W9-BME-133

THE AMERICAN HERITAGE COLLEGE DICTIONARY

dic·tio

THE AMERICAN HERITAGE COLLEGE DICTIONARY

THIRD EDITION

n·ar·y

HOUGHTON MIFFLIN COMPANY
Boston • New York

0-395-67161-2 (UPC)

Library of Congress Cataloging-in-Publication Data

The American heritage college dictionary. —3rd ed.
p. cm.
ISBN 0-395-66917-0 (plain edge). —ISBN 0-395-44638-4 (thumb edge). —ISBN 0-395-66918-9 (deluxe binding).
1. English language—Dictionaries. 2. Americanisms.
PE1628.A6227 1993
423—dc20 92-42124
CIP

Manufactured in the United States of America

Table of Contents

Preface

The American Heritage College Dictionary, Third Edition, embodies the belief that the ideal dictionary is a companion that not only answers questions about individual words accurately and carefully but also engages the mind in larger questions involving language, such as how best to express oneself or what our language tells us about ourselves.

The makers of the American Heritage dictionaries have always held this ideal. The immediate predecessor of the College Dictionary, *The American Heritage Dictionary of the English Language, Third Edition,* has been singled out by critics for its information about usage and the history of the language as well as for its accessibility and attractiveness. The College Edition displays these same virtues and assets in a more compact form.

The most evident of these virtues is the attractiveness of the Dictionary. The clear typography and design and the large number of photographs and line drawings in the margins are designed to appeal to the eye, to invite the reader into the Dictionary. This is a reference book that is meant to be readable and companionable, so the reader will be drawn within it to linger and learn.

The definitions match the expectations raised by the appealing design. They are written in a clear and full style to provide access to meaning unhindered by dictionary shorthand or jargon. Furthermore, the most frequently sought meanings are placed first so that the basic meanings of a word are grasped quickly. Finally, all entries in the Dictionary, including abbreviations and biographical and geographic entries, are found in a single convenient A–Z list.

The College Dictionary is designed to ensure that the reader knows what a word means and how it is used. Our usage program under the guidance of the noted linguist Geoffrey Nunberg discusses carefully chosen usage points to help the reader understand broader issues of usage. The Notes are additionally helpful in describing usage because they often report the opinions of our unique Usage Panel, a distinguished group of writers, teachers, and others who use the English language regularly and publicly and are noted for their command of it. The Panelists' advice is based on writing and speaking colored by the knowledge that their words receive wide and careful scrutiny.

American Heritage dictionaries are notable for the thoroughness of research and clarity of form of their etymologies, which place words in their historical contexts. Our unique Indo-European Roots Appendix lies at the heart of the etymological apparatus of the Dictionary, just as the ancestral hypothetical language of Indo-European underlies much of our vocabulary. Calvert Watkins's essay "Indo-European and the Indo-Europeans" on pages 1573–1579 explains the details of this language and how it bears on English. Suffice it to say that in entry after entry of the Dictionary the Appendix illustrates connections between seemingly unrelated words that not only take one by surprise but also deepen one's understanding of the words one uses.

We further enrich this understanding with extended essays on the history of the English language and its regional variety in the United States. The aim of both types of paragraphs is the same, to help readers better understand how language changes and develops over time and from place to place.

The American Heritage dictionaries are attentive to the heritage of the English language and of English dictionaries. At the same time, they have always been at the forefront in the use of technology. In preparing this dictionary we have used a structured database that has revolutionized the way we produce dictionaries. We have also had access to massive databases of text that we have searched for new words and meanings and for citational evidence.

The ideal dictionary takes full advantage of the resources of the present while at the same time carrying on the traditions of the past, reflecting the very pattern we see in language itself. In a single sentence we can use a word such as *I* that can be traced back to Indo-European and a word such as *nerd* that has been coined in the past few years of human existence. We have reason to believe that the College Dictionary will be the ideal companion for exploring the English language from its earliest beginnings to its use in our own time.

—David A. Jost

Editorial and Production Staff

EDITORIAL STAFF

Vice President, Director of Lexical Publishing, Production, and Manufacturing Services
Margery S. Berube

Executive Editor
Robert B. Costello

Senior Lexicographer
David A. Jost (Project Director)

Senior Coordinating Editor
Kaethe Ellis

Managing Editor
Marion Severynse

Senior Editors
Joseph P. Pickett (Assistant Project Director), David R. Pritchard, David M. Weeks (Etymology)

Editors
Donna Cremans (Physical Science), Paul G. Evenson, Joseph M. Patwell, Martha Fairman Phelps

Associate Editors
Jim A. Craig (Life Science), Ann-Marie Imbornoni (Pronunciation), Nina Judith Katz

Assistant Editor
Michael H. Choi (Life Science)

Editorial Assistants
Kenneth C. Carpenter, Laura P. Chesterton, Rachel King, Beth Gately Rowen

Administrative Assistance
Margaret M. May, Alisa Stepanian

Contributing Editor, Synonymy
Anne D. Steinhardt

Contributing Editors
Daniel Lepow, James P. Marciano, Hanna Schonthal

Citations Clerks
Shari Lynn Wheeler, Lily Moy

Proofreading
Kathryn Blatt, Judith L. Drummond, Valerie A. English, Bruce E. Frost II, Rebecca A. Parker, Thelma Prince

PRODUCTION STAFF

Production and Manufacturing Manager
Christopher Leonesio

Production Supervisor
Patricia McTiernan

Senior Art and Production Coordinator
Margaret Anne Miles

Database Production Supervisor
Scott Brigante

Database Keyboarding
Miriam E. Palmerola (Supervisor)

Lawrence Annucci, Edward Coleman, Lori Galvin, Britney K. Gress, M. Madeleine Newell, Meredith B. Phelan

Manufacturing Supervisor
Greg Mroczek

Production Coordinator
Nancy Priest

Production Assistant
Christina M. Granados

Administrative Assistance
Annmarie Baldelli, Elaine A. Gottlieb, Lauren B. Hunnewell

Contributors and Consultants

Usage
Geoffrey Nunberg, Ph.D.
Stanford University

Dialect
Sr. Mary Dominic Pitts, O.P., Ph.D.
Aquinas Junior College

Indo-European Roots Appendix
Calvert Watkins, Ph.D.
Harvard University

Language and Etymology Consultants

Patrick S. Diehl, Ph.D.
University of California, Berkeley

Deborah W. Anderson, Ph.D.
University of California, Los Angeles

Martin E. Huld, Ph.D.
Department of English, University of California, Los Angeles

Brian D. Joseph, Ph.D.
Department of Linguistics, Ohio State University

Reuven Merkin, Ph.D.
Professor, Academy of the Hebrew Language, Jerusalem, Israel

African Languages

George N. Clements, Ph.D.
Department of Modern Languages and Linguistics, Cornell University

Austronesian Languages

R. David Zorc, Ph.D.
Senior Linguist, MRM Language Research Center

Caribbean Languages

Richard Allsopp, Ph.D.
Caribbean Lexicography Project, University of the West Indies at Cave Hill, Barbados

Celtic Languages

Lionel S. Joseph, Ph.D.
Harvard University

Central and South American Languages

Richard F. Townsend, Ph.D.
Department of Africa, Oceania, and the Americas, Art Institute of Chicago

Hipólito Rafael Chacón, M.A.
Department of Art History, University of Chicago

Dialect

Craig M. Carver, Ph.D.
Dictionary of American Regional English

East Asian Languages

Stephen A. Bladey

Thomas Creamer, M.A.

English Language and Linguistics

G.W. Abernethy,
Middle English Dictionary

Sara E. Kimball, Ph.D.
Department of English, University of Texas at Austin

Henry Kučera, Ph.D.
Department of Linguistics, Brown University

Marilyn S. Miller, M.S.L.
Middle English Dictionary

Robert N. Mory, Ph.D.
Middle English Dictionary

Lee Pederson, Ph.D.
Department of English, Emory University

David W. Ruddy, M.A.
University of Michigan

David M. Yerkes, Ph.D.
Professor of English, Department of English, Columbia University

Greek and Latin

Vincent P. McCarren, Ph.D.
Middle English Dictionary

Rex E. Wallace, Ph.D.
Classics Department, University of Massachusetts, Amherst

Roger D. Woodard, Ph.D.
Classics Department, University of Southern California

North American Indian Languages

Ives Goddard, Ph.D.
Department of Anthropology, Smithsonian Institution

Russian, Persian, and Ural-Altaic Languages

Alexander Lehrman, Ph.D.
Department of Foreign Languages and Literatures, University of Delaware

Science Etymology

Sharon L. Marshall, Ph.D., M.D.
Harvard and Tufts Universities

Yiddish

Marvin I. Herzog, Ph.D.
Department of Linguistics, Columbia University

Special Consultants

Architecture

Edward F. Ford, M.Arch.
Associate Professor of Architecture, School of Architecture, University of Virginia

Art

H. Kristina Haugland, M.A.
Assistant Curator, Costume and Textiles, Philadelphia Museum of Art

Cinema

P. Adams Sitney, Ph.D.
Continuing Lecturer, Department of Visual Arts and Council of the Humanities, Princeton University

Dance

Mara Peets, M.A.
Teaching Fellow, Expository Writing Program, Columbia University; Writer/Researcher and Assistant Director, *Video Dictionary of Classical Ballet*

Economics, Business, and Finance

David L. Scott, Ph.D.
Professor of Accounting and Finance, Department of Accounting and Finance, Valdosta State College, Georgia

History and Government

John A. Garraty, Ph.D.
Gouverneur Morris Professor Emeritus, Department of History, Columbia University

Law

Timothy Stoltzfus Jost, J.D.
Newton D. Baker Professor of Law, Ohio State University

Robert M. Landis, J.D.
Partner and formerly Chair, Dechert Price & Rhoads

Meteorology

David B. Johnson, Ph.D.
National Center for Atmospheric Research, Boulder, Colorado

Military Science and Weapons

Daniel P. Bolger, Ph.D.
U.S. Army Infantry Officer

Music

Mary Davenport
Professor of Music, School for the Arts, Boston University

Mythology

William S. Bonds, Ph.D.
Associate Professor and Chair, Department of Classical Languages, University of the South

Philosophy

Hilary Kornblith, Ph.D.
Associate Professor, Department of Philosophy, University of Vermont

Religion

William A. Graham, Ph.D.
Professor of the History of Religion and Islamic Studies, Department of Near Eastern Languages and Civilizations, Harvard University

Van A. Harvey, Ph.D.
George Edwin Barnell Professor of Religious Studies, Department of Religious Studies, Stanford University

Martin E. Marty, Ph.D.
Fairfax M. Cone Distinguished Professor of the History of Modern Christianity, Divinity School, University of Chicago

Richard P. McBrien, S.T.D.
Crowley-O'Brien-Walter Professor of Theology, Department of Theology, University of Notre Dame

Paul Mendes-Flohr, Ph.D.
Professor, Department of Jewish Thought, Hebrew University, Jerusalem, Israel

Frank E. Reynolds, Ph.D.
Professor of the History of Religions and Buddhist Studies, Divinity School and Department of South Asian Languages and Civilizations, University of Chicago

Jack D. Van Horn, Ph.D.
Associate Professor, Department of Religion, College of William and Mary

Science and Technology

Donald C.S. Allison, Ph.D.
Professor and Head, Department of Computer Science, Virginia Polytechnic Institute and State University

William Ira Bennett, M.D.
Editor, *Harvard Health Letter,* Harvard Medical School

Sheila Ewing Browne, Ph.D.
Professor of Chemistry and Chair, Department of Chemistry, Mount Holyoke College

Neal D. Buffaloe, Ph.D.
Professor Emeritus of Biology, University of Central Arkansas

F.J. Collier
Collections Manager, Department of Paleobiology, National Museum of Natural History, Smithsonian Institution

Brooks B. Ellwood, Ph.D.
Professor and Acting Chair, Department of Geology, University of Texas at Arlington

R.J. Emry, Ph.D.
Curator, Division of Vertebrate Paleontology, Department of Paleobiology, National Museum of Natural History, Smithsonian Institution

Frank Espey, M.D.
Neurological Surgery (retired), Greenville, S.C.

William S. Haubrich, M.D.
Head, Division of Gastroenterology, Scripps Clinical Research Foundation

Nicholas Hotton III, Ph.D.
Curator, Division of Vertebrate Paleontology, Department of Paleobiology, National Museum of Natural History, Smithsonian Institution

Lynn Margulis, Ph.D.
Department of Botany, University of Massachusetts at Amherst

J.W. Pierce, Ph.D.
Chair, Department of Paleobiology, National Museum of Natural History, Smithsonian Institution

C.E. Ray, Jr.
Curator, Division of Vertebrate Paleontology, Department of Paleobiology, National Museum of Natural History, Smithsonian Institution

Richard Evans Schultes, Ph.D.
Jeffrey Professor of Biology and Director, Harvard Botanical Museum (Emeritus)

James Trefil, Ph.D.
Clarence J. Robinson Professor of Physics, George Mason University

Sociology

Mary Waters, Ph.D.
John L. Loeb Associate Professor of the Social Sciences, Harvard University

Sports

Robert W. Creamer
Formerly Senior Editor, *Sports Illustrated*

Trademarks

Ted J. Murphy
International and Information Services Manager, U.S. Trademark Association

The Usage Panel

Geoffrey Nunberg, Ph.D. Chair
Department of Linguistics, Stanford University

Edwin Newman Chair Emeritus
Journalist; lecturer; author

Elie Abel Educator; writer; Professor Emeritus, Stanford University

Shana Alexander Writer

Cleveland Amory Humorist; humanitarian; President, The Fund for Animals

Roger Angell Writer and Fiction Editor, *New Yorker*

Isaac Asimov* Writer; Professor of Biochemistry, Boston University School of Medicine

James Atlas Writer; Editor, *New York Times Magazine*

Margaret Atwood Writer

Kathryn H. Au Educational psychologist, Kamehameha (Hawaii) Schools

Louis Auchincloss Writer

Ralph Backlund Senior Contributing Editor, *Smithsonian*; formerly Producer and Executive Producer for news and public affairs, CBS; formerly Associate Editor and Managing Editor, *Horizon*

John Bainbridge Staff writer, *New Yorker*; columnist, *Gourmet*

Sheridan Baker Professor Emeritus of English, University of Michigan

Letitia Baldrige Author; lecturer on manners

Jacques Barzun Writer; literary consultant; educator

Carolyn Wilkerson Bell Susan Duval Adams Professor of English, Randolph-Macon Woman's College

Daniel Bell Henry Ford II Professor of Social Sciences Emeritus, Harvard University; Scholar in Residence, American Academy of Arts and Sciences

Pierre Berton Canadian writer and broadcaster

Alton Blakeslee Science Editor (retired), Associated Press

Harold Bloom Writer; Sterling Professor of Humanities, Yale University; Berg Professor of English, New York University; MacArthur Fellow

Roy Blount, Jr. Writer; Contributing Editor, *Atlantic*

Kallia H. Bokser Coordinator, Office for the Aging, New York City Housing Authority; proposal writer

Dwight Bolinger* Professor Emeritus of Romance Languages and Literatures, Harvard University; Visiting Professor Emeritus of Linguistics, Stanford University

The Hon. Julian Bond Formerly Georgia state legislator; Professor, American University and University of Virginia; lecturer; host, public affairs television program

The Hon. Daniel J. Boorstin Librarian of Congress Emeritus; recipient, Pulitzer Prize and National Book Award Medal for Distinguished Contribution to American Letters

Charles P. Boren Associate Editor (retired), *Lewiston* (Idaho) *Morning Tribune*

Barbara Taylor Bradford Novelist

The Hon. William W. Bradley U.S. Senator from New Jersey; formerly professional basketball player

Leo Braudy Bing Professor of English, University of Southern California

Paul Brooks Writer; formerly Editor in Chief, Houghton Mifflin Company

Heywood Hale Broun Writer; actor; television newsperson

Rachel M. Brownstein Professor of English, Brooklyn College and the Graduate Center, City University of New York

William F. Buckley, Jr. President, National Review Inc.

Gabrielle Burton Writer

Gerald Carson* Social historian; writer; advertising agency executive

Claudia Cassidy Writer; formerly music and drama critic, *Chicago Tribune*; formerly critic at large, *Chicago* magazine

Walter C. Clemens, Jr. Writer; Professor of Political Science, Boston University; Adjunct Research Fellow, Harvard University Center for Science and International Affairs

Pat Conroy Novelist

Claire Kehrwald Cook Formerly Editorial Director, Modern Language Association of America; author, *Line by Line: How to Edit Your Own Writing*

Robin Cook, M.D. Physician; writer

Alistair Cooke Journalist and broadcaster

Roy H. Copperud* Professor Emeritus of Journalism, University of Southern California; columnist, *Editor & Publisher*; author of works on English usage; recipient, Humanities Award, Association of American Publishers

Norman Cousins* Adjunct Professor, School of Medicine, University of California, Los Angeles; writer; formerly Editor, *Saturday Review*; formerly Chair, Pulitzer Prize jury in literature

Malcolm Cowley* Writer; literary adviser, Viking Press, Inc.; formerly Associate Editor, *New Republic*

Robert W. Creamer Writer; biographer; formerly Senior Editor, *Sports Illustrated*

Gene D. Dahmen Attorney; past President, Boston Bar Association

Marshall B. Davidson* Writer; Senior Editor, *Horizon*; formerly Editor of Publications, Metropolitan Museum of Art, New York

Robertson Davies Writer; founding Master, Massey College, University of Toronto; Professor of English and Drama

Lois DeBakey Writer, lecturer, and consultant; Professor of Scientific Communication, Baylor College of Medicine; Adjunct Professor of Scientific Communication, Tulane University School of Medicine

Vine Deloria, Jr. Standing Rock Sioux Tribe Professor of Law, Religious Studies, Political Science, and History, University of Colorado

Annie Dillard Writer

William K. Durr Professor of Education Emeritus, Michigan State University; past President, International Reading Association

Andrea Dworkin Writer

Freeman J. Dyson Writer; Professor of Physics, Institute for Advanced Study, Princeton, New Jersey

Anne Edwards Biographer and novelist; past President, Authors Guild

Gretel Ehrlich Writer; Guggenheim Fellow from Wyoming

Ralph Ellison Writer; educator

Carolly Erickson Historian; writer

Howard Fast Writer

Frances FitzGerald Writer; contributor, *New Yorker*; recipient, Pulitzer Prize

Elizabeth Frank Writer; Joseph E. Harry Professor of Modern Languages and Literature, Bard College; recipient, Pulitzer Prize

Reuven Frank Formerly President, NBC News; formerly Executive Producer, *Huntley-Brinkley Report*

John Kenneth Galbraith Economist; writer; formerly U.S. Ambassador to India; Paul M. Warburg Professor of Economics Emeritus, Harvard University

Sara Garnes Linguist; Associate Professor of English, Ohio State University

Michael G. Gartner President, NBC News; language columnist; past President, American Society of Newspaper Editors; member, Pulitzer Prize Board

J. Edward Gates Lexicographer; editor; Professor Emeritus of English, Indiana State University

A. Bartlett Giamatti* Sports executive; educator; Commissioner of Baseball; formerly President, National Baseball League; formerly President, Yale University

Francine du Plessix Gray Writer

Linda Gregerson William Wilhartz Assistant Professor of English, University of Michigan

Patricia Hampl Writer; Professor of English, University of Minnesota

The Hon. Mark O. Hatfield U.S. Senator from Oregon

The Hon. S.I. Hayakawa* Writer; educator; President Emeritus, San Francisco State University; formerly U.S. Senator from California

Mark Helprin Writer; Contributing Editor, *Wall Street Journal*; Senior Fellow, Hudson Institute

Douglas R. Hofstadter Professor of Cognitive Science and Computer Science, Indiana University, Bloomington; recipient, Pulitzer Prize

Gloria Hom Educator and consultant; Chair, Economics Department, Mission College; member, California State University Board of Trustees; member, Board of Trustees, Dominican College of San Rafael

Paul Horgan Novelist, biographer, and historian; Professor Emeritus and Author in Residence, Wesleyan University; recipient, Pulitzer Prize

The Hon. Shirley M. Hufstedler Attorney; formerly U.S. Secretary of Education; formerly Judge, U.S. Court of Appeals for the Ninth Circuit

John K. Hutchens Retired member, Editorial Board, Book-of-the-Month Club; retired literary and drama reviewer, *New York Times*, *New York Herald Tribune*, and *Boston Evening Transcript*

Jennifer James Cultural anthropologist; writer

Joyce Johnson Writer; recipient, National Book Critics Circle Award

William F. Johnston* Associate Professor and Newspaper Internship Coordinator, School of Communications, University of Washington

Erica Jong Poet and novelist; President, Authors Guild

The Hon. Barbara Jordan Educator, attorney, and writer; Lyndon B. Johnson Centennial Professor in National Policy, Lyndon B. Johnson School of Public Affairs, University of Texas at Austin; formerly U.S. Representative from Texas

June M. Jordan Poet; Professor of African American Studies and Women's Studies, University of California, Berkeley

Alfred E. Kahn Professor of Economics Emeritus, Cornell University; formerly Economic Adviser to the President of the United States

Roger Kahn Author; journalist

Justin Kaplan Writer; recipient, Pulitzer Prize and National Book Award

Stanley Kauffmann Film critic, *New Republic*; Distinguished Visiting Professor of Theater and Film, Adelphi University

Alfred Kazin Writer; Distinguished Professor of English Emeritus, the Graduate Center, City University of New York

Trudy Kehret-Ward Educator; writer

Garrison Keillor Author and host of *American Radio Company*

Elizabeth T. Kennan President, Mount Holyoke College

Walter Kerr Drama critic (retired), *New York Times*; formerly drama critic, *New York Herald Tribune*; past President, New York Drama Critics' Circle; recipient, Pulitzer Prize

Florence King Writer; critic

Maxine Hong Kingston Writer; recipient, National Book Award, National Book Critics Circle Award, and Anisfield-Wolf Race Relations Award

Galway Kinnell Poet; Erich Maria Remarque Professor of Creative Writing, New York University; recipient, Pulitzer Prize

The Hon. Jeremy K.B. Kinsman Sous-ministre adjoint, Affaires politiques et de la sécurité internationale, Affaires exterieures, Ottawa, Canada

The Hon. Jeane J. Kirkpatrick Diplomat; writer; educator; formerly U.S. Ambassador to the United Nations

Maxine Kumin Writer; formerly Consultant in Poetry, Library of Congress; recipient, Pulitzer Prize

Charles Kuralt News correspondent, CBS

J.J. Lamberts* Professor Emeritus of English, Arizona State University; author of works on English usage

Milton I. Levine, M.D. Formerly Professor of Clinical Pediatrics, New York Hospital — Cornell Medical Center; radio commentator, CBS; formerly syndicated columnist

Flora Lewis Senior Columnist, *New York Times*

Robert E. Lewis Lexicographer; Editor in Chief, *Middle English Dictionary*; Professor of English, University of Michigan

Sara Lawrence Lightfoot Professor of Education, Harvard University; writer; recipient, MacArthur Prize

J. Anthony Lukas Author; journalist; recipient, Pulitzer Prize

Russell Lynes* Writer; formerly Managing Editor, *Harper's*

Claudine B. Malone Management consultant; formerly Associate Professor, Harvard Business School

William Manchester Writer in Residence and Professor of History Emeritus, Wesleyan University; Fellow, Pierson College, Yale University

Robert Manning Writer; editor; formerly Editor in Chief, *Atlantic*

Richard Curry Marius Novelist and biographer; Director of Expository Writing, Harvard University

Suzanne R. Massie Writer; lecturer on Russian history and culture; Fellow, Harvard Russian Research Center

Alice E. Mayhew Editorial Director, Trade Division, Simon & Schuster

The Hon. Eugene McCarthy Writer, poet, and lecturer; formerly U.S. Senator from Minnesota

David McCord Poet; essayist; Honorary Curator of the Poetry and Farnsworth Rooms, Harvard University Library

Kenneth McCormick Senior Consulting Editor, Bantam Doubleday Dell; formerly Editor in Chief, Doubleday & Company, Inc.

Mary McGrory Journalist; columnist, *Washington Post* and Universal Press Syndicate; recipient, Pulitzer Prize

Leonard Michaels Professor of English, University of California, Berkeley

James A. Michener Writer; recipient, Pulitzer Prize and Presidential Medal of Freedom

Hassan Minor, Jr. Special Assistant to the President, Howard University

Richard Scott Mitchell* Mineralogist; educator; writer; Professor of Environmental Science, University of Virginia; Executive Editor, *Rocks and Minerals*

Jessica Mitford Writer

Lance Morrow Essayist and Senior Writer, *Time*; recipient, National Magazine Award

The Hon. Daniel Patrick Moynihan U.S. Senator from New York; formerly Professor of Political Science, Harvard University

Cullen Murphy Managing Editor, *Atlantic*

The Hon. Maurine Neuberger Formerly U.S. Senator from Oregon; formerly Oregon state legislator

His Excellency Thomas M.T. Niles Assistant Secretary of State for European and Canadian Affairs; formerly U.S. Representative to the European Community; formerly U.S. Ambassador to Canada

David Ogilvy, O.B.E. Advertising copywriter; Officer of the Order of Arts and Letters (France); past Chair, United Negro College Fund

Cynthia Ozick Novelist; essayist; member, American Academy of Arts and Letters; founding member, Académie Universelles des Cultures (Paris)

Robert S Pirie Chairman and Chief Executive Officer, Rothschild Inc.

Alvin F. Poussaint, M.D. Associate Professor of Psychiatry, Harvard Medical School

Ellen F. Prince Professor of Linguistics, University of Pennsylvania

Jane Bryant Quinn Journalist; syndicated financial columnist, *Newsweek* and *Woman's Day*

Tony Randall Actor

William James Raspberry Syndicated urban affairs columnist and broadcast commentator; formerly member, Pulitzer Prize Board

Edward W. Rosenheim Editor; writer; Professor of English, University of Chicago

Judith Rossner Novelist

Leo Rosten Writer; social scientist; editor

Berton Roueché Writer

Vermont Royster Writer; educator; William Rand Kenan, Jr., Professor of Journalism and Mass Communication, University of North Carolina at Chapel Hill; Editor Emeritus, *Wall Street Journal*; recipient, Pulitzer Prize

Carl Sagan David Duncan Professor of Astronomy and Space Sciences and Director, Laboratory for Planetary Studies, Cornell University; scientist; author; recipient, Pulitzer Prize

Robert Saudek Division Chief, Library of Congress; television producer; Lecturer on Visual Studies, Harvard University; founding President, Museum of Broadcasting

Arthur M. Schlesinger, Jr. Writer; historian; educator; formerly Special Assistant to the President of the United States; recipient, Pulitzer Prize

Glenn T. Seaborg University Professor of Chemistry, University of California, Berkeley; formerly Chair, U.S. Atomic Energy Commission; recipient, Nobel Prize

Art Seidenbaum* Journalist; Editor, Opinion Section, *Los Angeles Times*

Harvey Shapiro Poet; Deputy Editor, *New York Times Magazine*

Elaine Showalter Professor of English, Princeton University

John Simon Drama critic, *New York*; film critic, *National Review*

Carlota S. Smith Professor of Linguistics and Director, Center for Cognitive Science, University of Texas

Jack Smith Columnist, *Los Angeles Times*

Susan Sontag Writer

Theodore C. Sorensen Attorney; writer; formerly Special Counsel to the President of the United States

Susan Stamberg Special Correspondent, National Public Radio

Wallace Stegner Writer; founder and formerly Director, Stanford University Writing Program; recipient, Pulitzer Prize and National Book Award

Shane Templeton Foundation Professor of Curriculum and Instruction, University of Nevada, Reno

Paul Theroux Novelist; travel writer

Elizabeth Marshall Thomas Writer

Nina Totenberg Legal Affairs Correspondent, National Public Radio and NBC

Elizabeth C. Traugott Professor of Linguistics and English, Stanford University

Calvin Trillin Staff writer, *New Yorker*; syndicated columnist

Anne Tyler Novelist; recipient, Pulitzer Prize

The Hon. Stewart L. Udall Writer; Chairman of the Board, The Archaeological Conservancy, Santa Fe, New Mexico; formerly U.S. Secretary of the Interior and U.S. Representative from Arizona

Helen H. Vendler A. Kingsley Porter University Professor of English, Harvard University

Douglas Turner Ward Actor; playwright; recipient, Vernon Rice Award and Obie Award

Calvert Watkins Victor S. Thomas Professor of Linguistics and the Classics, Harvard University; past President, Linguistic Society of America

Fay Weldon Writer

Eudora Welty Writer

Jacqueline Grennan Wexler Writer; formerly President, Hunter College, City University of New York

Tom Wicker Author; journalist; Editor, *New York Times*

Alden S. Wood Lecturer on Editorial Procedures, Simmons College; national columnist on language and English usage

Richard A. Young Writer, editor, lecturer, and engineer; Publisher, *Pollution Engineering*; Executive Director, National Registry of Environmental Professionals

William Zinsser Writer, editor, and educator; author of *On Writing Well* and *Writing to Learn*

* We regret that these members of the Usage Panel died during the course of the project.

Usage in the American Heritage Dictionary: The Place of Criticism

Geoffrey Nunberg

Ever since the conception of "correctness" first emerged in the 18th century, there has never been a time when standards of usage were not controversial. Swift's proposals for improving English were derided by Whig pamphleteers. Noah Webster remonstrated with the influential Dr. Robert Lowth for defending a construction like *the King of England's hat,* and was in turn excoriated by later grammarians for countenancing the double negative. And so on, to the present day.

This litigious history may be disconcerting to those who would like to think of the English rules of correctness as long-settled standards from which we have lately fallen away. But a healthy tradition of language criticism requires controversy. This Dictionary contains over 400 Usage Notes and comments. That is a good deal more than what is found in most dictionaries. But at the most conservative estimate, an educated speaker of English knows around 100,000 words and constructions. And these can be combined in an infinite number of ways, most of them infelicitous—for there are many more ways to get a word wrong than to get it right. The number of possible mistakes in English is inexhaustibly vast, and no one could hope to catalog them all.

So traditional usage criticism has had to provide critical methods rather than lists. As a matter of convenience, of course, these methods are usually demonstrated in disputations over a body of canonical rules and dicta. When readers with an interest in these matters pick up a new usage book or a dictionary containing usage guidance, they invariably turn first to the entries dealing with the modification of *unique,* the proper use of *disinterested,* or the distinction between *shall* and *will.* These, however, are merely the traditional occasions for discussions of usage and scarcely exhaust the scope of the subject.

Modern controversies about usage are different from their predecessors. The earlier disputes were waged intramurally, with everyone tacitly agreed about the stakes and the ground rules. Between Webster and Lowth there was no disagreement about the central premise of language criticism: that some forms of expression are preferable to others. Now that assumption itself has become controversial.

Modern discussions of usage often take the form of engagements in a battle between irreconcilable camps. On one side of the field is ranged the party of science, the "descriptivists," who hold that all standards are ultimately based on the facts of use and that the business of dictionaries and usage books is simply to record those facts in a neutral way. On the other side stand the "prescriptivists," who insist that language is subject to a higher morality and that people who care about the state of the language have an obligation to defend traditional values in the face of growing laxity and permissiveness.

Certainly language criticism was not originally conceived as an apology for traditional values. The 18th-century founders of the tradition were champions of a new class of writers, freed by an expanded reading public from a direct dependence on aristocratic patronage. The object of their criticism, whether of language, literature, or life, was to usurp the authority of the court and the aristocracy as a source of social values. Hence their insistence that the spoken language must defer to the written and that custom must sometimes defer to criticism—for in that era "custom" was simply another name for the practices of the privileged. Serious language criticism since then has been more often than not an arm of traditional liberalism, which reserved its sternest admonitions for the transgressions of the educated and the powerful. Matthew Arnold could berate the *London Times* for its "orthographical antics." Edmund Wilson taxed Walter Lippmann, Lionel Trilling, and John F. Kennedy for their stylistic lapses.

Usage doctrines must change with the times, of course. The fundamental linguistic virtues—order, clarity, and conciseness—are unassailable, yet they must be constantly reinterpreted against an evolving social background. It is no longer permissible to pretend that the English language is a club for gentlemen who have "their" Latin authors at their fingertips. The language is too important to be left to nostalgic reveries. Nevertheless, it is also too important to be excused from responsible critical review.

Usage in this Dictionary

In the treatment of usage the editors of *The American Heritage College Dictionary, Third Edition,* have tried to construct each Usage Note as a miniature critical exercise and to provide, within the limits of space, the kinds of information that readers will require to resolve the question to their own satisfaction.

Naturally the Notes vary greatly in content and length according to the point at issue. Some provide no more than brief comments on relatively technical points. (What is the difference between *flotsam* and *jetsam*?) At the other end of the spectrum, longer Notes deal primarily with complex grammatical questions or with questions of particular social or critical interest (see *I, man, he, hopefully,* and *unique,* for example).

The material provided in the Notes falls into three broad categories: information about use, summaries and analyses of critical arguments, and observations about the opinions of writers and critics. Speaking very broadly, all questions of usage involve a weighing of one or more of these three considerations.

Use. The doctrine that correctness rests on use is hardly an invention of modern linguistics. Horace insisted that the laws of speech are fixed by custom, "whose arbitrary sway/Words and the forms of language must obey," a dictum quoted with approval by the grammarians of every succeeding era. Of course, the rules of the language are determined by use, but whose? Where use is uniform, the question does not arise. It is a curious fact of English that the phrase *more than one* takes a singular verb, despite its sense, as in *More than one student* has *left.* Doubtless it would be more logical to say *More than one student* have *left,* but it would not be English.

Still, usage is often divided, sometimes unaccountably but more often according to social or geographic differences. And in these cases Horace's dictum offers little by way of helpful advice, as Noah Webster observed with some impatience:

> But what kind of custom did Horace design to lay down as the standard of speaking? Was it a local custom? . . . Is it the practice of a court, or a few eminent scholars, that he designed to constitute a standard?

Webster's questions have no general answer. It depends on the word. Sometimes local custom is the only determinant, and we find as many standards as there are speech communities.

In other cases people do insist that there must be some one general standard, usually as determined by the practice of educated middle-class speakers. The Dictionary records facts about the use of items like these either in usage labels such as *Non-Standard* (see the Guide to the Dictionary) or, in particularly complicated cases, in the Usage Notes. Take the past tense form *snuck.* It originated as a nonstandard regional variant for *sneaked,* and many people still have a lingering prejudice against it: 67 percent of the Usage Panel disapproves of it. In recent years, however, *snuck* has become increasingly frequent in reputable writing (the *American Heritage Dictionary* files contain citations for it from the *New Republic* and the *San Francisco Chronicle,* as well as from the works of writers like Anne Tyler and Garrison Keillor). And while the files show that *sneaked* is by far more prevalent in edited prose by a factor of about 7 to 2, it is no longer possible to label *snuck* as nonstandard, even though many educated users of English continue to consider it informal.

While the practice of the educated middle class often determines what counts as "Standard English," it does not have the last word in all matters of divided usage. Not even the most assiduously "descriptivist" dictionary would think of basing its definitions of *annuity* or *zabaglione* simply on the way the words are used by educated speakers in general. Here readers do not expect to find a mirror of their own practice; they want to know how the words are used by experts in finance or Italian cooking. Of course, those are specialists' terms, but the point applies to many words in the general vocabulary as well. A great many educated speakers use *ironic* to mean simply "coincidental" or "improbable," as in *It's ironic that he was also using a borrowed bat when he hit a grand slam last week against the Dodgers.* The use, then, is unquestionably Standard English, and it is certainly the responsibility of a dictionary to record it. But the meaning of *ironic* is not at the disposition of the general public in quite the way the past tense of *sneak* is. *Ironic* is still a literary sort of word, and it is likely that a good many of the people who have used it to mean "coincidental" were reaching for a literary effect at the time. As long as literary folk continue to use *ironic* in a narrower sense—and what is no less important, as long as a large proportion of the general public continues to think of the word as literary—a dictionary has the responsibility to note that in this case the general use is sometimes at odds with the use of the writers and critics who have particular authority about the notion in question.

It is never easy to say which group has authority over any given usage, of course. Who owns *disinterested*? Is the word *kudos* by now a common or garden-variety English plural like *peas,* or is it still an elegant borrowing that should be held responsible to its origin as a Greek singular? We will want to take the facts of use into consideration when we approach these questions, but it is the height of scientistic self-deception to suppose that use provides an objective criterion for resolving them. Lexicographers invariably have to make critical evaluations of the raw facts of use. And where the verdict of use is equivocal, a dictionary should give readers the wherewithal to make up their own minds.

Criticism. Custom fixes the rules of language but does not justify them. Even complete uniformity of use doesn't make a practice exempt from critical review. After all, custom is partly determined by our beliefs about the world and society, and in these we might all be wrong. At one time everybody used *fish* to refer to whales, but the practice was abandoned in the light of new zoological evidence. And until quite recently, everybody used the words *man* and *men* to mean simply "human beings," but now many people have abandoned that practice in the light of new conceptions of social justice.

The prescriptive tradition had its origins in the Age of Criticism as a method no different in kind from the criticism of artistic works or of civil society in general. The 18th-century writers established the battery of principles to which usage might be held accountable—the familiar arguments from etymology, meaning, analogy, logic, and the rest. Granted, they often applied these principles with the overzealous love of rules and systems that they brought to all their critical enterprises, so that we may sometimes feel, as Leslie Stephen put it, that they "sanctioned the attempt to do by rule and compasses what ought to be done by the eye." And much of the "logic" they invoked was derived either from speculative philosophy or from inappropriate parallels to Latin grammar, with the result that it often turns out to be of dubious relevance to the facts of English. It is fair to criticize the double negative in a sentence like *I never got nothing* on the grounds that it is associated with nonstandard varieties of English. But one cannot fault the construction on logical grounds without also being willing to assert the illogicality of standard French and Italian.

Linguists of a generation or so ago were fond of citing examples such as these in an effort to undermine the entire prescriptive program, and some of them went on to argue that the rules of language are simply immune from criticism, since they answer to natural laws inaccessible to cursory reflection. But the fact that particular prescriptive arguments are sometimes unsound does not vitiate the case for criticism in general. If modern linguistics teaches us that the logic of language structure is a good deal more subtle and elusive than traditional grammarians supposed, it does not follow that the grammar of every variety has achieved complete consistency or functional perfection—particularly with regard to the relatively "unnatural" requirements of written public communication.

In fact there is no reason that the methods of scientific linguistics and of traditional criticism should be regarded as incompatible. Modern syntax and semantics have developed an impressive array of analytical tools, which often make it possible to capture distinctions and subtleties that elude the sometimes coarse apparatus of traditional, Latin-based school grammar. These techniques can be as useful in analyzing prescriptive rules as in describing the facts of actual speech, and we believe, along with an increasing number of linguists, that there is an important place for a "critical linguistics" in the study of usage.

Opinion: The Role of the Usage Panel. Custom can provide precedents and criticism can provide principles, but each has to be evaluated at the bar of opinion. Of course, dictionaries register received opinion at every turn (what else could justify labeling a usage as "offensive"?). But it is often useful to have a more explicit way of gauging the opinions of people who have a critical interest in the language. This, then, is the role of the Dictionary's Usage Panel, a group of 173 well-known writers, critics, and scholars. Panel members are regularly surveyed on a broad range of usage questions. The results of these surveys are included in many of the Usage Notes.

The Usage Panel should not be thought of as an Academy, charged with ruling on all questions of disputed usage. Indeed, the opinions of the Panel are often divided, even though at times the Panelists seem to speak with a single voice. In earlier surveys, for example, 99 percent of the Panelists rejected *between you and I* and *ain't I* in formal writing. But the Panel's judgment on questions like these merely reflects the hegemony of Standard English. The results of the surveys are far more interesting when they involve questions that are matters of dispute among educated speakers. In the most recent survey, for example, 49 percent of the Panel accepted the use of *alternative* to refer to one of three or more choices, as in *Of the three alternatives, the first is the least distasteful.*

One might think that faced with this sort of disagreement readers interested merely in knowing which usage is "correct" would be perplexed: if there is no agreement among so august a group as this, what hope is there of fixing standards? But this misses the point. In the first place, the variation may itself be instructive. In the most recent survey, for example, we included several questions about words of uncertain pronunciation, such as *banal, err, harass,* and *hegemony.* We were not surprised to find a lack of consensus—the Usage Panel was split exactly 50–50 on which syllable takes the emphasis in *harass,* for example—but the results did serve to make the no less useful point that on these matters, at least, there *is* no agreed-upon standard.

More important, the Panel's diverging opinions underscore the point that usage questions are always controversial—*must* be controversial, if discussions of usage are to be instructive. The Usage Panel surveys are most interesting in providing a rough indication of just how controversial an issue is, that is, how seriously the views of individual critics have been taken by people with a critical interest in the language. This fact becomes clear when we compare the Panel's reactions on different items. For instance, if you read what some critics have had to say about new forms like the use of *parent* as a verb, or the word *lifestyle,* you may be led to believe that they are all egregious New Age jargon. But collectively, the Panel was more discriminating. *Lifestyle,* for example, is acceptable to a large majority of the Panel, 70 percent, in the sentence *Salaries in the Bay Area may be higher, but it may cost employees as much as 30 percent more to maintain their lifestyles.* Readers, of course, will want to make up their own minds about each of these usages, but the opinions of the Panel may carry some weight, especially when taken together with the critical discussions in the Usage Notes.

Changing Attitudes. In preparing this edition of the Dictionary, we were able for the first time to use the results of the Usage Panel surveys to draw another kind of comparison, one that shows the shifts in critical attitudes over time. The Usage Panel was first polled in 1964, nearly a generation ago. That is not a long time on the linguistic scale of things, for language as a whole changes much more slowly than other social institutions. But it is time enough for usages to change significantly in their status, particularly when they involve the sorts of innovations and neologisms that criticism often focuses on.

One notable trend, for example, is that a number of words and constructions that were questionable a generation ago have become more acceptable. The verb *contact* was problematic to many language critics of the 1950's and 1960's, but resistance seems to have abated: between 1969 and the most recent survey the Panel's acceptance of *contact* rose from 34 to 65 percent. The pattern of increasing acceptability was repeated with the use of the verb *intrigue* to mean "arouse interest" (up from 52 to 78 percent) and with many others. The tendency is not surprising. Innovations rarely remain for long on the linguistic littoral; most either make their way onto dry land or are carried off with the receding tide.

But other shifts in the Panel's opinions may have less to do with changing patterns of usage than with changes in critical standards. In evaluating the most recent survey, for example, we were struck by the Panelists' increased indifference to traditional injunctions against using certain words in ways that appear to be inconsistent with their Latin origins. Fully 68 percent of the Panel now accepts the use of *aggravate* to mean "irritate," up from 43 percent in 1969. The same shift is evident with the use of *anxious* to mean "eager" (up from 23 to 48 percent), *transpire* to mean "happen" (up from 38 to 58 percent), *cohort* to refer to a single person (up from 31 to 71 percent), and several other words of this type.

Does this mean that the Panel has become generally more liberal or permissive? It is true that its composition has changed over the years. The membership of the current Panel is more numerous and younger than it was in 1969, and it includes a greater proportion of women and members of minority groups than before. Yet on many other canonical usage issues the current Panelists have proved to be no less conservative than their predecessors. For example, 89 percent rejects the use of *disinterested* to mean "uninterested," a figure not significantly different from the 93 percent who rejected this usage in 1969. And on a few issues, such as the use of *hopefully* as a sentence adverb, the Panel is actually more conservative now than it was a generation ago. Why then the shift in the Panelists' opinions on *aggravate* and the rest? Perhaps they have come to believe that it is no longer possible to expect adherence to general usage standards that presuppose a familiarity with classical languages, even if many of them note that they still observe the traditional strictures in their own writing. (See also the Usage Notes at *data* and *celibate.*)

The Scope of Coverage

The Traditional Canon. These changes in critical attitudes should not obscure the fact that most of the traditional canon of usage questions has emerged largely intact from the controversies of recent years. When people think about "usage questions," they still have in mind the same points of grammar and diction that occupied critics a century ago: the differences between *who* and *whom, between* and *among, enormity* and *enormousness*; the qualification of absolute terms such as *unique* and *parallel*; and so forth. These questions exemplify the consideration of usage in its most general form; they are ostensibly motivated by very broad critical principles that apply to writing of all sorts and about all subjects: criteria of logic, coherence, clarity, and concision. Over the years, to be sure, the traditional canon has accumulated a good deal of unexamined grammatical lore that does not hold up well under scrutiny; see, for example, the Notes at *and* and *preposition.* But we believe that canonical issues like these give language criticism its historical continuity; thus they still constitute the largest single category among the Usage Notes in the Dictionary. In some cases we have added Notes dealing with questions that, though not historically part of the canon, have much the quality of traditional issues, for example, the use of *specious* to mean "false" and the modification of *infinite.* The traditional canon has always been surrounded by a penumbra of items like these, introduced by individual writers or reference books in the interest of making particular points. What makes the canon central, after all, is not so much the particular words included but the broader linguistic questions raised.

New Words, New Issues. The Dictionary's treatment of usage has been extended to cover a variety of new issues. Notes are included for a host of new words that have attracted commentary. Some of these are drawn from the language of particular domains: new social movements (*lifestyle,* for example); publicity (*legend*); technology (*input* and *access*). Others have a more general provenance: the use of *go* to mean "say" or the use of *holocaust* to mean simply "disaster" or "misfortune." Of course the Dictionary's coverage of such items cannot be "comprehensive"—the class is far too fluid for that—but we have tried to cover items of particular critical interest.

In other cases, we have included Usage Notes for items not often touched on by criticism, which exemplify problems that might be considered appropriate elements in a revised usage canon. For example, there are Notes on several terms, such as *black English*, *nonstandard*, and *literacy*, that figure in recent public discussions of language questions. In including items like these, of course, we may be open to a charge of special pleading. But such words are only examples of a kind of scientific and technical terminology that has become increasingly important in public discussion. So we have also included Usage Notes on questions such as the difference between *methodology* and *method*, whether a *cross section* is necessarily "representative," and whether one can speak of a quantity as having been "reduced by 150 percent." Obviously the brief of usage criticism cannot be extended to cover all of the specialized discourse of the sciences. But the program of criticism can make at least a token effort to acknowledge the role that scientific and quantitative argumentation has come to play in general discourse.

Usage and Social Justice. Over the past 30 years the most radical change in the scope of language criticism has been its extension to a wide range of usages involving the relation between language and questions of social diversity and social justice. Discussion of these issues constitutes the most important and extensive additions to the treatment of usage in this Edition. One category includes the names of various social groups defined along lines of ethnicity, religion, race, physical capacity, and sexual preference, as discussed in the Notes at *Asian, black, Chicano, color, gay, handicapped, Hispanic, Jew, Jewess, Kanaka, Native American,* and *Negress*. In one sense, of course, these questions are not genuinely "new." But in the past they were not taken up as part of the public discussion of language standards. Only recently have these issues emerged as critical questions, whether as a result of the rise of official pluralism or of a more general tendency to emphasize the political and ideological aspects of usage.

In matters like these, of course, a dictionary has no authority to lay down standards of "correct" usage (at least not in the linguistic sense of the term). Most of these words are subject to a great deal of variation, even among members of the groups they apply to, and their connotations and use can change very rapidly. The Dictionary can help by providing information on the social and linguistic backgrounds of the questions. Thus the Note at *Hispanic* explains how that term is different in meaning from *Latino*. At the least, this information may spare some readers from resorting to unnecessary circumlocution or from giving inadvertent offense.

Usage and Gender. With a few exceptions (as with *black* and *gay*), the usage questions raised by the names of ethnic categories and the like are socially complex but linguistically simple. Replacement of one such word by another rarely causes grammatical difficulties or creates ancillary linguistic problems. But gender differences are so extensively and intricately woven into the fabric of the language that efforts to change usage often require a great deal of attentiveness and linguistic ingenuity. So it is not surprising that feminism has had more extensive consequences for questions of usage than any other recent social movement or that the debate over these issues has been particularly energetic. In this Edition we have greatly expanded coverage of these issues, which are discussed in the Usage Notes at *blond, brunette, –ess, –ette, feminist, gender, he, heroine, lady, man,* and *Ms.*

With these items, as with the names of ethnic and social categories, we have tried to present the linguistic and social background that readers will require to make informed decisions about the issues. Because the linguistic program of feminism has called for such extensive and varied changes in usage, we have also made an effort to gauge its overall effects on the attitudes and practice of writers, both in general and with regard to particular words and constructions. To this end, we included a number of questions about these issues in recent Usage Panel surveys. Generally speaking, we found that a great majority of the Panelists of both sexes have adopted at least a few of the recommendations of feminists. But virtually all the Panelists were discriminating in their revisions; they found some usages more objectionable than others. (In reporting the results on these items, we have sometimes broken down the Panelists' responses on the basis of gender. Not surprisingly, women were consistently more likely than men to reject usages that might be labeled sexist. But men and women showed roughly the same patterns in differentiating one item from the next. Thus both groups found *hostess* more acceptable than *sculptress,* and so forth.)

Fewer than 40 percent of the Panelists say they would use the masculine pronoun *his* to complete the sentence *A child who wants to become a doctor should be encouraged by ______ parents and teachers,* against 81 percent (including 58 percent of the women members) who accepted the generic use of *man* in *If early man suffered from a lack of information, modern man is tyrannized by an excess of it.*

Like most critical users of the language, the Panelists seem to have revised their usage on a case-by-case basis, evaluating each item in the light of the sometimes conflicting claims of syntax, established use, and social justice. In a sense, one can say that the feminist linguistic program has already succeeded, in requiring most literate people to reflect carefully on the ways in which usage might imply or reinforce gender stereotypes. Of course, the Panel's divisions reflect controversies about these usages that are not likely to be resolved in the near future. But these are precisely the kinds of controversies about particular words and principles that ensured the vitality of traditional language criticism in the 18th and 19th centuries. Here as elsewhere, what matters is not that we should expect to achieve uniformity but that we should discover in our differences the occasion for lively critical discussion.

Guide to the Dictionary

This Guide explains the conventions used in presenting the great array of information contained in the Dictionary, enabling you to find and understand that information quickly and easily.

Guidewords

A pair of boldface guidewords, together with the page number, appears on each page. The word on the top represents the first boldface entry on that page of the Dictionary. The word on the bottom represents the last boldface entry on that page. Thus, **bravery** and **break** and all the entries that fall alphabetically between them are entered and defined on page 171.

The Entry Words: Alphabetical Order

Each entry word, printed in boldface type, is set slightly to the left of the text column. All entries — including biographical and geographic names, abbreviations, symbols, and compounds of two or more words — are listed in strict alphabetical order:

abs.
Absaroka Range
Absaroke
abscess
abscise

For the sake of convenience, proper names are listed according to their most important element, such as a surname shared by a number of important people. In these cases, the alphabetical sequence applies only to those letters preceding the first comma:

George
George, Saint
George I^{1}
George I^{2}
. . . . . .
George VI
George, Henry
George, Lake
George River

Superscript numbers. Words with identical spellings but different etymologies are entered separately and have superscript, or raised, numbers. In most cases, these numbers reflect the frequency of use:

tick^{1} (tĭk) *n.* **1.** A light sharp clicking sound made repeatedly by a machine, such as a clock. . . . [ME *tek*, light tap.]

tick^{2} (tĭk) *n.* **1.** Any of numerous small bloodsucking parasitic arachnids of the family Ixodidae, many of which transmit febrile diseases, such as Lyme disease. . . . [ME *tik*, perh. < OE **ticca*.]

Syllabication

An entry word and its inflected and derived forms are divided into syllables by means of centered dots:

ac•e•tate (ăs′ĭ-tāt′) *n.*

In entries, such as *ethyl acetate,* that consist of two or more words separated by spaces, the words without centered dots are divided into syllables at their own places in the Dictionary.

Pronunciations are syllabicated for the sake of clarity. The syllabication of the pronunciation may not match the syllabication of the entry word because the division of the pronunciation follows phonological rules, while the division of the entry word reflects the long-established practices of printers and editors in breaking words at the end of a line of text.

Variants

Though standardization of English in the United States is more extensive than at any earlier time, many variant spellings and stylings remain in common use. All variants shown in this Dictionary are acceptable in any context unless indicated otherwise by a restrictive label, such as a dialect label. Variants, set in boldface type, are of two kinds: equal and unequal.

Equal variants. The word *or* joining an entry word and its variant form or forms indicates that these forms occur with virtually equal frequency in edited sources, based on our electronic and printed citational evidence:

ar•chae•ol•o•gy or **ar•che•ol•o•gy** (är′kē-ŏl′ə-jē) *n.*

Unequal variants. The word *also* joining an entry word and its variant form or forms indicates that the variant form occurs less frequently:

am•bi•ance also **am•bi•ence** (ăm′bē-əns, äN-byäNS′) *n.*

Variants that occur more than ten entries away from the main entry word in alphabetical order are entered as separate cross-references at the appropriate places in the alphabetical word list:

me•di•e•val also **me•di•ae•val** (mē′dē-ē′vəl, mĕd′ē-) *adj.*

me•di•ae•val (mē′dē-ē′vəl, měd′ē-) *adj.* Var. of **medieval.**

British variants. A number of variants consist of spellings preferred in British English. These variants, such as *defence* and *colour,* are labeled *Chiefly British.* They are entered at their own alphabetical places but are not given at the entries to which they relate:

de•fence (dĭ-fĕns′) *n. & v. Chiefly British.* Var. of **defense.**

Part-of-speech Labels

The following italicized labels indicate parts of speech:

adj.	adjective
adv.	adverb
conj.	conjunction
def.art.	definite article
indef.art.	indefinite article
interj.	interjection
n.	noun
prep.	preposition
pron.	pronoun
v.	verb

These italicized labels indicate inflected forms:

pl.	plural
sing.	singular

These italicized labels are used for the traditional classification of verbs:

tr.	transitive
intr.	intransitive
aux.	auxiliary

The labels for word elements are:

pref.	prefix
suff.	suffix

Entries that are abbreviations, such as *A.M.* and *blvd.,* are labeled *abbr.*

Certain entries do not carry labels. They include contractions (*I'll*), symbols (*I*^{2}, the symbol for *iodine*), trademarks (*Walkman*), and the word elements *–i–* and *–o–*, which never occur in initial or final position in a word.

Sometimes an entry word fulfills more than one grammatical function. For example, *current* can be an adjective (*current pricing*; *current negotiations*) and a noun (*a current of air*; *the swift current of a river*; *electric current*). In such cases the different parts of speech are defined within a single entry called a *combined entry.* The shift in grammatical function is indicated by a boldface dash followed by the appropriate part-of-speech label. If the syllabication or pronunciation differs, it is also included. Inflected forms are given if necessary and are followed by definitions:

re•bel (rĭ-bĕl′) *intr.v.* **-belled, -bel•ling, -bels. 1.** To refuse allegiance to and oppose by force an established government or ruling authority. **2.** To resist or defy an authority or a generally accepted convention. **3.** To feel or express strong unwillingness or repugnance: *rebelled at the suggestion.* —*n.* **reb•el.** (rĕb′əl). One who rebels or is in rebellion.

Inflected Forms

An inflected form of a word differs from the main entry form by the addition of a suffix or by a change in its base form to indicate grammatical features such as number, person, mood, or tense.

Inflected forms follow the part-of-speech label. They are set in boldface type, divided into syllables, and given pronunciations as necessary. Inflected forms are usually shortened to the last syllable of the entry word plus the inflectional ending. Irregular inflected forms are spelled out to the extent required for clarity. When inflected forms are shortened, each shortened inflected form is preceded by a boldface hyphen:

cap•i•tal•ize (kăp′ĭ-tl-īz′) *v.* **-ized, -iz•ing, -iz•es.**

Principal parts of verbs. The principal parts of verbs are entered in this order: *past tense, past participle, present participle,* and *third person singular present tense.* When the past tense and the past participle are identical, one form represents both:

fly[1] (flī) *v.* **flew** (flo͞o), **flown** (flōn), **fly•ing, flies** (flīz).

walk (wôk) *v.* **walked, walk•ing, walks.**

Comparison of adjectives and adverbs. Adjectives and adverbs whose comparative and superlative degrees can be formed by adding *–er* and *–est* to the unchanged word show these comparative and superlative suffixes immediately after the part-of-speech label:

high (hī) *adj.* **high•er, high•est.**

Irregular comparative and superlative forms are given in full, as in *bad, worse, worst.*

Plurals of nouns. Plurals of nouns other than those formed regularly by adding the suffixes *–s* or *–es* are shown and labeled *pl.*:

mouse (mous) *n., pl.* **mice** (mīs).

When a noun has a regular and an irregular plural form, both forms appear, with the most common shown first:

a•quar•i•um (ə-kwâr′ē-əm) *n., pl.* **-i•ums** or **-i•a** (-ē-ə).

Regular plurals are also shown when spelling might be a problem:

ra•di•o (rā′dē-ō) *n., pl.* **-os.**

hon•ey (hŭn′ē) *n., pl.* **-eys.**

A noun that is chiefly or exclusively plural in both form and meaning is labeled *pl.n.*:

cat•tle (kăt′l) *pl.n.* **1.** Any of various mammals of the genus *Bos,* including cows, steers, bulls, and oxen, often raised for meat and dairy products.

A noun that is always plural in form but is not necessarily used with a plural verb is labeled like this:

aer•o•bics (â-rō′bĭks) *n.* *(used with a sing. or pl. v.)* **1.** A system of physical conditioning designed to enhance circulatory and respiratory efficiency that involves vigorous, sustained exercise, such as jogging, swimming, or cycling. **2.** A program of physical fitness that involves such exercise. [< AEROBIC.]

pol•i•tics (pŏl′ĭ-tĭks) *n.* **1.** *(used with a sing. v.)* **a.** The art or science of government or governing, esp. the governing of a political entity, such as a nation, and the administration and control of its internal and external affairs. **b.** Political science.

Separate entries for inflected forms. Irregular inflected forms are entered separately in the Dictionary when they occur more than ten entries away from the main entry word:

men (mĕn) *n.* Pl. of **man.**

Such entries carry a part-of-speech label and are given pronunciations as necessary.

Some verbs, such as *do, be,* and *have,* have archaic inflected forms, such as *dost, art,* and *hadst,* that occur frequently enough to justify their inclusion in this Dictionary. These forms are also entered separately:

dost (dŭst) *v. Archaic.* A second pers. sing. pr.t. of **do**[1].

Labels

This Dictionary uses various labels to indicate entries related to particular subject areas, to provide guidance regarding various levels of usage, and to indicate words indigenous to specific geographic areas.

Subject labels. A subject label identifies the special area of knowledge to which an entry word or a definition applies:

tri•mor•phic (trī-môr′fĭk) also **tri•mor•phous** (-fəs) *adj.* **1.** *Biol.* Having or occurring in three differing forms. **2.** *Chem.* Crystallizing in three distinct forms.

Status labels. Status labels indicate that an entry word or a definition is limited to a particular level or style of usage. All words and definitions not restricted by such a label should be regarded as appropriate for use in all contexts.

Non-Standard. This, the most restrictive label in the Dictionary, is applied to forms and usages that educated speakers and writers consider unacceptable:

an•y•ways (ĕn′ē-wāz′) *adv. Non-Standard.* In any case.

Usage Problem. The label *Usage Problem* warns of possible difficulties involving grammar, diction, and writing style. A word or definition so labeled is discussed in a Usage Note:

snuck (snŭk) *v. Usage Problem.* A p.t. and p.part. of **sneak.** See Usage Note at **sneak.**

Offensive. This label is reserved for words and expressions such as racial, ethnic, or gender slurs that are not only derogatory and insulting to the person to whom they are directed but also a discredit to the one using them. This label may occur alone or in combination as *Offensive Slang.*

Vulgar. This label warns of social taboos attached to a word; it may appear alone or in combination as *Vulgar Slang.*

Obscene. A word that violates accepted standards of decency carries the label *Obscene.*

Slang. This label indicates a style of language that is distinguished by a striving for rhetorical effect through the use of extravagant, often facetious figures of speech. Some forms of slang occur in most cultivated speech but not in formal discourse. An example of a word labeled *Slang* is:

white-knuck•le (hwīt′nŭk′əl, wīt′-) *adj. Slang.* Characterized by tense nervousness or apprehension.

Informal. Those whose speech is standard use not only the language of formal discourse but also the language of conversation. The great majority of words are acceptable at both levels, though many words that are acceptable in conversation with friends and colleagues would be unsuitable in the formal prose of an article written for publication in the journal of a learned society, for example. An example of an entry labeled *Informal* is:

wish list *n. Informal.* An often mental list of things wanted.

Temporal labels. Temporal labels signal words or senses whose use in modern English is uncommon.

Archaic. This label is applied to words and senses that once were common but are now rare. Specifically, this label is attached to entry words and senses for which there is only sporadic evidence in print after 1755:

en•ter•tain•ment (ĕn′tər-tān′mənt) *n.* . . . **5.** *Archaic.* Maintenance; support. **6.** *Obsolete.* Employment.

Obsolete. The label *Obsolete* is used with entry words and senses no longer in active use, except, for example, in literary quotations. Specifically, this label is attached to entry words and senses for which there is little or no printed evidence since 1755. Sense 6 of *entertainment* is an example.

English-language labels. This Dictionary contains a number of labels noting the restriction of particular entry words and senses to specific areas of the English-speaking world. Here is a typical example of a word labeled *Chiefly British*:

win•kle[2] (wĭng′kəl) *tr.v.* **-kled, -kling, -kles.** *Chiefly British.* To pry, extract, or force from a place or position. Often used with *out.*

Other English-language labels are:

Australian	*Irish*
Canadian	*Scots*
Caribbean	*South African*

Dialect labels. When a word or sense is commonly used in a specific area of the United States and little used — even if known — in other areas, it has been given a dialect label.

> **bo•da•cious** also **bow•da•cious** (bō-dā′shəs) or **bar•da•cious** (bär-) *Southern & South Midland U.S.*

This Dictionary uses dialect labels singly and in various combinations ranging from the very general (*Regional*) to the very specific (*Cincinnati*). The very specific labels, which are self-explanatory, serve as descriptors of geographic regions such as cities, states, and interstate areas. For a list of these labels see page xxxi.

Cross-references

A cross-reference signals that additional information about one entry can be found at another entry. Cross-references have two main functions: to avoid needless duplication of information and to indicate where further discussion of a word occurs.

The entry referred to is printed in boldface type preceded by a brief descriptive or instructional phrase:

> **bade** (băd, bād) *v.* A p.t. of **bid.**

The cross-reference indicates that *bade* is a past tense at the entry *bid,* where further information about the entry can be found.

The word *See* is also used to introduce certain cross-references:

> **feath•er•edge** (fĕ*th*′ər-ĕj′) *n.* . . . **2.** See **deckle edge.**

A full definition is given at the entry referred to, in this case *deckle edge.*

A cross-reference referring to only one definition in an entry having two or more definitions contains that definition number:

> **tsar** (zär, tsär) *n.* Var. of **czar** 1.

Some cross-references refer to tables. The boldface term in the cross-reference is the entry at which the table can be found:

> **kro•na²** (krō′nə) *n., pl.* **-nor** (-nôr′, -nər). See table at **currency.**

> **lep•ton²** (lĕp′tŏn′) *n.* Any of a family of elementary particles that participate in the weak interaction, including the electron, the muon, and their associated neutrinos. See table at **subatomic particle.**

Order of Senses

Entries containing more than one sense are arranged for the convenience of contemporary dictionary users with the central and often the most commonly sought meanings first. Senses and subsenses are grouped to show their relationships with each other. For example, in the entry for *fatal* shown below, the commonly sought meaning "Causing or capable of causing death" appears first and the now obsolete sense "Having been destined; fated" comes last in the series of five:

> **fa•tal** (fāt′l) *adj.* **1.** Causing or capable of causing death. **2.** Causing ruin or destruction; disastrous. **3.** Of decisive importance; fateful. **4.** Concerned with or determining destiny. **5.** *Obsolete.* Having been destined; fated.

Division of senses. Boldface letters before senses indicate that two or more subsenses are closely related:

> **phe•nom•e•non** (fĭ-nŏm′ə-nŏn′, -nən) *n., pl.* **-na** (-nə). **1.** . . . **2.** *pl.* **-nons. a.** An unusual, significant, or unaccountable fact or occurrence; a marvel. **b.** A remarkable or outstanding person; a paragon. See Syns at **wonder.**

In a combined entry the senses are numbered in separate sequences after each part of speech:

> **ber•ry** (bĕr′ē) *n., pl.* **-ries. 1.a.** *Bot.* An indehiscent fruit derived from a single ovary and having the whole wall fleshy, such as the grape. **b.** A small, juicy, fleshy fruit, such as a raspberry, regardless of its botanical structure. **2.** The small dark egg of certain crustaceans or fishes. — *intr.v.* **-ried, -ry•ing, -ries. 1.** To hunt for or gather berries. **2.** To bear or produce berries.

Information applicable only to a particular sense or subsense is shown after the number or letter of that sense or subsense:

> **ra•dix** (rā′dĭks) *n.* . . . **1.** *Biol.* A root or point of origin. **2.** *Math.* The base of a system of numbers, such as 10 in the decimal system.

In this entry the subject label *Biology* applies only to the first sense; the subject label *Mathematics,* only to the second sense.

Labels and other information applicable to all senses in an entry with more than one part of speech appear before the first part of speech in that entry:

> **kedge** (kĕj) *Naut.* — *n.* A light anchor used to warp a vessel. — *v.* **kedged, kedg•ing, kedg•es.** — *tr.* To warp (a vessel) by using a light anchor. — *intr.* To move by using a light anchor.

The positioning of the label *Nautical* before the noun part-of-speech label, the first such label in the entry, indicates that *Nautical* applies to the entire combined entry — in this case, the noun and the verb.

Explanatory notes. Words whose meanings do not permit standard definitions have explanatory notes, beginning with *Used* or *Often used.* Words requiring notes of this kind include function words, interjections, intensives, some auxiliary verbs, and words labeled *Offensive* and *Offensive Slang.* An example is the explanatory note at the interjection *ugh:*

> Used to express horror, disgust, or repugnance.

Illustrative Examples

Illustrative examples, which follow the definitions and are set in italic type, show the entry words in typical contexts. Here is an instance of the use of a quoted illustration:

> **bloom¹** (blo͞om) *n.* . . . **3.** A fresh, rosy complexion: *"She was short, plump, and fair, with a fine bloom"* (Jane Austen).

Illustrative examples that are not direct quotations appear in entries such as the verb *speak*:

> **speak** (spēk) *v.* **spoke** (spōk), **spo•ken** (spō′kən), **speak•ing, speaks.** — *intr.* . . . **4.a.** To make a statement in writing: *The biography speaks of loneliness.*

Phrasal Verbs

A phrasal verb is an expression consisting of a verb and an adverb or a preposition with a unitary meaning that cannot be deduced from the sum total of the meanings of its constituent parts. Phrasal verbs, set in boldface type and introduced by the heading ***phrasal verbs,*** follow the main definitions and precede the idioms, if any are present. Phrasal verbs are listed in alphabetical order:

> **set**[1] (sĕt) *v.* **set, set•ting, sets.** — *tr.* **1.** To put in a specified position; place. . . . — ***phrasal verbs.*** **set about.** To begin or start. **set apart. 1.** To reserve for a specific use. **2.** To make noticeable. **set aside. 1.** To separate and reserve for a special purpose. **2.** To discard or reject. **3.** To declare invalid; annul or overrule. **set at.** To attack or assail. **set back. 1.** To slow down the progress of; hinder. **2.** *Informal.* To cost. **set by.** To reserve for future use.

Idioms

An idiom is an expression consisting of two or more words having a meaning that cannot be deduced from the sum total of the meanings of its constituent parts. Idioms, set in boldface type and introduced by the heading ***idioms,*** are fully defined in the last part of an entry. Idioms are listed in alphabetical order:

> **take** (tāk) *v.* **took** (to͝ok), **tak•en** (tā′kən), **tak•ing, takes.** — *tr.* **1.** To get into one's possession by force, skill, or artifice . . . — ***idioms.*** **on the take.** *Informal.* Taking or seeking to take bribes or illegal income. **take a bath.** *Informal.* To experience serious financial loss. **take account of.** To take into consideration. . . . **take it on the chin.** *Slang.* To endure punishment, suffering, or defeat. **take it or leave it.** To accept or reject unconditionally.

Etymologies

Etymologies appear in square brackets following the definitions. An etymology traces the history of a word from one language to another as far back in time as can be determined with reasonable certainty. The most recent stage before Modern English is given first, with each earlier stage following in sequence:

> **cab•in** (kăb′ĭn) *n.* **1.** A small, roughly built house. . . . [ME *caban* < OFr. *cabane* < OProv. *cabana* < LLat. *capanna.*]

A language name, linguistic form, and brief definition, or gloss, of that form are given for each stage of the derivation. In order to avoid redundancy, however, a language, form, or gloss is not repeated if it is identical to the corresponding item in the immediately preceding stage. In the example shown for *cabin,* the different Middle English, Old French, and Late Latin forms have the same gloss, which is the same as the first definition of the Modern English word *cabin*: "small, roughly built house."

Content of etymologies. The etymologies in this Dictionary are designed to be as readable as possible. The traditional language of descriptive grammar is used to identify parts of speech and various grammatical and morphological forms and processes, such as *diminutive, frequentative, variant, stem, past participle,* and *metathesis.* All of these terms are fully defined entries in the Dictionary. Likewise, every language that is cited in an etymology either is a Dictionary entry or is glossed in the etymology itself.

Sometimes a stage in the history of a word is not attested, yet there is reasonable certainty from comparative evidence about what the missing linguistic form looked like and what language it belonged to. These unattested forms are preceded by an asterisk indicating their hypothetical nature:

> **cer•tain** (sûr′tn) *adj.* **1.** Definite; fixed. **2.** Sure to come or happen; inevitable. **3.** Established beyond doubt or question; indisputable. . . . [ME < OFr. < VLat. **certānus* < Lat. *certus,* p.part. of *cernere,* to determine. See **krei-***.]

If a word is taken from the name of a person or place, such names are identified with pertinent information as to time or place. The etymology usually stops there, although a further etymology of the name itself is occasionally given.

Some words are not given etymologies. These include interjections, trademarks, and ethnic names that are Anglicizations of the group's name for itself. A large and important group of words not given explicit etymologies consists of compounds and derivatives, such as *sodium chloride, emergence,* and *euploid,* formed in English from words or word elements that are themselves entries in the Dictionary. If only a portion of an entry is used in an etymology, the unused portion of the entry is enclosed within parentheses:

> **bal•lis•to•car•di•o•gram** (bə-lĭs′tō-kär′dē-ə-grăm′) *n.* A recording made by a ballistocardiograph. [BALLIST(IC) + CARDIOGRAM.]

Derivatives such as *emergence,* from *emerge,* in which only the final vowel of one constituent has been deleted, are assumed to be sufficiently understandable not to need etymologies.

Indo-European roots. It is remarkable that the great bulk of the now vast vocabulary of English can be traced back to the reconstructed ancestral language called Proto-Indo-European. The etymologies in this Dictionary take many such words back to their earliest ascertainable origins either in Proto-Indo-European or in the prehistoric stage of one of its chief branches, such as Germanic or Celtic. Each word is traced back to its earliest documentary attestation in its own etymology, then cross-referred to the Appendix of Indo-European Roots found at the end of the Dictionary by a cross-reference like See **krei-***, as shown in the etymology of *certain.* An introductory essay by Professor Calvert Watkins discusses some of the cultural inferences that may be drawn from this material (see pages 1573–1579). Also included are an explanatory Guide to the Appendix (pages 1580–1581), a table of the principal sound correspondences, and a diagram of the Indo-European languages on the endpapers.

Style of etymologies. The etymologies present a great deal of complex information in a small space, and for this reason certain typographic and stylistic conventions are used. The symbol < indicates origin of any kind – by inheritance, borrowing, derivation, or composition. When a compound word is split into its component elements, a colon introduces these parts. Each element is traced in turn to its further origins. Parentheses enclose the further history of a part of a compound:

> **pseud•e•pig•ra•pha** (so͞o′dĭ-pĭg′rə-fə) *pl.n.* **1.** Spurious writings, esp. writings falsely attributed to biblical characters or times. . . . [Gk. < neut. pl. of *pseudepigraphos*, falsely ascribed : *pseudēs*, false; see PSEUDO– + *epigraphein*, to inscribe (*epi-*, epi- + *graphein*, to write; see **gerbh-***).]

At times it is necessary to cross-refer from one etymology to another, either to avoid repeating part of a lengthy and complex derivation or to indicate the close relationship between two different Modern English words:

> **bat**[3] (băt) *tr.v.* **bat•ted, bat•ting, bats.** To wink or flutter: *bat one's eyelashes.* [Prob. a var. of BATE[2].]

A word or word element in an etymology printed in small capitals is an entry in the Dictionary and should be referred to for more etymological information. Linguistic forms that are not Modern English words appear in italics, and glosses and language names appear in roman type.

The transliterations of Greek, Russian, Arabic, and Hebrew are shown at the Table of Alphabets on page xxxiii. Old English thorn (þ) and edh (ð) are both given as *th*, whereas Old Norse thorn is spelled as *th* and the phonemically distinct edh as *dh*. In Latin all long vowels are marked with macrons. Mandarin Chinese forms are given in the Pinyin system. The transcription of African and Native American languages occasionally requires the use of symbols – usually drawn from the International Phonetic Alphabet – whose values will be apparent to specialists but are not discussed here.

Undefined Forms

At the end of many entries additional boldface words appear without definitions – words either formed from the entry word by the addition of suffixes or otherwise closely and clearly related to the entry word or the entry word itself with a different part of speech. These *run-on entries* are related in basic meaning to the entry word but may have different grammatical functions, as indicated by their part-of-speech labels. Multisyllabic run-ons are divided into syllables and show primary and secondary stresses as needed. Pronunciations are included as required:

> **ex•cuse** (ĭk-skyo͞oz′) *tr.v.* . . . [ME *excusen* < OFr. *excuser* < Lat. *excūsāre* : *ex-*, ex- + *causa*, accusation; see CAUSE.] — **ex•cus′a•ble** *adj.* — **ex•cus′a•ble•ness** *n.* — **ex•cus′a•bly** *adv.* — **ex•cus′er** *n.*

Synonym Paragraphs

Synonyms of special interest are listed after the entry for the central word in the group. Synonym paragraphs are introduced by the heading ***Syns.*** There are two kinds of synonym paragraphs. The first consists of a group of undiscriminated, alphabetically ordered words sharing a single, irreducible meaning. Antonyms, if applicable, appear at the end of the paragraph, as seen at the entry for the adjective *close*:

> ***Syns:*** *close, immediate, near, nearby, nigh, proximate.* The central meaning shared by these adjectives is "not far from another in space, time, or relationship": *an airport close to town; her immediate family; his nearest relative; a nearby library; the nighest route; a proximate town.* **Ant:** *far.*

The second kind, exemplified at the adjective entry *curious*, consists of fully discriminated synonyms ordered in a way that reflects their interrelationship. A brief sentence explaining the initial point of comparison of the words is given, followed by explanations of connotations and varying shades of meaning:

> ***Syns:*** *curious, inquisitive, snoopy, nosy.* These adjectives apply to persons who show a marked desire for information or knowledge. *Curious* most often implies an avid desire to know or learn, though it can suggest prying: *a curious child. Inquisitive* frequently suggests excessive curiosity and the asking of many questions: *"Remember, no revolvers. The police are, I believe, proverbially inquisitive"* (Lord Dunsany). *Snoopy* suggests underhanded prying: *a snoopy neighbor. Nosy* implies impertinent curiosity likened to that of an animal using its nose to examine or probe: *He went through my mail in his nosy way.* See also Syns at **strange.**

In both kinds of paragraphs the synonyms are set in lightface italic type. Illustrative examples, many of them quoted, exemplify the use of the synonyms in context.

Synonym cross-references. Every synonym in a synonym paragraph is itself cross-referenced to that synonym paragraph. For instance, the word *inquisitive* is discussed in the synonym paragraph at the entry *curious*. Therefore, definition 1 of the entry *inquisitive* – the definition directly tied in with the synonym paragraph at *curious* – contains a cross-reference to the synonym paragraph at *curious*:

> **in•quis•i•tive** (ĭn-kwĭz′ĭ-tĭv) *adj.* **1.** Unduly curious and inquiring. See Syns at **curious.**

At times the entry word central to one synonym group is a synonym in a group of synonyms at another entry. Such is the case with the entry *curious*. At the end of the synonym paragraph at *curious*, a cross-reference directs you to another synonym paragraph at the entry *strange*.

Usage Notes

Usage Notes following many entries present important information and guidance on matters of grammar, diction, pronunciation, and registers and nuances of usage. For a discussion of usage and our Usage Panel, see Geoffrey Nunberg's essay on pages xvi–xxi.

Some Notes, such as the one at *finalize,* contain opinions of the Usage Panel:

> ***Usage Note:*** *Finalize* is frequently associated with the language of bureaucracy and so is objected to by many writers. The sentence *We will finalize plans for a class reunion* was unacceptable to 71 percent of the Usage Panel. A substitute can always be found from among *complete, conclude, make final,* and *put into final form.* See Usage Note at **-ize.**

An example of a Usage Note without an opinion of the Usage Panel is found at the entry *criterion*:

> ***Usage Note:*** Like the analogous etymological plurals *agenda* and *data, criteria* is widely used as a singular form. Unlike them, however, it is not yet acceptable in that use.

Usage Note cross-references. A Note containing information related to the content of another Note ends with a cross-reference:

> **well²** (wĕl) *adv.* **bet•ter** (bĕt′ər), **best** (bĕst).
> ***Usage Note:*** Used as an adjective applied to people, *well* usually refers to a state of health, whereas *good* has a much wider range of senses. . . .

If an entry without a Note is discussed in a Note elsewhere, that entry contains a cross-reference to the Note where a full discussion is to be found. For example, the Usage Note at the entry *-ess* is cross-referenced from the entry *stewardess*:

> **stew•ard•ess** (stōō′ər-dĭs, styōō′-) *n.* A woman flight attendant. See Usage Note at **-ess.**

Regional Notes

This Dictionary contains hundreds of words and meanings whose occurrence is restricted to certain areas of the United States. Some entries contain Regional Notes explaining in detail a point of dialect. For example, the word *dragonfly* is widespread in American English, but dialect terms for the insect abound. These dialect terms, listed at the entry for *dragonfly,* are discussed in the Regional Note at the end of the entry:

> **drag•on•fly** (drăg′ən-flī′) *n., pl.* **-flies.** Any of various insects of the order Odonata or suborder Anisoptera, having a long slender body and two pairs of net-veined wings. Also called regionally *darning needle, devil's darning needle, ear sewer, mosquito hawk, skeeter hawk, snake doctor, snake feeder, spindle.*
> ***Regional Note:*** Regional terms for the dragonfly are numerous, providing good evidence for dialect boundaries in the United States. The greatest variety of terms is to be found in the South, where the most widespread term is *snake doctor* (from a folk belief that dragonflies take care of snakes). The Midland equivalent is *snake feeder.* In the Lower South one hears *mosquito hawk* or, in the South Atlantic states, *skeeter hawk.* The imagery outside the South alludes to the insect's shape: Upper Northern speakers call it a *darning needle* or a *devil's darning needle*; those in Coastal New Jersey, a *spindle*; and Northern Californians, an *ear sewer.*

Regional Note cross-references. In the case of *snake doctor,* a term appropriately labeled to reflect its use in the South, the entry contains two cross-references — a "See" cross-reference directing the reader to the main entry at *dragonfly,* where the full definition and a list of synonymous terms are found, and a "Regional Note" cross-reference directing the reader to the Regional Note at *dragonfly* for full discussion of the distribution of these terms:

> **snake doctor** *n.* **1.** *Chiefly Southern U.S.* See **dragonfly.** See Regional Note at **dragonfly.**

Word Histories

In addition to etymologies, which necessarily contain information in a compressed form, this Dictionary provides word history paragraphs at some entries whose etymologies are of particular interest. In these paragraphs the bare facts of the etymology are expanded to give a fuller understanding of how important linguistic processes operate, how words move from one language to another, and how the history of an individual word can be related to historical and cultural developments.

> **al•li•ga•tor** (ăl′ĭ-gā′tər) *n.* . . . [Alteration of Sp. *el lagarto,* the lizard : *el,* the (< Lat. *ille,* that; see **al-¹***) + *lagarto,* lizard (< Lat. *lacertus*).]
> ***Word History:*** In *The Travailes of an Englishman,* published in 1568, Job Hortop says that "in this river we killed a monstrous Lagarto or Crocodile." This is the first recorded instance of *alligator* in English. *Alligator* comes to us from Spanish *el lagarto,* "the lizard," and was modified in pronunciation and form in several ways before taking on the form *alligator.* Such changes, referred to by linguists as taboo deformation, are not uncommon in a name for something that is feared. An interesting parallel case is Spanish *cocodrilo,* "crocodile," which shows a similar change in the position of the *r.* The earliest recorded form of *alligator* that is similar to ours appears in Shakespeare's *Romeo and Juliet* (First Folio, 1623): "In his needie shop a tortoyrs hung/An Allegater stuft."

Abbreviations and Labels Used in This Dictionary

Abbreviated Language Names Used in Etymologies

Afr.	Afrikaans
Am.E.	American English
Am.Sp.	American Spanish
AN	Anglo-Norman
Ar.	Arabic
Aram.	Aramaic
Balt.	Baltic
Brit.	British
Brit.E.	British English
Canadian Fr.	Canadian French
Celt.	Celtic
Chin.	Chinese
Dan.	Danish
Du.	Dutch
E.	English
Egypt.	Egyptian
Finn.	Finnish
Flem.	Flemish
Fr.	French
Gael.	Gaelic
Ger.	German
Gk.	Greek
Gmc.	Germanic
Goth.	Gothic
Heb.	Hebrew
HGer.	High German
Hung.	Hungarian
Icel.	Icelandic
IE	Indo-European
Ir.	Irish
Iran.	Iranian
Ir.Gael.	Irish Gaelic
Ital.	Italian
J.	Japanese
Lat.	Latin
LGer.	Low German
L.Gk.	Late Greek
LHeb.	Late Hebrew
Lith.	Lithuanian
LLat.	Late Latin
Louisiana Fr.	Louisiana French
MDu.	Middle Dutch
ME	Middle English
Med.Gk.	Medieval Greek
Med.Lat.	Medieval Latin
Mex. Sp.	Mexican Spanish
MFlem.	Middle Flemish
MHGer.	Middle High German
MIr.	Middle Irish
MLGer.	Middle Low German
Mod.E.	Modern English
Mod.Gk.	Modern Greek
Mod.Heb.	Modern Hebrew
Mod.Ir.	Modern Irish
MPers.	Middle Persian
N.Amer.Fr.	North American French
NHeb.	New Hebrew
NLat.	New Latin
Norman Fr.	Norman French
Norw.	Norwegian
ODan.	Old Danish
OE	Old English
OFr.	Old French
OHGer.	Old High German
OIcel.	Old Icelandic
OIr.	Old Irish
OIran.	Old Iranian
OItal.	Old Italian
OLat.	Old Latin
ON	Old Norse
ONFr.	Old North French
OPers.	Old Persian
OPort.	Old Portuguese
OProv.	Old Provençal
ORuss.	Old Russian
OSpan.	Old Spanish
OSwed.	Old Swedish
Penn. Dutch	Pennsylvania Dutch
Pers.	Persian
Pidgin E.	Pidgin English
Pol.	Polish
Port.	Portuguese
Prov.	Provençal
Rom.	Romanian
Russ.	Russian
Sc.	Scots
Scand.	Scandinavian
Sc. Gael.	Scottish Gaelic
Skt.	Sanskrit
Slav.	Slavic
Sp.	Spanish

Swed.	Swedish
Turk.	Turkish
VLat.	Vulgar Latin

Other Abbreviations and Symbols Used in This Dictionary

abbr.	abbreviation
adj.	adjective
adv.	adverb
approx.	approximately
aug.	augmentative
cent.	century, centuries
comp.	comparative
conj.	conjunction
dial.	dialectal
dim.	dimunitive
esp.	especially
ety.	etymology
fem.	feminine
freq.	frequentative
fut.	future
imit.	imitative
imper.	imperative
indic.	indicative
interj.	interjection
intr.	intransitive
M	Middle
masc.	masculine
Med.	Medieval
Mod.	Modern
n.	noun
naut.	nautical
neut.	neuter
O	Old
orig.	origin
p.	past
part.	participle, participial
p.part.	past participle
p.t.	past tense
perh.	perhaps
pers.	person
pl.	plural
pl.n.	plural noun
poss.	possibly
pr.	present
pr.part.	present participle
pr.t.	present tense
pref.	prefix
prep.	preposition
prob.	probably
pron.	pronoun
redup.	reduplication
sing.	singular
St.	Saint
suff.	suffix
superl.	superlative
t.	tense
tr.	transitive
transl.	translation
ult.	ultimately
usu.	usually
v.	verb
var.	variant, variants
*	unattested
<	derived from
+	combined with
?	Origin unknown

Field Labels

Accounting.	
Acoustics.	
Aerospace.	
Anat.	Anatomy
Anthro.	Anthropology
Archaeol.	Archaeology
Archit.	Architecture
Astron.	Astronomy
Astrophys.	Astrophysics
Baseball.	
Basketball.	
Bible.	
Biochem.	Biochemistry
Biol.	Biology
Bot.	Botany
Buddhism.	
Bus.	Business
Chem.	Chemistry
Christian Sci.	Christian Science
Color.	
Commerce.	
Comp. Sci.	Computer Science
Cytology.	
Dentistry.	
Eastern Orthodox Ch.	Eastern Orthodox Church
Eccles.	Ecclesiastical
Ecol.	Ecology
Econ.	Economics
Elect.	Electricity
Electron.	Electronics
Embryol.	Embryology
Engineering.	
Football.	
Games.	
Genet.	Genetics
Geog.	Geography
Geol.	Geology
Gram.	Grammar
Gk. Myth.	Greek Mythology
Gk. & Rom. Myth.	Greek and Roman Mythology
Her.	Heraldry
Hinduism.	
Immun.	Immunology

Islam.	
Judaism.	
Law.	
Ling.	Linguistics
Logic.	
Math.	Mathematics
Med.	Medicine
Metall.	Metallurgy
Meteorol.	Meteorology
Microbiol.	Microbiology
Mineral.	Mineralogy
Mormon Ch.	Mormon Church
Mus.	Music
Myth.	Mythology
Naut.	Nautical
Paleontol.	Paleontology
Pathol.	Pathology
Pharm.	Pharmacology
Philos.	Philosophy
Phys.	Physics
Physiol.	Physiology
Print.	Printing
Psychiat.	Psychiatry
Psychol.	Psychology
Rom. Cath. Ch.	Roman Catholic Church
Rom. Myth.	Roman Mythology
Sports.	
Statistics.	
Theol.	Theology
Vet. Medic.	Veterinary Medicine
Zool.	Zoology

Regional Labels

Major areas of distribution. Major, generalized areas of dialect distribution are labeled as follows and can occur in any number of combinations:

Northern U.S. From New Jersey and Pennsylvania north to New England and west to Washington and Oregon

Southern U.S. From southern Maryland along the coastal plains of Virginia, North and South Carolina, Georgia, Florida, Alabama, Mississippi, and Louisiana to eastern Texas and also including the "Upper South" as defined in the section "Midwestern and Midland"

Eastern U.S. The Atlantic states from Maine to Florida, also including Vermont, New Hampshire, and upstate New York

Western U.S. West of the 100th parallel, which extends southward from the Dakotas to western Oklahoma and Texas.

Subcategories of distribution. Within the major areas are these subcategories, the labels for which also can occur in various combinations:

New England. Maine, New Hampshire, Vermont, Massachusetts, Connecticut, and Rhode Island

Northeastern U.S. New England, New York State, Pennsylvania, and New Jersey

Upper Northern or *Inland Northern U.S.* Western upstate New York; northwest Pennsylvania; northern Ohio, Indiana, and Illinois; Michigan; Wisconsin; and Minnesota

Lower Northern or *North Midland U.S.* Southern New Jersey and Pennsylvania; northern Delaware, Maryland, and West Virginia; Ohio; Indiana; Illinois; Iowa; and Nebraska

Upper Midwest Minnesota, Iowa, North and South Dakota, and Nebraska

Northwestern U.S. or *Pacific Northwest* Washington, Oregon, Idaho, Montana, and Wyoming

Southeastern U.S. North and South Carolina, Georgia, Florida, Tennessee, Alabama, and Mississippi

Upper Southern or *South Midland U.S.* Southern Delaware, Maryland, West Virginia, Ohio, Indiana, and Illinois; western Virginia and North Carolina; northern Georgia, Alabama, Mississippi, and Louisiana; Tennessee; Kentucky; Arkansas; and eastern Oklahoma

Lower Southern U.S. Florida, Georgia, Alabama, Mississippi, Louisiana, and eastern Texas

Eastern Lower Southern or *South Atlantic U.S.* North and South Carolina, Georgia, and Florida

Central Atlantic U.S. Delaware; Washington, D.C.; eastern Virginia, Maryland, and Pennsylvania; and southern New Jersey

North Atlantic Coast Maine, Massachusetts, Rhode Island, Connecticut, southeast New York State, and northern New Jersey

Southwestern U.S. Oklahoma, Texas, New Mexico, Arizona, and southern California

Midwestern and Midland. In addition to the labels just described, two labels are used that overlap with but lie outside the overall scheme. *Midwestern U.S.* designates regional terms that occur throughout the area from Michigan westward to the Dakotas and from Ohio westward to Kansas, an area that includes parts of several dialect areas. *Midland U.S.*, a term previously used in American dialect geography, includes the *Lower North* and the *Upper South*. The collective label *Midland* is distinguished from *Midwestern*, which does not include the South.

Gullah. The label *Gullah* refers not to a region but to the distinctive dialect of English spoken by American Black people who lived on the coast and coastal islands of Georgia, South Carolina, and northern Florida.

Pronunciation

The pronunciation enclosed in parentheses follows the boldface entry word. If an entry word and a variant to that entry word have the same pronunciation, the pronunciation follows the variant. If the variant or variants do not have the same pronunciation as the entry word, pronunciations follow the forms to which they apply. Differing or variant pronunciations are given whenever necessary. If an entry or a variant requires more than one pronunciation, subsequent pronunciations show only those syllables that are different in sound quality or stress from the first pronunciation or that are necessary for clarity.

Pronunciation symbols. The symbols in this dictionary enable you to produce a satisfactory pronunciation with no more than a quick reference to the key. All pronunciations given here are acceptable in all circumstances. When more than one pronunciation is given, the first is assumed to be the most common, but the difference in frequency may be insignificant.

A list of the pronunciation symbols used in this Dictionary is given here in the column headed **SYMBOLS.** The column headed **EXAMPLES** contains words chosen to illustrate how the symbols are pronounced. The letters that correspond in sound to the symbols are shown in boldface. The nonalphabetical symbol (ə) is called a *schwa.* It is used in this Dictionary to represent a reduced vowel, a vowel that receives the weakest level of stress within a word. The schwa sound varies, sometimes according to the vowel it is representing and often according to the sounds surrounding it:

sis•ter (sĭs′tər)

a•bun•dant (ə-bŭn′dənt)

For most words a single set of symbols can represent the pronunciation found in each regional variety of American English. You will supply those features of your own regional speech that are called forth by the pronunciation key in this Dictionary. The pronunciations are exclusively those of educated speech.

Stress. The relative emphasis with which the syllables of a word or phrase are spoken, called *stress,* is indicated in three different ways. The strongest, or primary, stress is marked with a bold mark (**′**). An intermediate, or secondary, level of stress is marked with a similar but lighter mark (′). The weakest stress is unmarked. Words of one syllable show no stress mark.

Symbols	Examples
ă	pat
ā	pay
âr	care
ä	father
b	bib
ch	church
d	deed, milled
ĕ	pet
ē	bee
f	fife, phase, rough
g	gag
h	hat
hw	which
ĭ	pit
ī	pie, by

Symbols	Examples
îr	pier
j	judge
k	kick, cat, pique
l	lid, needle* (nēd′l)
m	mum
n	no, sudden* (sŭd′n)
ng	thing
ŏ	pot
ō	toe
ô	caught, paw, for, horrid, hoarse**
oi	noise
o͝o	took
o͞o	boot
ou	out

Symbols	Examples
p	pop
r	roar
s	sauce
sh	ship, dish
t	tight, stopped
th	thin
th	this
ŭ	cut
ûr	urge, term, firm, word, heard
v	valve
w	with
y	yes
z	zebra, xylem

Symbols	Examples
zh	vision, pleasure garage
ə	about, item, edible gallop, circus
ər	butter

Foreign

Symbols	Examples
œ	*French* feu *German* schön
ü	*French* tu *German* über
KH	*German* ich *Scottish* loch
N	*French* bon

*In English the consonants *l* and *n* often constitute complete syllables by themselves.

Regional pronunciations of *-or-* vary. In pairs such as **for, four; horse, hoarse; and **morning; mourning,** the vowel varies between (ô) and (ō). In this Dictionary these vowels are represented as follows: **for** (fôr), **four** (fôr, fōr); **horse** (hôrs), **hoarse** (hôrs, hōrs); and **morning** (môr′ning), **mourning** (môr′ning, mōr′-). A similar variant occurs in words such as **coral, forest,** and **horrid,** where the pronunciation of *o* before *r* varies between (ô) and (ŏ): **forest** (fôr′ĭst, fŏr′-).

Table of Alphabets

Because it is more convenient to use a single system of spelling to represent the speech sounds of many different languages, words from languages that use other writing systems are usually transliterated into Roman characters. The transliterations shown here are those used in the etymologies in this Dictionary for four of the most important non-Roman alphabets. The names of the Hebrew and Greek letters are also entered and defined in the Dictionary as English nouns. (In some cases the English spelling differs from the transliterated letter name shown here, chiefly in the absence of diacritical marks—for example English **omega** versus Greek **ōmega**.) The Cyrillic letters shown are those used in modern Russian. For the history of the English alphabet, see "Development of the Alphabet" overleaf.

HEBREW

FORMS	NAME	SOUND
א	'aleph	'
ב	bēth	b
ג	gimel	g
ד	dāleth	d
ה	hē	h
ו	vāv, wāw	w
ז	zayin	z
ח	ḥeth	ḥ
ט	ṭeth	ṭ
י	yodh	y
ך כ	kāph	k
ל	lāmedh	l
ם מ	mēm	m
ן נ	nūn	n
ס	samekh	s
ע	'ayin	'
ף פ	pē	p
ץ צ	ṣadhe	ṣ
ק	qōph	q
ר	rēsh	r
שׂ	sin	ś
שׁ	shin	š
ת	tāv, tāw	t

ARABIC

FORMS 1	2	3	4	NAME	SOUND
ا	ـا			'alif	'
ب	ـب	ـبـ	بـ	bā	b
ت	ـت	ـتـ	تـ	tā	t
ث	ـث	ـثـ	ثـ	thā	ṯ
ج	ـج	ـجـ	جـ	jīm	j
ح	ـح	ـحـ	حـ	ḥā	ḥ
خ	ـخ	ـخـ	خـ	khā	ḫ
د	ـد			dāl	d
ذ	ـذ			dhāl	ḏ
ر	ـر			rā	r
ز	ـز			zāy	z
س	ـس	ـسـ	سـ	sīn	s
ش	ـش	ـشـ	شـ	shīn	š
ص	ـص	ـصـ	صـ	ṣād	ṣ
ض	ـض	ـضـ	ضـ	ḍād	ḍ
ط	ـط	ـطـ	طـ	ṭā	ṭ
ظ	ـظ	ـظـ	ظـ	ẓā	ẓ
ع	ـع	ـعـ	عـ	'ayn	'
غ	ـغ	ـغـ	غـ	ghayn	ḡ
ف	ـف	ـفـ	فـ	fā	f
ق	ـق	ـقـ	قـ	qāf	q
ك	ـك	ـكـ	كـ	kāf	k
ل	ـل	ـلـ	لـ	lām	l
م	ـم	ـمـ	مـ	mīm	m
ن	ـن	ـنـ	نـ	nūn	n
ه	ـه	ـهـ	هـ	hā	h
و	ـو			wāw	w
ى	ـى	ـيـ	يـ	yā	y

GREEK

FORMS	NAME	SOUND
Α α	alpha	a
Β β	beta	b
Γ γ	gamma	g (n)
Δ δ	delta	d
Ε ϵ	epsilon	e
Ζ ζ	zēta	z
Η η	ēta	ē
Θ θ	thēta	th
Ι ι	iota	i
Κ κ	kappa	k
Λ λ	lambda	l
Μ μ	mu	m
Ν ν	nu	n
Ξ ξ	xi	x
Ο ο	omicron	o
Π π	pi	p
Ρ ρ	rhō	r (rh)
Σ σ	sigma	s
Τ τ	tau	t
Υ υ	upsilon	u
Φ φ	phi	ph
Χ χ	chi, khi	kh
Ψ ψ	psi	ps
Ω ω	ōmega	ō

CYRILLIC

FORMS	SOUND
А а	a
Б б	b
В в	v
Г г	g
Д д	d
Е е Ё ё	e, ё[1]
Ж ж	zh
З з	z
И и Й й	i, ĭ
К к	k
Л л	l
М м	m
Н н	n
О о	o
П п	p
Р р	r
С с	s
Т т	t
У у	u
Ф ф	f
Х х	kh
Ц ц	ts
Ч ч	ch
Ш ш	sh
Щ щ	shch
Ъ ъ	”[2]
Ы ы	y
Ь ь	’[3]
Э э	e
Ю ю	yu
Я я	ya

Vowels are not represented in normal Hebrew writing, but for certain purposes they are indicated by a system of subscript and superscript dots. The transliterations with subscript dots are pharyngeal consonants as in Arabic. The second forms shown are used when the letter falls at the end of a word.

The different forms in the four numbered columns are used when the letters are in: 1. isolation; 2. juncture with a previous letter; 3. juncture with letters on both sides; 4. juncture with a following letter.

Long vowels are represented by the consonants *'alif* (for *ā*), *wāw* (for *ū*), and *yā* (for *ī*). Short vowels are not usually written; they can, however, be indicated by the following signs: ʹ*fatha* (for *a*), ͵ *kesra* (for *i*), and ʼ *damma* (for *u*).

Transliterations with subscript dots represent "emphatic" or pharyngeal consonants, which are pronounced in the usual way except that the pharynx is tightly narrowed during articulation. When two dots are placed over the *hā*, the new letter thus formed is called *tā marbūta*, and is pronounced (t).

There are several other diacritical marks indicating such situations as the doubling of a consonant or the elision of a vowel.

The superscript ʽ on an initial vowel or *rhō* represents aspiration or "rough breathing," and is transliterated by h. Lack of aspiration on an initial vowel is indicated by the superscript ʼ, called the smooth breathing. When *gamma* precedes *kappa, xi, khi*, or another *gamma*, it has the value *n* and is so transliterated. The second lowercase form of *sigma* is used only in final position.

[1]The variant *ё* occurs only in stressed position, and is pronounced as a very short (ô) or (yô).

[2]This letter, called the "hard sign," is very rare in modern Russian. It indicates that the previous consonant remains hard even when followed by a front vowel.

[3]This letter, called the "soft sign," indicates that the previous consonant is palatalized even when a front vowel does not follow.

DEVELOPMENT OF THE ALPHABET

In early forms of writing such as hieroglyphics, pictorial signs represented whole words or syllables. By around 1500 B.C. the Canaanites, a Semitic-speaking people living in ancient Palestine and Syria, began to use such signs to stand for individual speech sounds, writing them from right to left. A version of this alphabet was adopted by their successors the Phoenicians, who simplified the forms and added several new ones. Trade with the Phoenicians brought the alphabet to the early Greeks, who reassigned some of the semitic consonant symbols to vowel sounds such as a, e, ē, and o. The Greeks also split the Semitic *wāw* into two letters, *wau* (later called *digamma*, "double gamma," whose sound [w] was lost in classical Greek but whose form survives in modern F) and *u* (later *u psilon*, "simple u"), the ancestor of modern U, V, W, and Y.

In Italy, a western variant of the Greek alphabet was adopted by the Etruscans. Our modern letters derive from the Romans, who adapted the Etruscan script for monumental inscriptions and wrote from left to right. Because Etruscan writing did not distinguish between the sounds of *c* and *g*, the Romans created the new letter G by adding a stroke to C. The classical Greek Y and Z were added to represent the sounds ü and z in words borrowed from Greek. The English alphabet reached its total of 26 letters only after medieval scribes added *w* (originally written *uu*) and Renaissance printers separated the variant pairs *i/j* and *u/v*.

During the Middle Ages, the Roman capitals evolved into uncials and then to Carolingian minuscules and Italic cursive script, which are the prototypes of many modern printed and handwritten letters.

PROTO-CANAANITE	SEMITIC NAMES	SEMITIC SOUNDS	PHOENICIAN	EARLY GREEK	GREEK NAMES	GREEK SOUNDS	ETRUSCAN	CLASSICAL ROMAN	UNCIAL	CAROLINGIAN MINUSCULE	ITALIC CURSIVE	MODERN PRINTED	MODERN SCRIPT
C. 1500 B.C.			C. 1000 B.C.	C. 800 B.C.			C. 500 B.C.		300-700	800	1400		
	'aleph 'ox'	[']			alpha	[a]		A	A	a	a	A a	Aa
	bēth 'house'	[b]			bēta	[b]		B	B	b	b	B b	Bb
	gaml, gīmel 'camel'	[g]			gamma	[g]		C	C	c	c	C c	Cc
	dag 'fish' dāleth 'door'	[d]			delta	[d]		D	D	d	d	D d	Dd
	hē	[h]			e (psilon)	[ĕ]		E	E	e	e	E e	Ee
	wāw	[w]			wau, digamma	[w]		F	F	f	f	F f	Ff
	zayin	[z]			zēta	[z]		G	G	g	g	G g	Gg
	hēth	[ḥ]			ēta	[h, ē]		H	h	h	h	H h	Hh
	yōdh 'arm'	[y]			iōta	[i,y]		I	I	i	i	I i	Ii
									J	j	j	J j	Jj
	kaph 'hand'	[k]			kappa	[k]		K	K	k	k	K k	Kk
	lāmedh	[l]			lambda	[l]		L	L	l	l	L l	Ll
	mēm 'water'	[m]			mu	[m]		M	m	m	m	M m	Mm
	naḥš 'snake' nūn 'fish'	[n]			nu	[n]		N	N	n	n	N n	Nn
	samekh	[s]			xi	[ks]	X						
	'ayin 'eye'	[']			o (micron)	[ŏ]		O	O	o	o	O o	Oo
	pē	[p]			pi	[p]		P	P	p	p	P p	Pp
	qōph	[q]			koppa	[q]		Q	q	q	q	Q q	Qq
	rōsh, rēsh 'head'	[r]			rhō	[r]		R	R	r	r	R r	Rr
	thann 'bow' shin 'tooth'	[th, š]			sigma	[s]		S	S	ſ	s	S s	Ss
	tāw 'mark'	[t]			tau	[t]		T	T	t	t	T t	Tt
											u	U u	Uu
					u (psilon)	[ü, w]		V	U	u	v	V v	Vv
											w	W w	Ww
								X	X	x	x	X x	Xx
								Y	Y	y	y	Y y	Yy
								Z	Z	z	z	Z z	Zz

A a

a[1] or **A** (ā) *n., pl.* **a's** or **A's. 1.** The first letter of the modern English alphabet. **2.** Any of the speech sounds represented by the letter *a.* **3.** The first in a series. **4.** The best or highest in quality or rank: *grade A milk.* **5.** Something shaped like the letter A. **6.** *Mus.* **a.** The sixth tone in the scale of C major or the first tone in the relative minor scale. **b.** A key or scale in which A is the tonic. **7. A.** One of four types of blood in the ABO system.

a[2] (ə; ā *when stressed*) *indef.art.* **1.** Used before nouns and noun phrases that denote a single but unspecified person or thing: *a region.* **2.** Used before terms that denote number, amount, quantity, or degree: *only a few of the voters; a bit more rest.* **3.a.** Used before a proper name to denote a type or a member of a class: *the wisdom of a Socrates.* **b.** Used before a mass noun to indicate a single type or example: *a dry wine.* **4.** The same: *birds of a feather.* **5.** Any: *not a drop to drink.* [ME, var. of *an,* an. See AN[1].]

Usage Note: In modern written English, the form *a* is used before a word beginning with a consonant sound, however it may be spelled (*a frog, a university*). The form *an* is used before a word beginning with a vowel sound (*an orange, an hour*). At one time *an* was an acceptable alternative before words beginning with a consonant sound but spelled with a vowel (*an one*), but this usage is now obsolete. • *An* was also once a common variant before words beginning with *h* in which the first syllable was unstressed; thus 18th-century authors wrote either *a historical* or *an historical* but *a history,* not *an history.* Nowadays the use of *an* before *h* survives primarily before the words *historical* and *historic.*

a[3] (ə) *prep.* In every; to each; per: *once a month; one dollar a pound.* [ME < OE *an,* in. See ON.]

a[4] (ə) *aux.v. Informal.* Have: *He'd a come if he could.* [ME, alteration of *haven,* to have. See HAVE.]

a[5] *abbr.* **1.** Also **a.** Absent. **2.** *Phys.* Acceleration. **3.** Also **a.** Are (measurement).

A *abbr.* **1.** Also **a.** or **A.** Acre. **2.** Ammeter. **3.** Ampere. **4.** Or **Å.** Angstrom. **5.** Also **a.** or **A.** Area.

a. *abbr.* **1.** About. **2.** Acreage. **3.** Acting. **4.** Adjective. **5.** Afternoon. **6.** Also **A.** Amateur. **7.** *Lat.* Anno (in the year). **8.** *Lat.* Annus (year). **9.** Anode. **10.** Anonymous. **11.** Also **A.** Answer. **12.** *Lat.* Ante (before). **13.** Anterior.

A. *abbr.* **1.** Academy. **2.** *Mus.* Alto. **3.** America; American.

a–[1] or **an–** *pref.* Without; not: *amoral.* [Gk. See **ne*.**]

a–[2] *pref.* **1.** On; in: *abed.* **2.** In the act of: *aborning.* **3.** In the direction of: *astern.* **4.** In a specified state or condition: *abuzz.* [ME < OE < *an,* on. See ON.]

A1C *abbr.* Airman first class.

AA *abbr.* **1.** Alcoholics Anonymous. **2.** Antiaircraft.

A.A. *abbr.* Associate in Arts.

AAA *abbr.* **1.** Agricultural Adjustment Administration. **2.** American Automobile Association. **3.** Antiaircraft artillery.

AAAL *abbr.* American Academy of Arts and Letters.

AAAS *abbr.* American Association for the Advancement of Science.

Aa•chen (ä′kən, ä′KHən) also **Aix-la-Cha•pelle** (āks′lä-shə-pĕl′, ĕks′-). A city of W Germany near the Belgian and Dutch borders. Pop. 239,801.

aah (ä) *interj.* Used to express pleasure, satisfaction, surprise, or great joy. **—aah** *v. & n.*

Aal•borg (ôl′bôrg′). See **Ålborg.**

Aalst (älst) also **A•lost** (ä-lôst′). A city of W-central Belgium WNW of Brussels; cap. of Austrian Flanders in the 18th cent. Pop. 78,068.

Aal•to (äl′tô), **Alvar.** 1898–1976. Finnish architect and furniture designer noted for his use of contrasting materials.

A and R *abbr.* Artists and repertory.

AAPSS *abbr.* American Academy of Political and Social Sciences.

AAR *abbr.* Against all risks.

aard•vark (ärd′värk′) *n.* A burrowing mammal *(Orycteropus afer)* of southern Africa, having a stocky, hairy body, large ears, and a long tubular snout. [Obsolete Afr. : *aarde,* earth (< MDu. *aerde;* see **er-[2]***) + *vark,* pig (< MDu. *varken;* see **porko-***).]

aard•wolf (ärd′wo͝olf′) *n.* A mammal *(Proteles cristatus)* native to southern and eastern Africa that resembles the hyena and feeds mainly on termites and insect larvae. [Afr. : *aarde,* earth (< MDu. *aerde;* see **er-[2]***) + *wolf,* wolf (< MDu.; see **wl̥kʷo-***).]

Aa•re (är′ə) or **Aar** (är). A river of central and N Switzerland flowing c. 295 km (183 mi) to the Rhine R.

Aar•hus (ôr′ho͞os′). See **Århus.**

Aar•on (âr′ən, ăr′-). In the Bible, the elder brother of Moses who helped lead the Hebrews out of Egypt.

Aaron, Henry ("Hank") Louis. b. 1934. Amer. baseball player who retired (1976) with a total of 755 home runs.

Aa•ron•ic (â-rŏn′ĭk, ă-rŏn′-) also **Aa•ron•i•cal** (-ĭ-kəl) *adj.* **1.** Of, having to do with, or characteristic of Aaron. **2.** *Mormon Ch.* Of or having to do with the lower order of priests.

Aa•ron's rod (âr′ənz, ăr′-) *n. Archit.* A rod-shaped molding decorated with a design of leaves, scrolls, or a twined serpent.

A.A.S. *abbr.* Associate in Applied Sciences.

AAU *abbr.* Amateur Athletic Union.

AAUP *abbr.* American Association of University Professors.

AAUW *abbr.* American Association of University Women.

Ab (ăb, äv, ôv) *n.* Var. of **Av.**

AB[1] (ā′bē′) *n.* One of four types of blood in the ABO system.

AB[2] *abbr.* **1.** Airman basic. **2.** Alberta.

ab. *abbr.* About.

A.B. *abbr.* **1.** Also **a.b.** Able-bodied seaman. **2.** *Lat.* Artium Baccalaureus (Bachelor of Arts).

ab–[1] *pref.* Away from: *aboral.* [Lat. See **apo-*.**]

ab–[2] *pref.* Used to indicate an electromagnetic unit in the centimeter-gram-second system: *abcoulomb.* [< ABSOLUTE.]

aardwolf
Proteles cristatus

a•ba (ə-bä′, ä′bə) *n.* **1.** A fabric woven of the hair of camels or goats. **2.** A loose-fitting sleeveless garment made of this fabric, traditionally worn by Arabs. [Ar. *'abā'.*]

A•ba (ä′bə). A city of SE Nigeria WNW of Lagos. Pop. 210,700.

ABA *abbr.* **1.** Abscisic acid. **2.** American Bankers Association. **3.** Also **A.B.A.** American Bar Association. **4.** American Booksellers Association.

ab•a•ca also **ab•a•cá** (ăb′ə-kä′) *n.* **1.** A bananalike plant *(Musa textilis)* native to the Philippines. **2.** The fibers obtained from the stalks of this plant. [Sp. *abacá* < Tagalog *abaká.*]

a•back (ə-băk′) *adv.* **1.** By surprise. **2.** *New England & Southern U.S.* Behind: *aback of the house.* **3.** *Upper Southern U.S.* Ago: *several years aback.* **4.** *Naut.* In such a way that the wind pushes against the forward side of a sail or sails. **5.** *Archaic.* Back; backward. **—***adj. New England.* Being at a standstill; unable to move: *"You run your business that way and first thing you know you're all aback"* (Dialect Notes).

A•ba•co and Cays (ăb′ə-kō′; kēz, kāz). An island group in the Atlantic Ocean E of S FL.

ab•a•cus (ăb′ə-kəs, ə-băk′əs) *n., pl.* **ab•a•cus•es** or **ab•a•ci** (ăb′ə-sī′, ə-băk′ī′). **1.** A computing device consisting of a frame holding parallel rods strung with movable counters. **2.** *Archit.* A slab on the top of the capital of a column. [ME < Lat. < Gk. *abax, abak-,* counting board, prob. < Heb. *'ābāq,* dust.]

abacus

Ab•a•dan (ä′bə-dän′, ăb′ə-dăn′). A city of SW Iran on **Abadan Island** at the head of the Persian Gulf. Pop. 296,081.

a•baft (ə-băft′) *prep. Naut.* Toward the stern from. [ME *on baft: on,* at; see ON + *baft,* to the rear (< OE *beæftan,* behind : *be,* by, at; see **ambhi*** + *æftan,* behind; see **apo-***).]

A•ba•kan (ä′bə-kän′). A city of S-central Russia ESE of Novosibirsk on the Yenisei R. Pop. 147,000.

ab•a•lo•ne (ăb′ə-lō′nē, ăb′ə-lō′-) *n.* Any of various large, edible marine gastropods of the genus *Haliotis,* having an ear-shaped shell with a row of holes along the outer edge and a pearly interior. [Am.Sp. *abulón.*]

ab•am•pere (ăb-ăm′pîr′) *n.* The centimeter-gram-second electromagnetic unit of current equal to ten amperes.

a•ban•don (ə-băn′dən) *tr.v.* **-doned, -don•ing, -dons. 1.** To withdraw one's support or help from, esp. in spite of duty; desert. **2.** To give up by leaving or ceasing to operate or inhabit, esp. as a result of danger: *abandoned the ship.* **3.** To surrender one's claim to, right to, or interest in; give up entirely. See Syns at **relinquish. 4.** To cease trying to continue; desist from: *abandoned the search.* **5.** To yield (oneself) completely, as to emotion. **—***n.* **1.** Unbounded enthusiasm; exuberance. **2.** A complete surrender of inhibitions. [ME *abandounen* < OFr. *abandoner* < *a bandon: a,* at (< Lat. *ad;* see

ă pat	oi boy
ā pay	ou out
âr care	o͝o took
ä father	o͞o boot
ĕ pet	ŭ cut
ē be	ûr urge
ĭ pit	th thin
ī pie	*th* this
îr pier	hw which
ŏ pot	zh vision
ō toe	ə about,
ô paw	item

Stress marks:
′ (primary);
′ (secondary), as in
dictionary (dĭk′sh-

AD–) + *bandon*, control; see **bhā-[2]***.] — **a•ban′don•ment** *n.*

a•ban•doned (ə-băn′dənd) *adj.* **1.** Deserted; forsaken. **2.** Exuberantly enthusiastic. **3.** Recklessly unrestrained.

ab•ap•i•cal (ăb-ăp′ĭ-kəl, -ā′pĭ-) *adj.* Being opposite to or directed away from the apex.

a•base (ə-bās′) *tr.v.* **a•based, a•bas•ing, a•bas•es.** To lower in rank, prestige, or esteem. See Syns at **degrade.** [ME *abassen* < OFr. *abaissier*: Lat. *ad-*, ad– + VLat. **bassiāre*(< Med. Lat. *bassus*, low).] — **a•base′ment** *n.*

a•bash (ə-băsh′) *tr.v.* **a•bashed, a•bash•ing, a•bash•es.** To make ashamed or uneasy; disconcert. [ME *abaishen*, to lose one's composure < OFr. *esbahir*, *esbahiss-* : *es-*, intensive pref. (< Lat. *ex-*; see EX–) + *baer*, to gape; see BAY[2].] — **a•bash′ment** *n.*

a•ba•sia (ə-bā′zhə) *n.* Impaired muscular coordination in walking. [A–[1] + Gk. *basis*, step; see **gʷā-*** + –IA[1].]

a•bate (ə-bāt′) *v.* **a•bat•ed, a•bat•ing, a•bates.** — *tr.* **1.** To reduce in amount, degree, or intensity; lessen. See Syns at **decrease. 2.** To deduct from an amount; subtract. **3.** *Law.* **a.** To put an end to. **b.** To make void. — *intr.* **1.** To fall off in degree or intensity; subside. **2.** *Law.* To become void. [ME *abaten* < OFr. *abattre*, to beat down : *a-*, to (< Lat. *ad-*; see AD–) + *batre*, to beat; see BATTER[1].]

a•bate•ment (ə-bāt′mənt) *n.* **1.** Diminution in degree or intensity; moderation. **2.** The amount lowered; a reduction.

ab•at•toir (ăb′ə-twär′) *n.* **1.** A slaughterhouse. **2.** Something likened to a slaughterhouse. [Fr. < *abattre*, to strike down < OFr. See ABATE.]

ab•ax•i•al (ăb-ăk′sē-əl) *adj. Biol.* Located away from or on the opposite side of the axis, as of an organ or organism.

abb. *abbr.* **1.** Abbess. **2.** Abbey. **3.** Abbot.

Ab•ba (ăb′ə, ä′bə) *n.* **1.** *Bible.* In the New Testament, God. **2. abba.** Used as a title of honor for bishops and patriarchs in some Christian churches of Egypt, Syria, and Ethiopia. [ME < LLat. *abbā* < Gk. *abba.* See ABBOT.]

ab•ba•cy (ăb′ə-sē) *n., pl.* **-cies.** The office, term, or jurisdiction of an abbot. [ME *abbatie* < LLat. *abbātia* < *abbās*, *abbāt-*, abbot. See ABBOT.]

Ab•bas•side also **Ab•bas•sid** (ăb′ə-sīd′, ə-băs′īd′). An Arabic dynasty (750–1258) named for al-Abbas (566?–652), paternal uncle of Muhammad.

ab•ba•tial (ə-bā′shəl) *adj.* Of or having to do with an abbey, abbot, or abbess. [ME *abbacyal* < LLat. *abbātiālis* < *abbās*, *abbāt-*, abbot. See ABBOT.]

ab•bé (ă-bā′, ă-bā′) *n. Rom. Cath. Ch.* **1.** Used as a title for the superior of a monastery in a French-speaking area. **2.** Used as a title for a cleric in major or minor orders in a French-speaking area. [Fr. < OFr. *abbe* < LLat. *abbās*, abbot. See ABBOT.]

ab•bess (ăb′ĭs) *n.* **1.** The superior of a convent. **2.** Used as a title for such a person. [ME *abesse* < OFr. < LLat. *abbātissa* < *abbās*, *abbāt-*, abbot. See ABBOT.]

Ab•be•vil•li•an (ăb′ə-vĭl′ē-ən) *adj.* Of or relating to the earliest Paleolithic archaeological sites in Europe, characterized by bifacial stone hand axes. [After *Abbeville*, a city of N France.]

ab•bey (ăb′ē) *n., pl.* **-beys. 1.** A monastery supervised by an abbot. **2.** A convent supervised by an abbess. **3.** A church that is or once was part of a monastery or convent. [ME < OFr. *abaie* < LLat. *abbātia.* See ABBACY.]

ab•bot (ăb′ət) *n.* **1.** The superior of a monastery. **2.** Used as a title for such a person. [ME *abbod* < OE < LLat. *abbās*, *abbāt-* < Gk. *abbā* < Aram. *abbā*, father.]

Ab•bot (ăb′ət), **Charles Greeley.** 1872–1973. Amer. astrophysicist noted for his pioneering study of solar radiation.

Ab•bott (ăb′ət), **Berenice.** 1898–1991. Amer. photographer known esp. for her black-and-white portraits of New York City.

Abbott, Grace. 1878–1939. Amer. social reformer noted for her opposition to child labor.

Abbott, Sir **John Joseph Caldwell.** 1821–93. Canadian politician who served as prime minister (1891–92).

Abbott, Lyman. 1835–1922. Amer. Congregational cleric, writer, and editor.

Abbott, Robert Sengstacke. 1868–1940. Amer. newspaper publisher who founded and edited (1905–40) the *Chicago Defender.*

Abbott, William ("Bud"). 1898–1974. Amer. comedian noted for his partnership with Lou Costello.

abbr. or **abbrev.** *abbr.* Abbreviation.

ab•bre•vi•ate (ə-brē′vē-āt′) *tr.v.* **-at•ed, -at•ing, -ates. 1.** To make shorter. **2.** To reduce (a word or phrase) to a shorter form intended to represent the full form. [ME *abbreviaten* < LLat. *abbreviāre*, *abbreviāt-* : *ab-*(var. of *ad-*, ad-) + *breviāre*, to shorten (< *brevis*, short; see **mregh-u-***).] — **ab•bre′vi•a′tor** *n.*

ab•bre•vi•a•tion (ə-brē′vē-ā′shən) *n.* **1.** The act or product of shortening. **2.** A shortened form of a word or phrase used chiefly in writing, such as *USMC* for *United States Marine Corps.* **3.** *Mus.* Any of various symbols used in notation to indicate that a series of notes is to be repeated.

ABC (ā′bē-sē′) *n., pl.* **ABC's. 1.** The alphabet. Often used in the plural. **2. ABC's.** The rudiments of reading and writing.

ab•cou•lomb (ăb-ko͞o′lŏm′, -lōm′) *n.* The centimeter-gram-second electromagnetic unit of charge, equal to ten coulombs.

ABC soil *n.* Soil in which three distinct layers can be seen in vertical section.

ABD (ā′bē-dē′) *n.* A candidate for a doctorate who has completed all requirements except the dissertation. [*a(ll) b(ut) d(issertation).*]

Ab•di•as (ăb-dī′əs). See **Obadiah** 1.

ab•di•cate (ăb′dĭ-kāt′) *v.* **-cat•ed, -cat•ing, -cates.** — *tr.* To relinquish (power or responsibility) formally. — *intr.* To relinquish formally a high office or responsibility. [Lat. *abdīcāre*, *abdīcāt-*, to disclaim : *ab-*, away; see AB–[1] + *dīcāre*, to proclaim; see **deik-***.] — **ab′di•ca•ble** (-kə-bəl) *adj.* — **ab′di•ca′tion** *n.* — **ab′di•ca′tor** *n.*

ab•do•men (ăb′də-mən, ăb-dō′mən) *n.* **1.** The part of the body that lies between the thorax and the pelvis and encloses the stomach, intestines, liver, spleen, and pancreas. **2.** The posterior segment of the body in arthropods. [Lat. *abdōmen*, belly.] — **ab•dom′i•nal** (ăb-dŏm′ə-nəl) *adj.* — **ab•dom′i•nal•ly** *adv.*

ab•du•cens (ăb-do͞o′sənz, -dyo͞o′-) *n., pl.* **ab•du•cen•tes** (ăb′do͞o-sĕn′tēz′, -dyo͞o-). Either of the sixth pair of cranial nerves that convey motor impulses to the rectus muscle on the lateral side of each eye. [< Lat. *abdūcēns*, pr.part. of *abdūcere*, to take away. See ABDUCT.]

ab•duct (ăb-dŭkt′) *tr.v.* **-duct•ed, -duct•ing, -ducts. 1.** To carry off by force; kidnap. **2.** *Physiol.* To draw away from the midline of the body or from an adjacent part or limb. [Lat. *abdūcere*, *abduct-* : *ab-*, away; see AB–[1] + *dūcere*, to lead; see **deuk-***.] — **ab•duc′tion** *n.*

ab•duc•tor (ăb-dŭk′tər) *n.* **1.** One, such as a kidnapper, that abducts. **2.** *Anat.* A muscle that draws a body part, such as a finger, away from the midline of the body or of an extremity.

Ab•dul-A•ziz (ăb′do͝ol-ä-zēz′). 1830–76. Turkish sultan (1861–76) whose absolutist rule led to his deposition.

Ab•dul Ha•mid II (ăb′do͝ol hä-mēd′, -mĭt′). 1842–1918. Turkish sultan (1876–1909) whose autocratic rule led to revolts by the Young Turks.

Ab•dul-Jab•bar (ăb-do͝ol′jə-bär′), **Kareem.** Lew Alcindor. b. 1947. Amer. basketball player and all-time leading scorer in the National Basketball Association.

Ab•dul•lah ibn-Hu•sein (ăb′do͞o-lä′ ĭb′n-ho͞o-sān′). 1882–1951. Transjordanian emir (1921–46) and first king of independent Jordan (1946–51).

Ab•dul-Me•djid I also **Ab•dul-Me•jid I** (ăb′do͝ol-mĕ-jēd′, -jĭt′). 1823–61. Turkish sultan (1839–61) whose extravagances contributed to the financial ruin of Turkey.

a•beam (ə-bēm′) *adv. Naut.* At right angles to the fore-and-aft line of a ship.

a•be•ce•dar•i•an (ā′bē-sē-dâr′ē-ən) *n.* **1.** One who teaches or studies the alphabet. **2.** One who is just learning; a beginner. — *adj.* **1.** Having to do with the alphabet. **2.** Being arranged alphabetically. **3.** Elementary or rudimentary. [ME < Med.Lat. *abecedārium*, alphabet < LLat. *abecedārius*, alphabetical : from the names of the letters A B C D + *-ārius*, -ary.]

a•bed (ə-bĕd′) *adv.* In bed.

A•bed•ne•go (ə-bĕd′nĭ-gō′). In the Bible, a young man who emerged unharmed from the fiery furnace of Babylon.

A•bel (ā′bəl). In the Bible, the son of Adam and Eve who was slain by his elder brother, Cain.

Abel, Sir **Frederick Augustus.** 1827–1902. British chemist who invented cordite (1889) with Sir James Dewar.

Ab•e•lard (ăb′ə-lärd′) also **A•bé•lard** (ä-bā-lär′), **Peter** or **Pierre.** 1079–1142. French theologian and philosopher whose application of the principles of ancient Greek logic to the doctrines of the medieval Catholic Church led to charges of heresy.

a•bele (ə-bēl′) *n.* See **white poplar.** [Du. *abeel* < OFr. *aubel* < Med.Lat. *albellus*, dim. of Latin *albus*, white. See **albho-***.]

a•bel•mosk (ā′bəl-mŏsk′) *n.* A hairy annual or biennial plant *(Abelmoschus moschatus)* native to tropical Asia and having yellow flowers with crimson centers. [NLat. *abelmoschus* < Ar. *ḥabbalmusk*, grain of musk : *ḥabb*, grain + *musk*, musk (< Pers. *mušk*; see MUSK).]

Ab•e•na•ki (ä′bə-nä′kē, ăb′ə-năk′ē) or **Ab•na•ki** (ăb-nä′kē, ăb-) *n., pl.* **Abenaki** or **-kis** or **Abnaki** or **-kis. 1.** A member of any of various Native American peoples formerly inhabiting northern New England and southeast Canada, with present-day populations in Maine and southern Quebec. **2.** A member of a confederacy of Abenaki and other peoples formed in the mid-18th century in opposition to the Iroquois confederacy and the English colonists. **3.** Either or both of the two Eastern Algonquian languages of the Abenaki peoples.

ABEND *abbr. Comp. Sci.* Abnormal end of task.

A•be•o•ku•ta (ăb′ē-ō-ko͞o′tə). A city of SW Nigeria N of Lagos. Pop. 301,000.

Ab•er•deen (ăb′ər-dēn′). **1.** (*also* ăb′ər-dēn′). A city of NE Scotland on the North Sea. Pop. 212,542. **2.** A city of NE SD NE of Pierre. Pop. 24,927. **3.** A city of W WA WSW of Tacoma. Pop. 16,565.

Aberdeen An•gus (ăng′gəs) *n.* A breed of black, hornless beef

Kareem Abdul-Jabbar

abelmosk
Abelmoschus moschatus

Aberdeen Angus

cattle that originated in Scotland. [After *Aberdeen* and *Angus*, former counties of Scotland.]

Ab•er•nath•y (ăb′ər-năth′ē), **Ralph David.** 1926–90. Amer. civil rights leader who was president (1968–77) of the Southern Christian Leadership Conference.

ab•er•rant (ă-bĕr′ənt, ăb′ər-) *adj.* **1.** Deviating from the proper or expected course. **2.** Deviating from what is normal; untrue to type. [Lat. *aberrāns, aberrant-*, pr.part. of *aberrāre*, to go astray. See ABERRATION.] **—ab•er′rance, ab•er′ran•cy** *n.* **—ab•er′rant•ly** *adv.*

ab•er•ra•tion (ăb′ə-rā′shən) *n.* **1.** A deviation from the proper or expected course. **2.** A departure from the normal or typical. **3.** *Psychol.* A disorder or abnormal alteration in one's mental state. **4.a.** A defect of focus, such as blurring in an image. **b.** A physical defect in an optical element, as in a lens, that causes such an imperfection. **5.** *Astron.* The apparent displacement of the position of a celestial body in the direction of motion of an observer on Earth, caused by the motion of Earth and the finite velocity of light. **6.** *Genet.* A deviation in the normal structure or number of chromosomes in an organism. [Lat. *aberrātiō, aberrātiōn-*, diversion < *aberrātus*, p.part. of *aberrāre*, to go astray : *ab-*, away from; see AB-[1] + *errāre*, to stray; see **ers-*.**]

a•bet (ə-bĕt′) *tr.v.* **a•bet•ted, a•bet•ting, a•bets. 1.** To approve, encourage, and support (an action or a plan of action); urge and help on. **2.** To urge, encourage, or help (a person). [ME *abetten* < OFr. *abeter*, to entice : *a-*, to (< Lat. *ad-*; see AD-) + *beter*, to bait; see **bheid-*.**] **—a•bet′ment** *n.* **—a•bet′tor, a•bet′ter** *n.*

ab ex•tra (ăb ĕk′strə) *adv.* From without. [Lat. *ab extrā*: *ab*, from + *extrā*, outside.]

a•bey•ance (ə-bā′əns) *n.* The condition of being temporarily set aside; suspension. [AN, var. of OFr. *abeance*, desire < *abaer*, to gape at : *a-*, at (< Lat. *ad-*; see AD-) + *baer*, to gape; see BAY[2].] **—a•bey′ant** *adj.*

ab•far•ad (ăb-făr′ăd′, -əd) *n.* The centimeter-gram-second electromagnetic unit of capacitance, equal to one billion farads.

ab•hen•ry (ăb-hĕn′rē) *n., pl.* **-ries.** The centimeter-gram-second electromagnetic unit of inductance, equal to one billionth of a henry.

ab•hor (ăb-hôr′) *tr.v.* **-horred, -hor•ring, -hors. 1.** To regard with horror or loathing; abominate. **2.** To reject vehemently; shun. [ME *abhorren* < Lat. *abhorrēre*, to shrink from : *ab-*, from; see AB-[1] + *horrēre*, to shudder.] **—ab•hor′rer** *n.*

ab•hor•rence (ăb-hôr′əns, -hŏr′-) *n.* **1.** One that is disgusting or loathsome. **2.** A feeling of repugnance or loathing.

ab•hor•rent (ăb-hôr′ənt, -hŏr′-) *adj.* **1.** Disgusting, loathsome, or repellent. **2.** Feeling repugnance or loathing. **3.** *Archaic.* Being strongly opposed. **—ab•hor′rent•ly** *adv.*

A•bib (ä-vēv′) *n.* The seventh month of the year in the Hebrew calendar, corresponding to Nisan. [Heb. *'ābîb*, spring.]

a•bid•ance (ə-bīd′ns) *n.* **1.** The act or condition of abiding; continuance. **2.** Adherence; compliance.

a•bide (ə-bīd′) *v.* **a•bode** (ə-bōd′) or **a•bid•ed, a•bid•ing, a•bides.** —*tr.* **1.** To put up with; tolerate: *can't abide delays.* See Syns at **bear[1]. 2.** To wait patiently for. **3.** To be in store for; await. **4.** To withstand. —*intr.* **1.** To remain in a place. **2.** To continue to be sure or firm; endure. See Syns at **stay[1]. 3.** To dwell or sojourn. **—*idiom.* abide by.** To conform to; comply with. [ME *abiden* < OE *ābīdan*: *ā-*, intensive pref. + *bīdan*, to remain; see **bheidh-*.**] **—a•bid′er** *n.*

a•bid•ing (ə-bī′dĭng) *adj.* Lasting for a long time; enduring: *an abiding love of music.* **—a•bid′ing•ly** *adv.*

Ab•i•djan (ăb′ĭ-jän′). The cap. of Ivory Coast, in the S part on the Gulf of Guinea. Pop. 1,500,000.

ab•i•et•ic acid (ăb′ē-ĕt′ĭk) *n.* A yellowish resinous powder, $C_{19}H_{29}COOH$, isolated from rosin and used in lacquers, varnishes, and soaps. [< Lat. *abiēs, abiet-*, silver fir.]

Ab•i•gail (ăb′ĭ-gāl′). In the Bible, the wife of David.

Ab•i•lene (ăb′ə-lēn′). A city of W-central Texas WSW of Fort Worth; founded 1881. Pop. 106,654.

a•bil•i•ty (ə-bĭl′ĭ-tē) *n., pl.* **-ties. 1.** The quality of being able to do something; the physical, mental, financial, or legal power to perform. **2.** A natural or acquired skill or talent. [ME *abilite* < OFr. *habilite* < Lat. *habilitās* < *habilis*, handy. See ABLE.]

-ability or **-ibility** *suff.* Ability, inclination, or suitability for a specified action or condition: *teachability.* [ME *-abilitie* < OFr. *-abilite* < Lat. *-ābilitās* < *-ābilis*, -able.]

ab in•i•ti•o (ăb′ ĭ-nĭsh′ē-ō′) *adv.* From the beginning. [Lat. *ab initiō*: *ab*, from + *initiō*, ablative of *initium*, beginning.]

ab in•tra (ăb ĭn′trə) *adv.* From within. [Lat. *ab intrā*: *ab*, from + *intrā*, within.]

a•bi•o•gen•e•sis (ā′bī-ō-jĕn′ĭ-sĭs) *n.* The supposed development of living organisms from nonliving matter. **—a′bi•o•ge•net′ic** (-jə-nĕt′ĭk), **a′bi•o•ge•net′i•cal** *adj.* **—a′bi•og′e•nist** (-ŏj′ə-nĭst) *n.*

a•bi•o•gen•ic (ā′bī-ō-jĕn′ĭk) *adj.* Not produced by living organisms. **—a′bi•o•gen′i•cal•ly** *adv.*

a•bi•o•log•i•cal (ā′bī-ə-lŏj′ĭ-kəl) *adj.* Not associated with or derived from living organisms. **—a′bi•o•log′i•cal•ly** *adv.*

a•bi•ot•ic (ā′bī-ŏt′ĭk) *adj.* Nonliving. **—a•bi•o′sis** (-ō′sĭs) *n.* **—a•bi•ot′ic•al•ly** *adv.*

Ab•i•tib•i Lake (ăb′ĭ-tĭb′ē). A lake of E Ontario and SW Quebec, Canada; source of the **Abitibi River,** which flows c. 370 km (230 mi) to an arm of James Bay.

ab•ject (ăb′jĕkt′, ăb-jĕkt′) *adj.* **1.** Brought low in condition or status. **2.** Being of the most contemptible kind: *abject cowardice.* **3.** Being of the most miserable kind; wretched: *abject poverty.* [ME, outcast < Lat. *abiectus*, p.part. of *abicere*, to cast away : *ab-*, from; see AB-[1] + *iacere*, to throw; see **yē-*.**] **—ab′ject′ly** *adv.* **—ab•ject′ness, ab•jec′tion** *n.*

ab•jure (ăb-jo͝or′) *tr.v.* **-jured, -jur•ing, -jures. 1.** To renounce under oath; forswear. **2.** To recant solemnly; repudiate: *abjure one's beliefs.* **3.** To give up (an action or practice, for example); abstain from. [ME *abjuren* < OFr. *abjurer* < Lat. *abiūrāre*: *ab-*, away; see AB-[1] + *iūrāre*, to swear; see **yewes-*.**] **—ab′ju•ra′tion** *n.* **—ab•jur′er** *n.*

abl. *abbr.* Ablative (grammar).

ab•late (ă-blāt′) *v.* **-lat•ed, -lat•ing, -lates.** —*tr.* To remove by erosion, melting, evaporation, or vaporization. —*intr.* To become ablated. [Back-formation < ABLATION.]

ab•la•tion (ă-blā′shən) *n.* **1.** Surgical excision or amputation of a body part or tissue. **2.** The erosive processes by which a glacier is reduced. **3.** *Aerospace.* The dissipation of heat generated by aerodynamic friction. [LLat. *ablātiō, ablātiōn-* < Lat. *ablātus*, p.part. of *auferre*, to carry away : *ab-*, away; see AB-[1] + *lātus*, carried; see **telə-*.**]

ab•la•tive[1] (ăb′lə-tĭv) *adj.* Of, relating to, or being a grammatical case indicating separation, direction away from, sometimes manner or agency, and the object of certain verbs. —*n.* **1.** The ablative case. **2.** A word in this case. [ME < Lat. *ablātīvus* < *ablātus*, carried away. See ABLATION.]

ab•la•tive[2] (ă-blā′tĭv) *adj.* **1.** Of, relating to, or capable of ablation. **2.** Tending to ablate. [< ABLATION.]

ab•la•tive absolute (ăb′lə-tĭv) *n.* In Latin grammar, an adverbial phrase syntactically independent from the rest of the sentence and containing a noun plus a participle, an adjective, or a noun, both in the ablative case.

ab•laut (äb′lout′, äp′-) *n.* A vowel change, characteristic of Indo-European languages, that accompanies a change in grammatical function. [Ger. : *ab*, off (< MHGer. < OHGer. *aba*; see **apo-***) + *Laut*, sound (< MHGer. *lūt* < OHGer. *hlūt*; see **kleu-***).]

a•blaze (ə-blāz′) *adj.* **1.** Being on fire. **2.** Radiant with bright color: *a maple tree ablaze in autumn.* **—a•blaze′** *adv.*

a•ble (ā′bəl) *adj.* **a•bler, a•blest. 1.** Having sufficient ability or resources. **2.** Especially capable or talented. [ME < OFr. < Lat. *habilis* < *habēre*, to handle. See **ghabh-*.**] **—a′bly** (ā′blē) *adv.*

Usage Note: The construction *able to* ascribes to its subject the ability to accomplish the action expressed in its complement: *The troupe was able to get a grant for the project from a large corporation.* One should avoid using *able to* with passive constructions involving forms of the verb *be*, as in *The problem was able to be solved*, since this sentence ascribes no capacity or ability to the problem itself. In such cases *can* or *could* can usually be substituted: *The problem could be solved.* By contrast, passives with *get* ascribe a more active role to their subjects, and here the *able to* construction can be used: *He was able to get himself accepted by a top law school.*

-able or **-ible** *suff.* **1.** Susceptible to, capable of, or worthy of a specified action: *debatable.* **2.** Inclined or given to a specified state or action: *changeable.* [ME < OFr. < Lat. *-ābilis*: *-ā-*and *-i-*, thematic vowels + *-bilis*, adj. suff.]

a•ble-bod•ied (ā′bəl-bŏd′ēd) *adj.* Physically strong and healthy.

able-bodied seaman *n.* A merchant seaman certified for all seaman's duties.

a•bloom (ə-blo͞om′) *adj.* Being in bloom; flowering.

ab•lu•tion (ə-blo͞o′shən, ă-blo͞o′-) *n.* **1.** A washing or cleansing of the body. **2.** The liquid so used. [ME *ablucioun* < Lat. *ablūtiō, ablūtiōn-* < *ablūtus*, p.part. of *abluere*, to wash away : *ab-*, away; see AB-[1] + *-luere*, to wash; see **leu(ə)-*.**] **—ab•lu′tion•ar′y** (-shə-nĕr′ē) *adj.*

ABM (ā′bē-ĕm′) *n.* See **antiballistic missile.**

abn *abbr.* Airborne.

Ab•na•ki (äb-nä′kē, ăb-) *n.* Var. of **Abenaki.**

ab•ne•gate (ăb′nĭ-gāt′) *tr.v.* **-gat•ed, -gat•ing, -gates. 1.** To give up (rights or a claim, for example); renounce. **2.** To deny (something) to oneself. [Lat. *abnegāre, abnegāt-*, to refuse : *ab-*, away; see AB-[1] + *negāre*, to deny; see **ne*.**] **—ab′ne•ga′tor** *n.*

ab•ne•ga•tion (ăb′nĭ-gā′shən) *n.* Self-denial.

ab•nor•mal (ăb-nôr′məl) *adj.* Not usual or regular; not normal; deviant. [Alteration (influenced by AB-[1]) of obsolete *anormal* < Med.Lat. *anormālis*, blend of LLat. *abnormis* (Lat. *ab-*, away from; see AB-[1] + Lat. *norma*, rule; see **gnō-***) and *anōmalus*; see ANOMALOUS.] **—ab•nor′mal•ly** *adv.*

ab•nor•mal•i•ty (ăb′nôr-măl′ĭ-tē) *n., pl.* **-ties. 1.** The condition of not being normal. **2.** A phenomenon or occurrence that is not normal.

abnormal psychology *n.* Psychopathology.

ă pat · ā pay · âr care · ä father · ĕ pet · ē be · ĭ pit · ī pie · îr pier · ŏ pot · ō toe · ô paw
oi boy · ou out · o͝o took · o͞o boot · ŭ cut · ûr urge · th thin · *th* this · hw which · zh vision · ə about, item

Stress marks:
′ (primary);
′ (secondary), as in dictionary (dĭk′shə-nĕr′ē)

Ab•o or **ab•o** (ăb′ō) *n., pl.* **-os.** *Offensive Slang.* Used as a disparaging term for an Australian aborigine.

a•board (ə-bôrd′, ə-bōrd′) *adv.* **1.** On board a passenger vehicle. **2.** In or into a group, organization, or business. **3.** *Baseball.* On base. —*prep.* On board of; on; in. [ME *abord*: *a-*, on; see A-^{2} + *bord*, ship (< OE *bord*).]

a•bode (ə-bōd′) *v.* A p.t. and p.part. of **abide.** —*n.* **1.** A dwelling place; a home. **2.** The act of abiding; a sojourn. [ME *abod*, home < *abiden*, to wait. See ABIDE.]

ab•ohm (ă-bōm′) *n.* The centimeter-gram-second electromagnetic unit of resistance, equal to one billionth of an ohm.

a•bol•ish (ə-bŏl′ĭsh) *tr.v.* **-ished, -ish•ing, -ish•es. 1.** To do away with; annul. **2.** To destroy completely. [ME *abolisshen* < OFr. *abolir*, *aboliss-* < Lat. *abolēre*. See **al-^{2}*.**] —**a•bol′ish•a•ble** *adj.* —**a•bol′ish•er** *n.* —**a•bol′ish•ment** *n.*

ab•o•li•tion (ăb′ə-lĭsh′ən) *n.* **1.** The act of doing away with or the state of being done away with; annulment. **2.** Abolishment of slavery. [Lat. *abolitiō*, *abolitiōn-* < *abolitus*, p.part. of *abolēre*, to abolish. See ABOLISH.] —**ab′o•li′tion•ar′y** (-lĭsh′ə-nĕr′ē) *adj.*

ab•o•li•tion•ism (ăb′ə-lĭsh′ə-nĭz′əm) *n.* Advocacy of the abolition of slavery. —**ab′o•li′tion•ist** *n.*

ab•o•ma•sum (ăb′ō-mā′səm) *n., pl.* **-sa** (-sə). The fourth division of the stomach in ruminant animals, in which digestion takes place. —**ab′o•ma′sal** (-səl) *adj.*

A-bomb (ā′bŏm′) *n.* See **atom bomb** 1.

a•bom•i•na•ble (ə-bŏm′ə-nə-bəl) *adj.* **1.** Unequivocally detestable; loathsome. **2.** Thoroughly unpleasant or disagreeable. [ME *abhominable* < OFr. < Lat. *abōminābilis* < *abōminārī*, to abhor. See ABOMINATE.] —**a•bom′i•na•bly** *adv.*

abominable snowman *n.* A hairy humanlike animal reportedly inhabiting the high Himalaya Mountains.

a•bom•i•nate (ə-bŏm′ə-nāt′) *tr.v.* **-nat•ed, -nat•ing, -nates.** To detest thoroughly; abhor. [Lat. *abōminārī*, *abōmināt-*, to deprecate as a bad omen : *ab-*, away; see AB-^{1} + *ōmen*, omen.] —**a•bom′i•na′tor** *n.*

a•bom•i•na•tion (ə-bŏm′ə-nā′shən) *n.* **1.** Abhorrence; disgust. **2.** A cause of abhorrence or disgust.

ab•o•ral (ă-bôr′əl, ăb-ōr′-) *adj.* Located opposite to or away from the mouth.

ab•o•rig•i•nal (ăb′ə-rĭj′ə-nəl) *adj.* **1.** Having existed in a region from the beginning. **2.** Of or relating to aborigines. —*n.* An aborigine. —**ab′o•rig′i•nal•ly** *adv.*

abracadabra

ab•o•rig•i•ne (ăb′ə-rĭj′ə-nē) *n.* **1.** A member of the indigenous or earliest known population of a region. **2. aborigines.** The flora and fauna native to a geographic area. [< Lat. *aborīgines*, orig.al inhabitants : *ab-*, from; see AB-^{1} + *orīgine*, ablative of *orīgō*, beginning; see ORIGIN.]

a•born•ing (ə-bôr′nĭng) *adv.* While coming into being or getting under way.

a•bort (ə-bôrt′) *v.* **a•bort•ed, a•bort•ing, a•borts.** —*intr.* **1.** To give birth before the embryo or fetus is capable of surviving on its own; miscarry. **2.** To cease growth before full development or maturation. **3.** To terminate an operation or procedure before completion. —*tr.* **1.a.** To cause to terminate pregnancy prematurely, before the embryo or fetus is viable. **b.** To cause the expulsion of (a nonviable embryo or fetus). **2.** To interfere with the development of; conclude prematurely: *abort plans for a corporate takeover.* **3.** To terminate before completion: *abort a takeoff.* **4.** To stop the progress of (a disease, for example). —*n.* **1.** The act of terminating an operation or procedure before completion. **2.** *Comp. Sci.* A procedure to terminate execution of a program when an unrecoverable error or malfunction occurs. [Lat. *abortāre*, freq. of *aborīrī*, *abort-*, to disappear, miscarry : *ab-*, away; see AB-^{1} + *orīrī*, to appear; see **er-^{1}*.**]

a•bor•ti•fa•cient (ə-bôr′tə-fā′shənt) *adj.* Causing abortion. —*n.* A substance or device used to induce abortion.

a•bor•tion (ə-bôr′shən) *n.* **1.** Induced termination of pregnancy and expulsion of an embryo or fetus that is incapable of survival. **2.** A miscarriage. **3.** Cessation of normal growth, esp. of a body part, prior to full development or maturation. **4.** An aborted organism. **5.** Something malformed or incompletely developed; a monstrosity.

a•bor•tion•ist (ə-bôr′shə-nĭst) *n.* One who performs abortions.

a•bor•tive (ə-bôr′tĭv) *adj.* **1.** Failing to accomplish an intended objective; fruitless. **2.** *Biol.* Partially or imperfectly developed. —**a•bor′tive•ly** *adv.* —**a•bor′tive•ness** *n.*

ABO system *n.* A classification system for human blood that identifies four major blood types, A, B, AB, and O, based on the presence or absence of two antigens, A and B, on red blood cells.

a•bou•li•a (ə-bo͞o′lē-ə, ə-byo͞o′-) *n.* Var. of **abulia.**

a•bound (ə-bound′) *intr.v.* **a•bound•ed, a•bound•ing, a•bounds. 1.** To be great in number or amount. **2.** To be fully supplied or filled. See Syns at **teem^1.** [ME *abounden* < OFr. *abonder* < Lat. *abundāre*, to overflow : *ab-*, away; see AB-^{1} + *undāre*, to flow (< *unda*, wave; see **wed-^{1}***).]

a•bout (ə-bout′) *adv.* **1.** Approximately; nearly: *about an hour.* **2.** Almost: *The job is about done.* **3.** To a reversed position or direction. **4.** In no particular direction: *wandering about.* **5.** All around; on every side: *look about for help.* **6.** In the area or vicinity; near: *spoke to spectators standing about.* **7.** In succession; one after another: *Turn about is fair play.* —*prep.* **1.** On all sides of; surrounding. **2.** In the vicinity of; around: *explored the streams about the estate.* **3.** Almost the same as; close to; near. **4.a.** In reference to; relating to; concerned with: *a book about snakes.* **b.** In the act or process of: *While you're about it, please clean your room.* **5.** In the possession or innate character of: *Keep your wits about you.* **6.a.** Ready or prepared to do something: *The chorus is about to sing.* **b.** Used with a negative to indicate strong intention. —*adj.* **1.** Moving here and there; astir: *The patient is up and about.* **2.** Being in evidence or existence: *Rumors are about concerning his resignation.* [ME < OE *onbūtan*: *on*, in; see ON + *būtan*, outside; see **ud-*.**]

a•bout-face (ə-bout′fās′) *n.* **1.a.** The act of pivoting to face in the opposite direction from the original. **b.** A military command to turn clockwise 180°. **2.** A total change of attitude or viewpoint. —**a•bout′-face′** *v.*

a•bove (ə-bŭv′) *adv.* **1.** On high; overhead: *the clouds above.* **2.** In heaven; heavenward. **3.a.** Upstairs: *in the dining room above.* **b.** To a degree that is over zero: *15° above.* **4.** In or to a higher place. **5.** In an earlier part of a given text. **6.** In or to a higher rank or position: *the ranks of major and above.* —*prep.* **1.** Over or higher than. **2.** Superior to in rank, position, or number; greater than: *put principles above expediency.* **3.** Beyond the level or reach of: *heard above the music.* **4.** In preference to. **5.** Too honorable to bend to: *above petty intrigue.* **6.** More than: *above normal temperature.* —*n. Usage Problem.* An earlier part of a given text. —*adj.* Appearing earlier in the same text: *the above interpretation.* [ME *aboven* < OE *abufan*: *a-*, on; see A-^{2} + *būfan*, above; see **upo*.**]

Usage Note: In general writing the use of *above* as an adjective in referring to a preceding text (*the above figures*) was accepted by a majority of the Usage Panel in an earlier survey, but its use as a noun (*read the above*) was accepted by only a minority. These uses are most common in business and legal writing.

above all *adv.* Over and above all other considerations.

a•bove•board (ə-bŭv′bôrd′, -bōrd′) *adv. & adj.* Without deceit or trickery; straightforward in manner. [Originally a gambling term referring to the fact that a gambler could not engage in trickery when the hands were above the gaming table.]

a•bove•ground (ə-bŭv′ground′) *adj.* **1.** Situated on or above the surface of the ground. **2.** Operating or existing within the establishment or in accordance with conventional standards: *the aboveground press.* —**a•bove′ground′** *adv.*

abp. or **Abp.** *abbr.* Archbishop.

abr. *abbr.* **1.** Abridged. **2.** Abridgment.

ab•ra•ca•dab•ra (ăb′rə-kə-dăb′rə) *n.* **1.** A magical charm or incantation having the power to ward off disease or disaster. **2.** Foolish or unintelligible talk. [LLat., magical formula.]

a•brad•ant (ə-brād′nt) *n.* An abrasive. —*adj.* Abrasive.

a•brade (ə-brād′) *tr.v.* **a•brad•ed, a•brad•ing, a•brades. 1.** To wear down or rub away by friction; erode. **2.** To make weary through constant irritation; wear down spiritually. [Lat. *abrādere*, to scrape off : *ab-*, away; see AB-^{1} + *rādere*, to scrape; see **rēd-*.**]

A•bra•ham (ā′brə-hăm′). In the Bible, the first patriarch and progenitor of the Hebrew people.

ab•ra•sion (ə-brā′zhən) *n.* **1.** The process of wearing down or rubbing away by means of friction. **2.a.** A scraped or worn area. **b.** A scraped area on the skin or on a mucous membrane, resulting from injury or irritation. [Med.Lat. *abrāsiō*, *abrāsiōn-* < Lat. *abrāsus*, p.part. of *abrādere*, to scrape off. See ABRADE.]

ab•ra•sive (ə-brā′sĭv, -zĭv) *adj.* **1.** Causing abrasion. **2.** Harsh and rough in manner. —*n.* A substance that abrades. —**a•bra′sive•ly** *adv.* —**a•bra′sive•ness** *n.*

ab•re•act (ăb′rē-ăkt′) *tr.v.* **-act•ed, -act•ing, -acts.** To release (repressed emotions) by acting out, as in behavior or the imagination, the situation causing the conflict. [Transl. of Ger. *abreagieren*: *ab-*, away + *reagieren*, to react.] —**ab′re•ac′tion** *n.*

a•breast (ə-brĕst′) *adv.* **1.** Side by side: *ships docked two abreast.* **2.** Up to date with: *keeping abreast of the news.*

a•bridge (ə-brĭj′) *tr.v.* **a•bridged, a•bridg•ing, a•bridg•es. 1.** To reduce the length of (a written text); condense. **2.** To cut short; curtail. [ME *abregen* < OFr. *abregier* < LLat. *abbreviāre*, to shorten. See ABBREVIATE.] —**a•bridg′er** *n.*

a•bridg•ment also **a•bridge•ment** (ə-brĭj′mənt) *n.* **1.** The act of abridging or the state of being abridged. **2.** A written text that has been abridged.

a•broach (ə-brōch′) *adj.* **1.** Opened or positioned so that a liquid, such as wine, can be let out. **2.** In a state of action; astir. [ME *abroche*: *a-*, on, in; see A-^{2} + *broche*, a pointed object, spigot; see BROACH^1.]

a•broad (ə-brôd′) *adv. & adj.* **1.** Out of one's own country. **2.** In a foreign country or countries. **3.** Away from one's home. **4.** In circulation; at large. **5.** Covering a large area; widely. **6.** Not on target; in error. —*n.* A foreign country or countries in which to live or travel: *"Do you like abroad or* *hate it?"* (John le Carré). [ME *abrod*: *a-*, in, on; see A-[2] + *brod*, broad; see BROAD.]

ab•ro•gate (ăb′rə-gāt′) *tr.v.* **-gat•ed, -gat•ing, -gates.** To abolish, do away with, or annul. [Lat. *abrogāre, abrogāt-* : *ab-*, away; see AB-[1] + *rogāre*, to ask; see **reg-***.] —**ab′ro•ga′tion** *n.*

a•brupt (ə-brŭpt′) *adj.* **1.** Unexpectedly sudden. **2.** Surprisingly and unceremoniously curt; brusque. **3.** Touching on one subject after another with sudden transitions. **4.** Steeply inclined. See Syns at **steep[1]**. **5.** *Bot.* Terminating suddenly rather than gradually; truncate. [Lat. *abruptus*, p.part. of *abrumpere*, to break off : *ab-*, away; see AB-[1] + *rumpere*, to break; see **reup-***.] —**a•brupt′ly** *adv.* —**a•brupt′ness** *n.*

a•brup•tion (ə-brŭp′shən) *n.* An instance of suddenly breaking away or off.

A•bruz•zi (ä-bro͞ot′sē, ə-bro͞ot′-) also **A•bruz•zi e Mo•li•se** (ā mô-lē′zĕ). A region of central Italy bordering on the Adriatic Sea.

abs *abbr.* Absolute temperature.

abs. *abbr.* **1.** Absence; absent. **2.** Absolute; absolutely. **3.** Abstract.

Ab•sa•ro•ka Range (ăb-sär′ə-kə). A section of the Rocky Mts. in NW WY and S MT, rising to 4,007.7 m (13,140 ft).

Ab•sa•ro•ke (ăb-sär′ə-kə) *n., pl.* **Absaroke** or **-kes.** See **Crow[1]**.

ab•scess (ăb′sĕs′) *n.* A localized collection of pus in part of the body, surrounded by an inflamed area. —*intr.v.* **-scessed, -scess•ing, -scess•es.** To form an abscess. [Lat. *abscessus* < p.part. of *abscēdere*, to go away : *ab-*, away; see AB-[1] + *cēdere*, to go; see **ked-***.]

ab•scise (ăb-sīz′) *v.* **-scised, -scis•ing, -scis•es.** —*tr.* To cut off; remove. —*intr.* To shed by abscission. [Lat. *abscindere, absciss-* : *ab-*, away; see AB-[1] + *caedere*, to cut; see **kaə-id-***.]

ab•scis•sa (ăb-sĭs′ə) *n., pl.* **-scis•sas** or **-scis•sae** (-sĭs′ē). *Symbol* **x** The coordinate representing the position of a point along a line perpendicular to the *y*-axis in a plane Cartesian coordinate system. [NLat. *(linea) abscissa*, (line) cut off < Lat. *abscissus*, p.part. of *abscindere*, to abscise. See ABSCISE.]

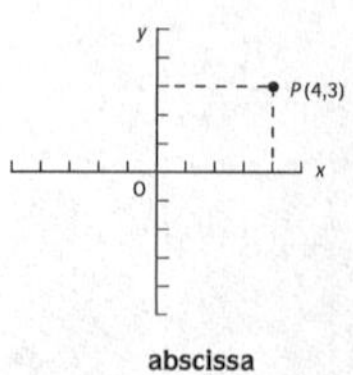

abscissa
P, abscissa 4; ordinate 3

ab•scis•sion (ăb-sĭzh′ən) *n.* **1.** The act of cutting off. **2.** *Bot.* The shedding of leaves, flowers, or fruits following the formation of the abscission zone.

abscission zone *n.* The region at the base of a plant part, such as a leaf, where the formation of a cork layer results in the separation of that part from the plant body.

ab•scond (ăb-skŏnd′) *intr.v.* **-scond•ed, -scond•ing, -sconds.** To leave quickly and secretly and hide, often to avoid arrest or prosecution. [Lat. *abscondere*, to hide : *abs-*, *ab-*, away; see AB-[1] + *condere*, to put; see **dhē-***.] —**ab•scond′er** *n.*

ab•sence (ăb′səns) *n.* **1.** The state of being away. **2.** The time during which one is away. **3.** Lack; want.

ab•sent (ăb′sənt) *adj.* **1.** Not present; missing: *absent friends.* **2.** Not existent; lacking: *Morality is absent.* **3.** Exhibiting or feeling inattentiveness: *an absent nod.* —*tr.v.* (ăb-sĕnt′) **-sent•ed, -sent•ing, -sents.** To keep (oneself) away: *They absented themselves from the debate.* —*prep.* Without. [ME < OFr. < Lat. *absēns, absent-*, pr.part. of *abesse*, to be away : *abs-*, *ab-*, away; see AB-[1] + *esse*, to be; see **es-***.] —**ab′sent•ly** *adv.*

ab•sen•tee (ăb′sən-tē′) *n.* One that is absent. —*adj.* **1.** Of or relating to one that is absent. **2.** Not in residence: *absentee landlords.* See Usage Note at **-ee[1]**.

absentee ballot *n.* A ballot marked and mailed in advance by a voter away from the place where he or she is registered.

ab•sen•tee•ism (ăb′sən-tē′ĭz′əm) *n.* **1.** Habitual failure to appear, esp. for work or other regular duty. **2.** The rate of occurrence of habitual absence from work or duty.

ab•sent-mind•ed (ăb′sənt-mīn′dĭd) *adj.* Deep in thought and heedless of present circumstances or activities; preoccupied. —**ab′sent-mind′ed•ly** *adv.* —**ab′sent-mind′ed•ness** *n.*

absent without leave *adj.* Absent from one's assigned military post or duties without official permission; AWOL.

ab•sinthe also **ab•sinth** (ăb′sĭnth) *n.* **1.** A perennial aromatic European herb *(Artemisia absinthium)*. **2.** A green liqueur having a bitter anise or licorice flavor and a high alcohol content, prepared from absinthe and other herbs. [ME, wormwood < OFr. < Lat. *absinthium* < Gk. *apsinthion*.]

ab•so•lute (ăb′sə-lo͞ot′, ăb′sə-lo͞ot′) *adj.* **1.** Perfect in quality or nature; complete. **2.** Not mixed; pure. See Syns at **pure.** **3.a.** Not limited by restrictions or exceptions; unconditional: *absolute trust.* **b.** Unqualified in extent or degree; total: *absolute silence.* See Usage Note at **infinite.** **4.** Unconstrained by constitutional or other provisions: *an absolute ruler.* **5.** Not to be doubted or questioned; positive: *absolute proof.* **6.** *Gram.* **a.** Of, relating to, or being a word, phrase, or construction that is isolated syntactically from the rest of a sentence. **b.** Of, relating to, or being a transitive verb when its object is implied but not stated. **c.** Of, relating to, or being an adjective or a pronoun that stands alone when the noun it modifies is implied but not stated. **7.** *Phys.* **a.** Relating to measurements or units of measurement derived from fundamental units of length, mass, and time. **b.** Relating to absolute temperature. —*n.* **1.** Something that is absolute. **2. Absolute.** *Philos.* **a.** Something regarded as the ultimate basis of all thought and being. Used with *the.* **b.** Something regarded as independent of and unrelated to anything else. [ME *absolut* < Lat. *absolūtus*, unrestricted, p.part. of *absolvere*, to absolve : *ab-*, away; see AB-[1] + *solvere*, to loosen; see **leu-***.] —**ab′so•lute′ness** *n.*

absolute alcohol *n.* Ethyl alcohol containing no more than one percent water.

absolute ceiling *n.* The maximum altitude above sea level at which an aircraft or missile can maintain horizontal flight under standard atmospheric conditions.

ab•so•lute•ly (ăb′sə-lo͞ot′lē, ăb′sə-lo͞ot′lē) *adv.* **1.** Definitely and completely; unquestionably. **2.** *Gram.* In a manner that does not take an object.

Usage Note: For some time *absolutely* has been used informally as a vague intensive, as in *an absolutely magnificent painting.* In an earlier survey a majority of the Usage Panel disapproved of this usage in formal writing.

absolute magnitude *n.* The intrinsic magnitude of a celestial body computed as if viewed from a distance of 10 parsecs, or 32.6 light-years.

absolute music *n.* Instrumental music that depends solely on its rhythmic, melodic, and contrapuntal structures.

absolute pitch *n.* **1.** The precise pitch of an isolated tone, as established by its rate of vibration measured on a standard scale. **2.** *Mus.* The ability to identify or sing any tone heard.

absolute scale *n.* **1.** A scale of temperature with absolute zero as the minimum. **2.** The Kelvin scale.

absolute temperature *n.* Temperature measured or calculated on an absolute scale.

absolute value *n.* **1.** The numerical value of a real number without regard to its sign. **2.** The modulus of a complex number, equal to the square root of the sum of the squares of the real and imaginary parts of the number.

absolute zero *n.* *Phys.* The temperature at which substances possess no thermal energy, equal to −273.15°C, or −459.67°F.

ab•so•lu•tion (ăb′sə-lo͞o′shən) *n.* The formal remission of sin imparted by a priest. [ME < OFr. < Lat. *absolūtiō*, acquittal < *absolūtus*, p.part. of *absolvere*, to absolve. See ABSOLUTE.]

ab•so•lut•ism (ăb′sə-lo͞o′tĭz′əm) *n.* **1.a.** A political theory holding that all power should be vested in one authority. **b.** A form of government in which all power is vested in a single authority. **2.** An absolute doctrine, principle, or standard. —**ab′so•lut′ist** *n.* —**ab′so•lu•tis′tic** (-lo͞o-tĭs′tĭk) *adj.*

ab•solve (əb-zŏlv′, -sŏlv′) *tr.v.* **-solved, -solv•ing, -solves.** **1.** To pronounce clear of guilt or blame. **2.** To relieve of a requirement or an obligation. **3.a.** To grant a remission of sin to. **b.** To pardon or remit (a sin). [ME *absolven* < Lat. *absolvere.* See ABSOLUTE.] —**ab•solv′a•ble** *adj.* —**ab•solv′er** *n.*

ab•sorb (əb-sôrb′, -zôrb′) *tr.v.* **-sorbed, -sorb•ing, -sorbs.** **1.** To take (something) in through or as through pores or interstices. **2.** To occupy the full attention, interest, or time of; engross. **3.** *Phys.* To retain (radiation, for example) wholly, without reflection or transmission. **4.** To take in; assimilate. **5.** To receive (an impulse) without echo or recoil: *a bumper that absorbs impact.* **6.** To take over (a cost or costs). **7.** To endure; accommodate. [ME, to swallow up < OFr. *absorber* < Lat. *absorbēre*: *ab-*, away; see AB-[1] + *sorbēre*, to suck.] —**ab•sorb′a•bil′i•ty** *n.* —**ab•sorb′a•ble** *adj.* —**ab•sorb′er** *n.* —**ab•sorb′ing•ly** *adv.*

ab•sorbed (əb-sôrbd′, -zôrbd′) *adj.* Wholly involved or occupied; engrossed. —**ab•sorb′ed•ly** (əb-sôr′bĭd-lē, -zôr′-) *adv.* —**ab•sorb′ed•ness** *n.*

ab•sor•be•fa•cient (əb-sôr′bə-fā′shənt, -zôr′-) *adj.* Inducing or causing absorption. —*n.* A medicine or an agent that induces absorption. [ABSORBE(NT) + -FACIENT.]

ab•sorb•ent (əb-sôr′bənt, -zôr′-) *adj.* Capable of absorbing. —*n.* A substance that is capable of absorbing. —**ab•sorb′en•cy** *n.*

absinthe
Artemisia absinthium

ab•sorp•tance (əb-sôrp′təns, -zôrp′-) *n.* The ratio of absorbed to incident radiation. [ABSORPT(ION) + -ANCE.]

ab•sorp•tion (əb-sôrp′shən, -zôrp′-) *n.* **1.** The act or process of absorbing or the condition of being absorbed. **2.** A state of mental concentration. [Lat. *absorptiō, absorptiōn-* < *absorptus*, p.part. of *absorbēre*, to absorb. See ABSORB.] —**ab•sorp′tive** (-tĭv) *adj.* —**ab′sorp•tiv′i•ty** *n.*

absorption spectrum *n.* *Phys.* The electromagnetic spectrum, broken by a specific pattern of dark lines or bands, observed when radiation traverses an absorbing medium.

ab•squat•u•late (ăb-skwŏch′ə-lāt′) *intr.v.* **-lat•ed, -lat•ing, -lates.** *Midland U.S.* **1.a.** To depart in a hurry; abscond: *"Your horse has absquatulated!"* (Robert M. Bird). **b.** To die. **2.** To argue. [Mock-Latinate formation, purporting to mean "to go off and squat elsewhere."]

Regional Note: The vibrant energy of American English sometimes appears in the use of Latin affixes to create jocular pseudo-Latin "learned" words. Midland *absquatulate* has a prefix *ab-*, "away from," and a suffix *-ate*, "to act upon in a specified manner," affixed to a nonexistent base form *-squatul-*, probably suggested by *squat.* Another such coinage is Northern *busticate*, which joins *bust* with *-icate* by

ă pat	oi boy
ā pay	ou out
âr care	o͝o took
ä father	o͞o boot
ĕ pet	ŭ cut
ē be	ûr urge
ĭ pit	th thin
ī pie	*th* this
îr pier	hw which
ŏ pot	zh vision
ō toe	ə about,
ô paw	item

Stress marks:
′ (primary);
′ (secondary), as in
dictionary (dĭk′shə-nĕr′ē)

analogy with verbs like *medicate.* Southern *argufy* joins *argue* to a redundant *–fy,* "to make, cause to become." These creations are largely confined to regions of the United States where the 19th-century love for Latinate words and expressions is still manifest. For example, Appalachian speech is characterized by the frequent use of words such as *recollect, aggravate,* and *oblige.*

ab•stain (ăb-stān′, əb-) *intr.v.* **-stained, -stain•ing, -stains.** To refrain from something by one's own choice. [ME *absteinen,* to avoid < OFr. *abstenir* < Lat. *abstinēre,* to hold back : *abs-, ab-,* away; see AB–[1] + *tenēre,* to hold; see **ten-***.] **—ab•stain′er** *n.*

ab•ste•mi•ous (ăb-stē′mē-əs, əb-) *adj.* **1.** Eating and drinking in moderation. **2.a.** Sparingly used or consumed. **b.** Restricted to bare necessities. [< Lat. *abstēmius: abs-, ab-,* away; see AB–[1] + **tēmum,* liquor, var. of *tēmētum.*] **—ab•ste′mi•ous•ly** *adv.* **—ab•ste′mi•ous•ness** *n.*

ab•sten•tion (ăb-stĕn′shən, əb-) *n.* The act or habit of deliberate self-denial. [LLat. *abstentiō, abstentiōn-* < *abstentus,* p.part. of Lat. *abstinēre,* to hold back. See ABSTAIN.]

ab•sti•nence (ăb′stə-nəns) *n.* **1.** The act or practice of refraining from indulging an appetite. **2.** Abstention from alcoholic beverages. [ME < OFr. *abstenance* < Lat. *abstinentia* < *abstinēns, abstinent-,* pr.part. of *abstinēre,* to hold back. See ABSTAIN.] **—ab′sti•nent** *adj.* **—ab′sti•nent•ly** *adv.*

ab•stract (ăb-străkt′, ăb′străkt′) *adj.* **1.** Considered apart from concrete existence. **2.** Not applied or practical; theoretical. **3.** Difficult to understand; abstruse: *abstract philosophical problems.* **4.** Thought of or stated without reference to a specific instance: *abstract words like* truth *and* justice. **5.** Impersonal, as in attitude or views. **6.** Having an intellectual and affective artistic content that depends solely on intrinsic form rather than on narrative content or pictorial representation. *—n.* (ăb′străkt′). **1.** A statement summarizing the important points of a text. **2.** Something abstract. *—tr.v.* (ăb-străkt′) **-stract•ed, -stract•ing, -stracts. 1.** To take away; remove. **2.** To remove without permission; filch. **3.** To consider (a quality, for example) without reference to a particular example or object. **4.** (ăb′străkt′). To summarize; epitomize. **5.** To create artistic abstractions of. [ME < Lat. *abstractus,* p.part. of *abstrahere,* to draw away : *abs-, ab-,* away; see AB–[1] + *trahere,* to draw.] **—ab•stract′er** *n.* **—ab•stract′ly** *adv.* **—ab•stract′ness** *n.*

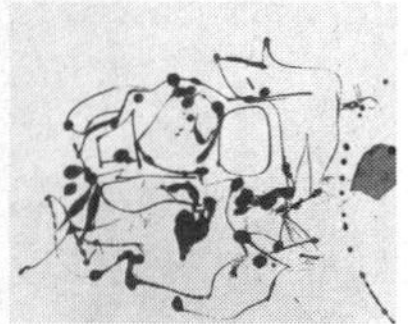

abstract expressionism
Asheville, 1948
by Willem de Kooning

ab•stract•ed (ăb-străk′tĭd, ăb′străk′-) *adj.* **1.** Removed or separated from something else; apart. **2.** Lost or deep in thought; preoccupied. **—ab•stract′ed•ly** *adv.* **—ab•stract′ed•ness** *n.*

abstract expressionism *n.* A school of painting that flourished after World War II until the early 1960's, characterized by the view that art is nonrepresentational.

ab•strac•tion (ăb-străk′shən, əb-) *n.* **1.a.** The act or process of abstracting or the state of having been abstracted. **b.** An abstract concept, idea, or term. **c.** An abstract quality. **2.** Preoccupation; absent-mindedness. **3.** An abstract work of art.

ab•strac•tion•ism (ăb-străk′shə-nĭz′əm) *n.* The theory and practice of abstract art. **—ab•strac′tion•ist** *n.*

ab•strac•tive (ăb-străk′tĭv, əb-) *adj.* Of or derived by abstraction.

abstract of title *n. Law.* A brief history of the transfers of a piece of land, including all claims that could be made against it.

ab•struse (ăb-stro͞os′, əb-) *adj.* Difficult to understand; recondite. See Syns at **ambiguous.** [Lat. *abstrūsus,* p.part. of *abstrūdere,* to hide : *abs-, ab-,* away; see AB–[1] + *trūdere,* to push; see **treud-***.] **—ab•struse′ly** *adv.* **—ab•struse′ness** *n.*

ab•surd (əb-sûrd′, -zûrd′) *adj.* **1.** Ridiculously incongruous or unreasonable. **2.** Of, relating to, or manifesting the view that there is no order or value in the universe. **3.** Of or relating to absurdism or the absurd. *—n.* The condition in which human beings exist in a meaningless, irrational universe. Used chiefly with *the.* [Lat. *absurdus.*] **—ab•surd′i•ty** (-sûr′dĭ-tē, -zûr′-), **ab•surd′ness** *n.* **—ab•surd′ly** *adv.*

ab•surd•ism (əb-sûr′dĭz-əm, -zûr′-) *n.* **1.** A philosophy holding that human beings exist in a meaningless, irrational universe. **2.** An act or an instance of the ridiculous. **—ab•surd′ist** *adj. & n.*

abt. *abbr.* About.

A•bu-Bakr (ä′bo͞o-bä′kər) also **A•bu Bekr** (ä′bo͞o bĕk′ər). 573–634. First caliph of the Muslim empire (632–634).

A•bu Dha•bi (ä′bo͞o dä′bē). A sheikdom and city of E Arabia on the Persian Gulf. The city is the cap. of the United Arab Emirates. Pop. 242,975.

a•build•ing (ə-bĭl′dĭng) *adj.* In the process of being built or of building.

Abu Simbel
Great Temple of
Rameses II

A•bu•ja (ä-bo͞o′jä). A city of central Nigeria NE of Lagos; designated cap. in 1982. Pop. 15,000.

A•bu•kir or **A•bu Qir** (ä′bo͞o-kîr′, ăb′o͞o-). A village of N Egypt in the Nile R. delta on the **Bay of Abukir;** site of Adm. Horatio Nelson's victory over a French fleet (1798).

a•bu•li•a also **a•bou•li•a** (ə-bo͞o′lē-ə, ə-byo͞o′-) *n.* Loss or impairment of the ability to make decisions or act independently. [NLat. < Gk. *aboulia,* indecision : *a-,* without; see A–[1] + *boulē,* will; see **g^welə-*.**] **—a•bu′lic** (-lĭk) *adj.*

a•bun•dance (ə-bŭn′dəns) *n.* **1.** A great or plentiful amount. **2.** Fullness to overflowing. **3.** Affluence; wealth.

a•bun•dant (ə-bŭn′dənt) *adj.* **1.** Occurring in or marked by abundance; plentiful. **2.** Abounding with; rich: *land abundant in wildlife.* [ME *aboundant* < OFr. *abondant* < Lat. *abundāns, abundant-,* pr.part. of *abundāre,* to overflow. See ABOUND.] **—a•bun′dant•ly** *adv.*

a•buse (ə-byo͞oz′) *tr.v.* **a•bused, a•bus•ing, a•bus•es. 1.** To use wrongly or improperly; misuse. **2.** To hurt or injure by maltreatment; ill-use. **3.** To assail with contemptuous, coarse, or insulting words; revile. *—n.* (ə-byo͞os′). **1.** Improper use or handling; misuse: *drug abuse.* **2.** Physical maltreatment. **3.** A corrupt practice or custom. **4.** Insulting or coarse language: *verbal abuse.* [ME *abusen* < OFr. *abuser* < *abus,* improper use < Lat. *abūsus,* p.part. of *abūtī,* to misuse : *ab-,* away; see AB–[1] + *ūtī,* to use.] **—a•bus′er** *n.*

Syns: *abuse, misuse, mistreat, ill-treat, maltreat.* These verbs mean to treat wrongfully or harmfully. *Abuse* applies to injurious or improper treatment: *"We abuse land because we regard it as a commodity belonging to us"* (Aldo Leopold). *Misuse* stresses incorrect or unknowledgeable handling: *"How often misused words generate misleading thoughts"* (Herbert Spencer). *Mistreat, ill-treat,* and *maltreat* all share the sense of inflicting injury, often intentionally: *"I had seen many more patients die from being mistreated for consumption than from consumption itself"* (Earl of Lytton). *The army had orders not to ill-treat the citizens. "We let ourselves maltreat* [a language other than our native tongue] *as though it naturally belonged to us"* (Manchester Guardian Weekly).

A•bu Sim•bel (ä′bo͞o sĭm′bəl, -bĕl). A village of S Egypt on the Nile R.; site of massive rock temples that were raised (1964–66) to avoid flooding from the Aswan High Dam.

a•bu•sive (ə-byo͞o′sĭv, -zĭv) *adj.* **1.** Of or relating to abuse. **2.a.** Characterized by abuse. **b.** Serving to abuse. **3.** Physically injurious to another. **—a•bu′sive•ly** *adv.*

a•but (ə-bŭt′) *v.* **a•but•ted, a•but•ting, a•buts.** *—intr.* To touch at one end or side of something; lie adjacent. *—tr.* To border upon; be next to. [ME *abutten* < OFr. *abouter,* to border on (*a-,* to < Lat. *ad-*; see AD– + *bouter,* to strike; see **bhau-***) and < OFr. *abuter,* to end at (< *but,* end; see BUTT[4]).] **—a•but′ter** *n.*

a•but•ment (ə-bŭt′mənt) *n.* **1.** The act or process of abutting. **2.a.** Something that abuts. **b.** The point of contact of two abutting objects or parts. **3.a.** The part of a structure that bears the weight or pressure of an arch. **b.** A structure that supports the end of a bridge. **c.** A structure that anchors the cables of a suspension bridge.

a•buzz (ə-bŭz′) *adj.* Filled with or as if with a buzzing sound.

ab•volt (ăb′vōlt′) *n.* The centimeter-gram-second electromagnetic unit of potential difference, equal to one hundred-millionth of a volt.

A•by•dos (ə-bī′dŏs). **1.** An ancient town of Asia Minor on the Asiatic coast of the Hellespont in modern-day Turkey; scene of the legendary tale of Hero and Leander. **2.** An ancient city of S Egypt on the Nile R. NW of Thebes; burial site for kings of the earliest dynasties.

a•bysm (ə-bĭz′əm) *n.* An abyss. [ME *abime* < OFr. *abisme* < VLat. **abissimus,* alteration of LLat. *abyssus.* See ABYSS.]

a•bys•mal (ə-bĭz′məl) *adj.* **1.** Resembling an abyss in depth; unfathomable. **2.** Very profound; limitless: *abysmal misery.* See Syns at **deep. 3.** Very bad. **—a•bys′mal•ly** *adv.*

a•byss (ə-bĭs′) *n.* **1.** An unfathomable chasm; a yawning gulf. **2.** An immeasurably profound depth or void. **3.a.** The primeval chaos out of which it was believed that the earth and sky were formed. **b.** The abode of evil spirits; hell. [ME *abissus* < LLat. *abyssus* < Gk. *abussos,* bottomless : *a-,* without; see A–[1] + *bussos,* bottom.]

a•bys•sal (ə-bĭs′əl) *adj.* **1.** Abysmal; unfathomable. **2.** Of or relating to the great depths of the oceans.

Ab•ys•sin•i•a (ăb′ĭ-sĭn′ē-ə). See **Ethiopia. —Ab′ys•sin′i•an** *adj. & n.*

Abyssinian cat *n.* A slender shorthaired cat of a breed developed from Near Eastern stocks, having a reddish-brown coat tipped with small black markings.

Ab•zug (ăb′zo͝og′, -zŭg′), **Bella.** b. 1920. Amer. politician noted for her support of feminism and the peace movement.

ac or **AC** *abbr.* Alternating current.

Ac[1] The symbol for the element **actinium.**

Ac[2] *abbr. Bible.* Acts of the Apostles.

ac. *abbr.* **1.** Acre. **2.** Air-cool.

a.c. *abbr. Lat.* Ante cibum (before meals).

a/c *abbr.* **1.** Account. **2.** Account current. **3.** Or **a.c.** Air conditioning.

ac– *pref.* Var. of **ad–** 1.

–ac *suff.* Used to form adjectives from nouns: *ammoniac.* [NLat. *-acus* < Gk. *-akos.*]

a•ca•cia (ə-kā′shə) *n.* **1.** Any of various often spiny trees or shrubs of the genus *Acacia* in the pea family, having heads or spikes of small flowers. **2.** Any of several other leguminous plants. **3.** See **gum arabic.** [ME < Lat. < Gk. *akakia.*]

acad. *abbr.* Academic; academy.

ac•a•deme (ăk′ə-dēm′) *n.* **1.a.** The academic environment, community, or world. **b.** Academic life. **2.** A place in which instruction is given to students. **3.** A scholar, esp. a pedant. [< Lat. *Acadēmīa*, the Academy. See ACADEMY.]

ac•a•de•mi•a (ăk′ə-dē′mē-ə) *n.* The academic community; academe. [NLat. *acadēmīa* < Lat., the Academy. See ACADEMY.]

ac•a•dem•ic (ăk′ə-dĕm′ĭk) *adj.* **1.** Of, relating to, or characteristic of a school, esp. one of higher learning. **2.a.** Relating to studies that are liberal or classical. **b.** Relating to scholarly performance. **3.** Relating or belonging to a scholarly organization. **4.** Scholarly to the point of being unaware of the outside world. **5.** Based on formal education. **6.** Formalistic or conventional. **7.** Theoretical or speculative. **8.** Having no practical purpose or use. — *n.* **1.** A member of an institution of higher learning. **2.** One who has an academic viewpoint or a scholarly background. — **ac′a•dem′i•cal•ly** *adv.*

academic freedom *n.* Liberty to teach and pursue knowledge and to discuss it openly without restriction or interference.

ac•a•de•mi•cian (ăk′ə-də-mĭsh′ən, ə-kăd′ə-) *n.* **1.** An academic. **2.** A member of an art, literary, or scientific academy or society.

ac•a•dem•i•cism (ăk′ə-dĕm′ĭ-sĭz′əm) also **a•cad•e•mism** (ə-kăd′ə-mĭz′əm) *n.* Traditional formalism, esp. in art.

ac•a•dem•ics (ăk′ə-dĕm′ĭks) *n.* *(used with a pl. v.)* College or university courses and studies.

a•cad•e•my (ə-kăd′ə-mē) *n., pl.* **-mies. 1.** A school for special instruction. **2.** A secondary or college-preparatory school, esp. a private one. **3.a.** The academic community; academe. **b.** Higher education in general. Used with *the*. **c.** A society of scholars, scientists, or artists. **4. Academy. a.** Plato's school for advanced education. **b.** Platonism. **c.** The disciples of Plato. [Lat. *Acadēmīa*, the school where Plato taught < Gk. *Akadēmia*.]

A•ca•di•a (ə-kā′dē-ə). A region and former French colony of E Canada, chiefly in Nova Scotia but also including New Brunswick, Prince Edward I., Cape Breton I., and the coastal area from the St. Lawrence R. S into ME.

A•ca•di•an (ə-kā′dē-ən) *adj.* Of or relating to Acadia or its people, language, or culture. — *n.* **1.a.** One of the early French settlers of Acadia. **b.** A descendant of these settlers, esp. a Cajun. **2.** A dialect of French spoken by the Acadians.

a•can•tha (ə-kăn′thə) *n., pl.* **-thae** (-thē). A sharp spiny part or structure, such as the spinous process of a vertebra. [Gk. *akantha*, thorn.]

acantho– or **acanth–** *pref.* Thorn: *acanthocephalan*. [< Gk. *akanthos*, thorn plant. See ACANTHUS.]

a•can•tho•ceph•a•lan (ə-kăn′thə-sĕf′ə-lən) also **a•can•tho•ceph•a•lid** (-lĭd) *n.* See **spiny-headed worm.** [< NLat. *Acanthocephala*, phylum name : ACANTHO– + Gk. *kephalē*, head; see –CEPHALOUS.] — **a•can′tho•ceph′a•lan** *adj.*

a•can•thoid (ə-kăn′thoid′) *adj.* Shaped like a thorn or spine.

ac•an•thop•ter•yg•i•an (ăk′ən-thŏp′tə-rĭj′ē-ən) *n.* Any of a large group of fishes of the superorder Acanthopterygii, having bony skeletons and spiny rays in the dorsal and anal fins. [< NLat. *Acanthopterygii*: ACANTHO– + Gk. *pterugion*, dim. of *pterux*, wing; see **pet-***.] — **ac′an•thop′ter•yg′i•an** *adj.*

a•can•thus (ə-kăn′thəs) *n., pl.* **-thus•es** or **-thi** (-thī′). **1.** Any of various perennial herbs or small shrubs of the genus *Acanthus*, native to the Mediterranean and having pinnately lobed basal leaves with spiny margins. **2.** *Archit.* A design patterned after the leaves of one of these plants, used esp. on the capitals of Corinthian columns. [NLat. *Acanthus*, genus name < Gk. *akanthos*, thorn plant < *akantha*, thorn.]

a•cap•ni•a (ā-kăp′nē-ə) *n.* A condition marked by the presence of less than the normal amount of carbon dioxide in the blood and tissues. [NLat. < Lat. *acapnos*, without smoke < Gk. *akapnos*: *a*-, not; see A–[1] + *kapnos*, smoke.]

a cap•pel•la (ä′ kə-pĕl′ə) *adv. Mus.* Without instrumental accompaniment. [Ital. : *a*, in the manner of + *cappella*, chapel, choir.]

Ac•a•pul•co (ăk′ə-po͝ol′kō, ä′kä-po͝ol′kô). A city of S Mexico on the Pacific Ocean. Pop. 301,902.

ac•a•ri•a•sis (ăk′ə-rī′ə-sĭs) *n.* Infestation with or disease caused by mites. [ACAR(ID) + –IASIS.]

ac•a•rid (ăk′ə-rĭd) *n.* An arachnid of the order Acarina, which includes the mites and ticks. [< NLat. *Acaridae*, family name < *Acarus*, type genus < Gk. *akari*, a mite.] — **ac′a•rid** *adj.*

a•car•pous (ā-kär′pəs) *adj. Bot.* **1.** Producing no fruit; sterile. **2.** Having no fruit.

ac•a•rus (ăk′ər-əs) *n., pl.* **-ri** (-rī′). A mite, esp. one of the genus *Acarus*. [NLat. *Acarus*. See ACARID.]

a•cat•a•lec•tic (ā-kăt′l-ĕk′tĭk) *adj.* Having a metrically complete pattern, esp. having the full number of syllables in the final foot. Used of verse. [LLat. *acatalēcticus* < Gk. *akatalēktikos*: *a*-, not; see A–[1] + *katalēktikos*, incomplete; see CATALECTIC.]

a•cau•date (ā-kô′dāt′) also **a•cau•dal** (ā-kôd′l) *adj.* Having no tail.

a•cau•les•cent (ā′kô-lĕs′ənt) *adj. Bot.* Stemless or apparently so.

acc. or **acc** *abbr.* Accusative.

Ac•cad (ăk′ăd′, ä′käd′). See **Akkad.**

ac•cede (ăk-sēd′) *intr.v.* **-ced•ed, -ced•ing, -cedes. 1.** To give one's consent, often at the insistence of another; concede. See Syns at **assent. 2.** To arrive at or come into an office or dignity. **3.** To become a party to an agreement. [ME *acceden*, to come near < Lat. *accēdere*, to go near : *ad*-, ad- + *cēdere*, to go; see **ked-***.] — **ac•ced′ence** (-sēd′ns) *n.* — **ac•ced′er** *n.*

ac•cel•er•an•do (ä-chĕl′ə-rän′dō) *adv. & adj. Mus.* Gradually accelerating in time. [Ital., pr.part. of *accelerare*, to hasten < Lat. *accelerāre*. See ACCELERATE.]

ac•cel•er•ant (ăk-sĕl′ər-ənt) *n.* A substance, such as a petroleum distillate, that is used as a catalyst.

ac•cel•er•ate (ăk-sĕl′ə-rāt′) *v.* **-at•ed, -at•ing, -ates.** — *tr.* **1.** To increase the speed of. **2.** To cause to occur sooner than expected. **3.** To cause to develop or progress more quickly. **4.a.** To speed up (an academic course, for example). **b.** To make it possible for (a student) to finish an academic course faster than usual. **5.** *Phys.* To cause a change of velocity. — *intr.* **1.** To move or act faster. **2.** To engage in an academic program that progresses faster than usual. [Lat. *accelerāre*, *accelerāt*- : *ad*-, intensive pref.; see AD– + *celerāre*, to quicken (< *celer*, swift).] — **ac•cel′er•a′tive** *adj.*

ac•cel•er•a•tion (ăk-sĕl′ə-rā′shən) *n.* **1.a.** The act of accelerating. **b.** The process of being accelerated. **2.** *Phys.* The rate of change of velocity with respect to time.

acceleration of gravity *n.* The acceleration of freely falling bodies under the influence of terrestrial gravity, equal to approx. 9.81 meters (32 feet) per second per second.

ac•cel•er•a•tor (ăk-sĕl′ə-rā′tər) *n.* **1.** A device, esp. the gas pedal of a motor vehicle, for increasing speed. **2.** *Chem.* A substance that increases the speed of a reaction. **3.** *Phys.* A device, such as a cyclotron or linear accelerator, that accelerates charged subatomic particles or nuclei to high energies.

ac•cel•er•o•graph (ăk-sĕl′ər-ə-grăf′) *n.* An accelerometer equipped to measure and record ground motion during an earthquake.

ac•cel•er•om•e•ter (ăk-sĕl′ə-rŏm′ĭ-tər) *n.* An instrument used to measure acceleration. [ACCELER(ATION) + –METER.]

ac•cent (ăk′sĕnt′) *n.* **1.** The relative prominence of a particular syllable of a word by greater intensity or by variation or modulation of pitch or tone. **2.** Vocal prominence or emphasis given to a particular syllable, word, or phrase. **3.** A characteristic pronunciation, esp.: **a.** One determined by the regional or social background of the speaker. **b.** One determined by the phonetic habits of the speaker's native language carried over to his or her use of another language. **4.** A mark or symbol used in the printing and writing of certain languages to indicate the vocal quality to be given to a particular letter: *an acute accent*. **5.** A mark or symbol used in printing and writing to indicate the stressed syllables of a spoken word. **6.** Rhythmically significant stress in a line of verse. **7.** *Mus.* **a.** Special stress given to a note within a phrase. **b.** A mark representing this stress. **8.** *Math.* **a.** A mark used as a superscript to distinguish among variables represented by the same symbol. **b.** A mark used as a superscript to indicate the first derivative of a variable. **9.** A mark or one of several marks used as a superscript to indicate a unit, such as feet (′) and inches (″) in linear measurement. **10.** A distinctive feature or quality. **11.** Particular importance or interest; emphasis. See Syns at **emphasis.** — *tr.v.* (ăk′sĕnt′, ăk-sĕnt′) **-cent•ed, -cent•ing, -cents. 1.** To stress or emphasize the pronunciation of. **2.** To mark with a printed accent. **3.** To focus attention on; accentuate. [ME < OFr. < Lat. *accentus*, accentuation : *ad*-, ad- + *cantus*, song (< *canere*, to sing; see **kan-***).]

ac•cen•tu•al (ăk-sĕn′cho͞o-əl) *adj.* **1.** Of or relating to accent. **2.** Based on stress accents: *accentual rhythm*. [< Lat. *accentus*, accent. See ACCENT.] — **ac•cen′tu•al•ly** *adv.*

ac•cen•tu•ate (ăk-sĕn′cho͞o-āt′) *tr.v.* **-at•ed, -at•ing, -ates. 1.** To stress or emphasize; intensify. **2.** To pronounce with a stress or an accent. **3.** To mark with an accent. [Med.Lat. *accentuāre*, *accentuāt*- < Lat. *accentus*, accent. See ACCENT.] — **ac•cen′tu•a′tion** *n.*

ac•cept (ăk-sĕpt′) *v.* **-cept•ed, -cept•ing, -cepts.** — *tr.* **1.** To receive (something offered), esp. with gladness. **2.** To admit to a group, an organization, or a place. **3.a.** To regard as proper, usual, or right: *widely accepted customs*. **b.** To regard as true; believe in: *accepted the new theory*. **c.** To understand as having a specific meaning. **4.** To endure resignedly or patiently. **5.a.** To answer affirmatively: *accept an invitation*. **b.** To agree to take (a duty or responsibility). **6.** To be able to hold (something applied or inserted). **7.** To receive officially: *accept the report*. **8.** To consent to pay, as by a signed agreement. — *intr.* To receive something, esp. with favor. Often used with *of*. [ME *accepten* < Lat. *acceptāre*, freq. of *accipere*, to receive : *ad*-, ad- + *capere*, to take; see **kap-***.]

ac•cept•a•ble (ăk-sĕp′tə-bəl) *adj.* **1.** Worthy of being accepted. **2.** Adequate to satisfy a need, requirement, or standard; satisfactory. — **ac•cept′a•bil′i•ty, ac•cept′a•ble•ness** *n.* — **ac•cept′a•bly** *adv.*

ac•cep•tance (ăk-sĕp′təns) *n.* **1.** The act or process of accepting. **2.** The state of being accepted or acceptable. **3.** Favorable

acanthus

ă pat	oi boy
ā pay	ou out
âr care	o͝o took
ä father	o͞o boot
ĕ pet	ŭ cut
ē be	ûr urge
ĭ pit	th thin
ī pie	*th* this
îr pier	hw which
ŏ pot	zh vision
ō toe	ə about, item
ô paw	

Stress marks:
′ (primary);
′ (secondary), as in
dictionary (dĭk′shə-nĕr′ē)

reception; approval. **4.** Belief in something; agreement. **5.a.** A formal indication by a debtor of willingness to pay a time draft or bill of exchange. **b.** A written instrument so accepted. **6.** *Law.* Compliance by one party with the terms and conditions of another's offer so that a contract becomes legally binding between them.

ac•cep•tant (ăk-sĕp′tənt) *adj.* Accepting willingly.

ac•cep•ta•tion (ăk′sĕp-tā′shən) *n.* **1.** The usual or accepted meaning, as of a word or expression. See Syns at **meaning. 2.** Favorable reception; approval.

ac•cept•ed (ăk-sĕp′tĭd) *adj.* Widely encountered, used, or recognized.

ac•cept•er (ăk-sĕp′tər) *n.* One that accepts.

ac•cep•tor (ăk-sĕp′tər) *n.* **1.** Also **ac•cept•er.** One who signs a time draft or bill of exchange. **2.** *Chem.* **a.** The reactant in an induced reaction that has an increased rate of reaction in the presence of the inductor. **b.** The atom that contributes no electrons to a covalent bond.

ac•cess (ăk′sĕs) *n.* **1.** A means of approaching, entering, exiting, or making use of; a passage. **2.** The act of approaching. **3.** The right to approach, enter, exit, or make use of. **4.** Increase by addition. **5.** An outburst or onset: *an access of rage.* — *tr.v.* **-cessed, -cess•ing, -cess•es. 1.** *Comp. Sci.* To obtain access to (data or processes). **2.** *Usage Problem.* To obtain access to (goods or information), usu. by technological means. [ME *acces*, a coming to < OFr. < Lat. *accessus*, p.part. of *accēdere*, to arrive : *ad-*, ad- + *cēdere*, to come; see **ked-***.]

Usage Note: The verb *access* is well established in its computational sense "to obtain access to (data or processes)." In recent years it has come to be used in nontechnical contexts with the more general sense "to obtain access to (goods or information), usually by technological means," as in *You can access your cash at any of 300 automatic tellers throughout the area.* This example was judged unacceptable by 82 percent of the Usage Panel.

ac•ces•si•ble (ăk-sĕs′ə-bəl) *adj.* **1.** Easily approached or entered. **2.** Easily obtained: *accessible money.* **3.** Easy to talk to or get along with. **4.** Easily swayed or influenced. — **ac•ces′si•bil′i•ty, ac•ces′si•ble•ness** *n.* — **ac•ces′si•bly** *adv.*

ac•ces•sion (ăk-sĕsh′ən) *n.* **1.** The attainment of a dignity or rank: *the queen's accession to the throne.* **2.a.** Something that has been acquired or added; an acquisition. **b.** An increase by means of something added. **3.** *Law.* **a.** The addition to or increase in value of property by means of improvements or natural growth. **b.** The right of a proprietor to ownership of such addition or increase. **4.** Agreement or assent. **5.** Access; admittance. **6.** A sudden outburst. — *tr.v.* **-sioned, -sion•ing, -sions.** To record (paintings, for example) in the order of acquisition. — **ac•ces′sion•al** *adj.*

ac•ces•sor•ize (ăk-sĕs′ə-rīz′) *tr.v.* **-ized, -iz•ing, -iz•es.** *Usage Problem.* To furnish with accessories. See Usage Note at **-ize.**

ac•ces•so•ry (ăk-sĕs′ə-rē) *n., pl.* **-ries. 1.a.** A subordinate or supplementary item; an adjunct. **b.** Something nonessential but desirable that contributes to an effect or result. **2.** *Law.* **a.** One who incites, aids, or abets a lawbreaker in the commission of a crime but is not present at the time of the crime. **b.** One who aids a criminal after the commission of a crime but was not present at the time of the crime. — *adj.* **1.** Having a secondary, supplementary, or subordinate function. **2.** *Law.* Serving to aid or abet a lawbreaker, either before or after the commission of the crime, without being present at the time the crime was committed. [ME *accessorie* < Med.Lat. *accessōrius* < *accessor*, helper < Lat. *accessus*, approach. See ACCESS.] — **ac′ces•so′ri•al** (-sə-sôr′ē-əl, -sōr-) *adj.* — **ac•ces′so•ri•ly** *adv.* — **ac•ces′so•ri•ness** *n.*

accessory after the fact *n., pl.* **accessories after the fact.** *Law.* See **accessory** 2b.

accessory before the fact *n., pl.* **accessories before the fact.** *Law.* See **accessory** 2a.

accessory fruit *n.* A fruit, such as the pear or strawberry, that develops from a ripened ovary or ovaries but includes a significant portion derived from nonovarian tissue.

accessory nerve *n.* Either of the 11th pair of cranial nerves, which convey motor impulses to the pharynx and muscles of the upper thorax, back, and shoulders.

access time *n.* *Comp. Sci.* The time lag between a request for information stored in a computer and its delivery.

acciaccatura
A. Grace note
B. Principal note

ac•ciac•ca•tu•ra (ä-chä′kə-to͝or′ə) *n.* *Mus.* A short grace note one half step below a principal note, sounded immediately before or at the same time as the principal note to add sustained dissonance. [Ital. < *acciaccare*, to crush.]

ac•ci•dence (ăk′sĭ-dəns, -dĕns′) *n.* *Gram.* The section of morphology that deals with the inflections of words. [ME < LLat. *accidentia* < Lat. *accidēns*, *accident-*, accident. See ACCIDENT.]

ac•ci•dent (ăk′sĭ-dənt, -dĕnt′) *n.* **1.a.** An unexpected, undesirable event. **b.** An unforeseen incident. **2.** Lack of intention; chance: *met by accident.* **3.** *Logic.* A circumstance or an attribute that is not essential to the nature of something. [ME, chance event < OFr. < Lat. *accidēns*, *accident-*, pr.part. of *accidere*, to happen : *ad-*, ad- + *cadere*, to fall; see **kad-***.]

ac•ci•den•tal (ăk′sĭ-dĕn′tl) *adj.* **1.** Occurring unexpectedly, unintentionally, or by chance. **2.** *Mus.* Of or relating to a sharp, flat, or natural not indicated in the key signature. — *n.* **1.** A property, a factor, or an attribute that is not essential. **2.** *Mus.* A chromatically altered note not belonging to the key signature. — **ac′ci•den′tal•ly** *adv.*

accident insurance *n.* Insurance against injury or death because of accident.

ac•ci•dent-prone (ăk′sĭ-dənt-prōn′) *adj.* Having or susceptible to having a greater than average number of accidents or mishaps.

ac•cip•i•ter (ăk-sĭp′ĭ-tər) *n.* A hawk of the genus *Accipiter*, characterized by short wings and a long tail. [Lat., hawk. See **ōku-***.] — **ac•cip′i•trine′** (-trīn′, -trĭn) *adj.*

ac•claim (ə-klām′) *v.* **-claimed, -claim•ing, -claims.** — *tr.* To praise enthusiastically and often publicly; applaud. See Syns at **praise.** — *intr.* To shout approval. — *n.* Enthusiastic applause; acclamation. [< Lat. *acclāmāre*: *ad-*, ad- + *clāmāre*, to shout; see **kelə-**[2]***.] — **ac•claim′er** *n.*

ac•cla•ma•tion (ăk′lə-mā′shən) *n.* **1.** A shout or salute of enthusiastic approval. **2.** An oral vote, esp. an enthusiastic vote of approval without formal ballot. [Lat. *acclāmātiō*, *acclāmātiōn-* < *acclāmātus*, p.part. of *acclāmāre*, to shout at. See ACCLAIM.] — **ac•clam′a•to′ry** (ə-klăm′ə-tôr′ē, -tōr′ē) *adj.*

ac•cli•mate (ə-klī′mĭt, ăk′lə-māt′) *tr. & intr.v.* **-mat•ed, -mat•ing, -mates.** To accustom or become accustomed to a new environment or situation; adapt. [Fr. *acclimater*: *a-*, to (< Lat. *ad-*; see AD–) + *climat*, climate (< OFr.; see CLIMATE).]

ac•cli•ma•tion (ăk′lə-mā′shən) *n.* **1.** The process of acclimating or of becoming acclimated. **2.** Acclimatization.

ac•cli•ma•ti•za•tion (ə-klī′mə-tĭ-zā′shən) *n.* The physiological adaptation of an animal or a plant to changes in climate or environment, such as light, temperature, or altitude.

ac•cli•ma•tize (ə-klī′mə-tīz′) *v.* **-tized, -tiz•ing, -tiz•es.** — *tr.* **1.** To acclimate. **2.** To adapt (oneself), esp. to environmental or climatic changes. — *intr.* To become acclimated or adapted. — **ac•cli′ma•tiz′er** *n.*

ac•cliv•i•ty (ə-klĭv′ĭ-tē) *n., pl.* **-ties.** An upward slope. [Lat. *acclīvitās* < *acclīvis*, uphill : *ad-*, ad- + *clīvus*, slope; see **klei-***.]

ac•co•lade (ăk′ə-lād′, -läd′) *n.* **1.a.** An expression of approval; praise. **b.** A special acknowledgment; an award. **2.** A ceremonial embrace, as of greeting. **3.** Ceremonial bestowal of knighthood. — *tr.v.* **-lad•ed, -lad•ing, -lades.** To praise or honor. [Fr., an embrace, accolade < *accoler*, to embrace < OFr. *acoler* < VLat. **accolāre*: Lat. *ad-*, ad- + Lat. *collum*, neck; see **k^{w}el-**[1]***.]

ac•com•mo•date (ə-kŏm′ə-dāt′) *v.* **-dat•ed, -dat•ing, -dates.** — *tr.* **1.** To do a favor or service for; oblige. **2.** To provide for; supply with. **3.** To hold comfortably without crowding. See Syns at **contain. 4.** To make suitable; adapt. See Syns at **adapt. 5.** To allow for; consider. **6.** To settle; reconcile. — *intr. Physiol.* To become adjusted, as the eye to focusing on objects at a distance. [Lat. *accomodāre*, *accomodāt-*, to fit : *ad-*, ad- + *commodus*, suitable; see COMMODIOUS.] — **ac•com′mo•da′tive** *adj.* — **ac•com′mo•da′tive•ness** *n.* — **ac•com′mo•da′tor** *n.*

ac•com•mo•dat•ing (ə-kŏm′ə-dā′tĭng) *adj.* Helpful and obliging. — **ac•com′mo•dat′ing•ly** *adv.*

ac•com•mo•da•tion (ə-kŏm′ə-dā′shən) *n.* **1.** The act of accommodating or the state of being accommodated; adjustment. **2.** Something that meets a need; a convenience. **3. accommodations. a.** Room and board; lodgings. **b.** A seat, compartment, or room on a public vehicle. **4.** Reconciliation or settlement of opposing views. **5.** *Physiol.* The automatic adjustment in the focal length of the lens of the eye to permit retinal focus of images of objects at varying distances. **6.** A financial favor.

ac•com•mo•da•tion•ist (ə-kŏm′ə-dā′shə-nĭst) *n.* One that compromises with or adapts to the viewpoint of the opposition. — **ac•com′mo•da′tion•ist** *adj.*

accommodation ladder *n.* *Naut.* A portable ladder hung from the side of a ship.

ac•com•pa•ni•ment (ə-kŭm′pə-nē-mənt, ə-kŭmp′nē-) *n.* **1.** *Mus.* A vocal or instrumental part that supports another, often solo, part. **2.** Something that accompanies something else; a concomitant. **3.** Something added for embellishment, completeness, or symmetry; a complement.

ac•com•pa•nist (ə-kŭm′pə-nĭst, ə-kŭmp′nĭst) *n.* *Mus.* A performer, such as a pianist, who plays an accompaniment.

ac•com•pa•ny (ə-kŭm′pə-nē, ə-kŭmp′nē) *v.* **-nied, -ny•ing, -nies.** — *tr.* **1.** To be or go with as a companion. **2.** To add to; supplement. **3.** To coexist or occur with. **4.** *Mus.* To perform an accompaniment to. — *intr. Mus.* To play an accompaniment. [ME *accompanien* < OFr. *acompagnier*: *a-*, to (< Lat. *ad-*; see AD–) + *compaignon*, companion; see COMPANION[1].]

Syns: *accompany, conduct, escort, chaperon.* These verbs mean to be with or to go with another or others. *Accompany* suggests going on an equal basis: *She went accompanied by her colleague. Conduct* implies guidance of others: *The usher conducted us to our seats. Escort* stresses protective guidance:

escorting the candidate through the crowd. Chaperon specifies adult supervision of young persons: *teachers chaperoning students.*

ac•com•plice (ə-kŏm′plĭs) *n.* One who aids or abets a lawbreaker in a criminal act, either as a principal or an accessory. [Alteration of COMPLICE.]

ac•com•plish (ə-kŏm′plĭsh) *tr.v.* **-plished, -plish•ing, -plish•es. 1.** To succeed in doing; bring to pass. **2.** To reach the end of; complete. [ME *accomplisshen* < OFr. *acomplir, accompliss-*, to complete : *a-*, to (< Lat. *ad-*; see AD-) + *complir*, to complete (< Lat. *complēre*, to fill out; see COMPLETE).] **—ac•com′plish•a•ble** *adj.* **—ac•com′plish•er** *n.*

ac•com•plished (ə-kŏm′plĭsht) *adj.* **1.** Skilled; expert: *an accomplished pianist.* **2.** Unquestionable; indubitable.

ac•com•plish•ment (ə-kŏm′plĭsh-mənt) *n.* **1.** The act of accomplishing or the state of being accomplished; completion. **2.** Something completed successfully; an achievement. **3.** Social poise and grace.

ac•cord (ə-kôrd′) *v.* **-cord•ed, -cord•ing, -cords.** *—tr.* **1.** To cause to conform or agree; bring into harmony. **2.** To grant, esp. as being due or appropriate. **3.** To bestow upon: *I accord you my blessing.* *—intr.* To be in agreement, unity, or harmony. *—n.* **1.** Agreement; harmony. **2.** A settlement or compromise of conflicting opinions. **3.** A settlement of points at issue between nations. **4.** Spontaneous or voluntary desire to take a certain action: *on their own accord.* [ME *accorden* < OFr. *acorder* < VLat. **accordāre*: Lat. *ad-*, ad- + Lat. *cor, cord-*, heart; see **kerd-***.]

ac•cor•dance (ə-kôr′dns) *n.* **1.** Agreement; conformity: *in accordance with your instructions.* **2.** The act of granting.

ac•cor•dant (ə-kôr′dnt) *adj.* Being in agreement or harmony; consonant. **—ac•cor′dant•ly** *adv.*

ac•cord•ing as (ə-kôr′dĭng) *conj.* **1.** Corresponding to the way in which; precisely as. **2.** Depending on whether; if.

ac•cord•ing•ly (ə-kôr′dĭng-lē) *adv.* **1.** In accordance; correspondingly. **2.** So; consequently.

according to *prep.* **1.** As stated or indicated by; on the authority of. **2.** In keeping with; in agreement with. **3.** As determined by: *a list arranged according to the alphabet.*

ac•cor•di•on (ə-kôr′dē-ən) *n. Mus.* A portable instrument with a small keyboard and free metal reeds that sound when air is forced past them by pleated bellows operated by the player. *—adj.* Having folds or bends like the bellows of an accordion: *accordion pleats.* [Ger. *Akkordion* < *Akkord*, chord < Fr. *accord*, harmony < OFr. *acorder*, to accord < Med.Lat. *accordāre*. See ACCORD.] **—ac•cor′di•on•ist** *n.*

ac•cost (ə-kôst′, ə-kŏst′) *tr.v.* **-cost•ed, -cost•ing, -costs.** To approach and speak to in an aggressive, hostile, or suggestive manner. [Fr. *accoster* < OFr. < Med.Lat. *accostāre*, to adjoin : Lat. *ad-*, ad- + Lat. *costa*, side; see **kost-***.]

ac•couche•ment (ä′ko͞osh-mäN′) *n.* A confinement during childbirth; lying-in. [Fr. < *accoucher*, to assist in childbirth < OFr. : *a-*, to (< Lat. *ad-*; see AD-) + *coucher*, to lay down; see COUCH.]

ac•count (ə-kount′) *n.* **1.a.** A narrative or record of events. **b.** A reason given for a particular action. **2.a.** A formal banking, brokerage, or business relationship established to provide for financial transactions. **b.** A precise list or enumeration of financial transactions. **c.** Money deposited for checking, savings, or brokerage use. **d.** A customer having a business or credit relationship with a firm. **3.** Worth, standing, or importance. **4.** Profit or advantage. *—tr.v.* **-count•ed, -count•ing, -counts.** To consider as being; deem. See Usage Note at **as**[1]. ***—phrasal verb.* account for. 1.** To constitute the governing or primary factor for. **2.** To provide an explanation or justification for: *couldn't account for my time.* ***—idioms.* call to account. 1.** To challenge or contest. **2.** To hold answerable for. **on account.** On credit. **on account of. 1.** Because of; for the sake of: *"We got married on account of the baby"* (Anne Tyler). **2.** *Chiefly Southern U.S.* Because. **on no account.** Under no circumstances. **on (one's) own account. 1.** For oneself. **2.** On one's own; by oneself. **take into account.** To take into consideration; allow for. [ME < OFr. *acont* < *aconter*, to reckon : *a-*, to (< Lat. *ad-*; see AD-) + *cunter*, to count (ult. < Lat. *computāre*, to sum up; see COMPUTE).]

ac•count•a•ble (ə-koun′tə-bəl) *adj.* **1.** Liable to being called to account; answerable. See Syns at **responsible. 2.** That can be explained: *an accountable phenomenon.* **—ac•count′a•bil′i•ty, ac•count′a•ble•ness** *n.* **—ac•count′a•bly** *adv.*

ac•count•ant (ə-koun′tənt) *n.* One that keeps, audits, and inspects financial records and prepares financial and tax reports. **—ac•count′an•cy** (-tən-sē) *n.*

account executive *n.* A person, as in an advertising or a public relations firm, who manages clients' accounts.

ac•count•ing (ə-koun′tĭng) *n.* The bookkeeping methods involved in making a financial record of business transactions and in the preparation of statements concerning the assets, liabilities, and operating results of a business.

ac•cou•ter or **ac•cou•tre** (ə-ko͞o′tər) *tr.v.* **-tered, -ter•ing, -ters** or **-tred, -tre•ing, -tres.** To outfit and equip, as for military duty. [Fr. *accoutrer* < OFr. *acoustrer*, arrange, equip : *a-*, to (< Lat. *ad-*; see AD-) + *coustrer*, sew; see COUTURE.]

ac•cou•ter•ment or **ac•cou•tre•ment** (ə-ko͞o′tər-mənt, -trə-) *n.* **1.a.** An ancillary item of equipment or dress. Often used in the plural. **b.** Military equipment other than uniforms and weapons. Often used in the plural. **2. accouterments.** Outward forms of recognition; trappings. **3.** *Archaic.* The act of accoutering.

Ac•cra (ăk′rə, ə-krä′). The cap. of Ghana, in the SE part on the Gulf of Guinea. Pop. 859,640.

ac•cred•it (ə-krĕd′ĭt) *tr.v.* **-it•ed, -it•ing, -its. 1.** To ascribe or attribute to; credit with. **2.a.** To supply with credentials or authority; authorize. **b.** To appoint as an ambassador to a foreign government. **3.a.** To attest to and approve as meeting a prescribed standard. See Syns at **approve. b.** To recognize (an institution of learning) as maintaining those standards requisite for its graduates to gain admission to other reputable institutions of higher learning or achieve credentials for professional practice. **4.** To believe. [Fr. *accréditer*: *a-*, to (< Lat. *ad-*; see AD-) + *crédit*, credit (< OFr.; see CREDIT).] **—ac•cred′i•ta′tion** *n.*

ac•crete (ə-krēt′) *v.* **-cret•ed, -cret•ing, -cretes.** *—tr.* To make larger or greater, as by increased growth. *—intr.* **1.** To grow together; fuse. **2.** To grow or increase gradually, as by addition. [Back-formation < ACCRETION.]

ac•cre•tion (ə-krē′shən) *n.* **1.a.** Growth or increase in size by gradual external addition, fusion, or inclusion. **b.** Something added externally to promote such growth or increase. **2.** *Biol.* The growing together or adherence of parts that are normally separate. **3.** *Geol.* **a.** Slow addition to land by deposition of water-borne sediment. **b.** An increase of land along the shores of a body of water. **4.** *Astron.* An increase in the mass of a celestial object by the collection of surrounding interstellar gases and objects by gravity. [Lat. *accrētiō, accrētiōn-* < *accrētus*, p.part. of *accrēscere*, to grow. See ACCRUE.] **—ac•cre′tion•ar′y** (-shə-nĕr′ē), **ac•cre′tive** *adj.*

accordion

Ac•cring•ton (ăk′rĭng-tən). A borough of NW England N of Manchester. Pop. 79,200.

ac•cru•al (ə-kro͞o′əl) *n.* **1.** The act or process of accumulating; an increase. **2.** Something that accumulates or increases.

ac•crue (ə-kro͞o′) *v.* **-crued, -cru•ing, -crues.** *—intr.* **1.** To come to one as a gain, an addition, or an increment. **2.** To increase, accumulate, or come about as a result of growth. **3.** To come into existence as a claim that is legally enforceable. *—tr.* To accumulate over time: *I have accrued 15 days of sick leave.* [ME *acreuen*, ult. < Lat. *accrēscere*, to grow : *ad-*, ad- + *crēscere*, to arise; see **ker-**[2]*****.] **—ac•crue′ment** *n.*

acct. *abbr.* **1.** Account. **2.** Accountant.

ac•cul•tur•ate (ə-kŭl′chə-rāt′) *v.* **-at•ed, -at•ing, -ates.** *—tr.* To cause (a society, for example) to change by the process of acculturation. *—intr.* To change by acculturation.

ac•cul•tur•a•tion (ə-kŭl′chə-rā′shən) *n.* **1.** The modification of the culture of a group or an individual as a result of contact with a different culture. **2.** The process by which the culture of a particular society is instilled in a human being from infancy onward. **—ac•cul′tur•a′tion•al** *adj.* **—ac•cul′tur•a′tive** *adj.*

ac•cum•bent (ə-kŭm′bənt) *adj.* Lying down; reclining. [Lat. *accumbēns, accumbent-*, pr.part. of *accumbere*, to recline at table : *ad-*, ad- + *cumbere*, to recline.]

ac•cu•mu•late (ə-kyo͞om′yə-lāt′) *v.* **-lat•ed, -lat•ing, -lates.** *—tr.* To gather or pile up; amass. See Syns at **gather.** *—intr.* To mount up; increase. [Lat. *accumulāre, accumulāt-* : *ad-*, ad- + *cumulāre*, to pile up (< *cumulus*, heap; see **keuə-***).] **—ac•cu′mu•la•ble** (-lə-bəl) *adj.*

ac•cu•mu•la•tion (ə-kyo͞om′yə-lā′shən) *n.* **1.** The act of gathering or amassing, as into a heap. **2.** The process of growing into a large amount or heap. **3.** A mass heaped up or collected.

ac•cu•mu•la•tive (ə-kyo͞om′yə-lā′tĭv, -lə-tĭv) *adj.* **1.** Characterized by or showing the effects of accumulation; cumulative. **2.** Tending to accumulate. **—ac•cu′mu•la•tive•ly** *adv.* **—ac•cu′mu•la•tive•ness** *n.*

ac•cu•mu•la•tor (ə-kyo͞om′yə-lā′tər) *n.* **1.** One that accumulates. **2.** A register or electric circuit in a calculator or computer, in which the results of arithmetical and logical operations are formed. **3.** *Chiefly British.* An automobile storage battery.

ac•cu•ra•cy (ăk′yər-ə-sē) *n.* **1.** Conformity to fact. **2.** Precision; exactness.

ac•cu•rate (ăk′yər-ĭt) *adj.* **1.** Conforming exactly to fact; errorless. **2.** Deviating only slightly or within acceptable limits from a standard. **3.** Capable of providing a correct reading or measurement. [Lat. *accūrātus*, done with care, p.part. of *accūrāre*, to do with care : *ad-*, ad- + *cūrāre*, to care for (< *cūra*, care; see CURE).] **—ac′cu•rate•ly** *adv.* **—ac′cu•rate•ness** *n.*

ac•curs•ed (ə-kûr′sĭd, ə-kûrst′) also **ac•curst** (ə-kûrst′) *adj.* **1.** Abominable; hateful. **2.** Being under a curse; doomed. [ME *acursed*, p.part. of *acursen*, to put a curse on : *a-*, intensive pref. (< OE *ā-*) + OE *cursian*, to curse (< *curs*, curse).] **—ac•curs′ed•ly** *adv.* **—ac•curs′ed•ness** *n.*

accus *abbr.* Accusative.

ac•cu•sa•tion (ăk′yo͞o-zā′shən) *n.* **1.** An act of accusing or

ă **pat**	oi **boy**
ā **pay**	ou **out**
âr **care**	o͝o **took**
ä **father**	o͞o **boot**
ĕ **pet**	ŭ **cut**
ē **be**	ûr **urge**
ĭ **pit**	th **thin**
ī **pie**	*th* **this**
îr **pier**	hw **which**
ŏ **pot**	zh **vision**
ō **toe**	ə **about, item**
ô **paw**	

Stress marks:
′ (primary);
′ (secondary), as in
dictionary (dĭk′shə-nĕr′ē)

the state of being accused. **2.** A charge of wrongdoing that is made against a person or other party.

ac•cu•sa•tive (ə-kyo͞o′zə-tĭv) *adj.* Of, relating to, or being the case of a noun, pronoun, adjective, or participle that is the direct object of a verb or the object of certain prepositions. —*n.* The accusative case. [ME *acusatif* < OFr. < Lat. *(casus) accūsātīvus*, (case) of accusation < *accūsātus*, p.part. of *accūsāre*, to accuse. See ACCUSE.] —**ac•cu′sa•tive•ly** *adv.*

ac•cu•sa•to•ri•al (ə-kyo͞o′zə-tôr′ē-əl, -tōr′-) also **ac•cu•sa•to•ry** (-tôr′ē, -tōr′ē) *adj.* Containing or implying accusation: *an accusatorial glare.* —**ac•cu′sa•to′ri•al•ly** *adv.*

ac•cuse (ə-kyo͞oz′) *v.* **-cused, -cus•ing, -cus•es.** —*tr.* **1.** To charge with a shortcoming or an error. **2.** To charge formally with a wrongdoing. —*intr.* To make a charge of wrongdoing against another. [ME *acusen* < Lat. *accūsāre*: *ad-*, ad- + *causa*, lawsuit.] —**ac•cus′er** *n.* —**ac•cus′ing•ly** *adv.*

ac•cused (ə-kyo͞ozd′) *n. Law.* The defendant or defendants in a criminal case.

ac•cus•tom (ə-kŭs′təm) *tr.v.* **-tomed, -tom•ing, -toms.** To familiarize, as by constant practice, use, or habit. [ME *accustomen* < OFr. *acostumer*: *a-*, to (< Lat. *ad-*; see AD–) + *costume*, custom; see CUSTOM.]

ac•cus•tomed (ə-kŭs′təmd) *adj.* **1.** Frequently practiced, used, or experienced; customary. See Syns at **usual. 2.** Being in the habit of: *I am accustomed to sleeping late.* **3.** Having been adapted to the existing environment and conditions.

AC/DC (ā′sē-dē′sē) *adj. Offensive Slang.* Engaging in or practicing bisexuality. [From the likening of a bisexual person to an appliance that works on either alternating or direct current.]

ace (ās) *n.* **1.** *Games.* **a.** A single spot or pip on a playing card, die, or domino. **b.** A playing card, die, or domino having one spot or pip. **2.** *Sports.* In racket games: **a.** A serve that one's opponent fails to return. **b.** A point scored by such a serve. **3.** *Sports.* The act of hitting a golf ball in the hole with one's first shot. **4.** A military aircraft pilot who has destroyed five or more enemy aircraft. **5.** An expert in a given field. —*adj.* Topnotch; first-rate. —*tr.v.* **aced, ac•ing, ac•es. 1.** *Sports.* To serve an ace against. **2.** *Sports.* To hit an ace in golf. **3.** *Slang.* To get the better of (someone). **4.** *Slang.* To receive a grade of A on: *She aced the exam.* —**idioms. ace in the hole.** A hidden advantage or resource kept in reserve until needed. **within an ace of.** On the verge of; very near to. [ME *as* < OFr. < Lat., unit.]

–acean *suff.* **1.** Var. of **–aceous. 2.** An organism belonging to a taxonomic group: *cetacean.* [< NLat. *-ācea*, neut. pl. of *-āceus*, -aceous.]

a•ce•di•a (ə-sē′dē-ə) *n.* Spiritual torpor and apathy; ennui. [LLat. < Gk. *akēdeia*, indifference : *a-*, a-; see A–[1] + *kēdos*, care.]

a•cel•lu•lar (ā-sĕl′yə-lər) *adj.* Containing no cells; not made of cells.

–aceous or **–acean** *suff.* **1.a.** Of or relating to: *amylaceous.* **b.** Resembling or having the nature of: *amentaceous.* **2.** Belonging to a taxonomic group: *orchidaceous.* [< Lat. *-āceus.*]

a•ceph•a•lous (ā-sĕf′ə-ləs) *adj.* **1.** *Biol.* Headless or lacking a clearly defined head. **2.** Having no leader. [< Med.Lat. *acephalus* < Gk. *akephalos*: *a-*, without; see A–[1] + *kephalē*, head; see –CEPHALOUS.]

a•ce•qui•a (ə-sā′kē-ə, ä-sā′-) *n. Southwestern U.S.* An irrigation canal. [Sp. < Ar. *as-sāqīyah.*]

ac•er•ate (ăs′ə-rāt′) also **ac•er•at•ed** (-rā′tĭd) *adj.* Acerose. [< Lat. *ācer*, sharp. See **ak-***.]

ac•er•bate (ăs′ər-bāt′) *tr.v.* **-bat•ed, -bat•ing, -bates.** To vex or annoy. [Lat. *acerbāre, acerbāt-*, to make harsh < *acerbus*, harsh. See ACERBIC.]

a•cer•bic (ə-sûr′bĭk) also **a•cerb** (ə-sûrb′) *adj.* Sour or bitter, as in taste, character, or tone. [< Lat. *acerbus.* See **ak-***.] —**a•cer′bi•cal•ly** *adv.*

a•cer•bi•ty (ə-sûr′bĭ-tē) *n., pl.* **-ties.** Sourness of taste, character, or tone.

ac•er•ose (ăs′ə-rōs′) *adj.* Needlelike, as the leaves of pine; acerate. [NLat. *acerōsus*, incorrect use (as if < Lat. *acus*, needle, or *ācer*, sharp) of Lat. *acerōsus*, full of chaff < Lat. *acus*, *acer-*, chaff. See **ak-***.]

acerose
Needles of the whitebark pine
Pinus albicaulis

acet. *abbr.* Acetone.

acet– *pref.* Var. of **aceto–.**

ac•e•tab•u•lum (ăs′ĭ-tăb′yə-ləm) *n., pl.* **-la** (-lə). **1.** *Anat.* The cup-shaped cavity at the base of the hipbone into which the head of the femur fits. **2.** *Zool.* The cavity in the body of an insect into which the leg fits. **3.** *Zool.* A cup-shaped structure, such as the sucker of a tapeworm. [Lat., vinegar cup < *acētum*, vinegar. See ACETUM.] —**ac′e•tab′u•lar** (-lər) *adj.*

ac•e•tal (ăs′ĭ-tăl′) *n.* **1.** A colorless, flammable, volatile liquid, $CH_3CH(OC_2H_5)_2$, used in cosmetics and as a solvent. **2.** Any of the class of compounds formed from aldehydes combined with alcohol. [ACET(O)– + AL(COHOL).]

ac•et•al•de•hyde (ăs′ĭ-tăl′də-hīd′) *n.* A colorless flammable liquid, C_2H_4O, used in perfumes and drugs.

a•cet•a•mide (ə-sĕt′ə-mīd′, ăs′ĭt-ăm′īd′) *n.* The crystalline amide of acetic acid, CH_3CONH_2, used as a solvent and wetting agent and in lacquers and explosives.

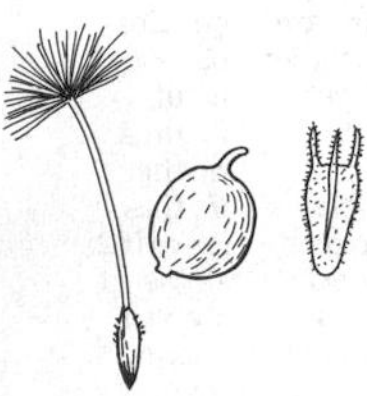

achene
Left to right: Buttercup, dandelion, and swamp beggar ticks

a•cet•a•min•o•phen (ə-sē′tə-mĭn′ə-fən, ăs′ə-) *n.* A crystalline compound, $C_8H_9NO_2$, used in chemical synthesis and to relieve pain and reduce fever. [ACET(O)– + AMINO– + PHEN(OL).]

ac•et•an•i•lide (ăs′ĭt-ăn′l-īd′) also **ac•et•an•i•lid** (-ăn′l-ĭd) *n.* A white crystalline compound, $C_6H_5NH(COCH_3)$, used to relieve pain and reduce fever. [ACET(O)– + ANIL(INE) + –IDE.]

ac•e•tate (ăs′ĭ-tāt′) *n.* **1.** A salt or ester of acetic acid. **2.** Cellulose acetate or any of various products, esp. fibers, derived from it.

a•ce•tic (ə-sē′tĭk) *adj.* Of, relating to, or containing acetic acid or vinegar. [< Lat. *acētum*, vinegar. See ACETUM.]

acetic acid *n.* A clear colorless organic acid, CH_3COOH, with a distinctive pungent odor, used as a solvent and in the manufacture of rubber, plastics, and acetate fibers, for example.

a•ce•ti•fy (ə-sē′tə-fī′, ə-sĕt′ə-) *tr. & intr.v.* **-fied, -fy•ing, -fies.** To convert or become converted to acetic acid or vinegar. —**a•ce′ti•fi•ca′tion** (-fĭ-kā′shən) *n.* —**a•ce′ti•fi•er** *n.*

aceto– or **acet–** *pref.* **1.** Acetic acid: *acetify.* **2.** Acetyl: *acetanilide.* [< Lat. *acētum*, vinegar. See ACETUM.]

ac•e•to•a•ce•tic acid (ăs′ĭ-tō-ə-sē′tĭk, ə-sē′tō-) *n.* A ketone body, CH_3COCH_2COOH, excreted in the urine in certain diabetic conditions.

ac•e•tone (ăs′ĭ-tōn′) *n.* A colorless, volatile, extremely flammable liquid ketone, CH_3COCH_3, widely used as an organic solvent. —**ac′e•ton′ic** (-tŏn′ĭk) *adj.*

acetone body *n.* See **ketone body.**

ac•e•to•phe•net•i•din (ăs′ĭ-tō-fə-nĕt′ĭ-dĭn, ə-sē′tō-) *n.* A white powder or crystalline solid, $CH_3CONHC_6H_4OC_2H_5$, derived from coal tar and used to reduce fever and relieve pain. [ACETO– + PHEN(O)– + E(THYL) + –ID(E) + –IN.]

a•ce•tous (ə-sē′təs, ăs′ĭ-təs) *adj.* **1.** Of, relating to, or producing acetic acid or vinegar. **2.** Having an acetic taste; sourtasting. [ME, sour < Med.Lat. *acētōsus*, vinegary < Lat. *acētum*, vinegar. See ACETUM.]

a•ce•tum (ə-sē′təm) *n.* **1.** Vinegar. **2.** An acetic acid solution of a drug. [Lat. *acētum.* See **ak-***.]

a•ce•tyl (ə-sēt′l, ăs′ĭ-tl) *n.* The acetic acid radical CH_3CO. —**ac′e•tyl′ic** (ăs′ĭ-tĭl′ĭk) *adj.*

a•cet•y•late (ə-sĕt′l-āt′) *tr.v.* **-lat•ed, -lat•ing, -lates.** To bring an acetyl group into (an organic molecule). —**a•cet′y•la′tion** *n.*

a•ce•tyl•cho•line (ə-sēt′l-kō′lēn′) *n.* A white crystalline derivative of choline, $C_7H_{17}NO_3$, that is involved in the transmission of nerve impulses in the body.

a•ce•tyl•cho•lin•es•ter•ase (ə-sēt′l-kō′lə-nĕs′tə-rās′, -rāz′) *n.* An enzyme found in nerve synapses that cleaves acetylcholine into acetate and choline.

a•ce•tyl-co•A (ə-sēt′l- kō′ā′, ăs′ĭ-tl-) *n.* See **acetyl coenzyme A.**

acetyl coenzyme A *n.* A compound, $C_{25}H_{38}N_7O_{17}P_3S$, that functions as a coenzyme in many biological acetylation reactions and is formed as an intermediate in the oxidation of carbohydrates, fats, and proteins.

a•cet•y•lene (ə-sĕt′l-ēn′, -ən) *n.* A colorless, highly flammable or explosive gas, C_2H_2, used for metal welding and cutting and as an illuminant. —**a•cet′y•len′ic** (ə-sĕt′l-ĕn′ĭk) *adj.*

acetylene series *n.* A series of unsaturated aliphatic hydrocarbons having chemical properties resembling acetylene and the general formula C_nH_{2n-2}.

a•ce•tyl•sal•i•cyl•ic acid (ə-sēt′l-săl′ĭ-sĭl′ĭk) *n.* See **aspirin 1.**

ace•y-deuc•y (ā′sē-do͞o′sē, -dyo͞o′-) *n. Games.* A variation of backgammon. [< ACE + DEUCE[1].]

A•chae•a (ə-kē′ə) also **A•cha•ia** (ə-kī′ə, ə-kā′ə). An ancient region of S Greece in the Peloponnesus on the Gulf of Corinth. The **Achaean League,** formed in the early 3rd cent. B.C., defeated Sparta but was eventually beaten by the Romans, who annexed Achaea in 146 B.C.

A•chae•an (ə-kē′ən) also **A•cha•ian** (ə-kā′ən, ə-kī′-) *n.* **1.** A native or inhabitant of Achaea. **2.** One of a Hellenic people believed to have inhabited the Peloponnesus and created the Mycenaean civilization. **3.** A Greek, esp. of the Mycenaean era. —**A•chae′an** *adj.*

ach•a•la•sia (ăk′ə-lā′zhə) *n.* The failure of a ring of muscle fibers, such as a sphincter of the esophagus, to relax. [NLat. : A–[1] + Gk. *khalasis*, relaxation (< *khalan*, to loosen).]

A•cha•tes (ə-kā′tēz) *n.* **1.** *Myth.* The faithful companion of Aeneas in Virgil's *Aeneid.* **2.** A loyal friend.

ache (āk) *intr.v.* **ached, ach•ing, aches. 1.** To suffer a dull, sustained pain. **2.** To feel sympathy or compassion. **3.** To yearn painfully. —*n.* **1.** A dull, steady pain. **2.** A longing or desire; a yen. [ME *aken* < OE *acan.*]

A•che•be (ä-chā′bā), **Chinua.** b. 1930. Nigerian writer whose works include the novel *Things Fall Apart* (1958).

a•chene (ā-kēn′) *n.* A small, dry, indehiscent one-seeded fruit with a thin wall. [NLat. *achenium*: Gk. *a-*, without; see A–[1] + Gk. *khainein*, to yawn.] —**a•che′ni•al** (-nē-əl) *adj.*

A•cher•nar (ā′kər-när′) *n.* A star in the constellation Eridanus that is one of the brightest stars in the sky. [< Ar. *'āḫir an-nahr*, the end of the river.]

Ach•er•on (ăk′ə-rŏn′, -rən) *n. Gk. Myth.* The river of woe, one of the five rivers of Hades.

Ach•e•son (ăch′ĭ-sən), **Dean Gooderham.** 1893–1971. Amer. public official who helped establish NATO.

A•cheu•li•an also **A•cheu•le•an** (ə-sho͞o′lē-ən) *adj.* Of or relating to a stage of tool culture of the European Lower Paleolithic Age between the second and third interglacial periods, characterized by symmetrical stone hand axes. [Fr. *acheuléen*, after St. *Acheul*, a hamlet in N France.]

a•chieve (ə-chēv′) *v.* **a•chieved, a•chiev•ing, a•chieves.** — *tr.* **1.** To perform or carry out with success; accomplish. **2.** To attain with effort or despite difficulty. See Syns at **reach.** — *intr.* To accomplish something successfully. [ME *acheven* < OFr. *achever* < *a chief (venir)*, (to come) to a head. See CHIEF.] — **a•chiev′a•ble** *adj.* — **a•chiev′er** *n.*

a•chieve•ment (ə-chēv′mənt) *n.* **1.** The act of accomplishing or finishing. **2.** Something accomplished successfully, esp. by means of exertion, skill, or perseverance.

Ach•ill (ăk′ĭl). A mountainous and barren island off the NW coast of Ireland. At its W end is **Achill Head.**

ach•il•le•a (ăk′ə-lē′ə, ə-kĭl′ē-ə) *n.* See **yarrow.** [NLat. *achillēa* < Lat., a plant that healed wounds < Gk. *achilleios*, of Achilles < *Achilleus*, Achilles.]

A•chil•les (ə-kĭl′ēz) *n. Gk. Myth.* The hero of Homer's *Iliad*, the son of Peleus and Thetis and slayer of Hector.

A•chil•les′ heel (ə-kĭl′ēz) *n.* A seemingly small but actually mortal weakness. [From Achilles being vulnerable only in the heel.]

Achilles tendon *n.* The large tendon connecting the heel bone to the calf muscle of the leg.

ach•la•myd•e•ous (ăk′lə-mĭd′ē-əs, ā′klə-) *adj.* Having no perianth, as the flowers of a willow.

a•chlor•hy•dri•a (ā′klôr-hī′drē-ə, ā′klōr-) *n.* Absence of hydrochloric acid in the gastric secretions of the stomach. [A-[1] + CHLOR(O)- + HYDR(O)- + -IA[1].] — **a•chlor•hy′dric** *adj.*

a•cho•li•a (ā-kō′lē-ə) *n.* A decrease in or an absence of bile secretion. [NLat. : A-[1] + Gk. *kholē*, bile; see **ghel-**[2]*.]

A•cho•ma•wi (ə-chō′mə-wē′) *n., pl.* **Achomawi** or **-wis. 1.** A member of a native American people inhabiting northeast California. **2.** The Hokan language of the Achomawi.

a•chon•drite (ā-kŏn′drīt′) *n.* A stony meteorite that contains no chondrules. — **a′chon•drit′ic** (-drĭt′ĭk) *adj.*

a•chon•dro•pla•sia (ā-kŏn′drō-plā′zhə, -zhē-ə) *n.* Improper development of cartilage at the ends of the long bones, resulting in a form of congenital dwarfism. — **a•chon′dro•plas′tic** (-plăs′tĭk) *adj.*

ach•ro•mat•ic (ăk′rə-măt′ĭk) *adj.* **1.** Of or relating to color having zero saturation or hue, such as white or black. **2.** Refracting light without spectral color separation. **3.** *Biol.* Difficult to stain with standard dyes. Used of cells or tissues. **4.** *Mus.* Having only the diatonic tones of the scale. [< Gk. *akhrōmatos*: *a-*, without; see A-[1] + *khrōma*, color.] — **ach′ro•mat′i•cal•ly** *adv.* — **a•chro′ma•tism** (ā-krō′mə-tĭz′əm), **ach′ro•ma•tic′i•ty** (ăk′rō-mə-tĭs′ĭ-tē) *n.*

achromatic lens *n.* A combination of lenses made of different glass, used to produce images free of chromatic aberrations.

a•chro•ma•tin (ā-krō′mə-tĭn) *n.* The part of a cell nucleus that remains less colored than the rest when stained or dyed. [ACHROMAT(IC) + -IN.] — **a•chro′ma•tin′ic** *adj.*

a•chro•ma•tize (ā-krō′mə-tīz′) *tr.v.* **-tized, -tiz•ing, -tiz•es.** To rid of color; render achromatic.

a•chro•mic (ā-krō′mĭk) *adj.* Having no color; colorless. [A-[1] + CHROM(O)- + -IC.]

ach•y (ā′kē) *adj.* **-i•er, -i•est.** Experiencing aches. — **ach′i•ness** *n.*

a•cic•u•la (ə-sĭk′yə-lə) *n., pl.* **-lae** (-lē′). A slender needlelike part or structure, such as the crystals of certain minerals. [Lat., hairpin, dim. of *acus*, needle. See **ak-***.] — **a•cic′u•late** (-lĭt, -lāt′), **a•cic′u•lat′ed** (-lā′tĭd) *adj.*

a•cic•u•lar (ə-sĭk′yə-lər) *adj.* Having the shape of a needle.

ac•id (ăs′ĭd) *n.* **1.** *Chem.* **a.** Any of a large class of sour-tasting substances whose aqueous solutions are capable of turning blue litmus indicators red, dissolving certain metals to form salts, and reacting with bases or alkalis to form salts. **b.** A substance that ionizes in solution to give the positive ion of the solvent. **c.** A substance capable of yielding hydrogen ions. **d.** A proton donor. **e.** An electron acceptor. **f.** A molecule or ion that can combine with another by forming a covalent bond with two electrons of the other. **2.** A substance having a sour taste. **3.** The quality of being sarcastic, bitter, or scornful. **4.** *Slang.* See **LSD**[1]. — *adj.* **1.** *Chem.* **a.** Of or relating to an acid. **b.** Having a high concentration of acid. **2.** Having a sour taste. **3.** Biting, sarcastic, or scornful. [< Lat. *acidus*, sour < *acēre*, to be sour. See **ak-***.] — **ac′id•ly** *adv.* — **ac′id•ness** *n.*

ac•i•dan•the•ra (ăs′ĭ-dăn′thər-ə) *n.* Any of several ornamental African plants of the genus *Acidanthera*, having fibrous corms, swordlike leaves, and large fragrant flowers. [NLat. : Gk. *akis*, *akid-*, needle; see **ak-*** + NLat. *anthera*; see ANTHER.]

ac•i•de•mi•a (ăs′ĭ-dē′mē-ə) *n.* Abnormal acidity of the blood.

ac•id-fast (ăs′ĭd-făst′) *adj.* Not decolorized by acid after staining, as bacteria that retain dye after an acid rinse. — **ac′id-fast′ness** *n.*

a•cid•ic (ə-sĭd′ĭk) *adj.* **1.** Acid. **2.** Tending to form an acid.

a•cid•i•fy (ə-sĭd′ə-fī′) *tr. & intr.v.* **-fied, -fy•ing, -fies.** To make or become acid. — **a•cid′i•fi′a•ble** *adj.* — **a•cid′i•fi•ca′tion** (-fĭ-kā′shən) *n.* — **a•cid′i•fi′er** *n.*

ac•i•dim•e•ter (ăs′ĭ-dĭm′ĭ-tər) *n.* A hydrometer used to determine the specific gravity of acid solutions. — **a•cid′i•met′ric** (ə-sĭd′ə-mĕt′rĭk) *adj.* — **ac′i•dim′e•try** *n.*

a•cid•i•ty (ə-sĭd′ĭ-tē) *n.* **1.** The state, quality, or degree of being acid. **2.** Hyperacidity.

ac•i•do•phil•ic (ăs′ĭ-dō-fĭl′ĭk) also **ac•i•doph•i•lus** (-dŏf′ə-ləs) *adj. Microbiol.* **1.** Growing well in an acid medium. **2.** Easily stained with acid dyes. — **a•cid′o•phil′** (ə-sĭd′ə-fĭl′), **a•cid′o•phile′** (-fīl′) *n.*

acidophilus milk *n.* Milk fermented by bacterial cultures that thrive in dilute acid. [NLat. *acidophilus*, specific epithet of several species of bacteria : ACID + *-philus*, -philous.]

ac•i•do•sis (ăs′ĭ-dō′sĭs) *n.* An abnormal increase in the acidity of the body's fluids, caused either by accumulation of acids or by depletion of bicarbonates. — **ac′i•dot′ic** (-dŏt′ĭk) *adj.*

acid precipitation *n.* Precipitation having an abnormally high acidity as a result of interactions with atmospheric pollutants.

acid rain *n.* Acid precipitation falling as rain.

acid rock *n. Mus.* Rock music having a prominent repetitive beat and lyrics that suggest psychedelic experiences.

acid test *n.* A decisive or critical test, as of worth or quality. [From the testing of gold in nitric acid.]

a•cid•u•late (ə-sĭj′ə-lāt′) *tr. & intr.v.* **-lat•ed, -lat•ing, -lates.** To make or become slightly acid. [ACIDUL(OUS) + -ATE[1].] — **a•cid′u•la′tion** *n.*

a•cid•u•lous (ə-sĭj′ə-ləs) *adj.* Slightly sour in taste or in manner. [< Lat. *acidulus*, dim. of *acidus*, sour. See ACID.]

ac•i•dur•i•a (ăs′ĭ-do͝or′ē-ə, -dyo͝or′-) *n.* A condition marked by the presence of acid in the urine.

acid washing *n.* A washing process in which stones soaked in chlorine acid are used to soften and bleach fabric, esp. denim. — **ac′id-washed′** (ăs′ĭd-wŏsht′, -wôsht′) *adj.*

ac•i•nar (ăs′ĭ-nər, -när′) *adj.* Of or relating to an acinus.

ac•i•nus (ăs′ə-nəs) *n., pl.* **-ni** (-nī′). *Anat.* One of the small saclike dilations composing a compound gland. [Lat., berry.] — **a•cin′ic** (ə-sĭn′ĭk), **ac′i•nous** *adj.*

ack. *abbr.* Acknowledge; acknowledgment.

ack-ack (ăk′ăk′) *n. Slang.* **1.** An antiaircraft gun. **2.** Antiaircraft fire. [British telephone code for AA, abbreviation for ANTIAIRCRAFT.]

ac•knowl•edge (ăk-nŏl′ĭj) *tr.v.* **-edged, -edg•ing, -edg•es. 1.a.** To admit the existence, reality, or truth of. **b.** To recognize as being valid or having force or power. **2.a.** To express recognition of. **b.** To express thanks or gratitude for. **3.** To report the receipt of. **4.** *Law.* To certify or notarize as legally binding. [Prob. blend of ME *knowlechen*, to acknowledge (< *knowen*, to know; see KNOW) and ME *aknouen*, to recognize (< OE *oncnāwan*, to know : *on-*, on; see ON + *cnāwan*, to know; see KNOW).] — **ac•knowl′edge•a•ble** *adj.*

ac•knowl•edged (ăk-nŏl′ĭjd) *adj.* Commonly accepted or recognized.

ac•knowl•edg•ment or **ac•knowl•edge•ment** (ăk-nŏl′ĭj-mənt) *n.* **1.** The act of admitting or owning to something. **2.** Recognition of another's existence, validity, authority, or right. **3.** A response in return for something done. **4.** An expression of thanks or a token of appreciation. **5.** A formal declaration made to authoritative witnesses to ensure legal validity.

a•clin•ic line (ā-klĭn′ĭk) *n.* See **magnetic equator.** [< Gk. *aklinēs*, not inclining to either side : *a-*, not; see A-[1] + *klinein*, to lean; see **klei-***.]

ACLU *abbr.* American Civil Liberties Union.

ac•me (ăk′mē) *n.* The highest point, as of perfection. [Gk. *akmē*. See **ak-***.]

ac•ne (ăk′nē) *n.* An inflammatory disease of the sebaceous glands and hair follicles of the skin that is marked by pimples or pustules, esp. on the face. [NLat., prob. < misreading of Gk. *akmē*, point, facial eruption. See ACME.] — **ac′ned** *adj.*

acne rosacea *n.* See **rosacea.**

a•coe•lo•mate (ə-sē′lə-māt′) *n.* An animal that lacks a coelom, exhibits bilateral symmetry, and possesses a digestive cavity. — **a•coe′lo•mate** (-lə-mĭt) *adj.*

a•coe•lous (ā-sē′ləs) *adj.* Lacking a true body cavity or digestive tract. [A-[1] + COEL(OM) + -OUS.]

ac•o•lyte (ăk′ə-līt′) *n.* **1.** One who assists the celebrant in the performance of liturgical rites. **2.** A devoted follower or attendant. [ME *acolit* < OFr. < Med.Lat. *acolytus* < Gk. *akolouthos*, attendant. See ANACOLUTHON.]

A•co•ma[1] (ăk′ə-mə, -mô′, ä′kə-) *n., pl.* **Acoma** or **-mas. 1.** A member of a Pueblo people, the founders and inhabitants of Acoma. **2.** The Keresan language of the Acoma.

A•co•ma[2] (ăk′ə-mə, -mô′, ä′kə-). A pueblo of W-central NM W of Albuquerque; founded c. 1100–1250. Pop. 975.

A•con•ca•gua (ăk′ən-kä′gwə, ä′kən-). A mountain, 7,025.4 m (23,034 ft), in the Andes of W Argentina.

ă pat	oi boy
ā pay	ou out
âr care	o͝o took
ä father	o͞o boot
ĕ pet	ŭ cut
ē be	ûr urge
ĭ pit	th thin
ī pie	*th* this
îr pier	hw which
ŏ pot	zh vision
ō toe	ə about, item
ô paw	

Stress marks:
′ (primary);
′ (secondary), as in **dictionary** (dĭk′shə-nĕr′ē)

ac•o•nite (ăk′ə-nīt′) *n.* **1.** Any of various, usu. poisonous perennial herbs of the genus *Aconitum.* **2.** The dried poisonous roots of these plants, used as a source of drugs. [Fr. *aconit* < Lat. *aconītum* < Gk. *akoniton.*]

a•corn (ā′kôrn′, ā′kərn) *n.* The fruit of an oak, consisting of a single-seeded, thick-walled nut set in a woody, cuplike base. [ME *akorn* < OE *æcern.*]

acorn squash *n.* A type of winter squash shaped somewhat like an acorn and having yellow to orange flesh.

acorn worm *n.* Any of a class (Enteropneusta) of hemichordate, wormlike animals that are equipped with an acornlike proboscis used for digging and collecting food.

aconite

a•cous•tic (ə-ko͞o′stĭk) *adj.* also **a•cous•ti•cal** (-stĭ-kəl). **1.** Of or relating to sound, the sense of hearing, or the science of sound. **2.** Designed to carry sound or to aid in hearing. **3.** *Mus.* Of, relating to, or being an instrument that does not feature electronically modified sound. —*n. Mus.* An acoustic instrument. [Gk. *akoustikos*, pertaining to hearing < *akouein*, to hear. See **keu-***.] —**a•cous′ti•cal•ly** *adv.*

ac•ous•ti•cian (ăk′o͞o-stĭsh′ən) *n.* A specialist in acoustics.

acoustic nerve *n.* Either of the eighth pair of cranial nerves that divides to form the cochlear nerve and the vestibular nerve.

a•cous•tics (ə-ko͞o′stĭks) *n.* **1.** *(used with a sing. v.)* The scientific study of sound. **2.** *(used with a pl. v.)* The total effect of sound, esp. as produced in an enclosed space.

ACP *abbr.* American College of Physicians.

acpt. *abbr.* Acceptance.

ac•quaint (ə-kwānt′) *tr.v.* **-quaint•ed, -quaint•ing, -quaints. 1.a.** To cause to come to know: *Let me acquaint you with my family.* **b.** To make familiar: *acquainted myself with the controls.* **2.** To inform: *Acquaint us with your plans.* [ME *aqueinten* < OFr. *acointier* < Med.Lat. *adcognitāre* < Lat. *accognitus*, p.part. of *accognoscere*, to know perfectly : *ad-*, intensive pref.; see AD– + *cognoscere*, to know; see COGNITION.]

ac•quain•tance (ə-kwān′təns) *n.* **1.** Knowledge of a person that is less intimate than friendship. **2.** A person whom one knows. **3.** Knowledge or information. —**ac•quain′tance•ship′** *n.*

ac•quaint•ed (ə-kwān′tĭd) *adj.* **1.** Known by or familiar with another. **2.** Informed or familiar: *acquainted with the facts.*

ac•qui•esce (ăk′wē-ĕs′) *intr.v.* **-esced, -esc•ing, -esc•es.** To consent or comply passively or without protest. See Syns at **assent.** [Lat. *acquiēscere*: *ad-*, ad- + *quiēscere*, to rest (< *quiēs*, rest; see **kʷeiə-***).]

Usage Note: When *acquiesce* takes a preposition, it is usually used with *in* (*acquiesced in the ruling*) but sometimes with *to* (*acquiesced to her parents' wishes*). *Acquiesced with* is obsolete.

acorn

ac•qui•es•cence (ăk′wē-ĕs′əns) *n.* **1.** Passive assent or agreement without protest. **2.** The state of being acquiescent.

ac•qui•es•cent (ăk′wē-ĕs′ənt) *adj.* Disposed or willing to acquiesce. —**ac′qui•es′cent•ly** *adv.*

ac•quire (ə-kwīr′) *tr.v.* **-quired, -quir•ing, -quires. 1.** To gain possession of: *acquire stock.* **2.** To get by one's own efforts: *acquire knowledge.* **3.** *Aerospace.* To locate (a satellite, for example) with a detector, esp. radar. [ME *acquere* < OFr. *aquerre* < Lat. *acquīrere*, to add to : *ad-*, ad- + *quaerere*, to seek, get.] —**ac•quir′a•ble** *adj.* —**ac•quir′er** *n.*

ac•quired character (ə-kwīrd′) *n.* A nonhereditary change in a plant or animal in response to the environment.

acquired immune deficiency syndrome *n.* AIDS.

acquired immunity *n.* Immunity obtained either from the development of antibodies in response to exposure to an antigen, as from vaccination, or from the transmission of antibodies, as from mother to fetus.

acrobat
Members of the National China Acrobats performing on unicycles

ac•quire•ment (ə-kwīr′mənt) *n.* **1.** The act of acquiring. **2.** An attainment, such as a skill.

ac•qui•si•tion (ăk′wĭ-zĭsh′ən) *n.* **1.** The act of acquiring. **2.** Something acquired. **3.** *Aerospace.* The process of locating a moving target so that its track can be determined. [ME *adquisicioun*, attainment < Lat. *acquīsitiō*, *acquīsitiōn-* < *acquīsitus*, p.part. of *acquīrere*, to acquire. See ACQUIRE.]

ac•quis•i•tive (ə-kwĭz′ĭ-tĭv) *adj.* **1.** Characterized by a strong desire to gain and possess. **2.** Tending to acquire and retain information: *an acquisitive mind.* —**ac•quis′i•tive•ly** *adv.* —**ac•quis′i•tive•ness** *n.* —**ac•quis′i•tor** (-tər) *n.*

ac•quit (ə-kwĭt′) *tr.v.* **-quit•ted, -quit•ting, -quits. 1.** *Law.* To clear from a charge or accusation. **2.** To release or discharge from a duty. **3.** To conduct (oneself) in a specified manner. **4.** *Obsolete.* To repay. [ME *aquiten* < OFr. *aquiter*: *a-*, to (< Lat. *ad-*; see AD–) + *quite*, free, clear (< Med.Lat. *quittus*, var. of Lat. *quiētus*, p.part. of *quiēscere*, to rest; see QUIET).] —**ac•quit′ter** *n.*

acropolis
As reconstructed by Friedrich Ritter von Thiersch (1852–1921)

ac•quit•tal (ə-kwĭt′l) *n.* *Law.* **1.** Judgment by a court that a defendant is not guilty of a crime. **2.** The state of being found not guilty.

ac•quit•tance (ə-kwĭt′ns) *n.* A written release from an obligation, specifically a receipt indicating payment in full.

acr– *pref.* Var. of **acro–.**

a•cre (ā′kər) *n.* **1.** A unit of area in the U.S. Customary System, equal to 160 square rods, 4,840 square yards, or 43,560 square feet. See table at **measurement. 2. acres.** Property in the form of land; estate. **3.** A large quantity. Often used in the plural. **4.** *Archaic.* A field or plot of arable land. [ME *āker*, field, acre < OE *æcer.* See **agro-***.]

A•cre (ä′krə, ā′kər) also **Ak•ko** (ä-kō′, ä′kō). A port of N Israel on the Bay of Haifa; ceded to the Arabs in the 1948 partition of Palestine but captured by Israel shortly thereafter. Pop. 37,700.

a•cre•age (ā′kər-ĭj, ā′krĭj) *n.* Area of land measured in acres.

a•cre-foot (ā′kər-fo͝ot′) *n.* The volume of water, 43,560 cubic feet, that will cover an area of one acre to a depth of one foot.

a•cre-inch (ā′kər-ĭnch′) *n.* One twelfth of an acre-foot, equal to 3,630 cubic feet.

ac•rid (ăk′rĭd) *adj.* **1.** Unpleasantly sharp or bitter to the taste or smell. **2.** Caustic in language or tone. [< Lat. *ācer*, sharp (prob. modeled on ACID). See **ak-***.] —**a•crid′i•ty** (ə-krĭd′ĭ-tē), **ac′rid•ness** *n.* —**ac′rid•ly** *adv.*

ac•ri•dine (ăk′rĭ-dēn′) *n.* A coal tar derivative, $C_{13}H_9N$, that is used in the manufacture of dyes and synthetics.

ac•ri•fla•vine (ăk′rə-flā′vēn′, -vĭn) *n.* A brown or orange powder, $C_{14}H_{14}N_3Cl$, used as a topical antiseptic. [ACRI(DINE) + FLAVIN.]

ac•ri•mo•ni•ous (ăk′rə-mō′nē-əs) *adj.* Bitter and sharp in language or tone; rancorous: *an acrimonious debate.* —**ac′ri•mo′ni•ous•ly** *adv.* —**ac′ri•mo′ni•ous•ness** *n.*

ac•ri•mo•ny (ăk′rə-mō′nē) *n.* Bitter or sharp animosity, esp. in speech or behavior. [Lat. *ācrimōnia*, sharpness < *ācer*, sharp. See **ak-***.]

A•cris•i•us (ə-krĭz′ē-əs) *n.* *Gk. Myth.* A king of Argos and father of Danaë who was killed by his grandson Perseus.

acro– or **acr–** *pref.* **1.a.** Top; summit: *acropetal.* **b.** Height: *acrophobia.* **2.a.** Tip; beginning: *acronym.* **b.** Extremity of the body: *acromegaly.* [< Gk. *akros*, extreme. See **ak-***.]

ac•ro•bat (ăk′rə-băt′) *n.* One who is skilled in feats of balance and agility in gymnastics. [Fr. *acrobate* < Gk. *akrobatēs* < *akrobatein*, to walk on tiptoe : *akros*, high; see ACRO– + *bainein*, *bat-*, to walk; see **gʷā-***.] —**ac′ro•bat′ic** *adj.* —**ac′ro•bat′i•cal•ly** *adv.*

ac•ro•bat•ics (ăk′rə-băt′ĭks) *n.* *(used with a sing. or pl. v.)* **1.** The art, skill, or moves of an acrobat. **2.** A display of great skill and agility: *vocal acrobatics.*

ac•ro•cen•tric (ăk′rō-sĕn′trĭk) *adj.* Having the centromere near one end of the chromosome so that one chromosomal arm is long and the other is short. —**ac′ro•cen′tric** *n.*

ac•ro•ceph•a•ly (ăk′rə-sĕf′ə-lē) *n.* See **oxycephaly.** —**ac′ro•ce•phal′ic** (-sə-făl′ĭk) *adj.*

a•cro•le•in (ə-krō′lē-ĭn) *n.* A colorless, flammable, poisonous liquid aldehyde, CH_2CHCHO, having an acrid odor and vapors irritating to the eyes. [ACR(ID) + OLEIN.]

ac•ro•meg•a•ly (ăk′rō-mĕg′ə-lē) *n.* A disease marked by enlargement of the bones of the extremities and face, caused by overactivity of the pituitary gland. [Fr. *acromégalie*: Gk. *akron*, extremity (< *akros*, extreme; see ACRO–) + Gk. *megas*, *megal-*, big; see **meg-***.] —**ac′ro•me•gal′ic** (-mĭ-găl′ĭk) *adj.* & *n.*

a•cro•mi•on (ə-krō′mē-ən) *n.* The outer end of the scapula. [NLat. *acrōmion* < Gk. *akrōmion*: *akros*, extreme; see **ak-*** + *ōmion*, dim. of *ōmos*, shoulder.]

ac•ro•nym (ăk′rə-nĭm′) *n.* A word formed from the initial letters or parts of a word, such as *PAC* for *p*olitical *a*ction *c*ommittee. [ACR(O)– + –ONYM.] —**ac′ro•nym′ic, a•cron′y•mous** (ə-krŏn′ə-məs) *adj.*

a•crop•e•tal (ə-krŏp′ĭ-tl) *adj.* Developing from the base toward the apex of a plant. —**a•crop′e•tal•ly** *adv.*

ac•ro•pho•bi•a (ăk′rə-fō′bē-ə) *n.* An abnormal fear of high places.

a•crop•o•lis (ə-krŏp′ə-lĭs) *n.* The fortified height or citadel of an ancient Greek city. [Gk. *akropolis*: *akron*, top (< *akros*, extreme; see ACRO–) + *polis*, city; see **pelə-³***.]

ac•ro•some (ăk′rə-sōm′) *n.* A caplike structure at the end of a spermatozoon that produces enzymes aiding in egg penetration. [ACRO– + –SOME³.] —**ac′ro•so′mal** (-sō′məl) *adj.*

a•cross (ə-krôs′, ə-krŏs′) *prep.* **1.** On, at, or from the other side of: *across the street.* **2.** So as to cross; through: *drew lines across the paper.* **3.** From one side of to the other. **4.** Into contact with: *came across my old friend.* —*adv.* **1.** From one side to the other. **2.** On or to the opposite side. **3.** Crosswise; crossed. **4.** So as to be comprehensible or successful: *put our idea across.* [ME *acrois* < AN *an croiz*: *an*, in (< Lat. *in*; see IN–²) + *croiz*, cross (< Lat. *crux*; see CROSS).]

a•cross-the-board (ə-krôs′thə-bôrd′, -bōrd′, ə-krŏs′-) *adj.* **1.** Including all categories or members. **2.** *Sports & Games.* Of or relating to a bet that wins if a contestant finishes first, second, or third.

a•cros•tic (ə-krô′stĭk, ə-krŏs′tĭk) *n.* **1.** A poem or series of lines in which certain letters, usu. the first, form a name or motto. **2.** See **word square.** [Fr. *acrostiche* < OFr. < Gk. *akrostikhis*: *akron*, head, end (< *akros*, extreme; see ACRO–) + *stikhos*, line; see **steigh-***.] —**a•cros′tic** *adj.* —**a•cros′ti•cal•ly** *adv.*

ACRR *abbr.* American Council on Race Relations.

ac•ry•late resin (ăk′rə-lāt′) *n.* Any of a class of acrylic resins used esp. in emulsion paints, adhesives, and plastics.

a•cryl•ic (ə-krĭl**′**ĭk) *n.* **1.** An acrylic resin. **2.** A paint containing acrylic resin. **3.** A painting done in acrylic resin. **4.** An acrylic fiber. [ACR(OLEIN) + -YL + -IC.] **— a•cryl′ic** *adj.*

acrylic acid *n.* An easily polymerized, colorless corrosive liquid, H_2C:CHCOOH, used as a monomer for acrylate resins.

acrylic fiber *n.* Any of numerous synthetic fibers polymerized from acrylonitrile.

acrylic resin *n.* Any of numerous thermoplastic polymers of acrylic acid, methacrylic acid, esters of these acids, or acrylonitrile, used esp. to produce paints and plastics.

ac•ry•lo•ni•trile (ăk′rə-lō-nī**′**trəl, -trēl, -trīl) *n.* A colorless liquid organic compound, H_2C:CHCN, used in the manufacture of acrylic rubber and fibers. [ACRYL(IC RESIN) + NITRILE.]

ACS *abbr.* **1.** American Chemical Society. **2.** American College of Surgeons.

act (ăkt) *n.* **1.** The process of doing or performing something: *the act of thinking.* **2.** Something done or performed; a deed: *a charitable act.* **3.** A decision, such as a statute or decree, delivered by a legislative or judicial body. **4.** A written record of proceedings or transactions. **5.a.** One of the major divisions of a play or an opera. **b.** A theatrical performance that forms part of a longer presentation. **6.** A manifestation of insincerity; a pose. *— v.* **act•ed, act•ing, acts.** *— tr.* **1.** To play the part of; assume the dramatic role of: *act Lady Macbeth.* **2.** To perform (a role) on the stage. **3.a.** To behave like or pose as. **b.** To behave in a manner suitable for: *Act your age.* *— intr.* **1.** To behave or comport oneself: *act like a born leader.* **2.** To perform in a dramatic role or roles. **3.** To be suitable for performance: *This scene acts well.* **4.** To behave affectedly or unnaturally; pretend. **5.** To appear or seem to be: *The dog acted ferocious.* **6.** To carry out an action: *The governor acted on the bill.* **7.** To operate or function in a specific way: *His mind acts quickly.* **8.** To serve or function as a substitute: *A coin can act as a screwdriver.* **9.** To produce an effect: *The drug acts slowly.* ***— phrasal verbs.*** **act out. 1.a.** To perform in or as if in a play; dramatize: *act out a story.* **b.** To realize in action: *act out a theory.* **2.** To express (unconscious impulses, for example) without awareness or understanding. **act up. 1.** To misbehave. **2.** To malfunction. **3.** *Informal.* To become painful or troublesome again. ***— idioms.*** **clean up (one's) act.** *Slang.* To improve one's behavior or performance. **get (one's) act together.** *Slang.* To get organized. [ME < OFr. *acte* < Lat. *āctus*, a doing, and *āctum*, a thing done, both < *agere*, *āct-*, to drive, do. See **ag-***.] **— ac′ta•bil′i•ty** *n.* **— act′a•ble** *adj.*

Usage Note: The words *act* and *action* both mean "a deed" and "the process of doing." However, *act* tends to refer to a deed while *action* tends to refer to the process of doing. The demands of meaning or idiom will often require one word or the other: *class act* and *class action,* for example, are not interchangeable. In cases where either *act* or *action* can be used, either is acceptable: *My act* (or *action*) *was premature.*

Ac•tae•on (ăk-tē**′**ən) *n. Gk. Myth.* A hunter who, having seen Artemis bathing, was turned into a stag and killed by his own dogs.

actg. *abbr.* Acting.

ACTH (ā′sē′tē-āch**′**) *n.* A hormone produced by the anterior lobe of the pituitary gland that stimulates the secretion of hormones by the adrenal cortex. [A(DRENO)C(ORTICO)T(ROPIC) H(ORMONE).]

ac•tin (ăk**′**tĭn) *n.* A protein found in muscle that together with myosin functions in muscle contraction. [Lat. *āctus*, motion (< *agere*, *āct-*, to drive, do; see ACT) + -IN.]

ac•ti•nal (ăk**′**tĭ-nəl, ăk-tī**′**-) *adj.* Of or relating to the part of a radially symmetric animal from which the tentacles radiate or the side where the oral area is found. **— ac′ti•nal•ly** *adv.*

act•ing (ăk**′**tĭng) *adj.* **1.** Temporarily assuming the duties of another. **2.** Appropriate for dramatic performance: *an acting comedy.* *— n.* **1.** The occupation of an actor or actress. **2.** Performance as an actor or actress.

ac•tin•i•a (ăk-tĭn**′**ē-ə) also **ac•tin•i•an** (-ən) *n., pl.* **-i•ae** (-ē-ē′) also **-i•ans.** A sea anemone or a related animal. [NLat. *Actinia*, genus name < Gk. *aktis*, *aktin-*, ray. See ACTINO-.]

ac•tin•ic (ăk-tĭn**′**ĭk) *adj.* Of, relating to, or exhibiting actinism. **— ac•tin′i•cal•ly** *adv.*

actinic ray *n.* Photochemically active radiation, as of the sun.

ac•ti•nide (ăk**′**tə-nīd′) *n.* Any of a series of chemically similar, radioactive elements with atomic numbers ranging from 89 (actinium) through 103 (lawrencium).

ac•ti•nism (ăk**′**tə-nĭz′əm) *n.* The intrinsic property in radiation that produces photochemical activity.

ac•tin•i•um (ăk-tĭn**′**ē-əm) *n. Symbol* **Ac** A radioactive element found in uranium ores. Its longest lived isotope is Ac 227 with a half-life of 21.7 years. Atomic number 89; melting point 1,050°C; boiling point (estimated) 3,200°C; specific gravity (calculated) 10.07; valence 3. See table at **element.** [ACTIN(O)- + -IUM.]

actino- or **actin-** *pref.* **1.** Radial in form: *actinoid.* **2.** Actinic radiation: *actinometer.* [< Gk. *aktis*, *aktin-*, ray.]

ac•ti•noid (ăk**′**tə-noid′) *adj.* Having a radial form, as a starfish.

ac•tin•o•lite (ăk-tĭn**′**ə-līt′) *n.* A greenish variety of amphibole.

ac•ti•no•mere (ăk-tĭn**′**ə-mîr′) *n.* One of the segments forming the body of a radially symmetric animal.

ac•ti•nom•e•ter (ăk′tə-nŏm**′**ĭ-tər) *n.* Any of several radiometric instruments used chiefly for meteorological measurements of terrestrial and solar radiation. **— ac′ti•no•met′ric** (-nō-mĕt**′**rĭk), **ac′ti•no•met′ri•cal** *adj.* **— ac′ti•nom′e•try** *n.*

ac•ti•no•mor•phic (ăk′tə-nō-môr**′**fĭk) also **ac•ti•no•mor•phous** (-fəs) *adj.* Having radial form, as a tulip flower. **— ac′ti•no•mor′phy** *n.*

ac•ti•no•my•ces (ăk′tə-nō-mī**′**sēz′) *n., pl.* **actinomyces.** Any of various filamentous, mostly anaerobic microorganisms of the genus *Actinomyces,* which includes the causative agents of actinomycosis. [NLat., genus name : ACTINO- + Gk. *mukēs*, fungus.]

ac•ti•no•my•cete (ăk′tə-nō-mī**′**sēt′, -mī-sēt**′**) *n.* Any of various filamentous or rod-shaped, often pathogenic microorganisms of the order Actinomycetales that are found in soil. **— ac′ti•no•my•ce′•tal** (-mī-sēt**′**l), **ac′ti•no•my′ce•tous** *adj.*

ac•ti•no•my•cin (ăk′tə-nō-mī**′**sĭn) *n.* Any of various red, often toxic polypeptide antibiotics obtained from soil bacteria.

ac•ti•no•my•co•sis (ăk′tə-nō-mī-kō**′**sĭs) *n.* An inflammatory disease of cattle, hogs, and sometimes human beings, caused by microorganisms of the genus *Actinomyces* and characterized by lumpy tumors. **— ac′ti•no•my•cot′ic** (-kŏt**′**ĭk) *adj.*

ac•ti•non (ăk**′**tə-nŏn′) *n.* A radioactive, inert gaseous isotope of radon, with a half-life of 3.92 seconds. [ACTIN(IUM) + -ON[2].]

ac•ti•no•u•ra•ni•um (ăk′tə-nō-yo͝o-rā**′**nē-əm) *n.* The isotope of uranium with mass number 235, fissionable with relatively low-energy neutrons. [ACTIN(IUM) + URANIUM.]

ac•tion (ăk**′**shən) *n.* **1.** The state or process of acting or doing. **2.** A deed. See Usage Note at **act. 3.** A movement or a series of movements. **4.** Manner of movement: *a gearshift with smooth action.* **5.** Habitual, vigorous activity. **6.** Behavior or conduct. Often used in the plural. **7.a.** The operating parts of a mechanism. **b.** The manner in which such parts operate. **8.** Effect or influence: *the action of a drug.* **9.** A change that occurs in the body or in a bodily organ as a result of its functioning. **10.** A physical change, as in mass or energy, that an object or a system undergoes. **11.** The series of events that form the plot of a story or play. **12.** The appearance of animation of a figure in painting or sculpture. **13.** *Law.* A judicial proceeding undertaken against another. **14.** Armed encounter; combat. **15.** Activity or excitement.

ac•tion•a•ble (ăk**′**shə-nə-bəl) *adj. Law.* Giving cause for legal action: *an actionable statement.* **— ac′tion•a•bly** *adv.*

action painting *n.* A style of abstract painting that uses techniques such as the dribbling or splashing of paint to achieve a spontaneous effect. **— action painter** *n.*

action potential *n.* A momentary change in electrical potential on the surface of a nerve or muscle cell that takes place when it is stimulated, esp. by the transmission of a nerve impulse.

Ac•ti•um (ăk**′**shē-əm, -tē-). A promontory and ancient town of W Greece; site of Octavian's victory over Mark Antony and Cleopatra (31 B.C.).

ac•ti•vate (ăk**′**tə-vāt′) *v.* **-vat•ed, -vat•ing, -vates.** *tr.v.* **1.** To set in motion; make active or more active. **2.** To organize or create (a military unit, for example). **3.** To treat (sewage) with air and bacteria in order to accelerate decomposition. **4.** *Chem.* To accelerate a reaction in, as by heat. **5.** *Phys.* To make (a substance) radioactive. **6.** *Biol.* To convert (compounds) into biologically active derivatives. **— ac′ti•va′tion** *n.* **— ac′ti•va′tor** *n.*

ac•ti•vat•ed charcoal (ăk**′**tə-vā′tĭd) *n.* A highly absorbent form of carbon made by heating granulated charcoal and used primarily for purifying gases and deodorization.

ac•ti•va•tion analysis (ăk′tə-vā**′**shən) *n.* A method for analyzing a material for its component chemical elements by bombarding it with nuclear particles or gamma rays and identifying the resultant radiations.

ac•tive (ăk**′**tĭv) *adj.* **1.** Being in physical motion. **2.** Functioning or capable of functioning. **3.** Disposed to take action or effectuate change. **4.a.** Engaged in activity; participating: *an active member of a club.* **b.** Busy: *active markets.* **c.** Being in continuous use. **5.** Being in a state of action: *an active volcano.* **6.a.** Characterized by energetic action or activity; lively. **b.** Requiring physical exertion and energy: *active sports.* **7.** *Gram.* **a.** Indicating that the subject of the sentence is performing or causing the action of the verb. Used of a verb form or voice. **b.** Expressing action rather than a state of being. Used of verbs such as *run* or *speak.* **8.** Being on full military duty and receiving full pay. *— n.* **1.** *Gram.* **a.** The active voice. **b.** A construction or form in the active voice. **2.** A participating member of an organization: *union actives.* [ME *actif* < OFr. < Lat. *āctīvus* < *agere*, *āct-*, to drive, do. See **ag-***.] **— ac′tive•ly** *adv.* **— ac′tive•ness** *n.*

active immunity *n.* Immunity resulting from the development of antibodies in response to the presence of an antigen.

actinoid
A starfish
Asterias forbesii

action painting
c. 1950 untitled India ink on paper, 17½" x 22¼" (irregular), by Jackson Pollock.
The Museum of Modern Art, New York. Gift of Mr. and Mrs. Ronald Lauder in honor of Eliza Parkinson Cobb.

ă **pat**	oi **boy**
ā **pay**	ou **out**
âr **care**	o͝o **took**
ä **father**	o͞o **boot**
ĕ **pet**	ŭ **cut**
ē **be**	ûr **urge**
ĭ **pit**	th **thin**
ī **pie**	*th* **this**
îr **pier**	hw **which**
ŏ **pot**	zh **vision**
ō **toe**	ə **about,**
ô **paw**	**item**

Stress marks:
′ (primary);
′ (secondary), as in
dictionary (dĭk**′**shə-nĕr′ē)

Abigail Adams
Detail of portrait by Gilbert Stuart

John Adams
Detail of portrait by Gilbert Stuart

John Quincy Adams
Detail of 1864 portrait by George Peter Alexander Healy (1813–1894)

addax
Addax nasomaculatus

active site *n.* The part of an enzyme at which catalysis of the substrate occurs.

active transport *n.* The movement of a substance across a cell membrane by means of chemical energy in the direction opposite to normal diffusion.

ac•tiv•ism (ăk**′**tə-vĭz′əm) *n.* The doctrine or practice of assertive, often militant action, such as strikes, as a means of achieving a political or social goal. **—ac′tiv•ist** *n. & adj.* **—ac•tiv•ist′ic** *adj.*

ac•tiv•i•ty (ăk-tĭv**′**ĭ-tē) *n., pl.* **-ties. 1.** The state of being active. **2.** Energetic action or movement; liveliness. **3.a.** A specified pursuit or action. **b.** An educational procedure intended to stimulate learning through experience. **4.** The intensity of a radioactive source. **5.** The ability to take part in a chemical reaction. **6.** A physiological process: *respiratory activity.*

act of God *n., pl.* **acts of God.** An unusual or unforeseeable manifestation of the forces of nature that could not be prevented, such as a tornado.

ac•to•my•o•sin (ăk′tə-mī**′**ə-sĭn) *n.* The system of actin and myosin that, with other substances, constitutes muscle fiber and is responsible for muscular contraction. [ACT(IN) + MYOSIN.]

Ac•ton (ăk**′**tən). A town of NE MA, a suburb of Boston. Pop. 17,872.

Acton, 1st Baron. John Emerich Edward Dalberg Acton. 1834–1902. British historian and educator.

ac•tor (ăk**′**tər) *n.* **1.** A theatrical performer. **2.** One who takes part; a participant. [ME *actour,* doer, prob. < Lat. *āctor* < *agere, āct-,* to drive, do. See **ag-***.]

ac•tress (ăk**′**trĭs) *n.* A woman who is an actor. See Usage Note at **–ess.**

Acts of the Apostles (ăkts) *pl.n. (used with a sing. v.)* See table at **Bible.**

ac•tu•al (ăk**′**cho͞o-əl) *adj.* **1.** Existing and not merely potential or possible. **2.** Being, existing, or acting at the present moment; current. **3.** Based on fact: *an actual account of the accident.* [ME < OFr., active < LLat. *āctuālis* < Lat. *agere, āct-,* to drive, do. See **ag-***.] **—ac′tu•al•ly** *adv.*

ac•tu•al•i•ty (ăk′cho͞o-ăl**′**ĭ-tē) *n., pl.* **-ties. 1.** The state or fact of being actual; reality. **2.** An actual condition or fact. Often used in the plural.

ac•tu•al•ize (ăk**′**cho͞o-ə-līz′) *v.* **-ized, -iz•ing, -iz•es.** —*tr.* **1.** To realize in action or make real. **2.** To describe or portray realistically. —*intr.* To become actual. **—ac′tu•al•i•za′tion** (-ə-lĭ-zā**′**shən) *n.*

ac•tu•ar•y (ăk**′**cho͞o-ĕr′ē) *n., pl.* **-ies.** A statistician who computes insurance risks and premiums. [Lat. *āctuārius,* secretary of accounts < *ācta,* records < *agere, āct-,* to drive, do. See **ag-***.] **—ac′tu•ar′i•al** *adj.* **—ac′tu•ar′i•al•ly** *adv.*

ac•tu•ate (ăk**′**cho͞o-āt′) *tr.v.* **-at•ed, -at•ing, -ates. 1.** To put into motion or action. **2.** To move to action: *a speech that actuated dissent.* [Med.Lat. *āctuāre, āctuāt-* < Lat. *āctus,* act. See ACT.] **—ac′tu•a′tion** *n.* **—ac′tu•a′tor** *n.*

a•cu•i•ty (ə-kyo͞o**′**ĭ-tē) *n.* Acuteness of vision or perception. [ME *acuite* < OFr., ult. < Lat. *acūtus,* sharp. See ACUTE.]

a•cu•le•ate (ə-kyo͞o**′**lē-ĭt, -āt′) *adj.* **1.** *Biol.* Having a stinger, as a bee or wasp. **2.** *Bot.* Having sharp prickles. [Lat. *aculeātus* < *acūleus,* sting, dim. of *acus,* needle. See ACUMEN.]

a•cu•men (ə-kyo͞o**′**mən, ăk**′**yə-) *n.* Quickness, accuracy, and keenness of judgment or insight. [Lat. *acūmen* < *acuere,* to sharpen < *acus,* needle. See **ak-***.]

a•cu•mi•nate (ə-kyo͞o**′**mə-nĭt, -nāt′) *adj.* Tapering to a point: *acuminate leaves.* —*tr.v.* (ə-kyo͞o**′**mə-nāt′) **-nat•ed, -nat•ing, -nates.** To make sharp; taper. [Lat. *acūminātus,* p.part. of *acūmināre,* to sharpen < *acūmen,* acuteness. See ACUMEN.] **—a•cu′mi•na′tion** *n.*

ac•u•pres•sure (ak**′**yə-prĕsh′ər) *n.* See **shiatsu.** [ACU(PUNCTURE) + PRESSURE.]

ac•u•punc•ture (ăk**′**yo͝o-pŭngk′chər) *n.* A technique, as for relieving pain or inducing regional anesthesia, in which needles are inserted into the body at specific points. [Lat. *acus,* needle; see **ak-*** + PUNCTURE.] **—ac′u•punc′tur•ist** *n.*

a•cute (ə-kyo͞ot**′**) *adj.* **1.** Having a sharp point or tip. **2.** Keenly perceptive or discerning. See Syns at **sharp. 3.** Reacting readily to impressions; sensitive. **4.** Of great importance or consequence; crucial: *an acute lack of funds.* **5.** Extremely sharp or severe; intense: *acute pain.* **6.** *Medic.* **a.** Having a rapid onset and a short, severe course: *acute disease.* **b.** Afflicted with an acute disease. **7.** *Mus.* High in pitch; shrill. **8.** *Geometry.* Being angles less than 90°. [Lat. *acūtus,* p.part. of *acuere,* to sharpen < *acus,* needle. See **ak-***.] **—a•cute′ly** *adv.* **—a•cute′ness** *n.*

acute accent *n.* A mark (´) indicating: **a.** A vowel that is close or tense, such as *é* in French *été.* **b.** A high or rising pitch of a vowel or syllable, as in Chinese or Ancient Greek. **c.** A long vowel, as in Czech *dobrý.* **d.** Stress of a syllable in which a vowel appears, as in Spanish *fácil.*

acv *abbr.* Actual cash value.

ACV *abbr.* Air-cushion vehicle.

a•cy•clic (ā-sī**′**klĭk, ā-sĭk**′**lĭk) *adj.* **1.** *Bot.* Not cyclic: *an acyclic flower.* **2.** *Chem.* Having an open-chain molecular structure.

a•cy•clo•vir (ā-sī**′**klō-vîr, -klə-) *n.* A synthetic purine nucleoside analog, $C_8H_{10}N_5O_3$, used topically in the treatment of herpes simplex infections. [A-¹ + CYCLO- + VIR(AL) or VIR(US).]

ac•yl (ăs**′**əl) *n. Chem.* A radical having the general formula RCO-, derived from an organic acid. [AC(ID) + -YL.]

ad¹ (ăd) *n.* An advertisement.

ad² (ăd) *n. Sports.* An advantage in tennis.

AD *abbr.* **1.** Active duty. **2.** Air-dried.

ad. *abbr.* Adapter.

A.D. *abbr.* Often A.D. Anno Domini.

ad– *pref.* **1. ac–** or **af–** or **ag–** or **al–** or **ap–** or **as–** or **at–.** Toward; to. Before *c, f, g, k, l, p, q, s,* and *t, ad-* is usually assimilated to *ac-, af-, ag-, ac-, al-, ap-, ac-, as-,* and *at-,* respectively. **2.** Near; at: *adrenal.* [Lat. < *ad,* to. See **ad-***.]

–ad *suff.* In the direction of; toward: *cephalad.* [< Lat. *ad,* to. See **ad-***.]

A•da¹ (ā**′**də). A city of S-central OK SE of Oklahoma City. Pop. 15,820.

A•da² (ā**′**də) *n. Comp. Sci.* A programming language, based on Pascal and developed for the U.S. Department of Defense. [After Augusta *Ada* Byron, Countess of Lovelace (1815–52).]

ADA *abbr.* **1.** American Dental Association. **2.** American Diabetes Association. **3.** Americans for Democratic Action.

ad•age (ăd**′**ĭj) *n.* A traditional saying; a proverb. [Fr. < OFr. < Lat. *adagium.*]

Usage Note: It is sometimes claimed that the expression *old adage* is redundant, inasmuch as a saying must have a certain tradition behind it to count as an *adage* in the first place. But the word *adage* is first recorded by the *Oxford English Dictionary* in the phrase *old adage,* showing that this redundancy itself is very old. Such idiomatic redundancy is paralleled by similar phrases such as *young whelp.*

a•da•gio (ə-dä**′**jō, -jē-ō′, -zhō, -zhē-ō) *adv. & adj. Mus.* In a slow tempo. —*n., pl.* **-gios. 1.** *Mus.* A slow passage, movement, or work. **2.** A section of a pas de deux requiring great skill in lifting, balancing, and turning. [Ital. : *ad-,* at (< Lat.; see AD-) + *agio,* ease (< OProv. *aize* < VLat. **adiacēs* < Lat. *adiacēns,* convenient; see ADJACENT).]

A•dak (ā**′**dăk′). An island of W AK in the central Aleutian Is.

Ad•am¹ (ăd**′**əm). In the Bible, the first man and the husband of Eve.

Ad•am² (ăd**′**əm) *adj.* Of or relating to the neoclassic style of furniture and architecture originated by Robert and James Adam.

Adam, Robert. 1728–92. British neoclassic architect and designer who collaborated with his brother **James** (1730–94).

Ad•am-and-Eve (ăd′əm-ənd-ēv**′**) *n.* See **puttyroot.**

ad•a•mant (ăd**′**ə-mənt, -mănt′) *adj.* Impervious to pleas or reason; stubbornly unyielding. —*n.* **1.** A stone once believed to be impenetrable in its hardness. **2.** An extremely hard substance. [< ME, a hard precious stone < OFr. *adamaunt* < Lat. *adamās, adamant-,* hard steel, diamond, anything inflexible < Gk. *adamas, adamant-,* hard steel, diamond, anything fixed or unalterable, unconquerable. See **demə-***.]

ad•a•man•tine (ăd′ə-măn**′**tēn′, -tīn′, -tĭn) *adj.* **1.** Made of or resembling adamant. **2.** Having the hardness or luster of a diamond. **3.** Unyielding; inflexible.

Ad•ams (ăd**′**əmz), **Abigail Smith.** 1744–1818. First Lady of the U.S. (1797–1801).

Adams, Ansel. 1902–84. Amer. photographer noted for his black-and-white photographs of the wilderness.

Adams, Brooks. 1848–1927. Amer. historian who theorized that civilizations rise and fall according to a pattern of economic growth and decline.

Adams, Charles Francis. 1807–86. Amer. public official who served as ambassador to Great Britain during the Civil War.

Adams, Franklin Pierce. "F.P.A." 1881–1960. Amer. humorist who wrote "The Conning Tower" column.

Adams, Henry Brooks. 1838–1918. Amer. historian noted for his autobiography, *The Education of Henry Adams* (1918).

Adams, John. 1735–1826. The first Vice President (1789–97) and second President (1797–1801) of the U.S. He was a major figure during the drafting of the Declaration of Independence and the Constitution.

Adams, John Quincy. 1767–1848. The sixth President of the U.S. (1825–29). He later served in the House of Representatives (1831–48), where he advocated antislavery measures.

Adams, Mount. A peak, 3,753.6 m (12,307 ft), in the Cascade Range of SW WA.

Adams, Samuel. 1722–1803. Amer. Revolutionary leader whose agitations spurred Bostonians toward rebellion against British occupation and rule.

Ad•am's apple (ăd**′**əmz) *n.* The slight projection at the front of the throat formed by the largest cartilage of the larynx.

Adam's Bridge also **Ra•ma's Bridge** (rä**′**məz). A chain of shoals between India and Sri Lanka.

Ad•am's-nee•dle (ăd**′**əmz-nēd**′**l) *n.* Any of several related, stemless plants of the genus *Yucca.* [From the spines on its leaves.]

Adam's Peak. A mountain, 2,244.8 m (7,360 ft), in S-central Sri Lanka; a pilgrimage site for Buddhists, Hindus, and Muslims.

A·da·na (ä′də-nə, ə-dä′nə). A city of S Turkey near the Mediterranean; probably founded by the Hittites. Pop. 574,515.
a·dapt (ə-dăpt′) *v.* **a·dapt·ed, a·dapt·ing, a·dapts.** — *tr.* To make suitable to a specific use or situation. — *intr.* To become adapted. [ME *adapten* < Lat. *adaptāre*: *ad-*, ad- + *aptāre*, to fit (< *aptus*, fitting; see APT).]
Syns: *adapt, accommodate, adjust, conform, fit, reconcile.* The central meaning shared by these verbs is "to make suitable to or consistent with a particular situation or use": *adapted themselves to city life; can't accommodate myself to the new requirements; adjusting their behavior to the rules; conforming her life to the church's teachings; fit the punishment to the crime; couldn't reconcile his gentle words with his hostile actions.* ***Ant:*** *unfit.*
a·dapt·a·ble (ə-dăp′tə-bəl) *adj.* Capable of adapting or of being adapted. —**a·dapt′a·bil′i·ty, a·dapt′a·ble·ness** *n.*
ad·ap·ta·tion (ăd′ăp-tā′shən) *n.* **1.a.** The act or process of adapting. **b.** The state of being adapted. **2.a.** Something that is changed or changes to become suitable to a new situation. **b.** A composition recast into a new form: *an adaptation of a novel for the stage.* **3.** *Biol.* A usu. hereditary alteration in an organism that facilitates its survival and reproduction. **4.** *Physiol.* The responsive adjustment of a sense organ, such as the eye, to varying conditions, such as light intensity. **5.** Change in behavior in response to new surroundings. —**ad′ap·ta′tion·al** *adj.* —**ad′ap·ta′tion·al·ly** *adv.*
a·dapt·er also **a·dap·tor** (ə-dăp′tər) *n.* One that adapts, such as a device used to connect different pieces of apparatus.
a·dap·tion (ə-dăp′shən) *n.* Adaptation.
a·dap·tive (ə-dăp′tĭv) *adj.* Showing or capable of adaptation. —**a·dap′tive·ly** *adv.* —**a·dap′tive·ness** *n.*
adaptive radiation *n.* Diversification of a species or single ancestral type into several forms that are each adaptively specialized to a specific environmental niche.
A·dar (ä-där′, ä′där) *n.* The sixth month of the year in the Jewish calendar. [Heb. *'ădār* < Akkadian *adaru*, a month of the Akkadian calendar corresponding to parts of February and March.]
Adar She·ni (shā-nē′) *n.* An extra month of the Hebrew year, having 29 days, added in leap years after the regular month of Adar. [Heb. *'ădār šēnî*, second Adar.]
ad·ax·i·al (ăd-ăk′sē-əl) *adj.* Located on the side nearest to the axis of an organ or organism.
ADC *abbr.* **1.** Also **a.d.c.** Aide-de-camp. **2.** Aid to Dependent Children. **3.** Air Defense Command.
add (ăd) *v.* **add·ed, add·ing, adds.** — *tr.* **1.** To combine into a sum. **2.** To join or unite so as to increase in size, quantity, quality, or scope: *added 12 inches to the deck.* **3.** To say or write further. — *intr.* **1.** To find a sum in arithmetic. **2.** To constitute an addition: *an exploit that will add to her reputation.* **3.** To make or create an addition. —***phrasal verb.*** **add up. 1.** To be reasonable, plausible, or consistent; make sense. **2.** To amount to an expected total. —***idiom.*** **add up to.** To constitute; amount to: *This movie adds up to a lot of tears.* [ME *adden* < Lat. *addere*: *ad-*, ad- + *dare*, to give; see **dō-***.] —**add′a·ble, add′i·ble** *adj.*
ADD *abbr.* Attention deficit disorder.
add. *abbr.* **1.** Addendum. **2.** Addition.
Ad·dams (ăd′əmz), **Jane.** 1860–1935. Amer. social reformer who shared the 1931 Nobel Peace Prize.
ad·dax (ăd′ăks′) *n.* An antelope *(Addax nasomaculatus)* of northern Africa having long twisted horns. [Lat., of African orig.]
ad·dend (ăd′ĕnd′, ə-dĕnd′) *n.* Any of a set of numbers to be added. [Short for ADDENDUM.]
ad·den·dum (ə-dĕn′dəm) *n., pl.* **-da** (-də). Something added or to be added, esp. a supplement to a book. [Lat., neut. gerundive of *addendus*, gerundive of *addere*, to add. See ADD.]
add·er¹ (ăd′ər) *n.* One that adds, esp. a computational device that performs arithmetic addition.
ad·der² (ăd′ər) *n.* **1.** See **viper** 1. **2.** Any of several nonvenomous snakes popularly believed to be harmful. [ME < *an addre*, alteration of *a naddre*: *a*, a; see A² + *naddre*, snake (< OE *nǣdre*).]
Word History: The biblical injunction to be wise as serpents and innocent as doves looks somewhat alien in Middle English "Loke ye be prudent as neddris and symple as dowves." *Neddris* would be *adders* in Modern English, with a different meaning and form. *Adder*, an example of specialization in meaning, no longer refers to just any serpent or snake, as it once did, but now denotes only specific kinds of snakes. *Adder* also illustrates a process known as false splitting, or juncture loss: the word came from Old English *nǣdre* and kept its *n* into the Middle English period, but later during that stage of the language people started writing the phrase *a naddre* as *an addre*, which has given us *adder*.
ad·der's-mouth (ăd′ərz-mouth′) *n.* Any of various chiefly terrestrial orchids of the genus *Malaxis*, having small, often greenish flowers. [From the resemblance of its flowers to the open mouths of snakes.]
ad·der's-tongue (ăd′ərz-tŭng′) *n.* **1.** See **adder's-tongue fern. 2.** See **dogtooth violet.**
adder's-tongue fern *n.* Any of various ferns in the genus *Ophioglossum*, having leaves divided into a simple sterile blade and a slender, spikelike spore-bearing segment. [From the resemblance of the spike at the base of the frond to a snake's tongue.]
ad·dict (ə-dĭkt′) *tr.v.* **-dict·ed, -dict·ing, -dicts. 1.** To devote or give (oneself) habitually or compulsively. **2.** To cause to become compulsively and physiologically dependent on a habit-forming substance. —*n.* (ăd′ĭkt). **1.** One who is addicted, as to narcotics. **2.** A devoted believer or follower. [Lat. *addīcere, addict-*, to sentence : *ad-*, ad- + *dīcere*, to adjudge; see **deik-***.] —**ad·dic′tive** *adj.*
ad·dic·tion (ə-dĭk′shən) *n.* The quality or condition of being addicted, esp. to a habit-forming substance.
Ad·dis Ab·a·ba (ăd′ĭs ăb′ə-bə, ä′dĭs ä′bə-bä′). The cap. of Ethiopia, in the center on a high plateau; held by the Italians from 1936 to 1941. Pop. 1,408,068.
Ad·di·son (ăd′ĭ-sən). A village of NE IL, a suburb of Chicago. Pop. 32,058.
Addison, Joseph. 1672–1719. English essayist whose works appeared in *The Tatler* and *The Spectator.* —**Ad′di·so′ni·an** (-sō′nē-ən) *adj.*
Ad·di·son's disease (ăd′ĭ-sənz) *n.* A disease caused by failure of adrenocortical function and characterized by bronze pigmentation of the skin, anemia, weakness, and low blood pressure. [After Thomas *Addison* (1793–1860), British physician.]
ad·di·tion (ə-dĭsh′ən) *n.* **1.** The act or process of adding, esp. of combining numbers into a sum. **2.** Something added, such as a room to a building. —***idioms.*** **in addition.** Also; as well as. **in addition to.** Over and above; besides. [ME < OFr. < Lat. *additiō, additiōn-* < *additus*, p.part. of *addere*, to add. See ADD.] —**ad·di′tion·al** *adj.* —**ad·di′tion·al·ly** *adv.*
ad·di·tive (ăd′ĭ-tĭv) *n.* A substance added in small amounts to something else to improve, strengthen, or otherwise alter it. —*adj.* Marked by or involving addition.
additive identity *n. Math.* An identity element that in a given mathematical system leaves unchanged any element to which it is added.
additive inverse *n. Math.* See **inverse** 2b.
ad·dle (ăd′l) *v.* **-dled, -dling, -dles.** — *tr.* To muddle; confuse: *The heat addled his brain.* See Syns at **confuse.** — *intr.* **1.** To become confused. **2.** To become rotten; spoil. [< ME *adel*, rotten < OE *adel*, pool of excrement.]
ad·dle·pat·ed (ăd′l-pā′tĭd) *adj.* Muddled; confused.
add-on (ăd′ŏn′, -ôn′) *n.* One thing added to another, esp. a component that enhances a device.
ad·dress (ə-drĕs′) *tr.v.* **-dressed, -dress·ing, -dress·es. 1.** To speak to, esp. when using a formal name. **2.** To make a formal speech to. **3.** To direct (a spoken or written comment) to someone's attention: *Address your remarks to the manager.* **4.** To mark with a destination: *address a letter.* **5.a.** To direct the efforts of (oneself): *address oneself to a task.* **b.** To deal with; manage. **6.** *Sports.* To adjust the club behind (a golf ball) before a stroke. —*n.* **1.** A formal communication: *used the proper address for a priest.* **2.** A formal speech. **3.** (*also* ăd′rĕs′). The written directions on mail indicating destination. **4.** (*also* ăd′rĕs′). The location at which a person or organization may be found or reached. **5.** Courteous attention. Often used in the plural. **6.** The manner or bearing of a person, esp. in conversation. **7.** Skill and grace in dealing with people or situations. **8.** *Comp. Sci.* A number that designates a specific memory location. [ME *adressen*, to direct < OFr. *adresser* < VLat. **addīrēctiāre*: Latin *ad-*, ad- + VLat. **dīrēctiāre*, to straighten (< Lat. *dīrēctus*, p.part. of *dīrigere*, to direct; see DIRECT).] —**ad·dress′er, ad·dres′sor** *n.*
ad·dress·a·ble (ə-drĕs′ə-bəl) *adj.* Accessible through an address, as in computer memory.
ad·dress·ee (ăd′rĕ-sē′, ə-drĕs′ē′) *n.* The one to whom something is addressed.
ad·duce (ə-do͞os′, ə-dyo͞os′) *tr.v.* **-duced, -duc·ing, -duc·es.** To cite as an example or means of proof in an argument. [Lat. *addūcere*, to bring to : *ad-*, ad- + *dūcere*, to lead; see **deuk-***.] —**ad·duce′a·ble, ad·duc′i·ble** *adj.*
ad·duct (ə-dŭkt′, ă-dŭkt′) *tr.v.* **-duct·ed, -duct·ing, -ducts.** *Physiol.* To draw inward toward the median axis of the body or toward an adjacent part or limb. [Back-formation < ADDUCTOR.] —**ad·duc′tion** *n.* —**ad·duc′tive** *adj.*
ad·duc·tor (ə-dŭk′tər) *n.* A muscle that adducts a body part. [< Lat. *addūcere*, to bring to. See ADDUCE.]
Ade (ād), **George.** 1866–1944. Amer. humorist whose works include *Fables in Slang* (1899).
-ade *suff.* A sweetened beverage of: *limeade.* [ME < OFr., ult. < Lat. *-āta*, fem. of *-ātus*, -ate. See -ATE¹.]
Ad·e·laide (ăd′l-ād′). A city of S Australia NW of Melbourne; founded 1836. Met. area pop. 983,200.
A·dé·lie Coast also **A·dé·lie Land** (ə-dā′lē). A region of Antarctica near George V Coast, under French sovereignty.
Adélie penguin *n.* A common Antarctic penguin *(Pygoscelis adeliae)* that has white underparts and a black back and head.
a·demp·tion (ə-dĕmp′shən) *n. Law.* The disposal by a testator of property bequeathed in a will so as to invalidate the

adder's-tongue fern
Ophioglossum vulgatum

Adélie penguin
Pygoscelis adeliae

ă pat	oi boy
ā pay	ou out
âr care	o͝o took
ä father	o͞o boot
ĕ pet	ŭ cut
ē be	ûr urge
ĭ pit	th thin
ī pie	*th* this
îr pier	hw which
ŏ pot	zh vision
ō toe	ə about, item
ô paw	

Stress marks:
′ (primary);
′ (secondary), as in dictionary (dĭk′shə-nĕr′ē)

bequest. [Lat. *ademptiō*, *ademptiōn-*, a taking away < *ademptus*, p.part. of *adimere*, to take away : *ad-*, ad- + *emere*, to buy, take; see **em-***.]

A•den (ăd′n, äd′n). **1.** A former British colony and protectorate of S Arabia, part of Southern Yemen (now Yemen) since 1967. **2.** A city of S Yemen on the Gulf of Aden; cap. of Southern Yemen (1967–90). Pop. 271,600.

Aden, Gulf of. An arm of the Arabian Sea between Yemen on the Arabian Peninsula and Somalia in E Africa.

Ad•en•au•er (ăd′n-ou′ər, äd′-), **Konrad.** 1876–1967. First chancellor of West Germany (1949–63).

ad•e•nec•to•my (ăd′n-ĕk′tə-mē) *n.* Surgical excision of a gland.

ad•e•nine (ăd′n-ēn′, -ĭn) *n.* A purine base, $C_5H_5N_5$, that is a constituent of DNA and RNA.

ad•e•ni•tis (ăd′n-ī′tĭs) *n.* Inflammation of a lymph node or gland.

adeno– or **aden–** *pref.* Gland: *adenectomy.* [< Gk. *adēn*, *aden-*.]

ad•e•no•car•ci•no•ma (ăd′n-ō-kär′sə-nō′mə) *n.* A malignant tumor originating in glandular tissue. **—ad′e•no•car′ci•nom′a•tous** (-nŏm′ə-təs, -nō′mə-təs) *adj.*

ad•e•no•hy•poph•y•sis (ăd′n-ō-hī-pŏf′ĭ-sĭs) *n.* The anterior lobe of the pituitary gland. **—ad′e•no•hy•poph′y•se′al, ad′e•no•hy•poph′y•si′al** (-pŏf′ĭ-sē′əl) *adj.*

ad•e•noid (ăd′n-oid′) *n.* A lymphoid tissue growth in the upper part of the throat at the back of the nose that when swollen may obstruct breathing. Often used in the plural. *—adj.* Of or relating to lymphatic glands or lymphoid tissue.

ad•e•noi•dal (ăd′n-oid′l) *adj.* **1.** Of or relating to the adenoids. **2.** Suggestive of the vocal sound caused by enlarged adenoids.

ad•e•no•ma (ăd′n-ō′mə) *n., pl.* **-mas** or **-ma•ta** (-mə-tə). A benign epithelial tumor having a glandular origin and structure. **—ad′e•nom′a•toid′** (ăd′n-ŏm′ə-toid′) *adj.* **—ad′e•nom′a•tous** (-ŏm′ə-təs) *adj.*

a•den•o•sine (ə-dĕn′ə-sēn′) *n.* A nucleoside, $C_{10}H_{13}N_5O_4$, that is a structural component of nucleic acids and the major molecular component of ADP, AMP, and ATP. [Blend of AD-ENINE and RIBOSE.]

adenosine diphosphate *n.* ADP.

adenosine mon•o•phos•phate (mŏn′ō-fŏs′fāt′) *n.* **1.** AMP. **2.** Cyclic AMP.

adenosine triphosphate *n.* ATP.

ad•e•no•sis (ăd′n-ō′sĭs) *n.* A disease of a gland, esp. one marked by abnormal formation or enlargement.

ad•e•no•vi•rus (ăd′n-ō-vī′rəs) *n.* Any of a group of DNA-containing viruses that cause conjunctivitis and respiratory infections in humans. **—ad′e•no•vi′ral** *adj.*

a•den•yl•ate cy•clase (ə-dĕn′l-ĭt sī′klās, -klāz, ăd′n-ĭl′ĭt) *n.* An enzyme that catalyzes the formation of cylic AMP from ATP. [ADEN(INE) + -YL + -ATE[2] + CYCL(O)- + -ASE.]

a•de•nyl cyclase (ăd′n-ĭl) *n.* See **adenylate cyclase.**

ad•e•nyl•ic acid (ăd′n-ĭl′ĭk) *n.* See **AMP.** [ADEN(INE) + -YL + -IC + ACID.]

a•dept (ə-dĕpt′) *adj.* Very skilled. See Syns at **proficient.** *—n.* (ăd′ĕpt′). A highly skilled person; an expert. [Lat. *adeptus*, p.part. of *adipīscī*, to attain : *ad-*, ad- + *apīscī*, to grasp.] **—a•dept′ly** *adv.* **—a•dept′ness** *n.*

ad•e•quate (ăd′ĭ-kwĭt) *adj.* **1.** Sufficient to meet a need. **2.** Barely satisfactory or sufficient. [Lat. *adaequātus*, p.part. of *adaequāre*, to equalize : *ad-*, ad- + *aequāre*, to make equal < *aequus*, equal.] **—ad′e•qua•cy** (-kwə-sē), **ad′e•quate•ness** *n.* **—ad′e•quate•ly** *adv.*

à deux (ä′ dœ′) *adj.* Involving two persons. *—adv.* With only two persons involved. [Fr.]

ad fem•i•nam (ăd fĕm′ĭ-năm′, -nəm) *adj.* Appealing to irrelevant personal considerations concerning women. [Lat. *ad*, to + *fēminam*, accusative of *fēmina*, woman.] **—ad fem′i•nam′** *adv.*

ADH *abbr.* Antidiuretic hormone.

ad•here (ăd-hîr′) *intr.v.* **-hered, -her•ing, -heres. 1.** To stick fast; remain attached. **2.** To be a devoted follower or supporter. [Fr. *adhérer* < Lat. *adhaerēre*, to stick to : *ad-*, ad- + *haerēre*, to stick.]

ad•her•ence (ăd-hîr′əns, -hĕr′-) *n.* **1.** The process or condition of adhering. **2.** Faithful attachment; devotion.

ad•her•ent (ăd-hîr′ənt, -hĕr′-) *n.* A supporter, as of a cause or an individual. *—adj.* **1.** Sticking or holding fast. **2.** *Bot.* Joined but not united. **—ad•her′ent•ly** *adv.*

ad•he•sion (ăd-hē′zhən) *n.* **1.** The act or state of adhering. **2.** Attachment or devotion; loyalty. **3.** Assent or agreement to join. **4.** *Phys.* The molecular force that attracts or binds dissimilar substances. **5.** *Medic.* **a.** A fibrous band of scar tissue that binds together normally separate anatomical structures. **b.** The binding together of bodily tissues that are normally separate. [Fr. *adhésion* < Lat. *adhaesiō*, *adhaesiōn-* < *adhaesus*, p.part. of *adhaerēre*, to adhere. See ADHERE.]

ad•he•si•o•to•my (ăd-hē′zē-ŏt′ə-mē) *n., pl.* **-mies.** Surgical division or separation of adhesions.

ad•he•sive (ăd-hē′sĭv, -zĭv) *adj.* **1.** Tending to adhere; sticky. **2.** Gummed so as to adhere. *—n.* A substance, such as paste or cement, that provides adhesion. **—ad•he′sive•ly** *adv.* **—ad•he′sive•ness** *n.*

adhesive tape *n.* A tape lined on one side with an adhesive.

ad hoc (ăd hŏk′, hōk′) *adv.* For the specific purpose or situation at hand. *—adj.* **1.** Formed for or concerned with one specific purpose: *an ad hoc committee.* **2.** Improvised; impromptu. [Lat. *ad*, to + *hoc*, this.]

ad hom•i•nem (hŏm′ə-nĕm′, -nəm) *adj.* Appealing to personal considerations rather than to logic or reason. [Lat. : *ad*, to + *hominem*, accusative of *homō*, man.] **—ad hom′i•nem′** *adv.*

ad•i•a•bat•ic (ăd′ē-ə-băt′ĭk, ā′dī-ə-) *adj.* Of or relating to a thermodynamic process occurring without gain or loss of heat. [< Gk. *adiabatos*, impassable : *a-*, not; see A-[1] + *diabatos*, passable (*dia*, dia- + *batos*, passable < *bainein*, to go; see **g^{w}ā-***.)] **—ad′i•a•bat′i•cal•ly** *adv.*

a•dieu (ə-dyo͞o′, ə-do͞o′) *interj.* Used to express farewell. *—n., pl.* **a•dieus** or **a•dieux** (ə-dyo͞oz′, ə-do͞oz′). A farewell. [ME < OFr. *a dieu*, (I commend you) to God : *a*, to (< Lat. *ad*; see AD-) + *Dieu*, God (< Lat. *deus*; see **deiw-***).]

A•di•ge (ä′dĭ-jā′, ä′dē-jĕ′). A river of NE Italy rising in the Alps and flowing c. 410 km (255 mi) to the Adriatic Sea.

ad in•fi•ni•tum (ăd ĭn′fə-nī′təm) *adv. & adj.* To infinity; having no end. [Lat. *ad*, to + *infīnītum*, accusative of *infīnītus*, infinite.]

ad in•ter•im (ĭn′tər-əm) *adv.* In or for the meantime; temporarily. *—adj.* Acting or done ad interim; temporary. [Lat. *ad*, to, for + *interim*, the meantime.]

ad•i•os (ăd′ē-ōs′, ä′dē-) *interj.* Used to express farewell. [Sp. *adiós*, prob. translated < French *à dieu*. See ADIEU.]

ad•i•po•cere (ăd′ə-pō-sîr′) *n.* A brown, fatty waxlike substance that forms on dead animal tissues in response to moisture. [ADIPO(SE) + Lat. *cēra*, wax.]

ad•i•po•cyte (ăd′ə-pō-sīt′) *n.* See **fat cell.**

ad•i•pose (ăd′ə-pōs′) *adj.* Of, relating to, or composed of animal fat; fatty. *—n.* The fat found in adipose tissue. [NLat. *adipōsus* < Lat. *adeps*, *adip-*, fat.] **—ad′i•pose′ness, ad′i•pos′i•ty** (-pŏs′ĭ-tē) *n.*

adipose tissue *n.* A type of connective tissue that contains stored cellular fat.

Ad•i•ron•dack Mountains (ăd′ə-rŏn′dăk′). A group of mountains in NE NY between the St. Lawrence R. and the Mohawk R. Part of the Appalachian system, the range rises to 1,629.9 m (5,344 ft).

ad•it (ăd′ĭt) *n.* An almost horizontal entrance to a mine. [Lat. *aditus*, access < p.part. of *adīre*, to approach : *ad-*, ad- + *īre*, to go; see **ei-***.]

adj. *abbr.* **1.** *Gram.* Adjective. **2.** Adjunct. **3.** Adjustment. **4.** Also **Adj.** Adjutant.

ad•ja•cen•cy (ə-jā′sən-sē) *n., pl.* **-cies. 1.** The state of being adjacent; contiguity. **2.** A thing that is adjacent.

ad•ja•cent (ə-jā′sənt) *adj.* **1.** Close to; lying near: *adjacent cities.* **2.** Next to; adjoining: *adjacent garden plots.* [ME < Lat. *adiacēns*, *adiacent-*, pr.part. of *adiacēre*, to lie near : *ad-*, ad- + *iacēre*, to lie; see **yē-***.] **—ad•ja′cent•ly** *adv.*

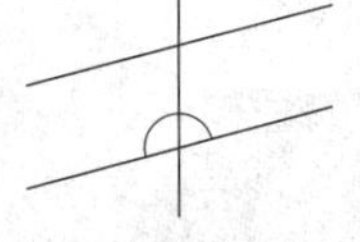
adjacent angle

adjacent angle *n. Math.* Either of two angles having a common side and a common vertex.

ad•jec•tive (ăj′ĭk-tĭv) *n. Gram.* Any of a class of words used to modify a noun or other substantive by limiting, qualifying, or specifying and distinguished in English by one of several suffixes, such as *-ous*, *-er*, and *-est*, or by preceding a noun or nominal phrase. *—adj.* **1.** *Gram.* Of, relating to, or functioning as an adjective. **2.** Not standing alone; derivative or dependent. [ME < OFr. *adjectif* < LLat. *adiectīvus* < *adiectus*, p.part. of *adiicere*, to add to : *ad-*, ad- + *iacere*, to throw; see **yē-***.] **—ad′jec•ti′val** (-tī′vəl) *adj.* **—ad′jec•ti′val•ly** *adv.* **—ad′jec•tive•ly** *adv.*

ad•join (ə-join′) *v.* **-joined, -join•ing, -joins.** *—tr.* **1.** To be next to; be contiguous to. **2.** To attach; append. *—intr.* To be contiguous. [ME *ajoinen* < OFr. *ajoindre*, *ajoin-* < Lat. *adiungere*, to join to : *ad-*, ad- + *iungere*, to join; see **yeug-***.]

ad•join•ing (ə-joi′nĭng) *adj.* Neighboring; contiguous.

ad•journ (ə-jûrn′) *v.* **-journed, -journ•ing, -journs.** *—tr.* To suspend until a later stated time. *—intr.* **1.** To suspend proceedings to another time or place. **2.** To move from one place to another: *We adjourned to the living room.* [ME *ajournen* < OFr. *ajourner*: *a-*, to (< Lat. *ad-*; see AD-) + *jour*, day (< LLat. *diurnum* < Lat. *diurnus*, daily < *diēs*, day; see **deiw-***).] **—ad•journ′ment** *n.*

adjt. also **Adjt.** *abbr.* Adjutant.

ad•judge (ə-jŭj′) *tr.v.* **-judged, -judg•ing, -judg•es. 1.** *Law.* **a.** To determine or decide by judicial procedure; adjudicate. **b.** To order judicially; rule. **c.** To award by law. **d.** To sentence; condemn. **2.** To regard or deem. [ME *ajugen* < OFr. *ajuger* < Lat. *adiūdicāre*. See ADJUDICATE.]

ad•ju•di•cate (ə-jo͞o′dĭ-kāt′) *tr.v.* **-cat•ed, -cat•ing, -cates. 1.** *Law.* To hear and settle (a case). **2.** To study and settle (a dispute). [Lat. *adiūdicāre*, *adiūdicāt-*, to award to (judicially) : *ad-*, ad- + *iūdicāre*, to judge (< *iūdex*, judge; see JUDGE).] **—ad•ju′di•ca′tion** *n.* **—ad•ju′di•ca′tive** *adj.* **—ad•ju′di•ca′tor** *n.*

ad•junct (ăj′ŭngkt′) *n.* **1.** Something attached to another in a dependent or subordinate position. **2.** A person associated with another in a subordinate or auxiliary capacity. **3.** *Gram.* A clause or phrase added to a sentence that amplifies its meaning. — *adj.* **1.** Added or connected in a subordinate or auxiliary capacity. **2.** Attached to a faculty or staff in a temporary or auxiliary capacity: *an adjunct professor of history.* [< Lat. *adiūnctus*, p.part. of *adiungere*, to join to. See ADJOIN.] **— ad•junc′tion** (ə-jŭngk′shən) *n.* **— ad•junc′tive** *adj.*

ad•ju•ra•tion (ăj′ə-rā′shən) *n.* An earnest, solemn appeal. **— ad•jur′a•to′ry** (ə-jo͝or′ə-tôr′ē, -tōr′ē) *adj.*

ad•jure (ə-jo͝or′) *tr.v.* **-jured, -jur•ing, -jures. 1.** To command or enjoin solemnly, as under oath. **2.** To appeal to or entreat earnestly. [ME *adjuren* < Lat. *adiūrāre*, to swear to : *ad-*, ad- + *iūrāre*, to swear; see **yewes-***.] **— ad•jur′er, ad•ju′ror** *n.*

ad•just (ə-jŭst′) *v.* **-just•ed, -just•ing, -justs.** — *tr.* **1.** To change so as to match or fit. **2.** To bring into proper relationship. **3.** To adapt or conform, as to new conditions. See Syns at **adapt. 4.** To make more effective or efficient: *adjust the timing of a car.* **5.** To settle; resolve. **6.** To decide how much is to be paid on (an insurance claim). — *intr.* To adapt oneself; conform. [Obsolete Fr. *adjuster* < OFr. *ajoster* < VLat. **adiuxtāre*, to put close to : Lat. *ad-*, ad- + Lat. *iuxtā*, near; see **yeug-***.] **— ad•just′a•ble** *adj.* **— ad•just′a•bly** *adv.* **— ad•just′er, ad•jus′tor** *n.*

ad•just•ment (ə-jŭst′mənt) *n.* **1.** The act of adjusting or the state of being adjusted. **2.** A means of adjusting. **3.** Settlement of a debt or claim. **4.** A modification, fluctuation, or correction: *an adjustment on a bill.*

ad•ju•tant (ăj′ə-tənt) *n.* **1.** A staff officer who helps a commanding officer with administrative affairs. **2.** An assistant. **3.** See **marabou** 1. [< Lat. *adiūtāns*, *adiūtant-*, pr.part. of *adiūtāre*, to help. See AID.] **— ad′ju•tan•cy** *n.*

adjutant general *n., pl.* **adjutants general. 1.** An adjutant of a unit having a general staff. **2.** An officer in charge of the National Guard in one of the U.S. states. **3. Adjutant General.** The chief administrative officer, a major general, of the U.S. Army.

adjutant stork *n.* See **marabou** 1.

ad•ju•vant (ăj′ə-vənt) *n.* **1.** An agent added to a drug to increase or aid its effect. **2.** An immunological agent that increases antigenic response. [< Lat. *adiuvāns*, *adiuvant-*, pr.part. of *adiuvāre*, to help. See AID.]

Ad•ler (ăd′lər, ăd′-), **Alfred.** 1870–1937. Austrian psychiatrist who theorized that neurotic behavior is an overcompensation for feelings of inferiority. **— Ad•le′ri•an** (ăd-lîr′ē-ən) *adj.*

Ad•ler (ăd′lər), **Cyrus.** 1863–1940. Amer. religious leader who was president of the Jewish Theological Seminary (1924–40).

Ad•ler (ăd′lər, ăd′-), **Felix.** 1851–1933. German-born Amer. educator who founded the Society for Ethical Culture (1876).

Ad•ler (ăd′lər), **Mortimer Jerome.** b. 1902. Amer. philosopher and educator whose works include *How to Read a Book* (1940).

ad lib (ăd lĭb′) *adv.* In an unrestrained manner; spontaneously. [Short for AD LIBITUM.]

ad-lib (ăd-lĭb′) *v.* **-libbed, -lib•bing, -libs.** — *tr.* To improvise and deliver extemporaneously. — *intr.* To engage in improvisation, as in a speech. — *n.* (ăd′lĭb′). Something, such as a joke, that is improvised. — *adj.* Improvised; extemporaneous. **— ad-lib′ber** *n.*

ad lib•i•tum (ăd lĭb′ĭ-təm) *adj. Mus.* At the discretion of the performer. Used chiefly as a direction giving license to alter or omit a part. [Lat. *ad*, according to + *libitum*, p.part. of *libēre*, to please.]

ad loc. *abbr. Lat.* Ad locum (to, or at, the place).

adm. *abbr.* **1.** Administration. **2.** Administrative. **3.** Administrator.

ad•meas•ure (ăd-mĕzh′ər) *tr.v.* **-ured, -ur•ing, -ures.** To divide and distribute proportionally; apportion. [ME *amesuren* < OFr. *amesurer*: *a-*, to (< Lat. *ad-*; see AD-) + *mesurer*, to measure (< LLat. *mēnsūrāre*, to measure < Lat. *mēnsūra*, measure; see MEASURE).] **— ad•meas′ure•ment** *n.* **— ad•meas′ur•er** *n.*

Ad•me•tus (ăd-mē′təs) *n. Gk. Myth.* A king of Thessaly and husband of Alcestis.

admin. *abbr.* **1.** Administration. **2.** Administrative. **3.** Administrator.

ad•min•is•ter (ăd-mĭn′ĭ-stər) *v.* **-tered, -ter•ing, -ters.** — *tr.* **1.** To have charge of; manage. **2.a.** To give or apply in a formal way: *administer the last rites.* **b.** To apply as a remedy: *administer a sedative.* **3.** To mete out; dispense: *administer justice.* **4.** To manage or dispose of (a trust or an estate) under a will or an official appointment. **5.** To impose, offer, or tender (an oath, for example). — *intr.* **1.** To manage as an administrator. **2.** To minister: *administering to every whim.* [ME *administren* < OFr. *administrer* < Lat. *administrāre*: *ad*, ad- + *ministrāre*, to manage; see MINISTER.] **— ad•min′is•tra•ble** (-ĭ-strə-bəl) *adj.* **— ad•min′is•trant** *adj. & n.*

ad•min•is•trate (ăd-mĭn′ĭ-strāt′) *tr.v.* **-trat•ed, -trat•ing, -trates.** To administer.

ad•min•is•tra•tion (ăd-mĭn′ĭ-strā′shən) *n.* **1.** Management, esp. of business affairs. **2.** The activity of a sovereign state in the exercise of its powers or duties. **3.** Often **Administration.** Those who constitute the executive branch of a government. **4.** Those who manage an institution. **5.** The term of office of an executive officer or a body. **6.** *Law.* Management and disposal of a trust or an estate. **7.** The administering of something, such as medicine or an oath. **— ad•min′is•tra′tive** (-strā′tĭv, -strə-) *adj.* **— ad•min′is•tra′tive•ly** *adv.*

ad•min•is•tra•tor (ăd-mĭn′ĭ-strā′tər) *n.* **1.** One who administers, esp. business or public affairs; an executive. **2.** One appointed to administer an estate.

ad•mi•ra•ble (ăd′mər-ə-bəl) *adj.* Deserving admiration. **— ad′mi•ra•ble•ness** *n.* **— ad′mi•ra•bly** *adv.*

ad•mi•ral (ăd′mər-əl) *n.* **1.** The commander in chief of a fleet. **2.** A flag officer. **3.a.** A commissioned rank in the U.S. Navy or Coast Guard that is above vice admiral and below Admiral of the Fleet. **b.** One who holds the rank of admiral, Admiral of the Fleet, rear admiral, or vice admiral. **4.** Any of various brightly colored butterflies of the genera *Limenitis* and *Vanessa.* **5.** *Archaic.* The ship carrying an admiral; a flagship. [ME *amiral, admiral* < OFr. and < Med.Lat. *amīrālis, admīrālis*, both < Ar. *'amīr a 'ālī*, high commander.]

admiral
Red admiral
Vanessa atalanta

Ad•mi•ral of the Fleet (ăd′mər-əl) *n.* **1.** The highest rank in the U.S. Navy, equivalent to General of the Army. **2.** One who holds this rank.

ad•mi•ral•ty (ăd′mər-əl-tē) *n., pl.* **-ties. 1.a.** A court exercising jurisdiction over all maritime cases. **b.** Maritime law. **2. Admiralty.** The department of the British government that once had control over all naval affairs.

Admiralty Islands. A group of volcanic islands of Papua New Guinea in the SW Pacific.

Admiralty Range. A mountain group of Antarctica on the N coast of Victoria Land NW of Ross Sea.

ad•mi•ra•tion (ăd′mə-rā′shən) *n.* **1.** A feeling of pleasure, wonder, and approval. **2.** An object of wonder and esteem; a marvel. **3.** *Archaic.* Wonder.

ad•mire (ăd-mīr′) *v.* **-mired, -mir•ing, -mires.** — *tr.* **1.** To regard with pleasure, wonder, and approval. **2.** To have a high opinion of; esteem or respect. **3.** *Chiefly New England & Upper Southern U.S.* To enjoy (something). **4.** *Archaic.* To marvel or wonder at. — *intr. New England & Upper Southern U.S.* To marvel at something. [Fr. *admirer* < OFr. *amirer* < Lat. *admīrārī*, to wonder at : *ad-*, ad- + *mīrārī*, to wonder (< *mīrus*, wonderful; see **smei-***).] **— ad•mir′er** *n.* **— ad•mir′ing•ly** *adv.*

ad•mis•si•ble (ăd-mĭs′ə-bəl) *adj.* **1.** Acceptable; allowable: *admissible evidence.* **2.** Worthy of admission. **— ad•mis′si•bil′i•ty, ad•mis′si•ble•ness** *n.* **— ad•mis′si•bly** *adv.*

ad•mis•sion (ăd-mĭsh′ən) *n.* **1.a.** The act of admitting or allowing to enter. **b.** The state of being allowed to enter. **2.** Right to enter; access. **3.** The price required or paid for entering. **4.** A confession, as of having committed a crime. **5.** A voluntary acknowledgment of truth. **6.** A fact or statement granted or admitted; a concession. [ME < Lat. *admissiō, admissiōn-* < *admissus*, p.part. of *admittere*, to admit. See ADMIT.] **— ad•mis′sive** (-mĭs′ĭv) *adj.*

ad•mit (ăd-mĭt′) *v.* **-mit•ted, -mit•ting, -mits.** — *tr.* **1.** To permit to enter. **2.** To entitle to entrance: *A ticket that admits four.* **3.** To permit to exercise the rights, functions, or privileges of: *admitted to the bar.* **4.** To have room for; accommodate. **5.** To afford opportunity for; permit. **6.** To grant to be real, valid, or true; acknowledge: *admit the truth.* **7.** To grant as true or valid; concede. — *intr.* **1.** To afford possibility: *The problem admits of no solution.* **2.** To allow entrance: *a door admitting to the hall.* **3.** To make acknowledgment. [ME *amitten, admitten* < OFr. *amettre, admettre* < Lat. *admittere*: *ad-*, ad- + *mittere*, to send.]

ad•mit•tance (ăd-mĭt′ns) *n.* **1.** The act of admitting or entering. **2.** Permission or right to enter. **3.** *Symbol* **Y** *Elect.* The reciprocal of impedance.

ad•mit•ted•ly (ăd-mĭt′ĭd-lē) *adv.* By general admission; confessedly.

ad•mix (ăd-mĭks′) *tr. & intr.v.* **-mixed, -mix•ing, -mix•es.** To mix; blend. [Back-formation < obsolete *admixt*, mixed into < ME < Lat. *admixtus*, p.part. of *admiscēre*, to mix into : *ad-*, ad- + *miscēre*, to mix; see **meik-***.]

ad•mix•ture (ăd-mĭks′chər) *n.* **1.** The act of mixing or the state of being mixed. **2.** Something produced by mixing; a mixture. **3.** Something added in mixing. See Syns at **mixture.**

ad•mon•ish (ăd-mŏn′ĭsh) *tr.v.* **-ished, -ish•ing, -ish•es. 1.** To reprove gently. **2.** To caution; warn. **3.** To remind of an obligation or a duty. [ME *amonishen, admonishen*, alteration of *amonesten* < OFr. *amonester, admonester* < VLat. **admonestāre* < Lat. *admonēre*: *ad-*, ad- + *monēre*, to warn; see **men-**[1]***.**] **— ad•mon′ish•er** *n.* **— ad•mon′ish•ing•ly** *adv.* **— ad•mon′ish•ment** *n.*

***Syns:** admonish, reprove, rebuke, reprimand, reproach.* These verbs refer to criticism intended as a corrective or caution. *Admonish* implies the giving of advice or a warning: *"A gallows erected on an eminence admonished the offenders of the fate that awaited them"* (William Hickling Prescott). *Reprove* usually suggests gentle criticism: *With a quick look the*

ă pat	oi boy
ā pay	ou out
âr care	o͝o to͝ok
ä father	o͞o bo͞ot
ĕ pet	ŭ cut
ē be	ûr urge
ĭ pit	th thin
ī pie	*th* this
îr pier	hw which
ŏ pot	zh vision
ō toe	ə about, item
ô paw	

Stress marks:
′ (primary);
′ (secondary), as in
dictionary (dĭk′shə-nĕr′ē)

teacher reproved the child for interrupting. Rebuke and *reprimand* both refer to sharp, often angry criticism: *"Some of the most heated criticism . . . has come from the Justice Department, which rarely rebukes other agencies in public"* (Howard Kurtz). *"A committee at* [the university] *asked its president to reprimand a scientist who tested gene-altered bacteria on trees"* (New York Times). *Reproach* usually refers to regretful or unhappy criticism: *"Even if I had done wrong you should not have reproached me in public — people wash their dirty linen at home"* (Napoleon Bonaparte).

ad•mo•ni•tion (ăd′mə-nĭsh′ən) *n.* **1.** Mild reproof. **2.** Cautionary advice or warning. [ME *amonicioun* < OFr. *amonition* < Lat. *admonitiō, admonitiōn-* < *admonitus,* p.part. of *admonēre,* to admonish. See ADMONISH.]

ad•mon•i•to•ry (ăd-mŏn′ĭ-tôr′ē, -tōr′ē) *adj.* Expressing admonition.

ad•nate (ăd′nāt′) *adj. Biol.* United to a different part or organ. [Lat. *adnātus,* var. of *agnātus,* p.part. of *agnāscī,* to grow upon. See AGNATE.] **—ad•na′tion** *n.*

ad nau•se•am (ăd nô′zē-əm) *adv.* To a disgusting or ridiculous degree. [Lat. *ad,* to + *nauseam,* accusative of *nausea,* sickness.]

ad•nex•a (ăd-nĕk′sə) *pl.n.* Accessory or adjoining anatomical parts. [Lat., neut. pl. of *adnexus,* p.part. of *adnectere,* to bind to. See ANNEX.] **—ad•nex′al** *adj.*

a•do (ə-do͞o′) *n.* Bustle; fuss; bother. [ME < the phrase *at do*: *at,* to (used with infinitive) (< ON *at*; see **ad-***) + *do,* do; see DO[1].]

adobe
Saint Francis Mission in Ranchos de Taos, New Mexico

a•do•be (ə-dō′bē) *n.* **1.a.** A sun-dried brick of clay and straw. **b.** The clay or soil from which this brick is made. **2.** A structure built with this brick. [Sp. < Ar. *aṭ-ṭūbah,* the brick : *al,* the + *ṭūbah,* brick.]

a•do•bo (ä-dō′bō) *n., pl.* **-bos.** A Philippine dish of marinated vegetables and meat or fish seasoned with garlic and spices. [Sp. < OSp. *adobar,* to stew < OFr. *adouber,* to dub, arm, prepare, of Gmc. orig.]

ad•o•les•cence (ăd′l-ĕs′əns) *n.* **1.** The period of development from the onset of puberty to maturity. **2.** A period of development between youth and maturity.

ad•o•les•cent (ăd′l-ĕs′ənt) *adj.* Of or relating to adolescence. *—n.* A person who has undergone puberty but not reached maturity. [ME < OFr. < Lat. *adolēscēns, adolēscent-,* pr.part. of *adolēscere,* to grow up : *ad-,* ad- + *alēscere,* to grow, inchoative of *alere,* to nourish; see **al-**[2]*.]

Ad•o•nai (ä′dō-nī′, -noi′) *n.* Lord. Used in Judaism as a spoken substitute for the ineffable name of God. [Heb. *'ădōnāy,* my lord < *'ādôn,* lord.]

A•don•is (ə-dŏn′ĭs, ə-dō′nĭs) *n.* **1.** *Gk. Myth.* A beautiful young man loved by Aphrodite. **2.** Often **adonis.** A very handsome young man. [Gk. *Adōnis* < Phoenician *adōn,* lord.]

a•dopt (ə-dŏpt′) *tr.v.* **a•dopt•ed, a•dopt•ing, a•dopts. 1.** To take into one's family through legal means and raise as one's own child. **2.a.** To take and follow (a course of action, for example). **b.** To take up and make one's own: *adopt a new idea.* **3.** To vote to accept: *adopt a resolution.* **4.** To choose as standard or required in a course. [ME *adopten* < OFr. *adopter* < Lat. *adoptāre*: *ad-,* ad- + *optāre,* to choose.] **—a•dopt′a•ble** *adj.* **—a•dop′tee** *n.* **—a•dopt′er** *n.* **—a•dop′tion** *n.*

Usage Note: One refers to an *adopted* child but to *adoptive* parents.

a•dop•tive (ə-dŏp′tĭv) *adj.* **1.** Of or having to do with adoption. **2.** Related by adoption: *adoptive parents.* See Usage Note at **adopt. —a•dop′tive•ly** *adv.*

a•dor•a•ble (ə-dôr′ə-bəl, ə-dōr′-) *adj.* **1.** Delightful, lovable, and charming. **2.** Worthy of adoration. **—a•dor′a•bil′i•ty, a•dor′a•ble•ness** *n.* **—a•dor′a•bly** *adv.*

ad•o•ra•tion (ăd′ə-rā′shən) *n.* **1.** The act of worship. **2.** Profound love or regard.

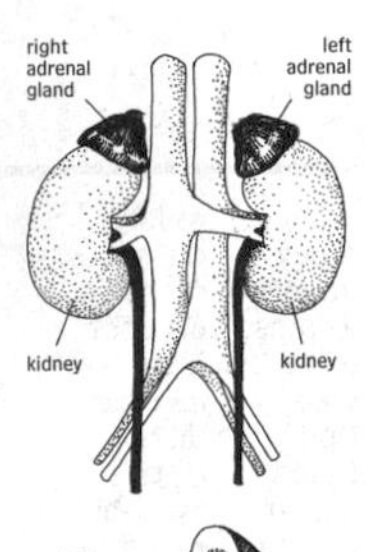

adrenal gland

a•dore (ə-dôr′, ə-dōr′) *v.* **a•dored, a•dor•ing, a•dores.** *—tr.* **1.** To worship as God or a god. **2.** To regard with deep, often rapturous love. See Syns at **revere**[1]. **3.** To like very much: *adores mink coats.* *—intr.* To worship. [ME *adouren* < OFr. *adourer* < Lat. *adōrāre,* to pray to : *ad-,* ad- + *ōrāre,* to pray.] **—a•dor′er** *n.* **—a•dor′ing•ly** *adv.*

a•dorn (ə-dôrn′) *tr.v.* **a•dorned, a•dorn•ing, a•dorns. 1.** To make beautiful or attractive. **2.** To put ornaments on; decorate. [ME *adornen* < OFr. *adourner* < Lat. *adōrnāre*: *ad-,* ad- + *ōrnāre,* to decorate; see **ar-***.] **—a•dorn′er** *n.*

a•dorn•ment (ə-dôrn′mənt) *n.* **1.** The act of adorning. **2.** Something that adorns; an ornament.

A•dour (ə-do͝or′). A river of SW France rising in the Pyrenees and flowing c. 338 km (210 mi) to the Bay of Biscay.

ADP[1] (ā′dē′pē′) *n.* An ester of adenosine, $C_{10}H_{15}N_5O_{10}P_2$, that is converted to ATP for the storage of energy. [A(DENOSINE) D(I)P(HOSPHATE).]

ADP[2] *abbr. Comp. Sci.* Automatic data processing.

ad•re•nal (ə-drē′nəl) *adj.* **1.** At, near, or on the kidneys. **2.** Of or relating to the adrenal glands or their secretions. *—n.* An adrenal gland. [AD– + RENAL.] **—ad•re′nal•ly** *adv.*

adrenal gland *n.* Either of two small endocrine glands, one located above each kidney, consisting of the cortex, which secretes several steroid hormones, and the medulla, which secretes epinephrine.

A•dren•a•lin (ə-drĕn′ə-lĭn). A trademark used for a medicinal preparation of adrenaline.

a•dren•a•line (ə-drĕn′ə-lĭn) *n.* See **epinephrine** 1.

ad•re•nal•ize (ə-drē′nə-līz′, ə-drĕn′ə-) *tr.v.* **-ized, -iz•ing, -izes.** To stir up and spur to action.

ad•re•ner•gic (ăd′rə-nûr′jĭk) *adj.* Producing or activated by epinephrine or an epinephrinelike substance: *an adrenergic nerve fiber.* [ADREN(ALINE) + Gk. *ergon,* work; see **werg-***.] **—ad′re•ner′gi•cal•ly** *adv.*

a•dre•no•chrome (ə-drē′nō-krōm′, -nə-) *n.* A naturally occurring chemical formed during the oxidation of epinephrine. [ADREN(ALINE) + CHROME.]

a•dre•no•cor•ti•cal (ə-drē′nō-kôr′tĭ-kəl) *adj.* Of, relating to, or derived from the cortex of an adrenal gland. [ADREN(AL) + CORTICAL.]

ad•re•no•cor•ti•co•ster•oid (ə-drē′nō-kôr′tĭ-kō-stîr′oid, -stĕr′-) *n.* Any of various steroids derived from the cortex of an adrenal gland. [ADREN(AL) + CORTICOSTEROID.]

ad•re•no•cor•ti•co•trop•ic (ə-drē′nō-kôr′tĭ-kō-trŏp′ĭk, -trō′pĭk) also **ad•re•no•cor•ti•co•troph•ic** (-trŏf′ĭk, -trō′fĭk) *adj.* Stimulating or otherwise acting on the cortex of an adrenal gland. [ADREN(AL) + CORTICO– + –TROPIC.]

adrenocorticotropic hormone also **adrenocorticotrophic hormone** *n.* ACTH.

ad•re•no•cor•ti•co•trop•in (ə-drē′nō-kôr′tĭ-kō-trŏp′ĭn, -trō′pĭn) also **ad•re•no•cor•ti•co•troph•in** (-trŏf′ĭn, trō′fĭn) *n.* See **ACTH.** [ADREN(AL) + CORTICOTROPIN.]

A•dri•a•my•cin (ā′drē-ə-mī′sən). A trademark for an antibiotic used as an antineoplastic agent.

A•dri•an (ā′drē-ən). A city of SE MI SW of Detroit. Pop. 22,097.

Adrian IV. Nicholas Breakspear. 1100?–59. English-born pope (1154–59).

Adrian, Edgar Douglas. 1st Baron Adrian. 1889–1977. British physiologist who shared a 1932 Nobel Prize.

A•dri•a•no•ple (ā′drē-ə-nō′pəl). See **Edirne.**

A•dri•at•ic Sea (ā′drē-ăt′ĭk). An arm of the Mediterranean Sea between Italy and the Balkan Peninsula.

a•drift (ə-drĭft′) *adv. & adj.* **1.** Drifting or floating freely; not anchored. **2.** Without direction or purpose.

a•droit (ə-droit′) *adj.* **1.** Dexterous; deft. **2.** Skillful and adept under pressing conditions. See Syns at **dexterous.** [Fr. < *à droit*: *à,* to (< Lat. *ad*; see AD–) + *droit,* right (< Lat. *dīrēctus*; see DIRECT).] **—a•droit′ly** *adv.* **—a•droit′ness** *n.*

ad•sci•ti•tious (ăd′sĭ-tĭsh′əs) *adj.* Not inherent or essential; derived from something outside. [< Lat. *adscītus,* p.part. of *adscīscere,* to adopt : *ad-,* ad- + *scīscere,* to accept, inchoative of *scīre,* to know; see **skei-***.]

ad•sorb (ăd-sôrb′, -zôrb′) *tr.v.* **-sorbed, -sorb•ing, -sorbs.** To take up by adsorption. [AD– + Lat. *sorbēre,* to suck.] **—ad•sorb′a•ble** *adj.*

ad•sor•bate (-sôr′bĭt, -bāt′, ăd-zôr′-) *n.* An adsorbed substance.

ad•sor•bent (ăd-sôr′bənt, -zôr′-) *adj.* Capable of adsorption. *—n.* An adsorptive material, such as activated charcoal.

ad•sorp•tion (ăd-sôrp′shən, -zôrp′-) *n.* The accumulation of gases, liquids, or solutes on the surface of a solid or liquid. [< ADSORB.] **—ad•sorp′tive** (-tĭv) *adj.*

ad•su•ki bean (ăd-so͞o′kē, -zo͞o′-) *n.* Var. of **adzuki bean.**

ad•u•lar•i•a (ăj′ə-lâr′ē-ə, -lăr′-) *n.* A variety of transparent or translucent orthoclase. [Ital. < Fr. *adulaire,* after *Adula,* a mountain group of SE Switzerland.]

ad•u•late (ăj′ə-lāt′) *tr.v.* **-lat•ed, -lat•ing, -lates.** To praise or admire excessively. [Back-formation < ADULATION.] **—ad′u•la′tor** *n.* **—ad′u•la•to′ry** (-lə-tôr′ē, -tōr′ē) *adj.*

ad•u•la•tion (ăj′ə-lā′shən) *n.* Excessive flattery or admiration. [ME *adulacioun* < OFr. < Lat. *adūlātiō, adūlātiōn-* < *adūlātus,* p.part. of *adūlārī,* to flatter.]

a•dult (ə-dŭlt′, ăd′ŭlt) *n.* **1.** One who has attained maturity or legal age. **2.** *Biol.* A fully grown, mature organism. *—adj.* **1.** Fully developed and mature. **2.** Intended for or befitting adults: *adult education.* **3.** Containing or dealing in explicitly sexual material; pornographic: *adult movies.* [< Lat. *adultus,* p.part. of *adolēscere,* to grow up. See ADOLESCENT.] **—a•dult′hood′** *n.* **—a•dult′ness** *n.*

a•dul•ter•ant (ə-dŭl′tər-ənt) *n.* A substance that adulterates. *—adj.* Serving to adulterate.

a•dul•ter•ate (ə-dŭl′tə-rāt′) *tr.v.* **-at•ed, -at•ing, -ates.** To make impure by adding extraneous, improper, or inferior ingredients. *—adj.* (-tər-ĭt). **1.** Spurious; adulterated. **2.** Adulterous. [Lat. *adulterāre, adulterāt-,* to pollute. See **al-**[1]*.] **—a•dul′ter•a′tion** *n.* **—a•dul′ter•a′tor** *n.*

a•dul•ter•er (ə-dŭl′tər-ər) *n.* One who commits adultery.

a•dul•ter•ess (ə-dŭl′trĭs, -tər-ĭs) *n.* A woman who commits adultery.

a•dul•ter•ine (ə-dŭl′tə-rīn′, -rēn′) *adj.* **1.** Characterized by adulteration; spurious. **2.** Unauthorized by law; illegal. **3.** Born of adultery. [Lat. *adulterīnus* < *adulter,* adulterer, perh. back-formation < *adulterāre,* to pollute. See ADULTERATE.]

a•dul•ter•ous (ə-dŭl′tər-əs, -trəs) *adj.* Relating to, inclined to, or marked by adultery. **— a•dul′ter•ous•ly** *adv.*

a•dul•ter•y (ə-dŭl′tə-rē, -trē) *n., pl.* **-ies.** Voluntary sexual intercourse between a married person and a partner other than the lawful spouse. [ME < OFr. *adultere* < Lat. *adulterium* < *adulter*, adulterer. See ADULTERATE.]

a•dult-on•set diabetes (ə-dŭlt′ŏn′sĕt, -ôn′-) *n.* Non-insulin-dependent diabetes mellitus.

ad•um•brate (ăd′əm-brāt′, ə-dŭm′-) *tr.v.* **-brat•ed, -brat•ing, -brates. 1.** To give a sketchy outline of. **2.** To prefigure indistinctly; foreshadow. **3.** To disclose partially or guardedly. [Lat. *adumbrāre, adumbrāt-*, to represent in outline : *ad-*, ad- + *umbra*, shadow.] **— ad′um•bra′tion** *n.* **— ad•um′bra•tive** (ə-dŭm′brə-tĭv) *adj.* **— ad•um′bra•tive•ly** *adv.*

a•dust (ə-dŭst′) *adj.* **1.** Burned; scorched. **2.** *Archaic.* Browned by the sun; sunburned. **3.** *Archaic.* Melancholy in appearance; gloomy. [ME < Lat. *adūstus*, p.part. of *adūrere*, to set fire to : *ad-*, ad- + *ūrere*, to burn.]

adv. *abbr.* **1.** *Gram.* Adverb; adverbial. **2.** *Lat.* Adversus (against). **3.** Advertisement. **4.** Advisory.

ad va•lo•rem (ăd′ və-lôr′əm, -lōr′-) *adj.* In proportion to the value: *ad valorem duties on imported goods.* [Lat. *ad*, to + *valorem*, value.]

ad•vance (ăd-văns′) *v.* **-vanced, -vanc•ing, -vanc•es.** *— tr.* **1.** To move or cause to move forward. **2.** To put forward; propose or suggest. **3.** To aid the growth or progress of. **4.** To raise in rank; promote. **5.** To cause to occur sooner: *advance a deadline.* **6.** To raise in amount or rate; increase. **7.** To pay (money or interest) before due. **8.** To supply or lend, esp. on credit. *— intr.* **1.** To go or move forward or onward. **2.** To make progress; improve. **3.** To rise in rank, position, or value. *— n.* **1.** The act or process of moving or going forward. **2.** A forward move, an improvement: *an advance in research.* **3.** An increase of price or value. **4. advances.** Opening approaches to secure acquaintance or favor. **5.a.** The furnishing of funds or goods on credit. **b.** The funds or goods so furnished. **6.** Payment of money before due. *— adj.* **1.** Made or given ahead of time: *an advance payment.* **2.** Going before, in front, or forward. **— *idioms.* in advance.** Ahead of time; beforehand. **in advance of.** In front of; ahead of. [ME *avauncen* < OFr. *avauncer* < VLat. **abantiāre* < Lat. *abante*, from before : *ab-*, ab- + *ante*, before; see **ant-***.] **— ad•vanc′er** *n.*

Syns: *advance, forward, foster, further, promote.* The central meaning shared by these verbs is "to cause to move ahead, as toward a goal": *advance a worthy cause; forwarding their own interests; fostered friendly relations; furthering your career; efforts to promote sales.* ***Ant:*** *retard.*

Usage Note: *Advance* as a noun is used for forward movement (*the advance of the army*) or for progress or improvement in a figurative sense. *Advancement* is used mainly in the figurative sense: *career advancement.* In this use, moreover, there is a distinction between the two terms deriving from the transitive and intransitive forms of the verb *advance.* Thus, *the advance of science* means simply the progress of science, whereas *the advancement of science* implies progress resulting from the action of an agent or force: *The purpose of the legislation was the advancement of science.*

ad•vanced (ăd-vănst′) *adj.* **1.** Highly developed or complex. **2.** Being at a higher level than others: *an advanced textbook.* **3.** Ahead of the times; progressive. **4.** Far along in course or time: *an advanced stage of illness.*

advanced standing *n.* The status of a college student granted credit for courses taken elsewhere.

advance guard *n.* A detachment of troops sent ahead of a main force to reconnoiter and provide protection.

advance man or **ad•vance•man** (ăd-văns′măn′) *n.* A man who travels ahead to arrange scheduling, publicity, and security for someone making a public appearance.

ad•vance•ment (ăd-văns′mənt) *n.* **1.** A forward step; an improvement. **2.** Development; progress: *the advancement of knowledge.* **3.** A promotion, as in rank. **4.** The act of moving forward. See Usage Note at **advance.**

advance person *n.* A person who travels ahead to arrange scheduling, publicity, and security for someone making a public appearance.

ad•van•tage (ăd-văn′tĭj) *n.* **1.** A beneficial factor or combination of factors. **2.** Benefit or profit; gain: *It is to your advantage to invest wisely.* **3.** A relatively favorable position: *Good education gave us the advantage.* **4.** *Sports.* **a.** The first point scored in tennis after deuce. **b.** The resulting score. *— tr.v.* **-taged, -tag•ing, -tag•es.** To afford profit or gain to; benefit. **— *idioms.* take advantage of. 1.** To put to good use; avail oneself of: *take advantage of all opportunities.* **2.** To profit selfishly by; exploit: *took advantage of the customer.* **to advantage.** To good effect; favorably. [ME *avauntage* < OFr. < *avant*, before < Lat. *abante*, from before. See ADVANCE.]

ad•van•ta•geous (ăd′văn-tā′jəs, -vən-) *adj.* Affording advantage; beneficial. See Syns at **beneficial. — ad′van•ta′geous•ly** *adv.* **— ad′van•ta′geous•ness** *n.*

ad•vect (ăd-vĕkt′) *tr.v.* **-vect•ed, -vect•ing, -vects. 1.** To convey horizontally by advection. **2.** To transport (a substance) by advection. [Back-formation < ADVECTION.]

ad•vec•tion (ăd-vĕk′shən) *n.* The transfer of an atmospheric property, such as temperature, by the movement of air, esp. horizontally. [Lat. *advectiō, advectiōn-*, act of conveying < *advectus*, p.part. of *advehere*, to carry to : *ad-*, ad- + *vehere*, to carry; see **wegh-***.]

ad•vent (ăd′vĕnt′) *n.* **1.** A coming or arrival: *the advent of the computer.* **2.** Also **Advent. a.** The period including the four Sundays before Christmas, observed by many Christians as a season of penitence. **b.** *Theol.* The coming of Jesus at the Incarnation. **c.** *Theol.* See **Second Coming.** [ME, the Advent season < OFr. < Lat. *adventus*, arrival < p.part. of *advenīre*, to come to : *ad-*, ad- + *venīre*, to come; see **gʷā-***.]

Ad•vent•ist (ăd′vĕn′tĭst, ăd-vĕn′-) *n.* A member of any of several Christian denominations that believe the Second Coming and the end of the world are near. **— Ad′vent′ism** *n.*

ad•ven•ti•tia (ăd′vĕn-tĭsh′ə, -vən-) *n.* The membranous outer covering of an organ or a blood vessel. [NLat. < Lat. *adventīcius*, foreign. See ADVENTITIOUS.] **— ad′ven•ti′tial** *adj.*

ad•ven•ti•tious (ăd′vĕn-tĭsh′əs, -vən-) *adj.* **1.** Not inherent but added extrinsically. **2.** *Biol.* Of or belonging to a structure that develops in an unusual place. [< Lat. *adventīcius*, foreign < *adventus*, arrival. See ADVENT.] **— ad′ven•ti′tious•ly** *adv.* **— ad′ven•ti′tious•ness** *n.*

ad•ven•tive (ăd-vĕn′tĭv) *Biol.* *— adj.* Not native to and not fully established in a new habitat or environment: *an adventive weed.* *— n.* An adventive organism. [< Lat. *adventus*, arrival. See ADVENT.] **— ad•ven′tive•ly** *adv.*

Advent Sunday *n.* The first Sunday of Advent.

ad•ven•ture (ăd-vĕn′chər) *n.* **1.** A hazardous or uncertain undertaking. **2.** An unusual or exciting experience. **3.** Participation in hazardous or exciting experiences: *the love of adventure.* **4.** A financial speculation or business venture. *— v.* **-tured, -tur•ing, -tures.** *— tr.* To hazard or risk. *— intr.* To engage in hazardous activities; take risks. [ME *aventure* < OFr. < Lat. *adventūrus*, fut.part. of *advenīre*, to arrive. See ADVENT.]

ad•ven•tur•er (ăd-vĕn′chər-ər) *n.* **1.** One that seeks adventure. **2.** A soldier of fortune. **3.** A heavy speculator in stocks, business, or trade. **4.** One that attempts to gain wealth and social position by unscrupulous means.

ad•ven•ture•some (ăd-vĕn′chər-səm) *adj.* Disposed to engage in risky activities or enterprises. **— ad•ven′ture•some•ly** *adv.* **— ad•ven′ture•some•ness** *n.*

ad•ven•tur•ess (ăd-vĕn′chər-ĭs) *n.* A woman who seeks social and financial advancement by unscrupulous means.

ad•ven•tur•ism (ăd-vĕn′chə-rĭz′əm) *n.* Involvement in risky enterprises, esp. in international affairs. **— ad•ven′tur•ist** *adj. & n.*

ad•ven•tur•ous (ăd-vĕn′chər-əs) *adj.* **1.** Inclined to undertake new and daring enterprises. **2.** Hazardous; risky. **— ad•ven′tur•ous•ly** *adv.* **— ad•ven′tur•ous•ness** *n.*

ad•verb (ăd′vûrb) *n.* *Gram.* **1.** A part of speech comprising a class of words that modify a verb, an adjective, or another adverb. **2.** A word belonging to this class, such as *rapidly* in *The dog runs rapidly.* [ME *adverbe* < OFr. < Lat. *adverbium*: *ad-*, in relation to; see AD- + *verbum*, word; see **wer-**[5]*.]

ad•ver•bi•al (ăd-vûr′bē-əl) *adj.* *Gram.* Of, relating to, or being an adverb. **— ad•ver′bi•al•ly** *adv.*

ad ver•bum (ăd vûr′bəm) *adv.* Word for word; verbatim. [Lat. : *ad*, in accordance with + *verbum*, word.]

ad•ver•sar•i•al (ăd′vər-sâr′ē-əl) *adj.* Relating to or characteristic of an adversary.

ad•ver•sar•y (ăd′vər-sĕr′ē) *n., pl.* **-ies.** An opponent; an enemy. [ME *adversarie* < Lat. *adversārius*, enemy < *adversus*, against. See ADVERSE.]

ad•ver•sa•tive (ăd-vûr′sə-tĭv) *adj.* Expressing antithesis or opposition: *the adversative conjunction* but. *— n.* A word that expresses antithesis or opposition. [Lat. *adversātīvus* < *adversātus*, p.part. of *adversārī*, to oppose < *adversus*, against. See ADVERSE.] **— ad•ver′sa•tive•ly** *adv.*

ad•verse (ăd-vûrs′, ăd′vûrs′) *adj.* **1.** Acting or serving to oppose; antagonistic: *adverse criticism.* **2.** Contrary to one's interests or welfare; harmful or unfavorable: *adverse circumstances.* **3.** Moving in an opposite or opposing direction: *adverse currents.* **4.** *Archaic.* Placed opposite. [ME < OFr. *advers* < Lat. *adversus*, p.part. of *advertere*, to turn toward : *ad-*, ad- + *vertere*, to turn; see **wer-**[2]*.] **— ad•verse′ly** *adv.* **— ad•verse′ness** *n.*

ad•ver•si•ty (ăd-vûr′sĭ-tē) *n., pl.* **-ties. 1.** A state of hardship or affliction; misfortune. **2.** A calamitous event.

ad•vert[1] (ăd-vûrt′) *intr.v.* **-vert•ed, -vert•ing, -verts.** To call attention; refer: *advert to a problem.* [ME *adverten* < OFr. *advertir*, to notice < Lat. *advertere*, to turn toward. See ADVERSE.]

ad•vert[2] (ăd′vûrt) *n.* *Chiefly British.* An advertisement.

ad•ver•tise (ăd′vər-tīz′) *v.* **-tised, -tis•ing, -tis•es.** *— tr.* **1.** To make public announcement of, esp. to proclaim the qualities or advantages of (a product or business) so as to increase sales. **2.** To make known; call attention to: *advertised my intention to resign.* **3.** To warn or notify: *"This event advertises me that there is such a fact as death"* (Henry David Thoreau). *— intr.* **1.** To call the attention of the public to a

ă pat	oi boy
ā pay	ou out
âr care	ŏŏ took
ä father	ōō boot
ĕ pet	ŭ cut
ē be	ûr urge
ĭ pit	th thin
ī pie	*th* this
îr pier	hw which
ŏ pot	zh vision
ō toe	ə about, item
ô paw	

Stress marks:
′ (primary);
′ (secondary), as in
dictionary (dĭk′shə-nĕr′ē)

product or business. **2.** To inquire or seek in a public notice, as in a newspaper. [ME *advertisen*, to notify < OFr. *advertir*, *advertiss-*, to notice. See ADVERT[1].] **—ad′ver·tis′er** *n.*

ad·ver·tise·ment (ăd′vər-tīz′mənt, ăd-vûr′tĭs-, -tĭz-) *n.* **1.** The act of advertising. **2.** A notice, such as a poster, newspaper display, or paid announcement in the electronic media, designed to attract public attention or patronage.

ad·ver·tis·ing (ăd′vər-tī′zĭng) *n.* **1.** The activity of attracting public attention to a product or business, as by paid announcements in print or on the air. **2.** The business of designing and writing advertisements for publication or broadcast. **3.** Advertisements considered as a group.

ad·vice (ăd-vīs′) *n.* **1.** Opinion about what could or should be done about a situation or problem; counsel. **2.** Information communicated; news. Often used in the plural: *advices from an ambassador.* [ME *avis*, *advice* < OFr. *avis* < *(ester) a vis*, to seem : *a*, to (< Lat. *ad*; see AD–) + *vis*, seen (< Lat. *vīsum*, what seems (good) < neut. p.part. of *vidēre*, to see; see **weid-***).] **—ad·vis′er, ad·vis′or** (ăd-vī′zər) *n.*

Syns: *advice, counsel, recommendation.* The central meaning shared by these nouns is "an opinion as to a decision or course of action": *sound advice for the unemployed; accepted the counsel of her attorney; will follow his recommendation.*

ad·vis·a·ble (ăd-vī′zə-bəl) *adj.* Worthy of being recommended or suggested; prudent. **—ad·vis′a·bil′i·ty, ad·vis′a·ble·ness** *n.* **—ad·vis′a·bly** *adv.*

ad·vise (ăd-vīz′) *v.* **-vised, -vis·ing, -vis·es.** *—tr.* **1.** To offer advice to; counsel. **2.** To recommend; suggest: *advised patience.* **3.** *Usage Problem.* To inform; notify. *—intr.* **1.** To take counsel; consult: *advised with her boss.* **2.** To offer advice. [ME *avisen*, *advisen* < OFr. *aviser* < *avis*, advice. See ADVICE.]

Usage Note: The use of *advise* in the sense of "inform, notify," was found acceptable by a majority of the Usage Panel in an earlier survey, but many members would prefer that this usage be restricted to business correspondence and legal contexts. Thus one may say *The suspects were advised of their rights,* but it would be considered pretentious to say *You'd better advise your friends about the date of the picnic.*

ad·vised (ăd-vīzd′) *adj.* **1.** Thought out; considered. Often used in combination: *well-advised; ill-advised.* **2.** Informed: *Keep me advised of further developments.*

adz
Top: XVIII Dynasty Egyptian adz with bronze blade, wood handle, and leather binding
Bottom: Carpenter's adz (*top*), shipbuilder's adz (*bottom left*), and curved-blade adz (*bottom right*)

ad·vis·ed·ly (ăd-vī′zĭd-lē) *adv.* With careful consideration.

ad·vi·see (ăd-vī-zē′) *n.* One that is advised.

ad·vise·ment (ăd-vīz′mənt) *n.* Careful consideration: *Your request will be taken under advisement.*

ad·vi·so·ry (ăd-vī′zə-rē) *adj.* **1.** Empowered to advise: *an advisory committee.* **2.** Relating to or containing advice: *an advisory memorandum.* *—n., pl.* **-ries.** A report giving information, esp. a warning: *a weather advisory.*

ad·vo·ca·cy (ăd′və-kə-sē) *n.* The act of pleading or arguing in favor of something, such as a cause; active support.

ad·vo·cate (ăd′və-kāt′) *tr.v.* **-cat·ed, -cat·ing, -cates.** To speak, plead, or argue in favor of. See Syns at **support.** *—n.* (-kĭt, -kāt′). **1.** One that argues for a cause; a supporter or defender: *an advocate of civil rights.* **2.** One that pleads in another's behalf; an intercessor. **3.** A lawyer. [< ME *advocat*, lawyer < OFr. *advocat* < Lat. *advocātus*, p.part. of *advocāre*, to summon for counsel : *ad-*, ad- + *vocāre*, to call; see **wek^{w}-***.] **—ad′vo·ca′tor** *n.* **—ad·voc′a·to′ry** (ăd-vŏk′ə-tôr′ē, -tōr′ē, ăd′və-kə-) *adj.*

aerialist

ad·vow·son (ăd-vou′zən) *n.* The right in English ecclesiastical law of presentation to a vacant benefice. [ME *avouson* < OFr. *avoeson* < Med.Lat. *advocātia* < Lat. *advocātiō*, a summoning < *advocāre*, to summon. See ADVOCATE.]

advt. *abbr.* Advertisement.

ad·y·tum (ăd′ĭ-təm) *n., pl.* **-ta** (-tə). The sanctum in an ancient temple. [Lat. < Gk. *aduton* < *adutos*, not to be entered : *a-*, not; see A–[1] + *duein*, to enter.]

adz or **adze** (ădz) *n.* An axlike tool with a curved blade at right angles to the handle, used for dressing wood. [ME *adese* < OE *adesa.*]

Ad·zhar·i·a (ə-jär′ē-ə) or **Ad·zhar·i·stan** (ə-jär′ĭ-stăn′, ŭj′-ə-ryĭ-stän′). A region of SW Georgia bordering on the Black Sea and Turkey. **—Ad·zhar′** (ə-jär′) *n.* **—Ad·zhar′i·an** *adj. & n.*

ad·zu·ki bean (ăd-zo͞o′kē) also **ad·su·ki bean** (-so͞o′-, -zo͞o′-) *n.* **1.** An erect or twining East Asian herb (*Vigna angularis*) of the pea family, having edible sprouts and reddish seeds used to make flour. **2.** A seed of this plant. [J. *azuki* < Chin. *xiăo dòu*: *xiăo*, small + *dòu*, bean.]

a·e·des (ā-ē′dēz) *n., pl.* **aedes.** A mosquito of the genus *Aēdes*, including *A. aegypti*, which transmits diseases such as yellow fever and dengue. [NLat. *Aēdēs*, genus name < Gk. *aēdēs*, unpleasant : *a-*, not; see A–[1] + *ēdos*, pleasure; see **swād-***.] **—a·e′dine** (-dīn, -dēn) *adj.*

ae·dile (ē′dīl′) *n.* An elected official of ancient Rome who was responsible for public works and games, markets, the grain supply, and the water supply. [Lat. *aedīlis* < *aedēs*, house.]

Ae·ga·de·an Isles (ē-gā′dē′ən) also **Ae·ga·tes** (-tēz). See **Egadi Islands.**

Ae·ge·an (ĭ-jē′ən) *adj.* Of or relating to the Bronze Age civilization that flourished in the Aegean area, as at Crete.

Aegean Sea. An arm of the Mediterranean off SE Europe between Greece and Turkey. The **Aegean Islands** include the Cyclades, the Dodecanese, and the Sporades.

Ae·geus (ē′jo͞os, ē′jē-əs) *n. Gk. Myth.* A king of Athens and the father of Theseus.

Ae·gi·na (ĭ-jī′nə). An island off SE Greece in the Saronic Gulf of the Aegean Sea near Athens.

Aeg·ir (ăg′ər, ĕj′ĭr) *n. Myth.* The Norse god of the sea.

ae·gis also **e·gis** (ē′jĭs) *n.* **1.** Protection: *a child under the aegis of the courts.* **2.** Sponsorship; patronage: *a concert held under the aegis of the parents' association.* **3.** *Gk. Myth.* The shield or breastplate of Zeus, later of Athena, carrying at its center the head of Medusa. [Lat. < Gk. *aigis.*]

Ae·gis·thus (ĭ-jĭs′thəs) *n. Gk. Myth.* The son of Thyestes and lover of Clytemnestra who helped Clytemnestra kill Agamemnon upon Agamemnon's return from the Trojan War.

Ae·gos·pot·a·mi (ē′gəs-pŏt′ə-mī′) or **Ae·gos·pot·a·mos** (-mŏs′). A river and ancient town of S Thrace in present-day W Turkey; site of the final battle of the Peloponnesian War, in which the Spartans destroyed the Athenian fleet (405 B.C.).

Ael·fric (ăl′frĭk). "Grammaticus." 955?–1020? Anglo-Saxon abbot whose works include *Lives of the Saints* and a Latin grammar.

–aemia *suff.* Var. of **–emia.**

Ae·ne·as (ĭ-nē′əs) *n. Gk. & Rom. Myth.* The Trojan hero of the *Aeneid* who escaped the sack of Troy and wandered for seven years before settling in Italy.

a·e·ne·ous or **a·e·ne·us** (ā-ē′nē-əs) *adj.* Brassy or golden green in color. [< Lat. *aēneus*, of bronze < *aes*, bronze. See **ayes-***.]

Ae·o·li·an (ē-ō′lē-ən) *adj.* **1.** Of or relating to Aeolis or its people or culture. **2.** *Gk. Myth.* Of or relating to Aeolus. **3. aeolian.** Var. of **eolian.** *—n.* **1.** One of a Hellenic people of central Greece that occupied Aeolis and Lesbos around 1100 B.C. **2.** See **Aeolic** 1.

Aeolian harp *n. Mus.* An instrument consisting of an open box over which are stretched strings that sound when struck by the wind. [< AEOLIAN, relating to Aeolus, god of the winds.]

Ae·ol·ic (ē-ŏl′ĭk) *n.* **1.** A group of dialects of ancient Greek spoken by the Aeolians. **2.** Any of several verse forms built around a central choriamb, used esp. by Sappho and Alcaeus.

Ae·o·lis (ē′ə-lĭs) or **Ae·o·li·a** (ē-ō′lē-ə). An ancient region of W Asia Minor in present-day Turkey.

Ae·o·lus (ē′ə-ləs) *n.* **1.** *Gk. Myth.* The god of the winds. **2.** A king of Thessaly and ancestor of the Aeolians.

ae·on (ē′ŏn′, ē′ən) *n.* Var. of **eon.**

ae·o·ni·an (ē-ō′nē-ən) *adj.* Var. of **eonian.**

ae·py·or·nis (ē′pē-ôr′nĭs) *n.* A genus of extinct, large, flightless birds native to Madagascar. [NLat. *Aepyornis*, genus name : Gk. *aipus*, high + Gk. *ornis*, bird; see **or-***.]

aer·ate (âr′āt) *tr.v.* **-at·ed, -at·ing, -ates.** **1.** To supply or charge (liquid) with a gas, esp. to charge with carbon dioxide. **2.** To expose to the circulation of air for purification. **3.** To expose to oxygen, as in the oxygenation of the blood by respiration. **—aer·a′tion** *n.*

aer·a·tor (âr′ā′tər) *n.* One that aerates, as a machine for aerating turf or a device for aerating liquids.

aer·i·al (âr′ē-əl, ā-îr′ē-əl) *adj.* **1.** Of, in, or caused by the air. **2.** Living in the air. **3.** Reaching high into the air; lofty. **4.** Suggestive of air, as in lightness; airy. **5.** Unsubstantial; imaginary. **6.** Of, for, or by means of aircraft: *aerial photography.* **7.** *Bot.* Growing or borne above the ground or water: *aerial roots.* *—n.* (âr′ē-əl). A radio antenna, esp. one suspended in or extending into the air. [< Lat. *āerius* < Gk. *aerios* < *aēr*, air. See **wer-**[1]*.]

aer·i·al·ist (âr′ē-ə-lĭst) *n.* An acrobat who performs in the air, as on a trapeze or tightrope.

aerial ladder *n.* A ladder that can be extended to reach high places, esp. one mounted on a fire engine.

aerial yam *n.* See **air potato.**

aer·ie or **aer·y** also **ey·rie** or **eyr·y** (âr′ē, îr′ē) *n., pl.* **-ies.** **1.** The nest of a bird, such as an eagle, built on a cliff or other high place. **2.** A house or stronghold perched on a height. [Med.Lat. *aeria* < OFr. *aire* < Lat. *ārea*, open space, threshing-floor.]

aero– or **aer–** *pref.* **1.a.** Air; atmosphere: *aeroballistics.* **b.** Gas: *aerosol.* **2.** Aviation: *aeronautics.* [Gk. < *aēr*, air. See **wer-**[1]*.]

aer·o·al·ler·gen (âr′ō-ăl′ər-jən) *n.* Any of various airborne substances, such as pollen or spores, that can cause an allergic response.

aer·o·bal·lis·tics (âr′ō-bə-lĭs′tĭks) *n.* (*used with a sing. v.*) Ballistics, esp. of missiles, in the atmosphere. **—aer′o·bal·lis′tic** *adj.*

aer·o·bat·ics (âr′ə-băt′ĭks) *n.* (*used with a sing. or pl. v.*) Stunts, such as rolls and loops, performed in an aircraft. [AERO– + (ACRO)BATICS.] **—aer′o·bat′** *n.* **—aer′o·bat′ic** *adj.*

aer·obe (âr′ōb′) *n.* An organism, such as a bacterium, requiring oxygen to live. [Fr. *aérobie*: Gk. *aēr*, air; see AERO– + Gk. *bios*, life; see **g^{w}ei-***.]

aer•o•bic (â-rō**′**bĭk) *adj.* **1.** *Biol.* **a.** Living or occurring only in the presence of oxygen: *aerobic bacteria.* **b.** Of or relating to aerobes. **2.** Involving or improving oxygen consumption by the body: *aerobic exercise.* **3.** Relating to or used in aerobics: *aerobic shoes.* **—aer•o′bi•cal•ly** *adv.*

aer•o•bics (â-rō**′**bĭks) *n.* *(used with a sing. or pl. v.)* **1.** A system of physical conditioning designed to enhance circulatory and respiratory efficiency that involves vigorous, sustained exercise, such as jogging, swimming, or cycling. **2.** A program of physical fitness that involves such exercise. [< AEROBIC.]

aer•o•bi•ol•o•gy (âr′ō-bī-ŏl**′**ə-jē) *n.* The study of the sources, dispersion, and effects of airborne biological materials, such as pollen, spores, and microorganisms. **—aer′o•bi•o•log′i•cal** (-ə-lŏj**′**ĭ-kəl) *adj.* **—aer′o•bi•o•log′i•cal•ly** *adv.*

aer•o•bi•um (â-rō**′**bē-əm) *n.* See **aerobe.** [NLat. < AEROBE.]

aer•o•cul•ture (âr**′**ə-kŭl′chər) *n.* See **aeroponics.** [AERO– + (AGRI)CULTURE.]

aer•o•drome (âr**′**ə-drōm′) *n.* *Chiefly British.* An airdrome.

aer•o•dy•nam•ic (âr′ō-dī-năm**′**ĭk) also **aer•o•dy•nam•i•cal** (-ĭ-kəl) *adj.* **1.** Of or relating to aerodynamics. **2.** Styled to reduce wind drag. **—aer′o•dy•nam′i•cal•ly** *adv.*

aer•o•dy•nam•ics (âr′ō-dī-năm**′**ĭks) *n.* *(used with a sing. v.)* The dynamics of bodies moving relative to gases, esp. the interaction of moving objects with the atmosphere. **—aer′o•dy•nam′i•cist** (-ĭ-sĭst) *n.*

aer•o•dyne (âr**′**ə-dīn′) *n.* A heavier-than-air aircraft deriving lift from motion. [AERO– + Gk. *dunamis,* power (< *dunasthai,* to be able; see **deu-^{2}***).]

aer•o•em•bo•lism (âr′ō-ĕm**′**bə-lĭz′əm) *n.* Embolism that occurs as a result of the entrance of air bubbles into a blood vessel after surgical procedures or trauma.

aer•o•foil (âr**′**ə-foil′) *n.* *Chiefly British.* Var. of **airfoil.**

aer•o•gram also **aer•o•gramme** (âr**′**ə-grăm′) *n.* An airmail letter in the form of a lightweight sheet of stationery that folds into its own envelope.

aer•o•lite (âr**′**ə-līt′) also **aer•o•lith** (-lĭth′) *n.* A chiefly siliceous meteorite. **—aer′o•lit′ic** (-lĭt**′**ĭk) *adj.*

aer•ol•o•gy (â-rŏl**′**ə-jē) *n.* Meteorology of the total vertical extent of the atmosphere as opposed to the study of the atmosphere near Earth's surface. **—aer′o•log′ic** (âr′ə-lŏj**′**ĭk), **aer′o•log′i•cal** *adj.* **—aer•ol′o•gist** *n.*

aer•o•mag•net•ics (âr′ō-măg-nĕt**′**ĭks) *n.* *(used with a sing. v.)* The science of magnetic characteristics associated with atmospheric conditions. **—aer′o•mag•net′ic** *adj.* **—aer′o•mag•net′i•cal•ly** *adv.*

aer•o•me•chan•ics (âr′ō-mĭ-kăn**′**ĭks) *n.* *(used with a sing. v.)* The science of the motion and equilibrium of air and other gases, comprising aerodynamics and aerostatics. **—aer′o•me•chan′i•cal** *adj.* **—aer′o•me•chan′i•cal•ly** *adv.*

aer•o•med•i•cine (âr′ō-mĕd**′**ĭ-sĭn) *n.* The medical study and treatment of physiological and psychological disorders associated with atmospheric or space flight. **—aer′o•med′i•cal** (-kəl) *adj.*

aer•o•me•te•or•o•graph (âr′ō-mē′tē-ôr**′**ə-grăf′, -ŏr′-) *n.* An aircraft instrument for simultaneously recording temperature, atmospheric pressure, and humidity.

aer•om•e•ter (â-rŏm**′**ĭ-tər) *n.* An instrument for determining the weight and density of air or another gas.

aer•o•naut (âr**′**ə-nôt′) *n.* A pilot of a lighter-than-air craft, such as a balloon. [AERO– + Gk. *nautēs,* sailor; see **nāu-***.]

aer•o•nau•tic (âr′ə-nô**′**tĭk) also **aer•o•nau•ti•cal** (-tĭ-kəl) *adj.* Of or relating to aeronautics. **—aer′o•nau′ti•cal•ly** *adv.*

aer•o•nau•tics (âr′ə-nô**′**tĭks) *n.* *(used with a sing. v.)* **1.** The design and construction of aircraft. **2.** The theory and practice of aircraft navigation.

aer•o•neu•ro•sis (âr′ō-no͝o-rō′sĭs, -nyo͝o-) *n.* Nervous exhaustion from prolonged piloting of aircraft.

aer•on•o•my (â-rŏn**′**ə-mē) *n.* The study of the upper atmosphere, esp. of regions of ionized gas. **—aer•on′o•mer** *n.* **—aer′o•nom′ic, aer′o•nom′i•cal** *adj.* **—aer•on′o•mist** *n.*

aer•o•pause (âr**′**ō-pôz′) *n.* The region of the atmosphere above which aircraft cannot fly.

aer•o•pha•gia (âr′ə-fā**′**jə) *n.* The abnormal, spasmodic swallowing of air, esp. as a symptom of hysteria.

aer•o•pho•bi•a (âr′ə-fō**′**bē-ə) *n.* An abnormal fear of air, esp. drafts.

aer•o•phore (âr**′**ə-fôr′, -fōr′-) *n.* A device that supplies air to the lungs, as for a person in a closed mine.

aer•o•phyte (âr**′**ə-fīt′) *n.* See **epiphyte.**

aer•o•plane (âr**′**ə-plān′) *n.* *Chiefly British.* Var. of **airplane.**

aer•o•pon•ics (âr′ə-pŏn**′**ĭks) *n.* *(used with a sing. v.)* A technique for growing plants without soil by suspending them and constantly misting the roots with nutrient-laden water. [AERO– + (HYDRO)PONICS.]

aer•o•sol (âr**′**ə-sôl′, -sŏl′) *n.* **1.** A gaseous suspension of fine solid or liquid particles. **2.** A substance, such as paint, packaged under pressure with a gaseous propellant for release as a spray of fine particles. [AERO– + SOL(UTION).]

aer•o•space (âr**′**ō-spās′) *adj.* **1.** Of or relating to Earth's atmosphere and the space beyond. **2.** Of or relating to the science or technology of flight. **—aer′o•space′** *n.*

aerospace medicine *n.* See **aeromedicine.**

aer•o•sphere (âr**′**ō-sfîr′) *n.* The lower portion of the atmosphere in which both uncrewed and crewed flight is possible.

aer•o•stat (âr**′**ō-stăt′) *n.* An aircraft, esp. a balloon or dirigible, deriving its lift from the buoyancy of surrounding air. [Fr. *aérostat:* Gk. *aēr,* air; see AERO– + Gk. *statos,* standing; see STATO–.] **—aer′o•stat′ic, aer′o•stat′i•cal** *adj.*

aer•o•stat•ics (âr′ō-stăt**′**ĭks) *n.* *(used with a sing. v.)* The science of gases in equilibrium and of the equilibrium of balloons or aircraft under changing atmospheric flight conditions.

aer•o•ther•mo•dy•nam•ics (âr′ō-thûr′mō-dī-năm**′**ĭks) *n.* **1.** *(used with a sing. v.)* The study of the thermodynamics of gases, esp. at high relative velocities. **2.** *(used with a pl. v.)* The thermodynamics of such gases.

aer•y^1 (âr**′**ē, ā**′**ə-rē) *adj.* **-i•er, -i•est.** Ethereal. [Lat. *āerius,* of the air. See AERIAL.]

aer•y^2 (âr**′**ē, îr**′**ē) *n.* Var. of **aerie.**

Aes•chy•lus (ĕs**′**kə-ləs, ē**′**skə-). 525–456 B.C. Greek dramatist whose surviving plays include the *Oresteia* trilogy (458). **—Aes′chy•le′an** (-lē**′**ən) *adj.*

Aes•cu•la•pi•an (ĕs′kyə-lā**′**pē-ən) *adj.* Relating to the healing arts; medical.

Aes•cu•la•pi•us (ĕs′kyə-lā**′**pē-əs) *n.* *Rom. Myth.* The god of medicine and healing. [Lat., Gk. *Asklēpios.*]

Ae•sir (ā**′**sîr′, ā**′**zîr′) *pl.n.* *Myth.* The Norse gods. [ON, pl. of *āss,* god. See **ansu-***.]

Ae•sop (ē**′**səp, -sŏp′). 6th cent. B.C. Greek fabulist traditionally considered the author of *Aesop's Fables.* **—Ae•so′pi•an** (ē-sō**′**pē-ən), **Ae•sop′ic** (ē-sŏp**′**ĭk) *adj.*

aes•the•sia or **es•the•sia** (ĕs-thē**′**zhə) *n.* The ability to feel or perceive. [Back-formation < ANESTHESIA.]

aes•thete or **es•thete** (ĕs**′**thēt) *n.* **1.** One who cultivates an unusual sensitivity to beauty, as in art or nature. **2.** One whose admiration of beauty is regarded as excessive or affected. [Back-formation < AESTHETIC.]

aes•thet•ic or **es•thet•ic** (ĕs-thĕt**′**ĭk) *—adj.* **1.** Relating to aesthetics. **2.** Of or concerning the appreciation of beauty or good taste: *the aesthetic faculties.* **3.** Characterized by a heightened sensitivity to beauty. *—n.* A conception of what is artistically valid or beautiful. [Ger. *ästhetisch* < NLat. *aesthēticus* < Gk. *aisthētikos,* of sense perception < *aisthēta,* perceptible things < *aisthanesthai,* to perceive. See **au-***.] **—aes•thet′i•cal•ly** *adv.*

aes•the•ti•cian or **es•the•ti•cian** (ĕs′thĭ-tĭsh**′**ən) *n.* **1.** One versed in the theory of beauty and artistic expression. **2.** One skilled in giving facials and other beauty treatments.

aes•thet•i•cism or **es•thet•i•cism** (ĕs-thĕt**′**ĭ-sĭz′əm) *n.* **1.** Devotion to and pursuit of the beautiful; sensitivity to artistic beauty and refined taste. **2.** The doctrine that beauty is the basic principle from which all other principles are derived.

aes•thet•ics or **es•thet•ics** (ĕs-thĕt**′**ĭks) *n.* **1.** *(used with a sing. v.)* **a.** The branch of philosophy that deals with the nature and expression of beauty, as in the fine arts. **b.** In Kantian philosophy, the branch of metaphysics concerned with the laws of perception. **2.** *(used with a sing. v.)* The study of the psychological responses to beauty and artistic experiences. **3.** *(used with a sing. or pl. v.)* A conception of what is artistically valid or beautiful: *minimalist aesthetics.* **4.** *(used with a sing. or pl. v.)* An artistically beautiful or pleasing appearance: *"They're looking for quality construction, not aesthetics"* (Ron Schram).

aes•ti•val (ĕs**′**tə-vəl) *adj.* Var. of **estival.**

aes•ti•vate (ĕs**′**tə-vāt′) *v.* Var. of **estivate.**

aes•ti•va•tion (ĕs′tə-vā**′**shən) *n.* Var. of **estivation.**

Aeth•el•red II (ĕth**′**əl-rĕd′). See **Ethelred II.**

Ae•ther (ē**′**thər) *n.* *Gk. Myth.* The personification of the clear upper air breathed by the Olympians. [Lat. < Gk. *aithēr,* upper air.]

ae•ti•ol•o•gy (ē′tē-ŏl**′**ə-jē) *n.* Var. of **etiology.**

Aet•na (ĕt**′**nə), **Mount.** See **Mount Etna.**

Ae•to•li•a (ē-tō**′**lē-ə, -tōl**′**yə). An ancient region of central Greece. The **Aetolian League,** a military confederation formed in 290 B.C., was defeated by the Achaeans later in the 3rd cent. **—Ae•to′li•an** *adj.* & *n.*

AF *abbr.* **1.** Air force. **2.** Audio frequency.

af– *pref.* Var. of **ad–** 1.

a•far (ə-fär**′**) *adv.* From, at, or to a great distance: *saw it afar off; traveled afar.* *—n.* A long distance: *Tales from afar.* [ME *afer* < *on fer,* far, and < *of fer,* from afar < OE *feor,* far. See FAR.]

A•fars and Is•sas (ə-färs**′**; ī**′**səs). See **Djibouti** 1.

AFB *abbr.* Air force base.

AFC *abbr.* American Football Conference.

AFDC *abbr.* Aid to Families with Dependent Children.

a•feard also **a•feared** (ə-fîrd**′**) *adj.* *New England, Upper Southern U.S.,* & *Ozarks.* Afraid. [ME *afered* < OE *āfǣred,* p.part. of *āfǣran,* to frighten : *ā-,* intensive pref. + *fǣran,* to frighten (< *fǣr,* danger; see FEAR).]

a•feb•rile (ā-fĕb**′**rəl, ā-fē**′**brəl) *adj.* Having no fever.

ă pat	oi boy
ā pay	ou out
âr care	o͝o took
ä father	o͞o boot
ĕ pet	ŭ cut
ē be	ûr urge
ĭ pit	th thin
ī pie	*th* this
îr pier	hw which
ŏ pot	zh vision
ō toe	ə about, item
ô paw	

Stress marks:
′ (primary);
′ (secondary), as in
dictionary (dĭk**′**shə-nĕr′ē)

af•fa•ble (ăf′ə-bəl) *adj.* **1.** Easy and pleasant to speak to; approachable. **2.** Gentle and gracious: *an affable smile.* [ME *affabil* < OFr. *affable* < Lat. *affābilis* < *affārī*, to speak to : *ad-*, ad- + *fārī*, to speak; see **bhā-[2]***.] — **af′fa•bil′i•ty** *n.* — **af′fa•bly** *adv.*

af•fair (ə-fâr′) *n.* **1.** Something done or to be done; business. **2. affairs.** Transactions and other matters of professional or public business: *affairs of state.* **3.a.** An occurrence, an object, or a matter: *The senator's death was a tragic affair.* **b.** A social function. **4.** A matter of personal concern. **5. affairs.** Personal business: *get one's affairs in order.* **6.** A matter causing public scandal and controversy: *the Dreyfus affair.* **7.** A sexual relationship between two people who are not married to each other. [ME *affaire* < OFr. *afaire* < *a faire*, to do : *a*, to (< Lat. *ad*; see AD-) + *faire*, to do (< *facere*; see **dhē-***).]

af•faire d'a•mour (ä-fâr′ dä-mo͝or′) *n., pl.* **af•faires d'a•mour** (ä-fâr′ dä-mo͝or′). A love affair. [Fr. : *affaire*, affair + *de*, of + *amour*, love.]

af•faire de coeur (ä-fâr′ də kœr′) *n., pl.* **af•faires de coeur** (ä-fâr′ də kœr′). A love affair. [Fr. : *affaire*, affair + *de*, of + *cœur*, heart.]

af•faire d'hon•neur (ä-fâr′ dô-nœr′) *n., pl.* **af•faires d'hon•neur** (ä-fâr′ dô-nœr′). An affair of honor; a duel. [Fr. : *affaire*, affair + *de*, of + *honneur*, honor.]

af•fect[1] (ə-fĕkt′) *tr.v.* **-fect•ed, -fect•ing, -fects. 1.** To have an influence on or effect a change in: *Inflation affects buying power.* **2.** To act on the emotions of; touch or move. **3.** To attack or infect, as a disease. — *n.* (ăf′ĕkt′). **1.** *Psychol.* **a.** A feeling or emotion as distinguished from cognition, thought, or action. **b.** A strong feeling having active consequences. **2.** *Obsolete.* A disposition, feeling, or tendency. [Lat. *afficere*, *affect-* : *ad-*, ad- + *facere*, to do; see **dhē-***.]

Usage Note: *Affect*[1] and *effect* have no senses in common. As a verb *affect*[1] is most commonly used in the sense of "to influence" (*how smoking affects health*). *Effect* means "to bring about or execute": *measures designed to effect savings.*

af•fect[2] (ə-fĕkt′) *tr.v.* **-fect•ed, -fect•ing, -fects. 1.** To put on a false show of; simulate: *affected a British accent.* **2.a.** To have or show a liking for: *affects dramatic clothes.* **b.** *Archaic.* To fancy; love. **3.** To tend to by nature; tend to assume: *a substance that affects crystalline form.* **4.** To imitate; copy: *"Spenser, in affecting the ancients, writ no language"* (Ben Jonson). [ME *affecten* < Lat. *affectāre*, to strive after, freq. of *afficere*, *affect-*, to affect, influence. See AFFECT[1].] — **af•fect′er** *n.*

Afghan hound

af•fec•ta•tion (ăf′ĕk-tā′shən) *n.* **1.** A show, pretense, or display. **2.a.** Behavior that is assumed rather than natural; artificiality. **b.** A particular habit adopted to give a false impression. [Lat. *affectātiō*, *affectātiōn-* < *affectātus*, p.part. of *affectāre*, to strive after. See AFFECT[2].]

Syns: *affectation, pose, air, mannerism.* These nouns refer to personal behavior assumed for effect. An *affectation* is an artificial habit, often adopted in imitation of an admired person, that is perceived as being unnatural: *"His* [Arthur Rubinstein's] *playing stripped away . . . the affectations and exaggerations that characterized Chopin interpretation before his arrival"* (Michael Kimmelman). *Pose* denotes an attitude adopted in order to call favorable attention to oneself or make an impression on other people: *His humility is only a pose. Air*, meaning a distinctive but intangible quality, does not always imply sham: *an air of authority.* In the plural, however, it suggests affectation and self-importance: *putting on airs. Mannerism* denotes an idiosyncratic trait or quirk, often one that others find obtrusive and distracting: *a mannerism of closing his eyes as he talked.*

af•fect•ed[1] (ə-fĕk′tĭd) *adj.* **1.** Acted upon, influenced, or changed. **2.** Emotionally stirred or moved. **3.** Infected or attacked, as by disease. [< AFFECT[1].]

af•fect•ed[2] (ə-fĕk′tĭd) *adj.* **1.** Assumed or simulated to impress others: *an affected accent.* **2.** Speaking or behaving in an artificial way to make an impression. **3.** Disposed or inclined. [< AFFECT[2].] — **af•fect′ed•ly** *adv.* — **af•fect′ed•ness** *n.*

af•fect•ing (ə-fĕk′tĭng) *adj.* Inspiring or capable of inspiring strong emotion; moving. [< AFFECT[1].] — **af•fect′ing•ly** *adv.*

af•fec•tion (ə-fĕk′shən) *n.* **1.** A tender feeling toward another; fondness. See Syns at **love. 2.** Feeling or emotion. Often used in the plural. **3.** A disposition to feel, do, or say; a propensity. [ME *affeccioun* < OFr. *affection* < Lat. *affectiō*, *affectiōn-* < *affectus*, p.part. of *afficere*, to affect, influence. See AFFECT[1].] — **af•fec′tion•al** *adj.* — **af•fec′tion•al•ly** *adv.*

Afghanistan

af•fec•tion•ate (ə-fĕk′shə-nĭt) *adj.* **1.** Having or showing fond feelings or affection; loving and tender. **2.** *Obsolete.* Inclined or disposed. — **af•fec′tion•ate•ly** *adv.* — **af•fec′tion•ate•ness** *n.*

af•fec•tive (ə-fĕk′tĭv) *adj.* **1.** *Psychol.* Influenced by or resulting from the emotions: *affective disorders.* **2.** Concerned with or arousing feelings or emotions; emotional. — **af•fec′tive•ly** *adv.* — **af′fec•tiv′i•ty** (ăf′ĕk-tĭv′ĭ-tē) *n.*

af•fect•less (ăf′fĕkt′lĭs) *adj.* Having or showing no emotion; unfeeling. — **af′fect′less•ness** *n.*

af•fen•pin•scher (ăf′ən-pĭn′shər) *n.* Any of a breed of small dogs of European origin, having wiry shaggy hair and a tufted muzzle. [Ger. : *Affe*, ape (< MHGer. < OHGer. *affo*) + *Pinscher*, a type of dog with ears operated on or "pinched" to make them stand up (< E. PINCH).]

af•fer•ent (ăf′ər-ənt) *adj.* Carrying inward to a central organ or section, as nerves that conduct impulses from the periphery of the body to the spinal cord. [Lat. *afferēns*, *afferent-*, pr.part. of *afferre*, to bring toward : *ad-*, ad- + *ferre*, to bring; see **bher-[1]***.] — **af′fer•ent•ly** *adv.*

af•fi•ance (ə-fī′əns) *tr.v.* **-anced, -anc•ing, -anc•es.** To bind in a pledge of marriage; betroth. [< ME *affiaunce*, assurance < OFr. < *affier*, to trust to < Med.Lat. *affīdāre*: Lat. *ad-*, ad- + Lat. *fīdus*, faithful; see **bheidh-***.]

af•fi•ant (ə-fī′ənt) *n.* *Law.* One who makes an affidavit. [< *affy*, to make affidavit < ME *affien*, to trust < OFr. *affier*, to promise. See AFFIANCE.]

af•fi•da•vit (ăf′ĭ-dā′vĭt) *n.* *Law.* A written declaration made under oath before an authorized official. [Med.Lat. *affīdāvit* < third pers. sing. p.t. of Lat. *affīdāre*, to pledge. See AFFIANCE.]

af•fil•i•ate (ə-fĭl′ē-āt′) *v.* **-at•ed, -at•ing, -ates.** — *tr.* **1.** To adopt or accept as a member, subordinate, or branch. **2.** To associate (oneself) as a member, subordinate, or employee: *affiliated herself with a new law firm.* **3.** To assign the origin of. — *intr.* To become closely connected or associated. — *n.* (-ē-ĭt, -āt′). A person or an organization associated with another as a subordinate, subsidiary, or member: *network affiliates.* [Med.Lat. *affiliāre*, to adopt : Lat. *ad-*, ad- + Lat. *fīlius*, son; see **dhē(i)-***.] — **af•fil′i•a′tion** *n.*

af•fine (ə-fīn′) *adj.* *Math.* **1.** Of or relating to a transformation, such as a rotation or expansion, that carries parallel lines into parallel lines but may change the distances between points. **2.** Of or relating to the geometry of affine transformations. [Fr. *affin*, closely related < OFr. See AFFINED.]

af•fined (ə-fīnd′) *adj.* **1.** Linked by a very close relationship. **2.** Beholden to another; bound. [Fr. *affiné* < OFr. *affin*, closely related < Lat. *affīnis*, related by marriage : *ad-*, ad- + *fīnis*, boundary.]

af•fin•i•ty (ə-fĭn′ĭ-tē) *n., pl.* **-ties. 1.** A natural attraction or feeling of kinship. **2.** Relationship by marriage. **3.** An inherent similarity between persons or things. See Syns at **likeness. 4.** *Biol.* A relationship or resemblance in structure between species that suggests a common origin. **5.** *Immunol.* The attraction between an antigen and an antibody. **6.** *Chem.* An attraction or force between particles that causes them to combine. [ME *affinite* < OFr. *afinite* < Lat. *affīnitās* < *affīnis*, related by marriage. See AFFINED.]

af•firm (ə-fûrm′) *v.* **-firmed, -firm•ing, -firms.** — *tr.* **1.** To declare positively or firmly; maintain to be true. **2.** To support or uphold the validity of; confirm. — *intr.* *Law.* To declare solemnly and formally but not under oath. [ME *affermen* < OFr. *afermer* < Lat. *affirmāre*: *ad-*, ad- + *firmāre*, to strengthen (< *firmus*, strong; see **dher-***).] — **af•firm′a•ble** *adj.* — **af•firm′a•bly** *adv.* — **af•fir′mant** *adj. & n.* — **af•firm′er** *n.*

af•fir•ma•tion (ăf′ər-mā′shən) *n.* **1.** The act of affirming or the state of being affirmed; assertion. **2.** Something declared to be true; a positive statement or judgment. **3.** *Law.* A solemn declaration given in place of a statement made under oath.

af•fir•ma•tive (ə-fûr′mə-tĭv) *adj.* **1.** Asserting that something is true or correct. **2.** Giving assent or approval; confirming: *an affirmative vote.* **3.** Positive; optimistic: *an affirmative outlook.* **4.** *Logic.* Of, relating to, or being a proposition that affirms something about the subject, such as the statement *Apples have seeds.* — *n.* **1.** A word or statement of agreement or assent, such as the word *yes.* **2.** The side in a debate that upholds the proposition. — *adv.* *Informal.* Used in place of the response "yes" to express confirmation or consent. — **af•fir′ma•tive•ly** *adv.*

Usage Note: The expressions *in the affirmative* and *in the negative*, as in *She answered in the affirmative*, are generally regarded as pompous. *She answered yes* would be more acceptable even at the most formal levels of style.

affirmative action *n.* A policy or a program that seeks to redress past discrimination by increasing opportunities for underrepresented groups, as in employment.

af•fix (ə-fĭks′) *tr.v.* **-fixed, -fix•ing, -fix•es. 1.** To secure to something; attach: *affix a label to a package.* **2.** To impute; attribute: *affix blame.* **3.** To place at the end; append: *affix a postscript to a letter.* **4.** *Gram.* To add as an affix. — *n.* (ăf′ĭks′). **1.** Something that is attached, joined, or added. **2.** *Ling.* A word element, such as a prefix or suffix, that can only occur attached to a base, stem, or root. [Med.Lat. *affixāre*, freq. of Lat. *affīgere*, *affix-* : *ad-*, ad- + *fīgere*, to fasten; see **dhīg[w]-***.] — **af•fix′a•ble** *adj.* — **af•fix′er** *n.*

af•fla•tus (ə-flā′təs) *n.* A strong creative impulse; divine inspiration. [Lat. *afflātus* < p.part. of *afflāre*, to breathe on : *ad-*, ad- + *flāre*, to blow; see **bhlē-***.]

af•flict (ə-flĭkt′) *tr.v.* **-flict•ed, -flict•ing, -flicts.** To inflict grievous physical or mental suffering on. [ME *afflighten* < *afflight*, disturbed, frightened < Lat. *afflictum*, p.part. of *afflīgere*, to cast down : *ad-*, ad- + *flīgere*, to strike.] — **af•flict′er** *n.* — **af•flic′tive** *adj.* — **af•flic′tive•ly** *adv.*

af•flic•tion (ə-flĭk′shən) *n.* **1.** A condition of pain, suffering, or distress. **2.** A cause of pain, suffering, or distress. See Syns at **burden**[1].

af•flu•ence (ăf′lo͞o-əns, ə-flo͞o′-) *n.* **1.** A plentiful supply of material goods; wealth. **2.** A great quantity; an abundance. **3.** A flowing to or toward a point; afflux.

af•flu•en•cy (ăf′lo͞o′ən-sē, ə-flo͞o′-) *n.* Affluence.

af•flu•ent (ăf′lo͞o-ənt, ə-flo͞o′-) *adj.* **1.** Generously supplied with money, property, or possessions; prosperous or rich. **2.** Plentiful; abundant. **3.** Flowing freely; copious. *—n.* **1.** A stream or river that flows into a larger one; a tributary. **2.** A person who is well-off financially. [ME, abundant, flowing < OFr. < Lat. *affluēns, affluent-*, pr.part. of *affluere*, to abound in : *ad-*, ad- + *fluere*, to flow; see **bhleu-***.] **—af′flu•ent•ly** *adv.*

af•flux (ăf′lŭks′) *n.* A flow to or toward an area, esp. of blood or other fluid toward a body part. [Med.Lat. *affluxus* < Lat., p.part. of *affluere*, to flow to. See AFFLUENT.]

af•ford (ə-fôrd′, ə-fōrd′) *tr.v.* **-ford•ed, -ford•ing, -fords. 1.** To have the financial means for; bear the cost of: *I can afford a new car.* **2.** To be able to spare or give up: *can't afford an hour for lunch.* **3.** To manage or bear without serious risk: *can afford to be tolerant.* **4.** To make available; provide: *a sport affording good exercise.* [ME *afforthen* < OE *geforthian*, to carry out : *ge-*, perfective pref.; see YCLEPT + *forthian*, to further (< *forth*, forth, forward; see **per**[1]***.)] **—af•ford′a•bil′i•ty** *n.* **—af•ford′a•ble** *adj.* **—af•ford′a•bly** *adv.*

af•for•est (ə-fôr′ĭst, -fŏr′-) *tr.v.* **-est•ed, -est•ing, -ests.** To convert (open land) into a forest. [Med.Lat. *afforēstāre*: Lat. *ad-*, ad- + Med.Lat. *forēstāre*(< *forēsta*, forest; see FOREST).] **—af•for′es•ta′tion** *n.*

af•fray (ə-frā′) *n.* A noisy quarrel or brawl. See Syns at **conflict.** *—tr.v.* **-frayed, -fray•ing, -frays.** *Archaic.* To frighten. [ME < OFr. *effrei, esfrei* < *esfraier, esfreer*, to disturb. See **prī-***.]

af•fri•cate (ăf′rĭ-kĭt) *n. Ling.* A speech sound consisting of a stop consonant followed by a fricative; for example, the initial sounds of *child* and *joy.* [Lat. *affricātus*, p.part. of *affricāre*, to rub against : *ad-*, ad- + *fricāre*, to rub.]

af•fric•a•tive (ə-frĭk′ə-tĭv) *Ling. —adj.* Of, relating to, or forming an affricate. *—n.* See **affricate.**

af•fright (ə-frīt′) *tr.v.* **-fright•ed, -fright•ing, -frights.** To arouse fear in; terrify. *—n.* **1.** Great fear; terror. **2.** A cause of terror. [ME *afrighten* < OE *āfyrhtan*: *ā-*, intensive pref. + *fyrhtan*, to frighten (< *fyrhto*, fright).] **—af•fright′ment** *n.*

af•front (ə-frŭnt′) *tr.v.* **-front•ed, -front•ing, -fronts. 1.** To insult intentionally, esp. openly. **2.a.** To meet defiantly; confront. **b.** *Obsolete.* To meet or encounter face to face. *—n.* An open or intentional offense or insult. [ME *afrounten* < OFr. *afronter*: Lat. *ad-*, ad- + Lat. *frōns, front-*, face; see FRONT.]

Aff•ton (ăf′tən). A city of E MO, a suburb of St. Louis. Pop. 21,106.

af•fu•sion (ə-fyo͞o′zhən) *n.* A pouring on of liquid, as in baptism. [LLat. *affūsiō, affūsiōn-* < Lat. *affūsus*, p.part. of *affundere*, to pour on : *ad-*, ad- + *fundere*, to pour; see **gheu-***.]

Afg. *abbr.* Afghanistan.

Af•ghan (ăf′găn′, -gən) *adj.* Of or relating to Afghanistan or its people, language, or culture. *—n.* **1.** A native or inhabitant of Afghanistan. **2.** See **Pashto. 3. afghan.** A coverlet or shawl of wool, knitted or crocheted in colorful geometric designs. **4.** An Afghan hound. [Pers. *afghān*, an Afghan.]

Afghan hound *n.* A large, slender hunting dog having long thick hair, a pointed muzzle, and drooping ears.

af•ghan•i (ăf-găn′ē, -gä′nē) *n.* See table at **currency.** [Pashto.]

Af•ghan•i•stan (ăf-găn′ĭ-stăn′). A country of SW-central Asia; crisscrossed by invasion routes since ancient times. Cap. Kabul. Pop. 13,051,358.

a•fi•cio•na•do (ə-fĭsh′ē-ə-nä′dō, ə-fĭs′ē-, ə-fē′sē-) *n., pl.* **-dos.** An enthusiastic admirer or follower; a devotee or fan. [Sp., p.part. of *aficionar*, to induce a liking for < *afición*, liking < Lat. *affectiō, affectiōn-*. See AFFECTION.]

a•field (ə-fēld′) *adv.* **1.** Off the usual or desired track. See Syns at **amiss. 2.** Away from one's home or usual environment. **3.** To or on a field.

a•fire (ə-fīr′) *adv. & adj.* **1.** On fire. **2.** Intensely interested.

AFL *abbr.* **1.** American Federation of Labor. **2.** American Football League.

a•flame (ə-flām′) *adv. & adj.* **1.** On or as if on fire. **2.** Keenly excited and interested.

af•la•tox•in (ăf′lə-tŏk′sĭn) *n.* Any of a group of toxic compounds produced by certain molds, esp. *Aspergillus flavus*, that contaminate stored food supplies such as animal feed and peanuts. [NLat. *A(spergillus) fla(vus)*, species name (ASPERGILLUS + Lat. *flavus*, yellow; see FLAVO–) + TOXIN.]

AFL-CIO *abbr.* American Federation of Labor and Congress of Industrial Organizations.

a•float (ə-flōt′) *adv. & adj.* **1.** In a floating position or condition. **2.** On a boat or ship away from the shore; at sea. **3.** In circulation; prevailing: *Rumors are afloat.* **4.** Awash; flooded. **5.** Drifting about; moving without guidance. **6.** Free or out of difficulty, esp. financial difficulty.

a•flut•ter (ə-flŭt′ər) *adj.* **1.** Being in a flutter; fluttering: *with flags aflutter.* **2.** Nervous and excited.

A.F. of L. *abbr.* American Federation of Labor.

a•foot (ə-fo͝ot′) *adv. & adj.* **1.** On foot; walking. **2.** In the process of being carried out; astir: *plans afoot to resign.*

a•fore (ə-fôr′, ə-fōr′) *adv., prep., & conj. Chiefly Southern & Midland U.S.* Before. [ME < OE *onforan*: *on*, at; see ON + *fōran*, before (< *fore*; see FORE).]

a•fore•men•tioned (ə-fôr′mĕn′shənd, -fōr′-) *adj.* Mentioned previously.

a•fore•said (ə-fôr′sĕd′, -fōr′-) *adj.* Spoken of earlier.

a•fore•thought (ə-fôr′thôt′, -fōr′-) *adj.* Planned or intended beforehand; premeditated: *malice aforethought.*

a•fore•time (ə-fôr′tīm′, -fōr′-) *Archaic. —adv.* At a former or past time; previously. *—adj.* Earlier; former.

a for•ti•o•ri (ä fôr′tē-ôr′ē, ā fōr′tē-ō′rī′) *adv.* For a still stronger reason; all the more. [Lat. : *ā, ab*, from + *fortiōrī*, ablative of *fortior*, stronger.]

a•foul of (ə-foul′) *prep.* **1.** In or into collision, entanglement, or conflict with. **2.** In trouble with: *ran afoul of the law.*

AFP *abbr.* Alpha-fetoprotein.

Afr. *abbr.* Africa; African.

a•fraid (ə-frād′) *adj.* **1.** Filled with fear: *afraid of ghosts; afraid to die.* **2.** Having feelings of aversion or unwillingness: *afraid to show emotion.* **3.** Filled with regret or concern: *I'm afraid you're wrong.* [ME *affraied*, p.part. of *affraien*, to frighten < OFr. *esfraier, esfreer*, to disturb, of Gmc. orig. See **prī-***.]

Syns: *afraid, apprehensive, fearful.* The central meaning shared by these adjectives is "filled with fear": *afraid of snakes; feeling apprehensive before surgery; fearful of criticism.* ***Ant:*** *unafraid.*

A-frame

A-frame (ā′frām′) *n.* A structure, such as a house, with steeply angled sides that meet at the top in the shape of the letter A.

af•reet also **af•rit** (ăf′rēt′, ə-frēt′) *n. Myth.* A powerful evil spirit or monstrous demon in Arabic mythology. [Ar. *'ifrīt.*]

a•fresh (ə-frĕsh′) *adv.* Once more; anew; again: *start afresh.*

Af•ri•ca (ăf′rĭ-kə). A continent S of Europe between the Atlantic and Indian oceans.

Af•ri•can (ăf′rĭ-kən) *adj.* Of or relating to Africa or its peoples, languages, or cultures. *—n.* **1.** A native or inhabitant of Africa. **2.** A person of African descent.

Af•ri•can-A•mer•i•can or **African American** (ăf′rĭ-kən-ə-mĕr′ĭkən) *—adj.* Of or relating to Americans of African ancestry; Afro-American. *—n.* **1.** An American of African ancestry; an Afro-American. **2.** See Usage Note at **black.**

African daisy *n.* Any of several African plants in the composite family, esp. those in the genera *Arctotis, Gerbera,* and *Lonas,* that have showy flower heads.

Af•ri•can•ism (ăf′rĭ-kə-nĭz′əm) *n.* **1.** A characteristically African cultural feature. **2.** A linguistic feature of an African language occurring in a non-African language.

Af•ri•can•ist (ăf′rĭ-kə-nĭst) *n.* A specialist in African affairs, cultures, or languages.

Af•ri•can•ized bee (ăf′rĭ-kə-nīzd′) *n.* A hybrid strain of honeybee introduced into Brazil in the mid-1950's and distinguished by aggressive traits such as the tendency to mass swarm and sting with great frequency.

African lily *n.* A South African rhizomatous plant *(Agapanthus africanus)* having funnel-shaped flowers grouped in umbels.

African marigold *n.* An aromatic annual Mexican plant *(Tagetes erecta)* in the composite family, having pinnately lobed leaves and showy, solitary yellow to orange flower heads.

African oil palm *n.* See **oil palm** 1.

African sleeping sickness *n.* See **sleeping sickness** 1.

African swine fever *n.* See **hog cholera.**

African violet

African violet *n.* Any of various East African herbs of the genus *Saintpaulia*, having a basal leaf rosette and a showy cluster of violet or sometimes pink or white flowers.

Af•ri•kaans (ăf′rĭ-käns′, -känz′) *n.* A language that developed from 17th-century Dutch and is an official language of South Africa. *—adj.* Of or relating to Afrikaans or Afrikaners. [*Afrikaans* < Du. *Afrikaansch*, African < Lat. *Āfricānus.* See AFRIKANER.]

Af•ri•ka•ner (ăf′rĭ-kä′nər) *n.* An Afrikaans-speaking South African of European ancestry, esp. one descended from 17th-century Dutch settlers. [Afr., an African < Du. < Lat. *Āfricānus* < *Āfrica*, Africa < *Āfer, Āfr-*, an African.]

af•rit (ăf′rēt′, ə-frēt′) *n. Myth.* Var. of **afreet.**

Af•ro (ăf′rō) *n., pl.* **-ros.** A rounded, tightly curled hair style. *—adj.* African in style or origin. [Prob. short for AFRO-AMERICAN.]

Afro– *pref.* African: *Afro-Asiatic.* [< Lat. *Āfer, Āfr-*, an African.]

Af•ro-A•mer•i•can (ăf′rō-ə-mĕr′ĭ-kən) *adj.* Of or relating to Americans of African ancestry or to their history or culture. *—n.* An American of African ancestry. See Usage Note at **black.**

Af•ro-A•si•at•ic (ăf′rō-ā′zhē-ăt′ĭk, -shē-, -zē-) *n.* A large family of languages spoken in northern Africa and southwest Asia, comprising the Semitic, Chadic, Cushitic, Berber, and

ă pat	oi boy
ā pay	ou out
âr care	o͝o took
ä father	o͞o boot
ĕ pet	ŭ cut
ē be	ûr urge
ĭ pit	th thin
ī pie	*th* this
îr pier	hw which
ŏ pot	zh vision
ō toe	ə about, item
ô paw	

Stress marks:
′ (primary);
′ (secondary), as in dictionary (dĭk′shə-nĕr′ē)

ancient Egyptian languages; formerly known as Hamito-Semitic. —**Af′ro-A′si•at′ic** *adj.*

aft (ăft) *adv. & adj. Naut.* At, in, toward, or close to the stern of a vessel or the rear of an aircraft or a spacecraft. [ME *afte,* back < OE *æftan,* behind. See **apo-***.]

AFT *abbr.* American Federation of Teachers.

aft. *abbr.* Afternoon.

af•ter (ăf′tər) *prep.* **1.a.** Behind in place or order: *Z comes after Y.* **b.** Next to or lower than in order or importance. **2.** In quest or pursuit of: *He is after your job.* **3.** Concerning: *asked after you.* **4.** Subsequent in time to; at a later time than: *come after dinner.* **5.** Subsequent to and because of or regardless of: *They are still friends after all their differences.* **6.** Following continually: *year after year.* **7.** In the style of or in imitation of: *satires after Horace.* **8.** In honor or commemoration of: *named after her mother.* **9.** In accordance with; in conformity to: *a tenor after my own heart.* **10.** Past the hour of: *five minutes after three.* —*adv.* **1.** Behind; in the rear. **2.** At a later or subsequent time; afterward: *departed shortly after.* —*adj.* **1.** Subsequent in time or place; later; following: *in after years.* **2.** *Naut.* Nearer the stern of a vessel. —*conj.* Following or subsequent to the time that: *I saw them after I arrived.* [ME < OE *æfter.* See **apo-***.]

after all also **af•ter•all** (ăf′tər-ôl′) *adv.* In spite of everything to the contrary; nevertheless: *We took a plane after all.*

af•ter•birth (ăf′tər-bûrth′) *n.* The placenta and fetal membranes expelled from the uterus following childbirth.

af•ter•burn•er (ăf′tər-bûr′nər) *n.* **1.** A device for augmenting the thrust of a jet engine by burning additional fuel with the uncombined oxygen in the hot exhaust gases. **2.** A device for burning or chemically altering unburned or partially burned carbon compounds in exhaust gases.

af•ter•care (ăf′tər-kâr′) *n.* Treatment or care given to convalescent patients after release from a hospital.

af•ter•damp (ăf′tər-dămp′) *n.* An asphyxiating mixture of gases, primarily nitrogen and carbon dioxide, left in a mine after a fire or an explosion. [AFTER + DAMP, gas.]

af•ter•deck (ăf′tər-dĕk′) *n. Naut.* The part of a ship's deck past amidships toward the stern.

af•ter•ef•fect (ăf′tər-ĭ-fĕkt′) *n.* An effect following its cause after some delay.

af•ter•glow (ăf′tər-glō′) *n.* **1.** The atmospheric glow that remains for a short time after sunset. **2.** The light emitted after removal of a source of energy, esp. the emission of light from a phosphor after removal of excitation. **3.** A lingering impression of past glory or success.

agaric

af•ter-hours (ăf′tər-ourz′) *adj.* **1.** Occurring after closing time: *after-hours socializing.* **2.** Open after a legal or established closing time: *an after-hours club.*

af•ter•im•age (ăf′tər-ĭm′ĭj) *n.* A visual image that persists after the visual stimulus causing it has ceased to act.

af•ter•life (ăf′tər-līf′) *n.* **1.** A life believed to follow death. **2.** The part of one's life that follows a particular event.

af•ter-mar•ket (ăf′tər-mär′kĭt) *n.* The demand for goods and services, such as parts and repairs, associated with the upkeep of a previous purchase.

af•ter•math (ăf′tər-măth′) *n.* **1.** A consequence, esp. of a disaster: *famine as an aftermath of drought.* **2.** A period of time following a disaster: *in the aftermath of war.* **3.** A second growth or crop in the same season, as of grass after mowing. [AFTER + obsolete *math,* mowing (< OE *mǣth*; see **mē-**[4]*).]

af•ter•most (ăf′tər-mōst′) *adj.* **1.** *Naut.* Nearest the stern; farthest aft. **2.** Nearest the end or rear; hindmost or last.

af•ter•noon (ăf′tər-no͞on′) *n.* **1.** The part of day from noon until sunset. **2.** The latter part: *in the afternoon of life.*

af•ter•pains (ăf′tər-pānz′) *pl.n.* Cramps or pains following childbirth, caused by contractions of the uterus.

af•ter•piece (ăf′tər-pēs′) *n.* A short comic piece performed after a play.

af•ter-shave (ăf′tər-shāv′) *n.* A usu. fragrant lotion for use on the face after shaving.

af•ter•shock (ăf′tər-shŏk′) *n.* **1.** A quake of lesser magnitude following a large earthquake in the same area. **2.** A further reaction following the shock of a disturbing occurrence.

af•ter•taste (ăf′tər-tāst′) *n.* **1.** A taste persisting in the mouth after the substance that caused it is no longer present. **2.** A feeling that remains after an event or experience.

af•ter-tax also **af•ter•tax** (ăf′tər-tăks) *adj.* Remaining after payment, esp. of income taxes: *after-tax profits.*

agave

af•ter•thought (ăf′tər-thôt′) *n.* An idea, a response, or an explanation that occurs to one after an event or a decision.

af•ter•time (ăf′tər-tīm′) *n.* The time to come; the future.

af•ter•ward (ăf′tər-wərd) also **af•ter•wards** (-wərdz) *adv.* At a later time; subsequently.

af•ter•word (ăf′tər-wûrd′) *n.* See **epilogue** 2.

af•ter•world (ăf′tər-wûrld′) *n.* A world thought to exist after death.

aft•most (ăft′mōst′) *adj. Naut.* Farthest aft; aftermost.

Ag The symbol for the element **silver** 1. [< Lat. *argentum,* silver. See ARGENT.]

A.G. also **AG** *abbr.* **1.** Adjutant general. **2.** *Law.* Attorney general.

ag– *pref.* Var. of **ad–** 1.

a•ga also **a•gha** (ä′gə, ăg′ə) *n.* Used as a title for a male civil or military leader, esp. in Turkey. [Turk. *ağa* < Old Turkic *aqa,* older brother.]

A•ga•de (ə-gä′də). See **Akkad** 2.

a•gain (ə-gĕn′) *adv.* **1.** Once more; anew: *try again.* **2.** To a previous place, position, or state: *left home but went back again.* **3.** Furthermore; moreover. **4.** On the other hand: *She might go, and again she might not.* **5.** In return; in response. [ME (influenced by ON *i gegn,* again) < OE *ongeagn,* against.]

a•gainst (ə-gĕnst′) *prep.* **1.** In a direction or course opposite to: *row against the current.* **2.** So as to come into forcible contact with: *waves dashing against the shore.* **3.** In contact with so as to rest or press on: *leaned against the tree.* **4.** In hostile opposition or resistance to: *struggle against fate.* **5.** Contrary to; opposed to: *against my better judgment.* **6.** In contrast with the background of: *dark colors against a fair skin.* **7.** In preparation for; in anticipation of: *food stored against winter.* **8.** As a defense or safeguard from: *protection against the cold.* **9.** To the account or debt of: *drew a check against my bank balance.* **10.** Directly opposite to; facing. [ME, alteration of *againes* < OE *ongeagn.*]

A•ga Khan III (ä′gə kän′). 1877–1957. Indian leader of the Ismaili Muslim sect. His grandson Prince Karim (b. 1936) succeeded him as **Aga Khan IV.**

a•ga•lac•ti•a (ā-gə-lăk′tē-ə, -shē-ə, ăg′ə-) *n.* Absence of or faulty secretion of milk following childbirth. [NLat. < Gk. *agalaktia,* lack of milk : *a-,* without; see A–[1] + *gala, galakt-,* milk; see **melg-***.]

a•ga•ma (ə-gā′mə, ăg′ə-) *n.* Any of various small, long-tailed, insect-eating lizards of the family Agamidae, found in the Old World tropics. [Am.Sp., of Cariban orig.]

Ag•a•mem•non (ăg′ə-mĕm′nŏn′, -nən) *n. Gk. Myth.* The king of Mycenae and leader of the Greeks in the Trojan War and the father of Orestes, Electra, and Iphigenia; killed by his wife Clytemnestra upon returning from Troy.

a•gam•ete (ā-găm′ēt′, ā′gə-mēt′) *n.* An asexual reproductive cell, such as a spore. [< Gk. *agametos,* unmarried, var. of *agamos.* See AGAMIC.]

a•gam•ic (ā-găm′ĭk) also **ag•a•mous** (ăg′ə-məs) *adj. Biol.* Occurring or reproducing without the union of male and female cells; asexual or parthenogenetic. [< LLat. *agamus,* unmarried < Gk. *agamos*: *a-,* not; see A–[1] + *gamos,* marriage; see –GAMY.] —**a•gam′i•cal•ly** *adv.*

a•gam•o•gen•e•sis (ā-găm′ə-jĕn′ĭ-sĭs, ăg′ə-mō-) *n.* Asexual reproduction, as by budding, cell division, or parthenogenesis. [Gk. *agamos,* unmarried; see AGAMIC + –GENESIS.]

A•ga•na (ə-gä′nyə, ä-gä′nyä). The cap. of Guam, on the W coast of the island. Pop. 896.

ag•a•pan•thus (ăg′ə-păn′thəs) *n.* See **African lily.** [NLat. *Agapanthus,* genus name : Gk. *agapē,* love + Gk. *anthos,* flower.]

a•gape[1] (ə-gāp′, ə-găp′) *adv. & adj.* **1.** In a state of wonder or amazement, as with the mouth wide open. **2.** Wide open.

a•ga•pe[2] (ä-gä′pā, ä′gə-pā′) *n.* **1.** *Theol.* Disinterested, superabundant love. **2.** Divine love and Christian love for others. **3.** In the early Christian Church, the love feast accompanied by Eucharistic celebration. [Gk. *agapē,* love.]

a•gar (ā′gär′, ä′gär′) also **a•gar-a•gar** (ā′gär-ā′gär′, ä′gär-ä′-) *n.* **1.** A gelatinous material derived from certain marine algae and used as a base for bacterial culture media and a stabilizer and thickener in many food products. **2.** A culture medium containing this material. [Short for Malay *agar-agar.*]

ag•a•ric (ăg′-ər-ĭk, ə-găr′ĭk) *n.* **1.** Any of various mushrooms of the genera *Agaricus, Fomes,* or related genera, having large umbrellalike caps with numerous gills beneath. **2.** The dried fruiting body of certain fungal species in the genus *Fomes,* formerly used in medicine. [ME *agarik,* a kind of fungus < Lat. *agaricum* < Gk. *agarikon* < *Agaria,* a town in Sarmatia.]

Ag•as•siz (ăg′ə-sē), **(Jean) Louis (Rodolphe).** 1807–73. Swiss-born Amer. naturalist and geologist noted for his study of fossil fish.

Agassiz, Lake. A glacial lake of the Pleistocene Epoch extending across NW MN, NE ND, S Manitoba, and SW Ontario.

ag•ate (ăg′ĭt) *n.* **1.** A fine-grained fibrous variety of chalcedony with colored bands or irregular clouding. **2.** *Games.* A playing marble made of agate or a glass imitation of it. **3.** A tool with agate parts, such as a burnisher tipped with agate. **4.** *Print.* A type size, approximately 5½ points. [ME *achate, agaten* < OFr. *acate, agate,* alteration (influenced by Gk. *agathē,* good) of Lat. *achātēs* < Gk. *akhatēs.*]

agate line *n. Print.* A measure of space, usu. one column wide and 1/14 inch deep, used esp. for classified advertisements.

a•ga•ve (ə-gä′vē, ə-gā′-) *n.* Any of numerous plants of the genus *Agave,* native to hot, dry regions of the New World and having basal rosettes of tough sword-shaped leaves. [NLat. *Agave,* genus name < Gk. *agauē,* fem. of *agauos,* noble.]

Ag•a•wam (ăg′ə-wŏm′). A town of SW MA on the Connecticut R. near Springfield; settled in 1635. Pop. 27,323.

agcy. *abbr.* Agency.

age (āj) *n.* **1.** The length of time that one has existed; duration of life. **2.** The time of life when a person becomes qualified to assume certain civil and personal rights and responsibilities; legal age: *under age; of age.* **3.** One of the stages of life: *at an awkward age.* **4.** The state of being old; old age: *hair white with age.* **5.** Often **Age. a.** A period in the history of humankind marked by a distinctive characteristic or person: *the computer age.* **b.** A period in the history of the earth, usu. shorter than an epoch: *the Ice Age.* **6.a.** The period of history during which a person lives: *a product of his age.* **b.** A generation: *ages yet unborn.* **7. ages.** *Informal.* An extended period of time: *left ages ago.* — *v.* **aged, ag•ing, ag•es.** — *tr.* **1.** To cause to become old. **2.** To cause to mature or ripen under controlled conditions: *aging wine.* — *intr.* **1.** To become old. **2.** To manifest traits associated with old age. **3.** To develop a certain quality of ripeness; become mature: *cheese aging at room temperature.* See Syns at **mature.** [ME < OFr. *aage* < VLat. **aetāticum* < Lat. *aetās, aetāt-*, age. See **aiw-*.**] — **ag′er** *n.*

–age *suff.* **1.** Collection; mass: *sewerage.* **2.** Relationship; connection: *parentage.* **3.** Condition; state: *vagabondage.* **4.a.** An action: *blockage.* **b.** Result of an action: *breakage.* **5.** Residence or place of: *vicarage.* **6.** Charge or fee: *cartage.* [ME < OFr. < VLat. **-āticum*, abstract n. suff. < Lat. *-āticum*, n. and adj. suff.]

ag•ed (ā′jĭd) *adj.* **1.** Being of advanced age; old. **2.** Characteristic of old age. **3.** (ājd). Having reached the age of: *aged three.* **4.** (ājd). Brought to a desired ripeness or maturity: *aged cheese.* **5.** *Geol.* Approaching the base level of erosion. — *n.* Elderly people considered as a group. — **ag′ed•ly** *adv.* — **ag′ed•ness** *n.*

A•gee (ā′jē), **James.** 1909–55. Amer. writer noted esp. for his novel *A Death in the Family* (1957).

age group *n.* All the people of a particular age or range of ages.

age•ing (ā′jĭng) *n. Chiefly British.* Var. of **aging.**

age•ism also **ag•ism** (ā′jĭz′əm) *n.* Discrimination based on age. — **age′ist** *adj. & n.*

age•less (āj′lĭs) *adj.* **1.** Seeming never to grow old. **2.** Existing forever; eternal. — **age′less•ly** *adv.* — **age′less•ness** *n.*

Ag•e•nais (ä′zhə-nā′) or **Ag•e•nois** (-nwä′). A historical region of SW France.

a•gen•cy (ā′jən-sē) *n., pl.* **-cies. 1.** The condition of being in action; operation. **2.** The means or mode of acting; instrumentality. **3.** A business or service authorized to act for others: *an employment agency.* **4.** An administrative division of a government or an international body. [Med.Lat. *agentia* < Lat. *agēns, agent-*, pr.part. of *agere*, to do. See AGENT.]

agency shop *n.* An establishment in which a union represents all employees regardless of union membership but requires that nonmembers pay union dues or fees.

a•gen•da (ə-jĕn′də) *n., pl.* **-das.** A list or program of things to be done or considered. [Lat., pl. of *agendum*, agendum. See AGENDUM.]

Usage Note: In Modern English a phrase such as *item on the agenda* expresses the sense of the Latin singular form *agendum*, and the plural form *agenda* is used as a singular noun to denote the set or list of such items, as in *The agenda for the meeting has not yet been set.* If a plural of *agenda* is required, the form should be *agendas.*

a•gen•dum (ə-jĕn′dəm) *n., pl.* **-da** (-də) also **-dums.** Something to be done, esp. an item on a program or list. [Lat., neut. gerundive of *agere*, to do. See **ag-*.**]

a•gen•e•sis (ā-jĕn′ĭ-sĭs) *n.* Absence or incomplete development of an organ or body part.

a•gent (ā′jənt) *n.* **1.** One that acts or has the power or authority to act. **2.** One empowered to act for or represent another: *an insurance agent.* **3.** A means by which something is done or caused; an instrument. **4.** A force or substance that causes a change: *a chemical agent.* **5.** A representative or official of a government: *an FBI agent.* **6.** A spy. [ME < Lat. *agēns, agent-*, pr.part. of *agere*, to do. See **ag-*.**]

a•gen•tial (ā-jĕn′shəl) *adj.* Of, relating to, or acting as an agent or agency.

A•gent Orange (ā′jənt) *n.* A herbicide containing trace amounts of the toxic contaminant dioxin that was used in the Vietnam War to defoliate areas of forest. [From the orange identifying strip on drums in which it was stored.]

a•gent pro•vo•ca•teur (ä-zhäN′ prô-vô′kä-tœr′) *n., pl.* **a•gents pro•vo•ca•teurs** (ä-zhäN′ prô-vô′kä-tœr′). A person employed to incite suspected persons to commit acts that will make them liable to punishment. [Fr. : *agent*, agent + *provocateur*, instigator.]

age of consent *n. Law.* The age at which a person is legally considered competent to give consent, as to sexual intercourse.

age of reason *n.* **1.** An era in which rationalism prevails, esp. the period of the Enlightenment in England, France, and the United States. **2.** An age at which a person is considered capable of making reasoned judgments.

age-old (āj′ōld′) *adj.* Very old or of long standing.

ag•er•a•tum (ăj′ə-rā′təm) *n.* **1.** Any of various New World plants of the genus *Ageratum* in the composite family, esp. *A. houstonianum*, having showy, colorful flower heads. **2.** Any of several other plants having flower clusters similar to the ageratum. [NLat. *Agēratum*, genus name < Gk. *agēratos*, ageless : *a-*, without; see A-[1] + *gēras*, old age; see **gerə-[1]*.**]

A•ges•i•la•us II (ə-jĕs′ə-lā′əs). 444?–360? B.C. Spartan king (399?–360?) who defended Sparta during the Corinthian War (394–387).

ag•gie[1] (ăg′ē) *n. Games.* A playing marble. [AG(ATE) + -IE.]

ag•gie[2] (ăg′ē) *n. Informal.* **1.** An agricultural school or college. **2.** A student enrolled at such a school or college. [AG(RICULTURAL) + -IE.]

ag•gior•na•men•to (ə-jôr′nə-mĕn′tō) *n., pl.* **-tos.** The process of bringing an institution or organization up to date; modernization. [Ital. < *aggiornare*, to update : *a-*, to (< Lat. *ad-*; see AD-) + *giorno*, day (< Lat. *diurnus*, daily; see DIURNAL).]

ag•glom•er•ate (ə-glŏm′ə-rāt′) *tr. & intr.v.* **-at•ed, -at•ing, -ates.** To form or collect into a rounded mass. — *adj.* (-ər-ĭt). Gathered into a rounded mass. — *n.* (-ər-ĭt). **1.** A confused or jumbled mass; a heap. **2.** A volcanic rock consisting of rounded and angular fragments fused together. [Lat. *agglomerāre, agglomerāt-*, to mass together : *ad-*, ad- + *glomerāre*, to form into a ball (< *glomus*, ball).] — **ag•glom′er•a′tive** (-ə-rā′tĭv, -ər-ə-tĭv) *adj.* — **ag•glom′er•a′tor** *n.*

James Agee

ag•glom•er•a•tion (ə-glŏm′ə-rā′shən) *n.* **1.** The act or process of gathering into a mass. **2.** A confused or jumbled mass.

ag•glu•ti•nate (ə-glo͞ot′n-āt′) *v.* **-nat•ed, -nat•ing, -nates.** — *tr.* **1.** To cause to adhere, as with glue. **2.** *Ling.* To form (words) by combining words or words and word elements. **3.** *Physiol.* To cause (red blood cells or bacteria) to clump together. — *intr.* **1.** To join together into a group or mass. **2.** *Ling.* To form words by agglutination. **3.** *Physiol.* To clump together; undergo agglutination. — *n.* See **agglutination** 2. [Lat. *agglūtināre, agglūtināt-* : *ad-*, ad- + *glūtināre*, to glue (< *glūten*, glue).] — **ag•glu′ti•nant** *adj. & n.*

ag•glu•ti•na•tion (ə-glo͞ot′n-ā′shən) *n.* **1.** The act or process of agglutinating; adhesion of distinct parts. **2.** A clumped mass of material formed by agglutination. **3.** *Ling.* The formation of words from morphemes that retain their original forms and meanings with little change during the combination process. **4.** The clumping together of red blood cells or bacteria, usu. in response to a particular antibody.

ag•glu•ti•na•tive (ə-glo͞ot′n-ā′tĭv, -ə-tĭv) *adj.* **1.** Tending toward, concerning, or characteristic of agglutination. **2.** *Ling.* Of, relating to, or being a language in which words are formed primarily by means of agglutination.

ag•glu•ti•nin (ə-glo͞ot′n-ĭn) *n. Physiol.* A substance, such as an antibody, that causes agglutination. [AGGLUTIN(ATION) + -IN.]

ag•glu•tin•o•gen (ăg′lo͞o-tĭn′ə-jən, ə-glo͞ot′n-) *n. Physiol.* An antigen that stimulates the production of a particular agglutinin, such as an antibody. [AGGLUTIN(IN) + -GEN.] — **ag′glu•tin′o•gen′ic** (ăg′lo͞o-tĭn′ə-jĕn′ĭk, ə-glo͞ot′n-) *adj.*

ag•grade (ə-grād′) *tr.v.* **-grad•ed, -grad•ing, -grades.** To fill and raise the level of (the bed of a stream) by deposition of sediment. — **ag′gra•da′tion** (ăg′rə-dā′shən) *n.* — **ag′gra•da′tion•al** *adj.*

ag•gran•dize (ə-grăn′dīz′, ăg′rən-) *tr.v.* **-dized, -diz•ing, -diz•es. 1.** To increase the scope of; extend. **2.** To make greater in power, influence, stature, or reputation. **3.** To make appear greater; exaggerate: *aggrandize an argument.* [Fr. *agrandir, agrandiss-* < OFr. : *a-*, to (< Lat. *ad-*; see AD-) + *grandir*, to grow larger (< Lat. *grandīre* < *grandis*, large).] — **ag•gran′dize•ment** (ə-grăn′dĭz-mənt, -dīz′-) *n.* — **ag•gran′diz′er** *n.*

ag•gra•vate (ăg′rə-vāt′) *tr.v.* **-vat•ed, -vat•ing, -vates. 1.** To make worse or more troublesome. **2.** To rouse to exasperation or anger; provoke. [Lat. *aggravāre, aggravāt-* : *ad-*, ad- + *gravāre*, to burden (< *gravis*, heavy; see **gʷerə-[1]***).] — **ag′gra•vat′ing•ly** *adv.* — **ag′gra•va′tive** *adj.* — **ag′gra•va′tor** *n.*

Usage Note: It is sometimes claimed that *aggravate* should be used only to mean "to make worse" and not "to irritate." But the latter use dates back as far as the 17th century and is accepted by 67 percent of the Usage Panel. As H.W. Fowler wrote, "the extension from aggravating a person's temper to aggravating the person himself is slight and natural."

ag•gra•vat•ed assault (ăg′rə-vā′tĭd) *n. Law.* An assault that is more serious than a common assault, esp. one performed with an intent to commit a crime.

ag•gra•va•tion (ăg′rə-vā′shən) *n.* **1.** The act of aggravating or the state of being aggravated. **2.** A source of continuing, increasing irritation or trouble. **3.** Exasperation.

ag•gre•gate (ăg′rĭ-gĭt) *adj.* **1.** Constituting or amounting to a whole; total: *aggregate sales.* **2.** *Bot.* Crowded or massed into a dense cluster. **3.** Composed of a mixture of minerals separable by mechanical means. — *n.* **1.** A total considered with reference to its constituent parts. **2.** The mineral materials used in making concrete. — *tr.v.* (-gāt′) **-gat•ed, -gat•ing, -gates. 1.** To gather into a mass, sum, or whole. **2.** To amount to; total. — ***idiom.* in the aggregate.** Taken into account as a whole. [ME *aggregat* < Lat. *aggregātus*, p.part. of

ă pat	oi boy
ā pay	ou out
âr care	o͝o took
ä father	o͞o boot
ĕ pet	ŭ cut
ē be	ûr urge
ĭ pit	th thin
ī pie	*th* this
îr pier	hw which
ŏ pot	zh vision
ō toe	ə about, item
ô paw	

Stress marks:
′ (primary);
′ (secondary), as in
dictionary (dĭk′shə-nĕr′ē)

aggregāre, to add to : *ad-,* ad- + *gregāre,* to collect (< *grex, greg-,* flock; see **ger-***).] **— ag′gre•gate•ly** *adv.* **— ag′gre•ga′tion** *n.* **— ag′gre•ga′tive** *adj.* **— ag′gre•ga′tor** *n.*

aggregate fruit *n.* A fruit, such as the raspberry, consisting of many individual small fruits derived from separate ovaries within a single flower, borne on a common receptacle.

ag•gress (ə-grĕs′) *intr.v.* **-gressed, -gress•ing, -gress•es.** To initiate an attack, a war, or a fight. [Fr. *agresser* < Lat. *aggredī, aggress-,* to attack : *ad-,* ad- + *gradī,* to go; see **ghredh-***.]

ag•gres•sion (ə-grĕsh′ən) *n.* **1.** The act of initiating hostilities or invasion. **2.** The practice or habit of launching attacks. **3.** *Psychol.* Hostile or destructive behavior or actions.

ag•gres•sive (ə-grĕs′ĭv) *adj.* **1.** Inclined toward hostile behavior. **2.** Assertive, bold, and enterprising. **3.** Intense or harsh, as in color. **4.** Fast growing; tending to spread quickly: *an aggressive tumor.* **— ag•gres′sive•ly** *adv.* **— ag•gres′sive•ness** *n.*

ag•gres•sor (ə-grĕs′ər) *n.* One that engages in aggression.

ag•grieve (ə-grēv′) *tr.v.* **-grieved, -griev•ing, -grieves. 1.** To distress; afflict. **2.** To inflict an injury or injuries on. [ME *agreven* < OFr. *agrever* < Lat. *aggravāre,* to make worse. See AGGRAVATE.]

ag•grieved (ə-grēvd′) *adj.* **1.** Feeling distress or affliction. **2.** Treated wrongly; offended. **3.** *Law.* Treated unjustly, as by denial of one's legal rights. **— ag•griev′ed•ly** (ə-grē′vĭd-lē) *adv.* **— ag•griev′ed•ness** *n.*

ag•gro (ăg′rō) *n., pl.* **-gros.** *Chiefly British.* **1.** Irritation and exasperation. **2.** Aggressive behavior. [Short for AGGRAVATION and AGGRESSION.] **— ag′gro** *adj.*

a•gha (ä′gə, ăg′ə) *n.* Var. of **aga.**

a•ghast (ə-găst′) *adj.* Struck by shock, terror, or amazement. [ME *agast,* p.part. of *agasten,* to frighten : *a-,* intensive pref. (< OE *ā-*) + *gasten,* to frighten (< OE *gǣstan* < *gāst,* ghost).]

ag•ile (ăj′əl, -īl′) *adj.* **1.** Characterized by quickness, lightness, and ease of movement; nimble. **2.** Mentally alert: *an agile mind.* [Fr. < Lat. *agilis* < *agere,* to drive, do. See **ag-***.] **— ag′ile•ly** *adv.* **— ag′ile•ness** *n.*

a•gil•i•ty (ə-jĭl′ĭ-tē) *n.* The state or quality of being agile; nimbleness. [ME *agilite* < OFr. < Med.Lat. *agilitās* < Lat. *agilis.* See AGILE.]

a•gin (ə-gĭn′) *Chiefly Upper Southern U.S.* **—** *prep.* **1.** Against. **2.** Opposed to: *I'm agin him.* **3.** Next to; beside; near. **4.** By or before (a specified time). **—** *conj.* By the time that. [Regional var. of AGAINST.]

A•gin•court (ăj′ĭn-kôrt′, -kōrt′). A village of N France; site of Henry V of England's decisive defeat of the French (1415).

ag•ing (ā′jĭng) *n.* **1.** The process of growing old or maturing. **2.** A process for imparting the properties of age.

ag•ism (ā′jĭz′əm) *n.* Var. of **ageism.**

ag•i•ta (ăj′ĭ-tə) *n.* Acid indigestion. [Ital. < *agitare,* to agitate < Lat. *agitāre.* See AGITATE.]

ag•i•tate (ăj′ĭ-tāt′) *v.* **-tat•ed, -tat•ing, -tates. —** *tr.* **1.** To cause to move with violence or sudden force. **2.** To upset; disturb: *agitated by the news.* **3.** To arouse interest in (a cause, for example). **—** *intr.* To stir up interest: *agitate for a tax reduction.* [Lat. *agitāre, agitāt-,* freq. of *agere,* to drive, do. See **ag-***.] **— ag′i•tat′ed•ly** (-tā′tĭd-lē) *adv.* **— ag′i•ta′tive** *adj.*

ag•i•ta•tion (ăj′ĭ-tā′shən) *n.* **1.** The act of agitating or the state of being agitated. **2.** Extreme emotional disturbance; perturbation. **3.** The stirring up of public interest in a matter of controversy. **— ag′i•ta′tion•al** *adj.*

ag•i•ta•to (ăj′ĭ-tä′tō) *adv. & adj. Mus.* In a restless, agitated style. [Ital., p.part. of *agitare* < Lat. *agitāre,* to agitate. See AGITATE.]

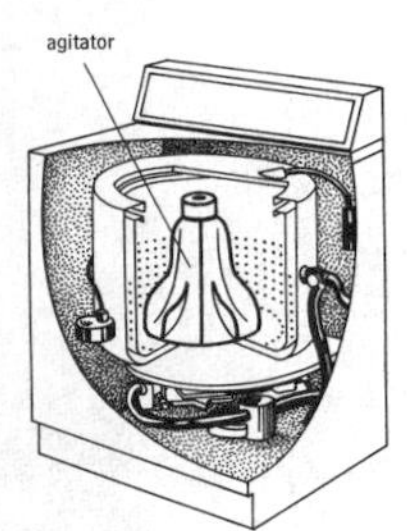

agitator
Cutaway view of a washing machine

ag•i•ta•tor (ăj′ĭ-tā′tər) *n.* **1.** One who agitates, esp. one who engages in political agitation. **2.** An apparatus that shakes or stirs.

ag•it•prop (ăj′ĭt-prŏp′) *n.* **1.** Political propaganda, esp. for Communism. **2.** A government department or similar agency that disseminates such propaganda. [Russ., short for *otdel agitatsii i propagandy,* incitement and propaganda section (of the central and local committees of the Russian Communist Party); name changed in 1934.]

A•gla•ia (ə-glā′ə, ə-glī′ə) *n. Gk. Myth.* One of the three Graces.

a•gleam (ə-glēm′) *adv. & adj.* Brightly shining.

ag•let (ăg′lĭt) *n.* **1.** A tag or metal sheath on the end of a lace, cord, or ribbon to help it pass through eyelet holes. **2.** A similar ornamental device. [ME < OFr. *aguillette,* dim. of *aguille,* needle < VLat. **acūcula* < LLat. *acucula,* dim. of Lat. *acus,* needle. See **ak-***.]

a•gley (ə-glī′, ə-glā′, ə-glē′) *adv. Scots.* Off to one side; awry. [A-[2] + Sc. *gley,* to squint (< ME *glien,* poss. of Scand. orig.).]

a•glit•ter (ə-glĭt′ər) *adv. & adj.* Glittering; sparkling.

a•glow (ə-glō′) *adv. & adj.* In a glow; glowing.

a•gly•cone (ə-glī′kōn′) or **a•gly•con** (-kŏn) *n.* The nonsugar component of a glycoside molecule. [*a-,* together (< Gk. *ha-;* see HAPLOID) + GLYC(O)- + -ONE.]

ag•nail (ăg′nāl′) *n.* **1.** A hangnail. **2.** A painful sore or swelling around a fingernail or toenail. [ME *angnail,* corn < OE *angnægl: ang-,* painful; see **angh-*** + *nægel,* peg, nail; see NAIL.]

agouti

ag•nate (ăg′nāt′) *adj.* **1.** Related on the male side. **2.** Coming from a common source; akin. **—** *n.* A relative on the male side only. [Lat. *agnātus,* p.part. of *agnāscī,* to become an agnate : *ad-,* ad- + *nāscī,* to be born; see **genə-***.] **— ag•nat′ic** (ăg-năt′ĭk) *adj.* **— ag•nat′i•cal•ly** *adv.* **— ag•na′tion** *n.*

Ag•nes (ăg′nĭs), Saint. d. c. A.D. 304. Roman Christian martyr and traditional patron saint of young girls.

Ag•new (ăg′no͞o′, -nyo͞o′), **Spiro Theodore.** b. 1918. Vice President of the U.S. (1969–73); resigned.

Ag•ni (ŭg′nē) *n. Hinduism.* The Vedic god of fire.

ag•no•men (ăg-nō′mən) *n., pl.* **-nom•i•na** (-nŏm′ə-nə). An additional cognomen given to a Roman citizen, often in honor of military victories. [Lat. : *ad-,* ad- (influenced by *agnōscere,* to recognize) + *nōmen,* name; see **nō-men-***.]

Ag•non (äg′nôn′), **Shmuel Yosef.** 1888–1970. Polish-born Israeli writer who shared the 1966 Nobel Prize for literature.

ag•no•sia (ăg-nō′zhə) *n.* Loss of the ability to interpret sensory stimuli. [Gk. *agnōsia,* ignorance : *a-,* without; see A-[1] + *gnōsis,* knowledge (< *gignōskein,* to know; see **gnō-***).]

ag•nos•tic (ăg-nŏs′tĭk) *n.* One who believes that there is no proof of the existence of God but does not deny the possibility that God exists. **—** *adj.* **1.** Relating to or being an agnostic. **2.** Noncommittal: *"I favored European unity, but I was agnostic about the form it should take"* (Henry A. Kissinger). [A-[1] + GNOSTIC.] **— ag•nos′ti•cal•ly** *adv.* **— ag•nos′ti•cism** (-tĭ-sĭz′əm) *n.*

Ag•nus De•i (ăg′nəs dē′ī′, än′yo͞os dā′ē, äg′no͞os′) *n.* **1.** Lamb of God; Jesus. **2.** A liturgical prayer to Jesus or its musical setting. [LLat. : Lat. *agnus,* lamb + Lat. *dei,* genitive of *deus,* god.]

a•go (ə-gō′) *adv. & adj.* **1.** Gone by; past: *two years ago.* **2.** In the past: *ages ago.* [ME, p.part. of *agon,* to go away < OE *āgān: ā-,* intensive pref. + *gān,* to go; see **ghē-***.]

a•gog (ə-gŏg′) *adj.* Full of anticipation or excitement; eager. [ME *agogge* < OFr. *en gogue,* in merriment : *en,* in (< Lat. *in;* see IN-[2]) + *gogue,* merriment.] **— a•gog′** *adv.*

à go•go or **à•go-go** (ə-gō′gō′) **—** *adv.* In a fast and lively manner; freely: *dancing à gogo.* **—** *n.* A nightclub. [Fr. *à gogo,* galore < OFr. *a gogo: a,* to (< Lat. *ad;* see AD-) + *gogo*(prob. reduplicated form of *gogue,* merriment).]

-agogue or **-agog** *suff.* A substance that stimulates the flow of: *emmenagogue.* [Fr. < LLat. *-agōgus* < Gk. *-agōgos* < *agōgos,* drawing off < *agein,* to lead, drive. See **ag-***.]

ag•on (ăg′ŏn, -ōn, ä-gōn′) *n., pl.* **a•gon•es** (ə-gō′nēz). **1.** A conflict, esp. between the protagonist and antagonist in literature or drama. **2.** The part of an ancient Greek drama, esp. a comedy, in which two characters engage in verbal dispute. [Gk. *agōn.* See AGONY.]

ag•o•nal (ăg′ə-nəl) *adj.* Associated with or relating to great pain, esp. the agony of death.

a•gone (ə-gôn′, ə-gŏn′) *adv. & adj. Archaic.* Gone by; past. [ME *agon,* p.part. of *agon,* to go away. See AGO.]

a•gon•ic (ā-gŏn′ĭk, ə-gŏn′-) *adj.* Having no angle. [< Gk. *agōnos: a-,* without; see A-[1] + *gōnia,* angle; see DIAGONAL.]

agonic line *n.* An imaginary line on the earth's surface connecting points where the magnetic variation is zero.

ag•o•nist (ăg′ə-nĭst) *n.* **1.** One involved in a struggle. **2.** *Physiol.* A contracting muscle that is resisted by another muscle. **3.** *Biochem.* A substance that can combine with a nerve receptor to produce a reaction typical for that substance. [LLat. *agōnista,* contender < Gk. *agōnistēs* < *agōn,* contest. See AGONY.]

ag•o•nis•tic (ăg′ə-nĭs′tĭk) also **ag•o•nis•ti•cal** (-tĭ-kəl) *adj.* **1.** Striving to overcome in argument; combative. **2.** Struggling to achieve effect. **3.** Of or relating to contests, originally those of the ancient Greeks. **— ag′o•nis′ti•cal•ly** *adv.*

ag•o•nize (ăg′ə-nīz′) *v.* **-nized, -niz•ing, -niz•es. —** *intr.* **1.** To suffer extreme pain or great anguish. **2.** To make a great effort; struggle. **—** *tr.* To cause great pain or anguish to. [Med. Lat. *agōnizāre* < Gk. *agōnizesthai,* to struggle < *agōn,* contest. See AGONY.] **— ag′o•niz′ing•ly** *adv.*

ag•o•ny (ăg′ə-nē) *n., pl.* **-nies. 1.** The suffering of intense physical or mental pain. **2.** The struggle that precedes death. **3.** A sudden or intense emotion: *an agony of doubt.* **4.** A violent, intense struggle. [ME *agonie* < OFr. < LLat. *agōnia* < Gk. < *agōn,* struggle < *agein,* to drive. See **ag-***.]

ag•o•ra[1] (ăg′ər-ə) *n., pl.* **-o•rae** (-ə-rē′) or **-o•ras.** A gathering place, esp. an ancient Greek marketplace. [Gk. See **ger-***.]

a•go•ra[2] (ä′gə-rä′) *n., pl.* **-rot** or **-roth** (-rōt′). See table at **currency.** [Heb. *'ăgôrâ* < *'āgar,* to hire.]

ag•o•ra•pho•bi•a (ăg′ər-ə-fō′bē-ə) *n.* Fear of open or public places. [Gk. *agora,* marketplace; see **ger-*** + -PHOBIA.] **— ag•o•ra•pho′bi•ac′** (-ăk′) *n.* **— ag′o•ra•pho′bic** (-fō′bĭk, -fŏb′ĭk) *adj. & n.*

a•gou•ti (ə-go͞o′tē) *n., pl.* **-tis** or **-ties. 1.** A burrowing rodent of the genus *Dasyprocta,* native to tropical America and usu. having brown fur streaked with gray. **2.** The alternation of light and dark bands of color in some furs. [Fr. < Am.Sp. *agutí* < Guarani *acutí.*]

agr– *pref.* Var. of **agro–**.

A•gra (ä′grə). A city of N-central India on the Jumna R. SE of New Delhi; site of the Taj Mahal. Pop. 694,191.

a•graffe also **a•grafe** (ə-grăf′) *n.* **1.** A clasp on armor and clothing. **2.** A cramp iron for holding stones together in building. [Fr. *agrafe* < *agrafer*, to hook onto : *a-*, to (< Lat. *ad-*; see AD–) + *grafer*, to hook (< *grafe*, hook < OHGer. *krāpfo*).]

a•gran•u•lo•cy•to•sis (ā-grăn′yə-lō-sī-tō′sĭs) *n.* An acute disease marked by high fever and loss of circulating granular white blood cells.

ag•ra•pha also **Ag•ra•pha** (ăg′rə-fə) *pl.n.* The sayings of Jesus not in the Bible. [Gk. < neut. pl. of *agraphos*, unwritten : *a-*, not; see A–[1] + *graphein*, to write; see **gerbh-***.]

a•graph•i•a (ā-grăf′ē-ə) *n.* Loss of the ability to write. [A–[1] + Gk. *graphein*, to write; see **gerbh-*** + –IA[1].] **— a•graph′ic** *adj.*

a•grar•i•an (ə-grâr′ē-ən) *adj.* **1.** Relating to the land and its ownership, cultivation, and tenure. **2.** Relating to agricultural or rural matters. **—** *n.* A person who favors equitable distribution of land. [< Lat. *agrārius* < *ager, agr-*, field. See **agro-***.] **— a•grar′i•an•ly** *adv.*

a•grar•i•an•ism (ə-grâr′ē-ə-nĭz′əm) *n.* A movement for equitable distribution of land and for agrarian reform.

a•gree (ə-grē′) *v.* **a•greed, a•gree•ing, a•grees.** — *intr.* **1.** To grant consent; accede. **2.** To come into or be in accord. **3.** To be of one opinion; concur. See Syns at **assent. 4.** To come to an understanding. **5.** To be compatible or in correspondence: *The copy agrees with the original.* **6.** To be suitable, pleasing, or healthful: *Spicy food does not agree with me.* **7.** *Gram.* To correspond in gender, number, case, or person. — *tr.* To grant or concede: *They agreed that we should go.* [ME *agreen* < OFr. *agreer* < VLat. **aggrātāre*: Lat. *ad-*, ad- + Lat. *grātus*, pleasing; see **gʷerə-²***.]

a•gree•a•ble (ə-grē′ə-bəl) *adj.* **1.** To one's liking; pleasing. **2.** Suitable; conformable. **3.** Ready to consent or submit. **— a•gree′a•bil′i•ty, a•gree′a•ble•ness** *n.* **— a•gree′a•bly** *adv.*

a•gree•ment (ə-grē′mənt) *n.* **1.** The act of agreeing. **2.** Harmony of opinion; accord. **3.** An arrangement regarding a method of action; a covenant. **4.** *Law.* **a.** A properly executed and legally binding compact. **b.** The writing or document embodying this compact. **5.** *Gram.* Correspondence in gender, number, case, or person between words.

agri. *abbr.* **1.** Agricultural. **2.** Agriculture.

agri– *pref.* Var. of **agro–**.

ag•ri•a (ăg′rē-ə) *n.* An extensive pustular eruption. [< Gk. *agrios*, wild. See **agro-***.]

ag•ri•busi•ness (ăg′rə-bĭz′nĭs) *n.* Farming engaged in as a large-scale business operation.

agric. *abbr.* **1.** Agriculture. **2.** Agriculturist.

A•gric•o•la (ə-grĭk′ə-lə), **Gnaeus Julius.** A.D. 37–93. Roman soldier and governor of Britain (77–84).

ag•ri•cul•ture (ăg′rĭ-kŭl′chər) *n.* The science, art, and business of farming. [ME < Lat. *agrīcultūra*: *agrī*, genitive of *ager*, field; see **agro-*** + *cultūra*, cultivation; see CULTURE.] **— ag′ri•cul′tur•al** *adj.* **— ag′ri•cul′tur•al•ly** *adv.* **— ag′ri•cul′tur•ist, ag′ri•cul′tur•al•ist** *n.*

A•gri•gen•to (ä′grĭ-jĕn′tō, ăg′rĭ-). A city of SW Sicily, Italy, overlooking the Mediterranean; founded c. 580 B.C. Pop. 51,931.

ag•ri•mo•ny (ăg′rə-mō′nē) *n., pl.* **-nies. 1.** Any of various perennial herbaceous plants of the genus *Agrimonia*, having pinnately compound leaves and spikelike clusters of small yellow flowers. **2.** Any of several similar or related plants, such as the hemp agrimony. [ME < OFr. *aigremoine* < Lat. *agrimōnia* (influenced by OFr. *aigre*, sour), alteration of *argemōnia* < Gk. *argemōnē*, poppy, poss. < *argos*, white. See **arg-***.]

A•grip•pa (ə-grĭp′ə), **Marcus Vipsanius.** 63–12 B.C. Roman soldier who commanded the victorious fleet at Actium (31).

Ag•rip•pi•na¹ (ăg′rə-pī′nə, -pē′-). "the Elder." 13 B.C.?–A.D. 33. Roman matron and mother of Caligula.

Ag•rip•pi•na² (ăg′rə-pī′nə, -pē′-). "the Younger." A.D. 15?–59. Roman empress who murdered her husband, Claudius, so that her son by a previous marriage, Nero, would become emperor.

agro– or **agri–** or **agr–** *pref.* **1.** Field; soil: *agrology.* **2.** Agriculture: *agroindustrial.* [< Gk. *agros*, field. See **agro-***.]

ag•ro•bi•ol•o•gy (ăg′rō-bī-ŏl′ə-jē) *n.* The study of plant nutrition and growth as related to soil condition. **— ag′ro•bi′o•log′ic** (-ə-lŏj′ĭk), **ag′ro•bi′o•log′i•cal** *adj.* **— ag′ro•bi′o•log′i•cal•ly** *adv.* **— ag′ro•bi•ol′o•gist** *n.*

ag•ro•chem•i•cal (ăg′rə-kĕm′ĭ-kəl) also **ag•ri•chem•i•cal** (ăg′rĭ-) *n.* **1.** A chemical, such as an insecticide, that improves the production of crops. **2.** A chemical or product derived from plants.

ag•ro•in•dus•tri•al (ăg′rō-ĭn-dŭs′trē-əl) *n.* Of or relating to the production or supply of various needs, such as water or power, for agriculture and industry.

a•grol•o•gy (ə-grŏl′ə-jē) *n.* The applied science of soils in relation to crops. **— ag′ro•log′ic** (ăg′rə-lŏj′ĭk), **ag′ro•log′i•cal** *adj.* **— ag′ro•log′i•cal•ly** *adv.* **— a•grol′o•gist** *n.*

a•gron•o•my (ə-grŏn′ə-mē) *n.* Scientific agriculture. **— ag′ro•nom′ic** (ăg′rə-nŏm′ĭk), **ag′ro•nom′i•cal** *adj.* **— a•gron′o•mist** *n.*

ag•ros•tol•o•gy (ăg′rə-stŏl′ə-jē) *n.* The study of grasses. [Gk. *agrōstis*, a kind of wild grass (< *agros*, field; see AGRO–) + –LOGY.] **— ag′ros•tol′o•gist** *n.*

a•ground (ə-ground′) *adv. & adj.* **1.** Onto or on a shore, reef, or the bottom of a body of water: *a ship that ran aground.* **2.** On the ground: *combat aircraft aloft and aground.*

agt. *abbr.* **1.** Agent. **2.** Agreement.

a•gua•ca•te (ä′gwə-kä′tē) *n.* The avocado. [Am.Sp. < Nahuatl *ahuacatl.*]

A•gua•dil•la (ä′gwə-dē′ə, ä′gwä-*thē′*ä). A town of NW Puerto Rico on Mona Passage. Pop. 22,039.

A•guas•ca•lien•tes (ä′gwäs-kä-lyĕn′tĕs). A city of central Mexico NE of Guadalajara; built over an intricate system of ancient tunnels. Pop. 293,152.

a•gue (ā′gyo͞o) *n.* **1.** A febrile condition in which there are alternating periods of chills, fever, and sweating. **2.** A chill or fit of shivering. [ME < OFr. *(fievre) ague*, sharp (fever) < Med.Lat. *(febris) acūta* < Lat., fem. of *acūtus*. See ACUTE.] **— a′gu•ish** (ā′gyo͞o-ĭsh) *adj.* **— a′gu•ish•ly** *adv.* **— a′gu•ish•ness** *n.*

A•gui•nal•do (ä′gē-näl′dō), **Emilio.** 1869–1964. Philippine revolutionary leader.

A•gul•has (ə-gŭl′əs), **Cape.** A rugged headland of South Africa, the southernmost point of Africa.

ah (ä) *interj.* Used to express various emotions, such as satisfaction, surprise, or pain.

A.h. *abbr.* Ampere-hour.

A.H. *abbr.* **1.** *Lat.* Anno Hebraico (in the Hebrew year). **2.** *Lat.* Anno Hegirae (in the year of the Hegira).

a•ha (ä-hä′) *interj.* Used to express surprise or pleasure.

AHA *abbr.* **1.** American Heart Association. **2.** American Hospital Association.

A•hab (ā′hăb′). 9th cent. B.C. King of Israel and husband of Jezebel.

a•head (ə-hĕd′) *adv.* **1.** At or to the front or head. **2.a.** In advance; before: *pay ahead.* **b.** In or into the future; for the future: *planned ahead.* **3.a.** In an advanced position registering the future: *Set the clock ahead.* **b.** At or to a different time; earlier or later: *moved the appointment ahead.* **4.a.** In a forward direction; onward: *The train moved ahead.* **b.** In the prescribed direction for normal use: *Roll the tape ahead.* **5.** In or into a more advantageous position: *get ahead in life.* **—** ***idiom.*** **be ahead.** To be winning or in a superior position.

ahead of *prep.* **1.** In front of. **2.** In advance of; at an earlier time than: *arrived ahead of the others.* **3.** In a superior or advanced position to; more successful than.

a•hem (ə-hĕm′) *interj.* Used to attract attention or express doubt or warning.

AHF *abbr.* Antihemophilic factor.

a•him•sa (ə-hĭm′sä′) *n.* A Jain, Buddhist, and Hindu doctrine of nonviolence expressing belief in the sacredness of all living creatures. [Skt. *ahiṁsā*: *a-*, not; see **ne*** + *hiṁsā*, injury (< *hiṁsati*, he injures).]

a•his•tor•i•cal (ā′hĭ-stôr′ĭ-kəl, -stŏr′-) *adj.* Unconcerned with or unrelated to history.

Ah•ma•da•bad or **Ah•me•da•bad** (ä′mə-də-bäd′). A city of NW India N of Bombay; founded 1412. Pop. 2,059,725.

a•hold (ə-hōld′) *n.* Hold; grip: *took ahold of my arm.*

–aholic *suff.* One that is addicted to or compulsively in need of: *workaholic.* [< (ALC)OHOLIC.]

A-ho•ri•zon (ā′hə-rī′zən) *n.* In ABC soil, the topsoil.

a•hoy (ə-hoi′) *interj. Naut.* Used to hail a ship or person.

Ah•ri•man (ä′rĭ-mən) *n.* The spirit of evil in Zoroastrianism. [Pers. *ahriman* < MPers. *ahraman* < Avestan *angrō mainiiuš*, the evil spirit : *angrō*, evil + *mainiiuš*, spirit; see **men-¹***.]

A•hu•ra Maz•da (ä-ho͝or′ə măz′də) *n.* Ormazd. [Avestan *ahurō mazdå*, the Wise Lord : *ahura-*, lord; see **ansu-*** + *mazdā-*, wise; see **men-¹***.]

Ah•vaz or **Ah•waz** (ä-wäz′). A city of SW Iran NNE of Basra, Iraq; built on ruins of an ancient Persian city. Pop. 471,000.

Ah•ven•an•maa (ä′və-nän-mä′) also **Å•land Islands** (ä′lənd, ō′lănd′). A Finnish archipelago in the Baltic Sea at the entrance to the Gulf of Bothnia.

ai¹ (ī) *n.* See **sloth** 28. [Port., of Tupian orig.]

ai² *abbr.* Airborne intercept.

AI *abbr.* **1.** Artificial insemination. **2.** *Comp. Sci.* Artificial intelligence.

a.i. *abbr. Lat.* Ad interim (in the meantime).

aid (ād) *intr. & tr.v.* **aid•ed, aid•ing, aids.** To help or furnish with help, support, or relief. See Syns at **help.** — *n.* **1.** The act or result of helping; assistance. **2.a.** An assistant or a helper. **b.** A device that assists: *visual aids.* **c.** A hearing aid. **3.** An aide or aide-de-camp. **4.** A payment to a lord by a vassal in medieval England. [ME *aiden* < OFr. *aider* < Lat. *adiūtāre*, freq. of *adiuvāre*, *adiūt-*, to help : *ad-*, to; see **ad-*** + *iuvāre*, to help.] **— aid′er** *n.*

aide (ād) *n.* **1.** An aide-de-camp. **2.** An assistant; a helper: *a nurse's aide.* [Fr. < *aider*, to aid. See AID.]

Agrippina the Younger

ă **pat**	oi **boy**
ā **pay**	ou **out**
âr **care**	o͝o **took**
ä **father**	o͞o **boot**
ĕ **pet**	ŭ **cut**
ē **be**	ûr **urge**
ĭ **pit**	th **thin**
ī **pie**	*th* **this**
îr **pier**	hw **which**
ŏ **pot**	zh **vision**
ō **toe**	ə **about,** item
ô **paw**	

Stress marks:
′ (primary);
′ (secondary), as in
dictionary (dĭk′shə-nĕr′ē)

aide-de-camp (ăd′dĭ-kămp′) *n., pl.* **aides-de-camp.** A military officer acting as secretary and confidential assistant to a superior officer of general or flag rank. [Fr. : *aide*, assistant + *de*, of + *camp*, camp.]

aide-mé•moire (ăd′măm-wär′, ĕd-) *n., pl.* **aide-mémoire** or **aide-mémoires. 1.** A memorandum setting forth the major points of a proposed discussion or agreement. **2.** Something that serves as an aid to memory. [Fr. : *aide*, aid + *memoire*, memory.]

AIDS (ādz) *n.* A severe immunological disorder caused by HIV, resulting in a defect in cell-mediated immune response causing increased susceptibility to opportunistic infections and certain rare cancers. [A(CQUIRED) I(MMUNE) D(EFICIENCY) S(YNDROME).]

AIDS-re•lat•ed complex (ādz′rĭ-lā′tĭd) *n.* ARC.

ai•grette or **ai•gret** (ā-grĕt′, ā′grĕt′) *n.* **1.** An ornamental tuft of upright plumes, esp. the tail feathers of an egret. **2.** An ornament resembling a tuft of plumes. [Fr., egret < OFr. See EGRET.]

ai•guille (ā-gwēl′) *n.* **1.** A sharp, pointed mountain peak. **2.** A needle-shaped drill for boring holes in rock or masonry. [Fr., needle < OFr. See AGLET.]

ai•guil•lette (ā′gwə-lĕt′) *n.* An ornamental cord worn on the shoulder of a military uniform. [Fr. See AGLET.]

Ai•ken (ā′kən), **Conrad Potter.** 1889–1973. Amer. writer who won a 1930 Pulitzer Prize for *Selected Poems.*

ai•ki•do (ī′kē-dō′, ī-kē′dō) *n. Sports.* A Japanese art of self-defense that uses holds and locks to exploit an opponent's strength to one's own advantage. [J. *aikidō*: *ai*, mutual + *ki*, spirit + *dō*, art.]

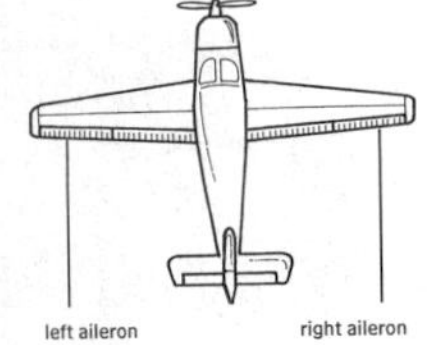

aileron

ail (āl) *v.* **ailed, ail•ing, ails.** *—intr.* To feel ill or have pain. *—tr.* To cause physical or mental pain or uneasiness to; trouble. See Syns at **trouble.** [ME *eilen* < OE *eglian* < *egle*, troublesome.]

ai•lan•thus (ā-lăn′thəs) *n.* Any of several deciduous Asian trees of the genus *Ailanthus*, esp. the tree of heaven. [NLat. *Ailanthus*, genus name, alteration (influenced by Gk. *anthos*, flower) of Ambonese *ai lanto*.]

ai•le•ron (ā′lə-rŏn′) *n.* Either of two movable flaps on the wings of an airplane, used to control rolling and banking. [Fr., dim. of *aile*, wing < OFr. < Lat. *āla*.]

Ai•ley (ā′lē, ī′lē), **Alvin, Jr.** 1931–89. Amer. choreographer whose works combine modern dance, ballet, and African ethnic dance.

ail•ment (āl′mənt) *n.* A physical or mental disorder, esp. a mild illness.

ai•lu•ro•phile (ī-lo͝or′ə-fīl′, ā-lo͝or′-) *n.* One who loves cats. [Gk. *ailouros*, cat + -PHILE.]

ai•lu•ro•phobe (ī-lo͝or′ə-fōb′, ā-lo͝or′-) *n.* One who hates or fears cats. [Gk. *ailouros*, cat + -PHOBE.] **—ai•lu′ro•pho′bi•a** *n.*

aim (ām) *v.* **aimed, aim•ing, aims.** *—tr.* To direct (a weapon or remark, for example) toward an intended goal or mark. *—intr.* **1.** To direct a weapon. **2.** To determine a course: *aim for a better education.* **3.** To propose to do something; intend. *—n.* **1.a.** The act of aiming. **b.** Skill at hitting a target: *perfect aim.* **2.a.** The line of fire of an aimed weapon. **b.** The degree of accuracy of a weapon. **3.** A purpose or intention toward which one's efforts are directed. See Syns at **intention. 4.** *Obsolete.* A target; a mark. **5.** *Obsolete.* A conjecture; a guess. [ME *aimen* < OFr. *esmer*, to estimate (< Lat. *aestimāre*) and < OFr. *aesmer*(< VLat. **ad estimāre* : Lat. *ad-*, ad- + Lat. *aestimāre*, to estimate).]

aim•less (ām′lĭs) *adj.* Devoid of direction or purpose. **—aim′less•ly** *adv.* **—aim′less•ness** *n.*

ain (ān) *adj. Scots.* Own.

ain't (ānt). *Non-Standard.* **1.** Am not. **2.** Used also as a contraction for *are not, is not, has not,* and *have not.*

Usage Note: The use of *ain't* as a contraction of *am not, are not, is not, has not,* and *have not* has a long history, but *ain't* has by now acquired such a stigma that it is beyond any possibility of rehabilitation. However, it is used by educated speakers, for example, when they want to strike a jocular or popular note, as in fixed expressions such as *Say it ain't so.* • The stigmatization of *ain't* leaves us with no happy alternative for use in first-person questions. The widely used *Aren't I?,* though illogical, was found acceptable for use in speech by a majority of the Usage Panel in an earlier survey, but in writing there is no acceptable substitute for the admittedly stilted *Am I not?*

Airedale

Ain•tab (īn-tăb′). See **Gaziantep.**

Ai•nu (ī′no͞o) *n., pl.* **Ainu** or **-nus. 1.** A member of an indigenous people of Japan. **2.** The language of the Ainu.

ai•o•li (ī-ō′lē, ā-ō′-) *n.* A sauce of garlic, egg yolks, lemon juice, and olive oil. [Prov. : *ai*, garlic (< Lat. *allium*) + *oli*, oil (< Lat. *oleum*; see OIL).]

air (âr) *n.* **1.a.** A colorless, odorless, gaseous mixture, mainly nitrogen (approx. 78 percent) and oxygen (approx. 21 percent) with lesser amounts of other gases. **b.** This mixture with varying amounts of moisture and particulate matter, enveloping Earth; the atmosphere. **2.a.** The sky; the firmament. **b.** A giant void; nothingness: *vanished into thin air.* **3.** A breeze or wind. **4.** Aircraft: *travel by air.* **5.a.** Public utterance; vent: *gave air to their grievances.* **b.** The electronic broadcast media. **6.** A characteristic impression; an aura. **7.** Personal bearing, appearance, or manner; mien. **8. airs.** An affected pose; affectation. See Syns at **affectation. 9.** *Mus.* A melody or tune, esp.: **a.** The soprano or treble part in a harmonized composition. **b.** A solo with or without accompaniment. **10.** Air conditioning. **11.** *Archaic.* Breath. *—v.* **aired, air•ing, airs.** *—tr.* **1.** To expose so that air can dry or freshen; ventilate. **2.** To give vent to publicly: *airing my pet peeves.* See Syns at **vent**[1]. **3.** To broadcast on television or radio. *—intr.* To be broadcast on television or radio. ***—idioms.* in the air.** Abroad; prevalent: *Excitement was in the air.* **up in the air.** Not yet decided; uncertain. [Partly < ME *air*, gas, atmosphere (< OFr. < Lat. *āēr* < Gk. *aēr*; see **wer-**[1]*) and partly < Fr. *air*, nature, quality, place of origin (< Lat. *ager*, place, field; see AGRICULTURE, and Lat. *ārea*, open space, threshing floor; see AREA). N., sense 9 < Fr. *air*, tune < Ital. *aria*. See ARIA.]

air bag *n.* **1.** An automotive restraint consisting of a bag that is designed to inflate upon collision. **2.** A large, strong, rubber inflatable bag used to lift a vehicle or heavy machinery or debris that has trapped a person.

air base *n.* A base for military aircraft.

air bladder *n. Biol.* **1.** An air-filled structure in many fishes that functions to maintain buoyancy or aid in respiration. **2.** See **float** 2.

air•boat (âr′bōt′) *n. Naut.* See **swamp boat.**

air•borne (âr′bôrn′, -bōrn′) *adj.* **1.** Carried by or through the air: *airborne pollen.* **2.** Transported in aircraft. **3.** In flight; flying.

air brake *n.* **1.** A brake operated by compressed air. **2.** A surface that can be projected into the airflow to increase drag; a spoiler.

air•brush (âr′brŭsh′) *n.* An atomizer using compressed air to spray a liquid on a surface. *—tr.v.* **-brushed, -brush•ing, -brush•es.** To spray with an airbrush.

air•burst (âr′bûrst′) *n.* Explosion of a bomb or shell in the atmosphere.

air chamber *n.* **1.** An enclosure filled with air for a special purpose. **2.** A chamber in which air elastically compresses and expands to regulate the flow of a fluid.

air-con•di•tion (âr′kən-dĭsh′ən) *tr.v.* **-tioned, -tion•ing, -tions.** To provide with or ventilate by air conditioning.

air conditioner *n.* An apparatus for controlling, esp. lowering, the temperature and humidity of an enclosed space.

air conditioning *n.* **1.** The state of temperature and humidity produced by an air conditioner. **2.** A system of air conditioners.

air-cool (âr′ko͞ol′) *tr.v.* **-cooled, -cool•ing, -cools. 1.** To cool by a flow of air. **2.** To air-condition.

air cover *n.* **1.** Protective use of military aircraft during ground operations. **2.** The aircraft used to support ground troops.

air•craft (âr′krăft′) *n., pl.* **aircraft.** A machine or device that is capable of atmospheric flight.

aircraft carrier *n.* A large naval vessel designed as a mobile air base.

air•crew (âr′kro͞o′) *n.* The crew operating an aircraft.

air cushion *n.* **1.** Trapped air that supports a vehicle a short distance above land or water. **2.** A device that uses trapped air to absorb the shock of motion. **—air′-cush′ion** (âr′ko͝osh′ən), **air′-cush′ioned** (-ənd) *adj.*

air-cush•ion vehicle (âr′ko͝osh′ən) *n.* A usu. propeller-driven vehicle for traveling over land or water on a supportive cushion of air.

air dam *n.* A strip of metal or plastic, running the width of a car and fitted beneath the front bumper, intended to enhance aerodynamics by blocking the flow of turbulent air under the vehicle.

air•date (âr′dāt′) *n.* The date on which a program is scheduled to be broadcast.

air door *n.* A strong current of air that is used instead of a door.

air•drome (âr′drōm′) *n.* An airport.

air•drop (âr′drŏp′) *n.* A delivery by parachute. *—tr. & intr.v.* **-dropped, -drop•ping, -drops.** To drop or be dropped from an aircraft.

air-dry (âr′drī′) *tr.v.* **-dried, -dry•ing, -dries.** To dry by exposure to the air. *—adj.* Sufficiently dry so that further exposure to air does not yield more moisture to be evaporated.

Aire•dale (âr′dāl′) *n.* A large terrier of a breed having long legs and a wiry tan coat marked with black. [After *Airedale*, a valley of N-central England.]

air•fare (âr′fâr′) *n.* Fare for travel by aircraft.

air•field (âr′fēld′) *n.* **1.** The area of fields and runways where aircraft can take off and land. **2.** An airport.

air•flow (âr′flō′) *n.* **1.** A flow of air. **2.** The air currents caused by the motion of an object.

air•foil (âr′foil′) *n.* A part or surface, such as a wing or rudder, that controls stability or lift.

air force *n.* **1.** The aviation branch of a country's armed forces. **2.** A unit of the U.S. Air Force larger than a division and smaller than a command.

air•frame (âr′frām′) *n.* The structure of an aircraft, such as an airplane, a helicopter, or a rocket, exclusive of its power plant.

air•freight (âr′frāt') *n.* **1.** A system of transporting freight by air. **2.** The amount charged for transporting freight by air. **—air′freight′** *v.*

air gas *n.* See **producer gas.**

air•glow (âr′glō') *n.* A faint photochemical luminescence in the upper atmosphere.

air gun *n.* A gun discharged by compressed air.

air•head¹ (âr′hĕd') *n. Slang.* A silly, unintelligent person.

air•head² (âr′hĕd') *n.* An area of hostile or enemy-controlled territory secured by paratroops. [AIR + (BEACH)HEAD.]

air hole *n.* **1.** A hole through which gas or air may pass. **2.** An opening in the frozen surface of water. **3.** See **air pocket.**

air hunger *n.* See **dyspnea.**

air•ing (âr′ĭng) *n.* **1.** Exposure to air for freshening or drying. **2.** Exposure to open air for exercise or health-promoting activity. **3.** Exposure to public attention. **4.** A broadcast.

air lane *n.* A regular route of travel for aircraft.

air•less (âr′lĭs) *adj.* **1.** Having no air. **2.** Lacking fresh air; stuffy. **3.** Lacking movement of air; still. **—air′less•ness** *n.*

air letter *n.* See **aerogram.**

air•lift (âr′lĭft') *n.* **1.** A system of transporting troops, passengers, or supplies by air, as when surface routes are blocked. **2.** A flight in such a system. **—*tr.v.* -lift•ed, -lift•ing, -lifts.** To transport by air, as when ground routes are blocked.

air•line (âr′līn') *n.* **1.** A system for scheduled air transport of passengers and freight. **2.** A business providing such a system.

air•lin•er (âr′lī'nər) *n.* A passenger airplane operated by an airline.

air lock *n.* **1.** An airtight chamber in which air pressure can be regulated. **2.** A bubble or pocket of air or vapor that stops the normal flow of fluid, as in a pipe.

air•mail (âr′māl') *tr.v.* **-mailed, -mail•ing, -mails.** To send (a letter, for example) by air. **—*adj.*** Of, relating to, or for use with air mail. **—*n.* air mail** also **airmail. 1.** The system of conveying mail by aircraft. **2.** Mail conveyed by aircraft.

air•man (âr′mən) *n.* **1.** An enlisted person in the U.S. Air Force ranking above airman basic and below airman first class. **2.** An enlisted person in the U.S. Navy working with aircraft. **3.** An aviator.

airman basic *n.* An enlisted person in the U.S. Air Force ranking below airman.

airman first class *n.* An enlisted person in the U.S. Air Force ranking above airman and below sergeant.

air mass *n.* A large body of air with only small horizontal variations of temperature, pressure, and moisture.

air mattress *n.* An inflatable airtight sack on which to sleep or float in water.

Air Medal (âr) *n.* A decoration awarded by the U.S. Army, Air Force, or Navy for meritorious airborne conduct.

air mile *n.* A unit of distance in air travel, equal to one international nautical mile (6,076.115 feet).

air•mo•bile also **air-mo•bile** (âr′mō'bəl, -bēl, -bīl) *adj.* Capable of being transported and deployed to a combat zone or between sites.

air piracy *n.* The forcible seizure of an aircraft in flight. **—air pirate** *n.*

air•plane (âr′plān') *n.* A winged vehicle capable of flight, generally heavier than air and driven by jet engines or propellers.

air plant *n.* See **epiphyte.**

air•play (âr′plā') *n.* The radio broadcast of a recording.

air pocket *n.* A downward air current that causes an aircraft to lose altitude abruptly.

air police *n.* The military police branch of an air force.

air•port (âr′pôrt', -pōrt') *n.* A place where aircraft can take off and land, usu. having hangars, refueling facilities, and accommodations for passengers and cargo.

air potato or **air-po•ta•to** (âr′pə-tā'tō) *n.* A tropical Old World yam *(Dioscorea bulbifera)* having potatolike tubers.

air•pow•er or **air power** (âr′pou'ər) *n.* The tactical and strategic strength of a country's air force.

air pump *n.* Equipment for compressing, removing, or forcing a flow of air.

air raid *n.* An attack by military aircraft.

air rifle *n.* A low-powered rifle that uses manually compressed air to fire small pellets.

air rights *pl.n.* The rights to develop further the heretofore unused space above a building or other structure.

air sac *n.* **1.** An air-filled space in the body of a bird that forms a connection between the lungs and bone cavities. **2.** See **alveolus** 3. **3.** A saclike thin-walled enlargement in the trachea of an insect.

air•screw (âr′skro͞o') *n. Chiefly British.* An airplane propeller.

air shed *n.* **1.** The air supply of a given region. **2.** The geographic region that shares an air supply. [AIR + (WATER)SHED.]

air•ship (âr′shĭp') *n.* A self-propelled lighter-than-air craft with directional control surfaces.

air•sick (âr′sĭk') *adj.* Suffering from airsickness.

air•sick•ness (âr′sĭk'nĭs) *n.* Nausea, vomiting, or dizziness induced by the motion that occurs during air flight.

air•space or **air space** (âr′spās') *n.* **1.** The portion of the atmosphere above a particular land area. **2.a.** The space occupied by an aircraft. **b.** A designated sector of space. **3.** See **airtime** 1.

air speed *n.* The speed, esp. of an aircraft, relative to the air.

air splint *n.* An inflatable cylinder used to immobilize injured limbs.

air spring *n.* See **air cushion** 2.

air strike *n.* An air attack on a ground or naval target.

air•strip (âr′strĭp') *n.* See **landing strip.**

airt (ârt) *n. Scots.* A cardinal point on the compass; a direction. [ME *art* < Sc.Gael. *aird* < OIr. *aird*, point of the compass.]

air taxi *n.* A small aircraft that makes short local flights.

air•tight (âr′tīt') *adj.* **1.** Impermeable by air. **2.** Having no weak points; sound: *an airtight excuse.*

air•time (âr′tīm') *n.* **1.** The time that a radio or television station is broadcasting. **2.** The time of a broadcast.

air-to-air (âr′tə-âr′) *adj.* Operating between or designed to be fired from rockets or aircraft in flight.

air-to-sur•face (âr′tə-sûr′fĭs) *adj.* Operating from or designed to be fired from aircraft at targets on the ground.

air vesicle *n. Biol.* See **float** 2.

air walk *n.* An aboveground passageway connecting two buildings.

air•wave (âr′wāv') *n.* The medium used for the transmission of radio and television signals. Often used in the plural.

air•way (âr′wā') *n.* **1.** A passageway or shaft in which air circulates. **2.a.** See **air lane. b.** See **airline** 2.

air•wor•thy (âr′wûr'*thē*) *adj.* **-thi•er, -thi•est.** Being in fit condition to fly: *airworthy avionics.* **—air′wor'thi•ness** *n.*

air•y (âr′ē) *adj.* **-i•er, -i•est. 1.** Of, relating to, or having the constitution of air. **2.** High in the air; lofty. **3.** Open to the air: *airy chambers.* **4.** Performed in the air; aerial. **5.** Immaterial; illusory; unreal: *an airy apparition.* **6.** Speculative and often impractical: *airy theories.* **7.** Light; delicate. **8.** Displaying lofty nonchalance: *an airy wave of the hand.* **9.** Lighthearted; gay: *an airy mood.* **—air′i•ly** *adv.* **—air′i•ness** *n.*

Syns: *airy, diaphanous, ethereal, filmy, gauzy, gossamer, sheer, transparent, vaporous.* The central meaning shared by these adjectives is "so light and insubstantial as to resemble air or a thin film": *an airy organdy blouse; a diaphanous veil; ethereal mist; the filmy wings of a moth; gauzy clouds; gossamer cobwebs; sheer silk stockings; transparent chiffon; vaporous muslin.*

air•y-fair•y (âr′ē-fâr′ē) *Chiefly British.* **—*n.*, *pl.* -ies.** An intellectual. **—*adj.*** Speculative and impractical; unrealistic.

A•i•sha also **A•ye•sha** (ä′ē-shä'). 611–678. The wife of Muhammad who led a revolt against his successor, Ali.

aisle (īl) *n.* **1.** A part of a church separated from the nave by pillars or columns. **2.** A passageway between rows of seats. **3.** A passageway for indoor traffic. [Alteration (influenced by ISLE and more recently by Fr. *aile*, wing < Lat. *āla*) of ME *ele* < OFr., wing of a building < Lat. *āla*.]

Aisne (ān). A river of N France rising in the Argonne Forest and flowing c. 266 km (165 mi) to the Oise R.

ait (āt) *n. Chiefly British.* A small island. [ME *eit* < OE *īgeth*, dim. of *īg*, *īeg*, island. See ISLAND.]

aitch (āch) *n.* The letter *h*. [Fr. *hache*.]

aitch•bone (āch′bōn') *n.* **1.** The rump bone, esp. of cattle. **2.** The cut of beef containing the rump bone. [ME *hach-boon* < the phrase **an hach-boon*, an aitchbone, alteration of **a nachebon*: *nache*, buttock (< OFr. < LLat. *naticas*, accusative pl. of *natica*, buttock < Lat. *natis*) + *bōn*, bone (< OE *bān*).]

Aix-en-Pro•vence (āk'sän-prō-väns′, ĕk'-). A city of SE France N of Marseilles; founded 123 B.C. Pop. 121,327.

Aix-la-Cha•pelle (āks'lä-shä-pĕl′, ĕks'-). See **Aachen.**

A•jac•cio (ä-yä′chō). A city of W Corsica, France, on the **Gulf of Ajaccio**, an inlet of the Mediterranean Sea; birthplace of Napoleon Bonaparte. Pop. 54,089.

A•jan•ta (ə-jŭn′tə). A village of W-central India SW of Amravati. Nearby caves dating from c. 200 B.C. to A.D. 650 contain remarkable examples of Buddhist art.

a•jar (ə-jär′) *adv. & adj.* Partially opened: *left the door ajar.* [ME *on char*: *on*, in; see ON + *char*, turn (< OE *cierr*).]

A•jax¹ (ā′jăks') *n. Gk. Myth.* **1.** The son of Telamon of Salamis and a warrior of great stature and prowess who fought against Troy. **2.** The son of Ileus of Locris and a warrior of small stature and arrogant character who fought against Troy.

A•jax² (ā′jăks'). A town of SE Ontario, Canada, on Lake Erie NE of Toronto. Pop. 25,475.

Aj•man (ăj-män′). A sheikdom of E Arabia, part of the United Arab Emirates on the Persian Gulf. Pop. 3,725.

Aj•mer (ŭj-mîr′). A city of NW India SW of Delhi; founded c. A.D. 145. Pop. 375,593.

A•jodh•ya (ə-yōd′yə). A village of N India near Faizabad; a pilgrimage center sacred to Hindus.

AK *abbr.* Alaska.

a.k.a. or **aka** *abbr.* Also known as.

A•kan (ä′kän') *n.*, *pl.* **Akan** or **A•kans. 1.** A Niger-Congo language spoken in parts of Ghana and the Ivory Coast. **2.** A member of a people of Ghana and the Ivory Coast. **—A′kan′** *adj.*

air rifle

ă pat	oi boy
ā pay	ou out
âr care	o͝o took
ä father	o͞o boot
ĕ pet	ŭ cut
ē be	ûr urge
ĭ pit	th thin
ī pie	*th* this
îr pier	hw which
ŏ pot	zh vision
ō toe	ə about, item
ô paw	

Stress marks: ′ (primary); ' (secondary), as in **dictionary** (dĭk′shə-nĕr'ē)

a•kar•y•o•cyte (ā-kăr′ē-ō-sīt′) *n.* A cell having no nucleus.

A•ka•shi (ä-kä′shē). A city of SW Honshu, Japan, on **Akashi Strait,** the E end of the Inland Sea. Pop. 263,365.

Ak•bar (ăk′bär). "the Great." 1542–1605. Emperor of India (1556–1605) who conquered most of N India.

AKC *abbr.* American Kennel Club.

ak•ee also **ac•kee** (ăk′ē, ə-kē′) *n.* **1.** A tropical western African evergreen tree *(Blighia sapida)* having leathery red and yellow fruits. **2.** The edible ripe aril of this tree. [Poss. Kru *akee*or Akan (Twi) *aŋkyẽ*, wild cashew.]

A•khe•na•ton or **A•khe•na•ten** (ä′kə-nät′n, äk-nät′n) also **Ikh•na•ton** (ĭk-nät′n). Orig. **A•men•ho•tep IV** (ä′mən-hō′tĕp, ăm′ən-). d. c. 1358 B.C. King of Egypt (1375?–1358?) who initiated a new form of sun worship.

A•ki•ba ben Jo•seph (ä-kē′bä bĕn jō′zəf, -səf, ə-kē′və). A.D. 50?–132. Jewish religious leader whose works include a reinterpretation of the Halakah.

A•ki•hi•to (ä′kē-hē′tō). b. 1933. Emperor of Japan (since 1989).

a•kim•bo (ə-kĭm′bō) *adv.* In or into a position in which the hands are on the hips and the elbows are bowed outward: *standing akimbo.* —*adj.* **1.** Placed in such a way as to have the hands on the hips and the elbows bowed outward: *with arms akimbo.* **2.** Being in a bent, bowed, or arched position. [ME *in kenebowe.*]

Akbar the Great
Detail from *The Emperor Akbar Hunting,* c. 1600–1610

a•kin (ə-kĭn′) *adj.* **1.** Of the same kin; related by blood. **2.** Having a similar quality or character; analogous. **3.** *Ling.* Sharing a common origin or an ancestral form.

a•ki•ne•sia (ā′kĭ-nē′zhə, -kī-) *n.* Loss of normal motor function, resulting in impaired muscle movement. [Gk. *akinēsia*: *a-*, without; see A-[1] + *-kinēsia*, motion (< *kinēsis*; see -KINESIS).] —**a′ki•net′ic** (-nĕt′ĭk) *adj.*

A•ki•ta (ä-kē′tə, ä′kĭ-tä′). A city of NW Honshu, Japan, on the Sea of Japan. Pop. 296,381.

Ak•kad also **Ac•cad** (ăk′ăd′, ä′käd′). **1.** An ancient region of Mesopotamia in N Babylonia; reached the height of its power in the 3rd millennium B.C. **2.** Also **A•ga•de** (ə-gä′də). An ancient city of Mesopotamia; cap. of the Akkadian empire.

Ak•ka•di•an (ə-kā′dē-ən) *n.* **1.** A native or inhabitant of ancient Akkad. **2.** The Semitic language of Mesopotamia. —**Ak•ka′di•an** *adj.*

Ak•ko (ä-kō′, ä′kō). See **Acre.**

Ak•ron (ăk′rən). A city of NE Ohio SSE of Cleveland. Its first rubber factory was estab. in 1869 by B.F. Goodrich (1841–88). Pop. 223,019.

Ak•sum or **Ax•um** (äk′so͞om′). A town of N Ethiopia; cap. of an empire that controlled much of N Ethiopia (1st–8th cent. A.D.).

Ak•tyu•binsk (äk-tyo͞o′bĭnsk). A city of W Kazakhstan NW of Astrakhan; founded 1869. Pop. 231,000.

Al The symbol for the element **aluminum.**

AL *abbr.* **1.** Alabama. **2.** American League.

al. *abbr.* Alcohol; alcoholic.

al– *pref.* Var. of **ad–** 1.

–al[1] *suff.* Of, relating to, or characterized by: *parental.* [ME < OFr. < Lat. *-ālis*, adj. suff.]

–al[2] *suff.* Action; process: *retrieval.* [ME *-aille* < OFr. < Lat. *-ālia* < neut. pl. of *-ālis.*]

–al[3] *suff.* Aldehyde: *citronellal.* [< AL(DEHYDE).]

Akhenaton

a•la (ā′lə) *n., pl.* **a•lae** (ā′lē). A winglike structure or part, such as the external ear or the flattened border of some stems, fruits, and seeds. [Lat. *āla*, wing.]

Ala. *abbr.* Alabama.

à la also **a la** (ä′ lä, ä′ lə, ăl′ə) *prep.* In the style or manner of. [Fr., short for *à la mode de*, in the manner of.]

Al•a•bam•a[1] (ăl′ə-băm′ə) *n., pl.* **Alabama** or **-as. 1.** A member of a tribe of the Creek confederacy formerly inhabiting southern Alabama and now located in eastern Texas. **2.** The Muskogean language of the Alabama.

Al•a•bam•a[2] (ăl′ə-băm′ə). A state of the SE U.S.; admitted as the 22nd state in 1819. Cap. Montgomery. Pop. 4,062,608. —**Al′a•ba′mi•an** (-bā′mē-ən), **Al′a•bam′an** *adj. & n.*

Alabama River. A river formed in central AL N of Montgomery and flowing c. 507 km (315 mi) to the Tombigbee R. N of Mobile.

al•a•bas•ter (ăl′ə-băs′tər) *n.* **1.** A dense translucent, white or tinted fine-grained gypsum. **2.** A variety of hard calcite, translucent and sometimes banded. **3.** *Color.* A pale yellowish pink to yellowish gray. [ME *alabastre* < OFr. < Lat. *alabaster* < Gk. *alabastros, alabastos*, poss. of Egypt. orig.]

à la carte also **a la carte** (ä′lə kärt′, ăl′ə) *adv. & adj.* With a separate price for each item on the menu. [Fr. : *à*, by + *la*, the + *carte*, menu.]

Albania

a•lack (ə-lăk′) *interj.* Used to express sorrow, regret, or alarm. [On the model of ALAS. See LACK.]

a•lac•ri•ty (ə-lăk′rĭ-tē) *n.* **1.** Cheerful willingness; eagerness. **2.** Speed or quickness; celerity. [Lat. *alacritās* < *alacer*, lively.] —**a•lac′ri•tous** (-təs) *adj.*

A•lad•din (ə-lăd′n) *n.* In the *Arabian Nights*, a boy who acquires a magic lamp and a magic ring with which he can summon two jinn to fulfill any desire.

a•lae (ā′lē) *n.* Pl. of **ala.**

A•lai or (ä′lī′). A mountain range of SW Kirghiz extending c. 322 km (200 mi) W from the Chinese border and rising to 5,880.4 m (19,280 ft).

à la king (ä′lə kĭng′, ăl′ə) *adj.* Cooked in a cream sauce with green pepper or pimiento and mushrooms.

al•a•me•da (ăl′ə-mē′də, -mā′-) *n. Southwestern U.S.* A tree-shaded promenade or public park. [Sp. < *álamo*, poplar, alamo.]

Al•a•me•da (ăl′ə-mē′də). A city of W-central CA on an island in San Francisco Bay near Oakland. Pop. 76,459.

Al•a•mein (ăl′ə-mān′), **El.** See **El Alamein.**

al•a•mo (ăl′ə-mō′) *n., pl.* **-mos.** *Southwestern U.S.* A poplar tree, esp. a cottonwood. [Sp. *álamo.*]

Al•a•mo (ăl′ə-mō′). A chapel built after 1744 as part of a mission in San Antonio TX; besieged and taken by Mexico (1836) during the Texas Revolution.

a•la•mode (ä′lə-mōd′, ăl′ə-) *n.* A lustrous plain-weave silk fabric for head coverings and scarfs. [< À LA MODE.]

à la mode (ä′lə mōd′, ăl′ə) *adj.* **1.** According to the prevailing style. **2.** Served with ice cream. [Fr. : *à*, in + *la*, the + *mode*, fashion.]

Al•a•mo•gor•do (ăl′ə-mə-gôr′dō). A city of S-central NM NE of Las Cruces; first atomic bomb detonated nearby on Jul. 16, 1945. Pop. 27,596.

Å•land Islands (ä′lənd, ō′lănd′). See **Ahvenanmaa.**

al•a•nine (ăl′ə-nēn′) *n.* A crystalline amino acid, $C_3H_7NO_2$, that is a constituent of many proteins. [Ger. *Alanin*, ult. < *Aldehyd*, aldehyde. See ALDEHYDE.]

a•lar (ā′lər) or **a•la•ry** (ā′lə-rē) *adj.* **1.** Resembling, containing, or composed of wings or alae. **2.** *Anat.* Concerned with the armpit; axillary. [Lat. *ālāris* < *āla*, wing.]

A•lar (ăl′är). A trademark used for daminozide.

A•lar•cón (ä′lär-kôn′), **Pedro Antonio de.** 1833–1891. Spanish writer whose novels include *The Three-Cornered Hat* (1874).

Al•ar•ic (ăl′ər-ĭk). A.D. 370?–410. King of the Visigoths (395–410) who plundered Greece in 395 and conquered Rome in 410.

a•larm (ə-lärm′) *n.* **1.** A sudden fear caused by the realization of danger. **2.** A warning of danger. **3.** A device that serves to warn of danger by a sound or signal. **4.** The sounding mechanism of an alarm clock. **5.** A call to arms. —*tr.v.* **a•larmed, a•larm•ing, a•larms. 1.** To fill with alarm; frighten. **2.** To give warning to. [ME < OFr. *alarme* < OItal. *allarme* < *all'arme*, to arms : *alla*, to the (< Lat. *ad illa* : *ad-*, ad- + *illa*, pl. of *illud*, the; see **al-**[1]*) + *arme*, arms (< Lat. *arma*; see **ar-***).] —**a•larm′ing•ly** *adv.*

Syns: *alarm, alert, tocsin, warning.* The central meaning shared by these nouns is "a signal that warns of imminent danger": *a burglar alarm; sirens signaling a bomb alert; a tocsin ringing from church steeples; factory whistles sounding a forest-fire warning.* See also Syns at **fear.**

alarm clock *n.* A clock that can be set to sound a bell or buzzer at a desired hour.

a•larm•ist (ə-lär′mĭst) *n.* A person who needlessly alarms others, as by inventing false rumors of impending danger. —**a•larm′ism** *n.*

a•la•rum (ə-lär′əm, ə-lăr′-) *n.* A warning or an alarm, esp. a call to arms. [ME *alarom*, var. of *alarm*, alarm. See ALARM.]

a•las (ə-lăs′) *interj.* Used to express sorrow, regret, grief, compassion, or apprehension of danger or evil. [ME < OFr. *a las, helas*, ah (I am) miserable < Lat. *lassus*, weary. See **lē-***.]

A•las•ka (ə-lăs′kə). A state of the U.S. in extreme NW North America, separated from the other mainland states by British Columbia, Canada; admitted as the 49th state in 1959. Cap. Juneau. Pop. 551,947. —**A•las′kan** *adj. & n.*

Alaska, Gulf of. An inlet of the Pacific Ocean between the Alaska Peninsula and Alexander Archipelago.

Alaska Highway. Formerly **Al•can Highway** (ăl′kăn′). A road extending 2,450.5 km (1,523 mi) from Dawson Creek, British Columbia, to Fairbanks AK; built in 1942.

Alaskan king crab *n.* See **king crab** 1.

Alaskan malamute *n.* Malamute.

Alaska Peninsula. A peninsula of S-central to SW AK between the Bering Sea and the Pacific Ocean.

Alaska Range. A mountain range of S-central AK rising to 6,197.6 m (20,320 ft) at Mt. McKinley.

Alaska Standard Time *n.* Standard time in the ninth time zone west of Greenwich, England, reckoned at 135° west and used throughout Alaska except for the western Aleutian Islands.

A•la-Tau (ăl′ə-tou′, ä′lə-). Several mountain ranges of the Tien Shan in central Asia, E Kirghiz, and S Russia.

a•late (ā′lāt′) also **a•lat•ed** (ā′lā′tĭd) *adj.* Having winglike extensions or parts; winged. [Lat. *ālātus* < *āla*, wing.]

Al•a•va (ăl′ə-və), **Cape.** A cape of NW WA; the westernmost point of the coterminous U.S.

alb (ălb) *n.* A long white linen robe with tapered sleeves worn by a priest at Mass. [ME *albe* < OE < Med.Lat. *alba* < *(vestis) alba*, white (garment), fem. of Lat. *albus*, white. See **albho-***.]

Alb. *abbr.* Albania; Albanian.

Al•ba (ăl′bə), Duke of. See Duke of **Alva.**

Al•ba•ce•te (ăl′bə-sä′tē, äl′vä-thĕ′tĕ). A city of SE Spain WSW of Valencia. Pop. 121,909.

al•ba•core (ăl′bə-kôr′, -kōr′) *n., pl.* **albacore** or **-cores.** A large marine fish *(Thunnus alalunga)* having edible flesh. [Port. *albacor* < Ar. *al-bakrah*: *al*, the + *bakrah*, young camel.]

Al•ba Lon•ga (ăl′bə lông′gə, lŏng′-). A city of ancient Latium in central Italy SE of Rome; founded before 1100 B.C. and the legendary birthplace of Romulus and Remus.

Al•ba•ni•a (ăl-bā′nē-ə, -bān′yə, ôl-). A country of SE Europe on the Adriatic Sea; became a republic in 1925. Cap. Tiranë. Pop. 2,841,300.

Al•ba•ni•an (ăl-bā′nē-ən, -bān′yən, ôl-) *adj.* Of or relating to Albania or its people, language, or culture. *—n.* **1.** A native or an inhabitant of Albania. **2.** The Indo-European language of the Albanians.

Al•ba•no (äl-bä′nō). A lake of central Italy SE of Rome in an extinct volcanic crater.

Al•ba•ny (ôl′bə-nē). **1.** A city of SW GA SE of Columbus. Pop. 78,122. **2.** The cap. (since 1797) of NY, in the E part on the Hudson R.; founded in the early 17th cent. as Fort Orange and renamed Albany in 1664. Pop. 101,082. **3.** A city of NW OR on the Willamette R. S of Salem. Pop. 29,462.

Albany River. A river rising in W Ontario, Canada, and flowing c. 982 km (610 mi) to James Bay.

al•ba•tross (ăl′bə-trôs′, -trŏs′) *n., pl.* **albatross** or **-tross•es.** **1.** Any of several large web-footed birds constituting the family Diomedeidae, chiefly of the oceans of the Southern Hemisphere. **2.a.** A constant, worrisome burden. **b.** An obstacle to success. [Prob. alteration (influenced by Lat. *albus*, white) of *alcatras*, pelican < Port. or Sp. *alcatraz* < Ar. *al-ġaṭṭās*: *al*, the + *ġaṭṭās*, white-tailed sea eagle. Sense 2, after the *albatross* in *The Rime of the Ancient Mariner* by Samuel Taylor Coleridge, which the mariner killed and had to wear around his neck as a penance.]

al•be•do (ăl-bē′dō) *n., pl.* **-dos.** The fraction of incident electromagnetic radiation reflected by a surface. [LLat. *albēdō*, whiteness < Lat. *albus*, white. See **albho-*.**]

Al•bee (ôl′bē, ŏl′-, ăl′-), **Edward Franklin.** b. 1928. Amer. playwright best known for *Who's Afraid of Virginia Woolf?* (1962).

al•be•it (ôl-bē′ĭt, ăl-) *conj.* Even though; although; notwithstanding: *a clear albeit cold day.* [ME *al be it*: *al*, even if; see ALL + *be*, subjunctive of *ben*, to be; see BE + *it*, it; see IT.]

Al•be•marle Sound (ăl′bə-märl′). A large body of generally fresh water in NE NC separated from the Atlantic by a narrow barrier island.

Al•bé•niz (äl-bā′nēs′, äl-), **Isaac.** 1860–1909. Spanish composer of piano works based on Spanish folk music.

Al•bers (ăl′bərz, ŏl′-), **Josef.** 1888–1976. German-born Amer. painter whose works include *Homage to the Square* (1950–59).

Al•bert (ăl′bərt), Prince. 1819–61. German-born consort (1840–61) of Victoria.

Albert I. 1875–1934. King of the Belgians (1909–34) who led the forces that reconquered Belgium (1918) during World War I.

Albert, Lake. Also **Mo•bu•to Lake** (mō-bo͞o′tō) or **Albert Nyan•za** (nī-ăn′zə, nyän′-). A shallow lake of E-central Africa in the Great Rift Valley between Uganda and Zaire.

Al•ber•ta (ăl-bûr′tə). A province of W Canada between British Columbia and Saskatchewan; joined the confederation in 1905. Cap. Edmonton. Pop. 2,237,724. **—Al•ber′tan** *adj. & n.*

Albert Lea (lē). A city of S MN near the IA border S of Minneapolis. Pop. 18,310.

Albert Nile (nīl). Part of the upper Nile R. in NW Uganda.

Al•ber•tus Mag•nus (ăl-bûr′təs măg′nəs), Saint. 1206?–80. German religious philosopher.

al•bes•cent (ăl-bĕs′ənt) *adj.* Becoming white; whitish. [Lat. *albēscēns, albēscent-*, pr.part. of *albēscere*, to become white < *albus*, white. See **albho-*.**]

Al•bi•gen•ses (ăl′bə-jĕn′sēz′) *pl.n.* The members of a Catharist religious sect of southern France in the 12th and 13th centuries, condemned for heresy and persecuted during the Inquisition. [Med.Lat., pl. of *Albigēnsis*, inhabitant of *Albiga*, Albi, a town of S France.] **—Al′bi•gen′sian** (-shən, -sē-ən) *adj.* **—Al′bi•gen′sian•ism** *n.*

al•bi•nism (ăl′bə-nĭz′əm) *n.* **1.** Congenital absence of normal pigmentation or coloration. **2.** The condition of being an albino. [Fr. *albinisme* < Ger. *Albinismus* < *Albino*, albino < Port. See ALBINO.] **—al′bi•nis′tic** *adj.*

al•bi•no (ăl-bī′nō) *n., pl.* **-nos.** **1.** A person or an animal lacking normal pigmentation, so that the skin and hair are abnormally white and the eyes have a pink or blue iris and a deep-red pupil. **2.** A plant that lacks chlorophyll. [Port. < *albo*, white < Lat. *albus*. See **albho-*.**]

Al•bi•on (ăl′bē-ən). England or Great Britain.

al•bite (ăl′bīt) *n.* A white feldspar, $NaAlSi_3O_8$, that is one of the common rock-forming plagioclase group. [Lat. *albus*, white; see **albho-*** + -ITE[1].] **—al•bit′ic** (-bĭt′ĭk), **al•bit′i•cal** (-ĭ-kəl) *adj.*

Al•boin (ăl′boin, -bō-ĭn). d. 572. King of the Lombards (565?–572) who led the Germanic invasion of Italy.

Ål•borg also **Aal•borg** (ôl′bôrg′). A city of N Denmark NNE of Århus; chartered 1342. Pop. 154,840.

Al•bright (ôl′brīt, ŏl′-), **Horace Marden.** 1890–1987. Amer. conservationist and cofounder of the National Park Service.

al•bum (ăl′bəm) *n.* **1.** A book with blank pages for the insertion and preservation of collections, as of stamps. **2.a.** A set of phonograph records stored together. **b.** The holder for such records. **c.** One or more 12-inch long-playing records. **3.** A printed collection of musical compositions, pictures, or literary selections. **4.** A tall printed book, often having profuse illustrations and short, sentimental texts. [Lat., blank tablet < neut. of *albus*, white. See **albho-*.**]

al•bu•men (ăl-byo͞o′mən) *n.* **1.** The white of an egg. **2.** See **albumin.** [Lat. *albūmen* < *albus*, white. See **albho-*.**]

al•bu•min (ăl-byo͞o′mĭn) *n.* A class of simple water-soluble proteins found in egg white, blood serum, milk, and other animal and plant juices and tissues. [ALBUM(EN) + -IN.] **—al•bu′mi•nous** *adj.*

al•bu•mi•noid (ăl-byo͞o′mə-noid′) *n.* See **scleroprotein.** *—adj.* also **al•bu•mi•noi•dal** (-byo͞o′mə-noid′l). Composed of or resembling albumin.

al•bu•mi•nu•ri•a (ăl-byo͞o′mə-no͝or′ē-ə, -nyo͝or-) *n.* The presence of albumin in the urine. **—al•bu′mi•nu′ric** (-no͝or′ĭk, -nyo͝or′-) *adj.*

al•bu•mose (ăl′byə-mōs′, -mōz′) *n.* A class of substances derived from albumins and formed by the enzymatic breakdown of proteins during digestion. [Fr. : *albumine*, albumin; see ALBUMIN + *-ose*, -ose; see -OSE[2].]

Al•bu•quer•que (ăl′bə-kûr′kē). A city of central NM on the Rio Grande SW of Santa Fe; founded 1706. Pop. 384,736.

Al•bu•quer•que (ăl′bə-kûr′kē, äl′bə-kûr′-), **Affonso de.** "Affonso the Great." 1453–1515. Portuguese colonial administrator considered the founder of the E Portuguese empire.

alc. *abbr.* Alcohol; alcoholic.

Al•cae•us (ăl-sē′əs). fl. 611?–580 B.C. Greek poet who reputedly invented Alcaic verse.

Al•ca•ic (ăl-kā′ĭk) *adj.* Of or relating to a verse form consisting of strophes having four tetrametric lines. [LLat. *Alcaicus*, of Alcaeus < Gk. *Alkaïkos* < *Alkaios*, Alcaeus.] **—Al•ca′ic** *n.*

al•cai•de also **al•cay•de** (ăl-kī′dē) *n.* The commander or governor of a fortress in Spain or Portugal. [Sp. < Ar. *al-qā'id*, the commander : *al*, the + *qā'id*, commander (< *qāda*, to command).]

Al•ca•lá de He•na•res (ăl′kə-lä′ dā hĕ-när′əs, äl′kä-lä′ *thĕ* ĕ-nä′rĕs). A town of central Spain ENE of Madrid; birthplace of Cervantes. Pop. 146,994.

al•cal•de (ăl-kăl′dē, äl-) *n.* The mayor or chief judicial official of a Spanish town. [Sp. < Ar. *al-qāḍī*: *al*, the + *qāḍī*, judge (< *qaḍā*, to judge).]

Al•can Highway (ăl′kăn′). See **Alaska Highway.**

Al•ca•traz (ăl′kə-trăz′). "the Rock." A rocky island of W CA in San Francisco Bay; a military prison from 1859 to 1933 and a federal prison until 1963.

al•caz•ar (ăl-kăz′ər, -kä′zər, ăl′kə-zär′) *n.* A Spanish palace or fortress, originally one built by the Moors. [Sp. *alcázar* < Ar. *alqaṣr*: *al*, the + *qaṣr*, castle (< Lat. *castra*, fort, pl. of *castrum*, camp; see **kes-*.**)]

Al•ces•tis (ăl-sĕs′tĭs) *n. Gk. Myth.* The wife of Admetus, who agreed to die in his place and was later rescued from Hades by Hercules.

al•che•mist (ăl′kə-mĭst) *n.* A practitioner of alchemy. **—al′che•mis′tic, al′che•mis′ti•cal** *adj.*

al•che•my (ăl′kə-mē) *n.* **1.** A medieval chemical philosophy having as its asserted aims the transmutation of base metals into gold, the discovery of the panacea, and the preparation of the elixir of longevity. **2.** A seemingly magical power or process of transmuting. [ME *alkamie* < OFr. *alquemie* < Med. Lat. *alchymia* < Ar. *al-kīmiyā'*: *al*, the + *kīmiyā'*, chemistry (< LGk. *khēmeia, khumeia*, perh. < Gk. *Khēmia*, Egypt).] **—al•chem′i•cal** (ăl-kĕm′ĭ-kəl), **al•chem′ic** *adj.* **—al′che•mize′** (ăl′kə-mīz′) *v.*

Al•ci•bi•a•des (ăl′sə-bī′ə-dēz′). 450?–404 B.C. Athenian politician and general who changed allegiance three times during the Peloponnesian War (431–404).

Al•cin•dor (ăl-sĭn′dər), **Lew.** See Kareem **Abdul-Jabbar.**

Alc•me•ne (ălk-mē′nē) *n. Gk. Myth.* Amphitryon's wife and mother of Hercules by Zeus.

al•co•hol (ăl′kə-hôl′, -hŏl′) *n.* **1.** A colorless, volatile, flammable liquid, C_2H_5OH, synthesized or obtained by fermentation of sugars and starches and used as a solvent and in drugs and intoxicating beverages. **2.** Intoxicating liquor containing alcohol. **3.** Any of a series of hydroxyl compounds having the general formula $C_nH_{2n+1}OH$, including ethanol and methanol. [Med.Lat., fine metallic powder, esp. of antimony < Ar. *al-kuḥl*: *al*, the + *kuḥl*, powder of antimony.]

Word History: The *al–* in *alcohol* may alert some readers to the fact that this is a word of Arabic descent, as is the case with *algebra* and *alkali*. *Al* is the Arabic definite article cor-

albatross
Top: Wandering albatross
Diomedea exulans
Bottom: Laysan albatross
Diomedea immutabilis

alcazar
Segovia, Spain

ă pat	oi boy
ā pay	ou out
âr care	o͝o took
ä father	o͞o boot
ĕ pet	ŭ cut
ē be	ûr urge
ĭ pit	th thin
ī pie	*th* this
îr pier	hw which
ŏ pot	zh vision
ō toe	ə about, item
ô paw	

Stress marks:
′ (primary);
′ (secondary), as in
dictionary (dĭk′shə-nĕr′ē)

responding to *the* in English. The origin of *–cohol* is less obvious, however. Its Arabic ancestor was *kuḥl,* a fine powder most often made from antimony and used by women to darken their eyelids. Arabic chemists came to use *al-kuḥl* to mean "any fine powder produced in a number of ways, including the process of heating a substance to a gaseous state and then recooling it." The English word *alcohol,* derived through Medieval Latin from Arabic, is first recorded in 1543 in this sense. Arabic chemists also used *al-kuḥl* to refer to other substances such as essences that were obtained by distillation. This sense of *alcohol* is first found in English in 1672. One of these distilled essences, known as "alcohol of wine," is the constituent of fermented liquors that causes intoxication. This essence took over the term *alcohol* for itself, and it has since come to refer to the liquor that contains this essence as well as to a class of chemical compounds such as methanol.

al•co•hol•ic (ăl′kə-hô′lĭk, -hŏl′ĭk) *adj.* **1.** Related to or resulting from alcohol. **2.** Containing or preserved in alcohol. **3.** Suffering from alcoholism. — *n.* A person who suffers from alcoholism.

Louisa May Alcott

al•co•hol•ism (ăl′kə-hô-lĭz′əm, -hŏ-) *n.* **1.** Psychophysiological dependence on alcoholic beverages. **2.** A chronic disease, mainly affecting the nervous and digestive systems, caused by the excessive and habitual consumption of alcohol.

al•co•hol•om•e•ter (ăl′kə-hô-lŏm′ĭ-tər) also **al•co•hol•me•ter** (ăl′kə-hôl-mē′tər, -hŏl-) *n.* An instrument used to determine the amount of alcohol in a liquid. — **al′co•hol•om′e•try** *n.*

Al•cott (ôl′kət, -kŏt, ŏl′-), **Amos Bronson.** 1799–1888. Amer. educator and transcendentalist philosopher.

Alcott, Louisa May. 1832–88. Amer. writer and reformer best known for her novel *Little Women* (1868–69).

al•cove (ăl′kōv′) *n.* **1.** A recess or partly enclosed extension connected to or forming part of a room. **2.** A secluded structure, such as a bower, in a garden. [Fr. *alcôve* < Sp. *alcoba* < Ar. *al-qubbah*, the vault : *al*, the + *qubbah*, vault.]

Al•cuin (ăl′kwĭn). 735?–804. Anglo-Saxon prelate and scholar who was a leader in the revival of learning.

Al•cy•o•ne (ăl-sī′ə-nē) *n.* **1.** *Gk. Myth.* The daughter of Aeolus who in grief over the death of her husband threw herself into the sea and was changed into a kingfisher. **2.** *Gk. Myth.* A nymph, one of the Pleiades. **3.** *Astron.* The brightest star in the Pleiades. [Lat. < Gk. *Alkuonē* < *alkuōn*, kingfisher.]

Ald. *abbr.* Alderman.

Al•dan (ăl-dän′). A river of SE Russia rising in the Stanovoy Range and flowing c. 2,253 km (1,400 mi) around the **Aldan Plateau** to the Lena R. N of Yakutsk.

alembic

Al•deb•a•ran (ăl-dĕb′ər-ən) *n.* A bright double star in the constellation Taurus. [ME *Aldeboran* < Med.Lat. *Aldebaran* < Ar. *ad-dabarān*: *al*, the + *dabarān*, following (the Pleiades) (< *dabara*, to follow).]

al•de•hyde (ăl′də-hīd′) *n.* **1.** Any of a class of highly reactive organic chemical compounds obtained by oxidation of primary alcohols, characterized by the common group CHO, and used in resins, dyes, and organic acids. **2.** See **acetaldehyde.** [Ger. *Aldehyd* < NLat., short for *alcohol dehydrogenātum*, dehydrogenized alcohol.]

Al•den (ôl′dən), **John.** 1599?–1687. Pilgrim colonist known for his courtship of Priscilla Mullins (b. c. 1602).

al den•te (äl dĕn′tē, äl dĕn′tā) *adj.* Cooked just enough to be firm. [Ital. : *al*, to the + *dente*, tooth.] — **al den′te** *adv.*

Alexander the Great
As depicted on an ancient coin

al•der (ôl′dər) *n.* **1.** Any of various deciduous shrubs or trees of the genus *Alnus,* native chiefly to northern temperate regions and having toothed leaves and fruits in woody conelike catkins. **2.** The wood of these plants, used in carvings and furniture. [ME < OE *alor.*]

Al•der (äl′dər), **Kurt.** 1902–58. German chemist who shared a 1950 Nobel Prize.

al•der•man (ôl′dər-mən) *n.* **1.** A member of a municipal legislative body in many jurisdictions. **2.** A member of the higher branch of the municipal or borough council in England and Ireland before 1974. **3.a.** A noble of high rank or authority in Anglo-Saxon England. **b.** The chief officer of a shire in Anglo-Saxon England. [ME, a person of high rank < OE *ealdorman*: *ealdor*, elder, chief (< *eald*, old; see **al-**[2*]) + *man*, man; see MAN.] — **al′der•man•cy** (-sē) *n.* — **al′der•man′ic** (-măn′ĭk) *adj.*

Al•der•ney[1] (ôl′dər-nē). A British island in the Channel Is. separated from the French coast by the **Race of Alderney.**

Al•der•ney[2] (ôl′dər-nē) *n.*, *pl.* **-neys.** One of a breed of dairy cattle originally raised in the Channel Islands.

alfalfa
Medicago sativa

Al•der•shot (ôl′dər-shŏt′). A municipal borough of S-central England SW of London. Pop. 80,800.

al•di•carb (ăl′dĭ-kärb′) *n.* A crystalline compound, $C_7H_{14}N_2O_2S$, used in agriculture as a pesticide. [*(propion)al-d(ehyde)*, C_2H_5CHO (PROPION(IC ACID), ALDEHYDE) + *(methyl)-carb(amoyloxime)*, $C_2H_{14}N_2O_2S$.]

al•dol (ăl′dôl′, -dōl′, -dŏl′) *n.* **1.** A thick colorless to yellow liquid, $C_4H_8O_2$, obtained from acetaldehyde and used in perfumery and as a solvent. **2.** A similar aldehyde. [ALD(EHYDE) + -OL[1].]

al•dol•ase (ăl′də-lās′) *n.* An enzyme in certain living tissues that catalyzes the breakdown of a fructose ester into triose sugars.

al•dose (ăl′dōs′, -dōz′) *n. Chem.* Any of a class of monosaccharide sugars containing an aldehyde group. [ALD(EHYDE) + -OSE[1].]

al•dos•ter•one (ăl-dŏs′tə-rōn′) *n.* A steroid hormone secreted by the cortex of an adrenal gland that regulates the salt and water balance in the body. [ALD(EHYDE) + STER(OL) + -ONE.]

al•dos•ter•on•ism (ăl-dŏs′tə-rō-nĭz′əm, ăl′dō-stĕr′ə-) *n.* A disorder marked by excessive secretion of aldosterone, which can cause weakness, cardiac irregularities, and abnormally high blood pressure.

Al•drich (ôl′drĭch, ŏl′-), **Thomas Bailey.** 1836–1907. Amer. writer and editor whose works include *The Story of a Bad Boy* (1870).

al•drin (ôl′drĭn) *n.* An insecticide containing a naphthalene-derived compound, $C_{12}H_8Cl_6$. [After Kurt ALDER.]

Al•drin (ôl′drĭn, ŏl′-), **Edwin Eugene, Jr.** "Buzz." b. 1930. Amer. astronaut who was the second person to walk on the moon (Jul. 20, 1969).

Al•dus Ma•nu•tius (ôl′dəs mə-nōō′shəs, -shē-əs, -nyōō′-, ŏl′-). See Aldus **Manutius.**

ale (āl) *n.* A fermented alcoholic beverage similar to but heavier than beer. [ME < OE *ealu, alu.* See **alu-*.**]

a•le•a•to•ry (ā′lē-ə-tôr′ē, -tōr′ē) *adj.* **1.** Dependent on chance, luck, or an uncertain outcome. **2.** Of or characterized by gambling. **3.** Also **a•le•a•to•ric** (ā′lē-ə-tôr′ĭk, -tōr′-). *Mus.* Using or consisting of sounds chosen by the performer or left to chance: *aleatory music.* [Lat. *āleātōrius* < *āleātor*, gambler < *ālea*, dice.]

a•lec•i•thal (ă-lĕs′ə-thəl) *adj.* Having little or no yolk: *an alecithal egg.* [A-[1] + LECITH(IN) + -AL[1].]

A•lec•to (ə-lĕk′tō) *n. Gk. & Rom. Myth.* One of the Furies.

a•lee (ə-lē′) *adv. Naut.* At, on, or to the leeward side.

al•e•gar (ăl′ĭ-gər, ā′lĭ-) *n.* Vinegar made from ale. [ME, blend of *ale*, ale; see ALE, and *vinegar*, vinegar; see VINEGAR.]

ale•house (āl′hous′) *n.* A place where ale is sold and served.

A•lei•chem (ä-lā′kĕm, -KHĕm), **Shalom** or **Sholem.** Solomon Rabinowitz. 1859–1916. Russian-born Jewish humorist noted for his stories and plays.

A•leix•an•dre (ä′lĕk-sän′drə), **Vicente.** 1898–1984. Spanish poet who won the 1977 Nobel Prize for literature.

A•lek•san•drovsk (ăl′ĭk-săn′drəfsk, ə-lĭk-sän′-). See **Zaporozhe.**

A•le•mán (ä′lā-män′), **Mateo.** 1547–1610? Mexican writer whose works include *Guzmán de Alfarache* (1599).

Al•e•man•ni (ăl′ə-măn′ī) *pl.n.* A group of Germanic tribes that settled in and near Alsace during the fourth century A.D. and were defeated by the Franks in 496. [Lat., of Gmc. orig. See **man-**[1*].]

Al•e•man•nic (ăl′ə-măn′ĭk) *n.* **1.** A group of High German dialects spoken in Alsace, Switzerland, and parts of southern Germany. **2.** The Germanic dialect of the Alemanni. — *adj.* **1.** Of or relating to the Alemannic dialects. **2.** Of or relating to the Alemanni or their language.

A•lem•bert (ăl′əm-bâr′, ä-län-bĕr′), **Jean Le Rond d′.** 1717–83. French mathematician and philosopher who defined the laws of dynamics governing equilibrium and centrifugal force.

a•lem•bic (ə-lĕm′bĭk) *n.* **1.** An apparatus consisting of two vessels connected by a tube, formerly used for distilling. **2.** A device that purifies or alters by a process comparable to distillation. [ME *alambic* < OFr. < Med.Lat. *alembicus* < Ar. *al-'anbīq*: *al*, the + *'anbīq*, still (< Gk. *ambix*, cup).]

Al•en•çon (ăl-äN-sôN′). A town of NW France on the Sarthe R. WSW of Paris. Pop. 31,608.

a•leph (ä′lĕf, -ləf) *n.* The first letter of the Hebrew alphabet. [Heb. *'alep* < *'elep*, ox < Canaanite *'alp.*]

a•leph-null (ä′lĕf-nŭl′, -ləf-) *n. Math.* The first transfinite number.

A•lep•po (ə-lĕp′ō) also **A•lep** (ə-lĕp′). A city of NW Syria near the Turkish border; inhabited perhaps as early as the 6th millennium B.C. Pop. 985,413.

a•lert (ə-lûrt′) *adj.* **1.** Vigilantly attentive: *alert to danger.* See Syns at **aware. 2.** Mentally responsive and perceptive. **3.** Brisk or lively in action: *the bird's alert hopping.* — *n.* **1.** A signal that warns of danger: *Sirens sounded the alert.* See Syns at **alarm. 2.** A condition or period of heightened watchfulness or preparation for action. — *tr.v.* **a•lert•ed, a•lert•ing, a•lerts.** To notify of approaching danger or action. — ***idiom.* on the alert.** Watchful and prepared for danger, emergency, or opportunity. [Fr. *alerte* < Ital. *all' erta*, on the lookout : *alla*, to the, on the (< Lat. *ad illam*, to that : *ad-*, ad- + *illam*, accusative of *illa*, that; see **al-**[1*]) + *erta*, lookout < p.part. of *ergere*, to raise (< Lat. *ērigere*; see ERECT).]

Al•es•san•dri•a (ăl′ĭ-săn′drē-ə, ä′lĕs-sän′-). A city of NW Italy ESE of Turin; founded c. 1168. Pop. 100,518.

A•leut (ə-lōōt′, ăl′ē-ōōt′) *n.*, *pl.* **Aleut** or **A•leuts. 1.** A member of a Native American people inhabiting the Aleutian Islands and coastal areas of southwest Alaska. **2.** Either or both of the two languages of the Aleut. See Usage Note at **Native American.** [Russ.]

A•leu•tian (ə-lo͞o′shən) *adj.* Of or relating to the Aleut, their language, or their culture. — *n.* A native or inhabitant of the Aleutian Islands, esp. an Aleut.

Aleutian Islands. A chain of rugged volcanic islands of SW AK curving c. 1,931 km (1,200 mi) W from the Alaska Peninsula; under Russian control from 1741 until 1867.

Aleutian Range. A mountain chain of SW AK extending W along the Alaska Peninsula and the Aleutian Is. to Attu I.

A level *n. Chiefly British.* The later of two standardized tests in a secondary school subject, used for university admissions. [*A(dvanced) level.*]

ale•wife[1] (āl′wīf′) *n.* A fish *(Alosa pseudoharengus)* closely related to the herrings and native to North American Atlantic waters and some inland lakes. [Perh. < ALEWIFE[2].]

ale•wife[2] (āl′wīf′) *n.* A woman who keeps an alehouse.

al•ex•an•der also **Al•ex•an•der** (ăl′ĭg-zăn′dər) *n.* A cocktail made with crème de cacao, sweet cream, and brandy or gin. [< the name *Alexander.*]

Alexander I[1] (ăl′ĭg-zăn′dər). 1777–1825. Czar of Russia (1801–25) whose plans to liberalize his country's government were forestalled by wars with Napoleon I.

Alexander I[2]. Orig. **Alexander O•bre•no•vić** (ō-brĕn′ə-vĭch′). 1876–1903. King of Serbia (1889–1903) whose efforts to increase his power at the expense of the national assembly led to his assassination.

Alexander I[3]. 1888–1934. King of Yugoslavia (1921–34) who unified the peoples of Serbia, Croatia, and Slovenia (1929).

Alexander I Island. An island in Bellingshausen Sea off the coast of the Antarctic Peninsula.

Alexander II. 1818–81. Czar of Russia (1855–81) who emancipated the serfs in 1861.

Alexander III[1]. "Alexander the Great." 356–323 B.C. King of Macedonia (336–323) and conqueror of Asia Minor, Syria, Egypt, Babylonia, and Persia.

Alexander III[2]. d. 1181. Pope (1159–81) who established papal supremacy.

Alexander VI. Rodrigo Borgia. 1431–1503. Pope (1492–1503) noted as a patron of the arts.

Alexander Archipelago. A group of more than 1,000 islands off SE AK.

Alexander Nev•ski (nĕv′skē, nĕf′-). 1220?–63. Russian national hero who defeated the Swedes (1240).

Alexander of Tu•nis (to͞o′nĭs, tyo͞o′-), 1st Earl. Harold Rupert Leofric George Alexander. 1891–1969. British field marshal in World War II.

Alexander Se•ve•rus (sə-vîr′əs). A.D. 208?–235. Emperor of Rome (222–235) who succeeded his cousin Heliogabalus.

Al•ex•an•der•son (ăl′ĭg-zăn′dər-sən), **Ernst Frederick Werner.** 1878–1975. Swedish-born Amer. electrical engineer who demonstrated the first practical television system (1930).

Alexander the Great. See **Alexander III[1].**

Al•ex•an•dra (ăl′ĭg-zăn′drə, -zän′-). 1872–1918. Last czarina of Russia (1894–1917).

Al•ex•an•dret•ta (ăl′ĭg-zăn-drĕt′ə). See **Iskenderun.**

Al•ex•an•dri•a (ăl′ĭg-zăn′drē-ə). **1.** A city of N Egypt on the Mediterranean Sea at the W tip of the Nile Delta. Founded in 332 B.C., it was famous for its libraries and pharos (lighthouse), one of the Seven Wonders of the World. Pop. 2,821,000. **2.** A city of central LA NW of Baton Rouge. Pop. 49,188. **3.** An independent city of N VA on the Potomac R. opposite Washington DC; laid out in 1749. Pop. 111,183.

Al•ex•an•dri•an (ăl′ĭg-zăn′drē-ən) *adj.* **1.** Of or relating to Alexander the Great. **2.** Of or relating to Alexandria, Egypt. **3.** Of, characteristic of, or belonging to a school of Hellenistic literature, science, and philosophy located at Alexandria in the last three centuries B.C.

al•ex•an•drine also **Al•ex•an•drine** (ăl′ĭg-zăn′drĭn) — *n.* **1.** A line of English verse in iambic hexameter, usu. with a caesura after the third foot. **2.** A line of French verse consisting of 12 syllables, usu. with a caesura after the sixth syllable. — *adj.* Characterized by or composed of alexandrines. [Fr. *alexandrin* < OFr. < *Alexandre*, title of a romance about Alexander the Great written in this meter.]

al•ex•an•drite (ăl′ĭg-zăn′drīt′) *n.* A greenish chrysoberyl that appears red in artificial light, used as a gemstone. [Ger. *Alexandrit*, after ALEXANDER I[1].]

a•lex•i•a (ə-lĕk′sē-ə) *n.* Loss of the ability to read, usu. caused by brain lesions. [A-[1] + Gk. *lexis*, speech (< *legein*, to speak; see **leg-***) + -IA[1].]

a•lex•in (ə-lĕk′sĭn) *n.* See **complement** 6. [Gk. *alexein*, to ward off + -IN.]

A•lex•is I Mi•khai•lo•vich (ä-lĕk′sĭs; mĭ-kī′lə-vĭch, mə-KHĪ′-). 1629–76. Czar of Russia (1645–76) who implemented a code of law that established serfdom (1649).

A•lex•i•us I Com•ne•nus (ə-lĕk′sē-əs; kŏm-nē′nəs). 1048–1118. Emperor of Byzantium (1081–1118) whose reign was marked by the First Crusade (1096–99).

al•fal•fa (ăl-făl′fə) *n.* A southwest Asian perennial herb *(Medicago sativa)* with compound leaves and clusters of usu. blue-violet flowers, cultivated as a pasture and hay crop. [Sp. < Ar. *al-faṣfaṣah.*]

Al Fay•yam (äl′ fä-o͞om′, fī-, ĕl′). A city of N Egypt on the Nile R. SSW of Cairo. Pop. 218,500.

Al•fie•ri (ăl-fē-âr′ē, äl-fyâr′ē), Conte **Vittorio.** 1749–1803. Italian playwright and poet whose works influenced Italian nationalism.

al•fil•a•ri•a or **al•fil•e•ri•a** (ăl-fĭl′ə-rē′ə) *n.* An annual Mediterranean plant *(Erodium cicutarium)* having pinnately dissected leaves and small pink or purple flowers and used for spring forage in the western United States. [Am.Sp. *alfilerillo*, any of various cacti < Sp., dim. of *alfiler*, pin < Ar. *al-ḫilal*, the thorn : *al*, the + *ḫilal*, thorn.]

Al•föld (ôl′föld) also **Great Alföld.** An extensive plain of central Hungary extending into N Serbia and W Romania. The **Little Alföld** lies in NW Hungary and S Slovakia.

Al•fon•so I (ăl-fŏn′sō, -zō). 1110?–85. King of Portugal (1139–85) who won Portuguese independence from Castile (1139).

Alfonso XIII. 1886–1941. King of Spain (1886–1931) who abdicated on the establishment of a republican government.

Al•fred (ăl′frĭd). "the Great." 849–899. King of the West Saxons (871–899) noted as a scholar and lawmaker.

al•fres•co (ăl-frĕs′kō) *adv.* In the fresh air: *dining alfresco.* — *adj.* Taking place outdoors: *an alfresco conference.* [Ital. *al fresco*, in the fresh (air) : *a il*, in the + *fresco*, fresh.]

alg. *abbr. Math.* Algebra.

Alg. *abbr.* Algeria.

al•ga (ăl′gə) *n., pl.* **-gae** (-jē). Any of various chiefly aquatic, eukaryotic, photosynthetic organisms, ranging from single-celled forms to the giant kelp. [Lat., seaweed.] — **al′gal** (ăl′gəl) *adj.*

alga
Irish moss
Chondrus crispus

al•gar•ro•ba or **al•ga•ro•ba** (ăl′gə-rō′bə) *n.* **1.** See **mesquite** b. **2.** See **carob** 2. **3.** The edible pod of either the mesquite or the carob tree. [Sp. < Ar. *al-ḫarrūbah*: *al*, the + *ḫarrūbah*, carob.]

Al•gar•ve (äl-gär′və). A medieval Moorish kingdom in present-day S Portugal.

al•ge•bra (ăl′jə-brə) *n. Math.* **1.** A generalization of arithmetic in which symbols, usu. letters, represent numbers or members of a set of numbers to which the same operations apply. **2.** A set together with operations defined in the set that obey specified laws. [ME, bone-setting, and Ital., algebra, both < Med. Lat. < Ar. *al-jabr*, the (science of) reuniting : *al*, the + *jabr*, reunification, bone-setting.] — **al′ge•bra′ist** (-brā′ĭst) *n.*

al•ge•bra•ic (ăl′jə-brā′ĭk) *adj. Math.* **1.** Of or relating to algebra. **2.** Of or relating to an expression, an equation, or a function in which only numbers, variables, and a finite number of arithmetic operations are contained or used. — **al′ge•bra′i•cal•ly** *adv.*

algebraic number *n. Math.* A number that is a root of a polynomial equation with rational coefficients.

Al•ge•ci•ras (ăl′jĭ-sîr′əs, äl′hĕ-thē′räs). A city of S Spain on the **Bay of Algeciras** opposite Gibraltar. Pop. 92,474.

Al•ger (ăl′jər), **Horatio.** 1832–99. Amer. writer of inspirational adventure books, such as *Ragged Dick* (1867).

Al•ge•ri•a (ăl-jîr′ē-ə). A country of NW Africa on the Mediterranean; gained independence from France in 1962. Cap. Algiers. Pop. 16,948,000. — **Al•ge′ri•an** *adj. & n.*

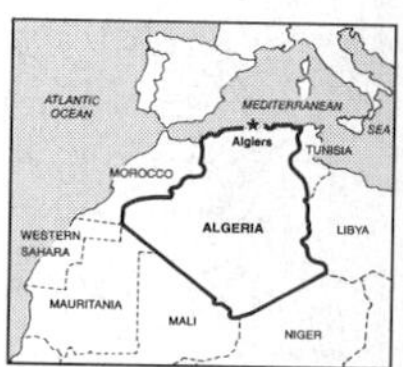

Algeria

-algia *suff.* Pain: *neuralgia.* [Gk. < *algos*, pain.]

al•gi•cide (ăl′jĭ-sīd′) *n.* A substance used to kill or inhibit the growth of algae. [ALG(A) + -CIDE.]

al•gid (ăl′jĭd) *adj.* Cold; chilly. [Lat. *algidus* < *algēre*, to be cold.] — **al•gid′i•ty** (-jĭd′ĭ-tē) *n.*

Al•giers (ăl-jîrz′). The cap. of Algeria, in the N on the **Bay of Algiers**, an arm of the Mediterranean. Pop. 1,523,000.

al•gin (ăl′jĭn) *n.* Any of several derivatives of a gelatinous substance extracted from brown algae and widely used to thicken, stabilize, emulsify, or suspend. [ALG(A) + -IN.]

algo– *pref.* Pain: *algophobia.* [< Gk. *algos*, pain.]

al•goid (ăl′goid′) *adj.* Of or resembling algae.

Al•gol (ăl′gŏl′, -gôl′) *n.* A double, eclipsing variable star in the constellation Perseus. [Ar. *al-ġūl*: *al*, the + *ġūl*, ghoul; see GHOUL.]

AL•GOL also **Al•gol** (ăl′gŏl′, -gôl′) *n. Comp. Sci.* An algebraic computer language for solving problems using algorithms. [*alg(orithmic)-o(riented) l(anguage).*]

al•go•lag•ni•a (ăl′gō-lăg′nē-ə) *n.* Sexual gratification derived from inflicting or experiencing pain. [NLat. : ALGO- + Gk. *lagneia*, lust (< *lagnos*, lustful; see **slēg-***).] — **al′go•lag′nic** *adj.* — **al′go•lag′nist** *n.*

al•gol•o•gy (ăl-gŏl′ə-jē) *n.* See **phycology.** [ALG(A) + -LOGY.] — **al′go•log′i•cal** (ăl′gə-lŏj′ĭ-kəl) *adj.* — **al′go•log′i•cal•ly** *adv.* — **al•gol′o•gist** *n.*

Al•gon•ki•an (ăl-gŏng′kē-ən) *n., pl.* **Algonkian** or **-ans.** *Geol.* Late Proterozoic. [After the *Algonkin* Indians,. See ALGONQUIN.]

Al•gon•qui•an (ăl-gŏng′kwē-ən, -kē-ən) also **Al•gon•ki•an** (-kē-ən) *n., pl.* **Algonquian** or **-ans** also **Algonkian** or **-ans. 1.** A family of North American Indian languages spoken from Labrador to the Carolinas between the Atlantic coast and the Rocky Mountains. **2.** A member of a people traditionally speaking an Algonquian language. [< ALGONQUIN.] — **Al•gon′qui•an** *adj.*

ă pat	oi boy
ā pay	ou out
âr care	o͝o took
ä father	o͞o boot
ĕ pet	ŭ cut
ē be	ûr urge
ĭ pit	th thin
ī pie	*th* this
îr pier	hw which
ŏ pot	zh vision
ō toe	ə about, item
ô paw	

Stress marks:
′ (primary);
′ (secondary), as in
dictionary (dĭk′shə-nĕr′ē)

Al•gon•quin (ăl-gŏng′kwĭn, -kĭn) also **Al•gon•kin** (-kĭn) *n., pl.* **Algonquin** or **-quins** also **Algonkin** or **-kins. 1.** A member of any of various Native American peoples inhabiting the Ottawa River valley of Quebec and Ontario. **2.** Any of the varieties of Ojibwa spoken by the Algonquin. [Canadian Fr.]

al•go•pho•bi•a (ăl′gə-fō′bē-ə) *n.* An abnormal fear of pain.

al•go•rism (ăl′gə-rĭz′əm) *n.* **1.** The Arabic system of numeration; the decimal system. **2.** Computation with Arabic figures. [ME *algorisme* < OFr. < Med.Lat. *algorismus*, after Muhammad ibn-Musa al- KHWARIZMI.]

al•go•rithm (ăl′gə-rĭth′əm) *n. Math.* A step-by-step problem-solving procedure, esp. an established, recursive computational procedure with a finite number of steps. [Var. (prob. influenced by ARITHMETIC) of ALGORISM.] **— al′go•rith′mic** (-rĭth′mĭk) *adj.*

algorithmic language *n. Comp. Sci.* A programming language in which an algorithm can be expressed accurately.

al•gor mor•tis (ăl′gər môr′tĭs) *n.* The cooling of the body after death. [Lat. *algor*, coolness + *mortis*, genitive of *mors*, death.]

Muhammad Ali

Al•gren (ôl′grĭn), **Nelson.** 1909–81. Amer. writer whose works include *The Man with the Golden Arm* (1949).

Al•ham•bra[1] (ăl-hăm′brə). A citadel overlooking Granada, Spain; built by Moorish kings in the 12th and 13th cent.

Alhambra[2]. A city of S CA, a suburb of Los Angeles. Pop. 82,106.

Al Hil•lah (ăl hĭl′ə, ĕl). A city of central Iraq S of Baghdad; built c. 1100. Pop. 215,249.

A•li (ä-lē′). 600?–661. Muslim caliph (656–661) after whose assassination Islam was divided into Sunnite and Shiite sects.

Ali, Muhammad. Cassius Marcellus Clay. b. 1942. Amer. prizefighter who won the world heavyweight title (1964, 1974, and 1978).

A•li•ák•mon (äl-yäk′môn, ä′lē-äk′-). A river, c. 322 km (200 mi), of N Greece.

a•li•as (ā′lē-əs, āl′yəs) *n.* **1.** An assumed name: *worked under an alias.* **2.** *Electron.* A false signal in telecommunication links from beats between signal frequency and sampling frequency. *— adv.* Also known as: *Johnson, alias Johns.* [Lat., otherwise < *alius*, other. See **al-[1]***.]

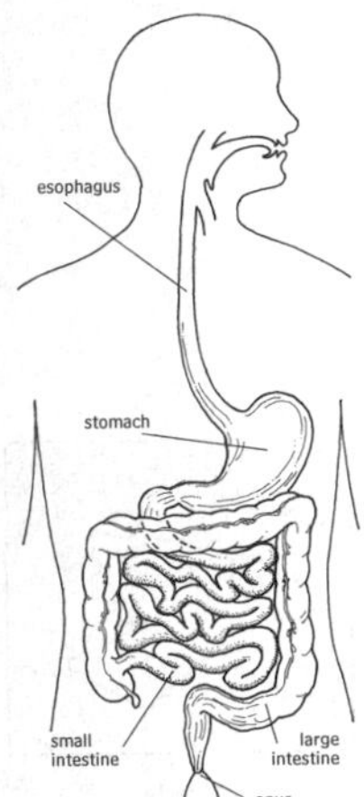

alimentary canal

A•li Ba•ba (ä′lē bä′bə, ăl′ē) *n.* A poor woodcutter in the *Arabian Nights* who enters a thieves' treasure cave by saying "Open, Sesame!"

al•i•bi (ăl′ə-bī′) *n., pl.* **-bis. 1.** *Law.* **a.** A form of defense whereby a defendant attempts to prove absence from the scene of the crime. **b.** The fact of absence when a crime was committed. **2.** *Usage Problem.* An explanation offered to avoid blame or justify action; an excuse. *— intr.v.* **-bied, -bi•ing, -bis.** *Usage Problem.* To make an excuse for oneself. [Lat., elsewhere : *alius*, other; see **al-[1]*** + *ubi*, where; see **kʷo-***.]

Usage Note: *Alibi* (noun) in its nonlegal sense of "an excuse" is acceptable in written usage to almost half of the Usage Panel. As an intransitive verb (*They never alibi*), it is unacceptable in written usage to a large majority of the Panel.

al•i•ble (ăl′ə-bəl) *adj.* Having nutrients; nourishing. [Lat. *alibilis* < *alere*, to nourish. See **al-[2]***.]

Al•i•can•te (ăl′ĭ-kăn′tē, ä′lē-kän′tĕ). A city of SE Spain on the Mediterranean Sea S of Valencia. Pop. 253,722.

Al•ice (ăl′ĭs). A city of S TX W of Corpus Christi. Pop. 19,788.

Alice Springs. A town of central Australia. Pop. 22,000.

al•i•cy•clic (ăl′ĭ-sī′klĭk, -sĭk′lĭk) *adj.* Of or relating to organic compounds having both aliphatic and cyclic characteristics or structures. [ALI(PHATIC) + CYCLIC.]

al•i•dade (ăl′ĭ-dād′) also **al•i•dad** (-dăd′) *n.* **1.** An indicator or a sighting apparatus on a plane table for angular measurement. **2.** A topographic surveying and mapping instrument for determining directions, consisting of a telescope and attached parts. [Fr. < Med.Lat. *alidada*, sighting rod < Ar. *al-'iḍādah*, the revolving radius of a circle < *'aḍud*, humerus.]

a•li•en (ā′lē-ən, āl′yən) *adj.* **1.** Owing political allegiance to another country or government; foreign: *alien residents.* **2.** Belonging to, characteristic of, or constituting another and very different place, society, or person; strange. **3.** Dissimilar, inconsistent, or opposed: *emotions alien to her temperament.* *— n.* **1.** An unnaturalized foreign resident of a country. **2.** A person from another and very different family, people, or place. **3.** A person not included in a group; an outsider. **4.** A creature from outer space: *an invasion of aliens.* **5.** *Ecol.* A plant or an animal in a region to which it is not native. *— tr.v.* **-ened, -en•ing, -ens.** *Law.* To transfer (property) to another; alienate. [ME < OFr. < Lat. *aliēnus* < *alius*, other. See **al-[1]***.] **— al′ien•a•bil′i•ty** *n.* **— al′•ien•a•ble** *adj.* **— al′ien•ee′** *n.*

al•ien•ate (āl′yə-nāt′, ā′lē-ə-) *tr.v.* **-at•ed, -at•ing, -ates. 1.** To make unfriendly or hostile; estrange. **2.** To make withdrawn or unresponsive; isolate or dissociate emotionally: *The numbing labor alienated the workers.* **3.** To cause to be transferred; turn away: *alienate someone's affections.* **4.** *Law.* To transfer (property or a right) to another, esp. by an act of the owner rather than by inheritance. [Lat. *aliēnāre*, *aliēnāt-* < Lat. *aliēnus*, alien. See ALIEN.] **— al′ien•a′tor** *n.*

al•ien•a•tion (āl′yə-nā′shən, ā′lē-ə-) *n.* **1.** The act of alienating or the condition of being alienated. **2.** Emotional isolation or dissociation. **3.** *Psychol.* A state of estrangement between the self and the objective world or between different parts of the personality. **4.** *Law.* The act of propery transfer.

a•li•form (ā′lə-fôrm′, ăl′ə-) *adj. Biol.* Shaped like a wing; alar. [Lat. *āla*, wing + -FORM.]

A•li•garh (ăl′ĭ-gär′, ä′lē-gŭr′). A city of N-central India SE of Delhi. Pop. 320,861.

a•light[1] (ə-līt′) *intr.v.* **a•light•ed** or **a•lit** (ə-lĭt′), **a•light•ing, a•lights. 1.** To land, as after flight: *a sparrow alighting on a branch.* **2.** To set down, as from a vehicle; dismount: *alight from a carriage.* **3.** To come by chance: *alight on a solution.* [ME *alighten* < OE *ālīhtan*: *ā-*, intensive pref. + *līhtan*, to relieve of a burden (< *līht*, light; see LIGHT[2]).]

a•light[2] (ə-līt′) *adj.* **1.** Burning; lighted. **2.** Illuminated: *The sky was alight with stars.* [ME, p.part. of *alighten*, to set on fire < OE *ālīhtan*, to illuminate : *ā-*, intensive pref. + *līhtan*, to shine (< *lēoht*, a light; see LIGHT[1]).] **— a•light′** *adv.*

a•lign also **a•line** (ə-līn′) *— v.* **a•ligned, a•lign•ing, a•ligns** also **a•lined, a•lin•ing, a•lines.** *— tr.* **1.** To arrange in a line or make parallel: *align the car with the curb.* **2.** To adjust to produce a proper relationship or orientation: *align the truck wheels.* **3.** To ally (oneself, for example) with one party or cause: *aligned themselves with the traders.* *— intr.* To fall into line. [Fr. *aligner* < OFr. : *a-*, to (< Lat. *ad-*; see AD-) + *ligne*, line (< Lat. *līnea*; see LINE[1]).] **— a•lign′er** *n.*

a•lign•ment also **a•line•ment** (ə-līn′mənt) *n.* **1.** Linear or parallel positioning. **2.a.** The process of adjusting parts so that they are in proper relative position: *Gears need alignment.* **b.** The condition of having parts so adjusted. **3.** A ground plan: *Building blueprints include an alignment.* **4.** The act of aligning or the condition of being aligned.

a•like (ə-līk′) *adj.* Resembling closely; similar: *The twins are alike.* *— adv.* In the same manner or to the same degree: *They dress alike.* [ME *alich* (influenced by ON *ālīkr*), blend of *ilich* (< OE *gelīc*) and *anlich* (< OE *onlīc*; see **līk-***).] **— a•like′ness** *n.*

al•i•ment (ăl′ə-mənt) *n.* **1.** Something that nourishes; food. **2.** Something that supports or sustains. *— tr.v.* (-mĕnt′) **-ment•ed, -ment•ing, -ments.** To provide sustenance, such as food. [ME < Lat. *alimentum* < *alere*, to nourish. See **al-[2]***.] **— al′i•men′tal** (-mĕn′tl) *adj.* **— al′i•men′tal•ly** *adv.*

al•i•men•ta•ry (ăl′ə-mĕn′tə-rē, -trē) *adj.* **1.** Concerned with food, nutrition, or digestion. **2.** Providing nourishment.

alimentary canal *n.* The mucous membrane-lined tube of the digestive system extending from the mouth to the anus and including the pharynx, esophagus, stomach, and intestines.

al•i•men•ta•tion (ăl′ə-mĕn-tā′shən) *n.* **1.** The act or process of giving or receiving nourishment. **2.** Support; sustenance. **— al′i•men′ta•tive** (-tə-tĭv) *adj.*

al•i•mo•ny (ăl′ə-mō′nē) *n., pl.* **-nies. 1.** *Law.* An allowance for support made under court order to a divorced or separated person by the former partner, usu. the chief provider prior to separation. **2.** A means of livelihood; maintenance. [Lat. *alimōnia*, sustenance < *alere*, to nourish. See **al-[2]***.]

A-line (ā′līn′) *adj.* Having a fitted top and a flared bottom: *an A-line dress.* [From garments being shaped like a capital *A.*]

al•i•phat•ic (ăl′ə-făt′ĭk) *adj.* Of or relating to a group of organic chemical compounds with carbon atoms linked in open chains. [< Gk. *aleiphar*, *aleiphat-*, oil < *aleiphein*, to anoint with oil. See **leip-***.]

al•i•quot (ăl′ĭ-kwŏt′, -kwət) *Math.* *— adj.* Of or relating to an exact divisor of a quantity, esp. of an integer. *— n.* An aliquot part. [Lat. *aliquot*, some number : *alius*, some; see **al-[1]*** + *quot*, how many; see **kʷo-***.]

a•lit (ə-lĭt′) *v.* A p.t. and p.part. of **alight[1]**.

a•live (ə-līv′) *adj.* **1.** Having life; living. **2.** In existence or operation; active: *keep hopes alive.* **3.** Full of living or moving things: *a pool alive with trout.* **4.** Active; animated; lively: *a face alive with mischief.* **— *idiom.* alive to.** Aware of; sensitive to. [ME : *a-*, in a specified state; see A-[2] + *live*, life (< OE *līf*; see LIFE).] **— a•live′ness** *n.*

a•li•yah (ä′lē-ä′, ə-lē′ə) *n., pl.* **al•li•yot** (ä′lē-ōt′) or **a•li•yahs** (ə-lē′əz). **1.** Immigration of Jews to Israel. **2.** Going up to the Torah to recite the blessings for the Torah reading. [Heb. *'alīyâ*, ascent.]

a•liz•a•rin (ə-lĭz′ər-ĭn) also **a•liz•a•rine** (-ĭn, -ə-rēn′) *n.* An orange-red crystalline compound, $C_{14}H_6O_2(OH)_2$, used in making dyes. [Fr. *alizarine* < *alizari*, madder root < Sp., prob. < Ar. *al-'aṣārah*, the juice : *al*, the + *'aṣārah*, juice (< *'aṣara*, to squeeze).]

al•ka•hest (ăl′kə-hĕst′) *n.* The hypothetical universal solvent sought by alchemists. [Med.Lat. *alchahest.*]

al•ka•les•cent (ăl′kə-lĕs′ənt) *adj.* Becoming alkaline; slightly alkaline. [ALKAL(I) + -ESCENT.] **— al′ka•les′cence, al′ka•les′cen•cy** *n.*

al•ka•li (ăl′kə-lī′) *n., pl.* **-lis** or **-lies.** *Chem.* **1.** A carbonate or hydroxide of an alkali metal, the aqueous solution of which is bitter, slippery, caustic, and usu. basic in reactions. **2.** Any of various soluble mineral salts found in natural water and arid soils. **3.** Alkali metal. [ME, alkaline substance from calcined plant ashes < Med.Lat. < Ar. *al-qalīy*, the ashes of saltwort : *al*, the + *qalīy*, ashes (< *qalā*, to fry).]

alkali metal *n.* Any of a group of soft, white, low-density, low-melting, highly reactive metallic elements, including lithium, sodium, potassium, rubidium, cesium, and francium.

al•ka•lim•e•ter (ăl′kə-lĭm′ĭ-tər) *n.* An apparatus for measuring alkalinity. **—al′ka•lim′e•try** *n.*

al•ka•line (ăl′kə-lĭn, -līn′) *adj.* **1.** Of, relating to, or containing an alkali. **2.** Having a pH greater than 7.

alkaline earth *n.* An oxide of an alkaline-earth metal.

al•ka•line-earth metal (ăl′kə-lĭn-ûrth′, -līn′-) *n.* Any of the metallic elements, esp. calcium, strontium, magnesium, barium, and usu. beryllium and radium.

al•ka•lin•i•ty (ăl′kə-lĭn′ĭ-tē) *n.* The alkali concentration or alkaline quality of an alkali-containing substance.

al•ka•lize (ăl′kə-līz′) also **al•ka•lin•ize** (-lə-nīz′) — *v.* **-lized, -liz•ing, -liz•es** also **-ized, -iz•ing, -iz•es.** — *tr.* To make alkaline. — *intr.* To become an alkali. **—al′ka•li•za′tion** (-lĭ-zā′shən) *n.*

al•ka•loid (ăl′kə-loid′) *n.* Any of various nitrogenous organic compounds occurring chiefly in vascular plants and often having toxic, stimulant, or analgesic properties. [ALKAL(I) + -OID.] **—al′ka•loi′dal** (-loid′l) *adj.*

al•ka•lo•sis (ăl′kə-lō′sĭs) *n.* Abnormally high alkalinity of the body fluids. [ALKAL(I) + -OSIS.] **—al′ka•lot′ic** (-lŏt′ĭk) *adj.*

al•kane (ăl′kān′) *n.* Any member of the alkane series. [ALK(YL) + (METH)ANE.]

alkane series *n.* *Chem.* A group of saturated open-chain hydrocarbons having the general formula C_nH_{2n+2}, the most abundant of which is methane.

al•kene (ăl′kēn′) *n.* Any of a series of unsaturated, open chain hydrocarbons with one or more carbon-carbon double bonds, having the general formula C_nH_{2n}. [ALK(YL) + -ENE.]

Alk•maar (älk′mär′). A town of N Netherlands NNW of Amsterdam; chartered 1254. Pop. 83,892.

al•ky (ăl′kē) *n.*, *pl.* **-kies.** *Slang.* An alcoholic. [Shortening and alteration of ALCOHOLIC + -Y[3].]

alky. *abbr.* Alkalinity.

al•kyd (ăl′kĭd) *n.* A widely used durable synthetic resin derived from glycerol and phthalic anhydride. [ALKY(L) + (ACI)D.]

al•kyl (ăl′kəl) *n.* *Chem.* A monovalent radical, such as ethyl, having the general formula C_nH_{2n+1}. [Ger. *Alkohol*, alcohol (< Med.Lat. *alcohol*, antimony; see ALCOHOL) + -YL.]

al•kyl•ate (ăl′kə-lāt′) *tr.v.* **-at•ed, -at•ing, -ates.** *Chem.* To add one or more alkyl groups to (a compound).

al•kyl•a•tion (ăl′kə-lā′shən) *n.* *Chem.* A process in which an alkyl group is added to or substituted in a compound, as in the reaction of alkenes with alkanes to make high-octane fuels.

al•kyne also **al•kine** (ăl′kīn′) *n.* Any of a series of open chain hydrocarbons with a carbon-carbon triple bond and the general formula C_nH_{2n-2}. [ALKY(L) + -(I)NE[2].]

all (ôl) *adj.* **1.** Being or representing the entire number, amount, or quantity: *All the windows are open.* See Syns at **whole. 2.** Constituting, being, or representing the total extent or the whole. **3.** Being the utmost possible of: *in all seriousness.* **4.** Every. **5.** Any whatsoever: *beyond all doubt.* **6.** *Pennsylvania.* Finished; used up: *The apples are all.* See Regional Note at **gum band. 7.** *Informal.* Being more than one: *Who all came?* See Regional Note at **you-all.** — *n.* The whole of one's resources or energy; everything one has: *They gave their all.* — *pron.* **1.** The entire number, amount, or quantity; totality. **2.** Everyone; everything: *justice for all.* — *adv.* **1.** Wholly; completely: *all wrong.* **2.** Each; apiece: *five all.* **3.** So much: *all the better.* **—*idioms.* all along.** From the beginning; throughout. **all but.** Nearly; almost: *all but crying with relief.* **all in.** Tired; exhausted. **all in all.** Everything being taken into account: *All in all, it seemed fair.* **all of.** *Informal.* Not more than: *all of five minutes.* **all that.** *Informal.* To the degree expected. **at all. 1.** In any way. **2.** To any extent. [ME *al* < OE *eall.* See **al-**[3*].]

all– *pref.* Var. of **allo–.**

al•la breve (ăl′ə brĕv′, ä′lə brĕv′ā) *adv.* & *adj.* *Mus.* In duple or quadruple meter with the half note being the unit of time. [Ital. : *alla*, according to the + *breve*, breve.]

Al•lah (ăl′ə, ä′lə) *n.* God, esp. in Islam. [Ar. *Allāh.*]

Al•la•ha•bad (ăl′ə-hə-băd′, ä′lə-hə-bäd′). A city of N-central India E of Varanasi; a pilgrimage site for Hindus. Pop. 616,051.

Al•lais (ä-lā′), **Maurice.** b. 1911. French economist who won a 1988 Nobel Prize.

all-A•mer•i•can (ôl′ə-mĕr′ĭ-kən) *adj.* **1.** Typical or representative of the people of the United States or their ideals. **2.** *Sports.* Chosen as the best United States amateur at a particular position or event. **3.** Composed entirely of people or materials from the United States. **4.** Of all the American nations: *an all-American conference.* — *n.* Often **All-American.** An all-American athlete.

al•lan•toid (ə-lăn′toid′) also **al•lan•toi•dal** (ăl′ən-toid′l) — *adj.* **1.** Of or having an allantois. **2.** Shaped like a sausage. — *n.* See **allantois.** [NLat. *allantoīdes.* See ALLANTOIS.]

al•lan•to•in (ə-lăn′tō-ĭn) *n.* A crystalline oxidation product, $C_4H_6N_4O_3$, of uric acid that is the metabolic end product of vertebrate purine oxidation and promotes tissue growth. [ALLANTO(IS) + -IN.]

al•lan•to•is (ə-lăn′tō-ĭs) *n.*, *pl.* **al•lan•to•i•des** (ăl′ən-tō′ĭ-dēz′). A membranous sac in the embryos of mammals, birds, and reptiles that helps form the umbilical cord and placenta in mammals. [NLat. < *allantoīdes* < Gk. *allantoeidēs*, sausage-shaped : *allas, allant-*, sausage + *-oeidēs*, -oid.] **—al′lan•to′ic** (ăl′ən-tō′ĭk) *adj.*

al•lar•gan•do (ä′lär-gän′dō) *adv.* & *adj.* *Mus.* In a gradually broadening style and slowing tempo. [Ital., pr.part. of *allargare*, to broaden : *al-*, to (< Lat. *ad-*; see AD–) + *largare*, to broaden (< *largo*, broad < Lat. *largus*).]

all-a•round (ôl′ə-round′) also **all-round** (ôl′round′) *adj.* **1.** Comprehensive in extent or depth. **2.** Able to do many things well; versatile.

al•lay (ə-lā′) *tr.v.* **-layed, -lay•ing, -lays. 1.** To reduce the intensity of; relieve: *allay back pains.* See Syns at **relieve. 2.** To calm or pacify; set to rest: *allay fears.* [ME *aleien* < OE *ālecgan*, to lay down : *ā-*, intensive pref. + *lecgan*, to lay; see LAY[1].] **—al•lay′er** *n.*

all clear *n.* A signal, usu. by siren, that a danger has passed.

al•le•ga•tion (ăl′ĭ-gā′shən) *n.* **1.** Something affirmed; an assertion. **2.** The act of alleging. **3.** An unproven assertion: *The charges were mere allegations.* **4.** *Law.* An assertion that must be proved or supported with evidence. [Fr. *allégation* < Lat. *allēgātiō, allēgātiōn-* < *allēgātus*, p.part. of *allēgāre*, to dispatch, adduce : *ad-*, ad- + *lēgāre*, to depute; see LEGATE.]

al•lege (ə-lĕj′) *tr.v.* **-leged, -leg•ing, -leg•es. 1.** To assert; affirm: *alleged innocence.* **2.** To assert without or before proof: *The indictment alleges bribery.* **3.** To state in support or denial of a claim or accusation: *allege insanity.* **4.** *Archaic.* To present as an authority. [ME *alleggen* < OFr. *alegier*, to vindicate, justify (influenced by *aleguer*, to give a reason) < *esligier*, to pay a fine, justify oneself < LLat. **exlītigāre*, to clear at law : Lat. *ex-*, out; see EX– + Lat. *lītigāre*, to sue; see LITIGATE.] **—al•lege′a•ble** *adj.* **—al•leg′er** *n.*

al•leged (ə-lĕjd′, ə-lĕj′ĭd) *adj.* Represented in a certain way without proof; supposed. **—al•leg′ed•ly** (ə-lĕj′ĭd-lē) *adv.*

Usage Note: In their zeal to protect the rights of the accused, newspapers and law enforcement officials sometimes misuse *alleged.* A man arrested for murder may be only an *alleged* murderer, for example, because no charge has been proved, but he is a real, not an *alleged*, suspect in that his status as a suspect is not in doubt. Similarly, if the money from a safe is known to have been stolen and not merely mislaid, then we may safely speak of a theft without having to qualify our description with *alleged.*

Al•le•ghe•ny Mountains (ăl′ĭ-gā′nē) also **Al•le•ghe•nies** (-nēz). A range forming the W part of the Appalachian Mts., extending from N PA to SW VA and rising to c. 1,483 m (4,862 ft).

Allegheny River. A river rising in N-central PA and flowing c. 523 km (325 mi) to join the Monongahela at Pittsburgh and form the Ohio R.

al•le•giance (ə-lē′jəns) *n.* **1.** Loyalty or the obligation of loyalty, as to a cause. **2.** The obligations of a vassal. [ME *alligeaunce*, alteration of *ligeaunce* < OFr. *ligeance* < *lige*, liege. See LIEGE.] **—al•le′giant** *adj.*

al•le•gor•i•cal (ăl′ĭ-gôr′ĭ-kəl, -gŏr′-) also **al•le•gor•ic** (-ĭk) *adj.* Of, like, characteristic of, or containing allegory. **—al′le•gor′i•cal•ly** *adv.*

al•le•go•rize (ăl′ĭ-gô-rīz′, -gō-, -gə-) *v.* **-rized, -riz•ing, -riz•es.** — *tr.* **1.** To express as an allegory. **2.** To interpret allegorically. — *intr.* To use allegory. **—al′le•go′ri•za′tion** (-gôr′ĭ-zā′shən, -gŏr′-, -gŏr′-) *n.* **—al′le•go•riz′er** *n.*

al•le•go•ry (ăl′ĭ-gôr′ē, -gŏr′ē) *n.*, *pl.* **-ries. 1.a.** The use of characters or events to represent ideas or principles in a story, play, or picture. **b.** A story, picture, or play in which such representation occurs. **2.** A symbolic representation. [ME *allegorie* < Lat. *allēgoria* < Gk. < *allēgorein*, to interpret allegorically : *allos*, other; see **al-**[1*] + *agoreuein*, to speak publicly (< *agora*, marketplace; see **ger-***).] **—al′le•go′rist** *n.*

al•le•gret•to (ăl′ĭ-grĕt′ō, ä′lĭ-) *Mus.* — *adv.* & *adj.* In a moderately quick tempo. — *n.*, *pl.* **-tos.** An allegretto passage or movement. [Ital., dim. of *allegro*, allegro. See ALLEGRO.]

al•le•gro (ə-lĕg′rō, ə-lā′grō) *Mus.* — *adv.* & *adj.* In a quick, lively tempo. — *n.*, *pl.* **-gros.** An allegro passage or movement. [Ital. < Lat. *alacer*, lively.]

al•lele (ə-lēl′) *n.* One member of a pair or series of genes that occupy a specific position on a specific chromosome. [Ger. *Allel*, short for *Allelomorph*, allelomorph. See ALLELOMORPH.] **—al•le′lic** (ə-lē′lĭk, ə-lĕl′ĭk) *adj.* **—al•le′lism** *n.*

al•le•lo•morph (ə-lē′lə-môrf′, ə-lĕl′ə-) *n.* An allele. [Gk. *allēlōn*, mutually (< *allos*, other; see **al-**[1*]) + -MORPH.] **—al•le′lo•mor′phic** *adj.* **—al•le′lo•mor′phism** *n.*

al•le•lop•a•thy (ə-lē-lŏp′ə-thē, ăl′ə-) *n.* The inhibition of growth in one species of plants by chemicals from another species. [Gk. *allēlōn*, reciprocally (< *allos*, another; see **al-**[1*]) + -PATHY.] **—al•le′lo•path′ic** (ə-lē′lə-păth′ĭk, ə-lĕl′ə-) *adj.*

al•le•lu•ia (ăl′ə-lōō′yə) *interj.* Hallelujah. [ME < Med.Lat.

ă pat	oi boy
ā pay	ou out
âr care	ŏŏ took
ä father	ōō boot
ĕ pet	ŭ cut
ē be	ûr urge
ĭ pit	th thin
ī pie	*th* this
îr pier	hw which
ŏ pot	zh vision
ō toe	ə about, item
ô paw	

Stress marks:
′ (primary);
′ (secondary), as in **dictionary** (dĭk′shə-nĕr′ē)

alleluia < LGk. *allelouia* < Heb. *hallĕlûyāh*, praise God. See HALLELUJAH.]

al•le•mande (ăl′ə-mănd′, -mänd′, ăl′ə-mănd′, -mänd′) *n.* **1.a.** A stately 16th-century dance in 2/2 time. **b.** A composition written to or as if to accompany this dance, often beginning a suite. **2.** A lively late 18th-century dance in 3/4 time. [Fr., fem. of *allemand*, German < Lat. *Alemanni*, an ancient Germanic tribe. See ALEMANNI.]

Al•len (ăl′ən), **Ethan.** 1738–89. Amer. Revolutionary soldier whose Green Mountain Boys helped capture Fort Ticonderoga (1775).

Allen, Frederick Lewis. 1890–1954. Amer. editor and historian whose works include *The Big Change* (1952).

Allen, Grace Ethel Cecile Rosalie. "Gracie." 1906–64. Amer. comedienne best remembered as the confused but unflappable foil to her husband and stage partner, George Burns.

Allen, Richard. 1760–1831. Amer. cleric who was the first bishop of the African Methodist Episcopal Church (1816–31).

Allen, William. 1532–94. English Roman Catholic cardinal who directed the work on the Douay Bible.

Allen, Woody. b. 1935. Amer. actor, writer, and filmmaker whose films include *Annie Hall* (1977).

Gracie Allen

Al•len•by (ăl′ən-bē), 1st Viscount. Edmund Henry Hynman. 1861–1936. British field marshal during World War I.

Al•len•de Gos•sens (ä-yĕn′dā gô′sĕns), **Salvador.** 1908–73. Chilean president (1970–73) who was killed in a coup d'état.

Allen Park. A city of SE MI, a suburb of Detroit. Pop. 31,092.

Al•len•ti•ac (ə-lĕn′tē-ăk′) *n., pl.* **Allentiac** or **-acs. 1.** A member of a South American Indian people inhabiting west-central Argentina. **2.** The extinct language of the Allentiac. [Sp. *alentiaco*.] **—Al•len′ti•ac′** *adj.*

Al•len•town (ăl′ən-toun′). A city of E PA NNW of Philadelphia; founded 1762. Pop. 105,090.

al•ler•gen (ăl′ər-jən) *n.* A substance, such as pollen, that causes an allergy. [Ger. *Allergen*: *Allergie*, allergy; see ALLERGY + *-gen*, -gen.] **—al′ler•gen′ic** (-jĕn′ĭk) *adj.*

al•ler•gic (ə-lûr′jĭk) *adj.* **1.** Of, characterized by, or caused by an allergy. **2.** Having an allergy. **3.** *Informal.* Having a dislike; averse: *allergic to work.*

al•ler•gist (ăl′ər-jĭst) *n.* A physician specializing in the diagnosis and treatment of allergies.

al•ler•gy (ăl′ər-jē) *n., pl.* **-gies. 1.** An abnormally high sensitivity to certain substances, such as pollens or foods, often causing sneezing, itching, and skin rashes. **2.** *Informal.* An aversion; an antipathy: *an allergy to cocktail parties.* [Ger. *Allergie*: Gk. *allos*, other; see ALLO- + Gk. *ergon*, action; see **werg-***.]

al•le•thrin (ăl′ə-thrĭn′) *n.* A synthetic clear or amber-colored viscous insecticide, $C_{19}H_{26}O_3$, similar to pyrethrin. [ALL(YL) + (PYR)ETHRIN.]

Woody Allen
Photographed in 1987

al•le•vi•ate (ə-lē′vē-āt′) *tr.v.* **-at•ed, -at•ing, -ates.** To make more bearable. See Syns at **relieve.** [LLat. *alleviāre, alleviāt-*, to lighten : Lat. *ad-*, ad- + *levis*, light; see **leg^{w}h-***.] **—al•le′vi•a′tion** *n.* **—al•le′vi•a′tor** *n.*

al•le•vi•a•tive (ə-lē′vē-ā′tĭv) also **al•le•vi•a•to•ry** (-ə-tôr′ē, -tōr′ē) *adj.* Reducing pain or severity; palliative.

al•ley[1] (ăl′ē) *n., pl.* **-leys. 1.** A narrow street or passageway between or behind city buildings. **2.** A path between rows or trees in a garden or park. **3.** A straight narrow course or track; a lane. **4.** *Sports.* Either of the parallel lanes on a tennis court, which widen the inbounds area for doubles play. ***—idiom.* up (one's) alley.** *Informal.* Compatible with one's interests or qualifications. [ME *alei* < OFr. *alee* < *aller*, to walk < Lat. *ambulāre*. See AMBULATE.]

al•ley[2] (ăl′ē) *n., pl.* **-leys.** *Games.* A large playing marble, often used as the shooter. [Short for ALABASTER.]

alley cat *n.* A homeless or stray cat.

al•ley•way (ăl′ē-wā′) *n.* A narrow passage between buildings.

all-fired (ôl′fīrd′) *adv. Informal.* Used as an intensive: *Don't be so all-fired aggressive.* [Alteration of *hell-fired*.]

All Fools' Day (ôl fo͞olz) *n.* See **April Fools' Day.**

all fours *pl.n. (used with a sing. v.) Games.* Any of several card games in which points are scored in four ways: for the high trump, the low trump, the jack of trumps, and the game.

all get-out also **all get out** (gĕt′out′) *n. Informal.* The utmost degree imaginable: *raced like all get-out.*

all hail *interj.* Used to express acclamation, a welcome, or a greeting.

All•hal•low•mas (ôl′hăl′ō-məs) *n. Archaic.* All Saints' Day. [ME *Alhalwemesse* < OE *ealra hālgena mæsse*: *ealra*, genitive pl. of *eall*, all; see ALL + *hālgena*, genitive pl. of *hālga*, saint (< *hālig*, holy; see HOLY) + *mæsse*, Mass; see MASS.]

All•hal•lows (ôl′hăl′ōz) *n.* See **All Saints' Day.** [ME *al halwes*: *al*, all; see ALL + *halwes*, pl. of *halwe*, saint (< OE *hālga*; see ALLHALLOWMAS).]

alligator
American alligator
Alligator mississipiensis

all-heal or **all•heal** (ôl′hēl′) *n.* Any of several plants, such as the valerian, once thought to have broad healing powers.

al•li•a•ceous (ăl′ē-ā′shəs) *adj.* Of or resembling onion, garlic, or similar plants of the genus *Allium*, esp. in taste and smell. [Lat. *allium*, garlic + -ACEOUS.]

al•li•ance (ə-lī′əns) *n.* **1.a.** A close association of nations or other groups, formed to advance common interests: *an alliance of labor unions.* **b.** A formal agreement establishing such an association, esp. an international treaty. **2.** A connection based on kinship or marriage. **3.** Close similarity in nature or type; affinity: *the alliance between mathematics and music.* **4.** The act of becoming allied or the condition of being allied. [ME < OFr. *aliance* < *alier*, to ally. See ALLY.]

Al•li•ance (ə-lī′əns). A city of NE OH SW of Youngstown; settled by Quakers in 1805. Pop. 23,376.

al•lied (ə-līd′, ăl′īd′) *adj.* **1.** Joined or united: *allied tribes.* **2.** Similar; related: *art and allied studies.* **3. Allied.** Of or relating to the Allies.

Al•lier (ä-lyā′). A river rising in S-central France and flowing c. 410 km (255 mi) to the Loire R.

al•li•ga•tor (ăl′ĭ-gā′tər) *n.* **1.** Either of two large reptiles, *Alligator mississipiensis* of the southeast United States or *A. sinensis* of China, having sharp teeth, powerful jaws, and a broader, shorter snout than the crocodile. **2.** Leather from the hide of one of these reptiles. **3.** A tool or fastener with strong, adjustable, often toothed jaws. [Alteration of Sp. *el lagarto*, the lizard : *el*, the (< Lat. *ille*, that; see **al-[1]***) + *lagarto*, lizard (< Lat. *lacertus*).]

Word History: In *The Travailes of an Englishman*, published in 1568, Job Hortop says that "in this river we killed a monstrous Lagarto or Crocodile." This is the first recorded instance of *alligator* in English. *Alligator* comes to us from Spanish *el lagarto*, "the lizard," and was modified in pronunciation and form in several ways before taking on the form *alligator*. Such changes, referred to by linguists as taboo deformation, are not uncommon in a name for something that is feared. An interesting parallel case is Spanish *cocodrilo*, "crocodile," which shows a similar change in the position of the *r*. The earliest recorded form of *alligator* that is similar to ours appears in Shakespeare's *Romeo and Juliet* (First Folio, 1623): "In his needie shop a tortoyrs hung/An Allegater stuft."

alligator pear *n.* See **avocado** 1. [By folk ety. < Am.Sp. *aguacate*, avocado (the trees are said to grow in areas infested by alligators). See AGUACATE.]

alligator snapper *n.* See **alligator snapping turtle.**

alligator snapping turtle *n.* A large freshwater snapping turtle *(Macrochelys temmincki)* of the south-central United States, having a rough carapace and powerful hooked jaws.

all-im•por•tant (ôl′ĭm-pôr′tnt) *adj.* Of the greatest importance; crucial. **—all′-im•por′tance** *n.*

all-in•clu•sive (ôl′in-klo͞o′sĭv) *adj.* Including everything; comprehensive.

al•lit•er•ate (ə-lĭt′ə-rāt′) *v.* **-at•ed, -at•ing, -ates.** *—intr.* **1.** To use alliteration in speech or writing. **2.** To have or contain alliteration. *—tr.* To form or arrange with alliteration. [Back-formation < ALLITERATION.]

al•lit•er•a•tion (ə-lĭt′ə-rā′shən) *n.* The repetition of the same sounds, usu. consonants, esp. at the beginning of words, as in *the zany zone.* [< AD- + Lat. *littera*, letter.]

al•lit•er•a•tive (ə-lĭt′ə-rā′tĭv, -ər-ə-) *adj.* Of, showing, or characterized by alliteration. **—al•lit′er•a′tive•ly** *adv.* **—al•lit′er•a′tive•ness** *n.*

al•li•um (ăl′ē-əm) *n.* Any of numerous, usu. bulbous plants of the genus *Allium* in the lily family, with long stalks bearing variously colored flowers and including onions and garlic. [Lat. *allium*, garlic.]

all-night (ôl′nīt′) *adj.* **1.** Continuing all through the night: *an all-night party.* **2.** Open all during the night.

all night•er or **all-night•er** (ôl′nī′tər) *n. Informal.* A project or event lasting all through the night.

allo *abbr.* Allegro.

allo- or **all-** *pref.* **1.** Other; different: *allopatric.* **2.** Isomeric: *allocholesterol.* [Gk. < *allos*, other. See **al-[1]***.]

al•lo•an•ti•bod•y (ăl′ō-ăn′tĭ-bŏd′ē) *n.* See **isoantibody.**

al•lo•an•ti•gen (ăl′ō-ăn′tĭ-jən) *n.* See **isoantigen.**

al•lo•cate (ăl′ə-kāt′) *tr.v.* **-cat•ed, -cat•ing, -cates. 1.** To reserve for a purpose; designate: *allocate room for books.* **2.** To distribute by a plan; allot: *allocate rations.* [Med.Lat. *allocāre, allocāt-* : Lat. *ad-*, ad- + Lat. *locāre*, to place (< *locus*, place).] **—al′lo•ca•ble** (-kə-bəl) *adj.* **—al′lo•ca′tion** *n.*

Syns: *allocate, appropriate, designate, earmark.* The central meaning shared by these verbs is "to set aside for a specified purpose": *allocated time for recreation; appropriated funds for public education; designated a location for the new hospital; money earmarked for a vacation.*

al•lo•cu•tion (ăl′ə-kyo͞o′shən) *n.* A formal authoritative speech; an address. [Lat. *allocūtiō, allocūtiōn-* < *allocūtus*, p.part. of *alloquī*, to speak to : *ad-*, ad- + *loquī*, to speak; see **tolk^w-***.]

al•log•a•my (ə-lŏg′ə-mē) *n. Biol.* See **cross-fertilization** 1.

al•lo•ge•ne•ic (ăl′ə-jə-nē′ĭk) also **al•lo•gen•ic** (-jĕn′ĭk) *adj.* Being genetically different but from the same species. [ALLO- + Gk. *genea*, race; see **genə-*** + -IC.]

al•lo•graft (ăl′ə-grăft′) *n.* A graft of tissue from an allogeneic donor.

al•lo•graph (ăl′ə-grăf′) *n.* **1.** A variant shape of a letter. **2.** A letter or letters that can represent one phoneme, as *f* and *gh* can represent the phoneme /f/. **3.** Writing, esp. a signature, made by one person for another.

al•lom•er•ism (ə-lŏm′ə-rĭz′əm) *n.* Consistency in crystalline form with variation in chemical composition. **—al•lom′er•ous** *adj.*

al•lom•e•try (ə-lŏm′ĭ-trē) *n.* The study of the change in proportion of various parts of an organism as a consequence of growth. **—al′lo•met′ric** (ăl′ə-mĕt′rĭk) *adj.*

al•lo•morph[1] (ăl′ə-môrf′) *n.* See **paramorph.** **—al′lo•mor′phic** *adj.* **—al′lo•mor′phism** *n.*

al•lo•morph[2] (ăl′ə-môrf′) *n.* Any of the variant forms of a morpheme. [ALLO– + MORPH(EME).] **—al′lo•mor′phic** *adj.* **—al′lo•mor′phism** *n.*

al•lo•nym (ăl′ə-nĭm′) *n.* The name of a person, usu. historical, assumed by a writer. [Fr. *allonyme*: Gk. *allos*, other; see ALLO– + Gk. *onoma*, name; see **nŏ-men-*.**] **—al•lon′y•mous** (ə-lŏn′ə-məs) *adj.* **—al•lon′y•mous•ly** *adv.*

al•lo•path (ăl′ə-păth′) also **al•lop•a•thist** (ə-lŏp′ə-thĭst) *n.* One who practices or advocates allopathy.

al•lop•a•thy (ə-lŏp′ə-thē) *n.* A method of treating disease with remedies causing effects different from those of the disease itself. **—al′lo•path′ic** (ăl′ə-păth′ĭk) *adj.* **—al′lo•path′i•cal•ly** *adv.*

al•lo•pat•ric (ăl′ə-păt′rĭk) *adj. Ecol.* Occurring in separate, nonoverlapping geographic areas, esp. when unable to crossbreed because of the separation. [ALLO– + Gk. *patra*, fatherland (< *patēr*, father; see **pəter-***) + –IC.] **—al′lo•pat′ri•cal•ly** *adv.* **—al•lop′a•try** (ə-lŏp′ə-trē) *n.*

al•lo•phane (ăl′ə-fān′) *n.* An amorphous translucent mineral, essentially hydrous aluminum silicate. [< Gk. *allophanēs*, appearing otherwise : *allos*, other; see ALLO– + *phainesthai*, to appear, passive of *phainein*, to show; see FANTASY.]

al•lo•phone (ăl′ə-fōn′) *n. Ling.* A predictable phonetic variant of a phoneme. For example, the aspirated *t* of *top* and the unaspirated *t* of *stop* are allophones of the English phoneme /t/. [ALLO– + PHONE(ME).] **—al′lo•phon′ic** (-fŏn′ĭk) *adj.*

al•lo•pol•y•ploid (ăl′ə-pŏl′ē-ploid′) *adj.* Having three or more complete sets of chromosomes derived from different species. **—al•lo•pol′•y•ploid′** *n.* **—al′lo•pol′y•ploi′dy** *n.*

al•lo•pu•ri•nol (ăl′ō-pyo͝or′ə-nôl′, -nōl′, -nŏl′) *n.* A drug, $C_5H_4N_4O$, used to treat gout because it promotes the excretion of uric acid. [ALLO– + PURIN(E) + –OL[2].]

all-or-none (ôl′ər-nŭn′) *adj.* Characterized by either a complete response or a total lack of response or effect.

all-or-noth•ing (ôl′ər-nŭth′ĭng) *adj.* **1.** Involving either complete success or failure, with no intermediate result. **2.** Refusing to accept less than all demands; uncompromising.

al•lo•ster•ic (ăl′ə-stĕr′ĭk) *adj.* Of or involving molecular binding to an enzyme at a site other than the enzymatically active one. **—al′lo•ster′i•cal•ly** *adv.* **—al•los′ter•y** (ə-lŏs′tə-rē) *n.*

al•lot (ə-lŏt′) *tr.v.* **-lot•ted, -lot•ting, -lots. 1.** To parcel out; distribute or apportion: *allot land.* **2.** To assign as a portion; allocate: *allot time to each speaker.* [ME *alotten* < OFr. *aloter*: *a-*, to (< Lat. *ad-*; see AD–) + *lot*, portion (of Gmc. orig.).] **—al•lot′tee′** *n.* **—al•lot′ter** *n.*

al•lot•ment (ə-lŏt′mənt) *n.* **1.** The act of allotting. **2.** Something allotted. **3.** A portion of military pay regularly deducted and set aside, as for insurance.

al•lo•trans•plant (ăl′ō-trăns′plănt′) *tr.v.* **-plant•ed, -plant•ing, -plants.** To transfer (an organ or body tissue) between two genetically different individuals of the same species. *—n.* An organ or tissue so transferred. **—al′lo•trans′plan•ta′tion** *n.*

al•lo•trope (ăl′ə-trōp′) *n.* A structurally differentiated form of an element that exhibits allotropy. [Back-formation < ALLOTROPY.]

al•lot•ro•py (ə-lŏt′rə-pē) *n.* The existence, esp. in the solid state, of two or more crystalline or molecular structural forms of an element. **—al′lo•trop′ic** (ăl′ə-trŏp′ĭk, -trō′pĭk), **al′lo•trop′i•cal** *adj.* **—al′lo•trop′i•cal•ly** *adv.*

all' ot•ta•va (ăl′ə-tä′və, äl′ō-) *adv. & adj. Mus.* Ottava. [Ital. : *all'*, at the + *ottava*, octave.]

all out *adv.* With every possible effort: *worked all out.*

all-out (ôl′out′) *adj.* Using all available means or resources.

all over *adv.* **1.** Over the whole area or extent: *embroidered all over.* **2.** Everywhere: *searched all over.* **3.** In all respects.

all-o•ver also **all•o•ver** (ôl′ō′vər) *adj.* Covering an entire surface: *wallpaper with an all-over pattern.*

all-o•vers (ôl′ō′vərz) *pl.n. Informal.* A feeling of great unease or extreme nervousness.

al•low (ə-lou′) *v.* **-lowed, -low•ing, -lows.** *—tr.* **1.** To let do or happen; permit: *We allow smoking only in restricted areas.* **2.** To permit the presence of: *No pets allowed.* **3.** To permit to have: *allow oneself a treat.* **4.** To make provision for; assign: *Allow time for a break.* **5.** To plan for in case of need: *allowed room for shrinkage.* **6.** To grant as a discount or in exchange: *allowed me 20 dollars on my old word processor.* **7.** *Chiefly Upper Southern U.S.* **a.** To admit; grant: *I allowed as how he was right.* **b.** To suppose. **c.** To assert. *—intr.* **1.** To offer a possibility; admit: *The poem allows of several interpretations.* **2.** To take a possibility into account; make allowance. [ME *allouen*, to approve, permit < OFr. *allouer* < Lat. *allaudāre*, to praise (*ad-*, intensive pref.; see AD– + *laudāre*, to praise; see LAUD) and < Med.Lat. *allocāre*, to assign; see ALLOCATE.] **—al•low′a•ble** *adj.* **—al•low′a•bly** *adv.*

al•low•ance (ə-lou′əns) *n.* **1.** The act of allowing. **2.** An amount allowed or granted: *a weekly allowance of two eggs.* **3.** Something, such as money, given regularly or for a specific purpose: *a travel allowance.* **4.** A price reduction, esp. in exchange for used merchandise: *an allowance on an old car.* **5.** A consideration for possibilities or modifying circumstances: *made allowances for rush-hour traffic.* **6.** An allowed difference in dimension of closely mating machine parts. *—tr.v.* **-anced, -anc•ing, -anc•es. 1.** To put on a fixed allowance. **2.** To dispense in fixed quantities; ration.

al•low•ed•ly (ə-lou′ĭd-lē) *adv.* By general admission.

al•loy (ăl′oi′, ə-loi′) *n.* **1.** A homogeneous mixture or solid solution of two or more metals, the atoms of one replacing or occupying interstitial positions between the atoms of the other. **2.** A mixture; an amalgam. **3.** The relative degree of mixture with a base metal; fineness. **4.** Something added that lowers value or purity. *—tr.v.* (ə-loi′, ăl′oi′) **-loyed, -loy•ing, -loys. 1.** To combine (metals) to form an alloy. **2.** To combine; mix: *idealism alloyed with skill.* **3.** To debase by adding an inferior element. [Alteration (influenced by Fr. *aloi*, alloy) of obsolete *allay* < ME *alay* < ONFr. *allai* < *allayer*, to alloy < Lat. *alligāre*, to bind : *ad-*, ad- + *ligāre*, to bind; see **leig-*.**]

all-pur•pose (ôl′pûr′pəs) *adj.* Serving many purposes.

all right *adj.* **1.a.** In proper or satisfactory operational or working order: *Were the tires all right?* **b. all-right** (ôl′rīt′). *Informal.* Satisfactory; good: *an all-right movie.* **2.** Correct. **3.** Average; mediocre: *The show was just all right, not great.* **4.** Uninjured; safe. **5.** Fairly healthy; well: *I feel all right.* *—adv.* **1.** Satisfactorily; adequately: *did all right.* **2.** Very well; yes. Used as a reply to a question or to introduce a declaration: *Will you join us? All right. All right, here's the plan.* **3.** Without a doubt: *It's cold, all right.*

Usage Note: *All right,* usually pronounced as if it were a single word, probably should have followed the same orthographic development as *already* and *altogether.* But despite its use by a number of reputable authors, the spelling *alright* has never been accepted as a standard variant.

all-round (ôl′round′) *adj.* Var. of **all-around.**

All Saints' Day (sānts) *n.* November 1, the day on which a Christian feast honoring all the saints is observed.

All Souls' Day (sōlz) *n. Rom. Cath. Ch.* November 2, when special prayers are offered for souls in purgatory.

all•spice (ôl′spīs′) *n.* **1.** A tropical American evergreen tree (*Pimenta dioica*) having opposite simple leaves and small white flowers clustered in cymes. **2.** The dried, nearly ripe berries of this plant used as a spice, esp. in baking.

all-star (ôl′stär′) *adj.* Made up wholly of star performers. *—n. Sports.* One chosen for a team of star players.

all the same *adv.* Nevertheless: *I was ill but went all the same.*

all-time (ôl′tīm′) *adj.* Exceeding all others up to the present.

all told *adv.* Counting everything; in all.

al•lude (ə-lo͞od′) *intr.v.* **-lud•ed, -lud•ing, -ludes.** To make an indirect reference. [Lat. *allūdere*, to play with : *ad-*, ad- + *lūdere*, to play (< *lūdus*, game; see **leid-*.**)]

Usage Note: *Allude* and *allusion* are often used where the more general terms *refer* and *reference* would be preferable. *Allude* and *allusion* apply to indirect references in which the source is not specifically identified: *"Well, we'll always have Paris," he told the travel agent, in an allusion to* Casablanca. *Refer* and *reference,* unless qualified, usually imply specific mention of a source: *I will refer to* Hamlet *for my conclusion: As Polonius says, "Though this be madness, yet there is method in't."* See Usage Note at **refer.**

al•lure (ə-lo͝or′) *v.* **-lured, -lur•ing, -lures.** *—tr.* To attract with something desirable; entice: *Promises allure the unwary.* *—intr.* To be highly, often subtly attractive. *—n.* The power to attract; enticement. [ME *aluren* < OFr. *alurer*: *a-*, to (< Lat. *ad-*; see AD–) + *loirre*, bait (of Gmc. orig.).] **—al•lure′ment** *n.* **—al•lur′er** *n.* **—al•lur′ing•ly** *adv.*

al•lu•sion (ə-lo͞o′zhən) *n.* **1.** The act of alluding; indirect reference: *The candidate criticized them by allusion.* **2.** An instance of indirect reference. See Usage Note at **allude.** [LLat. *allūsiō*, *allūsiōn-*, a playing with < Lat. *allūsus*, p.part. of *allūdere*, to play with. See ALLUDE.]

al•lu•sive (ə-lo͞o′sĭv) *adj.* Characterized by indirect references. **—al•lu′sive•ly** *adv.* **—al•lu′sive•ness** *n.*

al•lu•vi•al (ə-lo͞o′vē-əl) *adj.* Of, relating to, or found in alluvium: *alluvial soil; alluvial gold.*

alluvial fan *n.* A fan-shaped accumulation of alluvium deposited at the mouth of a ravine or at the juncture of a tributary stream with the main stream.

al•lu•vi•on (ə-lo͞o′vē-ən) *n.* **1.** See **alluvium. 2.** The flow of water against a shore or bank. **3.** Inundation by water; flood. **4.** *Law.* The increasing of land area along a shore by deposited alluvium or water recession. [Lat. *alluviō*, *alluviōn-* < *alluere*, to wash against : *ad-*, ad- + *-luere*, to wash; see **leu(ə)-*.**]

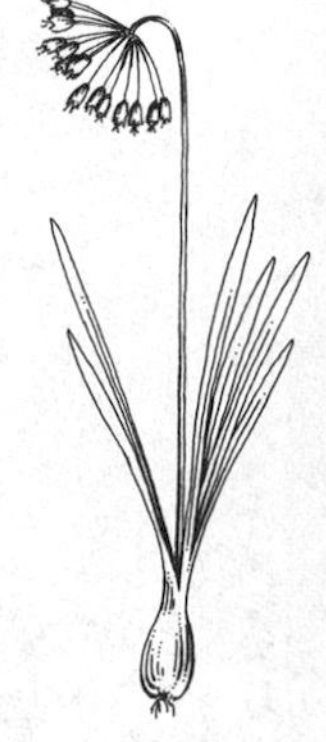

allium
Nodding wild onion
Allium cernuum

allspice
Pimenta dioica

ă pat	oi boy
ā pay	ou out
âr care	o͝o took
ä father	o͞o boot
ĕ pet	ŭ cut
ē be	ûr urge
ĭ pit	th thin
ī pie	*th* this
îr pier	hw which
ŏ pot	zh vision
ō toe	ə about, item
ô paw	

Stress marks:
′ (primary);
′ (secondary), as in
dictionary (dĭk′shə-nĕr′ē)

al•lu•vi•um (ə-lo͞o′vē-əm) *n., pl.* **-vi•ums** or **-vi•a** (-vē-ə). Sediment deposited by flowing water, as in a riverbed or delta. [Med.Lat., flood < neut. of Lat. *alluvius*, alluvial < *alluere*, to wash against. See ALLUVION.]

al•ly (ə-lī′, ăl′ī) *v.* **-lied, -ly•ing, -lies.** *—tr.* **1.** To place in a friendly association, as by treaty. **2.** To unite or connect in a personal relationship, as in friendship or marriage. *—intr.* To enter into an alliance. *—n., pl.* **-lies. 1.** One allied with another, esp. by treaty: *an ally of France.* **2.** One in helpful association with another. See Syns at **partner. 3. Allies. a.** The nations allied against the Central Powers of Europe during World War I, including Russia, France, Great Britain, and later the United States. **b.** The nations, primarily Great Britain, France, the Soviet Union, and the United States, allied against the Axis during World War II. [ME *allien* < OFr. *alier* < Lat. *alligāre*, to bind to. See ALLOY.]

al•lyl (ăl′əl) *n.* The univalent unsaturated organic radical C_3H_5. [Lat. *allium*, garlic + -YL (so called because it was first obtained from garlic).] **—al•lyl′ic** (ə-lĭl′ĭk) *adj.*

alm *abbr.* Alarm.

Al•ma (ăl′mə). A city of S-central Quebec, Canada, on the Saguenay R. Pop. 26,322.

Al•ma-A•ta (ăl′mə-ä′tə, əl-mä′ə-tä′). The cap. of Kazakhstan, in the SE part S of Lake Balkash; founded in the 1850's. Pop. 1,068,000.

Al•ma•gest (ăl′mə-jĕst′) *n.* **1.** A comprehensive treatise on astronomy, geography, and mathematics compiled by Ptolemy about A.D. 150. **2. almagest.** Any of several medieval treatises on astronomy or alchemy. [ME *almageste* < OFr. < Ar. *al-majisti*: *al*, the + Gk. *megistē*, greatest, fem. of *megistos*, greatest, superl. of *megas*, great; see **meg-***.]

al•ma ma•ter or **Al•ma Ma•ter** (ăl′mə mä′tər, äl′mə) *n.* **1.** The school, college, or university that one has attended. **2.** The anthem of an institution of higher learning. [Lat. *alma*, nourishing + *mater*, mother.]

almond
Prunus dulcis

al•ma•nac (ôl′mə-năk′, ăl′-) *n.* **1.** An annual publication including weather forecasts, astronomical information, tide tables, and other tabular information. **2.** An annual publication composed of various lists, charts, and tables of information in one or many fields. [ME *almenak* < Med.Lat. *almanach*, perh. < LGk. *almenikhiaka*, ephemeris.]

Al Ma•na•mah (ăl′ mə-năm′ə, mă-). See **Manama.**

al•man•dine (ăl′mən-dēn′) also **al•man•dite** (-dīt′) *n.* A deep violet-red garnet, $FeAl_2Si_3O_{12}$, found in metamorphic rocks and used as a gemstone. [Alteration of obsolete *alabandyne* < ME *alabandine* < LLat. *(gemma) alabandina*, (gem) of Alabanda < *Alabanda*, a town of ancient Asia Minor.]

Al•ma-Tad•e•ma (ăl′mə-tăd′ə-mə), Sir **Lawrence.** 1836–1912. British painter noted for his romantic works.

Al•me•lo (äl′mə-lō′). A city of E Netherlands near the German border. Pop. 62,941.

al•me•mar (äl-mē′mär) *n. Judaism.* See **bema** 1. [Heb. *'almēmār* < Ar. *al-minbar*, the pulpit.]

Al•me•rí•a (ăl′mə-rē′ə, äl′mĕ-). A city of SE Spain on the **Gulf of Almería**, an arm of the Mediterranean. Pop. 149,310.

alpaca
Lama pacos

al•might•y (ôl-mī′tē) *adj.* **1.** Having absolute power: *almighty God.* **2.** *Informal.* Great; extreme: *an almighty din.* *—adv. Informal.* Used as an intensive: *almighty scared.* *—n.* **Almighty.** God. Used with *the.* [ME *almighti* < OE *ealmihtig*: *eall*, all; see ALL + *mihtig*, mighty (< *miht*, might; see MIGHT[1]).] **—al•might′i•ly** *adv.*

al•mond (ä′mənd, ăm′ənd) *n.* **1.a.** A deciduous tree *(Prunus dulcis)* native to Asia and northern Africa and having alternate simple leaves, pink flowers, and leathery fruits. **b.** The ellipsoidal kernel of this tree, either eaten as a nut or used for extraction of an oil. **2.** Any of several other plants, esp. those with almondlike fruits or seeds. **3.** Something having the oval form of an almond. **4.** *Color.* A pale tan. [ME *almande* < OFr. < LLat. *amandula*, alteration of Lat. *amygdala* < Gk. *amugdalē*.]

al•mo•ner (ăl′mə-nər, ä′mə-) *n.* **1.** One who distributes alms. **2.** *Chiefly British.* A hospital social worker. [ME *aumoner* < OFr. *aumonier* < *amosne*, alms < LLat. *eleēmosyna*, alms. See ALMS.]

altar
Saint Joseph's Church,
Winsted, Connecticut

al•most (ôl′mōst′, ôl-mōst′) *adv.* Slightly short of; not quite; nearly: *almost time.* See Usage Note at **none.** [ME < OE *ealmǣst*: *eall*, all; see ALL + *mǣst*, most; see MOST.]

alms (ämz) *pl.n.* Money or goods given to the poor. [ME *almes* < OE *ælmesse* < LLat. *eleēmosyna* < Gk. *eleēmosunē* < *eleēmōn*, pitiful < *eleos*, pity.]

alms•house (ämz′hous′) *n.* A poorhouse.

alms•man (ämz′mən) *n.* One, usu. a man, dependent on alms.

al•ni•co (ăl′nĭ-kō′) *n.* Any of several hard, strong alloys of iron, aluminum, nickel, cobalt, and sometimes copper, niobium, or tantalum, used to make strong permanent magnets. [AL(UMINUM) + NI(CKEL) + CO(BALT).]

al•oe (ăl′ō) *n.* **1.** Any of various chiefly African plants of the genus *Aloe*, having rosettes of succulent leaves and long stalks bearing tubular flowers. **2.** See **aloe vera. 3. aloes.** *(used with a sing. v.)* A laxative drug obtained from the juice of a certain species of aloe. [ME < OE *aluwe* < Lat. *aloē* < Gk.] **—al′o•et′ic** (ăl′ō-ĕt′ĭk) *adj.*

aloe ver•a (vĕr′ə, vîr′ə) *n.* **1.** A species of aloe *(Aloe vera)* native to the Mediterranean region. **2.** The mucilaginous juice or gel from the leaves of this plant, used for its soothing and healing properties. [Lat. *aloē*, aloe plant + *vera*, fem. of *verus*, true.]

a•loft (ə-lôft′, ə-lŏft′) *adv.* **1.** In or into a high place; high or higher up. **2.** *Naut.* At or toward the upper rigging. *—prep.* On or above. [ME < ON *ā lopt*: *ā*, in; see **an-*** + *lopt*, air.]

a•log•i•cal (ā-lŏj′ĭ-kəl) *adj.* Beyond the bounds of logic. **—a•log′i•cal•ly** *adv.* **—a•log′i•cal•ness** *n.*

a•lo•ha (ə-lō′ə, -hə, ä-lō′ä′, -hä′) *interj. Chiefly Hawaii.* Used as a traditional greeting or farewell. [Hawaiian.]

al•o•in (ăl′ō-ĭn) *n.* A bitter, yellow crystalline compound obtained from the aloe and used as a laxative. [ALO(E) + -IN.]

a•lone (ə-lōn′) *adj.* **1.** Being apart from others; solitary. **2.** Being without anyone or anything else; only. **3.** Considered separately from all others of the same class. **4.** Being unequaled. *—adv.* **1.** Without others. **2.** Without help: *cooked alone.* **3.** Exclusively; only: *The credit is hers alone.* [ME : *al*, all; see ALL + *one*, one; see ONE.] **—a•lone′ness** *n.*

***Syns:** alone, lonely, lonesome, solitary.* These adjectives describe lack of companionship. *Alone* emphasizes being apart from others but does not necessarily imply unhappiness: *"I am never less alone, than when I am alone"* (James Howell). *Lonely* connotes painful awareness of being alone: *" 'No doubt they are dead,' she thought, and felt . . . sadder and . . . lonelier for the thought"* (Ouida). *Lonesome* emphasizes a plaintive desire for companionship: *"You must . . . not be lonesome because I'm not at home"* (Charles Dickens). *Solitary* often stresses physical isolation that is self-imposed: *She enjoyed a solitary meal.*

a•long (ə-lông′, ə-lŏng′) *prep.* **1.** Over the length of: *walked along the path.* **2.** On a line or course parallel and close to; continuously beside: *trees along the avenue.* **3.** In accordance with: *split along party lines.* *—adv.* **1.** Forward; onward: *Farther along, we passed a hitchhiker.* **2.** As a companion: *Bring a friend along.* **3.** In accompaniment or association; together: *packed an atlas along with other books.* See Usage Note at **together. 4.** With one; at hand. **5.** *Informal.* Advanced to some degree: *along in years.* [ME < OE *andlang*, extending opposite : *and-*, facing; see **ant-*** + *lang*, long; see LONG[1].]

a•long•shore (ə-lông′shôr′, -shōr′, ə-lŏng′-) *adv.* Along, near, or by the shore.

a•long•side (ə-lông′sīd′, ə-lŏng′-) *adv.* Along, near, at, or to the side. *—prep.* By the side of; side by side with.

Usage Note: In its prepositional use *alongside* may be accompanied by *of*: *The barge lay alongside, or alongside of, the pier.*

a•loof (ə-lo͞of′) *adj.* Distant physically or emotionally; reserved and remote: *stood apart with aloof dignity.* *—adv.* At a distance but within view; apart. [A-[2] + LUFF, windward part of a ship (obsolete).] **—a•loof′ly** *adv.* **—a•loof′ness** *n.*

al•o•pe•cia (ăl′ə-pē′shə, -shē-ə) *n.* Loss of hair; baldness. [Lat. *alōpecia*, fox mange < Gk. *alōpekia* < *alōpēx*, fox. See **wl̥p-ē-***.] **—al′o•pe′cic** (-pē′sĭk) *adj.*

A•lost (ä-lôst′). See **Aalst.**

a•loud (ə-loud′) *adv.* **1.** By voice; orally: *Read aloud.* **2.** Loudly: *crying aloud for help.*

alp (ălp) *n.* **1.** A high mountain. **2.** A very large mound or mass. [Back-formation < the ALPS.]

ALPA *abbr.* Air Line Pilots Association.

al•pac•a (ăl-păk′ə) *n., pl.* **alpaca** or **-as. 1.** A domesticated South American mammal *(Lama pacos)*, related to the llama and having fine long wool. **2.a.** The wool of this mammal. **b.** Cloth made from alpaca. **c.** A coat made of this cloth. **3.** A glossy cotton or rayon and wool fabric. [Am.Sp. < Aymara *allpaca*.]

al•pen•glow (ăl′pən-glō′) *n.* A rosy glow that suffuses snow-covered mountain peaks at dawn or dusk on a clear day. [Partial transl. of Ger. *Alpenglühen*: *Alpen*, Alps + *glühen*, to glow.]

al•pen•horn (ăl′pən-hôrn′) *n.* A curved wooden horn, sometimes as long as 6 meters (approx. 20 feet), used by Alpine herders to call cows. [Ger. : *Alpen*, Alps + *Horn*, horn (< MHGer. < OHGer.; see **ker-[1]***).]

al•pen•stock (ăl′pən-stŏk′) *n.* A mountaineer's long, iron-pointed staff. [Ger. : *Alpen*, Alps + *Stock*, staff (< MHGer. *stoc* < OHGer.).]

al•pes•trine (ăl-pĕs′trĭn) *adj.* Growing at high altitudes; alpine or subalpine. [< Med.Lat. *alpestris* < Lat. *Alpēs*, the Alps.]

al•pha (ăl′fə) *n.* **1.** The first letter of the Greek alphabet. **2.** The first one; the beginning. **3.** *Chem.* The first position from a designated carbon atom in an organic molecule at which an atom or radical may be substituted. **4.** *Astron.* The brightest or main star in a constellation. **5.** The mathematical estimate of the return on a security when the return on the market as a whole is zero. *—adj.* **1.** First in order of importance. **2.** *Chem.* Closest to the functional group of atoms in an organic molecule. **3.** Alphabetical. [Gk. < Canaanite *'alp*, ox.]

al•pha-ad•re•ner•gic (ăl′fə-ăd′rə-nûr′jĭk) *adj.* Of, relating to, or being an alpha-receptor.
alpha-adrenergic block•ing agent (blŏk′ĭng) *n.* See **alpha-blocker.**
alpha-adrenergic receptor *n.* See **alpha-receptor.**
alpha and omega *n.* **1.** The first and the last. **2.** The most important part.
al•pha•bet (ăl′fə-bĕt′, -bĭt) *n.* **1.** The letters of a language, arranged in the order fixed by custom. **2.** A system of characters or symbols representing sounds or things. **3.** The basic or elementary principles; rudiments. [ME *alphabete* < Lat. *alphabētum* < Gk. *alphabētos*: *alpha*, alpha; see ALPHA + *bēta*, beta; see BETA.]
al•pha•bet•i•cal (ăl′fə-bĕt′ĭ-kəl) also **al•pha•bet•ic** (-bĕt′ĭk) *adj.* **1.** Arranged in the customary order of the letters of a language. **2.** Of, relating to, or expressed by an alphabet. — **al′pha•bet′i•cal•ly** *adv.*
al•pha•bet•ize (ăl′fə-bĭ-tīz′) *tr.v.* **-ized, -iz•ing, -iz•es. 1.** To arrange alphabetically. **2.** To supply with an alphabet. — **al′pha•bet′i•za′tion** (-bĕt′ĭ-zā′shən) *n.* — **al′pha•bet•iz′er** *n.*
al•pha-block•er (ăl′fə-blŏk′ər) *n. Physiol.* A drug that opposes the excitatory effects of norepinephrine released from sympathetic nerve endings at alpha receptors.
Al•pha Cen•tau•ri (ăl′fə sĕn-tôr′ē) *n.* A multiple star in the constellation Centaurus, 4.4 light-years from Earth.
Alpha Cru•cis (kro͞o′sĭs) *n.* A double star in the constellation Southern Cross.
al•pha-fe•to•pro•tein (ăl′fə-fē′tō-prō′tēn, -tē-ĭn) *n.* An antigen produced in the liver of a fetus that can appear in certain diseases of adults, such as liver cancer.
alpha helix *n.* A structure of proteins, characterized by a spiral chain of amino acids. — **al′pha-hel′i•cal** (ăl′fə-hĕl′ĭ-kəl, -hē′lĭ-) *adj.*
al•pha-naph•thol (ăl′fə-năf′thôl, -thōl, -năp′-) *n.* An isomeric form of naphthol, $C_{10}H_7OH$, used in making dyes and perfumes and in organic synthesis.
al•pha•nu•mer•ic (ăl′fə-no͞o-mĕr′ĭk, -nyo͞o-) also **al•pha•mer•ic** (-fə-mĕr′ĭk) *adj.* Consisting of or utilizing letters and numbers and usu. punctuation marks, mathematical symbols, and other conventional symbols: *an alphanumeric code.* [AL-PHA(BETIC) + NUMERIC(AL).] — **al′pha•nu•mer′i•cal** *adj.* — **al′pha•nu•mer′i•cal•ly** *adv.*
alpha particle *n.* A positively charged particle, consisting of two protons and two neutrons.
alpha privative *n.* The prefix *a-* or *an-* before vowels, used in Greek and in English words borrowed from Greek to express absence or negation.
alpha ray *n.* A stream of alpha particles.
al•pha-re•cep•tor (ăl′fə-rĭ-sĕp′tər) *n.* A site in the autonomic nervous system in which excitatory responses occur when adrenergic agents, such as epinephrine, are released.
alpha rhythm *n.* A pattern of smooth, regular electrical oscillations in the human brain, having a frequency of 8 to 13 hertz, that occur when a person is awake and relaxed.
Al•phe•us (ăl-fē′əs). A river of the Peloponnesus in S Greece flowing c. 113 km (70 mi) to the Ionian Sea.
al•pine (ăl′pīn′) *adj.* **1. Alpine.** Of or relating to the Alps or their inhabitants. **2.** Of or relating to high mountains. **3.** *Biol.* Living or growing above the timberline. **4.** *Sports.* **a.** Intended for or concerned with mountaineering. **b. Alpine.** Of or relating to downhill racing and slalom skiing events. [ME < Lat. *Alpīnus* < *Alpēs*, the Alps.]
al•pin•ist also **Al•pin•ist** (ăl′pə-nĭst) *n. Sports.* A mountain climber. — **al′pin•ism** *n.*
Alps (ălps). A mountain system of S-central Europe, c. 805 km (500 mi) long and 161 km (100 mi) wide, extending from the Riviera to Albania and rising to 4,810.2 m (15,771 ft).
al•read•y (ôl-rĕd′ē) *adv.* **1.** By this or a specified time; before. **2.** So soon: *Are you quitting already?* **3.** *Non-Standard.* Used as an intensive: *Enough already.* [ME *alredi*: *al*, all; see ALL + *redi*, ready; see READY.]
al•right (ôl-rīt′) *adv. Non-Standard.* All right. See Usage Note at **all right.**
ALS *abbr.* Amyotrophic lateral sclerosis.
a.l.s. or **A.L.S.** *abbr.* Autograph letters, signed.
Al•sace (ăl-săs′, -sās′). A region and former province of E France. Along with neighboring Lorraine, it was annexed by Germany in 1871 and returned to France by the Treaty of Versailles (1919).
Al•sa•tian (ăl-sā′shən) *adj.* Of or relating to Alsace or its inhabitants or culture. — *n.* **1.** A native or inhabitant of Alsace. **2.** *Chiefly British.* A German shepherd.
Al•sek (ăl′sĕk′). A river of NW Canada and SE AK flowing c. 418 km (260 mi) to the Pacific Ocean.
al•sike clover (ăl′sīk′) *n.* A perennial European clover *(Trifolium hybridum)* grown as a pasture and hay plant. [After *Alsike*, near Uppsala in E Sweden.]
Al•sip (ôl′sĭp). A village of NE IL, a suburb of Chicago. Pop. 18,227.
al•so (ôl′sō) *adv.* **1.** In addition; besides. **2.** Likewise; too. — *conj.* And in addition: *It's a pretty cat, also friendly.* [ME < OE *ealswā*: *eall*, all; see **al-**[3]* + *swā*, so; see so[1].]
al•so-ran (ôl′sō-răn′) *n.* **1.** A horse that does not win, place, or show in a race. **2.** A loser in a competition. **3.** One that has little talent or success.
al•stroe•me•ri•a (ăl′strə-mîr′ē-ə) *n.* Any of several South American perennial herbs of the genus *Alstroemeria*, having showy, variously colored blooms. [NLat., genus name, after Baron Clas *Alstroemer* (1736–94), Swedish naturalist.]
alt (ălt) *Mus.* — *adj.* Pitched in the first octave above the treble staff. — *n.* **1.** The first octave above the treble staff. **2.** A note or tone in the alt octave. [Lat. *altus*, high. See **al-**[2]*.]
alt. *abbr.* **1.** Alteration. **2.** Alternate. **3.** Altitude.
Alta. *abbr.* Alberta.
Al•ta Cal•i•for•nia (ăl′tə kăl′ĭ-fôr′nyə, -fôr′nē-ə). Also **Up•per California** (ŭp′ər). The Spanish possessions along the Pacific coast N of the peninsula of Baja California.
Al•ta•ic (ăl-tā′ĭk) *n.* A language family of Europe and Asia that includes the Turkic, Tungusic, and Mongolian subfamilies. — *adj.* **1.** Of or relating to the Altai Mountains. **2.** Of or relating to Altaic.
Al•tai Mountains or **Al•tay Mountains** (ăl′tī′). A mountain system of central Asia, mostly in E Kazakhstan, S-central Russia, and W Mongolia, rising to 4,508.8 m (14,783 ft).
Al•tair (ăl-tīr′, -târ′, ăl′tīr′, -târ′) *n.* A variable double star in the constellation Aquila. [Ar. *(an-nasr) aṭ-ṭā'ir*, the flying (eagle), Altair : *an-nasr*, the eagle (*al*, the + *nasr*, eagle) + *aṭ-ṭā'ir* (*al*, the + *ṭā'ir*, flying).]
Al•ta•mi•ra (ăl′tə-mîr′ə, äl′tä-mē′rä). A group of caverns of N Spain WSW of Santander; noted for specimens of Paleolithic art (discovered 1879).
Al•ta•monte Springs (ăl′tə-mŏnt′). A city of E-central FL, a suburb of Orlando. Pop. 34,879.
al•tar (ôl′tər) *n.* **1.** An elevated place or structure before which religious ceremonies may be enacted or upon which sacrifices may be offered. **2.** A structure, typically a table, before which the divine offices are recited and upon which the Eucharist is celebrated in Christian churches. [ME *auter* < OE *altar* and OFr. *auter*, both < Lat. *altāre*.]
altar boy *n.* An attendant to an officiating cleric in the performance of a liturgical service; an acolyte.
altar call *n.* A time at the end of a Protestant service when worshipers may come forward to profess their faith. Also called regionally *invitation.*
al•tar•piece (ôl′tər-pēs′) *n.* A piece of artwork that is placed above and behind an altar.
altar rail *n.* A railing in front of the altar that separates the chancel from the rest of a church.
alt•az•i•muth (ăl-tăz′ə-məth) *n.* **1.** A mounting for astronomical telescopes that permits both horizontal and vertical rotation. **2.** A telescope having such a mounting. [ALT(ITUDE) + AZIMUTH.]
Alt•dorf (ält′dôrf). A town of central Switzerland near the SE tip of the Lake of Lucerne; site of the legendary exploits of William Tell. Pop. 8,200.
al•ter (ôl′tər) *v.* **-tered, -ter•ing, -ters.** — *tr.* **1.** To change or make different; modify. **2.** To adjust (a garment) for a better fit. **3.** To castrate or spay (an animal). — *intr.* To change or become different. [ME *alteren* < OFr. *alterer* < Med.Lat. *alterāre* < Lat. *alter*, other. See **al-**[1]*.]
al•ter•a•ble (ôl′tər-ə-bəl) *adj.* That can be altered: *alterable clothing.* — **al′ter•a•bil′i•ty, al′ter•a•ble•ness** *n.* — **al′ter•a•bly** *adv.*
al•ter•a•tion (ôl′tə-rā′shən) *n.* **1.** The act or procedure of altering. **2.** The condition resulting from altering.
al•ter•a•tive (ôl′tə-rā′tĭv, -tər-ə-tĭv) *adj.* **1.** Tending to alter. **2.** *Medic.* Tending to restore health. — *n. Medic.* A medication that restores health.
al•ter•cate (ôl′tər-kāt′) *intr.v.* **-cat•ed, -cat•ing, -cates.** To argue or dispute vehemently; wrangle. [Lat. *altercārī*, *altercāt-*, to quarrel < *alter*, other. See **al-**[1]*.]
al•ter•ca•tion (ôl′tər-kā′shən) *n.* A vehement quarrel.
alter ego *n.* **1.** Another side of oneself; a second self. **2.** An intimate friend or a constant companion. [Lat. : *alter*, other + *ego*, I, self.]
al•ter•nate (ôl′tər-nāt′, ăl′-) *v.* **-nat•ed, -nat•ing, -nates.** — *intr.* **1.** To occur in successive turns. **2.** To pass back and forth from one state, action, or place to another. — *tr.* **1.** To do or execute by turns. **2.** To cause to follow in turns; interchange regularly. — *adj.* (-nĭt). **1.** Happening or following in turns; succeeding each other continuously: *alternate seasons.* See Usage Note at **alternative. 2.** Relating to or being every other one of a series: *alternate lines.* **3.** Serving or used in place of another: *an alternate plan.* **4.** *Bot.* **a.** Arranged singly at each node, as leaves on a stem. **b.** Arranged regularly between other parts. — *n.* (-nĭt). **1.** A person acting in the place of another; a substitute. **2.** An alternative. [Lat. *alternāre*, *alternāt-* < *alternus*, by turns < *alter*, other. See **al-**[1]*.] — **al′ter•nate•ly** *adv.* — **al′ter•nate•ness** *n.*
al•ter•nate angle (ôl′tər-nĭt, ăl′-) *n. Math.* One of a pair of nonadjacent, nonvertical angles on opposite sides of a transversal that cuts two parallel lines.
al•ter•nat•ing current (ôl′tər-nā′tĭng, ăl′-) *n.* An electric

altazimuth
Mid 18th-century Russian telescope built by Mikhail V. Lomonosov (1711–1765)

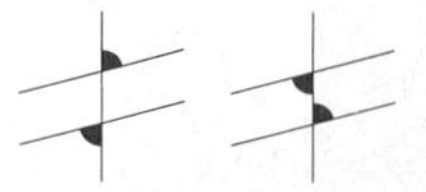

alternate angle
Exterior (*left*) and interior (*right*) alternate angles

ă pat	oi boy
ā pay	ou out
âr care	o͝o took
ä father	o͞o boot
ĕ pet	ŭ cut
ē be	ûr urge
ĭ pit	th thin
ī pie	*th* this
îr pier	hw which
ŏ pot	zh vision
ō toe	ə about,
ô paw	item

Stress marks:
′ (primary);
′ (secondary), as in
dictionary (dĭk′shə-nĕr′ē)

current that reverses direction at regular intervals.

al•ter•na•tion (ôl′tər-nā′shən, ăl′-) *n.* Successive change from one thing or state to another and back again.

alternation of generations *n.* The regular alternation of forms of reproduction in the life cycle of an organism, such as between sexual and asexual reproductive cycles.

al•ter•na•tive (ôl-tûr′nə-tĭv, ăl-) *n.* **1.a.** The choice between two mutually exclusive possibilities. **b.** Either of these possibilities. See Syns at **choice. 2.** *Usage Problem.* One of a number of things from which one must be chosen. —*adj.* **1.** Allowing or necessitating a choice between two or more things. **2.** Existing outside traditional or established institutions or systems: *an alternative school.* —**al•ter′na•tive•ly** *adv.*

Usage Note: Some traditionalists hold that *alternative* should be used only in situations where the number of choices involved is exactly two, because of the word's historical relation to Latin *alter,* "the other of two." The Usage Panel is evenly divided on the issue, with 49 percent accepting the sentence *Of the three alternatives, the first is the least distasteful.* • *Alternative* should not be confused with *alternate.* Correct usage requires *The class will meet on alternate* (not *alternative*) *Tuesdays.*

al•ter•na•tor (ôl′tər-nā′tər, ăl′-) *n.* An electric generator that produces alternating current.

al•the•a also **al•thae•a** (ăl-thē′ə) *n.* **1.** See **rose of Sharon** 1. **2.** See **hollyhock.** [Lat., mallows < Gk. *althaia* < *althainein,* to heal. See **al-[2]*.**]

alt•horn or **Alt•horn** (ălt′hôrn′) *n. Mus.* Any of several upright, valved brass wind instruments. [Ger. : *alt,* alto (< Ital. *alto;* see ALTO) + *Horn,* horn (< MHGer. < OHGer.; see **ker-[1]*.**)]

al•though also **al•tho** (ôl-*thō*′) *conj.* Regardless of the fact that; even though. [ME : *al,* all; see ALL + *though,* though; see THOUGH.]

Usage Note: As conjunctions *although* and *though* are generally interchangeable: *Although* (or *though*) *she smiled, she was angry. Although* is usually placed at the beginning of its clause (as in the preceding example), whereas *though* may occur elsewhere and is the more common term when used to link words or phrases, as in *wiser though poorer,* or in constructions such as *Fond though* (not *although*) *I am of opera, I'd rather not attend tonight.*

al•tim•e•ter (ăl-tĭm′ĭ-tər) *n.* An instrument for determining elevation, esp. one used in aircraft. [Lat. *altus,* high; see **al-[2]*** + -METER.] —**al′ti•met′ric** (ăl′tə-mĕt′rĭk) *adj.* —**al•tim′e•try** *n.*

al•ti•pla•no (äl′tĭ-plä′nō) *n., pl.* **-nos.** A high plateau. [Am. Sp. : Lat. *altus,* high; see **al-[2]*** + Lat. *planum,* plain; see PLANE[1].]

al•ti•tude (ăl′tĭ-to͞od′, -tyo͞od′) *n.* **1.** The height of a thing above a reference level, esp. above sea level. **2.** A high location or area. **3.** *Astron.* The angular distance of a celestial object above the horizon. **4.** The perpendicular distance from the base of a geometric figure to the opposite vertex, parallel side, or parallel surface. **5.** High position or rank. [ME < Lat. *altitūdō* < *altus,* high. See **al-[2]*.**] —**al′ti•tu′di•nal** (-to͞od′-n-əl, -tyo͞od′-) *adj.*

altitude sickness *n.* A collection of symptoms, including shortness of breath and headache, brought on by decreased oxygen in the atmosphere.

al•to (ăl′tō) *n., pl.* **al•tos.** *Mus.* **1.** A low female singing voice; a contralto. **2.** A countertenor. **3.** The range between soprano and tenor. **4.** A singer whose voice lies within this range. **5.** An instrument that sounds within this range. **6.** A part written for a voice or an instrument within this range. [Ital. < Lat. *altus,* high. See **al-[2]*.**]

alto clef *n. Mus.* The C clef positioned to indicate that the third line from the bottom of a staff represents middle C.

al•to•cu•mu•lus (ăl′tō-kyo͞o′myə-ləs) *n.* A cloud formation of rounded, fleecy, white or gray masses. [Lat. *altus,* high; see **al-[2]*** + CUMULUS.]

al•to•geth•er (ôl′tə-gĕ*th*′ər) *adv.* **1.** Entirely; completely; utterly: *an altogether new approach.* **2.** With all included or counted: *Altogether 20 people came.* **3.** On the whole; with everything considered: *Altogether, I'm sorry it happened.* —*n.* A state of nudity. Often used with *the.* [ME *al togeder: al,* all; see ALL + *togeder,* together; see TOGETHER.]

Al•ton (ôl′tən). A city of SW IL on the Mississippi R. N of St. Louis MO. Pop. 32,905.

Al•too•na (ăl-to͞o′nə). A city of central PA near the Allegheny Mts. E of Pittsburgh; laid out in 1849. Pop. 51,881.

al•to-re•lie•vo also **al•to-ri•lie•vo** (ăl′tō-rĭ-lē′vō, äl′tō-rēl-yā′vō) *n., pl.* **al•to-re•lie•vos** also **al•to-ri•lie•vi** (äl′tō-rēl-yā′vē). See **high relief.** [Ital. *altorilievo: alto,* high; see ALTO + *rilievo,* relief; see BAS-RELIEF.]

al•to•stra•tus (ăl′tō-strā′təs, -străt′əs) *n.* An extended cloud formation of bluish or gray sheets or layers. [Lat. *altus,* high; see **al-[2]*** + STRATUS.]

al•tri•cial (ăl-trĭsh′əl) *adj.* Helpless, naked, and blind when hatched. [< Lat. *altrix, altrīc-,* fem. of *altor,* nourisher < *alere,* to nourish. See **al-[2]*.**]

al•tru•ism (ăl′tro͞o-ĭz′əm) *n.* Unselfish concern for the welfare of others; selflessness. [Fr. *altruisme,* prob. < Ital. *altrui,* someone else < Lat. *alter,* other. See **al-[1]*.**] —**al′tru•ist** *n.* —**al′tru•is′tic** *adj.* —**al′tru•is′ti•cal•ly** *adv.*

Al•tus (ăl′təs). A city of SW OK near the TX border SW of Oklahoma City. Pop. 21,910.

Al U•bay•yid (ăl′ o͞o-bā′ĭd) also **El O•beid** (ĕl′ ō-bād′). A city of central Sudan SW of Khartoum; founded in the 1820's. Pop. 140,000.

al•u•la (ăl′yə-lə) *n., pl.* **-lae** (-lē′). A small joint in the middle of a bird's wing that is homologous with the thumb. [NLat., dim. of Latin *āla,* wing.] —**al′u•lar** (-lər) *adj.*

al•um (ăl′əm) *n.* Any of various double sulfates of a trivalent metal, such as aluminum, chromium, or iron, and a univalent metal, such as potassium or sodium, esp. aluminum potassium sulfate, $AlK(SO_4)_2 \cdot 12H_2O$. [ME < OFr. < Lat. *alūmen.*]

a•lu•mi•na (ə-lo͞o′mə-nə) *n.* Any of several forms of aluminum oxide, Al_2O_3, occurring naturally as corundum, in bauxite, and with various impurities as ruby, sapphire, and emery. [NLat. *alūmina* < Lat. *alūmen, alūmin-,* alum.]

a•lu•mi•nate (ə-lo͞o′mə-nāt′, -nĭt) *n.* A chemical compound containing aluminum as part of a negative ion.

a•lu•mi•nif•er•ous (ə-lo͞o′mə-nĭf′ər-əs) *adj.* Containing or yielding aluminum, alumina, or alum. [Lat. *alūmen, alūmin-,* alum + -FEROUS.]

al•u•min•i•um (ăl′yə-mĭn′ē-əm) *n. Chiefly British.* Var. of **aluminum.**

a•lu•mi•nize (ə-lo͞o′mə-nīz′) *tr.v.* **-nized, -niz•ing, -niz•es.** To coat or cover with aluminum or aluminum paint.

a•lu•mi•nous (ə-lo͞o′mə-nəs) *adj.* Of, relating to, or containing aluminum or alum.

a•lu•mi•num (ə-lo͞o′mə-nəm) *n. Symbol* **Al** A silvery-white, ductile metallic element, found chiefly in bauxite. A good conductor, it is used in light, corrosion-resistant alloys. Atomic number 13; atomic weight 26.98; melting point 660.2°C; boiling point 2,467°C; specific gravity 2.69; valence 3. See table at **element.** [ALUMIN(A) + -(I)UM.]

aluminum oxide *n.* See **alumina.**

aluminum plant *n.* A succulent herb *(Pilea cadierei)* often grown as a houseplant for its silver-colored leaves.

aluminum sulfate *n.* A crystalline compound, $Al_2(SO_4)_3$, used in papermaking and water purification.

a•lum•na (ə-lŭm′nə) *n., pl.* **-nae** (-nē′). A woman graduate or former student of a school, college, or university. See Usage Note at **alumnus.** [Lat., fem. of *alumnus,* pupil. See ALUMNUS.]

a•lum•nus (ə-lŭm′nəs) *n., pl.* **-ni** (-nī′). A male graduate or former student of a school, college, or university. [Lat., pupil < *alere,* to nourish. See **al-[2]*.**]

Usage Note: The fact that the plural *alumni* of the masculine *alumnus* differs from the plural *alumnae* of the feminine *alumna* has created a certain amount of awkwardness for coeducational institutions. Most commonly, *alumni* is used for graduates of both sexes. But those who object to the choice of masculine forms in such cases may prefer the phrase *alumni and alumnae* or the form *alumnae/i;* this is the choice, for example, of many women's colleges that have begun to admit men.

al•um•root (ăl′əm-ro͞ot′, -ro͝ot′) *n.* Any of various North American perennials of the genus *Heuchera* having palmately lobed basal leaves and leafless stalks.

al•u•nite (ăl′yə-nīt′) *n.* A gray mineral, chiefly $K_2Al_3(OH)_6(SO_4)_3$. [Fr. < *alun,* alum < Lat. *alūmen.*]

Al•va (ăl′və, äl′vä) also **Al•ba** (ăl′bə), Duke of. Fernando Álvarez de Toledo. 1508–82. Spanish colonial administrator of the Netherlands (1567–73).

Al•va•ra•do (ăl′və-rä′dō, äl′vä-rä′*th*ô), **Pedro de.** 1485–1541. Spanish governor of Guatemala.

Al•va•rez (ăl′və-rĕz′), **Luis Walter.** 1911–88. Amer. physicist who won a 1968 Nobel Prize.

Ál•va•rez Quin•te•ro (äl′vä-rĕ*th*′ kēn-tĕ′rō), **Serafín.** 1871–1938. Spanish dramatist who collaborated with his brother **Joaquín** (1873–1944) on nearly 200 plays.

al•ve•o•lar (ăl-vē′ə-lər) *adj.* **1.** Of or relating to an alveolus. **2.** *Anat.* **a.** Relating to the jaw section containing the tooth sockets. **b.** Relating to the alveoli of the lungs. **3.** *Ling.* Formed with the tip of the tongue touching or near the inner ridge of the gums of the upper front teeth, as the English *t.* —*n. Ling.* An alveolar sound. —**al•ve′o•lar•ly** *adv.*

al•ve•o•late (ăl-vē′ə-lĭt) *adj.* Having a honeycombed surface. —**al•ve′o•la′tion** (-lā′shən) *n.*

al•ve•o•lus (ăl-vē′ə-ləs) *n., pl.* **-li** (-lī′). **1.** A small angular cavity or pit. **2.** A tooth socket in the jawbone. **3.** A tiny, thin-walled, capillary-rich sac in the lungs where the exchange of oxygen and carbon dioxide takes place. [Lat., small hollow, dim. of *alveus,* a hollow < *alvus,* belly.]

Al•vin (ăl′vĭn). A city of SE TX S of Houston. Pop. 19,220.

al•ways (ôl′wāz, -wĭz, -wēz) *adv.* **1.** At all times; invariably: *always late.* **2.** For all time; forever: *They will always be friends.* **3.** At any time; in any event: *You can always resign if you're unhappy.* [ME *alweis: alwei,* always (< OE *ealne weg: ealne,* accusative of *eall,* all; see ALL + *weg,* way; see **wegh-*)** + *-es,* adv. suff.; see -s[3].]

Al•yce clover or **al•yce clover** (ăl′ĭs) *n.* A tropical Asiatic herb

(*Alysicarpus vaginalis*) with alternate simple leaves and reddish flowers. [Prob. by folk ety. < NLat. *Alysicarpus*, genus name : Gk. *halusis*, chain; see **wel-**[2]* + Gk. *karpos*, fruit; see -CARP.]

a•lys•sum (ə-lĭsʹəm) *n.* **1.** See **sweet alyssum. 2.** Any of various chiefly Mediterranean weeds or ornamentals of the genus *Alyssum* in the mustard family. **3.** See **hoary alyssum.** [NLat. *Alyssum*, genus name < Lat. *alysson*, kind of madder < Gk. *alusson*, a plant believed to cure rabies : *a-*, not; see A-[1] + *lussa*, rabies; see **wḷkʷo-***.]

Alz•heim•er's disease (ältsʹhī-mərz, ăltsʹ-, ôltsʹ-, ôlzʹhī-mərs) *n.* A disease marked by progressive loss of mental capacity. [After Alois *Alzheimer* (1864–1915), German neurologist.]

am[1] (ăm) *v.* First pers. sing. pr. indic. of **be.** [ME < OE *eom.* See **es-***.]

am[2] or **AM** *abbr.* Amplitude modulation.

Am[1] The symbol for the element **americium.**

Am[2] *abbr. Bible.* Amos.

Am. *abbr.* America; American.

A.M. *abbr.* **1.** Airmail. **2.** Or A.M. *Lat.* Anno mundi (in the year of the world). **3.** Also **a.m.** or A.M. Ante meridiem. See Usage Note at **ante meridiem. 4.** *Lat.* Artium magister (Master of Arts).

AMA also **A.M.A.** *abbr.* American Medical Association.

A•ma•do (ə-mäʹdo͝o), **Jorge.** b. 1912. Brazilian writer whose works include *Doña Fior and Her Two Husbands* (1966).

A•ma•ga•sa•ki (äʹmə-gä-säʹkē). A city of S Honshu, Japan, on Osaka Bay. Pop. 509,115.

a•mah also **a•ma** (äʹmə, äʹmä) *n.* A housemaid, esp. a wet nurse, in Asia. [Port. *ama*, nurse < Med.Lat. *amma*, mother.]

Am•a•lek•ite (ămʹə-lĕkʹ-īt', ə-mălʹĭ-kīt') *n.* A member of an ancient nomadic people of Canaan. [Heb. *'ămālēqî* < *'ămālēq*, Amalek.]

a•mal•gam (ə-mălʹgəm) *n.* **1.** Any of various alloys of mercury with other metals. **2.** A combination of diverse elements; a mixture. See Syns at **mixture.** [ME < OFr. *amalgame* < Med.Lat. *amalgama*, prob. ult. < Gk. *malagma*, soft mass.]

a•mal•ga•mate (ə-mălʹgə-māt') *v.* **-mat•ed, -mat•ing, -mates.** —*tr.* **1.** To combine into a unified or integrated whole; unite. **2.** To alloy (a metal) with mercury. —*intr.* **1.** To become combined; unite. **2.** To blend with another metal. —**a•malʹga•maʹtive** *adj.* —**a•malʹga•maʹtor** *n.*

a•mal•ga•ma•tion (ə-măl'gə-māʹshən) *n.* **1.** The act of amalgamating or the condition resulting from this act. **2.** A consolidation or merger. **3.** The production of an alloy of mercury.

Am•al•the•a (ăm'əl-thēʹə) *n.* A satellite of Jupiter. [Lat. *Amalthēa*, nymph who nursed the infant Jupiter with goat's milk < Gk. *Amaltheia*.]

a•man•dine (äʹmən-dēn', ămʹən-) *adj.* Prepared or garnished with almonds: *sole amandine.* [Fr. < *amande*, almond < OFr. *almande.* See ALMOND.]

am•a•ni•ta (ăm'ə-nīʹtə, -nēʹ-) *n.* Any of various mushrooms in the genus *Amanita.* [NLat. *Amanīta*, genus name < Gk. *amanitai*, a fungus.]

a•man•ta•dine (ə-mănʹtə-dēn') *n.* An antiviral drug, $C_{10}H_{17}N{\cdot}HCl$, also used in the treatment of Parkinson's disease. [Alteration of *adamantane*, a hydrocarbon + -INE[2].]

a•man•u•en•sis (ə-măn'yo͞o-ĕnʹsĭs) *n., pl.* **-ses** (-sēz). One who is employed to take dictation or copy manuscripts. [Lat. *āmanuēnsis* < (*servus*) *ā manū*, (slave) at handwriting : *ā, ab*, by; see AB-[1] + *manū*, ablative of *manus*, hand; see **man-**[2]*.]

am•a•ranth (ămʹə-rănth') *n.* **1.** Any of various annuals of the genus *Amaranthus*, including several weeds, ornamentals, and food plants. **2.** An imaginary flower that never fades. **3.** *Color.* A deep reddish purple to dark or grayish purplish red. **4.** A dark red to purple azo dye. [NLat. *amaranthus*, genus name, alteration of Lat. *amarantus* < Gk. *amarantos*, unfading : *a-*, not; see A-[1] + *marainein*, to wither; see **mer-***.]

am•a•ran•thine (ăm'ə-rănʹthĭn, -thīn') *adj.* **1.** Of, relating to, or resembling the amaranth. **2.** Eternally beautiful and unfading; everlasting. **3.** *Color.* Deep purple-red.

am•a•relle (ăm'ə-rĕlʹ) *n.* A type of sour cherry. [Ger. < Med. Lat. *amarellum* < Lat. *amārus*, bitter.]

am•a•ret•to (ăm'ə-rĕtʹō) *n., pl.* **-tos.** An Italian liqueur flavored with almond. [Ital., dim. of *amaro*, bitter < Lat. *amārus*.]

Am•a•ril•lo (ăm'ə-rĭlʹō, -rĭlʹə). A city of N TX in the Panhandle N of Lubbock. Pop. 157,615.

am•a•ryl•lis (ăm'ə-rĭlʹĭs) *n.* **1.** Any of several chiefly tropical American bulbous plants of the genus *Hippeastrum*, grown as ornamentals. **2.** See **belladonna lily. 3.** Any of several similar or related plants. [NLat. *Amaryllis*, genus name < Lat., name of a shepherdess < Gk. *Amarullis*.]

a•mass (ə-măsʹ) *tr.v.* **a•massed, a•mass•ing, a•mass•es.** To gather together for oneself, as for one's pleasure or profit; accumulate. See Syns at **gather.** [ME, to accumulate < OFr. *amasser*, to assemble : *a-*, to (< Lat. *ad-*; see AD-) + *masser*, to gather together (< Lat. *massa*, lump, mass; see MASS).] —**a•massʹa•ble** *adj.* —**a•massʹer** *n.* —**a•massʹment** *n.*

am•a•teur (ămʹə-tûr', -tər, -ə-cho͝or', -chər, -tyo͝orʹ) *n.* **1.** A person who engages in an art, a science, a study, or an athletic activity as a pastime rather than a profession. **2.** *Sports.* An athlete who has never competed for money. **3.** One lacking the skill of a professional. —*adj.* **1.** Of, relating to, or performed by an amateur. **2.** Made up of amateurs. **3.** Not professional; unskillful. [Fr. < Lat. *amātor*, lover < *amāre*, to love.] —**amʹa•teur•ism** *n.*

am•a•teur•ish (ăm'ə-tûrʹĭsh, -cho͝orʹ-, -tyo͝orʹ-) *adj.* Characteristic of an amateur; not professional. —**am'a•teurʹish•ly** *adv.* —**am'a•teurʹish•ness** *n.*

A•ma•ti (ä-mäʹtē), **Nicolò** or **Nicola.** 1596–1684. Italian violin maker who succeeded his father and grandfather in the family business.

am•a•tive (ămʹə-tĭv) *adj.* Inclined toward love; amorous. [Med. Lat. *amātīvus*, capable of love < *amātus*, p.part. of Lat. *amāre*, to love.] —**amʹa•tive'•ly** *adv.* —**amʹa•tive'•ness** *n.*

am•a•tol (ămʹə-tôl', -tŏl') *n.* An explosive mixture of ammonium nitrate and trinitrotoluene. [< AM(MONIUM) + (TRINITRO)TOL(UENE).]

am•a•to•ry (ămʹə-tôr'ē, -tōr'ē) *adj.* Of, relating to, or expressive of love, esp. sexual love. [Lat. *amātōrius* < *amātor*, lover. See AMATEUR.]

am•au•ro•sis (ăm'ô-rōʹsĭs) *n.* Total loss of vision, esp. when occurring without pathological changes to the eye. [Gk. *amaurōsis* < *amauros*, dark.] —**am'au•rotʹic** (-rŏtʹĭk) *adj.*

a•maze (ə-māzʹ) *tr.v.* **a•mazed, a•maz•ing, a•maz•es. 1.** To affect with great wonder; astonish. See Syns at **surprise. 2.** *Obsolete.* To bewilder; perplex. —*n.* Amazement; wonder. [< ME *masen*, to bewilder, and < *amased*, bewildered (< OE *āmasod*), both < OE *āmasian*, to bewilder : *ā-*, intensive pref. + **masian*, to confuse.] —**a•mazʹed•ly** (ə-māʹzĭd-lē) *adv.* —**a•mazʹed•ness** *n.*

a•maze•ment (ə-māzʹmənt) *n.* **1.** A state of extreme surprise or wonder; astonishment. **2.** *Obsolete.* Bewilderment; perplexity.

Am•a•zon (ămʹə-zŏn', -zən) *n.* **1.** *Gk. Myth.* A member of a nation of women warriors reputed to have lived in Scythia. **2.** Often **amazon.** A tall, aggressive, strong-willed woman. [ME < Lat. *Amāzōn* < Gk., prob. of Iran. orig.]

Am•a•zo•ni•a (ăm'ə-zōʹnē-ə). The vast basin of the Amazon R. in N South America.

Am•a•zo•ni•an (ăm'ə-zōʹnē-ən) *adj.* **1.** Of or relating to the Amazon River or Amazonia. **2.** Characteristic of or resembling an Amazon. **3.** Often **amazonian.** Strong and aggressive. Used of women.

am•a•zon•ite (ămʹə-zə-nīt') *n.* A green variety of microcline. [After the AMAZON (RIVER).]

Amazon River. A river flowing c. 6,275 km (3,900 mi) from N Peru across N Brazil to a wide delta on the Atlantic Ocean.

amazon stone *n.* See **amazonite.**

am•bage (ămʹbĭj) *n. Archaic.* **1.** Ambiguity. Often used in the plural. **2. ambages.** Winding ways or indirect proceedings. [Back-formation < ME *ambages*, equivocation < Lat. *ambāges*: *ambi-*, around; see AMBI- + *agere*, to drive; see **ag-***.] —**am•baʹgious** (ăm-bāʹjəs) *adj.*

am•bas•sa•dor (ăm-băsʹə-dər, -dôr') *n.* **1.** A diplomatic official of the highest rank appointed and accredited as representative in residence by one government or sovereign to another. **2.** A diplomatic official heading his or her country's permanent mission to certain international organizations. **3.** An authorized messenger or representative. **4.** An unofficial representative: *ambassadors of goodwill.* [ME *ambassadour* < OFr. *ambassadeur* < Med.Lat. *ambactia*, mission < Lat. *ambactus*, servant, ult. of Celt. orig. See **ag-***.] —**am•basʹsa•doʹri•al** (-dôrʹē-əl, -dōrʹ-) *adj.* —**am•basʹsa•dor•shipʹ** *n.*

am•bas•sa•dress (ăm-băsʹə-drĭs) *n. Usage Problem.* A woman ambassador. See Usage Note at **-ess.**

Am•ba•to (äm-bäʹtō). A city of central Ecuador in a high Andean valley S of Quito. Pop. 100,454.

am•beer (ămʹbîr) *n. Chiefly Southern U.S.* Tobacco juice. [Alteration (influenced by BEER with reference to color and foam of the spittle) of AMBER with reference to color.]

am•ber (ămʹbər) *n.* **1.** A hard, translucent yellow, orange, or brownish-yellow fossil resin, used for making jewelry. **2.** *Color.* A brownish yellow. —*adj.* **1.** *Color.* Having the color of amber; brownish-yellow. **2.** Made of or resembling amber. [ME *ambre* < OFr. < Med.Lat. *ambra, ambar* < Ar. *'anbar*, ambergris, amber.]

am•ber•gris (ămʹbər-grĭs', -grēs') *n.* A waxy substance formed in the intestines of sperm whales and used in perfume. [ME < OFr. *ambre gris*: *ambre*, amber; see AMBER + *gris*, gray; see GRIZZLE.]

am•ber•jack (ămʹbər-jăk') *n., pl.* **amberjack** or **-jacks.** A food and game marine fish of the genus *Seriola*. [AMBER + JACK, a fish.]

ambi– *pref.* Both: *ambiversion.* [Lat., around. See **ambhi***.]

am•bi•ance also **am•bi•ence** (ămʹbē-əns, äN-byäNsʹ) *n.* The special atmosphere or mood created by a particular environment. [Fr. < *ambiant*, surrounding < Lat. *ambiēns, ambient-*. See AMBIENT.]

am•bi•dex•ter•i•ty (ăm'bĭ-dĕk-stĕrʹĭ-tē) *n.* **1.** The state or

amanita

amaryllis

ă pat	oi boy
ā pay	ou out
âr care	o͝o took
ä father	o͞o boot
ĕ pet	ŭ cut
ē be	ûr urge
ĭ pit	th thin
ī pie	*th* this
îr pier	hw which
ŏ pot	zh vision
ō toe	ə about, item
ô paw	

Stress marks: ʹ (primary); ' (secondary), as in dictionary (dĭkʹshə-nĕr'ē) quality of being ambidextrous. **2.** Deceit or hypocrisy.

am•bi•dex•trous (ăm′bĭ-dĕk′strəs) *adj.* **1.** Able to use both hands with equal facility. **2.** Unusually skillful; adroit. **3.** Deceptive or hypocritical. [< *ambidexter*, ambidextrous (archaic) < ME, double dealer < Med.Lat. : Lat. *ambi-*, on both sides; see AMBI- + Lat. *dexter*, right-handed.] **—am′bi•dex′trous•ly** *adv.*

am•bi•ent (ăm′bē-ənt) *adj.* Surrounding; encircling: *ambient sound.* [Lat. *ambiēns*, *ambient-*, pr.part. of *ambīre*, to surround : *ambi-*, around; see AMBI- + *īre*, to go; see **ei-***.]

am•bi•gu•i•ty (ăm′bĭ-gyo͞o′ĭ-tē) *n.*, *pl.* **-ties. 1.** Doubtfulness or uncertainty as regards interpretation: *moral ambiguity.* **2.** Something of doubtful meaning: *a poem full of ambiguities.*

am•big•u•ous (ăm-bĭg′yo͞o-əs) *adj.* **1.** Open to more than one interpretation: *an ambiguous reply.* **2.** Doubtful or uncertain. [< Lat. *ambiguus*, uncertain < *ambigere*, to go about : *ambi-*, around; see AMBI- + *agere*, to drive; see **ag-***.]

Syns: *ambiguous, equivocal, obscure, recondite, abstruse, vague, cryptic, enigmatic.* These adjectives mean lacking clarity of meaning. *Ambiguous* indicates the presence of two or more possible meanings: *Frustrated by ambiguous instructions, the parents were never able to assemble the new toy.* Something *equivocal* is unclear or misleading: *"The polling had a complex and equivocal message for potential female candidates"* (David S. Broder). *Obscure* implies that meaning is hidden, either from lack of clarity of expression or from inherent difficulty of comprehension: *Some say that Kafka's style is obscure and complex. Recondite* and *abstruse* connote the erudite obscurity of the scholar: *"some recondite problem in historiography"* (Walter Laqueur). *His lectures are so abstruse that students avoid them.* What is *vague* is expressed in indefinite form or reflects imprecision of thought: *"Vague . . . forms of speech . . . have so long passed for mysteries of science"* (John Locke). *Cryptic* suggests an often deliberately puzzling terseness: *a policy full of cryptic phrases.* Something *enigmatic* is mysterious, puzzling, and often challenging: *an enigmatic comment.*

am•bi•po•lar (ăm′bĭ-pō′lər) *adj.* Operating in two directions simultaneously.

am•bi•sex•u•al (ăm′bĭ-sĕk′sho͞o-əl) *adj.* **1.** Sexually attracted to either sex indiscriminately. **2.** Suited to either sex: *ambisexual fashion.* —*n.* An ambisexual person or thing. **—am′bi•sex′u•al′i•ty** (-ăl′ĭ-tē) *n.*

am•bit (ăm′bĭt) *n.* **1.** An external boundary; a circuit. **2.** Sphere or scope. [Lat. *ambitus* < p.part. of *ambīre*, to go around. See AMBIENT.]

am•bi•tion (ăm-bĭsh′ən) *n.* **1.a.** An eager or strong desire to achieve something. **b.** The object or goal desired. **2.** Desire for exertion or activity; energy: *no ambition for dancing.* [ME *ambicioun*, excessive desire for honor, power, or wealth < OFr. *ambition* < Lat. *ambitiō*, *ambitiōn-* < *ambitus*, p.part. of *ambīre*, to go around (for votes). See AMBIENT.]

am•bi•tious (ăm-bĭsh′əs) *adj.* **1.** Full of, characterized by, or motivated by ambition. **2.** Greatly desirous; eager: *"I am not ambitious of ridicule"* (Edmund Burke). **3.** Requiring or showing much effort; challenging. **—am•bi′tious•ly** *adv.* **—am•bi′tious•ness** *n.*

am•biv•a•lence (ăm-bĭv′ə-ləns) *n.* **1.** The coexistence of opposing attitudes or feelings. **2.** Uncertainty or indecisiveness as to which course to follow. [Ger. *Ambivalenz*: Lat. *ambi-*, ambi- + Lat. *valentia*, vigor (< *valēns*, *valent-*, pr.part. of *valēre*, to be strong; see **wal-***).]

am•biv•a•lent (ăm-bĭv′ə-lənt) *adj.* Exhibiting or feeling ambivalence.

am•bi•ver•sion (ăm′bĭ-vûr′zhən, -shən) *n.* A personality trait including the qualities of both introversion and extroversion. [AMBI- + (INTRO)VERSION or (EXTRA)VERSION.] **—am′bi•vert′** (-vûrt′) *n.*

am•ble (ăm′bəl) *intr.v.* **-bled, -bling, -bles. 1.** To walk slowly or leisurely; stroll. **2.** To move along at an easy gait by using both legs on one side alternately with both on the other. Used of a horse. —*n.* **1.** An unhurried or leisurely walk. **2.** An easy gait, esp. that of a horse. [ME *amblen* < OFr. *ambler* < Lat. *ambulāre*, to walk.] **—am′bler** *n.*

Am•bler (ăm′blər), **Eric.** b. 1909. British writer noted for his suspense novels, including *A Passage of Arms* (1959).

am•blyg•o•nite (ăm-blĭg′ə-nīt′) *n.* A white or greenish mineral, $(Li,Na)Al(PO_4)(F,OH)$, that is an important source of lithium. [Ger. *Amblygonit* < Gk. *amblugōnios*, obtuse-angled : *amblus*, blunt; see **mel-**[1]* + *gōnia*, angle; see **genu-**[1]*.]

am•bly•o•pi•a (ăm′blē-ō′pē-ə) *n.* Dimness of vision, esp. when occurring in one eye without apparent physical defect. [NLat. < Gk. *ambluōpia* < *ambluōpos*, dim-sighted : *amblus*, dim; see **mel-**[1]* + *ōps*, eye; see MYOPIA.] **—am′bly•o′pic** (-ō′pĭk, -ŏp′ĭk) *adj.*

am•bo (ăm′bō′) *n.*, *pl.* **am•bos** or **am•bo•nes** (ăm-bō′nēz). One of the two pulpits or raised stands in early Christian churches from which parts of the service were chanted or read. [Med.Lat. < Gk. *ambōn*, raised edge.]

Am•bon (ăm′bôn) also **Am•boi•na** (ăm-boi′nə). An island of E Indonesia in the Moluccas near Ceram.

Am•bo•nese (ăm′bə-nēz′, -nēs′, ăm′-) or **Am•boi•nese** (-boi-) *n.*, *pl.* **Ambonese** or **Amboinese. 1.** A native or inhabitant of Ambon. **2.** The Austronesian language of Ambon.

Am•brose (ăm′brōz′), Saint. A.D. 340?–397. Bishop of Milan (374–397) who imposed orthodoxy on the early Christian Church. **—Am•bro′sian** (ăm-brō′zhən) *adj.*

am•bro•sia (ăm-brō′zhə, -zhē-ə) *n.* **1.** *Gk. & Rom. Myth.* The food of the gods, thought to confer immortality. **2.** Something with an especially delicious flavor or fragrance. [Lat. < Gk. < *ambrotos*, immortal, immortalizing : *a-*, not; see A-[1] + *-mbrotos*, mortal; see **mer-***.]

am•bro•sial (ăm-brō′zhəl, -zhē-əl) also **am•bro•sian** (-zhən, -zhē-ən) *adj.* **1.** Suggestive of ambrosia; fragrant or delicious. **2.** Of or worthy of the gods. **—am•bro′sial•ly** *adv.*

am•bro•type (ăm′brō-tīp′) *n.* An early type of photograph made by imaging a negative on glass backed by a dark surface. [Gk. *ambrotos*, immortal; see AMBROSIA + TYPE.]

am•bry (ăm′brē) *n.*, *pl.* **-bries. 1.** *Chiefly British.* A pantry. **2.** A niche near the altar of a church for keeping sacred vessels and vestments. [ME *almerie*, place for safekeeping < OFr. *almarie* < Med.Lat. *almārium* < Lat. *armārium*, closet < *arma*, tools. See ARM[2].]

ambs•ace (ām′zās′) *n.* **1.** *Games.* Double aces. **2.** Bad luck; misfortune. **3.** The smallest amount possible or the most worthless thing. [ME *ambes as* < OFr. < Lat. *ambās ās*: *ambō*, both + *ās*, unit.]

am•bu•lac•rum (ăm′byə-lăk′rəm, -lā′krəm) *n.*, *pl.* **-lac•ra** (-lăk′rə, -lā′krə). One of the areas on the undersurface of echinoderms, from which the tube feet project. [Lat., walk planted with trees < *ambulāre*, to walk.] **—am′bu•lac′ral** *adj.*

am•bu•lance (ăm′byə-ləns) *n.* A specially equipped vehicle used to transport the sick or injured. [Fr. < *(hôpital) ambulant*, mobile (hospital) < Lat. *ambulāns*, *ambulant-*, pr.part. of *ambulāre*, to walk.]

ambulance chaser *n. Slang.* **1.** A lawyer who obtains clients by persuading accident victims to sue for damages. **2.** A lawyer avid for clients.

am•bu•lant (ăm′byə-lənt) *adj.* Moving or walking about. [Fr. < Lat. *ambulāns*, *ambulant-*, pr.part. of *ambulāre*, to walk.]

am•bu•late (ăm′byə-lāt′) *intr.v.* **-lat•ed, -lat•ing, -lates.** To walk from place to place; move about. [Lat. *ambulāre*, *ambulāt-*, to walk. See **ambhi***.]

am•bu•la•to•ry (ăm′byə-lə-tôr′ē, -tōr′ē) *adj.* **1.** Of, relating to, or adapted for walking. **2.** Capable of walking: *an ambulatory patient.* **3.** Moving about. **4.** *Law.* That can be changed or revoked. —*n.*, *pl.* **-ries.** A covered place for walking. **—am′bu•la•to′ri•ly** *adv.*

am•bus•cade (ăm′bə-skād′, ăm′bə-skād′) *n.* An ambush. —*tr.v.* **-cad•ed, -cad•ing, -cades.** To attack suddenly and without warning from a concealed place; ambush. [< Fr. *embuscade*(< OFr. *embuschier*, to ambush) and < OItal. *imboscata* < fem. p.part. of *imboscare*, to ambush, both < Old Frankish **boscu*, bush, woods.] **—am′bus•cad′er** *n.*

am•bush (ăm′bo͝osh) *n.* **1.** The act of lying in wait to attack by surprise. **2.** A sudden attack made from a concealed position. **3.a.** Those hiding in order to attack by surprise. **b.** The hiding place used for this. **4.** A hidden peril or trap. —*tr.v.* **-bushed, -bush•ing, -bush•es.** To attack from a concealed position. [ME *embush* < OFr. *embusche* < *embuschier*, to ambush < Old Frankish **boscu*, bush, woods.] **—am′bush′er** *n.*

Am•chit•ka (ăm-chĭt′kə). An island off W AK in the W Aleutians.

a•me•ba (ə-mē′bə) *n.* Var. of **amoeba.**

am•e•bi•a•sis also **am•oe•bi•a•sis** (ăm′ə-bī′ə-sĭs) *n.* An infection caused by amoebas, esp. *Entamoeba histolytica.*

a•me•bic dysentery or **a•moe•bic dysentery** (ə-mē′bĭk) *n.* An acute disease caused by the amoeba *Entamoeba histolytica* and characterized by severe diarrhea.

a•me•bo•cyte (ə-mē′bə-sīt′) *n.* Var. of **amoebocyte.**

a•me•lio•rate (ə-mēl′yə-rāt′) *tr. & intr.v.* **-rat•ed, -rat•ing, -rates.** To make or become better; improve. See Syns at **improve.** [Alteration of MELIORATE.]

a•me•lio•ra•tion (ə-mēl′yə-rā′shən) *n.* **1.** The act or an instance of ameliorating. **2.** The state of being ameliorated.

a•men (ā-mĕn′, ä-mĕn′) *interj.* Used at the end of a prayer or a statement to express assent or approval. [ME < OE < LLat. *āmēn* < Gk. *amēn* < Heb. *'āmēn*, certainly, verily.]

A•men also **A•mon** (ä′mən) *n. Myth.* The Egyptian god of life and reproduction, represented as a man with a ram's head.

a•me•na•ble (ə-mē′nə-bəl, ə-mĕn′ə-) *adj.* **1.** Responsive to advice, authority, or suggestion; tractable. **2.** Responsible to higher authority; accountable. See Syns at **responsible. 3.** Open to testing, criticism, or judgment. [Prob. alteration of ME *menable* < OFr. < *mener*, to lead < Lat. *mināre*, to drive < *minārī*, to threaten < *minae*, threats. See **men-**[2]*.] **—a•me′na•bil′i•ty, a•me′na•ble•ness** *n.* **—a•me′na•bly** *adv.*

a•mend (ə-mĕnd′) *v.* **a•mend•ed, a•mend•ing, a•mends.** —*tr.* **1.** To change for the better; improve: *amended the earlier proposal.* **2.** To remove the faults or errors in; correct. See Syns at **correct. 3.** To alter (a legislative measure, for example) formally by adding, deleting, or rephrasing. — *intr.* To better one's conduct; reform. [ME *amenden* < OFr. *amender* < Lat. *ēmendāre*: *ē-*, *ex-*, ex- + *mendum*, fault.]

a•men•da•to•ry (ə-měn′də-tôr′ē, -tōr′ē) *adj.* Serving or tending to amend; corrective.

a•mend•ment (ə-měnd′mənt) *n.* **1.** The act of changing for the better; improvement. **2.** A correction or an alteration. **3.a.** Formal revision of, addition to, or change. **b.** A statement of such a change: *the 19th Amendment to the Constitution.*

a•mends (ə-měndz′) *pl.n. (used with a sing. or pl. v.)* Recompense for grievance or injury. [ME *amendes* < OFr., pl. of *amende*, reparation < *amender*, to amend. See AMEND.]

A•men•ho•tep III (ä′mən-hō′těp, ăm′ən-) also **Am•e•no•phis III** (ăm′ə-nō′fĭs). King of Egypt (1411?–1375 B.C.) who sponsored the building of many monuments.

Amenhotep IV. See **Akhenaton.**

a•men•i•ty (ə-měn′ĭ-tē, ə-mē′nĭ-) *n., pl.* **-ties. 1.** The quality of being pleasant or attractive; agreeableness. **2.** Something that contributes to physical or material comfort. **3.** A feature that increases attractiveness or value. **4. amenities.** Social courtesies; pleasantries. [ME *amenite* < OFr. < Lat. *amoenitās* < *amoenus*, pleasant.]

a•men•or•rhe•a or **a•men•or•rhoe•a** (ā-měn′ə-rē′ə) *n.* Abnormal suppression or absence of menstruation. [A-[1] + Gk. *mēn*, month; see **mē-**[2]* + -RRHEA.] — **a•men′or•rhe′ic** *adj.*

a•men•sa•lism (ā-měn′sə-lĭz′əm) *n.* A relationship between organisms in which one species is harmed and the other species is unaffected. [Prob. A-[1] + (COM)MENSALISM.]

am•ent[1] (ăm′ənt, ā′mənt) *n.* See **catkin.** [Lat. *āmentum*, strap.]

a•ment[2] (ā′měnt′, ā′mənt) *n.* A person whose intellectual capacity remains undeveloped. [< Lat. *āmēns*, *āment-*, insane : *ā-*, *ab-*, out of; see AB-[1] + *mēns*, mind; see **men-**[1]*.]

am•en•ta•ceous (ăm′ən-tā′shəs, ā′mən-) *adj. Bot.* **1.** Resembling or consisting of a catkin. **2.** Bearing catkins.

a•men•tia (ā-měn′shə, -shē-ə) *n.* Insufficient mental development. [Lat. *āmentia*, madness, senselessness < *āmēns*, *āment-*, insane. See AMENT[2].]

Amer. *abbr.* America; American.

Am•er•a•sian (ăm′ə-rā′zhən, -shən) *n.* A person of American and Asian descent. [AMER(ICAN) + ASIAN.] — **Am′er•a′sian** *adj.*

A•mer•i•ca (ə-měr′ĭ-kə). **1.** The United States. **2.** Also **the A•mer•i•cas** (-kəz). The landmasses and islands of North America, South America, Mexico, and Central America included in the Western Hemisphere.

A•mer•i•can (ə-měr′ĭ-kən) *adj.* **1.** Of or relating to the United States of America or its people, language, or culture. **2.** Of or relating to North or South America, the West Indies, or the Western Hemisphere. **3.** Of or relating to any of the Native American peoples. **4.** Indigenous to North or South America. Used of plants and animals. — *n.* **1.** A native or inhabitant of America. **2.** A citizen of the United States. — **A•mer′i•can•ness** *n.*

A•mer•i•ca•na[1] (ä-mĕ′rē-kä′nä). A city of SE Brazil, a suburb of São Paulo. Pop. 121,743.

A•mer•i•ca•na[2] (ə-mĕr′ə-kä′nə, -kăn′ə, -kā′nə) *n.* **1.** *(used with a pl. v.)* Materials relating to American history, folklore, or geography or considered to be typical of American culture. **2.** *(used with a sing. v.)* The culture of America.

American Beauty *n.* A type of rose bearing large, long-stemmed purplish-red flowers.

American cheese *n.* A mild, white to yellow cheddar.

American chestnut *n.* An eastern North American deciduous tree *(Castanea dentata).*

American eagle *n.* See **bald eagle.**

American elk *n.* See **wapiti.**

American elm *n.* A North American deciduous tree *(Ulmus americana)* having double serrate leaves and winged fruits.

American English *n.* The English language as used in the United States.

American Falls. A section, 50.9 m (167 ft) high, of Niagara Falls in W NY N of Buffalo.

American foxhound *n.* Any of a breed of foxhounds having drooping ears and usu. a black, tan, and white coat.

American Indian *n.* See **Native American.** See Usage Note at **Native American.**

A•mer•i•can•ism (ə-měr′ĭ-kə-nĭz′əm) *n.* **1.** A custom, trait, or tradition originating in the United States. **2.** A word, phrase, or idiom characteristic of American English. **3.** Allegiance to the United States and its customs and institutions.

A•mer•i•can•ist (ə-měr′ĭ-kə-nĭst) *n.* **1.** One who studies a facet of America. **2.** A specialist in American aboriginal cultures or languages. **3.** One that is sympathetic to the United States and its policies.

A•mer•i•can•ize (ə-měr′ĭ-kə-nīz′) *v.* **-ized, -iz•ing, -iz•es.** — *tr.* To assimilate into American culture. — *intr.* To become American, as in spirit. — **A•mer′i•can•i•za′tion** (-kə-nĭ-zā′shən) *n.*

American kestrel *n.* See **sparrow hawk** 2.

American plan *n.* A system of hotel management in which a guest pays a fixed daily rate for room and meals.

American Revolution *n.* The war between the American colonies and Great Britain (1775–1783), leading to the formation of the independent United States.

American saddle horse *n.* A three- or five-gaited high-stepping saddle horse of a breed originating in Kentucky.

American Sa•mo•a (sə-mō′ə). An unincorp. territory of the U.S. in the S Pacific NE of Fiji comprising the E islands of the Samoan archipelago; administered by the U.S. since 1899. Cap. Pago Pago. Pop. 32,279.

American Sign Language *n.* An American system of communication for the hearing-impaired that uses manual signs.

American Spanish *n.* The Spanish language as used in the Western Hemisphere.

American Staf•ford•shire terrier (stăf′ərd-shîr′, -shər) *n.* A strong, muscular terrier of an American breed, originally developed for dogfighting.

American Standard Version *n. Bible.* A revised version of the King James Bible published in the United States in 1901.

A•mer•i•cas (ə-měr′ĭ-kəz), **the.** See **America** 2.

am•er•i•ci•um (ăm′ə-rĭsh′ē-əm) *n. Symbol* **Am** A white metallic synthetic element of the actinide series; its longest-lived isotopes, Am 241 and Am 243, are used as radiation sources in research. Atomic number 95; specific gravity 11.7; valence 3, 4, 5, 6. See table at **element.** [After AMERICA.]

A•mer•i•cus (ə-měr′ĭ-kəs). A city of SW-central GA SE of Columbus. Pop. 16,512.

Am•er•in•di•an (ăm′ə-rĭn′dē-ən) also **Am•er•ind** (ăm′ə-rĭnd′) *n.* See **Native American.** See Usage Note at **Native American.** [AMER(ICAN) + IND(IAN).] — **Am′er•in′di•an, Am′er•ind′, Am′er•in′dic** *adj.*

A•mers•foort (ä′mərz-fôrt′, -fōrt′, ä′mərs-). A city of central Netherlands NE of Utrecht. Pop. 86,896.

Ames (āmz). A city of central IA N of Des Moines. Pop. 47,198.

Am•es•lan (ăm′ĭ-slăn′) *n.* See **American Sign Language.**

Ames test *n.* A test used to determine the mutagenic potential of a substance. [After *Bruce Ames* (b. 1928), Amer. biochemist.]

am•e•thop•ter•in (ăm′ə-thŏp′tə-rĭn′) *n.* Methotrexate. [A(MINO)- + METH- + *pter(oyl)*, a chemical radical + -IN.]

am•e•thyst (ăm′ə-thĭst) *n.* **1.** A purple transparent quartz used as a gemstone. **2.** *Color.* A moderate purple to grayish reddish purple. [ME *amatist* < OFr. < Lat. *amethystus* < Gk. *amethustos*: *a-*, not; see A-[1] + **methustos*, intoxicated (< *methuskein*, to intoxicate < *methuein*, to be drunk (from the belief that it was a remedy for drunkenness) < *methu*, wine).] — **am′e•thys′tine** (-thĭs′tĭn, -tīn′) *adj.*

am•e•tro•pi•a (ăm′ĭ-trō′pē-ə) *n.* Any of various eye abnormalities resulting from faulty refraction. [Gk. *ametros*, without measure (*a-*, without; see A-[1] + *metron*, measure; see METER[1]) + -OPIA.] — **am′e•trop′ic** (-trŏp′ĭk, -trō′pĭk) *adj.*

Amex *abbr.* American Stock Exchange.

Am•ga (äm-gä′). A river rising in E Russia and flowing c. 1,287 km (800 mi) to the Aldan R. E of Yakutsk.

Am•gun (äm-gōōn′). A river of SE Russia flowing c. 788 km (490 mi) to the Amur R.

Am•har•ic (ăm-hăr′ĭk, äm-hä′rĭk) *n.* A Semitic language that is the official language of Ethiopia. [After *Amhara*, a former kingdom of NW Ethiopia.] — **Am•har′ic** *adj.*

Am•herst (ăm′ərst, -hərst). A town of W MA NE of Northampton; birthplace of Emily Dickinson. Pop. 35,228.

Am•herst (ăm′ərst), **Jeffrey** also **Jeffery.** Baron Amherst. 1717–97. British general in North America during the French and Indian War.

a•mi•a•ble (ā′mē-ə-bəl) *adj.* **1.** Friendly and agreeable in disposition; good-natured and likable. **2.** Cordial; sociable; congenial. [ME < OFr. < LLat. *amīcābilis*. See AMICABLE.] — **a′mi•a•bil′i•ty, a′mi•a•ble•ness** *n.* — **a′mi•a•bly** *adv.*

am•i•an•thus (ăm′ē-ăn′thəs) also **am•i•an•tus** (-təs) *n.* A fine silky asbestos. [Lat. *amiantus* < Gk. *amiantos*, undefiled : *a-*, not; see A-[1] + *miantos*, defiled (< *miainein*, to defile).]

am•i•ca•ble (ăm′ĭ-kə-bəl) *adj.* Characterized by or exhibiting friendliness or goodwill. [ME < LLat. *amīcābilis* < Lat. *amīcus*, friend.] — **am′i•ca•bil′i•ty, am′i•ca•ble•ness** *n.* — **am′i•ca•bly** *adv.*

am•ice (ăm′ĭs) *n.* A liturgical vestment consisting of an oblong piece of white linen worn around the neck and shoulders and partly under the alb. [ME, prob. < OFr. *amis*, pl. of *amit* < Lat. *amictus*, mantle < p.part. of *amicīre*, to wrap around : *ambi-*, around; see AMBI- + *iacere*, to throw; see **yē-***.]

a•mi•cus cu•ri•ae (ə-mē′kəs kyōōr′ē-ī′) *n., pl.* **a•mi•ci cu•riae** (ə-mē′kē). *Law.* A party uninvolved in a particular litigation but allowed to advise the court on a matter of law concerning the litigation. [Lat. *amīcus*, friend + *curiae*, genitive of *curia*, court.]

a•mid (ə-mĭd′) also **a•midst** (ə-mĭdst′) *prep.* Surrounded by; in the middle of. [ME : *a-*, in; see A-[2] + *mid*, middle (< OE *midde*, middle; see **medhyo-***).]

am•ide (ăm′īd′, -ĭd) *n.* **1.** An organic compound containing the $CONH_2$ radical. **2.** A compound with a metal replacing hydrogen in ammonia. [AM(MONIA) + -IDE.] — **a•mid′ic** (ə-mĭd′ĭk, ă-mĭd′-) *adj.*

ă pat	oi boy
ā pay	ou out
âr care	ŏŏ took
ä father	ōō boot
ĕ pet	ŭ cut
ē be	ûr urge
ĭ pit	th thin
ī pie	*th* this
îr pier	hw which
ŏ pot	zh vision
ō toe	ə about, item
ô paw	

Stress marks:
′ (primary);
′ (secondary), as in
dictionary (dĭk′shə-nĕr′ē)

am•i•dol (ăm′ĭ-dôl′, -dōl′, -dŏl′) *n.* A colorless crystalline compound, $C_6H_3(NH_2)_2OH{\cdot}2HCl$, used as a photographic developer. [Ger. *Amidol*, a trademark.]

a•mid•ships (ə-mĭd′shĭps′) also **a•mid•ship** (-shĭp′) *adv. Naut.* Midway between the bow and the stern or between the port and starboard sides.

a•midst (ə-mĭdst′) *prep.* Var. of **amid.** [ME *amiddes*: *amidde*; see AMID + *-es*, adverbial suffix; see –s³.]

Am•i•ens (ăm′ē-ənz, ä-myăɴ′). A city of N France on the Somme R. N of Paris; settled in pre-Roman times. Pop. 131,332.

a•mi•go (ə-mē′gō) *n., pl.* **-gos.** A friend. [Sp. < Lat. *amīcus.*]

A•min Da•da (ä-mēn′ dä-dä′, dä′dä), **Idi.** b. c. 1925. Ugandan dictator (1971–79) who fled the country after a coup d'état.

A•min•di•vi Islands (ä′mĭn-dē′vē). A group of islands in the Arabian Sea off SW India.

ammonite
Cross section of
a Jurassic ammonite

a•mine (ə-mēn′, ăm′ēn) *n.* Any of a group of organic compounds derived from ammonia by replacing one or more hydrogen atoms by a hydrocarbon radical. [AM(MONIUM) + –INE².]

–amine *suff.* Amine: *diamine.* [< AMINE.]

a•mi•no (ə-mē′nō, ăm′ə-nō′) *adj.* Relating to an amine or other chemical compound containing an NH_2 group combined with a nonacid organic radical. [< AMINO–.]

amino– *pref.* Containing NH_2 combined with a nonacid organic radical: *aminopyrine.* [< AMINE.]

amino acid *n.* An organic compound containing both an amino group (NH_2) and a carboxylic acid group (COOH), esp. any of the 20 compounds that link together to form proteins.

a•mi•no•ac•i•de•mi•a (ə-mē′nō-ăs′ĭ-dē′mē-ə, ăm′ə-nō-) *n.* A condition in which excessive amounts of amino acids are present in the blood.

a•mi•no•ac•i•du•ri•a (ə-mē′nō-ăs′ĭ-dŏŏr′ē-ə, -dyŏŏr′-, ăm′ə-nō-) *n.* A disorder of protein metabolism in which excessive amounts of amino acids are excreted in the urine.

a•mi•no•ben•zo•ic acid (ə-mē′nō-bĕn-zō′ĭk, ăm′ə-nō-) *n.* Any of three benzoic acid derivatives, $C_7H_7NO_2$, esp. the para form, which is part of the vitamin B complex.

a•mi•no•phe•nol (ə-mē′nō-fē′nôl, -nōl, ăm′ə-nō-) *n.* One of three organic compounds with composition $C_6H_4NH_2OH$.

a•mi•no•py•rine (ə-mē′nō-pī′rēn′, ăm′ə-nō-) *n.* A crystalline compound, $C_{13}H_{17}N_3O$, used to reduce fever and relieve pain. [AMINO– + (ANTI)PYRINE.]

a•mir (ə-mîr′, ā-mîr′) *n.* Var. of **emir.**

A•mis (ā′mĭs), Sir **Kingsley.** b. 1922. British writer whose novels include *Lucky Jim* (1954).

A•mish (ä′mĭsh, ăm′ĭsh) *n.* An orthodox Anabaptist sect that exists today primarily in southeast Pennsylvania. [Ger. *amisch*, after Jacob *Amman*, 17th-cent. Swiss Mennonite bishop.] **—A′mish** *adj.*

a•miss (ə-mĭs′) *adj.* **1.** Out of proper order. **2.** Not in perfect shape; faulty. *—adv.* In an improper, defective, unfortunate, or mistaken way. [ME *amis*, prob. < ON *ā mis*, so as to miss : *ā*, on; see **an-*** + *mis*, act of missing; see **mei-¹*.**]

Syns: *amiss, afield, astray, awry, wrong.* The central meaning shared by these adverbs is "not in the right way or the proper order": *spoke amiss; research extending far afield; afraid the letter would go astray; thinking awry; plans that went wrong.* ***Ant:*** *aright.*

am•i•trip•tyl•ine (ăm′ĭ-trĭp′tə-lēn′) *n.* An antidepressant drug, $C_{20}H_{23}N$. [Perh. AMI(NO)– + *tript*-(alteration and shortening of TRYPTOPHAN) + –YL + –INE².]

am•i•ty (ăm′ĭ-tē) *n., pl.* **-ties.** Peaceful relations; friendship. [ME *amite* < OFr. < VLat. **amīcitās* < Lat. *amīcus*, friend.]

Am•man (ä-män′, ä′män). The cap. of Jordan, in the N-central part; known as Philadelphia during Roman and Byzantine times. Pop. 777,500.

am•me•ter (ăm′mē′tər) *n.* An instrument that measures electric current. [AM(PERE) + –METER.]

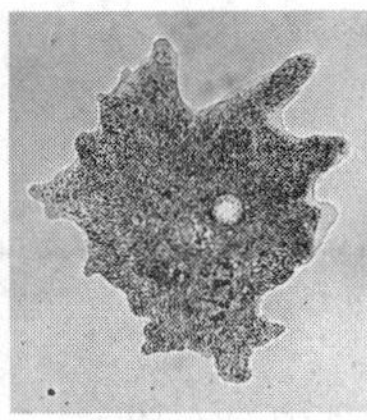

amoeba

am•mine (ăm′ēn′, ă-mēn′) *n.* Any of a class of inorganic coordination compounds of ammonia and a metallic salt. [AM-M(ONIA) + –INE².] **—am′mi•no′** (ăm′ə-nō′, ə-mē′nō) *adj.*

am•mo (ăm′ō) *n. Informal.* Ammunition.

am•mo•nia (ə-mōn′yə) *n.* **1.** A colorless pungent gas, NH_3, used to manufacture fertilizers and nitrogen-containing chemicals. **2.** See **ammonium hydroxide.** [NLat. < Lat. *(sāl) ammōniacus*, (salt) of Amen < Gk. *Ammōniakos*, from *Ammōn*, Amen (from its having been obtained from a region near the temple of Amen in Libya).]

am•mo•ni•ac¹ (ə-mō′nē-ăk′) also **am•mo•ni•a•cal** (ăm′ə-nī′ə-kəl) *adj.* Of, containing, or similar to ammonia.

am•mo•ni•ac² (ə-mō′nē-ăk′) *n.* A strong-smelling gum resin from a plant *(Dorema ammoniacum)*, formerly used in perfume and in medicine. [ME *ammoniak* < Lat. *ammōniacum* < *Ammōniacus*, of Amen < Gk. *Ammōniakos.* See AMMONIA.]

am•mo•ni•ate (ə-mō′nē-āt′) *tr.v.* **-at•ed, -at•ing, -ates.** To treat or combine with ammonia. *—n.* A compound that contains ammonia. **—am•mo′ni•a′tion** *n.*

ammonia water *n.* See **ammonium hydroxide.**

am•mon•i•fi•ca•tion (ə-mŏn′ə-fĭ-kā′shən, ə-mō′nə-) *n.* **1.** Impregnation with ammonia or an ammonium compound. **2.** Production of ammonia or ammonium compounds in the decomposition of organic matter.

am•mon•i•fy (ə-mŏn′ə-fī′, ə-mō′nə-) *tr. & intr.v.* **-fied, -fy•ing, -fies.** To subject or be subjected to ammonification. **—am•mon′i•fi′er** *n.*

am•mo•nite (ăm′ə-nīt′) also **am•mo•noid** (-noid′) *n.* The coiled fossil shell of an extinct mollusk abundant in the Cretaceous Period. [NLat. *Ammōnītēs* < Lat. *(cornū) Ammōnis*, (horn) of Amen, ammonite, genitive of *Ammōn*, Amen < Gk.] **—am′mo•nit′ic** (-nĭt′ĭk) *adj.*

Am•mon•ite (ăm′ə-nīt′) *n.* **1.** A member of an ancient Semitic people living east of the Jordan River. **2.** The Semitic language of the Ammonites. [< LLat. *Ammōnītēs*, the Ammonites < Heb. *'ammônî*, Ammonite < *'ammôn*, Ammon < Canaanite *'amm*, people, kinsman.] **—Am′mon•ite′** *adj.*

am•mo•ni•um (ə-mō′nē-əm) *n.* The univalent chemical ion NH_4+, derived from ammonia. [AMMON(IA) + –IUM.]

ammonium bicarbonate *n.* A crystalline salt, NH_4HCO_3, used in fire-extinguishing compounds and in baking powder.

ammonium carbamate *n.* A salt, a carbonate of ammonium, $NH_4NH_2CO_2$, that is a component of smelling salts.

ammonium carbonate *n.* **1.** A carbonate of ammonium, $(NH_4)_2CO_3$. **2.** The commercially produced double salt of ammonium bicarbonate and ammonium carbamate, $NH_4HCO_3{\cdot}NH_2COONH_4$, used in smelling salts.

ammonium chloride *n.* A slightly hygroscopic white crystalline compound, NH_4Cl, used in dry cells.

ammonium hydroxide *n.* A colorless, basic, aqueous solution of ammonia, NH_4OH, used as a cleanser and in the manufacture of textiles, rayon, rubber, fertilizer, and plastic.

ammonium nitrate *n.* A colorless crystalline salt, NH_4NO_3, used in fertilizers, explosives, and solid rocket propellants.

ammonium sulfate *n.* A brownish-gray to white crystalline salt, $(NH_4)_2SO_4$, used in fertilizers and water purification.

ammonium thiocyanate *n.* A colorless crystalline compound, NH_4SCN, used in dyeing fabrics and electroplating.

am•mo•noid (ăm′ə-noid′) *n.* Var. of **ammonite.**

am•mu•ni•tion (ăm′yə-nĭsh′ən) *n.* **1.** All projectiles, such as bullets and shot, that can be fired from guns or otherwise propelled. **2.** Nuclear, biological, chemical, or explosive materiel that are used as weapons. **3.** An object used as a missile in offense or defense. **4.** A means of attacking or defending an argument, thesis, or point of view. [Obsolete Fr. *amunition* < *l'amunition*, the provisioning, alteration of *la munition* < OFr. < Lat. *mūnītiō, mūnītiōn-*, fortification. See MUNITION.]

Amn *abbr.* Airman.

Am•ne Ma•chin Shan (ăm′nē mə-jĭn′ shän). A range of mountains of W-central China, rising to 7,164.5 m (23,490 ft) at **Amne Machin.**

am•ne•sia (ăm-nē′zhə) *n.* Partial or total loss of memory. [Gk. *amnēsia*, forgetfulness, prob. < *amnēstia*: *a-*, not; see A–¹ + *mimnēskein*, to remember; see **men-¹*.**] **—am•ne′si•ac′** (-nē′zē-ăk′, -zhē-ăk′), **am•ne′sic** (-zĭk, -sĭk) *n. & adj.* **—am•nes′tic** (-nĕs′tĭk) *adj.*

am•nes•ty (ăm′nĭ-stē) *n., pl.* **-ties.** A general pardon granted by a government, esp. for political offenses. *—tr.v.* **-tied, -ty•ing, -ties.** To grant a general pardon to. [Lat. *amnestia* < Gk. *amnēstia* < *amnēstos*, not remembered : *a-*, not; see A–¹ + *mimnēskein*, to remember; see **men-¹*.**]

am•ni•o•cen•te•sis (ăm′nē-ō-sĕn-tē′sĭs) *n., pl.* **-ses** (-sēz). A procedure in which amniotic fluid is drawn out of the uterus and analyzed to determine genetic abnormalities in or the sex of the fetus. [NLat. *amniocentēsis*: AMNION + Gk. *kentēsis*, act of pricking (< *kentein*, to prick; see **kent-***).]

am•ni•og•ra•phy (ăm′nē-ŏg′rə-fē) *n., pl.* **-phies.** Radiographic examination of the fetus following injection of a radiopaque substance into the amnion. [AMNIO(N) + –GRAPHY.]

am•ni•on (ăm′nē-ən, -ŏn′) *n., pl.* **-ni•ons** or **-ni•a** (-nē-ə). A thin, fluid-filled membranous sac that encloses the embryo or fetus of a mammal, bird, or reptile. [Gk. *amniŏn.*] **—am′ni•ot′ic** (-ŏt′ĭk), **am′ni•on′ic** (-ŏn′ĭk) *adj.*

am•ni•os•co•py (ăm′nē-ŏs′kə-pē) *n., pl.* **-pies.** Examination of the fetus using an optical instrument that is inserted directly into the amniotic cavity. [AMNIO(N) + –SCOPY.] **—am′ni•o•scope′** (-ə-skōp′) *n.*

am•o•bar•bi•tal (ăm′ō-bär′bĭ-tăl′, -tôl′) *n.* A barbiturate, $C_{11}H_{18}N_2O_3$, used as a sedative and a hypnotic. [AM(YL) + BARBITAL.]

a•moe•ba also **a•me•ba** (ə-mē′bə) *n., pl.* **-bas** or **-bae** (-bē). A protozoan of the genus *Amoeba* or related genera having no definite form and moving by means of pseudopods. [NLat., genus name < Gk. *amoibē*, change < *ameibein*, to change. See **mei-¹*.**] **—a•moe′bic** (-bĭk) *adj.*

am•oe•bae•an or **am•oe•be•an** (ăm′ə-bē′ən) *adj.* Answering alternately in prosody. [< LLat. *amoebaeus* < Gk. *amoibaios* < *amoibē*, change. See AMOEBA.]

am•oe•bi•a•sis (ăm′ə-bī′ə-sĭs) *n.* Var. of **amebiasis.**

amoebic dysentery *n.* Var. of **amebic dysentery.**

a•moe•bo•cyte also **a•me•bo•cyte** (ə-mē′bə-sīt′) *n.* A cell having amoeboid form or motion. [AMOEB(A) + –CYTE.]

a•moe•boid (ə-mē′boid′) *adj.* **1.** Of or resembling an amoeba, esp. in changeability of form and means of locomotion.

2. Having an irregular or asymmetrical shape.

a•mok (ə-mŭk′, ə-mŏk′) *adv. & adj.* Var. of **amuck.**

a•mo•le (ə-mō′lē) *n.* **1.** The root, bulb, or another plant part of several North American plants, such as species of *Agave, Chlorogalum,* and *Yucca,* used as a soap. **2.** A plant so used. [Am.Sp. < Nahuatl *amolli.*]

A•mon (ä′mən) *n. Myth.* Var. of **Amen.**

a•mong (ə-mŭng′) also **a•mongst** (ə-mŭngst′) *prep.* **1.** In the midst of; surrounded by. **2.** In the group, number, or class of: *She is among the wealthy.* **3.** In the company of; in association with: *traveling among a group of tourists.* **4.** By many or the entire number of; with many: *a custom among the Greeks.* **5.** By the joint action of: *Among us, we will finish.* **6.** With portions to each of: *Distribute this among you.* **7.** Each with the other: *Don't fight among yourselves.* See Usage Note at **between.** [ME < OE *āmang*: *ā*, in; see A–[2] + *gemang*, throng; see **mag-*.**]

a•mon•til•la•do (ə-mŏn′tl-ä′dō, -tē-ä′-) *n., pl.* **-dos.** A pale dry sherry. [Sp. : *a-*, to (< Lat. *ad-*; see AD–) + *Montilla*, a town of S Spain.]

a•mor•al (ā-môr′əl, ā-mŏr′-) *adj.* **1.** Not admitting of moral distinctions or judgments; neither moral nor immoral. **2.** Lacking moral sensibility; not caring about right and wrong. **—a•mor′al•ism, a′mo•ral′i•ty** (ā′mô-răl′ĭ-tē, -mə-) *n.* **—a•mor′al•ly** *adv.*

am•o•ret•to (ăm′ə-rĕt′ō, ä′mə-) *n., pl.* **-ti** (-tē) or **-tos.** A cupid. [Ital., dim. of *Amore*, Cupid < Lat. *Amor* < *amor*, love. See AMOROUS.]

am•o•rist (ăm′ər-ĭst) *n.* **1.** One dedicated to love, esp. sexual love. **2.** One who writes about love. [Lat. *amor*, love; see AMOROUS + –IST.]

Am•o•rite (ăm′ə-rīt′) *n.* A member of one of several ancient Semitic peoples primarily inhabiting Canaan and Babylonia. [< Heb. *'ĕmōrî*, Amorite < Akkadian *amurru*, westerner, Amorite.] **—Am′o•rite′** *adj.*

am•o•rous (ăm′ər-əs) *adj.* **1.** Strongly attracted or disposed to love, esp. sexual love. **2.** Indicative of love or sexual desire: *an amorous glance.* **3.** Of or associated with love. **4.** Being in love; enamored. [ME < OFr. *amoureus* < Med.Lat. *amōrōsus* < Lat. *amor*, love < *amāre*, to love.] **—am′or•ous•ly** *adv.* **—am′or•ous•ness** *n.*

a•mor•phism (ə-môr′fĭz′əm) *n.* The state or quality of being amorphous.

a•mor•phous (ə-môr′fəs) *adj.* **1.** Lacking definite form; shapeless. **2.** Of no particular type; anomalous. **3.** Lacking organization; formless. **4.** Lacking distinct crystalline structure. [< Gk. *amorphos*: *a-*, without; see A–[1] + *morphē*, shape.] **—a•mor′phous•ly** *adv.* **—a•mor′phous•ness** *n.*

am•or•ti•za•tion (ăm′ər-tĭ-zā′shən, ə-môr′tĭ-) *n.* **1.a.** The act or process of amortizing. **b.** The money set aside for this purpose. **2.** For a bond bought at a premium, the periodic subtraction from its current yield of a proportionate share of the premium between the purchase date and the maturity date.

am•or•tize (ăm′ər-tīz′, ə-môr′-) *tr.v.* **-tized, -tiz•ing, -tiz•es.** **1.** To liquidate (a debt) by installment payments or payment into a sinking fund. **2.** To write off an expenditure for (office equipment, for example) by prorating over a certain period. [ME *amortisen*, to alienate in mortmain < OFr. *amortir*, *amortiss-* < VLat. **admortīre*, to deaden : Lat. *ad-*, ad- + Lat. *mors, mort-*, death; see **mer-*.**] **—am′or•tiz′a•ble** *adj.*

A•mos (ā′məs) *n. Bible.* **1.** A Hebrew prophet of the 8th cent. B.C. **2.** See table at **Bible.**

a•mount (ə-mount′) *n.* **1.** The total of two or more quantities; the aggregate. **2.** A number; a sum. **3.** A principal plus its interest. **4.** The full effect or meaning; import. **5.** Quantity: *a great amount.* —*intr.v.* **a•mount•ed, a•mount•ing, a•mounts. 1.** To add up in number or quantity. **2.** To add up in import or effect: *That plan will never amount to much.* **3.** To be equivalent or tantamount: *accusations that amount to an indictment.* [< ME *amounten*, to ascend < OFr. *amonter* < *amont*, upward < Lat. *ad montem*, to the hill : *ad*, to; see **ad-*** + *mōns, mont-*, hill; see **men-[2]*.**]

a•mour (ə-mo͝or′) *n.* A love affair, esp. an illicit one. [ME < OFr. < OProv. < Lat. *amor*, love. See AMOROUS.]

a•mour-pro•pre (ä-mo͝or-prôp′rə) *n.* Respect for oneself; self-esteem. [Fr. : *amour*, love + *propre*, own.]

A•moy[1] (ä-moi′). See **Xiamen.**

A•moy[2] (ä-moi′, ə-moi′) *n.* The dialect of Chinese spoken in and around Xiamen in southeast China. [After *Amoy* (Xiamen).]

amp (ămp) *n. Informal.* **1.** An ampere. **2.** An amplifier.

AMP (ā′em-pē′) *n.* A mononucleotide, $C_{10}H_{14}N_5O_7P$, found in animal cells and reversibly convertible to ADP and ATP; adenosine monophosphate. [A(DENOSINE) M(ONO)P(HOSPHATE).]

am•per•age (ăm′pər-ĭj, ăm′pîr′-) *n.* The strength of an electric current expressed in amperes.

am•pere (ăm′pîr′) *n.* **1.** A unit of electric current in the meter-kilogram-second system, equal to the current that, flowing in two parallel wires one meter apart, produces a force of 2 × 10^{-7} newtons per meter. **2.** A unit specified as one International coulomb per second and equal to 0.999835 ampere. See table at **measurement.** [After André Marie AMPÈRE.]

Am•père (ăm′pîr, äɴ-pĕr′), **André Marie.** 1775–1836. French physicist and mathematician.

am•pere-hour (ăm′pîr-our′) *n.* The electric charge transferred by a current of one ampere in one hour.

am•pere-turn (ăm′pîr-tûrn′) *n.* A unit of magnetomotive force in the meter-kilogram-second system equal to the force of one turn of a conducting loop carrying a current of one ampere.

am•per•sand (ăm′pər-sănd′) *n.* The character or sign (&) representing the word *and.* [Alteration of *and per se and*, & (the sign) by itself (is the word) and.]

am•phet•a•mine (ăm-fĕt′ə-mēn′, -mĭn) *n.* **1.** A colorless volatile liquid, $C_9H_{13}N$, used primarily as a central nervous system stimulant. **2.** A derivative of amphetamine, such as dextroamphetamine, used as a central nervous system stimulant. [A(LPHA) + M(ETHYL) + PH(ENYL) + ET(HYL) + AMINE.]

amphi– *pref.* **1.** Both: *amphibiotic.* **2.** On both sides: *amphistylar.* **3.** Around: *amphithecium.* [Lat. < Gk. < *amphi*, on both sides, around. See **ambhi*.**]

am•phi•ar•thro•sis (ăm′fē-är-thrō′sĭs) *n., pl.* **-ses** (-sēz). A type of articulation between bony surfaces that permits limited motion and is connected by ligaments or elastic cartilage.

am•phib•i•an (ăm-fĭb′ē-ən) *n.* **1.** A cold-blooded smooth-skinned vertebrate of the class Amphibia that hatches as an aquatic larva with gills and transforms into an adult having air-breathing lungs. **2.** An animal capable of living both on land and in water. **3.** An aircraft that can take off and land on either land or water. **4.** A vehicle that can operate both on land and in water. [< NLat. *Amphibia*, class name < Gk., neut. pl. of *amphibios*, amphibious : *amphi-*, amphi- + *bios*, life; see **g^wei-*.**]

am•phi•bi•ot•ic (ăm′fə-bī-ŏt′ĭk) *adj.* Living in water during an early stage of development and on land during the adult stage.

am•phib•i•ous (ăm-fĭb′ē-əs) *adj.* **1.** *Biol.* Living or able to live on land and in water. **2.** Able to operate both on land and in water: *amphibious tanks.* **3.** Relating to or organized for a military landing by naval and land forces. **4.** Of a mixed or twofold nature. [< Lat. *amphibius* < Gk. *amphibios*. See AMPHIBIAN.] **—am•phib′i•ous•ly** *adv.* **—am•phib′i•ous•ness** *n.*

am•phi•bole (ăm′fə-bōl′) *n.* Any of a large group of structurally similar hydrated double silicate minerals, such as hornblende. [Fr. < LLat. *amphibolus*, ambiguous < Gk. *amphibolos*, doubtful < *amphiballein*, to throw on either side : *amphi-*, amphi- + *ballein*, to throw; see **g^welə-*.**] **—am′phi•bol′ic** (-bŏl′ĭk) *adj.*

am•phib•o•lite (ăm-fĭb′ə-līt′) *n.* A chiefly amphibole rock with minor plagioclase and little quartz. **—am•phib′o•lit′ic** (-lĭt′ĭk) *adj.*

am•phib•o•lous (ăm-fĭb′ə-ləs) *adj.* Having a grammatical structure that allows of two interpretations; equivocal. [< LLat. *amphibolus*. See AMPHIBOLE.]

am•phi•brach (ăm′fə-brăk′) *n.* A trisyllabic metrical foot having one accented or long syllable between two unaccented or short syllables, as in *remember.* [Lat. *amphibrachys* < Gk. *amphibrakhus*: *amphi-*, amphi- + *brakhus*, short; see **mregh-u-*.**]

am•phic•ty•o•ny (ăm-fĭk′tē-ə-nē) *n., pl.* **-nies.** A league of neighboring ancient Greek states sharing a common religious center or shrine, esp. the one at Delphi. [Gk. *Amphiktuonia* < *amphiktuones*, var. of *amphiktiones*, neighbors : *amphi-*, on the periphery; see AMPHI– + *ktizein*, to settle; see **tkei-*.**] **—am•phic′ty•on′ic** (-ŏn′ĭk) *adj.*

am•phi•dip•loid (ăm′fĭ-dĭp′loid) *adj. Genet.* Having a diploid set of chromosomes derived from each parent. **—am′phi•dip′loid** *n.* **—am′phi•dip′loid•y** *n.*

am•phim•a•cer (ăm-fĭm′ə-sər) *n.* A trisyllabic metrical foot having an unaccented or short syllable between two accented or long syllables, as in *Peter Pan.* [Lat. *amphimacrus* < Gk. *amphimakros*: *amphi-*, amphi- + *makros*, long; see **māk-*.**]

am•phi•mix•is (ăm′fə-mĭk′sĭs) *n., pl.* **-mix•es** (-mĭk′sēz′). The union of the sperm and egg in sexual reproduction. [AMPHI– + Gk. *mixis*, a mingling (< *mignunai*, *mik-*, to mingle; see **meik-***).] **—am′phi•mic′tic** (-mĭk′tĭk) *adj.*

Am•phi•on (ăm-fī′ən) *n. Gk. Myth.* The son of Zeus and twin brother of Zethus, with whom he built a wall around Thebes by charming the stones into place with his lyre.

am•phi•ox•us (ăm′fē-ŏk′səs) *n.* See **lancelet.** [AMPHI– + Gk. *oxus*, sharp; see **ak-*.**]

am•phi•pod (ăm′fə-pŏd′) *n.* A crustacean of the order Amphipoda with a laterally compressed body and no carapace. [< NLat. *Amphipoda*, order name : AMPHI– + NLat. *-poda*, -pod.]

amphipod

am•phip•ro•style (ăm-fĭp′rō-stīl′, ăm′fĭ-prō′stīl′) *adj. Archit.* Having a set of columns at each end but none along the sides. [Lat. *amphiprostȳlos* < Gk. *amphiprostulos*: *amphi-*, amphi- + *prostulos*, with pillars in front; see PROSTYLE.] **—am•phip′ro•style′** *n.*

am•phis•bae•na (ăm′fĭs-bē′nə) *n. Myth.* A serpent having a head at each end of its body. [ME *amphibena* < Lat. *am-*

ă **pat**	oi **boy**
ā **pay**	ou **out**
âr **care**	o͝o **took**
ä **father**	o͞o **boot**
ĕ **pet**	ŭ **cut**
ē **be**	ûr **urge**
ĭ **pit**	th **thin**
ī **pie**	*th* **this**
îr **pier**	hw **which**
ŏ **pot**	zh **vision**
ō **toe**	ə **about,** item
ô **paw**	

Stress marks:
′ (primary);
′ (secondary), as in **dictionary** (dĭk′shə-nĕr′ē)

phisbaena < Gk. *amphisbaina*: *amphis*, both ways (< *amphi-*, on both sides; see AMPHI–) + *bainein*, to go; see **gʷā-***.]

am•phi•sty•lar (ăm′fĭ-stī′lər) *adj. Archit.* Having columns at both front and back or on each side. [< AMPHI– + Gk. *stulos*, pillar; see **stā-***.]

am•phi•the•a•ter (ăm′fə-thē′ə-tər) *n.* **1.** An oval or round structure having tiers of seats rising gradually outward from an open space or arena. **2.** An arena for contests and spectacles. **3.** A level area surrounded by upward sloping ground. **4.** An upper, sloping gallery with seats for spectators, as in a theater. [ME *amphitheatre* < Lat. *amphitheātrum* < Gk. *amphitheatron*: *amphi-*, amphi- + *theatron*, theater; see THEATER.] —**am′phi•the•at′ric** (-ăt′rĭk), **am′phi•the•at′ri•cal** *adj.* —**am′phi•the•at′ri•cal•ly** *adv.*

am•phi•the•ci•um (ăm′fə-thē′shē-əm, -sē-əm) *n., pl.* **-ci•a** (-shē-ə, -sē-ə). The outer layer of cells of the spore-containing capsule of a moss. [NLat. : AMPHI– + Gk. *thēkion*, dim. of *thēkē*, receptacle; see **dhē-***.]

Am•phi•tri•te (ăm′fĭ-trī′tē) *n. Gk. Myth.* A Nereid, goddess of the sea and the wife of Poseidon.

am•phit•ro•pous (ăm-fĭt′rə-pəs) *adj. Bot.* Partly inverted and attached near the center to the funiculus.

Am•phit•ry•on (ăm-fĭt′rē-ən) *n. Gk. Myth.* A king of Thebes and the husband of Alcmene.

am•pho•ra (ăm′fər-ə) *n., pl.* **-pho•rae** (-fə-rē′) or **-pho•ras.** A two-handled, narrow-necked Greek or Roman jar for wine or oil. [ME < Lat. < Gk. *amphoreus*, short for *amphiphoreus*: *amphi-*, amphi- + *phoreus*, bearer (< *pherein*, to bear; see **bher-¹***).] —**am′pho•ral** *adj.*

amphitheater
Théâtre Antique, Orange, France

am•pho•ter•ic (ăm′fə-tĕr′ĭk) *adj.* Having the characteristics of an acid and a base and capable of reacting chemically as either. [< Gk. *amphoteros*, each of two < *amphō*, both.]

am•pho•ter•i•cin B (ăm′fə-tĕr′ĭ-sĭn) *n.* An antibiotic derived from the actinomycete *Streptomyces nodosus* and used in treating systemic fungal infections. [AMPHOTERIC + –IN.]

amp hr *abbr.* Ampere-hour.

am•pi•cil•lin (ăm′pĭ-sĭl′ĭn) *n.* A type of penicillin effective against gram-negative and gram-positive bacteria and used to treat gonorrhea and infections of the intestinal, urinary, and respiratory tracts. [Blend of AMINO– and PENICILLIN.]

am•ple (ăm′pəl) *adj.* **-pler, -plest. 1.** Of large size, amount, extent, or capacity. **2.a.** Large in degree, kind, or quantity: *an ample reward.* **b.** More than enough: *ample evidence.* **3.** Fully sufficient for a purpose: *ample food for all.* [ME < OFr. < Lat. *amplus*.] —**am′ple•ness** *n.* —**am′ply** (-plē) *adv.*

amphora
c. 540 B.C. neck amphora painted by Exekias

am•plex•i•caul (ăm-plĕk′sĭ-kôl′) *adj. Bot.* Clasping the stem, as the base of a leaf. [Lat. *amplexus*, an embracing < p.part. of *amplectī*, to embrace (*ambi-*, amphi- + *plectere*, to twine; see **plek-***) + Lat. *caulis*, stem.]

am•pli•fi•ca•tion (ăm′plə-fĭ-kā′shən) *n.* **1.** The act or result of amplifying, enlarging, or extending. **2.a.** An addition to or expansion of a statement or an idea. **b.** A statement with such an addition. **3.** *Phys.* **a.** The process of increasing the magnitude of a variable quantity, esp. voltage, power, or current, without altering any other quality. **b.** The result of such a process. **4.** *Electron.* See **gain¹** 4.

am•pli•fi•er (ăm′plə-fī′ər) *n.* **1.** One that amplifies, enlarges, or extends. **2.** *Electron.* A device, esp. one using transistors or electron tubes, that amplifies an electrical signal.

am•pli•fy (ăm′plə-fī′) *v.* **-fied, -fy•ing, -fies.** —*tr.* **1.** To make larger or more powerful; increase. **2.** To add to, as by illustrations; make complete. **3.** To exaggerate. **4.** To produce amplification of: *amplify an electrical signal.* —*intr.* To write or discourse at length; expatiate. [ME *amplifien* < OFr. *amplifier* < Lat. *amplificāre*: *amplus*, large + *-ficāre*, -fy.]

am•pli•tude (ăm′plĭ-to͞od′, -tyo͞od′) *n.* **1.** Greatness of size; magnitude. **2.** Fullness; copiousness. **3.** Breadth or range, as of intelligence. **4.** *Astron.* The angular distance along the horizon from true east or west to the intersection of the vertical circle of a celestial body with the horizon. **5.** *Phys.* The maximum absolute value of a periodically varying quantity. **6.** *Math.* **a.** The maximum absolute value of a periodic curve measured along its vertical axis. **b.** The angle made with the positive horizontal axis by the vector representation of a complex number. **7.** *Electron.* The maximum absolute value reached by a voltage or current waveform. [Lat. *amplitūdō* < *amplus*, large.]

amplitude modulation *n. Electron.* **1.** The encoding of a carrier wave by variation of its amplitude in accordance with an input signal. **2.** A broadcast system that uses amplitude modulation.

am•poule also **am•pule** or **am•pul** (ăm′po͞ol, -pyo͞ol) *n.* A small glass vial that is sealed after filling and used chiefly as a container for a hypodermic injection solution. [Fr. < OFr. < Lat. *ampulla*. See AMPULLA.]

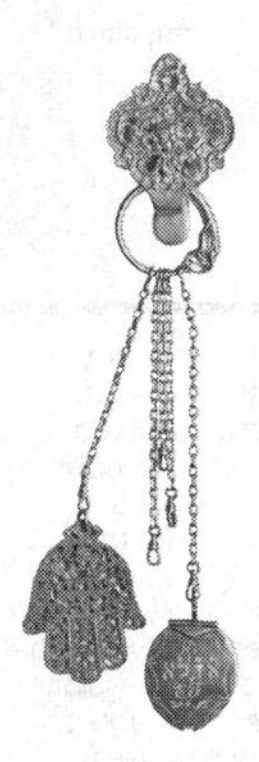

amulet
Late 19th-century Tunisian amulets suspended from a belt clip

am•pul•la (ăm-po͝ol′ə, -pŭl′ə) *n., pl.* **-pul•lae** (-po͝ol′ē, -pŭl′ē). **1.** A nearly round bottle with two handles used by the ancient Romans for wine, oil, or perfume. **2.** *Eccles.* A vessel for consecrated wine or holy oil. **3.** *Anat.* A small dilatation in a canal or duct, esp. in the semicircular canal. [ME < OE < Lat., dim. of *amphora*. See AMPHORA.] —**am•pul′lar** *adj.*

am•pu•tate (ăm′pyo͝o-tāt′) *tr.v.* **-tat•ed, -tat•ing, -tates.** To cut off (a part of the body), esp. by surgery. [Lat. *amputāre*, *amputāt-*, to cut around : *ambi-*, around; see AMBI– + *putāre*, to cut; see **peu-***.] —**am′pu•ta′tion** *n.* —**am′pu•ta′tor** *n.*

am•pu•tee (ăm′pyo͝o-tē′) *n.* A person with one or more amputated limbs.

Am•ra•va•ti (əm-rä′və-tē, äm-). A town of central India W of Nagpur. Pop. 261,404.

am•ri•ta also **am•ree•ta** (ŭm-rē′tə) *n. Myth.* **1.** The ambrosia, prepared by the Hindu gods, that bestows immortality. **2.** The immortality thus bestowed. [Skt. *amṛtam*: *a-*, without; see **ne*** + *mṛtam*, death; see **mer-***.]

Am•rit•sar (əm-rĭt′sər). A city of NW India near the Pakistan border; founded 1577. Pop. 594,844.

AMS *abbr.* **1.** Agricultural Marketing Service. **2.** Auditory memory span.

Am•ster•dam (ăm′stər-dăm′). **1.** The constitutional cap. of the Netherlands, in the W part on an inlet of the Ijsselmeer. Pop. 676,439. **2.** A city of E-central NY on the Mohawk R. NW of Albany; settled in 1783. Pop. 20,714.

amt. *abbr.* Amount.

am•trac also **am•track** (ăm′trăk′) *n.* A small, flatbottom amphibious vehicle that moves along finned tracks and carries troops from ship to shore. [AM(PHIBIOUS) + TRAC(TOR).]

amu *abbr. Phys.* Atomic mass unit.

a•muck (ə-mŭk′) also **a•mok** (ə-mŭk′, ə-mŏk′) —*adv.* **1.** In a frenzy to do violence or kill: *Rioters ran amuck.* **2.** In or into a confused state: *The plans went amuck.* —*adj.* Crazed with murderous frenzy. [Malay *amok*.]

A•mu Dar•ya (ä′mo͞o där′yə, ə-mo͞o′ dŭr-yä′). Formerly **Ox•us** (ŏk′səs). A river of central Asia flowing c. 2,574 km (1,600 mi) from the Pamir Mts. to the S Aral Sea.

am•u•let (ăm′yə-lĭt) *n.* An object worn esp. around the neck as a charm against evil or injury. [Lat. *amulētum*.]

A•mund•sen (ä′mənd-sən, ä′mo͝on-), **Roald.** 1872–1928. Norwegian explorer who reached the South Pole in 1911.

Amundsen Gulf. An inlet of the Arctic Ocean in Northwest Terrs., Canada; navigated by Roald Amundsen during his 1903–05 expedition.

Amundsen Sea. An arm of the S Pacific off the coast of Marie Byrd Land, Antarctica.

A•mur River (ä-mo͝or′) also **Hei•long Jiang** (hā′lông′ jyäng′). A river of NE Asia flowing c. 2,896 km (1,800 mi) mainly along the border between China and Russia.

a•muse (ə-myo͞oz′) *tr.v.* **a•mused, a•mus•ing, a•mus•es. 1.** To occupy in an agreeable, pleasing, or entertaining fashion. **2.** To cause to laugh or smile from pleasure. **3.** *Archaic.* To delude or deceive. [ME < OFr. *amuser*, to stupefy : *a-*, to (< Lat. *ad-*; see AD–) + *muser*, to stare stupidly; see MUSE.] —**a•mus′a•ble** *adj.* —**a•mus′er** *n.* —**a•mu′sive** *adj.*

a•muse•ment (ə-myo͞oz′mənt) *n.* **1.** The state of being amused, entertained, or pleased. **2.** Something that amuses, entertains, or pleases.

amusement park *n.* A commercial enterprise that offers rides, games, and other entertainment.

a•mus•ing (ə-myo͞o′zĭng) *adj.* **1.** Entertaining or pleasing. **2.** Arousing laughter. —**a•mus′ing•ly** *adv.* —**a•mus′ing•ness** *n.*

AMVETS *abbr.* American Veterans.

a•myg•da•la (ə-mĭg′də-lə) *n., pl.* **-lae** (-lē). *Anat.* An almond-shaped mass of gray matter in the anterior portion of the temporal lobe. [Lat., almond < Gk. *amugdalē*.]

a•myg•dale (ə-mĭg′dāl) *n.* An amygdule. [< Lat. *amygdala*, almond. See AMYGDALA.]

a•myg•da•lin (ə-mĭg′də-lĭn) *n.* A glycoside, $C_{20}H_{27}NO_{11}$, found in plant parts of many members of the rose family. [< LLat. *amygdalus*, almond tree < Gk. *amygdalos*.]

a•myg•da•line (ə-mĭg′də-lĭn, -līn′) *adj.* Of, relating to, or like an almond. [Lat. *amygdalīnus* < Gk. *amugdalinos* < *amugdalē*, almond.]

a•myg•da•loid (ə-mĭg′də-loid′) *n.* A volcanic rock containing many amygdules. —*adj.* also **a•myg•da•loi•dal** (ə-mĭg′də-loi′dl). **1.** Shaped like an almond. **2.** *Anat.* Of or relating to the amygdala. **3.** Resembling a volcanic rock that contains amygdules. [Lat. *amygdala*, almond; see AMYGDALA + –OID.]

amygdaloid nucleus *n.* See **amygdala.**

a•myg•dule (ə-mĭg′dyo͞ol) *n.* A small gas bubble in igneous rock filled with secondary minerals such as quartz. [Lat. *amygdala*, almond (from its shape); see AMYGDALA + (NOD)ULE.]

am•yl (ăm′əl) *n.* The univalent organic radical, C_5H_{11}, occurring in many organic compounds in eight isomeric forms. [Blend of AMYL(O)– and –YL.]

amyl– *pref.* Var. of **amylo–.**

am•y•la•ceous (ăm′ə-lā′shəs) *adj.* Of, relating to, or resembling starch; starchy.

amyl acetate *n.* An organic compound, $CH_3COOC_5H_{11}$, used as a flavoring agent.

amyl alcohol *n.* Any of eight isomers of the alcohol composition $C_5H_{11}OH$, one of which is the principal constituent of fusel oil.

am•y•lase (ăm′ə-lās′, -lāz′) *n.* A group of enzymes that help convert starch to sugar in plants and animals.

amyl nitrite *n.* A volatile yellow liquid, $C_5H_{11}NO_2$, used in medicine as a vasodilator.
amylo– or **amyl–** *pref.* Starch: *amylose.* [< Lat. *amylum,* starch. See AMYLUM.]
am•y•loid (ăm′ə-loid′) *n.* **1.** A starchlike substance. **2.** *Pathol.* A hard waxy deposit of protein and polysaccharides resulting from tissue degeneration. — *adj.* Starchlike.
am•y•loid•o•sis (ăm′ə-loi-dō′sĭs) *n.* A disorder marked by the deposition of amyloid in various organs and tissues of the body.
am•y•lol•y•sis (ăm′ə-lŏl′ĭ-sĭs) *n.* Conversion of starch to sugars by the action of enzymes or acids. — **am′y•lo•lyt′ic** (-lō-lĭt′ĭk) *adj.*
am•y•lop•sin (ăm′ə-lŏp′sĭn) *n.* The starch-digesting amylase produced by the pancreas. [AMYLO– + (TRY)PSIN.]
am•y•lose (ăm′ə-lōs′, -lōz′) *n.* **1.** The inner portion of a starch granule, consisting of relatively soluble polysaccharides. **2.** A polysaccharide.
am•y•lum (ăm′ə-ləm) *n.* Starch. [Lat. < Gk. *amulon,* starch < neut. of *amulos,* not ground at a mill : *a-,* not; see A–[1] + *mulē,* mill; see **melə-*.**]
a•my•o•to•ni•a (ā′mī-ə-tō′nē-ə) *n.* Lack of muscle tone.
a•my•o•tro•phic lateral sclerosis (ā′mī-ə-trō′fĭk, -trŏf′ĭk, ā-mī′-) *n.* A chronic, progressive, and usu. terminal disease marked by gradual degeneration of the nerve cells in the central nervous system that control voluntary muscle movement.
an[1] (ən; ăn *when stressed*) *indef.art.* The form of *a* used before words beginning with a vowel or with an unpronounced *h*: *an hour.* See Usage Notes at **a**[2], **every.** [ME < OE *ān,* one. See **oi-no-*.**]
an[2] also **an'** (ən, ăn *when stressed*) *conj. Archaic.* And if; if. [ME, short for *and,* and < OE. See AND.]
AN *abbr.* Airman, Navy.
an. *abbr. Lat.* **1.** Anno (in the year). **2.** Ante (before).
an– *pref.* Var. of **a–**[1].
–an[1] *suff.* **1.** Of, relating to, or resembling: *brachyuran.* **2.** One relating to, belonging to, or resembling: *librarian.* [ME < OFr. < Lat. *-ānus,* adj. and n. suff.]
–an[2] *suff.* **1.** Unsaturated carbon compound: *urethan.* **2.** Anhydride of a carbohydrate: *dextran.* [Alteration of –ANE.]
an•a[1] (ăn′ə, ä′nə) *n., pl.* **ana** or **-as. 1.** A collection of various materials that reflect the character of a person or place: *ana of Oman.* **2.** An item in such a collection. [< NLat. *-āna,* as in titles of such collections. See –ANA.]
an•a[2] (ăn′ə) *adv.* Both in the same quantity. Used in prescriptions. [ME < Med.Lat. < Gk., at the rate of. See **an-*.**]
ANA *abbr.* **1.** American Newspaper Association. **2.** American Nurses Association. **3.** Association of National Advertisers.
ana– *pref.* **1.** Upward; up: *anabolism.* **2.** Backward; back: *anaplasia.* **3.** Again; anew: *anaphylaxis.* [Gk. < *ana,* up. See **an-*.**]
–ana or **–iana** *suff.* A collection of items relating to a specified person or place: *Americana.* [NLat. *-āna* < Lat. *-āna,* neut. pl. of *-ānus,* adj. and n. suff. See –AN[1].]
an•a•bae•na (ăn′ə-bē′nə) *n.* Any of various freshwater algae of the genus *Anabaena* that can give drinking water a bad taste and odor. [NLat. *Anabaena,* genus name < Gk. *anabainein,* to go up : *ana-,* ana- + *bainein,* to go; see **gʷā-*.**]
An•a•bap•tist (ăn′ə-băp′tĭst) *n.* A member of a 16th-century Reformation movement believing in baptism as a witness of faith and in separation of church from state. [< LGk. *anabaptizein,* to baptize again : Gk. *ana-,* ana- + Gk. *baptizein,* to baptize (< *baptein,* to dip).] — **An′a•bap′tism** *n.*
an•a•bas (ăn′ə-băs′) *n.* A freshwater fish of the family Anabantidae, native to Africa and southeast Asia. [Gk. *anabas,* climbing, aorist part. of *anabainein,* to go up. See ANABAENA.]
a•nab•a•sis (ə-năb′ə-sĭs) *n., pl.* **-ses** (-sēz′). **1.** An advance; an expedition. **2.** A large-scale military advance, specifically the unsuccessful Greek mercenary expedition across Asia Minor in 401 B.C. led by Cyrus the Younger, as described by Xenophon. [Gk. < *anabainein,* to go up. See ANABAENA.]
an•a•bat•ic (ăn′ə-băt′ĭk) *adj.* Of or relating to rising wind currents. [Gk. *anabatikos,* skilled in mounting < *anabainein,* to rise. See ANABAENA.]
an•a•bi•o•sis (ăn′ə-bī-ō′sĭs) *n.* **1.** A restoration to life from a deathlike condition; resuscitation. **2.** A state of suspended animation, esp. one in which certain aquatic invertebrates can survive long droughts. [Gk. *anabiōsis* < *anabioun,* to return to life : *ana-,* ana- + *bioun,* to live (< *bios,* life; see **gʷei-*).**] — **an′a•bi•ot′ic** (-ŏt′ĭk) *adj.*
anabolic steroid *n.* A group of synthetic hormones that promote the storage of protein and the growth of tissue.
a•nab•o•lism (ə-năb′ə-lĭz′əm) *n.* The phase of metabolism in which simple substances are synthesized into the complex materials of living tissue. [ANA– + (META)BOLISM.] — **an′a•bol′ic** (ăn′ə-bŏl′ĭk) *adj.*
a•nach•ro•nism (ə-năk′rə-nĭz′əm) *n.* **1.** Representation of someone as existing or something as happening in other than the chronological, proper, or historical order. **2.** One that is out of its proper or chronological order. [Fr. *anachronisme* < NLat. *anachronismus* < LGk. *anakhronismos* < *anakhronizesthai,* to be an anachronism : Gk. *ana-,* ana- + Gk. *khronizein,* to take time (< *khronos,* time).] — **a•nach′ro•nis′tic, a•nach′ro•nous** (-nəs) *adj.* — **a•nach′ro•nis′ti•cal•ly, a•nach′ro•nous•ly** *adv.*
an•a•cli•sis (ăn′ə-klī′sĭs, ə-năk′lĭ-) *n.* Psychological dependence on others. [Gk. *anaklisis,* a leaning back < *anaklinein,* to lean on : *ana-,* on-; see ANA– + *klinein,* to lean; see **klei-*.**] — **an′a•clit′ic** (-klĭt′ĭk) *adj.*
an•a•co•lu•thon (ăn′ə-kə-lo͞o′thŏn′) *n., pl.* **-thons** or **-tha** (-thə). An abrupt change within a sentence to a second construction inconsistent with the first; for example, *I warned that if he drinks, what will become of him?* [LLat. < LGk. *anakolouthon,* inconsistency in logic < Gk., neut. of *anakolouthos,* inconsistent : *an-,* not; see A–[1] + *akolouthos,* following (*a-,* together; see **sem-[1]*** + *keleuthos,* path).] — **an′a•co•lu′thic** *adj.*
an•a•con•da (ăn′ə-kŏn′də) *n.* **1.** A large nonvenomous arboreal snake *(Eunectes murinus)* of tropical South America that suffocates its prey. **2.** A similar or related snake. [Perh. alteration of Singhalese *henakandayā,* whip snake.]
A•nac•re•on (ə-năk′rē-ən). 563?–478? B.C. Greek poet noted for his songs praising love and wine.
A•nac•re•on•tic (ə-năk′rē-ŏn′tĭk) *adj.* Of or resembling the poems of Anacreon. — *n.* A poem in the style of Anacreon.
an•a•cru•sis (ăn′ə-kro͞o′sĭs) *n.* **1.** One or more unstressed syllables at the beginning of a line of verse, before the reckoning of the normal meter begins. **2.** *Mus.* An upbeat. [NLat. < Gk. *anakrousis,* beginning of a tune < *anakrouein,* to strike up a song : *ana-,* ana- + *krouein,* to push.]
an•a•dam•a bread (ăn′ə-dăm′ə) *n. New England.* A loaf of bread made of white flour, cornmeal, and molasses. [?]
an•a•dem (ăn′ə-dĕm′) *n. Archaic.* A wreath or garland for the head. [Lat. *anadēma* < Gk. < *anadein,* to bind up : *ana-,* ana- + *dein,* to bind.]
an•a•di•plo•sis (ăn′ə-də-plō′sĭs) *n., pl.* **-ses** (-sēz). Rhetorical repetition at the beginning of a phrase of the word or words with which the previous phrase ended. [LLat. *anadiplōsis* < Gk. < *anadiploun,* to redouble : *ana-,* ana- + *diploun,* to double (< *diplous,* double; see **dwo-*).**]

Roald Amundsen

a•nad•ro•mous (ə-năd′rə-məs) *adj.* Migrating up rivers from the sea to breed in fresh water. Used of fish. [< Gk. *anadromos,* running up < *anadromē,* a running back : *ana-,* ana- + *dromos,* a running.]
A•na•dyr (ä′nə-dîr′). A river of NE Russia rising in the **Anadyr Plateau** and flowing c. 1,118 km (695 mi) to **Anadyr Bay,** an inlet of the Bering Sea.
a•nae•mi•a (ə-nē′mē-ə) *n.* Var. of **anemia.**
a•nae•mic (ə-nē′mĭk) *adj.* Var. of **anemic.**
an•aer•obe (ăn′ə-rōb′, ăn-âr′ōb′) *n.* An organism, such as a bacterium, that can live without oxygen. — **an′aer•o′bic** (ăn′ə-rō′bĭk, -âr-ō′bĭk) *adj.* — **an′aer•o′bi•cal•ly** *adv.*
an•aer•o•bi•o•sis (ăn′ə-rō′bī-ō′sĭs, ăn′âr-ō′-) *n.* Life sustained without oxygen. — **an′aer•o′bi•ot′ic** (-ŏt′ĭk) *adj.*
an•aes•the•sia (ăn′ĭs-thē′zhə) *n.* Var. of **anesthesia.**
an•aes•the•si•ol•o•gist (ăn′ĭs-thē′zē-ŏl′ə-jĭst) *n.* Var. of **anesthesiologist.**
an•aes•the•si•ol•o•gy (ăn′ĭs-thē′zē-ŏl′ə-jē) *n.* Var. of **anesthesiology.**
an•aes•thet•ic (ăn′ĭs-thĕt′ĭk) *adj. & n.* Var. of **anesthetic.**
a•naes•the•tist (ə-nĕs′thĭ-tĭst) *n.* Var. of **anesthetist.**
a•naes•the•tize (ə-nĕs′thĭ-tīz′) *v.* Var. of **anesthetize.**
an•a•gen•e•sis (ăn′ə-jĕn′ĭ-sĭs) *n.* A pattern of evolution resulting in linear descent with no splitting of the population.
an•a•glyph (ăn′ə-glĭf′) *n.* An ornament carved in low relief. [< LLat. *anaglyphus,* carved in low relief < Gk. *anagluphos*: *ana-,* ana- + *gluphein,* to carve; see **gleubh-*.**] — **an′a•glyph′ic, an′a•glyp′tic** (-glĭp′tĭk) *adj.*

amusement park

an•a•go•ge also **an•a•go•gy** (ăn′ə-gō′jē) *n., pl.* **-ges** also **-gies.** A mystical interpretation of a word, passage, or text, esp. scriptural exegesis that detects allusions to heaven or the afterlife. [LLat. *anagōgē* < LGk., spiritual uplift < *anagein,* to lift up : *ana-,* ana- + *agein,* to lead; see **ag-*.**] — **an′a•gog′ic** (-gŏj′ĭk), **an′a•gog′i•cal** *adj.* — **an′a•gog′i•cal•ly** *adv.*
an•a•gram (ăn′ə-grăm′) *n.* **1.** A word or phrase formed by reordering the letters of another word or phrase, such as *satin* to *stain.* **2. anagrams.** *(used with a sing. v.) Games.* A game whose object is to form words from randomly picked letters. [NLat. *anagramma* < Gk. *anagrammatismos* < *anagrammatizein,* to rearrange letters in a word : *ana-,* from bottom to top; see ANA– + *gramma, grammat-,* letter; see **gerbh-*.**] — **an′a•gram•mat′ic** (-grə-măt′ĭk) *adj.* — **an′a•gram•mat′i•cal•ly** *adv.*
an•a•gram•ma•tize (ăn′ə-grăm′ə-tīz′) *tr.v.* **-tized, -tiz•ing, -tiz•es.** To make an anagram of. [LGk. *anagrammatizein,* to rearrange letters in a word. See ANAGRAM.]
An•a•heim (ăn′ə-hīm′). A city of S CA SE of Los Angeles; site of Disneyland (opened in 1955). Pop. 266,406.
A•ná•huac (ə-nä′wäk′). An extensive plateau of central Mexico; center of a pre-Columbian Aztec civilization.
a•nal (ā′nəl) *adj.* **1.** Of, relating to, or near the anus. **2.a.** In psychoanalytic theory, of or relating to the second stage of psychosexual development when gratification derives from sensations associated with the anus. **b.** Anal-expulsive or

ă pat	oi boy
ā pay	ou out
âr care	o͝o took
ä father	o͞o boot
ĕ pet	ŭ cut
ē be	ûr urge
ĭ pit	th thin
ī pie	*th* this
îr pier	hw which
ŏ pot	zh vision
ō toe	ə about, item
ô paw	

Stress marks:
′ (primary);
′ (secondary), as in
dictionary (dĭk′shə-nĕr′ē)

anal-retentive. [< Lat. *ānus*, anus.] —**a'nal•ly** *adv.*

anal. *abbr.* **1.** Analogous; analogy. **2.** Analysis; analytic.

a•nal•cime (ə-năl'sēm') also **a•nal•cite** (-sīt') *n.* A zeolite, $NaAlSi_2O_6 \cdot H_2O$, found in certain basalts. [Fr. < Gk. *analkimos*, weak (from its weak electric power) : *an-*, not; see A-[1] + *alkimos*, brave (< *alkē*, strength).] —**a•nal•cim'ic** *adj.*

an•a•lects (ăn'ə-lĕkts') also **an•a•lec•ta** (ăn'ə-lĕk'tə) *pl.n.* Selections from or parts of a literary work or group of works. [Gk. *analekta*, selected things < neut. pl. of *analektos*, gathered together < *analegein*, to gather : *ana-*, ana- + *legein*, to gather; see **leg-***.] —**an'a•lec'tic** *adj.*

an•a•lem•ma (ăn'ə-lĕm'ə) *n.* A graduated scale in the shape of a figure eight, indicating the sun's declination and the equation of time for every day of the year. [Lat., sundial < Gk. *analēmma* < *analambanein*, to take up. See ANALEPTIC.]

an•a•lep•tic (ăn'ə-lĕp'tĭk) *adj.* Restorative or stimulating, as a drug or medication. —*n.* A medication used as a central nervous system stimulant. [Gk. *analēptikos* < *analambanein*, to take up : *ana-*, ana- + *lambanein*, *lēp-*, to take.]

a•nal-ex•pul•sive (ā'nəl-ĭk-spŭl'sĭv) *adj. Psychol.* In psychoanalytic theory, of or relating to personality traits, such as conceit, suspicion, ambition, and generosity, originating in infantile pleasure in expelling feces.

an•al•ge•si•a (ăn'əl-jē'zē-ə, -zhə) *n. Pathol.* A deadening or absence of pain without loss of consciousness. [Gk. *analgēsia*: *an-*, without; see A-[1] + *algēsia*, pain (< *algein*, to feel pain < *algos*, pain).] —**an'al•get'ic** (-jĕt'ĭk) *adj.*

an•al•ge•sic (ăn'əl-jē'zĭk, -sĭk) *n.* A medication that reduces or eliminates pain. —*adj.* Of or causing analgesia.

an•a•log (ăn'ə-lôg', -lŏg') *n. & adj.* Var. of **analogue.**

analog computer also **analogue computer** *n. Comp. Sci.* A computer in which numerical data are represented by measurable physical variables, such as electrical signals.

an•a•log•i•cal (ăn'ə-lŏj'ĭ-kəl) *adj.* Of, expressing, composed of, or based on an analogy. —**an'a•log'i•cal•ly** *adv.*

a•nal•o•gist (ə-năl'ə-jĭst) *n.* One who seeks or reasons by analogy.

a•nal•o•gize (ə-năl'ə-jīz') *v.* **-gized, -giz•ing, -giz•es.** —*tr.* To make an analogy to. —*intr.* To seek or reason by analogy.

a•nal•o•gous (ə-năl'ə-gəs) *adj.* **1.** Similar in such a way as to permit analogy. **2.** *Biol.* Similar in function but not in structure and evolutionary origin. [< Lat. *analogus* < Gk. *analogos*, proportionate : *ana-*, according to; see ANA- + *logos*, proportion; see **leg-***.] —**a•nal'o•gous•ly** *adv.* —**a•nal'o•gous•ness** *n.*

an•a•logue also **an•a•log** (ăn'ə-lôg', -lŏg') —*n.* **1.** Something that bears an analogy to something else. **2.** *Biol.* An organ or structure similar in function to one in another kind of organism but of dissimilar evolutionary origin. **3.** *Chem.* A structural derivative of a parent compound that often differs from it by a single element. —*adj.* **1.** Often **analog.** Of, relating to, or being a device in which data are represented by variable measurable physical quantities. **2.** Often **analog.** *Comp. Sci.* Of or relating to an analog computer. [Fr., analogous, analogue < Med.Lat. *analogus* < Gk. *analogos*, proportionate. See ANALOGOUS.]

a•nal•o•gy (ə-năl'ə-jē) *n., pl.* **-gies. 1.a.** Similarity in some respects between things that are otherwise dissimilar. **b.** A comparison based on such similarity. See Syns at **likeness. 2.** *Biol.* Correspondence in function or position between organs of dissimilar evolutionary origin or structure. **3.** A form or instance of logical inference, based on the assumption that if two things are alike in some respects, they must be alike in other respects. **4.** *Ling.* The process by which words and morphemes are re-formed or created on the model of existing grammatical patterns, as *name : names* for Old English *nama : naman* on the model of nouns like *stone : stones.* [ME *analogie* < OFr. < Lat. *analogia* < Gk. < *analogos*, proportionate. See ANALOGOUS.]

an•al•pha•bet•ic (ăn-ăl'fə-bĕt'ĭk) *adj.* **1.** Not alphabetical. **2.** Unable to read; illiterate. —*n.* One who is unable to read; an illiterate. [< Gk. *analphabētos*, not knowing the alphabet : *an-*, not; see A-[1] + *alphabētos*, alphabet; see ALPHABET.]

a•nal-re•ten•tive (ā'nəl-rĭ-tĕn'tĭv) *adj.* In psychoanalytic theory, of or relating to personality traits, such as meticulousness, avarice, and obstinacy, originating in infantile pleasure in retention of feces.

a•nal•y•sand (ə-năl'ĭ-sănd') *n.* A person who is being psychoanalyzed. [< ANALYZE, on the model of MULTIPLICAND.]

a•nal•y•sis (ə-năl'ĭ-sĭs) *n., pl.* **-ses** (-sēz'). **1.** The separation of a whole into its constituent parts for individual study. **2.** *Chem.* **a.** The separation of a substance into its constituent elements to determine either their nature (qualitative analysis) or their proportions (quantitative analysis). **b.** The stated findings of such a procedure. **3.** *Math.* **a.** A branch of mathematics principally involving calculus, sequences, and series and concerned with limits and convergence. **b.** The method of proof in which a known truth is sought as a consequence of deductions from that which is to be proved. **4.** *Ling.* The use of function words such as prepositions instead of inflectional endings to express a grammatical relationship; for example, *the paw of the dog* instead of *the dog's paw.* **5.** Psychoanalysis. **6.** Systems analysis. [Med.Lat. < Gk. *analusis*, a dissolving < *analuein*, to undo : *ana-*, throughout; see ANA- + *luein*, to loosen; see **leu-***.]

an•a•lyst (ăn'ə-lĭst) *n.* **1.** One that analyzes. **2.** A licensed practitioner of psychoanalysis. **3.** A systems analyst.

an•a•lyt•ic (ăn'ə-lĭt'ĭk) or **an•a•lyt•i•cal** (-ĭ-kəl) *adj.* **1.** Of or relating to analysis or analytics. **2.** Dividing into elemental parts or basic principles. **3.** Reasoning from a perception of the parts and interrelations of a subject. **4.** Expert in or using analysis, esp. in thinking: *an analytic mind.* **5.** *Logic.* Following necessarily; tautologous. **6.** *Math.* **a.** Using or capable of being subjected to a methodology involving algebra and calculus. **b.** Proving a known truth by reasoning from that which is to be proved. **7.** *Ling.* Expressing a grammatical category with two or more words instead of an inflected form. **8.** Psychoanalytic. [Med.Lat. *analyticus* < Gk. *analutikos* < *analuein*, to resolve. See ANALYSIS.] —**an'a•lyt'i•cal•ly** *adv.*

analytical balance *n.* A balance for chemical analysis.

analytic geometry *n. Math.* The analysis of geometric structures and properties principally by algebraic operations on variables defined in terms of position coordinates.

an•a•lyt•ics (ăn'ə-lĭt'ĭks) *n. (used with a sing. or pl. v.)* The branch of logic dealing with analysis.

an•a•lyze (ăn'ə-līz') *tr.v.* **-lyzed, -lyz•ing, -lyz•es. 1.** To separate into parts or basic principles so as to determine the nature of the whole; examine methodically. **2.** *Chem.* To make a chemical analysis of. **3.** *Math.* To make a mathematical analysis of. **4.** To psychoanalyze. [Perh. < Fr. *analyser* < *analyse*, analysis < Gk. *analusis.* See ANALYSIS.] —**an'a•lyz'a•ble** *adj.* —**an'a•ly•za'tion** *n.* —**an'a•lyz'er** *n.*

Syns: *analyze, anatomize, dissect, resolve.* The central meaning shared by these verbs is "to separate into constituent parts for study": *analyzed a chemical substance; anatomizing the doctrine of free enterprise; medical students dissecting cadavers; vapor resolved into water.*

an•am•ne•sis (ăn'ăm-nē'sĭs) *n., pl.* **-ses** (-sēz). **1.** *Psychol.* A recalling to memory; recollection. **2.** *Medic.* The complete case history of a patient. [Gk. *anamnēsis* < *anamimnēskein*, to remind : *ana-*, ana- + *mimnēskein*, to recall; see **men-**[1]*.] —**an'am•nes'tic** (-nĕs'tĭk) *adj.* —**an'am•nes'ti•cal•ly** *adv.*

an•a•mor•phic (ăn'ə-môr'fĭk) *adj.* Having, producing, or being different optical magnifications along mutually perpendicular radii. [< ANAMORPHOSIS.]

an•a•mor•pho•sis (ăn'ə-môr'fə-sĭs) *n., pl.* **-ses** (-sēz'). **1.a.** An image that appears distorted unless viewed from a special angle or with a special instrument. **b.** The production of such an image. **2.** Evolutionary increase in complexity of form and function. [NLat. < LGk. *anamorphoun*, to transform : Gk. *ana-*, ana- + Gk. *morphē*, shape.]

An•a•ni•as (ăn'ə-nī'əs). In the Bible, a liar who died when Peter rebuked him.

An•an•ke (ə-năng'kē, ə-năn'-) *n.* A satellite of Jupiter. [Gk. *Anankē*, mother of Adrasteia, distributor of rewards and punishments, by Jupiter < *anankē*, necessity.]

an•a•pest also **an•a•paest** (ăn'ə-pĕst') *n.* **1.** A metrical foot of two short syllables followed by one long one, as in *at the park.* **2.** A line of verse using this meter. [Lat. *anapestus* < Gk. *anapaistos*: *ana-*, ana- + *paiein*, *pais-*, to strike (so called because an anapest is a reversed dactyl); see **peu-***.] —**an'a•pes'tic** *adj.*

an•a•phase (ăn'ə-fāz') *n. Biol.* The stage of mitosis and meiosis in which the chromosomes move to opposite ends of the nuclear spindle.

a•naph•o•ra (ə-năf'ər-ə) *n.* The repetition of a word or phrase at the beginning of several successive verses, clauses, or paragraphs. [LLat. < Gk. < *anapherein*, to bring back : *ana-*, ana- + *pherein*, to carry; see **bher-**[1]*.]

an•aph•ro•dis•i•a (ăn-ăf'rə-dĭz'ē-ə, -dĭzh'ə) *n.* Decline or absence of sexual desire. [Gk., want of power to inspire love : *an-*, without; see A-[1] + *aphrodisia*, sexual pleasures; see APHRODISIAC.] —**an•aph'ro•dis'i•ac'** (ăn-ăf'rə-dĭz'ē-ăk') *adj. & n.*

anaphylactic shock *n.* A sudden, severe and sometimes fatal allergic reaction marked by a sharp drop in blood pressure, urticaria, and breathing difficulties caused by exposure to a foreign substance after a preliminary exposure.

an•a•phy•lax•is (ăn'ə-fə-lăk'sĭs) *n.* **1.** Hypersensitivity esp. in animals to a substance, induced by a small preliminary exposure to the substance. **2.** See **anaphylactic shock.** [ANA- + (PRO)PHYLAXIS.] —**an'a•phy•lac'tic** (-lăk'tĭk), **an'a•phy•lac'toid** (-toid) *adj.* —**an'a•phy•lac'ti•cal•ly** *adv.*

an•a•pla•sia (ăn'ə-plā'zhə) *n.* Reversion of cells to an immature or a less differentiated form, as in most malignant tumors.

an•a•plas•tic (ăn'ə-plăs'tĭk) *adj.* **1.** *Medic.* Relating to the surgical restoration of a lost or absent part. **2.** Of or characterized by cells that have become less differentiated.

A•ná•po•lis (ä-nä'po͝o-lĭs). A city of central Brazil SE of Brasília. Pop. 160,571.

an•arch (ăn'ärk') *n.* An adherent of anarchy or a leader practicing it. [Back-formation < ANARCHY.]

an•ar•chic (ăn-är′kĭk) or **an•ar•chi•cal** (-kĭ-kəl) *adj.* **1.a.** Of, like, or supporting anarchy. **b.** Likely to produce or result in anarchy. **2.** Lacking order or control. **—an•ar′chi•cal•ly** *adv.*

an•ar•chism (ăn′ər-kĭz′əm) *n.* **1.** The theory or doctrine that all forms of government are unnecessary, oppressive, and undesirable and should be abolished. **2.** Advocacy of or an active attempt to realize anarchism. **—an′ar•chis′tic** (-kĭs′tĭk) *adj.*

an•ar•chist (ăn′ər-kĭst) *n.* An advocate of or a participant in anarchism.

an•ar•cho-syn•di•cal•ism (ăn-är′kō-sĭn′dĭ-kə-lĭz′əm) *n.* Syndicalism. [ANARCH(Y) + SYNDICALISM.]

an•ar•chy (ăn′ər-kē) *n., pl.* **-chies. 1.** Absence of political authority. **2.** Political disorder and confusion. **3.** Absence of any cohesive principle, such as a common purpose. [NLat. *anarchia* < Gk. *anarkhia* < *anarkhos*, without a ruler : *an-*, without; see A-[1] + *arkhos*, ruler; see -ARCH.]

an•ar•thri•a (ăn-är′thrē-ə) *n.* Loss of the motor ability that enables speech. [NLat. < Gk. *anarthros*, not articulated. See ANARTHROUS.] **—an•ar′thric** (-thrĭk) *adj.*

an•ar•throus (ăn-är′thrəs) *adj.* **1.** *Ling.* Lacking an article. Used esp. of Greek nouns. **2.** *Zool.* Lacking joints. [< Gk. *anarthros*, not articulated : *an-*, without; see A-[1] + *arthron*, joint; see **ar-***.]

an•a•sar•ca (ăn′ə-sär′kə) *n.* A general accumulation of serous fluid in various tissues and body cavities. [ME < Med. Lat. : Gk. *ana*, throughout; see ANA- + Gk. *sarx*, *sark-*, flesh.] **—an′a•sar′cous** (-sär′kəs) *adj.*

A•na•sa•zi (ä′nə-sä′zē) *n., pl.* **Anasazi.** A member of a Native American people inhabiting southern Colorado and Utah and northern New Mexico and Arizona from about A.D. 100 and whose descendants are the present-day Pueblo peoples. [Navajo *'anaasází*, inhabitants of the now ruined Pueblos.]

an•as•tig•mat (ăn-ăs′tĭg-măt′) *n.* An anastigmatic lens.

an•as•tig•mat•ic (ăn-ăs′tĭg-măt′ĭk) *adj.* Free from astigmatism. Used of a compound lens.

a•nas•to•mose (ə-năs′tə-mōz′, -mōs′) *v.* **-mosed, -mos•ing, -mos•es.** *—tr.* To join by anastomosis. *—intr.* To be connected by anastomosis, as blood vessels. [Prob. back-formation < ANASTOMOSIS.]

a•nas•to•mo•sis (ə-năs′tə-mō′sĭs) *n., pl.* **-ses** (-sēz). **1.** The connection of separate parts of a branching system in a network. **2.** *Medic.* The surgical connection of separate or severed tubular hollow organs in a continuous channel. [LLat. *anastomōsis* < Gk., outlet < *anastomoun*, to furnish with a mouth : *ana-*, ana- + *stoma*, mouth.] **—a•nas′to•mot′ic** (-mŏt′ĭk) *adj.*

a•nas•tro•phe (ə-năs′trə-fē) *n.* Inversion of the normal syntactic order of words. [LLat. *anastrophē* < Gk. < *anastrephein*, to turn upside-down : *ana-*, ana- + *strephein*, to turn; see **streb(h)-***.]

anat. *abbr.* Anatomical; anatomist; anatomy.

an•a•tase (ăn′ə-tās′, -tāz′) *n.* A blue or light yellow to brown crystalline mineral, the rarest form of titanium dioxide, TiO_2, used as a pigment, esp. in paint. [Fr. < Gk. *anatasis*, extension (from its long crystals) < *anateinein*, to extend : *ana-*, ana- + *teinein*, to stretch; see **ten-***.]

a•nath•e•ma (ə-năth′ə-mə) *n., pl.* **-mas. 1.** An ecclesiastical ban, curse, or excommunication. **2.** A vehement denunciation; a curse. **3.** One that is cursed or damned. **4.** One that is reviled, loathed, or shunned. [LLat., an accursed thing < Gk. *anathēma* < *anatithenai*, to dedicate : *ana-*, ana- + *tithenai*, to put; see **dhē-***.]

a•nath•e•ma•tize (ə-năth′ə-mə-tīz′) *tr.v.* **-tized, -tiz•ing, -tiz•es.** To proclaim an anathema on; curse. [LLat. *anathematīzāre* < Gk. *anathematizein* < *anathema*, *anathemat-*, anathema. See ANATHEMA.] **—a•nath′e•ma•ti•za′tion** (-tĭ-zā′shən) *n.*

An•a•to•li•a (ăn′ə-tō′lē-ə, -tōl′yə). The Asian part of Turkey, usu. considered synonymous with Asia Minor.

An•a•to•li•an (ăn′ə-tō′lē-ən) *adj.* **1.** Of or relating to Anatolia or its people, language, or culture. **2.** Of or relating to a branch of Indo-European that includes Hittite and other languages of ancient Anatolia. *—n.* **1.** A native or inhabitant of Anatolia. **2.** The Anatolian languages.

an•a•tom•i•cal (ăn′ə-tŏm′ĭ-kəl) also **an•a•tom•ic** (-tŏm′ĭk) *adj.* **1.** Concerned with anatomy. **2.** Concerned with dissection. **3.** Related to the structure of an organism. **—an′a•tom′i•cal•ly** *adv.*

a•nat•o•mist (ə-năt′ə-mĭst) *n.* An expert in or a student of anatomy.

a•nat•o•mize (ə-năt′ə-mīz′) *tr.v.* **-mized, -miz•ing, -miz•es. 1.** To dissect (an organism) to study the structure and relation of its parts. **2.** To analyze minutely. **3.** See Syns at **analyze.** **—a•nat′o•mi•za′tion** (-mĭ-zā′shən) *n.*

a•nat•o•my (ə-năt′ə-mē) *n., pl.* **-mies. 1.** The bodily structure of a plant or an animal or of any of its parts. **2.** The science of the shape and structure of organisms and their parts. **3.** A treatise on anatomic science. **4.** Dissection of a plant or an animal to study the structure and interrelation of its parts. **5.** A skeleton. **6.** The human body. **7.** A detailed examination or analysis. [ME *anatomie* < LLat. *anatomia* < Gk. *anatomē*, dissection : *ana-*, ana- + *tomē*, a cutting (< *temnein*, to cut; see **tem-***).]

a•nat•ro•pous (ə-năt′rə-pəs) *adj. Bot.* Completely inverted so that the micropyle faces downward and is near the base of the funiculus: *an anatropous ovule.*

An•ax•ag•o•ras (ăn′ăk-săg′ər-əs). 500?–428 B.C. Greek philosopher who believed matter to be composed of atoms.

A•nax•i•man•der (ə-năk′sə-măn′dər). 611–547 B.C. Greek philosopher and astronomer who postulated the existence of a single primordial substance.

anc. *abbr.* Ancient.

-ance *suff.* **1.** State or condition: *absorptance.* **2.** Action: *continuance.* [ME < OFr. < Lat. *-antia*, n. suff. (*-ant*, -ant + *-ia*, n. suff.) and < Lat. *-entia* (*-ent*, -ent + *-ia*, n. suff.).]

an•ces•tor (ăn′sĕs′tər) *n.* **1.** A person from whom one is descended, esp. more remote than a grandparent; a forebear. **2.** A forerunner or predecessor. **3.** *Law.* The person from whom one inherits an estate. **4.** *Biol.* The organism or stock from which later kinds evolved. [ME *auncestre* < OFr. < Lat. *antecessor*, predecessor < *antecessus*, p.part. of *antecēdere*, to precede : *ante-*, ante- + *cēdere*, to go; see **ked-***.]

Syns: *ancestor, forebear, forefather, progenitor.* The central meaning shared by these nouns is "a person from whom one is descended": *ancestors who were farmers; land once owned by his forebears; methods as old as our forefathers; the wisdom of our progenitors. Ant: descendant.*

an•ces•tral (ăn-sĕs′trəl) *adj.* Of, relating to, or evolved from an ancestor or ancestors. **—an•ces′tral•ly** *adv.*

an•ces•try (ăn′sĕs′trē) *n., pl.* **-tries. 1.** Ancestral descent or lineage. **2.** Ancestors as a group. [ME *auncestrie*, alteration (influenced by *auncestre*) of OFr. *ancesserie* < *ancessour*, ancestor < Lat. *antecessor*. See ANCESTOR.]

an•chor (ăng′kər) *n.* **1.** *Naut.* A heavy object attached to a vessel and lowered overboard to keep the vessel in place either by its weight or by its flukes, which grip the bottom. **2.** A rigid point of support, as for securing a rope. **3.** A source of security or stability. **4.** *Sports.* **a.** An athlete who performs the last stage of a competition. **b.** The end of a tug-of-war team. **5.** An anchorperson. *—v.* **-chored, -chor•ing, -chors.** *—tr.* **1.** To hold fast by or as if by an anchor. **2.** *Sports.* To serve as anchor for (a team or competition). **3.** To narrate or coordinate (a newscast). *—intr. Naut.* To drop anchor or lie at anchor. [ME *anker*, *ancher* < OE *ancor* < Lat. *ancora*, *anchora* < Gk. *ankura*.]

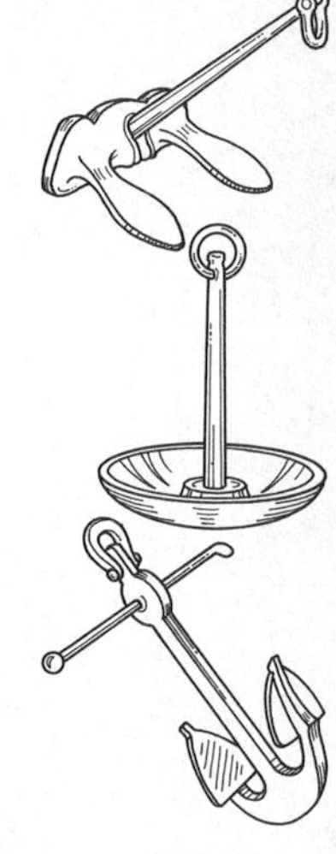

anchor
Top: Stockless
Center: Mushroom
Bottom: Admiralty

an•chor•age (ăng′kər-ĭj) *n.* **1.** A place for anchoring. **2.** A fee charged for anchoring. **3.** The act of anchoring or the condition of being at anchor. **4.** A means of securing or stabilizing.

An•chor•age (ăng′kər-ĭj). A city of S AK SSW of Fairbanks; founded 1915. Pop. 226,338.

an•cho•ress (ăng′kər-ĭs) *n.* A woman who has retired into religious seclusion. [ME *anchoryse*, *ankres* < *ancre*, anchorite < OE *ancra* < OIr. *anchara* < LLat. *anachōrēta*. See ANCHORITE.]

an•cho•rite (ăng′kə-rīt′) also **an•cho•ret** (-rĕt′) *n.* One who has retired into religious seclusion. [ME < Med.Lat. *anchōrīta* < LLat. *anachōrēta* < LGk. *anakhōrētēs* < *anakhōrein*, to retire : *ana-*, ana- + *khōrein*, to withdraw; see **ghē-***.] **—an′cho•rit′ic** (-rĭt′ĭk) *adj.*

an•chor•man (ăng′kər-măn′) *n.* **1.** A man who narrates or coordinates a newscast. **2.** *Sports.* See **anchor** 4.

an•chor•per•son (ăng′kər-pûr′sən) *n.* An anchorman or an anchorwoman.

an•chor•wom•an (ăng′kər-wo͝om′ən) *n.* A woman who narrates or coordinates a newscast.

an•cho•vy (ăn′chō′vē, ăn-chō′vē) *n., pl.* **anchovy** or **-vies.** A herringlike marine fish of the family Engraulidae, esp. the European fish *Engraulis encrasicholus*, widely used in cooking. [Sp. *anchova*, poss. < VLat. **apiuva*, var. of Lat. **aphyē* < Gk. *aphuē*.]

an•chy•lose (ăng′kə-lōs′, -lōz′) *v.* Var. of **ankylose.**

an•chy•lo•sis (ăng′kə-lō′sĭs) *n.* Var. of **ankylosis.**

an•cien ré•gime (äN-syăN′ rā-zhēm′) *n.* **1.** The French political and social system prior to the Revolution of 1789. **2.** A former sociopolitical or other system. [Fr. : *ancien*, old + *régime*, regime.]

an•cient[1] (ān′shənt) *adj.* **1.** Of great age; very old. **2.** Of or relating to the far past, esp. before the fall of the Western Roman Empire (A.D. 476). See Syns at **old. 3.** Old-fashioned; antiquated. **4.** Having the qualities associated with age, wisdom, or long use; venerable. *—n.* **1.** A very old person. **2.** A person who lived long ago. **3. ancients. a.** The ancient Greeks and Romans. **b.** The ancient Greek and Roman authors. [ME *auncien* < OFr. < VLat. **anteānus*: Lat. *ante*, before; see **ant-*** + *-ānus*, adj. and n. suff.] **—an′cient•ly** *adv.* **—an′cient•ness** *n.*

an•cient[2] (ān′shənt) *n.* **1.** *Archaic.* An ensign; a flag. **2.** *Obsolete.* A flag-bearer or lieutenant. [Alteration of ENSIGN.]

ancient history *n.* **1.** The history of times long past. **2.** *Informal.* Common knowledge, esp. of a recent event that has lost its original impact or importance.

ă **pat**	oi **boy**
ā **pay**	ou **out**
âr **care**	o͝o **took**
ä **father**	o͞o **boot**
ĕ **pet**	ŭ **cut**
ē **be**	ûr **urge**
ĭ **pit**	th **thin**
ī **pie**	*th* **this**
îr **pier**	hw **which**
ŏ **pot**	zh **vision**
ō **toe**	ə **a**bout,
ô **paw**	it**e**m

Stress marks:
′ (primary);
′ (secondary), as in
dictionary (dĭk′shə-nĕr′ē)

an•cil•lar•y (ăn′sə-lĕr′ē) *adj.* **1.** Subordinate; secondary. **2.** Auxiliary; helping: *an ancillary pump.* —*n., pl.* **-ies. 1.** Something subordinate to something else, as a workbook to a textbook. **2.** *Archaic.* A servant. [< Lat. *ancilla*, maidservant, fem. dim. of *anculus*, servant. See **kʷel-**[1]*.]

An•co•hu•ma (ăng′kə-ho͞o′mə, äng′kō-o͞o′mä). A mountain, c. 6,554 m (21,490 ft), of W Bolivia.

an•con (ăng′kŏn′) *n., pl.* **-con•es** (-kō′nēz). A projecting bracket that carries the upper elements of a cornice in classical architecture; a console. [Lat. *ancōn* < Gk. *ankōn*, elbow.]

An•co•na (ăng-kō′nə, ăn-, än-). A city of central Italy on the Adriatic Sea. Pop. 106,421.

–ancy *suff.* Condition or quality: *buoyancy*; *pliancy.* [Lat. *-antia* and *-entia*; see -ANCE.]

an•cy•lo•sto•mi•a•sis (ăn′sə-lō-stō-mī′ə-sĭs, ăng′kə-lō-) *n.* A disease caused by hookworm infestation and marked by progressive anemia. [NLat. *Ancylostoma*, hookworm genus (Gk. *ankulos*, curved + Gk. *stoma*, mouth) + -IASIS.]

An•cy•ra (ăn-sī′rə). See **Ankara.**

and (ənd, ən; ănd *when stressed*) *conj.* **1.** Together with; in addition to; as well as. Used to connect words, phrases, or clauses with the same grammatical function. **2.** Added to; plus: *Two and two makes four.* **3.** Used to indicate result. **4.** *Usage Problem.* To. Used between finite verbs, such as *go, come, try, write,* or *see*: *try and find it; come and see.* **5.** *Archaic.* If: *and it pleases you.* [ME < OE. See **en***.]

Usage Note: It is frequently asserted that sentences beginning with *and* or *but* express "incomplete thoughts" and are therefore incorrect. But this rule was ridiculed by grammarians like Wilson Follett and H.W. Fowler, and the stricture has been ignored by writers from Shakespeare to Virginia Woolf. Members of the Usage Panel were asked whether they paid attention to the rule in their own writing: 24 percent answered "always or usually," 36 percent answered "sometimes," and 40 percent answered "rarely or never." See Usage Notes at **both, but, try, with.**

AND (ănd) *n. Comp. Sci.* A logic operator equivalent to "and." [< AND.]

and. *abbr. Mus.* Andante.

And. *abbr.* Andorra.

An•da•lu•sia (ăn′də-lo͞o′zhə, -zhē-ə, -shē-ə). A region of S Spain on the Mediterranean Sea, the Strait of Gibraltar, and the Atlantic Ocean. —**An′da•lu′sian** (-zhən, -shən) *adj. & n.*

an•da•lu•site (ăn′də-lo͞o′sīt′) *n.* An aluminum silicate mineral, Al_2SiO_5, usu. found in prisms of various colors. [After ANDALUSIA.]

An•da•man•ese (ăn′də-mə-nēz′, -nēs′) *n., pl.* **Andamanese. 1.** Also **An•da•man** (ăn′də-mən). A member of an indigenous people of the Andaman Islands. **2.** The language of the Andamanese, of no known linguistic affiliation. —**An′da•man•ese′** *adj.*

Andaman Islands. A group of Indian islands in the E Bay of Bengal S of Burma; separated from the Malay Peninsula by the **Andaman Sea,** an arm of the Bay of Bengal.

an•dan•te (än-dän′tā, ăn-dăn′tē) *Mus.* —*adv. & adj.* In a moderately slow tempo. —*n.* An andante passage or movement. [Ital. < pr.part. of *andare*, to walk, ult. perh. < Lat. *ambulāre*.]

an•dan•ti•no (än′dän-tē′nō, ăn′dăn-) *Mus.* —*adv. & adj.* In a tempo either slightly faster or slower than andante. —*n., pl.* **-nos.** An andantino passage or movement. [Ital., dim. of *andante*, andante. See ANDANTE.]

An•der•lecht (än′dər-lĕkt′, -lĕKHT′). A commune of central Belgium, a suburb of Brussels. Pop. 92,912.

An•der•sen (ăn′dər-sən), **Hans Christian.** 1805–75. Danish writer whose fairy tales include "The Ugly Duckling."

Marian Anderson
Photographed in 1943

An•der•son (ăn′dər-sən). **1.** A city of E-central IN NE of Indianapolis. Pop. 59,459. **2.** A city of NW SC SW of Greenville near the GA border. Pop. 26,184.

Anderson, Carl David. b. 1905. Amer. physicist who won a 1936 Nobel Prize.

Anderson, Dame **Judith.** 1898–1992. Australian-born actress noted for her roles in the plays of Shakespeare and Eugene O'Neill.

Anderson, Marian. 1897–1993. Amer. contralto who was the first Black singer to perform at the Metropolitan (1955).

Anderson, Maxwell. 1888–1959. Amer. playwright whose works include *Winterset* (1935).

Anderson, Sherwood. 1876–1941. Amer. writer noted for his autobiographical *Winesburg, Ohio* (1919).

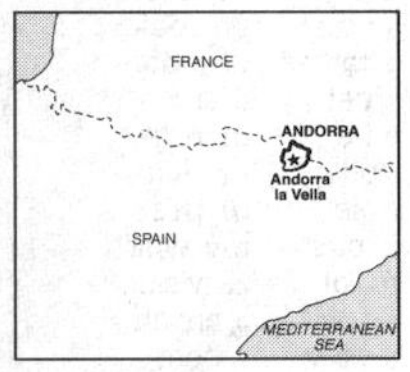

Andorra

Anderson River. A river of NW Northwest Terrs., Canada, meandering c. 748 km (465 mi) to an arm of the Arctic Ocean.

An•der•son•ville (ăn′dər-sən-vĭl′). A village of SW-central GA NNE of Americus; site of a notorious Confederate prison during the Civil War.

An•des (ăn′dēz). A mountain system of W South America extending c. 8,045 km (5,000 mi) along the Pacific coast from Venezuela to Tierra del Fuego and rising to more than 6,710 m (22,000 ft). —**An′de•an** (ăn′dē-ən, ăn-dē′ən) *adj. & n.*

an•de•site (ăn′dĭ-zīt′) *n.* A gray, fine-grained volcanic rock, chiefly plagioclase and feldspar. [After ANDES.]

AND gate *n. Comp. Sci.* A logic circuit that emits a signal only if all input wires receive coincident signals.

and•i•ron (ănd′ī′ərn) *n.* One of a pair of metal supports for logs in a fireplace. Also called regionally *dog iron, firedog.* [ME *aundiren*, alteration (influenced by ME *īren*, iron) of OFr. *andier*, of Celt. orig.]

An•di•zhan (ăn′dĭ-zhăn′, än-dĭ-zhän′). A city of E Uzbekistan ESE of Tashkent. Pop. 275,000.

AND NOT gate *n. Comp. Sci.* A logic circuit that emits a signal only if input A is true and input B is not.

and/or (ăn′dôr′) *conj.* Used to indicate that either or both of the items connected by it are involved.

Usage Note: *And/or* is widely used in legal and business writing. Its use in general writing to mean "one or the other or both" is acceptable but can appear stilted. See Usage Note at **or**[1].

AND-OR circuit (ănd′ôr′) *n. Comp. Sci.* A gating circuit that produces an output signal only if one of several possible combined input signals is received.

An•dor•ra (ăn-dôr′ə, -dŏr′ə). A country of SW Europe between France and Spain in the E Pyrenees. Cap. Andorra la Vella (pop. 14,928). Pop. 38,051. —**An•dor′ran** *adj. & n.*

an•dou•ille (ăn-do͞o′ē) *n.* A spicy smoked sausage made with pork and garlic, used esp. in Cajun cooking. [Fr. < OFr. *andoille* < Med.Lat. **indūctilia*, things to be introduced < *indūctilis, indūct-*, introduceable < Lat. *indūcere*, to introduce into a casing. See INDUCE.]

An•do•ver (ăn′dō′vər, -də-). A town of NE MA S of Lawrence. Pop. 29,151.

andr– *pref.* Var. of **andro–.**

An•dra•da e Sil•va (ăN-drä′də ĕ sēl′və), **José Bonifácio de.** 1763?–1838. Brazilian politician, scientist, and poet who led the movement for independence from Portugal.

an•dra•dite (ăn-drä′dīt) *n.* A green to brown or black calcium-iron garnet, $Ca_3Fe_2(SiO_4)_3$. [After José Bonifácio de ANDRADA E SILVA.]

An•dré (än′drā, ăn′drē), **John.** 1751–80. British army officer hanged as a spy in the American Revolution for conspiring with Benedict Arnold.

An•dre•a del Sar•to (än-drā′ə dĕl sär′tō). 1486–1531. Italian painter whose works epitomize Florentine classicism.

An•dre•a•nof Islands (ăn′drē-ăn′əf, -ôf, än′drē-ä′nəf). A group of islands of SW AK in the central Aleutian Is.

An•dre•ev or **An•dre•yev** (ăn-drā′əf, -yəf), **Leonid Nikolaevich.** 1871–1919. Russian writer noted for his pessimism.

An•drew (ăn′dro͞o), Saint. One of the 12 Apostles. According to legend, he was martyred at Patrai (c. A.D. 60).

An•drews (ăn′dro͞oz), **Roy Chapman.** 1884–1960. Amer. naturalist noted for his contributions to paleontology.

An•dri•a (än′drē-ə). A city of S Italy WNW of Bari. Pop. 83,319.

An•drić (än′drĭch), **Ivo.** 1892–1975. Yugoslavian writer who won the 1961 Nobel Prize for literature.

andro– or **andr–** *pref.* **1.** Male; masculine: *androgen.* **2.** Stamen or anther: *androecium.* [Gk. < *anēr, andr-*, man. See **ner-**[2]*.]

An•dro•cles (ăn′drə-klēz′) also **An•dro•clus** (-kləs) *n.* A legendary Roman spared in the arena by a lion that remembered him for having removed a thorn from its paw.

an•droe•ci•um (ăn-drē′shē-əm, -shəm) *n., pl.* **-ci•a** (-shē-ə, -shə). The stamens of a flower considered as a group. [NLat. : ANDR(O)- + Gk. *oikion*, dim. of *oikos*, house; see **weik-**[1]*.] —**an•droe′cial** (-shəl) *adj.*

an•dro•gen (ăn′drə-jən) *n.* A steroid hormone, such as testosterone or androsterone, that develops and maintains masculine characteristics. —**an′dro•gen′ic** (-jĕn′ĭk) *adj.*

an•drog•e•nize (ăn-drŏj′ə-nīz′) *tr.v.* **-nized, -niz•ing, -niz•es.** To treat with male hormones, usu. in large doses. —**an•drog′e•ni•za′tion** (-nĭ-zā′shən) *n.*

an•dro•gyne (ăn′drə-jīn′) *n.* An androgynous individual. [Fr. < OFr. < Lat. *androgynus.* See ANDROGYNOUS.]

an•drog•y•nous (ăn-drŏj′ə-nəs) *adj.* **1.** *Biol.* Having both female and male characteristics; hermaphroditic. **2.** Being neither distinguishably masculine nor feminine; unisex. [< Lat. *androgynus*, hermaphrodite < Gk. *androgunos*: *andro-*, andro- + *gunē*, woman; see -GYNOUS.] —**an•drog′y•nous•ly** *adv.* —**an•drog′y•ny** (-ə-nē) *n.*

an•droid (ăn′droid′) *adj.* Having human features. —*n.* An automaton made from biological materials to resemble a human being.

An•drom•a•che (ăn-drŏm′ə-kē) *n. Gk. Myth.* The wife of Hector, captured by the Greeks at the fall of Troy.

an•drom•e•da (ăn-drŏm′ĭ-də) *n.* Any of several shrubs of the genera *Pieris* or *Andromeda* or their relatives. [< ANDROMEDA.]

An•drom•e•da (ăn-drŏm′ĭ-də) *n.* **1.** *Gk. Myth.* The daughter of Cepheus and Cassiopeia and wife of Perseus, who rescued her from a sea monster. **2.** A constellation in the Northern Hemisphere, containing a spiral galaxy visible to the naked eye. [Lat. < Gk. *Andromedē*.]

An•dro•pov (ăn-drŏp′ŏf, -ŏv), **Yuri.** 1914–84. Soviet politician who was general secretary of the Communist Party (1982–84).

An•dros (ăn′drəs). **1.** The largest island of the Bahamas, in the W part of the archipelago. **2.** (*also* än′drôs′). An island of SE Greece in the Aegean; colonized by Athens in the 5th cent. B.C.

An•dros (ăn′drŏs, -drəs), Sir **Edmund.** 1637–1714. English colonial administrator in America.

An•dros•cog•gin (ăn′drə-skŏg′ĭn). A river of NE NH and SW ME flowing c. 253 km (157 mi) to the Kennebec R. near the ME coast.

an•dros•ter•one (ăn-drŏs′tə-rōn′) *n.* An androgen excreted in urine. [ANDRO– + STER(OL) + –ONE.]

–androus *suff.* Having a specified number or kind of stamens: *monandrous.* [< NLat. *-andrus* < Gk. *-andros,* having men < *anēr, andr-,* man. See **ner-**[2]*.]

–andry *suff.* **1.** The condition of having a specified kind or number of husbands: *monandry.* **2.** The condition of having a specified kind or number of stamens: *polyandry.* [Gk. *-andria* < *anēr, andr-,* man. See **ner-**[2]*.]

–ane *suff.* A saturated hydrocarbon: *hexane.* [Var. of –ENE, –INE[2], and –ONE.]

an•ec•dot•al (ăn′ĭk-dōt′l) *adj.* Of, characterized by, or full of anecdotes. **— an′ec•dot′al•ist** *n.* **— an′ec•dot′al•ly** *adv.*

an•ec•dote (ăn′ĭk-dōt′) *n.* **1.** A short account of an interesting or humorous incident. **2.** *pl.* **-dotes** or **-do•ta** (-dō′tə). Secret or hitherto undivulged particulars of history or biography. [Fr. < Gk. *anekdota,* unpublished items : *an-,* not; see A–[1] + *ekdota,* neut. pl. of *ekdotos,* published (< *ekdidonai,* to publish : *ek-,* out; see ECTO– + *didonai,* to give; see **dō-***).] **— an′ec•do′tist** *n.*

an•ec•dot•ic (ăn′ĭk-dŏt′ĭk) also **an•ec•dot•i•cal** (-ĭ-kəl) *adj.* **1.** Given to telling anecdotes. **2.** Anecdotal. **— an′ec•dot′i•cal•ly** *adv.*

an•e•cho•ic (ăn′ĕ-kō′ĭk) *adj.* Neither having nor producing echoes: *an anechoic chamber.*

a•ne•mi•a also **a•nae•mi•a** (ə-nē′mē-ə) *n.* A pathological deficiency in the oxygen-carrying component of the blood, measured in unit volume concentrations of hemoglobin, red blood cell volume, or red blood cell number. [NLat. < Gk. *anaimia: an-,* without; see A–[1] + *haima,* blood.]

a•ne•mic also **a•nae•mic** (ə-nē′mĭk) *adj.* **1.** Of, relating to, or suffering from anemia. **2.** Lacking vitality; listless and weak. **— a•ne′mi•cal•ly** *adv.*

anemo– *pref.* Wind: *anemometer.* [< Gk. *anemos,* wind. See **anə-***.]

a•nem•o•cho•ry (ə-nĕm′ə-kôr′ē, -kōr′ē) *n.* Dispersal of seeds, fruits, or other plant parts by wind.

an•e•mom•e•ter (ăn′ə-mŏm′ĭ-tər) *n.* An instrument for indicating and measuring wind force and velocity.

an•e•mom•e•try (ăn′ə-mŏm′ĭ-trē) *n.* Measurement of wind force and velocity. **— an′e•mo•met′ri•cal** *adj.*

a•nem•o•ne (ə-nĕm′ə-nē) *n.* **1.** Any of various perennial herbs of the genus *Anemone,* having palmately lobed leaves and large flowers. **2.** A sea anemone. [Lat. *anemōnē* < Gk.]

anemone fish *n.* A small, brightly colored marine fish of the genus *Amphiprion,* found near sea anemones.

an•e•moph•i•lous (ăn′ə-mŏf′ə-ləs) *adj.* Pollinated by wind-dispersed pollen.

an•en•ceph•a•ly (ăn′ən-sĕf′ə-lē) *n., pl.* **-lies.** Congenital absence of most of the brain and spinal cord. **— an′en•ce•phal′ic** (-sə-făl′ĭk) *adj.*

a•nent (ə-nĕnt′) *prep.* Regarding; concerning. [ME < OE *onefn,* near : *on,* on; see ON + *efn,* even.]

an•er•oid (ăn′ə-roid′) *adj.* Not using liquid. [Fr. *anéroïde:* Gk. *a-,* without; see A–[1] + LGk. *nērон,* water; see **newo-***.]

aneroid barometer *n.* A barometer in which variations of atmospheric pressure are indicated by the relative bulges of a thin elastic metal disk covering a partially evacuated chamber.

an•es•the•sia also **an•aes•the•sia** (ăn′ĭs-thē′zhə) *n.* **1.** Loss of sensation, esp. tactile sensibility, induced by disease, injury, acupuncture, or an anesthetic. **2.** Insensibility to pain, induced by an anesthetic. [NLat. *anaesthesia* < Gk. *anaisthēsia,* insensibility : *an-,* without; see A–[1] + *aisthēsis,* feeling (< *aisthanesthai,* to feel; see **au-***).]

an•es•the•si•ol•o•gist also **an•aes•the•si•ol•o•gist** (ăn′ĭs-thē′zē-ŏl′ə-jĭst) *n.* A physician specializing in anesthesiology.

an•es•the•si•ol•o•gy also **an•aes•the•si•ol•o•gy** (ăn′ĭs-thē′zē-ŏl′ə-jē) *n.* The medical study and application of anesthetics.

an•es•thet•ic also **an•aes•thet•ic** (ăn′ĭs-thĕt′ĭk) *— adj.* **1.** Relating to or resembling anesthesia. **2.** Causing anesthesia. **3.** Insensitive. *— n.* An agent that causes loss of sensation with or without the loss of consciousness. [< Gk. *anaisthētos,* without feeling : *an-,* without; see A–[1] + *aisthētos,* perceptible (< *aisthanesthai,* to feel; see ANESTHESIA).] **— an′es•thet′i•cal•ly** *adv.*

a•nes•the•tist also **a•naes•the•tist** (ə-nĕs′thĭ-tĭst) *n.* A person trained to administer anesthetics.

a•nes•the•tize also **a•naes•the•tize** (ə-nĕs′thĭ-tīz′) *tr.v.* **-tized, -tiz•ing, -tiz•es.** To induce anesthesia in. **— an•es′the•ti•za′tion** (-tĭ-zā′shən) *n.*

an•es•trus (ăn-ĕs′trəs) *n.* An interval of sexual inactivity between two periods of estrus in mammals that breed cyclically.

A•ne•to (ə-nā′tō, ä-nĕ′-), **Pico de.** A peak, 3,406.2 m (11,168 ft), in the Pyrenees of NE Spain near the French border.

an•eu•ploid (ăn′yōō-ploid′) *adj.* Having a chromosome number that is not a multiple of the haploid number for the species. *— n.* An aneuploid cell or organism. **— an′eu•ploi′dy** (-yə-ploi′dē) *n.*

an•eu•rysm also **an•eu•rism** (ăn′yə-rĭz′əm) *n.* A localized, pathological, blood-filled dilatation of a blood vessel caused by a disease or weakening of the vessel's wall. [ME *aneurisme,* ult. < Gk. *aneurusma* < *aneurein,* to dilate : *ana-,* throughout; see ANA– + *eurus,* wide.] **— an′eu•rys′mal** (-məl) *adj.*

a•new (ə-nōō′, ə-nyōō′) *adv.* **1.** Once more; again. **2.** In a new and different way or form. [ME : *a,* of (< OE *of;* see OF) + *new,* new thing (< OE *nīwe;* see NEW), or : *a-,* on; see A–[2] + *new.*]

ANF *abbr.* Atrial natriuretic factor.

an•frac•tu•os•i•ty (ăn-frăk′chōō-ŏs′ĭ-tē) *n., pl.* **-ties. 1.** The condition or quality of having many twists and turns. **2.** A winding channel, passage, or crevice. **3.** A complicated or involved process.

an•frac•tu•ous (ăn-frăk′chōō-əs) *adj.* Full of twists and turns; tortuous. [< LLat. *anfrāctuōsus* < Lat. *anfrāctus,* winding : *an-* (< *ambi-,* around; see AMBI–) + *frāctus,* p.part. of *frangere,* to break; see **bhreg-***.]

Ang. *abbr.* Angola.

An•ga•ra (än′gə-rä′). A river of E-central Russia flowing c. 1,850 km (1,150 mi) from Lake Baikal to the Yenisei R.

An•garsk (än-gärsk′). A city of SE-central Russia on the Angara R. near Irkutsk. Pop. 256,000.

an•ga•ry (ăng′gə-rē) also **an•gar•i•a** (ăng-gâr′ē-ə) *n.* The legal right of a belligerent to seize, use, or destroy a neutral's property if full compensation is made. [LLat. *angaria,* service to a lord < Gk. *angareia,* impressment for public service < *angaros,* conscript courier.]

an•gel (ān′jəl) *n.* **1.a.** *Theol.* An immortal spiritual being attendant upon God. **b.** The conventional representation of such a being as a human with a halo and wings. **2.** A guardian spirit or guiding influence. **3.a.** A kind and lovable person. **b.** One who manifests goodness, purity, and selflessness. **4.** *Informal.* A financial backer of an enterprise. [ME < OE *engel*or OFr. *angele,* both < LLat. *angelus* < LGk. *angelos* < Gk., messenger.] **— an•gel′ic** (ăn-jĕl′ĭk), **an•gel′i•cal** *adj.* **— an•gel′i•cal•ly** *adv.*

angel cake *n.* Angel food cake.

angel dust *n. Slang.* Phencyclidine.

An•ge•le•no (ăn′jə-lē′nō) *n., pl.* **-nos.** A native or inhabitant of Los Angeles. [Am.Sp. *Angeleño,* after LOS ANGELES.]

An•gel Fall or **Falls** (ān′jəl). A waterfall, c. 980 m (3,212 ft), in SE Venezuela; highest uninterrupted waterfall in the world.

an•gel•fish (ān′jəl-fĭsh′) *n., pl.* **angelfish** or **-fish•es. 1.** A brightly colored fish of the family Pomacanthidae, having a laterally compressed body. **2.** A South American freshwater fish *(Pterophyllum scalare)* having a laterally compressed, usu. striped body.

angel food cake *n.* An almond-flavored sponge cake.

an•gel•i•ca (ăn-jĕl′ĭ-kə) *n.* **1.a.** Any of various herbs of the genus *Angelica* in the parsley family, having pinnately compound leaves and flowers in compound umbels, esp. *A. archangelica.* **b.** The edible stem, leaf, or root of *Angelica archangelica.* **2.** Often **Angelica.** A sweet white wine or liqueur. [Med.Lat. *(herba) angelica,* angelic (herb), angelica < LLat., fem. of *angelicus,* angelic < LGk. *angelikos* < Gk., of a messenger < *angelos,* messenger.]

angelica tree *n.* See **Hercules' club** 1.

An•gel•i•co (ăn-jĕl′ĭ-kō′), Fra. Also known as **Giovanni da Fie•so•le** (fyĕ′zō-lā, -zô-lĕ). 1400?–55. Italian Dominican friar and painter of the Florentine school.

An•gell (ān′jəl), Sir **Norman.** 1872–1967. British economist who won the 1933 Nobel Peace Prize.

an•gel•ol•o•gy (ān′jəl-ŏl′ə-jē) *n.* The branch of theology having to do with angels.

angel shark *n.* Any of several raylike sharks of the genus *Squatina,* having a broad flat head and body.

an•gel's trumpet (ān′jəlz) *n.* Any of several New World plants of the genera *Brugmansia* or *Datura,* having large, variously colored trumpet-shaped flowers and containing belladonna.

An•ge•lus also **an•ge•lus** (ăn′jə-ləs) *n. Rom. Cath. Ch.* **1.** A devotional prayer at morning, noon, and night to commemorate the Annunciation. **2.** A bell rung as a call to recite this prayer. [Med.Lat. < LLat., angel, first word of the devotion. See ANGEL.]

an•ger (ăng′gər) *n.* A strong feeling of displeasure or hostility. *— v.* **-gered, -ger•ing, -gers.** *— tr.* To make angry; enrage or provoke. *— intr.* To become angry. [ME < ON *angr,* sorrow. See **angh-***.]

Syns: *anger, rage, fury, ire, wrath, resentment, indignation.* These nouns denote varying degrees of marked displeasure. *Anger,* the most general, is strong displeasure: *threw a book in a fit of anger. Rage* and *fury* apply to intense, explosive, often destructive emotion: *"Heaven has no rage like love to hatred turned"* (William Congreve). *"Beware the fury*

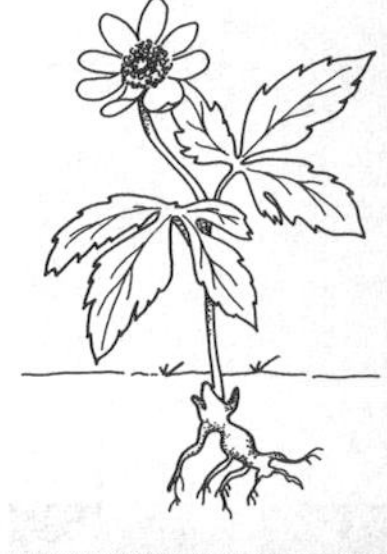

anemone
Top: Wood anemone
Anemone quinquefolia
Bottom: American warty sea anemone
Bunodosoma cavernata

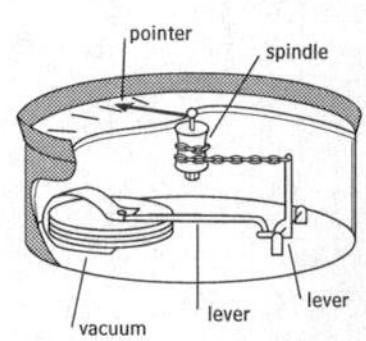

aneroid barometer

angelfish
Arabian angelfish

ă pat	oi boy
ā pay	ou out
âr care	ŏŏ took
ä father	ōō boot
ĕ pet	ŭ cut
ē be	ûr urge
ĭ pit	th thin
ī pie	*th* this
îr pier	hw which
ŏ pot	zh vision
ō toe	ə about, item
ô paw	

Stress marks:
′ (primary);
′ (secondary), as in **dictionary** (dĭk′shə-nĕr′ē)

of a patient man" (John Dryden). *Ire* is frequently encountered in literature: *"The best way to escape His ire/Is, not to seem too happy"* (Robert Browning). *Wrath* applies especially to fervid anger that seeks vengeance or punishment: *the wrath of God. Resentment* refers to ill will and smoldering anger generated by a sense of grievance: *The workers' resentment led to a strike. Indignation* is righteous anger at something wrongful, unjust, or evil: *"public indignation about takeovers causing people to lose their jobs"* (Allan Sloan).

an•ger•ly (ăng**′**gər-lē) *adv. Archaic.* Angrily.

An•gers (ăn**′**jərz, äɴ-zhā**′**). A city of W France ENE of Nantes; historical cap. of Anjou. Pop. 136,038.

An•ge•vin (ăn**′**jə-vĭn) *adj.* **1.** Of or relating to the historical region and former province of Anjou, France. **2.** Of or relating to the House of Anjou, esp. the Plantagenets, who descended from Geoffrey, Count of Anjou (died 1151). [Fr. < OFr. < Med.Lat. *Andegavīnus* < *Andegavia*, Anjou, France.]

an•gi•na (ăn-jī**′**nə, ăn**′**jə-) *n.* **1.** Angina pectoris. **2.** A condition, such as severe sore throat, marked by spasmodic attacks of suffocating pain. [Lat., quinsy < Gk. *ankhonē*, a strangling. See **angh-***.] **—an•gi′nal** *adj.* **—an′gi•nose′** (-jə-nōs′) *adj.*

angina pec•to•ris (pĕk**′**tər-ĭs) *n.* Severe paroxysmal pain in the chest associated with an insufficient blood supply to the heart. [NLat. : Lat. *angina*, quinsy + *pectoris*, genitive of *pectus*, chest.]

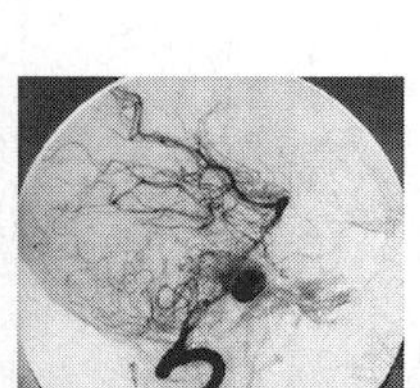

angiogram
Showing an aneurysm and hemorrhaging in the basal artery

angio– *pref.* **1.** Blood and lymph vessel: *angiogram.* **2.** Pericarp: *angiosperm.* [NLat. < Gk. *angeio-* < *angeion*, vessel, blood vessel, dim. of *angos*, vessel.]

an•gi•o•car•di•og•ra•phy (ăn′jē-ō-kär′dē-ŏg**′**rə-fē) *n.* Examination of the heart and associated blood vessels using x-rays following the injection of a radiopaque substance. **—an′gi•o•car′di•o•graph′ic** (-ə-grăf**′**ĭk) *adj.*

an•gi•o•gram (ăn**′**jē-ə-grăm′) *n.* An x-ray by angiography used in diagnosing pathological conditions of the cardiovascular system.

an•gi•og•raph•y (ăn′jē-ŏg**′**rə-fē) *n.* Examination of the blood vessels using x-rays following the injection of a radiopaque substance. **—an′gi•o•graph′ic** (-grăf**′**ĭk) *adj.*

an•gi•ol•o•gy (ăn′jē-ŏl**′**ə-jē) *n.* The study of blood and lymph vessels.

an•gi•o•ma (ăn′jē-ō**′**mə) *n., pl.* **-mas** or **-ma•ta** (-mə-tə). A tumor composed chiefly of lymph and blood vessels. **—an′gi•o′ma•tous** (-ō**′**mə-təs, -ŏm**′**ə-) *adj.*

an•gi•op•a•thy (ăn′jē-op**′**ə-thē) *n., pl.* **-thies.** Any of several diseases of the blood or lymph vessels.

an•gi•o•plas•ty (ăn**′**jē-ə-plăs′tē) *n., pl.* **-ties.** A procedure in which a catheter with a tiny balloon is inserted into an artery narrowed by fatty deposits that clear when the balloon is inflated to widen the artery.

an•gi•o•sar•co•ma (ăn′jē-ō-sär-kō**′**mə) *n.* A malignant tumor arising from vascular tissue.

an•gi•o•sperm (ăn**′**jē-ə-spûrm′) *n.* A plant whose ovules are enclosed in an ovary; a flowering plant.

an•gi•o•ten•sin (ăn′jē-ō-tĕn**′**sĭn) *n.* Either of two polypeptide hormones, one of which is a powerful vasoconstrictor, that function in the body in controlling arterial pressure. [ANGIO– + TENS(ION) + –IN.]

Ang•kor (ăng**′**kôr, -kōr). A region in NW Cambodia including two Hindu temple complexes, Angkor Wat (12th cent.) and Angkor Thom (13th cent.).

Angl. *abbr.* Anglican.

an•gle[1] (ăng**′**gəl) *intr.v.* **-gled, -gling, -gles. 1.** To fish with a hook and line. **2.** To try to get something by artful means: *angle for a promotion.* **—***n. Obsolete.* A fishhook or fishing tackle. [ME *anglen* < *angel*, fishhook < OE.]

an•gle[2] (ăng**′**gəl) *n.* **1.** *Math.* **a.** The figure formed by two lines diverging from a common point. **b.** The figure formed by two planes diverging from a common line. **c.** The rotation required to superimpose either of two such lines or planes on the other. **d.** The space between such lines or surfaces. **e.** A solid angle. **2.** A sharp or projecting corner, as of a building. **3.a.** The place, position, or direction from which an object is presented to view. **b.** An aspect, as of a problem, seen from a specific point of view. **4.** *Slang.* A devious method; a scheme. **—***v.* **-gled, -gling, -gles.** **—***tr.* **1.** To turn or direct (something) at an angle: *angled the chair toward the window.* **2.** *Informal.* To impart a biased point of view to: *angled the story so as to criticize.* **—***intr.* To continue along or turn at an angle or by angles: *The path angled through the woods.* [ME < OFr. < Lat. *angulus.*]

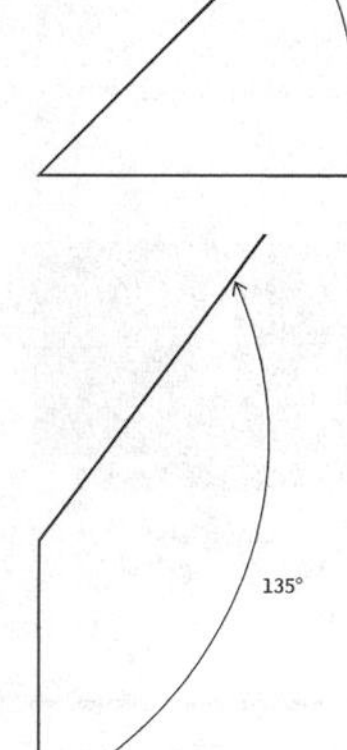

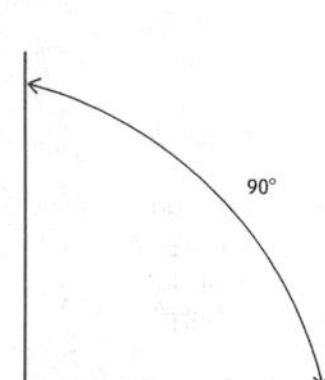

angle[2]
Top: Acute angle
Center: Obtuse angle
Bottom: Right angle

An•gle (ăng**′**gəl) *n.* A member of a Germanic people that migrated to England from southern Jutland in the fifth and sixth centuries A.D. [< Lat. *Anglī*, the Angles, of Gmc. orig.]

angle bracket *n.* **1.** Either of a pair of symbols, < >, used to enclose written material. **2.** *Math.* Either of these symbols, used esp. together to indicate the average of a contained quantity.

angle iron *n.* A length of steel or iron bent at a right angle along its long side, used as a support or structural framework.

angle of attack *n.* The acute angle between the chord of an airfoil and a line representing the undisturbed relative airflow.

angle of incidence *n. Phys.* The angle formed by a ray incident on a surface and a perpendicular to the surface at the point of incidence.

angle of reflection *n. Phys.* The angle formed by a reflected ray and a perpendicular to the surface at the point of reflection.

angle of refraction *n. Phys.* The angle formed by a refracted ray and a perpendicular to the refracting surface at the point of refraction.

angle of yaw *n.* The angle between an aircraft's longitudinal axis and its line of travel, as seen from above.

angle plate *n.* A right-angled metal bracket that is used on the faceplate of a lathe to hold the pieces that are being worked.

an•gler (ăng**′**glər) *n.* **1.** One who fishes with a hook. **2.** A schemer. **3.** An anglerfish.

an•gler•fish (ăng**′**glər-fĭsh′) *n., pl.* **anglerfish** or **-fish•es.** A marine fish of the order Lophiiformes or Pediculati, having a long dorsal fin ray suspended over the mouth that serves to attract prey.

An•gle•sey or **An•gle•sea** (ăng**′**gəl-sē). An island of NW Wales in the Irish Sea; site of druidic ruins, esp. dolmens.

an•gle•site (ăng**′**glĭ-sīt′) *n.* A lead sulfate mineral, $PbSO_4$, occurring in colorless or tinted crystals and formed by the weathering of lead ore. [After ANGLESEY.]

an•gle•worm (ăng**′**gəl-wûrm′) *n.* A worm used as bait.

An•gli•a (ăng**′**glē-ə). England.

An•gli•an (ăng**′**glē-ən) *adj.* Of or relating to East Anglia or to the Angles. **—***n.* **1.** An Angle. **2.** The Old English dialects of Mercia and Northumbria.

An•gli•can (ăng**′**glĭ-kən) *adj.* **1.** Of, relating to, or characteristic of the Church of England or any related church, such as the Protestant Episcopal Church. **2.** Of or relating to England or the English. **—***n.* A member of the Church of England or of any related church. [Med.Lat. *Anglicānus*, English < *Anglicus* < LLat. *Anglī*, the Angles. See ANGLE.]

Anglican Church *n.* The Church of England and other churches in complete agreement with it as to doctrine and discipline and in communion with the Archbishop of Canterbury.

An•gli•can•ism (ăng**′**glĭ-kə-nĭz′əm) *n.* The faith, doctrine, system, and practice of the Anglican Church.

An•gli•ce (ăng**′**glĭ-sē′) *adv.* In the English form: *Firenze,* Anglice Florence. [Med.Lat. *Anglicē* < *Anglicus*, English. See ANGLICAN.]

An•gli•cism also **an•gli•cism** (ăng**′**glĭ-sĭz′əm) *n.* **1.** A word, a phrase, or an idiom peculiar to English, esp. as spoken in England; a Briticism. **2.** A typically English quality. [< Med. Lat. *Anglicus*, English. See ANGLICAN.]

An•gli•cist (ăng**′**glĭ-sĭst) *n.* A specialist in English linguistics.

An•gli•cize also **an•gli•cize** (ăng**′**glĭ-sīz′) **—***v.* **-cized, -ciz•ing, -ciz•es.** **—***tr.* To make English or similar to English in form, idiom, style, or character. **—***intr.* To become English in form or character. **—An′gli•ci•za′tion** (-sĭ-zā**′**shən) *n.*

an•gling (ăng**′**glĭng) *n.* Fishing with a hook and line and usu. a rod.

An•glo also **an•glo** (ăng**′**glō) *n., pl.* **-glos. 1.** *Informal.* An Anglo-American. **2.** An English-speaking person, esp. a white North American who is not of Hispanic or French descent. [Short for ANGLO-AMERICAN.] **—An′glo** *adj.*

Anglo– *pref.* England; English: *Anglo-Saxon.* [NLat. < Med. Lat. *Anglī*, the English people < LLat., the Angles. See ANGLE.]

An•glo-A•mer•i•can (ăng′glō-ə-mĕr**′**ĭ-kən) *n.* An American, esp. one from the United States, whose language and ancestry are English. **—***adj.* **1.** Of, relating to, or between England and America, esp. the United States. **2.** Of or relating to Anglo-Americans.

An•glo-Cath•o•lic (ăng′glō-kăth**′**lĭk, -kăth**′**ə-lĭk) *n.* An Anglican whose convictions stress sacramental worship. **—An′glo-Cath′o•lic** *adj.*

An•glo-French (ăng**′**glō-frĕnch**′**) *adj.* Of, relating to, or between England and France or their peoples; English and French. **—***n.* See **Anglo-Norman** 2.

An•glo-In•di•an (ăng**′**glō-ĭn**′**dē-ən) *adj.* Of, relating to, or between England and India. **—***n.* **1.** A person of English and Indian descent. **2.** A person of English birth or ancestry living in India. **3.** The variety of English used in India.

An•glo-I•rish (ăng′glō-ī**′**rĭsh) *n.* **1.** An English native living in Ireland. **2.** An Irish native living in England. **3.** One of mixed Irish and English ancestry. **4.** See **Irish English. —An′glo-I′rish** *adj.*

An•glo-Nor•man (ăng′glō-nôr**′**mən) *n.* **1.** One of the Normans who lived in England after the Norman Conquest of England in 1066 or a descendant of these settlers. **2.a.** The dialect of Old French, derived chiefly from Norman French, that was used by the Anglo-Normans. **b.** The form of this dialect used in English law until the 17th century. **—An′glo-Nor′man** *adj.*

An•glo•phile (ăng**′**glə-fīl′) also **An•glo•phil** (-fĭl) *n.* One who admires England, its people, and its culture. **—An′glo•phile, An′glo•phil′ic** (ăng′glə-fĭl**′**ĭk) *adj.* **—An′glo•phil′i•a** (-fĭl′-ē-ə) *n.*

An•glo•phobe (ăng**′**glə-fōb′) *n.* One who dislikes or fears

England, its people, or its culture. —**An′glo•pho′bi•a** *n.* —**An′glo•pho′bic** (-fō′bĭk) *adj.*

An•glo•phone also **an•glo•phone** (ăn′glə-fōn′) *n.* An English-speaking person, esp. one in a country where two or more languages are spoken. —**An′glo•phon′ic** (-fŏn′ĭk) *adj.*

An•glo-Sax•on (ăng′glō-săk′sən) *n.* **1.** A member of one of the Germanic peoples who settled in Britain in the fifth and sixth centuries A.D. **2.** A descendant of the Anglo-Saxons, who were dominant in England until the Norman Conquest of 1066. **3.** See **Old English** 1. **4.** A person of English ancestry. —*adj.* Of, relating to, or characteristic of Anglo-Saxons, their descendants, or their language or culture; English.

An•go•la (ăng-gō′lə, ăn-). A country of SW Africa on the Atlantic Ocean; achieved independence from Portugal in 1975. Cap. Luanda. Pop. 8,140,000. —**An•go′lan** *adj. & n.*

An•go•ra[1] (ăng-gôr′ə, -gōr′ə, ăng′gər-ə). See **Ankara.**

An•go•ra[2] (ăng-gôr′ə, -gōr′ə) *n.* **1.** Often **angora. a.** The hair of the Angora goat. **b.** The hair of the Angora rabbit. **c.** A yarn or fabric made from either of these fibers. **2.** An Angora cat. **3.** An Angora goat. **4.** An Angora rabbit. [After *Angora* (Ankara), Turkey.]

Angora cat *n.* A domestic cat having long silky hair.

Angora goat *n.* A domestic goat having long silky hair.

Angora rabbit *n.* A domestic rabbit having long, soft, usu. white hair.

an•gos•tu•ra bark (ăng′gə-stŏŏr′ə, -styŏŏr′ə) *n.* The bitter, aromatic bark of either of two South American trees *(Galipea officinalis* or *Cusparia trifoliata),* used as a flavoring in bitters and as a tonic. [After *Angostura* (Ciudad Bolívar), Venezuela.]

An•gou•mois (än′gōō-mwä′). A historical region and former province of W France; occupied by Gallic peoples in pre-Roman times and a French duchy after 1515.

an•gry (ăng′grē) *adj.* **-gri•er, -gri•est. 1.** Feeling or showing anger; incensed or enraged: *an angry customer.* **2.** Indicative of or resulting from anger: *an angry silence.* **3.** Having a menacing aspect; threatening: *angry clouds moving in.* **4.** Inflamed and painful: *an angry sore.* [ME *angri* < *anger*, anger. See ANGER.]

angry young man also **Angry Young Man** *n.* **1.** One of a group of English writers of the 1950's whose works are characterized by social protest. **2.** A critic of economic or social injustice.

angst[1] (ängkst) *n.* A feeling of anxiety or apprehension often accompanied by depression. [Ger. < MHGer. *angest* < OHGer. *angust.* See **angh-*.**]

angst[2] *abbr.* Angstrom.

ang•strom or **ång•strom** (ăng′strəm) *n.* A unit of length equal to one hundred-millionth (10^{-8}) of a centimeter, used esp. to specify radiation wavelengths. See table at **measurement.** [After Anders Jonas ÅNGSTRÖM.]

Ång•ström (ăng′strəm, ông′strœm), **Anders Jonas.** 1814–74. Swedish physicist and astronomer who founded the science of spectography.

angstrom unit *n.* See **angstrom.**

An•guil•la (ăng-gwĭl′ə, ăn-). An island of the British West Indies in the N Leeward Is.; settled by the British in the 17th cent. A bid for independence led to the landing of British troops in 1969.

an•guish (ăng′gwĭsh) *n.* Agonizing physical or mental pain; torment. See Syns at **regret.** —*v.* **-guished, -guish•ing, -guish•es.** —*tr.* To cause to feel or suffer anguish. —*intr.* To feel or suffer anguish. [ME *angwisshe* < OFr. *anguisse* < Lat. *angustiae*, distress < *angustus*, narrow. See **angh-*.**]

an•guished (ăng′gwĭsht) *adj.* Feeling, expressing, or caused by anguish: *anguished screams for help.*

an•gu•lar (ăng′gyə-lər) *adj.* **1.** Having, forming, or consisting of an angle or angles. **2.** Measured by an angle or by degrees of an arc. **3.** Bony and lean; gaunt: *an angular face.* **4.** Lacking grace or smoothness; awkward: *an angular gait.* [Lat. *angulāris* < *angulus*, angle.] —**an′gu•lar•ly** *adv.* —**an′gu•lar•ness** *n.*

angular acceleration *n.* The rate of change of angular velocity with respect to time.

an•gu•lar•i•ty (ăng′gyə-lăr′ĭ-tē) *n., pl.* **-ties. 1.** The quality or condition of being angular. **2. angularities.** Angular forms, outlines, or corners.

angular momentum *n.* The vector product of the position vector and the linear momentum of a particle.

angular velocity *n.* The rate of change of angular displacement with respect to time.

an•gu•late (ăng′gyə-lĭt, -lāt′) *adj.* Having angles or an angular shape. —*tr. & intr.v.* (-lāt′) **-lat•ed, -lat•ing, -lates.** To make or become angular. —**an′gu•late•ly** *adv.*

an•gu•la•tion (ăng′gyə-lā′shən) *n.* **1.** The formation of angles. **2.** An angular part, position, or formation.

an•hin•ga (ăn-hĭng′gə) *n.* Any of a genus *(Anhinga)* of long-necked birds having a pointed bill and inhabiting tropical and subtropical America. [Port. < Tupi *ayingá.*]

An•hui (än′hwē′) also **An•hwei** (-hwā′, -wā′). A province of E-central China; given provincial status in the 17th cent. Cap. Hefei. Pop. 51,560,000.

an•hy•dride (ăn-hī′drīd′) *n.* A chemical compound formed from another by the removal of water. [ANHYDR(OUS) + -IDE.]

an•hy•drite (ăn-hī′drīt) *n.* A colorless to white mineral of anhydrous calcium sulfate, $CaSO_4$. [ANHYDR(OUS) + -ITE[1].]

an•hy•drous (ăn-hī′drəs) *adj.* Without water, esp. water of crystallization. [< Gk. *anudros*: *an-*, without; see A-[1] + *hudōr*, water; see **wed-**[1]***.**]

a•ni (ä-nē′) *n.* Any of several chiefly tropical American birds of the genus *Crotophaga*, related to the cuckoo and having black plumage and a long tail. [Am.Sp. *aní*or Port. *ani*, both < Tupi *ani.*]

an•il (ăn′ĭl) *n.* The indigo plant or the blue dye obtained from it. [Fr. < Port. < Ar. *an-nīl*, the indigo plant < Pers. *nīl* < Skt. *nīlī* < *nīla-*, dark blue.]

an•ile (ăn′īl′, ā′nīl′) *adj.* **1.** Of or like an old woman. **2.** Senile. [Lat. *anīlis* < *anus*, old woman.] —**a•nil′i•ty** (ə-nĭl′ĭ-tē) *n.*

an•i•line also **an•i•lin** (ăn′ə-lĭn) —*n.* A colorless, oily, poisonous benzene derivative, $C_6H_5NH_2$, used in the manufacture of rubber, dyes, resins, pharmaceuticals, and varnishes. —*adj.* Derived from aniline. [ANIL + -INE[2].]

a•ni•lin•gus (ā′nə-lĭng′gəs) *n.* Oral stimulation of the anus. [NLat. : Lat. *ānus*, anus + Lat. *lingere*, to lick; see **leigh-*.**]

anim. *abbr. Mus.* Animato.

an•i•ma (ăn′ə-mə) *n.* **1.** The inner self of an individual; the soul. **2.** In Jungian psychology: **a.** The unconscious or true inner self of an individual as opposed to the persona. **b.** The feminine inner personality, as present in men. [Lat. See **anə-*.**]

an•i•mad•ver•sion (ăn′ə-măd-vûr′zhən, -shən) *n.* **1.** Strong criticism. **2.** A critical or censorious remark. [Lat. *animadversiō, animadversiōn-* < *animadversus*, p.part. of *animadvertere*, to turn the mind toward. See ANIMADVERT.]

an•i•mad•vert (ăn′ə-măd-vûrt′) *intr.v.* **-vert•ed, -vert•ing, -verts.** To remark or comment critically, usu. with strong disapproval or censure. [ME *animadverten*, to notice < Lat. *animadvertere*: *animus*, mind; see **anə-*** + *advertere*, to turn toward; see ADVERSE.]

an•i•mal (ăn′ə-məl) *n.* **1.** A multicellular organism of the kingdom Animalia, characterized by a capacity for locomotion, nonphotosynthetic metabolism, pronounced response to stimuli, restricted growth, and fixed bodily structure. **2.** An animal organism other than a human being, esp. a mammal. **3.** A person who behaves in a bestial or brutish manner. **4.** A person considered with respect to the physical nature. **5.** A person having a specified aptitude or set of interests: *"that rarest of musical animals, an instrumentalist who is as comfortable on a podium with a stick as he is playing his instrument"* (Lon Tuck). —*adj.* **1.** Relating to, characteristic of, or derived from an animal or animals: *animal fat.* **2.** Relating to the physical nature of people: *animal instincts.* [ME < Lat. < *animāle*, neut. of *animālis*, living < *anima*, soul. See **anə-*.**]

animal cracker *n.* A small, animal-shaped cookie.

an•i•mal•cule (ăn′ə-măl′kyōōl) also **an•i•mal•cu•lum** (-kyə-ləm) *n., pl.* **-cules** also **-cu•la** (-kyə-lə). **1.** A microscopic or minute organism, such as an amoeba or a paramecium. **2.** *Archaic.* A tiny animal, such as a mosquito. [NLat. *animalculum*, dim. of Lat. *animal*, animal < *anima*, soul. See ANIMA.]

animal heat *n.* The heat generated in the body of a warm-blooded vertebrate.

animal husbandry *n.* The branch of agriculture concerned with the care and breeding of domestic animals.

an•i•mal•ism (ăn′ə-mə-lĭz′əm) *n.* **1.** Enjoyment of vigorous health and physical drives. **2.** Indifference to all but the physical appetites. **3.** The doctrine that humans are all animal with no spiritual nature. —**an′i•mal•ist** *n.* —**an′i•mal•is′tic** (-lĭs′tĭk) *adj.*

an•i•mal•i•ty (ăn′ə-măl′ĭ-tē) *n.* **1.** The characteristics or nature of an animal. **2.** The animal kingdom. **3.** The animal instincts of humans.

an•i•mal•ize (ăn′ə-mə-līz′) *tr.v.* **-ized, -iz•ing, -iz•es. 1.** To cause (another) to behave like an animal. **2.** To depict or represent as an animal. —**an′i•mal•i•za′tion** (-mə-lĭ-zā′shən) *n.*

animal kingdom *n.* A main classification of living organisms that includes all animals.

animal magnetism *n.* **1.** A special presence held to aid in hypnotism. **2.** Magnetic personal charm. **3.** Sex appeal.

animal pole *n. Embryol.* The portion of an egg, opposite the vegetal pole, that contains the nucleus and most of the cytoplasm.

animal spirits *pl.n.* The vitality of good health.

animal starch *n.* See **glycogen.**

an•i•mate (ăn′ə-māt′) *tr.v.* **-mat•ed, -mat•ing, -mates. 1.** To give life to; fill with life. **2.** To impart interest or zest to; enliven. **3.** To fill with spirit, courage, or resolution; encourage. **4.** To inspire to action; prompt. **5.** To impart motion or activity to. **6.** To make, design, or produce so as to create the illusion of motion. —*adj.* (ăn′ə-mĭt). **1.** Possessing life; living. **2.** Of or relating to animal life as distinct from plant life. **3.** Belonging to the class of nouns that stand for living things: *The word* dog *is animate; the word* car *is inanimate.* [Lat. *animāre, animāt-* < *anima*, soul. See **anə-*.**]

Angola

Angora goat

anhinga

ă pat	oi boy
ā pay	ou out
âr care	ŏŏ took
ä father	ōō boot
ĕ pet	ŭ cut
ē be	ûr urge
ĭ pit	th thin
ī pie	*th* this
îr pier	hw which
ŏ pot	zh vision
ō toe	ə about, item
ô paw	

Stress marks:
′ (primary);
′ (secondary), as in
dictionary (dĭk′shə-nĕr′ē)

an•i•mat•ed (ăn′ə-mā′tĭd) *adj.* **1.** Having life; alive. **2.** Filled with activity, vigor, or spirit; lively. **3.** Made in the form of an animated cartoon. **—an′i•mat′ed•ly** *adv.*

animated cartoon *n.* A motion picture consisting of a photographed series of drawings that simulates motion with very slight, continuous changes in the drawings.

an•i•ma•tion (ăn′ə-mā′shən) *n.* **1.** The act, process, or result of imparting life, interest, spirit, motion, or activity. **2.** The quality or condition of being alive, active, spirited, or vigorous. **3.a.** The preparation of animated cartoons. **b.** An animated cartoon.

a•ni•ma•to (ä′nē-mä′tō) *adv. & adj. Mus.* In an animated or lively manner. [Ital. < *animare*, to animate < Lat. *animāre*. See ANIMATE.]

an•i•ma•tor (ăn′ə-mā′tər) *n.* **1.** One that provides or imparts life, interest, spirit, or vitality. **2.** One who designs, develops, or produces an animated cartoon.

an•i•mism (ăn′ə-mĭz′əm) *n.* **1.** The attribution of conscious life to nature. **2.** The belief in the existence of spiritual beings that are separate from bodies. **3.** The theory that an immaterial force animates the universe. [< Lat. *anima*, soul. See **anə-***.] **—an′i•mist** *n.* **—an′i•mis′tic** *adj.*

an•i•mos•i•ty (ăn′ə-mŏs′ĭ-tē) *n., pl.* **-ties.** Bitter hostility or open enmity; active hatred. [ME *animosite* < OFr. < LLat. *animōsitās*, courage < Lat. *animōsus*, bold < *animus*, soul, spirit. See **anə-***.]

Anne of Cleves

an•i•mus (ăn′ə-məs) *n.* **1.** An attitude that informs one's actions; disposition. **2.** A feeling of animosity; ill will. **3.** In Jungian psychology, the masculine inner personality, as present in women. [Lat. See **anə-***.]

an•i•on (ăn′ī′ən) *n.* A negatively charged ion, esp. the ion that migrates to an anode in electrolysis. [< Gk., neut. pr.part. of *anienai*, to go up : *ana-*, ana- + *ienai*, to go; see **ei-***.] **—an′i•on′ic** (-ŏn′ĭk) *adj.* **—an′i•on′i•cal•ly** *adv.*

an•ise (ăn′ĭs) *n.* **1.** An annual Mediterranean herb *(Pimpinella anisum)* in the parsley family, cultivated for its seedlike fruits and oil. **2.** Anise seed. [ME *anis* < OFr. < Lat. *anīsum* < Gk. *anison*.]

an•i•sei•ko•ni•a (ăn-ī′sī-kō′nē-ə) *n.* A condition in which the shape and size of the ocular image differ in each eye. [< ANIS(O)- + Gk. *eikōn*, image.] **—an•i′sei•kon′ic** (-kŏn′ĭk) *adj.*

anise seed or **an•i•seed** (ăn′ĭ-sēd′) *n.* The seedlike fruit of the anise.

an•i•sette (ăn′ĭ-sĕt′, -zĕt′) *n.* A liqueur flavored with anise. [Fr., dim. of *anis*, anise < OFr. See ANISE.]

aniso– or **anis–** *pref.* Unequal; dissimilar: *anisogamy.* [< Gk. *anisos*: *an-*, not; see A-[1] + *isos*, equal.]

an•i•so•gam•ete (ăn-ī′sō-găm′ēt, -gə-mēt′, ăn′ĭ-) *n.* See **heterogamete.**

an•i•sog•a•my (ăn′ī-sŏg′ə-mē) *n.* A union between two gametes that differ in size or form. **—an′i•so•gam′ic** (-sə-găm′ĭk) *adj.*

an•i•so•me•tro•pi•a (ăn-ī′sə-mĭ-trō′pē-ə) *n.* A condition in which the refractive power of one eye differs from that of the other. [ANISO- + Gk. *metron*, measure; see METER[1] + -OPIA.] **—an•i′so•me•trop′ic** (-trŏp′ĭk, -trō′pĭk) *adj.*

an•i•so•trop•ic (ăn-ī′sə-trŏp′ĭk, -trō′pĭk) *adj.* **1.** Not isotropic. **2.** *Phys.* Having different properties in different directions. **—an•i′so•trop′i•cal•ly** *adv.* **—an′i•sot′ro•pism** (-sŏt′rə-pĭz′əm), **an′i•sot′ro•py** (-sŏt′rə-pē) *n.*

An•jou[1] (ăn′jo͞o′, äN-zho͞o′). **1.** A historical region and former province of NW France; annexed to the French crown lands in the 1480's. **2.** A town of S Quebec, Canada, a suburb of Montreal. Pop. 37,346.

An•jou[2] (ăn′zho͞o, -jo͞o) *n.* A variety of pear with green skin and firm, smooth flesh.

An•ka•ra (ăng′kər-ə, äng′-). Formerly **An•cy•ra** (ăn-sī′rə) and **An•go•ra** (ăng-gôr′ə, -gōr′ə, ăng′gər-ə). The cap. of Turkey, in the W-central part; replaced Istanbul as the cap. in 1923. Pop. 1,877,755.

annual ring
Cross section from the trunk of a white pine
Pinus strobus

an•ker•ite (ăng′kə-rīt′) *n.* A white, gray, or red iron-rich dolomitic or carbonate mineral, $Ca(Fe,Mg,Mn)(CO_3)_2$. [After Matthias Joseph *Anker* (1771–1843), Austrian mineralogist.]

ankh (ăngk) *n.* An ansate cross. [Egypt. *'nḫ*, life.]

an•kle (ăng′kəl) *n.* **1.** The joint formed by the articulation of the lower leg bones with the talus. **2.** The slender section of the leg immediately above the foot. [ME *ancle, ankel*, partly < OE *anclēow*, and partly of Scand. orig.]

an•kle•bone (ăng′kəl-bōn′) *n.* See **talus**[1] 1.

an•klet (ăng′klĭt) *n.* **1.** An ornament worn around the ankle. **2.** A sock that reaches just above the ankle.

an•ky•lose also **an•chy•lose** (ăng′kə-lōs′, -lōz′) *—v.* **-losed, -los•ing, -los•es.** *—tr.* To join or consolidate by ankylosis. *—intr.* To become joined or consolidated by ankylosis. [Back-formation < ANKYLOSIS.]

an•ky•lo•sis also **an•chy•lo•sis** (ăng′kə-lō′sĭs) *n.* **1.** *Anat.* The consolidation of bones to form a single unit. **2.** *Pathol.* The stiffening and immobility of a joint as the result of disease, trauma, surgery, or abnormal bone fusion. [NLat. < Gk. *ankulōsis*, stiffening of the joints < *ankuloun*, to crook, bend < *ankulos*, crooked, bent.] **—an′ky•lot′ic** (-lŏt′ĭk) *adj.*

an•la•ge also **An•la•ge** (än′lä′gə) *n., pl.* **-ges** or **-gen** (-gən). **1.** *Biol.* The initial clustering of embryonic cells from which a part or an organ develops; a primordium. **2.** A fundamental principle; the foundation for a future development. [Ger., fundamental principle < MHGer. *anlāge*, request : *ane-*, on (< OHGer. *ana-*; see **an-***) + *lāge*, act of laying (< OHGer. *lāga*; see **legh-***).]

Ann (ăn), **Cape.** A peninsula of NE MA NE of Gloucester.

ann. *abbr.* **1.** Annals. **2.** Annual. **3.** Annuity.

An•na•ba (ə-nä′bə, ă-nä′-). A city of NE Algeria on the Mediterranean Sea; founded by the Carthaginians. Pop. 222,607.

An•na I•va•nov•na (ä′nə ē-vä′nəv-nə). 1693–1740. Empress of Russia (1730–40) who ordered an attack on Turkey (1736).

An Na•jaf (ăn năj′ăf′). A city of S-central Iraq on a lake near the Euphrates R. Pop. 242,603.

an•nal•ist (ăn′ə-lĭst) *n.* One who writes annals; a chronicler.

an•nals (ăn′əlz) *pl.n.* **1.** A chronological record of the events of successive years. **2.** A descriptive account or record; a history. **3.** A journal in which the records and reports of a learned field are compiled. [Lat. *(lībrī) annālēs*, yearly (books), annals, pl. of *annālis*, yearly < *annus*, year. See **at-***.]

An•nam (ə-năm′, ăn′ăm′). A region and former kingdom of central Vietnam on the South China Sea; ruled by China from 111 B.C. to A.D. 939. **—An′na•mese′** (ăn′ə-mēz′, -mēs′), **An′nam•ite′** *adj. & n.*

An•nan•dale (ăn′ən-dāl′). A city of NE VA, a suburb of Washington DC. Pop. 50,975.

An•nap•o•lis (ə-năp′ə-lĭs). The cap. of MD, in the central part on an inlet of Chesapeake Bay. Pop. 33,187.

Annapolis Roy•al (roi′əl). A town of W Nova Scotia, Canada, on an arm of the Bay of Fundy; founded as **Port Royal** by the French in 1605 and renamed by the British after 1710.

An•na•pur•na (ăn′ə-po͝or′nə, -pûr′-). A massif of the Himalaya Mts. in N-central Nepal rising to 8,083.7 m (26,504 ft) at **Annapurna I. Annapurna II** is 7,942.5 m (26,041 ft).

Ann Ar•bor (är′bər). A city of SE MI W of Detroit; seat of the University of Michigan (founded 1817). Pop. 109,592.

an•nat•to (ə-nä′tō) *n., pl.* **-tos. 1.** A tropical American evergreen shrub or small tree *(Bixa orellana)*, having heart-shaped leaves and showy flowers. **2.** The seed of this plant, used as a coloring and as a flavoring. **3.** A yellowish-red dyestuff obtained from the seed aril of this plant. [Of Cariban orig.]

Anne (ăn). 1665–1714. Queen of Great Britain and Ireland (1702–14); last monarch of the Stuart line.

an•neal (ə-nēl′) *v.* **-nealed, -neal•ing, -neals.** *—tr.* **1.** To subject (glass or metal) to a process of heating and slow cooling to reduce brittleness. **2.** To strengthen or harden. *—intr.* To become strengthened or hardened. [ME *anelen* < OE *onǣlan*, to set fire to : *on*, on; see ON + *ǣlan*, to kindle.]

An•ne•cy (ăn′ə-sē′, än-sē′). A city of S France in the Alps on **Lake Annecy** ENE of Lyons. Pop. 49,965.

an•ne•lid (ăn′ə-lĭd) also **an•nel•i•dan** (ə-nĕl′ĭ-dən) *—n.* Any of various worms or wormlike animals of the phylum Annelida, characterized by an elongated, cylindrical, segmented body. *—adj.* Of or belonging to the phylum Annelida. [< NLat. *Annelida*, phylum name < Fr. *annelés*, pl. p.part. of *anneler*, to ring < OFr. *anel*, ring < Lat. *ānellus*, dim. of *ānus*, ring.]

Anne of Aus•tri•a (ô′strē-ə). 1601–66. Wife of Louis XIII of France and regent (1643–61) for her son Louis XIV.

Anne of Cleves (klēvz). 1515–57. Queen of England (Jan.–Jul. 1540) as the fourth wife of Henry VIII.

an•nex (ə-nĕks′, ăn′ĕks′) *tr.v.* **-nexed, -nex•ing, -nex•es. 1.** To append or attach, especially to a larger or more significant thing. **2.** To incorporate (territory) into an existing political unit. **3.** To add or attach, as an attribute, a condition, or a consequence. *—n.* (ăn′ĕks′, ăn′ĭks). **1.** A building added on to or situated near a main one. **2.** An addition that is made to a record or other document. [ME *annexen* < OFr. *annexer* < Lat. *annectere, annex-*, to connect : *ad-*, ad- + *nectere*, to bind; see **ned-***.] **—an′nex•a′tion** (ăn′ĭk-sā′shən) *n.* **—an′nex•a′tion•al** *adj.* **—an′nex•a′tion•ism** *n.* **—an′nex•a′tion•ist** *n.*

an•nexe (ăn′ĭks) *n. Chiefly British.* Var. of **annex.**

An•nie Oak•ley (ăn′ē ōk′lē) *n.* A free ticket or pass. [After Annie OAKLEY (from the association of the punched ticket with one of her bullet-riddled targets).]

an•ni•hi•late (ə-nī′ə-lāt′) *v.* **-lat•ed, -lat•ing, -lates.** *—tr.* **1.a.** To destroy completely. **b.** To reduce to nonexistence. **c.** To defeat decisively; vanquish. **2.** To nullify or render void; abolish. *—intr. Phys.* To participate in annihilation. [LLat. *annihilāre, annihilāt-* : Lat. *ad-*, ad- + Lat. *nihil*, nothing; see **ne***.] **—an•ni′hi•la•bil′i•ty** (-lə-bĭl′ĭ-tē) *n.* **—an•ni′hi•la•ble** (-lə-bəl) *adj.* **—an•ni′hi•la′tive** (-lā′tĭv, -lə-) *adj.* **—an•ni′hi•la′tor** *n.*

an•ni•hi•la•tion (ə-nī′ə-lā′shən) *n.* **1.a.** The act or process of annihilating. **b.** Utter destruction. **2.** *Phys.* The phenomenon in which a particle and an antiparticle meet and are converted to energy approx. equivalent to the sum of their masses.

An•nis•ton (ăn′ĭ-stən). A city of NE AL ENE of Birmingham; founded 1872. Pop. 26,623.

an•ni•ver•sa•ry (ăn′ə-vûr′sə-rē) *n., pl.* **-ries. 1.** The annually recurring date of a past event. **2.** A celebration commemorating such a date. [ME *anniversarie* < Med.Lat. *(diēs) anniversāria*, anniversary (day) < Lat., fem. of *anniversārius*, returning yearly : *annus*, year; see **at-*** + *versus*, p.part. of *vertere*, to turn; see **wer-²***.]

an•no Dom•i•ni (ăn′ō dŏm′ə-nī′, dŏm′ə-nē) *adv.* In a specified year of the Christian era. [Med.Lat. : *annō*, in the year + *Domini*, genitive of *Dominus*, Lord.]

an•no•tate (ăn′ō-tāt′) *v.* **-tat•ed, -tat•ing, -tates.** — *tr.* To add commentary or notes to; gloss. — *intr.* To gloss a text. [Lat. *annotāre, annotāt-*, to note down : *ad-*, ad- + *notāre*, to write (< *nota*, note; see **gnō-***).] — **an′no•ta′tor** *n.*

an•no•ta•tion (ăn′ō-tā′shən) *n.* **1.** The act or process of adding commentary or notes. **2.** A critical or explanatory note.

an•nounce (ə-nouns′) *v.* **-nounced, -nounc•ing, -nounc•es.** — *tr.* **1.** To make known publicly. **2.** To proclaim the presence of: *announce a caller.* **3.** To provide an indication of beforehand; foretell. **4.** To provide running comments on: *announce a football game.* — *intr.* **1.** To declare one's candidacy. **2.** To provide running comments. [ME *announcen* < OFr. *anoncier* < Lat. *annūntiāre*: *ad-*, ad- + *nūntiāre*, to report (< *nūntius*, messenger; see **neu-***).] — **an•nounc′er** *n.*

an•nounce•ment (ə-nouns′mənt) *n.* **1.a.** The act of making known publicly. **b.** Something announced. **2.** An engraved or printed statement or notice.

an•noy (ə-noi′) *v.* **-noyed, -noy•ing, -noys.** — *tr.* **1.** To cause irritation to by troublesome acts. **2.** To harass or disturb by repeated attacks. — *intr.* To be annoying. [ME *anoien* < OFr. *anoier, ennuyer* < VLat. **inodiāre*, to make odious < Lat. *in odio*, odious : *in*, in; see IN-² + *odiō*, ablative of *odium*, hatred; see **od-***.]

an•noy•ance (ə-noi′əns) *n.* **1.** The act of annoying or the state of being annoyed. **2.** A cause of irritation or vexation.

an•noy•ing (ə-noi′ĭng) *adj.* Causing vexation or irritation; troublesome: *an annoying cough.* — **an•noy′ing•ly** *adv.*

an•nu•al (ăn′yo͞o-əl) *adj.* **1.** Happening every year; yearly: *an annual trip to Paris.* **2.** Of, relating to, or determined by a year: *an annual income.* **3.** *Bot.* Living or growing for one year or season. — *n.* **1.** A periodical published yearly; a yearbook. **2.** *Bot.* A plant that completes its life cycle in one growing season. [ME *annuel* < OFr. < LLat. *annuālis*, ult. < Lat. *annus*, year. See **at-***.] — **an′nu•al•ly** *adv.*

an•nu•al•ize (ăn′yo͞o-ə-līz′) *tr.v.* **-ized, -iz•ing, -iz•es.** To calculate to reflect a rate based on a full year.

annual ring *n. Bot.* The layer of wood formed in a plant during a single year.

an•nu•i•tant (ə-no͞o′ĭ-tənt, ə-nyo͞o′-) *n.* One that receives or is qualified to receive an annuity.

an•nu•i•ty (ə-no͞o′ĭ-tē, ə-nyo͞o′-) *n., pl.* **-ties. 1.a.** The annual payment of an income. **b.** The right to receive this payment or the obligation to make this payment. **2.** An investment on which one receives fixed payments for a lifetime or for a number of years. [ME *annuite* < AN < Med.Lat. *annuitās* < Lat. *annuus*, yearly < *annus*, year. See **at-***.]

an•nul (ə-nŭl′) *tr.v.* **-nulled, -nul•ling, -nuls. 1.** To make or declare void or invalid; nullify. **2.** To obliterate: *a memory annulled by time.* [ME *annullen* < OFr. *annuller* < LLat. *annullāre*: Lat. *ad-*, ad- + Lat. *nullus*, none; see **ne***.]

an•nu•lar (ăn′yə-lər) *adj.* Shaped like or forming a ring. [Lat. *ānulāris* < *ānulus*, ring. See ANNULUS.]

annular eclipse *n.* A solar eclipse in which the moon covers all but a bright ring around the circumference of the sun.

annular ligament *n.* The fibrous band of tissue that surrounds the ankle joint or the wrist joint.

an•nu•late (ăn′yə-lĭt, -lāt′) also **an•nu•lat•ed** (-lā′tĭd) *adj.* Having or consisting of rings or ringlike segments. [Lat. *ānulātus* < *ānulus*, ring. See ANNULUS.]

an•nu•la•tion (ăn′yə-lā′shən) *n.* **1.** The act or process of forming rings. **2.** A ringlike structure, segment, or part.

an•nu•let (ăn′yə-lĭt) *n. Archit.* A ringlike molding around the capital of a pillar. [Lat. *ānulus*, ring; see ANNULUS + -ET.]

an•nul•ment (ə-nŭl′mənt) *n.* **1.** An act of making or declaring void. **2.** The invalidation of a marriage by means of a declaration stating that the marriage was never valid.

an•nu•lus (ăn′yə-ləs) *n., pl.* **-lus•es** or **-li** (-lī′). **1.** A ringlike figure, part, structure, or marking. **2.a.** A ring of cells around the sporangia of many ferns that functions in spore release. **b.** A ring found around the stipes of certain mushrooms. **3.** *Math.* The region bounded by two concentric circles. [Lat. *ānulus*, ring, dim. of *ānus*.]

an•nun•ci•ate (ə-nŭn′sē-āt′) *tr.v.* **-at•ed, -at•ing, -ates.** To announce; proclaim: *annunciate a policy.* [Lat. *annūntiāre, annūntiāt-*. See ANNOUNCE.]

an•nun•ci•a•tion (ə-nŭn′sē-ā′shən) *n.* **1.** The act of announcing. **2.** An announcement; a proclamation. **3. Annunciation. a.** The angel Gabriel's announcement to the Virgin Mary of the Incarnation. **b.** The Christian feast celebrating this event, traditionally observed on March 25.

an•nun•ci•a•tor (ə-nŭn′sē-ā′tər) *n.* One that announces, esp. an electrical signaling device on a switchboard.

an•nus mi•rab•i•lis (ăn′əs mĭ-răb′ə-lĭs) *n., pl.* **an•ni mi•ra•bi•les** (ăn′ī mĭ-răb′ə-lēz, ăn′ē). A year of wonders. [NLat. : Lat. *annus*, year + Lat. *mīrābilis*, wondrous.]

an•ode (ăn′ōd′) *n.* **1.** A positively charged electrode, as of a storage battery. **2.** The negatively charged terminal of a primary cell or of a storage battery that is supplying current. [Gk. *anodos*, a way up : *ana-*, ana- + *hodos*, way.]

an•o•dize (ăn′ə-dīz′) *tr.v.* **-dized, -diz•ing, -diz•es.** To coat (a metal) electrolytically with a protective or decorative oxide. [ANOD(E) + -IZE.] — **an′o•di•za′tion** (-dĭ-zā′shən) *n.*

an•o•dyne (ăn′ə-dīn′) *adj.* **1.** Capable of soothing or eliminating pain. **2.** Watered-down; insipid: *"that passage was pretty anodyne"* (Conor Cruise O'Brien). — *n.* A comforter or a reliever of pain. [Lat. *anōdynus* < Gk. *anōdunos*, free from pain : *an-*, without; see A-¹ + *odunē*, pain; see **ed-***.]

a•noint (ə-noint′) *tr.v.* **a•noint•ed, a•noint•ing, a•noints. 1.** To apply oil, ointment, or a similar substance to. **2.** To put oil on during a religious ceremony. **3.** To choose by or as if by divine intervention. [ME *enointen* < OFr. *enoint*, p.part. of *enoindre* < Lat. *inunguere, inūnct-* : *in-*, on; see IN-² + *unguere*, to smear.] — **a•noint′ment** *n.*

a•noint•ing of the sick (ə-noin′tĭng) *n. Rom. Cath. Ch.* The sacrament of anointing a critically ill or weak person, with prayers for recovery and an act of penance or confession.

a•no•le (ə-nō′lē) *n.* Any of various chiefly tropical New World lizards of the genus *Anolis,* characterized by the ability to change color. [Fr. *anolis*, of Cariban orig.]

a•nom•a•lous (ə-nŏm′ə-ləs) *adj.* **1.** Deviating from the usual or common order, form, or rule. **2.** Equivocal, as in classification or nature. [< LLat. *anōmalos* < Gk., uneven : prob. < *an-*, not; see A-¹ + *homalos*, even (< *homos*, same; see **sem-¹***).]

a•nom•a•ly (ə-nŏm′ə-lē) *n., pl.* **-lies. 1.** Deviation or departure from the usual or common order, form, or rule. **2.** One that is peculiar, irregular, abnormal, or difficult to classify. **3.** *Astron.* The angular deviation, as observed from the sun, of a planet from its perihelion. — **a•nom′a•lis′tic** (-lĭs′tĭk), **a•nom′a•lis′ti•cal** *adj.* — **a•nom′a•lis′ti•cal•ly** *adv.*

an•o•mie or **an•o•my** (ăn′ə-mē) *n.* **1.** Social instability caused by erosion of standards and values. **2.** Alienation and purposelessness as a result of a lack of standards and values. **3.** Personal disorganization resulting in unsocial behavior. [Fr. < Gk. *anomia*, lawlessness < *anomos*, lawless : *a-*, without; see A-¹ + *nomos*, law; see **nem-***.] — **an•o′mic** (ə-nŏm′ĭk, ə-nō′mĭk) *adj.*

a•non (ə-nŏn′) *adv.* **1.** At another time; later. **2.** In a short time; soon. **3.** *Archaic.* At once; forthwith. — ***idiom.*** **ever (or now) and anon.** Time after time; now and then. [ME, at once < OE *on ān*: *on*, in; see ON + *ān*, one; see **oi-no-***.]

anon. *abbr.* Anonymous.

an•o•nym (ăn′ə-nĭm′) *n.* **1.** An anonymous person. **2.** A pseudonym. [Fr. *anonyme* < LLat. *anōnymus*, anonymous. See ANONYMOUS.]

an•o•nym•i•ty (ăn′ə-nĭm′ĭ-tē) *n., pl.* **-ties. 1.** The quality or state of being unknown or unacknowledged. **2.** One that is unknown or unacknowledged.

a•non•y•mous (ə-nŏn′ə-məs) *adj.* **1.** Having an unknown or unacknowledged name: *an anonymous author.* **2.** Having an unknown or withheld authorship or agency: *an anonymous letter.* **3.** Having no distinctive character or individuality. [< LLat. *anōnymus* < Gk. *anōnumos*, nameless : *an-*, without; see A-¹ + *onuma*, name; see **nō-men-***.]

a•noph•e•les (ə-nŏf′ə-lēz′) *n.* Any of various mosquitoes of the genus *Anopheles*, which can carry the malaria parasite. [< Gk. *anōphelēs*, useless : *an-*, without; see A-¹ + *ōpheleia*, advantage.] — **a•noph′e•line′** (-līn′, -lĭn) *adj.*

an•o•rak (ăn′ə-răk′) *n.* A heavy jacket with a hood; a parka. [Greenlandic Eskimo *annoraaq*, formerly spelled *ánorâk*.]

an•o•rec•tic (ăn′ə-rĕk′tĭk) also **an•o•ret•ic** (-rĕt′ĭk) — *adj.* **1.** Marked by loss of appetite. **2.** Causing loss of appetite. **3.** Of or affected with anorexia nervosa. — *n.* **1.** One who is affected with anorexia nervosa. **2.** An anorectic drug. [< Gk. *anorektos*: *an-*, not; see A-¹ + *orektos*, desired (< *oregeom*, to reach out for; see **reg-***).]

an•o•rex•i•a (ăn′ə-rĕk′sē-ə) *n.* Loss of appetite. [Gk. : *an-*, without; see A-¹ + *orexis*, appetite (< *oregein*, to reach out for; see **reg-***).]

anorexia nerv•o•sa (nûr-vō′sə) *n.* A disorder usu. occurring in teenage women, characterized by a fear of obesity, a distorted self-image, an aversion to food, and severe weight loss. [NLat. : *anorexia*, anorexia + *nervosa*, nervous.]

an•o•rex•ic (ăn′ə-rĕk′sĭk) *adj.* **1.** Afflicted with anorexia nervosa. **2.** Anorectic. — **an′o•rex′ic** *n.*

an•or•thite (ăn-ôr′thīt′) *n.* A rare plagioclase feldspar with high calcium oxide content occurring in igneous rocks. [< Gk. *an-*, not; see A-¹ + *orthos*, straight (from its oblique crystals).]

an•or•tho•site (ăn-ôr′thə-sīt′) *n.* A variety of diorite consisting chiefly of feldspar. [Fr. *anorthose*, a kind of feldspar (Gk. *an-*, not; see A-¹ + Gk. *orthos*, straight) + -ITE¹.]

an•os•mi•a (ăn-ŏz′mē-ə) *n.* Loss of the sense of smell. [NLat. : Gk. *an-*, without; see A-¹ + Gk. *osmē*, odor.] — **an•os′mic** *adj.*

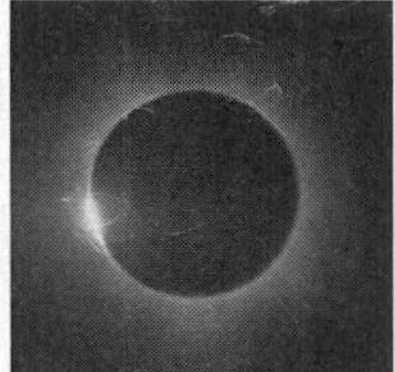

annular eclipse
Solar eclipse,
March 7, 1970

anorak

ă pat	oi **boy**
ā pay	ou **out**
âr care	o͝o t**oo**k
ä father	o͞o b**oo**t
ĕ pet	ŭ cut
ē be	ûr **urge**
ĭ pit	th **thin**
ī pie	*th* **this**
îr pier	hw **which**
ŏ pot	zh vision
ō toe	ə about,
ô paw	item

Stress marks:
′ (primary);
′ (secondary), as in
dictionary (dĭk′shə-nĕr′ē)

an•oth•er (ə-nŭth′ər) *adj.* **1.** One more; an additional: *another cup of coffee.* **2.** Distinctly different from the first. **3.** Some other: *another day.* —*pron.* **1.** An additional one. **2.** A different one. **3.** One of an undetermined number or group: *one reason or another.* [ME *on other*: *on*, one; see ONE + *other*, other; see OTHER.]

A•nou•ilh (ä-no͞o′ē), **Jean.** 1910–87. French playwright whose works include *Antigone* (1944).

an•ov•u•lant (ăn′ŏv′yə-lənt) *n.* A drug that suppresses ovulation. [AN– + OVUL(ATION) + –ANT.] —**an•ov′u•lant** *adj.*

an•o•vu•la•tion (ăn-ō′vyə-lā′shən, -ŏv′yə-) *n.* The failure, cessation, or suppression of ovulation.

an•o•vu•la•to•ry (ăn-ō′vyə-lə-tôr′ē, -tōr′ē, -ŏv′yə-) *adj.* **1.** Relating to or causing the suppression of ovulation. **2.** Not associated with or influenced by ovulation.

an•ox•e•mi•a (ăn′ŏk-sē′mē-ə) *n.* An abnormal reduction in the oxygen content of the blood. [AN– + OX(O)– + –EMIA.] —**an′ox•e′mic** *adj.*

an•ox•i•a (ăn-ŏk′sē-ə) *n.* **1.** Absence of oxygen. **2.** A pathological deficiency of oxygen, esp. hypoxia. [AN– + OX(O)– + –IA[1].] —**an•ox′ic** (-ŏk′sĭk) *adj.*

ans. *abbr.* Answer.

an•sate (ăn′sāt′) *adj.* Having a handle or a part resembling a handle. [Lat. *ānsātus* < *ānsa*, handle.]

ansate cross *n.* A cross shaped like a T with a loop at the top.

ansate cross
Held in right hand

An•schluss (än′shlo͝os′) *n.* A political union, esp. the one unifying Nazi Germany and Austria in 1938. [Ger., annexation < *anschliessen*, to enclose, annex : *an*, on (< MHGer. *ane* < OHGer. *ana*; see **an-***) + *schliessen*, to close (< MHGer. *sliezen* < OHGer. *sliozan*).]

An•selm (ăn′sĕlm), Saint. 1033–1109. Italian-born English philosopher and theologian who founded Scholasticism.

an•ser•ine (ăn′sə-rīn′, -rĭn) *adj.* **1.** Of or belonging to the subfamily Anserinae, which comprises the geese. **2.** Of or resembling a goose; gooselike. [Lat. *ānserīnus*, pertaining to geese < *ānser*, goose. See **ghans-***.]

An•shan (än′shän′). A city of NE China SSW of Shenyang. Pop. 1,280,000.

An•so•ni•a (ăn-sō′nē-ə, -sōn′yə). A city of SW CT WNW of New Haven; first settled in 1651. Pop. 18,403.

an•swer (ăn′sər) *n.* **1.a.** A spoken or written reply. **b.** A correct reply. **2.a.** A solution. **b.** A correct solution. **3.** An act in retaliation or response: *Our only possible answer was to sue.* **4.** Something markedly similar to another of the same class. **5.** *Law.* A defendant's defense against charges. —*v.* **-swered, -swer•ing, -swers.** —*intr.* **1.** To speak, write, or act as a return. **2.** To be liable or accountable: *answer for your actions.* **3.** To serve the purpose; suffice: *"Often I do use three words where one would answer"* (Mark Twain). **4.** To correspond; match: *a dog answering to that description.* —*tr.* **1.** To speak, write, or act as a return to; respond to. **2.** To respond correctly to. **3.** To fulfill the demands or needs of; serve. **4.** To conform or correspond to: *The suspect answers the description.* [ME *answere* < OE *andswaru.* See **swer-***.]

Syns: *answer, respond, reply, retort.* These verbs relate to action taken in return to a stimulus. *Answer, respond,* and *reply,* the most general, all mean to speak, write, or act in response: *Please answer my question. Did you expect the President to respond personally to your letter? The opposing team scored three runs; the home team replied with two of their own. Respond* also denotes a reaction, either voluntary (*A bystander responded to the victim's need for help*) or involuntary (*She responded in spite of herself to the antics of the puppy*). To *retort* is to answer verbally in a quick, caustic, or witty manner: *"You don't need to worry about appearing too intelligent," retorted his opponent.* See also Syns at **satisfy.**

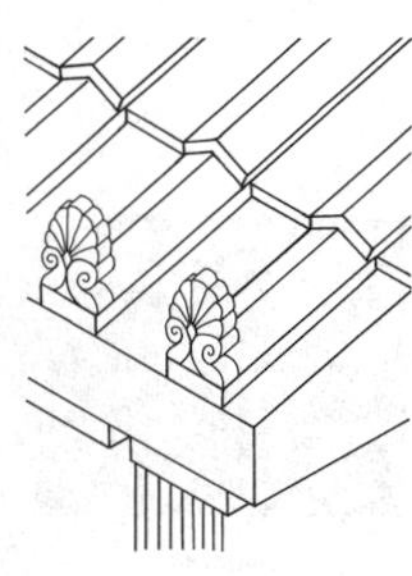

antefix

an•swer•a•ble (ăn′sər-ə-bəl) *adj.* **1.** Subject to being called to answer; accountable. See Syns at **responsible. 2.** That can be answered or refuted: *an answerable charge.* **3.** *Archaic.* **a.** Suitable. **b.** Corresponding. —**an′swer•a•bil′i•ty, an′swer•a•ble•ness** *n.* —**an′swer•a•bly** *adv.*

an•swer•back (ăn′sər-băk′) *n.* A response to a transmission made over a two-way radio.

an•swer•ing machine (ăn′sər-ĭng) *n.* A device for answering one's telephone and recording callers' messages.

answering service *n.* A business service that answers its clients' telephones and conveys messages to the clients.

ant (ănt) *n.* Any of various social insects of the family Formicidae, living in colonies that have a complex social organization. —***idiom.* ants in (one's) pants.** *Slang.* A state of restless impatience. [ME *amte* < OE *ǣmete.*]

ant. *abbr.* **1.** Antenna. **2.** Antiquarian; antiquary; antiquity. **3.** Antonym.

Ant. *abbr.* Antarctica.

ant– *pref.* Var. of **anti–.**

anthemion
Detail from the frieze of the Erechtheum in Athens, Greece, showing two anthemions and one palmette

–ant *suff.* **1.a.** Performing, promoting, or causing a specified action: *acceptant.* **b.** Being in a specified state or condition: *flippant.* **2.a.** One that performs, promotes, or causes a specified action: *deodorant.* **b.** One that undergoes a specified action: *inhalant.* [ME < OFr. < Lat. *-āns, -ant-*, pr.part. suff. of verbs in *-āre.*]

an•ta (ăn′tə) *n., pl.* **-tae** (-tē). *Archit.* A pier or rectangular column formed by thickening the end of a wall. [< Lat. *antae*, pilasters.]

ant•ac•id (ănt-ăs′ĭd) *adj.* Counteracting or neutralizing acidity, esp. of the stomach. —*n.* A substance that neutralizes acid.

an•tag•o•nism (ăn-tăg′ə-nĭz′əm) *n.* **1.** Hostility that results in active resistance, opposition, or contentiousness. **2.** The condition of being an opposing principle, force, or factor: *the antagonism of capitalism and socialism.* **3.** *Biochem.* Interference in the physiological action of a chemical substance by another having a similar structure.

an•tag•o•nist (ăn-tăg′ə-nĭst) *n.* **1.** One who contends against another; an adversary. **2.** The principal character in opposition to the protagonist or hero of a narrative or drama. **3.** *Physiol.* A muscle that counteracts the action of another muscle. **4.** *Biochem.* A chemical substance that interferes with the physiological action of another. —**an•tag′o•nis′tic** *adj.* —**an•tag′o•nis′ti•cal•ly** *adv.*

an•tag•o•nize (ăn-tăg′ə-nīz′) *tr.v.* **-nized, -niz•ing, -niz•es.** **1.** To incur the dislike of. **2.** To counteract. [Gk. *antagōnizesthai*, to struggle against : *anti-*, anti- + *agōnizesthai*, to struggle (< *agōn*, contest; see AGONY).]

An•ta•kya (än-täk′yä). See **Antioch** 2.

An•tal•ya (än-täl′-yä). A city of SW Turkey on the **Gulf of Antalya**, an inlet of the Mediterranean Sea. Pop. 173,501.

An•ta•na•na•ri•vo (ăn′tə-năn′ə-rē′vō, än′tə-nä′nə-). Formerly **Ta•nan•a•rive** (tə-năn′ə-rēv′, tä-nä-nä-rēv′). The cap. of Madagascar, in the E-central part; founded in the 17th cent. Pop. 700,000.

Ant•arc•ti•ca (ănt-ärk′tĭ-kə, -är′tĭ-). A continent lying chiefly within the Antarctic Circle and asymmetrically centered on the South Pole; first explored in the early 1800's. —**Ant•arc′tic** *adj. & n.*

Antarctic Archipelago. See **Palmer Archipelago.**

Antarctic Circle. The parallel of latitude approx. 66°33′ S that forms the boundary between the South Temperate and South Frigid zones.

Antarctic Ocean. The waters surrounding Antarctica, the S extensions of the Atlantic, Pacific, and Indian oceans.

Antarctic Peninsula also **Palm•er Peninsula** (pä′mər). A region of Antarctica extending N toward South America.

An•tar•es (ăn-târ′ēz, -tăr′-) *n.* A giant, red, double and variable star, the brightest in the constellation Scorpio. [Gk. *antarēs*: *anti*, instead of; see ANTI– + *Arēs*, Mars.]

ant bear *n.* A large anteater *(Myrmecophaga jubata),* native to South America and having white stripes that run along both sides of its body.

ant cow *n.* An aphid that yields a substance on which ants feed.

an•te (ăn′tē) *n.* **1.** *Games.* The stake that each poker player puts into the pool. See Syns at **bet. 2.** A price to be paid, esp. as one's share; cost. —*v.* **-ted** or **-teed, -te•ing, -tes.** —*tr.* **1.** *Games.* To put (one's stake) into the pool in poker. **2.** To pay. —*intr.* To pay up. [< Lat., before. See **ant-***.]

ante– *pref.* **1.** Prior to; earlier: *antenatal.* **2.** In front of; before: *anteroom.* [Lat. < *ante*, before. See **ant-***.]

ant•eat•er (ănt′ē′tər) *n.* **1.** Any of several tropical American mammals of the family Myrmecophagidae, which feed on ants and termites, esp. *Myrmecophaga tridactyla.* **2.** Any of several other animals that feed on ants.

an•te•bel•lum (ăn′tē-bĕl′əm) *adj.* Belonging to the period before a war, esp. the American Civil War. [Lat. *ante bellum*: *ante*, before + *bellum*, war.]

an•te•cede (ăn′tĭ-sēd′) *tr.v.* **-ced•ed, -ced•ing, -cedes.** To precede. [Lat. *antecēdere*: *ante-*, ante- + *cēdere*, to go; see **ked-***.] —**an′te•ce′dence** (-sēd′ns) *n.*

an•te•ce•dent (ăn′tĭ-sēd′nt) *adj.* Going before; preceding. —*n.* **1.** One that precedes another. **2.a.** A preceding occurrence, cause, or event. **b. antecedents.** The important events and occurrences in one's early life. **3. antecedents.** One's ancestors. **4.** *Gram.* The word, phrase, or clause to which a pronoun refers. **5.** *Math.* The first term of a ratio. **6.** *Logic.* The conditional member of a hypothetical proposition. —**an′te•ce′dent•ly** *adv.*

an•te•cham•ber (ăn′tē-chām′bər) *n.* An anteroom. [Fr. *antichambre*: *anti*, before (< Lat. *ante-*, ante-) + *chambre*, chamber (< OFr. *chaumbre*; see CHAMBER).]

an•te•choir (ăn′tĭ-kwīr′) *n.* A place in front of the choir reserved for the clergy and choir members.

an•te•date (ăn′tĭ-dāt′) *tr.v.* **-dat•ed, -dat•ing, -dates.** **1.** To precede in time. **2.a.** To assign to a date earlier than that of the actual occurrence. **b.** To date as of a time before that of actual execution: *antedate a check.* —*n.* A date given to an event or a document that is earlier than the actual date.

an•te•di•lu•vi•an (ăn′tĭ-də-lo͞o′vē-ən) *adj.* **1.** Extremely old and antiquated. See Syns at **old. 2.** Occurring or belonging to the era before the Flood in the Bible. [< ANTE– + Lat. *dīluvium*, flood; see DILUVIAL.] —**an′te•di•lu′vi•an** *n.*

an•te•fix (ăn′tē-fĭks′) *n., pl.* **-fix•es** or **-fix•a** (-fĭk′sə). *Archit.* An ornament on the eaves of a tiled roof meant to conceal the joints between the rows of tiles. [< Lat. *antefixa*, pl. of *antefixum*, something fastened in front < *antefixus*, fastened in front : *ante-*, ante- + *fīxus*, fastened, p.part. of *fīgere*, to fasten; see **dhīgʷ-***.] **—an′te•fix′al** *adj.*

an•te•lope (ăn′tl-ōp′) *n., pl.* **antelope** or **-lopes. 1.a.** Any of various swift-running ruminant mammals of the family Bovidae, having long horns. **b.** An animal that resembles a true antelope. **2.** Leather made from the hide of the antelope. [ME, heraldic beast, prob. < OFr. *antelop*, savage beast with saw-like horns < Med.Lat. *anthalopus* < LGk. *antholops*.]

an•te•me•rid•i•an (ăn′tē-mə-rĭd′ē-ən) *adj.* Of, relating to, or taking place in the morning. [Lat. *antemerīdiānus*: *ante-*, ante- + *merīdiānus*, of noon; see MERIDIAN.]

an•te me•rid•i•em (ăn′tē mə-rĭd′ē-əm) *adv. & adj.* Before noon. Used chiefly to specify the hour. [Lat. *ante*, before + *merīdiem*, accusative of *merīdiēs*, noon.]

Usage Note: Strictly speaking, *12* A.M. denotes midnight and *12* P.M. denotes noon, but there is sufficient confusion over these uses to make it advisable to use *12 noon* and *12 midnight* where clarity is required.

an•te•mor•tem (ăn′tē-môr′təm) *adj.* Preceding death. [Lat. *ante*, before; see ANTE– + *mortem*, accusative of *mors*, *mort-*, death. See MORTAL.]

an•te•na•tal (ăn′tē-nāt′l) *adj.* Occurring before birth; prenatal: *antenatal diagnostic procedures.* **—an′te•na′tal•ly** *adv.*

an•ten•na (ăn-tĕn′ə) *n., pl.* **-ten•nae** (-tĕn′ē). **1.a.** *Zool.* One of the paired, flexible, segmented sensory appendages on the head of an insect, a myriapod, or a crustacean. **b.** Something likened to this sensory appendage: *sensitive public relations antennae.* **2.** *pl.* **-nas.** An apparatus for sending or receiving electromagnetic waves. [Med.Lat. < Lat., sail yard, transl. of Gk. *keraia*, insect feeler, yardarm.] **—an•ten′nal** *adj.*

an•ten•nule (ăn-tĕn′yo͞ol) *n. Zool.* A small antenna or similar organ. [Fr., dim. of *antenne*, antenna < Med.Lat. *antenna*, sail yard. See ANTENNA.]

an•te•pen•di•um (ăn′tē-pĕn′dē-əm) *n., pl.* **-di•a** (-dē-ə). A hanging for an altar, a lectern, or a pulpit. [Med.Lat. : Lat. *ante-*, ante- + Lat. *pendēre*, to hang; see **(s)pen-***.]

an•te•pe•nult (ăn′tē-pē′nŭlt′, -pĭ-nŭlt′) *n.* The third syllable from the end in a word, such as *te* in *antepenult.* [Short for LLat. *antepaenultima* < fem. of *antepaenultimus*, antepenultimate. See ANTEPENULTIMATE.]

an•te•pe•nul•ti•mate (ăn′tē-pĭ-nŭl′tə-mĭt) *adj.* Coming before the next to the last in a series. *—n.* An antepenult. [< LLat. *antepaenultimus*: Lat. *ante-*, ante- + Lat. *paenultimus*, next to last; see PENULT.]

an•te•ri•or (ăn-tîr′ē-ər) *adj.* **1.** Placed before or in front. **2.** Occurring before in time; earlier. **3.** *Anat.* **a.** Located near or toward the head in lower animals. **b.** Located on or near the front of the body in higher animals. **c.** Located on or near the ventral surface of the body in human beings. **4.** *Bot.* Facing away from the axis or stem. [Lat., comp. of *ante*, before. See **ant-***.] **—an•te′ri•or•ly** *adv.*

An•te•ro (ăn-târ′ō), **Mount.** A peak, 4,352 m (14,269 ft), in the Sawatch Mts. of central CO.

an•te•room (ăn′tē-ro͞om′, -ro͝om′) *n.* An outer room that opens into another room, often used as a waiting room.

ant•he•li•on (ănt-hē′lē-ən, ăn-thē′-) *n., pl.* **-li•a** (-lē-ə) or **-ons.** A luminous white area occasionally seen opposite the sun on the parhelic circle. [Gk. *anthēlion* < neut. of *anthēlios*, opposite the sun : *anti-*, anti- + *hēlios*, sun; see **sāwel-***.]

ant•hel•min•tic (ănt′hĕl-mĭn′tĭk, ăn′thĕl-) also **ant•hel•min•thic** (-thĭk) *adj.* Acting to expel or destroy parasitic intestinal worms. [ANT(I)– + Gk. *helmins*, *helminth-*, worm; see **wel-²***.] **—ant′hel•min′tic** *n.*

an•them (ăn′thəm) *n.* **1.** A hymn of praise or loyalty. **2.** A sacred composition set to words from the Bible. [ME *anteme* < OE *antefn* < LLat. *antiphōna* < LGk. < neut. pl. of *antiphōnos*, sounding in answer : *anti-*, in return; see ANTI– + *phōnē*, voice; see **bhā-²***.]

an•the•mi•on (ăn-thē′mē-ən) *n., pl.* **-mi•a** (-mē-ə). A pattern of honeysuckle or palm leaves in a radiating cluster, used as a motif in Greek art. [Gk., dim. of *anthemon*, flower < *anthos*.]

an•ther (ăn′thər) *n. Bot.* The pollen-bearing part of the stamen. [Med.Lat. *anthēra*, pollen < Lat., a medicine extracted from flowers < Gk. < fem. of *anthēros*, flowery < *anthos*, flower.]

an•ther•id•i•um (ăn′thə-rĭd′ē-əm) *n., pl.* **-i•a** (-ē-ə). *Bot.* A sperm-producing organ occurring in seedless plants, fungi, and algae. [NLat. : *anthēra*, anther; see ANTHER + *-idium*, dim. suff. (< Gk. *-idion*).]

an•ther•o•zoid (ăn′thər-ə-zō′ĭd) *n. Bot.* A male gamete produced by an antheridium.

an•the•sis (ăn-thē′sĭs) *n. Bot.* The period during which a flower is fully open and functional. [Gk. *anthēsis*, flowering < *anthein*, to bloom < *anthos*, flower.]

ant•hill (ănt′hĭl′) *n.* A mound of soil, sand, or dirt formed by ants or termites in digging or building a nest.

antho– *pref.* Flower: *anthozoan.* [Gk. < *anthos*, flower.]

an•thol•o•gize (ăn-thŏl′ə-jīz′) *v.* **-gized, -giz•ing, -giz•es.** *—intr.* To compile or publish an anthology. *—tr.* To include (material) in an anthology. **—an•thol′o•gist** *n.*

an•thol•o•gy (ăn-thŏl′ə-jē) *n., pl.* **-gies. 1.** A collection of literary pieces. **2.** A miscellany, an assortment, or a catalog. [Med.Gk. *anthologia*, collection of epigrams < Gk., flower gathering < *anthologein*, to gather flowers : *antho-*, antho- + *logos*, a gathering (< *legein*, to gather; see **leg-***).] **—an′tho•log′i•cal** (ăn′thə-lŏj′ĭ-kəl) *adj.*

An•tho•ny (ăn′thə-nē), Saint. A.D. 250?–350? Egyptian ascetic monk considered the founder of Christian monasticism.

Anthony, Susan Brownell. 1820–1906. Amer. feminist leader; cofounded the National Woman Suffrage Association (1869).

Anthony of Pad•u•a (păj′o͞o-ə, păd′yo͞o-ə), Saint. 1195–1231. Portuguese-born Franciscan monk.

an•tho•zo•an (ăn′thə-zō′ən) *n.* Any of a class (Anthozoa) of marine organisms, such as the corals and sea anemones, that have radial segments and grow singly or in colonies. **—an′tho•zo′an, an′tho•zo′ic** (-zō′ĭk) *adj.*

an•thra•cene (ăn′thrə-sēn′) *n.* A crystalline hydrocarbon, $C_{14}H_{10}$, extracted from coal tar and used in making dyes and organic chemicals. [Gk. *anthrax*, *anthrak-*, charcoal + –ENE.]

an•thra•cite (ăn′thrə-sīt′) *n.* A coal that has a high carbon content and little volatile matter and burns with a clean flame. [Prob. ult. < Gk. *anthrakitis*, a kind of coal < *anthrax*, *anthrak-*, charcoal.] **—an′thra•cit′ic** (-sĭt′ĭk) *adj.*

an•thra•co•sis (ăn′thrə-kō′sĭs) *n.* See **black lung.** [NLat. : Gk. *anthrax*, *anthrak-*, charcoal + –OSIS.]

an•thrax (ăn′thrăks′) *n.* **1.** An infectious, usu. fatal disease of warm-blooded animals that can be transmitted to human beings and is caused by the bacterium *Bacillus anthracis.* **2.** *pl.* **-thra•ces** (-thrə-sēz′). A lesion caused by anthrax. [ME *antrax*, malignant boil < Lat. *anthrax*, carbuncle < Gk.]

anthrop. *abbr.* **1.** Anthropological. **2.** Anthropology.

an•throp•ic (ăn-thrŏp′ĭk) also **an•throp•i•cal** (-ĭ-kəl) *adj.* Of or relating to human beings or the era of human life. [Gk. *anthrōpikos* < *anthrōpos*, human being.]

anthropo– *pref.* Human being: *anthropometry.* [Gk. < *anthrōpos*, human being.]

an•thro•po•cen•tric (ăn′thrə-pə-sĕn′trĭk) *adj.* Regarding human beings as the central element of the universe. **—an′thro•po•cen′tri•cal•ly** *adv.* **—an′thro•po•cen′trism** *n.*

an•thro•po•gen•e•sis (ăn′thrə-pə-jĕn′ĭ-sĭs) *n.* The scientific study of the origin and development of human beings. **—an′thro•po•gen′ic** (-jĕn′ĭk) *adj.*

an•thro•poid (ăn′thrə-poid′) *adj.* **1.** Resembling a human being, esp. in shape or outward appearance. **2.** Of or belonging to the group of great apes of the family Pongidae. **3.** Resembling or characteristic of an ape; apelike. *—n.* An ape of the family Pongidae. **—an′thro•poid′al** (-poid′l) *adj.*

an•thro•pol•o•gy (ăn′thrə-pŏl′ə-jē) *n.* The scientific study of the origin, the behavior, and the physical, social, and cultural development of human beings. **—an′thro•po•log′i•cal** (-pə-lŏj′ĭ-kəl), **an′thro•po•log′ic** (-ĭk) *adj.* **—an′thro•po•log′i•cal•ly** *adv.* **—an′thro•pol′o•gist** *n.*

an•thro•pom•e•try (ăn′thrə-pŏm′ĭ-trē) *n.* The study of human body measurement for use in anthropological classification and comparison. **—an′thro•po•met′ric** (-pə-mĕt′rĭk), **an′thro•po•met′ri•cal** (-rĭ-kəl) *adj.* **—an′thro•po•met′ri•cal•ly** *adv.* **—an′thro•pom′e•trist** *n.*

an•thro•po•mor•phism (ăn′thrə-pə-môr′fĭz′əm) *n.* Attribution of human characteristics to inanimate objects, animals, or natural phenomena. **—an′thro•po•mor′phic** *adj.* **—an′thro•po•mor′phi•cal•ly** *adv.*

an•thro•po•mor•phize (ăn′thrə-pə-môr′fīz′) *v.* **-phized, -phiz•ing, -phiz•es.** *—tr.* To ascribe human characteristics to. *—intr.* To ascribe human characteristics to things not human.

an•thro•po•mor•phous (ăn′thrə-pə-môr′fəs) *adj.* **1.** Having or suggesting human form and appearance. **2.** Ascribing human characteristics to things not human.

an•thro•pop•a•thism (ăn′thrə-pŏp′ə-thĭz′əm) *n.* Attribution of human feelings to things not human. [LGk. *anthrōpopathēs*, involved in human suffering (< Gk., having human feelings < *anthrōpopathein*, to have human feelings : *anthrōpo-*, anthropo- + *pathos*, feeling; see PATHOS) + –ISM.]

an•thro•poph•a•gus (ăn′thrə-pŏf′ə-gəs′) *n., pl.* **-gi** (-jī′). A cannibal. [Lat. *anthrōpophagus* < Gk. *anthrōpophagos*, man-eating : *anthrōpo-*, anthropo- + *-phagos*, -phagous.] **—an′thro•po•phag′ic** (-pə-făj′ĭk), **an′thro•poph′a•gous** (-pŏf′ə-gəs) *adj.* **—an′thro•poph′a•gy** (-jē) *n.*

an•thro•pos•o•phy (ăn′thrə-pŏs′ə-fē) *n.* The doctrines and beliefs of a modern religious sect derived from theosophy. [ANTHROPO– + (THEO)SOPHY.] **—an′thro•po•soph′i•cal** (-pə-sŏf′ĭ-kəl) *adj.* **—an′thro•pos′o•phist** *n.*

an•thur•i•um (ăn-tho͝or′ē-əm) *n.* Any of various evergreen tropical American plants of the genus *Anthurium*, grown as ornamentals. [NLat. *Anthurium*, genus name : ANTH(O)– + Gk. *oura*, tail; see **ors-***.]

an•ti (ăn′tī, -tē) *n., pl.* **-tis.** A person who is opposed to something, such as a group, policy, proposal, or practice. *—prep.* Opposed to; against. [< ANTI–.] **—an′ti** *adj.*

anti– or **ant–** *pref.* **1.a.** Opposite: *antimere.* **b.** Opposing; against: *antibusiness.* **c.** Counteracting; neutralizing: *antibody.* **2.** Inverse: *antilogarithm.* [Gk. < *anti*, opposite. See **ant-***.]

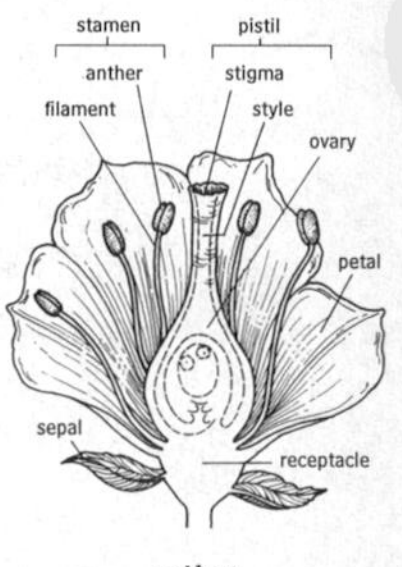

anther

Susan B. Anthony
Photographed in 1896 by
Theodore C. Marceau
(1868?–1922)

anthurium

ă pat	oi boy
ā pay	ou out
âr care	o͝o took
ä father	o͞o boot
ĕ pet	ŭ cut
ē be	ûr urge
ĭ pit	th thin
ī pie	*th* this
îr pier	hw which
ŏ pot	zh vision
ō toe	ə about,
ô paw	item

Stress marks:
′ (primary);
′ (secondary), as in
dictionary (dĭk′shə-nĕr′ē)

an•ti•air•craft (ăn′tē-âr′krăft′, ăn′tī-) *adj.* Designed for defense against aircraft or missile attack. —*n.* An antiaircraft weapon.

an•ti-A•mer•i•can (ăn′tē-ə-mĕr′ĭ-kən, ăn′tī-) *adj.* Opposed or hostile to the government, official policies, or people of the United States. —**an′ti-A•mer′i•can•ism** *n.*

an•ti•a•part•heid (ăn′tē-ə-pärt′hīt′, -hāt′, ăn′tī-) *adj.* Opposing the system of official racial segregation in South Africa: *antiapartheid activism.*

an•ti•ar•rhyth•mic (ăn′tē-ə-rĭ*th*′mĭk, ăn′tī-) *adj.* Preventing or alleviating irregularities in the force or rhythm of the heart. —*n.* An antiarrhythmic substance.

an•ti-art (ăn′tē-ärt′, ăn′tī-) *n.* Art, specifically Dada, that rejects traditional art forms and theories.

an•ti•at•om (ăn′tē-ăt′əm, ăn′tī-) *n.* An atom composed of antiparticles.

an•ti•bal•lis•tic missile (ăn′tĭ-bə-lĭs′tĭk, ăn′tī-) *n.* A defensive missile designed to intercept and destroy a ballistic missile in flight.

an•ti•bar•y•on (ăn′tē-băr′ē-ŏn′, ăn′tī-) *n.* The antiparticle of a baryon.

An•tibes (äɴ-tēb′). A city of SE France on the Riviera between Nice and Cannes. Pop. 62,859.

an•ti•bi•o•sis (ăn′tē-bī-ō′sĭs, ăn′tī-) *n.* **1.** An association between two or more organisms that is detrimental to at least one of them. **2.** The antagonistic association between an organism and the metabolic substances produced by another.

an•ti•bi•ot•ic (ăn′tĭ-bī-ŏt′ĭk, ăn′tī-) *n.* A substance, such as penicillin, produced by or derived from certain fungi, bacteria, and other organisms, that can destroy or inhibit the growth of other microorganisms. —*adj.* **1.** Of or relating to antibiotics. **2.** Of or relating to antibiosis. **3.** Destroying life or preventing the inception or continuance of life. —**an′ti•bi•ot′i•cal•ly** *adv.*

antibody

an•ti-Black or **an•ti-black** (ăn′tē-blăk′, ăn′tī-) *adj.* Hostile or opposed to Black people.

an•ti•bod•y (ăn′tĭ-bŏd′ē, ăn′tī-) *n.* **1.** A protein substance produced in the blood or tissues in response to a specific antigen. **2.** An object composed of antimatter.

an•ti•busi•ness (ăn′tē-bĭz′nĭs, ăn′tī-) *adj.* Hostile to business, esp. to big corporations.

an•tic (ăn′tĭk) *n.* **1.** A ludicrous or extravagant act; a caper. **2.** *Archaic.* A buffoon, esp. a performing clown. —*adj.* Ludicrously odd; fantastic. [< Ital. *antico,* ancient (used of grotesque designs on some ancient Roman artifacts) < Lat. *antīquus,* former, old. See **ant-***.] —**an′ti•cal•ly** *adv.*

an•ti•cat•a•lyst (ăn′tē-kăt′l-ĭst, ăn′tī-) *n.* **1.** A substance that retards or arrests a chemical reaction. **2.** A substance that reduces or destroys the effectiveness of a catalyst.

an•ti•cath•ode (ăn′tē-kăth′ōd′, ăn′tī-) *n.* An electrode that is the target in a cathode-ray tube, esp. in an x-ray tube.

an•ti•chlor (ăn′tĭ-klôr′, -klōr′, ăn′tī-) *n.* A substance used to neutralize the excess chlorine or hypochlorite left after bleaching textiles, fiber, or paper pulp. [ANTI- + CHLOR(INE).] —**an′ti•chlo•ris′tic** (-klə-rĭs′tĭk) *adj.*

an•ti-choice (ăn′tē-chois′, ăn′tī-) *adj.* Opposed to the right of women to choose or reject abortion.

an•ti•cho•lin•er•gic (ăn′tē-kō′lə-nûr′jĭk, ăn′tī-) *adj.* Inhibiting or blocking the physiological action of acetylcholine at a receptor site. —**an′ti•cho′lin•er′gic** *n.*

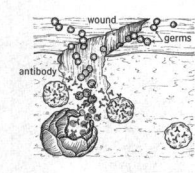

anticipation
Harmonic anticipation

an•ti•christ (ăn′tĭ-krīst′, ăn′tī-) *n.* **1.** An enemy of Christ. **2. Antichrist.** The great antagonist expected by the early Church to cause chaos and corruption in the last days before the Second Coming. **3.** A false Christ. [ME *Antecrist* < OFr. and < OE, both < LLat. *Antichrīstus* < LGk. *Antikhristos*: Gk. *anti-,* anti- + Gk. *Khristos,* Christ; see CHRIST.]

an•tic•i•pant (ăn-tĭs′ə-pənt) *adj.* **1.** Coming or acting in advance: *clouds anticipant of a storm.* **2.** Expectant; anticipating: *anticipant of victory.* —*n.* One who anticipates.

an•tic•i•pate (ăn-tĭs′ə-pāt′) *tr.v.* **-pat•ed, -pat•ing, -pates. 1.** To feel or realize beforehand; foresee. **2.** To look forward to, esp. with pleasure; expect. **3.** To act in advance so as to prevent; forestall. **4.** To foresee and fulfill in advance. See Syns at **expect. 5.** To cause to happen in advance; accelerate. **6.** To use in advance. **7.** To pay (a debt) before it is due. [Lat. *anticipāre, anticipāt-,* to take before : *ante-,* ante- + *capere,* to take; see **kap-***.] —**an•tic′i•pat′a•ble** *adj.* —**an•tic′i•pa′tor** *n.* —**an•tic′i•pa•to′ry** (-pə-tôr′ē, -tōr′ē) *adj.*

an•tic•i•pa•tion (ăn-tĭs′ə-pā′shən) *n.* **1.** The act of anticipating. **2.** An expectation. **3.** Foreknowledge, intuition, and presentiment. **4.** The use or assignment of funds before they are legitimately available for use. **5.** *Mus.* Introduction of one note of a new chord before the previous chord is resolved.

an•tic•i•pa•tive (ăn-tĭs′ə-pā′tĭv, -pə-tĭv) *adj.* Expectant. —**an•tic′i•pa′tive•ly** *adv.*

an•ti•cler•i•cal (ăn′tē-klĕr′ĭ-kəl, ăn′tī-) *adj.* Opposed to the influence of the church or the clergy in political affairs. —**an′ti•cler′i•cal•ism** *n.*

an•ti•cli•max (ăn′tē-klī′măks′, ăn′tī-) *n.* **1.** A decline viewed in disappointing contrast to previous events: *the anticlimax of a brilliant career.* **2.** Something trivial that concludes a series of significant events: *all that followed was anticlimax.* **3.** A sudden descent from the impressive or significant to the ludicrous or inconsequential. —**an′ti•cli•mac′tic** (-klī-măk′tĭk) *adj.* —**an′ti•cli•mac′ti•cal•ly** *adv.*

an•ti•cli•nal (ăn′tē-klī′nəl, ăn′tī-) *adj.* **1.** Sloping downward in opposite directions. **2.** *Bot.* Of or relating to the plane of a cell division perpendicular to the surface of a plant organ.

an•ti•cline (ăn′tĭ-klīn′) *n. Geol.* A fold with strata sloping downward on both sides from a common crest.

an•ti•clock•wise (ăn′tē-klŏk′wīz, ăn′tī-) *adv. & adj.* Counterclockwise.

an•ti•co•ag•u•lant (ăn′tē-kō-ăg′yə-lənt, ăn′tī-) *n.* A substance that prevents the clotting of blood. —*adj.* Acting as an anticoagulant.

an•ti•co•don (ăn′tē-kō′dŏn, ăn′tī-) *n.* A triplet of adjacent nucleotides in transfer RNA that binds to a complementary codon in messenger RNA during protein synthesis.

an•ti-col•li•sion also **an•ti•col•li•sion** (ăn′tē-kə-lĭzh′ən, ăn′tī-) *adj.* Serving to prevent midair collisions.

an•ti•com•pet•i•tive (ăn′tē-kəm-pĕt′ĭ-tĭv, ăn′tī-) *adj.* Discouraging competition among businesses.

an•ti•con•vul•sant (ăn′tē-kən-vŭl′sənt, ăn′tī-) *n.* A drug that prevents or relieves convulsions. —**an′ti•con•vul′sive** (-sĭv) *adj.*

An•ti•cos•ti (ăn′tĭ-kô′stē, -kŏs′tē). An island of E Quebec, Canada, at the head of the Gulf of St. Lawrence.

an•ti•cy•clone (ăn′tē-sī′klōn′, ăn′tī-) *n.* An extensive system of winds spiraling outward from a high-pressure center, circling clockwise in the Northern Hemisphere and counterclockwise in the Southern Hemisphere. —**an′ti•cy•clon′ic** (-klŏn′ĭk) *adj.*

an•ti•de•pres•sant (ăn′tē-dĭ-prĕs′ənt, ăn′tī-) *n.* A drug used to prevent or relieve mental depression. —**an′ti•de•pres′sive** (-prĕs′ĭv) *adj.*

an•ti•deu•ter•on (ăn′tē-do͞o′tə-rŏn′, -dyo͞o′-, ăn′tī-) *n.* The antimatter equivalent of deuteron.

an•ti•di•u•ret•ic hormone (ăn′tē-dī′ə-rĕt′ĭk, ăn′tī-) *n.* See **vasopressin.**

an•ti•dote (ăn′tĭ-dōt′) *n.* **1.** A remedy or other agent used to neutralize or counteract the effects of a poison. **2.** An agent that relieves or counteracts: *jogging as an antidote to nervous tension.* [ME < Lat. *antidotum* < Gk. *antidoton* < *antididonai,* to give as a remedy against : *anti-,* anti- + *didonai, do-,* to give; see **dō-***.] —**an′ti•dot′al** (ăn′tĭ-dōt′l) *adj.* —**an′ti•dot′al•ly** *adv.*

Usage Note: *Antidote* may be followed by *to, for,* or *against*: *an antidote to boredom; an antidote for snakebite; an antidote against inflation.*

an•ti•e•lec•tron (ăn′tē-ĭ-lĕk′trŏn′, ăn′tī-) *n.* See **positron.**

an•ti•en•zyme (ăn′tē-ĕn′zīm′, ăn′tī-) *n.* A substance that neutralizes or counteracts the actions of an enzyme. —**an′ti•en′zy•mat′ic** (-zĭ-măt′ĭk, -zī-), **an′ti•en•zy′mic** (-zī′mĭk) *adj.*

an•ti•es•tab•lish•ment (ăn′tē-ĭ-stăb′lĭsh-mənt, ăn′tī-) *adj.* Marked by opposition or hostility to conventional principles.

An•tie•tam (ăn-tē′təm). A creek of N-central MD emptying into the Potomac R.; site of a major Civil War battle (1862).

an•ti•feb•rile (ăn′tē-fĕb′rəl, -fē′brəl, -brĭl′, ăn′tī-) *n.* An agent that reduces fever. —**an′ti•feb′rile** *adj.*

an•ti•fed•er•al•ist also **An•ti•fed•er•al•ist** (ăn′tē-fĕd′ər-ə-lĭst, -fĕd′rə-lĭst, ăn′tī-) *n.* An opponent of the ratification of the U.S. Constitution. —**an′ti•fed′er•al•ist** *adj.* —**an′ti•fed′er•al•ism** *n.*

an•ti•fer•til•i•ty (ăn′tē-fər-tĭl′ĭ-tē, ăn′tī-) *adj.* Capable of reducing or eliminating fertility; contraceptive.

---

an′ti•a•bor′tion *adj.*
an′ti•a•bor′tion•ist *n.*
an′ti•al•ler′gic *adj.*
an′ti•anx•i′e•ty *adj.*
an′ti•a•part′heid′ *adj.*
an′ti•bac•te′ri•al *adj. & n.*
an′ti•bus′ing *adj.*
an′ti•can′cer *adj.*
an′ti•can′cer•ous *adj.*
an′ti•cho′lin•es′ter•ase′ *n.*
an′ti•cit′y *adj.*
an′ti•crime′ *adj.*
an′ti•di′ar•rhe′al *n. & adj.*
an′ti•fem′i•nism *n.*
an′ti•fem′i•nist *adj. & n.*
an′ti•fluor′i•da′tion•ist *n.*
an′ti•fun′gal *adj. & n.*
an′ti•green′mail′ *adj.*
an′ti-in•fec′tive *adj. & n.*
an′ti-in•flam′ma•to′ry *adj. & n.*
an′ti-in′tel•lec′tu•al *adj. & n.*
an′ti-in′tel•lec′tu•al•ism *n.*
an′ti•mi•tot′ic *adj. & n.*
an′ti•noise′ *adj.*
an′ti•ox′i•dant *n.*
an′ti•par′a•sit′ic *adj. & n.*
an′ti•pol•lu′tion *adj.*
an′ti•pol•lu′tion•ist *n.*
an′ti•pov′er•ty *adj.*
an′ti•psy•chot′ic *adj. & n.*
an′ti•slav′er•y *adj. & n.*
an′ti•smog′ *adj.*
an′ti•sub′ma•rine′ *adj.*
an′ti•take′o′ver *adj.*
an′ti•tank′ *adj.*
an′ti•ter′ror•ism *n.*
an′ti•ter′ror•ist *adj.*
an′ti•theft′ *adj.*
an′ti•tu′mor *adj.*
an′ti•vi′ral *adj. & n.*
an′ti•war′ *adj.*

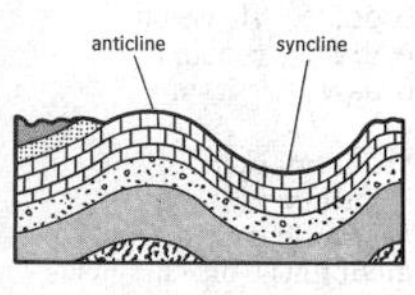

anticline

an•ti•foul•ing paint (ăn′tē-fou′lĭng, ăn′tī-) *n.* Paint that counteracts or prevents the fouling of underwater surfaces.

an•ti•freeze (ăn′tĭ-frēz′) *n.* A substance, such as ethylene glycol, mixed with another liquid to lower its freezing point.

an•ti•gal•ax•y (ăn′tē-găl′ək-sē, ăn′tī-) *n.* A galaxy that is made up of antimatter.

an•ti•gen (ăn′tĭ-jən) also **an•ti•gene** (-jēn′) *n.* A substance that when introduced into the body stimulates the production of an antibody. — **an′ti•gen′ic** (-jĕn′ĭk) *adj.* — **an′ti•gen′i•cal•ly** *adv.* — **an′ti•ge•nic′i•ty** (-jə-nĭs′ĭ-tē) *n.*

An•tig•o•ne (ăn-tĭg′ə-nē) *n. Gk. Myth.* The daughter of Oedipus and Jocasta who performed funeral rites over her brother's body in defiance of Creon.

An•tig•o•nus I (ăn-tĭg′ə-nəs). 382–301 B.C. King of Macedonia (306–301) who was one of Alexander III's generals.

an•ti•grav•i•ty (ăn′tē-grăv′ĭ-tē, ăn′tī-) *n.* The hypothetical effect of reducing or canceling a gravitational field. — **an′ti•grav′i•ty** *adj.*

An•ti•gua and Bar•bu•da (ăn-tē′gə; bär-bōō′də). A country in the N Leeward Is. of the Caribbean comprising **Antigua**, Barbuda, and Redonda; achieved independence in 1981. Cap. St. John's. Pop. 72,000. — **An•ti′guan** *adj. & n.*

an•ti•he•li•um (ăn′tē-hē′lē-əm, ăn′tī-) *n.* The antimatter equivalent of helium.

an•ti•he•mo•phil•ic factor (ăn′tē-hē′mə-fĭl′ĭk, ăn′tī-) *n.* A protein substance in blood plasma that participates in and is essential for the blood-clotting process.

an•ti•he•ro also **an•ti-he•ro** (ăn′tē-hîr′ō, ăn′tī-) *n., pl.* **-roes.** A main character in a dramatic or narrative work who lacks traditional heroic qualities, such as idealism or courage. — **an′ti•her•o′ic** (-hĭ-rō′ĭk) *adj.* — **an′ti•her′o•ism** (-hĕr′ō-ĭz′əm) *n.*

an•ti•her•o•ine or **an•ti-her•o•ine** (ăn′tē-hĕr′ō-ĭn, ăn′tī-) *n.* A woman protagonist who lacks the qualities of a traditional hero or who acts counter to traditional expectations of women.

an•ti•his•ta•mine (ăn′tē-hĭs′tə-mēn′, -mĭn) *n.* A drug used to counteract the physiological effects of histamine production, as in allergic reactions. — **an′ti•his′ta•min′ic** (-mĭn′ĭk) *adj.*

an•ti•hy•dro•gen (ăn′tē-hī′drə-jən, ăn′tī-) *n.* The antimatter equivalent of hydrogen.

an•ti•hy•per•ten•sive (ăn′tē-hī′pər-tĕn′sĭv, an′tī-) *adj.* Reducing or controlling high blood pressure. — **an′ti•hy′per•ten′sive** *n.*

an•ti•knock (ăn′tĭ-nŏk′) *n.* A substance, such as tetraethyl lead, added to gasoline to reduce engine knock.

An•ti-Leb•a•non Range (ăn′tē-lĕb′ə-nən). A mountain range on the Syria-Lebanon border, rising to 2,815.8 m (9,232 ft).

an•ti•lep•ton (ăn′tē-lĕp′tŏn, ăn′tī-) *n.* The antiparticle of a lepton.

An•til•les (ăn-tĭl′ēz). The islands of the West Indies except for the Bahamas, separating the Caribbean from the Atlantic and divided into the **Greater Antilles** to the N and the **Lesser Antilles** to the E.

an•ti•log (ăn′tē-lôg′, -lŏg′, ăn′tī-) *n.* An antilogarithm.

an•ti•log•a•rithm (ăn′tē-lô′gə-rĭth′əm, -lŏg′ə-, ăn′tī-) *n.* The number for which a given logarithm stands; for example, where log *x* equals *y*, the *x* is the antilogarithm of *y*. — **an′ti•log′a•rith′mic** *adj.*

an•ti•ma•cas•sar (ăn′tē-mə-kăs′ər) *n.* A protective covering for the backs of chairs and sofas. [ANTI- + *Macassar*, a brand of hair oil.]

an•ti•mag•net•ic (ăn′tē-măg-nĕt′ĭk, ăn′tī-) *adj.* Impervious to the effect of a magnetic field; resistant to magnetization.

an•ti•ma•lar•i•al (ăn′tē-mə-lâr′ē-əl, ăn′tī-) *adj.* Preventing or relieving the symptoms of malaria. — *n.* A drug used to treat malaria.

an•ti•mat•ter (ăn′tĭ-măt′ər, ăn′tī-) *n.* A hypothetical form of matter that is identical to physical matter except that its atoms are composed of antielectrons, antiprotons, and antineutrons.

an•ti•mere (ăn′tĭ-mîr′) *n. Zool.* A part in the body of a bilaterally or radially symmetric animal that corresponds to an opposite or similar part. — **an′ti•mer′ic** (-mĕr′ĭk) *adj.*

an•ti•me•tab•o•lite (ăn′tē-mĭ-tăb′ə-līt′, ăn′tī-) *n.* A substance that closely resembles an essential metabolite and therefore interferes with physiological reactions involving it.

an•ti•mi•cro•bi•al (ăn′tē-mī-krō′bē-əl, ăn′tī-) also **an•ti•mi•cro•bic** (-bĭk) *adj.* Capable of destroying or inhibiting the growth of microorganisms. — **an′ti•mi•cro′bial** *n.*

an•ti•mo•ni•al (ăn′tə-mō′nē-əl) *adj.* Of or containing antimony. — *n.* A medicine containing antimony.

an•ti•mo•ny (ăn′tə-mō′nē) *n. Symbol* **Sb** An element having several allotropes, the most common of which is a brittle, silver-white crystalline metal. It is used in alloys, esp. with lead in battery plates, and in flame-proofing compounds. Atomic number 51; atomic weight 121.75; melting point 630.5°C; boiling point 1,380°C; specific gravity 6.691; valence 3, 5. See table at **element.** [ME *antimonie* < Med.Lat. *antimōnium*, perh. < Ar. *al-'itmid*, perh. < Gk. *stimmi.*]

an•ti•ne•o•plas•tic (ăn′tē-nē′ə-plăs′tĭk, ăn′tī-) *adj.* Inhibiting or preventing the growth or development of malignant cells. — **an′ti•ne′o•plas′tic** *n.*

an•ti•neu•tri•no (ăn′tē-nōō-trē′nō, -nyōō-, ăn′tī-) *n., pl.* **-nos.** The antiparticle of the neutrino.

an•ti•neu•tron (ăn′tē-nōō′trŏn′, -nyōō′-, ăn′tī-) *n.* The antiparticle of the neutron.

an•ti•node (ăn′tĭ-nōd′) *n.* For a standing wave, the region or point of maximum amplitude between adjacent nodes.

an•ti•nome (ăn′tə-nōm′) *n.* One that is contradictory or opposite to another. [ANTI- + Gk. *nomos*, law; see ANTINOMY.]

an•ti•no•mi•an (ăn′tĭ-nō′mē-ən) *n.* An adherent of antinomianism. — *adj.* **1.** Of or relating to antinomianism. **2.** Opposed to the fixed meaning or universality of moral law. [< Med.Lat. *Antinomī*, antinomians, pl. of *antinomus*, opposed to the moral law : Gk. *anti-*, anti- + Gk. *nomos*, law; see **nem-*.**]

an•ti•no•mi•an•ism (ăn′tĭ-nō′mē-ə-nĭz′əm) *n.* **1.** *Theol.* The doctrine or belief that the Gospel frees Christians from obedience to any law, whether scriptural, civil, or moral, and that salvation is attained solely through faith and divine grace. **2.** The belief that moral laws are relative rather than fixed or universal.

an•tin•o•my (ăn-tĭn′ə-mē) *n., pl.* **-mies. 1.** Contradiction or opposition, esp. between two laws or rules. **2.** A contradiction between equally reasonable principles or conclusions; a paradox. [Lat. *antinomia* < Gk. : *anti-*, anti- + *nomos*, law; see **nem-*.**] — **an′ti•nom′ic** (ăn′tĭ-nŏm′ĭk) *adj.*

an•ti•nov•el also **an•ti-nov•el** (ăn′tē-nŏv′əl, ăn′tī-) *n.* A fictional work that lacks traditional elements of the novel, such as a coherent plot. — **an′ti•nov′el•ist** *n.*

an•ti•nu•cle•ar (ăn′tē-nōō′klē-ər, -nyōō′-, ăn′tī-) *adj.* **1.** Opposed to nuclear power or nuclear weaponry. **2.** Reacting with the components of a cell nucleus.

an•ti•nu•cle•on (ăn′tē-nōō′klē-ŏn′, -nyōō′-, ăn′tī-) *n.* The antiparticle of a nucleon.

an•ti-nuke or **an•ti•nuke** (ăn′tē-nōōk′, -nyōōk′, ăn′tī-) *adj.* Antinuclear. — **an′ti-nuk′er** *n.*

An•ti•och (ăn′tē-ŏk′). **1.** An ancient town of Phrygia N of present-day Antalya, Turkey. **2.** Also **An•ta•kya** (än-täk′yä). A city of S Turkey near the Mediterranean; founded c. 300 B.C. Pop. 94,942. **3.** A city of W CA NE of Oakland on the San Joaquin R. Pop. 62,195.

An•ti•o•chus (ăn-tī′ə-kəs). A Seleucid dynasty ruling in Syria (280–264 B.C.), including **Antiochus III** (242–187, ruled 223–187), known as "the Great," who conquered much of Asia Minor before 190.

an•ti•ox•i•dant (ăn′tē-ŏk′sĭ-dənt, ăn′tī-) *n.* A chemical compound or substance that inhibits oxidation.

an•ti•par•ti•cle (ăn′tē-pär′tĭ-kəl, ăn′tī-) *n.* A subatomic particle, such as an antiproton, having the same mass, lifetime, and spin as its corresponding particle but having the opposite electric charge, intrinsic parity, and direction of magnetic moment. See table at **subatomic particle.**

an•ti•pas•to (än′tē-päs′tō) *n., pl.* **-tos** or **-ti** (-tē). An appetizer usu. consisting of an assortment of ingredients, such as smoked meats, cheese, fish, and vegetables. [Ital. : *anti-*, before (< Lat. *ante-*; see ANTE-) + *pasto*, food (< Lat. *pastus*, p.part. of *pāscere*, to feed; see **pā-***).]

An•tip•a•ter (ăn-tĭp′ə-tər). 398?–319 B.C. Macedonian general and regent (334–323 and 321–319).

an•tip•a•thet•ic (ăn-tĭp′ə-thĕt′ĭk) also **an•tip•a•thet•i•cal** (-ĭ-kəl) *adj.* **1.a.** Having or showing a strong aversion or repugnance. **b.** Opposed in nature or character; antagonistic: *antipathetic factions.* **2.** Causing a feeling of antipathy; repugnant. — **an•tip′a•thet′i•cal•ly** *adv.*

an•tip•a•thy (ăn-tĭp′ə-thē) *n., pl.* **-thies. 1.** A strong feeling of aversion or repugnance. **2.** An object of aversion. [Lat. *antipathīa* < Gk. *antipatheia* < *antipathēs*, of opposite feelings : *anti-*, anti- + *pathos*, feeling; see PATHOS.]

an•ti•pe•ri•od•ic (ăn′tē-pîr′ē-ŏd′ĭk, ăn′tī-) *adj.* Preventing regular recurrence of disease symptoms, as in malaria. — **an′ti•pe′ri•od′ic** *n.*

an•ti•per•son•nel (ăn′tē-pûr′sə-nĕl′, ăn′tī-) *adj.* Designed to inflict death or bodily injury rather than material destruction: *antipersonnel grenades.*

an•ti•per•spi•rant (ăn′tē-pûr′spər-ənt, ăn′tī-) *n.* An astringent preparation for decreasing perspiration. — **an′ti•per′spi•rant** *adj.*

an•ti•phlo•gis•tic (ăn′tē-flə-jĭs′tĭk, ăn′tī-) *adj.* Reducing inflammation or fever; anti-inflammatory. — **an′ti•phlo•gis′tic** *n.*

an•ti•phon (ăn′tə-fŏn′) *n.* **1.** A liturgical text sung responsively. **2.** A short liturgical text sung responsively preceding or following a psalm or canticle. **3.** A response; a reply. [LLat. *antiphōna*, sung responses. See ANTHEM.]

an•tiph•o•nal (ăn-tĭf′ə-nəl) *adj.* **1.** Of or like an antiphon. **2.** Responsive, as in antiphony. **3.** Occurring or responding in turns; alternating. — *n.* An antiphonary. — **an•tiph′o•nal•ly** *adv.*

an•tiph•o•nar•y (ăn-tĭf′ə-nĕr′ē) *n., pl.* **-ies.** A bound collection of antiphons, esp. of the Divine Office.

an•tiph•o•ny (ăn-tĭf′ə-nē) *n., pl.* **-nies. 1.** Responsive or an-

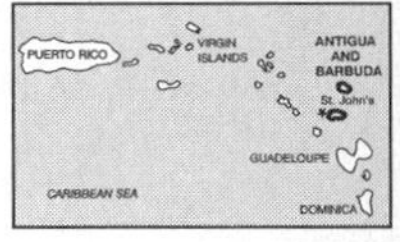

Antigua and Barbuda

ă pat	oi boy
ā pay	ou out
âr care	ŏŏ took
ä father	ōō boot
ĕ pet	ŭ cut
ē be	ûr urge
ĭ pit	th thin
ī pie	*th* this
îr pier	hw which
ŏ pot	zh vision
ō toe	ə about, item
ô paw	

Stress marks:
′ (primary);
′ (secondary), as in **dictionary** (dĭk′shə-nĕr′ē)

tiphonal singing or chanting. **2.** A composition that is sung responsively; an antiphon. **3.** A responsive or reciprocal interchange, as of ideas or opinions.

an•tiph•ra•sis (ăn-tĭf′rə-sĭs) *n.* The ironic or humorous use of a word or phrase in a sense contrary to its normal meaning, as in *a babe of 40 years.* [LLat. < Gk. < *antiphrazein,* to express by the opposite : *anti-,* anti- + *phrazein,* to speak; see PHRASE.]

an•tip•o•dal (ăn-tĭp′ə-dəl) *adj.* **1.** Of, on, or relating to the opposite side or sides of the earth. **2.** Diametrically opposed; exactly opposite.

an•ti•pode (ăn′tĭ-pōd′) *n.* A direct or diametrical opposite. [Back-formation < ANTIPODES.]

an•tip•o•des (ăn-tĭp′ə-dēz′) *pl.n.* **1.** Any two places or regions on opposite sides of the earth. **2.** *(used with a sing. or pl. v.)* The exact opposite or contrary of something; an antipode. [ME, people with feet opposite ours < Lat. < Gk. < pl. of *antipous,* with the feet opposite : *anti-,* anti- + *pous, pod-,* foot; see **ped-***.] **—an•tip′o•de′an** *adj.*

An•tip•o•des (ăn-tĭp′ə-dēz′). **1.** Australia and New Zealand. Usu. used informally. **2.** A group of rocky islands of the S Pacific Ocean SE of New Zealand; so named by 19th-cent. British sailors because the islands are diametrically opposite Greenwich, England.

an•ti•pope (ăn′tĭ-pōp′) *n.* A person claiming to be or elected pope in opposition to the one chosen by church law, as during a schism. [ME < OFr. *antipape* < Med.Lat. *antipāpa*: Lat. *anti-,* anti- + *pāpa,* pope; see POPE.]

an•ti•pro•ton (ăn′tē-prō′tŏn′, ăn′tī-) *n.* The antiparticle of the proton.

an•ti•pru•rit•ic (ăn′tē-prōō-rĭt′ĭk, ăn′tī-) *adj.* Preventing or relieving itching: *an antipruritic agent.* **—an′ti•pru•rit′ic** *n.*

an•ti•py•ret•ic (ăn′tē-pī-rĕt′ĭk, ăn′tī-) *adj.* Reducing fever. *—n.* A medication that reduces fever. **—an′ti•py•re′sis** (-rē′sĭs) *n.*

an•ti•py•rine (ăn′tē-pī′rēn) *n.* A toxic white powder, $C_{11}H_{12}N_2O$, formerly used to reduce fever and relieve pain. [Originally a trademark.]

antiq. *abbr.* **1.** Antiquarian; antiquary. **2.** Antiquities. **3.** Antiquity.

an•ti•quar•i•an (ăn′tĭ-kwâr′ē-ən) *adj.* **1.** Of or relating to the study or collecting of antiquities. **2.** Dealing in or having to do with old or rare books. *—n.* One who studies, collects, or deals in antiquities. **—an′ti•quar′i•an•ism** *n.*

an•ti•quark (ăn′tē-kwôrk′, ăn′tī-) *n.* The antiparticle of a quark.

an•ti•quar•y (ăn′tĭ-kwĕr′ē) *n., pl.* **-ies.** An antiquarian. [Lat. *antīquārius* < *antīquus,* old. See ANTIQUE.]

an•ti•quate (ăn′tĭ-kwāt′) *tr.v.* **-quat•ed, -quat•ing, -quates. 1.** To make obsolete or old-fashioned. **2.** To antique. [LLat. *antīquāre, antīquāt-,* to make old < Lat., to leave in an old state < *antīquus,* old. See ANTIQUE.] **—an′ti•qua′tion** *n.*

an•ti•quat•ed (ăn′tĭ-kwā′tĭd) *adj.* **1.** Too old to be fashionable, suitable, or useful; outmoded. See Syns at **old. 2.** Very old; aged. **—an′ti•quat′ed•ness** *n.*

an•tique (ăn-tēk′) *adj.* **1.** Belonging to, made in, or typical of an earlier period. See Syns at **old. 2.** Of, from, or characteristic of ancient times, esp. of ancient Greece or Rome. **3.** Of or dealing in antiques. **4.** Old-fashioned: *an antique appearance.* *—n.* **1.** An object, esp. a piece of furniture, esteemed for its age. **2.** The style or manner of ancient times. *—v.* **-tiqued, -tiqu•ing, -tiques.** *—tr.* To give the appearance of an antique to: *antique an oak chest.* *—intr.* To hunt or shop for antiques. [Fr. < Lat. *antīquus.* See **ant-***.] **—an•tique′ly** *adv.* **—an•tique′ness** *n.*

an•tiqu•er (ăn-tē′kər) *n.* One who treats or finishes new furniture so as to make it appear antique.

an•tiq•ui•ty (ăn-tĭk′wĭ-tē) *n., pl.* **-ties. 1.** Ancient times, esp. the times preceding the Middle Ages. **2.** The people, esp. the writers and artisans, of ancient times. **3.** The quality of being old or ancient; considerable age. **4.** Something, such as an object, from ancient times. Often used in the plural.

an•ti•ra•chit•ic (ăn′tē-rə-kĭt′ĭk, ăn′tī-) *adj.* Curing or preventing rickets: *antirachitic drugs.* **—an′ti•ra•chit′ic** *n.*

an•ti-roll bar (ăn′tē-rōl′, ăn′tī-) *n.* See **anti-sway bar.**

An•ti•sa•na (ăn′tĭ-sä′nə). An active volcano, c. 5,760 m (18,885 ft), of N-central Ecuador in the Andes SE of Quito.

an•ti-sat•el•lite or **an•ti•sat•el•lite** (ăn′tē-săt′l-īt, ăn′tī-) *adj.* Directed against enemy satellites: *anti-satellite weapons.*

an•ti•scor•bu•tic (ăn′tē-skôr-byōō′tĭk, ăn′tī-) *adj.* Curing or preventing scurvy. **—an′ti•scor•bu′tic** *n.*

an•ti•se•cre•to•ry (ăn′tē-sĭ-krē′tə-rē, ăn′tī-) *adj.* Inhibiting or decreasing secretion, esp. gastric secretions. **—an′ti•se•cre′to•ry** *n.*

an•ti-Sem•ite (ăn′tē-sĕm′īt′, ăn′tī-) *n.* One who discriminates against or is hostile or prejudiced toward Jews. **—an′ti-Se•mit′ic** (-sə-mĭt′ĭk) *adj.*

an•ti-Sem•i•tism (ăn′tē-sĕm′ĭ-tĭz′əm, ăn′tī-) *n.* **1.** Hostility or prejudice toward Jews or Judaism. **2.** Discrimination against Jews.

an•ti•sep•sis (ăn′tĭ-sĕp′sĭs) *n.* Destruction of disease-causing microorganisms to prevent infection.

an•ti•sep•tic (ăn′tĭ-sĕp′tĭk) *adj.* **1.** Of, relating to, or producing antisepsis. **2.** Capable of preventing infection by inhibiting the growth of microorganisms. **3.** Thoroughly clean; aseptic. See Syns at **clean. 4.** Of or associated with the use of antiseptics. **5.a.** Devoid of enlivening or enriching qualities. **b.** Free of disturbing or unpleasant features; sanitized: *an antiseptic version of history.* *—n.* A substance that inhibits the growth of disease-causing microorganisms. **—an′ti•sep′ti•cal•ly** *adv.*

an•ti•se•rum (ăn′tĭ-sîr′əm) *n., pl.* **-se•rums** or **-se•ra** (-sîr′-rə). Human or animal serum containing antibodies that are specific for one or more antigens.

an•ti•smok•ing (ăn′tē-smō′kĭng, ăn′tī-) *adj.* Opposed to or prohibiting the smoking of tobacco, esp. in public.

an•ti•so•cial (ăn′tē-sō′shəl, ăn′tī-) *adj.* **1.** Shunning the society of others; not sociable. **2.** Hostile to or disruptive of the established social order; violating accepted mores. **3.** Disrespectful of others; rude. **—an′ti•so′cial•ly** *adv.*

an•ti•spas•mod•ic (ăn′tē-spăz-mŏd′ĭk, ăn′tī-) *adj.* Relieving or preventing spasms, esp. of smooth muscle. *—n.* An antispasmodic agent.

an•ti•stat•ic (ăn′tē-stăt′ĭk, ăn′tī-) also **an•ti•stat** (-tē-stăt′, -tī-) *adj.* Preventing or inhibiting the buildup of static electricity. **—an′ti•stat′ic** *n.*

An•tis•the•nes (ăn-tĭs′thə-nēz′). 444?–371? B.C. Greek philosopher who founded the Cynic school.

an•tis•tro•phe (ăn-tĭs′trə-fē) *n.* **1.** The second stanza, and those like it, in a poem with alternating stanzas in contrasting metric form. **2.** The second division of the triad of a Pindaric ode, having the same form as the strophe. **3.a.** The choral movement in classical Greek drama in the opposite direction from that of the strophe. **b.** The part of a choral ode sung during this movement and in the same meter as the strophe. [LLat. *antistrophē,* antistrophe of Gk. tragedy < Gk., strophic correspondence < *antistrephein,* to turn back : *anti-,* back; see ANTI- + *strephein,* to turn; see STROPHE.] **—an′ti•stroph′ic** (ăn′tĭ-strŏf′ĭk) *adj.* **—an′ti•stroph′i•cal•ly** *adv.*

an•ti-sway bar (ăn′tē-swā′, ăn′tī-) *n.* A metal bar connecting the left and right suspension systems at the front or rear of an automobile or a truck, used to stabilize the chassis against sway.

an•ti•ter•ror•ist (ăn′tē-tĕr′ər-ist, ăn′tī-) *adj.* Intended to prevent or counteract terrorism. **—an′ti•ter′ror•ism** *n.*

an•tith•e•sis (ăn-tĭth′ĭ-sĭs) *n., pl.* **-ses** (-sēz′). **1.** Direct contrast; opposition. **2.** The direct or exact opposite. **3.a.** A figure of speech in which contrasting ideas are juxtaposed in balanced or parallel grammatical structures. **b.** The second and contrasting part of such a juxtaposition. **4.** The second stage of the Hegelian dialectic, representing the opposite of the thesis. [LLat. < Gk. < *antitithenai,* to oppose : *anti-,* anti- + *tithenai, the-,* to set; see **dhē-***.]

an•ti•thet•i•cal (ăn′tĭ-thĕt′ĭ-kəl) also **an•ti•thet•ic** (-ĭk) *adj.* **1.** Of, relating to, or marked by antithesis. **2.** Diametrically opposed. [< Med.Lat. *antitheticus* < Gk. *antithetikos* < *antitithenai,* to oppose. See ANTITHESIS.] **—an′ti•thet′i•cal•ly** *adv.*

an•ti•tox•ic (ăn′tē-tŏk′sĭk) *adj.* **1.** Counteracting a toxin or poison. **2.** Of, relating to, or containing an antitoxin.

an•ti•tox•in (ăn′tē-tŏk′sĭn) *n.* **1.** An antibody formed in response to and capable of neutralizing a specific biological toxin. **2.** An animal or human antitoxic serum used to prevent or treat diseases caused by biological toxins, such as tetanus and diphtheria.

an•ti•trade (ăn′tĭ-trād′) *n.* The westerly winds above the surface trade winds of the tropics, which become the prevailing westerly winds of the middle latitudes. Often used in the plural.

an•ti•trust (ăn′tē-trŭst′, ăn′tī-) *adj.* Opposing or intended to regulate business monopolies, such as trusts or cartels.

an•ti•tus•sive (ăn′tē-tŭs′ĭv, ăn′tī-) *adj.* Capable of relieving or suppressing coughing. **—an′ti•tus′sive** *n.*

an•ti•type (ăn′tĭ-tīp′) *n.* **1.** One that is foreshadowed by or identified with an earlier symbol or type. **2.** An opposite or contrasting type. [Med.Lat. *antitypus* < LGk. *antitupos,* copy, antitype < Gk., corresponding, representing : *anti-,* equal to, like; see ANTI- + *tupos,* print, impression.] **—an′ti•typ′i•cal** (-tĭp′ĭ-kəl) *adj.*

an•ti-u•to•pi•a (ăn′tē-yōō-tō′pē-ə, ăn′tī-) *n.* **1.** An imaginary place or society marked by misery and oppression; a dystopia. **2.** A work describing an anti-utopia. **—an′ti-u•to′pi•an** *adj. & n.*

an•ti•ven•in (ăn′tē-vĕn′ĭn, ăn′tī-) *n.* **1.** An antitoxin active against animal or insect venom. **2.** An animal serum containing antivenins, used to treat poisoning caused by animal or insect venom. [ANTI- + VEN(OM) + -IN.]

an•ti•vi•ta•min (ăn′tē-vī′tə-mĭn, ăn′tī-) *n.* A substance that destroys or inhibits the metabolic action of a vitamin.

an•ti-white (ăn′tē-hwīt′, wīt′, ăn′tī-) *adj.* Hostile to or prejudiced against white people.

ant•ler (ănt′lər) *n.* One of a pair of bony deciduous growths, usu. elongated and branched, on the head of a member of the deer family. [ME *aunteler* < OFr. *antoillier* < VLat. **antocu-*

antler
Top: Moose
Alces alces
Center: Reindeer
Rangifer tarandus
Bottom: White-tailed deer
Odocoileus virginianus

lāre, anteoculāre: Lat. *ante-*, ante- + Lat. *oculāris*, of the eye; see OCULAR.] — **ant′lered** *adj.*

Ant•li•a (ănt′lē-ə) *n.* A constellation in the Southern Hemisphere near Hydra and Vela. [Lat. *antlia*, pump < Gk., ship's hold, bilge water < *antlos*.]

ant lion *n.* **1.** Any of various insects of the family Myrmeleontidae, the adults of which resemble dragonflies. **2.** The large-jawed larva of the ant lion, which digs a conical crater in the sand to trap insects for food.

An•to•fa•gas•ta (än′tō-fə-gä′stə). A city of N Chile on the Pacific Ocean. Pop. 185,486.

An•to•ni•nus Pi•us (ăn′tə-nī′nəs pī′əs). A.D. 86–161. Emperor of Rome (138–161) who was the successor of Hadrian.

An•to•ni•on•i (ăn-tō′nē-ō′nē), **Michelangelo.** b. 1912. Italian filmmaker whose works include *L'Avventura* (1959).

An•to•ni•us (ăn-tō′nē-əs), **Marcus.** See **Mark Antony.**

an•to•no•ma•sia (ăn′tə-nə-mā′zhə) *n.* **1.** The substitution of a title or epithet for a proper name. **2.** The substitution of a personal name for a common noun in order to designate a member of a group, as in calling a traitor a "Benedict Arnold." [Lat. < Gk. *antonomazein*, to name instead : *anti-*, instead of; see ANTI- + *onomazein*, to name (< *onoma*, name; see **nō-men-***).]

an•to•nym (ăn′tə-nĭm′) *n.* A word having a meaning opposite to that of another word: *The word* wet *is an antonym of the word* dry. [ANT(I)- + -ONYM.] — **an′to•nym′ic** *adj.* — **an•ton′y•mous** (ăn-tŏn′ə-məs) *adj.* — **an•ton′y•my** *n.*

an•tre (ăn′tər) *n.* A cavern; a cave. [Fr. < Lat. *antrum*. See ANTRUM.]

an•trorse (ăn′trôrs′) *adj. Biol.* Directed forward and upward, as the hairs on certain plant stems. [NLat. *antrōrsum* < Lat. *anterior*, before (perh. after *intrōrsum*, inwards < *interior*, inside). See ANTERIOR.] — **an′trorse′ly** *adv.*

an•trum (ăn′trəm) *n., pl.* **-tra** (-trə). **1.** A cavity or chamber, esp. one in a bone. **2.** Either of the sinuses in the bones of the upper jaw, opening into the nasal cavity. [LLat., cavity in the body < Lat., cave < Gk. *antron*.] — **an′tral** *adj.*

ant•sy (ănt′sē) *adj.* **-si•er, -si•est.** *Slang.* **1.** Restless or impatient; fidgety: *The wait made the children antsy.* **2.** Nervous; apprehensive. [Perh. from the incessant motions of ants.]

An•tung (än′to͝ong′). See **Dandong.**

Ant•werp (ăn′twərp) also **An•vers** (äN-vâr′). A city of N Belgium on the Scheldt R. N of Brussels; a center of the diamond industry since the 15th cent. Pop. 490,524.

A•nu•bis (ə-no͞o′bĭs, ə-nyo͞o′-) *n. Myth.* The jackal-headed Egyptian god who conducted the dead to judgment.

A•nu•ra•dha•pur•a (ŭn′ə-rä′də-po͝or′ə, ə-no͝or′ə-). A town of N-central Sri Lanka NNE of Colombo; ancient cap. of Singhalese kings. Pop. 36,000.

a•nu•ran (ə-no͝or′ən, ə-nyo͝or′-) *n.* See **salientian.** [< NLat. *Anura*, order of frogs and toads : A-[1] + Gk. *oura*, tail; see **ors-***.]

an•u•re•sis (ăn′yə-rē′sĭs) *n.* **1.** Inability to urinate. **2.** See **anuria.** [A-[1] + Gk. *ourēsis*, urination (< *ourein*, to urinate < *ouron*, urine).] — **an′u•ret′ic** (-rĕt′ĭk) *adj.*

a•nu•ri•a (ə-no͝or′ē-ə, ə-nyo͝or′-) *n.* The absence of urine formation. — **a•nu′ric** (ə-no͝or′ĭk, ə-nyo͝or′-) *adj.*

a•nu•rous (ə-no͝or′əs, ə-nyo͝or′-) *adj.* Having no tail; tailless.

a•nus (ā′nəs) *n., pl.* **a•nus•es.** The opening at the lower end of the alimentary canal through which solid waste is eliminated. [ME < Lat. *ānus*.]

an•vil (ăn′vĭl) *n.* **1.** A heavy block of iron or steel with a smooth, flat top on which metals are shaped by hammering. **2.** The fixed jaw in a set of calipers. **3.** *Anat.* See **incus** 1. [ME *anfilt* < OE. See **pel-**[5]*.]

anx•i•e•ty (ăng-zī′ĭ-tē) *n., pl.* **-ties. 1.a.** A state of uneasiness and apprehension. **b.** A cause of anxiety: *Air travel can be an anxiety.* **2.** *Psychiat.* A state of intense, often disabling apprehension, uncertainty, and fear caused by the anticipation of something threatening. **3.** Eager, often agitated desire: *anxiety to make a good impression.* [Lat. *ānxietās* < *ānxius*, anxious. See ANXIOUS.]

Syns: *anxiety, worry, care, concern, solicitude.* These nouns refer to troubled states of mind. *Anxiety* suggests feelings of fear and apprehension unrelated to objective sources: *"Resentment and rage over this devious form of manipulation cannot surface in the child . . . At the most, he will experience feelings of anxiety, shame, insecurity, and helplessness"* (Alice Miller). *Worry* implies persistent doubt or fear: *"Rich people have about as many worries as poor ones"* (Louisa May Alcott). *Care* denotes a state of mind burdened by responsibilities: *We slept without care. Concern* stresses serious thought combined with emotion: *"Concern for man himself and his fate must always form the chief interest of all technical endeavors"* (Albert Einstein). *Solicitude* is active and sometimes excessive concern for another's well-being: *"Animosity had given way . . . to worried solicitude for Lindbergh's safety"* (Warren Trabant).

anx•ious (ăngk′shəs, ăng′shəs) *adj.* **1.** Uneasy and apprehensive about something uncertain; worried. **2.** Attended with, showing, or causing anxiety: *an anxious night.* **3.** *Usage Problem.* Eagerly or earnestly desirous. [< Lat. *ānxius* < *angere*, to torment. See **angh-***.] — **anx′ious•ly** *adv.* — **anx′ious•ness** *n.*

Usage Note: *Anxious* has a long history of use roughly as a synonym for *eager*, but many would prefer that *anxious* be used only when its subject is worried or uneasy about the anticipated event. Fifty-two percent of the Usage Panel rejects *anxious* in the sentence *We are anxious to see the new show of British sculpture at the museum.* But general adoption of *anxious* to mean "eager" is understandable, at least in colloquial discourse, since it provides a means of adding emotional urgency to an assertion. Note, in this connection, the analogous use of sentences such as *I'm dying to see your new baby* in informal style.

an•y (ĕn′ē) *adj.* **1.** One, some, every, or all without specification: *Are there any messages for me? Any child would love that.* **2.** Exceeding normal limits, as in size or duration: *I never stay for any length of time.* — *pron. (used with a sing. or pl. v.)* Any one or more persons, things, or quantities. — *adv.* To any degree or extent; at all: *didn't feel any better.* [ME *ani* < OE *ǣnig*. See **oi-no-***.]

Usage Note: Used as a pronoun *any* can take either a singular or plural verb, depending on how it is construed: *Any of these books is suitable* (that is, *any one*). *But are any* (that is, *some*) *of them available?* • The construction *of any* is often used in informal contexts to mean "of all," as in *He is the best known of any living playwright.* In an earlier survey this example was unacceptable in writing to 67 percent of the Usage Panel. • *Any* is also used to mean "at all" before a comparative adjective or adverb in questions and negative sentences: *Is she any better?* This usage is entirely acceptable. The related use of *any* to modify a verb, as in *It didn't hurt any,* is considered informal and should be avoided in writing. See Usage Notes at **every, he**[1].

An•yang (än′yäng′). A city of E China NNE of Zhengzhou; one of the earliest centers of Chinese civilization. Pop. 250,000.

an•y•bod•y (ĕn′ē-bŏd′ē, -bŭd′ē) *pron.* Any person; anyone. See Usage Notes at **anyone, every, he**[1]. — *n.* A person of consequence: *Everybody who is anybody was at the party.*

an•y•how (ĕn′ē-hou′) *adv.* **1.** In whatever way or manner; however: *I'll cook it anyhow you like.* **2.** Carelessly; haphazardly. **3.a.** In any case; at least: *I think they're asleep; anyhow, they're quiet.* **b.** Nevertheless: *It's crazy, but I believe it anyhow.*

an•y•more (ĕn′ē-môr′, -mōr′) *adv.* **1.a.** Any longer; now: *Do they make this model anymore?* **b.** From now on: *We won't quarrel anymore.* **2.** *Regional.* Nowadays.

Regional Note: In standard American English the word *anymore* is often found in negative sentences: *They don't live here anymore.* But *anymore* is widely used in regional American English in positive sentences with the meaning "nowadays": *"We use a gas stove anymore"* (Oklahoma informant in DARE). Its use is centered in the South Midland and Midwestern states — Tennessee, Kentucky, Indiana, Oklahoma, and Iowa — and the Western states that received settlers from those areas.

an•y•one (ĕn′ē-wŭn′, -wən) *pron.* Any person.

Usage Note: The one-word form *anyone* is used to mean "any person." The two-word form *any one* is used to mean "whatever one (person or thing) of a group." *Anyone may join* means that admission is open to everybody. *Any one may join* means that admission is open to one person only. When followed by *of,* only *any one* can be used: *Any one* (not *anyone*) *of you may join.* • *Anyone* is often used in place of *everyone,* as in *She is the most thrifty person of anyone I know.* In an earlier survey 64 percent of the Usage Panel found this sentence unacceptable in writing. • *Anyone* and *anybody* are singular terms and always take a singular verb. See Usage Note at **he**[1].

an•y•place (ĕn′ē-plās′) *adv.* To, in, or at any place; anywhere. See Usage Note at **everyplace.**

an•y•thing (ĕn′ē-thĭng′) *pron.* Any object, occurrence, or matter whatever. — *adv.* To any degree or extent; at all: *They aren't anything like last year's team.* — *n.* Something or someone of importance: *"Jeremy never was anything"* (Anne Tyler). — ***idiom.* anything but.** By no means; not at all: *anything but happy.*

an•y•time (ĕn′ē-tīm′) *adv.* At any time.

an•y•way (ĕn′ē-wā′) *adv.* **1.** In any way or manner whatever: *Do the job anyway you can.* **2.** In any case; at least: *I don't know why; anyway, it's gone.* **3.** Nevertheless; regardless: *It rained but they played anyway.*

an•y•ways (ĕn′ē-wāz′) *adv. Non-Standard.* In any case.

an•y•where (ĕn′ē-hwâr′, -wâr′) *adv.* **1.** To, in, or at any place. **2.** To any extent or degree; at all: *not anywhere near completion.* **3.** Used to indicate limits of variation: *anywhere from 300 to 400.* — *n.* Any place whatsoever.

an•y•wise (ĕn′ē-wīz′) *adv. Non-Standard.* In any case.

An•zac (ăn′zăk′) *n.* A soldier from New Zealand or Australia. [*A(ustralian and) N(ew) Z(ealand) A(rmy) C(orps).*] — **An′zac′** *adj.*

An•zi•o (ăn′zē-ō, än′tsyô). A town of central Italy on the

Anubis
From XXI Dynasty funerary papyrus

ă **pat**	oi **boy**
ā **pay**	ou **out**
âr **care**	o͝o **took**
ä **father**	o͞o **boot**
ĕ **pet**	ŭ **cut**
ē **be**	ûr **urge**
ĭ **pit**	th **thin**
ī **pie**	*th* **this**
îr **pier**	hw **which**
ŏ **pot**	zh **vision**
ō **toe**	ə **about,**
ô **paw**	**item**

Stress marks:
′ (primary);
′ (secondary), as in
dictionary (dĭk′shə-nĕr′ē)

Tyrrhenian Sea SSE of Rome; site of Allied landing (1944). Pop. 27,094.

a/o *abbr.* Account of.

ao dai (ouʹ dī, ôʹ) *n., pl.* **ao dais.** The traditional dress of Vietnamese women, consisting of a long tunic slit on the sides and worn over loose trousers. [Vietnamese *áo dài*: *áo*, tunic (of Chin. orig.) + *dài*, long.]

ao dai

AOH *abbr.* Ancient Order of Hibernians.

A-OK also **A-O•kay** (āʹō-kāʹ) *adj. Informal.* Being in perfect condition or order. —**A-OK** *adv. & n.*

Ao•mo•ri (ouʹmə-rē, äʹô-môrʹē). A city of N Honshu, Japan, on **Aomori Bay.** Pop. 294,050.

A-one also **A-1** (āʹwŭnʹ) *adj. Informal.* First-class; excellent. [From classification for ships in The Lloyd's Register of Shipping.]

A•o•rang•i (äʹō-rängʹgē). See Mount **Cook.**

a•o•rist (āʹər-ĭst) *Gram. n.* **1.** A verb form in some languages, such as Classical Greek, that expresses action without indicating its completion or continuation. **2.** A verb form in some languages, such as Classical Greek, that in the indicative mood expresses past action. [< Gk. *aoristos*, indefinite, aorist tense : *a-*, not; see A–¹ + *horistos*, definable (< *horizein*, to define; see HORIZON).] —**aʹo•risʹtic** *adj.* —**aʹo•risʹti•cal•ly** *adv.*

a•or•ta (ā-ôrʹtə) *n., pl.* **-tas** or **-tae** (-tē). *Anat.* The main trunk of the systemic arteries, carrying blood from the left side of the heart to the arteries of all limbs and organs except the lungs. [NLat. < Gk. *aortē* < *aeirein*, to lift. See **wer-¹*.**] —**a•orʹtal, a•orʹtic** *adj.*

aortic arch *n. Anat.* One of a series of paired arteries in a vertebrate embryo that connects the ventral arterial system to the dorsal arterial system.

a•ou•dad (äʹo͞o-dădʹ, ouʹdădʹ) *n.* A wild sheep *(Ammotragus lervia)* of northern Africa having long curved horns and beardlike hair on the neck and chest. [Fr. < Berber *audad.*]

AP *abbr.* **1.** Advanced placement. **2.** Airplane. **3.** Air police. **4.** American plan. **5.** Antipersonnel. **6.** Also **A.P.** Associated Press.

ap. *abbr.* Apothecary.

a.p. *abbr.* **1.** Additional premium. **2.** Author's proof.

ap–¹ *pref.* Var. of **ad–** 1.

ap–² *pref.* Var. of **apo–.**

APA *abbr.* **1.** American Philological Association. **2.** American Philosophical Association. **3.** American Psychiatric Association. **4.** American Psychological Association.

a•pace (ə-pāsʹ) *adv.* **1.** Rapidly; swiftly. **2.** So as to keep up the requisite momentum; abreast. [ME *a pas* < OFr. : *a*, to (< Lat. *ad*; see AD–) + *pas*, step; see PACE¹.]

a•pache (ə-păshʹ, ä-păshʹ) *n., pl.* **a•paches** (ə-păshʹ, ä-păshʹ). **1.** A member of the Parisian underworld. **2.** A thug; a ruffian. [Fr. < *Apache*, Apache Indian. See APACHE.]

A•pach•e (ə-păchʹē) *n., pl.* **Apache** or **-es. 1.** A member of a Native American people inhabiting the southwest United States and northern Mexico. **2.** Any of the Apachean languages of the Apache. [Am.Sp.]

A•pach•e•an (ə-păchʹē-ən) *n.* **1.** The subgroup of Athabaskan comprising the languages of the Apache and Navajo. **2.** A speaker of any of these languages.

Ap•a•lach•i•co•la (ăpʹə-lăchʹĭ-kōʹlə). A river of NW FL flowing c. 180 km (112 mi) from the GA border to **Apalachicola Bay,** an inlet of the Gulf of Mexico.

ap•a•nage (ăpʹə-nĭj) *n.* Var. of **appanage.**

Ap•a•po•ris (äʹpə-pōrʹēs, -pôrʹ-). A river rising in S-central Colombia and flowing c. 805 km (500 mi) to the Japurá R.

ap•a•re•jo (ăpʹə-rāʹhō, -rāʹō) *n., pl.* **-jos.** *Southwestern U.S.* A packsaddle made of a stuffed leather pad. [Am.Sp. < Sp., equipment < *aparejar*, to prepare < VLat. **appariculāre*. See APPAREL.]

a•part (ə-pärtʹ) *adv.* **1.a.** At a distance in place, position, or time: *two feet apart.* **b.** Away from another or others: *live apart.* **2.** In or into parts or pieces: *split apart.* **3.** One from another: *I can't tell the twins apart.* **4.** Aside or in reserve, as for a separate use or purpose. **5.** As a distinct item or entity: *Quality sets it apart.* **6.** So as to except or exclude from consideration: *Joking apart, I think you're crazy.* —*adj.* Set apart; isolated. Used after a noun or in the predicate: *a people existing as a world apart.* [ME < OFr. *a part*: *a*, to (< Lat. *ad-*; see AD–) + *part*, side (< Lat. *pars, part-*; see PART).] —**a•partʹness** *n.*

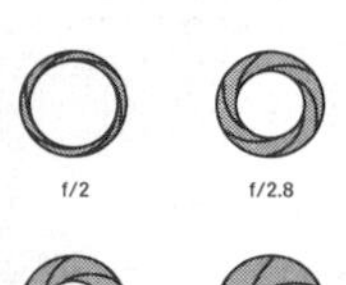

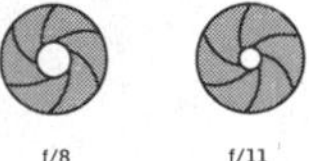

aperture

apart from *prep.* With the exception of; besides: *Apart from a few scratches, the car was undamaged.*

a•part•heid (ə-pärtʹhītʹ, -hātʹ) *n.* **1.** A policy of racial segregation practiced in South Africa against nonwhites. **2.** Any policy or practice of separating or segregating groups. **3.** The condition of being separated from others; segregation. [Afr. : Du. *apart*, separate (< Fr. *à part*, apart; see APART) + *-heid*, -hood.]

a•part•ment (ə-pärtʹmənt) *n.* **1.** A room or suite designed as a residence and usu. located in a building occupied by more than one household. **2.** An apartment house: *high-rise apartments.* **3.** A room. **4. apartments.** *Chiefly British.* A suite of rooms set aside for a particular purpose or person. [Fr. *appartement* < Ital. *appartamento* < *appartare*, to separate < *a parte*, apart : *a*, to (< Lat. *ad-*; see AD–) + *parte*, side (< Lat. *pars, part-*; see PART).]

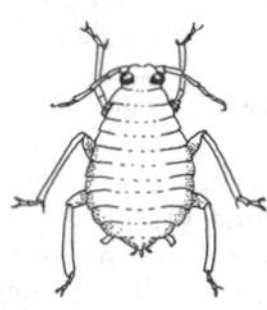
aphid

apartment building *n.* An apartment house.

apartment house *n.* A building divided into apartments.

ap•a•tet•ic (ăpʹə-tĕtʹĭk) *adj. Zool.* Relating to or characterized by coloration serving as natural camouflage. [Gk. *apatētikos*, deceptive < *apatētēs*, deceiver < *apateuein*, to cheat < *apatē*, deceit.]

ap•a•thet•ic (ăpʹə-thĕtʹĭk) also **ap•a•thet•i•cal** (-ĭ-kəl) *adj.* **1.** Lacking interest or concern; indifferent. **2.** Lacking emotion; unresponsive. [< APATHY, on the model of PATHETIC.] —**apʹa•thetʹi•cal•ly** *adv.*

ap•a•thy (ăpʹə-thē) *n.* **1.** Lack of interest or concern, esp. in matters of general importance or appeal; indifference. **2.** Lack of emotion or feeling; impassiveness. [Lat. *apathīa* < Gk. *apatheia* < *apathēs*, without feeling : *a-*, without; see A–¹ + *pathos*, feeling; see **kʷent(h)-*.**]

ap•a•tite (ăpʹə-tītʹ) *n.* A natural, variously colored calcium phosphate, $Ca_5(PO_4)_3(F,Cl,OH)$, used in the manufacture of fertilizers. [< Gk. *apatē*, deceit (from its often being mistaken for other minerals).]

APB *abbr.* All points bulletin.

ape (āp) *n.* **1.a.** Any of various large, tailless Old World primates of the family Pongidae, including the chimpanzee, gorilla, and orangutan. **b.** A monkey. **2.** A mimic or an imitator. **3.** *Informal.* A clumsy or boorish person. —*tr.v.* **aped, ap•ing, apes.** To mimic slavishly but often with an absurd result. See Syns at **imitate.** —*adj. Informal.* Wildly enthusiastic. —***idiom.* go ape.** *Informal.* To become wildly excited or enthusiastic. [ME < OE *apa.*] —**apʹer** *n.*

A•pel•doorn (ăpʹəl-dôrnʹ, -dōrnʹ, äʹpəl-). A city of E-central Netherlands N of Arnhem. Pop. 144,108.

A•pel•les (ə-pĕlʹēz). fl. 4th cent. B.C. Greek painter whose works are known only from descriptions in ancient writings.

ape-man (āpʹmănʹ) *n.* **1.** Any of various extinct primates sometimes considered intermediate in evolution between the anthropoid apes and modern human beings. **2.** A person or creature held to combine characteristics of apes and humans.

Ap•en•nines (ăpʹə-nīnzʹ). A mountain system extending from NW Italy to the Strait of Messina and rising to 2,915.8 m (9,560 ft).

a•per•çu (äʹpĕr-süʹ) *n., pl.* **-çus** (-süʹ). **1.** A discerning perception; an insight. **2.** A short outline or summary; a synopsis. [Fr. < p.part. of *apercevoir*, to perceive : *a-*, to (< Lat. *ad-*; see AD–) + *perceivre*, to perceive; see PERCEIVE.]

a•pe•ri•ent (ə-pîrʹē-ənt) *adj.* Gently stimulating evacuation of the bowels; laxative. —*n.* A mild laxative. [Lat. *aperiēns, aperient-*, pr.part. of *aperīre*, to open. See **wer-⁴*.**]

a•pe•ri•od•ic (āʹpîr-ē-ŏdʹĭk) *adj.* **1.** Lacking periodicity; irregular. **2.** *Phys.* Without periodic vibrations. —**aʹpe•ri•odʹi•cal•ly** *adv.* —**a•peʹri•o•dicʹi•ty** (-ə-dĭsʹĭ-tē) *n.*

a•pé•ri•tif (ä-pĕrʹĭ-tēfʹ) *n.* An alcoholic drink taken before a meal. [Fr. < OFr. *aperitif*, purgative < Med.Lat. *aperitīvus* < LLat. *apertīvus* < Lat. *apertus*, p.part. of *aperīre*, to open. See **wer-⁴*.**]

ap•er•ture (ăpʹər-chər) *n.* **1.** An opening, such as a hole, gap, or slit. **2.** A usu. adjustable opening in an optical instrument, such as a camera, that limits the amount of light that can enter. [ME < Lat. *apertūra* < *apertus*, p.part. of *aperīre*, to open. See **wer-⁴*.**] —**apʹer•turʹal** *adj.*

a•pet•al•ous (ā-pĕtʹl-əs) *adj. Bot.* Having no petals. —**a•petʹal•y** (ā-pĕtʹl-ē) *n.*

a•pex (āʹpĕks) *n., pl.* **a•pex•es** or **a•pi•ces** (āʹpĭ-sēzʹ, ăpʹĭ-). **1.** The highest point; the vertex: *the apex of a hill.* **2.** The point of culmination. **3.** The usu. pointed end of an object; the tip: *the apex of a leaf.* [Lat.]

Ap•gar score (ăpʹgär) *n.* A system of assessing the health of a newborn by rating heart rate, respiration, muscle tone, skin color, and response to stimuli, with a perfect score being 10. [After Virginia *Apgar* (1909–74), Amer. physician.]

a•phaer•e•sis or **a•pher•e•sis** (ə-fĕrʹĭ-sĭs) *n., pl.* **-ses** (-sēzʹ). *Ling.* The loss of one or more sounds from the beginning of a word, as in *till* for *until.* [LLat. < Gk. *aphairesis* < *aphairein*, to take away : *apo-*, apo- + *hairein*, to take.] —**aphʹae•retʹic** (ăfʹə-rĕtʹĭk) *adj.*

a•pha•gi•a (ə-fāʹjē-ə, -jə) *n.* Loss of the ability to swallow.

aph•a•nite (ăfʹə-nītʹ) *n.* A dense homogeneous rock with constituents too fine to be seen by the naked eye. [< Gk. *aphanēs*, unseen : *a-*, not; see A–¹ + *phainesthai, phan-*, to appear (< *phainein*, to show; see PHENOMENON).] —**aphʹa•nitʹic** (-nĭtʹĭk) *adj.*

a•pha•sia (ə-fāʹzhə) *n.* Partial or total loss of the ability to articulate ideas or comprehend language, resulting from brain damage caused by injury or disease. [Gk. < *aphatos*, speechless : *a-*, not; see A–¹ + *phatos*, spoken, speakable (< *phanai*, to speak; see –PHASIA).] —**a•phaʹsi•acʹ** (-zē-ăkʹ) *n.* —**a•phaʹsic** (-zĭk, -sĭk) *adj. & n.*

a•phe•li•on (ə-fēʹlē-ən, ə-fēlʹyən) *n., pl.* **-li•a** (-lē-ə). The point on the orbit of a celestial body that is farthest from the sun. [< NLat. *aphēlium*: Gk. *apo-*, apo- + Gk. *hēlios*, sun; see **sāwel-*.**]

a•pher•e•sis (ə-fĕr′ĭ-sĭs) *n. Medic.* A procedure in which blood is drawn from a donor and separated into its components, some of which are retained, such as plasma or platelets, and the remainder returned by transfusion to the donor. [Var. of APHAERESIS.]

aph•e•sis (ăf′ĭ-sĭs) *n., pl.* **-ses** (-sēz′). *Ling.* The loss of an initial, usu. unstressed vowel, as in *cute* from *acute.* [Gk., a release < *aphienai,* to let go : *apo-,* apo- + *hienai, he-,* to send; see DIESIS.] —**a•phet′ic** (ə-fĕt′ĭk) *adj.* —**a•phet′i•cal•ly** *adv.*

a•phid (ā′fĭd, ăf′ĭd) *n.* Any of various small soft-bodied insects of the family Aphididae that feed by sucking sap from plants. [NLat. *Aphis, Aphid-,* type genus. See APHIS.] —**a•phid′i•an** (ə-fĭd′ē-ən) *adj. & n.*

aphid lion *n.* The larva of any of several insects of the family Chrysopidae, such as the lacewing, that feed on aphids.

a•phis (ā′fĭs, ăf′ĭs) *n., pl.* **a•phi•des** (ā′fĭ-dēz′, ăf′ĭ-). An aphid, esp. of the genus *Aphis.* [NLat. *Aphis,* genus name.]

a•pho•ni•a (ā-fō′nē-ə) *n.* Loss of the voice resulting from disease, injury to the vocal cords, or various psychological causes. [NLat. < Gk. *aphōnia,* speechlessness < *aphōnos,* voiceless : *a-,* without; see A–[1] + *phōnē,* voice; see **bhā-**[2]*.] —**a•phon′ic** (ā-fŏn′ĭk, ā-fō′nĭk) *adj.*

aph•o•rism (ăf′ə-rĭz′əm) *n.* **1.** A terse statement of a truth or opinion; an adage. **2.** A brief statement of a principle. [Fr. *aphorisme* < OFr. < LLat. *aphorismus* < Gk. *aphorismos* < *aphorizein,* to delimit, define : *apo-,* apo- + *horizein,* to delimit, define; see HORIZON.] —**aph′o•rist** *n.* —**aph′o•ris′tic** (-rĭs′tĭk) *adj.* —**aph′o•ris′ti•cal•ly** *adv.*

aph•o•rize (ăf′ə-rīz′) *intr.v.* **-rized, -riz•ing, -riz•es.** To express oneself in or as if in aphorisms.

a•pho•tic (ā-fō′tĭk) *adj.* **1.** Having no light. **2.** Of or relating to the region of a body of water that is not reached by sunlight and in which photosynthesis is unable to occur.

aph•ro•dis•i•ac (ăf′rə-dĭz′ē-ăk′, -dē′zē-) *adj.* Arousing or intensifying sexual desire. —*n.* Something, such as a drug or food, having such an effect. [Gk. *aphrodisiakos* < *aphrodisia,* sexual pleasures < *Aphroditē,* Aphrodite.] —**aph′ro•di•si′a•cal** (-dĭ-zī′ĭ-kəl) *adj.*

aph•ro•di•te (ăf′rə-dī′tē) *n.* A brightly colored butterfly *(Argynnis aphrodite)* of North America. [< APHRODITE.]

Aph•ro•di•te (ăf′rə-dī′tē) *n. Gk. Myth.* The goddess of love and beauty. [Gk. *Aphroditē.*]

A•pi•a (ə-pē′ə, ä′pē-ä′). The cap. of Western Samoa, on the N coast of Upolo I. Pop. 33,170.

a•pi•an (ā′pē-ən) *adj.* Of, relating to, or having the characteristics of bees. [< Lat. *apis,* bee.]

a•pi•ar•i•an (ā′pē-âr′ē-ən) *adj.* Relating to bees or the keeping and care of bees.

a•pi•ar•y (ā′pē-ĕr′ē) *n., pl.* **-ies.** A place where bees are kept, esp. a place where bees are raised for honey. [Lat. *apiārium,* beehive < *apis,* bee.] —**a′pi•a•rist** (ā′pē-ə-rĭst, -ĕr′ĭst) *n.*

a•pi•cal (ā′pĭ-kəl, ăp′ĭ-) *adj.* **1.** Of, relating to, located at, or constituting an apex. **2.** *Ling.* Of, relating to, or articulated with the tip of the tongue, as *t, d,* and *s.* [< Lat. *apex, apic-,* top.] —**ap′i•cal•ly** *adv.*

a•pi•ces (ā′pĭ-sēz′, ăp′ĭ-) *n.* Pl. of **apex.**

a•pic•u•late (ə-pĭk′yə-lĭt) *adj.* Ending abruptly with a sharp flexible tip: *an apiculate leaf.* [< NLat. *apiculus,* sharp point, dim. of Lat. *apex, apic-,* point.]

a•pi•cul•ture (ā′pĭ-kŭl′chər) *n.* The raising and care of bees for commercial or agricultural purposes. [Lat. *apis,* bee + CULTURE.] —**a′pi•cul′tur•al** *adj.* —**a′pi•cul′tur•ist** *n.*

a•piece (ə-pēs′) *adv.* To or for each one; each: *an apple apiece.* [ME *a pece: a,* a; see A[2] + *pece,* piece; see PIECE.]

A•pis (ā′pĭs) *n.* A sacred bull of the ancient Egyptians.

ap•ish (ā′pĭsh) *adj.* **1.** Resembling an ape. **2.** Slavishly or foolishly imitative. **3.** Silly; outlandish. —**ap′ish•ly** *adv.* —**ap′ish•ness** *n.*

a•piv•o•rous (ā-pĭv′ər-əs) *adj. Zool.* Feeding on bees. [Lat. *apis,* bee + -VOROUS.]

APL (ā′pē-ĕl′) *n. Comp. Sci.* A programming language that can handle arrays and is designed for use at remote terminals. [*A P(rogramming) L(anguage).*]

a•pla•cen•tal (ā′plə-sĕn′tl) *adj.* Having no placenta, as marsupials and monotremes.

ap•la•nat•ic (ăp′lə-năt′ĭk) *adj.* Of or relating to optical systems that correct for spherical aberration. [< A–[1] + Gk. *planasthai,* to wander; see **pelə-**[2]*.]

a•plas•tic anemia (ā-plăs′tĭk) *n.* A form of anemia caused by bone marrow disease or exposure to toxic agents and impairing the capacity of the bone marrow to generate red blood cells.

a•plen•ty (ə-plĕn′tē) *adj.* In plentiful supply; abundant. —**a•plen′ty** *adv.*

ap•lite (ăp′līt′) also **hap•lite** (hăp′līt′) *n.* A fine-grained, light-colored granitic rock consisting primarily of orthoclase and quartz. [Ger. *Aplit* < Gk. *haplous,* single. See HAPLOID.] —**ap•lit′ic** (ă-plĭt′ĭk) *adj.*

a•plomb (ə-plŏm′, ə-plŭm′) *n.* Self-confident assurance. [Fr. < OFr. *a plomb,* perpendicularly : *a,* according to (< Lat. *ad-;* see AD–) + *plomb,* lead weight (< Lat. *plumbum,* lead).]

ap•ne•a also **ap•noe•a** (ăp′nē-ə, ăp-nē′ə) *n.* Temporary absence or cessation of breathing. [NLat. < Gk. *apnoia: a-,* without; see A–[1] + *pnoia,* breathing (< *pnein,* to breathe; see **pneu-***).] —**ap•ne′ic** *adj. & n.*

A•po (ä′pō). The highest mountain, 2,956.1 m (9,692 ft), of the Philippines, an active volcano on SE Mindanao.

APO or **A.P.O.** *abbr.* Army Post Office.

apo– or **ap–** *pref.* **1.a.** Away from; off: *aphelion.* **b.** Separate: *apocarpous.* **2.** Without; not: *apogamy.* **3.** Related to; derived from: *apomorphine.* **4.** Metasomatic: *apophyllite.* [Gk. < *apo,* away from. See **apo-***.]

Apoc. *abbr. Bible.* **1.** Apocalypse. **2.** Apocrypha; Apocryphal.

a•poc•a•lypse (ə-pŏk′ə-lĭps′) *n.* **1.a. Apocalypse.** *Bible.* The Book of Revelation. **b.** Any of various anonymous Jewish or Christian texts from around the second century B.C. to the second century A.D. containing prophetic or symbolic visions, esp. of the imminent destruction of the world. **2.** Great or total devastation: *nuclear apocalypse.* **3.** A prophetic disclosure; a revelation. [ME *Apocalipse* < LLat. *Apocalypsis* < Gk. *apokalupsis,* revelation, Apocalypse < *apokaluptein,* to uncover : *apo-,* apo- + *kaluptein,* to cover; see **kel-**[1]*.]

a•poc•a•lyp•tic (ə-pŏk′ə-lĭp′tĭk) also **a•poc•a•lyp•ti•cal** (-tĭ-kəl) *adj.* **1.** Of or relating to an apocalypse. **2.** Involving or portending doom or vast devastation. **3.** Marked by usu. exaggerated predictions of or allusions to a disastrous outcome. **4.** Revelatory or prophetic. —**a•poc′a•lyp′ti•cal•ly** *adv.*

ap•o•car•pous (ăp′ə-kär′pəs) *adj.* Having carpels that are free from one another. Used of a single flower with two or more separate pistils. —**ap′o•car′py** (ăp′ə-kär′pē) *n.*

ap•o•chro•mat•ic (ăp′ə-krō-măt′ĭk) *adj.* Corrected for both chromatic and spherical aberration, as a lens.

a•poc•o•pe (ə-pŏk′ə-pē) *n. Ling.* The loss of one or more sounds from the end of a word, as in Modern English *sing* from Middle English *singen.* [LLat. < Gk. *apokopē* < *apokoptein,* to cut off : *apo-,* apo- + *koptein,* to cut.]

ap•o•crine (ăp′ə-krĭn, -krīn′, -krēn′) *adj.* Of or relating to a type of glandular secretion in which the apical portion of the secreting cell is released along with the secretory products. [Prob. < Gk. *apokrinein,* to set apart : *apo-,* apo- + *krinein,* to separate; see **krei-***.]

A•poc•ry•pha (ə-pŏk′rə-fə) *n. (used with a sing. or pl. v.)* **1.** *Bible.* The 14 books of the Septuagint excluded from the Jewish and Protestant canons, 11 of which are part of the Roman Catholic canon. See table at **Bible. 2.** Various early Christian writings proposed as additions to the New Testament but rejected by the major canons. **3. apocrypha.** Writings or statements of questionable authorship or authenticity. [ME *apocripha,* not authentic < LLat. *Apocrypha,* the Apocrypha < Gk. *Apokrupha,* neut. pl. of *apokruphos,* secret, hidden < *apokruptein,* to hide away : *apo-,* apo- + *kruptein, kruph-,* to hide.]

a•poc•ry•phal (ə-pŏk′rə-fəl) *adj.* **1.** Of questionable authorship or authenticity. **2.** Erroneous; fictitious. **3. Apocryphal.** Of or relating to the Apocrypha. —**a•poc′ry•phal•ly** *adv.*

ap•o•dal (ăp′ə-dl) also **ap•o•dous** (-dəs) *adj.* Having no limbs, feet, or footlike appendages. [< Gk. *apous: a-,* without; see A–[1] + *pous, pod-,* foot; see **ped-***.]

ap•o•dic•tic (ăp′ə-dĭk′tĭk) *adj.* Necessarily or demonstrably true; incontrovertible. [Lat. *apodīcticus* < Gk. *apodeiktikos* < *apodeiktos,* demonstrable < *apodeiknunai,* to demonstrate : *apo-,* apo- + *deiknunai,* to show; see **deik-***.] —**ap′o•dic′ti•cal•ly** *adv.*

a•pod•o•sis (ə-pŏd′ə-sĭs) *n., pl.* **-ses** (-sēz′). The main clause of a conditional sentence, as *We'll go* in *We'll go if we can.* [LLat. < Gk. < *apodidonai,* to give back : *apo-,* apo- + *didonai,* to give; see **dō-***.]

ap•o•en•zyme (ăp′ō-ĕn′zīm) *n.* The protein part of an enzyme, to which the coenzyme attaches to form an active enzyme.

a•pog•a•my (ə-pŏg′ə-mē) *n. Bot.* The development of an embryo without the occurrence of fertilization. —**ap′o•gam′ic** (ăp′ə-găm′ĭk), **a•pog′a•mous** *adj.*

ap•o•gee (ăp′ə-jē) *n.* **1.a.** The point in the orbit of the moon or of an artificial satellite most distant from the center of the earth. **b.** The point in an orbit most distant from the body being orbited. **2.** The farthest or highest point; the apex. [Fr. *apogée* < NLat. *apogaeum* < Gk. *apogaion* < neut. of *apogaios,* far from the earth : *apo-,* apo- + *gaia,* earth.] —**ap′o•ge′an** (-jē′ən) *adj.*

a•po•lit•i•cal (ā′pə-lĭt′ĭ-kəl) *adj.* **1.** Having no interest in or association with politics. **2.** Having no political importance: *an apolitical event.* —**a′po•lit′i•cal•ly** *adv.*

A•pol•li•naire (ə-pŏl′ə-nâr′), **Guillaume.** 1880–1918. French poet and leading figure in avant-garde circles.

A•pol•lo (ə-pŏl′ō) *n. Gk. & Rom. Myth.* **1.** The god of prophecy, music, medicine, and poetry, sometimes identified with the sun. **2. apollo,** *pl.* **-los.** A young man of great physical beauty. [Lat. < Gk. *Apollōn.*]

Ap•ol•lo•ni•an (ăp′ə-lō′nē-ən) *adj.* **1.** *Gk. & Rom. Myth.* Of or relating to Apollo or his cult. **2.** Often **apollonian.** Clear, harmonious, and restrained.

apiary
Apiarist extracting frames from a hive

Apis

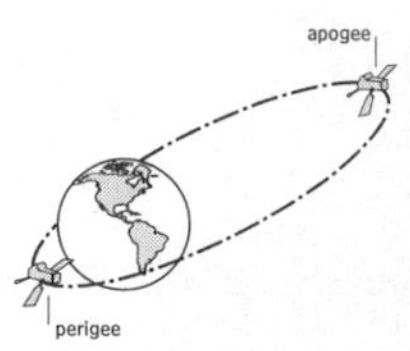

apogee

ă pat	oi boy
ā pay	ou out
âr care	ŏŏ took
ä father	ōō boot
ĕ pet	ŭ cut
ē be	ûr urge
ĭ pit	th thin
ī pie	*th* this
îr pier	hw which
ŏ pot	zh vision
ō toe	ə about, item
ô paw	

Stress marks:
′ (primary);
′ (secondary), as in **dictionary** (dĭk′shə-nĕr′ē)

a•pol•o•get•ic (ə-pŏl′ə-jĕt′ĭk) also **a•pol•o•get•i•cal** (-ĭ-kəl) —*adj.* **1.** Offering or expressing an apology or excuse: *an apologetic smile.* **2.** Self-deprecating; humble: *an apologetic manner.* **3.** Justifying or defending in speech or writing. —*n.* A formal defense or apology. [ME, formal defense < Lat. *apologēticus* < Gk. *apologētikos*, suitable for defense < *apologeisthai*, to defend oneself verbally < *apologos*, apology, story. See APOLOGUE.] —**a•pol′o•get′i•cal•ly** *adv.*

a•pol•o•get•ics (ə-pŏl′ə-jĕt′ĭks) *n.* *(used with a sing. v.)* **1.** The branch of theology that is concerned with defending or proving Christian doctrines. **2.** Formal argumentation in defense of something, such as a position or system.

ap•o•lo•gi•a (ăp′ə-lō′jē-ə, -jə) *n.* A formal defense or justification. [Lat., apology < Gk. *apologia.* See APOLOGY.]

a•pol•o•gist (ə-pŏl′ə-jĭst) *n.* A person who defends or justifies something, such as a doctrine, a policy, or an institution.

a•pol•o•gize (ə-pŏl′ə-jīz′) *intr.v.* **-gized, -giz•ing, -giz•es.** **1.** To excuse or regretfully acknowledge a fault or offense. **2.** To defend or justify formally. —**a•pol′o•giz′er** *n.*

ap•o•logue (ăp′ə-lôg′, -lŏg′) *n.* A moral fable, esp. one having animals or inanimate objects as characters. [Fr. < Lat. *apologus* < Gk. *apologos*: *apo-*, apo- + *logos*, speech; see **leg-***.]

a•pol•o•gy (ə-pŏl′ə-jē) *n., pl.* **-gies. 1.** An acknowledgment expressing regret or asking pardon for a fault or offense. **2.a.** A formal justification or defense. **b.** An explanation or excuse. **3.** An inferior substitute: *The cot was a poor apology for a bed.* [Lat. *apologia* < Gk. : *apo-*, apo- + *logos*, speech; see **leg-***.]

a•po•lune (ăp′ə-lo͞on′) *n.* The point of an orbit around the moon farthest from the moon's center. [APO– + Lat. *luna*, moon; see LUNE.]

ap•o•mict (ăp′ə-mĭkt′) *n.* A plant that reproduces or is reproduced by apomixis. [Back-formation < *apomictic*, produced by apomixis : APO– + Gk. *miktos*, mixed (< *mignunai*, to mix; see APOMIXIS).] —**ap′o•mic′tic** *adj.* —**ap′o•mic′tic•al•ly** *adv.*

ap•o•mix•is (ăp′ə-mĭk′sĭs) *n.* Reproduction without meiosis or formation of gametes. [APO– + Gk. *mixis*, a mingling (< *mignunai*, to mingle; see **meik-***).]

ap•o•mor•phine (ăp′ə-môr′fēn′) *n.* A poisonous white crystalline alkaloid, $C_{17}H_{17}NO_2$, derived from morphine and used medicinally to induce vomiting.

ap•o•neu•ro•sis (ăp′ə-no͝o-rō′sĭs, -nyo͝o-) *n., pl.* **-ses** (-sēz′). A fibrous membrane, resembling a flattened tendon, that serves to bind muscles together or connect muscle to bone. [Gk. *aponeurōsis* < *aponeurousthai*, to become tendinous : *apo-*, apo- + *neuron*, sinew; see **(s)neəu-***.] —**ap′o•neu•rot′ic** (-rŏt′ĭk) *adj.*

a•poph•a•sis (ə-pŏf′ə-sĭs) *n.* Allusion to something by denying that it will be mentioned, as in *I will not mention their corruption.* [LLat. < Gk. < *apophanai*, to say no : *apo-*, apo- + *phanai*, to say; see **bhā-[2]***.]

ap•o•phthegm (ăp′ə-thĕm′) *n.* Var. of **apothegm.**

a•poph•y•ge (ə-pŏf′ə-jē) *n.* *Archit.* The outward curve at the top and bottom of a column where the shaft joins the capital or base. [Gk. *apophugē* < *apopheugein*, to flee : *apo-*, apo- + *pheugein, phug-*, to flee.]

a•poph•yl•lite (ə-pŏf′ə-līt′, ăp′ə-fĭl′īt′) *n.* A white crystalline mineral, essentially $KCa_4Si_8O_{20}(F,OH)\cdot 8H_2O$.

a•poph•y•sis (ə-pŏf′ĭ-sĭs) *n., pl.* **-ses** (-sēz′). **1.** *Anat.* A natural swelling, projection, or outgrowth of an organ or a part. **2.** *Geol.* A branch from a dike or vein. [NLat. < Gk. *apophusis* < *apophuein*, to send out branches : *apo-*, apo- + *phuein*, to grow; see **bheuə-***.] —**a•poph′y•sate′** (-sāt′), **a•poph′y•se′al** (-sē′əl) *adj.*

ap•o•plec•tic (ăp′ə-plĕk′tĭk) *adj.* **1.** Of, resembling, or produced by apoplexy: *an apoplectic fit.* **2.a.** Having or inclined to have apoplexy. **b.** Exhibiting symptoms associated with apoplexy. **3.** Extremely angry; furious. —**ap′o•plec′ti•cal•ly** *adv.*

ap•o•plex•y (ăp′ə-plĕk′sē) *n.* **1.** Sudden impairment of neurological function, esp. when resulting from a cerebral hemorrhage; a stroke. **2.** A sudden effusion of blood into an organ or tissue. **3.** A fit of extreme anger; rage. [ME *apoplexie* < OFr. < LLat. *apoplēxia* < Gk. < *apoplēssein*, to cripple by a stroke : *apo-*, intensive pref.; see APO– + *plēssein, plēk-*, to strike; see **plāk-[2]***.]

ap•o•se•mat•ic coloration (ăp′ə-sə-măt′ĭk) *n.* See **warning coloration.**

ap•o•si•o•pe•sis (ăp′ə-sī′ə-pē′sĭs) *n., pl.* **-ses** (-sēz). A sudden breaking off of a thought in the middle of a sentence, as though the speaker were unwilling or unable to continue. [LLat. *aposiōpēsis* < Gk. < *aposiōpan*, to become silent : *apo-*, intensive pref.; see APO– + *siōpan*, to be silent (< *siōpē*, silence).] —**ap′o•si′o•pet′ic** (-pĕt′ĭk) *adj.*

ap•o•spor•y (ăp′ə-spôr′ē, -spōr′ē, ə-pŏs′pə-rē) *n.* The development of a gametophyte from a sporophyte without meiosis. —**a•pos′por•ous** (ə-pŏs′pər-əs) *adj.*

a•pos•ta•sy (ə-pŏs′tə-sē) *n., pl.* **-sies.** Abandonment of one's beliefs, as in a religion or a cause. [ME *apostasie* < OFr. < LLat. *apostasia*, defection < LGk. < Gk. *apostasis*, revolt < *aphistanai*, to revolt : *apo-*, apo- + *histanai*, to stand, place; see **stā-***.]

a•pos•tate (ə-pŏs′tāt′, -tĭt) *n.* One who practices apostasy. [ME < OFr. < LLat. *apostata* < Gk. *apostatēs* < *aphistanai*, to revolt. See APOSTASY.] —**a•pos′tate′** *adj.* —**a•pos′ta•tize′** (-tə-tīz′) *v.*

a pos•te•ri•o•ri (ä′ pŏ-stîr′ē-ôr′ē, -ôr′ī, -ōr′ē, -ōr′ī, ā′) *adj.* Derived by or relating to the process of reasoning from facts or particulars to general principles or from effects to causes; empirical. [Med.Lat. : Lat. *a*, from + Lat. *posteriōrī*, ablative of *posterior*, later.]

a•pos•tle (ə-pŏs′əl) *n.* **1.a. Apostle.** One of a group made up esp. of the 12 disciples chosen by Jesus to preach the gospel. **b.** A missionary of the early Christian Church. **c.** A leader of the first Christian mission to a country or region. **2.** *Mormon Ch.* A member of the administrative council. **3.** One who pioneers a movement or belief: *an apostle of conservation.* [ME < OE *apostol*and < OFr. *apostle*, both < LLat. *apostolus* < Gk. *apostolos*, messenger < *apostellein*, to send off : *apo-*, apo- + *stellein*, to send; see **stel-***.] —**a•pos′tle•hood′** *n.* —**a•pos′tle•ship′** *n.*

A•pos•tles' Creed (ə-pŏs′əlz) *n.* A Christian creed ascribed to the 12 Apostles and used in public worship services.

a•pos•to•late (ə-pŏs′tə-lāt′, -lĭt) *n.* **1.** The office or duties of an apostle. **2.** An association for the dissemination of a religion or a doctrine. [LLat. *apostolātus* < *apostolus*, apostle. See APOSTLE.]

ap•os•tol•ic (ăp′ə-stŏl′ĭk) *adj.* **1.** Of or relating to an apostle or the 12 Apostles. **2.a.** Of or relating to a succession of spiritual authority from the 12 Apostles. **b.** *Rom. Cath. Ch.* Of or relating to the pope; papal.

apostolic delegate *n.* *Rom. Cath. Ch.* A representative of the Vatican to a country having no formal relations with it.

Ap•os•tol•ic Father (ăp′ə-stŏl′ĭk) *n.* A church father of the first or second century A.D. said to have received instruction from the 12 Apostles or from their disciples.

a•pos•tro•phe[1] (ə-pŏs′trə-fē) *n.* The superscript sign (') used to indicate the omission of a letter or letters from a word, the possessive case, and the plurals of numbers, letters, and abbreviations. [Fr. < LLat. *apostrophus* < Gk. *apostrophos* < *apostrephein*, to turn away : *apo-*, apo- + *strephein*, to turn; see **streb(h)-***.] —**ap′os•troph′ic** (ăp′ə-strŏf′ĭk) *adj.*

a•pos•tro•phe[2] (ə-pŏs′trə-fē) *n.* A rhetorical device in which a speaker or writer addresses an absent person, an abstraction, or an inanimate object. [LLat. *apostrophē* < Gk. < *apostrephein*, to turn away. See APOSTROPHE[1].] —**ap′os•troph′ic** (ăp′ə-strŏf′ĭk) *adj.* —**a•pos′tro•phize′** (ə-pŏs′-trə-fīz′) *v.*

a•poth•e•car•ies' measure (ə-pŏth′ĭ-kĕr′ēz) *n.* A system of liquid volume measure used in pharmacy.

apothecaries' weight *n.* A system of weights used in pharmacy and based on an ounce equal to 480 grains and a pound equal to 12 ounces.

a•poth•e•car•y (ə-pŏth′ĭ-kĕr′ē) *n., pl.* **-ies. 1.** One that prepares and sells medicines; a pharmacist. **2.** See **pharmacy** 2. [ME *apotecarie* < OFr. *apotecaire*and < Med.Lat. *apothēcārius*, both < LLat., clerk < Lat. *apothēca*, storehouse < Gk. *apothēkē*: *apo-*, away; see APO– + *thēkē*, receptacle; see **dhē-***.]

ap•o•the•ci•um (ăp′ə-thē′sē-əm, -shē-) *n., pl.* **-ci•a** (-sē-ə, -shē-ə). A disk-shaped or cup-shaped ascocarp of some lichens and the fungi Ascomycetes. [< Lat. *apothēca*, storehouse. See APOTHECARY.] —**ap′o•the′cial** (-shəl) *adj.*

ap•o•thegm also **ap•o•phthegm** (ăp′ə-thĕm′) *n.* A terse, witty, instructive saying; a maxim. [Gk. *apophthegma* < *apophthengesthai*, to speak plainly : *apo-*, intensive pref.; see APO– + *phthengesthai, phtheg-*, to speak.] —**ap′o•theg•mat′ic** (-thĕg-măt′ĭk), **ap′o•theg•mat′i•cal** (-ĭ-kəl) *adj.* —**ap′o•theg•mat′i•cal•ly** *adv.*

ap•o•them (ăp′ə-thĕm′) *n.* *Math.* The perpendicular distance from the center of a regular polygon to any of its sides. [APO– + Gk. *thema*, something laid down; see THEME.]

a•poth•e•o•sis (ə-pŏth′ē-ō′sĭs, ăp′ə-thē′ə-sĭs) *n., pl.* **-ses** (-sēz′). **1.** Exaltation to divine rank or stature; deification. **2.** An exalted or glorified example: *the apotheosis of courage.* [LLat. *apotheōsis* < Gk. < *apotheoun*, to deify : *apo-*, change; see APO– + *theos*, god; see **dhēs-***.]

ap•o•the•o•size (ăp′ə-thē′ə-sīz′, ə-pŏth′ē-ə-sīz′) *tr.v.* **-sized, -siz•ing, -siz•es.** To glorify; exalt.

ap•o•tro•pa•ic (ăp′ə-trō-pā′ĭk) *adj.* Intended to ward off evil. [< Gk. *apotropaios* < *apotrepein*, to ward off : *apo-*, apo- + *trepein*, to turn; see **trep-***.] —**ap′o•tro•pa′i•cal•ly** *adv.*

app. *abbr.* **1.** Apparatus. **2.** Appendix. **3.** Applied. **4.a.** Appoint. **b.** Appointed. **5.** Apprentice.

Ap•pa•la•chi•a (ăp′ə-lā′chē-ə, -chə, -lăch′ē-ə, -lăch′ə). A region of the E U.S. including the Appalachian Mts. —**Ap′pa•la′chi•an** *adj.*

Appalachian Mountains. A mountain system of E North America extending c. 2,574 km (1,600 mi) from E Canada to central AL and rising to 2,038.6 m (6,684 ft).

Appalachian tea *n.* See **withe rod.**

Appalachian Trail. A hiking path of the E U.S. extending c. 3,298 km (2,050 mi) from central ME to N GA.

ap•pall (ə-pôl′) *tr.v.* **-palled, -pall•ing, -palls.** To fill with consternation or dismay. See Syns at dismay. [ME *apallen*, to grow faint < OFr. *apalir*: *a-*, to (< Lat. *ad-*; see AD–) + *palir*, to grow pale (< *pale*, pale < Lat. *pallidus* < *pallēre*, to grow pale; see pel-[1]*).]

ap•pall•ing (ə-pô′lĭng) *adj.* Causing consternation or dismay; frightful: *appalling conditions.* —**ap•pall′ing•ly** *adv.*

ap•pa•loo•sa (ăp′ə-lo͞o′sə) *n.* A breed of saddle horse characteristically having a spotted rump. [?]

ap•pa•nage also **ap•a•nage** (ăp′ə-nĭj) *n.* **1.** A source of revenue given by a sovereign for the maintenance of a member of the ruling family. **2.** Something extra offered to or claimed as due to a party; a perquisite. **3.** A rightful or customary accompaniment or adjunct. [Fr. *apanage* < OFr. < *apaner*, to make provisions for, poss. < Med.Lat. *appānāre*: Lat. *ad-*, ad- + Lat. *pānis*, bread; see pā-*.]

ap•pa•rat (ăp′ə-răt′, ä′pə-rät′) *n.* See apparatus 1. [Russ., the government organization < Ger. *Apparat*, a political organization < Lat. *apparātus*, preparation. See APPARATUS.]

ap•pa•ra•tchik (ä′pə-rä′chĭk) *n.*, *pl.* **-tchiks** or **-tchi•ki** (-chĭ-kē). **1.** A member of a Communist apparat. **2.** An unquestioningly loyal subordinate, esp. of a political leader or organization. [Russ. < *apparat*, apparat. See APPARAT.]

ap•pa•ra•tus (ăp′ə-rā′təs, -răt′əs) *n.*, *pl.* **apparatus** or **-tus•es. 1.a.** The means by which a function is performed or executed. **b.** A political organization or an underground political movement. **2.a.** An appliance or device for a particular purpose. **b.** An integrated group of materials or devices used for a particular purpose. **3.** *Physiol.* A group of organs that collectively perform a specific function or process: *the digestive apparatus.* [Lat. *apparātus*, preparation < p.part. of *apparāre*, to prepare : *ad-*, ad- + *parāre*, to prepare; see perə-[1]*.]

ap•par•el (ə-păr′əl) *n.* **1.** Clothing, esp. outer garments; attire. **2.** A covering or an adornment. —*tr.v.* **-eled, -el•ing, -els** or **-elled, -el•ling, -els. 1.** To clothe or dress. **2.** To adorn or embellish. [ME *appareil* < OFr. *apareil*, preparation < *apareillier*, to prepare, poss. < VLat. **appariculāre* < Lat. *apparāre*. See APPARATUS.]

ap•par•ent (ə-păr′ənt, ə-pâr′-) *adj.* **1.** Readily seen; visible. **2.** Readily understood; clear or obvious. **3.** Appearing as such; seeming: *an apparent advantage.* [ME < OFr. *aparant*, pr.part. of *aparoir*, to appear. See APPEAR.] —**ap•par′ent•ly** *adv.* —**ap•par′ent•ness** *n.*

Syns: apparent, clear, clear-cut, distinct, evident, manifest, obvious, patent, plain. The central meaning shared by these adjectives is "readily seen, perceived, or understood": *angry for no apparent reason; a clear danger; clear-cut evidence of tampering; distinct fingerprints; evident hostility; manifest pleasure; obvious errors; patent advantages; making my meaning plain.*

apparent horizon *n.* See horizon 1.

apparent magnitude *n. Astron.* See magnitude 2.

ap•pa•ri•tion (ăp′ə-rĭsh′ən) *n.* **1.** A ghostly figure; a specter. **2.** A sudden or unusual sight. **3.** The act of appearing; appearance. [ME *apparicioun* < OFr. *apparition* < LLat. *appāritiō*, *appāritiōn-*, an appearance < Lat. *appāritus*, p.part. of *appārēre*, to appear. See APPEAR.] —**ap′pa•ri′tion•al** *adj.*

ap•par•i•tor (ə-păr′ĭ-tər) *n.* An official formerly sent to carry out the orders of a civil or ecclesiastical court. [ME < Lat. *appāritor* < *appārēre*, to appear. See APPEAR.]

ap•peal (ə-pēl′) *n.* **1.** An earnest or urgent request, entreaty, or supplication. **2.** A resort or an application to a higher authority, as for sanction: *an appeal to reason.* **3.** *Law.* **a.** The transfer of a case from a lower to a higher court for a review of the lower court's decision. **b.** A case so transferred. **c.** A request for such a review. **4.** The power of attracting interest: *a city with appeal for tourists.* —*v.* **-pealed, -peal•ing, -peals.** —*intr.* **1.** To make an earnest or urgent request. **2.** To have recourse, as for corroboration; resort. **3.** *Law.* To make or apply for an appeal. **4.** To be attractive or interesting. —*tr. Law.* To transfer or apply to transfer (a case) to a higher court for an appeal. [ME *apel* < OFr. < *apeler*, to appeal < Lat. *appellāre*, to entreat. See pel-[5]*.] —**ap•peal′a•bil′i•ty** *n.* —**ap•peal′a•ble** *adj.* —**ap•peal′er** *n.*

ap•pear (ə-pîr′) *intr.v.* **-peared, -pear•ing, -pears. 1.** To become visible. **2.** To come into existence: *New viruses appear periodically.* **3.** To seem or look to be: *appeared unhappy.* **4.** To seem likely. **5.** To come before the public: *has appeared in plays.* **6.** *Law.* To present oneself formally before a court. [ME *aperen* < OFr. *aparoir*, *aper-* < Lat. *appārēre*: *ad-*, ad- + *pārēre*, to show.]

ap•pear•ance (ə-pîr′əns) *n.* **1.** The act or an instance of coming into sight. **2.** The act or an instance of coming into public view: *a rare personal appearance.* **3.** Outward aspect: *an untidy appearance.* **4.** Something that appears; a phenomenon. **5.** A superficial aspect; a semblance: *an appearance of wealth.* **6. appearances.** Outward indications; circumstances.

ap•pease (ə-pēz′) *tr.v.* **-peased, -peas•ing, -peas•es. 1.** To bring peace or calm to; soothe. **2.** To satisfy or relieve: *appease thirst.* **3.** To pacify or attempt to pacify (an enemy) by granting concessions, often at the expense of principle. See Syns at pacify. [ME *appesen* < OFr. *apesier*: *a-*, to (< Lat. *ad-*; see AD–) + *pais*, peace (< Lat. *pāx*; see pag-*).] —**ap•peas′a•ble** *adj.* —**ap•peas′a•bly** *adv.* —**ap•peas′er** *n.*

ap•pease•ment (ə-pēz′mənt) *n.* **1.a.** An act of appeasing. **b.** The condition of being appeased. **2.** The policy of granting concessions to potential enemies to maintain peace.

ap•pel•lant (ə-pĕl′ənt) *Law.* —*adj.* Of or relating to an appeal; appellate. —*n.* One that appeals a court decision. [ME < OFr. *apelant* < pr.part. of *apeler*, to appeal. See APPEAL.]

ap•pel•late (ə-pĕl′ĭt) *adj. Law.* Having the power to hear appeals and review court decisions. [Lat. *appellātus*, p.part. of *appellāre*, to entreat. See APPEAL.]

ap•pel•la•tion (ăp′ə-lā′shən) *n.* **1.** A name, title, or designation. **2.** The act of naming. [ME *appelacion* < OFr. *appelation* < Lat. *appellātiō*, *appellātiōn-* < *appellātus*, p.part. of *appellāre*, to entreat. See APPEAL.]

ap•pel•la•tive (ə-pĕl′ə-tĭv) *adj.* **1.** Of or relating to the assignment of names. **2.** *Gram.* Of or relating to a common noun. —*n.* A name or descriptive epithet. [ME, common (noun) < OFr. *appelatif* < LLat. *appellātīvus* < Lat. *appellātus*, p.part. of *appellāre*, to call upon, entreat. See APPEAL.]

ap•pel•lee (ăp′ə-lē′) *n. Law.* One against whom an appeal is taken. [Fr. *appelé* < OFr. *apele* < p.part. of *apeler*, to appeal. See APPEAL.]

ap•pend (ə-pĕnd′) *tr.v.* **-pend•ed, -pend•ing, -pends. 1.** To add as a supplement or an appendix: *appended a note to the report.* **2.** To fix to; attach: *append a charm to the bracelet.* [Lat. *appendere*, to hang upon : *ad-*, ad- + *pendere*, to hang; see (s)pen-*.]

ap•pend•age (ə-pĕn′dĭj) *n.* **1.** Something added or attached to a larger or more important entity; an adjunct. **2.** *Biol.* A part or an organ that is joined to the axis or trunk of a body.

ap•pen•dant (ə-pĕn′dənt) *adj.* **1.** Affixed as an appendage. **2.** Accompanying; attendant. **3.** Belonging to a land grant as a subsidiary right in English law. —**ap•pen′dant** *n.*

ap•pen•dec•to•my (ăp′ən-dĕk′tə-mē) *n.*, *pl.* **-mies.** Surgical removal of the vermiform appendix. [APPEND(IX) + –ECTOMY.]

appaloosa
Dreamfinder,
National Grand Champion

ap•pen•di•ci•tis (ə-pĕn′dĭ-sī′tĭs) *n.* Inflammation of the vermiform appendix. [NLat. < Lat. *appendix*, *appendic-*, appendage. See APPENDIX.]

ap•pen•dic•u•lar (ăp′ən-dĭk′yə-lər) *adj.* Of, relating to, or consisting of an appendage or appendages, esp. the limbs. [< Lat. *appendicula*, dim. of *appendix*, *appendic-*, appendix. See APPENDIX.]

ap•pen•dix (ə-pĕn′dĭks) *n.*, *pl.* **-dix•es** or **-di•ces** (-dĭ-sēz′). **1.a.** An appendage. **b.** A collection of supplementary material, usu. at the end of a book. **2.** The vermiform appendix. **3.** *Anat.* A supplementary or accessory part of a body organ or structure. [Lat. < *appendere*, to hang upon. See APPEND.]

ap•per•ceive (ăp′ər-sēv′) *tr.v.* **-ceived, -ceiv•ing, -ceives.** *Psychol.* To perceive in terms of past experiences. [Back-formation < APPERCEPTION.]

ap•per•cep•tion (ăp′ər-sĕp′shən) *n. Psychol.* **1.** Conscious perception with full awareness. **2.** The process of understanding by which newly observed qualities of an object are related to past experience. [NLat. *apperceptiō*, *apperceptiōn-* : Lat. *ad-*, ad- + Lat. *perceptiō*, perception; see PERCEPTION.] —**ap′per•cep′tive** (-sĕp′tĭv) *adj.*

ap•per•tain (ăp′ər-tān′) *intr.v.* **-tained, -tain•ing, -tains.** To belong as a proper function or part; pertain. [ME *appertenen* < OFr. *apartenir* < VLat. **appartenēre* < LLat. *appertinēre*: *ad-*, ad- + *pertinēre*, to belong; see PERTAIN.]

ap•pe•stat (ăp′ĭ-stăt′) *n.* The area in the brain that is believed to regulate appetite and food intake. [APPE(TITE) + –STAT.]

ap•pe•tence (ăp′ĭ-təns) *n.* **1.** A strong craving or desire. **2.** A tendency or propensity. **3.** A natural attraction or affinity. [Prob. Fr. *appétence* < Lat. *appetentia* < *appetēns*, *appetent-*, pr.part. of *appetere*, to strive after. See APPETITE.] —**ap′pe•ten•cy** *n.*

ap•pe•tite (ăp′ĭ-tīt′) *n.* **1.** An instinctive physical desire, esp. for food or drink. **2.** A strong wish or urge. [ME *apetit* < OFr. < Lat. *appetītus*, strong desire < p.part. of *appetere*, to strive after : *ad-*, ad- + *petere*, to seek; see pet-*.] —**ap′pe•ti′tive** (ăp′ĭ-tī′tĭv, ə-pĕt′ĭ-tĭv) *adj.*

ap•pe•tiz•er (ăp′ĭ-tī′zər) *n.* A food or drink served usu. before a meal to stimulate the appetite.

ap•pe•tiz•ing (ăp′ĭ-tī′zĭng) *adj.* Appealing to or stimulating the appetite. —**ap′pe•tiz′ing•ly** *adv.*

Ap•pi•an Way (ăp′ē-ən). An ancient Roman road between Rome and Capua, later extended to Brindisi.

appl. *abbr.* Applied.

ap•plaud (ə-plôd′) *v.* **-plaud•ed, -plaud•ing, -plauds.** —*intr.* To express approval, esp. by clapping. —*tr.* **1.** To express approval of, esp. by clapping. **2.** To commend highly; praise: *applauded her decision.* [ME *applauden* < Lat. *applaudere*: *ad-*, ad- + *plaudere*, to clap.] —**ap•plaud′a•ble** *adj.* —**ap•plaud′a•bly** *adv.* —**ap•plaud′er** *n.*

ap•plause (ə-plôz′) *n.* **1.** Approval expressed esp. by clapping. **2.** Praise; commendation. [Med.Lat. *applausus* < p.part. of Lat. *applaudere*, to applaud. See APPLAUD.]

ă pat	oi boy
ā pay	ou out
âr care	o͝o took
ä father	o͞o boot
ĕ pet	ŭ cut
ē be	ûr urge
ĭ pit	th thin
ī pie	*th* this
îr pier	hw which
ŏ pot	zh vision
ō toe	ə about, item
ô paw	

Stress marks:
′ (primary);
′ (secondary), as in
dictionary (dĭk′shə-nĕr′ē)

ap•ple (ăp′əl) *n.* **1.a.** A deciduous tree *(Malus pumila)* having alternate simple leaves and white or pink flowers. **b.** The firm, edible, usu. rounded fruit of this tree. **2.a.** Any of several other plants, esp. those with fruits like the apple. **b.** The fruit of any of these plants. — ***idiom.* apple of (one's) eye.** One that is treasured. [ME *appel* < OE *æppel.*]

apple green *n. Color.* A moderate or vivid yellow green to light or strong yellowish green. — **ap′ple-green′** (ăp′əl-grēn′) *adj.*

ap•ple•jack (ăp′əl-jăk′) *n.* **1.** Brandy distilled from hard cider. **2.** An alcoholic drink made from frozen hard cider.

ap•ple-pie (ăp′əl-pī′) *adj. Informal.* **1.** Nearly perfect: *apple-pie order.* **2.** Often **apple pie.** Of or relating to values regarded as typically American.

ap•ple-pol•ish (ăp′əl-pŏl′ĭsh) *v.* **-ished, -ish•ing, -ish•es.** — *intr.* To seek favor by toadying. — *tr.* To seek favor with. — **apple polisher, ap′ple-pol′ish•er** *n.*

ap•ple•sauce (ăp′əl-sôs′) *n.* **1.** Apples stewed to a pulp and sometimes sweetened or spiced. **2.** *Slang.* Nonsense.

Ap•ple•seed (ăp′əl-sēd′), **Johnny.** See John **Chapman.**

Ap•ple•ton (ăp′əl-tən). A city of E WI on the Fox R. SW of Green Bay. Pop. 65,695.

Appleton, Sir **Edward Victor.** 1892–1965. British physicist who won a 1947 Nobel Prize.

Ap•ple Valley (ăp′əl). A city of SE MN, a suburb of Minneapolis–St. Paul. Pop. 34,598.

ap•pli•ance (ə-plī′əns) *n.* **1.** A device that performs a specific function, esp. an electrical device for household use. See Syns at **tool. 2.** A dental or surgical device that performs a therapeutic or corrective function. [< APPLY.]

ap•pli•ca•ble (ăp′lĭ-kə-bəl, ə-plĭk′ə-) *adj.* That can be applied; appropriate. — **ap′pli•ca•bil′i•ty** *n.* — **ap′pli•ca•bly** *adv.*

ap•pli•cant (ăp′lĭ-kənt) *n.* One that applies, as for a job. [ME < Lat. *applicāns*, pr.part. of *applicāre*, to affix. See APPLY.]

ap•pli•ca•tion (ăp′lĭ-kā′shən) *n.* **1.** The act of applying. **2.** Something applied, such as a curative agent. **3.a.** The act of putting something to a special use. **b.** A specific use to which something is put: *the application of science to industry.* **4.** The capacity of being usable; relevance. **5.** Close attention; diligence: *application to her work.* **6.a.** A request, as for employment. **b.** The form or document on which such a request is made. — *adj.* also **applications.** *Comp. Sci.* Of or being a computer program designed for a specific task or use: *applications software.* [ME *applicacion* < OFr. < Lat. *applicātiō, applicātiōn-* < *applicātus*, p.part. of *applicāre*, to affix. See APPLY.]

ap•pli•ca•tive (ăp′lĭ-kā′tĭv, ə-plĭk′ə-) *adj.* **1.** Characterized by actual application; applied. **2.** Practical; applicatory.

ap•pli•ca•tor (ăp′lĭ-kā′tər) *n.* An instrument for applying something, such as medicine or glue.

ap•pli•ca•to•ry (ăp′lĭ-kə-tôr′ē, -tōr′ē, ə-plĭk′ə-) *adj.* Readily applicable; practical.

ap•plied (ə-plīd′) *adj.* Put into practice: *applied physics.*

ap•pli•qué (ăp′lĭ-kā′) *n.* A decoration or an ornament made by cutting pieces of one material and applying them to the surface of another. [Fr., p.part. of *appliquer*, to apply < Lat. *applicāre*, to affix. See APPLY.] — **ap′pli•qué′** *v.*

appliqué
Stitching a piece of fabric on a quilt

ap•ply (ə-plī′) *v.* **-plied, -ply•ing, -plies.** — *tr.* **1.** To bring into nearness or contact with something; put on, upon, or to. **2.** To put to or adapt for a special use: *applies all her money to her mortgage.* **3.** To put into action: *applied the brakes.* **4.** To devote (oneself or one's efforts) to something: *applied myself to my studies.* — *intr.* **1.** To be pertinent or relevant. **2.** To request or seek, as employment: *will apply to college.* [ME *applien* < OFr. *aplier* < Lat. *applicāre*, to affix : *ad-*, ad- + *plicāre*, to fold together; see **plek-*.**]

ap•pog•gia•tu•ra (ə-pŏj′ə-to͝or′ə) *n. Mus.* An embellishing note, usu. one step above or below the note it precedes. [Ital. < *appoggiato*, p.part. of *appoggiare*, to lean on < VLat. **appodiāre*: Lat. *ad-*, ad- + Lat. *podium*, support (< Gk. *podion*, base < *pous, pod-*, foot; see **ped-***).]

ap•point (ə-point′) *tr.v.* **-point•ed, -point•ing, -points. 1.** To select or designate to fill a position. **2.** To set by authority or by mutual agreement: *will appoint a date for the examination.* **3.** To furnish; equip. **4.** *Law.* To direct the disposition of (property) to a person in exercise of a power granted by a preceding deed. [ME *appointen* < OFr. *apointier*, to arrange < *a point*, to the point : *a*, to (< Lat. *ad*; see AD-) + *point*, point; see POINT.]

ap•point•ee (ə-poin′tē′, ăp′oin-) *n.* **1.** One who is appointed to a position. **2.** *Law.* One granted a power of appointment of property.

ap•point•ive (ə-poin′tĭv) *adj.* Relating to or filled by appointment: *an appointive office.*

ap•point•ment (ə-point′mənt) *n.* **1.a.** The act of appointing to a position. **b.** The position to which one has been appointed. **2.** An arrangement to do something or meet someone at a particular time and place. See Syns at **engagement. 3. appointments.** Furnishings, fittings, or equipment. **4.** *Law.* The act of directing the disposition of property by virtue of a power granted for this purpose.

ap•poin•tor (ə-poin′tər, ə-poin′tôr′) *n. Law.* One that executes a power of appointment of property.

Ap•po•mat•tox (ăp′ə-măt′əks). A town of S-central VA E of Lynchburg. Robert E. Lee surrendered to Ulysses S. Grant at **Appomattox Courthouse** on Apr. 9, 1865, ending the Civil War.

ap•por•tion (ə-pôr′shən, ə-pōr′-) *tr.v.* **-tioned, -tion•ing, -tions.** To divide and assign according to a plan; allot. [Fr. *apportioner* < OFr. : *a-*, to (< Lat. *ad-*, ad-) + *portionner*, to divide into portions (< *portion*, portion; see PORTION).]

ap•por•tion•ment (ə-pôr′shən-mənt, ə-pōr′-) *n.* **1.a.** The act of apportioning. **b.** The condition of having been apportioned. **2.a.** The proportional distribution of the number of members of the U.S. House of Representatives on the basis of the population of each state. **b.** Allotment of direct taxes on the basis of state population.

ap•pose (ă-pōz′) *tr.v.* **-posed, -pos•ing, -pos•es.** To place in proximity; juxtapose. [Prob. AD- + *-pose*(as in COMPOSE).]

ap•po•site (ăp′ə-zĭt) *adj.* Strikingly appropriate and relevant. [Lat. *appositus*, p.part. of *appōnere*, to put near : *ad-*, ad- + *pōnere*, to put; see **apo-*.**] — **ap′po•site•ly** *adv.* — **ap′po•site•ness** *n.*

ap•po•si•tion (ăp′ə-zĭsh′ən) *n.* **1.** *Gram.* **a.** A construction in which a noun or noun phrase is placed with another as an explanatory equivalent, both having the same syntactic relation to the other elements in the sentence; for example, *Copley* and *the painter* in *The painter Copley was born in Boston.* **b.** The relationship between such nouns or noun phrases. **2.** A placing side by side or next to each other. **3.** *Biol.* The growth of successive layers of a cell wall. [ME *apposicioun* < Lat. *appositiō, appositiōn-* < *appositus*, p.part. of *appōnere*, to put near. See APPOSITE.] — **ap′po•si′tion•al** *adj.* — **ap′po•si′tion•al•ly** *adv.*

ap•pos•i•tive (ə-pŏz′ĭ-tĭv) *adj.* Of, relating to, or being in apposition. — *n. Gram.* A word or phrase that is in apposition. — **ap•pos′i•tive•ly** *adv.*

ap•prais•al (ə-prā′zəl) *n.* **1.** The act or an instance of appraising. **2.** An expert or official valuation, as for taxation.

ap•praise (ə-prāz′) *tr.v.* **-praised, -prais•ing, -prais•es. 1.** To evaluate, esp. in an official capacity. **2.** To estimate the quality, amount, size, and other features of; judge. See Syns at **estimate.** [ME *appreisen*, poss. < OFr. *aprisier* < LLat. *appretiāre*: Lat. *ad-*, ad- + Lat. *pretium*, price; see **per-5*.**] — **ap•prais′a•ble** *adj.* — **ap•praise′ment** *n.* — **ap•prais′er** *n.*

ap•pre•cia•ble (ə-prē′shə-bəl) *adj.* Possible to estimate, measure, or perceive: *appreciable changes in temperature.* See Syns at **perceptible.** — **ap•pre′cia•bly** *adv.*

ap•pre•ci•ate (ə-prē′shē-āt′) *v.* **-at•ed, -at•ing, -ates.** — *tr.* **1.** To recognize the quality, significance, or magnitude of: *appreciated their freedom.* **2.** To be fully aware of; realize. **3.** To be thankful or show gratitude for: *I appreciate your help.* **4.** To admire greatly; value. **5.** To raise in value, esp. over time. — *intr.* To increase in value, esp. over time. [LLat. *appretiāre, appretiāt-*, to appraise. See APPRAISE.] — **ap•pre′ci•a′tor** *n.* — **ap•pre′cia•to′ry** (-shə-tôr′ē, -tōr′ē) *adj.*

Syns: *appreciate, value, prize, esteem, treasure, cherish.* These verbs mean to have a favorable opinion of someone or something. *Appreciate* applies especially to high regard based on critical assessment, comparison, and judgment: *As immigrants they appreciated their newfound freedom. Value* implies high regard for the importance or worth of the object: *"In principle, the modern university values . . . the free exchange of ideas"* (Eloise Salholz). *Prize* often suggests pride of possession: *"the nonchalance prized by teen-agers"* (Elaine Louie). *Esteem* implies formal respect: *"If he had never esteemed my opinion before, he would have thought highly of me then"* (Jane Austen). *Treasure* and *cherish* stress solicitous care and affectionate regard: *We treasure our freedom. "They seek out the Salish Indian woman . . . to learn the traditions she cherishes"* (Tamara Jones).

ap•pre•ci•a•tion (ə-prē′shē-ā′shən) *n.* **1.** Recognition of the quality, value, significance, or magnitude of people and things. **2.** A judgment or opinion, esp. a favorable one. **3.** An expression of gratitude. **4.** Awareness or delicate perception, esp. of aesthetic qualities or values. **5.** A rise in value, esp. over time.

ap•pre•cia•tive (ə-prē′shə-tĭv, -shē-ā′tĭv) *adj.* Showing gratitude or recognition of worth. — **ap•pre′cia•tive•ly** *adv.*

ap•pre•hend (ăp′rĭ-hĕnd′) *v.* **-hend•ed, -hend•ing, -hends.** — *tr.* **1.** To take into custody; arrest. **2.** To grasp mentally; understand: *apprehends geopolitical issues.* **3.** To become conscious of, as through the senses; perceive. — *intr.* To understand something. [ME *apprehenden* < OFr. *apprehender* < Lat. *apprehendere*, to seize : *ad-*, ad- + *prehendere*, to grasp; see **ghend-*.**]

Syns: *apprehend, comprehend, understand, grasp.* These verbs denote perception of the nature and significance of something. *Apprehend* denotes both mental and intuitive awareness but often with less than full understanding: *"Intelligence is quickness to apprehend"* (Alfred North Whitehead). Both *comprehend* and *understand* stress complete realization and knowledge: *"To comprehend is to know a thing as well as that thing can be known"* (John Donne). *"No one who has not had the responsibility can really understand what it is like to be President"* (Harry S. Truman). To *grasp* is to seize an idea firmly: *"We have grasped the mystery of the atom and rejected the Sermon on the Mount"* (Omar N. Bradley).

ap•pre•hen•si•ble (ăp′rĭ-hĕn′sə-bəl) *adj.* Capable of being understood: *apprehensible truths.* **—ap′pre•hen′si•bly** *adv.*

ap•pre•hen•sion (ăp′rĭ-hĕn′shən) *n.* **1.** Fearful or uneasy anticipation of the future; dread. **2.** The act of seizing or capturing; arrest. **3.** The ability to apprehend; understanding. [ME *apprehencioun*, perception < OFr. *apprehension* < LLat. *apprehēnsiō, apprehēnsiōn-* < Lat. *apprehēnsus*, p.part. of *apprehendere*, to seize. See APPREHEND.]

ap•pre•hen•sive (ăp′rĭ-hĕn′sĭv) *adj.* **1.** Anxious or fearful about the future; uneasy. See Syns at **afraid. 2.** Capable of understanding and quick to apprehend. **—ap′pre•hen′sive•ly** *adv.* **—ap′pre•hen′sive•ness** *n.*

ap•pren•tice (ə-prĕn′tĭs) *n.* **1.** One bound by legal agreement to work in return for instruction, as in a trade. **2.** One who is learning a trade or occupation, esp. as a member of a labor union. **3.** A beginner; a learner. —*tr.v.* **-ticed, -tic•ing, -tic•es.** To place or take on as a beginner or learner. [ME *apprentis* < OFr. *aprentis* < VLat. **apprenditīcius* < **apprenditus*, alteration of Lat. *apprehēnsus*, p.part. of *apprehendere*, to seize. See APPREHEND.] **—ap•pren′tice•ship′** *n.*

ap•pressed (ə-prĕst′) *adj.* Lying flat or pressed closely against something, as hairs on certain plant stems. [< Lat. *appressus*, p.part. of *apprimere*, to press down : *ad-*, ad- + *premere*, to press; see **per-**[4]***.**]

ap•prise (ə-prīz′) *tr.v.* **-prised, -pris•ing, -pris•es.** To give notice to; inform: *apprised us of our rights.* [Fr. *apprendre, appris-* < OFr. *aprendre*, to learn < VLat. **apprendere* < Lat. *apprehendere.* See APPRENTICE.]

ap•prize (ə-prīz′) *tr.v.* **-prized, -priz•ing, -priz•es.** To appreciate; value.

ap•proach (ə-prōch′) *v.* **-proached, -proach•ing, -proach•es.** —*intr.* **1.** To come near or nearer, as in space or time. **2.** *Sports.* To make an approach in golf. —*tr.* **1.** To come or go near or nearer to. **2.** To come close to, as in appearance or quality; approximate: *The performance approaches perfection.* **3.** To make a proposal or overtures to with a specific end in view. **4.** To begin to deal with or work on: *approached the task.* —*n.* **1.** The act of approaching. **2.** A fairly close resemblance; an approximation. **3.** A means of reaching something; an access. **4.** The method used in dealing with or accomplishing. **5.** An advance or overture made by one person to another. **6.** *Sports.* **a.** The golf stroke following the drive from the tee. **b.** The steps taken by a bowler before delivering the ball. **c.** The part of the area behind the foul line in a bowling alley. [ME *approchen* < OFr. *aprochier* < LLat. *appropiāre*: Lat. *ad-*, ad- + Lat. *propius*, nearer, comp. of *prope*, near; see **per**[1]***.**]

ap•proach•a•ble (ə-prō′chə-bəl) *adj.* **1.** Possible to approach; accessible. **2.** Easy to talk to or deal with; friendly. **—ap•proach′a•bil′i•ty** *n.*

ap•pro•bate (ăp′rə-bāt′) *tr.v.* **-bat•ed, -bat•ing, -bates.** To sanction officially; authorize. [ME *approbaten* < Lat. *approbāre, approbāt-*, to approve. See APPROVE.] **—ap′pro•ba′tive, ap•pro′ba•to′ry** (ə-prō′bə-tôr′ē, -tōr′ē) *adj.*

ap•pro•ba•tion (ăp′rə-bā′shən) *n.* **1.** An expression of warm approval; praise. **2.** Official approval.

ap•pro•pri•a•ble (ə-prō′prē-ə-bəl) *adj.* That can be appropriated: *appropriable funds.*

ap•pro•pri•ate (ə-prō′prē-ĭt) *adj.* Suitable for a particular person, condition, occasion, or place; fitting. —*tr.v.* (-āt′) **-at•ed, -at•ing, -ates. 1.** To set apart for a specific use. See Syns at **allocate. 2.** To take possession of or make use of exclusively for oneself, often without permission. [ME *appropriat* < LLat. *appropriātus*, p.part. of *appropriāre*, to make one's own : Lat. *ad-*, ad- + Lat. *proprius*, own; see **per**[1]***.**] **—ap•pro′pri•ate•ly** *adv.* **—ap•pro′pri•ate•ness** *n.* **—ap•pro′pri•a′tive** (-ā′tĭv) *adj.* **—ap•pro′pri•a′tor** *n.*

ap•pro•pri•a•tion (ə-prō′prē-ā′shən) *n.* **1.** The act of appropriating. **2.a.** Something appropriated, esp. public funds. **b.** A legislative act authorizing the expenditure of an amount of public funds.

ap•prov•al (ə-pro͞o′vəl) *n.* **1.** The act of approving. **2.** An official approbation; sanction. **3.** Favorable regard; commendation. **—*idiom.* on approval.** For examination or trial by a customer without the obligation to buy: *took the dress on approval.*

ap•prove (ə-pro͞ov′) *v.* **-proved, -prov•ing, -proves.** —*tr.* **1.** To consider right or good; think or speak favorably of. **2.** To consent to officially or formally; confirm or sanction. **3.** *Obsolete.* To prove or attest. —*intr.* To show, feel, or express approval. [ME *approven* < OFr. *aprover* < Lat. *approbāre*: *ad-*, ad- + *probāre*, to test (< *probus*, good; see **per**[1]*****).] **—ap•prov′a•ble** *adj.* **—ap•prov′ing•ly** *adv.*

Syns: *approve, endorse, sanction, certify, accredit, ratify.* These verbs mean to express a favorable opinion or signify satisfaction or acceptance. Though *approve* means simply to consider right or good, it also denotes official consent: *"The colonel or commanding officer approves the sentence of a regimental court-martial"* (Charles James). *Endorse* often implies the public expression of support: *a speech endorsing her party's candidate. Sanction* often implies official authorization: *The privilege of voting is a right sanctioned by law. Certify* and *accredit* imply official approval based on compliance with requirements or standards: *"The proper officers, comparing every article with its voucher, certified them to be right"* (Benjamin Franklin). *The board will not accredit every school.* To *ratify* is to invest officially with legal authority: *"Amendments . . . shall be valid . . . when ratified by the Legislatures of three fourths of the several States"* (U.S. Constitution, Article V).

approx. *abbr.* **1.** Approximate. **2.** Approximately.

ap•prox•i•mate (ə-prŏk′sə-mĭt) *adj.* **1.** Almost exact or correct: *the approximate time.* **2.** Very similar; closely resembling: *sketched an approximate likeness.* **3.** *Bot.* Close together but not united. —*v.* (-māt′) **-mat•ed, -mat•ing, -mates.** —*tr.* **1.** To come close to; be nearly the same as: *approximates the real thing.* **2.** To bring near or together. —*intr.* To come near or close, as in degree or quality. [ME < LLat. *approximātus*, p.part. of *approximāre*, to approach : Lat. *ad-*, ad- + *proximāre*, to come near (< *proximus*, nearest; see **per**[1]*****).] **—ap•prox′i•mate•ly** *adv.*

ap•prox•i•ma•tion (ə-prŏk′sə-mā′shən) *n.* **1.** The act, process, or result of approximating. **2.** *Math.* An inexact result adequate for a given purpose. **—ap•prox′i•ma′tive** (-mā′tĭv) *adj.* **—ap•prox′i•ma′tive•ly** *adv.*

appt. *abbr.* Appoint; appointment.

ap•pur•te•nance (ə-pûr′tn-əns) *n.* **1.** Something added to a more important thing; an appendage. **2. appurtenances.** Equipment, such as clothing or tools, used for a specific purpose; gear. **3.** *Law.* A right, privilege, or property that is considered incident to the principal property for purposes such as passage of title. [ME *appurtenaunce* < AN *apurtenance* < VLat. **appertinentia* < LLat. *appertinēns, appertinent-*, pr.part. of *appertinēre*, to appertain. See APPERTAIN.] **—ap•pur′te•nant** *adj.*

Apr. or **Apr** *abbr.* April.

a•prax•i•a (ā-prăk′sē-ə) *n.* Loss of the ability to perform coordinated movements or manipulate objects in the absence of motor or sensory impairment. [Gk., inaction : *a-*, without; see A-[1] + *praxis*, action; see PRAXIS.] **—a•prac′tic** (ā-prăk′tĭk), **a•prax′ic** (ā-prăk′sĭk) *adj.*

a•près (ä′prā, ăp′rā) *prep.* After. Often used in combination: *an après-dinner entertainment; a concert après dinner.* [Fr. < OFr. < LLat. *ad pressum*: *ad*, to; see AD- + *pressum*, nearby (< neut. of Lat. *pressus*, p.part. of *premere*, to press closely; see PRESS[1]).]

a•près-ski (ä′prā-skē′, ăp′rā-) *adj.* Concerned with or designed for use after skiing: *après-ski wear.* [Fr. : *après*, after + *ski*, skiing.] **—a′près-ski′** *n.*

a•pri•cot (ăp′rĭ-kŏt′, ā′prĭ-) *n.* **1.a.** A deciduous tree *(Prunus armeniaca)* having alternate leaves and clusters of flowers. **b.** The edible yellow-orange fruit of this tree. **2.** *Color.* A moderate, light, or strong orange to strong orange yellow. [Alteration of earlier *abrecock*, ult. < Ar. *al-barqūq*, the plum : *al*, the + Gk. *praikokion*, apricot (< Lat. *praecoquus*, ripe early : *prae-*, pre- + *coquere*, to cook, ripen; see **pekʷ-***).]

apricot
Prunus armeniaca

A•pril (ā′prəl) *n.* The fourth month of the year in the Gregorian calendar. [ME < Lat. *aprīlis.*]

April fool *n.* **1.** The victim of a joke or trick played on April Fools' Day. **2.** The joke or trick so played.

April Fools' Day (fo͞olz) *n.* April 1, celebrated in various countries and marked by the playing of practical jokes.

a pri•o•ri (ä′ prē-ôr′ē, -ōr′ē, ā′ prī-ôr′ī, -ōr′ī′) *adj.* **1.** Proceeding from a known or assumed cause to a necessarily related effect; deductive. **2.** Based on a hypothesis or theory rather than on experiment or experience. **3.** Made before or without examination; not supported by factual study. [Med. Lat. *ā priōrī*: *ā*, from + *priōrī*, former.] **—a′ pri•o′ri** *adv.* **—a′ pri•or′i•ty** (-ôr′ĭ-tē, -ŏr′-) *n.*

a•pron (ā′prən) *n.* **1.a.** A garment worn over the front of the body to protect clothing. **b.** Something that resembles this garment in appearance or function. **2.** The paved strip in front of and around airport hangars and terminal buildings. **3.** The part of a stage in a theater extending in front of the curtain. **4.** A covering or structure, as along a shoreline or below a dam, for protection against erosion. **5.** A continuous conveyor belt. **6.** An area covered by sand and gravel deposited at the front of a glacial moraine. —*tr.v.* **a•proned, a•pron•ing, a•prons.** To cover, protect, or provide with an apron. [ME < *an apron*, alteration of *a napron* < OFr. *naperon*, dim. of *nape*, tablecloth < Lat. *mappa*, napkin. See MAP.]

apron string *n.* The string of an apron. Usu. used with *tied* to indicate control: *tied to her mother's apron strings.*

ap•ro•pos (ăp′rə-pō′) *adj.* Being opportune and to the point. —*adv.* **1.** At an appropriate time; opportunely. **2.** By the way; incidentally. —*prep.* With regard to; concerning: *Apropos our date, I can't go.* [Fr. *à propos*: *à*, to (< Lat. *ad-*; see AD-)

ă pat	oi boy
ā pay	ou out
âr care	o͝o took
ä father	o͞o boot
ĕ pet	ŭ cut
ē be	ûr urge
ĭ pit	th thin
ī pie	*th* this
îr pier	hw which
ŏ pot	zh vision
ō toe	ə about, item
ô paw	

Stress marks:
′ (primary);
′ (secondary), as in
dictionary (dĭk′shə-nĕr′ē)

Aquarius

+ *propos*, purpose (< Lat. *prōpositum* < *prōponere*, *prōposit-*, to intend; see PROPOSE).]

apropos of *prep.* With reference to; speaking of.

apse (ăps) *n.* **1.** *Archit.* A semicircular or polygonal, usu. domed projection of a building, esp. of a church. **2.** *Astron.* Apsis. [Var. of APSIS.] — **ap′si•dal** (ăp′sĭ-dəl) *adj.*

ap•sis (ăp′sĭs) *n., pl.* **-si•des** (-sĭ-dēz′). **1.** *Archit.* An apse. **2.** *Astron.* The point of greatest or least distance of the orbit of a celestial body from a center of attraction. [< Lat., arch, vault < Gk. *hapsis* < *haptein*, to fasten.]

apt (ăpt) *adj.* **1.** Exactly suitable; appropriate: *an apt reply.* **2.** Having a natural tendency; inclined: *apt to take offense.* See Usage Notes at **liable, likely. 3.** Quick to learn or understand: *an apt student.* [ME < OFr. *apte* < Lat. *aptus*, p.part. of *apere*, to fasten.] — **apt′ly** *adv.* — **apt′ness** *n.*

APT (ā′pē-tē′) *n. Comp. Sci.* A language designed for programming numerically controlled machine tools. [*A(utomatically) P(rogrammed) T(ool).*]

apt. *abbr.* Apartment.

ap•ter•al (ăp′tər-əl) *adj. Archit.* Having no columns along the sides. [< Gk. *apteros*, wingless : *a-*, without; see A-[1] + *pteron*, wing; see -PTER.]

ap•ter•ous (ăp′tər-əs) *adj. Biol.* Having no wings or winglike extensions: *an apterous insect.*

ap•ter•yx (ăp′tə-rĭks′) *n.* See **kiwi** 1. [NLat. : A-[1] + Gk. *pterux*, wing; see **pet-***.]

ap•ti•tude (ăp′tĭ-to͞od′, -tyo͞od′) *n.* **1.** An inherent ability, as for learning; a talent. **2.** Quickness in understanding; intelligence. **3.** The condition of being suitable; appropriateness. [ME, tendency < LLat. *aptitūdō*, aptitude < Lat. *aptus*, apt. See APT.]

aptitude test *n.* A standardized test designed to measure the ability of a person to develop skills or acquire knowledge.

Ap•u•lei•us (ăp′yə-lē′əs), **Lucius.** fl. 2nd cent. A.D. Roman philosopher and satirist best known for *The Golden Ass.*

A•pu•lia (ə-po͞ol′yə) also **Pu•glia** (po͞o′lyä). A region of SE Italy on the Adriatic Sea. Its S portion is the heel of the Italian "boot."

A•pu•re (ə-po͝or′ā). A river of W-central Venezuela rising in the Andes of Colombia and flowing c. 805 km (500 mi) to the Orinoco R.

A•pu•rí•mac (ä′pə-rē′mäk). A river of S Peru rising in the Andes and flowing c. 885 km (550 mi) to the Ucayali R.

A•pus (ā′pəs) *n.* A constellation in the Southern Hemisphere near Musca and Pavo. [Lat. *apus*, a kind of swallow < Gk. *apous*, without feet, sand martin : *a-*, without; see A-[1] + *pous*, foot; see **ped-***.]

ap•y•rase (ăp′ə-rās′, -rāz′) *n.* Any of various enzymes that catalyze the hydrolysis of ATP, causing the release of phosphate and energy. [A(DENOSINE) + PYR(O)- + (PHOSPHAT)ASE.]

A•qa•ba (ä′kə-bə, ăk′ə-), **Gulf of.** An arm of the Red Sea between the Sinai Peninsula and NW Saudi Arabia.

aq•ua (ăk′wə, ä′kwə) *n., pl.* **aq•uae** (ăk′wē, ä′kwī′) or **aq•uas. 1.** Water. **2.** An aqueous solution. **3.** *Color.* A light bluish green to light greenish blue. [ME < Lat. See **ak^w-ā-***.] — **aq′ua** *adj.*

aqua– *pref.* Water: *aquacade.* [< Lat. *aqua*, water. See AQUA.]

aq•ua•cade (ăk′wə-kād′, ä′kwə-) *n.* An entertainment spectacle of swimmers and divers. [AQUA- + (CAVAL)CADE.]

aq•ua•cul•ture (ăk′wə-kŭl′chər, ä′kwə-) *n.* **1.** The cultivation of food fish or shellfish under controlled conditions. **2.** *Bot.* Hydroponics. — **aq′ua•cul′tur•al** *adj.* — **aq′ua•cul′tur•ist** *n.*

aqua for•tis also **aq•ua•for•tis** (ăk′wə-fôr′tĭs, ä′kwə-) *n.* See **nitric acid.** [NLat. : Lat. *aqua*, water + Lat. *fortis*, strong.]

Aq•ua-Lung (ăk′wə-lŭng′, ä′kwə-). A trademark used for an underwater breathing apparatus.

aq•ua•ma•rine (ăk′wə-mə-rēn′, ä′kwə-) *n.* **1.** A transparent blue-green variety of beryl, used as a gemstone. **2.** *Color.* A pale blue to light greenish blue. [Lat. *aqua marīna*, sea water : *aqua*, water; see AQUA + *marīna*, of the sea; see MARINE.]

aq•ua•naut (ăk′wə-nôt′, ä′kwə-) *n.* A person trained to live underwater and take part in scientific research. [AQUA- + Gk. *nautēs*, sailor; see **nāu-***.]

aqua re•gi•a (rē′jē-ə, rē′jə) *n.* A corrosive, fuming, volatile mixture of hydrochloric and nitric acids, used for testing and dissolving metals. [NLat. : Lat. *aqua*, water + Lat. *rēgia*, royal (because it dissolves gold, the "royal metal").]

aq•ua•relle (ăk′wə-rĕl′, ä′kwə-) *n.* A drawing done in transparent watercolors. [Fr. < obsolete Ital. *acquarella*, water color, dim. of *acqua*, water < Lat. *aqua*. See **ak^w-ā-***.] — **aq′ua•rel′list** *n.*

a•quar•ist (ə-kwâr′ĭst) *n.* One who maintains an aquarium.

a•quar•i•um (ə-kwâr′ē-əm) *n., pl.* **-i•ums** or **-i•a** (-ē-ə). **1.** A water-filled enclosure in which living fish or other aquatic animals and plants are kept. **2.** A place for the public exhibition of aquatic life. [Lat. *aquārium*, source of water < neut. of *aquārius*, of water < *aqua*, water. See **ak^w-ā-***.]

A•quar•i•us (ə-kwâr′ē-əs) *n.* **1.** A constellation in the equatorial region of the Southern Hemisphere near Pisces and Aquila. **2.a.** The 11th sign of the zodiac in astrology. **b.** One who is born under this sign. [ME < Lat., water carrier, the constellation Aquarius < *aqua*, water. See AQUA.]

a•quat•ic (ə-kwăt′ĭk, ə-kwŏt′-) *adj.* **1.** Consisting of, relating to, or being in water. **2.** Living or growing in, on, or near the water: *aquatic animals.* **3.** Taking place in or on the water: *an aquatic sport.* — *n.* **1.** An organism that lives in, on, or near the water. **2. aquatics.** *Sports.* Athletic activities performed in or on the water. [ME *aquatique* < OFr. < Lat. *aquāticus* < *aqua*, water. See **ak^w-ā-***.] — **a•quat′i•cal•ly** *adv.*

aq•ua•tint (ăk′wə-tĭnt′, ä′kwə-) *n.* **1.** A process of etching that produces several tones by varying the etching time of different areas of a copper plate. **2.** An etching made by this process. [Fr. *aquatinte* < Ital. *acquatinta*: *acqua*, water (< Lat. *aqua*; see AQUA) + *tinta*, dyed (< Lat. *tincta*, fem. p.part. of *tingere*, to dye).] — **aq′ua•tint′** *v.* — **aq′ua•tint′er, aq′ua•tint′ist** *n.*

a•qua•vit (ä′kwə-vēt′) *n.* A strong liquor distilled from potato or grain mash and flavored with caraway seed. [Swed., Dan., and Norw. *akvavit* < Med.Lat. *aqua vītae*, highly distilled spirits : Lat. *aqua*, water; see AQUA + Lat. *vītae*, genitive of *vīta*, life; see VITAL.]

aqua vi•tae (vī′tē) *n.* Strong distilled alcohol. [ME *aqua vite* < Med.Lat. *aqua vītae*. See AQUAVIT.]

aq•ue•duct (ăk′wĭ-dŭkt′) *n.* **1.a.** A pipe or channel that transports water from a remote source, usu. by gravity. **b.** A bridgelike structure supporting a conduit or canal. **2.** *Anat.* A channel or passage in an organ or a body part, esp. for conveying fluid. [Lat. *aquaeductus*: *aquae*, genitive of *aqua*, water; see AQUA + *ductus*, a leading; see DUCT.]

aqueduct
Pont du Gard
near Nîmes, France

a•que•ous (ā′kwē-əs, ăk′wē-) *adj.* **1.** Relating to, similar to, containing, or dissolved in water; watery. **2.** *Geol.* Formed from matter deposited by water. [< Med.Lat. *aqueus* < Lat. *aqua*, water. See AQUA.]

aqueous humor *n. Anat.* The clear, watery fluid circulating in the chamber of the eye between the cornea and the lens.

aqui– *pref.* Water: *aquifer.* [Lat. < *aqua*, water. See **ak^w-ā-***.]

aq•ui•fer (ăk′wə-fər, ä′kwə-) *n.* An underground layer, as of earth, that yields water. — **a•quif′er•ous** (ə-kwĭf′ər-əs) *adj.*

A•qui•la[1] (ăk′wə-lə, ä′kwē-lä). See **L'Aquila.**

Aq•ui•la[2] (ăk′wə-lə) *n.* A constellation in the Northern Hemisphere and the Milky Way near Aquarius and Serpens Cauda. [ME < Lat. *aquila*, eagle, the constellation Aquila.]

aq•ui•le•gi•a (ăk′wə-lē′jē-ə, -lē′jə) *n.* See **columbine.** [Med. Lat. *aquilēgia*.]

aq•ui•line (ăk′wə-līn′, -lĭn) *adj.* **1.** Of or relating to an eagle. **2.** Curved or hooked like an eagle's beak. [Lat. *aquilīnus* < *aquila*, eagle.] — **aq′ui•lin′i•ty** (-lĭn′ĭtē) *n.*

A•qui•nas (ə-kwī′nəs), Saint **Thomas.** 1225–74. Italian theologian and philosopher best known for his *Summa Theologica* (1266–73).

A•qui•no (ä-kē′nō), **Corazón Cojuangco.** b. 1933. Philippine politician and president (1986–92).

Aq•ui•taine (ăk′wĭ-tān′). A historical region of SW France between the Pyrenees and the Garonne R.

Aq•ui•ta•ni•a (ăk′wĭ-tā′nē-ə). A Roman division of SW Gaul extending from the Pyrenees to the Garonne R.

a•quiv•er (ə-kwĭv′ər) *adj.* Marked by quivering.

ar[1] (är) *n.* Var. of **are**[2].

ar[2] (är) *n.* The letter *r.* [ME *arre* < LLat. *er.*]

Ar The symbol for the element **argon.**

AR *abbr.* **1.** Also **A/R.** Account receivable. **2.** Arkansas.

ar. *abbr.* Arrival; arrive.

Ar. *abbr.* **1.** Arabia; Arabian. **2.** Arabic. **3.** Arabist.

A.R. *abbr.* Army regulation.

–ar *suff.* Of, relating to, or resembling: *polar.* [ME < OFr. *-er* < Lat. *-āris*, alteration of *-ālis*, -al.]

A•ra (âr′ə) *n.* A constellation in the Southern Hemisphere near Norma and Telescopium. [Lat. *āra*, altar, Ara. See **as-***.]

Ar•ab (ăr′əb) *n.* **1.** A member of a Semitic people inhabiting Arabia, whose language and Islamic religion spread widely throughout the Middle East and northern Africa from the seventh century. **2.** A member of an Arabic-speaking people. **3.** An Arabian horse. **4.** *Offensive Slang.* A waif. [Fr. *Arabe* < Lat. *Arabs* < Gk. *Araps*, *Arab-* < Ar. *'arab.*] — **Ar′ab** *adj.*

Arab. *abbr.* **1.** Arabian. **2.** Arabic. **3.** Arabist.

ar•a•besque (ăr′ə-bĕsk′) *n.* **1.** A ballet position in which the dancer stands on one leg with the other extended to the back. **2.** A complex, ornate design of intertwined floral, foliate, and geometric figures. **3.** *Mus.* A usu. short, whimsical composition esp. for the piano. **4.** An intricate or elaborate pattern or design: *"the complex arabesque of a camera movement"* (Nigel Andrews). — *adj.* In the fashion of or formed as an arabesque. [Fr. < Ital. *arabesco*, in Arabian fashion < *Arabo*, an Arab < Lat. *Arabus* < *Arabs*. See ARAB.]

arabesque
Carla Stallings in
Concerto Barocco

A•ra•bi•a (ə-rā′bē-ə) also **A•ra•bi•an Peninsula** (-bē-ən). A peninsula of SW Asia between the Red Sea and the Persian Gulf. Politically, it includes Saudi Arabia, Yemen, Oman, the United Arab Emirates, Qatar, Bahrain, and Kuwait.

Arabian *adj.* Of or concerning Arabia or the Arabs; Arab. — *n.* **1.** A native or inhabitant of Arabia. **2.** An Arabian horse.

Arabian camel *n.* See **dromedary.**

Arabian Desert. A desert of E Egypt between the Nile Valley and the Red Sea.

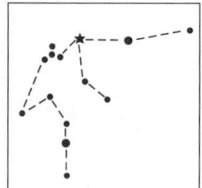

Arabian horse
Arabian stallion

Arabian Gulf. See **Persian Gulf.**

Arabian horse *n.* Any of a breed of swift horses native to Arabia.

Arabian Sea. The NW part of the Indian Ocean between Arabia and W India.

Ar•a•bic (ăr′ə-bĭk) *adj.* Of or relating to Arabia, the Arabs, their language, or their culture. —*n.* A Semitic language consisting of numerous dialects that is the principal language of Arabia, Jordan, Syria, Iraq, Lebanon, Egypt, and parts of northern Africa.

Arabic numeral *n.* One of the numerical symbols 1, 2, 3, 4, 5, 6, 7, 8, 9, or 0.

a•rab•i•nose (ə-răb′ə-nōs′, ăr′ə-bə-) *n.* A crystalline pentose sugar, $C_5H_{10}O_5$, obtained from plant polysaccharides such as gums and hemicelluloses. [(GUM) ARAB(IC) + -IN + -OSE[2].]

Ar•ab•ist (ăr′ə-bĭst) *n.* **1.** A specialist in the Arabic language or culture. **2.** One favorably disposed to Arab concerns.

ar•a•ble (ăr′ə-bəl) *adj.* Fit for cultivation, as by plowing. —*n.* Land fit to be cultivated. [ME < OFr. < Lat. *arābilis* < *arāre*, to plow.] —**ar′a•bil′i•ty** *n.*

A•ra•ca•ju (ä-rä′kä-zho͞o′). A city of E-central Brazil near the Atlantic Ocean SSE of Recife. Pop. 287,934.

ar•a•chi•don•ic acid (ăr′ə-kĭ-dŏn′ĭk) *n.* An unsaturated fatty acid, $C_{20}H_{32}O_2$, found in animal fats that is essential in human nutrition. [< *arachidic*, of the groundnut < NLat. *Arachis*, groundnut genus < Gk. *arakis*, *arakid-*, dim. of *arakos*, a leguminous plant.]

A•rach•ne (ə-răk′nē) *n. Gk. Myth.* A young woman who challenged Athena to a weaving contest and was turned into a spider.

a•rach•nid (ə-răk′nĭd) *n.* Any of various arthropods of the class Arachnida, characterized by four pairs of segmented legs and a body divided into two regions. [< NLat. *Arachnida*, class name < Gk. *arakhnē*, spider.] —**a•rach′ni•dan** (-nĭ-dən) *adj. & n.*

a•rach•noid (ə-răk′noid′) *adj.* **1.** *Anat.* Of, relating to, or being a delicate membrane enclosing the spinal cord and brain. **2.** Of, relating to, or resembling arachnids. —*n.* **1.** See **arachnid. 2.** *Anat.* The arachnoid membrane. [NLat. *arachnoidēs* < Gk. *arakhnoeidēs*, cobweblike : *arakhnē*, spider + *-oeidēs*, -oid.]

a•rach•no•pho•bi•a (ə-răk′nə-fō′bē-ə, -nō-) *n.* An abnormal fear of spiders. [ARACHN(ID) + -PHOBIA.]

A•rad (ä-räd′). A city of W Romania on the Mureşul R.; part of Romania since 1920. Pop. 183,774.

Ar•a•fat (ăr′ə-făt′, ăr′ə-făt′), **Yasir.** b. 1929. Leader of Al Fatah and the Palestine Liberation Organization.

A•ra•fu•ra Sea (ä′rə-fo͞o′rə). A shallow part of the W Pacific Ocean separating New Guinea from Australia.

Ar•a•gon (ăr′ə-gŏn′). A region and former kingdom of NE Spain; united with Castile in 1479 to form the nucleus of modern Spain. —**Ar′a•go•nese′** (ăr′ə-gə-nēz′, -nēs′) *adj. & n.*

A•ra•gon (ăr-ä-gôN′), **Louis.** 1897–1982. French writer who was a founder of literary surrealism.

a•rag•o•nite (ə-răg′ə-nīt′, ăr′ə-gə-) *n.* An orthorhombic mineral form of crystalline calcium carbonate. [After ARAGON.]

A•ra•guai•a or **A•ra•gua•ya** (ăr′ə-gwī′ə). A river rising in central Brazil and flowing c. 2,092 km (1,300 mi) to the Tocantins R.

Ar•al Sea (ăr′əl). An inland sea E of the Caspian Sea between S Kazakhstan and NW Uzbekistan. Once the fourth-largest inland body of water, it is fast disappearing because of diversion of its two sources, the Amu Darya and the Syr Darya.

Ar•am (âr′əm, ăr′-, ā′răm). In the Bible, an ancient country of SW Asia, roughly coextensive with present-day Syria.

Ar•a•ma•ic (ăr′ə-mā′ĭk) *n.* A Semitic language comprising several dialects, originally of the ancient Arameans. —**Ar′a•ma′ic** *adj.*

ar•a•me (ăr′ə-mā, ə-rä′-) *n.* An edible, mild-flavored seaweed. [J.]

Ar•a•me•an or **Ar•a•mae•an** (ăr′ə-mē′ən) —*adj.* Of or relating to Aram, its inhabitants, their language, or their culture. —*n.* **1.** One of a group of Semitic peoples inhabiting Aram and parts of Mesopotamia from the 11th to the 8th century B.C. **2.** See **Aramaic.**

Ar•an Islands (ăr′ən). Three small islands of W Ireland at the entrance to Galway Bay.

A•rap•a•ho also **A•rap•a•hoe** (ə-răp′ə-hō′) *n., pl.* **Arapaho** or **-hos** also **Arapahoe** or **-hoes. 1.** A member of a Native American people formerly inhabiting eastern Colorado and southeast Wyoming, with present-day populations in Oklahoma and central Wyoming. **2.** The Algonquian language of the Arapaho. [Crow *aaraxpéahu*, those with many tattoos.]

ar•a•pai•ma (ăr′ə-pī′mə) *n.* A large South American freshwater food fish *(Arapaima gigas)*, up to 3 meters (10 feet) in length. [Am.Sp. or Portuguese, both prob. of Tupian orig.]

Ar•a•rat (ăr′ə-răt′), **Mount.** A massif, c. 5,168 m (16,945 ft), of extreme E Turkey; traditional resting place of Noah's ark.

A•ras (ə-räs′). Formerly **A•rax•es** (ə-răk′sēz). A river rising in NE Turkey and flowing c. 965 km (600 mi) along the Turkey-Armenia and Azerbaijan-Iran borders.

A•rau•ca (ə-rou′kə). A river rising in N Colombia and flowing c. 805 km (500 mi) to the Orinoco R. in Venezuela.

Ar•au•ca•ni•an (ăr′ô-kā′nē-ən) also **A•rau•can** (ə-rô′kən) *n.* **1.** A member of a group of South American Indian peoples of south-central Chile and western Argentina. **2.** The language of the Araucanians, which constitutes an independent language family. [Sp. *araucano* < *Arauco*, a former province of S-central Chile.] —**Ar′au•ca′ni•an** *adj.*

ar•au•car•i•a (ăr′ô-kâr′ē-ə) *n.* Any of several evergreen trees of the genus *Araucaria*, having awl-shaped leaves and whorled branches. [< Sp. *araucaria*, (tree) of Arauco, a former province of S-central Chile.]

Ar•a•wak (ăr′ə-wäk′) *n., pl.* **Arawak** or **-waks. 1.** A member of a South American Indian people formerly inhabiting much of the Greater Antilles and now living chiefly in certain regions of Guiana. **2.** The Arawakan language of the Arawak.

Ar•a•wa•kan (ăr′ə-wä′kən) *n., pl.* **Arawakan** or **-kans. 1.** A member of a group of Indian peoples living in parts of Colombia, Venezuela, Guiana, the Amazon basin of Brazil, Paraguay, Bolivia, Peru, and formerly most of the Greater Antilles. **2.** The family of languages spoken by the Arawakan peoples. —**Ar′a•wa′kan** *adj.*

ar•ba•lest also **ar•ba•list** (är′bə-lĭst) *n.* A medieval missile launcher designed on the principle of the crossbow. [ME *arblast* < OE < OFr. *arbaleste* < LLat. *arcuballista*: Lat. *arcus*, bow + Lat. *ballista*, ballista; see BALLISTA.] —**ar′ba•lest′er** (-lĕs′tər) *n.*

Ar•be•la (är-bē′lə). An ancient town of Assyria in present-day N Iraq. Its name is sometimes given to the battle fought at Gaugamela, c. 97 km (60 mi) away, in which Alexander the Great defeated Darius III in 331 B.C.

ar•bi•ter (är′bĭ-tər) *n.* **1.** One chosen to judge or decide a disputed issue; an arbitrator. **2.** One who has the power to judge or ordain at will: *an arbiter of fashion.* [ME *arbitre* < OFr. < Lat. *arbiter*.]

ar•bi•tra•ble (är′bĭ-trə-bəl) *adj.* **1.** Subject to arbitration. **2.** Appropriate for referral to an arbitrator.

ar•bi•trage (är′bĭ-träzh′) *n.* The purchase of securities on one market for immediate resale on another market. —*intr.v.* **-traged, -trag•ing, -trag•es.** To be involved in arbitrage. [ME, arbitration < OFr. < *arbitrer*, to judge < Lat. *arbitrārī*, to give judgment. See ARBITRATE.]

ar•bi•tra•geur (är′bĭ-trä-zhûr′) *n.* One that engages in arbitrage. [Fr. < *arbitrage*, arbitration. See ARBITRAGE.]

ar•bit•ra•ment (är-bĭt′rə-mənt) *n.* **1.** The act of arbitrating; arbitration. **2.** The judgment of an arbitrator. [ME *arbitrement* < OFr. < *arbitrer*, to judge. See ARBITRAGE.]

ar•bi•trar•y (är′bĭ-trĕr′ē) *adj.* **1.** Determined by chance, whim, or impulse: *arbitrary division of the group into halves.* **2.** Based on or subject to individual judgment or preference. **3.** Established by a court or judge rather than a specific law or statute. **4.** Not limited by law; despotic: *the arbitrary rule of a dictator.* [ME *arbitrarie* < Lat. *arbitrārius* < *arbiter*, *arbitr-*, arbiter.] —**ar′bi•trar′i•ly** (-trâr′ə-lē) *adv.* —**ar′bi•trar′i•ness** *n.*

ar•bi•trate (är′bĭ-trāt′) *v.* **-trat•ed, -trat•ing, -trates.** —*tr.* **1.** To judge or decide in or as in the manner of an arbitrator. **2.** To submit to settlement or judgment by arbitration. —*intr.* **1.** To serve as an arbitrator. **2.** To submit a dispute to arbitration. [Lat. *arbitrārī*, *arbitrāt-*, to give judgment < *arbiter*, *arbitr-*, arbiter.]

ar•bi•tra•tion (är′bĭ-trā′shən) *n.* The process by which the parties to a dispute submit their differences to the judgment of an impartial person or group appointed by mutual consent or statutory provision.

ar•bi•tra•tor (är′bĭ-trā′tər) *n.* **1.** A person chosen to settle the issue between parties engaged in a dispute. **2.** One having the ability or power to make authoritative decisions; an arbiter.

ar•bor[1] (är′bər) *n.* A shady place in a garden or park, often made of rustic work or latticework on which plants are grown. [ME *erber* < OFr. *erbier*, garden < *erbe*, herb. See HERB.]

ar•bor[2] (är′bər) *n.* **1.** An axis or shaft supporting a rotating part on a lathe. **2.** A bar for supporting cutting tools. **3.** A spindle of a wheel, as in clocks. **4.** *pl.* **ar•bo•res** (är′bə-rēz′). A tree, as opposed to a shrub. [Fr. *arbre* < Lat. *arbor*, tree.]

Ar•bor Day (är′bər) *n.* An unofficial holiday observed in the United States, usu. in April, for the public planting of trees.

ar•bo•re•al (är-bôr′ē-əl, -bōr′-) *adj.* **1.** Relating to or resembling a tree. **2.** Living in trees; arboreous: *arboreal apes.* [< Lat. *arboreus* < *arbor*, tree.] —**ar•bo′re•al•ly** *adv.*

ar•bo•re•ous (är-bôr′ē-əs, -bōr′-) *adj.* **1.** Having many trees; wooded. **2.** Characteristic of a tree; treelike. **3.** Arboreal.

ar•bo•res•cent (är′bə-rĕs′ənt) *adj.* Having the size, form, or characteristics of a tree; treelike. [Lat. *arborēscēns*, *arborēscent-*, pr.part. of *arborēscere*, to grow to be a tree < *arbor*, tree.] —**ar′bo•res′cence** *n.*

ar•bo•re•tum (är′bə-rē′təm) *n., pl.* **-tums** or **-ta** (-tə). A place where an extensive variety of woody plants are cultivated for scientific, educational, and ornamental purposes. [Lat. *arborētum*, a place grown with trees < *arbor*, tree.]

FORMS 1	2	3	4	NAME	SOUND
ا	ـا			ʼalif	ʼ
ب	ـب	ـبـ	بـ	bā	b
ت	ـت	ـتـ	تـ	tā	t
ث	ـث	ـثـ	ثـ	thā	ṯ
ج	ـج	ـجـ	جـ	jīm	j
ح	ـح	ـحـ	حـ	ḥā	ḥ
خ	ـخ	ـخـ	خـ	khā	ḫ
د	ـد			dāl	d
ذ	ـذ			dhāl	ḏ
ر	ـر			rā	r
ز	ـز			zāy	z
س	ـس	ـسـ	سـ	sīn	s
ش	ـش	ـشـ	شـ	shīn	š
ص	ـص	ـصـ	صـ	ṣād	ṣ
ض	ـض	ـضـ	ضـ	ḍād	ḍ
ط	ـط	ـطـ	طـ	ṭā	ṭ
ظ	ـظ	ـظـ	ظـ	ẓā	ẓ
ع	ـع	ـعـ	عـ	ʻayn	ʻ
غ	ـغ	ـغـ	غـ	ghayn	ğ
ف	ـف	ـفـ	فـ	fā	f
ق	ـق	ـقـ	قـ	qāf	q
ك	ـك	ـكـ	كـ	kāf	k
ل	ـل	ـلـ	لـ	lām	l
م	ـم	ـمـ	مـ	mīm	m
ن	ـن	ـنـ	نـ	nūn	n
ه	ـه	ـهـ	هـ	hā	h
و	ـو			wāw	w
ى	ـى	ـيـ	يـ	yā	y

Arabic

Yasir Arafat

ă pat	oi boy
ā pay	ou out
âr care	o͝o took
ä father	o͞o boot
ĕ pet	ŭ cut
ē be	ûr urge
ĭ pit	th thin
ī pie	*th* this
îr pier	hw which
ŏ pot	zh vision
ō toe	ə about, item
ô paw	

Stress marks:
′ (primary);
′ (secondary), as in
dictionary (dĭk′shə-nĕr′ē)

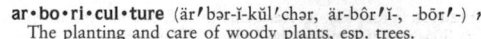

ar•bo•ri•cul•ture (är′bər-ĭ-kŭl′chər, är-bôr′ĭ-, -bōr′-) *n.* The planting and care of woody plants, esp. trees.
ar•bor•ist (är′bər-ĭst) *n.* A specialist in the care of woody plants, esp. trees. [< Lat. *arbor*, tree.]
ar•bo•ri•za•tion (är′bər-ĭ-zā′shən) *n.* **1.** A branching treelike shape or arrangement, as that of the dendrite of a nerve cell. **2.** The formation of a treelike shape or arrangement.
ar•bo•rize (är′bə-rīz′) *intr.v.* **-rized, -riz•ing, -riz•es.** To have or produce branching formations, as the capillaries. [< Lat. *arbor*, tree.]
ar•bor•vi•tae also **ar•bor vi•tae** (är′bər-vī′tē) *n.* **1.a.** Any of several North American or eastern Asian evergreen trees or shrubs of the genus *Thuja,* having flattened branchlets with opposite scalelike leaves. **b.** Any similar plant of the genus *Platycladus* or *Thujopsis.* **2.** *Anat.* The white nerve tissue of the cerebellum. [Lat. *arbor*, tree + *vītae*, genitive of *vīta*, life; see VITAL.]
ar•bour (är′bər) *n. Chiefly British.* Var. of **arbor**[1].
ar•bo•vi•rus (är′bə-vī′rəs) *n.* Any of a large group of viruses transmitted by arthropods that include the causative agents of encephalitis and dengue. [*ar(thropod-)bo(rne) virus.*] **—ar′bo•vi′ral** *adj.* **—ar′bo•vi•rol′o•gy** (är′bō-vĭ-rŏl′ə-jē) *n.*
Ar•buth•not (är-bŭth′nət, är′bəth-nŏt′), **John.** 1667–1735. Scottish physician noted for his anti-Whig pamphlets.
ar•bu•tus (är-byo͞o′təs) *n.* **1.** Any of various broad-leaved evergreen trees or shrubs of the genus *Arbutus* that are native chiefly to warm regions in the Americas and Europe. **2.** The trailing arbutus. [Lat. *arbutus*, arbutus.]
arc (ärk) *n.* **1.** Something shaped like a curve or an arch: *the arc of a rainbow.* **2.** *Math.* A segment of a circle. **3.** *Elect.* A luminous discharge that is formed when a current jumps a gap in a circuit or between two electrodes. **4.** *Astron.* The apparent path of a celestial body as it rises above and falls below the horizon. *—intr.v.* **arced** or **arcked** (ärkt), **arc•ing** or **arck•ing** (är′kĭng), **arcs. 1.** To form an arc. **2.** To move or seem to move in a curved path. [ME *ark* < OFr. *arc* < Lat. *arcus.*]
ARC[1] (ärk) *n.* A combination of symptoms, including blood abnormalities and susceptibility to opportunistic infections, that is now considered a milder form of AIDS. [**A**(IDS)-R(ELATED) C(OMPLEX).]
ARC[2] *abbr.* American Red Cross.
ar•cade (är-kād′) *n.* **1.** An arched roofed building or part of a building. **2.** A series of arches supported by piers or pillars. **3.** A roofed passageway or lane, esp. one with shops on either side. **4.** A commercial establishment featuring coin-operated games. *—tr.v.* **-cad•ed, -cad•ing, -cades.** To provide with or form into an arcade. [Fr. < Ital. *arcata* < *arco*, arch < Lat. *arcus.*]
Ar•ca•di•a[1] (är-kā′dē-ə). **1.** Also **Ar•ca•dy** (är′kə-dē). A region of ancient Greece in the Peloponnesus. Its isolated inhabitants proverbially lived a simple, pastoral life. **2.** A city of S CA at the foot of the San Gabriel Mts. Pop. 48,290.
Ar•ca•di•a[2] also **ar•ca•di•a** (är-kā′dē-ə) *n.* A region offering rural simplicity and contentment.
Ar•ca•di•an (är-kā′dē-ən) *adj.* **1.** Of or relating to the ancient Greek region of Arcadia or its people, language, or culture. **2.** Often **arcadian.** Rustic, peaceful, and simple; pastoral. *—n.* **1.** A native or inhabitant of ancient Arcadia. **2.** Often **arcadian.** One who leads or prefers a simple, rural life. **3.** The dialect of ancient Greek used in Arcadia.
ar•cane (är-kān′) *adj.* Known or understood by only a few. See Syns at **mysterious.** [Lat. *arcānus*, secret < *arca*, chest.]
ar•ca•num (är-kā′nəm) *n., pl.* **-na** (-nə) or **-nums. 1.** A deep secret; a mystery. **2.** Often **arcana.** Specialized knowledge that is mysterious to the average person: *"knows the arcana of police procedure"* (George F. Will). **3.** A secret essence or remedy; an elixir. [Lat. *arcānum* < neut. of *arcānus*, secret. See ARCANE.]
arc-bou•tant (är′bo͞o-täɴ′) *n., pl.* **arcs-bou•tants** (är′bo͞o-täɴ′). *Archit.* See **flying buttress.** [Fr. : *arc*, arch (< OFr.; see ARC) + *boutant*, pr.part. of *bouter*, to thrust (< OFr.; see BUTT[1]).]
arc cosecant *n. Math.* The inverse function of the cosecant.
arc cosine *n. Math.* The inverse function of the cosine.
arc cotangent *n. Math.* The inverse function of the cotangent.
arch[1] (ärch) *n.* **1.** A structure forming the curved, pointed, or flat upper edge of an open space and supporting the weight above it, as in a doorway. **2.** A structure shaped like an inverted U. **3.** A curve with the ends down and the middle up: *the arch of a raised eyebrow.* **4.** *Anat.* A curved or bowlike structure, esp. either of two arched sections of the bony structure of the foot. *—v.* **arched, arch•ing, arch•es.** *—tr.* **1.** To provide with an arch: *arch a passageway.* **2.** To cause to form an arch or similar curve. **3.** To bend backward. **4.** To span: *"the rude bridge that arched the flood"* (Ralph Waldo Emerson). *—intr.* To form an arch or archlike curve. [ME < OFr. *arche* < VLat. **arca* < Lat. *arcus.*]
arch[2] (ärch) *adj.* **1.** Chief; principal. **2.** Mischievous; roguish. [< ARCH-[1].] **—arch′ly** *adv.* **—arch′ness** *n.*
arch. *abbr.* **1.** Archaic; archaism. **2.** Archery. **3.** Archipelago. **4.a.** Architect; architecture. **b.** Architectural.
Arch. *abbr.* Archbishop.

arch[1]
Top: Arc de Triomphe, Paris, France
Bottom: Gateway Arch, St. Louis, Missouri

archaeopteryx

arch–[1] *pref.* **1.** Chief; highest; most important: *archenemy.* **2.** Extreme or most characteristic of its kind: *archconservative.* [ME *arche-* < OE *ærce-* and < OFr. *arche-*, both < Lat. *archi-* < Gk. *arkhi-*, archi-.]
arch–[2] *pref.* Var. of **archi–.**
–arch *suff.* Ruler; leader: *matriarch.* [ME *-arche* < OFr. < LLat. *-archa* < Lat. *-archēs* < Gk. *-arkhēs* < *arkhos*, ruler < *arkhein*, to rule.]
Ar•chae•an (är-kē′ən) *adj.* Var. of **Archean.**
archaeo– or **archeo–** *pref.* Ancient; earlier; primitive: *archaeopteryx.* [NLat. < Gk. *arkhaio-* < *arkhaios*, ancient. See ARCHAIC.]
ar•chae•ol•o•gy or **ar•che•ol•o•gy** (är′kē-ŏl′ə-jē) *n.* The study of material remains, such as graves, tools, and pottery, from past human life and culture. [Fr. *archéologie* < NLat. *archaeologia* < Gk. *arkhaiologia*, antiquarian lore : *arkhaio-*, archaeo- + *-logia*, -logy.] **—ar′chae•o•log′i•cal** (-ə-lŏj′ĭ-kəl), **ar′chae•o•log′ic** *adj.* **—ar′chae•ol′o•gist** *n.*
ar•chae•op•ter•yx (är′kē-ŏp′tər-ĭks) *n.* An extinct primitive bird (genus *Archaeopteryx*) of the Jurassic Period, having lizardlike characteristics, such as a long, bony tail. [NLat. : ARCHAEO– + Gk. *pterux*, bird, wing; see **pet-*.**]
Ar•chae•o•zo•ic (är′kē-ə-zō′ĭk) *adj. & n.* Var. of **Archeozoic.**
ar•cha•ic (är-kā′ĭk) also **ar•cha•i•cal** (-ĭ-kəl) *adj.* **1.** Of, relating to, or characteristic of a much earlier, often more primitive period. **2.** No longer current or applicable; antiquated. See Syns at **old. 3.** Of or characteristic of words and language that are used chiefly to suggest an earlier style or period. [Gk. *arkhaikos*, old-fashioned < *arkhaios*, ancient < *arkhē*, beginning < *arkhein*, to begin.] **—ar•cha′i•cal•ly** *adv.*
archaic smile *n.* A representation of the human mouth with slightly upturned corners, characteristic of early Greek sculpture.
ar•cha•ism (är′kē-ĭz′əm, -kā-) *n.* **1.** An archaic word, phrase, or other expression. **2.** An archaic style, quality, or usage. [NLat. *archaeismus* < Gk. *arkhaismos* < *arkhaios*, ancient. See ARCHAIC.] **—ar′cha•ist** *n.* **—ar′cha•is′tic** (-ĭs′tĭk) *adj.*
ar•cha•ize (är′kē-īz′, -kā-) *v.* **-ized, -iz•ing, -iz•es.** *—tr.* To give an archaic quality to; make archaic. *—intr.* To use archaisms in order to suggest the past. **—ar′cha•iz′er** *n.*
arch•an•gel (ärk′ān′jəl) *n.* **1.** A high-ranking angel. **2. archangels.** The eighth of the nine orders of spiritual beings in medieval angelology. [ME < OFr. *archangele* < LLat. *archangelus* < LGk. *arkhangelos*: Gk. *arkh-*, archi- + Gk. *angelos*, angel.] **—arch′an•gel′ic** (-ăn-jĕl′ĭk) *adj.*
Arch•an•gel (ärk′ān′jəl). See **Arkhangelsk.**
arch•bish•op (ärch-bĭsh′əp) *n.* A bishop of the highest rank, heading an archdiocese or a province. [ME *archebishop* < OE *arcebisceop* < LLat. *archiepiscopus* < LGk. *arkhiepiskopos*: Gk. *arkhi-*, archi- + LGk. *episkopos*, bishop; see BISHOP.]
arch•bish•op•ric (ärch-bĭsh′əp-rĭk) *n.* **1.** The rank, office, or term of an archbishop. **2.** The area under an archbishop's jurisdiction; an archdiocese.
Archbp. *abbr.* Archbishop.
arch•con•ser•va•tive (ärch′kən-sûr′və-tĭv) *adj.* Highly conservative, esp. politically. **—arch′con•ser′va•tive** *n.*
arch•dea•con (ärch-dē′kən) *n.* A church official with powers delegated from a bishop. [ME *archedeken* < OE *arcediakon* < LLat. *archidiāconus* < LGk. *arkhidiakonos*: Gk. *arkhi-*, archi- + LGk. *diakonos*, deacon.] **—arch•dea′con•ate** (-kə-nĭt) *n.* **—arch•dea′con•ship′** *n.*
arch•dea•con•ry (ärch-dē′kən-rē) *n., pl.* **-ries. 1.** The rank or office of an archdeacon. **2.** The district or residence of an archdeacon.
arch•di•o•cese (ärch-dī′ə-sĭs, -sēs′, -sēz′) *n.* The district under an archbishop's jurisdiction. **—arch′di•oc′e•san** (-ŏs′ĭ-sən) *adj.*
arch•du•cal (ärch-do͞o′kəl, -dyo͞o′-) *adj.* Of or having to do with an archduke or an archduchy. [Fr. *archiducal* < *archiduc*, archduke. See ARCHDUKE.]
arch•duch•ess (ärch-dŭch′ĭs) *n.* **1.** The wife or widow of an archduke. **2.** A woman holding an archduchy in her own right. **3.** Used as a title for such a noblewoman. [Fr. *archiduchesse*, fem. of *archiduc*, archduke. See ARCHDUKE.]
arch•duch•y (ärch-dŭch′ē) *n., pl.* **-ies.** The territory over which an archduke or an archduchess has authority. [Fr. *archiduché* < obsolete Fr. *archeduché*: *arche-*, arch- + *duché*, duchy; see DUCHY.]
arch•duke (ärch-do͞ok′, -dyo͞ok′) *n.* **1.** In certain royal families, a nobleman having a rank equivalent to that of a sovereign prince. **2.** Used as a title for such a nobleman. [Obsolete Fr. *archeduc*: *arche-*, arch- + *duc*, duke; see DUKE.]
Ar•che•an also **Ar•chae•an** (är-kē′ən) *adj.* Of or relating to the oldest known rocks, those of the Precambrian. [< Gk. *arkhaios*, ancient. See ARCHAIC.]
arched (ärcht) *adj.* **1.** Forming an arch or a curve like that of an arch. **2.** Provided, made, or covered with an arch.
ar•che•go•ni•um (är′kĭ-gō′nē-əm) *n., pl.* **-ni•a** (-nē-ə). An egg-producing organ occurring in mosses, ferns, and most gymnosperms. [NLat. < Gk. *arkhegonos*, original : *arkhe-*, *arkhi-*, archi- + *gonos*, offspring; see **genə-*.**] **—ar′che•go′ni•al** *adj.* **—ar′che•go′ni•ate** (-ĭt) *adj.*

arch•en•ceph•a•lon (är′kĕn-sĕf′ə-lŏn′) *n.* The part of the embryonic brain from which the forebrain and midbrain develop.

arch•en•e•my (ärch-ĕn′ə-mē) *n.* **1.** A principal enemy. **2.** Often **Archenemy.** *Theol.* The Devil; Satan. Used with *the.*

ar•chen•ter•on (är-kĕn′tə-rŏn′, -tər-ən) *n.* The central cavity of the gastrula. —**ar′chen•ter′ic** (är′kĕn-tĕr′ĭk) *adj.*

archeo– *pref.* Var. of **archaeo–.**

ar•che•ol•o•gy (är′kē-ŏl′ə-jē) *n.* Var. of **archaeology.**

Ar•che•o•zo•ic also **Ar•chae•o•zo•ic** (är′kē-ə-zō′ĭk) —*adj.* Of or relating to the earlier of two divisions of the Precambrian Era. —*n.* The Archeozoic Era.

arch•er (är′chər) *n.* One that shoots with a bow and arrow. [ME < OFr. *archier* < LLat. *arcārius,* alteration of *arcuārius,* maker of bows < Lat. *arcus,* bow.]

Arch•er (är′chər) *n.* See **Sagittarius.**

arch•er•fish (är′chər-fĭsh′) *n., pl.* **archerfish** or **-fish•es.** Any of various freshwater fishes of the family Toxotidae that spit at insects and prey on those knocked into the water.

arch•er•y (är′chə-rē) *n.* **1.** The art, sport, or skill of shooting with a bow and arrow. **2.** The equipment of an archer. **3.** A group of archers.

ar•che•type (är′kĭ-tīp′) *n.* **1.** An original model or type after which other similar things are patterned; a prototype. **2.** An ideal example of a type; quintessence. [Lat. *archetypum* < Gk. *arkhetupon* < neut. of *arkhetupos,* original : *arkhe-, arkhi-,* archi- + *tupos,* model, stamp.] —**ar′che•typ′al** (-tī′pəl), **ar′che•typ′ic** (-tĭp′ĭk), **ar′che•typ′i•cal** *adj.* —**ar′che•typ′i•cal•ly** *adv.*

arch•fiend (ärch-fēnd′) *n.* **1.** A principal fiend. **2. Archfiend.** *Theol.* The Devil; Satan. Used with *the.*

archi– or **arch–** *pref.* **1.** Chief; highest; most important: *archiepiscopal.* **2.** Earlier; primitive: *archenteron.* [Fr. *archi-* and Ital. *arci-,* both < Lat. *archi-* < Gk. *arkhi-, arkh-* < *arkhein,* to begin, rule.]

ar•chi•di•ac•o•nal (är′kĭ-dī-ăk′ə-nəl) *adj.* Of or having to do with an archdeacon or an archdeacon's office. [ME < LLat. *archidiāconus,* archdeacon. See ARCHDEACON.]

ar•chi•di•ac•o•nate (är′kĭ-dī-ăk′ə-nĭt) *n.* The office or position of an archdeacon. [Med.Lat. *archidiāconātus* < LLat. *archidiāconus,* archdeacon. See ARCHDEACON.]

ar•chi•e•pis•co•pal (är′kē-ĭ-pĭs′kə-pəl) *adj.* Of or having to do with an archbishop or an archbishopric. [Med.Lat. *archiepiscopālis* < LLat. *archiepiscopus,* archbishop. See ARCHBISHOP.] —**ar′chi•e•pis′co•pal′i•ty** (-păl′ĭ-tē) *n.* —**ar′chi•e•pis′co•pal•ly** *adv.* —**ar′chi•e•pis′co•pate** *n.*

ar•chil (är′kĭl, -chĭl) *n.* Var. of **orchil.**

ar•chi•man•drite (är′kə-măn′drīt′) *n. Eastern Orthodox Ch.* **1.** A cleric ranking below a bishop. **2.** The head of a monastery or a group of monasteries. [LLat. *archimandrīta* < LGk. *arkhimandritēs*: Gk. *arkhi-,* archi- + LGk. *mandra,* monastery (< Gk., cattle pen).]

Archimedean screw *n.* An ancient apparatus for raising water, consisting of either an inclined spiral tube or a broad-threaded screw.

Ar•chi•me•des (är′kə-mē′dēz). 287?–212 B.C. Greek mathematician, engineer, and physicist, one of the most important intellectual figures of antiquity. —**Ar′chi•me′de•an** (-mē′dē-ən, -mĭ-dē′-) *adj.*

Ar•chi•me•des' screw (är′kə-mē′dēz) *n.* See **Archimedean screw.**

ar•chine also **ar•shin** (är-shēn′) *n.* A unit of length formerly used in Russia and Turkey, equal to about 71 centimeters (28 inches). [Russ. *arshin* < Tatar *arshyn,* an ell; akin to Turk. *arşin,* of Pers. orig.]

ar•chi•pel•a•go (är′kə-pĕl′ə-gō′) *n., pl.* **-goes** or **-gos. 1.** A large group of islands. **2.** A sea containing many scattered islands. [Ital. *Arcipelago,* the Aegean Sea : *arci-* (< Gk. *arkhi-,* archi-) + Ital. *pelago,* sea (< Lat. *pelagus* < Gk. *pelagos,* sea; see **plāk-**[1]***.**)] —**ar′chi•pe•lag′ic** (-pə-lăj′ĭk) *adj.*

Ar•chi•pen•ko (är′kə-pĕng′kō), **Alexander Porfirievich.** 1887–1964. Russian-born Amer. sculptor noted for his cubist works.

archit. *abbr.* Architecture.

ar•chi•tect (är′kĭ-tĕkt′) *n.* **1.** One who designs and supervises the construction of buildings or other large structures. **2.** One that plans or devises: *the chief architect of war.* [Lat. *architectus* < Gk. *arkhitektōn*: *arkhi-,* archi- + *tektōn,* builder; see **teks-*.**]

ar•chi•tec•ton•ic (är′kĭ-tĕk-tŏn′ĭk) also **ar•chi•tec•ton•i•cal** (-ĭ-kəl) *adj.* **1.** Of or relating to architecture or design. **2.** Having qualities, such as design and structure, that are characteristic of architecture. **3.** *Philos.* Of or relating to the scientific systematization of knowledge. [Lat. *architectonicus,* architectural < Gk. *arkhitektonikos* < *arkhitektōn,* architect. See ARCHITECT.] —**ar′chi•tec•ton′i•cal•ly** *adv.*

ar•chi•tec•ton•ics (är′kĭ-tĕk-tŏn′ĭks) *n.* (*used with a sing. v.*) **1.** The science of architecture. **2.** Structural design: *the architectonics of a fugue.* **3.** *Philos.* The systematization of knowledge.

ar•chi•tec•ture (är′kĭ-tĕk′chər) *n.* **1.** The art and science of designing and erecting buildings. **2.** Buildings and other large structures: *brick-and-adobe architecture.* **3.** A style and method of design and construction: *Byzantine architecture.* **4.** Orderly arrangement of parts; structure: *computer architecture.* [Lat. *architectūra* < *architectus,* architect. See ARCHITECT.] —**ar′chi•tec′tur•al** *adj.* —**ar′chi•tec′tur•al•ly** *adv.*

ar•chi•trave (är′kĭ-trāv′) *n.* **1.** The lowermost part of an entablature in classical architecture. **2.** The molding around a door or window. [Fr. < OFr. < OItal. : *archi-,* archi- + *trave,* beam (< Lat. *trabs, trab-*; see **treb-***).]

ar•chi•val (är-kī′vəl) *adj.* Of, relating to, kept in, or suitable for archives.

ar•chive (är′kīv′) *n.* **1.** A place or collection containing records, documents, or other materials of historical interest. Often used in the plural. **2.** A repository for memories or information: *the archive of the mind.* [< Fr. *archives* < Lat. *archīva* < Gk. *arkheia,* pl. of *arkheion,* town hall < *arkhē,* government < *arkhein,* to rule.] —**ar′chive′** *v.*

ar•chi•vist (är′kə-vĭst, -kī′-) *n.* One who is in charge of archives.

ar•chi•volt (är′kə-vōlt′) *n. Archit.* A decorative molding carried around an arched wall opening. [Fr. *archivolte*or Ital. *archivolto* (Fr. < Ital.) : *arco,* arch (< Lat. *arcus*) + *volta,* vault (< Lat. *volūta*; see VAULT[1]).]

arch•lib•er•al (ärch′lĭb′ər-əl, -lĭb′rəl) *adj.* Highly liberal, esp. politically. —**arch′lib′er•al** *n.*

ar•chon (är′kŏn′, -kən) *n.* **1.** A high official; a ruler. **2.** One of the nine principal magistrates of ancient Athens. **3.** An authoritative figure; a leader. [Lat. *archōn* < Gk. *arkhōn* < pr.part. of *arkhein,* to rule.] —**ar′chon•ship′** *n.*

arch•priest (ärch′prēst′) *n. Rom. Cath. Ch.* **1.a.** Used formerly as a title for a priest holding first rank among the members of a cathedral chapter. **b.** An honorific title applied to a priest. **2.** *Eastern Orthodox Ch.* The highest rank a married priest can hold. [ME *archeprest* < OFr. *archeprestre* < LLat. *archipresbyter* < LGk. *arkhipresbuteros*: Gk. *arkhi-,* archi- + LGk. *presbuteros,* priest; see PRESBYTER.]

arch•ri•val (ärch′rī′vəl) *n.* A principal rival.

archt. *abbr.* Architect.

arch•way (ärch′wā′) *n.* **1.** A passageway under an arch. **2.** An arch over an entrance or a passageway.

–archy *suff.* Rule; government: *oligarchy.* [< words such as (MON)ARCHY.]

ar•ci•form (är′sə-fôrm′) *adj.* Formed in the shape of an arc. [Lat. *arci-*(< *arcus,* bow) + -FORM.]

arcked (ärkt) *v.* A p.t. and p.part. of **arc.**

arck•ing (är′kĭng) *v.* A pr.part. of **arc.**

arc lamp *n.* An electric light in which a current traverses a gas between two electrodes and generates an arc that produces light.

arc secant *n. Math.* The inverse function of the secant.

arc sine *n. Math.* The inverse function of the sine.

arc tangent *n. Math.* The inverse function of the tangent.

arc•tic (ärk′tĭk, är′tĭk) *adj.* Extremely cold; frigid. See Syns at **cold.** —*n.* A warm, waterproof overshoe. [Alteration (influenced by Lat. *arcticus*) of ME *artic,* northern < Med.Lat. *articus* < Lat. *arcticus* < Gk. *arktikos* < *arktos,* bear, the northern constellation Ursa Major. See **r̥tko-*.**]

Arc•tic (ärk′tĭk, är′tĭk). A region between the North Pole and the N timberlines of North America and Eurasia. —**Arc′tic** *adj.*

Arctic Archipelago. A group of more than 50 large islands of Northwest Terrs., Canada, in the Arctic Ocean.

arctic char *n.* A char *(Salvelinus alpinus)* native to the fresh waters of Alaska and northern Canada.

Arctic Circle. The parallel of latitude approx. 66°33′ N that forms the boundary between the North Temperate and North Frigid zones.

arctic fox *n.* A fox *(Alopex lagopus)* of Arctic regions, having fur that is white or light gray in winter and brown or blue-gray in summer.

Arctic Ocean. The waters surrounding the North Pole between North America and Eurasia; covered year-round by pack ice.

Arctic Red River (rĕd). A river rising in W Northwest Terrs., Canada, and flowing c. 499 km (310 mi) to the Mackenzie R.

arctic tern *n.* A tern *(Sterna paradisaea)* that typically migrates from the Arctic to the Antarctic and back each year.

Arc•tu•rus (ärk-to͝or′əs, -tyo͝or′-) *n.* The fourth-brightest star in the sky and the brightest in the constellation Boötes. [ME < Lat. *Arctūrus* < Gk. *Arktouros*: *arktos,* bear; see **r̥tko-*** + *ouros,* guard, from its position behind Ursa Major; see **wer-**[3]***.**]

ar•cu•ate (är′kyo͞o-ĭt, -āt′) also **ar•cu•at•ed** (-ā′tĭd) *adj.* Having the form of a bow; curved. [Lat. *arcuātus,* p.part. of *arcuāre,* to bend like a bow < *arcus,* bow.] —**ar′cu•ate•ly** *adv.*

ar•cu•a•tion (är′kyo͞o-ā′shən) *n.* **1.** The process of curving or the condition of being curved. **2.** The use of arches or vaults in building.

–ard or **–art** *suff.* One that habitually or excessively is in a specified condition or performs a specified action: *drunkard.* [ME < OFr., of Gmc. orig. See **kar-*.**]

ar•deb (är′dĕb′) *n.* A unit of dry measure in the Middle East,

archery

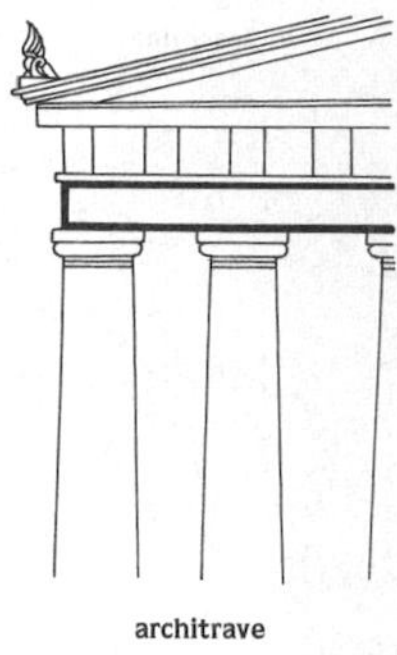

architrave

arctic fox
Alopex lagopus

ă pat	oi boy
ā pay	ou out
âr care	o͝o took
ä father	o͞o boot
ĕ pet	ŭ cut
ē be	ûr urge
ĭ pit	th thin
ī pie	*th* this
îr pier	hw which
ŏ pot	zh vision
ō toe	ə about, item
ô paw	

Stress marks:
′ (primary);
′ (secondary), as in **dictionary** (dĭk′shə-nĕr′ē)

standardized in Egypt to equal 198 liters (5.62 U.S. bushels). [Ar. dial. *'ardabb* < Aram. *'rdbor* < Coptic *artabor* < Gk. *artabē*, all prob. of OPers. orig.]

Ar•den (är′dn), **Elizabeth.** 1884?–1966. Canadian-born Amer. business executive whose original beauty salon was founded in 1910.

Arden, Forest of. A wooded area of central England W of Stratford-upon-Avon; setting for Shakespeare's *As You Like It.*

Ar•dennes (är-dĕn′). A plateau region of N France, SE Belgium, and N Luxembourg; site of heavy fighting in World War I and World War II.

ar•dent (är′dnt) *adj.* **1.** Expressing or characterized by warmth of feeling; passionate. **2.** Displaying or characterized by strong enthusiasm or devotion; fervent. **3.a.** Burning; fiery. **b.** Glowing; shining: *ardent eyes.* [ME *ardaunt* < OFr. *ardant* < Lat. *ārdēns, ārdent-*, pr.part. of *ārdēre*, to burn. See **as-***.] **—ar′den•cy** (-dn-sē) *n.* **—ar′dent•ly** *adv.*

ardent spirits *pl.n.* Strong alcoholic liquors.

Ard•more (ärd′môr, -mōr). A city of S OK SSE of Oklahoma City. Pop. 23,079.

ar•dor (är′dər) *n.* **1.** Fiery intensity of feeling. **2.** Strong enthusiasm or devotion; zeal. **3.** Intense heat or glow. [ME *ardour* < OFr. < Lat. *ārdor* < *ārdēre*, to burn. See **as-***.]

ar•dour (är′dər) *n. Chiefly British.* Var. of **ardor.**

ar•du•ous (är′jo͞o-əs) *adj.* **1.** Demanding great effort or labor; difficult: *"the arduous work of preparing a Dictionary of the English Language"* (Macaulay). **2.** Testing severely the powers of endurance; strenuous: *an arduous war.* **3.** Hard to traverse, climb, or surmount. [< Lat. *arduus*, high, steep.] **—ar′du•ous•ly** *adv.* **—ar′du•ous•ness** *n.*

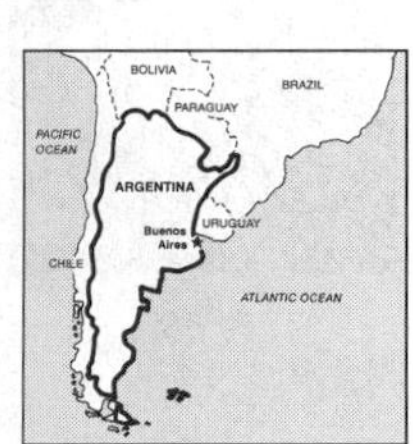

Argentina

are[1] (är) *v.* Second pers. sing. and pl. and first and third pers. pl. pr. indic. of **be.** [ME *aren* < OE *aron.* See **er-**[1]*.]

are[2] (âr, är) also **ar** (är) *n.* A metric unit of area equal to 100 square meters (119.6 square yards). [Fr. < Lat. *ārea*, open space. See AREA.]

ar•e•a (âr′ē-ə) *n.* **1.** A roughly bounded part of a surface; a region: *the New York area.* **2.** A surface, esp. an open, unoccupied piece of ground: *a landing area.* **3.** A distinct part or section set aside for a specific function: *a storage area.* **4.** A division of experience, activity, or knowledge; a field: *the area of finance.* **5.** An open, sunken space next to a building; an areaway. **6.** The extent of a planar region or of the surface of a solid measured in square units. **7.** *Comp. Sci.* A section of storage set aside for a particular purpose. [Lat. *ārea*, open space; poss. akin to *ārēre*, to be dry. See ARID.]

Ar•e•a Code (âr′ē-ə) also **area code** *n.* A number, usu. three-digit, used when calling its assigned telephone area.

ar•e•a•way (âr′ē-ə-wā′) *n.* **1.** A small, sunken area allowing access or light and air to basement doors or windows. **2.** An often narrow passageway between buildings.

a•re•ca (ə-rē′kə, ăr′ĭ-kə) *n.* Any of certain tropical Old World palms, such as those in the genus *Areca.* [Port. < Malayalam *aṭekka*, areca nut < Tamil *aṭaikkāy.*]

areca nut *n.* See **betel nut.**

A•re•ci•bo (ä′rə-sē′bō). A city of N Puerto Rico on the Atlantic Ocean. Pop. 48,779.

a•re•na (ə-rē′nə) *n.* **1.** A large modern building for the presentation of sports events and spectacles. **2.** A place or scene where forces contend or events unfold: *the political arena.* **3.** The area in the center of an ancient Roman amphitheater where contests and other spectacles were held. [Lat. *harēna, arēna*, sand, a sand-strewn place of combat in an amphitheater, perh. of Etruscan orig.]

ar•e•na•ceous (ăr′ə-nā′shəs) *adj.* **1.** Resembling, derived from, or containing sand. **2.** Growing in sandy areas. [< Lat. *harēnāceus, arēnāceus*: *harēna, arēna*, sand; see ARENA + *-āceus*, -aceous.]

arena theater *n.* A theater in which the stage is at the center of the auditorium and is surrounded by seats.

A•rendt (âr′ənt, är′-), **Hannah.** 1906–75. German-born Amer. historian whose works include *The Origins of Totalitarianism* (1951).

aren't (ärnt, är′ənt). Are not. See Usage Note at **ain't.**

a•re•o•la (ə-rē′ə-lə) also **ar•e•ole** (âr′ē-ōl′) *n., pl.* **-lae** (-lē′) or **-las** also **-oles** (-ōlz′). **1. areole.** *Biol.* A small space or interstice in a tissue or part. **2.** *Anat.* A small ring of color around a center portion, as about the nipple of the breast. [Lat. *āreola*, small open space, dim. of *ārea*, open place. See AREA.] **—a•re′o•lar, a•re′o•late** (-lĭt) *adj.* **—a•re′o•la′tion** *n.*

Ar•e•op•a•gite (ăr′ē-ŏp′ə-jīt′, -gīt′) *n.* A member of the Areopagus. **—Ar′e•op•a•git′ic** (-jĭt′ĭk, gĭt′-) *adj.*

Ar•e•op•a•gus (ăr′ē-ŏp′ə-gəs) *n.* The highest judicial and legislative council of ancient Athens. [Lat. < Gk. *Areios pagos*, Areopagus, hill of Ares (where the tribunal met) : *Areios*, of Ares (< *Arēs*, Ares) + *pagos*, stiff mass, hill (< *pēgnunai, pag-*, to stick, stiffen; see **pag-***).]

A•re•qui•pa (ăr′ə-kē′pə, ä′rĕ-kē′pä). A city of S Peru at the foot of El Misti; founded 1540. Pop. 108,023.

Ar•es (âr′ēz) *n. Gk. Myth.* The god of war.

a•rête (ə-rāt′) *n.* A sharp, narrow mountain ridge or spur. [Fr. < OFr. *areste*, fishbone, spine < LLat. *arista*, awn, fishbone < Lat., awn.]

ar•e•thu•sa (ăr′ə-tho͞o-zə, -sə) *n.* See **swamp pink.** [< Lat., a wood nymph < Gk. *Arethousa.*]

A•re•ti•no (ăr′ə-tē′nō, är′-), **Pietro.** 1492–1556. Italian writer and satirist best known for his six volumes of letters.

A•rez•zo (ä-rĕt′sō). A city of central Italy on the Arno R. SE of Florence; orig. an Etruscan settlement. Pop. 91,535.

arg. *abbr. Her.* Argent.

Arg. *abbr.* **1.** Argentina. **2.** Argentine.

ar•gal (är′gəl) *n.* Var. of **argol.**

ar•ga•li (är′gə-lē) *n., pl.* **argali** or **-lis.** A wild sheep *(Ovis ammon)* of central and northern Asia having large, spirally curved horns. [Mongolian, mountain ewe.]

ar•gent (är′jənt) *n.* **1.** *Her.* The metal silver, represented by the color white. **2.** *Archaic.* Silver or something resembling it. [ME < OFr. < Lat. *argentum*, silver. See **arg-***.]

Ar•gen•teuil (är-zhäN-tœ′yə). A city of N France, a suburb of Paris on the Seine R. Pop. 95,347.

ar•gen•tic (är-jĕn′tĭk) *adj.* Of or containing silver.

ar•gen•tif•er•ous (är′jən-tĭf′ər-əs) *adj.* Bearing or producing silver.

Ar•gen•ti•na (är′jən-tē′nə). A country of SE South America extending from Bolivia to Tierra del Fuego, an island it shares with Chile; proclaimed its independence from Spain in 1816. Cap. Buenos Aires. Pop. 27,947,446. **—Ar′gen•tine′** (-tēn′, -tīn′), **Ar′gen•tin′e•an** (-tĭn′ē-ən) *adj. & n.*

ar•gen•tine (är′jən-tīn′, -tēn′) *adj.* Relating to or resembling silver; silvery. —*n.* **1.** Silver. **2.** Any of various silvery metals. [ME < OFr. *argentin* < Lat. *argentīnus* < *argentum*, silver. See **arg-***.]

ar•gen•tite (är′jən-tīt′) *n.* A valuable silver ore, Ag_2S, with a lead-gray color and metallic luster.

ar•gil (är′jĭl) *n.* Clay, esp. a white clay used by potters. [ME *argilla* < Lat. < Gk. *argillos.* See **arg-***.]

ar•gil•la•ceous (är′jə-lā′shəs) *adj.* Containing, made of, or resembling clay; clayey. [< Lat. *argillāceus*: *argilla*, argil; see ARGIL + *-āceus*, -aceous.]

ar•gil•lite (är′jə-līt′) *n.* A metamorphic rock, intermediate in structure between shale and slate. [Lat. *argilla*, argil; see ARGIL + -ITE[1].]

ar•gi•nase (är′jə-nās′, -nāz) *n.* An enzyme found primarily in the liver that catalyzes the hydrolysis of arginine to form urea and ornithine. [< Ger. *Arginin*, arginine. See ARGININE.]

ar•gi•nine (är′jə-nēn′) *n.* An amino acid, $C_6H_{14}N_4O_2$, obtained from plant and animal protein. [Ger. *Arginin*, poss. < Gk. *arginoeis*, bright. See **arg-***.]

Ar•give (är′jīv′, -gīv′) *adj.* **1.** Of or relating to Argos or Argolis. **2.** Of or relating to Greece or the Greeks. —*n.* A Greek, esp. an inhabitant of Argos or Argolis. [Lat. *Argīvus* < Gk. *Argeios* < ARGOS.]

Ar•go (är′gō′) *n.* **1.** *Gk. Myth.* The ship in which Jason sailed in search of the Golden Fleece. **2.** Formerly, a constellation in the Southern Hemisphere, now divided into the constellations Carina, Puppis, Pyxis, and Vela. [Lat. *Argō* < Gk.]

ar•gol (är′gôl′) also **ar•gal** (-gəl) *n.* Crude potassium bitartrate, a byproduct of winemaking. [ME *argoile* < AN *argoil*, ult. < Lat. *argilla*, clay. See ARGIL.]

Ar•go•lis (är′gə-lĭs). An ancient region of S Greece in the E Peloponnesus on the **Gulf of Argolis**, an inlet of the Aegean Sea.

ar•gon (är′gŏn′) *n. Symbol* **Ar** A colorless, inert gaseous element constituting approx. one percent of Earth's atmosphere, used in electric bulbs and fluorescent tubes and as an inert gas shield in arc welding. Atomic number 18; atomic weight 39.948; melting point −189.2°C; boiling point −185.7°C. See table at **element.** [< Gk., neut. of *argos*, idle, inert : *a-*, without; see A-[1] + *ergon*, work; see **werg-***.]

ar•go•naut (är′gə-nôt′) *n.* See **paper nautilus.** [Lat. *Argonauta*, Argonaut. See ARGONAUT.]

Ar•go•naut (är′gə-nôt′) *n.* **1.** *Gk. Myth.* One who sailed with Jason on the *Argo* in search of the Golden Fleece. **2.** Also **argonaut.** A person who is engaged in a dangerous but rewarding quest; an adventurer. [Lat. *Argonauta* < Gk. *Argonautēs*: *Argō*, the ship Argo + *nautēs*, sailor (< *naus*, ship; see **nāu-***).]

Ar•gonne (är-gŏn′, är′gŏn). A wooded region of NE France between the Meuse and Aisne rivers; site of major battles during World War I and World War II.

Ar•gos (är′gŏs, -gəs). A city of ancient Greece in the E Peloponnesus near the head of the Gulf of Argolis; inhabited since the early Bronze Age.

ar•go•sy (är′gə-sē) *n., pl.* **-sies. 1.** *Naut.* **a.** A large merchant ship. **b.** A fleet of ships. **2.** A rich source or supply: *an argosy of adventure lore.* [Alteration of obsolete *ragusye* < Ital. *ragusea*, vessel of Ragusa (Dubrovnik).]

ar•got (är′gō, -gət) *n.* A specialized vocabulary or set of idioms used by a particular group: *thieves' argot.* [Fr.]

ar•gu•a•ble (är′gyo͞o-ə-bəl) *adj.* **1.** Open to argument: *an arguable question.* **2.** That can be argued plausibly; defensible in argument: *arguable points of law.* **—ar′gu•a•bly** *adv.*

ar•gue (är′gyo͞o) *v.* **-gued, -gu•ing, -gues.** —*tr.* **1.** To put forth reasons for or against; debate. **2.** To attempt to prove by reasoning; maintain or contend. **3.** To give evidence of; indicate: *"Similarities cannot always be used to argue descent"* (Isaac Asimov). **4.** To persuade or influence (another), as by presenting reasons. —*intr.* **1.** To put forth reasons for or against something: *argued for dismissal of the case.* **2.** To engage in a quarrel; dispute. [ME *arguen* < OFr. *arguer* < Lat. *argūtāre*, to babble, chatter, freq. of *arguere*, to make clear. See **arg-***.] —**ar′gu·er** *n.*

ar·gu·fy (är′gyə-fī′) *v.* **-fied, -fy·ing, -fies.** —*tr.* To dispute (a point). —*intr.* To argue aimlessly; wrangle. See Regional Note at **absquatulate.** —**ar′gu·fi′er** *n.*

ar·gu·ment (är′gyə-mənt) *n.* **1.a.** A discussion in which disagreement is expressed; a debate. **b.** A quarrel; a dispute. **c.** *Archaic.* A reason or matter for dispute or contention: *"sheath'd their swords for lack of argument"* (Shakespeare). **2.a.** A course of reasoning aimed at demonstrating truth or falsehood. **b.** A fact or statement put forth as proof or evidence; a reason: *an argument for buying a house.* **3.a.** A summary or short statement of the plot or subject of a literary work. **b.** A topic; a subject. **4.** *Logic.* The minor premise in a syllogism. **5.** *Math.* **a.** The independent variable of a function. **b.** The amplitude of a complex number. **6.** *Comp. Sci.* A value used to evaluate a procedure or subroutine. [ME < OFr. < Lat. *argūmentum* < *arguere*, to make clear. See ARGUE.]

ar·gu·men·ta·tion (är′gyə-měn-tā′shən) *n.* **1.** The presentation and elaboration of an argument or arguments. **2.** Deductive reasoning in debate. **3.** A debate.

ar·gu·men·ta·tive (är′gyə-měn′tə-tĭv) *adj.* **1.** Given to arguing; disputatious. **2.** Of or marked by argument. —**ar′gu·men′ta·tive·ly** *adv.* —**ar′gu·men′ta·tive·ness** *n.*

Syns: *argumentative, combative, contentious, disputatious, quarrelsome, scrappy.* The central meaning shared by these adjectives is "given to or fond of arguing": *an argumentative child; combative impulses; a contentious mood; a disputatious lawyer; a quarrelsome boy; a scrappy litigator.*

ar·gu·men·tum (är′gyə-měn′təm) *n., pl.* **-ta** (-tə). *Logic.* An argument, demonstration, or appeal to reason. [Lat. *argūmentum.* See ARGUMENT.]

Ar·gun River (är-go͞on′) also **Er·gun He** (ĕr′go͞on′ hĕ′, œr′-gün′ hə′). A river of E-central Asia rising in NE China and flowing c. 1,529 km (950 mi) along the Russia-China border.

Ar·gus (är′gəs) *n.* **1.** *Gk. Myth.* A giant with 100 eyes who was made guardian of Io and was later slain by Hermes. **2.** An alert or watchful person; a guardian. [Lat. < Gk. *Argos.*]

Ar·gus-eyed (är′gəs-īd′) *adj.* Extremely observant; vigilant.

ar·gus pheasant (är′gəs) *n.* A large bird *(Argusianus argus)* of southeast Asia having tail feathers with eyelike spots. [After ARGUS, whose hundred eyes were given to a peacock's tail.]

ar·gy-bar·gy (är′gē-bär′gē) *n., pl.* **-gies.** *Chiefly British.* A lively or disputatious discussion. [Sc., redup. of *argie*, argument < ARGUE.]

ar·gyle also **ar·gyll** (är′gīl′) *n.* **1.** A knitting pattern of varicolored diamond shapes on a solid background. **2.** A sock knit in this pattern. [After Clan Campbell of *Argyle, Argyll*, a former county of W Scotland, originally from the pattern of their tartan.]

ar·hat (är′hət) *n. Buddhism.* In Hinayana, one who has attained enlightenment. [Skt. < pr.part. of *arhati*, he deserves.] —**ar′hat·ship′** *n.*

År·hus also **Aar·hus** (ôr′ho͞os′). A city of central Denmark on **Århus Bay,** an arm of the Kattegat. Pop. 250,404.

a·ri·a (ä′rē-ə) *n. Mus.* **1.** A solo vocal piece with instrumental accompaniment, as in an opera. **2.** An air; a melody. [Ital. < Lat. *āera*, accusative of *āēr*, air < Gk. *aēr.* See **wer-**[1]*.]

Ar·i·ad·ne (ăr′ē-ăd′nē) *n. Gk. Myth.* The daughter of Minos and Pasiphaë who gave Theseus the thread with which he found his way out of the Minotaur's labyrinth.

Ar·i·an[1] (âr′ē-ən, ăr′-) *adj.* **1.** Of or relating to Arianism. **2.** Of or relating to Arius. —*n.* A believer in Arianism.

Ar·i·an[2] (ăr′ē-ən, âr′-) *n.* One who is born under the sign of Aries. —**Ar′i·an** *adj.*

-arian *suff.* Believer in; advocate of: *utilitarian.* [Lat. *-ārius*, -ary + -AN[1].]

Ar·i·an·ism (âr′ē-ə-nĭz′əm, ăr′-) *n. Theol.* The doctrines of Arius, denying that Jesus was of the same substance as God and holding instead that he was only the highest of created beings.

A·ri·as San·chez (ä′rē-äs sän′chĕs), **Oscar.** b. 1941. Costa Rican politician who won the 1987 Nobel Peace Prize.

a·ri·bo·fla·vi·no·sis (ā-rī′bō-flā′və-nō′sĭs, -bə-) *n.* A condition caused by the dietary deficiency of riboflavin, characterized by mouth lesions and seborrhea.

A·ri·ca (ə-rē′kə, ä-rē′kä). A city of N Chile on the Pacific Ocean near the Peruvian border. Pop. 139,320.

ar·id (ăr′ĭd) *adj.* **1.** Lacking moisture, esp. having insufficient rainfall to support trees or woody plants. **2.** Lacking interest or feeling; lifeless and dull: *an arid performance.* [Lat. *āridus* < *ārēre*, to be dry. See **as-***.] —**a·rid′i·ty** (ə-rĭd′ĭ-tē), **ar′id·ness** *n.*

Ar·i·el (âr′ē-əl) *n.* **1.** A mischievous spirit in Shakespeare's *Tempest.* **2.** A satellite of Uranus.

Ar·ies (âr′ēz, âr′ē-ēz′) *n.* **1.** A constellation in the Northern Hemisphere near Taurus and Pisces. **2.a.** The first sign of the zodiac in astrology. **b.** One who is born under this sign. [ME, zodiacal sign Aries < Lat. *ariēs*, ram, zodiacal sign Aries.]

a·ri·et·ta (ä′rē-ĕt′ə) also **a·ri·ette** (-ĕt′) *n. Mus.* A short aria. [Ital., dim. of *aria*, aria. See ARIA.]

a·right (ə-rīt′) *adv.* In a proper manner; correctly. [ME < OE *ariht*: *a-*, on; see A-[2] + *riht*, right; see RIGHT.]

A·rik·a·ra (ə-rĭk′ər-ə) *n., pl.* **Arikara** or **-ras. 1.** A member of a Native American people formerly inhabiting the Missouri River valley from Kansas into the Dakotas and now located in western North Dakota. **2.** The Caddoan language of the Arikara.

ar·il (ăr′əl) *n.* A fleshy, usu. brightly colored cover of a seed. [Med.Lat. *arillus*, grape seed.] —**ar′iled, ar′il·late′** (-lāt′, -lĭt) *adj.*

a·ri·o·so (ä′rē-ō′sō, -zō) *Mus.* —*n., pl.* **-sos. 1.a.** A declamatory style used in opera and oratorio, similar to recitative but more melodic. **b.** A passage rendered in this style. **2.** A usu. short vocal solo having the melodic style but not the form of an aria. —*adv. & adj.* In a melodic style like that of an aria. [Ital. < *aria*, aria. See ARIA.]

A·ri·os·to (är′ē-ŏs′tō, -ō′stō, ăr′-), **Ludovico** or **Lodovico.** 1474–1533. Italian writer best known for *Orlando Furioso* (1532).

a·rise (ə-rīz′) *intr.v.* **a·rose** (ə-rōz′), **a·ris·en** (ə-rĭz′ən), **a·ris·ing, a·ris·es. 1.** To get up, as from a sitting or prone position; rise. **2.** To move upward; ascend. **3.** To come into being; originate. **4.** To result, issue, or proceed. See Syns at **stem**[1]. [ME *arisen* < OE *ārīsan*: *ā-*, intensive pref. + *rīsan*, to rise.]

a·ris·ta (ə-rĭs′tə) *n., pl.* **-tae** (-tē) or **-tas.** A bristlelike part or appendage, such as the awn of grains and grasses. [Lat., beard of grain, spike.] —**a·ris′tate** (-tāt) *adj.*

Ar·is·tar·chus (ăr′ĭ-stär′kəs). 217?–145? B.C. Greek grammarian and critic.

Aristarchus of Sa·mos (sā′mŏs′, săm′ŏs′, sä′môs). fl. 270 B.C. Greek astronomer who was among the first to propose that the earth moves around the sun.

Ar·is·ti·des also **Ar·is·tei·des** (ăr′ĭ-stī′dēz). "the Just." 530?–468? B.C. Athenian statesman and general who fought at Marathon (490) and Salamis (480).

Ar·is·tip·pus of Cy·re·ne (ăr′ĭ-stĭp′əs; sī-rē′nē). 435?–366? B.C. Greek philosopher who founded the Cyrenaic school.

ar·is·toc·ra·cy (ăr′ĭ-stŏk′rə-sē) *n., pl.* **-cies. 1.** A hereditary ruling class; nobility. **2.a.** Government by a ruling class. **b.** A state or country having this form of government. **3.a.** Government by the citizens deemed to be best qualified to lead. **b.** A state having such a government. **4.** A group or class considered superior to others. [LLat. *aristocratia*, government by the best < Gk. *aristokratia*: *aristos*, best; see **ar-*** + *kratos*, power; see -CRACY.]

a·ris·to·crat (ə-rĭs′tə-krăt′, ăr′ĭs-) *n.* **1.** A member of a ruling class or of the nobility. **2.** A person having the tastes, manners, or other characteristics of the aristocracy. **3.** A person who advocates government by an aristocracy. **4.** One considered the best of its kind: *the aristocrat of cars.* [Fr. *aristocrate* < *aristocratie*, aristocracy < OFr. < LLat. *aristocratia.* See ARISTOCRACY.] —**a·ris′to·crat′ic, a·ris′to·crat′i·cal** *adj.* —**a·ris′to·crat′i·cal·ly** *adv.*

Ar·is·toph·a·nes (ăr′ĭ-stŏf′ə-nēz). 448?–388? B.C. Athenian playwright whose works include *Lysistrata* (411).

Ar·is·to·te·li·an also **Ar·is·to·te·le·an** (ăr′ĭ-stə-tē′lē-ən, -tēl′yən, ə-rĭs′tə-) —*adj.* Of or relating to Aristotle or to his philosophy. —*n.* **1.** A follower of Aristotle or his teachings. **2.** A person whose thinking and methods tend to be empirical, scientific, or commonsensical. —**Ar′is·to·te′li·an·ism** *n.*

Aristotelian logic *n.* **1.** Aristotle's deductive method of logic, esp. the theory of the syllogism. **2.** The formal logic based on Aristotle's and dealing with the relations between propositions in terms of their form instead of their content.

Ar·is·tot·le (ăr′ĭ-stŏt′l). 384–322 B.C. Greek philosopher who studied under Plato and tutored Alexander the Great.

a·rith·me·tic (ə-rĭth′mĭ-tĭk) *n.* **1.** The mathematics of integers, rational numbers, real numbers, or complex numbers under addition, subtraction, multiplication, and division. **2.** A book on arithmetic. [ME *arsmetike, arithmetic* < OFr. *arismetique* < LLat. *arismetica*, alteration of Lat. *arithmētica* < Gk. *arithmētikē (tekhnē)*, (the art) of counting < *arithmein*, to count < *arithmos*, number. See **ar-***.] —**ar′ith·met′ic** (ăr′ĭth-mĕt′ĭk), **ar′ith·met′i·cal** (-ĭ-kəl) *adj.* —**ar′ith·met′i·cal·ly** *adv.* —**a·rith′me·ti′cian** (-tĭsh′ən) *n.*

arithmetic mean *n. Math.* The value obtained by dividing the sum of a set of quantities by the number of those quantities.

arithmetic progression *n. Math.* A sequence in which each term is formed by adding a constant to the preceding term.

-arium *suff.* A place or device containing or associated with: *planetarium.* [Lat., neut. of *-ārius*, -ary.]

A·ri·us (ə-rī′əs, ăr′ē-, âr′-). A.D. 256?–336. Greek Christian

argyle

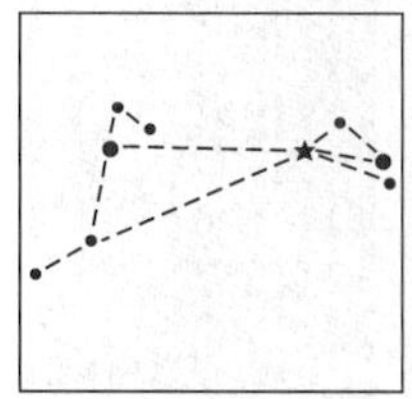
Aries

ă pat	oi boy
ā pay	ou out
âr care	o͝o took
ä father	o͞o boot
ĕ pet	ŭ cut
ē be	ûr urge
ĭ pit	th thin
ī pie	*th* this
îr pier	hw which
ŏ pot	zh vision
ō toe	ə about, item
ô paw	

Stress marks:
′ (primary);
′ (secondary), as in **dictionary** (dĭk′shə-nĕr′ē)

theologian and founder of Arianism who was condemned as a heretic.

Ariz. Arizona.

Ar•i•zo•na (ăr′ĭ-zō′nə). A state of the SW U.S. on the Mexican border; admitted as the 48th state in 1912. Cap. Phoenix. Pop. 3,677,985. **—Ar′i•zo′nan, Ar′i•zo′ni•an** *adj. & n.*

Ar•ju•na (är′jə-nə, -jo͞o-) *n. Hinduism.* The prince in the *Bhagavad-Gita* to whom Krishna expounds the nature of being and the way human beings can come to know God.

ark (ärk) *n.* **1.** Often **Ark.** *Bible.* The chest containing the Ten Commandments written on stone tablets, carried by the Hebrews during their desert wanderings. **2.** Often **Ark.** *Judaism.* The Holy Ark. **3.** *Bible.* The boat built by Noah for survival during the Flood. **4.** A shelter or refuge. [ME < OE *arc* < Gmc. **arca* < Lat. *arca*, chest.]

Ark. Arkansas.

Ar•kan•sas (är′kən-sô′). A state of the S-central U.S. on the Mississippi R.; admitted as the 25th state in 1836. Cap. Little Rock. Pop. 2,362,239. **—Ar•kan′san** (är-kăn′zən) *adj. & n.*

Ar•kan•sas River (är′kən-sô′, är-kăn′zəs). A river of the S-central U.S. rising in central CO and flowing c. 2,333 km (1,450 mi) to the Mississippi R. in SE AR.

Armenia^1

Ar•kan•sas stone (är′kən-sô′) *n.* A stone used for sharpening and grinding metals, esp. the metal blades of knives.

Ark•han•gelsk (är-kăn′gĕlsk, -KHän′-) or **Arch•an•gel** (ärk′ān′jəl). A city of NW Russia on the Northern Dvina R. near its mouth on the White Sea. Pop. 408,000.

Ark of the Covenant *n. Bible.* See **ark** 1.

Ark•wright (ärk′rīt′), Sir **Richard.** 1732–92. British inventor who patented a machine for spinning cotton thread (1769).

Ar•len (är′lən), **Harold.** 1905–86. Amer. composer whose songs include "Over the Rainbow."

Arlen, Michael. 1895–1956. Armenian-born British writer best known for his novel *The Green Hat* (1924).

Arles (ärlz, ärl). **1.** A medieval kingdom (933–1246) of E and SE France. **2.** A city of S-central France on the Rhone R. delta; founded in Roman times. Pop. 37,571.

Ar•ling•ton (är′lĭng-tən). **1.** A town of E MA, a suburb of Boston. Pop. 44,630. **2.** A city of N TX midway between Dallas and Fort Worth. Pop. 261,721. **3.** A county and unincorp. city of N VA across the Potomac R. from Washington DC; site of **Arlington National Cemetery,** where American war dead and other notables are buried. Pop. 170,936.

Arlington Heights. A village of NE IL, a suburb of Chicago. Pop. 75,460.

armoire
Early 18th-century French

arm^1 (ärm) *n.* **1.** An upper limb of the human body, connecting the hand and wrist to the shoulder. **2.** A part similar to a human arm, such as the projection from a central support in a machine. **3.** Something, such as a sleeve on a garment, that is designed to cover or support the human arm. **4.** A relatively narrow extension jutting out from a large mass: *an arm of the sea.* **5.** An administrative or functional branch. **6.** Power or authority: *the long arm of the law.* **—*idioms.* an arm and a leg.** *Slang.* An excessively high price. **at arm's length.** At such a distance that physical or social contact is discouraged: *kept the newcomer at arm's length.* **with open arms.** With great cordiality. [ME < OE *earm.* See **ar-*.**]

arm^2 (ärm) *n.* **1.** A weapon, esp. a firearm: *nuclear arms.* **2.** A branch of a military force. **3. arms. a.** Warfare: *a call to arms.* **b.** Military service: *volunteers under arms.* **4. arms. a.** *Her.* Bearings. **b.** Insignia, as of a state, an official, a family, or an organization. **—*v.* armed, arm•ing, arms. —*intr.*** **1.** To supply or equip oneself with weaponry. **2.** To prepare oneself for warfare or conflict. **—*tr.*** **1.** To equip with weapons. **2.** To equip with what is needed for effective action. **3.** To provide with something that strengthens or protects. **4.** To prepare (a weapon) for use or operation. **—*idiom.* up in arms.** Extremely upset; indignant. [< ME *armes*, weapons < OFr. < Lat. *arma.* V. < ME *armen* < OFr. *armer* < Lat. *armāre* < *arma*, arms. See **ar-*.**] **—arm′er** *n.*

Arm. *abbr.* Armenia; Armenian.

armor
16th-century German

ar•ma•da (är-mä′də, -mā′-) *n.* **1.** A fleet of warships. **2.** A large group of moving things. [Sp. < Med.Lat. *armāta.* See ARMY.]

ar•ma•dil•lo (är′mə-dĭl′ō) *n., pl.* **-los.** Any of several burrowing edentate mammals (family Dasypodidae) with armorlike bony plates, native to southern North America and South America. [Sp., dim. of *armado*, armored, p.part. of *armar*, to arm < Lat. *armāre* < *arma*, arms. See **ar-*.**]

Ar•ma•ged•don (är′mə-gĕd′n) *n.* **1.** *Bible.* The scene of a final battle between the forces of good and evil, prophesied to occur at the end of the world. **2.** A decisive or catastrophic conflict. [LLat. *Armagedōn* < Gk. < Heb. *har mĕgiddô, mĕgiddōn*, the mountain region of Megiddo.]

Ar•magh (är-mä′, är′mä′). An urban district of S Northern Ireland; reputedly founded by St. Patrick. Pop. 12,700.

Ar•ma•gnac^1 (är′mən-yăk′). A historical region of SW France; noted for its viniculture.

Ar•ma•gnac^2 (är′mən-yăk′) *n.* A dry brandy.

ar•ma•ment (är′mə-mənt) *n.* **1.** The weapons and supplies of war with which a military unit is equipped. **2.** All the military forces and war equipment of a country. Often used in the plural. **3.** A military force equipped for war. **4.** The process of arming for war. [Lat. *armāmenta*, tools < *arma*, arms. See ARM^2.]

ar•ma•men•tar•i•um (är′mə-mĕn-târ′ē-əm) *n., pl.* **-i•ums** or **-i•a** (-ē-ə). The complete equipment of a physician or medical institution, including books, supplies, and instruments. [Lat. *armāmentārium*, arsenal < *armāmenta*, tools. See ARMAMENT.]

ar•ma•ture (är′mə-cho͝or′, -chər) *n.* **1.** *Elect.* **a.** The rotating part of a dynamo. **b.** The moving part of an electromagnetic device such as a relay, buzzer, or loudspeaker. **c.** A piece of soft iron connecting the poles of a magnet. **2.** *Biol.* A protective covering, structure, or organ of an animal or a plant, such as the shell of a turtle. **3.** A framework serving as a supporting core for clay sculpture. [ME, armor < OFr. < Lat. *armātūra*, equipment < *armātus*, p.part. of *armāre*, to arm < *arma*, arms. See **ar-*.**]

arm•chair (ärm′châr′) *n.* A chair with side structures to support the arms. **—*adj.*** Remote from active involvement.

armed forces (ärmd) *pl.n.* The military forces of a country.

Ar•me•ni•a^1 (är-mē′nē-ə, -mēn′yə). A republic and former kingdom of Asia Minor S of Georgia; a constituent republic of the U.S.S.R. from 1936 to 1991. Cap. Yerevan. Pop. 3,317,000.

Ar•me•nia^2 (är-mē′nē-ə, -nyə, -nyä). A city of W-central Colombia W of Bogotá. Pop. 179,727.

Ar•me•ni•an (är-mē′nē-ən, -mēn′yən) *adj.* Of or relating to Armenia or its people, language, or culture. **—*n.* 1.a.** A native or inhabitant of Armenia. **b.** A person of Armenian ancestry. **2.** The Indo-European language of the Armenians.

Armenian Church *n.* An autonomous Christian church established in Armenia in the fourth century A.D.

Ar•men•tières (är′mən-tîrz′, -mäN-tyĕr′). A city of N France WNW of Lille. Pop. 24,834.

arm•ful (ärm′fo͝ol′) *n.* The amount that an arm or arms can hold.

arm•hole (ärm′hōl′) *n.* An opening in a garment for an arm.

ar•mi•ger (är′mə-jər) *n.* **1.** A bearer of armor for a knight; a squire. **2.** A person entitled to bear heraldic arms. [Med.Lat. < Lat., arms-bearing : *arma*, arms; see ARM^2 + *gerere*, to carry.]

ar•mil•lar•y sphere (är′mə-lĕr′ē, är-mĭl′ə-rē) *n.* An old astronomical model used to display the principal celestial circles. [Transl. of Fr. *sphère armillaire* < Lat. *armilla*, bracelet < *armus*, shoulder. See **ar-*.**]

Ar•min•i•an (är-mĭn′ē-ən) *adj.* Of or relating to the theology of Jacobus Arminius and his followers, who believed that predestination was conditioned by God's foreknowledge of human free choices. **—Ar•min′i•an** *n.* **—Ar•min′i•an•ism** *n.*

Ar•min•i•us (är-mĭn′ē-əs) also **Ar•min** (-mēn′). 17? B.C.–A.D. 21. German hero who defeated the Romans in A.D. 9.

Arminius, Jacobus. 1560–1609. Dutch theologian who opposed the predestinarianism of John Calvin.

ar•mi•stice (är′mĭ-stĭs) *n.* A temporary cessation of fighting by mutual consent; a truce. [Fr. < NLat. *armistitium*: Lat. *arma*, arms; see ARM^2 + Lat. *-stitium*, a stopping; see **stā-*.**]

Ar•mi•stice Day (är′mĭ-stĭs) *n.* November 11, formerly observed in the United States in commemoration of the signing of the armistice ending World War I in 1918. Since 1954 it has been incorporated into the observances of Veterans Day.

arm•let (ärm′lĭt) *n.* **1.** A band worn on the arm for ornament or identification. **2.** A small arm, as of the sea.

arm•load (ärm′lōd′) *n.* The amount that can be carried in one arm or both arms: *an armload of laundry.*

ar•moire (ärm-wär′, ärm′wär) *n.* A large, often ornate cabinet or wardrobe. [Fr. *armoire* < OFr. *armaire* < Lat. *armārium*, chest < *arma*, tools. See **ar-*.**]

ar•mor (är′mər) *n.* **1.** A defensive covering worn to protect the body against weapons. **2.** A tough, protective covering, such as the metallic plates on tanks or warships. **3.** A safeguard or protection. **4.a.** The combat arm that deploys armored vehicles, such as tanks. **b.** The armored vehicles of an army. **—*tr.v.* -mored, -mor•ing, -mors.** To cover with armor. [ME *armure* < OFr. *armeure* < Lat. *armātūra*, equipment. See ARMATURE.] **—ar′mored** *adj.*

ar•mor-clad (är′mər-klăd′) *adj.* Covered with or wearing armor: *armor-clad warships.*

ar•mor•er (är′mər-ər) *n.* **1.** A manufacturer of weapons, esp. firearms. **2.** An enlisted person in charge of maintenance and repair of the small arms of a military unit. **3.** One that makes or repairs armor.

ar•mo•ri•al (är-môr′ē-əl, -mōr′-) *adj. Her.* Of or relating to heraldry or heraldic arms. **—*n.*** A book or treatise on heraldry. [< ME *armorie*, arms < OFr. *armeurerie* < *armeure*, armor. See ARMOR.]

Ar•mor•ic (är-môr′ĭk, -mŏr′-) also **Ar•mor•i•can** (-ĭ-kən) **—*adj.*** Of or relating to Armorica or its people, language, or culture. **—*n.* 1.** A native or inhabitant of Armorica. **2.** See **Breton** 2.

Ar•mor•i•ca (är-môr′ĭ-kə, -mōr′-). The NW part of France, esp. Brittany.

armor plate *n.* Specially formulated hard steel plate used to cover warships, vehicles, and fortifications. —**ar′mor-plat′ed** (är′mər-plā′tĭd) *adj.*

ar•mor•y (är′mə-rē) *n., pl.* **-ies. 1.a.** A storehouse for arms; an arsenal. **b.** A building for storing arms and military equipment, esp. one serving as headquarters for military reserve personnel. **2.** An arms factory.

ar•mour (är′mər) *n. & v. Chiefly British.* Var. of **armor.**

arm•pit (ärm′pĭt′) *n.* The hollow under the upper part of the arm at the shoulder.

arm•rest (ärm′rĕst′) *n.* A support for the arm, as on a piece of furniture or within a motor vehicle.

Arm•strong (ärm′strông′), **Edwin Howard.** 1890–1954. Amer. engineer who developed frequency modulation (1933).

Armstrong, Louis. "Satchmo." 1900–71. Amer. trumpeter who greatly influenced the development of jazz.

Armstrong, Neil Alden. b. 1930. Amer. astronaut who as commander of Apollo 11 became the first person to walk on the moon (Jul. 20, 1969).

arm-wres•tle (ärm′rĕs′əl) *intr. & tr.v.* **-tled, -tling, -tles.** *Sports.* To engage in or subject (another) to a form of wrestling in which two opponents sit facing each other with usu. right hands interlocked and elbows firmly planted and attempt to force each other's arm down. —**arm wrestler, arm′-wres′tler** *n.*

ar•my (är′mē) *n., pl.* **-mies. 1.a.** A large body of people organized and trained for land warfare. **b.** Often **Army.** The entire military land forces of a country. **c.** A tactical and administrative military unit consisting of a headquarters, two or more corps, and auxiliary forces. **2.** A large group of people organized for a specific cause: *the construction army that built the canal.* **3.** A multitude; a host: *an army of waiters.* [ME *armee* < OFr. < Med.Lat. *armāta* < Lat., fem. p.part. of *armāre*, to arm < *arma*, arms. See **ar-*.**]

army ant *n.* Any of various tropical ants of the family Formicidae that move in swarms and subsist on other insects.

ar•my•worm (är′mē-wûrm′) *n.* A caterpillar belonging to either of two genera of moth, *Pseudaletia* or *Spodoptera,* large groups of which destroy crops and other vegetation.

Arne (ärn), **Thomas Augustine.** 1710–78. British composer best known for his song "Rule, Britannia."

Arn•hem (ärn′hĕm′, är′nəm). A city of E Netherlands on the lower Rhine R. ESE of Utrecht. Pop. 128,598.

Arn•hem Land (är′nəm). A region of N Australia W of the Gulf of Carpentaria.

ar•ni•ca (är′nĭ-kə) *n.* **1.** Any of various perennial herbs of the genus *Arnica* in the composite family, having opposite simple leaves. **2.** A tincture of the dried flower heads of the European species *A. montana,* applied externally to reduce pain and inflammation. [NLat. *Arnica*, genus name.]

Ar•no (är′nō). A river of central Italy rising in the N Apennines and flowing c. 241 km (150 mi) to the Ligurian Sea.

Ar•nold (är′nəld). A city of E MO, a suburb of St. Louis. Pop. 18,828.

Arnold, Benedict. 1741–1801. Amer. Revolutionary general and traitor who fled to England in 1781.

Arnold, Matthew. 1822–88. British poet and critic whose works include "Dover Beach" (1867).

Arnold, Thomas. 1795–1842. British educator and historian; headmaster of Rugby School (1827–42).

Ar•nold•son (är′nəld-sən), **Klas Pontus.** 1844–1916. Swedish politician who shared the 1908 Nobel Peace Prize.

Arns•berg (ärnz′bərg, ärns′bĕrk). A city of W-central Germany SSE of Münster; founded 1077. Pop. 75,135.

A•roe Islands (ä′ro͞o). See **Aru Islands.**

ar•oid (ăr′oid′, âr′-) *n.* Any of various perennial herbs in the arum family, including houseplants such as the dieffenbachia and philodendron. [AR(UM) + -OID.] —**ar′oid′** *adj.*

a•roint (ə-roint′) *tr.v.* **a•roint•ed, a•roint•ing, a•roints.** *Archaic.* Begone; avaunt. [?]

a•ro•ma (ə-rō′mə) *n.* **1.a.** A quality that can be perceived by the olfactory sense. See Syns at **smell. b.** A pleasant characteristic odor, as of a plant, spice, or food. **2.** A distinctive, intangible quality; an aura: *the aroma of success.* [Alteration (influenced by Lat. *arōma*, spice) of ME *aromat*, aromatic substance < OFr. < Lat. *arōmata*, pl. of *arōma* < Gk., aromatic herb.]

ar•o•mat•ic (ăr′ə-măt′ĭk) *adj.* **1.** Having an aroma; fragrant or sweet-smelling. **2.** *Chem.* Of, relating to, or containing one or more six-carbon rings characteristic of the benzene series and related organic groups. —*n.* An aromatic plant or substance. —**ar′o•mat′i•cal•ly** *adv.* —**ar′o•mat′ic•ness** *n.*

ar•o•ma•tic•i•ty (ăr′ə-mə-tĭs′ĭ-tē, ə-rō′mə-) *n.* Aromatic quality or character, esp. the distinctive structure or properties of the aromatic chemical compounds.

a•ro•ma•tize (ə-rō′mə-tīz′) *tr.v.* **-tized, -tiz•ing, -tiz•es. 1.** To make aromatic or fragrant. **2.** *Chem.* To convert a substance into an aromatic compound. —**a•ro′ma•ti•za′tion** (-tĭ-zā′shən) *n.*

A•roos•took (ə-ro͞os′tək, -ro͝os′-). A river rising in N ME and flowing c. 225 km (140 mi) to the St. John R. in New Brunswick, Canada.

a•rose (ə-rōz′) *v.* P.t. of **arise.**

a•round (ə-round′) *adv.* **1.a.** On all sides: *dirty clothes lying around.* **b.** In close to all sides from all directions: *a field bordered around with trees.* **2.** In a circle or with a circular motion: *spun around twice.* **3.** In circumference or perimeter: *two miles around.* **4.** In succession or rotation. **5.** In or toward the opposite direction or position: *wheeled around.* **6.a.** To or among various places; here and there: *wander around.* **b.** To a specific place: *Come around again.* **7.** In or near one's current location: *waited around for the next flight.* **8.** From the beginning to the end: *frigid weather the year around.* **9.** Approximately; about: *weighed around 30 pounds.* —*prep.* **1.** On all sides of: *trees around the field.* **2.** In such a position as to encircle or surround: *a sash around the waist.* **3.a.** Here and there within; throughout: *around the country.* **b.** In the immediate vicinity of; near: *She lives around Norfolk.* **4.** On or to the farther side of: *the house around the corner.* **5.** So as to pass, bypass, or avoid: *got around the difficulty.* **6.** Approximately at: *woke up around seven.* **7.** In such a way as to have a basis or center in: *an economy focused around farming.* —*adj.* **1.** Being in existence: *Our old dog is no longer around.* **2.** Being in evidence; present: *Is the store manager around?* —***idiom.* been around.** *Informal.* Having had many and varied experiences: *an executive who has been around.* [ME : prob. *a-*, in; see A-² + *round*, circle; see ROUND¹.]

a•round-the-clock (ə-round′thə-klŏk′) *adj.* Var. of **round-the-clock.**

a•rouse (ə-rouz′) *v.* **a•roused, a•rous•ing, a•rous•es.** —*tr.* **1.** To awaken from or as if from sleep. **2.** To stir up; excite. —*intr.* To be or become aroused; stir. [< ROUSE, on the model of pairs such as RISE, ARISE.] —**a•rous′al** *n.*

Arp (ärp), **Jean** or **Hans.** 1887–1966. French artist noted for his abstract reliefs and three-dimensional sculptures.

Ar•pád (är′päd). d. 907. Hungarian national hero who founded the first Hungarian dynasty (c. 884).

ar•peg•gi•o (är-pĕj′ē-ō′, -pĕj′ō) *n., pl.* **-os.** *Mus.* **1.** The playing of the tones of a chord in rapid succession rather than simultaneously. **2.** A chord played or sung in this manner. [Ital. < *arpeggiare*, to play the harp < *arpa*, harp, of Gmc. orig. See HARP.]

ar•pent (är-pän′) *n.* Any of various French units of land measurement, esp. one used in parts of Canada and the southern United States and equal to about 0.4 hectare (0.85 acre). [Fr. < OFr. < Lat. *arepennis*, half acre. See **per¹*.**]

ar•que•bus (är′kə-bəs, -kwə-) *n.* Var. of **harquebus.**

arr. *abbr.* **1.** Arranged. **2.a.** Arrival; arrive. **b.** Arrived.

ar•rack (ăr′ək, ə-răk′) *n.* A strong alcoholic drink of the Middle East and the Far East. [Ar. *'araq*, sweet juice, as in *'araq at-tamr*, fermented juice of the date.]

ar•raign (ə-rān′) *tr.v.* **-raigned, -raign•ing, -raigns. 1.** *Law.* To call (an accused person) before a court to answer the charge made against him or her by indictment, information, or complaint. **2.** To call to account; accuse. [ME *arreinen* < OFr. *araisnier* < VLat. **adratiōnāre*, to call to account : Lat. *ad-*, ad- + Lat. *ratiō-*, *ratiōn-*, account; see REASON.] —**ar•raign′er** *n.* —**ar•raign′ment** *n.*

Ar•ran (ăr′ən). An island of W Scotland in the Firth of Clyde.

ar•range (ə-rānj′) *v.* **-ranged, -rang•ing, -rang•es.** —*tr.* **1.** To put into a specific order or relation; dispose. **2.** To plan or prepare for. **3.** To bring about an agreement concerning; settle: *"It has been arranged for him by his family to marry a girl of his own class"* (Edmund Wilson). **4.** *Mus.* To reset (a composition) for other instruments or voices or for another style of performance. —*intr.* **1.** To come to an agreement. **2.** To make preparations; plan. [ME *arengen* < OFr. *arengier*: *a-*, to (< Lat. *ad-*; see AD-) + *rengier*, to put in a line (< *reng*, line; see **sker-²*).**] —**ar•rang′er** *n.*

Syns: arrange, marshal, order, organize, sort, systematize. The central meaning shared by these verbs is "to distribute or dispose persons or things properly or methodically": *arranging figures in numerical sequence; marshal all relevant facts for presentation; ordered my chaotic life; organizing fund-raising efforts; sorted the sweaters by color; systematizing rules into a cohesive whole.* **Ant:** *disarrange.*

ar•range•ment (ə-rānj′mənt) *n.* **1.** The act or process of arranging. **2.** The condition, manner, or result of being arranged; disposal. **3.** A collection of things that have been arranged. **4.** A provision or plan made in preparation for an undertaking. Often used in the plural. **5.** An agreement or settlement; a disposition. **6.** *Mus.* **a.** An adaptation of a composition for other instruments or voices or for another style of performance. **b.** A composition so arranged.

ar•rant (ăr′ənt) *adj.* Completely such; thoroughgoing: *an arrant fool.* [Var. of ERRANT.] —**ar′rant•ly** *adv.*

ar•ras (ăr′əs) *n.* **1.** A wall hanging; a tapestry. **2.** A curtain or a wall hanging, esp. one of Flemish origin. [ME, after ARRAS.]

Ar•ras (ăr′əs, ə-răs′). A city of N France SSW of Lille; noted in the Middle Ages for its tapestry. Pop. 41,736.

ar•ray (ə-rā′) *tr.v.* **-rayed, -ray•ing, -rays. 1.** To set out for display or use; place in an orderly arrangement. **2.** To dress in finery; adorn. —*n.* **1.** An orderly, often imposing arrange-

Louis Armstrong

Neil Armstrong

ă pat	oi boy
ā pay	ou out
âr care	o͝o took
ä father	o͞o boot
ĕ pet	ŭ cut
ē be	ûr urge
ĭ pit	th thin
ī pie	*th* this
îr pier	hw which
ŏ pot	zh vision
ō toe	ə about, item
ô paw	

Stress marks:
′ (primary);
′ (secondary), as in **dictionary** (dĭk′shə-nĕr′ē)

arrowhead
Top: From 8000 to 10,000 B.C.
Bottom: Broad-leaved arrowhead *Sagittaria latifolia*

Artemis

ment: *an array of royal jewels.* **2.** An impressively large number, as of persons or objects. **3.** Splendid attire; finery. **4.** *Math.* **a.** An arrangement of quantities in rows and columns, as in a matrix. **b.** Numerical data linearly ordered by magnitude. **5.** *Comp. Sci.* An arrangement of memory elements in one or several planes. [ME *arraien* < AN *arraier* < VLat. **arrēdāre.* See **reidh-*.**]

ar•ray•al (ə-rā′əl) *n.* **1.** The act or process of arranging in an orderly or imposing manner. **2.** Something so arranged.

ar•rear•age (ə-rîr′ĭj) *n.* **1.** The state of being behind in the fulfillment of obligations or of being overdue in payment. **2.** A payment owed.

ar•rears (ə-rîrz′) *pl.n.* **1.** An unpaid overdue debt or unfulfilled obligation. **2.** The state of being behind in fulfilling obligations: *in arrears.* [ME *arrers* < *arrere,* behind < OFr. *arere* < VLat. **ad retrō,* backward : Lat. *ad,* to; see AD- + Lat. *retrō,* behind; see **re-*.**]

ar•rest (ə-rĕst′) *v.* **-rest•ed, -rest•ing, -rests.** —*tr.* **1.** To stop; check: *arrested the growth of the tumor.* **2.** To seize and hold under the authority of law. **3.** To capture and hold briefly (the attention, for example); engage. —*intr.* To undergo cardiac arrest. —*n.* **1.a.** The act of detaining in legal custody. **b.** The state of being so detained: *a criminal under arrest.* **2.** A device for stopping motion, esp. of a moving part. [ME *aresten* < OFr. *arester* < VLat. **arrestāre*: Lat. *ad-,* ad- + Lat. *restāre,* to stand still (*re-,* re- + *stāre,* to stand; see **stā-***).] —**ar•rest′er, ar•res′tor** *n.* —**ar•rest′ment** *n.*

ar•rest•ee (ə-rĕs-tē′) *n.* One who is under arrest.

ar•rest•ing (ə-rĕs′tĭng) *adj.* Attracting and holding the attention; striking. —**ar•rest′ing•ly** *adv.*

Ar•rhe•ni•us (ə-rē′nē-əs, ə-rā′-), **Svante August.** 1859–1927. Swedish scientist who won a 1903 Nobel Prize.

ar•rhyth•mi•a (ə-rĭth′mē-ə) *n.* An irregularity in the force or rhythm of the heartbeat. [NLat. < Gk. *arruthmia,* lack of rhythm < *arruthmos,* unrhythmical : *a-,* without; see A-[1] + *rhuthmos,* rhythm; see RHYTHM.]

ar•rhyth•mic (ə-rĭth′mĭk) *adj.* Lacking rhythm or regularity of rhythm. —**ar•rhyth′mi•cal•ly** *adv.*

ar•ri•ba (ə-rē′bə) *interj.* Used as an exclamation of pleasure, approval, or elation. [Sp. < Lat. *ad rīpam,* on the shore : *ad,* to; see AD- + *rīpa,* shore.]

ar•ri•ère-ban (ăr′ē-âr-bän′, -băn′) *n.* **1.** A medieval royal proclamation by which vassals were summoned to military service. **2.** The vassals summoned. [Fr. < OFr. *ariere-ban,* alteration (influenced by *arere,* behind) of *herban.* See **koro-*.**]

ar•ri•ère-pen•sée (ăr′ē-âr′päN-sā′) *n.* A mental reservation. [Fr. : *arrière,* in back (< OFr. *arere;* see ARREARS) + *pensée,* thought (< *penser,* to think; see PENSIVE).]

ar•ris (ăr′ĭs) *n., pl.* **arris** or **-ris•es.** The sharp edge or ridge formed by two surfaces meeting at an angle, as in a molding. [Alteration of OFr. *areste,* fishbone, spine. See ARÊTE.]

ar•ri•val (ə-rī′vəl) *n.* **1.** The act of arriving. **2.** One that arrives or has arrived. **3.** The reaching of a goal or an objective as a result of effort or a process.

ar•rive (ə-rīv′) *intr.v.* **-rived, -riv•ing, -rives. 1.** To reach a destination. **2.** To come at length; take place: *The day of reckoning has arrived.* **3.** To achieve success or recognition. —***phrasal verb.*** **arrive at.** To reach through effort or a process. [ME *ariven* < OFr. *ariver* < VLat. **arrīpāre,* to reach the shore : Lat. *ad-,* ad- + Lat. *rīpa,* shore.] —**ar•riv′er** *n.*

ar•ri•viste (ă-rē-vēst′) *n.* **1.** A person who has recently attained high position or great power without due effort or merit; an upstart. **2.** An unscrupulous, vulgar social climber. [Fr. < *arriver,* to arrive < OFr. *ariver.* See ARRIVE.]

ar•ro•ba (ə-rō′bə) *n.* **1.** A unit of weight formerly used in Spanish-speaking countries, equal to about 11.3 kilograms (25 pounds). **2.** A unit of weight formerly used in Portuguese-speaking countries, equal to about 14.4 kilograms (32 pounds). [Sp. and Port., both < Ar. *ar-rub‘,* the quarter (of a quintal) : *al,* the + *rub‘,* quarter.]

Ar•roe Islands (ä′rō͞o). See **Aru Islands.**

ar•ro•gance (ăr′ə-gəns) *n.* The state or quality of being arrogant; overbearing pride.

ar•ro•gant (ăr′ə-gənt) *adj.* **1.** Making or disposed to make claims to unwarranted importance or consideration out of overbearing pride. **2.** Marked by or arising from arrogance. See Syns at **proud.** [ME *arrogaunt* < OFr. < Lat. *arrogāns, arrogant-,* pr.part. of *arrogāre,* to arrogate. See ARROGATE.] —**ar′ro•gant•ly** *adv.*

ar•ro•gate (ăr′ə-gāt′) *tr.v.* **-gat•ed, -gat•ing, -gates. 1.** To take or claim for oneself without right; appropriate. **2.** To ascribe on behalf of another in an unwarranted manner. [Lat. *arrogāre, arrogāt-* : *ad-,* ad- + *rogāre,* to ask; see **reg-*.**] —**ar′ro•ga′tion** *n.* —**ar′ro•ga′tive** *adj.* —**ar′ro•ga′tor** *n.*

ar•ron•disse•ment (ä-rôN′dēs-mäN′) *n.* **1.** The chief administrative subdivision of a department in France. **2.** A municipal subdivision in some large French cities. [Fr. < OFr., rounded projection on a wall < *arrondir, arrondiss-,* to round out : *a,* to (< Lat. *ad-;* see AD-) + *rondir,* to make round (< *rond,* round; see ROUND[1]).]

ar•row (ăr′ō) *n.* **1.** A straight thin shaft with a pointed head at one end and often flight-stabilizing vanes at the other, meant to be shot from a bow. **2.** Something that is similar to an arrow in form or function. [ME *arwe* < OE.]

Ar•row (ăr′ō), **Kenneth Joseph.** b. 1921. Amer. economist who shared a 1972 Nobel Prize.

ar•row•head (ăr′ō-hĕd′) *n.* **1.** The pointed, removable striking tip of an arrow. **2.** Something that is shaped like the head of an arrow. **3.a.** Any of various aquatic or wetland perennial plants of the genus *Sagittaria,* having arrowhead-shaped leaves. **b.** The edible tubers of the Eurasian species *S. sagittifolia* or of the North American species *S. latifolia.*

ar•row•root (ăr′ō-ro͞ot′, -ro͝ot′) *n.* **1.a.** A starch obtained from a tropical American perennial herb *(Maranta arundinacea).* **b.** The rhizome of this plant, eaten as a vegetable or used for starch extraction. **c.** The plant itself. **2.a.** The edible starch obtained from plants in the genera *Canna* and *Tacca.* **b.** Any of these plants. [By folk ety. < Arawak *aru-aru,* meal of meals (from its use in drawing poison from arrow wounds).]

ar•row-wood (ăr′ō-wo͝od′) *n.* Any of several North American species of viburnum having straight tough stems formerly used by certain Native American peoples to make arrows.

arrow worm *n.* Any of various small slender marine worms of the phylum Chaetognatha.

ar•roy•o (ə-roi′ō) *n., pl.* **-os. 1.** A deep gully cut by an intermittent stream; a dry gulch. **2.** A brook; a creek. [Sp. < VLat. **arrugiu,* gold mine, underground passage, masc. var. of Lat. *arrugia,* a galleried mine.]

ARS *abbr.* Agricultural Research Service.

arse (ärs) *n. Chiefly British.* Var. of **ass[2].**

ar•se•nal (är′sə-nəl) *n.* **1.** A governmental establishment for the storing, development, manufacturing, testing, or repairing of arms and other war materiel. **2.** A stock of weapons. **3.** A store or supply. [Ital. *arsenale* < obsolete Ital. *arzanale* < Ar. *dār-aṣ-ṣinā‘ah*: *dār,* house + *aṣ-,* the + *ṣinā‘ah,* manufacture (< *ṣana‘a,* to make).]

ar•se•nate (är′sə-nĭt, -nāt′) *n.* A salt or ester of arsenic acid.

ar•se•nic (är′sə-nĭk) *n.* **1.** *Symbol* **As** A poisonous metallic element having three allotropes, of which the gray form is the most common. Arsenic compounds are used in insecticides and solid-state doping agents. Atomic number 33; atomic weight 74.922; valence 3, 5. Gray arsenic melts at 817°C (at 28 atm pressure), sublimes at 613°C, and has a specific gravity of 5.73. See table at **element. 2.** Arsenic trioxide. —*adj.* **ar•sen•ic.** (är-sĕn′ĭk). Of or containing arsenic, esp. with valence 5. [ME *arsenik* < OFr. < Lat. *arsenicum* < Gk. *arsenikon,* yellow orpiment, alteration of Syriac *zarnīkā* < MPers. **zarnīk* < OIran. **zarna-,* golden. See **ghel-[2]*.**]

ar•sen•ic acid (är-sĕn′ĭk) *n.* A poisonous translucent crystalline compound, H_3AsO_4, used to manufacture arsenates.

ar•sen•i•cal (är-sĕn′ĭ-kəl) *adj.* Of or containing arsenic. —*n.* A drug or preparation containing arsenic.

ar•se•nic trioxide (är′sə-nĭk) *n.* A poisonous amorphous powder, As_2O_3, used in rat poisons.

ar•se•nide (är′sə-nīd′) *n.* A compound of arsenic with a more electropositive element.

ar•se•ni•ous (är-sē′nē-əs) *adj.* Of or containing arsenic, esp. with valence 3.

ar•se•no•py•rite (är′sə-nō-pī′rīt) *n.* An arsenic ore, FeAsS.

ar•shin (är-shēn′) *n.* Var. of **archine.**

ar•sine (är-sēn′, är′sēn′) *n.* A poisonous gas, H_3As, used as a solid-state doping agent. [ARS(ENIC) + -INE[2].]

ar•sis (är′sĭs) *n., pl.* **-ses** (-sēz′). **1.a.** The short or unaccented part of a metrical foot, esp. in quantitative verse. **b.** The accented or long part of a metrical foot, esp. in accentual verse. **2.** *Mus.* The upbeat or unaccented part of a measure. [ME, raising of the voice < LLat., accented part of a metrical foot < Gk., the unaccented part of a metrical foot < *aeirein,* to lift. See **wer-[1]*.**]

ar•son (är′sən) *n.* The crime of maliciously, voluntarily, and willfully setting fire to one's own or another's property for an improper purpose. [AN < LLat. *ārsiō, ārsiōn-* < Lat. *ārsus,* p.part. of *ārdēre,* to burn. See **as-*.**] —**ar′son•ist** *n.*

ars•phen•a•mine (ärs-fĕn′ə-mēn′) *n.* A hygroscopic powder, $C_{12}H_{12}As_2N_2O_2 \cdot 2HCl \cdot 2H_2O$, formerly used to treat syphilis. [ARS(ENIC) + PHEN(YL) + AMINE.]

art[1] (ärt) *n.* **1.** Human effort to imitate, supplement, alter, or counteract the work of nature. **2.a.** The conscious production or arrangement of sounds, colors, forms, or other elements in a manner that affects the sense of beauty, specifically the production of the beautiful in a graphic or plastic medium. **b.** The study of these activities. **c.** The product of these activities; human works of beauty considered as a group. **3.** High quality of conception or execution; aesthetic value. **4.** A field or category of art, such as music. **5.** A nonscientific branch of learning; one of the liberal arts. **6.a.** A system of principles and methods employed in the performance of a set of activities: *the art of building.* **b.** A trade or craft that applies such a system: *the art of the lexicographer.* **7.a.** Skill that is attained by study, practice, or observation: *the art of the baker.* **b.** Skill arising from the exercise of intuitive faculties: *"Self-criticism is an art not many are qualified to practice"* (Joyce Carol Oates). **8.a. arts.** Artful devices, stratagems, and tricks. **b.** Artful contrivance; cunning. **9.** *Print.* Illustrative material. [ME < OFr. < Lat. *ars, art-*. See **ar-***.]

art^{2} (ərt; ärt *when stressed*) *v. Archaic.* A second pers. sing. pr. indic. of **be.** [ME < OE *eart.* See **er-^{1}***.]

art. *abbr.* **1.** Article. **2.** Artificial. **3.** Artillery. **4.** Artist.

–art *suff.* Var. of **–ard.**

Ar•ta•xer•xes I (är′tə-zûrk′sēz′). d. 424 B.C. King of Persia (465–425) who sanctioned Judaism in Jerusalem.

Artaxerxes II. d. 359 B.C. King of Persia (404–359) whose reign was marked by a peace agreement with Sparta (386).

art dec•o also **Art Dec•o** (dĕk′ō) *n.* A decorative and architectural style of the period 1925–1940, characterized by geometric designs, bold colors, and the use of plastic and glass. [Fr. *Art Déco* < *Exposition Internationale des Arts Décoratifs et Industriels Modernes*, a 1925 exposition in Paris, France.]

ar•te•fact (är′tə-făkt′) *n.* Var. of **artifact.**

Ar•te•mis (är′tə-mĭs) *n. Gk. Myth.* The virgin goddess of the hunt and the moon and the twin sister of Apollo. [Gk.]

ar•te•mis•i•a (är′tə-mĭzh′ē-ə, -mĭzh′ə, -mĭz′ē-ə) *n.* Any of various aromatic plants of the genus *Artemisia* in the composite family, having green or grayish foliage. [ME *artemesie,* mugwort < OFr. < Lat. *artemisia* < Gk., wormwood, after ARTEMIS (to whom it was sacred).]

ar•te•ri•al (är-tîr′ē-əl) *adj.* **1.** Of, like, or in an artery or arteries. **2.** Of, relating to, or being the blood in the arteries that has absorbed oxygen in the lungs and is bright red. **3.** Being a main road or channel with many branches: *an arterial route.* —*n.* A through road or street. **—ar•te′ri•al•ly** *adv.*

ar•te•ri•al•ize (är-tîr′ē-ə-līz′) *tr.v.* **-ized, -iz•ing, -iz•es.** To convert (venous blood) into arterial blood. **—ar•te′ri•al•i•za′tion** (-ĭ-zā′shən) *n.*

arterio– *pref.* Artery: *arteriovenous.* [Gk. *artērio-* < *artēria,* artery. See **wer-^{1}***.]

ar•te•ri•og•ra•phy (är-tîr′ē-ŏg′rə-fē) *n.* Examination of the arteries using x-rays following injection of a radiopaque substance. **—ar•te′ri•o•gram′** (-ə-grăm′) *n.* **—ar•te′ri•o•graph′ic** (-ə-grăf′ĭk) *adj.*

ar•te•ri•ole (är-tîr′ē-ōl′) *n.* One of the small terminal branches of an artery, esp. one connected to a capillary. [NLat. *arteriola,* dim. of Lat. *artēria,* artery < Gk. See **wer-^{1}***.] **—ar•te′ri•o′lar** (-ō′lər, -ə-lər) *adj.*

ar•te•ri•o•scle•ro•sis (är-tîr′ē-ō-sklə-rō′sĭs) *n.* A chronic disease in which thickening, hardening, and loss of elasticity of the arterial walls result in impaired blood circulation. **—ar•te′ri•o•scle•rot′ic** (-rŏt′ĭk) *adj.*

ar•te•ri•o•ve•nous (är-tîr′ē-ō-vē′nəs) *adj.* Of, relating to, or connecting both arteries and veins.

ar•te•ri•tis (är′tə-rī′tĭs) *n.* Inflammation of an artery.

ar•ter•y (är′tə-rē) *n., pl.* **-ies. 1.** *Anat.* Any of a branching system of muscular elastic tubes that carry blood from the heart to cells, tissues, and organs. **2.** A major route of transportation into which local routes flow. See Syns at **way.** [ME *arterie* < Lat. *artēria* < Gk. See **wer-^{1}***.]

ar•te•sian well (är-tē′zhən) *n.* A well drilled through impermeable strata to reach water capable of rising to the surface by internal hydrostatic pressure. [Fr. *artésien* < OFr., of Artois < *Arteis,* Artois, France.]

Ar•te•vel•de (är′tə-vĕl′də), **Jacob van.** "Brewer of Ghent." 1290?–1345. Flemish political leader who maintained the neutrality of Flanders during Anglo-French hostilities.

art film *n.* **1.a.** A foreign film or one with limited distribution. **b.** A film about art or an artist. **2.** A serious film intended to be artistic, often experimental and not for mass appeal.

art form *n.* An activity or a piece of artistic work that can be regarded as a medium of artistic expression.

art•ful (ärt′fəl) *adj.* **1.** Exhibiting art or skill. **2.** Skillful in accomplishing a purpose, esp. with cunning or craft. **3.** Artificial. **—art′ful•ly** *adv.* **—art′ful•ness** *n.*

ar•thral•gia (är-thrăl′jə, -jē-ə) *n.* Neuralgic pain in a joint or joints. **—ar•thral′gic** (-jĭk) *adj.*

ar•thri•tis (är-thrī′tĭs) *n.* Joint inflammation causing pain and swelling. **—ar•thrit′ic** (-thrĭt′ĭk) *adj. & n.* **—ar•thrit′i•cal•ly** *adv.*

arthro– or **arthr–** *pref.* Joint: *arthropathy.* [Gk. < *arthron,* joint. See **ar-***.]

ar•throd•e•sis (är-thrŏd′ĭ-sĭs) *n.* The surgical fixation of a joint by artificially induced ankylosis, resulting in bone fusion. [ARTHRO– + Gk. *desis,* binding together (< *dein,* to bind).]

ar•throg•ra•phy (är-thrŏg′rə-fē) *n.* Examination of the interior of a joint using x-rays following the injection of a radiopaque substance. **—ar′thro•gram′** (är′thrə-grăm′) *n.*

ar•thro•gry•po•sis (är′thrə-grə-pō′sĭs) *n.* **1.** The permanent fixation of a joint in a contracted position. **2.** A congenital disorder marked by generalized stiffness of the joints. [ARTHRO– + LLat. *grypōsis,* hooking (< LGk. *grupōsis* < Gk. *grupousthai,* to become hooked < *grupos,* hook-nosed).]

ar•thro•mere (är′thrə-mîr′) *n.* One of the segments or divisions in the body of a jointed animal, such as an arthropod. **—ar′thro•mer′ic** (är′thrə-mĕr′ĭk, -mîr′ĭk) *adj.*

ar•throp•a•thy (är-thrŏp′ə-thē) *n.* A disease or an abnormality of a joint.

ar•thro•pod (är′thrə-pŏd′) *n.* Any of numerous invertebrate animals of the phylum Arthropoda, including insects and arachnids, that are characterized by a chitinous exoskeleton and a segmented body with jointed appendages. [< NLat. *Arthropoda,* phylum name : ARTHRO– + NLat. *-poda,* -pod.] **—ar′thro•pod** *adj.* **—ar•throp′o•dous** (är-thrŏp′ə-dəs), **ar•throp′o•dal** (-dəl) *adj.*

ar•thros•co•py (är-thrŏs′kə-pē) *n., pl.* **-pies.** Examination of a joint using an endoscope that is inserted through a small incision. **—ar′thro•scope′** (är′thrə-skōp′) *n.* **—ar′thro•scop′ic** (-skŏp′ĭk) *adj.* **—ar′thro•scop′ic•al•ly** *adv.*

ar•thro•sis (är-thrō′sĭs) *n., pl.* **-ses** (-sēz). **1.** *Anat.* An articulation or a joint between bones. **2.** A degenerative disease of a joint. [Gk. *arthrōsis* < *arthroun,* to be jointed < *arthron,* joint. See ARTHRO–.]

ar•throt•o•my (är-thrŏt′ə-mē) *n.* Surgical incision into a joint.

Ar•thur (är′thər) *n.* The legendary sixth-century king of the Britons who held court at Camelot.

Arthur, Chester Alan. 1829–86. The 21st President of the U.S. (1881–85) who became President after the assassination of James A. Garfield.

Ar•thu•ri•an (är-thŏŏr′ē-ən) *adj.* Of or relating to King Arthur and his Knights of the Round Table.

ar•ti•choke (är′tĭ-chōk′) *n.* **1.a.** A Mediterranean thistlelike plant *(Cynara scolymus)* in the composite family, having pinnately divided leaves. **b.** The edible immature flower head of this plant. **2.** The Jerusalem artichoke. [Ult. < OSp. *alcarchofa* < Ar. *al-ḫaršūf.*]

ar•ti•cle (är′tĭ-kəl) *n.* **1.** An individual thing or element of a class; a particular item: *articles of food.* **2.** A given section or item of a series in a written document. **3.** A nonfiction literary composition that forms an independent part of a publication, as of a newspaper. **4.** *Gram.* Any of a class of words used to signal nouns and to specify their application. In English the articles are *a, an,* and *the.* **5.** A particular part or subject; a specific matter or point. —*tr.v.* **-cled, -cling, -cles.** To bind by articles in a contract. [ME < OFr. < Lat. *articulus,* part, dim. of *artus,* joint. See **ar-***.]

article of faith *n., pl.* **articles of faith.** A very basic belief not to be doubted.

ar•tic•u•la•ble (är-tĭk′yə-lə-bəl) *adj.* That can be articulated: *articulable doubts.*

ar•tic•u•lar (är-tĭk′yə-lər) *adj.* Of or relating to a joint or joints. [ME *articuler* < Lat. *articulāris* < *articulus,* small joint. See ARTICLE.] **—ar•tic′u•lar•ly** *adv.*

ar•tic•u•late (är-tĭk′yə-lĭt) *adj.* **1.** Endowed with the power of speech. **2.** Composed of distinct meaningful syllables or words. **3.** Expressing oneself easily in clear and effective language: *an articulate speaker.* **4.** Marked by the use of clear, expressive language. **5.** *Anat.* Consisting of sections united by joints; jointed. —*v.* (är-tĭk′yə-lāt′) **-lat•ed, -lat•ing, -lates.** —*tr.* **1.** To pronounce distinctly and carefully; enunciate. **2.** To utter (a sound) by making the necessary movements of the speech organs. **3.** To express in coherent verbal form; give words to. **4.** To fit together into a coherent whole; unify. **5.** *Anat.* To unite by forming joints or a joint. —*intr.* **1.** To speak clearly and distinctly. **2.** To utter a speech sound. **3.** *Anat.* To form a joint; be jointed. [Lat. *articulātus,* p.part. of *articulāre,* to divide into joints, utter distinctly < *articulus,* small joint. See ARTICLE.] **—ar•tic′u•late•ly** *adv.* **—ar•tic′u•late•ness, ar•tic′u•la•cy** *n.*

ar•tic•u•la•tion (är-tĭk′yə-lā′shən) *n.* **1.** The act of vocal expression; utterance: *an articulation of the plan.* **2.a.** The act or manner of producing a speech sound. **b.** A speech sound, esp. a consonant. **3.a.** A jointing together or being jointed together. **b.** The method or manner of jointing. **4.** *Anat.* **a.** A joint between bones. **b.** A movable joint between inflexible parts of the body of an animal. **5.** *Bot.* **a.** A joint between two separable parts, as a leaf and a stem. **b.** A node or space on a stem between two nodes. **—ar•tic′u•la•to′ry** (-lə-tôr′ē, -tōr′ē), **ar•tic′u•la′tive** (-lā′tĭv, -lə-tĭv) *adj.*

ar•tic•u•la•tor (är-tĭk′yə-lā′tər) *n.* **1.** One that articulates. **2.** One of the organs of speech, such as the lips or tongue.

ar•ti•fact also **ar•te•fact** (är′tə-făkt′) *n.* **1.** An object produced or shaped by human craft, esp. one of archaeological or historical interest. **2.** A typical product or result: *"The act of looking at a naked model was an artifact of male supremacy"* (Philip Weiss). **3.** *Biol.* A structure or substance not normally present but produced by an external agent or action. [Lat. *arte,* ablative of *ars,* art; see ART^{1} + *factum,* something made < neut. p.part. of *facere,* to make; see **dhē-***.] **—ar′ti•fac′tu•al** (-făk′chōō-əl) *adj.*

ar•ti•fice (är′tə-fĭs) *n.* **1.** An artful or crafty expedient; a stratagem. **2.** Subtle but base deception; trickery. **3.** Cleverness or skill; ingenuity. [Fr. < OFr., craftsmanship < Lat. *artificium* < *artifex, artific-,* craftsman : *ars, art-,* art; see ART^{1} + *-fex,* maker; see **dhē-***.]

ar•tif•i•cer (är-tĭf′ĭ-sər) *n.* **1.** A skilled worker; a craftsperson. **2.** One that contrives, devises, or constructs something.

ar•ti•fi•cial (är′tə-fĭsh′əl) *adj.* **1.a.** Made by human beings; produced rather than natural. **b.** Brought about or caused by

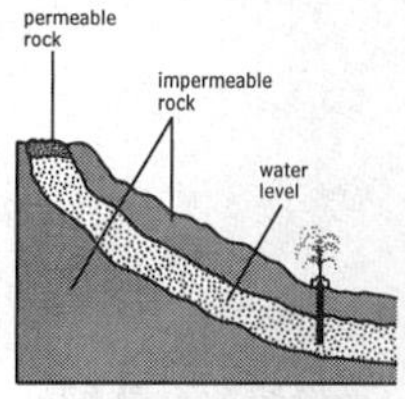

artesian well

Chester A. Arthur

artichoke
Cynara scolymus

ă pat	oi boy
ā pay	ou out
âr care	ŏŏ took
ä father	ōō boot
ĕ pet	ŭ cut
ē be	ûr urge
ĭ pit	th thin
ī pie	*th* this
îr pier	hw which
ŏ pot	zh vision
ō toe	ə about, item
ô paw	

Stress marks:
′ (primary);
′ (secondary), as in
dictionary (dĭk′shə-nĕr′ē)

sociopolitical or other human-generated forces or influences: *artificial barriers against women and minorities.* **2.** Imitating something natural; simulated. **3.** Not genuine or natural: *an artificial smile.* [ME < OFr. < Lat. *artificiālis,* belonging to art < *artificium,* craftsmanship. See ARTIFICE.] **—ar′ti•fi′ci•al′i•ty** (-fish′ē-ăl′ĭ-tē) *n.* **—ar′ti•fi′cial•ly** *adv.*

Syns: *artificial, synthetic, ersatz, simulated.* These adjectives refer to what is made by human beings rather than natural in origin. *Artificial* is broadest in meaning and connotation: *an artificial sweetener; artificial flowers. Synthetic* often implies the use of a chemical process to produce a substance that will look or function like the original, often with certain advantages: *synthetic rubber.* An *ersatz* product is a transparently inferior imitation: *ersatz mink. Simulated* often refers to a substitute for or an imitation of a costlier substance: *simulated mahogany paneling.*

artificial horizon *n.* An instrument showing a line about which an aircraft's pitching and banking movements appear on a flight indicator.

artificial insemination *n.* Introduction of semen into the vagina or uterus without sexual contact.

artificial intelligence *n. Comp. Sci.* **1.** The ability of a machine to perform activities thought to require intelligence. **2.** The branch of computer science concerned with developing machines with this ability.

artificial language *n.* **1.** An invented language based on prescribed rules. **2.** *Comp. Sci.* A language designed for use in a specific field.

artificial respiration *n.* A mechanical or manual procedure used to restore or maintain respiration in a person who has stopped breathing.

artificial selection *n.* Human intervention in animal or plant reproduction to ensure that desirable traits are represented in successive generations.

ar•til•ler•ist (är-tĭl′ər-ĭst) *n.* An artillery soldier; a gunner.

ar•til•ler•y (är-tĭl′ə-rē) *n.* **1.** Large-caliber crew-operated weapons, such as cannon and missile launchers. **2.** The combat arm that specializes in the use of such weapons. **3.** The science of the use of guns; gunnery. **4.** Early weapons, such as catapults, for discharging missiles. [ME *artillerie* < OFr. < *artillier,* to equip, perh. alteration of *atiller* < VLat. **apticulāre* < Lat. *aptāre,* to fit, adapt < *aptus,* apt. See APT.]

ar•til•ler•y•man (är-tĭl′ə-rē-mən) *n.* An artillery soldier.

ar•ti•o•dac•tyl (är′tē-ō-dăk′təl) *n.* Any of various hoofed mammals of the order Artiodactyla that have an even number of toes on each foot. [< NLat. *Artiodactyla,* order name : Gk. *artios,* even; see **ar-*** + Gk. *daktulos,* toe.] **—ar′ti•o•dac′tyl, ar′ti•o•dac′ty•lous** (-tə-ləs) *adj.*

ar•ti•san (är′tĭ-zən, -sən) *n.* A skilled manual worker; a craftsperson. [Prob. Fr. < Ital. *artigiano* < VLat. **artitiānus* < Lat. *artītus,* skilled in the arts, p.part. of *artīre,* to instruct in the arts < *ars, art-,* art. See **ar-***.] **—ar′ti•san•ship′** *n.*

art•ist (är′tĭst) *n.* **1.** One who creates imaginative works of aesthetic value, esp. in the fine arts. **2.** One whose work shows great creativity or skill: *a culinary artist.* **3.** One who works in the performing arts. **4.** One who is adept at an activity, esp. trickery or deceit: *a con artist.* [Fr. *artiste* < OFr., lettered person < Med.Lat. *artista* < Lat. *ars, art-,* art. See **ar-***.]

ar•tiste (är-tēst′) *n.* **1.** A public performer, esp. a singer or dancer. **2.** A person with artistic pretensions. [Fr. See ARTIST.]

ar•tis•tic (är-tĭs′tĭk) *adj.* **1.** Of or relating to art or artists. **2.** Sensitive to or appreciative of art or beauty. **3.** Showing imagination and skill. **—ar•tis′ti•cal•ly** *adv.*

art•ist•ry (är′tĭ-strē) *n.* **1.** Artistic ability: *a sculptor of great artistry.* **2.** Artistic quality or craft: *the artistry of a poem.*

art•less (ärt′lĭs) *adj.* **1.** Having or displaying no guile, cunning, or deceit. See Syns at **naive. 2.** Free of artificiality; natural: *artless charm.* **3.** Lacking art, knowledge, or skill; uncultured and ignorant. **4.** Poorly made or done; crude. **—art′less•ly** *adv.* **—art′less•ness** *n.*

art nou•veau also **Art Nou•veau** (är′ no͞o-vō′, ärt′) *n.* A style of decoration and architecture of the late 19th and early 20th centuries, marked by the depiction of leaves and flowers in flowing, sinuous lines. [Fr. : *art,* art + *nouveau,* new.]

art nouveau
Late 19th- to early 20th-century American vase made by the Alvin Manufacturing Company

Ar•tois (är-twä′). A historical region and former province of N France near the English Channel.

art song *n. Mus.* A lyric song intended to be sung in recital, usu. accompanied by a piano.

art•sy-craft•sy (ärt′sē-krăft′sē) *adj. Informal.* **1.** Decorative rather than functional. **2.** Pretentiously or self-consciously artistic.

art•work (ärt′wûrk′) *n.* **1.** Work in the graphic or plastic arts, esp. small decorative objects. **2.** An illustrative and decorative element used in a printed work.

art•y (är′tē) *adj.* **-i•er, -i•est.** *Informal.* Showily or affectedly artistic. **—art′i•ly** *adv.* **—art′i•ness** *n.*

arty. *abbr.* Artillery.

A•ru•ba (ə-ro͞o′bə). An island of the Netherlands in the Leeward Is. of the Caribbean N of the Venezuela coast.

a•ru•gu•la (ə-ro͞o′gə-lə) *n.* See **rocket² 1.** [Prob. Ital. dial. < Lat. *ērūca,* colewort.]

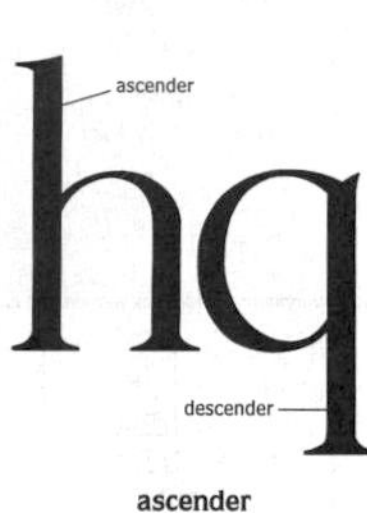

ascender

A•ru Islands also **A•roe Islands** or **Ar•roe Islands** (ä′ro͞o). An island group of E Indonesia, part of the Moluccas in the Arafura Sea SW of New Guinea.

ar•um (ăr′əm, âr′-) *n.* **1.** Any of several Old World plants, such as the cuckoopint, of the genus *Arum,* having basal arrowhead-shaped leaves. **2.** Any of several related plants, such as the water arum. [Lat. < Gk. *aron.*]

a•rus•pex (ə-rŭs′pĕks′) *n.* Var. of **haruspex.**

A•ru•wi•mi (är′ə-wē′mē, ăr′-). A river of central Africa rising in NE Zaire near Lake Albert and flowing c. 1,287 km (800 mi) to the Congo R.

ARV *abbr. Bible.* American Revised Version.

Ar•vad•a (är-văd′ə). A city of N-central CO, a suburb of Denver. Pop. 89,235.

ARVIN *abbr.* Army of the Republic of Vietnam.

-ary *suff.* **1.** Of or relating to: *bacillary.* **2.** One that relates to or is connected with: *boundary.* [ME *-arie* < OFr. < Lat. *-ārius,* adj. and n. suff.]

Ar•y•an (âr′ē-ən, ăr′-) *n.* **1.** See **Indo-Iranian. 2.** A member of the people who spoke Proto-Indo-European. **3.** A member of any people speaking an Indo-European language. **4.** In Nazism, a Caucasian Gentile, esp. of Nordic type. *—adj.* **1.** Of or relating to Indo-Iranian. **2.** Of or relating to the Indo-European languages or Proto-Indo-European. **3.** Of or relating to a speaker of an Indo-European language. **4.** In Nazism, of or relating to a Caucasian Gentile. [< Skt. *ārya-,* noble, Aryan.]

ar•y•te•noid (ăr′ĭ-tē′noid′, ə-rĭt′n-oid′) *Anat. n.* **1.** Either of two small pitcher-shaped cartilages at the back of the larynx to which the vocal cords are attached. **2.** A muscle connected to either of these cartilages. **3.** Any of several small mucous glands in front of these cartilages. [NLat. *arytaenoīdēs* < Gk. *arutainoeidēs,* shaped like a ladle : *arutaina,* ladle (< *aruein,* to draw water) + *-oeidēs,* -oid.] **—ar′y•te′noid′, ar′y•te•noid′al** *adj.*

as¹ (ăz; əz *when unstressed*) *adv.* **1.** To the same extent or degree; equally: *sings as sweetly as a nightingale.* **2.** For instance: *large carnivores, as the lion.* **3.** When taken into consideration in a specified relation or form: *this as distinguished from that.* *—conj.* **1.** To the same degree or quantity that. Often used as a correlative after *so* or *as*: *as sweet as sugar.* **2.** In the same manner or way that: *Think as I think.* **3.** At the same time that; while: *slipped as I ran.* **4.** For the reason that; because. **5.** With the result that: *so foolish as to lie.* **6.** Though: *Ridiculous as it seems, it's true.* **7.** In accordance with which or with the way in which: *The cafe is fine as such places go.* **8.** *Informal.* That: *I don't know as I can answer.* *—pron.* **1.** That; which; who. Used after *same* or *such*: *I received the same grade as you did.* **2.** *Chiefly Upper Southern U.S.* Who, whom, which, or that: *Those as want to can come.* *—prep.* **1.** In the role, capacity, or function of: *acting as mediator.* **2.** In a manner similar to; the same as: *They thought as one.* **—*idioms.* as is.** *Informal.* Just the way it is, with no changes or modifications. **as it were.** In a manner of speaking; as if such were so. [ME < OE *ealswā.* See ALSO.]

Usage Note: Traditionally, a distinction has been drawn between the constructions *as . . . as* and *so . . . as.* The *so . . . as* construction was required in negative sentences (as in Shakespeare's *" 'tis not so deep as a well"*), in questions (as in *Is it so bad as that?*), and in certain *if* clauses (as in *If it is so bad as you say, leave*). But in American English the use of *as . . . as* is now acceptable in all contexts. • In a comparison involving both *as . . . as* and *than,* one should write *He is as smart as, or smarter than, his brother,* not *He is as smart or smarter than his brother,* which remains unacceptable in formal style. • *As* should be preceded by a comma when it expresses a causal relation, as in *She won't be coming, as we didn't invite her.* When used to express a time relation, *as* is not preceded by a comma: *She was finishing the painting as I walked into the room.* • *As* is sometimes used superfluously to introduce the complements of verbs like *consider, deem,* and *account,* as in *They considered it as folly.* This usage may have arisen by analogy to *regard* and *esteem,* with which *as* is standardly used in this way. But the use of *as* with verbs like *consider* is not sufficiently well established to be acceptable in writing. See Usage Notes at **like², so¹, than.**

as² (ăs) *n., pl.* **as•ses** (ăs′ēz′, ăs′ĭz). **1.** An ancient Roman coin of copper or copper alloy. **2.** An ancient Roman unit of weight equal to about one troy pound. [Lat. *ās.*]

As The symbol for the element **arsenic** 1.

AS *abbr.* **1.** Also **a/s.** Air speed. **2.** American Samoa **3.** Also **A.S.** Anglo-Saxon. **4.** Antisubmarine. **5.** Associate in Science.

As. *abbr.* Asia; Asian.

as- *pref.* Var. of **ad-** 1.

as•a•fet•i•da also **as•a•foet•i•da** (ăs′ə-fĕt′ĭ-də) *n.* A bitter, foul-smelling resinous material from the roots of several plants of the genus *Ferula* in the parsley family, formerly used in medicine. [ME < Med.Lat. : *asa,* gum (< Pers. *azā,* mastic) + Lat. *fetida,* fem. of *fetidus,* stinking; see FETID.]

A•sa•hi•ka•wa (ä′sə-hē-kä′wə, ä′sä-hē′kä-wä) also **A•sa•hi•ga•wa** (ä′sə-hē-gä′wə, ä′sä-hē′gä-wä). A city of W-central Hokkaido, Japan. Pop. 363,630.

A•sa•ma (ə-sä′mə), **Mount.** An active volcano, 2,543.7 m (8,340 ft), of central Honshu, Japan, near Nagano.
A•san•te (ə-sän′tē) *n.* Var. of **Ashanti[1].**
ASAP or **asap** *abbr.* As soon as possible.
as•bes•tos also **as•bes•tus** (ăs-bĕs′təs, ăz-) *n.* Either of two incombustible, chemical-resistant, fibrous mineral forms of impure magnesium silicate. [ME *asbestus* < Lat. *asbestos,* mineral or gem < Gk., mineral or gem, unslaked lime < *asbestos,* unquenchable : *a-,* not; see A-[1] + *sbennunai, sbes-,* to quench.] **—as•bes′tine** (-tĭn), **as•bes′tic** (-tĭk) *adj.*
as•bes•to•sis (ăs′bĕs-tō′sĭs, ăz′-) *n.* A chronic, progressive lung disease caused by prolonged inhalation of asbestos particles. [ASBEST(OS) + -OSIS.] **—as′bes•tot′ic** (-tŏt′ĭk) *adj.*
As•bur•y (ăz′bə-rē), **Francis.** 1745–1816. British-born Amer. Methodist Episcopal bishop.
As•bur•y Park (ăz′bĕr′ē, -bə-rē). A city of E NJ on the Atlantic Ocean. Pop. 16,799.
ASCAP *abbr.* American Society of Composers, Authors, and Publishers.
a•scared (ə-skârd′) *adj. Chiefly Upper Southern U.S.* Afraid. [Prob. *a-* (var. of *y-,* p.part. pref.; see YCLEPT) + *scared,* p.part. of SCARE.]
as•ca•ri•a•sis (ăs′kə-rī′ə-sĭs) *n.* Infestation or disease caused by the parasitic roundworm *Ascaris lumbricoides.* [ASCAR(ID) + -IASIS.]
as•ca•rid (ăs′kə-rĭd) *n.* Any of various nematode worms of the family Ascaridae. [Sing. of *ascarides,* intestinal worms < LLat. < Gk. *askarides,* pl. of *askaris,* intestinal worm.]
ASCE *abbr.* American Society of Civil Engineers.
as•cend (ə-sĕnd′) *v.* **-cend•ed, -cend•ing, -cends.** —*intr.* **1.** To go or move upward; rise. **2.** To slope upward. —*tr.* **1.** To move upward upon or along; climb. **2.** To succeed to; occupy: *ascended the throne upon her father's death.* [ME *ascenden* < OFr. *ascendre* < Lat. *ascendere*: *ad-,* ad- + *scandere,* to climb; see **skand-*.**] **—as•cend′a•ble, as•cend′i•ble** *adj.*
as•cen•dance also **as•cen•dence** (ə-sĕn′dəns) *n.* Ascendancy.
as•cen•dan•cy also **as•cen•den•cy** (ə-sĕn′dən-sē) *n.* Superiority or decisive advantage; domination.
as•cen•dant also **as•cen•dent** (ə-sĕn′dənt) —*adj.* **1.** Inclining or moving upward; rising. **2.** Dominant in position or influence; superior. —*n.* **1.** The state of being dominant or in control. **2.** The point of the ecliptic or the zodiac sign that rises in the east at a given time, esp. a birth. **3.** An ancestor.
as•cend•er (ə-sĕn′dər) *n.* **1.** *Print.* The part of the tall lowercase letters, such as *b* and *h,* that extends above the other lowercase letters. **2.** A letter with such a part.
as•cend•ing (ə-sĕn′dĭng) *adj.* **1.** Moving, going, or growing upward. **2.** *Bot.* Growing or directing upward from a curved or slanted base. **—as•cend′ing•ly** *adv.*
ascending rhythm *n.* See **rising rhythm.**
as•cen•sion (ə-sĕn′shən) *n.* **1.** The act or process of ascending; ascent. **2.** *Astron.* The rising of a star above the horizon. **3. Ascension.** *Theol.* The bodily rising of Jesus into heaven 40 days after the Resurrection. [ME *ascensioun* < OFr. *ascention* < Lat. *ascēnsiō, ascēnsiōn-* < *ascēnsus,* p.part. of *ascendere,* to ascend. See ASCEND.] **—as•cen′sion•al** *adj.*
Ascension Day *n.* The 40th day after Easter, on which the Christian feast of the Ascension is observed.
Ascension Island. A British island in the S Atlantic NW of St. Helena; named by Portuguese explorers (1501).
as•cent (ə-sĕnt′) *n.* **1.** The act or process of rising or going upward. **2.** An advancement, esp. in social status. **3.** An upward slope or incline. **4.** A going back in time or genealogical succession. [< ASCEND, on the model of DESCENT.]
as•cer•tain (ăs′ər-tān′) *v.* **-tained, -tain•ing, -tains.** —*tr.* **1.** To discover with certainty, as through examination or experimentation. See Syns at **discover. 2.** *Archaic.* To make certain and precise. [ME *acertainen,* to inform < OFr. *acertener, ascertain-* : *a-,* to (< Lat. *ad-*; see AD-) + *certain,* certain; see CERTAIN.] **—as′cer•tain′a•ble** *adj.* **—as′cer•tain′a•ble•ness** *n.* **—as′cer•tain′a•bly** *adv.* **—as′cer•tain′ment** *n.*
as•cet•ic (ə-sĕt′ĭk) *n.* One who renounces material comforts for austere self-discipline, esp. as an act of religious devotion. —*adj.* **1.** Leading a life of self-discipline and self-denial, esp. for spiritual improvement. See Syns at **severe. 2.** Relating to or characteristic of an ascetic; self-denying and austere. [LGk. *askētikos* < Gk. *askētēs,* practitioner, hermit, monk < *askein,* to work.] **—as•cet′i•cal•ly** *adv.*
as•cet•i•cism (ə-sĕt′ĭ-sĭz′əm) *n.* **1.** The principles and practices of an ascetic; self-denial and austerity. **2.** The doctrine that the ascetic life releases the soul from bondage to the body and permits union with the divine.
Asch (ăsh), **Sholem** or **Shalom.** 1880–1957. Polish-born Amer. Yiddish writer whose works include *The Nazarene* (1939).
As•cham (ăs′kəm), **Roger.** 1515–68. English scholar who advocated the use of the vernacular in literature.
as•ci (ăs′ī′, -kī′) *n. Bot.* Pl. of **ascus.**
as•cid•i•an (ə-sĭd′ē-ən) *n.* See **sea squirt.** [< NLat. *Ascidia,* genus name < Gk. *askidion,* dim. of *askos,* wineskin.]
as•cid•i•um (ə-sĭd′ē-əm) *n., pl.* **-i•a** (ə-sĭd′ē-ə). *Bot.* A pitcher-shaped or bottle-shaped part or organ. [NLat. < Gk. *askidion,* dim. of *askos,* wineskin.] **—as•cid′i•ate′** *adj.* **—as•cid′i•form′** (-ə-fôrm′) *adj.*
ASCII (ăs′kē) *n. Comp. Sci.* **1.** A standard for defining codes for information exchange between equipment produced by different manufacturers. **2.** A code that follows this standard. [*A(merican) S(tandard) C(ode for) I(nformation) I(nterchange).*]
as•ci•tes (ə-sī′tēz) *n., pl.* **ascites.** An abnormal accumulation of serous fluid in the abdominal cavity. [ME *aschites* < LLat. *ascītēs* < Gk. *askitēs* < *askos,* belly, wineskin.] **—as•cit′ic** (-sĭt′ĭk) *adj.*
As•cle•pi•us (ə-sklē′pē-əs) *n. Gk. Myth.* Apollo's son, the god of medicine.
asco– *pref.* Ascus: *ascospore.* [NLat. < Gk. *askos,* bag, wineskin.]
as•co•carp (ăs′kə-kärp′) *n. Bot.* An ascus-bearing structure found in ascomycetous fungi.
as•co•go•ni•um (ăs′kə-gō′nē-əm) *n., pl.* **-ni•a** (-nē-ə). *Bot.* The female reproductive organ of ascomycetous fungi.
as•co•my•cete (ăs′kō-mī′sēt′, -mī-sēt′) *n. Bot.* Any of various fungi characterized by the presence of sexually produced spores formed within an ascus. **—as′co•my•ce′tous** (-sē′təs) *adj.*
a•scor•bate (ə-skôr′bāt, -bĭt) *n.* A salt of ascorbic acid. [ASCORB(IC ACID) + -ATE[2].]
a•scor•bic acid (ə-skôr′bĭk) *n.* A crystalline vitamin, $C_6H_8O_6$, found in citrus fruits, tomatoes, potatoes, and leafy green vegetables and used to prevent scurvy. [A-[1] + SCORB(UT)IC.]
as•co•spore (ăs′kə-spôr′, -spōr′) *n.* A sexually produced fungal spore in an ascus. **—as′co•spo′rous** (-spôr′əs, -spōr′-, ăs-kŏs′pər-əs), **as′co•spor′ic** (-spôr′ĭk, -spōr′-) *adj.*
as•cot (ăs′kət, -kŏt′) *n.* A broad neck scarf knotted so that one end lies flat on the other. [After the racetrack near ASCOT.]
As•cot (ăs′kət). A village of S-central England SW of London; site of the Royal Ascot horse races since 1711.
as•cribe (ə-skrīb′) *v.* **-cribed, -crib•ing, -cribes.** —*tr.* **1.** To attribute to a specified cause, source, or origin. **2.** To assign as a quality or characteristic: *ascribed jealousy to the critics.* [ME *ascriben* < OFr. *ascrivre* < Lat. *ascrībere*: *ad-,* ad- + *scrībere,* to write; see **skrībh-*.**]
as•crip•tion (ə-skrĭp′shən) *n.* **1.** The act of ascribing. **2.** A statement that ascribes. [Lat. *ascrīptiō, ascrīptiōn-,* addendum < *ascrīptus,* p.part. of *ascrībere,* to ascribe. See ASCRIBE.] **—as•crip′tive** *adj.*
ASCU *abbr.* Association of State Colleges and Universities.
As•cu•lum (ăs′kyə-ləm). An ancient Roman town of SE Italy; site of Pyrrhus's victory (279 B.C.).
as•cus (ăs′kəs) *n., pl.* **as•ci** (ăs′ī′, -kī′). *Bot.* A membranous, often club-shaped structure in which typically eight ascospores form through sexual reproduction of ascomycetes. [NLat. < Gk. *askos,* bag.]
ASE *abbr.* American Stock Exchange.
-ase *suff.* Enzyme: *amylase.* [< DIASTASE.]
a•sep•sis (ə-sĕp′sĭs, ā-) *n.* **1.** The state of being free of pathogenic microorganisms. **2.** The process of removing pathogenic microorganisms or protecting against infection by such organisms.
a•sep•tic (ə-sĕp′tĭk, ā-) *adj.* **1.a.** Free of pathogenic microorganisms. **b.** Protecting against infection by pathogenic microorganisms: *aseptic surgery.* **2.** Lacking animation or emotion. **—a•sep′ti•cal•ly** *adv.* **—a•sep′ti•cism** *n.*
a•sex•u•al (ā-sĕk′sho͞o-əl) *adj.* **1.** Having no evident sex or sex organs; sexless. **2.** Relating to, produced by, or involving reproduction without the union of male and female gametes, as in binary fission. **3.** Lacking interest in or desire for sex. **—a•sex′u•al′i•ty** (-ăl′ĭ-tē) *n.* **—a•sex′u•al•ly** *adv.*
as far as *conj.* To the degree or extent that.
as for *prep.* With regard to.
asg. *abbr.* **1.** Assigned. **2.** Assignment.
As•gard (ăs′gärd′, ăz′-) *n. Myth.* The heavenly residence of the Norse gods and slain heroes of war.
asgd. *abbr.* Assigned.
asgmt. *abbr.* Assignment.
ash[1] (ăsh) *n.* **1.** The grayish-white to black powdery residue from something that is burned. **2.** *Geol.* Pulverized particulate matter ejected by volcanic eruption. **3. ashes.** Ruins. **4. ashes.** Human remains, esp. after cremation or decay. [ME *asshe* < OE *æsce.* See **as-*.**]
ash[2] (ăsh) *n.* **1.** Any of various chiefly deciduous trees of the genus *Fraxinus,* having opposite, pinnately compound leaves. **2.** The strong elastic wood of this tree. **3.** *Ling.* The letter *æ* in Old English and some phonetic alphabets, representing the vowel sound of *ash.* [ME *asshe* < OE *æsc.*]
a•shamed (ə-shāmd′) *adj.* **1.** Feeling shame or guilt. **2.** Feeling inferior, inadequate, or embarrassed. **3.** Reluctant through fear of humiliation or shame: *ashamed to ask.* [ME < OE *āsceamod,* p.part. of *āsceamian,* to feel shame : *ā-,* intensive pref. + *sceamian,* to feel shame.]
A•shan•ti[1] (ə-shăn′tē, ə-shän′-) also **A•san•te** (-sän′tē) *n., pl.* **Ashanti** or **-tis** also **Asante** or **-tes. 1.** A member of an Akan people of Ghana, formerly united in the Ashanti kingdom. **2.** The Twi language of the Ashanti.

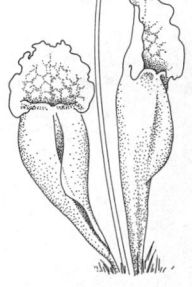

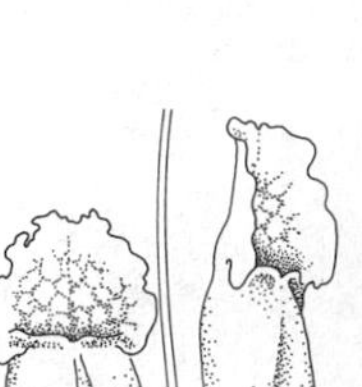
ascidium
Pitcher plant
Sarracenia purpurea

ash[2]
White ash
Fraxinus americana

ă pat	oi boy
ā pay	ou out
âr care	o͝o took
ä father	o͞o boot
ĕ pet	ŭ cut
ē be	ûr urge
ĭ pit	th thin
ī pie	*th* this
îr pier	hw which
ŏ pot	zh vision
ō toe	ə about, item
ô paw	

Stress marks:
′ (primary);
′ (secondary), as in
dictionary (dĭk′shə-nĕr′ē)

A•shan•ti[2] (ə-shăn′tē, -shän′-). A region and former kingdom of W Africa in present-day central Ghana; formed in the late 17th cent. and annexed to the British Gold Coast in 1901.

ash•cake (ăsh′kāk′) *n. Chiefly Southern U.S.* See **johnnycake.** See Regional Note at **johnnycake.** [From its being baked in hot ashes.]

ash•can or **ash can** (ăsh′kăn′) *n.* **1.** A large, usu. metal receptacle for trash. **2.** *Slang.* A depth change.

Ash•can school (ăsh′kăn′) *n.* A group of early 20th-century U.S. painters of everyday urban life.

Ash•dod (ăsh′dŏd′, äsh-dōd′). A city of SW Israel on the Mediterranean W of Jerusalem near the site of ancient **Ashdod,** an important Philistine city-state. Pop. 68,900.

Ashe (ăsh), **Arthur Robert, Jr.** 1943–93. Amer. tennis player who won singles titles at the U.S. Open (1968) and Wimbledon (1975).

ash•en[1] (ăsh′ən) *adj.* **1.** Consisting of ashes. **2.** Resembling ashes, esp. in color; very pale: *A face ashen with grief.*

ash•en[2] (ăsh′ən) *adj.* Of or relating to wood from the ash tree.

Ash•er (ăsh′ər). In the Bible, a son of Jacob and the forebear of one of the tribes of Israel.

Ashe•ville (ăsh′vĭl′). A city of W NC in the Blue Ridge WNW of Charlotte; site of Thomas Wolfe's home. Pop. 61,607.

Ash•ke•naz•i (äsh′kə-nä′zē) *n., pl.* **-naz•im** (-năz′ĭm, -nä′zĭm). A member of the branch of European Jews, historically Yiddish-speaking, who settled in central and northern Europe. [< Medieval Heb. *Ashkenaz,* Germany < Heb. *Ashkĕnāz,* one of Noah's grandsons, name of a neighboring but unidentified nation.] **—Ash′ke•naz′ic** (-nä′zĭk) *adj.*

Ash•kha•bad (äsh′kä-bäd′, -KHä-bät′). The cap. of Turkmenistan, in the S-central part near the Iranian border; founded as a fortress in 1881. Pop. 356,000.

Ash•land (ăsh′lənd). **1.** A city of NE KY on the OH–WV border; settled in 1786. Pop. 23,622. **2.** A city of N-central OH SE of Cleveland. Pop. 20,079.

ash•lar (ăsh′lər) *n.* **1.a.** A squared block of building stone. **b.** Masonry of such stones. **2.** A thin dressed rectangle of stone for facing walls. [ME *assheler* < OFr. *aisselier,* board < *aissele* < Med.Lat. *axicellus* < Lat. *assis.*]

a•shore (ə-shôr′, ə-shōr′) *adv.* **1.** To or onto the shore: *driven ashore by the wind.* **2.** On land: *spent the day ashore.*

as how *conj. Informal.* That: *The child allowed as how he had already done his homework.*

Ash•qe•lon or **Ash•ke•lon** (äsh′kə-lŏn′, äsh′kĕ-lôn′). An ancient city of SW Palestine on the Mediterranean Sea; inhabited as early as the 3rd millennium B.C.

ash•ram (äsh′rəm) *n. Hinduism.* **1.** A usu. secluded residence of a religious community and its guru. **2.** One of the four stages of an individual's life. [Skt. *āśramaḥ*: *ā-,* to + *śramaḥ,* toil, penance, austerity (< *śramati,* he toils, practices austerity).]

Ash•ta•bu•la (ăsh′tə-byōō′lə). A city of NE OH on Lake Erie NE of Cleveland. Pop. 21,633.

Ash•ton (ăsh′tən), Sir **Frederick.** 1904–88. British choreographer whose ballets include *The Dream* (1964).

Ash•ton-un•der-Lyne (ăsh′tən-ŭn-dər-līn′). A borough of NW England, a suburb of Manchester. Pop. 218,800.

Ash•to•reth (ăsh′tə-rĕth′) *n. Myth.* The ancient Syrian and Phoenician goddess of sexual love and fertility.

ash•tray (ăsh′trā′) *n.* A receptacle for tobacco ashes and cigarette butts.

A•shur (ä′shŏŏr′) also **As•sur** (ä′sŏŏr′, ä′shŏŏr′) *n.* The principal Assyrian deity.

A•shur•ba•ni•pal (ä′shŏŏr-bä′nə-päl′) also **As•sur•ba•ni•pal** (ä′sŏŏr-). fl. 7th cent. B.C. King of Assyria (669–626) who was a noted patron of literature and the arts.

Ash Wednesday (ăsh) *n.* The seventh Wednesday before Easter and the first day of Lent, when many Christians receive a mark of ashes on the forehead to indicate penitence and mortality.

ash•y (ăsh′ē) *adj.* **-i•er, -i•est. 1.** Of, relating to, or covered with ashes. **2.** Of the color of ashes; pale. **—ash′i•ness** *n.*

ASI *abbr.* Air speed indicator.

A•sia (ā′zhə, ā′shə). A continent occupying the E part of the Eurasian landmass and its adjacent islands; separated from Europe by the Ural Mts.

Asia Minor. A peninsula of W Asia between the Black Sea and the Mediterranean; generally coterminous with Asian Turkey.

A•sian (ā′zhən, ā′shən) *adj.* Of or relating to Asia or its peoples, languages, or cultures. *—n.* **1.** A native or inhabitant of Asia. **2.** A person of Asian descent.

Usage Note: The term *Asian* is now preferred for persons of South and East Asian ancestry, such as Indians, Southeast Asians, Chinese, Koreans, and Japanese, in place of *Oriental,* an older term for some of these groups. *Oriental* has been objected to because it suggests racial rather than cultural identity and identifies the place of origin in terms of its location relative to the West (that is, "from the East"), rather than in absolute terms.

Asian American also **A•sian-A•mer•i•can** (ā′zhən-ə-mĕr′ĭ-kən, ā′shən-) *n.* A U.S. citizen or resident of Asian descent. **—A′sian-A•mer′i•can** *adj.*

asparagus
Asparagus officinalis

Asian influenza *n.* Influenza caused by the most common influenza virus (type A), first isolated in China in 1957.

A•sian•i•za•tion (ā′zhə-nĭ-zā′shən) *n.* The act or process of making or becoming Asian in character, culture, or outlook.

Asian pear *n.* See **sand pear.**

Asian tiger mosquito *n.* A mosquito *(Aeder albopictus),* once confined to Asia but now present in parts of tropical and subtropical America, that transmits dengue and yellow fever.

A•si•at•ic (ā′zhē-ăt′ĭk, -shē-, -zē-) *adj.* Asian. Offensive when used of people.

Asiatic cholera *n.* See **cholera** 1.

a•side (ə-sīd′) *adv.* **1.** To or toward the side: *step aside.* **2.** Out of one's thoughts or mind: *put doubt aside.* **3.** Apart: *time set aside for fun.* **4.** In reserve; away. **5.** Set out of the way; dispensed with: *Joking aside, can you swim 15 miles? —n.* **1.** A piece of dialogue supposedly not heard by the other actors on stage. **2.** A remark made in an undertone so as to be inaudible. **3.** A parenthetical departure; a digression.

aside from *prep.* Excluding; except for.

as if *conj.* **1.** In the same way that it would be if: *ran as if she were chased.* **2.** That: *It seemed as if the work would never end.*

As•i•mov (ăz′ĭ-môf′, -mŏf′), **Isaac.** 1920–92. Russian-born Amer. scientist and writer whose works include *The Foundation Trilogy* (1963).

as•i•nine (ăs′ə-nīn′) *adj.* **1.** Utterly stupid or silly. **2.** Of or like an ass. [Lat. *asinīnus,* of an ass < *asinus,* ass.]

ask (ăsk) *v.* **asked, ask•ing, asks.** *—tr.* **1.** To put a question to. **2.** To seek an answer to. **3.** To seek information about: *asked directions.* **4.** To make a request of or for. **5.** To require or call for as a price or condition: *asked ten dollars for the book.* **6.** To expect or demand: *ask too much.* **7.** To invite. **8.** *Archaic.* To publish, as marriage banns. *—intr.* **1.** To inquire; seek information. **2.** To make a request: *asked for help.* ***—idiom.*** **ask for it** (or **trouble).** *Informal.* To persist in an action although it may result in difficulty or punishment. [ME *asken* < OE *āscian.* See **ais-*.**]

Syns: *ask, question, inquire, query, interrogate, examine, quiz.* These verbs mean to seek information. *Ask* is the most neutral term: *asked her what was wrong; ask too many questions. Question* often implies careful and continuous asking: *The prosecutor questioned the witness. Inquire* refers to a simple request for information: *will inquire how we can help. Query* usually suggests settling a doubt: *The proofreader queried the spelling of the word. Interrogate* applies especially to official questioning: *The suspects were interrogated by detectives. Examine* refers particularly to close and detailed questioning to ascertain a person's knowledge or qualifications: *Only lawyers who have been examined and certified by the bar association are admitted to practice. Quiz* often denotes the informal examination of students: *The teacher quizzed the pupils on the multiplication tables.*

a•skance (ə-skăns′) also **a•skant** (ə-skănt′) *adv.* **1.** With disapproval, suspicion, or distrust. **2.** With a sideways glance; obliquely. [?]

a•skew (ə-skyōō′) *adv. & adj.* To one side; awry: *rugs lying askew.* [Prob. A-[2] + SKEW.]

ask•ing price (ăs′kĭng) *n.* The price asked for an item.

ASL *abbr.* American Sign Language.

a•slant (ə-slănt′) *adv. & adj.* At a slant; obliquely. *—prep.* Obliquely over or across.

a•sleep (ə-slēp′) *adj.* **1.** In a state of sleep; sleeping. **2.a.** Inactive; dormant. **b.** Indifferent: *politicians asleep to minority needs.* **3.** Numb: *My leg is asleep.* **4.** Dead. *—adv.* **1.** In or into a state of sleep. **2.** In or into a state of apathy or indifference. **3.** Into death.

as long as *conj.* **1.** Since: *As long as you've offered, I accept.* **2.** On the condition that.

a•slope (ə-slōp′) *adv. & adj.* At a slope or slant.

a•slosh (ə-slŏsh′) *adv. & adj.* Awash.

As•ma•ra (ăz-mä′rə). A city of N Ethiopia near the Red Sea at an altitude of c. 2,227 m (7,300 ft). Pop. 474,241.

ASME *abbr.* American Society of Mechanical Engineers.

As•mo•de•us (ăz′mə-dē′əs, ăs′-) *n. Judaism.* The king of demons.

As•nières-sur-Seine (ä-nyĕr′sür-sān′, -sĕn′). A city of N-central France, a suburb of Paris. Pop. 71,077.

A•so (ä′sō′), **Mount.** Also **A•so-san** (ä′sō-sän′). A volcanic mountain of central Kyushu, Japan, topped by one of the world's largest calderas and rising to 1,593 m (5,223 ft).

a•so•cial (ā-sō′shəl) *adj.* **1.** Not social. **2.** Avoiding or averse to the society of others; not sociable. **3.** Unable or unwilling to conform to normal standards of social behavior; antisocial. **4.** Inconsiderate of others; self-centered. *—n.* One that exhibits behavior and characteristics deemed asocial.

as of *prep.* On; at: *The project was terminated as of January 1.*

A•so•ka (ə-sō′kə). "the Great." d. 232 B.C. King of Magadha (273–232) who adopted Buddhism as the state religion.

asp (ăsp) *n.* Any of several venomous snakes of Africa, Asia, and Europe, such as the small cobra *Naja haje.* [ME *aspis* < Lat. < Gk.]

as•par•a•gin•ase (ə-spăr′ə-jə-nās′, -nāz′) *n.* An enzyme isolated from bacteria that catalyzes the hydrolysis of asparagine.

as•par•a•gine (ə-spăr′ə-jēn′) *n.* A crystalline amino acid, $C_4H_8N_2O_3$, found in plants and easily hydrolyzed to aspartic acid. [ASPARAG(US) + -INE[2].]

as•par•a•gus (ə-spăr′ə-gəs) *n.* **1.** The tender shoots of a Eurasian plant *(Asparagus officinalis),* eaten as a vegetable. **2.** Any of various perennial plants of the Old World genus *Asparagus* with leaflike stems, scalelike leaves, and small flowers. [Lat. < Gk. *asparagos.*]

asparagus beetle *n.* A small spotted beetle *(Crioceris asparagi)* that infests and damages asparagus plants.

asparagus pea *n.* An Asiatic twining herb *(Psophocarpus tetragonolobus)* having tuberous roots and long four-angled pods.

as•par•tame (ăs′pər-tām′, ə-spär′-) *n.* An artificial sweetener, $C_{14}H_{18}N_2O_5$, formed from aspartic acid. [ASPART(IC ACID) + (PHENYL)A(LANINE) + M(ETHYL) + E(STER).]

a•spar•tate (ə-spär′tāt) *n.* A salt or ester of aspartic acid. [ASPART(IC ACID) + -ATE[2].]

as•par•tic acid (ə-spär′tĭk) *n.* A nonessential amino acid, $C_4H_7NO_4$, found esp. in young sugar cane and sugar-beet molasses. [< ASPARAGUS (from its being obtained from an amino acid found in asparagus).]

as•par•to•kin•ase (ə-spär′tō-kī′nās) *n.* An enzyme that catalyzes aspartic acid phosphorylation by ATP. [ASPART(IC ACID) + KINASE.]

As•pa•sia (ă-spā′zhə). fl. c. 440 B.C. Greek courtesan and lover of Pericles who was noted for her wisdom, wit, and beauty.

A.S.P.C.A. *abbr.* American Society for the Prevention of Cruelty to Animals.

as•pect (ăs′pĕkt) *n.* **1.** A particular look or facial expression; mien. **2.** Appearance to the eye, esp. from a specific vantage point. **3.** A way in which something can be viewed by the mind: *all aspects of the situation.* **4.** A position facing or commanding a given direction; an exposure. **5.** A side or surface facing a particular direction. **6.** The configuration of the stars or planets in relation to one another, thought by astrologers to influence human affairs. **7.** *Gram.* A property of verbs that indicates inception, duration, completion, habituality, or other modes of action or being. **8.** *Archaic.* An act of looking or gazing. [ME < Lat. *aspectus,* a view < p.part. of *aspicere,* to look at : *ad-,* ad- + *specere,* to look; see **spek-***.]

aspect ratio *n.* **1.** The width-to-height ratio of a photographic or television image. **2.** The span-to-mean-chord ratio of an airfoil.

as•pen (ăs′pən) *n.* Any of several trees of the genus *Populus* having leaves attached by flat leafstalks so that they flutter in the wind. —*adj.* **1.** Of or relating to one of these trees. **2.** Shaking like aspen leaves. [ME *aspe* < OE *æspe.*]

As•pen (ăs′pən). A city of W-central CO in the Sawatch Range of the Rocky Mts.; founded c. 1879. Pop. 5,049.

as•per•ate (ăs′pə-rāt′) *tr.v.* **-at•ed, -at•ing, -ates.** To make uneven; roughen. [Lat. *asperāre, asperāt-* < *asper,* rough.]

as•per•ges (ə-spûr′jēz) *n. Rom. Cath. Ch.* The ceremony of sprinkling the altar, clergy, and congregation with holy water. [< Lat. *asperges (me),* you will sprinkle (me), the first words of the rite < *aspergere,* to sprinkle. See ASPERSE.]

as•per•gil•lo•sis (ăs′pər-jə-lō′sĭs) *n.* An infection caused by fungi of the genus *Aspergillus.* [ASPERGILL(US) + -OSIS.]

as•per•gil•lum (ăs′pər-jĭl′əm) or **as•per•gill** (-jĭl) *n., pl.* **-gil•la** (-jĭl′ə) or **-gil•lums.** *Rom. Cath. Ch.* An instrument, such as a brush, used for sprinkling holy water. [NLat. < Lat. *aspergere,* to sprinkle. See ASPERSE.]

as•per•gil•lus (ăs′pər-jĭl′əs) *n., pl.* **-gil•li** (-jĭl′ī′). Any of various fungi of the genus *Aspergillus,* which includes many common molds. [NLat. < *aspergillum,* aspergill (from its resemblance to an aspergillum brush). See ASPERGILLUM.]

as•per•i•ty (ă-spĕr′ĭ-tē) *n.* **1.a.** Roughness or harshness, as of surface, sound, or climate. **b.** Severity; rigor. **2.** Harshness of manner; ill temper or irritability. [ME *asperite* < OFr. *asprete* < Lat. *asperitās* < *asper,* rough.]

as•perse (ə-spûrs′) *tr.v.* **-persed, -pers•ing, -pers•es. 1.** To spread false or damaging charges or insinuations against. **2.** To sprinkle, esp. with holy water. [ME, to besprinkle < Lat. *aspergere, aspers-* : *ad-,* ad- + *spargere,* to strew.]

as•per•sion (ə-spûr′zhən, -shən) *n.* **1.a.** An unfavorable or damaging remark; slander: *Don't cast aspersions.* **b.** The act of defaming or slandering. **2.** A sprinkling, esp. with holy water.

as•phalt (ăs′fôlt′) *n.* **1.** A brownish-black solid or semisolid mixture of bitumens obtained from native deposits or as a petroleum byproduct, used in paving, roofing, and waterproofing. **2.** Mixed asphalt and crushed stone gravel or sand, used for paving or roofing. —*tr.v.* **-phalted, -phalt•ing, -phalts.** To pave or coat with this mixture. [ME *aspalt* < Med.Lat. *asphaltus* < Gk. *asphaltos.*] —**as•phal′tic** *adj.*

as•phal•tite (ăs′fôl-tīt′) *n.* A solid dark-colored complex of hydrocarbons found in natural veins and deposits.

asphalt jungle *n.* An urban area, usu. having a high population and crime rate.

a•spher•ic (ā-sfîr′ĭk, ā-sfĕr′-) also **a•spher•i•cal** (-ĭ-kəl) *adj.* Varying slightly from sphericity with only slight aberration, as a lens.

as•pho•del (ăs′fə-dĕl′) *n.* **1.a.** Any of several chiefly Mediterranean plants of the genera *Asphodeline* and *Asphodelus* in the lily family, having linear leaves and elongate flower clusters. **b.** Any of several other plants, such as the bog asphodel. **2.** In Greek poetry and mythology, the flowers of Hades and the dead, sacred to Persephone. **3.** In early English and French poetry, the daffodil. [Lat. *asphodelus* < Gk. *asphodelos.*]

as•phyx•i•a (ăs-fĭk′sē-ə) *n.* An extreme decrease in the amount of oxygen in the body accompanied by excess carbon dioxide leading to unconsciousness or death. [NLat. < Gk. *asphuxia,* stopping of the pulse : *a-,* not; see A-[1] + *sphuxis,* heartbeat (< *sphuzein, sphug-,* to throb).]

as•phyx•i•ant (ăs-fĭk′sē-ənt) *adj.* Inducing or tending to induce asphyxia. —**as•phyx′i•ant** *n.*

as•phyx•i•ate (ăs-fĭk′sē-āt′) *v.* **-at•ed, -at•ing, -ates.** —*tr.* To cause asphyxia in; smother. —*intr.* To undergo asphyxia; suffocate. —**as•phyx′i•a′tion** *n.* —**as•phyx′i•a′tor** *n.*

as•pic[1] (ăs′pĭk) *n.* A clear jelly usu. made of stock and gelatin and used as a garnish or to make a mold. [Fr. < *aspic,* asp (from the resemblance of the jelly's coloration to an asp's). See ASPIC[2].]

as•pic[2] (ăs′pĭk) *n. Archaic.* An asp. [Fr. < OFr., alteration of *aspe* < Lat. *aspis.* See ASP.]

as•pi•dis•tra (ăs′pĭ-dĭs′trə) *n.* Any of several eastern Asian plants of the genus *Aspidistra* in the lily family, esp. *A. elatior,* cultivated as a houseplant for its evergreen basal leaves and bell-shaped flowers. [NLat. *Aspidistra,* genus name < Gk. *aspis, aspid-,* shield.]

as•pi•rant (ăs′pər-ənt, ə-spīr′-) *n.* One who aspires, as to advancement, honors, or a high position. —**as′pi•rant** *adj.*

as•pi•rate (ăs′pə-rāt′) *tr.v.* **-rat•ed, -rat•ing, -rates. 1.** *Ling.* **a.** To pronounce (a vowel or word) with the initial release of breath associated with English *h,* as in *hurry.* **b.** To follow (a consonant, esp. a stop) with a clearly audible puff of breath, as in English *pit.* **2.** To draw (something) into the lungs; inhale. **3.** *Medic.* To remove (liquids or gases) by means of a suction device. —*n.* (-pər-ĭt). **1.** *Ling.* **a.** The speech sound represented by English *h.* **b.** The puff of air accompanying the release of a stop. **c.** A speech sound followed by a puff of breath. **2.** *Medic.* Matter removed by aspiration. [Lat. *aspīrāre, aspīrāt-,* to breathe on : *ad-,* ad- + *spīrāre,* to breathe.]

as•pi•ra•tion (ăs′pə-rā′shən) *n.* **1.** Expulsion of breath in speech. **2.** *Ling.* **a.** Aspirated pronunciation of a consonant. **b.** A speech sound produced with an aspirate. **3.** The act of breathing in; inhalation. **4.** *Medic.* The process of removing fluids or gases from the body with a suction device. **5.a.** A desire for high achievement. **b.** An object of such desire.

as•pi•ra•tor (ăs′pə-rā′tər) *n.* **1.** A device for removing liquids or gases by suction, esp. from a body cavity. **2.** A suction pump used to create a partial vacuum.

as•pir•a•to•ry (ə-spīr′ə-tôr′ē, -tōr′ē) *adj.* Of, relating to, or suited for breathing or suction.

as•pire (ə-spīr′) *intr.v.* **-pired, -pir•ing, -pires. 1.** To have a great ambition or ultimate goal; desire strongly: *aspired to stardom.* **2.** To strive toward an end. **3.** To soar. [ME *aspiren* < *aspirer* < Lat. *aspīrāre,* to desire. See ASPIRATE.] —**as•pir′er** *n.* —**as•pīr′ing•ly** *adv.*

as•pi•rin (ăs′pər-ĭn, -prĭn) *n.* **1.** A crystalline compound, $CH_3COOC_6H_4COOH$, derived from salicylic acid and used to relieve pain and reduce fever and inflammation. **2.** A tablet of aspirin. [Originally a trademark.]

a•squint (ə-skwĭnt′) *adv. & adj.* With a sidelong glance. [ME : *a-,* on; see A-[2] + *-squint;* akin to *-skwyn,* in ME *of skwyn,* obliquely.]

As•quith (ăs′kwĭth), **Herbert Henry.** 1st Earl of Oxford and Asquith. 1852–1928. British prime minister (1908–16).

ASR *abbr.* Air-sea rescue.

as regards *prep.* In regard to.

ass[1] (ăs) *n., pl.* **ass•es** (ăs′ĭz). **1.** Any of several hoofed mammals of the genus *Equus,* closely related to the horses but with smaller build and longer ears and including the domesticated donkey. **2.** A vain, silly, or aggressively stupid person. [ME *asse* < OE *assa,* perh. of Celt. orig., ult. < Lat. *asinus.*]

ass[2] (ăs) *n., pl.* **ass•es** (ăs′ĭz). *Vulgar Slang.* **1.a.** The buttocks. **b.** The anus. **2.** Sexual intercourse. [ME *ars* < OE *ears.* See **ors-***.]

As•sad (ä-säd′), **Hafez al-.** b. c. 1928. Syrian politician who seized control in 1970 and was elected president in 1971.

as•sa•gai (ăs′ə-gī′) *n.* Var. of **assegai.**

as•sai[1] (ä-sī′) *n.* **1.** Any of several feather-leaved South American palms, esp. *Euterpe edulis* and *E. oleracea,* which are sources of heart of palm. **2.** A beverage made from the fleshy purple fruit of one of these palms. [Port. *assaí* < Tupi *assahi.*]

as•sai[2] (ä-sī′) *adv. Mus.* Very. [Ital. < VLat. **ad satis,* to sufficiency. See ASSET.]

as•sail (ə-sāl′) *tr.v.* **-sailed, -sail•ing, -sails. 1.** To attack with or as if with violent blows; assault. **2.** To attack verbally. **3.** To trouble; beset: *assailed by doubts.* [ME *assailen* < OFr. *asalir, asaill-* < VLat. **assalīre,* var. of Lat. *assilīre,* to jump on : *ad-,* onto; see AD- + *salīre,* to jump; see **sel-***.] —**as•**

aspergillum
Priest with aspergillum in right hand

ass[1]
Somali ass
Equus africanus somalicus

ă pat	oi boy
ā pay	ou out
âr care	o͝o took
ä father	o͞o boot
ĕ pet	ŭ cut
ē be	ûr urge
ĭ pit	th thin
ī pie	*th* this
îr pier	hw which
ŏ pot	zh vision
ō toe	ə about, item
ô paw	

Stress marks:
′ (primary);
′ (secondary), as in
dictionary (dĭk′shə-nĕr′ē)

sail′a•ble *adj.* —**as•sail′a•ble•ness** *n.* —**as•sail′ant, as•sail′er** *n.* —**as•sail′er** *n.* —**as•sail′ment** *n.*

As•sam (ă-săm′). A former kingdom of extreme NE India, now a state separated from the rest of the country by Bangladesh.

As•sam•ese (ăs′ə-mēz′, -mēs′) *adj.* Of or relating to Assam or its people, language, or culture. —*n., pl.* **Assamese. 1.** A native or inhabitant of Assam. **2.** The Indic language of the Assamese.

as•sas•sin (ə-săs′ĭn) *n.* **1.** One who murders by surprise attack, esp. one who carries out a plot to kill a prominent person. **2. Assassin.** A member of a secret Muslim order that killed Crusaders and others. [Fr. < Med.Lat. *assassīnus* < Ar. *ḥaššāšīn*, pl. of *ḥaššāš*, hashish user < *ḥašīš*, hashish.]

as•sas•si•nate (ə-săs′ə-nāt′) *tr.v.* **-nat•ed, -nat•ing, -nates. 1.** To murder (a prominent person) by surprise attack, as for political reasons. **2.** To destroy or injure treacherously. —**as•sas′si•na′tion** *n.* —**as•sas′si•na′tive** *adj.* —**as•sas′si•na′tor** *n.*

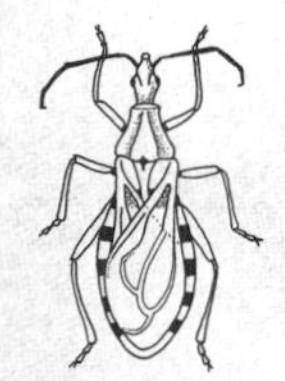

assassin bug
Bloodsucking conenose
Triatoma sanguisuga

assassin bug *n.* Any of various predatory bugs of the family Reduviidae, which have powerful beaks used to prey on other insects or modified to suck blood from mammals.

As•sa•teague Island (ăs′ə-tēg′). An island off MD and VA separating Chincoteague Bay from the Atlantic Ocean.

as•sault (ə-sôlt′) *n.* **1.** A violent physical or verbal attack. **2.a.** A military attack, such as one launched against a fortified place. **b.** The concluding stage of an attack at which close combat occurs. **3.** *Law.* **a.** An unlawful threat or attempt to do bodily injury to another. **b.** The act or an instance of unlawfully threatening or attempting to injure another. **4.a.** *Law.* Sexual assault. **b.** Rape. —*v.* **-sault•ed, -sault•ing, -saults.** —*tr.* **1.** To make an assault upon; attack. **2.** To rape. —*intr.* To make an assault. [ME *assaut* < OFr. < VLat. **assaltus*, var. of Lat. *assultus* < p.part. of *assilīre*, to jump on. See ASSAIL.] —**as•sault′er** *n.*

assault and battery *n. Law.* An assault upon a victim that is carried out by striking the victim, knocking the victim down, or otherwise doing violence to the victim.

as•saul•tive (ə-sôl′tĭv) *adj.* Inclined to or suggestive of violent attack.

as•say (ăs′ā′, ă-sā′) *n.* **1.a.** Qualitative or quantitative analysis of a substance, esp. of an ore or drug, to determine its components. **b.** A substance to be so analyzed. **c.** The result of such an analysis. **2.** An analysis or examination. **3.** *Archaic.* An attempt; an essay. —*v.* (ă-sā′, ăs′ā′) **-sayed, -say•ing, -says.** —*tr.* **1.** To subject to chemical analysis. **2.** To examine by trial or experiment; put to a test: *assay one's ability to speak Chinese.* **3.** To evaluate; assess. See Syns at **estimate. 4.** To attempt; try. —*intr.* To be shown by analysis to contain a certain proportion of usu. precious metal. [ME < OFr. *essai, assai.* See ESSAY.] —**as•say′a•ble** *adj.* —**as•say′er** *n.*

as•se•gai or **as•sa•gai** (ăs′ə-gī′) *n.* **1.** A light spear or lance, esp. one with a short shaft and long blade for close combat, used by southern Africans. **2.** A southern African tree *(Curtisia dentata)* having wood used for spears or lances. [Obsolete Fr. *azagaie*, prob. < OSp. *azagaya* < Ar. *az-zaġāyah*: *al*, the + Berber *zaghāyah*, spear.]

as•sem•blage (ə-sĕm′blĭj) *n.* **1.a.** The act of assembling. **b.** The state of being assembled. **2.** A collection of people or things; a gathering. **3.** A fitting together of parts, as in a machine. **4.** A sculptural composition of miscellaneous objects. —**as•sem′blag•ist** *n.*

as•sem•ble (ə-sĕm′bəl) *v.* **-bled, -bling, -bles.** —*tr.* **1.** To bring or call together into a group or whole: *assembled the jury.* **2.** To fit together the parts or pieces of. —*intr.* To gather together; congregate. See Syns at **gather.** [ME *assemblen* < OFr. *assembler* < VLat. **assimulāre*: Lat. *ad-*, ad- + Lat. *simul*, together; see **sem-**[1]***.**]

as•sem•bler (ə-sĕm′blər) *n.* **1.** One that assembles. **2.** *Comp. Sci.* A program that translates symbolic code into the equivalent executable machine code. **3.** *Comp. Sci.* See **assembly language.**

as•sem•bly (ə-sĕm′blē) *n., pl.* **-blies. 1.a.** The act of assembling. **b.** The state of being assembled. **2.** A group gathered for a common reason, as for a religious or social purpose. **3. Assembly.** The lower house of certain U.S. state legislatures. **4.a.** The putting together of manufactured parts to make a completed product. **b.** A set of parts so assembled. **5.** A signal for troops to come together in formation. **6.** *Comp. Sci.* The automatic translation of symbolic code into machine code.

assembly language *n. Comp. Sci.* A programming language that approximates the binary machine code.

assembly line *n.* **1.** An arrangement of workers, machines, and equipment in which the product being assembled passes consecutively from operation to operation until completed. **2.** A process in which finished products are turned out in a mechanically efficient, though impersonal manner.

as•sem•bly•man (ə-sĕm′blē-mən) *n.* A man who is a member of a legislative assembly.

Assembly of God *n.* A Pentecostal congregation founded in the United States in 1914.

as•sem•bly•wom•an (ə-sĕm′blē-wo͝om′ən) *n.* A woman who is a member of a legislative assembly.

as•sent (ə-sĕnt′) *intr.v.* **-sent•ed, -sent•ing, -sents.** To agree, as to a proposal; concur. —*n.* **1.** Agreement; concurrence. **2.** Acquiescence; consent. [ME *assenten* < OFr. *assentir* < Lat. *assentārī*: *ad-*, ad- + *sentīre*, to feel; see **sent-*.**] —**as•sent′er, as•sen′tor** *n.* —**as•sent′ing•ly** *adv.* —**as•sen′tive** *adj.* —**as•sen′tive•ness** *n.*

Syns: assent, agree, accede, acquiesce, consent, concur, subscribe. These verbs denote acceptance of and often belief in another's views, proposals, or actions. *Assent* implies agreement, especially as a result of deliberation: *assented to our suggestion. Agree* and *accede* are related in the sense that assent has been reached after discussion or persuasion, but *accede* implies that one person or group has yielded to the other: *"It was not possible to agree to a proposal so extraordinary and unexpected"* (William Robertson). *"In an evil hour this proposal was acceded to"* (Mary E. Herbert). *Acquiesce* suggests passive assent because of inability or unwillingness to oppose: *I acquiesced despite my private opinion. Consent* implies voluntary agreement: *Her parents consented to her marriage. Concur* may suggest that one has reached the same conclusion as another independently: *"I concurred with our incumbent in getting up a petition against the Reform Bill"* (George Eliot). *Subscribe* indicates hearty approval: *"I am contented to subscribe to the opinion of the best-qualified judge of our time"* (Sir Walter Scott).

as•sen•ta•tion (ăs′ĕn-tā′shən) *n.* Hasty, typically servile agreement with another's opinions.

As•ser (ä′sər), **Tobias Michael Carel.** 1838–1913. Dutch jurist who shared the 1911 Nobel Peace Prize.

as•sert (ə-sûrt′) *tr.v.* **-sert•ed, -sert•ing, -serts. 1.** To state or express positively; affirm. **2.** To defend or maintain (one's rights, for example). **3.** To put (oneself) forward boldly or forcefully in an effort to make an opinion known, for example: *I asserted myself in order to ensure action.* [Lat. *asserere, assert-* : *ad-*, ad- + *serere*, to join; see **ser-**[2]***.**] —**as•sert′a•ble, as•sert′i•ble** *adj.* —**as•sert′er, as•ser′tor** *n.*

as•sert•ed (ə-sûr′tĭd) *adj.* Confidently stated to be so but without proof; alleged. —**as•sert′ed•ly** *adv.*

as•ser•tion (ə-sûr′shən) *n.* **1.** The act of asserting. **2.** Something declared or stated positively, often with no support or attempt at proof. —**as•ser′tion•al** *adj.*

as•ser•tive (ə-sûr′tĭv) *adj.* Inclined to bold or confident assertion; aggressively self-assured. —**as•ser′tive•ly** *adv.* —**as•ser′tive•ness** *n.*

as•ses[1] (ăs′ēz′, ăs′ĭz) *n.* Pl. of **as**[2].

ass•es[2] (ăs′ĭz) *n.* Pl. of **ass**[1].

ass•es[3] (ăs′ĭz) *n. Vulgar Slang.* Pl. of **ass**[2].

as•sess (ə-sĕs′) *tr.v.* **-sessed, -sess•ing, -sess•es. 1.** To estimate the value of (property) for taxation. **2.** To set or determine the amount of (a payment). **3.** To charge with a special payment. **4.** To determine the value, significance, or extent of; appraise. See Syns at **estimate.** [ME *assessen* < OFr. *assesser* < Lat. *assidēre, assess-*, to sit by as an assistant judge : *ad-*, ad- + *sedēre*, to sit; see **sed-*.**] —**as•sess′a•ble** *adj.*

as•sess•ment (ə-sĕs′mənt) *n.* **1.** The act of assessing; appraisal. **2.** An amount assessed, as for taxation.

as•ses•sor (ə-sĕs′ər) *n.* **1.** An official who evaluates property for taxation. **2.** An assistant to a judge or magistrate, usu. selected for special knowledge in a particular area. —**as′ses•so′ri•al** (ăs′ə-sôr′ē-əl, -sōr′-) *adj.*

as•set (ăs′ĕt′) *n.* **1.** A useful or valuable quality, person, or thing; an advantage or a resource. **2.** A valuable item that is owned. **3. assets. a.** *Accounting.* The entries on a balance sheet showing all properties and claims against others that may be applied to cover the liabilities of a person or business, such as cash, stock, and goodwill. **b.** The entire property owned by a person, esp. a bankrupt, that can be used to settle debts. [Back-formation < E. *assets*, sufficient goods to settle a testator's debts and legacies < AN *asetz* < *asez*, enough < VLat. **ad satis*, to sufficiency : Lat. *ad-*, ad- + Lat. *satis*, enough; see **sā-*.**]

as•sev•er•ate (ə-sĕv′ə-rāt′) *tr.v.* **-at•ed, -at•ing, -ates.** To declare seriously or positively; affirm. [Lat. *assevērāre, assevērāt-* : *ad-*, ad- + *sevērus*, serious; see **wēro-*.**] —**as•sev′er•a′tion** *n.*

ass•hole (ăs′hōl′) *n. Vulgar Slang.* **1.** The anus. **2.** A thoroughly contemptible, detestable person. [ASS[2] + HOLE.]

as•sib•i•late (ə-sĭb′ə-lāt′) *tr.v.* **-lat•ed, -lat•ing, -lates.** To pronounce with a hissing sound; make sibilant. [AD- + SIBILATE.] —**as•sib′i•la′tion** *n.*

as•si•du•i•ty (ăs′ĭ-do͞o′ĭ-tē, -dyo͞o′-) *n., pl.* **-ties. 1.** Persistent diligence; unflagging effort. **2.** Constant personal attention and often obsequious solicitude. Often used in the plural.

as•sid•u•ous (ə-sĭj′o͞o-əs) *adj.* **1.** Constant in application or attention; diligent. **2.** Unceasing; persistent. [< Lat. *assiduus* < *assidēre*, to attend to : *ad-*, ad- + *sedēre*, to sit; see **sed-*.**] —**as•sid′u•ous•ly** *adv.* —**as•sid′u•ous•ness** *n.*

as•sign (ə-sīn′) *tr.v.* **-signed, -sign•ing, -signs. 1.** To set apart for a purpose; designate. **2.** To select for a duty or office; appoint. **3.** To give out as a task; allot. **4.** To ascribe; attribute. **5.** *Law.* To transfer (property, rights, or interests) from one to another. **6.** To place (a person or a military unit) under a specific command. — *n. Law.* An assignee. [ME *assignen* < OFr. *assigner* < Lat. *assignāre*: *ad-*, ad- + *signāre*, to mark (< *signum*, sign; see **sek^{w}-^{1}***).] — **as•sign′a•bil′i•ty** *n.* — **as•sign′a•ble** *adj.* — **as•sign′a•bly** *adv.* — **as•sign′er** *n.*

as•sig•na•tion (ăs′ĭg-nā′shən) *n.* **1.** The act of assigning. **2.** Something assigned, esp. an allotment. **3.** An appointment for a meeting between lovers; a tryst. See Syns at **engagement.** — **as′sig•na′tion•al** *adj.*

as•signed risk (ə-sīnd′) *n.* A poor risk that an insurance company is compelled to cover under state laws.

as•sign•ee (ə-sī′nē′, ăs′ĭ-nē′) *n. Law.* **1.** A party to which a transfer of property, rights, or interest is made. **2.** One appointed to act for another; a deputy or an agent.

as•sign•ment (ə-sīn′mənt) *n.* **1.** The act of assigning. **2.** Something, such as a task, that is assigned. See Syns at **task. 3.** A position to which one is assigned. **4.** *Law.* **a.** The transfer of a claim, right, interest, or property from one to another. **b.** The instrument by which this transfer is effected.

as•sign•or (ə-sī′nôr′, ə-sī′nər, ăs′ə-nôr′) *n. Law.* One that makes an assignment.

as•sim•i•la•ble (ə-sĭm′ə-lə-bəl) *adj.* That can be assimilated. — **as•sim′i•la•bil′i•ty** *n.*

as•sim•i•late (ə-sĭm′ə-lāt′) *v.* **-lat•ed, -lat•ing, -lates.** — *tr.* **1.** *Physiol.* **a.** To consume and incorporate (nutrients) into the body after digestion. **b.** To transform (food) into living tissue by the process of anabolism; metabolize constructively. **2.** To incorporate and absorb into the mind. **3.** To make similar; cause to resemble. **4.** *Ling.* To alter (a sound) by assimilation. **5.** To absorb (a minority) into the prevailing culture. — *intr.* To become assimilated. [ME *assimilaten* < Lat. *assimilāre*, *assimilāt-*, to make similar to : *ad-*, ad- + *similis*, like; see **sem-^{1}***.] — **as•sim′i•la′tor** *n.*

as•sim•i•la•tion (ə-sĭm′ə-lā′shən) *n.* **1.a.** The act or process of assimilating. **b.** The state of being assimilated. **2.** *Physiol.* The conversion of nutriments into living tissue; constructive metabolism. **3.** *Ling.* The process by which a sound becomes similar or identical to an adjacent or nearby sound. **4.** The process whereby a minority group gradually adopts the customs and attitudes of the majority.

as•sim•i•la•tion•ism (ə-sĭm′ə-lā′shə-nĭz′əm) *n.* A policy of furthering cultural or racial assimilation. — **as•sim′i•la′tion•ist** *adj. & n.*

as•sim•i•la•tive (ə-sĭm′ə-lā′tĭv) also **as•sim•i•la•to•ry** (-lə-tôr′ē, -tōr′ē) *adj.* Marked by or causing assimilation.

As•sin•i•boin also **As•sin•i•boine** (ə-sĭn′ə-boin′) *n., pl.* **Assiniboin** or **-boins** also **Assiniboine** or **-boines. 1.** A member of a Native American people formerly inhabiting southern Manitoba and now located in Montana, Alberta, and Saskatchewan. **2.** The Siouan language of the Assiniboin. [Fr. *Assiniboine*, of Ojibwa orig.] — **As•sin′i•boin′** *adj.*

As•sin•i•boine (ə-sĭn′ə-boin′). A river of S-central Canada rising in S Saskatchewan and flowing c. 949 km (590 mi) to the Red R. at Winnipeg, Manitoba.

As•si•si (ə-sē′zē, -sē, ə-sĭs′ē). A town of central Italy ESE of Perugia; home of St. Francis of Assisi. Pop. 19,000.

as•sist (ə-sĭst′) *v.* **-sist•ed, -sist•ing, -sists.** — *tr.* To help or support, esp. as a subordinate or supplement; aid. — *intr.* **1.** To give aid or support. See Syns at **help. 2.** To be present, as at a conference. — *n.* **1.** An act of giving aid; help. **2.** *Sports.* **a.** A fielding and throwing of a baseball that enables a teammate to put out a runner. **b.** A pass of a basketball or an ice hockey puck that enables a teammate to score a goal. **c.** The action of a soccer player who enables a teammate to score by presenting the ball for a goal. **d.** Official credit given for such an act. **3.** A mechanical device providing aid. [ME *assisten* < OFr. *assister* < Lat. *assistere*: *ad-*, ad- + *sistere*, to stand; see **stā-***.] — **as•sist′er** *n.*

as•sis•tance (ə-sĭs′təns) *n.* **1.** The act of assisting. **2.** Aid; help: *financial assistance.*

as•sis•tant (ə-sĭs′tənt) *n.* One that assists; a helper. — *adj.* **1.** Holding an auxiliary position; subordinate. **2.** Giving aid; auxiliary.

assistant professor *n.* A college or university teacher who ranks above an instructor and below an associate professor.

as•sis•tant•ship (ə-sĭs′tənt-shĭp′) *n.* An academic position that carries a stipend and usu. involves part-time teaching or research, given to a qualified graduate student.

as•size (ə-sīz′) *n.* **1.a.** A session of a court. **b.** A decree or edict rendered at such a session. **2.a.** An ordinance regulating weights and measures and the weights and prices of articles of consumption. **b.** The standards so established. **3.** *Law.* A judicial inquest, the writ by which it is instituted, or the verdict of the jurors. **4. assizes. a.** One of the periodic county court sessions formerly held in England and Wales. **b.** The time or place of such sessions. [ME *assise* < OFr. < p.part. of *asseoir*, to seat < Lat. *assidēre*, to sit beside : *ad-*, ad- + *sedēre*, to sit; see ASSIDUOUS.]

assn. *abbr.* Association.

assoc. *abbr.* **1.** Associate. **2.** Association.

as•so•ci•a•ble (ə-sō′shē-ə-bəl, -shə-bəl) *adj.* That can be associated. — **as•so′ci•a•bil′i•ty, as•so′ci•a•ble•ness** *n.*

as•so•ci•ate (ə-sō′shē-āt′, -sē-) *v.* **-at•ed, -at•ing, -ates.** — *tr.* **1.** To join as a partner, ally, or friend. **2.** To connect or join together; combine. **3.** To connect in the mind or imagination. — *intr.* **1.** To join in or form a league, union, or association. See Syns at **join. 2.** To keep company. — *n.* (-ĭt, -āt′). **1.** A person united with another or others in an act or a business; a partner or colleague. **2.** A companion; a comrade. **3.** An attendant circumstance. **4.** A member of an institution or society with only partial status or privileges. **5.** Often **Associate.** A degree conferred by a two-year college after the prescribed course of study has been successfully completed. — *adj.* (-ĭt, -āt′). **1.** Joined with another or others and having equal or nearly equal status: *an associate editor.* **2.** Having partial status or privileges. **3.** Following or accompanying; concomitant. [ME *associaten* < Lat. *associāre*, *associāt-* : *ad-*, ad- + *socius*, companion; see **sek^{w}-^{1}***.]

associate professor *n.* A college or university professor who ranks above an assistant professor and below a professor.

as•so•ci•a•tion (ə-sō′sē-ā′shən, -shē-) *n.* **1.** The act of associating or the state of being associated. **2.** An organized body of people who have an interest in common; a society. **3.a.** A mental connection or relation between thoughts, feelings, ideas, or sensations. **b.** A remembered or imagined feeling, emotion, idea, or sensation linked to a person, object, or idea. **4.** *Chem.* Any of various processes of combination depending on relatively weak chemical bonding. **5.** *Ecol.* A large number of organisms in a specific geographic area constituting a community with one or two dominant species. — **as•so′ci•a′tion•al** *adj.*

association area *n.* An area of the cerebral cortex where motor and sensory functions are integrated.

association football *n. Chiefly British.* Soccer.

as•so•ci•a•tion•ism (ə-sō′sē-ā′shə-nĭz′əm, ə-sō′shē-) *n.* The psychological theory that association is the basis of all mental activity. — **as•so′ci•a′tion•ist** *adj. & n.* — **as•so′ci•a′tion•is′tic** *adj.*

as•so•ci•a•tive (ə-sō′shē-ā′tĭv, -sē-, -shə-tĭv) *adj.* **1.** Of, marked by, resulting from, or causing association. **2.** *Math.* Independent of grouping. For example, if $a + (b + c) = (a + b) + c$, the operation indicated by + is associative. — **as•so′ci•a′tive•ly** *adv.*

as•soil (ə-soil′) *tr.v.* **-soiled, -soil•ing, -soils.** *Archaic.* **1.** To absolve; pardon. **2.** To atone for. [ME *assoilen* < OFr. *assoldre*, *assoil-* < Lat. *absolvere*, to set free : *ab-*, away; see AB-^{1} + *solvere*, to loosen; see **leu-***.]

as•so•nance (ăs′ə-nəns) *n.* **1.** Resemblance of sound, esp. of vowels in stressed syllables, as in *swarms of arms.* **2.** Rough similarity; approximate agreement. [Fr. < Lat. *assonāre*, to respond to : *ad-*, ad- + *sonāre*, to sound; see **swen-***.] — **as′so•nant** *adj. & n.* — **as′so•nan′tal** (-năn′tl) *adj.*

as•sort (ə-sôrt′) *v.* **-sort•ed, -sort•ing, -sorts.** — *tr.* **1.** To separate into groups according to kind; classify. **2.** To supply with (a variety, as of goods). — *intr.* **1.** To agree in kind; fall into the same class. **2.** To associate with others. [ME *assorte* < OFr. *assorter*: *a-*, to (< Lat. *ad-*; see AD-) + *sorte*, kind (< Lat. *sors*, *sort-*, chance, lot; see **ser-^{2}***).] — **as•sort′a•tive** (ə-sôr′tə-tĭv) *adj.* — **as•sort′er** *n.*

as•sort•ed (ə-sôr′tĭd) *adj.* **1.** Consisting of a number of different kinds: *assorted sizes.* See Syns at **miscellaneous. 2.** Separated according to kind or class. **3.** Suited or matched. Often used in combination: *well-assorted accessories.*

as•sort•ment (ə-sôrt′mənt) *n.* **1.** The act of assorting; separation into classes. **2.** A collection of various kinds; a variety.

A.S.S.R. or **ASSR** *abbr.* Autonomous Soviet Socialist Republic.

asst. *abbr.* Assistant.

asstd. *abbr.* **1.** Assisted. **2.** Assorted.

as•suage (ə-swāj′) *tr.v.* **-suaged, -suag•ing, -suag•es. 1.** To make (something unpleasant) less intense or severe: *assuage grief.* See Syns at **relieve. 2.** To satisfy or appease (thirst, for example). **3.** To pacify or calm: *assuage insecurity.* [ME *aswagen* < OFr. *assuagier* < VLat. **assuāviāre*: Lat. *ad-*, ad- + Lat. *suāvis*, delightful, sweet; see **swād-***.] — **as•suage′ment** *n.*

as•sua•sive (ə-swā′sĭv, -zĭv) *adj.* Soothing; calming. [AD- + SUASIVE (sense influenced by ASSUAGE).]

as•sume (ə-so͞om′) *tr.v.* **-sumed, -sum•ing, -sumes. 1.** To take upon oneself: *assume responsibility.* **2.** To undertake the duties of (an office). **3.** To take on; adopt. **4.** To put on; don. **5.** To affect the appearance or possession of; feign. **6.** To take for granted; suppose: *assumed that prices would rise.* See Syns at **presume. 7.** To take over without justification; seize: *assume control.* **8.** *Theol.* To take up or receive into heaven. [ME *assumen* < Lat. *assūmere*: *ad-*, ad- + *sūmere*, to take; see **em-***.] — **as•sum′a•ble** *adj.* — **as•sum′a•bly** *adv.* — **as•sum′er** *n.*

as•sumed (ə-so͞omd′) *adj.* **1.** Adopted or used so as to deceive; pretended. **2.** Taken for granted; supposed. — **as•sum′ed•ly** (ə-so͞o′mĭd-lē) *adv.*

as•sum•ing (ə-so͞o′mĭng) *adj.* Presumptuous; arrogant. — *conj.* On the assumption that; supposing: *Assuming the house is for sale, would you buy it?* — **as•sum′ing•ly** *adv.*

ă pat	oi **boy**
ā pay	ou **out**
âr care	o͝o **took**
ä father	o͞o **boot**
ĕ pet	ŭ cut
ē be	ûr **urge**
ĭ pit	th **thin**
ī pie	*th* **this**
îr pier	hw **which**
ŏ pot	zh vision
ō toe	ə about, item
ô paw	

Stress marks:
′ (primary);
′ (secondary), as in
dictionary (dĭk′shə-nĕr′ē)

as•sump•sit (ə-sŭmp′sĭt) *n. Law.* **1.** An agreement or promise made orally or in writing not under seal; a contract. **2.** A legal action to enforce or recover damages for a breach of such an agreement. [NLat. < third pers. sing. p.t. of Lat. *assūmere*, to undertake. See ASSUME.]

as•sump•tion (ə-sŭmp′shən) *n.* **1.** The act of taking to or upon oneself: *assumption of an obligation.* **2.** The act of taking over. **3.** The act of taking for granted. **4.** Something taken for granted or accepted as true without proof; a supposition. **5.** Presumption; arrogance. **6.** *Logic.* A minor premise. **7. Assumption. a.** *Theol.* The bodily taking up of the Virgin Mary into heaven after her death. **b.** The Christian feast commemorating this event, traditionally observed on August 15. [ME *assumpcion* < Lat. *assumptiō*, *assumptiōn-*, adoption < *assumptus*, p.part. of *assūmere*, to adopt. See ASSUME.]

as•sump•tive (ə-sŭmp′tĭv) *adj.* **1.** Characterized by assumption. **2.** Taken for granted; assumed. **3.** Presumptuous; assuming. **—as•sump′tive•ly** *adv.*

Fred Astaire

As•sur (ä′so͝or′, ä′sho͝or′) *n.* Var. of **Ashur.**

as•sur•ance (ə-sho͝or′əns) *n.* **1.** The act of assuring. **2.** A statement or indication that inspires confidence; a guarantee or pledge. **3.** Freedom from doubt; certainty. See Syns at **certainty. 4.** Self-confidence. **5.** Excessive self-confidence; presumption. **6.** *Chiefly British.* Insurance, esp. life insurance.

As•sur•ba•ni•pal (ä′so͝or-bä′nə-päl′). See **Ashurbanipal.**

as•sure (ə-sho͝or′) *tr.v.* **-sured, -sur•ing, -sures. 1.** To state positively, as to remove doubt. **2.** To cause to feel sure. **3.** To give confidence to; reassure. **4.** To make certain; ensure. **5.** To make safe or secure. **6.** *Chiefly British.* To insure, as against loss. [ME *assuren* < OFr. *assurer* < VLat. **assēcūrāre*, to make sure : Lat. *ad-*, ad- + Lat. *sēcūrus*, secure; see SECURE.] **—as•sur′a•ble** *adj.* **—as•sur′er** *n.*

Usage Note: *Assure, ensure,* and *insure* all mean "to make secure or certain." Only *assure* is used with reference to a person in the sense of "to set the mind at rest": *assured the leader of my loyalty.* Although *ensure* and *insure* are generally interchangeable, only *insure* is now widely used in American English in the commercial sense of "to guarantee financially against risk."

as•sured (ə-sho͝ord′) *adj.* **1.** Made certain; guaranteed. **2.** Exhibiting confidence or authority. **3.** *Chiefly British.* Insured. —*n., pl.* **assured** or **assureds.** Insured. **—as•sur′ed•ly** (-ĭd-lē) *adv.* **—as•sur′ed•ness** *n.*

as•sur•gent (ə-sûr′jənt) *adj.* **1.** Rising or tending to rise. **2.** *Bot.* Slanting or curving upward; ascending. [Lat. *assurgēns, assurgent-*, pr.part. of *assurgere*, to rise up to : *ad-*, ad- + *surgere*, to rise; see SURGE.] **—as•sur′gen•cy** *n.*

assy. *abbr.* Assembly.

As•syr•i•a (ə-sîr′ē-ə). An ancient empire and civilization of W Asia in the upper valley of the Tigris R.; reached the height of its power between the 9th and 7th cent. B.C.

As•syr•i•an (ə-sîr′ē-ən) *adj.* Of or relating to Assyria or its people, language, or culture. —*n.* **1.** A native or inhabitant of Assyria. **2.** See **Akkadian** 2. **3.** The Assyrian dialects of Akkadian.

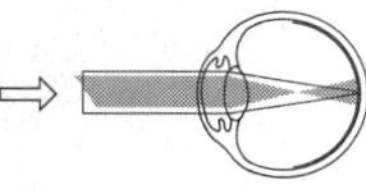

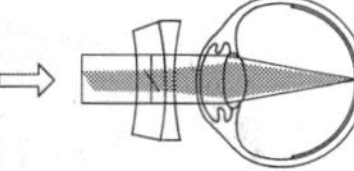

astigmatism
Top: Before correction
Bottom: After correction

As•syr•i•ol•o•gy (ə-sîr′ē-ŏl′ə-jē) *n.* The study of the civilization and language of Assyria. **—As•syr′i•ol′o•gist** *n.*

-ast *suff.* One associated with: *ecdysiast.* [< Lat. *-astēs*, n. suff. < Gk.]

A•staire (ə-stâr′), **Fred.** 1899–1987. Amer. dancer and actor whose films include *Top Hat* (1935).

As•tar•te (ə-stär′tē) *n. Myth.* A Near Eastern goddess traditionally associated with love and fertility.

a•sta•sia (ə-stā′zhə) *n.* Inability to stand because of motor incoordination. [Gk., unsteadiness < *astatos*, unsteady : *a-*, not; see A-[1] + *statos*, standing; see **stā-*.**]

a•stat•ic (ā-stăt′ĭk) *adj.* **1.** Unsteady; unstable. **2.** *Phys.* Having no particular directional characteristics. **—a•stat′i•cal•ly** *adv.* **—a•stat′i•cism** *n.*

astragal

as•ta•tine (ăs′tə-tēn′, -tĭn) *n. Symbol* **At** A radioactive halogen element. Its longest lived isotope has a mass number of 210 and a half-life of 8.3 hours. Atomic number 85; melting point 302°C; boiling point 337°C; valence probably 1, 3, 5, 7. See table at **element.** [Gk. *astatos*, unstable; see ASTASIA + -INE[2].]

as•ter (ăs′tər) *n.* **1.** Any of various plants of the genus *Aster* in the composite family, having radiate flower heads and a usu. yellow disk. **2.** The China aster. **3.** *Biol.* A star-shaped structure formed in the cytoplasm of a cell and having raylike fibers that surround the centrosome during mitosis. [Lat. *astēr*, a plant, star < Gk. *astēr*, star. See **ster-[3]*.**]

astrolabe
17th-century astrolabe

as•te•ri•at•ed (ă-stîr′ē-ā′tĭd) *adj. Mineral.* Exhibiting asterism. [< Gk. *asterios*, starry < *astēr*, star. See **ster-[3]*.**]

as•ter•isk (ăs′tə-rĭsk′) *n.* **1.** A star-shaped figure (*) used in print to indicate an omission or a footnote. **2.** *Ling.* Such a figure used to indicate an unattested sound, affix, or word. —*tr.v.* **-isked, -isk•ing, -isks.** To mark with an asterisk. [ME < LLat. *asteriscus* < Gk. *asteriskos*, dim. of *astēr*, star. See **ster-[3]*.**]

as•ter•ism (ăs′tə-rĭz′əm) *n.* **1.** *Print.* Three asterisks in triangular form used to call attention to a following passage. **2.** *Astron.* A cluster of stars smaller than a constellation. **3.** *Mineral.* A six-rayed figure produced in some crystal structures by reflected or transmitted light. [Gk. *asterismos*, constellation < *astēr*, star. See **ster-[3]*.**] **—as′ter•is′mal** *adj.*

a•stern (ə-stûrn′) *adv. & adj. Naut.* **1.** Behind a vessel. **2.** At or to the stern of a vessel. **3.** With or having the stern foremost; backward.

a•ster•nal (ā-stûr′nəl) *adj. Anat.* **1.** Not connected to the sternum. **2.** Lacking a sternum.

as•ter•oid (ăs′tə-roid′) *n.* **1.** *Astron.* Any of numerous small celestial bodies that revolve around the sun, with characteristic diameters between a few and several hundred kilometers. **2.** *Zool.* See **starfish.** —*adj.* also **as•ter•oi•dal** (ăs′tə-roid′l). Star-shaped. [< Gk. *asteroeidēs*, starlike : *astēr*, star; see **ster-[3]*** + *-oeidēs*, -oid.]

as•the•ni•a (ăs-thē′nē-ə) *n.* Loss or lack of bodily strength; weakness; debility. [NLat. < Gk. *astheneia* < *asthenēs*, weak : *a-*, without; see A-[1] + *sthenos*, strength.]

as•then•ic (ăs-thĕn′ĭk) *adj.* **1.** Relating to or exhibiting asthenia; weak. **2.** Having a slender, lightly muscled physique. —*n.* A person having such a physique.

as•the•no•pi•a (ăs′thə-nō′pē-ə) *n.* Weakness or fatigue of the eyes, usu. accompanied by headache and dimming of vision. [ASTHEN(IA) + -OPIA.] **—as′the•nop′ic** (-nŏp′ĭk) *adj.*

as•then•o•sphere (ăs-thĕn′ə-sfîr′) *n.* A zone of the earth's mantle that lies beneath the lithosphere and consists of several hundred kilometers of deformable rock. [Gk. *asthenēs*, weak; see ASTHENIA + SPHERE.]

asth•ma (ăz′mə, ăs′-) *n.* A chronic respiratory disease, often arising from allergies, marked by sudden recurring attacks of labored breathing, chest constriction, and coughing. [ME *asma* < Med.Lat. < Gk. *asthma.*] **—asth•mat′ic** (-măt′ĭk) *adj. & n.* **—asth•mat′i•cal•ly** *adv.*

as though *conj.* As if: *looked as though they were mad.*

As•ti (ä′stē). A city of NW Italy SE of Turin; noted for its sparkling wines. Pop. 76,950.

a•stig•ma•tism (ə-stĭg′mə-tĭz′əm) *n.* **1.** A refractive defect of a lens that prevents light rays from converging at a single point. **2.** A visual defect in which the unequal curvature of one or more refractive surfaces of the eye, usu. the cornea, prevents light rays from focusing at one point on the retina, resulting in blurred vision. [A-[1] + Gk. *stigma, stigmat-*, point (< *stizein, stig-*, to tattoo; see **steig-***).] **—as′tig•mat′ic** (ăs′tĭg-măt′ĭk) *adj. & n.* **—as′tig•mat′i•cal•ly** *adv.*

a•stir (ə-stûr′) *adj.* **1.** Moving about; being in motion. **2.** Having gotten out of bed.

ASTM *abbr.* American Society for Testing and Materials.

as to *prep.* **1.** With regard to: *We are puzzled as to how it happened.* **2.** According to: *chosen as to ability.*

a•stom•a•tous (ā-stŏm′ə-təs, ā-stō′mə-) also **as•tom•ous** (ăs′tə-məs) or **a•stom•a•tal** (ā-stŏm′ə-təl, ā-stō′mə-) *adj.* Having no mouth or oral opening.

As•ton (ăs′tən), **Francis William.** 1877–1945. British chemist and physicist who won a 1922 Nobel Prize.

a•ston•ish (ə-stŏn′ĭsh) *tr.v.* **-ished, -ish•ing, -ish•es.** To fill with sudden wonder or amazement. See Syns at **surprise.** [Prob. alteration of ME *astonien* < OFr. *estoner* < VLat. **extonāre*: Lat. *ex-*, ex- + Lat. *tonāre*, to thunder; see **(s)tenə-*.**] **—a•ston′ish•ing•ly** *adv.*

a•ston•ish•ment (ə-stŏn′ĭsh-mənt) *n.* **1.** Great surprise or amazement. **2.** A cause of amazement; a marvel.

As•tor (ăs′tər), **John Jacob.** 1763–1848. German-born Amer. fur trader.

Astor, Nancy Witcher Langhorne. Viscountess Astor. 1879–1964. Amer.-born British politician who was the first woman elected to the House of Commons (1919–45).

As•to•ri•a (ă-stôr′ē-ə, -stōr′-). A city of NW OR near the mouth of the Columbia R.; founded as a fur-trading post in 1811. Pop. 10,069.

a•stound (ə-stound′) *tr.v.* **a•stound•ed, a•stound•ing, a•stounds.** To astonish and bewilder. See Syns at **surprise.** [< ME *astoned*, p.part. of *astonen, astonien*, to amaze. See ASTONISH.] **—a•stound′ing•ly** *adv.*

astr- *pref.* Var. of **astro-.**

a•strad•dle (ə-străd′l) *adv.* **1.** In a straddling position; astride. **2.** Across or over both sides. —*prep.* So as to straddle or bridge; astride.

as•tra•gal (ăs′trə-gəl) *n. Archit.* A narrow convex molding often having the form of beading. [Lat. *astragalus* < Gk. *astragalos.* See **ost-*.**]

as•trag•a•lus (ə-străg′ə-ləs) *n., pl.* **-li** (-lī′). See **talus[1]** 1. [NLat. < Gk. *astragalos*, vertebra. See **ost-*.**] **—as•trag′a•lar** *adj.*

as•tra•khan also **as•tra•chan** (ăs′trə-kăn′, -kən) *n.* **1.** The curly, wavy fur made of the skins of young lambs from Astrakhan. **2.** A fabric with a curly looped pile, made to resemble this fur.

As•tra•khan (ăs′trə-kăn′, ä-strä-KHän′). A city of SW Russia on the Volga R. delta. Pop. 493,000.

as•tral (ăs′trəl) *adj.* **1.** Of, relating to, or resembling the stars. **2.** *Biol.* Of, relating to, or shaped like the mitotic aster; star-shaped. [LLat. *astrālis* < Lat. *astrum*, star < Gk. *astron.* See **ster-[3]*.**] **—as′tral•ly** *adv.*

astral body *n.* A supersensible body believed by theosophists to coexist with and survive the death of the human physical body.

a•stray (ə-strā′) *adv.* **1.** Away from the correct path or direction. See Syns at **amiss. 2.** Away from the right or good, as in thought or behavior. [ME < OFr. *estraie,* p.part. of *estraier,* to stray. See STRAY.] — **a•stray′** *adj.*

a•stride (ə-strīd′) *adv.* **1.** With a leg on each side: *riding astride.* **2.** With the legs wide apart. — *prep.* **1.** On or over and with a leg on each side of. **2.** Situated on both sides of. **3.** Lying across or over; spanning.

as•trin•gent (ə-strĭn′jənt) *adj.* **1.** *Medic.* Tending to draw together or constrict tissues; styptic. **2.** Sharp and penetrating; pungent or severe: *astringent remarks.* — *n.* A substance that draws together body tissues and stops the flow of blood or other secretions. [Lat. *astringēns, astringent-,* pr.part. of *astringere,* to bind fast : *ad-,* ad- + *stringere,* to bind; see **streig-*.**] — **as•trin′gen•cy** *n.* — **as•trin′gent•ly** *adv.*

astro– or **astr–** *pref.* **1.a.** Star: *astrophysics.* **b.** Celestial body: *astrometry.* **c.** Outer space: *astronaut.* **2.** The aster of a cell: *astrosphere.* [Gk. < *astron,* star. See **ster-^{3}*.**]

as•tro•bi•ol•o•gy (ăs′trō-bī-ŏl′ə-jē) *n.* See **exobiology.** — **as′tro•bi′o•log′i•cal** (-ə-lŏj′ĭ-kəl) *adj.*

as•tro•bleme (ăs′trə-blĕm′, -blēm′) *n.* A scar on the earth's surface left from the impact of a meteorite. [ASTRO– + Gk. *blēma,* missile, wound (< *ballein,* to throw; see **g^{w}elə-*.**)]

as•tro•chem•is•try (ăs′trō-kĕm′ĭ-strē) *n.* The chemistry of stars and interstellar space. — **as′tro•chem′ist** *n.*

as•tro•cyte (ăs′trə-sīt′) *n.* A star-shaped cell, esp. a neuroglial cell of nervous tissue. — **as′tro•cyt′ic** (-sĭt′ĭk) *adj.*

as•tro•dome (ăs′trə-dōm′) *n.* A transparent dome on the top of an aircraft, through which celestial observations are made.

as•tro•ge•ol•o•gy (ăs′trō-jē-ŏl′ə-jē) *n.* The geology of celestial bodies. — **as′tro•ge•ol′o•gist** *n.*

astrol. *abbr.* **1.** Astrologer; astrological. **2.** Astrology.

as•tro•labe (ăs′trə-lāb′) *n.* A medieval instrument used to determine the altitude of the sun or other celestial bodies. [ME *astrelabie* < OFr. *astrelabe* < Med.Lat. *astrolabium* < Gk. *astrolabon,* planisphere : *astro-,* astro- + *lambanein, lab-,* to take.]

as•trol•o•gy (ə-strŏl′ə-jē) *n.* **1.** The study of the positions and aspects of celestial bodies in the belief that they have an influence on the course of natural earthly occurrences and human affairs. **2.** *Obsolete.* Astronomy. [ME *astrologie* < OFr. < Lat. *astrologia* < Gk. : *astro-,* astro- + *-logia,* -logy.] — **as•trol′o•ger** *n.* — **as′tro•log′i•cal** (ăs′trə-lŏj′ĭ-kəl), **as′tro•log′ic** *adj.* — **as′tro•log′i•cal•ly** *adv.*

as•trom•e•try (ə-strŏm′ĭ-trē) *n.* The scientific measurement of the positions and motions of celestial bodies. — **as′tro•met′ric** (ăs′trō-mĕt′rĭk), **as′tro•met′ri•cal** *adj.*

astron. *abbr.* Astronomer; astronomical; astronomy.

as•tro•naut (ăs′trə-nôt′) *n.* A person trained to pilot, navigate, or participate in the flight of a spacecraft. [ASTRO– + Gk. *nautēs,* sailor (< *naus,* ship; see **nāu-***).]

as•tro•nau•tics (ăs′trə-nô′tĭks) *n. (used with a sing. or pl. v.)* The science and technology of space flight. — **as′tro•nau′tic, as′tro•nau′ti•cal** *adj.* — **as′tro•nau′ti•cal•ly** *adv.*

as•tro•nav•i•ga•tion (ăs′trō-năv′ĭ-gā′shən) *n.* See **celestial navigation.** — **as′tro•nav′i•ga′tor** *n.*

as•tron•o•mer (ə-strŏn′ə-mər) *n.* One that specializes in astronomy.

as•tro•nom•i•cal (ăs′trə-nŏm′ĭ-kəl) also **as•tro•nom•ic** (-nŏm′ĭk) *adj.* **1.** Of or relating to astronomy. **2.** Of enormous magnitude; immense. — **as′tro•nom′i•cal•ly** *adv.*

astronomical unit *n.* A unit of length equal to the mean distance from Earth to the sun, approx. 150 million kilometers (93 million miles).

as•tron•o•my (ə-strŏn′ə-mē) *n.* The scientific study of matter in outer space, such as the positions, dimensions, energy, and evolution of stars and planets. [ME *astronomie* < OFr. < Lat. *astronomia* < Gk. : *astro-,* astro- + *-nomia,* -nomy.]

as•tro•pho•tog•ra•phy (ăs′trō-fə-tŏg′rə-fē) *n.* Astronomical photography. — **as′tro•pho′to•graph′ic** *adj.*

as•tro•phys•ics (ăs′trō-fĭz′ĭks) *n. (used with a sing. v.)* The branch of astronomy that deals with the physics of stellar phenomena. — **as′tro•phys′i•cal** *adj.* — **as′tro•phys′i•cist** (-fĭz′ĭ-sĭst) *n.*

as•tro•sphere (ăs′trō-sfîr′) *n.* **1.** The central portion of a cell aster exclusive of the rays. **2.** The entire cell aster with the exception of the centrosome.

As•tro•Turf (ăs′trō-tûrf′). A trademark used for an artificial grasslike ground covering.

As•tu•ri•as (ăs-to͝or′ē-əs, -tyo͝or′-, äs-to͞o′ryäs). A region and former kingdom of NW Spain; conquered by Rome in the 2nd cent. B.C. — **As•tu′ri•an** *adj. & n.*

As•tu•ri•as (ə-sto͝or′ē-əs, ä-sto͝or′yäs), **Miguel Angel.** 1899–1974. Guatemalan writer who won the 1966 Nobel Prize for literature.

as•tute (ə-sto͞ot′, ə-styo͞ot′) *adj.* Having or showing shrewdness and discernment, esp. with respect to one's own concerns. [Lat. *astūtus* < *astus,* craft. See **wes-^{1}*.**] — **as•tute′ly** *adv.* — **as•tute′ness** *n.*

As•ty•a•nax (ə-stī′ə-năks′) *n. Gk. Myth.* The son of Hector and Andromache, killed when the Greeks conquered Troy.

a•sty•lar (ā-stī′lər) *adj. Archit.* Not having columns or pilasters. [A-^{1} + Gk. *stulos,* pillar; see **stā-*** + -AR.]

A•sun•ción (ä-so͞on′syôn′). The cap. of Paraguay, in the S part on the Paraguay R. Pop. 455,517.

a•sun•der (ə-sŭn′dər) *adv.* **1.** Into separate parts. **2.** Apart from each other. [ME < OE *on sundran: on,* on; see ON + *sundran,* separately (< *sunder,* apart).] — **a•sun′der** *adj.*

ASV *abbr. Bible.* American Standard Version.

As•wan (ăs′wän, ăs-wän′, äs-). A city of S Egypt at the First Cataract of the Nile R. near the **Aswan High Dam** (dedicated 1971). Pop. 182,700.

a•swarm (ə-swôrm′) *adj.* Filled or overrun, as with moving objects or beings; teeming.

as well as *conj.* And in addition: *courageous as well as strong.* — *prep.* In addition to.

a•swirl (ə-swûrl′) *adj.* Moving with a swirling motion.

a•swoon (ə-swo͞on′) *adv. & adj.* In a faint or swoon. [ME *aswowne,* ult. < OE *geswōgen,* fainted, p.part. of **swōgan,* to lose consciousness.]

a•sy•lum (ə-sī′ləm) *n.* **1.** An institution for the care of people who require organized supervision or assistance. **2.** A place offering protection and safety; a shelter. **3.** A place formerly constituting an inviolable refuge for criminals or debtors. **4.** The protection afforded by a sanctuary. **5.** Protection and immunity from extradition granted by a government to a political refugee from another country. [ME *asilum,* refuge < Lat. *asȳlum* < Gk. *asulon,* sanctuary < neut. of *asulos,* inviolable : *a-,* without; see A-^{1} + *sulon,* right of seizure.]

a•sym•met•ri•cal (ā′sĭ-mĕt′rĭ-kəl) also **a•sym•met•ric** (-rĭk) *adj.* Having no balance or symmetry. — **a′sym•met′ri•cal•ly** *adv.*

a•sym•me•try (ā-sĭm′ĭ-trē) *n.* Lack of balance or symmetry.

a•symp•to•mat•ic (ā′sĭmp-tə-măt′ĭk) *adj.* Causing or showing no disease symptoms. — **a′symp•to•mat′i•cal•ly** *adv.*

as•ymp•tote (ăs′ĭm-tōt′, -ĭmp-) *n. Math.* A line considered a limit to a curve in that the perpendicular distance from a moving point on the curve to the line approaches zero as the point moves an infinite distance from the origin. [Ult. < Gk. *asumptōtos,* not intersecting : *a-,* not; see A-^{1} + *sumptōtos,* intersecting (< *sumpiptein,* to converge : *sun-,* syn- + *piptein, ptō-,* to fall; see **pet-***).] — **as′ymp•tot′ic** (-tŏt′ĭk), **as′ymp•tot′i•cal** *adj.* — **as′ymp•tot′i•cal•ly** *adv.*

a•syn•ap•sis (ā′sĭ-năp′sĭs) *n.* The failure of homologous chromosomes to pair during meiosis.

a•syn•chro•nism (ā-sĭng′krə-nĭz′əm) or **a•syn•chron•y** (-krə-nē) *n.* Lack of concurrence; absence of synchronism. — **a•syn′chro•nous** (-nəs) *adj.* — **a•syn′chro•nous•ly** *adv.*

a•syn•de•ton (ə-sĭn′dĭ-tŏn′) *n.* The omission of conjunctions from constructions in which they would normally be used, as in *"Are all thy conquests, glories, triumphs, spoils/Shrunk to this little measure?"* (Shakespeare). [LLat. < Gk. *asundeton* < neut. of *asundetos,* without conjunctions : *a-,* not; see A-^{1} + *sundetos,* bound together (< *sundein,* to bind together : *sun-,* syn- + *dein,* to bind).] — **as′yn•det′ic** (ăs′ĭn-dĕt′ĭk) *adj.* — **as′yn•det′i•cal•ly** *adv.*

a•syn•tac•tic (ā′sĭn-tăk′tĭk) *adj.* Not conforming to accepted patterns of syntax.

As•yut (ä-syo͞ot′). A city of E-central Egypt on the Nile R. Pop. 274,400.

at^1 (ăt; ət *when unstressed*) *prep.* **1.a.** In or near the area occupied by; in or near the location of: *at the market.* **b.** In or near the position of: *at the center of the page.* **2.** To or toward the direction of, esp. for a specific purpose: *Questions came at us from all sides.* **3.** Present during; attending: *at the dance.* **4.** Within the interval or span of: *at a glance.* **5.** In the state of: *at peace.* **6.** In the activity or field of: *good at math.* **7.** To or using the rate, extent, or amount of; to the point of: *at 350°F.* **8.** On, near, or by the time or age of: *at three o'clock.* **9.** On account of; because of. **10.** By way of; through: *exited at the rear gate.* **11.** In accord with; following: *at my request.* **12.** Dependent upon: *at the mercy of the court.* **13.** Occupied with: *at work.* — ***idiom.* at it.** *Informal.* Engaged in verbal or physical conflict. [ME < OE *æt.* See **ad-*.**]

at^2 (ät) *n., pl.* **at.** See table at **currency.** [Thai.]

At^1 The symbol for the element **astatine.**

At^2 *abbr.* Ampere-turn.

AT *abbr.* **1.** Air temperature. **2.** Automatic transmission.

at. *abbr.* **1.** Airtight. **2.** Atomic.

at– *pref.* Var. of **ad–** 1.

At•a•brine (ăt′ə-brĭn, -brēn′). A trademark used for an antimalarial preparation of quinacrine hydrochloride.

At•a•ca•ma Desert (ăt′ə-kăm′ə, ä′tä-kä′mä). An arid region of NW Chile, one of the driest areas in the world.

A•ta•hual•pa (ä′tə-wäl′pə) also **A•ta•ba•li•pa** (-bä′lĭ-pä′). 1502?–33. Last Incan emperor of Peru (1525–33).

At•a•lan•ta (ăt′ə-lăn′tə) *n. Gk. Myth.* A virgin hunter who, having agreed to marry any man who could defeat her in a footrace, was outrun by Hippomenes, who dropped three golden apples, which she paused to pick up.

at•a•man (ăt′ə-măn′) *n., pl.* **-mans.** A Cossack chief. [Russ.

astronaut
Edwin E. Aldrin, Jr., on the moon

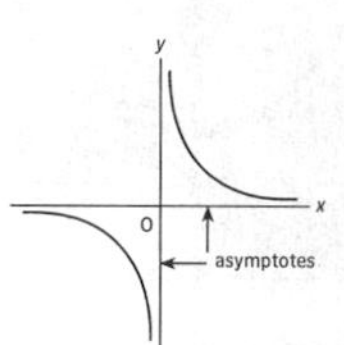

asymptote
Asymptotes of a hyperbola; $xy = 1$

ă pat	oi boy
ā pay	ou out
âr care	o͝o took
ä father	o͞o boot
ĕ pet	ŭ cut
ē be	ûr urge
ĭ pit	th thin
ī pie	*th* this
îr pier	hw which
ŏ pot	zh vision
ō toe	ə about, item
ô paw	

Stress marks:
′ (primary);
′ (secondary), as in **dictionary** (dĭk′shə-nĕr′ē)

< South Turkic, leader of an armed band : *ata*, father + *-man*, aug. suff.]

at•a•mas•co lily (ăt′ə-măs′kō) *n.* A bulbous plant *(Zephyranthes atamasco)* of the southeast United States, having a solitary flower on a long stalk. [Virginia Algonquian *attamusco*.]

at•a•rac•tic (ăt′ə-răk′tĭk) also **at•a•rax•ic** (-răk′sĭk) *—adj.* Relating to or producing calmness and peace of mind. *—n.* A drug that reduces nervous tension; a tranquilizer. [< Gk. *ataraktos*, undisturbed : *a-*, not; see A-¹ + *taraktos*, disturbed (< *tarassein*, *tarak-*, to disturb).]

at•a•rax•i•a (ăt′ə-răk′sē-ə) *n.* Peace of mind or tranquillity; calmness. [Gk. < *ataraktos*, undisturbed. See ATARACTIC.]

At•a•türk (ăt′ə-tûrk′, ä-tä-tûrk′), **Kemal.** See **Kemal Atatürk.**

at•a•vism (ăt′ə-vĭz′əm) *n.* **1.** The reappearance of a characteristic after several generations of absence, usu. caused by the chance recombination of genes. **2.** An individual or a part that exhibits atavism. **3.** The return of a trait or previous behavior after a period of absence. [Fr. *atavisme* < Lat. *atavus*, ancestor : *atta*, father + *avus*, grandfather; see **awo-***.] **—at′a•vist** *n.* **—at′a•vis′tic** *adj.* **—at′a•vis′ti•cal•ly** *adv.*

a•tax•i•a (ə-tăk′sē-ə) also **a•tax•y** (ə-tăk′sē) *n.* Loss of the ability to coordinate muscular movement. [Gk., disorder : *a-*, not; see A-¹ + *taxis*, order.] **—a•tax′ic** *adj. & n.*

At•ba•ra (ăt′bər-ə, ät′-). A river of NE Africa rising in NW Ethiopia and flowing c. 805 km (500 mi) to the Nile R. in E Sudan.

at bat or **at-bat** (ăt-băt′) *n. Baseball.* A player's official turn to bat, not counted for batting average if the player is hit by the ball, makes a sacrifice hit, is walked, or is interfered with.

At•chi•son (ăch′ĭ-sən). A city of NE KS NW of Kansas City; terminus for the Atchison, Topeka, and Santa Fe Railroad after 1859. Pop. 10,656.

ate (āt) *v.* P.t. of **eat.**

A•te (ā′tē, ä′tē, ä′tā) *n. Gk. Myth.* The personification of criminal rashness and consequent punishment.

-ate¹ *suff.* **1.a.** Having: *nervate.* **b.** Characterized by: *Latinate.* **c.** Resembling: *lyrate.* **2.a.** One characterized by: *laminate.* **b.** Rank; office: *rabbinate.* **3.** To act upon in a specified way: *acidulate.* [Ult. < Lat. *-ātus*, p.part. suff. of verbs in *-āre*.]

-ate² *suff.* **1.** A derivative of a specified chemical compound or element: *aluminate.* **2.** A salt or ester of a specified acid whose name ends in *-ic*: *acetate.* [NLat. *-ātum* < Lat., neut. of *-ātus*, p.part. suff. of verbs in *-āre*.]

at•e•lec•ta•sis (ăt′l-ĕk′tə-sĭs) *n.* **1.** Total or partial collapse of the lung. **2.** Incomplete expansion of the lungs at birth. [NLat. : Gk. *atelēs*, incomplete (*a-*, not; see A-¹ + *telos*, end; see TELO-) + Gk. *ektasis*, stretching out (< *ekteinein*, to stretch out : *ek-*, out; see ECTO- + *teinein*, to stretch; see EPITASIS).]

at•el•ier (ăt′l-yā′) *n.* A workshop or studio. [Fr. < OFr. *astelier*, carpenter's shop < *astele*, splinter < LLat. *astella*, alteration of Lat. *astula*, dim. of *assis*, board.]

a tem•po (ä tĕm′pō) *adv. & adj. Mus.* In the time originally designated; resuming the initial tempo of a section or movement after a deviation from it. [Ital. : *a*, in + *tempo*, time.]

a•tem•po•ral (ā-tĕm′pər-əl) *adj.* Independent of time.

A•ten (ät′n) *n. Myth.* Var. of **Aton.**

A•te•ri•an (ə-tîr′ē-ən) *adj.* Of or relating to a northern African Paleolithic culture using leaf-shaped spearheads. [Fr. *atérien*, after Bir el *Ater* (Constantine), a city of NE Algeria.]

Ath•a•bas•ca or **Ath•a•bas•ka** (ăth′ə-băs′kə). A river rising in the Rocky Mts. of SW Alberta, Canada, and flowing c. 1,231 km (765 mi) to **Lake Athabasca** on the border between N Alberta and Saskatchewan.

Ath•a•bas•kan or **Ath•a•bas•can** (ăth′ə-băs′kən) also **Ath•a•pas•can** (-păs′-) *n.* **1.** A group of related North American Indian languages including the Apachean languages and languages of Alaska, northwest Canada, and coastal Oregon and California. **2.** A member of an Athabaskan-speaking people. [After Lake ATHABASCA < Cree *athapaskaaw*, there is scattered grass.] **—Ath′a•bas′kan** *adj.*

Athanasian Creed *n.* A Christian creed of the early fifth century, originally attributed to Athanasius.

Ath•a•na•sius (ăth′ə-nā′shəs), Saint. A.D. 293?–373. Greek patriarch of Alexandria. **—Ath′a•na′sian** (-zhən) *adj. & n.*

a•the•ism (ā′thē-ĭz′əm) *n.* **1.a.** Disbelief in or denial of the existence of God or gods. **b.** The doctrine that there is no God or gods. **2.** Godlessness; immorality. [Fr. *athéisme* < *athée*, atheist < Gk. *atheos*, godless : *a-*, without; see A-¹ + *theos*, god; see **dhēs-***.] **—a′the•ist** *n.* **—a′the•is′tic** (-ĭs′tĭk), **a′the•is′ti•cal** (-tĭ-kəl) *adj.* **—a′the•is′ti•cal•ly** *adv.*

ath•e•ling (ăth′ə-lĭng, ăth′-) *n.* An Anglo-Saxon nobleman or prince. [ME < OE *ætheling*.]

Ath•el•stan (ăth′əl-stăn′). 895?–939. King of Mercia and Wessex (924?–939) who established control over England.

A•the•na (ə-thē′nə) also **A•the•ne** (-nē) *n. Gk. Myth.* The goddess of wisdom, the practical arts, and warfare.

ath•e•nae•um also **ath•e•ne•um** (ăth′ə-nē′əm) *n.* **1.** An institution, such as a literary club, for the promotion of learning. **2.** A place, such as a library, where printed materials are available. [LLat. *Athēnaeum*, a Roman school, after Gk. *Athēnaion*, the temple of Athena < *Athēna*, Athena.]

Athena
Mourning Athena, c. 460 B.C.

Atlas
Atlas, 1937, by Lee Lawrie (1877–1963), in forecourt of the International Building, Rockefeller Center, New York City

ă pat	oi boy
ā pay	ou out
âr care	o͝o to͝ok
ä father	o͞o bo͞ot
ĕ pet	ŭ cut
ē be	ûr urge
ĭ pit	th thin
ī pie	*th* this
îr pier	hw which
ŏ pot	zh vision
ō toe	ə about, item
ô paw	

Stress marks:
′ (primary);
′ (secondary), as in **dictionary** (dĭk′shə-nĕr′ē)

A•the•ni•an (ə-thē′nē-ən) *adj.* Of or relating to Athens, Greece, or its people. *—n.* A citizen of Athens, Greece.

Ath•ens (ăth′ənz). **1.** The cap. of Greece, in the E part near the Saronic Gulf; reached the height of its power in the 5th cent. B.C. and became the cap. of modern Greece in 1834. Pop. 885,737. **2.** A city of NE GA ENE of Atlanta; founded 1785. Pop. 45,734. **3.** A city of SE OH in the foothills of the Appalachian Mts.; settled c. 1797. Pop. 21,265.

ath•er•o•gen•e•sis (ăth′ər-ō-jĕn′ĭ-sĭs) *n.* Formation of atheromatous deposits. [ATHERO(MA) + -GENESIS.] **—ath′er•o•gen′ic** (-jĕn′ĭk) *adj.* **—ath′er•o•gen•i′ci•ty** (-jə-nĭs′ĭtē) *n.*

ath•er•o•ma (ăth′ə-rō′mə) *n., pl.* **-mas** or **-ma•ta** (-mə-tə). A deposit or degenerative accumulation of lipid-containing plaques on the innermost layer of the wall of an artery. [Lat. *atherōma*, tumor full of pus that is like gruel < Gk. < *athēra*, gruel.] **—ath′er•o•ma•to′sis** (-tō′sĭs) *n.* **—ath′er•om′a•tous** (-rŏm′ə-təs, -rō′mə-) *adj.*

ath•er•o•scle•ro•sis (ăth′ə-rō-sklə-rō′sĭs) *n.* A form of arteriosclerosis characterized by the deposit of atheromatous plaques on the innermost layer of the walls of large and medium-sized arteries. [ATHERO(MA) + SCLEROSIS.] **—ath′er•o•scle•rot′ic** (-rŏt′ĭk) *adj.* **—ath′er•o•scle•rot′i•cal•ly** *adv.*

a•thirst (ə-thûrst′) *adj.* **1.** Strongly desirous; eager: *athirst for freedom.* **2.** *Archaic.* Thirsty.

athl. *abbr.* Athlete; athletic; athletics.

ath•lete (ăth′lēt′) *n.* A person possessing the natural or acquired traits necessary for physical exercise or sports, esp. those performed in competitive contexts. [ME < Lat. *athlēta* < Gk. *athlētēs*, contestant < *athlein*, to contend, poss. < *athlos*, contest.]

ath•lete's foot (ăth′lēts) *n.* A fungal infection of the skin usu. affecting the feet, characterized by itching and scaling.

ath•let•ic (ăth-lĕt′ĭk) *adj.* **1.** Of or relating to athletics or athletes. **2.** Physically strong; muscular. See Syns at **muscular.** **3.** *Anthro.* Having a large skeletal structure and well-developed muscles; mesomorphic. **—ath•let′i•cal•ly** *adv.* **—ath•let′i•cism** (-lĕt′ĭ-sĭz′əm) *n.*

ath•let•ics (ăth-lĕt′ĭks) *n.* *(used with a sing. or pl. v.)* **1.** Activities that require physical skill and stamina. **2.** The principles or system of training and practice for such activities.

athletic supporter *n.* An elastic support for the male genitals, worn esp. in athletic or other strenuous activity.

ath•o•dyd (ăth′ə-dĭd′) *n.* A simple, essentially tubular jet engine, such as a ramjet. [A(ERO)- + TH(ERM)ODY(NAMIC) + D(UCT).]

at-home or **at home** (ət-hōm′, ăt-) *—n.* An informal reception in one's home. *—adj.* **1.** Being or occurring in one's home: *at-home care.* **2.** Designed for or appropriate for one's home.

Ath•os (ăth′ŏs, ā′thŏs, ä′thôs), **Mount.** A peak, c. 2,034 m (6,670 ft), of NE Greece; site of the monastic community of **Mount Athos,** founded in the 10th cent.

a•thwart (ə-thwôrt′) *adv.* **1.** From side to side; crosswise or transversely. **2.** So as to thwart or oppose; perversely. *—prep.* **1.** From one side to the other of; across: *"the Stars that shoot athwart the Night"* (Alexander Pope). **2.** Contrary to; against. [ME : *a-*, on; see A-² + *thwert*, across; see THWART.]

a•tilt (ə-tĭlt′) *adv. & adj.* **1.** In a tilted position; inclined upward. **2.** Tilting or as if tilting with a lance.

a•tin•gle (ə-tĭng′gəl) *adj.* Experiencing a prickling sensation, as from excitement.

-ation *suff.* **1.a.** Action or process: *strangulation.* **b.** The result of an action or process: *acculturation.* **2.** State, condition, or quality of: *eburnation.* [ME *-acioun* < OFr. *-ation* < Lat. *-ātiō*, *-ātiōn-*, n. suff. : *-ā-*, stem vowel of verbs in *-āre* + *-tiō*, *-tiōn-*, abstract n. suff.]

A•ti•tlán (ä′tē-tlän′). A lake of SW Guatemala amid three inactive volcanoes, including **Atitlán,** 3,539.2 m (11,604 ft).

-ative *suff.* Of, relating to, or associated with: *talkative.* [ME < OFr. *-atif, -ative* < Lat. *-ātīvus* < *-ātus*, p.part. suff. See -ATE¹.]

At•ka Island (ăt′kə, ät′-). An island of SW AK in the central Aleutian Is.; site of a major World War II military base.

Atka mackerel *n.* A food fish *(Pleurogrammus monopterygius)* native to northern Pacific waters.

Atl. *abbr.* Atlantic.

At•lan•ta (ăt-lăn′tə). The cap. of GA, in the NW part; founded in 1837. Pop. 394,017. **—At•lan′tan** *n.*

At•lan•te•an¹ (ăt′lăn-tē′ən, ăt-lăn′tē-) *adj.* Of, relating to, or like Atlas. [< Gk. *Atlas*, *Atlant-*, Atlas. See ATLAS.]

At•lan•te•an² (ăt′lăn-tē′ən, ăt-lăn′tē-) *adj.* Of or relating to Atlantis.

at•lan•tes (ăt-lăn′tēz) *n. Archit.* Pl. of **atlas²** 1.

At•lan•tic (ăt-lăn′tĭk) *adj.* **1.** Of, in, near, upon, or relating to the Atlantic Ocean. **2.** Of, on, near, or relating to the eastern coast of the United States. **3.** Of or concerning countries bordering the Atlantic Ocean. [ME *Atlantik* < Lat. *(mare) Atlanticum*, Atlantic (sea) < Gk. *(pelagos) Atlantikos* < *Atlas*, *Atlant-*, Atlas. See **telə-***.]

Atlantic City. A resort city of SE NJ on the Atlantic Ocean. Pop. 37,986.

Atlantic croaker *n.* A small silvery food fish *(Micropogonias undulatus)* common in Atlantic waters south of Massachusetts.

Atlantic In•tra•coast•al Waterway (ĭn′trə-kō′stəl). A system of inland waterways along the Atlantic coast of the U.S. extending from Cape Cod to S FL and forming part of the Intracoastal Waterway.

At•lan•ti•cism (ăt-lăn′tĭ-sĭz′əm) *n.* A policy of cooperation between western Europe and North America. — **At•lan′ti•cist** *n.*

Atlantic Ocean. The second-largest ocean, divided into the **North Atlantic** and the **South Atlantic** and extending from the Arctic to the Antarctic between the E Americas and W Europe and Africa.

Atlantic Provinces. The E Canadian provinces of New Brunswick, Prince Edward I., Nova Scotia, and Newfoundland.

Atlantic salmon *n.* A species of salmon *(Salmo salar)* native to northern Atlantic waters and valued as a food fish.

Atlantic Standard Time *n.* Standard time in the fourth time zone west of Greenwich, England, reckoned at 60° west and used, for example, in Puerto Rico.

At•lan•tis (ăt-lăn′tĭs) *n. Myth.* A legendary island in the Atlantic Ocean, said to have sunk during an earthquake.

at•las[1] (ăt′ləs) *n., pl.* **-las•es. 1.** A book or bound collection of maps, sometimes with supplementary illustrations and graphic analyses. **2.** A volume of tables, charts, or plates illustrating a particular subject: *an anatomical atlas.* [After *Atlas,* legendary king of N Africa, sometimes identified with, or considered descended from, the Titan Atlas.]

at•las[2] (ăt′ləs) *n., pl.* **-es. 1.** *pl.* **at•lan•tes** (ăt-lăn′tēz). *Archit.* A figure of a man used as a supporting column for an entablature. **2.** *Anat.* The top or first cervical vertebra of the neck, which supports the skull. [< ATLAS.]

At•las (ăt′ləs) *n.* **1.** *Gk. Myth.* A Titan condemned by Zeus to support the heavens upon his shoulders. **2.** A satellite of Saturn. **3. atlas.** A person who supports a great burden. [Gk. See **telə-*.**]

Atlas Mountains. A system of ranges and plateaus of NW Africa extending from SW Morocco to N Tunisia and rising to 4,167.8 m (13,665 ft).

at•la•tl (ät-lät′l) *n.* A spear-throwing device usu. consisting of a stick with a thong or socket to steady the butt of the spear. [Nahuatl < *atla,* to throw.]

At•li (ät′lē) *n.* In the *Volsunga Saga,* a husband of Gudrun.

atm or **atm.** *abbr. Phys.* Atmosphere; atmospheric.

ATM *abbr.* Automated teller machine.

at•man (ät′mən) *n. Hinduism.* **1.** The individual soul or essence. **2. Atman.** The eternal, unchanging essence that is indistinguishable from that of the universe. [Skt. *ātman,* breath, spirit.]

at•mom•e•ter (ăt-mŏm′ĭ-tər) *n.* An instrument that measures the rate of water evaporation. [Gk. *atmos,* vapor; see ATMOSPHERE + -METER.]

atmos. *abbr. Phys.* Atmosphere; atmospheric.

at•mos•phere (ăt′mə-sfîr′) *n.* **1.** The gaseous mass surrounding a celestial body, esp. the one surrounding Earth. **2.** The air or climate in a specific place. **3.** *Phys.* A unit of pressure equal to the air pressure at sea level, approx. equal to 1.01325 × 10^5 pascals. See table at **measurement. 4.** A dominant intellectual or emotional tone or attitude: *an atmosphere of distrust.* **5.** The dominant tone or mood of a work of art. **6.** An aesthetic quality or effect associated with a particular place. [NLat. *atmosphaera:* Gk. *atmos,* vapor; see **wet-**[1]***** + Lat. *sphaera,* sphere; see SPHERE.]

at•mos•pher•ic (ăt′mə-sfĕr′ĭk, -sfîr′-) also **at•mos•pher•i•cal** (-ĭ-kəl) *adj.* **1.** Of, relating to, or existing in the atmosphere. **2.** Produced by, dependent on, or coming from the atmosphere. **3.** Resembling or suggestive of the atmosphere: *a painting with an atmospheric glow.* **4.** Intended to evoke a particular emotional tone or aesthetic quality. — **at′mos•pher′i•cal•ly** *adv.*

atmospheric pressure *n.* Pressure caused by the weight of the atmosphere, a maximum at sea level and reducing with increasing altitude.

at•mos•pher•ics (ăt′mə-sfĕr′ĭks, -sfîr′-) *n.* **1.** *(used with a sing. v.)* **a.** Electromagnetic radiation produced by natural phenomena such as lightning. **b.** Radio interference produced by electromagnetic radiation. **2.** *(used with a pl. v.)* **a.** Actions intended to create a particular mood. **b.** The mood so created.

at. no. also **at no** *abbr.* Atomic number.

a•toll (ăt′ôl′, -ŏl′, ā′tôl′, ā′tŏl′) *n.* A ringlike coral island and reef that nearly or entirely encloses a lagoon. [Perh. ult. < Tamil *aṭar,* to be close together, thick, crowded.]

at•om (ăt′əm) *n.* **1.a.** A part or particle considered to be an irreducible constituent of a specified system. **b.** The irreducible indestructible material unit postulated by ancient atomism. **2.** An extremely small part, quantity, or amount. **3.** *Phys. & Chem.* **a.** The smallest unit of an element, characteristically remaining undivided in chemical reactions and consisting of a dense, central, positively charged nucleus surrounded by a system of electrons. **b.** This unit regarded as a source of nuclear energy. See table at **subatomic particle.** [ME *attome* < Lat. *atomus* < Gk. *atomos,* indivisible, atom : *a-,* not; see A-[1] + *tomos,* cutting (< *temnein,* to cut; see **tem-***).]

atom bomb *n.* **1.** An explosive weapon of great destructive power derived from the release of energy in the fission of atomic nuclei. **2.** A bomb deriving its destructive power from the release of nuclear energy.

a•tom•ic (ə-tŏm′ĭk) *adj.* **1.** Of or relating to an atom or atoms. **2.** Of or employing nuclear energy: *atomic weapons.* **3.** Very small; infinitesimal. — **a•tom′i•cal•ly** *adv.*

atomic age also **Atomic Age** *n.* The era defined by the discovery, applications, and consequences of nuclear energy.

atomic bomb *n.* See **atom bomb** 1.

atomic clock *n.* An extremely precise timekeeping device regulated in correspondence with a characteristic invariant frequency of an atomic or molecular system.

atomic energy *n.* See **nuclear energy.**

at•o•mic•i•ty (ăt′ə-mĭs′ĭ-tē) *n.* **1.** The state of being composed of atoms. **2.** *Chem.* **a.** The number of atoms in a molecule. **b.** Valence.

atomic mass *n.* The mass of an atom, usu. expressed in atomic mass units.

atomic mass unit *n.* A unit of mass equal to 1⁄12 the mass of an atom of carbon 12, which is assigned a mass of 12.

atomic number *n. Symbol* **Z** The number of protons in an atomic nucleus.

atomic weight *n.* The average mass of an atom of an element, usu. expressed relative to the atomic mass of carbon 12.

at•om•ism (ăt′ə-mĭz′əm) *n.* **1.** *Philos.* The ancient theory that simple, minute, indivisible, and indestructible particles are the components of the entire universe. **2.** *Philos.* A theory that social institutions, values, and processes arise solely from individuals, who are thus the only true subject of analysis. — **at′om•ist** *n.*

at•om•is•tic (ăt′ə-mĭs′tĭk) also **at•om•is•ti•cal** (-tĭ-kəl) *adj.* **1.** Of or relating to atoms or atomism. **2.** Consisting of many separate, often disparate elements. — **at′om•is′ti•cal•ly** *adv.*

at•om•ize (ăt′ə-mīz′) *tr.v.* **-ized, -iz•ing, -iz•es. 1.** To reduce to or separate into atoms. **2.** To reduce to tiny particles or a fine spray. **3.** To break into small fragments. **4.** To subject to bombardment with atomic weapons. — **at′om•i•za′tion** (-ĭ-zā′shən) *n.*

at•om•iz•er (ăt′ə-mī′zər) *n.* A device for converting a substance, esp. a perfume or medicine, to a fine spray.

atom smasher *n.* See **accelerator** 3.

at•o•my[1] (ăt′ə-mē) *n., pl.* **-mies.** *Archaic.* **1.** A tiny particle. **2.** A tiny being. [< Lat. *atomī,* pl. of *atomus,* atom. See ATOM.]

at•o•my[2] (ăt′ə-mē) *n., pl.* **-mies.** *Archaic.* A gaunt person; a skeleton. [< *an atomy,* respelling of ANATOMY.]

A•ton also **A•ten** (ät′n) *n. Myth.* An Egyptian god of the sun, regarded during the reign of Akhenaton as the only god.

a•to•nal (ā-tō′nəl) *adj. Mus.* Lacking a tonal center or key; characterized by atonality. — **a•to′nal•ly** *adv.*

a•to•nal•ism (ā-tō′nə-lĭz′əm) *n. Mus.* Atonal composition or the theory of atonal composition. — **a•to′nal•ist** *adj. & n.* — **a•to′nal•is′tic** *adj.*

a•to•nal•i•ty (ā′tō-năl′ĭ-tē) *n., pl.* **-ties.** *Mus.* The absence of a tonal center and of harmonies derived from a diatonic scale corresponding to such a center; lack of tonality.

a•tone (ə-tōn′) *v.* **a•toned, a•ton•ing, a•tones.** — *intr.* **1.** To make amends, as for a sin or fault. **2.** *Archaic.* To agree. — *tr.* **1.** To expiate. **2.** *Archaic.* To conciliate; appease. **3.** *Obsolete.* To reconcile or harmonize. [ME *atonen,* to be reconciled < *at one,* in agreement : *at,* at; see AT[1] + *one,* one; see ONE.] — **a•ton′a•ble, a•tone′a•ble** *adj.* — **a•ton′er** *n.*

a•tone•ment (ə-tōn′mənt) *n.* **1.** Amends or reparation made for an injury or wrong; expiation. **2.** *Theol.* also **Atonement** Reconciliation between God and human beings, brought about by the life and death of Jesus. **3.** *Obsolete.* Reconciliation; concord.

a•ton•ic (ā-tŏn′ĭk) *adj.* **1.** Not accented: *an atonic syllable.* **2.** *Pathol.* Relating to, caused by, or exhibiting lack of muscle tone. — *n.* A word, syllable, or sound that is unaccented. [< Gk. *atonos.* See ATONY.] — **at′o•nic′i•ty** (ăt′ə-nĭs′ĭ-tē, ăt′-n-ĭs-) *n.*

at•o•ny (ăt′ə-nē, ăt′n-ē) *n.* **1.** Lack of normal muscle tone. **2.** Lack of accent or stress. [LLat. *atonia* < Gk. < *atonos,* slack : *a-,* without; see A-[1] + *tonos,* stretching, tone; see TONE.]

a•top (ə-tŏp′) *adv.* To, on, or at the top. — *prep.* On top of. — **a•top′** *adj.*

a•top•ic (ā-tŏp′ĭk) *adj.* Of, relating to, or caused by a hereditary predisposition toward certain hypersensitivity reactions, such as hay fever or asthma, upon exposure to specific antigens. [< Gk. *atopia,* unusualness < *atopos,* out of the way : *a-,* not; see A-[1] + *topos,* place.] — **at′o•py** (ăt′ə-pē) *n.*

–ator *suff.* One that acts in a specified manner: *radiator.* [Lat. *-ātor: -ā-,* stem vowel of verbs in *-āre* + *-tor,* agent n. suff. (later reanalyzed as *-ātus,* -ate + *-or,* -or).]

–atory *suff.* **1.a.** Of or relating to: *perspiratory.* **b.** Tending to: *amendatory.* **2.** One that is connected with: *reformatory.* [< Lat. *-ātōrius*and *-ātōrium,* both < *-ātor,* -ator.]

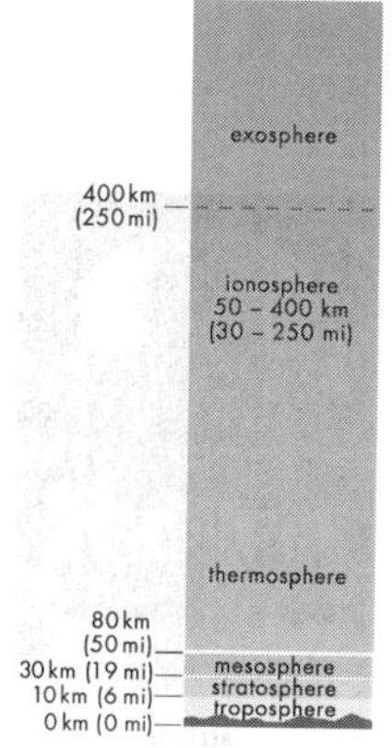

atmosphere

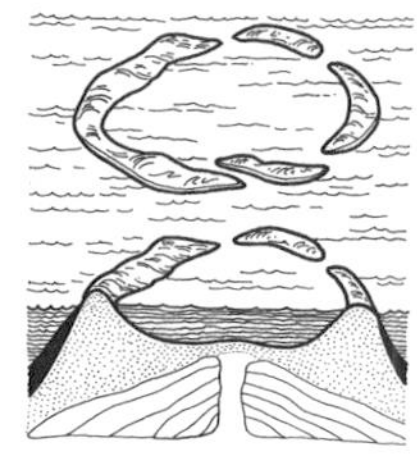
atoll
Top: Aerial view
Bottom: Cutaway drawing

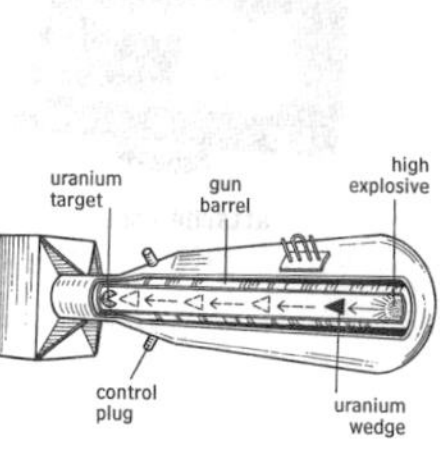

atom bomb

made in excess of the contract are scored toward game.

auc•tion•eer (ôk′shə-nîr′) *n.* One that conducts an auction. — *tr.v.* **-eered, -eer•ing, -eers.** To sell at auction.

auc•to•ri•al (ôk-tôr′ē-əl, -tōr′-) *adj.* Of or relating to an author. [< Lat. *auctor*, author. See AUTHOR.]

au•cu•ba (ô′kyə-bə) *n.* Any of several Asian evergreen shrubs of the genus *Aucuba*, esp. *A. japonica*, grown as an ornamental. [NLat. : poss. < J. *auku*, green + J. *ba*, leaved.]

aud. *abbr.* **1.** Audit; auditor. **2.** Audition.

au•da•cious (ô-dā′shəs) *adj.* **1.** Fearlessly, often recklessly daring; bold. See Syns at **brave. 2.** Unrestrained by propriety; insolent. **3.** Spirited and original. [Fr. *audacieux* < OFr. *audace*, boldness < Lat. *audācia* < *audāx, audāc-*, bold < *audēre*, to dare < *avidus*, avid. See AVID.] — **au•da′cious•ly** *adv.*

au•dac•i•ty (ô-dăs′ĭ-tē) *n., pl.* **-ties. 1.** Fearless daring; intrepidity. **2.** Bold or insolent heedlessness of restraints, as of those imposed by propriety. **3.** An act or instance of intrepidity or insolent heedlessness.

Au•den (ôd′n), **W(ystan) H(ugh).** 1907–73. British-born Amer. poet whose works include *The Dance of Death* (1933).

au•di•ble (ô′də-bəl) *adj.* That is heard or that can be heard. — *n. Football.* An offensive play or a defensive formation called at the line of scrimmage. [LLat. *audībilis* < Lat. *audīre*, to hear. See **au-***.] — **au′di•bil′i•ty, au′di•ble•ness** *n.* — **au′di•bly** *adv.*

John James Audubon
c. 1822 self-portrait

au•di•ence (ô′dē-əns) *n.* **1.a.** Those assembled at a performance, for example, or attracted by a radio or television program. **b.** The readership for printed matter. **2.** A body of adherents; a following. **3.** A formal hearing, as with a state dignitary. **4.** An opportunity to be heard or to express one's views. **5.** The act of hearing or attending. [ME < OFr. < Lat. *audientia* < *audiēns*, pr.part. of *audīre*, to hear. See **au-***.]

au•dile (ô′dīl′) *adj.* **1.** Capable of learning chiefly from auditory, rather than tactile or visual stimuli. **2.** Auditory. — *n.* An audile person. [< Lat. *audīre*, to hear. See **au-***.]

au•di•o (ô′dē-ō′) *adj.* **1.** Of or relating to humanly audible sound. **2.** Of or relating to the broadcasting, reception, or reproduction of sound. — *n., pl.* **-di•os. 1.** The part of television or movie equipment that has to do with sound. **2.** The broadcasting, reception, or reproduction of sound. **3.** Audible sound. **4.** A sound signal. [< AUDIO–.]

audio– *pref.* **1.** Hearing: *audio-lingual.* **2.** Sound: *audiophile.* [< Lat. *audīre*, to hear. See **au-***.]

audio frequency *n.* A range of frequencies, usu. from 15 hertz to 20,000 hertz, audible to the normal human ear.

au•di•o•gram (ô′dē-ə-grăm′) *n.* A graphic record of hearing ability for sound frequencies, used to measure hearing loss.

au•di•o-lin•gual (ô′dē-ō-lĭng′gwəl) *adj.* Relating to a system of language acquisition that stresses speaking and listening.

au•di•ol•o•gy (ô′dē-ŏl′ə-jē) *n.* The study of hearing, esp. hearing defects and their treatment. — **au′di•o•log′i•cal** (-ə-lŏj′ĭ-kəl) *adj.* — **au′di•ol′o•gist** *n.*

au•di•om•e•ter (ô′dē-ŏm′ĭ-tər) *n.* An instrument for measuring hearing activity for tones of normally audible frequencies. — **au′di•o•met′ric** (-ō-mĕt′rĭk) *adj.* — **au′di•om′e•try** *n.*

au•di•o•phile (ô′dē-ə-fīl′) *n.* A person having an ardent interest in stereo or high-fidelity sound reproduction.

au•di•o•tape (ô′dē-ō-tāp′) *n.* **1.** A relatively narrow magnetic tape used to record sound for subsequent playback. **2.** A tape recording of sound. — *tr.v.* **-taped, -tap•ing, -tapes.** To record (sound) on magnetic tape.

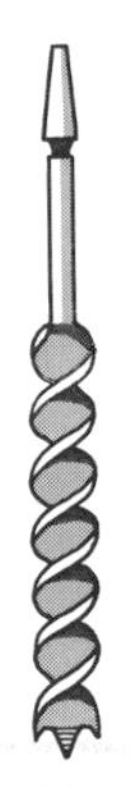

auger
Double twist auger bit

au•di•o-vis•u•al also **au•di•o•vis•u•al** (ô′dē-ō-vĭzh′o͞o-əl) — *adj.* **1.** Both audible and visible. **2.** Of or relating to materials, such as films, that present information in audible and pictorial form. — *n.* An aid, other than printed matter, that uses sight or sound to present information.

au•dit (ô′dĭt) *n.* **1.** An examination of records or financial accounts to check their accuracy. **2.** An adjustment or correction of accounts. **3.** An examined and verified account. — *v.* **-dit•ed, -dit•ing, -dits.** — *tr.* **1.** To examine, verify, or correct the financial accounts of. **2.** To attend (a course) without requesting or receiving academic credit. — *intr.* To examine financial accounts. [ME (influenced by *auditor*, auditor) < Lat. *audītus*, a hearing < p.part. of *audīre*, to hear. See **au-***.]

au•di•tion (ô-dĭsh′ən) *n.* **1.** The sense or power of hearing. **2.** The act of hearing. **3.** A trial performance, as by an actor, to demonstrate suitability or skill. — *v.* **-tioned, -tion•ing, -tions.** — *intr.* To take part in an audition. — *tr.* To evaluate (a person) in an audition. [Lat. *audītiō, audītiōn-* < *audītus*, p.part. of *audīre*, to hear. See **au-***.]

au•di•tive (ô′dĭ-tĭv) *adj.* Of or relating to hearing; auditory.

au•di•tor (ô′dĭ-tər) *n.* **1.** One that audits accounts. **2.** One who audits a course. **3.** One who hears; a listener. [ME < AN *auditour* < Lat. *audītor*, listener < *audīre*, to hear. See **au-***.]

au•di•to•ri•um (ô′dĭ-tôr′ē-əm, -tōr′-) *n., pl.* **-ri•ums** or **-ri•a** (-tôr′ē-ə, -tōr′-). **1.** A large room to accommodate an audience in a building. **2.** A large building for public meetings or performances. [Lat. < *audīre*, to hear. See **au-***.]

au•di•to•ry (ô′dĭ-tôr′ē, -tōr′ē) *adj.* Of or relating to hearing, the organs of hearing, or the sense of hearing. [LLat. *audītōrius* < Lat. *audīre*, to hear. See **au-***.]

auditory nerve *n. Anat.* See **acoustic nerve.**

Au•du•bon (ô′də-bŏn′, -bən), **John James.** 1785–1851. Haitian-born Amer. ornithologist and artist best known for *The Birds of America* (1827–38).

Auf•klä•rung (ouf′klā′ro͝ong) *n.* The Enlightenment. [Ger. : *auf*, up (< MHGer. *ūf* < OHGer.; see **upo***) + *Klärung*, a making clear (< *klären*, to make clear < MHGer. *klæren* < *klār*, clear < Lat. *clārus*; see CLEAR).]

auf Wie•der•seh•en (ouf vē′dər-zā′ən) *interj.* Used to express farewell. [Ger. : *auf*, until + *Wiedersehen*, seeing again.]

aug. *abbr. Gram.* Augmentative.

Aug. *abbr.* August.

Au•ge•an (ô-jē′ən) *adj.* **1.** Exceedingly filthy from long neglect. **2.** Requiring heroic efforts of cleaning or correction. [After *Augeas*, legendary Greek king who did not clean his stable for 30 years.]

au•gend (ô′jĕnd′) *n. Math.* A quantity to which the addend is added. [Lat. *augendum*, a thing to be increased < neut. gerundive of *augēre*, to increase. See **aug-***.]

au•ger (ô′gər) *n.* **1.** A tool for boring holes in wood or ice. **2.** A large tool for boring into the earth. [ME < *an auger*, alteration of *a nauger* < OE *nafogār*, auger. See **nobh-***.]

aught[1] also **ought** (ôt) — *pron.* Anything whatever: *"Neither of his parents had aught but praise for him"* (Louis Auchincloss). — *adv. Archaic.* In any respect; at all. [ME < OE *āuht*. See **aiw-***.]

aught[2] also **ought** (ôt) *n.* **1.** A cipher; zero. **2.** *Archaic.* Nothing. [< *an aught*, alteration of *a naught*. See NAUGHT.]

au•gite (ô′jīt′) *n.* A dark-green to black pyroxene mineral, $(Ca,Na)(Mg,Fe,Al)(Si,Al)_2O_6$, that contains large amounts of aluminum, iron, and magnesium. [Lat. *augītis*, a precious stone < Gk. *augītēs* < *augē*, brightness.]

aug•ment (ôg-mĕnt′) *v.* **-ment•ed, -ment•ing, -ments.** — *tr.* **1.** To make (something already developed or well under way) greater, as in size or extent: *Rain augmented the floodwaters.* **2.** To add an augment to. — *intr.* To become augmented. See Syns at **increase.** — *n.* (ôg′mĕnt′). The prefixation of a vowel accompanying a past tense, esp. of Greek and Sanskrit verbs. [ME *augmenten* < OFr. *augmenter* < LLat. *augmentāre* < Lat. *augmentum*, an increase < *augēre*, to increase. See **aug-***.] — **aug•ment′a•ble** *adj.* — **aug•ment′er** *n.*

aug•men•ta•tion (ôg′mĕn-tā′shən) *n.* **1.** The act or process of augmenting. **2.** The condition of being augmented. **3.** Something that augments. **4.** *Mus.* The repetition of a theme in notes of usu. double time value.

aug•men•ta•tive (ôg-mĕn′tə-tĭv) *adj.* **1.** Having the ability or tendency to augment. **2.** *Gram.* Increasing the size, force, or intensity of the meaning of an adjacent word, as *up* does in *eat up.* — *n. Gram.* An augmentative word.

aug•ment•ed (ôg-mĕn′tĭd) *adj. Mus.* Larger by a semitone than the corresponding major or perfect interval.

au gra•tin (ō grät′n, grăt′n, grä-tăN′) *adj.* Covered with bread crumbs and sometimes butter and grated cheese and then browned in an oven. [Fr. : *au*, with the + *gratin*, scrapings from the pan.]

Augs•burg (ôgz′bûrg′, ouks′bo͝ork′). A city of S Germany WNW of Munich; founded c. 14 B.C. Pop. 244,400.

au•gur (ô′gər) *n.* **1.** One of a group of ancient Roman religious officials who foretold events by interpreting signs and omens. **2.** A seer or prophet; a soothsayer. — *v.* **-gured, -gur•ing, -gurs.** — *tr.* **1.** To predict, esp. from signs or omens; foretell. **2.** To serve as an omen of; betoken. — *intr.* **1.** To make predictions from signs or omens. **2.** To be a sign or omen. [ME < Lat. See **aug-***.] — **au′gu•ral** (ô′gyə-rəl) *adj.*

au•gu•ry (ô′gyə-rē) *n., pl.* **-ries. 1.** The art, ability, or practice of auguring; divination. **2.** A sign of something coming; an omen. [ME *augurie* < OFr. < Lat. *augurium* < *augur*, augur. See AUGUR.]

au•gust (ô-gŭst′) *adj.* **1.** Inspiring awe or admiration; majestic. See Syns at **grand. 2.** Venerable because of age or rank. [Lat. *augustus*. See **aug-***.] — **au•gust′ly** *adv.* — **au•gust′ness** *n.*

Au•gust (ô′gəst) *n.* The eighth month of the year in the Gregorian calendar. [ME < OE < Lat. *(mēnsis) Augustus*, (month) of Augustus, after AUGUSTUS.]

Au•gus•ta (ô-gŭs′tə, ə-gŭs′-). **1.** A city of E GA on the SC border NNW of Savannah. Pop. 44,639. **2.** The cap. of ME, in the SW part on the Kennebec R. NNE of Portland; first settled in 1628. Pop. 21,325.

Au•gus•tan (ô-gŭs′tən) *adj.* **1.** Of or characteristic of Augustus or his reign or times. **2.** Of or characteristic of English literature during the early 18th century. — **Au•gus′tan** *n.*

Au•gus•tine[1] (ô′gə-stēn′, ô-gŭs′tĭn), Saint. A.D. 354–430. Early Christian church father and philosopher who served (396–430) as the bishop of Hippo (in present-day Algeria).

Au•gus•tine[2] (ô′gə-stēn′, ô-gŭs′tĭn) also **Aus•tin** (ô′stən), Saint. "Apostle of the English." d. c. 604. Italian-born missionary and first archbishop of Canterbury (ordained 598).

Au•gus•tin•i•an (ô′gə-stĭn′ē-ən) *adj.* **1.** Of or relating to Saint Augustine of Hippo or his doctrines. **2.** Of or being any religious order following or influenced by the rule of Saint

Augustine. — *n.* **1.** A follower of the principles and doctrines of Saint Augustine. **2.** A monk or friar of an Augustinian order. — **Au′gus•tin′i•an•ism, Au•gus′tin•ism** (ô-gŭs′tĭ-nĭz′əm) *n.*

Au•gus•tus (ô-gŭs′təs). Orig. **Oc•ta•vi•an** (ŏk-tā′vē-ən). 63 B.C.–A.D. 14. First emperor of Rome (27 B.C.–A.D. 14).

au jus (ō zho͞os′, zhü′) *adj.* Served with the natural juices or gravy: *roast beef au jus.* [Fr. : *au*, with the + *jus*, juice.]

auk (ôk) *n.* Any of several northern diving sea birds in the family Alcidae, such as the razor-billed auk, having a chunky body, short wings, and webbed feet. [Norw. *alk* < ON *ālka.*]

auk•let (ôk′lĭt) *n.* Any of various small auks (genus *Aethia* and related genera) of northern Pacific coasts and waters.

auld (ôld) *adj. Scots.* Old.

auld lang syne (ôld′ lăng zīn′, sīn′) *n.* The good old days. [Sc. : *auld*, old + *lang*, long + *syne*, since.]

Aum (ōm) *n. Hinduism & Buddhism.* Var. of **Om**[2].

au na•tu•rel (ō′ năch′ə-rĕl′, ô′ nä-tü-rĕl′) *adj.* **1.a.** Nude. **b.** In a natural state: *an au naturel hairstyle.* **2.** Cooked simply. [Fr. : *au*, in the + *naturel*, natural (state).]

Au•nis (ō-nēs′). A historical region and former province of W France on the Atlantic Ocean; became part of the crown lands in 1373.

aunt (ănt, änt) *n.* **1.** The sister of one's father or mother. **2.** The wife of one's uncle. [ME *aunte* < AN < Lat. *amita*, paternal aunt.] — **aunt′hood** *n.*

aunt•ie also **aunt•y** (ăn′tē, än′-) *n., pl.* **-ies.** *Informal.* Aunt.

au pair (ô pâr′) *n.* A young foreigner who does domestic work for a family in exchange for room and board and a chance to learn the family's language. [Fr. : *au*, at the + *pair*, equal.]

au•ra (ôr′ə) *n., pl.* **au•ras** or **au•rae** (ôr′ē). **1.** An invisible breath, emanation, or radiation. **2.** A distinctive but intangible quality that seems to surround a person or thing; atmosphere. **3.** *Pathol.* A sensation that precedes the onset of certain disorders, such as an attack of migraine. [ME, gentle breeze < Lat. < Gk., breath. See **wer-**[1]***.**]

au•ral[1] (ôr′əl) *adj.* Of, relating to, or perceived by the ear. [< Lat. *auris*, ear. See **ous-*.**] — **au′ral•ly** *adv.*

au•ral[2] (ôr′əl) *adj.* Characterized by or relating to an aura.

Au•rang•a•bad (ou-rŭng′gə-bäd′, -ə-bäd′). A town of W India ENE of Bombay; founded 1610. Pop. 284,607.

Au•rang•zeb also **Au•rung•zeb** or **Au•rung•zebe** (ôr′əng-zĕb′). 1618–1707. Hindustani emperor (1658–1707) who expanded the empire.

au•rar (ou′rär′, œ′rär′) *n.* Pl. of **eyrir.**

au•re•ate (ôr′ē-ĭt) *adj.* **1.** Of a golden color; gilded. **2.** Inflated and pompous in style. [ME *aureat* < LLat. *aureātus* < *aureus*, golden < *aurum*, gold.] — **au′re•ate•ly** *adv.* — **au′re•ate•ness** *n.*

Au•re•lian (ô-rēl′yən, ô-rē′lē-ən). A.D. 212?–275. Emperor of Rome (270–275) who regained Britain, Gaul, Spain, Syria, and Egypt for the empire.

au•re•ole (ôr′ē-ōl′) also **au•re•o•la** (ô-rē′ə-lə) *n.* **1.** A circle of light or radiance surrounding the head or body of a representation of a deity or holy person; a halo. **2.** *Astron.* See **corona** 1a. [ME < LLat. *(corōna) aureola*, golden (crown), fem. of Lat. *aureolus*, golden < *aureus* < *aurum*, gold.]

Au•re•o•my•cin (ôr′ē-ō-mī′sĭn). A trademark used for chlortetracycline.

au re•voir (ō′ rə-vwär′) *interj.* Used to express farewell. [Fr. : *au*, till the + *revoir*, seeing again.]

au•ric (ôr′ĭk) *adj.* Of, relating to, derived from, or containing gold, esp. with valence 3. [< Lat. *aurum*, gold.]

au•ri•cle (ôr′ĭ-kəl) *n.* **1.** *Anat.* **a.** The outer projecting portion of the ear. **b.** See **atrium** 2. **2.** *Biol.* An earlobe-shaped part, process, or appendage, esp. at the base of an organ. [ME, auricle of the heart < OFr., little ear < Lat. *auricula* < dim. of *auris*, ear. See **ous-*.**] — **au′ri•cled** (-kəld) *adj.*

au•ric•u•la (ô-rĭk′yə-lə) *n., pl.* **-las** or **-lae** (-lē′). **1.** A central European primrose *(Primula auricula)* having large yellow flowers grouped in umbels. **2.** Any of numerous hybrids of this species with other primroses. [Lat., auricle. See AURICLE.]

au•ric•u•lar (ô-rĭk′yə-lər) *adj.* **1.** Of or relating to the sense of hearing or the organs of hearing. **2.** Perceived by or spoken into the ear. **3.** Shaped like an ear or an earlobe; having earlike parts or extensions. **4.** Of or relating to an auricle of the heart. [ME *auriculer*, spoken into the ear < LLat. *auriculāris* < Lat. *auricula*, ear. See AURICLE.] — **au•ric′u•lar•ly** *adv.*

au•ric•u•late (ô-rĭk′yə-lĭt, -lāt′) also **au•ric•u•lat•ed** (-lāt′ĭd) *adj.* **1.** Having ears, auricles, or earlobe-shaped parts or extensions. **2.** Shaped like an earlobe. [< Lat. *auricula*, auricle. See AURICLE.] — **au•ric′u•late•ly** *adv.*

au•rif•er•ous (ô-rĭf′ər-əs) *adj.* Containing gold; gold-bearing. [< Lat. *aurifer*, gold-bearing : *aurum*, gold + *-fer*, -fer.]

au•ri•form (ôr′ə-fôrm′) *adj.* Shaped like an ear. [Lat. *auris*, ear; see **ous-*** + -FORM.]

Au•ri•ga (ô-rī′gə) *n.* A constellation in the Northern Hemisphere near Lynx and Perseus that contains the bright star Capella. [Lat. *aurīga*, charioteer, Auriga. See **ōs-*.**]

Au•ri•gnac (ô′rēn-yăk′). A village of S France at the foot of the Pyrenees; site of caves containing prehistoric relics.

Au•rig•na•cian (ôr′ĭg-nā′shən, ôr′ēn-yā′-) *adj.* Of or relating to the Old World Upper Paleolithic culture between Mousterian and Solutrean, associated with early *Homo sapiens.* [After AURIGNAC.]

au•rochs (ou′rŏks′, ôr′ŏks′) *n., pl.* **aurochs. 1.** See **urus. 2.** See **wisent.** [Obsolete Ger., var. of Ger. *Auerochs* < MHGer. *ūrohse* < OHGer. *ūrohso*: *ūro*, aurochs + *ohso*, ox.]

au•ro•ra (ô-rôr′ə, ô-rōr′ə, ə-rôr′ə, ə-rōr′ə) *n.* **1.** Aurora borealis. **2.** Aurora australis. **3.** The dawn. [ME, dawn < Lat. *aurōra.* See **aus-*.**] — **au•ro′ral, au•ro′re•an** (-ē-ən) *adj.* — **au•ro′ral•ly** *adv.*

Au•ro•ra[1] (ô-rôr′ə, ô-rōr′ə, ə-rôr′ə, ə-rōr′ə) *n. Rom. Myth.* The goddess of the dawn. [Lat. *Aurōra.* See AURORA.]

Au•ro•ra[2] (ô-rôr′ə, ô-rōr′ə, ə-rôr′ə, ə-rōr′ə). **1.** A town of S Ontario, Canada, N of Toronto. Pop. 16,267. **2.** A city of N-central CO, a suburb of Denver. Pop. 222,103. **3.** A city of NE IL on the Fox R. W of Chicago. Pop. 99,581.

aurora aus•tra•lis (ô-strā′lĭs) *n.* A southern luminous phenomenon corresponding to the northern aurora borealis. [NLat. *aurōra austrālis*: Lat. *aurōra*, dawn + Lat. *austrālis*, southern.]

aurora bo•re•al•is (bôr′ē-ăl′ĭs, bōr′-) *n.* Luminous bands or streamers of light sometimes visible in northern night skies and thought to be caused by the ejection of charged particles into the magnetic field of the earth. [NLat. *aurōra boreālis*: Lat. *aurōra*, dawn + Lat. *boreālis*, northern.]

au•rous (ôr′əs) *adj.* Of or relating to gold, esp. with valence 1. [Lat. *aurum*, gold + -OUS.]

Au•rung•zeb or **Au•rung•zebe** (ôr′əng-zĕb′). See **Aurangzeb.**

AUS *abbr.* Army of the United States.

Aus. *abbr.* **1.a.** Australia. **b.** Australian. **2.a.** Austria. **b.** Austrian.

Ausch•witz (oush′vĭts′). See **Oświęcim.**

aus•cul•tate (ô′skəl-tāt′) *tr.v.* **-tat•ed, -tat•ing, -tates.** *Medic.* To examine by auscultation. [Back-formation < AUSCULTATION.] — **aus′cul•ta′tive, aus•cul′ta•to′ry** (ô-skŭl′tə-tôr′ē, -tōr′ē) *adj.*

aus•cul•ta•tion (ô′skəl-tā′shən) *n.* **1.** The act of listening. **2.** *Medic.* The act of listening for sounds made by internal organs to help diagnose certain disorders. [Lat. *auscultātiō*, *auscultātiōn-* < *auscultātus*, p.part. of *auscultāre*, to listen to. See **ous-*.**]

aus•form (ôs′fôrm′) *tr.v.* **-formed, -form•ing, -forms.** To subject (esp. steel) to deformation, quenching, and tempering to improve its wear properties. [AUS(TENITIC) + (DE)FORM.]

aus•land•er (ou′slĕn′dər, -slăn′-) *n.* A foreigner. [Ger. *Ausländer* < *Ausland*, outland : *aus*, out (< MHGer. *ūz* < OHGer.; see **ud-***) + *Land*, land (< MHGer. *lant* < OHGer.; see **lendh-***).]

aus•pex (ô′spĕks′) *n., pl.* **aus•pi•ces** (ô′spĭ-sēz′). An augur of ancient Rome, esp. one who interpreted omens derived from the observation of birds. [Lat. See AUSPICE.]

aus•pi•cate (ô′spĭ-kāt′) *tr.v.* **-cat•ed, -cat•ing, -cates.** To begin or inaugurate with a ceremony for good luck. [Lat. *auspicārī*, *auspicāt-* < *auspex*, *auspic-*, bird augur. See AUSPICE.]

aus•pice (ô′spĭs) *n., pl.* **aus•pi•ces** (ô′spĭ-sĭz, -sēz′). **1.** Protection or support; patronage. Often used in the plural. **2.** A sign indicative of future prospects; an omen. **3.** Observation of and divination from birds. [Lat. *auspicium*, bird divination, auspices < *auspex*, *auspic-*, bird augur. See **awi-*.**]

aus•pi•cious (ô-spĭsh′əs) *adj.* **1.** Attended by favorable circumstances; propitious. See Syns at **favorable. 2.** Successful; prosperous. — **aus•pi′cious•ly** *adv.* — **aus•pi′cious•ness** *n.*

Aus•sie (ô′sē, ô′zē) *n. Informal.* A native or inhabitant of Australia. [< AUS(TRALIAN).] — **Aus′sie** *adj.*

Aust. *abbr.* **1.a.** Australia. **b.** Australian. **2.a.** Austria. **b.** Austrian.

Aus•ten (ô′stən), **Jane.** 1775–1817. British writer whose novels include *Pride and Prejudice* (1813) and *Emma* (1816).

aus•ten•ite (ô′stə-nīt′) *n.* A nonmagnetic solid solution of ferric carbide or carbon in iron, used in making corrosion-resistant steel. [After Sir William Chandler Roberts-*Austen* (1843–1902), British metallurgist.] — **aus′ten•it′ic** (-ĭt′ĭk) *adj.*

aus•tere (ô-stîr′) *adj.* **-ter•er, -ter•est. 1.** Severe or stern in disposition or appearance; somber and grave. **2.** Strict or severe in discipline; ascetic. **3.** Having no adornment or ornamentation; bare. See Syns at **severe.** [ME < OFr. < Lat. *austērus* < Gk. *austēros.*] — **aus•tere′ly** *adv.* — **aus•tere′ness** *n.*

aus•ter•i•ty (ô-stĕr′ĭ-tē) *n., pl.* **-ties. 1.** The quality of being austere. **2.** Severe and rigid economy: *wartime austerity.* **3.** An austere habit or practice.

Aus•ter•litz (ô′stər-lĭts′, ous′tər-). A town of SE Czech Republic; site of Napoleon's decisive defeat of the Russian and Austrian armies (Dec. 2, 1805).

Aus•tin[1] (ô′stən). See Saint **Augustine**[2].

Aus•tin[2] (ô′stən, ŏs′tən). **1.** A city of SE MN near the IA border SW of Rochester. Pop. 21,907. **2.** The cap. of TX, in the S-central part; chosen as cap. in 1870. Pop. 465,622.

Austin, Alfred. 1835–1913. British writer who became poet laureate in 1896.

auk
Razor-billed auk
Alca torda

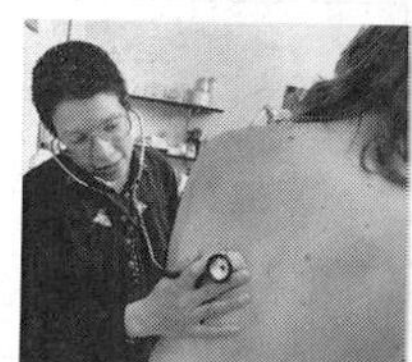

auscultation

ă pat	oi boy
ā pay	ou out
âr care	o͝o took
ä father	o͞o boot
ĕ pet	ŭ cut
ē be	ûr urge
ĭ pit	th thin
ī pie	*th* this
îr pier	hw which
ŏ pot	zh vision
ō toe	ə about, item
ô paw	

Stress marks:
′ (primary);
′ (secondary), as in
dictionary (dĭk′shə-nĕr′ē)

Austin, John. 1790–1859. British legal theorist who maintained that law is distinct from moral principles.

Austin, Stephen Fuller. 1793–1836. Amer. colonizer who helped Texas gain its independence from Mexico (1836).

Aus•tin•town (ô′stən-toun′). A community of NE OH, a suburb of Youngstown. Pop. 32,371.

Austl. *abbr.* Australia; Australian.

aus•tral¹ (ô′strəl) *adj.* Of, relating to, or coming from the south. [Lat. *austrālis* < *auster, austr-*, south.]

aus•tral² (ous-träl′) *n., pl.* **-tral•es** (-trä′lĕs). See table at **currency.** [Am.Sp. < Sp., from the south < Lat. *austrālis.* See AUSTRAL¹.]

Aus•tral•a•sia (ô′strə-lā′zhə, -shə). **1.** The islands of the S Pacific, including Australia, New Zealand, and New Guinea. **2.** Broadly, all of Oceania. — **Aus′tral•a′sian** *adj. & n.*

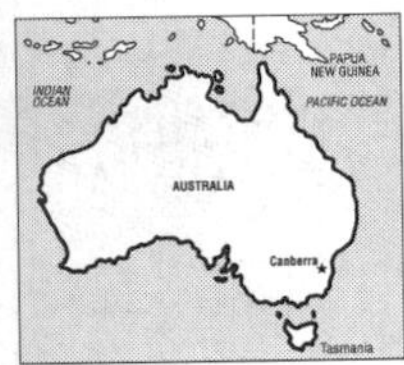

Australia

Aus•tra•lia (ô-strāl′yə). **1.** The world's smallest continent, SE of Asia between the Pacific and Indian oceans. **2.** A commonwealth comprising the continent of Australia, Tasmania, two external territories, and several dependencies; first formed as a federation in 1901. Cap. Canberra. Pop. 15,544,500.

Aus•tra•lian (ô-strāl′yən) *adj.* **1.** Of or relating to Australia or its peoples, languages, or cultures. **2.** *Ecol.* Of, relating to, or being the zoogeographic region that includes Australia and the islands adjacent to it. — *n.* **1.** A native or inhabitant of Australia. **2.** A member of any of the aboriginal peoples of Australia. **3.** Any of the aboriginal languages of Australia.

Australian Alps. A chain of mountain ranges of SE Australia in the Great Dividing Range, rising to 2,231.4 m (7,316 ft).

Australian ballot *n.* A printed ballot that bears the names of all candidates and the texts of propositions and is distributed to the voter at the polls and marked in secret.

Australian crawl *n. Sports.* A crawl stroke in swimming that is executed with a flutter kick to each arm stroke.

Australian terrier *n.* A small dog of a breed originally bred in Australia, having a coarse blackish coat with tan markings.

Aus•tra•loid (ô′strə-loid′) *adj. Anthro.* Of or relating to a purported human racial classification distinguished by dark skin and curly hair and including peoples indigenous to Australia and southeast Asia. No longer in scientific use. [AUSTRAL(IAN) + -OID.] — **Aus′tra•loid′** *n.*

aus•tra•lo•pith•e•cine (ô-strā′lō-pĭth′ĭ-sīn′, -sēn′) *n.* Any of several extinct humanlike primates of the genus *Australopithecus,* known chiefly from Pleistocene fossil remains found in southern and eastern Africa. [< NLat. *Australopithēcus*: Lat. *austrālis,* southern; see AUSTRAL¹ + *pithēcus,* ape (< Gk. *pithēkos*).] — **aus•tra′lo•pith′e•cine** *adj.*

Aus•tra•sia (ô-strā′zhə, -shə). The E portion of the kingdom of the Franks from the 6th to the 8th cent., including parts of E France, W Germany, and the Netherlands. — **Aus•tra′sian** *adj. & n.*

Austria

Aus•tri•a (ô′strē-ə). A landlocked country of central Europe; orig. a Roman and Carolingian territory and later a powerful empire ruled by the Hapsburgs. Cap. Vienna. Pop. 7,555,338. — **Aus′tri•an** *adj. & n.*

Aus•tri•a-Hun•ga•ry (ô′strē-ə-hŭng′gə-rē). A former dual monarchy (1867–1918) of central Europe consisting of Austria, Hungary, Bohemia, Slovenia, Croatia, and parts of Poland, Romania, Dalmatia, and Italy. — **Aus′tro-Hun•gar′i•an** (ô′strō-hŭng-gâr′ē-ən) *adj. & n.*

Austro–¹ *pref.* Southern: *Austro-Asiatic.* [< Lat. *auster, austr-,* south. See **aus-*.**]

Austro–² *pref.* Austria; Austrian: *Austro-Hungarian.*

Aus•tro-A•si•at•ic (ô′strō-ā′zhē-ăt′ĭk, -shē-, -zē-) *n.* A family of languages of southeast Asia once dominant in northeast India and Indochina, including Mon-Khmer and Munda. — **Aus′tro-A′si•at′ic** *adj.*

Aus•tro•ne•sia (ô′strō-nē′zhə, -shə). The islands of the Pacific Ocean, including Indonesia, Melanesia, Micronesia, and Polynesia.

Aus•tro•ne•sian (ô′strō-nē′zhən, -shən) *adj.* Of or relating to Austronesia or its peoples, languages, or cultures. — *n.* A family of languages that includes the Formosan, Indonesian, Malay, Melanesian, Micronesian, and Polynesian subfamilies.

aut– *pref.* Var. of **auto–.**

au•ta•coid (ô′tə-koid′) *n.* An organic substance from one part of an organism transported by blood, lymph, or sap to another part where it exerts a physiologic effect. [AUT(O)- + Gk. *akos,* cure + -OID.] — **au′ta•coid′al** (-koid′l) *adj.*

au•tarch (ô′tärk) *n.* An absolute ruler; a despot. [Gk. *autarkhos,* self-governing, autarch. See AUTARCHY¹.]

au•tar•chy¹ (ô′tär′kē) *n., pl.* **-chies. 1.** Absolute rule or power; autocracy. **2.** A country under such rule. [< Gk. *autarkhos,* self-governing, autarch : *aut-, auto-,* auto- + *arkhos,* ruler (< *arkhein,* to rule).] — **au•tar′chic, au•tar′chi•cal** *adj.*

au•tar•chy² (ô′tär′kē) *n.* Var. of **autarky.**

au•tar•ky or **au•tar•chy** (ô′tär′kē) *n., pl.* **-kies** or **-chies. 1.** A policy of national self-sufficiency and nonreliance on imports or economic aid. **2.** A self-sufficient region or country. [Gk. *autarkeia,* self-sufficiency < *autarkēs,* self-sufficient : *aut-, auto-,* auto- + *arkein,* to suffice.] — **au•tar′kic, au•tar′ki•cal** *adj.*

au•te•col•o•gy (ô′tĭ-kŏl′ə-jē) *n.* The branch of ecology that studies the biological relationship between an individual organism or species and its environment. — **au′te•co•log′i•cal** (-kə-lŏj′ĭ-kəl) *adj.*

au•teur (ō-tûr′, ō-tœr′) *n.* A filmmaker, usu. a director, who exercises creative control and has a strong personal style. [Fr. < OFr. *autor,* author. See AUTHOR.] — **au•teur′ist** *adj. & n.*

au•teur•ism (ō-tûr′ĭz′əm) *n.* Belief in the primary creative importance of the director in filmmaking.

auteur theory *n.* See **auteurism.**

auth. *abbr.* **1.** Authentic. **2.** Author. **3.** Authority. **4.** Authorized.

au•then•tic (ô-thĕn′tĭk) *adj.* **1.** Conforming to fact and therefore worthy of trust, reliance, or belief. **2.** Having a claimed and verifiable origin or authorship; not counterfeit or copied. **3.** *Mus.* **a.** Of or being a medieval mode having a range from its final tone to the octave above it. **b.** Of or being a cadence with the dominant chord immediately preceding the tonic chord. **4.** *Obsolete.* Authoritative. [ME *autentik* < OFr. *autentique* < LLat. *authenticus* < Gk. *authentikos* < *authentēs,* author.] — **au•then′ti•cal•ly** *adv.*

Syns: *authentic, bona fide, genuine, real, true, undoubted, unquestionable.* The central meaning shared by these adjectives is "not counterfeit or copied": *an authentic painting by Corot; a bona fide transfer of property; genuine crabmeat; a real diamond; true courage; undoubted evidence; an unquestionable antique.* **Ant:** *counterfeit.*

au•then•ti•cate (ô-thĕn′tĭ-kāt′) *tr.v.* **-cat•ed, -cat•ing, -cates.** To establish the authenticity of; prove genuine. — **au•then′ti•ca′tion** *n.* — **au•then′ti•ca′tor** *n.*

au•then•tic•i•ty (ô′thĕn-tĭs′ĭ-tē) *n.* The quality or condition of being authentic, trustworthy, or genuine.

au•thor (ô′thər) *n.* **1.a.** The original writer of a literary work. **b.** One who writes professionally. **2.** An originator or creator. **3. Author.** God. — *tr.v.* **-thored, -thor•ing, -thors.** To assume responsibility for the content of (a published or an unpublished text). [ME *auctour* < OFr. *autor* < Lat. *auctor,* creator < *auctus,* p.part. of *augēre,* to create. See **aug-*.**] — **au•thor′i•al** (ô-thôr′ē-əl, ô-thŏr′-) *adj.*

au•thor•i•tar•i•an (ə-thôr′ĭ-târ′ē-ən, ə-thŏr′-, ô-thôr′-, ô-thŏr′-) *adj.* **1.** Characterized by or favoring absolute obedience to authority, as against individual freedom. **2.** Of, relating to, or expecting unquestioning obedience. — **au•thor′i•tar′i•an** *n.* — **au•thor′i•tar′i•an•ism** *n.*

au•thor•i•ta•tive (ə-thôr′ĭ-tā′tĭv, ə-thŏr′-, ô-thôr′-, ô-thŏr′-) *adj.* **1.** Having or arising from authority; official. **2.** Known to be accurate or excellent; highly reliable. **3.** Wielding authority; commanding. — **au•thor′i•ta′tive•ly** *adv.* — **au•thor′i•ta′tive•ness** *n.*

au•thor•i•ty (ə-thôr′ĭ-tē, ə-thŏr′-, ô-thôr′-, ô-thŏr′-) *n., pl.* **-ties. 1.a.** The power to enforce laws, exact obedience, command, determine, or judge. **b.** One that is invested with this power, esp. a government or government officials. **2.** Power assigned to another; authorization. **3.** A public agency or corporation with administrative powers in a specified field. **4.a.** An accepted source of expert information or advice. **b.** A quotation or citation from such a source. **5.** Justification; grounds. **6.** A conclusive statement or decision that may be taken as a guide or precedent. **7.** Power to influence or persuade resulting from knowledge or experience. **8.** Confidence derived from experience or practice; firm self-assurance. [ME *auctorite* < OFr. *autorite* < Lat. *auctōritās, auctōritāt-* < *auctor,* creator. See AUTHOR.]

au•thor•i•za•tion (ô′thər-ĭ-zā′shən) *n.* **1.** The act of authorizing. **2.** Something that authorizes; sanction.

au•thor•ize (ô′thə-rīz′) *tr.v.* **-ized, -iz•ing, -iz•es. 1.** To grant authority or power to. **2.** To give permission for; sanction. **3.** To be sufficient grounds for; justify. [ME *auctorisen* < OFr. *autoriser* < Med.Lat. *auctōrizāre* < Lat. *auctor,* author. See AUTHOR.] — **au′thor•iz′er** *n.*

Au•thor•ized Version (ô′thə-rīzd′) *n.* See **King James Bible.**

au•thor•ship (ô′thər-shĭp′) *n.* **1.** The act, fact, or occupation of writing. **2.** Source or origin, as of a book or idea.

au•tism (ô′tĭz′əm) *n.* **1.** Abnormal introversion and egocentricity; acceptance of fantasy rather than reality. **2.** *Psychol.* Infantile autism. — **au′tist** *n.* — **au•tis′tic** (-tĭk) *adj. & n.* — **au•tis′ti•cal•ly** *adv.*

au•to (ô′tō) *n., pl.* **-tos.** An automobile. — *intr.v.* **-toed, -to•ing, -tos.** To go by or ride in a car. [Short for AUTOMOBILE.]

auto. *abbr.* **1.** Automatic. **2.** Automotive.

auto– or **aut–** *pref.* **1.** Self; same: *autogamy.* **2.** Automatic: *autopilot.* [Gk. < *autos,* self.]

au•to•an•ti•bod•y (ô′tō-ăn′tĭ-bŏd′ē) *n.* An antibody that attacks the cells and tissues of the organism in which it is formed.

au•to•bahn (ô′tə-bän′, ou′tō-) *n.* An expressway in Germany and German-speaking countries. [Ger. : *Auto,* automobile; see AUTO + *Bahn,* road < MHGer. *ban.* See **gʷhen-*.**]

au•to•bi•og•ra•phy (ô′tō-bī-ŏg′rə-fē, -bē-) *n., pl.* **-phies.** The biography of a person by that person. — **au′to•bi•og′ra•pher** *n.* — **au′to•bi′o•graph′ic** (-bī′ə-grăf′ĭk), **au′to•bi′o•graph′i•cal** *adj.* — **au′to•bi′o•graph′i•cal•ly** *adv.*

au•to•bus (ô′tō-bŭs′) *n., pl.* **-bus•es** or **-bus•ses.** A motor coach; a bus.

au•to•ca•tal•y•sis (ô′tō-kə-tăl′ĭ-sĭs) *n., pl.* **-ses** (-sēz′). Catalysis of a chemical reaction by one of the products of the reaction. **—au′to•cat′a•lyt′ic** (-kăt′l-ĭt′ĭk) *adj.* **—au′to•cat′a•lyt′i•cal•ly** *adv.*

au•toch•thon (ô-tŏk′thən) *n., pl.* **-thons** or **-tho•nes** (-thə-nēz′). **1.** One of the earliest known inhabitants of a place; an aborigine. **2.** *Ecol.* An indigenous plant or animal. [Gk. *autokhthōn*: *auto-*, auto- + *khthōn*, earth; see **dhghem-***.]

au•toch•tho•nous (ô-tŏk′thə-nəs) also **au•toch•tho•nal** (-thə-nəl) or **au•toch•thon•ic** (ô′tŏk-thŏn′ĭk) *adj.* **1.** Originating where found; indigenous. **2.** *Biol.* Originating or formed in the place where found. **—au•toch′thon•ism, au•toch′tho•ny** *n.* **—au•toch′tho•nous•ly** *adv.*

au•to•clave (ô′tō-klāv′) *n.* A strong, pressurized, steam-heated vessel, as for sterilization or cooking. [Fr. : Gk. *auto-*, auto- + Lat. *clāvis*, key.]

au•toc•ra•cy (ô-tŏk′rə-sē) *n., pl.* **-cies. 1.** Government by a single person having unlimited power; despotism. **2.** A country or state governed by a person with unlimited power.

au•to•crat (ô′tə-krăt′) *n.* **1.** A ruler having unlimited power; a despot. **2.** A person with unlimited power or authority: *a corporate autocrat.* [Fr. *autocrate* < Gk. *autokratēs*, ruling by oneself : *auto-*, auto- + *-kratēs*, -crat.] **—au′to•crat′ic, au′to•crat′i•cal** *adj.* **—au′to•crat′i•cal•ly** *adv.*

au•to-da-fé (ô′tō-də-fā′, ou′tō-) *n., pl* **au•tos-da-fé** (ô′tōz-, ou′tōz-). **1.** Public announcement of the sentences imposed by the Inquisition. **2.** The public execution of those sentences, esp. burning at the stake by secular authorities. [Port. *auto da fé*: *auto*, act + *da*, of the + *fé*, faith.]

au•to-de•struct (ô′tō-dĭ-strŭkt′) *intr.v.* **-struct•ed, -struct•ing, -structs.** To destroy itself or oneself; self-destruct. [AUTO– + (SELF-)DESTRUCT.]

au•to•di•dact (ô′tō-dī′dăkt′) *n.* A self-taught person. [< Gk. *autodidaktos*, self-taught : *auto-*, auto- + *didaktos*, taught; see DIDACTIC.] **—au′to•di•dac′tic** *adj.*

au•to•dyne (ô′tə-dīn′) *n.* A heterodyne radio device in which one tube serves simultaneously as oscillator and detector. [AUTO– + (HETERO)DYNE.] **—au′to•dyne′** *adj.*

au•toe•cious (ô-tē′shəs) *adj. Biol.* Having all stages of a life cycle occurring on the same host. [< AUTO– + Gk. *oikos*, house; see **weik-**[1]*.] **—au•toe′cism** (-sĭz′əm) *n.*

au•to•er•o•tism (ô′tō-ĕr′ə-tĭz′əm) or **au•to•e•rot•i•cism** (-ĭ-rŏt′ĭ-sĭz′əm) *n.* **1.** Self-satisfaction of sexual desire, as by masturbation. **2.** The arousal of sexual feeling without an external stimulus. **—au′to•e•rot′ic** (-ĭ-rŏt′ĭk) *adj.*

au•tog•a•my (ô-tŏg′ə-mē) *n.* **1.** *Bot.* Self-fertilization in plants. **2.** *Biol.* The union of nuclei within and arising from a single cell, as in certain protozoans and fungi. **—au′to•gam′ic** (ô′tō-găm′ĭk), **au•tog′a•mous** *adj.*

au•to•gen•e•sis (ô′tō-jĕn′ĭ-sĭs) also **au•tog•e•ny** (ô-tŏj′ə-nē) *n.* See **abiogenesis. —au′to•ge•ne′tic** (-jə-nĕt′ĭk) *adj.* **—au′to•ge•net′i•cal•ly** *adv.*

au•tog•e•nous (ô-tŏj′ə-nəs) also **au•to•gen•ic** (ô′tə-jĕn′ĭk) *adj.* **1.** Produced from within. **2.** *Medic.* Originating with the one to whom applied. **—au•tog′e•nous•ly** *adv.*

au•to•gi•ro also **au•to•gy•ro** (ô′tō-jī′rō) *n., pl.* **-ros.** An aircraft powered by a conventional propeller and supported in flight by a freewheeling horizontal rotor that provides lift. [A former trademark.]

au•to•graph (ô′tə-grăf′) *n.* **1.** A person's own signature or handwriting. **2.** A manuscript in the author's handwriting. *—tr.v.* **-graphed, -graph•ing, -graphs. 1.** To write one's name or signature on or in; sign. **2.** To write in one's own handwriting. *—adj.* Written in the writer's own handwriting. [LLat. *autographum* < neut. of Lat. *autographus*, written with one's own hand < Gk. *autographos*: *auto-*, auto- + *graphein*, to write; see -GRAPH.] **—au′to•graph′ic, au′to•graph′i•cal** *adj.* **—au′to•graph′i•cal•ly** *adv.*

au•tog•ra•phy (ô-tŏg′rə-fē) *n.* **1.** The writing of something in one's own handwriting. **2.** Autographs considered as a group.

Au•to•harp (ô′tō-härp′). A trademark used for a musical instrument similar to a zither.

au•to•hyp•no•sis (ô′tō-hĭp-nō′sĭs) *n.* **1.** The act or process of hypnotizing oneself. **2.** A self-induced hypnotic state. **—au′to•hyp•not′ic** (-nŏt′ĭk) *adj.*

au•to•im•mune (ô′tō-ĭ-myōōn′) *adj.* Of or relating to an immune response by the body against one of its own tissues or types of cells. **—au′to•im•mu′ni•ty** *n.* **—au′to•im′mu•ni•za′tion** (-ĭm′yə-nə-zā′shən) *n.*

au•to•in•fec•tion (ô′tō-ĭn-fĕk′shən) *n.* Infection, such as recurrent boils, caused by bacteria, viruses, or parasites that persist on or in the body.

au•to•in•oc•u•la•tion (ô′tō-ĭ-nŏk′yə-lā′shən) *n.* **1.** Inoculation with a vaccine made from microorganisms obtained from the recipient's body. **2.** An infection by a disease that has spread from a different part of the body. **—au′to•in•oc′u•la•ble** *adj.*

au•to•in•tox•i•ca•tion (ô′tō-ĭn-tŏk′sĭ-kā′shən) *n.* Self-poisoning caused by endogenous microorganisms, metabolic wastes, or other toxins produced within the body.

au•to•load•ing (ô′tō-lō′dĭng) *adj.* Semiautomatic.

au•tol•o•gous (ô-tŏl′ə-gəs) *adj.* Derived or transferred from the same individual's body. [AUTO– + *-logous*, as in HOMOLOGOUS.]

au•tol•y•sate (ô-tŏl′ĭ-sāt′, -zāt′) *n. Biochem.* An end product of autolysis.

au•tol•y•sin (ô-tŏl′ĭ-sĭn, ô′tə-lī′sĭn) *n. Biochem.* A substance, such as an enzyme, that is capable of destroying the cells or tissues of an organism within which it is produced.

au•tol•y•sis (ô-tŏl′ĭ-sĭs) *n. Biochem.* The destruction of tissues or cells of an organism by the action of substances produced within the organism. **—au′to•lyt′ic** (ô′tə-lĭt′ĭk) *adj.*

au•to•mak•er (ô′tō-mā′kər) *n.* A manufacturer of automotive vehicles; a carmaker.

au•tom•a•ta (ô-tŏm′ə-tə) *n.* Pl. of **automaton.**

au•to•mate (ô′tə-māt′) *v.* **-mat•ed, -mat•ing, -mates.** *—tr.* **1.** To convert to automatic operation: *automate a factory.* **2.** To control or operate by automation. *—intr.* To convert to or make use of automation. [Back-formation < AUTOMATION.]

au•to•mat•ed teller machine (ô′tə-mā′tĭd) *n.* An unattended computer terminal that provides banking services.

au•to•mat•ic (ô′tə-măt′ĭk) *adj.* **1.a.** Acting or operating in a manner essentially independent of external influence or control: *an automatic switch.* **b.** Self-regulating. **2.a.** Acting or done without volition or conscious control; involuntary. **b.** Acting or done as if by machine; mechanical: *an automatic reply to a question.* **3.a.** Capable of firing continuously until ammunition is exhausted or the trigger is released. **b.** Semiautomatic: *an automatic pistol.* *—n.* **1.** An automatic machine or device. **2.a.** An automatic firearm. **b.** A semiautomatic firearm. **3.** A transmission or a motor vehicle with an automatic gear-shifting mechanism. [< Gk. *automatos*: *auto-*, auto- + *-matos*, willing; see **men-**[1]*.] **—au′to•mat′i•cal•ly** *adv.* **—au′to•ma•tic′i•ty** (-mə-tĭs′ĭ-tē) *n.*

automatic pilot *n.* A navigation mechanism, as on an aircraft, that automatically maintains a preset course.

au•to•ma•tion (ô′tə-mā′shən) *n.* **1.** The automatic operation or control of equipment, a process, or a system. **2.** The techniques and equipment used to achieve automatic operation or control. **3.** The condition of being automatically controlled or operated. [< AUTOMATIC.]

au•tom•a•tism (ô-tŏm′ə-tĭz′əm) *n.* **1.a.** The state or quality of being automatic. **b.** Automatic mechanical action. **2.** *Philos.* The theory that the body is a machine whose functions are accompanied but not controlled by consciousness. **3.** *Physiol.* **a.** The involuntary functioning of a body structure that is not under conscious control, such as the beating of the heart. **b.** The reflexive action of a body part. **4.** *Psychol.* **a.** Suspension of consciousness in order to express subconscious ideas and feelings. **b.** Mechanical, seemingly aimless behavior characteristic of various mental disorders. [< Lat. *automaton*, automaton. See AUTOMATON.] **—au•tom′a•tist** *n.*

au•tom•a•ti•za•tion (ô-tŏm′ə-tĭ-zā′shən) *n.* Automation.

au•tom•a•tize (ô-tŏm′ə-tīz′) *tr.v.* **-tized, -tiz•ing, -tiz•es. 1.** To make automatic. **2.** To turn into an automaton. [< AUTOMATIC.]

au•tom•a•ton (ô-tŏm′ə-tən, -tŏn′) *n., pl.* **-tons** or **-ta** (-tə). **1.** A self-operating machine or mechanism, esp. a robot. **2.** One that behaves or responds in a mechanical way. [Lat., self-operating machine < Gk. < neut. of *automatos*, self-acting. See AUTOMATIC.] **—au•tom′a•tous** *adj.*

au•to•mo•bile (ô′tə-mō-bēl′, -mō′bēl′) *n.* A self-propelled passenger vehicle that usu. has four wheels and an internal-combustion engine, used for land transport. [Fr. : Gk. *auto-*, auto- + Fr. *mobile*, mobile (< OFr.; see MOBILE).] **—au′to•mo•bile′** *adj.* **—au′to•mo•bil′ist** *n.*

au•to•mo•tive (ô′tə-mō′tĭv) *adj.* **1.** Moving by itself; self-propelling or self-propelled. **2.** Of or relating to self-propelled vehicles.

au•to•nom•ic (ô′tə-nŏm′ĭk) *adj.* **1.** *Physiol.* **a.** Of, relating to, or controlled by the autonomic nervous system. **b.** Occurring involuntarily; automatic. **2.** Resulting from internal stimuli; spontaneous. **—au′to•nom′i•cal•ly** *adv.*

autonomic nervous system *n.* The part of the vertebrate nervous system that regulates involuntary action, as of the intestines, heart, and glands.

au•ton•o•mous (ô-tŏn′ə-məs) *adj.* **1.** Not controlled by others or by outside forces; independent. **2.** Independent in mind or judgment; self-directed. **3.a.** Independent of the laws of another state or government; self-governing. **b.** Of or relating to a self-governing entity. **c.** Self-governing with respect to local or internal affairs: *an autonomous region of a country.* **4.** Autonomic. [< Gk. *autonomos*: *auto-*, auto- + *nomos*, law; see **nem-***.] **—au•ton′o•mous•ly** *adv.*

au•ton•o•my (ô-tŏn′ə-mē) *n., pl.* **-mies. 1.** The condition or quality of being autonomous. **2.a.** Self-government or the right of self-government; self-determination. **b.** Self-government with respect to local or internal affairs. **3.** A self-governing state, community, or group. [Gk. *autonomia* < *autonomos*, self-ruling. See AUTONOMOUS.] **—au•ton′o•mist** *n.*

au•to•pen (ô′tō-pĕn′) *n.* A mechanical device used for writing imitations of a personal signature.

ă pat	oi boy
ā pay	ou out
âr care	ŏŏ took
ä father	ōō boot
ĕ pet	ŭ cut
ē be	ûr urge
ĭ pit	th thin
ī pie	*th* this
îr pier	hw which
ŏ pot	zh vision
ō toe	ə about, item
ô paw	

Stress marks:
′ (primary);
′ (secondary), as in
dictionary (dĭk′shə-nĕr′ē)

au•toph•a•gy (ô-tŏf′ə-jē) *n.* The process of self-digestion of a cell through the action of its own enzymes.

au•to•pil•er (ô′tō-pī′lər) *n.* *Comp. Sci.* A specific automatic compiler. [AUTO– + (COM)PILER.]

au•to•pi•lot (ô′tō-pī′lət) *n.* Automatic pilot.

au•to•plas•ty (ô′tō-plăs′tē) *n.* Surgical repair or reconstruction of a body part using tissue taken from another part of the body. **—au′to•plas′tic** *adj.* **—au′to•plas′ti•cal•ly** *adv.*

au•to•pol•y•ploid (ô′tō-pŏl′ə-ploid′) *adj.* Having more than two sets of chromosomes all derived from the same species. —*n.* An autopolyploid organism. **—au′to•pol′y•ploid′y** *n.*

au•top•sy (ô′tŏp′sē, ô′təp-) *n., pl.* **-sies. 1.** Examination of a cadaver to determine or confirm the cause of death. **2.** A critical assessment or examination after the fact. [Gk. *autopsia*, a seeing for oneself : *auto-*, auto- + *opsis*, sight; see **okʷ-***.] **—au•top′sic, au•top′si•cal** *adj.* **—au′top′sist** *n.*

au•to•ra•di•o•gram (ô′tō-rā′dē-ō-grăm′) *n.* See **autoradiograph.**

au•to•ra•di•o•graph (ô′tō-rā′dē-ō-grăf′) *n.* An image recorded on a photographic film or plate produced by the radiation emitted from a specimen containing a radioactively labeled isotope. **—au′to•ra′di•o•graph′ic** *adj.* **—au′to•ra′di•og′ra•phy** (-ŏg′rə-fē) *n.*

au•to•route (ô′tō-ro͞ot′) *n.* An expressway in France and French-speaking countries. [Fr. : *auto*, automobile; see AUTO + *route*, road (< OFr.; see ROUTE).]

au•to•some (ô′tə-sōm′) *n.* A chromosome that is not a sex chromosome. **—au′to•so′mal** (-sō′məl) *adj.* **—au′to•so′mal•ly** *adv.*

au•to•stra•da (ô′tō-strä′də, ou′tō-) *n.* An expressway in Italy. [Ital. : *auto*, automobile; see AUTO + *strada*, street (< LLat. *strāta*, paved road; see STREET).]

au•to•sug•ges•tion (ô′tō-səg-jĕs′chən) *n.* *Psychol.* The process by which a person induces self-acceptance of an opinion, belief, or plan of action. **—au′to•sug•gest′** *v.* **—au′to•sug•gest′i•bil′i•ty** (-ə-bĭl′ĭ-tē) *n.* **—au′to•sug•gest′i•ble** *adj.* **—au′to•sug•ges′tive** (-tĭv) *adj.*

au•tot•o•mize (ô-tŏt′ə-mīz′) *tr. & intr.v.* **-mized, -miz•ing, -miz•es.** To cause the autotomy of or undergo autotomy.

au•tot•o•my (ô-tŏt′ə-mē) *n.* The spontaneous casting off of a body part, such as the tail of certain lizards, esp. when the organism is injured or under attack. **—au′to•tom′ic** (ô′tə-tŏm′ĭk) *adj.*

au•to•tox•e•mi•a also **au•to•tox•ae•mi•a** (ô′tō-tŏk-sē′mē-ə) *n.* See **autointoxication.**

au•to•tox•in (ô′tō-tŏk′sĭn) *n.* A poison that acts on the organism in which it is generated. **—au′to•tox′ic** *adj.*

au•to•trans•form•er (ô′tō-trăns-fôr′mər) *n.* An electrical transformer in which the primary and secondary coils have some or all windings in common.

au•to•troph (ô′tə-trŏf′, -trōf′) *n.* An organism capable of synthesizing its own food from inorganic substances, using light or chemical energy. **—au′to•troph′ic** (-trŏf′ĭk, -trō′fĭk) *adj.* **—au′to•troph′i•cal•ly** *adv.* **—au•tot′ro•phy** (ô-tŏt′rə-fē) *n.*

au•to•work•er (ô′tō-wûr′kər) *n.* A worker in the automobile industry.

au•tumn (ô′təm) *n.* **1.** The season of the year between summer and winter, lasting from the autumnal equinox to the winter solstice and from September to December in the Northern Hemisphere; fall. **2.** A period of maturity verging on decline. —*adj.* **1.** Of, having to do with, occurring in, or appropriate to the season of autumn. **2.** Grown during the season of autumn. [ME *autumpne* < OFr. *autompne* < Lat. *autumnus.*] **—au•tum′nal** (-tŭm′nəl) *adj.* **—au•tum′nal•ly** *adv.*

autumnal equinox *n.* **1.** The point at which the ecliptic intersects the celestial equator, the sun having a southerly motion. **2.** The moment at which the sun passes through the autumnal equinox, about September 23, marking the beginning of autumn.

autumn crocus *n.* A corm-producing European and North African plant *(Colchicum autumnale)* with flowers in the fall.

au•tun•ite (ō-tŭn′īt′, ô′tə-nīt) *n.* A yellowish fluorescent minor ore of uranium with the composition $Ca(UO_2)_2(PO_4)_2 \cdot 10-12H_2O$. [After *Autun*, a city of E-central France.]

Au•vergne (ō-vûrn′, ō-vĕrn′). A historical region and former province of central France traversed by the **Auvergne Mountains,** a chain of extinct volcanoes.

aux. *abbr.* **1.** Auxiliary. **2.** *Gram.* Auxiliary verb.

aux•e•sis (ôg-zē′sĭs, ôk-sē′-) *n.* Growth resulting from increase in cell size without cell division. [Gk. *auxēsis*, growth < *auxanein, auxē-*, to grow. See **aug-***.] **—aux•et′ic** (ôg-zĕt′ĭk) *adj.* **—aux•et′i•cal•ly** *adv.*

aux•il•ia•ry (ôg-zĭl′yə-rē, -zĭl′ə-rē) *adj.* **1.** Giving assistance or support; helping. **2.** Acting as a subsidiary; supplementary. **3.** Held in or used as a reserve. **4.** *Naut.* Equipped with a motor as well as sails. **5.** *Gram.* Of, relating to, or being an auxiliary verb. —*n., pl.* **-ries. 1.** An individual or a group that assists or functions in a supporting capacity. **2.** A member of a foreign body of troops serving a country in war. **3.** *Gram.* An auxiliary verb. **4.** *Naut.* **a.** A sailing vessel equipped with a motor. **b.** A vessel that is designed for and used in instances and services other than combat. [ME < Lat. *auxiliārius* < *auxilium*, help. See **aug-***.]

auxiliary verb *n.* *Gram.* A verb, such as *have, can,* or *will,* that accompanies the main verb in a clause and helps make distinctions in mood, voice, aspect, and tense.

aux•in (ôk′sĭn) *n.* Any of several plant hormones that regulate various functions, including cell elongation. [< Gk. *auxein*, to grow. See **aug-***.] **—aux•in′ic** *adj.* **—aux•in′i•cal•ly** *adv.*

aux•o•troph (ôk′sə-trŏf, -trōf′) *n.* An auxotrophic organism. [Back-formation < AUXOTROPHIC.]

aux•o•troph•ic (ôk′sə-trŏf′ĭk, -trō′fĭk) *adj.* Requiring one or more specific substances for growth and metabolism that can no longer be synthesized because of mutational changes. [Gk. *auxein*, to increase; see AUXIN + –TROPHIC.]

aux. v. *abbr.* *Gram.* Auxiliary verb.

Av (äv, ôv) also **Ab** (äb, äv, ôv) *n.* A month in the Jewish calendar. [Heb. *'āb* < Canaanite *'ab.*]

AV or **A.V.** *abbr.* **1.** Audio-visual. **2.** *Bible.* Authorized Version.

av. *abbr.* **1.** Also **Av.** Avenue. **2.** Average. **3.** Avoirdupois.

a.v. or **a/v** *abbr.* Ad valorem.

a•vail (ə-vāl′) *v.* **a•vailed, a•vail•ing, a•vails.** —*tr.* To be of use or advantage to; help. —*intr.* To be of use, value, or advantage; serve. —*n.* Use, benefit, or advantage: *labored to no avail.* —***idiom.*** **avail (oneself) of.** To make use of. [ME *availen*: *a-*, intensive pref. (< Lat. *ad-*; see AD–) + OFr. *valoir, vail-*, to be worth (< Lat. *valēre*, to be strong; see **wal-***).] **—a•vail′ing•ly** *adv.*

a•vail•a•ble (ə-vā′lə-bəl) *adj.* **1.** Present and ready for use; at hand; accessible. **2.** Capable of being gotten; obtainable. **3.** Qualified and willing to serve. **—a•vail′a•bil′i•ty, a•vail′a•ble•ness** *n.* **—a•vail′a•bly** *adv.*

av•a•lanche (ăv′ə-lănch′) *n.* **1.** A fall or slide of a large mass, as of snow or rock, down a mountainside. **2.** A massive or overwhelming amount; a flood. —*v.* **-lanched, -lanch•ing, -lanch•es.** —*intr.* To fall or slide in a massive or overwhelming amount. —*tr.* To overwhelm; inundate. [Fr.; akin to Prov. *lavanca*, ravine; perh. akin to Lat. *lābī*, to slip.]

avalanche lily *n.* A western North American corm-producing plant *(Erythronium grandiflorum)* in the lily family. [So called because it grows near the snow line and blooms when the snow begins to melt.]

Av•a•lon (ăv′ə-lŏn′) *n.* In Arthurian legend, an island paradise in the western seas to which King Arthur went at his death.

Avalon Peninsula. A large, irregularly shaped peninsula of SE Newfoundland, Canada.

a•vant-garde (ä′vänt-gärd′, ăv′änt-) *n.* A group active in the invention and application of new techniques in a given field, esp. in the arts. —*adj.* Of, relating to, or being part of the avant-garde. [Fr. < OFr., vanguard. See VANGUARD.] **—a′vant-gard′ism** *n.* **—a′vant-gard′ist** *n.*

av•a•rice (ăv′ə-rĭs) *n.* Immoderate desire for wealth; cupidity. [ME < OFr. < Lat. *avāritia* < *avārus*, greedy < *avēre*, to desire.]

av•a•ri•cious (ăv′ə-rĭsh′əs) *adj.* Immoderately desirous of wealth or gain; greedy. **—av′a•ri′cious•ly** *adv.* **—av′a•ri′cious•ness** *n.*

a•vas•cu•lar (ā-văs′kyə-lər) *adj.* Not associated with or supplied by blood vessels. **—a•vas′cu•lar′i•ty** (-lăr′ĭ-tē) *n.*

a•vast (ə-văst′) *interj.* *Naut.* Used as a command to stop or desist. [< MDu. *hou vast*, hold fast : *hou, houd*, imper. of *houden*, to hold + *vast*, fast; see **past-***.]

av•a•tar (ăv′ə-tär′) *n.* **1.** The descent to earth of a Hindu deity, esp. Vishnu, in human or animal form. **2.** An embodiment, as of a quality or concept; an archetype. **3.** A temporary manifestation or aspect of a continuing entity. [Skt. *avatāraḥ*: *ava*, down + *tarati*, he crosses; see **terə-²***.]

a•vaunt (ə-vônt′, ə-vänt′) *adv.* Hence; away. [ME, forward < OFr. *avant* < Lat. *abante*: *ab-*, from; see AB–¹ + *ante*, before; see ANTE–.]

AVC *abbr.* American Veterans Committee.

avdp. *abbr.* Avoirdupois.

a•ve (ä′vā) *n.* **1.** An expression of greeting or farewell. **2. Ave.** *Rom. Cath. Ch.* Hail Mary. [ME < Lat.]

ave. or **Ave.** or **AVE** *abbr.* Avenue.

A•vel•la•ne•da (ä-vĕl′yä-nĕ′dä, ä-vĕ′yä-, ä-vĕ′zhä-nĕ′*th*ä). A city of E Argentina near Buenos Aires. Pop. 330,654.

A•ve Ma•ri•a (ä′vā mə-rē′ə) *n.* *Rom. Cath. Ch.* Hail Mary. [ME < Med.Lat.]

a•venge (ə-vĕnj′) *tr.v.* **a•venged, a•veng•ing, a•veng•es. 1.** To inflict a punishment or penalty in return for; revenge: *avenge a murder.* **2.** To take vengeance on behalf of. [ME *avengen* < OFr. *avengier*: *a-*, to (< Lat. *ad-*; see AD–) + *vengier*, to vindicate (< Lat. *vindicāre*, to claim; see VINDICATE).] **—a•veng′er** *n.* **—a•veng′ing•ly** *adv.*

av•ens (ăv′ənz) *n., pl.* **avens. 1.** Any of various perennial herbs of the genus *Geum* in the rose family. **2.** The mountain avens. [ME *avence* < OFr. < Med.Lat. *avencia.*]

Av•en•tine (ăv′ən-tīn′, -tēn′). One of the seven hills of ancient Rome; settled by plebes in 456 B.C. **—Av′en•tine′** *adj.*

a•ven•tu•rine (ə-vĕn′chə-rēn′, -rĭn) also **a•ven•tu•rin** (-rĭn) *n.* **1.** An opaque or semitranslucent brown glass flecked with small metallic particles, often of copper or chromic oxide. **2.** Any of several varieties of quartz or feldspar flecked with particles of mica, hematite, or other materials. [Fr. < *aventure*, accident. See ADVENTURE.] — **a•ven′tu•rine′** *adj.*

av•e•nue (ăv′ə-no͞o′, -nyo͞o′) *n.* **1.** A wide street or thoroughfare. **2.a.** A broad roadway lined with trees. **b.** *Chiefly British.* The drive leading from the main road up to a country house. **3.** A means of access or approach. [Fr. < OFr., arrival < fem. p.part. of *avenir*, to approach < Lat. *advenīre*, to come to. See ADVENT.]

Av•en•zo•ar (ăv′ən-zō′ər). 1090?–1162. Spanish-Arab physician and writer.

a•ver (ə-vûr′) *tr.v.* **a•verred, a•verr•ing, a•vers. 1.** To affirm positively; declare. **2.** *Law.* **a.** To assert formally as a fact. **b.** To justify or prove. [ME *averren* < OFr. *averer* < VLat. **adverāre*: Lat. *ad-*, ad- + Lat. *vērus*, true; see **wēro-***.] — **a•ver′ment** *n.* — **a•ver′ra•ble** *adj.*

av•er•age (ăv′ər-ĭj, ăv′rĭj) *n.* **1.** *Math.* **a.** A number that typifies a set of numbers of which it is a function. **b.** See **arithmetic mean. 2.a.** An intermediate level or degree. **b.** The usual or ordinary kind or quality. **3.** *Sports.* The ratio of successful performances divided by total opportunities for successful performance: *a batting average of .274.* **4.** *Law.* **a.** The loss of a ship or cargo, caused by damage at sea. **b.** The incurrence of such damage or loss. **c.** The equitable distribution of such a loss. **d.** A charge incurred through such a loss. **5.** *Naut.* Small expenses or charges that are usu. paid by the master of a ship. — *adj.* **1.** *Math.* Of, relating to, or being an average. **2.** Intermediate between extremes, as on a scale. **3.** Usual or ordinary in kind or character. **4.** Assessed according to the law of averages. — *v.* **-aged, -ag•ing, -ag•es.** — *tr.* **1.** *Math.* To calculate the average of. **2.** To do or have an average of: *averaged an hour a day.* **3.** To distribute proportionately. — *intr.* **1.** To be or amount to an average: *Costs averaged out to 5 dollars per day.* **2.** To buy or sell more goods or shares to obtain more than an average price. [< ME *averay*, charge above the cost of freight < OFr. *avarie* < OItal. *avaria*, duty < Ar. *'awārīyah*, damaged goods < *'awar*, blemish.] — **av′er•age•ly** *adv.* — **av′er•age•ness** *n.*

Syns: *average, medium, mediocre, fair, middling, indifferent, tolerable.* These adjectives indicate a middle position on a scale of evaluation. *Average* and *medium* apply to what is midway between extremes and usually imply both sufficiency and lack of distinction: *a novel of average merit; an orange of medium size. Mediocre* stresses the undistinguished aspect of what is average: *"The caliber of the students . . . has gone from mediocre to above average"* (Judy Pasternak). What is *fair* is passable but substantially below excellent: *in fair health. Middling* refers to a ranking between average and mediocre: *gave a middling performance. Indifferent* suggests neutrality: *"One and the same thing can at the same time be good, bad, and indifferent"* (Spinoza). Something that is *tolerable* is merely acceptable: *prepared a tolerable dinner.*

A•ver•no (ä-vĕr′nō). Ancient name **A•ver•nus** (ə-vûr′nəs). A small crater lake of S Italy near the Tyrrhenian Sea W of Naples; regarded by the ancient Romans as the entrance to the underworld.

A•ver•ro•ës or **A•ver•rho•ës** (ə-vĕr′ō-ēz′, ăv′ə-rō′ēz). 1126–98. Spanish-Arab physician and philosopher best known for his commentaries on Aristotle.

a•verse (ə-vûrs′) *adj.* Having a feeling of opposition, distaste, or aversion; strongly disinclined. [Lat. *āversus*, p.part. of *āvertere*, to turn away. See AVERT.] — **a•verse′ly** *adv.* — **a•verse′ness** *n.*

a•ver•sion (ə-vûr′zhən, -shən) *n.* **1.** A fixed, intense dislike; repugnance. **2.** One that is intensely disliked and avoided. **3.** A feeling of extreme repugnance accompanied by avoidance or rejection. **4.** *Obsolete.* The act of turning away or averting.

aversion therapy *n.* A type of behavior therapy designed to modify antisocial habits or addictions by creating a strong association with a disagreeable or painful stimulus.

a•ver•sive (ə-vûr′sĭv, -zĭv) *adj.* Causing avoidance of an unpleasant or punishing stimulus, as in techniques of behavior modification. — **a•ver′sive•ly** *adv.* — **a•ver′sive•ness** *n.*

a•vert (ə-vûrt′) *tr.v.* **a•vert•ed, a•vert•ing, a•verts. 1.** To turn away: *avert one's eyes.* **2.** To ward off (something about to happen); prevent. [ME *averten* < OFr. *avertir* < Lat. *āvertere*: *ā-*,*ab-*, away from; see AB-[1] + *vertere*, to turn; see **wer-[2]***.] — **a•vert′i•ble, a•vert′a•ble** *adj.*

A•ves•ta (ə-vĕs′tə) *n.* A body of ancient Persian writings that is a sacred text of Zoroastrianism. [MPers. *apastāk*, the basic (text), and *apastāk*, the (hymns of) praise.]

A•ves•tan (ə-vĕs′tən) *n.* The eastern dialect of Old Iranian, in which the Avesta is written. — *adj.* Of or relating to the Avesta or Avestan.

avg. *abbr.* Average.

a•vi•an (ā′vē-ən) *adj.* Of, relating to, or characteristic of birds. [< Lat. *avis*, bird. See **awi-***.]

a•vi•ar•y (ā′vē-ĕr′ē) *n.*, *pl.* **-ies.** A large enclosure for confining birds. [Lat. *aviārium* < *avis*, bird. See **awi-***.] — **a′vi•a•rist** (-ə-rĭst, -ĕr′ĭst) *n.*

a•vi•ate (ā′vē-āt′, ăv′ē-) *intr.v.* **-at•ed, -at•ing, -ates.** To operate an aircraft; fly. [Back-formation < AVIATION.]

a•vi•a•tion (ā′vē-ā′shən, ăv′ē-) *n.* **1.** The operation of aircraft. **2.** The design, development, and production of aircraft. **3.** Military aircraft. [Fr. < Lat. *avis*, bird. See **awi-***.]

aviation medicine *n.* See **aeromedicine.**

a•vi•a•tor (ā′vē-ā′tər, ăv′ē-) *n.* One who operates an aircraft; a pilot. [Fr. *aviateur* < *aviation*, aviation. See AVIATION.]

aviator glasses *pl.n.* Eyeglasses having a lightweight metal frame and oval lenses that narrow toward the bridge of the nose.

a•vi•a•trix (ā′vē-ā′trĭks, ăv′ē-) *n.* A woman who operates an aircraft; a woman pilot.

Av•i•cen•na (ăv′ĭ-sĕn′ə). 980–1037. Persian physician and philosopher noted for his *Canon of Medicine.*

a•vi•cul•ture (ā′vĭ-kŭl′chər, ăv′ĭ-) *n.* The raising, keeping, and care of birds. [Lat. *avis*, bird; see **awi-*** + CULTURE.] — **a′vi•cul′tur•ist** *n.*

av•id (ăv′ĭd) *adj.* **1.** Having an ardent desire or craving; greedy. **2.** Marked by keen interest and enthusiasm. [Lat. *avidus* < *avēre*, to desire.] — **av′id•ly** *adv.*

av•i•din (ăv′ĭ-dĭn) *n.* A protein found in uncooked egg white that binds to and inactivates biotin, sometimes causing a deficiency. [AVID + (BIOT)IN, from its affinity for biotin.]

a•vid•i•ty (ə-vĭd′ĭ-tē) *n.* **1.** Ardent desire or craving; eagerness. **2.** Keen interest or enthusiasm: *followed the tournament with avidity.* **3.** *Chem.* **a.** The dissociation-dependent strength of an acid or base. **b.** Degree of affinity.

a•vi•fau•na (ā′və-fô′nə, ăv′ə-) *n.* The birds of a specific region or period. [Lat. *avis*, bird; see **awi-*** + FAUNA.] — **a′vi•fau′nal** *adj.*

A•vi•gnon (ä-vē-nyôN′). A city of SE France on the Rhone R.; seat of the papacy from 1309 to 1378. Pop. 89,132.

Á•vi•la (ä′və-lə, ä′vē-lä). A town of central Spain WNW of Madrid. Pop. 42,165.

Á•vi•la Ca•ma•cho (ä′vē-lä′ kə-mä′chō), **Manuel.** 1897–1955. Mexican general and president (1940–46).

A•vi•lés (ä′-və-lās′, ä′vē-lĕs′). A town of NW Spain on an inlet of the Bay of Biscay. Pop. 89,992.

a•vi•on•ics (ā′vē-ŏn′ĭks, ăv′ē-) *n.* **1.** *(used with a sing. v.)* The science and technology of the development and use of electronic devices in aeronautics and astronautics. **2.** *(used with a pl. v.)* The electronic systems, equipment, and other devices so developed. [AVI(ATION) + (ELECTR)ONICS.] — **a′vi•on′ic** *adj.*

a•vir•u•lent (ā-vîr′yə-lənt, ā-vîr′ə-) *adj.* Not virulent. — **a•vir′u•lence** *n.*

a•vi•ta•min•o•sis (ā-vī′tə-mĭ-nō′sĭs) *n.* A disease, such as scurvy, beriberi, or pellagra, caused by deficiency of one or more essential vitamins. — **a•vi′ta•min•ot′ic** (-nŏt′ĭk) *adj.*

avn. *abbr.* Aviation.

AV node (ā′vē′) *n.* See **atrioventricular node.** [A(TRIO)V(ENTRICULAR) NODE.]

a•vo (ä′vo͞o) *n.*, *pl.* **a•vos.** See table at **currency.** [Port., shortened < *oitavo*, eighth < Lat. *octāvus*. See OCTAVE.]

av•o•ca•do (ăv′ə-kä′dō, ä′və-) *n.*, *pl.* **-dos. 1.** A tropical American tree *(Persea americana)* having oval or pear-shaped fruit with leathery skin, yellowish-green flesh, and a large seed. **2.** The edible fruit of this tree. **3.** *Color.* A dull green. [Am.Sp., alteration (influenced by Sp. *avocado*, earlier form of *abogado*, lawyer) of Nahuatl *ahuacatl*.]

av•o•ca•tion (ăv′ō-kā′shən) *n.* **1.** An activity taken up in addition to one's regular work or profession, usu. for enjoyment; a hobby. **2.** One's regular work or profession. **3.** *Archaic.* A distraction or diversion. [Lat. *āvocātiō*, *āvocātiōn-*, diversion < *āvocātus*, p.part. of *āvocāre*, to call away : *ā-*, *ab-*, away; see AB-[1] + *vocāre*, to call; see **wekʷ-***.] — **av′o•ca′tion•al** *adj.* — **av′o•ca′tion•al•ly** *adv.*

av•o•cet (ăv′ə-sĕt′) *n.* Any of several long-legged shore birds of the genus *Recurvirostra*, characterized by a long, slender, upturned beak. [Fr. *avocette* < Ital. *avocetta*.]

A•vo•ga•dro (ä′və-gä′drō, ä′vō-), **Amedeo.** 1776–1856. Italian chemist and physicist.

A•vo•ga•dro's law (ä′və-gä′drōz, ä′vō-) *n.* The principle that equal volumes of all gases under identical conditions of pressure and temperature contain the same number of molecules.

Avogadro's number also **Avogadro number** *n.* *Symbol* **N** The number of molecules in a mole of a substance, approx. 6.0225×10^{23}.

a•void (ə-void′) *tr.v.* **a•void•ed, a•void•ing, a•voids. 1.** To stay clear of; shun. **2.** To keep from happening: *avoid illness.* **3.** *Law.* To annul or make void; invalidate. **4.** *Obsolete.* To void or expel. [ME *avoiden* < AN *avoider*, to empty out, var. of OFr. *esvuidier*: *es-*, out (< Lat. *ex-*; see EX-) + *vuidier*, to empty (< *voide*, empty; see VOID).] — **a•void′a•ble** *adj.* — **a•void′a•bly** *adv.* — **a•void′ance** (ə-void′ns) *n.* — **a•void′er** *n.*

av•oir•du•pois (ăv′ər-də-poiz′) *n.* **1.** Avoirdupois weight. **2.** *Informal.* Weight or heaviness, esp. of a person. [ME *avoir de pois*, commodities sold by weight, alteration of OFr. *aveir de peis*, goods of weight : *aveir*, *avoir*, to have (< Lat. *habēre*; see ABLE) + *de*, of (< Lat. *dē-*, from; see DE-) + *peis*, *pois*,

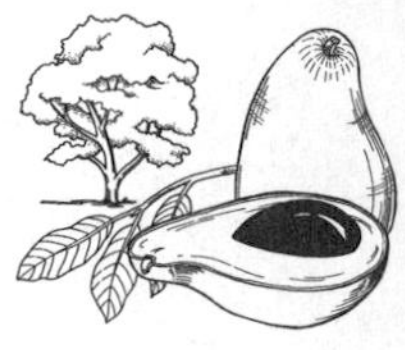

avocado
Persea americana

avocet
American avocet
Recurvirostra americana

ă pat	oi boy
ā pay	ou out
âr care	o͝o took
ä father	o͞o boot
ĕ pet	ŭ cut
ē be	ûr urge
ĭ pit	th thin
ī pie	*th* this
îr pier	hw which
ŏ pot	zh vision
ō toe	ə about, item
ô paw	

Stress marks:
′ (primary);
′ (secondary), as in
dictionary (dĭk′shə-nĕr′ē)

weight (< VLat. *pēsum < Lat. pēnsum, p.part. of pendere, to hang; see **(s)pen-***.)]

avoirdupois weight *n.* A system of weights and measures based on a pound containing 16 ounces or 7,000 grains and equal to 453.59 grams.

A•von (ā′vŏn, ā′vən, ăv′ən) also **Up•per Avon** (ŭp′ər). A river of S-central England flowing 154.5 km (96 mi) to the Severn R.; known for its associations with Shakespeare.

a•vouch (ə-vouch′) *tr.v.* **a•vouched, a•vouch•ing, a•vouch•es. 1.** To declare the provable truth or validity of; affirm. **2.** To vouch for. **3.** To accept responsibility for (an action, for example); acknowledge. **4.** To avow; confess. [ME *avouchen*, to cite as a warrant < OFr. *avochier* < Lat. *advocāre*, to summon. See ADVOCATE.]

a•vow (ə-vou′) *tr.v.* **a•vowed, a•vow•ing, a•vows. 1.** To acknowledge openly, boldly, and unashamedly; confess: *avow guilt.* **2.** To state positively. [ME *avowen* < OFr. *avouer* < Lat. *advocāre*, to call upon. See ADVOCATE.] **—a•vow′a•ble** *adj.* **—a•vow′a•bly** *adv.* **—a•vow′ed•ly** (-ĭd-lē) *adv.* **—a•vow′er** *n.*

a•vow•al (ə-vou′əl) *n.* A frank admission or acknowledgment.

a•vulse (ə-vŭls′) *tr.v.* **a•vulsed, a•vuls•ing, a•vuls•es.** To separate, cut, or tear off by avulsion. [Lat. *āvellere, āvuls-*, to tear off : *ā-, ab-*, away; see AB-[1] + *vellere*, to pull.]

a•vul•sion (ə-vŭl′shən) *n.* **1.** *Medic.* The forcible tearing away of a body part by trauma or surgery. **2.** The sudden movement of soil from one property to another as a result of a flood or a shift in the course of a boundary stream.

a•vun•cu•lar (ə-vŭng′kyə-lər) *adj.* **1.** Of or having to do with an uncle. **2.** Similar to an uncle, esp. in benevolence. [< Lat. *avunculus*, maternal uncle. See **awo-***.]

aw (ô) *interj.* Used to express sympathy, disgust, or disbelief.

AW *abbr.* **1.** Aircraft warning. **2.** Articles of War. **3.** Automatic weapon.

a.w. *abbr.* **1.** Also **A/W.** Actual weight. **2.** All water.

AWACS (ā′wăks) *n., pl.* **AWACS.** An airborne surveillance system that is capable of tracking a large number of aircraft from a great distance. [*A(irborne) W(arning) A(nd) C(ontrol) S(ystem).*]

a•wait (ə-wāt′) *v.* **a•wait•ed, a•wait•ing, a•waits.** *—tr.* **1.a.** To wait for. See Syns at **expect. b.** To be in a state of abeyance until: *a contract awaiting signature.* **2.** To be in store for: *Death awaits us all.* **3.** *Obsolete.* To lie in ambush for. *—intr.* **1.** To wait. **2.** To be in store. [ME *awaiten* < ONFr. *awaitier*: *a-*, on (< Lat. *ad-*; see AD-) + *waitier*, to watch; see WAIT.]

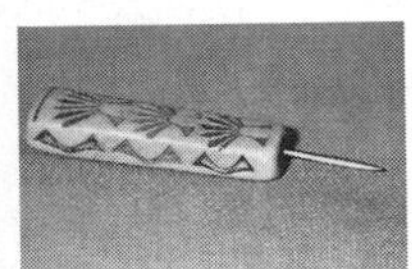

awl
Carved bone handle on a Native American awl

a•wake (ə-wāk′) *v.* **a•woke** (ə-wōk′) or **a•waked, a•waked** or **a•wok•en** (ə-wō′kən), **a•wak•ing, a•wakes.** *—tr.* **1.** To rouse from sleep; waken. **2.** To stir the interest of; excite. **3.** To stir up (memories, for example). *—intr.* **1.** To wake up. **2.** To become alert. **3.** To become aware or cognizant: *awoke to reality.* See Usage Note at **wake[1]**. *—adj.* **1.** Conscious; not asleep. **2.** Vigilant; watchful. See Syns at **aware.** [ME *awaken* < OE *āwacan*: *ā-*, intensive pref. + *wacan*, wake; see WAKE[1].]

a•wak•en (ə-wā′kən) *v.* **-ened, -en•ing, -ens.** *—tr.* To cause to wake up. *—intr.* To wake up. See Usage Note at **wake[1]**. [ME *awakenen* < OE *āwæcnian*: *ā-*, on, up; see A-[2] + *wæcnian*, to waken; see WAKEN.] **—a•wak′en•er** *n.*

a•ward (ə-wôrd′) *tr.v.* **a•ward•ed, a•ward•ing, a•wards. 1.** To grant as merited or due: *awarded prizes.* **2.** To give as legally due: *awarded damages to the plaintiff.* *—n.* **1.** Something awarded or granted, as for merit. **2.** A decision, such as one made by a judge or arbitrator. [ME *awarden* < AN *awarder*, to decide (a legal case), var. of ONFr. *eswarder*: *es-*, out (< Lat. *ex*; see EX-) + *warder*, to judge, guard; see **wer-[3]***.] **—a•ward′a•ble** *adj.* **—a•ward′er** *n.*

a•ward•ee (ə-wôr-dē′) *n.* The recipient of an award.

a•ware (ə-wâr′) *adj.* **1.** Having knowledge or cognizance: *aware of a sound.* **2.** *Archaic.* Vigilant; watchful. [ME, var. of *iwar* < OE *gewær*. See **wer-[3]***.] **—a•ware′ness** *n.*

Syns: *aware, cognizant, conscious, sensible, awake, alert, watchful, vigilant.* These adjectives mean mindful or heedful. *Aware* implies knowledge gained through one's own perceptions or by means of information: *I am aware that the legislation passed. Cognizant* is a rather formal equivalent of *aware*: *"Our research indicates that the nation's youth are cognizant of the law"* (Jerry D. Jennings). *Conscious* emphasizes the recognition of something sensed or felt: *"an importance . . . of which even Americans are barely conscious"* (William Stanley Jevons). *Sensible* implies knowledge gained through intuition or intellectual perception: *"I am sensible that the mention of such a circumstance may appear trifling"* (Henry Hallam). To be *awake* is to have full consciousness of something: *"as much awake to the novelty of attention in that quarter as Elizabeth herself"* (Jane Austen). *Alert* stresses quickness to recognize and respond: *alert to career opportunities. Watchful* and *vigilant* imply looking out for what is dangerous or potentially so: *the toddler's watchful parent; keeping a vigilant eye out for forest fires.*

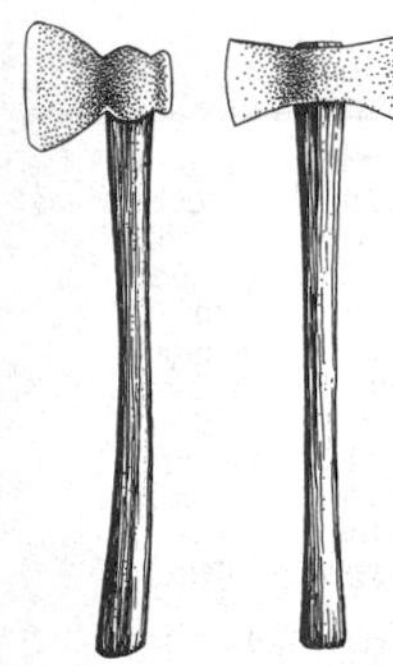

ax
Left: Broadax
Right: Full double-bitted ax

a•wash (ə-wŏsh′, ə-wôsh′) *adv.* **1.** Washed by the sea. **2.** At the surface level of a body of water, so as to be washed by waves. *—adj.* **1.** Level with or washed by waves. **2.** Overflowing with or as if with water: *awash in cash.* **3.** Floating on or as if on waves.

A•wash River (ä′wäsh′) also **Ha•wash River** (hä′-). A river of E Ethiopia flowing c. 805 km (500 mi) to the Danakil Desert.

a•way (ə-wā′) *adv.* **1.** From a particular thing or place: *Go away!* **2.a.** At or to a distance in space or time: *We live a block away from the park.* **b.** At or by a considerable interval: *away back in time.* **3.a.** In a different direction; aside: *glanced away.* **b.** On the way: *get away early.* **4.** In or into storage or safekeeping: *put the toys away.* **5.** Out of existence or notice: *The music faded away.* **6.** So as to remove, separate, or eliminate: *cleared away the debris.* **7.** From one's possession: *gave the tickets away.* **8.** Continuously; steadily: *toiling away.* **9.** Freely; at will: *Fire away!* *—adj.* **1.** Absent: *The neighbors are away.* **2.** Distant, as in space or time: *The city is miles away.* **3.** Played on an opponent's field or grounds: *an away game.* **4.** *Baseball.* Out. [ME < OE *aweg*: *a-*, on; see A-[1] + *weg*, way; see **wegh-***.]

awe (ô) *n.* **1.** A mixed emotion of reverence, respect, dread, and wonder inspired as by authority, genius, great beauty, or might. **2.** *Archaic.* **a.** The power to inspire dread. **b.** Dread. *—tr.v.* **awed, aw•ing, awes.** To inspire with awe. [ME < ON *agi.*]

a•wea•ry (ə-wîr′ē) *adj.* *Archaic.* Tired; weary.

a•weath•er (ə-wĕth′ər) *adv.* *Naut.* To the windward side.

a•weigh (ə-wā′) *adj.* *Naut.* Hanging clear of the bottom. Used of an anchor.

awe•some (ô′səm) *adj.* **1.** Inspiring awe: *an awesome thunderstorm.* **2.** Expressing awe. **3.** *Slang.* Remarkable; outstanding. **—awe′some•ly** *adv.* **—awe′some•ness** *n.*

awe•struck (ô′strŭk′) also **awe•strick•en** (-strĭk′ən) *adj.* Full of awe.

aw•ful (ô′fəl) *adj.* **1.** Extremely bad or unpleasant; terrible. **2.** Commanding or inspiring awe. **3.** Filled with awe, esp.: **a.** Filled with or displaying great reverence. **b.** *Obsolete.* Afraid. **4.** Formidable in nature or extent. *—adv.* *Informal.* Extremely; very. [ME *aweful*, awe-inspiring, blend of *awe*, awe; see AWE, and **ayfull*, awful (< OE *egefull*: *ege*, dread + *-full*, -ful).] **—aw′ful•ly** *adv.* **—aw′ful•ness** *n.*

a•while (ə-hwīl′, ə-wīl′) *adv.* For a short time.

Usage Note: *Awhile*, an adverb, is never preceded by a preposition, such as *for*, but the two-word form *a while* may be preceded by a preposition. In writing each of the following is acceptable: *stay awhile; stay for a while; stay a while* (but not *stay for awhile*).

a•whirl (ə-hwûrl′, ə-wûrl′) *adj.* **1.** Having a whirling motion; spinning: *leaves awhirl in the wind.* **2.** Being in a state of excitement or confusion. **—a•whirl′** *adv.*

awk•ward (ôk′wərd) *adj.* **1.** Not graceful; ungainly. **2.a.** Not dexterous; clumsy. **b.** Clumsily or unskillfully performed. **3.a.** Difficult to handle or manage. **b.** Difficult to effect; uncomfortable: *an awkward pose.* **4.a.** Marked by or causing embarrassment or discomfort. **b.** Requiring great tact and skill. [ME *awkeward*, in the wrong way : *awke*, wrong (< ON *öfugr*, backward; see **apo-***) + *-ward*, -ward.] **—awk′ward•ly** *adv.* **—awk′ward•ness** *n.*

awl (ôl) *n.* A pointed tool used for making holes, as in wood or leather. [ME *aul*, prob. blend of OE *æl* and OE *awel*, fleshhook.]

awn (ôn) *n.* A slender, bristlelike appendage found on the spikelets of many grasses. [ME *awne* < ON *ögnor* < OE *agen*; see **ak-***.] **—awned** *adj.* **—awn′less** *adj.*

awn•ing (ô′nĭng) *n.* A rooflike structure, often made of canvas or plastic, that serves as a shelter, as over a storefront, window, door, or deck. [?]

a•woke (ə-wōk′) *v.* A p.t. of **awake.**

a•wok•en (ə-wō′kən) *v.* A p.part. of **awake.**

AWOL or **awol** (ā′wôl′) *—adj.* Absent without leave. *—n.* One who is absent without leave.

a•wry (ə-rī′) *adv.* **1.** In a position that is turned or twisted toward one side; askew. **2.** Away from the correct course; amiss. See Syns at **amiss. —a•wry′** *adj.*

ax or **axe** (ăks) *—n., pl.* **ax•es** (ăk′sĭz). **1.** A tool with a bladed head mounted crosswise on a handle, used for felling trees or chopping wood. **2.** A similar implement used as a cutting tool or weapon. **3.** *Informal.* A sudden termination of employment. **4.** *Slang.* A musical instrument, esp. a guitar. *—tr.v.* **axed, ax•ing, ax•es. 1.** To chop or fell with an ax. **2.** *Informal.* To remove ruthlessly or suddenly. ***—idiom.* ax to grind.** A selfish or subjective aim. [ME < OE *æx.*]

ax. *abbr.* **1.** *Math. & Logic.* Axiom. **2.** Axis.

ax•el (ăk′səl) *n.* *Sports.* A jump in figure skating in which the skater leaps from the outer forward edge of one skate, makes 1½ turns, and lands on the outer backward edge of the other skate. [After *Axel* Paulsen (1855–1938), Norwegian figure skater.]

Ax•el Hei•berg (ăk′səl hī′bûrg′). An island of N Northwest Terrs., Canada, in the Arctic Ocean W of Ellesmere I.

Ax•el•rod (ăk′səl-räd′), **Julius.** b. 1912. Amer. biochemist who shared a 1970 Nobel Prize.

a•xen•ic (ā-zĕn′ĭk, ā-zē′nĭk) *adj.* Not contaminated by or associated with any other living organisms. Usu. used of cultures of microorganisms. —**a•xen′i•cal•ly** *adv.*

ax•es¹ (ăk′sēz′) *n.* Pl. of **axis.**

ax•es² (ăk′sĭz) *n.* Pl. of **ax.**

ax•i•al (ăk′sē-əl) *adj.* **1.** Relating to, characterized by, or forming an axis. **2.** Located on, around, or in the direction of an axis. —**ax′i•al′i•ty** (-ăl′ĭ-tē) *n.* —**ax′i•al•ly** *adv.*

axial skeleton *n.* The bones constituting the head and trunk of a vertebrate body.

ax•il (ăk′sĭl) *n.* The upper angle between a lateral organ, such as a leafstalk, and the stem that bears it. [Lat. *axilla*, armpit.]

ax•ile (ăk′sīl) *adj.* Situated along the central axis of an ovary having two or more locules: *axile placentation.* [AX(IS) + -ILE¹.]

ax•il•la (ăk-sĭl′ə) *n., pl.* **-il•lae** (-sĭl′ē). *Anat.* **1.** The armpit. **2.** A body part analogous to the armpit, such as the hollow under a bird's wing. [Lat.]

ax•il•lar (ăk-sĭl′ər, ăk′sə-lər) or **ax•il•lar•y** (ăk′sə-lĕr′ē) *n., pl.* **axillars** or **-ies.** One of the feathers in the axilla of a bird's wing.

ax•il•lar•y (ăk′sə-lĕr′ē) *adj.* **1.** *Anat.* Of, relating to, or located near the axilla. **2.** *Bot.* Of, relating to, or located in an axil.

axillary bud *n.* A lateral bud.

ax•i•ol•o•gy (ăk′sē-ŏl′ə-jē) *n. Philos.* The study of the nature of values and value judgments. [Gk. *axios*, worth; see **ag-*** + -LOGY.] —**ax′i•o•log′i•cal** (-ə-lŏj′ĭ-kəl) *adj.* —**ax′i•o•log′i•cal•ly** *adv.* —**ax′i•ol′o•gist** *n.*

ax•i•om (ăk′sē-əm) *n.* **1.** A self-evident or universally recognized truth. **2.** An established rule, principle, or law. **3.** A principle that is accepted as true without proof as the basis for argument; a postulate. [ME < OFr. *axiome* < Lat. *axiōma, axiōmat-* < Gk. < *axios*, worthy. See **ag-***.] —**ax′i•o•mat′ic** (-ə-măt′ĭk), **ax′i•o•mat′i•cal** (-ĭ-kəl) *adj.* —**ax′i•o•mat′i•cal•ly** *adv.*

ax•is (ăk′sĭs) *n., pl.* **ax•es** (ăk′sēz′). **1.** A straight line about which a body or geometric object rotates or may be conceived to rotate. **2.** *Math.* **a.** A line serving to orient a geometric object, esp. a line about which the object is symmetric. **b.** A reference line along which coordinates are measured. **3.** A center line to which parts of a structure or body may be referred. **4.** An imaginary line to which elements of a work of art are referred for measurement or symmetry. **5.** *Anat.* **a.** The second cervical vertebra. **b.** Any of various central structures, such as the spinal column or standard abstract lines used as a positional referent. **6.** *Bot.* The main stem or central part about which plant parts are arranged. **7.** One of three mutually perpendicular lines that define the orientation of an aircraft. **8.** A line through the optical center of a lens that is perpendicular to both its surfaces. **9.** One of three or four imaginary lines used to define the faces of a crystal. **10.a.** An alliance of powers, such as nations, to promote mutual interests and policies. **b. Axis.** The alliance of Germany and Italy in 1936, later including Japan and other nations, that opposed the Allies in World War II. [ME < Lat.]

axis deer *n.* A deer *(Axis axis)* of central Asia having a brown coat with white spots. [Lat. *axis*, a spotted Indian quadruped.]

ax•i•sym•met•ric (ăk′sē-sĭ-mĕt′rĭk) also **ax•i•sym•met•ri•cal** (-rĭ-kəl) *adj.* Having symmetry around an axis. —**ax′i•sym•met′ri•cal•ly** *adv.*

ax•le (ăk′səl) *n.* **1.** A supporting shaft or member on or with which a wheel or a set of wheels revolves. **2.a.** The spindle of an axletree. **b.** Either end of an axletree. [ME *axel* < ON *öxull.*]

ax•le•tree (ăk′səl-trē′) *n.* A crossbar or rod supporting a vehicle, such as a cart, that has terminal spindles on which the wheels revolve. [Blend of ME *axel*, axle; see AXLE, and ME *axtre*, axletree (*ax* < OE *eax* + *tre*, tree; see TREE).]

ax•man (ăks′mən) *n.* A man who wields an ax.

Ax•min•ster (ăks′mĭn′stər) *n.* A carpet with stiff backing and a soft, colorful cut pile usu. arranged in a complex pattern. [After *Axminster*, a town of SW England.]

ax•o•lotl (ăk′sə-lŏt′l) *n.* Any of several salamanders of the genus *Ambystoma*, native to Mexico and the western United States, that become sexually mature without undergoing metamorphosis. [Nahuatl.]

ax•on (ăk′sŏn′) also **ax•one** (-sōn′) *n.* The process of a nerve fiber that conducts impulses away from the body of the nerve cell. [Gk. *axōn*, axis.] —**ax′on•al** (ăk′sə-nəl, ăk-sŏn′əl) *adj.*

ax•o•neme (ăk′sə-nēm′) *n.* **1.** The bundle of fibrils that constitutes the central core of a cilium or flagellum. **2.** The axial thread of a chromosome. [Gk. *axōn*, axis + *nēma*, thread; see **(s)nē-***.] —**ax′o•ne′mal** *adj.*

ax•o•no•met•ric (ăk′sə-nō-mĕt′rĭk) *adj.* Of or relating to a projection in which an object is drawn with its horizontal and vertical axes to scale but with its curved lines and diagonals distorted. [< *axonometry*: Gk. *axōn*, axis + -METRY.]

ax•o•plasm (ăk′sə-plăz′əm) *n.* The cytoplasm of an axon. [Gk. *axōn* + -PLASM.] —**ax′o•plas′mic** (-plăz′mĭk) *adj.*

Ax•um (äk′so͞om′). See **Aksum.**

ay¹ (ī) *interj.* Used before *me* to express distress or regret.

ay² (ī) *n. & adv.* Var. of **aye¹.**

ay³ (ā) *adv.* Var. of **aye².**

a•yah (ä′yə, ā′ə, ī′ə) *n.* A maid or nurse native to India. [Hindi *āyā* < Port. *aia*, nursemaid < Lat. *avia*, grandmother. See **awo-***.]

a•ya•tol•lah (ī′ə-tō′lə, -tō-lä′) *n. Islam.* **1.** A high-ranking male Shiite religious authority generally assuming a political role and regarded as worthy of imitation. **2.** Used as a title for such a leader. [Pers. *ayātullah* < Ar. *'āyatullāh*: *'āyah*, Koranic verse, miracle + *allāh*, Allah.]

aye¹ also **ay** (ī) —*n.* An affirmative vote or voter. —*adv.* Yes; yea. [Perh. < ME **ayye*: *ay*, always; see AYE² + *ye*, yes; see YEA.]

aye² also **ay** (ā) *adv.* Always; ever. [ME *ai* < ON *ei.* See **aiw-***.]

aye-aye (ī′ī′) *n.* A nocturnal lemur *(Daubentonia madagascariensis)* native to Madagascar, having a long bushy tail and rodentlike teeth. [Fr. < Malagasy *aiay*, prob. imit. of its cry.]

A•ye•sha (ä′ē-shä′). See **Aisha.**

AYH *abbr.* American Youth Hostels.

a•yin (ī′ĭn) *n.* The 16th letter of the Hebrew alphabet. [Heb. *'ayin.*]

Ayl•mer (āl′mər). A town of SW Quebec, Canada, on the Ottawa R. W of Hull. Pop. 26,695.

Ay•ma•ra (ī′mä-rä′, ī′mə-) *n., pl.* **Aymara** or **-ras. 1.** A member of a South American Indian people inhabiting parts of Bolivia and Peru. **2.** The Aymaran language of the Aymara.

Ay•ma•ran (ī′mä-rän′) *n.* A subgroup of the Quechumaran languages, the most important language being Aymara. —*adj.* Of or relating to the Aymara or their language or culture.

Ayr (âr). A burgh of SW Scotland at the mouth of the **Ayr River** on the Firth of Clyde. Pop. 48,600.

Ayr•shire (âr′shîr, -shər) *n.* Any of various brown and white dairy cattle of a breed that originated in Ayr, Scotland.

a-yuh (ā′yə, ī′yə, ā-yŭ′) *interj. New England.* Used to express agreement.

A•yut•thay•a (ä-yo͞o′tə-yä′). A city of S-central Thailand on an island in the Chao Phraya R. N of Bangkok; founded c. 1350. Pop. 55,319.

AZ *abbr.* Arizona.

az. *abbr.* **1.** Azimuth. **2.** Azure.

az– *pref.* Var. of **azo–.**

a•zal•ea (ə-zāl′yə) *n.* Any of various shrubs of the genus *Rhododendron*, having showy, variously colored flowers. [Gk. < fem. of *azaleos*, dry (so called because it grows in dry soil or from the texture of its wood). See **as-***.]

a•zan (ä-zän′) *n. Islam.* The summons to a prayer service. [Ar. *'adān* < *'addana*, to call to prayer < *'udn*, ear.]

A•za•ni•a (ə-zā′nē-ə, ə-zān′yə). South Africa. —**A•za′ni•an** *adj. & n.*

az•a•thi•o•prine (ăz′ə-thī′ə-prēn′) *n.* An immunosuppressive agent used esp. to prevent organ rejection in kidney transplant recipients. [Prob. < AZ(O)– + THIO– + P(U)RINE.]

A•za•zel (ə-zā′zəl, ăz′ə-zĕl′) *n. Bible.* The evil spirit in the wilderness to whom a scapegoat was sent on the Day of Atonement. [Heb. *'ăzā'zēl*, removal, scapegoat (ritually sent into the wilderness), perh. orig.ally a divine name.]

a•ze•o•trope (ə-zē′ə-trōp′, ā′zē-) *n.* A mixture of two or more substances that retains the same composition in the vapor state as in the liquid state. [A–¹ + Gk. *zein*, to boil; see ZEOLITE + Gk. *-tropos*, turning; see –TROPOUS.] —**a′ze•o•trop′ic** (a′zē-ə-trŏp′ĭk, -trō′pĭk) *adj.* —**a′ze•ot′ro•py** (-ŏt′rə-pē) *n.*

A•zer•bai•jan (ăz′ər-bī-jän′, ä′zər-). A republic and former kingdom of Transcaucasia N of Iran; a constituent republic of the U.S.S.R. from 1936 to 1991. Cap. Baku. Pop. 6,614,000.

A•zer•bai•ja•ni (ăz′ər-bī-jä′nē, äz′ər-) *adj.* Of or relating to Azerbaijan or its people, language, or culture. —*n., pl.* **Azerbaijani** or **-nis. 1.** A native or inhabitant of Azerbaijan. **2.** The Turkic language of Azerbaijan.

az•ide (ăz′īd, ā′zīd) *n.* A chemical compound that contains the group N_3. —**az•i•do** (az′ĭ-dō′) *adj.*

a•z•i•do•thy•mi•dine (ə-zī′dō-thī′mĭ-dēn′, ə-zē′-, ăz′ĭ-) *n.* An antiviral drug that inhibits replication of the retrovirus that causes AIDS; AZT.

A•zil•ian (ə-zĭl′yən) *adj. Archaeol.* Of or relating to a Mesolithic western European culture. [After Le Mas d'*Azil*, a village of S France.]

az•i•muth (ăz′ə-məth) *n.* **1.** The horizontal angular distance from a reference direction, usu. the northern point of the horizon, to the point where a vertical circle through a celestial body intersects the horizon, usu. measured clockwise. **2.** The horizontal angle of the observer's bearing in surveying, measured clockwise from a referent direction. **3.** The lateral deviation of a projectile or bomb. [ME *azimut* < OFr. < Ar. *as-sumūt*, pl. of *as-samt*, the way, compass bearing < Lat. *sēmita*, path.] —**az′i•muth′al** (-mŭth′əl) *adj.* —**az′i•muth′al•ly** *adv.*

azimuthal equidistant projection *n.* A map projection of the earth designed so that a straight line from the central point on the map to any other point gives the shortest distance between the two points.

az•ine (ăz′ēn′, ā′zēn′) *n.* A six-membered heterocyclic com-

azalea
Flame azalea
Rhododendron calendulaceum

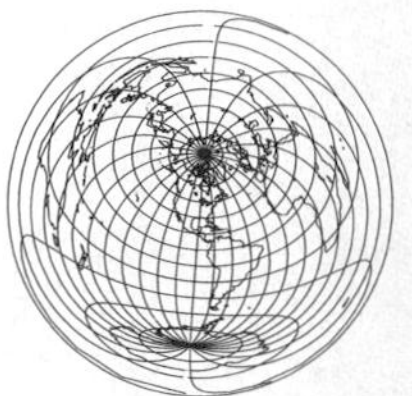

azimuthal equidistant projection

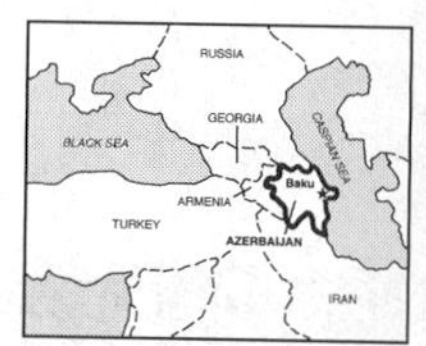

Azerbaijan

ă pat	oi boy
ā pay	ou out
âr care	o͝o took
ä father	o͞o boot
ĕ pet	ŭ cut
ē be	ûr urge
ĭ pit	th thin
ī pie	*th* this
îr pier	hw which
ŏ pot	zh vision
ō toe	ə about, item
ô paw	

Stress marks:
′ (primary);
′ (secondary), as in
dictionary (dĭk′shə-nĕr′ē)

pound that contains nitrogen and carbon atoms.

azine dye *n.* Any of various dyes derived from phenazine.

az•o (ăz′ō, ā′zō) *adj.* Containing a nitrogen group, esp. N=N. [< AZO-.]

azo- or **az-** *pref.* Containing a nitrogen group, esp. one attached at both ends in a covalent bond to other groups: *azole.* [< Fr. *azote,* nitrogen : Gk. *a-,* not; see A-[1] + Gk. *zōē,* life (from the fact that nitrogen does not support respiration); see **g^wei-***.]

azo dye *n.* Any of various red, brown, or yellow acidic or basic dyes derived from amino compounds.

a•zo•ic (ā-zō′ĭk) *adj.* Of or relating to geologic periods that precede the appearance of life.

az•ole (ăz′ōl′, ā′zōl′) *n.* A class of organic compounds having a five-membered heterocyclic ring with two double bonds.

a•zon•al (ā-zō′nəl) *adj.* Not divided into zones.

a•zon•ic (ā-zŏn′ĭk, ā-zō′nĭk) *adj.* Not restricted to a particular zone or region; not local.

A•zores (ā′zôrz, ā′zōrz, ə-zôrz′, ə-zōrz′). A group of volcanic islands in the N Atlantic Ocean c. 1,448 km (900 mi) W of mainland Portugal, of which they are administrative districts. **—A•zor′e•an, A•zor′i•an** *adj. & n.*

az•o•te•mi•a (ăz′ə-tē′mē-ə, ā′zə-) *n.* See **uremia.** [Fr. *azote,* nitrogen; see AZO- + -EMIA.] **—az′o•te′mic** (-mĭk) *adj.*

az•oth (ăz′ŏth, -ôth) *n.* Mercury considered in alchemy to be the primary source of all metals. [ME *azoc* < OFr. < Ar. *az-zā'uq,* the mercury < Syriac *zīwag* < MPers. **zhīwak* < OIran. **jīvaka-,* lively; akin to Skt. *jīvaka-,* lively < *jīva-,* alive. See **g^wei-***.]

a•zo•to•bac•ter (ā-zō′tə-băk′tər) *n.* Any of various rod-shaped, nitrogen-fixing bacteria of the genus *Azotobacter,* found in soil and water. [Fr. *azote,* nitrogen; see AZO- + BACTER(IA).]

az•o•tu•ri•a (ăz′ə-to͝or′ē-ə, -tyo͝or′-) *n.* Increase of nitrogenous substances, esp. urea, in the urine. [Fr. *azote,* nitrogen; see AZO- + -URIA.]

A•zov (ăz′ôf, ā′zôf, ə-zôf′), **Sea of.** The N arm of the Black Sea between Russia and the Ukraine.

AZT (ā′zē-tē′) *n.* Azidothymidine. [AZ(IDO)T(HYMIDINE).]

Az•tec (ăz′tĕk′) *n.* **1.** A member of a people of central Mexico whose civilization was at its height at the time of the Spanish conquest in the early 16th century. **2.** The Nahuatl language of the Aztecs. *—adj.* also **Az•tec•an** (-tĕk′ən). Of or relating to the Aztecs or their language, culture, or empire. [Sp. *Azteca* < Nahuatl *Aztecatl*: *aztatl-,* cranes + *lan-,* near + *ztecatl,* place.]

az•ure (ăzh′ər) *n.* **1.a.** *Color.* A light purplish blue. **b.** *Her.* The color blue. **2.** The blue sky. [ME < OFr. *azur* < Med.Lat. *azura* < Ar. *al-lāzaward* < Pers. *lājvard,* lapis lazuli.]

az•ur•ite (ăzh′ə-rīt′) *n.* An azure blue vitreous mineral, $Cu_3(CO_3)_2(OH)_2$, used as a copper ore and as a gemstone.

A•zu•sa (ə-zo͞o′sə). A city of S CA E of Pasadena. Pop. 41,333.

a•zy•gous (ā-zī′gəs) *adj. Anat.* Occurring singly; not one of a pair, as a vein or muscle.

B b

b[1] (bē) or **B** (bē) *n., pl.* **b's** or **B's. 1.** The second letter of the modern English alphabet. **2.** Any of the speech sounds represented by the letter *b.* **3.** The second in a series. **4.** *Mus.* **a.** The seventh tone in the scale of C major or the second tone in the relative minor scale. **b.** A key or scale in which B is the tonic. **5.** One of four types of blood in the ABO system. **6.** The second best or second highest in quality or rank: *a mark of B in English.*

b[2] *abbr. Phys.* **1.** Barn. **2.** Or **B.** Bel. **3.** Bottom quark.

B[1] **1.** The symbol for the element **boron. 2.** The symbol for **magnetic flux density.**

B[2] or **b** *abbr.* **1.** Baryon number. **2.** *Games.* Bishop.

b. or **B.** *abbr.* **1.** Base. **2.** *Mus.* Basso. **3.** Bay. **4.** Billion. **5.** Bolivar. **6.** Book. **7.** Born. **8.** Breadth. **9.** Brother.

B. *abbr.* **1.** Bachelor. **2.** Bacillus. **3.** Baumé scale. **4.** Bible. **5.** Brotherhood.

Ba The symbol for the element **barium.**

B.A. *abbr.* **1.** Bachelor of Arts. **2.** British Academy.

baa (bă, bä) *intr.v.* **baaed, baa•ing, baas.** To make a bleating sound, as a goat. *—n.* The bleat of a sheep or goat. [Imit.]

Ba•al (bā′əl) *n., pl.* **-als** or **-al•im** (-ə-lĭm). **1.** Any of various local fertility and nature gods of the ancient Semitic peoples considered to be false idols by the Hebrews. **2.** Often **baal.** A false god or idol. [Heb. *ba'al,* lord, Baal.]

Baal•bek (bäl′bĕk′, bā′əl-). Formerly **He•li•op•o•lis** (hē′lē-ŏp′ə-lĭs). A town of E Lebanon NE of Beirut; noted for its extensive Roman ruins. Pop. 24,000.

Baal Shem Tov (bäl′ shĕm′ tōv′). Orig. Israel ben Eliezer. 1700?–60. Polish-born Jewish leader who founded Hasidism.

Bab (bäb, băb), **the.** Ali Mohammad of Shiraz. 1819?–50. Persian founder of Babism, a religion that forbade polygamy, begging, and trading in slaves.

Bab. *abbr.* Babylonian.

ba•ba (bä′bə) *n.* A leavened rum cake, usu. made with raisins. [Fr. < Pol., old woman.]

Ba•bar (bä′bər). See **Baber.**

ba•bas•su (bä′bə-so͞o′) *n.* A Brazilian feather-leaved palm *(Orbignya barbosiana)* bearing seeds that yield an edible vegetable oil. [Port. *babaçú* < Tupi *babassú, oauaussu.*]

Bab•bage (băb′ĭj), **Charles.** 1792–1871. British mathematician and inventor of a forerunner to the digital computer.

Bab•bitt (băb′ĭt) *n.* A self-satisfied person concerned chiefly with business and middle-class ideals like material success. [After George F. *Babbitt,* the main character in the novel *Babbitt* by Sinclair Lewis.] **—Bab′bitt•ry** *n.*

Babbitt, Irving. 1865–1933. Amer. humanist and scholar who founded the New Humanism movement.

Babbitt, Isaac. 1799–1862. Amer. inventor who patented (1839) a bearing housing lined with alloy.

Babbitt, Milton Byron. b. 1916. Amer. composer whose works combine serial music and electronic effects.

bab•bitt metal (băb′ĭt) *n.* Any of several soft, silvery antifriction alloys composed of tin usu. with small amounts of copper and antimony. [After Isaac BABBITT.]

babirusa
Babyrousa babyrussa

bab•ble (băb′əl) *v.* **-bled, -bling, -bles.** *—intr.* **1.** To utter a meaningless confusion of words or sounds. **2.** To talk foolishly or idly; chatter. **3.** To make a low, murmuring sound, as flowing water. *—tr.* **1.** To utter rapidly and indistinctly. **2.** To utter carelessly; blurt out. *—n.* **1.** Inarticulate or meaningless talk or sounds. **2.** Idle talk; prattle. **3.** A low, murmuring sound. [ME *babelen.*] **—bab′bler** *n.*

babe (bāb) *n.* **1.** A baby; an infant. **2.** An innocent or naive person. **3.** *Slang.* A young woman. [ME.]

ba•bel also **Ba•bel** (băb′əl, bā′bəl) *n.* **1.** A confusion of sounds or voices. See Syns at **noise. 2.** A scene of noise and confusion. [After BABEL.]

Ba•bel (bā′bəl, băb′əl). In the Bible, a city (now thought to be Babylon) in Shinar where construction of a tower intended to reach heaven was ended when the builders became unable to understand each other's language.

Bab el Man•deb (băb′ ĕl män′dĕb). A strait, 27.4 km (17 mi) wide, between the Arabian Peninsula and E Africa linking the Red Sea with the Gulf of Aden.

Ba•ber also **Ba•bar** or **Ba•bur** (bä′bər). Orig. Zahir ud-Din Mohammed. 1483–1530. Mongol conqueror of India who founded the Mogul dynasty.

ba•be•sia (bə-bē′zhə) *n.* A genus of parasitic sporozoans of the family Babesiidae that infect mammalian red blood cells. [NLat. *Babesia,* genus name, after Victor *Babeş* (1854–1926), Romanian bacteriologist.]

ba•be•si•o•sis (bə-bē′zē-ō′sĭs) also **bab•e•si•a•sis** (băb′ĭ-zī′ə-sĭs) *n.* **1.** A tick-borne infection of animals that is caused by species of *Babesia.* **2.** A disease of human red blood cells caused by *Babesia* species.

Ba•bian Jiang (bä′byän′ jyäng′). See **Black River** 1.

bab•i•ru•sa also **bab•i•rus•sa** or **bab•i•rous•sa** (băb′ə-ro͞o′sə, bä′bə-) *n.* A wild pig *(Babyrousa babyrussa)* of the East Indies, having upward-curving tusks in the male. [Malay *bābīrūsa*: *bābī,* hog + *rūsa,* deer.]

Ba•bi Yar (bä′bē yär′, bä′byē). A ravine outside Kiev in N-central Ukraine where the Jews of the city were killed by German troops (1941).

bab•ka (bäb′kə) *n.* A coffee cake flavored with orange rind, rum, almonds, and raisins. [Pol., dim. of *baba,* old woman.]

ba•boon (bă-bo͞on′) *n.* **1.** Any of several large, terrestrial African and Asian monkeys of the family Cercopithecidae, esp. of the genus *Papio* and related genera, characterized by a doglike muzzle and a short tail. **2.** *Slang.* A brutish person; a boor. [ME *babewin* < OFr. *babuin,* gaping figure, gargoyle, baboon, perh. blend of OFr. *babine,* muzzle, and *babau,* grimace.] **—ba•boon′er•y** *n.* **—ba•boon′ish** *adj.*

ba•bu also **ba•boo** (bä′bo͞o) *n.* **1.** Used as a Hindi courtesy title for a man, equivalent to *Mr.* **2.a.** A Hindu clerk who is literate in English. **b.** *Offensive.* A native of India who has acquired some education in English. [Hindi *bābū,* father.]

ba•bul (bə-bo͞ol′) *n.* A tropical African tree *(Acacia nilotica)* that yields a gum similar to gum arabic and has a bark used in tanning. [Pers. *bābul.*]

ba•bush•ka (bə-bo͝osh′kə) *n.* A woman's head scarf, folded triangularly and worn tied under the chin. [Russ., grandmother, dim. of *baba*, woman.]

Ba•bu•yan Islands (bä'bo͞o-yän′). An island group of the Philippines separated from the N coast of Luzon by the **Babuyan Channel.**

ba•by (bā′bē) *n., pl.* **-bies. 1.a.** A very young child; an infant. **b.** The youngest member of a family or group. **c.** A very young animal. **2.** An adult or a young person who behaves in an infantile way. **3.** *Slang.* A girl or young woman. **4.** *Slang.* An object of personal concern: *That boat is your baby.* — *adj.* **-i•er, -iest. 1.** Of or having to do with a baby. **2.** Infantile or childish. **3.** Smaller than others of the same kind: *baby vegetables.* — *tr.v.* **-bied, -by•ing, -bies.** To treat with indulgence and solicitude. [ME.] — **ba′by•hood'** *n.* — **ba′by•ish** *adj.*

baby blue *n. Color.* A very light to very pale greenish or purplish blue.

ba•by-blue-eyes (bā'bē-blo͞o′īz') *pl.n. (used with a sing. or pl. v.)* An annual plant *(Nemophila menziesii)* native to California and having blue flowers with white centers.

baby boom *n.* A large increase in the birthrate, esp. the one in the United States from 1947 through 1961. — **ba′by-boom'** (bā′bē-bo͞om') *adj.*

ba•by boom•er also **ba•by-boom•er** (bā′bē-bo͞o'mər) *n.* A member of a baby-boom generation.

baby bust *n.* A sudden decline in the birthrate.

baby carriage *n.* A four-wheeled carriage, often with a hood that folds back, used for wheeling an infant about.

baby grand *n. Mus.* A small grand piano about 1.5 meters (5 feet) long.

Bab•y•lon[1] (băb′ə-lən, -lŏn'). The cap. of ancient Babylonia, in Mesopotamia on the Euphrates R.; estab. as cap. c. 1750 B.C. and site of the Hanging Gardens, one of the Seven Wonders of the World.

Bab•y•lon[2] (băb′ə-lən, -lŏn') *n.* **1.** A city or place of great luxury, sensuality, and often vice and corruption. **2.** A place of captivity or exile.

Bab•y•lo•ni•a (băb'ə-lō′nē-ə, -lōn′yə). An ancient empire of Mesopotamia in the Euphrates R. valley; fell to the Persians in 539 B.C.

Bab•y•lo•ni•an (băb'ə-lō′nē-ən) *adj.* **1.** Of or relating to Babylonia or Babylon or their people, culture, or language. **2.** Marked by a luxurious, pleasure-seeking, and often immoral way of life. — *n.* **1.** A native or inhabitant of Babylon or Babylonia. **2.** The form of Akkadian used in Babylonia.

ba•by's breath (bā′bēz) *n.* Any of several Eurasian plants of the genus *Gypsophila,* such as *G. paniculata,* having numerous small white flowers in profusely branched panicles.

ba•by-sit (bā′bē-sĭt') *v.* **-sat** (-săt'), **-sit•ting, -sits.** — *intr.* To act as a babysitter. — *tr.* To take care of.

Word History: One normally would expect the agent noun *baby sitter* with its *–er* suffix to come from the verb *baby-sit,* as *diver* comes from *dive,* but in fact *baby sitter* is first recorded in 1937, ten years earlier than the first appearance of *baby sit.* Thus, the verb was shortened from the agent noun and presents a good example of back-formation.

baby sitter *n.* **1.** A person engaged to care for one or more children when the parents or guardians are not at home. **2.** A person who watches over someone or something.

baby tooth *n.* See **milk tooth.**

Ba•cău (bə-kou′). A city of E Romania NNE of Bucharest. Pop. 165,655.

bac•ca•lau•re•ate (băk'ə-lôr′ē-ĭt) *n.* **1.** See **bachelor's degree. 2.** A farewell address delivered to a graduating class. [Med.Lat. *baccalaureātus* (influenced by *bacca,* berry + *laureātus,* crowned with laurel) < *baccalārius,* bachelor. See BACHELOR.]

bac•ca•rat (bä'kə-rä′, băk'ə-) *n. Games.* A card game in which the winner is the player who holds two or three cards totaling closest to nine. [Fr. *baccara* < Prov.]

bac•cate (băk′āt') *adj.* **1.** Resembling a berry in texture or form; berrylike. **2.** Bearing berries. [< Lat. *bacca,* berry.]

Bac•chae (băk′ē) *pl.n. Gk. & Rom. Myth.* The priestesses and women followers of Bacchus. [Lat. < Gk. *Bakkhai,* pl. of *Bakkhē,* female worshiper of Bacchus < *Bakkhos,* Bacchus.]

bac•cha•nal (băk'ə-năl′, -näl′, băk′ə-nəl) *n.* **1.** A participant in the Bacchanalia. **2.** The Bacchanalia. Often used in the plural. **3.** A drunken or riotous celebration. **4.** A reveler. — *adj.* Of or relating to the worship of Bacchus. [< Lat. *bacchānālis,* of Bacchus, prob. < *Bacchānālia,* Bacchanalia < *Bacchus,* Bacchus < Gk. *Bakkhos.*]

Bac•cha•na•lia (băk'ə-nāl′yə, -nā′lē-ə) *n., pl.* **Bacchanalia. 1.** The ancient Roman festival in honor of Bacchus. **2. bacchanalia.** A riotous drunken festivity; a revel. [Lat. < *Bacchus,* Bacchus < Gk. *Bakkhos.*] — **Bac'cha•na′lian** *adj. & n.*

bac•chant (bə-kănt′, -känt′, băk′ənt) *n., pl.* **bac•chants** or **bac•chan•tes** (bə-kăn′tēz, -kän′-, -kănts′, -känts′). **1.** *Gk. & Rom. Myth.* A priest or votary of Bacchus. **2.** A boisterous reveler. [Lat. *bacchāns, bacchant-,* pr.part. of *bacchārī,* to celebrate the festival of Bacchus < *Bacchus,* Bacchus < Gk. *Bakkhos.*] — **bac•chan•tic** (-kăn′tĭk) *adj.*

bac•chan•te (bə-kăn′tē, -kän′-, -kănt′, -känt′) *n. Gk. & Rom. Myth.* A priestess or female votary of Bacchus. [Fr. < Lat. *bacchāns, bacchant-.* See BACCHANT.]

Bac•chic (băk′ĭk) *adj.* **1.** *Gk. & Rom. Myth.* Of or relating to Bacchus. **2. bacchic.** Drunken and carousing; bacchanalian.

Bac•chus (băk′əs) *n. Gk. & Rom. Myth.* See **Dionysus.**

bach also **batch** (băch) *intr.v.* **bached, bach•ing, bach•es** also **batched, batch•ing, batch•es.** *Informal.* To live alone and keep house as a bachelor. [Short for BACHELOR.] — **bach** *n.*

Bach (bäKH, bäk), **Johann Sebastian.** 1685–1750. German composer and organist of the late baroque period. Four of his children also became noted musicians: **Wilhelm Friedemann** (1710–84); **Carl Philipp Emanuel** (1714–88); **Johann Christoph Friedrich** (1732–95); and **Johann Christian** (1735–82).

bach•e•lor (băch′ə-lər, băch′lər) *n.* **1.** An unmarried man. **2.** A person who has completed the undergraduate curriculum of a college or university and holds a bachelor's degree. **3.** A male animal, esp. a young fur seal, that does not mate during the breeding season. **4.** A young knight in the service of another knight in feudal times. [ME *bacheler,* squire, youth, bachelor < OFr. < Med.Lat. *baccalārius,* tenant farmer, perh. of Celt. orig.] — **bach′e•lor•dom, bach′e•lor•hood', bach′e•lor•ship'** *n.*

bachelor's but•ton *n., pl.* **bachelor's buttons. 1.** See **cornflower. 2.** Any of several plants that have buttonlike flowers or flower heads.

bachelor's degree *n.* An academic degree conferred by a college or university upon those who complete the undergraduate curriculum.

bac•il•lar•y (băs′ə-lĕr'ē, bə-sĭl′ə-rē) also **ba•cil•lar** (bə-sĭl′ər, băs′ə-lər) *adj.* **1.** Shaped like a rod or rods. **2.a.** Consisting of small rods or rodlike structures. **b.** Caused by, relating to, or resembling bacilli: *bacillary dysentery.* [< BACILLUS.]

ba•cil•lus (bə-sĭl′əs) *n., pl.* **-cil•li** (-sĭl′ī'). **1.** Any of various rod-shaped, spore-forming aerobic bacteria of the genus *Bacillus* that often occur in chains. **2.** Any of various bacteria. [LLat., dim. of Lat. *baculum,* rod. See **bak-*.**]

Ba•cil•lus Cal•mette-Gué•rin vaccine (bə-sĭl′əs kăl-mĕt′-gā-răn′) *n.* A preparation consisting of attenuated human tubercle bacilli that is used for immunization against tuberculosis. [After Albert L.C. *Calmette* (1863–1933) and Camille *Guérin* (1872–1961), French bacteriologists.]

bac•i•tra•cin (băs'ĭ-trā′sĭn) *n.* A polypeptide antibiotic obtained from a strain of a bacterium *(Bacillus subtilis)* and used as a topical ointment to treat certain bacterial infections, esp. those caused by cocci. [BACI(LLUS) + Margaret *Tracy,* an Amer. child in whose blood it was first isolated + –IN.]

back[1] (băk) *n.* **1.a.** The posterior portion of the human body between the neck and the pelvis. **b.** The analogous dorsal region in other animals. **2.** The backbone or spine. **3.** The part or area farthest from the front. **4.** The part that is less seen or used: *the back of a photograph.* **5.** The reverse side, as of a coin. **6.** A part that supports or strengthens from the rear: *the back of a couch.* **7.a.** The part of a book where the pages are stitched or glued together into the binding. **b.** The binding itself. **8.** *Sports.* **a.** A player who takes a position behind the front line in certain games, such as football. **b.** This playing position. — *v.* **backed, back•ing, backs.** — *tr.* **1.** To cause to move backward or in a reverse direction: *Back the car up.* **2.** To furnish or strengthen with a back or backing. **3.** To provide with financial or spiritual help; support or sustain. See Syns at **support. 4.** To bet or wager on. **5.** To adduce evidence in support of; substantiate. **6.** To form the back or background of. — *intr.* **1.** To move backward. **2.** To shift in a counterclockwise direction. Used of the wind. — *adj.* **1.** Located or placed in the rear. **2.** Distant from a center of activity; remote. **3.** Of a past date; not current: *a back issue.* **4.** Being owed or due from an earlier time: *back pay.* **5.** Being in a backward direction. **6.** *Ling.* Pronounced with the back of the tongue, as *oo* in *cool.* — *adv.* **1.** At, to, or toward the rear or back; backward. **2.** In, to, or toward a former location. **3.** In, to, or toward a former condition. **4.** In, to, or toward a past time. **5.** In reserve or concealment. **6.** In check or under restraint: *held the crowd back.* **7.** In reply or return. — ***phrasal verbs.*** **back away.** To withdraw from a position; retreat. **back down.** To withdraw from a position, opinion, or commitment. **back off.** To retreat or draw away. **back out. 1.** To withdraw from an enterprise or a plan before completion. **2.** To fail to keep a commitment or promise. **back up. 1.** To cause to stop and accumulate. **2.** To accumulate or be stopped. **3.** *Comp. Sci.* To make a backup of (a program or file). — ***idiom.*** **back and fill. 1.** *Naut.* To maneuver a vessel in a narrow channel by adjusting the sails so as to let the wind in and out of them in alteration. **2.** To vacillate in one's actions or decisions. [ME *bak* < OE *bæc.*] — **back′less** *adj.*

Usage Note: The expression *back of* is an informal variant of *in back of* and is best avoided in writing: *There was a small stable in back of* (not simply *back of*) *the house.*

back[2] (băk) *n.* A shallow vat or tub used chiefly by brewers. [Du. *bak* < Fr. *bac* < OFr., boat < VLat. **baccus,* vessel, prob. of Celt. orig.]

Johann Sebastian Bach

ă pat	oi boy
ā pay	ou out
âr care	o͝o took
ä father	o͞o boot
ĕ pet	ŭ cut
ē be	ûr urge
ĭ pit	th thin
ī pie	*th* this
îr pier	hw which
ŏ pot	zh vision
ō toe	ə about, item
ô paw	

Stress marks:
′ (primary);
' (secondary), as in
dictionary (dĭk′shə-nĕr'ē)

back•ache (băk′āk′) *n.* Discomfort or a pain in the region of the back or spine.
back and forth *adv.* Backward and forward; to and fro. —**back′-and-forth′** (băk′ăn-fôrth′, -fōrth′) *n. & adj.*
Back Bay (băk). An area of Boston MA largely consisting of filled-in land reclaimed from mud flats after the 1850's.
back•beat (băk′bēt′) *n. Mus.* A loud, steady rhythmic beat characteristic of rock music. [BACK(GROUND) + BEAT.]
back•bench (băk′bĕnch′) *n.* **1.** *Chiefly British.* The rear benches in the House of Commons where junior members of Parliament sit. **2.** New members of Congress considered as a group. —**back•bench′er** *n.*
back•bite (băk′bīt′) *v.* **-bit** (-bĭt′), **-bit•ten** (-bĭt′n), **-bit•ing, -bites.** —*tr.* To speak spitefully or slanderously about (another). —*intr.* To speak spitefully or slanderously. —**back′bit′er** *n.*
back•board (băk′bôrd′, -bōrd′) *n.* **1.** A board placed under or behind for firmness or support. **2.** *Basketball.* The elevated vertical board from which the basket projects.
back•bone (băk′bōn′) *n.* **1.** The vertebrate spine or spinal column. **2.** Something that resembles a backbone in appearance or position. **3.** A main support or sustaining factor. **4.** Strength of character; determination. —**back′boned′** *adj.*
back•break•ing (băk′brā′kĭng) *adj.* Demanding great exertion; arduous and exhausting. —**back′break′er** *n.*
back burner *n. Informal.* A position of little importance.
back•cloth (băk′klôth, -klŏth) *n.* See **backdrop** 1.
back•coun•try (băk′kŭn′trē) *n.* A sparsely inhabited rural region.
back•court (băk′kôrt′, -kōrt′) *n.* **1.** *Sports.* The part of a court between the service line and the base line in tennis and other net games. **2.** *Basketball.* **a.** The half of the court that a team defends. **b.** The two guards on one team.
back•cross (băk′krôs′, -krŏs′) *tr.v.* **-crossed, -cross•ing, -cross•es.** To cross (a hybrid) with one of its parents or with an individual genetically identical to one of its parents. —*n.* **1.** The act of making such a cross. **2.** An individual resulting from such a cross. —**back′cross′** *n.*
back dive *n. Sports.* A dive performed from a board or platform with the diver's back to the water.
back•door (băk′dôr′, -dōr′) *adj.* Secret or surreptitious; clandestine: *a backdoor romance.* —**back′door′** *adv.*
back•drop (băk′drŏp′) *n.* **1.** A painted curtain hung at the back of a stage set. **2.** The setting, as of a historical event; the background.
backed (băkt) *adj.* Having or furnished with a back or backing.
back•er (băk′ər) *n.* **1.** One that supports a person, a group, or an enterprise. **2.** A person who bets on a contestant.
back•field (băk′fēld′) *n. Football.* **a.** The players stationed behind the line of scrimmage. **b.** The positions filled by them.
back•fire (băk′fīr′) *n.* **1.** An explosion of prematurely ignited fuel or of unburned exhaust gases in an internal-combustion engine. **2.** The backward escape of gases or cartridge fragments when a gun is fired. **3.** Fire started to control an oncoming forest or prairie fire by burning an area in its path. —*intr.v.* **-fired, -fir•ing, -fires. 1.** To explode in the manner of or make the sound of a backfire. **2.** To start or use a backfire. **3.** To produce an unexpected, undesired result.
back-for•ma•tion or **back formation** (băk′fôr-mā′shən) *n.* **1.** A new word created by removing an affix from another word, as *vacuum clean* from *vacuum cleaner,* or by removing what is thought to be an affix, as *pea* from the earlier English plural *pease.* **2.** The process of forming words in this way.
back•gam•mon (băk′găm′ən) *n. Games.* A board game for two persons, played with pieces whose moves are determined by throws of dice. [BACK[1] + GAMMON[1].]
back•ground (băk′ground′) *n.* **1.** The ground or scenery located behind something. **2.a.** The part of a pictorial representation that provides relief for the objects in the foreground. **b.** The general scene or surface against which designs, patterns, or figures are represented or viewed. **3.** A position or an area of relative inconspicuousness or unimportance. **4.** The circumstances and events surrounding or leading up to an event or occurrence. **5.** A person's experience, training, and education. **6.** Subdued music played esp. as an accompaniment to dialogue. **7.** Sound or radiation present at a low level at a specific location. —**back′ground′** *v.*
back•hand (băk′hănd′) *n.* **1.** *Sports.* A stroke or motion made with the back of the hand facing outward and the arm moving forward. **2.** Handwriting characterized by letters that slant to the left. —*adj.* Backhanded. —*adv.* With a backhanded stroke or motion. —*tr.v.* **-hand•ed, -hand•ing, -hands.** *Sports.* To perform, catch, or hit with a backhand.
back•hand•ed (băk′hăn′dĭd) *adj.* **1.** *Sports.* Made with or using a backhand. **2.** Oblique or roundabout. —**back′hand′ed•ly** *adv.* —**back′hand′ed•ness** *n.*
back•hoe (băk′hō′) *n.* An excavator whose bucket is attached to a hinged pole on a boom and drawn backward to the machine when in operation. —**back′hoe′** *v.*
back•ing (băk′ĭng) *n.* **1.** Something forming a back: *the backing of a carpet.* **2.a.** Support or aid: *financial backing.* **b.** Approval or endorsement.

backgammon
Detail of a late 15th-century Austrian illuminated page from *Der Renner* by Hugo von Trimberg

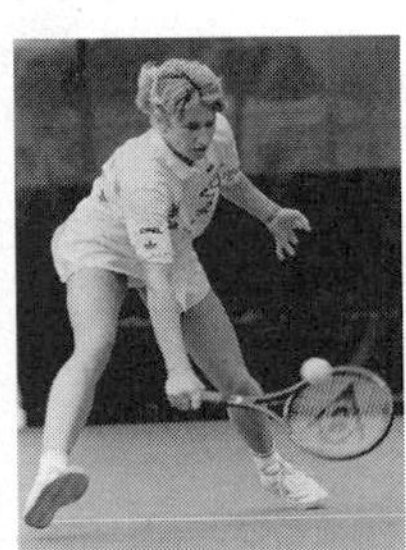
backhand
German tennis player Steffi Graf

backsaw

back•lash (băk′lăsh′) *n.* **1.** A sudden or violent backward whipping motion. **2.** An antagonistic reaction to an earlier action. **3.** A snarl formed in the part of a fishing line that is wound around the reel. **4.** The play resulting from loose connections between gears or other mechanical elements. —**back′lash′** *v.*
back•light (băk′līt′) *n.* A type of spotlight, used in photography, that illuminates a subject from behind. —*tr.v.* **-light•ed** or **-lit** (-lĭt′), **-light•ing, -lights.** To illuminate from behind.
back•list (băk′lĭst′) *n.* A publisher's list of older titles kept in print. —**back′list′** *v.*
back•log (băk′lŏg′, -lôg′) *n.* **1.** A reserve supply or source. **2.** An accumulation, esp. of unfinished work or unfilled orders. **3.** A large log at the back of a fire in a fireplace. —*v.* **-logged, -log•ging, -logs.** —*tr.* To acquire (something) as a backlog. —*intr.* To become a backlog.
back matter *n.* Material, such as an index or appendix, that follows the main body of a book.
back mutation *n.* A reversal process whereby a gene that has undergone mutation returns to its previous state.
back•pack (băk′păk′) *n.* **1.** A knapsack, often mounted on a lightweight frame, that is worn on a person's back, as to carry camping supplies. **2.** A piece of equipment designed to be used while being carried on the back. —*v.* **-packed, -pack•ing, -packs.** —*intr.* To hike while carrying a backpack. —*tr.* To carry in a backpack. —**back′pack′er** *n.* —**back′pack′ing** *n.*
back•ped•al (băk′pĕd′l) *v.* **-aled, -al•ing, -als** or **-alled, -al•ling, -als.** —*intr.* **1.** *Sports.* To move backward, esp. in boxing or football. **2.** To retreat or withdraw from a previous stand. —*tr.* To pedal (a bicycle, for example) backward in order to brake it.
back•rest (băk′rĕst′) *n.* A rest or support for the back.
Back River. A river of central Northwest Terrs., Canada, flowing c. 965 km (600 mi) to an inlet S of Boothia Peninsula.
back•room or **back room** (băk′ro͞om′, -ro͝om′) —*n.* **1.** A room located at the rear. **2.** The meeting place used by an inconspicuous controlling group. —*adj.* **1.** Of, relating to, or taking place in a backroom. **2.** Marked by inconspicuous control and maneuvering: *backroom politics.*
back•rush (băk′rŭsh′) *n.* The seaward return of water after the landward motion of a wave.
back•saw (băk′sô′) *n.* A saw that is reinforced by a metal band along its back edge.
back•scat•ter (băk′skăt′ər) *n.* The deflection of waves or particles by electromagnetic or nuclear forces through angles greater than 90° to the initial direction of travel. —**back′scat′ter** *v.*
back seat *n.* **1.** A seat in the back, esp. of a vehicle. **2.** A subordinate position, as in a group or hierarchy.
back-seat driver (băk′sēt′) *n.* **1.** A passenger who gives unsolicited advice to the driver of a motor vehicle. **2.** A person who persists in giving unsolicited advice.
back•set (băk′sĕt′) *n.* **1.** A setback or reversal. **2.** An eddy or countercurrent in water.
back•shore (băk′shôr′, -shōr′) *n.* The part of a shore between the foreshore and the landward edge that is above high water except in the most severe storms.
back•side (băk′sīd′) *n. Informal.* The buttocks; the rump.
back•slap (băk′slăp′) *v.* **-slapped, -slap•ping, -slaps.** —*intr.* To demonstrate effusive goodwill. —*tr.* To demonstrate effusive goodwill toward (another). —**back′slap′per** *n.*
back•slide (băk′slīd′) *intr.v.* **-slid** (-slĭd′), **-slid•ing, -slides.** To revert to sin or wrongdoing. —**back′slid′er** *n.*
back•space (băk′spās′) *v.* **-spaced, -spac•ing, -spac•es.** —*intr.* To move the carriage of a typewriter or the cursor of a computer back one or more spaces by striking the key used for this purpose. —*n.* The backspacing key.
back•spin (băk′spĭn′) *n.* A spin that tends to retard, arrest, or reverse the linear motion of an object, esp. of a ball.
back•stab (băk′stăb′) *v.* **-stabbed, -stab•bing, -stabs.** —*tr.* To attack (someone) unfairly, esp. in an underhand, deceitful manner. —**back′stab′ber** *n.*
back•stage (băk′stāj′) *adv.* **1.** In or toward the area behind the performing space in a theater, esp. the dressing rooms. **2.** In secret; privately. —*adj.* (băk′stāj′). **1.** Of, relating to, occurring in, or situated behind the performing area of a theater. **2.** Concealed from the public; private.
back•stairs (băk′stârz′) also **back•stair** (-stâr′) *adj.* Furtively carried on; clandestine: *backstairs gossip.*
back•stay (băk′stā′) *n.* **1.** *Naut.* A stay extending from the top of a mast aft to a ship's side or stern to help support the mast. **2.** A supporting device at or for the back of something else.
back•stitch (băk′stĭch′) *n.* A stitch made by inserting the needle at the midpoint of a preceding stitch so that the stitches overlap by half lengths. —**back′stitch′** *v.*
back•stop (băk′stŏp′) *n. Sports.* A screen or fence used to prevent a ball from going far out of a playing area. —*tr.v.* **-stopped, -stop•ping, -stops.** To serve as a backstop for.
back•stretch (băk′strĕch′) *n. Sports.* The part of an oval racecourse opposite the homestretch.
back•stroke (băk′strōk′) *n.* **1.** *Sports.* A swimming stroke ex-

ecuted with the swimmer lying on the back. **2.** A backhanded stroke or motion. — **backʹstrokeʹ** *v.* — **backʹstrokʹer** *n.*

back•swept (băkʹswĕptʹ) *adj.* Swept, angled, or slanting backward: *a backswept hairstyle.*

back•swim•mer (băkʹswĭmʹər) *n.* Any of various aquatic bugs of the family Notonectidae that swim on their backs by means of broadened, oarlike hind legs.

back•sword (băkʹsôrdʹ, -sōrdʹ) *n.* **1.** A sword with only one cutting edge. **2.** A one-handed fencing stick; a singlestick.

back talk *n.* Insolent or impudent retorts.

back-to-back (băkʹtə-băkʹ) *adj.* Consecutive.

back•track (băkʹtrăkʹ) *intr.v.* **-tracked, -track•ing, -tracks. 1.** To go back over the course by which one has come. **2.** To reverse one's position or policy.

back•up (băkʹŭpʹ) *n.* **1.a.** A reserve or substitute. **b.** *Comp. Sci.* A copy of a program or file stored separately from the original. **2.a.** Support or backing. **b.** *Mus.* A background accompaniment. **3.** An overflow or accumulation caused by clogging or by a stoppage. — *adj.* Extra; standby.

back•ward (băkʹwərd) *adj.* **1.** Directed or facing toward the back or rear. **2.** Done or arranged so as to be opposite to previous occurrence or normal use. **3.** Unwilling to act; reluctant; shy. **4.** Behind in progress or development: *backward technology.* — *adv.* or **back•wards** (-wərdz). **1.** To or toward the back or rear. **2.** With the back leading. **3.** In a reverse manner or order. **4.** To, toward, or into the past. **5.** Toward a worse or less advanced condition. — ***idiom.*** **bend (or lean) over backward.** To make an effort greater than is required. — **backʹward•ly** *adv.* — **backʹward•ness** *n.*

Usage Note: The adverb forms *backward* and *backwards* are interchangeable: *stepped backward; a mirror facing backwards.* Only *backward* is an adjective: *a backward view.*

back•wash (băkʹwŏshʹ, -wôshʹ) *n.* **1.a.** A backward flow of water, as from oars. **b.** See **backrush. 2.** A backward flow of air, as from an aircraft propeller. **3.** A result of an event.

back•wa•ter (băkʹwôʹtər, -wŏtʹər) *n.* **1.** Water held or pushed back, as by a dam or current. **2.** A place or situation regarded as isolated, stagnant, or backward.

back•woods (băkʹwŏŏdzʹ) *pl.n.* *(used with a sing. or pl. v.)* **1.** Heavily wooded, uncultivated, thinly settled areas. **2.** An area that is far from population centers or that is held to be culturally backward.

back yard also **back•yard** (băkʹyärdʹ) *n.* A yard at the rear of a house.

Ba•co•lod (bä-kōʹlôdʹ). A city of NW Negros I. in the S-central Philippines. Pop. 262,415.

ba•con (bāʹkən) *n.* The salted and smoked meat from the back and sides of a pig. [ME < OFr., of Gmc. orig.]

Ba•con (bāʹkən), **Francis[1].** 1st Baron Verulam and Viscount Saint Albans. 1561–1626. English philosopher and essayist who proposed a theory of scientific knowledge based on observation and experiment that came to be known as the inductive method. — **Ba•coʹni•an** (bā-kōʹnē-ən) *adj. & n.*

Bacon, Francis[2]. 1909–1992. Irish-born British painter whose works are often invested with feelings of terror.

Bacon, Nathaniel. 1647–76. English-born Amer. colonist in Virginia who led Bacon's Rebellion (1676).

Bacon, Roger. "the Admirable Doctor." 1214?–92. English scientist and philosopher who wrote *Opus Majus* (1267).

bact. *abbr.* Bacteria; bacterial.

bac•te•re•mi•a (băkʹtə-rēʹmē-ə) *n.* The presence of bacteria in the blood. — **bacʹte•reʹmic** (-mĭk) *adj.* — **bacʹte•reʹmi•cal•ly** *adv.*

bac•te•ri•a (băk-tîrʹē-ə) *n.* Pl. of **bacterium.**

bac•te•ri•al (băk-tîrʹē-əl) *adj.* Relating to or caused by bacteria. — **bac•teʹri•al** *n.* — **bac•teʹri•al•ly** *adv.*

bac•te•ri•cide (băk-tîrʹĭ-sīdʹ) *n.* An agent that destroys bacteria. — **bac•teʹri•cidʹal** (-sīdʹl) *adj.*

bacterio– or **bacteri–** or **bacter–** *pref.* Bacteria; bacterial: *bacteriology.* [< NLat. *bacterium,* bacterium. See BACTERIUM.]

bac•te•ri•ol•o•gy (băk-tîrʹē-ŏlʹə-jē) *n.* The study of bacteria, esp. in relation to medicine and agriculture. — **bac•teʹri•o•logʹic** (-ə-lŏjʹĭk), **bac•teʹri•o•logʹi•cal** *adj.* — **bac•teʹri•o•logʹi•cal•ly** *adv.* — **bac•teʹri•olʹo•gist** *n.*

bac•te•ri•ol•y•sis (băk-tîrʹē-ŏlʹĭ-sĭs) *n., pl.* **-ses** (-sēzʹ). Dissolution or destruction of bacteria. — **bac•teʹri•o•lytʹic** (-ə-lĭtʹĭk) *adj.*

bac•te•ri•o•phage (băk-tîrʹē-ə-fājʹ) *n.* A virus that infects and lyses certain bacteria. — **bac•teʹri•o•phagʹic** (-fājʹĭk) *adj.* — **bac•teʹri•ophʹa•gy** (-ŏfʹə-jē) *n.*

bac•te•ri•o•sta•sis (băk-tîrʹē-ō-stāʹsĭs) *n., pl.* **-ses** (-sēz). The inhibition of growth, but not the killing, of bacteria.

bac•te•ri•o•stat (băk-tîrʹē-ə-stătʹ) *n.* An agent, such as a chemical or biological material, that inhibits bacterial growth. — **bac•teʹri•o•statʹic** *adj.*

bac•te•ri•um (băk-tîrʹē-əm) *n., pl.* **-te•ri•a** (-tîrʹē-ə). Any of the one-celled prokaryotic microorganisms of the class Schizomycetes, which vary in morphology and nutritional requirements and may be free-living, saprophytic, or pathogenic. [NLat. < Gk. *baktērion,* dim. of *baktron,* rod. See **bak-*.**]

bac•te•ri•u•ri•a (băk-tîrʹē-yŏŏrʹē-ə) *n.* The presence of bacteria in urine.

bac•te•rize (băkʹtə-rīzʹ) *tr.v.* **-rized, -riz•ing, -riz•es.** To change the composition of (something) by means of bacterial action. — **bacʹte•ri•zaʹtion** (-rĭ-zāʹshən) *n.*

bac•te•roid (băkʹtə-roidʹ) *adj.* Resembling bacteria in appearance or action. — *n.* Any of various structurally modified bacteria, such as those occurring on the root nodules of leguminous plants.

Bac•tra (băkʹtrə). See **Balkh.**

Bac•tri•a (băkʹtrē-ə). An ancient country of SW Asia; destroyed c. 130 B.C. by nomadic tribes. — **Bacʹtri•an** *adj. & n.*

Bactrian camel *n.* A two-humped camel *(Camelus bactrianus)* native to central and southwest Asia.

bac•u•li•form (băkʹyə-lə-fôrmʹ, bə-kyōōʹlə-) *adj.* Rod-shaped. [Lat. *baculum,* stick; see **bak-*** + -FORM.]

bad[1] (băd) *adj.* **worse** (wûrs), **worst** (wûrst). **1.** Not achieving an adequate standard; poor. **2.** Evil; sinful. **3.** Disobedient or naughty. **4.** Disagreeable, unpleasant, or disturbing: *bad news.* **5.** Unfavorable: *bad reviews.* **6.** Not fresh; rotten or spoiled. **7.** Injurious in effect; detrimental: *bad habits.* **8.** Not working properly; defective. **9.** Full of or exhibiting faults or errors: *bad grammar.* **10.** Having no validity; void: *bad checks.* **11.** Severe; intense: *a bad cold.* **12.a.** Being in poor health or in pain: *I feel bad today.* **b.** Being in poor condition; diseased: *bad lungs.* **13.** Sorry; regretful: *She feels bad about it.* **14. bad•der, bad•dest.** *Slang.* Very good; great. — *n.* Something that is below standard or expectations. — *adv. Usage Problem.* Badly. — ***idioms.*** **in bad.** *Informal.* In trouble or disfavor. **not half (or so) bad.** *Informal.* Reasonably good. [ME *badde.*] — **badʹness** *n.*

Syns: *bad, evil, wicked.* These adjectives mean departing from moral or ethical standards. *Bad,* the most inclusive, applies to what is regarded as being unpleasant, offensive, or blameworthy: *"A bad book is as much of a labor to write as a good one"* (Aldous Huxley). *Evil* has connotations of depravity and corruption: *"The unconscious is not just evil by nature, it is also the source of the highest good"* (Carl Jung). *Wicked* suggests conscious moral transgression: *"this wicked man Hitler, the repository and embodiment of many forms of soul-destroying hatred, this monstrous product of former wrongs and shame"* (Winston S. Churchill).

Usage Note: *Bad* is often used as an adverb in sentences such as *We need water bad.* This usage is common in informal speech but is widely regarded as unacceptable in formal writing. In an earlier survey the sentence *His tooth ached so bad he could not sleep* was unacceptable to 92 percent of the Usage Panel. • The adverb *badly* is often used as the complement of verbs such as *feel,* as in *I felt badly about the whole affair,* where the choice of *badly* as opposed to *bad* may convey an implication that the distress is emotional, rather than physical. This usage is now widespread and is supported by analogy to the use of other adverbs with *feel* (as in *We feel strongly about this issue*). In an earlier survey a majority of the Usage Panel accepted this use of *badly* in speech, though *bad* is less likely to occasion objections.

bad[2] (băd) *v. Archaic.* A p.t. of **bid.**

Ba•da•joz (bäʹdə-hōzʹ, *-thä-*hôthʹ). A city of SW Spain on the Guadiana R. near the Portugal border. Pop. 92,800.

Ba•da•lo•na (bäʹdə-lōʹnə, *-thä-*lôʹnä). A city of NE Spain, a suburb of Barcelona. Pop. 229,281.

bad•ass (bădʹăsʹ) *Vulgar Slang.* — *n.* A mean-tempered or belligerent person. — *adj.* Mean; belligerent.

bad blood *n.* Enmity or bitterness.

bade (băd, bād) *v.* A p.t. of **bid.**

Ba•den (bädʹn). A historical region of SW Germany.

Ba•den-Ba•den (bädʹn-bädʹn). A city of SW Germany in the Black Forest near the French border; founded as a Roman garrison in the 3rd cent. A.D. Pop. 48,622.

Ba•den-Pow•ell (bādʹn-pōʹəl), Sir **Robert Stephenson Smyth.** 1857–1941. British soldier who founded the Boy Scouts (1908) and with his sister **Agnes** (1858–1945) the Girl Guides (1910).

badge (băj) *n.* **1.a.** A device or emblem worn as an insignia of rank, office, or membership in an organization. **b.** An emblem given as an award or honor. **2.** A characteristic mark. [ME *bagge* < Norman Fr. *bage.*] — **badge** *v.*

badg•er (băjʹər) *n.* **1.** Any of several carnivorous burrowing mammals of the family Mustelidae, such as *Taxidea taxus* of North America, having short legs and long claws on the front feet. **2.** The fur or hair of this mammal. **3.** Any of several similar mammals, such as the ratel. — *tr.v.* **-ered, -er•ing, -ers.** To harry or pester persistently. See Syns at **harass.** [Perh. < BADGE.]

Bad Hom•burg (bätʹ hŏmʹbûrgʹ, -bŏŏrkʹ). A city of W-central Germany at the foot of the Taunus Mts. near Frankfurt. Pop. 50,647.

bad•i•nage (bădʹn-äzhʹ) *n.* Light, playful banter. [Fr. < *badin,* joker < Prov. *badar,* to gape < Lat. **batāre.*]

bad•lands (bădʹlăndzʹ) *pl.n.* Barren land characterized by roughly eroded ridges, peaks, and mesas.

Bad•lands also **Bad Lands** (bădʹlăndzʹ). A heavily eroded arid region of SW SD and NW NE.

bad•ly (bădʹlē) *adv. Usage Problem.* **1.** In a bad manner.

CLOSTRIDIUM TETANI

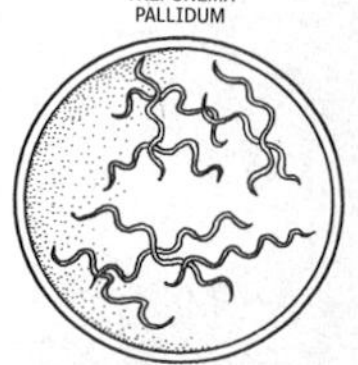

TREPONEMA PALLIDUM

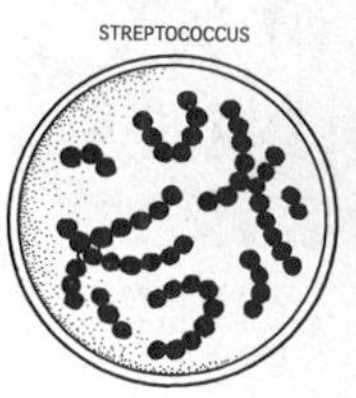

STREPTOCOCCUS

bacterium

Robert Baden-Powell

ă pat	oi boy
ā pay	ou out
âr care	ŏŏ took
ä father	ōō boot
ĕ pet	ŭ cut
ē be	ûr urge
ĭ pit	th thin
ī pie	*th* this
îr pier	hw which
ŏ pot	zh vision
ō toe	ə about, item
ô paw	

Stress marks:
ʹ (primary);
ʹ (secondary), as in
dictionary (dĭkʹshə-nĕrʹē)

Joan Baez
At a 1977 Kent State University rally

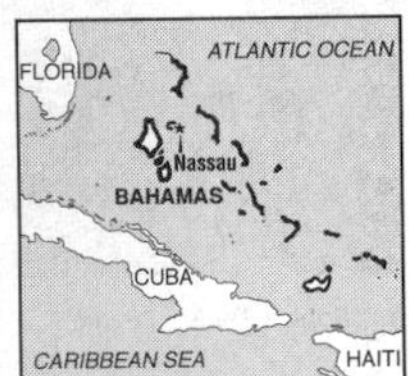

Bahamas

Bahrain

2. Very much; greatly. See Usage Note at **bad**[1].

bad•min•ton (băd′mĭn′tən) *n. Sports.* A sport played by volleying a shuttlecock over a high net by means of a light racket. [After *Badminton,* the Duke of Beaufort's country seat in W England.]

bad•mouth or **bad-mouth** (băd′mouth′, -mouth′) *tr.v.* **-mouthed, -mouth•ing, -mouths.** *Slang.* To criticize or disparage, often spitefully or unfairly; run down.

B.A.E. *abbr.* **1.** Bachelor of Aeronautical Engineering. **2.** Bachelor of Agricultural Engineering. **3.** Bachelor of Architectural Engineering. **4.** Bachelor of Art Education. **5.** Bachelor of Arts in Education.

Bae•da (bē′də). See **Bede.**

bae•de•ker (bā′dĭ-kər) *n.* A guidebook to countries or a country. [After Karl BAEDEKER.]

Bae•de•ker (bā′dĭ-kər), **Karl.** 1801–59. German publisher who originated his series of guidebooks in 1829.

B.A.Ed. *abbr.* Bachelor of Arts in Education.

B.Ae.E. *abbr.* Bachelor of Aeronautical Engineering.

Ba•ez (bī-ĕz′, bī′ĕz′), **Joan.** b. 1941. Amer. folk singer and political activist.

Baf•fin (băf′ĭn). A region of NE Northwest Terrs., Canada.

Baffin, William. 1584?–1622. English explorer who led expeditions (1612–16) in search of the Northwest Passage.

Baffin Bay. An ice-clogged body of water between NE Canada and Greenland connecting the Arctic Ocean with the Atlantic.

Baffin Island. An island of NE Northwest Terrs., Canada, W of Greenland.

baf•fle (băf′əl) *tr.v.* **-fled, -fling, -fles. 1.** To frustrate or check (a person) by confusing or perplexing; stymie. **2.** To impede the force or movement of. —*n.* **1.** A usu. static device that regulates the flow of a fluid or light. **2.** A partition that prevents interference between sound waves in a loudspeaker. [Perh. blend of Sc.Gael. *bauchle,* to denounce, revile publicly, and Fr. *bafouer,* to ridicule.] —**baf′fle•ment** *n.* —**baf′fler** *n.*

bag (băg) *n.* **1.a.** A container of flexible material that is used for carrying or storing items. **b.** A handbag; a purse. **c.** A piece of hand luggage. **d.** An organic sac or pouch, such as an udder. **2.** An object that resembles a pouch. **3.** The amount that a bag can hold. **4.** An amount of game taken or legally permitted to be taken. **5.** *Baseball.* A base. **6.** *Slang.* An area of interest or skill. **7.** *Slang.* A woman considered ugly or unkempt. —*v.* **bagged, bag•ging, bags.** —*tr.* **1.** To put into a bag. **2.** To cause to bulge like a pouch. **3.** To capture or kill (game). —*intr.* **1.** To hang loosely. **2.** To swell out; bulge. —***idiom.* in the bag.** Assured of a successful outcome; virtually accomplished or won. [ME *bagge* < ON *baggi.*] —**bag′ful** *n.* —**bag′ger** *n.*

bag and baggage *adv.* **1.** With all one's belongings. **2.** To a complete degree; entirely.

ba•gasse (bə-găs′) *n.* The dry fibrous residue remaining after the extraction of juice from sugar cane, used as a source of cellulose. [Fr. < Sp. *bagazo,* dregs < Lat. *bāca,* berry.]

bag•a•telle (băg′ə-tĕl′) *n.* **1.** An insignificant thing. **2.** A short piece of verse or music. **3.** *Games.* A game played on an oblong table with a cue and balls. [Fr. < Ital. *bagatella,* dim. of dialectal *bagata,* little property, poss. < Lat. *bāca,* berry.]

Bage•hot (băj′ət), **Walter.** 1826–77. British economist and social scientist who wrote *The English Constitution* (1867).

ba•gel (bā′gəl) *n.* A glazed ring-shaped roll with a chewy texture, made from dough that is dropped into nearly boiling water and then baked. [Yiddish *beygl* < MHGer. **bögel,* dim. of *bouc,* ring < OHGer. *boug.* See **bheug-*.**]

bag•gage (băg′ĭj) *n.* **1.** The trunks, bags, and parcels of a traveler; luggage. **2.** The movable equipment and supplies of an army. **3.** Superfluous or burdensome practices, regulations, ideas, or traits. **4.a.** A wanton or immoral woman. **b.** An impudent or saucy girl or woman. [ME *bagage* < OFr. *bague,* bundle, perh. of Gmc. orig.]

bag•ging (băg′ĭng) *n.* Material used for making bags.

bag•gy (băg′ē) *adj.* **-gi•er, -gi•est.** Bulging or hanging loosely: *baggy trousers.* —**bag′gi•ly** *adv.* —**bag′gi•ness** *n.*

Bagh•dad or **Bag•dad** (băg′dăd′). The cap. of Iraq, in the central part on the Tigris R.; founded in the 8th cent. Pop., 2,200,000.

bag lady *n. Slang.* A homeless woman, esp. one in a big city, who carries her possessions in a shopping bag.

bag•man (băg′mən) *n.* **1.** *Slang.* A person who collects money, as for racketeers. **2.** *Chiefly British.* A traveling salesman.

ba•gnio (băn′yō, bän′-) *n., pl.* **-gnios. 1.** A brothel. **2.** *Obsolete.* A prison for slaves in Asian countries. **3.** *Obsolete.* A public bathhouse in Italy or Turkey. [Ital. *bagno,* bath < Lat. *balneum* < Gk. *balaneion.*]

bag of waters *n.* See **water bag.**

bag•pipe (băg′pīp′) *n. Mus.* An instrument having a flexible bag inflated either by a tube with valves or by bellows, a double-reed melody pipe, and from one to four drone pipes. Often used in the plural. —**bag′pipe′** *v.* —**bag′pip′er** *n.*

ba•guette (bă-gĕt′) *n.* **1.a.** A gem cut in the form of a narrow rectangle. **b.** The form of such a gem. **2.** *Archit.* A narrow, convex molding. **3.** A small narrow loaf of French bread. [Fr., rod < Ital. *bacchetta,* dim. of *bacchio,* rod < Lat. *baculum,* stick. See **bak-*.**]

Ba•gui•o (bä′gē-ō′). A city of NW Luzon, Philippines; summer cap. of the country. Pop. 119,009.

bag•wig (băg′wĭg′) *n.* A wig with the back hair encased in a small silk sack, worn in the 18th century.

bag•worm (băg′wûrm′) *n.* Any of several moths of the family Psychidae that construct fibrous cases of silk in which the plant-feeding larvae and wingless adult females live.

bah (bä, bă) *interj.* Used to express rejection or contempt.

Ba•ha'i (bä-hä′ē, bə-hī′) *adj.* Of or relating to a religion founded in 1863 in Iran and emphasizing the spiritual unity of all humankind. —*n.* A teacher of or a believer in this faith. [Pers. *bahā'ī,* a follower of *Bahā'ullāh* (see BAHAULLAH), "the Splendor of God" < *bahā',* splendor < Ar.] —**Ba•ha′ism** (bə-hä′ĭz′əm, -hī′-) *n.* —**Ba•ha′ist** *n.*

Ba•ha•mas (bə-hä′məz, -hā′-) also **Ba•ha•ma Islands** (-mə). An island country in the Atlantic E of FL; gained independence from Great Britain in 1973. Cap. Nassau. Pop. 218,000. —**Ba•ha′mi•an** (-hā′mē-ən, -hä′-), **Ba•ha′man** (-hä′mən, -hā′-) *adj. & n.*

Ba•ha•sa Indonesia (bä-hä′sə) *n.* See **Indonesian** 4. [Indonesian, Indonesian language < Skt. *bhāṣā,* speech, language.]

Bahasa Ma•lay (mə-lā′, mā′lā) also **Bahasa Me•la•yo** (mə-lä′yo͞o) *n.* See **Malay** 2. [Malay, Malay language < Skt. *bhāṣā,* speech, language.]

Ba•ha•ul•lah (bä-hä′o͞o-lä′). 1817–92. Persian religious leader who founded the Baha'i sect (1863).

Ba•ha•wal•pur (bə-hä′wəl-po͝or′, -hä′wəl-po͝or′). A region and former princely state of E-central Pakistan between the Sutlej R. and the Indian border.

Ba•hi•a (bə-hē′ə, bä-ē′ə). See **Salvador.** —**Ba•hi′an** *adj. & n.*

Ba•hí•a Blan•ca (bə-hē′ə blăng′kə, bä-ē′ä vläng′kä). A city of E Argentina on the **Bahía Blanca,** an inlet of the Atlantic SW of Buenos Aires. Pop. 223,818.

Ba•hi•a grass (bə-hē′ə) *n.* A perennial tropical American grass *(Paspalum notatum)* grown in warm regions for forage, soil binding, and turf. [After *Bahia* (Salvador), Brazil.]

Bah•rain or **Bah•rein** (bä-rān′). A country comprising an archipelago of low sandy islands in the Persian Gulf between Qatar and Saudi Arabia; gained independence from Great Britain in 1971. Cap. Manama, on **Bahrain Island.** Pop. 350,798. —**Bah•rain′i** *adj. & n.*

Bahr el Gha•zal (bär′ ĕl′ gə-zăl′, bär′ ĕl′ gä-zĭl′). A river of SW Sudan flowing c. 805 km (500 mi) to Lake No.

Bahr el Jeb•el (jĕb′əl). A river, c. 956 km (594 mi), of S Sudan, a section of the White Nile.

baht (bät) *n., pl.* **bahts** or **baht.** See table at **currency.** [Thai *bāt.*]

bai•gnet (bĕn-yā′) *n. Southern Louisiana.* Var. of **beignet.**

Bai•kal or **Bay•kal** (bī-kôl′, -kŏl′), **Lake.** A lake of S-central Russia, with a maximum depth of 1,742.2 m (5,712 ft).

bail[1] (bāl) *n.* **1.** Security, usu. a sum of money, exchanged for the release of an arrested person as a guarantee of that person's appearance for trial. **2.** Release from imprisonment provided by the payment of such money. **3.** A person who provides this security. —*tr.v.* **bailed, bail•ing, bails. 1.** To secure the release of by providing security. **2.** To release (a person) for whom security has been paid. **3.** *Informal.* To extricate from a difficult situation: *bailed me out.* **4.** To transfer (property) to another for a special purpose but without permanent transference of ownership. [ME, custody < OFr. < *baillier,* to take charge of < Lat. *bāiulāre,* to carry a load < *bāiulus,* carrier of a burden.] —**bail′er** *n.*

bail[2] (bāl) *v.* **bailed, bail•ing, bails.** —*tr.* **1.** To remove (water) from a boat with a container. **2.** To empty (a boat) of water by bailing. —*intr.* To empty a boat of water by bailing. —*n.* A container used for bailing. —***phrasal verb.* bail out. 1.** To parachute from an aircraft; eject. **2.** To abandon a project. [< ME *baille,* bucket < OFr. < VLat. **bāiulā,* water container < Lat. *bāiulāre,* to carry a load.] —**bail′er** *n.*

bail[3] (bāl) *n.* **1.** The arched hooplike handle of a container, such as a pail. **2.** An arch or hoop, such as one of those used to support the top of a covered wagon. **3.** A hinged bar on a typewriter that holds the paper against the platen. [ME *beil,* perh. < OE **bēgel*or of Scand. orig.; see **bheug-*.**]

bail[4] (bāl) *n.* **1.** *Chiefly British.* A pole or bar used to confine or separate animals. **2.** *Sports.* One of the two crossbars that form the top of a wicket used in the game of cricket. [OFr. dial., prob. < Lat. *baculum,* stick. See BACILLUS.]

bail•a•ble (bā′lə-bəl) *adj.* **1.** Eligible for bail: *a bailable defendant.* **2.** Allowing or admitting of bail: *a bailable offense.*

bail•ee (bā-lē′) *n.* A person to whom property is bailed.

bai•ley (bā′lē) *n.* **-leys. 1.** The outer wall of a castle. **2.** The space enclosed by this outer wall. [ME *bailli* < OFr. *baille,* prob. < Lat. *bacula,* pl. of *baculum,* log, stick. See BACILLUS.]

Bai•ley (bā′lē), **Nathan** or **Nathaniel.** d. 1742. British lexicographer who compiled the *Universal Etymological English Dictionary* (1721).

Bailey bridge *n.* A steel bridge designed to be shipped in parts and assembled rapidly. [After Sir Donald *Bailey* (1901–85), British engineer.]

bail•ie (bā′lē) *n.* **1.** A Scottish municipal officer similar to an English alderman. **2.** *Obsolete.* A bailiff. [ME *baillie*, town official < OFr. *bailiff* < Med.Lat. **bāiulīvus.* See BAILIFF.]

bail•iff (bā′lĭf) *n.* **1.** A court attendant entrusted with duties such as the maintenance of order in court. **2.** An official who assists a British sheriff, able to execute writs, processes, and arrests. **3.** *Chiefly British.* An overseer of an estate; a steward. [ME *baillif* < OFr. *baillis, baillif-*, overseer of an estate, steward < Med.Lat. **bāiulīvus* < Lat. *bāiulus*, carrier.]

bail•i•wick (bā′lə-wĭk′) *n.* **1.** A person's specific area of interest, skill, or authority. **2.** The office or district of a bailiff. [ME *bailliwik*: *baillif*, bailiff; see BAILIFF + *wik*, town (< OE *wīc* < Lat. *vīcus*; see VICINITY).]

bail•ment (bāl′mənt) *n.* **1.** The process of providing bail for an accused person. **2.** The act of delivering goods or personal property to another in trust.

bail•or (bā′lər, bā-lôr′) *n.* One who bails property to another.

bail•out (bāl′out′) *n.* A rescue from financial difficulties.

bails•man (bālz′mən) *n.* One who provides bail or security.

Baird (bârd), **John Logie.** 1888–1946. British electrical engineer and pioneer in the development of television.

Bai•ri•ki (bī-rē′kē). The administrative center of Kiribati, on Tarawa atoll in the N Gilbert Is. of the W-central Pacific Ocean. Pop. 1,956.

bairn (bârn) *n. Scots.* A child. [ME *barn* < OE *bearn.* See **bher-¹*.**]

bait¹ (bāt) *n.* **1.a.** Food or other lure placed on a hook or in a trap and used in the taking of fish, birds, or other animals. **b.** Something, such as a worm, used for this purpose. **2.** An enticement; a temptation. **3.** *Archaic.* A stop for food or rest during a trip. —*v.* **bait•ed, bait•ing, baits.** —*tr.* **1.** To place a lure in (a trap) or on (a fishing hook). **2.** To entice, esp. by trickery or strategy. **3.** To set dogs upon (a chained animal, for example) for sport. **4.** To attack or torment, esp. with insults or ridicule. **5.** To tease. See Syns at **harass. 6.** To feed (an animal), esp. on a journey. —*intr. Archaic.* To stop for food or rest during a trip. [ME < ON *beita*, food, fodder, fish bait. V. < ON *beita*, to put animals to pasture, hunt with dogs. See **bheid-*.**] —**bait′er** *n.*

bait² (bāt) *v.* Var. of **bate².**

bait and switch *n.* A sales tactic in which a bargain-priced item is used to attract customers who are then encouraged to purchase a more expensive similar item.

bait•fish (bāt′fĭsh′) *n. Chiefly Chesapeake Bay & North Atlantic Coast.* A small fish used for fishing bait.

bai•za (bī′zä) *n.* See table at **currency.** [Ar. < Hindi *paisā.*]

baize (bāz) *n.* An often bright-green cotton or woolen material used chiefly as a cover for gaming tables. [Fr. *baies* < pl. of *bai*, bay-colored < Lat. *badius.*]

Ba•ja Cal•i•for•nia (bä′hä kăl′ĭ-fôr′nyə, -fôr′nē-ə) also **Low•er California** (lō′ər). A mountainous peninsula of W Mexico extending SSE between the Pacific Ocean and the Gulf of California S of the U.S. border.

Ba•jer (bī′ər), **Fredrik.** 1837–1922. Danish pacifist who shared the 1908 Nobel Peace Prize.

bake (bāk) *v.* **baked, bak•ing, bakes.** —*tr.* **1.** To cook (food) with dry heat, esp. in an oven. **2.** To harden or dry (something) by subjecting to heat. —*intr.* **1.** To bake food. **2.** To become hardened or dry by baking. —*n.* **1.a.** The act or process of baking. **b.** An amount baked. **2.** A social gathering at which food is baked and served. [ME *baken* < OE *bacan.*]

bak•er (bā′kər) *n.* **1.** One that bakes bread, cakes, or pastries. **2.** A portable oven.

Ba•ker (bākər), **Ella.** 1903–1986. Amer. social reformer during the civil rights movement of the 1950's and 1960's.

Baker, Josephine. 1906–75. Amer.-born French entertainer who became a popular jazz dancer and singer in Paris during the 1920's and 1930's.

Baker, Mount. A peak, 3,287.3 m (10,778 ft), of NW WA in the Cascade Range E of Bellingham.

Baker, Russell Wayne. b. 1925. Amer. writer and columnist noted for his autobiography *Growing Up* (1982).

Baker, Sir **Samuel White.** 1821–93. British explorer who was the first European to sight Lake Albert (1864).

Baker Lake. A lake of E Northwest Terrs., Canada.

bak•er's dozen (bā′kərz) *n.* A group of 13. [From the custom of adding an extra roll so that 12 would not weigh light.]

Ba•kers•field (bā′kərz-fēld′). A city of S-central CA at the S end of the San Joaquin Valley NNW of Los Angeles. Pop. 105,611.

bak•er•sheet (bā′kər-shēt′) *n. Maine.* See **drip pan.**

bak•er•y (bā′kə-rē) *n., pl.* **-ies.** A place where products such as bread, cake, and pastries are baked or sold.

bake•shop (bāk′shŏp′) *n.* See **bakery.**

Bakh•ta•ran (băk′tə-rän′, bäKH′tä-). A city of W Iran WSW of Tehran; founded in the 4th cent. A.D. Pop. 532,000.

bak•ing powder (bā′kĭng) *n.* A mixture of baking soda, starch, and an acidic compound such as cream of tartar that acts as a leavening agent when mixed with a liquid.

baking soda *n.* A white crystalline compound, $NaHCO_3$, with a slightly alkaline taste, used in effervescent salts and beverages, in fire extinguishers, and as an antacid.

ba•kla•va (bä′klə-vä′, bä′klə-vä′) *n.* A dessert made of paper-thin layers of pastry, chopped nuts, and honey. [Turk.]

bak•sheesh (băk′shēsh′, băk-shēsh′) *n., pl.* **baksheesh.** A gratuity or tip, esp. in some Near Eastern countries. [Pers. *bakhshish*, present < MPers. *bakhshishn* < *bakhshīdan, bakhsh-*, to give presents < Avestan *bakhsh-*. See **bhag-*.**]

Bakst (bäkst), **Léon Nikolaevich.** 1866–1924. Russian painter and scenic designer who modernized theater design.

Ba•ku (bä-ko͞o′). The cap. of Azerbaijan in the E on the Caspian Sea; acquired by Russia in 1806. Pop. 1,104,000.

Ba•ku•nin (bə-ko͞o′nĭn, -nyĭn), **Mikhail Aleksandrovich.** 1814–76. Russian anarchist and political theorist.

bal•a•cla•va (băl′ə-klä′və) *n.* A woolen hood covering most of the head and neck, worn in cold climates. [After BALAKLAVA.]

Ba•la•ki•rev (bə-lä′kĭ-rəf), **Mili Alekseevich.** 1837–1910. Russian composer whose works include the symphonic poems *Tamara* and *Russia.*

Bal•a•kla•va also **Bal•a•cla•va** (băl′ə-klăv′ə, -klä′və). A section of Sevastopol in the Crimea of S Ukraine; site of the charge of the Light Brigade (1854) during the Crimean War.

bal•a•lai•ka (băl′ə-lī′kə) *n. Mus.* A Russian instrument with a triangular body and three strings. [Russ. *balalaĭka*, of Turkic orig.]

balalaika
20th-century Russian

bal•ance (băl′əns) *n.* **1.** A weighing device, esp. one consisting of a rigid beam horizontally suspended at its center, with identical pans hung at either end. **2.** A state of equilibrium or parity. **3.** The power or means to decide. **4.** A state of bodily equilibrium. **5.** A stable mental or psychological state. **6.** A harmonious arrangement of parts or elements, as in a design. See Syns at **proportion. 7.** An influence or force tending to produce equilibrium; counterpoise. **8.** The difference in magnitude between opposing forces or influences. **9.** *Accounting.* **a.** Equality of totals in the debit and credit sides of an account. **b.** The difference between such totals, either on the credit or the debit side. **10.** Something that is left over; a remainder. **11.** *Chem.* Equality of mass and net electric charge of reacting species on each side of an equation. **12.** *Math.* Equality with respect to the net number of reduced symbolic quantities on each side of an equation. **13.** A balance wheel. —*v.* **-anced, -anc•ing, -anc•es.** —*tr.* **1.** To determine the weight of (something) in a weighing device. **2.** To compare by turning over in the mind. **3.** To bring into or maintain in a state of equilibrium. **4.** To act as an equalizing weight or force to; counterbalance. **5.** *Accounting.* **a.** To compute the difference between the debits and credits of (an account). **b.** To reconcile or equalize the sums of the debits and credits of (an account). **c.** To settle by paying what is owed. **6.** To bring into or keep in equal or satisfying proportion or harmony. **7.** *Math.* To bring (an equation) into balance. **8.** *Chem.* To bring (an equation) into balance. **9.** To move toward and then away from (a dance partner). —*intr.* **1.** To be in or come into equilibrium. **2.** To be equal or equivalent. **3.** To sway or waver as if losing or regaining equilibrium. **4.** To balance a dance partner. —***idioms.* in the balance.** In an undetermined and often critical position. **on balance.** Taking everything into consideration; all in all. [ME *balaunce* < OFr. < VLat. **bilancia*, having two scale pans < Lat. *bilanx*: *bi-*, two; see **dwo-*** + *lanx*, scale.]

balance beam

Bal•ance (băl′əns) *n.* See **Libra** 1, 2a.

balance beam *n. Sports.* **1.** A horizontal raised beam used in gymnastic competition for balancing exercises. **2.** A competitive gymnastics event performed on this beam.

balance of payments *n.* A systematic record of a nation's total payments to and receipts from foreign countries.

balance of power *n.* Distribution of power in which no single nation is able to dominate or interfere with others.

balance of trade *n.* The difference in value between the total exports and total imports of a nation during a specific period.

bal•anc•er (băl′ən-sər) *n.* See **halter².**

balance sheet *n.* A dated statement of a business or institution that lists the assets, debts, and owners' investment.

balance wheel *n.* **1.** A wheel that regulates rate of movement in machine parts, as in a watch. **2.** A stabilizing influence.

Bal•an•chine (băl′ən-chēn′, băl′ən-chēn′), **George.** 1904–83. Russian-born Amer. ballet director who choreographed more than 100 ballets, including *Firebird* (1950).

bal•as (băl′əs) *n.* A rose-red to orange spinel used as a semiprecious gem. [ME < OFr. *balais* and < OSp. *balax*; both akin to Med.Lat. *balascus* < Ar. *balakhš* < Pers. *Badakhshān*, a region of NE Afghanistan.]

ba•la•ta (bə-lä′tə) *n.* The nonelastic rubber obtained from the latex of the South American tree *Manilkara bidentata.* [Am. Sp. < Tupi and Galibi.]

Bal•a•ton (băl′ə-tŏn′, bŏl′ŏ-tôn′), **Lake.** A lake of W-central Hungary SW of Budapest.

bal•bo•a (băl-bō′ə) *n.* See table at **currency.** [After Vasco Núñez de BALBOA.]

Bal•bo•a (băl-bō′ə), **Vasco Núñez de.** 1475–1517. Spanish explorer and colonial governor who claimed the Pacific Ocean for Spain (1513).

bal•brig•gan (băl-brĭg′ən) *n.* A knitted, unbleached cotton

ă pat	oi boy
ā pay	ou out
âr care	o͝o took
ä father	o͞o boot
ĕ pet	ŭ cut
ē be	ûr urge
ĭ pit	th thin
ī pie	*th* this
îr pier	hw which
ŏ pot	zh vision
ō toe	ə about,
ô paw	item

Stress marks:
′ (primary);
′ (secondary), as in
dictionary (dĭk′shə-nĕr′ē)

Bal•tic (bôl′tĭk) *adj.* **1.** Of or relating to the Baltic Sea, the Baltic States, or a Baltic-speaking people. **2.** Of or relating to the branch of the Indo-European language family that contains Latvian, Lithuanian, and Old Prussian. — *n.* The Baltic language branch.

Baltic Sea. An arm of the Atlantic in N Europe bounded by Denmark, Sweden, Finland, Russia, Estonia, Latvia, Lithuania, Poland, and Germany.

Baltic States. Estonia, Latvia, and Lithuania.

Bal•ti•more (bôl′tə-môr′, -mōr′). A city of N MD on an arm of Chesapeake Bay NE of Washington DC. Pop. 736,014. — **Bal′ti•mor′e•an** *n.*

Baltimore, Lord. See **Calvert.**

Baltimore oriole *n.* An eastern subspecies of the northern oriole, of which the male is bright orange and black and the female olive brown with white wing bars. [After Lord BALTIMORE.]

Bal•to-Sla•vic (bôl′tō-slä′vĭk, -slăv′ĭk) *n.* A subfamily of the Indo-European language family that consists of the Baltic and Slavic branches. — **Bal′to-Sla′vic** *adj.*

Ba•lu•chi (bə-lo͞o′chē) also **Ba•luch** (-lo͞och′) *n., pl.* **Baluchi** or **-chis** also **Baluch** or **-lu•ches** (-lo͞o′chəz). **1.** A member of a traditionally nomadic Muslim people of Baluchistan. **2.** The Iranian language of the Baluchi.

Ba•lu•chi•stan (bə-lo͞o′chĭ-stăn′). A desert region of W Pakistan bounded by Iran, Afghanistan, and the Arabian Sea.

bal•us•ter (băl′ə-stər) *n.* **1.a.** One of the upright, usu. rounded supports of a balustrade. **b.** An upright support, such as a furniture leg, having a similar shape. **2.** One of the supporting posts of a handrail. [Fr. *balustre* < Ital. *balaustro* < *balaustra,* pomegranate flower (from a resemblance to the post) < Lat. *balaustium* < Gk. *balaustion.*]

balustrade

bal•us•trade (băl′ə-strād′) *n.* A rail and the row of balusters or posts that support it, as along the front of a gallery. [Fr. < Ital. *balaustrata* < *balaustro,* baluster. See BALUSTER.]

Bal•zac (bôl′zăk′, băl′-, bäl-zäk′), **Honoré de.** 1799–1850. French writer who portrayed the panorama of French society in *La Comédie Humaine.* — **Bal•zac′i•an** *adj.*

Honoré de Balzac
1845 drawing by Carl Christian Vogel von Vogelstein (1788–1868)

B.A.M. *abbr.* **1.** Bachelor of Applied Mathematics. **2.** Bachelor of Arts in Music.

Ba•ma•ko (bä′mə-kō′). The cap. of Mali, in the SW on the Niger R.; a center of Muslim learning during the Mali empire (c. 11th–15th cent.). Pop. 502,000.

Bam•ba•ra (bäm-bä′rä) *n., pl.* **-ra** or **-ras. 1.** A member of a people of the upper Niger River valley. **2.** The Mandingo language of the Bambara, used as a lingua franca in Mali.

bam•bi•no (băm-bē′nō, bäm-) *n., pl.* **-nos** or **-ni** (-nē). **1.** A child; a baby. **2.** A representation of the infant Jesus. [Ital., dim. of *bambo,* child.]

bam•boo (băm-bo͞o′) *n., pl.* **-boos. 1.** Any of various usu. woody, temperate or tropical grasses of the genera *Arundinaria, Bambusa, Dendrocalamus, Phyllostachys,* or *Sasa.* **2.** The stems of these plants, used in construction and crafts. [Malay *bambu,* of Indic orig.]

Bam•boo Curtain (băm-bo͞o′) *n.* A political and ideological barrier between the West and the Communist countries of Asia after the Chinese revolution of 1949.

bamboo shoot *n.* The young shoot of certain species of the bamboo genera *Dendrocalamus* and *Phyllostachys,* sliced, cooked, and eaten as a vegetable, esp. in East Asian cuisine.

bam•boo•zle (băm-bo͞o′zəl) *tr.v.* **-zled, -zling, -zles.** *Informal.* To take in by elaborate methods of deceit; hoodwink. [?] — **bam•boo′zle•ment** *n.*

ban[1] (băn) *tr.v.* **banned, ban•ning, bans. 1.** To prohibit, esp. by official decree. See Syns at **forbid. 2.** *South African.* To deprive (one suspected of illegal activity) of the right of free movement and association with others. **3.** *Archaic.* To curse. — *n.* **1.** An excommunication or condemnation by church officials. **2.** A prohibition imposed by law or official decree. **3.** Censure, condemnation, or disapproval, esp. by the public. **4.** A curse; an imprecation. **5.** A summons to arms in feudal times. [ME *bannen,* to summon, banish, curse < OE *bannan,* to summon, and < ON *banna,* to prohibit, curse; see **bhā-[2]*.**]

ban[2] (bän) *n., pl.* **ba•ni** (bä′nē). See table at **currency.** [Romanian < Serbo-Croatian *bān,* lord < Turkic *bayan,* very rich person : *bay,* rich; akin to Turk. *bay,* rich, gentleman + *-an,* intensive suff.]

ba•nal (bə-năl′, bā′nəl, bə-näl′) *adj.* Drearily commonplace and often predictable; trite. [Fr. < OFr., shared by tenants in a feudal jurisdiction < *ban,* summons to military service, of Gmc. orig. See **bhā-[2]*.**] — **ba•nal′ize′** *v.* — **ba•nal′ly** *adv.*

Usage Note: The pronunciation of *banal* is not settled among educated American English speakers. BANE-al (rhyming with *anal*) is preferred by 38 percent of the Usage Panel; ba-NAL (rhyming with *canal*), by 46 percent; ba-NAHL (the last syllable rhyming with *doll*), by 14 percent (this last pronunciation is more common in British English); and BAN-al (rhyming with *panel*), by only 2 percent. None of the first three pronunciations is incorrect.

ba•nal•i•ty (bə-năl′ĭ-tē, bā-) *n.* **1.** The condition or quality of being banal; triviality. **2.** Something that is trite, obvious, or predictable; a commonplace.

ba•nan•a (bə-năn′ə) *n.* **1.** Any of several treelike Asian herbs of the genus *Musa,* esp. *M. acuminata,* having a crown of large leaves and a hanging fruit cluster. **2.** The elongated, edible fruit of these plants, having a thick yellow to red skin and white, aromatic, seedless pulp. [Port. and Sp. < Wolof, Mandingo, and Fulani.]

banana oil *n.* **1.** A liquid mixture of amyl acetate and usu. nitrocellulose, having a bananalike odor and used as a solvent or flavoring agent. **2.** See **amyl acetate. 3.** *Slang.* Insincere flattery; nonsensical exaggeration.

banana republic *n.* A small country that is economically dependent on a single product or crop, such as bananas, and often governed by the armed forces or a dictator.

ba•nan•as (bə-năn′əz) *adj. & adv. Slang.* Crazy; nuts.

banana seat *n.* An elongated bicycle seat that usu. curves upward in the back. [From its shape.]

banana split *n.* Ice cream and usu. flavored sauces, nuts, fruit, and whipped cream served on two halves of a banana.

Ba•na•ras (bə-när′əs, -ēz). See **Varanasi.**

Ba•nat (bə-nät′, bä′nät′). A region of SE-central Europe extending across W Romania, NE Serbia, and S Hungary.

ba•nau•sic (bə-nô′sĭk, -zĭk) *adj.* **1.** Merely mechanical; routine. **2.** Of or relating to a mechanic. [Gk. *banausikos* < *banausos,* mechanic.]

Ban•croft (băn′krôft′, -krŏft′, băng′-), **George.** 1800–91. Amer. historian and diplomat who founded (1845) the naval academy at Annapolis.

band[1] (bănd) *n.* **1.** A thin strip of flexible material used to encircle and bind one object or hold a number of objects together. **2.** A strip or stripe that contrasts with something else in color, texture, or material. **3.** A narrow strip of fabric used to trim, finish, or reinforce clothing. **4.** Something that constrains or binds morally or legally. **5.** A simple ungrooved ring, esp. a wedding ring. **6.a.** A neckband or collar. **b. bands.** The two strips hanging from the front of a collar as part of the dress of certain clerics, scholars, and lawyers. **c.** A high collar popular in the 16th and 17th centuries. **7.a.** *Biol.* A chromatically, structurally, or functionally differentiated strip or stripe in or on an organism. **b.** *Anat.* A cordlike tissue that connects or holds structures together. **8.** *Phys.* **a.** A specific range of wavelengths or frequencies of electromagnetic radiation. **b.** A range of closely spaced electron energy levels in solids, the distribution and nature of which determine the electrical properties of a material. **9.** *Comp. Sci.* Circular tracks on a storage device such as a disk. **10.** The cords across the back of a book to which the sheets or quires are attached. — *tr.v.* **band•ed, band•ing, bands. 1.** To tie, bind, or encircle with or as if with a band. **2.** To mark or identify with or as if with a band. [ME < ON *band,* band, fetter, and < OFr. *bande,* band, strip, of Gmc. orig. See **bhendh-*.**]

band[2] (bănd) *n.* **1.a.** A group of people. **b.** A group of animals. **2.** *Mus.* A group of ensemble players. — *v.* **band•ed, band•ing, bands.** — *tr.* To assemble or unite in a group. — *intr.* To form a group; unite. [OFr., prob. of Gmc. orig.]

band•age (băn′dĭj) *n.* A strip of material such as gauze used to protect, immobilize, compress, or support an injured body part. — *tr.v.* **-aged, -ag•ing, -ag•es.** To apply a bandage to. [Fr. < OFr. *bande,* band, strip. See BAND[1].] — **band′ag•er** *n.*

Band-Aid (bănd′ād′). A trademark used for a small adhesive bandage with gauze in the center.

ban•dan•na or **ban•dan•a** (băn-dăn′ə) *n.* A large handkerchief usu. figured and brightly colored. [Prob. Port. < Hindi *bāndhnū,* tie-dyeing < *bāndhnā,* to tie < Skt. *bandhati,* he ties. See **bhendh-*.**]

Ban•dar Se•ri Be•ga•wan (bŭn′dər sĕr′ē bə-gä′wən). The cap. of Brunei, on the N coast of Borneo. Pop. 63,868.

Ban•da Sea (băn′də, bän′-). An arm of the Pacific Ocean in E Indonesia SE of Sulawesi and N of Timor. It includes the **Banda Islands,** a group of volcanic islands S of Ceram.

B & B *abbr.* Bed-and-breakfast.

band•box (bănd′bŏks′) *n.* A lightweight cylindrical box used to hold small articles of apparel.

B and E *abbr. Law.* Breaking and entering.

ban•deau (băn-dō′) *n., pl.* **-deaux** (-dōz′) or **-deaus. 1.** A narrow hair band. **2.** A brassiere. [Fr. < OFr. *bandel,* dim. of *bande,* band, strip. See BAND[1].]

ban•de•ri•lla (băn′də-rē′ə, -rēl′yə) *n.* A barbed dart that is thrust into the bull's neck or shoulder muscles in a bullfight. [Sp., dim. of *bandera,* banner < VLat. **bandāria.* See BANNER.]

ban•de•ri•lle•ro (băn′də-rē-âr′ō, -rēl-yâr′ō) *n., pl.* **-ros.** One who implants banderillas during a bullfight. [Sp. < *banderilla,* banderilla. See BANDERILLA.]

ban•de•role or **ban•de•rol** (băn′də-rōl′) also **ban•ne•rol** (băn′ə-rōl′) *n.* **1.** A narrow forked flag or streamer. **2.** An inscribed representation of a ribbon or scroll. [Fr. < Ital. *banderuola,* dim. of *bandiera,* banner < VLat. **bandāria.* See BANNER.]

ban•di•coot (băn′dĭ-ko͞ot′) *n.* **1.** Any of several large Indian rats of the genera *Bandicota* and *Nesokia.* **2.** Any of several ratlike marsupials of the family Peramelidae of Australia and adjacent islands. [Telugu *bantikoku*: *banti,* ball + *kokku,* long beak.]

ă pat	oi boy
ā pay	ou out
âr care	o͝o took
ä father	o͞o boot
ĕ pet	ŭ cut
ē be	ûr urge
ĭ pit	th thin
ī pie	*th* this
îr pier	hw which
ŏ pot	zh vision
ō toe	ə about, item
ô paw	

Stress marks:
′ (primary);
′ (secondary), as in
dictionary (dĭk′shə-nĕr′ē)

ban•dit (băn′dĭt) *n.* **1.** A robber, esp. with a gun. **2.** An outlaw; a gangster. **3.** One who cheats or exploits others. **4.** *Slang.* A hostile aircraft, esp. a fighter. **—*idiom.* make out like a bandit (**or **like bandits).** *Slang.* To be highly successful in a given enterprise. [Ital. *bandito* < *bandire,* to band together, prob. of Gmc. orig. See **bhā-[2]*.**] **—ban′dit•ry** *n.*

Ban•djar•ma•sin (băn′jər-mä′sĭn, bän′-). See **Banjarmasin.**

band•lead•er (bănd′lē′dər) *n. Mus.* One who conducts a band, esp. a dance band.

band•mas•ter (bănd′măs′tər) *n. Mus.* One who conducts a band.

ban•dog (băn′dôg′, -dŏg′) *n.* A dog kept chained as a watchdog or because of its ferocious aggressiveness. [ME *banddogge*: *band,* leash, chain; see BAND[1] + *dogge,* dog; see DOG.]

ban•do•leer or **ban•do•lier** (băn′də-lîr′) *n.* A soldier's belt with small pockets or loops for cartridges that is worn across the chest. [Fr. *bandoulière* < Sp. *bandolera,* dim. of *banda,* band, of Gmc. orig. See **bhā-[1]*.**]

ban•do•ne•on (băn-dō′nē-ŏn′) *n. Mus.* A small accordion esp. popular in Latin America. [Am.Sp. *bandoneón* < Ger. *Bandonion, Bandoneon*: after H. *Band* (1821–60), German inventor, + *Akkordion,* accordion; see ACCORDION.] **—ban•do′ne•on•ist** (-ə-nĭst) *n.*

ban•dore (băn′dôr′, -dōr′) also **ban•do•ra** (băn-dôr′ə, -dōr′ə) *n. Mus.* An ancient instrument resembling a guitar. [Port. *bandurra* < LLat. *pandūra* < Gk. *pandoura.*]

band saw *n.* A power saw for woodworking, consisting of a toothed metal band coupled to and driven around two wheels.

band shell also **band•shell** (bănd′shĕl′) *n. Mus.* A bandstand with a concave, almost hemispheric wall at the rear that serves as a sounding board.

bands•man (băndz′mən) *n. Mus.* A male player in a band.

band•stand (bănd′stănd′) *n. Mus.* **1.** A stand or platform, often roofed, for a band or orchestra. **2.** An indoor stand or platform for musicians and other performers.

Ban•dung (bän′dŏŏng′). A city of Indonesia in W Java SE of Jakarta; founded by the Dutch in 1810. Pop. 1,462,637.

band•wag•on (bănd′wăg′ən) *n.* **1.** *Mus.* An elaborately decorated wagon used to transport musicians in a parade. **2.** *Informal.* A cause or party that attracts increasing numbers of adherents. **3.** *Informal.* A current trend. **—band′wag′on•ing** *n.*

band•width (bănd′wĭdth′, -wĭth′) *n.* The numerical difference between the upper and lower frequencies of an electromagnetic radiation band, esp. an assigned range of radio frequencies.

ban•dy (băn′dē) *tr.v.* **-died, -dy•ing, -dies. 1.a.** To toss or throw back and forth. **b.** To hit (a ball, for example) back and forth. **2.a.** To give and receive (words, for example); exchange. **b.** To discuss in a casual or frivolous manner. —*adj.* Bowed or bent in an outward curve: *bandy legs.* —*n., pl.* **-dies.** *Sports.* **1.** A game similar to modern field hockey. **2.** A stick, bent at one end, used in this game. [?]

ban•dy-leg•ged (băn′dē-lĕg′ĭd, -lĕgd′) *adj.* Bowlegged.

bane (bān) *n.* **1.** Fatal injury or ruin. **2.** A cause of death, destruction, or ruin. **3.** A deadly poison. [ME, destroyer < OE *bana.* See **g^when-*.**]

bane•ber•ry (bān′bĕr′ē) *n.* **1.** Any of several perennial herbs of the genus *Actaea,* native to northern temperate regions and having terminal berry clusters. **2.** The poisonous berry of such an herb.

bane•ful (bān′fəl) *adj.* Causing death, destruction, or ruin; harmful. See Usage Note at **baleful. —bane′ful•ly** *adv.*

Banff (bămf). A town of SW Alberta, Canada, in the Rocky Mts. near Lake Louise. Pop. 4,208.

bang[1] (băng) *n.* **1.** A sudden loud noise, as of an explosion. **2.** A sudden loud blow or bump. **3.** *Informal.* A sudden burst of action. **4.** *Slang.* A sense of excitement; a thrill. —*v.* **banged, bang•ing, bangs.** —*tr.* **1.** To strike heavily and often repeatedly; bump. **2.** To close suddenly and loudly; slam. **3.** To handle noisily or violently. **4.** *Vulgar Slang.* To have sexual intercourse with. —*intr.* **1.** To make a sudden loud, explosive noise. **2.** To crash noisily against or into something. —*adv.* Exactly; precisely: *bang on the target.* **—*phrasal verbs.* bang away. 1.** To assail insistently, esp. with questions. **2.** To work diligently and often at length. **bang up.** To damage extensively. [Prob. < ON *bang,* a hammering.]

bang[2] (băng) *n.* A fringe of short hair cut straight across the forehead. Often used in the plural. —*tr.v.* **banged, bang•ing, bangs.** To cut (hair) in bangs. [Perh. short for *bangtail,* racehorse : BANG[1] + TAIL[1].]

bang[3] (băng) *n.* Var. of **bhang.**

bang[4] (bĕn-yā′) *n. Southern Louisiana.* Var. of **beignet.**

Ban•ga•lore (băng′gə-lôr′, -lōr′). A city of S-central India W of Madras; founded 1537. Pop. 2,476,355.

ban•ga•lore torpedo (băng′gə-lôr′, -lōr′) *n.* A piece of metal pipe filled with an explosive, used to clear a path through barbed wire or to detonate land mines. [After BANGALORE.]

bang•er (băng′ər) *n. Chiefly British.* **1.** A sausage. **2.** A noisy old car. **3.** A firework that explodes with a sudden loud noise.

Bang•ka or **Ban•ka** (băng′kə). An island of W Indonesia in the Java Sea separated from Sumatra by the **Strait of Bangka.**

bang•kok (băng′kŏk′, băng-kŏk′) *n.* A hat made of finely woven straw. [After BANGKOK.]

Bang•kok (băng′kŏk′, băng-kŏk′) also **Krung Thep** (grŏŏng tĕp′). The cap. of Thailand, in the SW near the Gulf of Siam. Pop. 5,174,682.

Bang•la•desh (bäng′glə-dĕsh′, băng′-). A country of S Asia on the Bay of Bengal; once a province of Pakistan (1947–71). Cap. Dacca. Pop. 87,052,000. **—Bang′la•desh′i** *adj. & n.*

ban•gle (băng′gəl) *n.* **1.** A rigid bracelet or anklet, esp. one with no clasp. **2.** An ornament that hangs from a bracelet or necklace. [Hindi *baṅgrī,* glass bracelet.]

Ban•gor (băng′gôr, -gər). A city of S-central ME on the Penobscot R.; settled in 1769. Pop. 33,181.

Bang's disease (băngz) *n.* See **brucellosis** 2. [After Bernhard L.F. *Bang* (1848–1932), Danish veterinarian.]

Ban•gui (bäng-gē′, bäɴ-). The cap. of Central African Republic, in the S part on the Ubangi R. Pop. 340,000.

bang-up (băng′ŭp′) *adj. Informal.* Very good; excellent. [< BANG[1].]

Bang•we•u•lu (băng′wē-ōō′lōō), **Lake.** A shallow lake on a plateau of NE Zambia.

ba•ni (bä′nē) *n.* Pl. of **ban[2].**

ban•ian (băn′yən) *n.* Var. of **banyan.**

ban•ish (băn′ĭsh) *tr.v.* **-ished, -ish•ing, -ish•es. 1.** To force to leave a place by official decree; exile. **2.** To drive away; expel: *banished fear.* [ME *banishen* < OFr. *banir, baniss-,* of Gmc. orig. See **bhā-[2]*.**] **—ban′ish•er** *n.* **—ban′ish•ment** *n.*

Syns: *banish, exile, expatriate, deport, transport, extradite.* These verbs mean to send away from a country or state. *Banish* applies to forced departure by official decree: *banished from the kingdom. Exile* specifies either voluntary or involuntary departure from one's own country because of adverse circumstances: *The royal family was exiled after the uprising. Expatriate* pertains to departure that is sometimes forced but often voluntary and may imply change of citizenship: *expatriated because of political beliefs. Deport* denotes the official act of expelling an alien: *deported for entering the country illegally. Transport* pertains to sending a convict abroad, usually to a penal colony: *Offenders were transported to Australia. Extradite* applies to the delivery of an accused or convicted person to the state or country having jurisdiction over him or her: *will extradite the terrorists.*

ban•is•ter also **ban•nis•ter** (băn′ĭ-stər) *n.* **1.** A handrail, along with all of its supporting structures. **2.** One of the vertical supports of a handrail on a staircase. [Var. of BALUSTER.]

Ban•ja Lu•ka (bän′yə lōō′kə). A city of NW Bosnia and Herzegovina NW of Sarajevo; became part of Yugoslavia after World War I. Pop. 104,000.

Ban•jar•ma•sin also **Ban•djar•ma•sin** (băn′jər-mä′sĭn, bän′-). A city of Indonesia on a delta island of S Borneo; part of a Hindu kingdom in the 14th cent. Pop. 381,286.

ban•jo (băn′jō) *n., pl.* **-jos** or **-joes.** *Mus.* A fretted stringed instrument having a narrow neck and a hollow circular body with a covering of skin or plastic under the bridge. [Akin to Jamaican E. *banja,* fiddle; prob. akin to Kimbundu, Tshiluba *mbanza,* a plucked stringed instrument.] **—ban′jo•ist** *n.*

Ban•jul (bän′jōōl′). Formerly **Bath•urst** (băth′ərst). The cap. of Gambia, on an island at the mouth of the Gambia R. Pop. 44,536.

bank[1] (băngk) *n.* **1.** A piled-up mass, as of snow or clouds. **2.** A steep natural incline. **3.** An artificial embankment. **4.** The slope of land adjoining a body of water. Often used in the plural. **5.** A large elevated area of a sea floor. Often used in the plural. **6.** *Games.* The cushion of a billiard or pool table. **7.** The lateral inward tilting, as of a vehicle, in turning or negotiating a curve. —*v.* **banked, bank•ing, banks.** —*tr.* **1.** To border or protect with a ridge or embankment. **2.** To pile up; amass: *banked earth along the wall.* **3.** To cover (a fire), as with ashes, to ensure continued low burning. **4.** To construct with a slope rising to the outside edge. **5.a.** To tilt (an aircraft) laterally and inwardly in flight. **b.** To tilt (a motor vehicle) laterally and inwardly when negotiating a curve. **6.** *Games.* To strike (a billiard ball) so that it rebounds from the table cushion. **7.** *Sports.* To play (a ball) in such a way as to make it glance off a surface. —*intr.* **1.** To rise in or take the form of a bank. **2.** To tilt an aircraft or a motor vehicle laterally when turning. [ME, of Scand. orig.]

bank[2] (băngk) *n.* **1.a.** A business establishment where money is kept for saving or commercial purposes or is invested, supplied for loans, or exchanged. **b.** The offices or building housing such an establishment. **2.** *Games.* **a.** The funds of a gambling establishment. **b.** The funds held by a dealer or banker in some gambling games. **c.** The reserve pieces, cards, chips, or play money in some games from which players may draw. **3.a.** A stock for future or emergency use. **b.** *Medic.* A supply of human tissues or other materials, such as blood, held in reserve for future use. **4.** A place of safekeeping or storage. **5.** *Obsolete.* A moneychanger's table or place of business. —*v.* **banked, bank•ing, banks.** —*tr.* To deposit in or as if in a bank. —*intr.* **1.** To transact business with or maintain an account in a bank. **2.** To operate a bank. **—*phrasal verb.* bank on.** To have confidence in; rely on. [Fr. *banque* < OItal.

banana

band shell
Concert at the Hatch Shell, Boston

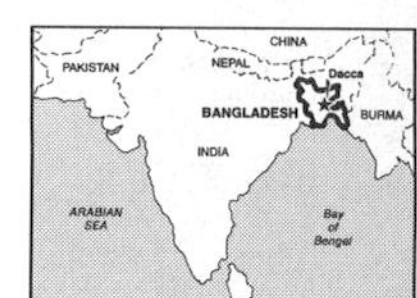

Bangladesh

banjo

banca, bench, moneychanger's table < OHGer. *banc.*]

bank[3] (băngk) *n.* **1.** A set of similar or matched things arranged in a row, esp.: **a.** A set of elevators. **b.** A row of keys on a keyboard. **2.** *Naut.* **a.** A bench for rowers in a galley. **b.** A row of oars in a galley. **3.** *Print.* The lines of type under a headline. — *tr.v.* **banked, bank•ing, banks.** To arrange in a row. [ME, bench < OFr. *banc* < LLat. *bancus,* of Gmc. orig.]

Ban•ka (băng′kə). See **Bangka.**

bank•a•ble (băng′kə-bəl) *adj.* **1.** Acceptable to or at a bank. **2.** Guaranteed to bring profit. — **bank′a•bil′i•ty** *n.*

bank acceptance *n.* A draft or bill of exchange drawn upon and accepted by a bank.

bank account *n.* Funds deposited in a bank that are credited to and subject to withdrawal by the depositor.

bank annuity *n. Chiefly British.* See **consol.**

bank bill *n.* See **bank note.**

bank•book (băngk′bo͝ok′) *n.* A book in which a depositor's withdrawals and deposits are recorded by the bank.

bank•card (băngk′kärd′) *n.* A card issued by a bank esp. for identification, credit, and access to an automated teller machine.

bank discount *n.* The interest on a loan computed in advance and deducted at the time the loan is made.

bank•er[1] (băng′kər) *n.* **1.** One serving as a bank officer or owner. **2.** *Games.* The player in charge of the bank in some gambling games. — **bank′er•ly** *adj.*

bank•er[2] (băng′kər) *n.* One engaged in cod fishing off Newfoundland.

bank•er[3] (băng′kər) *n.* A workbench used by a mason or sculptor. [< BANK[3], bench (obsolete).]

bank•er's acceptance (băng′kərz) *n.* See **bank acceptance.**

bank•ers' hours (băng′kərz) *pl.n.* A short working day.

bank holiday *n.* **1.** A day on which banks are legally closed. **2.** *Chiefly British.* A legal holiday when banks must stay closed.

bank•ing (băng′kĭng) *n.* **1.** The business of a bank. **2.** The occupation of a banker.

ban•kit (băng′kĭt) *n. Southern Louisiana & East Texas.* Var. of **banquette** 2.

bank note *n.* A note issued by a bank promising to pay a sum to the bearer on demand and acceptable as money.

bank paper *n.* **1.** Bank notes considered as a group. **2.** Securities, drafts, and other commercial paper acceptable by a bank.

bank rate *n.* The rate of discount established by a country's central bank.

bank•roll (băngk′rōl′) *n.* **1.** A roll of paper money. **2.** *Informal.* One's ready cash. — *tr.v.* **-rolled, -roll•ing, -rolls.** *Informal.* To underwrite the expense of (a business venture, for example). — **bank′roll′er** *n.*

bank•rupt (băngk′rŭpt′, -rəpt) *n.* **1.** *Law.* A debtor judged legally insolvent. **2.** A person who is totally lacking in a specified resource or quality. — *adj.* **1.a.** Having been legally declared financially insolvent. **b.** Financially ruined; impoverished. **2.a.** Depleted of valuable qualities or characteristics. **b.** Totally depleted; destitute. **c.** Being in a ruined state. — *tr.v.* **-rupt•ed, -rupt•ing, -rupts. 1.** To cause to become financially bankrupt. **2.** To ruin: *bankrupted their credibility.* [Fr. *banqueroute* < Ital. *bancarotta*: *banca,* moneychanger's table; see BANK[2] + *rotta,* p.part. of *rompere,* to break (< Lat. *rumpere*; see **reup-***).] — **bank′rupt•cy** (-rəpt-sē, -rəp-sē) *n.* — **bank•rup′tive** *adj.*

Banks (băngks), Sir **Joseph.** 1743–1820. British botanist who circumnavigated the globe (1768–71) with James Cook and cataloged many species of plant and animal life.

bank•si•a (băngk′sē-ə) *n.* Any of various Australian evergreen shrubs or trees of the genus *Banksia,* with narrow leaves, usu. yellow flowers, and small fruits in conelike clusters. [After Sir Joseph BANKS.]

Banks Island. An island of NW Northwest Terrs., Canada, in the Arctic Ocean W of Victoria I.

Ban•ne•ker (băn′ĭ-kər), **Benjamin.** 1731–1806. Amer. mathematician and astronomer noted for his almanac (1792–1802).

ban•ner (băn′ər) *n.* **1.a.** A piece of cloth on a staff used as a standard by a monarch, military commander, or knight. **b.** The flag of a nation, a state, or an army. **2.** A piece of cloth bearing a motto or legend, as of a club. **3.** A headline spanning the width of a newspaper page. **4.** *Bot.* See **standard** 8. — *adj.* Unusually good; outstanding. — *tr.v.* **-nered, -ner•ing, -ners.** *Informal.* To give a banner headline to in a newspaper. [ME *banere* < OFr. *baniere* < VLat. **bandāria* < LLat. *bandum,* of Gmc. orig. See **bhā-[1]*.**]

ban•ner•et[1] (băn′ər-ĭt, -ə-rĕt′) also **ban•ner•ette** (băn′ə-rĕt′) *n.* A small banner. [ME *baneret* < OFr. *banerete,* dim. of *baniere,* banner. See BANNER.]

ban•ner•et[2] (băn′ər-ĭt, -ə-rĕt′) *n.* A feudal knight ranking between a knight bachelor and a baron. [ME *baneret* < OFr. < *baniere,* banner. See BANNER.]

ban•ne•rol (băn′ə-rōl′) *n.* Var. of **banderole.**

ban•nis•ter (băn′ĭ-stər) *n.* Var. of **banister.**

Ban•nis•ter (băn′ĭ-stər), **Roger.** b. 1929. British runner who was the first person to run the mile in under four minutes (1954).

ban•nock (băn′ək) *n.* **1.** A flat, usu. unleavened bread made of oatmeal or barley flour. **2.** *New England.* Thin cornbread baked on a griddle. [ME *bannok* < OE *bannuc,* of Celt. orig.]

Ban•nock (băn′ək) *n., pl.* **Bannock** or **-nocks. 1.** A member of a Native American people inhabiting southeast Idaho and western Wyoming. **2.** The variety of Northern Paiute spoken by the Bannock.

Ban•nock•burn (băn′ək-bûrn′, băn′ək-bûrn′). A town of central Scotland NNE of Glasgow on the **Bannock River,** a tributary of the Forth; site of Robert the Bruce's defeat of the English under Edward II (1314).

banns also **bans** (bănz) *pl.n.* An announcement, esp. in a church, of an intended marriage. [ME *banes,* pl. of *ban,* proclamation < OE *gebann* and < OFr. *ban* (of Gmc. orig.; see **bhā-[2]***).]

ban•quet (băng′kwĭt) *n.* **1.** An elaborate, sumptuous repast. **2.** A ceremonial dinner honoring a particular guest or occasion. — *tr. & intr.v.* **-quet•ed, -quet•ing, -quets.** To honor at or partake of a banquet. [OFr., dim. of *banc,* bench. See BANK[3].] — **ban′quet•er** *n.*

banquet room *n.* A large room suitable for banquets.

ban•quette (băng-kĕt′) *n.* **1.** A platform lining a trench or parapet wall on which soldiers may stand when firing. **2.** Also **ban•kit** (băng′kĭt). *Southern Louisiana & East Texas.* A sidewalk. See Regional Note at **beignet. 3.** A long upholstered bench placed against or built into a wall. **4.** A ledge or shelf, as on a buffet. [Fr. < Prov. *banqueta,* dim. of *banca,* bench, of Gmc. orig.]

bans (bănz) *pl.n.* Var. of **banns.**

ban•shee also **ban•shie** (băn′shē) *n.* A female spirit in Gaelic folklore believed to presage, by wailing, a death in a family. [Ir.Gael. *bean sídhe,* woman of the fairies, banshee : *bean,* woman (< OIr. *ben*; see **g^{w}en-***) + *sídhe,* fairy (< OIr. *síde*).]

ban•tam (băn′təm) *n.* **1.** Any of various breeds of small domestic fowl that are often miniatures of larger breeds. **2.** A small but aggressive and spirited person. — *adj.* **1.** Diminutive; miniature. **2.** Aggressive and spirited. [After *Bantam,* a region of W Java, Indonesia.]

ban•tam•weight (băn′təm-wāt′) *n. Sports.* **1.** A professional boxer weighing more than 112 and not more than 118 pounds (approx. 51–53.5 kilograms), heavier than a flyweight and lighter than a featherweight. **2.** A contestant of a similar weight in various sports.

ban•ter (băn′tər) *n.* Good-humored, playful conversation. — *v.* **-tered, -ter•ing, -ters.** — *tr.* To speak to in a playful or teasing way. — *intr.* To exchange mildly teasing remarks. [?] — **ban′ter•er** *n.* — **ban′ter•ing•ly** *adv.*

Ban•ting (băn′tĭng), Sir **Frederick Grant.** 1891–1941. Canadian physiologist who shared a 1923 Nobel Prize.

bant•ling (bănt′lĭng) *n.* A young child. [?]

Ban•tu (băn′to͞o) *n., pl.* **Bantu** or **-tus. 1.** A member of any of numerous linguistically related peoples of central and southern Africa. **2.** A group of more than 400 closely related languages spoken in central, east-central, and southern Africa, belonging to the South Central subgroup of the Niger-Congo language family. [< Proto-Bantu **bantu,* people : *ba-,* pl. human pref. + *ntu,* entity.] — **Ban′tu** *adj.*

ban•yan also **ban•ian** (băn′yən) *n.* A tropical Indian fig tree *(Ficus benghalensis)* with aerial roots that descend from the branches and develop into additional trunks. [Short for *banyan tree,* merchants' tree < Port. *banian,* Hindu merchant < Gujarati *vāṇiyo* < Skt. *vāṇijaḥ.* See **wen-[1]*.**]

ban•zai (bän-zī′) *n.* A Japanese battle cry or patriotic cheer. [J., (may you live) ten thousand years < Chin. (Mandarin) *wàn sui*: *wàn,* ten thousand + *sui,* years.]

ba•o•bab (bā′ō-băb′, bä′-) *n.* A tropical African tree *(Adansonia digitata)* with a water-filled trunk, palmately compound leaves, and long hard-shelled fruits. [Poss. < North African Ar. *bū ḥibab,* fruit of many seeds.]

Bao•ding also **Pao•ting** (bou′dĭng′). A city of NE China SSW of Beijing. Pop. 400,000.

Bao•tou also **Pao•tow** (bou′tō′). A city of N China on the Huang He (Yellow R.) W of Hohhot. Pop. 866,200.

Bap. *abbr.* Baptist.

Bapt. *abbr.* Baptist.

bap•tism (băp′tĭz′əm) *n.* **1.** A Christian sacrament marked by the symbolic use of water and resulting in the recipient's admission into the Christian community. **2.** An initiation, purification, or naming ceremony or experience. [ME *baptisme* < OFr. < LLat. *baptismus* < Gk. *baptismos* < *baptizein,* to baptize. See BAPTIZE.] — **bap•tis′mal** *adj.* — **bap•tis′mal•ly** *adv.*

baptism of fire *n.* **1.** A soldier's first experience of combat conditions. **2.** A severe ordeal experienced for the first time.

Bap•tist (băp′tĭst) *n.* **1.** A member of an evangelical Protestant church of congregational polity, believing in baptism of voluntary, conscious believers. **2. baptist.** One that baptizes. [ME, baptizer < OFr. *baptiste* < LLat. *baptista* < Gk. *baptistēs* < *baptizein,* to baptize. See BAPTIZE.] — **Bap′tist** *adj.*

banquette
Louis XVI style banquette by Jean Baptiste Claude Sene (1748–1803)

baobab
Adansonia digitata

baptistery
15th-century German

bap•tis•ter•y also **bap•tis•try** (băp′tĭ-strē) *n., pl.* **-ies** also **-tries. 1.** A part of a church or a separate building used for baptizing. **2.** A font used for baptism. [ME *baptisterie* < OFr. < LLat. *baptistērium* < Gk. *baptistērion* < *baptizein*, to baptize. See BAPTIZE.]

bap•tize (băp-tīz′, băp′tīz′) *v.* **-tized, -tiz•ing, -tiz•es.** — *tr.* **1.** To admit into Christianity through baptism. **2.a.** To cleanse or purify. **b.** To initiate. **3.** To give a Christian name to; christen. — *intr.* To administer baptism. [ME *baptizen* < OFr. *baptiser* < LLat. *baptizāre* < Gk. *baptizein* < *baptein*, to dip.] — **bap•tiz′er** *n.*

bar[1] (bär) *n.* **1.** A relatively long, straight, rigid piece of solid material used as a fastener, support, barrier, or structural or mechanical member. **2.a.** A solid oblong block of a substance, such as soap or candy. **b.** A rectangular block of a precious metal. **3.** Something that impedes or prevents action or progress. **4.** A ridge, as of sand on a shore, that is formed by the action of tides or currents. **5.** A narrow marking, such as a stripe. **6.** *Her.* A pair of horizontal parallel lines across a shield. **7.** *Law.* **a.** The nullification, defeat, or prevention of a claim or action. **b.** The process by which nullification, defeat, or prevention is achieved. **8.** The railing in a courtroom enclosing the area where the judges and lawyers sit, witnesses are heard, and prisoners are tried. **9.** A place of judgment; a tribunal. **10.** *Law.* **a.** Attorneys considered as a group. **b.** The profession of law. **11.** *Mus.* **a.** A vertical line dividing a staff into equal measures. **b.** A measure. **12.a.** A counter for serving drinks, esp. alcoholic drinks, and sometimes food. **b.** An establishment or room with such a counter. — *tr.v.* **barred, bar•ring, bars. 1.** To fasten securely with a long, straight, rigid piece of material. **2.** To shut in or out with or as if with bars. **3.** To obstruct or impede; block. **4.** To keep out; exclude. **5.** To rule out; except. **6.** To mark with stripes or bands. **7.** *Law.* To stop (a claim or action) by objection. — *prep.* Except for; excluding. — ***idiom.* behind bars.** In prison. [ME *barre* < OFr. < VLat. **barra*.]

bar[2] (bär) *n.* A unit of pressure equal to one million (10^6) dynes per square centimeter. [Gk. *baros*, weight. See **g^{w}erə-**[1]***.**]

BAR *abbr.* Browning automatic rifle.

bar. *abbr.* **1.a.** Barometer. **b.** Barometric. **2.** Barrel.

bar– *pref.* Var. of **baro–.**

Ba•rab•bas (bə-răb′əs). In the Bible, the condemned thief whose release, instead of that of Jesus, was demanded of Pilate by the multitude.

Ba•ra•cal•do (băr′ə-käl′dō, bä′rä-). A city of N Spain, a suburb of Bilbao. Pop. 118,692.

Ba•ra•co•a (băr′ə-kō′ə, bä′rä-). A city of SE Cuba on the Atlantic coast; the oldest settlement in Cuba. Pop. 35,754.

Ba•ra•ka (bə-rä′kə), **Imamu Amiri.** Orig. LeRoi Jones. b. 1934. Amer. writer whose works focus on racial conflict.

Ba•ra•nof Island (băr′ə-nôf′, -nŏf′, bə-rä′nəf). An island off SE AK in the Alexander Archipelago.

Ba•ra•nov (bə-rä′nəf), **Aleksandr Andreevich.** 1746–1819. Russian fur trader and first governor of the Russian colony of Alaska.

bar•a•the•a (băr′ə-thē′ə) *n.* A soft fabric of silk and cotton, silk and wool, or all wool. [?]

barb[1] (bärb) *n.* **1.** A sharp point projecting in reverse direction to the main point of a weapon or tool, as on an arrow. **2.** A cutting remark. **3.** *Zool.* One of the parallel filaments projecting from the main shaft of a feather. **4.** *Bot.* A short, sharply hooked bristle or hairlike projection. **5.** See **barbel**[1]**. 6.** Any of various Old World freshwater fishes of the genus *Barbus* or *Puntius* and related genera. **7.** A linen covering for a woman's head, throat, and chin worn in medieval times. — *tr.v.* **barbed, barb•ing, barbs.** To provide or furnish with a barb. [ME *barbe* < OFr., beard < Lat. *barba*. See **bhardh-ā-*.**]

barb[2] (bärb) *n.* **1.** A horse of a breed introduced by the Moors into Spain from northern Africa that resembles the Arabians. **2.** One of a breed of domestic pigeons that is similar to the carrier and has dark plumage. [Fr. *barbe* < Ital. *barbero*, Berber < VLat. **Barbaria*, Barbary States < Lat. *barbarus*, barbarian. See BARBARIAN.]

Barb. *abbr.* Barbados.

Bar•ba•dos (bär-bā′dōs′, -dōz′, -dəs). An island country of the E West Indies; achieved independence from Great Britain in 1966. Cap. Bridgetown. Pop. 248,983. — **Bar•ba′di•an** *adj. & n.*

Barbados cherry *n.* A tropical American evergreen shrub *(Malpighia glabra)* having red cherrylike edible fruits.

bar•bar•i•an (bär-bâr′ē-ən) *n.* **1.** A member of a people considered by another nation or group to have a primitive civilization. **2.** A fierce, brutal, or cruel person. **3.** An insensitive, uncultured person; a boor. [Fr. *barbarien* < *barbare* < Lat. *barbarus*, barbarous. See BARBAROUS.] — **bar•bar′i•an** *adj.* — **bar•bar′i•an•ism** *n.*

bar•bar•ic (bär-băr′ĭk) *adj.* **1.** Of, relating to, or characteristic of barbarians. **2.** Marked by crudeness or lack of restraint in taste, style, or manner. [Lat. *barbaricus* < Gk. *barbarikos* < *barbaros*, foreign.] — **bar•bar′i•cal•ly** *adv.*

bar•ba•rism (bär′bə-rĭz′əm) *n.* **1.** An act, trait, or custom characterized by ignorance or crudity. **2.a.** The use of words, forms, or expressions considered incorrect or unacceptable. **b.** A specific word, form, or expression so used. [Lat. *barbarismus*, incorrect use of a language, barbarism < Gk. *barbarismos* < *barbarizein*, to behave or speak like a barbarian < *barbaros*, non-Greek, foreign.]

bar•bar•i•ty (bär-băr′ĭ-tē) *n., pl.* **-ties. 1.** Savage brutality or cruelty in actions or conduct. **2.** A cruel or savage act. **3.** Crudity; coarseness.

bar•ba•rize (bär′bə-rīz′) *tr. & intr.v.* **-rized, -riz•ing, -riz•es.** To make or become crude, savage, or barbarous. — **bar′ba•ri•za′tion** (-rĭ-zā′shən) *n.*

Bar•ba•ros•sa[1] (bär′bə-rŏs′ə, -rôs′ə). Khair ed-Din. d. 1546. Greek-born Turkish corsair who with his brother **Arouj** (d. 1518) ravaged the coasts of Spain, Italy, and Greece.

Bar•ba•ros•sa[2] (bär′bə-rŏs′ə, -rôs′ə). See **Frederick I.**

bar•ba•rous (bär′bər-əs) *adj.* **1.** Primitive in culture and customs; uncivilized. **2.** Lacking refinement or culture; coarse. **3.** Characterized by savagery; very cruel. See Syns at **cruel. 4.** Marked by the use or occurrence of barbarisms in language. [< Lat. *barbarus* < Gk. *barbaros*, non-Greek, foreign.] — **bar′ba•rous•ly** *adv.* — **bar′ba•rous•ness** *n.*

Bar•ba•ry (bär′bə-rē, -brē). A region of N Africa on the Mediterranean coast between Egypt and the Atlantic Ocean; used as a base by pirates from the 16th to the 19th cent.

Barbary ape *n.* A tailless monkey *(Macaca sylvana)* of Gibraltar and northern Africa.

Barbary Coast. 1. The Mediterranean coastal area of Barbary and the Barbary States. **2.** A waterfront area of San Francisco CA in the years after the 1849 gold rush.

Barbary sheep *n.* See **aoudad.**

Barbary States. The North African states of Algeria, Tunisia, Tripoli, and Morocco, esp. from the 16th to the 19th cent.

bar•bas•co (bär-bäs′kō) *n., pl.* **-cos. 1.** Any of several tropical American plants containing a substance that can stun or paralyze fish. **2.** Any of several plants of the genus *Dioscorea*, native to Mexico and having a root that yields an extract used for synthetic steroid hormones. [Am.Sp. < Sp. *barbasco*, mullein, alteration (poss. influenced by *barba*, beard) of *verbasco* < Lat. *verbascum*.]

bar•bate (bär′bāt′) *adj.* Having a beard; bearded. [Lat. *barbātus* < *barba*, beard. See BARB[1].]

bar•be•cue (bär′bĭ-kyo͞o′) *n.* **1.** A grill, pit, or outdoor fireplace for roasting meat. **2.a.** A whole animal carcass or section thereof cooked over an open fire or on a spit. **b.** A social gathering, usu. outdoors, at which food is cooked over an open flame. — *tr.v.* **-cued, -cu•ing, -cues.** To cook over live coals or an open fire. [Am.Sp. *barbacoa*, of Taino orig.]

barbed (bärbd) *adj.* **1.** Having barbs. **2.** Cutting; stinging: *barbed criticism.* — **barb′ed•ness** (bär′bĭd-nĭs) *n.*

barbed wire *n.* Twisted strands of fence wire with barbs at regular intervals.

bar•bel[1] (bär′bəl) *n.* One of the slender, whiskerlike tactile organs extending from the head of certain fishes. [Obsolete Fr. < OFr. < Med.Lat. *barbula*, dim. of LLat. *barbus*, beard < Lat. *barba*. See **bhardh-ā-*.**]

bar•bel[2] (bär′bəl) *n.* Any of several Old World freshwater fish of the genus *Barbus*, esp. *B. barbus*, having usu. four barbels on the upper jaw. [ME < OFr. < Med.Lat. **barbellus*, dim. of *barbus* < Lat. *barba*, beard. See BARBEL[1].]

bar•bell (bär′bĕl′) *n.* A bar with adjustable weights at each end, lifted for sport or exercise. [BAR[1] + (DUMB)BELL.]

bar•bel•late (bär′bə-lāt′, bär-bĕl′ĭt, -āt′) *adj. Bot.* Finely or minutely barbed. [< NLat. *barbella*, dim. of Latin *barba*, beard. See **bhardh-ā-*.**]

bar•ber (bär′bər) *n.* One who cuts hair and shaves or trims beards professionally. — *v.* **-bered, -ber•ing, -bers.** — *tr.* **1.** To cut the hair of. **2.** To shave or trim the beard of. — *intr.* To work as a barber. [ME < OFr. *barbour* < Med.Lat. *barbātōr* < Lat. *barba*, beard. See **bhardh-ā-*.**]

Bar•ber (bär′bər), **Samuel.** 1910–81. Amer. composer whose works include the opera *Vanessa* (1958).

bar•ber•ry (bär′bĕr′ē) *n.* Any of various shrubs of the genus *Berberis* having often clustered leaves, small yellow flowers, and red, orange, or blackish berries. [ME *berberie* < Med. Lat. *berberis*.]

bar•ber•shop (bär′bər-shŏp′) *n.* A barber's place of business. — *adj. Mus.* Of, consisting of, or relating to the performance of sentimental songs in four-part harmony.

bar•ber's itch (bär′bərz) *n.* Any of various skin eruptions on the face and neck, esp. ringworm of the beard.

Bar•ber•ton (bär′bər-tən). A city of NE OH, a suburb of Akron. Pop. 27,623.

bar•bet (bär′bĭt) *n.* Any of various brightly colored tropical birds of the family Capitonidae that have a broad bristled bill and are related to the toucans. [Prob. < BARB[1].]

bar•bette (bär-bĕt′) *n.* **1.** A platform or mound of earth within a fort from which guns are fired over the parapet. **2.** An armored protective cylinder around a revolving gun turret on a warship. [Fr., dim. of *barbe*, beard. See BARB[1].]

bar•bi•can (bär′bĭ-kən) *n.* A tower or other fortification on the approach to a castle or town, esp. one at a gate or draw-

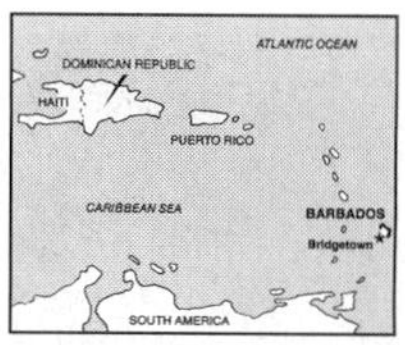

Barbados

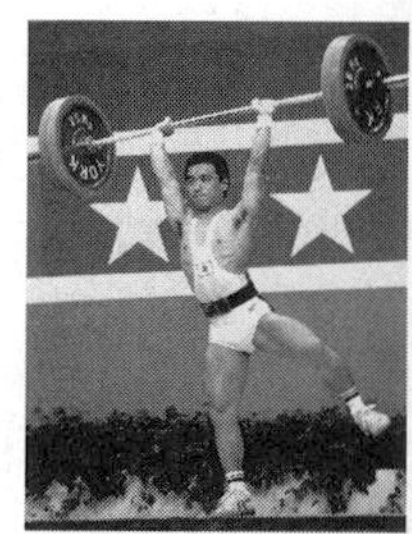
barbell
Kazushito Manabe of Japan at the 1984 Summer Olympics, Los Angeles

ă **pat**	oi **boy**
ā **pay**	ou **out**
âr **care**	o͝o **took**
ä **father**	o͞o **boot**
ĕ **pet**	ŭ **cut**
ē **be**	ûr **urge**
ĭ **pit**	th **thin**
ī **pie**	*th* **this**
îr **pier**	hw **which**
ŏ **pot**	zh **vision**
ō **toe**	ə **a**bout,
ô **paw**	item

Stress marks:
′ (primary);
′ (secondary), as in
dictionary (dĭk′shə-nĕr′ē)

bridge. [ME < OFr. *barbacane* < Med.Lat. *barbacana* < Pers. *barbārkhāna*: *barbār*, guard (< OIran. **parivāraka-*, protective; see **wer-⁴***) + *khāna*, house (< MPers. *khānak*).]

bar•bi•cel (bär′bĭ-sĕl′) *n. Zool.* One of the minute hooked projections extending from and interlocking the barbules of a feather. [NLat. *barbicella*, dim. of Latin *barba*, beard. See **bhardh-ā-***.]

bar•bi•tal (bär′bĭ-tôl′, -tăl′) *n.* A barbiturate, $C_8H_{12}N_2O_3$, a crystalline powder used as a sedative and hypnotic esp. in the form of sodium barbital. [< BARBITURIC ACID.]

bar•bi•tu•rate (bär-bĭch′ər-ĭt, -ə-rāt′, bär′bĭ-to͝or′ĭt, -āt′, -tyo͝or′-) *n.* **1.** A salt or ester of barbituric acid. **2.** Any of a group of barbituric acid derivatives that act as central nervous system depressants and are used as sedatives or hypnotics. [BARBITUR(IC ACID) + -ATE².]

bar•bi•tu•ric acid (bär′bĭ-to͝or′ĭk, -tyo͝or′-) *n.* An organic acid, $C_4H_4O_3N_2$, used in the manufacture of barbiturates and some plastics. [Partial transl. of German *Barbitursäure*.]

Bar•bi•zon (bär′bĭ-zŏn′) *adj.* Of, relating to, or typical of a 19th-century group of landscape painters in France that included Millet. [After *Barbizon*, a village of N-central France.]

Bar•bour (bär′bər), **Philip Pendleton.** 1783–1841. Amer. jurist; associate justice of the U.S. Supreme Court (1836–41).

Bar•bu•da (bär-bo͞o′də). An island of Antigua and Barbuda in the West Indies N of Antigua; privately owned from 1691 to 1872. —**Bar•bu′dan** *adj. & n.*

bar•bule (bär′byo͞ol) *n. Zool.* A small barb or pointed projection, esp. fringing the edges of the barbs of feathers. [Lat. *barbula*, dim. of *barba*, beard. See **bhardh-ā-***.]

bard²

barb•wire (bärb′wīr′) *n.* Barbed wire.

bar•ca (bär′kə) *n. Naut.* A double-ended boat, skiff, or barge used in the Mediterranean. [Ital. *barca*. See BARK³.]

bar•ca•role also **bar•ca•rolle** (bär′kə-rōl′) *n. Mus.* **1.** A Venetian gondolier's song with a rhythm suggestive of rowing. **2.** A composition imitating such a song. [Fr. < Ital. *barcaruola* < *barcaruolo*, gondolier < *barca*, boat < Lat.]

Bar•ce•lo•na (bär′sə-lō′nə). A city of NE Spain on the Mediterranean; long a center of Catalan separatism. Pop. 1,770,296.

Barcelona chair A trademark used for a wide armless chair with leather cushions on a double X-shaped steel frame.

B.Arch. *abbr.* Bachelor of Architecture.

bar chart *n.* See **bar graph.**

Bar•clay (bär′klē), **Robert.** 1648–90. Scottish Quaker apologist who wrote *Truth Triumphant* (1692).

bar code *n.* See **Universal Product Code.**

bard¹ (bärd) *n.* **1.** One of an ancient Celtic order of minstrel poets who composed and recited verses celebrating heroic exploits. **2.** A poet, esp. a lyric poet. [ME < Ir. and Sc.Gael. *bard* and < Welsh *bardd*; see **gʷerə-²***.] —**bard′ic** *adj.*

bard² also **barde** (bärd) —*n.* A piece of armor used to protect or ornament a horse. —*tr.v.* **bard•ed, bard•ing, bards.** To equip (a horse) with bards. [ME *barde* < OFr. < OItal. *barda* < Ar. *barda'ah*, packsaddle < Pers. *pardah*. See PURDAH.]

bar•da•cious (bär′dā′shəs) *adj. & adv. Southern & South Midland U.S.* Var. of **bodacious.**

Bar•deen (bär-dēn′), **John.** 1908–91. Amer. physicist who shared a Nobel Prize in 1956 and in 1972.

Bar•do•li•no (bär′dl-ē′nō) *n., pl.* **-nos.** A dry red Italian wine. [After *Bardolino*, a village of N Italy.]

Bar•dot (bär-dō′), **Brigitte.** b. 1935? French actress whose films include *And God Created Woman* (1956).

bargeboard
Kingscote,
Newport, Rhode Island

bare¹ (bâr) *adj.* **bar•er, bar•est. 1.** Lacking the usual or appropriate covering or clothing; naked. **2.** Exposed to view; undisguised. **3.** Lacking the usual furnishings, equipment, or decoration. **4.** Having no addition, adornment, or qualification. **5.** Just sufficient; mere. **6.** *Obsolete.* Bareheaded. —*tr.v.* **bared, bar•ing, bares. 1.** To make bare; uncover or reveal. **2.** To expose: *bared its teeth.* [ME *bar* < OE *bær*. See **bhoso-***.] —**bare′ness** *n.*

bare² (bâr) *v. Archaic.* A p.t. of **bear¹.**

bare•back (bâr′băk′) also **bare•backed** (-băkt′) *adv. & adj.* On a horse, pony, or other animal with no saddle.

bare bones *pl.n. Informal.* The basic elements or essentials: *bare bones of a plan.* —**bare′-bones′** (bâr′bōnz′) *adj.*

bare•faced (bâr′fāst′) *adj.* **1.a.** Having no face covering. **b.** Having no beard. **2.** Without disguise; unconcealed. **3.** Undisguisedly bold; brazen. —**bare′fac′ed•ly** (-fā′sĭd-lē, -fāst′lē) *adv.* —**bare′fac′ed•ness** *n.*

bare•foot (bâr′fo͝ot′) also **bare•foot•ed** (-fo͝ot′ĭd) *adv. & adj.* With nothing on the feet: *walking barefoot in the grass.*

barefoot doctor *n.* A lay health care worker, esp. in rural China, trained in such activities as first aid.

ba•rege also **ba•rège** (bə-rĕzh′) *n.* A sheer fabric woven of silk or cotton and wool, used for women's apparel. [Fr. *barège*, after *Barèges*, a town in France.]

bare•hand•ed (bâr′hăn′dĭd) *adv. & adj.* With no covering on the hands: *fought barehanded.* —**bare′hand′ed•ness** *n.*

bare•head•ed (bâr′hĕd′ĭd) *adv. & adj.* With no covering on the head. —**bare′head′ed•ness** *n.*

Ba•reil•ly also **Ba•re•li** (bə-rā′lē). A city of N India ESE of Delhi; founded in the 16th cent. Pop. 386,734.

bare-knuck•le (bâr′nŭk′əl) *adv.* Without gloves: *fought bare-knuckle.* —*adj.* **1.** Wearing no gloves. **2.** *Slang.* Of a fiercely implacable character.

bare-knuck•led (bâr′nŭk′əld) *adv. & adj.* Bare-knuckle.

bare•leg•ged (bâr′lĕg′ĭd, -lĕgd′) *adv. & adj.* With the legs uncovered: *ran barelegged.* —**bare′leg′ged•ness** *n.*

bare•ly (bâr′lē) *adv.* **1.** By a very little; hardly: *barely saw the road in the fog.* **2.** In a scanty manner; sparsely.

bare-na•ked (bâr′nā′kĭd, -nĕk′ĭd) *adv. & adj. Chiefly Northern U.S.* With no clothes on.

Regional Note: The chiefly Northern U.S. expression *bare-naked* illustrates the linguistic process of redundancy productive in regional dialect speech. A redundant expression combines words having the same meaning, thereby intensifying the effect. In *buck-naked*, used chiefly in the South Atlantic and Gulf States, *buck* is possibly an alteration of *butt*, "buttocks." If so, *bum-naked* and *bare-ass(ed)*, attested in the Northeastern U.S., represent the same idea.

Bar•ents (băr′ənts, bär′-), **Willem.** 1550?–97. Dutch Arctic explorer who led several expeditions (1594–97) in search of the Northeast Passage.

Barents Sea. A shallow section of the Arctic Ocean N of Norway and NW Russia.

barf (bärf) *tr. & intr.v.* **barfed, barf•ing, barfs.** *Slang.* To vomit. [Prob. imit.] —**barf** *n.*

bar•fly (bär′flī′) *n. Slang.* One who frequents bars.

bar•gain (bär′gĭn) *n.* **1.** An agreement between parties fixing obligations that each promises to carry out. **2.a.** An agreement establishing the terms of a sale or exchange of goods or services. **b.** Property acquired or services rendered as a result of such an agreement. **3.** Something offered or acquired at a price advantageous to the buyer. —*v.* **-gained, -gain•ing, -gains.** —*intr.* **1.** To negotiate the terms of an agreement, as to sell. **2.** To engage in collective bargaining. **3.** To arrive at an agreement. —*tr.* To exchange; trade. —***phrasal verb.* bargain for** (or **on**). To count on; expect. —***idiom.* into** (or **in**) **the bargain.** Over and above what is expected; in addition. [ME < OFr. *bargaigne*, haggling < *bargaignier*, to haggle, of Gmc. orig. See **bhergh-¹***.] —**bar′gain•er** *n.*

bargain basement *n.* A store basement where goods are sold at reduced prices. —**bar′gain-base′ment** (bär′gĭn-bās′mənt) *adj.*

bar•gain•ing chip (bär′gə-nĭng) *n.* Leverage, typically in the form of an inducement or a concession, useful in successful negotiations.

barge (bärj) *n. Naut.* **1.a.** A large, usu. flatbottom freight boat that is generally unpowered and towed or pushed by other craft. **b.** A large, open pleasure boat used for parties or formal ceremonies. **2.** An admiral's powerboat. —*v.* **barged, barg•ing, barg•es.** —*tr. Naut.* To carry by barge. —*intr.* **1.** To move clumsily. **2.** To enter rudely and abruptly; intrude: *barged into the meeting.* [ME < OFr. < Lat. *barca*, boat.]

barge•board (bärj′bôrd′, -bōrd′) *n. Archit.* A board, often ornately carved, attached to a gable roof. [?]

barg•ee (bär-jē′) *n. Chiefly British.* A bargeman. [BARGE + -EE².]

bar•gel•lo (bär-zhĕl′ō) *n., pl.* **-los.** A needlepoint stitch that produces zigzag lines. [After the *Bargello*, a museum in Florence, Italy.]

barge•man (bärj′mən) *n.* The captain or a crew member of a barge.

bar graph *n.* A graph consisting of parallel bars with lengths proportional to the frequency of specified quantities in a data set.

Bar Harbor (bär). A resort town of SE ME on Mount Desert I. Pop. 2,768.

bar•hop (bär′hŏp′) *intr.v.* **-hopped, -hop•ing, -hops.** *Slang.* To patronize a series of bars during an evening.

Ba•ri (bä′rē). A city of SE Italy on the Adriatic Sea; became part of the kingdom of Naples in 1557. Pop. 370,781.

bar•i•at•rics (băr′ē-ăt′rĭks) *n.* *(used with a sing. v.)* The branch of medicine that deals with obesity. [BAR(O)- + -IATRICS.] —**bar′i•at′ric** *adj.* —**bar′i•a•tri′cian** (-ə-trĭsh′ən) *n.*

ba•ril•la (bə-rēl′yə, -rē′yə) *n.* **1.** Either of two Mediterranean saltworts *(Salsola kali* or *S. soda)* or a similar plant *(Halogeton sativus)*. **2.** The crude sodium carbonate ash obtained from these plants. [Sp. *barrilla*.]

Bar•ing (bâr′ĭng), **Alexander.** 1st Baron Ashburton. 1774–1848. British public official who concluded the treaty between Great Britain and the U.S. that defined the border between Canada and ME (1842).

Ba•ri•sal (băr′ĭ-sôl′, bŭr′ĭ-säl′). A city of S Bangladesh on the Ganges R. delta. The phenomenon known as "the Barisal guns," unexplained sounds resembling distant thunder or cannon fire, may be seismic in origin. Pop. 159,298.

bar•ite (bâr′ĭt, băr′-) also **ba•ry•tes** (bə-rī′tēz) *n.* A crystalline mineral of barium sulfate, $BaSO_4$, used in paint and as the chief source of barium chemicals. [Gk. *barus*, heavy; see **gʷerə-¹*** + -ITE¹.]

bar•i•tone also **bar•y•tone** (băr′ĭ-tōn′) *n. Mus.* **1.a.** A male singer or voice with a range higher than a bass and lower than a tenor. **b.** A part written for such a voice. **2.** A brass wind instrument with a range similar to that of a baritone voice. [Ital. *baritono* < Gk. *barutonos*, deep sounding : *barus*, heavy; see **gʷerə-¹*** + *tonos*, tone; see TONE.]

bar•i•um (bâr′ē-əm, băr′-) *n. Symbol* **Ba** A soft alkaline-earth metal used to deoxidize copper. Atomic number 56; atomic weight 137.34; melting point 725°C; boiling point 1,140°C; specific gravity 3.50; valence 2. See table at **element.** [BAR(YTA) + -IUM.] **—bar′ic** (-ĭk) *adj.*

barium sulfate *n.* A fine white powder, $BaSO_4$, used as a pigment, a filler for textiles, rubbers, and plastics, and a contrast medium in x-ray photography of the digestive tract.

bark¹ (bärk) *n.* **1.** The harsh, abrupt sound uttered by a dog. **2.** A sound similar to a dog's bark. *—v.* **barked, bark•ing, barks.** *—intr.* **1.** To utter the harsh, abrupt sound of a dog. **2.** To make a sound similar to a bark. **3.** To speak sharply; snap. **4.** To work as a barker. *—tr.* To utter in a loud, harsh voice. **—*idiom.* bark up the wrong tree.** To misdirect one's energies. [< ME *berken*, to bark < OE *beorcan*.]

bark² (bärk) *n.* **1.** The tough outer covering of the stems and roots of trees and other woody plants. **2.** A specific kind of bark used for a special purpose, as in medicine. *—tr.v.* **barked, bark•ing, barks. 1.** To remove bark from (a tree or log). **2.** To rub the skin off of; abrade. **3.** To treat medically, tan, or dye using bark. [ME < ON *börkr*.]

bark³ also **barque** (bärk) *n. Naut.* **1.** A sailing ship with from three to five masts, all of them square-rigged except the aftermost mast, which is fore-and-aft rigged. **2.** A small vessel propelled by oars or sails. [ME *barke*, boat < OFr. *barque* < OItal. *barca* < Lat.]

bark beetle *n.* Any of various beetles of the family Scolytidae that burrrow beneath the bark of trees, causing extensive damage.

bar•keep•er (bär′kē′pər) also **bar•keep** (-kēp′) *n.* **1.** One who owns a bar that sells alcoholic drinks. **2.** See **bartender.**

bar•ken•tine also **bar•quen•tine** (bär′kən-tēn′) *n. Naut.* A sailing ship with from three to five masts of which only the foremost mast is square-rigged, the others being fore-and-aft rigged. [Prob. BARK³ + (BRIG)ANTINE.]

bark•er¹ (bär′kər) *n.* **1.** One that makes a bark or a barking sound. **2.** An employee who stands before the entrance to a show and solicits customers with a loud, colorful sales spiel.

bark•er² (bär′kər) *n.* One that removes bark from trees or logs or prepares it for tanning.

Bar•kley (bär′klē), **Alben William.** 1877–1956. Vice President of the U.S. (1949–53).

bar-le-duc also **Bar-le-Duc** (bär′lĭ-do͝ok′) *n.* A savory preserve made of white currants or gooseberries. [After *Bar-le-Duc*, a town of NE France.]

Bar•let•ta (bär-lĕt′ə). A city of S Italy on the Adriatic WNW of Bari. Pop. 83,719.

bar•ley (bär′lē) *n.* **1.** A grass in the genus *Hordeum*, native to temperate regions and having flowers in terminal, often long-awned spikes. **2.** The grain of *H. vulgare* or its varieties, used for malt and cereal. [ME *barli* < OE *bærlic*. See **bhares-*.**]

bar•ley•corn (bär′lē-kôrn′) *n.* **1.** The grain of barley. **2.** A unit of measure equal to the width of a grain of barley, or about ⅓ inch (0.85 centimeter).

barley sugar *n.* A clear, hard candy made by boiling down sugar, formerly with an extract of barley added.

Bar•low (bär′lō′), **Joel.** 1754–1812. Amer. poet and diplomat whose works include "The Hasty Pudding" (1796).

Barlow knife *n.* A pocketknife with one short prying and gouging blade and one long slicing and carving blade. [After *Barlow*, the family name of its makers.]

barm (bärm) *n.* The yeasty foam that rises to the surface of fermenting malt liquors. [ME *berme* < OE *beorma*, yeast. See **bhreu-*.**]

bar•maid (bär′mād′) *n.* A woman who serves drinks in a bar.

bar•man (bär′mən) *n.* A man who serves drinks in a bar.

Bar•me•cid•al (bär′mĭ-sīd′l) also **Bar•me•cide** (bär′mĭ-sīd′) *adj.* Plentiful or abundant in appearance only; illusory. [After *Barmecide*, a nobleman in *The Arabian Nights* who served an imaginary feast to a beggar.]

bar mitz•vah or **bar miz•vah** (bär mĭts′və) *—n.* **1.** *Judaism.* The ceremony that initiates and recognizes a 13-year-old Jewish boy as an adult responsible for his moral and religious duties. **2.** A boy so recognized. *—tr.v.* **-vahed, -vah•ing, -vahs.** To confirm in the ceremony of bar mitzvah. [Heb. *bar miṣwâ*: *bar*, son + *miṣwâ*, command, commandment.]

barm•y (bär′mē) *adj.* **-i•er, -i•est. 1.** Full of barm; foamy. **2.** Eccentric; daft.

barn (bärn) *n.* **1.** A farm building used to store farm products and shelter livestock. **2.** A large shed for the housing of vehicles. **3.** A particularly large, typically bare building. **4.** *Phys.* A unit of area equal to 10^{-24} square centimeter, used to measure collision cross sections. [ME *bern* < OE *berærn*: *bere*, barley; see **bhares-*** + *ærn*, house.]

Bar•na•bas (bär′nə-bəs), Saint. fl. 1st cent. A.D. Christian convert and missionary with St. Paul to Cyprus and Asia Minor.

bar•na•cle (bär′nə-kəl) *n.* **1.** Any of various marine crustaceans of the subclass Cirripedia that in the adult stage form a hard shell and remain attached to submerged surfaces, such as rocks. **2.** The barnacle goose. [ME, barnacle goose < OFr. *bernacle* < Med.Lat. *bernacula*, dim. of *bernaca*, perh. < OIr. *báirneach*, limpet.] **—bar′na•cled** *adj.*

barnacle goose *n.* A waterfowl *(Branta leucopsis)* of northern Europe and Greenland that breeds in the Arctic and has a white face with a black streak between the eyes and bill.

Bar•nard (bär′nərd, bär-närd′), **Christiaan Neethling.** b. 1923. South African surgeon who performed the first human heart transplant (1967).

Barnard, George Grey. 1863–1938. Amer. sculptor noted for his colossal statue of Abraham Lincoln (1917).

Bar•na•ul (bär′nə-o͞ol′). A city of S-central Russia on the Ob R. S of Novosibirsk. Pop. 578,000.

barn•burn•er (bärn′bûr′nər) *n. Informal.* An extremely impressive event or successful outcome.

barn dance *n.* A social gathering, often held in a barn, with music and square dancing.

Bar•ne•veldt or **Bar•ne•veld** (bär′nə-vĕlt′), **Jan van Olden.** 1547–1619. Dutch public official who negotiated a treaty with Spain (1609) and opposed certain Calvinist doctrines; executed for treason.

barn owl *n.* A predatory nocturnal bird *(Tyto alba)* having a white heart-shaped face, buff-brown upper plumage, and pale underparts, often nesting in buildings.

Barns•ley (bärnz′lē). A municipal borough of N England N of Sheffield. Pop. 225,800.

Barn•sta•ble (bärn′stə-bəl). A town of SE MA on central Cape Cod. Pop. 30,898.

barn•storm (bärn′stôrm′) *v.* **-stormed, -storm•ing, -storms.** *—intr.* **1.** To travel around the countryside making political speeches, giving lectures, or performing plays. **2.** To appear, as at fairs, in exhibitions of stunt flying and parachute jumping. *—tr.* To travel in this manner. **—barn′storm′er** *n.*

barn swallow *n.* A widely distributed bird *(Hirundo rustica)* that nests in barns and caves and has a deeply forked tail, a dark-blue back, and tan underparts.

Bar•num (bär′nəm), **P(hineas) T(aylor).** 1810–91. Amer. circus impresario who produced The Greatest Show on Earth (after 1871).

barn•yard (bärn′yärd′) *n.* The area surrounding a barn, often enclosed by a fence. *—adj.* Smutty; earthy.

barnyard grass *n.* Any of certain grasses in the genus *Echinochloa*, esp. the Old World annual species *E. crusgalli*, used sometimes for forage and widespread as a weed.

baro- or **bar-** *pref.* Weight; pressure: *barometer.* [< Gk. *baros*, weight. See **gʷerə-¹*.**]

Ba•ro•da (bə-rō′də). A city of W-central India SE of Ahmadabad; former cap. of the princely state of **Baroda.** Pop. 734,473.

bar•o•graph (băr′ə-grăf′) *n.* A recording barometer. **—bar′o•graph′ic** *adj.*

Ba•ro•ja y Nes•si (bə-rō′hə ē nĕs′ē, bä-rô′hä), **Pío.** 1872–1956. Spanish writer whose novels largely concern the intellectual and political climate of his homeland.

Ba•ro•lo (bä-rō′lō′, bə-rō′-) *n.* A full-bodied red wine produced in Italy. [After *Barolo* in the Piedmont region of Italy.]

ba•rom•e•ter (bə-rŏm′ĭ-tər) *n.* **1.** An instrument for measuring atmospheric pressure, used esp. in weather forecasting. **2.** Something that shows fluctuations; an indicator. **—bar′o•met′ric** (băr′ə-mĕt′rĭk), **bar′o•met′ri•cal** *adj.* **—bar′o•met′ri•cal•ly** *adv.* **—ba•rom′e•try** *n.*

bar•on (băr′ən) *n.* **1.a.** A British nobleman of the lowest rank. **b.** A nobleman, ranked differently in various countries. **c.** Also **Baron.** Used as the title for such a nobleman. **2.a.** A male feudal tenant holding his rights and title directly from a superior. **b.** A lord or nobleman; a peer. **3.** A man with great wealth and influence in a specified sphere of activity. [ME < OFr., prob. of Gmc. orig.]

bar•on•age (băr′ə-nĭj) *n.* **1.** Peers considered as a group. **2.** Barons and baronesses considered as a group. **3.** The rank or dignity of a baron or baroness.

bar•on•ess (băr′ə-nĭs) *n.* **1.** The wife or widow of a baron. **2.a.** A British noblewoman of the lowest rank. **b.** A noblewoman, ranked differently in various countries. **3.** Also **Baroness.** Used as the title for such a noblewoman.

bar•on•et (băr′ə-nĭt, băr′ə-nĕt′) *n.* **1.** A man holding a British hereditary title reserved for commoners, ranking immediately below the barons. **2.** Also **Baronet.** Used as the title for such a man. [ME, dim. of *baron*, baron. See BARON.]

bar•on•et•age (băr′ə-nĭ-tĭj, -nĕt′ĭj) *n.* **1.** Baronets and baronetesses considered as a group. **2.** Baronetcy.

bar•on•et•cy (băr′ə-nĭt-sē, -nĕt′sē) *n., pl.* **-cies.** The rank or dignity of a baronet or a baronetess.

bar•on•et•ess (băr′ə-nĭ-tĭs, băr′ə-nĕt′ĭs) *n.* **1.** A woman holding a British hereditary title of honor reserved for commoners, ranking immediately below the barons. **2.** Also **Baronetess.** Used as the title for such a woman.

ba•rong (bə-rông′, -rŏng′) *n.* A large, broad-bladed knife used by the Moros. [Native word in the Philippines.]

ba•ro•ni•al (bə-rō′nē-əl) *adj.* **1.** Of or relating to a baron or barony. **2.** Suited for or befitting a baron; stately and grand.

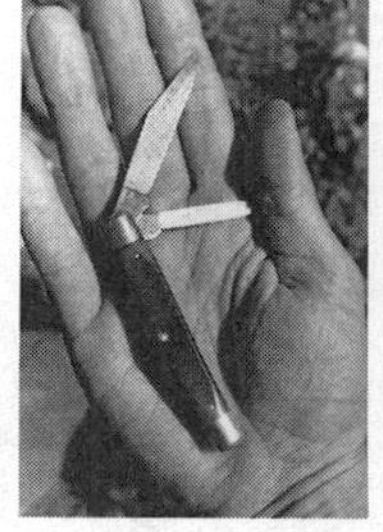
Barlow knife

Christiaan Barnard

ă pat	oi **boy**
ā pay	ou **out**
âr care	o͝o t**oo**k
ä father	o͞o b**oo**t
ĕ pet	ŭ cut
ē be	ûr **urge**
ĭ pit	th **thin**
ī pie	*th* **this**
îr pier	hw **which**
ŏ pot	zh vision
ō toe	ə about, item
ô paw	

Stress marks:
′ (primary);
′ (secondary), as in
dictionary (dĭk′shə-nĕr′ē)

bar·o·ny (băr′ə-nē) *n., pl.* **-nies. 1.** The domain of a baron or baroness. **2.** The rank or dignity of a baron or baroness.

ba·roque (bə-rōk′) *adj.* **1.** Also **Baroque.** Of, relating to, or characteristic of a style in art and architecture developed in Europe from about 1550 to 1700, emphasizing dramatic effect and typified by elaborate ornamentation and balance of disparate parts. **2.** Also **Baroque.** *Mus.* Of, relating to, or characteristic of a composition style that flourished in Europe from about 1600 to 1750, marked by chromaticism, strict forms, and elaborate ornamentation. **3.** Marked by rich and sometimes incongruous ornamentation. **4.** Irregular in shape. — *n.* also **Baroque.** The baroque style or period in art, architecture, or music. [Fr. < Ital. *barocco* and < Port. *barroco.*] — **ba·roque′ly** *adv.*

bar·o·re·cep·tor (băr′ə-rĭ-sĕp′tər) *n.* A sensory nerve ending that is stimulated by pressure changes, esp. one in the blood vessel walls.

Ba·rot·se·land (bə-rŏt′sē-lănd′). A former kindgom of central Africa, now the W part of Zambia.

ba·rouche (bə-ro͞osh′) *n.* A four-wheeled carriage with a collapsible top, two double seats opposite each other, and a box seat outside for the driver. [Ger. *Barutsche* < Ital. *biroccio* < VLat. **birotium* < LLat. *birotus*, two-wheeled : Lat. *bi-*, bi-; see **dwo-*** + Lat. *rota*, wheel; see **ret-*.**]

barouche
c. 1870

barque (bärk) *n. Naut.* Var. of **bark³.**

bar·quen·tine (bär′kən-tēn′) *n. Naut.* Var. of **barkentine.**

Bar·qui·si·me·to (bär′kə-sə-mā′tō, -kē-sē-mĕ′tô). A city of NW Venezuela WSW of Caracas; founded 1552. Pop. 504,000.

bar·rack¹ (băr′ək) *tr.v.* **-racked, -rack·ing, -racks.** To house (soldiers, for example) in quarters. — *n.* **1.** Quarters for military personnel. Often used in the plural. **2.** A large building for temporary occupancy. Often used in the plural. [< Fr. *baraques*, barracks < Sp. *barracas*, soldiers' tents.]

bar·rack² (băr′ək) *v.* **-racked, -rack·ing, -racks.** — *intr.* **1.** *Chiefly British.* To jeer or shout at a player, speaker, or team. **2.** *Australian.* To shout support for a team. — *tr. Chiefly British.* To shout against; jeer at. [Perh. < Ir. dial. *barrack*, to brag; akin to *brag.*] — **bar′rack·er** *n.*

barracuda
Great barracuda
Sphyraena barracuda

barracks bag *n.* A cloth bag, usu. with a drawstring, for the storage of clothing or laundry.

bar·ra·coon (băr′ə-ko͞on′) *n.* A barracks in which slaves or convicts were formerly held in temporary confinement. [Sp. *barracón*, aug. of *barraca*, hut. See BARRACK¹.]

bar·ra·cu·da (băr′ə-ko͞o′də) *n., pl.* **barracuda** or **-das.** Any of various fierce, mostly tropical marine fishes of the genus *Sphyraena* that resemble pike and have a projecting lower jaw with fanglike teeth. [Am.Sp. < Sp. dial. *barraco*, overlapping tooth.]

bar·rage¹ (bär′ĭj) *n.* An artificial obstruction built in a watercourse to increase its depth or to divert its flow. [Fr. < *barrer*, to bar < *barre*, bar < OFr. See BAR¹.]

bar·rage² (bə-räzh′) *n.* **1.a.** A heavy curtain of artillery fire directed in front of allies to protect them. **b.** A rapid, concentrated missile discharge. **2.** An overwhelming outpouring, as of words. [Fr. *(tir de) barrage*, barrier (fire). See BARRAGE¹.] — **bar·rage′** *v.*

bar·rage balloon (bə-räzh′) *n.* A balloon anchored over a military objective to support nets that hinder enemy aircraft.

bar·ra·mun·da (băr′ə-mŭn′də) also **bar·ra·mun·di** (-dē) *n., pl.* **barramunda** or **-das** also **barramundi** or **-dis.** Any of several Australian food fishes, such as the lungfish. [Prob. of Aborig.al orig.]

bar·ran·ca (bə-răng′kə) also **bar·ran·co** (-kō) *n. Southwestern U.S.* **1.** A deep ravine or gorge. **2.** A bluff. [Sp., prob. of Iberian orig.]

bartizan
El Morro fortress,
San Juan, Puerto Rico

Bar·ran·quil·la (băr′ən-kē′ə, -yä, bä′rän-). A city of N Colombia on the Magdalena R.; founded 1629. Pop. 891,545.

bar·ra·tor also **bar·ra·ter** (băr′ə-tər) *n. Law.* One that persistently instigates lawsuits. [ME *baratour* < OFr. *barateour*, swindler < *barater*, to cheat, perh. < VLat. **prattāre* < Gk. *prattein*, to do.]

bar·ra·try (băr′ə-trē) *n., pl.* **-tries. 1.** *Law.* The offense of persistently instigating lawsuits, typically groundless ones. **2.** Sale or purchase of positions in church or state. [ME *barratrie*, the sale of church offices < OFr. *baraterie*, deception, malversation < *barater*, to cheat. See BARRATOR.] — **bar′ra·trous** (-trəs) *adj.* — **bar′ra·trous·ly** *adv.*

Barr body (bär) *n. Genet.* The condensed, inactive, single X chromosome found in the nuclei of somatic cells of most female mammals. [After Murray L. *Barr* (b. 1908), Canadian anatomist.]

Clara Barton

barred (bärd) *adj.* Marked with bars or stripes.

barred owl *n.* A large North American owl *(Strix varia)* having barred brownish breast plumage, a streaked belly, and a strident hoot.

bar·rel (băr′əl) *n.* **1.** A large cylindrical container, usu. made of staves bound with hoops, with a flat top and bottom of equal diameter. **2.** The quantity that a barrel with a given or standard capacity will hold. **3.** Any of various units of volume or capacity. In the U.S. Customary System it varies, as a liquid measure, from 31 to 42 gallons (120 to 159 liters) as established by law or usage. See table at **measurement. 4.** The cylindrical part or hollow shaft of any of various mechanisms, as: **a.** The cylindrical metal part of a firearm through which the bullet travels. **b.** A cylinder that contains a movable piston. **c.** The drum of a capstan. **d.** The cylinder within the mechanism of a timepiece that contains the mainspring. **5.** *Informal.* A large quantity. **6.** *Slang.* An act or an instance of moving rapidly, often recklessly, in a motor vehicle. — *adj.* Likened to a barrel, as in shape: *a barrel chest.* — *v.* **-reled, -rel·ing, -rels** or **-relled, -rel·ling, -rels.** — *tr.* To put or pack in a barrel. — *intr. Slang.* To move at a high speed. — ***idioms.* on the barrel** (or **barrelhead).** Giving, or requesting no credit: *paid cash on the barrel.* **over a barrel.** In an awkward position from which extrication is difficult. [ME *barel* < OFr. *baril.*]

barrel cactus *n.* Any of several cacti, esp. in the genera *Ferocactus* and *Echinocactus,* having unbranched, globular to columnar, ribbed spiny stems.

barrel chair *n.* A large upholstered chair having a high rounded back resembling a half barrel.

bar·rel·ful (băr′əl-fo͝ol′) *n., pl.* **-fuls.** The amount that a barrel can hold.

bar·rel·head (băr′əl-hĕd′) *n.* The flat top of a barrel.

bar·rel·house (băr′əl-hous′) *n.* **1.** A disreputable old-time saloon or house of prostitution. **2.** *Mus.* An early jazz style characterized by free group improvisation and an accented two-beat rhythm.

barrel organ *n. Mus.* A mechanical instrument on which a tune is played by the action of a revolving cylinder fitted with pegs or pins that open pipe valves supplied by a bellows.

barrel roll *n.* A flight maneuver in which an airplane makes a complete rotation on its longitudinal axis while approximately maintaining its original direction.

bar·ren (băr′ən) *adj.* **1.a.** Not producing offspring. **b.** Incapable of producing offspring. **2.** Lacking vegetation. **3.** Unproductive of results or gains; unprofitable. See Syns at **futile. 4.** Devoid of something specified. **5.** Lacking in liveliness or interest. — *n.* A tract of unproductive land, often with a scrubby growth of trees. Often used in the plural. [ME *barreine* < OFr. *brahaigne*, perh. of Gmc. orig.] — **bar′ren·ly** *adv.* — **bar′ren·ness** *n.*

Bar·ren Grounds (băr′ən). A treeless region of N Canada NW of Hudson Bay and E of the Mackenzie R. basin.

barren strawberry *n.* A low-growing, eastern North American perennial herb *(Waldsteinia fragarioides)* having strawberrylike leaves, yellow flowers, and small, dry, inedible fruit.

Bar·rès (bä-rĕs′), **Auguste Maurice.** 1862–1923. French writer and politician whose works trace his metamorphosis from egocentric to nationalist.

bar·rette (bə-rĕt′) *n.* A small clasp for holding hair in place. [Fr., dim. of *barre*, bar < OFr. See BAR¹.]

bar·ri·cade (băr′ĭ-kād′, băr′ĭ-kād′) *n.* **1.** A structure set up to obstruct the passage of an enemy. **2.** Something that serves as an obstacle; a barrier. — *tr.v.* **-cad·ed, -cad·ing, -cades. 1.** To close off or block with a barricade. **2.** To keep in or out by such means. [Fr. < *barrique*, barrel < OProv. *barrica* < VLat. **barrīca.* See EMBARGO.] — **bar′ri·cad′er** *n.*

Bar·rie (băr′ē). A city of S Ontario, Canada, on Lake Simcoe NNW of Toronto. Pop. 38,423.

Barrie, Sir **J(ames) M(atthew).** 1860–1937. British writer whose works include the play *Peter Pan* (1904).

bar·ri·er (băr′ē-ər) *n.* **1.** A structure built to bar passage. **2.** Something immaterial that obstructs or impedes. **3.** *Ecol.* A physical or biological factor that limits the migration, interbreeding, or free movement of individuals or populations. **4.** A boundary or limit. **5.** Something that separates or holds apart. **6.** A movable gate that keeps racehorses in line before a race. **7.** The palisades or fences enclosing the lists of a medieval tournament. Often used in the plural. **8.** *Geol.* An ice barrier. [ME *barrer* < OFr. *barriere* < VLat. **barrāria* < **barra*, bar.]

barrier reef *n.* A long narrow ridge of coral or rock parallel to and near a coastline from which it is separated by a lagoon too deep for coral growth.

bar·ring (bär′ĭng) *prep.* Assuming no occurrence of; excepting.

bar·ri·o (bä′rē-ō′, băr′-) *n., pl.* **-os. 1.** An urban district or quarter in a Spanish-speaking country. **2.** A chiefly Spanish-speaking community or neighborhood in a U.S. city. [Sp. < Ar. *barrī*, of an open area < *barr*, open area.]

bar·ris·ter (băr′ĭ-stər) *n. Chiefly British.* A lawyer admitted to the bar in the superior courts. [Prob. blend of BAR¹ and obsolete *legister*, legist; see LEGIST.]

bar·room (bär′ro͞om′, -ro͝om′) *n.* A room or building in which alcoholic beverages are sold at a bar.

bar·row¹ (băr′ō) *n.* **1.** A flat, rectangular tray or cart with handles at each end. **2.** A wheelbarrow. [ME *barowe* < OE *bearwe.* See **bher-¹*.**]

bar·row² (băr′ō) *n.* A large mound of earth or stones placed over a burial site. [ME *bergh* < OE *beorg*, hill. See **bhergh-²*.**]

bar·row³ (băr′ō) *n.* A male pig castrated prior to sexual maturity. [ME *barow* < OE *bearg.*]

Bar•row (băr′ō), **Point.** The northernmost point of Alaska, in the NW on the Arctic Ocean. The nearby city of **Barrow** has research and government facilities. Pop. 3,469.
Bar•row-in-Fur•ness (băr′ō-ĭn-fûr′nĭs). A borough of NW England on an inlet of the Irish Sea NW of Manchester. Pop. 72,800.
Bar•ry (băr′ē), **Leonora Marie Kearney.** "Mother Lake." 1849–1930. Irish-born Amer. labor leader.
Barry, Philip. 1896–1949. Amer. playwright whose works include *The Philadelphia Story* (1939).
Bar•ry•more (băr′ĭ-môr′, -mōr′). Family of Amer. actors, including **Lionel** (1878–1954), his sister **Ethel** (1879–1959), and their brother **John** (1882–1942), "the Great Profile."
bar sinister *n.* **1.** *Her.* A bend or baton sinister held to signify birth out of wedlock. **2.** A hint or proof of such birth.
bar•stool (bär′sto͞ol′) *n.* A usu. high stool with a cushioned seat, used chiefly as seating for patrons at a bar.
Bar•stow (bär′stō). A city of SE CA NE of Los Angeles; founded in the 1880's. Pop. 21,472.
Bart. *abbr.* Baronet.
bar•tend•er (bär′tĕn′dər) *n.* One who mixes and serves alcoholic drinks at a bar.
bar•ter (bär′tər) *v.* **-tered, -ter•ing, -ters.** —*intr.* To trade goods or services without money. —*tr.* To trade (goods or services) without money. —*n.* **1.** The act or practice of bartering. **2.** Something bartered. —*adj.* Of, relating to, or being based on bartering. [ME *barteren*, prob. < OFr. *barater.* See BARRATOR.] —**bar′ter•er** *n.*
Barth (bärth), **John Simmons.** b. 1930. Amer. writer whose novels often examine the relationship between language and reality.
Barth (bärt, bärth), **Karl.** 1886–1968. Swiss Protestant theologian who advocated a return to the principles of the Reformation. —**Barth′i•an** *adj.*
Barthes (bärt), **Roland.** 1915–80. French critic who applied semiology to literary and social criticism.
Bar•thol•di (bär-thŏl′dē, -tôl-dē′), **Frédéric Auguste.** 1834–1904. French sculptor best known for the Statue of Liberty in New York Harbor (dedicated 1886).
Bar•tho•lin's gland (bär′tl-ĭnz, -thə-lĭnz) *n. Anat.* Either of two small glands located on either side of the vaginal orifice that secrete a lubricating mucus. [After Caspar *Bartholin* (1585–1629), Danish physician.]
Bar•thol•o•mew (bär-thŏl′ə-myo͞o′), Saint. Sometimes called **Na•than•ael** (nə-thăn′yəl). One of the 12 Apostles, who according to tradition was martyred in Armenia.
bar•ti•zan also **bar•ti•san** (bär′tĭ-zən, bär′tĭ-zăn′) *n.* A small overhanging turret on a wall or tower. [Alteration of *bratticing*, timberwork < BRATTICE.] —**bar′ti•zaned** *adj.*
Bar•tles•ville (bär′tlz-vĭl′). A city of NE OK N of Tulsa. Pop. 34,256.
Bart•lett¹ (bärt′lĭt). A town of SW TN, a suburb of Memphis. Pop. 26,989.
Bart•lett² (bärt′lĭt) *n.* A comon variety of pear with yellowish skin and juicy flesh. [After Enoch *Bartlett* (1779–1860).]
Bartlett, John. 1820–1905. Amer. publisher and editor who compiled *Familiar Quotations* (1855).
Bar•tók (bär′tŏk′, -tôk′), **Béla.** 1881–1945. Hungarian pianist and composer whose works combine Eastern European folk music with dissonant harmonies. —**Bar•tók′i•an** *adj.*
Bar•to•lom•me•o (bär-tŏl′ə-mā′ō, -tô′lô-), **Fra.** 1475?–1517. Italian painter of the Florentine school whose works include *Madonna della Misericordia* (1515).
Bar•ton (bär′tn), **Clara.** 1821–1912. Amer. administrator who did battlefield relief work during the Civil War and organized the American Red Cross (1881).
Barton, Sir **Derek Harold Richard.** b. 1918. British chemist who shared a 1969 Nobel Prize.
Bar•tram (bär′trəm), **John.** 1699–1777. Amer. botanist who established the first botanical garden in the colonies (1728). His son **William Bartram** (1739–1823) was also a botanist.
Bar•uch (bâr′ək, bə-ro͞ok) *n.* See table at **Bible.**
Ba•ruch (bə-ro͞ok′), **Bernard Mannes.** 1870–1965. Amer. financier, public official, and political adviser.
bar•ware (bär′wâr′) *n.* The glassware and other items used to prepare alcoholic drinks.
bar•y•cen•ter (băr′ĭ-sĕn′tər) *n.* See **center of mass.** [Gk. *barus*, heavy; see **gʷerə-¹*** + CENTER.]
bar•y•on (băr′ē-ŏn′) *n.* Any of a family of subatomic particles that participate in strong interactions, are composed of three quarks, and are generally more massive than mesons. See table at **subatomic particle.** [Gk. *barus*, heavy; see **gʷerə-¹*** + -ON¹.] —**bar′y•on′ic** *adj.*
baryon number *n.* A quantum number equal to the difference between the number of baryons and the number of antibaryons in a system of subatomic particles.
Ba•rysh•ni•kov (bə-rĭsh′nĭ-kôf′), **Mikhail Nikolayavich.** b. 1948. Russian-born ballet dancer and choreographer who performed with the Kirov Ballet in Leningrad and later with the American Ballet Theater.
bar•y•sphere (băr′ĭ-sfîr) *n.* See **centrosphere** 2. [Gk. *barus*, heavy; see **gʷerə-¹*** + SPHERE.]
ba•ry•ta (bə-rī′tə) *n.* Any of several barium compounds. [NLat. < Gk. *barutēs*, weight < *barus*, heavy. See **gʷerə-¹*.**]
ba•ry•tes (bə-rī′tēz) *n.* Var. of **barite.**
bar•y•tone (băr′ĭ-tōn′) *n. Mus.* Var. of **baritone.**
B.A.S. *abbr.* **1.** Bachelor of Agricultural Science. **2.** Bachelor of Applied Science.
bas•al (bā′səl, -zəl) *adj.* **1.a.** Of, at, relating to, or forming a base. **b.** *Bot.* Located at or near the base of any plant part. **2.** Of primary importance; basic. —**bas′al•ly** *adv.*
basal body *n.* A cellular organelle associated with the formation of cilia and flagella and similar to the centriole in structure.
basal cell *n. Biol.* A type of cell found in the deepest layer of the epithelium.
basal ganglion *n. Anat.* Any of several masses of gray matter embedded in the cerebral hemispheres that are involved in the regulation of voluntary movement.
basal granule *n.* See **basal body.**
basal metabolic rate *n. Physiol.* The rate at which energy is used by an organism at complete rest, measured in human beings by the heat given off per unit time and expressed as the calories released per kilogram of body weight or per square meter of body surface per hour.
basal metabolism *n. Physiol.* The minimum amount of energy required to maintain vital functions in an organism at complete rest, measured by the basal metabolic rate in a fasting individual who is awake, resting, and comfortably warm.
ba•salt (bə-sôlt′, bā′sôlt′) *n.* **1.** A hard, dense, dark volcanic rock composed chiefly of plagioclase, pyroxene, and olivine and often having a glassy appearance. **2.** A kind of hard unglazed pottery. [Lat. *basaltēs*, alteration of *basanītēs*, touchstone < Gk. *basanitēs (lithos)* < *basanos*, of Egypt. orig.] —**ba•sal′tic** (-sôl′tĭk) *adj.*
B.A.Sc. *abbr.* **1.** Bachelor of Agricultural Science. **2.** Bachelor of Applied Science.
bas•cule (băs′kyo͞ol) *n.* A device or structure, such as a drawbridge, counterbalanced so that when one end is lowered the other is raised. [Fr., seesaw : *bas*, low (< Med.Lat. *bassus*) + *cul*, bottom (< Lat. *cūlus*, rump; see **(s)keu-***).]
base¹ (bās) *n.* **1.a.** The lowest or bottom part. **b.** *Biol.* The part of an animal or plant organ nearest its point of attachment. **2.a.** A supporting part or layer; a foundation. **b.** A basic or underlying element; an infrastructure. **3.** The fundamental principle or underlying concept of a system or theory; a basis. **4.** A fundamental ingredient; a chief constituent. **5.** The fact, observation, or premise from which a reasoning process is begun. **6.a.** *Games.* A starting point, safety area, or goal. **b.** *Baseball.* Any one of the four corners of an infield, marked by a bag or plate. **7.** A center of organization, supply, or activity; a headquarters. **8.a.** A fortified center of operations. **b.** A supply center for a large force of military personnel. **9.** *Archit.* The lowest part of a structure, such as a wall, considered as a separate unit. **10.** *Her.* The lower part of a shield. **11.** *Ling.* A morpheme or morphemes regarded as a form to which affixes or other bases may be added. **12.** *Math.* **a.** The side or face of a geometric figure to which an altitude is or is thought to be drawn. **b.** The number that is raised to various powers to generate the principal counting units of a number system. **c.** The number raised to the logarithm of a designated number in order to produce that designated number. **13.** A line used as a reference for measurement or computations. **14.** *Chem.* **a.** Any of a large class of compounds, including the hydroxides and oxides of metals, having the ability to react with acids to form salts. **b.** A molecular or ionic substance capable of combining with a proton to form a new substance. **c.** A substance that provides a pair of electrons for a covalent bond with an acid. **15.** *Electron.* **a.** The region in a transistor between the emitter and the collector. **b.** The electrode attached to this region. **16.** One of the purines (adenine and guanine) or pyrimidines (cystosine, thymine, and uracil) in DNA or RNA. —*adj.* **1.** Forming or serving as a base: *a base layer of soil.* **2.** Situated at or near the base or bottom: *a base camp.* —*tr.v.* **based, bas•ing, bas•es.** **1.** To form or provide a base for: *based the new company in Portland.* **2.** To find a basis for; establish: *based her conclusions on the report.* **3.** To assign to a base; station. —***idiom.* off base.** Badly mistaken. [ME < OFr. < Lat. *basis* < Gk. See **gʷā-*.**]
base² (bās) *adj.* **bas•er, bas•est.** **1.a.** Having or showing a contemptible, mean-spirited, or selfish lack of human decency. **b.** Devoid of high values or ethics. **c.** Inferior in value or quality. **2.** Containing inferior substances. **3.** *Archaic.* Of low birth, rank, or position. —*n. Obsolete.* A bass singer or voice. [ME *bas*, low < OFr. < Med.Lat. *bassus.*] —**base′ly** *adv.*
base•ball (bās′bôl′) *n. Sports.* **1.** A game played with a bat and ball by two teams of nine players, each team playing alternately in the field and at bat, the players at bat having to run a course of four bases laid out in a diamond pattern in order to score. **2.** The ball used in this game.
base•board (bās′bôrd′, -bōrd′) *n.* A molding that conceals the joint between an interior wall and a floor.

Mikhail Baryshnikov

bascule
Tower Bridge, London

ă pat	oi boy
ā pay	ou out
âr care	o͝o took
ä father	o͞o boot
ĕ pet	ŭ cut
ē be	ûr urge
ĭ pit	th thin
ī pie	*th* this
îr pier	hw which
ŏ pot	zh vision
ō toe	ə about, item
ô paw	

Stress marks:
′ (primary);
′ (secondary), as in **dictionary** (dĭk′shə-nĕr′ē)

base•born (bās′bôrn′) *adj.* **1.** Ignoble; contemptible. **2.a.** Born to unmarried parents. **b.** Of humble birth.

base•burn•er (bās′bûr′nər) *n.* A coal stove with a hopper that replenishes itself from above as fuel is burned.

base hit *n. Baseball.* A hit by which the batter reaches base safely without an error, a fielder's choice, or a force play.

Ba•sel (bä′zəl) also **Basle** (bäl). A city of N Switzerland on the Rhine R. Pop. 176,200.

base•less (bās′lĭs) *adj.* Having no basis or foundation in fact.

base level *n.* The lowest level to which a land surface can be reduced by the action of running water.

base line *n.* **1.** A line serving as a basis, as for measurement. **2.** *Baseball.* An area within which a base runner must stay when running between bases. **3.** *Sports.* The boundary line at either end of a court, as in tennis.

basenji

base•ment (bās′mənt) *n.* **1.** The substructure or foundation of a building. **2.** The lowest habitable story of a building, usu. below ground level. **3.** *New England.* A public toilet, esp. one in a school. [Perh. obsolete Du., foundation, poss. < Ital. *basamento,* base of a column < *basare,* to found < *base,* bottom < Lat. *basis.* See BASIS.]

basement membrane *n.* A thin delicate layer of connective tissue underlying the epithelium of many organs.

base•ness (bās′nĭs) *n.* The quality or state of being contemptible, mean-spirited, or selfish.

ba•sen•ji (bə-sĕn′jē) *n.* A dog of a breed from Africa, having a short reddish-brown coat and characterized by the absence of a bark. [Of Bantu orig.; akin to Tshiluba, inhabitants of the hinterland : *ba-,* pl. pref. + *-senji.*]

base on balls *n. Baseball.* An advance to first base that is awarded to a batter who takes four pitches that are balls.

base pair *n.* The pair of nitrogenous bases, consisting of a purine linked by hydrogen bonds to a pyrimidine, that connects the complementary strands of a DNA molecule or of a double-stranded RNA molecule.

base pay *n.* An amount or a rate of compensation for a specified position of employment or activity excluding any other payments or allowances.

Count Basie

base runner *n. Baseball.* A member of the team at bat who has safely reached or is trying to reach a base.

ba•ses (bā′sēz′) *n.* Pl. of **basis.**

bash (băsh) *v.* **bashed, bash•ing, bash•es.** —*tr.* **1.** To strike with a heavy crushing blow. **2.** *Informal.* To criticize (another) harshly, accusatorially, and threateningly. —*intr. Informal.* To engage in harsh, accusatory, threatening criticism. —*n.* **1.** *Informal.* A heavy crushing blow. **2.** *Slang.* A celebration; a party. [?] —**bash′er** *n.*

Ba•shan (bā′shən). An ancient region of Palestine NE of the Sea of Galilee.

ba•shaw (bə-shô′) *n.* A pasha. [Ar. *bāšā* < Turk. *paşa* < Pers. *pādshāh.* See PADISHAH.]

bash•ful (băsh′fəl) *adj.* **1.** Shy, self-conscious, and awkward in the presence of others. See Syns at **shy**[1]. **2.** Characterized by, showing, or resulting from shyness, self-consciousness, or awkwardness. [< ME *basshe* < *basshed,* p.part. of *basshen,* to be discomfited, prob. var. of *abaishen.* See ABASH.] —**bash′ful•ly** *adv.* —**bash′ful•ness** *n.*

Bash•kir•i•a (băsh-kîr′ē-ə). A region of SW Russia in the southern Ural Mts.; part of Russia since the 16th cent.

basi– or **baso–** *pref.* **1.** Base; lower part: *basipetal.* **2.** Chemical base; chemically basic: *basophil.* [< Lat. *basis,* base. See BASIS.]

ba•sic (bā′sĭk) *adj.* **1.** Of, relating to, or forming a base; fundamental. **2.** Of, being, or serving as a starting point or basis. **3.** *Chem.* **a.** Producing, resulting from, or relating to a base. **b.** Containing a base, esp. in excess of acid. **c.** Containing oxide or hydroxide anions. Used of a salt. **4.** *Geol.* Containing little silica, as igneous rocks. —*n.* **1.** An essential, fundamental element or entity: *the basics of math.* **2.** Basic training. —**ba′si•cal•ly** *adv.* —**ba•sic′i•ty** (-sĭs′ĭ-tē) *n.*

BA•SIC or **Ba•sic** (bā′sĭk) *n. Comp. Sci.* A simplified user-level programming language. [*b(eginner's) a(ll-purpose) s(ymbolic) i(nstruction) c(ode).*]

basic process *n.* A method of steel production that uses a furnace lined with a basic refractory material.

ba•sid•i•o•carp (bə-sĭd′ē-ō-kärp′) *n.* A basidium-bearing structure found in basidiomycetous fungi. [BASIDI(UM) + -CARP.]

ba•sid•i•o•my•cete (bə-sĭd′ē-ō-mī′sēt′, -mī-sēt′) *n.* Any of a large group of fungi bearing sexually produced spores on a basidium. [BASIDI(UM) + -MYCETE.] —**ba•sid′i•o•my•ce′tous** (-mī-sē′təs) *adj.*

ba•sid•i•o•spore (bə-sĭd′ē-ə-spôr′, -spōr′) *n.* A sexually produced fungal spore borne on a basidium. —**ba•sid′i•o•spo′rous** *adj.*

ba•sid•i•um (bə-sĭd′ē-əm) *n., pl.* **-i•a** (-ē-ə). A small, specialized club-shaped structure typically bearing four basidiospores at the tips of minute projections. [BAS(I)- + *-idium,* dim. suff. (< Gk. *-idion*).] —**ba•sid′i•al** *adj.*

Ba•sie (bā′sē), **William.** "Count Basie." 1904–84. Amer. jazz pianist, band leader, and composer famous for his Big Band sound.

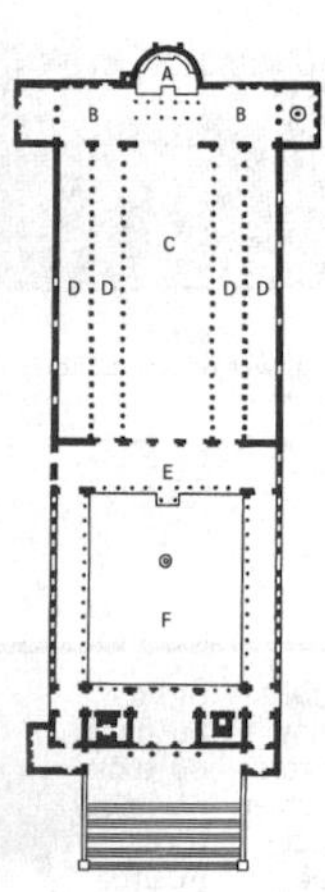

basilica
Plan of fourth-century A.D. Saint Peter's, Rome
A. Apse
B. Transept
C. Nave
D. Aisle
E. Narthex
F. Atrium

ba•si•fixed (bā′sə-fĭkst′) *adj. Bot.* Attached by the base.

ba•si•fy (bā′sə-fī′) *tr.v.* **-fied, -fy•ing, -fies.** *Chem.* **1.** To convert into a base. **2.** To make alkaline. —**ba′si•fi•ca′tion** (-fĭ-kā′shən) *n.* —**ba′si•fi′er** *n.*

bas•il (băz′əl, bā′zəl) *n.* **1.** An Old World aromatic annual herb *(Ocimum basilicum)* in the mint family, cultivated for its leaves that are used as a seasoning. **2.** Any of various plants in the genus *Ocimum,* native to warm regions and having aromatic foliage. [ME < OFr. *basile* < Med.Lat. *basilicum* < Gk. *basilikon* < neut. of *basilikos,* royal. See BASILICA.]

Bas•il (băz′əl, băs′-, bā′zəl, -səl), Saint. "Basil the Great." A.D. 330?–379? Greek Christian leader who was bishop of Caesarea after A.D. 370.

Ba•si•lan Islands (bä-sē′län′). A group of islands in the S Philippines separated from SW Mindanao by the narrow **Basilan Strait. Basilan Island** is the largest in the group.

bas•i•lar (băs′ə-lər) also **bas•i•lar•y** (-lĕr′ē) *adj.* Of, relating to, or located at or near the base, esp. the base of the skull. [NLat. *basilāris* < Lat. *basis,* base. See BASIS.]

Bas•il•don (băz′əl-dən, bā′zəl-). An urban district of SE England ENE of London. Pop. 153,200.

ba•sil•i•ca (bə-sĭl′ĭ-kə) *n.* **1.a.** An ancient Roman public building having a central nave with an apse at one or both ends and two side aisles formed by rows of columns. **b.** A Christian church of a similar design. **2.** *Rom. Cath. Ch.* A church that has been accorded certain privileges by the pope. [Lat. < Gk. *basilikē* < fem. of *basilikos,* royal < *basileus,* king.] —**ba•sil′i•can** (-kən) *adj.*

Ba•si•li•ca•ta (bə-zĭl′ĭ-kä′tə, bä-zē′lē-kä′tä). A region of S Italy bordering on the Tyrrhenian Sea and the Gulf of Taranta and forming the instep of the Italian "boot."

bas•i•lisk (băs′ə-lĭsk′, băz′-) *n.* **1.** A legendary serpent or dragon with lethal breath and glance. **2.** Any of various tropical American lizards of the genus *Basiliscus,* having a crest on the head, back, and tail. [ME < OFr. *basilisc* < Lat. *basiliscus* < Gk. *basiliskos,* dim. of *basileus,* king.]

ba•sin (bā′sĭn) *n.* **1.a.** An open, shallow, usu. round container used esp. for holding liquids. **b.** The amount that such a vessel can hold. **2.** A washbowl; a sink. **3.a.** An enclosed area of a river or harbor designed so that water level is unaffected by tidal changes. **b.** A small enclosed or partly enclosed body of water. **4.** A region drained by a single river system: *the Amazon basin.* **5.** *Geol.* **a.** A tract of land in which the rock strata are tilted toward a common center. **b.** A large bowl-shaped depression in the surface of the land or ocean floor. [ME < OFr. *bacin* < VLat. **baccīnum* < **baccus,* container, of Celt. orig.] —**ba′sin•al** *adj.*

bas•i•net (băs′ə-nĕt′, băs′ə-nĭt) *n.* A small steel helmet having a point and often a visor. [ME < OFr. *bacinet,* dim. of *bacin,* basin. See BASIN.]

ba•sip•e•tal (bā-sĭp′ĭ-tl, -zĭp′-) *adj. Bot.* Of or relating to growth or movement from the apex down to the base. —**ba•sip′e•tal•ly** *adv.*

ba•sis (bā′sĭs) *n., pl.* **-ses** (-sēz′). **1.** A foundation upon which something rests. **2.** The chief constituent; the fundamental ingredient. **3.** The fundamental principle. [ME < Lat. < Gk. See **gʷā-*.**]

basis point *n.* One hundredth of a percent, used in measuring yield differences among bonds.

bask (băsk) *intr.v.* **basked, bask•ing, basks. 1.** To expose oneself to pleasant warmth. **2.** To take great pleasure or satisfaction. [ME *basken.*]

Bas•ker•ville (băs′kər-vĭl′), **John.** 1706–75. British printer and typographer who produced a notable edition of Virgil (1757) and designed the typeface that bears his name.

bas•ket (băs′kĭt) *n.* **1.a.** A container made of interwoven material, such as rushes. **b.** The amount that a basket can hold. **2.** An item resembling such a container in shape or function. **3.** A usu. open gondola suspended from a hot-air balloon. **4.** *Basketball.* **a.** Either of the two elevated goals, each having a metal hoop and a suspended, open-bottomed circular net. **b.** The score made by throwing the ball through this goal. **5.** *Sports.* A circular structure at the base of a ski pole, used to prevent the pole from sinking into the snow. [ME < AN < VLat. **baskauta,* of Celt. orig.] —**bas′ket•ful′** *n.*

bas•ket•ball (băs′kĭt-bôl′) *n. Sports.* **1.** A game played between two teams of five players each, the object being to throw the ball through an elevated basket on the opponent's side of the rectangular court. **2.** The ball used in this game.

basket case *n. Informal.* **1.** One that is in a completely hopeless or useless condition. **2.** A person, esp. a soldier, who has had all four limbs amputated.

basket fish *n.* See **basket star.**

basket hilt *n.* A sword hilt with a basket-shaped guard.

Bas•ket Maker (băs′kĭt) *n.* **1.** Any of several early periods of Anasazi culture characterized by the use of basketry, dry farming, and coiled pottery. **2.** A member of the people of this culture.

bas•ket-of-gold (băs′kĭt-əv-gōld′) *n.* A shrubby perennial European herb *(Aurinia saxatilis)* with golden-yellow flowers.

bas•ket•ry (băs′kĭ-trē) *n.* **1.** The craft or process of making baskets. **2.** Baskets considered as a group.

basket star *n.* Any of various marine organisms of the class Ophiuroidea, having slender, branching, interlaced arms.

basket weave *n.* A textile weave of double threads interlaced to produce a checkered pattern like that of a woven basket.

bask•ing shark (băsʹkĭng) *n.* A shark *(Cetorhinus maximus)* that measures up to about 12 meters (40 feet) in length, feeds on plankton, and often floats near the surface of water.

Basle (bäl). See **Basel.**

bas mitz•vah or **bas miz•vah** (bäs mĭtsʹvə) *n. & v.* Var. of **bat mitzvah.**

baso– *pref.* Var. of **basi–.**

ba•so•phil (bāʹsə-fĭl, -zə-) *n.* A cell, esp. a white blood cell, having granules that stain readily with basic dyes. **—baʹso•philʹic, ba•sophʹi•lous** (bə-sŏfʹə-ləs) *adj.*

basque (băsk) *n.* A woman's close-fitting bodice. [Fr., skirt of a garment, alteration (perh. influenced by *Basque,* Basque; see BASQUE) of OFr. *baste* < Ital. *basta,* tuck, poss. of Gmc. orig.]

Basque (băsk) *n.* **1.** A member of a people of unknown origin inhabiting the western Pyrenees and the Bay of Biscay. **2.** The Basque language, of no known linguistic affiliation. [Fr., prob. < Lat. *Vascō,* perh. < Basque *Euskadi.*] **— Basque** *adj.*

Basque Provinces. A region comprising three provinces of N Spain on the Bay of Biscay.

Bas•ra (bäsʹrə, bŭsʹ-). A port city of SE Iraq on the Shatt al Arab near the Persian Gulf. Pop. 616,700.

bas-re•lief (bäʹrĭ-lēfʹ) *n.* See **low relief.** [Fr. < Ital. *bassorilievo*: *basso,* low (< Med.Lat. *bassus*) + *rilievo,* relief (< *rilevare,* to raise < Lat. *relevāre*; see RELIEVE).]

bass[1] (băs) *n., pl.* **bass** or **bass•es. 1.** Any of several North American freshwater fishes of the family Centrarchidae. **2.** Any of various marine fishes of the family Serranidae, such as the sea bass. [ME **bars,* perch < OE *bærs.*]

bass[2] (bās) *n. Mus.* **1.** A low-pitched sound or tone. **2.** The tones in the lowest register of an instrument. **3.** The lowest part in vocal or instrumental part music. **4.a.** A male singing voice of the lowest range. **b.** A singer who has such a voice. **5.** An instrument that produces tones in a low register. [ME *bas,* lowest musical part < *bas,* low. See BASE[2].] **— bass** *adj.*

bass clef (bās) *n. Mus.* A symbol showing that the fourth line from the bottom of a staff represents the F below middle C.

bass drum (bās) *n. Mus.* A large drum having a cylindrical body and two heads and producing a low resonant sound.

Basse•terre (băs-târʹ, bäs-). The cap. of St. Christopher–Nevis, on St. Christopher I. in the Leeward Is. of the West Indies. Pop. 14,725.

Basse-Terre (băs-târʹ, bäs-). The cap. of the French overseas department of Guadeloupe, on the S end of **Basse-Terre Island** in the Leeward Is. of the West Indies. Pop. 13,656.

basset hound (băsʹĭt) *n.* A hunting dog of a breed originating in France, with a long body, short legs, and long ears. [Fr., dim. of *basse,* fem. of *bas,* low. See BASE[2].]

bass fiddle (bās) *n. Mus.* See **double bass.**

bas•si•net (băsʹə-nĕtʹ, băsʹə-nĕtʹ) *n.* An oblong basketlike bed for an infant. [Fr., small basin, dim. of *bassin,* basin < OFr. *bacin.* See BASIN.]

bass•ist (bāʹsĭst) *n. Mus.* One who plays a bass instrument.

bas•so (băsʹō, bäʹsō) *n., pl.* **bas•sos** or **bas•si** (bäʹsē). *Mus.* A bass singer, esp. operatic. [Ital. < Med.Lat. *bassus,* low.]

bas•soon (bə-so͞onʹ, bă-) *n. Mus.* A low-pitched woodwind instrument having a double reed, a long wooden body, and a U-shaped tube leading to the mouthpiece. [Fr. *basson* < Ital. *bassone,* aug. of *basso,* bass. See BASSO.] **— bas•soonʹist** *n.*

bas•so pro•fun•do (băsʹō prə-fŭnʹdō, bäʹsō prə-fo͞onʹdō) *n., pl.* **basso pro•fun•dos** or **bas•si pro•fun•di** (bäʹsē prə-fo͞onʹdē). *Mus.* **1.** A deep bass singing voice. **2.** A singer who has such a voice. [Ital. : *basso,* bass + *profondo,* deep.]

bas•so-re•lie•vo (băsʹō-rĭ-lēʹvō) *n., pl.* **-vos.** See **low relief.** [Ital. *bassorilievo.* See BAS-RELIEF.]

Bass Strait (băs). A channel between Tasmania and SE Australia connecting the Indian Ocean with the Tasman Sea.

bass viol (bās) *n. Mus.* **1.** See **double bass. 2.** See **viola da gamba.**

bass•wood (băsʹwo͝odʹ) *n.* **1.** See **linden. 2.** The soft, light-colored wood of any species of linden. [*bass,* linden bark (alteration of BAST) + WOOD[1].]

bast (băst) *n. Bot.* Bast fiber. [ME < OE *bæst.*]

bas•tard (băsʹtərd) *n.* **1.** A child born to parents not married to each other. **2.** Something of irregular, inferior, or dubious origin. **3.** *Vulgar Slang.* A person, esp. one held to be mean or disagreeable. *—adj.* **1.** Born to unmarried parents. **2.** Not genuine; spurious. **3.** Resembling a known kind or species but not truly such. [ME < OFr., prob. of Gmc. orig.; akin to Old Frisian *bōst,* marriage.] **— basʹtard•ly** *adj.*

bas•tard•ize (băsʹtər-dīzʹ) *tr.v.* **-ized, -iz•ing, -iz•es.** To lower in quality or character; debase. **— basʹtard•i•zaʹtion** (-tər-dĭ-zāʹshən) *n.*

bastard toadflax *n.* Any of various hemiparasitic plants of the genus *Comandra,* having clusters of small flowers.

bastard wing *n.* See **alula.**

bas•tard•y (băsʹtər-dē) *n.* **1.** The condition of being born to unmarried parents. **2.** The begetting of a bastard.

baste[1] (bāst) *tr.v.* **bast•ed, bast•ing, bastes.** To sew with large running stitches to hold together temporarily. [ME *basten* < OFr. *bastir,* of Gmc. orig.] **— bastʹer** *n.*

baste[2] (bāst) *tr.v.* **bast•ed, bast•ing, bastes.** To moisten (meat, for example) periodically with a liquid, esp. while cooking. [ME *basten.*] **— bastʹer** *n.*

baste[3] (bāst) *tr.v.* **bast•ed, bast•ing, bastes. 1.** To beat vigorously; thrash. **2.** To lambaste. [Prob. of Scand. orig.; akin to ON *beysta.* See **bhau-*.**]

bast fiber *n. Bot.* Any of various durable fibers from the phloem or from tissues outside the phloem, including flax.

bas•tille (bă-stēlʹ) *n.* A prison; a jail. [Fr. < OFr., fortress, alteration of *bastide* < OProv. *bastida* < *bastir,* to build, of Gmc. orig.]

Bas•tille Day (bă-stēlʹ) *n.* July 14, observed in France in commemoration of the storming of the Paris Bastille in 1789.

bas•ti•na•do (băsʹtə-nāʹdō, -näʹ-) also **bas•ti•nade** (-nādʹ, -nädʹ) *—n., pl.* **-does** also **-nades. 1.** A beating with a stick or cudgel, esp. on the soles of the feet. **2.** A stick or cudgel. *—tr.v.* **-doed, -do•ing, -does** also **-nad•ed, -nad•ing, -nades.** To subject to a beating; thrash. [Alteration of Sp. *bastonada* < *baston,* stick < VLat. **bastō, *bastōn-.*]

bas•tion (băsʹchən, -tē-ən) *n.* **1.** A projecting part of a fortification. **2.** A well-fortified position. **3.** One that is considered similar to a defensive stronghold. [Fr. < OFr. *bastillon* < *bastille,* fortress. See BASTILLE.] **— basʹtioned** *adj.*

bast•naes•ite (băstʹnə-sītʹ) *n.* A yellowish to reddish-brown mineral, $(Ce,La)CO_3(F,OH)$, that is a source of rare-earth elements. [After *Bastnäs,* a mine in S-central Sweden.]

Bas•togne (bă-stōnʹ, bă-stônʹyə). A town of SE Belgium near the Luxembourg border; a crucial point in the Battle of the Bulge (Dec. 1944–Jan. 1945). Pop. 11,386.

Ba•su•to•land (bə-so͞oʹtō-lăndʹ). See **Lesotho.**

bat[1] (băt) *n.* **1.** A stout wooden stick; a cudgel. **2.** A blow, such as one delivered with a stick. **3.** *Baseball.* A rounded club, wider at the hitting end, used to strike the ball. **4.** *Sports.* **a.** A club used in cricket, having a broad, flat-surfaced hitting end and a narrow handle. **b.** The racket used in various games, such as table tennis. *—v.* **bat•ted, bat•ting, bats.** *—tr.* **1.** To hit with or as if with a bat. **2.** *Baseball.* **a.** To cause (a run) to be scored while at bat: *batted in a run.* **b.** To have (a certain percentage) as a batting average. **3.** *Informal.* To produce in a hurried or an informal manner: *bat out a speech.* **4.** *Informal.* To discuss or consider at length. *—intr.* **1.** *Baseball.* **a.** To use a bat. **b.** To have a turn at bat. **2.** *Slang.* To wander about aimlessly. ***—idioms.*** **at bat.** *Sports.* Taking one's turn to bat, as in baseball or cricket. **go to bat for.** To give assistance to; defend. **off the bat.** Without hesitation; immediately. [ME, perh. partly of Celt. orig., and partly < OFr. *batte,* pounding implement, flail (< *batre,* to beat; see BATTER[1]).]

bat[2] (băt) *n.* Any of various nocturnal flying mammals of the order Chiroptera, having membranous wings that extend from the forelimbs to the hind limbs or tail and anatomical adaptations for echolocation. ***—idiom.*** **have bats in (one's) belfry.** To behave in an eccentric, bizarre manner. [Alteration of ME *bakke,* of Scand. orig.]

bat[3] (băt) *tr.v.* **bat•ted, bat•ting, bats.** To wink or flutter: *bat one's eyelashes.* [Prob. a var. of BATE[2].]

bat[4] (băt) *n. Slang.* A binge; a spree. [Prob. < *batter,* spree.]

bat. *abbr.* Battalion.

B.A.T. *abbr.* Bachelor of Arts in Teaching.

Ba•taan (bə-tănʹ, -tänʹ). A peninsula of W Luzon, Philippines, between Manila Bay and the South China Sea. U.S. and Philippine World War II troops surrendered to the Japanese here in 1942.

Ba•ta•vi•a (bə-tāʹvē-ə). **1.** A city of W NY WSW of Rochester. Pop. 16,310. **2.** See **Jakarta.**

bat•boy (bătʹboiʹ) *n. Baseball.* A boy who is employed by a baseball team to look after its equipment, esp. the bats.

batch[1] (băch) *n.* **1.** An amount produced at one baking. **2.** The quantity produced as the result of one operation: *a batch of cement.* **3.** The quantity needed for one operation. **4.** A group of persons or things. **5.** *Comp. Sci.* A set of data or jobs to be processed in a single program run. *—tr.v.* **batched, batch•ing, batch•es.** To assemble or process as a batch. [ME *bache,* prob. < OE **bæcce* < *bacan,* to bake.]

batch[2] (băch) *v. Informal.* Var. of **bach.**

bate[1] (bāt) *tr.v.* **bat•ed, bat•ing, bates. 1.** To lessen the force or intensity of; moderate. **2.** To take away; subtract. [ME *baten,* short for *abaten.* See ABATE.]

bate[2] also **bait** (bāt) *intr.v.* **bat•ed, bat•ing, bates** also **bait•ed, bait•ing, baits.** To flap the wings wildly. Used of a falcon. [ME *baten* < OFr. *batre,* to beat. See BATTER[1].]

ba•teau (bă-tōʹ) *n., pl.* **-teaux** (-tōzʹ). *Naut.* **1.** A long, light, flatbottom boat with a sharply pointed bow and stern. **2.** A small, light, flatbottom rowboat. [Canadian and Louisiana Fr. < Fr., boat < OFr. *batel* < OE *bāt.* See **bheid-*.**]

Bates (bāts), **Katherine Lee.** 1859–1929. Amer. educator and writer best known for her poem "America the Beautiful."

Bates•i•an mimicry (bātʹsē-ən) *n.* A form of protective mimicry in which a species closely resembles an unpalatable or harmful species and therefore is avoided by predators. [After

basket star
Astrophyton muricatum

bass clef

bat[2]
Mouse-eared bat

ă pat	oi boy
ā pay	ou out
âr care	o͝o took
ä father	o͞o boot
ĕ pet	ŭ cut
ē be	ûr urge
ĭ pit	th thin
ī pie	*th* this
îr pier	hw which
ŏ pot	zh vision
ō toe	ə about, item
ô paw	

Stress marks:
ʹ (primary);
ʹ (secondary), as in **dictionary** (dĭkʹshə-nĕrʹē)

Henry W. *Bates* (1825–92), British naturalist.]

Bate•son (bāt′sən), **William.** 1861–1926. British biologist who experimentally proved Mendel's theories on heredity.

bat•fish (băt′fĭsh′) *n., pl.* **batfish** or **-fish•es.** Any of various marine anglerfishes of the family Ogcocephalidae, having a retractable appendage above the mouth.

bat•fowl (băt′foul′) *intr.v.* **-fowled, -fowl•ing, -fowls.** To catch roosting birds at night by blinding them with a light and then hitting or netting them.

bat•girl (băt′gûrl′) *n. Baseball.* A girl who is employed by a baseball team to look after its equipment, esp. the bats.

bath[1] (băth, bäth) *n., pl.* **baths** (bă*th*z, bä*th*z, băths, bäths). **1.a.** The act of soaking or cleansing the body, as in water or steam. **b.** The water used for cleansing the body. **2.a.** A bathtub. **b.** A bathroom. **3.** A building equipped for bathing. **4.** A resort providing therapeutic baths; a spa. Often used in the plural. **5.** A liquid in which something is dipped or soaked in order to process it: *an acid bath.* [ME < OE *bæth.*]

bath[2] (băth) *n.* An ancient Hebrew unit of liquid measure, equal to about 38 liters (10 U.S. gallons). [Heb.]

Bath (băth, bäth). A city of SW England SE of Bristol; famous for its Georgian architecture and its hot mineral springs. Pop. 84,100.

Bath chair (băth, bäth) *n.* A hooded wheelchair used esp. for invalids, typically at a spa. [After BATH.]

bathe (bā*th*) *v.* **bathed, bath•ing, bathes.** —*intr.* **1.** To take a bath. **2.** To go into the water, as for swimming. **3.** To become immersed in or as if in liquid. —*tr.* **1.** To immerse in liquid; wet. **2.** To wash in a liquid. **3.** To apply a liquid to for healing or soothing purposes. **4.** To seem to wash or pour over; suffuse. [ME *bathen* < OE *bathian.*] —**bath′er** *n.*

bathyscaph
The *Trieste*

ba•thet•ic (bə-thĕt′ĭk) *adj.* Characterized by bathos. [Prob. a blend of BATHOS and PATHETIC.]

bath•house (băth′hous′, bäth′-) *n.* A building with bathing facilities or with dressing rooms for swimmers.

Bath•i•nette (băth′ə-nĕt′, bä′thə-). A trademark used for portable bathing devices for infants.

bath•ing cap (bā′*th*ĭng) *n.* An elastic cap worn by swimmers.

bathing suit *n.* See **swimsuit.**

bath•mat (băth′măt′, bäth′-) *n.* A mat used in front of a bathtub or shower to absorb water or prevent slipping.

batho– *pref.* Var. of **bathy–.**

bath•o•lith (băth′ə-lĭth′) *n.* A mass of igneous rock that has melted and intruded surrounding strata. —**bath′o•lith′ic** *adj.*

ba•thom•e•ter (bə-thŏm′ĭ-tər) *n.* An instrument used to measure the depth of water.

ba•thos (bā′thŏs′, -thôs′) *n.* **1.a.** An abrupt, unintended transition in style from the exalted to the commonplace, producing a ludicrous effect. **b.** An anticlimax. **2.a.** Insincere or grossly sentimental pathos. **b.** Banality; triteness. [Gk., depth < *bathus,* deep.]

bath•robe (băth′rōb′, bäth′-) *n.* A loose-fitting robe worn before and after bathing and for lounging.

bath•room (băth′rōōm′, -rŏŏm′, bäth′-) *n.* A room with facilities for bathing and usu. also containing a sink and toilet.

bath salts (băth, bäth) *pl.n.* A perfumed crystalline substance for softening bathwater.

Bath•she•ba (băth-shē′bə, băth′shə-). In the Bible, the wife of Uriah and later of David.

bath•tub (băth′tŭb′, bäth′-) *n.* A tub for bathing.

Bath•urst (băth′ərst). See **Banjul.**

bathy– or **batho–** *pref.* **1.** Deep; depth: *batholith.* **2.** Deep-sea: *bathysphere.* [< Gk. *bathus,* deep, and < Gk. *bathos,* depth (< *bathus*).]

battering ram

ba•thym•e•try (bə-thĭm′ĭ-trē) *n.* Measurement of the depth of large bodies of water. —**bath′y•met′ric** (băth′ə-mĕt′rĭk), **bath′y•met′ri•cal** *adj.* —**bath′y•met′ri•cal•ly** *adv.*

bath•y•pe•lag•ic (băth′ə-pə-lăj′ĭk) *adj.* Of, relating to, or living in the depths of the ocean, esp. between about 600 and 3,000 meters (2,000 and 10,000 feet).

bath•y•scaph (băth′ĭ-skăf′) also **bath•y•scaphe** (-skăf′, -skāf′) *n.* A free-diving deep-sea research vessel having a large flotation hull and an observation capsule, capable of reaching depths of 10 kilometers (6.2 miles) or more. [BATHY– + Gk. *skaphos,* boat.]

bath•y•sphere (băth′ĭ-sfîr′) *n.* A reinforced spherical deep-diving chamber in which persons study the oceans.

ba•tik (bə-tēk′, băt′ĭk) *n.* **1.a.** A dyeing method by which the parts of fabric not dyed are covered with removable wax. **b.** A design created by this method. **2.** Fabric dyed by this method. [Malay *batek,* of Javanese orig. < Proto-Austronesian **beCik,* tattoo (from the fact that the original process was similar to tattooing).]

Ba•tis•ta y Zal•dí•var (bə-tēs′tə ē zäl-dē′vär′, bä-tē′stä), **Fulgencio.** 1901–73. Cuban dictator (1933–40) and president (1940–44 and 1954–58); overthrown by Fidel Castro (1959).

ba•tiste (bə-tēst′, bă-) *n.* A fine plain-woven fabric made from various fibers and used esp. for clothing. [Fr. < OFr., perh. after *Baptiste* of Cambrai, 13th-cent. textile maker.]

bat•man (băt′mən) *n.* A British military officer's orderly. [Obsolete *bat,* packsaddle (< Fr. *bât* < OFr. *bast* < LLat. *bastum*) + MAN.]

bat mitz•vah or **bat miz•vah** (bät mĭts′və) or **bas mitz•vah** or **bas miz•vah** (bäs) —*n. Judaism.* **1.** The ceremony that initiates and recognizes a 12- to 14-year-old Jewish girl as an adult responsible for her moral and religious duties. **2.** A girl so recognized. —*tr.v.* **-vahed, -vah•ing, -vahs.** To confirm in the ceremony of bat mitzvah. [Heb. *bat miṣwâ*: *bat,* daughter + *miṣwâ,* commandment.]

ba•ton (bə-tŏn′, bă-, băt′n) *n.* **1.** *Mus.* A wooden stick or rod used to conduct an orchestra or a band. **2.** A hollow metal rod with a heavy rubber tip or tips wielded and twirled by a drum major or drum majorette. **3.** A short staff carried by certain public officials as a symbol of office. **4.** *Sports.* The hollow cylinder that is carried by each member of a relay team. **5.** A club or truncheon. **6.** *Her.* A shortened narrow bend, often signifying bastardy. [Fr. *bâton* < OFr. *baston,* stick < VLat. **bastō, *bastōn-.*]

Bat•on Rouge (băt′n rōōzh′). The cap. of LA, in the SE-central part on a bluff above the Mississippi R. Pop. 219,531.

ba•tra•chi•an (bə-trā′kē-ən) *adj.* Of or relating to vertebrate amphibians without tails. [< Gk. *batrakhos,* frog.] —**ba•tra′chi•an** *n.*

bats (băts) *adj. Slang.* Crazy; insane. [< *bats in the belfry.*]

bats•man (băts′mən) *n. Sports.* The player at bat in cricket and baseball.

Bat•swa•na (bŏt-swä′nə) *n., pl.* **Batswana** or **-nas.** See **Tswana** 1.

batt (băt) *n.* Pieces of fabric used for stuffing; batting. [Var. of BAT[1], cotton or wool fiber wadded into rolls or sheets.]

bat•tal•ion (bə-tăl′yən) *n.* **1.a.** An army unit typically having a headquarters and two or more companies, batteries, or similar subdivisions. **b.** A large body of organized troops. **2.** A great number. [Fr. *bataillon* < OFr. < Ital. *battaglione,* aug. of *battaglia* < VLat. **battalia.* See BATTLE.]

Bat•ta•ni (bə-tä′nē), **al-.** 858?–929. Arab astronomer and mathematician who introduced an organized table of sines.

bat•ten[1] (băt′n) *intr.v.* **-tened, -ten•ing, -tens. 1.** To become fat. **2.** To thrive and prosper, esp. at another's expense. [Ult. < ON *batna,* to improve. See **bhad-*.**]

bat•ten[2] (băt′n) *n.* **1.** *Naut.* **a.** One of several flexible strips of wood placed in pockets at the outer edge of a sail to keep it flat. **b.** A strip of wood used to fasten the edges of the material that covers hatches. **2.** *Chiefly British.* A narrow strip of wood used esp. for flooring. —*tr.v.* **-tened, -ten•ing, -tens.** *Naut.* To furnish, fasten, or secure with battens. [ME *batent* < OFr. *bataunt,* wooden strip, clapper < pr.part. of *batre,* to beat. See BATTER[1].]

Bat•ten (băt′n), **Jean.** 1909–82. New Zealand aviator who was the first woman to fly a solo round trip between England and Australia (1935).

bat•ter[1] (băt′ər) *v.* **-tered, -ter•ing, -ters.** —*tr.* **1.** To hit repeatedly with violent blows. **2.** To damage, as by heavy wear. **3.** To abuse physically or mentally on a regular basis. —*intr.* To pound repeatedly with heavy blows. —*n. Print.* A damaged area on the face of type or on a plate. [ME *bateren* < OFr. *batre* < LLat. *battere* < Lat. *battuere.*]

bat•ter[2] (băt′ər) *n. Sports.* The player at bat in baseball and cricket.

bat•ter[3] (băt′ər) *n.* A liquid or semiliquid mixture, as of flour, milk, and eggs, used in cooking. [ME *bater,* prob. < OFr. *bateure,* a beating < *batre,* to beat. See BATTER[1].]

bat•ter[4] (băt′ər) *n.* A slope, as of the outer face of a wall, that recedes from bottom to top. —*tr.v.* **-tered, -ter•ing, -ters.** To construct so as to create an upwardly receding slope. [?]

bat•ter•cake (băt′ər-kāk′) *n. Chiefly Southern U.S.* **1.** See **pancake. 2.** See **johnnycake.** See Regional Note at **johnnycake.**

battering ram *n.* **1.** A heavy metal bar used to break down walls and doors. **2.** A heavy beam used in ancient warfare to batter down the walls and gates of a place under siege.

bat•ter•y (băt′ə-rē) *n., pl.* **-ies. 1.a.** The act of beating or pounding. **b.** *Law.* The unlawful and unwanted touching or striking of one person by another, with the intention of bringing about a harmful or offensive contact. **2.a.** An emplacement for one or more pieces of artillery. **b.** A set of guns or other heavy artillery. **c.** An army artillery unit, corresponding to a company in the infantry. **3.a.** An array of similar things intended for use together. **b.** An impressive body or group. **4.** *Baseball.* The pitcher and catcher. **5.** *Mus.* The percussion section of an orchestra. **6.** *Elect.* **a.** Two or more connected cells that produce a direct current by converting chemical energy to electrical energy. **b.** A single cell that produces an electric current. [ME *batri,* forged metal ware < OFr. *baterie,* a beating < *batre,* to batter. See BATTER[1].]

bat•ting (băt′ĭng) *n.* **1.** The act of a batter. **2.** Cotton, wool, or synthetic fiber wadded into rolls or sheets, used for stuffing furniture and mattresses and for lining quilts. [Sense 2, from the beating of raw cotton to clean it.]

batting average *n. Baseball.* A measure of a batter's performance obtained by dividing the total of base hits by the number of times at bat.

bat•tle (băt′l) *n.* **1.a.** An encounter between opposing forces. **b.** Armed fighting; combat. **2.** A match between two combatants. **3.a.** A protracted controversy or struggle. **b.** An intense competition. — *v.* **-tled, -tling, -tles.** — *intr.* To engage in or as if in battle. — *tr.* To fight against. [ME *batel* < OFr. *bataille* < VLat. *battālia < LLat. *battuālia*, fighting and fencing exercises < Lat. *battuere*, to beat.] — **bat′tler** *n.*

Bat•tle (băt′l). A town of SE England; site of the Battle of Hastings (1066). Pop. 4,987.

bat•tle-ax or **bat•tle-axe** (băt′l-ăks′) *n.* **1.** A heavy broad-headed ax formerly used as a weapon. **2.** *Informal.* A woman held to be antagonistic or overbearing.

Battle Creek. A city of S MI E of Kalamazoo. Pop. 53,540.

battle cry *n.* **1.** A rallying cry uttered in combat, esp. while attacking. **2.** A slogan used by the proponents of a cause.

bat•tle•dore (băt′l-dôr′) *n. Sports.* **1.a.** An early form of badminton played with a flat wooden paddle and a shuttlecock. **b.** The paddle used in this game. **2.** A badminton racket. [ME *batildore*, perh. blend of *betel*, bat; see BEETLE[3], and OProv. *batedor*, bat (< *battre*, to beat < LLat. *battere*; see BATTER[1]).]

battle fatigue *n.* The debilitating psychiatric breakdown caused by the stress of combat.

bat•tle•field (băt′l-fēld′) *n.* **1.** An area where a battle is fought. **2.** A sphere of contention.

bat•tle•front (băt′l-frŭnt′) *n.* **1.** The sector in which armed forces engage in combat. **2.** The area where opponents meet.

bat•tle•ground (băt′l-ground′) *n.* See **battlefield.**

battle group *n.* **1.** A U.S. army unit usu. composed of five companies. **2.** A naval force composed of a variable number of warships, escorts, and supply vessels.

bat•tle•ment (băt′l-mənt) *n.* A parapet built on top of a wall, with indentations for decoration or defense. [ME *batelment*, alteration (influenced by *batel*, battle; see BATTLE) of OFr. *batillement*, tower, turret < *bastille.* See BASTILLE.] — **bat′tle•ment′ed** (-mĕn′tĭd) *adj.*

battle royal *n.*, *pl.* **battles royal. 1.** An intense altercation. **2.** A battle involving many combatants. **3.** A fight to the finish. [BATTLE + ROYAL, grand in scale.]

bat•tle•ship (băt′l-shĭp′) *n.* Any one of a class of warships of the largest size, carrying the greatest number of weapons and clad with the heaviest armor. [Short for *line-of-battle ship.*]

bat•tle•wag•on (băt′l-wăg′ən) *n.* See **battleship.**

bat•ty (băt′ē) *adj.* **-ti•er, -ti•est.** *Slang.* Crazy; insane. [< *bats in the belfry.*] — **bat′ti•ness** *n.*

Ba•tu•mi (bə-to͞o′mē) also **Ba•tum** (-to͞om′). A city of SW Georgia on the Black Sea near Turkey. Pop. 132,000.

Bat Yam (bät′ yäm′). A city of W-central Israel on the Mediterranean near Tel Aviv–Jaffa. Pop. 131,200.

bau•ble (bô′bəl) *n.* **1.** A small showy ornament of little value; a trinket. **2.** *Archaic.* A mock scepter carried by a court jester. [ME *babel* < OFr., plaything.]

Bau•cis (bô′sĭs) *n. Gk. Myth.* A peasant woman of Phrygia who with her husband Philemon was honored for their hospitality to Zeus and Hermes disguised as men.

baud (bôd) *n. Comp. Sci.* A unit of speed in data transmission usu. equal to one bit per second. [After Jean Maurice Emile *Baudot* (1845–1903), French engineer.]

Baude•laire (bōd-lâr′), **Charles Pierre.** 1821–67. French writer, translator, and critic known for his only volume of poetry, *Les Fleurs du Mal* (1857, expanded 1861).

Bau•douin I (bō-dwăN′). b. 1930. King of Belgium (since 1951).

Bau•haus (bou′hous′) *adj.* Of or relating to a 20th-century school of design influenced by and derived from techniques and materials esp. of industrial manufacture. [Ger., an architecture school founded by Walter Gropius (1883–1969).]

bau•hin•i•a (bō-hĭn′ē-ə, bō-ĭn′-) *n.* Any of various tropical or subtropical trees, shrubs, or woody vines of the genus *Bauhinia* in the pea family. [NLat., after Jean *Bauhin* (1541–1612) and Gaspard *Bauhin* (1560–1624), Swiss botanists.]

baulk (bôk) *v.* & *n.* Var. of **balk.**

Baum (bôm, bäm), **Lyman Frank.** 1856–1919. Amer. writer known esp. for *The Wonderful Wizard of Oz* (1900).

Bau•mé (bō-mā′), **Antoine.** 1728–1804. French pharmacist who in 1768 devised an improved hydrometer using the scale that now bears his name.

Baumé scale *n.* A hydrometer scale used to measure the specific gravity of liquids. [After Antoine BAUMÉ.]

Bau•ru (bou-ro͞o′). A city of SE Brazil NW of São Paulo. Pop. 180,093.

baux•ite (bôk′sīt′) *n.* The principal ore of aluminum, composed mainly of hydrous aluminum oxides and aluminum hydroxides. [After Les *Baux*, a village of SE France.] — **baux•it′ic** (-sĭt′ĭk) *adj.*

Ba•var•i•a (bə-vâr′ē-ə). A region and former duchy of S Germany.

Ba•var•i•an (bə-vâr′ē-ən) *n.* **1.** A native or inhabitant of Bavaria. **2.** The High German dialect of Bavaria and Austria. — **Ba•var′i•an** *adj.*

Bavarian Alps. A range of the Alps between S Bavaria in Germany and the Tyrol in W Austria rising to 2,964.9 m (9,721 ft) in S Germany.

bawd (bôd) *n.* **1.** A woman who runs a house of prostitution. **2.** A prostitute. [ME, prob. < OFr. *baud*, gay, licentious < Old LGer. *bald*, bold, merry. See **bhel-**[2]*.]

bawd•ry (bô′drē) *n.* Risqué, coarse, or obscene language. [ME *bawdery*, pandering < *bawd*, bawd. See BAWD.]

bawd•y (bô′dē) *adj.* **-i•er, -i•est. 1.** Humorously coarse; risqué. **2.** Vulgar; lewd. — **bawd′i•ly** *adv.* — **bawd′i•ness** *n.*

bawd•y•house (bô′dē-hous′) *n.* A house of prostitution.

bawl (bôl) *v.* **bawled, bawl•ing, bawls.** — *intr.* **1.** To cry or sob loudly; wail. **2.** To cry out loudly and vehemently; shout. — *tr.* To utter in a loud, vehement voice. See Syns at **shout.** — *n.* A loud, bellowing cry; a wail. — ***phrasal verb.*** **bawl out.** *Informal.* To reprimand loudly or harshly. [ME *bawlen*, to bark < Med.Lat. *baulāre*, to bark (prob. of Scand. orig.) or < ON *baula*, to low (of imit. orig.).] — **bawl′er** *n.*

bay[1] (bā) *n.* **1.** A body of water partially enclosed by land but with a wide mouth, affording access to the sea. **2.** An area of land that resembles a bay of the sea. [ME < OFr. *baie*, perh. < *baer*, to open out, gape. See BAY[2].]

bay[2] (bā) *n.* **1.** *Archit.* A part of a building marked off by vertical elements, such as columns. **2.** *Archit.* **a.** A bay window. **b.** An opening or a recess in a wall. **3.** A section or compartment that is set off for a specific purpose: *a cargo bay.* **4.** A sickbay. [ME < OFr. *baee*, an opening < *baer*, to gape < VLat. *badāre.*]

bay[3] (bā) *adj. Color.* Reddish-brown. — *n.* **1.** *Color.* A reddish brown. **2.** A reddish-brown animal, esp. a horse having a black mane and tail. [ME < OFr. *bai* < Lat. *badius.*]

bay[4] (bā) *n.* **1.** A deep prolonged bark, such as the sound made by hounds. **2.** The position of one cornered by pursuers and forced to turn and fight at close quarters. **3.** The position of having been checked or held at a distance. — *v.* **bayed, bay•ing, bays.** — *intr.* To utter a deep, prolonged bark. — *tr.* **1.** To pursue or challenge with barking. **2.** To express by barking or howling. **3.** To bring to bay. [ME < *abai*, cornering a hunted animal < OFr. < *abaiier*, to bark, perh. < VLat. **abbaiāre*: Lat. *ad-*, ad- + VLat. *badāre*, to gape, yawn. V. < ME *baien*, to bark < *abaien* < OFr. *abaiier.*]

bay[5] (bā) *n.* **1.** See **laurel** 1. **2.** Any of certain other trees or shrubs with aromatic foliage, such as the California laurel. **3.** A crown or wreath made esp. of the leaves and branches of the laurel and given as a sign of honor or victory. **4.** Honor; renown. Often used in the plural. [ME < OFr. *baie*, berry < Lat. *bāca.*]

ba•ya•dere (bī′ə-dîr′, -dâr′) *n.* A fabric with contrasting horizontal stripes. [Fr. *bayadère* < Port. *bailadeira*, dancer < *bailar*, to dance < LLat. *ballāre* < Gk. *ballizein.* See **gʷelə-***.]

Ba•ya•món (bä′yä-môn′). A town of NE Puerto Rico, a suburb of San Juan. Pop. 185,087.

Bay•ard (bā′ərd, bī′-, bä-yär′), Seigneur de. Orig. Pierre Terrail. 1473–1524. French military hero active in the Italian campaigns of Charles VII, Louis XII, and Francis I.

bay•ber•ry (bā′bĕr′ē) *n.* **1.** A deciduous eastern North American shrub *(Myrica pensylvanica)* having aromatic foliage and small waxy fruits. **2.** The fruit of this tree.

Bay City (bā). **1.** A city of E MI on Saginaw Bay NNW of Detroit. Pop. 38,936. **2.** A city of SE TX near the Colorado R. and the Gulf of Mexico SW of Houston. Pop. 18,170.

Ba•yeux (bī-yo͞o′, bā-, bä-yœ′). A town of NW France near the English Channel. The Bayeux tapestry depicts incidents in the Norman Conquest (1066). Pop. 14,721.

Bay•kal (bī-kôl′, -kŏl′), **Lake.** See Lake **Baikal.**

bay laurel *n.* See **laurel** 1.

Bayle (bāl, bĕl), **Pierre.** 1647–1706. French philosopher who compiled the *Dictionnaire Historique et Critique* (1697).

bay leaf *n.* The dried aromatic leaf of the laurel or bay *(Laurus nobilis)* used as a seasoning in cooking.

bay lynx *n.* See **bobcat.**

Bay of. For names of actual bays, see the specific element of the name; for example, **Biscay, Bay of.**

bay•o•net (bā′ə-nĭt, -nĕt′, bā′ə-nĕt′) *n.* A blade adapted to fit the muzzle end of a rifle, used as a weapon. — *tr.v.* **-net•ed, -net•ing, -nets** or **-net•ted, -net•ting, -nets.** To prod, stab, or kill with this weapon. [Fr. *baïonnette*, after BAYONNE[1].]

Ba•yonne[1] (bä-ōn′, bä-yôn′). A town of SW France near the Bay of Biscay and the Spanish border. Pop. 41,381.

Bay•onne[2] (bā-yōn′). A city of NE NJ on a peninsula in Upper New York Bay across from Staten I. Pop. 61,444.

bay•ou (bī′o͞o, bī′ō) *n.* **1.** A body of water that is a tributary of a larger body of water. **2.** A sluggish stream that meanders through lowlands, marshes, or plantation grounds. [Louisiana Fr. *bayouque, bayou*, poss. < Choctaw *bayuk.*]

Bay•reuth (bī-roit′, bī′roit). A city of E-central Germany NE of Nuremberg; home of Richard Wagner from 1872 to 1883. Pop. 71,811.

bay rum *n.* An aromatic liquid originally prepared by distilling the leaves of the bay rum tree in rum and water but now usu. made by mixing the oil from those leaves with other solvents.

bay rum tree *n.* A tropical American evergreen tree *(Pimenta racemosa)* having leathery leaves that yield a fragrant oil.

Bay•town (bā′toun′). A city of SE TX at the head of Galveston Bay on the Houston Ship Channel. Pop. 63,850.

ă pat — oi boy
ā pay — ou out
âr care — o͝o took
ä father — o͞o boot
ĕ pet — ŭ cut
ē be — ûr urge
ĭ pit — th thin
ī pie — *th* this
îr pier — hw which
ŏ pot — zh vision
ō toe — ə about, item
ô paw

Stress marks:
′ (primary);
′ (secondary), as in **dictionary** (dĭk′shə-nĕr′ē)

Bay Village. A city of NE Ohio, a suburb of Cleveland. Pop. 17,000.

bay window *n.* **1.** *Archit.* A large window or series of windows projecting from the outer wall of a building and forming a recess within. **2.** *Slang.* A protruding belly; a paunch.

bay window

ba•zaar also **ba•zar** (bə-zär′) *n.* **1.** A market consisting of a street lined with shops and stalls, esp. one in the Middle East. **2.** A shop or a part of a store in which miscellaneous articles are sold. **3.** A fair or sale at which miscellaneous articles are sold, often for charitable purposes. [< Ital. *bazarro* and < Urdu *bāzār,* both < Pers. See **wes-^{3}*.**]

ba•zoo•ka (bə-zo͞o′kə) *n.* A weapon consisting of a metal smoothbore tube for firing rockets at short range. [After the *bazooka,* a crude wind instrument made of pipes, invented and named by Bob Burns (1896–1956), Amer. comedian, prob. < *bazoo,* kazoo.]

bb also **b.b.** *abbr.* Ball bearing.

BB (bē′bē) *n.* A standard size of lead pellet that measures 7/40 of an inch (.44 centimeter) and is used in air rifles.

B.B.A. *abbr.* Bachelor of Business Administration.

BBC (bē′bē-sē′) *abbr.* British Broadcasting Corporation.

BBC English *n.* See **Received Pronunciation.**

bbl or **bbl.** *abbr.* Barrel.

B.C. *abbr.* **1.** Bachelor of Chemistry. **2.** Also B.C. Before Christ. **3.** Or **BC** British Columbia.

B.C.E. *abbr.* **1.** Bachelor of Chemical Engineering. **2.** Bachelor of Civil Engineering. **3.** Or B.C.E. Before the Common Era.

B cell *n.* A lymphocyte that synthesizes antibodies that circulate in the blood and react with foreign antigens. [*b(ursa-dependent) cell.*]

BCG *abbr.* Bacillus Calmette-Guérin vaccine.

B.Ch.E. *abbr.* Bachelor of Chemical Engineering.

B.C.L. *abbr.* **1.** Bachelor of Canon Law. **2.** Bachelor of Civil Law.

B complex *n.* See **vitamin B complex.**

bd *abbr.* Bundle.

BD *abbr.* **1.** Bank draft. **2.** Bomb disposal.

bd. *abbr.* **1.** Board. **2.** Bond. **3.** Bound.

B.D. *abbr.* Bachelor of Divinity.

b/d *abbr.* Barrels per day.

bdel•li•um (dĕl′ē-əm) *n.* An aromatic gum resin produced by certain Asian and African shrubs or trees of the genus *Commiphora.* [ME < Lat. < Gk. *bdellion;* akin to Heb. *bĕdōlaḥ.*]

bd. ft. *abbr.* Board foot.

bdl *abbr.* Bundle.

bdrm. *abbr.* Bedroom.

B.D.S. *abbr.* Bachelor of Dental Surgery.

be (bē) *v.* First and third pers. sing. p. indic. **was** (wŭz, wŏz; wəz *when unstressed*), second pers. sing. and pl. and first and third pers. pl. p. indic. **were** (wûr), p. subjunctive **were,** p.part. **been** (bĭn), pr.part. **be•ing** (bē′ĭng), first pers. sing. pr. indic. **am** (ăm), second pers. sing. and pl. and first and third pers. pl. pr. indic. **are** (är), third pers. sing. pr. indic. **is** (ĭz), pr. subjunctive **be.** —*intr.* **1.** To exist in actuality; have life or reality: *I think, therefore I am.* **2.a.** To occupy a specified position: *The food is on the table.* **b.** To remain in a certain state or situation undisturbed, untouched, or unmolested: *Let the children be.* **3.** To take place; occur: *The test was yesterday.* **4.** To go or come: *Have you been home?* **5.** Used as a copula in such senses as: **a.** To equal in identity: *"To be a Christian was to be a Roman"* (James Bryce). **b.** To have a specified significance: *A is excellent.* **c.** To belong to a specified class or group: *The human being is a primate.* **d.** To have or show a specified quality or characteristic: *She is lovely.* **e.** To seem to consist or be made of: *The yard is all snow.* **6.** To belong; befall: *Woe is me.* —*aux.* **1.** Used with the past participle of a transitive verb to form the passive voice: *The election is held annually.* **2.** Used with the present participle of a verb to express a continuing action: *We are trying to improve.* **3.** Used with the infinitive of a verb to express intention, obligation, or future action: *She was to call.* **4.** *Archaic.* Used with the past participle of certain intransitive verbs to form the perfect tense: *"Where be those roses gone?"* (Philip Sidney). [ME *ben* < OE *bēon.* See **bheuə-*.** See AM[1], IS, etc. for links to other Indo-European roots.]

beagle

Usage Note: Traditional grammar requires the nominative form of the pronoun in the predicate of the verb *be: It is I* (not *me*). The stigmatization of *It is me* is by now so deeply lodged among the canons of correctness that there is little likelihood that the construction will ever be entirely acceptable in formal writing. Adherence to the traditional rule in informal speech, however, has come to sound increasingly pedantic. • The traditional rule creates particular problems when the pronoun following *be* also functions as the object of a verb or preposition in a relative clause, as in *It is not them/they that we have in mind,* where the plural pronoun serves as both the predicate of *is* and the object of *have.* Writers can usually find a way to avoid this problem: *We have someone else in mind.* See Usage Notes at **I[1], we.**

Be The symbol for the element **beryllium.**

BE *abbr.* **1.** Also **B.E.** Bachelor of Education. **2.** Also **B.E.** Bachelor of Engineering. **3.** Board of Education.

B/E *abbr.* **1.** Bill of entry. **2.** Bill of exchange.

be– *pref.* **1.** Completely; thoroughly; excessively. Used as an intensive: *bemuse.* **2.** On; around; over: *besmear.* **3.** About; to: *bespeak.* **4.** Used to form transitive verbs from nouns, adjectives, and intransitive verbs, as: **a.** To make; cause to become: *bedim.* **b.** To affect, cover, or provide: *bespectacled.* [ME *bi-, be-* < OE *be-, bi-.* See **ambhi*.**]

Bé *abbr.* Baumé scale.

beach (bēch) *n.* **1.** The shore of a body of water, esp. when sandy or pebbly. **2.** The sand or pebbles on a shore. —*tr.v.* **beached, beach•ing, beach•es.** To haul or run ashore: *beached the rowboat.* [Perh. ME *beche,* stream < OE *bece.*]

Beach (bēch), **Alfred Ely.** 1826–96. Amer. editor and inventor who built (1870) a demonstration pneumatic subway under Broadway in New York City.

Beach, Moses Yale. 1800–68. Amer. publisher who established the *New York Sun* as a leading daily newspaper.

Beach, Sylvia Woodbridge. 1887–1962. Amer. bookseller in Paris who published the first edition of James Joyce's *Ulysses* in 1922.

beach ball *n.* A large inflatable ball used for games.

beach buggy *n.* See **dune buggy.**

beach bum *n. Informal.* A person who habitually loafs or idles on beaches.

beach-burn•er (bēch′ bûr′nər) *n. Informal.* A small self-propelled watercraft for recreational use close to shore.

beach•comb•er (bēch′kō′mər) *n.* **1.** One who scavenges along beaches or in wharf areas. **2.** A seaside vacationer.

beach flea *n.* Any of various small, jumping crustaceans of the family Orchestiidae, living on sandy beaches.

beach•front (bēch′frŭnt′) *n.* A strip of land facing or running along a beach. —**beach′front′** *adj.*

beach grass *n.* A perennial grass of the genus *Ammophila,* esp. *A. breviligulata,* native to sandy shores of eastern and central North America and having spikelets in long, erect, crowded clusters.

beach•head (bēch′hĕd′) *n.* **1.** A position on an enemy shoreline captured by troops in advance of an invading force. **2.** A first achievement that opens the way for further developments.

Beach-la-Mar (bēch′lə-mär′) *n.* See **Bislama.**

beach pea or **beach-pea** (bēch′pē′) *n.* Any of certain perennial herbs of the genus *Lathyrus* in the pea family, esp. *L. japonicus,* native to shores in the Northern Hemisphere.

beach plum *n.* A seacoast shrub *(Prunus maritima)* in the rose family, native to northeast North America and having edible plumlike fruits.

beach•wear (bēch′wâr′) *n.* Clothing appropriate for swimming, boating, or sunning.

beach wormwood *n.* An Asian perennial seacoast plant *(Artemisia stelleriana)* in the composite family, densely covered with felty hairs.

bea•con (bē′kən) *n.* **1.** A signaling or guiding device, such as a lighthouse, located on a coast. **2.** A radio transmitter that emits a characteristic guidance signal for aircraft. **3.** A source of guidance or inspiration. **4.** A signal fire, esp. one used to warn of an enemy's approach. —*tr. & intr.v.* **-coned, -con•ing, -cons.** To provide with or shine as a beacon. [ME *beken* < OE *bēacen.* See **bhā-^{1}*.**]

Bea•con Hill (bē′kən). An area of Boston MA noted for its historic residences, brick sidewalks, and picturesque mews.

Bea•cons•field (bē′kənz-fēld′). A town of S Quebec, Canada, a suburb of Montreal. Pop. 19,613.

bead (bēd) *n.* **1.a.** A small, often round piece of material, such as glass, plastic, or wood, that is pierced for stringing or threading. **b. beads.** A necklace made of such pieces. **c. beads.** *Rom. Cath. Ch.* A rosary. **d.** *Obsolete.* A prayer. Often used in the plural. **2.** A small, round object, esp.: **a.** A drop of moisture: *beads of sweat.* **b.** A bubble of gas in a liquid. **c.** A small metal knob on the muzzle of a firearm used for sighting. **3.** A strip of material, usu. wood, with one molded edge placed flush against the inner part of a door or window frame. **4.** *Archit.* **a.** A decoration consisting of a usu. continuous series of small spherical shapes, as on a convex molding. **b.** Beading. **5.** A projecting rim or lip, as on a pneumatic tire. **6.** A line of continuously applied ductile material, such as solder or caulking compound. **7.** *Chem.* A globule of fused borax or other flux covered with a mineral to be analyzed, heated in a flame as a test for the presence of metals. —*tr. & intr.v.* **bead•ed, bead•ed, beads.** To furnish with or collect into beads. —***idiom.*** **draw** (or **get**) **a bead on.** To take careful aim at. [ME *bede,* rosary bead, prayer < OE *bed, bedu, gebed,* prayer. See **gʷhedh-*.**]

bead•ing (bē′dĭng) *n.* **1.** Beads or the material used for making them. **2.** Ornamentation with beads. **3.** *Archit.* A narrow, half-rounded molding; a bead. **4.** A narrow piece of openwork lace through which ribbon may be run. **5.** Tiny drops of condensation, as on the outside of a glass.

bea•dle (bēd′l) *n.* A minor parish official formerly employed in an English church to usher and keep order during services. [ME *bedel,* herald (< OE *bydel*) and < OFr. *bedel* (< Med. Lat. *bedellus* < OHGer. *butil;* see **bheudh-***).]

Bea•dle (bēd′l), **Erastus Flavel.** 1821–94. Amer. publisher who in 1860 published the first dime novel.
bead plant *n.* An evergreen plant *(Nertera granadensis)* chiefly of the Southern Hemisphere, grown esp. as a houseplant for its orange drupes.
bead•work (bēd′wûrk′) *n.* **1.** See **beading** 2. **2.** *Archit.* Beaded molding.
bead•y (bē′dē) *adj.* **-i•er, -i•est. 1.** Small, round, and shiny: *beady eyes.* **2.** Decorated or covered with beads.
bea•gle (bē′gəl) *n.* One of a breed of hounds having short legs, drooping ears, and white, black, and tan markings. [ME *begle,* poss. < OFr. *bee gueule,* loudmouth : *beer,* to gape (var. of *baer;* see BAY[2]) + *gueule,* gullet (< Lat. *gula*).]
beak (bēk) *n.* **1.a.** The horny projecting structure forming the mandibles of a bird, esp. one that is useful in striking and tearing; a bill. **b.** A similar structure in other animals, such as turtles. **2.** A usu. firm, tapering tip on certain plant structures. **3.** A beaklike structure or part, as: **a.** The spout of a pitcher. **b.** A metal or metal-clad ram projecting from the bow of an ancient warship. **4.** *Informal.* The human nose. **5.** *Chiefly British.* **a.** A schoolmaster. **b.** A judge. [ME *bek* < OFr. *bec* < Lat. *beccus,* of Celt. orig.] **—beaked** *adj.*
beaked salmon *n.* See **sandfish** 2.
beak•er (bē′kər) *n.* **1.** A wide cylindrical glass vessel with a pouring lip, used as a laboratory container and mixing jar. **2.** A large drinking cup with a wide mouth. [MDu. *bēker,* drinking vessel, and ME *bekir,* both < Med.Lat. *bicārius, bicārium,* prob. < Gk. *bikos,* jug, poss. of Egypt. orig.]
be all and end all or **be-all and end-all** (bē′ôl′ ənd ĕnd′ôl′) *n.* The quintessential or all-important element.
beam (bēm) *n.* **1.** A squared-off log or a large oblong piece of timber, metal, or stone used esp. as a horizontal support in construction. **2.** *Naut.* **a.** A transverse structural member of a ship's frame, used to support a deck and brace the sides against stress. **b.** The breadth of a ship at the widest point. **c.** The side of a ship. **3.** *Informal.* The widest part of a person's hips. **4.** A steel tube or wooden roller on which the warp is wound in a loom. **5.** An oscillating lever connected to an engine piston rod and used to transmit power to the crankshaft. **6.a.** The bar of a balance from which weighing pans are suspended. **b.** *Sports.* A balance beam. **7.** The main horizontal bar on a plow to which the share, colter, and handles are attached. **8.** One of the main stems of a deer's antlers. **9.a.** A ray or shaft of light. **b.** A concentrated stream of particles or a similar propagation of waves: *a beam of light.* **10.** A radio beam. **—*v.* beamed, beam•ing, beams. —*intr.* 1.** To radiate light; shine. **2.** To smile expansively. **—*tr.* 1.** To emit or transmit: *beam a message via satellite.* **2.** To express by means of a radiant smile. **—*idiom.* on the beam. 1.** Following a radio beam. Used of aircraft. **2.** On the right track; operating correctly. [ME *bem* < OE *bēam.* See **bheuə-*.**]
beam•ish (bē′mĭsh) *adj.* Smiling, as with happiness or optimism. **—beam′ish•ly** *adv.*
beam•y (bē′mē) *adj.* **-i•er, -i•est. 1.** Broad in the beam: *a beamy boat.* **2.** Emitting beams, as of light; radiant.
bean (bēn) *n.* **1.a.** Any of various New World herbs of the genus *Phaseolus* in the pea family, having leaves with three leaflets and edible pods and seeds. **b.** A seed or pod of any of these plants. **2.** Any of several related plants or their seeds or pods, such as the adzuki bean. **3.** Any of various other plants or their seeds or fruits, esp. those suggestive of beans, such as the coffee bean. **4.** *Slang.* A person's head. **5. beans.** *Slang.* A small amount. **6.** *Chiefly British.* A fellow; a chap. **—*tr.v.* beaned, bean•ing, beans.** *Slang.* To hit (another) on the head with a thrown object, esp. a pitched baseball. **—*idioms.* full of beans. 1.** Energetic; frisky. **2.** Badly mistaken. **spill the beans.** To disclose a secret. [ME *ben,* broad bean < OE *bēan.* See **bha-bhā-*.**]
bean•bag (bēn′băg′) *n.* **1.** A small bag filled with dried beans and used for throwing in games. **2.** An article, such as a chair, that is constructed as a bag filled with small pellets.
bean ball *n. Baseball.* A pitch aimed at the batter's head.
bean counter *n. Slang.* A financial executive, esp. an accountant.
bean curd *n.* Tofu.
bean•er•y (bē′nə-rē) *n., pl.* **-ies.** *Informal.* An inexpensive restaurant or café.
bean family *n.* The pea family.
bean•ie (bē′nē) *n.* A small brimless cap. [Prob. < BEAN, head.]
bean•o (bē′nō) *n., pl.* **-os.** *Games.* A form of bingo, esp. one using beans as markers. [Blend of BEAN and (BING)O.]
bean•pole (bēn′pōl′) *n.* **1.** A thin pole used to support bean vines. **2.** *Informal.* A very tall, thin person.
bean sprouts *pl.n.* The tender edible seedlings of certain bean plants, esp. those of the mung bean.
bean•stalk (bēn′stôk′) *n.* The stem of a bean plant.
bear[1] (bâr) *v.* **bore** (bôr, bōr), **borne** (bôrn, bōrn) or **born** (bôrn), **bear•ing, bears. —*tr.* 1.** To hold up; support. **2.** To carry on one's person; convey. **3.** To carry in the mind; harbor. **4.** To transmit at large; relate: *bearing glad tidings.* **5.** To have as a visible characteristic: *bore a scar.* **6.** To have as a quality; exhibit: *"A thousand different shapes it bears"* (Abraham Cowley). **7.** To carry (oneself) in a specified way; conduct. **8.** To be accountable for; assume: *bearing heavy responsibilities.* **9.** To have a tolerance for; endure: *couldn't bear lying.* **10.** To call for; warrant: *This case bears investigation.* **11.** To give birth to. **12.** To produce; yield: *plants bearing flowers.* **13.** To offer; render: *I will bear witness to the deed.* **14.** To move by or as if by steady pressure; push. **—*intr.* 1.** To yield fruit; produce. **2.** To have relevance; apply: *news bearing on the trial.* **3.** To exert pressure, force, or influence. **4.a.** To force oneself along; forge. **b.** To endure something with tolerance and patience: *Bear with me.* **5.** To extend or proceed in a specified direction: *bears to the right.* **—*phrasal verbs.* bear down. 1.** To overwhelm; vanquish. **2.** To apply maximum effort and concentration. **bear out.** To prove right or justified; confirm. **bear up.** To withstand stress, difficulty, or attrition. **—*idioms.* bear down on.** To effect in a harmful or adverse way. **bear fruit.** To come to a satisfactory conclusion or to fruition. **bear in mind.** To hold in one's mind; remember. [ME *beren* < OE *beran.* See **bher-[1]*.**]

Syns: *bear, endure, stand, abide, suffer, tolerate.* These verbs mean to undergo something difficult or painful without giving way. *Bear* pertains broadly to capacity to withstand: *"Man performs, engenders, so much more than he can or should have to bear"* (William Faulkner). *Endure* specifies a continuing capacity to face pain or hardship: *"Human life is everywhere a state in which much is to be endured and little to be enjoyed"* (Samuel Johnson). *Stand* implies resoluteness: *He can't stand criticism. Abide* and *suffer* suggest resignation and forbearance: *She couldn't abide fools. He suffered their insults in silence. Tolerate,* when applied to something other than pain, connotes reluctant acceptance: *He tolerated the noise.* See also Syns at **produce.**

bear[2] (bâr) *n.* **1.a.** Any of various usu. omnivorous mammals of the family Ursidae, having a shaggy coat and a short tail. **b.** Any of various other animals, such as the koala, that resemble a true bear. **2.** A large, clumsy, or ill-mannered person. **3.a.** One that sells securities or commodities in expectation of falling prices. **b.** A pessimist, esp. regarding business conditions. **4.** *Slang.* Something that is difficult or unpleasant. [ME *bere* < OE *bera.* See **bher-[2]*.** Sense 3, prob. < proverb *To sell the bear's skin before catching the bear.*]
Bear (bâr), **Mount.** A peak, 4,523.5 m (14,831 ft), in the Wrangell Mts. of S AK near the British Columbia border.
bear•a•ble (bâr′ə-bəl) *adj.* That can be endured: *a bearable schedule.* **—bear′a•bil′i•ty** *n.* **—bear′a•bly** *adv.*
bear•bait•ing (bâr′bā′tĭng) *n.* The practice of setting dogs on a chained bear.
bear•ber•ry (bâr′bĕr′ē) *n.* Any of certain shrubs of the genus *Arctostaphylos,* esp. *A. uva-ursi,* native to North America and Eurasia and having leathery leaves and red fruits.
bear•cat (bâr′kăt′) *n.* See **binturong.**
beard (bîrd) *n.* **1.** The hair on a man's chin, cheeks, and throat. **2.** A hairy or hairlike growth such as that on or near the face of certain mammals. **3.** A tuft or group of hairs or bristles on certain plants, such as barley and wheat. **4.** One that serves to divert suspicion or attention from another. **—*tr.v.* beard•ed, beard•ing, beards. 1.** To furnish with a beard. **2.** To confront boldly. [ME *berd* < OE *beard.* See **bhardh-ā-*.**] **—beard′ed** *adj.* **—beard′ed•ness** *n.* **—beard′less** *adj.* **—beard′less•ness** *n.*
Beard (bîrd), **Charles Austin.** 1874–1948. Amer. historian who explored the economic aspects of history in works such as *An Economic Interpretation of the Constitution* (1913).
Beard, Daniel ("Dan") Carter. 1850–1941. Amer. writer and illustrator who founded the first Boy Scout organization in the U.S. (1910).
Beard, Mary Ritter. 1876–1958. Amer. historian who collaborated with her husband, Charles, on *The Rise of American Civilization* (first volume 1927).
beard•ed iris (bîr′dĭd) *n.* Any of various irises having hairs or hairlike structures on the lower parts of the three outer perianth segments.
bearded vulture *n.* See **lammergeier.**
Beards•ley (bîrdz′lē), **Aubrey Vincent.** 1872–98. British illustrator whose black and white drawings were both highly individual and typical of the art nouveau style.
beard•tongue or **beard-tongue** (bîrd′tŭng′) *n.* See **penstemon.** [After its bearded, tonguelike stamen.]
bear•er (bâr′ər) *n.* **1.** One that carries or supports, as: **a.** A porter. **b.** A pallbearer. **2.** One that holds a redeemable note for payment. **3.** A fruit- or flower-bearing plant.
bear grass *n.* **1.** A western North American perennial herb *(Xerophyllum tenax)* in the lily family, having a dense clump of grasslike leaves and a tall stalk. **2.** Any of several similar North American plants.
bear hug *n.* A rough, tight hug.
bear•ing (bâr′ĭng) *n.* **1.** The manner in which one carries or conducts oneself: *regal bearing.* **2.a.** A machine or structural part that supports another part. **b.** A device that supports, guides, and reduces the friction of motion between fixed and moving machine parts. **3.** Something that supports weight. **4.** The part of an arch or beam that rests on a support.

beak
Bald eagle
Haliaeetus leucocephalus (*top left*);
evening grosbeak
Hesperiphona vespertina (*top right*); and
black skimmer
Rynchops niger (*bottom*)

beaker
Measuring liquid into a beaker

ă pat	oi boy
ā pay	ou out
âr care	o͝o took
ä father	o͞o boot
ĕ pet	ŭ cut
ē be	ûr urge
ĭ pit	th thin
ī pie	*th* this
îr pier	hw which
ŏ pot	zh vision
ō toe	ə about, item
ô paw	

Stress marks:
′ (primary);
′ (secondary), as in
dictionary (dĭk′shə-nĕr′ē)

5.a. The act, power, or period of producing fruit or offspring. **b.** The quantity produced; yield. **6.** Direction, esp. angular direction measured from one position to another using geographical or celestial reference lines. **7.** Awareness of one's position or situation relative to one's surroundings. Often used in the plural. **8.** Relevant relationship or interconnection. **9.** *Her.* A charge or device on a field.

bearing rein *n.* A rein for a horse; a checkrein.

bear•ish (bâr′ĭsh) *adj.* **1.** Clumsy, boorish, and surly. **2.a.** Causing, expecting, or characterized by falling stock market prices. **b.** Pessimistic. —**bear′ish•ly** *adv.* —**bear′ish•ness** *n.*

Bé•arn (bā-ärn′). A historical region and former province of SW France in the W Pyrenees; autonomous until 1620.

bé•ar•naise sauce (bâr-nāz′, bā′är-, -ər-) *n.* A sauce of butter and egg yolks flavored with vinegar, wine, shallots, tarragon, and chervil. [Fr. *béarnaise*, fem. of *béarnais*, of Béarn.]

Bear River. A river rising in NE UT and flowing c. 563 km (350 mi) in a U-shaped course.

bear's breech (bârz) *n.* See **acanthus** 1.

bear's ear *n.* See **auricula** 1.

bear•skin (bâr′skĭn′) *n.* **1.** Something made from the skin of a bear. **2.** A tall military hat made of black fur.

bearskin

Be•as (bē′äs′). A river, c. 402 km (250 mi), of N India rising in the Himalaya Mts.; one of the five rivers of the Punjab.

beast (bēst) *n.* **1.a.** An animal other than a human being, esp. a large four-footed mammal. **b.** *New England & Southern U.S.* A large domestic animal, esp. a horse or bull. **2.** Animal nature as opposed to intellect or spirit. **3.** A brutal, contemptible person. [ME *beste* < OFr. < Lat. *bēstia*.]

beast•ings (bē′stĭngz) *pl.n. (used with a sing. or pl. v.)* Var. of **beestings.**

beast•ly (bēst′lē) *adj.* **-li•er, -li•est. 1.** Of or resembling a beast; bestial. **2.** Very disagreeable; unpleasant. —*adv. Chiefly British.* To an extreme degree; very. —**beast′li•ness** *n.*

beast of burden *n., pl.* **beasts of burden.** An animal, such as a donkey, used to transport loads or do other heavy work.

beat (bēt) *v.* **beat, beat•en** (bēt′n) or **beat, beat•ing, beats.** —*tr.* **1.a.** To strike repeatedly. **b.** To punish by hitting or whipping; flog. **2.a.** To strike against repeatedly and with force; pound: *waves beating the shore.* **b.** To flap, esp. wings. **c.** To strike so as to produce music or a signal: *beat a drum.* **d.** *Mus.* To mark or count (time or rhythm) with the hands or with a baton. **3.a.** To shape or break by repeated blows; forge. **b.** To make by pounding or trampling: *beat a path.* **4.** To mix rapidly with a utensil: *beat two eggs.* **5.a.** To defeat or subdue, as in a contest. See Syns at **defeat. b.** To force to withdraw or retreat: *beat back the enemy.* **c.** To dislodge from a position: *I beat him down to a lower price.* **6.** *Informal.* To be superior to or better than: *Riding beats walking.* **7.** *Slang.* To perplex or baffle. **8.** *Informal.* **a.** To avoid or counter the effects of; circumvent: *beat the traffic.* **b.** To arrive or finish before (another): *We beat you home.* **c.** To deprive, as by craft or ability: *beat me out of 20 dollars.* —*intr.* **1.** To inflict repeated blows. **2.** To pulsate; throb. **3.** *Phys.* To cause pulsating by superposing waves of different but nearly equal frequencies. **4.a.** To emit sound when struck. **b.** To strike a drum. **5.** To flap repeatedly. **6.** To be victorious or successful; win. **7.** To hunt through woods or underbrush in search of game. **8.** *Naut.* To sail in the direction from which the wind blows. —*n.* **1.** A stroke or blow, esp. one that produces a sound or serves as a signal. **2.** A pulsation or throb. **3.** *Phys.* A pulsation produced by beating. Often used in the plural. **4.** *Mus.* **a.** A regular, rhythmical unit of time. **b.** The gesture used by a conductor to indicate a beat. **c.** The symbol representing a beat. **5.** The measured rhythmical sound of verse; meter. **6.a.** The area regularly covered by a reporter, a police officer, or a sentry. **b.** The reporting of a news item obtained ahead of one's competitors. —*adj.* **1.** *Informal.* Worn-out; fatigued. **2.** Of, relating to, or being a beatnik: *the beat generation.* —***phrasal verbs.*** **beat off. 1.** To drive away. **2.** *Vulgar Slang.* To masturbate. **beat out.** *Baseball.* To reach base safely on (a bunt or ground ball). —***idioms.*** **beat a retreat.** To make a hasty withdrawal. **beat around (or about) the bush.** To fail to confront a subject directly. **beat it.** *Slang.* To leave hurriedly. **beat the bushes.** To make an exhaustive search. **beat the drum (or drums).** To give enthusiastic public support or promotion. **to beat the band.** With great vigor; in a fast and furious manner. [ME *beten* < OE *bēaten.* See **bhau-*.**]

Beatrix
Photographed in 1982

beat•en (bēt′n) *adj.* **1.** Formed or made thin by hammering: *beaten gold.* **2.** Worn by continuous use; familiar and much traveled. **3.** Totally worn-out; exhausted.

beat•er (bē′tər) *n.* **1.** One that beats, esp. a device for beating. **2.** A person who drives game from under cover for a hunter.

be•a•tif•ic (bē′ə-tĭf′ĭk) *adj.* Showing or producing exalted joy or blessedness; angelic: *a beatific smile.* [Lat. *beātificus*: *beātus*, happy < p.part. of *beāre*, to bless; see **deu-²*** + *-ficus*, -fic.] —**be′a•tif′i•cal•ly** *adv.*

be•at•i•fy (bē-ăt′ə-fī′) *tr.v.* **-fied, -fy•ing, -fies. 1.** To make blessedly happy. **2.** *Rom. Cath. Ch.* To proclaim (a deceased person) to be one of the blessed and thus worthy of public veneration in a particular region or congregation. **3.** To exalt above all others. [Fr. *beatifier* < LLat. *beātificāre*: Lat. *beātus*, happy; see BEATIFIC + Lat. *-ficāre*, -fy.] —**be•at′i•fi•ca′tion** (-fĭ-kā′shən) *n.*

beat•ing (bē′tĭng) *n.* **1.** Punishment by whipping or flogging. **2.** A sound defeat. **3.** A throbbing or pulsation. **4.** *Phys.* The periodic variation in amplitude of a wave produced by the superposition of two waves of different frequencies.

be•at•i•tude (bē-ăt′ĭ-to͞od′, -tyo͞od′) *n.* **1.** Supreme blessedness or happiness. **2. Beatitude.** Any of the declarations of blessedness made by Jesus in the Sermon on the Mount. [ME < OFr. < Lat. *beātitūdō* < *beātus*, happy. See BEATIFIC.]

Beat•les (bēt′lz). A former British pop group comprising John Lennon, Ringo Starr, Paul McCartney, and George Harrison.

beat•nik (bēt′nĭk) *n.* A person who acts with disregard for what is generally thought proper and is given to social criticism and self-expression. [< *beat generation*, a group of unconventional young people of the 1950's + -NIK.]

Bea•ton (bēt′n), **Cecil Walter Hardy.** 1904–80. British photographer, diarist, and theatrical designer.

Be•a•trix (bā′ə-trĭks′, bē′-). b. 1938. Queen of the Netherlands who ascended the throne (1980) after the abdication of her mother, Juliana.

Beat•tie (bā′tē, bē′-), **James.** 1735–1803. Scottish philosopher and poet who wrote *The Minstrel* (1771–74).

beat-up (bēt′ŭp′) *adj. Slang.* Damaged or worn because of neglect or heavy use.

beau (bō) *n., pl.* **beaus** or **beaux** (bōz). **1.** The boyfriend of a woman or girl. **2.** A dandy; a fop. [Fr. < *beau, bel*, handsome < Lat. *bellus.* See **deu-²*.**]

Beau Brum•mell (bō brŭm′əl) *n.* A dandy; a fop. [After George Bryan *("Beau")* BRUMMELL.]

beau•coup (bō′ko͞o, bo͞o′-, bō-ko͞o′) also **boo•coo** or **boo•koo** (bo͞o′-) *Chiefly Southern U.S.* —*adj.* Many; much: *beaucoup money.* —*n., pl.* **-coups** also **-coos** or **-koos.** An abundance; a lot. —*adv.* In abundance; galore. [Fr. : *beau, bel*, fine, handsome; see BEAU + *coup*, stroke; see COUP.]

Beaufort scale (bō′fərt) *n.* A scale on which successive ranges of wind velocities are assigned code numbers from 0 (calm) to 12 (hurricane), corresponding to wind speeds of from less than 1 mile per hour (0–1 kilometer per hour) to over 74 miles per hour (over 117 kilometers per hour). [After Sir Francis *Beaufort* (1774–1857), British naval officer.]

Beaufort Sea. A part of the Arctic Ocean N of NE AK and NW Canada extending from Point Barrow to the Canadian Arctic Archipelago.

beau geste (bō zhĕst′) *n., pl.* **beaux gestes** or **beau gestes** (bō zhĕst′). **1.** A gracious gesture. **2.** A gesture noble in form but meaningless in substance. [Fr. : *beau*, noble + *geste*, gesture.]

Beau•har•nais (bō-är-nā′), **Eugène de.** 1781–1824. French soldier who was adopted by Napoleon I and became heir apparent to the throne of Italy (1806).

Beauharnais, Josephine de. 1763–1814. Empress of the French (1804–09) as the wife of Napoleon I.

beau i•de•al (bō′ ī-dē′əl) *n., pl.* **beau ideals. 1.** The concept of perfect beauty. **2.** An idealized type or model. [Fr. *beau idéal*: *beau*, perfect + *ideal*, ideal.]

Beau•jo•lais¹ (bō′zhə-lā′). A hilly region of E-central France W of the Saône R. between Mâcon and Lyons.

Beau•jo•lais² (bō′zhə-lā′) *n.* A light red table wine. [After BEAUJOLAIS¹.]

Beau•mar•chais (bō-mär-shā′), **Pierre Augustin Caron de.** 1732–99. French writer whose comic plays *Le Barbier de Séville* (1775) and *Le Mariage de Figaro* (1784) inspired operas by Rossini and Mozart.

beau monde (bō mŏnd′, môɴd′) *n., pl.* **beaux mondes** (bō môɴd′) or **beau mondes** (bō mŏndz′). The world of fashionable society. [Fr. : *beau*, good + *monde*, world, society.]

Beau•mont (bō′mŏnt′). A city of SE TX NNE of Houston. Pop. 114,323.

Beau•mont (bō′mŏnt′, -mənt), **Francis.** 1584–1616. English poet and playwright whose major works, including *The Maid's Tragedy* (1611), were written with John Fletcher.

Beau•port (bō-pôr′). A city of S Quebec, Canada, a suburb of Quebec City. Pop. 60,447.

Beau•re•gard (bō′rĭ-gärd′, bō-rə-gär′), **Pierre Gustave Toutant.** 1818–93. Amer. Confederate general who ordered the bombardment of Fort Sumter (1861).

beaut (byo͞ot) *n. Slang.* Something outstanding of its kind. [Short for BEAUTY.]

beau•te•ous (byo͞o′tē-əs) *adj.* Beautiful, esp. to the sight. —**beau′te•ous•ly** *adv.* —**beau′te•ous•ness** *n.*

beau•ti•cian (byo͞o-tĭsh′ən) *n.* A cosmetician.

beau•ti•ful (byo͞o′tə-fəl) *adj.* **1.** Having qualities that delight the senses, esp. sight. **2.** Exciting intellectual or emotional admiration. —**beau′ti•ful•ly** *adv.* —**beau′ti•ful•ness** *n.*

beautiful people also **Beautiful People** *n.* Wealthy, prominent people, esp. those in international society.

beau•ti•fy (byo͞o′tə-fī′) *tr. & intr.v.* **-fied, -fy•ing, -fies.** To make or become beautiful. —**beau′ti•fi•ca′tion** (-fĭ-kā′shən) *n.* —**beau′ti•fi′er** *n.*

beau•ty (byo͞o′tē) *n., pl.* **-ties. 1.** A delightful quality associated with such things as harmony of form or color, truthfulness, or originality. **2.** One that is beautiful. **3.** A quality or feature that is most effective, gratifying, or telling. **4.** An outstanding or conspicuous example. [ME *beaute* < OFr. *biaute* < VLat. **bellitās* < Lat. *bellus*, pretty. See **deu-²*.**]

beau•ty•ber•ry (byōō′ tē-bĕr′ē) *n.* Any of various shrubs of the genus *Callicarpa* cultivated for their berrylike fruits.

beau•ty•bush (byōō′tē-bōōsh′) *n.* A deciduous Chinese ornamental shrub (*Kolkwitzia amabilis*) cultivated for its pink flowers.

beauty mark *n.* See **beauty spot** 1.

beauty parlor *n.* An establishment providing services that include hair treatment, manicures, and facials.

beauty quark *n.* See **bottom quark.**

beauty salon *n.* See **beauty parlor.**

beauty shop *n.* See **beauty parlor.**

beauty spot *n.* **1.** A mole or birthmark. **2.** A small black mark penciled or glued on the face or shoulders to accentuate fairness of skin or to conceal a blemish.

Beau•vais (bō-vā′). A town of N France NNW of Paris; long noted for its tapestry works. Pop. 52,365.

Beau•voir (bō-vwär′), **Simone de.** 1908–86. French writer and existentialist whose works include *The Second Sex* (1949).

beaux (bōz) *n.* Pl. of **beau.**

Beaux (bō), **Cecilia.** 1863–1942. Amer. artist who excelled in portraits, esp. those of women and children.

beaux-arts (bō-zär′, -zärt′) *pl.n.* The fine arts. [Fr. : *beau*, fine + *art*, art.]

beaux es•prits (bō′zĕ-sprē′) *n.* Pl. of **bel esprit.**

beaux gestes (bō zhĕst′) *n.* Pl. of **beau geste.**

beaux mondes (bō mônd′) *n.* Pl. of **beau monde.**

bea•ver¹ (bē′vər) *n.* **1.a.** A large aquatic rodent of the genus *Castor*, having thick brown fur, webbed hind feet, a broad flat tail, and sharp incisors adapted for gnawing bark, felling trees, and constructing dams and underwater lodges. **b.** The fur of this rodent. **c.** A top hat originally made of the fur of this rodent. **2.** A napped wool fabric, similar to felt, used for outer garments. **3.** *Offensive & Vulgar Slang.* The female genitalia. —*intr.v.* **-vered, -ver•ing, -vers.** To work diligently and energetically. [ME *bever* < OE *beofor.* See **bher-²*.**]

bea•ver² (bē′vər) *n.* **1.** A piece of armor attached to a helmet or breastplate to protect the mouth and chin. **2.** The visor on a helmet. [ME *bavier* < OFr. *baviere*, child's bib, beaver < *bave*, saliva.]

bea•ver•board (bē′vər-bôrd′, -bōrd′) *n.* A light building material of compressed wood pulp. [Originally a trademark.]

Bea•ver•brook (bē′vər-brōōk′), 1st Baron **William Maxwell Aitken.** 1879–1964. Canadian-born British publisher, financier, and politician.

Bea•ver•creek (bē′vər-krēk′). A village of SW OH, a suburb of Dayton. Pop. 33,626.

Bea•ver River (bē′vər). **1.** A river rising in central Alberta, Canada, and flowing c. 491 km (305 mi) to the headwaters of the Churchill R. **2.** A name for the North Canadian R. as it flows c. 450 km (280 mi) through NW OK.

Bea•ver•ton (bē′vər-tən). A city of NW OR W of Portland; founded 1868. Pop. 53,310.

Be•bel (bā′bəl), **(Ferdinand) August.** 1840–1913. German socialist leader who was a cofounder and leader of the Social Democratic Party (organized 1869).

be•bop (bē′bŏp′) *n. Mus.* Bop. [Imitation of a two-note phrase in this music.] —**be′bop′per** *n.*

be•calm (bĭ-käm′) *tr.v.* **-calmed, -calm•ing, -calms. 1.** To render motionless for lack of wind. **2.** To make calm or still.

be•came (bĭ-kām′) *v.* P.t. of **become.**

be•cause (bĭ-kôz′, -kŭz′) *conj.* For the reason that; since. [ME. See BECAUSE OF.]

because of *prep.* On account of; by reason of. [ME *bi cause of*, by reason of : *bi*, by; see BY¹ + *cause*, reason; see CAUSE + *of*, of; see OF.]

bec•ca•fi•co (bĕk′ə-fē′kō) *n., pl.* **-cos.** A small songbird or warbler of various genera, esp. the European garden warbler *(Sylvia hortensis).* [Ital. : *beccare*, to peck (< *becco*, beak < Lat. *beccus*; see BEAK) + *fico*, fig (< Lat. *fīcus*).]

bé•cha•mel sauce (bā′shə-mĕl′) *n.* A white sauce of butter, flour, and milk or cream. [Fr. *sauce béchamel*, after Louis de *Béchamel* (1603–1703), chief steward of Louis XIV.]

be•chance (bĭ-chăns′) *intr. & tr.v.* **-chanced, -chanc•ing, -chanc•es.** *Archaic.* To happen or happen to.

bêche-de-mer (bĕsh′də-mâr′) *n., pl.* **bêches-de-mer** (bĕsh′də-mâr′). See **trepang.** [Fr., alteration (influenced by *bêche*, grub) of *biche-de-mer* < Port. *bicho do mar*: *bicho*, worm (< LLat. *bēstulus*, dim. of Lat. *bēstia*, beast) + *do*, of the + *mar*, sea (< Lat. *mare*; see **mori-*.**)]

Bêche-de-Mer (bĕsh′də-mâr′) *n.* See **Bislama.** [From the commercial importance of BÊCHE-DE-MER where the language is spoken.]

Bech•u•a•na (bĕch′ōō-ä′nə) *n., pl.* **Bechuana** or **-nas.** See **Tswana** 1.

Bech•u•a•na•land (bĕch′wä′nə-lănd′, bĕch′ōō-ä′nə-). See **Botswana.**

beck¹ (bĕk) *n.* A gesture of beckoning or summons. —*idiom.* **at (one's) beck and call.** Ready to fulfill any wish or order. [ME *bek* < *bekken*, to beckon, alteration of *bekenen.* See BECKON.]

beck² (bĕk) *n. Chiefly British.* A small brook; a creek. [ME < ON *bekkr.* See **bhegʷ-*.**]

Beck•et (bĕk′ĭt), Saint **Thomas à.** 1118?–70. English Roman Catholic martyr who was appointed archbishop of Canterbury (1162) but fell into disfavor with Henry II over religious matters and was later murdered.

Beck•ett (bĕk′ĭt), **Samuel.** 1906–89. Irish-born writer known esp. for his absurdist plays, such as *Waiting for Godot* (1952). He won the 1969 Nobel Prize for literature.

Beck•ford (bĕk′fərd), **William.** 1759?–1844. British writer and collector noted for his Arabian tale *Vathek* (1782).

Beck•ley (bĕk′lē). A city of S WV SE of Charleston. Pop. 18,290.

Beck•mann (bĕk′män), **Max.** 1884–1950. German artist whose works include *Night* (1919).

beck•on (bĕk′ən) *v.* **-oned, -on•ing, -ons.** —*tr.* **1.** To signal or summon, as by nodding or waving. **2.** To attract because of an inviting or enticing appearance. —*intr.* **1.** To make a signaling or summoning gesture. **2.** To be inviting or enticing. —*n.* A gesture of summons. [ME *bekenen* < OE *bēcnan.* See **bhā-¹*.**] —**beck′on•er** *n.* —**beck′on•ing•ly** *adv.*

be•cloud (bĭ-kloud′) *tr.v.* **-cloud•ed, -cloud•ing, -clouds.** To darken with or as if with clouds; obscure.

be•come (bĭ-kŭm′) *v.* **-came** (-kām′), **-come, -com•ing, -comes.** —*intr.* To grow or come to be. —*tr.* **1.** To be appropriate or suitable to. **2.** To show to advantage; look good with. —*phrasal verb.* **become of.** To be the fate of; happen to. [ME *bicomen* < OE *becuman.* See **gʷā-*.**]

be•com•ing (bĭ-kŭm′ĭng) *adj.* **1.** Appropriate, suitable, or proper. **2.** Pleasing or attractive to the eye. —**be•com′ing•ly** *adv.* —**be•com′ing•ness** *n.*

Bec•que•rel (bĕ-krĕl′, bĕk′ə-rĕl′). Family of French physicists, including **Antoine César** (1788–1878), one of the first investigators of electrochemistry; his son **Alexandre Edmond** (1820–91), noted for his research on phosphorescence; and his grandson **Antoine Henri** (1852–1908), who shared a 1903 Nobel Prize.

bed (bĕd) *n.* **1.a.** A piece of furniture for reclining and sleeping, typically consisting of a flat rectangular frame and a mattress on springs. **b.** A bedstead. **c.** A mattress. **2.a.** A place where one may sleep; lodging. **b.** Accommodations for a single person at a hospital or institution. **3.** A time at which one goes to sleep. **4.** A place for lovemaking. **5.** A marital relationship with its rights and intimacies. **6.a.** A small plot of cultivated or planted land. **b.** An underwater or intertidal area in which a particular organism is established in large numbers. **7.** The bottom of a body of water. **8.** A supporting, underlying, or securing part, esp.: **a.** A layer of food surmounted by another kind of food. **b.** A foundation of crushed rock or a similar substance for a road or railroad; a roadbed. **c.** A layer of mortar upon which stones or bricks are laid. **9.** *Print.* The heavy table of a printing press in which the type form is placed. **10.** The part of a truck, trailer, or freight car designed to carry loads. **11.** *Geol.* **a.** A rock mass of large horizontal extent bounded, esp. above, by physically different material. **b.** A deposit, as of ore, parallel to local stratification. **12.** A heap of material. —*v.* **bed•ded, bed•ding, beds.** —*tr.* **1.** To furnish with a bed or sleeping quarters. **2.** To put or send to bed. **3.** To have sexual relations with. **4.** To plant in a prepared plot of soil. **5.** To lay flat or arrange in layers. **6.a.** To embed. **b.** To establish; base. —*intr.* **1.** To go to bed. **2.** *Geol.* To form layers or strata. [ME < OE.]

B.Ed. *abbr.* Bachelor of Education.

bed-and-break•fast or **bed and breakfast** (bĕd′n-brĕk′fəst) *n.* A private home that provides rooms and breakfast for paying guests. —**bed′-and-break′fast** *adj.*

be•daub (bĭ-dôb′) *tr.v.* **-daubed, -daub•ing, -daubs. 1.** To smear; soil. **2.** To ornament in a vulgar, showy fashion.

be•daz•zle (bĭ-dăz′əl) *tr.v.* **-zled, -zling, -zles. 1.** To dazzle so completely as to make blind. **2.** To please irresistibly; enchant. —**be•daz′zle•ment** *n.*

bed•bug also **bed bug** (bĕd′bŭg′) *n.* A wingless odorous insect *(Cimex lectularius)* that infests dwellings and bedding and feeds on human blood. Also called regionally *chinch, chinch bug.*

bed•cham•ber (bĕd′chām′bər) *n.* A bedroom.

bed•clothes (bĕd′klōz′, -klōthz′) *pl.n.* Coverings, such as sheets and blankets, that are ordinarily used on a bed.

bed•ding (bĕd′ĭng) *n.* **1.** Bedclothes. **2.** Material, esp. straw, on which animals sleep. **3.** A bottom layer; a foundation. **4.** *Geol.* Stratification of rocks into beds.

Bed•does (bĕd′ōz′), **Thomas Lovell.** 1803–49. British poet whose works include *The Bride's Tragedy* (1822).

Bede (bēd) also **Bae•da** or **Be•da** (bē′də). "the Venerable Bede." 673?–735. Anglo-Saxon historian who introduced the method of dating events from the birth of Christ.

be•deck (bĭ-dĕk′) *tr.v.* **-decked, -deck•ing, -decks.** To adorn or ornament in a showy fashion.

Simone de Beauvoir

Thomas à Becket
The Martyrdom of Thomas à Becket, mid 13th-century miniature from the Carrow Psalter

ă pat	oi boy
ā pay	ou out
âr care	ŏŏ took
ä father	ōō boot
ĕ pet	ŭ cut
ē be	ûr urge
ĭ pit	th thin
ī pie	*th* this
îr pier	hw which
ŏ pot	zh vision
ō toe	ə about, item
ô paw	

Stress marks:
′ (primary);
′ (secondary), as in
dictionary (dĭk′shə-nĕr′ē)

be•dev•il (bĭ-dĕv′əl) *tr.v.* **-iled, -il•ing, -ils** or **-illed, -il•ling, -ils. 1.** To torment mercilessly; plague. **2.** To worry, annoy, or frustrate. **3.** To possess with or as if with a devil; bewitch. **4.** To spoil; ruin. — **be•dev′il•ment** *n.*

be•dew (bĭ-do͞o′, -dyo͞o′) *tr.v.* **-dewed, -dew•ing, -dews.** To wet with or as if with dew.

bed•fast (bĕd′făst′) *adj.* Confined to bed; bedridden.

bed•fel•low (bĕd′fĕl′ō) *n.* **1.** A bedmate. **2.** One that is closely associated or allied with another.

Bed•ford (bĕd′fərd). **1.** A municipal borough of S-central England on the Ouse R. W of Cambridge; site of a British victory over the Saxons in 571. Pop. 74,500. **2.** A city of N TX NE of Fort Worth; settled c. 1843. Pop. 43,762.

Bedford, Duke of. See **John of Lancaster.**

Bedford cord *n.* A heavy fabric with a lengthwise ribbed weave that resembles corduroy. [After BEDFORD, England.]

be•dight (bĭ-dīt′) *tr.v.* **-dight** or **-dight•ed, -dight•ing, -dights.** *Archaic.* To dress or array.

be•dim (bĭ-dĭm′) *tr.v.* **-dimmed, -dim•ming, -dims.** To dim.

be•di•zen (bĭ-dī′zən, -dĭz′ən) *tr.v.* **-zened, -zen•ing, -zens.** To ornament or dress in a showy or gaudy manner. [BE– + DIZEN.] — **be•di′zen•ment** *n.*

bed•lam (bĕd′ləm) *n.* **1.** A place or situation of noisy uproar and confusion. **2.** Often **Bedlam.** *Archaic.* An insane asylum. [ME *Bedlem*, Hospital of St. Mary of *Bethlehem*, an insane asylum in London.] — **bed′lam•ite′** (-lə-mīt′) *n.*

Bedlington terrier

Bed•ling•ton terrier (bĕd′lĭng-tən) *n.* A gray- or brown-haired dog of a breed developed in England. [After *Bedlington*, a town of NE England.]

Bed•loe's Island (bĕd′lōz). See **Liberty Island.**

bed•mate (bĕd′māt′) *n.* One with whom a bed is shared.

bed molding *n.* **1.** The molding between the corona and frieze of an entablature. **2.** A molding below a projecting part.

bed of roses *n.* A state of great comfort or luxury.

Bed•ou•in also **Bed•u•in** (bĕd′o͞o-ĭn, bĕd′wĭn) *n., pl.* **Bedouin** or **-ins** also **Beduin** or **-ins.** An Arab of any of various nomadic desert tribes. [ME *Bedoin* < OFr. *beduin* < Ar. *badāwīn*, pl. of *badāwī* < *badw*, desert.]

bed•pan (bĕd′păn′) *n.* A metal, glass, or plastic receptacle for the urinary and fecal discharges of persons confined to bed.

bed•plate (bĕd′plāt′) *n.* A plate, frame, or platform serving as a base or support for a machine.

bed•post (bĕd′pōst′) *n.* A vertical post at the corner of a bed.

be•drag•gle (bĭ-drăg′əl) *tr.v.* **-gled, -gling, -gles.** To make wet and limp. [BE– + DRAGGLE.]

be•drag•gled (bĭ-drăg′əld) *adj.* **1.a.** Wet; limp. **b.** Soiled by or as if by having been dragged through mud. **2.** Being in a condition of deterioration; dilapidated.

bed•rid•den (bĕd′rĭd′n) also **bed•rid** (-rĭd′) *adj.* Confined to bed because of infirmity.

bed•rock (bĕd′rŏk′) *n.* **1.** The solid rock that underlies loose material, such as soil, sand, clay, or gravel. **2.a.** The very basis; the foundation. **b.** The lowest point.

bed•roll (bĕd′rōl′) *n.* A portable roll of bedding used esp. by campers and others who sleep outdoors.

bed•room (bĕd′ro͞om′, -ro͝om′) *n.* A room in which to sleep. — *adj.* **1.** Sexually suggestive. **2.** Relating to commuters.

bed•side (bĕd′sīd′) *n.* The side of a bed or the space alongside it. — *adj.* **1.** Near a bed. **2.** Of or relating to a bed.

bedside manner *n.* The attitude and conduct of a physician in the presence of a patient.

bed-sit•ter (bĕd′sĭt′ər) *n.* *Chiefly British.* A one-room apartment that serves as a bedroom and a living room. [< BED + SITTING ROOM.]

bed•sore (bĕd′sôr′, -sōr′) *n.* A pressure-induced ulceration of the skin of persons confined to bed for long periods of time.

bed•spread (bĕd′sprĕd′) *n.* A usu. decorative bed covering.

bed•spring (bĕd′sprĭng′) *n.* One of the springs supporting the mattress of a bed. Often used in the plural.

bed•stead (bĕd′stĕd′) *n.* The frame supporting a bed.

bed•straw (bĕd′strô′) *n.* Any of several plants of the genus *Galium*, having whorled leaves, small flower clusters, and prickly stems. [Short for *Our Lady's Bedstraw*, a plant whose foliage was once used in mattresses.]

bed•time (bĕd′tīm′) *n.* The time at which one goes to bed.

Bed•u•in (bĕd′o͞o-ĭn, bĕd′wĭn) *n.* Var. of **Bedouin.**

bed-wet•ting (bĕd′wĕt′ĭng) *n.* Enuresis, esp. during sleep.

Bę•dzin (bĕn′jēn′). A town of S Poland NE of Katowice; part of Russia from 1815 to 1919. Pop. 77,100.

bee[1] (bē) *n.* **1.a.** Any of several winged, hairy-bodied, usu. stinging insects of the superfamily Apoidea in the order Hymenoptera, marked by sucking and chewing mouthparts for gathering nectar and pollen. **b.** A bumblebee. **c.** A honeybee. **2.** A social gathering where people also work in competition. — ***idiom.* a bee in (one's) bonnet.** An impulsive, often eccentric turn of mind; a notion. [ME < OE *bēo*. See **bhei-*.** Sense 2, perh. also alteration of dial. *bean*, neighborly help to a farmer < ME *bene*, extra service by a tenant < OE *bēn*, prayer. See **bhā-[2]*.**]

bee[2] (bē) *n.* *Naut.* A bee block. [ME *be*, a ring < OE *bēag*. See **bheug-*.**]

bee[3] (bē) *n.* The letter *b.*

beefeater
Yeoman Warder at the Tower of London

bee balm *n.* An aromatic eastern North American herb *(Monarda didyma)* in the mint family, having variously colored, tubular bilabiate flowers grouped in dense showy heads.

Bee•be (bē′bē), **(Charles) William.** 1877–1962. Amer. naturalist and explorer who helped design the bathysphere.

bee block *n.* *Naut.* A piece of hardwood on either side of a bowsprit through which forestays are reeved.

bee•bread (bē′brĕd′) *n.* A brownish substance consisting of a mixture of pollen and honey and used by bees as food.

beech (bēch) *n.* **1.** A deciduous tree of the genus *Fagus* having smooth gray bark, alternate simple leaves, and three-angled nuts enclosed in prickly burs. **2.** The wood of a beech. [ME *beche* < OE *bēce*. See **bhāgo-*.**]

Bee•cham (bē′chəm), Sir **Thomas.** 1879–1961. British conductor who founded the London Philharmonic (1932) and the Royal Philharmonic (1947) orchestras.

beech•drops or **beech-drops** (bēch′drŏps′) *pl.n. (used with a sing. or pl. v.)* A brownish eastern North American annual plant *(Epifagus virginiana)* having scalelike leaves and whitish tubular flowers with brown-purple stripes.

Bee•cher (bē′chər), **Lyman.** 1775–1863. Amer. cleric and father of the abolitionist editor **Henry Ward Beecher** (1813–87) and the novelist Harriet Beecher Stowe.

beech mast *n.* The nuts of the beech tree; beechnuts.

beech•nut (bēch′nŭt′) *n.* The three-angled beech tree nut.

bee-eat•er (bē′ē′tər) *n.* Any of various chiefly tropical Old World birds of the family Meropidae that have brightly colored plumage and feed on bees and wasps.

beef (bēf) *n., pl.* **beeves** (bēvz) or **beef. 1.a.** A full-grown steer, bull, ox, or cow, esp. one intended for use as meat. **b.** The flesh of slaughtered full-grown cattle. **2.** *Informal.* Human muscle; brawn. **3.** *pl.* **beefs.** *Slang.* A complaint. — *intr.v.* **beefed, beef•ing, beefs.** *Slang.* To complain. — ***phrasal verb.*** **beef up.** *Informal.* To make or become greater or stronger. [ME < OFr. *buef* < Lat. *bōs*, *bov-*. See **g[w]ou-*.**]

beef•a•lo (bē′fə-lō′) *n., pl.* **beefalo** or **-los** or **-loes.** A hybrid from a cross between the American buffalo, or bison, and beef cattle. [BEEF + (BUFF)ALO.]

beef bour•gui•gnon (bo͝or′gēn-yôn′, -yôɴ′) *n.* Braised beef cubes simmered in a seasoned red wine sauce with mushrooms, carrots, and onions. [Fr. *boeuf bourguignon* < *Bourgogne*, Burgundy, a region of E France.]

beef•cake (bēf′kāk′) *n.* *Informal.* Minimally attired men with muscular physiques, as in pictures. [BEEF + (CHEESE)CAKE.]

beef•eat•er (bēf′ē′tər) *n.* A yeoman of the British monarch's royal guard.

bee fly *n.* Any of various beelike flies of the family Bombyliidae that feed on nectar and pollen and have parasitic larvae.

beef•steak (bēf′stāk′) *n.* A slice of beef, such as one taken from the loin, suitable for broiling or frying.

beefsteak fungus *n.* An edible fungus *(Fistulina hepatica)*, growing on living tree trunks, such as oak and ash, and having a large, irregularly shaped reddish cap.

beef stro•ga•noff (strō′gə-nôf′, -nŏf′) *n.* Thinly sliced sautéed beef with onions, mushrooms, sour cream, and herbs. [After Count Paul *Stroganoff*, 19th-cent. Russian diplomat.]

beef Well•ing•ton (wĕl′ĭng-tən) *n.* A beef fillet covered with pâté de foie gras and encased in pastry. [Prob. < the name *Wellington*.]

beef•y (bē′fē) *adj.* **-i•er, -i•est. 1.a.** Muscular in build; brawny. **b.** Substantial; filling. **2.** Filled with beef. — **beef′i•ness** *n.*

bee gum *n.* *Chiefly Southern U.S.* **1.** A beehive located in a hollow tree or log. **2.** Any beehive. [BEE[1] + *gum*, a hollowed-out log (< GUM[1]).]

bee•hive (bē′hīv′) *n.* A hive for bees.

bee•keep•er (bē′kē′pər) *n.* An apiarist. — **bee′keep•ing** *n.*

bee•line (bē′līn′) *n.* A direct straight course. [From the belief that a bee returns to its hive in a straight course.]

Be•el•ze•bub (bē-ĕl′zə-bŭb′) *n.* *Theol.* **1.** The Devil; Satan. **2.** One of the fallen angels in Milton's *Paradise Lost.* **3.** An evil spirit; a demon. [Prob. ult. alteration of *ba'al zebûl*, exalted Baal : *ba'al*, Baal + *zebûl*, exalted.]

bee moth *n.* A moth *(Galleria mellonella)* that lays its eggs in beehives, where the larvae feed on wax and debris.

been (bĭn) *v.* P.part. of **be.**

beep (bēp) *n.* A sound or a signal, as from a horn. — *v.* **beeped, beep•ing, beeps.** — *intr.* To make a beep. — *tr.* **1.** To cause to make a beep. **2.** To call or warn with a beeper. [Imit.]

beep•er (bē′pər) *n.* **1.** One that beeps. **2.** A portable electronic device that beeps when the person carrying it is being paged.

bee plant *n.* Any of numerous plants that attract bees.

beer (bîr) *n.* **1.** A fermented alcoholic beverage brewed from malt and flavored with hops. **2.** A beverage made from extracts of roots and plants. [ME *ber* < OE *bēor* < West Gmc., prob. < Lat. *bibere*, to drink. See **pō(i)-*.**]

Beer•bohm (bîr′bōm′), Sir **Henry Maximilian ("Max").** 1872–1956. British caricaturist, writer, and wit.

Beer•naert (bâr′närt), **Auguste Marie François.** 1829–1912. Belgian diplomat who shared the 1909 Nobel Peace Prize.

Beer•she•ba (bîr-shē′bə, bĕr-shĕv′ə). A city of S Israel SW of Jerusalem; the S border of biblical Palestine. Pop. 114,300.

beer•y (bîr′ē) *adj.* **-i•er, -i•est. 1.** Smelling or tasting of beer: *beery breath.* **2.** Affected or produced by beer: *beery humor.*
beest•ings also **beast•ings** (bē′stĭngz) *pl.n. (used with a sing. or pl. v.)* The first milk secreted by a mammal, esp. a cow, after parturition; colostrum. [ME *bestinggis*, pl. of *besting* < OE *bȳsting* < *bēost*, beestings.]
bees•wax (bēz′wăks′) *n.* **1.** The wax secreted by the honeybee for constructing honeycombs. **2.** Commercial wax obtained by processing and purifying the crude wax of the honeybee.
beet (bēt) *n.* **1.** A biennial Eurasian plant *(Beta vulgaris)* grown as a crop plant for its edible roots and leaves. **2.** The swollen root of this plant eaten as a vegetable. **3.** The sugar beet. [ME *bete* < OE *bēte* < Lat. *bēta.*]
beet armyworm *n.* An armyworm *(Spodoptera exigua)* that feeds primarily on the foliage of beets and other crops.
Bee•tho•ven (bā′tō′vən), **Ludwig van.** 1770–1827. German composer whose music formed a transition from classical to romantic composition.
bee•tle[1] (bēt′l) *n.* **1.** Any of numerous insects of the order Coleoptera, having biting mouthparts and forewings that form horny coverings to protect the underlying hind wings when at rest. **2.** An insect resembling a beetle. *—intr.v.* **-tled, -tling, -tles.** To make one's way or move like a beetle. [ME *betil* < OE *bitela* < *bītan*, to bite. See **bheid-*.**]
bee•tle[2] (bēt′l) *adj.* Jutting; overhanging. *—intr.v.* **-tled, -tling, -tles.** To jut; overhang. [< ME *bitel-brouwed*, grim-browed : *bitel*, sharp (prob. < OE **bitol*, biting < OE *bite*, bite; see BIT[2]) + *brouwed* (< *brow*, brow; see BROW).]
bee•tle[3] (bēt′l) *n.* **1.** A heavy mallet with a large wooden head. **2.** A small wooden household mallet. **3.** A machine with revolving wooden hammers that gives fabrics a lustrous sheen. [ME *betel* < OE *bȳtl.* See **bhau-*.**]
beet leafhopper *n.* A small insect *(Eutettix tenellus)* that transmits a destructive viral disease to plants, esp. sugar beets, in the western United States.
bee tree *n.* **1.** Any of various trees having nectar-rich flowers attractive to bees. **2.** A hollow tree in which bees form nests.
beeves (bēvz) *n.* A pl. of **beef.**
bef. *abbr.* Before.
be•fall (bĭ-fôl′) *v.* **-fell** (-fĕl′), **-fall•en** (-fô′lən), **-fall•ing, -falls.** *—intr.* To come to pass; happen. *—tr.* To happen to. [ME *bifallen* < OE *befeallan*, to fall.]
be•fit (bĭ-fĭt′) *tr.v.* **-fit•ted, -fit•ting, -fits.** To be suited to.
be•fit•ting (bĭ-fĭt′ĭng) *adj.* Appropriate; suitable; proper. **—be•fit′ting•ly** *adv.*
be•fog (bĭ-fôg′, -fŏg′) *tr.v.* **-fogged, -fog•ging, -fogs. 1.** To cover or obscure with or as if with fog. **2.** To cause confusion in; muddle.
be•fool (bĭ-fo͞ol′) *tr.v.* **-fooled, -fool•ing, -fools. 1.** To make a fool of. **2.** To hoodwink; deceive.
be•fore (bĭ-fôr′, -fōr′) *adv.* **1.** Earlier in time. **2.** In front; ahead. *—prep.* **1.** Previous to in time. **2.** In front of. **3.** In store for; awaiting. **4.** Into or in the presence of. **5.** Under the consideration or jurisdiction of. **6.** In a position superior to. *—conj.* **1.** In advance of the time when. **2.** Rather than; sooner than. [ME *bifore* < OE *beforan.* See **per[1]*.**]
before Christ *adv.* In a given year of the pre-Christian era.
be•fore•hand (bĭ-fôr′hănd′, -fōr′-) *adv. & adj.* **1.** In anticipation. **2.** In advance; early.
be•fore•time (bĭ-fôr′tīm′, -fōr′-) *adv. Archaic.* Formerly.
be•foul (bĭ-foul′) *tr.v.* **-fouled, -foul•ing, -fouls. 1.** To make dirty; soil. **2.** To cast aspersions upon; speak badly of.
be•friend (bĭ-frĕnd′) *tr.v.* **-friend•ed, -friend•ing, -friends.** To behave as a friend to.
be•fud•dle (bĭ-fŭd′l) *tr.v.* **-dled, -dling, -dles. 1.** To confuse; perplex. See Syns at **confuse. 2.** To stupefy with or as if with alcoholic drink.
beg (bĕg) *v.* **begged, beg•ging, begs.** *—tr.* **1.** To ask for as charity. **2.** To ask earnestly for or of; entreat. **3.a.** To evade; dodge: *a speech that begged the real issues.* **b.** To take for granted without proof: *beg the point in a dispute.* *—intr.* **1.** To solicit alms. **2.** To make a humble or urgent plea. ***—phrasal verb.* beg off.** To ask to be released from something, such as an obligation. [ME *beggen*, poss. < AN *begger* < OFr. *begart*, lay brother, one who prays. See BEGGAR.]
be•get (bĭ-gĕt′) *tr.v.* **-got** (-gŏt′), **-got•ten** (-gŏt′n) or **-got, -get•ting, -gets. 1.** To father; sire. **2.** To cause to exist or occur; produce: *Violence begets violence.* [ME *biyeten, bigeten* < OE *begetan.* See **ghend-*.**] **—be•get′ter** *n.*
beg•gar (bĕg′ər) *n.* **1.** One who solicits alms for a living. **2.** An impoverished person; a pauper. **3.** *Informal.* A man or a boy. *—tr.v.* **-gared, -gar•ing, -gars. 1.** To make a beggar of; impoverish. **2.** To exceed the limits, resources, or capabilities of. [ME < OFr. *begart*, ult. < MDu. *beggaert*, one who rattles off prayers.]
beg•gar•ly (bĕg′ər-lē) *adj.* **1.** Of, relating to, or befitting a beggar; very poor. **2.** So mean, petty, or paltry as to deserve contempt. **—beg′gar•li•ness** *n.*
beg•gar's lice (bĕg′ərz) *n. (used with a sing. or pl. v.)* **1.** Any of several plants having small, often prickly fruits that cling to clothing or animal fur. **2.** The fruit of any of these plants.
beggar ticks also **beggar's ticks** *pl.n. (used with a sing. or pl. v.)* **1.a.** Any of various weeds of the genus *Bidens* in the composite family. **b.** The fruit of these plants, typically having barbed awns and clinging to clothing and animal fur. **2.** Any of certain other plants or their clinging fruits.
beg•gar•y (bĕg′ə-rē) *n.* **1.** Extreme poverty; penury. **2.** The state of being a beggar. **3.** Beggars considered as a group.
be•gin (bĭ-gĭn′) *v.* **-gan** (-găn′), **-gun** (-gŭn′), **-gin•ning, -gins.** *—intr.* **1.** To take the first step in performing an action; start. **2.** To come into being. **3.** To do or accomplish in the least degree: *That does not even begin to address the problem.* *—tr.* **1.** To take the first step in doing; start. **2.** To cause to come into being; originate. **3.** To come first in: *1 begins the sequence.* [ME *biginnen* < OE *beginnan.*]
Be•gin (bā′gĭn), **Menachem.** b. 1913. Russian-born Israeli politician who shared the 1978 Nobel Peace Prize.
be•gin•ner (bĭ-gĭn′ər) *n.* One who is just starting to learn or do something; a novice.
be•gin•ning (bĭ-gĭn′ĭng) *n.* **1.** The act or process of bringing or being brought into being; a start. **2.** The time when something begins or is begun. **3.** The place where something begins or is begun. **4.** A source; an origin. **5.** The first part. **6.** An early or rudimentary phase. Often used in the plural.
Syns: *beginning, birth, dawn, genesis, nascence, rise.* The central meaning shared by these nouns is "the initial stage of a developmental process": *the beginning of a new era; the birth of generative grammar; the dawn of civilization; the genesis of algebra; the nascence of classical sculpture; the rise of an ancient city-state.* ***Ant:*** *end.*
beginning rhyme *n.* Rhyme at the beginning of consecutive lines of verse.
be•gird (bĭ-gûrd′) *tr.v.* **-girt** (-gûrt′) or **-gird•ed, -girt, -gird•ing, -girds.** To encircle with or as if with a band.
be•gone (bĭ-gôn′, -gŏn′) *v.* Used chiefly in the imperative to express an order of dismissal.
be•go•nia (bĭ-gōn′yə) *n.* Any of various tropical or subtropical plants of the genus *Begonia,* having usu. asymmetrical leaves. [NLat. *Begonia*, genus name, after Michel *Bégon* (1638–1710), French governor in the West Indies.]
be•gor•ra (bĭ-gôr′ə, -gŏr′ə) *interj. Irish.* Used as a mild oath. [Alteration of *by God.*]
be•got (bĭ-gŏt′) *v.* P.t. and p.part. of **beget.**
be•got•ten (bĭ-gŏt′n) *v.* A p.part. of **beget.**
be•grime (bĭ-grīm′) *tr.v.* **-grimed, -grim•ing, -grimes.** To smear or soil with or as if with dirt.
be•grudge (bĭ-grŭj′) *tr.v.* **-grudged, -grudg•ing, -grudg•es. 1.a.** To envy the possession or enjoyment of. **b.** To envy for the possession of. See Syns at **envy. 2.** To give or expend with reluctance. **—be•grudg′er** *n.* **—be•grudg′ing•ly** *adv.*
be•guile (bĭ-gīl′) *tr.v.* **-guiled, -guil•ing, -guiles. 1.** To deceive by guile; delude. See Syns at **deceive. 2.** To take away from by or as if by guile; cheat. **3.** To distract the attention of; divert. **4.** To pass (time) pleasantly. **5.** To amuse or charm; delight. See Syns at **charm. —be•guile′ment** *n.* **—be•guil′er** *n.* **—be•guil′ing•ly** *adv.*
be•guine (bĭ-gēn′) *n.* A ballroom dance similar to the rumba, based on a dance of Martinique and St. Lucia. [Fr. (West Indies) *béguine* < Fr. *béguin*, hood, flirtation < *beguine*, Beguine. See BEGUINE.]
Beg•uine (bā′gēn′, bā-gēn′) *n. Rom. Cath. Ch.* A member of any of several lay sisterhoods founded in the Netherlands in the 13th century. [ME *begine* < OFr. *beguine* < MDu. *beg-*, root of *beggaert*, one who rattles off prayers.]
be•gum (bā′gəm, bē′-) *n.* **1.** A Muslim woman of rank. **2.** Used as a form of address for such a woman. [Urdu *begam* < East Turkic *begüm*, first pers. sing. possessive of *beg*, master, mistress < Old Turkic.]
be•gun (bĭ-gŭn′) *v.* P.part. of **begin.**
be•half (bĭ-hăf′, -häf′) *n.* Interest, support, or benefit. ***—idioms.* in behalf of.** For the benefit of; in the interest of. **on behalf of.** As the agent of; on the part of. [ME < OE *be healfe*, by (his) side : *be*, by, at; see BY[1] + *healf*, side, half; see HALF.]
Usage Note: Traditionally, *in behalf of* and *on behalf of* have distinct senses. *In behalf of* means "for the benefit of," as in *We raised money in behalf of the earthquake victims. On behalf of* means "as the agent of, on the part of," as in *The guardian signed the contract on behalf of the minor child.* The two senses are often confused, even by reputable writers.
Be•han (bē′ən), **Brendan Francis.** 1923–64. Irish writer whose works include *The Quare Fellow* (1954).
be•have (bĭ-hāv′) *v.* **-haved, -hav•ing, -haves.** *—intr.* **1.a.** To conduct oneself in a specified way: *behave well.* **b.** To conduct oneself in a proper way: *I told the child to behave.* **2.** To act, react, function, or perform in a particular way. *—tr.* **1.** To conduct (oneself) properly. **2.** To conduct (oneself) in a specified way. [ME *behaven*: *be-*, be- + *have*, have; see HAVE.]
be•hav•ior (bĭ-hāv′yər) *n.* **1.** The manner in which one behaves. **2.** *Psychol.* The actions or reactions of persons or things in response to external or internal stimuli. [ME *behavour* < *behaven*, to behave. See BEHAVE.] **—be•hav′ior•al** *adj.* **—be•hav′ior•al•ly** *adv.*
Syns: *behavior, conduct, deportment.* These nouns all

Ludwig van Beethoven

ă pat	oi boy
ā pay	ou out
âr care	o͝o took
ä father	o͞o boot
ĕ pet	ŭ cut
ē be	ûr urge
ĭ pit	th thin
ī pie	*th* this
îr pier	hw which
ŏ pot	zh vision
ō toe	ə about, item
ô paw	

Stress marks:
′ (primary);
′ (secondary), as in
dictionary (dĭk′shə-nĕr′ē)

pertain to a person's actions as they constitute a means of evaluation by others. *Behavior* is the most general: *guilty of contemptible behavior. Conduct* applies to actions considered from the standpoint of morality and ethics: *"Life, not the parson, teaches conduct"* (Oliver Wendell Holmes, Jr.). *Deportment* more narrowly pertains to actions measured by a prevailing code of social behavior: "[Old Mr. Turveydrop] *was not like anything in the world but a model of Deportment"* (Charles Dickens).

behavioral medicine *n.* The application of behavior therapy to the prevention and treatment of medical and psychosomatic disorders and to the treatment of undesirable behaviors.

behavioral science *n.* A scientific discipline that studies the actions and reactions of human beings and animals through scientific procedures. **— behavioral scientist** *n.*

behavioral therapy *n.* See **behavior therapy.**

be•hav•ior•ism (bĭ-hāv′yə-rĭz′əm) *n. Psychol.* A school of psychology that confines itself to the study of observable and quantifiable aspects of behavior and excludes subjective phenomena. **— be•hav′ior•ist** *n.* **— be•hav′ior•is′tic** *adj.*

behavior medicine *n.* See **behavioral medicine.**

behavior modification *n. Psychol.* **1.** The use of basic learning techniques, such as conditioning, biofeedback, reinforcement, or aversion therapy, to alter human behavior. **2.** See **behavior therapy. — behavior modifier** *n.*

behavior therapy *n. Psychol.* A form of psychotherapy that seeks to modify maladaptive behavior by substituting new responses to given stimuli. **— behavior therapist** *n.*

be•hav•iour (bĭ-hāv′yər) *n. Chiefly British.* Var. of **behavior.**

be•head (bĭ-hĕd′) *tr.v.* **-head•ed, -head•ing, -heads.** To sever the head from; decapitate. [ME *biheden* < OE *behēafdian*: *be-*, away from; see BE- + *hēafod*, head; see HEAD.]

be•he•moth (bĭ-hē′məth, bē′ə-məth) *n.* **1.** Something enormous in size or power. **2.** Often **Behemoth.** *Bible.* A huge animal, possibly the hippopotamus, described in the Book of Job. [Heb. *bĕhēmôt*, intensive pl. of *bĕhēmâ*, beast.]

be•hest (bĭ-hĕst′) *n.* **1.** An authoritative command. **2.** An urgent request. [ME *bihest*, vow < OE *behǣs*. See **kei-[2]*.**]

be•hind (bĭ-hīnd′) *adv.* **1.** In, to, or toward the rear. **2.** In a place or condition that has been passed or left. **3.** In arrears; late. **4.** Below the standard level; in or into an inferior position: *behind in class.* **5.** Slow: *My watch is running behind.* **6.** *Archaic.* Yet to come. *— prep.* **1.** At the back of or in the rear of. **2.** On the farther side or other side of; beyond: *behind the door.* **3.** In a place or time that has been passed or left by: *Their worries are behind them.* **4.a.** Later than. **b.** Used to indicate deficiency in performance: *behind us in technology.* **5.a.** Hidden or concealed by. **b.** In the background of; underlying. **6.** In a position of support; at the back of. **7.** In pursuit of. *— n. Informal.* The buttocks. [ME *bihinde* < OE *behindan.* See **ko-*.**]

be•hind•hand (bĭ-hīnd′hănd′) *adj.* **1.** Being in arrears. **2.** Being behind time; slow. **— be•hind′hand′** *adv.*

be•hind-the-scenes (bĭ-hīnd′*thə*-sēnz′) *adj.* Done, maintained, or held in secret.

be•hold (bĭ-hōld′) *v.* **-held** (-hĕld′), **-hold•ing, -holds.** *— tr.* **1.a.** To perceive by the visual faculty; see. **b.** To perceive through use of the mental faculty; comprehend. **2.** To look upon; gaze at. See Syns at **see[1].** *— intr.* Used in the imperative in order to call attention. **— be•hold′er** *n.*

be•hold•en (bĭ-hōl′dən) *adj.* Owing something to another; indebted. [ME *biholden*, p.part. of *biholden*, to observe < OE *behaldan*: *be-*, bi- + *haldan*, to hold; see HOLD[1].]

be•hoof (bĭ-ho͞of′) *n.* Benefit; advantage. [ME *bihove* < OE *behōf.* See **kap-*.**]

be•hoove (bĭ-ho͞ov′) *v.* **-hooved, -hoov•ing, -hooves.** *— tr.* To be necessary or proper for. *— intr.* To be necessary or proper. [ME *behōven* < OE *behōfian.* See **kap-*.**]

Beh•ring (bâr′ĭng, bĕr′-, bā′rĭng), **Emil Von.** 1854–1917. German physiologist who won a 1901 Nobel Prize.

Behr•man (bâr′mən), **S(amuel) N(athaniel).** 1893–1973. Amer. playwright whose works include *The Second Man* (1927).

Bei•der•becke (bī′dər-bĕk′), **Leon Bismark ("Bix").** 1903–31. Amer. jazz composer and musician.

beige (bāzh) *n.* **1.** *Color.* A light grayish brown or yellowish brown to grayish yellow. **2.** A soft fabric of undyed, unbleached wool. [Fr., fine woolen fabric left in its natural color < OFr. *bege*, perh. < OItal. *bambagia*, cotton wool < fem. of LLat. *bombax.* See BOMBAST.] **— beige** *adj.*

bei•gnet also **bai•gnet** or **bei•gné** or **bang** (bĕn-yā′) *n. Southern Louisiana.* **1.** A square doughnut with no hole. **2.** A seafood fritter. [Fr., fritter, of Celt. orig.]

Regional Note: New Orleans, Louisiana, has been a rich contributor of French loan words and local expressions to American English. Many of the words, such as *beignet, café au lait, faubourg, lagniappe,* and *krewe,* reflect the New World French cuisine and culture characterizing this city and much of southern Louisiana. Words such as *banquette, camelback,* and *shotgun* reflect distinctive physical characteristics and architectural styles found in the city.

Bei•jing (bā′jĭng′) also **Pe•king** (pē′kĭng′, pā′-). Formerly (1928–49) **Pei•ping** (pā′pĭng′). The cap. of China, in the NE part; founded c. 700 B.C. Pop. 5,860,000.

be•ing (bē′ĭng) *n.* **1.** The state or quality of having existence. **2.a.** Something that exists, is thought to exist, or is represented as existing. **b.** The totality of all things that exist. **3.a.** A person: *"The artist after all is a solitary being"* (Virginia Woolf). **b.** All the qualities constituting one that exists; the essence. **c.** One's basic or essential nature; personality.

Bei•ra (bā′rə). A city of E-central Mozambique on the Mozambique Channel, an arm of the Indian Ocean. Pop. 230,744.

Bei•rut[1] (bā-ro͞ot′). The cap. of Lebanon, in the W part on the Mediterranean Sea. Pop. 509,000.

Bei•rut[2] (bā-ro͞ot′, bā′ro͞ot′) *n.* A place or situation characterized by ongoing, highly destructive strife.

Be•ja (bā′jə) *n., pl.* **Beja. 1.** A member of a people living primarily as pastoral nomads in the area between the Nile River and the Red Sea. **2.** The Cushitic language of the Beja.

be•je•sus (bĭ-jē′zəs, -jā′-) *n. Slang.* Used as an intensive: *The bear scared the bejesus out of us.* [Alteration of *by Jesus.*]

be•jew•eled (bĭ-jo͞o′əld) *adj.* Decorated with or as if with jewels.

bel (bĕl) *n.* Ten decibels. [After Alexander Graham BELL.]

be•la•bor (bĭ-lā′bər) *tr.v.* **-bored, -bor•ing, -bors. 1.** To attack with blows; hit, beat, or whip. **2.** To assail verbally. **3.** To discuss repeatedly or at length; harp on.

be•la•bour (bĭ-lā′bər) *v. Chiefly British.* Var. of **belabor.**

Bel•a•rus (bĕl′ə-ro͞os′, bĕl′ä-ro͞os′). See **Belorussia.**

Be•las•co (bə-lăs′kō), **David.** 1853–1931. Amer. playwright and theatrical producer known for his realistic stage settings and innovative lighting effects.

be•lat•ed (bĭ-lā′tĭd) *adj.* Having been delayed; done or sent too late: *a belated birthday card.* [BE- + LATED.] **— be•lat′ed•ly** *adv.* **— be•lat′ed•ness** *n.*

Be•lau (bə-lou′) also **Pa•lau** (pä-, pə-). A group of volcanic islands and islets in the Caroline Is. of the W Pacific; a republic in free association with the U.S. until 1996.

be•lay (bĭ-lā′) *v.* **-layed, -lay•ing, -lays.** *— tr.* **1.** *Naut.* To secure or make fast (a line, for example) by winding on a cleat or pin. **2.** To secure (a mountain climber, for example) at the end of a length of rope. **3.** To cause to stop. *— intr.* **1.** To be made secure. **2.** Used in the imperative as an order to stop. *— n.* **1.** The securing of a rope on a rock or other projection during mountain climbing. **2.** An object thus used. [ME *bileggen*, to surround < OE *belecgan.* See **legh-*.**]

Be•la•ya (bĕl′ə-yə). A river of SW Russia rising in the Ural Mts. and flowing c. 1,416 km (880 mi) to the Kama R.

be•lay•ing pin (bĭ-lā′ĭng) *n. Naut.* A short, removable wooden or metal pin fitted in a rail of a ship and used for securing rigging.

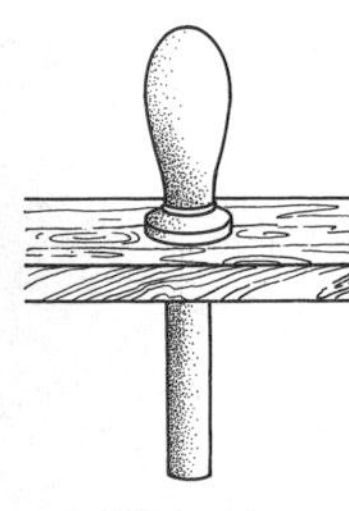

belaying pin

bel can•to (bĕl kän′tō) *n. Mus.* A style of singing characterized by legato, beauty of tone, and evenness and agility in passagework. [Ital. : *bel, bello,* beautiful + *canto,* singing.]

belch (bĕlch) *v.* **belched, belch•ing, belch•es.** *— intr.* **1.** To expel stomach gas noisily through the mouth. **2.** To erupt or explode. **3.** To gush forth. *— tr.* **1.** To expel (stomach gas) noisily through the mouth. **2.** To eject violently. [ME *belchen* < OE *bealcettan*or < **bealcian*; akin to *bealcan.*] **— belch** *n.*

bel•dam or **bel•dame** (bĕl′dəm, -dăm′) *n.* An old woman, esp. one who is considered ugly. [ME, grandmother : *bel*, indicating respect (< OFr. *bel*, fine < Lat. *bellus*; see **deu-[2]***) + *dame*, lady; see DAME.]

be•lea•guer (bĭ-lē′gər) *tr.v.* **-guered, -guer•ing, -guers. 1.** To harass; beset. **2.** To surround with troops; besiege. [Prob. Du. *belegeren*: *be-*, around (< MDu. *bie*; see **ambhi***) + *leger*, camp; see **legh-*.**] **— be•lea′guer•ment** *n.*

Be•lém (bə-lĕm′, -lāɴ′). Formerly **Pa•rá** (pə-rä′). A city of N Brazil in the Amazon delta. Pop. 933,287.

bel•em•nite (bĕl′əm-nīt′) *n.* A cone-shaped, fossilized internal shell of any of an extinct genus of cephalopods related to the cuttlefish. [NLat. *belemnītēs* < Gk. *belemnon*, dart. See **gʷelə-*.**]

bel es•prit (bĕl′ ĕ-sprē′) *n., pl.* **beaux es•prits** (bō′zĕ-sprē′). A cultivated, intelligent person. [Fr. : *bel*, fine + *esprit*, mind.]

Bel•fast (bĕl′făst′, bĕl-făst′). The cap. of Northern Ireland, in the E part on **Belfast Lough,** an inlet of the Irish Sea. Pop. 318,600.

Bel•fort (bĕl-fôr′). A city of NE France commanding the strategic **Belfort Gap** between the Vosges and the Jura Mts. Pop. 51,206.

bel•fry (bĕl′frē) *n., pl.* **-fries. 1.** A bell tower, esp. one attached to a building. **2.** The part of a tower or steeple in which bells are hung. [ME *belfrei* < ONFr. *belfroi*, alteration of OFr. *berfrei, berfroi.* See **bhergh-[2]*.**] **— bel′fried** *adj.*

belfry

Belg. *abbr.* Belgian; Belgium.

Bel•gae (bĕl′gī′, -jē′) *pl.n.* A people who formerly inhabited northeast Gaul and areas of southeast England. [Lat.]

Bel•gian (bĕl′jən) *adj.* Of or relating to Belgium or its people or culture. *— n.* **1.** A native or inhabitant of Belgium. **2.** Any of a breed of typically large draft horses.

Belgian Con•go (kŏng′gō). See **Zaire.**

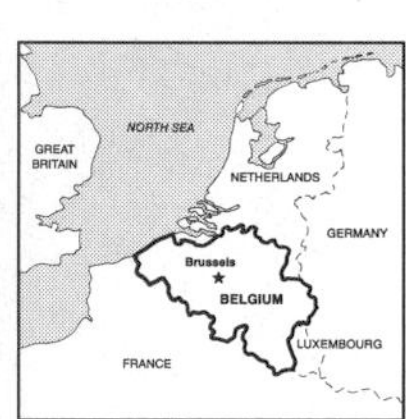

Belgium

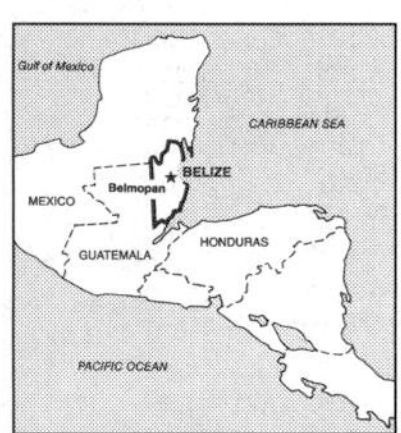

Belize

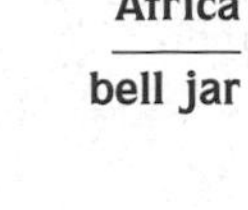

Belgian East Af•ri•ca (ăf′rĭ-kə). The former Belgian trust territory of Ruanda-Urundi, now divided into the independent countries of Rwanda and Burundi.

Belgian hare *n.* A large reddish-brown rabbit of a domestic breed developed in England from Belgian stock.

Belgian Mal•in•ois (măl′ən-wä′) *n.* See **Belgian sheep dog** 2.

Belgian sheep dog *n.* **1.** Any of a breed of hardy sheep dogs developed in Belgium. **2.** Any of a breed of working dogs closely related to the Belgian sheep dog.

Belgian Ter•vu•ren (tĕr-vyo͝or′ən, tər-) *n.* See **Belgian sheep dog** 2.

Bel•gic (bĕl′jĭk) *adj.* **1.** Of or relating to Belgium or the Belgians. **2.** Of or relating to the Belgae.

Bel•gium (bĕl′jəm). A country of NW Europe on the North Sea; culturally divided into Dutch-speaking Flanders in the N and French-speaking Wallonia in the S. Cap. Brussels. Pop. 9,858,017.

Bel•go•rod (bĕl′gə-rŏd′, byĕl′gə-rət). A city of SW Russia on the Donets R. Pop. 280,000.

Bel•grade (bĕl′grād′, -gräd′, bĕl-grād′) also **Be•o•grad** (bĕ′ô-gräd). The cap. of Serbia and of Yugoslavia, in the N-central part of Serbia at the confluence of the Danube and Sava rivers; founded in the 3rd cent. B.C. Pop. 936,200.

Bel•gra•vi•a (bĕl-grā′vē-ə). A fashionable residential district of SW London, England, centered on Belgrave Square.

Be•li•al (bē′lē-əl, bel′yəl) *n.* **1.** *Bible.* A personification of wickedness and ungodliness. **2.** One of the fallen angels who rebelled against God in Milton's *Paradise Lost.*

be•lie (bĭ-lī′) *tr.v.* **-lied, -ly•ing, -lies. 1.** To picture falsely; misrepresent. **2.** To show to be false: *His smile belied his ire.* **3.** To be counter to; contradict. [ME *bilien* < OE *belēogan,* to deceive with lies. See **leugh-***.] **— be•li′er** *n.*

be•lief (bĭ-lēf′) *n.* **1.** The mental act, condition, or habit of placing trust or confidence in another. **2.** Mental acceptance of and conviction in the truth, actuality, or validity of something. **3.** Something believed or accepted as true, esp. a particular tenet or a body of tenets accepted by a group of persons. [ME *bileve,* alteration (influenced by *belȳfan, belēfan,* to believe; see BELIEVE) of OE *gelēafa.* See **leubh-***.]

be•liev•a•ble (bĭ-lē′və-bəl) *adj.* Capable of eliciting belief or trust. See Syns at **plausible. — be•liev′a•bil′i•ty** *n.* **— be•liev′a•bly** *adv.*

be•lieve (bĭ-lēv′) *v.* **-lieved, -liev•ing, -lieves.** *— tr.* **1.** To accept as true or real. **2.** To credit with veracity: *I believe you.* **3.** To expect or suppose; think. *— intr.* **1.** To have firm faith, esp. religious faith. **2.** To have faith, confidence, or trust. **3.** To have confidence in the truth or value of something. **4.** To have an opinion; think. [ME *bileven* < OE *belȳfan, belēfan, gelēfan.* See **leubh-***.] **— be•liev′er** *n.*

be•like (bĭ-līk′) *adv. Archaic.* Probably; perhaps. [Prob. *be-* (< BY[1]) + LIKE[2], what is likely; see LIKE.]

Bel•i•sar•i•us (bĕl′ĭ-sâr′ē-əs). 505?–565. Byzantine general who led campaigns against the barbarians in North Africa and Italy.

be•lit•tle (bĭ-lĭt′l) *tr.v.* **-tled, -tling, -tles. 1.** To represent or speak of as contemptibly small or unimportant; disparage. **2.** To cause to seem less than another or little. **— be•lit′tle•ment** *n.* **— be•lit′tler** *n.*

Be•li•tung (bə-lē′to͝ong) also **Bil•li•ton** (bə-lē′tŏn′). An island of W Indonesia in the Java Sea between Sumatra and Borneo.

Be•lize (bə-lēz′). **1.** Formerly **Brit•ish Hon•du•ras** (brĭt′ĭsh hŏn-do͝or′əs, -dyo͝or′-). A country of Central America on the Caribbean Sea; achieved independence in 1981. Cap. Belmopan. Pop. 145,353. **2.** Also **Belize City.** The former cap. (until 1970) of Belize, in the E part at the mouth of the **Belize River.** Pop. 39,771.

bell[1] (bĕl) *n.* **1.** A hollow metal instrument, usu. cup-shaped with a flared opening, that emits a metallic tone when struck. **2.** Something resembling a bell in shape or sound, as: **a.** *Mus.* The round flared mouth of a wind instrument. **b. bells.** *Mus.* A percussion instrument consisting of metal tubes or bars that emit tones when struck. **c.** A hollow, usu. inverted vessel. **d.** The corolla of a flower. **3.** *Naut.* **a.** A stroke on a bell to mark the hour. **b.** The time indicated by these strokes, divided into half hours. *— v.* **belled, bell•ing, bells.** *— tr.* **1.** To put a bell on. **2.** To cause to flare like a bell. *— intr.* To assume the form of a bell; flare. **— *idiom.* bell the cat.** To perform a daring act. [ME *belle* < OE.]

bell[2] (bĕl) *n.* The bellowing or baying cry of certain animals. *— intr.v.* **belled, bell•ing, bells.** To utter long, deep, resonant sounds; bellow. [< ME *bellen,* to bellow < OE *bellan.*]

Bell (bĕl). A city of S CA, a suburb of Los Angeles. Pop. 34,365.

Bell, Alexander Graham. 1847–1922. Scottish-born Amer. inventor of the telephone (first demonstrated 1876).

Bell, (Arthur) Clive (Howard). 1881–1964. British critic who proposed his aesthetic theories in *Art* (1914).

Bel•la Coo•la (bĕl′ə ko͞o′lə) *n., pl.* **Bella Coola** or **-las. 1.** A member of a Native American people inhabiting the coast of British Columbia along the Bella Coola River, a stream flowing into a channel of Queen Charlotte Sound. **2.** The Salishan language of the Bella Coola.

bel•la•don•na (bĕl′ə-dŏn′ə) *n.* **1.** A poisonous Eurasian perennial herb *(Atropa belladonna)* having usu. solitary, nodding, bell-shaped flowers and glossy black berries. **2.** A medicinal alkaloidal extract or tincture derived from this plant. [Ital. : *bella,* fem. of *bello,* beautiful (< Lat. *bellus;* see **deu-[2]***) + *donna,* lady; see DONNA.]

belladonna alkaloids *pl.n.* A group of alkaloids found in plants such as belladonna and used in medicine.

belladonna lily *n.* A bulbous, perennial southern African herb *(Amaryllis belladonna)* with trumpet-shaped flowers.

Bel•la•my (bĕl′ə-mē), **Edward.** 1850–98. Amer. writer and utopian socialist noted for *Looking Backward* (1888).

Bel•lay (bə-lā′, bĕ-lā′), **Joachim du.** 1522?–60. French poet who was a founder of a group of poets known as the Pléiade.

bell•bird (bĕl′bûrd′) *n.* Any of various tropical American birds of the family Cotingidae, having a bell-like call.

bell-bot•tom (bĕl′bŏt′əm) *adj.* Having legs that flare out at the bottom: *bell-bottom trousers.* **— bell-bottoms** *pl.n.*

bell•boy (bĕl′boi′) *n.* A bellhop.

bell buoy *n. Naut.* A buoy fitted with a warning bell that is activated by the movement of the waves.

bell captain *n.* The supervisor of a group of bellhops.

belle (bĕl) *n.* A popular, attractive girl or woman, esp. the most attractive in a group: *the belle of the ball.* [Fr., beautiful, belle < Lat. *bella,* fem. of *bellus.* See **deu-[2]***.]

Bel•leau Wood (bĕ-lō′, bĕl′ō). A forested area of N France E of Château-Thierry; site of a major World War I battle (Jun. 1918).

belle é•poque (ā-pŭk′) *n.* An era of artistic and cultural refinement in a society, esp. in France at the beginning of the 20th century. [Fr. : *belle,* beautiful + *époque,* era.]

Belle Fourche (bĕl′ fo͞osh′). A river rising in NE WY and flowing c. 467 km (290 mi) to the Cheyenne R. in W SD.

Belle Glade. A city of SE FL on Lake Okeechobee W of West Palm Beach. Pop. 16,177.

Belle Isle, Strait of. A channel between SE Labrador and NW Newfoundland, Canada.

Bel•ler•o•phon (bə-lĕr′ə-fən, -fŏn′) *n. Gk. Myth.* The Corinthian hero who with the aid of Pegasus slew the Chimera.

belles-let•tres (bĕl-lĕt′rə) *pl.n. (used with a sing. v.)* **1.** Literature regarded for its aesthetic value rather than its didactic or informative content. **2.** Light, stylish writings, usu. on literary or intellectual subjects. [Fr. : *belles,* fine + *lettres,* letters, literature.]

bel•let•rist (bĕl-lĕt′rĭst) *n.* A writer of belles-lettres. **— bel•let′rism** *n.* **— bel′le•tris′tic** (bĕl′ĭ-trĭs′tĭk) *adj.*

Belle•ville (bĕl′vĭl′). **1.** A city of SE Ontario, Canada, near Lake Ontario ENE of Toronto; founded 1790. Pop. 34,881. **2.** A city of SW IL SE of East St. Louis. Pop. 42,875. **3.** A town of NE NJ on the Passaic R. near Newark; settled by the Dutch c. 1680. Pop. 34,213.

Belle•vue (bĕl′vyo͞o′). **1.** A city of E NE, a suburb of Omaha. Pop. 30,982. **2.** A city of W-central WA on Lake Washington opposite Seattle. Pop. 86,874.

bell•flow•er (bĕl′flou′ər) *n.* **1.** Any of various herbs of the genus *Campanula,* native chiefly to the Northern Hemisphere and often having bell-shaped violet or blue flowers. **2.** Any of several other plants, esp. one with bell-shaped flowers.

Bell•flow•er (bĕl′flou′ər). A city of S CA, a suburb in the Los Angeles–Long Beach area. Pop. 61,815.

Bell Gardens. A city of S CA, a suburb of Los Angeles. Pop. 42,355.

bell•hop (bĕl′hŏp′) *n.* A person employed by a hotel to assist guests, as by carrying luggage. [Prob. short for *bell-hopper.*]

bel•li•cose (bĕl′ĭ-kōs′) *adj.* Warlike in manner or temperament; pugnacious. [ME < Lat. *bellicōsus* < *bellicus,* of war < *bellum,* war.] **— bel′li•cose′ly** *adv.* **— bel′li•cos′i•ty** (-kŏs′ĭ-tē), **bel′li•cose′ness** *n.*

bel•lig•er•ence (bə-lĭj′ər-əns) *n.* A hostile or warlike attitude, nature, or inclination.

bel•lig•er•en•cy (bə-lĭj′ər-ən-sē) *n.* **1.** The state of being at war or being engaged in a warlike conflict. **2.** Belligerence.

bel•lig•er•ent (bə-lĭj′ər-ənt) *adj.* **1.** Inclined or eager to fight; hostile or aggressive. **2.** Of, relating to, or engaged in warfare. *— n.* One that is hostile or aggressive, esp. one engaged in war. [Lat. *belligerāns, belligerant-,* pr.part. of *belligerāre,* to wage war < *belliger,* warlike : *bellum,* war + *gerere,* to make.] **— bel•lig′er•ent•ly** *adv.*

bell•ing (bĕl′ĭng) *n. Pennsylvania, West Virginia, & Ohio.* See **shivaree.** See Regional Note at **shivaree.** [< BELL[1].]

Bel•ling•ham (bĕl′ĭng-hăm′). A city of NW WA on **Bellingham Bay** S of the Canadian border. Pop. 52,179.

Bel•lings•hau•sen Sea (bĕl′ĭngz-hou′zən). An arm of the S Pacific Ocean off the coast of Antarctica.

Bel•li•ni (bə-lē′nē). Family of Venetian painters, including **Jacopo** (1400?–70?) and his two sons, **Gentile** (1429?–1507) and **Giovanni** (1430?–1516).

Bellini, Vincenzo. 1801–35. Italian composer whose operas include *La Sonnambula* and *Norma* (both 1831).

bell jar *n.* A cylindrical glass vessel with a rounded top and an open base, used to protect and display fragile objects or establish a controlled atmosphere in scientific experiments.

Alexander Graham Bell
Calling Chicago from New York City, 1892

Bellerophon

ă pat	oi boy
ā pay	ou out
âr care	o͝o took
ä father	o͞o boot
ĕ pet	ŭ cut
ē be	ûr urge
ĭ pit	th thin
ī pie	*th* this
îr pier	hw which
ŏ pot	zh vision
ō toe	ə about, item
ô paw	

Stress marks:
′ (primary);
′ (secondary), as in
dictionary (dĭk′shə-nĕr′ē)

bell•man (bĕl′mən) *n.* **1.** A bellhop. **2.** A town crier.

bell metal *n.* An alloy of tin and copper used to make bells.

Bel•loc (bĕl′ŏk′, -ək), **Hilaire.** 1870–1953. French-born British writer.

Bel•lo•na (bə-lō′nə) *n. Rom. Myth.* The goddess of war.

bel•low (bĕl′ō) *v.* **-lowed, -low•ing, -lows.** —*intr.* **1.** To roar deeply, as does a bull. **2.** To shout in a deep voice. —*tr.* To utter in a loud, powerful voice. See Syns at **shout.** —*n.* **1.** The roar of a large animal, such as a bull. **2.** A very loud utterance or other sound. [ME *belwen,* perh. < OE *belgan,* to be enraged, and *bylgan,* to bellow.] —**bel′low•er** *n.*

Bel•low (bĕl′ō), **Saul.** b. 1915. Canadian-born Amer. writer who won the 1976 Nobel Prize for literature.

bel•lows (bĕl′ōz, -əz) *pl.n. (used with a sing. or pl. v.)* **1.a.** An apparatus for producing a strong current of air, consisting of a flexible valved air chamber that is contracted and expanded by pumping to force the air through a nozzle. **b.** Something that resembles a bellows. **2.** The lungs. [ME *belowes* < OE *belgas,* pl. of *belg.* See **bhelgh-*.**]

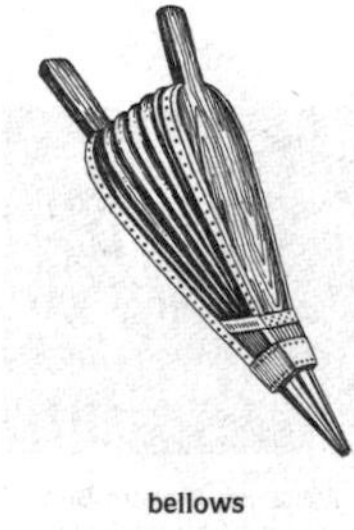

bellows

Bel•lows (bĕl′ōz), **George Wesley.** 1882–1925. Amer. artist noted for his energetic paintings of sporting scenes.

bell pepper *n.* **1.** An annual pepper *(Capsicum annuum)* widely cultivated for its edible fruit. **2.** Its bell-shaped fruit.

Bell's Law (bĕlz) *n. Anat.* **1.** An axiom stating that the anterior or ventral roots of the spinal nerves are motor and the posterior or dorsal roots sensory. **2.** The neurological law that, in any reflex arc, nerve impulses are conducted in only one direction. [After Sir Charles *Bell* (1774–1842), Scottish anatomist.]

bells of Ire•land (īr′lənd) *n.* An annual western Asian plant *(Moluccella laevis)* in the mint family, having long stems covered with shell-shaped calyxes.

Bell's palsy *n.* A unilateral facial muscle paralysis of sudden onset, resulting from trauma, compression, or infection of the facial nerve and characterized by a distorted facial expression. [After Sir Charles *Bell* (1774–1842), Scottish anatomist.]

bell•weth•er (bĕl′wĕ*th*′ər) *n.* One that serves as a leader or as a leading indicator of future trends. [ME *bellewether,* wether with a bell hung from its neck, leader of the flock : *belle,* bell; see BELL[1] + *wether,* wether; see WETHER.]

Bell•wood (bĕl′wo͝od′). A village of NE IL, a suburb of Chicago. Pop. 20,241.

bell•wort (bĕl′wûrt′, -wôrt′) *n.* Any of various perennial plants of the genus *Uvularia* in the lily family, native to eastern North America and having yellow bell-shaped flowers.

bel•ly (bĕl′ē) *n., pl.* **-lies. 1.** See **abdomen** 1. **2.** The underside of the body of certain vertebrates, such as fish. **3.** *Informal.* **a.** The stomach. **b.** An appetite for food. **4.** The womb; the uterus. **5.a.** A part that bulges or protrudes. **b.** *Anat.* The bulging central part of a muscle. **6.** A deep, hollow interior. —*intr. & tr.v.* **-lied, -ly•ing, -lies.** To bulge or cause to bulge. [ME *beli* < OE *belg,* bag. See **bhelgh-*.**]

bel•ly•ache (bĕl′ē-āk′) *n.* **1.** Stomach pain; colic. **2.** *Slang.* A whining complaint. —*intr.v.* **-ached, -ach•ing, -aches.** *Slang.* To complain, esp. by whining. —**bel′ly•ach′er** *n.*

bel•ly•band (bĕl′ē-bănd′) *n.* **1.** A band passed around the belly of an animal to secure something. **2.** An encircling band for holding in a baby's protruding navel.

bel•ly•but•ton (bĕl′ē-bŭt′n) *n. Informal.* The navel; the umbilicus.

belly dance *n.* A dance in which the performer makes sinuous hip and abdominal movements. —**bel′ly-dance′** (bĕl′ē-dăns′) *v.* —**belly dancer** *n.*

belly flop *n. Informal.* A dive in which the front of the body hits flat against a surface. —**bel′ly-flop′** (bĕl′ē-flŏp′) *v.*

bel•ly•ful (bĕl′ē-fo͝ol′) *n. Informal.* An undesirable or unendurable amount: *a bellyful of criticism.*

bel•ly-land (bĕl′ē-lănd′) *intr.v.* **-land•ed, -land•ing, -lands.** To land an aircraft on its underside without aid of landing gear.

belly laugh *n.* A deep laugh.

Bel•mont (bĕl′mŏnt′). **1.** A city of W CA, a suburb between San Francisco and San Jose. Pop. 24,127. **2.** A town of E MA, a suburb of Boston. Pop. 24,720.

bench press

Belmont, Alva Ertskin Smith Vanderbilt. 1853–1933. Amer. suffragist who was president of the National Women's Party (1921–33).

Bel•mo•pan (bĕl′mō-păn′). The cap. of Belize, in the N-central part. Pop. 2,935.

Bel•oeil (bə-lĭl′, bĕl-œy′). A town of S Quebec, Canada, on the Richelieu R. NE of Montreal. Pop. 17,540.

Be•lo Ho•ri•zon•te (bĕl′ō hôr′ĭ-zŏn′tē, bĕ′lo͞o ô′rĭ-zôN′-tĭ). A city of E Brazil N of Rio de Janeiro; built (1895–97) as the first of Brazil's planned communities. Pop. 1,780,855.

Be•loit (bə-loit′). A city of S WI on the IL border SSE of Madison. Pop. 35,573.

bel•o•ne•pho•bi•a (bĕl′ə-nə-fō′bē-ə) *n.* An abnormal fear of sharply pointed objects, esp. needles. [Gk. *belonē,* needle; see **gʷelə-*** + -PHOBIA.]

be•long (bĭ-lông′, -lŏng′) *intr.v.* **-longed, -long•ing, -longs. 1.a.** To be proper or suitable. **b.** To be in an appropriate situation or environment. **2.a.** To be a member of a group. **b.** To fit into a group naturally. **3.** To be owned; pertain. Often used with *to.* **4.** To be a part of something else. [ME *bilongen:* prob. *bi-,* be- + *longen,* to belong (prob. < *long,* dependent < OE *gelang,* along, depending; see **del-[1]*.**)]

be•long•ing (bĭ-lông′ĭng, -lŏng′-) *n.* **1.** Personal items that one owns; possessions. Often used in the plural. **2.** Close, secure relationship: *a sense of belonging.*

Be•lo•rus•sia (bĕl′ō-rŭsh′ə) also **Bye•lo•rus•sia** (byĕl′ō-) or **Bel•a•rus** (bĕl′ə-ro͞os′, bĕl′ä-ro͞os′). Popularly known as **White Rus•sia** (rŭsh′ə). A republic of E Europe E of Poland; a constituent republic of the U.S.S.R. from 1922 to 1991. Cap. Minsk. Pop. 9,942,000.

Be•lo•rus•sian (bĕl′ō-rŭsh′ən) *adj.* Of or relating to Belorussia or its people, language, or culture. —*n.* **1.** A native or inhabitant of Belorussia. **2.** The Slavic language of the Belorussians.

be•lov•ed (bĭ-lŭv′ĭd, -lŭvd′) *adj.* Dearly loved; adored. —**be•lov′ed** *n.*

be•low (bĭ-lō′) *adv.* **1.** In or to a lower place; beneath. **2.a.** On or to a lower floor; downstairs. **b.** *Naut.* On or to a lower deck. **3.** In a later part of a given text. **4.** Farther down, as along a slope or valley. **5.** In or to hell or Hades. **6.** On earth. **7.a.** In a lower rank or class. **b.** Below zero in temperature: *40° below.* —*prep.* **1.** Underneath; beneath. **2.** Lower than, as on a graduated scale. **3.** Unsuitable to the rank or dignity of. [ME *biloogbe: bi,* by; see BY[1] + *loghe,* low; see LOW[1].]

be•low•ground (bĭ-lō′ground′) *adv. & adj.* Into or under the ground.

Bel•sen (bĕl′zən). In full **Ber•gen-Bel•sen** (bûr′gən-bĕl′sən, bĕr′gən-bĕl′zən). A village of N Germany N of Hanover; site of a Nazi concentration camp during World War II.

Bel•shaz•zar (bĕl-shăz′ər). Son of Nebuchadnezzar II and last king of Babylon, who in the Bible was warned of his doom by handwriting on the wall that was interpreted by Daniel.

belt (bĕlt) *n.* **1.a.** A flexible band worn around the waist to support clothing, secure tools, or serve as decoration. **b.** Something resembling a belt. **2.** An encircling route. **3.** A seat belt. **4.** A continuous band or chain for transferring motion or power or conveying materials. **5.** A band of tough reinforcing material beneath the tread of a tire. **6.** A geographic region that is distinctive in a specific respect. **7.** *Slang.* A powerful blow; a wallop. **8.** *Slang.* A strong emotional reaction. **9.** *Slang.* A drink of hard liquor. —*tr.v.* **belt•ed, belt•ing, belts. 1.** To encircle; gird. **2.** To attach with or as if with a belt. **3.** To mark with or as if with a belt. **4.** *Slang.* To strike forcefully; punch. **5.** *Slang.* To sing in a loud and forceful manner: *belt out a song.* **6.** *Slang.* To swig (an alcoholic beverage). —***idioms.* below the belt.** Not according to the rules; unfairly. **tighten (one's) belt.** To begin to exercise thrift and frugality. **under (one's) belt.** In one's possession or experience. [ME < OE, ult. < Lat. *balteus.*]

Bel•tane (bĕl′tān, -tən) *n.* An ancient Celtic feast marked by bonfires and various rites of purification, traditionally observed on May 1. [ME < Sc.Gael. *bealltainn.*]

belt highway *n.* See **beltway.**

belt•ing (bĕl′tĭng) *n.* **1.** Belts considered as a group. **2.** The material used to make belts.

belt•way (bĕlt′wā′) *n.* A high-speed highway that encircles or skirts an urban area.

be•lu•ga (bə-lo͞o′gə) *n.* **1.** See **white whale. 2.** A large white sturgeon *(Huso huso)* of the Black and Caspian seas, whose roe is processed into caviar. [Russ. *byelukha,* white whale, and *byeluga,* sturgeon : *byeliĭ,* white; see **bhel-[1]*** + *-uga, -ukha,* aug. suff.]

bel•ve•dere (bĕl′vĭ-dîr′) *n.* A structure, such as a summerhouse, situated so as to command a view. [Ital. : *bel, bello,* beautiful (< Lat. *bellus;* see **deu-[2]***) + *vedere,* to see, view (< Lat. *vidēre,* to see; see **weid-*.**)]

Bel•ve•dere (bĕl′vĭ-dîr′). A city of NW GA, a suburb of Atlanta. Pop. 18,089.

be•ma (bē′mə) *n., pl.* **-ma•ta** (-mə-tə). **1.** *Judaism.* The platform for services in a synagogue. **2.** *Eastern Orthodox Ch.* The area of a church in which the altar is located; the sanctuary. [Ult. < Gk. *bēma,* step, platform. See **gʷā-*.**]

Bem•ba (bĕm′bə) *n.* A Bantu language spoken in Zambia.

be•med•aled or **be•med•alled** (bĭ-mĕd′ld) *adj.* Decorated with or wearing medals.

Be•mel•mans (bē′məl-mənz, bĕm′əl-), **Ludwig.** 1898–1962. Austrian-born Amer. illustrator and writer.

be•mire (bĭ-mīr′) *tr.v.* **-mired, -mir•ing, -mires. 1.** To soil with mud. **2.** To cause to sink into mud.

be•moan (bĭ-mōn′) *tr.v.* **-moaned, -moan•ing, -moans. 1.** To mourn over; lament. **2.** To express pity or grief for. [ME *bimonen,* alteration (influenced by *mone,* moan; see MOAN) of *bimenen* < OE *bemǣnan: be-,* be- + *mǣnan,* to complain of; see **mei-no-*.**]

be•muse (bĭ-myo͞oz′) *tr.v.* **-mused, -mus•ing, -mus•es. 1.** To cause to be bewildered; confuse. **2.** To cause to be engrossed in thought. —**be•mus′ed•ly** (-myo͞o′zĭd-lē) *adv.* —**be•muse′ment** *n.*

ben (bĕn) *Scots.* —*n.* The inner room or parlor of a house with two rooms. —*adv.* Inside; within. —*prep.* Within. [ME, var. of *binne,* within < OE *binnan.* See **en*.**]

Be•na•res (bə-närʹəs, -ĕz). See **Varanasi.**

Be•na•ven•te y Mar•tí•nez (bĕnʹə-vĕnʹtē ē mär-tēʹnəs, bĕʹnä-vĕnʹtĕ ē mär-tēʹnĕth), **Jacinto.** 1866–1954. Spanish playwright who won the 1922 Nobel Prize for literature.

Ben Bel•la (bĕn bĕlʹə), **Ahmed.** b. 1919. Algerian revolutionary leader.

Bence-Jones protein (bĕnsʹjōnzʹ) *n.* A protein occurring in the serum and urine of patients with certain diseases, esp. multiple myeloma. [After Henry *Bence-Jones* (1813–73), British physician.]

bench (bĕnch) *n.* **1.** A long seat for two or more persons. **2.** *Law.* **a.** A judge's seat in a courtroom. **b.** A judge's office or position. **c.** Often **Bench.** The judge or judges composing a court. **3.a.** A seat occupied by a person in an official capacity. **b.** The office of such a person. **4.** A strong worktable. **5.** A platform on which animals, esp. dogs, are exhibited. **6.** *Sports.* **a.** The place where the players on a team sit when not playing. **b.** The reserve players on a team. **7.a.** A level, narrow stretch of land interrupting a declivity. **b.** A level elevation of land along a shore or coast, esp. one marking a former shoreline. —*tr.v.* **benched, bench•ing, bench•es. 1.** To furnish with benches. **2.** To seat on a bench. **3.** *Sports.* To keep out of or remove from a game. [ME < OE *benc.*]

bench•er (bĕnʹchər) *n.* **1.** One that sits on a bench. **2.** *Chiefly British.* A member of the inner or higher bar who acts as a governor of one of the Inns of Court. **3.** An official who occupies a bench.

Bench•ley (bĕnchʹlē), **Robert Charles.** 1889–1945. Amer. humorist, critic, and actor whose works include the book *My Ten Years in a Quandary* (1936).

bench•mark (bĕnchʹmärkʹ) *n.* **1.** A standard by which something can be measured or judged. **2.** Often **bench mark.** A surveyor's mark made on a stationary object of previously determined position and elevation and used as a reference point in tidal observations and surveys. [From the use of the mark as a place to insert an angle iron that serves as a support for a leveling rod.]

bench press *n. Sports.* A lift executed from a horizontal position on a bench, in which the weight is lifted from the chest to arm's length and then lowered back to the chest.

bench warrant *n. Law.* A warrant issued by a judge or court ordering the apprehension of an offender.

bend[1] (bĕnd) *v.* **bent** (bĕnt), **bend•ing, bends.** —*tr.* **1.** To bring (something) into a state of tension: *bend a bow.* **2.a.** To cause to assume a curved or angular shape. **b.** To force to assume a different direction or shape, according to one's own purpose: *bend the course of events.* **3.** To cause to swerve from a straight line; deflect. **4.** To render submissive; subdue. **5.** To apply (the mind) closely. **6.** *Naut.* To fasten. —*intr.* **1.a.** To deviate from a straight line or position. **b.** To assume a curved, crooked, or angular form or direction. **2.** To incline the body; stoop. **3.** To make a concession; yield. **4.** To apply oneself closely; concentrate. —*n.* **1.a.** The act or fact of bending. **b.** The state of being bent. **2.** Something bent. **3. bends.** *(used with a sing. or pl. v.)* A manifestation of decompression sickness caused by the formation of nitrogen bubbles in the blood and tissues after a rapid reduction in the surrounding pressure and characterized by pain in the joints and abdomen. —***idioms.*** **around the bend.** *Slang.* Insane; crazy. **bend (someone's) ear.** *Slang.* To talk to at length, usu. excessively. [ME *benden* < OE *bendan.* See **bhendh-*.**]

Syns: *bend, crook, curve, round.* The central meaning shared by these verbs is "to swerve or cause to swerve from a straight line": *bent his knees and knelt; crooks her little finger when she holds a teacup; claws that curve under; rounding the lips to articulate an "o."* ***Ant:*** *straighten.*

bend[2] (bĕnd) *n.* **1.** *Her.* A band passing from the upper dexter corner of an escutcheon to the lower sinister corner. **2.** *Naut.* A knot that joins a rope to a rope or another object. [ME < OE *bend,* band, and < OFr. *bende,* band (of Gmc. orig.; see **bhendh-***).]

Bend (bĕnd). A city of central Oregon at the E foot of the Cascade Range E of Eugene. Pop. 20,469.

Ben Day also **ben•day** or **Ben•day** (bĕn-dāʹ) *n.* A method of adding a tone to a printed image by imposing a transparent sheet of dots or other patterns on the image at some stage of a photographic reproduction process. [After Benjamin *Day* (1838–1916), Amer. printer.]

bend•er (bĕnʹdər) *n.* **1.** One that bends: *a bender of iron bars; a bender of the truth.* **2.** *Slang.* A drinking spree.

Ben•di•go (bĕnʹdĭ-gōʹ). A city of SE Australia NNW of Melbourne; founded 1851. Pop. 31,841.

bend sinister *n. Her.* A band passing from the upper sinister corner of an escutcheon to the lower dexter corner.

be•neath (bĭ-nēthʹ) *adv.* **1.** In a lower place; below. **2.** Underneath. —*prep.* **1.** Lower than; below. **2.** Covered or concealed by. **3.** Under the force, control, or influence of. **4.a.** Lower than, as in rank or station. **b.** Unworthy of; unbefitting. [ME *binethe* < OE *beneothan: be,* by; see BY[1] + *neothan,* below.]

ben•e•dict (bĕnʹĭ-dĭktʹ) *n.* A newly married man who was previously considered a confirmed bachelor. [After *Benedick,* a character in *Much Ado About Nothing* by Shakespeare.]

Ben•e•dict XIV (bĕnʹĭ-dĭktʹ). 1675–1758. Pope (1740–58) who enlarged the Vatican Library.

Benedict XV. 1854–1922. Pope (1914–22) who sponsored World War I relief efforts.

Benedict, Ruth Fulton. 1887–1948. Amer. anthropologist noted for her study of Native American and Japanese cultures.

Ben•e•dic•tine (bĕnʹĭ-dĭkʹtĭn, -tēnʹ) *n. Rom. Cath. Ch.* A monk or nun of the order founded by Saint Benedict of Nursia. —**Benʹe•dicʹtine** *adj.*

ben•e•dic•tion (bĕnʹĭ-dĭkʹshən) *n.* **1.** A blessing. **2.** An invocation of divine blessing. **3.** Often **Benediction.** A short Christian service consisting of prayers, the singing of a Eucharistic hymn, and the blessing of the congregation with the host. [ME *benediccioun* < OFr. *benedicion* < Lat. *benedictiō, benedictiōn-* < *benedictus,* p.part. of *benedicere,* to bless : *bene,* well; see **deu-[2]*** + *dīcere,* to speak; see **deik-*.**] —**benʹe•dicʹtive, benʹe•dicʹto•ry** (-dĭkʹtə-rē) *adj.*

Benedict of Nur•si•a (nûrʹshē-ə, -shə), Saint. A.D. 480?–547? Italian monk who founded the Benedictine order (c. 529).

Ben•e•dict's solution (bĕnʹĭ-dĭkts) *n.* A solution of sodium citrate, sodium carbonate, and copper sulfate that is changed from blue to yellow or red by reducing sugars. [After Stanley Rossiter *Benedict* (1884–1936), Amer. chemist.]

Ben•e•dic•tus (bĕnʹĭ-dĭkʹtəs) *n.* **1.** A canticle that begins "Blessed is he that cometh in the name of the Lord" (Matthew 21:9). **2.** A canticle that begins "Blessed be the Lord God of Israel" (Luke 1:68). [Lat., p.part. of *benedīcere,* to bless. See BENEDICTION.]

ben•e•fac•tion (bĕnʹə-făkʹshən, bĕnʹə-făkʹ-) *n.* **1.** The act of conferring aid. **2.** A charitable gift or deed. [LLat. *benefactiō, benefactiōn-* < Lat. *benefactus,* p.part. of *benefacere,* to do a service : *bene,* well; see **deu-[2]*** + *facere,* to do; see **dhē-*.**]

ben•e•fac•tor (bĕnʹə-făkʹtər) *n.* One that gives aid, esp. financial aid. [ME < LLat. < Lat. *benefacere,* to do a service. See BENEFACTION.]

ben•e•fac•tress (bĕnʹə-făkʹtrĭs) *n.* A woman who gives aid, esp. financial aid.

be•nef•ic (bə-nĕfʹĭk) *adj.* Beneficent. [Lat. *beneficus: bene,* well; see BENEFACTION + *-ficus,* -fic.]

ben•e•fice (bĕnʹə-fĭs) *n.* **1.** *Eccles.* **a.** A church office endowed with assets that provide a living. **b.** The revenue from such assets. **2.** A landed estate granted in feudal tenure. [ME < OFr. < Lat. *beneficium,* benefit < *beneficus,* benefic. See BENEFIC.] —**benʹe•fice** *v.*

be•nef•i•cence (bə-nĕfʹĭ-səns) *n.* **1.** The state or quality of being kind, charitable, or beneficial. **2.** A charitable act or gift. [Lat. *beneficentia* < *beneficus, beneficent-,* benefic. See BENEFIC.]

be•nef•i•cent (bə-nĕfʹĭ-sənt) *adj.* **1.** Characterized by or performing acts of kindness or charity. **2.** Producing benefit; beneficial. [Prob. < BENEFICENCE, on the model of such pairs as BENEVOLENT, BENEVOLENCE.] —**be•nefʹi•cent•ly** *adv.*

ben•e•fi•cial (bĕnʹə-fĭshʹəl) *adj.* **1.** Producing or promoting a favorable result; advantageous. **2.** *Law.* Receiving or having the right to receive proceeds or other advantages. [ME < OFr. *beneficial* < LLat. *beneficiālis* < Lat. *beneficium,* benefit. See BENEFICE.] —**benʹe•fiʹcial•ly** *adv.* —**benʹe•fiʹcial•ness** *n.*

Syns: *beneficial, profitable, advantageous.* These adjectives apply to what promotes a favorable result or gain. *Beneficial* is said of what enhances well-being: *a beneficial trade agreement. Profitable* refers to what yields material gain or useful compensation: *a profitable business on the stock market.* Something *advantageous* affords improvement in relative position or in chances of success: *socially advantageous.*

ben•e•fi•ci•ar•y (bĕnʹə-fĭshʹē-ĕrʹē, -fĭshʹə-rē) *n., pl.* **-ies. 1.** One that receives a benefit. **2.** The recipient of funds, property, or other benefits, as from an insurance policy or will. **3.** *Eccles.* The holder of a benefice. [Med.Lat. *beneficiārius,* holder of a feudal benefice < Lat., soldier granted privileges < *beneficium,* benefit. See BENEFICE.] —**benʹe•fiʹci•arʹy** *adj.*

ben•e•fit (bĕnʹə-fĭt) *n.* **1.a.** Something that promotes or enhances well-being; an advantage. **b.** Help; aid. **2.** A payment made or an entitlement available in accordance with a wage agreement, an insurance policy, or a public assistance program. **3.** A public entertainment or social event held to raise funds for a cause. **4.** *Archaic.* A kindly deed. —*v.* **-fit•ed, -fit•ing, -fits** also **-fit•ted, -fit•ting, -fits.** —*tr.* To be helpful or useful to. —*intr.* To derive benefit. [ME < OFr. *bienfait,* good deed < Lat. *benefactum* < *benefacere,* to do a service. See BENEFACTION.]

benefit of clergy *n.* **1.** The authorized sanction of a religious rite. **2.** Exemption from trial or punishment in a civil court, given to the clergy in the Middle Ages.

benefit of the doubt *n.* A favorable judgment granted in the absence of full evidence.

Be•ne•lux (bĕnʹə-lŭksʹ). An economic union of Belgium, the Netherlands, and Luxembourg.

Be•neš (bĕnʹĕshʹ), **Eduard.** 1884–1948. Czechoslovakian politician who served as president (1935–38 and 1946–48).

Be•nét (bĭ-nāʹ), **William Rose.** 1886–1950. Amer. writer and editor whose works include *The Reader's Encyclopedia*

bend[2]

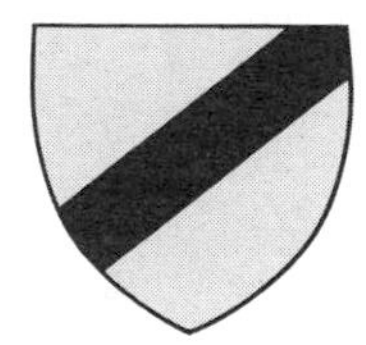

bend sinister

ă pat	oi boy
ā pay	ou out
âr care	ŏŏ took
ä father	ōō boot
ĕ pet	ŭ cut
ē be	ûr urge
ĭ pit	th thin
ī pie	*th* this
îr pier	hw which
ŏ pot	zh vision
ō toe	ə about, item
ô paw	

Stress marks:
ʹ (primary);
ʹ (secondary), as in
dictionary (dĭkʹshə-nĕrʹē)

(1948). His brother **Stephen Vincent Benét** (1898–1943) is best known for his Civil War narrative poem *John Brown's Body* (1928).

be•nev•o•lence (bə-nĕv′ə-ləns) *n.* **1.** An inclination to perform generous acts. **2.** An act of generosity. **3.** A compulsory payment exacted by an English monarch without parliamentary consent.

be•nev•o•lent (bə-nĕv′ə-lənt) *adj.* **1.** Characterized by or suggestive of doing good. **2.** Of, concerned with, or organized for the benefit of charity. [ME < OFr. < Lat. *benevolēns, benevolent-* : *bene*, well; see **deu-**[2]* + *volēns*, pr.part. of *velle*, to wish; see **wel-**[1]*.] — **be•nev′o•lent•ly** *adv.*

Ben•fleet (bĕn′flēt′). An urban district of SE England on an inlet of the Thames estuary E of London. Pop. 86,000.

B.Eng. *abbr.* Bachelor of Engineering.

Ben•gal (bĕn-gôl′, bĕng-, bĕn′gəl, bĕng′-). A region of E India and Bangladesh. — **Ben′ga•lese′** (bĕn′gə-lēz′, -lēs′, bĕng′-) *adj.* & *n.*

Bengal, Bay of. An arm of the Indian Ocean bordered by Sri Lanka and India on the W, Bangladesh on the N, and Burma and Thailand on the E.

Ben•ga•li (bĕn-gô′lē, bĕng-) *adj.* Of or relating to Bengal or its people, language, or culture. — *n.* **1.** A native or inhabitant of Bengal. **2.** The modern Indic language of western Bengal and Bangladesh.

ben•ga•line (bĕng′gə-lēn′) *n.* A fabric of silk, wool, or synthetic fibers having a crosswise ribbed effect. [Fr. < *Bengale*, Bengal.]

Bengal light *n.* **1.** A colored flare or light. **2.** A blue light, formerly used for signaling.

Beng•bu (bŭng′bo͞o′) also **Peng•pu** (pŭng′po͞o′). A city of E China NW of Nanjing. Pop. 425,000.

Ben•gha•zi also **Ben•ga•si** (bĕn-gä′zē, bĕng-). A city of NE Libya on the Gulf of Sidra; formerly cap. of Libya (1951–72). Pop. 367,600.

B.Engr. *abbr.* Bachelor of Engineering.

B.Eng.Sci. *abbr.* Bachelor of Engineering Science.

David Ben Gurion

Ben Gur•i•on (bĕn go͝or′ē-ən), **David.** 1886–1973. Polish-born Israeli prime minister (1948–53 and 1955–63).

Be•ni (bĕ′nē). A river of central and NW Bolivia rising in the Andes and flowing c. 1,599 km (994 mi) to the Mamoré R.

be•night•ed (bĭ-nī′tĭd) *adj.* **1.** Overtaken by night or darkness. **2.** Being in a state of moral or intellectual darkness. — **be•night′ed•ly** *adv.* — **be•night′ed•ness** *n.*

be•nign (bĭ-nīn′) *adj.* **1.** Of a kind and gentle disposition. **2.** Showing gentleness and mildness. **3.** Tending to exert a beneficial influence; favorable. See Syns at **favorable.** **4.** *Medic.* Of no danger to health; not recurrent or progressive; not malignant. [ME *benigne* < OFr. < Lat. *benignus*. See **genə-***.] — **be•nign′ly** *adv.*

be•nig•nan•cy (bĭ-nĭg′nən-sē) *n.*, *pl.* **-cies.** Benignity.

be•nig•nant (bĭ-nĭg′nənt) *adj.* **1.** Favorable; beneficial. **2.** Kind and gracious. — **be•nig′nant•ly** *adv.*

be•nig•ni•ty (bĭ-nĭg′nĭ-tē) *n.*, *pl.* **-ties. 1.** The quality or condition of being kind and gentle. **2.** A kindly or gracious act.

Benin

Be•nin (bə-nĭn′, bĕ-nēn′). **1.** A former kingdom of W Africa, now part of Nigeria. **2.** Formerly **Da•ho•mey** (də-hō′mē, dä-ô-mā′). A country of W Africa; achieved independence in 1960. Cap. Porto-Novo. Pop. 3,567,000. **3.** Also **Benin City.** A city of S Nigeria on the **Benin River,** c. 161 km (100 mi) long. Pop. 161,700.

Benin, Bight of. A wide indentation of the Gulf of Guinea in W Africa.

ben•i•son (bĕn′ĭ-zən, -sən) *n.* A blessing; a benediction. [ME < OFr. *beneison* < Lat. *benedictiō, benedictiōn-*, praising. See BENEDICTION.]

ben•ja•min (bĕn′jə-mən) *n.* See **benzoin** 1. [Alteration of *benjoin, bengewyne*, early forms of BENZOIN.]

Ben•ja•min (bĕn′jə-mən). In the Bible, the younger son of Jacob and Rachel and the forebear of one of the tribes of Israel.

Benjamin, Judah Philip. 1811–84. British-born Amer. politician who served as Confederate secretary of war (1861–62).

Ben Lo•mond (lō′mənd). A mountain, 973.6 m (3,192 ft), of S-central Scotland on the E shore of Loch Lomond.

ben•net (bĕn′ĭt) *n.* Herb bennet.

Ben•nett (bĕn′ĭt), **(Enoch) Arnold.** 1867–1931. British writer whose plays and novels were influenced by the French realists.

Bennett, James Gordon. 1795–1872. Amer. journalist who founded and edited (1835–67) the *New York Herald.*

Bennett, Richard Bedford. Viscount Bennett. 1870–1947. Canadian prime minister (1930–35) who convened the 1932 economic conference in Ottawa.

Ben Ne•vis (nē′vĭs, nĕv′ĭs). The highest mountain of Great Britain, rising to 1,343.8 m (4,406 ft) in the Grampian Mts. of W Scotland.

Ben•ning•ton (bĕn′ĭng-tən). A town of SW VT E of Brattleboro. Pop. 16,451.

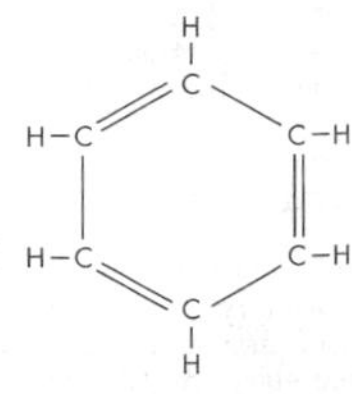

benzene ring

ben•ny (bĕn′ē) *n.*, *pl.* **-nies.** *Slang.* An amphetamine tablet taken as a stimulant. [< BENZEDRINE.]

Ben•ny (bĕn′ē), **Jack.** 1894–1974. Amer. comedian known for his shows on radio (1932–55) and television (1950–65).

Be•noît de Sainte-Maure (bən-wä′ də săNt-môr′). fl. 12th cent. French trouvère whose *Roman de Troie* was a source for works such as Chaucer's *Troilus and Criseyde.*

Ben•sen•ville (bĕn′sən-vĭl′). A village of NE IL, a suburb of Chicago. Pop. 17,767.

bent[1] (bĕnt) *v.* P.t. and p.part. of **bend**[1]. — *adj.* **1.** Altered from a straight or even condition. **2.** Set on a course of action. **3.** *Chiefly British.* Corrupt; venal. — *n.* **1.** A tendency, disposition, or inclination. **2.** A transverse structural member or framework for strengthening a bridge or trestle.

bent[2] (bĕnt) *n.* **1.** Bent grass. **2.** The stiff stalk of various grasses. **3.** An area of grassland unbounded by hedges or fences. [ME < OE *beonet* (attested only in place names).]

bent grass also **bent•grass** (bĕnt′grăs′) *n.* Any of various grasses of the genus *Agrostis*, native to chiefly temperate regions.

Ben•tham (bĕn′thəm), **Jeremy.** 1748–1832. British writer and philosopher who systematically analyzed law and legislation, thereby laying the foundations of utilitarianism.

Ben•tham•ism (bĕn′thə-mĭz′əm) *n.* *Philos.* Utilitarianism. — **Ben′tham•ite′** (-mīt′) *n.*

ben•thos (bĕn′thŏs′) *n.* **1.** The collection of organisms living on or in sea or lake bottoms. **2.** The bottom of a sea or a lake. [Gk.] — **ben′thic** (-thĭk), **ben•thon′ic** (bĕn-thŏn′ĭk) *adj.*

ben•to (bĕn′tō) *n.* Var. of **obento.**

Ben•ton (bĕn′tən). A city of central AR SW of Little Rock. Pop. 18,177.

Benton, Thomas Hart[1]. "Old Bullion." 1782–1858. Amer. legislator who staunchly opposed the use of paper currency.

Benton, Thomas Hart[2]. 1889–1975. Amer. artist whose paintings and murals, such as *The History of Missouri,* were executed in a flat, realistic style known as regionalism.

ben•ton•ite (bĕn′tə-nīt′) *n.* A silicate clay formed from volcanic ash and used in various adhesives and cements. [After *Benton* Formation (formerly Fort Benton Formation) of the Rock Creek district in E WY.] — **ben′ton•it′ic** (-nĭt′ĭk) *adj.*

bent•wood (bĕnt′wo͝od′) *n.* Wood that has been steamed until pliable and then bent into shape.

Be•nue (bān′wā) also **Bin•ue** (bĭn′-). A river of W Africa rising in Cameroon and flowing c. 1,078 km (670 mi) to the Niger R. in central Nigeria.

be•numb (bĭ-nŭm′) *tr.v.* **-numbed, -numb•ing, -numbs. 1.** To make numb, esp. by cold. **2.** To make inactive; dull. [ME *binomen* < p.part. of *binimen*, to take away < OE *beniman*: *be-*, away; see BE- + *niman*, to take; see NUMB.] — **be•numb′ment** *n.*

Ben•xi (bŭn′shē′) also **Pen•ki** (-jē′). A city of NE China SSE of Shenyang. Pop. 678,500.

benz•al•de•hyde (bĕn-zăl′də-hīd′) *n.* An aromatic oil, C_6H_5CHO, obtained from the bitter almond or made synthetically and used in perfumes and flavorings.

ben•zal•ko•ni•um chloride (bĕn′zăl-kō′nē-əm) *n.* A water-soluble powder used as a detergent, fungicide, bactericide, and spermicide. [BENZ(O)- + ALK(YL) + (AMM)ONIUM.]

Ben•ze•drine (bĕn′zĭ-drēn′). A trademark used for a brand of amphetamine.

ben•zene (bĕn′zēn′, bĕn-zēn′) *n.* A clear, highly refractive flammable liquid, C_6H_6, derived from petroleum and used in detergents, insecticides, and motor fuels.

benzene hexachloride *n.* A musty-smelling crystalline substance, $C_6H_6Cl_6$, prepared by the chlorination of benzene and used as a powerful insecticide.

benzene ring *n.* The six-carbon hexagonal ring structure in the benzene molecule, C_6H_6, and its substitutional derivatives.

ben•zi•dine (bĕn′zĭ-dēn′) *n.* A crystalline powder, $NH_2C_6H_4C_6H_4NH_2$, used in the detection of blood stains. [BENZ(ENE) + -ID(E) + -INE[2].]

ben•zim•id•az•ole (bĕn′zə-mĭ-dăz′ōl′, -mĭd′ə-zōl′) *n.* A crystalline compound, $C_7H_6N_2$, that is used in organic synthesis and inhibits the growth of certain microorganisms.

ben•zine (bĕn′zēn′, bĕn-zēn′) also **ben•zin** (bĕn′zĭn) *n.* **1.** A liquid mixture of hydrocarbons obtained in distilling petroleum, used in cleaning and dyeing. **2.** See **benzene.**

benzo– or **benz–** *pref.* Benzene; benzoic acid: *benzophenone.* [< BENZOIN.]

ben•zo•ate (bĕn′zō-āt′) *n.* A salt or ester of benzoic acid.

benzoate of soda *n.* See **sodium benzoate.**

ben•zo•caine (bĕn′zə-kān′) *n.* A crystalline ester, ethyl-para-aminobenzoate ($C_6H_4NH_2CO_2C_2H_5$), used as a local anesthetic.

ben•zo•di•az•e•pine (bĕn′zō-dī-ăz′ə-pēn′, -pĭn) *n.* Any of a group of chemical compounds with a common structure and similar effects, used as antianxiety agents, muscle relaxants, sedatives, and hypnotics. [BENZO- + DIAZEP(AM) + -INE[2].]

ben•zo•ic acid (bĕn-zō′ĭk) *n.* An aromatic white crystalline acid, C_6H_5COOH, used to season tobacco and in perfumes, dentifrices, and germicides. [< BENZOIN.]

ben•zo•in (bĕn′zō-ĭn, -zoin′) *n.* **1.** A balsamic resin obtained from certain tropical Asian trees of the genus *Styrax* and used in perfumery and medicine. **2.** A crystalline compound, $C_{14}H_{12}O_2$, derived from benzaldehyde. [Fr. *benjoin*and Ital. *benzoino*, both < Ar. *lubān jāwīy*, frankincense of Java.]

ben•zol (bĕn′zôl′, -zōl′, -zŏl′) *n.* See **benzene.** [BENZ(O)- + -OL[1].]

ben•zo•phe•none (bĕn′zō-fĭ-nōn′, -fē′nōn) *n.* A crystalline compound, $C_6H_5COC_6H_6$, used in perfumery.

ben•zo•py•rene (bĕn′zō-pī′rēn′, -pī-rēn′) *n.* A carcinogenic aromatic hydrocarbon, $C_{20}H_{12}$, found in cigarette smoke.

ben•zo•yl (bĕn′zō-ĭl′) *n.* The univalent radical $C_6H_5ICO^-$, derived from benzoic acid.

benzoyl peroxide *n.* A granular solid, $(C_6H_5CO)_2O_2$, used as a bleaching agent for flour, fats, waxes, and oils, as a polymerization catalyst, and in pharmaceuticals.

ben•zyl (bĕn′zĭl, -zēl′) *n.* The univalent radical $C_6H_5CH_2-$, derived from toluene.

Be•o•grad (bĕ′ô-gräd). See **Belgrade.**

Be•o•wulf (bā′ə-wo͝olf′) *n.* The hero of an Old English epic poem probably composed in the early eighth century.

be•queath (bĭ-kwēth′, -kwēth′) *tr.v.* **-queathed, -queath•ing, -queathes. 1.** *Law.* To leave or give (property) by will. **2.** To pass (something) on to another; hand down. [ME *biquethen* < OE *becwethan*: *be-*, be- + *cwethan*, to say; see **g^wet-***.] **—be•queath′al, be•queath′ment** *n.* **—be•queath′er** *n.*

be•quest (bĭ-kwĕst′) *n.* **1.** The act of giving, leaving by will, or passing on to another. **2.** Something that is bequeathed; a legacy. [ME *biquest* (influenced by *biquethen*, to bequeath) : *bi-*, be- + *quist*, will (< OE *-cwis*, as in *andcwis*, answer; see **g^wet-***).]

Be•rar (bā-rär′, bə-). A region of W-central India, one of the early kingdoms of the Deccan.

be•rate (bĭ-rāt′) *tr.v.* **-rat•ed, -rat•ing, -rates.** To rebuke or scold angrily and at length.

Ber•ber (bûr′bər) *n.* **1.** A member of a North African, primarily Muslim people living in settled or nomadic tribes from Morocco to Egypt. **2.** Any of the Afro-Asiatic languages of the Berbers. [Ar. *Barbar.*] **—Ber′ber** *adj.*

ber•ber•ine (bûr′bə-rēn′) *n.* An alkaloid, $C_{20}H_{19}NO_5$, obtained from plants such as goldenseal and used as an antipyretic and antibacterial agent. [NLat. *Berberis*, barberry genus (< Med.Lat. *berberis*, barberry < Ar. *barbārīs*) + -INE[2].]

ber•ceuse (bĕr-sœz′) *n., pl.* **-ceuses** (-sœz′). *Mus.* **1.** A lullaby. **2.** A soothing composition. [Fr., fem. of *berceur*, cradle rocker < *bercer*, to rock < VLat. **bertiāre.*]

Berch•tes•ga•den (bĕrk′təs-gäd′n, bĕrKH′-). A town of SE Germany in the Bavarian Alps. The site of Adolf Hitler's wartime villa is on a peak overlooking the town. Pop. 8,126.

ber•dache (bər-dăsh′) *n.* Among certain Native American peoples, a person, usu. a male, who assumes the sexual identity and social roles of the opposite sex. [N.Amer.Fr. < Fr. *bardache*, catamite < Ital. dial. *bardascia* < Ar. *bardaj*, slave < Pers. *bardah*, prisoner < MPers. *vartak* < OIran. **varta-*. See **welə-***.] **—ber•dach′ism** *n.*

Ber•dya•ev (bər-dyä′yəf), **Nikolai Aleksandrovich.** 1874–1948. Russian philosopher whose works include *The Spiritual Crisis of the Intelligentsia* (1910).

Be•re•a (bə-rē′ə). A city of NE OH, a suburb of Cleveland. Pop. 19,051.

be•reave (bĭ-rēv′) *tr.v.* **-reaved** or **-reft** (-rĕft′), **-reav•ing, -reaves. 1.** To leave desolate or alone, esp. by death. **2.** *Archaic.* To take (something valuable or necessary), esp. by force. [ME *bireven*, to deprive < OE *berēafian*. See **reup-***.] **—be•reave′ment** *n.* **—be•reav′er** *n.*

be•reaved (bĭ-rēvd′) *adj.* Suffering the loss of a loved one. **—** *n.* One or those bereaved.

be•reft (bĭ-rĕft′) *adj.* **1.a.** Deprived of something: *They are bereft of dignity.* **b.** Lacking something needed or expected. **2.** Suffering the death of a loved one; bereaved.

Ber•e•ni•ce's Hair (bĕr′ə-nī′sēz) *n.* See **Coma Berenices.**

Ber•en•son (bĕr′ĭn-sən), **Bernard** also **Bernhard.** 1865–1959. Lithuanian-born Amer. art critic and historian noted for his writings on the Italian Renaissance.

be•ret (bə-rā′, bĕr′ā′) *n.* A round, soft, brimless cap that fits snugly and is often worn angled to one side. [Fr. *béret* < Fr. dial. *berret*and < OProv. *berret*, cap, both < LLat. *birrus*, hooded cloak. See BIRETTA.]

be•ret•ta or **ber•ret•ta** (bə-rĕt′ə) *n.* Var. of **biretta.**

Be•re•zi•na (bə-rĕ′zĭ-nə, byə-ryĕ-zyĭ-nä′). A river rising in NW Belorussia and flowing c. 611 km (380 mi) to the Dnieper R.

Be•rez•ni•ki (bə-rĕz′nĭ-kē, byə-ryôz′nyĭ-kē′). A city of W Russia on the Kama R. Pop. 195,000.

berg (bûrg) *n.* A mass of floating or stationary ice; an iceberg.

Berg (bĕrg, bĕrk), **Alban.** 1885–1935. Austrian composer who applied an atonal manner to classical forms.

Ber•ga•ma (bər-gä′mə, bûr′gə-). A town of W Turkey N of Izmir on the site of ancient Pergamum. Pop. 34,716.

Ber•ga•mo (bĕr′gə-mō′). A city of N Italy in the foothills of the Alps NE of Milan. Pop. 121,846.

ber•ga•mot (bûr′gə-mŏt′) *n.* **1.a.** A tree *(Citrus aurantium* subsp. *bergamia)* grown chiefly in southern Italy for its fruits, the rinds of which yield an aromatic oil. **b.** The oil itself, used extensively in perfumery. **2.** See **bee balm.** [Fr. *bergamote* < Ital. *bergamotta* < Turk. dial. *beg-armudu*, bey's pear : *beg*, bey; see BEY + *armud*, pear + *-u*, possessive suff.]

Ber•gen (bûr′gən, bĕr′-). A city of SW Norway on inlets of the North Sea; founded c. 1070. Pop. 207,232.

Ber•gen-Bel•sen (bûr′gən-bĕl′sən, bĕr′gən-bĕl′zən). See **Belsen.**

Ber•gen•field (bûr′gən-fēld′). A borough of NE NJ E of Paterson. Pop. 24,458.

Bergh (bûrg), **Henry.** 1811–88. Amer. reformer who founded the American Society for the Prevention of Cruelty to Animals (1866).

Ber•gisch-Glad•bach (bĕr′gĭsh-glät′bäk′, -bäKH′). A town of W Germany near Cologne; chartered 1856. Pop. 100,749.

Berg•man (bûrg′mən), **Ingmar.** b. 1918. Swedish director whose films include *The Silence* (1963).

Bergman, Ingrid. 1915–82. Swedish actress whose films include *Gaslight, Anastasia,* and *Murder on the Orient Express.*

Berg•mann's rule (bûrg′mənz) *n. Ecol.* The principle holding that in a warm-blooded, polytypic, wide-ranging animal species, the body size of the members of each geographic group varies inversely with the average environmental temperature. [After Karl *Bergmann* (d. 1865), German biologist.]

Berg•son (bĕrg′sən, bĕrg-sôN′), **Henri Louis.** 1859–1941. French philosopher and writer who won the 1927 Nobel Prize for literature. **—Berg•so′ni•an** (-sō′nē-ən) *adj. & n.*

Berg•son•ism (bĕrg′sə-nĭz′əm) *n.* The philosophy of Henri Bergson, which asserts that all living forms arise from a persisting natural force, the élan vital.

Ber•i•a (bĕr′ē-ə), **Lavrenti Pavlovich.** 1899–1953. Soviet secret police chief (1938–53) during the regime of Joseph Stalin; convicted of conspiracy and executed.

ber•i•ber•i (bĕr′ē-bĕr′ē) *n.* A disease caused by a deficiency of thiamine, characterized by neuropathy, heart abnormalities, and edema. [Singhalese, redup. of *beri*, weakness.]

Ber•ing (bîr′ĭng, bâr′-, băr′- bā′rĭng), **Vitus.** 1681–1741. Danish navigator and explorer who in 1728 sailed through the Bering Strait.

Bering Sea. A northward extension of the Pacific Ocean between Siberia and AK, lying N of the Aleutian Is. and connected with the Arctic Ocean by the Bering Strait.

Bering Standard Time *n.* Standard time in the 11th time zone west of Greenwich, England, reckoned at 165° west and used, for example, in the Midway Islands. [After the BERING (SEA) or BERING (STRAIT).]

Bering Strait. A narrow stretch of water separating AK from Siberia and connecting the Arctic Ocean with the Bering Sea. It is believed that during prehistoric times the strait formed a land bridge by which the original inhabitants of North America arrived from Asia.

Bering Time *n.* See **Bering Standard Time.**

Berke•le•ian•ism (bärk′lē-ə-nĭz′əm, bûr′-) *n.* George Berkeley's philosophy of subjective idealism, which holds that material objects exist as concepts in God's mind and as perceptions of those concepts in other minds.

Berke•ley (bûrk′lē). A city of W CA on San Francisco Bay N of Oakland. Pop. 102,724.

Berkeley, Busby. 1895–1976. Amer. choreographer and film director noted for lavish dance routines in films such as *42nd Street* (1933).

Berke•ley (bärk′lē, bûrk′-), **George.** 1685–1753. Irish philosopher who wrote *Treatise Concerning the Principles of Human Knowledge* (1710). **—Berke′le•ian** *adj. & n.*

Berke•ley (bûrk′lē, bärk′-), Sir **William.** 1606–77. English colonial governor of Virginia (1641–49 and 1660–77).

ber•ke•li•um (bər-kē′lē-əm, bûrk′lē-əm) *n. Symbol* **Bk** A synthetic radioactive element. Its most stable isotope is Bk 247 with a half-life of 1,380 years. Atomic number 97; melting point 986°C; valence 3, 4. See table at **element.** [After BERKELEY.]

Berk•ley (bûrk′lē). A city of SE MI, a suburb of Detroit. Pop. 16,960.

Berk•shire (bûrk′shîr′, -shər) *n.* One of a domestic breed of medium-sized black swine with white markings. [After *Berkshire*, a county of S-central England.]

Berkshire Hills also **Berk•shires** (bûrk′shîrz′, -shərz). A region of wooded hills in W MA rising to 1,064.8 m (3,491 ft).

ber•lin (bər-lĭn′) *n.* **1.** Berlin wool. **2.** Often **berline.** A four-wheeled closed carriage having an open, hooded seat behind. [After BERLIN.]

Ber•lin (bûr-lĭn′). The cap. of Germany, in the NE part; divided (1945–90) into **East Berlin** and **West Berlin.** The **Berlin Wall,** a wire and concrete barrier, was erected by the East German government in 1961 and dismantled in 1989. Pop. 3,034,118. **—Ber•lin′er** *n.*

Berlin, Irving. 1888–1989. Russian-born Amer. songwriter whose musical comedies include *Annie Get Your Gun* (1946).

Ber•lin•er (bûr′lə-nər), **Emile.** 1851–1929. German-born Amer. inventor of the gramophone (1887).

Berlin wool *n.* A light wool yarn, esp. used in gloves.

Ber•li•oz (bĕr′lē-ōz′, -ōs′), **(Louis) Hector.** 1803–69. French composer whose works include *Symphonie Fantastique* (1830).

berm also **berme** (bûrm) *n.* **1.a.** A narrow ledge or shelf, as along the top or bottom of a slope. **b.** The shoulder of a road.

beret

ă **pat**	oi **boy**
ā **pay**	ou **out**
âr **care**	o͝o **to͝ok**
ä **father**	o͞o **bo͞ot**
ĕ **pet**	ŭ **cut**
ē **be**	ûr **urge**
ĭ **pit**	th **thin**
ī **pie**	*th* **this**
îr **pier**	hw **which**
ŏ **pot**	zh **vision**
ō **toe**	ə **about,**
ô **paw**	**item**

Stress marks:
′ (primary);
′ (secondary), as in
dictionary (dĭk′shə-nĕr′ē)

c. A raised bank or path, such as one along a canal. **2.** A terrace formed by wave action along the backshore of a beach. **3.** A mound or bank of earth placed against the wall of a building to provide protection or insulation. [Fr. *berme* < Du. *berm* < MDu. *bærm, berme.*]

Ber·me·jo (bər-mā′hō, bĕr-). A river of N Argentina rising near the Bolivian border and flowing c. 1,046 km (650 mi) to the Paraguay R. at the Paraguay border.

Ber·mu·da (bər-myo͞o′də). A self-governing British colony comprising c. 300 coral islands in the Atlantic Ocean SE of Cape Hatteras. Cap. Hamilton, on **Bermuda Island.** Pop. 56,000. — **Ber·mu′di·an, Ber·mu′dan** *adj. & n.*

Bermuda grass *n.* A mat-forming perennial grass *(Cynodon dactylon),* widespread in warm regions and important as a lawn and pasturage grass in the southern United States.

Bermuda lily *n.* See **Easter lily.**

Bermuda onion *n.* Any of several varieties of mild-flavored onions shaped like a flattened sphere.

Bermuda petrel *n.* See **cahow.**

Bermuda rig *n. Naut.* A fore-and-aft rig with a tall triangular mainsail and jib, used on cruising and racing vessels.

Bermuda shorts *pl.n.* Short pants that end slightly above the knee.

Bern or **Berne** (bûrn, bĕrn). The cap. of Switzerland, in the W-central part on the Aare R.; founded as a military post in 1191. Pop. 140,600.

Bernese mountain dog

Ber·na·dette of Lourdes (bûr′nə-dĕt′; lo͝ord, lo͝ordz), Saint. 1844–79. French peasant girl whose visions of the Virgin Mary led to the establishment of the shrine at Lourdes.

Bernadotte (bûr′nə-dŏt′), Count **Folke.** 1895–1948. Swedish diplomat who was a leader of the Red Cross (1943–48).

Ber·nard (bĕr-när′), **Claude.** 1813–78. French physiologist noted for his study of the digestive and nervous systems.

Ber·nar·din de Saint-Pierre (bĕr-när-dăN′ də săN-pyĕr′), **Jacques Henri.** 1737–1814. French writer whose works include *Paul et Virginie* (1787).

Ber·nard of Clair·vaux (bər-närd′, bĕr-när′; klâr-vō′), Saint. 1090–1153. French monastic reformer who rallied support for the Second Crusade.

Ber·nese Alps (bûr′nēz, -nēs, bûr-nēz′, -nēs′). A range of the Alps in S-central Switzerland rising to 4,276.7 m (14,022 ft).

Ber·nese mountain dog (bûr′nēz, -nēs, bûr-nēz′, -nēs′) *n.* Any of a Swiss breed of large muscular dogs having a black coat with russet or tan markings and a white chest.

Sarah Bernhardt
Photographed by
Napoleon Sarony
(1821–1896)

Bern·hardt (bûrn′härt′, bĕr-när′), **Sarah.** "the Divine Sarah." 1844–1923. French actress who first achieved fame for her performance in *Phèdre* (1874).

Ber·ni·na Alps (bər-nē′nə, bĕr-). A mountain group of SE Switzerland in the Rhaetian Alps on the Swiss-Italian border, rising to 4,051.6 m (13,284 ft).

Ber·ni·ni (bər-nē′nē, bĕr-), **Giovanni Lorenzo** or **Gianlorenzo.** 1598–1680. Italian sculptor, painter, and architect whose sculptures include *Apollo and Daphne* (1622–24).

Ber·noul·li (bər-no͞o′lē). Family of Swiss mathematicians and scientists, including **Jakob** or **Jacques** (1654–1705), an important theorist of the calculus of variations. His brother **Johann** or **Jean** (1667–1748) developed integral and exponential calculus. Johann's son **Daniel** (1700–82) did pioneering work in the molecular theory of gases.

Bernoulli distribution *n.* See **binomial distribution.** [After Jakob BERNOULLI.]

Bernoulli effect *n.* The phenomenon of internal pressure reduction with increased stream velocity in a fluid. [After Daniel BERNOULLI.]

Ber·noul·li's law (bər-no͞o′lēz) *n. Statistics.* See **law of large numbers.** [After Jakob BERNOULLI.]

Bern·stein (bûrn′stīn′, -stēn′), **Leonard.** 1918–90. Amer. conductor and composer whose works include *West Side Story* (1957).

Ber·ra (bĕr′ə), **Lawrence Peter.** "Yogi." b. 1925. Amer. athlete considered among the best catchers in baseball history.

ber·ried (bĕr′ēd) *adj.* **1.** Having or bearing berries. **2.** Resembling a berry or berries. **3.** Bearing eggs. Used esp. of crustaceans or fishes.

ber·ry (bĕr′ē) *n., pl.* **-ries. 1.a.** *Bot.* An indehiscent fruit derived from a single ovary and having the whole wall fleshy, such as the grape. **b.** A small, juicy, fleshy fruit, such as a raspberry, regardless of its botanical structure. **2.** The small dark egg of certain crustaceans or fishes. — *intr.v.* **-ried, -ry·ing, -ries. 1.** To hunt for or gather berries. **2.** To bear or produce berries. [ME *berye* < OE *berie.* See **bhā-¹*.**]

Leonard Bernstein

Ber·ry (bĕ-rē′). A historical region and former province of central France.

Ber·ry (bĕr′ē), **Charles ("Chuck") Edward Anderson.** b. 1926. Amer. musician considered among the earliest and most influential rock 'n' roll performers.

Ber·ry·man (bĕr′ē-mən), **John.** 1914–72. Amer. poet whose works include *Homage to Mistress Bradstreet* (1956).

ber·seem (bər-sēm′) *n.* A yellowish-flowered annual clover *(Trifolium alexandrinum),* grown for forage in warm areas. [Ar. *birsīm* < Coptic *bersīm.*]

ber·serk (bər-sûrk′, -zûrk′) *adj.* **1.** Destructively or frenetically violent. **2.** Mentally or emotionally upset; deranged. **3.** *Informal.* Unrestrained, as with enthusiasm; wild. — *n.* **1.** One that is violent, upset, or unrestrained. **2.** A berserker. — **ber·serk′** *adv.* — **ber·serk′ly** *adv.*

ber·serk·er (bər-sûr′kər, -zûr′-) *n.* One of a band of ancient Norse warriors legendary for their savagery and reckless frenzy in battle. [ON *berserkr:* **bera,* fem. of *björn,* bear; see **bher-²*** + *serkr,* shirt.]

berth (bûrth) *n.* **1.** Sufficient space for a ship to maneuver; sea room. **2.** A space for a ship to dock or anchor. **3.a.** Employment on a ship. **b.** A job. **4.a.** A built-in bed or bunk, as on a ship or train. **b.** A place to sleep or stay; accommodations. **5.** A space where a vehicle can be parked, as for loading. — *v.* **berthed, berth·ing, berths.** — *tr.* **1.** To bring (a ship) to a berth. **2.** To provide with a berth. — *intr.* To come to a berth; dock. — ***idiom.* a wide berth.** Ample space or distance to avoid an unwanted consequence. [ME *birth;* perh. akin to *beren,* to bear. See BEAR¹.]

ber·tha (bûr′thə) *n.* A wide, deep collar, often of lace, that covers the shoulders of a dress. [Fr. *berthe,* after *Bertha* (d. 783), Carolingian queen as the wife of Pepin the Short.]

Ber·til·lon (bûr′tl-ŏn′, bĕr-tē-yôN′), **Alphonse.** 1853–1914. French criminologist who devised the Bertillon system (1880).

Bertillon system *n.* A former system used for identifying persons by means of body measurements, physical description, and photographs. [After Alphonse BERTILLON.]

Ber·wyn (bûr′wĭn). A city of NE IL, a suburb of Chicago. Pop. 45,426.

ber·yl (bĕr′əl) *n.* A transparent to translucent glassy mineral, $Be_3Al_2Si_6O_{18}$, constituting the chief source of beryllium and in its transparent varieties valued as gems. [ME < OFr. < Lat. *bēryllus* < Gk. *bērullos* < *bērullion* < Prakrit *veruliya* < Pali *veḷuriya.*] — **ber′yl·line** (-ə-lĭn, -līn′) *adj.*

be·ryl·li·um (bə-rĭl′ē-əm) *n. Symbol* **Be** A lightweight, corrosion-resistant metallic element used as an aerospace structural material, as a moderator and reflector in nuclear reactors, and in a copper alloy for springs and electrical contacts. Atomic number 4; atomic weight 9.0122; melting point 1,278°C; boiling point 2,970°C; specific gravity 1.848; valence 2. See table at **element.** [< BERYL.]

Ber·ze·li·us (bər-zē′lē-əs, bĕr-sā′lē-o͝os′), Baron **Jöns Jakob.** 1779–1848. Swedish chemist who published a table of atomic weights (1828).

Bes (bĕs) *n. Myth.* The Egyptian god of music and revelry.

Be·san·çon (bĭ-zäN-sôN′). A city of E France E of Dijon. Pop. 113,283.

Bes·ant (bĕz′ənt), **Annie Wood.** 1847–1933. English theosophist, philosopher, and political figure who advocated home rule and educational reforms in India.

be·seech (bĭ-sēch′) *tr.v.* **-sought** (-sôt′) or **-seeched, -seech·ing, -seech·es. 1.** To address an earnest or urgent request to; implore: *beseech him for help.* **2.** To request earnestly; beg for: *beseech help.* [ME *bisechen* < OE *besēcan: be-,* be- + *sēcan,* to seek; see SEEK.] — **be·seech′er** *n.*

be·seem (bĭ-sēm′) *tr.v.* **-seemed, -seem·ing, -seems.** *Archaic.* To be appropriate for; befit. [ME *bisemen: bi-,* be- + *semen,* to seem; see SEEM.]

be·set (bĭ-sĕt′) *tr.v.* **-set, -set·ting, -sets. 1.** To attack from all sides. **2.** To trouble persistently; harass; beleaguer. **3.** To hem in; surround. **4.** To stud, as with jewels. [ME *bisetten* < OE *besettan.* See **sed-*.**] — **be·set′ment** *n.*

be·set·ting (bĭ-sĕt′ĭng) *adj.* Constantly troubling or attacking.

be·shrew (bĭ-shro͞o′) *tr.v.* **-shrewed, -shrew·ing, -shrews.** *Archaic.* To invoke evil upon; curse.

be·side (bĭ-sīd′) *prep.* **1.** At the side of; next to. **2.a.** In comparison with. **b.** On an equal footing with. **3.** In addition to. See Usage Note at **besides. 4.** Except for. See Usage Note at **besides. 5.** Not relevant to. — *adv. Archaic.* **1.** In addition. **2.** Nearby. — ***idiom.* beside (oneself).** In a state of extreme excitement or agitation. [ME *biside* < OE *be sīdan: be,* by; see BY¹ + *sīde,* side.]

be·sides (bĭ-sīdz′) *adv.* **1.** In addition; also. **2.** Moreover; furthermore. **3.** Otherwise; else. — *prep.* **1.** In addition to. **2.** Except for; other than. [ME : *biside,* at the side; see BESIDE + *-es,* adv. suff.; see -s³.]

Usage Note: In modern usage the senses "in addition to" and "except for" are conveyed more often by *besides* than *beside.* See Usage Note at **together.**

be·siege (bĭ-sēj′) *tr.v.* **-sieged, -sieg·ing, -sieg·es. 1.** To surround with hostile forces. **2.** To crowd around; hem in. **3.** To harass or importune, as with requests. **4.** To cause to feel distressed or worried. [ME *besegen,* prob. (with substitution of *bi-,* be-) < *assegen* < OFr. *assegier* < VLat. **assedicāre:* Lat. *ad-,* ad- + VLat. **sedicāre,* to sit (< Lat. *sedēre;* see SIEGE).] — **be·siege′ment** *n.* — **be·sieg′er** *n.*

Bes·kids (bĕs′kĭdz′, bĕs-kēdz′). A mountain range of the W Carpathians extending c. 322 km (200 mi) along the Polish-Slovakian border and rising to 1,726 m (5,659 ft). The range is divided into the **East Beskids** and the **West Beskids.**

be·smear (bĭ-smîr′) *tr.v.* **-smeared, -smear·ing, -smears.** To smear.

be•smirch (bĭ-smûrch′) *tr.v.* **-smirched, -smirch•ing, -smirch•es. 1.** To stain; sully: *besmirched by slander.* **2.** To make dirty; soil. **— be•smirch′er** *n.* **— be•smirch′ment** *n.*

be•som (bē′zəm) *n.* **1.** A bundle of twigs attached to a handle and used as a broom. **2.** *Sports.* The broom used to sweep the ice in curling. [ME < OE *besma.*]

besom pocket *n.* A pocket trimmed with welting or reinforced stitching. [*besom*, reinforcement around pocket opening.]

be•sot (bĭ-sŏt′) *tr.v.* **-sot•ted, -sot•ting, -sots.** To muddle or stupefy, as with alcohol. [BE- + *sot*, to stupefy (< *sot*, fool; see SOT) or < *assot*, to befool (< OFr. *assoter* (< *sot*, foolish).]

be•sought (bĭ-sôt′) *v.* A p.t. and p.part. of **beseech.**

be•spake (bĭ-spāk′) *v. Archaic.* A p.t. of **bespeak.**

be•spat•ter (bĭ-spăt′ər) *tr.v.* **-tered, -ter•ing, -ters.** To spatter with or as if with mud.

be•speak (bĭ-spēk′) *tr.v.* **-spoke** (-spōk′), **-spo•ken** (-spō′kən) or **-spoke, -speak•ing, -speaks. 1.** To be or give a sign of; indicate. **2.** To engage, hire, or order in advance. **3.** To foretell; portend. **4.** *Archaic.* To speak to; address. [ME *bispeken*, to speak out < OE *besprecan*, to speak about.]

be•spec•ta•cled (bĭ-spĕk′tə-kəld) *adj.* Wearing eyeglasses.

be•sprent (bĭ-sprĕnt′) *adj. Archaic.* Sprinkled over. [ME *bispreint*, p.part. of *bisprengen*, to besprinkle < OE *besprengan*: *be-*, be- + *sprengan*, to sprinkle.]

be•sprin•kle (bĭ-sprĭng′kəl) *tr.v.* **-kled, -kling, -kles.** To sprinkle. [Prob. < ME *bisprenklen* < *bisprengen*. See BESPRENT.]

Bes•sa•ra•bi•a (bĕs′ə-rā′bē-ə). A region of Moldavia and W Ukraine; became part of Russia in 1812 but declared itself independent in 1918 and later voted for union with Romania, which was forced to cede it to the U.S.S.R. in 1940. **— Bes′sa•ra′bi•an** *adj. & n.*

Bes•se•mer (bĕs′ə-mər). A city of N-central AL SSW of Birmingham. Pop. 33,497.

Bessemer, Sir **Henry.** 1813–98. British inventor and metallurgist who patented the Bessemer process.

Bessemer process *n.* A method for making steel by blasting compressed air through molten iron to burn out excess carbon and impurities. [After Sir Henry BESSEMER.]

best (bĕst) *adj.* Superl. of **good. 1.** Surpassing all others in excellence, achievement, or quality; most excellent. **2.** Most satisfactory, suitable, or useful; most desirable. **3.** Greatest; most: *for the best part of an hour.* — *adv.* Superl. of **well**[2]. **1.** In a most excellent way; most creditably or advantageously. **2.** To the greatest degree or extent; most. — *n.* **1.** One that surpasses all others. **2.** The best part, moment, or value: *The best is still to come.* **3.** The optimum condition or quality: *look your best.* **4.** One's nicest or most formal clothing. **5.** The supreme effort one can make: *doing our best.* **6.** One's warmest wishes or regards. — *tr.v.* **best•ed, best•ing, bests.** To get the better of; beat. **— *idioms.* at best. 1.** Interpreted most favorably; at the most. **2.** Under the most favorable conditions. **for the best.** With an ultimately positive or preferable result. **get (or have) the best of.** To outdo or outwit; defeat. [ME < OE *betst.* See **bhad-*.**]

Usage Note: According to rule, *better* should be used in comparisons between two things: *Which house of Congress has the better* (not *best*) *attendance record?* In certain fixed expressions, however, *best* is used idiomatically for comparisons between two: *Put your best foot forward.* See Usage Notes at **better**[1]**, rather.**

Best (bĕst), **Charles Herbert.** 1899–1978. Amer.-born Canadian physiologist noted for his work on insulin.

best boy *n.* The chief assistant to the gaffer on a movie or television set.

best-case (bĕst′kas′) *adj.* Most favorable; optimum.

be•stead (bĭ-stĕd′) *Archaic.* — *tr.v.* **-stead•ed** or **-stead, -stead•ing, -steads. 1.** To be of service to; aid. **2.** To be of use to; avail. — *adj.* Having been placed; located. [Prob. BE- + STEAD, to help. Adj. < ME *bistad*, placed : *bi-*, be- + *-stad* (ult. < ON *staddr*, placed, p.part. of *stedhja*, to stop, fix, appoint < *stadhr*, place; see **stā-***).]

bes•tial (bĕs′chəl, bēs′-) *adj.* **1.** Beastly. **2.** Marked by brutality or depravity. **3.** Lacking in intelligence or reason; subhuman. [ME < OFr. < LLat. *bēstiālis* < Lat. *bēstia*, beast.] **— bes′tial•ly** *adv.*

bes•ti•al•i•ty (bĕs′chē-ăl′ĭ-tē, bēs′-) *n., pl.* **-ties. 1.** The quality or condition of being an animal or like an animal. **2.** Conduct or an action marked by depravity or brutality. **3.** Sexual relations between a human being and an animal.

bes•ti•ar•y (bĕs′chē-ĕr′ē, bēs′-) *n., pl.* **-ies.** A collection of stories providing descriptions of real and imaginary animals along with moral interpretations of their behavior. [Med.Lat. *bēstiārium* < Lat. *bēstia*, beast.]

be•stir (bĭ-stûr′) *tr.v.* **-stirred, -stir•ring, -stirs.** To cause to become active; rouse: *bestirred himself to look for work.* [ME *bistiren*: prob. *bi-*, be- + *stiren*, to rouse; see STIR[1].]

best man *n.* The bridegroom's chief attendant at a wedding.

be•stow (bĭ-stō′) *tr.v.* **-stowed, -stow•ing, -stows. 1.** To present as a gift or an honor; confer: *bestowed praise on the winners.* **2.** To apply; use. **3.** To store or house. **— be•stow′a•ble** *adj.* **— be•stow′al, be•stow′ment** *n.*

be•strew (bĭ-strōō′) *tr.v.* **-strewed, -strewed** or **-strewn** (-strōōn′), **-strew•ing, -strews. 1.** To strew (a surface) with things so as to cover it. **2.** To lie scattered over or about.

be•stride (bĭ-strīd′) *tr.v* **-strode** (-strōd′), **-strid•den** (-strĭd′n), **-strid•ing, -strides. 1.** To sit or stand on with the legs astride; straddle. **2.** To dominate by position; tower over. **3.** *Archaic.* To step or stride across.

best•sell•er (bĕst′sĕl′ər) *n.* A product, such as a book, that is among those sold in the largest numbers. **— best′sell′er•dom** *n.* **— best′-sell′ing** *adj.*

bet (bĕt) *n.* **1.** An agreement that one who has made an incorrect prediction about an uncertain outcome will forfeit something stipulated to another; a wager. **2.** An amount or object risked in a wager; a stake. **3.** One on which a stake is or can be placed. **4.a.** A plan or an option considered with regard to its probable consequence. **b.** *Informal.* A view; an opinion. — *v.* **bet** or **bet•ted, bet•ting, bets.** — *tr.* **1.** To stake (an amount, for example) in a bet. **2.** To make a bet with. **3.** To make a bet on (a contestant or an outcome). **4.** To maintain confidently, as if making a bet. — *intr.* To make or place a bet. **— *idiom.* you bet.** *Informal.* Of course; surely. [?]

Syns: *bet, ante, pot, stake, wager.* The central meaning shared by these nouns is "something valuable risked on an uncertain outcome": *placed a 50-dollar bet in the first race; raising the ante in a poker game; won the whole pot at cards; played for high stakes; laid a wager on who would win.*

bet. *abbr.* Between.

be•ta (bā′tə, bē′) *n.* **1.** The second letter of the Greek alphabet. **2.** The second item in a series or system of classification. **3.** A mathematical measure of the sensitivity of rates of return on a portfolio or a given stock compared with rates of return on the market as a whole. **4.** *Phys.* A beta particle. **5.** *Chem.* **a.** The second position from a designated carbon atom in an organic molecule at which an atom or a radical may be substituted. **b.** An isomeric variation of a chemical compound. Used in combination: *beta-estradiol.* [Gk. *bēta* < Canaanite *bêt*, house. See BETH.]

be•ta-ad•re•ner•gic (bā′tə-ăd′rə-nûr′jĭk, bē′-) *adj.* Of, relating to, or being a beta-receptor.

beta-adrenergic blocking agent *n.* See **beta-blocker.**

beta-adrenergic receptor *n.* See **beta-receptor.**

be•ta-block•er (bā′tə-blŏk′ər, bē′-) *n. Physiol.* A drug that opposes the excitatory effects of norepinephrine released from sympathetic nerve endings at beta-receptors, used to treat angina, hypertension, arrhythmia, and migraine.

be•ta-car•o•tene (bā′tə-kăr′ə-tēn′, bē′-) *n.* One of the isomeric forms of carotene that is widely distributed in nature.

beta cell *n. Physiol.* **1.** Any of the insulin-producing cells of the islets of Langerhans in the pancreas. **2.** Any of the basophilic chromophil cells located in the adenohypophysis.

be•ta•ine (bē′tə-ēn′, -ĭn) *n.* **1.** An alkaloid, $C_5H_{11}NO_2$, in sugar beets, used to treat muscular degeneration. **2.** Any of several similar alkaloids. [Lat. *bēta*, beet + -INE[2].]

be•take (bĭ-tāk′) *tr.v.* **-took** (-tŏŏk′), **-tak•en** (-tā′kən), **-tak•ing, -takes. 1.** To make (oneself) move. **2.** *Archaic.* To commit.

be•ta•meth•a•sone (bā′tə-mĕth′ə-sōn′, bē′-) *n.* A synthetic glucocorticoid, $C_{22}H_{29}FO_5$, used as a topical anti-inflammatory agent. [BETA + METH(YL) + (PREDNI)S(OL)ONE.]

be•ta-naph•thol (bā′tə-năf′thôl′, -thōl′, -năp′-) *n.* An isomeric crystalline form of naphthol, $C_{10}H_7OH$, used as an antioxidant.

beta particle *n.* A high-speed electron or positron, esp. one emitted in radioactive decay.

beta ray *n.* A stream of beta particles, esp. of electrons.

be•ta-re•cep•tor (bā′tə-rĭ-sĕp′tər, bē′-) *n.* A site in the autonomic nervous system in which inhibitory responses occur when adrenergic agents are released.

beta rhythm *n.* See **beta wave.**

be•ta•tron (bā′tə-trŏn′, bē′-) *n.* A magnetic induction particle accelerator capable of producing high-energy electrons.

beta wave *n.* A waveform in electroencephalograms of the adult brain, characteristically of a frequency from 13 to 30 hertz and accompanying an alert or anxious waking state.

be•tel (bēt′l) *n.* An evergreen Indo-Malayan climbing or trailing shrub *(Piper betle)* having leaves used to wrap betel nuts. [Port. < Malayalam *vettila, verrila* < Tamil *verrilai.*]

Be•tel•geuse (bēt′l-jōōz′, bĕt′l-jœz′) *n.* A bright-red intrinsic variable star in the constellation Orion. [Fr. *Bételgeuse*, prob. < alteration of Ar. *yad al-jawzā′*: *yad*, hand + *al*, of + *jawzā′*, Orion.]

betel nut also **be•tel•nut** (bēt′l-nŭt′) *n.* The seed of the betel palm, chewed with betel leaves and lime as a mild stimulant.

betel palm *n.* A tropical Asian feather-leaved palm *(Areca catechu)* cultivated for its seeds.

bête noire (bĕt nwär′) *n.* One that is particularly disliked or that is to be avoided. [Fr. : *bête*, beast + *noire*, black.]

beth (bĕt) *n.* The second letter of the Hebrew alphabet. [Heb. *bêt* < *bayit*, house.]

be•than•e•chol (bĕ-thăn′ĭ-kôl′, -kōl′) *n.* A cholinergic drug, $C_7H_{17}CLN_2O_2$, used in the form of its chloride to treat abdominal distention and urinary retention. [Perh. *beth* (blend of BETA and METHYL) + -ANE + CHOL(INE).]

ă pat	oi **boy**
ā pay	ou **out**
âr care	ŏŏ **took**
ä father	ōō **boot**
ĕ pet	ŭ cut
ē be	ûr **urge**
ĭ pit	th **thin**
ī pie	*th* **this**
îr pier	hw **which**
ŏ pot	zh vision
ō toe	ə about, item
ô paw	

Stress marks:
′ (primary);
′ (secondary), as in **dictionary** (dĭk′shə-nĕr′ē)

Beth·a·ny (bĕth′ə-nē). **1.** A village of ancient Palestine at the foot of the Mount of Olives near Jerusalem. According to the Bible, it was the site of the resurrection of Lazarus. **2.** A city of central OK W of Oklahoma City. Pop. 20,075.

Be·the (bā′tə), **Hans Albrecht.** b. 1906. German-born Amer. physicist who won a 1967 Nobel Prize.

beth·el (bĕth′əl) *n.* **1.** A hallowed or holy place. **2.a.** A chapel for seafarers. **b.** *Chiefly British.* A Nonconformist chapel, esp. a Baptist or Methodist one. [Heb. *bêt'el*, house of God : *bêt*, house + *'el*, God.]

Beth·el (bĕth′əl). **1.** (*also* bĕth′ĕl′). A town of ancient Palestine N of Jerusalem; now a major archaeological site. **2.** A town of SW CT SE of Danbury. Pop. 17,541.

Bethel Park. A borough of SW PA, a suburb of Pittsburgh. Pop. 33,823.

Be·thes·da (bə-thĕz′də). An unincorp. city of W-central Maryland, a suburb of Washington DC. Pop. 62,936.

be·think (bĭ-thĭngk′) *v.* **-thought** (-thôt′), **-think·ing, -thinks.** —*tr.* **1.** To make (oneself) consider. **2.** To remind (oneself); remember. See Syns at **remember.** —*intr. Archaic.* To meditate. [ME *bithinken* < OE *bethencan.* See **tong-***.]

Beth·le·hem (bĕth′lĭ-hĕm′, -lē-əm). **1.** A town in the West Bank S of Jerusalem; traditional birthplace of Jesus. Pop. 25,000. **2.** A city of E PA on the Lehigh R. NNW of Philadelphia. Pop. 71,428.

Beth·mann-Holl·weg (bĕt′mən-hôl′vāg′, -män-), **Theobald von.** 1856–1921. German chancellor (1909–17) who opposed unrestricted submarine warfare during World War I.

Mary McLeod Bethune

Be·thune (bə-thōōn′, -thyōōn′), **Mary McLeod.** 1875–1955. Amer. educator who sought improved racial relations and educational opportunities for Black Americans.

be·tide (bĭ-tīd′) *v.* **-tid·ed, -tid·ing, -tides.** —*tr.* To happen to. —*intr.* To take place; befall. [ME *bitiden*: *bi-*, be- + *tiden*, to happen (< OE *tīdan*; see TIDE[2]).]

be·times (bĭ-tīmz′) *adv.* **1.** In good time; early. **2.** Once in a while. **3.** *Archaic.* Quickly; soon. [ME *bitimes*: *bi*, by; see BY[1] + *time*, time; see TIME + *-es*, adv. suff.; see -s[3].]

bê·tise (bā-tēz′) *n., pl.* **-tises** (-tēz′). **1.** Stupidity; folly. **2.** A stupid or foolish act or remark. [Fr. < *bête*, beast, fool, foolish < OFr. *beste*, beast. See BEAST.]

Bet·je·man (bĕch′ə-mən), Sir **John.** 1906–84. British writer and poet laureate (1972–84) whose works include *A Few Late Chrysanthemums* (1955).

be·to·ken (bĭ-tō′kən) *tr.v.* **-kened, -ken·ing, -kens.** To be or give a sign or portent of. [ME *bitokenen*: *bi-*, be- + *toknen*, to signify (< OE *tācnian*; see **deik-***).]

betony
Stachys officinalis

bet·o·ny (bĕt′n-ē) *n., pl.* **-nies. 1.** Any of several plants of the widespread genus *Stachys* in the mint family, esp. *S. officinalis* native chiefly to Europe and once used in medicine. **2.** The lousewort. [ME < OFr. *betoine* < Med.Lat. *betōnia*, both < Lat. *vettōnica*, prob. < *Vettōnēs*, an ancient Iberian tribe.]

be·took (bĭ-tŏŏk′) *v.* P.t. of **betake.**

be·tray (bĭ-trā′) *tr.v.* **-trayed, -tray·ing, -trays. 1.a.** To give aid or information to an enemy of; commit treason against. **b.** To deliver into the hands of an enemy in violation of a trust or allegiance. **2.** To be false or disloyal to. **3.** To divulge in a breach of confidence. **4.** To make known unintentionally. **5.** To reveal against one's desire or will. **6.** To lead astray; deceive. See Syns at **deceive.** [ME *bitrayen*: *bi-*, be- + *trayen*, to betray (< OFr. *trair* (< Lat. *trādere*, to hand over; see TRADITION).] —**be·tray′al** *n.* —**be·tray′er** *n.*

be·troth (bĭ-trōth′, -trôth′) *tr.v.* **-trothed, -troth·ing, -troths. 1.** To promise to give (someone) in marriage. **2.** To promise to marry (someone). [ME *bitrouthen*: *bi-*, be- + *trouth*, troth (< OE *trēowth*; see **deru-***).] —**be·trothed′** (-trōthd′, -trôtht′) *adj. & n.*

be·troth·al (bĭ-trō′thəl, -trô′thəl) *n.* **1.** The act of betrothing or the fact of being betrothed. **2.** A mutual promise to marry.

bet·ta (bĕt′ə) *n.* Any of various species of small, brightly colored, long-finned freshwater fishes of the genus *Betta*, found in southeast Asia. [NLat. *Betta*, genus name.]

Bet·ten·dorf (bĕt′n-dôrf′). A city of E IA, a suburb of Davenport. Pop. 28,132.

bet·ter[1] (bĕt′ər) *adj.* Comp. of **good. 1.** Greater in excellence or higher in quality than another or others. **2.** More useful, suitable, or desirable than another or others. **3.** More highly skilled or adept than another or others. **4.** Greater or larger: *the better part of an hour.* **5.** More advantageous or favorable than others; improved. **6.** Healthier or more fit than before. —*adv.* Comp. of **well[2]. 1.** In a more excellent way. **2.a.** To a greater extent or degree. **b.** To greater advantage; preferably: *better left undone.* **3.** More: *better than a year.* —*n.* **1.** One that is greater in excellence or higher in quality than another or others. **2.** A superior, as in standing, competence, or intelligence. —*v.* **-tered, -ter·ing, -ters.** —*tr.* **1.** To make better; improve. See Syns at **improve. 2.** To surpass or exceed. —*intr.* To become better. —***idioms.* for the better.** Resulting in or aiming at an improvement. **had better.** *Usage Problem.* Ought to; must. **think better of.** To change one's mind about (a course of action) after reconsideration. [ME < OE *betera.* See **bhad-***.]

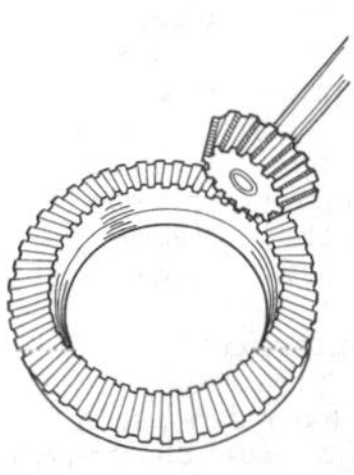
bevel gear

Usage Note: The phrase *had better* is acceptable, as long as the *had* or its contraction is preserved: *You had better do it* or *You'd better do it,* but not *You better do it.* See Usage Notes at **best, rather.**

bet·ter[2] (bĕt′ər) *n.* Var. of **bettor.**

better half *n. Informal.* One's spouse. [< *my better half*, the larger part of me, that is, a close friend.]

bet·ter·ment (bĕt′ər-mənt) *n.* **1.** An improvement over what has been the case. **2.** *Law.* An improvement beyond normal upkeep that adds to the value of real property.

bet·ter-off (bĕt′ər-ôf′, -ŏf′) *adj.* Being in a better or more prosperous condition.

bet·tor also **bet·ter** (bĕt′ər) *n.* One that bets or places a bet.

be·tween (bĭ-twēn′) *prep.* **1.a.** In or through the position or interval separating. **b.** Intermediate to, as in quantity, amount, or degree: *between 15 and 20 dollars.* **2.** Connecting spatially. **3.** Associating or uniting in a reciprocal action or relationship. **4.a.** By the combined effort or effect of. **b.** In the combined ownership of: *a few dollars between them.* **5.** As measured against. Often used to express a reciprocal relationship: *choose between riding and walking.* —*adv.* In an intermediate space, position, or time; in the interim. —***idioms.* between you and me.** In the strictest confidence. **in between.** In an intermediate situation. **in between times.** During an intervening period; in the meantime. [ME *bitwene* < OE *betwēonum.* See **dwo-***.] —**between′ness** *n.*

Usage Note: According to a widely repeated tradition, "*between* is used for two and *among* for more than two." It is true that *between* is the only choice when exactly two entities are specified: *the choice between good and evil.* When more than two entities are involved, however, or when the number of entities is unspecified, *between* is used when the entities are considered as distinct individuals; *among,* when they are considered as a mass or collectivity. Thus in the sentence *The bomb landed between the houses,* the houses are seen as points that define the boundaries of the area of impact. In *The bomb landed among the houses,* the area of impact is considered to be the general location of the houses, taken together. *Among* is most appropriate to indicate inclusion in a group: *She is among the best of our young sculptors. Between* is preferred when the entities are seen as determining the limits or endpoints of a range: *The plane went down somewhere between Quito, Lima, and La Paz.*

be·tween·brain (bĭ-twēn′brān′) *n.* See **diencephalon.**

be·tween·times (bĭ-twēn′tīmz′) *adv.* At or during pauses.

be·twixt (bĭ-twĭkst′) *adv. & prep.* Between. —***idiom.* betwixt and between.** In an intermediate position. [ME *bitwixt* < OE *betwix.* See **dwo-***.]

Beu·lah (byōō′lə) *n.* **1.** *Bible.* The land of Israel. **2.** The land of peace described in John Bunyan's *Pilgrim's Progress.*

beurre blanc (bûr′ blängk′, bœr bläN′) *n.* A sauce made with butter, shallots, and vinegar or lemon juice, often served with seafood. [Fr. : *beurre*, butter + *blanc*, white, not browned.]

Beuys (boiz, bois), **Joseph.** 1921–86. German artist who helped organize the German Green Party.

Bev·an (bĕv′ən), **Aneurin.** 1897–1960. Welsh-born British politician who as minister of health (1945–51) was the chief architect of the National Health Service.

bev·el (bĕv′əl) *n.* **1.** The angle or inclination of a line or surface that meets another at any angle but 90°. **2.** Two rules joined together as adjustable arms used to measure or draw angles of any size or to fix a surface at an angle. —*v.* **-eled, -el·ing, -els** or **-elled, -el·ling, -els.** —*tr.* To cut at an inclination that forms an angle other than a right angle. —*intr.* To be inclined; slant. [Poss. < OFr. **bevel*, perh. < *baif*, open-mouthed < *baer*, to gape < VLat. **badāre.*]

bevel gear *n.* Either of a pair of gears with teeth surfaces cut so that they can connect unparallel gear shafts.

bevel square *n.* See **bevel** 2.

bev·er·age (bĕv′ər-ĭj, bĕv′rĭj) *n.* Any one of various liquids for drinking, usu. excluding water. [ME < OFr. *bevrage* < *beivre*, to drink < Lat. *bibere.* See **pō(i)-***.]

Bev·er·idge (bĕv′ər-ĭj, bĕv′rĭj), **Albert Jeremiah.** 1862–1927. Amer. politician and historian whose works include *The Life of John Marshall* (1916–19).

Bev·er·ly (bĕv′ər-lē). A city of NE MA NE of Boston; settled in 1626. Pop. 38,195.

Beverly Hills. A city of S CA surrounded by Los Angeles. Pop. 31,971.

Bev·in (bĕv′ĭn), **Ernest.** 1884–1951. British labor leader and politician who helped draft the NATO treaty of 1949.

bev·y (bĕv′ē) *n., pl.* **-ies. 1.** A group of animals or birds, esp. larks or quail. **2.** A group or an assemblage. [ME < AN *bevee.*]

be·wail (bĭ-wāl′) *tr.v.* **-wailed, -wail·ing, -wails. 1.** To cry over; lament: *bewail the dead.* **2.** To express sorrow or unhappiness over. —**be·wail′er** *n.* —**be·wail′ment** *n.*

be·ware (bĭ-wâr′) *v.* **-wared, -war·ing, -wares.** —*tr.* To be on guard against; be cautious of. —*intr.* To be cautious; exert caution: *Beware of the dog.* [ME *ben war*: *ben*, to be; see BE + *war*, on one's guard; see WARE[2].]

be·whis·kered (bĭ-hwĭs′kərd, -wĭs′-) *adj.* Having whiskers.

be·wigged (bĭ-wĭgd′) *adj.* Wearing a wig.

be•wil•der (bĭ-wĭl′dər) *tr.v.* **-dered, -der•ing, -ders. 1.** To confuse or befuddle, esp. with numerous conflicting situations, objects, or statements. **2.** To cause to lose one's bearings; disorient. **—be•wil′dered•ly** *adv.* **—be•wil′dered•ness** *n.* **—be•wil′der•ing•ly** *adv.*

be•wil•der•ment (bĭ-wĭl′dər-mənt) *n.* **1.** The condition of being confused. **2.** A situation of confusion; a tangle.

be•witch (bĭ-wĭch′) *tr.v.* **-witched, -witch•ing, -witch•es. 1.** To place under one's power by magic; cast a spell over. **2.** To captivate completely; entrance. See Syns at **charm. —be•witch′er** *n.* **—be•witch′er•y** *n.*

be•witch•ing (bĭ-wĭch′ĭng) *adj.* Enchanting as if with a magic spell; fascinating. **—be•witch′ing•ly** *adv.*

be•witch•ment (bĭ-wĭch′mənt) *n.* **1.a.** The act of bewitching. **b.** The power to bewitch. **c.** The state of being bewitched. **2.** A bewitching spell.

be•wray (bĭ-rā′) *tr.v.* **-wrayed, -wray•ing, -wrays.** *Archaic.* To disclose or betray. [ME *biwreien*: *bi-*, be- + *wreien*, to accuse (< OE *wrēgan*).]

bey (bā) *n.* **1.** A provincial governor in the Ottoman Empire. **2.** A ruler of the former kingdom of Tunis. **3.** Used formerly as a title for various Turkish and Egyptian dignitaries. [Turk. < Old Turkic *beg*, ruler, prince.]

be•yond (bē-ŏnd′, bĭ-yŏnd′) *prep.* **1.** On the far side of; past. **2.** Later than; after. **3.** To a degree that is past the understanding, reach, or scope of: *beyond remedy.* **4.** To a degree or amount greater than. **5.** In addition to. *—adv.* **1.** Farther along or away. **2.** In addition; more. *—n.* **1.** That which is unknown or unexplored. **2.** The afterlife; the hereafter. [ME *biyonde* < OE *begeondan*: *be*, by; see BY[1] + *geondan*, on the far side of; see **i-*.**]

bez•ant (bĕz′ənt, bə-zănt′) *n.* **1.** See **solidus** 1. **2.** *Archit.* A flat disk used as an ornament. [ME *besant* < OFr. < Med. Lat. *Byzantius* < Lat., of Byzantium.]

bez•el (bĕz′əl) *n.* **1.** A slanting surface or bevel on the edge of a cutting tool. **2.** The upper, faceted portion of a cut gem. **3.** A groove or flange designed to hold a beveled edge, as of a watch crystal or a gem. [Prob. Fr. dial.,; akin to Fr. *biseau* < *bis*, two times < Lat. See **dwo-*.**]

Bé•ziers (bāz-yā′). A city of S France SW of Montpellier. Pop. 76,647.

be•zique (bə-zēk′) *n. Games.* A card game similar to pinochle that is played with a deck of 64 cards. [Fr. *bésigue*, poss. < Ital. *bazzica*, a kind of card game.]

be•zoar (bē′zôr′, -zōr′) *n.* A hard mass of indigestible material found in the stomachs or intestines of human beings and animals, once considered a poison antidote. [ME *bezear*, stone poison antidote, prob. < OFr. *bezahar*, gastric or intestinal mass used as poison antidote < Ar. *bāzahr* < Pers. *pādzahr*: *pād-*, protector (< Avestan *pātar-*; see **pā-***) + *zahr*, poison (< MPers.; see **gʷhen-***).]

Bez•wa•da (bĕz-wä′də). See **Vijayawada.**

bf *abbr.* also **b.f.** or **bf. 1.** Board foot. **2.** Boldface.

b.f. or **B/F** *abbr. Accounting.* Brought forward.

B.F.A. *abbr.* Bachelor of Fine Arts.

BG or **B.G.** *abbr.* Brigadier general.

bg. *abbr.* **1.** Background. **2.** Bag.

BGH *abbr.* Bovine growth hormone.

B-girl (bē′gûrl′) *n.* A woman employed by a bar to encourage customers to spend money freely. [B(AR)[1] + GIRL.]

BH *abbr.* Bill of health.

BHA (bē′āch-ā′) *n.* A white, waxy phenolic antioxidant, $C_{11}H_{16}O_2$, used to preserve fats and oils, esp. in foods. [B(UTYLATED) H(YDROXY)A(NISOLE).]

Bha•ga•vad-Gi•ta (bä′gə-väd-gē′tə) *n. Hinduism.* A sacred Hindu text in which Krishna instructs the prince Arjuna. [Skt. *bhagavad-gītā*, song of the Blessed One (Krishna) : *bhagavant-*, fortunate, blessed (< *bhagaḥ*, good fortune; see **bhag-***) + *gītā*, song (< *gāyati*, he sings).]

bhak•ti (bŭk′tē) *n. Hinduism.* The devotional way of achieving salvation, emphasizing loving faith for a deity and open to all. [Skt. *bhaktiḥ*, devotion < *bhajati*, he apportions < *bhagaḥ*, good fortune, share. See BHAGAVAD-GITA.]

bhang also **bang** (băng) *n.* A preparation from the leaves and seed capsules of the cannabis plant, smoked or ingested to obtain mild euphoria. [Ult. < Skt. *bhaṅgā*.]

Bhat•pa•ra (bät-pä′rə). A city of NE India on the Hooghly R. N of Calcutta. Pop. 260,761.

Bhav•na•gar (bou-nŭg′ər, bäv-). A city of W India on the Gulf of Cambay S of Ahmadabad. Pop. 307,121.

BHC *abbr.* Benzene hexachloride.

bhd. *abbr.* Bulkhead.

Bhn. *abbr.* Brinell hardness number.

Bho•lan Pass (bō-län′). See **Bolan Pass.**

Bho•pal[1] (bō-päl′). A city of central India NNW of Nagpur; site of a 1984 toxic gas leak that killed more than 2,000 people. Pop. 671,018.

Bho•pal[2] (bō-päl′). An industrial disaster.

B-ho•ri•zon (bē′hə-rī′-zən) *n.* In ABC soil, the second or subsurface zone of soil made of clay and oxidized materials and organic matter leached from the A-horizon; subsoil.

bhp or **b.hp.** *abbr.* Brake horsepower.

BHT (bē′āch-tē′) *n.* A crystalline phenolic antioxidant, $C_{15}H_{24}O$, used to preserve fats and oils, esp. in foods. [B(UTYLATED) H(YDROXY)T(OLUENE).]

Bhu. *abbr.* Bhutan.

Bhu•ba•nes•war (bo͞o′bə-nĕsh′wər). A city of E-central India SW of Calcutta; known for its Hindu and Buddhist shrines. Pop. 219,211.

Bhu•tan (bo͞o-tăn′, -tän′). An isolated country of central Asia in the E Himalaya Mts. Cap. Thimbu. Pop. 1,232,000.

Bhu•tan•ese (bo͞o′tə-nēz′, -nēs′) *adj.* Of or relating to Bhutan or its people, language, or culture. *—n., pl.* **Bhutanese. 1.** A native or inhabitant of Bhutan. **2.** The Sino-Tibetan language of Bhutan.

Bhut•to (bo͞o′tō), **Benazir.** b. 1953. Pakistani politician who served as prime minister (1988–90).

Bhutto, Zulfikar Ali. 1928–79. Pakistani prime minister (1973–77); deposed by a coup d'état and later executed.

bi (bī) *Slang. —n., pl.* **bi's.** A bisexual person. *—adj.* Bisexual.

Bi The symbol for the element **bismuth.**

bi–[1] or **bin–** *pref.* **1.a.** Two: *biform.* **b.** Both: *binaural.* **c.** Both sides, parts, or directions: *biconcave.* **2.a.** Occurring at intervals of two: *bicentennial.* **b.** *Usage Problem.* Occurring twice during: *biweekly.* **3.a.** Containing twice the proportion of a specified chemical element or group necessary for stability: *bicarbonate.* **b.** Containing two chemical atoms, radicals, or groups: *biphenyl.* [Lat. *bis*, *bi-*, twice, and *bīnī*, two by two; see **dwo-*.**]

Usage Note: *Bimonthly* and *biweekly* mean "once every two months" and "once every two weeks." For "twice a month" and "twice a week," the words *semimonthly* and *semiweekly* should be used. A writer is well advised to substitute expressions like *twice a month* where possible. The words with *bi–* are unavoidable to denote publications that appear at intervals of two.

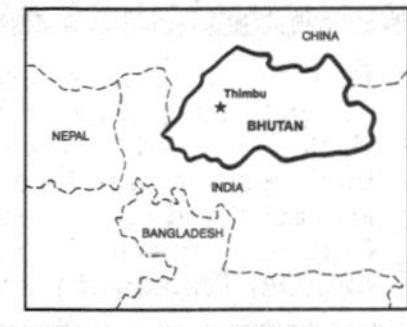

Bhutan

bi–[2] *pref.* Var. of **bio–.**

BIA *abbr.* Bureau of Indian Affairs.

Bi•a•fra (bē-ăf′rə, -ä′frə). A region of E Nigeria on the **Bight of Biafra,** an arm of the Gulf of Guinea stretching from the Niger R. delta to N Gabon. It formed a secessionist state from May 1967 to Jan. 1970. **—Bi•a′fran** *adj. & n.*

Bi•ak (bē-yăk′). The largest of the Schouten Is. of Indonesia off the NW coast of New Guinea.

bi•a•ly (bē-ä′lē) *n., pl.* **-lys.** A flat, round baked roll topped with onion flakes. [After BIALYSTOK.]

Bia•ly•stok (bē-ä′lĭ-stôk′, byä′wĭ-). A city of NE Poland near the border of Belorussia. About half the city's population was killed by Nazi occupation forces (1941–44). Pop. 245,400.

bi•an•nu•al (bī-ăn′yo͞o-əl) *adj.* Happening twice each year; semiannual. **—bi•an′nu•al•ly** *adv.*

Biar•ritz (bē′ə-rĭts′, bē′ə-rĭts′). A city of SW France on the Bay of Biscay near the Spanish border. Pop. 26,598.

bi•as (bī′əs) *n.* **1.** A line going diagonally across the grain of fabric. **2.a.** A preference or an inclination, esp. one that inhibits impartial judgment. See Syns at **predilection. b.** An unfair act or policy stemming from prejudice. **3.** A statistical sampling or testing error caused by systematically favoring some outcomes over others. **4.** *Sports.* **a.** A weight or irregularity in a ball that causes it to swerve. **b.** The tendency of such a ball to swerve. **5.** The fixed voltage applied to an electrode. *—adj.* Slanting or diagonal; oblique: *a bias fold. —tr.v.* **-ased, -as•ing, -as•es** or **-assed, -as•sing, -as•ses. 1.** To influence in a particular, typically unfair direction; prejudice. See Syns at **incline. 2.** To apply a small voltage to (a grid). [Fr. *biais*, slant < Prov., perh. ult. < Gk. *epikarsios*, slanted.]

bias-ply tire

bi•ased also **bi•assed** (bī′əst) *adj.* Marked by bias.

bi•as-ply tire (bī′əs-plī′) *n.* A pneumatic tire having crossed layers of ply cord running diagonally to the tread.

bi•ath•lon (bī-ăth′lən, -lŏn′) *n. Sports.* **1.** A competition that combines events in cross-country skiing and rifle shooting. **2.** An athletic contest in which participants compete in two successive events, such as long-distance swimming and running. [BI–[1] + Gk. *athlon*, prize of contest.] **—bi•ath′lete** (-lēt) *n.*

bi•ax′i•al *adj.*
bi•ax′i•al′i•ty *n.*
bi•ax′i•al•ly *adv.*
bi•cel′lu•lar *adj.*
bi•cen′tric *adj.*
bi′cen•tric′i•ty *n.*
bi′col′or *adj.*
bi′col′ored *adj.*
bi•cul′tur•al *adj.*
bi•cul′tur•al•ism *n.*
bi′di•a•lec′tal *adj.*
bi•flag′el•late *adj.*
bi•lo′bate′ *adj.*
bi•lob′u•lar *adj.*
bi•loc′u•lar *adj.*
bi•loc′u•late *adj.*
bi•man′u•al *adj.*
bi•max′il•lar′y *adj.*
bi′mo•lec′u•lar *adj.*
bi′mor•phe′mic *adj.*
bi•na′tion•al *adj.*
bi′pa•ren′tal *adj.*
bi•ra′cial *adj.*
bi•ra′cial•ism *n.*
bi•ra′mous *adj.*
bi•se′ri•ate *adj.*
bi′state′ *adj.*

ă pat
ā pay
âr care
ä father
ĕ pet
ē be
ĭ pit
ī pie
îr pier
ŏ pot
ō toe
ô paw
oi boy
ou out
o͝o took
o͞o boot
ŭ cut
ûr urge
th thin
th this
hw which
zh vision
ə about, item

Stress marks:
′ (primary);
′ (secondary), as in
dictionary (dĭk′shə-nĕr′ē)

bib (bĭb) *n.* **1.** A piece of cloth or plastic secured under the chin and worn to protect the clothing while eating. **2.a.** The part of an apron or pair of overalls worn over the chest. **b.** Bibbed overalls worn while skiing. — *tr. & intr.v.* **bibbed, bib•bing, bibs.** To drink or to indulge in drinking. [Prob. < ME *bibben,* to drink heartily < Lat. *bibere.* See **pō(i)-*.**]
bib. or **Bib.** *abbr.* Biblical.
Bib. *abbr.* Bible.
bib and tucker *n. Informal.* Clothing.
bibb (bĭb) *n.* A bibcock. [Alteration of BIB.]
bibbed (bĭbd) *adj.* Having a bib: *bibbed overalls.*
bib•ber (bĭb′ər) *n.* A tippler; a drinker. [< BIB.]
Bibb lettuce (bĭb) *n.* A kind of lettuce forming a small, loose head and having tender, dark green leaves. [After Jack Bibb, 19th-cent. Amer. vegetable grower.]
bib•cock (bĭb′kŏk′) *n.* A faucet with a nozzle that is bent downward. [Prob. BIB + COCK[1].]
bi•be•lot (bē′bə-lō′, bē-blō′) *n.* **1.** A small decorative object; a trinket. **2.** A miniature book, esp. one that is finely crafted. [Fr. < OFr. *beubelet* < a redup. of *bel,* beautiful < Lat. *bellus,* handsome. See BELLE.]
bibl. or **Bibl.** *abbr.* Biblical.
Bi•ble (bī′bəl) *n.* **1.a.** The sacred book of Christianity, a collection of ancient writings including both the Old Testament and the New Testament. **b.** The Hebrew Scriptures; the Tanakh. **c.** A particular copy of a Bible. **d.** A book or collection of writings constituting the sacred text of a religion. **2.** Often **bible.** A book considered authoritative in its field. [ME < OFr. < LLat. *biblia* < Gk., pl. of *biblion,* book, dim. of *biblos,* papyrus, book < *Bublos,* Byblos.]
Bible belt. Those sections of the U.S., esp. in the South and Midwest, where Protestant fundamentalism is widely practiced.
Bible paper *n.* A thin, strong, opaque printing paper used for Bibles and reference books.
bib•li•cal also **Bib•li•cal** (bĭb′lĭ-kəl) *adj.* **1.** Of, relating to, or contained in the Bible. **2.** Being in keeping with the nature of the Bible. [< Med.Lat. *biblicus* < LLat. *biblia,* Bible. See BIBLE.] — **Bib′li•cal•ly** *adv.*
Bib•li•cist (bĭb′lĭ-sĭst) *n.* **1.** An expert on the Bible. **2.** One who interprets the Bible literally. — **Bib′li•cism** *n.*
biblio– *pref.* Book: *bibliophile.* [< Gk. *biblion,* book. See BIBLE.]
bibliog. *abbr.* Bibliographer; bibliography.
bib•li•og•ra•pher (bĭb′lē-ŏg′rə-fər) *n.* **1.** One trained in the description and cataloging of printed matter. **2.** One who compiles a bibliography.
bib•li•og•ra•phy (bĭb′lē-ŏg′rə-fē) *n., pl.* **-phies. 1.** A list of the works of a specific author or publisher. **2.a.** A list of writings relating to a given subject. **b.** A list of writings used or considered by an author in preparing a particular work. **3.a.** The description and identification of the editions, dates of issue, authorship, and typography of books or other written material. **b.** A compilation of such information. — **bib′li•o•graph′i•cal** (-ə-grăf′ĭ-kəl), **bib′li•o•graph′ic** (-ĭk) *adj.* — **bib′li•o•graph′i•cal•ly** *adv.*
bib•li•ol•a•try (bĭb′lē-ŏl′ə-trē) *n.* **1.** Excessive adherence to a literal interpretation of the Bible. **2.** Extreme devotion to books. — **bib′li•ol′a•ter** *n.* — **bib′li•ol′a•trous** *adj.*
bib•li•o•man•cy (bĭb′lē-ə-măn′sē) *n., pl.* **-cies.** Divination by interpretation of a passage chosen at random from a book.
bib•li•o•ma•ni•a (bĭb′lē-ə-mā′nē-ə, -mān′yə) *n.* An exaggerated liking for the ownership of books. — **bib′li•o•ma′ni•ac′** (-ăk′) *n.* — **bib′li•o•ma•ni′a•cal** (-mə-nī′ə-kəl) *adj.*
bib•li•o•phile (bĭb′lē-ə-fīl′) also **bib•li•o•phil** (-fĭl′) *n.* **1.** A lover of books. **2.** A collector of books. — **bib′li•oph′i•lism** *n.* — **bib′li•oph′i•lis′tic** *adj.*
bib•li•o•pole (bĭb′lē-ə-pōl′) also **bib•li•op•o•list** (bĭb′lē-ŏp′ə-lĭst) *n.* A dealer in rare books. [Lat. *bibliopōla,* bookseller < Gk. *bibliopōlēs: biblio-,* biblio- + *pōlein,* to sell; see **pel-[4]*.**] — **bib′li•o•pol′ic** (-pŏl′ĭk), **bib′li•o•pol′i•cal** *adj.*
bib•li•o•the•ca (bĭb′lē-ə-thē′kə) *n.* **1.** A collection of books; a library. **2.** A catalog of books. [Lat. *bibliothēca* < Gk. *bibliothēkē: biblio-,* biblio- + *thēkē,* case; see **dhē-*.**]
bib•li•o•ther•a•py (bĭb′lē-ō-thĕr′ə-pē) *n.* The use of selected reading materials as a form of supportive psychotherapy.
bib•li•ot•ics (bĭb′lē-ŏt′ĭks) *n. (used with a sing. v.)* Examination of written documents to determine authorship or authenticity.
bib•u•lous (bĭb′yə-ləs) *adj.* **1.** Given to or marked by the consumption of alcoholic drink: *a bibulous evening.* **2.** Very absorbent, as paper or soil. [< Lat. *bibulus* < *bibere,* to drink. See **pō(i)-*.**] — **bib′u•lous•ly** *adv.* — **bib′u•lous•ness** *n.*
bi•cam•er•al (bī-kăm′ər-əl) *adj.* Composed of or based on two legislative chambers or branches. [BI-[1] + Lat. *camera,* chamber; see CAMERA + -AL[1].] — **bi•cam′er•al•ism** *n.*
bi•car•bon•ate (bī-kär′bə-nāt′, -nĭt) *n.* The radical group HCO_3^- or a compound containing it.
bicarbonate of soda *n.* See **baking soda.**
bi•cau•dal (bī-kôd′l) *adj. Zool.* Having two tails.
bice blue (bīs) *n. Color.* A moderate blue. [ME *bis,* blue-gray (sense uncertain) < OFr. *bis,* dark.]
bice green *n. Color.* A moderate yellow green. [See BICE BLUE.]
bi•cen•ten•a•ry (bī′sĕn-tĕn′ə-rē, bī-sĕn′tə-nĕr′ē) *n., pl.* **-ries.** A bicentennial. — **bi′cen•ten′a•ry** *adj.*
bi•cen•ten•ni•al (bī′sĕn-tĕn′ē-əl) *adj.* **1.** Happening once every 200 years. **2.** Lasting for 200 years. **3.** Relating to a 200th anniversary. — **bi′cen•ten′ni•al** *n.*
bi•ceph•a•lous (bī-sĕf′ə-ləs) *adj. Zool.* Having two heads.
bi•ceps (bī′sĕps′) *n., pl.* **biceps** or **-ceps•es** (-sĕp′sĭz). **1.** A muscle with two heads or points of origin. **2.a.** The large muscle at the front of the upper arm that flexes the forearm. **b.** The large muscle at the back of the thigh that flexes the knee joint. [Lat., two-headed : *bi-,* two; see BI-[1] + *caput,* head; see **kaput-*.**]
bi•chlo•ride (bī-klôr′īd, -klōr′-) *n.* See **dichloride.**
bichon frisé (bē-shŏn′ frē-zā′, frēz, bē′shŏn) *n., pl.* **bi•chons fri•sés** (bē-shŏn′ frē-zā′, frēz, bē′shŏn). Any of a European breed of small dogs having a wavy white coat, drooping ears, and a curved tail. [Fr. : *bichon,* lapdog + *frisé,* curly.]
bi•chro•mate (bī-krō′māt′, -mĭt) *n.* See **dichromate.**
bi•cip•i•tal (bī-sĭp′ĭ-tl) *adj.* **1.** Having two heads or points of origin, as a muscle. **2.** Of or relating to a biceps. [< NLat. *biceps, bicipit-,* biceps. See BICEPS.]
bick•er (bĭk′ər) *intr.v.* **-ered, -er•ing, -ers. 1.** To engage in a petty, bad-tempered quarrel; squabble. **2.** To flicker; quiver. — *n.* A petty quarrel; a squabble. [ME *bikeren,* to attack.]

BOOKS OF THE BIBLE

Books of the Hebrew Scriptures appear as listed in the translation by the Jewish Publication Society of America. Books of the Christian Bible appear as listed in the Jerusalem Bible, a 1966 translation of the 1956 French Roman Catholic version. The Old Testament books shown in italic are considered aprocryphal in most Christian churches, but they are accepted as canonical in the Roman Catholic Church, the Eastern Orthodox Churches, and the Armenian and the Ethiopian Oriental Orthodox Churches. The Christian Old Testament parallels the Hebrew Scriptures with the exception of these books.

HEBREW	CHRISTIAN	
THE TORAH	**OLD TESTAMENT**	**NEW TESTAMENT**
Genesis	Genesis	Matthew
Exodus	Exodus	Mark
Leviticus	Leviticus	Luke
Numbers	Numbers	John
Deuteronomy	Deuteronomy	Acts of the Apostles
	Joshua	Romans
THE PROPHETS	Judges	I Corinthians
	Ruth	II Corinthians
Joshua	I Samuel	Galatians
Judges	II Samuel	Ephesians
I Samuel	I Kings	Philippians
II Samuel	II Kings	Colossians
I Kings	I Chronicles	I Thessalonians
II Kings	II Chronicles	II Thessalonians
Isaiah	Ezra	I Timothy
Jeremiah	Nehemiah	II Timothy
Ezekiel	*Tobit*	Titus
Hosea	*Judith*	Philemon
Joel	Esther	Hebrews
Amos	*I Maccabees*	James
Obadiah	*II Maccabees*	I Peter
Jonah	Job	II Peter
Micah	Psalms	I John
Nahum	Proverbs	II John
Habakkuk	Ecclesiastes	III John
Zephaniah	Song of Songs	Jude
Haggai	(Song of Solomon)	Revelation
Zechariah	*Wisdom of Solomon*	
Malachi	*Ecclesiasticus*	
	Isaiah	
THE WRITINGS	Jeremiah	
Psalms	Lamentations	
Proverbs	*Baruch*	
Job	Ezekiel	
Song of Songs	Daniel	
Ruth	Hosea	
Lamentations	Joel	
Ecclesiastes	Amos	
Esther	Obadiah	
Daniel	Jonah	
Ezra	Micah	
Nehemiah	Nahum	
I Chronicles	Habakkuk	
II Chronicles	Zephaniah	
	Haggai	
	Zechariah	
	Malachi	

bi•coas•tal or **bi-coast•al** (bī-kō′stəl) *adj.* Relating to or occurring on the east and west coasts of the United States.

bi•con•cave (bī′kŏn-kāv′, bī-kŏn′kāv′) *adj.* Concave on both sides or surfaces. — **bi′con•cav′i•ty** (-kăv′ĭ-tē) *n.*

bi•con•vex (bī′kŏn-vĕks′, bī-kŏn′vĕks′) *adj.* Convex on both sides or surfaces. — **bi′con•vex′i•ty** (-vĕk′sĭ-tē) *n.*

bi•cor•nu•ate (bī-kôr′nyo͞o-ĭt, -āt′) also **bi•corn** (bī′kôrn′) *adj.* **1.** Having two horns or horn-shaped parts. **2.** Shaped like a crescent. [< BI-[1] + Lat. *cornū*, horn; see **ker-[1]*.**]

bi•cus•pid (bī-kŭs′pĭd) *adj.* Having two points or cusps, as the crescent moon. — *n.* A bicuspid tooth, esp. a premolar. [NLat. *bicuspis, bicuspid-* : Lat. *bi-*, two; see BI-[1] + Lat. *cuspis*, sharp point.]

bicuspid valve *n.* See **mitral valve.**

bi•cy•cle (bī′sĭk′əl, -sĭ-kəl, -sī′kəl) *n.* **1.** A vehicle consisting of a light frame mounted on two wheels one behind the other and having a seat, handlebars for steering, brakes, and two pedals or a small motor by which it is driven. **2.** An exercise bicycle. — *intr.v.* **-cled, -cling, -cles.** To ride or travel on a bicycle. [Prob. BI-[1] + *-cycle*(on the model of TRICYCLE, three-wheeled coach).] — **bi′cy•cler** (-klər), **bi′cy•clist** (-klĭst) *n.*

bi•cy•clic (bī-sī′klĭk, -sĭk′lĭk) also **bi•cy•cli•cal** (-sī′klĭ-kəl, -sĭk′lĭ-) *adj.* **1.** Consisting of or having two cycles. **2.** *Bot.* Composed of or arranged in two distinct whorls. **3.** *Chem.* Containing molecules consisting of two fused rings.

bid (bĭd) *v.* **bade** (băd, bād) or **bid, bid•den** (bĭd′n) or **bid, bid•ding, bids.** — *tr.* **1.** To issue a command to; direct. **2.** To utter (a greeting or salutation). **3.** To invite to attend; summon. **4.** *p.t. and p.part.* **bid.** *Games.* To state one's intention to take (tricks in cards). **5.** *p.t. and p.part.* **bid.** To offer or propose (an amount) as a price. **6.** *p.t. and p.part.* **bid.** To offer (someone) membership, as in a club. — *intr.* **1.** *p.t. and p.part.* **bid.** To make an offer to pay or accept a specified price. **2.** *p.t. and p.part.* **bid.** To seek to win or attain something; strive. — *n.* **1.a.** An offer or proposal of a price. **b.** The amount offered or proposed. **2.** An invitation, esp. one offering membership in a group or club. **3.** *Games.* **a.** The act of bidding in cards. **b.** The number of tricks or points declared. **c.** The trump or no-trump declared. **d.** The turn of a player to bid. **4.** An earnest effort to win or attain something. — ***phrasal verbs.*** **bid in.** To outbid on one's own property at an auction in order to raise the final selling price. **bid up.** To increase (the amount) bid. — ***idiom.*** **bid fair.** To appear likely. [ME *bidden*, to ask, command (< OE *biddan*; see **g^{w}hedh-***) and ME *beden*, to offer, proclaim (< OE *bēodan*; see **bheudh-***).] — **bid′der** *n.*

b.i.d. *abbr. Lat.* Bis in die (twice a day).

bid•da•ble (bĭd′ə-bəl) *adj.* **1.** *Games.* Strong enough to be bid. Used of a hand of cards. **2.** Following directions or obeying commands; docile.

Bid•de•ford (bĭd′ə-fərd). A city of SW ME on the Saco R. SW of Portland. Pop. 20,710.

bid•ding (bĭd′ĭng) *n.* **1.** A demand that something be done; a command. **2.** A request to appear; a summons. **3.** Bids considered as a group, as at an auction or in card games.

Bid•dle (bĭd′l), **John.** 1615–62. English theologian and founder of English Unitarianism.

Biddle, Nicholas. 1786–1844. Amer. financier who was president of the Bank of the United States (1822–39).

bid•dy[1] (bĭd′ē) *n., pl.* **-dies.** A hen; a fowl. [?]

bid•dy[2] (bĭd′ē) *n., pl.* **-dies.** *Slang.* A woman, esp. a garrulous old one. [Nickname for *Bridget*.]

bide (bīd) *v.* **bid•ed** or **bode** (bōd), **bid•ed, bid•ing, bides.** — *intr.* **1.** To remain in a condition or state. **2.a.** To wait; tarry. **b.** To stay; dwell. — *tr. p.t.* **bided.** To await; wait for. — ***idiom.*** **bide (one's) time.** To wait for further developments. [ME *biden* < OE *bīdan*. See **bheidh-***.]

bi•den•tate (bī-dĕn′tāt′) *adj.* Having two teeth or toothlike parts.

bi•det (bē-dā′) *n.* A fixture similar in design to a toilet that is straddled for bathing the genitals and the posterior parts. [Fr., pony, bidet, prob. < OFr. *bider*, to trot.]

bi•don•ville (bē′dôN-vēl′) *n.* A shantytown on the outskirts of a city, esp. in France or North Africa. [Fr. : *bidon*, gas can, oildrum (< OFr., bottle, tankard, prob. of Scand. orig.) + *ville*, town; see VILLAGE.]

Bie•der•mei•er (bē′dər-mī′ər) *adj.* Of or relating to a type of furniture developed in Germany during the first half of the 19th century and modeled after French Empire styles. [After Gottlieb *Biedermeier*, the unsophisticated imaginary author of poems written by Ludwig Eichrodt (1827–92) and others.]

Biel (bēl) also **Bi•enne** (bē-ĕn′). A city of NW Switzerland at the NE end of the **Lake of Biel** at the foot of the Jura Mts. Pop. 52,600.

Bie•le•feld (bē′lə-fĕlt′). A city of NW Germany E of Münster. Pop. 301,460.

Biel•sko-Bia•la (byĕl′skô-byä′lä, -byä′wä). A city of S Poland S of Katowice; passed to Austria in 1772 and was returned to Poland in 1919. Pop. 174,100.

bi•en•ni•al (bī-ĕn′ē-əl) *adj.* **1.** Lasting or living for two years. **2.** Happening every second year. **3.** *Bot.* Having a life cycle normally of two growing seasons. — *n.* **1.** An event that occurs every two years. **2.** *Bot.* **a.** A biennial plant. **b.** A perennial plant cultivated as a biennial. — **bi•en′ni•al•ly** *adv.*

bi•en•ni•um (bī-ĕn′ē-əm) *n., pl.* **-en•ni•ums** or **-en•ni•a** (-ĕn′ē-ə). A two-year period. [Lat. : *bi-*, two; see BI-[1] + *annus*, year; see **at-***.]

Bien•ville (byĕn′vĭl′, byăN-vēl′), **Jean Baptiste Lemoyne de.** 1680–1768. French colonial administrator who as governor of Louisiana founded New Orleans (1718).

bier (bîr) *n.* **1.** A stand on which a corpse or a coffin is placed before burial. **2.** A coffin along with its stand. [Alteration (influenced by Fr. *bière*, coffin < OFr. *biere*, bier, of Gmc. orig.) of ME *ber* < OE *bēr*. See **bher-[1]*.**]

Bierce (bîrs), **Ambrose Gwinett.** 1842–1914? Amer. writer whose satiric works include *The Devil's Dictionary* (1906).

Bier•stadt (bîr′stăt′, -shtät′), **Albert.** 1830–1902. German-born Amer. landscape painter noted for his romanticized works, including *Domes of the Yosemite* (1864).

Bierstadt, Mount. A peak, 4,288.3 m (14,000 ft), of N-central CO in the Front Range of the Rocky Mts.

bi•fa•cial (bī-fā′shəl) *adj.* **1.** Having two faces, fronts, or façades. **2.** Having two opposing surfaces that are alike.

biff[1] (bĭf) *Informal.* — *tr.v.* **biffed, biff•ing, biffs.** To strike or punch. — *n.* A blow or punch. [< E. *biff*, interjection, prob. of imit. orig.]

biff[2] (bĭf) *n. Upper Midwest.* Var. of **biffy.**

bif•fy (bĭf′ē) also **biff** (bĭf) *n., pl.* **-fies** also **biffs.** *Upper Midwest.* **1.** An outdoor toilet; an outhouse. **2.** An indoor toilet. [Perh. alteration of PRIVY.]

bi•fid (bī′fĭd) *adj.* Forked or cleft into two parts: *a bifid petal.* — **bi•fid′i•ty** (-fĭd′ĭ-tē) *n.* — **bi′fid•ly** *adv.*

bi•fi•lar (bī-fī′lər) *adj.* Fitted with or involving the use of two threads or wires. — **bi•fi′lar•ly** *adv.*

bi•fo•cal (bī-fō′kəl, bī′fō′-) *adj.* **1.** Having two focal lengths. **2.** Having one section that corrects for distant vision and another that corrects for near vision, as an eyeglass lens. — *pl.n.* **bi•fo•cals.** (bī-fō′kəlz, bī′fō′-). Eyeglasses with bifocal lenses. — **bi•fo′cal•ism** *n.*

bi•fo•caled (bī-fō′kəld) *adj.* Wearing bifocals.

bi•fo•li•o•late (bī-fō′lē-ə-lāt′, -lĭt) *adj. Bot.* Having two leaflets.

bi•form (bī′fôrm′) *adj.* Having a combination of features or qualities of two distinct forms. [Lat. *biformis*: *bi-*, two; see BI-[1] + *forma*, form; see FORM.]

bi•func•tion•al (bī-fŭngk′shə-nəl) *adj.* **1.** Having two functions: *bifunctional neurons.* **2.** *Chem.* Having or involving two functional groups or binding sites: *bifunctional reagents.*

bi•fur•cate (bī′fər-kāt′, bī-fûr′-) *tr. & intr.v.* **-cat•ed, -cat•ing, -cates.** To divide or be divided into two parts or branches. — *adj.* (-kāt′, -kĭt). Forked or divided into two parts or branches. [Med.Lat. *bifurcāre, bifurcāt-*, to divide < Lat. *bifurcus*, two-pronged : *bi-*, two; see BI-[1] + *furca*, fork.] — **bi′fur•cate′ly** *adv.* — **bi′fur•ca′tion** *n.*

big (bĭg) *adj.* **big•ger, big•gest. 1.** Of considerable size, number, quantity, magnitude, or extent; large. See Syns at **large. 2.a.** Of great force; strong: *a big wind.* **b.** *Obsolete.* Of great strength. **3.** Grown-up; adult. **4.** Pregnant. **5.** Filled up; brimming over. **6.** Having or exercising considerable authority, control, or influence. **7.** Conspicuous in position, wealth, or importance; prominent. **8.** Of great significance; momentous. **9.** *Informal.* Self-important; cocky. **10.** Loud and firm; resounding: *a big voice.* **11.** Bountiful; generous: *a big heart.* — *adv.* **1.** In a pretentious or boastful way. **2.** *Informal.* **a.** With considerable success: *made it big.* **b.** In a thorough or unmistakable way; emphatically. — ***idiom.*** **big on.** Enthusiastic about; partial to. [ME, perh. of Scand. orig.] — **big′gish** *adj.* — **big′ly** *adv.* — **big′ness** *n.*

big•a•mous (bĭg′ə-məs) *adj.* **1.** Involving bigamy. **2.** Guilty of bigamy. — **big′a•mous•ly** *adv.*

big•a•my (bĭg′ə-mē) *n., pl.* **-mies.** *Law.* The criminal offense of marrying one person while still legally married to another. [ME *bigamie* < OFr. < Med.Lat. *bigamia* < LLat. *bigamus*, twice married : Lat. *bi-*, two; see BI-[1] + Gk. *gamos*, marriage; see -GAMOUS.] — **big′a•mist** *n.*

bi•ga•rade (bē′gä-räd′) *n.* **1.** See **sour orange. 2.** A rich sauce served with duck, consisting of duck stock and flavorings. [Fr. < Prov. *bigarrado* < p.part. of *bigarrar*, to variegate < OFr. *bigarrer*: *bi-*, two (< Lat. *bi-*; see BI-[1]) + *garrer*, to variegate (< *garre*, of two colors).]

big band or **Big Band** (bĭg) *n.* A large dance or jazz band.

big bang *n.* The cosmic explosion that marked the origin of the universe according to the big bang theory.

big bang theory *n.* A cosmological theory holding that the universe originated approx. 10 to 15 billion years ago from the explosion of a very small agglomeration of hot, dense matter.

Big Bend (bĕnd). A region of SW TX on the Mexican border in a triangle formed by a bend in the Rio Grande.

Big Black River (blăk). A river rising in N-central MS and flowing c. 531 km (330 mi) to the Mississippi R.

Big Blue River (blo͞o). A river rising in SE NE and flowing c. 483 km (300 mi) to the Kansas R. in NE KS.

big brother *n.* **1.** An older brother. **2.** A man who assumes this

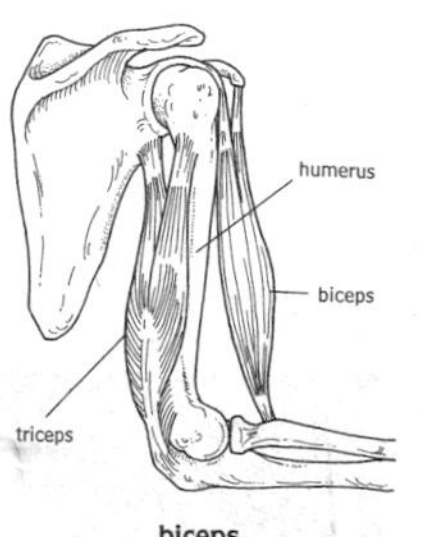

biceps

bicycle

ă pat	oi boy
ā pay	ou out
âr care	o͝o took
ä father	o͞o boot
ĕ pet	ŭ cut
ē be	ûr urge
ĭ pit	th thin
ī pie	*th* this
îr pier	hw which
ŏ pot	zh vision
ō toe	ə about,
ô paw	item

Stress marks:
′ (primary);
′ (secondary), as in
dictionary (dĭk′shə-nĕr′ē)

role. **3.** Also **Big Brother.** A ruthlessly oppressive or authoritarian state, organization, or leader. [Sense 3, after *Big Brother*, a character in the novel *Nineteen Eighty-Four* by George Orwell.]
big bucks *pl.n. Slang.* A large amount of money.
big business *n.* Commercial operations organized and financed on a large scale.
big daddy or **Big Daddy** *n. Slang.* **1.** One that is predominant, as in size, influence, or priority. **2.** One that exercises a paternalistic authority or control.
big deal *n. Slang.* **1.** Something of great importance. **2.** An important person. **—big′-deal′** (bĭg′dēl′) *adj.*
Big Di•o•mede Island (dī′ə-mēd′). See **Diomede Islands.**
Big Dipper *n.* A cluster of seven stars in the constellation Ursa Major, forming a dipper-shaped configuration.
bi•gem•i•nal (bī-jĕm′ə-nəl) *adj.* Occurring in pairs; doubled or twinned: *a bigeminal pulse.* [Poss. < LLat. *bigeminus*, doubled : Lat. *bi-*, two; see BI-[1] + Lat. *geminus*, double.]
bi•gem•i•ny (bī-jĕm′ə-nē) *n. Medic.* **1.** An association in pairs. **2.** An abnormal pulse characterized by two beats in rapid succession followed by a pause.
big enchilada or **Big Enchilada** *n. Slang.* **1.** One who is in charge. **2.** Something of the highest value or importance.
bi•ge•ner•ic (bī′jə-nĕr′ĭk) *adj.* **1.** Relating to a hybrid that results from a cross between plants of different genera. **2.** Having the characteristics of two different genera.
big•eye (bĭg′ī′) *n.* Any of several small, tropical marine fishes of the family Priacanthidae, having large eyes and reddish scales.
Big•foot (bĭg′fo͝ot′) *n.* A very large, hairy, humanlike creature purported to inhabit the Pacific Northwest and Canada.
big game *n.* **1.** Large animals or fish hunted or caught for sport. **2.** *Informal.* An important objective. **—big′-game′** (bĭg′gām′) *adj.*
big•gie (bĭg′ē) *n. Slang.* **1.** A very important person. **2.** Something that is considered big or important.
big•gi•ty also **big•ge•ty** (bĭg′ĭ-tē) *adj. Informal.* Self-important; conceited. [Prob. alteration of BIG + -Y[1].]
big gun *n. Slang.* One that is powerful or influential.
big•head (bĭg′hĕd′) *n.* **1.** *Informal.* Conceit; egotism. **2.** Also **big head.** Any of various diseases of animals, esp. rams, characterized by swelling of the head, face, or neck. **—big′-head′ed** *adj.* **—big′head′ed•ness** *n.*
big-heart•ed (bĭg′här′tĭd) *adj.* Generous; kind. **—big′-heart′ed•ly** *adv.* **—big′-heart′ed•ness** *n.*
big•horn (bĭg′hôrn′) *n., pl.* **bighorn** or **-horns.** A wild sheep *(Ovis canadensis)* of the mountains of western North America, the male of which has massive curved horns.

bighorn
American bighorn
Ovis canadensis

Big•horn Mountains (bĭg′hôrn′). A section of the Rocky Mts. of N WY and S MT rising to 4,018.4 m (13,175 ft).
Bighorn River. A river rising in W-central WY and flowing c. 742 km (461 mi) to join the Yellowstone R. in S MT.
big house *n. Slang.* A penitentiary.
bight (bīt) *n.* **1.a.** A loop in a rope. **b.** The middle or slack part of an extended rope. **2.a.** A bend or curve, esp. in a shoreline. **b.** A wide bay formed by such a bend or curve. [ME, bend, angle < OE *byht.* See **bheug-*.**]
big league *n.* **1.** *Sports.* A major league. **2.** *Informal.* The most prestigious level of accomplishment. **—big′-league′** (bĭg′lēg′) *adj.* **—big leaguer** *n.*
big lie *n.* Intentional distortion of the truth, esp. for political or official purposes.
big money *n. Slang.* **1.** A large amount of money, as in profits or salary: *made big money on the transaction.* **2.** A large-scale commercial enterprise. **—big′-mon′ey** (bĭg′mŭn′ē) *adj.*
big•mouth (bĭg′mouth′) *n.* **1.** *Slang.* A loudmouthed or gossipy person. **2.** Any of various fishes having unusually large mouths.
big•mouthed (bĭg′mouthd′, -moutht′) *adj.* **1.** *Slang.* Speaking loudly or indiscreetly. **2.** Having a large mouth.
Big Mud•dy River (mŭd′ē). A river of SW IL flowing c. 217 km (135 mi) to the Mississippi R.
big•no•ni•a (bĭg-nō′nē-ə) *n.* An evergreen woody vine *(Bignonia capreolata)* native chiefly to the southeast United States and having trumpet-shaped flowers. [NLat. *Bignonia*, genus name, after Jean Paul *Bignon* (d. 1743), French royal librarian.]
bigos (bē′gōs) *n.* A Polish stew made with meat and cabbage, traditionally simmered for several days before serving. [Pol.]
big•ot (bĭg′ət) *n.* One who is strongly partial to one's own group, religion, race, or politics and is intolerant of those who differ. [Fr. < OFr.]
big•ot•ed (bĭg′ə-tĭd) *adj.* Being or characteristic of a bigot. **—big′ot•ed•ly** *adv.* **—big′ot•ed•ness** *n.*
big•ot•ry (bĭg′ə-trē) *n.* The attitude, state of mind, or behavior characteristic of a bigot; intolerance.
big shot *n. Slang.* An important or influential person.
Big Sioux River (so͞o). A river rising in NE SD and flowing c. 676 km (420 mi) to the Missouri R. at Sioux City IA.
Big Spring. A city of W-central TX WSW of Abilene. Pop. 23,093.
big stick *n.* A display or threat, esp. of military force: *a policy that relied on the big stick.* **—big′stick′** (bĭg′stĭk′) *adj.*
Big Sur (sûr). A rugged, picturesque resort region along the Pacific coast of CA S of Carmel and Monterey.
big-tick•et (bĭg′tĭk′ĭt) *adj. Informal.* Having a high price.
big time *n. Informal.* The most prestigious level of attainment in a competitive field. **—big′ time′, big′-time′** (bĭg′tīm′) *adj.* **—big′-tim′er** *n.*
big toe *n.* The largest and innermost toe of the human foot.
big top *n.* **1.** The main tent of a circus. **2.** The circus.
big tree *n.* See **giant sequoia.**
big wheel *n. Slang.* A very important person.
big•wig (bĭg′wĭg′) *n. Slang.* A very important person.
Bi•har (bē-här′). A region of E-central India crossed by the Ganges R. Buddha spent his early days in the area.
Bi•ha•ri (bĭ-hä′rē) *n., pl.* **Bihari** or **-ris. 1.** A native or inhabitant of Bihar. **2.** The Indic language of the Bihari.
bi•jou (bē′zho͞o′) *n., pl.* **-joux** (-zho͞o′, -zho͞oz′). A small, exquisitely wrought trinket. [Fr. < Breton *bizou*, jeweled ring < *biz*, finger.]
bi•jou•te•rie (bē-zho͞o′tə-rē) *n.* **1.** A collection of trinkets or jewelry. **2.** Decoration.
bi•ju•gate (bī′jə-gāt′, -gĭt, -bī-jo͞o′-) also **bi•ju•gous** (bī′jə-gəs, bī-jo͞o′-) *adj. Bot.* Relating to a pinnate leaf with two pairs of leaflets.
Bi•ka•ner (bē′kə-nîr′, -nâr′). A city of NW India in the Thar Desert near the Pakistan border WSW of Delhi. Pop. 253,174.
bike (bīk) *n.* **1.** A bicycle. **2.** A motorcycle. **3.** A motorbike. **—***v.* **biked, bik•ing, bikes.** **—***intr.* To ride a bike. [Shortening and alteration of BICYCLE.]
bik•er (bī′kər) *n.* **1.** One who rides a bicycle or a motorbike. **2.** A motorcyclist, esp. a member of a motorcycle gang.
bike•way (bīk′wā′) *n.* A bicycle lane or path.
bi•ki•ni (bĭ-kē′nē) *n.* **1.** A very brief, close-fitting bathing suit. **2.** Brief underpants that reach only to the hips. Often used in the plural. [Fr., after BIKINI.] **—bi•ki′nied** (-nēd) *adj.*
Bi•ki•ni (bĭ-kē′nē). An atoll in the Ratak Chain of the Marshall Is. in the W-central Pacific; site of U.S. nuclear tests (1946–58).
bi•la•bi•al (bī-lā′bē-əl) *adj.* **1.** Pronounced with both lips, as the consonants *b, p, m,* and *w.* **2.** Relating to both lips. **—***n.* A bilabial sound or consonant. **—bi•la′bi•al•ly** *adv.*
bi•la•bi•ate (bī-lā′bē-ĭt, -āt′) *adj. Bot.* Having two lips.
bi•lat•er•al (bī-lăt′ər-əl) *adj.* **1.** Having or formed of two sides; two-sided. **2.** Affecting or undertaken by two sides equally; binding on both parties: *a bilateral agreement.* **3.** Having or marked by bilateral symmetry. **—bi•lat′er•al•ism, bi•lat′er•al•ness** *n.* **—bi•lat′er•al•ly** *adv.*
bilateral symmetry *n.* Symmetry along a central axis, so that a body is divided into right and left halves by only one plane.
bi•lay•er (bī′lā′ər) *n.* A structure, such as a film or membrane, consisting of two molecular layers.
Bil•ba•o (bĭl-bä′ō, -bou′). A city of N Spain near the Bay of Biscay; founded c. 1300. Pop. 397,541.
bil•ber•ry (bĭl′bĕr′ē) *n.* See **blueberry.** [*bil-*, prob. of Scand. orig.; see **bhel-[2]*** + BERRY.]
bil•bo[1] (bĭl′bō) *n., pl.* **-boes.** An iron bar with sliding fetters, formerly used to shackle the feet of prisoners. [?]
bil•bo[2] (bĭl′bō) *n., pl.* **-boes.** *Archaic.* A sword, esp. one having a well-tempered blade. [After BILBAO.]
bil•dungs•ro•man (bĭl′do͝ongz-rō-män′, -do͝ongks-) or **Bil•dungs•ro•man** *n.* A novel whose subject is the moral, psychological, and intellectual development of a usu. youthful main character. [Ger. : *Bildung*, formation + *Roman*, novel.]
bile (bīl) *n.* **1.** A bitter, alkaline, yellowish fluid that is secreted by the liver, stored in the gallbladder, and discharged into the duodenum to aid in the digestion of fats. **2.** Bitterness of temper; ill humor. **3.** Either of two bodily humors, black bile or yellow bile, in medieval physiology. [Fr. < Lat. *bīlis.*]
bile acid *n.* Any of the liver-generated steroid acids that occur in the bile with glycine and taurine as sodium salts.
bile duct *n.* Any of the excretory passages in the liver that carry bile to the hepatic duct.
bile salt *n.* **1.** Any of the sodium salts of the bile acids occurring in bile. **2.** A mixture, such as that derived from the bile of the ox, used medicinally as a hepatic stimulant or laxative.
bi-lev•el or **bi•lev•el** (bī′lĕv′əl) **—***adj.* **1.** Having or existing on two levels: *a bi-level passenger coach.* **2.** Divided vertically into two ground-floor levels. **—***n.* A bi-level dwelling.
bilge (bĭlj) *n.* **1.** *Naut.* The lowest inner part of a ship's hull. **2.** Bilgewater. **3.** *Slang.* Stupid talk or writing; nonsense. **4.** The bulging part of a barrel or cask. **—***v.* **bilged, bilg•ing, bilg•es.** **—***intr. Naut.* To bulge or swell. [Prob. alteration of BULGE.] **—bilg′y** *adj.*
bilge water *n.* **1.** Stagnant water that collects in a ship's bilge. **2.** *Slang.* Nonsense.
bil•har•zi•a (bĭl-här′zē-ə) *n.* See **schistosome.** [NLat. *Bilharzia*, genus name, after Theodor *Bilharz* (1825–62), German physician.]
bil•har•zi•a•sis (bĭl′här-zī′ə-sĭs) *n.* See **schistosomiasis.** [BILHARZ(IA) + -IASIS.]
bil•i•ar•y (bĭl′ē-ĕr′ē) *adj.* **1.** Of or relating to bile, the bile ducts, or the gallbladder. **2.** Transporting bile.

bi•lin•e•ar (bī-lĭn′ē-ər) *adj. Math.* Linear with respect to each of two variables or positions.

bi•lin•gual (bī-lĭng′gwəl) *adj.* **1.a.** Using or able to use two languages, esp. with nearly equal fluency. **b.** Using two languages to facilitate learning by students who have a proficiency in one language and are acquiring proficiency in the other: *bilingual education.* **2.** Of, relating to, or expressed in two languages: *a bilingual dictionary.* —*n.* A person who uses or is able to use two languages, esp. with equal fluency. —**bi•lin′gual•ism** *n.* —**bi•lin′gual•ly** *adv.*

bil•ious (bĭl′yəs) *adj.* **1.** Of, relating to, or containing bile. **2.a.** Characterized by an excess secretion of bile. **b.** Of or relating to gastric distress caused by a disorder of the liver or gallbladder. **c.** Appearing as if affected by such a disorder; sickly. **3.** Resembling bile, esp. in color. **4.** Having a peevish disposition. —**bil′ious•ly** *adv.* —**bil′ious•ness** *n.*

bil•i•ru•bin (bĭl′ĭ-ro͞o′bĭn, bĭl′ĭ-ro͞o′-) *n.* A reddish-yellow bile pigment, $C_{33}H_{36}N_4O_6$, derived from the degradation of heme. [Lat. *bīlis*, bile + *ruber*, red; see **reudh-*** + -IN.]

bil•i•ver•din (bĭl′ĭ-vûr′dĭn, bĭl′ĭ-vûr′-) *n.* A green pigment, $C_{33}H_{34}N_4O_6$, occurring in bile and sometimes formed by oxidation of bilirubin. [Ger. : Lat. *bīlis*, bile + Ger. *verd-* (< Fr. *verdir*, to make green; see VERDANT).]

bilk (bĭlk) *tr.v.* **bilked, bilk•ing, bilks. 1.a.** To defraud or swindle. **b.** To evade payment of. **2.** To thwart or frustrate. **3.** To elude. —*n.* **1.** One who cheats. **2.** *Obsolete.* A hoax or swindle. [Perh. an alteration of BALK.] —**bilk′er** *n.*

bill[1] (bĭl) *n.* **1.** An itemized list or statement of fees or charges. **2.** A statement or list of particulars, such as a menu. **3.** The entertainment offered by a theater. **4.** A public notice, such as a poster. **5.a.** A piece of legal paper money. **b.** *Slang.* One hundred dollars. **6.a.** A bill of exchange. **b.** *Obsolete.* A promissory note. **7.a.** A draft of a proposed law presented for approval to a legislative body. **b.** The law enacted from such a draft. **8.** *Law.* A document presented to a court and containing a formal statement of a case, complaint, or petition. —*tr.v.* **billed, bill•ing, bills. 1.** To present a statement of costs or charges to. **2.** To enter on a statement of costs or on a particularized list. **3.a.** To advertise or schedule by public notice or as part of a program. **b.** To declare or describe officially; proclaim. [ME *bille* < Norman Fr. < Med.Lat. *billa*, alteration of *bulla*, seal on a document < Lat., bubble.] —**bill′a•ble** *adj.*

bill[2] (bĭl) *n.* **1.** The horny part of the jaws of a bird; a beak. **2.** A beaklike mouth part, such as that of a turtle. **3.** The visor of a cap. —*intr.v.* **billed, bill•ing, bills.** To touch beaks together. [ME < OE *bile.*]

bill[3] (bĭl) *n.* **1.** A billhook. **2.** A halberd or similar weapon with a hooked blade. [ME *bil* < OE *bill.*]

bil•la•bong (bĭl′ə-bông′, -bŏng′) *n. Australian.* A stagnant pool or backwater filled with water only in the rainy season. [Wiradhuri (Aboriginal language of SE Australia) *bila*, river + *-baŋ*, watercourse filled only after rain.]

bill•board[1] (bĭl′bôrd′, -bōrd′) *n.* **1.** A panel for the display of advertisements in public places, as alongside highways. **2.** The advertisement or message on a billboard. **3.** An introductory list of highlights from the program or text that follows. —*tr.v.* **-board•ed, -board•ing, -boards.** To advertise or proclaim on or as if on a billboard. [BILL[1] + BOARD.]

bill•board[2] (bĭl′bôrd′, -bōrd′) *n. Naut.* A ledge on the bow of a ship on which the bill of an anchor rests when the anchor is secured to the cathead. [BILL[2] + BOARD.]

bill•bug (bĭl′bŭg′) *n.* Any of several weevils, esp. of the genera *Calendra* and *Sitophilus,* whose larvae feed on cereal grasses. [BILL[2] + BUG.]

bill•er (bĭl′ər) *n.* One that bills, as: **a.** A clerk who prepares bills. **b.** A machine used in preparing bills.

Bille•ric•a (bĭl-rĭk′ə, bĕl′ə-). A town of NE MA S of Lowell; settled in 1637. Pop. 37,609.

bil•let[1] (bĭl′ĭt) *n.* **1.a.** Lodging for troops. **b.** A written order directing that such lodging be provided. **2.** A position of employment; a job. **3.** *Archaic.* A short letter; a note. —*v.* **-let•ed, -let•ing, -lets.** —*tr.* **1.a.** To lodge (soldiers). **b.** To serve (a person) with a written order to provide lodging for soldiers. **2.** To assign lodging to. —*intr.* To be quartered; lodge. [ME, official register < OFr. *billette* < *bullette*, dim. of *bulle*, document < Med.Lat. *bulla*, document, seal. See BILL[1].]

bil•let[2] (bĭl′ĭt) *n.* **1.** A short, thick piece of wood, esp. one used as firewood. **2.** One of a series of regularly spaced, log-shaped segments used in the moldings of Norman architecture. **3.a.** A small, usu. rectangular bar of iron or steel in an intermediate stage of manufacture. **b.** A small ingot of nonferrous metal. **4.a.** The part of a harness strap that passes through a buckle. **b.** A loop or pocket for securing the end of a buckled harness strap. [ME < OFr. *billette*, dim. of *bille*, log < VLat. **bilia*, poss. of Celt. orig.]

bil•let-doux (bĭl′ā-do͞o′) *n., pl.* **bil•lets-doux** (bĭl′ā-do͞oz′). A love letter. [Fr. : *billet*, short note; see BILLET[1] + *doux*, sweet (< Lat. *dulcis*).]

bill•fish (bĭl′fĭsh′) *n., pl.* **billfish** or **-fish•es. 1.** Any of various fishes of the family Istiophoridae, such as a marlin, having an elongated swordlike or spearlike snout and upper jaw. **2.** Any of various other fishes having long pointed jaws.

bill•fold (bĭl′fōld′) *n.* A folding pocket-sized case for carrying paper money, small personal documents, and change.

bill•head (bĭl′hĕd′) *n.* A letterhead used for billing.

bill•hook (bĭl′ho͝ok′) *n.* An implement with a curved blade on a handle, used esp. for pruning and clearing brush.

bil•liard (bĭl′yərd) *Games. n.* See **carom** 17.

bil•liards (bĭl′yərdz) *pl.n. (used with a sing. v.) Games.* **1.** A game on a rectangular table, in which a cue is used to hit three small, hard balls against one another or the sides of the table. **2.** One of several similar games, sometimes using a table with pockets. [Fr. *billard* < *bille*, log. See BILLET[2].]

bill•ing (bĭl′ĭng) *n.* **1.** The relative importance of performers as indicated by the position and type size in which their names are listed. **2.** Advertising; promotion. **3.** The amount of business done in a period, as by an advertising agency. Often used in the plural.

Bil•lings (bĭl′ĭngz). A city of S MT on the Yellowstone R. ESE of Helena. Pop. 81,151.

Billings, Josh. See Henry Wheeler **Shaw.**

bil•lings•gate (bĭl′ĭngz-gāt′, -gĭt) *n.* Foul, abusive language. [After *Billingsgate*, a former fish market in London, England.]

bil•lion (bĭl′yən) *n.* **1.** The cardinal number equal to 10^9. **2.** *Chiefly British.* The cardinal number equal to 10^{12}. **3.** A huge number. [Fr., a million million : blend of *bi-*, second power; see BI-[1], and MILLION.] —**bil′lion** *adj. & pron.*

bil•lion•aire (bĭl′yə-nâr′, bĭl′yə-nâr′) *n.* A person whose wealth amounts to at least a billion dollars, pounds, or the equivalent in other currency. [BILLION + (MILLION)AIRE.]

bil•lionth (bĭl′yənth) *n.* **1.** The ordinal number matching the number one billion in a series. **2.** One of a billion equal parts. —**bil′lionth** *adj. & adv.*

Bil•li•ton (bə-lē′tŏn′). See **Belitung.**

bill of attainder *n., pl.* **bills of attainder.** A legislative act pronouncing a person guilty of a crime, usu. treason, without trial and subject to capital punishment and attainder.

bill of entry *n., pl.* **bills of entry.** A listing of goods received at a customhouse as imports or for export.

bill of exchange *n., pl.* **bills of exchange.** A written order directing that a sum of money be paid to a specified person.

bill of fare *n., pl.* **bills of fare. 1.** A list of dishes offered; a menu. **2.** A list of items in a presentation; a program.

bill of goods *n., pl.* **bills of goods. 1.** A consignment of items for sale. **2.** *Informal.* A plan, promise, or offer, esp. one that is dishonest or misleading.

bill of health *n., pl.* **bills of health. 1.** A certificate stating whether there is infectious disease aboard a ship or in a port of departure, to be presented at the next port of arrival. **2.** *Informal.* An attestation as to condition, esp. a favorable one.

bill of lading *n., pl.* **bills of lading.** A document issued by a carrier to a shipper, listing and acknowledging receipt of goods and specifying terms of delivery.

bill of particulars *n., pl.* **bills of particulars.** *Law.* An itemization of charges, claims, or counterclaims in an action.

bill of rights *n., pl.* **bills of rights. 1.** A summary of those rights considered essential to a group of people. **2.** Also **Bill of Rights.** The first ten amendments to the U.S. Constitution, added in 1791. **3.** Also **Bill of Rights.** A declaration of certain rights of subjects, enacted by the English Parliament in 1689.

bill of sale *n., pl.* **bills of sale.** A document that attests a transfer of the ownership of personal property.

bil•lon (bĭl′ən) *n.* **1.** An alloy of gold or silver with a greater proportion of another metal, such as copper, used in making coins. **2.** An alloy of silver with a high percentage of copper, used in making medals and tokens. [Fr. < OFr., ingot < *bille*, log. See BILLET[2].]

bil•low (bĭl′ō) *n.* **1.** A large wave or swell of water. **2.** A great swell, surge, or undulating mass. —*v.* **-lowed, -low•ing, -lows.** —*intr.* **1.** To surge or roll in billows. **2.** To swell out or bulge. —*tr.* To cause to billow. [< ON *bylgja*, a wave. See **bhelgh-***.] —**bil′low•i•ness** *n.* —**bil′low•y** *adj.*

bill•post•er (bĭl′pō′stər) *n.* One that posts notices, posters, or advertisements. —**bill′post′ing** *n.*

bil•ly[1] (bĭl′ē) *n., pl.* **-lies.** A billy club.

bil•ly[2] (bĭl′ē) *n., pl.* **-lies.** *Australian.* A metal pot or kettle used in camp cooking. [Prob. short for *billypot* < *Billy*, nickname for *William.*]

billy club *n.* A short wooden club, esp. a police officer's club. [Perh. alteration of **bully club*; see BULLY[1], or < BILLET[2].]

bil•ly•cock (bĭl′ē-kŏk′) *n. Chiefly British.* A felt hat with a low rounded crown, similar to a derby. [Perh. alteration of *bullycocked*, tilted like a bully's : BULLY[1] + COCK[1].]

billy goat *n. Informal.* A male goat.

Bil•ly the Kid (bĭl′ē). See William H. **Bonney.**

bi•lo•ca•tion (bī′lō-kā′shən) *n.* Existence or the ability to exist simultaneously in two places.

Bi•lox•i[1] (bə-lŭk′sē, -lŏk′-) *n., pl.* **Biloxi** or **-is. 1.** A member of a Native American people formerly inhabiting territory around Biloxi Bay in southeast Mississippi. **2.** The extinct Siouan language of the Biloxi.

Bi•lox•i[2] (bə-lŭk′sē, -lŏk′-). A city of SE MS on a peninsula between **Biloxi Bay** and Mississippi Sound. Pop. 46,319.

billy club

ă pat	oi boy
ā pay	ou out
âr care	o͝o to͝ok
ä father	o͞o bo͞ot
ĕ pet	ŭ cut
ē be	ûr urge
ĭ pit	th thin
ī pie	*th* this
îr pier	hw which
ŏ pot	zh vision
ō toe	ə about, item
ô paw	

Stress marks:
′ (primary);
′ (secondary), as in **dictionary** (dĭk′shə-nĕr′ē)

bil•tong (bĭl′tŏng′, -tông′) *n. South African.* Narrow strips of meat dried in the sun. [Afr. : *bil,* buttock (< MDu. *bille;* see **bhel-**[2]*****) + *tong,* tongue (< MDu. *tonghe;* see **dn̥ghū-***).]

bim•bo (bĭm′bō) *n., pl.* **-bos. 1.** *Offensive Slang.* A woman, esp. one perceived as vacuous or overly interested in sex. **2.** *Slang.* A vacuous person. [Perh. < Ital. *bimbo,* baby.]

bi•mes•tri•al (bī-mĕs′trē-əl) *adj.* **1.** Occurring every two months; bimonthly. **2.** Lasting two months. [< Lat. *bimēstris: bi-,* two; see BI–[1] + *mēnsis,* month; see **mē-**[2]*****.]

bi•me•tal•lic (bī′mə-tăl′ĭk) *adj.* **1.** Consisting of two metals, often bonded together and having different rates of thermal expansion. **2.** Of or based on bimetallism.

bi•met•al•lism (bī-mĕt′l-ĭz′əm) *n.* **1.** The use of a monetary standard consisting of two metals, esp. gold and silver, in a fixed ratio of value. **2.** The doctrine advocating bimetallism. **— bi•met′al•list** *n.* **— bi•met′al•lis′tic** *adj.*

bi•mil•le•nar•y (bī-mĭl′ə-nĕr′ē, bī′mə-lĕn′ə-rē) *n., pl.* **-ies.** A bimillennium. **— bi•mil•len•a•ry** *adj.*

bi•mil•len•ni•um (bī′mə-lĕn′ē-əm) *n., pl.* **-len•ni•ums** or **-len•ni•a** (-lĕn′ē-ə). **1.** A 2,000-year span. **2.** A 2,000th anniversary. **— bi•mil•len•ni•al** *adj.*

Bim•i•nis (bĭm′ə-nēz). A group of small islands of the W Bahamas in the Straits of Florida; legendary site of the Fountain of Youth sought by Juan Ponce de León.

bi•mod•al (bī-mōd′l) *adj.* **1.** Having two distinct statistical modes. **2.** Designed for operation on either railroads or highways. Used of vehicles. **— bi′mo•dal′i•ty** (bī′mō-dăl′ĭ-tē) *n.*

bi•month•ly (bī-mŭnth′lē) *adj.* **1.** Happening every two months. **2.** Happening twice a month; semimonthly. *— n., pl.* **-lies.** A bimonthly publication. See Usage Note at **bi–**[1]. **— bi•month′ly** *adv.*

bin (bĭn) *n.* A container or enclosed space for storage. *— tr.v.* **binned, bin•ning, bins.** To place or store in a bin. [ME *binne* < OE, prob. of Celt. orig.]

bin– *pref.* Var. of **bi–**[1].

bi•nal (bī′nəl) *adj.* Twofold; double. [NLat. *bīnālis,* twin < Lat. *bīnī,* two by two. See **dwo-***.]

bi•na•ry (bī′nə-rē) *adj.* **1.** Characterized by or consisting of two parts or components; twofold. **2.** Of or relating to the binary number system. **3.** *Chem.* Consisting of or containing only molecules consisting of two kinds of atoms. **4.** Of or employing two comparatively nontoxic chemicals that combine to produce a deadly poison: *binary weapons.* **5.** *Mus.* Having two sections or subjects. *— n., pl.* **-ries.** Something that is binary, esp. a binary star. [ME *binarie* < LLat. *bīnārius* < Lat. *bīnī,* two by two. See **dwo-***.]

binary cod•ed decimal (kō′dĭd) *n. Comp. Sci.* A code in which a four-bit binary number represents a decimal digit.

binary fission *n.* A method of asexual reproduction that involves the splitting of a parent cell into two approximately equal parts.

binary number system *n.* A method of representing numbers having two as its base and using the digits 0 and 1.

binary star *n.* A stellar system consisting of two stars orbiting about a common center of mass and often appearing as a single visual or telescopic object.

bin•au•ral (bī-nôr′əl, bĭn-ôr′-) *adj.* **1.a.** Having or relating to two ears. **b.** Having to do with the perception of sound with both ears: *binaural hearing.* **2.** Of or relating to sound transmission from two sources, which may vary acoustically to give a stereophonic effect. **— bin•au′ral•ly** *adv.*

bind (bīnd) *v.* **bound** (bound), **bind•ing, binds.** *— tr.* **1.** To tie or secure, as with a rope. **2.** To fasten or wrap by encircling, as with a belt. **3.** To bandage: *bound up their wounds.* **4.** To hold or restrain with or as if with bonds. **5.** To compel, obligate, or unite. **6.** *Law.* To place under legal obligation by contract or oath. **7.** To make certain or irrevocable. **8.** To apprentice or indenture: *was bound out as a servant.* **9.** To cause to cohere or stick together in a mass. **10.** To enclose and fasten (a book or other printed material) between covers. **11.** To furnish with an edge or border, as for protection. **12.** To constipate. **13.** To form a chemical bond with. *— intr.* **1.** To tie up or fasten something. **2.** To stick or become stuck. **3.** To be uncomfortably tight or restricting, as clothes. **4.** To become compact or solid; cohere. **5.** To be compelling or unifying: *the ties that bind.* **6.** To form a chemical bond. *— n.* **1.a.** The act of binding. **b.** The state of being bound. **c.** Something that binds. **d.** A place where something binds: *a bind in the seam.* **2.** *Informal.* A difficult, restrictive, or unresolvable situation: *in a bind.* **3.** *Mus.* A tie, slur, or brace. ***— phrasal verbs.*** **bind off.** To cast off in knitting. **bind over.** *Law.* To hold on bail or place under bond. [ME *binden* < OE *bindan.* See **bhendh-***.]

binocular

bind•er (bīn′dər) *n.* **1.** One that binds, esp. a bookbinder. **2.** Something used to bind. **3.** A notebook cover with rings or clamps for holding paper. **4.** Something, such as the latex in certain paints, that creates uniform consistency, solidification, or cohesion. **5.a.** A machine that reaps and ties grain. **b.** An attachment on a reaping machine that ties grain in bundles. **6.** *Law.* A payment or written statement making an agreement legally binding until the completion of a contract, esp. an insurance contract.

bind•er•y (bīn′də-rē) *n., pl.* **-ies.** A place where books are bound.

bind•ing (bīn′dĭng) *n.* **1.** The action of one that binds. **2.** Something that binds or is used as a binder. **3.** The cover that holds together the pages of a book. **4.** A strip sewn or attached over or along an edge, as for protection. **5.** *Sports.* Fastenings on a ski for securing the boot. *— adj.* **1.** Serving to bind. **2.** Uncomfortably tight and confining. **3.** Imposing or commanding adherence to a commitment, an obligation, or a duty. **— bind′ing•ly** *adv.* **— bind′ing•ness** *n.*

binding energy *n.* **1.** The net energy required to decompose a molecule, an atom, or a nucleus into its components. **2.** The net energy required to remove an atomic electron to an infinitely remote position from its orbit.

bin•dle•stiff (bĭn′dl-stĭf′) *n.* A hobo, esp. one who carries a bedroll. [E. *bindle,* bundle (prob. < Ger. dial. *bindel* < MHGer. *bündel* < *binden,* to bind < OHGer. *binten;* see **bhendh-***) + STIFF.]

bind•weed (bīnd′wēd′) *n.* **1.** Any of various trailing or twining plants of the genera *Calystegia* and *Convolvulus,* having bell-shaped or funnel-shaped flowers. **2.** Any of various similar trailing or twining plants, such as the black bindweed.

bine (bīn) *n.* The flexible twining or climbing stem of certain plants, such as the hop or woodbine. [Alteration of BIND, vine.]

Bi•net-Si•mon scale (bĭ-nā′sē-mōN′, -sī′mən) *n.* An evaluation of the relative mental development of children by psychological tests of intellectual ability. [After Alfred *Binet* (1857–1911) and Théodore *Simon* (1873–1961), French psychologists.]

Bing cherry (bĭng) *n.* A variety of cherry with sweet, red to nearly black fruit.

binge (bĭnj) *n.* **1.** A drunken spree or revel. **2.a.** A period of unrestrained, immoderate self-indulgence. **b.** A period of excessive indulgence in food or drink. *— intr.v.* **binged, bing•ing** or **binge•ing, bing•es. 1.** To be immoderately self-indulgent and unrestrained. **2.** To indulge excessively in food or drink. [Dial. *binge,* to soak.] **— bing′er** *n.*

Syns: *binge, fling, jag, orgy, spree.* The central meaning shared by these nouns is "a period of uncontrolled self-indulgence": *a gambling binge; had a fling between commencement and graduate school; a crying jag; an eating orgy; a shopping spree.*

binge-eat•ing syndrome (bĭnj′ē′tĭng) *n.* See **bulimia** 2.

binge-purge syndrome (bĭnj′pûrj′) *n.* See **bulimarexia.**

binge-vom•it syndrome (bĭnj′vŏm′ĭt) *n.* See **bulimarexia.**

Bing•ham (bĭng′əm), **George Caleb.** 1811–79. Amer. painter noted for his portraits and genre paintings of the frontier.

Bing•ham•ton (bĭng′əm-tən). A city of S-central NY near the PA border SSE of Syracuse; settled in 1787. Pop. 53,008.

bin•go (bĭng′gō) *n., pl.* **-gos.** *Games.* A game in which each player has one or more cards printed with differently numbered squares on which to place markers when the respective numbers are drawn and announced, the winner being the first player to mark a complete row of numbers. *— interj.* Used to express the sudden occurrence of an event. [?]

bin•na•cle (bĭn′ə-kəl) *n. Naut.* A case that supports and protects a ship's compass, located near the helm. [Alteration of ME *bitakille* < OSp. *bitáculaor* < OPort. *bitácola,* both < Lat. *habitāculum,* habitation < *habitāre,* to inhabit. See **ghabh-***.]

bin•oc•u•lar (bə-nŏk′yə-lər, bī-) *adj.* **1.** Relating to, used by, or involving both eyes at the same time. **2.** Having two eyes arranged to produce stereoscopic vision. *— n.* An optical device consisting of two small telescopes joined with a single focusing device. Often used in the plural. **— bin•oc′u•lar′i•ty** (-lăr′ĭ-tē) *n.* **— bin•oc′u•lar•ly** *adv.*

bi•no•mi•al (bī-nō′mē-əl) *adj.* Consisting of or relating to two names or terms. *— n.* **1.** *Math.* A polynomial with two terms. **2.** *Biol.* A taxonomic name in binomial nomenclature. [< NLat. *binōmius,* having two names : BI–[1] + Fr. *nom,* name (< Lat. *nōmen;* see NOMINAL).] **— bi•no′mi•al•ly** *adv.*

binomial distribution *n.* The frequency distribution of the probability of a possible number of specified outcomes in an arbitrary number of repeated independent trials.

binomial nomenclature *n.* The scientific naming of species whereby each species receives a Latin or Latinized name of two parts, the first indicating the genus and the second being the specific epithet.

binomial theorem *n. Math.* A theorem that specifies the expansion of a binomial to any power without requiring the explicit multiplication of the binomial terms.

bint (bĭnt) *n. Chiefly British & Offensive.* A woman or girl. [Ar., daughter.]

bin•tu•rong (bĭn-tŏŏr′ông, -ŏng) *n.* A civet *(Arctictis binturong)* of southeast Asia with a long prehensile tail. [Malay *bĕnturong, binturong.*]

bi•nu•cle•ate (bī-nōō′klē-ĭt, -āt′, -nyōō′-) also **bi•nu•cle•at•ed** (-ā′tĭd) or **bi•nu•cle•ar** (-klē-ər, -nyōō′-) *adj.* Having two nuclei.

Bin•ue (bĭn′wā). See **Benue.**

bi•o (bī′ō) *n., pl.* **-os.** *Informal.* **1.** A biography. **2.** A biographical sketch or outline.

bio– or **bi–** *pref.* **1.** Life; living organism: *biome.* **2.** Biology; biological: *biophysics.* [Gk. < *bios,* life. See **gʷei-***.]
bi•o•a•cous•tics (bī'ō-ə-ko͞o'stĭks) *n.* *(used with a sing. v.)* The study of sounds produced by or affecting living organisms, esp. those sounds involved in communication.
bi•o•ac•tive (bī'ō-ăk'tĭv) *adj.* Of or relating to a substance that affects living tissue. **—bi'o•ac•tiv'i•ty** *n.*
bi•o•as•say (bī'ō-ăs'ā', -ă-sā') *n.* Determination of the strength or biological activity of a substance by comparing its effects with those of a standard preparation on a test organism.
bi•o•as•tro•nau•tics (bī'ō-ăs'trə-nô'tĭks) *n.* *(used with a sing. v.)* The study of the biological and medical effects of space flight on living organisms. **—bi'o•as'tro•nau'ti•cal** *adj.*
bi•o•a•vail•a•bil•i•ty (bī'ō-ə-vā'lə-bĭl'ĭ-tē) *n.* The degree to which a drug or other substance becomes available at the physiological site of activity after administration.
Bí•o-Bí•o (bē'ō-bē'ō). A river of central Chile flowing c. 386 km (240 mi) from the Andes to the Pacific near Concepción.
bi•o•ce•no•sis also **bi•o•coe•no•sis** (bī'ō-sĭ-nō'sĭs) or **bi•o•ce•nose** (-sē'nōs) *n., pl.* **-ses** (-sēz). A group of interacting organisms that live in a habitat and form an ecological community.
biochemical oxygen demand *n. Microbiol.* See **biological oxygen demand.**
bi•o•chem•is•try (bī'ō-kĕm'ĭ-strē) *n.* **1.** The study of the chemical substances and vital processes occurring in living organisms; biological chemistry; physiological chemistry. **2.** The chemical composition of a particular living system or biological substance. **—bi'o•chem'i•cal** (-ĭ-kəl) *adj. & n.* **—bi'o•chem'i•cal•ly** *adv.* **—bi'o•chem'ist** *n.*
bi•o•chip (bī'ō-chĭp') *n. Comp. Sci.* A computer chip made from organic molecules rather than silicon or germanium.
bi•o•cide (bī'ə-sīd') *n.* A chemical agent capable of destroying living organisms. **—bi'o•cid'al** (-sīd'l) *adj.*
bi•o•com•pat•i•bil•i•ty (bī'ō-kəm-păt'ə-bĭl'ĭ-tē) *n.* The property of being biologically compatible by not producing a toxic, injurious, or immunological response in living tissue. **—bi'o•com•pat'i•ble** *adj.*
bi•o•con•ver•sion (bī'ō-kən-vûr'zhən, -shən) *n.* The conversion of organic materials, such as plant waste, into usable products or energy sources by biological processes or agents.
bi•o•de•grad•a•ble (bī'ō-dĭ-grā'də-bəl) *adj.* Capable of being decomposed by biological agents, esp. bacteria: *a biodegradable detergent.* **—bi'o•de•grad'a•bil'i•ty** *n.* **—bi'o•deg'ra•da'tion** (-dĕg'rə-dā'shən) *n.* **—bi'o•de•grade'** *v.*
bi•o•dy•nam•ic (bī'ō-dī-năm'ĭk, -dĭ-) *adj.* **1.** Of or relating to the study of the effects of dynamic processes on living organisms. **2.** Of or relating to a system of organic crop cultivation.
bi•o•dy•nam•ics (bī'ō-dī-năm'ĭks, -dĭ-) *n.* *(used with a sing. v.)* **1.** The study of the effects of dynamic processes on living organisms. **2.** The science of the force or energy of living matter and physiological processes.
bi•o•e•lec•tric (bī'ō-ĭ-lĕk'trĭk) also **bi•o•e•lec•tri•cal** (-trĭ-kəl) *adj.* **1.** Of or having to do with the electric current generated by living tissue. **2.** Of or relating to the effects of electricity on living tissue.
bi•o•e•lec•tric•i•ty (bī'ō-ĭ-lĕk-trĭs'ĭ-tē, -ē'lĕk-) *n.* An electric current that is generated by living tissue, such as nerve.
bi•o•e•lec•tron•ics (bī'ō-ĭ-lĕk-trŏn'ĭks, -ē-lĕk-) *n.* *(used with a sing. v.)* **1.** The application of the principles of electronics to biology and medicine. **2.** The study of the role of intermolecular electron transfer in physiological processes. **—bi'o•e•lec•tron'ic** *adj.*
bi•o•en•er•get•ics (bī'ō-ĕn'ər-jĕt'ĭks) *n.* *(used with a sing. v.) Biochem.* The study of the flow and transformation of energy in and between living organisms and between living organisms and their environment. **—bi'o•en•er•get'ic** *adj.*
bi•o•en•gi•neer•ing (bī'ō-ĕn'jə-nîr'ĭng) *n.* **1.** The application of engineering principles to the fields of biology and medicine. **2.** Genetic engineering. **—bi'o•en'gi•neer'** *n.*
bi•o•eth•ics (bī'ō-ĕth'ĭks) *n.* *(used with a sing. v.)* The study of the ethical and moral implications of discoveries and advances, as in the fields of genetic engineering. **—bi'o•eth'i•cal** *adj.* **—bi'o•eth'i•cist** (-ĭ-sĭst) *n.*
bi•o•feed•back (bī'ō-fēd'băk') *n.* The technique of using monitoring devices to gain some voluntary control over autonomic bodily functions, such as heart rate.
bi•o•fla•vo•noid (bī'ō-flā'və-noid') *n.* Any of a group of biologically active substances found in plants and functioning in the maintenance of the walls of small blood vessels in mammals.
biog. *abbr.* Biographer; biographical; biography.
bi•o•gas (bī'ō-găs') *n.* A mixture of methane and carbon dioxide produced by bacterial degradation of organic matter and used as a fuel.
bi•o•gen•e•sis (bī'ō-jĕn'ĭ-sĭs) also **bi•og•e•ny** (bī-ŏj'ə-nē) *n.* **1.** The principle that living organisms develop only from other living organisms and not from nonliving matter. **2.** Generation of living organisms from other living organisms. **3.** See **biosynthesis. 4.** The supposed recurrence of the evolutionary stages of a species during ontogeny. **—bi'o•ge•net'ic** (-jə-nĕt'ĭk), **bi'o•ge•net'i•cal** (-ĭ-kəl) *adj.* **—bi'o•ge•net'i•cal•ly** *adv.*
biogenetic law *n.* The theory that ontogeny recapitulates phylogeny.
bi•o•gen•ic (bī'ō-jĕn'ĭk) *adj.* Produced by or necessary for the maintenance of living organisms or biological processes.
bi•o•ge•o•chem•is•try (bī'ō-jē'ō-kĕm'ĭ-strē) *n.* The study of the relationship between regional geochemistry and animal and plant life. **—bi'o•ge'o•chem'i•cal** (-ĭ-kəl) *adj.*
bi•o•ge•og•ra•phy (bī'ō-jē-ŏg'rə-fē) *n.* The study of the geographic distribution of organisms. **—bi'o•ge•og'ra•pher** *n.* **—bi'o•ge'o•graph'ic** (-jē'ə-grăf'ĭk), **bi'o•ge'o•graph'i•cal** (-ĭ-kəl) *adj.*
bi•og•ra•phee (bī-ŏg'rə-fē', bē-) *n.* The subject of a biography.
bi•og•ra•pher (bī-ŏg'rə-fər, bē-) *n.* One who writes, composes, or produces biography.
bi•o•graph•i•cal (bī'ə-grăf'ĭ-kəl) also **bi•o•graph•ic** (-grăf'ĭk) *adj.* **1.** Containing, consisting of, or relating to the facts or events in a person's life. **2.** Of or relating to biography as a literary form. **—bi'o•graph'i•cal•ly** *adv.*
bi•og•ra•phy (bī-ŏg'rə-fē, bē-) *n., pl.* **-phies. 1.** An account of a person's life written, composed, or produced by another. **2.** Biographies considered as a group, esp. as a genre. **3.** The writing, composition, or production of biographies. [LGk. *biographia*: Gk. *bio-*, bio- + Gk. *-graphia*, -graphy.]
bi•o•haz•ard (bī'ō-hăz'ərd) *n.* **1.** A biological agent, such as an infectious microorganism, or a condition that constitutes a threat to human beings, esp. in biological research. **2.** The potential danger from a biohazard.
bi•o•in•stru•men•ta•tion (bī'ō-ĭn'strə-mĕn-tā'shən) *n.* **1.** Use of instruments for the recording or transmission of physiological information, such as heart rate. **2.** The instruments so used.
Bi•o•ko (bē-ō'kō). Formerly **Fer•nan•do Po** (fər-năn'dō pō'). An island of Equatorial Guinea in the Gulf of Guinea.
biol. *abbr.* **1.** Biological; biology. **2.** Biologist.
bi•o•log•i•cal (bī'ə-lŏj'ĭ-kəl) also **bi•o•log•ic** (-lŏj'ĭk) —*adj.* **1.** Of, relating to, caused by, or affecting life or living organisms. **2.** Having to do with biology. **3.** Related by blood: *his biological sister.* —*n.* A preparation synthesized from living organisms and used medically. **—bi'o•log'i•cal•ly** *adv.*
biological clock *n.* A mechanism in organisms that controls the periodicity or rhythm of physiological functions or activities.
biological control *n.* Control of pests through the use of organisms that are natural predators, parasites, or pathogens.
biological half-life *n. Biol.* See **half-life** 2a.
biological oxygen demand *n. Microbiol.* The amount of oxygen required by aerobic microorganisms to decompose the organic matter in a sample of water, used as a measure of the degree of water pollution.
biological warfare *n.* The use of disease-producing microorganisms, toxic biological products, or organic biocides to cause death or injury to humans, animals, or plants.
bi•ol•o•gy (bī-ŏl'ə-jē) *n.* **1.** The science of life and of living organisms, including their structure, function, growth, origin, evolution, and distribution. **2.** The life processes or characteristic phenomena of a group or category of living organisms. **3.** The plant and animal life of a specific area. **—bi•ol'o•gist** *n.*
bi•o•lu•mi•nes•cence (bī'ō-lo͞o'mə-nĕs'əns) *n.* Emission of visible light by living organisms. **—bi'o•lu'mi•nes'cent** *adj.*
bi•ol•y•sis (bī-ŏl'ĭ-sĭs) *n.* **1.** Death of a living organism or tissue caused or accompanied by lysis. **2.** The decomposition of organic material by living organisms, such as microorganisms. **—bi'o•lyt'ic** (bī'ə-lĭt'ĭk) *adj.*
bi•o•mark•er (bī'ō-mär'kər) *n. Medic.* **a.** See **marker** 9. **b.** A specific physical trait used to measure or indicate the effects or progress of a disease or condition.
bi•o•mass (bī'ō-măs') *n.* **1.** The total mass of living matter within a given unit of environmental area. **2.** Plant material, vegetation, or agricultural waste used as an energy source.
bi•o•ma•ter•i•al (bī'ō-mə-tîr'ē-əl) *n.* A biocompatible material used in the replacement of body organs or tissues and in prosthetics. [BIO(COMPATIBLE) + MATERIAL.]
bi•o•math•e•mat•ics (bī'ō-măth'ə-măt'ĭks) *n.* *(used with a sing. v.)* The application of mathematical principles to biological processes. **—bi'o•math'e•mat'i•cal** *adj.* **—bi'o•math'e•ma•ti'cian** (-mə-tĭsh'ən) *n.*
bi•ome (bī'ōm') *n.* A major regional or global biotic community, such as a desert, characterized chiefly by the dominant forms of plant life and the prevailing climate.
bi•o•me•chan•ics (bī'ō-mĭ-kăn'ĭks) *n.* **1.** *(used with a sing. v.)* The study of the mechanics of a living body. **2.** *(used with a pl. v.)* The mechanics of a part or function of a living body. **—bi'o•me•chan'i•cal** *adj.* **—bi'o•me•chan'i•cal•ly** *adv.*
biomedical engineering *n.* See **bioengineering.**
bi•o•med•i•cine (bī'ō-mĕd'ĭ-sĭn) *n.* **1.** The branch of medical science that deals with the ability of human beings to tolerate environmental stresses and variations, as in space

ă pat	oi boy
ā pay	ou out
âr care	o͝o took
ä father	o͞o boot
ĕ pet	ŭ cut
ē be	ûr urge
ĭ pit	th thin
ī pie	*th* this
îr pier	hw which
ŏ pot	zh vision
ō toe	ə about, item
ô paw	

Stress marks:
' (primary);
' (secondary), as in **dictionary** (dĭk'shə-nĕr'ē)

travel. **2.** The application of the principles of the natural sciences to clinical medicine. — **bi′o•med′i•cal** (-ĭ-kəl) *adj.*

bi•o•me•te•or•ol•o•gy (bī′ō-mē′tē-ə-rŏl′ə-jē) *n.* The study of the relationship between atmospheric conditions, such as temperature and humidity, and living organisms.

bi•o•met•rics (bī′ō-mĕt′rĭks) *n.* *(used with a sing. v.)* The statistical study of biological phenomena. — **bi′o•met′ric, bi′o•met′ri•cal** *adj.* — **bi′o•met′ri•cal•ly** *adv.*

bi•om•e•try (bī-ŏm′ĭ-trē) *n.* Biometrics.

bi•on•ic (bī-ŏn′ĭk) *adj.* **1.** Of or relating to bionics. **2.** Having electronically or mechanically enhanced or replaced anatomical structures or physiological processes. **3.** Having extraordinary strength, powers, or capabilities. [BI(O)– + (ELECTR)ONIC.]

bi•on•ics (bī-ŏn′ĭks) *n.* *(used with a sing. v.)* Application of biological principles to the study and design of engineering systems, esp. electronic systems. [BI(O)– + (ELECTR)ONICS.]

bi•o•nom•ics (bī′ə-nŏm′ĭks) *n.* *(used with a sing. v.)* See **ecology** 1a. [< Fr. *bionomique*, pertaining to ecology < *bionomie*, ecology : Gk. *bio-*, bio- + Gk. *-nomia*, -nomy.] — **bi′o•nom′ic, bi′o•nom′i•cal** *adj.* — **bi′o•nom′i•cal•ly** *adv.*

–bi•ont (bī′ŏnt′) *suff.* Living organism; mode of living: *symbiont.* [BI(O)– + –ONT.]

bi•o•or•gan•ic (bī′ō-ôr-găn′ĭk) *adj.* Of or having to do with organic compounds and their role in biochemical processes.

bi•o•phys•ics (bī′ō-fĭz′ĭks) *n.* *(used with a sing. v.)* The science that deals with the application of physics to biological processes and phenomena. — **bi′o•phys′i•cal** *adj.* — **bi′o•phys′i•cal•ly** *adv.* — **bi′o•phys′i•cist** *n.*

bi•o•pol•y•mer (bī′ō-pŏl′ə-mər) *n.* A macromolecule, such as a protein, formed in a living organism.

bi•o•proc•ess (bī′ō-prŏs′ĕs, -prō′sĕs) *n.* **a.** A technique that produces a biological material for commercial use. **b.** Production of a commercially useful chemical or fuel by a biological process. — **bi′o•proc′ess** *v.*

bi•op•sy (bī′ŏp′sē) *n., pl.* **-sies.** The removal and examination of a sample of tissue from a living body for diagnostic purposes. — **bi•op′sic** (bī-ŏp′sĭk), **bi•op′tic** (-tĭk) *adj.*

bi•o•psy•chol•o•gy (bī′ō-sī-kŏl′ə-jē) *n.* See **psychobiology** 1.

bi•o•re•ac•tor (bī′ō-rē-ăk′tər) *n.* **1.** A container for growing living organisms used in the industrial production of substances such as vaccines. **2.** A living organism so used.

birch
Paper birch
Betula papyrifera

bi•o•re•search (bī′ō-rĭ-sûrch′, -rē′sûrch) *n.* Research in the biological sciences.

bi•o•rhythm (bī′ō-rĭth′əm) *n.* An innate, cyclical biological process or function. — **bi′o•rhyth′mic** (-rĭth′mĭk) *adj.*

bi•o•sat•el•lite (bī′ō-săt′l-īt′) *n.* An artificial, recoverable satellite designed to carry humans, animals, or other life.

bi•o•sci•ence (bī′ō-sī′əns) *n.* See **life science.** — **bi′o•sci′en•tif′ic** (-sī′ən-tĭf′ĭk) *adj.* — **bi′o•sci′en•tist** *n.*

bi•os•co•py (bī-ŏs′kə-pē) *n., pl.* **-pies.** Medical examination of a body to determine the presence or absence of life.

–biosis *suff.* A way of living: *parabiosis.* [< Gk. *biōsis*, way of life < *bioun*, to live < *bios*, life. See BIO–.]

bi•o•so•cial (bī′ō-sō′shəl) *adj.* Of or relating to the interaction of biological and social forces. — **bi′o•so′cial•ly** *adv.*

bi•o•sphere (bī′ə-sfîr′) *n.* **1.** The part of the earth and its atmosphere capable of supporting life. **2.** The living organisms and their environment composing the biosphere. — **bi′o•spher′ic** (-sfîr′ĭk, -sfĕr′-) *adj.*

bireme

bi•o•sta•tis•tics (bī′ō-stə-tĭs′tĭks) *n.* *(used with a sing. v.)* Application of statistics to biological and medical data.

bi•o•syn•the•sis (bī′ō-sĭn′thĭ-sĭs) *n.* Formation of a chemical compound by a living organism. — **bi′o•syn•thet′ic** (-thĕt′ĭk) *adj.* — **bi′o•syn•thet′i•cal•ly** *adv.*

bi•o•sys•tem•at•ics (bī′ō-sĭs′tə-măt′ĭks) *n.* *(used with a sing. v.)* The use of data obtained from cytogenetic, biochemical, and other experimental studies to assess the taxonomic relationships of organisms or populations, esp. within an evolutionary framework. — **bi′o•sys′tem•at′ic** *adj.*

bi•o•ta (bī-ō′tə) *n.* The combined flora and fauna of a region. [NLat. < Gk. *biotē*, way of life < *bios*, life. See **g^wei-*.**]

bi•o•tech•nol•o•gy (bī′ō-tĕk-nŏl′ə-jē) *n.* **1.** The use of microorganisms or biological substances to perform specific industrial or manufacturing processes. **2.a.** The application of engineering and technology to the life sciences; bioengineering. **b.** See **ergonomics** 1. — **bi′o•tech′ni•cal** (-nĭ-kəl) *adj.* — **bi′o•tech′no•log′i•cal** (-nə-lŏj′ĭ-kəl) *adj.*

bi•o•te•lem•e•try (bī′ō-tə-lĕm′ĭ-trē) *n.* The monitoring, recording, and measuring of a living organism's physiological functions, such as heart rate, by telemetry.

bi•o•ther•a•py (bī′ō-thĕr′ə-pē) *n., pl.* **-pies.** Treatment of disease with biologicals, such as certain drugs or antitoxins.

bi•ot•ic (bī-ŏt′ĭk) *adj.* **1.** Of or having to do with life or living organisms. **2.** Produced or caused by living organisms. [Prob. Gk. *biōtikos* < *biōtos*, life < *bioun*, to live < *bios*, life. See **g^wei-*.**]

–biotic *suff.* A mode of living: *endobiotic.* [Prob. NLat. *-biōticus* < Gk. *biōtikos.* See BIOTIC.]

biretta

bi•o•tin (bī′ə-tĭn) *n.* A colorless crystalline vitamin, $C_{10}H_{16}N_2O_3S$, of the vitamin B complex, essential for the activity of many enzyme systems. [Gk. *biotos*, life; see BIOTIC + –IN.]

bi•o•tite (bī′ə-tīt′) *n.* A dark-brown to black mica, $K_2(Mg,Fe,Al)_6(Si,Al)_8O_{20}(OH)_4$, found in igneous and metamorphic rocks. [After Jean Baptiste *Biot* (1774–1862), French physicist.] — **bi′o•tit′ic** (-tĭt′ĭk) *adj.*

bi•o•tope (bī′ə-tōp′) *n.* An area that is uniform in environmental conditions and in its distribution of animal and plant life. [BIO– + Gk. *topos*, place.]

bi•o•trans•for•ma•tion (bī′ō-trăns′fər-mā′shən) *n.* Chemical alteration of a substance within the body.

bi•o•tron (bī′ə-trŏn′) *n.* A climate-control chamber used to study an organism's response to environmental conditions.

bi•o•type (bī′ə-tīp′) *n.* A group of organisms having the same genotype. — **bi′o•typ′ic** (-tĭp′ĭk) *adj.*

bip•a•rous (bĭp′ər-əs) *adj.* *Zool.* Producing two offspring in a single birth.

bi•par•ti•san (bī-pär′tĭ-zən, -sən) *adj.* Of, consisting of, or supported by members of two parties, esp. two major political parties. — **bi•par′ti•san•ism** *n.* — **bi•par′ti•san•ship′** *n.*

bi•par•tite (bī-pär′tīt′) *adj.* **1.** Having or consisting of two parts. **2.a.** Having two corresponding parts, one for each party. **b.** Having two participants; joint. **3.** *Bot.* Divided into two portions almost to the base, as certain leaves. [Lat. *bipartītus*, p.part. of *bipartīre*, to divide into two parts : *bi-*, two; see BI–[1] + *partīre*, to part (< *pars*, a share; see **perə-[2]*).] — **bi•par′tite′ly** *adv.* — **bi′par•ti′tion** (-tĭsh′ən) *n.*

bi•ped (bī′pĕd′) *n.* An animal with two feet. — *adj.* also **bi•ped•al** (bī-pĕd′l). Having two feet. [Lat. *bipēs*, *biped-*, two-footed : *bi-*, two; see BI–[1] + *pēs*, foot; see PEDESTRIAN.]

bi•phen•yl (bī-fĕn′əl, -fē′nəl) *n.* A colorless crystalline compound, $C_{12}H_{10}$, used as a heat-transfer agent, in fungicides, and in organic synthesis.

bi•pin•nate (bī-pĭn′āt′) *adj.* *Bot.* Decompound. — **bi•pin′nate′ly** *adv.*

bi•plane (bī′plān′) *n.* An airplane having two pairs of wings at different levels, esp. one above and one below the fuselage.

bi•pod (bī′pŏd′) *n.* A stand having two legs.

bi•po•lar (bī-pō′lər) *adj.* **1.** Relating to or having two poles. **2.** Relating to or involving both of the earth's polar regions. **3.** Having two opposite or contradictory ideas or natures. **4.** *Biol.* Having two poles or opposite extremities. **5.** *Psychol.* Relating to a major affective disorder marked by episodes of mania and depression. — **bi′po•lar′i•ty** (-lăr′ĭ-tē) *n.*

bipolar disorder *n.* *Psychiat.* See **manic-depressive illness.**

bipolar illness *n.* *Psychiat.* See **manic-depressive illness.**

bi•pro•pel•lant (bī′prə-pĕl′ənt) *n.* A two-component rocket propellant, such as liquid hydrogen and liquid oxygen, fed separately to the combustion chamber as fuel and oxidizer.

bi•quad•rat•ic (bī′kwŏ-drăt′ĭk) *Math.* — *adj.* Of or relating to the fourth degree. — *n.* A biquadratic algebraic equation.

bi•quar•ter•ly (bī-kwôr′tər-lē) *adj.* Happening or appearing twice quarterly. — **bi•quar′ter•ly** *adv.*

birch (bûrch) *n.* **1.a.** Any of various deciduous trees or shrubs of the genus *Betula*, native to the Northern Hemisphere and having toothed leaves and bark that often peels in thin papery layers. **b.** The hard close-grained wood of any of these trees. **2.** A rod from a birch, used to administer a whipping. — *tr.v.* **birched, birch•ing, birch•es.** To whip with or as if with a birch. [ME < OE *birce.* See **bherəg-*.**]

Birch•er (bûr′chər) also **Birch•ist** (-chĭst) or **Birch•ite** (-chīt′) *n.* A member or supporter of the John Birch Society, an anti-Communist organization founded in 1958. [After John *Birch* (d. 1945), Amer. missionary and intelligence officer.] — **Birch′ism** *n.* — **Birchist, Birchite** *adj.*

birch partridge *n.* See **ruffed grouse.**

bird (bûrd) *n.* **1.a.** Any of the class Aves of warm-blooded, egg-laying feathered vertebrates with forelimbs modified to form wings. **b.** Such an animal hunted as game. **c.** Such an animal, esp. a chicken or turkey, used as food. **2.** See **clay pigeon.** **3.** *Sports.* See **shuttlecock.** **4.** *Slang.* A rocket, guided missile, satellite, or airplane. **5.** *Slang.* A person, esp. one who is odd or remarkable. **6.** *Chiefly British.* A young woman. **7.** *Slang.* **a.** A loud sound expressing disapproval; a raspberry. **b.** Discharge from employment. **8.** An obscene gesture, as of anger, made by pointing the middle finger upward. — *intr.v.* **bird•ed, bird•ing, birds.** **1.** To observe and identify birds in their natural surroundings. **2.** To trap, shoot, or catch birds. — ***idiom.*** **for the birds.** Objectionable or worthless. [ME < OE *brid*, young bird.] — **bird′ing** *n.*

bird•bath (bûrd′băth′, -bäth′) *n.* A basin filled with water for birds to drink and bathe in.

bird•brain (bûrd′brān′) *n.* *Slang.* A person regarded as silly or stupid. — **bird′brained′** *adj.*

bird•cage (bûrd′kāj′) *n.* A cage for birds.

bird•call (bûrd′kôl′) *n.* **1.** The song or cry of a bird. **2.a.** An imitation of a birdcall. **b.** A small device for producing a birdcall.

bird cherry *n.* Any of several cherry trees, esp. the Eurasian *Prunus padus* having white flowers and small black fruits.

bird dog *n.* **1.** A dog used to hunt game birds; a gun dog. **2.** *Informal.* One that bird-dogs.

bird-dog also **bird•dog** (bûrd′dôg′, -dŏg′) —*v.* **-dogged, -dog•ging, -dogs.** —*intr.* To follow a subject of interest, such as a person or trend, with persistent attention. —*tr.* **1.** To observe or follow closely; monitor: *bird-dogged the suspect's movements.* **2.** To seek out (talent or clients, for example).
bird•er (bûr′dər) *n.* **1.** A bird watcher. **2.a.** A breeder of birds. **b.** A hunter of birds.
bird feed or **bird•feed** (bûrd′fēd′) *n.* Birdseed.
bird-foot violet (bûrd′fo͝ot′) *n.* Var. of **bird's-foot violet.**
bird•house (bûrd′hous′) *n.* **1.** A box with one or more small entry holes, made as a nesting place for birds. **2.** An aviary.
bird•ie (bûr′dē) *n.* **1.** *Informal.* A small bird. **2.** *Sports.* **a.** One stroke under par for a hole in golf. **b.** See **shuttlecock.** —*tr.v.* **-ied, -ie•ing, -ies.** *Sports.* To shoot (a hole in golf) in one stroke under par.
bird•lime (bûrd′līm′) *n.* **1.** A sticky substance that is smeared on branches or twigs to capture small birds. **2.** Something that captures or ensnares. —*tr.v.* **-limed, -lim•ing, -limes. 1.** To smear with birdlime. **2.** To catch with or as if with birdlime.
bird louse *n.* See **biting louse.**
bird•man (bûrd′mən) *n.* **1.** (*also* -măn′). One, such as an ornithologist, who works with birds. **2.** *Slang.* An aviator.
bird of paradise *n., pl.* **birds of paradise. 1.** Any of various birds of the family Paradisaeidae, native to New Guinea and adjacent islands and usu. having brilliant plumage and long tail feathers in the male. **2.** Any of several southern African herbs of the genus *Strelitzia,* esp. *S. reginae* having orange and blue flowers.
bird of passage *n., pl.* **birds of passage. 1.** A migratory bird. **2.** A person who moves from place to place frequently.
bird of prey *n., pl.* **birds of prey.** Any of various predatory carnivorous birds such as the eagle or hawk.
bird pepper *n.* **1.** A variety of pepper *(Capsicum annum* var. *glabriusculum)* that includes the wild forms native to the southern United States and from Mexico south to Colombia. **2.** The small, pungent fruit of this plant.
bird•seed (bûrd′sēd′) *n.* A mixture of various kinds of seeds used for feeding birds.
Birds•eye (bûrd′zī′), **Clarence.** 1886–1956. Amer. inventor who received more than 300 patents, most notably for methods of quick-freezing food.
bird's-eye (bûrdz′ī′) *n.* **1.** A fabric woven with a pattern of small diamonds, each having a dot in the center. **2.** The pattern of such a fabric. —*adj.* **1.** Marked with a spot or spots resembling a bird's eye or eyes, as the bird's-eye maple. **2.** Derived from or as if from an altitude or distance.
bird's-eye maple *n.* A form of wood, chiefly of the sugar maple, that is patterned with small rounded figures.
bird's-foot trefoil (bûrdz′fo͝ot′) *n.* A perennial Old World herb *(Lotus corniculata)* in the pea family, having golden-yellow flowers and clusters of pods arranged like bird claws.
bird's-foot violet also **bird-foot violet** (bûrd′fo͝ot′) *n.* An eastern North American violet *(Viola pedata)* having large flowers and leaves shaped somewhat like a bird's foot.
bird's-nest fern (bûrdz′nĕst′) *n.* An Old World tropical fern *(Asplenium nidus)* having leaves resembling a bird's nest.
bird's-nest fungus *n.* Any of various fungi having a cuplike body containing round egglike stuctures that enclose the spores.
bird watcher or **bird•watch•er** also **bird-watch•er** (bûrd′-wŏch′ər) *n.* A person who observes and identifies birds in their natural surroundings. —**bird watching** *n.*
bi•re•frin•gence (bī′rĭ-frĭn′jəns) *n.* The resolution or splitting of a light wave into two unequally reflected waves by an optically anisotropic medium. —**bi′re•frin′gent** *adj.*
bi•reme (bī′rēm′) *n.* An ancient galley equipped with two tiers of oars on each side. [Lat. *birēmis*: *bi-*, two; see BI-[1] + *rēmus*, oar; see **erə-*.**]
bi•ret•ta also **be•ret•ta** or **ber•ret•ta** (bə-rĕt′ə) *n.* A stiff square cap with three or four ridges across the crown, worn esp. by Roman Catholic clergy. [Ital. *berretta* < OProv. *berret*, cap < LLat. *birrus*, hooded cloak, prob. of Celt. orig.]
bi•ri•a•ni (bĭ′rē-ä′nē) *n.* Var. of **biryani.**
birk (bûrk) *n. Scots.* Birch. [ME *birk* < OE *birce.* See BIRCH.]
Bir•ken•head (bûr′kən-hĕd′). A borough of NW England at the mouth of the Mersey R. near Liverpool. Pop. 341,000.
birl (bûrl) *v.* **birled, birl•ing, birls.** —*tr.* To cause (a floating log) to spin rapidly by rotating with the feet. —*intr.* **1.** To participate in birling. **2.** To spin. —*n.* A whirring noise; a hum. [Blend of BIRR[1] and WHIRL.] —**birl′er** *n.*
birl•ing (bûr′lĭng) *n.* A game, esp. among loggers, in which two competitors try to birl a floating log.
Bir•ming•ham (bûr′mĭng-hăm′). **1.** (*also* -əm). A city of central England NW of London. Pop. 1,022,300. **2.** A city of N-central AL NE of Tuscaloosa. Pop. 265,968. **3.** A city of SE MI, a suburb of Detroit. Pop. 19,997.
birr[1] (bûr) *n.* **1.** A whirring sound. **2.** Strong forward momentum; driving force. —*intr.v.* **birred, birr•ing, birrs.** To make a whirring sound. [ME *bir*, favorable wind < ON *byrr.* See **bher-[1]*.**]
birr[2] (bîr) *n., pl.* **birr** or **birrs.** See table at **currency.** [Prob. of Amharic orig.]
birth (bûrth) *n.* **1.a.** The emergence and separation of offspring from the body of the mother. **b.** The act or process of bearing young; parturition. **c.** The circumstances or conditions relating to this event: *a Bostonian by birth.* **2.a.** The set of characteristics or circumstances received from one's ancestors; inheritance. **b.** Origin; extraction: *of humble birth.* **c.** Noble or high status. **3.** A beginning or commencement. See Syns at **beginning.** —*tr.v.* **birthed, birth•ing, births.** *Chiefly Southern U.S.* **1.** To deliver (a baby). **2.** To bear (a child). [ME, prob. of Scand. orig. See **bher-[1]*.**]
birth canal *n.* The passageway through which the fetus is expelled during parturition, leading from the uterus through the cervix, vagina, and vulva.
birth certificate *n.* An official record of the date and place of a person's birth, usu. including the names of the parents.
birth control *n.* Limitation or control of the number of children born, as by the use of contraception or other devices.
birth control pill *n.* See **oral contraceptive.**
birth•day (bûrth′dā′) *n.* **1.** The day of one's birth. **2.** The anniversary of one's birth.
birthday suit *n.* The state of being nude; nakedness.
birth defect *n.* A physiological or structural abnormality that develops at or before birth and is present at birth, esp. as a result of faulty development, infection, heredity, or injury.
birth•ing (bûr′thĭng) *adj.* Having to do with or used during birth: *a birthing counselor.* —*n.* The act of giving birth.
birth•mark (bûrth′märk′) *n.* A mole or blemish present on the skin from birth; a nevus.
birth pang *n.* **1.** One of the repetitive pains occurring in childbirth. Often used in the plural. **2. birth pangs.** Difficulty or turmoil associated with a development or transition.
birth parent also **birth•par•ent** (bûrth′pâr′ənt, -păr′-) *n.* A biological parent.
birth•place (bûrth′plās′) *n.* The place where someone is born or where something originates.
birth•rate also **birth rate** (bûrth′rāt′) *n.* The ratio of total live births to total population in a specified community or area over a specified period of time.
birth•right (bûrth′rīt′) *n.* **1.** A right, possession, or privilege that is one's due by birth. See Syns at **right. 2.** A special privilege accorded a first-born.
birth•root (bûrth′ro͞ot′, -ro͝ot′) *n.* See **trillium.**
birth•stone (bûrth′stōn′) *n.* A gemstone associated with a month and customarily worn by persons born in that month.
birth•wort (bûrth′wûrt′, -wôrt′) *n.* Any of several herbs or woody vines of the genus *Aristolochia,* having malodorous flowers with unusual shapes.
bi•ry•a•ni also **bi•ri•a•ni** (bĭ′rē-ä′nē) *n.* An Indian dish containing meat, fish, or vegetables and rice flavored with saffron or turmeric. [Hindi or Urdu.]
bis (bĭs) *adv. Mus.* Again; twice. —*interj.* Used to request an additional performance. [Fr. or Ital., both < Lat. See **dwo-*.**]
Bis•cay (bĭs′kā), **Bay of.** An arm of the Atlantic Ocean indenting the W coast of Europe from Brittany in NW France to NW Spain.
Bis•cayne Bay (bĭs-kān′, bĭs′kān′). A narrow inlet of the Atlantic Ocean in SW FL.
bis•cot•to (bĭ-skŏt′ō, bē-skôt′tô) *n., pl.* **bis•cot•ti** (bĭ-skŏt′-ē, bē-skôt′tē). A crisp Italian cookie flavored with anise and often containing almonds or filberts. [Ital. < Med.Lat. *bis coctus*, twice cooked. See BISCUIT.]
bis•cuit (bĭs′kĭt) *n., pl.* **-cuits. 1.** A small cake of shortened bread leavened with baking powder or soda. **2.** *Chiefly British.* **a.** A thin, crisp cracker. **b.** A cookie. **3.** *Color.* A pale brown. **4.** *pl.* **biscuit.** Clay that has been fired once but not glazed. [Middle English *bisquit* < OFr. *biscuit* < Med.Lat. *bis coctus*: Lat. *bis*, twice; see **dwo-*** + Lat. *coctus*, p.part. of *coquere*, to cook; see **pekʷ-*.**]
bise (bēz) *n.* A cold north wind of the Swiss Alps and nearby regions of France and Italy. [ME < OFr., of Gmc. orig.]
bi•sect (bī′sĕkt′, bī-sĕkt′) *v.* **-sect•ed, -sect•ing, -sects.** —*tr.* To cut or divide into two parts, esp. two equal parts. —*intr.* To split; fork. —**bi•sec′tion** *n.* —**bi•sec′tion•al** *adj.* —**bi•sec′tion•al•ly** *adv.*
bi•sec•tor (bī′sĕk′tər, bī-sĕk′-) *n.* Something that bisects, esp. a ray that bisects an angle.
bi•ser•rate (bī-sĕr′āt′) *adj.* **1.** *Bot.* Having serrations that are themselves serrated. **2.** *Zool.* Serrated on both sides.
bi•sex•u•al (bī-sĕk′sho͞o-əl) *adj.* **1.** Of or relating to both sexes. **2.a.** Having both male and female reproductive organs; hermaphroditic. **b.** *Bot.* Of or relating to a single flower that contains functional staminate and pistillate structures. **3.** Of, relating to, or having a sexual orientation to persons of either sex. —*n.* **1.** A bisexual organism; a hermaphrodite. **2.** A bisexual person. —**bi′sex•u•al′i•ty** (-ăl′ĭ-tē) *n.* —**bi•sex′-u•al•ly** *adv.*
Bish•kek (bĭsh′kĕk, bēsh′-). Formerly **Frun•ze** (fro͞on′zə). The cap. of Kirghiz, in the N-central part on the Chu R. Pop. 604,000.
bish•op (bĭsh′əp) *n.* **1.** A high-ranking Christian cleric, in modern churches usu. in charge of a diocese. **2.** *Games.* A usu. miter-shaped chess piece that can move diagonally across

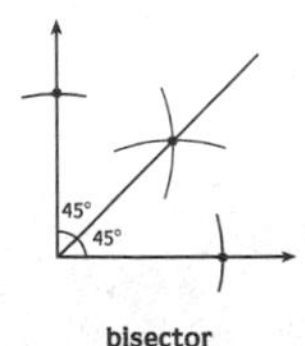

bisector

bishop
Chess piece

ă pat	oi boy
ā pay	ou out
âr care	o͝o took
ä father	o͞o boot
ĕ pet	ŭ cut
ē be	ûr urge
ĭ pit	th thin
ī pie	*th* this
îr pier	hw which
ŏ pot	zh vision
ō toe	ə about, item
ô paw	

Stress marks:
′ (primary);
′ (secondary), as in
dictionary (dĭk′shə-nĕr′ē)

any number of unoccupied spaces. **3.** Mulled port spiced with oranges, sugar, and cloves. [ME < OE *bisceope* < VLat. **ebiscopus* < LLat. *episcopus* < LGk. *episkopos* < Gk., overseer : *epi-*, epi- + *skopos*, watcher; see **spek-***.]

Bish•op (bĭsh′əp), **Elizabeth.** 1911–79. Amer. poet noted for works such as "Filling Station" (1965).

bish•op•ric (bĭsh′ə-prĭk) *n.* **1.** The office or rank of a bishop. **2.** The diocese of a bishop. [ME *bishoprik* < OE *bisceoprīce*, the diocese of a bishop : *bisceop*, bishop; see BISHOP + *rīce*, realm; see **reg-***.]

bish•op's cap (bĭsh′əps) *n.* See **miterwort.**

Bisk (bĭsk, bēsk). See **Biysk.**

Bis•la•ma (bĭs-lä′mə) *n.* A lingua franca that combines Malay and English, spoken in the southwest Pacific. [Pidgin or native variant of BÊCHE-DE-MER.]

Bis•marck (bĭz′märk′). The cap. of ND, in the S-central part on hills overlooking the Missouri R. Pop. 49,256.

Bismarck, Prince **Otto Eduard Leopold von.** "the Iron Chancellor." 1815–98. Creator and first chancellor of the German Empire (1871–90). — **Bis•marck′i•an** *adj.*

Otto von Bismarck

Bismarck Archipelago. A group of volcanic islands and islets of Papua New Guinea in the SW Pacific.

Bismarck Sea. A section of the SW Pacific NE of New Guinea and NW of New Britain; site of a major World War II naval battle (1943).

bis•muth (bĭz′məth) *n. Symbol* **Bi** A highly diamagnetic metallic element used in various low-melting alloys in castings, solders, and fire-safety devices. Atomic number 83; atomic weight 208.980; melting point 271.3°C; boiling point 1,560°C; specific gravity 9.747; valence 3, 5. See table at **element.** [Obsolete Ger. *Bismut* < NLat. *bisemūtum*, ult. < obsolete Ger. *Wismut*: MHGer. *wise*, meadow (< OHGer. *wisa*) + *Mut, Muth*, claim to a mine (< *muten*, to stake a claim, demand, ult. < OHGer. *muot*, mind, spirit; see **mē-¹***).] — **bis′muth•al** *adj.*

bi•son (bī′sən, -zən) *n.* **1.** A bovine mammal *(Bison bison)* of western North America, having large forequarters, a shaggy mane, and a massive head with short curved horns; a buffalo. **2.** An animal *(B. bonasus)* of Europe, similar to but somewhat smaller than the bison; a wisent. [Lat. *bisōn*, of Gmc. orig.; akin to OHGer. *wisunt*.]

bisque¹ (bĭsk) *n.* **1.a.** A rich creamy soup made from meat, fish, or shellfish. **b.** A thick cream soup made of puréed vegetables. **2.** Ice cream mixed with crushed macaroons or nuts. [Perh. < Fr. dial., sour soup < *Biscaye*, Bay of Biscay.]

bisque² (bĭsk) *n.* **1.** See **biscuit** 4. **2.** *Color.* **a.** A pale orange-yellow to yellowish gray. **b.** A color ranging from moderate yellowish pink to grayish yellow. [< BISCUIT.]

bisque³ (bĭsk) *n. Sports.* An advantage allowed an inferior player in certain games, as in tennis, croquet, or golf. [Fr.]

bison
American Plains bison
Bison bison

Bis•sau (bĭ-sou′). The cap. of Guinea-Bissau, on an estuary of the Atlantic; founded 1687. Pop. 109,486.

bis•sex•tile (bī-sĕk′stĭl, -stīl′, bĭ-) *adj.* **1.** Of or relating to a leap year. **2.** Of or relating to the extra day falling in a leap year. —*n.* A leap year. [LLat. *bissextilis*, containing an intercalary day < Lat. *bissextus*, an intercalary day : *bis*, twice; see BIS + *sextus*, sixth, because the sixth day before the Calends of March (February 24) occurred twice every leap year; see SEXT.]

bis•ter or **bis•tre** (bĭs′tər) *n.* **1.** A water-soluble yellowish-brown pigment. **2.** *Color.* A grayish to yellowish brown. [Fr. *bistre*.] — **bis′tered** *adj.*

bis•tort (bĭs′tôrt′) *n.* **1.** A Eurasian perennial herb *(Polygonum bistorta)* having cylindrical flower spikes and a rhizome used as an astringent in folk medicine. **2.** Any of certain related plants of the genus *Polygonum.* [Fr. *bistorte* < OFr. < Med.Lat. **bistorta*: Lat. *bis*, twice; see BIS + *torta*, p.part. of *torquēre*, to twist; see TORQUE¹.]

bis•tro (bē′strō, bĭs′trō) *n., pl.* **-tros. 1.** A small bar, tavern, or nightclub. **2.** A small informal restaurant serving wine. [Fr. *bistro* or *bistrot*, tavern owner, tavern.]

bi•sul•cate (bī-sŭl′kāt′) *adj.* Cleft or cloven, as a hoof.

bi•sul•fate (bī-sŭl′fāt′) *n.* The univalent inorganic acid group HSO_4 or a salt of sulfuric acid containing it.

bi•sul•fide (bī-sŭl′fīd′) *n.* See **disulfide.**

bi•sul•fite (bī-sŭl′fīt′) *n.* The univalent inorganic acid group HSO_3 or a salt of sulfurous acid containing it.

bit¹ (bĭt) *n.* **1.** A small portion, degree, or amount. **2.** A brief amount of time; a moment. **3.a.** A short scene or episode in a theatrical performance. **b.** A bit part. **4.** An entertainment routine given regularly by a performer; an act. **5.** *Informal.* **a.** A particular kind of action, situation, or behavior. **b.** A matter being considered. **6.** *Informal.* An amount equal to ⅛ of a dollar: *two bits.* **7.** *Chiefly British.* A small coin: *a threepenny bit.* —***idioms.* a bit.** To a small degree; somewhat: *a bit warm.* **bit by bit.** Little by little; gradually. [ME *bite*, morsel < OE *bita*. See **bheid-***.]

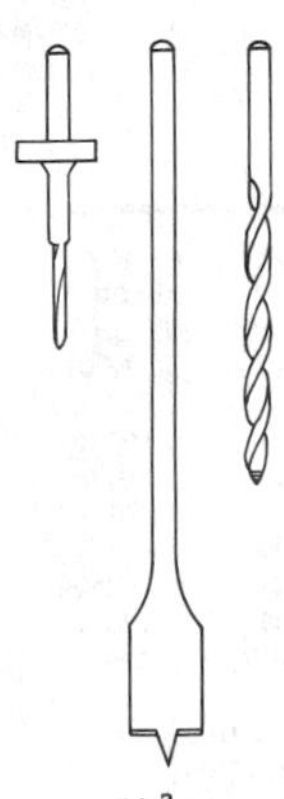
bit²
Left to right: Pilot, spade, and twist bits

bit² (bĭt) *n.* **1.** The sharp part of a tool, such as the cutting edge of an ax. **2.** A pointed and threaded tool for drilling and boring that is secured in a brace, bitstock, or drill press. **3.** The part of a key that engages the bolt and tumblers of a lock. **4.** The tip of the mouthpiece on a pipe or a cigarette or cigar holder. **5.** The metal mouthpiece of a bridle, serving to control, curb, and direct an animal. **6.** Something that controls, guides, or curbs. —*tr.v.* **bit•ted, bit•ting, bits. 1.** To place a bit in the mouth of (a horse, for example). **2.** To check or control with or as if with a bit. **3.** To make or grind a bit on (a key). —***idiom.* have (**or **take) the bit in one's teeth.** To be uncontrollable; to cast off or refuse restraint. [ME *bite* < OE, act of biting. See **bheid-***.]

bit³ (bĭt) *n. Comp. Sci.* **1.** Either of the digits 0 or 1 in the binary number system. **2.** A unit of information equivalent to the choice of either of two equally likely alternatives. **3.** A unit of information storage capacity, as of memory. [Blend of B(INARY) and (DIG)IT.]

bit⁴ (bĭt) *v.* P.t. and p.part. of **bite.**

bi•tar•trate (bī-tär′trāt′) *n.* The group $C_4H_5O_6{}_-$ or a salt of tartaric acid containing it.

bitch (bĭch) *n.* **1.** A female canine animal, esp. a dog. **2.** *Offensive.* **a.** A woman considered to be spiteful or overbearing. **b.** A woman considered to be lewd. **3.** *Slang.* A complaint. **4.** *Slang.* Something very unpleasant or difficult. —*v.* **bitched, bitch•ing, bitch•es.** —*intr.* To complain; grumble. —*tr.* To botch; bungle. [ME *bicche* < OE *bicce*.]

bitch•er•y (bĭch′ə-rē) *n.* Mean remarks or spiteful behavior.

bitch•y (bĭch′ē) *adj.* **-i•er, -i•est.** *Slang.* Malicious, spiteful, or overbearing. — **bitch′i•ly** *adv.* — **bitch′i•ness** *n.*

bite (bīt) *v.* **bit** (bĭt), **bit•ten** (bĭt′n) or **bit, bit•ing, bites.** —*tr.* **1.** To cut, grip, or tear with or as if with the teeth. **2.a.** To pierce the skin of with the teeth, fangs, or mouthparts. **b.** To sting with a stinger. **3.** To cut into with or as if with a sharp instrument. **4.** To grip, grab, or seize: *bitten by a sudden desire to travel.* **5.** To eat into; corrode. **6.** To cause to sting or be painful: *cold that bites the skin.* —*intr.* **1.** To grip, cut into, or injure something with or as if with the teeth. **2.** To have a stinging effect. **3.** To have a sharp taste. **4.** To take or swallow bait. **5.** To be taken in by a ploy or deception. —*n.* **1.** The act of biting. **2.** A skin wound or puncture produced by an animal's teeth or mouthparts. **3.a.** A stinging or smarting sensation. **b.** An incisive, penetrating quality. **4.** An amount removed by or as if by an act of biting. **5.a.** An amount of food taken into the mouth at one time; a mouthful. **b.** *Informal.* A light meal or snack. **6.** The act or an instance of taking bait. **7.a.** A secure grip or hold applied by a tool or machine upon a working surface. **b.** The part of a tool or machine that presses against and maintains a firm hold on a working surface. **8.** *Dentistry.* The angle at which the upper and lower teeth meet; occlusion. **9.** The corrosive action of acid upon an etcher's metal plate. **10.** *Slang.* An amount of money appropriated or withheld. —***idioms.* bite off more than one can chew.** To decide or agree to do more than one can finally accomplish. **bite the bullet.** *Slang.* To face a painful situation bravely and stoically. **bite the dust.** *Slang.* **1.** To fall dead, esp. in combat. **2.** To be defeated. **3.** To come to an end. **bite the hand that feeds (one).** To repay generosity or kindness with ingratitude and injury. [ME *biten* < OE *bītan*. See **bheid-***.] — **bit′a•ble, bite′a•ble** *adj.* — **bit′er** *n.*

bite•plate also **bite plate** (bīt′plāt′) *n.* A removable dental appliance worn in the palate and used as a diagnostic or therapeutic aid.

bite•wing (bīt′wĭng′) *n.* A dental x-ray film with a central projection on which the teeth can close.

Bi•thyn•i•a (bĭ-thĭn′ē-ə). An ancient country of NW Asia Minor in present-day Turkey; orig. inhabited by Thracians and absorbed into the Roman Empire by the end of the 1st cent. B.C. — **Bi•thyn′i•an** *adj. & n.*

bit•ing (bī′tĭng) *adj.* **1.** Causing a stinging sensation. **2.** Capable of gripping and affecting or wounding: *a biting aphorism.* — **bit′ing•ly** *adv.*

biting louse *n.* Any of several small, wingless, biting insects of the order Mallophaga that are external parasites on birds.

biting midge *n.* See **punkie.**

bi•tok (bē′tŏk) *n.* A dish made from ground meat mixed with milk, bread, and onions to form patties that are fried and served with a sour cream sauce. [Russ. < Fr. *bifteck (haché)*, (ground) beef < BEEFSTEAK.]

Bi•to•la (bēt′l-yä′, bē′tôl-yä′). A city of S Macedonia near the Greek border; an important military and commercial center in the 15th and 16th cent. Pop. 72,900.

bit part *n.* A small or insignificant role, as in a play or movie, usu. having a few spoken lines.

bit•stock (bĭt′stŏk′) *n.* A handle used to secure and turn a drilling or boring bit; a brace.

bitt (bĭt) *Naut.* —*n.* A vertical post, usu. one of a pair, set on the deck of a ship and used to secure lines or cables. —*tr.v.* **bitt•ed, bitt•ing, bitts.** To wind (a cable) around a bitt. [Perh. of Du. or LGer. orig.; akin to ON *biti*, crossbeam.]

bit•ten (bĭt′n) *v.* A p.part. of **bite.**

bit•ter (bĭt′ər) *adj.* **-er, -est. 1.** Having or being a taste that is sharp, acrid, and unpleasant. **2.** Causing a sharply unpleasant, painful, or stinging sensation; harsh. **3.** Difficult or distasteful to accept, admit, or bear. **4.** Proceeding from or exhibiting strong animosity: *bitter foes.* **5.** Resulting from or expressive of severe grief, anguish, or disappointment. **6.** Marked by resentment or cynicism. — *adv.* In an intense or harsh way. — *tr.v.* **-tered, -ter•ing, -ters.** To make bitter. — *n.* **1.** That which is bitter. **2. bitters.** A bitter, usu. alcoholic liquid made with herbs or roots and used in cocktails or as a tonic. **3.** *Chiefly British.* A sharp-tasting beer made with hops. [ME < OE. See **bheid-*.**] — **bit′ter•ly** *adv.* — **bit′ter•ness** *n.*

bitter almond *n.* A variety of almond *(Prunus dulcis* var. *amara)* having kernels that yield an oil used for flavoring.

bitter aloes *pl.n.* *(used with a sing. v.)* See **aloe** 3.

bitter apple *n.* See **colocynth.**

bit•ter•brush (bĭt′ər-brŭsh′) *n.* A shrub of the genus *Purshia,* esp. *P. tridentata* of western North America.

bitter cress *n.* Any of several herbs of the genus *Cardamine* in the mustard family, having usu. divided leaves and pods that dehisce explosively.

bitter end *n.* **1.** A final, painful, or disastrous extremity. **2.** *Naut.* The inboard end of a chain, line, or cable, esp. the end of a rope or cable that is wound around a bitt. [E. *bitter,* bitt (BITT + -ER¹) + END. Sense 1, influenced by BITTER.]

bit•ter•end•er or **bit•ter-end•er** (bĭt′ər-ĕn′dər) *n.* One who persists until it becomes impossible to continue.

bit•tern¹ (bĭt′ərn) *n.* Any of several wading birds of the genera *Botaurus* and *Ixobrychus,* having brownish plumage and a deep cry in the male. [ME *bitour* (with *-n* perh. from HERON) < OFr. *butor,* poss. < VLat. **buti-taurus:* Lat. *būtiō,* buzzard + Lat. *taurus,* bull (after its cry); see **tauro-*.**]

bit•tern² (bĭt′ərn) *n.* The bitter water solution of bromides, magnesium, and calcium salts remaining after sodium chloride is crystallized out of seawater. [< BITTER.]

bit•ter•nut (bĭt′ər-nŭt′) *n.* A hickory tree *(Carya cordiformis)* of eastern North America having bitter thin-shelled nuts.

bitter orange *n.* See **sour orange.**

bit•ter•root (bĭt′ər-ro͞ot′, -ro͝ot′) *n.* A perennial herb *(Lewisia rediviva)* of western North America having an edible root.

Bit•ter•root Range (bĭt′ər-ro͞ot′, -ro͝ot′). A chain of the Rocky Mts. along the ID–MT border rising to 3,474.9 m (11,393 ft).

bit•ter•sweet (bĭt′ər-swēt′) *n.* **1.** A vine of the genus *Celastrus,* esp. the North American species *C. scandens* and the eastern Asian species *C. orbiculata,* having yellow-orange fruits that open at maturity to expose red seeds. **2.** See **bittersweet nightshade. 3.** *Color.* A dark to deep reddish orange. — *adj.* **1.** Bitter and sweet at the same time: *bittersweet chocolate.* **2.** Producing or expressing a mixture of pain and pleasure. **3.** *Color.* Dark to deep reddish-orange. [After its roots, which are said to taste bitter, then sweet when chewed.]

bittersweet nightshade *n.* A poisonous climbing or trailing plant *(Solanum dulcamara)* native to Eurasia and having violet flowers and red berries. [After its roots, which are said to taste bitter, then sweet when chewed.]

bit•ty (bĭt′ē) *adj.* **-ti•er, -ti•est. 1.** *Informal.* Tiny. **2.** *Chiefly British.* Composed of small segments lacking cohesion; fragmented. — **bit′ti•ness** *n.*

bi•tu•men (bĭ-to͞o′mən, -tyo͞o′-, bī-) *n.* Any of various flammable mixtures of hydrocarbons and other substances, occurring naturally or obtained by distillation from coal or petroleum, that are a component of asphalt and tar. [ME *bithumen,* a mineral pitch < Lat. *bitūmen,* perh. of Celt. orig.] — **bi•tu′mi•noid′** (-mə-noid′) *adj.* — **bi•tu′mi•nize′** *v.* — **bi•tu′mi•ni•za′tion** (-nĭzā′shən) *n.*

bi•tu•mi•nous (bĭ-to͞o′mə-nəs, -tyo͞o′-, bī-) *adj.* **1.** Like or containing bitumen. **2.** Of or relating to bituminous coal.

bituminous coal *n.* A mineral coal with a high percentage of volatile matter that burns with a smoky yellow flame.

bi•va•lent (bī-vā′lənt) *adj.* **1.** *Chem.* Divalent. **2.** *Biol.* Consisting of a pair of homologous synapsed chromosomes, associated together during meiosis; double. — *n. Biol.* A pair of bivalent chromosomes. — **bi•va′lence, bi•va′len•cy** *n.*

bi•valve (bī′vălv′) *n.* A mollusk, such as an oyster or a clam, that has a shell consisting of two hinged valves. — *adj.* **1.** Having a shell consisting of two hinged valves. **2.** Consisting of two similar separable parts. — **bi′valved′** *adj.*

biv•ou•ac (bĭv′o͞o-ăk′, bĭv′wăk′) *n.* A temporary encampment often in an unsheltered area. — *intr.v.* **-acked, -ack•ing, -acs** also **-acks.** To camp in a bivouac. [Fr. < Ger. dial. *beiwacht,* supplementary night watch : *bei-,* beside (< MHGer. *bi-* (< OHGer.; see **ambhi***) + *Wacht,* watch, vigil (< MHGer. *wahte* < OHGer. *wahta;* see **weg-***).]

Bi•wa (bē′wä). A lake of S Honshu, Japan, W of Nagoya.

bi•week•ly (bī-wēk′lē) *adj.* **1.** Happening every two weeks. **2.** Happening twice a week; semiweekly. — *n., pl.* **-lies.** A publication issued every two weeks. See Usage Note at **bi-¹.** — **bi•week′ly** *adv.*

bi•year•ly (bī-yîr′lē) *adj.* **1.** Happening every two years. **2.** Happening twice a year; semiyearly. — **bi•year′ly** *adv.*

Bi•ysk (bē′ĭsk, bēsk) or **Bisk** (bĭsk, bēsk). A city of S-central Russia ESE of Barnaul; founded 1709. Pop. 226,000.

biz (bĭz) *n. Slang.* Business.

bi•zarre (bĭ-zär′) *adj.* Strikingly unconventional and far-fetched in style or appearance; odd. See Syns at **fantastic.** [Fr. < Sp. *bizarro,* brave, prob. < Basque *bizar,* beard.] — **bi•zarre′ly** *adv.* — **bi•zarre′ness** *n.*

Bi•zer•te (bĭ-zûr′tē, bē-zĕrt′). A city of N Tunisia on the Mediterranean NW of Tunis. Pop. 62,856.

Bi•zet (bē-zā′), **Alexandre César Léopold.** "Georges Bizet." 1838–75. French composer of the opera *Carmen* (1875).

B.J. *abbr.* Bachelor of Journalism.

Björn•son (byûrn′sən), **Björnstjerne.** 1832–1910. Norwegian writer who won the 1903 Nobel Prize for literature.

Bk The symbol for the element **berkelium.**

bk. *abbr.* **1.** Bank. **2.** Book.

bkg. *abbr.* Banking.

bkgd. *abbr.* Background.

bklr. *abbr. Print.* Black letter.

bkpg. *abbr.* Bookkeeping.

bkpt. *abbr.* Bankrupt.

bks. *abbr.* **1.** Barracks. **2.** Books.

bl. *abbr.* **1.** Barrel. **2.** Black. **3.** Blue.

B.L. *abbr.* **1.** Bachelor of Laws. **2.** Bachelor of Letters. **3.** Bachelor of Literature.

B/L *abbr.* Bill of lading.

B.L.A. *abbr.* Bachelor of Liberal Arts.

blab (blăb) *v.* **blabbed, blab•bing, blabs.** — *tr.* To reveal (secret matters) esp. through indiscreet or unreserved talk. — *intr.* **1.** To reveal secret matters. **2.** To chatter thoughtlessly or indiscreetly. — *n.* **1.** An incessant or indiscreet talker. **2.** Lengthy chatter. [ME *blabben,* to talk foolishly, back-formation < *blaberen.*] — **blab′by** *adj.*

blab•ber (blăb′ər) *intr.v.* **-bered, -ber•ing, -bers.** To chatter; babble. — *n.* **1.** Idle chatter. **2.** A blabbermouth. [ME *blaberen.*]

bittern¹
American bittern
Botaurus lentiginosus

blab•ber•mouth (blăb′ər-mouth′) *n. Informal.* One who talks indiscreetly or incessantly.

black (blăk) *adj.* **black•er, black•est. 1.** *Color.* Being of the color black, producing or reflecting comparatively little light and having no predominant hue. **2.** Having little or no light: *a black, moonless night.* **3.** Often **Black. a.** Of, relating to, or belonging to a racial group having brown to black skin, esp. one of African origin. **b.** Of, relating to, or belonging to an American ethnic group descended from African peoples having dark skin; African American; Afro-American. **4.** Very dark in color: *rich black soil.* **5.** Soiled, as from soot. **6.** Evil; wicked. **7.** Cheerless and depressing; gloomy: *black thoughts.* **8.** Marked by anger or sullenness: *a black look.* **9.** Often **Black.** Attended with disaster; calamitous. **10.** Deserving of, indicating, or incurring censure or dishonor. **11.** Wearing clothing of the darkest visual hue: *the black knight.* **12.** Served without milk or cream. **13.** *Chiefly British.* Boycotted as part of a labor union action. — *n.* **1.** *Color.* **a.** The achromatic color value of minimum lightness or maximum darkness; the color of objects that absorb nearly all light of all visible wavelengths; one extreme of the neutral gray series, the opposite being white. **b.** A pigment or dye having this color value. **2.** Complete or almost complete absence of light; darkness. **3.** Clothing of the darkest hue, esp. such clothing worn for mourning. **4.** Often **Black. a.** A member of a racial group having brown to black skin, esp. one of African origin. **b.** An American descended from peoples of African origin having brown to black skin; an African American; an Afro-American. **5.** Something that is colored black. **6.** *Games.* **a.** The black-colored pieces, as in chess or checkers. **b.** The player using these pieces. — *v.* **blacked, black•ing, blacks.** — *tr.* **1.** To make black. **2.** To apply blacking to. **3.** *Chiefly British.* To boycott as part of a labor union action. — *intr.* To become black. — ***phrasal verb.*** **black out. 1.a.** To lose consciousness or memory temporarily. **b.** To suppress (a fact or memory, for example) from conscious recognition. **2.** To prohibit the dissemination of, esp. by censorship. **3.** To extinguish or conceal all lights that might help enemy aircraft find a target during an air raid. **4.** To extinguish all the lights on (a stage). **5.** To cause a failure of electrical power in. **6.a.** To withhold (a televised event or program) from a broadcast area. **b.** To withhold a televised event or program from. — ***idiom.*** **in the black.** On the credit side of a ledger; prosperous. [ME *blak* < OE *blæc.* See **bhel-¹*.**] — **black′ish** *adj.* — **black′ly** *adv.* — **black′ness** *n.*

Usage Note: *Black* is often capitalized in its use to denote persons, though the lowercased form *black* is still widely used by authors of all races: *"Together, blacks and whites can move our country beyond racism"* (Whitney Moore Young, Jr.). Use of the capitalized form has the advantage of acknowledging the parallel with other ethnic groups and nationalities. Although *Black* is best given in its uppercase form for the reasons given here, it is probably best not to capitalize the term *white,* because that might be taken to imply that whites constitute a single ethnic group, an issue that is certainly debatable. See Usage Note at **color.**

Black (blăk), **Hugo La Fayette.** 1886–1971. Amer. jurist; associate justice of the U.S. Supreme Court (1937–71).

Black, Joseph. 1728–99. British chemist who rediscovered carbon dioxide (1756).

Black, Shirley Temple. b. 1927? Amer. actress and public official. As Shirley Temple she was an immensely popular child actress of the 1930's.

ă **pat**	oi **boy**
ā **pay**	ou **out**
âr **care**	o͝o **took**
ä **father**	o͞o **boot**
ĕ **pet**	ŭ **cut**
ē **be**	ûr **urge**
ĭ **pit**	th **thin**
ī **pie**	*th* **this**
îr **pier**	hw **which**
ŏ **pot**	zh **vision**
ō **toe**	ə **about,**
ô **paw**	**item**

Stress marks:
′ (primary);
′ (secondary), as in
dictionary (dĭk′shə-nĕr′ē)

black alder *n.* **1.** A widespread North American deciduous shrub or small tree *(Ilex verticillata)* of the holly family. **2.** A Eurasian alder tree *(Alnus glutinosa).*

black•a•moor (blăk′ə-mo͝or′) *n. Offensive.* A dark-skinned person, esp. a person from northern Africa. [BLACK + *-a-*, of unknown orig. + MOOR.]

black-and-blue (blăk′ən-blo͞o′) *adj.* Discolored from coagulation of blood below the surface of the skin.

black-and-tan (blăk′ən-tăn′) *adj.* **1.** Having a black coat with tannish markings. Used of a dog. **2.** Involving, recognizing, or admitting Black and white people equally.

Black and Tan *n., pl.* **Black and Tans.** A member of the Royal Irish Constabulary, a force of British soldiers sent to Ireland to suppress the Sinn Fein rebellion of 1919 to 1921. [From the color of their uniform.]

black-and-tan terrier *n.* See **Manchester terrier.**

black and white *n.* **1.** Writing or print. **2.** A visual medium, as in photography, employing only black and white or black, white, and values of gray.

black-and-white (blăk′ən-hwīt′, -wīt′) *adj.* **1.** Partially black and partially white. **2.** Being in writing or print. **3.a.** Rendered in black and white or in achromatic colors. **b.** Of or relating to the reproduction or presentation of visual images in black and white. **4.** Expressing, recognizing, or based on two mutually exclusive sets of ideas or values.

Black Ang•us (ăng′gəs) *n.* See **Aberdeen Angus.**

black art *n.* Sorcery; witchcraft.

black bear
American black bear
Ursus americanus

black•ball (blăk′bôl′) *n.* **1.** A negative vote, esp. one that blocks the admission of an applicant to an organization. **2.** A small black ball used as a negative ballot. —*tr.v.* **-balled, -ball•ing, -balls. 1.** To vote against, esp. to veto the admission of. **2.** To shut out from social or commercial participation; ostracize or boycott. — **black′ball′er** *n.*

black bass (băs) *n.* Any of several North American freshwater game fishes of the genus *Micropterus.*

black bear *n.* **1.** The common North American bear *(Euarctos* or *Ursus americanus)* that lives in forests, is omnivorous, and has a black or dark brown coat. **2.** Any of several black or dark brown Asiatic bears, esp. *Selenarctos thibetanus* with a pointed snout and a white V-shaped mark on the chest.

Black•beard (blăk′bîrd′). See Edward **Teach.**

black belt *n.* **1.a.** The black sash that symbolizes the rank of expert in a martial art such as judo or karate. **b.** A person who has attained this rank. **2.** A region of rich, black soil.

black•ber•ry (blăk′bĕr′ē) *n.* **1.** Any of various shrubs of the genus *Rubus,* having usu. prickly stems and an aggregate fruit of drupelets. **2.** The edible fruit of these plants.

black bile *n.* One of the four humors of medieval physiology, supposed to cause melancholy.

black bindweed or **black-bind•weed** (blăk′bīnd′wēd′) *n.* A twining annual vine *(Polygonum convolvulus)* native to Eurasia and having heart-shaped leaves.

black birch *n.* See **sweet birch.**

black•bird (blăk′bûrd′) *n.* **1.** Any of various New World birds of the family Icteridae, the male of which has black or predominantly black plumage. **2.** An Old World songbird *(Turdus merula),* the male of which is black with a yellow bill.

black•board (blăk′bôrd′, -bōrd′) *n.* A smooth, hard, dark-colored panel for writing on with chalk.

blackberry

black•bod•y (blăk′bŏd′ē) *n.* A theoretically perfect absorber of all incident radiation.

black book *n.* A book containing names of people and organizations to blacklist.

black box *n.* **1.** A device or theoretical construct whose means of operation is unknown. **2.** See **flight recorder.**

black bryony *n.* A poisonous, perennial twining herb *(Tamus communis)* native to Eurasia and having red berries.

black•buck (blăk′bŭk′) *n.* An antelope *(Antilope cervicapra)* of India that inhabits open grasslands and in the male has long spiraled horns and a black coat with white underparts.

Black•burn (blăk′bûrn′). A borough of NW England NNW of Manchester. Pop. 141,700.

Blackburn, Mount. A peak, 5,039.5 m (16,523 ft), of the Wrangell Mts. in S AK.

black•cap (blăk′kăp′) *n.* **1.** See **black raspberry** 1. **2.a.** A small European warbler *(Sylvia atricapilla),* the male of which is gray with a black crown. **b.** Any of various other black-crowned birds, such as the chickadee.

black cherry *n.* **1.a.** A deciduous North American tree *(Prunus serotina)* having drooping elongate clusters of white flowers and blackish fruits. **b.** The reddish-brown wood of this tree. **2.** Any of various dark-fruited kinds of cherry.

black•cock (blăk′kŏk′) *n.* The male of the black grouse.

black cod *n.* See **sablefish.**

black cohosh *n.* An eastern North American perennial herb *(Cimicifuga racemosa)* having large, pinnately compound leaves and racemes of small white flowers.

black-eyed Susan
Rudbeckia hirta

black comedy *n.* Comedy that uses black humor.

black cow *n. Chicago.* A float made with root beer and vanilla ice cream. [BLACK + COW[1] (from the ice cream).]

black crappie *n.* An edible North American sunfish *(Pomoxis nigromaculatus)* having dark mottled coloring.

black cumin *n.* An annual Eurasian herb *(Nigella sativa)* having bluish-white flowers and pungent black seeds used as a seasoning in Asian cuisines.

black•damp (blăk′dămp′) *n.* A suffocating gas that consists of a mixture of carbon dioxide and nitrogen, found in mines after fires or explosions. [BLACK + DAMP, gas.]

Black Death *n.* A form of bubonic plague, caused by the bacillus *Yersinia* (or *Pasturella*) *pestis,* that was pandemic throughout Europe and much of Asia in the 14th century. [From the dark splotches it causes on its victims.]

black diamond *n.* **1.** See **carbonado[2]. 2. black diamonds.** Coal.

black duck *n.* A common duck *(Anas rubripes)* of the northeast United States and Canada, characterized by dark plumage.

black•en (blăk′ən) *v.* **-ened, -en•ing, -ens.** —*tr.* **1.** To make black. **2.** To sully or defame: *a scandal that blackened his name.* **3.** To sear in a hot skillet until black. —*intr.* To become dark or black. — **black′en•er** *n.*

Black English *n.* The range of varieties of English spoken by American Black people.

Usage Note: In linguistic usage *Black English* refers to the entire range of varieties of English spoken by American Black people of any educational or social level. When reference is made to the nonstandard varieties of English used by certain Black speakers, the preferred terms are *Vernacular Black English* or *Black English Vernacular.*

Black•ett (blăk′ĭt), Baron **Patrick Maynard Stuart.** 1897–1974. British physicist who won a 1948 Nobel Prize.

black eye *n.* **1.** A bruised discoloration of the flesh surrounding the eye. **2.** A dishonored reputation; a bad name.

black-eyed pea (blăk′īd′) *n.* See **cowpea.**

black-eyed Su•san (so͞o′zən) *n.* Any of several North American herbs of the genus *Rudbeckia* in the composite family, having flower heads with yellow rays and dark centers.

black•face (blăk′fās′) *n.* **1.** Makeup for a comic travesty of Black people, esp. in a minstrel show. **2.** An actor wearing such makeup in a minstrel show.

black•fish (blăk′fĭsh′) *n., pl.* **blackfish** or **-fish•es. 1.** Any of various dark-colored fishes, such as: **a.** A small, edible freshwater fish *(Dallia pectoralis)* of Alaska and Siberia, noted for its ability to withstand freezing. **b.** See **tautog. 2.** See **pilot whale.**

black flag *n.* A Jolly Roger.

black fly *n.* Any of various small, dark-colored biting flies of the family Simuliidae, the larvae of which attach to rocks in running streams.

Black•foot (blăk′fo͝ot′) *n., pl.* **Blackfoot** or **-feet** (-fēt′). **1.** A member of a Native American confederacy located on the northern Great Plains, composed of the Blackfoot, Blood, and Piegan tribes. **2.** A member of the northernmost tribe of the Blackfoot confederacy, inhabiting central Alberta. **3.** The Algonquian language of the Blackfoot, Blood, and Piegan. **4.** See **Sihasapa.** — **Black′foot′** *adj.*

black-foot•ed albatross (blăk′fo͝ot′ĭd) *n.* An albatross *(Diomedea nigripes)* of the Pacific coastal islands that is blackish and dusky with black feet and a whitish face.

black-footed ferret *n.* A North American weasel *(Mustela nigripes)* that has a blackish mask and feet.

Blackfoot Sioux *n., pl.* **Blackfoot Sioux.** See **Sihasapa.**

Black Forest. A mountainous region of SW Germany between the Rhine and Neckar rivers.

black frost *n.* A dry freeze that results in the internal freezing and death of vegetation.

black gold *n. Informal.* Petroleum.

black grouse *n.* A Eurasian game bird *(Lyrurus tetrix)* with black plumage in the male.

black•guard (blăg′ərd, -ärd′) *n.* **1.** An unprincipled person; a scoundrel. **2.** A foul-mouthed person. —*tr.v.* **-guard•ed, -guard•ing, -guards.** To abuse verbally; revile. — **black′guard•ism** *n.* — **black′guard•ly** *adj. & adv.*

black gum *n.* See **sour gum.**

Black Hand *n.* A secret society organized for acts of terrorism and blackmail that was active in the United States in the early 20th century.

black haw *n.* Either of two deciduous plants *(Viburnum lentago* or *V. prunifolium)* native to the eastern United States and having white flowers and blue-black berrylike fruits.

Black Hawk. 1767–1838. Sauk leader. Resenting an 1804 treaty that ceded all Sauk and Fox lands E of the Mississippi R. to the U.S., he led 1,000 Sauk and Fox warriors in the Black Hawk War (1832).

black•head (blăk′hĕd′) *n.* **1.** *Medic.* A plug of keratin and sebum within a hair follicle that is blackened at the surface. **2.** An infectious disease of turkeys and some wildfowl that is caused by a protozoan *(Histomonas meleagridis)* and results in lesions of the intestine and liver. **3.** Any of various birds, such as the scaup, with dark head markings.

Black Hills. A group of rugged mountains of SW SD and NE WY rising to 2,208.8 m (7,242 ft).

black hole *n.* **1.** An extremely small region of space-time with a gravitational field so intense that nothing can escape, not even light. **2.** A great void; an abyss.

black humor *n.* The juxtaposition, as in writing or drama, of morbid or absurd elements with comical or farcical ones. — **black humorist** *n.*
black ice *n.* A thin, nearly invisible coating of ice.
black•ing (blăk′ĭng) *n.* **1.** See **lampblack. 2.** A preparation, such as a shoe or stove polish, used to impart a black color.
black•jack (blăk′jăk′) *n.* **1.** A leather-covered bludgeon with a short shaft or strap, used as a hand weapon. **2.** The blackjack oak. **3.** *Games.* A card game in which the object is to accumulate cards with a higher count than that of the dealer but not exceeding 21. **4.** Sphalerite. — *tr.v.* **-jacked, -jack•ing, -jacks. 1.** To hit or beat with a blackjack. **2.** To coerce by threats. [BLACK + JACK.]
blackjack oak *n.* A deciduous oak tree *(Quercus marilandica)* native mostly to the southeastern United States and having blackish bark.
black knot *n.* A disease of the plum, the cherry, and related plants caused by the fungus *Apiosporina morbosa* and resulting in black knotlike swellings on the branches.
black lead (lĕd) *n.* See **graphite.**
black•leg (blăk′lĕg′) *n.* **1.** An infectious, usu. fatal bacterial disease of cattle and other animals, characterized by gas-filled swellings in the musculature. **2.** A bacterial or fungal disease of certain plants that turns the stems black at the soil line. **3.** One who cheats at cards; a cardsharp. **4.** *Chiefly British.* A worker opposed to trade unions; a scab.
black letter *n. Print.* A heavy typeface with very broad counters and thick ornamental serifs.
black light *n.* Invisible ultraviolet or infrared radiation that is used to take pictures in the dark.
black•light trap (blăk′līt′) *n.* An insect trap that attracts a wide variety of insects by the use of a form of black light.
black•list (blăk′lĭst′) *n.* A list of persons or organizations that have incurred disapproval or suspicion or are to be boycotted or otherwise penalized. — *tr.v.* **-list•ed, -list•ing, -lists.** To place on or as if on a blacklist. — **black′list′er** *n.*
black locust *n.* A deciduous tree *(Robinia pseudoacacia)* in the pea family, native to the United States and having alternate, pinnately compound leaves and fragrant white flowers.
black lung *n.* Pneumoconiosis caused by the long-term inhalation of coal dust.
black magic *n.* Magic practiced for evil purposes or in league with supposed evil spirits; witchcraft.
black•mail (blăk′māl′) *n.* **1.a.** Extortion, as of money, from a person by the threat of exposing a criminal act or discreditable information. **b.** Something of value extorted in this manner. **2.** Tribute formerly paid to freebooters along the Scottish border for protection from pillage. [BLACK + MAIL[3].] — **black′mail′** *v.* — **black′mail′er** *n.*
Black Ma•ri•a (mə-rī′ə) *n.* A patrol wagon. [BLACK + the name *Maria.*]
black market *n.* **1.** The illegal business of buying or selling goods or currency in violation of restrictions such as price controls or rationing. **2.** A place where these illegal operations are carried on. — **black′-mar′ket** (blăk′mär′kĭt) *adj.* — **black′-mar′ket•er, black′-mar′ket•eer′** (-mär′kĭ-tîr′) *n.* — **black′-mar′ket•eer′ing** *n.*
black-mar•ket (blăk′mär′kĭt) *tr.v.* **-ket•ed, -ket•ing, -kets.** To trade (something) in the black market.
black mass *n.* **1.** A travesty of the Roman Catholic Mass, ascribed to reputed worshipers of Satanism. **2. Black Mass.** *Informal.* A Requiem Mass.
black measles *n. (used with a sing. or pl. v.)* A severe form of measles characterized by dark, hemorrhagic skin eruptions.
black medic or **black medick** *n.* A cloverlike Eurasian plant *(Medicago lupulina)* in the pea family, having dense clusters of small yellow flowers and black pods. [BLACK + MEDIC[1].]
black money *n.* Income, as from illegal activities, that is not reported to the government for tax purposes.
Black Mountains. A range of the Blue Ridge in W NC rising to 2,038.6 km (6,684 ft).
Black•mun (blăk′mən), **Harry Andrew.** b. 1908. Amer. jurist; associate justice of the U.S. Supreme Court (since 1970).
Black Muslim *n.* A member of a chiefly Black American group, the Nation of Islam, that professes Islamic religious beliefs.
black mustard *n.* A weedy, annual Eurasian plant *(Brassica nigra)* in the mustard family, having racemes of yellow flowers and pungent seeds.
Black Nationalist *n.* A member of a group of militant Black people who urge separatism from white people and self-government for Black communities. — **Black Nationalism** *n.*
black nightshade *n.* A poisonous annual Eurasian plant *(Solanum nigrum),* widespread as a weed and having clusters of white star-shaped flowers and usu. blackish berries.
black oak *n.* A deciduous North American tree *(Quercus velutina)* having a blackish bark and durable wood.
black•out (blăk′out′) *n.* **1.** The concealment or extinguishment of lights that might be visible during an air raid. **2.** Lack of illumination caused by an electrical power failure. **3.a.** The extinguishing of all stage lights in a theater to indicate the passage of time or mark the end of a scene. **b.** A short, comic vaudeville skit that ends with lights off. **4.** A temporary loss of memory or consciousness. **5.a.** A suppression, as of news, by censorship. **b.** Restriction or prohibition of telecasting a sports event to ensure ticket sales.
Black Panther *n.* A member of a militant Black American organization.
black pepper *n.* The small, dark, unripe fruit of the pepper plant *(Piper nigrum),* used whole or ground as a spice.
black•poll (blăk′pōl′) *n.* A North American warbler *(Dendroica striata),* the male of which has a black cap. [BLACK + POLL, head.]
Black•pool (blăk′po͞ol′). A borough of NW England on the Irish Sea N of Liverpool. Pop. 148,700.
black poplar *n.* A Eurasian shade tree *(Populus nigra)* with spreading branches.
Black Power *n.* A movement among Black Americans emphasizing racial pride and social equality.
black pudding *n.* A French black sausage made of pork and seasoned pig's blood.
black racer *n.* A North American blacksnake *(Coluber constrictor)* commonly found in the eastern United States.
black raspberry *n.* **1.** A prickly eastern North American shrub *(Rubus occidentalis)* having an aggregate, edible, juicy purple-black fruit. **2.** The fruit of this plant.
Black River. 1. Or in China **Ba•bian Jiang** (bä′byän′ jyäng′) and in Vietnam **Song Da** (sông′ dä′). A river of SE Asia rising in S China and flowing c. 805 km (500 mi) to the Red R. in N Vietnam. **2.** A river rising in SE MO and flowing c. 483 km (300 mi) to the White R. in NE AR.
Black Rod *n.* The chief usher of the British House of Lords. [After the rod carried as symbol of the office.]
black rot *n.* Any of several fungal or bacterial plant diseases resulting in dark discoloration and decay of affected parts.
black salsify *n.* A European plant *(Scorzonera hispanica)* in the composite family, having heads of yellow ray flowers and a large, edible, fleshy root.
black sa•po•te (sə-pō′tē, -tā) *n.* **1.** A tropical American tree *(Diospyros digyna)* related to the persimmon, with fruit that blackens when ripe. **2.** The fruit of this plant. [BLACK + Am. Sp. *zapote,* persimmonlike fruit (< Nahuatl *tzapotl*).]
Blacks•burg (blăks′bûrg′). A town of SW VA in the Allegheny Mts. W of Roanoke. Pop. 34,590.
Black Sea. An inland sea between Europe and Asia connected with the Aegean by the Bosporus, Sea of Marmara, and Dardanelles.
black sheep *n.* A member of a family or other group who is considered undesirable or disreputable.
Black Shirt *n.* A member of a fascist party organization having a black shirt as part of its uniform, esp. an Italian fascist.
black skimmer *n.* A skimmer *(Rynchops niger)* of North and South America that is black above and white below.
black•smith (blăk′smĭth′) *n.* **1.** One that forges and shapes iron with an anvil and hammer. **2.** One that makes, repairs, and fits horseshoes. [From the color of iron.] — **black′smith′ing** *n.*
black•snake (blăk′snāk′) *n.* **1.** Any of various dark-colored, chiefly nonvenomous snakes, such as the black racer of North America. **2.** A long braided rawhide or leather whip.
black snakeroot *n.* See **black cohosh.**
black spot *n.* Any of various fungal or bacterial diseases of plants, resulting in small black spots, as on the leaves.
black spruce *n.* A northern North American spruce *(Picea mariana)* having blue-green needles and egg-shaped cones.
Black•stone (blăk′stōn′, -stən), Sir **William.** 1723–80. British jurist and educator who wrote *Commentaries on the Laws of England* (1765–69).
black•strap (blăk′străp′) *n.* A dark, thick molasses, esp. a residual product of sugar refining. [From its color and texture.]
black studies also **Black Studies** *pl.n.* Studies that deal with Afro-American culture.
black-tailed deer (blăk′tāld′) also **black•tail deer** (-tāl′) *n.* See **mule deer.**
black tea *n.* A dark tea prepared from fresh tea leaves that have been fully fermented before being dried.
black•thorn (blăk′thôrn′) *n.* A thorny, deciduous Eurasian shrub *(Prunus spinosa)* having white flowers and small bluish-black fruits used for flavoring alcoholic beverages.
black tie *n.* **1.** A black bow tie worn with a dinner jacket. **2.** Semiformal evening wear typically for men, usu. requiring a dinner jacket. — **black′-tie′** (blăk′tī′) *adj.*
black•top (blăk′tŏp′) *n.* A bituminous material, such as asphalt, used to pave roads. — *v.* **-topped, -top•ping, -tops.** — *tr.* To pave with a bituminous material.
Black Vol•ta (vŏl′tə, vōl′-, vôl′-). A river of W Africa rising in W Burkina Faso and flowing c. 1,352 km (840 mi) to the White Volta in Ghana.
black vomit *n.* **1.** Dark vomit consisting of digested blood and gastric contents. **2.** Severe yellow fever with regurgitation of dark matter.
black vulture *n.* A carrion-eating bird *(Coragyps atratus)* of central North America and South America, having black plumage and a bald black head.

black letter

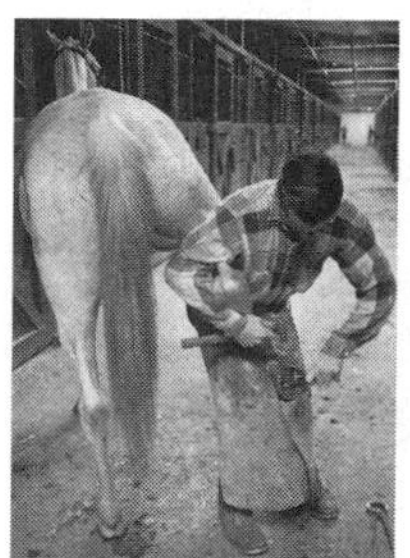
blacksmith

ă pat	oi boy
ā pay	ou out
âr care	o͝o took
ä father	o͞o boot
ĕ pet	ŭ cut
ē be	ûr urge
ĭ pit	th thin
ī pie	*th* this
îr pier	hw which
ŏ pot	zh vision
ō toe	ə about, item
ô paw	

Stress marks:
′ (primary);
′ (secondary), as in
dictionary (dĭk′shə-nĕr′ē)

black walnut *n.* **1.** An eastern North American tree *(Juglans nigra)* having dark brown wood and a deeply furrowed nut. **2.** The wood of this tree. **3.** The nut of this tree.

black•wa•ter fever (blăk′wô′tər, -wŏt′ər) *n.* A serious, often fatal complication of chronic malaria, characterized by the passage of bloody, dark red or black urine.

Black•well (blăk′wĕl′, -wəl), **Antoinette Louisa Brown.** 1825–1921. Amer. social reformer who was the first formally appointed (1852) woman pastor in America.

Blackwell, Elizabeth. 1821–1910. British-born Amer. physician who was the first woman to be awarded a medical doctorate in modern times (1849).

black widow *n.* A poisonous New World spider *(Latrodectus mactans),* the female of which has a shiny black body with red markings. [From the fact that the female eats its mate.]

Black•wood (blăk′wo͝od′), **William.** 1776–1834. Scottish publisher and editor (1817–34) of *Blackwood's Magazine,* a Tory literary review.

blad•der (blăd′ər) *n.* **1.a.** *Anat.* Any of various distensible membranous sacs, such as the urinary bladder, that serve as receptacles for fluid or gas. **b.** An item resembling a bladder. **2.** *Bot.* Any of various hollow or inflated saclike organs or structures. **3.** *Pathol.* A blister, pustule, or cyst filled with fluid or air; a vesicle. [ME *bladdre* < OE *blǣdre.* See **bhlē-*.**]

bladder campion *n.* A weedy Eurasian perennial herb *(Silene vulgaris)* having white flowers and an inflated calyx.

bladder fern *n.* Any of various ferns of the widespread genus *Cystopteris,* having pinnately compound fronds and often growing in rocky areas. [After its bladderlike indusium.]

blad•der•nose (blăd′ər-nōz′) *n.* See **hooded seal.**

blad•der•nut (blăd′ər-nŭt′) *n.* **1.** Any of various deciduous shrubs or small trees of the genus *Staphylea,* native to northern temperate regions and having opposite compound leaves and bladderlike fruits. **2.** The fruit of such a plant.

bladder worm *n.* The bladderlike encysted larva of the tapeworm that is characteristic of the cysticercus stage.

blad•der•wort (blăd′ər-wûrt′, -wôrt′) *n.* Any of various mostly aquatic carnivorous plants of the genus *Utricularia,* having bladders that trap minute insects and crustaceans.

bladder wrack *n.* Any of certain rockweeds, esp. *Fucus vesiculosus,* having forked brownish-green branches with gas-filled bladders.

blad•der•y (blăd′ə-rē) *adj.* **1.** Resembling or like a bladder. **2.** Possessing a bladder or bladders.

blade (blād) *n.* **1.** The flat-edged cutting part of a sharpened weapon or tool. **2.a.** A sword. **b.** A swordsman. **3.** A dashing youth. **4.** A flat, thin part or section: *the blade of an oar.* **5.** The metal runner of an ice skate. **6.** A wide flat bone or bony part. **7.** The flat upper surface of the tongue just behind the tip. **8.** *Bot.* **a.** The expanded part of a leaf or petal. **b.** The leaf of grasses and similar plants. [ME < OE *blæd.* See **bhel-[3]*.**] — **blad′ed** *adj.*

black widow
Latrodectus mactans

blaff (blăf) *n. Caribbean.* A West Indian stew consisting of fish or pork, seasonings such as lime and garlic, and often fruits and vegetables. [Prob. < Dominican E. *braff* < BROTH.]

blag•ging (blăg′ĭng) *n. Caribbean.* Informal talk, usu. among men, occurring in a public place. [< Fr. *blaguer,* to talk through one's hat < *blague,* bladder, pouch, of Gmc. orig., ult. < Lat. *bulga,* leather bag. See BULGE.]

Bla•go•vesh•chensk (blä′gə-vĕsh′chĕnsk, blə-gə-vyĕsh′chĭsk). A city of E Russia at the confluence of the Amur and Zeya rivers. Pop. 195,000.

blah (blä) *Informal.* —*n.* **1.** Worthless nonsense; drivel. **2. blahs.** A general feeling of discomfort, dissatisfaction, or depression. —*adj.* **1.** Dull and uninteresting. **2.** Low in spirit or health; down. [Imit. of meaningless talk.] — **blah** *adv.*

blain (blān) *n.* A skin swelling or sore; a blister; a blotch. [ME < OE *blegen.*]

Blaine (blān). A city of E Minnesota, a suburb of St. Paul. Pop. 38,975.

Blaine, James Gillespie. "the Plumed Knight." 1830–93. Amer. politician who served as U.S. secretary of state (1881 and 1889–92) and lost the 1884 presidential election.

Blair (blâr), **John.** 1732–1800. Amer. jurist; associate justice of the U.S. Supreme Court (1789–96).

Blake (blāk), **James Herbert ("Eubie").** 1883–1983. Amer. pianist and composer noted for his Broadway productions, such as *Shuffle Along* (1921).

Blake, Robert. 1599–1657. English Parliamentarian admiral who defeated the Royalist fleet in the Mediterranean Sea (1650) during the English Civil War.

Blake, William. 1757–1827. British poet and artist whose paintings and poetic works, such as *Songs of Innocence* (1789), have a mystical, visionary quality.

blam•a•ble also **blame•a•ble** (blā′mə-bəl) *adj.* Deserving blame. — **blam′a•ble•ness** *n.* — **blam′a•bly** *adv.*

blame (blām) *tr.v.* **blamed, blam•ing, blames. 1.** To hold responsible. **2.** To find fault with; censure. **3.** To place responsibility for. —*n.* **1.** The state of being responsible for a fault or an error; culpability. **2.** Censure; condemnation. —***idiom.*** **to blame. 1.** Deserving censure; at fault. **2.** Being the cause or source of something. [ME *blamen* < OFr. *blasmer, blamer* < VLat. **blastēmāre,* alteration of LLat. *blasphēmāre,* to reproach. See BLASPHEME.] — **blam′er** *n.*

Syns: *blame, fault, guilt.* These nouns refer to placing responsibility for an offense. *Blame* stresses censure or punishment for something for which one is held accountable: *The police laid the blame for the accident on the driver. Fault* is culpability for causing or failing to prevent the occurrence of something detrimental: *That he failed the exam was his own fault. Guilt* applies to willful wrongdoing and stresses moral culpability: *The prosecution had evidence of the defendant's guilt.* See also Syns at **criticize.**

blamed (blāmd) *adv. & adj. Informal.* Used as an intensive: *called me a blamed fool.*

blame•ful (blām′fəl) *adj.* Deserving of blame; blameworthy. — **blame′ful•ly** *adv.* — **blame′ful•ness** *n.*

blame•less (blām′lĭs) *adj.* Free of blame or guilt; innocent. — **blame′less•ly** *adv.* — **blame′less•ness** *n.*

blame•wor•thy (blām′wûr′thē) *adj.* **-thi•er, -thi•est.** Deserving blame; reprehensible. — **blame′wor′thi•ness** *n.*

Blanc (blăngk, bläN), **Mont.** The highest peak of the Alps, rising to 4,810.2 m (15,771 ft) in the Savoy Alps of SE France.

Blan•ca Peak (blăng′kə). A mountain, 4,375.2 m (14,345 ft), in the Sangre de Cristo Mts. of S CO.

blanc fixe (blăngk′ fĭks′, bläN fēks′) *n.* Powdered barium sulfate used as a base for watercolor pigments and as a filler in paper. [Fr. : *blanc,* white + *fixe,* fixed.]

blanch (blănch) also **blench** (blĕnch) —*v.* **blanched, blanch•ing, blanch•es** also **blenched, blench•ing, blench•es.** —*tr.* **1.** To take the color from; bleach. **2.** To whiten (a growing plant or plant part) by excluding light. **3.** To whiten (a metal) by soaking in acid or by coating with tin. **4.** To boil (food) briefly, as to loosen skin. **5.** To cause to turn white or become pale. —*intr.* To turn white or become pale. [ME *blaunchen,* to whiten < OFr. *blanchir* < *blanche,* fem. of *blanc,* white, of Gmc. orig. See **bhel-[1]*.**] — **blanch′er** *n.*

blanc•mange (blə-mänj′, -mäNzh′) *n.* A flavored and sweetened milk pudding thickened with cornstarch. [ME *blankmanger,* a dish made with almond milk < OFr. *blanc mangier*: *blanc,* white (of Gmc. orig.; see **bhel-[1]***) + *mangier,* to eat, food (< Lat. *mandūcāre*; see MANGER).]

bland (blănd) *adj.* **bland•er, bland•est. 1.a.** Pleasant in manner; smooth: *a bland smile.* **b.** Not irritating or stimulating; soothing: *a bland diet.* **c.** Exhibiting no embarrassment or concern: *bland lies.* **2.** Dull and insipid: *a bland drama.* [Lat. *blandus,* caressing, flattering. See **mel-[1]*.**] — **bland′ly** *adv.* — **bland′ness** *n.*

blan•dish (blăn′dĭsh) *tr.v.* **-dished, -dish•ing, -dish•es.** To coax by flattery or wheedling; cajole. [ME *blandishen* < OFr. *blandir, blandiss-* < Lat. *blandīrī* < *blandus,* flattering. See **mel-[1]*.**] — **blan′dish•er** *n.* — **blan′dish•ment** *n.*

blank (blăngk) *adj.* **blank•er, blank•est. 1.a.** Devoid of writing, images, or marks: *a blank page.* **b.** Containing no information; unrecorded or erased: *a blank tape.* **2.** Not completed or filled in: *a blank questionnaire.* **3.** Not having received final processing; unfinished: *a blank key.* **4.a.** Lacking expression; expressionless. **b.** Appearing or seeming to appear dazed or confused. **5.** Devoid of thought or impression: *a blank mind.* **6.** Devoid of activity, interest, or distinctive character; empty. **7.** Absolute; complete: *a blank refusal.* —*n.* **1.** An empty space or place; a void: *My mind was a blank.* **2.a.** An empty space on a document to be filled in. **b.** A document with one or more such spaces. **3.** A manufactured article of a standard shape or form that is ready for final processing: *a key blank.* **4.** A gun cartridge with a charge of powder but no bullet. **5.** Something worthless, such as a losing lottery ticket. **6.** A mark, usually a dash (—), indicating the omission of a word or of a letter or letters. **7.** The white circle in the center of a target; a bull's-eye. —*v.* **blanked, blank•ing, blanks.** —*tr.* **1.** To remove, as from view; obliterate. **2.** To block access to: *blank off a subway tunnel.* **3.** *Sports.* To prevent (an opponent) from scoring. **4.** To punch or stamp from flat stock, esp. with a die. —*intr.* **1.** To become abstracted: *My mind blanked out.* **2.** To fade away: *The music gradually blanked out.* [ME, white, having spaces to be filled in < OFr. *blanc,* white, of Gmc. orig. See **bhel-[1]*.**] — **blank′ly** *adv.* — **blank′ness** *n.*

blank check *n.* **1.** A signed check with no amount to be paid filled in. **2.** Total freedom of action; carte blanche.

blank endorsement *n.* An endorsement on a check or note that names no payee, making it payable to the bearer.

blan•ket (blăng′kĭt) *n.* **1.** A large piece of woven material used as a covering for warmth, esp. on a bed. **2.** A layer that covers or encloses. —*adj.* Applying to or covering all conditions, instances, or members of a class: *a blanket insurance policy.* —*tr.v.* **-ket•ed, -ket•ing, -kets. 1.** To cover with or as if with a blanket. **2.** To cover so as to inhibit, suppress, or extinguish. **3.** To apply to generally and uniformly without exception. [ME < OFr., an unbleached soft cloth < *blanc,* white, of Gmc. orig. See **bhel-[1]*.**]

blanket flower *n.* See **gaillardia.**

blanket stitch *n.* A buttonhole stitch used for edging around heavy material.

blan•ket-stitch (blăng′kĭt-stĭch′) *tr.v.* **-stitched, -stitch•ing, -stitch•es.** To sew with a buttonhole stitch.

blank verse *n.* Verse consisting of unrhymed lines, usu. of iambic pentameter.

Blan•tyre (blăn-tīr′). A city of S Malawi. Pop. 229,000.

blare (blâr) *v.* **blared, blar•ing, blares.** —*intr.* To sound loudly and stridently. —*tr.* **1.** To cause to blare. **2.** To proclaim loudly and flamboyantly. —*n.* **1.** A loud, strident noise. **2.** Flamboyance. [ME *bleren.*]

blar•ney (blär′nē) *n.* **1.** Smooth, flattering talk. **2.** Deceptive nonsense. [After the BLARNEY Stone in Blarney Castle, Blarney, Ireland.] —**blar′ney** *v.*

Blar•ney (blär′nē). A village of S Ireland near Cork. Blarney Castle (dating from the 15th cent.) is the site of the Blarney Stone, said to impart powers of eloquence and persuasion.

Blas•co I•bá•ñez (blä′skō ē-bän′yās, ē-vän′yĕth), **Vicente.** 1867–1928. Spanish writer of naturalistic novels.

bla•sé (blä-zā′) *adj.* **1.** Uninterested because of frequent exposure or indulgence. **2.** Unconcerned; nonchalant. **3.** Very sophisticated. [Fr. < p.part. of *blaser,* to cloy < Fr. dial., to be chronically hung over, prob. < MDu. *blāsen,* to blow up, swell. See **bhlē-*.**]

blas•pheme (blăs-fēm′, blăs′fēm′) *v.* **-phemed, -phem•ing, -phemes.** —*tr.* **1.** To speak of (God or a sacred entity) in an irreverent, impious manner. **2.** To revile; execrate. —*intr.* To speak blasphemy. [ME *blasfemen* < OFr. *blasfemer* < LLat. *blasphēmāre* < Gk. *blasphēmein: blas-,* of unknown meaning + *phēmē,* speech; see **bhā-²*.**] —**blas•phem′er** (blăs-fē′mər, blăs′fə-) *n.*

blas•phe•mous (blăs′fə-məs) *adj.* Impiously irreverent. —**blas′phe•mous•ly** *adv.* —**blas′phe•mous•ness** *n.*

blas•phe•my (blăs′fə-mē) *n., pl.* **-mies. 1.** A contemptuous or profane act, utterance, or writing concerning God or a sacred entity. **2.** An irreverent or impious act, attitude, or utterance. [ME *blasfemie* < LLat. *blasphēmia* < Gk. < *blasphēmein,* to blaspheme. See BLASPHEME.]

blast (blăst) *n.* **1.a.** A very strong gust of wind or air. **b.** The effect of such a gust. **2.** A forcible stream of air, gas, or steam from an opening, as in a blast furnace. **3.** A sudden loud sound. **4.a.** A violent explosion, as of dynamite. **b.** The violent effect of such an explosion, consisting of a wave of increased atmospheric pressure followed by a wave of decreased pressure. **c.** An explosive charge. **5.** *Bot.* Any of several plant diseases, resulting in sudden death of buds, flowers, foliage, or young fruits. **6.** A destructive or damaging influence. **7.** A powerful hit, blow, or shot. **8.** A violent verbal assault or outburst. **9.** *Slang.* A highly exciting event, such as a big party. —*v.* **blast•ed, blast•ing, blasts.** —*tr.* **1.** To knock down or shatter by or as if by explosion; smash. **2.** To play or sound loudly. **3.a.** To hit with great force. **b.** To kill or destroy by hitting or shooting. **4.** To have a harmful or destructive effect on. **5.** To cause to shrivel, wither, or mature imperfectly by or as if by blast or blight. **6.** To make or open by or as if by explosion: *blast a tunnel through the mountains.* **7.** To criticize or attack vigorously. —*intr.* **1.** To use or detonate explosives. **2.** To emit a loud, intense sound; blare. **3.** To wither or shrivel or mature imperfectly. **4.** To criticize or attack with vigor. **5.** To shoot. —***phrasal verb.* blast off.** To take off, as a rocket. —***idiom.* full blast.** At full speed, volume, or capacity. [ME < OE *blǣst.* See **bhlē-*.**] —**blast′er** *n.*

-blast *suff.* An immature, embryonic stage in the development of cells or tissues: *erythroblast.* [< Gk. *blastos,* bud.]

blast cell *n.* **1.** A precursor of a human blood cell. **2.** An immature undifferentiated cell. [-BLAST + CELL.]

blast•ed (blăs′tĭd) *adj.* **1.** Used as an intensive: *I hate these blasted flies.* **2.** *Slang.* Intoxicated; drunk. **3.** Blighted, withered, or shriveled.

blas•te•ma (blă-stē′mə) *n., pl.* **-mas** or **-ma•ta** (-mə-tə). **1.** The undifferentiated material from which cells are formed. **2.** A mass of embryonic cells from which a body part develops, either normally or in regeneration. [Gk. *blastēma,* offspring, sprout < *blastos,* bud.] —**blas•te′mal, blas′te•mat′ic** (blăs′tə-măt′ĭk), **blas•te′mic** (blă-stē′mĭk) *adj.*

blast furnace *n.* A furnace in which combustion is intensified by a blast of air.

-blastic *suff.* Having a specified number or kind of formative elements such as buds, germs, cells, or cell layers: *meroblastic.* [< -BLAST.]

blasto– or **blast–** *pref.* Bud; germ; budding; germination: *blastocyst.* [< Gk. *blastos,* bud.]

blas•to•coel or **blas•to•coele** (blăs′tə-sēl′) *n.* The fluid-filled central cavity of a blastula. —**blas′to•coe′lic** *adj.*

blas•to•cyst (blăs′tə-sĭst′) *n.* *Embryol.* The modified blastula characteristic of placental mammals. —**blas′to•cys′tic** *adj.*

blas•to•derm (blăs′tə-dûrm′) *n.* *Embryol.* **1.** The layer of cells that gives rise to the germinal disk from which an avian or reptilian embryo develops. **2.** The layer of cells formed by the cleavage of a fertilized mammalian egg. —**blas′to•der′mic, blas′to•der•mat′ic** (-dər-măt′ĭk) *adj.*

blastodermic vesicle *n.* See **blastocyst.**

blas•to•disk or **blas•to•disc** (blăs′tə-dĭsk′) *n.* See **germinal disk.**

blast•off also **blast-off** (blăst′ôf′, -ŏf′) *n.* The launch, esp. of a rocket.

blas•to•gen•e•sis (blăs′tə-jĕn′ĭ-sĭs) *n.* **1.** The theory that inherited characteristics are transmitted from parent to offspring by germ plasm. **2.** Reproduction of an organism by budding. —**blas′to•ge•net′ic** (-jə-nĕt′ĭk), **blas′to•gen′ic** (-jĕn′ĭk) *adj.*

blas•to•ma (blă-stō′mə) *n., pl.* **-mas** or **-ma•ta** (-mə-tə). A neoplasm composed of immature and undifferentiated cells.

blas•to•mere (blăs′tə-mîr′) *n.* *Embryol.* A cell resulting from the cleavage of a fertilized ovum during early embryonic development. —**blas′to•mer′ic** (-mîr′ĭk, -mĕr′-) *adj.*

blas•to•my•cete (blăs′tə-mī′sēt, -mī-sēt′) *n.* Any of various yeastlike budding fungi of the genus *Blastomyces* that cause diseases in humans and animals.

blas•to•my•co•sis (blăs′tō-mī-kō′sĭs) *n.* A fungal infection caused by a blastomycete and characterized by multiple inflammatory lesions of the skin, mucous membranes, or internal organs.

blas•to•pore (blăs′tə-pôr′, -pōr′) *n.* *Embryol.* The opening of the archenteron. [BLASTO- + PORE².] —**blas′to•por′ic, blas′to•por′al** (-pôr′əl, -pōr′-) *adj.*

blas•to•sphere (blăs′tə-sfîr′) *n.* See **blastula.**

blas•to•spore (blăs′tə-spôr′, -spōr′) *n.* A fungal spore produced by budding.

blas•tu•la (blăs′chə-lə) *n., pl.* **-las** or **-lae** (-lē′). *Embryol.* An early embryonic form produced by cleavage of a fertilized ovum and consisting of a spherical layer of cells surrounding a fluid-filled cavity. [NLat. < Gk. *blastos,* bud.] —**blas′tu•lar** *adj.* —**blas′tu•la′tion** (-lā′shən) *n.*

blat (blăt) *v.* **blat•ted, blat•ting, blats.** —*tr.* To utter without thinking; blurt. —*intr.* **1.** To cry, esp. like a sheep; bleat. **2.** To make a harsh or raucous noise. [Imit.] —**blat** *n.*

bla•tant (blăt′nt) *adj.* **1.** Unpleasantly loud and noisy. **2.** *Usage Problem.* Totally or offensively conspicuous or obtrusive. [< Lat. *blatīre,* to blab (on the model of words such as RAMPANT).] —**bla′tan•cy** *n.* —**bla′tant•ly** *adv.*

Usage Note: It is natural that *blatant* and *flagrant* are often confused, since the words overlap in meaning. Both attribute conspicuousness and offensiveness to certain acts. But *blatant* emphasizes the failure to conceal the act: *blatant vanity. Flagrant,* on the other hand, tends to emphasize a serious wrongdoing in the offense itself: *flagrant child abuse. Blatant* should not be used to mean simply "obvious."

Blatch•ford (blăch′fərd), **Samuel.** 1820–93. Amer. jurist; associate justice of the U.S. Supreme Court (1882–93).

blath•er (blăth′ər) also **bleth•er** (blĕth′-) —*intr.v.* **-ered, -er•ing, -ers.** To talk nonsensically. —*n.* Nonsensical talk. [ON *bladhra.* See **bhlē-*.**] —**blath′er•er** *n.*

blath•er•skite (blăth′ər-skīt′) *n.* **1.** A babbling, foolish person. **2.** Blather. [BLATHER + dial. *skite,* a contemptible person (< ME *shit,* diarrhea < OE *scitte* < *scītan,* to shit; see SHIT).]

Bla•vat•sky (blə-văt′skē, -văt′-), **Helena Petrovna Hahn.** 1831–91. Russian-born theosophist who founded (1875) the Theosophical Society in New York City.

blaze¹ (blāz) *n.* **1.a.** A brilliant flame. **b.** A destructive fire. **2.** A bright or steady light or glare. **3.** A brilliant, striking display. **4.** A sudden outburst: *a blaze of anger.* **5. blazes.** Used as an intensive: *Where in blazes are my keys?* —*v.* **blazed, blaz•ing, blaz•es.** —*intr.* **1.** To burn with a bright flame. **2.** To shine brightly. **3.** To be resplendent: *a garden blazing with flowers.* **4.** To flare up suddenly: *My temper blazed.* **5.** To shoot rapidly and continuously. —*tr.* To shine or be resplendent with: *eyes that blazed hatred.* [ME *blase* < OE *blæse.* See **bhel-¹*.**] —**blaz′ing•ly** *adv.*

blaze² (blāz) *n.* **1.** A white or light-colored spot on the face of an animal, such as a horse. **2.** A mark cut or painted on a tree to indicate a trail. —*tr.v.* **blazed, blaz•ing, blaz•es. 1.** To mark (a tree) with or as if with blazes. **2.** To indicate (a trail) by marking trees with blazes. [Of Gmc. orig.]

blaze³ (blāz) *tr.v.* **blazed, blaz•ing, blaz•es.** To make known publicly; proclaim: *Headlines blazed the news.* [ME *blasen* < MDu. *blāsen,* to blow up, swell. See **bhlē-*.**]

blaz•er (blā′zər) *n.* A lightweight, often striped or brightly colored sports jacket having pockets and notched lapels.

blaz•ing star (blā′zĭng) *n.* **1.** A North American dioecious herb *(Chamaelirium luteum)* in the lily family, having long racemes of small flowers. **2.** Any of various North American plants of the genus *Liatris* in the composite family, having small discoid flower heads grouped in a dense raceme or panicle. **3.** A biennial plant *(Mentzelia laevicaulis)* of western North America, having large star-shaped flowers.

bla•zon (blā′zən) *tr.v.* **-zoned, -zon•ing, -zons. 1.** *Her.* **a.** To describe (a coat of arms) in proper terms. **b.** To paint or depict (a coat of arms) with accurate detail. **2.** To adorn or embellish with or as if with a coat of arms. **3.** To proclaim widely. —*n.* **1.** *Her.* **a.** A coat of arms. **b.** The description or representation of a coat of arms. **2.** An ostentatious display. [Prob. < ME *blasoun,* shield < OFr. *blason.*] —**bla′zon•er** *n.* —**bla′zon•ment** *n.*

bla•zon•ry (blā′zən-rē) *n., pl.* **-ries. 1.** *Her.* **a.** The art of properly and accurately describing or representing armorial bear-

blastoff
Apollo 16 voyage to the moon, April 16, 1972

ă pat	oi boy
ā pay	ou out
âr care	ŏŏ took
ä father	ōō boot
ĕ pet	ŭ cut
ē be	ûr urge
ĭ pit	th thin
ī pie	*th* this
îr pier	hw which
ŏ pot	zh vision
ō toe	ə about, item
ô paw	

Stress marks:
′ (primary);
′ (secondary), as in dictionary (dĭk′shə-nĕr′ē)

ings. **b.** A coat of arms. **2.** An ostentatious display.

bld. *abbr.* **1.** Blood. **2.** *Print.* Boldface.

bldg. *abbr.* Building.

bldr. *abbr.* Builder.

bleach (blēch) *v.* **bleached, bleach•ing, bleach•es.** *—tr.* **1.** To remove the color from, as by means of chemical agents or sunlight. **2.** To make white or colorless. *—intr.* To become white or colorless. *—n.* **1.** A chemical agent used for bleaching. **2.a.** The act of bleaching. **b.** The degree of bleaching obtained. [ME *blechen* < OE *blǣcan.* See **bhel-**[1]*.]

bleach•er (blē′chər) *n.* **1.** One that bleaches or is used in bleaching. **2.** An often unroofed outdoor grandstand for seating spectators. Often used in the plural.

bleach•ing powder (blē′chĭng) *n.* A powder containing calcium chloride and calcium hypochlorite, used as a bleach.

bleak[1] (blēk) *adj.* **bleak•er, bleak•est. 1.a.** Gloomy and somber; dreary. **b.** Providing no encouragement; depressing. **2.** Cold and cutting; raw. **3.** Exposed to the elements; unsheltered and barren. [ME *bleik,* pale < ON *bleikr,* white. See **bhel-**[1]*.] **—bleak′ly** *adv.* **—bleak′ness** *n.*

bleak[2] (blēk) *n., pl.* **bleak** or **bleaks.** A small European freshwater fish of the genus *Alburnus,* having silvery scales used in making artificial pearls. [ME *bleke,* prob. alteration (influenced by *bleke,* pale; see BLEAK[1]) of **blay* < OE *blǣge.*]

blear (blîr) *tr.v.* **bleared, blear•ing, blears. 1.** To blur or redden (the eyes). **2.** To blur; dim. *—adj.* Bleary. [ME *bleren.*]

blear•y (blîr′ē) *adj.* **-i•er, -i•est. 1.** Blurred or dimmed by or as if by tears: *bleary eyes.* **2.** Vaguely outlined; indistinct. **3.** Exhausted; worn-out. **—blear′i•ly** *adv.* **—blear′i•ness** *n.*

blear•y-eyed (blîr′ē-īd′) also **blear-eyed** (blîr′īd′) *adj.* With eyes blurred or reddened, as from lack of sleep.

bleeding heart

bleat (blēt) *n.* **1.a.** The cry of a goat or sheep. **b.** A sound like this. **2.** A whining complaint. *—v.* **bleat•ed, bleat•ing, bleats.** *—intr.* **1.** To utter the cry of a goat or sheep. **2.** To utter a sound like this. *—tr.* To utter in a whining way. [ME *blet* < *bleten,* to bleat < OE *blǣtan.*] **—bleat′er** *n.*

bleb (blĕb) *n.* **1.** A small blister or pustule. **2.** An air bubble. [Prob. alteration of BLOB.] **—bleb′by** *adj.*

bleed (blēd) *v.* **bled** (blĕd), **bleed•ing, bleeds.** *—intr.* **1.** To emit or lose blood. **2.** To be wounded, esp. in battle. **3.** To feel sympathetic grief or anguish. **4.** To exude a fluid such as sap. **5.** To pay out money, esp. an exorbitant amount. **6.a.** To run together or be diffused, as dyes in wet cloth. **b.** To undergo or be subject to such a diffusion of color. **7.** To show through a layer of paint. **8.** To be printed so as to go off the edge or edges of a page after trimming. *—tr.* **1.a.** To take or remove blood from. **b.** To extract sap or juice from. **2.a.** To draw liquid or gaseous contents from; drain. **b.** To draw off (liquid or gaseous matter) from a container. **3.** To obtain money from, esp. by improper means. **4.a.** To cause (an illustration, for example) to bleed. **b.** To trim (a page, for example) so as to mutilate the printed matter. *—n.* **1.** Illustrative matter that bleeds. **2.a.** A page trimmed so as to bleed. **b.** The part of the page that is trimmed off. [ME *bleden* < OE *blēdan* < *blōd,* blood. See **bhel-**[3]*.]

bleed•er (blē′dər) *n.* **1.** A person, such as a hemophiliac, who bleeds freely or is subject to hemorrhages. **2.** A person who draws blood from another; a phlebotomist.

bleed•ing heart (blē′dĭng) *n.* **1.** Any of various perennial herbs of the genus *Dicentra,* esp. *D. spectabilis,* having clusters of pink or red heart-shaped flowers. **2.** A person who is considered excessively sympathetic toward those who claim to be underprivileged. **—bleed′ing-heart′** (-härt′) *adj.*

bleep (blēp) *n.* A brief high-pitched sound, as from an electronic device. *—v.* **bleeped, bleep•ing, bleeps.** *—intr.* To emit a bleep or bleeps. *—tr.* To edit out (spoken material) from a broadcast or recording, esp. by replacing with a bleep. [Imit.] **—bleep′er** *n.*

blimp
The Goodyear blimp
Spirit of Akron

blem•ish (blĕm′ĭsh) *tr.v.* **-ished, -ish•ing, -ish•es.** To mar or impair by a flaw. *—n.* An imperfection that mars or impairs. [ME *blemisshen* < OFr. *blesmir, blemir, blemiss-,* to make pale, of Gmc. orig. See **bhel-**[1]*.] **—blem′ish•er** *n.*

blench[1] (blĕnch) *intr.v.* **blenched, blench•ing, blench•es.** To draw back or shy away, as from fear; flinch. [ME *blenchen* < OE *blencan,* to deceive. See **bhel-**[1]*.] **—blench′er** *n.*

blench[2] (blĕnch) *v.* Var. of **blanch.**

blend (blĕnd) *v.* **blend•ed** or **blent** (blĕnt), **blend•ing, blends.** *—tr.* **1.** To combine or mix so that the constituent parts are indistinguishable from one another. **2.** To combine (varieties or grades) to obtain a mixture of a particular character or consistency. *—intr.* **1.** To form a uniform mixture; intermingle. **2.** To become merged into one; unite. **3.** To create a harmonious effect or result: *The tie blended with the jacket.* *—n.* **1.a.** The act of blending. **b.** Something, such as an effect or a product, that is created by blending: *a blend of coffees.* See Syns at **mixture. 2.** *Ling.* A word produced by combining parts of other words, as *smog* from *smoke* and *fog.* [ME *blenden,* prob. < ON *blanda, blend-.* See **bhel-**[1]*.]

blende (blĕnd) *n.* **1.** Any of various shiny minerals composed chiefly of metallic sulfides. **2.** See **sphalerite.** [Ger. < *blenden,* to deceive (because it resembles lead ore) < MHGer. *blenden* < OHGer. *blentan,* to blind, deceive. See **bhel-**[1]*.]

blend•ed whiskey (blĕn′dĭd) *n.* Whiskey that is a blend of straight whiskeys or of whiskey and neutral spirits.

blend•er (blĕn′dər) *n.* One that blends, esp. an appliance with blades for chopping, mixing, or liquefying foods.

blend•ing inheritance (blĕn′dĭng) *n. Genet.* The inheritance pattern in which the inherited characters in the offspring are intermediate between those of the parents.

blen•ny (blĕn′ē) *n., pl.* **-nies.** Any of several chiefly marine fishes that are primarily of the families Blenniidae and Clinidae and have small elongated bodies. [Lat. *blennius,* a kind of sea fish < Gk. *blennos,* slime, blenny. See **mel-**[1]*.]

bleph•a•ri•tis (blĕf′ə-rī′tĭs) *n.* Inflammation of the eyelids.

blepharo– or **blephar–** *pref.* **1.** Eyelid; eyelids: *blepharospasm.* **2.** Cilium; flagellum: *blepharoplast.* [Gk. < *blepharon,* eyelid.]

bleph•a•ro•plast (blĕf′ər-ə-plăst′) *n.* A basal body in certain flagellated protozoans that consists of a minute mass of chromatin embedded in the cytoplasm at the base of the flagellum.

bleph•a•ro•plas•ty (blĕf′ər-ə-plăs′tē) *n.* Plastic surgery of the eyelids.

bleph•a•ro•spasm (blĕf′ə-rō-spăz′əm) *n.* Spasmodic winking caused by involuntary contraction of an eyelid muscle.

Blé•riot (blā′re-o, blā-ryō′), **Louis.** 1872–1936. French inventor and aviator who was the first to cross the English Channel by airplane (1909).

bles•bok (blĕs′bŏk′) *n., pl.* **blesbok** or **-boks.** A South African antelope (*Damaliscus albifrons*) having curved horns and a large white mark on its face. [Afr. : *bles,* white mark on an animal's face (< MDu.; see **bhel-**[1]*) + *bok,* buck (< MDu. *boc*).]

bless (blĕs) *tr.v.* **blessed** or **blest** (blĕst), **bless•ing, bless•es. 1.** To make holy by religious rite; sanctify. **2.** To make the sign of the cross over so as to sanctify. **3.** To invoke divine favor upon. **4.** To honor as holy; glorify. **5.** To confer well-being on. **6.** To endow, as with talent. [ME *blessen* < OE *blētsian,* to consecrate. See **bhel-**[3]*.] **—bless′er** *n.*

bless•ed (blĕs′ĭd) also **blest** (blĕst) *adj.* **1.a.** Worthy of worship; holy. **b.** Held in veneration; revered. **2. Blessed.** *Rom. Cath. Ch.* Used as a title before the name of one who has been beatified. **3.** Bringing happiness, pleasure, or contentment. **4. blessed.** Used as an intensive: *I don't have a blessed dime.* [Sense 4, alteration of BLASTED.] **—bless′ed•ly** *adv.* **—bless′ed•ness** *n.*

Blessed Sacrament *n. Rom. Cath. Ch.* The consecrated host.

Blessed Virgin Mary *n.* The Virgin Mary.

bless•ing (blĕs′ĭng) *n.* **1.** The act of one that blesses. **2.** A short prayer said before or after a meal. **3.** Something promoting or contributing to happiness, well-being, or prosperity; a boon. **4.** Approbation; approval.

bleth•er (blĕth′ər) *v. & n.* Var. of **blather.**

bleu cheese (blo͞o) *n.* See **blue cheese.** [Fr., blue < OFr. See BLUE.]

blew[1] (blo͞o) *v.* P.t. of **blow**[1].

blew[2] (blo͞o) *v.* P.t. of **blow**[3].

Bli•da (blē′də). A town of N Algeria at the foot of the Atlas Mts. SW of Algiers. Pop. 136,033.

Bligh (blī), **William.** 1754–1817. British naval officer who as captain of the H.M.S. *Bounty* was set adrift by his mutinous crew during a voyage to Tahiti (1789).

blight (blīt) *n.* **1.a.** Any of numerous plant diseases resulting in sudden conspicuous wilting and dying of affected parts. **b.** The causative agent, such as a fungus, that results in blight. **2.** An adverse environmental condition, such as air pollution. **3.** Something that frustrates hope or impedes progress and prosperity. *—v.* **blight•ed, blight•ing, blights.** *—tr.* **1.** To cause (a plant, for example) to undergo blight. **2.** To have a deleterious effect on; ruin. *—intr.* To suffer blight. [?]

blight•er (blī′tər) *n. Chiefly British.* A fellow, esp. one held in low esteem.

blimp (blĭmp) *n.* A nonrigid, buoyant airship. [Perh. < LIMP.]

Blimp (blĭmp) *n. Chiefly British.* A pompous ultranationalistic reactionary. [After Colonel *Blimp,* a cartoon character invented by David Low (1891–1963).] **—Blimp′ish** *adj.*

blind (blīnd) *adj.* **blind•er, blind•est. 1.a.** Unable to see; sightless. **b.** Of, relating to, or for sightless persons. **2.a.** Performed or made without information that might prejudice the result: *blind tests of a new drug.* **b.** Performed without preparation or knowledge: *a blind stab at the question.* **c.** Performed solely by instruments: *blind navigation.* **3.** Unable or unwilling to perceive or understand: *blind to her faults.* **4.** Not based on reason or evidence; unquestioning. **5.** *Slang.* Drunk. **6.** Independent of human control: *blind fate.* **7.a.** Difficult to comprehend or see; illegible. **b.** Incompletely or illegibly addressed: *blind mail.* **c.** Hidden from sight: *a blind driveway.* **8.** Closed at one end: *a blind passage.* **9.** Having no opening: *a blind wall.* **10.** *Bot.* Failing to produce flowers or fruits: *a blind bud.* *—n.* **1.** Something, such as a window shade, that hinders vision or shuts out light. **2.** A shelter for concealing hunters. **3.** Something intended to conceal the true nature, esp. of an activity; a subterfuge. *—adv.* **1.a.** Without seeing; blindly. **b.** Without the aid of visual reference: *flew blind.* **2.** Without forethought or provision; unawares: *entered into* *the scheme blind.* **3.** *Informal.* Into a stupor. **4.** Used as an intensive: *robbed us blind.* — *tr.v.* **blind•ed, blind•ing, blinds. 1.** To deprive of sight. **2.** To dazzle: *blinded by sunlight.* **3.** To deprive of perception or insight: *Prejudice blinded them.* **4.** To withhold light from. [ME < OE. See **bhel-**[1]*.] — **blind′ing•ly** *adv.* — **blind′ly** *adv.* — **blind′ness** *n.*

blind alley *n.* **1.** An alley or passage that is closed at one end. **2.** A mistaken, unproductive undertaking.

blind date *n.* **1.** A social engagement between two persons who have not previously met, usu. arranged by a mutual acquaintance. **2.** Either of the persons on a blind date.

blind•er (blīn′dər) *n.* **1. blinders.** A pair of leather flaps attached to a horse's bridle to curtail side vision. **2.** Something that serves to obscure clear perception and discernment.

blind•fish (blīnd′fĭsh′) *n., pl.* **blindfish** or **-fish•es.** Any of various small fishes with rudimentary nonfunctioning eyes, inhabiting cave waters and underground streams.

blind•fold (blīnd′fōld′) *tr.v.* **-fold•ed, -fold•ing, -folds. 1.** To cover the eyes of with or as if with a bandage. **2.** To prevent from seeing and esp. from comprehending. — *n.* **1.** A bandage to cover the eyes. **2.** Something that serves to obscure clear perception. [< ME *blindfolde,* p.part. of *blindfellen,* to strike blind, cover the eyes < OE *geblindfellian: blind,* blind; see BLIND + *fellian,* to strike down.] — **blind′fold′ed** *adj.*

blind gut *n.* **1.** A digestive cavity having only one opening. **2.** See **cecum** 2.

blind•man's buff (blīnd′mănz′) *n. Games.* A game in which a blindfolded player tries to catch and identify one of the other players. [*buff,* short for BUFFET[2].]

blindman's bluff *n. Games.* Blindman's buff.

blind pig *n. Pacific Northwest.* See **blind tiger.**

blind side *n.* **1.** The side on which one's vision is limited or obstructed. **2.** The side away from which one is looking.

blind-side or **blind•side** (blīnd′sīd′) *tr.v.* **-sid•ed, -sid•ing, -sides. 1.** To hit or attack on or from the blind side. **2.** To catch or take unawares, esp. with harmful results.

blind spot *n.* **1.** *Anat.* The small, circular, optically insensitive region in the retina where fibers of the optic nerve emerge from the eyeball. **2.** A part of an area that cannot be directly observed under existing circumstances. **3.** An area where radio reception is weak or nonexistent. **4.** A subject about which one is markedly ignorant or prejudiced.

blind staggers *pl.n. (used with a sing. v.)* See **stagger** 3.

blind tiger *n. Chiefly Southern & Midland U.S.* A place where alcoholic beverages are sold illegally; a speakeasy. Also called regionally *blind pig.* [After the early custom of exhibiting animal curiosities in speakeasies.]

blind trust *n.* An arrangement in which a person, such as a public official, relegates the management of certain financial assets to a trustee and agrees to be kept ignorant of their status so as to avoid conflict of interest.

blind•worm (blīnd′wûrm′) *n.* See **slowworm.** [From its small eyes.]

blink (blĭngk) *v.* **blinked, blink•ing, blinks.** — *intr.* **1.** To close and open one or both of the eyes rapidly. **2.** To look through half-closed eyes, as in a bright glare; squint. **3.** To shine with intermittent gleams; flash on and off. **4.** To be startled or dismayed. **5.** To look with feigned ignorance. — *tr.* **1.** To cause to blink. **2.** To hold back or remove (tears) by blinking. **3.** To refuse to recognize or face: *blink ugly facts.* **4.** To transmit (a message) with a flashing light. — *n.* **1.** The act or an instance of rapidly closing and opening the eyes or an eye. **2.** An instant. **3.** *Scots.* A quick look or glimpse; a glance. **4.** A flash of light; a twinkle. **5.** See **iceblink** 1. — ***idiom.* on the blink.** Out of working order. [Prob. ME *blinken,* to move suddenly, var. of *blenchen.* See BLENCH[1].]

blink•er (blĭng′kər) *n.* **1.** One that blinks, esp. a light that blinks in order to convey a message. **2. blinkers.** See **blinder** 1. — *tr.v.* **-ered, -er•ing, -ers.** To put blinders on.

blintz (blĭnts) also **blin•tze** (blĭn′tsə) *n.* A thin pancake, usu. filled with cottage cheese, that is folded and then sautéed or baked. [Yiddish *blintse* < Belorussian *blintsy,* pl. of *blinets,* dim. of *blin,* pancake < ORuss. *mlinŭ, blinŭ.* See **melə-***.]

blip (blĭp) *n.* **1.** A spot of light on a radar or sonar screen indicating the position of a detected object. **2.** A high-pitched electronic sound; a bleep. **3.** A brief departure from the normal. — *tr.v.* **blipped, blip•ping, blips.** To bleep. [Imit.]

bliss (blĭs) *n.* **1.** Extreme happiness; ecstasy. **2.** The ecstasy of salvation; spiritual joy. [ME *blisse* < OE *bliss* < *blīths* < *blīthe,* joyful. See BLITHE.] — **bliss′ful** *adj.* — **bliss′ful•ly** *adv.* — **bliss′ful•ness** *n.*

blis•ter (blĭs′tər) *n.* **1.a.** A local swelling of the skin that contains watery fluid and is caused by burning or irritation. **b.** A similar swelling on a plant. **2.a.** A raised bubble, as on a painted surface. **b.** A rounded, usu. transparent structure. — *v.* **-tered, -ter•ing, -ters.** — *tr.* **1.** To cause a blister to form on. **2.** To reprove harshly. — *intr.* To break out in or as if in blisters. [ME, prob. < OFr. *blestre,* of Gmc. orig.] — **blis′ter•y** *adj.*

blister beetle *n.* Any of various soft-bodied beetles of the family Meloidae, such as the cantharis, that secrete a substance capable of blistering the skin.

blister copper *n.* An almost pure copper produced in an intermediate stage of refining. [From its blistered appearance.]

blis•ter•ing (blĭs′tər-ĭng) *adj.* **1.** Intensely hot. **2.** Harsh; severe. **3.** Very rapid. **4.** Producing a blister or blisters. — **blis′ter•ing•ly** *adv.*

blister rust *n.* Any of several diseases of pine trees caused by certain fungi of the genus *Cronartium* and resulting in conspicuous blistering.

B.Lit. *abbr. Lat.* Baccalaureus Litterarum (Bachelor of Literature).

blithe (blīth, blīth) *adj.* **blith•er, blith•est. 1.** Carefree and lighthearted. **2.** Lacking due concern; casual. [ME < OE *blīthe.*] — **blithe′ly** *adv.* — **blithe′ness** *n.*

blith•er (blĭth′ər) *intr.v.* **-ered, -er•ing, -ers.** To blather. [Alteration of BLATHER.]

blithe•some (blīth′səm, blīth′-) *adj.* Cheerful; merry. — **blithe′some•ly** *adv.* — **blith′some•ness** *n.*

B.Litt. *abbr. Lat.* Baccalaureus Litterarum (Bachelor of Literature).

blitz (blĭts) *n.* **1.a.** A blitzkrieg. **b.** A heavy aerial bombardment. **2.** An intense campaign: *a media blitz.* **3.** *Football.* A defensive play in which one or more linebackers or defensive backs attempt to overwhelm the quarterback. — *v.* **blitzed, blitz•ing, blitz•es.** — *tr.* **1.** To subject to a blitz. **2.** *Football.* To rush (the quarterback) in a blitz. — *intr. Football.* To carry out a blitz. [Short for BLITZKRIEG.]

blitz•krieg (blĭts′krēg′) *n.* A swift, sudden military offensive, usu. by combined air and land forces. [Ger. : *Blitz,* lightning (< MHGer. *blitze* < *bliczen,* to flash < OHGer. *blëcchazzen;* see **bhel-**[1]*) + *Krieg,* war (< MHGer. *kriec* < OHGer. *chrēg,* stubbornness; see **gʷerə-**[1]*).]

Blitz•stein (blĭts′stīn′), **Marc.** 1905–64. Amer. composer whose works include the opera *Triple Sec* (1928).

Blix•en (blĕk′sən, blĭk′-), Baroness **Karen.** See Isak **Dinesen.**

bliz•zard (blĭz′ərd) *n.* **1.** A very heavy snowstorm with high winds. **2.** A torrent; a superabundance. [?]

blk. *abbr.* **1.** Black. **2.** Block. **3.** Bulk.

bloat (blōt) *v.* **bloat•ed, bloat•ing, bloats.** — *tr.* **1.** To cause to swell up or inflate, as with gas. **2.** To cure (fish) by soaking in brine and half-drying in smoke. — *intr.* To become swollen or inflated. — *n.* **1.** A swelling of the rumen or intestine of cattle and domestic animals caused by gas formation from eating watery legumes or green forage. **2.** An excess or surfeit, as of employees. [< ME *blout,* soft, puffed < ON *blautr,* soft, soaked. See **bhleu-***.]

bloat•ed (blō′tĭd) *adj.* **1.** Much bigger than desired. **2.** *Medic.* Swollen or distended by fluid or gaseous material.

bloat•er[1] (blō′tər) *n.* A large mackerel or herring, lightly smoked and salted. [< obsolete dial. *bloat,* a soft, moist cured fish, prob. < BLOAT.]

bloat•er[2] (blō′tər) *n.* A small whitefish *(Coregonus hoyi)* of the Great Lakes and the lakes of eastern Canada.

blob (blŏb) *n.* **1.** A soft amorphous mass. **2.** A daub, as of color. — *tr.v.* **blobbed, blob•bing, blobs.** To splash or daub with blobs; splotch. [< ME *blober,* bubble.]

bloc (blŏk) *n.* **1.** A group of nations, parties, or persons united for common action. **2.** A coalition of legislators acting for a common purpose. [Fr. < OFr., block. See BLOCK.]

Bloch (blŏk, blôk, blôKH), **Ernest.** 1880–1959. Swiss-born Amer. composer noted for his chamber music.

Bloch, Felix. 1905–83. Swiss-born Amer. physicist who shared a 1952 Nobel Prize.

Bloch, Konrad Emil. b. 1912. German-born Amer. biochemist who shared a 1964 Nobel Prize.

block (blŏk) *n.* **1.a.** A solid piece of a hard substance, such as wood, having one or more flat sides. **b.** A block used in construction or as a support. **c.** A block upon which chopping or cutting is done. **d.** A block upon which persons are beheaded. **e.** A small wooden or plastic cube used as a building toy. **f.** *Print.* A large amount of text. **g.** *Sports.* A starting block. **2.** A stand from which articles are displayed and sold at an auction. **3.** A mold or form on which an item is shaped or displayed. **4.** A substance, such as wood or stone, that has been prepared for engraving. **5.a.** A pulley or a system of pulleys set in a casing. **b.** An engine block. **6.** A bloc. **7.a.** A set of like items, such as shares of stock, sold or handled as a unit. **b.** *Comp. Sci.* A group of data that is handled as a unit. **8.** A group of four or more unseparated postage stamps forming a rectangle. **9.** *Canadian.* A group of townships in an unsurveyed area. **10.a.** A usu. rectangular section of a city or town bounded on each side by consecutive streets. **b.** A segment of a street bounded by cross streets and including its buildings and inhabitants. **11.** A large building divided into separate units, such as apartments. **12.** A length of railroad track controlled by signals. **13.** The act of obstructing. **14.** Something that obstructs; an obstacle. **15.** *Sports.* An act of bodily obstruction, as of a player or ball. **16.** *Medic.* Interruption, esp. obstruction, of a normal physiological function. **17.** *Psychol.* Sudden cessation of speech or a thought process without an observable cause, sometimes considered a consequence of repression. **18.** *Slang.* The human head. **19.** A blockhead. — *v.* **blocked, block•ing, blocks.** — *tr.* **1.** To

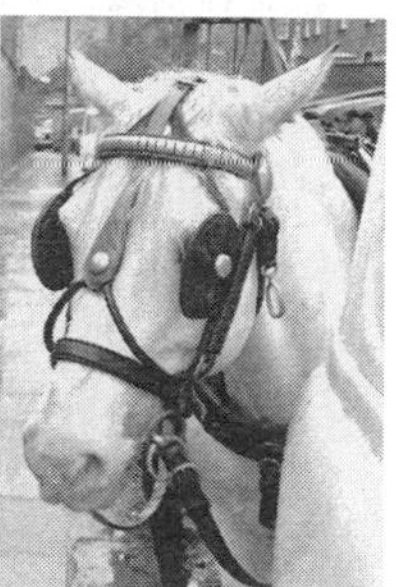

blinders

ă pat	oi boy
ā pay	ou out
âr care	o͝o to͝ok
ä father	o͞o bo͞ot
ĕ pet	ŭ cut
ē be	ûr urge
ĭ pit	th thin
ī pie	*th* this
îr pier	hw which
ŏ pot	zh vision
ō toe	ə about,
ô paw	item

Stress marks:
′ (primary);
′ (secondary), as in
dictionary (dĭk′shə-nĕr′ē)

shape into a block or blocks. **2.** To support, strengthen, or retain in place by means of a block. **3.** To shape, mold, or form with or on a block: *block a hat.* **4.a.** To stop or impede the passage of or movement through; obstruct. **b.** To shut out from view. **5.** To indicate broadly without great detail; sketch: *block out a plan.* **6.** *Sports.* To impede the movement of (an opponent or the ball) by physical interference. **7.** *Medic.* To interrupt the proper functioning of (a physiological process), esp. by the use of anesthesia. **8.** *Psychol.* To fail to remember. **9.** To run (trains) on a block system. — *intr. Sports.* To obstruct the movement of an opponent. [ME *blok* < OFr. < MDu.] — **block′er** *n.*

Syns: *block, hide, obscure, obstruct, screen, shroud.* The central meaning shared by these verbs is "to cut off from sight": *trees that block the view; a road hidden by brush; mist that obscures the mountain peak; skyscrapers obstructing the sky; a fence that screens the alley; a face shrouded by a veil.*

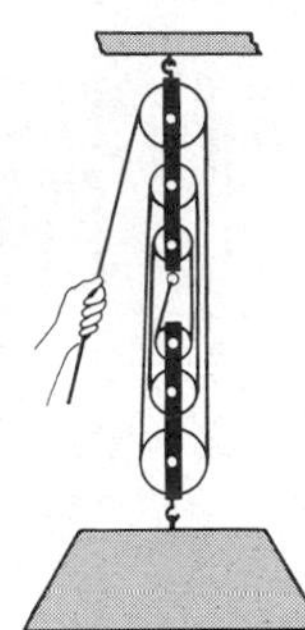
block and tackle
Multiple block and tackle

block•ade (blŏ-kād′) *n.* **1.** The isolation of a nation, an area, a city, or a harbor by hostile ships or forces in order to prevent the passage of traffic and commerce. **2.** The forces used to effect this isolation. — *tr.v.* **-ad•ed, -ad•ing, -ades.** To set up a blockade against. — **block•ad′er** *n.*

block•ade-run•ner (blŏ-kād′rŭn′ər) *n.* One that penetrates or evades a blockade. — **block•ade′-run′ning** *n.*

block•age (blŏk′ĭj) *n.* **1.** The act of obstructing. **2.** An obstruction.

block and tackle *n.* An apparatus of pulley blocks and ropes or cables used for hauling and hoisting heavy objects.

block•bust•er (blŏk′bŭs′tər) *n.* **1.** *Informal.* Something that sustains widespread popularity and achieves enormous sales. **2.** A high-explosive bomb used for demolition purposes. **3.** One that engages in the practice of blockbusting.

block•bust•ing (blŏk′bŭs′tĭng) *n.* *Informal.* The practice of persuading homeowners to sell by appealing to the fear that incoming minority groups will lower property values.

block grant *n.* An unrestricted federal grant, as to a locality.

block•head (blŏk′hĕd′) *n.* A person regarded as very stupid.

block•house (blŏk′hous′) *n.* **1.** A military fortification constructed of sturdy material, such as concrete, and designed for firing or observation. **2.** A heavily reinforced building used for launch operations of missiles and space launch vehicles. **3.** A fort made of squared timbers with a projecting upper story.

block•ish (blŏk′ĭsh) *adj.* Resembling a block, as in shape. — **block′ish•ly** *adv.* — **block′ish•ness** *n.*

Block Island (blŏk). An island of S RI at the E entrance to Long Island Sound; settled in 1661.

block letter *n. Print.* **1.** A letter printed or written sans serif. **2.** A sans-serif style of type.

block plane *n.* A small plane used by carpenters for cutting across the grain of wood.

blockhouse
On the site of Fort Neilson, New York

block signal *n.* A fixed signal at the entrance to a railroad block, indicating whether or not trains may enter.

block system *n.* A system for controlling and safeguarding the flow of railway trains in which track is divided into blocks, each controlled by automatic signals.

block•y (blŏk′ē) *adj.* **-i•er, -i•est.** Blockish.

Bloem•fon•tein (blo͞om′fŏn-tān′). A city of central South Africa ESE of Kimberley. Pop. 102,600.

Blois (blwä). A town of central France on the Loire R. NE of Tours; seat of the powerful counts of Blois. Pop. 47,243.

bloke (blōk) *n. Chiefly British.* A fellow; a man. [?]

blond also **blonde** (blŏnd) — *adj.* **blond•er, blond•est. 1.** Having fair hair and skin and usu. light eyes. **2.** Of a light color, such as auburn or yellowish brown. **3.** Light-colored through bleaching. — *n.* **1.** A blond person. **2.** *Color.* A light yellowish brown to dark grayish yellow. [ME *blounde* < OFr. *blonde,* of Gmc. orig. See **bhel-¹*.**] — **blond′ish** *adj.* — **blond′ness** *n.*

Usage Note: It is usual in English to treat *blond* as if it required gender marking, as in French, spelling it *blonde* when referring to women and *blond* elsewhere. But this practice is in fact a relatively recent innovation, and some have suggested that it has sexist implications and that the form *blond* should be used for both sexes. An association of hair color and a particular perception of feminine identity is suggested in phrases such as *dumb blonde* and *Is it true blondes have more fun?* See Usage Note at **brunette.**

blood (blŭd) *n.* **1.a.** The fluid consisting of plasma, blood cells, and platelets that is circulated by the heart through the vertebrate vascular system, carrying oxygen and nutrients to and waste materials away from all body tissues. **b.** A functionally similar fluid in animals other than vertebrates. **c.** The juice or sap of certain plants. **2.** A vital or animating force; lifeblood. **3.** Bloodshed; murder. **4.** Temperament or disposition: *a person of hot blood.* **5.a.** Descent from a common ancestor; parental lineage. **b.** Family relationship; kinship. **c.** Descent from noble or royal lineage. **d.** Recorded descent from purebred stock. **e.** National or racial ancestry. **6.a.** A dandy. **b.** *Slang.* A youth who is a gang member. — *tr.v.* **blood•ed, blood•ing, bloods. 1.** To give (a hunting dog) its first taste of blood. **2.** To subject (troops) to experience under fire. — ***idiom.* in cold blood.** Deliberately, coldly, and dispassionately. [ME *blod* < OE *blōd.* See **bhel-³*.**]

bloodhound

Blood (blŭd) *n., pl.* **Blood** or **Bloods.** A member of a tribe of the Blackfoot confederacy inhabiting southern Alberta.

blood bank *n.* **1.** A place where whole blood or plasma is typed, processed, and stored for future use in transfusion. **2.** Blood or plasma stored in such a place.

blood•bath also **blood bath** (blŭd′băth′, -bäth′) *n.* Savage indiscriminate killing; a massacre.

blood-brain barrier (blŭd′brān′) *n.* A physiological mechanism that alters the permeability of brain capillaries and prevents some substances, such as certain drugs, from entering brain tissue.

blood brother *n.* **1.** A brother by birth. **2.** One of two individuals who vow mutual fidelity by a ceremony involving the mingling of each other's blood. — **blood brotherhood** *n.*

blood cell *n.* Any of the cells contained in blood; an erythrocyte or leukocyte; a blood corpuscle.

blood clot *n. Physiol.* A semisolid gelatinous mass of coagulated blood that consists of red blood cells, white blood cells, and platelets entrapped in a fibrin network.

blood count *n.* **1.** The number of red blood cells, white blood cells, and platelets in a definite volume of blood. **2.** The determination of such a count. **3.** Complete blood count.

blood•cur•dling (blŭd′kûrd′lĭng) *adj.* Causing great horror; terrifying. — **blood′cur′dling•ly** *adv.*

blood dop•ing or **blood-dop•ing** (blŭd′dō′pĭng) *n.* The process of transfusing an athlete with red blood cells previously removed and stored, thereby increasing the oxygen-carrying capacity of the blood before a competition.

blood•ed (blŭd′ĭd) *adj.* **1.** Having blood or a temperament of a specified kind. Used only in combination: *a cold-blooded reptile.* **2.** Thoroughbred.

blood feud *n.* A feud involving the members of a family or clan.

blood fluke *n.* See **schistosome.**

blood group *n.* Any of several immunologically distinct classes of human blood that are based on the presence or absence of certain antigens and are identified by characteristic agglutination reactions.

blood•guilt (blŭd′gĭlt′) *n.* The fact or state of being guilty of murder or bloodshed.

blood heat *n.* The normal temperature (about 37.0°C or 98.6°F) of human blood.

blood•hound (blŭd′hound′) *n.* **1.** One of a breed of hounds with a smooth coat, drooping ears, sagging jowls, and a keen sense of smell. **2.** *Informal.* A relentless pursuer.

blood•less (blŭd′lĭs) *adj.* **1.** Deficient in or lacking blood. **2.** Pale and anemic in color: *bloodless lips.* **3.** Achieved without bloodshed: *a bloodless coup.* **4.** Lacking vivacity or spirit: *a long, bloodless speech.* **5.** Devoid of human emotion or feeling. — **blood′less•ly** *adv.* — **blood′less•ness** *n.*

blood•let•ting (blŭd′lĕt′ĭng) *n.* **1.** Bloodshed. **2.** The removal of blood, usu. from a vein, as a therapeutic measure. **3.** A sharp reduction or elimination. — **blood′let′ter** *n.*

blood•line (blŭd′līn′) *n.* Direct line of descent; pedigree.

blood meal *n.* The dried and powdered blood of animals, used in animal feeds and as a nitrogen-rich fertilizer for plants.

blood•mo•bile (blŭd′mə-bēl′) *n.* A motor vehicle equipped for collecting blood from donors. [BLOOD + (AUTO)MOBILE.]

blood money *n.* **1.** Money paid by a killer as compensation to the next of kin of a murder victim. **2.** Money gained at the cost of another's life or livelihood.

blood plasma *n.* The fluid portion of the blood in which the blood cells and platelets are normally suspended.

blood platelet *n.* See **platelet.**

blood poi•son•ing (poi′zə-nĭng) *n.* **1.** See **septicemia. 2.** See **toxemia.**

blood pressure *n.* The pressure exerted by the blood against the walls of the blood vessels, esp. the arteries.

blood profile *n.* See **complete blood count.**

blood red *n. Color.* A moderate to vivid red. — **blood′-red′** (blŭd′rĕd′) *adj.*

blood relation *n.* A person who is related to another by birth rather than by marriage. — **blood relationship** *n.*

blood•root (blŭd′ro͞ot′, -ro͝ot′) *n.* A perennial wildflower *(Sanguinaria canadensis)* native to forests in eastern North America and having a fleshy rootstock, a single lobed leaf, and a solitary white flower.

blood serum *n.* See **serum** 1.

blood•shed (blŭd′shĕd′) *n.* The shedding of blood, esp. the injury or killing of human beings.

blood•shot (blŭd′shŏt′) *adj.* Red and inflamed as a result of congested blood vessels: *bloodshot eyes.* [< obsolete *bloodshotten:* BLOOD + *shotten,* suffused, p.part. of SHOOT.]

blood•stain (blŭd′stān′) *n.* A stain caused by blood. — *tr.v.* **-stained, -stain•ing, -stains.** To stain with blood.

blood•stone (blŭd′stōn′) *n.* A variety of deep-green chalcedony flecked with red jasper.

blood•stream also **blood stream** (blŭd′strēm′) *n.* The flow of blood through the circulatory system of an organism.

blood•suck•er (blŭd′sŭk′ər) *n.* **1.** An animal, such as a leech, that sucks blood. **2.** An extortionist or a blackmailer. — **blood′suck′ing** *adj.*

blood sugar *n.* **1.** Sugar in the form of glucose in the blood.

2. The concentration of glucose in the blood.

blood test *n.* **1.** An examination of a sample of blood to determine its chemical, physical, or serologic characteristics. **2.** A serologic test for certain diseases, such as AIDS.

blood•thirst•y (blŭd′thûr′stē) *adj.* **1.** Eager to shed blood. **2.** Characterized by great carnage. **—blood′thirst′i•ly** *adv.* **—blood′thirst′i•ness** *n.*

blood type *n.* See **blood group.**

blood typ•ing or **blood-typ•ing** (blŭd′tī′pĭng) *n.* The process of identifying a person's blood group by serologic testing.

blood vessel *n.* An elastic tubular channel, such as an artery, a vein, or a capillary, through which the blood circulates.

blood•worm (blŭd′wûrm′) *n.* **1.** Any of various red, segmented marine worms of the genera *Polycirrus* and *Enoplobranchus.* **2.** The red freshwater larvae of certain midges.

blood•y (blŭd′ē) *adj.* **-i•er, -i•est. 1.** Stained with blood. **2.** Of, characteristic of, or containing blood. **3.** Accompanied by or giving rise to bloodshed: *a bloody fight.* **4.** Bloodthirsty. **5.** Suggesting the color of blood; blood-red. **6.** Used as an intensive: *Your desk is a bloody mess.* —*adv.* Used as an intensive: *bloody well right.* —*tr.v.* **-ied, -y•ing, -ies. 1.** To stain, spot, or color with or as if with blood. **2.** To make bleed. **—blood′i•ly** *adv.* **—blood′i•ness** *n.*

bloody mary also **Bloody Mary** *n., pl.* **bloody marys** or **bloody mary's.** A cocktail usu. made of vodka, tomato juice, and seasonings. [After MARY I.]

blood•y-mind•ed (blŭd′ē-mīn′dĭd) *adj.* **1.** Ready and willing to accept bloodshed or to resort to violence. **2.** *Chiefly British.* Perversely cantankerous. **—blood′y-mind′ed•ness** *n.*

bloom[1] (blo͞om) *n.* **1.** The flower of a plant. **2.a.** The condition of being in flower. **b.** A condition or time of vigor and beauty; prime: *"the radiant bloom of Greek genius"* (Edith Hamilton). **3.** A fresh, rosy complexion: *"She was short, plump, and fair, with a fine bloom"* (Jane Austen). **4.a.** A waxy or powdery coating sometimes occurring on the surface of plant parts, such as the fruits of certain plums. **b.** A similar coating, as on newly minted coins. **c.** *Chem.* See **efflorescence** 3a. **5.** Glare that is caused by a shiny object reflecting too much light into a television camera. **6.** A colored area on the surface of water caused by planktonic growth. —*v.* **bloomed, bloom•ing, blooms.** —*intr.* **1.a.** To bear a flower or flowers. **b.** To support plant life in abundance. **2.** To shine; glow. **3.** To grow or flourish with youth and vigor. **4.** To appear or expand suddenly. —*tr.* **1.** To cause to flourish. **2.** *Obsolete.* To cause to flower. [ME *blom* < ON *blōm.* See **bhel-[3]*.**] **—bloom′y** *adj.*

bloom[2] (blo͞om) *n.* **1.** A bar of steel prepared for rolling. **2.** A mass of wrought iron ready for further working. [ME *blome,* lump of metal < OE *blōma.* See **bhel-[3]*.**]

bloom•er[1] (blo͞o′mər) *n.* **1.a.** A plant that blooms. **b.** A person who attains full maturity and competence: *a late bloomer.* **2.** *Slang.* A blunder.

bloom•er[2] (blo͞o′mər) *n.* **1.** A costume formerly worn by women and girls that was composed of loose trousers gathered about the ankles. **2. bloomers. a.** Baggy trousers gathered at the knee and formerly worn by women and girls as an athletic costume. **b.** Girls' underpants of similar design. [After Amelia Jenks BLOOMER.]

Bloom•er (blo͞o′mər), **Amelia Jenks.** 1818–1894. Amer. social reformer who founded and edited the *Lily* (1849–55) and advocated a new style of dress for women.

Bloom•field (blo͞om′fēld′). **1.** A town of N-central CT, a suburb of Hartford. Pop. 19,483. **2.** A town of NE NJ, a suburb of Newark; settled c. 1660. Pop. 45,061.

Bloomfield, Leonard. 1887–1949. Amer. linguist who introduced a behavioristic approach in his text *Language* (1933).

bloom•ing (blo͞o′mĭng) *adv. & adj. Chiefly British.* Used as an intensive: *a blooming idiot.* [Prob. a euphemism for BLOODY.]

Bloo•ming•ton (blo͞o′mĭng-tən). **1.** A city of central IL ESE of Peoria. Pop. 51,972. **2.** A city of S-central IN SSW of Indianapolis. Pop. 60,633. **3.** A city of E MN, a suburb of Minneapolis. Pop. 86,335.

Blooms•bur•y (blo͞omz′bĕr′-ē, -bə-rē, -brē). A residential district of N-central London, England, famous for its associations with members of the intelligentsia, including Virginia Woolf and John Maynard Keynes, in the early 20th cent.

bloop (blo͞op) *Baseball.* —*n.* A blooper. —*tr.v.* **blooped, bloop•ing, bloops.** To hit (a ball) into the air just beyond the infield. —*adj.* Hit just beyond the infield.

bloop•er (blo͞o′pər) *n.* **1.** *Informal.* A clumsy mistake, esp. one made in public; a faux pas. **2.** *Baseball.* **a.** A weakly hit ball that carries just beyond the infield. **b.** A high pitch that is lobbed to the batter. [Prob. < BLOOP, a characteristic sound made by an early type of radio receiver.]

blos•som (blŏs′əm) *n.* **1.** A flower or cluster of flowers. **2.** The condition or time of flowering. **3.** A period or condition of maximum development. —*intr.v.* **-somed, -som•ing, -soms. 1.** To come into flower; bloom. **2.** To develop; flourish: *The child blossomed into a beauty.* [ME < OE *blōstm.* See **bhel-[3]*.**] **—blos′som•y** *adj.*

blot[1] (blŏt) *n.* **1.** A spot or a stain caused by a discoloring substance. **2.** A stain on one's character or reputation; a disgrace. —*v.* **blot•ted, blot•ting, blots.** —*tr.* **1.** To spot or stain, as with a discoloring substance. **2.** To bring moral disgrace to. **3.** To obliterate (writing, for example). **4.** To make obscure; hide. **5.** To destroy utterly; annihilate: *War blotted out their way of life.* **6.** To soak up or dry with absorbent material. —*intr.* **1.** To spill or spread in a spot or stain. **2.** To become blotted, soaked up, or absorbed. [ME.]

blot[2] (blŏt) *n.* **1.** *Games.* An exposed piece in backgammon. **2.** *Archaic.* A weak point. [Poss. < LGer. *blat,* naked, unprotected.]

blotch (blŏch) *n.* **1.** A spot or blot; a splotch. **2.** A discoloration on the skin; a blemish. **3.** Any of several plant diseases caused by fungi and resulting in dead areas on leaves or fruit. —*tr. & intr.v.* **blotched, blotch•ing, blotch•es.** To mark or become marked with blotches. [Prob. blend of BLOT[1] and BOTCH.] **—blotch′i•ly** *adv.* **—blotch′i•ness** *n.* **—blotch′y** *adj.*

blot•ter (blŏt′ər) *n.* **1.** A piece or pad of blotting paper. **2.** A book containing daily records of occurrences or transactions.

blot•ting paper (blŏt′ĭng) *n.* Absorbent paper used to blot a surface by soaking up excess ink.

blot•to (blŏt′ō) *adj. Slang.* Intoxicated; drunk.

blouse (blous, blouz) *n.* **1.** A woman's or child's loosely fitting shirt that extends to the waist or slightly below. **2.** A loosely fitting garment resembling a long shirt. **3.** The service coat or tunic worn by the members of some branches of the U.S. armed forces. —*intr. & tr.v.* **bloused, blous•ing, blous•es.** To hang or cause to hang loosely and fully. [Fr., poss. alteration (influenced by *blousse,* wool scraps, of Gmc. orig.) of obsolete Fr. *blaude* < OFr. *bliaut,* prob. of Gmc. orig.]

blou•son (blou′sŏn′, blo͞o′zŏn′) *n.* A woman's garment, such as a dress or blouse, with a fitted waistband over which material blouses. [Fr., dim. of *blouse,* blouse. See BLOUSE.]

blow[1] (blō) *v.* **blew** (blo͞o), **blown** (blōn), **blow•ing, blows.** —*intr.* **1.** To be in a state of motion. Used of the air or of wind. **2.** To move along or be carried by or as if by the wind. **3.** To expel a current of air, as from the mouth or from a bellows. **4.** To produce a sound by expelling a current of air, as in sounding a whistle. **5.** To breathe hard; pant. **6.** To storm. **7.** To melt or otherwise become disabled. Used of a fuse. **8.** To burst suddenly: *The tire blew.* **9.** To spout moist air from the blowhole. Used of a whale. **10.** *Informal.* To boast. **11.** *Slang.* To go away; depart. —*tr.* **1.** To cause to move by means of a current of air. **2.** To expel (air) from the mouth. **3.** To cause air to be expelled suddenly from: *blew a tire.* **4.** To drive a current of air on, in, or through: *blew my hair dry.* **5.** To clear out or make free of obstruction by forcing air through: *blew her nose.* **6.** To shape or form (glass, for example) by forcing air or gas through at the end of a pipe. **7.** *Mus.* **a.** To cause (a wind instrument) to sound. **b.** To sound: *a bugle blowing taps.* **8.** To cause to be out of breath. **9.** To demolish by the force of an explosion. **10.** To lay or deposit eggs in. Used of certain insects. **11.** To melt or otherwise disable (a fuse). **12.** *Slang.* **a.** To spend (money) freely and rashly. **b.** To spend money freely on; treat: *blew me to a sumptuous dinner.* **13.** *Vulgar Slang.* To perform fellatio on. **14.a.** *Slang.* To spoil or lose through ineptitude. See Syns at **botch. b.** To cause (a covert intelligence operation or operative) to be revealed. **15.** *Slang.* To depart (a place) in a great hurry. —*n.* **1.** The act or an instance of blowing. **2.a.** A blast of air or wind. **b.** A storm. **3.** *Informal.* An act of bragging. **4.** *Slang.* Cocaine. **—*phrasal verbs.* blow away.** *Slang.* **1.** To kill by shooting. **2.** To affect intensely; overwhelm. **blow in.** *Slang.* To arrive, esp. when unexpected. **blow off.** To relieve or release (pressure); let off. **blow out. 1.** To extinguish or be extinguished by a gust of air. **2.** To fail, as an electrical apparatus. **3.** To erupt in an uncontrolled manner. Used of a gas or oil well. **blow over.** To subside or pass over with little lasting effect. **blow up. 1.** To come into being: *A storm blew up.* **2.** To fill with air; inflate. **3.** To enlarge (a photographic image or print). **4.** To explode. **5.** To lose one's temper. **—*idioms.* blow a gasket.** *Slang.* To explode with anger. **blow hot and cold.** To change one's opinion often on a matter; vacillate. **blow off steam.** To give vent to pent-up emotion. **blow (one's) cool.** *Slang.* To lose one's composure. **blow (one's) mind.** *Slang.* To affect with intense emotion. **blow (one's) top** (or **stack).** *Informal.* To lose one's temper. [ME *blowen* < OE *blāwan.* See **bhlē-*.**]

blow[2] (blō) *n.* **1.** A sudden hard stroke or hit, as with the fist or an object. **2.** An unexpected shock or calamity. **3.** An unexpected attack; an assault. [ME *blaw.*]

blow[3] (blō) *n.* **1.** A mass of blossoms: *peach blow.* **2.** The state of blossoming. —*intr. & tr.v.* **blew** (blo͞o), **blown** (blōn), **blow•ing, blows.** To bloom or cause to bloom. [< ME *blowen,* to bloom < OE *blōwan.* See **bhel-[3]*.**]

blow-by-blow (blō′-bī-blō′) *adj.* Exhibiting great detail.

blow-dry (blō′drī′) *tr.v.* **-dried, -dry•ing, -dries.** To dry and often style (hair) with a hand-held dryer. **—blow dryer** *n.*

blow•er (blō′ər) *n.* **1.** One that blows, esp. a mechanical device, such as a fan, that produces a current of air. **2.** *Slang.* A braggart. **3.** *Chiefly British.* A telephone.

blow•fish (blō′fĭsh′) *n., pl.* **blowfish** or **-fish•es.** See **puffer.**

blow•fly (blō′flī′) *n.* Any of several flies of the family Calli-

bloomer[2]

ă pat	oi boy
ā pay	ou out
âr care	o͝o took
ä father	o͞o boot
ĕ pet	ŭ cut
ē be	ûr urge
ĭ pit	th thin
ī pie	*th* this
îr pier	hw which
ŏ pot	zh vision
ō toe	ə about,
ô paw	item

Stress marks:
′ (primary);
′ (secondary), as in
dictionary (dĭk′shə-nĕr′ē)

phoridae that deposit their eggs in carcasses or carrion or in open sores and wounds.

blow•gun (blō′gŭn′) *n.* A long narrow pipe through which darts or pellets may be blown.

blow•hard (blō′härd′) *n. Informal.* A boaster or braggart.

blow•hole (blō′hōl′) *n.* **1.** An opening or one of a pair of openings for breathing, on top of the head of cetaceans. **2.** A hole in ice to which aquatic mammals come to breathe. **3.** A vent to permit the escape of air or other gas.

blow•job (blō′jŏb′) *n. Vulgar Slang.* The act or an instance of fellatio.

blown¹ (blōn) *v.* P.part. of **blow¹**. —*adj.* **1.** Swollen or inflated; distended. **2.** Out of breath; panting. **3.** Flyblown. **4.** Formed by blowing: *blown glass.*

blown² (blōn) *v.* P.part. of **blow³**.

blow•off (blō′ôf′, -ŏf′) *n.* **1.** Something, such as a gas, that is blown off. **2.** A device or channel for blowing off something.

blow•out (blō′out′) *n.* **1.a.** A sudden rupture or bursting, as of an automobile tire. **b.** The hole made by such a rupture. **2.** A sudden escape of a confined gas or liquid, as from a well. **3.** *Slang.* A large party or other social affair.

blow•pipe (blō′pīp′) *n.* **1.** A metal tube in which a flow of gas is mixed with a controlled flow of air to concentrate the heat of a flame, used esp. in the identification of minerals. **2.** See **blowgun. 3.** A long narrow pipe used to work molten glass.

blow•torch (blō′tôrch′) *n.* A portable burner for mixing gas and oxygen to produce a very hot flame, used for soldering, welding, and glass blowing.

blow•up (blō′ŭp′) *n.* **1.** An explosion. **2.** An outburst of temper. **3.** A photographic enlargement.

blow•y (blō′ē) *adj.* **-i•er, -i•est.** Windy or breezy.

blow•zy also **blow•sy** (blou′zē) *adj.* **-zi•er, -zi•est** also **-si•er, -si•est. 1.** Having a coarsely ruddy and bloated appearance. **2.** Disheveled and frowzy; unkempt. [< obsolete *blowze,* beggar wench.] —**blow′zi•ly** *adv.* —**blow′zi•ness** *n.*

blueberry
Highbush blueberry
Vaccinium corymbosum

BLS *abbr.* Bureau of Labor Statistics.

B.L.S. *abbr.* Bachelor of Library Science.

BLT (bē′ĕl-tē′) *n., pl.* **BLT's** or **BLTs.** A bacon, lettuce, and tomato sandwich.

blub•ber¹ (blŭb′ər) *v.* **-bered, -ber•ing, -bers.** —*intr.* To sob noisily. See Syns at **cry.** —*tr.* **1.** To utter while crying and sobbing. **2.** To make wet and swollen by weeping. —*n.* A loud sobbing. [ME *bluberen,* to bubble < *bluber,* foam.] —**blub′ber•er** *n.* —**blub′ber•ing•ly** *adv.*

blub•ber² (blŭb′ər) *n.* **1.** The thick layer of fat between the skin and the muscle layers of whales and other marine mammals. **2.** Excessive body fat. **3.** A large sea nettle or medusa. —*adj.* Swollen and protruding: *blubber cheeks.* [ME *bluber,* foam.] —**blub′ber•y** *adj.*

blu•cher (blo͞o′chər, -kər) *n.* **1.** A high shoe or half boot. **2.** A shoe with the vamp and tongue of one piece and the quarters lapping over the vamp. [After G.L. von Blücher.]

Blü•cher (blo͞o′kər, -chər, -KHər), **Gebhard Leberecht von.** 1742–1819. Prussian field marshal who led the Prussian army in campaigns against Napoleon.

bludg•eon (blŭj′ən) *n.* A short, heavy club, usu. of wood, that is thicker or loaded at one end. —*tr.v.* **-eoned, -eon•ing, -eons. 1.** To hit with or as if with a heavy club. **2.** To overcome by or as if by using a heavy club. [?] —**bludg′eon•er, bludg′eon•eer′** (-ə-nîr′) *n.*

blue (blo͞o) *n.* **1.** *Color.* The hue of the portion of the visible spectrum between green and indigo, evoked in the human observer by radiant energy with wavelengths of approx. 450 to 490 nanometers; any of a group of colors whose hue is that of a clear daytime sky; one of the additive or light primaries; one of the psychological primary hues. **2.a.** A pigment or dye imparting this hue. **b.** Bluing. **3.a.** An object having this hue. **b.** Dress or clothing of this hue. **4.a.** A person who wears a blue uniform. **b. blues.** A dress blue uniform, esp. that of the U.S. Army. **5.** Often **Blue. a.** A member of the Union Army in the Civil War. **b.** The Union Army. **6.** A bluefish. **7.** A small blue butterfly of the family Lycaenidae. **8.a.** The sky. **b.** The sea. —*adj.* **blu•er, blu•est. 1.** *Color.* Of the color blue. **2.** Bluish or having parts that are blue or bluish, as the blue whale. **3.** Having a gray or purplish color, as from cold or contusion. **4.** Wearing blue. **5.a.** Gloomy; depressed. **b.** Dismal; dreary: *a blue day.* **6.** Puritanical; strict. **7.** Aristocratic; patrician. **8.** Indecent; risqué: *a blue movie.* —*tr. & intr.v.* **blued, blu•ing, blues.** To make or become blue. —***idioms.*** **blue in the face.** To the point or at the point of extreme exasperation. **out of the blue. 1.** From an unexpected or unforeseen source. **2.** At a completely unexpected time. [ME *blue, bleu* < OFr. *bleu,* of Gmc. orig. See **bhel-¹***.] —**blue′ly** *adv.* —**blue′ness** *n.*

blue grouse
Female blue grouse
Dendragapus obscurus

blue angel *n. Slang.* A blue devil.

blue baby *n.* An infant born with cyanosis as a result of a congenital cardiac or pulmonary defect.

blue•back salmon (blo͞o′băk′) *n.* See **sockeye salmon.**

blue•beard (blo͞o′bîrd′) *n.* A man who marries and murders one wife after another. [After *Blue Beard,* translation of French *Barbe Bleue,* a character in a story by Charles Perrault (1628–1703).]

blue•bell (blo͞o′bĕl′) also **blue•bells** (-bĕlz′) *n.* **1.** Any of several bulbous plants of the genus *Endymion* in the lily family, having usu. blue to pink bell-shaped flowers. **2.** Any of numerous plants of the genus *Mertensia,* esp. the Virginia cowslip. **3.** See **harebell. 4.** Any of several other plants having bluish, usu. bell-shaped flowers.

blue•ber•ry (blo͞o′bĕr′ē) *n.* **1.** Any of numerous plants of the genus *Vaccinium,* having edible blue to blue-black berries. **2.** The fruit of any of these plants.

blue•bill (blo͞o′bĭl′) *n.* See **scaup.**

blue•bird (blo͞o′bûrd′) *n.* Any of several North American songbirds of the genus *Sialia,* having blue plumage and usu. a rust-colored breast in the male.

blue-black (blo͞o′blăk′) *adj. Color.* Very dark blue.

blue blood also **blue•blood** (blo͞o′blŭd′) *n.* **1.** Noble or aristocratic descent. **2.** A member of the aristocracy. [Transl. of Sp. *sangre azul*: *sangre,* blood + *azul,* blue (prob. from the visible veins of fair-complexioned aristocrats).] —**blue′-blood′ed** *adj.*

blue•bon•net (blo͞o′bŏn′ĭt) *n.* **1.** Either of two annual lupines *(Lupinus texensis* and *L. subcarnosus)* native to Texas and having light blue flowers. **2.a.** A broad, blue woolen cap worn in Scotland. **b.** A person wearing such a cap.

blue book also **blue•book** (blo͞o′bo͝ok′) *n.* **1.** An official list of persons in the employ of the U.S. government. **2.** A book listing socially prominent people. **3.** A blank notebook with blue covers in which to answer examination questions.

blue•bot•tle (blo͞o′bŏt′l) *n.* Any of several flies of the genus *Calliphora* that have a bright metallic-blue body.

blue catfish *n.* A large bluish freshwater catfish *(Ictalurus furcatus)* of the Mississippi River valley.

blue cheese *n.* A semisoft cheese made of cow's milk and having a greenish-blue mold and flavor like Roquefort.

blue chip also **blue-chip•per** (blo͞o′chĭp′ər) *n.* **1.** A stock that sells at a high price because of public confidence in its long record of steady earnings. **2.** A valuable asset or property. **3.** A blue poker chip of high value. —**blue′-chip′** *adj.*

blue•coat (blo͞o′kōt′) *n.* A person who wears a blue uniform, esp. a police officer. —**blue′coat′ed** *adj.*

blue cohosh *n.* A perennial herb *(Caulophyllum thalictroides)* of eastern North America, having blue berrylike seeds.

blue-col•lar (blo͞o′kŏl′ər) *adj.* Of or relating to wage earners whose jobs are performed in work clothes and often involve manual labor. —**blue′-col′lar** *n.*

blue crab *n.* An edible bluish swimming crab *(Callinectes sapidus)* that has a wide distribution along the Atlantic and Gulf coasts of North America.

blue•curls also **blue curls** (blo͞o′kûrlz′) *pl.n. (used with a sing. or pl. v.)* Any of several North American plants of the genus *Trichostema* in the mint family, having clusters of mostly bluish or purplish flowers with long curved stamens.

blue devil *n.* **1.** *Slang.* A blue capsule or tablet containing barbiturate amobarbital or its sodium derivative. **2. blue devils.** *Informal.* A feeling of depression; despondency.

blue-eyed grass (blo͞o′īd′) *n.* Any of various New World perennial herbs of the genus *Sisyrinchium,* having grasslike leaves.

blue-eyed Mary *n.* An annual North American herb *(Collinsia verna)* having bicolored flowers with two lips.

blue•fin tuna (blo͞o′fĭn′) *n.* A very large tuna *(Thunnus thynnus)* of temperate waters.

blue•fish (blo͞o′fĭsh′) *n., pl.* **bluefish** or **-fish•es. 1.** A food and game fish *(Pomatomus saltatrix)* of the Atlantic and Indian oceans. **2.** Any of various predominantly blue fishes.

blue flag *n.* Any of several irises having blue or blue-violet flowers, esp. *Iris versicolor* of eastern North America.

blue flu *n.* A sickout, esp. by uniformed police officers. [From the blue color of most police officers' uniforms.]

blue fox *n.* **1.** An arctic fox whose fur is bluish gray during a color phase typically occurring in the summer or extending throughout the year. **2.** The fur of such a fox.

blue•gill (blo͞o′gĭl′) *n.* A common edible sunfish *(Lepomis macrochirus)* of North American lakes and streams.

blue•grass (blo͞o′grăs′) *n.* **1.** Also **blue grass.** Any of various grasses of the genus *Poa,* including Kentucky bluegrass. **2.** *Mus.* A type of folk music that originated in the southern United States, typically played on banjos and guitars.

Blue•grass also **Blue•grass Country** or **Blue•grass Region** (blo͞o′grăs′). A region of central KY noted for the breeding of thoroughbred horses.

blue-green alga (blo͞o′grēn′) *n.* See **cyanobacterium.**

blue grouse *n.* A wildfowl *(Dendragapus obscurus)* of western North America having predominantly gray plumage.

blue gum *n.* A tall timber tree *(Eucalyptus globulus)* of Australia having smooth bluish bark and lance-shaped leaves.

blue heaven *n. Slang.* A blue devil.

blue heron *n.* Any of several varieties of heron with blue or blue-gray plumage.

blue•ing (blo͞o′ĭng) *n.* Var. of **bluing.**

blue•ish (blo͞o′ĭsh) *adj.* Var. of **bluish.**

Blue Island. A city of NE IL, a suburb of Chicago. Pop. 21,203.

blue•jack•et (blo͞o′jăk′ĭt) *n.* An enlisted person in the U.S. or British Navy; a sailor.

blue jay *n.* A North American bird *(Cyanocitta cristata)* having a crested head, predominantly blue plumage, and a harsh cry.

blue jeans also **blue•jeans** (blo͞o′jēnz′) *pl.n.* Clothes, esp. pants, made of blue denim.

blue law *n.* **1.** A law regulating commercial business on Sunday. **2.** One of a body of laws in colonial New England enforcing strict moral standards.

blue moon *n. Informal.* A relatively long period of time.

Blue Mountains. A range of NE OR and SE WA rising to 2,777.3 m (9,106 ft).

Blue Nile (nīl). A river of NE Africa flowing c. 1,609 km (1,000 mi) from NW Ethiopia to Khartoum, where it merges with the White Nile.

blue•nose (blo͞o′nōz′) *n.* A puritanical person.

blue note *n. Mus.* A flatted note, esp. the third or seventh note of a chord, in place of an expected major interval. [From its use in blues music.]

blue-pen•cil (blo͞o′pĕn′səl) *tr.v.* **-ciled, -cil•ing, -cils** also **-cilled, -cil•ling, -cils.** To edit with or as if with a blue pencil.

blue pike *n.* A freshwater food and game fish *(Strizostedion vitreum glaucum)* found in the Great Lakes.

blue-plate (blo͞o′plāt′) *adj.* Being a main course of a restaurant meal usu. offered at a special price. [Perh. from the blue-patterned plate on which such meals were orig.ally served.]

blue•point also **blue point** (blo͞o′point′) *n.* A type of small oyster found chiefly in eastern coastal waters. [After *Blue Point,* a locality on Great S Bay, Long I., NY.]

blue point *n.* A variety of a domestic cat, esp. the Siamese, with a bluish-white coat and darker bluish-gray points.

blue•print (blo͞o′prĭnt′) *n.* **1.** A photographic reproduction, as of architectural plans or technical drawings, rendered as white lines on a blue background. **2.** A detailed plan of action. See Syns at **plan.** — **blue′print′** *v.*

blue racer *n.* A bluish-green harmless variety *(Coluber constrictor flaviventris)* of the blacksnake, found in the central United States.

blue ribbon *n.* **1.** An emblem, badge, or rosette of blue ribbon awarded as first prize in a competition. **2.** An award or honor for excellence. — **blue′-rib′bon** (blo͞o′rĭb′ən) *adj.*

blue-ribbon jury *n. Law.* A jury whose members have been selected for their special qualifications, such as higher education, that enable them to deal with complex legal issues.

Blue Ridge also **Blue Ridge Mountains.** A range of the Appalachian Mts. extending from S PA to N GA and rising to 2,038.6 m (6,684 ft).

blue runner *n.* See **runner** 16.

blues (blo͞oz) *pl.n. (used with a sing. or pl. v.)* **1.** A state of depression or melancholy. **2.** *Mus.* A style of music evolved from southern Black American secular songs and usu. distinguished by slow tempo and flatted thirds and sevenths. [Short for BLUE DEVILS.] — **blues′man** *n.* — **blues′y** *adj.*

blue shark *n.* A pelagic shark *(Prionace glauca)* of tropical and temperate oceans that is a brilliant dark blue on top.

blue shift *n.* A decrease in the wavelength of radiation emitted by an approaching celestial body as a consequence of the Doppler effect. [From the fact that the shorter wavelengths of light are at the blue end of the visible spectrum.]

blue-sky (blo͞o′skī′) *adj.* Unrealistic and impractical.

blue-sky law *n.* A law designed to protect the public from buying fraudulent securities.

Blue Springs. A city of W MO, a suburb of Kansas City. Pop. 40,153.

blue spruce *n.* A Rocky Mountain tree *(Picea pungens)* having silvery-blue or blue-green, four-angled needlelike leaves and cylindrical cones.

blues-rock (blo͞oz′rŏk′) *n. Mus.* A style of music that combines blues and rock 'n' roll.

blue•stem (blo͞o′stĕm′) *n.* Any of several chiefly North American grasses of the genera *Andropogon, Bothriochloa,* and *Schizachyrium,* some of which are important prairie grasses.

blue•stock•ing (blo͞o′stŏk′ĭng) *n.* A woman with strong scholarly or literary interests. [After the *Blue Stocking* Society, a nickname for a predominantly female literary club of 18th-cent. London.] — **blue′stock′ing** *adj.*

blue•stone (blo͞o′stōn′) *n.* **1.** A bluish-gray sandstone used for paving and building. **2.** A similar stone.

blue streak *n. Informal.* **1.** Something moving very fast. **2.** A rapid and seemingly interminable stream of words. [Prob. in allusion to a bolt of lightning.]

blue•tongue (blo͞o′tŭng′) *n.* A viral disease of sheep and cattle transmitted by biting insects and characterized by cyanosis of the lips and tongue.

blu•ets (blo͞o′ĭts) *pl.n. (used with a sing. or pl. v.)* Any of several herbs of the genus *Hedyotis,* esp. the low-growing *H. caerulea* of eastern North America that has blue flowers with yellow centers. [ME < *bleu,* blue. See BLUE.]

blue vitriol *n.* A blue crystalline hydrous solution of copper sulfate, $CuSO_4 \cdot 5H_2O$, used in fungicides, as a wood preservative, and in the processing of leather and textiles.

blue walleye *n.* See **blue pike.**

blue•weed (blo͞o′wēd′) *n.* A biennial Eurasian plant *(Echium vulgare)* having usu. blue flowers.

blue whale *n.* A large whalebone whale *(Sibbaldus musculus)* having a bluish-gray back, yellow underparts, and several ventral throat grooves.

bluff[1] (blŭf) *v.* **bluffed, bluff•ing, bluffs.** — *tr.* **1.** To mislead or deceive. **2.** To impress or deter by a false display of confidence. **3.** *Games.* To mislead (opponents) in a card game, as by heavy betting on a poor hand. — *intr.* To engage in a false display of strength or confidence. — *n.* **1.** The act or practice of bluffing. **2.** One that bluffs. [Prob. < Du. *bluffen* < LGer.] — **bluff′a•ble** *adj.* — **bluff′er** *n.*

bluff[2] (blŭf) *n.* A steep headland, promontory, riverbank, or cliff. — *adj.* **bluff•er, bluff•est. 1.** Rough and blunt but not unkind in manner. **2.** Having a broad steep front. [Prob. < obsolete Du. *blaf* or MLGer. *blaff,* broad.] — **bluff′ly** *adv.* — **bluff′ness** *n.*

blu•ing also **blue•ing** (blo͞o′ĭng) *n.* **1.** Any of various coloring agents that counteract yellowing of laundered fabrics. **2.** A rinsing agent used to tint gray or graying hair silver.

blu•ish also **blue•ish** (blo͞o′ĭsh) *adj.* Somewhat blue. — **blu′ish•ness** *n.*

Blum (blo͞om), **Léon.** 1872–1950. French socialist politician who served as premier (1936–37, 1938, and 1946–47).

blun•der (blŭn′dər) *n.* A usu. serious mistake typically caused by ignorance or confusion. — *v.* **-dered, -der•ing, -ders.** — *intr.* **1.** To move clumsily or blindly. **2.** To make a blunder. — *tr.* **1.** To make a blunder in; botch. **2.** To utter (something) stupidly or thoughtlessly. [< ME *blunderen,* to go blindly, perh. < OSwed. *blundra,* have one's eyes closed < ON *blunda.*] — **blun′der•er** *n.* — **blun′der•ing•ly** *adv.*

Syns: *blunder, bumble, flounder, lumber, lurch, stumble.* The central meaning shared by these verbs is "to move awkwardly or unsteadily": *blundered into the room; flies bumbling against the screen; floundered up the muddy trail; a wagon lumbering along a dirt road; twisted her ankle and lurched home; stumbled but regained his balance.*

blun•der•buss (blŭn′dər-bŭs′) *n.* **1.** A short musket of wide bore and flaring muzzle, formerly used to scatter shot at close range. **2.** A person regarded as clumsy and stupid. [Alteration of Du. *donderbus*: *donder,* thunder (< MDu. *doner*; see **(s)tenə-***) + *bus,* gun (< MDu. *busse,* tube < Lat. *buxis,* box; see BOX[1]).]

blunt (blŭnt) *adj.* **blunt•er, blunt•est. 1.** Having a dull edge or end; not sharp. **2.** Abrupt and often disconcertingly frank in speech. **3.** Slow to understand or perceive; dull. **4.** Lacking in feeling; insensitive. — *v.* **blunt•ed, blunt•ing, blunts.** — *tr.* **1.** To dull the edge of. **2.** To make less effective; weaken. — *intr.* To become blunt. [ME.] — **blunt′ly** *adv.* — **blunt′ness** *n.*

blur (blûr) *v.* **blurred, blur•ring, blurs.** — *tr.* **1.** To make indistinct and hazy in outline or appearance; obscure. **2.** To smear or stain; smudge. **3.** To lessen the perception of; dim. — *intr.* **1.** To become indistinct. **2.** To make smudges or stains by smearing. — *n.* **1.** A smear or blot. **2.** Something hazy and indistinct to the sight or mind. [Prob. akin to ME *bleren,* to blear.] — **blur′ri•ness** *n.* — **blur′ry** *adj.*

blurb (blûrb) *n.* A brief publicity notice, as on a book jacket. [Coined by Gelett Burgess (1866–1951), Amer. humorist.] — **blurb** *v.*

blurt (blûrt) *tr.v.* **blurt•ed, blurt•ing, blurts.** To utter suddenly and impulsively. [Prob. imit.] — **blurt′er** *n.*

blush (blŭsh) *intr.v.* **blushed, blush•ing, blush•es. 1.** To become red in the face, as from embarrassment; flush. **2.** To become red or rosy. **3.** To feel embarrassed or ashamed. — *n.* **1.** A reddening of the face, esp. as from embarrassment. **2.** A red or rosy color. **3.** A glance, look, or view: *seems so at first blush.* **4.** Blusher. [ME *blushen* < OE *blyscan.* See **bhel-**[1]***.**] — **blush′ful** *adj.* — **blush′ing•ly** *adv.*

blush•er (blŭsh′ər) *n.* Makeup used esp. on the cheekbones to give a usu. rosy tint.

blush wine *n.* Any of several wines having a slightly pink tinge, similar in style to a dry white wine.

blus•ter (blŭs′tər) *v.* **-tered, -ter•ing, -ters.** — *intr.* **1.** To blow in violent gusts, as the wind during a storm. **2.a.** To speak in a loudly arrogant or bullying manner. **b.** To brag or make loud, empty threats. — *tr.* To force or bully with swaggering threats. — *n.* **1.** A violent gusty wind. **2.** Turbulence or noisy confusion. **3.** Loud, arrogant speech, often full of empty threats. [ME *blusteren* < MLGer. *blüsteren.*] — **blus′ter•er** *n.* — **blus′ter•y, blus′ter•ous** *adj.*

blvd. or **Blvd.** *abbr.* Boulevard.

Bly (blī), **Nellie.** See Elizabeth Cochrane **Seaman.**

B lymphocyte also **B-lym•pho•cyte** (bē′lĭm′fə-sīt′) *n.* See **B cell.** [*b(ursa-dependent)* + LYMPHOCYTE.]

Blyth (blī, blīth). A municipal borough of NE England on the North Sea at the mouth of the **Blyth River.** Pop. 78,200.

Blythe•ville (blī′vəl, blīth′vĭl′). A city of NE AR near the Mississippi R. N of Memphis TN. Pop. 22,906.

BM *abbr. Physiol.* Basal metabolism.

bm. *abbr.* Beam.

b.m. *abbr.* **1.** Board measure. **2.** Bowel movement.

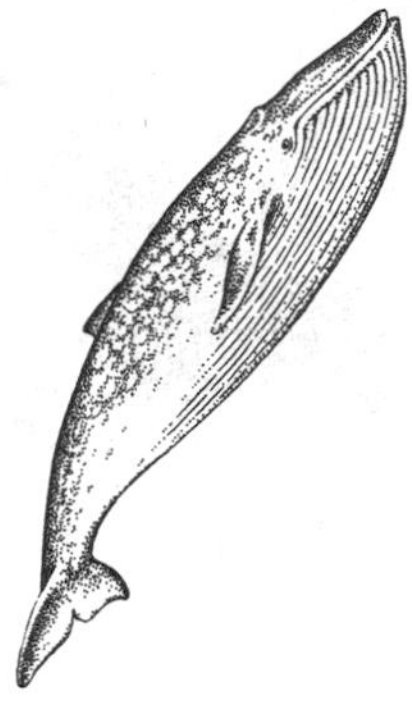

blue whale
Sibbaldus musculus

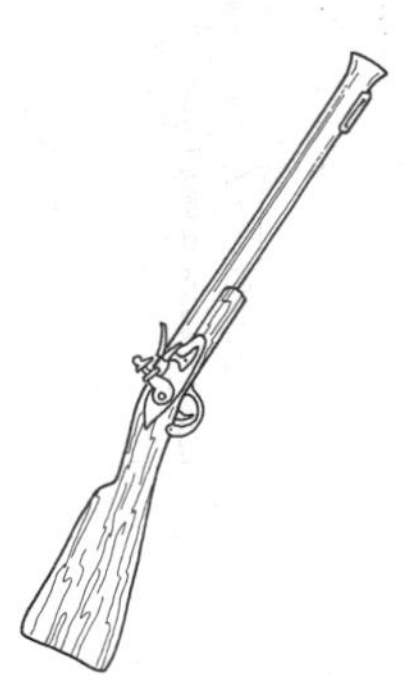

blunderbuss

ă pat	oi boy
ā pay	ou out
âr care	o͝o took
ä father	o͞o boot
ĕ pet	ŭ cut
ē be	ûr urge
ĭ pit	th thin
ī pie	*th* this
îr pier	hw which
ŏ pot	zh vision
ō toe	ə about, item
ô paw	

Stress marks:
′ (primary);
′ (secondary), as in
dictionary (dĭk′shə-nĕr′ē)

B.M. *abbr.* **1.** Bachelor of Medicine. **2.** Bachelor of Music.

B.M.E. *abbr.* **1.** Bachelor of Mechanical Engineering. **2.** Bachelor of Mining Engineering. **3.** Bachelor of Music Education.

B movie *n.* See **B picture.**

BMR *abbr. Physiol.* Basal metabolic rate.

B.M.S. *abbr.* Bachelor of Marine Science.

B.Mus. *abbr.* Bachelor of Music.

BMX *abbr. Sports.* Bicycle motocross.

Bn. or **bn.** *abbr.* **1.** Baron. **2.** Battalion.

B'nai B'rith (bnā′brĭth′) *n.* A Jewish international service organization. [Heb. *bĕnê bĕrît*, sons of the covenant.]

bo•a (bō′ə) *n.* **1.** Any of various large, nonvenomous, chiefly tropical snakes of the family Boidae, which coil around and suffocate their prey. **2.** A long fluffy scarf made of soft material, such as fur. [ME < Lat. *boa*, a large water snake.]

Bo•ab•dil (bō′əb-dēl′, bô′äb-*th*ēl′). d. c. 1527. Last Moorish king of Granada (1482–83 and 1486–92).

boa constrictor *n.* A large boa *(Constrictor constrictor)* of tropical America that kills its prey by constriction.

Bo•ad•i•ce•a (bō′ăd-ĭ-sē′ə). See **Boudicca.**

boar (bôr, bōr) *n.* **1.a.** An uncastrated male pig. **b.** The adult male of any of several mammals, such as the beaver or raccoon. **2.** The wild boar. [ME *bor* < OE *bār*.]

board (bôrd, bōrd) *n.* **1.** A long flat slab of sawed lumber; a plank. **2.** A flat piece of wood or similarly rigid material adapted for a special use. **3.** *Games.* A surface on which a game is played. **4.** The hard cover of a book. **5. boards.** A theater stage. **6.a.** A table, esp. one set for serving food. **b.** Food or meals considered as a whole. **7.** A table at which official meetings are held; a council table. **8.** An organized body of administrators or investigators. **9.** An electrical equipment panel. **10.** *Comp. Sci.* A circuit board. **11.** *Sports.* **a.** A scoreboard. **b.** *Basketball.* A backboard. **c. boards.** The wooden structure enclosing an ice hockey rink. **d.** A diving board. **e.** A surfboard. **12.** *Naut.* **a.** The side of a ship. **b.** A centerboard. **13.** *Obsolete.* A border or an edge. — *v.* **board•ed, board•ing, boards.** — *tr.* **1.** To cover or close with boards: *board up a window.* **2.a.** To furnish with meals for pay. **b.** To house where board is furnished. **3.** To enter or go abroad (a vehicle or ship). **4.** *Obsolete.* To approach. — *intr.* To receive meals for pay. — ***idiom.* on board. 1.** Aboard. **2.** On the job. [ME *bord* < OE.]

boa constrictor
Constrictor constrictor

board•er¹ (bôr′dər, bōr′-) *n.* One who boards, esp. one who pays for regular meals or for meals and lodging.

board•er² (bôr′dər, bōr′-) *n. Sports.* **1.** A person who skis. **2.** One who skateboards. **3.** One who snowboards.

board foot *n., pl.* **board feet.** A unit of cubic measure for lumber, equal to one foot square by one inch thick.

board game *n. Games.* A game of strategy, such as chess or backgammon, played by moving pieces on a board.

board•ing house also **board•ing•house** (bôr′dĭng-hous′, bōr′-) *n.* A house where paying guests are provided with meals and lodging.

boarding school *n.* A school where pupils are provided with meals and lodging.

board measure *n.* Measurement in board feet.

board of education *n., pl.* **boards of education.** A school board.

board of trade *n., pl.* **boards of trade.** An association of bankers and business people to promote common interests.

board•room (bôrd′ro͞om′, -ro͝om′, bōrd′-) *n.* The room where the members of a board meet.

board rule *n.* A measuring stick for determining board feet.

board•sail•ing (bôrd′sā′lĭng, bōrd′-) *n. Sports.* See **windsurfing.** — **board sailor** *n.*

board•walk (bôrd′wôk′, bōrd′-) *n.* **1.** A walk made of wooden planks. **2.** A promenade, esp. of planks, along a beach or waterfront.

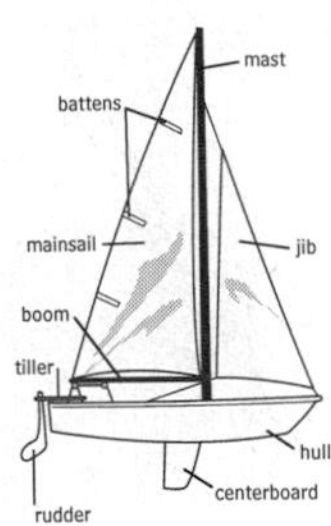

boat
Bermuda-rigged sloop

boar•fish (bôr′fĭsh, bōr′-) *n., pl.* **boarfish** or **-fish•es.** Any of several marine fishes of the genus *Antigonia*, having a deep flattened body, a projecting snout, and bright red coloring.

boar•hound (bôr′hound′, bōr′-) *n.* A large dog, such as the Great Dane, used originally for hunting wild boars.

Bo•as (bō′ăz), **Franz.** 1858–1942. German-born Amer. anthropologist who emphasized the systematic analysis of culture and language structures.

boast¹ (bōst) *v.* **boast•ed, boast•ing, boasts.** — *intr.* To glorify oneself in speech; talk in a self-admiring way. — *tr.* **1.** To speak of with excessive pride. **2.** To possess or own (a desirable feature). **3.** To contain; have. — *n.* **1.** The act or an instance of bragging. **2.** A source of pride. [ME *bosten* < *bost*, a brag.] — **boast′er** *n.* — **boast′ful** *adj.* — **boast′ful•ly** *adv.* — **boast′ful•ness** *n.*

boast² (bōst) *tr.v.* **boast•ed, boast•ing, boasts.** To shape or form (stone) roughly with a broad chisel. [?]

boat (bōt) *n.* **1.** *Naut.* **a.** A relatively small, usu. open craft of a size that might be carried aboard a ship. **b.** An inland vessel of any size. **c.** A ship or submarine. **2.** A dish shaped like a boat. — *intr.v.* **boat•ed, boat•ing, boats.** *Naut.* **1.** To travel by boat. **2.** To ride a boat for pleasure. — ***idiom.* in the same boat.** In the same situation as another or others. [ME *bot* < OE *bāt*. See **bheid-***.]

ă pat	oi boy
ā pay	ou out
âr care	o͝o took
ä father	o͞o boot
ĕ pet	ŭ cut
ē be	ûr urge
ĭ pit	th thin
ī pie	*th* this
îr pier	hw which
ŏ pot	zh vision
ō toe	ə about,
ô paw	item

Stress marks:
′ (primary);
′ (secondary), as in
dictionary (dĭk′shə-nĕr′ē)

boat•bill (bōt′bĭl′) *n.* A tropical American wading bird *(Cochlearius cochlearius)* having a large bill shaped like an inverted boat.

boat-billed heron (bōt′bĭld′) *n.* See **boatbill.**

boat•er (bō′tər) *n.* **1.** *Naut.* One that drives or rides in a boat, esp. a pleasure craft. **2.** A stiff straw hat with a flat crown.

boat hook *n.* A pole with a point and hook at one end used esp. to maneuver logs, rafts, and boats.

boat•house (bōt′hous′) *n.* A building at the water's edge in which boats are kept.

boat•lift (bōt′lĭft′) *n.* An unofficial system of transporting supplies and people, esp. refugees, by boats or ships. [BOAT + (AIR)LIFT.] — **boat′lift′** *v.*

boat•load (bōt′lōd′) *n.* The number of passengers or the amount of cargo that a boat can hold.

boat•man (bōt′mən) *n.* One who works on or operates boats. — **boat′man•ship′** *n.*

boat•swain also **bo's'n** or **bos'n** or **bo•sun** (bō′sən) *n.* A warrant officer or petty officer in charge of a ship's rigging, anchors, cables, and deck crew. [ME *botswein*: *bot*, boat; see BOAT + *swein*, mate; see SWAIN.]

boat•swain's chair (bō′sənz) *n. Naut.* A short board secured by ropes and used as a seat by sailors when working aloft or over a ship's side.

boat train *n.* A train that regularly carries passengers between a city and a port.

Bo•az (bō′ăz). In the Bible, the husband of Ruth.

bob¹ (bŏb) *v.* **bobbed, bob•bing, bobs.** — *tr.* **1.** To hit lightly and quickly; tap. **2.** To cause to move up and down. — *intr.* **1.** To move up and down: *a cork bobbing on the water.* **2.** To grab at floating or hanging objects with the teeth: *bobbed for apples.* **3.** To curtsy or bow. — *n.* **1.** A tap or light blow. **2.** A quick, jerky movement of the head or body. — ***phrasal verb.* bob up.** To appear or arise unexpectedly or suddenly. [ME *bobben*.]

bob² (bŏb) *n.* **1.** A small knoblike pendent object, such as a plumb bob. **2.** A fishing float or cork. **3.** A small lock or curl of hair. **4.** A woman's or child's short haircut. **5.** *Informal.* Surgical shortening or reshaping of the nose. **6.** The docked tail of a horse. **7.a.** A bobsled. **b.** A bob skate. — *v.* **bobbed, bob•bing, bobs.** — *intr.* To fish with a bob. — *tr.* To cut short or reshape. [ME *bobbe*, cluster of fruit.] — **bob′ber** *n.*

bob³ (bŏb) *n., pl.* **bob.** *Chiefly British.* A shilling. [?]

bob•bin (bŏb′ĭn) *n.* **1.** A spool or reel that holds thread or yarn. **2.** Narrow braid formerly used as trimming. [Fr. *bobine*.]

bob•bi•net (bŏb′ə-nĕt′) *n.* A machine-woven net fabric with hexagonal meshes. [BOBBI(N) + NET¹.]

bobbin lace *n.* A handmade lace made by interlacing thread around small notched pins or bobbins stuck into a pillow.

bob•ble (bŏb′əl) *v.* **-bled, -bling, -bles.** — *intr.* To bob up and down. — *tr.* To lose one's grip on (a ball, for example) momentarily. — *n.* A mistake or blunder. [< BOB¹.]

bob•by (bŏb′ē) *n., pl.* **-bies.** *Chiefly British.* A police officer. [After Sir Robert PEEL, home secretary of England when the Metropolitan Police Force was created in 1829.]

bobby pin *n.* A small metal hair clip with the ends pressed tightly together. [< BOB².]

bobby socks also **bobby sox** *pl.n. Informal.* Ankle socks worn by girls or women. [Poss. < BOB² (influenced by BOBBY PIN).]

bob•by•sox•er also **bobby sox•er** (bŏb′ē-sŏk′sər) *n. Informal.* A teenage girl.

bob•cat (bŏb′kăt′) *n.* A wild cat *(Lynx rufus)* of North America having spotted reddish-brown fur, tufted ears, and a short tail. [BOB(TAIL) + CAT.]

bob•o•link (bŏb′ə-lĭngk′) *n.* An American migratory songbird *(Dolichonyx oryzivorus)*, the male of which has black, white, and yellowish plumage. Also called regionally *ricebird*. [Imit. of its song.]

Bo•bruisk (bə-bro͞o′ĭsk). A city of S Belorussia SE of Minsk; founded in the 16th cent.. Pop. 223,000.

bob skate *n. Sports.* An ice skate with two parallel bearing edges. [Poss. BOB(SLED) + SKATE¹.]

bob•sled (bŏb′slĕd′) *Sports. n.* **1.** A long racing sled with a steering mechanism controlling the front runners. **2.a.** A long sled made of two shorter sleds joined in tandem. **b.** Either of these two smaller sleds. [BOB² + SLED.] — **bob′sled′** *v.*

bob•stay (bŏb′stā′) *n. Naut.* A rope or chain used to steady the bowsprit of a ship.

bob•tail (bŏb′tāl′) *n.* **1.** A short or shortened tail. **2.** An animal, such as a horse, having a short or shortened tail. **3.** Something that has been cut short or abbreviated. — **bob′tailed′** *adj.*

bob•white (bŏb-hwīt′, -wīt′) *n.* A small North American quail *(Colinus virginianus)* having brown plumage with white markings. [Imit. of its call.]

bo•cac•cio (bə-kä′chō, -chē-ō′) *n., pl.* **-cios.** A large rockfish *(Sebastes paucispinis)* of American Pacific waters. [Ital. *boccaccio*, ugly mouth, dim. of *bocca*, mouth < Lat. *bucca*.]

Bo•ca Ra•ton (bō′kə rə-tōn′). A city of SE FL on the Atlantic Ocean S of Palm Beach. Pop. 61,492.

Boc•cac•cio (bō-kä′chē-ō′, -chō′), **Giovanni.** 1313–75.

French-born Italian poet and writer best known for the *Decameron* (1351–53).

boc•ce or **boc•ci** or **boc•cie** (bŏch′ē) *n. Sports.* A game of Italian origin similar to bowling that is played with wooden balls on a long, narrow court covered with fine gravel. [Ital. *bocce*, bowls, pl. of *boccia*, ball.]

Boc•che•ri•ni (bŏ′kə-rē′nē, bŏk′ə-, bôk′kĕ-), **Luigi.** 1743–1805. Italian composer noted for his concertos.

Boc•cio•ni (bŏ-chō′nē, bôt-chô′-), **Umberto.** 1882–1916. Italian artist whose works embodied futurism.

Boche also **boche** (bŏsh, bôsh) *n. Offensive Slang.* Used as a disparaging term for a German. [Fr., alteration of *Alboche*, blend of *Allemand*, German; see ALLEMANDE, and Fr. dial. *caboche*, cabbage, blockhead; see CABBAGE.]

Bo•chum (bō′kəm, -KHŏŏm). A city of W-central Germany in the Ruhr Valley E of Essen; chartered 1321. Pop. 384,774.

bock beer (bŏk) *n.* A strong dark beer, the first that is drawn from the vats in springtime. [Ger. *Bockbier*, alteration of *Einbeckisch Bier*, after *Einbeck*, a town of N-central Germany.]

B.O.D. *abbr.* Biochemical oxygen demand.

bo•da•cious also **bow•da•cious** (bō-dā′shəs) or **bar•da•cious** (bär-) *Southern & South Midland U.S.* —*adj.* **1.** Remarkable; prodigious. **2.** Audacious; gutsy. —*adv.* **1.** Completely; extremely. **2.** Audaciously; boldly. [Prob. < dial. *boldacious*, blend of BOLD and AUDACIOUS.]

Regional Note: *Bodacious* is probably a blend of the words *bold* and *audacious*, whose combined senses are evident in the following description of Sevier County, Tennessee, as *"the most bodacious display of tourisma this side of Anaheim"* (Los Angeles Times). Black speech in New York City retains this Southernism as *bardacious.* The English dialect form *boldacious,* the likely source for *bodacious,* strengthens the theory that the speech of the American South preserves some archaic British expressions.

bode¹ (bōd) *tr.v.* **bod•ed, bod•ing, bodes. 1.** To be an omen of: *boded trouble.* **2.** *Archaic.* To predict; foretell. [ME *boden* < OE *bodian*, to announce. See **bheudh-***.]

bode² (bōd) *v.* A p.t. of **bide.**

bo•de•ga (bō-dā′gə) *n.* **1.** A small Hispanic grocery store, sometimes with a wineshop. **2.** A warehouse for storing wine. [Sp. < Lat. *apothēca*, storehouse. See APOTHECARY.]

Bo•den•see (bōd′n-zā′). See Lake of **Constance.**

bo•dhi•satt•va (bō′dĭ-sŭt′və) *n.* A future Buddha who, out of compassion, forgoes nirvana in order to save others. [Skt. *bodhisattvaḥ*, one whose essence is enlightenment : *bodhiḥ*, perfect knowledge; see **bheudh-*** + *sattvam*, essence, being (< *sat-*, existing; see **es-***).]

bod•ice (bŏd′ĭs) *n.* **1.** The fitted part of a dress that extends from the waist to the shoulder. **2.** A woman's laced outer garment, worn like a vest over a blouse. **3.** *Obsolete.* A corset. [Alteration of *bodies*, pl. of BODY.]

bod•ied (bŏd′ēd) *adj.* Having a body, esp. of a specified kind. Often used in combination: *strong-bodied; weak-bodied.*

bod•i•less (bŏd′ē-lĭs) *adj.* Having no body, form, or substance; incorporeal.

bod•i•ly (bŏd′l-ē) *adj.* **1.** Of, relating to, or belonging to the body. **2.** Physical as opposed to mental or spiritual: *bodily welfare.* —*adv.* **1.** In the flesh; in person: *bodily but not mentally present.* **2.** As a complete physical entity.

Syns: *bodily, corporal, corporeal, fleshly, physical, somatic.* The central meaning shared by these adjectives is "of or relating to the human body": *a bodily organ; a corporal defect; corporeal suffering; fleshly frailty; physical robustness; a somatic symptom.*

bod•ing (bō′dĭng) *n.* An omen or foreboding, esp. of evil.

bod•kin (bŏd′kĭn) *n.* **1.** A small, sharply pointed instrument for making holes in fabric or leather. **2.** A blunt needle for pulling tape or ribbon through a series of loops or a hem. **3.** A long hairpin, usu. with an ornamental head. **4.** *Print.* An awl or pick for extracting letters from set type. **5.** A dagger or stiletto. [ME *boidekin.*]

Bo•do•ni (bō-dō′nē, bə-), **Gianbattista.** 1740–1813. Italian printer and designer of the Bodoni typeface.

bod•y (bŏd′ē) *n., pl.* **-ies. 1.a.** The entire material or physical structure of an organism, esp. of a human being or an animal. **b.** The physical part of a person. **c.** A corpse or carcass. **2.a.** The trunk or torso of a human being or an animal. **b.** The part of a garment covering the torso. **3.a.** A human being; a person. **b.** A group of individuals regarded as an entity; a corporation. **4.** A number of persons, concepts, or things regarded as a group. **5.** The main or central part, as: **a.** *Anat.* The largest or principal part of an organ; corpus. **b.** The nave of a church. **c.** The content of a book or document exclusive of prefatory matter, codicils, indexes, or appendixes. **d.** The passenger- and cargo-carrying part of an aircraft, ship, or other vehicle. **e.** *Mus.* The sound box of an instrument. **6.** A mass or collection of material that is distinct from other masses: *a body of water.* **7.** Consistency of substance, as in paint: *a sauce with body.* **8.** *Print.* The part of a block of type underlying the impression surface. —*tr.v.* **-ied, -y•ing, -ies. 1.** To furnish with a body. **2.** To give shape to. [ME *bodi* < OE *bodig.*]

body bag *n.* A zippered bag, usu. of rubber, for transporting a human corpse.

body blow *n.* **1.** *Sports.* A blow delivered to the front of the torso above the waist in boxing. **2.** A serious setback.

bod•y•build•ing (bŏd′ē-bĭl′dĭng) *n. Sports.* The process of developing muscles through specific types of diet and physical exercise, such as weightlifting. —**bod′y•build′er** *n.*

body cavity *n.* See **coelom.**

body cell *n.* See **somatic cell.**

body clock *n.* An internal mechanism of the body that is thought to regulate physical and mental functions in rhythm with normal daily activities.

body corporate *n.* See **corporation** 2.

body count *n.* A count of individual bodies.

body English *n.* The tendency of a person to try to influence the movement of a propelled object, such as a ball, by twisting his or her body toward the desired goal.

body fluid *n.* **1.** A natural bodily fluid or secretion of fluid. **2.** Total body water, contained principally in blood plasma and in intracellular and interstitial fluids.

bod•y•guard (bŏd′ē-gärd′) *n.* A person or group of persons responsible for the physical safety of someone else.

body language *n.* The usu. unconscious bodily gestures, postures, and facial expressions of nonverbal communication.

body louse *n.* A parasitic louse *(Pediculus humanus corporis)* that infests the body and clothes of human beings.

body mechanics *n. (used with a sing. or pl. v.)* The application of kinesiology to help develop proper body movement, coordination, and endurance and to assist with posture problems.

body politic *n.* The people of a politically organized nation or state considered as a group.

body shirt *n.* **1.** A woman's garment for the torso with a sewn-in or snapped crotch. **2.** A tight-fitting shirt or blouse.

body shop *n.* A shop or garage where the bodies of automotive vehicles are repaired.

body snatcher *n.* **1.** A person who steals corpses from graves for sale, usu. for purposes of dissection. **2.** *Slang.* A corporate recruiter. —**bod′y•snatch′ing** (bŏd′ē-snăch′ĭng) *n.*

body stocking *n.* A tight-fitting, usu. one-piece garment that covers the torso and sometimes has sleeves and legs.

body suit *n.* A tight-fitting one-piece garment for the torso.

bod•y•surf (bŏd′ē-sûrf′) *intr.v.* **-surfed, -surf•ing, -surfs.** *Sports.* To ride the waves to shore without a surfboard. —**bod′y•surf′er** *n.*

body wall *n.* The portion of an animal body that consists of ectoderm and mesoderm, forms the external body surface, and encloses the body cavity.

body•work (bŏd′ē-wûrk′) *n.* **1.** The external structure of a motor vehicle. **2.** The repairing of motor vehicle bodies.

Boeh•me (bœ′mə) or **Boehm** (bœm), **Jakob.** See Jakob **Böhme.**

Boe•o•tia (bē-ō′shə, -shē-ə). An ancient region of Greece N of Attica and the Gulf of Corinth whose cities formed the **Boeotian League** in the 7th cent. B.C. —**Boe•o′tian** *adj. & n.*

Boer (bōr, bôr, bŏŏr) *n.* A Dutch colonist or descendant of a Dutch colonist in South Africa. [Afr. < Du., farmer < MDu. *gheboer*, peasant. See **bheuə-***.]

Bo•e•thi•us (bō-ē′thē-əs), **Anicius Manlius Severinus.** A.D. 480?–524? Roman philosopher who wrote *The Consolation of Philosophy.*

boff (bŏf) *n. Slang.* **1.** A line in a play or film, for example, that elicits a big laugh. **2.** A big laugh. **3.** A conspicuous success. [Prob. < B(OX) OFF(ICE).]

bof•fin also **Bof•fin** (bŏf′ĭn) *n. Chiefly British.* A scientist, esp. one engaged in research. [?]

bof•fo (bŏf′ō) *Slang.* —*adj.* Extremely successful; great. —*n.* See **boff.** [Alteration of BOFF.]

bof•fo•la (bŏf-ō′lə) *n. Slang.* See **boff.** [< BOFF.]

Bo•fors gun (bō′fôrz′, bŏŏ′-) *n.* A double-barreled automatic antiaircraft gun. [After *Bofors*, a city of S-central Sweden.]

bog (bôg, bŏg) *n.* **1.a.** An area having a wet, spongy, acidic substrate composed chiefly of sphagnum moss and peat in which characteristic shrubs and herbs and sometimes trees usu. grow. **b.** Any of certain other wetland areas, such as a fen, having a peat substrate. **2.** An area of soft, naturally waterlogged ground. —*v.* **bogged, bog•ging, bogs.** —*tr.* To cause to sink in or as if in a bog. —*intr.* To be hindered and slowed. [Ir.Gael. *bogach* < *bog*, soft. See **bheug-***.] —**bog′gi•ness** *n.* —**bog′gy** *adj.*

Bo•gart (bō′gärt), **Humphrey DeForest.** "Bogie." 1899–1957. Amer. actor who starred in *Casablanca* (1942) and *The African Queen* (1951).

bog asphodel or **bog-as•pho•del** (bôg′ăs′fə-dĕl′, bŏg′-) *n.* Any of several perennial herbs of the genus *Narthecium* in the lily family, native to boggy areas in northern temperate regions.

bo•gey *n.* also **bo•gy** or **bo•gie** (bō′gē), *pl.* **-geys** also **-gies. 1.** *(also* bŏŏg′ē, bŏŏ′gē). An evil or mischievous spirit; a hobgoblin. **2.** *(also* bŏŏg′ē, bŏŏ′gē). A cause of annoyance or harassment. **3.** *Sports.* **a.** An estimated standard golf score. **b.** One golf stroke over par on a hole. **4.** *Slang.* An unidentified flying aircraft. **5.** *Slang.* A detective or police officer.

boatbill
Cochlearius cochlearius

bobwhite
Male and female bobwhite quail
Colinus virginianus

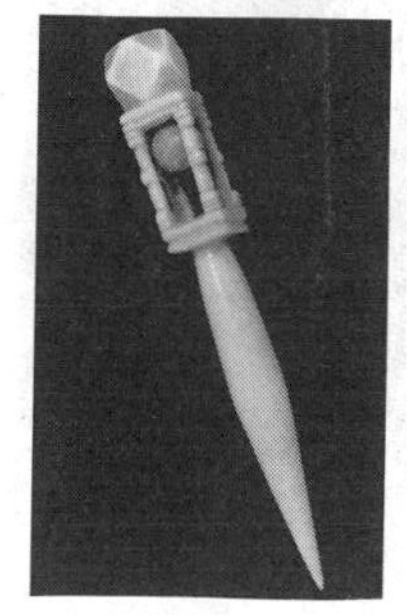

bodkin
Ivory sewing implement with "ball in cage" design

Humphrey Bogart

— *tr.v.* **-geyed, -gey•ing, -geys.** *Sports.* To shoot (a hole in golf) in one stroke over par. [Poss. var. of BOGLE.]

bog•ey•man or **bo•gy•man** also **boog•ey•man** or **boog•y•man** or **boog•ie•man** (bo͝og′ē-măn′, bō′gē-, bo͞o′gē-) *n.* A terrifying specter; a hobgoblin.

bog•gle (bŏg′əl) *v.* **bog•gled, bog•gling, bog•gles.** — *intr.* **1.** To hesitate as if in fear or doubt. **2.** To shy away or be overcome with fright or astonishment. **3.** To botch; bungle. — *tr.* To cause to be overcome, as with fright or astonishment. [Prob. < *boggle,* dialectal var. of BOGLE.] — **bog′gle** *n.* — **bog′gler** *n.*

bog hole *n.* A hole containing soft mud or quicksand.

bo•gie^1 also **bo•gy** (bō′gē) *n., pl.* **-gies. 1.** A railroad car or locomotive undercarriage with two, four, or six wheels that swivels so curves can be negotiated. **2.** One of several wheels or supporting and aligning rollers inside the tread of a tractor or tank. [?]

bo•gie^2 (bō′gē, bo͝og′ē, bo͞o′gē) *n.* A var. of **bogey.**

bo•gle (bō′gəl) *n.* A hobgoblin; a bogey. [Sc. *bogill.*]

Bo•gor (bō′gôr′). A city of W Java, Indonesia, S of Jakarta. Pop. 247,409.

Bo•go•tá (bō′gə-tä′). The cap. of Colombia, in the central part on a high plain in the E Andes; settled by the Spanish in 1538. Pop. 3,967,988.

bog rosemary *n.* Any of several evergreen shrubs of the genus *Andromeda,* having pink or white urn-shaped flowers.

bog•trot•ter (bôg′trŏt′ər, bŏg′-) *n.* **1.** A person who lives in or frequents bogs. **2.** *Offensive Slang.* Used as a disparaging term for an Irish person.

bo•gus (bō′gəs) *adj.* Counterfeit or fake. [< E. *bogus,* a device for making counterfeit money.]

bog•wood (bôg′wo͝od′, bŏg′-) *n.* Wood that has been preserved in a peat bog.

bo•gy^1 (bō′gē, bo͝og′ē, bo͞o′gē) *n.* Var. of **bogey.**

bo•gy^2 (bō′gē) *n.* Var. of **bogie^1.**

bo•gy•man (bo͝og′ē-măn′, bō′gē-, bo͞o′gē-) *n.* Var. of **bogeyman.**

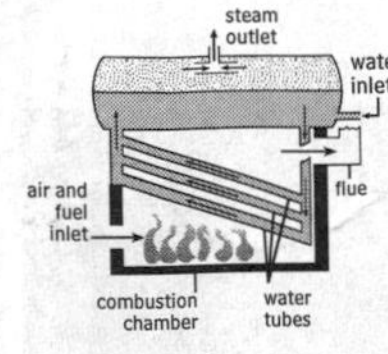

boiler
Water-tube boiler

Bo Hai also **Po Hai** (bō′ hī′). An inlet of the Yellow Sea on the NE coast of China.

bo•hea (bō-hē′) *n.* A black Chinese tea. [After the Fujian pronunciation of Chin. (Mandarin) *wŭ yí (shān),* the Wuyi mountain range on the border of Jiangxi and Fujian provinces.]

bo•he•mi•a (bō-hē′mē-ə) *n.* **1.** A community of persons with artistic or literary tastes who adopt unconventional manners and mores. **2.** The district in which bohemians live. [Back-formation < BOHEMIAN.]

Bo•he•mi•a (bō-hē′mē-ə). A historical region and former kingdom of present-day W Czech Republic; settled by Czechs between the 1st and 5th cent. A.D.

bo•he•mi•an (bō-hē′mē-ən) *n.* A person with artistic or literary interests who disregards conventional standards of behavior. [Fr. *bohémien* < *Bohême,* Bohemia (from the unconventional life style of its Gypsy inhabitants).] — **bo•he′mi•an** *adj.* — **bo•he′mi•an•ism** *n.*

Bo•he•mi•an (bō-hē′mē-ən) *n.* **1.** A native or inhabitant of Bohemia. **2.** A Gypsy. **3.** The Czech dialects of Bohemia. — **Bo•he′mi•an** *adj.*

Anne Boleyn
Detail of a portrait by an unknown artist

Bohemian Brethren *n.* A religious society organized in the 15th century by the Hussites.

Böh•me also **Boeh•me** (bœ′mə) or **Boehm** (bœm), **Jakob.** 1575–1624. German mystic considered the founder of modern theosophy.

Bo•hol (bō-hôl′). An island in the Visayan Is. of central Philippines N of Mindanao in the **Bohol Sea.**

Bohr (bôr, bōr), **Niels Henrik David.** 1885–1962. Danish physicist who won a 1922 Nobel Prize. His son **Aage Niels Bohr** (b. 1922), also a physicist, shared a 1975 Nobel Prize.

Bohr theory *n.* An early model of atomic structure in which electrons travel around the nucleus in a number of discrete stable orbits determined by quantum conditions. [After Niels Henrik David BOHR.]

bo•hunk (bō′hŭngk) *n.* *Offensive Slang.* Used as a disparaging term for a person from east-central Europe, esp. a laborer. [Blend of BO(HEMIAN) and HUNG(ARIAN).]

Bo•iar•do (boi-är′dō, bō-yär′-), **Matteo Maria.** 1440?–94. Italian lyric poet known for his unfinished romantic epic *Orlando Innamorato* (1487).

boil^1 (boil) *v.* **boiled, boil•ing, boils.** — *intr.* **1.a.** To change from a liquid to a vapor by the application of heat. **b.** To reach the boiling point. **c.** To undergo the action of boiling, esp. in being cooked. **2.** To be in a state of agitation; seethe: *a boiling river.* **3.** To be stirred up or greatly excited. — *tr.* **1.a.** To vaporize (a liquid) by the application of heat. **b.** To heat to the boiling point. **2.** To cook or clean by boiling. **3.** To separate by evaporation in the process of boiling. — *n.* **1.** The condition or act of boiling. **2.** *Lower Southern U.S.* A picnic featuring shrimp, crab, or crayfish boiled in large pots with spices and then shelled and eaten. **3.** An agitated, swirling, roiling mass of liquid. — ***phrasal verbs.* boil down. 1.** To reduce in bulk or size by boiling. **2.** To condense; summarize. **3.** To constitute the equivalent of in summary. **boil over. 1.** To overflow while boiling. **2.** To lose one's temper. [ME *boillen* < OFr. *boillir* < Lat. *bullīre.*]

Syns: *boil, simmer, seethe, stew.* To *boil* is to cook in a heated liquid that bubbles up and gives off vapor. Figuratively *boil* pertains to intense agitation: *She boiled with anger. Simmer* denotes gentle cooking just at or below the boiling point; figuratively it refers to a state of gentle ferment: *plans simmering in his mind. Seethe* emphasizes in both senses the turbulence of steady boiling: *"The city had . . . been seething with discontent"* (John R. Green). *Stew* refers literally to slow boiling and figuratively to a persistent but not violent state of agitation: *"They don't want a man to fret and stew about his work"* (William H. Whyte, Jr.).

boil^2 (boil) *n.* A painful, circumscribed pus-filled inflammation of the skin and subcutaneous tissue usu. caused by a local staphylococcal infection. [ME *bile* < OE *bȳle.*]

Boi•leau-Des•pré•aux (bwä-lō′dĕ-prā-ō′), **Nicolas.** 1636–1711. French critic who wrote *Art of Poetry* (1674).

boil•er (boi′lər) *n.* **1.** An enclosed vessel in which water is heated and circulated, either as hot water or as steam, for heating or power. **2.** A container, such as a kettle, for boiling liquids. **3.** A storage tank for hot water.

boil•er•mak•er (boi′lər-mā′kər) *n.* **1.** One that makes or repairs boilers. **2.** *Slang.* A drink of whiskey with a beer chaser.

boil•er•plate (boi′lər-plāt′) *n.* **1.** A steel plate used in making the shells of steam boilers. **2.** Journalistic material, such as syndicated features, available in plate or mat form. **3.** Inconsequential, formulaic, or stereotypical language.

boil•ing point (boi′lĭng) *n.* **1.** The temperature at which a liquid boils at a fixed pressure, esp. under standard atmospheric conditions. **2.** *Informal.* The point at which one loses one's temper.

boil•off (boil′ôf′, -ŏf′) *n.* The vaporization of liquid.

Bois de Bou•logne (bwä′ də bo͞o-lōn′, -lôn′yə). A park in Paris, France, bordering on Neuilly-sur-Seine; a popular recreation area since the 17th cent.

bois de rose (bwä′ də rōz′) *n.* *Color.* A grayish red. [Fr., rosewood : *bois,* wood + *de,* of + *rose,* rose.]

Boi•se (boi′sē, -zē). The cap. of ID, in the SW part on the **Boise River,** c. 257 km (160 mi); founded 1863. Pop. 102,160.

bois•ter•ous (boi′stər-əs, -strəs) *adj.* **1.** Rough and stormy; violent. **2.** Noisy and lacking in restraint or discipline. [ME *boistres,* var. of *boistous,* rude, rough, perh. < OFr. *boisteus,* lame, limping < *boiste,* knee joint.] — **bois′ter•ous•ly** *adv.* — **bois′ter•ous•ness** *n.*

boîte (bwät) *n.* A small restaurant or nightclub. [Fr. < OFr. *boiste,* box < LLat. *buxida* < *buxis.* See BOX^1.]

Bok (bŏk), **Edward William.** 1863–1930. Dutch-born Amer. editor and social reformer.

bok choy also **pak choi** (bŏk′ choi′) *n.* A Chinese vegetable *(Brassica rapa* var. *Chinensis)* in the mustard family, having a leafy head similar to that of the common cabbage. [Chin. (Mandarin) *bái cài*: *bái,* white + *cài,* vegetable.]

Bo•kha•ra (bō-kär′ə, -här′ə, -KHä′rə). See **Bukhara.**

Bok•mål (bo͝ok′môl′, bōk′-) *n.* See **Dano-Norwegian.** [Norw. : *bok,* book; see **bhāgo-*** + *mål,* language.]

Bol. *abbr.* **1.** Bolivia. **2.** Bolivian.

bo•la (bō′lə) also **bo•las** (-ləs) *n.* A rope with weights attached, used esp. in South America to catch cattle or game by entangling their legs. [< Am.Sp. *bolas,* pl. of Sp. *bola,* ball, prob. < Lat. *bulla.*]

Bo•lan Pass also **Bho•lan Pass** (bō-län′). A mountain pass of W Pakistan at an altitude of 1,793.4 m (5,880 ft).

bola tie *n.* Var. of **bolo tie.**

bold (bōld) *adj.* **bold•er, bold•est. 1.** Fearless and daring; courageous. **2.** Requiring or exhibiting courage and bravery. See Syns at **brave. 3.** Unduly forward and brazen in manner. **4.** Clear and distinct to the eye; conspicuous. **5.** Steep or abrupt in grade or terrain. **6.** *Print.* Boldface. [ME < OE *bald.* See **bhel-^{2}*.**] — **bold′ly** *adv.* — **bold′ness** *n.*

bold•face (bōld′fās′) *Print.* — *n.* Type with thick, heavy lines. — *adj.* Printed in thick, heavy type. — *tr.v.* **-faced, -fac•ing, -fac•es. 1.** To mark (copy) for printing in this type. **2.** To set or print in this type.

bold-faced (bōld′fāst′) *adj.* Impudent; brazen.

bole^1 (bōl) *n.* The trunk of a tree. [ME < ON *bolr.* See **bhel-^{2}*.**]

bole^2 (bōl) *n.* **1.** Any of various soft fine clays, esp. a reddish-brown variety used as a pigment. **2.** *Color.* A moderate reddish brown. [ME < Med.Lat. *bōlus.* See BOLUS.] — **bole** *adj.*

bo•lec•tion (bō-lĕk′shən) *n.* *Archit.* A molding that projects from the surface of a panel. [?]

bo•le•ro (bō-lâr′ō, bə-) *n., pl.* **-ros. 1.** A very short jacket worn open in the front. **2.a.** A Spanish dance in triple meter. **b.** The music for this dance. [Sp. < *bola,* ball. See BOLA.]

bo•le•tus (bō-lē′təs) *n., pl.* **-tus•es** or **-ti** (-tī′). A fungus of the genus *Boletus,* having an umbrella-shaped cap with spore-bearing tubules on the underside. [Lat. *bōlētus,* mushroom.]

Bol•eyn (bo͝ol′ĭn, bo͞o-lĭn′), **Anne.** 1507–36. Queen of England (1533–36) as the second wife of Henry VIII; accused of adultery and beheaded.

bo•lide (bō′līd, -lĭd) *n.* A meteoric fireball. [Fr. < Lat. *bolis,*

ă pat	oi boy
ā pay	ou out
âr care	o͝o took
ä father	o͞o boot
ĕ pet	ŭ cut
ē be	ûr urge
ĭ pit	th thin
ī pie	*th* this
îr pier	hw which
ŏ pot	zh vision
ō toe	ə about, item
ô paw	

Stress marks:
′ (primary);
′ (secondary), as in
dictionary (dĭk′shə-nĕr′ē)

bolid- < Gk., missile, javelin < *ballein*, to throw. See **gʷelə-*.**]

Bol•ing•broke (bŏl′ĭng-brŏŏk′, bŏŏl′-, bō′lĭng-), 1st Viscount. Henry Saint John. 1678–1751. English public official who wrote *The Idea of a Patriot King* (1749).

Bo•ling•brook (bō′lĭng-brŏŏk′). A village of NE IL, a suburb of Chicago. Pop. 40,843.

bo•li•var (bō-lē′vär, bŏl′ə-vər) *n.*, *pl.* **bo•li•vars** or **bo•li•var•es** (bō-lē′vä-rĕs′). See table at **currency.** [Am.Sp. *bolívar*, after Simón BOLÍVAR.]

Bo•lí•var (bō′lə-vär′, bŏl′ə-, bō-lē′vär), **Pico.** A mountain, 5,005.4 m (16,411 ft), of W Venezuela in the Cordillera Mérida S of Lake Maracaibo.

Bolívar, Simón. "the Liberator." 1783–1830. South American revolutionary leader who defeated the Spanish in 1819 and helped liberate (1823–34) Peru and Bolivia.

Bo•liv•i•a (bə-lĭv′ē-ə, bō-). A landlocked country of W South America; named after Simón Bolívar, who helped win its independence from Spain in 1825. Caps. Sucre and La Paz. Pop. 6,429,226. — **Bo•liv′i•an** *adj. & n.*

bo•li•vi•a•no (bə-lĭv′ē-ä′nō, bō-) *n.*, *pl.* **-nos.** See table at **currency.** [Sp., Bolivian, boliviano < BOLIVIA.]

boll (bōl) *n.* The seed-bearing capsule of certain plants, esp. cotton and flax. [ME < MDu. *bolle*, round object. See **bhel-[2]*.**]

Böll (bœl), **Heinrich.** 1917–85. German writer who won the 1972 Nobel Prize for literature.

bol•lard (bŏl′ərd) *n. Naut.* A thick post on a ship or wharf, used for securing lines and hawsers. [ME, prob. < *bole*, tree trunk. See BOLE[1].]

bol•li•to mis•to (bō-lē′tō mĭs′tō) *n.*, *pl.* **bol•li•ti mis•ti** (bō-lē′tē mĭs′tē). A mixture of vegetables and various meats cooked in a broth and usu. served with a mustard-fruit sauce. [Ital., mixed stew : *bollito*, stew + *misto*, mixed.]

bol•lix also **bol•lox** (bŏl′ĭks) *tr.v.* **-lixed, -lix•ing, -lix•es** also **-loxed, -lox•ing, -lox•es.** *Informal.* To throw into confusion; botch or bungle: *bollixed it up.* [Alteration of *ballocks*, testicles < ME *balloks* < OE *beallucas*. See **bhel-[2]*.**]

boll weevil *n.* **1.** A small, grayish, long-snouted beetle *(Anthonomus grandis)* of Mexico and the southern United States that damages cotton. **2.** *Informal.* A conservative Southern Democrat in the U.S. House of Representatives.

boll•worm (bōl′wûrm′) *n.* **1.** The pink bollworm. **2.** See **corn earworm.**

bo•lo (bō′lō) *n.*, *pl.* **-los.** A long, heavy, single-edged machete originally used in the Philippines. [Sp., of Philippine orig.]

bo•lo•gna (bə-lō′nē, -nə, -nyə) also **ba•lo•ney** or **bo•lo•ney** (-nē) *n.* A seasoned smoked sausage made of mixed meats, such as beef, pork, and veal. [After BOLOGNA.]

Bo•lo•gna (bə-lōn′yə). A city of N-central Italy at the foot of the Apennines NNE of Florence; orig. an Etruscan town. Pop. 455,853. — **Bo•lo′gnan, Bo′lo•gnese′** (bō′lə-nēz′, -nēs′, -lən-yēz′, -yēs′) *adj. & n.*

bo•lom•e•ter (bō-lŏm′ĭ-tər) *n.* An instrument that measures radiant energy by correlating the change in resistance of an electrical element with the amount of radiation absorbed. [Gk. *bolē*, ray; see **gʷelə-*** + -METER.] — **bo′lo•met′ric** (bō′lə-mĕt′rĭk) *adj.*

bolo tie also **bola tie** *n.* A necktie consisting of a piece of cord fastened with an ornamental bar or clasp. [Alteration of BOLA + TIE.]

Bol•she•vik (bōl′shə-vĭk′, bŏl′-) *n.*, *pl.* **-viks** or **-vi•ki** (-vē′kē). **1.a.** A member of the left-wing group of the Russian Social Democratic Workers' Party that adopted Lenin's theses on party organization (1903). **b.** A member of the Russian Social Democratic Workers' Party that seized power in November 1917. **c.** A member or a supporter of a Marxist-Leninist party; a Communist. **2.** Often **bolshevik.** A radical. [Russ. *Bol'shevik* < *bol'she*, comp. of *bol'shoĭ*, large. See **bel-*.**] — **Bol′she•vik′** *adj.*

Bol•she•vism also **bol•she•vism** (bōl′shə-vĭz′əm, bŏl′-) *n.* **1.** The strategy developed by the Bolsheviks between 1903 and 1917 with a view to seizing state power and establishing a dictatorship of the proletariat. **2.** Soviet Communism.

Bol•she•vist also **bol•she•vist** (bōl′shə-vĭst, bŏl′-) *n.* See **Bolshevik 1.** — **Bol′she•vis′tic** *adj.*

bol•son (bōl-sōn′) *n. Chiefly Southwestern U.S.* A flat arid valley surrounded by mountains and draining into a shallow central lake. [Am.Sp. *bolsón*, aug. of Sp. *bolsa*, purse, pouch < LLat. *bursa*. See BURSA.]

bol•ster (bōl′stər) *n.* A long narrow pillow or cushion. — *tr.v.* **-stered, -ster•ing, -sters. 1.** To support or prop up with or as if with a long narrow pillow or cushion. **2.** To buoy up. [ME < OE. See **bhelgh-*.**] — **bol′ster•er** *n.*

bolt[1] (bōlt) *n.* **1.** A bar made of wood or metal that slides into a socket and is used to fasten doors and gates. **2.** A metal bar or rod in the mechanism of a lock that is thrown or withdrawn by turning the key. **3.** A fastener consisting of a threaded pin or rod with a head at one end, designed to be inserted through holes in assembled parts and secured by a nut that is tightened by applying torque. **4.a.** A sliding metal bar that positions the cartridge in breechloading rifles, closes the breech, and ejects the spent cartridge. **b.** A similar device in any breech mechanism. **5.** A short heavy arrow with a thick head, used esp. with a crossbow. **6.** A flash of lightning; a thunderbolt. **7.** A sudden or unexpected event. **8.** A sudden movement toward or away. **9.** A large roll of cloth of a definite length, esp. as it comes from the loom. — *v.* **bolt•ed, bolt•ing, bolts.** — *tr.* **1.** To secure or lock with or as if with a bolt. **2.** To arrange or roll (lengths of cloth, for example) on or in a bolt. **3.** To eat (food) hurriedly. **4.** To desert or withdraw support from (a political party). **5.** To utter impulsively; blurt. **6.** *Archaic.* To shoot or discharge (a missile). — *intr.* **1.** To move or spring suddenly. **2.** To start suddenly and run away. **3.** To bolt a political party. **4.** *Bot.* To flower or produce seeds prematurely or develop a flowering stem from a rosette. — ***idiom.* bolt from the blue.** A sudden, shocking surprise. [ME < OE, heavy arrow.]

bolt[2] (bōlt) *tr.v.* **bolt•ed, bolt•ing, bolts.** To pass (flour, for example) through a sieve. [ME *bulten* < OFr. *buleter* < MHGer. *biuteln* < *biutel*, bag, purse.]

bolt-action (bōlt′ăk′shən) *adj.* Loaded by a manually operated bolt. Used of a firearm.

bolt•er[1] (bōl′tər) *n.* **1.** A horse given to bolting. **2.** One who withdraws support from a political party.

bolt•er[2] (bōl′tər) *n.* **1.** A machine used for sifting, esp. for sifting flour. **2.** One who operates a sifting machine.

bolt•hole (bōlt′hōl′) *n.* **1.** A hole through which to bolt. **2.** A means of escape.

Bol•ton (bōl′tən). A borough of NW England NW of Manchester. Pop. 263,000.

bol•to•ni•a (bōl-tō′nē-ə) *n.* Any of several perennial herbs of the genus *Boltonia* in the composite family, having flower heads with white to purplish rays and yellow centers. [NLat., genus name, after James Bolton, 18th-cent. British botanist.]

bolt•rope (bōlt′rōp′) *n. Naut.* A rope sewn into the outer edge of a sail to prevent it from tearing.

bo•lus (bō′ləs) *n.*, *pl.* **-lus•es. 1.** A round mass. **2.** *Pharm.* A round medicinal preparation that is usu. of a soft consistency and not prepackaged. **3.** A soft mass of chewed food within the mouth or alimentary canal. [Med.Lat. *bōlus* < Gk. *bōlos*, lump of earth.]

Bol•za•no (bōl-zä′nō, bôl-tsä′nô). A city of N Italy near the Austrian border NNW of Venice. Pop. 104,606.

bomb (bŏm) *n.* **1.a.** An explosive weapon detonated by impact, a timing mechanism, or other means. **b.** An atomic or a nuclear bomb. **2.** Any of various weapons detonated to release destructive material, such as smoke. **3.** *Football.* A very long forward pass. **4.a.** A container capable of withstanding high internal pressure. **b.** A vessel for storing compressed gas. **c.** A portable, manually operated container that ejects a spray, foam, or gas under pressure. **5.** *Slang.* A dismal failure. **6.** *Slang.* An old car. **7.** *Chiefly British.* A large amount of money. — *v.* **bombed, bomb•ing, bombs.** — *tr.* To attack, damage, or destroy with or as if with bombs. — *intr.* **1.** To drop bombs. **2.** *Slang.* To fail miserably. **3.** *Slang.* To paint a graffito. [Fr. *bombe* < Ital. *bomba*, prob. < Lat. *bombus*, a booming sound < Gk. *bombos*.]

bom•bard (bŏm-bärd′, bŏm′bärd′) *tr.v.* **-bard•ed, -bard•ing, -bards. 1.** To attack with bombs, shells, or missiles. **2.** To assail persistently, as with requests. **3.** To irradiate (an atom). **4.** To attack with a cannon firing stone balls. — *n.* An early form of cannon that fired stone balls. [< ME, a bombard < OFr. *bombarde* < Med.Lat. *bombarda*, prob. < Lat. *bombus*, a booming sound. See BOMB.] — **bom•bard′er** *n.* — **bom•bard′ment** *n.*

bom•bar•dier (bŏm′bər-dîr′) *n.* **1.** The member of a combat aircraft crew who drops the bombs. **2.** *Chiefly British.* A noncommissioned artillery officer. **3.** *Archaic.* An artillery soldier. [Fr. < OFr. *bombarde*, bombard. See BOMBARD.]

bombardier beetle *n.* Any of various beetles of the genus *Brachinus* and related genera that expel an acrid volatile secretion from the abdomen when disturbed.

bom•bar•don (bŏm′bər-dŏn′, bŏm-bär′dn) *n. Mus.* A bass or contrabass tuba. [Fr. < Ital. *bombardone*, aug. of *bombardo*, alteration of *bombarda*, bombard < Med.Lat. See BOMBARD.]

bom•bast (bŏm′băst′) *n.* Grandiloquent, pompous speech or writing. [Alteration of obsolete *bombace*, cotton padding < OFr. < LLat. *bombax*, cotton. See BOMBAZINE.] — **bom′bast′er** *n.* — **bom•bas′tic** *adj.* — **bom•bas′ti•cal•ly** *adv.*

Bom•bay (bŏm-bā′). A city of W-central India on coastal **Bombay Island** and adjacent Salsette I. Pop. 8,243,405.

Bombay duck *n.* **1.** A small edible lizardfish *(Harpodon nehereus)* of Asia having a thin, nearly transparent body. **2.** The dried, salted flesh of this fish that is used in India as a relish. [Alteration of Marathi *bombīla, bombil.*]

bom•ba•zine (bŏm′bə-zēn′) *n.* A fine twilled fabric of silk and worsted or cotton, often used for mourning clothes. [Fr. *bombasin* < LLat. *bambacīnum*, cotton fabric < *bombax*, cotton < Lat. *bombȳx*, silk, silkworm < Gk. *bombux*, silkworm.]

bombe (bŏm, bôɴb) *n.* A dessert consisting of two or more layers of variously flavored ice cream frozen in a round or

Simón Bolívar

Bolivia

bollard

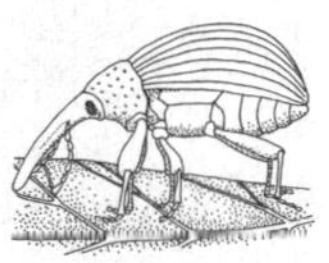

boll weevil
Anthonomus grandis

melon-shaped mold. [Fr. < its shape. See BOMB.]

bombed (bŏmd) *adj. Slang.* Intoxicated; drunk.

bomb•er (bŏm′ər) *n.* **1.** A combat aircraft designed to carry and drop bombs. **2.** One who makes and sets off bombs. **3.** *Upstate New York & Illinois.* See **submarine** 2. See Regional Note at **submarine.**

bomb•proof (bŏm′pro͞of′) *adj.* Designed and constructed to resist destruction by a bomb.

bomb•shell (bŏm′shĕl′) *n.* **1.** An explosive bomb. **2.** A shocking surprise.

bomb•sight (bŏm′sīt′) *n.* A device in a combat aircraft for determining the point at which to drop a bomb.

bom•by•cid (bŏm′bĭ-sĭd) *n.* A moth of the family Bombycidae, which includes the silkworms. [< NLat. *Bombycidae,* family name < Lat. *bombȳx,* silkworm. See BOMBAZINE.]

Bo•mu (bō′mo͞o). A river of central Africa rising in SE Central African Republic and flowing c. 805 km (500 mi) to join the Uele and form the Ubangi R.

Bo•na (bō′nə), **Mount.** A peak, 5,032.5 m (16,500 ft), of S AK at the S end of the Wrangell Mts.

bo•na fide (bō′nə fīd′, fī′dē, bŏn′ə) *adj.* **1.** Made or carried out in good faith; sincere. **2.** Authentic; genuine. See Syns at **authentic.** [Lat. *bonā fidē*: *bonā,* fem. ablative of *bonus,* good + *fidē,* ablative of *fidēs,* faith.]

Bo•naire (bô-nâr′). An island of the Netherlands Antilles in the Caribbean Sea off the N coast of Venezuela.

Bo•nam•pak (bō-näm′päk). A ruined Mayan city near present-day Tuxtla Gutiérrez in S Mexico.

bongo[1]
Boocercus eurycerus

bo•nan•za (bə-năn′zə) *n.* **1.** A rich mine, vein, or pocket of ore. **2.** A source of great wealth or prosperity. [Sp. < Med. Lat. *bonacia,* calm sea, blend of Lat. *bonus,* good; see **deu-**[2]*, and Med.Lat. *malacia,* calm sea (< Gk. *malakia* < *malakos,* soft; see **mel-**[1]*).]

Bo•na•parte (bō′nə-pärt′). Corsican family, all brothers of Napoleon I, including **Joseph** (1768–1844), king of Naples (1806–08) and Spain (1808–13); **Lucien** (1775–1840); **Louis** (1778–1846), king of Holland (1806–10); and **Jérôme** (1784–1860), king of Westphalia (1807–13). **—Bo′na•part′ism** *n.* **—Bo′na•part′ist** *n.*

Bon•a•ven•ture (bŏn′ə-vĕn′chər) also **Bon•a•ven•tu•ra** (bŏn′ə-vĕn-cho͝or′ə, -to͝or′ə, -tyo͝or′ə), Saint. "the Seraphic Doctor." 1217?–74. Italian theologian and philosopher who advocated direct contemplation of God as the highest goal.

bon•bon (bŏn′bŏn′) *n.* A candy that often has a center of fondant, fruit, or nuts and is coated with chocolate or fondant. [Fr., redup. of *bon,* good < Lat. *bonus.* See **deu-**[2]*.]

bond (bŏnd) *n.* **1.** Something, such as a band, that binds, ties, or fastens things together. **2.** Confinement in prison; captivity. Often used in the plural. **3.** A uniting force or tie; a link: *the familial bond.* **4.** A binding agreement; a covenant. **5.** An obligation, such as a promise, by which one is bound. **6.a.** A substance or an agent that causes two or more objects or parts to cohere. **b.** The union or cohesion brought about by such a substance or agent. **7.** A chemical bond. **8.** An overlapping arrangement of bricks or other masonry components in a wall. **9.** *Law.* **a.** A written and sealed obligation, esp. one requiring payment of a stipulated amount of money on or before a given day. **b.** A sum of money paid as bail or surety. **c.** A bail bondsman. **10.** A certificate of debt issued by a government or corporation guaranteeing payment of the original investment plus interest by a specified future date. **11.** The condition of taxable goods being stored in a warehouse until the taxes or duties owed on them are paid. **12.** An insurance contract in which an agency guarantees payment to an employer in the event of unforeseen financial loss through the actions of an employee. **13.** Bond paper. **—*v.* bond•ed, bond•ing, bonds. —*tr.*** **1.** To mortgage or place a guaranteed bond on. **2.** To furnish bond or surety for. **3.** To place (an employee, for example) under bond or guarantee. **4.** To join securely, as with glue or cement. **5.** To join (two or more individuals) in or as if in a nurturing relationship. **6.** To lay (bricks, for example) in an overlapping pattern for solidity. **—*intr.*** **1.** To cohere with or as if with a bond. **2.** To form a close personal relationship. [ME, var. of *band* < ON. See **bhendh-***.] **—bond′a•ble** *adj.* **—bond′er** *n.*

bongo[2]
Bongo drums

bond•age (bŏn′dĭj) *n.* **1.** The state of one who is bound as a slave or serf. **2.** A state of subjection to a force or an influence. **3.** The practice of being physically restrained as a means of attaining sexual gratification. **4.** Villeinage. [ME < AN < ME *bonde,* serf < OE *bōnda,* husbandman < ON *bōndi,* pr.part. of *būa,* to live. See **bheuə-***.]

bond•hold•er (bŏnd′hōl′dər) *n.* One that owns a bond certificate of a government or corporation.

bontebok
Damaliscus dorcas

bond•ing (bŏn′dĭng) *n.* **1.** The formation of close, specialized human relationships, such as those that link parent with offspring. **2.** *Dentistry.* A technique for the restoration, repair, or cosmetic improvement of a tooth that involves the application of a high-impact resinous material to the tooth surface.

bond•maid (bŏnd′mād′) *n.* A woman bondservant. [BOND(WOMAN) + MAID.]

bond•man (bŏnd′mən) *n.* A male bondservant. [ME < *bonde,* serf. See BONDAGE.]

bond paper *n.* A superior grade of strong white paper made wholly or in part from rag pulp.

bond•ser•vant (bŏnd′sûr′vənt) *n.* **1.** A person obligated to service without wages. **2.** A slave or serf. [BOND(MAN) + SERVANT.]

bonds•man (bŏndz′mən) *n.* **1.** A person who provides bond or surety for another. **2.** A male bondservant.

bond•wom•an (bŏnd′wo͝om′ən) *n.* A woman bondservant. [ME *bondewomman* < *bonde,* serf. See BONDAGE.]

bone (bōn) *n.* **1.a.** The dense, semirigid, porous, calcified connective tissue forming the major portion of the skeleton of most vertebrates. **b.** Any of numerous anatomically distinct structures making up the skeleton of a vertebrate animal. **c.** A piece of bone. **2. bones. a.** The skeleton. **b.** The body. **c.** Mortal remains. **3.** An animal structure or material, such as ivory, resembling bone. **4.** Something made of bone or of material resembling bone, esp.: **a.** A piece of whalebone or similar material used as a corset stay. **b. bones.** *Informal.* Dice. **5. bones.** The fundamental plan or design, as of the plot of a book. **6.** Flat clappers made of bone or wood. **—*v.* boned, bon•ing, bones. —*tr.*** **1.** To remove the bones from. **2.** To stiffen (a piece of clothing) with stays, as of whalebone. **—*intr.*** *Informal.* To study intensely, usu. at the last minute: *boning up on math.* **—*idioms.* bone of contention.** The subject of a dispute. **bone to pick.** Grounds for a complaint or dispute. [ME *bon* < OE *bān.*]

bone ash *n.* The white, powdery calcium phosphate ash of burned bones, used as a fertilizer and in making ceramics.

bone•black also **bone black** (bōn′blăk′) *n.* A black pigment containing about 10 percent charcoal, made by roasting bones in an airtight container.

bone china *n.* Porcelain made of clay mixed with bone ash.

bone-dry (bōn′drī′) *adj.* Having no trace of moisture.

bone•fish (bōn′fĭsh′) *n., pl.* **bonefish** or **-fish•es.** A marine game fish *(Albula vulpes)* of warm shallow waters, having silvery scales. [From its many small bones.]

bone•head (bōn′hĕd′) *n. Informal.* A stupid person; a dunce. **—bone′head′ed** *adj.* **—bone′head′ed•ness** *n.*

bone marrow *n.* The soft, fatty, vascular tissue that fills most bone cavities and is the source of red blood cells and many white blood cells.

bone meal *n.* A substance made of crushed and coarsely ground bones, used as a fertilizer and in animal feed.

bon•er (bō′nər) *n. Informal.* A blunder or an error. [BONE(HEAD) + -ER[1].]

bone•set (bōn′sĕt′) *n.* Any of several plants of the genus *Eupatorium* in the composite family, esp. the eastern North American species *E. perfoliatum* having clusters of small white flower heads. [From its use as a folk medicine.]

bon•ey (bō′nē) *adj.* Var. of **bony.**

bon•fire (bŏn′fīr′) *n.* A large outdoor fire. [ME *bonnefire*: *bon,* bone; see BONE + *fir,* fire; see FIRE.]

bong[1] (bŏng, bông) *n.* A deep ringing sound. **—*v.* bonged, bong•ing, bongs. —*tr.*** To cause to sound with a deep ringing noise. **—*intr.*** To make a deep ringing noise. [Imit.]

bong[2] (bŏng, bông) *n.* A water pipe that consists of a bottle or a vertical tube partially filled with liquid and a smaller tube ending in a bowl. [Thai *baung.*]

bon•go[1] (bŏng′gō, bông′-) *n.* **-gos.** A large antelope *(Boocercus eurycerus)* of central Africa having a reddish-brown coat with white stripes and spirally twisted horns. [Prob. of Bantu orig.; akin to Lingala *mongu,* antelope.]

bon•go[2] (bŏng′gō, bông′-) *n., pl.* **-gos** or **-goes.** *Mus.* One of a pair of connected tuned drums that are played by beating with the hands. [Am.Sp. *bongó.*]

Bon•heur (bô-nûr′, -nœr′), **Rosa.** 1822–99. French artist known for her animal paintings, such as *The Horse Fair.*

bon•ho•mie (bŏn′ə-mē′) *n.* A pleasant and affable disposition; geniality. [Fr. < *bonhomme,* good-natured man : *bon,* good (< Lat. *bonus*; see **deu-**[2]*) + *homme,* man (< Lat. *homō*; see **dhghem-***).]

Bon•i•face (bŏn′ə-fās′), Saint. 675?–754. English Roman Catholic missionary active in Germany.

Boniface VIII. 1235?–1303. Pope (1294–1303) who struggled to assert authority over England, France, and Sicily.

bon•ing knife (bō′nĭng) *n.* A knife with a narrow blade and a sharp point, used for removing animal bones.

Bo•nin Islands (bō′nĭn). An archipelago of volcanic islands in the W Pacific Ocean S of Japan.

bo•ni•to (bə-nē′tō) *n., pl.* **bonito** or **-tos. 1.** Any of several marine fishes of the genus *Sarda,* related to and resembling the tuna. **2.** Any of several similar fishes, such as the skipjack. [Sp., prob. < *bonito,* pretty < Lat. *bonus,* good. See **deu-**[2]*.]

bon•kers (bŏng′kərz) *adj. Informal.* Crazy. [?]

bon mot (bôn mō′) *n., pl.* **bons mots** (bôn mō′, mōz′). A clever saying; a witticism. [Fr. : *bon,* good + *mot,* word.]

Bonn (bŏn, bôn). The former cap. of West Germany, in the W part on the Rhine R.; founded as a Roman garrison in the 1st cent. A.D. and since 1990 the seat of the reunified German government. Pop. 291,291.

Bon•nard (bô-när′), **Pierre.** 1867–1947. French painter who adhered to an impressionistic style in works such as *The Bath.*

bon•net (bŏn′ĭt) *n.* **1.a.** A cloth or straw hat held in place by ribbons tied under the chin and worn by women and children. **b.** *Scots.* A brimless cap worn by men. **2.** A removable metal plate over a machine part. **3.** *Chiefly British.* The hood of an automobile. **4.a.** A windscreen for a chimney. **b.** A cover for a fireplace. —*tr.v.* **-net•ed, -net•ing, -nets.** To put a bonnet on. [ME *bonet*, cap < OFr., material for a headdress, perh. < Med.Lat. *obbonis*, prob. of Gmc. orig.]

Bon•ne•ville Salt Flats (bŏn′ə-vĭl′). A plain of NW UT W of Great Salt Lake in the bed of prehistoric **Lake Bonneville.**

Bon•ney (bŏn′ē), **William H.** "Billy the Kid." 1859–81. Amer. outlaw who murdered 21 men and was shot dead by Sheriff Pat Garrett (1850–1908).

bon•ny also **bon•nie** (bŏn′ē) *adj.* **-ni•er, -ni•est.** *Scots.* **1.** Physically attractive or appealing; pretty. **2.** Excellent. [?] —**bon′ni•ly** *adv.* —**bon′ni•ness** *n.*

bon•ny•clab•ber (bŏn′ē-klăb′ər) *n. New England & Central Atlantic U.S.* Thick soured milk eaten with cream and sugar, honey, or molasses. [Ir.Gael. *bainne clabair*: *bainne*, milk (< MIr., drop, milk < OIr. *bannae*, drop) + prob. *clabair*, genitive of *clabar*, dasher of a churn.]

bon•sai (bŏn-sī′, bŏn′sī′, -zī′) *n., pl.* **bonsai. 1.** The art of growing dwarfed ornamental trees or shrubs in shallow pots or trays. **2.** A tree or shrub so grown. [J., potted plant : *bon*, basin (< Chin. *pén*) + *sai*, to plant (< Chin. *zāi*).]

bon•spiel (bŏn′spēl′) *n. Scots.* A curling tournament or match. [Prob. Du. **bonspel*, league game : *bon*, league (perh. < *bonne*, precinct of a city) + *spel*, game < MDu.]

bon•te•bok (bŏn′tə-bŏk′) *n.* A rare South African antelope *(Damaliscus dorcas* or *D. pygargus)* having a dark reddish coat, a white rump, and a white mark on the face. [Afr. : *bont*, spotted (< MDu., prob. < Lat. *punctus*; see POINT) + *bok*, buck (< MDu. *boc*).]

Bon•temps (bôN-täN′), **Arna Wendell.** 1902–73. Amer. writer whose works explore Black life and heritage.

bon ton (bŏn tŏn′) *n.* **1.a.** A sophisticated manner or style. **b.** The proper thing to do. **2.** High society. [Fr. : *bon*, good + *ton*, tone.]

bo•nus (bō′nəs) *n., pl.* **-nus•es. 1.** Something given or paid beyond what is usual or expected. **2.** A sum of money or the equivalent given in addition to an employee's usual compensation. **3.** A government subsidy to an industry. **4.** A premium given by a corporation to another party. **5.** A sum of money paid by a corporation in excess of interest or royalties charged for a privilege or a loan. [< Lat., good. See **deu-**[2]***.**]

Syns: *bonus, bounty, subsidy, premium, prize, reward, gratuity.* Each of these nouns denotes a form of extra payment. *Bonus* usually applies to money in excess of what is strictly due, given especially in recognition of superior effort or as a share in profits: *Hard-working employees receive an annual bonus.* A *bounty* is a sum of money offered by a government for the performance of a special service: *a bounty of 15 dollars for every coyote pelt. Subsidy* refers to a grant from a government in support of an enterprise regarded as being in the public interest: *a subsidy for research.* A *premium* is generally something given as an incentive: *"[The company] has been a pioneer in direct mail since it began offering premiums"* (ADWEEK). A *prize* is awarded for superiority or victory: *won a prize. Reward* refers broadly to payment for a specific meritorious service: *a $10,000 reward for useful information.* A *gratuity* is a gift of money made in appreciation of services rendered: *left a gratuity for the porter.*

bon vi•vant (bôN′ vē-väN′) *n., pl.* **bons vi•vants** (bôN′ vē-väN′). One with refined taste, esp. for food and drink. [Fr. : *bon*, good + *vivant*, pr.part. of *vivre*, to live.]

bon voy•age (bôN′ vwä-yäzh′) *interj.* Used to express farewell and good wishes to a departing traveler. [Fr. : *bon*, good + *voyage*, journey.]

bon•y or **bon•ey** (bō′nē) *adj.* **-i•er, -i•est** or **-ey•er, -ey•est. 1.** Of, resembling, or consisting of bone. **2.** Having an internal skeleton of bones. **3.** Full of bones. **4.a.** Having prominent or protruding bones. **b.** Lean; scrawny. —**bon′i•ness** *n.*

bony fish *n.* A fish having a bony rather than cartilaginous skeleton; a teleost.

bonze (bŏnz) *n.* A Buddhist monk, esp. of Asia. [Fr. < Port. *bonzo* < J. *bonsō* < Chin. *fán sēng*: *fán*, ordinary + *sēng*, monk.]

boo[1] (bo͞o) *n., pl.* **boos. 1.** A sound uttered to show contempt or disapproval. **2.** *Informal.* Any sound or anything at all: *You never said boo to me about overtime.* —*interj.* Used to express contempt or disapproval or to frighten or surprise another. —*v.* **booed, boo•ing, boos.** —*intr.* To utter a boo. —*tr.* To express contempt or disapproval of by booing. [Imit.]

boo[2] (bo͞o) *n. Slang.* Marijuana. [?]

boob[1] (bo͞ob) *n. Slang.* A stupid or foolish person; a dolt. [Short for BOOBY[1].]

boob[2] (bo͝ob) *n. Vulgar Slang.* A woman's breast. [Short for BOOBY[2].]

boo-boo also **boo•boo** (bo͞o′bo͞o) *n., pl.* **-boos.** *Informal.* **1.** A stupid mistake; a blunder. **2.** A slight physical injury, such as a scratch. [Perh. alteration of *boohoo*, to weep noisily.]

boob tube *n. Slang.* Television. [BOOB[1] + TUBE, television set.]

boo•by[1] (bo͞o′bē) *n., pl.* **-bies. 1.** A person regarded as stupid. **2.** Any of several tropical sea birds of the genus *Sula*, resembling and related to the gannets. [Prob. Sp. *bobo* < Lat. *balbus*, stammering.]

boo•by[2] (bo͝ob′ē) *n., pl.* **-bies.** *Vulgar Slang.* A woman's breast. [Perh. alteration of obsolete E. *bubby*.]

booby hatch *n.* **1.** *Naut.* A raised covering over a small hatchway. **2.** *Slang.* A mental health facility.

booby prize *n.* **1.** *Sports & Games.* An award given to the one who scores lowest in a game or contest. **2.** *Informal.* Acknowledgment of great inferiority, as in ability.

booby trap *n.* **1.** A concealed, often explosive device that is triggered by an unsuspecting victim when a harmless-looking object is touched. **2.** A situation that catches one off guard; a pitfall. —**boo′by-trap′** (bo͞o′bē-trăp′) *v.*

boo•coo (bo͞o′ko͞o′) *adj., n., & adv. Chiefly Southern U.S.* Var. of **beaucoup.**

boo•dle (bo͞od′l) *n. Slang.* **1.a.** Money, esp. counterfeit money. **b.** Money accepted as a bribe. **2.** Stolen goods; swag. **3.** A crowd of people; caboodle. [Du. *boedel*, estate < MDu. *bōdel*. See **bheuə-*.**]

boog•er (bo͝og′ər) *n.* **1.** A bogeyman. **2.** *Slang.* Dried nasal mucus. **3.** *Slang.* An unnamed or unnameable item. **4.** *Slang.* **a.** A worthless, despicable person. **b.** A person. [?]

boog•ey•man (bo͝og′ē-măn′, bō′gē-, bo͞o′gē-) *n.* Var. of **bogeyman.**

boog•ie (bo͝og′ē, bo͞o′gē) *Slang.* —*intr.v.* **-ied, -y•ing, -ies.** To dance to the sound of rock music. —*n.* **1.** Strongly rhythmic rock music. **2.** Boogie-woogie. [< BOOGIE-WOOGIE.]

boog•ie•man (bo͝og′ē-măn′, bō′gē-, bo͞o′gē-) *n.* Var. of **bogeyman.**

boog•ie-woog•ie (bo͝og′ē-wo͝og′ē, bo͞o′gē-wo͞o′gē) *n. Mus.* A style of jazz piano characterized by a repeated rhythmic and melodic pattern in the bass and a series of improvised variations in the treble. [Poss. < Black West African E. (Sierra Leone) *bogi(-bogi)*, to dance.]

boog•y•man (bo͝og′ē-măn′, bō′gē-, bo͞o′gē-) *n.* Var. of **bogeyman.**

boo•jum tree (bo͞o′jəm) *n.* A deciduous tree *(Idria columnaris)* native to Baja California and having a tapering trunk and spiny branches. [After the *boojum*, an imaginary character in the poem *The Hunting of the Snark* by Lewis Carroll.]

book (bo͝ok) *n.* **1.** A set of pages fastened along one side and encased between protective covers. **2.a.** A printed or written literary work. **b.** A main division of a larger printed or written work: *a book of the* Iliad. **3.a.** A volume in which financial or business transactions are recorded. **b. books.** Financial or business records considered as a group. **4.a.** A libretto. **b.** The script of a play. **5. Book.** The Bible. **6.a.** A set of prescribed standards or rules on which decisions are based. **b.** Something regarded as a source of knowledge or understanding. **7.** A packet of like or similar items bound together: *a book of matches.* **8.** A record of bets placed on a race. **9.** *Games.* The number of card tricks needed before any tricks can have scoring value, as the first six tricks taken by the declaring side in bridge. —*tr.v.* **booked, book•ing, books. 1.** To list or register in or as if in a book. **2.** To record charges against (a person) on a police blotter. **3.** To arrange for (lodgings, for example) in advance; reserve. **4.** To hire or engage. **5.** To allocate time for. —***idioms.*** **bring to book.** To demand an explanation from; call to account. **in one's book.** In one's opinion. **like a book.** Thoroughly; completely. **one for the books.** A noteworthy act or occurrence. **throw the book at. 1.** To make all possible charges against (a lawbreaker, for example). **2.** To reprimand or punish severely. [ME *bok* < OE *bōc*. See **bhāgo-*.**] —**book′er** *n.*

book•bind•er•y (bo͝ok′bīn′də-rē) *n.* An establishment where books are bound.

book•bind•ing (bo͝ok′bīn′dĭng) *n.* The art, trade, or profession of binding books. —**book′bind′er** *n.*

book•case (bo͝ok′kās′) *n.* A cabinet with bookshelves.

book club *n.* A commercial organization that sells books to its members on a regular basis and typically at a discount.

book•end (bo͝ok′ĕnd′) *n.* A prop to keep books upright.

book•ie (bo͝ok′ē) *n.* See **bookmaker** 2.

book•ing (bo͝ok′ĭng) *n.* **1.** An engagement, as for a performance. **2.** A reservation, as for accommodations at a hotel.

book•ish (bo͝ok′ĭsh) *adj.* **1.** Of or resembling a book. **2.** Fond of books; studious. **3.** Relying chiefly on book learning. **4.** Pedantic; dull. **5.** Literary and formal in tone. Used of words. —**book′ish•ly** *adv.* —**book′ish•ness** *n.*

book•keep•ing (bo͝ok′kē′pĭng) *n.* The practice or profession of recording the accounts and transactions of a business. —**book′keep′er** *n.*

book•let (bo͝ok′lĭt) *n.* A small bound book or pamphlet.

book•lore (bo͝ok′lôr′, -lōr′) *n.* Knowledge gained from books.

book•louse or **book louse** (bo͝ok′lous′) *n.* Any of various insects of the order Psocoptera (or Corrodentia), some of which eat stored flour products, paper, or bookbindings.

book lung *n.* A sacculate respiratory organ found in some arachnids, such as scorpions and spiders, consisting of several parallel membranous folds arranged like the pages in a book.

booby[1]

boojum tree
Idria columnaris

ă pat	oi boy
ā pay	ou out
âr care	o͝o took
ä father	o͞o boot
ĕ pet	ŭ cut
ē be	ûr urge
ĭ pit	th thin
ī pie	*th* this
îr pier	hw which
ŏ pot	zh vision
ō toe	ə about, item
ô paw	

Stress marks:
′ (primary);
′ (secondary), as in dictionary (dĭk′shə-nĕr′ē)

book•mak•er (bo͝ok′mā′kər) *n.* **1.** One that edits, prints, publishes, or binds books. **2.** One who accepts and pays off bets, as on a horserace. — **book′mak′ing** *n.*

book•mark (bo͝ok′märk′) *n.* A strip of material or a metal clamp inserted between the pages of a book to mark a place.

book•mo•bile (bo͝ok′mō-bēl′) *n.* A truck, trailer, or van serving as a mobile lending library. [BOOK + (AUTO)MOBILE.]

Book of Common Prayer *n.* The book of services and prayers used in the Anglican Church.

boo•koo (bo͞o′ko͞o′) *adj., n., & adv. Chiefly Southern U.S.* Var. of **beaucoup.**

book•plate (bo͝ok′plāt′) *n.* A label with the owner's name or other identification, pasted usu. on a book's inside cover.

book•rack (bo͝ok′răk′) *n.* A rack for books or a book.

book•sell•er (bo͝ok′sĕl′ər) *n.* One that sells books, esp. the owner of a bookstore.

book•shelf (bo͝ok′shĕlf′) *n.* A shelf or set of shelves for books.

book•shop (bo͝ok′shŏp′) *n.* A bookstore.

book•stall (bo͝ok′stôl′) *n.* A stall where books are sold.

book•stand (bo͝ok′stănd′) *n.* **1.** A small counter where books are sold. **2.** A bookrack.

book•store (bo͝ok′stôr′, -stōr′) *n.* A store that sells books.

book value *n.* The monetary amount, not necessarily the open market price, by which an asset is valued in business records.

book•worm (bo͝ok′wûrm′) *n.* **1.** One who spends much time reading or studying. **2.** Any of various insects that infest books and feed on the paste in the bindings.

Boole (bo͞ol), **George.** 1815–64. British mathematician and logician who developed a calculus of symbolic logic.

Bool•e•an (bo͞o′lē-ən) *adj.* Of or relating to Boolean algebra. [After George BOOLE.]

Boolean algebra *n.* An algebra with two elements, usu. denoted 0 and 1, and the operations AND, OR, and NOT, used in symbolic logic and in logic circuits in computer science.

boom[1] (bo͞om) *v.* **boomed, boom•ing, booms.** — *intr.* **1.** To make a deep resonant sound. **2.** To grow or develop rapidly; flourish. — *tr.* **1.** To utter or give forth a boom. **2.** To cause to boom; boost. — *n.* **1.** A deep resonant sound, as of an explosion. **2.** A time of economic prosperity. **3.** A sudden increase. [ME *bomben*, imit. of a loud noise.]

boom[2] (bo͞om) *n.* **1.** *Naut.* A spar extending from a mast to hold or extend the foot of a sail. **2.** A long pole extending upward from the mast of a derrick to support or guide objects being lifted or suspended. **3.a.** A barrier composed of a chain of floating logs enclosing other free-floating logs. **b.** A floating barrier serving to contain an oil spill. **4.** A long movable arm used to support a microphone. **5.** A spar connecting the tail surfaces and the main structure of an airplane. [Du., tree, pole < MDu. See **bheuə-*.**]

boom box *n. Slang.* A portable audio system, usu. consisting of a cassette player, radio, and loudspeakers.

boom•er (bo͞o′mər) *n.* A transient worker, esp. in bridge construction.

boo•mer•ang (bo͞o′mə-răng′) *n.* **1.** A flat curved missile that returns to the thrower when hurled. **2.** A statement or course of action that backfires. — *intr.v.* **-anged, -ang•ing, -angs.** To have the opposite effect from that intended. [Dharuk (Aboriginal language of SE Australia) *bumarinʸ*.]

boom•let (bo͞om′lĭt) *n.* A small boom, as in business, politics, or the birth rate.

boom•town (bo͞om′toun′) *n.* A town experiencing an economic or a population boom.

boom vang *n. Naut.* See **vang** 1.

boon[1] (bo͞on) *n.* **1.** A benefit bestowed, esp. in response to a request. **2.** A timely blessing or benefit. [ME *bone* < ON *bōn*, prayer. See **bhā-²*.**]

boon[2] (bo͞on) *adj.* **1.** Convivial; jolly. **2.** *Archaic.* Favorable. [ME *bon*, good < OFr. < Lat. *bonus*. See **deu-²*.**]

boon•docks (bo͞on′dŏks′) *pl.n. Slang.* **1.** Wild and dense brush; jungle. **2.** Rural country; the backwoods. [< Tagalog *bundok*, mountain.]

boon•dog•gle (bo͞on′dô′gəl, -dŏg′əl) *Informal.* — *n.* Unnecessary, wasteful, and often counterproductive work. — *intr.v.* **-gled, -gling, -gles.** To waste time or money on unnecessary and often counterproductive work. [< *boondoggle*, a plaited leather cord worn by Boy Scouts.] — **boon′dog′gler** *n.*

Boone (bo͞on), **Daniel.** 1734–1820. Amer. pioneer, folk hero, and central figure in the settlement of Kentucky.

boon•ies (bo͞o′nēz) *pl.n. Slang.* Rural country or a jungle. [Shortening and alteration of BOONDOCKS.]

boor (bo͝or) *n.* **1.** A rude, clumsy person with little refinement. **2.** A peasant. [Du. *boer* < MDu. *gheboer*. See **bheuə-*.**] — **boor′ish** *adj.* — **boor′ish•ly** *adv.* — **boor′ish•ness** *n.*

boost (bo͞ost) *v.* **boost•ed, boost•ing, boosts.** — *tr.* **1.** To raise or lift by pushing up from behind or below. See Syns at **lift. 2.a.** To increase; raise: *boost prices.* **b.** To assist in further development or progress. **3.** To stir up enthusiasm for; promote vigorously. **4.** *Elect.* To increase the voltage of (a circuit). **5.** *Slang.* To shoplift. — *intr. Slang.* To engage in shoplifting. — *n.* **1.** A push upward or ahead. **2.** An increase. [Perh. < dial. *boostering*, bustling, active.]

boost•er (bo͞o′stər) *n.* **1.** One that boosts, as: **a.** A device for increasing power or effectiveness. **b.** An enthusiastic promoter. **c.** The primary stage of a multistage rocket that provides the main thrust for launch, liftoff, and initial flight. **2.** A booster shot. **3.** *Slang.* One who shoplifts.

booster cable *n.* An electric cable used to connect a discharged battery to a power source for charging.

booster dose *n.* See **booster shot.**

boost•er•ish (bo͞o′stər-ĭsh) *adj.* Highly supportive, as of a product, project, or cause.

boost•er•ism (bo͞o′stə-rĭz′əm) *n.* The highly supportive attitudes and activities of boosters.

booster shot *n.* An additional dose of an immunizing agent given at a time after the initial dose to sustain the immune response elicited by the previous dose.

boot[1] (bo͞ot) *n.* **1.** Protective footgear, as of leather or rubber, covering part or all of the leg. **2.** A protective covering, esp. a sheath for the base of a floor-mounted gear shift lever in a car or truck. **3.** *Chiefly British.* A car trunk. **4.a.** A kick. **b.** *Slang.* An unceremonious dismissal. **c.** *Slang.* A swift, pleasurable feeling; a thrill. **5.** A Denver boot. **6.** A marine or navy recruit in basic training. **7. boots.** A torture instrument, used to crush the foot and leg. — *tr.v.* **boot•ed, boot•ing, boots. 1.** To put boots on. **2.** To kick. **3.** *Slang.* To discharge unceremoniously; dismiss. **4.** *Comp. Sci.* To enter (a program) into a computer using a few initial instructions. [ME *bote* < OFr.]

boot[2] (bo͞ot) *intr.v.* **boot•ed, boot•ing, boots.** To be of help or advantage; avail. — *n.* **1.** *Chiefly Southern U.S.* See **lagniappe. 2.** *Archaic.* Advantage; avail. — ***idiom.* to boot.** In addition; besides. [ME *boten*, to be of help < OE *bōtian* < *bōt*, help. See **bhad-*.**]

boot•black (bo͞ot′blăk′) *n.* A person who cleans and polishes shoes for a living.

boot camp *n.* A training camp for military recruits.

boot•ed (bo͞o′tĭd) *adj.* Wearing boots.

boo•tee also **boo•tie** (bo͞o′tē) *n.* **1.** A soft, usu. knitted shoe for a baby. **2.** An ankle-length disposable foot covering, used by medical personnel and others in sterile environments.

Bo•ö•tes (bō-ō′tēz) *n.* A constellation in the Northern Hemisphere near Virgo and Canes Venatici, containing the bright star Arcturus. [Lat. *Boōtēs* < Gk. *boōtēs*, plowman, Boötes < *boōtein*, to plow < *bous*, ox. See **gʷou-*.**]

booth (bo͞oth) *n., pl.* **booths** (bo͞othz, bo͞oths). **1.a.** A small, often enclosed compartment, usu. accommodating only one person. **b.** A small enclosed compartment with a window, used to separate the occupant from others. **2.** A seating area in a restaurant that has a table and seats whose high backs serve as partitions. **3.** A small stall or stand for the display and sale of goods. [ME *bothe*, of Scand. orig. See **bheuə-*.**]

Booth[1] (bo͞oth). Family of Amer. Shakespearean actors, including **Junius Brutus** (1796–1852), born in Great Britain, and his sons **Edwin Thomas** (1833–93), noted for his portrayal of Hamlet, and **John Wilkes** (1838–65), the assassin of Abraham Lincoln.

Booth[2] (bo͞oth). Family of reformers, including **William** (1829–1912), a British religious leader who founded the Salvation Army (1878) with his wife, **Catherine Mumford Booth** (1829–90). Their children **William Bramwell** (1856–1929); **Ballington** (1857–1940), who with his wife, **Maud Ballington Booth** (1865–1948), founded the Volunteers of America (1896); and **Evangeline Cory** (1865–1950) were active in the Salvation Army.

Boo•thi•a Peninsula (bo͞o′thē-ə). The northernmost tip of the North American mainland, in NE Northwest Terrs., Canada; separated from Baffin I. by the **Gulf of Boothia,** an arm of the Arctic Ocean.

boot•jack (bo͞ot′jăk′) *n.* A forked device for holding a boot secure while the foot is being withdrawn.

boot•leg (bo͞ot′lĕg′) *v.* **-legged, -leg•ging, -legs.** — *tr.* **1.** To make, sell, or transport (alcoholic liquor) for illegal sale. **2.** To produce, distribute, or sell without permission or illegally. — *intr.* To engage in bootlegging. — *n.* **1.** A product, esp. alcoholic liquor, that is bootlegged. **2.** The part of a boot above the instep. [From a smuggler's practice of carrying liquor in the legs of boots.] — **boot′leg′ger** *n.*

boot•less (bo͞ot′lĭs) *adj.* Without advantage or benefit; useless. See Syns at **futile.** [BOOT² + -LESS.] — **boot′less•ly** *adv.* — **boot′less•ness** *n.*

boot•lick (bo͞ot′lĭk′) *v.* **-licked, -lick•ing, -licks.** — *tr.* To behave toward in a servile or obsequious manner. — *intr.* To behave in a servile or obsequious manner. — **boot′lick′er** *n.*

boot•strap (bo͞ot′străp′) *n.* **1.** A loop that is sewn at the side or the top rear of a boot to help in pulling the boot on. **2.** *Comp. Sci.* A subroutine used to establish the full routine or another routine. — *tr.v.* **-strapped, -strap•ping, -straps. 1.** To promote and develop by use of one's own initiative and work without outside help. **2.** *Comp. Sci.* To establish (a program) with a bootstrap. — *adj. Comp. Sci.* Being or relating to a self-initiating or self-sustaining process. — ***idiom.* by one's (own) bootstraps.** By one's own efforts.

boo•ty (bo͞o′tē) *n., pl.* **-ties. 1.** Plunder taken from an enemy in time of war. **2.** Goods or property seized by force. **3.** A

Daniel Boone

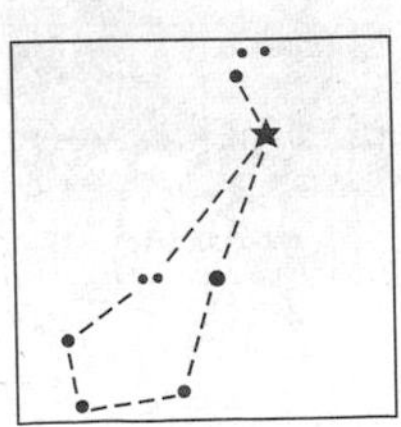

Boötes

John Wilkes Booth
Photographed c. 1862

valuable prize or award. [ME *botye* (influenced by *bote*, advantage; see BOOT²), prob. < MLGer. *būte*, exchange.]

booze (bo͞oz) *Slang.* —*n.* **1.a.** Hard liquor. **b.** An alcoholic beverage. **2.** A drinking spree. —*intr.v.* **boozed, booz•ing, booz•es.** To drink liquor to excess. [Alteration of obsolete *bouse*, liquor, drinking bout < ME *bousen*, to drink to excess < MDu. *būsen*.] —**booz′er** *n.* —**booz′y** *adj.*

bop¹ (bŏp) *Informal.* —*tr.v.* **bopped, bop•ping, bops.** To hit or strike. —*n.* A blow; a punch. [Imit.]

bop² (bŏp) *n. Mus.* A style of jazz characterized by rhythmic and harmonic complexity, improvised solo performances, and brilliant execution. —*intr.v.* **bopped, bop•ping, bops. 1.** To dance or move to the beat of this music. **2.** *Slang.* To go: *bopped off to the movies.* [Short for BEBOP.] —**bop′per** *n.*

Bo•phu•tha•tswa•na (bō′po͞o-tät-swä′nə). An autonomous Black homeland within South Africa; granted nominal independence in 1977. Cap. Mmabatho. Pop. 1,347,000.

Bopp (bŏp), **Franz.** 1791–1867. German philologist who illustrated the similarities among Indo-European languages.

BOQ *abbr.* Bachelor Officers' Quarters.

bor. *abbr.* Borough.

bor– *pref.* Var. of **boro–.**

bo•ra (bôr′ə, bōr′ə) *n.* A violent, cold, northeasterly winter wind on the Adriatic Sea. [Ital. dial. < Lat. *Boreās*, Boreas. See BOREAS.]

Bo•ra Bo•ra (bôr′ə bôr′ə, bōr′ə bōr′ə). A volcanic island of French Polynesia in the Society Is. of the S Pacific Ocean.

bo•rac•ic (bə-răs′ĭk) *adj.* Var. of **boric.** [< Med.Lat. *borāx*, *borāc-*, borax. See BORAX¹.]

bor•age (bôr′ĭj, bŏr′-) *n.* An annual, bristly European herb *(Borago officinalis)* having blue or purplish star-shaped flowers. [ME < OFr. *bourage* < Med.Lat. *borāgō*, prob. < Ar. *bū'araq* < *abū'araq*, father of sweat.]

Bo•rah (bôr′ə, bōr′ə), **William Edgar.** 1865–1940. Amer. politician who served as U.S. senator from ID (1907–40).

bo•rane (bôr′ān′, bōr′-) *n.* Any of a series of boron-hydrogen compounds or a substance such as BCL that may be considered a derivative of such a compound.

Bo•rås (bo͞o-rôs′). A city of SW Sweden E of Göteborg; founded 1632. Pop. 99,945.

bo•rate (bôr′āt′, bōr′-) *n.* A salt or an ester of boric acid.

bo•rax¹ (bôr′ăks′, -əks, bōr′-) *n.* **1.** A hydrated sodium borate, $Na_2B_4O_7 \cdot 10H_2O$, an ore of boron, used as a cleaning compound. **2.** An anhydrous sodium borate used in the manufacture of glass and various ceramics. [ME < Med.Lat. *bōrāx* < Ar. *būraq* < MPers. *būrak*.]

bo•rax² (bôr′ăks′, bōr′-) *n.* Cheap merchandise, esp. tasteless furnishings.

bor•bo•ryg•mus (bôr′bə-rĭg′məs) *n.*, *pl.* **-mi** (-mī′). The rumbling noise of gas moving through the intestines. [NLat. < Gk. *borborugmos*, of imit. orig.]

Bor•deaux¹ (bôr-dō′). A city of SW France on the Garonne R. Pop. 208,159.

Bor•deaux² (bôr-dō′) *n.*, *pl.* **Bor•deaux** (bôr-dō′, -dōz′). A wine originally produced in the region of Bordeaux, France.

Bordeaux mixture *n.* A fungicide mixture of copper sulfate, lime, and water. [Transl. of Fr. *bouillie bordelaise*: *bouillie*, gruel, mixture + *bordelaise*, of Bordeaux.]

bor•del•lo (bôr-dĕl′ō) *n.*, *pl.* **-los.** A house of prostitution. [Ital. < OFr. *bordel* < *borde*, wooden hut, of Gmc. orig.]

Bor•den (bôr′dn), **Lizzie Andrew.** 1860–1927. Amer. woman accused and acquitted of the ax murder of her parents (1892).

Borden, Sir **Robert Laird.** 1854–1937. Canadian politician who served as prime minister (1911–20).

bor•der (bôr′dər) *n.* **1.** A part that forms the outer edge of something. **2.** A decorative strip around the edge of something, such as fabric. **3.** A strip of ground, as at the edge of a walk, for ornamental plants. **4.** The line or frontier area separating political divisions or geographic regions. —*v.* **-dered, -der•ing, -ders.** —*tr.* **1.** To put a border on. **2.** To lie along or adjacent to the border of. —*intr.* **1.** To lie adjacent to another. **2.** To be almost like another in character. [ME *bordure* < OFr. *bordeure* < *border*, to border < *bort*, border, of Gmc. orig.] —**bor′der•er** *n.*

Syns: *border, margin, edge, verge, brink, rim, brim.* All these nouns refer to the line or narrow area that marks the outside limit of something such as a surface. *Border* refers either to the boundary line (*a fence along the border of the property*) or to the area immediately inside it (*a frame with a wide border*). *Margin* is a border of more or less precisely definable width: *notes in the margin of the page. Edge* refers to the bounding line formed by the continuous convergence of two surfaces: *sat on the edge of the chair. Verge* is an extreme terminating line or edge: *the sun's afterglow on the verge of the horizon. Brink* denotes the edge of a steep place: *the brink of the cliff. Rim* most often denotes the edge of something circular or curved: *a crack in the rim of the lens. Brim* applies to the upper edge or inner side of the rim of a container or something shaped like a basin: *lava issuing from the brim of the crater.*

Bor•der collie (bôr′dər) *n.* A British sheepdog used for herding. [From the border country of England and Scotland.]

bor•der•land (bôr′dər-lănd′) *n.* **1.a.** Land located on or near a frontier. **b.** The fringe. **2.** An indeterminate area, situation, or condition: *the borderland between sanity and insanity.*

bor•der•line (bôr′dər-līn′) *n.* **1.** A line that establishes or marks a border. **2.** An indefinite area intermediate between two qualities or conditions. —*adj.* **1.a.** Verging on a given quality or condition. **b.** Of a questionable nature or quality; dubious. **2.a.** *Psychol.* Relating to any phenomenon that is intermediate between two groups and therefore not clearly categorized. **b.** Relating to a condition characterized by instability, as in mood, and manifested by self-destructive, manipulative, and inconsistent behavior.

Border States. The slave states of DE, MD, VA, KY, and MO that were adjacent to the free states of the North during the Civil War.

Border terrier *n.* A small, hardy, rough-coated terrier bred to hunt foxes in the border country of England and Scotland.

Bor•det (bôr-dā′), **Jules Jean Baptiste Vincent.** 1870–1961. Belgian bacteriologist who won a 1919 Nobel Prize.

bor•de•tel•la (bôr′də-tĕl′ə) *n. Microbiol.* Any of various small gram-negative bacteria of the genus *Bordetella*, some of which are pathogenic in the human respiratory tract. [NLat. *Bordetella*, genus name, after Jules Jean Baptiste Vincent BORDET.]

bor•dure (bôr′jər) *n. Her.* A border around a shield. [ME. See BORDER.]

bore¹ (bôr, bōr) *v.* **bored, bor•ing, bores.** —*tr.* **1.** To make a hole in or through, with or as if with a drill. **2.** To form (a tunnel, for example) by drilling, digging, or burrowing. —*intr.* **1.** To make a hole in or through something by boring. **2.** To proceed or advance steadily or laboriously. —*n.* **1.** A hole or passage made by or as if by boring. **2.** A hollow, usu. cylindrical chamber or barrel, as of a firearm. **3.** The interior diameter of a hole, tube, or cylinder. **4.** The caliber of a firearm. **5.** A drilling tool. [ME *boren* < OE *borian*.]

bore² (bôr, bōr) *tr.v.* **bored, bor•ing, bores.** To weary by being dull. —*n.* One that bores. [?]

bore³ (bôr, bōr) *n.* A high, often dangerous wave caused by the surge of a flood tide up a narrowing estuary or by colliding tidal currents. [ME *bare*, wave < ON *bāra*. See **bher-¹***.]

bore⁴ (bôr, bōr) *v.* P.t. of **bear¹.**

bo•re•al (bôr′ē-əl, bōr′-) *adj.* **1.** Of or relating to the north; northern. **2.** Of or concerning the north wind. **3. Boreal.** Of or relating to the forest areas of the northern North Temperate Zone, dominated by coniferous trees. [ME < LLat. *Boreālis* < Lat. *Boreās*, Boreas. See BOREAS.]

Bo•re•as (bôr′ē-əs, bōr′-) *n.* **1.** *Gk. Myth.* The god of the north wind. **2. boreas.** The north wind. [ME < Lat. *Boreās* < Gk. < *boreios*, coming from the north.]

bore•cole (bôr′kōl′, bōr′-) *n.* See **kale** 1. [Du. *boerenkool*: *boren*, pl. of *boer*, peasant; see BOOR + *kool*, cabbage < MDu. *cōle* < Lat. *caulis*, stalk. See KALE.]

bore•dom (bôr′dəm, bōr′-) *n.* The condition of being bored.

bore•hole (bôr′hōl′, bōr′-) *n.* A hole drilled into the earth, as in exploratory well drilling.

bor•er (bôr′ər, bōr′-) *n.* **1.** A tool used for drilling. **2.** An insect or insect larva that bores into woody plant parts. **3.** Any of various mollusks that bore into soft rock or wood.

Bor•ges (bôr′hĕs), **Jorge Luis.** 1899–1986. Argentinian writer particularly known for his short stories.

Bor•gia (bôr′jə, -zhə). Italian family, influential from the 14th to the 16th cent., that included the son and daughter of Pope Alexander VI. **Cesare** (1475?–1507), a religious, military, and political leader, was the model for Machiavelli's *The Prince.* **Lucrezia** (1489–1519), the Duchess of Ferrara, was a patron of learning and the arts.

Bor•glum (bôr′gləm), **Gutzon.** 1867–1941. Amer. sculptor noted for the busts of four U.S. Presidents on Mt. Rushmore.

bo•ric (bôr′ĭk, bōr′-) also **bo•rac•ic** (bə-răs′ĭk) *adj.* Of, relating to, derived from, or containing boron.

boric acid *n.* A water-soluble crystalline compound, H_3BO_3, used as an antiseptic and a preservative and in detergents.

bo•ride (bôr′īd′, bōr′-) *n.* A binary compound of boron with a more electropositive element or radical.

bor•ing (bôr′ĭng, bōr′-) *adj.* Not interesting; tiresome; dull. —**bor′ing•ly** *adv.* —**bor′ing•ness** *n.*

Syns: *boring, monotonous, tedious, irksome, tiresome, humdrum.* These adjectives refer to what is so uninteresting as to cause mental weariness. *Boring* implies feelings of listlessness and discontent: *a boring book.* What is *monotonous* bores because of lack of variety: *a monotonous day. Tedious* suggests dull slowness or long-windedness: *spent tedious hours on the train. Irksome* describes what is demanding of time and effort and yet is dull and often unrewarding: *"I know and feel what an irksome task the writing of long letters is"* (Edmund Burke). Something *tiresome* fatigues because it seems to be interminable or marked by unremitting sameness: *"What a tiresome being is a man who is fond of talking"* (Benjamin Jowett). *Humdrum* refers to what is commonplace, trivial, or unexcitingly routine: *led a humdrum existence.*

Bor•laug (bôr′lôg′), **Norman Ernest.** b. 1914. Amer. agronomist who won the 1970 Nobel Peace Prize.

borage
Borago officinalis

Lizzie Borden

ă pat	oi boy
ā pay	ou out
âr care	o͝o took
ä father	o͞o boot
ĕ pet	ŭ cut
ē be	ûr urge
ĭ pit	th thin
ī pie	*th* this
îr pier	hw which
ŏ pot	zh vision
ō toe	ə about,
ô paw	item

Stress marks:
′ (primary);
′ (secondary), as in
dictionary (dĭk′shə-nĕr′ē)

Bor•mann (bôr′män′), **Martin Ludwig.** 1900–45? German Nazi official who served as Hitler's secretary (1941–45).
born (bôrn) *v.* A p.part. of **bear**[1]. — *adj.* **1.a.** Brought into life by birth. **b.** Brought into existence; created. **2.a.** Having from birth a particular quality or talent: *a born artist.* **b.** Destined, or seemingly destined, from birth. **3.** Resulting or arising. **4.** Native to a particular place. Often used in combination: *Irish-born.*
Born (bôrn), **Max.** 1882–1970. German-born physicist who shared a 1954 Nobel Prize.
born-a•gain (bôrn′ə-gĕn′) *adj.* **1.a.** Of, relating to, or being one who has converted to or renewed faith in Christianity. **b.** Of or relating to evangelical Christianity. **2.** Characterized by fervent renewal, resurgence, or return. [From *born again* in John 3:3 and 3:7.]
borne (bôrn, bōrn) *v.* A p.part. of **bear**[1].
Bor•ne•o (bôr′nē-ō′). An island of the W Pacific Ocean in the Malay Archipelago between the Sulu and Java seas SW of the Philippines. The sultanate of Brunei is on the NW coast; the rest of the island is divided between Indonesia and Malaysia. — **Bor′ne•an** *adj. & n.*
Born•holm (bôrn′hōm′, -hōlm′, -hôlm′). An island of E Denmark in the Baltic Sea near Sweden.
born•ite (bôr′nīt′) *n.* A brownish-bronze, lustrous copper ore, Cu_5FeS_4, that tarnishes to purple when exposed to air. [After Ignaz von *Born* (1742–91), Austrian mineralogist.]
Bor•nu (bôr′no͞o). A region and former Muslim kingdom of W Africa that became part of Nigeria in 1902.
boro– or **bor–** *pref.* Boron: *borosilicate.* [< BORON.]
Bo•ro•bu•dur (bôr′ə-bə-do͝or′, bōr′-). A ruined Buddhist shrine in central Java; dating probably from the 9th cent.
Bo•ro•din (bôr′ə-dēn′, bär′-, bə-rə-dēn′), **Aleksandr Porfirevich.** 1833–87. Russian composer whose works are based on folk themes.
Bo•ro•di•no (bôr′ə-dē′nō, bŏr′-, bə-rə-dyē-nô′). A village of W Russia W of Moscow. Nearby, Napoleon defeated the Russian troops defending Moscow in 1812.
bo•ron (bôr′ŏn′, bōr′-) *n. Symbol* **B** A soft, amorphous or crystalline nonmetallic element, used in flares and nuclear reactor control rods. Atomic number 5; atomic weight 10.811; melting point 2,300°C; sublimation point 2,550°C; specific gravity (crystal) 2.34; valence 3. See table at **element.** [BO-R(AX)[1] + (CARB)ON.]
boron carbide *n.* A compound of boron and carbon, esp. B_4C, an extremely hard crystalline compound used as an abrasive and a neutron absorber.
bo•ro•sil•i•cate (bôr′ō-sĭl′ĭ-kĭt, -kāt′, bōr′-, bŏr′-) *n.* A salt that is derived from both boric acid and silicic acid and occurs naturally in dumortierite.
borosilicate glass *n.* A strong heat-resistant glass that contains a minimum of 5 percent boric oxide.
bor•ough (bûr′ō, bŭr′ō) *n.* **1.** A self-governing incorporated town in some U.S. states. **2.** One of the five administrative units of New York City. **3.** A civil division of Alaska that is the equivalent of a county in most other U.S. states. **4.** *Chiefly British.* **a.** A town having a municipal corporation and certain rights. **b.** A town that sends a representative to Parliament. **5.** A medieval group of fortified houses that formed a town with special privileges and rights. [ME *burgh*, city < OE *burg*, fortified town. See **bhergh-**[2*].]
bor•ough-Eng•lish (bûr′ō-ĭng′glĭsh, bŭr′-) *n.* An old custom in certain boroughs whereby the right to inherit an estate intestate went to the youngest son or, in default of male issue, to the youngest brother. [Partial transl. of AN *tenure en burgh Engloys*, tenure in an English borough. See BOROUGH.]
bor•rel•i•a (bə-rĕl′ē-ə, -rē′lē-ə) *n. Microbiol.* Any of various irregularly coiled helical spirochetes of the genus *Borrelia*, some of which cause relapsing fever. [NLat., after Amédée *Borrel* (1867–1936), French bacteriologist.]
bor•row (bŏr′ō, bôr′ō) *v.* **-rowed, -row•ing, -rows.** — *tr.* **1.** To obtain or receive (something) on loan with the promise or understanding of returning it or its equivalent. **2.** To adopt or use as one's own. **3.** In subtraction, to take a unit from the next larger denomination in the minuend so as to make a number larger than the number to be subtracted. — *intr.* **1.** To obtain or receive something. **2.** *Ling.* To adopt words from one language for use in another. — ***idiom.* borrow trouble.** To take an unnecessary action that will probably have adverse effects. [ME *borwen* < OE *borgian.* See **bhergh-**[1*].]
bor•rowed time (bŏr′ōd, bôr′-) *n.* An uncertain, usu. uncontrolled extension of time: *living on borrowed time.*
bor•row•ing (bŏr′ō-ĭng, bôr′-) *n.* Something that is borrowed, esp. a word borrowed from one language to another.
borscht also **borsht** (bôrsht) or **borsch** (bôrsh) *n.* A beet soup often garnished with sour cream. [Yiddish *borsht* < Russ. *borshch*, cow parsnip (the original soup base), borscht.]
borscht belt *n. Informal.* The predominantly Jewish hotels of the Catskill Mountains, known for their vaudeville-type entertainment. [From the popularity of borscht in the cuisine.]
bort (bôrt) *n.* **1.** Poorly crystallized diamonds used for industrial cutting and abrasion. **2.** A carbonado. [Prob. < Du. *boort.*] — **bort′y** *adj.*

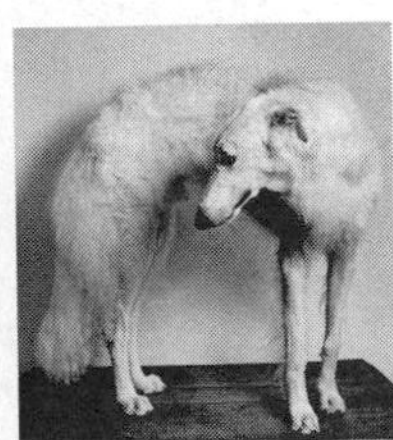
borzoi

boss[2]

Boston rocker

bor•zoi (bôr′zoi′) *n.* Any of a breed of tall slender dogs with a narrow pointed head and a silky coat, originally developed in Russia for hunting wolves. [< Russ. *borzoĭ*, swift.]
Bosc (bŏsk) *n.* A variety of pear with greenish-yellow skin overlaid with reddish-brown and juicy sweet flesh. [After Louis Auguste Guillaume *Bosc*, 19th-cent. Belgian horticulturist.]
bos•cage also **bos•kage** (bŏs′kĭj) *n.* A mass of trees or shrubs; a thicket. [ME *boskage* < OFr. *boscage* < *bosc*, forest, of Gmc. orig.]
Bosch (bŏsh, bôsh, bŏs, bôs), **Hieronymus.** 1450?–1516. Dutch painter whose largely religious works are characterized by grotesque, fantastic creatures mingling with human figures.
bosh (bŏsh) *Informal.* — *n.* Nonsense. — *interj.* Used to express disbelief or annoyance. [< Turk. *boş*, empty.]
bosk (bŏsk) *n.* A small wooded area. [Back-formation < BOSKY.]
bosk•y (bŏs′kē) *adj.* **-i•er, -i•est. 1.** Having many bushes, shrubs, or trees. **2.** Of or relating to woods. [< ME *bosk*, bush < Med.Lat. *bosca*, of Gmc. orig.] — **bosk′i•ness** *n.*
bo's'n or **bos'n** (bō′sən) *n.* Var. of **boatswain.**
Bos•ni•a (bŏz′nē-ə). The N section of Bosnia-Herzegovina; settled by Serbs in the 7th cent. — **Bos′ni•an** *adj. & n.*
Bos•ni•a-Her•ze•go•vi•na (bŏz′nē-ə-hĕrt′sə-gō-vē′nə, -hûrt′-) or **Bosnia and Herzegovina.** A region of the NW Balkans W of Serbia; a constituent republic of Yugoslavia from 1946 to 1991. Cap. Sarajevo. Pop. 3,710,965.
bos•om (bo͝oz′əm, bo͞o′zəm) *n.* **1.a.** The chest of a human being. **b.** A woman's breast or breasts. **2.** The part of a garment covering the chest or breasts. **3.** Security and closeness likened to being held in a warm familial embrace. **4.** The chest considered as the source of emotion. — *adj.* Beloved; intimate. [ME < OE *bōsm.*]
bo•son (bō′sŏn) *n.* Any of a class of particles that have zero or integral spin and obey statistical rules permitting any number of identical particles to occupy the same quantum state. [After Satyendra Nath *Bose* (1894–1974), Indian physicist.]
Bos•po•rus (bŏs′pər-əs). A narrow strait separating European and Asian Turkey and joining the Black Sea with the Sea of Marmara; an important trade route since ancient times.
bos•quet (bŏs′kĭt) *n.* A small grove; a thicket. [Fr. < Ital. *boschetto*, dim. of *bosco*, forest, of Gmc. orig.]
boss[1] (bôs, bŏs) *n.* **1.a.** An employer or a supervisor. **b.** One who makes decisions or exercises authority. **2.** A politician who controls a party or a political machine. — *v.* **bossed, boss•ing, boss•es.** — *tr.* **1.** To supervise or control. **2.** To give orders to, esp. arrogantly or domineeringly. — *intr.* To be or act as a supervisor or controlling element. — *adj. Slang.* First-rate; topnotch. [Du. *baas*, master.]
boss[2] (bôs, bŏs) *n.* **1.** A circular protuberance or knoblike swelling, as on animal horns. **2.** A raised area used as ornamentation. **3.** *Archit.* A raised ornament. **4.a.** An enlarged part of a shaft to which another shaft is coupled or to which a wheel or gear is keyed. **b.** A hub, esp. of a propeller. — *tr.v.* **bossed, boss•ing, boss•es.** To emboss. [ME *boce* < OFr.]
boss[3] (bôs, bŏs) *n.* A cow or calf. [Perh. ult. < Lat. *bōs.* See BOVINE.]
bos•sa no•va (bŏs′ə nō′və, bô′sə) *n.* **1.** A lively Brazilian dance similar to the samba. **2.** Music that is a blend of jazz and samba. [Port. : *bossa*, trend + *nova*, new.]
Bos•sier City (bō′zhər). A city of NW LA, a suburb of Shreveport. Pop. 52,721.
boss•ism (bô′sĭz′əm, bŏs′ĭz′-) *n.* The domination of a political organization by a boss.
Bos•suet (bô-swā′), **Jacques Bénigne.** 1627–1704. French prelate and historian noted for his philosophical treatise on history.
boss•y[1] (bô′sē, bŏs′ē) *adj.* **-i•er, -i•est.** Given to ordering others around. — **boss′i•ly** *adv.* — **boss′i•ness** *n.*
boss•y[2] (bô′sē, bŏs′ē) *adj.* Decorated with raised ornaments.
boss•y[3] (bô′sē, bŏs′ē) *n., pl.* **-ies.** *Informal.* A cow or calf. [< BOSS[3].]
Bos•ton (bô′stən, bŏs′tən). The cap. of MA, in the E part on **Boston Bay**, an arm of Massachusetts Bay; founded in the 17th cent. Pop. 574,283. — **Bos•to′ni•an** (bô-stō′nē-ən, bŏs-) *adj. & n.*
Boston bull *n.* See **Boston terrier.**
Boston cream pie *n.* A round cake with a custard or cream filling.
Boston fern *n.* **1.** A cultivar of sword fern *(Nephrolepis exaltata* cv. *Bostoniensis)* having arching or drooping pinnate fronds. **2.** Any of numerous ferns derived from the sword fern.
Boston ivy *n.* A high-climbing woody vine *(Parthenocissus tricuspidata)* from eastern Asia, with three-lobed deciduous leaves.
Boston lettuce *n.* A type of cultivated lettuce forming a rounded head and having soft, yellow-green inner leaves.
Boston rocker *n.* A rocking chair having a high back with spindles, a decorative panel at the top, and a seat and arms that curve downward in front.
Boston terrier *n.* Any of a breed of small dogs originating in New England as a cross between a bull terrier and a bulldog and having a brindled or black coat with white markings.

bo•sun (bō′sən) *n.* Var. of **boatswain.**

Bos•well (bŏz′wĕl′, -wəl), **James.** 1740–95. Scottish lawyer, diarist, and writer renowned as the biographer of Samuel Johnson. — **Bos•well′i•an** *adj. & n.*

Bos•worth Field (bŏz′wərth). A locality in central England near Leicester; site of the final battle (1485) of the Wars of the Roses.

bot also **bott** (bŏt) *n.* **1.** The parasitic larva of a botfly. **2. bots.** *(used with a sing. or pl. v.)* A disease of mammals caused by infestation of the stomach or intestines with botfly larvae. [ME, prob. of LGer. orig.]

bot. *abbr.* **1.** Botanical; botanist; botany. **2.** Bottle. **3.** Bottom.

bo•tan•i•cal (bə-tăn′ĭ-kəl) also **bo•tan•ic** (-tăn′ĭk) *— adj.* **1.** Of or relating to plants or plant life. **2.** Of or relating to botany. *— n.* A drug or similar substance obtained from a plant or plants. [< LLat. *botanicus* < Gk. *botanikos* < *botanē*, fodder, plants.] — **bo•tan′i•cal•ly** *adv.*

botanical garden or **botanic garden** *n.* A place where a wide variety of plants are cultivated for scientific, educational, and ornamental purposes.

bot•a•nist (bŏt′n-ĭst) *n.* One who specializes in botany.

bot•a•nize (bŏt′n-īz′) *v.* **-nized, -niz•ing, -niz•es.** *— intr.* **1.** To collect plants for scientific study. **2.** To investigate or study plants scientifically. *— tr.* To investigate or explore the plant life of (a region). — **bot′a•niz′er** *n.*

bot•a•ny (bŏt′n-ē) *n., pl.* **-nies. 1.a.** The science or study of plants. **b.** A book or scholarly work on this subject. **2.** The plant life of a particular area. **3.** The characteristic features and biology of a particular plant or plant group. [Back-formation < BOTANICAL.]

Bot•a•ny Bay (bŏt′n-ē). An inlet of the Tasman Sea in SE Australia S of Sydney.

botch (bŏch) *tr.v.* **botched, botch•ing, botch•es. 1.** To ruin through clumsiness. **2.** To make or perform clumsily; bungle. **3.** To repair or mend clumsily. *— n.* **1.** A ruined or defective piece of work. **2.** A hodgepodge. [ME *bocchen*, to mend.] — **botch′er** *n.* — **botch′y** *adj.*

Syns: *botch, blow, bungle, fumble, muff.* The central meaning shared by these verbs is "to harm or spoil through inept or clumsy handling": *botch a repair; blow an opportunity; a bungled performance; fumbled my chance; an actor muffing his lines.*

bot•fly also **bot fly** (bŏt′flī′) *n.* Any of various stout two-winged flies, chiefly of the genera *Gasterophilus* and *Oestrus*, having larvae that are parasitic on various animals.

both (bōth) *adj.* One and the other; relating to or being two in conjunction: *Both guests came. — pron.* The one and the other: *Both are mad. — conj.* Used with *and* to link two things in a coordinated phrase or clause: *both he and I.* [ME *bothe* < OE *bā thā*, both those : *bā*, neut. of *bēgen*, both + *thā*, pl. of *thæt*, that; see THAT.]

Usage Note: *Both* is used to indicate that the action or state denoted by the verb applies individually to each of two entities. *Both books weigh more than five pounds*, for example, means that each book weighs more than five pounds by itself, not that the two books weighed together come to more than five pounds. • In possessive constructions *of both* is usually preferred: *the mothers of both* (rather than *both their mothers*). • When *both* is used with *and* to link parallel elements in a sentence, the words or phrases that follow them should correspond grammatically: *in both India and China* or *both in India and in China* (not *both in India and China*).

Bo•tha (bō′tə, -tä′), **Louis.** 1862–1919. South African general and first prime minister of South Africa (1910–19).

Botha, Pieter Willem. b. 1916. South African prime minister (1978–89) who upheld apartheid.

both•er (bŏ*th*′ər) *v.* **-ered, -er•ing, -ers.** *— tr.* **1.** To disturb or anger, esp. by minor irritations; annoy. **2.a.** To make agitated or nervous; fluster. **b.** To make confused or perplexed; puzzle. **3.** To intrude on without warrant; disturb. **4.** To give trouble to. *— intr.* **1.** To take the trouble; concern oneself. **2.** To cause trouble. *— n.* A cause or state of disturbance. *— interj.* Used to express annoyance or mild irritation. [Prob. < dial. *bodder*, poss. of Celt. orig.]

both•er•a•tion (bŏ*th*′ə-rā′shən) *n.* The act of bothering or the state of being bothered. *— interj.* Used to express annoyance or irritation.

both•er•some (bŏ*th*′ər-səm) *adj.* Causing bother.

Both•ni•a (bŏth′nē-ə), **Gulf of.** An arm of the Baltic Sea between Sweden and Finland.

Both•well (bŏth′wĕl′, -wəl, bŏ*th*′-), 4th Earl of. James Hepburn. 1536?–78. Scottish noble and third husband of Mary Queen of Scots, whose second husband, Lord Darnley, he murdered (1567).

bo tree (bō) *n.* See **peepul.** [Partial transl. of Singhalese *bogaha*, tree of wisdom < Pali *bodhi* < Skt. *bodhiḥ*, enlightenment. See **bheudh-***.]

bot•ry•oi•dal (bŏt′rē-oid′l) also **bot•ry•oid** (bŏt′rē-oid′) *adj.* Shaped like a bunch of grapes. Used esp. of mineral formations: *botryoidal hematite.* [< Gk. *botruoeidēs*: *botrus*, bunch of grapes + *-oeidēs*, -oid.] — **bot′ry•oi′dal•ly** *adv.*

bo•try•tis (bō-trī′tĭs) *n.* **1.** Any of various fungi of the genus *Botrytis* responsible for numerous fruit and vegetable diseases. **2.** Noble rot. [NLat., genus name < Gk. *botrus*, bunch of grapes.]

Bot•swa•na (bŏt-swä′nə). Formerly **Bech•u•a•na•land** (bĕch′wä′nə-lănd′, bĕch′o͞o-ä′nə-). A country of S-central Africa; gained independence from Great Britain in 1966. Cap. Gaborone. Pop. 973,000.

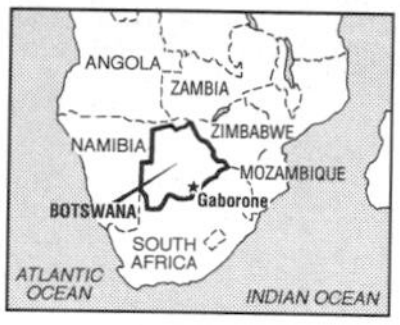

bott (bŏt) *n.* Var. of **bot.**

Bot•ti•cel•li (bŏt′ĭ-chĕl′ē), **Sandro.** 1444?–1510. Italian painter whose works include *Birth of Venus* (c. 1485).

bot•tle (bŏt′l) *n.* **1.** A receptacle having a narrow neck, usu. no handles, and a mouth that can be stopped. **2.** The quantity that a bottle holds. **3.** A receptacle filled with milk or formula that is fed to babies in place of breast milk. **4.** *Informal.* **a.** Intoxicating liquor. **b.** The practice of drinking large quantities of intoxicating liquor. *— tr.v.* **-tled, -tling, -tles. 1.** To place in a bottle. **2.** To hold in; restrain: *bottled up my emotions.* [ME *botel* < OFr. *botele* < Med.Lat. *butticula*, dim. of LLat. *buttis*, cask.] — **bot′tler** *n.*

bot•tle•brush (bŏt′l-brŭsh′) *n.* Any of various Australian shrubs or trees of the genera *Callistemon* and *Melaleuca*, having densely flowered cylindrical spikes with numerous protruding stamens that suggest a brush used to clean bottles.

bot•tled gas (bŏt′ld) *n.* Gas, such as butane or propane, stored under pressure in portable tanks.

bot•tle-feed (bŏt′l-fēd′) *tr.v.* **-fed** (-fĕd′), **-feed•ing, -feeds.** To feed (a baby, for example) with a bottle.

bottle gourd *n.* See **calabash** 1.

bottle green *n. Color.* A dark to moderate or grayish green. — **bot′tle-green′** (bŏt′l-grēn′) *adj.*

bot•tle•neck (bŏt′l-nĕk′) *n.* **1.a.** A narrow or obstructed section. **b.** A point or an area of traffic congestion. **2.** A hindrance to progress or production. **3.** The narrow part of a bottle near the top. **4.** *Mus.* A style of guitar playing in which an object is passed across the strings to achieve a gliding sound. *— tr.v.* **-necked, -neck•ing, -necks.** To obstruct.

bot•tle-nosed dolphin (bŏt′l-nōzd′) *n.* Any of several marine mammals of the genus *Tursiops*, esp. *T. truncatus*, of temperate and tropical waters and characterized by a short protruding beak, a large stocky body, and a falcate dorsal fin.

bottle tree *n.* Any of certain Australian trees of the genus *Brachychiton*, having a sometimes bottle-shaped trunk.

bot•tom (bŏt′əm) *n.* **1.** The deepest or lowest part. **2.** The underside. **3.** The supporting part; the base. **4.** The far end or part: *the bottom of the bed.* **5.a.** The last place, as on a list. **b.** The lowest or least favorable position. **6.** The basic underlying quality; the source. **7.** The solid surface under a body of water. **8.** Low-lying alluvial land adjacent to a river. Often used in the plural. **9.a.** *Naut.* The part of a ship's hull below the water line. **b.** A ship; a boat. **10.** Pajama pants. Often used in the plural. **11.** *Informal.* The buttocks. **12.** The seat of a chair. **13.** *Baseball.* The second or last half of an inning. **14.** Staying power; stamina. Used of a horse. *— v.* **-tomed, -tom•ing, -toms.** *— tr.* **1.** To provide with an underside. **2.** To provide with a foundation. **3.** To get to the bottom of; fathom. *— intr.* **1.** To be or become based or grounded. **2.** To rest on or touch the bottom. ***— phrasal verb.*** **bottom out.** To descend to the lowest point possible, after which only a rise may occur. ***— idiom.*** **at bottom.** Basically. [ME *botme* < OE *botm.*] — **bot′tom•er** *n.*

bottom break *n.* A branch arising from a plant stem base. [BOTTOM + BREAK, branch formed by pinching or disbudding.]

bot•tom•land (bŏt′əm-lănd′) *n.* See **bottom** 8.

bot•tom•less (bŏt′əm-lĭs) *adj.* **1.** Having no bottom. **2.** Too deep to be measured. **3.** Difficult or impossible to understand. **4.** Having no limitations or bounds. — **bot′tom•less•ly** *adv.*

bottom line *n.* **1.** The line in a financial statement for net income or loss. **2.** The final result. **3.** The main point.

bot•tom•most (bŏt′əm-mōst′) *adj.* **1.** Sited at the very bottom. **2.** Coming after all others. **3.** Forming the basis.

bottom quark *n.* A quark with a charge of −⅓ and a mass about 10,000 times that of the electron. See table at **subatomic particle.**

bottom round *n.* A cut of meat from the outer section of a round of beef.

Bot•trop (bŏt′rŏp′, bôt′rôp′). A city of NW Germany in the Ruhr Valley NW of Essen. Pop. 112,353.

bot•u•lin (bŏch′ə-lĭn) *n.* Any of several potent neurotoxins produced by botulinum and resistant to proteolytic digestion. [Lat. *botulus*, sausage + -IN.]

bot•u•li•num (bŏch′ə-lī′nəm) also **bot•u•li•nus** (-nəs) *n.* An anaerobic rod-shaped bacterium *(Clostridium botulinum)* that secretes botulin and inhabits soils. [NLat. < Lat. *botulus*, sausage.] — **bot′u•li′nal** *adj.*

bot•u•lism (bŏch′ə-lĭz′əm) *n.* A severe, sometimes fatal food poisoning caused by ingestion of food containing botulin and characterized by nausea, vomiting, disturbed vision, and fatigue. [Ger. *Botulismus* < Lat. *botulus*, sausage.]

Boua•ké (bwä′kā). A town of central Ivory Coast; once a crossroads for caravan trade. Pop. 230,000.

Bou•cher (bo͞o-shā′), **François.** 1703–70. French artist who painted in the rococo style.

Botswana

ă pat	oi boy
ā pay	ou out
âr care	o͝o took
ä father	o͞o boot
ĕ pet	ŭ cut
ē be	ûr urge
ĭ pit	th thin
ī pie	*th* this
îr pier	hw which
ŏ pot	zh vision
ō toe	ə about, item
ô paw	

Stress marks:
′ (primary);
′ (secondary), as in
dictionary (dĭk′shə-nĕr′ē)

Bou·cher·ville (bo͞o′shər-vĭl′, bo͞o′shā-vēl′). A town of S Quebec, Canada, a suburb of Montreal. Pop. 29,704.

Bou·ci·cault (bo͞o′sē-kō′), **Dion.** 1820?–90. Irish-born Amer. actor and playwright whose works include *The Octoroon* (1859).

bou·clé or **bou·cle** (bo͞o-klā′) *n.* **1.** A type of yarn, usu. three-ply and having one thread looser than the others. **2.** Fabric made from this yarn. [Fr. < p.part. of *boucler,* to curl < OFr. < *boucle,* buckle, curl of hair. See BUCKLE.]

Bou·dain (bo͞o-dăn′, -dăɴ′) *n.* Var. of **boudin.**

Bou·dic·ca (bo͞o-dĭk′ə) also **Bo·ad·i·ce·a** (bō′ăd-ĭ-sē′ə). 1st cent. A.D. Queen of ancient Britain who led a revolt against the Roman army.

bou·din also **Bou·dain** (bo͞o-dăn′, -dăɴ′) *n., pl.* **-dins** also **-dains** (-dăn′, -dănz′). A Louisiana Creole link sausage of pork, pork liver, and rice. [Fr. < OFr. *bodine,* intestines.]

boudin blanc (bläɴ) *n., pl.* **boudins blancs** (bläɴ). A French white sausage of pork, chicken, or veal. [Fr. : *boudin,* boudin + *blanc,* white.]

boudin noir (nwär) *n., pl.* **boudins noirs** (nwär). See **black pudding.** [Fr. : *boudin,* boudin + *noir,* black.]

bou·doir (bo͞o′dwär′, -dwôr′) *n.* A woman's private sitting room, dressing room, or bedroom. [Fr. < OFr. *bouder,* to sulk.]

bouf·fant (bo͞o-fänt′) *adj.* Puffed-out; full. [Fr. < pr.part. of *bouffer,* to puff up < OFr.]

bouffe (bo͞of) *n.* See **comic opera.** [Short for OPÉRA BOUFFE.]

Bou·gain·ville (bo͞o′gən-vĭl′, bo͞o-găɴ-vēl′). A volcanic island of Papua New Guinea in the Solomon Is. of the SW Pacific.

Bougainville, Louis Antoine de. 1729–1811. French explorer who circumnavigated the globe (1766–69).

bou·gain·vil·le·a also **bou·gain·vil·lae·a** (bo͞o′gən-vĭl′ē-ə, -vĭl′yə, -vē′ə, bō′-) *n.* Any of several South American woody shrubs or vines of the genus *Bougainvillea,* having groups of three petallike colored bracts attached to the flowers. [NLat. *Bougainvillea,* genus name, after Louis Antoine de BOUGAINVILLE.]

bough (bou) *n.* A tree branch, esp. a large or main branch. [ME < OE *bōh.* See **bhāghu-*.**]

bought (bôt) *v.* P.t. and p.part. of **buy.**

bought·en (bôt′n) *Chiefly Northern U.S.* —*v.* A p.part. of **buy.** —*adj.* **1.** Commercially made; purchased: *boughten bread.* **2.** Artificial; false. Used of teeth.

bou·gie (bo͞o′zhē, -jē) *n.* **1.** *Medic.* **a.** A slender, flexible, cylindrical instrument that is inserted into a body canal, such as the urethra. **b.** See **suppository. 2.** A wax candle. [Fr. < OFr., a fine wax, after *Bougie* (Bejaïa), a city of N Algeria.]

bouil·la·baisse (bo͞o′yə-bās′, bo͝ol′yə-bās′) *n.* **1.** A highly seasoned fish stew made of several kinds of fish and shellfish. **2.** A combination of various different, often incongruous elements. [Fr. < Prov. *bouiabaisso: boui,* imper. of *bouie,* to boil (< Lat. *bullīre* < *bulla,* bubble) + *abaisso,* imper. of *abeissa,* to lower (< VLat. **abbassiāre*: Lat. *ad-,* ad- + Med. Lat. *bassus,* low).]

bouil·lon (bo͝ol′yŏn′, -yən, bo͞o′yŏn′) *n.* A clear, thin broth made typically by simmering beef or chicken in water with seasonings. [Fr. < OFr. < *boulir,* to boil < Lat. *bullīre* < *bulla,* bubble.]

bouillon cube *n.* A small cube of evaporated seasoned meat, poultry, or vegetable stock, used in broths for flavor.

boul. *abbr.* Boulevard.

Bou·lan·ger (bo͞o-län-zhā′), **Nadia Juliette.** 1887–1979. French music teacher whose students included Virgil Thomson and Aaron Copland.

boul·der also **bowl·der** (bōl′dər) *n.* A large rounded mass of rock lying on the surface of the ground or embedded in the soil. [ME *bulder,* of Scand. orig. See **bhel-[2]*.**]

Boul·der (bōl′dər). A city of N-central CO NW of Denver. Pop. 83,312.

bou·le[1] (bo͞o′lē, bo͞o-lā′) *n.* **1.** The lower house of the modern Greek legislature. **2.a.** The senate of 400 founded by Solon in ancient Athens. **b.** A legislative assembly in any one of the ancient Greek states. [Gk. *boulē,* assembly. See **gʷelə-*.**]

boule[2] (bo͞ol) *n.* A pear-shaped synthetic gem, produced by fusing and tinting alumina. [Fr., ball < OFr., bubble < Lat. *bulla.*]

boule[3] (bo͞ol) *n.* Var. of **buhl.**

boul·e·vard (bo͝ol′ə-värd′, bo͞o′lə-) *n.* **1.** A broad city street, often tree-lined and landscaped. **2.** *Upper Midwest.* See **median strip.** See Regional Note at **neutral ground.** [Fr. < OFr. *bollevart,* rampart converted to a promenade < MDu. *bolwerc,* bulwark. See BULWARK.]

bou·le·vard·ier (bo͞o′lə-vär-dyā′, -dîr′) *n.* A man about town. [Obsolete Fr. < *boulevard,* boulevard. See BOULEVARD.]

boulevard strip *n. Upper Midwest.* See **median strip.** See Regional Note at **neutral ground.**

bou·le·ver·se·ment (bo͞o′lə-vĕr′sə-mäɴ′) *n.* **1.** A violent uproar; a tumult. **2.** A reversal. [Fr. < OFr. *bouleverser,* to overturn : *boule,* ball (< Lat. *bulla*) + *verser,* to overturn (< OFr. < Lat. *versāre,* freq. of *vertere,* to turn; see **wer-[2]*).]**

Bou·lez (bo͞o-lĕz′), **Pierre.** b. 1925. French conductor and composer of works such as *Le Marteau sans Maître* (1955).

boulle (bo͞ol) *n.* Var. of **buhl.**

Bou·logne (bo͞o-lōn′, -lôn′yə) also **Bou·logne-sur-Mer** (-sûr-mĕr′). A city of N France on the English Channel NNW of Amiens; of Celtic origin. Pop. 47,653.

Bou·logne-Bil·lan·court (bo͞o-lôn′yə-bē-yäɴ-ko͞or′). A city of N-central France, a suburb of Paris. Pop. 102,582.

bounce (bouns) *v.* **bounced, bounc·ing, bounc·es.** —*intr.* **1.** To rebound after having struck an object or a surface. **2.** To move jerkily; bump. **3.** To recover quickly, as from a setback. **4.** To bound. **5.** To be sent back by a bank as valueless: *a check bounced.* **6.** *Baseball.* To hit a ground ball that rebounds before reaching an infielder. —*tr.* **1.** To cause to strike an object or a surface and rebound. **2.** *Slang.* **a.** To expel by force. **b.** To dismiss from employment. **3.** To write (a check) on an overdrawn bank account. —*n.* **1.** A rebound. **2.** A sudden bound, spring, or leap. **3.** The capacity to rebound; spring. **4.** Spirit; liveliness. **5.** *Slang.* Expulsion; dismissal. **6.** *Chiefly British.* Loud, arrogant speech; bluster. [Prob. < ME *bounsen,* to beat.]

bounc·er (boun′sər) *n.* **1.** *Slang.* A person employed to expel disorderly persons from a public place, esp. a bar. **2.** *Baseball.* A ground ball hit in such a way that it bounces.

bounc·ing (boun′sĭng) *adj.* **1.** Vigorous; healthy. **2.** Spirited; lively: *a bouncing gait.* —**bounc′ing·ly** *adv.*

bouncing Bet (bĕt) *n.* A perennial Eurasian herb *(Saponaria officinalis)* having dense clusters of pink to whitish flowers. [< *Bet,* nickname for *Elizabeth.*]

bounc·y (boun′sē) *adj.* **-i·er, -i·est. 1.** Tending to bounce. **2.** Springy; elastic. **3.** Lively; energetic. —**bounc′i·ly** *adv.* —**bounc′i·ness** *n.*

bound[1] (bound) *intr.v.* **bound·ed, bound·ing, bounds. 1.** To leap forward or upward; spring. **2.** To progress by forward leaps or springs. —*n.* **1.** A leap; a jump. **2.** A rebound; a bounce. [Fr. *bondir,* to bounce < OFr., to resound, perh. ult. < Lat. *bombus,* a humming sound < Gk. *bombos.*]

bound[2] (bound) *n.* **1.** A boundary; a limit. Often used in the plural: *Our joy knew no bounds.* **2. bounds.** The territory on, within, or near limiting lines. —*v.* **bound·ed, bound·ing, bounds.** —*tr.* **1.** To set a limit to; confine. **2.** To constitute the boundary or limit of. **3.** To identify the boundaries of; demarcate. —*intr.* To border on another place, state, or country. [ME < OFr. *bodne, bonde* and AN *bunde,* both < Med.Lat. *bodina,* of Celt. orig.]

bound[3] (bound) *v.* P.t. and p.part. of **bind.** —*adj.* **1.** Confined by bonds; tied. **2.** Being under legal or moral obligation. **3.** Equipped with a cover or binding. **4.** Predetermined; certain: *bound to be late.* **5.** Determined; resolved: *She's bound to be mayor.* **6.** Constipated.

bound[4] (bound) *adj.* Headed or intending to head in a specified direction: *south-bound.* [Alteration of ME *boun,* ready < ON *būinn,* p.part. of *būa,* to get ready. See **bheuə-*.**]

bound·a·ry (boun′də-rē, -drē) *n., pl.* **-ries. 1.** Something indicating a border or limit. **2.** A border or limit so indicated.

boundary condition *n. Math.* The conditions specified for the solution to a set of differential equations.

boundary layer *n.* The layer of reduced velocity in fluids that is adjacent to the solid surface past which the fluid flows.

bound·en (boun′dən) *adj.* **1.** Obligatory: *their bounden duty.* **2.** *Archaic.* Being under obligation; obliged. [ME, p.part. of *binden,* to bind < OE *bindan.* See BIND.]

bound·er (boun′dər) *n. Chiefly British.* A cad.

bound form *n.* A linguistic element that always occurs as part of another word, such as *-ly* in *lovely.*

bound·less (bound′lĭs) *adj.* Being without boundaries or limits; infinite. See Syns at **infinite.** —**bound′less·ly** *adv.* —**bound′less·ness** *n.*

boun·te·ous (boun′tē-əs) *adj.* **1.** Giving or inclined to give generously. **2.** Generously and copiously given. See Syns at **liberal.** [ME *bountevous* < OFr. *bontive,* benevolent < *bonte,* bounty. See BOUNTY.] —**boun′te·ous·ly** *adv.* —**boun′te·ous·ness** *n.*

boun·ti·ful (boun′tə-fəl) *adj.* **1.** Giving freely and generously; liberal. **2.** Marked by abundance; plentiful. See Syns at **liberal.** —**boun′ti·ful·ly** *adv.* —**boun′ti·ful·ness** *n.*

Boun·ti·ful (boun′tə-fəl). A city of N-central UT, a suburb of Salt Lake City. Pop. 36,659.

boun·ty (boun′tē) *n., pl.* **-ties. 1.** Liberality in giving. **2.** Something given liberally. **3.** A reward, inducement, or payment, esp. from a government for acts deemed beneficial to the state. See Syns at **bonus.** [ME *bounte* < OFr. *bonte* < Lat. *bonitās,* goodness < *bonus,* good. See **deu-[2]*.**]

bounty hunter *n.* **1.** One who hunts predatory animals in order to collect a bounty. **2.** One who pursues a criminal or fugitive for whom a reward is offered.

bou·quet (bō-kā′, bo͞o-) *n.* **1.** A cluster of flowers; a nosegay. **2.** The fragrance typical of a wine or liqueur. [Fr. < OFr. *bosquet,* thicket, dim. of *bosc,* forest, of Gmc. orig.]

bouquet gar·ni (gär-nē′) *n., pl.* **bou·quets gar·nis** (bō-kāz′ gär-nē′, bo͞o-). A bunch of herbs tied together for cooking, wrapped in cheesecloth or enclosed in a small cloth sack. [Fr. : *bouquet,* bunch + *garni,* p.part. of *garnir,* to garnish.]

bour·bon (bûr′bən) *n.* A whiskey distilled from a fermented mash containing not less than 51 percent corn in addition to malt and rye. [After *Bourbon* County in NE KY.]

Bour•bon[1] (bo͝or′bən, bo͝or-bôɴ′). French royal family descended from Louis I, Duke of Bourbon (1270?–1342), whose members have ruled in France, Spain, and Sicily.

Bour•bon[2] (bûr′bən) *n.* A sociopolitical reactionary. [After the BOURBON family.]

Bour•bon (bo͝or′bən, bo͝or-bôɴ′), Duc **Charles de.** 1490–1527. French general who led a failed invasion of France (1524).

Bour•bon•nais (bo͝or-bôɴ-nā′). A historical region and former province of central France in the Massif Central; held by the Bourbons until 1527.

bour•don (bo͝or′dn) *n. Mus.* The monotonic drone bass of a bagpipe. [ME *burdoun,* bass < OFr. *bourdon.*]

bourg (bo͝org) *n.* **1.** A market town. **2.** A medieval village, esp. one near a castle. [Fr. < OFr. < LLat. *burgus,* fortress, of Gmc. orig. See **bhergh-**[2]***.**]

bour•geois (bo͝or-zhwä′, bo͝or′zhwä′) *n., pl.* **bourgeois. 1.** A member of the middle class. **2.** A person whose attitudes and behavior conform to that of the middle class. **3.** In Marxist theory, a member of the property-owning class; a capitalist. — *adj.* **1.** Of, relating to, or typical of the middle class. **2.** Preoccupied with respectability and material values. [Fr. < OFr. *burgeis,* citizen < *bourg,* bourg. See BOURG.]

Bour•geois (bo͝or-zhwä′), **Léon Victor Auguste.** 1851–1925. French politician who won the 1920 Nobel Peace Prize.

bour•geoise (bo͝or-zhwäz′, bo͝or′zhwäz′) *n., pl.* **-geois•es** (-zhwä′zĭz). A middle-class woman. [Fr., fem. of *bourgeois,* bourgeois. See BOURGEOIS.] — **bour•geoise′** *adj.*

bour•geoi•sie (bo͝or′zhwä-zē′) *n.* **1.** The middle class. **2.** In Marxist theory, the social group opposed to the proletariat in the class struggle. [Fr. < *bourgeois,* bourgeois. See BOURGEOIS.]

bour•geoi•si•fy (bo͝or-zhwä′zə-fī′) *tr.v.* **-fied, -fy•ing, -fies.** To cause to adopt the characteristics attributed to the bourgeoisie. — **bourg•eoi′si•fi•ca′tion** (-zə-fĭ-kā′shən) *n.*

bour•geon (bûr′jən) *v.* Var. of **burgeon.**

Bourges (bo͝orzh). A city of central France SSE of Orléans; a Roman provincial cap. under Augustus. Pop. 76,432.

Bour•gogne (bo͝or-gôn′yə). See **Burgundy**[2]**.**

Bourke-White (bûrk′hwīt′, -wīt′), **Margaret.** 1906–71. Amer. photographer and writer who was an editor of *Life* magazine (1936–69).

bourn[1] also **bourne** (bôrn, bōrn, bo͝orn) *n.* A small stream; a brook. [ME < OE *burna.* See **bhreu-*.**]

bourn[2] also **bourne** (bôrn, bōrn, bo͝orn) *n. Archaic.* **1.** A destination; a goal. **2.** A boundary; a limit. [Fr. *bourne* < Fr. dial. *bosne, borne* < OFr. *bodne,* limit, boundary marker < Med.Lat. *bodina,* of Celt. orig.]

Bourne•mouth (bôrn′məth, bōrn′-, bo͝orn′-). A borough of S England SW of Southampton. Pop. 143,000.

bour•rée (bo͞o-rā′, bo͞o-) *n.* **1.a.** An old French dance resembling the gavotte. **b.** The music for this dance. **2.** A pas de bourrée. [Fr. < *bourrer,* to stuff < *bourre,* hair, fluff < LLat. *burra,* a shaggy garment.]

bourse (bo͝ors) *n.* A stock exchange, esp. one in a continental European city. [Fr. < LLat. *bursa,* bag. See BURSA.]

bou•stro•phe•don (bo͞o′strə-fēd′n, -fē′dŏn′) *n.* An ancient method of writing in which the lines are inscribed alternately from right to left and from left to right. [< Gk. *boustrophēdon,* turning like an ox while plowing : *bous,* ox; see **g**ʷ**ou-*** + *strophē,* a turning (< *strephein,* to turn; see **streb(h)-***).] — **bou•stroph′e•don′ic** (-strŏf′ĭ-dŏn′ĭk) *adj.*

bout (bout) *n.* **1.** A contest between antagonists; a match. **2.** A period of time spent in a particular way; a spell: *a drinking bout.* [< obsolete E. *bought,* a turning (influenced by ABOUT) < ME < *bowen,* to bend, turn. See BOW[2].]

bou•tique (bo͞o-tēk′) *n.* **1.a.** A small retail shop that specializes in items such as gifts. **b.** A small shop located within a large department store or supermarket. **2.** An investment boutique. [Fr. < OFr. *botique,* small shop < OProv. *botica* < Lat. *apothēca,* storehouse. See APOTHECARY.]

bou•ton (bo͞o-tôn′) *n.* A knoblike enlargement at the end of an axon, where it synapses with other neurons. [Fr., button < OFr. See BUTTON.]

bou•ton•niere also **bou•ton•nière** (bo͞o′tə-nîr′, -tən-yâr′) *n.* A flower or nosegay worn in a buttonhole. [Fr. *boutonnière* < OFr., buttonhole < *bouton,* button. See BUTTON.]

bou•var•di•a (bo͞o-vär′dē ə) *n.* Any of several Mexican and Central American shrubs or herbs of the genus *Bouvardia,* having showy, narrowly tubular flowers. [NLat. *Bouvardia,* genus name, after Charles *Bouvard* (1572–1658), French physician.]

Bou•vier des Flan•dres (bo͞o-vyā′ də flăn′dərz, dā flăɴ′drə) *n.* Any of a breed of large shaggy dogs developed in Belgium, originally used for herding and guarding cattle. [Fr. : *bouvier,* cowherd + *des,* of + *Flandres,* Flanders.]

bou•zou•ki (bo͞o-zo͞o′kē, bə-) *n. Mus.* A Greek stringed instrument resembling a mandolin. [Mod.Gk. *mpouzouki,* prob. of Turk. orig.]

Bo•vet (bō-vā′, -vĕt′), **Daniel.** b. 1907. Swiss-born Italian physiologist who won a 1957 Nobel Prize.

bo•vid (bō′vĭd) *adj.* Of or belonging to the family Bovidae, which includes hoofed, hollow-horned ruminants such as cattle and sheep. [< NLat. *Bovidae,* family name < Lat. *bōs,* cow. See BOVINE.] — **bo′vid** *n.*

bo•vine (bō′vīn′, -vēn′) *adj.* **1.** Of, relating to, or resembling a ruminant mammal of the genus *Bos,* such as a cow. **2.** Sluggish, dull, and stolid. — *n.* An animal of the genus *Bos.* [LLat. *bovīnus* < Lat. *bōs,* cow. See **g**ʷ**ou-*.**]

bovine growth hormone *n.* A hormone of cattle that regulates growth and milk production.

bow[1] (bou) *n. Naut.* **1.** The front section of a ship or boat. **2.** The oar or the person wielding the oar closest to the bow. [ME *boue,* prob. of LGer. orig. See **bheug-*.**]

bow[2] (bou) *v.* **bowed, bow•ing, bows.** — *intr.* **1.** To bend or curve downward; stoop. **2.** To incline the body or head or bend the knee, as in greeting, consent, or courtesy. **3.** To yield in defeat or out of courtesy; submit. See Syns at **yield.** — *tr.* **1.** To bend (the head, knee, or body), as in greeting. **2.** To convey (greeting, for example) by bending the body. **3.** To escort deferentially. **4.** To cause to acquiesce; submit. **5.** To overburden. — *n.* An inclination of the head or body, as in greeting. — ***phrasal verb.*** **bow out.** To remove oneself; withdraw. — ***idiom.*** **bow and scrape.** To behave obsequiously. [ME *bowen* < OE *būgan.* See **bheug-*.**]

bow[3] (bō) *n.* **1.** A bent, curved, or arched object. **2.** A weapon made of a curved flexible strip of material, esp. wood, strung taut and used to launch arrows. **3.a.** An archer. **b.** Archers considered as a group. **4.a.** *Mus.* A rod having horsehair drawn tightly between its two raised ends, used in playing instruments of the violin and viol families. **b.** A stroke made by this rod. **5.** A knot usu. having two loops and two ends; a bowknot. **6.a.** A frame for eyeglass lenses. **b.** The part of such a frame passing over the ear. **7.** A rainbow. **8.** An oxbow. — *v.* **bowed, bow•ing, bows.** — *tr.* **1.** To bend (something) into the shape of a bow. **2.** *Mus.* To play (a stringed instrument) with a bow. — *intr.* **1.** To bend into a curve or bow. **2.** *Mus.* To play a stringed instrument with a bow. [ME *bowe* < OE *boga.* See **bheug-*.**]

Bow (bō), **Clara.** 1905–65. Amer. actress known for silent films such as *It* (1927).

bow compass *n.* A drawing compass with legs that are connected by an adjustable metal spring band.

bow•da•cious (bō′dā′shəs) *adj. & adv. Southern & South Midland U.S.* Var. of **bodacious.**

Bow•ditch (bou′dĭch), **Nathaniel.** 1773–1838. Amer. mathematician and astronomer noted for his works on navigation.

bowd•ler•ize (bōd′lə-rīz′, boud′-) *tr.v.* **-ized, -iz•ing, -iz•es. 1.** To expurgate (a book, for example) prudishly. **2.** To modify, as by shortening or simplifying or by skewing content. [After Thomas *Bowdler* (1754–1825), who expurgated Shakespeare.] — **bowd′ler•ism** *n.* — **bowd′ler•i•za′tion** (-lər-ĭ-zā′shən) *n.* — **bowd′ler•iz′er** *n.*

bow•el (bou′əl, boul) *n.* **1.a.** The intestine. Often used in the plural. **b.** A part or division of the intestine. **2. bowels.** The interior of something. **3. bowels.** *Archaic.* The seat of pity or the gentler emotions. [ME < OFr. *boel* < Lat. *botellus,* small intestine, dim. of *botulus,* sausage.]

Bow•ell (bō′əl), Sir **Mackenzie.** 1823–1917. British-born Canadian politician who served as prime minister (1894–96).

bowel movement *n.* **1.** The discharge of waste matter from the large intestine; defecation. **2.** The waste matter discharged from the large intestine; feces.

bow•er[1] (bou′ər) *n.* **1.** A shaded leafy recess; an arbor. **2.** A woman's private room in a medieval castle; a boudoir. **3.** A rustic cottage; a country retreat. — *tr.v.* **-ered, -er•ing, -ers.** To enclose in or as if in a bower; embower. [ME *bour,* a dwelling < OE *būr.* See **bheuə-*.**] — **bow′er•y** *adj.*

bow•er[2] (bou′ər) *n. Naut.* An anchor carried at the bow.

bow•er•bird (bou′ər-bûrd′) *n.* Any of various birds of the family Ptilonorhynchidae of Australia and New Guinea, the males of which build large elaborate structures.

Bow•er•y (bou′ə-rē, bou′rē). A section of lower Manhattan in New York City. The street that gives the area its name was once the road to Peter Stuyvesant's *bouwerij,* or farm.

bow•fin (bō′fĭn′) *n.* A primitive, bony freshwater fish *(Amia calva)* of central and eastern North America, with a long, spineless dorsal fin.

bow•front (bō′frŭnt′) *adj.* **1.** Having an outward-curving front. **2.** Designed with a bow window in front.

bow•head (bō′hĕd′) *n.* A whalebone whale *(Balaena mysticetus)* of Arctic seas, having a large head and an arched upper jaw.

Bow•ie (bo͞o′ē). A city of W-central MD NE of Washington DC. Pop. 37,589.

Bow•ie (bo͞o′ē, bō′ē), **James.** 1796–1836. Amer.-born Mexican colonist who died during the defense of the Alamo.

bow•ie knife (bō′ē, bo͞o′ē) *n.* A single-edged steel hunting knife, about 15 inches (38 centimeters) in length, having a hilt and a crosspiece. [After James BOWIE.]

bow•knot (bō′nŏt′) *n.* A knot with large decorative loops.

bowl[1] (bōl) *n.* **1.a.** A wide hemispherical vessel for holding food or fluids. **b.** The contents of such a vessel. **2.** A drinking

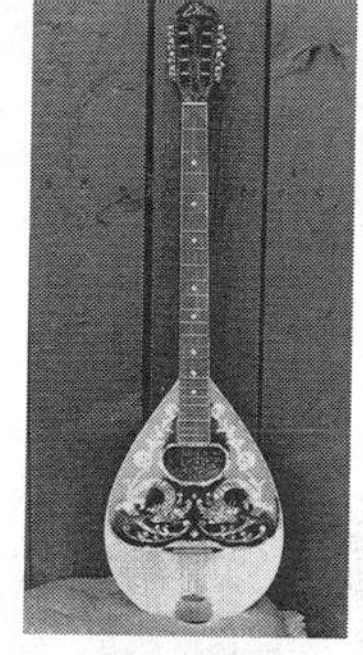

bouzouki

bowie knife

ă pat	oi boy
ā pay	ou out
âr care	o͝o took
ä father	o͞o boot
ĕ pet	ŭ cut
ē be	ûr urge
ĭ pit	th thin
ī pie	*th* this
îr pier	hw which
ŏ pot	zh vision
ō toe	ə about, item
ô paw	

Stress marks:
′ (primary);
′ (secondary), as in
dictionary (dĭk′shə-nĕr′ē)

goblet. **3.** A bowl-shaped part, as of a spoon or pipe. **4.a.** A bowl-shaped topographic depression. **b.** A bowl-shaped stadium or outdoor theater. **5.** *Football.* Any of various postseason games played between specially selected teams. [ME *bowle* < OE *bolla*. See **bhel-²***.]

bowl² (bōl) *n.* **1.** A large wooden ball weighted or slightly flattened so as to roll with a bias. **2.** *Sports.* A roll or throw of the ball, as in bowling. **3. bowls.** *(used with a sing. v.)* See **lawn bowling. 4.** A revolving cylinder or drum in a machine. —*v.* **bowled, bowl•ing, bowls.** —*intr.* **1.** *Sports.* **a.** To participate in a game of bowling. **b.** To throw or roll a ball in bowling. **c.** To hurl a cricket ball toward the batsman. **2.** To move quickly and smoothly, esp. by rolling: *bowling along on bicycles.* —*tr.* **1.** To throw or roll (a ball). **2.** *Sports.* To achieve (a score) or complete (a game, for example) in bowling. **3.** To move quickly and smoothly by or as if by rolling. —***phrasal verbs.* bowl out.** *Sports.* To retire (a batsman in cricket) with a bowled ball that knocks the bails off the wicket. **bowl over. 1.** To take by surprise. **2.** To make a powerful impression on; overwhelm. [ME *boule* < OFr. < Lat. *bulla*, round object.]

bowl•der (bōl′dər) *n.* Var. of **boulder.**

bow•leg (bō′lĕg′) *n.* **1.** A leg having an outward curvature in the knee region. **2.** The condition of such a curvature.

bow•leg•ged (bō′lĕg′ĭd, -lĕgd′) *adj.* Having bowlegs.

bowl•er¹ (bō′lər) *n. Sports.* One that bowls, as in bowling.

bowl•er² (bō′lər) *n.* A derby hat. [Prob. < BOWL².]

boxer³

bow•line (bō′lĭn, -līn′) *n. Naut.* A rope attached to the weather leech of a square sail to hold the leech forward when sailing close-hauled. [ME *bouline*, prob. < Middle Dan. *bovline* or MLGer. *bōlīne*, both < *bōch līne*: *bōch*, bow + *līne*, line (< Lat. *līnea*; see LINE¹).]

bowl•ing (bō′lĭng) *n. Sports & Games.* **1.a.** A game played by rolling a ball down a wooden alley in order to knock down ten pins. **b.** A similar game, such as duckpins or ninepins. **2.** Lawn bowling **3.** The playing of one of these games.

bowling alley *n. Sports.* **1.** A level wooden lane used in bowling. **2.** A building or room containing lanes for bowling.

bowling ball *n. Sports.* A large spherical ball, usu. of rubber or plastic, having indentations for the thumb and fingers.

bowling green *n. Sports & Games.* A level grassy area for lawn bowling.

Bowl•ing Green (bō′lĭng grēn′). **1.** A city of S KY SE of Owensboro. Pop. 40,641. **2.** A city of NW OH SSW of Toledo. Pop. 28,176.

bow•man¹ (bō′mən) *n.* An archer.

bow•man² (bou′mən) *n. Naut.* A person who oars, rows, or paddles at the bow of a boat.

Bow•man's capsule (bo′mənz) *n. Anat.* A double-walled cup-shaped structure around the glomerulus of each nephron of the kidney that filters out wastes, excess salts, and water. [After Sir William *Bowman* (1816–92), British surgeon.]

boxing²
Muhammad Ali and Jimmy Young at the Capital Centre in Landover, Maryland, on April 30, 1976

bow pen (bō) *n.* A bow compass with a pen at one leg end.

bow saw (bō) *n.* A slender-bladed saw with a narrow handle at each end curved outward like an archer's bow.

bow•shot (bō′shŏt′) *n.* The distance of an arrow shot.

bow•sprit (bou′sprĭt′, bō′-) *n. Naut.* A spar, extending forward from the stem of a ship, to which the stays of the foremast are fastened. [ME *bouspret*, poss. < MLGer. *bōchsprēt*: *bōch*, bow + *sprēt*, sprit; see **sper-***.]

bow•string (bō′strĭng′) *n.* The cord attached to both ends of an archer's bow.

bowstring hemp *n.* **1.** Any of several tropical African and Asian perennial plants of the genus *Sansevieria*, having thick swordlike leaves. **2.** The fibers of any of these plants, used for bowstrings, cordage, mats, and nets.

bow tie (bō) *n.* A short necktie fashioned into a bowknot close to the throat.

bow window (bō) *n.* A bay window built in a curve.

bow-wow or **bow•wow** (bou′wou′) *n.* **a.** The bark of a dog. **b.** *Informal.* A dog. [Imit.]

bow•yer (bō′yər) *n.* **1.** One who makes or sells bows for archery. **2.** *Archaic.* An archer.

box¹ (bŏks) *n.* **1.a.** A container typically constructed with four sides perpendicular to the base and often having a lid or cover. **b.** The amount or quantity that such a container can hold. **2.** A square or rectangle: *Draw a box around your answer.* **3.a.** A compartment in a place of entertainment, such as a theater or stadium, for the accommodation of a small group. **b.** An area of a public place, such as a courtroom or stadium, marked off for a specific function: *a jury box.* **4.** A small structure serving as a shelter: *a sentry box.* **5.** *Chiefly British.* A small country house used as a sporting lodge: *a shooting box.* **6.** A box stall. **7.** The raised seat for the driver of a coach or carriage. **8.** *Baseball.* One of various areas on a diamond marked by lines designating where the batter, catcher, or other team members may stand. **9.** *Sports.* A penalty box. **10.** *Print.* Featured printed matter enclosed by borders and placed within or between text columns. **11.** A hollow made in the side of a tree for the collection of sap. **12.** A post office box. **13.a.** An insulating, enclosing, or protective casing or part in a machine. **b.** A signaling device enclosed in a casing: *an alarm box.* **14.a.** *Informal.* A television. **b.** A very large portable radio. **15.** *Chiefly British.* A gift or gratuity, esp. one given at Christmas. **16.** An awkward or perplexing situation; a predicament. **17.** *Vulgar Slang.* The vulva and the vagina. —*tr.v.* **boxed, box•ing, box•es. 1.** To pack in a box. **2.** To confine or enclose in or as if in a box. **3.** *Sports.* To block (a competitor or opponent) from advancing and esp. from getting a rebound in basketball. **4.** To cut a hole in (a tree) for the collection of sap. **5.** To blend (paint) by pouring alternately between two containers. **6.** To change the shape of (a structure) by applying lath and plaster or boarding. —***idiom.* box the compass. 1.** To name the 32 points of the compass in proper order. **2.** To make a complete revolution or reversal. [ME < OE < LLat. *buxis* < Gk. *puxis* < *puxos*, box tree.]

box turtle
Eastern box turtle
Terrapene carolina

box² (bŏks) *n.* A slap or blow with the hand or fist. —*v.* **boxed, box•ing, box•es.** —*tr.* **1.** To hit with the hand or fist. **2.** *Sports.* To take part in a boxing match with. —*intr.* To fight with the fists or in a boxing match. [ME.]

box³ (bŏks) *n., pl.* **box** or **box•es. 1.a.** Any of several evergreen shrubs or trees of the genus *Buxus*, esp. *B. sempervirens*, having opposite leathery leaves and widely grown as a hedge plant. **b.** The hard yellow wood of these plants. **2.** Any of several other shrubs or trees with similar foliage or timber. [ME < OE < Lat. *buxus* < Gk. *puxos*.]

box•board (bŏks′bôrd′, -bōrd′) *n.* A firm cardboard used for making boxes.

box camera *n.* A simple camera shaped like a box and usu. having a fixed focus and a single shutter speed.

box•car (bŏks′kär′) *n.* **1.** A fully enclosed railroad car, typically having sliding side doors and used for freight. **2. boxcars.** *Games.* A pair of sixes on the first throw in craps.

box coat *n.* **1.** A coat designed to hang loosely from the shoulders. **2.** A heavy overcoat formerly worn by coachmen. [BOX¹ + COAT.]

box elder *n.* A North American maple tree *(Acer negundo)* having pinnately compound leaves with lobed leaflets.

box•er¹ (bŏk′sər) *n. Sports.* One who boxes as a sport.

box•er² (bŏk′sər) *n.* One that packs items in boxes.

box•er³ (bŏk′sər) *n.* A medium-sized short-haired dog of a breed developed in Germany, having a brownish coat and a short square-jawed muzzle. [Ger. < E. BOXER¹.]

Box•er (bŏk′sər) *n.* A member of a secret society in China that unsuccessfully attempted in 1900 to drive foreigners from the country by violence and to force Chinese Christians to renounce their religion. [Approx. transl. of Chin. (Mandarin) *yì hé quán*, righteous harmonious fists, alteration of *yì hé tuán*, righteous harmonious society.]

boxer shorts *pl.n.* Men's full-cut undershorts.

box•fish (bŏks′fĭsh′) *n., pl.* **boxfish** or **-fish•es.** See **trunkfish.**

box•haul (bŏks′hôl′) *tr.v.* **-hauled, -haul•ing, -hauls.** *Naut.* To turn (a square-rigged ship) about on the heel by bracing the sails aback. [BOX¹, to confine, reverse + HAUL.]

box•ing¹ (bŏk′sĭng) *n.* **1.** Material used for boxes. **2.** A boxlike covering or enclosure. **3.** The act of enclosing in a box.

box•ing² (bŏk′sĭng) *n. Sports.* The act, activity, or sport of fighting with the fists.

Box•ing Day (bŏk′sĭng) *n.* The first weekday after Christmas, celebrated as a holiday in parts of the British Commonwealth, when Christmas gifts are given to service workers.

boxing glove *n. Sports.* A heavily padded leather mitten worn for boxing.

box kite *n.* A tailless kite formed in the shape of open-ended boxes connected by shafts spanning an interval of open space.

box lunch *n.* An individually portioned lunch in a small box.

box office *n.* **1.** A booth, as in a theater, where tickets are sold. **2.a.** The drawing power of a theatrical entertainment or of a performer. **b.** A factor influencing this power. **3.** Total attendance or receipts for an entertainment. [Originally an office for the booking of boxes in a theater.] —**box′-of′fice** (bŏks′ô′fĭs, -ŏf′ĭs) *adj.*

box pleat *n.* A double pleat with two upper folds facing in opposite directions and two under folds pressed toward each other.

box score *n. Sports.* A tabular printed summary of a game, esp. in baseball, recording individual performance.

box seat *n.* **1.** A seat in a box at a public place of entertainment, such as a theater or stadium. **2.** A storage box on a coach, the lid of which serves as a seat for the driver.

box social *n.* A fund-raising event in which donated box lunches are auctioned off.

box spring *n.* A bedspring consisting of a cloth-covered frame containing rows of coil springs.

box stall *n.* A large enclosed stall for a single animal.

box•thorn (bŏks′thôrn′) *n.* See **matrimony vine.**

box turtle *n.* Any of several North American land turtles of the genus *Terrapene*, having a hinged plastron that pulls up against the carapace, completely closing the shell.

box•wood (bŏks′wo͝od′) *n.* **1.** The box plant. **2.** Its wood.

box•y (bŏk′sē) *adj.* **-i•er, -i•est.** Resembling a box, esp. in simplicity or rectangularity. —**box′i•ness** *n.*

boy (boi) *n.* **1.** A male child. **2.** An immature or inexperienced man, esp. a young man. **3.** A son. **4.** *Informal.* A grown man; a fellow. **5.** A male who comes from or belongs to a particular place: *a city boy.* **6.** *Offensive.* A male servant, such as a valet. —*interj.* Used to express mild astonishment, elation, or disgust: *Oh boy!* [ME *boi,* poss. < OFr. *embuié,* servant, p.part. of *embuier,* to fetter.] —**boy′hood′** *n.*

bo•yar (bō-yär′, boi′ər) *n.* A member of a class of higher Russian nobility that until the time of Peter I headed the civil and military administration. [< *boiaren* < Russ. *boyarin* < ORuss. *boljarin* < Turkic *baylar,* pl. of *bay,* rich; akin to Turk. *bay,* rich, gentleman.]

boy•cott (boi′kŏt′) *tr.v.* **-cott•ed, -cott•ing, -cotts.** To act together in abstaining from using, buying, or dealing with as an expression of protest or disfavor or as a means of coercion. —*n.* The act or an instance of boycotting. [After Charles C. *Boycott* (1832–97), English land agent in Ireland.] —**boy′cott′er** *n.*

Word History: Charles C. Boycott was the estate agent of the Earl of Erne in County Mayo, Ireland. The earl was one of the absentee landowners who as a group held most of the land in Ireland. Boycott was chosen in the fall of 1880 to be the test case for a new policy advocated by Charles Parnell, an Irish politician who wanted land reform. Parnell urged that any landlord who would not charge lower rents or any tenant who took over the farm of an evicted tenant should be given the complete cold shoulder. Boycott, a former British soldier, refused to charge lower rents and ejected his tenants. Boycott and his family found themselves without servants, farmhands, service in stores, or mail delivery. Boycott's name was quickly adopted as the term for this treatment, not just in English but in French, Dutch, German, and Russian as well.

Boyd Orr (boid′ ôr′, ōr′), Lord **John.** 1880–1971. British nutritionist who won the 1949 Nobel Peace Prize.

boy•friend also **boy friend** (boi′frĕnd′) *n.* **1.** A favored male companion or sweetheart. **2.** A male friend.

boy•ish (boi′ĭsh) *adj.* Characteristic of or befitting a boy: *boyish charm.* —**boy′ish•ly** *adv.* —**boy′ish•ness** *n.*

Boyle (boil), **Robert.** 1627–91. Irish-born British physicist and chemist who formulated Boyle's law (1622).

Boyle's law (boilz) *n.* The principle that at a constant temperature the volume of a confined ideal gas varies inversely with its pressure. [After Robert BOYLE.]

Boyne (boin). A river of E Ireland flowing c. 113 km (70 mi) to the Irish Sea; site of the Battle of the Boyne (1690).

Boyn•ton Beach (boin′tən). A city of SE FL on the Atlantic Ocean N of Boca Raton. Pop. 46,194.

Boy Scout (boi) *n.* A member of a worldwide organization of young men and boys, founded in England in 1908, for character development and citizenship training.

boy•sen•ber•ry (boi′zən-bĕr′ē) *n.* **1.** A prickly bramble derived from a western North American blackberry *(Rubus ursinus).* **2.** The edible dark red to nearly black fruit of this plant. [After Rudolph *Boysen* (d. 1950), Amer. botanist.]

boy wonder *n.* A very talented, accomplished young man.

Boz•ca•a•da (bŏz′jä-ä-dä′). An island of Turkey in the NE Aegean S of the Dardanelles; traditional site of a Greek naval station during the Trojan War.

Boze•man (bōz′mən). A city of SW MT ESE of Butte; settled in the 1860's. Pop. 22,660.

bo•zo (bō′zō) *n., pl.* **-zos.** *Slang.* **1.** A fellow; a guy. **2.** A dunce; a fool. [?]

bp[1] *abbr.* Boiling point.

bp[2] also **BP** *abbr.* Beautiful people.

BP *abbr.* **1.** Or **B/P** Bills payable. **2.** Or **B.P.** Blood pressure.

bp. *abbr.* **1.** Birthplace. **2.** *Games.* Bishop.

B.P. *abbr.* **1.** Bachelor of Pharmacy. **2.** Bachelor of Philosophy.

bpd *abbr.* Barrels per day.

B.Pd. *abbr.* Bachelor of Pedagogy.

B.P.E. *abbr.* Bachelor of Physical Education.

B.Ph. *abbr.* Bachelor of Philosophy.

B.Phil. *abbr.* Bachelor of Philosophy.

bpi *abbr. Comp. Sci.* **1.** Bits per inch. **2.** Bytes per inch.

B picture *n.* A movie produced on a low budget, originally made to accompany the main feature in a double billing.

bpl *abbr.* Birthplace.

BPOE or **B.P.O.E.** *abbr.* Benevolent and Protective Order of Elks.

Br The symbol for the element **bromine.**

BR *abbr.* **1.** Bedroom. **2.** Or **B/R** Bills receivable.

br. *abbr.* **1.** Branch. **2.** *Law.* Brief. **3.** Bronze. **4.** Or **Br.** Brother. **5.** Brown.

Br. *abbr.* **1.** Britain. **2.** British.

bra (brä) *n.* A brassiere.

Bra•bant (brə-bănt′, -bänt′, brä′bənt, -bänt′). A region and former duchy of the Netherlands now divided between the S Netherlands and N-central Belgium.

brab•ble (brăb′əl) *intr.v.* **-bled, -bling, -bles.** To quarrel noisily, esp. over a small matter; wrangle. —*n.* A petty dispute; a squabble. [Prob. < MDu. *brabbelen,* to squabble.] —**brab′bler** *n.*

brace (brās) *n.* **1.** A device that holds or fastens two or more parts together or in place; a clamp. **2.** A device, such as a supporting beam in a building, that steadies or holds something else erect. **3. braces.** *Chiefly British.* Suspenders. **4.** An orthopedic appliance used to support or align a body part. **5.** A dental appliance, constructed of bands and wires, that is fixed to the teeth to correct irregular alignment. Often used in the plural. **6.** An extremely stiff, erect posture. **7.** A cause or source of renewed physical or spiritual vigor. **8.** A protective pad strapped to the bow arm of an archer. **9.** *Naut.* A rope by which a yard is swung and secured on a square-rigged ship. **10.** A tool with an adjustable aperture for securing and turning a bit. **11.** *Mus.* A leather loop that slides to change the tension on the cord of a drum. **12.** *Mus.* **a.** A vertical line, usu. accompanied by the symbol {, connecting two or more staffs. **b.** A set of staffs connected in this way. **13.** A symbol, { or }, enclosing lines of text, listed items, or mathematical expressions that are considered as a unit. **14.** *pl.* **brace.** A pair of like things: *three brace of partridges.* —*v.* **braced, brac•ing, brac•es.** —*tr.* **1.** To furnish with a brace. **2.** To support or hold steady with or as if with a brace; reinforce. **3.** To prepare or position for impact or danger: *braced themselves for a confrontation.* **4.** To confront with questions or requests. **5.** To increase the tension of. **6.** To invigorate; stimulate. **7.** *Naut.* To turn (the yards of a ship) by the braces. —*intr.* To get ready; make preparations. —***phrasal verb.*** **brace up.** To summon one's strength or endurance. [ME < OFr., two arms < Lat. *brācchia,* pl. of *brācchium,* arm < Gk. *brakhiōn,* upper arm. See **mregh-u-*.**]

brace•let (brās′lĭt) *n.* **1.** An ornamental band or chain encircling the wrist or arm. **2.** Something, such as a handcuff, that resembles a wrist ornament. [ME < OFr., dim. of *bracel,* armlet < Lat. *brācchiāle* < *brācchium,* arm. See BRACE.]

brac•er[1] (brā′sər) *n.* **1.** One that braces, esp. one that supports. **2.** *Informal.* A stimulating drink, esp. alcoholic.

bra•cer[2] (brā′sər) *n.* An arm or wrist guard worn by archers and fencers. [ME, prob. < AN < OFr. *braceure* < *bras,* arm < Lat. *brācchium.* See BRACE.]

bra•ce•ro (brə-sâr′ō) *n., pl.* **-ros.** A Mexican laborer permitted to work in the United States for a limited period, esp. in agriculture. [Sp., laborer < *brazo,* arm < Lat. *brācchium* < Gk. *brakhiōn,* upper arm. See **mregh-u-*.**]

bra•chi•al (brā′kē-əl, brăk′ē-) *adj.* Of, relating to, or resembling the arm or a similar or homologous part. [< Lat. *brācchiālis* < *brācchium,* arm. See BRACHIUM.]

bra•chi•ate (brā′kē-ĭt, -āt′, brăk′ē-) *adj. Zool.* Having arms or armlike appendages. —*intr.v.* (-āt′) **-at•ed, -at•ing, -ates.** To move by swinging with the arms from one hold to another, as certain apes do. [Lat. *brācchiātus* < *brācchium,* arm. See BRACHIUM.] —**bra′chi•a′tion** *n.*

bra•chi•o•pod (brā′kē-ə-pŏd′, brăk′ē-) *n.* Any of various marine invertebrates of the phylum Brachiopoda, having bivalve dorsal and ventral shells enclosing a pair of armlike structures that sweep food particles into the mouth. [< NLat. *Brāchiopoda,* phylum name : Lat. *brācchium,* arm; see BRACHIUM + NLat. *-poda,* -pod.] —**brach′i•o•pod′** *adj.*

bra•chi•um (brā′kē-əm, brăk′ē-) *n., pl.* **bra•chi•a** (brā′kē-ə, brăk′ē-ə). **1.** The part of the upper arm or forelimb extending from the shoulder to the elbow. **2.** An arm or a homologous anatomical structure, such as a flipper or wing. **3.** The part of a limb or process corresponding to an arm. [Lat. *brācchium,* arm < Gk. *brakhiōn,* upper arm. See **mregh-u-*.**]

brachy– *pref.* Short: *brachycephalic.* [Gk. *brakhu-* < *brakhus,* short. See **mregh-u-*.**]

brach•y•ce•phal•ic (brăk′ĭ-sə-făl′ĭk) also **brach•y•ceph•a•lous** (-sĕf′ə-ləs) *adj.* Having a short, broad head with a cephalic index over 80. —**brach′y•ceph′a•ly** (-sĕf′ə-lē), **brach′y•ceph′a•lism** *n.*

bra•chyl•o•gy (bră-kĭl′ə-jē) *n., pl.* **-gies. 1.** Brevity of speech; conciseness. **2.** A shortened expression. [Med.Lat. *brachylogia* < Gk. *brakhulogia: brakhu-,* brachy- + *logos,* speech; see -LOGY.]

bra•chyp•ter•ous (bră-kĭp′tər-əs) *adj.* Having very short or rudimentary wings, as certain insects. [< Gk. *brakhupteros: brakhu-,* brachy- + *pteron,* wing; see -PTER.] —**bra•chyp′ter•ism** (-tə-rĭz′əm) *n.*

brach•y•u•ran (brăk′ē-yŏŏr′ən) also **brach•y•u•ral** (-yŏŏr′əl) or **brach•y•u•rous** (-yŏŏr′əs) —*adj.* Of or belonging to the Brachyura, a group of crustaceans including the true crabs, characterized by a short abdomen concealed under the cephalothorax. —*n.* A member of the Brachyura. [< NLat. *Brachyura,* suborder name : Gk. *brakhu-,* brachy- + Gk. *oura,* tail; see -UROUS.]

brac•ing (brā′sĭng) *adj.* Invigorating or refreshing; strengthening: *a bracing tonic.* —*n.* **1.** A support; a brace. **2.** Braces considered as a group. —**brac′ing•ly** *adv.*

bra•ci•o•la (brä′chē-ō′lə, brä-chō′-) or **bra•ci•o•le** (-lā′, -lĕ′) *n.* A thin slice of meat, usu. wrapped around a stuffing and cooked with wine. [Ital., prob. < dialectal *bras'ola* < *bras'a,* glowing ember, of Gmc. orig. See **bhreu-*.**]

brack•en (brăk′ən) *n.* **1.** A widespread fern *(Pteridium aquilinum)* having large, triangular, pinnately compound fronds. **2.** An area overgrown with this fern. [ME *braken,* prob. of Scand. orig. See **bhreg-*.**]

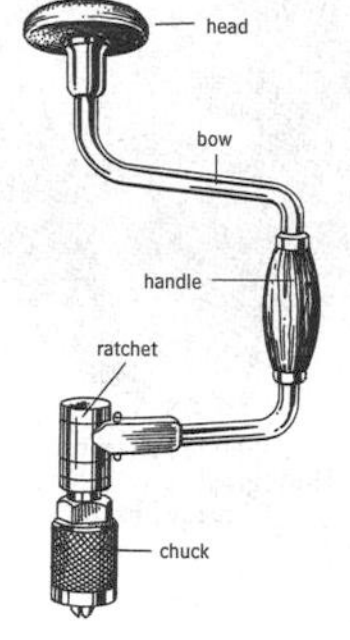

brace

ă pat	oi boy
ā pay	ou out
âr care	ŏŏ took
ä father	ōō boot
ĕ pet	ŭ cut
ē be	ûr urge
ĭ pit	th thin
ī pie	*th* this
îr pier	hw which
ŏ pot	zh vision
ō toe	ə about, item
ô paw	

Stress marks:
′ (primary);
′ (secondary), as in
dictionary (dĭk′shə-nĕr′ē)

Mathew Brady
Photographed in 1861

Johannes Brahms
Photographed c. 1880 by Fritz Luckhardt

A B C D E
F G H I J
K L M N O
P Q R S T
U V W X Y
Z and for the with
numeral sign
1 2 3 4 5
6 7 8 9 0

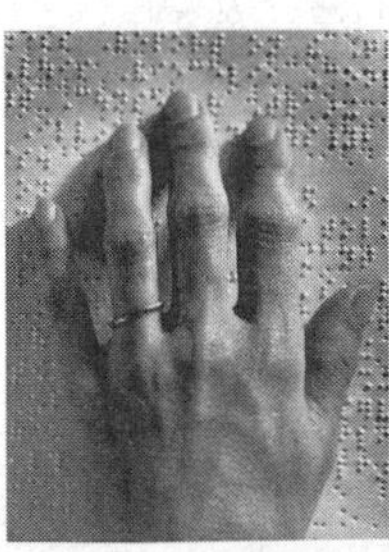
Braille
Top: Alphabet and numerals
Bottom: Printed material

brack•et (brăk′ĭt) *n.* **1.a.** A rigid structure in the shape of an L, used to support a shelf or other weight. **b.** A shelf or shelves supported by such structures. **2.** *Archit.* A usu. decorative wall fixture that supports something; a console or corbel. **3.** A wall fixture for gas or electricity. **4.a.** One of a pair of marks, [ ], used to enclose written or printed material or to indicate a mathematical expression considered as a single quantity. **b.** See **angle bracket. 5.** *Chiefly British.* One of a pair of parentheses. **6.** A classification or grouping, such as a category of incomes sharing the same tax rate. **7.a.** The distance between two impacting artillery shells, the first aimed beyond a target and the second aimed short of it, used to determine range. **b.** The shells fired in such a manner. —*tr.v.* **-et•ed, -et•ing, -ets. 1.** To furnish or support with a bracket or brackets. **2.** To place within or as if within brackets. **3.** To classify or group together. **4.** To include or exclude by establishing specific boundaries. **5.** To fire beyond and short of (a target) in order to determine artillery range. [Poss. Fr. *braguette*, codpiece, dim. of *brague*, breeches < OProv. *braga* < Lat. *brācae*, of Celt. orig.]

bracket creep *n. Informal.* A shift of personal income into a higher tax bracket when the taxable income increases.

bracket fungus *n.* Any of various fungi that form shelflike growths on tree trunks and wood structures.

brack•ish (brăk′ĭsh) *adj.* **1.** Having a somewhat salty taste, esp. from containing seawater. **2.** Distasteful; unpalatable: *brackish gruel.* [< Du. *brak.*] —**brack′ish•ness** *n.*

Brack•nell (brăk′nəl). A town of SE England; designated as a new town in 1949. Pop. 50,100.

bract (brăkt) *n.* A leaflike or scalelike plant part, usu. small, sometimes brightly colored, and located just below a flower, a flower stalk, or an inflorescence. [< Lat. *bractea*, gold leaf, perh. < Gk. *brakhein*, to rattle.] —**brac′te•al** (brăk′tē-əl) *adj.*

brac•te•ate (brăk′tē-ĭt, -āt′) *adj.* Bearing bracts. [NLat. *bracteātus* < Lat. *bractea*, gold leaf. See BRACT.]

brac•te•o•late (brăk′tē-ə-lĭt, -lāt′) *adj.* Bearing bracteoles.

brac•te•ole (brăk′tē-ōl′) *n.* A small bract. [Lat. *bracteola*, gold leaf, dim. of *bractea*. See BRACT.]

brad (brăd) *n.* A thin wire nail with a small head or a slight side projection instead of a head. [ME < ON *broddr*, spike.] —**brad** *v.*

brad•awl (brăd′ôl′) *n.* An awl with a beveled tip, used to make holes in wood for brads or screws.

Brad•bur•y (brăd′bĕr′ē, -bə-rē), **Ray Douglas.** b. 1920. Amer. writer whose works include *The Martian Chronicles* (1950).

Brad•dock (brăd′ək), **Edward.** 1695–1755. British general in America during the French and Indian War.

Bra•den•ton (brād′n-tən). A city of W-central FL on an inlet of Tampa Bay S of Tampa. Pop. 43,779.

Brad•ford (brăd′fərd). A borough of N-central England W of Leeds. Pop. 464,100.

Bradford, Roark. 1896–1948. Amer. writer whose works, such as *John Henry* (1931), reflect Black folklore.

Bradford, William[1]**.** 1590–1657. English Puritan colonist in America; a signer of the Mayflower Compact and governor of Plymouth Plantation for 30 one-year terms.

Bradford, William[2]**.** 1663–1752. English-born Amer. colonial printer who produced the first American Book of Common Prayer (1710).

Brad•ley (brăd′lē), **Joseph P.** 1813–92. Amer. jurist; associate justice of the U.S. Supreme Court (1870–92).

Bradley, Omar Nelson. 1893–1981. Amer. general who played a major part in the Allied victory in World War II.

Bradley, Thomas. b. 1917. Amer. politician who became the first Black mayor of Los Angeles in 1973.

Brad•street (brăd′strēt′), **Anne Dudley.** 1612–72. English-born colonial poet who wrote several collections of verse, including *The Tenth Muse Lately Sprung Up in America* (1650).

Bra•dy (brā′dē), **James Buchanan.** "Diamond Jim." 1856–1917. Amer. financier and philanthropist known for his extravagant lifestyle.

Brady, Mathew B. 1823–96. Amer. pioneer photographer who was appointed official Union photographer of the Civil War in 1861.

brady– *pref.* Slow: *bradycardia.* [Gk. *bradu-* < *bradus*, slow.]

brad•y•car•di•a (brăd′ĭ-kär′dē-ə) *n.* Slowness of the heart rate, usu. fewer than 60 beats per minute in an adult human being. [BRADY- + Gk. *kardia*, heart; see CARDIA.] —**brad′y•car′dic** (-dĭk) *adj.*

brad•y•ki•nin (brăd′ĭ-kī′nĭn, -kĭn′ĭn) *n.* A polypeptide that forms from a blood plasma globulin and stimulates pain receptors, increases vasodilation, and causes contraction of smooth muscle.

brae (brā) *n. Scots.* A hillside; a slope. [ME *bra* < ON *brā*, eyelash.]

brag (brăg) *v.* **bragged, brag•ging, brags.** —*intr.* To talk boastfully. —*tr.* To assert boastfully. —*n.* **1.** A boast. **2.** Arrogant or boastful speech or manner. **3.** Something boasted of. **4.** A braggart. **5.** *Games.* A card game similar to poker. —*adj.* **brag•ger, brag•gest.** Exceptionally fine. [ME *braggen* < *brag*, ostentatious.] —**brag′ger** *n.*

Bra•ga (brä′gə). A city of NW Portugal NNE of Oporto; probably founded by the Carthaginians. Pop. 63,033.

Bra•gan•za (brə-găn′zə) also **Bra•gan•ça** (-gäɴ′sä). A dynasty of Portuguese rulers (1640–1910) who also controlled Brazil (1822–89).

Bragg (brăg), **Braxton.** 1817–76. Amer. Confederate general in the Civil War who was defeated in the Chattanooga campaign (1863).

Bragg, Sir **William Henry.** 1862–1942. British physicist who shared a 1915 Nobel Prize with his son Sir **William Lawrence Bragg** (1890–1971).

brag•ga•do•ci•o (brăg′ə-dō′sē-ō′, -shē-ō′, -shō) *n., pl.* **-os. 1.** A braggart. **2.** Empty or pretentious bragging. [Alteration of *Braggadocchio* (prob. from BRAG), the personification of vainglory in *The Faerie Queene* by Edmund Spenser.]

brag•gart (brăg′ərt) *n.* One given to loud, empty boasting; a bragger. —*adj.* Boastful. [Fr. *bragard* < *braguer*, to brag, perh. < ME *braggen.* See BRAG.]

Brahe (brä, brä′hē, brä′ə), **Tycho.** 1546–1601. Danish astronomer whose astronomical observations formed the basis for Kepler's laws of planetary motion.

Brah•ma[1] (brä′mə) *n.* **1.** *Hinduism.* **a.** The creator god, conceived chiefly as a member of the triad including also Vishnu and Shiva. **b.** Var. of **Brahman** 1. **2.** Var. of **Brahman** 3. [Skt. *brahmā.*]

Brah•ma[2] also **brah•ma** (brä′mə, brā′-) *n.* A large domestic fowl of a breed originating in Asia and having feathered legs and small wings and tail. [After BRAHMAPUTRA.]

Brah•man (brä′mən) *n.* **1.** Also **Brah•ma** (-mə). *Hinduism.* The single absolute being pervading the universe and found within the individual; atman. **2.** *Hinduism.* Var. of **Brahmin** 1. **3.** Also **Brah•ma** (-mə) or **Brah•min** (-mĭn). One of a breed of domestic cattle developed in the southern United States from stock originating in India and having a hump between the shoulders and a pendulous dewlap. [Skt. Sense 2 < *brāhmaṇa-*, brahmanic < *brahman.*] —**Brah•man′ic** (-măn′ĭk), **Brah•man′i•cal** *adj.*

Brah•man•ism (brä′mə-nĭz′əm) also **Brah•min•ism** (brä′-mĭ-) *n. Hinduism.* **1.** The religious practices and beliefs of ancient India as reflected in the Vedas. **2.** The social and religious system of orthodox Hindus, esp. of the Brahmins, based on a caste structure and various forms of pantheism. —**Brah′man•ist** *n.*

Brah•ma•pu•tra (brä′mə-po͞o′trə). A river of S Asia rising in the Himalaya Mts. and flowing c. 2,896 km (1,800 mi) to the Ganges R. in central Bangladesh.

Brah•min (brä′mĭn) *n.* **1.** Also **Brah•man** (-mən). *Hinduism.* A member of the first of the four Hindu classes, responsible for officiating at religious rites and studying and teaching the Vedas. **2.** A member of a cultural and social elite: *a Boston Brahmin.* **3.** Var. of **Brahman** 3. [Prob. alteration of Skt. *brāhmaṇaḥ* < *brāhmaṇa-*, brahminic. See BRAHMAN.] —**Brah•min′ic** (-mĭn′ĭk), **Brah•min′i•cal** *adj.*

Brah•min•ism (brä′mə-nĭz′əm) *n.* **1.** The attitude or conduct of a social or cultural elite. **2.** *Hinduism.* **Brahmanism.**

Brahms (brämz), **Johannes.** 1833–97. German composer whose works blend classical tradition with romanticism.

braid (brād) *v.* **braid•ed, braid•ing, braids.** —*tr.* **1.a.** To interweave three or more lengths of: *braided the rags into a rope.* **b.** To create (something) by such interweaving: *braid a rug.* **c.** To style (the hair) by such interweaving. **2.** To decorate or edge (something) with a trim of interwoven strands. **3.** To fasten or decorate (hair) with a band or ribbon. —*intr.* To flow, twist, or wind as if interwoven. —*n.* **1.** A braided segment or length, as of hair, fabric, or fiber. **2.** Ornamental cord or ribbon, used esp. for decorating fabrics. **3.** A ribbon or band used to fasten the hair. [ME *braiden* < OE *bregdan*, to weave.] —**braid′er** *n.*

braid•ed (brā′dĭd) *adj.* **1.a.** Produced by or as if by braiding. **b.** Having braids. **2.** Decorated with braid. **3.** Flowing as if interwoven: *a braided stream.*

braid•ing (brā′dĭng) *n.* **1.** Braided embroidery or trim. **2.** Braids considered as a group.

brail (brāl) *Naut.* —*n.* **1.** One of several small lines attached to the leech of a sail for drawing the sail in or up. **2.** A small net for drawing fish from a trap or a larger net into a boat. —*tr.v.* **brailed, brail•ing, brails. 1.** To gather in (a sail) with brails. **2.** To haul in (fish) with a brail. [ME *braile* < OFr. *brail*, belt < Med.Lat. *brācale* < Lat. *brācae*, breeches, of Celt. orig.]

Bră•i•la (brə-ē′lə). A city of SE Romania on the Danube R. near the Moldavian and Ukrainian borders. Pop. 224,998.

Braille or **braille** (brāl) —*n.* A system of writing and printing for visually impaired or sightless people, in which varied arrangements of raised dots representing letters and numerals are identified by touch. —*tr.v.* **Brailled, Braill•ing, Brailles** or **brailled, braill•ing, brailles.** To print or transliterate using this system. [After Louis BRAILLE.]

Braille, Louis. 1809–52. French inventor of the Braille system of writing and printing (1829).

Braill•er or **braill•er** (brā′lər) *n.* A machine analogous to a typewriter, used for printing in Braille.

Braille·writ·er or **braille·writ·er** (brāl′rī′tər) *n.* See **Brailler.**

brain (brān) *n.* **1.a.** The portion of the vertebrate central nervous system that is enclosed within the cranium, continuous with the spinal cord, and composed of gray matter and white matter. It regulates and controls many bodily activities and is the seat of consciousness, memory, and emotion. **b.** A functionally similar portion of the invertebrate nervous system. **2.a.** Intellectual ability; mind: *a dull brain.* **b.** Intellectual power; intelligence. Often used in the plural. **3.** A highly intelligent person. **4.** The primary director or planner, as of an organization. Often used in the plural. **5.** The control center, as of a ship. —*tr.v.* **brained, brain·ing, brains.** *Slang.* **1.** To smash in the skull of. **2.** To hit on the head. —***idioms.*** **beat (one's) brains (out).** *Informal.* To exert or expend great mental effort. **on the brain.** Obsessively in mind. **pick (someone's) brain (or brains).** To explore another's ideas through questioning. **rack (one's) brain.** *Informal.* To think long and hard. [ME < OE *brægen.*]

brain·case also **brain case** (brān′kās′) *n.* The part of the skull that encloses the brain; the cranium.

brain·child (brān′chīld′) *n.* An original idea or plan attributed to a person or group.

brain coral *n.* Any of several reef-building corals of the genus *Meandrina,* forming rounded colonies that resemble the convolutions of the human brain.

brain death *n.* Irreversible brain damage and loss of brain function, as evidenced by cessation of breathing and other vital reflexes, unresponsiveness to stimuli, absence of muscle activity, and a flat electroencephalogram for a specific length of time. —**brain′-dead′** (brān′dĕd′) *adj.*

brain drain *n.* The loss of intellectual and technical labor, esp. through emigration to more appealing countries. —**brain-drain** (brān′drān′) *v.*

Braine (brān), **John.** 1922–86. British writer best known for his novel *Room at the Top* (1957).

brain fever *n.* Inflammation of the brain or meninges, as in encephalitis or meningitis.

brain·less (brān′lĭs) *adj.* Unintelligent; stupid. —**brain′less·ly** *adv.* —**brain′less·ness** *n.*

brain·pan (brān′păn′) *n.* See **braincase.**

brain·pow·er (brān′pou′ər) *n.* **1.** Intellectual capacity. **2.** People of well-developed mental abilities.

brain·sick (brān′sĭk′) *adj.* Of, relating to, or induced by a mental disorder; insane or mad. —**brain′sick′ly** *adv.* —**brain′sick′ness** *n.*

brain stem also **brain·stem** (brān′stĕm′) *n.* The portion of the brain, consisting of the medulla oblongata, pons Varolii, and mesencephalon, that connects the spinal cord to the forebrain and cerebrum.

brain·storm (brān′stôrm′) *n.* **1.** A sudden clever plan or idea. **2.** A sudden, violent disturbance of the mind. —*v.* **-stormed, -storm·ing, -storms.** —*intr.* To engage in or organize shared problem solving. —*tr.* To consider or come up with by brainstorming. —**brain′storm′er** *n.* —**brain′storm′ing** *n.*

brain·teas·er (brān′tē′zər) *n.* A mentally challenging problem or puzzle.

Brain·tree (brān′trē′). A town of E MA, a suburb of Boston. Pop. 33,836.

brain trust *n.* A group of experts who serve as unofficial advisers and policy planners, esp. in a government.

brain·wash (brān′wŏsh′, -wôsh′) *tr.v.* **-washed, -wash·ing, -wash·es.** To subject to brainwashing. —*n.* The process or an instance of brainwashing.

brain·wash·ing (brān′wŏsh′ĭng, -wô′shĭng) *n.* **1.** Intensive, forcible indoctrination aimed at replacing a person's basic convictions with an alternative set of beliefs. **2.** The application of a concentrated means of persuasion in order to develop a specific belief or motivation. [Transl. of Chin. (Mandarin) *xǐ naǒ*: *xǐ*, to wash + *naǒ*, brain.]

brain wave *n.* **1.** A rhythmic fluctuation of electric potential between parts of the brain, as seen on an electroencephalogram. **2.** *Informal.* A sudden inspiration.

brain·y (brā′nē) *adj.* **-i·er, -i·est.** *Informal.* Intelligent; smart. —**brain′i·ly** *adv.* —**brain′i·ness** *n.*

braise (brāz) *tr.v.* **braised, brais·ing, brais·es.** To cook (meat or vegetables) by browning in fat, then simmering in a small quantity of liquid in a covered container. [Fr. *braiser* < *braise*, hot charcoal < OFr. *brese*, of Gmc. orig. See **bhreu-*.**]

brake[1] (brāk) *n.* **1.** A device for slowing or stopping motion, as of a vehicle, esp. by contact friction. **2.** Something that slows or stops action. —*v.* **braked, brak·ing, brakes.** —*tr.* To reduce the speed of with or as if with a brake. —*intr.* **1.** To operate or apply a brake. **2.** To be slowed or stopped by or as if by a brake. [Prob. *brake*, bridle, curb < MDu. or MLGer., nose ring, curb, flax brake; see BRAKE[2].]

brake[2] (brāk) *n.* **1.** A toothed device for crushing and beating flax or hemp. **2.** A heavy harrow for breaking clods of earth. **3.** An apparatus for kneading large amounts of dough. **4.** A machine for bending and folding sheet metal. —*tr.v.* **braked, brak·ing, brakes. 1.** To crush (flax or hemp) in a toothed device. **2.** To break up (clods of earth) with a harrow. [ME < MDu. < MLGer. See **bhreg-*.**]

brake[3] (brāk) *n.* A lever or handle on a machine such as a pump. [ME < OFr. *brac* < oblique form of *bras*, arm. See BRACER[2].]

brake[4] (brāk) *n.* **1.** Any of various ferns of the genus *Pteris*, having pinnately compound leaves and including several popular houseplants. **2.** Any of certain other ferns, such as bracken. [ME, prob. back-formation < *braken*. See BRACKEN.]

brake[5] (brāk) *n.* An area overgrown with dense brushwood, briers, and undergrowth; a thicket. [ME < MLGer. See **bhreg-*.**]

brake[6] (brāk) *n.* Var. of **break** 27. —*v.* *Archaic.* A p.t. of **break.**

brake drum *n.* A metal cylinder to which pressure is applied by a braking mechanism in order to arrest rotation of the wheel or shaft to which the cylinder is attached.

brake horsepower *n.* The actual horsepower of an engine, usu. determined from the force exerted on a friction brake or dynamometer connected to the drive shaft.

brake lining *n.* The covering of a brake shoe.

brake·man (brāk′mən) *n.* One who operates, inspects, or repairs brakes, esp. on a train.

brake pad *n.* A flat block that presses against the disk of a disc brake.

brake shoe *n.* A curved metal block that presses against and arrests the rotation of a wheel or brake drum.

Bra·man·te (brə-män′tā, brä-män′tĕ), **Donato.** 1444–1514. Italian architect who evolved the High Renaissance style.

bram·ble (brăm′bəl) *n.* **1.** A prickly shrub of the genus *Rubus*, including the blackberry and the raspberry. **2.** A prickly shrub or bush. [ME *brembel* < OE *bræmbel.*] —**bram′bly** *adj.*

bram·ble·ber·ry (brăm′bəl-bĕr′ē) *n.* The fruit of a bramble.

bram·bling (brăm′blĭng) *n.* A finch *(Fringilla montifringilla)* of northern Eurasia having black, white, and rust-brown plumage. [Prob. < OE **bræmbling*: *bræmbel*, bramble + *-ling*, one connected with; see -LING[1].]

Bramp·ton (brămp′tən). A city of S Ontario, Canada, a suburb of Toronto. Pop. 149,030.

bran (brăn) *n.* The outer layers of the grain of cereals, removed during the process of milling and used as a source of dietary fiber. [ME < OFr., of Celt. orig.] —**bran′ny** *adj.*

Bran (brăn) *n.* *Myth.* A gigantic Celtic god and ruler of Britain.

branch (brănch) *n.* **1.a.** A secondary woody stem or limb growing from the trunk of a tree or shrub or from another secondary limb. **b.** A lateral division or subdivision of certain other plant parts, such as a root. **2.** Something that resembles a branch of a tree, as in form or function, as: **a.** A secondary outgrowth or subdivision of a main axis, such as the tine of a deer's antlers. **b.** *Anat.* An offshoot or a division of the main portion of a structure, such as a nerve or blood vessel. **3.** A limited part of a larger or more complex system, esp.: **a.** An area of skill or knowledge that is related to but separate from other areas. **b.** A division of a business or other organization. **c.** A division of a family, categorized by descent from a particular ancestor. **d.** *Ling.* A subdivision of a family of languages. **4.a.** A tributary of a river. **b.** *Chiefly Southern U.S.* See **creek** 1. See Regional Note at **run. c.** A divergent section of a river, esp. near the mouth. **5.** *Math.* A part of a curve that is separated, as by discontinuities. **6.** *Comp. Sci.* A sequence of program instructions to which the normal sequence of instructions relinquishes control, depending on the value of certain variables. —*v.* **branched, branch·ing, branch·es.** —*intr.* **1.** To put forth a branch or branches; spread by dividing. **2.a.** To come forth as a branch or subdivision; develop or diverge from. **b.** To enlarge the scope of one's interests or activities: *branch out into related fields.* **3.** *Comp. Sci.* To relinquish control to another set of instructions or another routine as a result of the presence of a branch. —*tr.* **1.** To separate (something) into or as if into branches. **2.** To embroider (something) with a design of foliage or flowers. [ME < OFr. *branche* < LLat. *branca*, paw, perh. of Celt. orig.] —**branch′less** *adj.* —**branch′y** *adj.*

bran·chi·a (brăng′kē-ə) *n., pl.* **-chi·ae** (-kē-ē). A gill or similar organ of respiration. [Lat. < Gk. *brankhia*, gills.] —**bran′chi·al** (-kē-əl) *adj.*

branchial arch *n.* See **gill arch.**

branchial cleft *n.* See **gill slit** 1.

branchial groove *n.* See **gill slit** 2.

bran·chi·o·pod (brăng′kē-ə-pŏd′) *n.* Any of various aquatic crustaceans of the subclass Branchiopoda, such as the fairy shrimp and water flea, characterized by a segmented body and flattened, leaflike thoracic appendages. [< NLat. *Branchiopoda*, subclass name : Lat. *branchia*, gills; see BRANCHIA + NLat. *poda*, -pod; see -POD.] —**bran′chi·o·pod′, bran′chi·op′o·dan** (-ŏp′ə-dən), **bran′chi·op′a·dous** (-dəs) *adj.*

branch·let (brănch′lĭt) *n.* A small branch or the terminal or ultimate subdivision of a branch.

branch water *n.* **1.** Plain water, esp. when mixed with a liquor such as whiskey. **2.** *Chiefly Southern U.S.* Water from a stream. [BRANCH, stream + WATER.]

Bran·cu·si (brän-ko͞o′zē, brăng-koosh′), **Constantin.** 1876–1957. Romanian-born sculptor of geometric, abstract metal and stone sculptures.

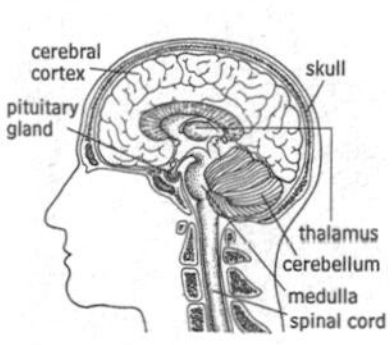

brain

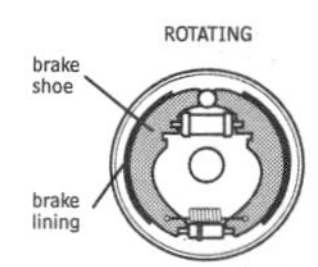

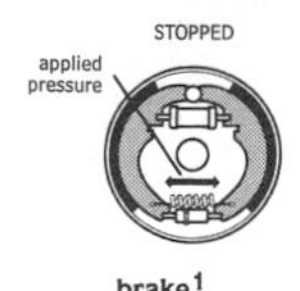

brake[1]
Shoe brake

ă pat	oi boy
ā pay	ou out
âr care	o͝o took
ä father	o͞o boot
ĕ pet	ŭ cut
ē be	ûr urge
ĭ pit	th thin
ī pie	*th* this
îr pier	hw which
ŏ pot	zh vision
ō toe	ə about, item
ô paw	

Stress marks:
′ (primary);
′ (secondary), as in **dictionary** (dĭk′shə-nĕr′ē)

brand (brănd) *n.* **1.a.** A trademark or distinctive name identifying a product or a manufacturer. **b.** A product line so identified. **c.** A distinctive category; a particular kind. **2.** A mark indicating identity or ownership, burned on the hide of an animal with a hot iron. **3.** A mark burned into the flesh of criminals. **4.** A mark of disgrace or notoriety; a stigma. **5.** A branding iron. **6.** A piece of burning or charred wood. **7.** A sword. — *tr.v.* **brand•ed, brand•ing, brands. 1.** To mark with or as if with a hot iron. See Syns at **mark**[1]. **2.** To mark with disgrace or infamy; stigmatize. **3.** To impress firmly; fix ineradicably. [ME, torch < OE. See **g^{w}her-***.] — **brand′er** *n.*

Bran•deis (brăn′dīs′, -dīz′), **Louis Dembitz.** 1856–1941. Amer. jurist; associate justice of the U.S. Supreme Court (1916–39).

Bran•den•burg (brăn′dən-bûrg′, brän′dən-bo͝ork′). **1.** A historical region and former duchy of N-central Germany now divided between Poland and Germany. **2.** A city of NE Germany on the Havel R. WSW of Berlin. Pop. 95,133.

brand•ing iron (brăn′dĭng) *n.* An iron that is heated and used for indicating identity or ownership.

bran•dish (brăn′dĭsh) *tr.v.* **-dished, -dish•ing, -dish•es. 1.** To wave or flourish (a weapon, for example) menacingly. **2.** To display ostentatiously. See Syns at **flourish.** — *n.* A menacing or defiant wave or flourish. [ME *brandissen* < OFr. *brandir, brandiss-* < *brand*, sword, of Gmc. orig. See **g^{w}her-***.] — **bran′dish•er** *n.*

brand•ling (brănd′lĭng) *n.* A common reddish-brown earthworm *(Eisenia foetida)* often used as fish bait. [BRAND (< its markings) + -LING[1].]

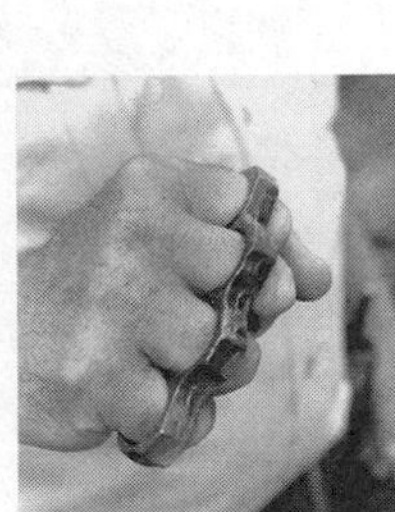

brass knuckles

brand name *n.* **1.** See **trade name** 1. **2.** A commodity, service, or process having a trade name. — **brand′-name′** (brănd′nām′) *adj.*

brand-new (brănd′no͞o′, -nyo͞o′) *adj.* Being in a fresh and unused condition; completely new.

Bran•do (brăn′dō), **Marlon.** b. 1924. Amer. actor who starred in *A Streetcar Named Desire* (1951).

Bran•don (brăn′dən). A city of SW Manitoba, Canada, on the Assiniboine R. W of Winnipeg. Pop. 36,242.

Brandt (brănt, bränt), **Willy.** 1913–92. German political leader who served as chancellor of West Germany (1969–74) and won the 1971 Nobel Peace Prize.

bran•dy (brăn′dē) *n., pl.* **-dies.** An alcoholic liquor distilled from wine or fermented fruit juice. — *tr.v.* **-died, -dy•ing, -dies.** To preserve, flavor, or mix with brandy. [Short for *brandy-wine* < Du. *brandewijn*: *brandende*, pr.part. of *branden*, to burn; see **g^{w}her-*** + *wijn*, wine; see WINE.]

Bran•dy•wine (brăn′dē-wīn′). A creek of SE PA and N DE; site of a major defeat of the Continental Army (1777) in the American Revolution.

brank (brăngk) *n.* A device consisting of a metal frame for the head and a bit to restrain the tongue, formerly used to punish scolds. Often used in the plural. [Poss. < Du. *branken*, legs (of a compass, scissors, etc.), pl. of *branke*, branch < LLat. *branca*, paw. See BRANCH.]

bran•ni•gan (brăn′ĭ-gən) *n.* **1.** A noisy or confused quarrel. **2.** A drinking spree. [Prob. < the name *Brannigan*.]

brant (brănt) *n., pl.* **brant** or **brants.** Any of several small dark wild geese of the genus *Branta* that breed in arctic regions, esp. *B. bernicla* having a long black neck and head. [Var. of *brent (-goose)*, poss. < ME *brende*, brindled. See BRINDLED.]

Brant (brănt), **Joseph.** 1742–1807. Mohawk leader who supported the British in the French and Indian War and the American Revolution.

Brant•ford (brănt′fərd). A city of S Ontario, Canada, SW of Toronto; named for Joseph Brant. Pop. 74,315.

Bran•ting (brăn′tĭng, brän′-), **Karl Hjalmar.** 1860–1925. Swedish politician who shared the 1921 Nobel Peace Prize.

Braque (bräk, brăk), **Georges.** 1882–1963. French painter who was a leading exponent of the cubist movement.

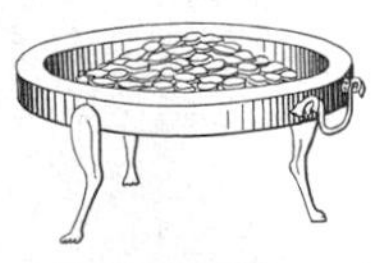

brazier[2]

brash[1] (brăsh) *adj.* **brash•er, brash•est. 1.a.** Hasty and unthinking; impetuous. **b.** Rash. **2.** Lacking in sensitivity or tact. **3.** Presumptuously forward; impudent. **4.** Brittle: *brash timbers.* [Poss. imit. (influenced by RASH[1]) or < *brash*, attack.] — **brash′ly** *adv.* — **brash′ness** *n.*

brash[2] (brăsh) *n.* A mass or pile of fragments, as of stone or ice. [Perh. an alteration of Fr. *brèche*, breach in a wall < Ital. *breccia*. See BRECCIA.]

bra•sier[1] (brā′zhər) *n.* Var. of **brazier**[1].

bra•sier[2] (brā′zhər) *n.* Var. of **brazier**[2].

Bra•sí•lia (brə-zĭl′yə). The cap. of Brazil (since 1960), in the central plateau NW of Rio de Janeiro. Pop. 1,176,935.

Bra•şov (brä-shôv′). A city of central Romania NNW of Bucharest; founded 1211. Pop. 331,240.

brass (brăs) *n.* **1.a.** A yellowish alloy of copper and zinc, sometimes including small amounts of other metals. **b.** Ornaments, objects, or utensils made of this alloy. **2.** *Mus.* **a.** The section of a band or an orchestra composed of brass instruments. Often used in the plural. **b.** Brass instruments or their players considered as a group. Often used in the plural. **3.** A memorial plaque or tablet made of brass. **4.** A bushing or similar lining for a bearing, made from a copper alloy. **5.** *Informal.* Bold self-assurance; effrontery. **6.** *Slang.* High-ranking military officers or other high officials. [ME *bras* < OE *bræs*.] — **brass** *adj.*

bras•sard (brə-särd′, brăs′ärd′) *n.* **1.** A band or badge worn around the upper arm. **2.** Also **bras•sart** (brə-särt′, brăs′ärt′). A piece of armor covering the arm. [Fr. < OFr. *bras*, arm < Lat. *brācchium* < Gk. *brakhīōn*, upper arm. See **mregh-u-***.]

brass band *n. Mus.* A band composed of brass and sometimes percussion instruments.

brass•bound (brăs′bound′) *adj.* **1.** Banded or trimmed with brass or a similar metal, such as bronze. **2.** Inflexible; rigid: *brassbound party loyalists.* **3.** Bold and impudent; brazen.

brass-col•lar (brăs′kŏl′ər) *adj.* Unwavering in political allegiance; consistently voting a straight party ticket.

bras•se•rie (brăs′ə-rē′, brăs-rē′) *n.* A restaurant serving alcoholic beverages, esp. beer, as well as food. [Fr. < *brasser*, to malt, brew < OFr. *bracier* < VLat. **braciāre* < Lat. *brace*, malt, of Celt. orig.]

brass hat *n. Slang.* A high-ranking military officer or civilian official. [From the gold braid on the hat.]

brass•ie also **brass•y** (brăs′ē) *n., pl.* **-ies.** *Sports.* A two wood used in golf.

bras•siere (brə-zîr′) *n.* A woman's undergarment worn to support and give contour to the breasts. [Fr., child's jacket with sleeves, brassiere : OFr. *bras*, arm (< Lat. *brācchium* < Gk. *brakhīōn*, upper arm; see **mregh-u-***) + OFr. *-iere*, one associated with; see -ER[1].]

brass instrument *n. Mus.* A wind instrument, such as the French horn, made of brass or other metal.

brass knuckles *pl.n. (used with a sing. or pl. v.)* A metal chain or a set of rings attached to a bar that can be fitted over the fingers to increase the impact of a blow with the fist.

brass tacks *pl.n. Informal.* Essential facts; basics.

brass•ware (brăs′wâr′) *n.* Articles made from brass.

brass•y[1] (brăs′ē) *adj.* **-i•er, -i•est. 1.** Made of or decorated with brass. **2.** Resembling brass, as in color. **3.** *Mus.* Resembling or characterized by the sound of brass instruments. **4.** Cheap and showy; flashy. **5.** *Informal.* Brazen; insolent. — **brass′i•ly** *adv.* — **brass′i•ness** *n.*

brass•y[2] (brăs′ē) *n. Sports.* Var. of **brassie.**

brat[1] (brăt) *n.* A child, esp. a spoiled or ill-mannered one. [Poss. < *brat*, coarse garment < ME < OE *bratt*, of Celt. orig.] — **brat′tish** *adj.* — **brat′tish•ness** *n.* — **brat′ty** *adj.*

brat[2] (brät) *n.* Bratwurst.

Bra•ti•sla•va (brăt′ĭ-slä′və, brä′tĭ-). The cap. of Slovakia, in the SW on the Danube R.; cap. of Hungary (1541–1784). Pop. 409,100.

Bratsk (brätsk). A city of S-central Russia NNW of Irkutsk. Pop. 240,000.

brat•tice (brăt′ĭs) *n.* **1.** A partition, typically of wood or cloth, erected in a mine for ventilation. **2.** A breastwork erected during a siege. [ME *bretice*, defensive structure < OFr. *bretesche* < Med.Lat. *bretescha (turris)*, British-style (tower), prob. < OE *bryttisc*, British.] — **brat′tice** *v.*

brat•tle (brăt′l) *Scots.* — *n.* **1.** A rattling or clattering sound. **2.** A movement that produces such a sound. — *intr.v.* **-tled, -tling, -tles.** To make a rattling or clattering sound. [Imit.]

brat•wurst (brăt′wûrst′, -vo͝orst′) *n.* A sausage of highly seasoned fresh pork. [Ger. < MHGer. *brātwurst* < OHGer. : *brāto*, meat; see **bhreu-*** + *wurst*, sausage; see WURST.]

Braun (broun), **Eva.** 1912–45. German lover and later wife of Adolf Hitler.

Braun (brôn, broun), **Wernher Magnus Maximilian von.** 1912–77. German-born Amer. rocket engineer who directed the development and launch of Explorer I (1958).

Braun•schwei•ger (broun′shwī′gər) *n.* A smoked liver sausage. [Ger., after *Braunschweig* (Brunswick), Germany.]

bra•va (brä′vä, brä-vä′) *interj.* Used to express approval of a woman, esp. for a performance. — *n.* A shout or cry of "brava." [Ital., fem. of *bravo*, bravo. See BRAVO[1].]

bra•va•do (brə-vä′dō) *n., pl.* **-dos** or **-does. a.** Defiant or swaggering behavior. **b.** A false show of bravery. [Sp. *bravada* < *bravo*, brave. See BRAVE.]

brave (brāv) *adj.* **brav•er, brav•est. 1.** Possessing or displaying courage; valiant. **2.** Making a fine display; impressive or showy. **3.** Excellent; great. — *n.* **1.** A Native American warrior. **2.** A courageous person. **3.** *Archaic.* A bully. — *v.* **braved, brav•ing, braves.** — *tr.* **1.** To undergo or face courageously. **2.** To challenge; dare. **3.** *Obsolete.* To make showy or splendid. — *intr. Archaic.* To make a courageous show. [ME < OFr. < OItal. or OSp. *bravo*, wild, brave, excellent, prob. < VLat. **brabus* < Lat. *barbarus*. See BARBAROUS.] — **brave′ly** *adv.* — **brave′ness** *n.*

Syns: brave, courageous, fearless, intrepid, bold, audacious, valiant, plucky, undaunted. These adjectives all mean having or showing courage under difficult or dangerous conditions. *Brave*, the least specific, is frequently associated with an innate quality: *"Familiarity with danger makes a brave man braver"* (Herman Melville). *Courageous* implies consciously rising to a specific test by drawing on a reserve of inner strength: *his courageous battle with cancer. Fearless* emphasizes absence of fear and resolute self-possession: *"world-*

class [boating] *races for fearless loners"* (Jo Ann Morse Ridley). *Intrepid* sometimes suggests invulnerability to fear: *Intrepid pioneers settled the American West. Bold* stresses readiness to meet danger or difficulty and often a tendency to seek it out: *"If we shrink from the hard contests ... then bolder and stronger peoples will pass us by"* (Theodore Roosevelt). *Audacious* implies extreme confidence and boldness: *"To demand these God-given rights is to seek black power — what I call audacious power"* (Adam Clayton Powell, Jr.). *Valiant* suggests the bravery of a hero or a heroine: *"a ... biography that sees Hemingway as a valiant and moral man"* (New York Times). *Plucky* emphasizes spirit and heart in the face of unfavorable odds: *"Everybody was ... anxious to show these Belgians what England thought of their plucky little country"* (H.G. Wells). *Undaunted* suggests persistent courage and resolve: *"We must be united, we must be undaunted, we must be inflexible"* (Winston S. Churchill).

brav•er•y (brā′və-rē, brāv′rē) *n., pl.* **-ies. 1.** The condition or quality of being brave. **2.** Splendor or magnificence; show.

bra•vis•si•mo (brä-vĭs′ə-mō′) *interj.* Used to express great approval, esp. of a performance. [Ital., superl. of *bravo*, fine. See BRAVO[1].]

bra•vo[1] (brä′vō, brä-vō′) *interj.* Used to express approval, esp. of a performance. *— n., pl.* **-vos.** A shout or cry of "bravo." [Ital. See BRAVE.] **— bra′vo** *v.*

bra•vo[2] (brä′vō) *n., pl.* **-voes** or **bra•vos.** A villain, esp. a hired killer. [Ital. < *bravo*, wild, excellent. See BRAVE.]

bra•vu•ra (brə-vo͝or′ə, -vyo͝or′ə) *n.* **1.** *Mus.* **a.** Brilliant technique or style in performance. **b.** A piece or passage that emphasizes a performer's virtuosity. **2.** A showy manner or display. [Ital. < *bravo*, excellent. See BRAVE.]

braw (brô) *adj.* **-er, -est.** *Scots.* **1.** Fine; splendid. **2.** Dressed in a fine or showy manner. [Sc., var. of BRAVE.]

brawl (brôl) *n.* **1.** A noisy quarrel or fight. **2.** A loud party. **3.** A loud, roaring noise. *— intr.v.* **brawled, brawl•ing, brawls. 1.** To quarrel or fight noisily. **2.** To flow noisily, as water. [ME *braul* < *braullen*, to quarrel.] **— brawl′er** *n.* **— brawl′ing•ly** *adv.* **— brawl′y** *adj.*

brawn (brôn) *n.* **1.** Solid and well-developed muscles. **2.** Muscular strength and power. **3.** *Chiefly British.* The meat of a boar. **4.** Headcheese. [ME, muscle < OFr. *braon*, meat, of Gmc. orig. See **bhreu-***.]

brawn•y (brô′nē) *adj.* **-i•er, -i•est. 1.** Strong and muscular. See Syns at **muscular. 2.** Hardened; calloused. **— brawn′i•ly** *adv.* **— brawn′i•ness** *n.*

bray[1] (brā) *v.* **brayed, bray•ing, brays.** *— intr.* **1.** To utter the bray of a donkey. **2.** To sound loudly and harshly. *— tr.* To emit (an utterance or a sound) loudly and harshly. *— n.* **1.** The loud, harsh cry of a donkey. **2.** A sound resembling a bray. [ME *braien* < OFr. *braire*, of Celt. orig.]

bray[2] (brā) *tr.v.* **brayed, bray•ing, brays. 1.** To crush and pound to a fine consistency, as in a mortar. **2.** To spread (ink) thinly over a surface. [ME *braien* < OFr. *breier*, of Gmc. orig. See **bhreg-***.]

bray•er[1] (brā′ər) *n.* One that brays, esp. a donkey.

bray•er[2] (brā′ər) *n. Print.* A small hand roller used to spread ink thinly and evenly.

Braz. *abbr.* **1.** Brazil. **2.** Brazilian.

braze[1] (brāz) *tr.v.* **brazed, braz•ing, braz•es. 1.** To make of or decorate with brass. **2.** To make hard like brass. [ME *brasen* < OE *brasian* < *bræs*, brass.]

braze[2] (brāz) *tr.v.* **brazed, braz•ing, braz•es.** To solder (two pieces of metal) together using a hard solder with a high melting point. [Prob. < Fr. *braser* < OFr., to burn < *brese*, hot coal, of Gmc. orig. See **bhreu-***.] **— braz′er** *n.*

bra•zen (brā′zən) *adj.* **1.** Marked by flagrant and insolent audacity. **2.** Having a loud, usu. harsh resonant sound. **3.** Made of brass. **4.** Resembling brass, as in color or strength. *— tr.v.* **-zened, -zen•ing, -zens.** To face or undergo with bold self-assurance. [ME *brasen*, made of brass < OE *bræsen* < *bræs*, brass.] **— bra′zen•ly** *adv.* **— bra′zen•ness** *n.*

bra•zen•faced (brā′zən-fāst′) *adj.* Flagrantly and insolently audacious.

bra•zier[1] also **bra•sier** (brā′zhər) *n.* One who works in brass. [ME *brasier* < *bras*, brass. See BRASS.]

bra•zier[2] also **bra•sier** (brā′zhər) *n.* **1.** A metal pan for holding burning coals or charcoal. **2.** A cooking device consisting of a charcoal or electric heating source over which food is grilled. [Fr. *brasier* < *braise*, hot coals. See BRAISE.]

Bra•zil (brə-zĭl′). A country of E South America; achieved independence from Portugal in 1822. Cap. Brasília. Pop. 119,002,706. **— Bra•zil′i•an** *adj. & n.*

Brazilian pepper tree *n.* An evergreen Brazilian tree *(Schinus terebinthifolius)* having aromatic foliage and clusters of red berrylike fruits used for Christmas decorations.

Brazil nut *n.* **1.** A tropical South American evergreen tree *(Bertholletia excelsa)* having edible dark brown seeds. **2.** The seed of this tree. [After BRAZIL.]

bra•zil•wood (brə-zĭl′wo͝od′) *n.* The reddish wood of certain tropical trees or shrubs in the pea family, esp. the Brazilian tree *Caesalpinia echinata* whose wood is used for violin bows and as a source of a red or purplish dye. [Obsolete *brazil*, brazilwood (< ME *brasil* < OFr. *bresil*, perh. < **bresiller*, to glow red < *brese*, hot coal; see BRAISE) + WOOD[1].]

Braz•os (brăz′əs). A river rising in E NM and flowing c. 1,400 km (870 mi) to the Gulf of Mexico SW of Galveston TX.

Braz•za•ville (brăz′ə-vĭl′, brä-zä-vēl′). The cap. of Congo, in the S part on the Congo R.; founded in the 1880's. Pop. 595,102.

B.R.E. *abbr.* Bachelor of Religious Education.

Bre•a (brā′ə). A city of S CA N of Anaheim. Pop. 32,873.

breach (brēch) *n.* **1.a.** An opening, a tear, or a rupture. **b.** A gap or rift, as in a dike or fortification. **2.** A violation or infraction, as of a law or a promise. **3.** A breaking up or disruption of friendly relations; an estrangement. **4.** A leap of a whale from the water. **5.** The breaking of waves or surf. *— v.* **breached, breach•ing, breach•es.** *— tr.* **1.** To make a hole or gap in; break through. **2.** To break or violate (an agreement, for example). *— intr.* To leap from the water. [ME *breche* < OE *brēc*. See **bhreg-***.]

Syns: *breach, infraction, violation, transgression, trespass, infringement.* These nouns denote an act or instance of breaking a law or regulation or failing to fulfill a duty, obligation, or promise. *Breach* and *infraction* are the least specific: *a breach of trust; infractions of the rules.* A *violation* is committed willfully and with complete lack of regard for legal, moral, or ethical considerations: *violation of her contract. Transgression* most often applies to divine or moral law: *"The children shall not be punished for the father's transgression"* (Daniel Defoe). *Trespass* implies willful intrusion on another's rights, possessions, or person: *committed trespass when hunting. Infringement* is most frequently used specifically to denote encroachment on another's rights: *"Necessity is the plea for every infringement of human freedom"* (William Pitt the Younger).

breach of promise *n.* Failure to fulfill a promise, esp. a promise to marry.

bread (brĕd) *n.* **1.** A staple food made from flour or meal mixed with other ingredients, usu. combined with a leavening agent, and baked. **2.** Food in general, regarded as necessary for sustaining life. **3.a.** Means of support; livelihood: *earn one's bread.* **b.** *Slang.* Money. *— tr.v.* **bread•ed, bread•ing, breads.** To coat with bread crumbs, as before cooking: *breaded the fillets.* [ME < OE *brēad*. See **bhreu-***.]

bread and butter *n.* **1.** Means of support; livelihood. **2.** The essential sustaining element or elements; the mainstay.

bread-and-but•ter (brĕd′n-bŭt′ər) *adj.* **1.a.** Influenced by or undertaken out of necessity: *a bread-and-butter job.* **b.** Reliable, esp. for producing income; basic. **2.** Expressive of gratitude for hospitality.

bread•bas•ket (brĕd′băs′kĭt) *n.* **1.** A basket for serving bread. **2.** A geographic region serving as a principal source of grain supply. **3.** *Slang.* The stomach.

bread•board (brĕd′bôrd′, -bōrd′) *n.* **1.** A board on which bread is sliced or dough is kneaded. **2.** An experimental model, esp. of an electric circuit; a prototype. *— tr.v.* **-board•ed, -board•ing, -boards.** To construct an experimental model of.

bread•box (brĕd′bŏks′) *n.* A container in which baked goods are stored to maintain their freshness.

bread•fruit (brĕd′fro͞ot′) *n.* **1.** A Malaysian evergreen timber tree *(Artocarpus altilis)* having large, round, yellowish edible fruits. **2.** The fruit of this tree.

bread line *n.* A line of people waiting to receive food given by a charitable organization or public agency.

bread mold *n.* Any of various fungi of the genus *Rhizopus*, forming a dense cottony growth on bread and other foods.

bread•nut (brĕd′nŭt′) *n.* **1.** A large tree *(Brosimum alicastrum)* native to Mexico, Central America, and the West Indies and having yellow fruits each with a large edible seed. **2.** The seed of this tree.

bread•root (brĕd′ro͞ot′, -ro͝ot′) *n.* A perennial herb *(Psoralea esculenta)* in the pea family, native to prairies and plains in central North America and having a tuberous starchy root.

bread•stuff (brĕd′stŭf′) *n.* **1.** Bread in any form or shape. **2.** Flour, meal, or grain used in the baking of bread.

breadth (brĕdth) *n.* **1.** The measure or dimension from side to side; width. **2.** A piece usu. produced in a standard width: *a breadth of canvas.* **3.a.** Wide range or scope: *breadth of knowledge.* **b.** Tolerance; broadmindedness. **4.** An effect of unified, encompassing vision in an artistic composition. [ME *breth* < *brede*, on the model of *length*, length.]

breadth•ways (brĕdth′wāz′) or **breadth•wise** (-wīz′) *adv. & adj.* In the direction of the breadth.

bread•win•ner (brĕd′wĭn′ər) *n.* One whose earnings are the primary source of support for one's dependents.

break (brāk) *v.* **broke** (brōk), **bro•ken** (brō′kən), **break•ing, breaks.** *— tr.* **1.** To cause to separate into pieces suddenly or violently; smash. **2.** To divide into pieces, as by bending or cutting: *break crackers.* **3.** To snap off or detach. **4.a.** To fracture a bone of: *I broke my leg.* **b.** To fracture (a bone). **5.** To crack without separating into pieces. **6.a.** To destroy the completeness of (a set or collection). **b.** To exchange for smaller monetary units: *break a dollar.* **7.** To disrupt the uniformity or continuity of: *a plain broken by low hills.* **8.** *Elect.*

Brazil

Brazil nut
Bertholletia excelsa

ă pat	oi boy
ā pay	ou out
âr care	o͝o took
ä father	o͞o boot
ĕ pet	ŭ cut
ē be	ûr urge
ĭ pit	th thin
ī pie	*th* this
îr pier	hw which
ŏ pot	zh vision
ō toe	ə about, item
ô paw	

Stress marks:
′ (primary);
′ (secondary), as in
dictionary (dĭk′shə-nĕr′ē)

To open: *break a circuit.* **9.a.** To puncture or penetrate: *The blade broke the skin.* **b.** To part or pierce the surface of: *a dolphin breaking water.* **10.** To cause to burst. **11.** To force one's way out of; escape from: *break jail.* **12.a.** To prove false: *They broke my alibi.* **b.** To uncover the basic elements and arrangement of: *break a code.* **13.** To make known, as news: *break a story.* **14.** To surpass or outdo: *broke the record.* **15.** To overcome (a force or resistance): *break the sound barrier.* **16.** To put an end to: *break a strike.* **17.** To lessen in force or effect: *break a fall.* **18.** To render useless or inoperative: *We broke the radio.* **19.** To weaken or destroy, as in spirit or health. **20.** To cause the ruin or failure of (an enterprise, for example). **21.** To reduce in rank; demote. **22.** To cause to be without money or go into bankruptcy. **23.** To fail to fulfill; cancel: *break one's plans.* **24.** To fail to conform to; violate: *break the law.* **25.** *Law.* To invalidate (a will) by judicial action. **26.a.** To give up (a habit). **b.** To cause to give up a habit. **27.** To train to obey; tame. — *intr.* **1.** To become separated into pieces or fragments. **2.** To become cracked or split. **3.** To become unusable or inoperative. **4.** To give way; collapse. **5.** To burst: *The balloon broke.* **6.a.** To become punctured or penetrated. **b.** To intrude on: *They broke in upon the conversation.* **c.** To filter in or penetrate: *Sunlight broke into the room.* **7.** To become fractured. **8.** To scatter or disperse; part: *The clouds broke.* **9.** *Games.* To make the opening shot that scatters the grouped balls in billiards or pool. **10.** *Sports.* To separate from a clinch in boxing. **11.** To move away or escape suddenly. **12.** To come forth or begin from a state of latency: *A storm was breaking over Miami.* **13.** To emerge above the surface of water. **14.** To become known or noticed: *The story broke on Friday.* **15.** To change direction suddenly. **16.** *Baseball.* To curve near or over the plate. **17.** To change suddenly, as in tone: *My voice broke to a whisper.* **18.** *Ling.* To undergo breaking. **19.** To change to a gait different from the one set. Used of a horse. **20.** To interrupt or cease an activity. **21.** To discontinue an association, an agreement, or a relationship. **22.** To diminish or discontinue abruptly: *The fever is breaking.* **23.** To lose physical or spiritual strength. **24.** To decrease sharply in value or quantity. **25.** To collapse or crash into surf or spray. **26.** *Informal.* To take place or happen; proceed. — *n.* **1.** The act or an occurrence of breaking. **2.** The result of breaking, as a crack or separation. **3.** A beginning or an opening: *the break of day.* **4.** A sudden movement; a dash. **5.** An escape: *a prison break.* **6.** An interruption or a disruption in continuity or regularity: *commercial breaks.* **7.** A pause or an interval, as from work: *a coffee break.* **8.** A sudden or marked change. **9.** A violation: *a security break.* **10.** An often sudden piece of luck: *finally got a break.* **11.** *Informal.* **a.** An allowance or indulgence; accommodating treatment. **b.** A favorable price or reduction: *a tax break.* **12.** A severing of ties: *a break between families.* **13.** *Informal.* A faux pas. **14.** A sudden decline in prices. **15.** A caesura. **16.** *Print.* **a.** The space between two paragraphs. **b.** A series of three dots (. . .) used to indicate an omission in a text. **c.** The place where a word is or should be divided at the end of a line. **17.** *Elect.* Interruption of a flow of current. **18.** *Geol.* A marked change in topography such as a fault or deep valley. **19.** *Mus.* **a.** The point at which one register or a tonal quality changes to another. **b.** The change itself. **c.** A short solo between the phrases or choruses of a melody. **20.** A change in the gait of a horse to one different from that set by the rider. **21.** *Sports.* The swerving of a ball from a straight path of flight, as in baseball. **22.** *Sports.* The beginning of a race. **23.** *Sports.* The separation after a clinch in boxing. **24.** *Games.* The opening shot that scatters the grouped balls in billiards or pool. **25.** *Games.* An unbroken series of successful shots, as in billiards. **26.** *Sports & Games.* Failure to score a strike or a spare in a given bowling frame. **27.** Also **brake.** A high horse-drawn carriage with four wheels. ***— phrasal verbs.*** **break down. 1.** To cause to collapse; destroy. **2.a.** To become or cause to become distressed or upset. **b.** To have a physical or mental collapse. **3.** To give up resistance; give way. **4.** To fail to function; cease to be useful or effective. **5.** To render weak or ineffective. **6.a.** To divide into or consider in parts; analyze. **b.** To be divisible; admit of analysis. **7.** To decompose or cause to decompose chemically. **8.** *Elect.* To undergo a breakdown. **break in. 1.** To train or adapt for a purpose. **2.** To loosen or soften with use: *break in new shoes.* **3.** To enter premises forcibly or illegally. **4.a.** To interrupt a conversation or discussion. **b.** To intrude. **break into. 1.** To interrupt. **2.** To begin suddenly: *The child broke into tears.* **3.** To enter (a field of activity): *broke into journalism.* **break off. 1.** To separate or become separated, as by twisting or tearing. **2.** To stop suddenly, as in speaking. **3.a.** To discontinue (a relationship). **b.** To cease to be friendly. **break out. 1.** To become affected with a skin eruption, such as pimples. **2.** To develop suddenly and forcefully: *Measles broke out.* **3.a.** To ready for action or use: *Break out the rifles!* **b.** To bring forth for consumption: *break out the champagne.* **4.** To emerge or escape. **5.** To separate or be separable into categories, as data. **break through.** To make a sudden, quick advance, as through obstruction or opposition. **break up. 1.a.** To separate into pieces; divide. **b.** To interrupt the uniformity or continuity of: *His visit broke up the afternoon.* **2.** To scatter; disperse: *The crowd broke up.* **3.** To bring or come to an end. **4.** *Informal.* To burst or cause to burst into laughter. ***— idioms.*** **break a leg.** Used to wish someone success in a performance. **break camp.** To pack up equipment and leave a campsite. **break even.** To gain an amount equal to that risked or invested. **break rank (**or **ranks). 1.** To fall into disorder, as a formation of soldiers. **2.** To fail to conform to a prevailing or expected pattern or order. **break (someone's) service.** *Sports.* To win a game, as in tennis, served by one's opponent. **break the ice. 1.** To make a start. **2.** To relax a tense or formal social situation. **break wind.** To expel intestinal gas. [ME *breken* < OE *brecan.* See **bhreg-*.**]

Syns: *break, crack, fracture, burst, split, splinter, shatter, shiver, smash.* These verbs mean to separate or cause to separate into parts or pieces, either by the sudden application of force or by the build-up of internal stress. *Break* is the most general: *vandals breaking windows.* To *crack* is to break, often with a sharp snapping sound, without dividing into parts: *I cracked the plate. Fracture* applies to a break or crack in a rigid body: *a vertebra that fractured in the fall. Burst* implies a sudden coming apart, esp. from internal pressure, and the dispersion of contents: *burst the balloon with a pin. Split* refers to a division made longitudinally or with the grain: *frost that caused the rock to split. Splinter* implies splitting into long, thin, sharp pieces: *Repeated blows splintered the door.* To *shatter* is to break into many scattered pieces: *The bottle shattered. Shiver* is mostly encountered in literary contexts; like *shatter,* it indicates sudden force that causes fragmentation: *"Every painted window* [was] *shivered to atoms"* (John Lothrop Motley). *Smash* stresses force of blow or impact and suggests complete destruction: *My glass smashed on the floor.*

break•a•ble (brā′kə-bəl) *adj.* Liable to break or to be broken. See Syns at **fragile.** — *n.* An article that can be broken easily. **— break′a•ble•ness** *n.*

break•age (brā′kĭj) *n.* **1.** The act of breaking. **2.** A quantity broken. **3.** Loss or damage as a result of breaking. **4.** A commercial allowance for loss or damage.

break•a•way (brāk′ə-wā′) *adj.* **1.** Designed to break, bend, or fall apart easily upon impact. **2.** Severing or having severed alliance with another entity, policy, or attitude. — *n.* **1.** One that breaks away. **2.** The act of breaking away. **3.** An object designed to break away.

break•bone fever (brāk′bōn′) *n.* See **dengue.**

break danc•ing also **break•danc•ing** (brāk′dăn′sĭng) *n.* A style of gymnastic dancing performed esp. to rap music. **— break dance** *n.* **— break′-dance′** *v.* **— break dancer, break′-danc′er** *n.*

break•down (brāk′doun′) *n.* **1.a.** The act or process of failing to function or continue. **b.** The condition resulting from this. **2.** *Elect.* The abrupt failure of an insulator or insulating medium to restrict the flow of current. **3.** A typically sudden collapse in physical or mental health. **4.** An analysis, an outline, or a summary consisting of itemized data or essentials. **5.** Disintegration or decomposition into parts or elements. **6.** An energetic American country dance.

break•er[1] (brā′kər) *n.* **1.** One that breaks, as a machine for crushing rock. **2.** A circuit breaker. **3.** A wave that crests or breaks into foam.

brea•ker[2] (brā′kər) *n.* *Naut.* A small water cask, often used in lifeboats. [Alteration of Sp. *barrica.* See BARRICADE.]

break-e•ven (brāk′ē′vən) *adj.* Also **break•e•ven.** Marked by or indicating a balance of investment and return; having or showing neither profit nor loss. — *n.* The break-even point.

break•fast (brĕk′fəst) *n.* The first meal of the day, usu. eaten in the morning. — *v.* **-fast•ed, -fast•ing, -fasts.** — *intr.* To eat breakfast. — *tr.* To provide breakfast for. [ME *brekfast: breken,* to break; see BREAK + *faste,* a fast (< ON *fasta,* to fast; see **past-***).] **— break′fast•er** *n.*

break•front (brāk′frŭnt′) *n.* A piece of furniture, such as a cabinet or bookcase, with a projecting central section.

break-in (brāk′ĭn′) *n.* **1.** Forcible entry, as into a building or room, for an illegal purpose. **2.** An initial, evaluative period of employment or operation.

break•ing[1] (brā′kĭng) *n.* *Ling.* The change of a simple vowel to a diphthong, often caused by the influence of neighboring consonants. [Transl. of Ger. *Brechung.*]

break•ing[2] (brā′kĭng) *n.* Break dancing.

breaking and en•ter•ing (ĕn′tər-ĭng) *n.* *Law.* The gaining of unauthorized illegal access to another's premises.

breaking point *n.* **1.** The point at which physical, mental, or emotional strength gives way under stress. **2.** The point at which a condition or situation becomes critical.

break•neck (brāk′nĕk′) *adj.* **1.** Dangerously fast: *a breakneck pace.* **2.** Likely to cause an accident: *a breakneck curve.*

break•out (brāk′out′) *n.* A forceful emergence from a restrictive condition or situation.

break•point (brāk′point′) *n.* **1.** Or **break point.** A point of discontinuity, change, or cessation. **2.** *Comp. Sci.* A point in a program at which manual intervention may occur.

break•through (brāk′thrōō′) *n.* **1.** An act of overcoming or penetrating an obstacle or restriction. **2.** A military offensive that penetrates an enemy's lines of defense. **3.** A major achievement or success that permits further progress.

break•up (brāk′ŭp′) *n.* **1.** The act or an instance of breaking up. **2.** The discontinuance of a relationship, as a marriage or a friendship. **3.** The cracking and shifting of ice in rivers or harbors during the spring. **4.** A loss of control or composure.

break•wa•ter (brāk′wô′tər, -wŏt′ər) *n.* A barrier that protects a harbor or shore from the full impact of waves.

bream[1] (brēm, brĭm) *n., pl.* **bream** or **breams. 1.** Any of several European freshwater fishes of the genus *Abramis,* esp. *A. brama,* having a flattened body. **2.a.** Any of various saltwater fishes in the family Sparidae. **b.** Any of various freshwater sunfishes of the genus *Lepomis* and related genera. [ME *breme* < OFr., of Gmc. orig.]

bream[2] (brēm) *tr.v.* **breamed, bream•ing, breams.** *Naut.* To clean (a wooden ship's hull) by applying heat to soften the pitch and then scraping. [< MDu. *brem(e),* furze, broom.]

breast (brĕst) *n.* **1.a.** Either of two milk-secreting glandular organs on the chest of a woman; the human mammary gland. **b.** A corresponding organ in other mammals. **c.** A corresponding rudimentary gland in the male. **2.a.** The surface of the human body extending from the neck to the abdomen. **b.** A corresponding part in other animals. **3.** The part of a garment that covers the chest. **4.** The seat of affection and emotion. **5.** A source of nourishment. **6.** Something likened to the human breast: *the breast of a hill.* **7.** The face of a mine or tunnel. —*tr.v.* **breast•ed, breast•ing, breasts. 1.** To rise over; climb. **2.** To encounter or advance against resolutely; confront boldly. [ME *brest* < OE *brēost.*]

breast-beat•ing (brĕst′bē′tĭng) *n.* A loud demonstration of emotion, esp. of remorse. —**breast′-beat′ing** *adj.*

breast•bone (brĕst′bōn′) *n.* See **sternum.**

breast-feed (brĕst′fēd′) *tr.v.* **-fed** (-fĕd′), **-feed•ing, -feeds.** To feed (a baby) mother's milk from the breast; suckle.

breast•plate (brĕst′plāt′) *n.* **1.** A piece of armor that covers the breast. **2.** *Judaism.* A square cloth set with 12 precious stones representing the 12 tribes of Israel, worn over the breast by ancient high priests.

breast•stroke (brĕst′strōk′) *n. Sports.* A swimming stroke in which a person lies face down in the water and extends the arms in front of the head, then sweeps them both back laterally under the surface of the water while performing a frog kick. —**breast′stroke′** *v.* —**breast′strok′er** *n.*

breast•work (brĕst′wûrk′) *n.* A temporary, quickly constructed fortification, usu. breast-high.

breath (brĕth) *n.* **1.** The air inhaled and exhaled in respiration. **2.** The act or process of breathing; respiration. **3.** The capacity to breathe, esp. in an unlabored manner. **4.** Spirit or vitality; life. **5.** A single respiration: *a deep breath.* **6.** Exhaled air, as evidenced by vapor, odor, or heat. **7.** A momentary pause or rest. **8.a.** A momentary stirring of air. **b.** A slight gust of fragrant air. **9.** A trace or suggestion. **10.** A softly spoken sound; a whisper. **11.** *Ling.* Exhalation of air without vibration of the vocal cords, as in the articulation of *p* and *s.* —***idioms.*** **in one (or the same) breath.** At or almost at the same time. **out of breath.** Breathing with difficulty, as from exertion; gasping. **under (one's) breath.** In a muted voice or whisper. [ME *breth* < OE *brǣth.* See **gʷhrē-*.**]

breath•a•ble (brē′thə-bəl) *adj.* **1.** Suitable or pleasant for breathing: *breathable air.* **2.** Permitting air to pass through: *a breathable fabric.* —**breath′a•bil′i•ty** *n.*

Breath•a•lyz•er (brĕth′ə-lī′zər). A trademark used for a device that measures alcohol in expired air so as to determine the concentration of alcohol in a person's blood.

breathe (brēth) *v.* **breathed, breath•ing, breathes.** —*intr.* **1.** To inhale and exhale air. **2.** To be alive; live. **3.** To pause to rest or regain breath. **4.** To move or blow gently, as air. **5.** To allow air to pass through: *a fabric that breathes.* **6.** To be exhaled or emanated, as a fragrance. **7.** To be manifested or suggested, as a feeling. **8.** To reach fullness of flavor and aroma through exposure to air. Used chiefly of wine. **9.** To require air in the combustion process. Used of an internal-combustion engine. —*tr.* **1.** To inhale and exhale (air, for example) during respiration. **2.** To inhale (an aroma, for example). **3.** To impart as if by breathing; instill. **4.** To exhale (something); emit. **5.** To utter, esp. quietly; whisper: *Don't breathe a word of this.* **6.** To make apparent or manifest, suggest. **7.** To allow (a person or animal) to rest or regain breath. **8.** *Ling.* To utter with a voiceless exhalation of air. **9.** To draw in (air) for the combustion process. Used of an internal-combustion engine. —***idioms.*** **breathe down (someone's) neck. 1.** To threaten by proximity, esp. by pursuing closely. **2.** To watch or monitor closely, often annoyingly. **breathe (one's) last.** To die. [ME *brethen* < *breth,* breath. See BREATH.]

breathed (brĕtht) *adj.* **1.** (*also* brēthd). *Ling.* Voiceless. **2.** Having breath of a specified kind. Often used in combination: *sour-breathed.*

breath•er (brē′thər) *n.* **1.** One that breathes, esp. in a specified manner: *a shallow breather.* **2.** *Informal.* A short rest period: *took a breather.* **3.** *Informal.* An activity, such as exercise, that causes difficult breathing. **4.** A small vent allowing the passage of gas or liquid to or from an enclosed area.

breath•ing (brē′thĭng) *n.* **1.a.** The act or process of respiration. **b.** A single breath. **2.** The time required to take one's breath. **3.a.** Either of two marks used in Greek to indicate aspiration of an initial vowel or diphthong (ʽ) or the absence of such aspiration (ʼ). **b.** The presence or absence of aspiration indicated by these marks.

breathing room *n.* Sufficient room to permit ease of breathing or movement: *no breathing room on the crowded bus.*

breathing space *n.* **1.** Breathing room. **2.** A breathing spell.

breathing spell *n.* An opportunity for rest or thought.

breath•less (brĕth′lĭs) *adj.* **1.** Breathing with difficulty; gasping. **2.** Marked by the suspension of regular breathing, as from tension. **3.** Causing the suspension of regular breathing; tense or exciting. **4.a.** Not breathing; without breath. **b.** Dead. **5.** Having no air or breeze; still. —**breath′less•ly** *adv.* —**breath′less•ness** *n.*

breath•tak•ing (brĕth′tā′kĭng) *adj.* Inspiring awe; exciting. —**breath′tak′ing•ly** *adv.*

breath•y (brĕth′ē) *adj.* **-i•er, -i•est.** Marked by audible or noisy breathing. —**breath′i•ly** *adv.* —**breath′i•ness** *n.*

brec•ci•a (brĕch′ē-ə, brĕch′ə, brĕsh′-) *n.* Rock composed of sharp-angled fragments embedded in a fine-grained matrix. [Ital., of Gmc. orig. See **bhreg-*.**]

brec•ci•ate (brĕch′ē-āt′, brĕsh′-) *tr.v.* **-at•ed, -at•ing, -ates.** To form (rock) into breccia. —**brec′ci•a′tion** *n.*

Brecht (brĕkt, brĕKHt), **Bertolt.** 1898–1956. German poet and playwright whose works include *The Threepenny Opera* (1928). —**Brecht′i•an** *adj.*

Breck•in•ridge (brĕk′ĭn-rĭj′), **John Cabell.** 1821–75. Vice President of the U.S. (1857–61).

bred (brĕd) *v.* P.t. and p.part. of **breed.**

Bre•da (brā-dä′). A city of S Netherlands SSE of Dordrecht; founded in the 11th cent. Pop. 118,662.

brede (brēd) *n. Archaic.* Ornamental embroidery or braiding. [Var. of BRAID.]

bred-in-the-bone (brĕd′n-thə-bōn′) *adj.* **1.** Deeply instilled; firmly established. **2.** Persistent; habitual.

breech (brēch) *n.* **1.** The lower rear portion of the human trunk; the buttocks. **2. breeches** (brĭch′ĭz, brē′chĭz). **a.** Trousers extending to the knee. **b.** *Informal.* Trousers. **3.** The part of a firearm behind the barrel. **4.** The lower part of a pulley block. [ME *brech* < OE *brēc,* pl. of *brōc,* leg covering; akin to Gaulish *brāca,* hose, trousers.]

breech birth *n.* See **breech delivery.**

breech•block (brēch′blŏk′) *n.* The metal part that closes the breech end of the barrel of a breechloading gun.

breech•cloth (brēch′klôth′, -klŏth′) also **breech•clout** (-klout′) *n.* A cloth worn to cover the loins; a loincloth.

breech delivery *n.* Delivery of a fetus with the buttocks or feet appearing first.

breech•ing (brē′chĭng, brĭch′ĭng) *n.* **1.** The strap of a harness that passes behind a draft animal's haunches. **2.** The short wool or hair on the rump and hind legs of a sheep, goat, or dog.

breech•load•er (brēch′lō′dər) *n.* A gun or other firearm loaded at the breech. —**breech′load′ing** (-lō′dĭng) *adj.*

breech presentation *n.* The position of a fetus during labor in which the buttocks or feet appear first.

breed (brēd) *v.* **bred** (brĕd), **breed•ing, breeds.** —*tr.* **1.** To produce (offspring); give birth to or hatch. **2.** To bring about; engender. **3.a.** To cause to reproduce, esp. by controlled mating. **b.** To mate with. **4.** To rear or train; bring up. **5.** To produce (fissionable material) in a breeder reactor. **6.** To be the place of origin of. —*intr.* **1.** To produce offspring. **2.** To originate and thrive. —*n.* **1.** A group of organisms having common ancestors and certain distinguishable characteristics, esp. when developed and maintained by controlled propagation. **2.** A kind; a sort. —***idioms.*** **breed a scab (or scabs) on (one's) nose.** *Regional.* To stir up trouble for oneself. **breed up a storm.** *New England.* To become cloudy. [ME *breden* < OE *brēdan.* See **bhreu-*.**]

breed•er (brē′dər) *n.* **1.** A person who breeds animals or plants. **2.** An animal or a plant that produces offspring.

breeder reactor *n.* A nuclear reactor that produces more fissionable material than it consumes.

breed•ing (brē′dĭng) *n.* **1.** One's line of descent; ancestry. **2.** Training in the proper forms of social and personal conduct. **3.** Production of offspring or young. **4.** The propagation of animals or plants.

breeding ground *n.* **1.** A place where animals breed. **2.** A place or set of circumstances that encourages the development of certain ideas or conditions.

Breed's Hill (brēdz). A hill in Charlestown, a section of Boston MA; site of the Battle of Bunker Hill on Jun. 17, 1775.

breeks (brēks) *pl.n. Scots.* Breeches. [ME, pl. of *brek* < OE *brēc.* See BREECH.]

breeze[1] (brēz) *n.* **1.** A light current of air; a gentle wind. **2.** *Meteorol.* A wind speed of from 4 to 31 miles (6 to 50 kilometers) per hour, according to the Beaufort scale. **3.** *In-*

breastplate

ă pat	oi boy
ā pay	ou out
âr care	ŏŏ took
ä father	ōō boot
ĕ pet	ŭ cut
ē be	ûr urge
ĭ pit	th thin
ī pie	*th* this
îr pier	hw which
ŏ pot	zh vision
ō toe	ə about, item
ô paw	

Stress marks:
′ (primary);
′ (secondary), as in **dictionary** (dĭk′shə-nĕr′ē)

formal. Something that is easy to do. —*intr.v.* **breezed, breez•ing, breez•es. 1.** To blow lightly. **2.** *Informal.* To progress swiftly and effortlessly. **3.** To sprint around a racetrack as a means of exercise. Used of a racehorse. —*idiom.* **shoot the breeze.** *Slang.* To engage in idle conversation. [Perh. < OSp. *briza,* northeast wind.]

breeze² (brēz) *n.* The refuse left when coke or charcoal is made. [Prob. < Fr. *braise,* hot coals < OFr. *brese,* of Gmc. orig. See **bhreu-*.**]

breeze•way (brēz′wā′) *n.* A roofed open-sided passageway connecting two structures, such as a house and a garage.

breez•y (brē′zē) *adj.* **-i•er, -i•est. 1.** Exposed to breezes; windy. **2.** Fresh and animated; lively: *a breezy prose style.* —**breez′i•ly** *adv.* —**breez′i•ness** *n.*

breg•ma (brĕg′mə) *n., pl.* **-ma•ta** (-mə-tə). The junction of the sagittal and coronal sutures at the top of the skull. [Lat., top of the head < Gk.] —**breg•mat′ic** (-măt′ĭk) *adj.*

Bre•men (brĕm′ən, brā′mən). A city of NW Germany on the Weser R. SW of Hamburg. Pop. 530,520.

Bre•mer•ha•ven (brĕm′ər-hä′vən, -hā′-, brā′mər-hä′fən). A city of NW Germany on the Weser R. Pop. 135,095.

Brem•er•ton (brĕm′ər-tən). A city of W-central WA on an arm of Puget Sound W of Seattle. Pop. 38,142.

brems•strah•lung (brĕm′shträ′ləng) *n.* The electromagnetic radiation produced by an accelerated charged particle, usu. an electron. [Ger. : *Bremse,* brake (< MLGer. *premse* < *pramen,* to press) + *Strahlung,* radiation (< *Strahl,* ray < MHGer. *strāle* < OHGer. *strāla,* arrow, stripe; see **ster-²*).**]

Leonid Brezhnev
Photographed in 1978

Bren•nan (brĕn′ən), **William Joseph, Jr.** b. 1906. Amer. jurist; associate justice of the U.S. Supreme Court (1956–90).

Bren•ner Pass (brĕn′ər). An Alpine pass, 1,371 m (4,495 ft) high, connecting Innsbruck, Austria, with Bolzano, Italy.

brent (brĕnt) *n. Chiefly British.* Var. of **brant.**

Brent (brĕnt), **Margaret.** 1600–71? English-born feminist; the first woman to obtain a land grant in the colony of Maryland.

Bre•scia (brĕsh′ə). A city of N Italy E of Milan; a free city from 936 to 1426. Pop. 206,460.

Bres•lau (brĕs′lou). See **Wroclaw.**

Brest (brĕst). **1.** A city of NW France on an inlet of the Atlantic. Pop. 156,060. **2.** Formerly **Brest-Li•tovsk** (-lĭ-tôfsk′). A city of SW Belorussia on the Bug R.; site of signing of the Treaty of Brest-Litovsk (1918). Pop. 222,000.

Bre•tagne (brə-tän′yə). See **Brittany.**

breth•ren (brĕth′rən) *n.* Pl. of **brother** 2, 3, 4c.

Bret•on (brĕt′n) *adj.* Of or relating to Brittany or its people, language, or culture. —*n.* **1.** A native or inhabitant of Brittany. **2.** The Celtic language of Brittany. [ME < OFr. See BRITON.]

Bre•ton (brĭ-tôN′), **André.** 1896–1966. French poet who wrote the first manifesto of surrealism (1924).

Breu•er (broi′ər), **Marcel Lajos.** 1902–81. Hungarian-born Amer. architect and furniture designer who was associated with the Bauhaus in the 1920's.

Breu•ghel (broi′gəl, brōō′-, brœ′-). See **Brueghel.**

breve (brĕv, brēv) *n.* **1.** A symbol (˘) placed over a vowel to show that it has a short sound, as the *a* in *bat.* **2.** A curved mark used to indicate a short or unstressed syllable of verse. **3.** *Mus.* A note equivalent to two whole notes. [ME, written communication < OFr. < Med.Lat., short syllable < Lat., neut. of *brevis,* short. See BRIEF.]

bre•vet (brə-vĕt′, brĕv′ĭt) *n.* A commission promoting a military officer in rank without an increase in pay. —*tr.v.* **-vet•ted, -vet•ting, -vets** or **-vet•ed, -vet•ing, -vets.** To promote by brevet. [ME, official letter < AN, dim. of *bref,* letter < Lat. *brevis,* short. See BRIEF.] —**bre•vet′cy** (brə-vĕt′sē) *n.*

bre•vi•ar•y (brē′vē-ĕr′ē, brĕv′ē-) *n., pl.* **-ies.** *Eccles.* A book containing the hymns, offices, and prayers for the canonical hours. [ME *breviarie* < OFr. *breviaire* < Med.Lat. *breviārium* < Lat., summary < *brevis,* short. See BRIEF.]

brev•i•ty (brĕv′ĭ-tē) *n.* **1.** The quality or state of being brief in duration. **2.** Concise expression; terseness. [Lat. *brevitās* < *brevis,* short. See BRIEF.]

bridge¹
Top: San Francisco–Oakland Bay suspension bridge
Bottom: Bridge of the Cunard *Princess*

brew (brōō) *v.* **brewed, brew•ing, brews.** —*tr.* **1.** To make (ale or beer) from malt and hops by infusion, boiling, and fermentation. **2.** To make (a beverage) by boiling, steeping, or mixing various ingredients. **3.** To concoct; devise. —*intr.* **1.** To make ale or beer as an occupation. **2.** To be imminent; impend. —*n.* **1.a.** A beverage made by brewing. **b.** A serving of such a beverage. **2.** Something produced as if by brewing; a mix. [ME *brewen* < OE *brēowan.* See **bhreu-*.**] —**brew′age** *n.* —**brew′er** *n.*

Brew•er (brōō′ər), **David Josiah.** 1837–1910. Amer. jurist; associate justice of the U.S. Supreme Court (1889–1910).

brew•er's yeast (brōō′ərz) *n.* A yeast of the genus *Saccharomyces,* used as a ferment and a source of B vitamins.

brew•er•y (brōō′ə-rē, brŏŏr′ē) *n., pl.* **-ies.** An establishment for the manufacture of malt liquors, such as beer and ale.

brew•is (brōō′ĭs, brōōz) *n. New England.* Bread soaked in liquid, usu. milk, and eaten as a pudding or a side dish. [ME *brewes* < OFr. *broez,* pl. of *broet,* dim. of *breu,* broth < VLat. **brodum,* of Gmc. orig. See **bhreu-*.**]

Brew•ster (brōō′stər), **William.** 1567–1644. English Pilgrim colonist who was the religious leader of Plymouth Colony.

Brezh•nev (brĕzh′nĕf, -nyĭf), **Leonid Ilyich.** 1906–82. Soviet leader; president of the U.S.S.R. (1960–64 and 1977–82) and secretary of the Communist Party (1964–82).

Bri•an Bo•ru (brī′ən bə-rōō′, bô-rō′, brēn). 926–1014. Irish king (1002–14) who defeated the Danes and the Norse.

Bri•and (brē-änd′, -äN′), **Aristide.** 1862–1932. French politician who shared the 1926 Nobel Peace Prize.

Bri•ansk (brē-änsk′). See **Bryansk.**

bri•ar¹ also **bri•er** (brī′ər) *n.* **1.** A Mediterranean shrub or small tree *(Erica arborea).* **2.** A tobacco pipe made from the hard, woody root of this plant or from a similar wood. [Fr. *bruyère,* heath < OFr. < VLat. **brūcāria* < LLat. *brūcus,* heather, of Celt. orig. See **wer-²*.**]

bri•ar² (brī′ər) *n.* Var. of **brier¹.**

bri•ard (brē-är′, -ärd′) *n.* Any of an ancient French breed of sturdily built dogs. [Fr. < *Brie,* a region of N France.]

bri•ar•root (brī′ər-rōōt′, -rŏŏt′) *n.* The hard, woody root of the briar.

bri•ar•wood (brī′ər-wŏŏd′) *n.* Wood from the briarroot.

bribe (brīb) *n.* **1.** Something offered or given to a person in a position of trust to influence that person's views or conduct. **2.** Something serving to influence or persuade. —*v.* **bribed, brib•ing, bribes.** —*tr.* **1.** To give, offer, or promise a bribe to. **2.** To gain influence over or corrupt by bribery. —*intr.* To give, offer, or promise bribes. [ME < OFr., piece of bread given as alms.] —**brib′a•ble** *adj.* —**brib′er** *n.*

brib•er•y (brī′bə-rē) *n., pl.* **-ies.** The act or practice of offering, giving, or taking a bribe.

bric-a-brac (brĭk′ə-brăk′) *n.* Small, usu. ornamental objects valued for their antiquity, rarity, originality, or sentimental associations. [Fr. *bric-à-brac,* expressive of confusion.]

Brice (brīs), **Fannie.** 1891–1951. Amer. entertainer known for her work in films, radio, and the Ziegfield Follies.

brick (brĭk) *n., pl.* **bricks** or **brick. 1.** A molded rectangular block of clay baked by the sun or in a kiln until hard and used as a building and paving material. **2.** An object shaped like such a block: *a brick of cheese.* **3.** *Informal.* A helpful, reliable person. —*tr.v.* **bricked, brick•ing, bricks. 1.** To construct, line, or pave with bricks. **2.** To close or wall with brick. [ME *brike* < MDu. *bricke.*] —**brick′y** *adj.*

brick•bat (brĭk′băt′) *n.* **1.** A piece, esp. of brick, used as a weapon or missile. **2.** An unfavorable remark; criticism. [BRICK + BAT¹, piece of brick.]

brick•lay•er (brĭk′lā′ər) *n.* A person skilled in building with bricks. —**brick′lay′ing** *n.*

brick red *n. Color.* A moderate to strong reddish brown. —**brick′-red′** (brĭk′rĕd′) *adj.*

brick•work (brĭk′wûrk′) *n.* **1.** The technique or work of constructing with bricks and mortar. **2.** A brick structure.

brick•yard (brĭk′yärd′) *n.* A place where bricks are made.

bri•co•lage (brē′kō-läzh′, brĭk′ō-) *n.* Something made or put together using whatever materials happen to be available. [Fr. < *bricole,* trifle < OFr., catapult < Ital. *briccola,* of Gmc. orig.]

bri•dal (brīd′l) *n.* A marriage ceremony; a wedding. —*adj.* **1.** Of or relating to a bride or a marriage ceremony; nuptial. **2.** Designed for a bride or a newly married couple: *a bridal shop.* [ME *bridale,* wedding, wedding feast < OE *brȳdealo*: *brȳd,* bride; see BRIDE + *ealu,* ale; see ALE.]

bridal wreath or **bri•dal-wreath** (brīd′l-rēth) *n.* Any of various shrubs of the genus *Spiraea,* having arching branches covered with white bloom and popular as an ornamental.

bride (brīd) *n.* A woman who is about to be married or has recently been married. [ME < OE *brȳd.*]

bride•groom (brīd′grōōm′, -grŏŏm′) *n.* A man who is about to be married or has recently been married. [Alteration (influenced by GROOM) of ME *bridegome* < OE *brȳdguma*: *brȳd,* bride; see BRIDE + *guma,* man; see **dhghem-*.**]

bride price *n.* A payment in the form of money, property, or other valuable asset made by or on behalf of a prospective husband to the bride's family in certain societies.

brides•maid (brīdz′mād′) *n.* A woman who attends the bride at a wedding.

bridge¹ (brĭj) *n.* **1.** A structure spanning and providing passage over a gap or barrier. **2.** Something resembling or analogous to this structure in form or function. **3.a.** The upper bony ridge of the human nose. **b.** The part of a pair of eyeglasses that rests against this ridge. **4.** A fixed or removable replacement for one or several of the natural teeth. **5.** *Mus.* **a.** A thin upright piece of wood in some stringed instruments that supports the strings above the soundboard. **b.** A transitional passage connecting two subjects or movements. **6.** *Naut.* A crosswise platform or enclosed area above the main deck of a ship from which the ship is controlled. **7.** *Games.* **a.** A piece of wood used to steady the cue in billiards. **b.** The hand used as a support to steady the cue. **8.** *Elect.* **a.** Any of various instruments for measuring the characteristics, such as impedance, of a conductor. **b.** An electrical shunt. **9.** *Chem.* An intramolecular connection that spans atoms or groups of atoms. —*tr.v.* **bridged, bridg•ing, bridg•es. 1.** To build a bridge over. **2.** To cross by or as if by a bridge. [ME *brigge*

< OE *brycg.* See **bhrū-*.**] — **bridge′a•ble** *adj.*

bridge² (brĭj) *n. Games.* Any of several card games derived from whist, usu. for two pairs of players. [< earlier *biritch-* (influenced by BRIDGE¹) < Russ. *birich*, a call.]

bridge•board (brĭj′bôrd′, -bōrd′) *n.* A notched board at either side of a staircase that supports the treads and risers.

bridge•head (brĭj′hĕd′) *n.* **1.a.** A fortified position from which troops defend the end of a bridge nearest the enemy. **b.** A forward position seized by advancing troops in enemy territory as a foothold for further advance. **2.** The area immediately adjacent to the end of a bridge.

bridge loan *n.* A short-term loan intended to provide or extend financing until a more permanent arrangement is made.

Bridge•port (brĭj′pôrt′, -pōrt′). A city of SW CT on Long Island Sound; settled in 1639. Pop. 141,686.

Bridg•es (brĭj′ĭz), **Robert Seymour.** 1844–1930. British poet and essayist who was appointed poet laureate in 1913.

Bridge•ton (brĭj′tən). **1.** A city of E MO on the Missouri R. NW of St. Louis. Pop. 17,779. **2.** A city of SW NJ near the mouth of the Delaware R. S of Philadelphia; settled by Quakers c. 1686. Pop. 18,942.

Bridge•town (brĭj′toun′). The cap. of Barbados; founded by the British in 1628. Pop. 7,466.

Bridge•wa•ter (brĭj′wô′tər, -wŏt′ər). A town of E MA S of Boston. Pop. 21,249.

bridge•work (brĭj′wûrk′) *n.* **1.** A dental bridge. **2.** Dental prosthetics involving a bridge or bridges.

Bridg•man (brĭj′mən), **Percy Williams.** 1882–1961. Amer. physicist who won a 1946 Nobel Prize.

bri•dle (brīd′l) *n.* **1.** A harness, consisting of a headstall, bit, and reins, fitted about a horse's head and used to restrain or guide the animal. **2.** A curb or check. —*v.* **-dled, -dling, -dles.** —*tr.* **1.** To put a bridle on. **2.** To control or restrain with or as if with a bridle. —*intr.* **1.** To lift the head and draw in the chin as an expression of scorn or resentment. **2.** To show anger or resentment; take offense: *bridling at the criticism.* [ME *bridel* < OE *brīdel.*] —**bri′dler** *n.*

bridle path *n.* A trail for horseback riding.

Brie (brē) *n.* A mold-ripened cheese with a whitish rind and a soft, light yellow center. [After *Brie*, a region of N France.]

brief (brēf) *adj.* **brief•er, brief•est. 1.** Short in time, duration, length, or extent. **2.** Succinct; concise. **3.** Curt; abrupt. —*n.* **1.** A short, succinct statement. **2.** A condensation or an abstract of a larger document or series of documents. **3.** *Law.* **a.** A formal outline listing main contentions along with supporting evidence. **b.** A document containing all the facts and points of law pertinent to a specific case, filed by an attorney before arguing the case in court. **4.** *Rom. Cath. Ch.* A papal letter that is not as formal as a bull. **5.** A briefing. **6. briefs.** Short, tight-fitting underpants. —*tr.v.* **briefed, brief•ing, briefs. 1.** To summarize. **2.** To give concise preparatory instructions, information, or advice to. —***idiom.* in brief.** In short. [ME *bref* < OFr. < Lat. *brevis.* See **mregh-u-*.**] —**brief′er** *n.* —**brief′ly** *adv.* —**brief′ness** *n.*

brief•case (brēf′kās′) *n.* A portable case with a handle, used for carrying papers or books. [BRIEF, document + CASE².]

brief•ing (brē′fĭng) *n.* **1.** The act or procedure of giving or receiving concise preparatory instructions, information, or advice. **2.** The information conveyed in this manner.

Bri•enz (brē-ĕnts′), **Lake of.** A scenic lake of central Switzerland near Interlaken.

bri•er¹ also **bri•ar** (brī′ər) *n.* Any of several prickly plants, such as certain rosebushes or the greenbrier. [ME *brer* < OE *brēr.*] —**bri′er•y** *adj.*

bri•er² (brī′ər) *n.* Var. of **briar¹.**

brig (brĭg) *n.* **1.** *Naut.* A two-masted sailing ship, square-rigged on both masts, carrying two or more headsails and a quadrilateral gaff sail or spanker aft of the mizzenmast. **2.** A jail or prison on board a U.S. Navy or Coast Guard vessel. **3.** A jail or guardhouse, esp. at a U.S. military installation. [Short for BRIGANTINE. Senses 2 and 3, from the use of ships as prisons.]

brig. *abbr.* Brigade.

bri•gade (brĭ-gād′) *n.* **1.a.** A military unit consisting of a variable number of combat battalions. **b.** A U.S. Army administrative and tactical unit composed of headquarters, infantry, armor, and designated support units. **2.** A group of persons organized for a specific purpose: *a bucket brigade.* —*tr.v.* **-gad•ed, -gad•ing, -gades.** To form into a brigade. [Fr. < OFr., company < OItal. *brigata* < *brigare*, to fight < *briga*, strife, of Celt. orig. See **gʷerə-¹*.**]

brig•a•dier (brĭg′ə-dîr′) *n.* A brigadier general. [Fr. < *brigade*, brigade. See BRIGADE.]

brigadier general *n., pl.* **brigadier generals.** A commissioned officer in the U.S. Army, Air Force, or Marine Corps ranking above colonel and below major general.

brig•and (brĭg′ənd) *n.* A robber or bandit, esp. one of an outlaw band. [ME *brigaunt* < OFr. < OItal. *brigante*, skirmisher < pr.part. of *brigare*, to fight. See BRIGADE.] —**brig′and•age** (-ən-dĭj), **brig′and•ism** *n.*

brig•an•tine (brĭg′ən-tēn′) *n. Naut.* A two-masted sailing ship, square-rigged on the foremast and having a fore-and-aft mainsail with square main topsails. [Fr. *brigantin* < OFr. *brigandin* < OItal. *brigantino*, skirmishing ship < *brigante*, skirmisher. See BRIGAND.]

Brig. Gen. *abbr.* Brigadier general.

Briggs (brĭgz), **Henry.** 1561–1630. English mathematician who devised the decimal-based system of logarithms.

bright (brīt) *adj.* **bright•er, bright•est. 1.a.** Emitting or reflecting light readily or in large amounts; shining. **b.** Comparatively high on the scale of brightness. **c.** Full of light or illumination. **2.** Characterizing a dyestuff that produces a highly saturated color; brilliant. **3.** Glorious; splendid. **4.** Full of promise and hope; auspicious: *a bright future.* **5.** Happy; cheerful. **6.** Animatedly clever; intelligent. **7.** High and clear: *the bright sound of trumpets.* [ME < OE *beorht.* See **bherəg-*.**] —**bright, bright′ly** *adv.*

Syns: *bright, brilliant, radiant, lustrous, lambent, luminous, incandescent, effulgent.* These adjectives refer to what emits or reflects light. *Bright* is the most general: *bright sunshine. Brilliant* implies intense brightness and often suggests sparkling or gleaming light: *a brilliant gemstone.* Something that is *radiant* emits or seems to emit light in rays: *a radiant smile.* A *lustrous* object simply reflects an agreeable sheen: *thick, lustrous auburn hair. Lambent* applies to a soft, flickering light: *"its tranquil streets, bathed in the lambent green of budding trees"* (James C. McKinley). *Luminous* especially refers to something that glows in the dark: *The watch has a luminous dial. Incandescent* stresses burning brilliance. *Flames consist of incandescent gases. Effulgent* suggests splendid radiance: *"The crocus, the snowdrop, and the effulgent daffodil are considered bright harbingers of spring"* (John Gould). See also Syns at **intelligent.**

Bright (brīt), **John.** 1811–89. British politician who was a founder of the Anti-Corn Law League (1839).

bright•en (brīt′n) *tr. & intr.v.* **-ened, -en•ing, -ens.** To make or become bright or brighter. —**bright′en•er** *n.*

bright•ness (brīt′nĭs) *n.* **1.** The state or quality of being bright. **2.** The effect or sensation by which an observer can distinguish differences in luminance. **3.** *Color.* The dimension of a color that represents its similarity to one of a series of achromatic colors ranging from very dim (dark) to very bright (dazzling).

Brigh•ton (brīt′n). A resort borough of SE England on the English Channel S of London. Pop. 150,200.

Bright's disease (brīts) *n.* Any of several diseases of the kidney marked by the presence of albumin in the urine. [After Richard *Bright* (1789–1858), British physician.]

bright•work (brīt′wûrk′) *n.* Metal parts or fixtures made bright by polishing.

brill (brĭl) *n., pl.* **brill** or **brills.** An edible flatfish *(Bothas rhombus)* of European waters. [?]

Bril•lat-Sa•va•rin (brē-yä′ sä-vä-răɴ′), **Anthelme.** 1755–1826. French politician and gourmet who wrote *Physiologie de Goût* (1825).

bril•liance (brĭl′yəns) *n.* **1.** The state or quality of being brilliant, as: **a.** Extreme brightness. **b.** Exceptional clarity and agility of intellect or invention. **2.** Splendor; magnificence. **3.** *Mus.* Sharpness and clarity of tone.

bril•lian•cy (brĭl′yən-sē) *n.* Brilliance, as of intellect.

bril•liant (brĭl′yənt) *adj.* **1.** Full of light; shining. See Syns at **bright. 2.** *Color.* Relating to or being a hue that has a combination of high lightness and strong saturation. **3.** Sharp and clear in tone. **4.** Glorious; magnificent. **5.** Superb; wonderful. **6.** Marked by unusual and impressive intellectual acuteness. See Syns at **intelligent.** —*n.* A precious gem finely cut with numerous facets. [Fr. *brillant*, pr.part. of *briller*, to shine < Ital. *brillare*, perh. < *brillo*, beryl < Lat. *beryllus.* See BERYL.] —**bril′liant•ly** *adv.* —**bril′liant•ness** *n.*

bril•lian•tine (brĭl′yən-tēn′) *n.* **1.** An oily perfumed hairdressing. **2.** A glossy fabric made from cotton and worsted or cotton and mohair. [Fr. *brillantine* < *brillant*, brilliant. See BRILLIANT.]

brim (brĭm) *n.* **1.** The rim or uppermost edge of a hollow container or natural basin. **2.** A projecting rim or edge: *the brim of a hat.* **3.** A border or an edge. See Syns at **border.** —*v.* **brimmed, brim•ming, brims.** —*intr.* **1.** To be full to the brim. **2.** To overflow. —*tr.* To fill to the brim. [ME *brimme.*]

brim•ful (brĭm′fo͝ol′) *adj.* Full to overflowing.

brim•stone (brĭm′stōn′) *n.* **1.** Sulfur. **2.a.** Damnation to hell. **b.** Fiery or passionate rhetoric. [ME *brimston* < OE *brynstān.* See **gʷher-*.**]

Brin•di•si (brĭn′dĭ-zē, brēn′-). A city of S Italy on the Adriatic Sea SE of Bari. Pop. 88,947.

brin•dle (brĭn′dl) *n.* **1.** A brindled color. **2.** A brindled animal. [Back-formation < BRINDLED.]

brin•dled (brĭn′dld) *adj.* Tawny or grayish with streaks or spots of a darker color. [Alteration of ME *brended*, prob. < *brende*, p.part. of *brennen*, to burn < ON *brenna.* See **gʷher-*.**]

brine (brīn) *n.* **1.** Water saturated with or containing large amounts of a salt, esp. of sodium chloride. **2.a.** The water of a sea or an ocean. **b.** A large body of salt water. **3.** Salt water used for preserving and pickling foods. —*tr.v.* **brined, brin•**

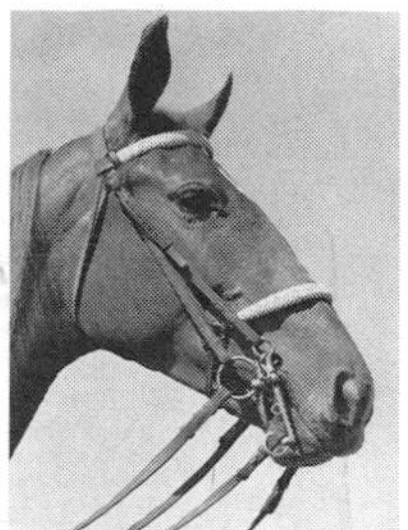

bridle

ă pat	oi boy
ā pay	ou out
âr care	o͝o took
ä father	o͞o boot
ĕ pet	ŭ cut
ē be	ûr urge
ĭ pit	th thin
ī pie	*th* this
îr pier	hw which
ŏ pot	zh vision
ō toe	ə about, item
ô paw	

Stress marks:
′ (primary);
′ (secondary), as in
dictionary (dĭk′shə-nĕr′ē)

ing, brines. To immerse, preserve, or pickle in salt water. [ME < OE *brīne*.] — **brin′er** *n.*

Bri•nell hardness (brĭ-nĕl′) *n.* The relative hardness of metals and alloys, determined by forcing a steel ball into a test piece. [After Johan August *Brinell* (1849–1925), Swedish engineer.]

Brinell hardness number *n.* The numerical value assigned to the Brinell hardness of metals and alloys.

brine shrimp *n.* Any of various small crustaceans of the genus *Artemia.*

bring (brĭng) *tr.v.* **brought** (brôt), **bring•ing, brings. 1.** To take with oneself to a place. **2.** To carry as an attribute or contribution. **3.** To lead or force into a specified state, situation, or location: *bring the water to a boil.* **4.a.** To persuade; induce. **b.** To get the attention of; attract. **5.** To cause to occur as a consequence or concomitant. **6.** To cause to become apparent to the mind; recall: *brings back memories.* **7.** *Law.* To advance or set forth (charges) in a court. **8.** To sell for: *brought five dollars.* **—*phrasal verbs.* bring around (**or **round). 1.** To cause to adopt an opinion or take a certain course of action. **2.** To cause to recover consciousness. **bring down. 1.** To cause to fall or collapse. **2.** To kill. **bring forth. 1.** To give rise to; produce. **2.** To give birth to (young). **bring forward. 1.** To present; produce. **2.** *Accounting.* To carry (a sum) from one page or column to another. **bring in.** To produce, yield, or earn (profits or income). **bring off.** To accomplish: *bring off a successful campaign.* **bring on.** To cause to appear. **bring out. 1.a.** To reveal or expose. **b.** To introduce (a debutante) to society. **2.** To produce or publish. **3.** To nurture and develop to best advantage: *bring out the best.* **bring to.** To cause to recover consciousness. **bring up. 1.** To take care of and educate (a child); rear. **2.** To introduce into discussion; mention. **3.** To vomit. **4.** To cause to come to a sudden stop. **—*idioms.* bring down the house.** To win overwhelming approval from an audience. **bring home.** To make perfectly clear. **bring to bear. 1.** To exert; apply: *bring pressure to bear.* **2.** To put (something) to good use. **bring to light.** To reveal or disclose. **bring to mind.** To cause to be remembered. **bring to terms.** To force (another) to agree. **bring up the rear.** To be the last in a line or sequence. [ME *bringen* < OE *bringan.* See **bher-¹***.] — **bring′er** *n.*

bring•down (brĭng′doun′) *n.* Something disappointing; a letdown.

brink (brĭngk) *n.* **1.a.** The upper edge of a steep or vertical slope. **b.** The margin of land bordering a body of water. **2.** The point at which something is likely to begin; the verge. See Syns at **border.** [ME, prob. of Scandinavian origin.]

brink•man•ship (brĭngk′mən-shĭp′) also **brinks•man•ship** (brĭngks′-) *n.* The practice of seeking advantage by pushing a highly dangerous situation to the limit.

Brin•ton (brĭn′tən), **Daniel Garrison.** 1837–99. Amer. anthropologist who first classified Native American languages.

brin•y (brī′nē) *adj.* **-i•er, -i•est.** Of, relating to, or resembling brine; salty. — **brin′i•ness** *n.*

bri•o (brē′ō) *n.* Vigor; vivacity. [Ital. < Sp. *brio*or Prov. *briu*, both of Celt. orig. See **gʷerə-¹***.]

bri•oche (brē-ôsh′, -ōsh′) *n.* A soft light-textured bread formed into a roll or bun. [Fr. < OFr. < *broyer, brier*, to knead, of Gmc. orig. See **bhreg-***.]

bri•o•lette (brē′ə-lĕt′) *n.* A pear-shaped or oval gem cut in triangular facets. [Fr., perh. alteration (influenced by *brillant*, brilliant) of *brignolette*, dim. of *brignole*, dried plum < *Brignoles*, a town of SE France.]

bri•quette also **bri•quet** (brĭ-kĕt′) *n.* A block of compressed coal dust, charcoal, or sawdust and wood chips, used for fuel. [Fr., dim. of *brique*, brick < MDu. *bricke.*]

bri•sance (brĭ-zäns′, -zäɴs′) *n.* The shattering effect of the sudden release of energy in an explosion. [Fr. < *brisant*, pr.part. of *briser*, to break < OFr. *brisier* < VLat. **brisiāre*, perh. of Celt. orig.] — **bri•sant′** (-zänt′, -zäɴt′) *adj.*

Bris•bane (brĭz′bən, -bān′). A city of E Australia on the **Brisbane River,** c. 346 km (215 mi), near its mouth on Moreton Bay; settled in 1824 as a penal colony. Pop. 734,750.

brisk (brĭsk) *adj.* **brisk•er, brisk•est. 1.** Marked by speed, liveliness, and vigor; energetic. **2.** Keen or sharp in speech or manner. **3.** Stimulating and invigorating: *a brisk wind.* **4.** Pleasantly zestful: *a brisk tea.* [Prob. of Scand. orig.] — **brisk′ly** *adv.* — **brisk′ness** *n.*

bris•ket (brĭs′kĭt) *n.* **1.** The chest of an animal. **2.** The ribs and meat taken from the chest of an animal. [ME *brusket*, perh. of Scand. orig.]

bris•ling (brĭz′lĭng, brĭs′-) *n.* See **sprat** 1. [Norw., alteration (influenced by Norw. *brisa*, to flash) of LGer. *bretling* < *bret*, broad.]

bris•tle (brĭs′əl) *n.* A stiff hair. —*v.* **-tled, -tling, -tles.** —*intr.* **1.** To stand stiffly on end like bristles. **2.** To raise the bristles. **3.** To react in an angry or offended manner. **4.** To be covered or thick with or as if with bristles. See Syns at **teem¹.** —*tr.* **1.** To cause to stand erect like bristles; stiffen. **2.** To furnish or supply with bristles. **3.** To ruffle; disturb. [ME *bristel*, prob. < OE **byrstel* < *byrst*, bristle.]

bris•tle•cone pine (brĭs′əl-kōn′) *n.* A small slow-growing pine *(Pinus aristata)* native to the western United States.

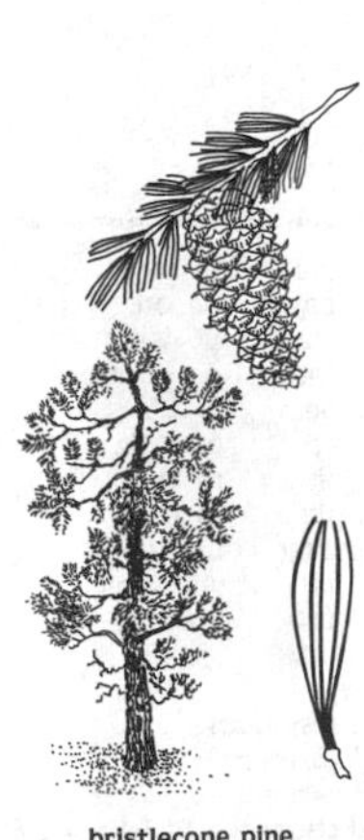

bristlecone pine
Pinus aristata

bris•tle•tail (brĭs′əl-tāl′) *n.* Any of various wingless insects of the order Thysanura, having bristlelike posterior appendages.

bris•tly (brĭs′lē) *adj.* **-tli•er, -tli•est. 1.a.** Consisting of or similar to bristles. **b.** Thick with bristles. **2.** Tending to react with agitation or anger; belligerent.

Bris•tol (brĭs′təl). **1.** A city of SW England W of London. Pop. 400,300. **2.** A city of central CT N of Waterbury. Pop. 60,640. **3.** A town of E RI on Narragansett Bay SE of Providence. Pop. 21,625. **4.** Two cities on the TN–VA line ENE of Kingsport TN that form an economic unit. Pop. 23,421 (TN) and 18,426 (VA).

Bristol Bay. An arm of the Bering Sea in SW AK.

Bristol board *n.* A smooth, heavy pasteboard of fine quality. [After Bʀɪsᴛᴏʟ, England.]

Bristol Channel. An inlet of the Atlantic stretching W from the Severn R. and separating Wales from SW England.

brit also **britt** (brĭt) *n.* **1.** The young of herring and similar fish. **2.** Minute marine organisms that are a major source of food for right whales. [Perh. < Cornish *brȳthel*, mackerel (< Old Cornish *breithil* < **breith*, speckled) or < Welsh *brithyll*, trout (< *brith*, speckled).]

Brit (brĭt) *n.* *Informal.* A British person.

Brit. *abbr.* Britain; British.

Brit•ain¹ (brĭt′n). The island of Great Britain during pre-Roman, Roman, and early Anglo-Saxon times.

Brit•ain² (brĭt′n). See **United Kingdom.**

Bri•tan•nia (brĭ-tăn′yə, -tăn′ē-ə) *n.* **1.** A female personification of Great Britain or the British Empire. **2.** Also **britannia.** Britannia metal. [Lat., Britain < *Brittannī*, the Britons. See Bʀɪᴛᴏɴ.]

bri•tan•nia metal (brĭ-tăn′yə, -tăn′ē-ə) *n.* An alloy of tin, copper, and antimony used in utensils and tableware.

Bri•tan•nic (brĭ-tăn′ĭk) *adj.* British.

britch•es (brĭch′ĭz) *pl.n.* Breeches. **—*idiom.* too big for (one's) britches.** Overconfident; cocky. [Alteration of *breeches*, pl. of ʙʀᴇᴇᴄʜ.]

Brit•i•cism (brĭt′ĭ-sĭz′əm) also **Brit•ish•ism** (-shĭz′əm) *n.* A word, a phrase, or an idiom characteristic of or peculiar to English as it is spoken in Great Britain. [< Bʀɪᴛɪ(sʜ), on the model of words such as Gᴀʟʟɪᴄɪsᴍ.]

Brit•ish (brĭt′ĭsh) *adj.* **1.a.** Of or relating to Great Britain or its people, language, or culture. **b.** Of or relating to the United Kingdom or the Commonwealth of Nations. **2.** Of or relating to the ancient Britons. —*n.* **1.** The people of Great Britain. **2.** British English. **3.** The Celtic language of the ancient Britons. [ME *Brittish* < OE *Bryttisc*, relating to the ancient Britons < *Bryttas*, Britons, of Celt. orig.]

British Ant•arc•tic Territory (ănt-ärk′tĭk, -är′tĭk). A British territory of the extreme Southern Hemisphere.

British an•ti-lew•is•ite (ăn′tē-lo͞o′ĭ-sīt′, ăn′tī-) *n.* See **dimercaprol.**

British Cam•e•roons (kăm′ə-ro͞onz′). A former territory of W Africa, divided in 1961 between Nigeria and Cameroon.

British Co•lum•bi•a (kə-lŭm′bē-ə). A province of W Canada bordering on the Pacific; joined the confederation in 1871. Cap. Victoria. Pop. 2,744,467.

British Com•mon•wealth (kŏm′ən-wĕlth′). See **Commonwealth of Nations.**

British Empire. The geographic and political units formerly under British control; at the height of its power in the late 19th and early 20th cent.

British English *n.* The English language as used in England.

Brit•ish•er (brĭt′ĭ-shər) *n.* *Informal.* A native or inhabitant of Great Britain.

British Gui•a•na (gē-ăn′ə, -ä′nə). See **Guyana.**

British Hon•du•ras (hŏn-do͝or′əs, -dyo͝or′-). See **Belize** 1.

British In•di•a (ĭn′dē-ə). The part of the Indian subcontinent under British administration until 1947.

British In•di•an Ocean Territory (ĭn′dē-ən). A British island colony in the W Indian Ocean; formed in 1965.

British Isles. A group of islands off the NW coast of Europe comprising Great Britain, Ireland, and adjacent islands.

Brit•ish•ism (brĭt′ĭ-shĭz′əm) *n.* Var. of **Briticism.**

British So•ma•li•land (sō-mä′lē-lănd′, sə-). A former protectorate of E Africa on the Gulf of Aden; part of Somaliland since 1960.

British thermal unit *n.* The heat equal to 1/180 of the heat required to raise the temperature of one pound of water from 32° to 212°F at a constant pressure of one atmosphere.

British Vir•gin Islands (vûr′jĭn). A British colony in the E Caribbean. Cap. Road Town, on Tortola I. Pop. 12,034.

British West In•dies (ĭn′dēz). The islands of the West Indies formerly under British control.

Brit•on (brĭt′n) *n.* **1.** A native or inhabitant of Great Britain. **2.** One of a Celtic people inhabiting Britain at the time of the Roman invasion. [ME *Britoun*, Celt, Briton < AN *Britun* < Lat. *Brittonēs*, Britons, of Celt. orig.]

britt (brĭt) *n.* Var. of **brit.**

Brit•ta•ny (brĭt′n-ē) also **Bre•tagne** (brə-tän′yə). A historical region and former province of NW France on a peninsula between the English Channel and the Bay of Biscay; settled c. 500 by Britons and incorporated into France in 1532.

Brittany spaniel *n.* A large pointing spaniel of a breed originating in France.

Brit•ten (brĭt′n), **(Edward) Benjamin.** 1913–76. British composer known for his song cycles and operas.

brit•tle (brĭt′l) *adj.* **-tler, -tlest. 1.a.** Likely to break, snap, or crack. **b.** Easily disrupted. See Syns at **fragile. 2.a.** Difficult to deal with; snappish. **b.** Lacking warmth of feeling; cold. **3.** Brilliantly sharp, as in percussive sound. **4.a.** Perishable. **b.** Fleeting; transitory. —*n.* A confection of caramelized sugar and nuts. [ME *britel*, prob. < OE **brytel* < *bryttian*, to shatter.] —**brit′tle•ly** (brĭt′l-ē) *adv.* —**brit′tle•ness** *n.*

brit•tle•bush (brĭt′l-bo͝osh′) *n.* A shrub *(Encelia farinosa)* in the composite family, native to Mexico and the southwest United States and having grayish foliage and flowers with yellow rays.

brittle star *n.* Any of various marine organisms of the class Ophiuroidea, related to and resembling the starfish but having long slender arms.

Brit•ton•ic (brĭ-tŏn′ĭk) also **Bry•thon•ic** (-thŏn′-) *n.* The branch of the Celtic languages that includes Welsh, Breton, and Cornish. [Ult. < Lat. *Brittonēs*, Britons. See BRITON.]

Brix scale (brĭks) *n.* A hydrometer scale for measuring the sugar content of a solution at a given temperature. [After Adolf F. *Brix* (1798–1870), German scientist.]

Br•no (bûr′nō). A city of SE Czech Republic SE of Prague; founded in the 10th cent. Pop. 383,443.

bro. *abbr.* Brother.

broach[1] (brōch) *tr.v.* **broached, broach•ing, broach•es. 1.a.** To bring up (a subject) for discussion or debate. **b.** To announce. **2.** To pierce in order to draw off liquid. **3.** To draw off (a liquid) by piercing a hole in a container. **4.** To shape or enlarge (a hole) with a tapered serrated tool. —*n.* **1.a.** A tapered serrated tool used to broach a hole. **b.** The hole made by such a tool. **2.** A spit for roasting meat. **3.** A mason's narrow chisel. **4.** A gimlet for tapping or broaching casks. **5.** Var. of **brooch.** [ME *brochen*, to pierce, prob. < *broche*, pointed weapon or implement < OFr. < VLat. **brocca* < Lat. *broccus*, projecting.] —**broach′er** *n.*

broach[2] (brōch) *intr. & tr.v.* **broached, broach•ing, broach•es.** *Naut.* To veer or cause to veer broadside to the wind and waves. [Prob. < BROACH[1].]

broad (brôd) *adj.* **broad•er, broad•est. 1.** Wide in extent from side to side: *a broad river.* **2.** Large in expanse; spacious. **3.** Having a certain width from side to side: *three feet broad.* **4.** Full; open: *broad daylight.* **5.** Covering a wide scope; general: *a broad rule.* **6.** Liberal; tolerant. See Syns at **broad-minded. 7.** Relating to or covering the main facts or the essential points. **8.** Plain and clear; obvious. **9.** *Obsolete.* Outspoken. **10.** Vulgar; ribald: *a broad joke.* **11.** Heavily regional: *a broad Southern accent.* **12.** *Ling.* Pronounced with the tongue placed low and flat and with the oral cavity wide open, like the *a* in *bath* when pronounced like the *a* in *father.* —*n.* **1.** A wide flat part, as of one's hand. **2.** *Offensive.* A woman or girl. —*adv.* Fully; completely. [ME *brod* < OE *brād.*] —**broad′ly** *adv.* —**broad′ness** *n.*

broad arrow *n.* **1.** An arrow with a wide barbed head. **2.** *Chiefly British.* A wide arrowhead mark identifying government property.

broad•ax also **broad•axe** (brôd′ăks′) *n.* An ax with a wide flat head and a short handle; a battle-ax.

broad•band (brôd′bănd′) *adj.* Of, relating to, or having a wide band of electromagnetic frequencies. —**broad′band′** *n.*

broad bean also **broad•bean** (brôd′bēn′) *n.* **1.** An annual Old World plant *(Vicia faba)* in the pea family, having pinnately compound leaves and long thick pods. **2.** The edible seed or green pod of this plant.

broad-brush (brôd′brŭsh′) *adj.* Sweepingly general in scope.

broad•cast (brôd′kăst′) *v.* **-cast** or **-cast•ed, -cast•ing, -casts.** —*tr.* **1.** To transmit (a radio or television program) for public or general use. **2.** To send out or communicate, esp. by radio or television. **3.** To make known over a wide area: *broadcast rumors.* **4.** To sow (seed) over a wide area, esp. by hand. —*intr.* **1.a.** To transmit a radio or television program for public or general use. **b.** To be on the air. **2.** To participate in a radio or television program. **3.** To send a transmission or signal; transmit. —*n.* **1.** Transmission of a radio or television program or signal for public use. **2.a.** A radio or television program. **b.** The duration of such a program. **3.** The act of scattering seed. —*adj.* **1.a.** Communicated by means of television or radio. **b.** Of or relating to television or radio communications. **2.** Widely known. **3.** Scattered over a wide area. —*adv.* In a scattered manner. —**broad′cast′er** *n.*

Broad-Church (brôd′chûrch′) *adj.* Of or relating to members of the Anglican Communion in the late 19th century who favored liberalization of ritual and doctrine.

broad•cloth (brôd′klôth′, -klŏth′) *n.* **1.** A densely textured woolen cloth with a plain or twill weave and a lustrous finish. **2.** A closely woven silk, cotton, or synthetic fabric with a narrow crosswise rib.

broad•en (brôd′n) *tr. & intr.v.* **-ened, -en•ing, -ens.** To make or become broad or broader. —**broad′en•er** *n.*

broad gauge *n.* **1.** A distance between the rails of a railroad track that is greater than the standard width of 56½ inches (143.5 centimeters). **2.** A locomotive, car, or railway line of this gauge.

broad-gauge (brôd′gāj′) *adj.* **1.** Having a broad gauge. Used of a railroad track. **2.** *Informal.* Having a wide scope.

broad jump *n. Sports.* See **long jump.**

broad•leaf (brôd′lēf′) *adj.* Broad-leaved.

broad-leaved (brôd′lēvd′) also **broad-leafed** (-lēft′) *adj.* Having broad leaves rather than needlelike or scalelike leaves.

broad•loom (brôd′lo͞om′) *adj.* Woven on a wide loom: *a broadloom carpet.* —**broad′loom′** *n.*

broad-mind•ed (brôd′mīn′dĭd) *adj.* Having or characterized by tolerant or liberal views. —**broad′-mind′ed•ly** *adv.* —**broad′-mind′ed•ness** *n.*

Syns: *broad-minded, broad, liberal, open-minded, tolerant.* The central meaning shared by these adjectives is "having or showing an inclination to respect views and beliefs that differ from one's own": *a broad-minded judge; showed broad sympathies; a liberal cleric; open-minded impartiality; a tolerant attitude.* **Ant:** *narrow-minded.*

Broads (brôdz). A low-lying region of E England with wide shallow lakes interconnected by rivers and small streams.

broad•sheet (brôd′shēt′) *n.* See **broadside** 4.

broad•side (brôd′sīd′) *n.* **1.** The side of a ship above the water line. **2.a.** All the guns on one side of a warship. **b.** The simultaneous discharge of these guns. **3.** A forceful verbal attack. **4.a.** A large sheet of paper usu. printed on one side. **b.** Something, such as an advertisement, that is printed on a broadside. **5.** A broad unbroken surface. —*adv.* With the side turned to a given object: *The wave caught the canoe broadside.* —*tr.v.* **-sid•ed, -sid•ing, -sides.** To strike or collide with full on the side.

Brittany spaniel

broad-spec•trum (brôd′spĕk′trəm) *adj.* Widely applicable or effective: *a broad-spectrum antibiotic.*

broad•sword (brôd′sôrd′, -sōrd′) *n.* A sword with a wide, usu. two-edged blade for slashing rather than thrusting.

broad•tail (brôd′tāl′) *n.* **1.** See **karakul. 2.** The black pelt of a prematurely born karakul sheep.

Broad•way (brôd′wā′). **1.** A thoroughfare of NY, the longest street in the world. It begins at the S tip of Manhattan and extends c. 241 km (150 mi) N to Albany. **2.** The principal theater and amusement district of New York City.

broad-winged hawk (brôd′wĭngd′) *n.* A crow-sized forest hawk *(Buteo platypterous)* of eastern North America.

Brob•ding•nag•i•an (brŏb′dĭng-năg′ē-ən) *adj.* Immense; enormous. [After *Brobdingnag*, a country in *Gulliver's Travels* by Jonathan Swift, where everything was enormous.]

bro•cade (brō-kād′) *n.* A heavy fabric interwoven with a rich, raised design. [Sp. or Port. *brocado* < Ital. *brocato* < *brocco*, twisted thread < VLat. **brocca*, spike < Lat. *brocchus*, projecting, of Celt. orig.] —**bro•cade′** *tr.v.*

broc•a•tel also **broc•a•telle** (brŏk′ə-tĕl′) *n.* A heavy fabric with highly raised designs. [Fr. *brocatelle* < Ital. *broccatello*, dim. of *broccato*, brocade. See BROCADE.]

broc•co•li (brŏk′ə-lē) *n.* **1.** A vegetable *(Brassica oleracea* var. *italica)* in the mustard family, related to the cauliflower and having clusters of green flower buds. **2.** The flower clusters of this plant, eaten as a vegetable before the buds open. [Ital., pl. of *broccolo*, flowering sprout of a turnip, dim. of *brocco*, shoot, sprout < VLat. **brocca*, spike. See BROCADE.]

broccoli
Brassica oleracea var. *italica*

broccoli raab or **broccoli rabe** (räb) *n.* A vegetable plant *(Brassica rapa)* related to the turnip. [Ital. *broccoli di rapa*: *broccoli*, pl. dim. of *brocco*, sprout, shoot; see BROCCOLI + *di*, of (< Lat. *dē*; see DE-) + *rapa*, turnip; see RAPE[2].]

bro•chette (brō-shĕt′) *n.* **1.** A small skewer or spit used to broil or roast meat, fish, or vegetables. **2.** Food broiled or roasted on a brochette. [Fr. < OFr., dim. of *broche*, spit. See BROACH[1].]

bro•chure (brō-sho͝or′) *n.* A small booklet or pamphlet. [Fr. < *brocher*, to stitch < *broche*, knitting needle < OFr., spit, needle. See BROACH[1].]

brock (brŏk) *n. Chiefly British.* A badger. [ME *brok* < OE *broc*, of Celt. orig.]

Brock•en (brŏk′ən). A granite peak, 1,142.8 m (3,747 ft), of the Harz Mts. in central Germany.

brock•et (brŏk′ĭt) *n.* **1.** A two-year-old red deer with its first horns. **2.** Any of several small South American deer of the genus *Mazama*, having short unbranched horns. [ME *broket* < OFr. *brocard* < *broque*, animal's horn, dialectal var. of *broche*, spit. See BROACH[1].]

Brock•ton (brŏk′tən). A city of E MA S of Boston; settled in 1700. Pop. 92,788.

Brock•ville (brŏk′vĭl′). A city of SE Ontario, Canada, on the St. Lawrence R. S of Ottawa. Pop. 19,896.

Brod•sky (brôd′skē), **Joseph.** b. 1940. Russian poet and essayist who won the 1987 Nobel Prize for literature.

bro•gan (brō′gən) *n.* A heavy, ankle-high work shoe. [Ir.Gael. *brōgan*, dim. of *brōg*, brogue. See BROGUE[1].]

Bro•glie (brô-glē′), **Louis Victor de.** 1892–1987. French physicist who won a 1929 Nobel Prize.

brogue[1] (brōg) *n.* **1.** A heavy shoe of untanned leather, formerly worn in Scotland and Ireland. **2.** A strong oxford shoe,

ă pat	oi boy
ā pay	ou out
âr care	o͝o took
ä father	o͞o boot
ĕ pet	ŭ cut
ē be	ûr urge
ĭ pit	th thin
ī pie	*th* this
îr pier	hw which
ŏ pot	zh vision
ō toe	ə about, item
ô paw	

Stress marks:
′ (primary);
′ (secondary), as in
dictionary (dĭk′shə-nĕr′ē)

usu. with ornamental perforations and wing tips. [Ir. and Sc. Gael. *brōg* < OIr. *brōc*, shoe, poss. < ON *brōk*, legging, or < OE *brōc*, sing. of *brēc*, trousers.]

brogue[2] (brōg) *n.* A strong dialectal accent, esp. a strong Irish accent. [Prob. from the brogues worn by peasants.]

broi•der (broi′dər) *tr.v.* **-dered, -der•ing, -ders.** To ornament with needlework; embroider. [Alteration (influenced by ME *broiden*, braided) of ME *brouderen* < OFr. *brosder, brouder.* See EMBROIDER.] **— broi′der•y** *n.*

broil[1] (broil) *v.* **broiled, broil•ing, broils.** *— tr.* **1.** To cook by direct radiant heat, as over a grill. **2.** To expose to great heat. *— intr.* To be exposed to great heat. *— n.* **1.** The act of broiling or the condition of being broiled. **2.** Food, esp. meat, that is broiled. [ME *broilen* < OFr. *brusler, bruler*, perh. < *usler*, to burn (with *br-* < *bruir*, to burn) < Lat. *ustulāre*, to scorch < *ūrere*, to burn.]

broil[2] (broil) *n.* A rowdy argument; a brawl. *— intr.v.* **broiled, broil•ing, broils.** To engage in a rowdy argument. [< obsolete *broil*, to brawl < ME *broilen* < AN *broiller*, to mix up, confuse < *breu*, broth, brew < VLat. **brodum*, of Gmc. orig. See **bhreu-*.**]

broil•er (broi′lər) *n.* **1.** One that broils, esp. a small oven or the part of a stove used for broiling food. **2.** A tender young chicken suitable for broiling.

broke (brōk) *v.* **1.** P.t. of **break. 2.** *Non-Standard.* A p.part. of **break.** *— adj. Informal.* **1.** Bankrupt. **2.** Lacking funds.

bro•ken (brō′kən) *v.* P.part. of **break.** *— adj.* **1.a.** Forcibly separated into two or more pieces; fractured. **b.** Sundered by divorce, separation, or desertion. **2.** Having been violated: *a broken promise.* **3.a.** Incomplete: *a broken set of books.* **b.** Being in a state of disarray; disordered. **4.a.** Intermittently stopping and starting; discontinuous. **b.** Varying abruptly, as in pitch: *broken sobs.* **c.** Spoken with gaps and errors: *broken English.* **5.** Topographically rough; uneven. **6.a.** Subdued totally; humbled. **b.** Weakened and infirm. **7.** Crushed by grief: *a broken heart.* **8.** Financially ruined; bankrupt. **9.** Not functioning; out of order. **— bro′ken•ly** *adv.* **— bro′ken•ness** *n.*

Bro•ken Arrow (brō′kən). A city of NE OK, a suburb of Tulsa. Pop. 58,043.

bro•ken-down (brō′kən-doun′) *adj.* **1.** Out of working order. **2.** In poor condition, as from old age; infirm.

bro•ken•heart•ed (brō′kən-här′tĭd) *adj.* Grievously sad.

bro•ker (brō′kər) *n.* **1.** One that acts as an agent for others, as in negotiating contracts, purchases, or sales, in return for a fee or commission. **2.** A stockbroker. **3.** A power broker. *— tr.v.* **-kered, -ker•ing, -kers.** To arrange or manage as a broker. [ME < AN *brocour, abrocour*; poss. akin to Sp. *alboroque*, ceremonial gift at conclusion of business deal.]

bro•ker•age (brō′kər-ĭj) *n.* **1.** The business of a broker. **2.** A fee or commission paid to a broker. **3.** A firm engaged in buying and selling stocks and bonds for clients.

brol•ly (brŏl′ē) *n., pl.* **-lies.** *Chiefly British.* An umbrella. [Shortening and alteration of UMBRELLA.]

bro•mate (brō′māt′) *n.* **1.** A salt of bromic acid. **2.** An ion of bromic acid, BrO_3. *— tr.v.* **-mat•ed, -mat•ing, -mates.** To treat (a substance) chemically with a bromate.

brome (brōm) *n.* Any of various grasses of the genus *Bromus*, native to temperate regions and including weed, ornamental, and forage species. [NLat. *Bromus*, genus name < Lat. *bromos*, oats < Gk.]

bro•me•li•ad (brō-mē′lē-ăd′) *n.* Any of various mostly epiphytic tropical American plants of the family Bromeliaceae, usu. having long stiff leaves, colorful flowers, and showy bracts. [< NLat. *Bromelia*, type genus, after Olaf *Bromelius* (1639–1705), Swedish botanist.]

bro•mic acid (brō′mĭk) *n.* A corrosive colorless liquid, $HBrO_3$, used in making dyes and pharmaceuticals.

bro•mide (brō′mīd′) *n.* **1.a.** A binary compound of bromine with another element. **b.** Potassium bromide. **2.a.** A commonplace remark or notion; a platitude. **b.** A tiresome person; a bore. **— bro•mid′ic** (-mĭd′ĭk) *adj.*

bro•mi•nate (brō′mə-nāt′) *tr.v.* **-nat•ed, -nat•ing, -nates.** To combine (a substance) with bromine or a bromine compound. **— bro′mi•na′tion** *n.*

bro•mine (brō′mēn) *n. Symbol* **Br** A volatile nonmetallic liquid element, having a highly irritating vapor. It is used in gasoline antiknock mixtures and photographic chemicals. Atomic weight 79.904; atomic number 35; melting point 7.2°C; boiling point 58.78°C; specific gravity 3.12; valence 1, 3, 5, 7. See table at **element.** [Fr. *brome* (< Gk. *brōmos*, stench) + -INE[2].]

bro•mism (brō′mĭz′əm) also **bro•min•ism** (brō′mə-nĭz′əm) *n.* A toxic condition caused by the chronic overuse of bromides, characterized by mental dullness, loss of muscular coordination, and sometimes skin eruptions.

bromo– or **brom–** *pref.* Bromine: *bromide.* [< BROMINE and BROMIDE.]

bron•chi (brŏng′kī′, -kē′) *n.* Pl. of **bronchus.**

bron•chi•al (brŏng′kē-əl) *adj.* Of or relating to the bronchi, the bronchia, or the bronchioles. **— bron′chi•al•ly** *adv.*

bronchial asthma *n.* Asthma that is caused by spasmodic contraction of the muscular walls of the bronchial tubes.

bronchial tube *n.* A bronchus or any of its branches.

bron•chi•ec•ta•sis (brŏng′kē-ĕk′tə-sĭs) *n.* Chronic dilatation of the bronchial tubes. [Gk. *bronkhia*, bronchial tubes (< *bronkhos*, windpipe) + Gk. *ektasis*, extension (*ek-*, out; see ECTO– + *tasis*, a stretching < *teinein*, to stretch; see **ten-***).]

bron•chi•ole (brŏng′kē-ōl′) *n.* Any of the fine thin-walled tubular extensions of a bronchus. [Fr. : *bronchi* (< NLat., pl. of *bronchus*) + *–ole*, dim. suff. (< Lat. *-ola*).] **— bron′chi•o′lar** (-ō′lər) *adj.*

bron•chi•tis (brŏn-kī′tĭs, brŏng-) *n.* **1.** Inflammation of the mucous membrane of the bronchial tubes. **2.** A disease marked by this inflammation. **— bron•chit′ic** (-kĭt′ĭk) *adj.*

bron•chi•um (brŏng′kē-əm) *n., pl.* **-chi•a** (-kē-ə). A bronchial tube that is smaller than a bronchus and larger than a bronchiole. [NLat., sing. of LLat. *bronchia*, bronchial tubes < Gk. *bronkhia* < *bronkhos*, windpipe.]

broncho– or **bronch–** *pref.* Bronchus; bronchial: *bronchoscope.* [LLat. < Gk. *bronkho-* < *bronkhos*, windpipe.]

bron•cho•di•la•tor (brŏng′kō-dī-lā′tər, -dĭ-, -dī′lā-) *n.* A drug that relaxes bronchial smooth muscle to ease breathing.

bron•cho•pneu•mon•ia (brŏng′kō-nōō-mōn′yə, -nyōō-) *n.* A pneumonia involving inflammation of the lungs that spreads from the bronchi.

bron•cho•scope (brŏng′kə-skōp′) *n.* A slender tubular instrument with a small light on the end for inspection of the interior of the bronchi. **— bron′cho•scop′ic** (-skŏp′ĭk) *adj.* **— bron′cho•scop′i•cal•ly** *adv.* **— bron•chos′co•pist** (brŏn-kŏs′kə-pĭst, brŏng-) *n.* **— bron•chos′co•py** (-kə-pē) *n.*

bron•chus (brŏng′kəs) *n., pl.* **-chi** (-kī′, -kē′). Either of two main branches of the trachea, leading directly to the lungs. [NLat. < Gk. *bronkhos*, windpipe.]

bron•co (brŏng′kō) *n., pl.* **-cos.** A wild or semiwild horse or pony of western North America. [Am.Sp. < Sp., wild, perh. < VLat. **bruncus*, knot in a tree, perh. < Lat. *broccus*, projecting (influenced by *truncus*, stump).]

bron•co•bust•er (brŏng′kō-bŭs′tər) *n.* One who breaks wild horses to the saddle.

Bron•të (brŏn′tē). Family of British novelists and poets, including **Charlotte** (1816–55), known for *Jane Eyre* (1847), **Emily** (1818–48), known for *Wuthering Heights* (1847), and **Anne** (1820–49), known for *Agnes Gray* (1847).

Brontë
Detail of a portrait of Anne, Emily, and Charlotte, painted by Patrick Branwell Brontë (1817–1848), who obliterated his image between Emily and Charlotte

bron•to•saur (brŏn′tə-sôr′) or **bron•to•sau•rus** (brŏn′tə-sôr′əs) *n.* A large herbivorous dinosaur of the genus *Apatosaurus* (or *Brontosaurus*) of the Jurassic Period. [NLat. *Brontosaurus*, genus name : Gk. *brontē*, thunder + Gk. *sauros*, lizard.]

brontosaur

Bronx (brŏngks). A borough of New York City in SE NY on the mainland N of Manhattan. Pop. 1,203,789.

Bronx cheer *n. Slang.* A loud sound expressing disapproval; a raspberry. [After the BRONX.]

bronze (brŏnz) *n.* **1.a.** Any of various alloys of copper and tin, sometimes with traces of other metals. **b.** Any of various alloys of copper, with or without tin, and antimony, phosphorus, or other components. **2.** A work of art made of one of these alloys. **3.a.** *Color.* A moderate yellowish to olive brown. **b.** A pigment of this color. *— adj.* **1.** Made of or consisting of bronze. **2.** *Color.* Of the color bronze. *— tr.v.* **bronzed, bronz•ing, bronz•es.** To give the color or appearance of bronze to. [Fr. < Ital. *bronzo.*] **— bronz′er** *n.* **— bronz′y** *adj.*

Bronze Age (brŏnz) *n.* A period of human culture between the Stone Age and the Iron Age, characterized by weapons and implements made of bronze.

Bronze Star *n.* A U.S. military decoration awarded either for heroism or for meritorious achievement in ground combat.

brooch (brōch, brōōch) also **broach** (brōch) *n.* A relatively large decorative pin or clasp. [ME *broche*, pointed tool, brooch, pin. See BROACH[1].]

brood (brōōd) *n.* **1.** The young of certain animals, esp. a group of young birds or fowl. **2.** The children in one family. *— v.* **brood•ed, brood•ing, broods.** *— tr.* **1.** To sit on or hatch (eggs). **2.** To protect (young) by or as if by covering with the wings. *— intr.* **1.** To sit on or hatch eggs. **2.** To hover envelopingly; loom. **3.a.** To be deep in thought; meditate. **b.** To focus the attention on a subject persistently and moodily; worry. **c.** To be depressed. *— adj.* Kept for breeding: *a brood hen.* [ME < OE *brōd.* See **bhreu-*.**] **— brood′ing•ly** *adv.*

Syns: *brood, dwell, fret, mope, stew, worry.* The central meaning shared by these verbs is "to turn over in the mind moodily and at length": *brooding about life; dwelled on defeat; fretting over the job; moping about illness; stewing over her; worrying about bills.*

brood•er (brōō′dər) *n.* **1.** One that broods. **2.** A heated enclosure in which fowls are raised.

brood•y (brōō′dē) *adj.* **-i•er, -i•est. 1.a.** Meditative; contemplative. **b.** Oppressive. **2.** Disposed to sit on eggs to hatch them. **— brood′i•ness** *n.*

brook[1] (brŏŏk) *n.* See **creek** 1. See Regional Note at **run.** [ME < OE *brōc.*]

brook[2] (brŏŏk) *tr.v.* **brooked, brook•ing, brooks.** To put up with; tolerate. [ME *brouken* < OE *brūcan*, to use, enjoy.]

Brooke (brŏŏk), **Rupert.** 1887–1915. British poet known esp. for his romantic war poetry.

Brook•field (brŏŏk′fēld′). **1.** A village of NE IL, a suburb of Chicago. Pop. 18,876. **2.** A city of SE WI, a suburb of Milwaukee. Pop. 35,184.

brook•ite (brŏŏk′īt′) *n.* A mineral form of titanium dioxide, TiO_2. [After Henry James *Brooke* (1771–1857), British mineralogist.]

brook•let (brŏŏk′lĭt) *n.* A small brook.

brook•lime (brŏŏk′līm′) *n.* Either of two trailing plants, *Veronica americana* of North America and *V. beccabunga* of Eurasia, having clusters of small blue or purplish flowers. [Alteration of ME *brokelemok*: *broke*, brook; see BROOK[1] + *lemok*, a kind of brooklime (< OE *hleomoc*).]

Brook•line (brŏŏk′līn′). A town of E MA, a suburb of Boston. Pop. 54,718.

Brook•lyn (brŏŏk′lĭn). A borough of New York City in SE NY on W Long I.; settled by Dutch colonists in 1645. Pop. 2,300,664.

Brooklyn Center. A city of SE MN, a suburb of Minneapolis. Pop. 28,887.

Brooklyn Park. A city of SE MN, a suburb of Minneapolis. Pop. 56,381.

Brook Park (brŏŏk). A city of NE OH, a suburb of Cleveland. Pop. 22,865.

Brooks (brŏŏks), **Gwendolyn Elizabeth.** b. 1917. Amer. poet known for her verses detailing the dreams and struggles of Black Americans.

Brooks, Phillips. 1835–93. Amer. Episcopal bishop who wrote the hymn "O Little Town of Bethlehem" (1868).

Brooks, Van Wyck. 1886–1963. Amer. literary historian whose works include *The Flowering of New England* (1936).

Brooks Range. A section of the Rocky Mts. in N AK within the Arctic Circle and rising to c. 2,763 m (9,060 ft).

brook trout *n.* A freshwater game fish *(Salvelinus fontinalis)* of eastern North America.

broom (brōōm, brŏŏm) *n.* **1.** A bunch of twigs, straw, or bristles bound together, attached to a stick or handle and used for sweeping. **2.a.** Any of various Mediterranean shrubs of the genus *Cytisus* in the pea family, esp. *C. scoparius,* usu. having compound leaves with bright yellow flowers. **b.** Any of several similar shrubs, esp. in the genera *Genista* and *Spartium.* — *tr.v.* **broomed, broom•ing, brooms.** To sweep with or as if with a broom. [ME < OE *brōm*.] — **broom′y** *adj.*

broom•corn (brōōm′kôrn′, brŏŏm′-) *n.* A variety of sorghum *(Sorghum bicolor),* the stalks of which are used to make brooms.

Broom•field (brōōm′fēld′). A city of N-central CO, a suburb of Denver. Pop. 24,638.

broom•rape (brōōm′rāp′, brŏŏm′-) *n.* Any of various parasitic herbs of the genus *Orobanche,* having purplish or yellowish flowers and small scalelike leaves that lack chlorophyll. [Transl. of Med.Lat. *rāpum genistae*: Lat. *rāpum,* underground stock of a tree + Lat. *genistae*, genitive of *genista,* broom (< growth of these tubers on broom roots).]

broom•stick (brōōm′stĭk′, brŏŏm′-) *n.* The handle of a broom.

bros. *abbr.* Brothers.

Bros•sard (brô-sär′, -särd′). A town of S Quebec, Canada, a suburb of Montreal on the St. Lawrence R. Pop. 52,232.

broth (brôth, brŏth) *n., pl.* **broths** (brôths, brŏths, brô*th*z, brŏ*th*z). **1.** The water in which meat, fish, or vegetables have been boiled; stock. **2.** A thin, clear soup based on stock. [ME < OE. See **bhreu-***.]

broth•el (brŏth′əl, brô′thəl) *n.* A house of prostitution. [Short for *brothel-house* < ME *brothel*, prostitute < *brothen*, p.part. of *brethen*, to go to ruin < OE *brēothan*, to decay.]

broth•er (brŭ*th*′ər) *n., pl.* **-ers. 1.** A male having the same parents as another or one parent in common with another. **2.** *pl. often* **breth•ren** (brĕ*th*′rən). One who shares a common ancestry, allegiance, character, or purpose with another or others, esp.: **a.** A kinsman. **b.** A fellow man. **c.** A fellow member, as of a fraternity or trade union. **d.** A close male friend. **e.** A soul brother. **3.** *pl. often* **brethren.** Something, such as a corporation or an institution, that is regarded as a member of a class. **4.** *Eccles.* **a.** A member of a men's religious order who is not in holy orders but engages in the work of the order. **b.** A lay member of a religious order of men. **c.** *pl. often* **brethren.** A fellow member of the Christian church. [ME < OE *brōthor*. See **bhrāter-***.]

broth•er•hood (brŭ*th*′ər-hŏŏd′) *n.* **1.** The state or relationship of being brothers. **2.** Fellowship. **3.** An association of men, such as a fraternity or union, united for common purposes. **4.** All the members of a profession or trade.

broth•er-in-law (brŭ*th*′ər-ĭn-lô′) *n., pl.* **broth•ers-in-law** (brŭ*th*′ərz-). **1.** The brother of one's husband or wife. **2.** The husband of one's sister. **3.** The husband of the sister of one's husband or wife.

broth•er•ly (brŭ*th*′ər-lē) *adj.* Characteristic of or befitting brothers. — **broth′er•li•ness** *n.* — **broth′er•ly** *adv.*

brougham (brōōm, brōō′əm, brōm, brō′əm) *n.* **1.** A closed four-wheeled carriage with an open driver's seat. **2.** An automobile with an open driver's seat. **3.** An electrically powered automobile resembling a coupé. [After Henry Peter *Brougham*, 1st Baron Brougham and Vaux (1778–1868), Scottish-born jurist.]

brought (brôt) *v.* P.t. and p.part. of **bring.**

brou•ha•ha (brōō′hä-hä′) *n.* An uproar; a hubbub. [Fr., of imit. orig.]

brow (brou) *n.* **1.a.** The superciliary ridge over the eyes. **b.** The eyebrow. **c.** The forehead. **2.** A facial expression; countenance. **3.** The projecting upper edge of a steep place: *the brow of a hill.* [ME < OE *brū*. See **bhrū-***.]

brow•beat (brou′bēt′) *tr.v.* **-beat, -beat•en** (-bēt′n), **-beat•ing, -beats.** To intimidate or subjugate by an overbearing manner or domineering speech; bully. — **brow′beat′er** *n.*

brown (broun) *n. Color.* Any of a group of colors between red and yellow in hue that are medium to low in lightness and low to moderate in saturation. — *adj.* **brown•er, brown•est. 1.** *Color.* Of the color brown. **2.** Deeply suntanned. **3.a.** Having a brownish or dark skin color. **b.** *Offensive.* Of or being a person of nonwhite origin. — *tr. & intr.v.* **browned, brown•ing, browns. 1.** To make or become brown. **2.** To cook until brown. [ME < OE *brūn*. See **bher-**[2]*.] — **brown′ish** *adj.* — **brown′ness** *n.*

Brown (broun), **Charles Brockden.** 1771–1810. Amer. writer and editor considered America's first professional novelist.

Brown, Henry Billings. 1836–1913. Amer. jurist; associate justice of the U.S. Supreme Court (1890–1906).

Brown, Herbert Charles. b. 1912. British-born Amer. chemist who shared a 1979 Nobel Prize.

Brown, James. b. 1933. Amer. singer often called the "Godfather of Soul."

Brown, John. 1800–59. Amer. abolitionist who captured the U.S. arsenal at Harper's Ferry as part of an effort to liberate Southern slaves (1859).

Brown, Olympia. 1835–1926. Amer. minister and suffragist who was the first woman in the U.S. to be ordained in the ministry of an established denomination (1863).

Brown, Robert. 1773–1858. Scottish botanist known for his discovery of the irregular movement of pollen grains.

brown alga *n.* Any of a group of chiefly marine plants of the division Phaeophyta, including rockweed and kelp, having brown and yellow pigments that mask the chlorophyll.

brown bagging *n.* The practice of taking one's lunch to work. — **brown bagger** *n.*

brown bear *n.* Any of several large bears of the genus *Ursus,* such as the grizzly and Kodiak bears, inhabiting western North America and northern Eurasia and having brown to yellowish fur.

brown Bet•ty (bĕt′ē) *n.* A baked pudding of chopped or sliced apples, bread crumbs, raisins, sugar, butter, and spices.

brown bread *n.* **1.** A bread made of a dark flour, such as graham or whole-wheat flour. **2.** A steamed bread usu. made of cornmeal, flour, and molasses.

brown coal *n.* See **lignite.**

Browne (broun), **Charles Farrar.** Artemus Ward. 1834–67. Amer. humorist who used backwoods characters and local dialect to comment on current events.

Browne, Sir **Thomas.** 1605–82. English physician and writer whose works include *Religio Medici* (1642).

brown fat *n.* A dark-colored mitochondrion-rich adipose tissue in many mammals that generates heat to regulate body temperature, esp. in hibernating animals.

Brown•i•an movement (brou′nē-ən) *n.* The random movement of microscopic particles suspended in a liquid or gas, caused by collisions with molecules of the surrounding medium. [After Robert BROWN.]

brown•ie (brou′nē) *n.* **1. Brownie.** A member of the Girl Scouts from six through eight years of age. **2.** A bar of moist, usu. chocolate cake, often with nuts. **3.** A small sprite thought to do helpful work at night. [Sense 3, from the notion of the sprite as a tiny brown man.]

Brownie point also **brownie point** *n.* Credit considered as earned, esp. by favorably impressing a superior.

Brown•ing (brou′nĭng), **Elizabeth Barrett.** 1806–61. British poet best known for *Sonnets from the Portuguese* (1850).

Browning, John Moses. 1855–1926. Amer. firearms inventor whose designs include repeating rifles, automatic pistols, and a machine gun dubbed "the Peacemaker."

Browning, Robert. 1812–89. British poet best known for dramatic monologues such as "My Last Duchess" (1846).

Browning automatic rifle *n.* A .30 caliber automatic or semiautomatic magazine-fed rifle used in World Wars I and II and the Korean War. [After John Moses BROWNING.]

Browning machine gun *n.* A .30 or .50 caliber automatic machine gun capable of firing ammunition at a rate of more than 500 rounds per minute, used in World War II and the Korean War. [After John Moses BROWNING.]

brown lung disease *n.* See **byssinosis.**

brown mustard *n.* **1.** See **Indian mustard. 2.** The black mustard.

brown•nose or **brown-nose** (broun′nōz′) *tr.v.* **-nosed, -nos•ing, -nos•es.** *Informal.* To curry favor with; fawn on. — **brown′nose′** *n.* — **brown′nos′er** *n.*

brown•out (broun′out′) *n.* A reduction or cutback in electric

Gwendolyn Brooks

brougham
c. 1901–1909

ă pat	oi boy
ā pay	ou out
âr care	ŏŏ took
ä father	ōō boot
ĕ pet	ŭ cut
ē be	ûr urge
ĭ pit	th thin
ī pie	*th* this
îr pier	hw which
ŏ pot	zh vision
ō toe	ə about, item
ô paw	

Stress marks:
′ (primary);
′ (secondary), as in
dictionary (dĭk′shə-nĕr′ē)

power, esp. as a result of a shortage, a mechanical failure, or overuse by consumers. [BROWN + (BLACK)OUT.]

brown rat *n.* See **Norway rat.**

brown recluse spider *n.* A venomous spider *(Loxosceles reclusa)* having a violin-shaped mark on the cephalothorax.

brown rice *n.* The whole grain of rice, including the germ and outer layers containing the bran; unpolished rice.

brown rot *n.* Any of several plant diseases, esp. a disease of peach, plum, and related plants, characterized by wilting and browning of the flowers and leaves and rotting of the fruits.

Brown Shirt or **brown•shirt** (broun′shûrt′) *n.* **1.** A Nazi, esp. a storm trooper. **2.** A racist, esp. a violent right-wing one. [Transl. of Ger. *Braunhemd*: *braun*, brown + *Hemd*, shirt.]

brown•stone (broun′stōn′) *n.* **1.** A brownish-red sandstone used as a building material. **2.** A house built or faced with brownish-red sandstone.

brown study *n.* A state of deep thought. [BROWN, gloomy + STUDY, mental state.]

brown sugar *n.* **1.** Unrefined or incompletely refined sugar that retains some molasses, which imparts a brownish color to it. **2.** A product made by the addition of molasses to white sugar.

Browns•ville (brounz′vĭl′, -vəl). A city of S TX on the Rio Grande near its mouth on the Gulf of Mexico. Pop. 98,962.

Brown Swiss *n.* One of a hardy breed of large brown dairy cattle that originated in Switzerland.

brown-tail moth (broun′tāl′) *n.* A small tussock moth *(Euproctis phaeorrhoea)* whose caterpillars defoliate shade trees and produce a poison capable of causing a skin rash on contact.

brown thrasher *n.* A North American bird *(Toxostoma rufum)* having a reddish-brown back and a dark-streaked breast.

brown trout *n.* A freshwater game fish *(Salmo trutta).*

Brown•wood (broun′wo͝od′). A city of central TX W of Waco. Pop. 18,387.

browse (brouz) *v.* **browsed, brows•ing, brows•es.** *—intr.* **1.a.** To inspect something in a leisurely and casual way. **b.** To read something superficially by selecting passages at random. **2.** To feed on leaves, young shoots, and other vegetation; graze. *—tr.* **1.** To look through or over (something) casually. **2.a.** To nibble; crop. **b.** To graze on. *—n.* **1.** Young twigs, leaves, and shoots fit for animals to eat. **2.** An act of browsing. [Prob. < obsolete Fr. *broust*, young shoot < OFr. *brost*, of Gmc. orig.] **—brows′er** *n.*

Broz (brōz, brôz), **Josip.** See Marshal **Tito.**

Bru•beck (bro͞o′bĕk), **David ("Dave") Warren.** b. 1920. Amer. jazz pianist and composer considered one of the foremost exponents of progressive jazz.

Bruce (bro͞os), **Blanche Kelso.** 1841–98. Amer. politician who was the first Black U.S. senator to serve a full term (1875–81).

Bruce, Sir **David.** 1855–1931. Australian physician and bacteriologist known for his description (1887) of the bacterium that causes brucellosis.

Bruce, Robert the. See **Robert I[2].**

Bruce, Stanley Melbourne. 1st Viscount Bruce of Melbourne. 1883–1967. Australian politician who served as prime minister (1923–29).

bru•cel•la (bro͞o-sĕl′ə) *n., pl.* **-cel•lae** (-sĕl′ē) or **-cel•las.** *Microbiol.* Any of various pathogenic aerobic bacteria of the genus *Brucella.* [After Sir David BRUCE.]

bru•cel•lo•sis (bro͞o′sə-lō′sĭs) *n.* **1.** An infectious disease of human beings caused by brucellae, transmitted by contact with infected animals and characterized by fever, malaise, and headache. **2.** A disease of domestic animals caused by brucellae and sometimes resulting in spontaneous abortions in newly infected animals. [BRUCELL(A) + -OSIS.]

bru•cine (bro͞o′sēn′, -sĭn) *n.* A poisonous alkaloid, $C_{23}H_{26}N_2O_4$, derived from the seeds of nux vomica and used to denature alcohol. [After James *Bruce* (1730–94), Scottish explorer.]

Bruck•ner (bro͝ok′nər), **Anton.** 1824–96. Austrian organist and composer whose works include a Requiem (1848–49).

Brue•ghel or **Brue•gel** also **Breu•ghel** (broi′gəl, bro͞o′-, brœ′-), **Pieter.** "the Elder." 1525?–69. Flemish painter noted for his landscapes and genre scenes, including *Peasant Wedding* (c. 1567). His son **Pieter** (1564–1638?), "the Younger," is primarily remembered for copies of his father's works; another son, **Jan** (1568–1625), is known for his still-life paintings.

Bruges (bro͞ozh). A city of NW Belgium connected by canal with the North Sea; founded in the 9th cent. Pop. 118,218.

bru•in (bro͞o′ĭn) *n.* A bear. [ME, name of the bear in *History of Reynard the Fox*, translated by William Caxton < MDu. *bruun, bruin*, brown, name of the bear in MDu. version of the fable. See **bher-[2]*.**]

bruise (bro͞oz) *v.* **bruised, bruis•ing, bruis•es.** *—tr.* **1.a.** To injure the underlying soft tissue or bone of (part of the body) without breaking the skin. **b.** To damage (plant tissue), as by abrasion or pressure. **2.** To dent or mar. **3.** To pound (berries, for example) into fragments; crush. **4.** To hurt, esp. psychologically. *—intr.* To experience or undergo bruising. *—n.* **1.** An injury to underlying tissues or bone in which the skin is not broken, often characterized by ruptured blood vessels and discolorations. **2.** A similar injury to plant tissue, often resulting in discoloration or spoilage. **3.** An injury, esp. to one's feelings. [ME *bruisen* < OE *brȳsan*, to crush, and < ONFr. *bruisier* (of Gmc. orig.).]

brown recluse spider
Loxosceles reclusa

brown thrasher
Toxostoma rufum

Pieter Brueghel the Elder
Self-portrait

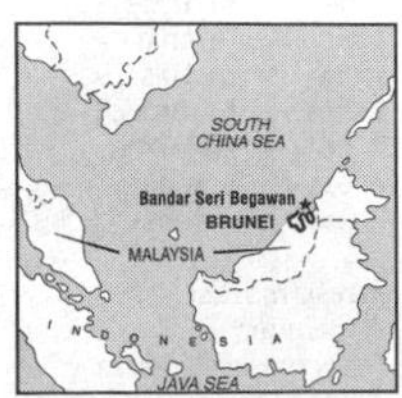

Brunei

bruis•er (bro͞o′zər) *n. Informal.* A large, heavyset man.

bruit (bro͞ot) *tr.v.* **bruit•ed, bruit•ing, bruits.** To spread news of; repeat. *—n.* **1.** (*also* bro͞o′ē). *Medic.* An abnormal sound heard in auscultation. **2.** *Archaic.* **a.** A rumor. **b.** A din; a clamor. [< ME, noise < OFr., p.part. of *bruire*, to roar < VLat. **brūgīre*, blend of Lat. *rūgīre*and VLat. **bragere.*]

Bru•lé (bro͞o-lā′) *n., pl.* **Brulé** or **-lés.** A member of a Native American people constituting a subdivision of the Teton Sioux, inhabiting Nebraska and South Dakota. [Fr. *brûlé*, burnt (partial transl. of their own name).]

bru•mal (bro͞o′məl) *adj.* Of, relating to, or occurring in winter. [Lat. *brūmālis* < *brūma*, winter < **brevima (diēs)*, the shortest (day), archaic superl. of *brevis*, short. See **mregh-u-*.**]

brume (bro͞om) *n.* Fog or mist. [Fr. < OFr., perh. < Prov. < Lat. *brūma*, winter. See BRUMAL.] **—bru′mous** (bro͞o′məs) *adj.*

brum•ma•gem (brŭm′ə-jəm) *adj.* Cheap and showy; meretricious. [Alteration of BIRMINGHAM, England (< 17th-cent. counterfeit coins made there).] **—brum′ma•gem** *n.*

Brum•mell (brŭm′əl), **George Bryan.** "Beau Brummell." 1778–1840. British dandy who popularized new men's fashions, including trousers.

brunch (brŭnch) *n.* A meal typically eaten late in the morning as a combination of a late breakfast and an early lunch. [BR(EAKFAST) + (L)UNCH.]

Bru•nei (bro͞o-nī′). A sultanate of NW Borneo on the South China Sea; gained independence from Great Britain in 1984. Cap. Bandar Seri Begawan. Pop. 191,765.

Bru•nel•le•schi (bro͞o′nə-lĕs′kē), **Filippo.** 1377–1446. Italian architect celebrated for his work during the Florentine Renaissance.

bru•net (bro͞o-nĕt′) *adj.* **1.** Of a dark complexion or coloring. **2.** Having dark brown or black hair or eyes. *—n.* A person with dark brown hair. See Usage Note at **brunette.** [Fr. < OFr., dim. of *brun*, brown, of Gmc. orig. See **bher-[2]*.**]

bru•nette (bro͞o-nĕt′) *adj.* Having dark or brown hair. *—n.* A girl or woman with dark or brown hair. [Fr., fem. of *brunet.* See BRUNET.]

Usage Note: *Brunette* is used chiefly in reference to hair color. The general practice is to use the form *brunette* to refer only to women, with *brunet* as a less frequently used variant that can be applied as well to men and mixed groups. It is unlikely that *brunette* could be pressed into service as a neutral term, since the suffix *-ette* is too closely associated with marked feminine gender. *Brunet* is rarely applied to men, whose corresponding coloration is typically described simply as "brown." See Usage Notes at **blond, -ette.**

brung (brŭng) *v. Usage Problem.* A p.t. and p.part. of **bring.**

Brun•hild (bro͞on′hĭlt′) *n.* A queen in the *Nibelungenlied* who is won as a bride by Gunther.

Bru•no (bro͞o′nō), **Giordano.** 1548?–1600. Italian philosopher who formulated a cosmic theory of an infinite universe.

Bruno of Co•logne (kə-lōn′), Saint. 1030?–1101. German monk who founded a monastery at Chartreuse in S France (1084) and founded the Carthusian order.

Bruns•wick (brŭnz′wĭk). **1.** A region and former duchy of N-central Germany; estab. in the 13th cent. **2.** A city of N-central Germany ESE of Hanover; founded 861. Pop. 253,057. **3.** A city of SE GA SSW of Savannah. Pop. 16,433. **4.** A city of NE OH, a suburb of Cleveland. Pop. 28,230.

Brunswick stew *n.* A stew that usu. contains chicken and rabbit or squirrel meat. [After *Brunswick*, a county of S VA.]

brunt (brŭnt) *n.* **1.** The main impact or force, as of an attack. **2.** The main burden. [ME, perh. of Scand. orig.]

brush[1] (brŭsh) *n.* **1.a.** A device consisting of bristles fastened into a handle, used in scrubbing, polishing, or painting. **b.** The act of using this device. **2.** A light touch in passing; a graze. **3.** A bushy tail. **4.** A sliding contact between a fixed and a moving conductor. **5.** A snub; a brushoff. *—v.* **brushed, brush•ing, brush•es.** *—tr.* **1.a.** To clean, polish, or groom with a brush. **b.** To apply with or as if with motions of a brush. **c.** To remove with or as if with motions of a brush. **2.** To dismiss abruptly or curtly: *brushed the matter aside.* **3.** To touch lightly in passing; graze against. *—intr.* **1.** To use or apply a brush. **2.** To move past something so as to touch it lightly. ***—phrasal verb.* brush up. 1.** To refresh one's memory. **2.** To renew a skill. [ME *brusshe* < OFr. *brosse*, brushwood, brush. See BRUSH[2].] **—brush′er** *n.* **—brush′y** *adj.*

brush[2] (brŭsh) *n.* **1.a.** A dense growth of bushes or shrubs. **b.** Land covered by such a growth. **2.** Cut or broken branches. [ME *brusshe* < OFr. *brosse*, brushwood < VLat. **bruscia*, perh. < Lat. *bruscum*, knot on a maple.] **—brush′y** *adj.*

brush[3] (brŭsh) *n.* A brief, often hostile or alarming encounter: *a brush with death.* [ME < *brushen*, to hasten, rush, prob. < *brusshe*, brush. See BRUSH[1].]

brush discharge *n.* A faintly visible, relatively slow crackling discharge of electricity without sparking.

brushed (brŭsht) *adj.* Having a nap produced by brushing.
brush•fire also **brush fire** (brŭsh′fīr′) *n.* **1.** A fire in low-growing scrubby trees and brush. **2.** A relatively minor crisis.
brush•off also **brush-off** (brŭsh′ôf′, -ŏf′) *n.* An abrupt dismissal or snub.
brush•wood (brŭsh′wo͝od′) *n.* **1.** Branches that have been cut or broken off. **2.a.** Dense undergrowth. **b.** An area covered by such growth.
brush•work (brŭsh′wûrk′) *n.* **1.** Work done with a brush. **2.** The manner in which a painter applies paint with a brush.
brusque also **brusk** (brŭsk) *adj.* Abrupt and curt in manner or speech; discourteously blunt. [Fr., lively, fierce < Ital. *brusco,* coarse, rough < LLat. *brūscum,* perh. blend of Lat. *rūscus,* butcher's broom, and LLat. *brūcus,* heather; see BRIAR[1].] **— brusque′ly** *adv.* **— brusque′ness** *n.*
brus•que•rie (brŭs′kə-rē′) *n.* Curtness or bluntness of manner. [Fr. < *brusque,* brusque. See BRUSQUE.]
Brus•sels (brŭs′əlz). The cap. of Belgium, in the central part; officially bilingual (Flemish and French). Met. area pop. 2,395,000.
Brussels carpet *n.* A machine-made carpet consisting of small, colored woolen loops that form a heavy patterned pile.
Brussels griffon *n.* See **griffon** 1.
Brussels lace *n.* Net lace with an appliqué design, formerly made by hand but now usu. made by machine.
Brussels sprouts *pl.n. (used with a sing. or pl. v.)* **1.** A vegetable *(Brassica oleracea* var. *gemmifera)* in the mustard family, having cabbagelike buds. **2.** The edible buds of this plant.
brut (bro͞ot) *adj.* Very dry. Used of champagne. [Fr. < OFr., rough < Lat. *brūtus,* heavy. See **g^werə-[1]***.]
bru•tal (bro͞ot′l) *adj.* **1.** Extremely ruthless or cruel. **2.** Crude or unfeeling in manner or speech. **3.** Harsh; unrelenting. **4.** Disagreeably precise or penetrating. **— bru′tal•ly** *adv.*
bru•tal•ism (bro͞ot′l-ĭz′əm) *n.* A style of architecture characterized by massive or monolithic forms typically unrelieved by exterior decoration. **— bru′tal•ist** *n.*
bru•tal•i•ty (bro͞o-tăl′ĭ-tē) *n., pl.* **-ties. 1.** The state or quality of being ruthless, cruel, harsh, or unrelenting. **2.** A ruthless, cruel, harsh, or unrelenting act.
bru•tal•ize (bro͞ot′l-īz′) *tr.v.* **-ized, -iz•ing, -iz•es. 1.** To make cruel, harsh, or unfeeling. **2.** To treat cruelly or harshly. **— bru′tal•i•za′tion** (-ĭ-zā′shən) *n.*
brute (bro͞ot) *n.* **1.** An animal; a beast. **2.** A brutal, crude, or insensitive person. *— adj.* **1.** Of or relating to beasts; animal. **2.** Characteristic of a brute, esp.: **a.** Entirely physical. **b.** Lacking or showing a lack of reason or intelligence. **c.** Savage; cruel: *brute coercion.* **d.** Unremittingly severe: *brute necessity.* **3.** Coarse; brutish. [< ME, nonhuman < OFr. *brut* < Lat. *brūtus,* stupid. See **g^werə-[1]***.] **— brut′ism** *n.*
brut•ish (bro͞o′tĭsh) *adj.* **1.** Of or characteristic of a brute. **2.** Crude in feeling or manner. **3.** Sensual; carnal. **4.** Rough; uncivilized. **— brut′ish•ly** *adv.* **— brut′ish•ness** *n.*
Brut•ti•um (bro͞ot′ē-əm, brŭt′-). An ancient region of S Italy roughly occupying present-day Calabria.
Bru•tus (bro͞o′təs), **Marcus Junius.** 85?–42 B.C. Roman politician and general who conspired to assassinate Julius Caesar.
brux•ism (brŭk′sĭz′əm) *n.* The habitual, involuntary grinding or clenching of the teeth, usu. during sleep, as from tension. [< NLat. *brūxis,* a gnashing < Gk. *brūkein,* to gnash.]
Bry•an (brī′ən). A city of E-central TX NW of Houston. Pop. 55,002.
Bryan, William Jennings. "the Great Commoner." 1860–1925. Amer. lawyer and politician famous for his "Cross of Gold" speech (1896).
Bry•ansk also **Bri•ansk** (brē-änsk′). A city of W Russia SW of Moscow; part of Lithuania until the 16th cent. Pop. 430,000.
Bry•ant (brī′ənt), **William Cullen.** 1794–1878. Amer. poet, critic, and editor known esp. for "Thanatopsis" (1817).
Bryce (brīs), **James.** 1838–1922. British diplomat and historian who wrote *American Commonwealth* (1888).
Bryn•hild (brĭn′hĭld′) *n.* A Valkyrie who is revived from an enchanted sleep by Sigurd.
bryo– *pref.* Moss: *bryology.* [NLat. < Gk. *bruon,* moss < *bruein,* to swell, teem.]
bry•ol•o•gy (brī-ŏl′ə-jē) *n.* The study of bryophytes. **— bry′o•log′i•cal** (-ə-lŏj′ĭ-kəl) *adj.*
bry•o•ny (brī′ə-nē) *n., pl.* **-nies. 1.** Any of various Eurasian vines of the genus *Bryonia,* having red or black berries and tuberous roots formerly used as medicine. **2.** The black bryony. [Lat. *bryōnia* < Gk. *bruōnia* < *bruein,* to swell, teem.]
bry•o•phyte (brī′ə-fīt′) *n.* A plant of the Bryophyta, a division of photosynthetic, chiefly terrestrial nonvascular plants, including the mosses. **— bry′o•phyt′ic** (-fĭt′ĭk) *adj.*
bry•o•zo•an (brī′ə-zō′ən) *n.* Any of various small aquatic animals of the phylum Bryozoa that reproduce by budding and form colonies attached to stones or seaweed. [< NLat. *Bryozoa,* phylum name : BRYO– + Gk. *zōia,* pl. of *zōion,* animal; see -ZOON.] **— bry′o•zo′an** *adj.*
Bryth•on (brĭth′ən, -ŏn′) *n.* **1.** An ancient Celtic Briton of Cornwall, Wales, or Cumbria. **2.** One who speaks a Brittonic language. [Welsh < Lat. *Brittonēs,* Britons. See BRITON.]
Bry•thon•ic (brĭ-thŏn′ĭk) *adj.* Of or relating to the Brythons or their language or culture. *— n.* Var. of **Brittonic.**
B.S. *abbr.* **1.** Bachelor of Science. **2.** Balance sheet. **3.** Bill of sale. **4.** *Obscene.* Bullshit.
BSA *abbr.* Boy Scouts of America.
B.Sc. *abbr.* Bachelor of Science.
B.S.Ed. *abbr.* Bachelor of Science in Education.
bsh. *abbr.* Bushel.
BSI *abbr.* British Standards Institution.
B-side (bē′sīd′) *n.* The reverse side of a phonograph record, esp. a single. [From the *B* on the record's label.]
bsk. *abbr.* Basket.
Bt. *abbr.* Baronet.
B.T. *abbr.* Bachelor of Theology.
B.Th. *abbr.* Bachelor of Theology.
btry. *abbr.* Battery.
Btss. *abbr.* Baronetess.
Btu *abbr.* British thermal unit.
bu. *abbr.* **1.** Bureau. **2.** Or **bu** Bushel.
bub (bŭb) *n. Slang.* Fellow. Used as a term of familiar address for a man or boy. [Prob. short for BROTHER.]
Bu•bas•tis (byo͞o-băs′tĭs). An ancient city of NE Egypt.
bub•ble (bŭb′əl) *n.* **1.** A thin, usu. spherical or hemispherical film of liquid filled with air or gas. **2.** A globular body of air or gas formed within a liquid. **3.** A pocket formed in a solid by trapped air or gas, as during cooling. **4.a.** The act or process of forming bubbles. **b.** A sound made by or as if by the forming and bursting of bubbles. **5.** Something insubstantial, groundless, or ephemeral, esp.: **a.** A fantastic or impracticable idea or belief; an illusion. **b.** A speculative scheme that comes to nothing. **6.** Something light or effervescent. **7.** A usu. transparent glass or plastic dome. **8.** A protective, often isolating envelope or cover. *— v.* **-bled, -bling, -bles.** *— intr.* **1.** To form or give off bubbles. **2.** To move or flow with a gurgling sound. **3.** To rise to or as if to the surface; emerge. **4.** To display irrepressible activity or emotion. *— tr.* To cause to form bubbles. [< ME *bubelen,* to bubble.]
bubble and squeak *n. Chiefly British.* Cabbage and potatoes fried together. [Imit. of the sounds made as it cooks.]
bubble bath *n.* **1.** A perfumed preparation added to bath water to make it foam. **2.** A bath containing such a preparation.
bubble chamber *n.* An apparatus in which the movement and collision of ionizing particles is seen as trails of gas bubbles that form as the particles move through a superheated liquid.
bubble gum *n.* Chewing gum that can be blown into bubbles.
bubble memory *n. Comp. Sci.* A memory in which binary digits are represented by the alignment of magnetic bubbles.
bub•bler (bŭb′lər) *n. Northern U.S.* A drinking fountain.
bubble top *n.* A transparent, often bulletproof enclosure forming the top of an automobile.
bub•bly (bŭb′lē) *adj.* **1.** Full of or producing bubbles. **2.** Resembling bubbles. **3.** Full of high spirits; effervescent. *— n., pl.* **-blies.** *Informal.* Champagne.
Bu•ber (bo͞o′bər), **Martin.** 1878–1965. Austrian-born Judaic scholar and philosopher who wrote *I and Thou* (1923).
bu•bo (bo͞o′bō, byo͞o′-) *n., pl.* **-boes.** An inflamed tender swelling of a lymph node, esp. of the armpit or groin, that is characteristic of certain infections such as plague. [ME < LLat. *bubō, bubōn-* < Gk. *boubōn.*]
bu•bon•ic plague (bo͞o-bŏn′ĭk, byo͞o-) *n.* A contagious, often fatal epidemic disease caused by the bacterium *Yersinia pestis,* transmitted from person to person or by the bite of fleas from an infected host, esp. a rat, and characterized by chills, fever, vomiting, diarrhea, and the formation of buboes.
bu•bon•o•cele (bo͞o-bŏn′ə-sēl′, byo͞o-) *n.* A partial hernia of the groin, characterized by swelling in the groin area. [Gk. *boubōnokēlē: boubōn,* groin + *kēlē,* rupture.]
Bu•ca•ra•man•ga (bo͞o′kə-rə-mäng′gə, -kä-rä-mäng′gä). A city of N-central Colombia in the Cordillera Oriental of the Andes; founded 1622. Pop. 342,169.
buc•cal (bŭk′əl) *adj.* Of or relating to the cheeks or the mouth cavity. [< Lat. *bucca,* cheek.]
buc•ca•neer (bŭk′ə-nîr′) *n.* **1.** A pirate, esp. one who preyed on Spanish shipping in the West Indies during the 17th century. **2.** A ruthless speculator or adventurer. [Fr. *boucanier* < *boucaner,* to cure meat < *boucan,* barbecue frame, poss. of Arawakan orig. or < Tupinamba (a Tupian language) *bocan,* rack.] **— buc′ca•neer′** *v.*
Bu•ceph•a•lus (byo͞o-sĕf′ə-ləs) *n.* Alexander the Great's war horse.
Buch•an (bŭk′ən, bŭKH′-), Sir **John.** 1st Baron Tweedsmuir. 1875–1940. Scottish writer and politician whose adventure novels include *The Thirty-Nine Steps* (1915).
Bu•chan•an (byo͞o-kăn′ən, bə-), **James.** 1791–1868. The 15th President of the U.S. (1857–61).
Bu•cha•rest (bo͞o′kə-rĕst′, byo͞o′-). The cap. of Romania, in the SE part on a tributary of the Danube R.; founded in the 14th cent. Pop. 1,995,156.
Bu•chen•wald (bo͞o′kən-wôld′, -KHən-vält′). A village of central Germany near Weimar; site of a Nazi concentration camp during World War II.
Buch•ner (bo͝ok′nər, bo͝oKH′-), **Eduard.** 1860–1917. German chemist who won a 1907 Nobel Prize.

Brussels sprouts
Brassica oleracea var. *gemmifera*

James Buchanan

ă pat	oi boy
ā pay	ou out
âr care	o͝o took
ä father	o͞o boot
ĕ pet	ŭ cut
ē be	ûr urge
ĭ pit	th thin
ī pie	*th* this
îr pier	hw which
ŏ pot	zh vision
ō toe	ə about, item
ô paw	

Stress marks:
′ (primary);
′ (secondary), as in
dictionary (dĭk′shə-nĕr′ē)

buck[1] (bŭk) *n.* **1.a.** The adult male of some animals, such as the deer, antelope, or rabbit. **b.** Antelope considered as a group. **2.a.** A robust or high-spirited young man. **b.** A fop. **3.** *Offensive.* Used as a disparaging term for a Native American or Black man. **4.** An act or instance of bucking. **5.a.** Buckskin. **b. bucks.** Buckskin breeches or shoes. — *v.* **bucked, buck•ing, bucks.** — *intr.* **1.** To leap upward arching the back. **2.** To charge with the head lowered; butt. **3.** To make sudden jerky movements; jolt. **4.** To resist stubbornly and obstinately; balk. **5.** *Informal.* To strive with determination. — *tr.* **1.** To throw or toss by bucking: *buck off a rider.* **2.** To oppose directly and stubbornly; go against. **3.** *Football.* To charge into (an opponent's line) carrying the ball. **4.** *Archaic.* To butt against with the head. — *adj.* Of the lowest rank in a specified military category. — ***phrasal verb.* buck up.** To summon one's courage or spirits; hearten. [ME *bukke* < OE *buc,* male deer, and *bucca,* male goat.] — **buck′er** *n.*

buck[2] (bŭk) *n.* **1.** A sawhorse or sawbuck. **2.** A leather-covered frame used for gymnastic vaulting. [Alteration (influenced by BUCK[1]) of Du. *bok,* male goat, trestle < MDu. *boc.*]

buck[3] (bŭk) *n. Informal.* **1.** A dollar. **2.** An amount of money. [Short for BUCKSKIN (from its use in trade).]

buck[4] (bŭk) *n. Games.* A counter or marker formerly passed from one poker player to another to indicate an obligation, esp. one's turn to deal. — ***idiom.* the buck stops here.** *Slang.* The ultimate responsibility rests here. [Short for *buckhorn knife* (from its use as a marker in poker).]

Buck (bŭk), **Pearl Sydenstricker.** 1892–1973. Amer. writer who won the 1938 Nobel Prize for literature.

buck•a•roo also **buck•er•oo** (bŭk′ə-ro͞o′) *n., pl.* **-roos** also **-oos.** *Chiefly California.* See **cowboy** 1. [Alteration (perh. influenced by BUCK[1]) of Sp. *vaquero* < *vaca,* cow < Lat. *vacca.*]

buck•bean (bŭk′bēn′) *n.* A perennial herb *(Menyanthes trifoliata)* of the Northern Hemisphere having trifoliate leaves and white, pink, or purplish flowers. [Transl. of Flem. *bocks boonen,* goat's beans : *bocks,* goat's + *boonen,* beans.]

buckboard
Adirondack buckboard

buck•board (bŭk′bôrd′, -bōrd′) *n.* A four-wheeled open carriage with the seat or seats attached to a flexible board running between the front and rear axles. [Obsolete *buck,* body of a wagon (< ME *bouk,* belly < OE *būc*) + BOARD.]

buck•er•oo (bŭk′ə-ro͞o′) *n. Chiefly California.* Var. of **buckaroo.**

buck•et (bŭk′ĭt) *n.* **1.a.** A cylindrical vessel used for holding or carrying liquids or solids; a pail. **b.** The amount that a bucket can hold. **2.** A unit of dry measure in the U.S. Customary System equal to 2 pecks (17.6 liters). See table at **measurement. 3.** A receptacle on various machines, such as the scoop of a power shovel, used to gather and convey material. **4.** *Basketball.* A basket. — *v.* **-et•ed, -et•ing, -ets.** — *tr.* **1.** To hold, carry, or put in a bucket. **2.** To ride (a horse) long and hard. — *intr.* **1.** To move or proceed rapidly and jerkily. **2.** To make haste; hustle. — ***idiom.* a drop in the bucket.** An insufficient or inconsequential amount in comparison with what is required. [ME < OFr. *buket,* of Gmc. orig.]

bucket brigade *n.* A line of people formed to fight a fire by passing buckets of water from a source to the fire.

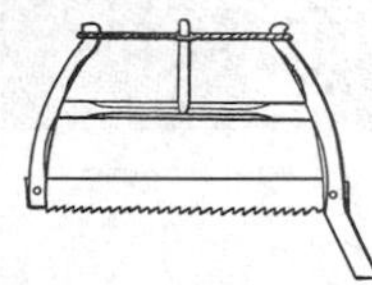
bucksaw

bucket seat *n.* A single, usu. low seat with a contoured back, typically used in some automobiles.

bucket shop *n.* A fraudulent brokerage operation in which orders to buy and sell are accepted but no executions take place. [< *bucket shop,* a saloon selling small amounts of liquor in buckets.]

buck•eye (bŭk′ī′) *n.* **1.** Any of various North American poisonous trees or shrubs of the genus *Aesculus,* having palmately compound opposite leaves and large shiny seeds. **2.** The fruit of any of these plants. **3.** The brown seed of such a fruit. [BUCK[1] + EYE.]

buck•hound (bŭk′hound′) *n.* A hound used for coursing deer.

Buck•ing•ham (bŭk′ĭng-əm, -hăm′), 1st Duke of. Orig. George Villiers. 1592–1628. English courtier and politician whose military and political policies caused continual friction with Parliament.

Buckingham, 2nd Duke of. Orig. George Villiers. 1628–87. English courtier who was a prominent member of the group known as the Cabal that formed the ministry of Charles II after the Restoration.

Buddha[1]
Sandstone carved Buddha, Yungang, China

buck•le (bŭk′əl) *n.* **1.** A clasp for fastening two ends, as of a belt, in which a device attached to one of the ends is fitted or coupled to the other. **2.** An ornament that resembles a buckle, such as a metal square on a hat. **3.** An instance of bending, warping, or crumpling; a bend or bulge. — *v.* **-led, -ling, -les.** — *tr.* **1.** To fasten with a buckle. **2.** To cause to bend, warp, or crumple. — *intr.* **1.** To become fastened with a buckle. **2.** To bend, warp, or crumple, as under pressure. **3.** To give way; collapse. **4.** To succumb, as to exhaustion or authority; give in. — ***phrasal verbs.* buckle down.** To apply oneself with determination. **buckle up.** To use a safety belt, esp. in an automobile. [ME *bokel* < OFr. *boucle* < Lat. *buccula,* cheek strap of a helmet, dim. of *bucca,* cheek.]

buck•ler (bŭk′lər) *n.* **1.** A small, round shield either carried or worn on the arm. **2.** A means of protection; a defense. — *tr.v.* **-lered, -ler•ing, -lers.** To shield; protect. [ME *bokeler* < OFr. *bouclier* < *boucle,* boss on a shield < Lat. *buccula,* dim. of *bucca,* cheek.]

buck•na•ked (bŭk′nĕk′ĭd) *adv. & adj. Chiefly Southern U.S.* Bare-naked. [?]

buck•o (bŭk′ō) *n., pl.* **-oes. 1.** A blustering or bossy person. **2.** *Irish.* A young man; a lad. [Alteration of BUCK[1].]

buck•ram (bŭk′rəm) *n.* **1.** A coarse cotton fabric heavily sized with glue, used for stiffening garments and in bookbinding. **2.** *Archaic.* Rigid formality. — *tr.v.* **-ramed, -ram•ing, -rams.** To stiffen with or as if with buckram. [ME *bukeram,* fine linen < OFr. *boquerantand* < OItal. *bucherame,* both after BUKHARA, from which fine linen was once imported.]

buck•saw (bŭk′sô′) *n.* A woodcutting saw, usu. set in an H-shaped frame. [< BUCK[2].]

buck•shee (bŭk′shē) *Chiefly British.* — *n.* **1.** Something extra or left over that is obtained free. **2.** An extra ration. — *adj.* **1.** Free of charge; gratis. **2.** Unsolicited; gratuitous. [Var. of BAKSHEESH.]

buck•shot (bŭk′shŏt′) *n.* A large lead shot for shotgun shells, used esp. in hunting big game.

buck•skin (bŭk′skĭn′) *n.* **1.a.** The skin of a male deer. **b.** A soft, grayish-yellow leather usu. having a suede finish. **2. buckskins.** Clothing, esp. breeches or shoes, made from buckskin. **3.** A person who wears buckskins. **4.** A grayish-yellow horse. — **buck′skin′** *adj.*

buck•thorn (bŭk′thôrn′) *n.* Any of various shrubs or small trees of the genus *Rhamnus,* including ornamentals and medicinal species. [Transl. of NLat. *cervī spīna*: *cervī,* genitive of *cervus,* buck + *spīna,* thorn.]

buck•tooth (bŭk′to͞oth′) *n.* A projecting upper front tooth. [BUCK[1] + TOOTH.] — **buck′toothed′** (-to͞otht′) *adj.*

buck•wheat (bŭk′hwēt′, -wēt′) *n.* **1.a.** An annual Asian plant *(Fagopyrum esculentum)* having small, seedlike triangular fruits. **b.** The edible fruits of this plant, used whole or ground into flour. **2.** Any of several similar or related plants. [Prob. partial transl. of MDu. *boecweite*: *boek,* beech; see **bhāgo-*** + *weite,* wheat.]

bu•col•ic (byo͞o-kŏl′ĭk) *adj.* **1.** Of or characteristic of the countryside or its people; rustic. **2.** Of or characteristic of shepherds or flocks; pastoral. — *n.* **1.** A pastoral poem. **2.** A farmer or shepherd; a rustic. [Lat. *būcolicus,* pastoral < Gk. *boukolikos* < *boukolos,* cowherd : *bous,* cow; see **gʷou-*** + *-kolos,* herdsman; see **kʷel-[1]***.] — **bu•col′i•cal•ly** *adv.*

Bu•co•vi•na (bo͞o′kə-vē′nə). See **Bukovina.**

bud[1] (bŭd) *n.* **1.** *Bot.* **a.** A small protuberance on a stem or branch, containing an undeveloped shoot, leaf, or flower. **b.** The stage or condition of having buds. **2.** *Biol.* **a.** An asexual reproductive structure, as in yeast, that consists of an outgrowth capable of developing into a new individual. **b.** A small rounded organic part, such as a taste bud, that resembles a plant bud. **3.** A person or thing that is not yet fully developed. — *v.* **bud•ded, bud•ding, buds.** — *intr.* **1.** To put forth or produce buds. **2.** To develop or grow from or as if from a bud. **3.** To be in an undeveloped stage or condition. **4.** To reproduce asexually by forming a bud. — *tr.* **1.** To cause to put forth buds. **2.** To graft a bud onto (a plant). [ME *budde.*] — **bud′der** *n.*

bud[2] (bŭd) *n. Informal.* Friend; chum. Used as a form of familiar address for a man or boy. [Short for BUDDY.]

Bu•da•pest (bo͞o′də-pĕst′, -pĕsht′). The cap. of Hungary, in the N-central part on the Danube R.; formed (1873) by the union of Buda on the right bank of the river with Pest on the left bank. Pop. 2,071,484.

Bud•dha[1] (bo͞o′də, bo͝od′ə). Orig. Siddhartha Gautama. 563?–483? B.C. Indian mystic and founder of Buddhism who began preaching after achieving supreme enlightenment at the age of 35.

Bud•dha[2] (bo͞o′də, bo͝od′ə) *n.* **1.** One who has achieved a state of perfect spiritual enlightenment in accordance with the teachings of Buddha. **2.** A representation or likeness of Buddha. [Skt. *buddha-,* enlightened, p.part. of *bodhati,* he awakes. See **bheudh-***.]

Bud•dhism (bo͞o′dĭz′əm, bo͝od′ĭz′-) *n.* **1.** The teaching of Buddha that life is permeated with suffering caused by desire, that suffering ceases when desire ceases, and that enlightenment obtained through meditation releases one from desire, suffering, and rebirth. **2.** The religion of the many groups that profess varying forms of this doctrine and that venerate Buddha. — **Bud′dhist** *adj. & n.* — **Bud•dhis′tic** *adj.*

bud•dle (bŭd′l) *n.* An inclined trough in which crushed ore is washed. [Prob. < LGer. *buddeln,* to agitate.]

bud•dle•ia (bŭd′lē-ə, bŭd-lē′ə) *n.* See **butterfly bush.** [NLat., after Adam *Buddle* (d. 1715), British botanist.]

bud•dy (bŭd′ē) *Informal.* — *n., pl.* **-dies. 1.** A good friend. **2.** A partner, esp. one of a pair or team associated under the buddy system. **3.** Friend or comrade; chum. Used as a form of familiar address, esp. for a man or boy. — *intr.v.* **-died, -dy•ing, -dies.** To associate as a buddy or buddies. — ***phrasal verb.* buddy up.** To ingratiate oneself, as by presuming friendship: *buddied up to the coach.* [Prob. alteration of BROTHER.]

bud•dy-bud•dy (bŭd′ē-bŭd′ē) *adj. Informal.* Showing or marked by great outward friendship.

buddy system *n.* An arrangement in which persons are paired, as for mutual safety or assistance.

budge[1] (bŭj) *v.* **budged, budg•ing, budg•es.** —*intr.* **1.** To move or stir slightly. **2.** To alter a position or attitude. —*tr.* **1.** To cause to move slightly. **2.** To cause to alter a position or attitude. [OFr. *bouger* < VLat. **bullicāre*, to bubble < Lat. *bullīre*, to boil.]

budge[2] (bŭj) *n.* Fur made from lambskin dressed with the wool outside, formerly used to trim academic robes. —*adj. Archaic.* Overformal; pompous. [ME *bouge* < AN < Med.Lat. *bugia*, prob. < Lat. *bulga*, leather bag. See BUDGET.]

budg•er•i•gar (bŭj′ə-rē-gär′, bŭj′ə-rē′-) *n.* A parakeet *(Melopsittacus undulatus)* of Australia having green, yellow, or blue plumage. [Yuwaalaraay (Aboriginal language of SE Australia) *gijirrigaa*.]

budg•et (bŭj′ĭt) *n.* **1.a.** An itemized summary of expenditures for a given period along with proposals for financing them. **b.** A plan for the expenditure of a usu. fixed resource, such as money or time, during a given period. **c.** The total sum of money allocated for a particular purpose or period of time. **2.** A stock or collection with definite limits. —*v.* **-et•ed, -et•ing, -ets.** —*tr.* **1.** To plan in advance the expenditure of. **2.** To enter or account for in a budget. —*intr.* To make or use a budget. —*adj.* **1.** Of or relating to a budget: *budget items.* **2.** Appropriate to a budget; inexpensive: *budget meals.* [ME *bouget*, wallet < OFr. *bougette*, dim. of *bouge*, leather bag < Lat. *bulga*, of Celt. orig. See **bhelgh-***.] —**budg′et•ar′y** (bŭj′ĭ-tĕr′ē) *adj.* —**budg′et•er, budg′et•eer′** (-ĭ-tîr′) *n.*

budg•ie (bŭj′ē) *n. Informal.* A budgerigar.

bud•worm (bŭd′wûrm′) *n.* A larva of several tortricid moths, esp. the spruce budworm, that devours plant buds.

Bue•na Park (bwā′nə). A city of S CA WNW of Anaheim. Pop. 68,784.

Bue•na•ven•tu•ra (bwā′nə-vĕn-to͝or′ə, -tyo͝or′ə, bwĕ′nä-vĕn-to͞o′rä). A city of W Colombia on **Buenaventura Bay**, an inlet of the Pacific. Pop. 157,528.

Bue•na Vis•ta (bwā′nə vĭs′tə, bwĕ′nä vēs′tä). A locality in N Mexico just S of Saltillo; site of a U.S. victory (1847) in the Mexican War.

Bue•nos Ai•res (bwā′nəs âr′ēz, ī′rĭz, bwĕ′nôs ī′rĕs). The cap. of Argentina, in the E part on the Río de la Plata; founded 1536. Pop. 2,922,829.

buff[1] (bŭf) *n.* **1.** A soft, thick, undyed leather made chiefly from the skins of buffalo, elk, or oxen. **2.** A military uniform coat made of such leather. **3.** *Color.* A pale, light, or moderate yellowish pink to yellow, including moderate orange yellow to light yellowish brown. **4.** *Informal.* Bare skin. **5.** A piece of soft material, such as leather, often mounted on a block and used for polishing. —*adj.* **1.** Made or formed of buff. **2.** *Color.* Of the color buff. —*tr.v.* **buffed, buff•ing, buffs. 1.** To polish or shine with a piece of soft material. **2.** To soften the surface of (leather) by raising a nap. **3.** To make the color of buff. [< obsolete *buffle*, buffalo < Fr. *buffle* < Ital. *bufalo*. See BUFFALO.]

buff[2] (bŭf) *n. Informal.* One that is enthusiastic and knowledgeable about a subject: *a Civil War buff.* [From the buff-colored uniform worn by New York volunteer firemen around 1920, originally applied to an enthusiast of fires.]

buf•fa•lo (bŭf′ə-lō′) *n., pl.* **buffalo** or **-loes** or **-los. 1.a.** Any of several oxlike Old World mammals of the family Bovidae, such as the water buffalo and Cape buffalo. **b.** The North American bison, *Bison bison.* **2.** The buffalo fish. —*tr.v.* **-loed, -lo•ing, -loes. 1.** To intimidate. **2.** To deceive; hoodwink. **3.** To confuse; bewilder. [Ital. *bufalo*or Port. or Sp. *búfalo* < LLat. *būfalus* < Lat. *būbalus* < Gk. *boubalos.*]

Word History: The buffalo is so closely associated with the Wild West that it would seem natural to assume that its name comes from a Native American word. In fact, however, *buffalo* can probably be traced back by way of one or more of the Romance languages through Latin ultimately to the Greek word *boubalos,* meaning "an antelope or a buffalo." The buffalo referred to by the Greek and Latin words was, of course, an Old World mammal, such as the water buffalo of southern Asia. Applied to the North American mammal, *buffalo* is in fact a misnomer, *bison* being the preferred scientific term. As far as everyday usage is concerned, however, *buffalo,* first recorded for the American mammal in 1635, is older than *bison,* first recorded in 1774.

Buf•fa•lo (bŭf′ə-lō′). A city of W NY at the E end of Lake Erie on the Canadian border. Pop. 328,123.

buffalo berry *n.* **1.** Any of three North American shrubs or small trees of the genus *Shepherdia*, having yellowish flowers, drupelike fruits, and silvery foliage. **2.** The berry of any of these plants.

Buffalo Bill (bĭl). See William Frederick **Cody.**

buffalo bug *n.* See **carpet beetle.**

buffalo fish *n.* Any of several suckers of the genus *Ictiobus,* mostly of the Mississippi Valley and having a humped back.

buffalo gnat *n.* See **black fly.**

buffalo grass *n.* A perennial grass *(Buchloe dactyloides)* of central North America, used for grazing and sometimes for lawns.

Buffalo Grove. A village of NE IL, a suburb of Chicago. Pop. 36,427.

buffalo robe *n.* The dressed skin of the North American bison, used as a lap robe, cape, or blanket.

Buffalo wings *pl.n.* Fried chicken wings served with hot sauce and blue cheese dressing. [After BUFFALO, where they were first served.]

buff•er[1] (bŭf′ər) *n.* **1.** One that buffs, esp. a piece of soft leather or cloth used to shine or polish. **2.** A buffing wheel.

buff•er[2] (bŭf′ər) *n.* **1.** Something that lessens or absorbs the shock of an impact. **2.** One that protects by intercepting or moderating adverse pressures or influences. **3.** Something that separates potentially antagonistic entities. **4.** *Chem.* A substance that minimizes change in the acidity of a solution when an acid or base is added to the solution. **5.** *Comp. Sci.* A device or area used to store data temporarily and deliver it at a rate different from that at which it was received. —*tr.v.* **-ered, -er•ing, -ers. 1.** To act as a buffer for or between. **2.** *Chem.* To treat (a solution) with a buffer. [Perh. < *buff*, blow, buffet < ME *buffe*, short for *buffet* < OFr. See BUFFET[2].]

buffer state *n.* A neutral state between two rival or potentially hostile states that serves to prevent conflict.

buffer zone *n.* A neutral area between hostile or belligerent forces that serves to prevent conflict.

buf•fet[1] (bə-fā′, bo͞o-) *n.* **1.** A large sideboard with drawers and cupboards. **2.a.** A counter or table from which meals or refreshments are served. **b.** A restaurant having such a counter. **3.** A meal at which guests serve themselves from various dishes on a table or sideboard. —*adj.* Informally served. [Fr.]

buf•fet[2] (bŭf′ĭt) *n.* A blow or cuff with or as if with the hand. —*v.* **-fet•ed, -fet•ing, -fets.** —*tr.* **1.** To hit or beat, esp. repeatedly. **2.** To strike against forcefully; batter. **3.** To drive or force with or as if with repeated blows. **4.** To force (one's way) with difficulty. —*intr.* To buffet one's way. [ME < OFr., dim. of *buffe*, blow.] —**buf′fet•er** *n.*

buff•ing wheel (bŭf′ĭng) *n.* A wheel covered with a soft material, such as velvet, for shining and polishing metal.

buffing wheel

buf•fle•head (bŭf′əl-hĕd′) *n.* A small North American diving duck *(Bucephala albeola)* having black and white plumage and a densely feathered, rounded head. [Obsolete *buffle*, buffalo (< Fr. < LLat. *būfalus*; see BUFFALO) + HEAD.]

buf•fo (bo͞o′fō) *n., pl.* **-fi** (-fē) or **-fos.** *Mus.* A man who sings comic opera roles. [Ital. < *buffare*, to puff, of imit. orig.]

Buf•fon (bo͞o-fôɴ′), Comte **Georges Louis Leclerc de.** 1707–88. French naturalist noted for his monumental *Histoire Naturelle* (1749–88 and 1804).

buf•foon (bə-fo͞on′) *n.* **1.** A clown; a jester. **2.** A person given to clowning and joking. **3.** A ludicrous or bumbling person. [Fr. *bouffon* < OItal. *buffone* < *buffa*, jest < *buffare*, to puff, of imit. orig.] —**buf•foon′er•y** (bə-fo͞o′nə-rē) *n.*

bug (bŭg) *n.* **1.** A true bug. **2.** An insect or similar organism, such as a centipede or an earwig. **3.a.** A disease-producing microorganism: *a flu bug.* **b.** The illness or disease so produced. **4.a.** A defect or difficulty, as in a system or design. **b.** *Comp. Sci.* A defect in the code or routine of a program. **5.** An enthusiasm or obsession. **6.** An enthusiast or devotee; a buff. **7.** An electronic listening device used in surveillance. —*v.* **bugged, bug•ging, bugs.** —*intr.* To grow large; bulge: *My eyes bugged when I saw the mess.* —*tr.* **1.a.** To annoy; pester. **b.** To prey on; worry. **2.** To equip (a room, for example) with a concealed electronic listening device. **3.** To make (the eyes) bulge or grow large. —***phrasal verbs.*** **bug off.** *Slang.* To leave someone alone; go away. **bug out.** *Slang.* **1.** To leave or quit, usu. in a hurry. **2.** To avoid a responsibility or duty. Often used with *on* or *of.* —***idiom.*** **put a bug in (someone's) ear.** *Informal.* To impart useful information to (another) in a subtle, discreet way. [?] —**bug′ger** *n.*

Bug (bo͞og, bo͝ok). **1.** Also **Western Bug.** A river of E Europe rising in the SW Ukraine and flowing c. 772 km (480 mi) through Poland to the Vistula R. near Warsaw. **2.** Also **Southern Bug.** A river rising in the SW Ukraine and flowing c. 853 km (530 mi) to the Black Sea.

bug•a•boo (bŭg′ə-bo͞o′) *n., pl.* **-boos. 1.** An object of obsessive, usu. exaggerated fear or anxiety. **2.** A recurring or persistent problem. [Perh. of Celt. orig.]

Bu•gan•da (bo͞o-găn′də, byo͞o-). A region and former kingdom of E Africa on the N shore of Lake Victoria in present-day Uganda; a British protectorate (1900–62).

bug•bane (bŭg′bān′) *n.* Any of several plants of the genus *Cimicifuga* of northern temperate regions, including the black cohosh.

bug•bear (bŭg′bâr′) *n.* **1.** A bugaboo. **2.** A fearsome imaginary creature, esp. one evoked to frighten children. [Obsolete *bug*, hobgoblin (< ME *bugge*) + BEAR[2].]

bug-eyed (bŭg′īd′) *adj.* **1.** Having protruding eyes. **2.** Wide-eyed, as with astonishment or curiosity; agog.

bug•ger (bŭg′ər, bo͝og′-) *n.* **1.** *Vulgar.* A sodomite. **2.** A contemptible or disreputable person. **3.** A fellow; a chap. —*v.* **-gered, -ger•ing, -gers.** —*intr.* To practice sodomy. —*tr.* To practice sodomy with. [ME *bougre*, heretic < OFr. *boulgre* < Med.Lat. *Bulgarus.* See BULGAR.]

bug•ger•y (bŭg′ə-rē, bo͝og′-) *n. Vulgar.* Sodomy.

ă pat	oi boy
ā pay	ou out
âr care	o͝o took
ä father	o͞o boot
ĕ pet	ŭ cut
ē be	ûr urge
ĭ pit	th thin
ī pie	*th* this
îr pier	hw which
ŏ pot	zh vision
ō toe	ə about, item
ô paw	

Stress marks:
′ (primary);
′ (secondary), as in
dictionary (dĭk′shə-nĕr′ē)

bug•gy[1] (bŭg′ē) *n., pl.* **-gies. 1.** A small, light, one-horse carriage usu. having four wheels or two wheels. **2.** A baby carriage. **3.** *Informal.* An automobile. **4.** *Chiefly Southern U.S.* A shopping cart, esp. for groceries. [?]

bug•gy[2] (bŭg′ē) *adj.* **-gi•er, -gi•est. 1.** Infested with bugs. **2.** *Slang.* Crazy. **— bug′gi•ness** *n.*

bug•house (bŭg′hous′) *n. Slang.* A mental health facility. [Prob. < BUG, enthusiast.]

bug juice *n. Slang.* A sweet flavored drink that is usu. not carbonated. [After its unattractive color and flavor.]

bu•gle[1] (byo͞o′gəl) *n. Mus.* A brass wind instrument somewhat shorter than a trumpet and lacking keys or valves. *— intr.v.* **-gled, -gling, -gles. 1.** *Mus.* To sound a bugle. **2.** To give forth a deep prolonged sound similar to the bay of a hound. [ME < OFr. < Lat. *būculus*, steer, dim. of *bōs*, ox. See **gʷou-*.**] **— bu′gler** *n.*

bu•gle[2] (byo͞o′gəl) *n.* A tubular glass or plastic bead used to trim clothing. [?]

bu•gle[3] (byo͞o′gəl) *n.* Bugleweed.

bu•gle•weed (byo͞o′gəl-wēd′) *n.* Any of several herbs of the genera *Ajuga* and *Lycopus* in the mint family, having opposite leaves, square stems, and axillary clusters of flowers. [< ME *bugle* < OFr. < LLat. *būgula* (perh. influenced by *būglōssa*, bugloss; see BUGLOSS) < Lat. *būgillō*.]

bu•gloss (byo͞o′glôs′, -glŏs′) *n.* Any of several usu. hairy Old World plants, esp. in the genera *Anchusa, Brunnera,* and *Echium,* having blue or violet flowers. [ME *buglosse* < OFr. < LLat. *būglōssa* < Lat. *būglōssos* < Gk. *bouglōssos*: *bous*, ox; see **gʷou-*** + *glōssa*, tongue.]

Bulgaria

buhl also **boule** or **boulle** (bo͞ol) *n.* An inlay of tortoiseshell, ivory, and metal, used esp. in decorating furniture. [After André Charles *Boulle* (1642–1732), French woodcarver.]

buhr•stone also **burr•stone** (bûr′stōn′) *n.* A tough silicified limestone once used for millstones. [Var. of BURR[1] + STONE.]

build (bĭld) *v.* **built** (bĭlt), **build•ing, builds.** *— tr.* **1.** To form by combining materials or parts; construct. **2.** To order, finance, or supervise the construction of. **3.** To develop or give form to according to a plan or process; create: *build a nation.* **4.** To increase or strengthen by adding gradually to: *build support.* **5.** To establish a basis for; found or ground: *build an argument.* *— intr.* **1.** To make something by combining materials or parts. **2.** To engage in the construction or design of buildings. **3.** To develop in magnitude or extent: *clouds building.* **4.** To progress toward a maximum, as of intensity: *suspense building.* *— n.* The physical makeup of a person or thing: *an athletic build.* See Syns at **physique.** *— phrasal verbs.* **build in (or into).** To construct or include as an integral part of. **build on (or upon).** To use as a basis or foundation. **build up. 1.** To develop or increase in stages or by degrees. **2.** To accumulate or collect. **3.** To bolster: *built up my hopes.* **4.** To fill up (an area) with buildings. [ME *bilden* < OE *byldan*. See **bheuə-*.**] **— build′a•ble** *adj.*

bull[1]
Longhorn bull

build•down also **build-down** (bĭld′doun′) *n.* A systematic numerical reduction, esp. of nuclear weapons, in which more than one weapon or warhead is destroyed for every new one built. [On the model of BUILDUP.] **— build′-down′** *adj.*

build•er (bĭl′dər) *n.* **1.** One that builds, esp. a person who contracts for and supervises the construction of a building. **2.** An abrasive or filler used in a soap or detergent.

build•ing (bĭl′dĭng) *n.* **1.** Something that is built, as for human habitation; a structure. **2.** The act, process, art, or occupation of constructing.

build•up also **build-up** (bĭld′ŭp′) *n.* **1.** The act or process of amassing or increasing: *a buildup of tension.* **2.** The result of building up. **3.a.** Widely favorable publicity, esp. by a systematic campaign. **b.** Extravagant praise.

built (bĭlt) *v.* P.t. and p.part. of **build.** *— adj.* **1.** Having a specified physique: *a heavily built boxer.* **2.** *Informal.* Having a well-developed or attractive body.

built-in (bĭlt′ĭn′) *adj.* **1.** Constructed as part of a larger unit; not detachable: *a built-in cabinet.* **2.** Forming a permanent or essential element or quality. **— built′-in′** *n.*

built-up (bĭlt′ŭp′) *adj.* **1.** Made by fastening several layers or sections one on top of the other: *a built-up roof.* **2.** Filled with buildings; developed: *a built-up neighborhood.*

Buis•son (bwē-sôɴ′), **Ferdinand Edouard.** 1841–1932. French educator who shared the 1927 Nobel Peace Prize.

Bu•jum•bu•ra (bo͞o′jəm-bo͝or′ə). The cap. of Burundi, in the W part on Lake Tanganyika. Pop. 229,980.

Bu•kha•ra (bo͞o-kär′ə, -här′ə, -KHÄ′rə) also **Bo•kha•ra** (bō-). A city of S Uzbekistan W of Samarkand; cap. of the former emirate of **Bukhara** from the 16th to the 19th cent. Pop. 209,000.

Bu•kha•rin (bo͞o-kär′ĭn, -KHär′-), **Nikolai Ivanovich.** 1888–1938. Bolshevik revolutionary and Soviet politician who advocated gradual agricultural collectivization.

Bu•ko•vi•na also **Bu•co•vi•na** (bo͞o′kə-vē′nə). A historical region of E Europe in W Ukraine and NE Romania.

bul. *abbr.* Bulletin.

Bu•la•wa•yo (bo͞o′lə-wā′yō, -wä′-). A city of SW Zimbabwe near the Botswana border; founded 1893. Pop. 413,814.

bulldozer

bulb (bŭlb) *n.* **1.** *Bot.* **a.** A short, modified underground stem surrounded by usu. fleshy modified leaves that contain stored food for the shoot within. **b.** A similar underground stem or root, such as a corm or rhizome. **c.** A plant that grows from a bulb. **2.** A rounded projection or part: *the bulb of a syringe.* **3.** An incandescent lamp or its glass housing. **4.** *Anat.* A rounded dilation or expansion of a canal, vessel, or organ. [Lat. *bulbus* < Gk. *bolbos*, bulbous plant.]

bul•bar (bŭl′bər, -bär′) *adj.* Of, relating to, or characteristic of a bulb, esp. of the medulla oblongata: *bulbar poliomyelitis.*

bul•bel (bŭl′bəl, -bĕl′) *n.* **1.** A smaller bulb produced from a larger bulb. **2.** A bulblet. [Fr. *bulbille*. See BULBIL.]

bul•bif•er•ous (bŭl-bĭf′ər-əs) *adj.* Bearing or producing bulbs or bulbils.

bul•bil (bŭl′bəl, -bĭl′) *n.* **1.** A small bulb or bulblike structure in the place of a flower or in a leaf axil. **2.** A bulblet. [Fr. *bulbille*, dim. of *bulbe*, bulb < Lat. *bulbus*. See BULB.]

bulb•let (bŭlb′lĭt) *n.* A small bulb.

bul•bo•u•re•thral gland (bŭl′bō-yo͞o-rē′thrəl) *n. Anat.* Either of two small glands below the prostate that discharge a component of the seminal fluid into the urethra. [BULBO(US) + URETHRAL + GLAND[1].]

bul•bous (bŭl′bəs) *adj.* **1.** Resembling a bulb in shape; rounded or swollen: *a bulbous stem base.* **2.** *Bot.* Bearing bulbs or growing from a bulb. **— bul′bous•ly** *adv.*

bul•bul (bo͝ol′bo͝ol′) *n.* **1.** Any of various passerine, chiefly tropical Old World songbirds of the family Pycnonotidae, having grayish or brownish plumage. **2.** A songbird mentioned in Persian poetry and thought to be a nightingale. [Pers. < Ar.]

Bul•finch (bo͝ol′fĭnch′), **Charles.** 1763–1844. Amer. architect who completed work on the U.S. Capitol (1830).

Bulfinch, Thomas. 1796–1867. Amer. writer best known for his books popularizing mythology.

Bulg. *abbr.* Bulgaria; Bulgarian.

Bul•ga•nin (bo͝ol-găn′ĭn, -gä′nyĭn), **Nikolai Aleksandrovich.** 1895–1975. Soviet politician who was premier from 1955 to 1958.

Bul•gar (bŭl′gär′, bo͝ol′-) *n.* See **Bulgarian** 1. [Med.Lat. *Bulgarus* < Gk. *Boulgaros* < Turkic *bulghar*, of mixed origin, promiscuous < *bulgamaq*, to mix.]

Bul•gar•i•a (bŭl-gâr′ē-ə, bo͝ol-). A country of SE Europe on the Black Sea; settled in the 6th cent. A.D. by Slavic tribes. Cap. Sofia. Pop. 8,960,679.

Bul•gar•i•an (bŭl-gâr′ē-ən, bo͝ol-) *adj.* Of or relating to Bulgaria or its people, language, or culture. *— n.* **1.** A native or inhabitant of Bulgaria. **2.** The Slavic language of the Bulgarians.

bulge (bŭlj) *n.* **1.** A protruding part; an outward curve or swelling. **2.** A sudden, usu. temporary increase in number or quantity: *a bulge in school enrollment.* **3.** An advantage. *— v.* **bulged, bulg•ing, bulg•es.** *— tr.* To cause to curve outward. *— intr.* **1.** To curve outward. **2.** To swell up. **3.** To stick out; protrude. [ME, pouch < OFr. *bulge, bouge* < Lat. *bulga*, bag, of Celt. orig. See **bhelgh-*.**] **— bulg′i•ness** *n.* **— bulg′y** *adj.*

bul•gur also **bul•ghur** (bo͝ol-go͝or′, bŭl′gər) *n.* Cracked wheat grains, often used in Middle Eastern dishes. [Ottoman Turk. *bulghūr*.]

bu•lim•a•rex•i•a (byo͞o-lĭm′ə-rĕk′sē-ə, -lē′mə-, bo͞o-) *n.* An eating disorder characterized by excessive food intake followed by fasting and self-induced vomiting or diarrhea. [BULIM(IA) + (AN)OREXIA.]

bu•lim•i•a (byo͞o-lĭm′ē-ə, -lē′mē-ə, bo͞o-) *n.* **1.** Insatiable appetite. **2.** An eating disorder characterized by episodic uncontrolled binge eating. [NLat. < Gk. *boulimia*: *bous*, ox; see **gʷou-*** + *limos*, hunger.] **— bu•lim′ic** *adj. & n.*

bulimia ner•vo•sa (nûr-vō′sə) *n.* See **bulimarexia.** [NLat. : BULIMIA + *nervosa*, consisting of nerves.]

bulk (bŭlk) *n.* **1.** Size, mass, or volume, esp. when very large. **2.a.** A distinct mass or portion of matter, esp. a large one. **b.** The body of a human being, esp. when large. **3.** The major portion or greater part. **4.** See **fiber** 6. **5.** Thickness of paper or cardboard in relation to weight. **6.** *Naut.* A ship's cargo. *— v.* **bulked, bulk•ing, bulks.** *— intr.* **1.** To be or appear to be massive in terms of size, volume, or importance; loom. **2.** To grow or increase in size or importance. **3.** To cohere or form a mass: *Certain paper bulks well.* *— tr.* **1.** To cause to swell or expand. **2.** To cause to cohere or form a mass. *— adj.* Being large in mass, quantity, or volume: *a bulk mailing.* *— idiom.* **in bulk. 1.** Unpackaged; loose. **2.** In large numbers, amounts, or volume. [ME, perh. partly alteration of *bouk*, belly, trunk of the body (< OE *būc*) and partly < ON *bulki*, cargo, heap; see **bhel-**[2]*.]

bulk•head (bŭlk′hĕd′) *n.* **1.a.** *Naut.* One of the upright partitions dividing a ship into compartments and serving to add structural rigidity and prevent the spread of leakage or fire. **b.** A partition or wall serving a similar purpose in a vehicle, such as an aircraft. **2.** A wall or an embankment, as in a mine, that acts as a protective barrier. **3.** *Chiefly New England.* A horizontal or sloping structure providing access to a cellar stairway. [*bulk*, stall, partition (perh. of Scand. orig.) + HEAD.]

bulk•y (bŭl′kē) *adj.* **-i•er, -i•est. 1.** Having considerable bulk; massive. **2.** Of large size for its weight. **3.** Clumsy to manage;

unwieldy. — **bulk′i•ly** *adv.* — **bulk′i•ness** *n.*

bull[1] (bo͝ol) *n.* **1.a.** An adult male bovine mammal. **b.** The uncastrated adult male of domestic cattle. **c.** The male of certain other large animals, such as the alligator. **2.** An exceptionally large, strong, and aggressive person. **3.a.** An optimist, esp. regarding business conditions. **b.** A person who buys commodities or securities in anticipation of a rise in prices or who tries by speculative purchases to effect such a rise. **4.** *Slang.* A police officer or detective. **5.** *Vulgar.* Empty, foolish, or pretentious talk. — *v.* **bulled, bull•ing, bulls.** — *tr.* To push; force. — *intr.* To push ahead or through forcefully. — *adj.* **1.** Male. **2.** Large and strong like a bull. **3.** Characterized by rising prices. — ***idiom.*** **grab (or take) the bull by the horns.** To deal with a problem directly and resolutely. [ME *bule* < OE *bula*, prob. < ON *boli.* See **bhel-[2]***.]

bull[2] (bo͝ol) *n.* **1.** An official document issued by the pope and sealed with a bulla. **2.** The bulla with which such a document is sealed. [ME *bulle* < OFr. < Med.Lat. *bulla.* See BULLA.]

bull[3] (bo͝ol) *n.* A gross blunder in logical speech or expression. [?]

Bull (bo͝ol) *n.* See **Taurus.**

bull. *abbr.* Bulletin.

bul•la (bo͝ol′ə) *n., pl.* **bul•lae** (bo͝ol′ē). **1.** A round seal affixed to a papal bull. **2.** *Pathol.* A large blister or vesicle. [Med.Lat. < Lat., bubble, seal.]

bul•lace plum (bo͝ol′ĭs) *n.* See **damson** 1. [ME *bolas* < AN *bullace* < Med.Lat. *bolluca.*]

bul•late (bo͝ol′āt′, bŭl′-) *adj.* Having a puckered or blistered appearance: *bullate leaves.* [Lat. *bullātus* < *bulla*, bubble.]

bull•bait•ing (bo͝ol′bā′tĭng) *n.* The formerly popular sport of setting dogs to attack a chained bull, esp. its nose.

bull•bat (bo͝ol′băt′) *n.* See **nighthawk** 1a. [From its roaring sound in flight.]

bull•dog (bo͝ol′dôg′, -dŏg′) *n.* **1.** Any of a breed of short-haired dog characterized by a large head, strong square jaws with dewlaps, and a stocky body, originally bred for bullbaiting. **2.** A short-barreled large-caliber revolver or pistol. **3.** A heat-resistant material used to line puddling furnaces. **4.** *Chiefly British.* A proctor's assistant at Oxford University or Cambridge University. — *adj.* Stubborn. — *tr.v.* **-dogged, -dog•ging, -dogs.** *Western U.S.* To throw (a calf or steer) by seizing its horns and twisting its neck until the animal falls. — **bull′dog′ger** *n.*

bull•doze (bo͝ol′dōz′) *v.* **-dozed, -doz•ing, -doz•es.** — *tr.* **1.** To clear, dig up, or move with a bulldozer. **2.** To treat in an abusive manner; bully. **3.** To coerce in an unsympathetic or cruel way. **4.** To do away with; demolish. — *intr.* **1.** To operate a bulldozer. **2.** To proceed forcefully or insensitively. [Perh. alteration of obsolete *bulldose*, severe beating : BULL[1] + DOSE.]

bull•doz•er (bo͝ol′dō′zər) *n.* **1.** A heavy machine for clearing and grading land, usu. having continuous treads and a broad hydraulic blade in front. **2.** An overbearing person; a bully.

bul•let (bo͝ol′ĭt) *n.* **1.a.** A usu. metal projectile in the shape of a pointed cylinder or a ball that is expelled from a firearm, esp. a rifle or handgun. **b.** Such a projectile in a metal casing; a cartridge. **2.** An object resembling a projectile in shape, action, or effect. **3.** *Print.* A heavy dot (•) used to highlight a particular passage. [Fr. *boulette*, dim. of *boule*, ball < OFr. < Lat. *bulla.*]

bul•le•tin (bo͝ol′ĭ-tn, -tĭn) *n.* **1.** A brief report, esp. an official statement on a matter of public interest issued for immediate publication or broadcast. **2.** A brief update or summary of current news, as on television or in a newspaper. **3.** A periodical, esp. one published by an organization or society. **4.** A printed program, esp. one listing the order of worship for a religious service. — *tr.v.* **-tined, -tin•ing, -tins.** To inform by bulletin. [Fr., prob. < Ital. *bullettino*, dim. of *bolletta*, bill, dim. of *bolla*, bubble, bull < Med.Lat. *bulla.* See BULL[2].]

bulletin board *n.* **1.** A board on which notices are posted. **2.** *Comp. Sci.* A system that enables users to send or read messages that are of general public interest.

bul•let•proof (bo͝ol′ĭt-pro͞of′) *adj.* Impenetrable by bullets. — *tr.v.* **-proofed, -proof•ing, -proofs.** To make bulletproof.

bullet train *n.* A high-speed passenger train.

bull fiddle *n.* See **double bass.**

bull•fight (bo͝ol′fīt′) *n.* A public spectacle, esp. in Spain, Portugal, and parts of Latin America, in which a bull after being engaged in a series of traditional maneuvers is usu. killed. — **bull′fight′er** *n.* — **bull′fight′ing** *n.*

bull•finch (bo͝ol′fĭnch′) *n.* **1.** A European bird *(Pyrrhula pyrrhula)* having a short thick bill and in the male a red breast, blue-gray back, and black head, wings, and tail. **2.** Any of several similar finches.

bull•frog (bo͝ol′frôg′, -frŏg′) *n.* Any of several large frogs, chiefly of the genus *Rana* and esp. *R. catesbeiana*, native to North America and having a deep resonant croak.

bull•head (bo͝ol′hĕd′) *n.* **1.** Any of several large-headed North American freshwater catfishes of the genus *Ictalurus.* **2.** Any of several fishes of the family Cottidae, such as the sculpin and the miller's thumb. **3.** *Upper Northern U.S.* See **catfish.**

bull•head•ed (bo͝ol′hĕd′ĭd) *adj.* Foolishly or irrationally stubborn; headstrong. See Syns at **obstinate.** — **bull′head′ed•ly** *adv.* — **bull′head′ed•ness** *n.*

bull•horn (bo͝ol′hôrn′) *n.* A portable device consisting of a microphone and a loudspeaker, used esp. to amplify the voice.

Bul•lins (bo͝ol′ĭnz), **Ed.** b. 1935. Amer. writer whose works explore the Black experience.

bul•lion (bo͝ol′yən) *n.* **1.a.** Gold or silver considered with respect to quantity rather than value. **b.** Gold or silver in the form of bars, ingots, or plates. **2.** A heavy lace trimming made of twisted gold or silver threads. [ME, ingot of precious metal < AN < OFr. *billon* (< *bille*, stick; see BILLON) and < OFr. *bouillon*, bubble (< *boilir*, to boil; see BOIL[1]).]

bull•ish (bo͝ol′ĭsh) *adj.* **1.a.** Having a heavy muscular physique. **b.** Bullheaded. **2.a.** Causing, expecting, or characterized by rising stock market prices. **b.** Optimistic or confident. — **bull′ish•ly** *adv.* — **bull′ish•ness** *n.*

bull•mas•tiff (bo͝ol′măs′tĭf) *n.* A large, heavy-set, powerful dog of a breed developed from the bulldog and the mastiff.

Bull Moose Party *n.* See **Progressive Party** 1.

bull•necked (bo͝ol′nĕkt′) *adj.* Having a short thick neck.

bul•lock (bo͝ol′ək) *n.* **1.** A castrated bull; a steer. **2.** A young bull. [ME *bullok* < OE *bulluc.* See **bhel-[2]***.]

bul•lock's heart (bo͝ol′əks) *n.* See **custard apple.**

Bul•lock's oriole (bo͝ol′əks) *n.* A subspecies of the northern oriole in its western range, the male of which has orange cheeks and large white wing patches. [After William *Bullock*, 19th-cent. British naturalist.]

bull•pen (bo͝ol′pĕn′) *n.* **1.** A fenced enclosure for confining bulls. **2.** A place for the temporary detention of prisoners. **3.** *Baseball.* **a.** An area where relief pitchers warm up during a game. **b.** The relief pitchers of a team considered as a group.

bull•ring (bo͝ol′rĭng′) *n.* A circular arena for bullfights.

bull•roarer (bo͝ol′rôr′ər, -rōr′-) *n.* A small wooden slat attached to a string that makes a roaring noise when whirled.

Bull Run. A small stream of NE VA SW of Washington DC near Manassas; site of two important Civil War battles (Jul. 1861 and Aug. 1862).

bull session *n.* *Informal.* An informal group discussion.

bull's-eye or **bull's eye** (bo͝olz′ī′) *n.* **1.a.** The small central circle on a target. **b.** A shot that hits this circle. **2.a.** A direct hit: *scored a bull's-eye.* **b.** The precise accomplishment of a goal. **3.** A thick circular piece of glass set, as in a ship's deck, to admit light. **4.** A circular opening or window. **5.a.** A plano-convex lens used to concentrate light. **b.** A lantern or lamp having such a lens. **6.** A piece of round hard candy.

bull•shit (bo͝ol′shĭt′) *Obscene.* — *n.* Foolish or insolent talk; nonsense. — *v.* **-shit** also **-shat** (-shăt) or **-shit•ted** (-shĭt′ĭd), **-shit•ting, -shits.** — *intr.* **1.** To speak foolishly or insolently. **2.** To engage in idle conversation. — *tr.* To attempt to mislead or deceive by talking nonsense. — *interj.* Used to express extreme displeasure or exasperation. — **bull′shit′ter** *n.*

bull snake *n.* Any of several large, nonvenomous North American snakes of the genus *Pituophis*, having yellow and brown or black markings and feeding chiefly on rodents.

bull terrier *n.* Any of a breed of dog having a short, usu. white coat and a tapering muzzle, developed by crossing a bulldog with a now extinct breed of terrier.

bull thistle *n.* A biennial Eurasian thistle *(Cirsium vulgare)* in the composite family, having heads of purplish flowers and spiny stems and leaves. [From its large head.]

bull tongue *n.* A large detachable plowshare with a single blade, used chiefly for breaking or clearing heavy soil.

bull•whip (bo͝ol′hwĭp′, -wĭp′) *n.* A long plaited rawhide whip with a knotted end. — *tr.v.* **-whipped, -whip•ping, -whips.** To whip or beat with a bullwhip.

bul•ly[1] (bo͝ol′ē) *n., pl.* **-lies. 1.** A person who is habitually cruel or overbearing, esp. to smaller or weaker people. **2.** A hired ruffian; a thug. **3.** A pimp. **4.** *Archaic.* A fine person. **5.** *Archaic.* A sweetheart. — *v.* **-lied, -ly•ing, -lies.** — *tr.* **1.** To treat in an overbearing or intimidating manner. **2.** To make (one's way) aggressively. — *intr.* **1.** To behave like a bully. **2.** To force one's way aggressively or by intimidation. — *adj.* Excellent; splendid. — *interj.* Used to express approval: *Bully for you!* [Poss. < MDu. *boele*, sweetheart, prob. alteration of *broeder*, brother. See **bhrāter-***.]

bul•ly[2] (bo͝ol′ē) *n.* Canned or pickled beef. [Perh. Fr. *bouilli*, boiled meat, label on canned beef < p.part. of *bouillir*, to boil < OFr. *boilir.* See BOIL[1].]

bul•ly•boy (bo͝ol′ē-boi′) *n.* A hired thug or ruffian.

bul•ly•rag (bo͝ol′ē-răg′) also **bal•ly•rag** (băl′ē-) *tr.v.* **-ragged, -rag•ging, -rags.** To mistreat or intimidate by bullying. [< dial. *ballarag.*]

Bü•low (byo͞o′lō), Prince **Bernhard Heinrich Martin Karl von.** 1849–1929. German politician and diplomat who served as chancellor (1900–09).

bul•rush (bo͝ol′rŭsh′) *n.* **1.** Any of various aquatic or wetland herbs of the genus *Scirpus*, having grasslike leaves and usu. small, often brown spikelets. **2.** Any of several similar wetland plants, such as the papyrus. [ME *bulrish*: perh. alteration (influenced by *bule*, bull; see BULL[1]) of *bole*, stem; see BOLE[1] + *rish*, rush; see RUSH[2].]

bul•wark (bo͝ol′wərk, -wôrk′, bŭl′-) *n.* **1.** A wall or an em-

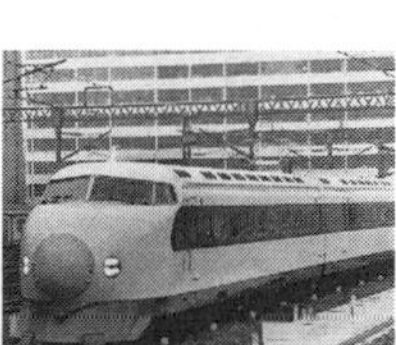

bullet train

bull terrier

ă pat	oi boy
ā pay	ou out
âr care	o͝o took
ä father	o͞o boot
ĕ pet	ŭ cut
ē be	ûr urge
ĭ pit	th thin
ī pie	*th* this
îr pier	hw which
ŏ pot	zh vision
ō toe	ə about,
ô paw	item

Stress marks:
′ (primary);
′ (secondary), as in
dictionary (dĭk′shə-nĕr′ē)

bankment raised as a defensive fortification; a rampart. **2.** Something serving as a defense or safeguard. **3.** A breakwater. **4.** *Naut.* The part of a ship's side that is above the upper deck. Often used in the plural. — *tr.v.* **-warked, -wark•ing, -warks. 1.** To fortify with a wall, an embankment, or a rampart. **2.** To provide defense or protection for. [ME *bulwerk* < MDu. *bolwerk* < MHGer. *bolwerc*: *bole*, plank; see **bhel-²*** + *werc*, work (< OHGer.; see **werg-***).]

Bul•wer (bo͝ol′wər), **William Henry Lytton Earle.** Baron Dalling and Bulwer. 1801–72. British politician and diplomat who negotiated the Clayton-Bulwer Treaty (1850).

Bul•wer-Lyt•ton (bo͝ol′wər-lĭt′n), **Edward George Earle Lytton.** 1st Baron Lytton. 1803–73. British writer known for his historical novels, esp. *The Last Days of Pompeii* (1834).

bum¹ (bŭm) *n.* **1.** A tramp; a vagrant. **2.** A lazy or shiftless person, esp. one who seeks to live solely by others' support. **3.** An incompetent, insignificant, or obnoxious person. **4.** One who is devoted to a particular activity or milieu. — *v.* **bummed, bum•ming, bums.** — *intr.* **1.** To live by begging and scavenging from place to place. Often used with *around.* **2.** To loaf. — *tr.* To acquire by begging; cadge. — *adj.* **1.** Inferior; worthless. **2.** Disabled; malfunctioning: *a bum shoulder.* **3.** Unfavorable or unfair. **4.** Unpleasant; lousy. — ***idiom.*** **on the bum. 1.** Living as a vagrant or a tramp. **2.** Out of order; broken. [Back-formation < BUMMER.]

bum² (bŭm) *n. Chiefly British.* The buttocks. [ME *bom.*]

bum•ber•shoot (bŭm′bər-sho͞ot′) *n.* An umbrella. [Alteration of UMBRELLA + alteration of (PARA)CHUTE.]

bum•ble¹ (bŭm′bəl) *v.* **-bled, -bling, -bles.** — *intr.* **1.** To speak in a faltering manner. **2.** To move or proceed clumsily. See Syns at **blunder.** — *tr.* To bungle; botch. [Perh. blend of BUNGLE and STUMBLE.]

bumblebee
Megabombus pennsylvanicus

bum•ble² (bŭm′bəl) *intr.v.* **-bled, -bling, -bles.** To make a humming or droning sound; buzz. — *n.* A humming or droning sound; a buzz. [ME *bomblen*, of imit. orig.]

bum•ble•bee (bŭm′bəl-bē′) *n.* Any of various large, hairy, social bees of the genus *Bombus* that nest underground. [BUMBLE² + BEE¹.]

bumf or **bumph** (bŭmf) *n. Chiefly British.* **1.** Printed matter, such as pamphlets or forms, esp. that deemed of little interest or importance. **2.** Toilet paper. [Short for *bum fodder.*]

bum•fuz•zle (bŭm′fŭz′əl) *tr.v.* **-zled, -zling, -zles.** *Chiefly Southern U.S.* To confuse. [Prob. *bum-* (prob. alteration of BAMBOOZLE) + *fuzzle* (perh. blend of FUDDLE (FUZZY).]

bum•ma•lo (bŭm′ə-lō) *n., pl.* **-los.** See **Bombay duck** 2. [Marathi *bombīla.*]

bum•mer (bŭm′ər) *n. Slang.* **1.a.** An adverse reaction to a hallucinogenic drug. **b.** A disagreeable person, experience, or situation. **2.** A failure. **3.** One who bums, esp. for a living. [< BUM¹, adj. Senses 2 and 3, prob. < Ger. *Bummler*loafer < *bummeln*, to loaf.]

Bunsen burner

bump (bŭmp) *v.* **bumped, bump•ing, bumps.** — *tr.* **1.** To strike or collide with. **2.** To cause to knock against an obstacle. **3.a.** To knock to a new position; shift. **b.** To shake up and down; jolt. **4.a.** To displace from a position within a group or organization. **b.** To deprive (a passenger) of a reserved seat because of overbooking. **5.** To raise; boost: *bump up the price.* — *intr.* **1.** To hit or knock against something. **2.** To proceed with jerks and jolts. — *n.* **1.a.** A blow, collision, or jolt. **b.** The sound of something bumping. **2.a.** A raised or rounded spot; a bulge. **b.** A slight swelling or lump. **c.** Something, such as a hole in a road, that causes a bump. **3.** A rise or increase, as in prices. **4.** One of the natural protuberances on the human skull, considered significant in phrenology. **5.** A forward thrust of the pelvis, as in an erotic dance. **6.** *Slang.* A shot of hard liquor, sometimes accompanied by a beer chaser. — ***phrasal verbs.*** **bump into.** To meet by chance. **bump off.** *Slang.* To murder. [Imit.]

bump•er¹ (bŭm′pər) *n.* **1.** A usu. metal or rubber bar attached to either end of a motor vehicle to absorb impact in a collision. **2.** A device for absorbing shocks or impeding contact.

bump•er² (bŭm′pər) *n.* **1.** A drinking vessel filled to the brim. **2.** Something extraordinarily large. — *adj.* Extraordinarily abundant or full: *a bumper crop of corn.* [Perh. < BUMP.]

bumper sticker *n.* A sticker bearing a printed message for display on a vehicle's bumper.

bump•kin¹ (bŭmp′kĭn, bŭm′-) *n.* An awkward unsophisticated person; a yokel. [Perh. < Flem. *boomken*, shrub, dim. of *boom*, tree; see **bheuə-***, or < MDu. *bommekijn*, dim. of *bomme*, barrel.]

Luis Buñuel

bump•kin² (bŭmp′kĭn, bŭm′-) *n. Naut.* A short spar projecting from the deck of a ship, used to extend a sail or secure a block or stay. [Prob. < Du. *boomken*, dim. of *boom*, tree. See BOOM².]

bump•tious (bŭmp′shəs) *adj.* Crudely or loudly assertive; pushy. [Perh. blend of BUMP and PRESUMPTUOUS.] — **bump′tious•ly** *adv.* — **bump′tious•ness** *n.*

bump•y (bŭm′pē) *adj.* **-i•er, -i•est. 1.** Covered with or full of bumps: *a bumpy country road.* **2.** Marked by bumps and jolts; rough. — **bump′i•ly** *adv.* — **bump′i•ness** *n.*

bun¹ (bŭn) *n.* **1.** A small bread roll, often sweetened or spiced and sometimes containing dried fruit. **2.** A tight roll of hair worn at the back of the head. [ME *bunne*, prob. < OFr. *bugne*, boil, of Celt. orig.]

bun² (bŭn) *n. Slang.* A drunken spree. [?]

bun³ (bŭn) *n. Slang.* One of the buttocks. [Dial., hind part of a rabbit or squirrel < Sc.Gael., stump, bottom < OIr.]

bu•na (bo͞o′nə, byo͞o′-) *n.* A synthetic rubber made from the polymerization of butadiene and sodium. [Originally a trademark.]

bunch (bŭnch) *n.* **1.a.** A group of things growing close together; a cluster or clump. **b.** A group of like items or individuals gathered or placed together. **2.** *Informal.* A group of people usu. having a common interest or association. **3.** *Informal.* A considerable number or amount; a lot. **4.** A small lump or swelling; a bump. — *v.* **bunched, bunch•ing, bunch•es.** — *tr.* **1.** To gather or form into a cluster. **2.** To gather together into a group. **3.** To gather (fabric) into folds. — *intr.* **1.** To form a cluster or group. **2.** To be gathered together in folds, as fabric. **3.** To swell; protrude. [ME *bonche*, prob. < Flem. *bondje*, dim. of *bont*, bundle < MDu. See BUNDLE.] — **bunch′i•ness** *n.* — **bunch′y** *adj.*

bunch•ber•ry (bŭnch′bĕr′ē) *n.* See **dwarf cornel.**

Bunche (bŭnch), **Ralph Johnson.** 1904–71. Amer. diplomat who won the 1950 Nobel Peace Prize.

bunch•flow•er (bŭnch′flou′ər) *n.* A perennial herb *(Melanthium virginicum)* in the lily family, native to the eastern United States and having a cluster of cream-colored or greenish flowers.

bunch grass or **bunch•grass** (bŭnch′grăs′) *n.* Any of various grasses in different genera that grow in clumplike fashion.

bunch•ing onion (bŭn′chĭng) *n.* Any of certain kinds of onion plants, such as the Welsh onion, that is grown for its multiple stems used as scallions.

bun•co also **bun•ko** (bŭng′kō) *Informal.* — *n., pl.* **-cos** also **-kos.** A swindle in which an unsuspecting person is cheated; a confidence game. — *tr.v.* **-coed, -co•ing, -cos** also **-koed, -ko•ing, -kos.** To swindle. [Prob. alteration of Sp. *banca*, card game < Ital. *banca*, bank, of Gmc. orig. See BANK².]

bun•combe (bŭng′kəm) *n.* Var. of **bunkum.**

bund¹ (bŭnd) *n.* **1.** An embankment or a dike, esp. in India. **2.** A street running along a harbor or waterway, esp. in the Far East. [Hindi *band* < Pers. < MPers. < Avestan *banda-* < OIran. See **bhendh-***.]

bund² (bo͝ond, bŭnd) *n.* **1.** An association, esp. a political association. **2.** Often **Bund.** A pro-Nazi German-American organization of the 1930's. **3.** Often **Bund.** A European Jewish socialist movement founded in Russia in 1897. [Ger. < MHGer. *bunt.* See **bhendh-***.] — **bund′ist** *n.*

bun•dle (bŭn′dl) *n.* **1.** A group of objects held together, as by tying or wrapping. **2.** Something wrapped or tied up for carrying; a package. **3.** *Biol.* A cluster or strand of closely bound muscle or nerve fibers. **4.** *Bot.* A vascular bundle. **5.** *Informal.* **a.** A large amount; a lot. **b.** A large sum of money. — *v.* **-dled, -dling, -dles.** — *tr.* **1.** To tie, wrap, or gather together. **2.** To dispatch or dispense of quickly and with little fuss; hustle. **3.** To dress (a person) warmly: *bundled them up in winter clothes.* — *intr.* **1.** To hurry; hasten. **2.** To dress oneself warmly. **3.** To sleep in the same bed with another while fully clothed. [ME *bundel*, prob. < MDu. *bondel.* See **bhendh-***.] — **bun′dler** *n.*

bundt cake (bŭnt, bo͝ont) *n.* A ring-shaped cake baked in a tube pan that has fluted sides. [Originally a trademark.]

bung (bŭng) *n.* **1.** A stopper esp. for the hole through which a cask, keg, or barrel is filled or emptied. **2.** A bunghole. — *tr.v.* **bunged, bung•ing, bungs. 1.** To close with or as if with a cork or stopper. **2.** *Informal.* To injure or damage. **3.** *Chiefly British.* To fling; toss. [ME *bunge* < MDu. *bonge* < LLat. *puncta*, hole < Lat., fem. p.part. of *pungere*, to prick. See **peuk-***.]

bun•ga•low (bŭng′gə-lō′) *n.* **1.** A small house or cottage usu. having a single story and sometimes an attic story. **2.** A thatched or tiled one-story house in India surrounded by a wide verandah. [Hindi *baṅglā*, Bengali (house) < *Bengali*, of Bengal.]

bung•hole (bŭng′hōl′) *n.* The hole in a cask, keg, or barrel through which liquid is poured in or drained out.

bun•gle (bŭng′gəl) *v.* **-gled, -gling, -gles.** — *intr.* To work or act ineptly or inefficiently. — *tr.* To handle badly; botch. See Syns at **botch.** — *n.* A clumsy or inept performance; a botch. [Perh. of Scand. orig.] — **bun′gler** *n.* — **bun′gling•ly** *adv.*

Bu•nin (bo͞o′nĭn, -nyĭn), **Ivan Alekseevich.** 1870–1953. Russian writer who won the 1933 Nobel Prize for literature.

bun•ion (bŭn′yən) *n.* A painful inflamed swelling of the bursa at the first joint of the big toe, characterized by enlargement of the joint and lateral displacement of the toe. [Prob. alteration of obsolete *bunny*, swelling < ME *bony*, perh. < OFr. *bugne.* See BUN¹.]

bunk¹ (bŭngk) *n.* **1.** A narrow bed built like a shelf into or against a wall, as in a ship's cabin. **2.** A bunk bed. **3.** A place for sleeping. — *v.* **bunked, bunk•ing, bunks.** — *intr.* **1.a.** To sleep in a bunk or bed. **b.** To stay the night; sleep. **2.** To go to bed: *bunked down early.* — *tr.* To provide with sleeping quarters. [Perh. short for BUNKER.]

bunk² (bŭngk) *n.* Empty talk; nonsense. [Short for BUNKUM.]
bunk bed *n.* Either of a pair of narrow beds stacked one on top of the other.
bun•ker (bŭng′kər) *n.* **1.** A bin or tank esp. for fuel storage, as on a ship. **2.a.** An underground defensive position with a fortified projection above ground level for gun emplacements. **b.** A protective chamber. **3.** *Sports.* A sand trap serving as an obstacle on a golf course. —*tr.v.* **-kered, -ker•ing, -kers. 1.** To store or place (fuel) in a bunker. **2.** *Sports.* To hit (a golf ball) into a bunker. [Sc. *bonker*, chest, perh. of Scand. orig.] —**bun′ker** *adj.*
Bun•ker Hill (bŭng′kər). A section of Charlestown MA. The first major Revolutionary War battle took place on nearby Breed's Hill (Jun. 17, 1775).
bunk•house (bŭngk′hous′) *n.* A building providing sleeping quarters on a ranch or in a camp.
bunk•mate (bŭngk′māt′) *n.* A person with whom one shares sleeping quarters.
bun•ko (bŭng′kō) *n.* & *v.* Var. of **bunco.**
bun•kum also **bun•combe** (bŭng′kəm) *n.* Empty or insincere talk; claptrap. [After *Buncombe*, a county of W N Carolina, from a remark made around 1820 by its congressman, who felt obligated to give a dull speech "for Buncombe."]
bun•ny (bŭn′ē) *n., pl.* **-nies.** A rabbit, esp. a young one. [< dial. *bun*, tail of a rabbit. See BUN³.]
Bun•ra•ku (bo͝on-rä′ko͞o, bo͝on′rä′-) *n.* A traditional Japanese puppet theater featuring large puppets and a narrative recited from off-stage. [J. : after the *Bunraku-za* theater built in the early 19th cent. by Bunraku-ken Oemurea (d. 1810).]
Bun•sen (bŭn′sən), **Robert Wilhelm.** 1811–99. German chemist who pioneered spectrum analysis.
Bunsen burner *n.* A small laboratory burner consisting of a vertical metal tube connected to a gas source and producing a very hot flame from a mixture of gas and air let in through adjustable holes at the base. [After Robert Wilhelm BUNSEN.]
bunt¹ (bŭnt) *v.* **bunt•ed, bunt•ing, bunts.** —*tr.* **1.** *Baseball.* To bat (a pitched ball) by tapping it lightly so that the ball rolls slowly in front of the infielders. **2.** To push or strike with or as if with the head; butt. —*intr.* **1.** *Baseball.* To make a bunt. **2.** To butt. —*n.* **1.** *Baseball.* **a.** The act of bunting. **b.** A bunted ball. **2.** A butt with or as if with the head. [Dial., to push, strike.] —**bunt′er** *n.*
bunt² (bŭnt) *n.* **1.** *Naut.* The middle portion of a sail, esp. a square one, that is shaped like a pouch to increase the effect of the wind. **2.** The pouchlike midsection of a fishing net in which the catch is concentrated. [Perh. < Swed. *bunt*or Dan. *bundt*, both of LGer. orig.]
bunt³ (bŭnt) *n.* A smut disease of wheat and other cereal grasses, caused by fungi of the genus *Tilletia* and resulting in grains filled with foul-smelling, sooty black spores. [?]
bunt•ing¹ (bŭn′tĭng) *n.* **1.** A light cotton or woolen cloth used for making flags. **2.** Flags considered as a group. **3.** Strips of cloth or material usu. in the colors of the national flag, used esp. as drapery or streamers for festive decoration. [Perh. < Ger. *bunt*, colored.]
bunt•ing² (bŭn′tĭng) *n.* Any of various birds of the family Fringillidae, having short cone-shaped bills and brownish or grayish plumage. [ME.]
bunt•ing³ (bŭn′tĭng) *n.* A snug-fitting hooded sleeping bag for infants. [Perh. < Sc. *buntin*, plump, short.]
Bunt•line (bŭnt′lĭn, -līn′), **Ned.** See E.Z.C. **Judson.**
Bu•ñu•el (bo͞o-nyo͞o-ĕl′), **Luis.** 1900–83. Spanish director known for films such as *The Discreet Charm of the Bourgeoisie* (1972).
bun•ya-bun•ya also **bun•ya•bun•ya** (bŭn′yə-bŭn′yə) *n.* An Australian evergreen tree *(Araucaria bidwilli)* having tiers of nearly whorled branches and large cones. [< Wiradhuri (Aboriginal language of SE Australia) *bunya.*]
Bun•yan (bŭn′yən), **John.** 1628–88. English preacher and writer celebrated for his *Pilgrim's Progress* (two parts, 1678 and 1684).
Bun•yan•esque (bŭn′yə-nĕsk′) *adj.* **1.** Of or relating to the allegorical writings of John Bunyan. **2.a.** Of or relating to the legend of Paul Bunyan. **b.** Of very large size.
bun•ya pine (bŭn′yə) *n.* See **bunya-bunya.**
buoy (bo͞o′ē, boi) *n.* **1.** *Naut.* A float, often having a bell or light, moored in water as a warning of danger or a marker for a channel. **2.** A life buoy. —*tr.v.* **buoyed, buoy•ing, buoys. 1.** To keep afloat or aloft. **2.a.** To maintain at a high level; support. **b.** To hearten or inspire; uplift. **3.** To mark with or as if with a buoy. [ME *boie* < OFr. *boue*, prob. of Gmc. orig. See **bhā-¹***.]
buoy•ance (boi′əns, bo͞o′yəns) *n.* Buoyancy.
buoy•an•cy (boi′ən-sē, bo͞o′yən-) *n.* **1.a.** The tendency or capacity to remain afloat in a liquid or rise in air or gas. **b.** The upward force that a fluid exerts on an object less dense than itself. **2.** Ability to recover quickly from setbacks; resilience. **3.** Lightness of spirit; cheerfulness.
buoy•ant (boi′ənt, bo͞o′yənt) *adj.* **1.** Having or marked by buoyancy. **2.** Lighthearted; gay: *in a buoyant mood.* [Sp. *boyante*, pr.part. of *boyar*, to refloat a boat < *boya*, buoy < OFr. *boue*. See BUOY.] —**buoy′ant•ly** *adv.*
bu•pres•tid (byo͞o-prĕs′tĭd) *n.* Any of various beetles of the family Buprestidae, which are destructive wood borers as larvae. [< NLat. *Būprēstidae*, family name < *Būprēstis*, type genus < Lat. *būprēstis*, beetle harmful to cattle < Gk. *bouprēstis*: *bous*, ox; see **gʷou-*** + *prēthein*, to swell up.]
bur¹ also **burr** (bûr) *n.* **1.a.** A rough prickly husk or covering surrounding the seeds or fruits of plants. **b.** A plant producing such husks or coverings. **2.** A persistently clinging or nettlesome person or thing. **3.** A rough protuberance, esp. a burl on a tree. **4.** Any of various rotary cutting tools designed to be attached to a drill. [ME *burre*, of Scand. orig.]
bur² (bûr) *n.* & *v.* Var. of **burr².**
bur³ (bûr) *n.* Var. of **burr³.**
bur. *abbr.* Bureau.
Bur. *abbr.* Burma; Burmese.
bu•ran (bo͞o-rän′) *n.* A violent windstorm of the Eurasian steppes. [Russ., prob. < Tatar.]
Bur•bage (bûr′bĭj), **Richard.** 1567?–1619. English actor and theater manager who was the first to play the title roles in Shakespeare's *Hamlet, King Lear, Othello,* and *Richard III.*
Bur•bank (bûr′băngk′). **1.** A city of S CA near Los Angeles. Pop. 93,643. **2.** A city of NE IL a suburb of Chicago. Pop. 27,600.
Burbank, Luther. 1849–1926. Amer. horticulturist who developed new varieties of fruits, vegetables, and flowers.
Bur•bidge (bûr′bĭj), **(Eleanor) Margaret.** b. 1919. British-born Amer. astronomer who directed the Royal Greenwich Observatory (1972–73).
bur•ble (bûr′bəl) *n.* **1.** A gurgling or bubbling sound, as of running water. **2.** A rapid, excited flow of speech. **3.** A breakdown in the smooth flow of fluid past a moving streamlined body, such as an airplane wing, resulting in turbulence. —*intr.v.* **-bled, -bling, -bles. 1.** To bubble; gurgle. **2.** To speak quickly and excitedly; gush. [ME *burblen*, to bubble.] —**bur′bler** *n.* —**bur′bly** *adj.*
bur•bot (bûr′bət) *n., pl.* **burbot** or **-bots.** A freshwater fish *(Lota lota)* of the Northern Hemisphere, having barbels on the nose and chin. [ME < OFr. *borbote* < *borbeter*, to move about in mud.]
Burch•field (bûrch′fēld′), **Charles Ephraim.** 1893–1967. Amer. painter whose works include somber urban scenes.
bur cucumber *n.* **1.** A weedy annual vine *(Sicyos angulatus)* of North America having whitish flowers and small fruits with long, slender prickles. **2.** The fruit of this vine.
bur•den¹ (bûr′dn) *n.* **1.** Something that is carried. **2.a.** Something that is emotionally difficult to bear. **b.** A source of great worry or stress; weight. **3.** A responsibility or duty. **4.** *Naut.* **a.** The amount of cargo that a vessel can carry. **b.** The weight of the cargo carried by a vessel at one time. —*tr.v.* **-dened, -den•ing, -dens. 1.** To weigh down; oppress. **2.** To load or overload. [ME < OE *byrthen*. See **bher-¹***.]
Syns: *burden, affliction, cross, trial, tribulation.* The central meaning shared by these nouns is "something that is onerous or troublesome": *the burden of guilt; indebtedness that is an affliction; illness that is her cross; such a trial to wait; domestic tribulations.*
bur•den² (bûr′dn) *n.* **1.** A principal or recurring idea; a theme. **2.** *Mus.* **a.** The chorus or refrain of a composition. **b.** The drone of a bagpipe. **c.** *Archaic.* The bass accompaniment to a song. [Var. of BOURDON.]
burden of proof *n.* *Law.* The responsibility of proving a disputed charge or allegation.
bur•den•some (bûr′dn-səm) *adj.* Of or like a burden; onerous. —**bur′den•some•ly** *adv.* —**bur′den•some•ness** *n.*
bur•dock (bûr′dŏk′) *n.* Any of several weedy, chiefly biennial plants of the genus *Arctium* in the composite family, having pink or purplish flower heads surrounded by prickly bracts and forming a bur in fruit. [BUR¹ + DOCK⁴.]
bu•reau (byo͝or′ō) *n., pl.* **-reaus** or **-reaux** (-ōz). **1.** A chest of drawers, esp. a dresser for holding clothes. **2.** *Chiefly British.* A writing desk or writing table with drawers. **3.a.** A government department or a subdivision of a department. **b.** An office, usu. of a large organization, that is responsible for a specific duty: *a news bureau.* **c.** A business that offers information of a specified kind: *a travel bureau.* [Fr., cloth cover for desks, desk, office < OFr. *burel*, woolen cloth, prob. < VLat. **būra* < LLat. *burra*, shaggy garment.]
bu•reauc•ra•cy (byo͝o-rŏk′rə-sē) *n., pl.* **-cies. 1.a.** Administration of a government chiefly through bureaus or departments staffed with nonelected officials. **b.** The departments and their officials as a group. **2.** Management or administration marked by diffuse authority and inflexible rules of operation. **3.** An administrative system in which the need or inclination to follow complex procedures impedes effective action. [Fr. *bureaucratie*: *bureau*, office; see BUREAU + *-cratie*, rule (< OFr.; see -CRACY).]
bu•reau•crat (byo͝or′ə-krăt′) *n.* **1.** An official of a bureaucracy. **2.** One who is rigidly devoted to the details of administrative procedure. —**bu′reau•crat′ic** *adj.* —**bu′reau•crat′i•cal•ly** *adv.* —**bu•reau′cra•ti•za′tion** (-tĭ-zā′shən) *n.* —**bu•reau′cra•tize′** (byo͝o-rŏk′rə-tīz′) *v.*
bu•rette also **bu•ret** (byo͝o-rĕt′) *n.* A uniform-bore glass tube

burdock
Smaller burdock
Arctium minus

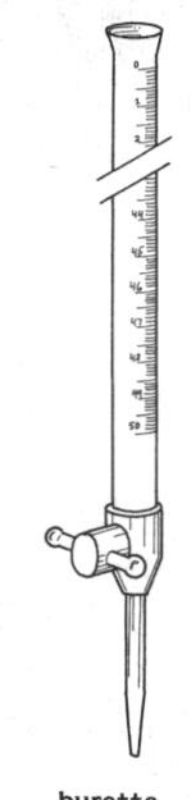
burette

ă pat	oi boy
ā pay	ou out
âr care	o͝o took
ä father	o͞o boot
ĕ pet	ŭ cut
ē be	ûr urge
ĭ pit	th thin
ī pie	*th* this
îr pier	hw which
ŏ pot	zh vision
ō toe	ə about, item
ô paw	

Stress marks:
′ (primary);
′ (secondary), as in
dictionary (dĭk′shə-nĕr′ē)

with fine gradations and a stopcock at the bottom, used esp. in laboratory procedures. [Fr., dim. of *buire*, vase for liquors < OFr., prob. of Gmc. orig.]

burg (bûrg) *n.* **1.** *Informal.* A city or town. **2.** A fortified or walled town in early or medieval Europe. [Prob. from *-burg* in place names < ME *burgh*, town < OE *burg*. Sense 2, ult. < Gmc. **burgs* hill fort. See **bhergh-**[2]*.]

bur•gage (bûr′gĭj) *n.* A tenure in England and Scotland under which property of the king or a lord in a town was held in return for a yearly rent or the rendering of a service. [ME < OFr. *bourgage* < Med.Lat. *burgāgium* < LLat. *burgus*, fortified town, of Gmc. orig. See BURGESS.]

bur•gee (bər-jē′, bûr′jē) *n. Naut.* A small distinguishing flag displayed by a yacht. [Perh. < Fr. dial. *bourgeais*, shipowner < OFr. *burgeis*, citizen < *bourg*, bourg. See BOURG.]

bur•geon also **bour•geon** (bûr′jən) *intr.v.* **-geoned, -geon•ing, -geons. 1.a.** To put forth new buds, leaves, or greenery. **b.** To begin to grow or blossom. **2.** To grow and flourish. [ME *burgeonen* < OFr. *borjoner* < *burjon*, a bud < VLat. **burriōnem* < LLat. *burra*, a shaggy garment.]

Usage Note: *Burgeon* has gained greater acceptance in recent years in its use to mean "to grow and flourish." In 1969 only 49 percent of the Usage Panel accepted the phrase *the burgeoning population of Queens* compared to the current 74 percent. However, it should be noted that in this use *burgeon* is more acceptable as a present participle.

burg•er (bûr′gər) *n.* **1.** A sandwich consisting of a bun, a cooked beef patty, and often other ingredients such as cheese. Often used in combination: *a cheeseburger.* **2.** A similar sandwich with a nonbeef filling. Often used in combination: *a crab burger.* [Short for HAMBURGER.]

Martha Jane Burk
"Calamity Jane"
Photographed in 1895

Bur•ger (bûr′gər), **Warren Earl.** b. 1907. Amer. jurist; chief justice of the U.S. Supreme Court (1969–86).

bur•gess (bûr′jĭs) *n.* **1.** A freeman or citizen of an English borough. **2.** A member of the English Parliament who once represented a town, borough, or university. **3.** A member of the lower house of the legislature of colonial Virginia or Maryland. [ME *burgeis* < OFr. < LLat. *burgēnsis* < *burgus*, fortified town. See **bhergh-**[2]*.]

Bur•gess (bûr′jĭs), **Anthony.** b. 1917. British writer and critic whose novels include *A Clockwork Orange* (1962).

Burgess, (Frank) Gelett. 1866–1951. Amer. writer and illustrator noted for *Are You a Bromide?* (1907).

burgh (bûrg) *n.* A chartered town or borough in Scotland. [Sc., var. of BOROUGH.]

burgh•er (bûr′gər) *n.* **1.** A citizen of a town or borough. **2.** A comfortable or complacent member of the middle class. **3.a.** A member of the mercantile class of a medieval European city. **b.** A citizen of a medieval European city. [Ger. *Bürger*or Du. *burger*, both < MHGer. *burgaere* < OHGer. *burgārī* < *burg*, city. See **bhergh-**[2]*.]

Burgh•ley (bûr′lē), 1st Baron. See William **Cecil.**

bur•glar (bûr′glər) *n.* One who burglarizes. [AN *burgler* (alteration of *burgesur*, prob. < OFr. *burg*, borough) and Med. Lat. *burgulātor* (alteration of *burgātor* < *burgāre*, to commit burglary in < LLat. *burgus*, fortified town), both of Gmc. orig. See **bhergh-**[2]*.]

bur•glar•i•ous (bər-glâr′ē-əs) *adj.* Of or relating to burglary.

bur•glar•ize (bûr′glə-rīz′) *v.* **-ized, -iz•ing, -iz•es.** —*tr.* **1.** To enter and steal from (a building or other premises). **2.** To commit burglary against. —*intr.* To commit burglary.

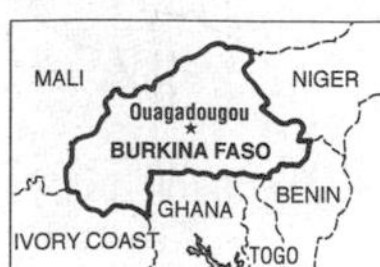

Burkina Faso

bur•gla•ry (bûr′glə-rē) *n., pl.* **-ries.** The act of entering a building or other premises with the intent to steal.

bur•gle (bûr′gəl) *tr.v.* & *intr.v.* **-gled, -gling, -gles.** To burglarize. [Back-formation < BURGLAR.]

bur•go•mas•ter (bûr′gə-măs′tər) *n.* The principal magistrate of a city or town in the Netherlands, Flanders, Austria, or Germany. [Partial transl. of Du. *burgemeester*: *burg*, town (< MDu. *burch*; see **bhergh-**[2]*) + *meester*, master.]

bur•go•net (bûr′gə-nĭt, bûr′gə-nĕt′) *n.* A light steel helmet with a peak and hinged flaps covering the cheeks, worn in the 16th century. [OFr. *bourguignotte*, prob. < *Bourgogne*, Burgundy, a region of E France.]

bur•goo (bûr′go͞o′, bər-go͞o′) *n., pl.* **-goos. 1.** *New England.* Any of several thick stews, originally an oatmeal porridge. **2.** *Kentucky.* **a.** A spicy stew made of poultry, game, other meats, and vegetables, usu. cooked outdoors. **b.** A picnic featuring such a stew. [Perh. alteration of RAGOUT.]

Bur•gos (bo͝or′gōs′). A city of N Spain on a high plateau SSW of Bilbao; founded c. 884. Pop. 155,849.

Bur•goyne (bûr-goin′, bûr′goin′), **John.** "Gentleman Johnny." 1722–92. British general and playwright who captured Fort Ticonderoga (Jul. 6, 1777).

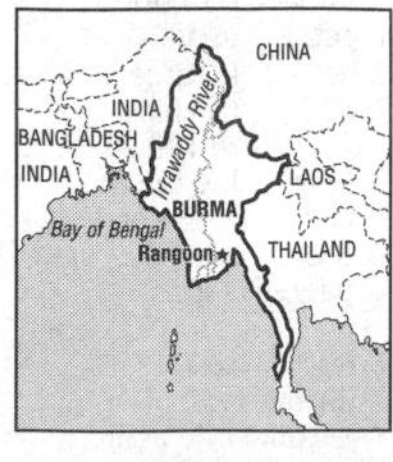

Burma

Bur•gun•dy[1] (bûr′gən-dē). **1.** A ducal house of Burgundy split into the Capetian line (1032–1361) and the Cadet, or Valois, line (1363–1477). **2.** A Portuguese dynasty (1139–1383) beginning with Alfonso I, who made Portugal an independent kingdom.

Bur•gun•dy[2] (bûr′gən-dē) also **Bour•gogne** (bo͝or-gôn′yə). A historical region and former province of E France; incorporated into the French crown lands by Louis XI in 1477. —**Bur•gun′di•an** (bər-gŭn′dē-ən) *adj.* & *n.*

Bur•gun•dy[3] (bûr′gən-dē) *n., pl.* **-dies. 1.a.** Any of various wines produced in Burgundy, France. **b.** Any of various similar wines produced elsewhere. **2. burgundy.** *Color.* A dark grayish or blackish red to dark purplish red or reddish brown.

bur•i•al (bĕr′ē-əl) *n.* The act or process of burying. [ME *buriel*, back-formation < *buriels* (taken as pl.) < OE *byrgels*. See **bhergh-**[1]*.] —**bur′i•al** *adj.*

bu•rin (byo͝or′ĭn, bûr′-) *n.* **1.** A steel cutting tool with a sharp beveled point, used in engraving or carving stone. **2.** The style or technique of an engraver's work. **3.** *Archaeol.* An early flint tool with a head like a chisel. [Fr., prob. < obsolete Ital. *burino*, of Gmc. orig.]

Burk or **Burke** (bûrk), **Martha Jane.** "Calamity Jane." 1852?–1903. Amer. frontierswoman and legendary figure of the Wild West; reputed to be a crack shot and an expert rider.

burke (bûrk) *tr.v.* **burked, burk•ing, burkes. 1.** To suppress or extinguish quietly; stifle. **2.** To avoid; disregard. **3.** To execute (someone) by suffocation so as to leave the body intact and suitable for dissection. [After William *Burke* (1792–1829), Irish-b. grave robber and murderer.]

Burke (bûrk), **Edmund.** 1729–97. Irish-born British politician and writer who was instrumental in developing the notion of a loyal opposition within the parliamentary system.

Bur•ki•na Fa•so (bər-kē′nə fä′sō). Formerly **Up•per Vol•ta** (ŭp′ər vŏl′tə, vōl′-, vôl′-). A landlocked country of W Africa; gained independence from France in 1960. Cap. Ouagadougou. Pop. 6,965,886.

Bur•kitt's lymphoma (bûr′kĭts) *n.* A malignant lymphoma usu. occurring among children in central Africa, associated with the Epstein-Barr virus. [After Denis Parsons *Burkitt*, 20th-cent. Ugandan physician.]

burl (bûrl) *n.* **1.** A knot, lump, or slub in yarn or cloth. **2.a.** A large, rounded outgrowth on a tree. **b.** The wood cut from a burl. —*tr.v.* **burled, burl•ing, burls.** To dress or finish (cloth) by removing burls. [ME *burle* < OFr. *bourle*, tuft of wool, dim. of *bourre*, coarse wool < LLat. *burra*, shaggy garment.] —**burl′er** *n.*

bur•lap (bûr′lăp′) *n.* A strong, coarsely woven cloth made of fibers of jute, flax, or hemp and used to make bags, to reinforce linoleum, and in interior decoration. [?]

Bur•leigh (bûr′lē), 1st Baron. See William **Cecil.**

bur•lesque (bər-lĕsk′) *n.* **1.** A literary or dramatic work that ridicules a subject either by presenting a solemn subject in an undignified style or an inconsequential subject in a dignified style. **2.** A ludicrous or mocking imitation; a travesty. **3.** A variety show characterized by broad ribald comedy, dancing, and striptease. —*v.* **-lesqued, -lesqu•ing, -lesques.** —*tr.* To imitate mockingly or humorously. —*intr.* To use the methods or techniques of burlesque. [< Fr., comical < Ital. *burlesco* < *burla*, joke, prob. < Sp. < VLat. **burrula*, dim. of LLat. *burrae*, nonsense < *burra*, wool.] —**bur•lesque′** *adj.* —**bur•lesque′ly** *adv.* —**bur•lesqu′er** *n.*

bur•ley (bûr′lē) *n., pl.* **-leys.** A light-colored tobacco grown chiefly in Kentucky and used esp. in making cigarettes. [Prob. < the name *Burley*.]

Bur•lin•game (bûr′lĭn-găm′, -lĭng-). A city of W CA on the W shore of San Francisco Bay. Pop. 26,801.

Bur•ling•ton (bûr′lĭng-tən). **1.** A city of S Ontario, Canada, a suburb of Hamilton on Lake Ontario. Pop. 114,853. **2.** A city of SE IA on hills overlooking the Mississippi R.; settled in the 1830's. Pop. 27,208. **3.** A town of NE MA, a suburb of Boston. Pop. 23,302. **4.** A city of N-central NC E of Greensboro. Pop. 39,498. **5.** A city of NW VT on Lake Champlain WNW of Montpelier. Pop. 39,127.

bur•ly (bûr′lē) *adj.* **-li•er, -li•est.** Heavy, strong, and muscular; husky. See Syns at **muscular.** [ME *burlich* < OE **borlic*, excellent. See **bher-**[1]*.] —**bur′li•ly** *adv.* —**bur′li•ness** *n.*

Bur•ma (bûr′mə). Officially (since 1989) **Myan•mar** (myän-mä′) A country of SE Asia on the Bay of Bengal and the Andaman Sea; gained independence from Great Britain in 1948. Cap. Rangoon. Pop. 35,313,905.

bur marigold *n.* See **beggar ticks** 1a.

Burma Road. A highway extending c. 1,126 km (700 mi) NE through mountainous country from NE Burma to Kunming, China. It was a vital transportation route for wartime supplies to the Chinese government from 1938 to 1946.

Bur•mese (bər-mēz′, -mēs′) *adj.* Also **Bur•man** (bûr′mən). Of or relating to Burma or its people, language, or culture. —*n., pl.* **Burmese. 1.** Also **Burman.** A native or inhabitant of Burma. **2.** The Sino-Tibetan language of Burma.

burn[1] (bûrn) *v.* **burned** or **burnt** (bûrnt), **burn•ing, burns.** —*tr.* **1.a.** To cause to undergo combustion. **b.** To destroy with fire. **c.** To consume (fuel or energy, for example). **2.** *Phys.* To cause to undergo nuclear fission or fusion. **3.** To damage or injure by fire, heat, radiation, electricity, or a caustic agent. **4.a.** To execute or kill with fire. **b.** To execute by electrocution. **5.a.** To make or produce by fire or heat: *burn a hole in the rug.* **b.** To dispel; dissipate: *The sun burned off the fog.* **6.a.** To use as a fuel. **b.** To metabolize (glucose, for example) in the body. **7.** To impart a sensation of intense heat to: *The chili burned my mouth.* **8.a.** To irritate or inflame, as by chafing or sunburn. **b.** To let (oneself or a part of one's body) become sunburned. **9.** To brand (an animal). **10.** To harden or impart a finish to by subjecting to intense heat; fire. **11.** To make angry. **12.a.** To defeat in a contest, esp. by a narrow margin. **b.** To inflict harm or hardship on; hurt. **c.** To swindle or deceive; cheat. — *intr.* **1.a.** To undergo combustion. **b.** To admit of burning: *Wood burns easily.* **2.** To consume fuel. **3.** *Phys.* To undergo nuclear fission or fusion. **4.a.** To emit heat or light by or as if by fire. **b.** To become dissipated or to be dispelled by or as if by heat. **5.** To give off light; shine. **6.** To be destroyed, injured, damaged, or changed by or as if by fire. **7.a.** To be very hot; bake. **b.** To feel or look hot: *a child burning with fever.* **c.** To impart a sensation of heat. **8.a.** To become irritated or painful, as by chafing or inflammation. **b.** To become sunburned or windburned. **9.** To be consumed with strong emotion, esp.: **a.** To be or become angry. **b.** To be very eager. **10.** To penetrate by or as if by intense heat or flames. **11.** To be vividly or painfully present: *shame burning in my heart.* **12.a.** To suffer punishment or death by or as if by fire. **b.** To be electrocuted. — *n.* **1.** An injury produced by fire, heat, radiation, electricity, or a caustic agent. **2.** A burned place or area. **3.** The process or result of burning. **4.** A stinging sensation. **5.** A sunburn or windburn. **6.** *Aerospace.* A firing of a rocket. **7.** A swindle. — ***phrasal verbs.*** **burn out. 1.** To stop burning from lack of fuel. **2.** To wear out or make or become inoperative as a result of heat or friction. **3.** To cause (a property owner or a resident) to have to evacuate the premises because of fire. **4.** To make or become exhausted, esp. as a result of long-term stress. **burn up. 1.** To make angry. **2.** To travel over or through at high speed: *burning up the track.* — ***idioms.*** **burn (one's) bridges.** To eliminate the possibility of return or retreat. **burn the (or one's) candle at both ends.** To exhaust oneself or one's resources by leading a hectic or extravagant life. **burn the midnight oil.** To work or study very late at night. **to burn.** In great amounts: *money to burn.* [ME *burnen* < OE *beornan*, to be on fire, and < *bærnan*, to set on fire; see **gʷher-***.]

burn² (bûrn) *n. Scots.* A small stream; a brook. [ME < OE *burna.* See **bhreu-***.]

Bur•na•by (bûr**′**nə-bē). A city of SW British Columbia, Canada, a suburb of Vancouver. Pop. 136,494.

burned-out (bûrnd**′**out**′**) or **burnt-out** (bûrnt**′**-) *adj.* Worn out or exhausted, esp. as a result of long-term stress.

Burne-Jones (bûrn**′**jōnz**′**), Sir **Edward Coley.** 1833–98. British painter known for the mystical dreamlike settings of his paintings and stained-glass designs.

burn•er (bûr**′**nər) *n.* **1.** One that burns, esp.: **a.** A device, as in a stove, that is lighted to produce a flame. **b.** A device on a stovetop that produces heat. **2.a.** A unit, such as a furnace, in which something is burned. **b.** An incinerator.

bur•net (bər-nĕt**′**, bûr**′**nĭt) *n.* A perennial plant of the genus *Sanguisorba*, having pinnately compound leaves and apetalous flowers. [ME < Med.Lat. *burneta* < OFr. *brunete*, dark brown, dim. of *brun*, brown, of Gmc. orig. See **bher-²***.]

Bur•nett (bûr-nĕt**′**, bûr**′**nĭt), **Frances Eliza Hodgson.** 1849–1924. British-born Amer. writer famous for her popular children's books, esp. *Little Lord Fauntleroy* (1886).

Bur•ney (bûr**′**nē), **Frances ("Fanny").** 1752–1840. British writer best known for her witty letters and diaries.

burn•ing (bûr**′**nĭng) *adj.* **1.** Marked by flames or intense heat: *a burning sun.* **2.** Characterized by intense emotion; passionate. **3.** Of immediate import; urgent. — **burn′ing•ly** *adv.*

burning bush also **burn•ing-bush** (bûr**′**nĭng-bo͝osh**′**) *n.* **1.** Any of several shrubs or shrubby plants having foliage that turns bright red in autumn. **2.** See **gas plant.**

bur•nish (bûr**′**nĭsh) *tr.v.* **-nished, -nish•ing, -nish•es. 1.** To make smooth or glossy by or as if by rubbing; polish. **2.** To rub with a tool that serves esp. to smooth or polish. — *n.* A smooth glossy finish or appearance; luster. [ME *burnishen* < OFr. *burnir, burniss-*, var. of *brunir* < *brun*, shining, of Gmc. orig. See **bher-²***.] — **bur′nish•er** *n.*

Burn•ley (bûrn**′**lē). A borough of NW England N of Manchester. Pop. 93,700.

bur•noose also **bur•nous** (bər-no͞os**′**) *n.* A hooded cloak worn esp. by Arabs. [Fr. *burnous* < Ar. *burnus* < Gk. *birros*, hooded cloak < LLat. *birrus*.]

burn•out (bûrn**′**out**′**) *n.* **1.** A failure in a device due to burning, excessive heat, or friction. **2.** *Aerospace.* **a.** The termination of rocket or jet-engine operation because of fuel exhaustion or shutoff. **b.** The point at which this termination occurs. **3.a.** Physical or emotional exhaustion, esp. as a result of long-term stress or dissipation. **b.** One who is burned out.

Burns (bûrnz), **George.** b. 1896. Amer. comedian and actor known for his comedy act (1922–64) with Gracie Allen and his later work in films.

Burns, Robert. 1759–96. Scottish poet renowned for his use of dialect and humor. — **Burns′i•an** *adj.*

Burn•side (bûrn**′**sīd**′**), **Ambrose Everett.** 1824–81. Amer. Union Army general; defeated at Fredericksburg (1862) and Petersburg (1864).

burn•sides (bûrn**′**sīdz**′**) *pl.n.* Heavy side whiskers worn with the chin clean-shaven. [After Ambrose Everett BURNSIDE.]

Burns•ville (bûrnz**′**vĭl**′**). A city of SE MN, a suburb of Minneapolis. Pop. 51,288.

burnt (bûrnt) *v.* A p.t. and p.part. of **burn¹.**

burnt offering *n.* A slaughtered animal or other offering burned on an altar as a religious sacrifice.

burnt-out (bûrnt**′**out**′**) *adj.* Var. of **burned-out.**

burnt sienna *n.* **1.** A reddish-brown pigment prepared by calcining raw sienna. **2.** *Color.* A dark reddish orange.

bur oak *n.* An oak tree *(Quercus macrocarpa)* of eastern North America, having pinnately lobed leaves, acorns enclosed within a deep fringed cup, and hard durable wood.

burp (bûrp) *n.* A belch. — *v.* **burped, burp•ing, burps.** — *intr.* To belch. — *tr.* To cause (a baby) to expel gas from the stomach, as by patting the back after feeding. [Imit.]

burp gun *n.* A lightweight portable submachine gun.

burr¹ (bûr) *n.* **1.** A rough edge or area remaining on material, such as metal, after it has been cast, cut, or drilled. **2.** Var. of **bur¹.** — *tr.v.* **burred, burr•ing, burrs. 1.** To form a burr on. **2.** To remove burrs from. [Var. of BUR¹.]

burr² also **bur** (bûr) — *n.* **1.** A trilling of the letter *r* characteristic of Scottish speech. **2.** A buzzing or whirring sound. — *v.* **burred, burr•ing, burrs** also **burs.** — *tr.* To pronounce with a burr. — *intr.* **1.** To speak with a burr. **2.** To make a buzzing or whirring sound. [Imit.]

burr³ also **bur** (bûr) *n.* A washer that fits around the smaller end of a rivet. [ME *burre*, ring, disk, alteration of *burwhe*, circle, disk.]

Burr (bûr), **Aaron.** 1756–1836. Vice President of the U.S. (1801–05) who mortally wounded Alexander Hamilton in a duel (1804).

bur reed or **bur-reed** (bûr**′**rēd**′**) *n.* Any of various aquatic or wetland plants of the genus *Sparganium*, having elongated leaves and ball-like clusters of tiny, beaked fruits.

bur•ri•to (bo͝o-rē**′**tō, bə-) *n., pl.* **-tos.** A flour tortilla wrapped around a filling, as of beef, beans, or cheese. [Am.Sp. < Sp., dim. of *burro*, burro. See BURRO.]

bur•ro (bûr**′**ō, bo͝or**′**ō, bŭr**′**ō) *n., pl.* **-ros.** A small donkey, esp. one used as a pack animal. [Sp., back-formation < *borrico*, donkey < LLat. *burrīcus*, small horse.]

Bur•roughs (bûr**′**ōz, bŭr**′**-), **Edgar Rice.** 1875–1950. Amer. writer best known for his novel *Tarzan of the Apes* (1914).

Burroughs, John. 1837–1921. Amer. naturalist and writer remembered for his vivid essays.

Burroughs, William Seward¹. 1855–98. Amer. inventor who patented the first practical adding machine.

Burroughs, William Seward². b. 1914. Amer. writer noted for *Naked Lunch* (1959).

bur•row (bûr**′**ō, bŭr**′**ō) *n.* **1.** A hole or tunnel dug in the ground by a small animal for habitation or refuge. **2.** A narrow or snug place. — *v.* **-rowed, -row•ing, -rows.** — *intr.* **1.a.** To dig a burrow. **b.** To live or hide in a burrow. **2.** To move or progress by or as if by digging or tunneling. — *tr.* **1.** To make by or as if by tunneling. **2.** To dig a hole or tunnel in or through. **3.** *Archaic.* To hide in or as if in a burrow. [ME *borow.*] — **bur′row•er** *n.*

burr•stone (bûr**′**stōn**′**) *n.* Var. of **buhrstone.**

bur•ry (bûr**′**ē) *adj.* **-ri•er, -ri•est.** Having burs; prickly.

bur•sa (bûr**′**sə) *n., pl.* **-sae** (-sē) or **-sas.** *Anat.* A sac or saclike body cavity, esp. one containing a viscous lubricating fluid and located between a tendon and a bone or at points of friction between moving structures. [LLat., purse, pouch < Gk., skin, wineskin.] — **bur′sal** *adj.*

Bur•sa (bûr**′**sə, bo͝or-sä**′**). A city of NW Turkey W of Ankara; estab. in the 3rd cent. B.C. Pop. 445,113.

bursa of Fa•bri•ci•us (fə-brĭsh**′**ē-əs, -brĭsh**′**əs) *n.* A thymuslike lymphoid gland in birds that is an outgrowth of the cloaca and the site of B cell maturation. [After Hieronymus *Fabricius* (1537–1619), Italian anatomist.]

bur•sar (bûr**′**sər, -sär**′**) *n.* An official in charge of funds, as at a college or university; a treasurer. [ME *burser* < Med.Lat. *bursārius* < LLat. *bursa*, purse. See BURSA.]

bur•sa•ry (bûr**′**sə-rē) *n., pl.* **-ries. 1.** A treasury, esp. of a public institution or religious order. **2.** *Chiefly British.* A university scholarship based on need. [Med.Lat. *bursāria* < *bursa*, purse. See BURSA.] — **bur•sar′i•al** (bər-sâr**′**ē-əl) *adj.*

burse (bûrs) *n.* **1.** A purse. **2.** *Eccles.* A flat cloth case for carrying the corporal. [LLat. *bursa.* See BURSA.]

bur•si•tis (bər-sī**′**tĭs) *n.* Inflammation of a bursa.

burst (bûrst) *v.* **burst, burst•ing, bursts.** — *intr.* **1.a.** To come open or fly apart suddenly or violently, esp. from internal pressure. **b.** To explode. **2.** To be or seem to be full to the point of breaking open. **3.** To emerge, come forth, or arrive suddenly. **4.** To come apart or seem to come apart because of overwhelming emotion. **5.** To give sudden expression: *burst out laughing.* — *tr.* **1.** To cause to burst. See Syns at **break. 2.** To exert strong pressure in order to force (something) open. **3.** *Comp. Sci.* To separate (a continuous form or printout) into individual sheets. — *n.* **1.** A sudden outbreak or outburst; an explosion. **2.** The result of bursting, esp. the explosion of a projectile or bomb. **3.a.** The number of bullets fired from an automatic weapon by one pull of the trigger. **b.** A volley of bullets from an automatic weapon. **4.** An

burnoose

George Burns
Photographed in 1986

ă **pat**	oi **boy**
ā **pay**	ou **out**
âr **care**	o͝o **took**
ä **father**	o͞o **boot**
ĕ **pet**	ŭ **cut**
ē **be**	ûr **urge**
ĭ **pit**	th **thin**
ī **pie**	*th* **this**
îr **pier**	hw **which**
ŏ **pot**	zh **vision**
ō **toe**	ə **about,**
ô **paw**	**item**

Stress marks:
′ (primary);
′ (secondary), as in **dictionary** (dĭk**′**shə-nĕr′ē)

abrupt, intense increase; a rush. [ME *bursten* < OE *berstan*.]

bur•then (bûr′*th*ən) *n.* A burden.

bur•ton (bûr′tn) *n. Naut.* A light tackle having double or single blocks, used to hoist or tighten rigging. [?]

Bur•ton (bûr′tn). A city of SE-central MI, a suburb of Flint. Pop. 27,617.

Burton, Harold Hitz. 1888–1964. Amer. jurist; associate justice of the U.S. Supreme Court (1945–58).

Burton, Sir **Richard Francis.** 1821–90. British explorer and Orientalist whose best-known work is a translation of *The Arabian Nights* (1855–88).

Burton, Robert. 1577–1640. English cleric and writer known chiefly for his *Anatomy of Melancholy* (1621).

Burton upon Trent or **Burton on Trent** (trĕnt′). A borough of W-central England SSW of Derby. Pop. 48,500.

Bu•ru (bo͝or′o͞o). An island of E Indonesia in the Moluccas.

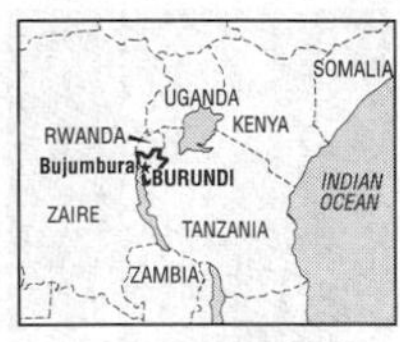

Burundi

Bu•run•di (bo͝o-ro͞on′dē, -ro͝on′-). A country of E-central Africa with a coastline on Lake Tanganyika; gained independence in 1962. Cap. Bujumbura. Pop. 4,523,513. **—Bu•run′di•an** *adj. & n.*

bur•y (bĕr′ē) *tr.v.* **-ied, -y•ing, -ies. 1.** To place in the ground. **2.** To place (a corpse) in a grave, a tomb, or the sea; inter. **3.** To conceal by or as if by covering over with earth; hide. See Syns at **hide**[1]. **4.** To occupy (oneself) with deep concentration; absorb. **5.** To put an end to; abandon. **—*idiom.* bury the hatchet.** To stop fighting. [ME *burien* < OE *byrgan.* See **bhergh-**[1]*.] **—bur′i•er** *n.*

Bur•y (bĕr′ē). A borough of NW England NNW of Manchester; founded on the site of a Saxon settlement. Pop. 177,600.

bur•y•ing beetle (bĕr′ē-ĭng) *n.* Any of various beetles of the genus *Nicrophorus* that bury small animals on which they feed and lay their eggs.

Bury Saint Ed•munds (ĕd′məndz). A municipal borough of E-central England E of Cambridge; chartered 1606. Pop. 28,914.

bus (bŭs) *n., pl.* **bus•es** or **bus•ses. 1.** A long motor vehicle for carrying passengers, usu. along a fixed route. **2.** *Informal.* A large or ungainly automobile. **3.** A four-wheeled cart for carrying dishes in a restaurant. **4.** *Elect.* A bus bar. **5.** *Comp. Sci.* A parallel circuit that connects the major components of a computer, allowing the transfer of electric impulses from one connected component to any other. **—*v.* bused, bus•ing, bus•es** or **bussed, bus•sing, bus•ses. —*tr.* 1.** To transport in a bus. **2.** To transport (schoolchildren) by bus to schools outside their neighborhoods, esp. for racial integration. **3.** To carry or clear (dishes) in a restaurant. **—*intr.* 1.** To travel in a bus. **2.** To work busing tables. [Short for OMNIBUS.]

bus. *abbr.* Business.

bus bar *n. Elect.* A conducting bar that carries heavy currents to supply several electric circuits.

burying beetle
Nicrophorus marginatus

bus•boy also **bus boy** (bŭs′boi′) *n.* A male employee who assists in a restaurant, as by busing tables. [(OMNI)BUS + BOY.]

bus•by (bŭz′bē) *n., pl.* **-bies.** A tall, full-dress fur hat worn in certain guards regiments of the British army. [Poss. < the name *Busby*.]

bush[1] (bo͝osh) *n.* **1.** A low shrub with many branches. **2.** A thick growth of shrubs; a thicket. **3.a.** Land covered with dense vegetation or undergrowth. **b.** Land remote from settlement. **4.** A shaggy mass, as of hair. **5.** A fox's tail. **6.a.** *Archaic.* A clump of ivy hung outside a tavern to indicate the availability of wine inside. **b.** *Obsolete.* A tavern. **—*v.* bushed, bush•ing, bushes. —*intr.* 1.** To grow or branch out like a bush. **2.** To extend in a bushy growth. **—*tr.*** To decorate, protect, or support with bushes. **—*adj. Slang.*** Bush-league; second-rate. [ME, partly < OE *busc,* partly < OFr. *bois,* wood (of Gmc. orig.), and partly of Scand. orig. (akin to Dan. *busk*). N., sense 3, poss. < Du. *bosch*.]

bush[2] (bo͝osh) *tr.v.* **bushed, bush•ing, bush•es.** To furnish or line with a bushing. [< *bush,* bushing, poss. alteration of Du. *bus,* box.]

Bush (bo͝osh), **Barbara.** b. 1925. First Lady of the U.S. (1989–93); active in promoting literacy.

Bush, George Herbert Walker. b. 1924. The 41st President of the U.S. (1989–93); previously Vice President (1981–89).

Bush, Vannevar. 1890–1974. Amer. electrical engineer who designed (1928) the differential analyzer, an early computer.

bush baby *n.* Any of several small nocturnal African primates of the genera *Galago* and *Euoticus,* having dense woolly fur, large round eyes, prominent ears, and a long tail.

bush bean *n.* **1.** A shrubby variety of the snap bean. **2.** Any upright bean plant not requiring an artificial support.

bush•buck (bo͝osh′bŭk′) *n.* An African antelope *(Tragelaphus scriptus)* having a brownish coat with white spots and twisted horns. [Transl. of Afr. *bosbok*: *bos,* bush + *bok,* buck.]

bush clover *n.* Any of various plants of the genus *Lespedeza* in the pea family, having compound leaves with three leaflets and various colored flowers.

bushed (bo͝osht) *adj. Informal.* Extremely tired; exhausted. [Poss. < Australian slang, lost in the bush.]

Barbara Bush
Photographed in 1989

bush•el[1] (bo͝osh′əl) *n.* **1.a.** A unit of volume or capacity in the U.S. Customary System, used in dry measure and equal to 4 pecks, 2,150.42 cubic inches, or 35.24 liters. **b.** A unit of volume or capacity in the British Imperial System, used in dry and liquid measure and equal to 2,219.36 cubic inches or 36.37 liters. See table at **measurement. 2.** A container with the capacity of a bushel. **3.** *Informal.* A large amount; a great deal. [ME < AN *bussel,* var. of OFr. *boissiel* < *boisse,* one sixth of a bushel, of Celt. orig.]

bush•el[2] (bo͝osh′əl) *tr.v.* **-eled, -el•ing, -els** or **-elled, -el•ling, -els.** To alter or mend (clothing). [Prob. < Ger. *bosseln,* to do odd jobs, alteration (perh. influenced by *bosseln,* to emboss) of *basteln,* to putter.] **—bush′el•er, bush′el•ler** *n.* **—bush′el•man** (-mən) *n.*

bush honeysuckle *n.* **1.** Any of three eastern North American shrubs of the genus *Diervilla,* having opposite deciduous leaves and clusters of yellow flowers. **2.** Any of several shrubby honeysuckle plants of the genus *Lonicera.*

Bu•shi•do also **bu•shi•do** (bo͝osh′ĭ-dō′, bo͞o′shĭ-) *n.* The traditional code of the Japanese samurai, stressing honor, self-discipline, bravery, and simple living. [J. *bushidō*: *bushi,* warrior (< Chin. *wǔ shì,* knight, warrior : *wǔ,* military + *shì,* brave warrior) + *dō,* way (< Chin. *dào*).]

bush•ing (bo͝osh′ĭng) *n.* **1.** A fixed or removable cylindrical metal lining used to constrain, guide, or reduce friction. **2.** *Elect.* An insulating lining for an aperture through which a conductor passes. **3.** An adapter threaded to permit joining of pipes with different diameters. [< BUSH[2].]

bush jacket *n.* A long, cotton shirtlike jacket usu. with four flat pockets and a belt.

bush league *n. Baseball.* A minor league. **—bush leaguer** *n.*

bush-league (bo͝osh′lēg′) *adj.* **1.** *Baseball.* Of or belonging to a minor league. **2.** *Slang.* Inferior or unprofessional.

Bush•man (bo͝osh′mən) *n.* **1.** See **San. 2. bushman.** *Australian.* One who lives or travels in the wilderness, esp. in the outback. [Transl. of Afr. *boschjeman.*]

bush•mas•ter (bo͝osh′măs′tər) *n.* A large venomous snake *(Lachesis mutus)* of tropical America having brown and grayish markings.

Bush•nell (bo͝osh′nəl), **David.** 1742–1824. Amer. inventor who designed (1775) a self-propelled submarine.

bush pilot *n.* A person who flies a small airplane to and from areas inaccessible by other means of transportation.

bush•rang•er (bo͝osh′rān′jər) *n.* **1.** One who lives in the wilderness. **2.** *Australian.* An outlaw living in the bush.

bush•tit (bo͝osh′tĭt′) *n.* Either of two small long-tailed birds *(Psaltriparus minimus* or *P. melanotis)* of western North America having predominantly gray plumage.

bush•whack (bo͝osh′hwăk′, -wăk′) *v.* **-whacked, -whack•ing, -whacks. —*intr.* 1.** To make one's way through thick woods by cutting away bushes and branches. **2.** To travel through or live in the woods. **3.** To fight as a guerrilla in the woods. **—*tr.*** To ambush. **—bush′whack′er** *n.*

bush•y (bo͝osh′ē) *adj.* **-i•er, -i•est. 1.** Overgrown with bushes. **2.** Thick and shaggy. **—bush′i•ly** *adv.* **—bush′i•ness** *n.*

busi•ness (bĭz′nĭs) *n.* **1.a.** The occupation, work, or trade in which a person is engaged. **b.** A specific occupation or pursuit. **2.** Commercial, industrial, or professional dealings. **3.** A commercial enterprise or establishment. **4.** Volume or amount of commercial trade. **5.** Commercial dealings; patronage. **6.a.** One's rightful or proper concern or interest. **b.** Something involving one personally. **7.** Serious work or endeavor: *down to business.* **8.** An affair or matter. **9.** An incidental action performed on the stage to fill a pause between lines or to provide detail. **10.** *Informal.* Verbal abuse; scolding. **11.** *Obsolete.* The condition of being busy. [ME *businesse* < *bisi,* busy. See BUSY.]

Syns: *business, industry, commerce, trade, traffic.* These nouns apply to forms of activity that have the objective of supplying commodities. *Business* pertains broadly to commercial, financial, and industrial activity: *decided to go into business. Industry* is the production and manufacture of goods or commodities, especially on a large scale: *the computer industry. Commerce* and *trade* refer to the exchange and distribution of goods or commodities: *interstate commerce; domestic trade. Traffic* pertains in particular to businesses engaged in the transportation of goods or passengers: *shipping traffic.* The word may also suggest illegal trade: *Traffic in stolen goods.*

business administration *n.* A college or university course of studies that offers instruction in business.

business card *n.* A small card printed or engraved with a person's name and business affiliation.

business cycle *n.* A sequence of economic activity typically marked by recession, recovery, growth, and decline.

busi•ness•like (bĭz′nĭs-līk′) *adj.* **1.** Showing or having characteristics useful in business; methodical and systematic. **2.** Purposeful; earnest. **3.** Practical; unemotional.

busi•ness•man (bĭz′nĭs-măn′) *n.* A man engaged in business. See Usage Note at **man.**

busi•ness•per•son (bĭz′nĭs-pûr′sən) *n.* One engaged in business. See Usage Note at **man.**

busi•ness•wom•an (bĭz′nĭs-wo͝om′ən) *n.* A woman engaged in business. See Usage Note at **man.**

busk•er (bŭs′kər) *n.* A street musician or public entertainer, esp. one who solicits money during a performance. [< *busk,* to entertain by singing and dancing.]

bus•kin (bŭs′kĭn) *n.* **1.** A usu. laced half boot. **2.a.** A thick-soled laced half boot worn by actors of Greek and Roman tragedies. **b.** Tragedy, esp. that which resembles a Greek tragedy. [Perh. alteration (influenced by BUCKSKIN) of obsolete Fr. *broisequin,* small leather boot.]

bus•load (bŭs′lōd′) *n.* The number of passengers or the quantity of cargo that a bus can carry.

bus•man (bŭs′mən) *n.* One who drives a bus.

bus•man's holiday (bŭs′mənz) *n. Informal.* A vacation during which one engages in activity similar to one's usual work.

Bu•so•ni (bo͞o-zō′nē, byo͞o-), **Ferruccio Benvenuto.** 1866–1924. Italian pianist, conductor, and composer.

buss (bŭs) *tr. & intr.v.* **bussed, buss•ing, buss•es.** To kiss. —*n.* A kiss. [Poss. blend of obsolete *bass* (akin to Fr. *baiser*) and obsolete *cuss* (akin to ME *kissen,* to kiss; see KISS), or < Sc.Gael. *bus,* lips, mouth; see PUSS[2].]

bus•ses (bŭs′ĭz) *n.* Pl. of **bus.**

bust[1] (bŭst) *n.* **1.** A sculpture representing a person's head, shoulders, and upper chest. **2.a.** A woman's bosom. **b.** The human chest. [Fr. *buste* < Ital. *busto,* poss. < Lat. *bustum,* sepulchral monument.]

bust[2] (bŭst) *v.* **bust•ed, bust•ing, busts.** —*tr.* **1.** *Slang.* **a.** To smash or break, esp. forcefully. **b.** To render inoperable or unusable. **2.** To cause to come to an end; break up. **3.** To break or tame (a horse). **4.** To cause to become bankrupt or short of money. **5.** *Slang.* To reduce in rank. **6.** To hit; punch. **7.** *Slang.* **a.** To place under arrest. **b.** To make a raid on. —*intr.* **1.** *Slang.* **a.** To undergo breakage. **b.** To burst; break. **2.** To become bankrupt or short of money. **3.** *Games.* To lose at blackjack by exceeding a score of 21. —*n.* **1.** A failure. **2.** A state of bankruptcy. **3.** A time of widespread financial depression. **4.** A punch; a blow. **5.** A spree. **6.** *Slang.* **a.** An arrest. **b.** A raid. [Var. of BURST.]

bus•tard (bŭs′tərd) *n.* Any of various large long-legged Old World game birds of the family Otididae that frequent dry grassy plains. [ME < blend of OFr. *bistarde* and *oustarde,* both < Lat. *avis tarda*: *avis,* bird; see **awi-*** + *tarda,* fem. of *tardus,* slow.]

bust•er (bŭs′tər) *n.* **1.** One that breaks up something: *a crime buster.* **2.** A broncobuster. **3.** A particularly robust child. **4.** *Informal.* Fellow; man. Used as a form of familiar address.

bus•ti•cate (bŭs′tĭ-kāt′) *tr.v.* **-cat•ed, -cat•ing, -cates.** *Northern U.S.* To break into pieces. See Regional Note at **absquatulate.** [BUST[2] + *-icate* (as in MEDICATE).]

bus•tier (bo͞os-tyā′, bŭs-) *n.* A formfitting sleeveless and usu. strapless woman's top, worn as lingerie and often as evening attire. [Fr. < *buste,* bust. See BUST[1].]

bus•tle[1] (bŭs′əl) *intr. & tr.v.* **-tled, -tling, -tles.** To move or cause to move energetically and busily. —*n.* Excited and often noisy activity; a stir. [Poss. var. of obsolete *buskle,* freq. of *busk,* to prepare oneself < ON *būask.* See **bheuə-*.**]

bus•tle[2] (bŭs′əl) *n.* A frame or pad formerly worn to expand the back of a woman's skirt. [?]

Bu•sto Ar•si•zio (bo͞o′stō är-sē′tsyō). A city of N Italy NW of Milan. Pop. 76,769.

bust•y (bŭs′tē) *adj.* **-i•er, -i•est.** Having large breasts.

bu•sul•fan (byo͞o-sŭl′fən) *n.* An alkylating agent, $C_6H_{14}O_6S_2$, used as an antineoplastic drug in the treatment of chronic myelocytic leukemia. [Blend of BUTANE and SULFONYL.]

bus•y (bĭz′ē) *adj.* **-i•er, -i•est. 1.** Engaged in activity; occupied. **2.** Sustaining much activity: *a busy street.* **3.** Meddlesome; prying. **4.** Being in use, as a telephone line. **5.** Cluttered with detail to the point of being distracting. —*tr.v.* **-ied, -y•ing, -ies.** To make busy; occupy. [ME *bisi, busi* < OE *bisig.*] —**bus′i•ly** *adv.* —**bus′y•ness** *n.*

bus•y•bod•y (bĭz′ē-bŏd′ē) *n.* A person who meddles or pries.

busy signal *n.* A series of sharp buzzing tones heard over a telephone when the line dialed is already in use.

bus•y•work (bĭz′ē-wûrk′) *n.* Activity meant to take up time but not necessarily yield productive results.

but (bŭt; bət *when unstressed*) *conj.* **1.** On the contrary: *caused not gain but loss.* **2.** Contrary to expectation; yet: *tired but happy.* **3.** *Usage Problem.* Used to indicate an exception: *No one but she.* **4.** With the exception that; except that. Used to introduce a dependent clause: *would have acted but that he fainted.* **5.** *Informal.* Without the result that: *It never rains but it pours.* **6.** *Informal.* That. Often used after a negative: *no doubt but right will prevail.* **7.** That . . . not. Used after a negative or question: *There never is a law but someone will oppose it.* **8.** If not; unless. **9.** *Informal.* Than. —*prep. Usage Problem.* Except. —*adv.* **1.** Merely; just; only: *lasted but a moment.* **2.** Used as an intensive: *Move but fast!* [ME < OE *būtan.* See **ud-*.**]

Usage Note: Some traditional grammarians have argued that *but* is a conjunction in sentences such as *No one but I has read it* and therefore should be followed by the nominative form *I.* If *but* were truly a conjunction here, however, the verb would agree in person and number with the noun or pronoun following *but*: *No one but I have read it.* What is more, if *but* were a true conjunction here, we would not expect that it could be moved to the end of a clause, as in *No one has read it but I.* These observations suggest that *but* is best considered as a preposition here and followed by accusative forms such as *me* and *them* in all positions: *No one but me has read it. No one has read it but me.* These recommendations are supported by 73 percent of the Usage Panel when the *but* phrase precedes the verb and by 93 percent when the *but* phrase follows the verb. • *But* is redundant when used together with *however,* as in *But the army, however, proceeded.* • *But* is generally not followed by a comma. Correct written style requires *Kim wanted to go, but we stayed.* • *But* may be used to begin a sentence at all levels of style. See Usage Notes at **and, however, I[1].**

but– *pref.* Containing a group of four carbon atoms: *butyl.* [< BUTYRIC.]

bu•ta•di•ene (byo͞o′tə-dī′ēn′, -dī-ēn′) *n.* A colorless, highly flammable hydrocarbon, C_4H_6, obtained from petroleum and used to make synthetic rubber. [BUTA(NE) + DI-[1] + -ENE.]

bu•tane (byo͞o′tān′) *n.* Either of two isomers of a gaseous hydrocarbon, C_4H_{10}, synthesized from petroleum and used as a fuel. [BUT(YL) + -ANE.]

bu•ta•no•ic acid (byo͞o′tə-nō′ĭk) *n.* See **butyric acid.** [BUTAN(E) + -OIC.]

bu•ta•nol (byo͞o′tə-nôl′, -nōl′, nŏl′) *n.* Either of two butyl alcohols derived from butane and used as solvents and in organic synthesis. [BUTAN(E) + -OL[1].]

bu•ta•none (byo͞o′tə-nōn′) *n.* A colorless flammable ketone, $CH_3COCH_2CH_3$, used as a solvent. [BUTAN(E) + -ONE.]

butch (bo͝och) *n.* A butch haircut. —*adj.* A woman, esp. a lesbian, exhibiting traits or appearance usu. associated with men. [Prob. < the male nickname *Butch.*] —**butch** *adj.*

butch•er (bo͝och′ər) *n.* **1.a.** One that slaughters and dresses animals for food or market. **b.** One that sells meats. **2.** One who kills brutally or indiscriminately. **3.** A vender, esp. one on a train or in a theater. **4.** One who bungles something. —*tr.v.* **-ered, -er•ing, -ers. 1.** To slaughter or prepare (animals) for market. **2.** To kill brutally or indiscriminately. **3.** To botch; bungle. [ME *bucher* < OFr. *bouchier* < *bouc, boc,* he-goat, prob. of Celt. orig.] —**butch′er•er** *n.*

butch•er•bird (bo͝och′ər-bûrd′) *n.* Any of various birds, esp. the shrike, that impale their prey on thorns.

butch•er-block (bo͝och′ər-blŏk′) *adj.* Made of or resembling a board of thick strips of hardwood like that on which butchers chop meat.

butcher knife *n.* A heavy-duty knife with a broad sharp blade used for cutting meat.

butch•er's broom (bo͝och′ərz) *n.* An evergreen shrub *(Ruscus aculeatus)* native to Europe and the Mediterranean region, with leaflike stems, greenish flowers, and usu. red berries.

butch•er•y (bo͝och′ə-rē) *n., pl.* **-ies. 1.** Wanton or cruel killing; carnage. **2.** Something botched; a bungle. **3.** The trade of a butcher. **4.** *Chiefly British.* A slaughterhouse.

butch haircut *n.* A haircut in which the hair is cropped close.

Bute (byo͞ot). An island of SW Scotland in the Firth of Clyde.

Bu•te•nandt (bo͞ot′n-änt′), **Adolf Friedrich.** b. 1903. German chemist who shared a 1939 Nobel Prize.

bu•te•o (byo͞o′tē-ō′) *n., pl.* **-os.** Any of various broad-winged, soaring hawks of the genus *Buteo.* [Lat. *būteō,* a kind of hawk or falcon.]

but•ler (bŭt′lər) *n.* A household head servant who is usu. in charge of food service and the deportment of the other servants. [ME < OFr. *bouteillier,* bottle bearer < *bouteille, botele,* bottle. See BOTTLE.]

But•ler (bŭt′lər), **Benjamin Franklin.** 1818–93. Amer. army officer and politician; military governor of New Orleans (May–Dec. 1862).

Butler, Nicholas Murray. 1862–1947. Amer. educator who shared the 1931 Nobel Peace Prize.

Butler, Pierce. 1866–1939. Amer. jurist; associate justice of the U.S. Supreme Court (1923–39).

Butler, Samuel[1]. 1612–80. English poet remembered primarily for his three-part work *Hudibras* (1663–78).

Butler, Samuel[2]. 1835–1902. British writer best known for his semiautobiographical novel *The Way of All Flesh* (1903).

but•ler's pantry (bŭt′lərz) *n.* A serving and storage room between a kitchen and dining room.

butt[1] (bŭt) *v.* **butt•ed, butt•ing, butts.** —*tr.* To hit or push against with the head or horns; ram. —*intr.* **1.** To butt something. **2.** To project forward or out. —*n.* A push or blow with the head or horns. ***—phrasal verb.* butt in.** To interfere or meddle in other people's affairs. [ME *butten* < OFr. *bouter,* to strike, of Gmc. orig. See **bhau-*.**] —**butt′er** *n.*

butt[2] (bŭt) *tr. & intr.v.* **butt•ed, butt•ing, butts.** To join or be joined end to end; abut. —*n.* **1.** A butt joint. **2.** A butt hinge. [ME *butten* < AN *butter* (var. of OFr. *bouter*; see BUTT[1]) and < *but,* end; see BUTT[4].]

butt[3] (bŭt) *n.* **1.** One that serves as an object of ridicule or contempt. **2.a.** A target. **b. butts.** A target range. **c.** An obstacle behind a target for stopping the shot. **3.** An embankment or hollow used as a blind by hunters of wildfowl. **4.a.** *Archaic.* A goal. **b.** *Obsolete.* A bound; a limit. [ME *butte,* target < OFr. < *but,* goal, end, target. See BUTT[4].]

George Bush

bustard
Kori bustard
Ardeotis kori

ă pat	oi boy
ā pay	ou out
âr care	o͞o took
ä father	o͞o boot
ĕ pet	ŭ cut
ē be	ûr urge
ĭ pit	th thin
ī pie	*th* this
îr pier	hw which
ŏ pot	zh vision
ō toe	ə about, item
ô paw	

Stress marks:
′ (primary);
′ (secondary), as in
dictionary (dĭk′shə-nĕr′ē)

butt[4] (bŭt) *n.* **1.** The larger or thicker end of an object. **2.a.** An unburned end, as of a cigarette. **b.** *Informal.* A cigarette. **3.** A short or broken remnant; a stub. **4.** *Informal.* The buttocks; the rear end. [ME *butte* < OFr. *but,* end, of Gmc. orig.]

butt[5] (bŭt) *n.* **1.** A large cask. **2.** A unit of volume equal to two hogsheads, usu. the equivalent of 126 U.S. gallons (about 477 liters). [ME < OFr. *boute* < LLat. **buttia,* var. of *buttis.*]

butte (byo͞ot) *n. Chiefly Western U.S.* A hill that rises abruptly from the surrounding area and has sloping sides and a flat top. [Fr. < OFr., mound behind targets. See BUTT[3].]

butte

Butte (byo͞ot). A city of SW MT SSW of Helena; settled in the 1860's. Pop. 37,205.

but•ter (bŭt′ər) *n.* **1.** A soft yellowish or whitish emulsion of butterfat, water, air, and sometimes salt, churned from milk or cream and processed for culinary use. **2.** Any of various substances similar to butter, esp.: **a.** A spread made from fruit, nuts, or other foods: *apple butter.* **b.** A vegetable fat having a nearly solid consistency at ordinary temperatures. **3.** Flattery. — *tr.v.* **-tered, -ter•ing, -ters.** To put butter on or in. — ***phrasal verb.*** **butter up.** To praise or flatter excessively. [ME *butere* < OE < Lat. *butyrum* < Gk. *bouturon: bous,* cow; see **gʷou-*** + *turos,* cheese; see **teuə-*.**]

but•ter-and-eggs (bŭt′ər-ən-ĕgz′) *pl.n. (used with a sing. or pl. v.)* A weedy perennial herb *(Linaria vulgaris)* native to Eurasia and having narrow leaves and racemes of showy, long-spurred yellow and orange flowers.

but•ter•ball (bŭt′ər-bôl′) *n.* **1.** *Informal.* A chubby or fat person. **2.** See **bufflehead.**

butter bean *n.* **1.** *Chiefly Southern & Midland U.S.* See **lima bean. 2.** *New England.* See **wax bean.**

but•ter•bur (bŭt′ər-bûr′) *n.* Any of several perennial herbs of the genus *Petasites* in the composite family, native to northern temperate regions and having large basal leaves.

butter clam *n.* A large clam of the genus *Saxidomus,* found on the Pacific coast of North America and having a distinctive shell formerly used as money by Native Americans.

but•ter•cup (bŭt′ər-kŭp′) *n.* Any of numerous herbs of the genus *Ranunculus,* native chiefly to temperate and cold regions and having usu. yellow or white flowers.

buttercup squash *n.* A round winter squash *(Cucurbita maxima)* shaped somewhat like a drum and having a dark green rind marked with silver or gray and yellowish to orange flesh.

but•ter•fat (bŭt′ər-făt′) *n.* The natural fat of milk from which butter is made, consisting largely of the glycerides of oleic, stearic, and palmitic acids.

but•ter•fin•gers (bŭt′ər-fĭng′gərz) *pl.n. (used with a sing. v.)* A person who drops things. — **but′ter•fin′gered** *adj.*

but•ter•fish (bŭt′ər-fĭsh′) *n., pl.* **butterfish** or **-fish•es. 1.** A marine food fish *(Poronotus triacanthus)* of the North American Atlantic coast, having a flattened body. **2.** Any of various similar or related fishes. [< its slippery mucous coating.]

but•ter•fly (bŭt′ər-flī′) *n.* **1.** Any of various insects of the order Lepidoptera, characteristically having slender bodies, knobbed antennae, and four broad, usu. colorful wings. **2.** A person interested principally in frivolous pleasure. **3.** *Sports.* A swimming stroke in which both arms are drawn upward out of the water and forward with a dolphin kick. **4. butterflies.** A feeling of unease or mild nausea caused esp. by fearful anticipation. — *tr.v.* **-flied, -fly•ing, -flies.** To cut and spread open and flat. [ME *butterflye* < OE *butorflēoge: butere,* butter; see BUTTER + *flēoge,* fly; see FLY[2].]

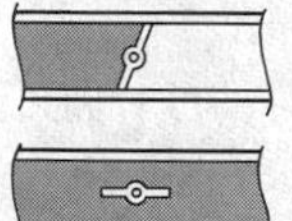
butterfly valve
Top: Closed
Bottom: Open

butterfly bush *n.* Any of various shrubs of the genus *Buddleja,* native chiefly to warm regions and cultivated for their clusters of small, variously colored flowers.

butterfly fish *n.* **1.** Any of various small, brightly colored tropical marine fishes of the family Chaetodontidae, having deep flattened bodies and a single dorsal fin. **2.** Any of various fishes with broad winglike fins.

butterfly orchid *n.* Any of certain orchids having showy, brightly colored flowers.

butterfly pea *n.* Any of several plants of the genera *Centrosema* and *Clitoria* in the pea family, having flat pods.

butterfly valve *n.* **1.** A disk turning on a diametrical axis inside a pipe, used as a throttle valve or damper. **2.** A valve composed of two semicircular plates hinged on a common spindle, used to permit flow in one direction only.

butterfly weed *n.* A North American milkweed *(Asclepias tuberosa)* having clusters of usu. bright orange flowers.

but•ter•milk (bŭt′ər-mĭlk′) *n.* **1.** The sour liquid that remains after the butterfat has been removed from whole milk or cream by churning. **2.** A cultured sour milk made by adding certain microorganisms to sweet milk.

buttermilk sky *n. Chiefly Southern U.S.* See **mackerel sky.** [< resemblance of clouds to texture of cultured milk.]

butternut
Juglans cinerea

but•ter•nut (bŭt′ər-nŭt′) *n.* **1.a.** An eastern North American walnut *(Juglans cinerea)* having light brown wood, pinnately compound leaves, and a furrowed nut. **b.** The nut of this tree. **c.** The wood of this tree. **d.** The bark of this tree. **e.** A brownish dye from the husks of the fruits of this tree. **2.a. butternuts.** Clothing dyed with butternut extract, esp. Confederate uniforms. **b.** *Informal.* A Confederate soldier or partisan. **3.** See **souari nut.** [From the nut's oiliness.]

butternut squash *n.* A bell-shaped winter squash *(Cucurbita moschata)* with a tan rind and yellowish to orange flesh.

but•ter•scotch (bŭt′ər-skŏch′) *n.* A syrup, sauce, candy, or flavoring made by melting butter, brown sugar, and sometimes artificial flavorings. [Alteration of *butterscot:* BUTTER + *scot,* of unknown orig.]

but•ter•weed (bŭt′ər-wēd′) *n.* **1.** A succulent annual or biennial plant *(Senecio glabellus)* native to the eastern United States and having pinnately divided leaves and bright yellow radiate flower heads. **2.** The horseweed.

but•ter•wort (bŭt′ər-wûrt′, -wôrt′) *n.* Any of numerous carnivorous plants of the genus *Pinguicula,* having basal leaves coated with a sticky secretion that traps small insects.

but•ter•y[1] (bŭt′ə-rē) *adj.* **1.** Resembling, containing, or spread with butter. **2.** Marked by effusive and insincere flattery. — **but′ter•i•ness** *n.*

but•ter•y[2] (bŭt′ə-rē, bŭt′rē) *n., pl.* **-ies. 1.** A room for storing liquors. **2.** *Chiefly British.* A store for provisions in colleges and universities. [ME *buttrie* < AN *buterie,* alteration of *botelerie* < OFr. *botele,* bottle. See BOTTLE.]

butt hinge *n.* A hinge of two plates attached to abutting surfaces of a door and door jamb and joined by a pin. [< BUTT[2].]

butt•in•sky (bŭt-ĭn′skē) *n., pl.* **-skies.** *Slang.* One who butts in; a meddler. [BUTT[1] + IN[1] + *-sky,* last syllable in many Slavic surnames.]

butt joint *n.* A joint formed by two abutting surfaces placed squarely together. [< BUTT[2].]

but•tock (bŭt′ək) *n.* **1.** Either of the two rounded prominences of the rear pelvic area. **2. buttocks.** The rear pelvic area of the human body. [ME < OE *buttuc,* strip of land, end. See **bhau-*.**]

but•ton (bŭt′n) *n.* **1.a.** A generally disk-shaped fastener used to join two parts of a garment by fitting through a buttonhole or loop. **b.** Such an object used for decoration. **2.** Any of various objects resembling a button, esp.: **a.** A push-button switch. **b.** The blunt tip of a fencing foil. **c.** A fused metal or glass globule. **3.** Any of various knoblike structures of a plant or animal, esp.: **a.** An immature, unexpanded mushroom. **b.** The tip of a rattlesnake's rattle. **4.** A usu. round flat pin that bears a design or printed information. *a campaign button.* **5.** *Informal.* The end of the chin, regarded as the point of impact for a punch. — *v.* **-toned, -ton•ing, -tons.** — *tr.* **1.** To fasten with buttons. **2.** To decorate or furnish with buttons. **3.** *Informal.* To close (the lips or mouth). — *intr.* To be or be capable of being fastened with buttons. — ***idiom.*** **on the button.** Exactly; precisely. [ME < OFr. *bouton* < *bouter,* to thrust, of Gmc. orig. See **bhau-*.**] — **but′ton•er** *n.* — **but′ton•y** *adj.*

but•ton•ball (bŭt′n-bôl′) *n.* See **sycamore** 1. [From its button-shaped fruit.]

but•ton•bush (bŭt′n-bo͝osh′) *n.* A deciduous North American shrub *(Cephalanthus occidentalis)* having opposite leaves and spherical clusters of small white flowers.

but•ton-down (bŭt′n-doun′) *adj.* **1.** Having the ends of the collar fastened down by buttons. **2.** Also **but•toned-down** (bŭt′nd-). Conservative, conventional, or unimaginative.

button fern *n.* A New Zealand fern *(Pellaea rotundifolia)* with round, dark green buttonlike leaflets.

but•ton•hole (bŭt′n-hōl′) *n.* **1.** A small slit in a garment or piece of fabric for fastening a button. **2.** *Chiefly British.* A boutonniere. — *tr.v.* **-holed, -hol•ing, -holes. 1.** To make a buttonhole in. **2.** To sew with a buttonhole stitch. **3.** To accost and detain (a person) in conversation by or as if by grasping the person's outer garments. — **but′ton•hol′er** *n.*

buttonhole stitch *n.* A loop stitch that forms a reinforced edge, as around a buttonhole.

but•ton•hook (bŭt′n-ho͝ok′) *n.* A small hook for fastening a button on shoes or gloves.

button mangrove *n.* See **buttonwood** 2.

but•ton•mold (bŭt′n-mōld′) *n.* A piece of wood, plastic, or metal that is covered with fabric to form a button.

but•ton•quail (bŭt′n-kwāl′) *n.* Any of various small quaillike Old World birds of the family Turnicidae, lacking a hind toe.

button snakeroot *n.* See **blazing star** 2.

but•ton•wood (bŭt′n-wo͝od′) *n.* **1.** See **sycamore** 1. **2.** An evergreen shrub or tree *(Conocarpus erectus)* growing in tropical America and western Africa and having alternate leathery leaves and small heads of greenish flowers.

but•tress (bŭt′rĭs) *n.* **1.** A structure, usu. brick or stone, built against a wall for support or reinforcement. **2.** Something resembling a buttress, as: **a.** The flared base of certain tree trunks. **b.** A horny growth on the heel of a horse's hoof. **3.** Something that serves to support, prop, or reinforce. — *tr.v.* **-tressed, -tress•ing, -tress•es. 1.** To support or reinforce with a buttress. **2.** To sustain, prop, or bolster. [ME *buteras* < OFr. *bouterez* < *bouter,* to strike against, of Gmc. orig. See **bhau-*.**]

butt weld *n.* A welded butt joint.

butt-weld (bŭt′wĕld′) *tr.v.* **-weld•ed, -weld•ing, -welds.** To join by a butt weld.

bu•tut (bo͞o′to͞ot′) *n., pl.* **butut** or **-tuts.** See table at **currency.** [Wolof.]

bu•tyl (byo͞ot′l) *n.* A hydrocarbon radical, C_4H_9, with the structure of butane and valence 1.

butyl alcohol *n.* Any of four isomeric alcohols, C_4H_9OH, widely used as solvents and in organic synthesis.

bu•tyl•ate (byo͞ot′l-āt′) *tr.v.* **-at•ed, -at•ing, -ates.** To bring a butyl group into (a compound). **—bu′tyl•a′tion** *n.*

bu•tyl•at•ed hy•drox•y•an•i•sole (byo͞ot′l-ā′tĭd hī-drŏk′-sē-ăn′ĭ-sōl′) *n.* BHA.

butylated hy•drox•y•tol•u•ene (hī-drŏk′sē-tŏl′yo͞o-ēn′) *n.* BHT.

bu•tyl•ene (byo͞ot′l-ēn′) *n.* Any of three gaseous isomeric ethylene hydrocarbons, C_4H_8, used principally in making synthetic rubbers.

butyl rubber *n.* A synthetic rubber produced by copolymerization of a butylene with isoprene.

bu•ty•ra•ceous (byo͞o′tə-rā′shəs) *adj.* Resembling butter in appearance, consistency, or chemical properties. [Lat. *butyrum*, butter; see BUTTER + -ACEOUS.]

bu•tyr•al•de•hyde (byo͞o′tə-răl′də-hīd′) *n.* A transparent, highly flammable liquid, C_4H_8O, used in synthesizing resins. [BUTYR(IC) + ALDEHYDE.]

bu•ty•rate (byo͞o′tə-rāt′) *n.* A salt or ester of butyric acid. [BUTYR(IC) + -ATE[2].]

bu•tyr•ic (byo͞o-tîr′ĭk) *adj.* **1.** Relating to, containing, or derived from butter. **2.** Relating to or derived from butyric acid. [< Lat. *butyrum*, butter. See BUTTER.]

butyric acid *n.* Either of two colorless isomeric acids, C_3H_7COOH, occurring in animal milk fats and used in disinfectants, emulsifying agents, and pharmaceuticals.

bu•ty•rin (byo͞o′tər-ĭn) *n.* Any of three isomeric glyceryl esters of butyric acid, naturally present in butter. [Fr. *butyrine* < Lat. *butyrum*, butter. See BUTTER.]

bu•ty•ro•phe•none (byo͞o-tîr′ō-fə-nōn′, byo͞o′tə-rō-) *n.* Any of a group of neuroleptic drugs, such as haloperidol, used to treat psychiatric disorders. [BUTYR(IC) + PHEN- + -ONE.]

bux•om (bŭk′səm) *adj.* **1.a.** Healthily plump and ample of figure. **b.** Having large breasts. **2.** *Archaic.* Lively, vivacious, and gay. **3.** *Obsolete.* Obedient; yielding; pliant. [ME, obedient < OE **būhsum* < *būgan*, to bend, submit. See **bheug-***.] **—bux′om•ly** *adv.* **—bux′om•ness** *n.*

Bux•te•hu•de (bo͝ok′stə-ho͞o′də), **Dietrich.** 1637–1707. Swedish-born organist and composer in Germany.

buy (bī) *v.* **bought** (bôt), **buy•ing, buys.** *—tr.* **1.** To acquire in exchange for money or its equivalent; purchase. **2.** To be capable of purchasing. Used of money, objects, and time. **3.** To acquire by sacrifice, exchange, or trade. **4.** To bribe. **5.** *Slang.* To accept the truth or feasibility of. *—intr.* **1.** To purchase goods; act as a purchaser. **2.** To believe in a person or movement or subscribe to an idea or theory. *—n.* **1.** Something bought or for sale; a purchase. **2.** *Informal.* Something that is underpriced; a bargain. ***—phrasal verbs.*** **buy off.** To bribe in order to avoid interference or be exempted from an obligation or from prosecution. **buy out.** To purchase the entire stock, business rights, or interests of. **buy up.** To purchase all that is available of. ***—idioms.*** **buy time.** To increase the time available for a specific purpose. **buy the farm.** *Slang.* To die, esp. suddenly or violently. [ME < OE *bycgan*.] **—buy′a•ble** *adj.*

buy•er (bī′ər) *n.* One that buys, esp. for a retail store.

buy•er's market also **buy•ers' market** (bī′ərz) *n.* A market marked by low prices and a supply exceeding demand.

buy•out also **buy-out** (bī′out′) *n.* **1.** The purchase of the entire holdings or interests of an owner or investor. **2.** The purchase of a company or business.

Bu•zău (bə-zou′, bo͞o-zü′o͞o). A city of SE Romania NE of Bucharest. Pop. 126,780.

buzz (bŭz) *v.* **buzzed, buzz•ing, buzz•es.** *—intr.* **1.** To make a low droning or vibrating sound like that of a bee. **2.a.** To talk, often excitedly, in low tones. **b.** To be abuzz; hum: *buzzing with rumors.* **3.** To move quickly and busily; bustle. **4.** To make a signal with a buzzer. *—tr.* **1.** To cause to buzz. **2.** To utter in a rapid, low voice. **3.** *Informal.* To fly low over. **4.** To signal with a buzzer. **5.** To make a telephone call to. *—n.* **1.** A vibrating, humming, or droning sound. **2.** A low murmur. **3.** A telephone call. **4.** *Slang.* Pleasant intoxication, as from alcohol. ***—phrasal verb.*** **buzz off.** *Informal.* To leave quickly; go away. [ME *bussen*, of imit. orig.]

buz•zard (bŭz′ərd) *n.* **1.** Any of various North American vultures, such as the turkey vulture. **2.** *Chiefly British.* A hawk of the genus *Buteo,* having broad wings and a broad tail. **3.** An avaricious or otherwise unpleasant person. [ME *busard*, hawk of the genus *Buteo* < OFr. < Lat. *būteō*.]

Buz•zards Bay (bŭz′ərdz). An inlet of the Atlantic in SE MA connected with Cape Cod Bay by the Cape Cod Canal.

buzz bomb *n.* See **robot bomb.**

buzz•er (bŭz′ər) *n.* An electric signaling device, such as a doorbell, that makes a buzzing sound.

buzz saw *n.* See **circular saw.**

buzz•word (bŭz′wûrd′) *n.* A word or phrase of a specialized field or group used primarily to impress laypersons.

B vitamin *n.* A member of the vitamin B complex group.

bvt. *abbr.* **1.** Brevet. **2.** Brevetted.

BW *abbr.* **1.** Biological warfare. **2.** Also **b/w** Black and white.

bwa•na (bwä′nə) *n.* Used as a form of respectful address in parts of Africa. [Swahili < Ar. *'abūnā*, our father.]

B.W.I. *abbr.* British West Indies.

bx. also **bx** *abbr.* Box.

by[1] (bī) *prep.* **1.** Close to; next to. **2.** With the use or help of; through: *by sea.* **3.** Up to and beyond; past: *drove by the house.* **4.** In the period of; during: *by day.* **5.** Not later than: *by 5:30* P.M. **6.a.** In the amount of: *by the thousands.* **b.** To the extent of: *by two inches.* **7.a.** According to: *by the rules.* **b.** With respect to: *siblings by blood.* **8.** In the name of. **9.** Through the agency or action of. **10.** Used to indicate a succession of specified individuals, groups, or quantities: *little by little.* **11.a.** Used in multiplication and division: *Multiply 4 by 6.* **b.** Used with measurements: *12 by 18 feet.* **c.** Used to express direction with points of the compass: *south by southeast.* *—adv.* **1.** On hand; nearby: *Stand by.* **2.** Aside; away: *We put it by.* **3.** Up to, alongside, and past: *racing by.* **4.** Into the past: *as days go by.* [ME < OE *bī, be.* See **ambhi*.**]

by[2] (bī) *n.* Var. of **bye.**

b.y. *abbr.* Billion years.

by- or **bye-** *pref.* **1.** By: *bygone.* **2.** Secondary, incidental: *byway.*

by and by *adv.* After a while; soon.

by-and-by (bī′ən-bī′) *n.* Some future time or occasion.

by and large *adv.* For the most part; generally.

Byb•los (bĭb′ləs, -lŏs′). An ancient city of Phoenicia NNE of present-day Beirut, Lebanon; chief city of Phoenicia in the 2nd millennium B.C.

by-blow (bī′blō′) *n.* **1.** An indirect or chance blow. **2.** A child born out of wedlock.

Byd•goszcz (bĭd′gôsh, -gôshch). A city of N-central Poland NE of Poznań; chartered 1346. Pop. 361,400.

bye also **by** (bī) *n.* **1.** A secondary matter; a side issue. **2.** *Sports.* The position of one who draws no opponent for a round in a tournament and so advances to the next round. ***—idiom.*** **by the bye.** By the way; incidentally. [< BY[1].]

bye-bye (bī′bī′, bī-bī′) *interj.* Used to express farewell. *—adv. Informal.* **1.** Away. **2.** To bed; to sleep. [Redup. of (GOOD-)BYE.]

by-e•lec•tion also **bye-e•lec•tion** (bī′ĭ-lĕk′shən) *n.* A special election held between general elections to fill a vacancy.

Bye•lo•rus•sia (byĕl′ō-rŭsh′ə). See **Belorussia.** **—Bye′lo•rus′sian** *adj. & n.*

by•gone (bī′gôn′, -gŏn′) *adj.* Gone by; past. *—n.* One, esp. a grievance, that is past: *Let bygones be bygones.*

by•law (bī′lô′) *n.* **1.** A law or rule governing the internal affairs of an organization. **2.** A secondary law. [ME *bilawe*, body of local regulations; akin to Dan. *by-lag*, township ordinance : ON *bȳr*, settlement; see **bheuə-*** + ON **lagu*, law; see **legh-*.**]

by•line also **by-line** (bī′līn′) *—n.* A line at the head of a newspaper or magazine article carrying the writer's name. *—tr.v.* **-lined, -lin•ing, -lines.** To write (a newspaper or magazine article) under a byline. **—by′lin′er** *n.*

by-name (bī′nām′) *n.* **1.** A surname. **2.** A nickname.

by•pass also **by-pass** (bī′păs′) *—n.* **1.** A highway that passes around or to one side of an obstructed or congested area. **2.** A pipe or channel used to conduct gas or liquid around another pipe or a fixture. **3.** A means of circumvention. **4.** *Elect.* See **shunt** 3. **5.** *Medic.* **a.** An alternative passage created surgically to divert a bodily fluid or circumvent an obstructed or diseased organ. **b.** A surgical procedure to create a bypass. *—tr.v.* **-passed, -pass•ing, -pass•es. 1.** To avoid (an obstacle) by using a bypass. **2.** To be heedless of; ignore. **3.** To channel (piped liquid, for example) through a bypass.

by•past (bī′păst′) *adj.* Past; bygone.

by-path (bī′păth′, -päth′) *n.* An indirect or rarely used path.

by-play (bī′plā′) *n.* Secondary action or speech taking place while the main action proceeds, as during a play.

by•prod•uct or **by-prod•uct** (bī′prŏd′əkt) *n.* **1.** Something produced in the making of something else. **2.** A secondary result; a side effect.

Byrd (bûrd), **Richard Evelyn.** 1888–1957. Amer. naval officer and explorer; first to fly over the North Pole (1926) and leader of five expeditions to Antarctica (1929–56).

Byrd, William. 1674–1744. Amer. planter and colonial official whose diaries depict daily life in Virginia.

byre (bīr) *n. Chiefly British.* A barn for cows. [ME < OE *bȳre*. See **bheuə-*.**]

Byrnes (bûrnz), **James Francis.** 1879–1972. Amer. politician; associate justice of the U.S. Supreme Court (1941–42) and secretary of state (1945–47).

by•road (bī′rōd′) *n.* See **byway** 1.

By•ron (bī′rən), **George Gordon.** 6th Baron Byron of Rochdale. 1788–1824. British poet whose works include *Childe Harold* (1812–18) and *Don Juan* (1819–24). **—By•ron′ic** (bī-rŏn′ĭk) *adj.*

bys•si•no•sis (bĭs′ĭ-nō′sĭs) *n.* A respiratory disease caused by the long-term inhalation of cotton, flax, or hemp dust and marked by shortness of breath, coughing, and wheezing. [LLat. *byssinum*, linen garment (< Lat. *byssus*, flax) + -OSIS.]

bys•sus (bĭs′əs) *n., pl.* **bys•sus•es** or **bys•si** (bĭs′ī′). **1.** *Zool.*

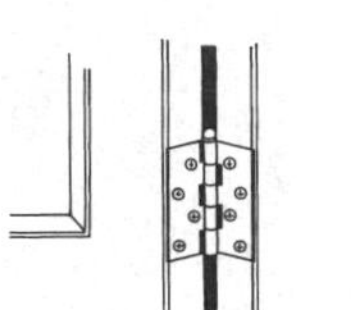

butt hinge

buzzard
Turkey vulture
Cathartes aura

Richard E. Byrd
Photographed c. 1933

ă pat	oi boy
ā pay	ou out
âr care	o͝o took
ä father	o͞o boot
ĕ pet	ŭ cut
ē be	ûr urge
ĭ pit	th thin
ī pie	*th* this
îr pier	hw which
ŏ pot	zh vision
ō toe	ə about, item
ô paw	

Stress marks:
′ (primary);
′ (secondary), as in dictionary (dĭk′shə-nĕr′ē)

A mass of strong silky filaments by which certain bivalve mollusks attach themselves to fixed surfaces. **2.** A fine-textured linen of ancient times, used by the Egyptians for wrapping mummies. [ME *bissus*, linen cloth < Lat., flax < Gk. *bussos*, linen, ult. < Egypt. *w'd*.]

by•stand•er (bī′stăn′dər) *n.* A person who is present at an event without participating in it.

by•street (bī′strēt′) *n.* A side street.

byte (bīt) *n.* **1.** A sequence of adjacent bits operated on as a unit by a computer. **2.** The amount of computer memory needed to store one character of a specified size, usu. 8 or 16 bits. [Alteration and blend of BIT[3] and BITE.]

by the way *adv.* Incidentally.

By•tom (bē′tôm′, bĭ′-). A city of SW Poland NW of Katowice; assigned to Poland in 1945. Pop. 239,200.

by•way (bī′wā′) *n.* **1.** A side road. **2.** A secondary or arcane field of study.

by•word also **by-word** (bī′wûrd′) *n.* **1.a.** A proverbial expression; a proverb. **b.** An often-used word or phrase. **2.** One that represents a type, class, or quality. **3.** An object of notoriety or interest. **4.** An epithet. [ME *byworde* < OE *bīword*, transl. of Lat. *prōverbium*.]

Byz•an•tine (bĭz′ən-tēn′, -tīn′, bĭ-zăn′tĭn) *adj.* **1.a.** Of or relating to the ancient city of Byzantium. **b.** Of or relating to the Byzantine Empire. **2.** Of or belonging to the architecture developed from the fifth century A.D. in the Byzantine Empire, characterized by a central dome resting on a cube and by the extensive use of surface decoration. **3.** Of the painting and decorative style developed in the Byzantine Empire, marked by frontal stylized figures, rich use of color, and religious subject matter. **4.** Of the Eastern Orthodox Church or its rites. **5.** Often **byzantine. a.** Of or relating to intrigue; scheming. **b.** Highly complicated. —*n.* A native or inhabitant of Byzantium or the Byzantine Empire.

Byzantine Empire. The E part of the later Roman Empire, dating from A.D. 330 to the fall of Constantinople to the Ottoman Turks in 1453.

By•zan•ti•um (bĭ-zăn′shē-əm, -tē-əm). **1.** The Byzantine Empire. **2.** An ancient city of Thrace on the site of present-day Istanbul, Turkey; founded by the Greeks in the 7th cent. B.C. and rebuilt by Constantine I in A.D. 330.

BZ (bē′zē′) *n.* Used by the U.S. Army as a code for a gas, $C_{21}H_{23}NO_3$, that produces incapacitating disorientation when inhaled. [Poss. abbr. of *benzilic* < BENZOIN.]

Cc

cab[1]

cable car

Mother Cabrini

c[1] or **C** (sē) *n., pl.* **c's** or **C's. 1.** The third letter of the modern English alphabet. **2.** Any of the speech sounds represented by the letter *c*. **3.** The third in a series. **4. C.** The third best or third highest in quality or rank. **5.** *Mus.* **a.** The first tone in the scale of C major or the third tone in the relative minor scale. **b.** A key or scale in which the tone of C is the tonic.

c[2] *abbr.* **1.** *Phys.* Candle. **2.** Carat. **3.** *Phys.* Charm quark. **4.** Also **C** *Math.* Constant. **5.** Cubic.

C[1] (sē) *n.* A computer programming language widely used on microcomputers.

C[2] **1.** The symbol for the element **carbon** 1. **2.** Also **c** The symbol for the Roman numeral one hundred. **3. c** The symbol for the speed of light in a vacuum. **4.** *Elect.* The symbol for **capacitance** 1, 2. **5.** *Phys.* The symbol for **charge conjugation.**

C[3] *abbr.* **1.** Celsius. **2.** Centigrade. **3.** Also **C.** *Phys.* Charm. **4.** *Slang.* Cocaine. **5.** Coulomb.

c. or **C.** *abbr.* **1.** Capacity. **2.** Cape. **3.** Carton. **4.** Case. **5.** Catcher. **6.** Cent. **7.** Centavo. **8.** Centime. **9.** Century. **10.** Chapter. **11.** Church. **12.** Circa. **13.** *Lat.* Congius (gallon). **14.** Consul. **15.** Copy. **16.** Copyright. **17.** Corps. **18.** Cup.

C. *abbr.* **1.** Catholic. **2.** Celtic. **3.** Chancellor. **4.** Chief. **5.** City. **6.** Companion. **7.** Congress. **8.** Conservative. **9.** Court.

ca *abbr.* **1.** Centare. **2.** Circa.

Ca The symbol for the element **calcium.**

CA *abbr.* **1.** California. **2.** Also **C.A.** Chronological age.

C.A. *abbr.* **1.** Central America. **2.** Central American.

CAA or **C.A.A.** *abbr.* Civil Aeronautics Administration.

cab[1] (kăb) *n.* **1.** A taxicab. **2.** The covered compartment for the operator or driver of a heavy vehicle or machine. **3.** A one-horse vehicle for public hire. —*v.* **cabbed, cab•bing, cabs.** —*intr.* **1.** To travel in a taxicab. **2.** To drive a taxicab. —*tr.* To transport in a taxicab. [Short for CABRIOLET.]

cab[2] also **kab** (kăb) *n.* An ancient Hebrew unit of measure equal to about 2 liters (2.1 quarts). [Heb. *qab*, hollow vessel.]

CAB *abbr.* Civil Aeronautics Board.

ca•bal (kə-băl′) *n.* **1.** A conspiratorial group. **2.** A secret scheme. —*intr.v.* **-balled, -bal•ling, -bals.** To form a cabal. [Fr. *cabale* < Med.Lat. *cabala*. See CABALA.]

cab•a•la or **cab•ba•la** also **kab•a•la** or **kab•ba•la** (kăb′ə-lə, kə-bä′-) *n.* **1.** Often **Cabala.** A body of mystical teachings of rabbinical origin, often based on an esoteric interpretation of the Hebrew Scriptures. **2.** A secret doctrine resembling these teachings. [Med.Lat. < Heb. *qabbālâ*, received doctrine, tradition < *qibbēl*, to receive.] —**cab′a•lism** *n.* —**cab′a•list** *n.*

ca•ba•let•ta (kăb′ə-lĕt′ə, kä′bə-) *n., pl.* **-let•tas** or **-let•te** (-lĕt′ē). *Mus.* **1.** A short aria that has a repetitive rhythm and a simple style. **2.** The final section of an aria or duet in a quick uniform rhythm. [Ital., alteration of *coboletta*, stanza, dim. of *cobola* < OProv. *cobla* < Lat. *cōpula*, link.]

cab•a•lis•tic (kăb′ə-lĭs′tĭk) *adj.* **1.** Having a secret or hidden meaning; occult. **2.** Of or relating to the cabala. —**cab′a•lis′ti•cal•ly** *adv.*

cab•al•le•ro (kăb′ə-lâr′ō, -əl-yâr′ō, kä′bä-yĕ′rō) *n., pl.* **-ros. 1.** A Spanish gentleman; a cavalier. **2.** A man skilled in riding and managing horses. [Sp. < LLat. *caballārius*, horse groom < Lat. *caballus*, horse.]

ca•ban•a also **ca•ba•ña** (kə-băn′ə, -băn′yə) *n.* A shelter on a beach or at a swimming pool used as a bathhouse. [Sp. *cabaña* < LLat. *capanna*, hut.]

Ca•ba•na•tuan (kä′bə-nə-twän′, -bä-nä-). A city of central Luzon, Philippines, N of Manila; site of a World War II Japanese prison camp. Pop. 38,400.

cab•a•ret (kăb′ə-rā′) *n.* **1.** A restaurant or nightclub providing short programs of live entertainment. **2.** The entertainment so provided. [Fr., taproom < MDu. *cabret* < ONFr. *camberette* < LLat. *camera*, room. See CHAMBER.]

cab•bage (kăb′ĭj) *n.* **1.** Any of several forms of a European vegetable *(Brassica oleracea* var. *capitata)* of the mustard family, having a globose head consisting of a short stem and tightly overlapping leaves. **2.** Any of several similar or related plants, such as Chinese cabbage. **3.** The terminal bud of several species of palm, eaten as a vegetable. **4.** *Slang.* Money, esp. bills. [ME *caboche* < ONFr., head, poss. < alteration of Lat. *caput*. See CAPITAL[1].] —**cab′bag•y** *adj.*

cabbage butterfly *n.* Any of several white butterflies of the genus *Pieris*, having larvae that feed on cabbage.

cabbage palm *n.* **1.** Any of several palms, such as the assai, with edible terminal buds. **2.** See **cabbage palmetto.**

cabbage palmetto *n.* A species of palmetto *(Sabal palmetto)* native to southeast North America and having an edible terminal bud.

cabbage rose *n.* A prickly shrub *(Rosa centifolia)* native to the Caucasus and having fragrant pink double-petaled flowers.

cab•bage•worm (kăb′ĭj-wûrm′) *n.* A larva that feeds on cabbage, esp. the bright green larva of the cabbage butterfly.

cab•ba•la (kăb′ə-lə, kə-bä′-) *n.* Var. of **cabala.**

cab•by or **cab•bie** (kăb′ē) *n., pl.* **-bies.** A cabdriver.

cab•driv•er also **cab driver** (kăb′drī′vər) *n.* One who drives a taxicab for hire.

Cab•ell (kăb′əl), **James Branch.** 1879–1958. Amer. writer best known for his satirical novels, including *Jurgen* (1919).

ca•ber (kā′bər) *n.* *Sports.* A long, heavy wooden pole tossed end over end as a demonstration of strength in Scottish highland games. [Sc.Gael. *cabar*, pole, beam, rafter < VLat. **capriō* < Lat. *capra*, she-goat. See CHEVRON.]

cab•er•net (kăb′ər-nā′) *n.* A dry red wine made from the black grape variety *Cabernet sauvignon*. [Fr.]

Ca•be•za de Va•ca (kə-bā′zə də vä′kə, kä-vĕ′thä *thĕ* vä′kä), **Álvar Núñez.** 1490?–1557? Spanish colonial administrator who explored parts of present-day FL, TX, and Mexico.

Ca•bi•mas (kə-bē′məs, kä-vē′mäs). A town of NW Venezuela on the NE shore of Lake Maracaibo. Pop. 183,000.

cab•in (kăb′ĭn) *n.* **1.** A small, roughly built house. **2.** *Naut.* **a.** A room in a ship used as living quarters. **b.** An enclosed compartment in a boat serving as a shelter or living quarters. **3.** The enclosed space in an aircraft or spacecraft for the crew, passengers, or cargo. —*tr. & intr.v.* **-ined, -in•ing, -ins.** To confine or live in or as if in a small space. [ME *caban* < OFr. *cabane* < OProv. *cabana* < LLat. *capanna*.]

cabin boy *n.* A boy servant aboard a ship.

cabin class *n.* *Naut.* A class of accommodations on passenger ships, below first class and above tourist class.

cabin cruiser *n.* *Naut.* A powerboat with a cabin that has living accommodations.

Ca•bin•da (kə-bĭn′də). A territory of Angola forming an exclave on the Atlantic Ocean between Congo and Zaire.

cab•i•net (kăb′ə-nĭt) *n.* **1.** An upright cupboardlike repository with shelves, drawers, or compartments. **2.** Often **Cabinet.** A body of persons appointed by a chief of state or prime minister to head the executive departments of the government and act as official advisers. **3.** *Archaic.* A small or private room set aside for a specific activity. **4.** *Rhode Island & Southeastern Massachusetts.* See **milk shake** 1. See Regional Note at **milk shake.** [Fr., partly < dim. of ONFr. *cabine*, gambling room (perh. alteration of OFr. *cabane*, small house; see CABIN) and partly < Ital. *gabinetto*, closet, chest of drawers; akin to ONFr. *cabine*.] **—cab′i•net** *adj.* **—cab′i•net•ful** *n.*

cab•i•net•mak•er (kăb′ə-nĭt-mā′kər) *n.* An artisan specializing in making fine articles of wooden furniture. **—cab′i•net•mak′ing** *n.*

cab•i•net•ry (kăb′ĭ-nĭ-trē) *n.* Cabinetwork.

cab•i•net•work (kăb′ə-nĭt-wûrk′) *n.* Finished woodwork fashioned by a cabinetmaker.

cabin fever *n.* Uneasiness or distress that results from living in a remote region or in a small enclosed space.

ca•ble (kā′bəl) *n.* **1.a.** A strong, heavy steel or fiber rope. **b.** Something that resembles such rope. **2.** *Elect.* A bound or sheathed group of insulated conductors. **3.** *Naut.* **a.** A heavy rope or chain for mooring or anchoring a ship. **b.** A cable length. **4.** A cablegram. **5.** Cable television. **—***v.* **-bled, -bling, -bles.** **—***tr.* **1.a.** To send a cablegram to. **b.** To transmit (a message) by telegraph. **2.** To supply or fasten with a cable. **—***intr.* To send a cablegram. [ME < ONFr. < LLat. *capulum*, lasso < Lat. *capere*, to seize. See **kap-***.] **—ca′bler** *n.*

Ca•ble (kā′bəl), **George Washington.** 1844–1925. Amer. writer whose works include *Grandissimes* (1880).

cable car *n.* A car designed to operate on a cableway or cable railway.

ca•ble•cast (kā′bəl-kăst′) *n.* A telecast by cable television. [CABLE + (BROAD)CAST.] **—ca′ble•cast′** *v.* **—ca′ble•cast′er** *n.*

ca•ble•gram (kā′bəl-grăm′) *n.* A telegram sent by submarine cable. [CABLE + (TELE)GRAM.]

ca•ble-laid (kā′bəl-lād′) *adj.* Made of three ropes of three strands each, twisted together counterclockwise.

cable length *n. Naut.* A unit of length equal to 720 feet (220 meters) in the United States and 608 feet (185 meters) in England.

cable railway *n.* A railroad on which the cars are moved by an endless cable driven by a stationary engine.

cable stitch *n.* A stitch in knitting that produces a twisted ropelike design.

ca•blet (kā′blĭt) *n.* A cable-laid rope with a circumference of less than 10 inches (25 centimeters).

cable television *n.* A television distribution system in which station signals are delivered by cable to subscribers.

ca•ble•way (kā′bəl-wā′) *n.* A suspended cable used as a track typically for a cable car.

cab•man (kăb′mən) *n.* A man who drives a taxicab.

cab•o•chon (kăb′ə-shŏn′) *n.* **1.** A highly polished, convex-cut, unfaceted gem. **2.** A convex style of cutting gems. [Fr. < ONFr., aug. of *caboche*, head. See CABBAGE.] **—cab′o•chon′** *adv.*

ca•bom•ba (kə-bŏm′bə) *n.* See **fanwort.** [Am.Sp.]

ca•boo•dle (kə-bo͝od′l) *n. Informal.* **1.** The lot or bunch. **2.** A crowd or collection of people. [Alteration of BOODLE.]

ca•boose (kə-bo͞os′) *n.* **1.** The last car on a freight train, having kitchen and sleeping facilities for the train crew. **2.** *Obsolete.* **a.** A ship's galley. **b.** A cast-iron cooking range used in such galleys. **c.** An outdoor oven or fireplace. [Poss. < obsolete Du. *cabūse*, ship's galley < MLGer. *kabūse* : perh. **kab-*, cabin; akin to OFr. *cabane*; see CABIN + MHGer. *hūs*, house.]

Cab•ot (kăb′ət), **John.** 1450?–98? Italian-born explorer who commanded the English expedition that explored the North American mainland (1497).

Cabot, Sebastian. 1476?–1557. Italian-born explorer who led an English expedition in search of the Northwest Passage (1509).

cab•o•tage (kăb′ə-täzh′) *n.* **1.** Trade or navigation in coastal waters. **2.** The exclusive right of a country to operate the air traffic within its territory. [Fr. < *caboter*, to sail along a coast, perh. < Sp. *cabo*, cape < Lat. *caput*, head. See CAPE[2].]

ca•bret•ta (kə-brĕt′ə) *n.* A soft kidlike leather made from sheepskin having coarse hairlike wool. [Sp. and Port. *cabra*, she-goat (both < Lat. *capra*, fem. of *caper*, goat) + Ital. *-etta*, dim. suff.]

ca•bril•la (kə-brē′yə, -brĭl′ə) *n.* Any of various sea basses, esp. *Epinephelus guttatus*, of tropical waters. [Sp., dim. of *cabra*, she-goat. See CABRETTA.]

Ca•bri•ni (kə-brē′nē), Saint **Frances Xavier.** "Mother Cabrini." 1850–1917. Italian-born religious leader who was the first American to be canonized (1946).

cab•ri•ole (kăb′rē-ōl′) *n.* A form of furniture leg that curves outward and then narrows downward into an ornamental foot. [Fr., caper. See CABRIOLET.]

cab•ri•o•let (kăb′rē-ə-lā′) *n.* **1.** A two-wheeled one-horse carriage that has two seats and a folding top. **2.** An automobile with a folding top; a convertible coupe. [Fr., dim. of *cabriole*, caper < obsolete *capriole* < Ital. *capriola* < *capriolo*, roebuck < Lat. *capreolus*, masc. dim. of *caprea*, roe deer < *caper*, he-goat.]

cab•stand (kăb′stănd′) *n.* A place for taxicabs to wait.

cac– *pref.* Var. of **caco–.**

ca•ca•o (kə-kä′ō, -kā′ō) *n., pl.* **-os. 1.** An evergreen tropical American tree *(Theobroma cacao)* having leathery, ellipsoid ten-ribbed fruits. **2.** The cacao seed, used in making chocolate, cocoa, and cocoa butter. [Sp. < Nahuatl *cacahuatl*.]

cacao butter *n.* See **cocoa butter.**

cach•a•lot (kăsh′ə-lŏt′, -lō′) *n.* See **sperm whale.** [Fr. < Sp. or Port. *cachalote*, aug. of *cachola*, big head.]

cache (kăsh) *n.* **1.a.** A hiding place used esp. for storing provisions. **b.** A place for concealment and safekeeping, as of valuables. **c.** The store of goods in a hiding place. **2.** *Comp. Sci.* A fast storage buffer in the central processing unit of a computer. **—***tr.v.* **cached, cach•ing, cach•es.** To hide or store in a cache. See Syns at **hide**[1]. [Fr. < *cacher*, to hide < OFr., to press, hide < VLat. **coācticāre*, to store, pack together, freq. of Lat. *coāctāre*, to constrain < *coāctus*, p.part. of *cōgere*, to force. See COGENT.]

cache memory *n. Comp. Sci.* See **cache** 2.

cache•pot (kăsh′pŏt′, -pō′) *n.* An ornamental container for a flowerpot. [Fr. : *cacher*, to hide; see CACHE + *pot*, pot (< OFr. < VLat. **pottus*).]

ca•chet (kă-shā′) *n.* **1.** A mark or a quality, as of distinction or authenticity. **2.** A seal on a document, such as a letter. **3.a.** A commemorative design stamped on an envelope. **b.** A motto on a postal cancellation. **4.** A wafer capsule formerly used by pharmacists to present an unpleasant-tasting drug. [Fr. < OFr. < *cacher*, to press. See CACHE.]

ca•chex•i•a (kə-kĕk′sē-ə) *n.* Weight loss, wasting of muscle, and debility that can occur during a chronic disease. [LLat. < Gk. *kakhexia* : *kako-*, caco- + *hexis*, condition (< *ekhein*, to have; see **segh-***).] **—ca•chec′tic** (kə-kĕk′tĭk) *adj.*

cach•in•nate (kăk′ə-nāt′) *intr.v.* **-nat•ed, -nat•ing, -nates.** To laugh hard, loudly, or convulsively; guffaw. [Lat. *cachinnāre, cachinnāt-*, prob. of imit. orig.] **—cach′in•na′tion** *n.* **—cach′in•na′tor** *n.*

ca•chou (kă-sho͞o′, kăsh′o͞o) *n.* A pastille that is used to sweeten the breath. [Fr. < Port. *cachu* < Malayalam *kāccu* < Tamil *kāyccu*.]

ca•chu•cha (kə-cho͞o′chə) *n.* An Andalusian solo dance in 3/4 time. [Sp., small boat, cachucha, poss. < dim. of *cacho*, shard, saucepan, prob. < VLat. **cacculus*, alteration of Lat. *caccabus*, pot < Gk. *kakkabos*, prob. of Semitic orig.; akin to Akkadian *kukubu*, vessel.]

ca•cique (kə-sēk′) *n.* **1.** An American Indian chief, esp. in Latin America during colonial and postcolonial times. **2.** A local political boss in Spain or Latin America. [Am.Sp. < Arawak *kassequa*, chieftain.]

cack•le (kăk′əl) *v.* **-led, -ling, -les.** **—***intr.* **1.** To make the shrill cry characteristic of a hen after laying an egg. **2.** To laugh or talk in a shrill manner. **—***tr.* To utter in cackles. **—***n.* **1.** The act or sound of cackling. **2.** Shrill laughter. **3.** Foolish chatter. [ME *cakelen*, prob. < MLGer. *kākeln*, of imit. orig.] **—cack′ler** *n.*

caco– or **cac–** *pref.* Bad: *cacography.* [Gk. *kako-* < *kakos*, bad. See **kakka-***.]

cac•o•dyl (kăk′ə-dĭl′) *n.* **1.** The arsenic group $(CH_3)_2As^-$. **2.** A foul-smelling poisonous oil, $As_2(CH_3)_4$. [Gk. *kakōdēs*, bad-smelling (*kakos*, bad; see **kakka-*** + *-ōdēs*, -smelling < *ozein*, *ŏd-*, to smell) + –YL.] **—cac′o•dyl′ic** *adj.*

cac•o•ë•thes (kăk′ō-ē′thēz) *n.* An irresistible compulsion; a mania. [Lat. *cacoēthes* < neut. of Gk. *kakoēthēs*, ill-disposed : *kakos*, bad; see **kakka-*** + *ēthos*, disposition; see **s(w)e-***.]

ca•cog•ra•phy (kə-kŏg′rə-fē) *n.* **1.** Bad handwriting. **2.** Bad spelling.

cac•o•mis•tle (kăk′ə-mĭs′əl) *n.* A small carnivorous raccoonlike mammal *(Bassariscus sumichrasti)* of Central America, having a black-banded tail. [Am.Sp. *cacomiztle* < Nahuatl *tlacomiztli* : *tlaco*, half, part + *miztli*, mountain lion.]

cac•o•nym (kăk′ə-nĭm) *n.* An erroneous name, esp. in taxonomy; a misnomer. **—ca•con′y•my** (kə-kŏn′ə-mē) *n.*

ca•coph•o•nous (kə-kŏf′ə-nəs) *adj.* Having a harsh unpleasant sound. [< Gk. *kakophōnos* : *kakos*, bad; see **kakka-*** + *phōnē*, sound; see **bhā-**[2]***.] **—ca•coph′o•nous•ly** *adv.*

ca•coph•o•ny (kə-kŏf′ə-nē) *n., pl.* **-nies. 1.** Jarring, discordant sound; dissonance. **2.** The use of harsh or discordant sounds in literary composition. [Fr. *cacophonie* < Gk. *kakophōnia* < *kakophōnos*, cacophonous. See CACOPHONOUS.]

cac•tus (kăk′təs) *n., pl.* **-ti** (-tī′) or **-tus•es. 1.** Any of various succulent spiny plants native mostly to arid regions of the New World, often having showy flowers. **2.** Any of several similar plants. [Lat., cardoon < Gk. *kaktos*.]

cactus pear *n.* See **tuna**[2].

ca•cu•mi•nal (kə-kyo͞o′mə-nəl) *adj.* Articulated with the tip of the tongue turned back and up toward the roof of the mouth; retroflex. [< Lat. *cacūmen*, *cacūmin-*, summit, point.]

cad (kăd) *n.* An unprincipled, ill-mannered man. [Short for CADDIE.] **—cad′dish** *adj.* **—cad′dish•ly** *adv.* **—cad′dish•ness** *n.*

cachepot
c. 1730 French

ă pat	oi boy
ā pay	ou out
âr care	o͝o took
ä father	o͞o boot
ĕ pet	ŭ cut
ē be	ûr urge
ĭ pit	th thin
ī pie	*th* this
îr pier	hw which
ŏ pot	zh vision
ō toe	ə about, item
ô paw	

Stress marks:
′ (primary);
′ (secondary), as in
dictionary (dĭk′shə-nĕr′ē)

CAD *abbr.* Computer-aided design.
ca•das•tre also **ca•das•ter** (kə-dăs′tər) *n.* A public record, survey, or map of the value, extent, and ownership of land as a basis of taxation. [Fr. < Prov. *cadastro* < Ital. *catastro*, alteration of OItal. *catastico* < LGk. *katastikhon*, register : Gk. *kata-*, by; see CATA- + Gk. *stikhos*, line; see **steigh-***.] — **ca•das′tral** *adj.*
ca•dav•er (kə-dăv′ər) *n.* A dead body, esp. one intended for dissection. [ME < Lat. *cadāver* < *cadere*, to fall, die. See **kad-***.] — **ca•dav′er•ic** (-ər-ĭk) *adj.*
ca•dav•er•ine (kə-dăv′ə-rēn′) *n.* A syrupy, colorless, fuming ptomaine, $C_5H_{14}N_2$, formed by the carboxylation of lysine by bacteria in decaying animal flesh.
ca•dav•er•ous (kə-dăv′ər-əs) *adj.* **1.** Suggestive of death; corpselike. **2.a.** Of corpselike pallor; pallid. **b.** Emaciated; gaunt. — **ca•dav′er•ous•ly** *adv.* — **ca•dav′er•ous•ness** *n.*
cad•die also **cad•dy** (kăd′ē) —*n., pl.* **-dies. 1.** One hired to assist a golfer, esp. to carry golf clubs. **2.** *Scots.* A boy who does odd jobs. —*intr.v.* **-died, -dy•ing, -dies.** To serve as a caddie. [Sc. < Fr. *cadet*, cadet, caddie. See CADET.]
cad•dis also **cad•dice** (kăd′ĭs) *n.* A coarse woolen fabric, yarn, or ribbon binding. [Prob. < ME *cadace*, cotton wool (< AN < OProv. *cadarz*) and < Fr. *cadis*, woolen cloth (< OProv.).]
caddis fly also **caddice fly** *n.* Any of various four-winged insects of the order Trichoptera, found near lakes and streams. [Perh. < obsolete *cad* (influenced by CADDIS) var. of COD[2].]
caddis worm also **caddice worm** *n.* The aquatic wormlike larva of the caddis fly, enclosed in a cylindrical case.

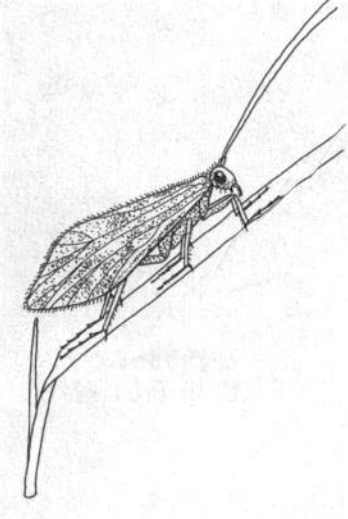
caddis fly

Cad•do (kăd′ō) *n., pl.* **Caddo** or **-dos. 1.** A member of a Native American confederacy formerly inhabiting the Red River area of Louisiana, Arkansas, and eastern Texas and now located in central Oklahoma. **2.** The Caddoan language of the Caddo. [Fr. < Caddo *kaduhdá·čuʔ*, a Caddo tribe.]
Cad•do•an (kăd′ō-ən) *n.* A family of North American Indian languages formerly spoken in the Dakotas, Kansas, Nebraska, Texas, Oklahoma, Arkansas, and Louisiana and presently spoken in North Dakota and Oklahoma.
cad•dy[1] (kăd′ē) *n., pl.* **-dies.** A small container, such as a box, used esp. for holding tea. [Alteration of CATTY[1].]
cad•dy[2] (kăd′ē) *n. & v.* Var. of **caddie.**
cade (kād) *adj.* Left by its mother and reared by hand: *a cade calf.* [ME, pet lamb.]
Cade (kād), **Jack.** d. 1450. English rebel who led an unsuccessful rebellion against Henry VI.
-cade *suff.* Procession: *motorcade.* [< CAVALCADE.]
ca•delle (kə-dĕl′) *n.* A small blackish beetle *(Tenebroides mauritanicus),* both the larval and adult forms of which damage stored grain. [Fr. < Prov. *cadello* < Lat. *catella*, fem. of *catellus*, puppy < *catulus*, the young of animals. See **kat-***.]
ca•dence (kād′ns) *n., pl.* **-denc•es. 1.** Balanced, rhythmic flow, as of poetry. **2.** The measure or beat of movement, as in dancing. **3.a.** A falling inflection of the voice. **b.** General inflection or modulation of the voice. **4.** *Mus.* A progression of chords moving to a harmonic close or point of rest. [ME < OFr. **cadence* < OItal. *cadenza* < VLat. **cadentia*, a falling < Lat. *cadēns*, *cadent-*, pr.part. of *cadere*, to fall. See **kad-***.] — **ca′denced** *adj.*
ca•den•cy (kād′n-sē) *n., pl.* **-den•cies.** Cadence.
ca•dent (kād′nt) *adj.* **1.** Having cadence or rhythm. **2.** *Archaic.* Falling, as water or tears. [Lat. *cadēns*, *cadent-*, pr.part. of *cadere*, to fall. See **kad-***.]
ca•den•tial (kə-dĕn′shəl) *adj.* **1.** Of or relating to a cadence. **2.** *Mus.* Of or having to do with a cadenza.
ca•den•za (kə-dĕn′zə) *n. Mus.* **1.** An elaborate melodic flourish interpolated into an aria or other vocal piece. **2.** An extended virtuosic section for the soloist near the end of a movement of a concerto. [Ital. < OItal., cadence. See CADENCE.]
ca•det (kə-dĕt′) *n.* **1.** A student at a military school who is training to be an officer. **2.a.** A younger son or brother. **b.** A youngest son. **3.** *Slang.* A pimp. [Fr. < dial. *capdet*, captain < LLat. *capitellum*, dim. of Lat. *caput*, *capit-*, head. See **kaput-***.] — **ca•det′ship′** *n.*
cadge (kăj) *intr. & tr.v.* **cadged, cadg•ing, cadg•es.** To beg or get by begging. [Perh. back-formation < obsolete *cadger*, peddler < ME *cadgear.*] — **cadg′er** *n.*
Cad•il•lac (kăd′l-ăk′, kä-dē-yäk′), Sieur **Antoine de la Mothe.** 1658–1730. French explorer and colonial administrator who founded Detroit (1701).

caduceus

Cá•diz (kə-dĭz′, kā′dĭz, kä′-, kä′thēth, -thēs). A city of SW Spain NW of Gibraltar on the **Gulf of Cádiz,** an inlet of the Atlantic; founded c. 1100 B.C. Pop. 160,839.
cad•mi•um (kăd′mē-əm) *n. Symbol* **Cd** A soft metallic element occurring primarily in zinc, copper, and lead ores that is used in low-friction fatigue-resistant alloys, solders, batteries, nuclear reactor shields, and electroplating. Atomic number 48; atomic weight 112.40; melting point 320.9°C; boiling point 765°C; specific gravity 8.65; valence 2. See table at **element.** [Lat. *cadmīa*, calamine (from its being found with calamine in zinc ore) (< Gk. *kadmeia (gē)*, Theban (earth) < *Kadmos*, Cadmus) + -IUM.] — **cad′mic** (-mĭk) *adj.*
Cad•mus (kăd′məs) *n. Gk. Myth.* A Phoenician prince who founded Thebes and introduced writing to the Greeks.
cad•re (kăd′rē, kä′drā) *n.* **1.** A nucleus of trained personnel around which a larger organization can be built. **2.a.** A tightly knit group of zealots in a revolutionary party. **b.** A member of a cadre. **3.** A framework. [Fr. < Ital. *quadro*, frame < Lat. *quadrum*, a square. See **kʷetwer-***.]
ca•du•ce•us (kə-do͞o′sē-əs, -shəs, -dyo͞o′-) *n., pl.* **-ce•i** (-sē-ī′). **1.a.** A herald's wand or staff. **b.** *Gk. Myth.* A winged staff with two serpents twined around it, carried by Hermes. **2.** An insignia modeled on Hermes's staff, used as the symbol of the medical profession. [Lat. *cādūceus*, alteration of Gk. *karukeion* < *karux*, herald.] — **ca•du′ce•an** *adj.*
ca•du•ci•ty (kə-do͞o′sĭ-tē, -dyo͞o′-) *n.* **1.** The frailty of old age; senility. **2.** The quality or state of being perishable; impermanence. [Fr. *caducité* < *caduc*, frail, falling < Lat. *cadūcus*. See CADUCOUS.]
ca•du•cous (kə-do͞o′kəs, -dyo͞o′-) *adj.* Dropping off or shedding at an early stage of development, as some sepals. [< Lat. *cadūcus*, falling < *cadere*, to fall. See **kad-***.]
cae•cil•ian (sə-sĭl′yən, -sĭl′ē-ən, -sēl′-) *n.* Any of various legless burrowing wormlike amphibians of the order Gymnophiona, of tropical regions. [< Lat. *caecilia*, a kind of lizard < *caecus*, blind (from its small eyes).]
cae•cum (sē′kəm) *n.* Var. of **cecum.**
Caed•mon (kăd′mən). d. c. 680. The earliest English poet, who supposedly received the power of song in a vision.
Cae•li•an (sē′lē-ən). One of the seven hills of ancient Rome; devastated by fire in A.D. 27. — **Cae′li•an** *adj.*
Cae•lum (sē′ləm) *n.* A constellation in the Southern Hemisphere near Columba and Eridanus. [Lat. *caelum*, sculptor's chisel. See **kaə-id-***.]
Caen (käN). A city of N France SW of Le Havre; a Huguenot stronghold in the 16th and 17th cent. Pop. 114,068.
caer•phil•ly (kär-fĭl′ē) *n.* A mild white Welsh cheese. [After *Caerphilly*, a district of SE Wales.]
cae•sar also **Cae•sar** (sē′zər) *n.* **1.** Used as a title and form of address for Roman emperors. **2.** A dictator or an autocrat. [ME *cesar* < Lat. *Caesar*, after Julius CAESAR.]
Caesar, Julius. In full Gaius Julius Caesar. 100–44 B.C. Roman general, statesman, and historian who invaded Britain (55), crushed the army of his political enemy Pompey (48), and was given a mandate by the people to rule as dictator for life (45). He was murdered by a group of republicans led by Cassius and Brutus. — **Cae•sar′e•an, Cae•sar′i•an** (sĭ-zâr′ē-ən) *adj.*
Cae•sa•re•a (sē′zə-rē′ə, sĕs′ə-, sĕz′ə-). **1.** Also **Caesarea Pal•e•sti•nae** (păl′ĭ-stī′nē). An ancient seaport of Palestine S of present-day Haifa, Israel; founded 30 B.C. by Herod the Great. **2.** Also **Caesarea Phil•ip•pi** (fĭl′ĭ-pī, fĭ-lĭp′ī). An ancient city of N Palestine near Mt. Hermon in present-day SW Syria. **3.** Also **Caesarea Maz•a•ca** (măz′ə-kə). An ancient city of Cappadocia on the site of Kayseri in central Turkey.
cae•sar•e•an (sĭ-zâr′ē-ən) *adj. & n.* Var. of **cesarean.**
caesarean section *n.* Var. of **cesarean section.**
cae•sar•i•an (sĭ-zâr′ē-ən) *adj. & n.* Var. of **cesarean.**
Cae•sar•ism (sē′zə-rĭz′əm) *n.* Military or imperial dictatorship; political authoritarianism. — **Cae′sar•ist** *n.* — **Cae′sar•is′tic** *adj.*
caesar salad *n.* A tossed salad of greens, anchovies, croutons, and grated cheese with a dressing of olive oil, lemon juice, and a raw or coddled egg. [Poss. after *Caesar's*, a restaurant in Tijuana, Mexico.]
cae•si•um (sē′zē-əm) *n.* Var. of **cesium.**
cae•su•ra also **ce•su•ra** (sĭ-zho͝or′ə, -zo͝or′ə) *n., pl.* **-su•ras** or **-su•rae** (-zho͝or′ē, -zo͝or′ē). **1.** A pause in a line of verse, esp. at a sense division. **2.** A pause or an interruption, as in conversation. **3.** In Latin and Greek prosody, a word ending within a foot. **4.** *Mus.* A pause or breathing at a point of rhythmic division in a melody. [Lat. *caesūra*, a cutting < *caesus*, p.part. of *caedere*, to cut off. See **kaə-id-***.] — **cae•su′ral, cae•su′ric** *adj.*
ca•fé also **ca•fe** (kă-fā′, kə-) *n.* A coffeehouse, restaurant, or bar. [Fr., coffee, café < Ital. *caffè*, coffee < Ottoman Turk. *qahveh*. See COFFEE.]
ca•fé au lait (kă-fā′ ō lā′) *n.* **1.** Coffee served with hot milk. See Regional Note at **beignet. 2.** *Color.* A light coffee hue. [Fr. : *café*, coffee + *à*, with + *lait*, milk.]
café fil•tre (fĭl′trə) *n.* A beverage made by passing boiling water through ground coffee held in a filtering device that fits on top of a cup or pot. [Fr. : *café*, coffee + *filtre*, filter.]
café noir (nwär′) *n.* Coffee served without cream or milk. [Fr. : *café*, coffee + *noir*, black.]
caf•e•te•ri•a (kăf′ĭ-tîr′ē-ə) *n.* A restaurant in which the customers are served at a counter and carry their meals on trays to tables. [Sp. *cafetería*, coffee shop, cafeteria < *café*, coffee < Ottoman Turk. *qahveh*. See COFFEE.]
caf•e•to•ri•um (kăf′ĭ-tôr′ē-əm, -tōr′-) *n., pl.* **-to•ri•ums** or **-to•ri•a** (-tôr′ē-ə, -tōr′-). A room, usu. in a school, doubling as cafeteria and auditorium. [CAFE(TERIA) + (AUDI)TORIUM.]
caf•feine also **caf•fein** (kă-fēn′, kăf′ēn′, kăf′ē-ĭn) *n.* A bitter white alkaloid, $C_8H_{10}N_4O_2$, often derived from tea or coffee and used in medicine chiefly as a mild stimulant. [Ger. *Kaffein* (< *Kaffee*, coffee) or Fr. *caféine*, both < Fr. *café*, coffee. See CAFÉ.] — **caf′fein•at′ed** (kăf′ə-nā′tĭd) *adj.*

caf·fe lat·te (käf′fĕ lät′tĕ, kăf′ā) *n.* See **latte.**

caf·tan or **kaf·tan** (kăf′tăn′, -tən, kăf-tăn′) *n.* **1.** A full-length garment with elbow-length or long sleeves, worn chiefly in eastern Mediterranean countries. **2.** A westernized version of this garment consisting of a loose, usu. brightly colored tunic. [Russ. *kaftan* < Ottoman Turk. *qaftān*.]

cage (kāj) *n.* **1.** A structure for confining animals, built in part with wires or bars. **2.** An enclosure for prisoners. **3.** An enclosing openwork structure. **4.** An elevator car. **5.a.** *Baseball.* A wire screen placed behind home plate to stop batting practice balls. **b.** *Sports.* A hockey or soccer goal made of a frame with a net. —*tr.v.* **caged, cag·ing, cag·es.** To put in or as if in a cage. [ME < OFr. < Lat. *cavea*.]

Cage (kāj), **John Milton, Jr.** 1912–92. Amer. composer of avant-garde works, such as *Sonatas and Interludes* (1948).

cage·ling (kāj′lĭng) *n.* A bird kept as a pet in a cage.

ca·gey also **ca·gy** (kā′jē) *adj.* **-gi·er, -gi·est. 1.** Wary; careful. **2.** Crafty; shrewd: *a cagey lawyer.* [?] —**ca′gi·ly** *adv.* —**ca′gi·ness** *n.*

Ca·glia·ri (käl′yə-rē′). A city of Sardinia, Italy, on the S coast on the **Gulf of Cagliari,** an inlet of the Mediterranean. Pop. 232,785.

Ca·glio·stro (kăl-yō′strō, kä-lyô′strô), Count **Alessandro di.** 1743–95. Italian adventurer famous as an alchemist.

Cag·ney (kăg′nē), **James ("Jimmy").** 1899–1986. Amer. actor whose films include *Public Enemy* (1931).

C.A.G.S. *abbr.* Certificate of Advanced Graduate Studies.

Ca·guas (kä′gwäs′). A city of E-central Puerto Rico SSE of San Juan. Pop. 87,214.

ca·hier (kä-yā′) *n.* A report, esp. on parliamentary matters. [Fr., notebook < OFr. *quaier* < VLat. **quaternum* < Lat. *quaterni*, foursome < *quater*, four times. See **kʷetwer-*.**]

Ca·ho·ki·a (kə-hō′kē-ə). A village of SW IL, a suburb of East St. Louis near the **Cahokia Mounds,** a group of prehistoric earthworks. Pop. 17,550.

ca·hoots (kə-ho͞ots′) *pl.n. Informal.* Questionable collaboration; secret partnership. [Perh. < Fr. *cahute*, cabin < OFr., poss. blend of *cabane*; see CABIN, and *hutte*; see HUT.]

ca·how (kə-hou′) *n.* An earth-burrowing nocturnal bird *(Pterodroma cahow),* once abundant in Bermuda but now nearly extinct. [Imit. of its cry.]

Ca·huil·la (kə-wē′ə) *n., pl.* **Cahuilla** or **-las. 1.** A member of a Native American people inhabiting parts of southeast California. **2.** The Uto-Aztecan language of the Cahuilla. [Am.Sp.]

CAI *abbr.* Computer-aided instruction.

Cai·a·phas (kā′ə-fəs, kī′-), **Joseph.** fl. 1st cent. A.D. The Jewish high priest who presided over the counsel that condemned Jesus.

Cai·cos Islands (kā′kəs, -kōs). One of the island groups constituting the Turks and Caicos Is. in the Atlantic Ocean.

cai·man also **cay·man** (kā′mən) *n., pl.* **-mans.** Any of various tropical American crocodilians of the genus *Caiman* and related genera, resembling and closely related to the alligators. [Sp. *caimán* < Carib *acayuman*.]

Cain (kān). The eldest son of Adam and Eve, who murdered his brother Abel and was condemned to be a fugitive.

–caine *suff.* A synthetic alkaloid anesthetic: *eucaine.* [< COCAINE.]

cai·no·to·pho·bi·a (kā-nō′tə-fō′bē-ə) *n.* An abnormal fear of newness. [Gk. *kainotēs*, newness (< *kainos*, new; see **ken-***) + -PHOBIA.]

ca·ïque (kä-ēk′) *n. Naut.* **1.** A long narrow rowboat used in the Middle East. **2.** A small sailing vessel used in the eastern Mediterranean. [Fr. < Ital. *caicco* < Ottoman Turk. *qayiq* < Old Turkic *qayghuq*.]

caird (kârd) *n. Scots.* An itinerant tinker. [Sc.Gael. *ceard*, tinker, smith < OIr. *cerd*, artisan, skill.]

cairn (kârn) *n.* A mound of stones erected as a memorial or marker. [ME *carne* < Sc.Gael. *carn* < OIr.] —**cairned** *adj.*

cairn·gorm (kârn′gôrm′) *n.* See **smoky quartz.**

Cairn·gorm Mountains (kârn′gôrm′). A range of the Grampian Mts. in central Scotland rising to 1,310.3 m (4,296 ft).

Cairn terrier (kârn) *n.* A small dog of a breed developed in Scotland, having a broad head and a rough shaggy coat.

Cai·ro (kī′rō). (kī′rō). The cap. of Egypt, in the NE part on the Nile R. Old Cairo was built c. 642; the new city was founded c. 968. Pop. 6,205,000. —**Cai′rene** *adj. & n.*

cais·son (kā′sŏn′, -sən) *n.* **1.** A watertight structure within which construction work is carried on under water. **2.** See **camel** 2. **3.** A large open box designed to fit against the side of a ship and used to repair damaged hulls under water. **4.** A floating structure used to close off the entrance to a dock or canal lock. **5.a.** A horse-drawn vehicle used to carry artillery ammunition and coffins at military funerals. **b.** A large box for ammunition. [Fr. < OFr., large box, alteration of *casson* < Ital. *cassone*, aug. of *cassa*, box < Lat. *capsa*.]

caisson disease *n.* See **decompression sickness.**

Caith·ness (kāth′nĕs, kāth-nĕs′). A historical region and former county of NE Scotland; settled by the Picts.

cai·tiff (kā′tĭf) *n.* A despicable coward; a wretch. [ME *caitif* < Norman Fr. < Lat. *captīvus*, prisoner. See CAPTIVE.] —**cai′tif** *adj.*

Ca·ius (kā′əs, kī′-). See **Gaius.**

ca·jan pea (kā′jən) *n.* **1.** A tropical African shrub *(Cajanus cajan)* of the pea family, having hairy pods and small edible seeds. **2.** A seed of this plant. [Malay *kachang*, bean, pea.]

ca·jole (kə-jōl′) *tr.v.* **-joled, -jol·ing, -joles.** To urge with gentle and repeated appeals, teasing, or flattery; wheedle. [Fr. *cajoler*, poss. blend of OFr. *cageoler*, to chatter like a jay (< *geai, jai*, jay; see JAY[2]) and OFr. *gaioler*, to lure into a cage (< *gaiole, jaiole*, cage; see JAIL).] —**ca·jol′er** *n.* —**ca·jol′er·y** (-jō′lə-rē) *n.* —**ca·jol′ing·ly** *adv.*

Ca·jun also **Ca·jan** (kā′jən) *n.* **1.** A member of a group of people in southern Louisiana descended from French colonists exiled from Acadia in the 18th century. **2.** Often **Cajan.** A member of a group living in southern Alabama and southeast Mississippi, of mixed white, Black, and Native American ancestry. [Alteration of ACADIAN.] —**Ca′jun** *adj.*

cake (kāk) *n.* **1.** A sweet baked food made of flour, liquid, eggs, and other ingredients and often served in rounded layer form. **2.** A flat rounded mass of dough or batter that is baked or fried. **3.** A flat rounded mass of hashed or chopped food that is baked or fried; a patty. **4.** A shaped or molded piece, as of soap or ice. **5.** A layer or deposit of compacted matter. —*v.* **caked, cak·ing, cakes.** —*tr.* To cover or fill with a thick layer, as of compacted matter. —*intr.* To become formed into a compact or crusty mass. [ME < ON *kaka*.]

cake·walk (kāk′wôk′) *n.* **1.** Something easily accomplished. **2.** A 19th-century entertainment among American Black people in which walkers performing the most accomplished or amusing steps won cakes. —**cake′walk′er** *n.*

cal or **Cal** *abbr.* **1. Cal.** Calorie (large calorie). **2.** Calorie (mean calorie). **3.** Calorie (small calorie).

cal. *abbr.* **1.** Calendar. **2.** Caliber.

Cal. *abbr.* California.

Cal·a·bar bean (kăl′ə-bär) *n.* The poisonous seed of a tropical western African woody vine *(Physostigma venenosum)* in the pea family, which is the source of the drug physostigmine. [After *Calabar*, a town of SE Nigeria.]

cal·a·bash (kăl′ə-băsh′) *n.* **1.** An annual vine *(Lagenaria siceraria)* having white flowers and smooth, large, hard-shelled gourds. **2.** A tropical American tree *(Crescentia cujete)* bearing hard-shelled gourdlike fruits. **3.** Any of certain similar or related plants. **4.** The fruit of a calabash. **5.** A utensil or container made from a calabash shell. **6.** A smoking pipe with a large bowl made from a gourd. [Fr. *calebasse*, gourd < Sp. *calabaza* < Catalan *carabaça*, perh. < Ar. *qar'ah yābisah*, dry gourd : *qar'ah*, gourd + *yābisah*, dry.]

Cal·a·bash (kăl′ə-băsh′) *n.* A style of cooking in the southeast United States in which various seafoods are deep-fried. [Perh. < *calabash*, a turtle cooked in its shell < CALABASH.]

calabash tree *n.* See **calabash** 2.

cal·a·boose (kăl′ə-bo͞os′) *n. Chiefly Southern & Western U.S.* A jail. [Louisiana Fr. *calabouse* < Sp. *calabozo*, dungeon.]

Ca·la·bri·a (kə-lā′brē-ə, kä-lä′brē-ä). A region of S Italy forming the toe of the Italian "boot."

ca·la·di·um (kə-lā′dē-əm) *n.* Any of various tropical American plants of the genus *Caladium*, cultivated for their ornamental foliage. [NLat. *Caladium*, genus name < Malay *kĕladi*, an aroid.]

Ca·lah (kā′lə) also **Ka·lakh** (kä′läkh). An ancient city of Assyria on the Tigris R. S of present-day Mosul, Iraq; probably founded in the 13th cent. B.C.

Ca·lais (kă-lā′, kăl′ā). A city of N France on the Strait of Dover opposite Dover, England. Pop. 76,527.

cal·a·man·co (kăl′ə-măng′kō) *n., pl.* **-coes.** A glossy woolen fabric with a checked pattern on one side. [Perh. < Sp. *calamaco* < LLat. *calamaucus*, felt cap.]

cal·a·man·der (kăl′ə-măn′dər) *n.* The hard black and brown striped wood of certain tropical trees of the genus *Diospyros*, esp. *D. quaesita* of Sri Lanka. [Prob. < Du. *kalamanderhout*, calamander wood, perh. < alteration of COROMANDEL (COAST).]

cal·a·mar·i (kä′lə-mä′rē, kăl′ə-) *n.* Squid as food. [Ital., pl. of *calamaro* < LLat. *calamārium*, pen-case < Lat. *calamārius*, of a reed pen < *calamus*, reed pen (perh. < squid "ink"). See CALAMUS.]

cal·a·mine (kăl′ə-mīn′, -mĭn) *n.* **1.** See **hemimorphite. 2.** A pink, odorless, tasteless powder of zinc oxide with a small amount of ferric oxide, dissolved in mineral oils and used in skin lotions. **3.** An alloy composed of lead, tin, and zinc. [Fr. < Med.Lat. *calamīna*, alteration of Lat. *cadmīa*. See CADMIUM.]

cal·a·mint (kăl′ə-mĭnt′) *n.* Any of several plants of the genera *Calamintha* and *Satureja* in the mint family, cultivated for their aromatic foliage and flower clusters. [ME *calaminte* < OFr. *calamente* < Med.Lat. *calamentum* < Lat. *calaminthē* < Gk. *kalaminthē*.]

cal·a·mite (kăl′ə-mīt′) *n.* Any of various extinct, chiefly carboniferous trees of the genus *Calamites*, related to the present-day horsetails *(Equisetum)*. [NLat. *Calamītēs*, genus name < LGk. *kalamitēs*, reedlike < Gk. *kalamos*, reed.]

ca·lam·i·tous (kə-lăm′ĭ-təs) *adj.* Causing or involving calamity. —**ca·lam′i·tous·ly** *adv.* —**ca·lam′i·tous·ness** *n.*

ca·lam·i·ty (kə-lăm′ĭ-tē) *n., pl.* **-ties. 1.** An event that brings

cairn

ă pat	oi boy
ā pay	ou out
âr care	o͝o took
ä father	o͞o boot
ĕ pet	ŭ cut
ē be	ûr urge
ĭ pit	th thin
ī pie	*th* this
îr pier	hw which
ŏ pot	zh vision
ō toe	ə about, item
ô paw	

Stress marks:
′ (primary);
′ (secondary), as in
dictionary (dĭk′shə-nĕr′ē)

terrible loss, lasting distress, or severe affliction; a disaster. **2.** Dire distress due to loss or tragedy. [ME *calamite* < OFr. < Lat. *calamitās*.]

Ca•lam•i•ty Jane (kə-lăm′ĭ-tē jān′). See Martha Jane **Burk.**

cal•a•mon•din (kăl′ə-mŏn′dĭn) *n.* **1.** A small evergreen citrus tree (×*Citrofortunella mitis*) having glossy foliage and ornamental fruits. **2.** Its sour fruit. [Tagalog *kalamunding*.]

cal•a•mus (kăl′ə-məs) *n., pl.* **-mi** (-mī′). **1.a.** See **sweet flag. b.** The aromatic underground stem of the sweet flag, yielding an oil used in perfumery. **2.** Any of various chiefly tropical Asian climbing palms of the genus *Calamus,* having strong flexible stems used as a source of rattan. **3.** See **quill** 1. [Lat., reed < Gk. *kalamos*.]

ca•lan•do (kə-län′dō) *adv. & adj. Mus.* With a gradual decrease in tempo and volume. [Ital., pr.part. of *calare,* to slacken < Lat. *calāre* < Gk. *khalan*.]

ca•lash (kə-lăsh′) also **ca•lèche** (-lĕsh′) *n.* **1.a.** A light carriage with low wheels and a collapsible top. **b.** A top for this or a similar carriage. **2.** A woman's folding bonnet of the late 18th century. [Fr. *calèche* < Ger. *Kalesche* < Czech *kolesa* < pl. of *kolo, koles-,* wheel < Slav. See **k**ʷ**el-**¹*.]

cal•a•thus (kăl′ə-thəs) *n., pl.* **-thi** (-thī′). A vase-shaped basket represented in Greek art. [Lat. < Gk. *kalathos*.]

calc. *abbr.* **1.** Calculation. **2.** *Math.* Calculus.

calc– *pref.* Var. of **calci–.**

cal•ca•ne•us (kăl-kā′nē-əs) also **cal•ca•ne•um** (-nē-əm) *n., pl.* **-ne•i** (-nē-ī′) also **-ne•a** (-nē-ə). The quadrangular bone at the back of the tarsus. [LLat. *calcāneus,* heel < Lat. *calcāneum* < *calx, calc-*.] **—cal•ca′ne•al** *adj.*

cal•car¹ (kăl′kär′) *n., pl.* **cal•car•i•a** (kăl-kâr′ē-ə). A spur or spurlike projection, as on the wing or leg of a bird. [Lat., spur < *calx, calc-,* heel.]

cal•car² (kăl′kär′) *n.* A furnace formerly used in glassmaking for calcination of materials into frit. [Ital. *calcara* < LLat. *calcāria (fornāx),* lime(-kiln) < Lat., fem. of *calcārius,* of lime. See CALCAREOUS.]

cal•car•e•ous (kăl-kâr′ē-əs) *adj.* Composed of, containing, or characteristic of calcium carbonate, calcium, or limestone; chalky. [< Lat. *calcārius* < *calx, calc-,* lime. See CALX.] **—cal•car′e•ous•ly** *adv.*

cal•car•ine sulcus (kăl′kə-rīn′) *n.* A sulcus on the occipital lobe of the brain. [CALCAR¹ + –INE¹.]

cal•ced•o•ny (kăl-sĕd′n-ē) *n.* Var. of **chalcedony.**

cal•ce•o•lar•i•a (kăl′sē-ə-lâr′ē-ə) *n.* Any of various plants of the genus *Calceolaria,* native from Mexico to South America and having speckled slipper-shaped flowers. [NLat. *Calceolaria,* genus name < Lat. *calceolus,* small shoe. See CALCEOLATE.]

cal•ce•o•late (kăl′sē-ə-lāt′) *adj.* Shaped like a slipper, as the pouchlike petal of the flower of the lady's slipper. [< Lat. *calceolus,* dim. of *calceus,* shoe < *calx, calc-,* heel.]

calash

cal•ces (kăl′sēz′) *n.* Pl. of **calx.**

calci– or **calc–** *pref.* Calcium; calcium salt; lime: *calciferous.* [< Lat. *calx, calc-,* lime. See CALX.]

cal•cic (kăl′sĭk) *adj.* Composed of, containing, derived from, or relating to calcium or lime.

cal•ci•cole (kăl′sĭ-kōl′) *n.* A plant that thrives in soil rich in lime. [Fr. : *calci-,* calcium (< Lat. *calx, calc-,* lime; see CALX) + *-cole,* -dwelling (< Lat. *-cola;* see –COLOUS).] **—cal•cic′o•lous** (-sĭk′ə-ləs) *adj.*

cal•cif•er•ol (kăl-sĭf′ə-rôl′, -rōl′, -rŏl′) *n.* See **vitamin D_2.** [CALCIFER(OUS) + –OL¹.]

cal•cif•er•ous (kăl-sĭf′ər-əs) *adj.* Of, forming, or containing calcium or calcium carbonate.

cal•cif•ic (kăl-sĭf′ĭk) *adj.* Producing salts of lime.

cal•ci•fi•ca•tion (kăl′sə-fĭ-kā′shən) *n.* **1.a.** Impregnation with calcium or calcium salts, as with calcium carbonate. **b.** Hardening, as of tissue, by such impregnation. **2.** A calcified substance or part. **3.** An inflexible, unchanging state.

cal•ci•fuge (kăl′sə-fyo͞oj′) *n.* A plant that does not grow well in lime-rich soil. **—cal•cif′u•gal** (-sĭf′yə-gəl), **cal•cif′u•gous** (-yə-gəs) *adj.*

cal•ci•fy (kăl′sə-fī′) *tr. & intr.v.* **-fied, -fy•ing, -fies. 1.** To make or become stony or chalky by deposition of calcium salts. **2.** To make or become inflexible and unchanging.

calceolaria

cal•ci•mine also **kal•so•mine** (kăl′sə-mīn′) *n.* A white or tinted liquid containing zinc oxide, water, and glue, used as a wash for walls and ceilings. [Originally a trademark.] **—cal′ci•mine′** *v.*

cal•cine (kăl-sīn′, kăl′sīn′) *v.* **-cined, -cin•ing, -cines.** —*tr.* To heat (a substance) to a high temperature but below the melting or fusing point, causing loss of moisture, reduction or oxidation, and the decomposition of carbonates and other compounds. —*intr.* To undergo calcination. [ME *calcinen* < OFr. *calciner* < Med.Lat. *calcīnāre* < LLat. *calcīna,* quicklime < Lat. *calx, calc-,* lime. See CALX.] **—cal′ci•na′tion** (-sə-nā′shən) *n.*

cal•ci•no•sis (kăl′sə-nō′sĭs) *n.* An abnormal condition in which calcium salts are deposited in a part or tissue of the body. [CALC(I)- (influenced by CALCINE) + –OSIS.]

cal•cite (kăl′sīt′) *n.* A common crystalline form of natural calcium carbonate, $CaCO_3$, that is the basic constituent of limestone, marble, and chalk. **—cal•cit′ic** (-sĭt′ĭk) *adj.*

cal•ci•to•nin (kăl′sĭ-tō′nĭn) *n.* A peptide hormone that lowers plasma calcium and phosphate levels without augmenting calcium accretion. [CALCI– + TON(E) + –IN.]

cal•ci•um (kăl′sē-əm) *n. Symbol* **Ca** A soft metallic element that is a basic component of animals and plants and constitutes approx. 3 percent of Earth's crust. It occurs naturally in limestone, gypsum, and fluorite. Atomic number 20; atomic weight 40.08; melting point 842 to 848°C; boiling point 1,487°C; specific gravity 1.55; valence 2. See table at **element.** [Lat. *calx, calc-,* lime; see CALX + –IUM.]

calcium carbide *n.* A crystalline compound, CaC_2, obtained by heating pulverized limestone or quicklime with carbon and used to generate acetylene gas.

calcium carbonate *n.* A crystalline compound, $CaCO_3$, occurring naturally as chalk, limestone, marble, and other forms and used in commercial chalk, medicines, and dentifrices.

calcium chloride *n.* A deliquescent compound, $CaCl_2$, used as a drying agent, refrigerant, and deicer and to control dust.

calcium cyanamide *n.* A gray-black compound, $CaCN_2$, used as a fertilizer.

calcium cyclamate *n.* An artificial salt of cyclamic acid, $C_{12}H_{24}O_6N_2S_2Ca_2H_2O$, formerly used as a low-calorie sweetener.

calcium fluoride *n.* A colorless powder, CaF_2, used in emery wheels, carbon electrodes, and cements.

calcium hydroxide *n.* A soft white powder, $Ca(OH)_2$, used in making mortar cements, paints, and petrochemicals.

calcium hypochlorite *n.* A crystalline solid, $Ca(OCl)_2{\cdot}4H_2O$, used as a bactericide, fungicide, and bleaching agent.

calcium light *n.* See **limelight** 2.

calcium oxide *n.* A caustic lumpy powder, CaO, used as a flux, in manufacturing steel and paper, and in glassmaking.

calcium phosphate *n.* **1.** A deliquescent powder, $Ca(H_2PO_4)_2$, used in baking powders and as a plant food. **2.** A crystalline powder, $CaHPO_4$, used in animal feed, glass, and toothpaste. **3.** An amorphous powder, $Ca_3(PO_4)_2$, used in fertilizers and as a nutritional supplement.

calc•spar or **calc-spar** (kălk′spär′) *n.* See **calcite.** [Partial transl. of Swed. *kalkspat* : *kalk,* lime (< OSwed. *kalker* < MLGer. *kalk* < Lat. *calx, calc-,* lime; see CALX) + *spat,* spar (mineral).]

cal•cu•la•ble (kăl′kyə-lə-bəl) *adj.* **1.** That can be calculated or estimated: *calculable odds.* **2.** Readily relied on; dependable: *a calculable assistant.* **—cal′cu•la•bil′i•ty** *n.*

cal•cu•late (kăl′kyə-lāt′) *v.* **-lat•ed, -lat•ing, -lates.** —*tr.* **1.** To ascertain by computation; reckon. **2.** To make an estimate of; evaluate. **3.** To make for a deliberate purpose; design. **4.** Also **cal′late** (kăl′āt′, -lāt′). *Chiefly New England & Upper Southern U.S.* **a.** To suppose: *"I cal'late she's a right smart cook"* (Dialect Notes). **b.** To plan, intend, or count on. —*intr.* **1.** To perform a mathematical process; figure. **2.** To predict consequences. **3.** *Regional.* **a.** To suppose; guess. **b.** To count, depend, or rely on someone or something. [LLat. *calculāre, calculāt-* < Lat. *calculus,* small stone used in reckoning, dim. of *calx, calc-,* small stone for gaming. See CALX.] **—cal′cu•la′tive** *adj.*

cal•cu•lat•ed (kăl′kyə-lā′tĭd) *adj.* **1.** Determined by mathematical calculation. **2.** Undertaken after careful estimation of the likely outcome. **3.** Made or planned to accomplish a certain purpose; deliberate: *insincere, calculated modesty.* **4.** Likely; apt. **—cal′cu•lat′ed•ly** *adv.*

cal•cu•lat•ing (kăl′kyə-lā′tĭng) *adj.* **1.** Capable of performing calculations: *a calculating machine.* **2.a.** Shrewd; crafty. **b.** Coldly scheming or conniving. **—cal′cu•lat′ing•ly** *adv.*

cal•cu•la•tion (kăl′kyə-lā′shən) *n.* **1.a.** The act, process, or result of calculating. **b.** An estimate based on probabilities. **2.** Careful, often cunning estimation and planning of outcomes, esp. to advance one's own interests.

cal•cu•la•tor (kăl′kyə-lā′tər) *n.* **1.** One that calculates, as: **a.** An electronic or a mechanical device for the performance of mathematical computations. **b.** A person who operates such a machine or otherwise makes calculations. **2.** A set of mathematical tables used to aid in calculating.

cal•cu•lous (kăl′kyə-ləs) *adj.* Relating to, caused by, or having a calculus or calculi.

cal•cu•lus (kăl′kyə-ləs) *n., pl.* **-li** (-lī′) or **-lus•es. 1.** *Pathol.* An abnormal concretion in the body, usu. formed of mineral salts, as in the kidney. **2.** *Dentistry.* Tartar. **3.** *Math.* **a.** The branch of mathematics that deals with limits and the differentiation and integration of functions of one or more variables. **b.** A method of analysis or calculation using a special symbolic notation. **4.** A system or method of calculation. [Lat., small stone used in reckoning. See CALCULATE.]

calculus of variations *n.* The study of maxima and minima of definite integrals whose integrands are functions of independent variables and dependent variables and their derivatives.

Cal•cut•ta (kăl-kŭt′ə). A city of E India on the Hooghly R. in the Ganges delta; founded c. 1690. Pop. 3,305,006.

Cal•der (kôl′der, kŏl′-), **Alexander.** 1898–1976. Amer. sculptor who created the mobile in Paris in the early 1930's.

cal•de•ra (kăl-dâr′ə, -dîr′ə, kôl-) *n.* A large crater formed by volcanic explosion or by collapse of a volcanic cone. [Sp., caldron, caldera < LLat. *caldāria*. See CALDRON.]

Cal•de•rón de la Bar•ca (kăl′də-rôn′ dā lə bär′kə, käl′thĕ-rôn′ thĕ lä bär′kä), **Pedro.** 1600–81. Spanish playwright whose plays include *Life Is a Dream* (1635).

cal•dron also **caul•dron** (kôl′drən) *n.* **1.** A large vessel used for boiling. **2.** A state or situation of great distress or unrest. [ME, alteration of *cauderon* < Norman Fr., dim. of *caudiere*, cooking pot < LLat. *caldāria* < fem. of Lat. *caldārius*, suitable for warming < *calidus*, warm. See **kelə-[1]***.]

Cald•well (kôld′wĕl′, -wəl, kŏld′-). A city of SW Idaho on the Boise R. W of Boise. Pop. 18,400.

Caldwell, Erskine Preston. 1903–87. Amer. writer best known for *Tobacco Road* (1932).

Caldwell, Sarah. b. 1928. Amer. conductor and opera producer noted for her staging of classical and modern works.

ca•lèche (kə-lĕsh′) *n.* Var. of **calash.**

Cal•e•don (kăl′ĭ-dən). A town of SE Ontario, Canada, NW of Toronto. Pop. 26,645.

Cal•e•do•ni•a (kăl′ĭ-dō′nē-ə, -dōn′yə). **1.** Roman Britain N of the Antonine Wall stretching from the Firth of Forth to the Firth of Clyde. **2.** Scotland. — **Cal′e•do′ni•an** *adj. & n.*

Caledonian Canal. A waterway, c. 97 km (60 mi), of N Scotland from Loch Linnhe to Moray Firth.

cal•en•dar (kăl′ən-dər) *n.* **1.** Any of various systems of reckoning time in which the beginning, length, and divisions of a year are defined. **2.** A table of the months, weeks, and days in at least one year. **3.** A schedule of events. **4.** An ordered list of matters to be considered. **5.** *Chiefly British.* A university catalog. — *tr.v.* **-dared, -dar•ing, -dars.** To enter in a calendar; schedule. [ME *calender* < OFr. *calendier* < LLat. *kalendārium* < Lat., account book < *kalendae*, calends (interest being due on the calends). See **kelə-[2]***.]

calendar month *n.* See **month** 2.

calendar year *n.* See **year** 1a.

cal•en•der (kăl′ən-dər) *n.* A machine in which paper or cloth is made smooth and glossy by being pressed through rollers. — *tr.v.* **-dered, -der•ing, -ders.** To press (paper or cloth) in such a machine. [Fr. *calandre* < VLat. **colendra*, alteration (poss. influenced by Lat. *columna*, column) of Lat. *cylindrus*, roller. See CYLINDER.] — **cal′en•der•er** *n.*

ca•len•dri•cal (kə-lĕn′drĭ-kəl) also **ca•len•dric** (-drĭk) *adj.* Of, relating to, or used in a calendar.

cal•ends also **kal•ends** (kăl′əndz, kā′ləndz) *n., pl.* **calends** also **kalends.** The day of the new moon and the first day of the month in the ancient Roman calendar. [ME *kalendes* < Lat. *kalendae*. See **kelə-[2]***.] — **ca•len′dal** (kə-lĕn′dəl) *adj.*

ca•len•du•la (kə-lĕn′jə-lə) *n.* A Mediterranean annual plant *(Calendula officinalis)* in the composite family, cultivated for its yellow or orange rayed flower heads. [Med.Lat., marigold < Lat. *kalendae*, calends. See CALENDS.]

cal•en•ture (kăl′ən-cho͝or′) *n.* A tropical fever once attributed to heat. [Sp. *calentura* < *calentar*, to heat < Lat. *calēns*, *calent-*, pr.part. of *calēre*, to be warm. See **kelə-[1]***.]

calf[1] (kăf, käf) *n., pl.* **calves** (kăvz, kävz). **1.a.** A young cow or bull. **b.** The young of certain other mammals, such as the elephant or whale. **2.** Calfskin leather. **3.** A large floating chunk of ice split off from a glacier, an iceberg, or a floe. **4.** An awkward, callow youth. [ME < OE *cealf*.]

calf[2] (kăf, käf) *n., pl.* **calves** (kăvz, kävz). The muscular back part of the human leg below the knee. [ME < ON *kālfi*.]

calf•skin (kăf′skĭn′, käf′-) *n.* **1.** The hide of a calf. **2.** Fine leather made from the hide of a calf.

Cal•ga•ry (kăl′gə-rē). A city of S Alberta, Canada, S of Edmonton; site of the annual Calgary Stampede, dating from 1912. Pop. 592,743. — **Cal•gar′i•an** (-gâr′ē-ən, -găr′-) *n.*

Cal•houn (kăl-ho͞on′), **John Caldwell.** 1782–1850. Vice President of the U.S. (1825–32) who maintained that states had the right to nullify federal legislation.

Ca•li (kä′lē). A city of W Colombia on the **Cali River** SW of Bogotá; founded 1536. Pop. 1,347,810.

Cal•i•ban (kăl′ə-băn′) *n.* The grotesque, deformed slave in Shakespeare's *The Tempest*.

cal•i•ber (kăl′ə-bər) *n.* **1.a.** The diameter of the inside of a cylinder. **b.** The diameter of the bore of a firearm, usu. in hundredths or thousandths of an inch and written as a decimal fraction. **c.** The diameter of a large projectile in millimeters or inches. **2.** Degree of worth; quality. [Fr. *calibre*.]

cal•i•brate (kăl′ə-brāt′) *tr.v.* **-brat•ed, -brat•ing, -brates.** **1.** To check, adjust, or determine the graduations of (a quantitative measuring instrument). **2.** To determine the caliber of (a tube). **3.** To correct; adjust. — **cal′i•bra′tor** *n.*

cal•i•bra•tion (kăl′ə-brā′shən) *n.* **1.** The act or process of calibrating; the state of being calibrated. **2.** Gradations showing positions or values. Often used in the plural.

cal•i•bre (kăl′ə-bər) *n.* *Chiefly British.* Var. of **caliber.**

ca•li•ces (kā′lĭ-sēz′, kăl′ĭ-) *n.* Pl. of **calix.**

ca•li•che (kə-lē′chē) *n.* **1.a.** A crude sodium nitrate occurring naturally in Chile, Peru, and the southwest United States, used as fertilizer. **b.** See **sodium nitrate.** **2.** See **hardpan** 1. [Am.Sp. < Sp., pebble in a brick, flake of lime < *cal*, lime < Lat. *calx*, *calc-*, lime. See CALX.]

cal•i•co (kăl′ĭ-kō′) *n., pl.* **-coes** or **-cos. 1.a.** A coarse, brightly printed cloth. **b.** *Chiefly British.* A white cotton cloth, heavier than muslin. **2.** An animal with a mottled coat in white tones with red and black. [After CALICUT.] — **cal′i•co** *adj.*

cal•i•co•back (kăl′ĭ-kō-băk′) *n.* See **harlequin bug.**

calico bass *n.* See **black crappie.** [< its colored spots.]

calico bush *n.* See **mountain laurel.**

Cal•i•cut (kăl′ĭ-kŭt′) also **Ko•zhi•kode** (kō′zhĭ-kōd′). A city of SW India on the Malabar Coast SW of Bangalore; site of Vasco da Gama's first landfall in India (1498). Pop. 394,447.

ca•lif (kā′lĭf, kăl′ĭf) *n.* Var. of **caliph.**

Calif. California.

Cal•i•for•nia (kăl′ĭ-fôr′nyə, -fôr′nē-ə). A state of the W U.S. on the Pacific Ocean; admitted as the 31st state in 1850. The area was colonized by the Spanish and formally ceded to the U.S. in 1848. Cap. Sacramento. Pop. 29,839,250. — **Cal′i•for′nian** *adj. & n.*

California, Gulf of. An arm of the Pacific Ocean in NW Mexico separating Baja California from the mainland.

California condor *n.* A very large vulture *(Gymnogyps californianus)* that is nearly extinct.

California laurel *n.* An aromatic evergreen tree *(Umbellularia californica)* native to California and southern Oregon and having clusters of yellowish-green flowers, olivelike fruits, and light brown wood.

California pepper tree *n.* See **pepper tree.**

California poppy *n.* An herb *(Eschscholzia californica)* native to western North America and having finely divided leaves and showy, often orange or yellow flowers.

cal•i•for•ni•um (kăl′ə-fôr′nē-əm) *n.* *Symbol* **Cf** A synthetic radioactive element produced in trace quantities by neutron bombardment of curium. Atomic number 98; mass numbers 244 to 254; half-lives varying from 25 minutes to 800 years. See table at **element.** [After CALIFORNIA.]

ca•lig•i•nous (kə-lĭj′ə-nəs) *adj.* Dark, misty, and gloomy. [< Lat. *cālīginōsus* < *cālīgō*, *cālīgin-*, darkness.]

Ca•lig•u•la (kə-lĭg′yə-lə). A.D. 12–41. Emperor of Rome (37–41) who succeeded his adoptive father, Tiberius.

Ca•li•na•go (kăl′ĭ-nä′gō, kä′lĭ-) *n., pl.* **Calinago** or **-gos. 1.** A member of a Caribbean Indian people inhabiting the Lesser Antilles. **2.** The language of the Calinago. [Sp. *calinago, calino, caribal*, alterations of *karinako* < Carib, brave men : *ka*, sky, spirit + *na*, group + *-ko*, group place.]

cal•i•per also **cal•li•per** (kăl′ə-pər) *n.* **1.** An instrument consisting of two curved hinged legs, used to measure thickness and distances. Often used in the plural. **2.** A large instrument with a fixed and a movable arm, used to measure diameters. **3.** A vernier caliper. [Alteration of CALIBER.] — **cal′i•per** *v.*

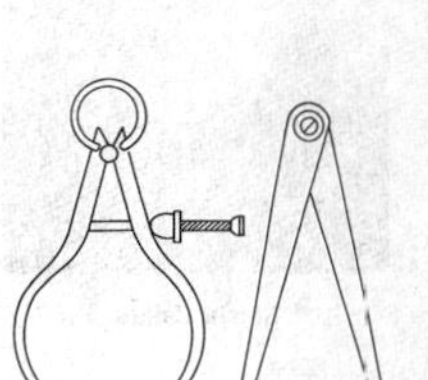

caliper
Left: Outside spring calipers
Right: Inside firm-joint calipers

ca•liph also **ca•lif** or **kha•lif** (kā′lĭf, kăl′ĭf) *n.* A male leader of an Islamic polity. [ME *calife* < OFr. < Ar. *ḫalīfah*, successor (to Muhammad), caliph < *ḫalafa*, to succeed.]

ca•liph•ate (kā′lĭ-fāt′, -fĭt, kăl′ĭ-) *n.* The office or jurisdiction of a caliph.

cal•is•then•ics (kăl′ĭs-thĕn′ĭks) *n.* *Sports.* **1.** *(used with a pl. v.)* Gymnastic exercises designed to develop muscular tone and promote physical well-being. **2.** *(used with a sing. v.)* The practice or art of such exercises. [< Gk. *kalli-*, beautiful (< *kallos*, beauty) + *sthenos*, strength.] — **cal′is•then′ic** *adj.*

ca•lix (kā′lĭks, kăl′ĭks) *n., pl.* **ca•li•ces** (kā′lĭ-sēz′, kăl′ĭ-). *Eccles.* A chalice. [Lat. *calix*, *calic-*, cup.]

Ca•lix•tus III (kə-lĭk′stəs). 1378–1458. Pope (1455–58) whose nepotism empowered the Borgia family in Italy.

calk[1] (kôk) *n.* **1.** A pointed extension on the toe or heels of a horseshoe to prevent slipping. **2.** A spiked plate on the bottom of a shoe to prevent slipping and preserve the sole. [Prob. back-formation < obsolete *calkin* < ME *kakun*, poss. < MDu. *kalkoen*, hoof, or < OFr. *calcain*, heel < Lat. *calcāneum*, heel bone. See CALCANEUS.] — **calk** *v.*

calk[2] (kôk) *v.* Var. of **caulk.**

call (kôl) *v.* **called, call•ing, calls.** — *tr.* **1.** To say in a loud voice; announce. **2.** To demand or ask for the presence of. **3.** To demand or ask for a meeting of; convene or convoke. **4.** To order or request to undertake a particular activity or work; summon: *called for jury duty.* **5.** To give the command for; order: *call a halt.* **6.** To communicate or try to communicate with by telephone. **7.** To lure (prey) by imitating the characteristic cry of an animal. **8.** To cause to come to the mind or to attention. **9.** To name. **10.** To regard as being of a particular type; characterize: *Let's call it a draw.* **11.** To designate; label. **12.a.** To demand payment of: *call a loan.* **b.** To require the presentation of (a bond) for redemption before maturity. **13.** *Sports.* **a.** To stop or postpone (a game) because of bad weather or other adverse conditions. **b.** To declare in the capacity of an umpire or referee. **c.** To indicate a decision in regard to: *called a close play.* **d.** To give the orders or signals for. **14.** *Games.* **a.** To describe the intended outcome of (one's billiard shot) before playing. **b.** To equal the bet of (the preceding bet or bettor) in poker. **15.** To indicate or characterize accurately in advance; predict. **16.** To challenge the truthfulness or genuineness of: *called her on that.* **17.** To shout directions in rhythm for (a square dance). — *intr.* **1.a.** To speak loudly; shout. **b.** To utter a character-

ă pat	oi boy
ā pay	ou out
âr care	o͝o took
ä father	o͞o boot
ĕ pet	ŭ cut
ē be	ûr urge
ĭ pit	th thin
ī pie	*th* this
îr pier	hw which
ŏ pot	zh vision
ō toe	ə about, item
ô paw	

Stress marks:
′ (primary);
′ (secondary), as in **dictionary** (dĭk′shə-nĕr′ē)

istic cry. Used of an animal. **2.** To communicate or try to communicate with someone by telephone. **3.** To pay a short visit. —*n.* **1.** A loud cry; a shout. **2.a.** The characteristic cry of an animal. **b.** A sound or an instrument made to imitate such a cry, used as a lure. **3.** A telephone communication or connection. **4.** Need or occasion: *call for an apology.* **5.** A claim on a person's time or life. **6.** A short visit, esp. a formal one. **7.** A summons or an invitation. **8.** A signal, such as that made by a horn. **9.a.** A strong inner urge or prompting; a vocation. **b.** Strong attraction or appeal. **10.** A roll call. **11.** A notice of rehearsal times posted in a theater. **12.** *Sports.* A decision made by an umpire or a referee. **13.** A direction or series of directions rhythmically called out to square dancers. **14.a.** A demand for payment of a debt. **b.** A demand to submit bonds to the issuer for redemption before maturity. **c.** An option to buy a certain quantity of a stock or commodity for a specified price within a specified time. **d.** A demand for payment due on stock bought on margin when the value has shrunk. —***phrasal verbs.*** **call back.** **1.** To communicate the need for (someone) to return from one situation or location to a previous one. **2.** To telephone or radio (a person) who has called previously. **3.** To recall (a defective product) for repair. **call down.** **1.** To find fault with; reprimand. **2.** To invoke, as from heaven. **call for.** **1.** To appear, as on someone else's premises, in order to get. **2.** To be an appropriate occasion for. **3.** To require; demand. **call forth.** To evoke; elicit. **call in.** **1.** To take out of circulation: *calling in silver dollars.* **2.** To summon for assistance or consultation. **3.** To communicate with another by telephone. **call off.** **1.** To cancel or postpone. **2.** To restrain or recall. **call out.** **1.** To cause to assemble; summon. **2.** To challenge to a duel. **call up.** **1.** To summon to active military service. **2.** To cause one to remember; bring to mind. **3.** To bring forth for action or discussion; raise. **call upon.** **1.** To order or require (a person). **2.** To make a demand or a series of demands on. —***idioms.*** **call a spade a spade.** To speak precisely and forthrightly. **call it a day.** *Informal.* To stop whatever one has been doing. **call it quits.** *Informal.* To stop working or trying; quit. **call the shots** (or **tune**). *Informal.* To exercise authority; be in charge. **on call.** **1.** Available when summoned for service or use. **2.** Subject to payment on demand. **within call.** Close enough to come if summoned. [ME *callen*, prob. < ON *kalla*. See **gal-***.]

Maria Callas

cal•la (kăl′ə) *n.* **1.** A calla lily. **2.** A marsh plant *(Calla palustris)* of the North Temperate Zone having small, densely clustered flowers in a spreading white spathe. [NLat. *Calla*, genus name < Gk. *kallaia*, wattle of a cock, perh. < *kallos*, beauty.]

Cal•la•ghan (kăl′ə-hən, -hăn′), **(Leonard) James.** b. 1912. British politician who served as prime minister (1976–79).

calla lily *n.* Any of several southern African plants of the genus *Zantedeschia*, having white, yellow, pink, or purple spathes.

Cal•la•o (kə-yä′ō, käyou′). A city of W-central Peru on the Pacific Ocean near Lima; founded 1537. Pop. 264,133.

Cal•las (kăl′əs, kä′ləs), **Maria Meneghini.** 1923–77. Amer. coloratura soprano known for her dramatic intensity.

cal'late (kăl′āt′, -lāt′) *v. Chiefly New England & Upper Southern U.S.* Var. of **calculate** 4.

call•back (kôl′băk′) *n.* **1.** The act or an instance of calling back from one location or situation to the previous one. **2.** A return telephone or radio call. **3.** A recall of a product by the manufacturer to correct a defect.

call•board (kôl′bôrd′, -bōrd′) *n.* A bulletin board backstage in a theater for posting instructions and notices.

call box *n.* **1.** A roadside telephone used for reporting motorists' emergencies. **2.** *Chiefly British.* A public telephone booth.

call•boy (kôl′boi′) *n.* **1.** One who prompts performers to go on stage. **2.** A bellhop. **3.** A male prostitute hired by telephone.

calliope

call•er¹ (kô′lər) *n.* **1.** One that calls, esp. a party placing a telephone call. **2.** A person paying a short social visit. **3.** A person who calls out numbers or directions, as at bingo.

cal•ler² (kăl′ər) *adj. Scots.* **1.** Fresh. **2.** Cool and refreshing. [ME *calour*, alteration of *calver*.]

call girl *n.* A female prostitute hired by telephone.

cal•lig•ra•phy (kə-lĭg′rə-fē) *n.* **1.a.** The art of fine handwriting. **b.** Works in fine handwriting considered as a group. **2.** Handwriting. [Fr. *calligraphie* < Gk. *kalligraphia*, beautiful writing : *kalli-*, beautiful (< *kallos*, beauty) + *-graphia*, -graphy.] —**cal•lig′ra•pher, cal•lig′ra•phist** *n.* —**cal′li•graph′ic** (kăl′ĭ-grăf′ĭk) *adj.*

Cal•lim•a•chus¹ (kə-lĭm′ə-kəs). 5th cent. B.C. Greek sculptor who reputedly designed the Corinthian column.

Cal•lim•a•chus² (kə-lĭm′ə-kəs). 3rd cent. B.C. Greek poet and scholar whose extant works include 64 epigrams.

call-in (kôl′ĭn′) *adj.* Being in a format such that listeners or viewers of a show are invited to have their telephone calls broadcast to other listeners. —*n.* **1.** A viewer or listener's telephone call to such a show. **2.** One making such a call.

call•ing (kô′lĭng) *n.* **1.** An inner urge; a strong impulse. **2.** An occupation, a profession, or a career.

calling card *n.* An engraved card bearing one's full name.

cal•li•o•pe (kə-lī′ə-pē′, kăl′ē-ōp′) *n. Mus.* An instrument fitted with steam whistles, played by a keyboard. [< CALLIOPE.]

Cal•li•o•pe (kə-lī′ə-pē′) *n. Gk. Myth.* The Muse of epic poetry. [Lat. < Gk. *Kalliopē* : *kalli-*, beautiful (< *kallos*, beauty) + *ops*, *op-*, voice; see **wekʷ-***.]

cal•li•op•sis (kăl′ē-ŏp′sĭs) *n.* A North American annual plant *(Coreopsis tinctoria)* having flower heads with yellow rays and dark centers. [NLat. : Gk. *kalli-*, beautiful (< *kallos*, beauty) + Gk. *opsis*, appearance; see -OPSIS.]

cal•li•per (kăl′ə-pər) *n.* Var. of **caliper.**

cal•li•pyg•i•an (kăl′ə-pĭj′ē-ən) also **cal•li•py•gous** (-pī′gəs) *adj.* Having beautiful buttocks. [< Gk. *kallipugos* : *kalli-*, beautiful (< *kallos*, beauty) + *pugē*, buttocks.]

Cal•lis•to (kə-lĭs′tō) *n.* **1.** *Gk. Myth.* A nymph beloved by Zeus whom Hera changed into a bear and Zeus then placed in the sky as the constellation Ursa Major. **2.** One of the four brightest satellites of Jupiter. [Lat. < Gk. *Kallistō*, perh. < *kallistos*, superl. of *kalos*, beautiful.]

call letters *pl.n.* The code letters or numbers of a radio or television transmitting station, assigned by a regulatory body.

call loan *n.* A loan repayable on demand at any time.

call number *n.* A number used in libraries to classify a book and indicate its location on the shelves.

cal•lose (kăl′ōs′) *n. Bot.* A complex branched carbohydrate commonly associated with sieve tube cells. [< Lat. *callōsus*, callous. See CALLOUS.]

cal•los•i•ty (kə-lŏs′ĭ-tē) *n., pl.* **-ties.** **1.** The condition of being calloused. **2.** Hardheartedness; insensitivity. **3.** See **callus** 1a. [ME *callosite* < OFr. < LLat. *callōsitās* < Lat. *callōsus*, callous. See CALLOUS.]

cal•lous (kăl′əs) *adj.* **1.** Having calluses; toughened. **2.** Emotionally hardened; unfeeling. —*tr. & intr.v.* **-loused, -lous•ing, -lous•es.** To make or become callous. [ME < OFr. *cailleux* < Lat. *callōsus* < *callum*, hard skin.] —**cal′lous•ly** *adv.* —**cal′lous•ness** *n.*

Usage Note: Do not confuse the adjective *callous*, as in *the callous criminal*, with the noun *callus*, as in *a callus on my thumb.*

cal•low (kăl′ō) *adj.* Lacking adult maturity or experience; immature. [ME *calwe*, bald < OE *calu*.] —**cal′low•ness** *n.*

Cal•lo•way (kăl′ə-wā′), **Cabell ("Cab").** b. 1907. Amer. jazz musician and bandleader noted for his scat singing.

call sign *n.* See **call letters.**

call-up (kôl′ŭp′) *n.* The summoning of reservists to active service.

cal•lus (kăl′əs) *n., pl.* **-lus•es.** **1.a.** A localized thickening and enlargement of the horny layer of the skin. **b.** The hard bony tissue that develops around the ends of a fractured bone during healing. **2.** *Bot.* **a.** Undifferentiated tissue that develops on or around an injured or cut plant surface or in tissue culture. **b.** The hardened, sometimes sharp base of the floret of certain grasses. —*intr.v.* **-lused, -lus•ing, -lus•es.** To form or develop such hardened tissue. See Usage Note at **callous.** [Lat., masc. of *callum*.]

calm (käm) *adj.* **calm•er, calm•est.** **1.** Nearly or completely motionless; undisturbed. **2.** Not excited or agitated; composed. —*n.* **1.** An absence or cessation of motion; stillness. **2.** Serenity; tranquillity; peace. —*tr. & intr.v.* **calmed, calm•ing, calms.** To make or become calm or quiet. [ME *calme* < OFr. < OItal. *calmo* < LLat. *cauma*, resting place in the heat of the day < Gk. *kauma*, burning heat < *kaiein*, to burn.] —**calm′ly** *adv.* —**calm′ness** *n.*

Syns: *calm, tranquil, placid, serene, halcyon, peaceful.* These adjectives denote absence of excitement or disturbance. *Calm* implies freedom from emotional agitation: *calm acceptance of the inevitable. Tranquil* suggests a more enduring calm: *a tranquil country life. Placid* suggests a pleasant, often phlegmatic calm: *"Not everyone shared his placid temperament"* (Samuel G. Freedman). *Serene* denotes a lofty, even spiritual repose: *remained serene in turbulence. Halcyon* suggests happy tranquillity: *halcyon days of youth. Peaceful* implies undisturbed serenity: *a peaceful night.*

calm•a•tive (kä′mə-tĭv, kăl′mə-) *adj.* Having relaxing or pacifying properties; sedative. —*n.* A sedative.

cal•o•mel (kăl′ə-mĕl′, -məl) *n.* A tasteless compound, Hg_2Cl_2, used as a purgative and an insecticide. [Prob. < NLat. *kalomelas* : Gk. *kalos*, beautiful + *melas*, black.]

cal•o•re•cep•tor (kăl′ə-rĭ-sĕp′tər) *n.* A sensory receptor that detects warmth. [Lat. *calor*, heat; see **kelə-¹*** + RECEPTOR.]

ca•lor•ic (kə-lôr′ĭk, -lŏr′-) *adj.* **1.** Of or relating to heat. **2.** Of or relating to calories. —*n.* A hypothetical fluid thought responsible for the phenomena of heat until Joule proved that heat is a form of energy. [Fr. *calorique* < Lat. *calor*, heat. See **kelə-¹***.] —**ca•lor′i•cal•ly** *adv.*

cal•o•rie (kăl′ə-rē) *n.* **1.** Any of several approx. equal units of heat, each measured as the quantity of heat required to raise the temperature of 1 gram of water by 1°C from a standard initial temperature, esp. from 3.98°C, 14.5°C, or 19.5°C, at 1 atmosphere pressure. **2.** The unit of heat equal to 1/100 the quantity of heat required to raise the temperature of 1 gram of water from 0 to 100°C at 1 atmosphere pressure. **3.a.** The unit of heat equal to the amount of heat required to raise the temperature of 1 kilogram of water by 1°C at 1 atmosphere pressure. **b.** A unit of energy-producing potential equal to this amount of heat that is contained in food and released upon oxidation by the body. [Fr. < Lat. *calor*, heat. See **kelə-[1]***.]

cal•o•rif•ic (kăl′ə-rĭf′ĭk) *adj.* Relating to or generating heat or calories. [Fr. *calorifique* < Lat. *calōrificus* : *calor*, heat; see **kelə-[1]*** + *-ficus*, -fic.]

calorific value *n.* The calories or thermal units contained in one unit of a substance and released by burning.

cal•o•rim•e•ter (kăl′ə-rĭm′ĭ-tər) *n.* **1.** An apparatus for calorimetry. **2.** The part of this apparatus in which the heat measured causes a change of state. [Lat. *calor*, heat; see **kelə-[1]*** + -METER.] —**ca•lor'i•met′ric** (kə-lôr'ə-mĕt′rĭk, -lŏr'-) *adj.* —**ca•lor'i•met′ri•cal•ly** *adv.*

cal•o•rim•e•try (kăl'ə-rĭm′ĭ-trē) *n.* Measurement of the amount of heat evolved or absorbed in a chemical reaction, change of state, or formation of a solution. [Lat. *calor*, heat; see **kelə-[1]*** + -METRY.]

ca•lotte (kə-lŏt′) *n.* A skullcap, esp. one worn by Roman Catholic priests. [Fr. < Prov. *calota* or Ital. *callotta*.]

cal•pac or **cal•pack** also **kal•pac** (kăl′păk', kăl-păk′) *n.* A large black cap, usu. of sheepskin or felt, worn in Turkey, the Caucasus, Iran, and neighboring regions. [Ottoman Turk. *qalpāq* < Old Turkic, prob. ult. < MPers. *kulāfak*, cap, dim. of *kulāf*, hat.]

Cal•pe (kăl′pē). Ancient Gibraltar, one of the Pillars of Hercules at the entrance to the Mediterranean Sea.

calque (kălk) *n.* See **loan translation.** [Fr. < *calquer*, to trace, copy < Ital. *calcare*, to press < Lat. *calcāre*, to tread on < *calx*, heel.]

cal•trop (kăl′trəp, kôl′-) *n.* **1.** Any of various plants of the genera *Tribulus* and *Kallstroemia*, having spiny or tuberculate fruits. **2.** A Mediterranean species of star thistle *(Centaurea calcitrapa)*. **3.** See **water chestnut** 1. **4.** A metal device with four spikes so arranged that when three are on the ground, the fourth points upward, used as a hazard to pneumatic tires or horses. [ME *calketrappe* < Norman Fr. and < OE *calcatrippe*, thistle, both < Med. Lat. *calcatrippa*.]

cal•u•met (kăl′yə-mĕt', -mĭt, kăl'yə-mĕt′) *n.* A long-stemmed ceremonial tobacco pipe used by certain Native Americans. [Canadian Fr. < Fr. dial., straw < LLat. *calamellus*, dim. of Lat. *calamus*, reed < Gk. *kalamos*.]

Cal•u•met (kăl′yə-mĕt', -mĭt). A major industrial region of NE IL and NW IN on Lake Michigan adjacent to Chicago.

Calumet City. A city of NE IL, a suburb of Chicago. Pop. 37,840.

ca•lum•ni•ate (kə-lŭm′nē-āt') *tr.v.* **-at•ed, -at•ing, -ates.** To make maliciously or knowingly false statements about. [Lat. *calumniārī*, *calumniāt-* < *calumnia*, calumny. See CALUMNY.] —**ca•lum'ni•a′tion** *n.* —**ca•lum′ni•a'tor** *n.*

ca•lum•ni•ous (kə-lŭm′nē-əs) *adj.* Containing or implying calumny; slanderous. —**ca•lum′ni•ous•ly** *adv.*

cal•um•ny (kăl′əm-nē) *n.*, *pl.* **-nies. 1.** A false statement maliciously made to injure another's reputation. **2.** The utterance of malicious falsehoods; slander. [ME *calumnie* < OFr. *calomnie* < Lat. *calumnia* < *calvī*, to deceive.]

cal•va•dos (kăl'və-dōs′, kăl′və-dōs') *n.* A French brandy made from apples. [Fr., after *Calvados*, a department of NW France.]

cal•var•i•um (kăl-vâr′ē-əm) *n.*, *pl.* **-i•ums** or **-i•a** (-ē-ə). A skull that lacks the lower jaw and sometimes the facial parts. [Lat. *calvāria*, skull < *calva*, scalp < *calvus*, bald.]

Cal•va•ry[1] (kăl′və-rē, kăl′vrē) also **Gol•go•tha** (gŏl′gə-thə, gŏl-gŏth′ə). A hill outside ancient Jerusalem where Jesus was crucified.

Cal•va•ry[2] also **cal•va•ry** (kăl′və-rē) *n.*, *pl.* **-ries. 1.** A sculptured depiction of the Crucifixion. **2. calvary.** A great ordeal.

Calvary cross *n. Her.* A Latin cross set on three steps.

calve (kăv, käv) *v.* **calved, calv•ing, calves.** —*intr.* **1.** To give birth to a calf. **2.** To break at an edge, so that a portion separates. Used of a glacier or an iceberg. —*tr.* **1.** To give birth to (a calf). **2.** To set loose (a mass of ice). Used of a glacier or an iceberg. [ME *calven* < OE **calfian* < *calf*, calf.]

Cal•vert (kăl′vərt). Family of English colonists in America, including **George** (1580?–1632), 1st Baron Baltimore, and his son **Leonard** (1606–47), who served as governor of Maryland (1634–47).

calves[1] (kăvz, kävz) *n.* Pl. of **calf[1]**.

calves[2] (kăvz, kävz) *n.* Pl. of **calf[2]**.

Cal•vin (kăl′vĭn), **John.** 1509–64. French-born Swiss Protestant theologian who founded Presbyterianism (1536).

Calvin, Melvin. b. 1911. Amer. chemist who won a 1961 Nobel Prize.

Cal•vin•ism (kăl′vĭ-nĭz'əm) *n.* The doctrines of John Calvin, emphasizing salvation by grace alone. —**Cal′vin•ist** *adj.* & *n.* —**Cal'vin•is′tic** *adj.* —**Cal'vin•is′ti•cal•ly** *adv.*

calx (kălks) *n.*, *pl.* **calx•es** or **cal•ces** (kăl′sēz'). The residue left after a mineral or metal has been calcined or roasted. [ME < Lat., lime, limestone, pebble < Gk. *khalix*, pebble.]

ca•ly•cine (kā′lĭ-sīn', -sĭn, kăl′ĭ-) *adj.* Of, relating to, or resembling a calyx.

ca•lyc•u•lus (kə-lĭk′yə-ləs) *n.*, *pl.* **-li** (-lī'). **1.** *Biol.* A small cup-shaped structure. **2.** *Bot.* A group of small bracts resembling a calyx. [Lat., dim. of *calyx*, *calyc-*, calyx. See CALYX.] —**ca•lyc′u•lar** *adj.* —**ca•lyc′u•late** (-lĭt, lāt') *adj.*

Cal•y•don (kăl′ĭ-dŏn', -dən). An ancient city of W-central Greece N of the Gulf of Patras. —**Cal'y•do′ni•an** (-dō′nē-ən, -dōn′yən) *adj.* & *n.*

ca•lyp•so (kə-lĭp′sō) *n.*, *pl.* **-sos.** A terrestrial orchid *(Calypso bulbosa)* native to northern and temperate regions and having a rose-pink flower with an inflated pouchlike lip. [Prob. Lat. *Calypsō*, Calypso. See CALYPSO[1].]

Ca•lyp•so[1] (kə-lĭp′sō) *n.* **1.** *Gk. Myth.* A sea nymph who delayed Odysseus for seven years. **2.** A satellite of Saturn. [Lat. *Calypsō* < Gk. *Kalupsō* < *kaluptein*, to conceal. See **kel-[1]***.]

Ca•lyp•so[2] or **ca•lyp•so** (kə-lĭp′sō) *n.*, *pl.* **-sos** also **-soes.** *Mus.* A type of music that originated in Trinidad and is marked by improvised topical or humorous lyrics. [?] —**Ca•lyp•so′ni•an** (kə-lĭp-sō′nē-ən, kăl'ĭp-) *n.*

ca•lyp•tra (kə-lĭp′trə) *n.* **1.** The protective cap or hood covering the spore case of a moss or related plant. **2.** A similar hoodlike, lidlike, or caplike structure, such as a root cap. [Med. Lat. < Gk. *kaluptra*, veil < *kaluptein*, to cover. See **kel-[1]***.] —**ca•lyp′trate'** (-trāt') *adj.*

ca•lyx (kā′lĭks, kăl′ĭks) *n.*, *pl.* **ca•lyx•es** or **ca•ly•ces** (kā′lĭ-sēz', kăl′ĭ-). **1.** The sepals of a flower considered as a group. **2.** A cuplike structure or organ. **3.** A collecting structure in the kidney. [Lat. *calyx*, *calyc-* < Gk. *kalux*.]

cal•zo•ne (kăl-zō′nē, -zōn′) *n.* An Italian turnover of pizza dough with a seasoned filling of cheese or meat. [Ital., pant leg, calzone < *calza*, sock < VLat. **calcea* < Lat. *calceus*, shoe. See DISCALCED.]

cam (kăm) *n.* An eccentric or multiply curved wheel mounted on a rotating shaft, used to produce variable or reciprocating motion in another part. [Du. *kam*, cog, comb. See **gembh-***.]

Cam (kăm). A river, c. 64 km (40 mi), of E-central England flowing past Cambridge to join the Ouse R. S of Ely.

CAM *abbr. Comp. Sci.* Computer-aided manufacturing.

Ca•ma•güey (kăm'ə-gwā′, kä'mä-). A city of E-central Cuba; founded 1514. Pop. 244,091.

ca•ma•ra•der•ie (kä'mə-rä′də-rē, kăm'ə-răd′ə-) *n.* Goodwill and lighthearted rapport between or among friends. [Fr. < *camarade*, comrade < OFr., roommate. See COMRADE.]

cam•a•ril•la (kăm'ə-rĭl′ə, -rē′yə) *n.* A group of confidential, often scheming advisers; a cabal. [Sp., dim. of *cámara*, room < LLat. *camera*. See CHAMBER.]

Cam•a•ril•lo (kăm'ə-rē′ō). A city of S CA W of Los Angeles. Pop. 52,303.

cam•as or **cam•ass** (kăm′əs) *n.* **1.** Any of several plants of the genus *Camassia* in the lily family, esp. *C. quamash* of western North America having blue flowers and an edible bulb. **2.** Death camas. [Chinook Jargon, perh. of Nootka orig.]

Cam•bay (kăm-bā′), **Gulf of.** An inlet of the Arabian Sea on the NW coast of India.

cam•ber (kăm′bər) *n.* **1.a.** A slightly arched surface, as of a road or snow ski. **b.** The condition of having an arched surface. **2.** A setting of automobile wheels in which they are closer together at the bottom than at the top. —*intr.* & *tr.v.* **-bered, -ber•ing, -bers.** To arch or cause to arch slightly. [< ME *caumber*, curved < ONFr. dial. *caumbre* < Lat. *camur*, perh. < Gk. *kamara*, vault.]

Cam•ber•well beauty (kăm′bər-wĕl', -wəl) *n. Chiefly British.* The mourning cloak. [After *Camberwell*, a former borough of London, England.]

cam•bi•um (kăm′bē-əm) *n.* A lateral meristem in most vascular plants that forms parallel rows of cells resulting in secondary tissues. [Med.Lat., exchange < LLat. *cambīre*, *cambiāre*, to exchange, of Celt. orig.] —**cam′bi•al** *adj.*

Cam•bo•di•a (kăm-bō′dē-ə) or **Kam•pu•che•a** (kăm'pōō-chē′ə). Formerly (1970–75) **Khmer Republic** (kmâr). A country of SE Asia on the Gulf of Siam. Part of French Indochina in the 19th cent., it proclaimed its independence in 1953. Cap. Phnom Penh. Pop. 5,756,141. —**Cam•bo′di•an** *adj.* & *n.*

Cam•bri•a (kăm′brē-ə). Wales during Roman times.

Cam•bri•an (kăm′brē-ən) *adj.* **1.** Of or relating to Wales; Welsh. **2.** Of, relating to, or belonging to the first period of the Paleozoic Era, characterized by warm seas and desert land areas. See table at **geologic time.** —*n.* **1.** A native of Wales. **2.** The Cambrian Period or its deposits. [< Med.Lat. *Cambria*, Wales, alteration of *Cumbria* < Welsh *Cymry*.]

cam•bric (kām′brĭk) *n.* A finely woven white linen or cotton fabric. [Obsolete Flem. *kameryk* < *Kameryk*, Cambrai, a city of N France.]

cambric tea *n.* A drink for children, made of hot water, milk, sugar, and usu. a small amount of tea. [So called because it is thin and white like cambric.]

Cam•bridge (kām′brĭj). **1.** A city of SE Ontario, Canada, WNW of Hamilton. Pop. 77,183. **2.** A municipal borough of E-central England on the Cam R. NNE of London; site of Cambridge University (estab. c. 13th cent.). Pop. 100,200. **3.** A city of E MA on the Charles R. opposite Boston; known for its universities and research facilities. Pop. 95,802.

Cam•by•ses (kăm-bī′sēz). d. 522 B.C. King of Persia (529–522) who extended Persian rule throughout the Nile Valley.

cam•cord•er (kăm′kôr'dər) *n.* A self-contained unit of com-

calumet
Mandan

Cambodia

ă pat	oi boy
ā pay	ou out
âr care	ŏŏ took
ä father	ōō boot
ĕ pet	ŭ cut
ē be	ûr urge
ĭ pit	th thin
ī pie	*th* this
îr pier	hw which
ŏ pot	zh vision
ō toe	ə about, item
ô paw	

Stress marks:
′ (primary);
' (secondary), as in **dictionary** (dĭk′shə-nĕr'ē)

munications equipment made up of a hand-held television camera and a videocassette recorder. [CAM(ERA) + (RE)CORDER.]

Cam•den (kăm′dən). A city of W NJ on the Delaware R. opposite Philadelphia. Pop. 87,492.

came[1] (kām) *n.* A grooved lead bar used to hold together windowpanes. [Poss. dial. *kame,* ridge. See KAME.]

came[2] (kām) *v.* P.t. of **come.**

cam•el (kăm′əl) *n.* **1.** A humped, long-necked ruminant mammal of the genus *Camelus,* domesticated in Old World desert regions as a beast of burden. **2.** A device used to raise sunken objects, consisting of a hollow structure that is submerged, attached to the object, and pumped free of water. **3.** *Sports.* An arabesque spin in figure skating. [ME < OE and < AN *cameil,* both < Lat. *camēlus* < Gk. *kamēlos,* of Semitic orig.]

cam•el•back (kăm′əl-băk′) *adj.* Shaped like a hump or an arching curve. — *n. New Orleans.* A narrow house with one story in front and two in the rear. See Regional Note at **beignet.**

cam•el•eer (kăm′ə-lîr′) *n.* One who drives or rides a camel.

ca•mel•lia (kə-mēl′yə) *n.* Any of several evergreen shrubs or small trees of the genus *Camellia,* esp. *C. japonica,* native to eastern Asia and having shiny leaves and roselike flowers. [NLat. *Camellia,* genus name, after Georg Josef *Kamel* (1661–1706), Moravian Jesuit missionary.]

ca•mel•o•pard (kə-mĕl′ə-pärd′) *n.* **1.** A giraffe. **2.** *Her.* A bearing resembling a giraffe but represented with long curved horns. [ME < Med.Lat. *camēlopardus* < Lat. *camēlopardalis* < Gk. *kamēlopardalis* : *kamēlos,* camel; see CAMEL + *pardalis,* pard.]

camel
Bactrian camel
Camelus bactrianus

Ca•mel•o•par•da•lis (kə-mĕl′ō-pär′dl-ĭs) *n.* A constellation in the Northern Hemisphere in the large space between Ursa Major, Ursa Minor, and Perseus. [Lat. *camēlopardalis,* camelopard. See CAMELOPARD.]

Cam•e•lot (kăm′ə-lŏt′) *n.* **1.** In Arthurian legend, the site of King Arthur's court. **2.** An idealized place or time.

cam•el's hair (kăm′əlz) *n.* **1.** The soft, fine hair of the camel or a substitute for it. **2.** A soft, heavy, usu. light tan cloth, made chiefly of the hair of camel.

Cam•em•bert (kăm′əm-bâr′) *n.* A creamy mold-ripened cheese that softens on the inside as it matures. [Fr., after *Camembert,* a village of NW France.]

cam•e•o (kăm′ē-ō′) *n., pl.* **-os. 1.a.** A gem or shell carved in relief, esp. one in which the raised design and the background consist of layers of contrasting colors. **b.** The technique of carving in this way. **c.** A medallion with a profile in raised relief. **2.** A brief, vivid portrayal or depiction. **3.** A brief appearance of an actor, as in a motion picture. [Ital. and ME *cameu* < OFr. *camaieu* < Med.Lat. *camahūtus.*]

cameo
Late 19th-century Italian

cam•er•a (kăm′ər-ə, kăm′rə) *n.* **1.** An apparatus for taking photographs, consisting of a lightproof enclosure having an aperture through which the image of an object is recorded on a photosensitive film or plate. **2.** The part of a television transmitter that receives the primary image on a light-sensitive cathode tube and transforms it into electrical impulses. **3.** Camera obscura. **4.** *pl.* **-er•ae** (-ə-rē). A judge's private chamber. — ***idiom.* in camera.** In private. [LLat., room. See CHAMBER.]

camera lu•ci•da (lo͞o′sĭ-də) *n., pl.* **camera lu•ci•das.** An optical device that projects a virtual image of an object onto a plane surface, esp. for tracing. [NLat. : Lat. *camera,* chamber + Lat. *lucida,* light.]

cam•er•a•man (kăm′ər-ə-măn′, kăm′rə-) *n.* A man who operates a movie or television camera.

camera ob•scu•ra (əb-skyo͝or′ə) *n., pl.* **camera ob•scu•ras.** A darkened chamber in which the image of an object is received through a small aperture and focused onto a facing surface. [NLat. : Lat. *camera,* chamber + Lat. *obscura,* dark.]

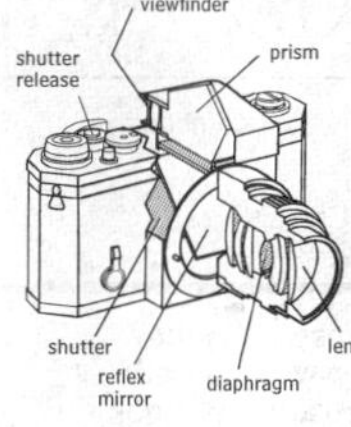

camera

cam•er•a•per•son (kăm′ər-ə-pûr′sən, kăm′rə-) *n.* One who operates a movie or television camera.

cam•er•a-read•y (kăm′ər-ə-rĕd′ē, kăm′rə-) *adj.* Prepared in such a way as to be appropriate for photographing prior to being made into a printing plate: *camera-ready art.*

cam•er•a•wom•an (kăm′ər-ə-wo͝om′ən, kăm′rə-) *n.* A woman who operates a movie or television camera.

cam•er•lin•go (kăm′ər-lĭng′gō) also **cam•er•len•go** (-lĕng′gō) *n., pl.* **-gos.** The cardinal who manages the pope's secular affairs. [Ital. *camarlingo,* of Gmc. orig.]

Cam•er•on (kăm′ər-ən), **Mount.** A peak, 4,342.6 m (14,238 ft), in the Rocky Mts. of central CO.

Cam•e•roon (kăm′ə-ro͞on′, kăm′rən) also **Came•roun** (kăm-ro͞on′). A country of W-central Africa on the Bight of Biafra; gained independence from France and Great Britain in 1960. Cap. Yaoundé. Pop. 9,542,400.

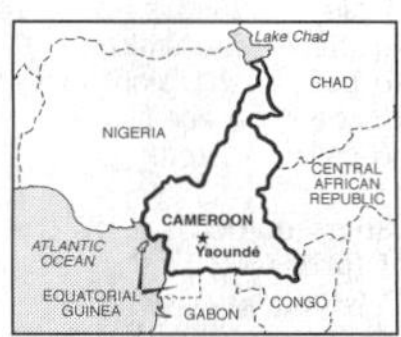

Cameroon

Cam•e•roons (kăm′ə-ro͞onz′). A region and former German protectorate of W-central Africa.

cam•i (kăm′ē) *n., pl.* **-is.** A camisole worn as an undergarment.

cam•i•on (kăm′ē-ən, käm-yôN′) *n.* **1.** A truck. **2.** A bus. [Fr. < OFr. *chamion,* three-wheeled cart.]

ca•mise (kə-mēz′, -mēs′) *n.* A loose shirt, shift, or tunic. [Ar. *qamīṣ* < LLat. *camisia, camīsa,* shirt.]

cam•i•sole (kăm′ĭ-sōl′) *n.* **1.** A woman's sleeveless undergarment. **2.** A short negligee. [Fr. (< Ital. *camiciola,* dim. of *camicia,* shirt) or < OProv. *camisolla,* dim. of *camisa,* shirt, both < LLat. *camisia, camīsa.*]

cam•let (kăm′lĭt) *n.* **1.** A rich cloth of Asian origin, generally made of camel's hair or goat's hair and silk. **2.** A garment made from this cloth. [ME *chamelet* < OFr. *chamelot,* perh. < Ar. *ḫamlah,* nap, fibers.]

cam•o (kăm′ō) *n., pl.* **-os.** *Informal.* Camouflage fabric or a garment made of it. [Short for CAMOUFLAGE.]

Ca•mões (kə-moiNsh′) also **Ca•mo•ëns** (kăm′ō-ənz, kə-mō′-), **Luiz Vaz de.** 1524?–80. Portuguese writer noted for his epic poem *Os Lusíadas* (1572).

cam•o•mile (kăm′ə-mīl′, -mēl′) *n.* Var. of **chamomile.**

Ca•mor•ra (kə-môr′ə, -mŏr′ə) *n.* **1.** A Neapolitan secret society organized about 1820, notorious for its violence and blackmail. **2. camorra.** An unscrupulous, clandestine group. [Ital., perh. < *camorra,* a kind of smock.]

cam•ou•flage (kăm′ə-fläzh′, -fläj′) *n.* **1.** The method or result of concealing personnel or equipment from an enemy by making them appear to be part of the natural surroundings. **2.** Concealment by disguise or protective coloring. **3.** Fabric or a garment dyed so as to make the wearer indistinguishable from the surrounding environment. — *v.* **-flaged, -flag•ing, -flag•es.** — *tr.* **1.** To conceal by the use of disguise or by protective coloring. **2.** To conceal, usu. through misrepresentation or other artifice. — *intr.* To use protective coloring or garments for concealment. [Fr. < *camoufler,* to disguise, alteration (influenced by *camouflet,* snub, smoke blown in one's face) of Ital. *camuffare.*] — **cam′ou•flag′er** *n.*

camp[1] (kămp) *n.* **1.a.** A place where tents, huts, or other temporary shelters are set up. **b.** A cabin or shelter or group of such buildings. **c.** The people using such shelters. **2.a.** A place in the country that offers simple group accommodations and organized recreation or instruction. **b.** *Sports.* A place where athletes engage in intensive training. **c.** The people attending a camp. **3.** Military service; army life. **4.** A group of people who think alike or share a cause; side. — *v.* **camped, camp•ing, camps.** — *intr.* **1.** To pitch or set up a camp. **2.** To live in or as if in a camp; settle. — *tr.* To shelter or lodge in a camp; encamp. [Obsolete Fr., perh. < Ital. or Sp. *campo,* all < Lat. *campus,* field.]

camp[2] (kămp) *n.* **1.** An affectation or appreciation of manners and tastes commonly thought artificial, vulgar, or banal. **2.** Banality, vulgarity, or artificiality when deliberately affected or appreciated for its humor. [?] — **camp** *adj. & v.* — **camp′y** *adj.*

Camp (kămp), **Walter Chauncey.** 1859–1925. Amer. football coach who developed many of the sport's basic rules.

Cam•pa•gna di Ro•ma (kăm-pän′yə dē rō′mə, -mä, käm-). A low-lying residential region surrounding Rome, Italy.

cam•paign (kăm-pān′) *n.* **1.** A series of military operations undertaken to achieve a large-scale objective. **2.** An operation energetically pursued to accomplish a purpose. — *intr.v.* **-paigned, -paign•ing, -paigns.** To engage in a campaign. [Fr. *campagne* < Ital. *campagna,* military operation < LLat. *campānia,* open country, battlefield < *campus,* field.] — **cam•paign′er** *n.*

Cam•pa•ni•a (kăm-pā′nē-ə, -pān′yə, käm-pä′nyä). A region of S Italy on the Tyrrhenian Sea.

cam•pa•ni•le (kăm′pə-nē′lē) *n., pl.* **-les** (-lēz) or **-li** (-lē). A bell tower, esp. one near but not attached to a church or other public building. [Fr. < Ital. < *campana,* bell < LLat. *campāna,* bell (made of metal produced in Campania) < Lat. *campānus,* of Campania < CAMPANIA.]

cam•pa•nol•o•gy (kăm′pə-nŏl′ə-jē) *n.* The art or study of bell casting and ringing. [LLat. *campāna,* bell; see CAMPANILE + -LOGY.] — **cam′pa•nol′o•gist** *n.*

cam•pan•u•la (kăm-păn′yə-lə) *n.* Any of various plants of the genus *Campanula,* which includes the harebell and bellflower. [NLat. *Campanula,* genus name, dim. of LLat. *campāna,* bell. See CAMPANILE.]

cam•pan•u•late (kăm-păn′yə-lĭt, -lāt′) *adj. Bot.* Bell-shaped.

Camp•bell (kăm′bəl). A city of W-central CA SW of San Jose. Pop. 36,048.

Campbell, John Archibald. 1811–89. Amer. jurist; associate justice of the U.S. Supreme Court (1853–61).

Campbell, Joseph. 1904–87. Amer. mythologist whose works include *Masks of God* (1959–67).

Campbell, Mrs. **Patrick.** 1865–1940. British actress who was the first to portray Eliza in Shaw's *Pygmalion.*

Campbell, Thomas[1]. 1763–1854. Irish-born Amer. religious leader who with his son **Alexander** (1788–1866) founded the Disciples of Christ (1809).

Campbell, Thomas[2]. 1777–1844. British poet and editor best known for his ballad "Lord Ullin's Daughter" (1809).

Camp•bell-Ban•ner•man (kăm′bəl-băn′ər-mən, kăm′əl-), Sir **Henry.** 1836–1908. British prime minister (1905–08).

Camp Da•vid (dā′vĭd). A presidential retreat in the Catoctin Mts. of N MD NNW of Washington DC.

Cam•pe•che (kăm-pē′chē, käm-pĕ′-). A city of SE Mexico on the **Bay of Campeche,** a section of the Gulf of Mexico W of Yucatán. Pop. 128,434.

camp•er (kăm′pər) *n.* **1.** One that camps, as in a tent. **2.a.** A motor vehicle used for camping and recreational travel. **b.** The rear compartment or attached trailer of such a vehicle.

cam•pe•si•no (kăm′pĭ-sē′nō, kăm′-) *n., pl.* **-nos.** A Latin-American farmer or farm worker. [Sp. < *campo,* field < Lat. *campus.*]

cam•pes•tral (kăm-pĕs′trəl) *adj.* Of, relating to, or growing in uncultivated land or open fields. [< Lat. *campester,* of a field < *campus,* field.]

camp•fire (kămp′fīr′) *n.* **1.** An outdoor fire in a camp, used for cooking or warmth. **2.** A meeting held around such a fire.

Camp Fire Girl *n.* A member of an organization for girls aged 7 through 18 that strives to teach good values and practical skills. [From *Camp Fire Girls,* Inc.]

camp follower *n.* A civilian who follows a military unit from place to place, esp. as a vender or a prostitute.

camp•ground (kămp′ground′) *n.* An area used for setting up a camp or holding a camp meeting.

cam•phene (kăm′fēn′) *n.* A crystalline terpene, $C_{10}H_{16}$, used to make synthetic camphor and insecticides. [CAMPH(OR) + -ENE.]

cam•phor (kăm′fər) *n.* An aromatic crystalline compound, $C_{10}H_{16}O$, obtained naturally from the camphor tree or synthesized and used in the manufacture of film and plastics and in medicine for mild pain and itching. [ME *caumfre* < AN < Med.Lat. *camphora* < Ar. *kāfūr,* poss. < Malay *kapur;* akin to Skt. *karpūraḥ.*] **— cam′phor•a′ceous** (kăm′fə-rā′shəs) *adj.* **— cam•phor′ic** (-fôr′ĭk, -fŏr′-) *adj.*

cam•phor•ate (kăm′fə-rāt′) *tr.v.* **-at•ed, -at•ing, -ates.** To treat or impregnate with camphor.

camphor oil *n.* The oil obtained by steam distillation from the wood of the camphor tree and used to produce natural camphor.

camphor tree *n.* An east Asian evergreen tree *(Cinnamomum camphora)* having wood and leathery leaves that are a source of camphor.

Cam•pi•na Gran•de (kăm′pē-nə grăn′də, -dē, käN-pē′nə gräN′də). A city of extreme E Brazil NW of Recife. Pop. 222,102.

Cam•pi•nas (kăm-pē′nəs, käN-). A city of SE Brazil NNW of São Paulo. Pop. 566,627.

cam•pi•on (kăm′pē-ən) *n.* Any of several plants of the genera *Lychnis* and *Silene,* native chiefly to the Northern Hemisphere and having notched or fringed flower petals. [?]

Cam•pi•on (kăm′pē-ən), **Thomas.** 1567–1620. English poet and composer of songs for voice and lute.

camp meeting *n.* An evangelistic gathering held in a tent or outdoors and often lasting several days.

cam•po (kăm′pō, käm′-) *n., pl.* **-pos.** A large grassy plain in South America, with scattered bushes and small trees. [Sp., field < Lat. *campus.*]

Cam•po•bel•lo Island (kăm′pə-bĕl′ō). An island of SW New Brunswick, Canada, off the coast of ME.

Cam•po Gran•de (kăm′pō grăn′də, -dē, kän′po͝o gräN′də). A city of SW Brazil WNW of São Paulo. Pop. 282,857.

camp•o•ree (kăm′pə-rē′) *n.* A local gathering of Boy Scouts or Girl Scouts. [Prob. CAMP[1] + (JAMB)OREE.]

Cam•pos (kăm′pəs, käN′po͞os). A city of SE Brazil NE of Rio de Janeiro; founded in the 17th cent. Pop. 178,457.

camp robber *n.* See **gray jay.**

camp•site (kămp′sīt′) *n.* An area for camping.

Camp Springs. A city of W-central Maryland, a suburb of Washington DC. Pop. 16,392.

cam•pus (kăm′pəs) *n., pl.* **-pus•es.** The grounds of a school, college, university, or hospital. [Lat., field.]

cam•py•lo•bac•ter•o•sis (kăm′pə-lō-băk′tə-rō′sĭs) *n.* A gastrointestinal condition characterized by diarrhea, abdominal cramps, and fever, caused by eating raw meat or unpasteurized milk contaminated with *Campylobacter jejuni.* [NLat. *Campylobacter,* genus name (Gk. *kampulos,* curved + BACTER(IUM)) + -OSIS.]

cam•py•lot•ro•pous (kăm′pə-lŏt′rə-pəs) *adj. Bot.* Having a partially inverted ovule such that the micropyle nearly meets the funiculus. [Gk. *kampulos,* curved + -TROPOUS.]

cam•shaft (kăm′shăft′) *n.* An engine shaft fitted with a cam or cams.

Ca•mus (kă-mo͞o′, -mü′), **Albert.** 1913–60. French existentialist who won the 1957 Nobel Prize for literature.

can[1] (kăn; kən *when unstressed*) *aux.v.* Past tense **could** (ko͝od). **1.a.** Used to indicate physical or mental ability: *I can lift it.* **b.** Used to indicate possession of a specified power, right, or privilege: *We can vote.* **c.** Used to indicate possession of a specified capability or skill: *I can sing.* **2.a.** Used to indicate possibility or probability: *Such things can happen.* **b.** Used to indicate that which is permitted, as by conscience or feelings: *One can hardly blame you.* **c.** Used to indicate probability or possibility under the specified circumstances: *They can hardly have intended that.* **3.** *Usage Problem.* Used to request or grant permission: *Can I be excused?* [ME, first and third pers. sing. pr.t. of *connen,* to know how < OE *cunnan.* See **gnō-*.**]

Usage Note: Generations of grammarians and schoolteachers have insisted that *can* should be used only to express the capacity to do something and that *may* must be used to express permission. Technically, correct usage therefore requires *May* (not *can*) *I take another week to submit the application?* Only 21 percent of the Usage Panel accepts *can* in this sentence. *Can* does have a long history of use by educated speakers to express permission, particularly in British English. But observance of the distinction is often advisable in the interests of clarity.

can[2] (kăn) *n.* **1.** A usu. cylindrical metal container. **2.a.** An airtight container, usu. made of tin-coated iron, in which foods or beverages are preserved. **b.** The contents of such a container. **3.** *Slang.* A jail or prison. **4.** *Slang.* A toilet or restroom. **5.** *Slang.* The buttocks. *— tr.v.* **canned, can•ning, cans. 1.** To seal (food) in an airtight container for future use; preserve. **2.** *Slang.* To make a recording of. **3.** *Slang.* To dismiss from employment or school. **4.** *Slang.* To put a stop to; quit: *Let's can the chatter.* [ME *canne,* a water container < OE.] **— can′ner** *n.*

can. *abbr.* **1.a.** Canceled. **b.** Cancellation. **2.** Cannon. **3.** Canon. **4.** Canto.

Can. *abbr.* **1.** Canada. **2.** Canadian.

Ca•na (kā′nə). A village of N Palestine near Nazareth where Jesus performed his first miracle, changing water into wine.

Ca•naan (kā′nən). An ancient region made up of Palestine or the part of it between the Jordan R. and the Mediterranean.

Ca•naan•ite (kā′nə-nīt′) *n.* **1.** A member of a Semitic people who inhabited Canaan from late prehistoric times and were conquered by the Israelites around 1000 B.C. **2.** The Semitic language of the Canaanites. *— adj.* Of or relating to ancient Canaan or its people, language, or culture.

Can•a•da (kăn′ə-də). A country of N North America; settled by English and French colonists and ceded to England in 1763. The Dominion of Canada was formed in 1867. Cap. Ottawa. Pop. 23,343,181. **— Ca•na′di•an** (kə-nā′dē-ən) *adj. & n.*

Canada balsam *n.* A viscous transparent resin obtained from the balsam fir and used as a cement for glass lenses and for mounting specimens on microscopic slides.

Canada Day *n.* July 1, observed in Canada in commemoration of the formation of the Dominion in 1867.

Canada goose or **Canadian goose** *n.* A common wild goose *(Branta canadensis)* of North America having grayish plumage, a black neck and head, and a white throat patch.

Canada jay *n.* See **gray jay.**

Canada thistle *n.* A perennial herb *(Cirsium arvense)* in the composite family, native to Europe and naturalized as a noxious weed in North America, having spiny-margined leaves.

Canadian bacon *n.* Cured rolled bacon from the loin of a pig.

Canadian Falls also **Horse•shoe Falls** (hôrs′sho͞o′, hôrsh′-). A section, c. 48 m (158 ft) high, of Niagara Falls within Ontario, Canada.

Canadian French *n.* The French language as used in Canada.

Canadian hemlock *n.* A coniferous evergreen monoecious tree *(Tsuga canadensis)* native from Nova Scotia to Alaska and valuable for its timber, as a pulpwood, and for tanning.

Canadian River. A river rising in NE NM and flowing c. 1,458 km (906 mi) E to the Arkansas R.

Canadian Shield. See **Laurentian Plateau.**

ca•naille (kə-nī′, -nāl′) *n.* **1.** The masses of the people; the proletariat. **2.** Rabble; riffraff. [Fr. < Ital. *canaglia,* pack of dogs, rabble < *cane,* dog < Lat. *canis.* See **kwon-*.**]

ca•nal (kə-năl′) *n.* **1.** An artificial waterway or artificially improved river used for travel, shipping, or irrigation. **2.** *Anat.* A tube, duct, or passageway. **3.** *Astron.* One of the faint hazy markings resembling straight lines on early telescopic images of the surface of Mars. *— tr.v.* **-nalled, -nal•ling, -nals** or **-naled, -nal•ing, -nals. 1.** To dig a canal through. **2.** To provide with a canal. [Partly Fr., channel, and partly ME, tube (< Med.Lat. *canāle*), both < Lat. *canālis,* prob. < *canna,* small reed. See CANE.]

Ca•na•let•to (kăn′ə-lĕt′ō). 1697–1768. Italian painter noted for his detailed views of Venice.

can•a•lic•u•late (kăn′ə-lĭk′yə-lĭt, -lāt′) *adj.* Having one or more longitudinal grooves or channels. [Lat. *canāliculātus* < *canāliculus,* dim. of *canālis,* channel. See CANAL.]

can•a•lic•u•lus (kăn′ə-lĭk′yə-ləs) *n., pl.* **-li** (-lī′). A small canal or duct in the body. [Lat. *canāliculus,* dim. of *canālis,* conduit. See CANAL.] **— can′a•lic′u•lar** (-lər) *adj.*

can•a•li•za•tion (kăn′ə-lĭ-zā′shən) *n.* **1.** The act or an instance of canalizing. **2.** A system of canals.

can•a•lize (kăn′ə-līz′) *tr.v.* **-lized, -liz•ing, -liz•es. 1.** To furnish with or convert into a canal or canals. **2.** To provide an outlet for; channel.

Ca•nal Zone (kə-năl′) also **Pan•a•ma Canal Zone** (păn′ə-mä′, -mô′). A strip of land, c. 16 km (10 mi) wide, across the Isthmus of Panama; formerly administered by the U.S. and turned over to Panama in 1979.

can•a•pé (kăn′ə-pā′, -pē) *n.* A cracker or a small piece of bread served with a spread as an appetizer. [Fr. < *canapé,* couch < Med.Lat. *canāpēum,* mosquito net. See CANOPY.]

ca•nard (kə-närd′) *n.* **1.** An unfounded or false, deliberately misleading story. **2.a.** A short winglike control surface projecting from the fuselage of an aircraft, mounted forward of

Albert Camus
Photographed in 1956

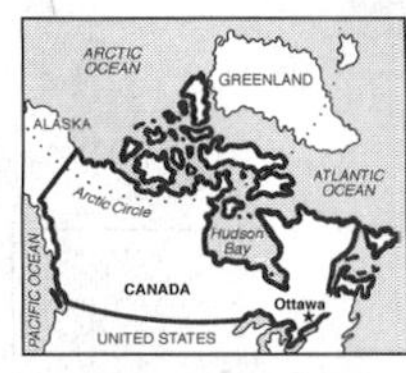

Canada

Canada goose
Branta canadensis

ă **pat**	oi **boy**
ā **pay**	ou **out**
âr **care**	o͝o **took**
ä **father**	o͞o **boot**
ĕ **pet**	ŭ **cut**
ē **be**	ûr **urge**
ĭ **pit**	th **thin**
ī **pie**	*th* **this**
îr **pier**	hw **which**
ŏ **pot**	zh **vision**
ō **toe**	ə **about, item**
ô **paw**	

Stress marks:
′ (primary);
′ (secondary), as in **dictionary** (dĭk′shə-nĕr′ē)

the main wing and serving as a horizontal stabilizer. **b.** An aircraft with canards. [Fr., duck, canard, prob. < the phrase *vendre un canard à moitié*, to swindle < OFr. *quanart*, duck < *caner*, to cackle, of imit. orig.]

ca•nar•y (kə-nâr′ē) *n.*, *pl.* **-ies. 1.** A small greenish to yellow finch *(Serinus canaria)* native to the Canary Islands. **2.** *Slang.* An informer; a stool pidgeon. **3.** A sweet white wine from the Canary Islands, similar to Madeira. **4.** A lively 16th-century court dance. **5.** *Color.* A light to vivid yellow. [Fr. *canari* < Sp. *canario*, of the Canary Islands < *(Islas) Canarias*, Canary (Islands) < LLat. *Canāriae (Īnsulae)*, (islands) of dogs < Lat. *canārius*, canine < *canis*, dog. See **kwon-***.]

ca•nar•y-bird flower (kə-nâr′ē-bûrd′) *n.* A Peruvian climbing plant *(Tropaeolum peregrinum)* with yellow flowers.

canary grass *n.* **1.** An annual Mediterranean grass *(Phalaris canariensis)* having grains used as food for caged birds, such as canaries. **2.** Any of several related grasses.

Ca•nar•y Islands (kə-nâr′ē). A group of Spanish islands in the Atlantic Ocean off the NW coast of Africa; part of Spain since 1479.

ca•nas•ta (kə-năs′tə) *n.* *Games.* A card game for two to six players, related to rummy and requiring two decks. [Sp. < *canasto*, basket < Lat. *canistrum*. See CANISTER.]

Ca•nav•er•al (kə-năv′ər-əl, -năv′rəl), **Cape.** Formerly (1963–73) **Cape Ken•ne•dy** (kĕn′ĭ-dē). A promontory extending into the Atlantic Ocean from a barrier island on the E-central coast of FL; launching area for U.S. space missions.

Can•ber•ra (kăn′bər-ə, -bĕr′ə). The cap. of Australia, in the SE part; settled in 1824 and designated cap. in 1908. Pop. 243,450.

canc. *abbr.* **1.** Canceled. **2.** Cancellation.

can•can (kăn′kăn′) *n.* A dance that originated in France, performed by women and marked by high kicking. [Fr.]

can•cel (kăn′səl) *v.* **-celed, -cel•ing, -cels** also **-celled, -cel•ling, -cels.** — *tr.* **1.** To cross out with lines or other markings. See Syns at **erase. 2.** To annul or invalidate. **3.** To mark or perforate (a check, for example) to indicate that it may not be used again. **4.** To equalize or make up for; offset. **5.** *Math.* **a.** To remove (a common factor) from the numerator and denominator of a fractional expression. **b.** To remove (a common factor or term) from both sides of an equation or inequality. **6.** *Print.* To omit or delete. — *intr.* To neutralize one another; counterbalance. — *n.* **1.** The act or an instance of canceling; a cancellation. **2.** *Print.* **a.** Deletion of typed or printed matter. **b.** The matter deleted. **c.** A replacement for deleted matter. [ME *cancellen* < OFr. *canceller* < Lat. *cancellāre*, to cross out < *cancellus*, lattice, dim. of *cancer*, lattice.] — **can′cel•a•ble** *adj.* — **can′cel•er** *n.*

can•cel•late (kăn-sĕl′ĭt, kăn′sə-lāt′) also **can•cel•lat•ed** (-lā′tĭd) *adj.* *Anat.* Cancellous. [Lat. *cancellātus*, p.part. of *cancellāre*, to make in a crisscross pattern. See CANCEL.]

can•cel•la•tion also **can•ce•la•tion** (kăn′sə-lā′shən) *n.* **1.** The act or an instance of canceling. **2.** A mark or a perforation indicating canceling. **3.** Something canceled.

can•cel•lous (kăn-sĕl′əs, kăn′sə-ləs) *adj.* *Anat.* Having an open, latticed, or porous structure. Used esp. of bone. [< Lat. *cancellus*, lattice. See CANCEL.]

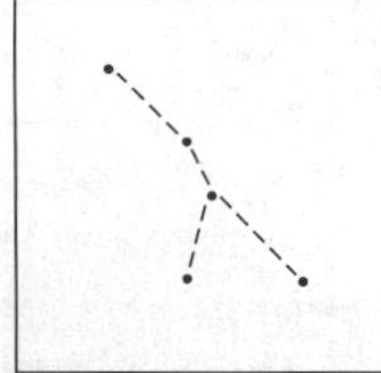
Cancer

can•cer (kăn′sər) *n.* **1.a.** Any of various malignant neoplasms marked by the proliferation of anaplastic cells that tend to invade surrounding tissue and metastasize to new body sites. **b.** The pathological condition characterized by such growths. **2.** A pernicious, spreading evil. [ME. See CANKER.] — **can′cer•ous** (kăn′sər-əs) *adj.*

Can•cer (kăn′sər) *n.* **1.** A constellation in the Northern Hemisphere near Leo and Gemini. **2.a.** The fourth sign of the zodiac in astrology. **b.** One born under this sign. [ME < Lat. See CANKER.]

Can•cún (kăn-kōōn′, käng-). An island resort community of SE Mexico off NE Yucatán. Pop. 33,273.

can•del•a (kăn-dĕl′ə) *n.* A unit of luminous intensity equal to 1/60 of the luminous intensity per square centimeter of a blackbody radiating at the temperature of solidification of platinum (2,046°K). See table at **measurement.** [Lat. *candēla*, candle. See CANDLE.]

can•de•la•bra (kăn′dl-ä′brə, -ăb′rə, -ā′brə) *n.* A candelabrum. [< Lat. *candēlābra*, pl. of *candēlābrum*. See CANDELABRUM.]

can•de•la•brum (kăn′dl-ä′brəm, -ăb′rəm, -ā′brəm) *n.*, *pl.* **-bra** (-brə) or **-brums.** A candlestick with several arms or branches. [Lat. *candēlābrum*, candlestick < *candēla*, candle. See CANDLE.]

can•de•lil•la (kăn′dl-ē′ə) *n.* A shrubby spurge *(Euphorbia antisyphilitica)* native to southwest Texas and Mexico and having leafless stems that yield a multipurpose wax. [Am.Sp., dim. of Sp. *candela*, candle < Lat. *candēla*. See CANDLE.]

can•dent (kăn′dənt) *adj.* Having a white-hot glow; incandescent. [Lat. *candēns*, *candent-*, pr.part. of *candēre*, to shine. See **kand-***.]

can•des•cence (kăn-dĕs′əns) *n.* The state of being white hot; incandescence. [< Lat. *candēscēns*, *candēscent-*, pr.part. of *candēscere*, inchoative of *candēre*, to shine. See CANDID.] — **can•des′cent** *adj.* — **can•des′cent•ly** *adv.*

Can•di•a[1] (kăn′dē-ə). The island of Crete.

Can•di•a[2] (kăn′dē-ə). See **Iráklion.**

can•did (kăn′dĭd) *adj.* **1.** Unprejudiced; impartial. **2.** Open and sincere, esp. in expression; straightforward. See Syns at **frank**[1]. **3.** Not posed or rehearsed. — *n.* A candid photograph. [Lat. *candidus*, guileless < *candēre*, to shine. See **kand-***.] — **can′did•ly** *adv.* — **can′did•ness** *n.*

can•di•da (kăn′dĭ-də) *n.* Any of the pathogenic yeastlike imperfect fungi of the genus *Candida.* [Lat., fem. of *candidus*, white. See CANDID.]

can•di•date (kăn′dĭ-dāt′, -dĭt) *n.* **1.** A person seeking an office, prize, or honor. **2.** One likely to gain a position or come to a certain fate. [Lat. *candidātus*, clothed in white, candidate < *candidus*, white. See CANDID.] — **can′di•da•cy** (-də-sē), **can′di•da•ture′** (-də-chŏŏr′, -chər) *n.*

candid camera *n.* A small simple camera with a fast lens for taking unposed photographs.

can•di•di•a•sis (kăn′dĭ-dī′ə-sĭs) *n.* A fungous infection caused by a member of the genus *Candida*, esp. *C. albicans*, that can involve various parts of the body.

can•died (kăn′dēd) *adj.* Covered or cooked with sugar.

can•dle (kăn′dl) *n.* **1.a.** A solid, usu. cylindrical mass of tallow, wax, or other fatty substance with an embedded wick, burned to provide light. **b.** Something resembling this. **2.** *Phys.* **a.** An obsolete unit of luminous intensity, originally defined in terms of a standard wax candle and equal to 1.02 candelas. **b.** See **candela.** — *tr.v.* **-dled, -dling, -dles.** To examine (an egg) for freshness or fertility before a bright light. [ME *candel* < OE and < AN *candele*, both < Lat. *candēla* < *candēre*, to shine. See **kand-***.] — **can′dler** *n.*

can•dle•ber•ry (kăn′dl-bĕr′ē) *n.* **1.** Any of certain bayberries, the wax myrtle, or the fruit of these plants. **2.** See **candlenut.**

can•dle•fish (kăn′dl-fĭsh′) *n.*, *pl.* **candlefish** or **-fish•es.** An oily edible fish *(Thaleichthys pacificus)* of northern Pacific waters, formerly used as a torch by Native Americans.

can•dle•light (kăn′dl-līt′) *n.* **1.** Illumination from a candle or candles. **2.** Dusk; twilight.

Can•dle•mas (kăn′dl-məs) *n.* A Christian feast commemorating the purification of the Virgin Mary and the presentation of the infant Jesus in the temple, traditionally observed on February 2. [ME *candelmasse* < OE *candelmæsse* : *candel*, candle; see CANDLE + *mæsse*, mass; see MASS.]

can•dle•nut (kăn′dl-nŭt′) *n.* **1.** A tropical southeast Asian tree *(Aleurites moluccana)* bearing seeds used to make candles and whose oil is used in paints, varnishes, lacquer, and soft soap. **2.** The seed of this tree.

can•dle•pin (kăn′dl-pĭn′) *n.* *Sports.* **1.** A slender bowling pin used in a variation of the game of tenpins. **2.** Also **candlepins.** *(used with a sing. v.)* A bowling game using candlepins.

can•dle•pow•er (kăn′dl-pou′ər) *n.* Luminous intensity expressed in candelas.

can•dle•snuff•er (kăn′dl-snŭf′ər) *n.* An implement with a bell-shaped cup used to extinguish the flame of a candle.

can•dle•stick (kăn′dl-stĭk′) *n.* A holder with a cup or spike for a candle.

can•dle•wick (kăn′dl-wĭk′) *n.* **1.** The wick of a candle. **2.a.** A soft, heavy cotton thread similar to that used to make wicks for candles. **b.** Embroidery made of tufts of this thread.

can•dle•wood (kăn′dl-wŏŏd′) *n.* **1.** Any of several trees or shrubs yielding a usu. resinous wood. **2.** The wood of such a plant, burned for light or fuel. **3.** The ocotillo.

can-do (kăn′dōō′) *adj.* *Informal.* Marked by a willingness to tackle a job and get it done.

can•dor (kăn′dər) *n.* **1.** Frankness or sincerity of expression; openness. **2.** Freedom from prejudice; impartiality. [ME < OFr. < Lat. < *candēre*, to shine. See **kand-***.]

C & W or **C and W** *abbr.* Country and western.

can•dy (kăn′dē) *n.*, *pl.* **-dies. 1.** A rich sweet confection made with sugar, often combined with fruits or nuts. **2.** A piece of candy. — *v.* **-died, -dy•ing, -dies.** — *tr.* **1.** To reduce to sugar crystals. **2.** To cook, preserve, saturate, or coat with sugar or syrup. **3.** To make pleasant or agreeable; sweeten. — *intr.* To become candied. [ME *candi*, crystallized cane sugar, short for *sugre-candi*, ult. < Ar. *sukkar qandīy* : *sukkar*, sugar; see SUGAR + *qandīy*, candied (< *qand*, cane sugar, prob. < Dravidian *kaṇṭu*, lump).]

can•dy-ass or **candy ass** (kăn′dē-ăs′) *n.* *Vulgar Slang.* A sissy; a wimp. — **can′dy-ass′** *adj.*

candy striper *n.* A volunteer worker in a hospital. [< the red and white striped uniform.]

can•dy•tuft (kăn′dē-tŭft′) *n.* Any of several plants of the genus *Iberis* in the mustard family, native to Europe and the Mediterranean region and widely cultivated for their showy flowers. [Obsolete *Candy* (var. of CANDIA[1]) + TUFT.]

cane (kān) *n.* **1.a.** A slender, strong but often flexible stem, as of certain reeds. **b.** A plant having such a stem. **c.** Cane used for wickerwork or baskets. **2.** A bamboo *(Arundinaria gigantea)* native to the southeast United States, having stiff stems and often forming canebrakes. **3.** The stem of a raspberry, blackberry, certain roses, or similar plants. **4.** Sugar cane. **5.** A stick used as an aid in walking or carried as an accessory. **6.** A rod used for flogging. — *tr.v.* **caned, can•ing,**

canes. **1.** To make, supply, or repair with flexible woody material. **2.** To hit or beat with a rod. [ME < OFr. < Lat. *canna*, small reed < Gk. *kanna*, of Semitic orig.] — **can′er** *n.*

cane•brake (kān′brāk′) *n.* A dense thicket of cane.

ca•nes•cent (kə-nĕs′ənt) *adj.* **1.** *Biol.* Covered with short, fine whitish or grayish hairs or down; hoary. **2.** Turning white or grayish. [Lat. *cānēscēns, cānēscent-*, pr.part. of *cānēscere*, inchoative of *cānēre*, to be white < *cānus*, white. See **kas-***.] — **ca•nes′cence** *n.*

cane sugar *n.* Sucrose obtained from sugar cane.

Ca•nes Ve•nat•i•ci (kā′nēz vĭ-năt′ĭ-sī′) *n.* A constellation in the Northern Hemisphere near Ursa Major and Boötes. [Lat. *canēs*, pl. of *canis*, dog + *vēnāticī*, pl. of *vēnāticus*, hunting.]

Ca•net•ti (kä-nĕt′ē), **Elias.** b. 1905. Bulgarian-born writer who won the 1981 Nobel Prize for literature.

can•field (kăn′fēld′) *n. Games.* A form of solitaire. [After Richard Albert *Canfield* (1855–1914), Amer. gambler.]

Can•i•a•pis•cau also **Kan•i•a•pis•kau** (kăn′ē-ə-pĭs′kō, -kou). A river of N Quebec, Canada, rising in **Lake Caniapiscau** (or **Lake Kaniapiskau**) and flowing c. 925 km (575 mi) to the Larch R.

ca•nic•u•lar (kə-nĭk′yə-lər) *adj.* **1.** Of or relating to Sirius or Procyon. **2.** Of or relating to the dog days. [LLat. *canīculāris*, of Sirius < Lat. *Canīcula*, Sirius, dim. of *canis*, dog. See **kwon-***.]

ca•nid (kā′nĭd, kăn′ĭd) *n.* Any of various widely distributed carnivorous mammals of the dog family Canidae. [< NLat. *Canidae*, family name < *Canis*, type genus < Lat. See CANINE.]

ca•nine (kā′nīn) *adj.* **1.** Of, relating to, or characteristic of the canids. **2.** Of, relating to, or being one of the pointed conical teeth located between the incisors and the first bicuspids. [Lat. *canīnus* < *canis*, dog. See **kwon-***.] — **ca′nine** *n.*

canine distemper *n.* See **distemper[1]** 1a.

Ca•nis Ma•jor (kā′nĭs mā′jər, kăn′ĭs) *n.* A constellation in the Southern Hemisphere near Puppis and Lepus, containing the star Sirius. [Lat. *canis*, dog + *maior*, larger.]

Canis Mi•nor (mī′nər) *n.* A constellation in the equatorial region of the Southern Hemisphere near Hydra and Monoceros, containing Procyon. [Lat. *canis*, dog + *minor*, smaller.]

can•is•tel (kăn′ĭ-stĕl′) *n.* **1.** A tree *(Pouteria campechiana)* native to Mexico, Central America, and the Caribbean and having sweet fruit. **2.** The fruit of this tree. [Am.Sp.]

can•is•ter (kăn′ĭ-stər) *n.* **1.** A box or can of thin metal or plastic used for holding dry cooking ingredients, such as flour. **2.** A metallic cylinder packed with shot that scatters on firing; case shot. **3.** The part of a gas mask containing the filter for removing toxic agents from the air. [Lat. *canistrum*, basket < Gk. *kanastron* < *kanna*, reed. See CANE.]

can•ker (kăng′kər) *n.* **1.** Ulceration of the mouth and lips. **2.** An inflammation or infection of the ear and auditory canal, esp. in dogs and cats. **3.** A condition in horses similar to but more advanced than thrush. **4.a.** A localized diseased or necrotic area on a plant part, usu. caused by fungi or bacteria. **b.** Any of several diseases of plants characterized by the presence of such lesions. **5.** A source of spreading corruption or decay. — *v.* **-kered, -ker•ing, -kers.** — *tr.* **1.** To attack or infect with canker. **2.** To infect with corruption or decay. — *intr.* To become infected with or as if with canker. [ME < OE *cancer* and < OFr. *cancre*, both < Lat. *cancer*. See **kar-***.]

canker brake *n.* See **Christmas fern.**

can•ker•ous (kăng′kər-əs) *adj.* **1.** Marked by or infected with canker; ulcerous. **2.** Causing canker; ulcerating.

canker sore *n.* A small painful ulcer or sore, usu. of the mouth.

can•ker•worm (kăng′kər-wûrm′) *n.* The larva of either of two moths *(Paleacrita vernata* or *Alsophila pometaria)*, destructive to fruit and shade trees.

can•na (kăn′ə) *n.* Any of various perennial tropical herbs of the genus *Canna*, having clusters of large showy flowers and including an edible variety. [Lat. *canna*, cane. See CANE.]

can•na•bin (kăn′ə-bĭn) *n.* A resinous material extracted from cannabis. [CANNAB(IS) + -IN.]

can•na•bis (kăn′ə-bĭs) *n.* **1.** An annual dioecious plant *(Cannabis sativa)* native to central Asia and having tough bast fibers. **2.** Any of several mildly euphoriant, intoxicating hallucinogenic drugs, such as marijuana, prepared from this plant. [Lat. < Gk. *kannabis*.] — **can′na•bic** (-bĭk) *adj.*

Can•nae (kăn′ē). An ancient town of SE Italy where Carthaginians defeated the Romans in 216 B.C..

canned (kănd) *adj.* **1.** Preserved and sealed in a can or jar. **2.** *Informal.* Recorded or taped for repeated use on television or radio. **3.** *Informal.* **a.** Used repeatedly with little or no change. **b.** Completely unoriginal.

can•nel (kăn′əl) *n.* A bituminous coal that burns brightly with much smoke. [Perh. short for *cannel coal*, dialectal var. of *candle coal* (< its bright flame).]

can•nel•lo•ni (kăn′ə-lō′nē) *n.* Large-sized tubes of pasta stuffed with meat or cheese and baked in a tomato or cream sauce. [Ital., pl. of *cannellone*, tubular soup noodle < *cannello*, small tube, dim. of *canna*, reed < Lat. See CANE.]

can•ner•y (kăn′ə-rē) *n.*, *pl.* **-ies.** A factory where fish, vegetables, or other foods are canned.

Cannes (kăn, kănz, kän). A resort city of SE France on the Mediterranean Sea near Nice. Pop. 72,259.

can•ni•bal (kăn′ə-bəl) *n.* **1.** A person who eats the flesh of other human beings. **2.** An animal that feeds on others of its own kind. [< Sp. *Caníbalis*, name of the man-eating Caribs of Cuba and Haiti, var. of *caríbalis* < Arawak *caniba, carib*, an ethnic name.] — **can′ni•bal•ism** *n.* — **can′ni•bal•is′tic** *adj.*

can•ni•bal•ize (kăn′ə-bə-līz′) *tr.v.* **-ized, -iz•ing, -iz•es. 1.** To remove parts from (damaged airplanes, for example) for use in repairing similar equipment. **2.** To deprive of vital elements or resources for use elsewhere. **3.** To draw on as a major source. — **can′ni•bal•i•za′tion** (-bə-lĭ-zā′shən) *n.*

can•ni•kin (kăn′ĭ-kĭn) *n.* **1.** A small can or cup. **2.** A small wooden bucket. [Du. *kanneken* (< MDu. *cannekijn*, dim. of *canne*, can) and Flem. *cannikin*, dim. of *cann*, can.]

Can•ning (kăn′ĭng), **George.** 1770–1827. British politician who served as foreign secretary (1807–09 and 1822–27) and prime minister (1827).

Can•nock (kăn′ək). An urban district of W-central England NNW of Birmingham; center of a mining area based at **Cannock Chase,** a nearby moorland. Pop. 84,900.

can•no•li (kə-nō′lē, kă-) *n.* A pastry roll with a creamy sweet filling. [Ital., pl. of *cannolo*, tube, dim. of *canna*, reed. See CANNELLONI.]

can•non (kăn′ən) *n.*, *pl.* **cannon** or **-nons. 1.** A large mounted weapon that fires heavy projectiles. **2.** The loop at the top of a bell by which it is hung. **3.** A round bit for a horse. **4.** *Zool.* The section of the lower leg in some hoofed mammals between the hock or knee and the fetlock, containing the cannon bone. **5.** *Chiefly British.* A carom made in billiards. — *v.* **-noned, -non•ing, -nons.** — *tr.* **1.** To bombard with cannon. **2.** *Chiefly British.* To cause to carom in billiards. — *intr.* **1.** To fire cannon. **2.** *Chiefly British.* To make a carom in billiards. [ME *canon* < OFr. < OItal. *cannone*, aug. of *canna*, tube < Lat., reed. See CANE.]

Can•non (kăn′ən), **Joseph Gurney.** "Uncle Joe." 1836–1926. Amer. politician who was speaker of the U.S. House of Representatives (1903–11).

can•non•ade (kăn′ə-nād′) *v.* **-ad•ed, -ad•ing, -ades.** *tr. & intr.v.* To assault with or deliver heavy artillery fire. — *n.* **1.** A long, usu. heavy discharge of artillery. **2.** A harsh verbal or physical attack. [< Fr. *canonade*, artillery discharge < Ital. *cannonata* < *cannone*, cannon < OItal. See CANNON.]

can•non•ball also **cannon ball** (kăn′ən-bôl′) — *n.* **1.** A round projectile fired from a cannon. **2.** A jump into water made with the arms grasping the upraised knees. **3.** Something, such as a fast train, moving with great speed. **4.** *Sports.* A fast low serve in tennis. — *intr.v.* **-balled, -ball•ing, -balls. 1.** To travel with great speed. **2.** To make a cannonball jump.

cannon bone *n.* A supporting bone of the leg in some hoofed mammals, analogous to the metatarsus in human beings.

can•non•eer (kăn′ə-nîr′) *n.* A soldier in the artillery.

cannon fodder *n.* Soldiers, sailors, or other military personnel regarded as likely to be killed or wounded in combat.

can•non•ry (kăn′ən-rē) *n.*, *pl.* **-ries. 1.** A battery of cannons; artillery. **2.** Artillery fire.

can•not (kăn′ŏt, kə-nŏt′, kă-) *aux.v.* The negative form of **can[1]**.

can•nu•la also **can•u•la** (kăn′yə-lə) *n.*, *pl.* **-las** or **-lae** (-lē′). A flexible tube, usu. containing a trocar at one end, that is inserted into a body cavity, duct, or vessel to drain fluid or administer a substance. [Lat., dim. of *canna*, reed. See CANE.]

can•nu•lar also **can•u•lar** (kăn′yə-lər) *adj.* Of, relating to, or resembling a tube; tubular.

can•nu•late also **can•u•late** (kăn′yə-lāt′) — *tr.v.* **-lat•ed, -lat•ing, -lates.** To insert a cannula into (a body cavity, duct, or vessel). — *adj.* Tubular; hollow. — **can′nu•la′tion** *n.*

can•ny (kăn′ē) *adj.* **-ni•er, -ni•est. 1.** Careful and shrewd, esp. in regard to one's own interests. **2.** Cautious with money; frugal. **3.** *Scots.* **a.** Steady, restrained, and gentle. **b.** Snug and quiet. [< CAN[1].] — **can′ni•ly** *adv.* — **can′ni•ness** *n.*

ca•noe (kə-no͞o′) *Naut.* — *n.* A light slender boat that has pointed ends and is propelled by paddles. — *v.* **-noed, -noe•ing, -noes.** — *tr.* To carry or send by canoe. — *intr.* To travel in or propel a canoe. [Fr. *canoe* and Sp. *canoa* (Fr. < Sp.), of Cariban orig.] — **ca•noe′ist** *n.*

canoe birch *n.* See **paper birch.**

can of worms *n.*, *pl.* **cans of worms.** *Informal.* A source of unforeseen and troublesome complexity.

ca•no•la (kə-nō′lə) *n.* A rapeseed oil that is very low in erucic acid content. [?]

can•on[1] (kăn′ən) *n.* **1.** A law or code of laws established by a church council. **2.** A secular law, rule, or code of law. **3.a.** An established principle. **b.** A basis for judgment; a standard or criterion. **4.** The books of the Bible officially accepted as Holy Scripture. **5.** The works of a writer that have been accepted as authentic. **6. Canon.** The part of the Mass beginning after the Preface and Sanctus and ending just before the Lord's Prayer. **7.** *Rom. Cath. Ch.* The calendar of saints. **8.** *Mus.* A composition or passage in which the same melody is repeated by one or more voices, overlapping in time in the same or a related key. [ME *canoun* < OE *canon* and < OFr., both <

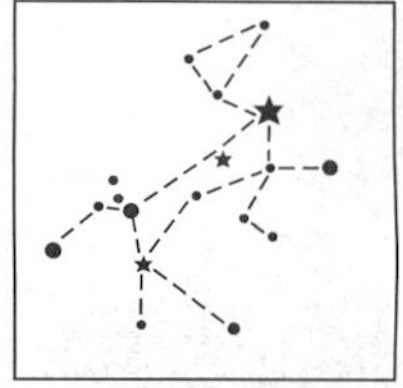
Canis Major

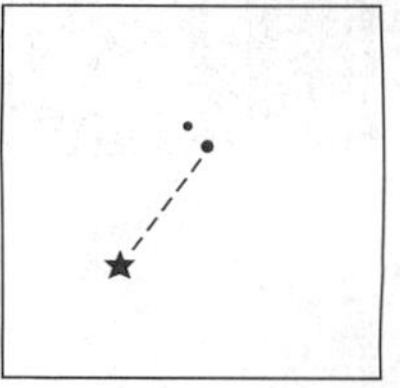
Canis Minor

canoe

ă pat	oi boy
ā pay	ou out
âr care	o͝o took
ä father	o͞o boot
ĕ pet	ŭ cut
ē be	ûr urge
ĭ pit	th thin
ī pie	*th* this
îr pier	hw which
ŏ pot	zh vision
ō toe	ə about, item
ô paw	

Stress marks:
′ (primary);
′ (secondary), as in **dictionary** (dĭk′shə-nĕr′ē)

Lat. *canōn*, rule < Gk. *kanōn*, measuring rod, rule.]

can•on[2] (kăn′ən) *n.* **1.** A member of a chapter of priests serving in a cathedral or collegiate church. **2.** A member of certain religious communities living under a common rule and bound by vows. [ME *canoun* < Norman Fr. *canun* < LLat. *canōnicus*, one living under a rule < *canōn*, rule. See CANON[1].]

ca•ñon (kăn′yən) *n.* Var. of **canyon.**

can•on•ess (kăn′ə-nĭs) *n.* A member of a religious community of women under a common rule but not bound by vows.

ca•non•i•cal (kə-nŏn′ĭ-kəl) also **ca•non•ic** (-ĭk) *adj.* **1.** Of, relating to, or required by canon law. **2.** Of the biblical canon. **3.** Conforming to orthodox rules. **4.** Of or belonging to a cathedral chapter. **5.** *Mus.* Having the form of a canon. **—ca•non′i•cal•ly** *adv.* **—can′on•ic′i•ty** (kăn′ə-nĭs′ĭ-tē) *n.*

canonical hours *pl.n.* **1.** *Eccles.* The times of day at which canon law prescribes certain prayers to be said. **2.** The prayers said at these times.

ca•non•i•cals (kə-nŏn′ĭ-kəlz) *pl.n.* The dress prescribed by canon for officiating clergy.

can•on•ist (kăn′ə-nĭst) *n.* A person specializing in canon law. **—can′on•is′tic, can′on•is′ti•cal** *adj.*

can•on•ize (kăn′ə-nīz′) *tr.v.* **-ized, -iz•ing, -iz•es. 1.** To declare (a deceased person) to be a saint and entitled to full honor as such. **2.** To include in the biblical canon. **3.** To approve as within canon law. **4.** To treat as sacred; glorify. **—can′on•i•za′tion** (-ĭ-zā′shən) *n.* **—can′on•iz′er** *n.*

canon law *n.* The body of rules for a Christian church.

can•on•ry (kăn′ən-rē) *n., pl.* **-ries. 1.** The office or dignity of a canon. **2.** Canons considered as a group.

Ca•no•pic or **ca•no•pic** (kə-nō′pĭk, -nŏp′ĭk) *adj.* Of, relating to, or being an ancient Egyptian vase, urn, or jar used to hold the viscera of an embalmed body. [After CANOPUS[1].]

Ca•no•pus[1] (kə-nō′pəs). An ancient city of N Egypt E of Alexandria; site of a temple honoring Serapis.

Ca•no•pus[2] (kə-nō′pəs) *n.* A star in the constellation Carina. [Lat. < Gk. *kanōpos*, perh. of Egypt. orig.]

canopy
Early 19th-century four-poster bed

can•o•py (kăn′ə-pē) *n., pl.* **-pies. 1.** A covering, usu. of cloth, suspended over a throne or bed or held aloft on poles. **2.** *Archit.* An ornamental rooflike projection over a niche, an altar, or a tomb. **3.** A protective rooflike covering over a walkway or door. **4.** A high, overarching covering, such as the sky. **5.** The uppermost layer in a forest, formed by the crowns of the trees. **6.** The transparent enclosure over the cockpit of an aircraft. **7.** The part of a parachute that opens up to catch the air. **—***tr.v.* **-pied, -py•ing, -pies.** To cover with or as if with a canopy. [ME *canape* < Med.Lat. *canāpēum*, mosquito net < Lat. *cōnōpēum* < Gk. *kōnōpeion*, bed with mosquito netting < *kōnōps*, mosquito.]

ca•no•rous (kə-nôr′əs, -nōr′-, kăn′ər-əs) *adj.* Richly melodious; tuneful. [< Lat. *canōrus* < *canor*, tune < *canere*, to sing. See **kan-***.] **—ca•no′rous•ly** *adv.* **—ca•no′rous•ness** *n.*

Ca•no•va (kə-nō′və), **Antonio.** 1757–1822. Italian sculptor who was important in the development of neoclassicism.

Can•so (kăn′sō), **Strait of.** A narrow channel between Cape Breton I. and the NE mainland of Nova Scotia, Canada.

canst (kănst) *aux.v. Archaic.* A second pers. sing. pr.t. of **can[1].**

cant[1] (kănt) *n.* **1.** Angular deviation from a vertical or horizontal plane or surface; an inclination or a slope. **2.** A slanted or oblique surface. **3.a.** A thrust or motion that tilts something. **b.** The tilt caused by such a thrust or motion. **4.** An outer corner, as of a building. **—***v.* **cant•ed, cant•ing, cants. —***tr.* **1.** To set at an oblique angle; tilt. **2.** To give a slanting edge to; bevel. **3.** To change the direction of suddenly. **—***intr.* **1.** To lean to one side; slant. **2.** To take an oblique direction or course; swing around. [ME, side < ONFr. < VLat. **cantus*, corner < Lat. *canthus*, rim of wheel, tire, of Celt. orig.]

cantaloupe
Cucumis melo var. *reticulatus*

cant[2] (kănt) *n.* **1.** Insincere speech full of platitudes or pious expressions. **2.** The special vocabulary peculiar to the members of a group. **3.** Whining or singsong speech, such as that of beggars. **—***intr.v.* **cant•ed, cant•ing, cants. 1.** To speak tediously or sententiously; moralize. **2.** To speak in argot or jargon. **3.** To speak in a whining, pleading tone. [AN *cant*, song, singing < *canter*, to sing < Lat. *cantāre*. See **kan-***.] **—cant′ing•ly** *adv.* **—cant′ing•ness** *n.*

Cant. *abbr. Bible.* Canticle of Canticles.

can't (kănt). Cannot.

can•ta•bi•le (kän-tä′bĭ-lā′) *Mus.* **—***adv. & adj.* In a smooth, lyrical, flowing style. **—***n.* A cantabile passage or movement. [Ital. < LLat. *cantābilis*, worthy to be sung < Lat. *cantāre*, to sing. See **kan-***.]

Can•ta•bri•an Mountains (kăn-tā′brē-ən). A range of N Spain extending c. 483 km (300 mi) along the coast of the Bay of Biscay.

Can•ta•brig•i•an (kăn′tə-brĭj′ē-ən) *adj.* **1.** Of or relating to Cambridge, England, or Cambridge, Massachusetts. **2.** Of or relating to Cambridge University. [< Med.Lat. *Cantabrigia*, Cambridge, England.] **—Can′ta•brig′i•an** *n.*

cantilever bridge

can•ta•la (kăn-tä′lə) *n.* **1.** A species of agave *(Agave cantula)* cultivated chiefly in warm regions of the Old World. **2.** The fiber of this plant, used for twine, rope, and nets. [?]

can•ta•loupe also **can•ta•loup** (kăn′tl-ōp′) *n.* **1.** A variety of melon *(Cucumis melo* var. *reticulatus)* having a tan rind with netlike ridges and a sweet, fragrant orange flesh. **2.** Any of several other related or similar melons. [Fr. *cantaloup*, perh. < Ital. *cantalupo* (< *Cantalupo*, a former papal villa near Rome) or < *Cantaloup*, a village of S France.]

can•tan•ker•ous (kăn-tăng′kər-əs) *adj.* Ill-tempered and quarrelsome; disagreeable. [Perh. alteration of ME *contek*, dissension < AN *contec*, poss. < Lat. *contāctus*, p.part. of *contingere*, to touch. See CONTACT.] **—can•tan′ker•ous•ly** *adv.* **—can•tan′ker•ous•ness** *n.*

can•ta•ta (kən-tä′tə) *n. Mus.* A vocal and instrumental piece composed of choruses, solos, and recitatives. [Ital. *(aria) cantata*, sung (aria), fem. p.part. of *cantare*, to sing < Lat. *cantāre*. See **kan-***.]

can•teen (kăn-tēn′) *n.* **1.a.** A snack bar or small cafeteria, as on a military installation. **b.** A bar or small general store formerly established for the patronage of soldiers. **2.** A recreation hall or social club where refreshments are available. **3.** A temporary or mobile eating place. **4.** A flask for carrying drinking water, as on a hike. **5.a.** A box with compartments for carrying cooking gear and eating utensils. **b.** A soldier's mess kit. **6.** *Chiefly British.* A box used to store silverware. [Fr. *cantine* < Ital. *cantina*, wine cellar.]

can•ter (kăn′tər) *n.* A smooth gait, esp. of a horse, that is slower than a gallop but faster than a trot. **—***v.* **-tered, -ter•ing, -ters. —***intr.* **1.** To ride a horse at a canter. **2.** To go or move at a canter. **—***tr.* To cause (a horse) to go at a canter. [Ult. < phrases such as *Canterbury gallop*, after CANTERBURY, toward which pilgrims rode at an easy pace.]

Can•ter•bur•y (kăn′tər-bĕr′ē, -brē, -tə-). A borough of SE England on the Stour R. ESE of London. Canterbury Cathedral (11th–16th cent.) is the seat of the archbishop and primate of the Anglican Communion. Pop. 36,000.

Canterbury bells *pl.n. (used with a sing. or pl. v.)* A European biennial herb *(Campanula medium)* widely cultivated for its showy flowers.

can•tha•ris (kăn′thər-ĭs) *n., pl.* **can•thar•i•des** (kăn-thăr′ĭ-dēz′). **1.** A green blister beetle *(Lytta vesicatoria* or *Cantharis vesicatoria)* of central and southern Europe. **2. cantharides.** *(used with a sing. or pl. v.)* A toxic preparation of the crushed dried bodies of this beetle, formerly used as a counterirritant for skin blisters and as an aphrodisiac. [Lat. *cantharis, cantharid-* < Gk. *kantharis* < *kantharos.*]

can•thi•tis (kăn-thī′tĭs) *n.* Inflammation of the canthus.

cant hook *n.* A wooden lever with a movable metal hook near one end, used for handling logs. [< CANT[1].]

can•thus (kăn′thəs) *n., pl.* **-thi** (-thī′). The angle formed by the meeting of the upper and lower eyelids at either side of the eye. [LLat. < Gk. *kanthos.*]

can•ti•cle (kăn′tĭ-kəl) *n.* **1.** *Mus.* A Christian hymn based on a psalm. **2. Canticles.** *Bible.* The Song of Songs. [ME < Lat. *canticulum*, dim. of *cantus*, song < p.part. of *canere*, to sing. See **kan-***.]

Canticle of Can•ti•cles (kăn′tĭ-kəlz) *n.* The Song of Songs.

Can•ti•gny (kän-tē-nyē′). A village of N France S of Amiens; site of the first U.S. World War I offensive (May 1918).

can•ti•le•na (kăn′tl-ē′nə) *n. Mus.* A sustained, smooth-flowing melodic line. [Ital. < Lat. *cantilēna*, song < *cantus.* See CANTICLE.]

can•ti•le•ver (kăn′tl-ē′vər, -ĕv′ər) *n.* **1.** A member, such as a beam, that projects beyond a fulcrum and is supported by a balancing member or a downward force behind the fulcrum. **2.** A bracket or block supporting a balcony or cornice. **—***v.* **-vered, -ver•ing, -vers. —***tr.* To construct as or in the manner of a cantilever. **—***intr.* To extend outward as or in the manner of a cantilever. [Perh. CANT[1] + LEVER.]

cantilever bridge *n.* A bridge formed by two projecting beams or trusses joined in the center by a connecting member and supported on piers and anchored by counterbalancing members.

can•til•late (kăn′tl-āt′) *tr. & intr.v.* **-lat•ed, -lat•ing, -lates.** To chant or recite in a musical monotone. [Lat. *cantillāre, cantillāt-*, to sing < *cantāre*. See **kan-***.] **—can′til•la′tion** *n.*

can•ti•na (kăn-tē′nə) *n. Southwestern U.S.* A bar; a tavern. [Sp., canteen < Ital., wine cellar.]

can•tle (kăn′tl) *n.* **1.** The raised rear part of a saddle. **2.** A corner, segment, or portion; a piece. [ME *cantel*, corner < OFr. < Med.Lat. *cantellus* < VLat. **cantus.* See CANT[1].]

can•to (kăn′tō) *n., pl.* **-tos.** One of the principal divisions of a long poem. [Ital. < Lat. *cantus*, song. See CANTICLE.]

can•ton (kăn′tən, -tŏn′) *n.* **1.a.** A small territorial division of a country. **b.** A subdivision of an arrondissement in France. **2.** *Her.* A small, square division of a shield, usu. in the upper right corner. **3.** A usu. rectangular division of a flag in the upper corner next to the staff. [Fr. < OFr. < OItal. *cantone*, aug. of *canto*, corner < VLat. **cantus.* See CANT[1].] **—can′ton•al** (kăn′tə-nəl, kăn-tŏn′əl) *adj.*

Can•ton (kăn′tən). **1.** A town of E MA, a suburb of Boston. Pop. 18,530. **2.** A city of NE OH SSE of Akron. Pop. 84,161. **3.** (kăn′tŏn′, kăn′tŏn′). See **Guangzhou.**

Can•ton crepe (kăn′tŏn′) *n.* A soft silk or rayon fabric with a crinkled texture. [After *Canton* (Guangzhou), China.]

Can•ton•ese (kăn′tə-nēz′, -nēs′) *n.* **1.** A native or inhabitant of Guangzhou. **2.** The Chinese dialect of Guangzhou (formerly Canton), China. **—Can′ton•ese′** *adj.*

Can•ton flannel (kăn′tŏn′) *n.* Flannelette. [After *Canton* (Guangzhou), China.]

can•ton•ment (kăn-tōn′mənt, -tŏn′-) *n.* **1.a.** A group of temporary billets for troops. **b.** Assignment of troops to temporary quarters. **2.** A permanent military installation in India. [< CANTON, to quarter soldiers.]

Can•ton River (kăn′tŏn′, kăn′tŏn′). See **Zhu Jiang.**

can•tor (kăn′tər) *n.* **1.** The religious official who leads the musical part of a Jewish service. **2.** The person who leads the singing in a church; a precentor. [Lat., singer < *canere,* to sing. See **kan-*.**] **—can•to′ri•al** (kăn-tôr′ē-əl, -tōr′-) *adj.*

can•trip (kăn′trĭp) *n.* **1.** *Scots.* A magic spell; a witch's trick. **2.** *Chiefly British.* A deceptive move; a sham. [?]

can•tus fir•mus (kăn′təs fîr′məs, fûr′-) *n. Mus.* A plainsong melody serving as the basis of a polyphonic composition. [Med. Lat. : Lat. *cantus,* song + Lat. *firmus,* fixed.]

Ca•nuck (kə-nŭk′) *n. Offensive Slang.* Used as a disparaging term for a Canadian, esp. a French Canadian. [Prob. alteration of CANADIAN.]

can•u•la (kăn′yə-lə) *n.* Var. of **cannula.**

can•u•lar (kăn′yə-lər) *adj.* Var. of **cannular.**

can•u•late (kăn′yə-lāt′) *v. & adj.* Var. of **cannulate.**

Ca•nute also **Cnut** or **Knut** (kə-no͞ot′, -nyo͞ot′). "the Great." 994?–1035. King of England (1016–35), Denmark (1018–35), and Norway (1028–35).

can•vas (kăn′vəs) *n.* **1.** A heavy, coarse fabric of cotton, hemp, or flax, used for tents and sails. **2.a.** A piece of canvas on which a painting is created. **b.** A painting thus created. **3.** A fabric of coarse open weave, used as a foundation for needlework. **4.** The background of events. **5.** *Naut.* A sail or set of sails. **6.a.** A tent or group of tents. **b.** A circus tent. **7.** *Sports.* The floor of a boxing or wrestling ring. **—*idiom.* under canvas. 1.** *Naut.* With sails spread. **2.** In a tent or tents. [ME *canevas* < OFr. and < Med.Lat. *canavāsium,* both ult. < Lat. *cannabis,* hemp. See CANNABIS.]

can•vas•back (kăn′vəs-băk′) *n.* A North American wild duck *(Aythya valisineria)* having a reddish-brown head and neck and a whitish back.

canvas duck *n.* A fabric made of lightweight cotton or linen.

can•vass (kăn′vəs) *v.* **-vassed, -vass•ing, -vass•es.** *—tr.* **1.** To examine carefully or discuss thoroughly; scrutinize. **2.a.** To go through (a region) or go to (persons) to solicit votes or orders. **b.** To survey (public opinion). *—intr.* **1.** To make or conduct a thorough canvass. **2.** To solicit voters, orders, or opinions. *—n.* **1.** An examination or discussion. **2.** A solicitation of votes or orders. **3.** A survey of public opinion. [< obsolete *canvass,* to toss in a canvas sheet as punishment < CANVAS.] **—can′vass•er** *n.*

can•yon also **ca•ñon** (kăn′yən) *n.* A narrow chasm with steep cliff walls, cut into the earth by running water; a gorge. [Sp. *cañon,* aug. of *caña,* tube, cane < Lat. *canna,* reed. See CANE.]

can•zo•ne (kăn-zō′nē, känt-sô′nĕ) *n., pl.* **-nes** (-nēz, -nāz) or **-ni** (-nē). **1.** A medieval Italian or Provençal lyric of varying stanzaic form. **2.** *Mus.* A polyphonic song evolving from this form of poetry. [Ital. < Lat. *cantiō, cantiōn-,* song < *cantus,* p.part. of *canere,* to sing. See **kan-*.**]

can•zo•net (kăn′zə-nĕt′) *n. Mus.* A short lighthearted song. [< Ital. *canzonetta,* dim. of *canzone.* See CANZONE.]

caou•tchouc (kou′cho͝ok′, -cho͞ok′) *n.* See **rubber[1] 1.** [Fr., prob. < Sp. *caucho* < Tupi *cau-ucha.*]

cap[1] (kăp) *n.* **1.** A usu. soft and close-fitting head covering. **2.a.** A head covering worn to indicate rank, occupation, or membership in a group. **b.** An academic mortarboard. **3.a.** A protective cover or seal, esp. one that closes off an end or a tip. **b.** A crown for covering or sealing a tooth. **c.** A tread for a worn pneumatic tire. **d.** A fitted covering used to seal a well or large pipe. **4.** A summit or top, as of a mountain. **5.** An upper limit; a ceiling. **6.** *Archit.* The capital of a column. **7.** *Bot.* **a.** The pileus of a mushroom. **b.** A calyptra. **8.a.** A percussion cap. **b.** A small explosive charge enclosed in paper for use in a toy gun. **9.** Any of several sizes of writing paper, such as foolscap. *—tr.v.* **capped, cap•ping, caps. 1.** To cover, protect, or seal with a cap. **2.** To award a special cap to as a sign of rank or achievement. **3.** To lie over or on top of; cover. **4.** To apply the finishing touch to; complete. **5.** To follow with something better; surpass or outdo. **6.** To set an upper limit on. **—*idioms.* cap in hand.** Respectfully or humbly; unpretentiously. **set (one's) cap for.** To attempt to attract and win as a mate. [ME *cappe* < OE *cæppe* < LLat. *cappa.*]

cap[2] (kăp) *Informal. —n.* A capital letter. *—tr.v.* **capped, cap•ping, caps.** To capitalize. [Shortened form of CAPITAL[1].]

CAP *abbr.* Civil Air Patrol.

cap. *abbr.* **1.** Capacity. **2.** Capital.

ca•pa•bil•i•ty (kā′pə-bĭl′ĭ-tē) *n., pl.* **-ties. 1.** The quality of being capable; ability. **2.** A talent or ability that has potential for development or use. Often used in the plural. **3.** The capacity to be used, treated, or developed for a specific purpose.

ca•pa•ble (kā′pə-bəl) *adj.* **1.** Having capacity or ability; efficient and able. **2.** Having the ability required for a specific task or accomplishment; qualified. **3.** Having the inclination or disposition. **4.** Susceptible; permitting: *capable of remedy.* [LLat. *capābilis* < *capere,* to take. See **kap-*.**] **—ca′pa•ble•ness** *n.* **—ca′pa•bly** *adv.*

ca•pa•cious (kə-pā′shəs) *adj.* Capable of containing a large quantity; spacious or roomy. [< Lat. *capāx, capāc-* < *capere,* to take. See **kap-*.**] **—ca•pa′cious•ly** *adv.* **—ca•pa′cious•ness** *n.*

ca•pac•i•tance (kə-păs′ĭ-təns) *n.* **1.** *Symbol* **C** The ratio of electric charge to potential on an isolated conductor. **2.** *Symbol* **C** The ratio of the electric charge on one of a pair of conductors to the potential difference between them. **3.a.** The property of a circuit element that permits it to store charge. **b.** The part of the circuit exhibiting capacitance. [CAPACIT(Y) + -ANCE.] **—ca•pac′i•tive** (-tĭv) *adj.* **—ca•pac′i•tive•ly** *adv.*

ca•pac•i•tate (kə-păs′ĭ-tāt′) *tr.v.* **-tat•ed, -tat•ing, -tates. 1.** To render fit or make qualified; enable. **2.** *Biol.* To cause (spermatozoa) to undergo the physical changes needed to fertilize an egg. [CAPACIT(Y) + -ATE[1].] **—ca•pac′i•ta′tion** *n.*

ca•pac•i•tor (kə-păs′ĭ-tər) *n.* An electric circuit element used to store charge temporarily, consisting in general of two metallic plates separated and insulated from each other by a dielectric.

ca•pac•i•ty (kə-păs′ĭ-tē) *n., pl.* **-ties. 1.a.** The ability to receive, hold, or absorb. **b.** A measure of this ability; volume. **2.** The maximum amount that can be contained. **3.a.** Ability to perform or produce; capability. **b.** The maximum or optimum amount that can be produced. **4.** The power to learn or retain knowledge; mental ability. **5.** Innate potential for development or accomplishment; faculty. **6.** The quality of being suitable for specified treatment. **7.** The position in which one functions; role. **8.** Legal qualification or authority. **9.** *Elect.* Capacitance. *—adj.* Filling a space to capacity. [ME *capacite* < OFr. < Lat. *capācitās* < *capāx, capāc-,* spacious. See CAPACIOUS.]

ca•par•i•son (kə-păr′ĭ-sən) *n.* **1.** An ornamental covering for a horse or for its saddle or harness; trappings. **2.** Richly ornamented clothing; finery. *—tr.v.* **-soned, -son•ing, -sons. 1.** To outfit (a horse) with an ornamental covering. **2.** To dress (another) in rich clothing. [Obsolete Fr. *caparasson* < OSp. *caparazón* < Med.Lat. *cappa,* cloak. See CAPE[1].]

Cap de la Ma•de•leine or **Cap-de-la-Ma•de•leine** (kăp′ də lä măd-lān′, -lĕn′). A city of S Quebec, Canada, on the St. Lawrence R. NE of Montreal. Pop. 32,626.

cape[1] (kāp) *n.* A sleeveless outer garment fastened at the throat and worn over the shoulders. [ME *cape,* partly var. of *cope,* cope; see COPE[2], and partly < AN *cape* (< Med.Lat. *cāpa,* var. of LLat. *cappa*).]

cape[2] (kāp) *n.* A point or head of land projecting into a body of water. [ME *cap* < OFr. < OProv. < Lat. *caput,* head. See **kaput-*.**]

Cape (kāp) or **Cape of.** For names of actual capes, see the specific element of the names, for example, **Hatteras, Cape; Good Hope, Cape of.**

Cape Bret•on Island (brĕt′n, brĭt′n). An island forming the NE part of Nova Scotia, Canada.

Cape buffalo *n.* A large, often fierce buffalo *(Syncerus caffer)* of Africa having massive downward-curving horns.

Cape Cod Canal (kŏd). A waterway, c. 28 km (17.5 mi), of SE MA connecting Buzzards Bay with **Cape Cod Bay,** the S part of Massachusetts Bay.

Cape Cod cottage *n.* A compact house of one or one-and-a-half stories with a gabled roof and a central chimney.

Cape Cor•al (kôr′əl, kŏr′-). A city of SW FL on the estuary of the Caloosahatchee R. SW of Fort Myers. Pop. 74,991.

Cape Fear River. A river rising in central NC and flowing c. 325 km (202 mi) SE to the Atlantic N of Cape Fear.

Cape Gi•rar•deau (jə-rär′dō, -rä′-). A city of SE MO on the Mississippi SSE of St. Louis; founded 1793. Pop. 34,438.

Cape gooseberry *n.* A tropical South American plant *(Physalis peruviana)* having an edible yellow berry.

Cape jasmine *n.* See **gardenia.**

Ča•pek (chä′pĕk′), **Karel.** 1890–1938. Czechoslovakian writer whose works include the play *R.U.R.* (1921).

cap•e•lin (kăp′ə-lĭn, kăp′lĭn) also **cap•lin** (kăp′lĭn) *n.* A small edible marine fish *(Mallotus villosus)* of northern Atlantic and Pacific waters. [Canadian Fr. *capelan* < Fr., codfish < OProv. < Med.Lat. *cappelānus.* See CHAPLAIN.]

Ca•pel•la (kə-pĕl′ə) *n.* A double star in Auriga, the brightest star in the constellation. [Lat., dim. of *caper,* goat.]

Cape primrose *n.* Any of various chiefly African plants of the genus *Streptocarpus,* having clusters of showy flowers.

Cape Province. Officially Cape of Good Hope Province; formerly (before 1910) Cape Colony. A province and historical region of S South Africa on the Atlantic and Indian oceans.

ca•per[1] (kā′pər) *n.* **1.** A playful leap or hop. **2.** A frivolous escapade or prank. **3.** *Slang.* An illegal plot or enterprise, esp. one involving theft. *—intr.v.* **-pered, -per•ing, -pers.** To leap or frisk about; frolic. [Alteration of CAPRIOLE.]

ca•per[2] (kā′pər) *n.* **1.** A usu. spiny Mediterranean shrub *(Capparis spinosa)* having dehiscent fruits with reddish pulp. **2.** A pickled flower bud of this plant, used as a pungent condiment. [ME *caperis, capar* < Lat. *capparis* < Gk. *kapparis.*]

canvasback
Male canvasback
Aythya valisineria

ă pat	oi boy
ā pay	ou out
âr care	o͝o took
ä father	o͞o boot
ĕ pet	ŭ cut
ē be	ûr urge
ĭ pit	th thin
ī pie	*th* this
îr pier	hw which
ŏ pot	zh vision
ō toe	ə about, item
ô paw	

Stress marks:
′ (primary);
′ (secondary), as in **dictionary** (dĭk′shə-nĕr′ē)

cap·er·cail·lie (kăp′ər-kāl′yē, -kā′lē) also **cap·er·cail·zie** (-kāl′zē) *n.* A large grouse *(Tetrao urogallus)* native to northern Europe with dark plumage and a fanlike tail. [Sc.Gael. *capull coille* : *capull*, horse (ult. < Lat. *caballus*, of Celt. orig.) + *coille*, forest (< OIr. *caill*).]
Ca·per·na·um (kə-pûr′nē-əm). A city of ancient Palestine on the NW shore of the Sea of Galilee.
cape·skin (kāp′skĭn′) *n.* Soft leather made from sheepskin, used esp. for gloves. [After Cape of Good Hope.]
Ca·pet (kā′pĭt, kăp′ĭt, kă-pā′). A dynasty of French kings (987–1328), including **Hugh Capet** (940?–996), who was elected king in 987. — **Ca·pe′tian** (kə-pē′shən) *adj. & n.*
Cape Town or **Cape·town** (kāp′toun′). The legislative cap. of South Africa, in the extreme SW part on the Atlantic Ocean; founded 1652. Pop. 859,940.
Cape Verde (vûrd). An island country of the Atlantic Ocean W of Senegal; gained independence from Portugal in 1975. Cap. Praia. Pop. 296,093.
Cape York Peninsula (yôrk). A peninsula of NE Australia between the Gulf of Carpentaria and the Coral Sea.
cap·ful (kăp′fo͝ol′) *n.*, *pl.* **-fuls.** The amount a cap can hold.
Cap Hai·tien (kăp′ hā′shən) or **Cap-Ha·ï·tien** (kä-pä-ē-syăN′). A city of N Haiti on the Atlantic Ocean; founded c. 1670. Pop. 64,406.
ca·pi·as (kā′pē-əs) *n. Law.* A warrant for arrest. [ME < Med. Lat. < Lat., second pers. sing. pr. subjunctive of *capere*, to seize (from the first word of the writ). See **kap-***.]
cap·il·lar·i·ty (kăp′ə-lăr′ĭ-tē) *n.*, *pl.* **-ties.** The interaction between contacting surfaces of a liquid and a solid that distorts the liquid surface from a planar shape.
cap·il·lar·y (kăp′ə-lĕr′ē) *adj.* **1.** Relating to or resembling a hair; fine and slender. **2.** Having a very small internal diameter. **3.** *Anat.* Of or relating to the capillaries. **4.** *Phys.* Of or relating to capillarity. — *n.*, *pl.* **-ies. 1.** *Anat.* One of the minute blood vessels that connect arterioles and venules. **2.** A capillary tube. [< Lat. *capillāris* < *capillus*, hair.]
capillary action *n.* See **capillarity.**
capillary attraction *n.* The force that results from greater adhesion of a liquid to a solid surface than internal cohesion of the liquid itself and causes the liquid to be raised against a vertical surface.
cap·i·tal[1] (kăp′ĭ-tl) *n.* **1.a.** A town or city that is the official seat of government in a political entity, such as a state or nation. **b.** A city that is the center of a specific activity or industry. **2.a.** Wealth in the form of money or property, used or accumulated in a business by a person, partnership, or corporation. **b.** Material wealth used or available for use in the production of more wealth. **c.** Human resources considered in terms of their contributions to an economy. **3.** *Accounting.* The remaining assets of a business after all liabilities have been deducted; net worth. **4.** Capital stock. **5.** Capitalists considered as a group or class. **6.** An asset or advantage. **7.** A capital letter. — *adj.* **1.** First and foremost; principal. **2.** First-rate; excellent: *a capital idea.* **3.** Relating to or being a seat of government. **4.** Extremely serious. **5.** Involving death or calling for the death penalty. **6.** Of, relating to, or being financial assets, esp. those that add to the net worth of a business. **7.** Relating to or being a capital letter. [< ME, principal < OFr. < Lat. *capitālis* < *caput*, head, money laid out. See **kaput-***.]

Usage Note: The term for a town or city that serves as a seat of government is spelled *capital.* The term for the building in which a legislative assembly meets is spelled *capitol.*

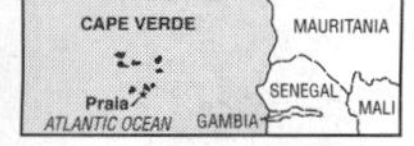

Cape Verde

cap·i·tal[2] (kăp′ĭ-tl) *n. Archit.* The top part of a pillar or column. [ME < AN < LLat. *capitellum*, dim. of Lat. *caput*, head. See **kaput-***.]
capital account *n.* **1.** An account stating the amount of funds and assets invested in a business by the owners or stockholders. **2.** A statement of the net worth of a business at a given time.
capital asset *n.* A long-term asset, such as land or a building.
capital expenditure *n.* Funds spent for the acquisition of a long-term asset.
capital gain *n.* The amount by which proceeds from the sale of a capital asset exceed the original cost.
capital goods *pl.n.* Producer goods.
cap·i·tal-in·ten·sive (kăp′ĭ-tl-ĭn-tĕn′sĭv) *adj.* Requiring a large expenditure of capital in comparison to labor.
cap·i·tal·ism (kăp′ĭ-tl-ĭz′əm) *n.* An economic system in which the means of production and distribution are privately or corporately owned and development is proportionate to the accumulation and reinvestment of profits gained in a free market.

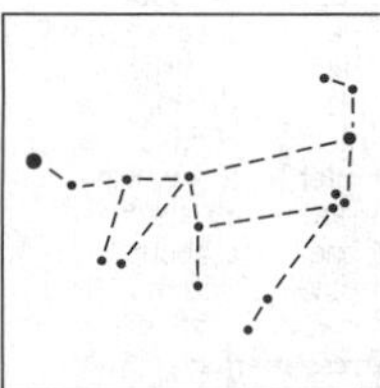
Capricorn

cap·i·tal·ist (kăp′ĭ-tl-ĭst) *n.* **1.** A supporter of capitalism. **2.** An investor of capital in business, esp. one having a major financial interest in an important enterprise. **3.** A person of great wealth. — *adj.* Capitalistic.
cap·i·tal·is·tic (kăp′ĭ-tl-ĭs′tĭk) *adj.* **1.** Of or relating to capitalism or capitalists. **2.** Favoring or practicing capitalism: *a capitalistic country.* — **cap′i·tal·is′ti·cal·ly** *adv.*
cap·i·tal·i·za·tion (kăp′ĭ-tl-ĭ-zā′shən) *n.* **1.a.** The practice or act of capitalizing. **b.** The sum that results from capitalizing. **2.a.** The amounts and types of long-term financing used by a firm. **b.** The total par value or stated value of no-par capital stock issues. **3.** The use of capital letters.
cap·i·tal·ize (kăp′ĭ-tl-īz′) *v.* **-ized, -iz·ing, -iz·es.** — *tr.* **1.** To use as or convert into capital. **2.** To supply with capital or investment funds. **3.** To authorize the issue of a certain amount of capital stock of. **4.** To convert (debt) into capital stock or shares. **5.** To calculate the current value of (a future stream of earnings or cash flows). **6.** To include (expenditures) in business accounts as assets instead of expenses. **7.a.** To write or print in capital letters. **b.** To begin a word with a capital letter. — *intr.* To turn something to one's advantage; benefit. — **cap′i·tal·iz′a·ble** *adj.*
capital letter *n.* A letter written or printed in a size larger than and often in a form differing from its lowercase form.
cap·i·tal·ly (kăp′ĭ-tl-ē) *adv.* Excellently; admirably.
capital stock *n.* **1.** The total amount of stock authorized for issue by a corporation. **2.** The total stated or par value of the permanently invested capital of a corporation.
cap·i·tate (kăp′ĭ-tāt′) *adj.* **1.** *Anat.* Enlarged and globular at the tip. **2.** *Bot.* Forming a headlike mass or dense cluster. [Lat. *capitātus*, having a head < *caput*, *capit-*, head. See **kaput-***.]
cap·i·ta·tion (kăp′ĭ-tā′shən) *n.* **1.** A poll tax. **2.** A payment or fee of a fixed amount per person. [LLat. *capitātiō*, *capitātiōn-* < Lat. *caput*, *capit-*, head. See **kaput-***.] — **cap′i·ta′tive** *adj.*
cap·i·tel·lum (kăp′ĭ-tĕl′əm) *n.*, *pl.* **-tel·la** (-tĕl′ə). *Anat.* The rounded protuberance at the lower end of the humerus that articulates with the radius. [LLat., dim. of Lat. *caput*, *capit-*, head. See **kaput-***.]
cap·i·tol (kăp′ĭ-tl) *n.* **1.** A building or complex of buildings in which a state legislature meets. **2. Capitol.** The building in Washington DC where the U.S. Congress meets. See Usage Note at **capital**[1]. [ME *Capitol*, Jupiter's temple in Rome < OFr. *capitole* < Lat. *Capitōlium*, after *Capitōlīnus*, Capitoline; perh. akin to *caput*, head. See capital[1].]
Capitol Hill *n. Informal.* The U.S. Congress.
Cap·i·to·line (kăp′ĭ-tə-līn′). The highest of the seven hills of ancient Rome. — **Cap′i·to·line′** *adj.*
Capitol Peak. A mountain, 4,309.7 m (14,130 ft), in the Rocky Mts. of W-central CO.
ca·pit·u·lar (kə-pĭch′ə-lər) *adj.* Of or relating to a chapter, esp. an ecclesiastical chapter. [Med.Lat. *capitulāris* < *capitulum*, chapter. See chapter.] — **ca·pit′u·lar·ly** *adv.*
ca·pit·u·lar·y (kə-pĭch′ə-lĕr′ē) *n.*, *pl.* **-ies. 1.** A member of an ecclesiastical or a similar chapter. **2.a.** An ecclesiastical or a civil ordinance. **b.** A set of such ordinances. [Med.Lat. *capitulārius* < *capitulum*, chapter. See chapter.]
ca·pit·u·late (kə-pĭch′ə-lāt′) *intr.v.* **-lat·ed, -lat·ing, -lates. 1.** To surrender under specified conditions; come to terms. **2.** To give up all resistance; acquiesce. [Med.Lat. *capitulāre*, *capitulāt-*, to draw up in chapters < *capitulum*, chapter. See chapter.] — **ca·pit′u·lant, ca·pit′u·la′tor** *n.* — **ca·pit′u·la·to′ry** (-lə-tôr′ē, -tōr′ē) *adj.*
ca·pit·u·la·tion (kə-pĭch′ə-lā′shən) *n.* **1.** The act of surrendering. **2.** A document with the terms of surrender. **3.** An enumeration of the main parts of a subject; a summary.
ca·pit·u·lum (kə-pĭch′ə-ləm) *n.*, *pl.* **-la** (-lə). **1.** *Bot.* See **flower head** 1. **2.** *Biol.* A small knob or head-shaped part. [Lat., dim. of *caput*, *capit-*, head. See **kaput-***.]
cap·let (kăp′lĭt) *n.* A smooth, coated, oval-shaped medicine tablet intended to be tamper-resistant. [cap(sule) + (tab)let.]
cap·lin (kăp′lĭn) *n.* Var. of **capelin.**
ca·po[1] (kā′pō) *n.*, *pl.* **-pos.** *Mus.* A small movable bar that is placed across the fingerboard of a guitar or similar instrument to raise the pitch of all the strings uniformly. [Ital. *capo (di tastiera)*, head (of the fingerboard) < Lat. *caput.* See **kaput-***.]
ca·po[2] (kä′pō, kăp′ō) *n.*, *pl.* **-pos.** The head of an organized crime syndicate branch. [Ital. < Lat. *caput*, head. See capo[1].]
ca·pon (kā′pŏn′, -pən) *n.* A male chicken castrated when young to improve its flesh for food. [ME *capoun* < OE *capūn* and < OFr. *capon*, both < Lat. *cāpō*, *cāpōn-*.]
ca·po·na·ta (kä′pə-nä′tə) *n.* A seasoned mixture of eggplant and other vegetables. [Ital., of Sicilian dial. orig.]
Ca·pone (kə-pōn′), **Alphonse ("Al").** 1899–1947. Italian-born Amer. gangster who ruthlessly ruled the Chicago underworld.
cap·o·ral (kăp′ər-əl, kăp′ə-răl′) *n.* A strong dark tobacco. [Fr., short for *(tabac de) caporal*, corporal('s tobacco) < Ital. *caporale* < *capo*, head. See capo[1].]
ca·pote (kə-pōt′) *n.* A long, usu. hooded cloak or coat. [Fr. < OFr. *capote*, *capette*, dim. of *cape*, cloak < Med.Lat. *cāpa.* See cape[1].]
Ca·po·te (kə-pō′tē), **Truman.** 1924–84. Amer. writer whose works include *In Cold Blood* (1966).
Cap·pa·do·cia (kăp′ə-dō′shə, -shē-ə). An ancient region of Asia Minor in present-day E-central Turkey; center of a Hittite state and a Persian satrapy. — **Cap′pa·do′cian** *adj. & n.*
cap·per (kăp′ər) *n.* **1.** One that caps or makes caps. **2.** *Informal.* Something that surpasses or completes; a finishing touch or finale. **3.** *Slang.* One who acts as a decoy.
cap·puc·ci·no (kăp′ə-chē′nō, kä′pə-) *n.*, *pl.* **-nos.** Espresso

coffee mixed or topped with steamed milk or cream. [Ital., Capuchin, cappuccino. See CAPUCHIN.]
Cap•ra (kăp′rə), **Frank.** 1897–1991. Amer. filmmaker whose works include *It Happened One Night* (1934).
Ca•pri (kə-prē′, kăp′rē, kä′prē). An island of S Italy on the S edge of the Bay of Naples; famous for its Blue Grotto.
cap•ric acid (kăp′rĭk) *n.* A fatty acid, $CH_3(CH_2)_8COOH$, obtained from animal fats and oils and used in the manufacture of perfumes and fruit flavors. [< Lat. *caper*, *capr-*, goat.]
ca•pric•cio (kə-prē′chō, -chē-ō′) *n.*, *pl.* **-cios. 1.** *Mus.* An instrumental work with an improvisatory style and a free form. **2.** A prank; a caper. **3.** A whim. [Ital. See CAPRICE.]
ca•pric•cio•so (kə-prē′chē-ō′sō, kä′prē-chō′sō) *adj. Mus.* Lively and free. [Ital. < *capriccio*, caprice. See CAPRICE.]
ca•price (kə-prēs′) *n.* **1.a.** An impulsive change of mind. **b.** An inclination to change one's mind impulsively. **c.** A sudden, unpredictable action, change, or series of actions or changes. **2.** *Mus.* A capriccio. [Fr. < Ital. *capriccio* < *caporiccio*, fright, sudden start : *capo*, head (< Lat. *caput*; see **kaput-***) + *riccio*, curly (< Lat. *ēricius*, hedgehog < *ēr*).]
ca•pri•cious (kə-prĭsh′əs, -prē′shəs) *adj.* Characterized by or subject to whim. **—ca•pri′cious•ly** *adv.* **—ca•pri′cious•ness** *n.*
Cap•ri•corn (kăp′rĭ-kôrn′) also **Cap•ri•cor•nus** (kăp′rĭ-kôr′nəs) *n.* **1.** A constellation in the equatorial region of the Southern Hemisphere, near Aquarius and Sagittarius. **2.a.** The tenth sign of the zodiac in astrology. **b.** One born under Capricorn. [ME *Capricorne* < Lat. *Capricornus* : *caper*, *capr-*, goat + *cornū*, horn; see **ker-¹***.]
cap•ri•fi•ca•tion (kăp′rə-fĭ-kā′shən) *n.* A method of pollination of edible figs in which wasps carry pollen from the flowers of the caprifig to those of the edible varieties. [Lat. *caprificātio*, *caprificātiōn-* < *caprificātus*, p.part. of *caprificāre*, to ripen figs by caprification < *caprificus*, caprifig. See CAPRIFIG.]
cap•ri•fig (kăp′rə-fĭg′) *n.* A wild fig *(Ficus carica* var. *sylvestris)* used in the caprification of edible figs. [ME < Lat. *caprificus* (influenced by ME *fig*, fig) : *caper*, *capr-*, goat + *fīcus*, fig; see FIG¹.]
cap•ri•ole (kăp′rē-ōl′) *n.* **1.** An upward leap made by a trained horse with the hind legs kicked out. **2.** A playful leap or jump; a caper. [Fr. < Ital. *capriola*, somersault < *capriolo*, roebuck, wild goat < Lat. *capreolus*, dim. of *caper*, *capr-*, goat.] **—cap′ri•ole′** *v.*
ca•pri pants (kə-prē′, kä′prē) *pl.n.* Tight-fitting calf-length women's pants. [After CAPRI.]
ca•pro•ic acid (kə-prō′ĭk, kă-) *n.* A liquid fatty acid, $CH_3(CH_2)_4COOH$, found in animal fats and oils or synthesized and used in the manufacture of pharmaceuticals and flavorings. [< Lat. *caper*, *capr-*, goat.]
ca•pryl•ic acid (kə-prĭl′ĭk, kă-) *n.* A liquid fatty acid, $C_8H_{16}0_2$, found in butter and other fats and oils and having a rancid taste. [CAPR(IC ACID) + -YL + -IC.]
cap•sa•i•cin (kăp-sā′ĭ-sĭn) *n.* A colorless, pungent, crystalline compound, $C_{18}H_{27}NO_3$, that is derived from capsicum and is a strong irritant to skin and mucous membranes. [CAPSIC(UM) (perh. influenced by Lat. *capsa*, box; see CAPSICUM) + -IN.]
cap screw *n.* A long-threaded bolt, usu. with a square head, used in fastening machine parts.
Cap•si•an (kăp′sē-ən) *adj.* Of, relating to, or being a Paleolithic culture of northern Africa and southern Europe. [Fr. *capsien* < Lat. *Capsa*, Gafsa, a town of W-central Tunisia.]
cap•si•cum (kăp′sĭ-kəm) *n.* **1.** Any of various tropical American pepper plants of the genus *Capsicum*, esp. of the species *C. annuum* and *C. frutescens*. **2.** The fruit of any of these plants, esp. the dried pungent types used as a condiment and in medicine. [NLat. *Capsicum*, genus name, perh. < Lat. *capsa*, box (from its podlike fruit).]
cap•sid (kăp′sĭd) *n.* The protein shell that surrounds a virus particle. [< Lat. *capsa*, box.]
cap•size (kăp′sīz′, kăp-sīz′) *intr. & tr.v.* **-sized, -siz•ing, -siz•es.** To overturn or cause to overturn. [?]
cap•so•mere (kăp′sə-mîr′) *n.* One of the individual subunits that makes up a capsid. [CAPS(ID) + -MERE.]
cap•stan (kăp′stən, -stăn′) *n.* **1.** *Naut.* An apparatus used for hoisting weights, consisting of a vertical spool-shaped cylinder around which a cable is wound. **2.** A shaft used to drive magnetic tape at a constant speed in a tape recorder. [ME < Norman Fr. < OProv. *cabestan* < *cabestre*, noose < Lat. *capistrum*, halter, prob. < *capere*, to seize. See **kap-***.]
cap•stone (kăp′stōn′) *n.* **1.** The top stone of a structure or wall. **2.** The crowning achievement or final stroke; the acme.
cap•su•late (kăp′sə-lāt′, -lĭt, -syo͞o-) also **cap•su•lat•ed** (-lā′tĭd) *adj.* Enclosed in or formed into a capsule. **—cap′su•la′tion** *n.*
cap•sule (kăp′səl, -so͞ol) *n.* **1.** A small soluble container, usu. made of gelatin, that encloses a dose of an oral medicine or a vitamin. **2.** *Anat.* A fibrous, membranous, or fatty sheath that encloses an organ or part. **3.** *Microbiol.* A mucopolysaccharide outer shell enveloping certain bacteria. **4.** *Bot.* **a.** A dry, dehiscent fruit that develops from two or more united carpels. **b.** The thin-walled spore-containing structure of mosses and related plants. **5.** A space capsule. **6.** A brief summary; a condensation. *—adj.* **1.** Highly condensed; very brief. **2.** Very small; compact. *—tr.v.* **-suled, -sul•ing, -sules. 1.** To enclose in or furnish with a capsule. **2.** To condense or summarize. [Fr. < Lat. *capsula*, dim. of *capsa*, box.] **—cap′su•lar** (-sə-lər, -syo͞o-) *adj.*
cap•sul•ize (kăp′sə-līz′, -syo͞o-) *tr.v.* **-ized, -iz•ing, -iz•es.** To capsule: *capsulized the news every 30 minutes.*
Capt. *abbr.* Captain.
cap•tain (kăp′tən) *n.* **1.** One who commands, leads, or guides others, esp.: **a.** The officer in command of a ship, an aircraft, or a spacecraft. **b.** A precinct commander in a police or fire department, usu. ranking above a lieutenant and below a chief. **c.** The designated leader of a team or crew in sports. **2.a.** A commissioned rank in the U.S. Army, Air Force, or Marine Corps that is above first lieutenant and below major. **b.** A commissioned rank in the U.S. Navy or Coast Guard that is above commander and below commodore. **c.** One who holds the rank of captain. **3.** A figure in the forefront; a leader. **4.** One who supervises or directs the work of others, esp.: **a.** A district official for a political party. **b.** A restaurant employee who is in charge of the servers and usu. attends to table seating. **c.** A bell captain. *—tr.v.* **-tained, -tain•ing, -tains.** To act as captain of; command or direct. [ME *capitain* < OFr. < LLat. *capitāneus*, chief < Lat. *caput*, *capit-*, head. See **kaput-***.] **—cap′tain•cy, cap′tain•ship′** *n.*
cap•tain's chair (kăp′tənz) *n.* A wooden chair having a low back with spindles that curve forward to provide armrests.
captain's mast *n.* A disciplinary hearing for enlisted personnel presided over by the commanding officer of a naval unit.
cap•tan (kăp′tən, -tăn′) *n.* A white solid agricultural fungicide, $C_9H_8O_2NSCl_3$. [Short for MERCAPTAN.]
cap•tion (kăp′shən) *n.* **1.** A title, short explanation, or description accompanying an illustration or a photograph. **2.** A motion picture subtitle. **3.** A title or heading, as of an article. **4.** *Law.* The heading of a pleading or other document that identifies the parties, court, term, and number of the action. *—tr.v.* **-tioned, -tion•ing, -tions.** To furnish a caption for. [ME *capcioun*, arrest < OFr. *capcion* < Lat. *captiō*, *captiōn-* < *captus*, p.part. of *capere*, to seize. See **kap-***.]
cap•tious (kăp′shəs) *adj.* **1.** Marked by a disposition to find and point out trivial faults. **2.** Intended to entrap or confuse, as in an argument. [ME *capcious* < OFr. *captieux* < Lat. *captiōsus* < *captiō*, seizure, sophism < *captus*, p.part. of *capere*, to seize. See **kap-***.] **—cap′tious•ly** *adv.* **—cap′tious•ness** *n.*
cap•ti•vate (kăp′tə-vāt′) *tr.v.* **-vat•ed, -vat•ing, -vates. 1.** To attract and hold by charm, beauty, or excellence. See Syns at **charm. 2.** *Archaic.* To capture. [LLat. *captivāre*, *captivāt-*, to capture < Lat. *captīvus*, prisoner. See CAPTIVE.] **—cap′ti•va′tion** *n.* **—cap′ti•va′tor** *n.*
cap•tive (kăp′tĭv) *n.* **1.** One that is forcibly confined, subjugated, or enslaved. **2.** One in the grip of a strong emotion or passion. *—adj.* **1.** Taken and held prisoner. **2.** Held in bondage; enslaved. **3.** Kept under restraint or control. **4.** Restrained from free choice. **5.** Enraptured, as by beauty; captivated. [ME *captif* < OFr. < Lat. *captīvus* < *captus*, p.part. of *capere*, to seize. See **kap-***.]
cap•tiv•i•ty (kăp-tĭv′ĭ-tē) *n.*, *pl.* **-ties.** The state or period of being imprisoned, confined, or enslaved.
cap•to•pril (kăp′tə-prĭl′) *n.* A drug used to treat hypertension that inhibits the enzymes that activate angiotensin. [(MER)CAPT(AN) + *pr(opano)*–, propane (< PROPANE) + -YL.]
cap•tor (kăp′tər, -tôr′) *n.* One that takes another as a captive. [LLat. *captor*, hunter < Lat. *capere*, to seize. See **kap-***.]
cap•ture (kăp′chər) *tr.v.* **-tured, -tur•ing, -tures. 1.** To take captive, as by force or craft; seize. **2.** To gain possession or control of, as in a game or contest. **3.** To attract and hold: *capture the imagination.* **4.** To succeed in preserving in lasting form: *capture a likeness.* *—n.* **1.** The act of catching, taking, or winning, as by force or skill. **2.** One that has been seized, caught, or won. **3.** *Phys.* The phenomenon in which an atom or a nucleus absorbs a subatomic particle. [< Fr., capture < OFr. < Lat. *captūra* < *captus*, p.part. of *capere*, to seize. See **kap-***.]
Cap•u•a (kăp′yo͞o-ə, kä′pwä). A town of S Italy N of Naples near the site of a strategically important ancient Roman city on the Appian Way. Pop. 18,053.
ca•puche (kə-po͞och′, -po͞osh′) *n.* A hood on a cloak, esp. the long pointed cowl worn by a Capuchin monk. [Ital. *cappuccio* < *cappa*, hood < LLat., cloak.]
cap•u•chin (kăp′yə-chĭn, -shĭn, kə-pyo͞o′-) *n.* **1. Capuchin.** A monk belonging to the Order of Friars Minor Capuchin. **2.** A hooded cloak worn by women. **3.** Any of several long-tailed monkeys of the genus *Cebus*, native to Central and South America and often having a hoodlike tuft of hair on the head. [Obsolete Fr. < Ital. *cappuccino*, pointed cowl, Capuchin < *cappuccio*, hood. See CAPUCHE.]
cap•y•ba•ra (kăp′ə-bär′ə, -băr′ə) *n.* A large rodent *(Hydrochoerus hydrochaeris)* of tropical South America having short limbs and a vestigial tail. [Port. *capybara* < Tupi *capivara*, *capibara* : *capii*, grass + *urara*, eater.]

capsule
Medicinal

capuchin
White-throated capuchin
Cebus capucinus

ă pat	oi boy
ā pay	ou out
âr care	o͝o took
ä father	o͞o boot
ĕ pet	ŭ cut
ē be	ûr urge
ĭ pit	th thin
ī pie	*th* this
îr pier	hw which
ŏ pot	zh vision
ō toe	ə about, item
ô paw	

Stress marks:
′ (primary);
′ (secondary), as in
dictionary (dĭk′shə-nĕr′ē)

car (kär) *n.* **1.** An automobile. **2.** A vehicle, such as a streetcar, that runs on rails. **3.** A boxlike enclosure for passengers and freight on a conveyance. **4.** The part of a balloon or airship that carries people and cargo. **5.** *Archaic.* A chariot, carriage, or cart. [ME *carre*, cart < ONFr. < Lat. *carra*, pl. of *carrus, carrum*, a Gallic type of wagon. See **kers-*.**]

car. *abbr.* Carat.

car•a•bao (kăr′ə-bou′, kä′rə-) *n., pl.* **-baos.** See **water buffalo.** [Sp. < Visayan *karabáw* < Malay *kêrbau.*]

car•a•bid (kăr′ə-bĭd, kə-răb′ĭd) *n.* Any of a large family (Carabidae) of chiefly black beetles that feed on other insects. [< NLat. *Cārabidae*, family name < Lat. *cārabus*, crustacean < Gk. *karabos*, horned beetle.] **—car′a•bid** *adj.*

car•a•bi•neer also **car•a•bi•nier** (kăr′ə-bə-nîr′) or **car•bi•neer** (kär′bə-) *n.* A soldier armed with a carbine. [Fr. *carabinier* < *carabine*, carbine. See CARBINE.]

car•a•bi•ner also **kar•a•bi•ner** (kăr′ə-bē′nər) *n.* An oblong metal ring with a spring clip, used in mountaineering to attach a running rope to a piton or similar device. [Ger. *Karabiner*, short for *Karabinerhaken*, hook for a carbine < *Karabiner*, carbine < Fr. *carabine.* See CARBINE.]

ca•ra•bi•nie•re (kăr′ə-bĭn-yâr′ē, kä′rä-bē-nyĕ′rĕ) *n., pl.* **-bi•nie•ri** (-bĭn-yâr′ē, -bē-nyĕ′rē). A member of the Italian police force. [Ital. < Fr. *carabinier.* See CARABINEER.]

car•a•cal (kăr′ə-kăl′) *n.* A wildcat *(Lynx caracal)* of Africa and southern Asia having short fur and long, tufted ears. [Fr. < Ottoman Turk. *qaraqūlāq* : *qara*, black + *qūlāq*, ear.]

Car•a•cal•la (kăr′ə-kăl′ə). A.D. 188–217. Emperor of Rome (211–217) whose brutal rule led to his assassination.

car•a•car•a (kăr′ə-kăr′ə, -kə-rä′) *n.* Any of several large carrion-eating or predatory hawks of the subfamily Caracarinae, native to South and Central America and the southern United States. [Sp. and Port. *caracará*, both < Tupi *caracara.*]

Ca•ra•cas (kə-rä′kəs). The cap. of Venezuela, in the N part near the Caribbean coast; founded by the Spanish in 1567. Pop. 3,041,000.

car•ack (kăr′ək) *n. Naut.* Var. of **carrack.**

car•a•cole (kăr′ə-kōl′) also **car•a•col** (-kŏl′) *n.* A half turn to right or left performed by a horse and rider. [Fr. < Sp. *caracol*, snail.] **—car′a•cole′** *v.*

car•a•cul (kăr′ə-kəl) *n.* Var. of **karakul.**

ca•rafe (kə-răf′) *n.* **1.** A glass or metal bottle, often with a flared lip, used for serving water or wine. **2.** A glass pot with a pouring spout, used in making coffee. [Fr. < Ital. *caraffa* < Sp. *garrafa*, prob. < Ar. *ġarafa*, to ladle, scoop.]

car•am•bo•la (kăr′əm-bō′lə) *n.* **1.** An ornamental evergreen tree *(Averrhoa carambola)* native to southeast Asia and having fruits that are star-shaped in cross section. **2.** The edible fruit of this plant. [Port., perh. < Marathi *karambal.*]

car•a•mel (kăr′ə-məl, -mĕl′, kär′məl) *n.* **1.** A smooth chewy candy made with sugar, butter, cream or milk, and flavoring. **2.** Burnt sugar, used for coloring and sweetening foods. **3.** *Color.* A moderate yellow brown. [Fr. < OFr. < OSp. *caramel, caramelo* < Port. *caramel* < LLat. *calamellus*, dim. of Lat. *calamus*, reed, cane < Gk. *kalamos.*]

car•a•mel•ize (kăr′ə-mə-līz′, kär′mə-) *tr. & intr.v.* **-ized, -iz•ing, -iz•es.** To convert or be converted into caramel. **—car′a•mel•i•za′tion** (-mə-lĭ-zā′shən) *n.*

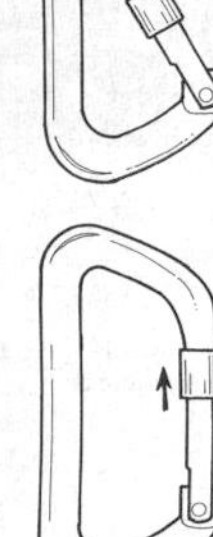

carabiner
Top: Open
Bottom: Closed

ca•ran•gid (kə-răn′jĭd, -răng′gĭd) *n.* Any of a family (Carangidae) of marine food and game fishes, such as the jacks. [< NLat. *Carangidae*, family name < Fr. *carangue*, mackerel < Sp. *caranga.*] **—ca•ran′gid** *adj.*

car•a•pace (kăr′ə-pās′) *n.* **1.** *Zool.* A hard bony or chitinous outer covering. **2.** A protective shell-like covering. [Fr. < Sp. *carapacho.*]

car•at (kăr′ət) *n.* **1.** A unit of weight for precious stones, equal to 200 milligrams. **2.** Var. of **karat.** [ME < OFr. < Med.Lat. *quarātus* < Ar. *qīrāṭ*, weight of four grains < Gk. *keration*, a weight, dim. of *keras*, horn. See **ker-¹*.**]

Ca•ra•vag•gio (kăr′ə-vä′jō, kä′rä-väd′jô), **Michelangelo Merisi da.** 1573–1610. Italian painter of the baroque whose works include *Deposition of Christ* (1604).

car•a•van (kăr′ə-văn′) *n.* **1.** A company of travelers journeying together, as across a desert. **2.** A single file of vehicles or pack animals. **3.** A large covered vehicle; a van. **4.** *Chiefly British.* A trailer or dwelling place on wheels. [Fr. *caravane* or Ital. *carovana*, both < Pers. *kārvān.*]

car•a•van•sa•ry (kăr′ə-văn′sə-rē) also **car•a•van•se•rai** (-rī′) *n., pl.* **-ries** also **-rais.** **1.** An inn built around a large court for caravans at night in the Near or Far East. **2.** A large inn or hostelry. [Fr. *caravanserai* < Pers. *kārvānsarāy* : *kārvān*, caravan + *sarāy*, camp, palace; see **terə-²*.**]

caravel

car•a•vel or **car•a•velle** (kăr′ə-vĕl′) also **car•vel** (kär′vəl, -vĕl′) *n. Naut.* Any of several types of small light sailing ships, esp. one with two or three masts and lateen sails used by the Spanish and Portuguese in the 15th and 16th centuries. [Fr. *caravelle* < OFr. < OPort. *caravela*, dim. of *cáravo*, ship < LLat. *cārabus*, a small wicker boat < LGk. *karabos*, light ship < Gk., horned beetle.]

car•a•way (kăr′ə-wā′) *n.* **1.** A biennial Eurasian herb *(Carum carvi)* in the parsley family, having finely divided leaves and white or pinkish flowers. **2.** The seedlike fruit of this plant, used as a flavoring and seasoning. [ME *carewei* < OFr. *carvi, caroi*, prob. < Med.Lat. *carvi, carwi*, ult. < Ar. *karāwiyā* < Gk. *karon.*]

car•ba•mate (kär′bə-māt′, kär-băm′āt′) *n.* A salt or an ester of carbamic acid, esp. one used as an insecticide. [CARBAM(IC ACID) + -ATE².]

car•bam•ic acid (kär-băm′ĭk) *n.* A hypothetical acid, NH_2COOH, that exists only in the form of its esters and salts. [CARBAM(IDE) + -IC.]

car•ba•mide (kär′bə-mīd′, kär-băm′ĭd) *n.* See **urea.**

car•bam•o•yl (kär-băm′ō-ĭl′) *n.* The radical NH_2CO. [CARBAM(IC ACID) + -YL.]

car•ban•i•on (kär-băn′ī′ən, -ī′ŏn′) *n.* An anion in which carbon carries a negative charge and an unshared pair of electrons.

car•ba•ryl (kär′bə-rĭl′) *n.* A carbamate, $C_{12}H_{11}NO_2$, used as an insecticide. [CARB(AMATE) + AR(OMATIC) + -YL.]

car•bide (kär′bīd′) *n.* **1.** A binary compound consisting of carbon and a more electropositive element, esp. calcium. **2.** A hard material made of compacted binary compounds of carbon and heavy metals, used to make tools that cut metal.

car•bine (kär′bēn′, -bīn′) *n.* A lightweight rifle with a short barrel. [Fr. *carabine* < OFr. *carabin*, soldier armed with a musket, perh. < *escarrabin*, gravedigger < *scarabee*, dung beetle. See SCARAB.]

car•bi•neer (kär′bə-nîr′) *n.* Var. of **carabineer.**

car•bi•nol (kär′bə-nôl′, -nōl′, -nŏl′) *n.* **1.** See **methanol. 2.** An alcohol derived from methanol.

carbo– or **carb–** *pref.* Carbon: *carbohydrate.* [Fr. < *carbone*, carbon. See CARBON.]

car•bo•cy•clic (kär′bō-sī′klĭk, -sĭk′lĭk) *adj. Chem.* Having a ring composed exclusively of carbon atoms, as benzene.

car•bo•hy•drase (kär′bō-hī′drās′, -drāz′) *n.* Any of various enzymes that catalyze the hydrolysis of a carbohydrate.

car•bo•hy•drate (kär′bō-hī′drāt′) *n.* Any of a group of organic compounds produced by photosynthetic plants that includes sugars, starches, celluloses, and gums and serves as a major energy source in the diet of animals.

car•bo•lat•ed (kär′bə-lā′tĭd) *adj.* Containing or treated with carbolic acid.

car•bol•ic acid (kär-bŏl′ĭk) *n.* See **phenol** 1. [CARB(O)- + -OL¹ + -IC.]

car•bon (kär′bən) *n.* **1.** *Symbol* **C** A nonmetallic element that occurs in many inorganic and in all organic compounds, exists freely as graphite and diamond and as a constituent of coal, limestone, and petroleum, and is capable of chemical self-bonding to form an enormous number of important molecules. Atomic number 6; atomic weight 12.01115; sublimation point above 3,500°C; boiling point 4,827°C; specific gravity of amorphous carbon 1.8 to 2.1, of diamond 3.15 to 3.53, of graphite 1.9 to 2.3; valence 2, 3, 4. See table at **element. 2.a.** A sheet of carbon paper. **b.** A copy made by using carbon paper. **3.** *Elect.* **a.** Either of two rods through which current flows to form an arc, as in lighting. **b.** A carbonaceous electrode in an electric cell. [Fr. *carbone* < Lat. *carbō, carbōn-*, a coal, charcoal. See **ker-³*.**] **—car′bon•ous** (-bə-nəs) *adj.*

carbon 14 *n.* A naturally radioactive carbon isotope with atomic mass 14 and half-life 5,780 years, used in carbon dating.

car•bo•na•ceous (kär′bə-nā′shəs) *adj.* Consisting of, containing, relating to, or yielding carbon.

car•bo•na•do¹ (kär′bə-nā′dō, -nä′-) *Archaic.* **—** *n., pl.* **-does** or **-dos.** A piece of scored and broiled fish, fowl, or meat. **—** *tr.v.* **-doed, -do•ing, -dos. 1.** To score and broil (fish, fowl, or meat). **2.** To slice or cut. [< Sp. *carbonada* < *carbón*, charcoal < Lat. *carbō, carbōn-.* See CARBON.]

car•bo•na•do² (kär′bə-nā′dō, -nä′-) *n., pl.* **-does.** A form of opaque or dark-colored diamond used for drills. [Port. < *carbone*, carbon < Fr. See CARBON.]

car•bo•na•ra (kär′bə-när′ə) *n.* A sauce for pasta containing eggs, minced bacon or ham, grated cheese, and seasonings. [Ital. *(alla) carbonara*, (from) a charcoal grill < *carbone*, charcoal < Lat. *carbō, carbōn-.* See CARBON.]

car•bon•ate (kär′bə-nāt′) *tr.v.* **-at•ed, -at•ing, -ates. 1.** To charge (a beverage, for example) with carbon dioxide gas. **2.** To burn to carbon; carbonize. **3.** To change into a carbonate. **—** *n.* (-nāt′, -nĭt). A salt or an ester of carbonic acid. **—car′bon•a′tion** *n.* **—car′bon•a′tor** *n.*

car•bon•at•ed water (kär′bə-nā′tĭd) *n.* See **soda water** 1a.

carbon black *n.* Any of various forms of carbon derived from the incomplete combustion of natural gas or petroleum oil and used to reinforce rubber and in inks, paints, crayons, and polishes.

carbon copy *n.* **1.** A duplicate, as of a letter, made with carbon paper. **2.** A person or thing that closely resembles another.

carbon cycle *n.* **1.** *Phys.* See **carbon-nitrogen cycle. 2.** *Ecol.* The combined processes, including photosynthesis, decomposition, and respiration, by which carbon as a component of various compounds cycles between its major reservoirs—the atmosphere, oceans, and living organisms.

Car•bon•dale (kär′bən-dāl′). A city of S IL SE of East St. Louis. Pop. 27,033.

carbon dating *n.* The determination of the approximate age of an ancient object, such as a geologic specimen, by the amount of carbon 14 it contains. — **car′bon-date′** (kär′bən-dāt′) *v.*

carbon dioxide *n.* A colorless, odorless, incombustible gas, CO_2, formed during respiration, combustion, and organic decomposition and used in food refrigeration, carbonated beverages, inert atmospheres, fire extinguishers, and aerosols.

carbon disulfide *n.* A clear flammable liquid, CS_2, used to make viscose rayon and cellophane, as a solvent, and in matches, fumigants, and pesticides.

car•bon•ic acid (kär-bŏn′ĭk) *n.* A weak unstable acid, H_2CO_3, present in solutions of carbon dioxide in water.

carbonic acid gas *n.* See **carbon dioxide.**

Car•bon•if•er•ous (kär′bə-nĭf′ər-əs) *adj.* **1.** Of, belonging to, or being a geologic division of the Paleozoic Era following the Devonian and preceding the Permian and characterized by swamp formation and deposition of plant remains later hardened into coal. **2. carboniferous.** Producing or containing carbon or coal. — *n.* The Carboniferous Period or its deposits. See table at **geologic time.**

car•bo•ni•um (kär-bō′nē-əm) *n.* An organic cation, such as H_3C, having one less electron than a corresponding free radical and with positive charge localized on the carbon atom.

car•bon•i•za•tion (kär′bə-nĭ-zā′shən) *n.* **1.** The process of carbonizing. **2.** The destructive distillation of coal to obtain coke and other fractions having a greater percentage of carbon than the original material.

car•bon•ize (kär′bə-nīz′) *tr.v.* **-ized, -iz•ing, -iz•es. 1.** To reduce or convert a carbon-containing substance to carbon. **2.** To coat or combine with carbon. — **car′bon•iz′er** *n.*

carbon monoxide *n.* A colorless, odorless, highly poisonous gas, CO, formed by the incomplete combustion of carbon or a carbonaceous material, such as gasoline.

car•bon-ni•tro•gen cycle (kär′bən-nī′trə-jən) *n. Phys.* A chain of thermonuclear reactions, thought to generate large amounts of energy in the sun and stars, in which four hydrogen atoms are converted into one helium atom.

carbon paper *n.* A lightweight paper coated on one side with a dark waxy pigment, used between two sheets of paper to copy what is on the top sheet to the bottom sheet.

carbon process *n.* A photographic printing process using permanent pigments, such as carbon, contained in a sensitized tissue or film of gelatin.

carbon star *n.* Any of a class of stars with high carbon-to-hydrogen ratios and primarily low temperatures.

carbon tetrachloride *n.* A poisonous nonflammable liquid, CCl_4, used as an industrial solvent.

car•bon•yl (kär′bə-nĭl′) *n.* **1.** The bivalent radical CO. **2.** A metal compound containing the CO group. — **car′bon•yl′ic** *adj.*

Car•bo•run•dum (kär′bə-rŭn′dəm). A trademark used for an abrasive of silicon carbide crystals.

carboxy– *pref.* Carboxyl: *carboxylase.* [< CARBOXYL.]

car•box•yl (kär-bŏk′səl) *n.* The univalent radical, COOH, the functional group characteristic of all organic acids. [CARB(O)– + OX(Y)– + –YL.] — **car′box•yl′ic** (-sĭl′ĭk) *adj.*

car•box•yl•ase (kär-bŏk′sə-lās′, -lāz′) *n.* An enzyme that catalyzes a carboxylation or decarboxylation reaction.

car•box•yl•a•tion (kär-bŏk′sə-lā′shən) *n.* The introduction of a carboxyl group into a compound or molecule.

car•box•yl•ic acid (kär′bŏk-sĭl′ĭk) *n.* An organic acid that contains one or more carboxyl groups.

car•box•y•meth•yl•cel•lu•lose (kär-bŏk′sē-mĕth′əl-sĕl′yə-lōs′) *n.* A derivative of cellulose whose sodium salt is used in the manufacture of processed foods and as a laxative.

car•boy (kär′boi′) *n.* A large glass or plastic bottle, usu. encased in a basket or crate and often used to hold corrosive liquids. [Pers. *qarābah* < Ar. *qarrābah*, big jug.]

car•bun•cle (kär′bŭng′kəl) *n.* **1.** A painful localized bacterial infection of the skin and subcutaneous tissue that usu. has several openings through which pus is discharged. **2.a.** A deep red garnet, unfaceted and convex. **b.** *Obsolete.* A red precious stone. [ME < OFr. < Lat. *carbunculus*, small glowing ember, carbuncle, dim. of *carbō, carbōn-*, coal. See **ker-**[3]*.] — **car′-bun′cled** *adj.* — **car•bun′cu•lar** (-kyə-lər) *adj.*

car•bu•ret (kär′bə-rāt′, -rĕt′, -byə-) *tr.v.* **-ret•ed, -ret•ing, -rets** or **-ret•ted, -ret•ting, -rets.** To combine or mix (a gas, for example) with volatile hydrocarbons, so as to increase available fuel energy. [< *carburet*, carbide < Fr. *carbure* < Lat. *carbō*, carbon. See CARBON.] — **car•bu•re′tion** *n.*

car•bu•re•tor (kär′bə-rā′tər, -byə-) *n.* A device used in internal-combustion engines to produce an explosive mixture of vaporized fuel and air. [< CARBURET.]

car•bu•rize (kär′bə-rīz′, -byə-) *tr.v.* **-rized, -riz•ing, -riz•es. 1.** To treat, combine, or impregnate with carbon, as when casehardening steel. **2.** To carburet. [CARBUR(ET) + –IZE.] — **car′bu•ri•za′tion** (-bər-ĭ-zā′shən, -byər-) *n.*

car•ca•jou (kär′kə-jo͞o′, -zho͞o′) *n.* See **wolverine** 1. [Canadian Fr. < Montagnais *kuàkuàtsheu.*]

car•ca•net (kär′kə-nĕt′, -nĭt) *n. Archaic.* A jeweled necklace, collar, or headband. [< OFr. *carcan*, collar, perh. < Med.Lat. *carcannum*, perh. of Gmc. orig.]

car•cass (kär′kəs) *n.* **1.** The dead body of an animal, esp. one slaughtered for food. **2.** The body of a human being. **3.** The remains of something, such as a ruined building. **4.** A framework or basic structure, as of a ship. [ME *carcas* < AN *carcais* and Med.Lat. *carcasium.*]

Car•cas•sonne (kär′-kə-sôn′, -sŏn′, -kä-). A city of S France SE of Toulouse. Pop. 41,153.

Car•che•mish (kär′kə-mĭsh′, kär-kē′mĭsh). An ancient Hittite and Assyrian city on the Euphrates R. in S Turkey.

carcino– *pref.* Cancer; cancerous: *carcinogen.* [Gk. *karkino-* < *karkinos*, crab, cancer. See **kar-***.]

car•cin•o•gen (kär-sĭn′ə-jən, kär′sə-nə-jĕn′) *n.* A cancer-causing substance or agent. — **car′ci•no•gen′e•sis** (kär′sə-nə-jĕn′ĭ-sĭs) *n.* — **car′cin•o•gen′ic** (-jĕn′ĭk) *adj.* — **car′ci•no•ge•nic′i•ty** (-jə-nĭs′ĭ-tē) *n.*

car•ci•noid (kär′sə-noid′) *n.* A small tumor, usu. found in the gastrointestinal tract, that secretes serotonin.

car•ci•no•ma (kär′sə-nō′mə) *n., pl.* **-mas** or **-ma•ta** (-mə-tə). An invasive malignant tumor derived from epithelial tissue that tends to metastasize to other areas of the body. [Lat., cancerous ulcer < Gk. *karkinōma* < *karkinos*, cancer. See **kar-***.] — **car′ci•no′ma•toid** (-nō′mə-toid′) *adj.* — **car′ci•nom′a•tous** (-nŏm′ə-təs, -nō′mə-) *adj.*

car•ci•no•ma•to•sis (kär′sə-nō′mə-tō′sĭs) *n.* A pathological condition characterized by the presence of carcinomas that have metastasized to many parts of the body. [Gk. *karkinōma*, *karkinōmat-*, cancerous ulcer; see CARCINOMA + –OSIS.]

car coat *n.* An overcoat extending to about midthigh.

card[1] (kärd) *n.* **1.** A flat, usu. rectangular piece of stiff paper, cardboard, or plastic, esp.: **a.** One of a set or pack bearing numbers, symbols, or figures, used in games and in divination. **b.** A greeting card. **c.** A post card. **d.** One bearing a person's name and other information, used for purposes of identification or classification. **e.** A business card. **f.** A credit card. **g.** A magnetic card. **h.** One used for recording information in a file. **2. cards.** *(used with a sing. or pl. v.) Games.* **a.** A game played with cards. **b.** The playing of cards. **3.** A program, esp. for a sports event. **4.a.** A menu, as in a restaurant. **b.** A wine list. **5.** *Comp. Sci.* **a.** A circuit board, esp. for use in a microcomputer. **b.** A punch card. **6.** A compass card. **7.** *Informal.* An eccentrically amusing person. **8.** Something that can be used to help gain an objective. — *tr.v.* **card•ed, card•ing, cards. 1.** To furnish with or attach to a card. **2.** To list (something) on a card; catalog. **3.** To check the identification of. — ***idioms.*** **card up (one's) sleeve.** A secret resource or plan held in reserve. **in the cards.** Likely or certain to happen. **put** (or **lay**) **(one's) cards on the table.** To reveal frankly one's thoughts, motives, or intentions. [ME *carde* < OFr. *carte* < Lat. *charta*, paper made from papyrus < Gk. *khartēs.*]

carboy

card[2] (kärd) *n.* **1.** A wire-toothed brush or a machine fitted with rows of wire teeth, used to disentangle fibers, as of wool, prior to spinning. **2.** A device used to raise the nap on a fabric. — *tr.v.* **card•ed, card•ing, cards.** To comb out or brush with a card. [ME *carde* < Med.Lat. *cardus* < Lat. *carduus*, thistle.] — **card′er** *n.*

car•da•mom (kär′də-məm) or **car•da•mon** (-mən) *n.* **1.a.** A rhizomatous Indian herb *(Elettaria cardamomum)* having aromatic seeds used as a spice or condiment. **b.** The seed of this plant. **2.** Any of several plants of the related genus *Amomum.* [ME *cardamome* < OFr. *cardemome* < Lat. *cardamōmum* < Gk. *kardamōmon* : *kardamon*, cress + *amōmon*, a spice.]

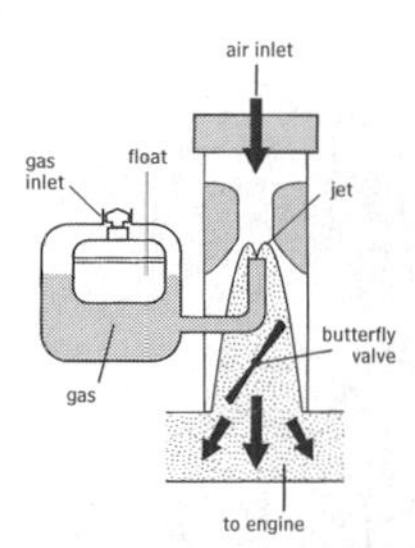

carburetor

card•board (kärd′bôrd′, -bōrd′) *n.* A stiff material made of pressed paper pulp or pasted sheets of paper and used for making cartons, for example. — *adj.* **1.** Made of or consisting of cardboard. **2.a.** Flimsy; insubstantial. **b.** Superficial.

card-car•ry•ing (kärd′kăr′ē-ĭng) *adj.* **1.** Being enrolled in an organization. **2.** Avidly devoted to a group or cause.

card catalog *n.* An alphabetical listing, esp. of books in a library, made with a separate card for each item.

Cár•de•nas (kär′dn-äs′, *-thĕ-*näs′). A city of N Cuba on the **Bay of Cárdenas,** an inlet of the Straits of Florida. Pop. 59,532.

card•hold•er (kärd′hōl′dər) *n.* One that holds a card, esp. a credit card. — **card′hold′ing** *adj.*

cardi– *pref.* Var. of **cardio–.**

car•di•a (kär′dē-ə) *n., pl.* **-di•ae** (-dē-ē′) or **-di•as. 1.** The opening of the esophagus into the stomach. **2.** The upper stomach adjoining the cardia. [Gk. *kardia.* See **kerd-***.]

car•di•ac (kär′dē-ăk′) *adj.* **1.** Of, near, or relating to the heart: *cardiac arteries.* **2.** Of or relating to the cardia. — *n.* A person with a heart disorder. [ME < Lat. *cardiacus* < Gk. *kardiakos* < *kardia*, heart. See **kerd-***.]

cardiac arrest *n.* Sudden cessation of heartbeat.

cardiac massage *n.* A resuscitative procedure using rhythmic compression of the chest to restore circulation.

car•di•al•gia (kär′dē-ăl′jə, -jē-ə) *n.* **1.** See **heartburn. 2.** Localized pain in the region of the heart. [Gk. *kardialgia* : *kardia*, heart; see CARDIA + *-algia*, -algia.]

Car•diff (kär′dĭf). The cap. of Wales, in the SE part on Bristol Channel. Pop. 281,300.

car•di•gan (kär′dĭ-gən) *n.* A knitted sweater or jacket that

ă pat	oi boy
ā pay	ou out
âr care	o͝o took
ä father	o͞o boot
ĕ pet	ŭ cut
ē be	ûr urge
ĭ pit	th thin
ī pie	*th* this
îr pier	hw which
ŏ pot	zh vision
ō toe	ə about, item
ô paw	

Stress marks:
′ (primary);
′ (secondary), as in
dictionary (dĭk′shə-nĕr′ē)

opens down the front. [After the 7th Earl of *Cardigan*, James Thomas Brudenell (1797–1868), British army officer.]

car•di•nal (kär′dn-əl, kärd′nəl) *adj.* **1.** Of foremost importance; paramount: *a cardinal rule.* **2.** *Color.* Dark to deep or vivid red. —*n.* **1.** *Rom. Cath. Ch.* A high church official, ranking just below the pope, who has been appointed by a pope to membership in the College of Cardinals. **2.** *Color.* A dark to deep or vivid red. **3.** A North American finch *(Cardinalis cardinalis)* having a crested head and bright red plumage in the male. **4.** A short hooded cloak, originally of scarlet cloth, worn by women in the 18th century. **5.** A cardinal number. [ME < LLat. *cardinālis* < Lat., serving as a hinge < *cardō, cardin-*, hinge.] —**car′di•nal•ship′** *n.*

car•di•nal•ate (kär′dn-ə-lĭt, -lāt′, kärd′nə-) *n. Rom. Cath. Ch.* **1.** The position, rank, dignity, or term of a cardinal. **2.** The College of Cardinals.

cardinal flower *n.* A perennial lobelia *(Lobelia cardinalis)* native to North America and having brilliant red flowers.

cardinal number *n.* A number, such as 3 or 11 or 412, used in counting to indicate quantity but not order.

cardinal point *n.* One of the four principal directions on a compass: north, south, east, or west.

cardinal virtue *n.* One of the four paramount virtues in classical philosophy: justice, prudence, fortitude, or temperance.

cardio– or **cardi–** *pref.* Heart: *cardiovascular.* [Gk. *kardio-* < *kardia*, heart. See **kerd-***.]

car•di•o•gen•ic (kär′dē-ō-jĕn′ĭk, -jē′nĭk) *adj.* **1.** Originating in the heart. **2.** Resulting from a heart disease or disorder.

car•di•o•gram (kär′dē-ə-grăm′) *n.* **1.** The curve traced by a cardiograph, used to diagnose heart disorders. **2.** See **electrocardiogram.**

car•di•o•graph (kär′dē-ə-grăf′) *n.* **1.** An instrument used to record the mechanical movements of the heart. **2.** See **electrocardiograph.** —**car′di•og′ra•phy** (-ŏg′rə-fē) *n.*

car•di•oid (kär′dē-oid′) *n.* A heart-shaped plane curve, the locus of a fixed point on a circle that rolls on the circumference of another circle with the same radius.

car•di•ol•o•gy (kär′dē-ŏl′ə-jē) *n.* The medical study of the structure, function, and disorders of the heart. —**car′di•o•log′i•cal** (-ə-lŏj′ĭ-kəl) *adj.* —**car′di•ol′o•gist** *n.*

cardinal
Cardinalis cardinalis

car•di•o•my•op•a•thy (kär′dē-ō-mī-ŏp′ə-thē) *n., pl.* **-thies.** A disease or disorder of the heart muscle, esp. of unknown or obscure cause.

car•di•op•a•thy (kär′dē-ŏp′ə-thē) *n., pl.* **-thies.** A disease or disorder of the heart.

car•di•o•pul•mo•nar•y (kär′dē-ō-po͝ol′mə-nĕr′ē, -pŭl′-) *adj.* Of, relating to, or involving both the heart and the lungs.

cardiopulmonary bypass *n.* A procedure using a heart-lung machine to circulate and oxygenate the blood while surgery is performed on the heart.

cardiopulmonary resuscitation *n.* An emergency procedure in which cardiac massage, artificial respiration, and drugs are used to maintain the circulation of blood to the brain.

car•di•o•res•pi•ra•to•ry (kär′dē-ō-rĕs′pər-ə-tôr′ē, -tōr′ē, -rĭ-spīr′ə-) *adj.* Of or relating to the heart and the respiratory system.

car•di•o•vas•cu•lar (kär′dē-ō-văs′kyə-lər) *adj.* Of, relating to, or involving the heart and the blood vessels.

car•di•tis (kär-dī′tĭs) *n.* Inflammation of the muscle tissue of the heart.

car•doon (kär-do͞on′) *n.* A Mediterranean plant *(Cynara cardunculus)* cultivated for its edible leafstalks and roots. [ME *cardoun* < OFr. *cardon* < OProv. < LLat. *cardō, cardōn-* < Lat. *carduus*, wild thistle.]

Car•do•zo (kär-dō′zō), **Benjamin Nathan.** 1870–1938. Amer. jurist; associate justice of the U.S. Supreme Court (1932–38).

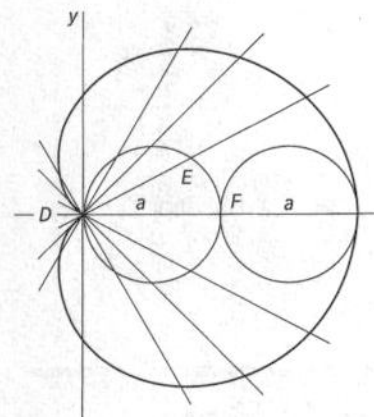

cardioid
Constructed from circle DEF and its secants through fixed point D

card•sharp (kärd′shärp′) also **card•sharp•er** (-shär′pər) *n.* An expert in cheating at cards. —**card′sharp′ing** *n.*

Car•duc•ci (kär-do͞o′chē), **Giosuè.** 1835–1907. Italian poet who won the 1906 Nobel Prize for literature.

care (kâr) *n.* **1.** A burdened state of mind, as that arising from heavy responsibilities; worry. **2.** Mental suffering; grief. **3.** An object or source of worry or concern. **4.** Caution in avoiding harm or danger. **5.a.** Close attention; painstaking application. **b.** Upkeep; maintenance: *lawn care.* **6.** Watchful oversight; charge or supervision. **7.** Attentive assistance or treatment to those in need. —*v.* **cared, car•ing, cares.** —*intr.* **1.** To be concerned or interested. **2.** To provide needed assistance or watchful supervision. **3.** To object or mind. **4.a.** To have a liking or attachment. **b.** To have a wish; be inclined. —*tr.* **1.** To wish; desire. **2.** To be concerned to the degree of: *I don't care a bit.* [ME < OE *cearu.*]

Syns: *care, charge, custody, keeping, supervision, trust.* The central meaning shared by these nouns is "the function of watching, guarding, or overseeing": *left the house keys in my care; has charge of these rare books; had custody of his friend's car during her absence; left the canary in the neighbors' keeping; assuming supervision of the students; documents committed to the bank's trust.* See also Syns at **anxiety.**

CARE *abbr.* Cooperative for American Relief Everywhere.

ca•reen (kə-rēn′) *v.* **-reened, -reen•ing, -reens.** —*intr.* **1.** To lurch or swerve while in motion. **2.** To rush headlong or carelessly; career. **3.** To lean to one side, as a ship sailing in the wind. —*tr. Naut.* **1.** To cause (a ship) to careen; tilt. **2.** To lean (a ship) on one side for cleaning, caulking, or repairing. —*n. Naut.* The position of a careened ship. [< Fr. *(en) carène*, (on) the keel < OFr. *carene* < OItal. *carena* < Lat. *carīna.* See **kar-***.] —**ca•reen′er** *n.*

Usage Note: The implication of rapidity that often accompanies the use of *careen* as a verb may have arisen by extension of the nautical sense of the verb to the motion of automobiles, which generally *careen*, that is, lurch or tip over, only at high speed. Whatever its origin, this use is by now well established.

ca•reer (kə-rîr′) *n.* **1.a.** A chosen pursuit; a profession or occupation. **b.** The general course or progression of one's working life. **2.** A path or course, as of the sun through the heavens. **3.** Speed. —*adj.* Doing what one does as a permanent occupation. —*intr.v.* **-reered, -reer•ing, -reers.** To move or run at full speed; rush. [Fr. *carrière* < OFr., racecourse < OProv. *carriera*, street < Med.Lat. *(via) carrāria*, (road) for carts < Lat. *carrus*, a Gallic type of wagon. See **kers-***.]

ca•reer•ism (kə-rîr′ĭz′əm) *n.* Pursuit of professional advancement as one's chief or sole aim. —**ca•reer′ist** *n.*

care•free (kâr′frē′) *adj.* Free of worries and responsibilities.

care•ful (kâr′fəl) *adj.* **1.** Attentive to potential danger, error, or harm; cautious. **2.** Thorough and painstaking in action or execution; conscientious. **3.** Protective; solicitous. **4.** Full of cares or anxiety. —**care′ful•ly** *adv.* —**care′ful•ness** *n.*

Syns: *careful, heedful, mindful, observant, watchful.* The central meaning shared by these adjectives is "cautiously attentive": *was careful not to get her shoes muddy; heedful of the danger; mindful of his health; observant to avoid giving offense; a watchful nurse.* ***Ant:*** *careless.*

care•giv•er (kâr′gĭv′ər) *n.* **1.** A person who assists a sick or disabled person. **2.** A person who attends to the needs of a child or dependent adult.

care•less (kâr′lĭs) *adj.* **1.** Taking insufficient care; negligent. **2.** Marked by or resulting from lack of forethought or thoroughness. **3.** Showing a lack of consideration. **4.** Unconcerned or indifferent; heedless. **5.** Unstudied or effortless. **6.** Free from cares; cheerful. —**care′less•ly** *adv.* —**care′less•ness** *n.*

ca•ress (kə-rĕs′) *n.* A gentle touch or gesture of tenderness or love. —*tr.v.* **-ressed, -ress•ing, -ress•es.** **1.** To touch or stroke in an affectionate or loving manner. **2.** To touch or move as if with a caress. **3.** To treat fondly, kindly, or favorably; cherish. [Fr. *caresse* < Ital. *carezza* < *caro*, dear < Lat. *cārus.* See **kā-***.] —**ca•ress′er** *n.* —**ca•ress′ing•ly** *adv.* —**ca•res′sive** *adj.*

car•et (kăr′ĭt) *n.* A proofreading symbol (∧) used to indicate an insertion in a line of printing or writing. [Lat., third pers. sing. pr.t. of *carēre*, to lack. See **kes-***.]

care•tak•er (kâr′tā′kər) *n.* **1.** One that is employed to look after or take charge of property or a person; a custodian. **2.** One that temporarily performs the duties of an office.

Ca•rew (kə-ro͞o′), **Thomas.** 1595?–1639? English poet whose amorous light lyrics were favored by Charles I.

care•worn (kâr′wôrn′, -wōrn′) *adj.* Showing worry.

car•fare (kär′fâr′) *n.* The fare a passenger pays, as on a bus.

car•go (kär′gō) *n., pl.* **-goes** or **-gos.** The freight carried by a ship, an aircraft, or another vehicle. [Sp. < *cargar*, to load < LLat. *carricāre* < Lat. *carrus*, a Gallic wagon. See **kers-***.]

car•hop (kär′hŏp′) *n.* One who waits on customers at a drive-in restaurant.

Car•i•a (kâr′ē-ə). An ancient region of SW Asia Minor with a coastline on the Aegean Sea. —**Car′i•an** *adj. & n.*

Car•ib (kăr′ĭb) *n., pl.* **Carib** or **-ibs.** **1.** Also **Car•i•ban** (kăr′ə-bən, kə-rē′bən′). A member of a group of American Indian peoples of northern South America, the Lesser Antilles, and the eastern coast of Central America. **2.** Any of the languages of the Carib. [Sp. *Caribe*, of Cariban orig.] —**Car′ib** *adj.*

Car•i•ban (kăr′ə-bən, kə-rē′bən) *n., pl.* **Cariban** or **-bans.** A language family comprising the Carib languages. —**Car′i•ban** *adj.*

Car•ib•be•an (kăr′ə-bē′ən, kə-rĭb′ē-ən) *adj.* **1.** Of or relating to the Caribbean Sea, its islands, or its Central or South American coasts or to the peoples or cultures of this region. **2.** Of or relating to the Carib or their language or culture. —*n.* A Carib.

Caribbean Sea. An arm of the W Atlantic bounded by the coasts of Central and South America and the West Indies.

ca•ri•be (kə-rē′bē) *n.* See **piranha.** [Am.Sp. < Sp. *Caribe*, Carib. See Carib.]

Car•i•boo Mountains (kăr′ə-bo͞o′). A range of E British Columbia, Canada, parallel to and W of the Rocky Mts.

car•i•bou (kăr′ə-bo͞o′) *n., pl.* **caribou** or **-bous.** Any of several large reindeer native to northern North America. [Micmac *ĝalipu* (influenced by Canadian Fr. *caribou*, also < Micmac) < Proto-Algonquin **mekālixpowa* : **mekāl-*, to scrape + **-ixpo-*, snow.]

car•i•ca•ture (kăr′ĭ-kə-cho͝or′, -chər) *n.* **1.a.** A representation in which the subject's distinctive features or peculiarities are exaggerated for comic or grotesque effect. **b.** The art of creating such representations. **2.** A grotesque imitation or misrepresentation: *The trial was a caricature of justice.* — *tr.v.* **-tured, -tur•ing, -tures.** To represent or imitate in an exaggerated, distorted manner. [Fr. < Ital. *caricatura* < *caricare*, to load, exaggerate < LLat. *carricāre* < Lat. *carrus*, a Gallic type of wagon. See **kers-*.**] — **car′i•ca•tur′ist** *n.*

car•ies (kâr′ēz) *n., pl.* **caries.** Decay of a bone or tooth, esp. dental caries. [Lat. *cariēs*.]

car•il•lon (kăr′ə-lŏn′, -lən) *n. Mus.* **1.** A stationary set of chromatically tuned bells in a tower, usu. played from a keyboard. **2.** A composition written or arranged for these bells. — *intr.v.* **-lonned, -lon•ning, -lons.** To play a carillon. [Fr., alteration of OFr. *quarregnon* < LLat. *quaterniō*, *quaterniōn-*, set of four. See QUATERNION.]

car•il•lon•neur (kăr′ə-lə-nûr′) *n. Mus.* A person who plays a carillon. [Fr. < *carillon*, carillon. See CARILLON.]

ca•ri•na (kə-rī′nə, -rē′-) *n., pl.* **-nae** (-nē). A keel-shaped ridge or structure, such as that on the breastbone of a bird. [Lat. *carīna*, keel. See **kar-*.**]

Ca•ri•na (kə-rī′nə) *n.* A constellation in the Southern Hemisphere near Volans and Vela. [Lat. *carīna*, keel. See CARINA.]

car•i•nate (kăr′ə-nāt′, -nĭt) also **car•i•nat•ed** (-nā′tĭd) *adj.* Shaped like or having a carina or keel; ridged.

car•ing (kâr′ĭng) *adj.* Feeling and exhibiting concern and empathy for others.

Ca•rin•thi•a (kə-rĭn′thē-ə). A region and former duchy of central Europe in S Austria. — **Ca•rin′thi•an** *adj.*

Car•i•o•ca (kăr′ē-ō′kə) *n.* **1.** A native or inhabitant of Rio de Janeiro, Brazil. **2. carioca. a.** A dance similar to the samba. **b.** The music for this dance. [Port., of Tupian orig.] — **Car′i•o′can** *adj.*

car•i•ole also **car•ri•ole** (kăr′ē-ōl′) *n.* **1.** A small, open, two- or four-wheeled carriage drawn by one horse. **2.** A light covered cart. [Fr. *carriole* < OProv. *carriola*, dim. of *carri*, chariot < Lat. *carrus*, a Gallic type of wagon. See **kers-*.**]

car•i•ous (kâr′ē-əs) *adj.* Having caries, esp. of the teeth; decayed. — **car′i•os′i•ty** (-ŏs′ĭ-tē), **car′i•ous•ness** *n.*

cark (kärk) *tr. & intr.v.* **carked, cark•ing, carks.** To burden or be burdened with trouble; worry. — *n.* A worry; a trouble. [ME *carken* < Norman Fr. *carquier*, to burden, load < LLat. *carricāre*. See CARGO.]

Carl XVI Gus•tav (kärl gŭs′täv, -täf, gŏŏs′-). b. 1946. King of Sweden (since 1973).

car•line or **car•lin** (kär′lĭn) *n. Scots.* A woman, esp. an old one. [ME *kerling* < ON < *karl*, man.]

Car•lisle (kär-līl′, kär′līl′). A borough of S PA WSW of Harrisburg. Pop. 18,419.

Car•list (kär′lĭst) *n.* A supporter of Don Carlos, the pretender to the Spanish throne, or his heirs. — **Car′list** *adj.*

car•load (kär′lōd′) *n.* **1.** The quantity that a car can hold. **2.** The minimum weight necessary to ship freight at a reduced rate.

Car•los (kär′ləs, -lôs), Don. Count of Molina. 1788–1855. Spanish pretender to the throne who claimed the title (1833) and waged an unsuccessful civil war until 1840.

Car•lo•ta (kär-lô′tə). 1840–1927. Belgian-born empress of Mexico (1864–67) as the wife of Maximilian of Austria.

Car•lo•vin•gian (kär′lə-vĭn′jən, -jē-ən) *adj. & n.* Var. of **Carolingian.**

Carls•bad (kärlz′băd′). **1.** A city of S CA NNW of San Diego. Pop. 63,126. **2.** A city of SE NM on the Pecos R. Pop. 24,952. **3.** (*also* kärls′bät′). See **Karlovy Vary.**

Carlsbad Caverns. A group of limestone caverns in the Guadalupe Mts. of SE NM.

Carls•ru•he (kärlz′rōō′ə, kärls′-). See **Karlsruhe.**

Car•lyle (kär-līl′, kär′līl), **Thomas.** 1795–1881. British historian whose works include *The French Revolution* (1837).

car•mak•er (kär′mā′kər) *n.* An automobile manufacturer.

Car•mel. 1. (kär-mĕl′). Also **Car•mel-by-the-Sea** (-bī-*th*ə-sē′). A city of W CA on **Carmel Bay** at the S end of the Monterey Peninsula. Pop. 4,707. **2.** (kär′məl). A city of central IN, a suburb of Indianapolis. Pop. 25,380.

Car•mel (kär′məl), **Mount.** A limestone ridge of NW Israel extending from the Plain of Esdraelon to the Mediterranean.

Car•mel•ite (kär′mə-līt′) *n.* **1.** A monk or mendicant friar belonging to the order of Our Lady of Mount Carmel, founded in 1155. **2.** A member of a community of nuns of this order, founded in 1452. — **Car′mel•ite′** *adj.*

Car•mi•chael (kär′mī′kəl), **Hoagland "Hoagy" Howard.** 1899–1981. Amer. songwriter whose popular works include "Stardust" (1929).

car•min•a•tive (kär-mĭn′ə-tĭv, kär′mə-nā′-) *adj.* Inducing the expulsion of gas from the stomach and intestines. — *n.* A carminative drug or agent. [ME *carminatif* < OFr. < Lat. *carminātus*, p.part. of *carmināre*, to card wool < **carmen*, card for wool < *cārere*, to card.]

car•mine (kär′mĭn, -mīn′) *n.* **1.** *Color.* A strong to vivid red. **2.** A crimson pigment derived from cochineal. — *adj. Color.* Strong to vivid red. [Fr. *carmin* < Med.Lat. *carminium*, prob. blend of Ar. *qirmiz*, kermes; see KERMES, and Lat. *minium*, cinnabar; see MINIUM.]

car•nage (kär′nĭj) *n.* **1.** Massive slaughter, as in war; a massacre. **2.** Corpses, esp. of those killed in battle. [Fr. < OFr. < OItal. *carnaggio* < Med.Lat. *carnāticum*, meat < Lat. *carō*, *carn-*, flesh. See **sker-[1]*.**]

car•nal (kär′nəl) *adj.* **1.** Relating to the physical and esp. sexual appetites. **2.** Worldly or earthly; temporal. **3.** Of or relating to the body or flesh. [ME < ONFr. *carnel* < Lat. *carnālis* < Lat. *carō*, *carn-*, flesh. See **sker-[1]*.**] — **car•nal′i•ty** (kär-năl′ĭ-tē) *n.* — **car′nal•ly** *adv.*

car•nall•ite (kär′nə-līt′) *n.* A white, brownish, or reddish mineral, $KCl \cdot MgCl_2 \cdot 6H_2O$, an ore of potassium, used to manufacture potash salts. [After Rudolf von *Carnall* (1804–74), German mining engineer.]

car•nas•si•al (kär-năs′ē-əl) *adj.* Adapted for tearing apart flesh. — *n.* A carnassial tooth. [< Fr. *carnassier*, carnivorous < Prov. < *carnasso*, meat in abundance < *carn*, flesh < Lat. *carō*, *carn-*. See **sker-[1]*.**]

car•na•tion (kär-nā′shən) *n.* **1.a.** Any of numerous cultivated forms of a perennial plant *(Dianthus caryophyllus)* having showy flowers with fringed petals. **b.** A flower of this plant. **2.** A pinkish tint once used in painting. [< obsolete Fr., flesh-colored < OFr. (< OItal. *carnagione*, skin, complexion < *carne*, flesh) or < LLat. *carnātiō*, *carnātiōn-*, flesh, both < Lat. *carō*, *carn-*. See **sker-[1]*.**]

car•nau•ba (kär-nô′bə, -nou′-, -nōō′-) *n.* **1.** A Brazilian palm tree *(Copernicia prunifera)* having waxy fan-shaped leaves. **2.** A hard wax obtained from the leaves of this plant. [Port. < Tupi *carnaúba*.]

Car•ne•gie (kär′nə-gē, kär-nā′gē, -nĕg′ē), **Andrew.** 1835–1919. Scottish-born Amer. industrialist and philanthropist who amassed a fortune in the steel industry.

car•nel•ian (kär-nēl′yən) also **cor•nel•ian** (kôr-) *n.* A pale to deep red or reddish-brown variety of clear chalcedony, used in jewelry. [ME *corneline* < OFr. < *cornel*, cornel < Lat. *cornus*.]

car•net (kär-nā′) *n.* **1.** An official pass or permit, esp. one for crossing national boundaries. **2.** A book of postage stamps. [Fr., notebook, carnet < OFr. *quernet*, pocket notebook < *quaer*, quire. See QUIRE[1].]

Car•nic Alps (kär′nĭk). A range of the E Alps in S Austria and NE Italy rising to c. 2,782 m (9,121 ft).

Car•ni•o•la (kär′nē-ō′lə, kärn-yō′-). A mountainous region roughly coextensive with Slovenia; first settled by Celtic peoples. — **Car′ni•o′lan** *adj. & n.*

car•ni•tine (kär′nĭ-tēn′) *n.* A betaine commonly occurring in the liver and in skeletal muscle. [Ger. *Karnitin* < *Karnin*, a meat derivative < Lat. *carō*, *carn-*, flesh. See CARNAL.]

car•ni•val (kär′nə-vəl) *n.* **1.a.** A festival marked by merrymaking and feasting during the season just before Lent. **b.** Merrymaking and feasting just before Lent. **2.** A traveling amusement show usu. including rides, games, and sideshows. **3.** A festival or revel. [Ital. *carnevale* < OItal. *carnelevare*, Shrovetide : *carne*, meat (< Lat. *carō*, *carn-*; see **sker-[1]***) + *levare*, to remove (< Lat. *levāre*, to raise; see **leg^{w}h-***).]

car•ni•vore (kär′nə-vôr′, -vōr′) *n.* **1.** A flesh-eating animal. **2.** Any of various predatory, flesh-eating mammals of the order Carnivora, including the dogs, cats, bears, weasels, hyenas, and raccoons. **3.** An insectivorous plant. [< Fr., meat-eating < Lat. *carnivorus*. See CARNIVOROUS.]

car•niv•o•rous (kär-nĭv′ər-əs) *adj.* **1.** Of or relating to carnivores. **2.** Flesh-eating or predatory: *a carnivorous bird.* **3.** *Bot.* Capable of trapping insects or other small organisms and absorbing nutrients from them; insectivorous. [< Lat. *carnivorus* : *carō*, *carn-*, flesh; see **sker-[1]*** + *-vorus*, -vorous.] — **car•niv′o•rous•ly** *adv.* — **car•niv′o•rous•ness** *n.*

Car•not (kär-nō′), **Lazare Nicolas Marguerite.** 1753–1823. French military strategist for the Republican armies during the French Revolution.

Carnot, Nicolas Léonard Sadi. 1796–1832. French physicist and engineer who founded the science of thermodynamics.

car•no•tite (kär′nə-tīt′) *n.* A yellow ore of uranium and radium with composition $K(UO_2)_2(VO_4)_2 \cdot 3H_2O$. [Fr., after Marie Adolphe *Carnot* (1839–1920), French mining engineer.]

car•ny also **car•ney** (kär′nē) *n., pl.* **-nies** also **-neys.** *Informal.* **1.** A carnival. **2.** A person who works with a carnival.

car•ob (kăr′əb) *n.* **1.** An eastern Mediterranean evergreen tree *(Ceratonia siliqua)* in the pea family, having pinnately compound leaves and large pods. **2.** The pod of this plant, containing an edible pulp and seeds that yield a gum used as a food stabilizer. **3.** An edible powder or flour made from the ground seeds and pods of this plant. [ME *carabe* < OFr. *carobe* < Med.Lat. *carrūbium* < Ar. *ḫarrūbah*.]

ca•roche (kə-rōch′, -rōsh′) *n.* A stately carriage of the late 16th and 17th centuries. [Obsolete Fr. *carroche* < OItal. *carrozza*, ult. < Lat. *carrus*, a Gallic wagon. See **kers-*.**]

car•ol (kăr′əl) *n.* **1.** *Mus.* A song of praise or joy, esp. for Christmas. **2.** An old round dance often with singing. — *v.* **-oled, -ol•ing, -ols** also **-olled, -ol•ling, -ols.** — *intr.* **1.** To sing in a loud, joyous manner. **2.** To go from house to house singing Christmas songs. — *tr.* **1.** To celebrate in or as if in song. **2.** To sing loudly and joyously. [ME *carole*, carol dance < OFr., prob. < LLat. *choraula*, choral song, ult. < Gk.

ă pat	oi boy
ā pay	ou out
âr care	ŏŏ took
ä father	ōō boot
ĕ pet	ŭ cut
ē be	ûr urge
ĭ pit	th thin
ī pie	*th* this
îr pier	hw which
ŏ pot	zh vision
ō toe	ə about, item
ô paw	

Stress marks:
′ (primary);
′ (secondary), as in
dictionary (dĭk′shə-nĕr′ē)

khoraulēs, accompanist : *khoros*, choral dance; see CHORUS + *aulos*, flute.] — **car′ol•er** *n.*

Car•o•le•an (kăr′ə-lē′ən) *adj.* Relating to Charles I or II of England. [< Med.Lat. *Carolus*, Charles.]

Car•o•li•na. 1. (kăr′ə-lī′nə). An English colony of SE North America, first settled in 1653 and divided into North Carolina and South Carolina in 1729. **2.** (kä′rô-lē′nä). A city of NE Puerto Rico ESE of San Juan. Pop. 147,835.

Carolina allspice *n.* A species of sweet shrub *(Calycanthus floridus)* native chiefly to the southeast United States.

Carolina jasmine also **Carolina jessamine** *n.* Any of several poisonous woody evergreen vines of the genus *Gelsemium,* esp. *G. sempervirens* of the southeast United States having fragrant yellow funnel-shaped flowers.

Car•o•li•nas (kăr′ə-lī′nəz). The colonies (after 1729) or present-day states of North Carolina and South Carolina.

Carolina yellow jasmine *n.* See **Carolina jasmine.**

Car•o•line (kăr′ə-līn′, -lĭn) *adj.* Relating to Charles I or II of England. [Med.Lat. *Carolīnus* < *Carolus*, Charles.]

Caroline Islands. An archipelago of the W Pacific Ocean E of the Philippines; included in the U.S. Trust Terr. of the Pacific Is. in 1947.

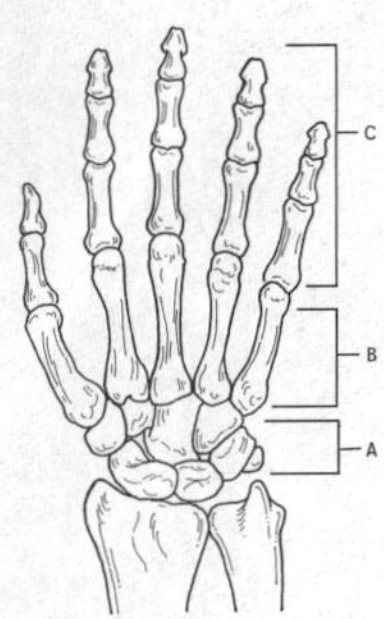

carpus
A. Carpus
B. Metacarpus
C. Phalanges

Car•o•lin•gian (kăr′ə-lĭn′-jən, -jē-ən) also **Car•lo•vin•gian** (kär′lə-vĭn′jən, -jē-ən) — *adj.* Of or relating to the Frankish dynasty founded by Pepin the Short in 751 and lasting until 987 in France and 911 in Germany. — *n.* A member of the Carolingian dynasty. [Fr. *Carolingien*, alteration of *Carlovingien*, blend of Med.Lat. *Carolus*, Charles, and Fr. *Mérovingien*, Merovingian.]

Car•o•lin•i•an (kăr′ə-lĭn′ē-ən) *adj.* **1.** Caroline. **2.** Of or relating to Charlemagne and his times. **3.** Of or relating to Carolina or the Carolinas. — *n.* A native or inhabitant of Carolina or the Carolinas.

car•om (kăr′əm) *n.* **1.** A collision followed by a rebound. **2.** *Games.* A shot, as in billiards, in which the cue ball successively strikes two other balls. — *v.* **-omed, -om•ing, -oms.** — *intr.* **1.** To collide and rebound; glance: *The car caromed off the guardrail.* **2.** *Games.* To make a carom, as in billiards. — *tr.* To cause to carom. [Short for *carambole*, a stroke at billiards < Fr., a billiard ball < Sp. *carambola*, a stroke at billiards, perh. < Port., carambola. See CARAMBOLA.]

Ca•ro•ní (kär′ə-nē′). A river rising in SE Venezuela and flowing 885 km (550 mi) N to join the Orinoco R.

car•o•tene (kăr′ə-tēn′) also **car•o•tin** (-tĭn) *n.* An orange-yellow to red crystalline pigment, $C_{40}H_{56}$, found in animal tissue and certain plants and converted to vitamin A in the liver. [Ger. *Karotin* < Lat. *carōta*, carrot. See CARROT.]

ca•rot•e•noid (kə-rŏt′n-oid′) *n.* Any of a class of yellow to red pigments, including the carotenes and the xanthophylls. — *adj.* Of or relating to such a pigment.

carrel

Ca•roth•ers (kə-rŭ*th*′ərz), **Wallace Hume.** 1896–1937. Amer. chemist who developed the synthetic material nylon.

ca•rot•id (kə-rŏt′ĭd) *n.* Either of the two major arteries, one on each side of the neck, that carry blood to the head. — *adj.* Of or relating to either of these arteries. [Fr. *carotide* < Gk. *karōtides*, carotid arteries < *karoun*, to stupefy. See **ker-**[1]***.**]

ca•rous•al (kə-rou′zəl) *n.* A riotous drinking party; boisterous merrymaking; revelry.

ca•rouse (kə-rouz′) *n.* Carousal. — *intr.v.* **-roused, -rous•ing, -rous•es. 1.** To engage in carousal. **2.** To drink excessively. [Ger. *garaus*, all out, drink up : *gar*, completely (< MHGer. < OHGer. *garo*) + *aus*, out, up (< MHGer. *ūz* < OHGer. *ūz*; see **ud-***).] — **ca•rous′er** *n.*

car•ou•sel or **car•rou•sel** (kăr′ə-sĕl′, -zĕl′) *n.* **1.** A merry-go-round. **2.** A circular conveyor to display or rotate objects. [Fr. *carrousel* < Ital. *carosello*, tilting match.]

carp[1] (kärp) *intr.v.* **carped, carp•ing, carps.** To find fault in a disagreeable manner; complain fretfully. [ME *carpen* < ON *karpa*, to boast.] — **carp′er** *n.*

carriage

carp[2] (kärp) *n., pl.* **carp** or **carps. 1.** An edible freshwater fish *(Cyprinus carpio)* of Europe and Asia. **2.** Any of various fishes of the family Cyprinidae. [ME *carpe* < OFr. *carpe* < Med. Lat. *carpa*, of Gmc. orig.]

–carp *suff.* Fruit; part of a fruit; fruitlike structure: *mesocarp.* [NLat. *-carpium* < Gk. *-karpion* < *karpos*, fruit. See **kerp-*.**]

car•pac•cio (kär-pä′chō) *n.* Very thinly sliced raw beef or tuna garnished with a sauce. [Ital., after Vittore CARPACCIO.]

Car•pac•cio (kär-pä′chē-ō, -chô), **Vittore.** 1460?–1525? Italian painter noted for his narrative series on religious subjects.

car•pal (kär′pəl) *adj.* Of, relating to, or near the carpus. — *n.* A bone of the carpus. [NLat. *carpālis* < Gk. *karpos*, wrist.]

carpal tunnel syndrome *n.* Pain, numbness, and muscular weakness in the thumb, index, and middle fingers, caused by compression of a major sensorimotor nerve at the wrist usu. due to inflammation or trauma.

Car•pa•thi•an Mountains (kär-pā′thē-ən). A major mountain system of central Europe extending in an arc c. 2,253 km (1,400 mi) long through Slovakia, S Poland, W Ukraine, and NE Romania.

carrick bend

car•pe di•em (kär′pĕ dē′ĕm′, -əm, dī′-) *n.* The admonition to seize the moment. [Lat. : *carpe*, seize + *diem*, day.]

car•pel (kär′pəl) *n.* One of the structural units of a pistil, representing a modified ovule-bearing leaf. [NLat. *carpellum* < Gk. *karpos*, fruit. See **kerp-*.**] — **car′pel•lar′y** (-pə-lĕr′ē) *adj.*

car•pel•late (kär′pə-lāt′, -lĭt) *adj. Bot.* Having carpels; pistillate.

Car•pen•tar•i•a (kär′pən-târ′ē-ə), **Gulf of.** A wide inlet of the Arafura Sea indenting the N coast of Australia.

car•pen•ter (kär′pən-tər) *n.* A worker who makes, finishes, and repairs wooden structures. — *v.* **-tered, -ter•ing, -ters.** — *tr.* To make, finish, or repair (wooden structures). — *intr.* To work as a carpenter. [ME < AN < Lat. *carpentārius (artifex)*, (maker) of a carriage < *carpentum*, a two-wheeled carriage, of Celt. orig. See **kers-*.**] — **car′pen•try** (-trē) *n.*

carpenter ant *n.* Any of various large ants of the genus *Camponotus* that nest in and are destructive to wood.

carpenter bee *n.* Any of various solitary bees of the family Apidae that bore tunnels into wood to lay their eggs.

Car•pen•ters•ville (kär′pən-tərz-vĭl′). A village of NE Illinois WNW of Chicago; settled in 1834. Pop. 23,049.

car•pet (kär′pĭt) *n.* **1.a.** A thick heavy covering for a floor, usu. made of woven wool or synthetic fibers; a rug. **b.** The fabric used for this floor covering. **2.** A surface or surface covering that is similar to a rug: *a carpet of leaves.* — *tr.v.* **-pet•ed, -pet•ing, -pets.** To cover with or as if with a carpet. — ***idiom.* on the carpet. 1.** In a position of being reprimanded by one in authority. **2.** Under discussion or consideration. [ME < OFr. *carpite* < Med.Lat. *carpīta* < OItal. *carpita* < *carpire*, to pluck < Lat. *carpere*. See **kerp-*.**]

car•pet•bag (kär′pĭt-băg′) *n.* A traveling bag made of carpet fabric. — *adj.* Of or relating to carpetbaggers.

car•pet•bag•ger (kär′pĭt-băg′ər) *n.* **1.** A Northerner who went to the South after the Civil War for political or financial advantage. **2.** An outsider who presumptuously seeks a position or success in a new locality. — **car′pet•bag′ger•y** *n.*

carpet beetle *n.* Any of various small beetles of the genera *Anthrenus* and *Attagenus,* having larvae that are injurious to fabrics and furs.

car•pet-bomb (kär′pĭt-bŏm′) *tr. & intr.v.* **-bombed, -bomb•ing, -bombs.** To bomb in a systematic pattern, so as to devastate a large area. — **car′pet-bomb′ing** *n.*

car•pet•ing (kär′pĭ-tĭng) *n.* **1.** Material used for carpets. **2.** A carpet or carpets.

car•pet•weed (kär′pĭt-wēd′) *n.* A widespread North American annual plant *(Mollugo verticillata)* having whorled leaves and greenish-white flowers.

carp•ing (kär′pĭng) *adj.* Naggingly critical or complaining. — **carp′ing•ly** *adv.*

carpo– *pref.* Fruit: *carpophore.* [Gk. *karpo-* < *karpos*, fruit. See **kerp-*.**]

car pool *n.* **1.** An arrangement whereby several people travel in one vehicle, sharing costs and often vehicles. **2.** A group in a car pool. — **car′-pool′** *v.* — **car′-pool′er** *n.*

car•poph•a•gous (kär-pŏf′ə-gəs) *adj.* Feeding on fruit.

car•po•phore (kär′pə-fôr′, -fōr′) *n.* A slender stalk that supports each half of a dehisced fruit in many members of the parsley family.

car•port (kär′pôrt′, -pōrt′) *n.* An open-sided shelter for an automotive vehicle, formed by a projecting roof.

–carpous or **–carpic** *suff.* A specified number or kind of carpel or fruit: *apocarpous.* [< NLat. *-carpus* < Gk. *karpos*, fruit. See **kerp-*.**]

car•pus (kär′pəs) *n., pl.* **-pi** (-pī′). **1.** The group of eight bones forming the joint between the forearm and the hand. **2.** A joint in quadrupeds corresponding to the wrist. [NLat. < Gk. *karpos*, wrist.]

Car•rac•ci (kə-rä′chē, kä-rät′-). Family of Bolognese painters, including **Agostino** (1557–1602), his brother **Annibale** (1560–1609), and their cousin **Lodovico** (1555–1619), whose works provided a transition to the baroque style.

car•rack also **car•ack** (kăr′ək) *n. Naut.* A large galleon used in the 14th, 15th, and 16th centuries. [ME *carike* < Med.Lat. *carrica* and < OFr. *caraque* (< OSp. *carraca*), both < Ar. *qarāqīr*, pl. of *qurqūr*.]

car•ra•geen also **car•ra•gheen** (kăr′ə-gēn′) *n.* See **Irish moss.** [After *Carragheen*, a village of SE Ireland.]

car•ra•geen•an also **car•ra•geen•in** (kăr′ə-gē′nən) *n.* Any of a group of colloids derived from Irish moss and several other red algae, used esp. as a thickening, stabilizing, or emulsifying agent in food products.

Car•ra•ra (kə-rär′ə, kär-rä′rä). A city of N Italy E of Genoa; famous for the marble quarried nearby. Pop. 68,460.

car•re•four (kăr′ə-fo͝or′) *n.* **1.** A crossroads. **2.** A public square; a plaza. [Fr. < OFr. *carrefor* < Lat. *quadrifurcus*, four-forked : *quadri-*, quadri- + *furca*, fork.]

car•rel also **car•rell** (kăr′əl) *n.* A partitioned nook in or near the stacks in a library, used for private study. [ME *carole*, round dance ring, circle, stall for study. See CAROL.]

Car•rel (kə-rĕl′, kăr′əl), **Alexis.** 1873–1944. French-born Amer. surgeon and biologist who won a 1912 Nobel Prize.

car•riage (kăr′ĭj) *n.* **1.** A wheeled vehicle, esp. a four-wheeled horse-drawn passenger vehicle. **2.** *Chiefly British.* A railroad passenger car. **3.** A baby carriage. **4.** A wheeled support or frame for carrying a heavy object, such as a cannon. **5.** A moving part of a machine for holding or shifting another part. **6.a.** The act or process of transporting or carrying. **b.** (kăr′ē-ĭj). The cost of or the charge for transporting. **7.** The manner of holding and moving one's head and body; bearing. **8.** *Archaic.* Management; administration. [ME *cariage* < ONFr. < *carier*, to carry. See CARRY.]

carriage dog *n.* See **Dalmatian** 2.

carriage trade *n.* Wealthy patrons or customers, as of a store.

car•rick bend (kăr′ĭk) *n. Naut.* A type of knot used to fasten two cables or hawsers together. [< obsolete *carrick*, var. of CARRACK.]

car•ri•er (kăr′ē-ər) *n.* **1.** One that transports or conveys: *baggage carriers.* **2.** One that deals in the transport of passengers or goods. **3.** A mechanism or device by which something is conveyed or conducted. **4.** *Medic.* A person or an animal that shows no symptoms of a disease but harbors the infectious agent and is capable of transmitting it. **5.** *Genet.* An individual that carries one gene for a particular recessive trait and when mated with another carrier can produce offspring that express the trait. **6.** *Electron.* **a.** A carrier wave. **b.** A charge-carrying entity, esp. an electron or a hole in a semiconductor. **7.** An aircraft carrier.

carrier pigeon *n.* **1.** A homing pigeon, esp. one trained to carry messages. **2.** Any of various large domestic pigeons having a prominent wattle.

carrier wave *n.* An electromagnetic wave that can be modulated, as in frequency, amplitude, or phase, to transmit speech, music, images, or other signals.

car•ri•ole (kăr′ē-ōl′) *n.* Var. of **cariole**.

car•ri•on (kăr′ē-ən) *n.* Dead and decaying flesh. — *adj.* **1.** Of or similar to carrion. **2.** Feeding on carrion. [ME *careine* < AN < VLat. **carōnia* < Lat. *carō*, flesh. See **sker-¹***.]

carrion crow *n.* A common European crow *(Corvus corone)* having glossy black plumage.

carrion flower *n.* Any of several North American plants of the genus *Smilax*, esp. *S. herbacea,* an herbaceous tendril-bearing vine having clusters of small greenish flowers with the odor of decaying flesh.

Car•roll (kăr′əl), **Charles.** "Carroll of Carrollton." 1737–1832. Amer. Revolutionary leader who signed the Declaration of Independence (1776).

Carroll, Lewis. See Charles Lutwidge **Dodgson.**

Car•roll•ton (kăr′əl-tən). A city of N TX, a suburb of Dallas. Pop. 82,169.

car•rot (kăr′ət) *n.* **1.** A biennial Eurasian plant *(Daucus carota* subsp. *sativus)* in the parsley family, widely cultivated as an annual for its edible taproot. **2.** The fleshy orange root of this plant, eaten as a vegetable. **3.** Queen Anne's lace. **4.** A reward offered for desired behavior; an inducement. [Fr. *carotte* < OFr. *garroite* < Lat. *carōta* < Gk. *karōton.* See **ker-¹***.]

car•rot-and-stick (kăr′ət-ən-stĭk′) *adj.* Combining a promised reward with a threatened penalty.

car•rot•y (kăr′ə-tē) *adj.* **1.** Bright orange in color. **2.** Having carrot-colored hair.

car•rou•sel (kăr′ə-sĕl′, -zĕl′) *n.* Var. of **carousel.**

car•ry (kăr′ē) *v.* **-ried, -ry•ing, -ries.** — *tr.* **1.** To hold or support while moving; bear. **2.a.** To take from one place to another; transport: *a train carrying freight.* **b.** *Chiefly Southern U.S.* To transport (someone) in a motor vehicle. **3.** To serve as a means for the conveyance of; transmit: *pipes that carry water.* **4.a.** To communicate; pass on. **b.** To express or contain: *Her words carried a threat.* **5.** To have (something) on the surface or skin; bear. **6.** To hold or be capable of holding. **7.** To support the weight or responsibility of. **8.** To keep or have on one's person. **9.** To be pregnant with. **10.a.** To hold and move (the body or a part of it) in a particular way. **b.** To behave or conduct (oneself) in a specified manner. **11.** To extend or continue in space, time, or degree: *carry a joke too far.* **12.a.** To give impetus to; propel. **b.** To take further; advance: *carry a cause.* **13.** To take or seize, esp. by force; capture. **14.a.** To be successful in; win. **b.** To gain victory, support, or acceptance for. **c.** To win a majority of the votes in: *carried ten states.* **d.** To gain the sympathy of; win over. **15.** To include or keep on a list: *carried six workers on the payroll.* **16.a.** To have as an attribute or accompaniment. **b.** To involve as a condition, consequence, or effect: *The crime carried a five-year sentence.* **17.** To transfer from one place, as a column or page, to another. **18.** To keep in stock; offer for sale. **19.** To keep in one's accounts as a debtor. **20.a.** To maintain or support (one that is less competent, for example). **b.** To compensate for (a weaker member or partner) by one's performance. **21.** To place before the public; print or broadcast. **22.** To produce as a crop. **23.** To provide forage for: *land that carries sheep.* **24.** To sing on key. **25.** *Sports.* **a.** To cover (a distance) or advance beyond (a point or object) in one golf stroke. **b.** *Football.* To hold and rush with (the ball). **c.** *Basketball.* To palm (the ball) in violation of the rules. — *intr.* **1.** To act as a bearer. **2.** To be transmitted or conveyed; cover a range: *a voice that carries well.* **3.** To admit of being transported. **4.** To hold the neck and head in a certain way. Used of a horse. **5.** To be accepted or approved. — *n., pl.* **-ries. 1.** The act or process of carrying.

2. A portage, as between two bodies of water. **3.a.** The range of a gun or projectile. **b.** The distance traveled by a hurled or struck ball. **c.** Reach; projection: *a voice with great carry.* **4.** *Football.* An act of rushing with the ball. ♦ *phrasal verbs.* **carry away.** To move or excite greatly. **carry forward.** *Accounting.* To transfer (an entry) to the next column, page, or book, or to ... **2.** To handle ... account. **carry off.** ... the death of. **2.** To handle ... **carry on. 1.** ... maintain. **2.** To engage in. ... persevere. **4.** To behave in an excited ... **carry out. 1.** To put into practice ... without ... obey. **3.** To bring to a conclusion; ... carry over. **1.** *Accounting.* **a.** To transfer (an amount) to the ... page, or book relating to the same account ... **b.** To ... merchandise or other goods) for a subsequent ... deduct (a loss, for example) in determining ... subsequent period. **3.** To persist to another ... **carry through. 1.** To accomplish; complete ... persist. **3.** To enable to endure; sustain. — *idiom* ... the) torch. To feel a painful, unreciprocated ... day. To be victorious; win. [ME *carien* < O... *carre*, cart. See CAR.]

car•ry•all (kăr′ē-ôl′) *n.* **1.** A large receptacle, such ... used to carry things around. **2.** A closed automobile ... lengthwise seats facing each other. **3.** A covered ... carriage with two seats. [Alteration of CARIOLE.]

car•ry•ing capacity (kăr′ē-ĭng) *n.* **1.** The maximum ... of persons or things that a vehicle or a receptacle can ... **2.** *Ecol.* The maximum number of individuals or inhabit... that an environment can support without detrimental effe...

carrying charge *n.* The interest charged on the balance ow... when paying in installments.

car•ry•on (kăr′ē-ŏn′) *adj.* Small or compact enough to be carried aboard an airplane, a train, or a bus by a passenger. — *n.* A piece of carryon luggage.

car•ry•out (kăr′ē-out′) *adj.* Intended to be consumed away from the place of sale; takeout. — *n.* A carryout item of food.

car•ry•o•ver (kăr′ē-ō′vər) *n.* **1.** Something that is transferred or extended from an earlier time or another place. **2.** *Accounting.* A sum transferred to a new column, page, or book relating to the same account.

car seat *n.* A small removable seat that fastens to the seat of a vehicle and is used for securing young children.

car•sick (kär′sĭk′) *adj.* Suffering from motion sickness caused by travel in a motor vehicle. — **car′sick′ness** *n.*

Car•son (kär′sən). A city of S CA, a suburb of Los Angeles. Pop. 83,995.

Carson, Christopher ("Kit"). 1809–68. Amer. pioneer who was a renowned guide and a Union general in the Civil War.

Carson, Johnny. b. 1925. Amer. comedian and long-time host of television's *The Tonight Show* (1962–92).

Carson, Rachel Louise. 1907–64. Amer. environmentalist whose works include *Silent Spring* (1962).

Carson City. The cap. of NV, in the W part near the CA border; laid out in 1858. Pop. 40,443.

cart (kärt) *n.* **1.** A small wheeled vehicle typically pushed by hand. **2.** A two-wheeled vehicle drawn by an animal and used in farm work and for transporting goods. **3.a.** An open two-wheeled carriage. **b.** A light motorized vehicle. — *tr.v.* **cart•ed, cart•ing, carts. 1.** To convey in a cart or truck: *cart away garbage.* **2.** To convey laboriously or unceremoniously; lug: *carted them off.* [ME, wagon < OE *cræt* and < ON *kartr.*] — **cart′a•ble** *adj.* — **cart′er** *n.*

cart•age (kär′tĭj) *n.* **1.** The act or process of carting. **2.** The cost of carting.

Car•ta•ge•na (kär′tə-gā′nə, -jē′-, -hĕ′nä). **1.** A city of NW Colombia on the **Bay of Cartagena**, an inlet of the Caribbean; founded 1533. Pop. 495,028. **2.** A city of SE Spain on the Mediterranean Sea SSE of Murcia; settled c. 225 B.C. Pop. 142,300.

Carte (kärt), **Richard D'Oyly.** 1844–1901. British producer, esp. of the works of W.S. Gilbert and Arthur Sullivan.

carte blanche (kärt blänsh′, blänch′, blănch′) *n., pl.* **cartes blanches** (kärt blänsh′, kärts blänch′, blănch′). Unrestricted power or authority. [Fr. : *carte*, ticket + *blanche*, blank.]

car•tel (kär-tĕl′) *n.* **1.** A combination of independent business organizations formed to regulate production, pricing, and marketing of goods. **2.** An official agreement between governments at war, esp. one concerning the exchange of prisoners. **3.** A group of factions or nations united in a common cause; a bloc. [Ger. *Kartell* < Fr. *cartel* < Ital. *cartello*, placard < Med.Lat. *cartellus*, charter, dim. of Lat. *charta, carta,* paper made from papyrus. See CARD¹.]

Car•ter (kär′tər), **James Earl, Jr.** "Jimmy." b. 1924. The 39th President of the U.S. (1977–81), who negotiated the Camp David accords between Egypt and Israel (1979).

Carter, Rosalynn Smith. b. 1928. First Lady of the U.S. (1977–81) who worked on better care for the elderly and emotionally disadvantaged.

Car•ter•et (kär′tə-rĕt′). An industrial borough of NE NJ S of Elizabeth opposite Staten I. Pop. 19,025.

Car•ter•et (kär′tər-ĭt), **John.** 1690–1763. British politician

Photo...

Jimmy Carter

Rosalynn Carter

ă pat	oi boy
ā pay	ou out
âr care	o͝o took
ä father	o͞o boot
ĕ pet	ŭ cut
ē be	ûr urge
ĭ pit	th thin
ī pie	*th* this
îr pier	hw which
ŏ pot	zh vision
ō toe	ə about,
ô paw	item

Stress marks:
′ (primary);
′ (secondary), as in
dictionary (dĭk′shə-nĕr′ē)

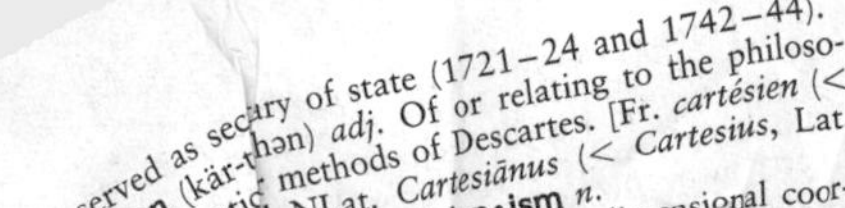

who served as sec[ret]ary of state (1721–24 and 1742–44).

Car•te•sian (kär-tē′zhən) *adj.* Of or relating to the philosophy, mathematical methods of Descartes. [Fr. *cartésien* (< René DESCARTES ... NLat. *Cartesiānus* (< *Cartesius*, Lat. form of D[escartes].] **—Car•te′sian•ism** *n.*

Cartesian [coordinate] system *n.* **1.** A two-dimensional coor[dinate system] in which the coordinates of a [point] in a plane [are its dist]ances from two perpendicul[ar lines] that intersect at an origin. **2.** A three-dimensional [coordinate system] in which the coordinates of a point [are] its distances from each [of three] perpendic[ular planes that] intersect at an origin.

Cartesian product [*n.*] ... all pairs of elements (x, y) ... given sets, X and Y, such that x ... to Y.

[Car•thage] ... An ancient city and state of N Africa on ... NE of modern Tunis; founded by Phoenicians ... 9th cent. B.C. **—Car′tha•gin′i•an** (kär′thə-jĭn′-...) *adj.* & *n.*

[Car•thu]•sian (kär-tho͞o′zhən) *Rom. Cath. Ch.* —*n.* A mem[be]r of a contemplative order founded in the 11th century by Saint Bruno. —*adj.* Of or relating to the Carthusian order. [Med.Lat. *Carthusiānus* < *Cartusia*, Chartreuse, France.]

Car•tier (kär-tyā′, kär′tē-ā′), Sir **George Étienne.** 1814–73. Prime minister of Canada (1858–62).

Cartier, Jacques. 1491–1557. French explorer who navigated the St. Lawrence R. (1535) and claimed the region for France.

Car•tier-Bres•son (kär-tyā′brĕ-sôN′), **Henri.** b. 1908. French photographer noted for his images of daily life.

car•ti•lage (kär′tl-ĭj) *n.* A tough, elastic, fibrous connective tissue found in body parts such as the joints, outer ear, and larynx. [ME < OFr. < Lat. *cartilāgō, cartilāgin-*.]

cartilage bone *n.* A bone developed from cartilage.

car•ti•lag•i•nous (kär′tl-ăj′ə-nəs) *adj.* **1.** Of, relating to, or consisting of cartilage. **2.** Having a skeleton consisting mainly of cartilage. **3.** Having the texture of cartilage.

cartilaginous fish *n.* A fish whose skeleton is mainly cartilage, esp. one of the class Chondrichthyes, such as a ray.

cart•load (kärt′lōd′) *n.* The amount that a cart can carry.

car•to•gram (kär′tə-grăm′) *n.* A presentation of statistical data in geographic distribution on a map. [Fr. *cartogramme* : *carte*, map (< OFr., card; see CARD[1]) + *-gramme*, a record (< LLat. *gramma*, something written; see -GRAM).]

car•tog•ra•phy (kär-tŏg′rə-fē) *n.* The art or technique of making maps or charts. [Fr. *cartographie* : *carte*, map (< OFr.; see CARD[1]) + *-graphie*, writing (< Gk. *graphia*; see -GRAPHY).] **—car•tog′ra•pher** *n.* **—car′to•graph′ic** (kär′tə-grăf′ĭk), **car′to•graph′i•cal** *adj.*

car•ton (kär′tn) *n.* **1.** Any of various containers made from cardboard or coated paper. **2.** The contents of a carton. —*tr.v.* **-toned, -ton•ing, -tons.** To place (something) in a carton. [Fr. < Ital. *cartone*, pasteboard, aug. of *carta*, card, paper < Lat. *charta, carta*, paper made from papyrus. See CARD[1].]

car•toon (kär-to͞on′) *n.* **1.** A drawing depicting a humorous situation, often accompanied by a caption. **2.** A drawing representing current public figures or issues symbolically and often satirically. **3.** A preliminary sketch similar in size to the work, such as a fresco, that is to be copied from it. **4.** An animated cartoon. **5.** A comic strip. —*v.* **-tooned, -toon•ing, -toons.** —*tr.* To draw a humorous or satirical representation of; caricature. —*intr.* To make humorous or satirical drawings. [Fr. *carton*, drawing < Ital. *cartone*, pasteboard. See CARTON.] **—car•toon′ish** *adj.* **—car•toon′ist** *n.*

car•touche or **car•touch** (kär-to͞osh′) *n.* **1.** A scrolllike or oval tablet or figure, used as an ornament or to bear an inscription. **2.** An oval or oblong figure in ancient Egyptian hieroglyphics that encloses characters expressing the names of rulers or gods. **3.** A heavy paper cartridge case. [Fr. < Ital. *cartoccio*, paper cornet < *carta*, card, paper. See CARTON.]

car•tridge (kär′trĭj) *n.* **1.a.** A cylindrical casing containing the primer and charge of ammunition for firearms. **b.** Such a casing fitted with a bullet. **2.** A case filled with high explosives, used in blasting. **3.** A modular unit designed to be inserted into a larger piece of equipment: *an ink cartridge.* **4.** A removable case containing the stylus and circuitry in a phonograph pickup. **5.** A case containing magnetic tape in a reel; a cassette. **6.** A lightproof case with photographic film that can be loaded directly into a camera. [Alteration of earlier *cartage*, alteration of Fr. *cartouche* < Ital. *cartuccio*, var. of *cartoccio*, roll of paper. See CARTOUCHE.]

cartridge belt *n.* A belt with loops or pockets for carrying ammunition or other kinds of equipment.

cartridge clip *n.* A metal container or frame for holding cartridges to be loaded into an automatic rifle or pistol.

car•tu•lar•y also **char•tu•lar•y** (kär′chə-lĕr′ē) *n.*, *pl.* **-ies.** A register of deeds or charters. [ME *cartularie*, collection of documents < Med.Lat. *cartulārium* < Lat. *cartula, chartula*, document. See CHARTER.]

cart•wheel (kärt′hwēl′, -wēl′) *n.* **1.** A handspring in which the body turns over sideways with the arms and legs spread like the spokes of a wheel. **2.** *Slang.* A large coin.

Cart•wright (kärt′rīt′), **Edmund.** 1743–1823. British cleric and inventor of the power loom (1785–90).

Enrico Caruso

George Washington Carver

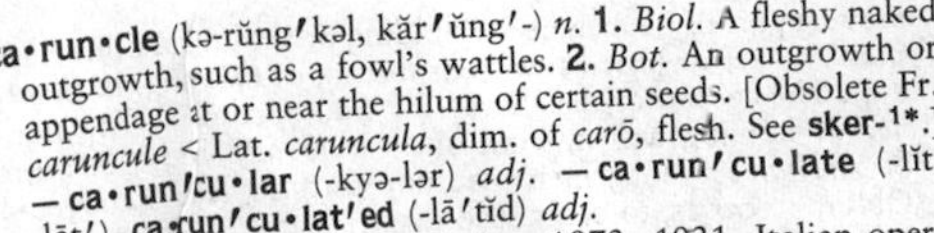

ca•run•cle (kə-rŭng′kəl, kăr′ŭng′-) *n.* **1.** *Biol.* A fleshy naked outgrowth, such as a fowl's wattles. **2.** *Bot.* An outgrowth or appendage at or near the hilum of certain seeds. [Obsolete Fr. *caruncule* < Lat. *caruncula*, dim. of *carō*, flesh. See **sker-**[1]*.] **—ca•run′cu•lar** (-kyə-lər) *adj.* **—ca•run′cu•late** (-lĭt, -lāt′), **ca•run′cu•lat′ed** (-lā′tĭd) *adj.*

Ca•ru•so (kə-ro͞o′sō, -zō), **Enrico.** 1873–1921. Italian operatic tenor who is considered one of the greatest singers ever.

car•va•crol (kär′və-krôl′, -krōl′) *n.* An aromatic phenol, $C_{10}H_4O$, used in flavorings and fungicides. [NLat. *carvi* (specific epithet of *(Carum) carvi*, caraway < Med.Lat.; see CARAWAY) + Lat. *ācer, acr-*, sharp; see **ak-*** + -OL[1].]

carve (kärv) *v.* **carved, carv•ing, carves.** —*tr.* **1.a.** To divide into pieces by cutting; slice. **b.** To divide by parceling out. **2.** To cut into a desired shape; fashion by cutting: *carve the wood into a figure.* **3.** To make or form by or as if by cutting: *carved out an empire.* **4.** To decorate by cutting and shaping carefully. —*intr.* **1.** To engrave or cut figures as an art, a hobby, or a trade. **2.** To slice and serve meat or poultry. [ME *kerven* < OE *ceorfan*. See **gerbh-***.] **—carv′er** *n.*

car•vel (kär′vəl, -vĕl′) *n.* Var. of **caravel.**

car•vel-built (kär′vəl-bĭlt′, -vĕl′-) *adj. Naut.* Built with the hull planks lying flush or edge to edge rather than overlapping: *a carvel-built ship.*

carv•en (kär′vən) *v. Archaic.* A p.t. and p.part. of **carve.** —*adj.* Wrought or decorated by carving.

Car•ver (kär′vər), **George Washington.** 1864?–1943. Amer. botanist, agricultural chemist, and educator who developed hundreds of uses for the peanut, soybean, and sweet potato.

Carver, John. 1576?–1621. English-born Pilgrim colonist who was the first governor of Plymouth Colony (1620–21).

carv•ing (kär′vĭng) *n.* **1.** The cutting of material such as stone or wood in order to form a figure or design. **2.** A figure or design formed by this kind of cutting.

car wash *n.* An area or business equipped for cleaning and washing motor vehicles.

Car•y (kăr′ē). A town of E-central NC, a suburb of Raleigh. Pop. 43,858.

Cary, (Arthur) Joyce (Lunel). 1888–1957. British writer whose novels include *The Horse's Mouth* (1944).

car•y•at•id (kăr′ē-ăt′ĭd) *n.*, *pl.* **-ids** or **-i•des** (-ĭ-dēz′). *Archit.* A supporting column sculptured in the form of a draped female figure. [< Lat. *Caryātides*, maidens of Caryae, caryatids < Gk. *Karuatides* < *Karuai*, Caryae, a village of Laconia in S Greece.] **—car′y•at′i•dal** (-ĭ-dəl), **car′y•at′i•de′an** (-ĭ-dē′ən), **car′y•a•tid′ic** (-ə-tĭd′ĭk) *adj.*

caryo– *pref.* Var. of **karyo–.**

car•y•op•sis (kăr′ē-ŏp′sĭs) *n.*, *pl.* **-op•ses** (-ŏp′sēz′) or **-op•si•des** (-ŏp′sĭ-dēz′). See **grain** 1a. [*cary(o)-*, var. of KARYO– + -OPSIS.]

ca•sa•ba also **cas•sa•ba** (kə-sä′bə) *n.* A variety of winter melon *(Cucumis melo* var. *Inodorus)* having a yellow rind and whitish flesh. [After *Kasaba* (Turgutlu), a city of W Turkey.]

Cas•a•blan•ca (kăs′ə-blăng′kə, kä′sə-bläng′kə). A city of NW Morocco on the Atlantic Ocean SSW of Tangier; a center of French influence in Africa after 1907. Pop. 2,139,204.

Ca•sals (kə-sălz′, -sälz′), **Pablo.** 1876–1973. Spanish cellist considered the greatest of his time.

Cas•a•no•va (kăs′ə-nō′və, kăz′-) *n.* **1.** A man who is amorously and gallantly attentive to women. **2.** A promiscuous man. [After Giovanni Jacopo CASANOVA DE SEINGALT.]

Cas•a•no•va de Sein•galt (kăs′ə-nō′və də săN-gält′, kăz′-, kä′sä-nô′vä), **Giovanni Jacopo.** 1725–98. Italian adventurer who established a legendary reputation as a lover.

Cas•bah also **Kas•bah** (kăz′bä′, käz′-) *n.* **1.** A castle or palace in northern Africa. **2.** Often **casbah.** The older section of a city in northern Africa or the Middle East. [Fr. < Ar. dial. *qaṣbah* < Ar. *qaṣabah*, fortress.]

cas•cade (kă-skād′) *n.* **1.** A waterfall or a series of small waterfalls over steep rocks. **2.** Something, such as lace, thought to resemble a cascade. **3.** A succession of stages, processes, or units. **4.** *Electron.* A series of components or networks, the output of each serving as the input for the next. —*intr.* & *tr.v.* **-cad•ed, -cad•ing, -cades.** To fall or cause to fall in or as if in a cascade. [Fr. < Ital. *cascata* < *cascare*, to fall < VLat. **casicāre* < Lat. *cadere*. See **kad-***.]

Cas•cade Range (kă-skād′). A mountain chain of W Canada and the U.S. extending c. 1,126 km (700 mi) S from British Columbia to N CA, where it joins the Sierra Nevada.

cas•car•a (kă-skăr′ə) *n.* A buckthorn *(Rhamnus purshiana)* native to northwest North America whose bark is the source of cascara sagrada. [Sp. *cáscara*, bark < *cascar*, to break off < VLat. **quassicāre* < Lat. *quassāre*, freq. of *quatere*, to shake. See **kwēt-***.]

cascara sa•gra•da (sə-grä′də) *n.* The dried bark of the cascara buckthorn, used as a laxative. [Am.Sp. *cáscara sagrada* : Sp. *cáscara*, bark + Sp. *sagrada*, sacred.]

cas•ca•ril•la (kăs′kə-rĭl′ə) *n.* **1.** A tropical shrub or tree *(Croton eluteria)* native to the West Indies and northern South America and having a bark that yields an aromatic oil used as a flavoring and fragrance. **2.** The bark of this plant. [Sp., dim. of *cáscara*, bark. See CASCARA.]

Cas•co Bay (kăsʹkō). A deep inlet of the Atlantic Ocean in SW Maine.

case[1] (kās) *n.* **1.** An instance of something; an occurrence; an example. **2.** An occurrence of a disease or disorder. **3.** A set of circumstances or a state of affairs; a situation. **4.** Actual fact; reality: *It proved to be the case.* **5.** A question or problem; a matter: *It is a case of honor.* **6.** A situation that requires investigation, esp. by an official body. **7.** *Law.* **a.** An action or a suit or just grounds for an action. **b.** The facts or evidence offered in support of a claim. **8.** A set of reasons or supporting facts; an argument. **9.** A person or group of persons being assisted, treated, or studied, as by a physician or social worker. **10.** *Informal.* A peculiar or eccentric person; a character. **11.** *Ling.* **a.** The syntactic relationship of a noun, a pronoun, or a determiner to the other words of a sentence, indicated by declensional endings, by the position of the words within the sentence, by prepositions, or by postpositions. **b.** The form or position of a word that indicates this relationship. **c.** Such forms, positions, and relationships considered as a group. **d.** A pattern of inflection of nouns, pronouns, and adjectives to express different syntactic functions in a sentence. **e.** The form of such an inflected word. —*tr.v.* **cased, cas•ing, cas•es.** *Informal.* To examine carefully, as in planning a crime. —***idioms.*** **in any case.** Regardless of what has occurred or will occur. **in case. 1.** If it happens that; if. **2.** As a precaution. **in case of.** If there should happen to be. [ME *cas* < OFr. < Lat. *cāsus* < p.part. of *cadere*, to fall. See **kad-***.]

case[2] (kās) *n.* **1.** A container; a receptacle. **2.** A container with its contents. **3.** A decorative or protective covering or cover. **4.** A set or pair: *a case of pistols.* **5.** The frame or framework, as of a door. **6.** The surface or outer layer of a metal alloy. —*tr.v.* **cased, cas•ing, cas•es.** To put into or cover with a case; encase. [ME < Norman Fr. *casse* < Lat. *capsa*.]

ca•se•ate (kāʹsē-āt′) *intr.v.* **-at•ed, -at•ing, -ates.** To undergo caseation. [Back-formation < CASEATION.]

ca•se•a•tion (kā′sē-āʹshən) *n.* Degeneration of body tissue into a soft cheeselike substance. [< Lat. *cāseus*, cheese.]

case•book (kāsʹbŏŏk′) *n.* A book containing source materials in a specific area, used as a reference and in teaching.

case goods *pl.n.* **1.a.** Furniture, such as bookcases or chests of drawers, that provide the user with interior storage space. **b.** Dining and bedroom furniture sold as sets. **2.** Food and beverage products sold by the case.

case•hard•en (kāsʹhär′dn) *tr.v.* **-ened, -en•ing, -ens. 1.** To harden the surface or case of (iron or steel) by high-temperature shallow infusion of carbon followed by quenching. **2.** To make callous or insensitive.

case history *n.* An account of the facts affecting the development or condition of a person or group under treatment or study.

ca•sein (kā-sēnʹ, -sē-ĭn) *n.* A protein precipitated from milk by rennin that is the basis of cheese and is used to make plastics, adhesives, paints, and foods. [Ult. < Lat. *cāseus*, cheese.]

case knife *n.* **1.** A knife kept in a sheath or case. **2.** A table knife.

case law *n.* Law based on judicial decision and precedent rather than on statutes.

case•load (kāsʹlōd′) *n.* The number of cases handled in a given period, as by a clinic or social services agency.

case•mate (kāsʹmāt′) *n.* **1.** A fortified enclosure for artillery on a warship. **2.** An armored compartment for artillery on a rampart. [Fr. < Ital. *casamatta* : perh. *casa*, house (< Lat. *cāsa*) + *matto*, mad, crazy (< Lat. *mattus*, drunk, p.part. of *madēre*, to be drunk).] —**caseʹmat′ed** *adj.*

case•ment (kāsʹmənt) *n.* **1.a.** A window sash that opens outward by means of hinges. **b.** A window with such sashes. **2.** A case or covering. [ME, a hollow molding, poss. < ME *case*, chest, frame. See CASE[2].] —**caseʹment•ed** *adj.*

Case•ment (kāsʹmənt), Sir **Roger David.** 1864–1916. British diplomat who sought German assistance in the Irish nationalist cause during World War I and was executed for treason.

ca•se•ous (kāʹsē-əs) *adj.* Resembling cheese. [< Lat. *cāseus*, cheese.]

ca•sern also **ca•serne** (kə-zûrnʹ) *n.* A military barracks or garrison. [Fr. *caserne* < OFr., small room for the night watch < OProv. *cazerna*, group of four men < Lat. *quaterna*, four together < Lat. *quaternī*, by four. See QUATERNION.]

case shot *n.* **1.** A shot-packed metallic cylinder used as ammunition in a firearm; a canister. **2.** The shot in such a cylinder.

case study *n.* **1.** An analysis of a person or group, esp. as a medical or social model. **2.a.** A study of a unit, such as a corporation, and causes of its success or failure. **b.** An exemplary or cautionary model; an instructive example.

case system *n.* A method of teaching law that emphasizes the study of selected cases rather than textbooks.

case•work (kāsʹwûrk′) *n.* Social work devoted to the needs of individual clients or cases. —**caseʹwork′er** *n.*

cash[1] (kăsh) *n.* **1.** Money in the form of bills or coins; currency. **2.** Payment for goods or services in currency or by check. —*tr.v.* **cashed, cash•ing, cash•es.** To exchange for or convert into ready money. —***phrasal verb.*** **cash in. 1.** To withdraw from a venture by or as if by settling one's account. **2.** *Informal.* To obtain an advantage by timely exploitation. **3.** *Slang.* To die. [Obsolete Fr. *casse*, money box (< Norman Fr.; see CASE[2]) or < Ital. *cassa* (< Lat. *capsa*, case).]

cash[2] (kăsh) *n., pl.* **cash.** Any of various Asian coins of small denomination. [Port. *caixa* < Tamil *kācu*, a small coin.]

cash-and-car•ry (kăshʹən-kărʹē) *adj.* Sold for cash, usu. without delivery service.

cash bar *n.* A bar, such as one at a large party, where drinks are sold by the glass.

cash•book (kăshʹbŏŏk′) *n.* A book in which a record of cash receipts and expenditures is kept.

cash cow *n.* *Slang.* A steady, dependable source of funds or income.

cash crop *n.* A crop, such as tobacco, grown for direct sale rather than for livestock feed.

cash discount *n.* A discount allowed if payment is made within a stipulated period.

cash•ew (kăshʹōō, kə-shōōʹ) *n.* **1.** A tropical American evergreen tree *(Anacardium occidentale)* having edible kernels. **2.** The kidney-shaped seed of this tree, eaten after roasting. [Prob. Port. *acajú* < Tupi < *cajú*, yellow fruit, acidic.]

cashew apple *n.* The soft, swollen, pear-shaped edible stalk of the fruit of the cashew, used for beverages, preserves, or jams.

cash flow *n.* **1.** The pattern of cash income and expenditures, as of a company or person, and the resulting availability of cash. **2.** The cash receipts from one or more assets for a given period, reckoned after taxes and other disbursements. —**cashʹ-flow′** (kăshʹflō′) *adj.*

cash•ier[1] (kă-shîrʹ) *n.* **1.** The officer of a bank or business concern in charge of paying and receiving money. **2.** A store employee who handles cash transactions with customers. [Du. *cassier* or Fr. *caissier*, both < Fr. *caisse*, money box < OProv. *caisa* < VLat. **capsea* < Lat. *capsa*, case.]

ca•shier[2] (kă-shîrʹ) *tr.v.* **-shiered, -shier•ing, -shiers.** To dismiss from a position of command or responsibility, esp. for disciplinary reasons. [Du. *casseren* < OFr. *casser*, to dismiss, annul. See QUASH[1].]

ca•shier's check (kă-shîrzʹ) *n.* A check drawn by a bank on its own funds and signed by the bank's cashier.

cash•mere (kăzhʹmîr′, kăshʹ-) *n.* **1.** Fine, downy wool growing beneath the outer hair of the Cashmere goat. **2.** A soft fabric made of this wool or of similar fibers. [After KASHMIR.]

Cash•mere (kăshʹmîr′, kăsh-mîrʹ). See **Kashmir.**

Cashmere goat also **Kashmir goat** *n.* A goat native to the Himalayan regions of India and Tibet and prized for its wool.

cash register *n.* A machine that tabulates the amount of sales transactions, makes a permanent record of them, and has a drawer in which cash can be kept.

cas•i•mere (kăzʹə-mîr′, kăsʹ-) *n.* Var. of **cassimere.**

cas•ing (kāʹsĭng) *n.* **1.** An outer cover: *a shell casing.* **2.** The frame or framework for a window or door. **3.** A metal pipe or tube used as a lining for a well. **4.** A membranous case used to contain sausage or other processed meat.

ca•si•no (kə-sēʹnō) *n., pl.* **-nos. 1.** A public room or building for gambling and other entertainment. **2.** Also **cas•si•no.** *Games.* A card game for two to four players in which cards on the table are matched by cards in the hand. **3.** A summer or country house in Italy. [Ital., dim. of *casa*, house < Lat.]

cask (kăsk) *n.* **1.** A sturdy cylindrical container for storing liquids; a barrel. **2.** The quantity that such a container can hold. [ME *caske*, poss. < OSp. *casco*, potsherd, helmet < *cascar*, to break. See CASCARA.]

cas•ket (kăsʹkĭt) *n.* **1.** A small case or chest. **2.** A coffin. —*tr.v.* **-ket•ed, -ket•ing, -kets.** To enclose in a case, chest, or coffin. [ME, poss. alteration of OFr. *cassette.* See CASSETTE.]

Cas•lon (kăzʹlən), **William.** 1692–1766. English type designer whose typefaces were widely used in the 18th cent.

Cas•par (kăsʹpär′, -pər) also **Gas•par** (găsʹ-). In the Bible, one of the three wise men from the East who came bearing gifts for the infant Jesus.

Cas•per (kăsʹpər). A city of E-central WY on the North Platte R. NW of Cheyenne; founded 1888. Pop. 46,742.

Cas•pi•an Sea (kăsʹpē-ən). A saline lake between SE Europe and W Asia.

casque (kăsk) *n.* **1.** A helmet, esp. an ornate visorless headpiece of the 16th century. **2.** *Zool.* A helmetlike structure or protuberance. [Fr. < Sp. *casco.* See CASK.] —**casqued** (kăskt) *adj.*

Cass (kăs), **Lewis.** 1782–1866. Amer. soldier and politician whose positions included U.S. secretary of war (1831–36).

cas•sa•ba (kə-säʹbə) *n.* Var. of **casaba.**

Cas•san•dra (kə-sănʹdrə) *n.* **1.** *Gk. Myth.* A daughter of Priam, the king of Troy, endowed with the gift of prophecy but fated by Apollo never to be believed. **2.** One that utters unheeded prophecies. [Lat. < Gk. *Kassandra.*]

cas•sa•tion (kă-sāʹshən) *n.* Abrogation or annulment by a higher authority. [ME *cassatioun* < OFr. *cassation* < LLat. *cassātiō, cassātiōn-* < *cassātus*, p.part. of *cassāre*, to annul. See QUASH[1].]

Cas•satt (kə-sătʹ), **Mary Stevenson.** 1844?–1926. Amer. painter whose works include *The Bath* (1891–92).

caryatid
Detail of *Porch of the Maidens* at the Erechtheum, Athens, Greece

cashew
Anacardium occidentale

Mary Cassatt
1880 self-portrait

ă pat	oi **boy**
ā pay	ou **out**
âr care	ŏŏ **took**
ä father	ōō **boot**
ĕ pet	ŭ cut
ē be	ûr **urge**
ĭ pit	th **thin**
ī pie	*th* **this**
îr pier	hw **which**
ŏ pot	zh vision
ō toe	ə about,
ô paw	item

Stress marks:
ʹ (primary);
′ (secondary), as in
dictionary (dĭkʹshə-nĕr′ē)

cas•sa•va (kə-sä′və) *n.* **1.** A shrubby tropical American plant *(Manihot esculenta)* widely grown for its large, tuberous, starchy roots. **2.** The root of this plant, eaten as a staple food in the tropics after leaching and drying to remove cyanide. [Ult. < Taino *casavi*, flour from manioc.]

Cas•sel (kăs′əl, kä′səl). See **Kassel.**

cas•se•role (kăs′ə-rōl′) *n.* **1.a.** A dish, usu. of earthenware or glass, in which food is baked and served. **b.** Food prepared and served in such a dish. **2.** *Chem.* A small-handled crucible used for heating and evaporating. [Fr., saucepan, dim. of OFr. *casse*, ladle, pan < OProv. *cassa* < Med.Lat. *cattia*, dipper < Gk. *kuathion*, dim. of *kuathos*, ladle.]

cas•sette (kə-sĕt′, kă-) *n.* **1.** A small flat case containing two reels and a length of magnetic tape that winds between them, used esp. in audio or video tape recorders or players. **2.** A lightproof cartridge containing photographic film or plates, used in specially designed cameras. [Fr., small box < OFr., dim. of Norman Fr. *casse*, case. See CASE[2].]

cas•sia (kăsh′ə) *n.* **1.** Any of various chiefly tropical or subtropical trees, shrubs, or herbs of the genus *Cassia* in the pea family, having pinnately compound leaves and long pods. **2.a.** A tropical Asian evergreen tree *(Cinnamomum cassia)* having aromatic bark used as a substitute for cinnamon. **b.** The bark of this tree. [ME < Lat., a kind of plant < Gk. *kassia*, of Semitic orig.]

cas•si•mere also **cas•i•mere** (kăz′ə-mîr′, kăs′-) *n.* A plain or twilled woolen cloth used for suits. [Var. of CASHMERE.]

Cas•sin (kä-săɴ′), **René.** 1887–1976. French jurist who won the 1968 Nobel Peace Prize.

cas•si•na also **cas•se•na** or **cas•se•ne** or **cas•si•ne** (kə-sē′nə) *n. Bot.* **1.** See **dahoon. 2.** See **yaupon.** [Am.Sp., yaupon < Timucua *kasine.*]

cas•si•no (kə-sē′nō) *n. Games.* Var. of **casino** 2.

Cas•si•no (kə-sē′nō, käs-). A town of central Italy in the Apennines NW of Naples. The town and nearby monastery of Monte Cassino were reduced to rubble during fierce German-Allied fighting (Feb.–May 1944). Pop. 26,300.

casserole
Pouring liquid sulfur from a porcelain casserole

Cas•si•o•pe•ia (kăs′ē-ə-pē′ə) *n.* A W-shaped constellation in the Northern Hemisphere between Andromeda and Cepheus. [Lat. *Cassiopēa* < Gk. *Kassiepeia.*]

Cas•sir•er (kə-sîr′ər, kä-), **Ernst.** 1874–1945. German philosopher who was concerned with the formation of concepts.

cas•sis (kə-sēs′) *n.* **1.** A Eurasian currant *(Ribes nigrum)* bearing black berries. **2.** A cordial made from the berries of this plant. [Fr. < Lat. *cassia*, a kind of plant. See CASSIA.]

cas•sit•er•ite (kə-sĭt′ə-rīt′) *n.* A light yellow, red-brown, or black mineral, SnO_2, that is an important tin ore. [Fr. *cassitérite* < Gk. *kassiteros*, tin.]

Cas•sius Lon•gi•nus (kăsh′əs lŏn-jī′nəs), **Gaius.** d. 42 B.C. Roman general and politician who was a leading member of the conspiracy to assassinate Julius Caesar.

cas•sock (kăs′ək) *n.* A long garment with a close-fitting waist and sleeves, worn by the clergy and others assisting in church services. [Fr. *casaque*, long coat < OFr., perh. < Ital. *casacca* < Pers. *kazhāgand*, padded garment : *kazh*, raw silk + *āgand*, stuffed.]

cas•sou•let (kăs′o͞o-lā′) *n.* A casserole of white beans, various meats, vegetables, and herbs, slowly simmered or baked. [Fr., stove dish, dim. of *cassolo*, earthenware vessel < *casso* < OProv. *cassa.* See CASSEROLE.]

cassowary
Southern cassowary
Casuarius casuarius

cas•so•war•y (kăs′ə-wĕr′ē) *n., pl.* **-ies.** Any of several large flightless birds of the genus *Casuarius* of Australia, New Guinea, and adjacent areas, having a large bony projection on the top of the head and brightly colored wattles. [Malay *kĕsuari.*]

cast (kăst) *v.* **cast, cast•ing, casts.** —*tr.* **1.** To throw; hurl. See Syns at **throw. 2.** To shed; molt. **3.** To throw on the ground, as in wrestling. **4.** To deposit or indicate (a ballot or vote). **5.** To turn or direct: *all eyes cast upon her.* **6.** To cause to fall onto or over something or in a certain direction, as if by throwing: *cast doubt.* **7.** To bestow; confer. **8.** To draw (lots). **9.** To give birth to prematurely. **10.** To cause (hounds) to scatter and circle in search of a lost scent. **11.a.** To choose actors for (a play, for example). **b.** To assign a certain role to (an actor). **c.** To assign an actor to (a part). **12.** To form (liquid metal, for example) into a particular shape by pouring into a mold. **13.** To give a form to; arrange. **14.** To contrive; devise. **15.** To calculate or compute; add up (a column of figures). **16.** To calculate astrologically. **17.** To warp; twist: *floorboards cast by age.* —*intr.* **1.** To throw something, esp. to throw out a baited fishing line. **2.** To add a column of figures; make calculations. **3.** To make a conjecture or a forecast. **4.** To receive form or shape in a mold. **5.** To search for a lost scent in hunting with hounds. **6.** To choose actors for parts, as in a play or movie. **7.** *Obsolete.* To estimate; conjecture. —*n.* **1.a.** The act or an instance of casting or throwing. **b.** The distance thrown. **2.a.** A throwing of a fishing line or net into the water. **b.** The line or net thrown. **3.a.** A throw of dice. **b.** The number thrown. **4.** A stroke of fortune or fate; lot. **5.a.** A direction or expression of the eyes. **b.** A slight squint. **6.** Something, such as molted skin, that is thrown off, out, or away. **7.** The addition of a column of figures; calculation. **8.** A conjecture; a forecast. **9.a.** The act of pouring molten material into a mold. **b.** The amount of molten material poured into a mold at a single operation. **c.** Something formed by this means. **10.** An impression formed in a mold or matrix; a mold. **11.** A rigid dressing, usu. made of gauze and plaster of Paris, used to immobilize an injured body part. **12.** The form in which something is made or constructed; arrangement. **13.** Outward form or look; appearance. **14.** Sort; type. **15.** An inclination; tendency. **16.** The actors in a theatrical presentation. **17.** A slight trace of color; a tinge. **18.** A distortion of shape. **19.** The circling of hounds to pick up a scent in hunting. **20.** A pair of hawks released by a falconer at one time. —***phrasal verbs.* cast about. 1.** To make a search; look. **2.** To devise means; contrive. **cast around.** To search about. **cast off. 1.** To discard; reject. **2.** To let go; set loose. **3.** To make the last row of stitches in knitting. **4.** *Print.* To estimate the space a manuscript will occupy when set into type. **cast on.** To make the first row of stitches in knitting. **cast out.** To drive out by force; expel. —***idiom.* cast (one's) lot with.** To join or side with for better or worse. [ME *casten* < ON *kasta.*]

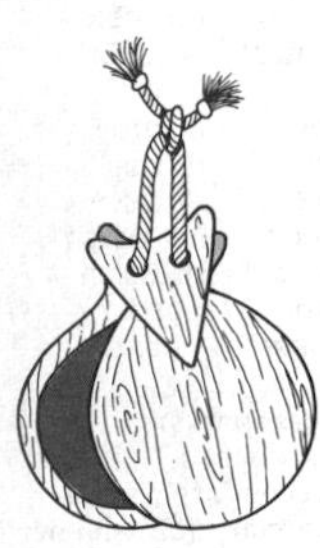
castanet

cas•ta•net (kăs′tə-nĕt′) *n. Mus.* A rhythm instrument consisting of two concave shells of ivory or hardwood, held in the palm by a connecting cord over the thumb and clapped with the fingers. Often used in the plural. [Sp. *castañeta* < *castaña*, chestnut < Lat. *castanea.* See CHESTNUT.]

cast•a•way (kăst′ə-wā′) *adj.* **1.** Cast adrift or ashore; shipwrecked. **2.** Discarded; thrown away. —*n.* **1.** A shipwrecked person. **2.** A rejected or discarded person or thing.

caste (kăst) *n.* **1.a.** Any of four classes, comprising numerous subclasses, constituting Hindu society. **b.** Any of numerous hereditary, endogamous social subclasses stratified according to Hindu ritual purity. **2.** A social class separated from others by distinctions of hereditary rank, profession, or wealth. **3.a.** A social system or the principle of grading society based on castes. **b.** The social position or status conferred by such a system. **4.** A level in a colony of social insects, such as ants, in which members carry out a specific function. [Sp. *casta*, race and Port. *casta*, race, caste, both < fem. of *casto*, pure < Lat. *castus.* See **kes-***.]

Cas•tel Gan•dol•fo (kä-stĕl′ gän-dôl′fō). A town of central Italy SE of Rome; papal summer residence. Pop. 3,600.

cas•tel•lan (kăs′tə-lən) *n.* The keeper or governor of a castle. [ME *castelain* < Norman Fr. < Med.Lat. *castellānus* < Lat., of a fortress < *castellum*, stronghold. See CASTLE.]

cas•tel•lat•ed (kăs′tə-lā′tĭd) *adj.* **1.** Furnished with turrets and battlements in the style of a castle. **2.** Having a castle. [Med.Lat. *castellātus*, p.part. of *castellāre*, to fortify as a castle < Lat. *castellum*, fort. See CASTLE.] —**cas′tel•la′tion** *n.*

Cas•tel•lón de la Pla•na (kăs′təl-yōn′ də lä plä′nə, kä′-stĕlyôn′ dĕ lä plä′nä). A city of E Spain on the Mediterranean NNE of Valencia. Pop. 129,518.

cast•er (kăs′tər) *n.* **1.** One that casts: *a caster of nets.* **2.** Also **cas•tor** (kăs′tər). A small wheel on a swivel, attached under a heavy object to make it easier to move. **3.** Also **castor. a.** A small bottle, pot, or shaker for holding a condiment. **b.** A stand for a set of condiment containers.

cas•ti•gate (kăs′tĭ-gāt′) *tr.v.* **-gat•ed, -gat•ing, -gates. 1.** To inflict severe punishment on. **2.** To criticize severely. [Lat. *castīgāre, castīgāt-* < *castus*, pure. See **kes-***.] —**cas′ti•ga′tion** *n.* —**cas′ti•ga′tor** *n.*

Cas•ti•glio•ne (kä′stĭl-yō′nā, kä′stē-lyô′nĕ), Count **Baldassare.** 1478–1529. Italian diplomat and writer best known for *Il Cortegiano* (1528), which describes the perfect courtier.

Cas•tile (kăs-tēl′). A region and former kingdom of central and N Spain; joined with Aragon after the marriage of Isabella and Ferdinand in 1479.

Castile soap also **cas•tile soap** (kăs-tēl′) *n.* A fine hard soap made with olive oil and sodium hydroxide. [After CASTILE.]

Cas•til•ian (kă-stĭl′yən) *n.* **1.** A native or inhabitant of Castile. **2.a.** The Spanish dialect of Castile. **b.** The standard form of Spanish, based on this dialect. —**Cas•til′ian** *adj.*

cast•ing (kăs′tĭng) *n.* **1.a.** The act or process of making casts or molds. **b.** Something cast in a mold. **2.** The act of throwing a fishing line. **3.** Something cast off or out. **4.** Selection of actors or performers for the parts of a presentation.

casting vote *n.* The vote of a presiding officer in an assembly or council, given to break a tie.

cast iron *n.* A hard, brittle, nonmalleable iron alloy, containing 2 to 4.5 percent carbon and cast into shape.

cast-i•ron (kăst′ī′ərn) *adj.* **1.** Made of cast iron. **2.** Rigid; inflexible. **3.** Exceptionally strong or resistant.

cast-iron plant *n.* See **aspidistra.**

cas•tle (kăs′əl) *n.* **1.a.** A large fortified building or group of buildings with thick walls, usu. dominating the surrounding country. **b.** A building similar to a fortified stronghold. **2.** A place of privacy, security, or refuge. **3.** *Games.* See **rook[2].** —*v.* **-tled, -tling, -tles.** —*intr. Games.* To move the king in chess from its own square two empty squares to one side and then, in the same move, bring the rook from that side to the square immediately past the new position of the king. —*tr.* **1.** To place in or as if in a castle. **2.** *Games.* To move (the king in chess) by castling. [ME *castel* < OE and < Norman Fr., both < Lat. *castellum*, dim. of *castrum*. See **kes-***.]

cas•tled (kăs′əld) *adj.* Castellated.

Ca•stle Peak (kăs′əl). A mountain, 4,350.8 m (14,265 ft), in the Elk Mts. of W-central CO.

Cas•tle•reagh (kăs′əl-rā′), Viscount. Robert Stewart, 2nd Marquis of Londonderry. 1769–1822. British politician who as chief secretary for Ireland (1798–1801) formed a political union between Ireland and Great Britain (1800).

cast•off (kăst′ôf′, -ŏf′) *n.* **1.** One that has been discarded. **2.** *Print.* A calculation of the amount of space a manuscript will occupy when set into type.

cas•tor[1] (kăs′tər) *n.* **1.** An oily, brown, odorous substance obtained from glands in the groin of the beaver and used as a perfume fixative. **2.** A hat made of beaver fur or an imitation. **3.** A heavy wool fabric used esp. for overcoats. [ME < Lat., beaver < Gk. *kastōr*.]

cas•tor[2] (kăs′tər) *n.* Var. of **caster** 2, 3.

Cas•tor (kăs′tər) *n.* **1.** *Gk. Myth.* One of the Dioscuri. **2.** A double star in Gemini. [Lat. < Gk. *Kastōr*, Castor.]

castor bean *n.* **1.** The castor-oil plant. **2.** The seed of this plant, from which castor oil is obtained. [CASTOR (OIL) + BEAN.]

castor oil *n.* An oil extracted from the seeds of the castor-oil plant, used as a laxative and skin softener and industrially as a lubricant.

cas•tor-oil plant (kăs′tər-oil′) *n.* A poisonous, ornamental tropical African herb or tree *(Ricinus communis)* having palmately lobed leaves and yielding castor oil.

cas•trate (kăs′trāt′) *tr.v.* **-trat•ed, -trat•ing, -trates. 1.** To remove the testicles of (a male); geld. **2.** To remove the ovaries of (a female); spay. **3.** To deprive of virility or spirit. —*n.* One who is sterile because of removal, destruction, or inactivation of the gonads. [Lat. *castrāre*, *castrāt-*. See **kes-***.] —**cas′trat•er, cas′tra•tor** *n.* —**cas•tra′tion** *n.*

ca•stra•to (kă-strä′tō, kə-) *n.*, *pl.* **-ti** (-tē) or **-tos.** *Mus.* A male singer castrated before puberty so as to retain a high voice. [Ital. < Lat. *castrātus*, p.part. of *castrāre*, to castrate. See CASTRATE.]

Cas•tries (käs′trēz′, -trēs′). The cap. of St. Lucia, in the Windward Is. of the British West Indies. Pop. 50,798.

Cas•tro (kăs′trō, kä′strō), **Fidel.** b. 1927. Cuban revolutionary leader who overthrew the regime of Fulgencio Batista in 1959. —**Cas′tro•ism** *n.* —**Cas′tro•ist, Cas′tro•ite′** (-īt′) *adj.* & *n.*

Cas•trop-Rau•xel (käs′trôp-rouk′səl). A city of W Germany in the Ruhr Valley SSW of Münster. Pop. 76,428.

ca•su•al (kăzh′o͞o-əl) *adj.* **1.** Occurring by chance. See Syns at **chance. 2.a.** Occurring at irregular or infrequent intervals; occasional. **b.** Unpremeditated; offhand. **3.a.** Being without formality; relaxed. **b.** Suited for everyday wear or use; informal. **4.** Not serious or thorough; superficial. **5.a.** Showing little interest; nonchalant. **b.** Lenient; permissive. **6.** Not close or intimate; passing. —*n.* **1.** One that serves or appears irregularly, esp. a temporary worker. **2.** A soldier temporarily attached to a unit, awaiting permanent assignment. [ME *casuel* < OFr. < Lat. *cāsuālis* < *cāsus*, event. See CASE[1].] —**ca′su•al•ly** *adv.* —**ca′su•al•ness** *n.*

ca•su•al•ty (kăzh′o͞o-əl-tē) *n.*, *pl.* **-ties. 1.** An accident, esp. one involving serious injury or loss of life. **2.** One injured or killed in an accident. **3.** One injured, killed, captured, or missing in action through engagement with an enemy. **4.** One harmed or eliminated as a result of a circumstance. [ME *casuelte* < OFr. < Med.Lat. *cāsuālitās*, chance, accident < Lat. *cāsuālis*, fortuitous. See CASUAL.]

ca•su•ist (kăzh′o͞o-ĭst) *n.* One who is expert in or given to casuistry. [Fr. *casuiste* < Sp. *casuista* < Lat. *cāsus*, case. See CASE[1].] —**ca′su•is′tic, ca′su•is′ti•cal** *adj.* —**ca′su•is′ti•cal•ly** *adv.*

ca•su•ist•ry (kăzh′o͞o-ĭ-strē) *n.*, *pl.* **-ries. 1.** Subtle but specious reasoning intended to rationalize or mislead. **2.** The determination of right and wrong by the application of general principles of ethics. [< CASUIST.]

ca•sus bel•li (kā′səs bĕl′ī, kä′səs bĕl′ē) *n.*, *pl.* **casus belli.** An act or event that provokes or is used to justify war. [NLat. *cāsus bellī* : Lat. *cāsus*, occasion + Lat. *bellī*, of war.]

cat (kăt) *n.* **1.a.** A small carnivorous mammal *(Felis catus* or *F. domesticus)* domesticated since early times as a catcher of rodents and as a pet and existing in several distinctive breeds and varieties. **b.** Any of various other carnivorous mammals of the family Felidae, such as the lion. **c.** The fur of a domestic cat. **2.** A woman regarded as spiteful. **3.** A cat-o'-nine-tails. **4.** A catfish. **5.** *Naut.* **a.** A cathead. **b.** A device for raising an anchor to the cathead. **c.** A catboat. **d.** A catamaran. **6.** *Slang.* **a.** A person, esp. a man. **b.** A player or devotee of jazz music. —*v.* **cat•ted, cat•ting, cats.** —*tr. Naut.* To hoist an anchor to (the cathead). —*intr. Slang.* To look for sexual partners; have an affair or affairs. —***idiom.* let the cat out of the bag.** To let a secret be known. [ME < OE *catt* < Gmc. **kattuz*.]

CAT (kăt) *abbr.* **1.** Clear-air turbulence. **2.** Computerized axial tomography.

cat. *abbr.* Catalog.

cata– *pref.* **1.** Down: *catadromous*. **2.** Reverse; backward; degenerative: *cataplasia*. [Gk. *kata-* < *kata*, down, downward, thoroughly. See **kat-***.]

ca•tab•o•lism (kə-tăb′ə-lĭz′əm) *n.* The metabolic breakdown of complex molecules into simpler ones, often resulting in a release of energy. [CATA– + (META)BOLISM.] —**cat′a•bol′ic** (kăt′ə-bŏl′ĭk) *adj.* —**cat′a•bol′i•cal•ly** *adv.*

ca•tab•o•lite (kə-tăb′ə-līt′) *n.* A substance produced by the process of catabolism. [CATABOL(ISM) + –ITE[2].]

ca•tab•o•lize (kə-tăb′ə-līz′) *intr.* & *tr.v.* **-lized, -liz•ing, -liz•es.** To undergo or cause to undergo catabolism.

cat•a•chre•sis (kăt′ə-krē′sĭs) *n.*, *pl.* **-ses** (-sēz). **1.** The misapplication of a word or phrase, as the use of *blatant* to mean "flagrant." **2.** The use of a strained figure of speech, such as a mixed metaphor. [Lat. *catachrēsis*, improper use of a word < Gk. *katakhrēsis*, excessive use < *katakhrēsthai*, to misuse : *kata-*, completely; see CATA– + *khrēsthai*, to use; see **gher-**[2]*.] —**cat′a•chres′tic** (-krĕs′tĭk), **cat′a•chres′ti•cal** (-tĭ-kəl) *adj.* —**cat′a•chres′ti•cal•ly** *adv.*

cat•a•clysm (kăt′ə-klĭz′əm) *n.* **1.** A violent upheaval that causes great destruction or brings about a fundamental change. **2.** A violent sudden change in the earth's crust. **3.** A devastating flood. [Fr. *cataclysme* < Lat. *cataclysmos*, deluge < Gk. *kataklusmos* < *katakluzein*, to inundate : *kata-*, intensive pref.; see CATA– + *kluzein*, to wash away.] —**cat′a•clys′mic** (-klĭz′mĭk), **cat′a•clys′mal** (-klĭz′məl) *adj.*

cat•a•comb (kăt′ə-kōm′) *n.* **1.** An underground cemetery consisting of chambers or tunnels with recesses for graves. Often used in the plural. **2.** An underground burial place. [Prob. Fr. *catacombe* < OFr. < LLat. *catacumba*.]

ca•tad•ro•mous (kə-tăd′rə-məs) *adj.* Living in fresh water but migrating to marine waters to breed. Used of fish.

cat•a•falque (kăt′ə-fălk′, -fôlk′) *n.* **1.** A decorative structure on which a coffin rests in state during a funeral. **2.** A coffin-shaped structure used to represent the corpse at a requiem Mass after the burial. [Fr. < Ital. *catafalco*.]

Cat•a•lan (kăt′l-ăn′, -ən, kăt′l-ăn′) *adj.* Of or relating to Catalonia or its people, language, or culture. —*n.* **1.** A native or inhabitant of Catalonia. **2.** The Romance language spoken esp. in Catalonia, the Balearic Islands, Andorra, and the Roussillon region of France.

cat•a•lase (kăt′l-ās′, -āz′) *n.* An enzyme in the blood and in most living cells that catalyzes the decomposition of hydrogen peroxide into water and oxygen. [CATAL(YSIS) + –ASE.]

cat•a•lec•tic (kăt′l-ĕk′tĭk) *adj.* Lacking one or more syllables, esp. in the final foot. Used of verse. [LLat. *catalēcticus* < Gk. *katalēktikos* < *katalēgein*, to leave off : *kata-*, intensive pref.; see CATA– + *lēgein*, to cease, terminate; see **slēg-***.]

cat•a•lep•sy (kăt′l-ĕp′sē) *n.*, *pl.* **-sies.** A condition characterized by muscular rigidity and occurring in a variety of physical and psychological disorders. [ME *catalempsi* < LLat. *catalēmpsia* < Gk. *katalēpsis* < *katalambanein*, to seize upon : *kata-*, intensive pref.; see CATA– + *lambanein*, *lēp-*, to seize.] —**cat′a•lep′tic** (kăt′l-ĕp′tĭk) *adj.*

cat•a•lex•is (kăt′l-ĕk′sĭs) *n.* The absence of one or more syllables in a line of verse, esp. in the last foot. [Gk. *katalēxis* < *katalēgein*, to leave off. See CATALECTIC.]

Cat•a•li•na Island (kăt′l-ē′nə). See **Santa Catalina Island.**

cat•a•lo (kăt′l-ō′) *n.* Var. of **cattalo.**

cat•a•log or **cat•a•logue** (kăt′l-ôg′, -ŏg′) —*n.* **1.a.** A list or itemized display, as of titles or articles for sale, usu. including descriptive information or illustrations. **b.** A publication, such as a book or pamphlet, containing such a list or display: *a seed catalog*. **2.** A list or enumeration. **3.** A card catalog. —*v.* **-loged, -log•ing, -logs** or **-logued, -logu•ing, -logues.** —*tr.* **1.** To make an itemized list of: *catalog a record collection.* **2.a.** To list or include in a catalog. **b.** To classify (a book, for example) according to a categorical system. —*intr.* **1.** To make a catalog. **2.** To be listed in a catalog. [ME *cathaloge*, list, register < OFr. *catalogue* < LLat. *catalogus* < Gk. *katalogos* < *katalegein*, to list : *kata-*, down, off; see CATA– + *legein*, to count; see **leg-***.] —**cat′a•log′er** *n.*

ca•ta•logue rai•son•né (kăt′l-ôg′ rā′zə-nā′, -ŏg′, kä-tä-lôg′ rĕ-zô-nā′) *n.*, *pl.* **ca•ta•logues rai•son•nés** (kăt′l-ôgz′ rā′zə-nā′, -ŏgz′, kä-tä-lôg′ rĕ-zô-nā′). A publication listing titles of articles or literary works, esp. of the contents of an exhibition, along with related descriptive or critical material. [Fr. : *catalogue*, catalog + *raisonné*, methodical, descriptive < p.part. of *raisonner*, to reason, analyze.]

Cat•a•lo•nia (kăt′l-ōn′yə, -ō′nē-ə). A region of NE Spain bordering on France and the Mediterranean Sea. —**Cat′a•lo′nian** *adj.* & *n.*

ca•tal•pa (kə-tăl′pə, -tôl′-) *n.* Any of various, usu. deciduous trees of the genus *Catalpa*, esp. *C. bignonioides* or *C. speciosa* native to the United States and having heart-shaped leaves, white flowers, and long slender cylindrical pods. [Creek *katałpa* : *ka-*, head + *tałpa*, wing (< flower shape).]

ca•tal•y•sis (kə-tăl′ĭ-sĭs) *n.*, *pl.* **-ses** (-sēz′). The action of a catalyst, esp. an increase in the rate of a chemical reaction. [Gk. *katalusis*, dissolution < *kataluein*, to dissolve : *kata-*, intensive pref.; see CATA– + *luein*, to loosen; see **leu-***.] —**cat′a•lyt′ic** (-ĭt′ĭk) *adj.* —**cat′a•lyt′i•cal•ly** *adv.*

cat•a•lyst (kăt′l-ĭst) *n.* **1.** *Chem.* A substance that modifies

castle
Neuschwanstein Castle, Germany

Fidel Castro
Photographed in 1978

ă **pat**	oi **boy**
ā **pay**	ou **out**
âr **care**	o͝o **took**
ä **father**	o͞o **boot**
ĕ **pet**	ŭ **cut**
ē **be**	ûr **urge**
ĭ **pit**	th **thin**
ī **pie**	*th* **this**
îr **pier**	hw **which**
ŏ **pot**	zh **vision**
ō **toe**	ə **a**bout,
ô **paw**	it**e**m

Stress marks:
′ (primary);
′ (secondary), as in **dictionary** (dĭk′shə-nĕr′ē)

whose works about frontier life include *One of Ours* (1922).

Cath•e•rine I (kăth′ər-ĭn, kăth′rĭn). 1684?–1727. Empress of Russia (1725–27) as successor to her husband, Peter I.

Catherine II. "Catherine the Great." 1729–96. Empress of Russia (1762–96) after her husband, Peter III (1728–62), was deposed by a group led by her lover.

Cath•e•rine de Mé•di•cis (kăth′ər-ĭn də mĕd′ĭ-chē′, kăth′rĭn, kät-rĕn′ də mā-dē-sēs′). 1519–89. Queen of France as the wife of Henry II and regent during the minority (1560–63) of her son Charles IX.

Cath•e•rine of Ar•a•gon (kăth′ər-ĭn, kăth′rĭn; ăr′ə-gŏn′). 1485–1536. The first wife of Henry VIII of England, whose divorce (1533) marked the start of the English Reformation.

Catherine of Aragon
c. 1530 portrait by an unknown artist

cath•er•ine wheel (kăth′ər-ĭn, kăth′rĭn) *n.* See **pinwheel** 2. [After St. *Catherine* of Alexandria (d. A.D. 307), who was condemned to be tortured on a wheel.]

cath•e•ter (kăth′ĭ-tər) *n.* A flexible tube inserted into a body cavity, duct, or vessel to allow fluids to pass or distend a passage. [LLat. < Gk. *kathetēr* < *kathienai*, to send down : *kat-, kata-*, cata- + *hienai, hē-*, to send; see **yē-*.**]

cath•e•ter•ize (kăth′ĭ-tə-rīz′) *tr.v.* **-ized, -iz•ing, -iz•es.** To put a catheter into. **— cath′e•ter•i•za′tion** (-rĭ-zā′shən) *n.*

ca•thex•is (kə-thĕk′sĭs) *n., pl.* **-thex•es** (-thĕk′sēz). *Psychol.* Concentration of emotional energy on an object or idea. [Gk. *kathexis*, holding, retention < *katekhein*, to hold fast : *kat-, kata-*, intensive pref.; see CATA- + *ekhein*, to hold; see **segh-*.**]

cath•ode (kăth′ōd′) *n.* **1.** A negatively charged electrode, as of an electrolytic cell or a storage battery. **2.** The positively charged terminal of a primary cell or a storage battery that is supplying current. [Gk. *kathodos*, descent : *kat-, kata-*, cata- + *hodos*, way, path.] **— ca•thod′ic** (kă-thŏd′ĭk) *adj.* **— ca•thod′i•cal•ly** *adv.*

cathode ray *n.* **1.** A stream of electrons emitted by the cathode in electrical discharge tubes. **2.** One of the electrons that is emitted in a stream from a cathode-ray tube.

cath•ode-ray tube (kăth′ōd-rā′) *n.* A vacuum tube in which a hot cathode emits electrons that are accelerated as a beam through an anode, then focused or deflected onto a phosphorescent screen.

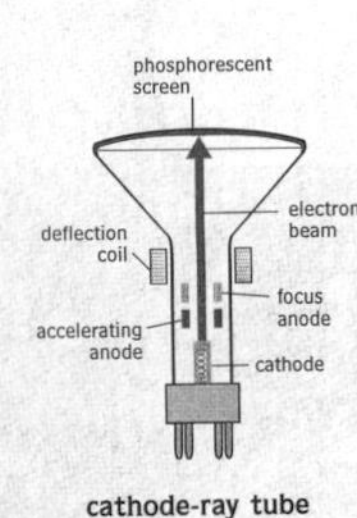

cathode-ray tube

cath•o•lic (kăth′ə-lĭk, kăth′lĭk) *adj.* **1.** Of broad or liberal scope; comprehensive. **2.** Including or concerning all humankind; universal. **3. Catholic. a.** Of or involving the Roman Catholic Church. **b.** Of or relating to the universal Christian church. **c.** Of or relating to the ancient undivided Christian church. **d.** Of or relating to those churches that have claimed to be representatives of the ancient undivided church. **—** *n.* **Catholic.** A member of a Catholic church, esp. a Roman Catholic. [ME *catholik*, universally accepted < OFr. *catholique* < Lat. *catholicus*, universal < Gk. *katholikos* < *katholou*, in general : *kat-, kata-*, down, along, according to; see CATA- + *holou* < neut. genitive of *holos*, whole; see **sol-*.**] **— ca•thol′i•cal•ly** (kə-thŏl′ĭk-lē) *adv.*

Ca•thol•i•cism (kə-thŏl′ĭ-sĭz′əm) *n.* The faith, doctrine, and practice of a Catholic church, esp. the Roman Catholic Church.

cath•o•lic•i•ty (kăth′ə-lĭs′ĭ-tē) *n.* **1.** The condition or quality of being catholic; inclusiveness. **2.** General application or acceptance; universality. **3. Catholicity.** Roman Catholicism.

ca•thol•i•cize (kə-thŏl′ĭ-sīz′) *tr. & intr.v.* **-cized, -ciz•ing, -ciz•es. 1.** To make or become catholic. **2.** To convert or be converted to Catholicism.

ca•thol•i•con (kə-thŏl′ĭ-kŏn′) *n.* A universal remedy; a panacea. [ME < OFr. < Med.Lat. < Gk. *katholikon*, generic description < neut. of *katholikos*, universal. See CATHOLIC.]

cat•house (kăt′hous′) *n. Slang.* A house of prostitution.

Cat•i•line (kăt′l-īn′). 108?–62 B.C. Roman politician who led an unsuccessful revolt against the Roman Republic.

cat•i•on (kăt′ī′ən) *n.* An ion or group of ions having a positive charge and characteristically moving toward the negative electrode in electrolysis. [Gk. *kation*, something going down < neut. pr.part. of *katienai* : *kat-, kata-*, cata- + *ienai*, to go; see **ei-*.**] **— cat′i•on′ic** (kăt′ī-ŏn′ĭk) *adj.*

cation exchange *n.* A chemical process in which cations of like charge are exchanged equally between a solid, such as zeolite, and a solution, such as water.

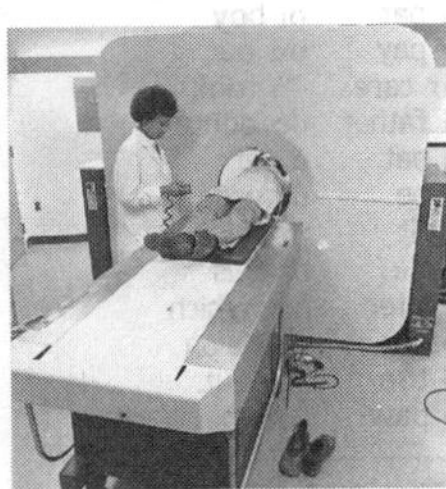

CAT scanner

cat•jang (kä-chăng′) *n.* **1.** See **cajan pea. 2.** See **cowpea.** [Du. *katjang* < Malay *kachang*, pea, bean.]

cat•kin (kăt′kĭn) *n.* A usu. dense cylindrical cluster of apetalous flowers found in willows, birches, and oaks. [< obsolete Du. *katteken*, kitten, dim. of *katte*, cat (from its resemblance to a kitten's tail) < Gmc. **kattuz*.]

cat•like (kăt′līk′) *adj.* Resembling a cat, esp. in being quiet or stealthy.

Cat•lin (kăt′lĭn), **George.** 1796–1872. Amer. artist noted for his portraits of Native Americans.

cat•mint (kăt′mĭnt′) *n. Chiefly British.* Catnip.

cat•nap (kăt′năp′) *n.* A short nap; a light sleep. **—** *intr.v.* **-napped, -nap•ping, -naps.** To take a short nap; doze.

cat•nip (kăt′nĭp′) *n.* **1.** An aromatic perennial herb *(Nepeta cataria)* in the mint family, native to Eurasia and containing an aromatic oil to which cats are strongly attracted. **2.** Any of various other mostly aromatic plants in the genus *Nepeta*, cultivated for their ornamental foliage and flowers. [CAT + *nip*, catnip (var. of *nep* < ME *nept, nep* < OE *nepte* < Lat. *nepeta*, aromatic herb, perh. of Etruscan orig.).]

Ca•to (kā′tō), **Marcus Porcius[1].** "the Elder." 234–149 B.C. Roman politician, censor, and general who wrote the first history of Rome.

Ca•to (kā′tō), **Marcus Porcius[2].** "the Younger." 95–46 B.C. Roman politician who supported Pompey against Caesar in the civil war and committed suicide after Caesar's victory.

Ca•toc•tin Mountains (kə-tŏk′tĭn). A section of the Blue Ridge in N MD extending from the PA border S to VA.

cat-o'-nine-tails (kăt′ə-nīn′tālz′) *n., pl.* **cat-o'-nine-tails.** A whip consisting of nine knotted cords fastened to a handle, used in flogging. [From its cat scratch marks.]

ca•top•tric (kə-tŏp′trĭk) also **ca•top•tri•cal** (-trĭ-kəl) *adj.* Of or relating to mirrors and reflected images. [Gk. *katoptrikos* < *katoptron*, mirror. See **ok^{w}-*.**] **— ca•top′trics** *n.*

cat rig *n. Naut.* The rig of a catboat.

Cat•ron (kăt′rən), **John.** 1786?–1865. Amer. jurist; associate justice of the U.S. Supreme Court (1837–65).

CAT scan (kăt) *n.* An image produced by a CAT scanner.

CAT scanner *n.* A device that produces cross-sectional views of a body structure using computerized axial tomography.

cat's cradle (kăts) *n.* A game in which a string is looped on the fingers to form an intricate pattern between a player's hands that can be varied or transferred to another player's hands.

cat scratch disease *n.* A disease thought to be transmitted to humans by the scratch or bite of a cat and characterized by fever and swollen lymph nodes.

cat's-eye (kăts′ī′) *n., pl.* **cat's-eyes. 1.** Any of various semiprecious gems such as chrysoberyl, $BeAl_2O_4$, reflecting a band of light that shifts position as the gem is turned. **2.** A glass or plastic reflector designed to glow in the beam of a headlight. **3.** A marble having an eyelike design.

Cats•kill Mountains (kăt′skĭl′). A range of the Appalachian Mts. in SE NY rising to 1,282.2 m (4,204 ft).

cat's-paw also **cats•paw** (kăts′pô′) *n., pl.* **cat's-paws** also **cats•paws. 1.** A person used by another as a dupe or tool. **2.** A light breeze that ruffles small areas of a water surface. **3.** *Naut.* A knot made by twisting a section of rope to form two adjacent eyes through which a hook is passed, used in hoisting. [From a fable about a monkey that used a cat's paw to pull chestnuts out of a fire.]

cat•sup (kăt′səp, kăch′əp, kĕch′-) *n.* Var. of **ketchup.**

Catt (kăt), **Carrie (Lane) Chapman.** 1859–1947. Amer. suffragist who organized the League of Women Voters in 1919.

cat•tail (kăt′tāl′) *n.* Any of various perennial herbs of the genus *Typha*, widespread in marshy places and having a dense cylindrical cluster of minute flowers and fruits.

cat•ta•lo also **cat•a•lo** (kăt′l-ō′) *n., pl.* **-loes** or **-los.** See **beefalo.** [CATT(LE) + (BUFF)ALO.]

cat•tle (kăt′l) *pl.n.* **1.** Any of various mammals of the genus *Bos*, including cows, steers, bulls, and oxen, often raised for meat and dairy products. **2.** Human beings, esp. when viewed contemptuously. [ME *catel*, property, livestock < ONFr. < OProv. *capdal* < Med.Lat. *capitāle*, funds < neut. of Lat. *capitālis*, principal < *caput*, head. See **kaput-*.**]

cattle call *n. Informal.* An audition in which a large number of often inexperienced actors or performers try out.

cattle egret *n.* A small egret *(Bubulus ibis)* native to Africa and southern Eurasia that feeds among grazing cattle.

cattle grub *n.* The larva of a warble fly, esp. of the genus *Hypoderma*, that parasitizes cattle.

cat•tle•man (kăt′l-mən, -măn′) *n.* A man who raises cattle.

cattle tick *n.* A brown tick *(Boophilus annulatus)* whose bite transmits the causative agent of Texas fever in cattle.

cat•tle•ya (kăt′lē-ə) *n.* Any of various tropical American orchids of the genus *Cattleya*, cultivated for their showy flowers. [NLat. *Cattleya*, genus name, after William *Cattley* (d. 1832), British patron of botany.]

Cat•ton (kăt′n), **(Charles) Bruce.** 1899–1978. Amer. historian and editor who wrote extensively on the Civil War.

cat•ty[1] (kăt′ē) *adj.* **-ti•er, -ti•est. 1.** Subtly cruel or malicious. **2.** Catlike; stealthy. **— cat′ti•ly** *adv.* **— cat′ti•ness** *n.*

cat•ty[2] also **cat•tie** (kăt′ē) *n., pl.* **-ties.** Any of various units of weight used in Southeast Asia, esp. a Chinese measure equal to 500 grams (approx. 1.1 pounds). [Malay *kati.*]

cat•ty-cor•nered (kăt′ē-kôr′nərd) or **cat•ty-cor•ner** (-nər) *adj. & adv.* Var. of **cater-cornered.**

Ca•tul•lus (kə-tŭl′əs), **Gaius Valerius.** 84?–54? B.C. Roman lyric poet known for his love poems to "Lesbia."

CATV *abbr.* Community antenna television.

cat•walk (kăt′wôk′) *n.* A narrow, often elevated walkway, as on the sides of a bridge or in the flies above a theater stage.

Cau•ca (kou′kə). A river rising in W Colombia and flowing c. 965 km (600 mi) N to the Magdalena R.

Cau•ca•sian (kô-kā′zhən, -kăzh′ən) *adj.* **1.** *Anthro.* Of, relating to, or being a racial classification traditionally distinguished by very light to brown skin pigmentation and straight to wavy or curly hair and including peoples indigenous to Europe, northern Africa, western Asia, and India. No longer in scientific use. **2.** Of or relating to the Caucasus region or its peoples, languages, or cultures. — *n.* **1.** *Anthro.* A member of the Caucasian racial classification. No longer in scientific use. **2.** A native or inhabitant of the Caucasus.

Cau•ca•soid (kô′kə-soid′) *Anthro. adj.* Of or relating to the Caucasian racial classification. — **Cau′ca•soid′** *n.*

Cau•ca•sus (kô′kə-səs) also **Cau•ca•sia** (kô-kā′zhə, -shə). A region between the Black and Caspian seas that includes Georgia, Azerbaijan, Armenia, and part of SW Russia.

Caucasus Mountains. A range in the Caucasus extending from the N to the SE and rising to 5,645.6 m (18,510 ft).

cau•cus (kô′kəs) *n., pl.* **-cus•es** or **-cus•ses. 1.a.** A meeting of the local members of a political party esp. to select delegates to a convention or register preferences for political candidates. **b.** A closed meeting of party members within a legislative body. **c.** A group within a legislative or decision-making body seeking to represent a specific interest or influence a policy area. **2.** *Chiefly British.* A committee within a political party to determine policy. — *v.* **-cused, -cus•ing, -cus•es** or **-cussed, -cus•sing, -cus•ses.** — *intr.* To assemble in or hold a caucus. — *tr.* To assemble or canvass (members of a caucus). [After the *Caucus* Club of Boston (in the 1760's), poss. < Med.Lat. *caucus,* drinking vessel.]

cau•dad (kô′dăd′) *adv. Anat.* Toward the tail or posterior end of the body; caudally. [Lat. *cauda,* tail + -AD.]

cau•dal (kôd′l) *adj. Anat.* **1.a.** Of, at, or near the tail or hind parts; posterior. **b.** Situated beneath or on the underside; inferior. **2.** *Zool.* Taillike. [NLat. *caudālis* < Lat. *cauda,* tail.] — **cau′dal•ly** *adv.*

cau•date (kô′dāt′) also **cau•dat•ed** (-dā′tĭd) *adj.* Having a tail or taillike appendage. [Med.Lat. *caudātus* < Lat. *cauda,* tail.] — **cau•da′tion** *n.*

cau•dex (kô′dĕks′) *n., pl.* **-di•ces** (-dĭ-sēz′) or **-dex•es. 1.** The thickened base of the stem of many perennial herbaceous plants, from which new leaves and flowering stems arise. **2.** The trunk of a palm or tree fern. [Lat. *caudex,* tree trunk.]

cau•dil•lo (kô-dēl′yō, -dē′yō, kou-*th*ē′-, -*th*ē′-) *n., pl.* **-los.** A leader or chief, esp. a military dictator. [Sp. < LLat. *capitellum,* dim. of Lat. *caput,* head. See **kaput-***.]

cau•dle (kôd′l) *n.* A warm drink of wine or ale mixed with sugar, eggs, bread, and various spices, sometimes given to ill persons. [ME *caudel* < ONFr. < Med.Lat. *caldellus* < Lat. *caldum,* hot drink < *caldus, calidus,* warm, hot. See **kelə-¹***.]

caught (kôt) *v.* P.t. and p.part. of **catch.**

caul (kôl) *n.* **1.** A portion of the amnion, esp. when it covers the head of a fetus at birth. **2.** See **greater omentum.** [ME *calle* < OE *cawl,* basket.]

caul•dron (kôl′drən) *n.* Var. of **caldron.**

cau•les•cent (kô-lĕs′ənt) *adj. Bot.* Having a well-developed aboveground stem. [Lat. *caulis,* stem + -ESCENT.]

cau•li•flow•er (kô′lĭ-flou′ər, kŏl′ĭ-) *n.* An herb *(Brassica oleracea* var. *botrytis)* in the mustard family, related to the cabbage and broccoli and having a whitish undeveloped flower with a large edible head. [Prob. alteration (influenced by FLOWER) of NLat. *cauliflora* : Lat. *caulis,* stem + Lat. *flōs, flōr-,* flower; see FLOWER.]

cauliflower ear *n.* An ear deformed by repeated blows.

cau•line (kô′līn′) *adj. Bot.* Of, having, or growing on a stem. [Lat. *caulis,* stem + -INE¹.]

caulk also **calk** (kôk) — *v.* **caulked, caulk•ing, caulks** also **calked, calk•ing, calks.** — *tr.* **1.** To make watertight or airtight by filling or sealing: *caulk a pipe joint.* **2.** *Naut.* To make (a boat) watertight by packing seams with a waterproof material, such as pitch. — *intr.* To apply caulking. — *n.* Caulking. [ME *cauken,* to press < ONFr. *cauquer* < Lat. *calcāre,* to tread < *calx,* heel.] — **caulk′er** *n.*

caulk•ing (kô′kĭng) *n.* An impermeable caulking substance.

caus. *abbr.* Causative.

caus•al (kô′zəl) *adj.* **1.** Of, involving, or being a cause. **2.** Indicative of a cause. — *n.* A word or grammatical element expressing a cause or reason. — **caus′al•ly** *adv.*

cau•sal•i•ty (kô-zăl′ĭ-tē) *n., pl.* **-ties. 1.** The principle of or relationship between cause and effect. **2.** A causal agency, force, or quality.

cau•sa•tion (kô-zā′shən) *n.* **1.** The act or process of causing. **2.** A cause. **3.** Causality.

caus•a•tive (kô′zə-tĭv) *adj.* **1.** Functioning as an agent or cause. **2.** Expressing causation. Used of a verb or verbal affix. — **caus′a•tive** *n.* — **caus′a•tive•ly** *adv.*

cause (kôz) *n.* **1.a.** The producer of an effect, result, or consequence. **b.** The one responsible for an action or a result. **2.** A basis for an action or a response; a reason. **3.** A goal or principle served with dedication. **4.** The interests of one engaged in a struggle. **5.** *Law.* **a.** A ground for legal action. **b.** A lawsuit. **6.** A subject under debate or discussion. — *tr.v.* **caused, caus•ing, caus•es. 1.** To be the cause of or reason for. **2.** To bring about or compel by authority or force. [ME < OFr. < Lat. *causa,* reason, purpose.] — **caus′a•ble** *adj.* — **cause′less** *adj.* — **caus′er** *n.*

'cause (kôz, kŭz) *conj. Informal.* Because.

cause cé•lè•bre (kōz′ sā-lĕb′rə) *n., pl.* **causes cé•lè•bres** (kōz′ sā-lĕb′rə). **1.** An issue arousing widespread controversy or heated public debate. **2.** A celebrated legal case. [Fr. : *cause,* case + *célèbre,* celebrated.]

cau•se•rie (kōz-rē′) *n.* **1.** An informal discussion or chat, esp. of an intellectual nature. **2.** A short, conversational piece of writing or criticism. [Fr. < *causer,* to talk < Lat. *causārī,* to plead, discuss < *causa,* case, cause.]

cause•way (kôz′wā′) *n.* **1.** A raised roadway, as across water or marshland. **2.** A paved highway. [ME *caucewei* : *cauce,* raised road (< Norman Fr. *caucie* < Med.Lat. *calciāta (via),* paved (road) < Lat. *calx, calc-,* limestone; see CALX) + *wei,* road (var. of *way;* see WAY).]

caus•tic (kô′stĭk) *adj.* **1.** Capable of burning, corroding, dissolving, or eating away by chemical action. **2.** Corrosive and bitingly trenchant; cutting. **3.** Causing a burning or stinging sensation, as from intense emotion. **4.** Of or relating to light emitted from a point source and reflected or refracted from a curved surface. — *n.* **1.** A caustic material or substance. **2.** A hydroxide of a light metal. **3.** A caustic curve or surface. [ME *caustik* < Lat. *causticus* < Gk. *kaustikos* < *kaustos* < *kaiein, kau-,* to burn.] — **caus′ti•cal•ly** *adv.* — **caus•tic′i•ty** (kô-stĭs′ĭ-tē) *n.*

caustic potash *n.* See **potassium hydroxide.**

caustic soda *n.* See **sodium hydroxide.**

cau•ter•ize (kô′tə-rīz′) *tr.v.* **-ized, -iz•ing, -iz•es. 1.** To burn or sear with a cautery. **2.** To deaden, as to feelings or moral scruples; callous. [ME *cauterizen* < LLat. *cautērizāre,* to cauterize, brand < Lat. *cautērium,* cautery. See CAUTERY.] — **cau′ter•i•za′tion** (-tər-ĭ-zā′shən) *n.*

cau•ter•y (kô′tə-rē) *n., pl.* **-ies. 1.** An agent or instrument, such as a laser or an electric current, used to destroy abnormal tissue by burning, searing, or scarring. **2.** The act or process of cauterizing. [ME *cauterie* < Lat. *cautērium,* branding iron, cautery < Gk. *kautērion* < *kaiein, kau-,* to burn.]

cau•tion (kô′shən) *n.* **1.a.** Careful forethought to avoid danger or harm. **b.** Close attention or vigilance to minimize risk: *went over the bridge with caution.* **2.** Prudence or restraint in action or decision. **3.** A warning or admonishment, esp. to take heed: *a caution about fat in my diet.* **4.** A cautious action; a precaution. **5.** *Informal.* One that is striking or alarming. — *tr.v.* **-tioned, -tion•ing, -tions.** To advise to take heed; warn or admonish. [ME *caucioun* < OFr. *caution* < Lat. *cautiō, cautiōn-* < *cautus,* p.part. of *cavēre,* to take care.]

cau•tion•ar•y (kô′shə-nĕr′ē) *adj.* Admonitory; warning.

cau•tious (kô′shəs) *adj.* **1.** Showing or practicing caution; careful. **2.** Tentative or restrained; guarded: *a cautious optimism.* — **cau′tious•ly** *adv.* — **cau′tious•ness** *n.*

cav. *abbr.* **1.** Cavalier. **2.** Cavalry. **3.** Cavity.

cav•al•cade (kăv′əl-kād′, kăv′əl-kād′) *n.* **1.** A procession of riders or horse-drawn carriages. **2.** A ceremonial procession or display. **3.** A succession or series. [Fr. < OFr. < OItal. *cavalcata* < *cavalcare,* to ride on horseback < Med.Lat. *caballicāre* < Lat. *caballus,* horse.]

cav•a•lier (kăv′ə-lîr′) *n.* **1.** A chivalrous man, esp. one serving as escort to a woman of high social position; a gentleman. **2.** A mounted soldier; a knight. **3. Cavalier.** A supporter of Charles I of England in his struggles against Parliament. — *adj.* **1.** Showing arrogant or offhand disregard; dismissive: *a cavalier attitude.* **2.** Carefree and nonchalant; jaunty. **3. Cavalier.** Of or relating to a group of English poets associated with the court of Charles I. [Fr., horseman < OItal. *cavaliere* < Med.Lat. *caballārius* < Lat. *caballus,* horse.]

ca•val•la (kə-văl′ə) *n., pl.* **-las** or **cavalla. 1.** Any of various tropical marine food fishes of the family Carangidae, which includes the jacks and pompanos. **2.** See **king mackerel.** [Sp. *caballa,* horse mackerel < LLat. < Lat. *caballus,* horse.]

cav•al•ry (kăv′əl-rē) *n., pl.* **-ries. 1.** A highly mobile army unit using vehicular transport. **2.** Troops trained to fight on horseback. [Fr. *cavalerie* < Ital. *cavalleria* < *cavaliere,* cavalier. See CAVALIER.] — **cav′al•ry•man** *n.*

cave (kāv) *n.* A hollow or natural passage under or into the earth, opening to the surface. — *v.* **caved, cav•ing, caves.** — *tr.* **1.** To dig or hollow out. **2.** To cause to collapse or yield. **3.** To crumple or smash: *The car was caved in.* — *intr.* **1.** To fall in; collapse. **2.** To give up all opposition: *caved in to me.* **3.** To explore caves. [ME < OFr. < Lat. *cava* < neut. pl. of *cavus,* hollow. See **keuə-***.] — **cav′er** *n.*

ca•ve•at (kā′vē-ăt′, kăv′ē-, kä′vē-ät′) *n.* **1.** A warning or caution. **2.** A qualification or explanation. [< Lat., let him beware, subjunctive of *cavēre,* to beware.]

caveat emp•tor (ĕmp′tôr′) *n.* The principle in commerce that the buyer is responsible for assessing the quality of a purchase before buying. [< Lat., let the buyer beware.]

cave dweller *n.* One that dwells in a cave, esp. a prehistoric human. — **cave′-dwell′ing** (kāv′dwĕl′ĭng) *adj.*

cave•fish (kāv′fĭsh′) *n., pl.* **cavefish** or **-fish•es.** Any of various freshwater fishes of the family Amblyopsidae, found in subterranean waters and having nonfunctioning eyes.

cave-in (kāv′ĭn′) *n.* **1.a.** A collapse, as of a tunnel. **b.** A place of a cave-in. **2.** An act of yielding.

Cav•ell (kăv′əl, kə-vĕl′), **Edith Louisa.** 1865–1915. British nurse who remained in Brussels after the German occupation (1915) to help smuggle Allied troops to the Dutch border.

causeway
Seven Mile Bridge crossing Pigeon Key in the Florida Keys

ă pat	oi boy
ā pay	ou out
âr care	ŏŏ took
ä father	ōō boot
ĕ pet	ŭ cut
ē be	ûr urge
ĭ pit	th thin
ī pie	*th* this
îr pier	hw which
ŏ pot	zh vision
ō toe	ə about, item
ô paw	

Stress marks:
′ (primary);
′ (secondary), as in
dictionary (dĭk′shə-nĕr′ē)

C clef

cecropia moth
Hyalophora cecropia

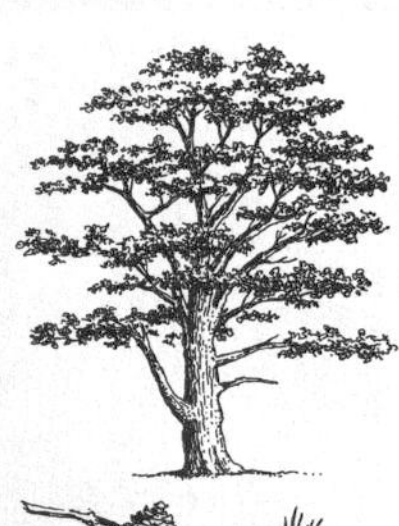
cedar of Lebanon
Cedrus libani

cedar waxwing
Bombycilla cedrorum

cave•man also **cave man** (kāv′măn′) *n.* **1.** A prehistoric or primitive human living in caves. **2.** *Informal.* A man who is crude or brutal. **— cave′man′, cave′-man′** *adj.*

Cav•en•dish (kăv′ən-dĭsh), **Henry.** 1731–1810. British chemist and physicist who established that water is a compound of hydrogen and oxygen.

cav•ern (kăv′ərn) *n.* **1.** A large cave. **2.** A large underground chamber, as in a cave. *— tr.v.* **-erned, -ern•ing, -erns. 1.** To enclose in or as if in a cavern. **2.** To hollow out. [ME *caverne* < OFr. < Lat. *caverna* < *cavus,* hollow. See **keuə-*.**]

cav•ern•ous (kăv′ər-nəs) *adj.* **1.** Filled with caverns. **2.** Resembling a cavern, as in depth or vastness. **3.** *Anat.* Filled with cavities or hollow areas. **— cav′ern•ous•ly** *adv.*

ca•vet•to (kə-vĕt′ō) *n., pl.* **-vet•ti** (-vĕt′ē) or **-vet•tos.** A concave molding with a cross section that approximates a quarter circle. [Ital., dim. of *cavo,* hollow < Lat. *cavus.* See **keuə-*.**]

cav•i•ar also **cav•i•are** (kăv′ē-är′, kä′vē-) *n.* The roe of a large fish, esp. sturgeon, eaten as a delicacy or relish. [Alteration of *caviarie* (prob. < obsolete Ital. *caviari,* pl. of *caviaro*) or < Fr. *caviare,* both < Turk. *havyar* < Pers. *khāvyār;* akin to *khāyah,* egg < MPers. *khāyak.* See **awi-*.**]

cav•il (kăv′əl) *v.* **-iled, -il•ing, -ils** also **-illed, -il•ling, -ils.** *— intr.* To find fault unnecessarily; raise trivial objections. *— tr.* To quibble about; detect petty flaws in. *— n.* A carping or trivial objection. [Fr. *caviller* < OFr. < Lat. *cavillārī,* to jeer < *cavilla,* a jeering.] **— cav′il•er** *n.*

cav•i•ta•tion (kăv′ĭ-tā′shən) *n.* **1.** The sudden formation and collapse of low-pressure bubbles in liquids by means of mechanical forces, such as those resulting from rotation of a propeller. **2.** The pitting of a solid surface. **3.** *Medic.* The formation of cavities in a tissue or an organ, esp. those formed in the lung as a result of tuberculosis. [< CAVITY.] **— cav′i•tate′** *v.*

Ca•vi•te (kə-vē′tē, kä-vē′tĕ). A city of SW Luzon, Philippines, on Manila Bay SW of Manila. Pop. 87,666.

cav•i•ty (kăv′ĭ-tē) *n., pl.* **-ties. 1.** A hollow; a hole. **2.** A hollow area within the body: *a sinus cavity.* **3.** A pitted area in a tooth caused by caries. [Fr. *cavité* < LLat. *cavitās* < Lat. *cavus,* hollow. See **keuə-*.**]

ca•vort (kə-vôrt′) *intr.v.* **-vort•ed, -vort•ing, -vorts. 1.** To bound or prance about in a sprightly manner; caper. **2.** To have lively fun; romp. [Poss. alteration of CURVET.]

Ca•vour (kə-vo͝or′, kä-vo͝or′), Conte **Camillo Benso di.** 1810–61. Italian political leader who was premier of Sardinia (1852–59 and 1860–61) and helped unify Italy.

ca•vy (kā′vē) *n., pl.* **-vies. 1.** Any of various tailless South American rodents of the family Caviidae, which includes the guinea pig. **2.** Any of various similar or related rodents, such as the coypu. [< NLat. *Cavia,* genus name, perh. < Galibi *cabiai.*]

caw (kô) *n.* The hoarse raucous sound characteristic of a crow or similar bird. [Imit.] **— caw** *v.*

Cawn•pore (kôn′pôr′, -pōr′). See **Kanpur.**

Ca•xi•as (kə-shē′əs), Duke of. 1803–80. Brazilian general and politician who served as minister of war.

Caxias do Sul (də so͞ol′). A city of S Brazil N of Pôrto Alegre. Pop. 198,683.

Cax•ton (kăk′stən), **William.** 1422?–91. English printer of the first book in English, a history of Troy (c. 1475).

cay (kē, kā) *n.* A small low island composed largely of coral or sand. [Alteration of Sp. *cayo,* prob. < Taino.]

Cay•enne (kī-ĕn′, kā-). The cap. of French Guiana, on **Cayenne Island** at the mouth of the **Cayenne River;** founded by the French in 1643. Pop. 38,093.

cay•enne pepper (kī-ĕn′, kā-) *n.* An orange-red to dark red condiment consisting of the ground ripe fruits of any of several pungent varieties of capsicum. [Alteration (by folk ety. < CAYENNE) of *kian, chian* < Tupi *quiínia,* hot pepper.]

cay•man (kā′mən) *n.* Var. of **caiman.**

Cay•man Islands (kā-măn′, kā′mən). A British-administered island group in the Caribbean Sea NW of Jamaica, including **Grand Cayman, Little Cayman,** and **Cayman Brac.** Cap. Georgetown. Pop. 16,677.

Ca•yu•ga (kā-yo͞o′gə, kī-) *n., pl.* **Cayuga** or **-gas. 1.** A member of a Native American people formerly inhabiting the shores of Cayuga Lake in west-central New York, with present-day populations in Ontario, western New York, Wisconsin, and Oklahoma. **2.** The Iroquoian language spoken by the Cayuga.

Cayuga Lake. A lake of W-central NY, the longest of the Finger Lakes.

cay•use (kī-yo͞os′, kī′yo͞os′) *n. Pacific Northwest.* A horse, esp. an Indian pony. [Short for *cayuse pony* < CAYUSE.]

Cay•use (kī-yo͞os′, kī′yo͞os′) *n., pl.* **Cayuse** or **-us•es. 1.** A member of a Native American people inhabiting northeast Oregon and southeast Washington. **2.a.** The extinct traditional language of the Cayuse. **b.** The dialect of Nez Perce spoken by the Cayuse in the 19th and 20th centuries.

CB (sē-bē′) *abbr.* Citizens band.

CBC *abbr.* **1.** Canadian Broadcasting Corporation. **2.** Complete blood count.

CBW *abbr.* Chemical and biological warfare.

cc *abbr.* **1.** Carbon copy. **2.** Cubic centimeter.

cc. *abbr.* Chapters.

C.C.A. *abbr. Law.* Circuit Court of Appeals.

CCC *abbr.* **1.** Civilian Conservation Corps. **2.** Commodity Credit Corporation.

CCD *abbr.* Confraternity of Christian Doctrine.

CCK *abbr.* Cholecystokinin.

C clef *n. Mus.* A symbol indicating which line of a staff represents the pitch of middle C. On the bottom line it becomes the soprano clef, on the middle line the alto clef, and on the third line above the bottom the tenor clef.

CCTV *abbr.* Closed-circuit television.

CCU *abbr.* Coronary care unit.

cd *abbr.* Candela.

Cd The symbol for the element **cadmium**

CD *abbr.* **1.** Also **C/D** Certificate of deposit. **2.** Also **C.D.** Civil defense. **3.** Compact disk. **4.** *Fr.* Corps diplomatique (diplomatic corps).

cd. *abbr.* Cord.

CDC *abbr.* Centers for Disease Control.

Cdr. or **CDR** *abbr.* Commander.

CD/ROM (sē′dē′rŏm′) *n. Comp. Sci.* A compact disk that functions as a read-only memory.

CDT or **C.D.T.** *abbr.* Central Daylight Time.

Ce The symbol for the element **cerium.**

C.E. *abbr.* **1.** Chemical engineer. **2.** Civil engineer. **3.** Common Era.

ce•a•no•thus (sē′ə-nô′thəs) *n.* Any of various shrubs or small trees of the genus *Ceanothus,* native to western North America and cultivated for their ornamental foliage and flowers. [NLat., genus name < Gk. *keanōthos,* corn thistle.]

cease (sēs) *v.* **ceased, ceas•ing, ceas•es.** *— tr.* To put an end to; discontinue. See Syns at **stop.** *— intr.* **1.** To come to an end; stop. **2.** To stop performing; desist. *— n.* Cessation; pause. [ME *cesen* < OFr. *cesser* < Lat. *cessāre,* to stop, freq. of *cēdere,* to yield. See **ked-*.**]

cease-fire or **cease•fire** (sēs′fīr′) *n.* **1.** An order to stop firing. **2.** Suspension of active hostilities; a truce.

cease•less (sēs′lĭs) *adj.* Without stop or pause. See Syns at **continual. — cease′less•ly** *adv.* **— cease′less•ness** *n.*

Ceau•ses•cu (chou-shĕs′ko͞o), **Nicolae.** 1918–89. Romanian politician who ruled as dictator (1965–89).

Ce•bu (sĕ-bo͞o′). An island of the central Philippines in the Visayan Is. between Leyte and Negros. The city of **Cebu** is an important harbor on the E coast. Pop. 490,281.

Cec•il (sĕs′əl), **(Edgar Algernon) Robert.** 1864–1958. British public official who won the 1937 Nobel Peace Prize.

Cecil, Robert Arthur Talbot Gascoyne. 3rd Marquis of Salisbury. 1830–1903. British politician who served as prime minister (1885–92 and 1895–1902).

Cecil, William. 1st Baron Burghley *or* Burleigh. 1520–98. English politician and chief adviser to Elizabeth I.

ce•cro•pi•a moth (sĭ-krō′pē-ə) *n.* A large North American silkworm moth *(Hyalophora cecropia)* having wings with red, white, and black markings. [NLat. *cecropia,* species name < Lat., fem. of *Cecropius,* Athenian < Gk. *Kekropios* < *Kekrops,* Cecrops, a legendary Athenian knight.]

ce•cum also **cae•cum** (sē′kəm) *n., pl.* **-ca** (-kə). **1.** A saclike cavity with only one opening. **2.** *Anat.* The large blind pouch forming the beginning of the large intestine. [ME < Lat. *(intestīnum) caecum,* blind (intestine) < *caecus,* blind.] **— ce′cal** *adj.* **— ce′cal•ly** *adv.*

ce•dar (sē′dər) *n.* **a.** Any of several Old World evergreen coniferous trees of the genus *Cedrus,* having stiff needles and large seed cones. **b.** Any of several other evergreen coniferous trees or shrubs, such as the incense cedar or red cedar. **c.** The durable aromatic wood of any of these plants. [ME *cedre* < OFr. < Lat. *cedrus* < Gk. *kedros.*]

ce•dar•bird (sē′dər-bûrd′) *n.* See **cedar waxwing.**

Ce•dar Falls (sē′dər). A city of NE IA, a suburb of Waterloo on the Cedar R. Pop. 36,322.

cedar of Lebanon *n., pl.* **cedars of Lebanon.** A large, long-lived cedar *(Cedrus libani)* native to Lebanon and Turkey.

Cedar Rapids. A city of E-central IA on the Cedar R. WNW of Davenport. Pop. 108,751.

Cedar River. A river rising in SE MN and flowing c. 531 km (330 mi) to the Iowa R. in SE IA.

cedar waxwing *n.* A North American bird *(Bombycilla cedrorum)* having a crested head, a yellow-tipped tail, and predominantly brown plumage.

cede (sēd) *tr.v.* **ced•ed, ced•ing, cedes. 1.** To surrender possession of, esp. by treaty. See Syns at **relinquish. 2.** To yield; grant. [Fr. *céder* < OFr. < Lat. *cēdere.* See **ked-*.**]

ce•di (sā′dē) *n., pl.* **cedi** or **-dis.** See table at **currency.** [Poss. < Akan (Fante) *sedį,* small shell, cowry.]

ce•dil•la (sĭ-dĭl′ə) *n.* A mark (¸) placed beneath the letter *c,* as in the French word *garçon,* to indicate that the letter is to be pronounced (s). [Obsolete Sp., dim. of *ceda,* the letter *z* (a small *z* having once been used to indicate that hard *c* was pronounced like *s* or *z*) < LLat. *zeta,* zeta. See ZETA.]

cee (sē) *n.* The letter *c.*

cei•ba (sā′bə) *n.* The silk-cotton tree. [Sp., prob. from Arawakan.]

ceil (sēl) *tr.v.* **ceiled, ceil•ing, ceils.** To provide or cover with a ceiling. [ME *celen,* prob. < OFr. **celer* < Lat. *caelāre,* to carve < *caelum,* chisel. See CAELUM.]

ceil•ing (sē′lĭng) *n.* **1.a.** The upper interior surface of a room. **b.** Material used to cover this surface. **2.** Something resembling a ceiling. **3.** An upper limit, esp. as set by regulation. **4.a.** The highest altitude under particular weather conditions from which the ground is still visible. **b.** The altitude of the lowest layer of clouds. **c.** Absolute ceiling. **5.** *Naut.* The planking applied to the interior framework of a ship. [ME *celing* < *celen,* to ceil. See CEIL.] **—ceil′inged** *adj.*

ceil•om•e•ter (sē-lŏm′ĭ-tər) *n.* An instrument for ascertaining cloud heights. [CEIL(ING) + -METER.]

cel•a•don (sĕl′ə-dŏn′) *n.* **1.** *Color.* A pale to very pale green. **2.** A type of pottery having a pale green glaze. [Fr., after *Céladon,* a character of Honoré d'Urfé (1568–1625), French writer.] **—cel′a•don′** *adj.*

cel•an•dine (sĕl′ən-dīn′, -dēn′) *n.* **1.** A perennial Eurasian herb *(Chelidonium majus)* having showy yellow flowers and yellow-orange latex. **2.** The lesser celandine. [ME *celidoine,* ult. < Gk. *khelidonion* < *khelidōn,* swallow (the blossoming of the plant being associated with the return of the swallows in spring). See **ghel-**[1]***.**]

celandine poppy *n.* A perennial herb *(Stylophorum diphyllum)* native to midwest North America similar to the celandine.

-cele[1] *suff.* Tumor; hernia: *cystocele.* [< Gk. *kēlē,* tumor.]

-cele[2] *suff.* Var. of **-coel.**

ce•leb (sə-lĕb′) *n. Informal.* A celebrity.

Cel•e•bes (sĕl′ə-bēz′, sə-lē′bēz′, sĕ-lā′bĕs) also **Su•la•we•si** (so͞o′lä-wā′sē). An island of central Indonesia E of Borneo.

Celebes Sea. A section of the W Pacific Ocean between Celebes and the S Philippines connected with the Java Sea by Makassar Strait.

cel•e•brant (sĕl′ə-brənt) *n.* **1.a.** A person who participates in a religious ceremony or rite. **b.** The priest officiating at the celebration of the Eucharist. **2.** A participant in a celebration.

Usage Note: Strictly speaking, *celebrant* should be reserved for an official participant in a religious ceremony or rite. In an earlier survey, however, a majority of the Usage Panel accepted the use of *celebrant* to mean "a participant in a celebration" (as in *New Year's Eve celebrants*). In this more general sense *celebrator* is an undisputed alternative.

cel•e•brate (sĕl′ə-brāt′) *v.* **-brat•ed, -brat•ing, -brates.** *—tr.* **1.** To observe (a day or event) with ceremonies of respect, festivity, or rejoicing. **2.** To perform (a religious ceremony). **3.** To extol or praise. **4.** To make widely known; display. *—intr.* **1.** To observe an occasion with appropriate ceremony or festivity. **2.** To perform a religious ceremony. **3.** To engage in festivities: *celebrated after the victory.* [ME *celebraten* < Lat. *celebrāre, celebrāt-,* to frequent, celebrate < *celeber, celebr-,* frequented, famous.] **—cel′e•bra′tion** *n.* **—cel′e•bra′tor** *n.* **—cel′e•bra•to′ry** (sĕl′ə-brə-tôr′ē, -tōr′ē, sə-lĕb′rə-) *adj.*

cel•e•brat•ed (sĕl′ə-brā′tĭd) *adj.* Known and praised widely; noted. See Syns at **noted.**

ce•leb•ri•ty (sə-lĕb′rĭ-tē) *n., pl.* **-ties. 1.** A famous person. **2.** Renown. [ME *celebrite,* fame < OFr. < Lat. *celebritās* < *celeber, celebr-,* famous.] **—ce•leb′ri•ty•hood′** *n.*

ce•le•ri•ac (sə-lîr′ē-ăk′, -lĕr′-) *n.* An edible variety of celery *(Apium graveolens* var. *rapaceum)* cultivated for its knobby root. [Alteration of CELERY.]

ce•ler•i•ty (sə-lĕr′ĭ-tē) *n.* Swiftness of action or motion; speed. See Syns at **haste.** [Fr. *célérité* < OFr. < Lat. *celeritās* < *celer,* swift.]

cel•er•y (sĕl′ə-rē) *n., pl.* **-ies. 1.** A biennial European plant *(Apium graveolens* var. *dulce)* in the parsley family, having edible roots, leafstalks, leaves, and fruits. **2.** The crisp thick leafstalks of this plant. **3.** The seedlike fruits of this plant used as a flavoring. [Fr. *céleri* < Ital. dial. *seleri,* pl. of *selero,* alteration of LLat. *selīnon,* parsley < Gk. *selinon.*]

celery cabbage *n.* See **Chinese cabbage.**

celery root *n.* See **celeriac.**

ce•les•ta (sə-lĕs′tə) also **ce•leste** (-lĕst′) *n. Mus.* An instrument with a keyboard and metal plates struck by hammers that produce bell-like tones. [Fr. *célesta* < *céleste,* celestial < Lat. *caelestis.* See CELESTIAL.]

ce•les•tial (sə-lĕs′chəl) *adj.* **1.** Of or relating to the sky or the heavens. **2.** Of or relating to heaven; divine. **3.** Supremely good; sublime. **4. Celestial.** Of or relating to the Chinese people or to the former Chinese Empire. *—n.* A heavenly being; a god or angel. [ME < OFr. < Med.Lat. *celestiālis* < Lat. *caelestis* < *caelum,* sky.] **—ce•les′tial•ly** *adv.*

celestial equator *n.* A great circle on the celestial sphere in the same plane as the earth's equator.

celestial globe *n.* A model of the celestial sphere showing the positions of the stars and other celestial bodies.

celestial horizon *n.* A great circle on the celestial sphere having a plane that passes through the center of the earth and is parallel to an observer's horizon.

celestial longitude *n.* The angular distance eastward from the vernal equinox to the great circle drawn through the pole of the ecliptic and a celestial body.

celestial mechanics *n. (used with a sing. v.)* The science of the motion of celestial bodies under the influence of gravitational forces.

celestial navigation *n.* Navigation of a ship or an aircraft based on the positions of celestial bodies.

celestial pole *n.* Either of two diametrically opposite points at which the extensions of the earth's axis intersect the celestial sphere.

celestial sphere *n.* An imaginary sphere of infinite extent with the earth at its center on which the stars, planets, and other heavenly bodies appear to be located.

cel•es•tine (sĕl′ĭ-stīn′, -stīn′, sə-lĕs′tĭn, -tīn) *n.* See **celestite.** [Ger. *Zölestin* < Lat. *caelestis,* celestial. See CELESTIAL.]

cel•es•tite (sĕl′ĭ-stīt′, sə-lĕs′tīt′) *n.* A white, red-brown, orange, or light blue strontium ore, essentially strontium sulfate, $SrSO_4$, found in sedimentary rock. [CELESTINE + -ITE[1].]

ce•li•ac also **coe•li•ac** (sē′lē-ăk′) *adj.* Of or relating to the abdomen or abdominal cavity. [Lat. *coeliacus* < Gk. *koiliakos* < *koilia,* abdomen < *koilos,* hollow. See **keuə-*.**]

celiac disease *n.* A chronic nutritional disturbance, usu. of young children, caused by the inability to metabolize gluten and resulting in malnutrition and a distended abdomen.

cel•i•ba•cy (sĕl′ə-bə-sē) *n.* **1.** Sexual abstinence, esp. for religious vows. **2.** The condition of being unmarried.

cel•i•bate (sĕl′ə-bĭt) *n. & adj.* **1.** Practicing sexual abstinence, esp. for religious vows. **2.** Unmarried; unwed. [Lat. *caelibātus* < *caelebs, caelib-,* unmarried.] **—cel′i•bate** *n.*

Usage Note: The use of *celibate* in its older sense "unmarried" is almost sure to invite misinterpretation in other than narrowly ecclesiastical contexts. Sixty-eight percent of the Usage Panel rejected the older use in the sentence *He remained celibate* [unmarried], *although he engaged in sexual intercourse.*

cell (sĕl) *n.* **1.** A narrow, confining room, as in a prison. **2.** A small enclosed cavity or space, as in a honeycomb. **3.** *Biol.* The smallest structural unit of an organism that is capable of independent functioning, consisting of one or more nuclei, cytoplasm, and various organelles, all surrounded by a semipermeable cell membrane. **4.** The smallest organizational unit of a centralized group or movement. **5.** *Elect.* **a.** A single unit for electrolysis or conversion of chemical into electric energy, usu. consisting of a container with electrodes and an electrolyte. **b.** A single unit that converts radiant energy into electric energy. **6.** *Comp. Sci.* A basic unit of storage in a computer memory that can hold one unit of information. **7.** A geographic area or zone surrounding a transmitter in a cellular telephone system. **8.** A small, humble abode, such as a hermit's hut. **9.** A small religious house dependent on a larger one. *—v.* **celled, cell•ing, cells.** *—tr.* **1.** To put or confine in a cell. **2.** To store in a honeycomb. *—intr.* To live in or share a cell. [ME *celle* < OE *cell* and < OFr., both < Lat. *cella,* chamber. See **kel-**[1]***.**]

cel•la (sĕl′ə) *n., pl.* **cel•lae** (sĕl′ē). The inner room or sanctuary of an ancient Greek or Roman temple. [Lat. See **kel-**[1]***.**]

cel•lar (sĕl′ər) *n.* **1.** A room or enclosed space used for storage, usu. beneath the ground or under a building. **2.** A basement. **3.** An underground shelter, as from storms. **4.** A wine cellar. **5.** *Slang.* The lowest level. *—tr.v.* **-lared, -lar•ing, -lars.** To store in a cellar. [ME *celer* < OFr. < LLat. *cellārium,* pantry < Lat. *cella,* storeroom. See **kel-**[1]***.**]

cel•lar•age (sĕl′ər-ĭj) *n.* **1.** A fee charged for storage in a cellar. **2.** A cellar or several cellars.

cel•lar•er (sĕl′ər-ər) *n.* A person, as in a monastic community, responsible for maintaining the supply of food and drink. [ME *celerer* < OFr. < Lat. *cellārius,* steward < *cella,* storeroom. See **kel-**[1]***.**]

cel•lar•ette also **cel•lar•et** (sĕl′ə-rĕt′) *n.* A cabinet for storing bottles of wine or liquor.

cell•block (sĕl′blŏk′) *n.* A group of cells in a prison.

cell body *n.* The portion of a nerve cell that contains the nucleus but does not incorporate the dendrites or axon.

cell cycle *n.* The series of events involving the growth, replication, and division of a eukaryotic cell.

cell division *n.* The process by which a cell divides to form two daughter cells, each of which contains the same genetic material as the original cell and roughly half of its cytoplasm.

Cel•li•ni (chə-lē′nē, chĕ-), **Benvenuto.** 1500–71. Italian writer and sculptor known for his *Autobiography.*

cell•mate (sĕl′māt′) *n.* A person sharing a cell, esp. in prison.

cell-med•i•at•ed immune response (sĕl′mē′dē-ā′tĭd) *n.* The immune response produced when sensitized T cells directly attack foreign antigens and secrete lymphokines that initiate the body's humoral immune response.

cell membrane *n.* The semipermeable membrane that encloses the cytoplasm of a cell.

cel•lo[1] (chĕl′ō) *n., pl.* **-los.** *Mus.* A four-stringed instrument of the violin family, lower than the viola but higher than the double bass. [Short for VIOLONCELLO.] **—cel′list** (chĕl′ĭst) *n.*

cel•lo[2] (sĕl′ō) *n.* Cellophane. **—cel•lo** *adj.*

cel•loi•din (sə-loid′n) *n.* A pure form of pyroxylin in which specimens for microscopic examination are embedded. [CEL-L(ULOSE) + -OID + -IN.]

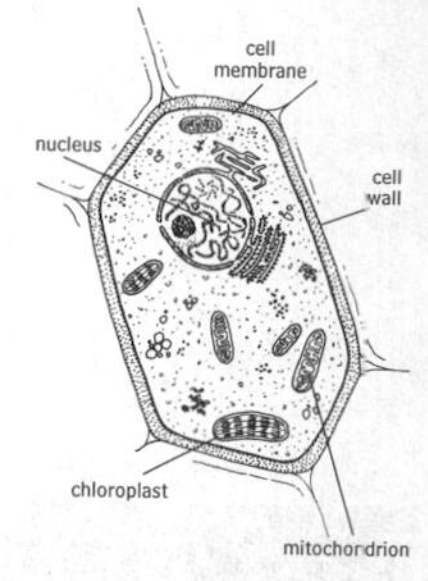

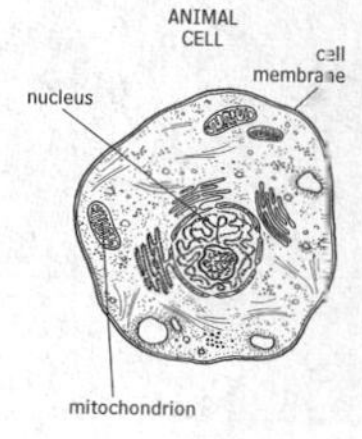

cell

cello[1]

ă pat	oi boy
ā pay	ou out
âr care	o͝o took
ä father	o͞o boot
ĕ pet	ŭ cut
ē be	ûr urge
ĭ pit	th thin
ī pie	*th* this
îr pier	hw which
ŏ pot	zh vision
ō toe	ə about, item
ô paw	

Stress marks:
′ (primary);
′ (secondary), as in **dictionary** (dĭk′shə-nĕr′ē)

cel•lo•phane (sĕl′ə-fān′) *n.* A thin, flexible, transparent cellulose material made from wood pulp and used as a moistureproof wrapping. [Originally a trademark.] — **cel′lo•phane′** *adj.*

cellophane noodle *n.* A thin transparent noodle.

cell plate *n.* A partition formed during cell division in plants and some algae that separates the two new daughter cells.

cell sap *n.* The liquid contained within a vacuole of a plant cell.

cel•lu•lar (sĕl′yə-lər) *adj.* **1.** Of, relating to, or resembling a cell. **2.** Consisting of or containing a cell or cells: *the cellular construction of a beehive.* **3.** Of or involving the cells of an organization or movement. [< Lat. *cellula*, cellule. See CELLULE.] — **cel′lu•lar′i•ty** (-lăr′ĭ-tē) *n.* — **cel′lu•lar•ly** *adv.*

cellular immune response *n.* See **cell-mediated immune response.**

cellular respiration *n.* The series of metabolic processes by which living cells produce energy through the oxidation of organic substances.

cellular slime mold *n.* See **slime mold** 1.

cellular telephone *n.* A mobile radiotelephone that uses a network of short-range transmitters in overlapping cells and a central station to connect to telephone lines.

cel•lu•lase (sĕl′yə-lās′, -lāz′) *n.* Any of several enzymes produced chiefly by fungi, bacteria, and protozoans that catalyze the hydrolysis of cellulose. [CELLUL(OSE) + -ASE.]

cel•lule (sĕl′yo͞ol) *n.* A small cell. [Fr. < Lat. *cellula*, dim. of *cella*, chamber. See CELLA.]

cel•lu•lite (sĕl′yə-līt′) *n.* A fatty deposit, as around the thighs. [Fr. : *cellule*, cellule; see CELLULE + *-ite*, disease (< NLat. *-itis*, -itis).]

cel•lu•li•tis (sĕl′yə-lī′tĭs) *n.* A spreading inflammation of subcutaneous or connective tissue. [CELLUL(E) + -ITIS.]

cel•lu•loid (sĕl′yə-loid′) *n.* **1.** A colorless flammable material made from nitrocellulose and camphor and used to make photographic film. **2.** The cinema. — *adj.* **1.** Made of or using celluloid. **2.** Of or portrayed on film or in motion pictures. **3.** Artificial; synthetic. [Originally a trademark.]

Celtic cross

cel•lu•lo•lyt•ic (sĕl′yə-lō-lĭt′ĭk) *adj.* Of, relating to, or causing the hydrolysis of cellulose. [CELLULO(SE) + -LYTIC.]

cel•lu•lose (sĕl′yə-lōs′, -lōz′) *n.* A complex carbohydrate, $(C_6H_{10}O_5)_n$, that is composed of glucose units, forms the main constituent of the cell wall in most plants, and is important in the manufacture of numerous products, such as paper and explosives. [Fr. < *cellule*, biological cell. See CELLULE.] — **cel′lu•lo′sic** (-lō′sĭk, -zĭk) *adj.*

cellulose acetate *n.* A cellulose resin used in lacquers, photographic film, transparent sheeting, and cigarette filters.

cellulose nitrate *n.* See **nitrocellulose.**

cell wall *n.* The rigid outermost cell layer found in plants and certain algae, bacteria, and fungi but characteristically absent from animal cells.

ce•lom (sē′ləm) *n.* Var. of **coelom.**

ce•lo•sia (sə-lō′zhə, -zhē-ə) *n.* See **cockscomb** 3. [NLat. *Celosia*, genus name < Gk. *kēlos*, burnt < *kaiein*, to burn.]

Cel•si•us (sĕl′sē-əs, -shəs) *adj.* Of or relating to a temperature scale that registers the freezing point of water as 0° and the boiling point as 100° under normal atmospheric pressure. See table at **measurement.** [After Anders CELSIUS.]

Celsius, Anders. 1701–44. Swedish astronomer who devised (1742) the centigrade thermometer.

celt (sĕlt) *n.* A common prehistoric tool of stone or metal, shaped like a chisel or ax head. [LLat. *celtis, chisel.]

censer

Celt (kĕlt, sĕlt) also **Kelt** (kĕlt) *n.* **1.** One of an Indo-European people originally of central Europe and spreading to western Europe and the British Isles and southeast to Galatia during pre-Roman times, esp. a Briton or Gaul. **2.** A speaker of a modern Celtic language or a descendant of such a speaker. [Fr. *Celte*, sing. of *Celtes* < Lat. *Celtae* < Gk. *Keltoi.*]

Celt•i•ber•i•an (kĕl′tĭ-bĕr′ē-ən, sĕl′-) *n.* **1.** One of an ancient Celtic people of northern Spain. **2.** The language of this people. — **Celt′i•ber′i•an** *adj.*

Celt•ic (kĕl′tĭk, sĕl′-) also **Kelt•ic** (kĕl′-) — *n.* A subfamily of the Indo-European language family comprising the Brittonic and the Goidelic branches. — *adj.* Of or relating to the Celtic people and languages.

Celtic cross *n.* A Latin cross with a circle superimposed on its center.

Celt•i•cism (kĕl′tĭ-sĭz′əm, sĕl′-) *n.* **1.** A Celtic custom. **2.** A Celtic idiom. **3.** A fondness for Celtic culture.

Celt•i•cist (kĕl′tĭ-sĭst, sĕl′-) *n.* A specialist in Celtic culture or Celtic languages.

cem•ba•lo (chĕm′bə-lō′) *n.*, *pl.* **-los.** *Mus.* A harpsichord. [Ital., short for *clavicembalo* < Med.Lat. *clāvicymbalum* : Lat. *clāvis*, key + Lat. *cymbalum*, cymbal; see CYMBAL.] — **cem′ba•list** (-bə-lĭst) *n.*

ce•ment (sĭ-mĕnt′) *n.* **1.a.** A building material made by grinding calcined limestone and clay to a fine powder, which can be mixed with water and poured to set as a solid mass or used in making mortar or concrete. **b.** Portland cement. **c.** Concrete. **2.** A substance that hardens to act as an adhesive; glue. **3.** Something that binds or unites. **4.** *Geol.* A chemically precipitated substance that binds particles of clastic rocks. **5.** *Dentistry.* A substance used for filling cavities or anchoring restorations. — *v.* **-ment•ed, -ment•ing, -ments.** — *tr.* **1.** To bind with or as if with cement. **2.** To cover or coat with cement. — *intr.* To become cemented. — ***idiom.* in cement.** Firmly settled; unalterable. [ME < OFr. *ciment* < Lat. *caementum*, rough-cut stone < *caedere*, to cut. See **kaə-id-*.**]

ce•men•ta•tion (sē′mĕn-tā′shən) *n.* **1.** The act, process, or result of cementing. **2.** A metallurgical coating process in which iron or steel is immersed in a powder of another metal, such as zinc or chromium, and heated to a temperature below the melting point of either.

ce•ment•ite (sĭ-mĕn′tīt′) *n.* A hard brittle iron carbide, Fe_3C, found in steel with more than 0.85 percent carbon. [< CEMENT.]

ce•men•ti•tious (sē′mĕn-tĭsh′əs) *adj.* Of or relating to a chemical precipitate having the characteristics of cement.

cement mixer *n.* A machine having a revolving drum in which cement, sand, gravel, and water are combined into concrete.

ce•men•tum (sĭ-mĕn′təm) also **ce•ment** (-mĕnt′) *n.* A bonelike substance covering the root of a tooth. [NLat. < Lat. *caementum*, rough stone. See CEMENT.]

cem•e•ter•y (sĕm′ĭ-tĕr′ē) *n.*, *pl.* **-ies.** A place for burying the dead; a graveyard. [ME *cimiterie* < OFr. *cimitiere* < Med. Lat. *cimitērium* < LLat. *coemētērium* < Gk. *koimētērion* < *koiman*, to put to sleep. See **kei-¹*.**]

cen. *abbr.* **1.** Central. **2.** Century.

cen•a•cle (sĕn′ə-kəl) *n.* **1.** A clique or circle, esp. of writers. **2.** A small dining room, usu. on an upper floor. [Fr. *cénacle* < OFr., the room where the Last Supper took place < Lat. *cēnāculum*, dining room < *cēna*, meal. See **sker-¹*.**]

Cen•ci (chĕn′chē), **Beatrice.** 1577–99. Italian noblewoman who was hanged for patricide.

-cene *suff.* Recent. Used in names of geological periods: *Oligocene.* [< Gk. *kainos*, new. See **ken-*.**]

Ce•nis (sə-nē′), **Mont.** A mountain pass, 2,083.5 m (6,831 ft), in the Alps on the French-Italian border.

ceno– *pref.* Var. of **coeno–.**

cen•o•bite also **coen•o•bite** (sĕn′ə-bīt′, sē′nə-) *n.* A member of a convent or other religious community. [ME < LLat. *coenobīta*, ult. < Gk. *koinobios*, living in community : *koinos*, common; see **kom*** + *bios*, life; see **gʷei-*.**] — **cen′o•bit′ic** (-bĭt′ĭk), **cen′o•bit′i•cal** *adj.*

ce•no•spe•cies (sē′nə-spē′shēz, -sēz, sĕn′ə-) *n.* A group of related ecospecies capable of interbreeding so as to produce at least partially fertile hybrids.

cen•o•taph (sĕn′ə-tăf′) *n.* A monument honoring a dead person whose remains lie elsewhere. [Fr. *cénotaphe* < OFr. < Lat. *cenotaphium* < Gk. *kenotaphion* : *kenos*, empty + *taphos*, tomb.] — **cen′o•taph′ic** *adj.*

Ce•no•zo•ic (sē′nə-zō′ĭk, sĕn′ə-) *adj.* Of, belonging to, or being the latest era of geologic time, during which modern continents were formed and animals and plants diversified. See table at **geologic time.** — *n.* The Cenozoic Era. [Gk. *kainos*, new; see **ken-*** + -ZOIC.]

cense (sĕns) *tr.v.* **censed, cens•ing, cens•es. 1.** To perfume with incense. **2.** To burn incense to. [ME *censen*, short for *encensen* < *encens*, incense. See INCENSE².]

cen•ser (sĕn′sər) *n.* A vessel for burning incense, esp. during religious services. [ME, short for *encenser* < AN *encensier* < *encens*, incense < OFr. See INCENSE².]

cen•sor (sĕn′sər) *n.* **1.** One authorized to examine books, films, or other material and suppress what is considered objectionable. **2.** An official who examines personal mail and official dispatches to remove information considered secret or a security risk. **3.** One that condemns or censures. **4.** One of two officials in ancient Rome responsible for the public census and public morals. **5.** *Psychol.* The agent in the unconscious that is responsible for censorship. — *tr.v.* **-sored, -sor•ing, -sors.** To examine and expurgate. [Lat. *cēnsor*, Roman censor < *cēnsēre*, to assess. See **kens-*.**] — **cen′sor•a•ble** *adj.* — **cen•so′ri•al** (sĕn-sôr′ē-əl, -sōr′-) *adj.*

cen•so•ri•ous (sĕn-sôr′ē-əs, -sōr′-) *adj.* **1.** Tending to censure; highly critical. **2.** Expressing censure. — **cen•so′ri•ous•ly** *adv.* — **cen•so′ri•ous•ness** *n.*

cen•sor•ship (sĕn′sər-shĭp′) *n.* **1.** The act, process, or practice of censoring. **2.** The office or authority of a Roman censor. **3.** *Psychol.* Prevention of disturbing thoughts or feelings from reaching consciousness except in a disguised form.

cen•sur•a•ble (sĕn′shər-ə-bəl) *adj.* Deserving of or open to censure. — **cen′sur•a•ble•ness, cen′sur•a•bil′i•ty** *n.* — **cen′sur•a•bly** *adv.*

cen•sure (sĕn′shər) *n.* **1.** An expression of strong disapproval or harsh criticism. **2.** An official rebuke, such as one by a legislature to a member. — *tr.v.* **-sured, -sur•ing, -sures. 1.** To criticize severely; blame. See Syns at **criticize. 2.** To express official disapproval of. [ME < Lat. *cēnsūra*, censorship < *cēnsor*, Roman censor. See CENSOR.] — **cen′sur•er** *n.*

cen•sus (sĕn′səs) *n.* **1.** An official enumeration of a population, often including related demographic information. **2.** In ancient Rome, a count of the citizens and a property evaluation for taxation purposes. [Lat. *cēnsus*, registration of citizens < *cēnsēre*, to assess. See **kens-*.**]

cent (sĕnt) *n.* See table at **currency.** [ME < OFr., hundred < Lat. *centum.* See **dekm̥*.**]
cent. *abbr.* **1.** Centigrade. **2.** Central. **3.** *Lat.* Centum (hundred). **4.** Century.
cen•tal (sĕn′tl) *n.* See **hundredweight** 1. [< Lat. *centum,* hundred. See **dekm̥*.**]
cen•taur (sĕn′tôr′) *n. Gk. Myth.* One of a race of monsters with a human upper and an equine lower male body. [ME < Lat. *Centaurus* < Gk. *Kentauros.*]
Cen•tau•rus (sĕn-tôr′əs) *n.* A constellation in the Southern Hemisphere near Vela and Lupus. [Lat. *Centaurus,* centaur. See CENTAUR.]
cen•tau•ry (sĕn′tôr′ē) *n., pl.* **-ries.** Any of several herbs of the genus *Centaurium,* esp. a Eurasian species *(C. erythraea)* long used in herbal medicine. [ME < OE *centaurie* < Lat. *centaurēum* < Gk. *kentaureion* < *Kentauros,* centaur.]
cen•ta•vo (sĕn-tä′vō) *n., pl.* **-vos.** See table at **currency.** [Sp., hundredth < Lat. *centum,* hundred. See **dekm̥*.**]
cen•te•nar•i•an (sĕn′tə-nâr′ē-ən) *n.* One that is 100 years old or older. [< Lat. *centēnārius,* of a hundred. See CENTENARY.] **— cen′te•nar′i•an** *adj.*
cen•ten•a•ry (sĕn-tĕn′ə-rē, sĕn′tə-nĕr′ē) *adj.* **1.** Of or relating to a 100-year period. **2.** Occurring once every 100 years. *— n., pl.* **-ries. 1.** A 100-year period. **2.** A centennial. [Lat. *centēnārius,* of a hundred < *centum,* hundred. See **dekm̥*.**]
cen•ten•ni•al (sĕn-tĕn′ē-əl) *adj.* **1.** Of or relating to an age or period of 100 years. **2.** Occurring once every 100 years. **3.** Of or relating to a 100th anniversary. *— n.* A 100th anniversary or a celebration of it. [Lat. *centum,* hundred; see **dekm̥*** + (BI)ENNIAL.] **— cen•ten′ni•al•ly** *adv.*
cen•ter (sĕn′tər) *n.* **1.** A point or place that is equally distant from the sides or outer boundaries of something; the middle. **2.a.** A point equidistant from the vertexes of a regular polygon. **b.** A point equidistant from all points on the circumference of a circle or on the surface of a sphere. **3.** A point around which something rotates or revolves. **4.** A part of an object that is surrounded by the rest; a core. **5.a.** A place where a particular activity or service is concentrated. **b.** A point of origin, as of influence, ideas, or actions. **c.** An area of dense population. **6.** A person or thing that is the chief object of attention, interest, activity, or emotion. **7.** A person, object, or group occupying a middle position. **8.** Often **Center.** A political group or a set of policies representing a moderate view. **9.** *Physiol.* A group of neurons in the central nervous system that control a particular function. **10.** *Sports.* A player who holds a middle position on the field, court, or forward line in some team sports. **11.** *Baseball.* Center field. **12.a.** A small conical hole made in a piece of work with a center punch so that a drill can be accurately positioned within it. **b.** A bar with a conical point used to support work, as during turning on a lathe. *— v.* **-tered, -ter•ing, -ters.** *— tr.* **1.** To place in or at the center. **2.** To direct toward a center or central point; concentrate or focus. **3.** *Football.* To pass (the ball) back between the legs to begin a down. *— intr.* **1.** To be concentrated; cluster. **2.** To have a central theme or concern; be focused. [ME *centre* < OFr. < Lat. *centrum* < Gk. *kentron,* center of a circle < *kentein,* to prick. See **kent-*.**]

Syns: *center, focus, headquarters, heart, hub, seat.* The central meaning shared by these nouns is "a region, person, or thing around which something concentrates": *a great cultural center; the focus of research efforts; the headquarters of a corporation; a town that is the heart of the colony; the hub of a steel empire; the seat of government.*

center bit *n.* A drill bit having a sharp center point, used in carpentry for boring holes.
cen•ter•board (sĕn′tər-bôrd′, -bōrd′) *n. Naut.* A keel in a sailboat that can be pivoted upward to reduce the boat's draft in shallow water.
Cen•ter•each (sĕn′tə-rēch′). A community of SE NY on central Long I. Pop. 26,720.
cen•tered (sĕn′tərd) *adj.* **1.** Being at or placed in the center. **2.** Having a specified center. Often used in combination: *soft-centered.* **3.** Self-confident and well-balanced.
center field *n. Baseball.* **1.** The middle third of the outfield. **2.** The position played there. **— center fielder** *n.*
cen•ter•fold (sĕn′tər-fōld′) *n.* A magazine center spread, esp. a foldout of an oversize photograph or feature.
cen•ter•line (sĕn′tər-līn′) *n.* A painted line dividing a road or highway into two sections.
center of gravity *n., pl.* **centers of gravity. 1.** The point in or near a body through which the resultant of the gravitational forces on the component particles of the body acts. **2.** The point of greatest importance or interest.
center of mass *n., pl.* **centers of mass.** The point in a body or system of bodies at which the total mass of the system may be considered to be concentrated and external forces may be considered to be applied.
cen•ter•piece (sĕn′tər-pēs′) *n.* **1.** Something in a central position, esp. a decorative object or arrangement placed at the center of a table. **2.** The central or most important feature.
center punch *n.* A tool with a sharp point used in metalworking to mark centers or center lines on pieces to be drilled.
center spread *n.* **1.** The two facing pages in the center of a magazine or newspaper. **2.** A feature located there.
cen•tes•i•mal (sĕn-tĕs′ə-məl) *adj.* Relating to or divided into hundredths. [< Lat. *centēsimus* < *centum,* hundred. See **dekm̥*.**] **— cen•tes′i•mal•ly** *adv.*
cen•tes•i•mo[1] (sĕn-tĕs′ə-mō′) *n., pl.* **-mos** or **-mi** (-mē). See table at **currency.** [Ital., hundredth < Lat. *centēsimus.* See CENTESIMAL.]
cen•tes•i•mo[2] (sĕn-tĕs′ə-mō′) *n., pl.* **-mos.** See table at **currency.** [Sp. *centésimo,* hundredth < Lat. *centēsimus.* See CENTESIMAL.]
centi– *pref.* **1.** One hundredth part (10^{-2}): *centiliter.* **2.** One hundred: *centipede.* [Fr. < Lat. *centi-,* hundred < *centum.* See **dekm̥*.**]
cen•ti•grade (sĕn′tĭ-grād′) *adj.* Celsius. See table at **measurement.** [Fr. : *centi-,* centi- + *grade,* degree (< Ital. *grado,* rank, degree < Lat. *gradus,* step; see **ghredh-*.**)]
cen•ti•gram (sĕn′tĭ-grăm′) *n.* A metric unit of mass equal to one hundredth (10^{-2}) of a gram.
cen•ti•li•ter (sĕn′tə-lē′tər) *n.* A metric unit of volume equal to one hundredth (10^{-2}) of a liter.
cen•time (sän′tēm′, säN-tēm′) *n.* See table at **currency.** [Fr. < OFr. *centisme* < Lat. *centēsimus,* hundredth < *centum,* hundred. See **dekm̥*.**]
cen•ti•me•ter (sĕn′tə-mē′tər) *n.* A unit of length equal to one hundredth (10^{-2}) of a meter. See table at **measurement.**
cen•ti•me•ter-gram-sec•ond system (sĕn′tə-mē′tər-grăm′sĕk′ənd) *n.* An absolute metric system in which the base units of length, mass, and time are the centimeter, gram, and second.
cen•ti•mo (sĕn′tə-mō′) *n., pl.* **-mos.** See table at **currency.** [Sp. *céntimo* < Fr. *centime.* See CENTIME.]
cen•ti•pede (sĕn′tə-pēd′) *n.* Any of various wormlike arthropods of the class Chilopoda, with a flat body composed of segments, each bearing a pair of jointed appendages. [Lat. *centipeda* : *centi-,* centi- + *pēs, ped-,* foot; see –PED.]
centipede grass *n.* A Southeast Asian perennial grass *(Eremochloa ophiuroides)* cultivated for lawns in warm regions.
cen•ti•poise (sĕn′tə-poiz′) *n.* A centimeter-gram-second unit of dynamic viscosity equal to one hundredth (10^{-2}) of a poise.
cent•ner (sĕnt′nər) *n.* **1.a.** A unit of weight in Germany and Scandinavia equal to 50 kilograms (110.23 pounds). **b.** A unit of weight equal to 100 kilograms (220.46 pounds) in parts of the former Soviet Union. **2.** An assaying unit equal to one dram. [Ger. *Zentner* < OHGer. *cëntenāri* < Lat. *centēnārius,* of a hundred. See CENTENARY.]
cen•to (sĕn′tō) *n., pl.* **-tos.** A literary work pieced together from the works of several authors. [Lat. *centō,* patchwork.]
centr– *pref.* Var. of **centro–.**
cen•tra (sĕn′trə) *n.* Pl. of **centrum.**
cen•tral (sĕn′trəl) *adj.* **1.** Situated at, in, or near the center. **2.** Forming the center. **3.** Having dominant or controlling power or influence. **4.** Of basic importance; essential or principal. **5.** Easily reached from various points. **6.** Of or constituting a single source controlling all components of a system. **7.** *Anat.* **a.** Of, relating to, or originating from the nervous system. **b.** Relating to a centrum. **8.** *Ling.* Neither front nor back. Used of vowels, as the *u* in *cut.* *— n.* **1.a.** A telephone exchange. **b.** An operator at a telephone exchange. **2.** A coordinating office or agency at the center of a group of related activities. [Lat. *centrālis* < *centrum,* center. See CENTER.] **— cen′tral•ly** *adv.*
Cen•tral Af•ri•can Republic (sĕn′trəl ăf′rĭ-kən). Formerly (1976–79) **Central African Empire.** A country of central Africa; gained independence from France in 1960. Cap. Bangui. Pop. 2,395,000.
Central A•mer•i•ca (ə-mĕr′ĭ-kə). A region of S North America extending from the S border of Mexico to the N border of Colombia. **— Central A•mer′i•can** *adj. & n.*
central angle *n. Math.* An angle having its vertex at the center of a circle.
Central A•sian U.S.S.R. (ā′zhən, ā′shən). A historical region of the S U.S.S.R. from the Caspian Sea to the Irtysh R.
central bank *n.* A nation's principal monetary authority, which regulates the money supply and credit, issues currency, and manages the rate of exchange.
central city *n.* A heavily populated city at the core of a large metropolitan area.
Central Falls. A city of NE RI near Providence. Pop. 17,637.
Central I•slip (ī′slĭp). A residential community of SE NY on central Long I. Pop. 26,028.
cen•tral•ism (sĕn′trə-lĭz′əm) *n.* Concentration of power in a central organization. **— cen′tral•ist** *n.* **— cen′tral•is′tic** *adj.*
cen•tral•i•ty (sĕn-trăl′ĭ-tē) *n.* **1.** The state or quality of being central. **2.** A tendency to be or remain at the center.
cen•tral•ize (sĕn′trə-līz′) *v.* **-ized, -iz•ing, -iz•es.** *— tr.* **1.** To draw into or toward a center; consolidate. **2.** To bring under a single, central authority. *— intr.* To come together at a center; concentrate. **— cen′tral•i•za′tion** (-trə-lĭ-zā′shən) *n.* **— cen′tral•iz′er** *n.*

centaur
Black marble statue by Aristeas and Papias of Aphrodisias (first half of second century A.D.)

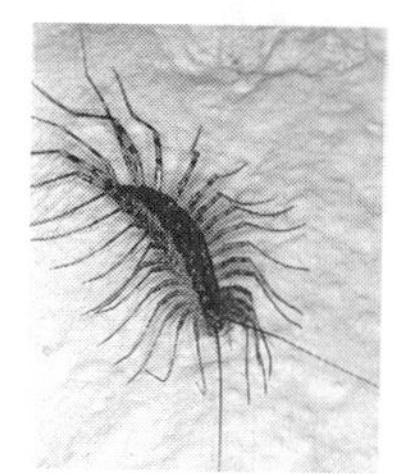

centipede

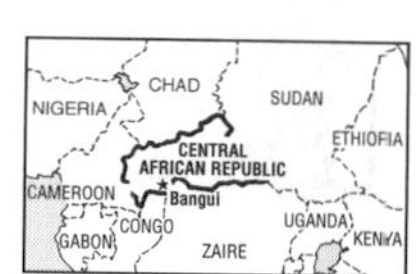

Central African Republic

ă pat	oi boy
ā pay	ou out
âr care	o͝o to͝ok
ä father	o͞o bo͞ot
ĕ pet	ŭ cut
ē be	ûr urge
ĭ pit	th thin
ī pie	*th* this
îr pier	hw which
ŏ pot	zh vision
ō toe	ə about, item
ô paw	

Stress marks:
′ (primary);
′ (secondary), as in
dictionary (dĭk′shə-nĕr′ē)

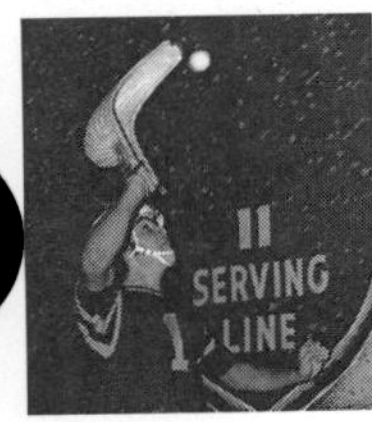

cesta

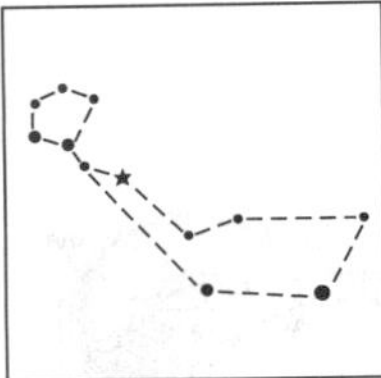
Cetus

Paul Cézanne
Self-portrait

Chad

chafing dish
Mid 18th-century silver chafing dish

cer•tif•i•cate (sər-tĭf′ĭ-kĭt) *n.* **1.** A document testifying to the truth of something. **2.** A document issued to a person completing a course of study not leading to a diploma. **3.** A document certifying that a person may officially practice in certain professions. **4.** A document certifying ownership. — *tr.v.* (-kāt′) **-cat•ed, -cat•ing, -cates.** To furnish with, testify to, or authorize by a certificate. [ME *certificat* < OFr. < Med. Lat. *certificātum*, something certified < neut. of LLat. *certificātus*, p.part. of *certificāre*, to certify. See CERTIFY.] — **cer•tif′i•ca•to′ry** (-kə-tôr′ē, -tōr′ē) *adj.*

certificate of deposit *n., pl.* **certificates of deposit.** A certificate from a bank stating that the named party has a specified sum on deposit, usu. for a given period of time at a fixed rate of interest.

cer•ti•fi•ca•tion (sûr′tə-fĭ-kā′shən) *n.* **1.a.** The act of certifying. **b.** The state of being certified. **2.** A certified statement.

cer•ti•fied check (sûr′tə-fīd′) *n.* A check guaranteed by a bank to be covered by sufficient funds on deposit.

certified mail *n.* Uninsured first-class mail for which proof of delivery is obtained.

certified public accountant *n.* A public accountant who has been certified by a state examining board.

cer•ti•fy (sûr′tə-fī′) *v.* **-fied, -fy•ing, -fies.** — *tr.* **1.a.** To confirm formally as true, accurate, or genuine. **b.** To guarantee as meeting a standard. See Syns at **approve. 2.** To acknowledge in writing on the face of (a check) that the signature of the maker is genuine and that sufficient funds are deposited for its payment. **3.** To issue a license or certificate to. **4.** To declare legally insane. **5.** *Archaic.* To inform positively; assure. — *intr.* To testify. [ME *certifien* < OFr. *certifier* < LLat. *certificāre* : Lat. *certus*, certain; see CERTAIN + Lat. *-ficāre*, -fy.] — **cer′ti•fi′er** *n.*

cer•ti•o•rar•i (sûr′shē-ə-râr′ē, -rä′rē) *n. Law.* A writ from a higher court to a lower one requesting a transcript of the proceedings of a case for review. [ME < Lat. *certiōrārī (volumus)*, (we wish) to be informed, passive of *certiōrāre*, to inform < *certior*, comp. of *certus*, certain. See CERTAIN.]

cer•ti•tude (sûr′tĭ-to͞od′, -tyo͞od′) *n.* **1.** The state of being certain; complete assurance. **2.** Sureness of occurrence; inevitability. **3.** Something assured. See Syns at **certainty.** [ME < LLat. *certitūdō* < Lat. *certus*, certain. See CERTAIN.]

ce•ru•le•an (sə-ro͞o′lē-ən) *adj. Color.* Azure; sky blue. [< Lat. *caeruleus*, dark blue; akin to *caelum*, sky.]

ce•ru•lo•plas•min (sə-ro͞o′lō-plăz′mĭn) *n.* A blood glycoprotein to which copper is bound during transport and storage. [CERUL(EAN) + PLASM(A) + -IN.]

ce•ru•men (sə-ro͞o′mən) *n.* See **earwax.** [NLat. < Lat. *cēra*, wax. See CERATE.] — **ce•ru′mi•nous** (-mə-nəs) *adj.*

ce•ruse (sə-ro͞os′, sîr′o͞os′) *n.* A white lead pigment, sometimes used in cosmetics. [ME < OFr. < Lat. *cērussa*.]

ce•rus•site (sə-rŭs′īt′) *n.* A colorless or white mineral, $PbCO_3$, that is an ore of lead; lead carbonate. [Ger. *Zerussit* < Lat. *cērussa*, ceruse.]

Cer•van•tes Sa•a•ve•dra (sər-văn′tēz sä′ə-vā′drə, thĕr-bän′tĕs sä′ä-bĕth′rä), **Miguel de.** 1547–1616. Spanish writer of the classic satirical novel *Don Quixote* (1605–15).

cer•vi•cal (sûr′vĭ-kəl) *adj.* Of or relating to a neck or a cervix. [< Lat. *cervīx*, *cervīc-*, neck. See CERVIX.]

cervical cap *n.* A small, rubber, cup-shaped contraceptive device that fits over the uterine cervix.

cer•vi•ci•tis (sûr′vĭ-sī′tĭs) *n.* Inflammation of the cervix of the uterus.

cer•vine (sûr′vīn′) *adj.* Of, like, or characteristic of deer. [Lat. *cervīnus* < *cervus*, deer. See **ker-**[1]*.]

cer•vix (sûr′vĭks) *n., pl.* **cer•vix•es** or **cer•vi•ces** (sûr′vĭ-sēz′, sər-vī′sēz). **1.** The neck. **2.** A neck-shaped anatomical structure. [Lat. *cervīx*, neck. See **ker-**[1]*.]

ce•sar•e•an also **cae•sar•e•an** or **cae•sar•i•an** or **ce•sar•i•an** (sĭ-zâr′ē-ən) — *adj.* Of or relating to a cesarean section. — *n.* A cesarean section.

cesarean section also **caesarean section** *n.* A surgical incision through the abdominal wall and uterus, performed to deliver a fetus. [From the traditional belief that Julius CAESAR (or his eponymous ancestor) was born by this operation.]

ce•si•um also **cae•si•um** (sē′zē-əm) *n. Symbol* **Cs** A soft ductile metal, liquid at room temperature, the most electropositive and alkaline of the elements, used in photoelectric cells. Atomic number 55; atomic weight 132.905; melting point 28.5°C; boiling point 690°C; specific gravity 1.87; valence 1. See table at **element.** [< Lat. *caesius*, bluish gray.]

Čes•ké Bu•dě•jo•vi•ce (chĕs′kĕ bo͝od′yə-yô-vĭ-tsĕ). A city of S-central Czech Republic on the Vltava R. S of Prague; founded in the 13th cent. Pop. 93,520.

ces•pi•tose (sĕs′pĭ-tōs′) *adj. Bot.* Growing in tufts or clumps. [NLat. *caespitōsus* < Lat. *caespes*, *caespit-*, turf.] — **ces′pi•tose′ly** *adv.*

cess (sĕs) *n. Irish.* Luck. [Poss. short for SUCCESS.]

ces•sa•tion (sĕ-sā′shən) *n.* A bringing or coming to an end; a ceasing. [ME *cessacioun* < OFr. *cessation* < Lat. *cessātiō*, *cessātiōn-* < *cessātus*, p.part. of *cessāre*, to stop. See CEASE.]

ces•sion (sĕsh′ən) *n.* **1.** A ceding or surrendering, as of territory. **2.** Something, such as territory, that is ceded. [ME < OFr. < Lat. *cessiō*, *cessiōn-* < *cessus*, p.part. of *cēdere*, to yield. See **ked-***.]

cess•pit (sĕs′pĭt′) *n.* A refuse or sewage pit. [CESS(POOL) + PIT[1].]

cess•pool (sĕs′po͞ol′) *n.* **1.** A covered hole or pit for drainage or sewage. **2.** A filthy, disgusting, or corrupt place. [Perh. alteration (influenced by POOL[1]) of obsolete *cesperalle*, drainpipe < ME *suspiral*, vent < OFr. *sospirail*, breathing hole < *souspirer*, to breathe < Lat. *suspīrāre*, to sigh. See SUSPIRE.]

ces•ta (sĕs′tə) *n. Sports.* A scoop-shaped wicker basket that is worn over the hand and used to catch and throw the ball in jai alai. [Sp., basket < Lat. *cista*, chest. See CHEST.]

ces•tode (sĕs′tōd′) *n.* Any of various parasitic flatworms of the class Cestoda, having a long flat body with a specialized organ of attachment at one end. [< NLat. *Cestoda*, class name < Lat. *cestus*, belt < Gk. *kestos*. See CESTUS[1].] — **ces′tode′** *adj.*

ces•tus[1] (sĕs′təs) *n., pl.* **-ti** (-tī). A woman's belt or girdle, esp. in ancient Greece. [Lat., belt < Gk. *kestos*. See **kent-***.]

ces•tus[2] (sĕs′təs) *n., pl.* **-tus•es.** A hand covering made of weighted leather straps and worn by boxers in ancient Rome. [Lat. *caestus* < *caedere*, to strike. See **kaə-id-***.]

ce•su•ra (sĭ-zho͝or′ə, -zo͝or′ə) *n.* Var. of **caesura.**

CET or **C.E.T.** *abbr.* Central European Time.

CETA *abbr.* Comprehensive Employment and Training Act.

ce•ta•cean (sĭ-tā′shən) *n.* Any of various aquatic, chiefly marine mammals of the order Cetacea, including the whales, characterized by a nearly hairless body, broad flippers, vestigial posterior limbs, and a flat notched tail. [< NLat. *Cētācea*, order name < Lat. *cētus*, whale. See CETUS.] — **ce•ta′cean, ce•ta′ceous** (sĭ-tā′shəs) *adj.*

ce•tane (sē′tān′) *n.* A liquid, $C_{16}H_{34}$, used as a solvent and in standardized hydrocarbons. [Lat. *cētus*, whale (so called because it is found in sperm whale oil); see CETUS + -ANE.]

cetane number *n.* The performance rating of a diesel fuel, the percentage of cetane in a cetane-methylnaphthalene mixture with the same ignition performance.

cete (sēt) *n.* A company of badgers. [ME, poss. < Med.Lat. *cetus*, assembly < Lat. *coetus*, var. of *coitus*. See COITUS.]

ce•ter•is par•i•bus (kā′tər-ĭs păr′ə-bəs) *adv.* With all other factors or things remaining the same. [NLat. *cēterīs pāribus*, with other things equal : Latin *cēterīs*, ablative pl. of *cēterus*, the other + Lat. *pāribus*, ablative pl. of *pārs*, equal.]

ce•tol•o•gy (sĭ-tŏl′ə-jē) *n.* The zoology of whales and related aquatic mammals. [Lat. *cētus*, whale; see CETUS + -LOGY.] — **ce′to•log′i•cal** (sēt′l-ŏj′ĭ-kəl) *adj.* — **ce•tol′o•gist** *n.*

cet. par. *abbr.* Ceteris paribus.

Ce•tus (sē′təs) *n.* A constellation in the Southern Hemisphere near Aquarius and Eridanus. [Lat. *cētus*, whale < Gk. *kētos*.]

ce•tyl alcohol (sēt′l) *n.* A waxy alcohol, $C_{15}H_{33}OH$, used in cosmetics and pharmaceuticals. [Lat. *cētus*, whale; see CETUS + -YL.]

Ceu•ta (syo͞o′tə, thĕ′o͞o-tä, sĕ′-). A Spanish city of NW Africa, an enclave in Morocco on the Strait of Gibraltar. Pop. 68,882.

Cé•vennes (sā-vĕn′). A mountain range of S France W of the Rhone R. and rising to 1,754.7 m (5,753 ft).

ce•vi•che or **se•vi•che** (sə-vē′chā, sĕ-) *n.* Raw fish marinated in lime or lemon juice and served usu. as an appetizer. [Am. Sp. < Sp. *cebiche*, fish stew < *cebo*, bait < Lat. *cibus*, food.]

Cey•lon (sĭ-lŏn′, sā-). See **Sri Lanka.** — **Cey′lo•nese′** (-nēz′, -nēs′) *adj. & n.*

Cé•zanne (sā-zăn′, -zän′), **Paul.** 1839–1906. French artist and leading postimpressionist whose paintings include *The Card Players* (1890–92). — **Cé•zan′nesque′** (-zăn′ĕsk′) *adj.*

Cf The symbol for the element **californium.**

CF *abbr.* **1.** *Baseball.* Center field; center fielder. **2.** Cystic fibrosis.

cf. *abbr.* **1.** Calfskin. **2.** *Lat.* Confer (compare).

CFC *abbr.* Chlorofluorocarbon.

cfm or **c.f.m.** *abbr.* Cubic feet per minute.

cfs or **c.f.s.** *abbr.* Cubic feet per second.

cg *abbr.* Centigram.

c.g. *abbr.* **1.** Center of gravity. **2.** Or **C.G.** Consul general.

C.G. *abbr.* **1.** Coast guard. **2.** Commanding general.

cgm *abbr.* Centigram.

cgs or **CGS** *abbr.* Centimeter-gram-second system.

ch. *abbr.* **1.** Or **Ch.** Chaplain. **2.** Chapter. **3.** Check (bank order). **4.** Or **Ch.** Chief. **5.** Child; children. **6.** Or **Ch.** Church.

Ch. *abbr.* China.

c.h. or **C.H.** *abbr.* **1.** Clearing-house. **2.** Courthouse. **3.** Customhouse.

Cha•blis (shă-blē′, shä-, shăb′lē) *n.* **1.** A dry white wine originally from east-central France. **2.** A blended white table wine of California. [After *Chablis*, a village of N-central France.]

cha-cha (chä′chä) *n.* A rhythmic ballroom dance that originated in Latin America. [Am.Sp. *chachachá*.] — **cha′-cha** *v.*

chach•ka or **tchotch•ke** (chŏch′kə) also **tsats•ke** (tsäts′kə) *n. Slang.* A cheap showy trinket. [Yiddish *tshatshke* < Pol. dial. *czaczka*.]

chac•ma (chăk′mə) *n.* A grayish-black baboon *(Papio ursinus)* of southern and eastern Africa. [Poss. of Khokhoin orig.]

Cha•co (chä′kō). See **Gran Chaco.**

cha•conne (shă-kôn′, -kŏn′) *n.* **1.** A slow stately dance of the 18th century or the music for it. **2.** *Mus.* A form consisting of variations based on a reiterated harmonic pattern. [Fr. < Sp. *chacona,* a kind of dance.]

Chad (chăd). A country of N-central Africa; achieved independence from France in 1960. Cap. Ndjamena. Pop. 4,405,000. **—Chad′i•an** *adj. & n.*

Chad, Lake. A shallow lake of N-central Africa in Chad, Cameroon, Niger, and Nigeria.

Chad•ic (chăd′ĭk) *n.* A branch of the Afro-Asiatic language family, spoken in west-central Africa and including Hausa.

cha•dor (chä-dôr′) *n.* A loose, usu. black robe worn by women, esp. Iranian Muslims, that covers the body from head to toe. [Urdu *chādar,* cover, cloth < Pers., screen, tent < Skt. *chattram,* screen, parasol. See CHUDDAR.]

Chad•wick (chăd′wĭk), Sir **James.** 1891–1974. British physicist who won a 1935 Nobel Prize.

Chaer•o•ne•a (kĕr′ə-nē′ə, kîr′-). An ancient city of E Greece where Philip of Macedon defeated a confederation of Greek states in 338 B.C.

chae•ta (kē′tə) *n., pl.* **-tae** (-tē′). A bristle or seta, esp. of an annelid worm. [NLat. < Gk. *khaitē,* long hair.]

chae•tog•nath (kē′tŏg-năth′) *n.* Any of various marine worms of the phylum Chaetognatha. [< NLat. *Chaetognatha,* phylum name : *chaeta,* chaeta; see CHAETA + Gk. *gnathos,* jaw; see **genu-**[2]*.] **—chae′tog•nath′, chae•tog′na•thous** (-nə-thəs) *adj.*

chafe (chāf) *v.* **chafed, chaf•ing, chafes.** *—tr.* **1.** To wear away or irritate by rubbing. **2.** To annoy; vex. **3.** To warm by rubbing. *—intr.* **1.** To rub and cause irritation or friction. **2.** To become worn or sore from rubbing. **3.** To feel irritated or impatient. *—n.* **1.** Warmth, wear, or soreness produced by friction. **2.** Annoyance; vexation. [ME *chafen* < OFr. *chaufer,* to warm < VLat. **calefāre,* alteration of Lat. *calefacere* : *calēre,* to be warm; see **kelə-**[1]* + *facere,* to make; see **dhē-***.]

cha•fer (chā′fər) *n.* Any of various beetles of the family Scarabaeidae. [ME, a kind of beetle < OE *ceafor.*]

chaff[1] (chăf) *n.* **1.** *Bot.* Thin, dry bracts or scales, esp.: **a.** The bracts enclosing mature grains of wheat and some other cereal grasses, removed during threshing. **b.** The scales or bracts borne on the receptacle among the flowers of many plants in the composite family. **2.** Finely cut straw or hay used as fodder. **3.** Trivial or worthless matter. **4.** Strips of metal, foil, or glass fiber with a metal content that are used to reflect electromagnetic energy as a radar countermeasure. [ME *chaf* < OE *ceaf.*] **—chaff′fy** *adj.*

chaff[2] (chăf) *v.* **chaffed, chaff•ing, chaffs.** *—tr.* To make fun of in a good-natured way; tease. *—intr.* To tease playfully. [Poss. alteration of CHAFE or CHAFF[1].] **—chaff** *n.*

chaff•er[1] (chăf′ər) *n.* One who engages in banter or good-natured teasing.

chaf•fer[2] (chăf′ər) *v.* **-fered, -fer•ing, -fers.** *—intr.* **1.** To bargain. **2.** *Chiefly British.* To bandy words. *—tr.* To bargain for. *—n. Archaic.* A bargaining. [ME *chaffaren,* to haggle < *chaffare, cheapfare,* bargaining : *chep,* purchase; see CHEAP + *fare,* journey, business (< OE *faru* < *faran,* to travel; see FARE).] **—chaf′fer•er** *n.*

chaf•finch (chăf′ĭnch) *n.* A small European songbird *(Fringilla coelebs),* the male of which has reddish-brown plumage. [ME *chaffinche* < OE *ceaffinc* : *ceaf,* chaff, husk + *finch,* finch.]

chaf•ing dish (chā′fĭng) *n.* A metal dish or pan mounted above a heating device and used to cook or warm food.

Cha•gall (shə-gäl′, -găl′, shä-), **Marc.** 1887–1985. Russian-born artist noted for his dreamlike fanciful imagery.

Cha•gas′ disease (shä′gəs) *n.* A South American form of trypanosomiasis caused by the protozoan *Trypanosoma cruzi* and characterized by fever and enlargement of the spleen and lymph nodes. [After Carlos *Chagas* (1879–1934), Brazilian physician.]

Chag•a•tai (chăg′ə-tī′). See **Jagatai.**

Cha•gres (chä′grĕs). A river rising in central Panama and flowing SW to Gatún Lake then NW to the Caribbean Sea.

cha•grin (shə-grĭn′) *n.* A keen feeling of mental unease caused by failure, disappointment, or a disconcerting event. *—tr.v.* **-grined, -grin•ing, -grins.** To cause to feel chagrin; mortify or discomfit. [Fr., poss. < dial. Fr. *chagraigner,* to distress < OFr. *graim,* gloomy, of Gmc. orig.]

chain (chān) *n.* **1.a.** A connected, flexible series of links, typically metal, used, for example, for binding or for transmitting mechanical power. **b.** Such a set of links, often of precious metal and with pendants attached, worn as an ornament or symbol of office. **2.** A restraining or confining agent or force. **3. chains. a.** Bonds, fetters, or shackles. **b.** Captivity or oppression; bondage. **4.** A series of closely linked or connected things. **5.** A number of establishments under common ownership or management. **6.** A mountain range. **7.** *Chem.* A group of atoms bonded in a spatial configuration like chain links. **8.a.** A surveying instrument consisting of 100 linked pieces of iron or steel and measuring 66 feet (20.1 meters). **b.** A similar instrument used in engineering, measuring 100 feet (30.5 meters). **c.** A unit of measurement equal to the length of either of these instruments. *—tr.v.* **chained, chain•ing, chains. 1.** To bind or make fast with a chain or chains. **2.** To restrain or confine as if with chains. [ME *chaine* < OFr. < Lat. *catēna.*]

Chain (chān), Sir **Ernst Boris.** 1906–79. German-born British biochemist who shared a 1945 Nobel Prize.

chain fern *n.* Any of various terrestrial ferns of the genus *Woodwardia,* native chiefly to the Northern Hemisphere and having leaves that bear chainlike rows of spore cases.

chain gang *n.* A group of convicts chained together.

chain letter *n.* A letter asking each recipient to send copies with the same request to a specified number of others.

chain•link fence (chān′lĭngk′) *n.* A fence made of thick steel wire interwoven in a diamond pattern.

chain mail *n.* Flexible armor made of metal links or scales.

chain•man (chān′mən) *n.* Either of the two persons who hold a surveyor's measuring chain.

chain pickerel *n.* A freshwater game and food fish *(Esox niger)* of eastern North America.

chain-re•act (chān′rē-ăkt′) *intr.v.* **-act•ed, -act•ing, -acts.** To undergo a chain reaction.

chain reaction *n.* **1.** A series of events in which each induces or influences the next. **2.** *Phys.* A multistage nuclear reaction, esp. a self-sustaining series of fissions in which the release of neutrons from the splitting of one atom leads to the splitting of others. **3.** *Chem.* A series of reactions in which one product of a reacting set is a reactant in the following set.

chain saw *n.* A portable power saw with teeth linked in an endless chain. **—chain′-saw′** (chān′sô′) *v.*

chain-smoke (chān′smōk′) *v.* **-smoked, -smok•ing, -smokes.** *—intr.* To smoke continually. *—tr.* To smoke (cigarettes, for example) in continuing succession. **—chain smoker** *n.*

chain stitch *n.* A decorative sewing stitch in which loops are connected like the links of a chain.

chain store *n.* A retail store that is part of a chain.

chair (châr) *n.* **1.** A piece of furniture consisting of a seat, legs, back, and often arms, holding one person. **2.** A seat of office, authority, or dignity. **3.a.** An office or position of authority. **b.** A person who holds an office or a position of authority; a chairperson. **4.** The position of a player in an orchestra. **5.** *Slang.* The electric chair. **6.** A seat carried about on poles; a sedan chair. **7.** Any of several devices that serve to support or secure. *—tr.v.* **chaired, chair•ing, chairs. 1.** To install in a position of authority. **2.** To preside over as chairperson. [ME *chaiere* < OFr. < Lat. *cathedra.* See CATHEDRA.]

chair car *n.* See **parlor car.**

chair lift *n.* A mechanized, cable-suspended, aerial chair assembly used as transport along a mountain slope.

chair•man (châr′mən) *n.* **1.** A man who is a chairperson. **2.** A chairperson. See Usage Note at **man. —chair′man** *v.*

chair•man•ship (châr′mən-shĭp′) *n.* The office or term of a chairman.

chair•per•son (châr′pûr′sən) *n.* **1.** The presiding officer of an assembly, a meeting, a committee, or a board. **2.** The administrative head of a department of instruction, as at a college. See Usage Note at **man.**

chair•wom•an (châr′wo͝om′ən) *n.* A woman who is a chairperson. See Usage Note at **man.**

chaise (shāz) *n.* **1.** Any of various light open carriages, often with a collapsible hood, esp. a two-wheeled carriage drawn by one horse. **2.** A post chaise. **3.** A chaise longue. [Fr., chair, var. of OFr. *chaiere.* See CHAIR.]

chaise longue (shāz lông′) *n., pl.* **chaise longues** or **chaises longues** (shāz lông′). A reclining chair with a lengthened seat that supports the outstretched legs. [Fr. : *chaise,* chair + *longue,* long.]

chak•ra (chŭk′rə) *n.* One of the seven centers of spiritual energy in the human body according to yoga philosophy. [Skt. *cakram,* wheel, circle. See **k**w**el-**[1]*.]

cha•lah (KHä′lə) *n.* Var. of **challah.**

cha•la•za (kə-lā′zə, -lăz′ə) *n., pl.* **-zae** (-zē) or **-zas. 1.** *Biol.* One of two spiral bands of tissue in an egg that connect the yolk to the lining membrane at either end of the shell. **2.** *Bot.* The region at the base of the nucellus of an ovule. [Gk. *khalaza,* hard lump, hailstone.] **—cha•la′zal** *adj.*

cha•la•zi•on (kə-lā′zē-ən, -ŏn′) *n., pl.* **-zi•a** (-zē-ə). A cyst of a tarsal gland. [Gk. *khalazion,* dim. of *khalaza,* lump.]

Chal•ce•don (kăl′sĭ-dŏn′, kăl-sēd′n). An ancient Greek city of NW Asia Minor on the Bosporus; founded 685 B.C.

chal•ced•o•ny also **cal•ced•o•ny** (kăl-sĕd′n-ē) *n., pl.* **-nies.** A translucent to transparent milky or grayish quartz with distinctive microscopic crystals arranged in slender fibers in parallel bands. [LLat. *chalcēdonius* < Gk. *khalkēdōn,* a mystical stone (Rev. 21:19), perh. < *Khalkēdōn,* Chalcedon.] **—chal′ce•don′ic** (kăl′sĭ-dŏn′ĭk) *adj.*

chal•cid (kăl′sĭd) *n.* Any of various minute wasps of the superfamily Chalcidoidea. [< NLat. *Chalcis,* type genus < Gk. *khalkos,* copper (from the wasp's metallic color).]

Chal•cid•i•ce (kăl-sĭd′ĭ-sē) also **Khal•ki•dhi•kí** (käl-kē′*th*ē-kē′, KHäl-). A mountainous peninsula of NE Greece projecting into the N Aegean Sea. **—Chal•cid′i•an** *adj. & n.*

Chal•cis (kăl′sĭs) also **Khal•kís** (käl-kēs′, KHäl-). An ancient city of SE Greece on the W coast of Euboea.

Marc Chagall
Photographed in the late 1970's

chain saw

chair lift
Mount Sunapee, New Hampshire

ă **pat**	oi **boy**
ā **pay**	ou **out**
âr **care**	o͝o **took**
ä **father**	o͞o **boot**
ĕ **pet**	ŭ **cut**
ē **be**	ûr **urge**
ĭ **pit**	th **thin**
ī **pie**	*th* **this**
îr **pier**	hw **which**
ŏ **pot**	zh **vision**
ō **toe**	ə **about, item**
ô **paw**	

Stress marks:
′ (primary);
′ (secondary), as in **dictionary** (dĭk′shə-nĕr′ē)

chal•co•cite (kăl′kə-sīt′) *n.* A dark gray mineral, essentially Cu_2S, that is an important ore of copper. [Alteration of obsolete *chalcosine* < Gk. *khalkos*, copper.]

chal•co•py•rite (kăl′kə-pī′rīt′) *n.* A yellow mineral, essentially $CuFeS_2$, that is an important ore of copper. [NLat. *chalcopyrites* : Gk. *khalkos*, copper + PYRITES.]

Chal•de•a or **Chal•dae•a** (kăl-dē′ə). An ancient region of S Mesopotamia; settled c. 1000 B.C.

Chal•de•an also **Chal•dae•an** (kăl-dē′ən) or **Chal•dee** (kăl′-dē′) *—adj.* Of or relating to Chaldea or its people, language, or culture. *—n.* **1.** A member of an ancient Semitic people who ruled in Babylonia. **2.** See **Aramaic. 3.** A person versed in occult learning. **—Chal•da′ic** (-dā′ĭk) *adj. & n.*

chal•dron (chôl′drən) *n.* A former unit of dry measure in England, equal to about 32 bushels for grain and 36 bushels of coal. [ME < OFr. *chauderon*, aug. of *chaudiere*, kettle < LLat. *caldāria*. See CALDRON.]

cha•let (shă-lā′, shăl′ā) *n.* **1.a.** A wooden dwelling with a sloping roof and widely overhanging eaves, common in Alpine regions. **b.** A cottage or lodge built in this style. **2.** The hut of a herder in the Swiss Alps. [Fr. < Swiss Fr.]

Cha•leur Bay (shə-lo͝or′, -lûr′). An inlet of the Gulf of St. Lawrence between E Quebec and N New Brunswick, Canada.

Cha•lia•pin (shä-lyä′pĭn), **Feodor Ivanovich.** 1873–1938. Russian-born French operatic basso.

chalice
Chalice of Tassilo, Merovingian, c. 780

chal•ice (chăl′ĭs) *n.* **1.** A cup or goblet. **2.** A cup for the Eucharistic wine. [ME < OFr. < Lat. *calix*, *calic-*.]

chal•i•co•there (kăl′ĭ-kə-thîr′) *n.* Any of various extinct ungulate mammals of the Eocene to Pleistocene epochs, having three-clawed, three-toed feet. [NLat. *Chalicotherium*, genus name : Gk. *khalix*, *khalik-*, pebble + Gk. *thērion*, dim. of *thēr*, beast; see **ghwer-***.]

chalk (chôk) *n.* **1.** A soft compact calcite, $CaCO_3$, with varying amounts of silica, quartz, feldspar, or other mineral impurities, generally gray-white or yellow-white and derived chiefly from fossil seashells. **2.a.** A piece of chalk or chalklike substance in crayon form, used for marking on a surface. **b.** *Games.* A small cube of chalk used in rubbing the tip of a billiard or pool cue to increase friction with the cue ball. **3.** A mark made with chalk. **4.** *Chiefly British.* A score or tally. *—tr.v.* **chalked, chalk•ing, chalks. 1.** To mark, draw, or write with chalk. **2.** To rub or cover with chalk. **3.** To make pale; whiten. **4.** To treat (soil, for example) with chalk. ***—phrasal verb.* chalk up. 1.** To earn or score. **2.** To credit or ascribe. [ME < OE *cealk* < Lat. *calx*, *calc-*, lime. See CALX.] **—chalk′i•ness** *n.* **—chalk′y** *adj.*

chalk•board (chôk′bôrd′, -bōrd′) *n.* A smooth hard panel, usu. green or black, for writing on with chalk; a blackboard.

chalk•stone (chôk′stōn′) *n. Pathol.* See **tophus** 1.

chal•lah also **cha•lah** or **hal•lah** (KHä′lə, hä′-) *n.* A loaf of yeast-leavened white egg bread, usu. braided, traditionally eaten by Jews on the Sabbath, holidays, and other ceremonial occasions. [Heb. *ḥallâ*.]

chameleon
Horned chameleon
Chamaeleo oweni

chal•lenge (chăl′ənj) *n.* **1.a.** A call to engage in a contest, fight, or competition. **b.** An act or statement of defiance; a call to confrontation. **2.** A demand for explanation or justification; a calling into question. **3.** A sentry's call to an unknown party for proper identification. **4.** A test of one's abilities or resources. **5.** A claim that a vote is invalid or that a voter is unqualified. **6.** *Law.* A formal objection to the inclusion of a prospective juror in a jury. **7.** *Immunol.* The challenging of an organism. *—v.* **-lenged, -leng•ing, -leng•es.** *—tr.* **1.a.** To call to engage in a contest, fight, or competition. **b.** To invite with defiance; dare. **2.** To take exception to; dispute. **3.** To order to halt and be identified. **4.** *Law.* To take formal objection to (a prospective juror). **5.** To question the qualifications of (a voter) or validity of (a vote). **6.** To have due claim to; call for. **7.** To summon to action, effort, or use; stimulate. **8.** *Immunol.* To induce or evaluate an immune response in (an organism) by administering a specific antigen to which it has been sensitized. *—intr.* **1.** To make or give voice to a challenge. **2.** To begin barking upon picking up the scent. Used of hunting dogs. [ME *chalenge* < OFr. < Lat. *calumnia*, trickery, false accusation. See CALUMNY.] **—chal′lenge•a•ble** *adj.*

chal•leng•er (chăl′ən-jər) *n.* **1.** One that challenges. **2.** *Sports.* One who competes against a champion.

chal•leng•ing (chăl′ən-jĭng) *adj.* **1.** Demanding all of one's abilities or resources in a stimulating way. **2.** Absorbing; intriguing.

chamois
Rupicapra rupicapra

chal•lis (shăl′ē) *n.* A soft, lightweight, usu. printed fabric made of wool, cotton, or rayon. [Poss. < the surname *Challis*.]

Chal•mette (shăl-mĕt′). A village of SE LA on the Mississippi R. just below New Orleans. Pop. 31,860.

cha•lone (kā′lōn′, kăl′ōn′) *n.* Any of several polypeptides produced by a body tissue that cause the reversible inhibition of mitosis in the tissue cells. [< Gk. *khalōn*, pr.part. of *khalan*, to slacken.]

Châ•lons-sur-Marne (shä-lôN′sûr′märn′, -sür-). A city of NE France E of Paris. The Huns under Attila were defeated here in A.D. 451. Pop. 51,137.

cha•lyb•e•ate (kə-lĭb′ē-ĭt, -lē′bē-) *adj.* **1.** Impregnated with or containing salts of iron. **2.** Tasting like iron, as water from a mineral spring. *—n.* Water or medicine containing iron in solution. [NLat. *chalybeātus* < Lat. *chalybs*, steel < Gk. *khalups*, *khalub-*, poss. < *Khalups*, sing. of *Khalubes*, Chalybes, people of Asia Minor famous for their steel.]

Cha•mae•leon also **Cha•me•leon** (kə-mēl′yən, -mē′lē-ən) *n.* A constellation in the southern polar region near Apus and Mensa. [Lat. *chamaeleōn*, chameleon. See CHAMELEON.]

cham•ae•phyte (kăm′ə-fīt′) *n.* A low-growing perennial plant with dormant overwintering buds borne near the ground. [Gk. *khamai*, on the ground; see **dhghem-*** + -PHYTE.]

cham•ber (chām′bər) *n.* **1.** A room in a house, esp. a bedroom. **2.** A room where a person of importance receives visitors. **3. chambers.** A room in which a judge may consult privately with attorneys or hear cases not taken into court. **4. chambers.** *Chiefly British.* A suite of rooms, esp. one used by lawyers. **5.** A hall for the meetings of a legislative or other assembly. **6.** A legislative or judicial body. **7.** A board or council. **8.** A place where municipal or state funds are received and held; a treasury. **9.a.** An enclosed space or compartment: *a compression chamber.* **b.** An enclosed space in the body of an organism; a cavity. **10.a.** A compartment in a firearm that holds the cartridge in readiness for firing. **b.** An enclosed space in the bore of a gun that holds the charge. *—tr.v.* **-bered, -ber•ing, -bers. 1.** To put in or as if in a chamber; enclose or confine. **2.** To furnish with a chamber. [ME *chaumbre* < OFr. *chambre* < LLat. *camera*, chamber < Lat., vault < Gk. *kamara*.]

cham•bered nautilus (chām′bərd) *n.* See **nautilus** 1.

cham•ber•lain (chām′bər-lən) *n.* **1.a.** An officer who manages the household of a sovereign or a noble; a chief steward. **b.** A high-ranking royal court official. **2.** An official who receives the rents and fees of a municipality; a treasurer. **3.** *Rom. Cath. Ch.* An often honorary papal attendant. [ME *chaumberlein* < OFr. *chamberlenc* < Frankish **kamerling* : LLat. *camera*, chamber; see CHAMBER + Gmc. **-linga-*, one connected with; see -LING[1].]

Cham•ber•lain (chām′bər-lĭn), **(Arthur) Neville.** 1869–1940. British prime minister (1937–40) who advocated a policy of appeasement toward the fascist regimes of Europe.

Chamberlain, Sir **(Joseph) Austen.** 1863–1937. British politician who won the 1925 Nobel Peace Prize.

cham•ber•maid (chām′bər-mād′) *n.* A woman who cleans and cares for bedrooms, as in a hotel.

chamber music *n. Mus.* Compositions traditionally intended for performance in a private room or small concert hall by an instrumental ensemble, with one player for each part.

chamber of commerce *n., pl.* **chambers of commerce.** An association of businesspersons and merchants for the promotion of commercial interests in the community.

chamber pot *n.* A portable vessel used as a toilet.

Cham•bers•burg (chām′bərz-bûrg′). A borough of S PA SW of Harrisburg. Pop. 16,647.

cham•bray (shăm′brā′) *n.* A fine lightweight fabric woven with white threads across a colored warp. [Alteration of Fr. *cambrai*, cambric, after *Cambrai*, a city of N France.]

cha•me•leon (kə-mēl′yən, -mē′lē-ən) *n.* **1.** Any of various tropical Old World lizards of the family Chamaeleonidae, marked by their ability to change color. **2.** See **anole. 3.** A changeable person. [ME *camelioun* < Lat. *chamaeleōn* < Gk. *khamaileōn* : *khamai*, on the ground; see **dhghem-*** + *leōn*, lion; see LION (loan transl. of Akkadian *nēš qaqqari*, ground lion, lizard).] **—cha•me′le•on′ic** (-lē-ŏn′ĭk) *adj.*

Cha•me•leon (kə-mēl′yən, -mē′lē-ən) *n.* Var. of **Chamaeleon.**

cham•fer (chăm′fər) *tr.v.* **-fered, -fer•ing, -fers. 1.** To cut off the edge or corner of; bevel. **2.** To cut a groove in; flute. *—n.* **1.** A flat surface made by cutting off the edge or corner of a block of wood or other material. **2.** A furrow or groove, as in a column. [Prob. back-formation < *chamfering* < Fr. *chanfrein*, beveled edge < p.part. of OFr. *chanfreindre*, to bevel : *chant*, edge (< Lat. *canthus*, iron tire; see CANT[1]) + *fraindre*, to break (< Lat. *frangere*; see **bhreg-***).]

cham•fron (chăm′frən) *n.* Armor used to protect the front of a war horse's head in medieval times. [ME *shamfron* < OFr. *chanfrein* : Lat. *cāmus*, horse muzzle, heavy necklace (< Gk. *kēmos*) + Lat. *frēnum*, bridle, bit; see FRENUM.]

cha•mi•se (chə-mēz′) also **cha•mi•so** (-mē′sō) *n., pl.* **-ses** also **-sos.** An evergreen shrub, *(Adenostoma fasciculatum)* in the rose family, native to California and having needlelike leaves in fascicles and small white flower clusters. [Sp. *chamisa* < Galician *chamiça*, dry brush, firewood < *chama*, flame < Lat. *flamma*. See FLAME.]

cham•ois (shăm′ē) *n., pl.* **cham•ois** (shăm′ēz). **1.** An extremely agile goat antelope *(Rupicapra rupicapra)* of mountainous regions of Europe, having upright horns with backward-hooked tips. **2.** Also **cham•my** or **sham•my** (shăm′ē)., *pl.* **-mies. a.** A soft leather made from the hide of this animal or other animals such as deer. **b.** A piece of such leather, or a similar cotton fabric. **3.** *Color.* A moderate to grayish yellow. [Fr. < OFr. < LLat. *camōx*.]

cham•o•mile or **cam•o•mile** (kăm′ə-mīl′, -mēl′) *n.* **a.** An aromatic perennial herb *(Chamaemelum nobile)* in the composite family, native to Europe and the Mediterranean and having feathery foliage and white and yellow flowers. **b.** A similar related Eurasian annual plant *(Matricaria recutita)*. **c.** The dried flower heads of either one of these plants, used in herbal tea, commercial flavorings, and perfumery. [ME *camomille* < OFr. < LLat. *chamomilla*, alteration of Lat. *chamaemēlon* < Gk. *khamaimēlon* : *khamai*, on the ground; see **dhghem-*** + *mēlon*, apple.]

Cha•mo•nix (shăm′ə-nē′, shä-mô-). A valley of E France at the foot of Mont Blanc; site of the 1924 Winter Olympics.

champ¹ (chămp) *v.* **champed, champ•ing, champs.** —*tr.* To bite or chew upon noisily. —*intr.* To work the jaws and teeth vigorously. —***idiom.* champ at the bit.** To show impatience at being held back or delayed. [Prob. imit.]

champ² (chămp) *n. Informal.* A champion.

cham•pagne (shăm-pān′) *n.* **1.a.** A sparkling white wine made in Champagne. **b.** A similar sparkling wine made elsewhere. **2.** *Color.* A pale orange yellow to grayish yellow or yellowish gray. [Fr., short for *(vin de) Champagne*, (wine from) Champagne < LLat. *campānia*, flat open country. See CAMPAIGN.]

Cham•pagne (shăm-pān′, shäN-pän′yə). A historical region and former province of NE France; noted for its sparkling wine (first produced here c. 1700).

cham•paign (shăm-pān′) *n.* A stretch of level and open country; a plain. [ME *champain* < OFr. *champaigne* < LLat. *campānia*. See CAMPAIGN.] —**cham•paign′** *adj.*

Cham•paign (shăm-pān′). A city of E-central IL adjoining Urbana; founded 1855. Pop. 63,502.

cham•pak also **cham•pac** (chăm′păk, chŭm′pŭk) or **cham•pa•ca** (chăm′pə-kə, chŭm′-) *n.* An evergreen timber tree *(Michelia champaca)* native to India and having fragrant orange-yellow flowers that yield an oil used in perfumery. [Hindi *campak* < Skt. *campakaḥ*.]

cham•per•ty (chăm′pər-tē) *n., pl.* **-ties.** *Law.* A sharing in the proceeds of a lawsuit by an outside party who has promoted the litigation. [ME *champartie* < OFr. *champart*, the lord's share of the tenant's crop < Med.Lat. *campars, campīpars* : Lat. *campī*, genitive of *campus*, field + Lat. *pars*, part; see PART.] —**cham′per•tous** (-təs) *adj.*

cham•pi•gnon (shăm-pĭn′yən) *n.* An edible mushroom, esp. *Agaricus bisporus*. [Fr., alteration of OFr. *champigneul*, prob. < VLat. **(fungus) campiniolus*, (fungus) growing in the fields < LLat. *campānia*, countryside. See CAMPAIGN.]

cham•pi•on (chăm′pē-ən) *n.* **1.** One that wins first place or first prize in a competition. **2.** One that is clearly superior or has the attributes of a winner. **3.** An ardent defender or supporter of a cause or another person. **4.** One who fights; a warrior. —*tr.v.* **-oned, -on•ing, -ons. 1.** To fight for, defend, or support as a champion. See Syns at **support. 2.** *Obsolete.* To defy or challenge. —*adj.* **1.** Holding first place or prize. **2.** Superior to all others. [ME *championn*, combatant, athlete < OFr. *champion* < Med.Lat. *campiō, campiōn-* < Lat. *campus*, field.]

cham•pi•on•ship (chăm′pē-ən-shĭp′) *n.* **1.** The position or title of a winner. **2.** Defense or support; advocacy. **3.** A competition or series of competitions held to determine a winner.

Cham•plain (shăm-plān′), **Lake.** A lake of NE NY, NW VT, and S Quebec, Canada.

Cham•plain (shăm-plān′, shäN-plăN′), **Samuel de.** 1567?–1635. French explorer who founded a settlement (1608) on the site of present-day Quebec.

champ•le•vé (shäN-lə-vā′) *n.* A technique of decorating metal in which hollowed-out areas are filled with colored enamel and fired. [Fr. : *champ*, field (< OFr. < Lat. *campus*) + *levé*, raised; see LEVEE².] —**champ′le•vé′** *adj.*

Cham•pol•lion (shäN-pô-lyôN′), **Jean François.** 1790–1832. French Egyptologist who first deciphered Egyptian hieroglyphics (1821).

Champs É•ly•sées (shäN zā-lē-zā′). A tree-lined thoroughfare of Paris, France, leading from the Place de la Concorde to the Arc de Triomphe.

chan. *abbr.* Channel.

chance (chăns) *n.* **1.a.** The unknown and unpredictable element in happenings that seems to have no assignable cause. **b.** A force assumed to cause events that cannot be foreseen or controlled; luck. **2.** The likelihood of something happening; possibility or probability. Often used in the plural. **3.** An accidental or unpredictable event. **4.** A favorable set of circumstances; an opportunity. **5.** A risk or hazard; a gamble. **6.** *Games.* A raffle or lottery ticket. **7.** *Baseball.* An opportunity to make a putout or an assist that counts as an error if unsuccessful. —*adj.* Caused by or ascribable to chance; unexpected, random, or casual. —*v.* **chanced, chanc•ing, chanc•es.** —*intr.* To come about by chance; occur. —*tr.* To take the risk or hazard of. —***phrasal verb.* chance on** (or **upon**). To find or meet accidentally; happen upon. —***idioms.* by chance. 1.** Without plan; accidentally. **2.** Possibly; perchance. **on the off chance.** In the slight hope or possibility. [ME, unexpected event < OFr. < VLat. **cadentia* < Lat. *cadēns, cadent-*, pr.part. of *cadere*, to fall, befall. See **kad-***.]

Syns: *chance, random, casual, haphazard, desultory.* These adjectives apply to what is determined by accident. *Chance* stresses lack of premeditation: *a chance meeting. Random* implies the absence of a specific pattern or objective: *a random guess. Casual* often suggests an absence of due concern: *a casual query. Haphazard* implies a carelessness or a willful leaving to chance: *a haphazard plan. Desultory* suggests a shifting about from one thing to another without method: *a desultory conversation.*

chance•ful (chăns′fəl) *adj.* **1.** Eventful. **2.** *Archaic.* Casual.

chan•cel (chăn′səl) *n.* The space around a church altar for the clergy and sometimes the choir, often enclosed by a lattice or railing. [ME *chauncel* < OFr. *chancel* < LLat. *cancellus*, latticework, sing. of Lat. *cancellī*. See CANCEL.]

chan•cel•ler•y or **chan•cel•lor•y** (chăn′sə-lə-rē, -slə-rē) *n., pl.* **-ies. 1.** A chancellor's rank or position. **2.a.** A chancellor's office or department. **b.** The building where such an office or department is located. **3.** The official place of business of an embassy or consulate. [ME *chancelrie* < OFr. *chancelerie* < *chancelier*, chancellor. See CHANCELLOR.]

chan•cel•lor (chăn′sə-lər, -slər) *n.* **1.** Any of various officials of high rank, esp.: **a.** A secretary to a monarch or noble. **b.** *Chiefly British.* The chief secretary of an embassy. **c.** The chief minister of state in some European countries. **2.a.** The president of certain American universities. **b.** *Chiefly British.* The honorary or titular head of a university. **3.** *Law.* The presiding judge of a court of chancery or equity in some states of the United States. [ME *chaunceler* < OFr. *chancelier* < LLat. *cancellārius*, doorkeeper < Lat. *cancellī*, bars, latticework. See CANCEL.] —**chan′cel•lor•ship′** *n.*

Chan•cel•lor of the Exchequer (chăn′sə-lər, -slər) *n.* The senior finance minister in the British government and a member of the prime minister's cabinet.

Chan•cel•lors•ville (chăn′sə-lərz-vĭl′, -slərz-). A former town of NE VA W of Fredericksburg; site of a major Civil War battle (May 2–4, 1863).

chance-med•ley (chăns′mĕd′lē) *n.* A random, haphazard action or occurrence. [ME *chaunce medley*, manslaughter < Norman Fr. *chance medlee*, mixed accident : OFr. *chance*, accident; see CHANCE + OFr. *medlee*, mixed; see MEDLEY.]

chan•cer•y (chăn′sə-rē) *n., pl.* **-ies. 1.** *Law.* **a.** A court of chancery. **b.** The proceedings and practice of a court of chancery; equity. **c.** A court of public record; an office of archives. **d.** One of the five divisions of the British High Court of Justice, presided over by the Lord High Chancellor. **2.** A chancellor's office or department; a chancellery. [ME *chancerie*, alteration of *chancelrie*. See CHANCELLERY.]

Chan Chan (chän′ chän′). A ruined pre-Incan city of N Peru; probably built after A.D. 800.

Chan•chiang (jän′jyäng′). See **Zhanjiang.**

chan•cre (shăng′kər) *n.* **1.** A dull red, hard, insensitive lesion that is the first manifestation of syphilis. **2.** An ulcer at the initial point of entry of a pathogen. [Fr. < OFr. < Lat. *cancer*, tumor, crab. See **kar-***.] —**chan′crous** (-krəs) *adj.*

chan•croid (shăng′kroid′) *n.* A soft, highly infectious, nonsyphilitic venereal ulcer of the genital region, caused by the bacillus *Hemophilus ducreyi.* [Fr. *chancroïde* < *chancre*, chancre. See CHANCRE.] —**chan′croid′al** (-kroid′l) *adj.*

chanc•y (chăn′sē) *adj.* **-i•er, -i•est. 1.** Uncertain as to outcome; risky; hazardous. **2.** Random; haphazard. **3.** *Scots.* Lucky; propitious. —**chanc′i•ness** *n.*

chan•de•lier (shăn′də-lîr′) *n.* A branched decorative lighting fixture that holds a number of bulbs or candles and is suspended from a ceiling. [ME *chandeler* < OFr. *chandelier*, ult. < Lat. *candēlābrum*, candelabrum. See CANDELABRUM.]

chandelier
c. 1870 American gas-burning chandelier

chan•delle (shăn-dĕl′) *n.* A sudden, steep climbing turn of an aircraft to alter flight direction while gaining altitude. [Fr. < *chandelle*, candle < OFr. < Lat. *candēla*. See CANDLE.]

Chan•di•garh (chŭn′dē-gər, chŭn′dĭ-gŭr′). A city of N India N of Delhi. Pop. 373,789.

chan•dler (chănd′lər) *n.* **1.** One that makes or sells candles. **2.** A retail dealer in specified goods or equipment. [ME *chaundeler* < OFr. *chandelier* < VLat. **candēlārius* < Lat. *candēla*, candle. See CANDLE.] —**chan′dler•y** (chănd′lə-rē) *n.*

Chan•dler (chănd′lər). A city of S-central AZ SE of Phoenix. Pop. 90,533.

Chandler, Raymond Thornton. 1888–1959. Amer. writer whose detective novels include *The Big Sleep* (1939).

Cha•nel (shə-nĕl′), **Gabrielle Bonheur.** "Coco." 1883–1971. French fashion designer famous for her tailored suits.

Chang•chow (chăng′jō′). See **Changzhou.**

Chang•chun (chăng′cho͞on′). Formerly **Hsin•king** (shĭn′kĭng′, -gĭng′). A city of NE China SSW of Harbin; cap. of Jilin province. Pop. 1,480,000.

change (chānj) *v.* **changed, chang•ing, chang•es.** —*tr.* **1.a.** To cause to be different. **b.** To give a completely different form or appearance to; transform. **2.** To give and receive reciprocally; interchange. **3.** To exchange for or replace with another, usu. of the same kind or category. **4.a.** To lay aside, abandon, or leave for another; switch: *change sides.* **b.** To transfer from (one conveyance) to another. **5.** To give or receive the equivalent of (money) in lower denominations or in foreign currency. **6.** To put a fresh covering on. —*intr.* **1.** To

ă pat	oi boy
ā pay	ou out
âr care	o͝o took
ä father	o͞o boot
ĕ pet	ŭ cut
ē be	ûr urge
ĭ pit	th thin
ī pie	*th* this
îr pier	hw which
ŏ pot	zh vision
ō toe	ə about, item
ô paw	

Stress marks:
′ (primary);
′ (secondary), as in dictionary (dĭk′shə-nĕr′ē)

become different or undergo alteration. **2.** To undergo transformation or transition. **3.** To go from one phase to another, as the moon. **4.** To make an exchange. **5.** To transfer from one conveyance to another. **6.** To put on other clothing. **7.** To become deeper in tone. — *n.* **1.** The act, process, or result of altering or modifying. **2.** The replacing of one thing for another; substitution. **3.** A transformation or transition from one state, condition, or phase to another. **4.** Something different; variety. **5.** A different or fresh set of clothing. **6.a.** Money of smaller denomination given or received in exchange for money of higher denomination. **b.** The balance of money returned when an amount given is more than what is due. **c.** Coins. **7.** *Mus.* A pattern or order in which bells are rung. **8.** A market or exchange where business is transacted. — ***phrasal verb.*** **change off. 1.** To alternate with another person in performing a task. **2.** To perform two tasks at once by alternating or a single task by alternate means. — ***idioms.*** **change hands.** To pass from one owner to another. **change (one's) mind.** To reverse a previously held opinion or an earlier decision. **change (one's) tune.** To alter one's approach or attitude. [ME *changen* < Norman Fr. *chaunger* < Lat. *cambiāre, cambīre*, to exchange, prob. of Celt. orig.] — **chang′er** *n.*

change•a•ble (chān′jə-bəl) *adj.* **1.** Liable to change; capricious. **2.** Being such that alteration is possible. **3.** Varying in color or appearance from different viewpoints. — **change′a•bil′i•ty, change′a•ble•ness** *n.* — **change′a•bly** *adv.*

change•ful (chānj′fəl) *adj.* Having the tendency or ability to change. — **change′ful•ly** *adv.* — **change′ful•ness** *n.*

change•less (chānj′lĭs) *adj.* Unchanging; constant.

change•ling (chānj′lĭng) *n.* **1.** A child secretly exchanged for another. **2.** *Archaic.* A changeable, fickle person. **3.** *Archaic.* A person of deficient intelligence.

change of heart *n.*, *pl.* **changes of heart.** A reversal of one's opinion, attitude, or feelings.

change of life *n.* Menopause.

change•o•ver (chānj′ō′vər) *n.* A conversion to a different purpose or from one system to another, as in equipment.

change ring•ing (rĭng′ĭng) *n.* *Mus.* The ringing of a set of chimes or bells with every possible unrepeated variation.

change•up (chānj′ŭp′) *n.* *Baseball.* A pitch that looks like a fastball but actually moves more slowly, thereby prompting a premature swing. [Alteration of *change-of-pace.*]

Chang Jiang (chäng′ jyäng′). See **Yangtze River.**

Chang•sha (chäng′shä′). A city of S China on the Xiang Jiang WSW of Shanghai; cap. of Hunan province. Pop. 1,123,900.

Chang•zhou also **Chang•chow** (chäng′jō′). A city of E China on the Grand Canal WNW of Shanghai. Pop. 425,000.

Chan•kiang (chän′kyäng′, jän′jyäng′). See **Zhanjiang.**

chan•nel¹ (chăn′əl) *n.* **1.** The bed of a stream or river. **2.** The deeper part of a river or harbor, esp. a deep navigable passage. **3.** A broad strait, esp. one that connects two seas. **4.** A trench, furrow, or groove. **5.** A tubular passage for liquids; a conduit. **6.** A course or passage through which something may move or be directed: *channels of thought.* **7.** A route of communication or access. Often used in the plural. **8.** *Electron.* A specified frequency band for the transmission and reception of electromagnetic signals, as for television. **9.** The medium through which a spirit guide purportedly communicates. **10.** A rolled metal bar with a bracket-shaped section. — *tr.v.* **-neled, -nel•ing, -nels** also **-nelled, -nel•ling, -nels. 1.** To make or cut channels in. **2.** To form a groove or flute in. **3.** To direct or guide along some desired course. **4.** To serve as a medium for (a spirit guide). [ME *chanel* < OFr. < Lat. *canālis.* See CANAL.] — **chan′nel•er** *n.*

chan•nel² (chăn′əl) *n.* *Naut.* A ledge projecting from a sailing ship's sides to spread the shrouds and keep them clear of the gunwales. [Alteration of obsolete *chainwale* : CHAIN + WALE.]

channel bass *n.* See **red drum.**

channel black *n.* A type of carbon black formed by exposing an iron plate to a natural gas flame. [< CHANNEL¹.]

channel catfish *n.* A freshwater food fish *(Ictalurus punctatus)* common to the central United States.

chan•nel•ing (chăn′ə-lĭng) *n.* Purported communication by a disembodied entity through a living person.

Chan•nel Islands (chăn′əl). A group of British islands in the English Channel off the coast of Normandy, France; orig. settled by Norse mariners.

chan•nel•ize (chăn′ə-līz′) *tr.v.* **-ized, -iz•ing, -iz•es. 1.** To make, form, or cut channels in. **2.** To direct through a channel. — **chan′nel•i•za′tion** (chăn′ə-lĭ-zā′shən) *n.*

Chan•nel•view (chăn′əl-vyōō′). A community of SE TX, a suburb of Houston. Pop. 25,564.

Chan•ning (chăn′ĭng), **William Ellery.** 1780–1842. Amer. religious leader and a founder of Unitarianism.

cha•no•yu (chä′nô-yōō′) *n.* An ancient Japanese ritual for the preparation, serving, and drinking of tea. [J. : *cha*, tea + *no*, possessive particle + *yu*, hot water.]

chan•son (shäɴ-sôɴ′) *n.*, *pl.* **-sons** (-sôɴ′, -sôɴz′). *Mus.* A song, esp. a French cabaret song. [Fr. < OFr. < Lat. *cantiō, cantiōn-* < *cantus*, p.part. of *cantāre*, to sing. See CHANT.]

chanson de geste (də zhĕst′) *n.*, *pl.* **chansons de geste.** An Old French epic poem of the 11th to the 14th century celebrating the deeds of historical or legendary figures. [Fr. : *chanson*, song + *de*, of + *geste*, heroic exploit.]

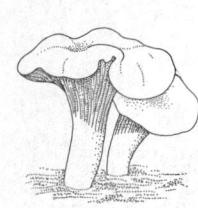

chanterelle
Cantharellus cibarius

chapel
Restored chapel,
Fort Ross, California

chant (chănt) *n.* **1.** *Mus.* **a.** A short simple melody in which syllables or words are sung on or intoned to the same note. **b.** A canticle or prayer sung or intoned in this manner. **c.** A song or melody. **2.** A monotonous rhythmic call or shout, as of a slogan. — *v.* **chant•ed, chant•ing, chants.** — *tr.* **1.** *Mus.* To sing or intone to a chant. **2.** *Mus.* To celebrate in song. **3.** To say in the manner of a chant. — *intr.* **1.** *Mus.* To sing, esp. in the manner of a chant. **2.** To speak monotonously. [Prob. < Fr., song < OFr. < Lat. *cantus* < p.part. of *canere*, to sing. See **kan-*.**] — **chant′ing•ly** *adv.*

chant•er (chăn′tər) *n.* **1.** *Mus.* A person who chants. **2.** *Mus.* The pipe of a bagpipe on which the melody is played. **3.** A priest who sings in a chantry.

chan•te•relle (shăn′tə-rĕl′, shän′-) *n.* A trumpet-shaped edible mushroom *(Cantharellus cibarius)* that is yellow to orange in color. [Fr. < NLat. *cantharella*, fem. dim. of Lat. *cantharus*, cup (< its shape) < Gk. *kantharos.*]

chan•teuse (shäɴ-tœz′) *n.* *Mus.* A woman singer, esp. a nightclub singer. [Fr., fem. of *chanteur*, singer < *chanter*, to sing. See CHANT.]

chan•tey also **chan•ty** (shăn′tē, chăn′-) or **shan•tey** or **shan•ty** (shăn′tē) *n.*, *pl.* **-teys** also **-ties.** *Mus.* A sailors' song sung to the rhythm of their work movements. [Prob. < Fr. *chantez*, imper. pl. of *chanter*, to sing < OFr. See CHANT.]

chan•ti•cleer (chăn′tĭ-klîr′, shăn′-) *n.* A rooster. [ME *chauntecler* < OFr. *chantecler*, the rooster in the tale of Reynard the Fox.]

Chan•til•ly (shăn-tĭl′ē, shäɴ-tē-yē′). A village of N France N of Paris; long noted for its delicate lace. Pop. 10,065.

chan•try (chăn′trē) *n.*, *pl.* **-tries.** *Eccles.* **1.** An endowment to cover expenses for the saying of masses and prayers, usu. for the soul of the founder of the endowment. **2.** An altar or chapel endowed for the saying of such masses and prayers. [ME *chanterie* < OFr. < *chanter*, to sing. See CHANT.]

Cha•nu•kah (ᴋʜä′nə-kə, hä′-) *n.* Var. of **Hanukkah.**

Chao K'uang-yin (jou′ kwäng′yĭn′). See **Zhao Kuangyin.**

Chao Phra•ya (chou prä-yä′). A river of Thailand formed by the Nan and Ping rivers and flowing c. 225 km (140 mi) S to the Gulf of Thailand.

cha•os (kā′ŏs′) *n.* **1.** A condition or place of great disorder or confusion. **2.** A disorderly mass; a jumble. **3.** Often **Chaos.** The disordered state of unformed matter and infinite space supposed in some cosmogonic views to have existed before the ordered universe. **4.** *Phys.* The aperiodic, unpredictable behavior arising in a system extremely sensitive to variations in initial conditions; phenomena and that exhibited by chaos include turbulent fluid flow, low-range weather patterns, and cardiac arrhythmias. **5.** *Obsolete.* An abyss; a chasm. [ME, formless primordial space < Lat. < Gk. *khaos.*] — **cha•ot′ic** (-ŏt′ĭk) *adj.* — **cha•ot′i•cal•ly** *adv.*

Chao Tzu-yang (jou′ dzōō-yäng′). See **Zhao Ziyang.**

chap¹ (chăp) *v.* **chapped, chap•ping, chaps.** — *tr.* To cause (the skin) to chap. — *intr.* To split or become rough and sore. — *n.* A chapping of the skin. [ME *chappen.*]

chap² (chăp) *n.* *Informal.* A man or boy; a fellow. [Short for CHAPMAN.]

chap. *abbr.* Chapter.

Cha•pa•la (chə-pä′lə). A lake of W-central Mexico SE of Guadalajara.

chap•ar•ral (shăp′ə-răl′) *n.* **1.** *Ecol.* A biome characterized by hot, dry summers and cool, moist winters and dominated by a dense growth of mostly small-leaved evergreen shrubs. **2.** A dense thicket of shrubs and small trees. [Sp. < *chaparro*, evergreen oak < Basque *txapar*, dim. of *saphar*, thicket.]

chaparral bird *n.* See **roadrunner.**

chaparral cock *n.* See **roadrunner.**

cha•pa•ti also **cha•pat•ti** (chə-pä′tē) *n.* A flat disk-shaped bread of northern India, made of wheat flour, water, and salt. [Hindi *capātī.*]

chap•book (chăp′bŏŏk′) *n.* A small book or pamphlet of poems, ballads, stories, or religious tracts. [CHAP(MAN) + BOOK.]

chape (chāp, chăp) *n.* A metal tip or mounting on a scabbard or sheath. [ME < OFr., hood, head covering < LLat. *cappa*, hooded cloak.]

cha•peau (shă-pō′) *n.*, *pl.* **-peaus** or **-peaux** (-pōz′). A hat. [Fr. < OFr. *chapel* < VLat. *cappellus*, dim. of LLat. *cappa*, hooded cloak.]

chap•el (chăp′əl) *n.* **1.a.** A place of worship that is smaller than and subordinate to a church. **b.** A place of worship in an institution, such as a hospital. **c.** A recess or room in a church set apart for special or small services. **d.** A place of worship for those not belonging to an established church. **e.** The services held at a chapel. **2.** *Mus.* A choir or orchestra connected with a place of worship at a royal court. **3.a.** A funeral home. **b.** A room in a funeral home for services. [ME *chapele* < OFr. < Med.Lat. *capella*, cape, canopy, chapel, dim. of *capa* < LLat. *cappa*, hooded cloak.]

Chap•el Hill (chăp′əl). A town of N-central NC at the edge of the Piedmont WNW of Raleigh. Pop. 38,719.

chap•er•on or **chap•er•one** (shăp′ə-rōn′) —*n.* **1.** A person, esp. an older or married woman, who accompanies a young unmarried woman in public. **2.** An older person who supervises a social gathering for young people. **3.** A guide or companion whose purpose is to ensure propriety or restrict activity. —*tr.v.* **-oned, -on•ing, -ones.** To act as chaperon to or for. See Syns at **accompany.** [Fr. < *chaperon,* hood < OFr., dim. of *chape,* cape, head covering. See CHAPE.] —**chap′er•on′age** (-rō′nĭj) *n.*

chap•fall•en (chăp′fô′lən) also **chop•fall•en** (chŏp′-) *adj.* Being in low spirits. [< obsolete *chaps,* alteration of CHOPS.]

chap•i•ter (chăp′ĭ-tər) *n. Archit.* The capital of a column. [ME *chapitre,* chapter, chapiter. See CHAPTER.]

chap•lain (chăp′lĭn) *n.* **1.** A member of the clergy attached to a chapel. **2.a.** A member of the clergy who conducts religious services for an institution, such as a hospital. **b.** A member of the clergy who is connected with a royal court or an aristocratic household. **3.** A member of the clergy attached to a branch of the armed forces. [ME *chapelein* < OFr. *chapelain* < Med.Lat. *capellānus* < *capella,* chapel. See CHAPEL.] —**chap′lain•cy, chap′lain•ship′** *n.*

chap•let (chăp′lĭt) *n.* **1.** A wreath or garland for the head. **2.** *Rom. Cath. Ch.* **a.** A rosary having beads for five decades of Hail Marys. **b.** The prayers counted on such a rosary. **3.** A string of beads. [ME *chapelet* < OFr., dim. of *chapel,* hat, wreath. See CHAPEAU.] —**chap′let•ed** *adj.*

Chap•lin (chăp′lĭn), Sir **Charles Spencer.** "Charlie." 1889–1977. British-born actor and filmmaker noted esp. for his role as a tramp in baggy trousers and a bowler hat.

chap•man (chăp′mən) *n.* **1.** *Chiefly British.* A peddler. **2.** *Archaic.* A dealer or merchant. [ME < OE *cēapman* : *cēap,* trade; see CHEAP + *man, mann,* man; see MAN.]

Chap•man (chăp′mən), **George.** 1559?–1634. English writer and dramatist noted for his translations of Homer.

Chapman, John. "Johnny Appleseed." 1775?–1845. Amer. pioneer who was legendary for planting apple seeds in the Ohio R. Valley.

chaps (chăps, shăps) *pl.n.* Heavy leather trousers without a seat, worn over ordinary trousers by ranch hands to protect their legs. [Short for Am.Sp. *chaparreras* < Sp. *chaparro,* chaparral. See CHAPARRAL.]

Chap Stick (chăp). A trademark used for a medicinal preparation for the prevention or treatment of chapped lips.

chap•ter (chăp′tər) *n.* **1.** One of the main divisions of a relatively lengthy piece of writing, such as a book, that is usu. numbered or titled. **2.** A distinct period or sequence of events. **3.** A local branch of an organization, such as a club or fraternity. **4.** *Eccles.* **a.** An assembly of the canons of a church or of the members of a religious residence. **b.** The canons of a church or the members of a religious residence considered as a group. **5.** A short scriptural passage read after the psalms in certain church services. [ME *chaptre,* var. of *chapitre,* chapter, chapiter < OFr., alteration of *chapitle* < Lat. *capitulum,* dim. of *caput,* head. See **kaput-*.**]

chapter house *n.* **1.** A building in which the chapter of a church or religious residence assembles. **2.** A house in which a chapter of a fraternity or sorority lives and meets.

Cha•pul•te•pec (chə-po͝ol′tə-pĕk′). A rocky hill S of Mexico City, Mexico; site of a major Amer. victory (Sep. 12–13, 1847) during the Mexican War.

char¹ (chär) *v.* **charred, char•ring, chars.** —*tr.* **1.** To burn the surface of; scorch. **2.** To reduce to carbon or charcoal by incomplete combustion. —*intr.* **1.** To become scorched. **2.** To become reduced to carbon or charcoal. —*n.* A charred substance. [Back-formation < CHARCOAL.]

char² also **charr** (chär) *n., pl.* **char** or **chars** also **charr** or **charrs.** Any of several fishes of the genus *Salvelinus,* esp. the arctic char. [?]

char³ (chär) *Chiefly British.* —*n.* A charwoman. —*intr.v.* **charred, char•ring, chars.** To work as a charwoman. [ME, a piece of work < OE *cierr,* a turning.]

char. *abbr.* Charter.

char•a•banc (shăr′ə-băng′) *n. Chiefly British.* A large sightseeing bus. [< Fr. *char à bancs* : *char,* coach, carriage + *à,* with + *bancs,* benches.]

char•a•cin (kăr′ə-sĭn) also **char•a•cid** (-sĭd) *n.* See **tetra.** [< NLat. *Characinidae,* former family name < Gk. *kharax, kharak-,* a kind of fish.]

char•ac•ter (kăr′ək-tər) *n.* **1.** The combination of qualities or features that distinguishes one person, group, or thing from another. **2.** A distinguishing feature or attribute, as of an individual, a group, or a category. **3.** *Genet.* A structure, function, or attribute determined by a gene or group of genes. **4.** Moral or ethical strength. **5.** A description of a person's attributes, traits, or abilities. **6.** A formal written statement as to competency and dependability, given by an employer to a former employee; a recommendation. **7.** Public estimation of someone; reputation. **8.** Status or role; capacity. **9.a.** A notable or well-known person; a personage. **b.** A person, esp. one who is peculiar or eccentric. **10.a.** A person portrayed in an artistic piece, such as a novel. **b.** Characterization in fiction or drama. **11.** A mark or symbol used in a writing system. **12.** *Comp. Sci.* **a.** One of a set of symbols, such as letters or numbers, that are arranged to express information. **b.** The multibit code representing such a character. **13.** A style of printing or writing. **14.** A symbol used in secret writing; a cipher or code. —*adj.* **1.** Of or relating to one's character. **2.** Of, relating to, or specializing in the interpretation of roles that emphasize fixed personality traits or specific physical characteristics. **3.** Dedicated to the portrayal of a person with regard to distinguishing psychological or physical features: *a character sketch.* **4.** *Law.* Of or relating to one who testifies as to the morals and ethics of one engaged in a lawsuit. —*tr.v.* **-tered, -ter•ing, -ters.** *Archaic.* **1.** To write, print, engrave, or inscribe. **2.** To portray or describe. —***idioms.*** **in character.** Consistent with someone's general character or behavior. **out of character.** Inconsistent with someone's general character or behavior. [ME *carecter,* distinctive mark, imprint on the soul < OFr. *caractere* < Lat. *charactēr* < Gk. *kharaktēr* < *kharassein,* to inscribe < *kharax,* pointed stick.] —**char′ac•ter•less** *adj.*

character assassination *n.* A vicious personal verbal attack, esp. one intended to destroy or damage a public figure's reputation. —**character assassin** *n.*

char•ac•ter•is•tic (kăr′ək-tə-rĭs′tĭk) *adj.* Being a feature that helps to distinguish a person or thing; distinctive. —*n.* **1.** A characteristic feature. **2.** *Math.* The integral part of a logarithm as distinguished from the mantissa: *The characteristic of the logarithm 6.3214 is 6.* —**char′ac•ter•is′ti•cal•ly** *adv.*

char•ac•ter•i•za•tion (kăr′ək-tər-ĭ-zā′shən) *n.* **1.** The act or an instance of characterizing. **2.** A description of qualities or peculiarities. **3.** Representation of a character or characters on the stage or in writing.

char•ac•ter•ize (kăr′ək-tə-rīz′) *tr.v.* **-ized, -iz•ing, -iz•es.** **1.** To describe the qualities or peculiarities of. **2.** To be a distinctive mark of; distinguish. —**char′ac•ter•iz′er** *n.*

char•ac•ter•y (kăr′ək-tə-rē, kə-răk′-) *n., pl.* **-ies.** A system of characters or symbols used to express thought and meaning.

cha•rade (shə-rād′) *n.* **1.** *Games.* **a. charades.** *(used with a sing. or pl. v.)* A game in which words or phrases are represented in pantomime until guessed. **b.** An episode in this game or a word or phrase so represented. **2.** A readily perceived pretense; a travesty. [Fr., prob. < Prov. *charrado,* chat < *charra,* perh. < Ital. *ciarlare.*]

char•broil (chär′broil′) *tr.v.* **-broiled, -broil•ing, -broils.** To broil over charcoal. [CHAR¹ + BROIL¹.]

char•coal (chär′kōl′) *n.* **1.** A black, porous, carbonaceous material produced by the destructive distillation of wood and used as a fuel, filter, and absorbent. **2.a.** A drawing pencil or crayon made from charcoal. **b.** A drawing executed with a charcoal. **3.** *Color.* A dark grayish brown to black or dark purplish gray. —*tr.v.* **-coaled, -coal•ing, -coals. 1.** To draw, write, or blacken with charcoal. **2.** To charbroil. [ME *charcol* : *char* (perh. < OFr. *charbon* < Lat. *carbō*; see CARBON) + *col,* charcoal, coal; see COAL.]

char•cu•ter•ie (shär-ko͞o′tə-rē′, -ko͞o′tə-rē) *n.* **1.** Sausages and other cooked or processed meat foods. **2.** A delicatessen specializing in such foods. [Fr. < *chaircuicterie* : *chair,* meat (< Lat. *carō,* flesh; see CARNAGE) + *cuict, cuit,* cooked (< Lat. *coctus,* p.part. of *coquere*; see COOK).]

chard (chärd) *n.* Swiss chard. [Alteration of Fr. *carde* < Prov. *cardon,* cardoon. See CARDOON.]

char•don•nay also **Char•don•nay** (shär′dn-ā′, shär′dn-ā′) *n.* A dry white table wine, originally from Burgundy, France.

Cha•rente (shə-ränt′, shä-räɴt′). A river of W France flowing c. 354 km (220 mi) to the Bay of Biscay.

charge (chärj) *v.* **charged, charg•ing, charg•es.** —*tr.* **1.** To impose a duty, responsibility, or obligation on. **2.** To set or ask (a given amount) as a price. **3.** To hold financially liable; demand payment from. **4.** To postpone payment on (a purchase) by recording as a debt. **5.a.** To load to capacity; fill. **b.** To saturate; impregnate. **6.** To load (a gun or other firearm) with a quantity of explosive. **7.** To instruct or urge authoritatively; command. **8.** *Law.* To instruct (a jury) about the law, its application, and the weighing of evidence. **9.** To make a claim of wrongdoing against; accuse or blame. **10.** To put the blame for; attribute or impute. **11.** To attack violently. **12.** *Elect.* **a.** To cause formation of a net electric charge on or in (a conductor, for example). **b.** To energize (a storage battery) by passing current through it in the direction opposite to discharge. **13.** To excite; rouse: *charged up the crowd.* **14.** To direct or put (a weapon) into position for use; level. **15.** *Her.* To place a bearing on. —*intr.* **1.** To rush forward in or as if in a violent attack. **2.** To demand or ask payment. **3.** To postpone payment for a purchase. **4.** *Accounting.* To consider or record as a loss. Often used with *off.* —*n.* **1.a.** Expense; cost. **b.** The price asked for something. **2.a.** A weight or burden; a load. **b.** The quantity that a container or apparatus can hold. **3.** A quantity of explosive to be set off at one time. **4.** An assigned duty or task; a responsibility. **5.** One that is entrusted to another's care or management. **6.a.** Supervision; management. **b.** Care; custody. See Syns at **care. 7.** An order, a command, or an injunction. **8.** *Law.* Instruction given by a judge to a jury about the law. **9.** A claim of wrongdoing; an

Charlie Chaplin
In character as *The Tramp*

ă **pat**	oi **boy**
ā **pay**	ou **out**
âr **care**	o͝o **took**
ä **father**	o͞o **boot**
ĕ **pet**	ŭ **cut**
ē **be**	ûr **urge**
ĭ **pit**	th **thin**
ī **pie**	*th* **this**
îr **pier**	hw **which**
ŏ **pot**	zh **vision**
ō **toe**	ə **about, item**
ô **paw**	

Stress marks:
′ (primary);
′ (secondary), as in
dictionary (dĭk′shə-nĕr′ē)

accusation. **10.a.** A rushing, forceful attack. **b.** The command to attack. **11.** A debt or an entry in an account recording a debt. **12.** A financial burden, such as a tax or lien. **13.** *Symbol* **q** *Phys.* **a.** The intrinsic property of matter responsible for all electric phenomena, in particular for the force of the electromagnetic interaction, occurring in two forms arbitrarily designated *negative* and *positive.* **b.** A measure of this property. **c.** The net measure of this property possessed by a body or contained in a bounded region of space. **14.** *Informal.* A feeling of pleasant excitement; a thrill. **15.** *Her.* A bearing or figure. **—*idiom.* in charge. 1.** In a position of leadership or supervision. **2.** *Chiefly British.* Under arrest. [ME *chargen,* to load < OFr. *chargier* < LLat. *carricāre* < Lat. *carrus,* cart, of Celt. orig. See **kers-*.**]

charge•a•ble (chär′jə-bəl) *adj.* **1.** Suitable to be charged, as to an account: *chargeable expenses.* **2.** Liable to be accused or indicted. **—charge′a•ble•ness** *n.*

charge account *n.* A credit arrangement in which a customer receives purchased goods or services before paying for them.

charge card *n.* See **credit card.**

charge conjugation *n.* *Symbol* **C** *Phys.* **1.** A mathematical operator that changes the sign of the charge and of the magnetic moment of every particle in the system to which it is applied. **2.** The theoretical conversion of matter to antimatter or of antimatter to matter.

char•gé d'af•faires (shär-zhā′ də-fâr′, dä-) *n., pl.* **char•gés d'affaires** (-zhā′, -zhāz′). **1.** A diplomat who temporarily substitutes for an absent ambassador or minister. **2.** A diplomat of the lowest rank, accredited by one government to the minister of foreign affairs of another. [Fr. : *chargé,* charged, in charge + *de,* with, of + *affaires,* affairs.]

charge density *n.* The electric charge per unit area or per unit volume of a body or of a region of space.

charg•er¹ (chär′jər) *n.* **1.** One that charges, such as an instrument that charges or replenishes storage batteries. **2.** A horse trained for battle; a cavalry horse.

charg•er² (chär′jər) *n.* A large shallow dish; a platter. [ME *chargeour* < OFr. *chargeor* < *chargier,* to load. See CHARGE.]

Cha•ri (shä′rē, shä-rē′). See **Shari.**

char•i•ot (chăr′ē-ət) *n.* **1.** An ancient horse-drawn two-wheeled vehicle. **2.** A light four-wheeled carriage used for ceremony or pleasure. [ME, vehicle < OFr. < *char,* cart < Lat. *carrus,* of Celt. orig. See **kers-*.**] **—char′i•ot** *v.*

chariot
Late sixth-century B.C. bronze Etruscan ceremonial chariot

char•i•o•teer (chăr′ē-ə-tîr′) *n.* The driver of a chariot.

Char•i•o•teer (chăr′ē-ə-tîr) *n.* See **Auriga.**

char•ism (kăr′ĭz′əm) *n.* *Theol.* Charisma.

cha•ris•ma (kə-rĭz′mə) *n., pl.* **-ma•ta** (-mə-tə). **1.a.** A rare personal quality of leaders who arouse fervent popular devotion and enthusiasm. **b.** Personal magnetism or charm. **2.** *Theol.* An extraordinary power, such as the ability to work miracles, granted by the Holy Spirit. [Gk. *kharisma,* divine favor < *kharizesthai,* to favor < *kharis,* favor. See **gher-²*.**]

char•is•mat•ic (kăr′ĭz-măt′ĭk) *adj.* **1.** Of, relating to, or characterized by charisma. **2.** *Theol.* Of, relating to, or being a type of Christianity that emphasizes personal religious experience and divinely inspired powers. **—*n.*** A member of a Christian charismatic group or movement.

char•i•ta•ble (chăr′ĭ-tə-bəl) *adj.* **1.** Generous in giving money or other help to the needy. **2.** Mild or tolerant in judging others; lenient. **3.** Of, for, or concerned with charity. **—char′i•ta•ble•ness** *n.* **—char′i•ta•bly** *adv.*

Charles
Photographed in 1981 by Lord Snowdon

Char•i•ton (shăr′ĭ-tn). A river rising in S IA and flowing c. 451 km (280 mi) to the Missouri R. in N MO.

char•i•ty (chăr′ĭ-tē) *n., pl.* **-ties. 1.** Provision of help or relief to the poor; almsgiving. **2.** Something given to help the needy; alms. **3.** A charitable institution, organization, or fund. **4.** Benevolence or generosity toward others. **5.** Indulgence or forbearance in judging others. See Syns at **mercy. 6.** Often **Charity.** *Theol.* The virtue defined as love directed first toward God but also toward oneself and one's neighbors as objects of God's love. [ME *charite* < OFr., Christian love < Lat. *cāritās,* affection < *cārus,* dear. See **kā-*.**]

cha•ri•va•ri (shĭv′ə-rē′, shĭv′ə-rē′) *n., pl.* **-ris.** See **shivaree.** See Regional Note at **shivaree.** [Fr. < OFr., perh. < LLat. *caribaria,* headache < Gk. *karēbaria* : *karē,* head; see **ker-¹*** + *barus,* heavy; see **gʷerə-¹*.**]

char•kha also **char•ka** (chûr′kə, chär′-) *n.* A spinning wheel used in India for spinning cotton. [Hindustani *carkhā* < Pers. *charkha,* dim. of *charkh,* wheel < OPers. **carka-.* See **kʷel-¹*.**]

char•la•tan (shär′lə-tən) *n.* A person who makes elaborate, fraudulent, and often voluble claims to skill or knowledge; a quack or fraud. [Fr. < Ital. *ciarlatano,* prob. alteration (influenced by *ciarlare,* to prattle) of *cerretano,* inhabitant of *Cerreto,* a city of Italy once famous for its quacks.] **—char′la•tan′ic** (-tăn′ĭk), **char′la•tan′i•cal** *adj.* **—char′la•tan•ism, char′la•tan•ry** *n.*

chasuble
Roman Catholic bishops

Char•le•magne (shär′lə-mān′). 742?–814. King of the Franks (768–814) and founder of the first empire in W Europe after the fall of Rome.

Char•le•roi (shär′lə-roi′, shär-lə-rwä′). A city of S Belgium S of Brussels; founded 1666. Pop. 216,144.

Charles (chärlz). Prince of Wales. b. 1948. The eldest son of Elizabeth II and heir to the British throne.

Charles I¹. 1600–49. King of England, Scotland, and Ireland (1625–49) who was defeated in the English Civil War (1642–48), tried for treason, and beheaded.

Charles I². 1887–1922. Emperor of Austria (1916–18) and king of Hungary as Charles IV (1916–18); deposed.

Charles II. 1630–85. King of England, Scotland, and Ireland (1660–85) who reigned during the Restoration.

Charles V. 1500–58. Holy Roman emperor (1519–58) and king of Spain as Charles I (1516–56); summoned the Diet of Worms (1521) and the Council of Trent (1545–63).

Charles VII. 1403–61. King of France (1422–61) who ended the Hundred Years' War (1453).

Charles IX. 1550–74. King of France (1560–74) who ordered the St. Bartholomew's Day Massacre (1752).

Charles X. 1757–1836. King of France (1824–30) who attempted to restore absolutism by abolishing the Chamber of Deputies and freedom of the press.

Charles XIV. 1763–1844. King of Sweden and Norway (1818–44) who founded the present Swedish royal dynasty.

Charles, Ray. b. 1930. Amer. musician and composer whose songs are rooted in gospel music, blues, and jazz.

Charles•bourg (chärlz′bûrg′, shärl-bo͞or′). A city of S Quebec, Canada, near Quebec City; settled in 1659. Pop. 68,326.

Charles Ed•ward Stu•art (ĕd′wərd sto͞o′ərt, styo͞o′-). See Charles Edward **Stuart.**

Charles Mar•tel (mär-tĕl′). "the Hammer." 688?–741. Frankish ruler of Austrasia (715–741) who in 732 halted the European invasion of the Moors.

Charles River. A river, c. 97 km (60 mi), of E MA flowing into Boston harbor.

Charles's law (chärl′zĭz) *n.* The physical law that the volume of a fixed mass of gas held at a constant pressure varies directly with the absolute temperature. [After Jacques Alexandre César *Charles* (1746–1823), French physicist.]

Charles's Wain *n.* See **Big Dipper.** [ME *charleswen,* Charles' (Charlemagne's) wain.]

Charles•ton¹ (chärl′stən). **1.** A city of E IL ESE of Decatur. Pop. 20,398. **2.** A city of SE SC NE of Savannah. Pop. 80,414. **3.** The cap. of WV, in the W-central part. Pop. 57,287.

Charles•ton² (chärl′stən) *n.* A fast ballroom dance popular during the 1920's and characterized by lively leg kicking and arm swinging. [After CHARLESTON¹ SC.]

Charles•town (chärlz′toun′). A former city of E MA, the oldest part of present-day Boston; settled c. 1629.

char•ley horse (chär′lē) *n.* *Informal.* A cramp or stiffness in a muscle, esp. of the upper leg, caused by strain. [?]

char•lock (chär′lək, -lŏk′) *n.* An annual weed *(Sinapis arvensis)* in the mustard family, native to Eurasia and having racemes of yellow flowers and hairy stems and foliage. [ME *cherlok* < OE *cerlic.*]

char•lotte (shär′lət) *n.* A dessert consisting of a mold of sponge cake or bread with a filling, as of fruits, whipped cream, or custard. [Fr. < the personal name *Charlotte.*]

Char•lotte (shär′lət). A city of S NC near the SC border SSW of Winston-Salem; settled c. 1750. Pop. 395,934.

Charlotte A•ma•lie (ə-mäl′yə). The cap. of the U.S. Virgin Islands, on St. Thomas I. in the West Indies. Pop. 11,842.

charlotte russe (ro͞os′) *n.* A cold dessert of Bavarian cream set in a mold lined with ladyfingers. [Fr. : *charlotte,* charlotte + *russe,* Russ.]

Char•lottes•ville (shär′ləts-vĭl′). An independent city of central VA NW of Richmond. Pop. 40,341.

Char•lotte•town (shär′lət-toun′). The cap. of Prince Edward I., Canada, on the S coast; founded c. 1720. Pop. 15,282.

charm (chärm) *n.* **1.** The power or quality of pleasing or delighting. **2.** A particular quality that attracts; a delightful characteristic. **3.** A small ornament, such as one worn on a bracelet. **4.** An item worn for its supposed magical benefit; an amulet. **5.** An action or formula thought to have magical power. **6.** The chanting of a magic word or verse; incantation. **7.** *Phys.* A quantum property of the charm quark whose conservation explains the absence of certain strange-particle decay modes and that accounts for the longevity of the J particle. **—*v.* charmed, charm•ing, charms. —*tr.* 1.** To attract or delight greatly. **2.** To induce by using strong personal attractiveness. **3.** To cast or seem to cast a spell on; bewitch. **—*intr.* 1.** To be alluring or pleasing. **2.** To function as an amulet or charm. **3.** To use magic spells. [ME *charme,* magic spell < OFr. < Lat. *carmen,* incantation. See **kan-*.**] **—charm′ing•ly** *adv.* **—charm′less** *adj.*

Syns: *charm, beguile, bewitch, captivate, enchant, entrance, fascinate.* The central meaning shared by these verbs is "to attract strongly or irresistibly": *manners that charmed us all; delicacies that beguile the gourmet; a performance that bewitched the audience; a novel that captivates its readers; an evening that enchanted the guests; music that entrances listeners; a host who fascinated his guests.* ***Ant:*** *repel.*

charmed life (chärmd) *n.* A life that seems to have been protected by a charm or spell.

charmed particle *n. Phys.* A particle with nonzero total charm.

charm•er (chär′mər) *n.* **1.** One that charms, esp. a disarmingly attractive person. **2.** One who casts spells; an enchanter.

char•meuse (shär-mo͞oz′, -mo͞os′, -mœz′) *n.* A satin-finished silk fabric. [Fr., trade name.]

char•mo•ni•um (chär-mō′nē-əm) *n.* Any of various elementary particles consisting of a charm quark and an antiquark. [< CHARM.]

charm quark *n.* A quark with a charge of +⅔, a mass about 2,900 times that of the electron, and a charm of +1. See table at **subatomic particle.**

char•nel (chär′nəl) *n.* A repository for the bones or bodies of the dead; a charnel house. — *adj.* Resembling or suitable for receiving the dead. [ME < OFr. < LLat. *carnāle* < neut. of Lat. *carnālis*, of the flesh < *carō, carn-*, flesh. See **sker-**[1]***.**]

charnel house *n.* A building, room, or vault in which the bones or bodies of the dead are placed; a charnel.

Char•on (kâr′ən) *n. Gk. Myth.* **1.** The ferryman who conveyed the dead to Hades over the river Styx. **2.** The only satellite of Pluto.

char•qui (chär′kē) *n.* See **jerky**[2]. [Am.Sp. < Quechua *ch'arki.*]

charr (chär) *n.* Var. of **char**[2].

chart (chärt) *n.* **1.** A map showing coastlines, water depths, or other information of use to navigators. **2.** An outline map on which specific information, such as scientific data, can be plotted. **3.** A sheet presenting information in the form of graphs or tables. **4.** See **graph**[1] 2. **5.** A listing of best-selling recorded music or other items. Often used in the plural. — *tr.v.* **chart•ed, chart•ing, charts. 1.** To make a chart of. **2.** To plan (something) in detail. [Obsolete Fr. *charte* < Lat. *charta*, sheet of paper made from papyrus. See CARD[1].]

char•ter (chär′tər) *n.* **1.** A document issued by a sovereign, legislature, or other authority, creating a public or private corporation, such as a city, college, or bank, and defining its privileges and purposes. **2.** A written grant from the sovereign power of a country conferring certain rights and privileges on a person, a corporation, or the people. **3.** A document outlining the principles, functions, and organization of a corporate body; a constitution. **4.** An authorization from a central organization to establish a local branch or chapter. **5.** Special privilege or immunity. **6.a.** A contract for the commercial leasing of a vessel or space on a vessel. **b.** The hiring or leasing of a vehicle, esp. for the exclusive, temporary use of a group of travelers. **7.** A written instrument given as evidence of agreement, transfer, or contract; a deed. — *tr.v.* **-tered, -ter•ing, -ters. 1.** To grant a charter to; establish by charter. **2.** To hire or lease by charter. **3.** To hire (a bus or an airplane, for example) for the exclusive, temporary use of a group of travelers. [ME *chartre* < OFr. < Lat. *chartula*, dim. of *charta*, paper made from papyrus. See CARD[1].] — **char′ter•er** *n.*

char•tered accountant (chär′tərd) *n. Chiefly British.* A member of one of the institutes of accountants granted a royal charter.

char•ter•house (chär′tər-hous′) *n.* A Carthusian monastery. [By folk ety. < AN *chartrouse* < OFr. *chartreus.*]

charter member *n.* An original member or a founder of an organization.

Chart•ism (chär′tĭz′əm) *n.* The principles and practices of a party of political reformers active in England (1838–1848). [< Med.Lat. *charta*, charter (referring to the "People's Charter" of 1837) < Lat., paper, document. See CARD[1].] — **Char′tist** *adj. & n.*

chart•ist (chär′tĭst) *n.* A stock-market specialist who uses charts and graphs.

Char•tres (shärt, shär′trə). A city of N France SW of Paris; noted for its 13th-cent. Gothic cathedral. Pop. 37,119.

char•treuse (shär-tro͞oz′, -tro͞os′, -trœz′) *n. Color.* A strong to brilliant greenish yellow to moderate or strong yellow green. [< CHARTREUSE.] — **char•treuse′** *adj.*

Char•treuse (shär-tro͞oz′, -tro͞os′, -trœz′). A trademark used for a usu. yellow or green liqueur.

char•tu•lar•y (kär′chə-lĕr′ē) *n.* Var. of **cartulary.**

char•wom•an (chär′wo͝om′ən) *n.* A woman hired to do cleaning or similar work, usu. in a large building.

char•y (châr′ē) *adj.* **-i•er, -i•est. 1.** Very cautious; wary. **2.** Not giving or expending freely; sparing. [ME *chari*, careful, sorrowful < OE *cearig*, sorrowful < *cearu*, sorrow. See CARE.] — **char′i•ly** *adv.* — **char′i•ness** *n.*

Cha•ryb•dis (kə-rĭb′dĭs) *n. Gk. Myth.* A whirlpool off the Sicilian coast opposite the cave of Scylla.

chase[1] (chās) *v.* **chased, chas•ing, chas•es.** — *tr.* **1.** To follow rapidly in order to catch or overtake; pursue. **2.** To follow (game) in order to capture or kill; hunt. **3.** *Informal.* To seek the favor or company of persistently. **4.** To put to flight; drive. — *intr.* **1.** To go or follow in pursuit. **2.** *Informal.* To go hurriedly; rush. — *n.* **1.** The act of chasing; pursuit. **2.a.** The hunting of game. **b.** Something that is hunted or pursued; quarry. **3.** *Chiefly British.* **a.** A privately owned, unenclosed game preserve. **b.** The right to hunt or keep game on the land of others. — ***idiom.* give chase.** To engage in pursuit of a quarry. [ME *chasen*, to hunt < OFr. *chacier* < VLat. **captiāre* < Lat. *captāre*, to catch. See CATCH.]

chase[2] (chās) *n. Print.* A rectangular frame into which pages or columns of type are locked for printing or plate making. [Perh. < Fr. *châsse*, case < OFr. *chasse* < Lat. *capsa.*]

chase[3] (chās) *n.* **1.a.** A groove cut in an object; a slot. **b.** A trench or channel for drainpipes or wiring. **2.** The part of a gun in front of the trunnions. **3.** The cavity of a mold. — *tr.v.* **chased, chas•ing, chas•es. 1.** To groove; indent. **2.** To cut (the thread of a screw). **3.** To decorate (metal) by engraving or embossing. [Poss. < obsolete Fr. *chas*, groove, enclosure < OFr. < Lat. *capsa*, box. V., var. of ENCHASE.]

Chase (chās), **Salmon Portland.** 1808–73. Amer. jurist; chief justice of the U.S. Supreme Court (1864–73).

Chase, Samuel. 1741–1811. Amer. jurist; associate justice of the U.S. Supreme Court (1796–1811).

chas•er[1] (chā′sər) *n.* **1.** One that chases or pursues another. **2.** *Informal.* A drink, as of beer, taken after hard liquor.

chas•er[2] (chā′sər) *n.* **1.** One who decorates metal by engraving or embossing. **2.** A steel tool for cutting or finishing screw threads.

chasm (kăz′əm) *n.* **1.** A deep, steep-sided opening in the earth's surface; an abyss or a gorge. **2.** A sudden interruption of continuity; a gap. **3.** A pronounced difference of opinion, interests, or loyalty. [Lat. *chasma* < Gk. *khasma.*] — **chas′mal** (kăz′məl) *adj.*

chas•sé (shă-sā′) *n.* A ballet movement consisting of one or more quick galloping steps with the same foot always leading. [Fr. < p.part. of *chasser*, to chase < OFr. *chacier*. See CHASE[1].] — **chas•sé′** *v.*

chasse•pot (shăs′pō′) *n.* A breechloading rifle introduced into the French army in 1866. [Fr., after Antoine Alphonse *Chassepot* (1833–1905), French gunsmith.]

chateau
Château de Chillon, Montreux, Switzerland

chas•seur (shă-sûr′) *n.* **1.** Any of certain light cavalry or infantry troops trained for rapid maneuvers. **2.** A hunter. **3.** A uniformed footman. [Fr. < OFr. *chaceor* < *chacier*, to pursue. See CHASE[1].]

Chas•sid (KHä′sĭd, KHô′-, hä′-) *n.* Var. of **Hasid.** — **Chas•si′dic** *adj.* — **Chas•si′dism** *n.*

chas•sis (shăs′ē, chăs′ē) *n., pl.* **chas•sis** (-ēz). **1.** The rectangular steel frame that holds the body and motor of an automotive vehicle. **2.** The landing gear of an aircraft. **3.** The frame on which a gun carriage moves forward and backward. **4.** The framework to which the components of a radio, television, or other electronic equipment are attached. [Fr. *châssis*, frame < OFr. < VLat. **capsīcium* < Lat. *capsa*, box.]

chaste (chāst) *adj.* **chast•er, chast•est. 1.** Morally pure in thought or conduct; decent and modest. **2.a.** Not having experienced sexual intercourse; virginal. **b.** Abstaining from sexual intercourse; celibate. **3.** Pure or simple in design or style; austere. [ME < OFr. < Lat. *castus*. See **kes-*.**] — **chaste′ly** *adv.* — **chaste′ness** *n.*

chas•ten (chā′sən) *tr.v.* **-tened, -ten•ing, -tens. 1.** To correct by punishment or reproof; take to task. **2.** To restrain; subdue. **3.** To rid of excess; refine or purify. [Alteration of obsolete *chaste* < ME *chasten, chastien* < OFr. *chastiier* < Lat. *castigāre*. See CASTIGATE.] — **chas′ten•er** *n.*

chas•tise (chăs-tīz′, chăs′tīz′) *tr.v.* **-tised, -tis•ing, -tis•es. 1.** To punish, as by beating. **2.** To criticize severely; rebuke. **3.** *Archaic.* To purify. [ME *chastisen*, alteration of *chasten*. See CHASTEN.] — **chas•tis′a•ble** *adj.* — **chas•tise′ment** (chăs-tīz′mənt, chăs′tĭz-mənt) *n.* — **chas•tis′er** *n.*

chas•ti•ty (chăs′tĭ-tē) *n.* **1.** The condition or quality of being pure or chaste. **2.a.** Virginity. **b.** Virtuous character. **c.** Celibacy. [ME *chastite* < OFr. *chastete* < Lat. *castitās* < *castus*, pure. See CHASTE.]

chastity belt *n.* A beltlike device of medieval times designed to prevent the woman wearing it from having sexual intercourse.

chas•u•ble (chăz′ə-bəl, chăzh′ə-, chăs′ə-) *n.* A long sleeveless vestment worn over the alb by a priest during services. [Fr. < OFr. < LLat. *casubla*, hooded garment < **casupula*, dim. of *casa*, house.]

chat (chăt) *intr.v.* **chat•ted, chat•ting, chats.** To converse in an easy, familiar manner; talk lightly and casually. — *n.* **1.** An informal, light conversation. **2.** Any of several birds known for their chattering call, as of the genera *Saxicola* or *Icteria*. [ME *chatten*, to jabber, alteration of *chateren*. See CHATTER.]

cha•teau also **châ•teau** (shă-tō′) *n., pl.* **-teaus** or **-teaux** (-tōz′). **1.a.** A French castle. **b.** A French manor house. **2.** A large country house. [Fr. *château* < OFr. *chastel* < Lat. *castellum*, castle. See CASTLE.]

Cha•teau•bri•and also **cha•teau•bri•and** (shă-tō′-brē-äN′) *n.* A double-thick, tender center cut of beef tenderloin, sometimes stuffed with seasonings before grilling. [After Vicomte François René de CHÂTEAUBRIAND.]

Châ•teau•bri•and (shä-tō′brē-äN′, shă-), Vicomte **François René de.** 1768–1848. French politician and writer whose works include *Atala* (1801).

Châ•teau•guay (shăt′ə-gā′, shä-tō-gā′). A town of S Quebec, Canada, SW of Montreal. Pop. 36,928.

Châ•teau-Thier•ry (shä-tō′tyĕ-rē′). A town of N France on the Marne R. ENE of Paris; site of the second Battle of the Marne (Jun. 3–4, 1918). Pop. 14,557.

chat•e•lain (shăt′l-ān′) *n.* The master of a castle; a castellan.

ă pat	oi boy
ā pay	ou out
âr care	o͝o took
ä father	o͞o boot
ĕ pet	ŭ cut
ē be	ûr urge
ĭ pit	th thin
ī pie	*th* this
îr pier	hw which
ŏ pot	zh vision
ō toe	ə about, item
ô paw	

Stress marks:
′ (primary);
′ (secondary), as in
dictionary (dĭk′shə-nĕr′ē)

[ME *chatelein* < OFr. *chastelain* < Lat. *castellānus* < *castellum*, castle. See CASTLE.]

chat•e•laine (shăt′l-ān′) *n.* **1.a.** The mistress of a castle. **b.** The mistress of a large, fashionable household. **2.** A clasp or chain worn at the waist for holding keys, a purse, or a watch. [Fr. *châtelaine*, fem. of *châtelain*, chatelain < OFr. *chastelain*. See CHATELAIN.]

chatelaine
18th-century German

Chat•ham (chăt′əm). **1.** A city of SE Ontario, Canada, on the Thames R. ENE of Windsor. Pop. 40,952. **2.** A municipal borough of SE England E of London. Pop. 142,800.

Chatham Islands. An island group of New Zealand in the SW Pacific Ocean E of South I.

cha•toy•ant (shə-toi′ənt) *adj.* Having a changeable luster. —*n.* A chatoyant stone or gemstone, such as the cat's-eye. [Fr., pr.part. of *chatoyer*, to shimmer like cats' eyes < *chat*, cat. See CAT.] —**cha•toy′an•cy** *n.*

chat show *n. Chiefly British.* A talk show.

Chat•ta•hoo•chee (chăt′ə-hōō′chē). A river rising in N GA and flowing c. 702 km (436 mi) generally S to the Flint R.

Chat•ta•noo•ga (chăt′ə-nōō′gə). A city of SE TN on the Tennessee R. and the GA border SE of Nashville. Pop. 152,466.

chat•tel (chăt′l) *n.* **1.** *Law.* An article of personal, movable property. **2.** A slave. [ME *chatel*, movable property < OFr. < Med.Lat. *capitāle*. See CATTLE.]

chat•ter (chăt′ər) *v.* **-tered, -ter•ing, -ters.** —*intr.* **1.** To talk rapidly, incessantly, and on trivial subjects; jabber. **2.** To utter a rapid series of short, inarticulate, speechlike sounds. **3.** To click quickly and repeatedly. **4.** To vibrate or rattle while in operation. —*tr.* To utter in a rapid, usu. thoughtless way. —*n.* **1.** Idle, trivial talk. **2.** The sharp rapid sounds made by some birds and animals. **3.** A series of quick rattling or clicking sounds. [ME *chateren*, of imit. orig.] —**chat′ter•er** *n.*

chat•ter•box (chăt′ər-bŏks′) *n.* A very talkative person.

chatter mark also **chat•ter•mark** (chăt′ər-märk′) *n.* **1.** A riblike marking on wood or metal, caused by vibration of a cutting tool. **2.** *Geol.* One of a series of short scars made by glacial drift on a surface of bedrock.

Chat•ter•ton (chăt′ər-tən), **Thomas.** 1752–70. British poet whose work influenced the romantic poets.

chat•ty (chăt′ē) *adj.* **-ti•er, -ti•est. 1.** Inclined to chat; friendly and talkative. **2.** Full of or in the style of light informal talk: *a chatty letter.* —**chat′ti•ly** *adv.* —**chat′ti•ness** *n.*

Chau•cer (chô′sər), **Geoffrey.** 1340?–1400. English poet regarded as the greatest literary figure of medieval England. His works include *The Canterbury Tales* (1387–1400). —**Chau•cer′i•an** (chô-sîr′ē-ən) *adj. & n.*

chauf•feur (shō′fər, shō-fûr′) *n.* One employed to drive a private automobile. —*v.* **-feured, -feur•ing, -feurs.** —*tr.* **1.** To serve as a chauffeur for (another). **2.** To transport in (a motor vehicle); drive. —*intr.* To serve as a chauffeur. [Fr., stoker < *chauffer*, to heat, stoke < OFr. *chaufer*. See CHAFE.]

chaul•moo•gra (chôl-mōō′grə) *n.* Any of several tropical Asian trees of the genus *Hydnocarpus*, whose seeds contain an oil formerly used to treat leprosy. [Bengali *cāulmugrā*.]

Cesar Chavez

chaunt (chônt, chänt) *n. & v. Archaic.* Var. of **chant.**

Chau•tau•qua Lake (shə-tô′kwə, chə-). A lake of SW NY.

chau•vin•ism (shō′və-nĭz′əm) *n.* **1.** Militant devotion to and glorification of one's country; fanatical patriotism. **2.** Prejudiced belief in the superiority of one's own gender, group, or kind. [Fr. *chauvinisme*, after Nicolas *Chauvin*, a legendary French soldier devoted to Napoleon.] —**chau′vin•ist** *n.* —**chau′vin•is′tic** *adj.* —**chau′vin•is′ti•cal•ly** *adv.*

Cha•vannes (shä-vän′), **Pierre Puvis de.** See Pierre **Puvis de Chavannes.**

Cha•vez (chä′vĕz′, shä′-), **Cesar Estrada.** 1927–93. Amer. labor organizer who founded the National Farm Workers Association (1962).

chaw (chô) *Regional.* —*intr. & tr.v.* **chawed, chaw•ing, chaws.** To chew. —*n.* A chew, esp. of tobacco. [Var. of CHEW.]

cha•yo•te (chä-yō′tā) *n.* **1.** A tropical American perennial herbaceous vine *(Sechium edule)* having tendrils, tuberous roots, and an edible pear-shaped fruit. **2.** The fruit of this plant. Also called regionally *mirliton.* [Sp. < Nahuatl *chayotli.*]

cha•zan or **haz•zan** also **chaz•zen** (KHä′zən) *n.* A cantor in a synagogue. [LHeb. *ḥazzān.*]

Ch.E. *abbr.* Chemical engineer.

cheap (chēp) *adj.* **cheap•er, cheap•est. 1.a.** Relatively low in cost. **b.** Charging low prices. **2.a.** Obtainable at a low rate of interest. Used esp. of money. **b.** Devalued, as in buying power. **3.** Achieved with little effort. **4.** Of or considered of small value. **5.** Of poor quality; inferior. **6.** Worthy of no respect; vulgar or contemptible. **7.** Stingy; miserly. —*adv.* **cheaper, cheapest.** Inexpensively. —***idioms.*** **cheap at twice the price.** Extremely inexpensive. **on the cheap.** By inexpensive means; cheaply. [< ME *(god) chep*, (good) price, purchase, bargain < OE *cēap*, trade < Lat. *caupō*, shopkeeper.] —**cheap′ly** *adv.* —**cheap′ness** *n.*

cheap•en (chē′pən) *v.* **-ened, -en•ing, -ens.** —*tr.* **1.** To make cheap or cheaper. **2.** To lower in public estimation; debase. —*intr.* To become cheap or cheaper. —**cheap′en•er** *n.*

cheap•ie (chē′pē) *n. Slang.* **1.** A cheap item. **2.** A stingy person.

cheap•jack (chēp′jăk′) *n.* A peddler or dealer of cheap goods. —*adj.* Inferior in quality or value; tawdry.

cheap shot *n.* An unfair or unsporting verbal attack on a vulnerable target.

Cheap•side (chēp′sīd′). A street and district in the City of London, England; the market center of medieval London.

cheap•skate (chēp′skāt′) *n. Slang.* A stingy person; a miser.

cheat (chēt) *v.* **cheat•ed, cheat•ing, cheats.** —*tr.* **1.** To deceive by trickery; swindle. **2.** To deprive by trickery; defraud. **3.** To mislead; fool. **4.** To elude; escape: *cheat death.* —*intr.* **1.** To act dishonestly; practice fraud. **2.** To violate rules deliberately, as in a game. **3.** *Informal.* To be sexually unfaithful. —*n.* **1.** An act of cheating; a fraud or swindle. **2.** One that cheats; a swindler. **3.** *Law.* Fraudulent acquisition of another's property. **4.** *Bot.* An annual European brome grass *(Bromus secalinus)* widely naturalized in temperate regions. [ME *cheten*, to confiscate, short for *acheten*, var. of *escheten* < *eschete*, escheat. See ESCHEAT.] —**cheat′er** *n.* —**cheat′ing•ly** *adv.*

Che•bok•sa•ry (chĭ-bŏk-sär′ē). A city of W-central Russia on the Volga R. W of Kazan. Pop. 389,000.

check (chĕk) *n.* **1.** An action or influence that stops motion or expression; a restraint. **2.** The condition of being stopped or held back; restraint. **3.** An abrupt stop in forward movement or progress; a halt. **4.** The act or an instance of inspecting or testing, as for accuracy; examination. **5.** A standard for inspecting or evaluating; a test. **6.** A check mark. **7.** A ticket or slip of identification. **8.** A bill at a restaurant or bar. **9.** *Games.* A chip or counter used in gambling. **10.** A written order to a bank to pay the amount specified from funds on deposit; a draft. **11.** A small crack; a chink. **12.a.** A pattern of small squares, as on a chessboard. **b.** One of the squares of such a pattern. **c.** A fabric patterned with squares. **13.** *Games.* **a.** A move in chess that directly attacks an opponent's king but does not constitute a checkmate. **b.** The position or condition of a king so attacked. **14.** *Sports.* The act of checking an opponent in ice hockey. —*interj.* **1.** *Games.* Used to declare that a chess opponent's king is in check. **2.** *Informal.* Used to express agreement or understanding. —*v.* **checked, check•ing, checks.** —*tr.* **1.** To arrest the motion of abruptly; halt. **2.** To hold in restraint; curb. **3.** To slow the growth of; retard. **4.** To rebuke; rebuff. **5.** To inspect so as to determine accuracy, quality, or other condition; test. **6.** To verify by consulting a source or authority. **7.** To put a check mark on or next to. **8.** To deposit for temporary safekeeping: *checked his coat.* **9.** To consign (luggage, for example) for shipment on a transportation vehicle. **10.** To make cracks or chinks in. **11.** *Games.* To move in chess so as to put (an opponent's king) under direct attack. **12.** *Sports.* To block or impede (an opposing player with the puck) in ice hockey by using one's body or one's stick. —*intr.* **1.** To come to an abrupt halt; stop. **2.** To agree point for point; correspond. **3.** To be verified or confirmed; pass inspection: *The story checked out.* **4.** To make an examination or investigation; inquire. **5.** To write a check on a bank account. **6.** To undergo cracking in a pattern of checks, as paint does. **7.** *Games.* To place a chess opponent's king in check. **8.a.** To pause to relocate a scent. Used of hunting dogs. **b.** To abandon the proper game and follow baser prey. Used of trained falcons. **9.** *Sports.* To check an opposing player in ice hockey. —***phrasal verbs.*** **check in.** To register, as at a hotel. **check out. 1.** To settle one's bill and leave a hotel or other place of lodging. **2.** To withdraw (an item) after recording the withdrawal: *check out books.* **3.** To record and total up the prices of and receive payment for (items being purchased) at a retail store. **check over.** To look over; examine. [ME *chek*, check in chess < OFr. *eschec* < Ar. *shāh* < Pers., king, king in chess. See SHAH.] —**check′a•ble** *adj.*

Word History: The words *check*, *chess*, and *shah* are all related. *Shah* is a borrowing into English of the Persian title for the monarch of that country. The Persian word *shāh* was also a term used in chess, a game played in Persia long before it was introduced to Europe. One said *shāh* as a warning when the opponent's king was under attack. The Persian word in this sense, after passing through Arabic, probably Old Spanish, and then Old French, came into Middle English as *chek* about seven hundred years ago. *Chess* itself comes from a plural form of the Old French word that gave us the word *check.*

check•book (chĕk′bo͝ok′) *n.* A book containing blank checks issued by a bank.

checked (chĕkt) *adj.* **1.** Having a pattern of checks or squares: *checked cloth.* **2.** Held in check; restrained. **3.** *Ling.* Situated in a stopped or closed syllable: *a checked vowel.*

check•er (chĕk′ər) *n.* **1.a.** One, such as an inspector or examiner, that checks. **b.** One that receives items for temporary safekeeping or for shipment: *a baggage checker.* **2.** *Games.* **a. checkers.** *(used with a sing. v.)* A game played on a checkerboard by two players, each using 12 pieces. **b.** One of the round, flat pieces used in this game. **3.a.** A pattern of checks or squares. **b.** One of the squares in such a pattern. **4.** A cashier. —*tr.v.* **-ered, -er•ing, -ers. 1.** To mark with a checked or squared pattern. **2.** To diversify (something) in color, shading, or character; variegate. [ME *cheker*, chessboard, alteration of *escheker* < OFr. *eschequier* < *eschec*, check in chess. See CHECK.]

check•er•ber•ry (chĕk′ər-bĕr′ē) *n.* See **wintergreen** 1a. [CHECKER(BOARD) + BERRY.]

check•er•bloom (chĕk′ər-blo͞om′) *n.* An ornamental herb *(Sidalcea malviflora)* native to western North America and having pink to purple flowers. [CHECKER(BOARD) + BLOOM[1].]

check•er•board (chĕk′ər-bôrd′, -bōrd′) *n. Games.* A board on which chess and checkers are played, divided into 64 squares of two alternating colors.

check•ered (chĕk′ərd) *adj.* **1.** Divided into squares. **2.** Marked by light and dark patches; diversified in color. **3.** Marked by great changes or shifts in fortune: *a checkered career.*

check•ing account (chĕk′ĭng) *n.* A bank account in which checks may be written against amounts on deposit.

check•list (chĕk′lĭst′) *n.* A list of items to be noted, checked, or remembered.

check mark *n.* A mark placed next to an item to show that it has been noted, verified, or approved.

check•mate (chĕk′māt′) *tr.v.* **-mat•ed, -mat•ing, -mates. 1.** *Games.* To attack (a chess opponent's king) in such a manner that no escape or defense is possible, thus ending the game. **2.** To defeat completely. —*n.* **1.** *Games.* **a.** A move that checkmates a chess opponent's king. **b.** The position or condition of a king so attacked. **2.** Utter defeat. —*interj. Games.* Used to checkmate. [ME *chekmat* < OFr. *eschec mat* < Ar. *shāh māt*, the king is dead : *shāh*, king (< Pers.; see SHAH) + *māt*, dead.]

check•off (chĕk′ôf′, -ŏf′) *n.* Collection of dues from members of a union by authorized deduction from their wages.

check•out (chĕk′out′) *n.* **1.** The act, time, or place of checking out, as at a hotel. **2.** A test, as of a machine, for proper functioning. **3.** An investigation; an inspection.

check•point (chĕk′point′) *n.* A point where a check is made.

check•rein (chĕk′rān′) *n.* **1.** A short rein that extends from a horse's bit to the saddle to keep the horse's head up. **2.** A rein joining the bit of one of a span of horses to the other's driving rein.

check•room (chĕk′ro͞om′, -ro͝om′) *n.* A place where hats, coats, packages, or other items can be stored temporarily.

check•up (chĕk′ŭp′) *n.* **1.** An examination or inspection. **2.** A general physical examination.

Ched•dar also **ched•dar** (chĕd′ər) *n.* Any of several types of smooth hard cheese varying in flavor from mild to extra sharp. [After *Cheddar*, a village of SW England.]

cheek (chēk) *n.* **1.** The fleshy part of either side of the face below the eye and between the nose and ear. **2.** Something resembling the cheek in shape or position. **3.** Either of the buttocks. **4.** Cool impertinence. —*tr.v.* **cheeked, cheek•ing, cheeks.** *Informal.* To speak impudently to. —***idiom.* cheek by jowl.** Side by side. [ME *cheke* < OE *cēace.*]

cheek•bone (chēk′bōn′) *n.* See **zygomatic bone.**

cheek pouch *n.* A pocketlike fold of skin in the cheeks of various animals in which food is carried.

cheek•y (chē′kē) *adj.* **-i•er, -i•est.** Impertinently bold; impudent and saucy. —**cheek′i•ly** *adv.* —**cheek′i•ness** *n.*

cheep (chēp) *n.* A faint shrill sound like that of a young bird; a chirp. —*intr.v.* **cheeped, cheep•ing, cheeps.** To make a faint shrill sound or sounds; chirp. [Imit.] —**cheep′er** *n.*

cheer (chîr) *n.* **1.** Lightness of spirits or mood; gaiety or joy. **2.** A source of joy or happiness; a comfort. **3.a.** A shout of approval, encouragement, or congratulation. **b.** A short rehearsed jingle or phrase, shouted in unison by a squad of cheerleaders. **4.** Festive food and drink; refreshment. —*v.* **cheered, cheer•ing, cheers.** —*tr.* **1.** To make happier or more cheerful. **2.** To encourage with or as if with cheers; urge: *cheered us on.* **3.** To salute or acclaim with cheers; applaud. —*intr.* **1.** To shout cheers. **2.** To become cheerful: *I cheered up.* [ME *chere*, expression, mood < OFr. *chiere*, face < LLat. *cara* < Gk. *kara*, head. See **ker-**[1]***.**] —**cheer′ing•ly** *adv.*

cheer•ful (chîr′fəl) *adj.* **1.** Being in good spirits; merry. See Syns at **glad**[1]. **2.** Promoting a feeling of cheer; pleasant: *a cozy, cheerful room.* **3.** Reflecting willingness or good humor: *cheerful labor.* —**cheer′ful•ly** *adv.* —**cheer′ful•ness** *n.*

cheer•i•o (chîr′ē-ō′) *interj. Chiefly British.* Used in greeting or parting. [Alteration of CHEER.]

cheer•lead (chîr′lēd′) *intr.v.* **-led** (-lĕd′), **-lead•ing, -leads.** To lead organized cheering, as at sports events.

cheer•lead•er (chîr′lē′dər) *n.* One who leads the cheering of spectators, as at a sports contest.

cheer•less (chîr′lĭs) *adj.* Lacking cheer; depressing. —**cheer′less•ly** *adv.* —**cheer′less•ness** *n.*

cheers (chîz) *interj.* Used as a toast.

cheer•y (chîr′ē) *adj.* **-i•er, -i•est.** Showing or suggesting good spirits; cheerful. —**cheer′i•ly** *adv.* —**cheer′i•ness** *n.*

cheese[1] (chēz) *n.* **1.a.** A solid food made from the pressed curd of milk, often seasoned and aged. **b.** A molded mass of this substance. **2.** Something resembling this substance. [ME *chese* < OE *cȳse* < Gmc. **kasjus* < Lat. *cāseus.*]

cheese[2] (chēz) *tr.v.* **cheesed, chees•ing, chees•es.** *Slang.* To stop. —***idiom.* cheese it.** *Slang.* **1.** To look out. **2.** To get away fast; get going. [?]

cheese[3] (chēz) *n. Slang.* An important person. [Perh. < Urdu *chīz*, thing < Pers. < OPers. *ciš-ciy*, something. See **kʷo-*.**]

cheese•burg•er (chēz′bûr′gər) *n.* A hamburger topped with melted cheese.

cheese•cake (chēz′kāk′) *n.* **1.** A cake made of sweetened cottage cheese or cream cheese, eggs, milk, sugar, and flavorings. **2.** *Informal.* Photographs of minimally attired women.

cheese•cloth (chēz′klôth′, -klŏth′) *n.* A coarse, loosely woven cotton gauze, originally used for wrapping cheese.

cheese-par•ing (chēz′pâr′ĭng) *adj.* Miserly; stingy. —*n.* **1.** Something of little or no value. **2.** Stinginess; parsimony.

chees•y (chē′zē) *adj.* **-i•er, -i•est. 1.** Containing or resembling cheese. **2.** *Informal.* **a.** Tasteless and showy, often in a vulgar manner. **b.** Having an appreciation for what is tasteless and showy. **3.** *Informal.* Of poor quality; shoddy. [Sense 2 and 3, poss. < CHEESE[3].] —**chees′i•ness** *n.*

chee•tah also **che•tah** (chē′tə) *n.* A long-legged swift-running wild cat *(Acinonyx jubatus)* of Africa and southwest Asia having black-spotted tawny fur and nonretractile claws. [Hindustani *cītā* < Skt. *citrakāyaḥ*, tiger, leopard : *citra-*, variegated + *kāyaḥ*, body; see **kʷei-**[2]***.**]

Chee•ver (chē′vər), **John.** 1912–82. Amer. writer who depicted suburban life with humor and compassion.

chef (shĕf) *n.* A cook, esp. the head of a large kitchen staff. [Fr., short for *chef (de cuisine)*, head (of the kitchen). See CHIEF.]

chef-d'oeu•vre (shā-dœ′vrə, -dûrv′) *n., pl.* **chefs-d'oeuvre** (shā-). A masterpiece, esp. in literature or art. [Fr. : *chef*, head, beginning + *de*, of + *oeuvre*, work.]

cheiro– *pref.* Var. of **chiro–.**

Che•ju (chĕ′jo͞o′). An island of South Korea separated from the SW coast of the mainland by **Cheju Strait**, a channel linking the Yellow Sea and Korea Strait.

Che•khov also **Che•kov** (chĕk′ôf, -ŏf, -ŏv, chyĕ′ᴋʜəf), **Anton Pavlovich.** 1860–1904. Russian writer whose works include *The Seagull* (1896). —**Che•kho′vi•an** (chĕ-kō′vē-ən) *adj.*

Che•kiang (chŭ′kyäng′, jə′gyäng′). See **Zhejiang.**

che•la (kē′lə) *n., pl.* **-lae** (-lē). A pincerlike claw of a crustacean or an arachnid. [NLat. < Gk. *khēlē*, claw.]

che•late (kē′lāt′) *adj. Zool.* Having chelae or resembling a chela. —*n. Chem.* A chemical compound in the form of a heterocyclic ring, containing a metal ion attached by coordinate bonds to at least two nonmetal ions. —*tr.v.* **-lat•ed, -lat•ing, -lates. 1.** *Chem.* To combine (a metal ion) with a chemical compound to form a ring. **2.** *Medic.* To remove (a heavy metal, such as lead or mercury) from the bloodstream by means of a chelate, such as EDTA. —**che′lat•a•ble** *adj.* —**che•la′tion** *n.* —**che′la′tor** *n.*

che•lic•er•a (kĭ-lĭs′ər-ə) *n., pl.* **-er•ae** (-ə-rē′). Either of the first pair of fanglike appendages near the mouth of an arachnid. [NLat. : CHELA + Gk. *keras*, horn; see **ker-**[1]***.**]

che•li•form (kē′lə-fôrm′) *adj.* Having the shape of a chela.

Chel•li•an or **Chel•le•an** (shĕl′ē-ən) *adj.* Abbevillian. [After *Chelles*, a city of N-central France.]

Chelms•ford (chĕmz′fərd). A town of NE MA near Lowell. Pop. 32,388.

che•loid (kē′loid′) *n.* Var. of **keloid.**

che•lo•ni•an (kĭ-lō′nē-ən) *adj.* Of, relating to, or belonging to the order Chelonia, which includes the turtles and tortoises. [< NLat. *Chelonia*, order name < Gk. *khelōnē*, tortoise.] —**che•lo′ni-an** *n.*

Chel•sea (chĕl′sē). **1.** A district of W London, England, on the N bank of the Thames R. **2.** A city of E MA, a suburb of Boston; settled in 1624. Pop. 28,710.

Chel•ten•ham (chĕlt′nəm, chĕl′tən-əm). A municipal borough of W-central England S of Birmingham. Pop. 86,100.

Che•lya•binsk (chĕl-yä′bĭnsk, chĭ-lyä′-). A city of S-central Russia S of Sverdlovsk; founded 1736. Pop. 1,096,000.

Che•lyus•kin (chĕl-yo͞o′skĭn, chĭ-lyo͞o′-), **Cape.** A cape of N-central Russia on the Taimyr Peninsula.

chem. *abbr.* Chemical; chemist; chemistry.

chem– or **chemi–** *pref.* Var. of **chemo–.**

chem•ic (kĕm′ĭk) *adj.* **1.** Chemical. **2.** *Archaic.* Alchemic. —*n. Obsolete.* An alchemist.

chem•i•cal (kĕm′ĭ-kəl) *adj.* **1.** Of or relating to chemistry. **2.** Of or relating to the properties or actions of chemicals. —*n.* **1.** A substance with a distinct molecular composition that is produced by or used in a chemical process. **2.** A drug, esp. an illicit or addictive one. [Obsolete *chimical* < *chimic*, alchemist < NLat. *chimicus* < Med.Lat. *alchimicus* < *alchymia*, alchemy. See ALCHEMY.] —**chem′i•cal•ly** *adv.*

chemical abuse *n.* See **substance abuse.**

chemical bond *n.* Any of several forces or mechanisms by which atoms or ions are bound in a molecule or crystal.

chemical dependency *n.* A physical and psychological habituation to a mood- or mind-altering drug.

chemical engineering *n.* The branch of engineering that deals with the manufacture of products through chemical processes. —**chemical engineer** *n.*

chemical warfare *n.* Warfare involving lethal and incapacitating munitions and agents, such as poisons.

cheetah
Acinonyx jubatus

ă pat	oi boy
ā pay	ou out
âr care	o͝o took
ä father	o͞o boot
ĕ pet	ŭ cut
ē be	ûr urge
ĭ pit	th thin
ī pie	*th* this
îr pier	hw which
ŏ pot	zh vision
ō toe	ə about, item
ô paw	

Stress marks:
′ (primary);
′ (secondary), as in
dictionary (dĭk′shə-nĕr′ē)

chem·i·lu·mi·nes·cence (kĕm′ə-lo͞o′mə-nĕs′əns) *n.* Emission of light as a result of a chemical reaction at environmental temperatures. — **chem′i·lu′mi·nes′cent** *adj.*

che·min de fer (shə-măɴ′ də fâr′) *n. Games.* A variation of baccarat. [Fr. *chemin de fer*, railroad : *chemin*, way + *de*, of + *fer*, iron.]

che·mise (shə-mēz′) *n.* **1.** A woman's loose shirtlike undergarment. **2.** A loosely fitting dress that hangs straight, sometimes belted; a shift. [ME < OFr., shirt < LLat. *camisia*.]

chem·i·sette (shĕm′ĭ-zĕt′) *n.* **1.** A short sleeveless bodice. **2.** A blouse front; a dickey. [Fr., dim. of *chemise*, shirt < OFr. See CHEMISE.]

chem·i·sorb (kĕm′ĭ-sôrb′) also **chem·o·sorb** (-ə-sôrb′) *tr.v.* **-sorbed, -sorb·ing, -sorbs.** To take up and chemically bind (a substance) onto the surface of another substance. [CHEMI– + (AB)SORB.] — **chem′i·sorp′tion** (-sôrp′shən) *n.*

chem·ist (kĕm′ĭst) *n.* **1.** A scientist specializing in chemistry. **2.** *Chiefly British.* A pharmacist. **3.** *Obsolete.* An alchemist. [Obsolete *chimist* < NLat. *chimista* < Med.Lat. *alchymista*, alchemist < *alchymia*, alchemy. See ALCHEMY.]

chem·is·try (kĕm′ĭ-strē) *n.*, *pl.* **-tries. 1.** The science of the composition, structure, properties, and reactions of matter, esp. of atomic and molecular systems. **2.** The composition, structure, properties, and reactions of a substance. **3.** The elements of a complex entity and their dynamic interrelation. **4.** Mutual attraction or sympathy; rapport.

Chem·nitz (kĕm′nĭts). Formerly **Karl-Marx-Stadt** (kärl-märk′shtät′). A city of E-central Germany SE of Leipzig. Pop. 318,917.

che·mo (kē′mō, kĕm′ō) *n. Informal.* Chemotherapy or a chemotherapeutic treatment.

chemo– or **chemi–** or **chem–** *pref.* Chemicals; chemical: *chemotherapy.* [< CHEMICAL.]

che·mo·au·to·troph (kē′mō-ô′tə-trŏf′, -trōf′, kĕm′ō-) *n.* An organism that obtains its nourishment by oxidation of inorganic chemical compounds as opposed to photosynthesis. — **che′mo·au′to·tro′phic** (-trō′fĭk, -trŏf′ĭk) *adj.* — **che′mo·au′to·tro′phi·cal·ly** *adv.* — **che′mo·au·tot′ro·phy** (-ô-tŏt′rə-fē) *n.*

che·mo·pre·ven·tion (kē′mō-prĭ-vĕn′shən, kĕm′ō-) *n.* The use of chemical agents, drugs, or food supplements to prevent disease. — **che′mo·pre·ven′tive** *adj. & n.*

che·mo·pro·phy·lax·is (kē′mō-prō′fə-lăk′sĭs, kĕm′ō-) *n.* See **chemoprevention.** — **che′mo·pro′phy·lac′tic** (-lăk′tĭk) *adj. & n.*

cherimoya
Annona cherimola

che·mo·re·cep·tion (kē′mō-rĭ-sĕp′shən, kĕm′ō-) *n.* The physiological response of a sense organ to a chemical stimulus. — **che′mo·re·cep′tive** *adj.* — **che′mo·re′cep·tiv′i·ty** (-rē′sĕp-tĭv′ĭ-tē) *n.*

che·mo·re·cep·tor (kē′mō-rĭ-sĕp′tər, kĕm′ō-) *n.* A sensory nerve cell or sense organ that responds to chemical stimuli.

che·mo·sen·so·ry (kē′mō-sĕn′sə-rē, kĕm′ō-) *adj.* Relating to the perception of a chemical stimulus by sensory means.

chem·o·sorb (kĕm′ə-sôrb′) *v.* Var. of **chemisorb.**

chess[1]

che·mo·sphere (kē′mə-sfîr′, kĕm′ə-) *n.* The region of the atmosphere from 30 to 190 kilometers (20 to 120 miles) above Earth's surface, in which photochemical reactions initiated by solar radiation occur.

che·mo·sur·ger·y (kē′mō-sûr′jə-rē, kĕm′ō-) *n.* Selective destruction of tissue by use of chemicals, as for removing malignant skin lesions. — **che′mo·sur′gi·cal** (-jĭ-kəl) *adj.*

che·mo·syn·the·sis (kē′mō-sĭn′thĭ-sĭs, kĕm′ō-) *n.* Synthesis of carbohydrate from carbon dioxide and water using energy obtained from the chemical oxidation of simple inorganic compounds. — **che′mo·syn·thet′ic** (-sĭn-thĕt′ĭk) *adj.* — **che′mo·syn·thet′i·cal·ly** *adv.*

che·mo·sys·tem·at·ics (kē′mō-sĭs′tə-măt′ĭks, kĕm′ō-) *n.* (*used with a sing. or pl. v.*) See **chemotaxonomy.**

che·mo·tax·is (kē′mō-tăk′sĭs, kĕm′ō-) *n.* The characteristic movement or orientation of an organism or cell along a chemical concentration gradient either toward or away from the chemical stimulus. — **che′mo·tac′tic** (-tăk′tĭk) *adj.* — **che′mo·tac′ti·cal·ly** *adv.*

che·mo·tax·on·o·my (kē′mō-tăk-sŏn′ə-mē, kĕm′ō-) *n.* Classification of organisms based on differences at the biochemical level. — **che′mo·tax′o·nom′ic** (-tăk′sə-nŏm′ĭk) *adj.* — **che′mo·tax′o·nom′i·cal·ly** *adv.* — **che′mo·tax·on′o·mist** *n.*

cheval glass
c. 1815 American, attributed to the workshop of Duncan Phyfe or to Charles Honoré Lannuier (fl. 1803–1819)

che·mo·ther·a·py (kē′mō-thĕr′ə-pē, kĕm′ō-) *n.* **1.** The treatment of cancer using specific chemical agents or drugs that are selectively destructive to malignant cells and tissues. **2.** The treatment of disease using chemical agents or drugs that are selectively toxic to the causative agent of the disease. — **che′mo·ther′a·peu′tic** (-pyo͞o′tĭk) *adj.* — **che′mo·ther′a·peu′ti·cal·ly** *adv.* — **che′mo·ther′a·pist** *n.*

che·mot·ro·pism (kĭ-mŏt′rə-pĭz′əm) *n.* Movement or growth of an organism in response to a chemical stimulus. — **che′mo·trop′ic** (kē′mō-trŏp′ĭk, kĕm′ō-) *adj.*

chem·ur·gy (kĕm′ər-jē, kĭ-mûr′-) *n.* The development of industrial chemical products from organic raw materials. — **che·mur′gic** (kĭ-mûr′jĭk), **che·mur′gi·cal** *adj.*

Chen also **Ch'ên** (chŭn). A Chinese dynasty (557–589).

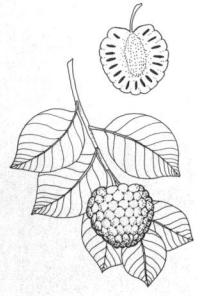

Che·nab (chə-näb′). A river, c. 1,086 km (675 mi), of N India and E Pakistan; one of the five rivers of the Punjab.

Cheng·chow (jŭng′jō′, jœng′-). See **Zhengzhou.**

Cheng·du also **Cheng·tu** (chŭng′do͞o′). A city of S-central China WNW of Chongqing. Pop. 1,590,000.

che·nille (shə-nēl′) *n.* **1.** A soft tufted cord of silk, cotton, or worsted used in embroidery or for fringing. **2.** Fabric made of this cord. [Fr. *chenille*, caterpillar, chenille < Lat. *canīcula*, dim. of *canis*, dog. See **kwon-*.**]

Che·nin Blanc (shĕn′ĭn blängk′) *n.* **1.** A grape used in making white wine. **2.** The white wine so made.

che·no·pod (kē′nə-pŏd′, kĕn′ə-) *n.* Any plant of the goosefoot family, which includes spinach, beets, and pigweed. [< NLat. *Chenopodiaceae*, family name < *Chenopodium*, type genus : Gk. *khēn*, goose; see **ghans-*** + *-podium*, neut. of *-podius*, -pod.]

Che·ops (kē′ŏps). Orig. **Khu·fu** (ko͞o′fo͞o′). 2590–2567 B.C. King of the IV Dynasty of Egypt; builder of the Great Pyramid at Giza.

cheque (chĕk) *n. Chiefly British.* Var. of **check.**

cheq·uer (chĕk′ər) *n. Chiefly British.* Var. of **checker.**

Cher (shĕr). A river of central France flowing c. 354 km (220 mi) to the Loire R. near Tours.

Cher·bourg (shâr′bo͝org′, shĕr-bo͞or′). A city of NW France on the English Channel. Pop. 28,442.

Che·ren·kov also **Ce·ren·kov** (chə-rĕng′kôf, -kəf, chĭ-ryĭn-kôf′), **Pavel Alekseevich.** b. 1904. Russian physicist who shared a 1958 Nobel Prize.

Che·ren·kov effect (chə-rĕng′kôf, -kəf) *n.* Var. of **Cerenkov effect.**

Che·re·po·vets (chĕr′ə-pə-vĕts′, chĭ-rĭ-pŭ-vyĕts′). A city of E-central Russia N of Moscow. Pop. 299,000.

cher·i·moy·a (chĕr′ə-moi′ə) *n.* **1.** A tropical American tree (*Annona cherimola*) having heart-shaped edible fruits with green skin and white aromatic flesh. **2.** The fruit of this plant. [Am.Sp. *chirimoya* < Quechua *chirimuya*.]

cher·ish (chĕr′ĭsh) *tr.v.* **-ished, -ish·ing, -ish·es. 1.** To treat with affection and tenderness. **2.** To keep fondly in mind; entertain. See Syns at **appreciate.** [ME *cherishen* < OFr. *cherir, cheriss-* < *cher*, dear < Lat. *cārus*. See **kā-*.**] — **cher′ish·a·ble** *n.* — **cher′ish·er** *n.* — **cher′ish·ing·ly** *adv.*

Cher·kas·sy (chər-kä′sē). A city of central Ukraine on the Dnieper R. SSE of Kiev. Pop. 273,000.

Cher·ni·gov (chər-nē′gəf, -nyē′-). A city of N-central Ukraine NNE of Kiev. Pop. 278,000.

Cher·no·byl (chər-nō′bəl, chyĭr-nô′bĭl). A city of N-central Ukraine NNW of Kiev; site of a major nuclear power plant accident in 1986.

Cher·nov·tsy (chər-nôft′sē, chyĭr-nŭf-tsĭ′). A city of SW Ukraine near the Romanian border. Pop. 244,000.

cher·no·zem (chĕr′nə-zĕm′, chîr′nə-zyôm′) *n.* A very black topsoil, rich in humus, typical of cool to temperate semiarid regions. [Russ. *chernozëm* : *chërnyĭ*, black + ORuss. *zemĭ*, earth; see **dhghem-*.**] — **cher′no·zem′ic** *adj.*

Cher·o·kee (chĕr′ə-kē′, chĕr′ə-kē′) *n.*, *pl.* **Cherokee** or **-kees. 1.** A member of a Native American people formerly inhabiting the southern Appalachian Mountains from the western Carolinas and eastern Tennessee to northern Georgia, with present-day populations in northeast Oklahoma and western North Carolina. **2.** The Iroquoian language of the Cherokee. [< Cherokee *tsalaki*.] — **Cher′o·kee′** *adj.*

Cherokee rose *n.* A prickly, climbing evergreen rose (*Rosa laevigata*) native to China, with white fragrant flowers.

Cherokee Strip or **Cherokee Outlet.** A plot of land in present-day N OK; opened to settlement in 1893.

che·root also **she·root** (shə-ro͞ot′) *n.* A cigar with square-cut ends. [Fr. *cheroute*, ult. < Tamil *curuttu* < *curi*, to be spiral.]

cher·ry (chĕr′ē) *n.*, *pl.* **-ries. 1.a.** Any of several trees or shrubs of the genus *Prunus*, esp. *P. avium* or *P. cerasus*, native chiefly to northern temperate regions and having small juicy drupes. **b.** The fruit of any of these plants. **c.** The wood of any of these plants, esp. black cherry. **d.** Any of various plants, such as the Barbados cherry, having fruits resembling a cherry. **2.** *Color.* A moderate or strong red to purplish red. **3.** *Vulgar Slang.* The hymen considered as a symbol of virginity. — *adj.* **1.** Containing or having the flavor of cherries. **2.** Made of the wood of a cherry tree. **3.** *Color.* Of the color cherry. [ME *cheri* < AN *cherise*, var. of OFr. *cerise* < VLat. **ceresia* < **cerasia* < Gk. *kerasia*, cherry tree < *kerasos*, of Semitic orig.; akin to Assyrian *karšu*.]

cherry birch *n.* See **sweet birch.**

cherry bomb *n.* A loud, red, ball-shaped firecracker.

Cher·ry Hill (chĕr′ē). An urban township of W-central NJ ESE of Camden. Pop. 69,319.

cherry laurel *n.* A frequently cultivated Eurasian evergreen shrub or small tree (*Prunus laurocerasus*) in the rose family, having showy clusters of white flowers and glossy foliage.

cherry picker *n.* A mobile crane having a maneuverable vertical boom that allows the passenger to do work such as pruning.

cherry plum *n.* A deciduous ornamental Eurasian shrub or small tree (*Prunus cerasifera*) in the rose family, having white flowers and small red to yellow edible fruits.

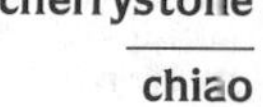

cher•ry•stone (chĕr′ē-stōn′) *n.* The quahog clam when half-grown and of comparatively small size.

cherry tomato *n.* A variety of tomato *(Lycopersicon esculentum* var. *cerasiforme)* having small red to yellow fruits.

cher•so•nese (kûr′sə-nēz′, -nēs′) *n.* A peninsula. [Lat. *chersonēsus* < Gk. *khersonēsos* : *khersos*, dry land + *nēsos*, island; see **snā-***.]

chert (chûrt) *n.* **1.** A variety of silica that contains microcrystalline quartz. **2.** A siliceous rock of chalcedonic or opaline silica occurring in limestone. [?] **—chert′y** *adj.*

cher•ub (chĕr′əb) *n.* **1.** *pl.* **cher•u•bim** (chĕr′ə-bĭm′, -yə-bĭm′). **a.** A winged celestial being. **b.** One of the second order of angels. **2.** *pl.* **cher•ubs. a.** A representation of a small angel, portrayed as a child with a chubby, rosy face. **b.** A person, esp. a child, with an innocent or chubby face. [ME < LLat. < Heb. *kĕrûb.*] **—che•ru′bic** (chə-ro͞o′bĭk) *adj.* **—che•ru′bi•cal•ly** *adv.*

Che•ru•bi•ni (kĕr′ə-bē′nē, kĕ′ro͞o-), **(Maria) Luigi Carlo Zenobio Salvatore.** 1760–1842. Italian composer whose operas include *Les Deux Journées* (1800).

cher•vil (chûr′vəl) *n.* **1.** An annual Eurasian herb *(Anthriscus cerefolium)* in the parsley family, having aromatic parsleylike leaves. **2.** Any of several related plants, such as those of the genus *Chaerophyllum*. [ME < OE *cerfille* < Lat. *chaerephyllum* < Gk. *khairephullon* : *khairein*, to greet, delight in; see **gher-²*** + *phullon*, leaf; see **bhel-³***.]

Ches•a•peake (chĕs′ə-pēk′). An independent city of SE VA S of Norfolk. Pop. 151,976.

Chesapeake Bay. An inlet of the Atlantic Ocean separating the Delmarva Peninsula from mainland MD and VA.

Chesapeake Bay retriever *n.* A hunting dog having a thick, short, wavy coat ranging from dark brown to tan in color.

Chesh•ire¹ (chĕsh′ər, -îr′). A town of S-central CT N of New Haven. Pop. 25,684.

Chesh•ire² also **chesh•ire** (chĕsh′ər) *n.* A hard yellow English cheese made from cow's milk. [After *Cheshire*, a county of W-central England.]

chess¹ (chĕs) *n. Games.* A board game for two players, each beginning with 16 pieces of six kinds that are moved according to individual rules, with the objective of checkmating the opposing king. [ME *ches*, short for OFr. *esches*, pl. of *eschec*, check in chess. See CHECK.]

chess² (chĕs) *n.* Any of several species of brome grass, esp. the cheat. [?]

chess³ (chĕs) *n.*, *pl.* **chess** or **chess•es.** One of the floorboards of a pontoon bridge. [ME *ches*, tier, perh. < OFr. *chasse*, frame < Lat. *capsa*, box.]

chess•board (chĕs′bôrd′, -bōrd′) *n. Games.* A board marked with 64 squares, used in playing chess.

chess•man (chĕs′măn′, -mən) *n. Games.* A chess piece.

ches•sy•lite (shĕs′ə-līt′, chĕs′-) *n.* See **azurite.** [After *Chessy*, a town of E-central France.]

chest (chĕst) *n.* **1.** The part of the body between the neck and the abdomen, enclosed by the ribs and the breastbone; the thorax. **2.a.** A sturdy box with a lid and often a lock, used esp. for storage. **b.** A small closet or cabinet with shelves for storing supplies. **3.a.** The treasury of a public institution. **b.** The funds kept there. **4.a.** A box for the shipping of certain goods, such as tea. **b.** The quantity packed in such a box. **5.** A sealed receptacle for liquid, gas, or steam. **6.** A bureau; a dresser. ***—idiom.* get (something) off (one's) chest.** To vent one's pent-up feelings. [ME < OE *cest*, box < West Gmc. **kistā* < Lat. *cista* < Gk. *kistē*.] **—chest′ed** (chĕs′tĭd) *adj.*

Ches•ter (chĕs′tər). **1.** A borough of W-central England on the Dee R. SSE of Liverpool. Pop. 58,100. **2.** A city of SE PA on the Delaware R., a suburb of Philadelphia. Pop. 41,856.

ches•ter•field (chĕs′tər-fēld′) *n.* **1.** A single- or double-breasted overcoat, usu. with concealed buttons and a velvet collar. **2.** *Chiefly Northern California & Canada.* A large overstuffed sofa with upright armrests. [After a 19th-cent. earl of *Chesterfield*.]

Ches•ter•field (chĕs′tər-fēld′). A city of N-central England S of Sheffield. Pop. 96,300.

Chesterfield, 4th Earl of. Philip Dormer Stanhope. 1694–1773. English politician known for *Letters to His Son* (1774).

Ches•ter•ton (chĕs′tər-tən), **Gilbert Keith.** 1874–1936. British writer whose works include a series of detective novels.

Chester White *n.* Any of a breed of large white hogs with drooping ears, originally bred in Pennsylvania.

chest•nut (chĕs′nŭt′, -nət) *n.* **1.a.** Any of several deciduous trees of the genus *Castanea*, native to northern temperate regions and having alternate simple toothed leaves and nuts enclosed in a prickly husk. **b.** The often edible nut of any of these trees. **c.** The wood of any of these trees. **2.** Any of several other plants, such as the horse chestnut. **3.** *Color.* A moderate to deep reddish brown. **4.** A reddish-brown horse. **5.** A small hard callus on the inner surface of a horse's foreleg. **6.** An old, frequently repeated joke, story, or song. *—adj. Color.* Of the color chestnut. [Earlier *chesten* (< ME *chesteine* < OFr. *chastaigne* < Lat. *castanea* < Gk. *kastanea*, chestnut tree) + NUT.]

chestnut blight *n.* A disease of chestnut trees caused by a fungus *(Cryphonectria parasitica)* and characterized by destructive cankers.

chestnut oak *n.* Either of two eastern North American deciduous oak trees *(Quercus prinus* and *Q. muehlenbergii)* having leaves that resemble those of the American chestnut.

chest of drawers *n.*, *pl.* **chests of drawers.** A piece of furniture consisting of a set of drawers that fit within a frame.

chest•y (chĕs′tē) *adj.* **-i•er, -i•est.** *Informal.* **1.** Having a large or well-developed chest or bust. **2.** Arrogant or proud; conceited. **—chest′i•ness** *n.*

che•tah (chē′tə) *n.* Var. of **cheetah.**

chet•rum (chē′trəm, chĕt′rəm) *n.* See table at **currency.** [Native word in Bhutan.]

che•val-de-frise (shə-văl′də-frēz′) *n.*, *pl.* **che•vaux-de-frise** (shə-vō′-). **1.** An obstacle of barbed wire or spikes on a wooden frame, used to block enemy advancement. **2.** An obstacle of jagged glass or spikes set into masonry on top of a wall. [Fr., Frisian horse : *cheval*, horse + *de*, of + *Frise*, Friesland.]

che•val•et (shə-văl′ā, shĕv′ə-lā′) *n. Mus.* The bridge of a stringed instrument. [Fr. < dim. of *cheval*, horse < Lat. *caballus*.]

che•val glass (shə-văl′) *n.* A long mirror mounted on swivels in a frame. [< Fr. *cheval*, support, horse. See CHEVALET.]

chev•a•lier (shĕv′ə-lîr′) *n.* **1.** A member of certain orders of knighthood or merit. **2.a.** A French nobleman of the lowest rank. **b.** Used as a title for such a nobleman. **3.** A knight. **4.** A chivalrous man. [ME *chevalier* < OFr. *chevalier* < LLat. *caballārius*, horseman < *caballus*, horse.]

che•ve•lure (shəv-lür′) *n.* A head of hair. [ME *cheveler* < OFr. *cheveleure* < Lat. *capillātūra* < *capillus*, hair.]

Chev•i•ot (shĕv′ē-ət, chĕv′-) *n.* **1.** Any of a breed of hornless sheep with short thick wool, originally raised in the Cheviot Hills. **2.** Also **cheviot.** A woolen fabric with a coarse twill weave originally made from Cheviot wool.

Cheviot Hills (chĕv′ē-ət, shĭv′-, chē′vē-). A range of hills extending along the border of England and Scotland.

chèv•re (shĕv′rə) *n.* Cheese made from goat's milk. [Fr. < OFr. < Lat. *capra*, she-goat, fem. of *caper*, goat.]

chev•ron (shĕv′rən) *n.* **1.** A badge or insignia consisting of stripes meeting at an angle, worn on the sleeve of a military or police uniform to indicate rank, merit, or length of service. **2.** *Her.* A device shaped like an inverted V. **3.** A V-shaped pattern, esp. a kind of fret used in architecture. [ME *cheveron* < OFr. *chevron*, rafter, prob. < VLat. **capriō*, *capriōn-* < Lat. *caper*, *capr-*, goat.]

chevron
On uniform of a 1980 West Point graduate

chev•ro•tain (shĕv′rə-tān′) *n.* Any of several small hornless ruminants of the genera *Hyemoschus* and *Tragulus* native to the tropical rain forests of central Africa, India, and southeast Asia. [Fr. *chevrotin* < OFr., dim. of *chevrot*, kid, dim. of *chevre*, goat < Lat. *capra*, she-goat, fem. of *caper*, goat.]

chew (cho͞o) *v.* **chewed, chew•ing, chews.** *—tr.* **1.** To bite and grind with the teeth. **2.** To meditate on. *—intr.* **1.** To make a crushing and grinding motion with the teeth. **2.** To meditate. **3.** *Informal.* To use chewing tobacco. *—n.* **1.** The act of chewing. **2.** Something held in the mouth and chewed, esp. a plug of tobacco. ***—phrasal verb.* chew out.** *Slang.* To reprimand; scold. ***—idioms.* chew the cud.** *Slang.* To ponder over. **chew the fat** (or **rag**). *Slang.* To talk together in a friendly, leisurely way; chat at length. [ME *cheuen* < OE *cēowan*.] **—chew′a•ble** *adj.* **—chew′er** *n.*

Che•wa (chā′wä) *n.* A Bantu language spoken in Malawi.

chew•ing gum (cho͞o′ĭng) *n.* A sweetened flavored preparation for chewing, usu. made of chicle.

che•wink (chĭ-wĭngk′) *n.* See **towhee** 1. [Imit. of its call.]

chew•y (cho͞o′ē) *adj.* **-i•er, -i•est.** Needing much chewing: *chewy candy.* **—chew′i•ness** *n.*

Chey•enne¹ (shī-ĕn′, -ăn′) *n.*, *pl.* **Cheyenne** or **-ennes. 1.** A member of a Native American people, divided after 1832 into the Northern and Southern Cheyenne, inhabiting respectively southeast Montana and southern Colorado, with present-day populations in Montana and Oklahoma. **2.** The Algonquian language of the Cheyenne. [Canadian Fr. < Dakota *šahíyela*.] **—Chey•enne′** *adj.*

Chey•enne² (shī-ăn′, -ĕn′). The cap. of WY, in the SE part near the NE and CO borders; founded 1867. Pop. 50,008.

Cheyenne River. A river rising in E WY and flowing c. 848 km (527 mi) to the Missouri R. in central SD.

chez (shā) *prep.* At the home of; at or by. [Fr. < OFr. < Lat. *casa*, cottage, hut.]

chg. *abbr.* **1.** Change. **2.** Charge.

chi also **khi** (kī) *n.* The 22nd letter of the Greek alphabet. [Gk. *khi*.]

Chia-ling (jyä′lĭng′). See **Jialing.**

Chia•mus•su (jyä′mo͞o′so͞o′). See **Jiamusi.**

Chiang Kai-shek (chăng′ kī′shĕk′, jyäng′). 1887–1975. Chinese military and political figure who led the Nationalists against the Communist forces and was driven to Taiwan (1949), where he became president of Nationalist China.

Chiang Kai-shek

Chi•an•ti (kē-än′tē, -ăn′-) *n.* A dry table wine, usu. red, originally produced in northwest Italy. [After the *Chianti* Mts., a range of the Apennines in central Italy.]

chiao (chyou) *n.*, *pl.* **chiao.** Var. of **jiao.**

ă **pat**	oi **boy**
ā **pay**	ou **out**
âr **care**	o͝o **took**
ä **father**	o͞o **boot**
ĕ **pet**	ŭ **cut**
ē **be**	ûr **urge**
ĭ **pit**	th **thin**
ī **pie**	*th* **this**
îr **pier**	hw **which**
ŏ **pot**	zh **vision**
ō **toe**	ə **about,**
ô **paw**	**item**

Stress marks:
′ (primary);
′ (secondary), as in **dictionary** (dĭk′shə-nĕr′ē)

chi•a•ro•scu•ro (kē-är′ə-sko͝or′ō, -skyo͝or′ō) *n.*, *pl.* **-ros.** **1.** The technique of using light and shade in pictorial representation. **2.** The arrangement of light and dark elements in a pictorial work of art. [Ital. : *chiaro*, bright, light (< Lat. *clārus*, clear; see **kelə-²***) + *oscuro*, dark (< Lat. *obscūrus*; see **(s)keu-***).] — **chi•a′ro•scu′rist** *n.*

chi•as•ma (kī-ăz′mə) also **chi•asm** (kī′ăz′əm) *n.*, *pl.* **-ma•ta** (-mə-tə) or **-mas** also **-asms.** **1.** *Anat.* A crossing or intersection of two tracts. **2.** *Genet.* The point of contact between paired chromatids during meiosis, resulting in a cross-shaped configuration and representing the cytological manifestation of crossing over. [Gk. *khiasma*, cross-piece < *khiazein*, to mark with an X < *khi*, chi (< the letter's shape).] — **chi•as′mal, chi•as′mic, chi′as•mat′ic** (-măt′ĭk) *adj.*

chi•as•ma•ty•py (kī-ăz′mə-tī′pē) *n.* The meiotic twisting between paired chromatids that produces chiasmata.

chi•as•mus (kī-ăz′məs) *n.*, *pl.* **-mi** (-mī′). A rhetorical inversion of the second of two parallel structures, as in *"Each throat/Was parched, and glazed each eye"* (Samuel Taylor Coleridge). [NLat. < Gk. *khiasmos*, syntactic inversion < *khiazein*, to invert or mark with an X. See CHIASMA.]

chi•as•to•lite (kī-ăs′tə-līt′) *n.* A mineral variety of andalusite with carbonaceous impurities regularly arranged along the longer axis of the crystal. [< Gk. *khiastos*, crossed, p.part. of *khiazein*, to mark with an X. See CHIASMA.]

chiaus (chous, choush) *n.* An official Turkish messenger or emissary. [Turk. *çāvuş* < Old Turkic *chāv*, announcement.]

Chi•ba (chē′bä′). A city of E-central Honshu, Japan, on the NE shore of Tokyo Bay. Pop. 788,920.

Chib•cha (chĭb′chə) *n.*, *pl.* **Chibcha** or **-chas.** **1.** A member of an extinct Indian people once inhabiting central Colombia. **2.** The extinct language of the Chibcha.

Chib•chan (chĭb′chən) *n.* **1.** A member of a widely scattered Indian people of Colombia and Central America. **2.** A language family comprising the Chibchan languages.

Chichén Itzá
El Castillo

Chi•bem•ba (chĭ-bĕm′bə) *n.* See **Bemba.**

chi•bouk also **chi•bouque** (chĭ-bo͞ok′, shĭ-) *n.* A Turkish tobacco pipe with a long stem and a red clay bowl. [Turk. dial. *çibuk* < *çubuk*, shoot, twig, staff < Old Turkic *chubuq*, *chibiq*, dim. of *chip*, *chib-*, branch.]

chic (shēk) *adj.* **chic•er, chic•est.** **1.** Conforming to the current fashion; stylish. **2.** Adopting or setting current fashions and styles; sophisticated. — *n.* **1.** The quality or state of being stylish; fashionableness. **2.** Sophistication in dress and manner; elegance. [Fr., prob. < Ger. *Schick*, skill, fitness, elegance < MHGer. *(sich) schicken*, to outfit (oneself); fit in.] — **chic′ly** *adv.* — **chic′ness** *n.*

Chi•ca•go (shĭ-kä′gō, -kô′-). A city of NE IL on Lake Michigan; nearly destroyed by a disastrous fire in 1871. Pop. 2,783,726. — **Chi•ca′go•an** *n.*

Chicago Heights. A city of NE IL S of Chicago. Pop. 33,072.

Chicago River. A river formed at Chicago by the junction of N and S branches that total c. 55 km (34 mi) in length.

Chi•ca•na (chĭ-kä′nə, shĭ-) *n.* *Usage Problem.* A Mexican-American woman or girl. See Usage Note at **Chicano.** [Am. Sp., fem. of *chicano*, chicano. See CHICANO.] — **Chi•ca′na** *adj.*

chi•cane (shĭ-kān′, chĭ-) *v.* **-caned, -can•ing, -canes.** — *intr.* To use chicanery. — *tr.* To trick; deceive. — *n.* Chicanery. [Fr. *chicaner* < OFr., to quibble.] — **chi•can′er** *n.*

chi•can•er•y (shĭ-kā′nə-rē, chĭ-) *n.*, *pl.* **-ies.** **1.** Deception by trickery or sophistry. **2.** A trick; a subterfuge.

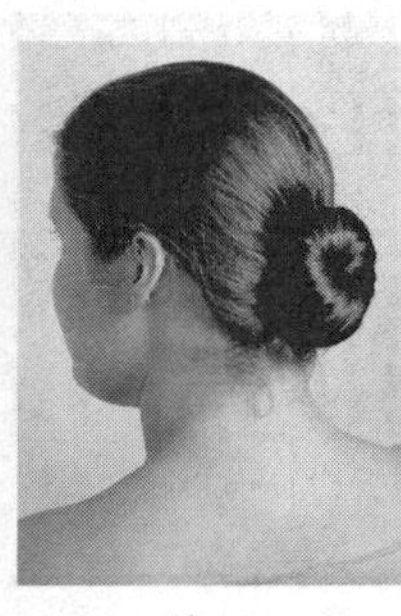
chignon

Chi•ca•no (chĭ-kä′nō, shĭ-) *n.*, *pl.* **-nos.** A Mexican-American, esp. a man or boy. [Am.Sp., dialectal var. of *Mexicano*, Mexican < *México*, Mexico.] — **Chi•ca′no** *adj.*

Usage Note: Care should be taken in using the term *Chicano* when referring to Mexican-Americans. In some regions of the Southwest the term suggests ethnic pride; in others it may be felt to be derogatory. See Usage Note at **Hispanic.**

Chi•chén It•zá (chē-chĕn′ ē-tsä′, ēt′sə). An ancient Mayan city of central Yucatán in Mexico; founded c. A.D. 514 and abandoned in 1194.

chi•chi (shē′shē) *adj.* **-chi•er, -chi•est.** Ostentatiously stylish; deliberately chic. [Fr.] — **chi′chi** *n.*

chick (chĭk) *n.* **1.a.** A young chicken. **b.** The young of any bird. **2.** A child. **3.** *Slang.* A girl or young woman. [ME *chike*, var. of *chiken*, chicken. See CHICKEN.]

chick•a•dee (chĭk′ə-dē′) *n.* Any of several small, plump North American birds of the genus *Parus*, having predominantly gray plumage and a dark-crowned head. [Imit. of its call.]

Chick•a•mau•ga (chĭk′ə-mô′gə). A city of extreme NW GA S of Chattanooga TN; site of a Union defeat (Sep. 19–20, 1863). Pop. 2,149.

chick•a•ree (chĭk′ə-rē′) *n.* A small squirrel *(Tamiasciurus douglasi)* of the evergreen forests of northwest North America, resembling and closely related to the red squirrel. [Imit.]

Chick•a•saw (chĭk′ə-sô′) *n.*, *pl.* **Chick•a•saw** or **-saws.** **1.** A member of a Native American people formerly inhabiting northeast Mississippi and northwest Alabama, now located in south-central Oklahoma. **2.** The Muskogean language of the Chickasaw. — **Chick′a•saw′** *adj.*

Chick•a•sa•whay (chĭk′ə-sô′wā). A river, c. 338 km (210 mi), of SE MS.

chick•en (chĭk′ən) *n.* **1.a.** The common domestic fowl *(Gallus domesticus)* or its young. **b.** Any of various similar or related birds. **c.** The flesh of the common domestic fowl. **2.** *Slang.* A coward. **3.** Any of various competitions in which the participants persist in a dangerous course of action until one loses nerve and stops. — *adj.* *Slang.* Afraid; cowardly. — *intr.v.* **-ened, -en•ing, -ens.** *Slang.* To act in a cowardly manner; lose one's nerve: *I chickened out.* [ME *chiken* < OE *cīcen*.]

chicken breast *n.* *Pathol.* See **pigeon breast.**

chicken feed *n.* *Slang.* A trifling amount of money.

chicken hawk *n.* Any of various hawks that prey on or have the reputation of preying on chickens.

chick•en-heart•ed (chĭk′ən-här′tĭd) *adj.* Lacking courage; cowardly. — **chick′en•heart′ed•ness** *n.*

chick•en-liv•ered (chĭk′ən-lĭv′ərd) *adj.* Cowardly.

chick•en•pox or **chicken pox** (chĭk′ən-pŏks′) *n.* An acute contagious disease, chiefly of children, caused by the varicella-zoster virus and marked by skin eruptions and slight fever.

chicken shit *Obscene.* — *n.* Contemptibly petty nonsense. — *adj.* **1.** Contemptibly petty. **2.** Cowardly; afraid.

chicken snake *n.* See **rat snake.**

chicken wire *n.* A light-gauge galvanized wire fencing usu. made with hexagonal mesh.

chick•pea (chĭk′pē′) *n.* **1.** An annual Asian plant *(Cicer arietinum)* in the pea family, widely cultivated for its edible seeds. **2.** A seed of this plant. [Obsolete *chichpease* : ME *chiche*, chickpea (< OFr. < Lat. *cicer*) + *pease*, pea; see PEA.]

chick•weed (chĭk′wēd′) *n.* Any of various herbs of the genera *Cerastium* and *Stellaria*, esp. *S. media*, a European weed with small white flowers and opposite leaves.

Chi•cla•yo (chĭ-klä′yō, chē-). A city of NW Peru NNW of Lima. Pop. 213,095.

chic•le (chĭk′əl) *n.* The coagulated milky juice of the sapodilla, used as the principal ingredient of chewing gum. [Sp. < Nahuatl *chictli*.]

Chi•co (chē′kō). A city of N CA NW of Oroville. Pop. 40,079.

Chic•o•pee (chĭk′ə-pē). A city of SW MA on the Connecticut R. near Springfield; founded c. 1641. Pop. 56,632.

chic•o•ry (chĭk′ə-rē) *n.*, *pl.* **-ries.** **1.** A perennial herb *(Cichorium intybus)* of the composite family, native to the Old World and having blue florets. **2.** Any of various forms of this plant having edible leaves, such as radicchio. **3.** The dried, roasted, and ground roots of this plant, used as an adulterant of or substitute for coffee. [ME *cicoree* and Fr. *chicorée*, both ult. < Gk. *kikhoreia*, pl. dim. of *kikhora*, *kikhorē*.]

Chi•cou•ti•mi (shĭ-ko͞o′tə-mē). A city of S-central Quebec, Canada, on the Saguenay R. N of Quebec City. Pop. 60,064.

chide (chīd) *v.* **chid•ed** or **chid** (chĭd), **chid•ed** or **chid** or **chid•den** (chĭd′n), **chid•ing, chides.** — *tr.* To scold mildly so as to correct or improve; reprimand: *chided the boy.* — *intr.* To express disapproval. [ME *chiden* < OE *cīdan* < *cīd*, strife, contention.] — **chid′er** *n.* — **chid′ing•ly** *adv.*

chief (chēf) *n.* **1.** One who is highest in rank or authority; a leader. **2.** Often **Chief. a.** A chief petty officer. **b.** *Naut.* The chief engineer of a ship. **3.** *Slang.* A boss. **4.** *Her.* The upper section of a shield. **5.** The most important or valuable part. — *adj.* **1.** Highest in rank, authority, or office. **2.** Most important or influential. — *adv.* *Archaic.* Chiefly. [ME *chef* < OFr. < Lat. *caput*, head. See **kaput-***.] — **chief′dom** *n.* — **chief′ship′** *n.*

chief executive *n.* **1. Chief Executive.** The President of the United States. **2.** A principal executive official.

chief executive officer *n.* The highest-ranking executive in a company or organization.

chief justice also **Chief Justice** *n.* The presiding judge of a high court having several judges, esp. the U.S. Supreme Court.

chief•ly (chēf′lē) *adv.* **1.** Above all; especially. **2.** Almost entirely; mainly. — *adj.* Of or relating to a chief.

chief master sergeant *n.* A noncommissioned officer in the U.S. Air Force, ranking above senior master sergeant.

chief of naval operations *n.*, *pl.* **chiefs of naval operations.** The ranking officer of the U.S. Navy, responsible to the secretary of the Navy and the President.

chief of staff *n.*, *pl.* **chiefs of staff. 1.** Often **Chief of Staff.** The ranking officer of the U.S. Army, Navy, or Air Force, responsible to the secretary of the branch and the President. **2.** The senior military staff officer at the division level or higher.

chief of state *n.*, *pl.* **chiefs of state.** The formal head of a nation, distinct from the head of the government.

chief petty officer *n.* An enlisted officer in the U.S. Navy, ranking above petty officer first class and below senior chief petty officer.

chief•tain (chēf′tən) *n.* The leader or head of a group, esp. a clan or tribe. [ME *cheftain* < OFr. *chevetain* < LLat. *capitāneus* < Lat. *caput*, head. See **kaput-***.] — **chief′tain•cy** *n.* — **chief′tain•ship′** *n.*

Ch'ien-lung (chyĕn′lo͝ong′). See **Qianlong.**

chiff•chaff (chĭf′chăf′) *n.* A small European warbler *(Phylloscopus collybita)* with yellowish-green plumage. [Imit. of its song.]

chif•fon (shĭ-fŏn′, shĭf′ŏn′) *n.* **1.** A fabric of sheer silk or rayon. **2.** Ornamental accessories, such as ribbons or laces, for women's clothing. — *adj.* **1.** Of, relating to, or resembling the fabric chiffon. **2.** Made light and fluffy by beaten egg whites or gelatin: *a lemon chiffon pie.* [Fr., rag, chiffon < *chiffe*, old rag, perh. var. of OFr. *chipe*, of Gmc. orig.]

chif•fo•nier (shĭf′ə-nîr′) *n.* A tall narrow chest of drawers or bureau, often with a mirror. [Fr. < *chiffon*, rag. See CHIFFON.]

chif•fo•robe (shĭf′ə-rōb′, shĭf′rōb′) *n. Regional.* A tall piece of furniture typically having drawers on one side and space for hanging clothes on the other. [CHIFFO(NIER) + (WARD)ROBE.]

chig•ger (chĭg′ər) *n.* **1.** Any of various small, six-legged mite larvae of the family Trombiculidae, parasitic on insects and vertebrates. **2.** See **chigoe** 1. [Alteration of CHIGOE.]

chi•gnon (shēn-yŏn′, shēn′yŏn′) *n.* A roll or knot of hair worn esp. at the nape of the neck. [Fr. < OFr. *chaignon*, chain, collar, nape < VLat. **catēniō* < Lat. *catēna*, chain.]

chig•oe (chĭg′ō, chē′gō) *n.* **1.** A small tropical flea *(Tunga penetrans),* the fertilized female of which burrows under the skin of animals and humans. **2.** See **chigger** 1. [Poss. < Galibi *chico*, or of African orig. See JIGGER[2].]

Chi•hua•hua[1] (chə-wä′wä, chē-). A city of N Mexico S of Ciudad Juárez. Pop. 385,603.

Chi•hua•hua[2] (chĭ-wä′wä, -wə) *n.* A very small dog of a breed originating in Mexico, having pointed ears and a smooth coat. [After *Chihuahua*, a city and state of N Mexico.]

chil•blain (chĭl′blān′) *n.* An inflammation followed by itchy irritation on the hands, feet, or ears, resulting from exposure to moist cold. [CHIL(L) + BLAIN.] — **chil′blained′** *adj.*

child (chīld) *n., pl.* **chil•dren** (chĭl′drən). **1.** A person between birth and puberty. **2.a.** A human fetus. **b.** An infant; a baby. **3.** One who is childish or immature. **4.** A son or daughter; an offspring. **5.** A member of a tribe; descendant. Often used in the plural. **6.** A person or thing regarded as strongly affected by another or by a specified time, place, or circumstance: *a child of nature.* — ***idiom.*** **with child.** Pregnant. [ME < OE *cild.*] — **child′less** *adj.* — **child′less•ness** *n.*

Child (chīld), **Lydia Maria Francis.** 1802–80. Amer. abolitionist and writer of novels and children's books.

child•bear•ing (chīld′bâr′ĭng) *n.* The human act or process of giving birth; parturition. — **child′bear′ing** *adj.*

child•bed (chīld′bĕd′) *n.* The condition of a woman in the process of giving birth.

childbed fever *n.* See **puerperal fever.**

child•birth (chīld′bûrth′) *n.* Parturition.

child-care or **child•care** (chīld′kâr′) *adj.* Of or providing care for children, esp. preschoolers. — **child′care′** *n.*

childe (chīld) *n. Archaic.* A child of noble birth. [ME.]

child•hood (chīld′ho͝od′) *n.* **1.** The time or state of being a child. **2.** The early stage in existence or development.

child•ish (chīl′dĭsh) *adj.* **1.** Of or suitable for a child or childhood. **2.a.** Marked by or indicating a lack of maturity. **b.** Not complicated; simple. **c.** Affected mentally by old age; senile. — **child′ish•ly** *adv.* — **child′ish•ness** *n.*

child labor *n.* The full-time employment of children under a minimum legal age.

child•like (chīld′līk′) *adj.* Like or befitting a child, as in innocence, trustfulness, or candor.

child•proof (chīld′pro͞of′) *adj.* **1.** Designed to resist tampering by young children: *a childproof bottle.* **2.** Made safe for young children. — **child′proof′** *v.*

chil•dren (chĭl′drən) *n.* Pl. of **child.**

child's play (chīldz) *n.* **1.** An easy task. **2.** A trivial matter.

Chil•e (chĭl′ē, chē′lĕ). A country of SW South America on the Pacific Ocean; declared independence from Spain in 1818. Cap. Santiago. Pop. 11,329,736. — **Chil′e•an** *adj. & n.*

Chil•e saltpeter (chĭl′ē) *n.* See **sodium nitrate.**

chil•i also **chil•e** or **chil•li** (chĭl′ē) *n., pl.* **chil•ies** also **chil•es** or **chil•lies. 1.** The pungent fruit of any of several cultivated varieties of capsicum, used esp. as a flavoring. **2.** Chili con carne. [Sp. *chile, chili* < Nahuatl *chilli.*]

chil•i•ad (kĭl′ē-ăd′, -əd) *n.* **1.** A group that contains 1,000 elements. **2.** One thousand years; a millennium. [LLat. *chilias, chiliad-* < Gk. *khilias* < *khilioi*, thousand. See **gheslo-*.**]

chil•i•asm (kĭl′ē-ăz′əm) *n.* The doctrine stating that Jesus will reign on earth for 1,000 years. [NLat. *chiliasmus* < LLat. *chilias*, chiliad. See CHILIAD.] — **chil′i•ast′** (-ăst′, -əst) *n.*

chili con car•ne (kŏn kär′nē) *n.* A highly spiced dish made of red peppers, meat, and often beans. [Sp. : *chili, chile*, chili + *con*, with + *carne*, meat.]

chil•i•dog (chĭl′ē-dôg′, -dŏg′) *n.* A hot dog covered with chili con carne, served in a long roll.

Chi•lin (jē′lĭn′). See **Jilin.**

chili pepper *n.* See **chili** 1.

chili powder *n.* A condiment consisting of ground chilies mixed with several seasonings, such as cumin, oregano, and garlic.

chili sauce *n.* A spiced sauce made with chilies and tomatoes.

chill (chĭl) *n.* **1.** A moderate but penetrating coldness. **2.** A sensation of coldness, often accompanied by shivering and pallor of the skin. **3.** A checking or dampening of enthusiasm, spirit, or joy. **4.** A sudden numbing fear or dread. — *adj.* **1.** Moderately cold; chilly. **2.** Not warm and friendly; distant: *a chill greeting.* **3.** Discouraging; dispiriting. — *v.* **chilled, chill•ing, chills.** — *tr.* **1.** To affect with or as if with cold. **2.** To lower in temperature; cool. **3.** To make discouraged; dispirit. **4.** *Metall.* To harden (a metallic surface) by rapid cooling. — *intr.* **1.** To be seized with cold. **2.** To become cold or set. **3.** *Metall.* To become hard by rapid cooling. [ME *chile* < OE *cele*. See **gel-*.**] — **chill′ing•ly** *adv.* — **chill′ness** *n.*

Chil•lán (chē-yän′). A city of central Chile ENE of Concepción; founded in the 16th cent. Pop. 118,163.

chill•er (chĭl′ər) *n.* **1.** One that chills. **2.** A frightening story, esp. one involving violence, evil, or the supernatural.

chill factor *n.* Wind-chill factor.

Chil•li•coth•e (chĭl′ĭ-kŏth′ē, -kô′thē). A city of S-central OH S of Columbus; settled in 1796. Pop. 21,923.

Chil•li•wack (chĭl′ə-wăk′). A city of SW British Columbia, Canada, on the Fraser R. E of Vancouver. Pop. 40,642.

chill•y (chĭl′ē) *adj.* **-i•er, -i•est. 1.** Cool or cold enough to cause shivering. See Syns at **cold. 2.** Seized with or feeling cold; shivering. **3.** Distant and cool; unfriendly: *a chilly look.* — **chill′i•ly** *adv.* — **chill′i•ness** *n.*

Chi•lo•é (chĭl′ō-ā′, chē′lô-ĕ′). An island off S-central Chile.

chi•lo•pod (kī′lə-pŏd′) *n.* Any of various arthropods of the class Chilopoda, which includes the centipedes. [< NLat. *Chīlopoda*, class name : Gk. *kheilos*, lip + *-poda*, -pod.]

Chiltern Hundreds (chĭl′tərn) *n.* *(used with a sing. v.) Chiefly British.* A merely formal office applied for by members of Parliament when they wish to resign from the House of Commons. [Short for *Stewardship of the Chiltern Hundreds*, tracts of crown lands in S-central England.]

Chi•lung (jē′lo͝ong′, chē′-). See **Keelung.**

chi•mae•ra (kī-mîr′ə, kĭ-) *n.* A deep-sea cartilaginous fish of the family Chimaeridae, having a tapering body and a whiplike tail. [NLat. *Chimaera*, type genus < Lat. *chimaera*, chimera. See CHIMERA.]

Chim•bo•ra•zo (chĭm′bə-rä′zō, -rä′-, chēm′bô-rä′sô). An inactive volcano, 6,271.1 m (20,561 ft), in central Ecuador.

Chim•bo•te (chĭm-bō′tē, chēm-bô′tĕ). A city of W Peru on the Pacific Ocean NNW of Callao. Pop. 223,341.

chime[1] (chīm) *n.* **1.** An apparatus for striking a bell or set of bells to produce a musical sound. **2.** *Mus.* A set of bells tuned to scale and used as an orchestral instrument. Often used in the plural. **3.** A single bell, as in a clock mechanism. **4.** The sound produced by or as if by a bell or bells. **5.** Agreement; accord. — *v.* **chimed, chim•ing, chimes.** — *intr.* **1.a.** To sound with a harmonious ring when struck. **b.** To make a musical sound by striking a bell or set of bells. **2.** To be in agreement or accord; harmonize. — *tr.* **1.** To produce (music) by striking bells. **2.** To strike (a bell) to produce music. **3.a.** To signal or make known by chiming. **b.** To call, send, or welcome by chiming. **4.** To repeat insistently. — ***phrasal verb.*** **chime in. 1.** To interrupt the speech of others, esp. with an unwanted opinion. **2.** To join in harmoniously. **3.** To go together harmoniously; agree. [< ME *chimbe (belle)* < OFr., var. of *cimble*, cymbal < Lat. *cymbalum*. See CYMBAL.] — **chim′er** *n.*

chime[2] (chīm) *n.* The rim of a cask. [ME *chimb* < OE *cim-, cimb-*. See **gembh-*.**]

chi•me•ra also **chi•mae•ra** (kī-mîr′ə, kĭ-) *n. Genet.* **1.** An organism consisting of two or more tissues of different genetic composition, produced by mutation, grafting, or the mixture of cell populations from different zygotes. **2.** A genetically engineered organism in which DNA from distinct parent species is combined to produce an individual with a double chromosome complement. [ME *chimere*, Chimera < OFr. < Lat. *chimaera* < Gk. *khimaira*, chimera, she-goat. See **ghei-*.**]

Chi•me•ra also **Chi•mae•ra** (kī-mîr′ə, kĭ-) *n.* **1.** *Gk. Myth.* A fire-breathing female monster usu. represented as a composite of a lion, goat, and serpent. **2.** An imaginary monster made up of grotesquely disparate parts.

chi•mer•i•cal (kī-mĕr′ĭ-kəl, -mîr′-, kĭ-) also **chi•mer•ic** (-mĕr′ĭk, -mîr′-) *adj.* **1.** Created by or as if by a wildly fanciful imagination; highly improbable. **2.** Given to unrealistic fantasies; fanciful. — **chi•mer′i•cal•ly** *adv.*

Chim•kent (chĭm-kĕnt′). A city of S-central Kazakhstan N of Tashkent; founded in the 12th cent. Pop. 369,000.

chim•ney (chĭm′nē) *n., pl.* **-neys. 1.a.** A passage through which smoke and gases escape from a fire or furnace; a flue. **b.** The usu. vertical structure containing a chimney. **c.** The part of such a structure that rises above a roof. **2.** *Chiefly British.* A smokestack, as of a ship. **3.** A glass tube for enclosing the flame of a lamp. **4.** Something resembling a chimney. [ME *chimenei* < OFr. *cheminee* < LLat. *camīnāta*, fireplace < Lat. *camīnus*, furnace < Gk. *kaminos.*]

chim•ney•piece (chĭm′nē-pēs′) *n.* **1.** The mantel of a fireplace. **2.** A decoration over a fireplace.

chimney pot *n.* A short, usu. earthenware pipe placed on the top of a chimney to improve the draft.

chimney sweep *n.* A worker who cleans chimneys.

chimney swift *n.* A small, dark, swallowlike New World bird *(Chaetura pelagica)* that frequently nests in chimneys.

chimp (chĭmp) *n. Informal.* A chimpanzee.

chim•pan•zee (chĭm′păn-zē′, -pən-, chĭm-păn′zē) *n.* A gregarious anthropoid ape *(Pan troglodytes)* of tropical Africa having dark hair, somewhat arboreal habits, and a high de-

Chihuahua[2]

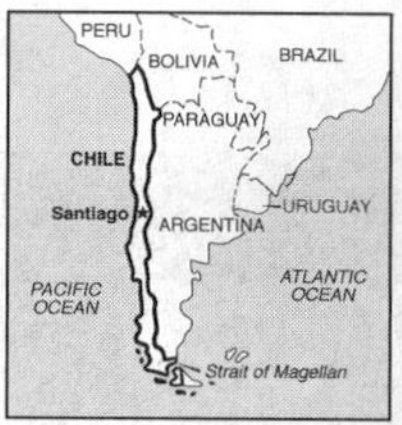

Chile

chimney sweep

ă pat	oi boy
ā pay	ou out
âr care	o͝o took
ä father	o͞o boot
ĕ pet	ŭ cut
ē be	ûr urge
ĭ pit	th thin
ī pie	*th* this
îr pier	hw which
ŏ pot	zh vision
ō toe	ə about, item
ô paw	

Stress marks:
′ (primary);
′ (secondary), as in
dictionary (dĭk′shə-nĕr′ē)

gree of intelligence. [Port. < Kongo *ci-mpenzi.*]

chin (chĭn) *n.* The central forward portion of the lower jaw. —*v.* **chinned, chin•ning, chins.** —*tr.* **1.** To pull (oneself) up with the arms on an overhead horizontal bar until the chin tops the bar. **2.** *Mus.* To place (a violin) under the chin before playing. —*intr.* **1.** To chin oneself. **2.** *Informal.* To chatter. [ME < OE *cin.* See **genu-[2]*.**] —**chin′less** *adj.*

Chin (jĭn). See **Jin.**

Chin. *abbr.* China; Chinese.

Ch'in (chĭn). See **Qin.**

chi•na (chī′nə) *n.* **1.** High-quality porcelain or ceramic ware, originally made in China. **2.** Porcelain or earthenware used for the table. [Short for *chinaware.*]

Chi•na (chī′nə). A country of E Asia whose civilization traditionally dates to c. 2700 B.C. After a bitter civil war (1946–49) a people's republic was established on the mainland, and the Nationalists fled to Taiwan. Cap. Beijing. Pop. 1,008,175,288.

China

China, Republic of. See **Taiwan.**

China aster *n.* An annual Chinese plant *(Callistephus chinensis)* in the composite family, grown for its showy flower heads.

chi•na•ber•ry (chī′nə-bĕr′ē) *n.* A deciduous Asian tree *(Melia azedarach)* having bipinnately compound leaves and yellow poisonous fruits.

Chi•na•man (chī′nə-mən) *n. Offensive.* Used as a disparaging term for a Chinese man.

China rose *n.* A Chinese rose *(Rosa chinensis)* having mostly red, pink, or white flowers.

China Sea. The W part of the Pacific Ocean extending along the E coast of Asia and divided by Taiwan into the **East China Sea** and the **South China Sea.**

Chi•na•town (chī′nə-toun′) *n.* A neighborhood or section of a city that is inhabited chiefly by Chinese people.

China tree *n.* See **chinaberry.**

chi•na•ware (chī′nə-wâr′) *n.* Tableware made of china.

Chi•na•wood oil (chī′nə-wo͝od′) *n.* See **tung oil.**

chinch (chĭnch) *n. Chiefly Southern & Midland U.S.* See **bedbug.** [Sp. *chinche* < Lat. *cimex, cīmic-,* bug.]

chinch bug also **cinch bug** *n.* **1.** A small black and white insect *(Blissus leucopterus)* that is very destructive to grains and grasses. **2.** *Chiefly Southern & Midland U.S.* See **bedbug.**

chin•che•rin•chee (chĭn′chə-rĭn-chē′, chĭng′kə-) *n.* A southern African plant *(Ornithogalum thyrsoides)* in the lily family whose blossom is popular as a cut flower. [Prob. Afr. *tjienkerientjee.*]

chin•chil•la (chĭn-chĭl′ə) *n.* **1.a.** A squirrellike rodent *(Chinchilla laniger)* of South America widely raised in captivity for its soft, pale gray fur. **b.** The fur of this animal. **2.** A thick twilled cloth of wool and cotton used for overcoats. [Sp., prob. alteration of a native word in Aymara.]

Chincoteague pony

Chin•chow (jĭn′jō′). See **Jinzhou.**

chinch•y (chĭn′chē) *adj.* **-i•er, -i•est.** *Chiefly Southern U.S.* Stingy; tightfisted; cheap. [Alteration of CHINTZY.]

Chin•co•teague Bay (shĭng′kə-tēg′, chĭng′-). A long narrow bay off NE VA and SE MD including **Chincoteague Island.**

Chincoteague pony *n.* A type of small, inbred North American horse. [After CHINCOTEAGUE ISLAND.]

Chin•dwin (chĭn′dwĭn′). A river rising in N Burma and flowing c. 1,158 km (720 mi) S to the Irrawaddy R.

chine (chīn) *n.* **1.a.** The backbone or spine, esp. of an animal. **b.** A cut of meat containing part of the backbone. **2.** A ridge or crest. **3.** *Naut.* The line of intersection between the side and bottom of a flatbottom or V-bottom boat. [ME < OFr. *eschine,* of Gmc. orig. See **skei-*.**]

chin-up

Chi•nese (chī-nēz′, -nēs′) *adj.* Of or relating to China or its peoples, languages, or cultures. —*n., pl.* **Chinese. 1.a.** A native or inhabitant of China. **b.** A person of Chinese ancestry. **c.** See **Han[1]. 2.a.** A branch of the Sino-Tibetan language family that consists of the various dialects spoken by the Chinese people. **b.** Any of these dialects. **3.** *Informal.* Chinese food.

Chinese anise *n.* An evergreen tree *(Illicium anisatum)* native to Japan and Korea having aromatic leaves and fragrant white or yellow flowers.

Chinese artichoke *n.* A perennial Chinese herb *(Stachys affinis)* in the mint family, cultivated for its edible stems.

Chinese black mushroom *n.* See **shiitake.**

Chinese cabbage *n.* Any of several forms of a plant *(Brassica rapa* var. *pekinensis)* of the mustard family, having an edible elongated head of overlapping, crinkled, broad-stalked leaves.

Chinese calendar *n.* The traditional lunisolar calendar of the Chinese people, based on 24 seasonal segments each about 15 days long and an occasional intercalary month.

Chinese checkers *pl.n. (used with a sing. or pl. v.) Games.* A board game in which each player tries to move a set of marbles arranged in holes from one point of a six-pointed star to the opposite point by means of single moves or jumps.

chipmunk
Eastern chipmunk
Tamias striatus

Chinese chestnut *n.* A chestnut *(Castanea mollissima)* native to China and Korea cultivated as an ornamental and for its edible nuts.

Chinese chive *n.* An eastern Asian herb *(Allium tuberosum)* having flat leaves, small white flowers, and elongated bulbs. Often used in the plural.

Chinese date *n.* See **jujube** 1.

Chinese evergreen *n.* A Chinese evergreen plant *(Aglaonena modestum)* with often dark green foilage.

Chinese gooseberry *n.* See **kiwi** 2.

Chinese houses *pl.n. (used with a sing. or pl. v.)* Any of several chiefly Californian plants of the genus *Collinsia,* esp. *C. heterophylla* having whorls of flowers resembling a pagoda.

Chinese ink *n.* See **India ink** 2.

Chinese kale *n.* A Chinese vegetable *(Brassica oleracea* var. *alboglabra)* of the mustard family.

Chinese lantern *n.* A decorative collapsible lantern of thin, brightly colored paper.

Chinese mustard *n.* Any of several cultivated varieties of the Indian mustard, eaten as a vegetable.

Chinese parsley *n.* See **coriander** 2.

Chinese pear *n.* See **sand pear.**

Chinese puzzle *n.* **1.** An intricate puzzle. **2.** Something complex.

Chinese radish *n.* See **daikon.**

Chinese red *n. Color.* See **vermilion** 2.

Chinese tallow tree *n.* An ornamental tree *(Sapium sebiferum),* native to China and Japan and having a waxy seed coat used in making candles and soap.

Chinese water chestnut *n.* See **water chestnut** 2.

Chinese white *n.* See **zinc oxide.**

Chinese windlass *n.* See **differential windlass.**

Ch'ing (chĭng). See **Qing.**

Ching•hai (chĭng′hī′). See **Qinghai.**

Chin Hills (chĭn). A range of hills in W Burma rising to 3,055.5 m (10,018 ft).

chink[1] (chĭngk) *n.* A narrow opening, such as a crack or fissure. —*tr.v.* **chinked, chink•ing, chinks. 1.** To make narrow openings in. **2.** To fill narrow openings in. [Prob. alteration of obsolete *chine* < ME, crack < OE *cine.*] —**chink′y** *adj.*

chink[2] (chĭngk) *n.* A slight, metallic sound. [Imit.] —**chink** *v.*

Chink (chĭngk) *n. Offensive Slang.* Used as a disparaging term for a Chinese person. [Prob. alteration of CHINESE.]

Chin•kiang (chĭn′kyăng′, jĭn′gyäng′). See **Zhenjiang.**

chi•no (chē′nō, shē′-) *n., pl.* **-nos. 1.** A coarse twilled cotton fabric used for uniforms and sometimes work or sports clothes. **2.** Trousers of a coarse twilled cotton. Often used in the plural. [Am.Sp., mestizo, yellowish (from its original tan color), prob. < Sp. *chino,* Chinese < *China,* China.]

Chi•no (chē′nō). A city of S CA E of Los Angeles; founded 1887. Pop. 59,682.

chi•noi•se•rie (shēn′wäz-rē′) *n.* **1.** A style in art reflecting Chinese influence through use of elaborate decoration and intricate patterns. **2.** An object reflecting Chinese artistic influence. [Fr. < *chinois,* Chin. < *Chine,* China.]

Chi•nook (shĭ-no͝ok′, chĭ-) *n., pl.* **Chinook** or **-nooks. 1.a.** A member of a Native American people formerly inhabiting the lower Columbia River valley and adjoining coastal regions of Washington and Oregon, now located in western Washington. **b.** The Chinookan language of the Chinook. **2.** A member of any of various Chinookan-speaking peoples formerly inhabiting the Columbia River valley eastward to The Dalles and now located in southern Washington and northern Oregon. **3. chinook. a.** A moist, warm wind blowing from the sea on the northwest U.S. coast. **b.** A warm, dry wind that descends from the eastern slopes of the Rocky Mountains. [Chehalis (Salishan) *c'inuk.*]

Chi•nook•an (shĭ-no͝ok′ən, chĭ-) *n.* A North American Indian language family of Washington and Oregon.

Chinook Jargon *n.* A pidgin language combining words from Nootka, Chinook, Salishan languages, French, and English.

Chinook salmon *n.* A very large, commercially valuable salmon *(Oncorhynchus tshawytscha)* of northern Pacific waters, characterized by irregular black spots on its back.

chin•qua•pin (chĭng′kə-pĭn′) *n.* **1.** Any of several deciduous shrubs or small trees related to the chestnut, esp. *Castanea pumila* of the eastern United States. **2.** A large evergreen tree *(Castanopsis chrysophylla)* of the Pacific Coast of North America. **3.** The chinquapin nut. [Of Algonquian orig.]

chintz (chĭnts) *n.* A printed and glazed cotton fabric, usu. of bright colors. [Obsolete *chints,* pl. of *chint,* calico cloth < Hindi *cīṇṭ* < Skt. *citra-,* shiny, variegated.]

chintz•y (chĭnt′sē) *adj.* **-i•er, -i•est. 1.** Of, relating to, or decorated with chintz. **2.a.** Gaudy and cheaply made. **b.** Stingy.

chin-up (chĭn′ŭp′) *n.* The act of chinning oneself.

Chin•wang•tao (chĭn′wäng′tou′). See **Qinhuangdao.**

Chi•os (kī′ŏs′, -ōs′, kē′-, KHē′ôs) also **Khí•os** (kē′ôs, KHē′-). An island of E Greece in the Aegean Sea off the W coast of Turkey; noted in antiquity for its school of epic poets.

chip[1] (chĭp) *n.* **1.** A small piece, as of wood or glass, broken or cut off. **2.** A crack or flaw caused by the removal of a small piece. **3.a.** *Games.* A small disk or counter used in poker and other games to represent money. **b. chips.** *Slang.* Money. **4.a.** *Electron.* A minute slice of a semiconducting material, such as silicon or germanium, processed to have specified electrical characteristics. **b.** An integrated circuit. **5.a.** A thin, usu. fried slice of food, esp. a potato chip. Often used in the plural. **b.** A very small piece of food or candy. Often used in the plural. **c. chips.** *Chiefly British.* French fries. **6.** Wood, palm leaves, straw, or similar material cut and dried for weaving. **7.** A fragment of dried animal dung used as fuel. **8.** Something worthless. **9.** *Sports.* A chip shot. — *v.* **chipped, chip•ping, chips.** — *tr.* **1.** To chop or cut, as with an ax. **2.a.** To break a small piece from. **b.** To break or cut off (a small piece). **3.** To shape or carve by cutting or chopping. — *intr.* **1.** To become broken off into small pieces. **2.** *Sports.* To make a chip shot in golf. ***— phrasal verb.*** **chip in. 1.** To contribute money or labor. **2.** To interrupt with comments; interject. **3.** *Games.* To put up chips or money as one's bet in poker and other games. ***— idioms.*** **chip off the old block.** A child who closely resembles a parent. **chip on (one's) shoulder.** A habitually hostile or combative attitude. [ME < OE *cyp*, beam < Lat. *cippus.*]

chip^{2} (chĭp) *intr.v.* **chipped, chip•ping, chips.** To cheep, as a bird. [Imit.] **— chip** *n.*

chip^{3} (chĭp) *n. Sports.* A trick method of throwing one's opponent in wrestling. [?]

Chip•e•wy•an (chĭp′ə-wī′ən) *n., pl.* **Chipewyan** or **-ans. 1.** A member of a Native American people inhabiting a large area of northern Canada north of the Churchill River. **2.** The Athabaskan language of the Chipewyan. [Cree *čīpwayān*, parka wearer : *cīpw-*, pointed + *ayān*, skin.]

chip•munk (chĭp′mŭngk′) *n.* Any of several small striped squirrels of the genera *Tamias* and *Eutamias,* esp. *T. striatus* of eastern North America. [Alteration of obsolete *chitmunk*, perh. < Ojibwa *ajidamoon*ʔ, red squirrel.]

chipped beef (chĭpt) *n.* Thinly sliced smoked dried beef.

Chip•pen•dale (chĭp′ən-dāl′) *adj.* Of an 18th-century English furniture style marked by flowing lines and often rococo ornamentation. [After Thomas CHIPPENDALE.]

Chippendale, Thomas. 1718–79. British cabinetmaker noted for his graceful neoclassical furniture.

chip•per^{1} (chĭp′ər) *n.* One that chips or cuts: *a wood chipper.*

chip•per^{2} (chĭp′ər) *intr.v.* **-pered, -per•ing, -pers. 1.** To chirp or twitter, as a bird. **2.** To babble. [Freq. of CHIP^{2}.]

chip•per^{3} (chĭp′ər) *adj.* In lively spirits; cheerful. [Poss. alteration of British dial. *kipper*, lively.]

Chip•pe•wa (chĭp′ə-wô′, -wä′, -wā′, -wə) *n., pl.* **Chippewa** or **-was.** See **Ojibwa.**

chip•ping sparrow (chĭp′ĭng) *n.* A small North American sparrow *(Spizella passerina)* having a reddish-brown crown.

chip•py (chĭp′ē) *n., pl.* **-pies. 1.** A chipping sparrow. **2.** *Slang.* A woman prostitute. [< CHIP^{2}.]

chip shot *n. Sports.* A short lofted golf shot.

chi•ral (kī′rəl) *adj.* Of or relating to the structural characteristic of a molecule that is impossible to superimpose on its own mirror image. [CHIR(O)- + -AL^{1}.] **— chi•ral′i•ty** (kī-răl′ĭ-tē) *n.*

Chi-Rho (kī′rō′, kē′-) *n.* A monogram and symbol for Christ, consisting of the superimposed Greek letters *chi* (X) and *rho* (P). [CHI + RHO, first two letters of Gk. *Khristos*, Christ.]

Chir•i•ca•hua (chĭr′ĭ-kä′wə) *n., pl.* **Chiricahua** or **-huas.** A member of a formerly nomadic Apache tribe inhabiting southern New Mexico, southeast Arizona, and northern Mexico, with present-day populations in Oklahoma and New Mexico.

Chi•ri•co (kîr′ĭ-kō′, kē′rē-kô′), **Giorgio de.** 1888–1978. Italian painter whose works are characterized by barren landscapes and elements of classical architecture and sculpture.

chirk (chûrk) *tr. & intr.v.* **chirked, chirk•ing, chirks.** To make or become cheerful. [ME *chirken*, to chirp < OE *cearcian*, to chatter, alteration of *cracian*, to resound. See CRACK.]

chiro– or **cheiro–** *pref.* Hand: *chiropractic.* [Lat. < Gk. *kheir*, hand. See **ghesor-*.**]

chi•rog•ra•phy (kī-rŏg′rə-fē) *n.* Penmanship. **— chi•rog′ra•pher** *n.* **— chi′ro•graph′ic** (kī′rə-grăf′ĭk), **chi′ro•graph′i•cal** *adj.*

chi•ro•man•cy (kī′rə-măn′sē) *n.* Palmistry. **— chi′ro•man′cer** *n.*

Chi•ron (kī′rŏn′) *n. Gk. Myth.* The wise centaur who tutored Achilles, Hercules, and Asclepius.

chi•rop•o•dy (kĭ-rŏp′ə-dē, shĭ-) *n.* See **podiatry.** [CHIRO- + -POD + -Y^{2}.] **— chi•rop′o•dist** *n.*

chi•ro•prac•tic (kī′rə-prăk′tĭk) *n.* A system of therapy usu. involving manipulation of the spinal column and other body structures. [CHIRO- + Gk. *praktikos*, practical; see PRACTICAL.] **— chi′ro•prac′tor** *n.*

chi•rop•ter•an (kī-rŏp′tər-ən) also **chi•rop•ter** (-rŏp′tər) *n.* A mammal, such as the bat, that is a member of the order Chiroptera and has forelimbs modified as wings. [< NLat. *Chiroptera*, order name : CHIRO- + -PTER.] **— chi•rop′ter•an** *adj.*

chirp (chûrp) *n.* A short high-pitched sound, such as that made by a small bird. [ME **chirpen*, of imit. orig.] **— chirp** *v.*

chirr (chûr) *n.* A harsh trilling sound, such as that made by crickets. [Imit.] **— chirr** *v.*

chir•ren (chĭr′ən) *n. Chiefly Southern U.S.* Children.

Regional Note: The linguistic process of ellipsis allows for the deletion within words of some internal sounds, such as weakly stressed syllables and less prominent consonants. This process is still active in American regional dialects. For example, in *chirren* both the *l* and the *d* of *children* are omitted in favor of the more conspicuous *r.*

chir•rup (chûr′əp, chĭr′-) *v.* **-ruped, -rup•ing, -rups.** — *intr.* **1.** To utter a series of chirps. **2.** To make clucking or clicking sounds with the lips, as in urging on a horse. — *tr.* **1.** To sound with chirps. **2.** To make clucking sounds to. [Var. of CHIRP.] **— chir′rup** *n.*

chi•rur•geon (kī-rûr′jən) *n. Archaic.* A surgeon. [ME *cirurgien* < OFr. < Lat. *chīrurgia*, surgery. See SURGERY.]

chis•el (chĭz′əl) *n.* A metal tool with a sharp beveled edge, used to cut and shape stone, wood, or metal. — *v.* **-eled, -el•ing, -els** or **-elled, -el•ling, -els.** — *tr.* **1.** To shape or cut with a chisel. **2.** *Informal.* **a.** To cheat or swindle. **b.** To obtain by deception. — *intr.* **1.** To use a chisel. **2.** *Informal.* **a.** To use unethical methods; cheat. **b.** To intrude oneself without welcome: *always tries to chisel in.* [ME < OFr. *cisiel* < VLat. **cīsellus*, cutting tool < dim. of Lat. *caesus*, p.part. of *caedere*, to cut. See **kaə-id-*.**] **— chis′el•er** *n.*

chis•eled or **chis•elled** (chĭz′əld) *adj.* Made or shaped with or as if with a chisel: *a finely chiseled nose.*

Chis•holm (chĭz′əm), **Shirley Anita Saint Hill.** b. 1924. Amer. politician who was a U.S. representative from NY (1969–83).

Chisholm Trail. A former cattle trail from San Antonio TX north to Abilene KS.

chi-square test (kī′skwâr′) *n.* A statistical test for the degree to which a theoretical frequency distribution corresponds to a frequency distribution of observed data.

chit^{1} (chĭt) *n.* **1.** A statement of an amount owed for food and drink; a check. **2.** A short letter; a note. [Obsolete *chitty* < Hindi *ciṭṭhī*, note, letter < Skt. **citrikā, *citritā*, note.]

chit^{2} (chĭt) *n.* **1.** A child. **2.** A girl or young woman considered saucy. [ME, young animal.]

Chi•ta (chĭ-tä′). A city of SE Russia E of Irkutsk; founded 1653. Pop. 336,000.

chit•chat (chĭt′chăt′) *n.* **1.** Casual conversation; small talk. **2.** Gossip. [Redup. of CHAT.] **— chit′chat′** *v.*

chi•tin (kīt′n) *n.* A tough semitransparent substance forming the principal component of arthropod exoskeletons and the cell walls of certain fungi. [Fr. *chitine* < NLat. *chitōn*, mollusk < Gk. *khitōn*, chiton. See CHITON.] **— chi′tin•ous** *adj.*

chi•ton (kīt′n, kī′tŏn′) *n.* **1.** Any of various marine mollusks of the class Polyplacophora that live on rocks and have shells consisting of eight overlapping calcareous plates. **2.** A tunic worn in ancient Greece. [Gk. *khitōn*, tunic, of Semitic orig.]

Chit•ta•gong (chĭt′ə-gông′, -gŏng′). A city of SE Bangladesh near the Bay of Bengal. Pop. 980,000.

chit•ter (chĭt′ər) *intr.v.* **-tered, -ter•ing, -ters.** To twitter or chatter, as a bird. [ME *chiteren*, of imit. orig.]

chit•ter•lings also **chit•lins** or **chit•lings** (chĭt′lĭnz) *pl.n.* The small intestines of pigs, esp. when cooked and eaten as food. [< ME *chiterling*, prob. dim. of OE **cieter*, intestines.]

chiv•al•rous (shĭv′əl-rəs) *adj.* **1.** Having the qualities attributed to an ideal knight. **2.** Of or relating to chivalry. **3.** Characterized by consideration and courtesy. **— chiv′al•rous•ly** *adv.* **— chiv′al•rous•ness** *n.*

chiv•al•ry (shĭv′əl-rē) *n., pl.* **-ries. 1.** The medieval system, principles, and customs of knighthood. **2.a.** The qualities idealized by knighthood, such as bravery, courtesy, honor, and gallantry toward women. **b.** A manifestation of any of these qualities. **3.** A group of knights or gallant gentlemen. [ME *chivalrie* < OFr. *chevalerie* < *chevalier*, knight. See CHEVALIER.] **— chi•val′ric** (shĭ-văl′rĭk, shĭv′əl-) *adj.*

chive (chīv) *n.* A Eurasian bulbous herb *(Allium schoenoprasum)* in the lily family, cultivated for its long hollow leaves used as a mild onion-flavored seasoning. Often used in the plural. [ME *chive* < AN < Lat. *cēpa*, onion.]

chiv•vy or **chiv•y** (chĭv′ē) — *v.* **-vied, -vy•ing, -vies** or **-ied, -y•ing, -ies.** — *tr.* **1.** To vex or harass with petty attacks. **2.** To maneuver or secure gradually. — *intr.* To scurry. — *n., pl.* **-vies** or **-ies. 1.** A hunt or chase. **2.** A hunting cry. [Var. of *chevy*, a hunt, hunting cry < *Chevy Chase*, title of a ballad about a border skirmish.]

Chka•lov (chə-kä′ləf, chkä′-). See **Orenburg.**

chlam•y•date (klăm′ĭ-dāt′) *adj.* Having a mantle. Used of mollusks. [Lat. *chlamydātus*, cloaked < *chlamys, chlamyd-*, mantle. See CHLAMYS.]

chla•myd•e•ous (klə-mĭd′ē-əs) *adj. Bot.* Having a perianth. [Lat. *chlamys, chlamyd-*, mantle; see CHLAMYS + -EOUS.]

chla•myd•i•a (klə-mĭd′ē-ə) *n., pl.* **-i•ae** (-ē-ē′). *Microbiol.* **1.** Any of various gram-negative coccoid microorganisms of the genus *Chlamydia*, esp. *C. psittaci* and *C. trachomatis*, that are pathogenic to human beings and animals. **2.** Any of several common, often asymptomatic, sexually transmitted diseases caused by the microorganism *Chlamydia trachomatis.* [NLat., genus name < Lat. *chlamys, chlamyd-*, mantle. See CHLAMYS.] **— chla•myd′i•al** *adj.*

chla•myd•o•spore (klə-mĭd′ə-spôr′, -spōr′) *n.* A thick-walled asexual fungal spore that can function as a resting spore. [Lat. *chlamys, chlamyd-*, mantle; see CHLAMYS + SPORE.]

chlam•ys (klăm′ĭs, klā′mĭs) *n., pl.* **chlam•ys•es** or **chlam•y•des** (klăm′ĭ-dēz′). A short mantle fastened at the shoulder, worn by men in ancient Greece. [Lat. < Gk. *khlamus.*]

Chi-Rho

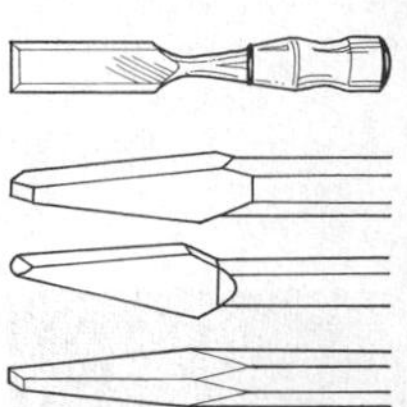
chisel
Top to bottom: Wood, cape, round-nose, and diamond-point chisels

chiton
Ceres wearing a chiton

ă **pat**	oi **boy**
ā **pay**	ou **out**
âr **care**	ŏŏ **took**
ä **father**	ōō **boot**
ĕ **pet**	ŭ **cut**
ē **be**	ûr **urge**
ĭ **pit**	th **thin**
ī **pie**	*th* **this**
îr **pier**	hw **which**
ŏ **pot**	zh **vision**
ō **toe**	ə **about,**
ô **paw**	**item**

Stress marks:
′ (primary);
′ (secondary), as in **dictionary** (dĭk′shə-nĕr′ē)

chlo•as•ma (klō-ăz′mə) *n., pl.* **-ma•ta** (-mə-tə). A patchy brown or dark brown skin discoloration that usu. occurs on a woman's face and may result from hormonal changes. [NLat. < Gk. *khloasma*, greenness < *khloazein*, to be green < *khloos*, greenish color. See **ghel-²***.]

chlor– *pref.* Var. of **chloro–**.

chlor•ac•ne (klôr-ăk′nē, klōr-) *n.* An acnelike skin disorder caused by prolonged exposure to chlorinated hydrocarbons.

chlo•ral (klôr′əl, klōr′-) *n.* A colorless, mobile, oily aldehyde, CCl_3CHO, a penetrating lung irritant used to manufacture DDT and chloral hydrate. [CHLOR(INE) + AL(COHOL).]

chloral hydrate *n.* A colorless crystalline compound, $CCl_3CH(OH)_2$, used medicinally as a sedative and hypnotic.

chlo•ra•mine (klôr′ə-mēn′, klōr′-) *n.* Any of several compounds containing nitrogen and chlorine, esp. an unstable colorless liquid, NH_2Cl, used to make hydrazine.

chlo•ram•phen•i•col (klôr′ăm-fĕn′ĭ-kôl′, -kōl′, -kŏl′, klōr′-) *n.* A broad-spectrum antibiotic, $C_{11}H_{12}Cl_2N_2O_5$, derived from the bacterium *Streptomyces venezuelae.* [CHLOR(O)– + AM(IDE) + PHE(NO)– + NI(TRO)– + (GLY)COL.]

chlo•rate (klôr′āt′, klōr′-) *n.* The inorganic group ClO_3 or a compound containing it.

chlor•dane (klôr′dān′, klōr′-) also **chlor•dan** (-dăn′) *n.* A toxic, odorless, viscous liquid, $C_{10}H_6Cl_8$, used as an insecticide. [CHLOR(O)– + (IN)D(ENE) + –ANE.]

chlor•di•az•e•pox•ide (klôr′dī-ăz′ə-pŏk′sīd′, klōr′-) *n.* A benzodiazepine drug, $C_{16}H_{14}ClN_3O$, used to treat anxiety, chronic alcoholism, and alcohol withdrawal. [CHLOR(O)– + DI–¹ + AZ(O) + EP(I)– + OXIDE.]

chlo•rel•la (klə-rĕl′ə) *n.* Any of various unicellular green algae of the genus *Chlorella,* often used in experiments. [NLat. *Chlorella*, genus name < Gk. *khlōros*, green. See CHLORO–.]

chlo•ren•chy•ma (klə-rĕng′kə-mə) *n.* Plant tissue consisting of parenchyma cells that contain chloroplasts. [CHLOR(OPHYLL) + –ENCHYMA.]

chlo•ric (klôr′ĭk, klōr′-) *adj.* Of or containing chlorine.

chloric acid *n.* A strongly oxidizing unstable acid, $HClO_3{\cdot}7H_2O$.

chlo•ride (klôr′īd′, klōr′-) *n.* A binary compound of chlorine. **—chlo•rid′ic** (klə-rĭd′ĭk) *adj.*

chloride of lime *n.* See **bleaching powder.**

chlo•ri•nate (klôr′ə-nāt′, klōr′-) *tr.v.* **-nat•ed, -nat•ing, -nates.** To treat or combine with chlorine or a chlorine compound. **—chlo′ri•na′tion** *n.* **—chlo′ri•na′tor** *n.*

chlo•ri•nat•ed lime (klôr′ə-nā′tĭd, klōr′-) *n.* See **bleaching powder.**

chlo•rine (klôr′ēn′, -ĭn, klōr′-) *n. Symbol* **Cl** A highly irritating poisonous halogen, capable of combining with nearly all other elements, produced principally by electrolysis of sodium chloride and used widely to purify water, as a disinfectant and bleaching agent, and in the manufacture of many important compounds. Atomic number 17; atomic weight 35.45; freezing point −100.98°C; boiling point −34.6°C; specific gravity 1.56 (−33.6°C); valence 1, 3, 5, 7. See table at **element.**

chock

chlo•rite¹ (klôr′īt′, klōr′-) *n.* A generally green or black secondary mineral, $(Mg,Fe,Al)_6(Si,Al)_4O_{10}(OH)_8$, often formed by metamorphic alteration of primary dark rock minerals. [Lat. *chlōrītis*, a green precious stone < Gk. *khlōritis* < *khlōros*, green. See **ghel-²***.]

chlo•rite² (klôr′īt′, klōr′-) *n.* The inorganic group ClO_2 or a salt containing it.

chloro– or **chlor–** *pref.* **1.** Green: *chlorosis.* **2.** Chlorine: *chloroform.* [< Gk. *khlōros*, green. See **ghel-²***.]

chlo•ro•ben•zene (klôr′ō-bĕn′zēn′, -bĕn-zēn′, klōr′-) *n.* A colorless volatile flammable liquid, C_6H_5Cl, used to prepare phenol, DDT, and aniline and as a general solvent.

chlo•ro•car•bon (klôr′ō-kär′bən, klōr′-) *n.* A compound that consists of chlorine and halocarbon.

chlo•ro•fluor•o•car•bon (klôr′ō-flo͝or′ō-kär′bən, -flôr′-, -flōr′-, klōr′-) *n.* Any of various halocarbon compounds consisting of carbon, hydrogen, chlorine, and fluorine, once used widely as aerosol propellants and refrigerants and now believed to cause depletion of the atmospheric ozone layer.

chlo•ro•form (klôr′ə-fôrm′, klōr′-) *n.* A clear, colorless, heavy, sweet-smelling liquid, $CHCl_3$, used in refrigerants, propellants, and resins, as a solvent, and sometimes as an anesthetic. *—tr.v.* **-formed, -form•ing, -forms. 1.** To treat with chloroform to anesthetize, render unconscious, or kill. **2.** To apply chloroform to. [CHLORO– + FORM(YL).]

chlo•ro•hy•drin (klôr′ō-hī′drĭn, klōr′-) *n.* Any of a group of aliphatic chemical compounds that are both alkyl chlorides and alcohols.

chlo•ro•phyll also **chlo•ro•phyl** (klôr′ə-fĭl, klōr′-) *n.* Any of a group of related green pigments found in photosynthetic organisms, esp.: **a.** A waxy blue-black microcrystalline green-plant pigment, $C_{55}H_{72}MgN_4O_5$. **b.** A similar green-plant pigment, $C_{55}H_{70}MgN_4O_6$.

chlo•ro•pic•rin (klôr′ə-pĭk′rĭn, klōr′-) *n.* An oily liquid, CCl_3NO_2, used in poison gas, dyestuffs, disinfectants, insecticides, and soil fumigants. [CHLORO– + PICR(O)– + –IN.]

chlo•ro•plast (klôr′ə-plăst′, klōr′-) also **chlo•ro•plas•tid** (klôr′ə-plăs′tĭd, klōr′-) *n. Bot.* A chlorophyll-containing plastid in algal and green plant cells. [CHLORO– + PLAST(ID).]

chlo•ro•prene (klôr′ə-prēn′, klōr′-) *n.* A liquid, C_4H_5Cl, that polymerizes to neoprene. [CHLORO– + (ISO)PRENE.]

chlo•ro•quine (klôr′ə-kwĭn′, -kwēn′, klōr′-) *n.* A drug, $C_{18}H_{26}ClN_3$, used to treat and prevent malaria. [CHLORO– + QUIN(OLIN)E.]

chlo•ro•sis (klə-rō′sĭs) *n.* **1.** *Bot.* The yellowing or whitening of normally green plant tissue because of a decreased amount of chlorophyll. **2.** *Pathol.* An iron-deficiency anemia characterized by a greenish-yellow discoloration of the skin. **—chlo•rot′ic** (-rŏt′ĭk) *adj.* **—chlo•rot′i•cal•ly** *adv.*

chlo•ro•thi•a•zide (klôr′ə-thī′ə-zīd′, klōr′-) *n.* A thiazide diuretic used to treat hypertension, heart failure, and edema.

chlor•prom•a•zine (klôr-prŏm′ə-zēn′, -prō′mə-, klōr-) *n.* A drug, $C_{17}H_{19}ClN_2S$, derived from phenothiazine and used to suppress vomiting and as a sedative and a tranquilizer. [CHLOR(O)– + PRO(PYL) + M(ETHYL) + AZINE.]

chlor•tet•ra•cy•cline (klôr′tĕt-rə-sī′klēn′, -klĭn, klōr′-) *n.* A broad-spectrum antibiotic, $C_{22}H_{23}ClN_2O_8$, obtained from the soil bacterium *Streptomyces aureofaciens.*

chm. *abbr.* **1.** Chairman. **2.** Checkmate.

chmn *abbr.* Chairman.

cho•an•o•cyte (kō-ăn′ə-sīt′) *n.* One of a layer of flagellated cells lining the body cavity of a sponge and characterized by a collar of cytoplasm surrounding the flagellum. [Gk. *khoanē*, funnel (< *khein*, to pour; see **gheu-***) + –CYTE.]

chock (chŏk) *n.* **1.** A block or wedge placed under something else to keep it from moving. **2.** *Naut.* A heavy fitting of metal or wood with two jaws curving inward, through which a rope or cable may be run. *—tr.v.* **chocked, chock•ing, chocks.** To fit with or secure by a chock. *—adv.* **1.** As completely as possible. **2.** As close as possible. [Poss. < ONFr. *choque*, log < Gaulish **tsukka*, stump, of Gmc. orig.]

chock-a-block or **chock•a•block** (chŏk′ə-blŏk′) *—adj.* **1.** Squeezed together; jammed. **2.** Completely filled; stuffed. **3.** *Naut.* Drawn so close as to have the blocks touching. Used of a ship's hoisting tackle. *—adv.* Chock. [Alteration of *block-a-block* : BLOCK + A–² + BLOCK.]

choc•o•late (chô′kə-lĭt, chôk′lĭt, chŏk′-) *n.* **1.** Fermented, roasted, shelled, and ground cacao seeds, often combined with a sweetener or flavoring agent. **2.** A beverage of water or milk and chocolate. **3.** A small chocolate-covered candy with a hard or soft center. **4.** *Color.* A grayish to deep reddish brown to deep grayish brown. *—adj.* **1.** Made or flavored with chocolate. **2.** *Color.* Of the color of chocolate. [Sp. < Nahuatl *xocolatl* : *xococ*, bitter + *atl*, water.]

chocolate tree *n.* See **cacao** 1.

Choc•taw (chŏk′tô) *n., pl.* **Choctaw** or **-taws. 1.** A member of a Native American people formerly inhabiting Mississippi and Alabama, with present-day populations in Mississippi and southeast Oklahoma. **2.** The Muskogean language of the Choctaw. [Choctaw *Chahta*.]

choice (chois) *n.* **1.** The act of choosing; selection. **2.** The power, right, or liberty to choose; option. **3.** One that is chosen. **4.** A number or variety from which to choose. **5.** The best or most preferable part. **6.** Care in choosing. **7.** An alternative. *—adj.* **choic•er, choic•est. 1.a.** Of very fine quality. **b.** Appealing to refined taste. **2.** Selected with care. **3.** Of the U.S. Government grade of meat higher than good and lower than prime. *—idiom.* **of choice.** Preferred above others of the same kind or set. [ME *chois* < OFr. < *choisir*, to choose < VLat. **causīre*, of Gmc. orig. See **geus-***.] **—choice′ly** *adv.*

Syns: *choice, alternative, option, preference, selection, election.* Each of these nouns denotes the act, power, or right of choosing. *Choice* implies broadly the freedom to choose from a set: *a wide choice of fruits. Alternative* emphasizes a choosing between only two possibilities: *"An unhappy alternative is before you, Elizabeth. . . . Your mother will never see you again if you do not marry Mr. Collins, and I will never see you again if you do"* (Jane Austen). *Option* often stresses a power or liberty to choose that has been granted: *The committee gave us several options. Preference* indicates choice based on one's values, bias, or predilections: *our preference of wines. Selection* suggests a variety of things or persons to choose from: *a wide selection of movies. Election* emphasizes the use of judgment: *The university recommends the election of courses in composition.* See also Syns at **delicate.**

choir (kwīr) *n.* **1.** An organized company of singers, esp. one performing church music or singing in a church. **2.** The part of a church used by a choir. **3.** *Mus.* **a.** A group of instruments of the same kind: *a string choir.* **b.** A division of some pipe organs, containing pipes suitable for accompanying a choir. **4.** An organized group: *a choir of dancers.* **5.** One of the orders of angels. *—intr.v.* **choired, choir•ing, choirs.** *Mus.* To sing in chorus. [ME *quer, quire* < OFr. *cuer* < Med. Lat. *chorus* < Lat., choral dance. See CHORUS.]

choir•boy (kwīr′boi′) *n. Mus.* A boy member of a choir.

choir•girl (kwīr′gûrl′) *n. Mus.* A girl member of a choir.

choir loft *n.* A gallery for a choir.

choir•mas•ter (kwīr′măs′tər) *n.* The director of a choir.

Choi•seul (shwä-zœl′). One of the Solomon Is. in the SW Pacific Ocean SE of Bougainville I.

choke (chōk) *v.* **choked, chok•ing, chokes.** —*tr.* **1.** To interfere with the respiration of by compression or obstruction of the larynx or trachea. **2.a.** To check or slow the movement, growth, or action of. **b.** To block up or obstruct by filling or clogging. **c.** To fill up; jam. **3.** To reduce the air intake of (a carburetor), thus enriching the fuel mixture. **4.** *Sports.* To grip (a bat, for example) nearer the hitting surface. —*intr.* **1.** To have difficulty in breathing, swallowing, or speaking. **2.** To become blocked up or obstructed. **3.** *Sports.* To shorten one's grip on the handle, as of a bat. **4.** To fail to perform effectively because of nervous tension. —*n.* **1.** The act or sound of choking. **2.a.** Something that constricts or chokes. **b.** A narrow part, such as a chokebore. **3.** A device used in an internal-combustion engine to enrich the fuel mixture by reducing the flow of air to the carburetor. —***phrasal verbs.*** **choke back.** To hold back; suppress. **choke off.** To bring to an end as if by choking. **choke up.** To be unable to speak because of emotion. [ME *choken*, short for *achoken* < OE *āceōcian* : *ā-*, intensive pref. + *cēoce*, jaw, cheek.]

choke•ber•ry (chōk′bĕr′ē) *n.* **1.** Any of various deciduous shrubs of the genus *Aronia* in the rose family, native to eastern North America and having tiny red to black applelike fruit. **2.** The fruit of any of these plants. [< its bitter fruit.]

choke•bore (chōk′bôr′, -bōr′) *n.* **1.** A shotgun bore that narrows toward the muzzle to prevent wide scattering of the shot. **2.** A gun with a narrowed bore near the muzzle.

choke chain *n.* See **choke collar.**

choke•cher•ry (chōk′chĕr′ē) *n.* **1.** A deciduous North American shrub or small tree *(Prunus virginiana)* in the rose family, having astringent, dark red to nearly black fruit. **2.** The fruit of this plant. [< its bitter fruit.]

choke coil *n. Electron.* A circuit element used to suppress or limit the flow of alternating current without affecting the flow of direct current.

choke collar *n.* A chain collar that tightens like a noose when the leash is pulled.

choke•damp (chōk′dămp′) *n.* See **blackdamp.**

choke•hold (chōk′hōld′) *n.* A restraining move in which one person seizes another around the neck in a tight grip.

choke•point or **choke point** (chōk′point′) *n.* **1.** A narrow passage through which shipping must pass. **2.** A point of congestion or obstruction.

chok•er (chō′kər) *n.* **1.** One that chokes or suffocates another. **2.** Something that fits closely around the neck or throat, as: **a.** A tight-fitting necklace. **b.** A high, tight collar. **c.** A narrow neckpiece of fur.

chok•ing (chō′kĭng) *adj.* **1.** Causing a choking or suffocating feeling. **2.** Having a husky sound. —**chok′ing•ly** *adv.*

chok•y (chō′kē) *adj.* **-i•er, -i•est. 1.** Likely to cause choking. **2.** Tending to become choked.

cho•lan•gi•og•ra•phy (kō-lăn′jē-ŏg′rə-fē) *n.* X-ray examination of the bile ducts following administration of a radiopaque contrast medium. [CHOL(E)– + ANGIOGRAPHY.] —**cho•lan′gi•o•graph′ic** (-ə-grăf′ĭk) *adj.*

chole– or **chol–** *pref.* Bile: *cholesterol.* [< Gk. *kholē*, bile. See **ghel-**[2]*.]

cho•le•cal•cif•er•ol (kō′lĭ-kăl-sĭf′ə-rôl′, -rōl′, -rŏl′) *n.* See **vitamin D_3.**

cho•le•cyst (kō′lĭ-sĭst′) *n.* The gallbladder.

cho•le•cys•tec•to•my (kō′lĭ-sĭ-stĕk′tə-mē) *n., pl.* **-mies.** Surgical removal of the gallbladder.

cho•le•cys•ti•tis (kō′lĭ-sĭ-stī′tĭs) *n.* Inflammation of the gallbladder.

cho•le•cys•to•ki•nin (kō′lĭ-sĭs′tə-kī′nĭn) *n.* A hormone produced principally by the small intestine in response to the presence of fats, causing contraction of the gallbladder, release of bile, and secretion of pancreatic digestive enzymes.

cho•le•li•thi•a•sis (kō′lə-lĭ-thī′ə-sĭs) *n.* The presence or formation of gallstones in the gallbladder or bile ducts.

chol•er (kŏl′ər, kō′lər) *n.* **1.** Anger; irritability. **2.a.** *Archaic.* One of the four humors of the body, thought in the Middle Ages to cause anger and bad temper when present in excess; yellow bile. **b.** *Obsolete.* The quality or condition of being bilious. [ME *colre* < OFr. < Lat. *cholera*, cholera, jaundice < Gk. *kholera* < *kholē*, bile. See **ghel-**[2]*.]

chol•er•a (kŏl′ər-ə) *n.* **1.** An acute infectious disease of the small intestine, caused by the bacterium *Vibrio cholerae* and characterized by profuse watery diarrhea, vomiting, muscle cramps, severe dehydration, and depletion of electrolytes. **2.** Any of various diseases of domesticated animals marked by severe gastroenteritis. [Lat., cholera, jaundice. See CHOLER.] —**chol′e•ra′ic** (-ə-rā′ĭk) *adj.* —**chol′e•roid′** (-ə-roid′) *adj.*

chol•er•ic (kŏl′ə-rĭk, kə-lĕr′ĭk) *adj.* **1.** Easily angered; bad-tempered. **2.** Showing or expressing anger. —**chol′er•i•cal•ly, chol′er•ic•ly** *adv.*

cho•le•sta•sis (kō′lĭ-stā′sĭs) *n.* Suppression of biliary flow.

cho•les•ter•in (kə-lĕs′tər-ĭn) *n.* Cholesterol.

cho•les•ter•ol (kə-lĕs′tə-rôl′, -rōl′) *n.* A white crystalline substance, $C_{27}H_{45}OH$, in animal tissues and various foods, normally synthesized by the liver and a constituent of cell membranes and precursor to steroid hormones. [CHOLE– + Gk. *stereos*, solid; see **ster-**[1]* + –OL[1].]

cho•le•styr•a•mine (kō′lĭ-stîr′ə-mēn′, kō-lĕs′tə-răm′ĕn) *n.* A drug used to lower serum cholesterol levels and treat itching associated with jaundice binding intestinal bile acids. [CHOLE– + *styr-*, poss. alteration of STER(OL) + AMINE.]

cho•lic acid (kō′lĭk) *n.* An abundant crystalline bile acid, $C_{24}H_{40}O_5$, derived from cholesterol. [Gk. *kholikos*, bilious < *kholē*, bile. See CHOLE–.]

cho•line (kō′lēn′) *n.* A natural amine, $C_5H_{15}NO_2$, often classed in the vitamin B complex and a constituent of many other biologically important molecules, such as lecithin.

cho•lin•er•gic (kō′lə-nûr′jĭk) *adj.* **1.** Activated by or capable of liberating acetylcholine, esp. as related to nerve fibers of the parasympathetic nervous system. **2.** Having physiological effects similar to acetylcholine. [(ACETYL)CHOLIN(E) + Gk. *ergon*, work; see **werg-***.]

cho•lin•es•ter•ase (kō′lə-nĕs′tə-rās′, -rāz′) *n.* An enzyme found chiefly at nerve terminals that inactivates acetylcholine by hydrolyzing it to form acetic acid and choline. [CHOLIN(E) + ESTERASE.]

chol•la (choi′ə) *n.* Any of several spiny, shrubby, or treelike cacti of the genus *Opuntia*, having cylindrical stem segments. [Am.Sp. < obsolete Sp., upper part of the head, poss. < OFr. *cholle*, round lump, head, of Gmc. orig.]

Cho•lu•la (chə-lo͞o′lə, chō-lo͞o′lä). A town of E-central Mexico W of Puebla; site of an ancient Toltec center and a city sacred to the Aztecs. Pop. 26,748.

Cho•mo Lha•ri (chō′mō lär′ē). A peak, 7,318.8 m (23,996 ft), of the SE Himalaya Mts. on the Bhutan-China border.

chomp (chŏmp) *v.* **chomped, chomp•ing, chomps.** —*tr.* To chew or bite on noisily. —*intr.* To chew or bite on something repeatedly: *chomping on a cigar.* —*n.* The act or an instance of vigorous biting. [Var. of CHAMP[1].]

Chom•sky (chŏm′skē), **Noam.** b. 1928. Amer. linguist noted for his theory of generative grammar.

chon (chŏn) *n., pl.* **chon.** See table at **currency.** [Korean.]

chon•dri•o•some (kŏn′drē-ə-sōm′) *n.* See **mitochondrion.**

chon•drite (kŏn′drīt′) *n.* A stone of meteoric origin characterized by chondrules. —**chon•drit′ic** (-drĭt′ĭk) *adj.*

chondro– or **chrondri–** or **chrondr–** *pref.* **1.** Cartilage: *chondrocranium.* **2.** Granule: *chondrite.* [< Gk. *khondros*, granule, cartilage. See **ghrendh-***.]

chon•dro•ma (kŏn-drō′mə) *n., pl.* **-mas** or **-ma•ta** (-mə-tə). A cartilaginous growth or tumor.

chon•dro•ma•la•cia (kŏn′drō-mə-lā′shə) *n.* Abnormal softening or degeneration of cartilage of the joints, esp. of the knee. [CHONDRO– + Gk. *malakia*, softness (< *malakos*, soft; see **mel-**[1]*).]

chon•drule (kŏn′dro͞ol) *n.* A small round granule of extraterrestrial origin found embedded in some meteorites.

Chong•jin (chông′jĭn′, chœng′-). A city of NE North Korea on the Sea of Japan. Pop. 490,000.

Chong•qing (chông′chĭng′, cho͝ong′-) also **Chung•king** (cho͝ong′kĭng′, jo͝ong′gĭng′). A city of S-central China on the Yangtze R. (Chang Jiang). Pop. 2,080,000.

Chon•ju (chôn′jo͞o′, chœn′-). A city of SW South Korea S of Seoul. Pop. 305,000.

choose (cho͞oz) *v.* **chose** (chōz), **cho•sen** (chō′zən), **choos•ing, choos•es.** —*tr.* **1.** To select from a number of possible alternatives. **2.a.** To prefer above others. **b.** To determine or decide. —*intr.* To make a choice; make a selection. —***phrasal verb.*** **choose up.** To choose players and form sides or teams for a game. [ME *chesen* < OE *cēosan.* See **geus-***.] —**choos′er** *n.*

choos•y also **choos•ey** (cho͞o′zē) *adj.* **-i•er, -i•est.** Very careful in choosing; highly selective. —**choos′i•ness** *n.*

Cho O•yu (chō′ ō-yo͞o′). A peak, 8,158.8 m (26,750 ft), of the central Himalaya Mts. on the Nepal-China border.

chop[1] (chŏp) *v.* **chopped, chop•ping, chops.** —*tr.* **1.a.** To cut by striking with a heavy sharp tool, such as an ax. **b.** To shape or form by chopping. **c.** To cut into small pieces. **d.** To curtail as if by chopping: *chop expenses.* **2.** *Sports.* To hit or hit at with a short, swift downward stroke. —*intr.* **1.** To make heavy cutting strokes. **2.** *Archaic.* To move roughly or suddenly. —*n.* **1.** The act of chopping. **2.a.** A swift, short, cutting blow or stroke. **b.** *Sports.* A short downward stroke. **3.** A piece that has been chopped off, esp. a cut of meat, usu. taken from the rib, shoulder, or loin and containing a bone. **4.a.** A short irregular motion of waves. **b.** An area of choppy water, as on an ocean. [ME *choppen*, prob. var. of *chappen*, to split. See CHAP[1].]

chop[2] (chŏp) *intr.v.* **chopped, chop•ping, chops.** To change direction suddenly, as a ship in the wind. [Obsolete, to exchange < ME *choppen*, to barter, bargain, var. of *chapen* < OE *cēapian* < *cēap*, bargain, trade. See CHEAP.]

chop[3] (chŏp) *n.* **1.** An official stamp or permit in the Far East. **2.a.** A mark stamped on goods or coins to indicate their identity or quality. **b.** Quality; class: *first chop.* [Hindi *chāp*, seal.]

chop-chop (chŏp′chŏp′) *adv. Informal.* Right away; quickly. [Pidgin E., redup. of *chop*, quick. See CHOPSTICK.]

chop•fall•en (chŏp′fô′lən) *adj.* Var. of **chapfallen.**

chop•house (chŏp′hous′) *n.* A restaurant that specializes in steaks and chops.

choker
Pearl necklace

ă pat	oi boy
ā pay	ou out
âr care	o͝o took
ä father	o͞o boot
ĕ pet	ŭ cut
ē be	ûr urge
ĭ pit	th thin
ī pie	*th* this
îr pier	hw which
ŏ pot	zh vision
ō toe	ə about, item
ô paw	

Stress marks:
′ (primary);
′ (secondary), as in
dictionary (dĭk′shə-nĕr′ē)

proteins in the cell nucleus that stains readily with basic dyes and condenses to form chromosomes during cell division. **— chro′ma•tin′ic** *adj.*

chromato– or **chromat–** *pref.* **1.** Color: *chromatophore.* **2.** Chromatin: *chromatolysis.* [Gk. *khrōma, khrōmat-,* color.]

chro•mat•o•gram (krō-măt′ə-grăm′) *n.* The pattern of separated substances obtained by chromatography.

chro•mat•o•graph (krō-măt′ə-grăf′) *n.* An instrument that produces a chromatogram. *—tr.v.* **-graphed, -graph•ing, -graphs.** To separate and analyze by chromatography. **— chro•mat′o•graph′ic** *adj.* **— chro•mat′o•graph′i•cal•ly** *adv.*

chro•ma•tog•ra•phy (krō′mə-tŏg′rə-fē) *n.* Any of various techniques for the separation of complex mixtures that rely on the differential affinities of substances for a gas or liquid mobile medium and for a stationary adsorbing medium. **— chro′ma•tog′ra•pher** *n.*

chro•ma•tol•y•sis (krō′mə-tŏl′ĭ-sĭs) *n. Biol.* The dissolution or disintegration of chromophil material, such as chromatin, within a cell. **— chro•mat′o•lyt′ic** (-măt′l-ĭt′ĭk) *adj.*

chro•mat•o•phil•ic (krō-măt′ə-fĭl′ĭk) *adj.* Staining readily. Used of a cell or cell structure.

chro•mat•o•phore (krō-măt′ə-fôr′, -fōr′) *n. Biol.* **1.** A pigment-containing or pigment-producing cell, esp. in certain lizards, that by expansion or contraction can change the color of the skin. **2.** A specialized pigment-bearing organelle in certain photosynthetic bacteria and cyanobacteria. **— chro•mat′o•phor′ic** (-fôr′ĭk, -fŏr′-) *adj.*

chrome (krōm) *n.* **1.a.** Chromium or a chromium alloy. **b.** Something plated with a chromium alloy. **2.** A pigment containing chromium. *—tr.v.* **chromed, chrom•ing, chromes. 1.** To plate with chromium. **2.** To tan or dye with a chromium compound. [Fr. < Gk. *khrōma,* color.]

–chrome *suff.* **1.** Colored: *polychrome.* **2.** Color; pigment: *urochrome.* [< Gk. *khrōma,* color.]

chrome alum *n.* A crystalline compound, $CrK(SO_4)_2{\cdot}12H_2O$, used in tanning and in photography.

chrome green *n.* **1.** Any of a class of green pigments consisting of chrome yellow and iron blue in various proportions. **2.** *Color.* A very dark yellowish green to moderate or strong green.

chrome red *n.* A light orange to red pigment consisting of basic lead chromate, $PbCrO_4$, with varying amounts of lead oxide, PbO.

chrome yellow *n.* Lead chromate, $PbCrO_4$, a yellow pigment often combined with lead sulfate, $PbSO_4$, for lighter hues.

chro•mic (krō′mĭk) *adj.* Of, relating to, or containing chromium, esp. with valence 3.

chromic acid *n.* **1.** A corrosive, oxidizing acid, H_2CrO_4, occurring only as salts or in solution. **2.** The anhydride of chromic acid, CrO_3, a crystalline material that reacts explosively with reducing agents and is used as an oxidizing agent.

chromic oxide *n.* A bright green crystalline powder, Cr_2O_3, used in metallurgy and as a paint pigment.

chro•mite (krō′mīt′) *n.* A widely distributed black to brownish-black chromium ore, $FeCr_2O_4$.

chro•mi•um (krō′mē-əm) *n. Symbol* **Cr** A lustrous hard metallic element, resistant to tarnish and corrosion and found primarily in chromite. It is used to harden steel alloys, in decorative platings, and as a pigment in glass. Atomic number 24; atomic weight 51.996; melting point 1,890°C; boiling point 2,482°C; specific gravity 7.18; valence 2, 3, 6. See table at **element.** [< Fr. *chrome.* See CHROME.]

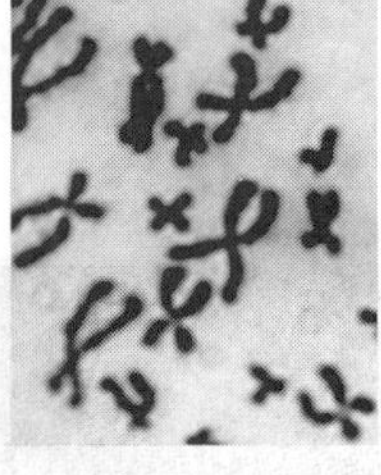
chromosome
Human chromosomes

chromo– or **chrom–** *pref.* **1.** Color: *chromoplast.* **2.** Chromium: *chromous.* [< Gk. *khrōma,* color.]

chro•mo•dy•nam•ics (krō′mō-dī-năm′ĭks) *n.* *(used with a sing. v.)* The theory of the strong interaction that postulates the exchange of gluons between color-carrying quarks.

chro•mo•gen (krō′mə-jən) *n.* **1.** *Chem.* A substance capable of conversion into a pigment or dye. **2.** *Biol.* A strongly pigmented or pigment-generating organelle, organ, or microorganism. **— chro′mo•gen′ic** (-jĕn′ĭk) *adj.*

chro•mo•lith•o•graph (krō′mə-lĭth′ə-grăf′) *n.* A colored print produced by chromolithography.

chro•mo•li•thog•ra•phy (krō′mə-lĭ-thŏg′rə-fē) *n.* The art or process of printing color pictures from a series of stone or zinc plates by lithography. **— chro′mo•li•thog′ra•pher** *n.* **— chro′mo•lith′o•graph′ic** (-lĭth′ə-grăf′ĭk) *adj.*

chro•mo•mere (krō′mə-mîr′) *n.* One of the serially aligned beadlike granules of concentrated chromatin that constitutes a chromosome during the early phases of cell division. **— chro′mo•mer′ic** (-mĕr′ĭk, -mîr′-) *adj.*

chro•mo•ne•ma (krō′mə-nē′mə) *n., pl.* **-ma•ta** (-mə-tə). The spirally coiled central filament of a chromatid along which the chromomeres are aligned. [CHROMO(SOME) + Gk. *nēma,* thread; see **(s)nē-***.] **— chro′mo•ne′mal** (-nē′məl), **chro•mo′ne•mat′al** (-nē-măt′l), **chro′mo•ne•mat′ic** (-nə-măt′ĭk), **chro′mo•ne′mic** (-nē′mĭk) *adj.*

chro•mo•phil (krō′mə-fĭl′) *adj.* Readily stained with dyes.

chro•mo•phore (krō′mə-fôr′, -fōr′) *n.* A chemical group capable of selective light absorption resulting in the coloration of certain organic compounds. **— chro′mo•phor′ic** *adj.*

chro•mo•plast (krō′mə-plăst′) *n. Bot.* A plastid that contains pigments other than chlorophyll, usu. yellow or orange carotenoids.

chro•mo•pro•tein (krō′mə-prō′tēn, -tē-ĭn) *n.* A conjugated protein, such as hemoglobin, that contains a colored metal-containing prosthetic group, such as heme.

chro•mo•some (krō′mə-sōm′) *n.* **1.** A threadlike linear strand of DNA and associated proteins in the nucleus of animal and plant cells that carries the genes and functions in the transmission of hereditary information. **2.** A circular strand of DNA in bacteria and cyanobacteria that contains the hereditary information necessary for cell life. **— chro′mo•so′mal** (-sō′məl), **chro′mo•so′mic** (-sō′mĭk) *adj.*

chro•mo•sphere (krō′mə-sfîr′) *n.* **1.** An incandescent transparent layer of gas, primarily hydrogen, several thousand miles in depth, lying above and surrounding the photosphere of the sun. **2.** A gaseous layer similar to a chromosphere around a star. **— chro′mo•spher′ic** (-sfîr′ĭk, -sfĕr′-) *adj.*

chro•mous (krō′məs) *adj.* Of, relating to, or containing chromium, esp. with valence 2.

chron. *abbr.* **1.** Chronicle. **2.** Chronological. **3.** Chronology.

Chron. *abbr. Bible.* Chronicles.

chro•nax•ie also **chro•nax•y** (krō′năk′sē, krŏn′ăk′-) *n., pl.* **-ies.** The minimum time necessary to electrically stimulate a muscle or nerve fiber, using twice the minimum current needed to elicit a threshold response. [Fr. : Gk. *khronos,* time + Gk. *axia,* value (< *axios,* worthy; see **ag-***).]

chron•ic (krŏn′ĭk) *adj.* **1.** Of long duration; continuing: *chronic problems.* **2.** Lasting for a long period of time or marked by frequent recurrence: *chronic colitis.* **3.** Subject to a habit or pattern of behavior for a long time. [Fr. *chronique* < Lat. *chronicus* < Gk. *khronikos,* of time < *khronos,* time.] **— chron′i•cal•ly** *adv.* **— chro•nic′i•ty** (krŏ-nĭs′ĭ-tē) *n.*

chron•i•cle (krŏn′ĭ-kəl) *n.* **1.** An account of historical events presented in chronological order. **2.** A detailed narrative record or report. **3. Chronicles.** *(used with a sing. v.)* See table at **Bible.** *—tr.v.* **-cled, -cling, -cles.** To record in or in the form of a historical record. [ME *cronicle* < AN, alteration of OFr. *cronique* < Lat. *chronica* < Gk. *khronika (biblia),* chronological (books), annals < *khronikos,* of time. See CHRONIC.] **— chron′i•cler** (-klər) *n.*

chrono– or **chron–** *pref.* Time: *chronometer.* [< Gk. *khronos,* time.]

chron•o•bi•ol•o•gy (krŏn′ō-bī-ŏl′ə-jē) *n.* The study of the effects of time and rhythmical phenomena on life processes.

chron•o•gram (krŏn′ə-grăm′, krō′nə-) *n.* **1.** The record produced by a chronograph. **2.** An inscribed phrase in which certain letters can be read as Roman numerals indicating a specific date. **— chron′o•gram•mat′ic** (-grə-măt′ĭk) *adj.* **— chron′o•gram•mat′i•cal•ly** *adv.*

chron•o•graph (krŏn′ə-grăf′, krō′nə-) *n.* An instrument that registers or graphically records time intervals. **— chron′o•graph′ic** *adj.* **— chron′o•graph′i•cal•ly** *adv.*

chronol. *abbr.* **1.** Chronological. **2.** Chronology.

chron•o•log•i•cal (krŏn′ə-lŏj′ĭ-kəl, krō′nə-) also **chron•o•log•ic** (-lŏj′ĭk) *adj.* **1.** Arranged in order of time of occurrence. **2.** Relating to or in accordance with chronology. **— chron′o•log′i•cal•ly** *adv.*

chro•nol•o•gy (krə-nŏl′ə-jē) *n., pl.* **-gies. 1.** The science that deals with the determination of dates and the sequence of events. **2.** The arrangement of events in time. **3.** A chronological list or table. **— chro•nol′o•gist** *n.*

chro•nom•e•ter (krə-nŏm′ĭ-tər) *n.* An exceptionally precise timepiece. **— chron′o•met′ric** (krŏn′ə-mĕt′rĭk, krō′nə-), **chron′o•met′ri•cal** *adj.* **— chron′o•met′ri•cal•ly** *adv.*

chro•nom•e•try (krə-nŏm′ĭ-trē) *n.* The scientific measurement of time.

chron•o•scope (krŏn′ə-skōp′, krō′nə-) *n.* An optical instrument for the precise measurement of very small time intervals. **— chron′o•scop′ic** (-skŏp′ĭk) *adj.*

chrys•a•lid (krĭs′ə-lĭd) *n.* A chrysalis. *—adj.* Relating to or resembling a chrysalis.

chrys•a•lis (krĭs′ə-lĭs) *n., pl.* **chrys•a•lis•es** or **chry•sal•i•des** (krĭ-săl′ĭ-dēz′). A pupa, esp. of a butterfly, enclosed in a firm case or cocoon. [Lat. *chrȳsallis* < Gk. *khrusallis, khrusallid-,* gold-colored pupa < *khrus-,* chryso-.]

chry•san•the•mum (krĭ-săn′thə-məm, -zăn′-) *n.* **1.** Any of numerous Eurasian plants of the genus *Chrysanthemum* in the composite family, many of which are cultivated for their showy flower heads. **2.** A flower head of one of these plants. [Lat. *chrȳsanthemum* < Gk. *khrusanthemon,* gold flower : *khrus-,* chryso- + *anthemon,* flower (< *anthos*).]

chrys•el•e•phan•tine (krĭ-sĕl′ə-făn′tēn′, -tīn′) *adj.* Made of gold and ivory. [Gk. *khruselephantinos* : *khrus-,* chryso- + *elephas, elephant-,* ivory; see ELEPHANT.]

chryso– or **chrys–** *pref.* Gold; golden: *chrysotherapy.* [Gk. *khrus-, khruso-* < *khrusos,* gold, of Semitic orig.]

chrys•o•ber•yl (krĭs′ə-bĕr′əl) *n.* A green to yellow vitreous mineral, $BeAl_2O_4$, used as a gemstone. [Lat. *chrȳsobēryllus* < Gk. *khrusobērullos* : *khruso-,* chryso- + *bērullos,* beryl; see BERYL.]

chrys•o•lite (krĭs′ə-līt′) *n.* See **olivine.** [ME *crisolite* < OFr. <

Med.Lat. *crīsolitus* < Lat. *chrȳsolithus* < Gk. *khrusolithos,* topaz : *khruso-*, chryso- + *lithos,* stone.]

chrys·o·mel·id (krĭs′ə-mĕl′ĭd, -mē′lĭd) *n.* Any of various beetles of the family Chrysomelidae. [< NLat. *Chrysomela,* type genus < Gk. *khrusomēlon,* quince : *khruso-*, chryso- + *mēlon,* apple.] **— chrys′o·mel′id** *adj.*

chrys·o·prase (krĭs′ə-prāz′) *n.* An apple-green chalcedony used as a gemstone. [ME *crisopase* < OFr. *crisopras* < Lat. *chrȳsoprasus* < Gk. *khrusoprasos* : *khruso-*, chryso- + *prason,* leek; see PRASEODYMIUM.]

Chry·sos·tom (krĭs′əs-təm, krĭ-sŏs′-), Saint **John.** A.D. 347?–407. Antioch-born patriarch of Constantinople (398–404).

chrys·o·ther·a·py (krĭs′ō-thĕr′ə-pē) *n.* The treatment of diseases, esp. rheumatoid arthritis, with gold compounds.

chrys·o·tile (krĭs′ə-tĭl′) *n.* A fibrous mineral variety of serpentine forming part of commercial asbestos. [Ger. *Chrysotil* : Gk. *khruso-*, chryso- + Gk. *tilos,* something plucked (< *tillein,* to pluck).]

chthon·ic (thŏn′ĭk) also **chtho·ni·an** (thō′nē-ən) *adj. Gk. Myth.* Of underworld gods and spirits. [< Gk. *khthonios,* earthly < *khthōn,* earth. See **dhghem-***.]

Chu (cho͞o). A river of S Kazakhstan flowing c. 1,126 km (700 mi) E into Issyk-Kul.

chub (chŭb) *n., pl.* **chub** or **chubs. 1.** Any of various freshwater fishes of the family Cyprinidae related to the carps and minnows, esp. a Eurasian species, *Leuciscus cephalus.* **2.** Any of various North American fishes, such as a freshwater whitefish of the genus *Coregonus.* [ME *chubbe.*]

chub·by (chŭb′ē) *adj.* **-bi·er, -bi·est.** Rounded and plump. See Syns at **fat.** [Prob. < CHUB (< the plumpness of the fish).] **— chub′bi·ly** *adv.* **— chub′bi·ness** *n.*

Chu·but (chə-bo͞ot′, cho͞o-). A river rising in SW Argentina and flowing c. 805 km (500 mi) E to the Atlantic Ocean.

chuck[1] (chŭk) *tr.v.* **chucked, chuck·ing, chucks. 1.** To pat or squeeze fondly or playfully, esp. under the chin. **2.a.** To throw or toss. **b.** *Informal.* To throw out; discard. **c.** *Informal.* To force out; eject: *chucking out the troublemakers.* **3.** *Informal.* To give up; quit. **—** *n.* **1.** An affectionate pat or squeeze under the chin. **2.** A throw, toss, or pitch. [Var. of *chock,* poss. < Fr. *choc,* knock, blow. See SHOCK[1].]

chuck[2] (chŭk) *n.* **1.** A cut of beef extending from the neck to the ribs and including the shoulder blade. **2.a.** A clamp that holds a tool or the material being worked in a machine such as a lathe. **b.** A clamping device for holding a drill bit. [Dial. *chuck,* lump, perh. var. of CHOCK.]

chuck[3] (chŭk) *intr.v.* **chucked, chuck·ing, chucks.** To make a clucking sound. **—** *n.* A clucking sound. [ME *chukken,* of imit. orig.]

chuck·hole (chŭk′hōl′) *n.* See **pothole** 1. [Prob. < CHUCK[1].]

chuck·le (chŭk′əl) *intr.v.* **-led, -ling, -les. 1.** To laugh quietly or to oneself. **2.** To cluck or chuck, as a hen. **—** *n.* A quiet laugh. [Prob. freq. of CHUCK[3].] **— chuck′ler** *n.* **— chuck′le·some** *adj.* **— chuck′ling·ly** (-lĭng-lē) *adv.*

chuck·le·head (chŭk′əl-hĕd′) *n. Informal.* A stupid, gauche person. [Poss. < CHUCK[2].] **— chuck′le·head′ed** *adj.*

chuck wagon *n.* A wagon equipped with food and cooking utensils, as on a ranch or in a lumber camp.

chuck·wal·la (chŭk′wŏl′ə) *n.* A large herbaceous lizard *(Sauromalus obesus)* of the southwest United States and Mexico. [Am.Sp. *chacahuala* < Cahuilla *tcáxxwal.*]

chuck-will's-wid·ow (chŭk′wĭlz-wĭd′ō) *n.* A bird *(Caprimulgus carolinensis)* of the southern and central United States, resembling the whippoorwill. [Imit. of its call.]

chud·dar (chŭd′ər) *n.* **1.** A chador. **2.** A cotton shawl traditionally worn in India. [Urdu *chaddar,* cloth < Skt. *chattram,* screen, parasol < *chadati,* he covers, protects.]

chu·fa (cho͞o′fə) *n.* An Old World sedge *(Cyperus esculentus* var. *sativus)* having edible nutlike tubers. [< Sp. *chufar,* to make fun of, alteration of *chuflar* < VLat. **sufilāre,* alteration of Lat. *sībilāre, sīfilāre,* whistle at. See SIBILANT.]

chuff[1] (chŭf) *n.* A rude, insensitive person; a boor. [ME *chuffe.*]

chuff[2] (chŭf) *intr.v.* **chuffed, chuf·fing, chuffs.** To produce or move with chuffs. **—** *n.* A noisy puffing or explosive sound. [Imit.]

chug (chŭg) *n.* A dull explosive sound made repeatedly by a laboring engine. **—** *intr.v.* **chugged, chug·ging, chugs. 1.** To make dull explosive sounds. **2.** To move or travel while chugging. [Imit.] **— chug′ger** *n.*

chug·a·lug (chŭg′ə-lŭg′) *Slang.* **—** *v.* **-lugged, -lug·ging, -lugs. —** *tr.* To drink (a container of beer, for example) without pausing. **—** *intr.* To drink a beverage without pausing. [Imit.]

chu·kar (chə-kär′) *n.* A Eurasian partridge *(Alectoris graeca)* with grayish-brown plumage and red legs and bill. [Hindi *cakor* < Skt. *cakoraḥ.*]

Chuk·chi also **Chuk·chee** (cho͝ok′chē) *n., pl.* **Chukchi** or **-chis** also **Chukchee** or **-chees. 1.** A member of a people of northeast Siberia. **2.** The language of the Chukchi. [Russ., pl. of *chukcha* < Chukchi *chawchəw.*]

Chukchi Peninsula. A peninsula of extreme NE Russia bordering on the **Chukchi Sea,** a section of the Arctic Ocean.

Chu Kiang (cho͞o′ kyäng′, jo͞o′ gyäng′). See **Zhu Jiang.**

chuk·ka (chŭk′ə) *n.* A short boot, usu. made of suede, having two or three pairs of eyelets. [Alteration of CHUKKER.]

chuk·ker also **chuk·kar** (chŭk′ər) *n. Sports.* One of the periods of play, lasting 7½ minutes, in a polo match. [Hindi *cakkar,* circle, turn < Skt. *cakram.* See **kʷel-[1]***.]

Chu·la Vis·ta (cho͞o′lə vĭs′tə). A city of S CA S of San Diego. Pop. 135,163.

Chu·lym also **Chu·lim** (chə-lĭm′, cho͞o-). A river of S-central Russia flowing c. 1,730 km (1,075 mi) to the Ob R.

chum[1] (chŭm) *n.* An intimate friend or companion. **—** *intr.v.* **chummed, chum·ming, chums. 1.a.** To be an intimate friend. **b.** To display good-natured friendliness. **2.** To share the same room, as in a dormitory. [Perh. short for *chamber fellow,* roommate.]

chum[2] (chŭm) *n.* Bait usu. consisting of oily fish ground up and scattered on the water. **—** *v.* **chummed, chum·ming, chums. —** *intr.* To fish with chum. **—** *tr.* To lure (fish) with chum. [?]

chum[3] (chŭm) *n.* A chum salmon.

Chu·mash (cho͞o′măsh) *n., pl.* **Chumash** or **-mash·es.** A member of a group of Hokan-speaking Native American peoples inhabiting the southern California coastal region around Santa Barbara.

chum·my (chŭm′ē) *adj.* **-mi·er, -mi·est.** Intimate; friendly. **— chum′mi·ly** *adv.* **— chum′mi·ness** *n.*

chump[1] (chŭmp) *n.* A stupid or foolish person; a dolt. [Perh. blend of CHUNK and LUMP[1] or STUMP.]

chump[2] (chŭmp) *tr. & intr.v.* **chumped, chump·ing, chumps.** To chew or make a chewing movement. [Var. of CHAMP[1].]

chum salmon *n.* A Pacific salmon *(Oncorhynchus keta)* with specks on its back. [Chinook Jargon *cam,* spotted, striped < Lower Chinook *c'ám(·),* variegated.]

Chung·king (cho͝ong′kĭng′, jo͝ong′gĭng′). See **Chongqing.**

chunk (chŭngk) *n.* **1.** A thick mass or piece. **2.** *Informal.* A substantial amount. **3.** A strong, stocky horse. **—** *v.* **chunked, chunk·ing, chunks. —** *tr.* To form into chunks. **—** *intr.* To make a dull clacking sound. [Perh. var. of CHUCK[2].]

chunk·y (chŭng′kē) *adj.* **-i·er, -i·est. 1.** Short and thick; stocky. **2.** Containing small thick pieces: *chunky soup.* **— chunk′i·ly** *adv.* **— chunk′i·ness** *n.*

chun·nel (chŭn′əl) *n.* A railroad tunnel under the English Channel. [CH(ANNEL)[1] + (T)UNNEL.]

church

church (chûrch) *n.* **1.** A building for public, esp. Christian worship. **2.** Often **Church. a.** The company of all Christians regarded as a mystic spiritual body. **b.** A specified Christian denomination. **c.** A congregation. **3.** Public divine worship in a church; a religious service. **4.** The clerical profession; clergy. **5.** Ecclesiastical power as distinguished from the secular. **—** *tr.v.* **churched, church·ing, church·es.** To conduct a church service for (a woman after childbirth). **—** *adj.* Of or relating to the church; ecclesiastical. [ME *chirche* < OE *cirice,* ult. < Med.Gk. *kurikon* < LGk. *kuriakon (dōma),* the Lord's (house) < Gk. *kuriakos,* of the lord < *kurios,* lord. See **keuə-***.]

Church (chûrch), **Frederick Edwin.** 1826–1900. Amer. painter who was a leader of the Hudson River School.

church father or **Church Father** *n.* Any of the authoritative early writers in the Christian church who formulated doctrines and codified religious observances.

church·go·er (chûrch′gō′ər) *n.* One who attends church. **— church′go′ing** *adj. & n.*

Chur·chill (chûr′chĭl′, chûrch′hĭl′), **John.** 1st Duke of Marlborough. 1650–1722. English general and public figure during the reigns of James II, Anne, and George I.

Churchill, Mount. A peak, 4,769.6 m (15,638 ft), in the Wrangell Mts. of S AK.

Churchill, Randolph Henry Spencer. 1849–95. British politician who advocated social and constitutional reform.

Winston S. Churchill

Churchill, Winston. 1871–1947. Amer. writer whose historical novels include *Richard Carvel* (1899).

Churchill, Sir **Winston Leonard Spenser.** 1874–1965. British politician who served as prime minister (1940–45 and 1951–55) and won the 1953 Nobel Prize for literature. **— Chur·chill′i·an** (chûr-chĭl′ē-ən) *adj.*

Churchill Falls. Formerly **Grand Falls** (grănd). A waterfall, 74.7 m (245 ft), of the Churchill R. in SW Labrador, Canada.

Churchill River. 1. A river of E Canada flowing c. 965 km (600 mi) across Labrador to the Atlantic Ocean. **2.** A river rising in NW Saskatchewan, Canada, and flowing c. 1,609 km (1,000 mi) to Hudson Bay in N Manitoba.

church key *n.* A can or bottle opener usu. having a triangular head.

church·ly (chûrch′lē) *adj.* **1.** Of or relating to a church. **2.** Appropriate for a church. **— church′li·ness** *n.*

church·man (chûrch′mən) *n.* **1.** A man who is a cleric. **2.** A man who is a member of a church. **— church′man·ly** *adj.* **— church′man·ship′** *n.*

Church of Christ, Scientist *n.* See **Christian Science.**

Church of England *n.* The episcopal and liturgical national church of England.

Church of Jesus Christ of Lat·ter-day Saints (lat′ər-dā′) *n.* See **Mormon Church.**

Church of Rome *n.* The Roman Catholic Church.

ă pat	oi boy
ā pay	ou out
âr care	o͝o took
ä father	o͞o boot
ĕ pet	ŭ cut
ē be	ûr urge
ĭ pit	th thin
ī pie	*th* this
îr pier	hw which
ŏ pot	zh vision
ō toe	ə about,
ô paw	item

Stress marks:
′ (primary);
′ (secondary), as in
dictionary (dĭk′shə-nĕr′ē)

from a given fixed point, the center. **2.** A planar region bounded by a circle. **3.** Something, such as a ring, shaped like such a plane curve. **4.** A circular course, circuit, or orbit. **5.** A curved section or tier of seats in a theater. **6.** A series or process that finishes at its starting point or repeats itself; a cycle. **7.** A group of people sharing an interest, activity, or achievement. **8.** A territorial or administrative division, esp. of a province, in some European countries. **9.** A sphere of influence or interest; domain. **10.** *Logic.* A vicious circle. — *v.* **-cled, -cling, -cles.** — *tr.* **1.** To make or form a circle around; enclose. **2.** To move in a circle around. — *intr.* To move in a circle. [ME *cercle* < OFr. < Lat. *circulus,* dim. of *circus,* circle < Gk. *kirkos, krikos.* See **sker-^{2}*.**] — **cir′cler** (-klər) *n.*

circle graph *n.* See **pie chart.**

cir•clet (sûr′klĭt) *n.* A small circle, esp. a circular ornament. [ME *cerclet* < OFr., dim. of *cercle,* circle. See CIRCLE.]

cir•cuit (sûr′kĭt) *n.* **1.a.** A closed, usu. circular line that goes around an object or area. **b.** The region enclosed by such a line. See Syns at **circumference. 2.a.** A path or route that returns to its starting point. **b.** The act of following such a path or route. **c.** A journey made on such a path or route. **3.** *Electron.* **a.** A closed path followed by an electric current. **b.** A configuration of electrically or electromagnetically connected components or devices. **4.a.** A regular or accustomed course from place to place; a round: *the lecture circuit.* **b.** The area or district thus covered, esp. a territory under the jurisdiction of a judge in which periodic court sessions are held. **5.a.** An association of theaters among which plays, acts, or films move for presentation. **b.** A group of nightclubs, show halls, or resorts at which entertainers appear in turn. **c.** An association of teams, clubs, or arenas of competition. — *intr.* & *tr.v.* **-cuit•ed, -cuit•ing, -cuits.** To make a circuit or circuit of. [ME, circumference < OFr. < Lat. *circuitus,* a going around < p.part. of *circumīre,* to go around : *circum-,* circum- + *īre,* to go; see **ei-*.**]

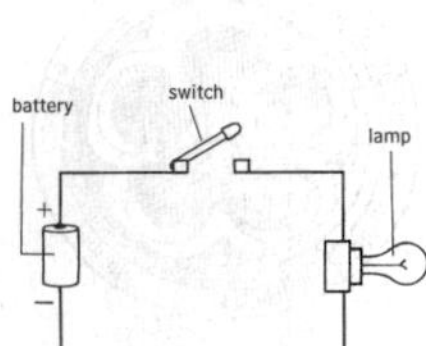

circuit
Electrical circuit

circuit board *n. Comp. Sci.* An insulated board on which interconnected circuits and components such as microchips are mounted or etched.

circuit breaker *n.* An automatic switch that stops the flow of electric current in an overloaded electric circuit.

circuit court *n. Law.* A state court that holds sessions at several different places within a judicial district.

cir•cu•i•tous (sər-kyo͞o′ĭ-təs) *adj.* Being or taking a roundabout, lengthy course. [< Med.Lat. *circuitōsus* < Lat. *circuitus,* a going around. See CIRCUIT.] — **cir•cu′i•tous•ly** *adv.* — **cir•cu′i•ty, cir•cu′i•tous•ness** *n.*

circuit rider *n.* A cleric who travels from church to church.

cir•cuit•ry (sûr′kĭ-trē) *n., pl.* **-ries. 1.** The design of or a detailed plan for an electric circuit. **2.** Electric circuits considered as a group.

cir•cu•lar (sûr′kyə-lər) *adj.* **1.** Of or relating to a circle. **2.a.** Shaped like or nearly like a circle; round. **b.** Moving in or forming a circle. **3.** Circuitous; roundabout. **4.** Marked by reasoning in a circle: *a circular theory.* **5.** Addressed or distributed to a large number of persons. — *n.* A circular printed advertisement, directive, or notice. [ME *circuler* < AN < Lat. *circulāris* < *circulus,* circle. See CIRCLE.] — **cir′cu•lar′i•ty** (-lăr′ĭ-tē) *n.* — **cir′cu•lar•ly** *adv.*

circular saw

circular function *n.* See **trigonometric function.**

cir•cu•lar•ize (sûr′kyə-lə-rīz′) *tr.v.* **-ized, -iz•ing, -iz•es. 1.** To publicize with circulars. **2.** To canvass or poll using a questionnaire. — **cir′cu•lar•i•za′tion** (-lər-ĭ-zā′shən) *n.*

circular saw *n.* A power saw for cutting wood or metal consisting of a toothed disk rotated at high speed.

cir•cu•late (sûr′kyə-lāt′) *v.* **-lat•ed, -lat•ing, -lates.** — *intr.* **1.** To move in or flow through a circle or circuit: *blood circulating through the body.* **2.** To move around, as from person to person or place to place. **3.** To move about or flow freely, as air. **4.** To spread widely among persons or places; disseminate. — *tr.* To cause to move about or be distributed. [< ME *circulat,* continuously distilled < *circulātus,* p.part. of *circulāre,* to make circular < *circulus,* circle. See CIRCLE.] — **cir′cu•la′tive** (-lā′tĭv) *adj.* — **cir′cu•la′tor** *n.*

cir•cu•lat•ing decimal (sûr′kyə-lā′tĭng) *n.* See **repeating decimal.**

circulating library *n.* See **lending library.**

cir•cu•la•tion (sûr′kyə-lā′shən) *n.* **1.** Movement in a circle or circuit, esp. the movement of blood through the circulatory system. **2.a.** Movement or passage through a system of vessels, as of water through pipes; flow. **b.** Free movement or passage. **3.** The passing of something, such as money, from place to place or person to person. **4.a.** The condition of being passed about and widely known; distribution. **b.** Dissemination of printed material among readers. **c.** The number of copies of a publication sold or distributed.

cirrocumulus

cir•cu•la•tor•y (sûr′kyə-lə-tôr′ē, -tōr′ē) *adj.* **1.** Of or relating to circulation. **2.** Of or relating to the circulatory system.

circulatory system *n.* The system of structures, consisting of the heart, blood vessels, and lymphatics, by which blood and lymph are circulated throughout the body.

circum. *abbr.* Circumference.

circum– *pref.* Around; about: *circumlunar.* [Lat. < *circum,* around, accusative of *circus,* circle. See CIRCLE.]

cir•cum•am•bi•ent (sûr′kəm-ăm′bē-ənt) *adj.* Encompassing on all sides; surrounding. — **cir′cum•am′bi•ence, cir′cum•am′bi•en•cy** *n.* — **cir′cum•am′bi•ent•ly** *adv.*

cir•cum•am•bu•late (sûr′kəm-ăm′byə-lāt′) *tr.v.* **-lat•ed, -lat•ing, -lates.** To walk around (something), esp. as part of a ritual. — **cir′cum•am′bu•la′tion** *n.*

cir•cum•bo•re•al (sûr′kəm-bôr′ē-əl, -bōr′-) *adj.* Distributed or occurring chiefly throughout the boreal regions of North America and Eurasia. Used esp. of plants.

cir•cum•cise (sûr′kəm-sīz′) *tr.v.* **-cised, -cis•ing, -cis•es. 1.** To remove the foreskin of (a male). **2.** To remove the foreskin or a part of the clitoris of (a female). [ME *circumcisen* < Lat. *circumcīdere, circumcīs-,* to cut around (transl. of Gk. *peritemnein*) : *circum-,* circum- + *caedere,* to cut; see **kaə-id-*.**] — **cir′cum•cis′er** *n.*

cir•cum•ci•sion (sûr′kəm-sĭzh′ən) *n.* **1.** The act of circumcising. **2.** A religious ceremony in which someone is circumcised. **3. Circumcision.** A Christian feast celebrating the circumcision of Jesus, celebrated on January 1.

cir•cum•duc•tion (sûr′kəm-dŭk′shən) *n.* The circular movement of a limb such that the distal end of the limb delineates an arc. [Ult. < Lat. *circumdūcere,* to lead around : *circum-,* circum- + *dūcere,* to lead; see **deuk-*.**]

cir•cum•fer•ence (sər-kŭm′fər-əns) *n.* **1.** The boundary line of a circle. **2.a.** The boundary line of a figure, area, or object. **b.** The length of such a boundary. [ME < OFr. *circonference* < Lat. *circumferentia* < *circumferēns, circumferent-,* pr.part. of *circumferre,* to carry around : *circum-,* circum- + *ferre,* to carry; see **bher-^{1}*.**] — **cir•cum′fer•en′tial** (-fə-rĕn′shəl) *adj.*

Syns: *circumference, circuit, compass, perimeter, periphery.* The meaning of these nouns is "a line around a closed figure or area": *the circumference of the earth; a park five miles in circuit; the compass of the schoolyard; the perimeter of a rectangle; a fence around the periphery.*

cir•cum•flex (sûr′kəm-flĕks′) *n.* A mark (ˆ) used over a vowel in certain languages or in phonetic keys to indicate quality of pronunciation. — *adj.* **1.** Having this mark. **2.** Curving around: *a circumflex blood vessel.* [< Lat. *circumflexus,* bent around, circumflex, p.part. of *circumflectere,* to bend around : *circum-,* circum- + *flectere,* to bend.]

cir•cum•flu•ent (sər-kŭm′flo͞o-ənt) also **cir•cum•flu•ous** (-əs) *adj.* Flowing around or surrounding.

cir•cum•fuse (sûr′kəm-fyo͞oz′) *tr.v.* **-fused, -fus•ing, -fus•es. 1.** To pour or diffuse around; spread. **2.** To surround, as with liquid; suffuse. [Lat. *circumfundere, circumfūs-* : *circum-,* circum- + *fundere,* to pour; see **gheu-*.**] — **cir′cum•fu′sion** *n.*

cir•cum•lo•cu•tion (sûr′kəm-lō-kyo͞o′shən) *n.* **1.** The use of unnecessarily wordy and indirect language. **2.** Evasion in speech or writing. **3.** A roundabout expression. [Ult. < Lat. *circumlocūtiō, circumlocūtiōn-* < *circumlocūtus,* p.part. of *circumloquī* : *circum-,* circum- + *loquī,* to speak; see **tolk^{w}-*.**] — **cir′cum•loc′u•to′ri•ly** (-lŏk′yə-tôr′ə-lē, -tōr′-) *adv.* — **cir′cum•loc′u•to′ry** (-tôr′ē, -tōr′ē) *adj.*

cir•cum•lu•nar (sûr′kəm-lo͞o′nər) *adj.* Revolving about or surrounding the moon.

cir•cum•nav•i•gate (sûr′kəm-năv′ĭ-gāt′) *tr.v.* **-gat•ed, -gat•ing, -gates. 1.** To proceed completely around: *circumnavigating the earth.* **2.** To go around; circumvent. — **cir′cum•nav′i•ga′tion** *n.* — **cir′cum•nav′i•ga′tor** *n.*

cir•cum•po•lar (sûr′kəm-pō′lər) *adj.* **1.** Located or found in one of the Polar Regions. **2.** *Astron.* Being a star that from a given observer's latitude does not go below the horizon.

cir•cum•ro•tate (sûr′kəm-rō′tāt′) *intr.v.* **-tat•ed, -tat•ing, -tat•es.** To turn like a wheel; revolve. — **cir′cum•ro•ta′tion** *n.* — **cir′cum•ro′ta•to′ry** (-tə-tôr′ē, -tōr′ē) *adj.*

cir•cum•scis•sile (sûr′kəm-sĭs′ĭl, -īl′) *adj. Bot.* Splitting or opening along a circumference, with the top coming off as a lid: *a circumscissile seed capsule.* [CIRCUM- + Lat. *scissilis,* easily split, splitting; see SCISSILE.]

cir•cum•scribe (sûr′kəm-skrīb′) *tr.v.* **-scribed, -scrib•ing, -scribes. 1.** To draw a line around; encircle. **2.** To limit narrowly; restrict. **3.** To determine the limits of; define. **4.a.** To enclose (a polygon or polyhedron) within a configuration of lines or surfaces so that every vertex of the enclosed object is incident on the enclosing configuration. **b.** To erect (such a configuration) around a polygon or polyhedron. [ME *circumscriben* < Lat. *circumscrībere* : *circum-,* circum- + *scrībere,* to write; see **skrībh-*.**] — **cir′cum•scrib′a•ble** *adj.* — **cir′cum•scrib′er** *n.*

cir•cum•scrip•tion (sûr′kəm-skrĭp′shən) *n.* **1.** The act of circumscribing or the state of being circumscribed. **2.** Something, such as a limit, that circumscribes. **3.** A circumscribed space or area. **4.** A circular inscription, as on a medallion. [Lat. *circumscrīptiō, circumscrīptiōn-* < *circumscrīptus,* p.part. of *circumscrībere,* to circumscribe. See CIRCUMSCRIBE.] — **cir′cum•scrip′tive** *adj.* — **cir′cum•scrip′tive•ly** *adv.*

cir•cum•so•lar (sûr′kəm-sō′lər) *adj.* Revolving around or surrounding the sun.

cir•cum•spect (sûr′kəm-spĕkt′) *adj.* Heedful of circumstances and potential consequences; prudent. [ME < Lat. *circumspec-*

tus, p.part. of *circumspicere*, to take heed : *circum-*, circum- + *specere*, to look; see **spek-***.] **—cir′cum·spect′ly** *adv.*

cir·cum·spec·tion (sûr′kəm-spĕk′shən) *n.* The state or quality of being circumspect. See Syns at **prudence.**

cir·cum·stance (sûr′kəm-stăns′) *n.* **1.** A condition or fact attending an event and having some bearing on it; a determining or modifying factor. **2.** A condition or fact that determines or must be considered in the determining of a course of action. **3.** The sum of determining factors beyond willful control. Often used in the plural. **4. circumstances.** Financial status or means. **5.** Detail accompanying or surrounding an event, as in a narrative or series of events. **6.** Formal display; ceremony: *pomp and circumstance.* **7.** A particular incident or occurrence. See Syns at **occurrence.** *—tr.v.* **-stanced, -stanc·ing, -stanc·es.** To place in particular circumstances or conditions; situate. **—*idioms.* under no circumstances.** In no case; never. **under (**or **in) the circumstances.** Given these conditions; such being the case. [ME < OFr. *circonstance* < Lat. *circumstantia* < *circumstāns, circumstant-*, pr.part. of *circumstāre*, to stand around : *circum-*, circum- + *stāre*, to stand; see **stā-***.]

Usage Note: Use of the idiom *under the circumstances* is justified by both logic and reputable precedent.

cir·cum·stan·tial (sûr′kəm-stăn′shəl) *adj.* **1.** Of, relating to, or dependent on circumstances. **2.** Of no primary significance; incidental. **3.** Complete and particular; full of detail: *a circumstantial report.* See Syns at **detailed. 4.** Full of ceremonial display. **—cir′cum·stan′tial·ly** *adv.*

circumstantial evidence *n. Law.* Evidence bearing on various attendant circumstances from which the judge or jury might infer the occurrence of a fact in dispute.

cir·cum·stan·ti·al·i·ty (sûr′kəm-stăn′shē-ăl′ĭ-tē) *n., pl.* **-ties. 1.** The quality of being fully or minutely detailed. **2.** A particular detail or circumstance.

cir·cum·stan·ti·ate (sûr′kəm-stăn′shē-āt′) *tr.v.* **-at·ed, -at·ing, -ates.** To set forth or verify with circumstances; give detailed proof or description of. **—cir′cum·stan′ti·a′tion** *n.*

cir·cum·ter·res·tri·al (sûr′kəm-tə-rĕs′trē-əl) *adj.* Revolving around or surrounding the earth.

cir·cum·val·late (sûr′kəm-văl′āt′) *tr.v.* **-lat·ed, -lat·ing, -lates.** To surround with or as if with a rampart. *—adj.* **1.** (*also* -ĭt). Surrounded with or as if with a rampart. **2.** *Anat.* Surrounded by a ridge or wall-like structure. [Lat. *circumvallāre, circumvallāt-* : *circum-*, circum- + *vallum*, rampart with palisades (< *vallus*, post, stake).] **—cir′cum·val·la′tion** *n.*

cir·cum·vent (sûr′kəm-vĕnt′) *tr.v.* **-vent·ed, -vent·ing, -vents. 1.** To surround (an enemy, for example); enclose or entrap. **2.** To go around; bypass. **3.** To avoid or get around by artful maneuvering. [ME *circumventen* < Lat. *circumvenīre, circumvent-* : *circum-*, circum- + *venīre*, to go, come; see **gʷā-***.] **—cir′cum·vent′er, cir′cum·ven′tor** *n.* **—cir′cum·ven′tion** *n.* **—cir′cu**[illegible]**′tive** *adj.*

cir·cum·vo·lu·tion ([illegible]və-lo͞o′shən, sûr′kəm-vō-) *n.* **1.** An act of turning, [illegible]folding about a center or an axis. **2.** A single turn, c[illegible] [Ult. < Lat. *circumvolvere, circumvolūt-*, to roll aro[illegible] CIRCUMVOLVE.]

cir·cum·volve (sûr′kəm-[illegible]*r. & tr.v.* **-volved, -volv·ing, -volves.** To revolve o[illegible]o revolve. [Lat. *circumvolvere* : *circum-*, circum- + [illegible], to roll; see **wel-²***.]

cir·cus (sûr′kəs) *n.* **1.a.** A pu[illegible]ntertainment consisting typically of a variety of perform[illegible]ces by acrobats, clowns, and trained animals. **b.** A traveling company that performs such entertainments. **c.** A circular arena, surrounded by tiers of seats and often covered by a tent, for such shows. **2.** A roofless oval enclosure surrounded by tiers of seats, used in antiquity for public spectacles. **3.** *Chiefly British.* An open circular place where several streets intersect. **4.** *Informal.* Something suggestive of a circus. [ME, round arena < Lat., circus, circle. See CIRCLE.] **—cir′cus·y** *adj.*

ci·ré also **cire** (sĭ-rā′) *—adj.* Having a highly glazed finish, usu. by the application of wax: *a ciré shirt.* *—n.* A fabric or garment with such a finish. [Fr., p.part. of *cirer*, to wax < Lat. *cērāre.* See CERATED.]

cirque (sûrk) *n.* A steep hollow occurring at the upper end of a mountain valley. [Fr. < Lat. *circus*, circle. See CIRCLE.]

cir·rate (sĭr′āt′) *adj. Biol.* Having or resembling a cirrus or cirri. [Lat. *cirrātus*, curled < *cirrus*, curl of hair.]

cir·rho·sis (sĭ-rō′sĭs) *n.* **1.** A chronic disease of the liver marked by replacement of normal tissue with fibrous tissue, resulting from alcohol abuse, nutritional deprivation, or infection. **2.** Chronic interstitial inflammation of any tissue or organ. [NLat. : Gk. *kirros*, tawny (from the color of the diseased liver) + -OSIS.] **—cir·rhot′ic** (-rŏt′ĭk) *adj.*

cir·ri·ped (sĭr′ə-pĕd′) also **cir·ri·pede** (-pēd′) *n.* Any of various crustaceans of the subclass Cirripedia, which includes the barnacles and related organisms that attach themselves to objects or become parasitic in the adult stage. [< NLat. *Cirripedia*, order name : CIRR(US) + -PED.] **—cir′ri·ped′** *adj.*

cirro– or **cirri–** *pref.* Cirrus cloud: *cirrostratus.* [< CIRRUS.]

cir·ro·cu·mu·lus (sĭr′ō-kyo͞om′yə-ləs) *n.* A high-altitude cloud composed of a series of small, regularly arranged cloudlets in the form of ripples or grains.

cir·ro·stra·tus (sĭr′ō-strā′təs, -străt′əs) *n.* A high-altitude, thin hazy cloud, usu. covering the sky and producing a halo effect.

cir·rus (sĭr′əs) *n., pl.* **cir·ri** (sĭr′ī′). **1.** A high-altitude cloud composed of narrow bands or patches of thin, generally white, fleecy parts. **2.** *Bot.* A tendril or similar part. **3.** *Zool.* A slender flexible appendage, such as the fused cilia of certain protozoans. [Lat., curl of hair.]

C.I.S. *abbr.* Commonwealth of Independent States.

cis– *pref.* **1.** On this side: *cisatlantic.* **2.** Having a pair of identical atoms or groups on the same side of a plane that passes through two carbon atoms linked by a double bond. Used of a geometric isomer: cis-*butene.* [Lat. < *cis*, on this side of. See **ko-***.]

cis·al·pine (sĭs-ăl′pīn′) *adj.* Relating to, living on, or coming from the southern side of the Alps. [Lat. *Cisalpīnus* : *cis-*, cis- + *alpīnus*, alpine; see ALPINE.]

Cis·al·pine Gaul (sĭs-ăl′pīn′ gôl′). A section of ancient Gaul S and E of the Alps in present-day Italy.

cis·at·lan·tic (sĭs′ət-lăn′tĭk) *adj.* Situated on this side of the Atlantic Ocean.

Cis·cau·ca·sia (sĭs′kô-kā′zhə, -shə). A steppeland of SW Russia in the Caucasus N of the main range of the Caucasus Mts.

cis·co (sĭs′kō) *n., pl.* **-coes** or **-cos.** Any of several North American freshwater fishes of the genus *Coregonus* or *Leucichthys.* [< Canadian Fr. *ciscoette* < Ojibwa *bemidewiskawed*, the (fish) with oily skin.]

Cis·kei (sĭs′kī). A Black homeland of SE South Africa; granted nominal independence in 1980. Cap. Zwelitsha. Pop. 645,000.

cis·lu·nar (sĭs-lo͞o′nər) *adj.* Situated between the earth and the moon.

cis·mon·tane (sĭs-mŏn′tān′) *adj.* Situated on this side of the mountains, esp. the Alps.

cist¹ (sĭst) *n.* A wicker receptacle used in ancient Rome for carrying sacred utensils in procession. [Lat. *cista* < Gk. *kistē.*]

cist² (sĭst, kĭst) also **kist** (kĭst) *n.* A Neolithic stone coffin. [Welsh, chest < Lat. *cista*, basket. See CIST¹.]

Cis·ter·cian (sĭ-stûr′shən) *n.* A member of a contemplative monastic order founded by reformist Benedictines in France in 1098. [Fr. *Cistertien* < Med.Lat. *Cistercium*, Cîteaux, a village of E France, site of an abbey.] **—Cis·ter′cian** *adj.*

cis·tern (sĭs′tərn) *n.* **1.** A receptacle for holding water or other liquid, esp. a tank for catching and storing rainwater. **2.** *Anat.* A cisterna. [ME *cisterne* < Lat. *cisterna* < *cista*, box < Gk. *kistē*, basket.] **—cis·tern′al** (sĭ-stûr′nəl) *adj.*

cis·ter·na (sĭ-stûr′nə) *n., pl.* **-nae** (-nē). **1.** *Anat.* A fluid-containing sac or cavity in the body of an organism. **2.** *Cytology.* One of the saclike vesicles of the endoplasmic reticulum. [Lat., cistern. See CISTERN.] **—cis·ter′nal** *adj.*

cis·tron (sĭs′trŏn′) *n.* A section of DNA that contains the genetic code for a single polypeptide and functions as a hereditary unit. [< *cis-trans test*, a genetic test (CIS- + TRANS-) + -ON¹.] **—cis·tron′ic** *adj.*

cit. *abbr.* **1.** Citation. **2.** Cited. **3.** Citizen.

cit·a·del (sĭt′ə-dəl, -dĕl′) *n.* **1.** A fortress in a commanding position in or near a city. **2.** A stronghold or fortified place; a bulwark. [Fr. *citadelle* < Ital. *cittadella*, dim. of *città*, city < Lat. *cīvitās.* See CITY.]

ci·ta·tion (sī-tā′shən) *n.* **1.** The act of citing. **2.** An authoritative source used for substantiation; a quotation. **3.** *Law.* A reference to previous court decisions or authoritative writings. **4.a.** An official commendation for meritorious action. **b.** A formal statement of the accomplishments of one being honored with an academic degree. **5.** An official summons, esp. one for appearance in court. **—ci·ta′tion·al** *adj.*

cite (sīt) *tr.v.* **cit·ed, cit·ing, cites. 1.** To quote as an authority or example. **2.** To mention or bring forward as support, illustration, or proof. **3.a.** To commend officially for meritorious action in military service. **b.** To honor formally. **4.** To summon before a court of law. [ME *citen*, to summon < OFr. *citer* < Lat. *citāre.* See **kei-²***.] **—cit′a·ble** *adj.* **—ci′ta·to′ry** (sī′tə-tôr′ē, -tōr′ē) *adj.*

cith·a·ra (sĭth′ər-ə, kĭth′-) *n. Mus.* An ancient instrument resembling the lyre. [Lat. < Gk. *kithara.*]

cith·er (sĭth′ər, sĭth′-) *n.* A cittern. [Fr. *cithare, kitaire* < Lat. *cithara*, cithara. See CITHARA.]

cith·ern (sĭth′ərn, sĭth′-) *n.* Var. of **cittern.**

cit·ied (sĭt′ēd) *adj.* Having a city or cities.

cit·i·fied (sĭt′ĭ-fīd′) *adj.* Having or pretending to have the sophisticated style or manner associated with the city.

cit·i·fy (sĭt′ĭ-fī′) *tr.v.* **-fied, -fy·ing, -fies. 1.** To cause to become urban. **2.** To impart the styles and manners of a city to. **—cit′i·fi·ca′tion** (-fĭ-kā′shən) *n.*

cit·i·zen (sĭt′ĭ-zən) *n.* **1.** A person owing loyalty to and entitled by birth or naturalization to the protection of a state or nation. **2.** A resident of a city or town, esp. one entitled to vote and enjoy other privileges there. **3.** A civilian. **4.** A native or inhabitant of a particular place. [ME *citisein* < AN *citesein*, prob. alteration of OFr. *citeain* < *cite*, city. See CITY.]

cit·i·zen·ry (sĭt′ĭ-zən-rē) *n., pl.* **-ries.** Citizens considered as a group.

cirrus

cithara
Detail from
mid fifth-century B.C.
Greek vase showing
Apollo holding a cithara

ă **pat**	oi **boy**
ā **pay**	ou **out**
âr **care**	o͝o **took**
ä **father**	o͞o **boot**
ĕ **pet**	ŭ **cut**
ē **be**	ûr **urge**
ĭ **pit**	th **thin**
ī **pie**	*th* **this**
îr **pier**	hw **which**
ŏ **pot**	zh **vision**
ō **toe**	ə **about,**
ô **paw**	**item**

Stress marks:
′ (primary);
′ (secondary), as in
dictionary (dĭk′shə-nĕr′ē)

cit•i•zen's arrest (sĭt**′**ĭ-zənz) *n.* An arrest made by a citizen, for whom legal authority arises from the fact of citizenship.
cit•i•zens band (sĭt**′**ĭ-zənz) *n.* A radio-frequency band officially allocated for private radio communications.
cit•i•zen•ship (sĭt**′**ĭ-zən-shĭp′) *n.* The status of a citizen with its attendant duties, rights, and privileges.
Ci•tlal•té•petl (sē′tläl-tā**′**pĕt-l). Also **Mount O•ri•za•ba** (ôr′ĭ-zä**′**bə, ōr′-, ô′rē-sä**′**vä). An extinct volcanic peak, 5,702.6 m (18,697 ft), of S Mexico E of Mexico City.
cit•ral (sĭt**′**răl) *n.* A mobile pale-yellow liquid, $C_9H_{15}COH$, derived from lemon-grass oil and used in perfume and as a flavoring. [CITR(US) + -AL[3].]
cit•rate (sĭt**′**rāt′) *n.* A salt or ester of citric acid.
cit•ric (sĭt**′**rĭk) *adj.* Of or relating to citric acid.
citric acid *n.* A colorless translucent crystalline acid, $C_6H_8O_7{\cdot}H_2O$, principally derived by fermentation of carbohydrates or from lemon, lime, and pineapple juices and used in preparing citrates and in flavorings and metal polishes.
citric acid cycle *n.* See **Krebs cycle.**
cit•ri•cul•ture (sĭt**′**rĭ-kŭl′chər) *n.* The cultivation of citrus fruits. [CITR(US) + CULTURE.] **— cit′ri•cul′tur•ist** *n.*
ci•trine (sĭ-trēn**′**, sĭt**′**rēn′) *n.* **1.** A pale yellow variety of crystalline quartz resembling topaz. **2.** *Color.* A light to moderate olive. [ME, reddish yellow < OFr. *citrin* < Med.Lat. *citrīnus* < Lat. *citrus*, citron tree.] **— ci•trine′** *adj.*
cit•ron (sĭt**′**rən) *n.* **1.a.** A thorny evergreen shrub or small tree *(Citrus medica)* native to India with large lemonlike fruits that have a thick warty rind. **b.** The fruit of this plant, whose rind is often candied. **2.** A globose watermelon *(Citrullus lanatus* var. *citroides)* having white flesh that is candied or pickled. **3.** *Color.* A grayish green yellow. [ME < OFr., alteration (influenced by *limon*, lemon; see LEMON) of Lat. *(mālum) citreum*, citron (fruit) < *citrus*, citron tree.] **— cit′ron** *adj.*
cit•ro•nel•la (sĭt′rə-nĕl**′**ə) *n.* **1.** A tropical Asian grass *(Cymbopogon nardus)* having lemon-scented leaves and an essential oil. **2.** The oil from this plant, used in perfumery, insect repellents, and commercial flavorings. [NLat. < Fr. *citronnelle*, lemon oil, dim. of *citron*, citron. See CITRON.]
cit•ro•nel•lal (sĭt′rə-nĕl**′**ăl′) *n.* An aromatic liquid, $C_{10}H_{18}O$, found in citronella and other essential oils and used in perfumes and flavorings. [CITRONELL(A) + -AL[3].]
cit•ro•nel•lol (sĭt′rə-nĕl**′**ôl, -ōl, -ŏl) *n.* A liquid, $C_{10}H_{20}O$, with a roselike odor, derived from any of several essential oils or synthesized and used in perfumery. [CITRONELL(A) + -OL[1].]
cit•rul•line (sĭt**′**rə-lēn′) *n.* An amino acid, $C_6H_{13}N_3O_3$ produced in the conversion of ornithine to arginine during urea formation in the liver. [NLat. *Citrullus*, watermelon genus (< Med.Lat. *citrullus*, watermelon < Ital. dial. *citrulo* < LLat. *citrium* < Lat. *citrus*, citron) + -INE[2].]
cit•rus (sĭt**′**rəs) *n.*, *pl.* **citrus** or **-rus•es. 1.** Any of various evergreen shrubs or trees of the genus *Citrus,* such as the grapefruit, native to southern and southeast Asia and having unifoliolate compound leaves and juicy edible fruits. **2.** The fruit of any citrus. [Lat., citron tree.] **— cit′rus** *adj.*
citrus canker *n.* A bacterial disease of citrus plants that causes defoliation and death.
Cit•rus Heights (sĭt**′**rəs). A community of N-central CA, a suburb of Sacramento. Pop. 107,439.
citrus red mite *n.* A large mite *(Panonychus citri)* that infests citrus plants and shrubs.
cit•tern (sĭt**′**ərn) also **cith•ern** (sĭth**′**ərn, sĭth**′**-) *n. Mus.* A 16th-century guitar with a flat pear-shaped body. [Perh. blend of Lat. *cithara*, cithara; see CITHARA, and obsolete E. *gittern* (< ME < OFr. *guiterne* < Lat. *cithara*).]

cittern
Mid 18th-century German

cit•y (sĭt**′**ē) *n.*, *pl.* **-ies. 1.** A center of population, commerce, and culture; a town of significant size and importance. **2.a.** An incorporated municipality in the United States with definite boundaries and legal powers set forth in a charter granted by the state. **b.** A Canadian municipality of high rank, usu. determined by population but varying by province. **c.** A large incorporated town in Great Britain, usu. the seat of a bishop, with its title conferred by the Crown. **3.** The inhabitants of a city. **4.** An ancient Greek city-state. [ME *cite* < OFr. < Lat. *cīvitās* < *cīvis*, citizen. See **kei-**[1]*.]
city council *n.* The governing body of a city.
city editor *n.* **1.** A newspaper editor responsible for local news and reporters' assignments. **2.** *Chiefly British.* A newspaper editor responsible for commercial and financial news.
city father *n.* A municipal official, such as a council member.
city hall *n.* **1.** The building housing municipal government offices. **2.** The municipal government, esp. its officials. **3.** *Slang.* An entrenched and insensitive bureaucracy.
city manager *n.* An administrator appointed by a city council to manage the affairs of the municipality.
cit•y•scape (sĭt**′**ē-skāp′) *n.* **1.** An artistic representation of a city. **2.** A city or section of a city regarded as a scene.
city slicker *n. Informal.* A person with the sophistication and dress traditionally linked by rural people with the city.
cit•y-state (sĭt**′**ē-stāt′) *n.* A sovereign state consisting of an independent city and its surrounding territory.
cit•y•wide (sĭt**′**ē-wīd′) *adj.* Including or occurring in all parts of a city: *citywide busing; a citywide strike.*

civet
Otter civet
Cynogale bennettii

Ci•u•dad Bo•lí•var (sē′o͞o-däd**′** bə-lē**′**vär, syo͞o-*thäth***′** bô-lē**′**vär). A city of E-central Venezuela on the Orinoco R. SE of Caracas; formerly known as Angostura. Pop. 151,000.
Ciudad Gua•ya•na (gwə-yä**′**nə, gwä-yä**′**nä). A city of E Venezuela on the Orinoco R.; founded 1961. Pop. 212,000.
Ciudad Juá•rez (wär**′**ĕz, hwä**′**rĕs) also **Juárez.** A city of N Mexico on the Rio Grande opposite El Paso TX. Pop. 544,496.
Ciudad Tru•jil•lo (tro͞o-hē**′**yō). See **Santo Domingo.**
Ciudad Vic•to•ri•a (vĭk-tôr**′**ē-ə, -tōr**′**-, vēk-tô**′**ryä). A city of E-central Mexico SSE of Monterrey; founded 1750. Pop. 140,161.
civ. *abbr.* Civil; civilian.
civ•et (sĭv**′**ĭt) *n.* **1.** Any of various carnivorous catlike mammals of the family Viverridae of Africa and Asia, having anal scent glands that secrete a fluid with a musky odor. **2.** The thick yellowish fluid so secreted, used in perfumes. **3.** The fur of one of these mammals. [Fr. *civette* < OFr. < Catalan *civetta* < Med.Lat. *zibethus* < Ar. *zabād*, civet perfume.]
civ•ic (sĭv**′**ĭk) *adj.* Of, relating to, or belonging to a city, a citizen, or citizenship; municipal or civil. [Lat. *cīvicus* < *cīvis*, citizen. See **kei-**[1]*.]
civ•ics (sĭv**′**ĭks) *n. (used with a sing. v.)* The branch of political science that deals with civic affairs and the rights and duties of citizens.
civ•ies (sĭv**′**ēz) *pl.n. Slang.* Var. of **civvies.**
civ•il (sĭv**′**əl) *adj.* **1.** Of, relating to, or befitting a citizen or citizens: *civil duties.* **2.** Of or relating to citizens and their interrelations with one another or with the state. **3.** Of ordinary citizens or ordinary community life as distinguished from the military or the ecclesiastical. **4.** Of or in accordance with organized society; civilized. **5.** Sufficiently observing or befitting accepted social usages; not rude. See Syns at **polite. 6.** Legally recognized as a division of time: *a civil year.* **7.** *Law.* Relating to the rights of private individuals and legal proceedings concerning these rights, as distinguished from criminal, military, or international regulations or proceedings. [ME < Lat. *cīvilis* < *cīvis*, citizen. See **kei-**[1]*.] **— civ′il•ly** *adv.*
civil death *n. Law.* Total deprivation of civil rights resulting from conviction for treason or other serious offense.
civil defense *n.* Protective measures for civilian volunteers to take in the event of natural disaster or enemy attack.
civil disobedience *n.* Refusal to obey civil laws in order to induce governmental change, characterized by nonviolence.
civil engineer *n.* An engineer trained in the design and construction of public works and other large facilities. **— civil engineering** *n.*
ci•vil•ian (sĭ-vĭl**′**yən) *n.* **1.** A person following the pursuits of civil life. **2.** A specialist in Roman or civil law. — *adj.* Of or relating to civilians or civil life. [ME, civil law judge < OFr. *civilien* < *civil*, civil < Lat. *cīvīlis.* See CIVIL.]
ci•vil•ian•ize (sĭ-vĭl**′**yə-nīz′) *tr.v.* **-ized, -iz•ing, -iz•es.** To convert to civilian operation or control. **— ci•vil′ian•i•za′tion** (-ĭ-zā**′**shən) *n.*
ci•vil•i•ty (sĭ-vĭl**′**ĭ-tē) *n.*, *pl.* **-ties. 1.** Courteous behavior; politeness. **2.** A courteous act or utterance.
civ•i•li•za•tion (sĭv′ə-lĭ-zā**′**shən) *n.* **1.** An advanced state of development in human society, marked by progress in the arts and sciences, the extensive use of writing, and complex political and social institutions. **2.** The type of culture and society developed by a particular nation or region or in a particular epoch. **3.** The act or process of civilizing or reaching a civilized state. **4.** Cultural or intellectual refinement; good taste. **5.** Modern society with its conveniences.
civ•i•lize (sĭv**′**ə-līz′) *tr.v.* **-lized, -liz•ing, -liz•es. 1.** To raise from barbarism to civilization. **2.** To educate in matters of culture and refinement; polish. **— civ′i•liz′a•ble** *adj.* **— civ′i•liz′er** *n.*
civ•i•lized (sĭv**′**ə-līzd′) *adj.* **1.** Having a highly developed society and culture. **2.** Showing evidence of moral and intellectual advancement; humane, ethical, and reasonable. **3.** Marked by refined taste and manners; cultured; polished.
civil law *n. Law.* **1.** The body of laws of a state or nation dealing with the rights of private citizens. **2.** The law of ancient Rome as embodied in the Justinian code, esp. that which applied to private citizens. **3.** A system of law having its origin in Roman law, as opposed to common law or canon law.
civil libertarian *n.* One actively concerned with protecting those rights guaranteed to the individual by law or principle.
civil lib•er•ties (lĭb**′**ər-tēz) *pl.n.* Fundamental individual rights, such as freedom of speech and religion, protected by law against unwarranted governmental or other interference.
civil marriage *n.* A marriage ceremony by a civil official.
civil rights *pl.n.* The rights belonging to an individual by virtue of citizenship, esp. those guaranteed by the 13th and 14th Amendments to the U.S. Constitution and by subsequent acts of Congress, including civil liberties and freedom from discrimination. — *adj.* or **civ•il-rights** (sĭv**′**əl-rīts**′**). **1.** Of or relating to civil rights. **2.** Of or relating to a political movement, esp. during the 1950's and 1960's, devoted to securing equal treatment of minority groups. **— civil righter** *n.*
civil servant *n.* A person employed in the civil service.

civil service *n.* **1.** Those branches of public service that are not legislative, judicial, or military and in which employment is usu. based on competitive examination. **2.** The entire body of persons employed by the civil branches of a government.

civil war *n.* **1.** A war between factions or regions of the same country. **2.** A state of hostility or conflict between elements within an organization. **3. Civil War.** The war in the United States between the Union and the Confederacy from 1861 to 1865. **4. Civil War.** The war in England between the Parliamentarians and the Royalists from 1642 to 1648.

civ•vies also **civ•ies** (sĭv**ʹ**ēz) *pl.n. Slang.* Civilian clothes.

C.J. *abbr. Law.* Chief Justice.

ck. *abbr.* **1.** Cask. **2.** Check.

cl *abbr.* Centiliter.

Cl The symbol for the element **chlorine.**

cl. *abbr.* **1.** Class; classification. **2.** Clause. **3.** Clearance. **4.** Closet. **5.** Cloth.

c.l. *abbr.* **1.** Carload. **2.** Or **C.L.** Civil law. **3.** Common law.

clab•ber (klăb**ʹ**ər) *n.* Sour, curdled milk. Also called regionally *thick milk.* — *tr. & intr.v.* **-bered, -ber•ing, -bers.** To curdle. [Short for BONNYCLABBER.]

clack (klăk) *v.* **clacked, clack•ing, clacks.** — *intr.* **1.** To make an abrupt sharp sound. **2.** To chatter thoughtlessly or at length. **3.** To cackle or cluck, as a hen. — *tr.* To cause to make an abrupt sharp sound. — *n.* **1.** A clacking sound. **2.** Something that makes a clacking sound. **3.** Thoughtless prolonged talk; chatter. [ME *clakken* < ON *klaka,* of imit. orig.] — **clack****ʹ****er** *n.*

clack valve *n.* A hinged valve that permits fluids to flow in only one direction and clacks when the valve closes.

Clac•to•ni•an (klăk-tō**ʹ**nē-ən) *adj. Archaeol.* Of or relating to a lower Paleolithic culture of northwest Europe. [After *Clacton,* an urban district of SE England.]

clad[1] (klăd) *tr.v.* **clad, clad•ding, clads. 1.** To sheathe or cover (a metal) with a metal. **2.** To cover with a protective or insulating layer of other material. [Back-formation < CLADDING.]

clad[2] (klăd) *v.* A p.t. and p.part. of **clothe.**

clad•ding (klăd**ʹ**ĭng) *n.* **1.** A metal coating bonded onto another metal under high pressure and temperature. **2.** A protective or insulating layer fixed to the outside of a building or another structure. [Earlier, clothing, poss. < CLAD[2].]

clade (klād) *n.* A group of organisms sharing homologous features from a common ancestor. [< Gk. *klados,* branch.]

cla•dist (klăd**ʹ**ĭst, klā**ʹ**dist) *n.* One who classifies organisms according to the principles of cladistics.

cla•dis•tics (klə-dĭs**ʹ**tĭks) *n. (used with a sing. v.)* A system of organism classification based on phylogeny. — **cla•dis****ʹ****tic** *adj.* — **cla•dis****ʹ****ti•cal•ly** *adv.*

cla•doc•er•an (klə-dŏs**ʹ**ər-ən) *n.* Any of various small, mostly freshwater crustaceans of the order Cladocera. [< NLat. *Cladocera,* order name : Gk. *klados,* branch + *keras,* horn; see **ker-**[1]*.] — **cla•doc****ʹ****er•an** *adj.*

clad•ode (klăd**ʹ**ōd**ʹ**) *n.* See **cladophyll.** [NLat. *cladōdium* < LGk. *kladōdēs,* many-branched < Gk. *klados,* branch.] — **cla•do****ʹ****di•al** (klə-dō**ʹ**dē-əl) *adj.*

clad•o•gen•e•sis (klăd**ʹ**ə-jĕn**ʹ**ĭ-sĭs) *n.* The evolutionary change resulting when taxa branch off from common ancestral lineages. [Gk. *klados,* branch + -GENESIS.] — **clad****ʹ****o•ge•net****ʹ****ic** (-jə-nĕt**ʹ**ĭk) *adj.* — **clad****ʹ****o•ge•net****ʹ****i•cal•ly** *adv.*

clad•o•gram (klăd**ʹ**ə-grăm**ʹ**, klā**ʹ**də-) *n.* A branching treelike diagram showing the phylogenetic relationships of specific species of organisms and indicating points of evolutionary diversification. [Gk. *klados,* branch + -GRAM.]

clad•o•phyll (klăd**ʹ**ə-fĭl**ʹ**) *n.* A branch or portion of a stem similar to a leaf. [Gk. *klados,* twig + -PHYLL.]

claim (klām) *tr.v.* **claimed, claim•ing, claims. 1.** To demand or ask for as one's own or one's due; assert one's right to. See Syns at **demand. 2.** To take in a violent manner as if by right: *a hurricane claimed two lives.* **3.** To state to be true, esp. when open to question; maintain. **4.** To deserve or call for; require: *problems that claim attention.* — *n.* **1.** A demand for something as rightful or due. **2.** A basis for demanding something; a title or right. **3.** Something claimed in a formal or legal manner, esp. a tract of public land staked out by a miner or homesteader. **4.a.** A demand for payment in accordance with an insurance policy or other formal arrangement. **b.** The sum of money demanded. **5.** A statement of something as a fact; an assertion of truth. — ***idiom.* lay claim to.** To assert one's right to or ownership of. [ME *claimen* < OFr. *clamer, claim-* < Lat. *clāmāre,* to call. See **kelə-**[2]*.] — **claim****ʹ****a•ble** *adj.* — **claim****ʹ****er** *n.*

claim•ant (klā**ʹ**mənt) *n.* A party that makes a claim.

Clair (klâr), **René.** 1898–1981. French filmmaker whose works include *Sous les Toits de Paris* (1929).

clair•au•di•ence (klâr-ô**ʹ**dē-əns) *n.* The supposed power to hear things outside the range of normal perception. [CLAIR(VOYANCE) + AUDIENCE.] — **clair•au****ʹ****di•ent** *adj. & n.*

clair de lune (klâr**ʹ** də lo͞on**ʹ**) *n.* **1.** A pale grayish-blue glaze applied to various kinds of Chinese porcelain. **2.** The color of such a glaze. [Fr. : *clair,* light + *de,* of + *lune,* moon.]

claire-ob•scure (klâr**ʹ**əb-skyo͝or**ʹ**) *n.* See **chiaroscuro.** [Fr. *clair-obscur,* transl. of Ital. *chiaroscuro.*]

clair•voy•ance (klâr-voi**ʹ**əns) *n.* **1.** The supposed power to see what cannot be perceived by the senses. **2.** Acute intuitive insight or perceptiveness.

clair•voy•ant (klâr-voi**ʹ**ənt) *adj.* Of, relating to, or having clairvoyance. — *n.* One possessing the supposed power of clairvoyance. [Fr. : *clair,* clear (< Lat. *clārus;* see **kelə-**[2]*) + *voyant,* pr.part. of *voir,* to see (< Lat. *vidēre;* see **weid-***).]

clam[1] (klăm) *n.* **1.a.** Any of various usu. burrowing marine and freshwater bivalve mollusks of the class Pelecypoda, some of which are edible. **b.** The soft body of an edible clam. **2.** *Informal.* A close-mouthed person. **3.** *Slang.* A dollar. — *intr.v.* **clammed, clam•ming, clams.** To hunt clams. — ***phrasal verb.* clam up.** *Informal.* To refuse to talk. [< obsolete *clamshell,* shell that clamps, clam < CLAM[2].] — **clam****ʹ****mer** *n.*

clam[2] (klăm) *n.* A clamp or vise. [ME < OE *clam,* bond.]

cla•mant (klā**ʹ**mənt, klăm**ʹ**ənt) *adj.* **1.** Clamorous; loud. **2.** Demanding attention; pressing. [Lat. *clāmāns, clāmant-,* pr.part. of *clāmāre,* to cry out. See **kelə-**[2]*.] — **cla****ʹ****mant•ly** *adv.*

clam•bake (klăm**ʹ**bāk**ʹ**) *n.* **1.** A seashore picnic where clams, fish, corn, and other foods are traditionally baked on heated stones covered with seaweed. **2.** *Informal.* A gathering, esp. a noisy and lively one.

clam•ber (klăm**ʹ**bər, klăm**ʹ**ər) *intr.v.* **-bered, -ber•ing, -bers.** To climb with difficulty, esp. on all fours; scramble. — *n.* A difficult, awkward climb. [ME *clambren,* prob. freq. of *climben,* to climb. See CLIMB.] — **clam****ʹ****ber•er** *n.*

clam•ber•ing (klăm**ʹ**bər-ĭng, klăm**ʹ**ər-) *adj.* Of or relating to a plant, often one without tendrils, that sprawls or climbs.

clam dig•gers or **clam•dig•gers** (klăm**ʹ**dĭg**ʹ**ərz) *pl.n.* Casual pants in a midcalf length.

clam-flat (klăm**ʹ**flăt**ʹ**) *n. New England.* A level stretch of soft tidal mud where clams burrow.

clam•my (klăm**ʹ**ē) *adj.* **-mi•er, -mi•est. 1.** Disagreeably moist, sticky, and cold to the touch. **2.** Damp and unpleasant. **3.** Uneasy; apprehensive. [ME, sticky, prob. < *clam* (< OE, mud, clay) or < MLGer. *klam,* stickiness.] — **clam****ʹ****mi•ly** *adv.* — **clam****ʹ****mi•ness** *n.*

clam•or (klăm**ʹ**ər) *n.* **1.** A loud outcry; a hubbub. **2.** A vehement expression of discontent or protest. **3.** A loud sustained noise. See Syns at **noise.** — *v.* **-ored, -or•ing, -ors.** — *intr.* **1.** To make a loud sustained noise or outcry. **2.** To make insistent demands or complaints. — *tr.* **1.** To exclaim insistently and noisily. **2.** To influence or force by clamoring. [ME *clamour* < OFr. < Lat. *clāmor,* shout < *clāmāre,* to cry out. See **kelə-**[2]*.] — **clam****ʹ****or•er** *n.*

clam•or•ous (klăm**ʹ**ər-əs) *adj.* **1.** Making or marked by outcry or sustained din. **2.** Insistently demanding attention; importunate. — **clam****ʹ****or•ous•ly** *adv.* — **clam****ʹ****or•ous•ness** *n.*

clam•our (klăm**ʹ**ər) *n. & v. Chiefly British.* Var. of **clamor.**

clamp (klămp) *n.* **1.** Any of various devices used to join, grip, support, or compress mechanical or structural parts. **2.** Any of various tools with opposing sides or parts for bracing objects or holding them together. — *tr.v.* **clamped, clamp•ing, clamps. 1.** To fasten, grip, or support with or as if with a clamp. **2.** To establish by authority; impose. — ***phrasal verb.* clamp down.** To become more strict or repressive; impose controls. [ME < MDu. *klampe.*]

clamp•down (klămp**ʹ**doun**ʹ**) *n.* An imposing of restrictions.

clamp•er (klăm**ʹ**pər) *n.* One that clamps, esp. a spiked plate attached to the sole of a shoe to prevent slipping on ice.

clam•shell (klăm**ʹ**shĕl**ʹ**) *n.* **1.** The shell of a clam. **2.** Any of various devices with two hinged jaws, used to dredge or dig.

clam•worm (klăm**ʹ**wûrm**ʹ**) *n.* Any of various segmented burrowing marine worms of the genus *Nereis,* used as bait.

clan (klăn) *n.* **1.** A traditional social unit in the Scottish Highlands, consisting of families claiming a common ancestor and following the same hereditary chieftain. **2.** A tribal division tracing descent from a common ancestor. **3.** A large group of relatives, friends, or associates. [ME < Sc.Gael. *clann,* family < OIr. *cland,* offspring < Lat. *planta,* sprout. See **plat-***.]

clan•des•tine (klăn-dĕs**ʹ**tĭn) *adj.* Kept or done in secret, often to conceal an illicit or improper purpose. [Lat. *clandestīnus,* prob. blend of **clam-de,* secretly (< *clam;* see **kel-**[1]*) and *intestīnus,* internal; see INTESTINE.] — **clan•des****ʹ****tine•ly** *adv.* — **clan•des****ʹ****tine•ness, clan****ʹ****des•tin****ʹ****i•ty** *n.*

clang (klăng) *n.* **1.** A loud, resonant, metallic sound. **2.** The strident call of a crane or goose. — *intr. & tr.v.* **clanged, clang•ing, clangs.** To make or cause a clang. [Prob. < Lat. *clangere,* to ring, clang.]

clang•er (klăng**ʹ**ər) *n. Chiefly British.* A blunder; a faux pas.

clan•gor (klăng**ʹ**ər, klăng**ʹ**gər) *n.* **1.** A clang or repeated clanging. **2.** A loud racket; a din. — *intr.v.* **-gored, -gor•ing, -gors.** To make a clangor. [Lat. < *clangere,* to clang.] — **clan****ʹ****gor•ous** *adj.* — **clan****ʹ****gor•ous•ly** *adv.*

clan•gour (klăng**ʹ**ər, klăng**ʹ**gər) *n. & v. Chiefly British.* Var. of **clangor.**

clank (klăngk) *n.* A sharp, hard metallic sound that is not resonant. — *intr.v.* **clanked, clank•ing, clanks.** To make a clank. [Prob. imit.] — **clank****ʹ****y** *adj.*

clan•nish (klăn**ʹ**ĭsh) *adj.* **1.** Of, relating to, or characteristic of a clan. **2.** Inclined to cling together as a group and exclude

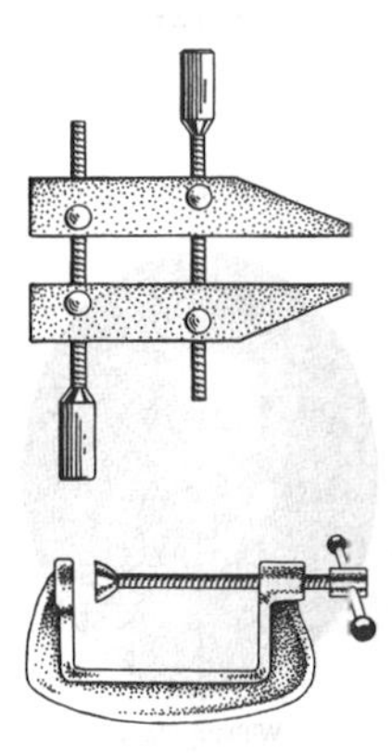

clamp
Top: Parallel clamp
Bottom: C-clamp

ă pat	oi boy
ā pay	ou out
âr care	o͝o took
ä father	o͞o boot
ĕ pet	ŭ cut
ē be	ûr urge
ĭ pit	th thin
ī pie	*th* this
îr pier	hw which
ŏ pot	zh vision
ō toe	ə about,
ô paw	item

Stress marks:
ʹ (primary);
ʹ (secondary), as in
dictionary (dĭk**ʹ**shə-nĕr**ʹ**ē)

— *idiom.* **clean house.** *Slang.* To eliminate or discard what is undesirable. [ME *clene* < OE *clǣne.*] — **clean′a•ble** *adj.* — **clean′ness** *n.*

Syns: *clean, antiseptic, cleanly, immaculate, spotless.* The central meaning shared by these adjectives is "free from dirt": *clean clothing; antiseptic instruments; cats, cleanly animals; an immaculate tablecloth; spotless gloves.* ***Ant:*** *dirty.*

clean and jerk *n. Sports.* A lift in weightlifting in which a weight is raised to shoulder height, held there briefly, and then pushed overhead in a rapid motion of the arms, typically accompanied by a spring or lunge from the legs.

clean-cut (klēn′kŭt′) *adj.* **1.** Clearly and sharply defined or outlined. **2.** Neat and trim in appearance.

clean•er (klē′nər) *n.* **1.** One whose work or business is cleaning. **2.** A machine or substance used in cleaning.

clean-hand•ed (klēn′hăn′dĭd) *adj.* Innocent; guiltless.

clean-limbed (klēn′lĭmd′) *adj.* Having well-formed limbs; well-proportioned.

clean•ly (klĕn′lē) *adj.* **-li•er, -li•est.** Habitually and carefully neat and clean. See Syns at **clean.** — *adv.* (klēn′lē). In a clean manner. — **clean′li•ness** (klĕn′lē-nĭs) *n.*

clean room *n.* A room that is maintained virtually free of contaminants, such as dust or bacteria, used in laboratory work and in electronic and aerospace production.

cleanse (klĕnz) *tr.v.* **cleansed, cleans•ing, cleans•es.** To free from dirt, defilement, or guilt; purge or clean. [ME *clensen* < OE *clǣnsian* < *clǣne,* pure, clean.]

cleans•er (klĕn′zər) *n.* **1.** A detergent or other agent that removes dirt or grease. **2.** A lotion or cream to clean the face.

clean-shav•en (klēn′shā′vən) *adj.* **1.** Having the beard or hair shaved off. **2.** Having recently shaved.

Cle•an•thes (klē-ăn′thēz). 331?–232? B.C. Greek philosopher who succeeded Zeno as head of the Stoic school.

clean•up (klēn′ŭp′) *n.* **1.** A thorough cleaning or ordering. **2.** *Informal.* The final, often routine tasks that complete a project. **3.** *Slang.* A very large profit; a killing. **4.** *Baseball.* The fourth position in the batting order. — **clean′up′** *adj.*

clean room

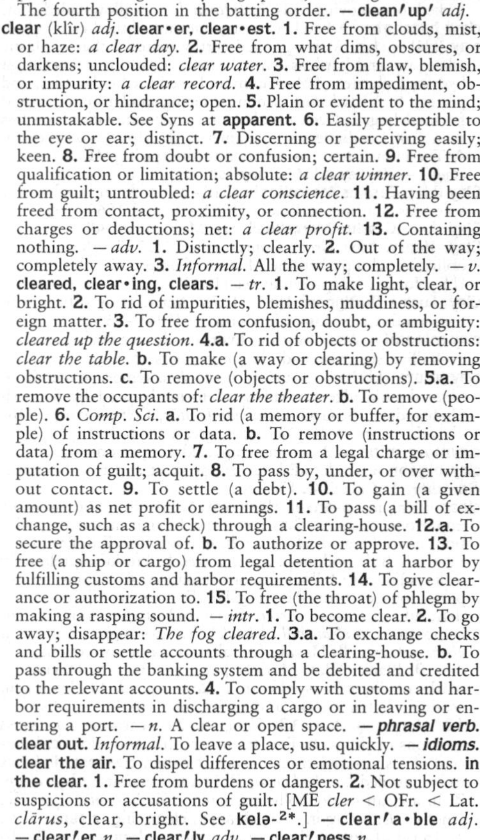

clear (klîr) *adj.* **clear•er, clear•est. 1.** Free from clouds, mist, or haze: *a clear day.* **2.** Free from what dims, obscures, or darkens; unclouded: *clear water.* **3.** Free from flaw, blemish, or impurity: *a clear record.* **4.** Free from impediment, obstruction, or hindrance; open. **5.** Plain or evident to the mind; unmistakable. See Syns at **apparent. 6.** Easily perceptible to the eye or ear; distinct. **7.** Discerning or perceiving easily; keen. **8.** Free from doubt or confusion; certain. **9.** Free from qualification or limitation; absolute: *a clear winner.* **10.** Free from guilt; untroubled: *a clear conscience.* **11.** Having been freed from contact, proximity, or connection. **12.** Free from charges or deductions; net: *a clear profit.* **13.** Containing nothing. — *adv.* **1.** Distinctly; clearly. **2.** Out of the way; completely away. **3.** *Informal.* All the way; completely. — *v.* **cleared, clear•ing, clears.** — *tr.* **1.** To make light, clear, or bright. **2.** To rid of impurities, blemishes, muddiness, or foreign matter. **3.** To free from confusion, doubt, or ambiguity: *cleared up the question.* **4.a.** To rid of objects or obstructions: *clear the table.* **b.** To make (a way or clearing) by removing obstructions. **c.** To remove (objects or obstructions). **5.a.** To remove the occupants of: *clear the theater.* **b.** To remove (people). **6.** *Comp. Sci.* **a.** To rid (a memory or buffer, for example) of instructions or data. **b.** To remove (instructions or data) from a memory. **7.** To free from a legal charge or imputation of guilt; acquit. **8.** To pass by, under, or over without contact. **9.** To settle (a debt). **10.** To gain (a given amount) as net profit or earnings. **11.** To pass (a bill of exchange, such as a check) through a clearing-house. **12.a.** To secure the approval of. **b.** To authorize or approve. **13.** To free (a ship or cargo) from legal detention at a harbor by fulfilling customs and harbor requirements. **14.** To give clearance or authorization to. **15.** To free (the throat) of phlegm by making a rasping sound. — *intr.* **1.** To become clear. **2.** To go away; disappear: *The fog cleared.* **3.a.** To exchange checks and bills or settle accounts through a clearing-house. **b.** To pass through the banking system and be debited and credited to the relevant accounts. **4.** To comply with customs and harbor requirements in discharging a cargo or in leaving or entering a port. — *n.* A clear or open space. — ***phrasal verb.*** **clear out.** *Informal.* To leave a place, usu. quickly. — ***idioms.*** **clear the air.** To dispel differences or emotional tensions. **in the clear. 1.** Free from burdens or dangers. **2.** Not subject to suspicions or accusations of guilt. [ME *cler* < OFr. < Lat. *clārus,* clear, bright. See **kelə-²*.**] — **clear′a•ble** *adj.* — **clear′er** *n.* — **clear′ly** *adv.* — **clear′ness** *n.*

Cleopatra
Roman sculpture

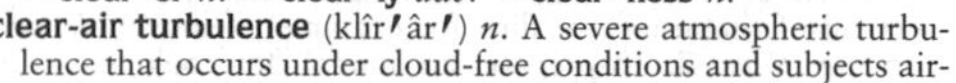

clear-air turbulence (klîr′âr′) *n.* A severe atmospheric turbulence that occurs under cloud-free conditions and subjects aircraft to strong updrafts and downdrafts.

clear•ance (klîr′əns) *n.* **1.** The act or process of clearing. **2.** A space cleared; a clearing. **3.a.** The amount of space by which a moving object clears something. **b.** The height or width of a passage. **4.** An intervening space or distance allowing free play, as between machine parts. **5.** Permission for a vehicle to proceed, as after an inspection. **6.** Official certification of blamelessness, trustworthiness, or suitability. **7.** A sale to dispose of old merchandise. **8.** The passage of checks and other bills of exchange through a clearing-house. **9.** *Physiol.* **a.** The removal by the kidneys of a substance from blood plasma. **b.** Renal clearance.

clerestory

Cle•ar•chus (klē-är′kəs). fl. 5th cent. B.C. Spartan military leader whose rule of Byzantium was so severe that the people surrendered the city to the Athenians in his absence (408).

clear-cut (klîr′kŭt′) *adj.* **1.** Distinctly and sharply defined or outlined. **2.** Not ambiguous; clear and obvious. See Syns at **apparent.** — *v.* **-cut, -cut•ting, -cuts.** — *tr.* To remove all of the trees in (a tract of timber) at one time. — *intr.* To clear-cut an area. — *n.* A clear-cut tract of timberland.

clear-eyed (klîr′īd′) *adj.* **1.** Having sharp, bright eyes; keen-sighted. **2.** Mentally acute or perceptive.

Clear•field (klîr′fēld′). A city of N-central UT N of Salt Lake City. Pop. 21,435.

clear-head•ed (klîr′hĕd′ĭd) *adj.* Having a clear, orderly mind. — **clear′-head′ed•ly** *adv.* — **clear′-head′ed•ness** *n.*

clear•ing (klîr′ĭng) *n.* **1.** The act or process of making or becoming clear. **2.** A tract of land within an overgrown area from which trees and other obstructions have been removed. **3.** An open space. **4.a.** The exchange among banks of checks, drafts, and notes and the settlement of consequent differences. **b. clearings.** The total of daily claims at a clearing-house.

clear•ing-house or **clear•ing•house** (klîr′ĭng-hous′) *n.* An office where banks engage in clearing.

clear-sight•ed (klîr′sī′tĭd) *adj.* **1.** Having sharp, clear vision. **2.** Perceptive; discerning. — **clear′-sight′ed•ly** *adv.* — **clear′-sight′ed•ness** *n.*

clear•sto•ry (klîr′stôr′ē, -stōr′ē) *n.* Var. of **clerestory.**

Clear•wa•ter (klîr′wô′tər, -wŏt′ər). A city of W-central FL W of Tampa. Pop. 98,784.

Clearwater Mountains. A range of N-central ID rising to c. 2,745 m (9,000 ft).

clear•weed (klîr′wēd′) *n.* Either of two eastern North American annual plants *(Pilea pumila* or *P. fontana)* having short drooping flower clusters and translucent stems and leaves.

clear•wing (klîr′wĭng′) *n.* Any of various wasplike moths of the family Sesiidae, with scaleless transparent wings.

cleat (klēt) *n.* **1.** A strip of wood or iron used to strengthen or support the surface to which it is attached. **2.a.** A projecting piece of metal or hard rubber attached to the underside of a shoe to provide traction. **b. cleats.** A pair of shoes with such projections on the soles. **3.** A piece of metal or wood having projecting arms or ends for winding or securing a line. **4.** A wedge-shaped piece of material that is fastened onto something to act as a support or prevent slippage. **5.** A spurlike device used to grip a tree or pole in climbing. — *tr.v.* **cleat•ed, cleat•ing, cleats.** To supply, support, secure, or strengthen with a cleat. [ME *clete* < OE **clēat,* lump, wedge.]

cleav•age (klē′vĭj) *n.* **1.** The act of splitting or cleaving. **2.** The state of being split or cleft; a fissure or division. **3.** *Mineral.* The splitting or tendency to split of a crystallized substance along definite crystalline planes, yielding smooth surfaces. **4.** *Embryol.* **a.** The series of mitotic cell divisions that produces a blastula from a fertilized ovum. **b.** Any single cell division in such a series. **5.** *Informal.* The hollow between a woman's breasts.

cleave¹ (klēv) *v.* **cleft** (klĕft) or **cleaved** or **clove** (klōv), **cleft** or **cleaved** or **clo•ven** (klō′vən), **cleav•ing, cleaves.** — *tr.* **1.** To split with or as if with a sharp instrument. See Syns at **tear¹. 2.** To make or accomplish by or as if by cutting. **3.** To pierce or penetrate. — *intr.* **1.** *Mineral.* To split or separate, esp. along a natural line of division. **2.** To make one's way; penetrate. [ME *cleven* < OE *clēofan.* See **gleubh-*.**] — **cleav′a•ble** *adj.*

cleave² (klēv) *intr.v.* **cleaved, cleav•ing, cleaves. 1.** To adhere or stick fast. **2.** To be faithful. [ME *cleven* < OE *cleofian.*]

cleav•er (klē′vər) *n.* A heavy broad-bladed knife or hatchet used esp. by butchers.

cleav•ers (klē′vərz) *pl.n. (used with a sing. or pl. v.)* See **bedstraw.** [ME *clivers,* prob. blend of *clife,* burdock (< OE *clīfe)* and *clivres,* claws (< OE *clifras,* pl. of *clifer*).]

Cle•burne (klē′bərn). A city of NE TX S of Fort Worth. Pop. 22,205.

cleek (klēk) *n.* **1.** *Sports.* **a.** A number one golf iron. **b.** A number four wood. **2.** *Scots.* A large hook. [ME *cleike,* large hook < *cleken,* to grasp, var. of *clechen* < OE **clǣcan.*]

clef (klĕf) *n. Mus.* A symbol indicating the pitch of one line of a staff, in relation to which the other pitches of the staff can be determined. [Fr., key < OFr. < Lat. *clāvis.*]

cleft (klĕft) *v.* A p.t. and p.part. of **cleave¹.** — *adj.* **1.** Divided; split. **2.** *Bot.* Having indentations that extend about halfway to the center. — *n.* **1.** A crack, crevice, or split. **2.** A split or indentation between two parts, as of the chin. [ME, p.part. of *cleven,* to split. See CLEAVE¹. N. < ME, alteration (influenced by *cleft*) of *clift* < OE *geclyft.* See **gleubh-*.**]

cleft lip *n.* A congenital deformity of the lip, usu. the upper one, characterized by a vertical fissure.

cleft palate *n.* A congenital fissure in the roof of the mouth, resulting from incomplete fusion of the palate during embryonic development.

Cleis•the•nes (klīs′thə-nēz′) or **Clis•the•nes** (klĭs′-). fl. 6th cent. B.C. Greek tyrant of Sicyon who led the Ionian population of the region in a revolt against the Dorians.

cleis•tog•a•mous (klī-stŏg′ə-məs) also **cleis•to•gam•ic** (klī′stə-găm′ĭk) *adj. Bot.* Of or relating to a flower that does not open and is self-pollinated in the bud. [Gk. *kleistos*, closed (< *kleiein*, to close) + -GAMOUS.] **— cleis•tog′a•mous•ly** *adv.* **— cleis•tog′a•my** (-mē) *n.*

cleis•to•the•ci•um (klī′stə-thē′sē-əm) *n., pl.* **-ci•a** (-sē-ə). *Bot.* A closed spherical ascocarp. [NLat. : Gk. *kleistos*, closed (< *kleiein*, to close) + Gk. *thēkion*, small case, dim. of *thēkē*, receptacle; see **dhē-*.**]

clem•a•tis (klĕm′ə-tĭs, klĭ-măt′ĭs) *n.* Any of various mostly climbing plants of the genus *Clematis*, native chiefly to northern temperate regions and having showy flowers or fruit clusters. [Lat. *clēmatis*, a creeping plant < Gk. *klēmatis* < *klēma, klēmat-*, twig.]

Cle•men•ceau (klĕm′ən-sō′, klĕ-mäɴ-), **Georges.** 1841–1929. French politician who served as premier (1906–09 and 1917–20) and played a key role in negotiating the Treaty of Versailles (1919).

clem•en•cy (klĕm′ən-sē) *n., pl.* **-cies. 1.** A disposition to show mercy, esp. to an offender or enemy. See Syns at **mercy. 2.** A merciful, kind, or lenient act. **3.** Mildness, esp. of weather.

Clem•ens (klĕm′ənz), **Samuel Langhorne.** Mark Twain. 1835–1910. Amer. author whose masterpieces of humor and sarcasm include *The Adventures of Huckleberry Finn* (1884).

clem•ent (klĕm′ənt) *adj.* **1.** Inclined to be lenient or merciful. **2.** Mild: *clement weather.* [ME < Lat. *clēmēns, clēment-.*] **— clem′ent•ly** *adv.*

Clem•ent I (klĕm′ənt), Saint. "Clement of Rome." Died c. A.D. 97. Pope (88–97) who was one of the Apostolic Fathers and the author of the First Epistle to the Corinthians (c. 96).

Clement V. 1264–1314. Pope (1305–14) befriended by Philip IV of France, who arranged his election.

Clement VII. 1475?–1534. Pope (1523–34) who refused to grant the divorce of Henry VIII from Catherine of Aragon.

clem•en•tine (klĕm′ən-tīn′, -tēn′) *n.* A deep red-orange, often seedless tangerinelike fruit. [Fr. *clémentine*, perh. after Père *Clément* (fl. 1902), French missionary in Africa.]

Clement of Al•ex•an•dri•a (ăl′ĭg-zăn′drē-ə), Saint. A.D. 150?–220? Greek Christian theologian considered the founder of the Alexandrian school of theology.

clench (klĕnch) *tr.v.* **clenched, clench•ing, clench•es. 1.** To close tightly: *clench one's teeth.* **2.** To grasp or grip tightly. **3.** To clinch (a bolt, for example). **4.** *Naut.* To fasten with a clinch. *— n.* **1.** A tight grip or grasp. **2.** Something, such as a mechanical device, that clenches or holds fast. **3.** *Naut.* See **clinch** 4. [ME *clenchen* < OE *beclencan.*]

cle•o•me (klē-ō′mē) *n.* Any of various often strong-smelling plants of the genus *Cleome*, native chiefly to warm regions. [NLat. *Cleome*, genus name.]

Cle•on (klē′ŏn). d. 422 B.C. Athenian politician who led the democratic faction after the death of Pericles (429).

Cle•o•pat•ra (klē′ə-păt′rə, -pä′trə, -pā′-). 69–30 B.C. Egyptian queen (51–49 and 48–30) who was defeated with Mark Antony by Octavian's forces at Actium (31).

clepe (klēp) *tr.v.* **cleped** (klēpt, klĕpt), **cleped** or **clept** (klĕpt) or **y•clept** (ĭ-klĕpt′) or **y•cleped** (ĭ-klēpt′, ĭ-klĕpt′), **clep•ing, clepes.** *Archaic.* To call; name. [ME *clepen* < OE *cleopian*, to cry out.]

clep•sy•dra (klĕp′sĭ-drə) *n., pl.* **-dras** or **-drae** (-drē′). An ancient device that measured time by marking the regulated flow of water through a small opening. [Lat. < Gk. *klepsudra* : *kleptein, kleps-*, to steal + *hudōr*, water; see **wed-[1]*.**]

clere•sto•ry also **clear•sto•ry** (klîr′stôr′ē, -stōr′ē) *n., pl.* **-ries. 1.** The upper part of the nave, transepts, and choir of a church, containing windows. **2.** An upper portion of a wall containing windows. [ME *clerestorie* : perh. *cler*, giving light, clear; see CLEAR + *storie*, tier; see STORY[2].]

cler•gy (klûr′jē) *n., pl.* **-gies.** The body of people ordained for religious service. See Usage Note at **collective noun.** [ME *clergie* < OFr. (< *clerc*, cleric < LLat. *clēricus*; see CLERK) and < OFr. *clerge*, clerks (< LLat. *clēricātus* < *clēricus*).]

cler•gy•man (klûr′jē-mən) *n.* A man who is a cleric.

cler•gy•wom•an (klûr′jē-wo͝om′ən) *n.* A woman who is a cleric.

cler•ic (klĕr′ĭk) *n.* A member of the clergy. [LLat. *clēricus*. See CLERK.]

cler•i•cal (klĕr′ĭ-kəl) *adj.* **1.** Of or relating to office workers or work. **2.** Of, relating to, or typical of the clergy. **3.** Advocating clericalism. *— n.* **1.** A cleric. **2. clericals.** Garments worn by clerics. **3.** An advocate of clericalism. **— cler′i•cal•ly** *adv.*

clerical collar *n.* A stiff white collar fastened at the back of the neck, worn by certain members of the Christian clergy.

cler•i•cal•ism (klĕr′ĭ-kə-lĭz′əm) *n.* A policy of supporting the power and influence of the clergy in political or secular matters. **— cler′i•cal•ist** *n.*

cler•i•hew (klĕr′ə-hyo͞o′) *n.* A humorous verse, usu. consisting of two unmatched rhyming couplets, about a person whose name generally serves as one of the rhymes. [After Edmund *Clerihew* Bentley (1875–1956), British writer.]

cler•i•sy (klĕr′ĭ-sē) *n.* Educated people considered as a group; the literati. [Ger. *Klerisei*, clergy < Med.Lat. *clēricia* < LLat. *clēricus*, priest. See CLERK.]

clerk (klûrk; *British* klärk) *n.* **1.** A person who works in an office handling such things as records, correspondence, or files. **2.a.** A person who keeps the records and performs the regular business of a court or legislative body. **b.** *Law.* A law clerk, as for a judge. **3.** A person who works at a sales counter or service desk. **4.** A cleric. **5.** *Archaic.* A scholar. *— intr.v.* **clerked, clerk•ing, clerks.** To work or serve as a clerk. [ME, clergyman, secretary < OE *clerc* and OFr. *clerc*, clergyman, both < LLat. *clēricus* < Gk. *klērikos*, belonging to the clergy < *klēros*, inheritance, lot.] **— clerk′dom** *n.* **— clerk′ship′** *n.*

clerk•ly (klûrk′lē) *adj.* **-li•er, -li•est. 1.** Of, relating to, or typical of a clerk. **2.** *Archaic.* Scholarly. **— clerk′li•ness** *n.*

Cler•mont-Fer•rand (klĕr-mōɴ′fə-räɴ′, -fĕ-). A city of central France W of Lyons. Pop. 147,361.

Cleve•land (klēv′lənd). **1.** A city of NE OH on Lake Erie; laid out in 1796. Pop. 505,616. **2.** A city of SE TN ENE of Chattanooga. Pop. 30,354.

Cleveland, (Stephen) Grover. 1837–1908. The 22nd and 24th President of the U.S. (1885–89 and 1893–97).

Cleveland Heights. A city of NE OH, a suburb of Cleveland. Pop. 54,052.

clev•er (klĕv′ər) *adj.* **-er•er, -er•est. 1.** Mentally quick and original; bright. **2.** Nimble; dexterous. **3.** Exhibiting quick-wittedness: *a clever story.* **4.** *New England.* Easily managed; docile. **5.** *New England.* Affable but not esp. smart. **6.** *Chiefly Southern U.S.* Good-natured; amiable. [ME *cliver*; akin to East Frisian *klifer, klüfer*, perh. < *klüfen*, to gnaw apart, work assiduously, of LGer. orig.; akin to Old Saxon *klioban*, to split, cleave. See **gleubh-*.**] **— clev′er•ly** *adv.* **— clev′er•ness** *n.*

Syns: clever, ingenious, shrewd. These adjectives refer to mental adroitness or to practical ingenuity and skill. *Clever* is the most comprehensive: *"As I was going into a room full of people, I would say to myself, 'You're the cleverest member of one of the cleverest families in the cleverest class of the cleverest nation in the world, why should you be frightened?' "* (Beatrice Webb). *Ingenious* implies originality and inventiveness: *"an ingenious solution to the storage problem"* (Linda Greider). *Shrewd* emphasizes mental astuteness and practical understanding: *a shrewd politician.*

Cleves (klēvz). See **Kleve.**

clev•is (klĕv′ĭs) *n.* A U-shaped metal fastening device with holes in each end for a pin or bolt. [< *clevi*, poss. of Scand. orig.; akin to ON *klofi*, cleft. See **gleubh-*.**]

clew[1] (klo͞o) *n.* **1.** A ball of yarn or thread. **2.** *Gk. Myth.* The ball of thread Theseus used to escape the labyrinth. **3. clews.** The cords used to suspend a hammock. **4.** Also **clue.** *Naut.* **a.** The lower aft corner of a fore-and-aft sail. **b.** One of the two lower corners of a square sail. *— tr.v.* **clewed, clew•ing, clews. 1.** To roll or coil into a ball. **2.** Also **clue.** *Naut.* To raise the lower corners of (a square sail) with ropes. Used with *up.* [ME *clewe* < OE *cliwen.*]

clew[2] (klo͞o) *n. & v. Chiefly British.* Var. of **clue[1].**

Cli•burn (klī′bərn), **Van.** b. 1934. Amer. pianist who was the first American to win the Tchaikovsky Prize (1958).

cli•ché (klē-shā′) *n.* A trite or overused expression or idea. [Fr., p.part. of *clicher*, to stereotype (imit. of sound of dropping a matrix into molten metal to make a stereotype plate).]

cli•chéd (klē-shād′) *adj.* Having become stale or commonplace through overuse; hackneyed.

Cli•chy (klē-shē′). A city of N-central France, a suburb of Paris. Pop. 46,895.

click (klĭk) *n.* **1.** A brief, sharp, nonresonant sound. **2.** A mechanical device that snaps into position. **3.** *Ling.* An implosive stop produced by raising the back of the tongue to make contact with the soft palate and simultaneously closing the lips or touching the teeth or alveolar ridge with the tip and sides of the tongue. *— v.* **clicked, click•ing, clicks.** *— intr.* **1.** To produce a click or series of clicks. **2.** *Slang.* **a.** To be a great success. **b.** To function well together; hit it off. **c.** To become clear; fall into place. *— tr.* To cause to click, as by striking together. [Imit.] **— click′er** *n.*

click beetle *n.* Any of various beetles of the family Elateridae, characterized by the ability to right themselves from an overturned position by flipping into the air with a clicking sound.

cli•ent (klī′ənt) *n.* **1.** The party for which professional services are rendered, as by an attorney. **2.** A customer or patron. **3.** One who uses a social services agency. **4.** One dependent on the protection of another. **5.** A client state. [ME < OFr. < Lat. *cliēns, client-*, dependent, follower. See **klei-*.**] **— cli′ent•age** (-ən-tĭj) *n.* **— cli•en′tal** (klī-ĕn′tl, klī′ən-) *adj.*

cli•en•tele (klī′ən-tĕl′, klē′än-) *n.* **1.** The clients of a professional practice considered as a group. **2.** A body of customers or patrons: *a restaurant's clientele.* [Fr. *clientèle* < Lat. *clientēla*, clientship < *cliēns*, client. See CLIENT.]

client state *n.* A country that is dependent on the economic or military support of a larger, more powerful country.

cliff (klĭf) *n.* A high, steep, or overhanging face of rock. [ME *clif* < OE.] **— cliff′y** *adj.*

clerical collar

Grover Cleveland

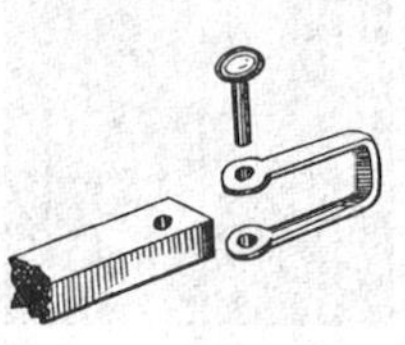

clevis

ă pat	oi boy
ā pay	ou out
âr care	o͝o took
ä father	o͞o boot
ĕ pet	ŭ cut
ē be	ûr urge
ĭ pit	th thin
ī pie	*th* this
îr pier	hw which
ŏ pot	zh vision
ō toe	ə about, item
ô paw	

Stress marks:
′ (primary);
′ (secondary), as in
dictionary (dĭk′shə-nĕr′ē)

cliff brake *n.* Any of several ferns in the genus *Pellaea,* typically growing in dry rocky areas or on cliffs and having pinnately compound, often leathery leaves.

cliff dweller *n.* A member of certain Anasazi groups of the southwest United States who built dwellings on sheltered ledges in the sides of cliffs. — **cliff dwelling** *n.*

cliff•hang•er (klĭf′hăng′ər) *n.* **1.** A melodramatic serial in which each episode ends in suspense. **2.** A suspenseful situation at the end of a chapter, a scene, or an episode. **3.** A contest in which the outcome is uncertain until the end. — **cliff′hang′ing** *adj.*

Clif•ford (klĭf′ərd), **Nathan.** 1803–81. Amer. jurist; associate justice of the U.S. Supreme Court (1858–81).

Cliff•side Park (klĭf′sīd′). A borough of NE NJ on the Palisades opposite New York City. Pop. 20,393.

cliff dweller
Cliff Palace, the largest cliff dwelling in Mesa Verde National Park, Colorado

cliff swallow *n.* A North American swallow *(Petrochelidon pyrrhonota)* that builds a bottle-shaped nest on the face of a cliff or bluff or under the eaves of a roof.

Clif•ton (klĭf′tən). A city of NE NJ near Paterson. Pop. 71,742.

cli•mac•ter•ic (klī-măk′tər-ĭk, klī′măk-tĕr′ĭk) *n.* **1.a.** A period of life characterized by physiological and psychological change that marks the end of a woman's reproductive capacity and terminates with the completion of menopause. **b.** A corresponding period in men marked by reduced sexual activity, although fertility is retained. **2.** A critical stage, period, or year. — *adj.* **1.** Of or relating to a climacteric. **2.** Critical; crucial. [< Lat. *clīmactēricus,* of a dangerous period in life < Gk. *klimaktērikos* < *klimaktēr,* dangerous point, rung of a ladder < *klimax,* ladder. See CLIMAX.]

cli•mac•tic (klī-măk′tĭk) also **cli•mac•ti•cal** (-tĭ-kəl) *adj.* Relating to or constituting a climax. — **cli•mac′ti•cal•ly** *adv.*

cli•mate (klī′mĭt) *n.* **1.** The characteristic meteorological conditions, including temperature, precipitation, and wind, of a particular region. **2.** A region of the earth having particular meteorological conditions. **3.** A prevailing condition or set of attitudes in human affairs. [ME *climat* < OFr. < LLat. *clīma, clīmat-* < Gk. *klima,* surface of the earth, region. See **klei-***.]

cli•mat•ic (klī-măt′ĭk) *adj.* **1.** Of or relating to climate. **2.** *Ecol.* Influenced or caused by the climate. — **cli•mat′i•cal•ly** *adv.*

Bill Clinton

cli•ma•tol•o•gy (klī′mə-tŏl′ə-jē) *n.* The meteorological study of climates and their phenomena. — **cli′ma•to•log′ic** (-mə-tl-ŏj′ĭk), **cli′ma•to•log′i•cal** (-ĭ-kəl) *adj.* — **cli′ma•to•log′i•cal•ly** *adv.* — **cli′ma•tol′o•gist** *n.*

cli•max (klī′măks′) *n.* **1.** The point of greatest intensity or force in an ascending series or progression; a culmination. **2.a.** A series of statements or ideas in an ascending order of rhetorical force. **b.** The final point in such a series. **3.a.** A moment of great or culminating intensity in a narrative or drama. **b.** The turning point in a plot or dramatic action. **4.** See **orgasm** 1. **5.** A stage in ecological development in which a community of organisms, esp. plants, is stable and capable of perpetuating itself. — *tr. & intr.v.* **-maxed, -max•ing, -max•es.** To bring to or reach a climax. [Lat. *clīmax,* rhetorical climax < Gk. *klimax,* ladder. See **klei-***.]

climb (klīm) *v.* **climbed, climb•ing, climbs.** — *tr.* **1.** To move upward on or mount, esp. with the hands and feet or the feet alone; ascend. **2.** To grow in an upward direction on or over. — *intr.* **1.** To move oneself upward, esp. with the hands and feet. **2.** To rise slowly, steadily, or effortfully; ascend. **3.** To move in a specified direction with the hands and feet. **4.** To slant or slope upward. **5.** To engage in mountain climbing. **6.** To grow in an upward direction, as some plants do, often with twining stems or tendrils. — *n.* **1.** An act of climbing; an ascent. **2.** A place to be climbed. [ME *climben* < OE *climban.*] — **climb′a•ble** (klī′mə-bəl) *adj.*

Hillary Rodham Clinton

climb•er (klī′mər) *n.* **1.** One that climbs, esp. a mountain climber. **2.** *Sports.* A device used in mountain climbing. **3.** A climbing plant. **4.** One avidly seeking a higher social or professional position.

climb•ing fern (klī′mĭng) *n.* Any of various terrestrial ferns of the genus *Lygodium,* having a single pinnately compound leaf that climbs by twining.

climbing iron *n. Sports.* See **crampon** 2.

climbing perch *n.* A freshwater fish *(Anabas testudineus)* of tropical Asia having modified gills allowing it to breathe air and pectoral fins adapted for traveling on land.

clime (klīm) *n.* Climate: *warmer climes.* [ME, region of the earth < LLat. *clīma* < Gk. *klima.* See CLIMATE.]

clin– *pref.* Var. of **clino–.**

–clinal *suff.* Sloping: *synclinal.* [< Gk. *klinein,* to lean. See **klei-***.]

clipper
The *Agenor*

cli•nan•dri•um (klĭ-năn′drē-əm) *n., pl.* **-dri•a** (-drē-ə). *Bot.* A hollow containing the anther in the upper part of the column of an orchid flower. [NLat. : Gk. *klinē,* couch (< *klinein,* to recline; see **klei-***) + NLat. *-andrium,* stamen (< Gk. *anēr, andr-,* man; see –ANDRY).]

clinch (klĭnch) *v.* **clinched, clinch•ing, clinch•es.** — *tr.* **1.a.** To fix or secure (a nail, for example) by bending down or flattening the protruding pointed end. **b.** To fasten together thus. **2.** To settle definitely and conclusively. **3.** *Naut.* To fasten with a clinch. — *intr.* **1.** To be held together securely. **2.** *Sports.* To hold a boxing opponent with one or both arms to prevent or hinder punches. **3.** *Slang.* To embrace amorously. — *n.* **1.** Something, such as a clamp, that clinches. **2.** The clinched part of a nail, bolt, or rivet. **3.** *Sports.* An act or instance of clinching in boxing. **4.** *Naut.* A half hitch in a rope with the end of the rope fastened back by seizing. **5.** *Slang.* An amorous embrace. [Var. of CLENCH.]

clinch•er (klĭn′chər) *n.* **1.** One that clinches, as: **a.** A nail, screw, or bolt for clinching. **b.** A tool for clinching nails, screws, or bolts. **2.** *Informal.* A decisive factor.

Clinch River (klĭnch). A river rising in SW VA and flowing c. 483 km (300 mi) generally SW to the Tennessee R.

cline (klīn) *n. Ecol.* A gradual change in a feature across the distributional range of a species or population, usu. correlated with an environmental or a geographic transition. [< Gk. *klinein,* to lean. See **klei-***.] — **clin′al** (klī′nəl) *adj.*

–cline *suff.* Slope: *anticline.* [Back-formation < –CLINAL.]

cling (klĭng) *intr.v.* **clung** (klŭng), **cling•ing, clings. 1.** To hold fast or adhere to something, as by grasping or embracing. **2.** To remain close; resist separation. **3.** To remain emotionally attached; hold on. — *n. Bot.* A clingstone. [ME *clingen* < OE *clingan.*] — **cling′er** *n.* — **cling′y** *adj.*

cling•fish (klĭng′fĭsh′) *n., pl.* **clingfish** or **-fish•es.** Any of various small marine fishes of the family Gobiesocidae, having a large sucking disk under the front part of the body by which they fasten themselves to rocks and seaweed.

Cling•mans Dome (klĭng′mənz). A mountain, 2,026.1 m (6,643 ft), in the Great Smoky Mts. on the TN–NC border.

cling•stone (klĭng′stōn′) *adj.* Of or relating to a fruit with flesh that adheres closely to the stone. — *n.* A clingstone fruit.

clin•ic (klĭn′ĭk) *n.* **1.** A facility devoted to the diagnosis and care of outpatients. **2.** A medical establishment run cooperatively by several specialists sharing the same facilities. **3.** A group session offering counsel or instruction in a particular field or activity. **4.** A training session with a patient for medical students. [Fr. *clinique* < Gk. *klinikē (tekhnē),* clinical (method), fem. of *klinikos* < *klinē,* couch. See **klei-***.]

–clinic *suff.* **1.** Sloping: *isoclinic.* **2.** Having a specified number of oblique axial intersections: *triclinic.*

clin•i•cal (klĭn′ĭ-kəl) *adj.* **1.** Of, relating to, or connected with a clinic. **2.** Involving or based on direct observation of the patient: *a clinical diagnosis.* **3.** Very objective and devoid of emotion; analytical. **4.** Suggestive of a medical clinic; austere and antiseptic: *a clinical style of decor.* — **clin′i•cal•ly** *adv.*

clinical thermometer *n.* A thermometer used to measure body temperature, esp. a small glass thermometer designed with a narrowing above the bulb so that the mercury column stays in position when the instrument is removed from the body.

cli•ni•cian (klĭ-nĭsh′ən) *n.* **1.** A physician, psychologist, or psychiatrist specializing in clinical studies or practice. **2.** One who conducts sessions or teaches at a clinic. [Fr. *clinicien* < *clinique,* clinic. See CLINIC.]

clink[1] (klĭngk) *intr. & tr.v.* **clinked, clink•ing, clinks.** To make or cause to make a clink. — *n.* A light sharp ringing sound. [ME *clinken,* prob. < MDu. *klinken,* of imit. orig.]

clink[2] (klĭngk) *n. Slang.* A prison or a prison cell; a jail. [After *Clink,* a district of London famous for its prison.]

clink•er (klĭng′kər) *n.* **1.** The incombustible residue, fused into an irregular lump, that remains after coal combustion. **2.** A partially vitrified brick or a mass of bricks fused together. **3.** An extremely hard burned brick. **4.** Vitrified matter expelled by a volcano. **5.** *Slang.* **a.** A sour note in a musical performance. **b.** A mistake; a blunder. **c.** Something of inferior quality; a conspicuous failure. **6.** *Chiefly British.* Something admirable or first-rate. — *intr.v.* **-ered, -er•ing, -ers.** To form clinkers in burning. [Obsolete Du. *klinckaerd* < MDu. *klinken,* to clink. See CLINK[1].]

clink•er-built (klĭng′kər-bĭlt′) *adj.* Built with overlapping planks or boards. [< obsolete *clinker,* clinch-nail < ME *clinken,* prob. var. of *clenchen,* to clench < OE *beclencan.*]

clino– or **clin–** *pref.* Slope; slant: *clinometer.* [NLat. < Gk. *klinein,* to slope. See **klei-***.]

cli•nom•e•ter (klī-nŏm′ĭ-tər) *n.* Any of various surveying instruments for measuring angles of elevation or incline. — **cli′no•met′ric** (-nə-mĕt′rĭk), **cli′no•met′ri•cal** *adj.* — **cli•nom′e•try** *n.*

clin•quant (klĭng′kənt, klăN-käN′) *adj.* Glittering with gold or tinsel. — *n.* Imitation gold leaf; tinsel; glitter. [Fr., glistening, tinkling, pr.part. of obsolete *clinquer,* to clink, perh. < MDu. *klinken.* See CLINK[1].]

Clin•ton (klĭn′tən). A city of E-central IA on the Mississippi R. NE of Davenport. Pop. 29,201.

Clinton, DeWitt. 1769–1828. Amer. politician who as governor of NY (1817–23 and 1825–28) was a principal supporter of the Erie Canal.

Clinton, George. 1739–1812. Vice President of the U.S. (1805–12).

Clinton, Sir **Henry.** 1738–95. British general in the American Revolution who was commander in chief of British forces in North America (1778–81).

Clinton, Hillary Rodham. b. 1947. First Lady of the U.S. (since 1993); attorney and noted spokesperson for children's rights.

Clinton, William Jefferson ("Bill"). b. 1946. The 42nd President of the U.S. (since 1993); previously governor of AR (1979–81 and 1983–93).

clin•to•ni•a (klĭn-tō′nē-ə) *n.* Any of various perennial herbs of the genus *Clintonia* in the lily family, native to North America and eastern Asia and having broad basal leaves, white, greenish-yellow, or purplish flowers, and blue or black berries. [NLat. *Clintonia*, genus name, after DeWitt CLINTON.]

Cli•o (klī′ō) *n. Gk. Myth.* The Muse of history. [Lat. *Clīo* < Gk. *Kleiō* < *kleiein*, to tell. See **kleu-***.]

cli•o•met•rics (klī′ə-mĕt′rĭks) *n. (used with a sing. v.)* The study of history using economic models and advanced mathematical methods of data processing and analysis. **—cli′o•met′ric** *adj.* **—cli′o•me•tri′cian** (-mĭ-trĭsh′ən) *n.*

clip¹ (klĭp) *v.* **clipped, clip•ping, clips.** *—tr.* **1.** To cut, cut off, or cut out with or as if with shears: *clip coupons.* **2.** To make shorter by cutting; trim. **3.** To cut off the edge of. **4.** To cut short; curtail. **5.a.** To shorten (a word) by leaving out letters or syllables. **b.** To enunciate clearly and precisely. **6.** *Informal.* To hit with a sharp blow. **7.** *Slang.* To cheat, swindle, or rob. *—intr.* **1.** To cut something. **2.** *Informal.* To move rapidly. *—n.* **1.** The act of clipping. **2.** Something clipped off, esp.: **a.** The wool shorn at one shearing. **b.** A season's shearing. **3.** A short extract from a film or videotape. **4.** *Informal.* A quick sharp blow. **5.** *Informal.* A pace or rate. **6.** A single occasion; a time. **7. clips.** A pair of shears or clippers. [ME *clippen* < ON *klippa.*]

clip² (klĭp) *n.* **1.** A device for gripping or holding things together; a clasp or fastener. **2.** A piece of jewelry that fastens with a clasp or clip; a brooch. **3.** A cartridge clip. **4.** *Football.* An act of clipping. *—tr.v.* **clipped, clip•ping, clips. 1.** To fasten with or as if with a clip; hold tightly. **2.** *Football.* To block (an opponent not carrying the ball) illegally from the rear. **3.** *Archaic.* To embrace or encompass. [ME, hook < *clippen*, to clasp, embrace < OE *clyppan.*]

clip•board (klĭp′bôrd′, -bōrd′) *n.* A small writing board with a spring clip at the top for holding papers or a writing pad.

clip joint *n. Slang.* A restaurant, nightclub, or other business where customers are regularly overcharged.

clipped form (klĭpt) *n.* A word formed by dropping one or more syllables from a polysyllabic word, such as *prof.*

clip•per (klĭp′ər) *n.* **1.** One that cuts, shears, or clips. **2.** An instrument or tool for cutting, clipping, or shearing. Often used in the plural: *nail clippers.* **3.** *Naut.* A sharp-bowed sailing vessel of the mid-19th century that was built for great speed. **4.** One that moves very fast. **5.** *Electron.* See **limiter** 2.

clip•ping (klĭp′ĭng) *n.* Something cut off or out, esp. from a newspaper or magazine.

clip•sheet (klĭp′shēt′) *n.* A sheet of paper containing news items and other newspaper material, usu. printed on only one side for convenience in clipping and reprinting.

clique (klēk, klĭk) *n.* A small, exclusive group of friends or associates. *—intr.v.* **cliqued, cliqu•ing, cliques.** *Informal.* To form, associate in, or act as a clique. [Fr. < OFr., latch, or < obsolete Fr. *cliquer*, to click, clink, of imit. orig.] **—cliqu′ey, cliqu′y, cliqu′ish** *adj.* **—cliqu′ish•ly** *adv.* **—cliqu′ish•ness** *n.*

Clis•the•nes (klĭs′thə-nēz′). See **Cleisthenes.**

cli•tel•lum (klī-tĕl′əm) *n., pl.* **-tel•la** (-tĕl′ə). A glandular epidermal region of certain annelid worms that secretes a fluid to form a cocoon for their eggs. [NLat. *clītellum*, sing. of Lat. *clītellae*, packsaddle. See **klei-***.]

clit•o•ris (klĭt′ər-ĭs, klī′tər-) *n.* A small, elongated erectile organ at the anterior part of the vulva. [NLat. < Gk. *kleitoris.* See **klei-***.] **—clit′o•ral** (-ər-əl) *adj.*

Clive (klīv), **Robert.** Baron Clive of Plassey. 1725–74. British soldier who was instrumental in securing Great Britain's interests in India.

clk. *abbr.* Clerk.

clm. *abbr.* Column.

clo•a•ca (klō-ā′kə) *n., pl.* **-cae** (-sē′). **1.** A sewer or latrine. **2.** *Zool.* **a.** The common cavity into which the intestinal, genital, and urinary tracts open in vertebrates such as fish, reptiles, birds, and some primitive mammals. **b.** The posterior part of the intestinal tract in various invertebrates. [Lat. *cloāca*, sewer, canal.] **—clo•a′cal** (-kəl) *adj.*

cloak (klōk) *n.* **1.** A loose outer garment, such as a cape. **2.** Something that covers or conceals. *—tr.v.* **cloaked, cloak•ing, cloaks.** To cover or conceal with or as if with a cloak. See Syns at **hide¹.** [ME *cloke* < ONFr. *cloque*, cloak, bell (< its shape) < Med.Lat. *clocca.* See CLOCK¹.]

cloak-and-dag•ger (klōk′ən-dăg′ər) *adj.* Marked by melodramatic intrigue and often espionage.

cloak fern *n.* Any of various ferns in the genus *Notholaena*, native chiefly to the temperate and tropical Americas and having pinnately compound leaves.

cloak•room (klōk′ro͞om′, -ro͝om′) *n.* **1.** A room where coats and other articles may be left temporarily, as in a theater. **2.** A private lounge adjacent to a legislative chamber.

clob•ber (klŏb′ər) *tr.v.* **-bered, -ber•ing, -bers.** *Slang.* **1.** To strike violently and repeatedly; batter or maul. **2.** To defeat decisively. **3.** To criticize harshly. [?]

clo•chard (klō-shär′) *n., pl.* **-chards** (-shär′). A tramp; a vagrant. [Fr. < *clocher*, to limp < OFr. < VLat. **cloppicāre* < *cloppus*, lame person, alteration of Lat. *claudus.*]

cloche (klōsh) *n.* **1.** A close-fitting woman's hat with a bell-like shape. **2.** A usu. bell-shaped cover, used to protect plants from frost. [Fr. < OFr., bell < Med.Lat. *clocca.* See CLOCK¹.]

clock¹ (klŏk) *n.* **1.** An instrument other than a watch for measuring or indicating time, esp. a mechanical or electronic device. **2.** A time clock. **3.** A source of regularly occurring pulses used to measure the passage of time, as in a computer. **4.** Any of various devices that indicate measurement, such as a speedometer. **5.** *Bot.* The downy flower head of a dandelion that has gone to seed. *—v.* **clocked, clock•ing, clocks.** *—tr.* **1.** To time, as with a stopwatch. **2.** To register or record with a mechanical device. *—intr.* To record working hours with a time clock: *clocks in at 8* A.M. ***—idiom.*** **clean (someone's) clock.** *Slang.* To beat or defeat decisively. [ME *clokke* < ONFr. *cloque*, bell, or < MDu. *clocke*, bell, clock, both < Med.Lat. *clocca*, of imit. orig.] **—clock′er** *n.*

clock² (klŏk) *n.* An embroidered or woven decoration on a stocking or sock. [Perh. < CLOCK¹, bell (obsolete).]

clock radio *n.* A radio having a built-in alarm clock that can be set to turn the radio on automatically.

clock•wise (klŏk′wīz′) *adv. & adj.* In the same direction as the rotating hands of a clock.

clock•work (klŏk′wûrk′) *n.* A mechanism of geared wheels driven by a wound spring, as in a mechanical clock. ***—idiom.*** **like clockwork.** With machinelike regularity and precision.

clod (klŏd) *n.* **1.** A lump or chunk, esp. of earth or clay. **2.** Earth or soil. **3.** A dull, stupid person; a dolt. [ME, var. of *clot*, lump. See CLOT.] **—clod′dish** *adj.* **—clod′dish•ly** *adv.* **—clod′dish•ness** *n.*

clod•hop•per (klŏd′hŏp′ər) *n.* **1.** A clumsy, coarse person; a bumpkin. **2.** A big heavy shoe.

clo•fi•brate (klō-fī′brāt, -fĭb′rāt) *n.* A synthetic drug, $C_{12}H_{15}ClO_3$, used primarily to reduce abnormally elevated levels of plasma cholesterol and triglyceride. [*clofibric acid* (perh. C(H)LO(RO)- + FIBR(O)- + -IC) + -ATE².]

clog (klôg, klŏg) *n.* **1.** An obstruction or hindrance. **2.** A weight attached to the leg of an animal to hinder movement. **3.** A heavy, usu. wooden-soled shoe. *—v.* **clogged, clog•ging, clogs.** *—tr.* **1.** To obstruct movement on or in; block up. **2.** To hamper the function or activity of; impede. *—intr.* **1.** To become obstructed or choked up. **2.** To thicken or stick together; clot. **3.** To do a clog dance. [ME.]

clog dance *n.* A dance performed while wearing clogs and characterized by heavy, stamping steps. **—clog dancer** *n.*

cloi•son•né (kloi′zə-nā′, klə-wä′zə-) *n.* **1.** Enamelware in which the surface decoration is formed by different colors of enamel separated by thin strips of metal. **2.** The process or method of producing such enamelware. [Fr., p.part. of *cloisonner*, to partition < OFr. *cloison*, partition < VLat. **clausiō, clausiōn-* < Lat. *clausus*, p.part. of *claudere*, to close, lock.] **—cloi•son•né′** *adj.*

clois•ter (kloi′stər) *n.* **1.** A covered walk with an open colonnade on one side, running along the walls of buildings that face a quadrangle. **2.a.** A place, esp. a monastery or convent, devoted to religious seclusion. **b.** Life in a monastery or convent. **3.** A secluded, quiet place. *—tr.v.* **-tered, -ter•ing, -ters. 1.** To shut away from the world in or as if in a cloister; seclude. **2.** To furnish (a building) with a cloister. [ME *cloistre* < OFr., alteration of *clostre* < Lat. *claustrum*, enclosed place < *claudere*, to close.]

clois•tral (kloi′strəl) also **claus•tral** (klô′strəl) *adj.* **1.** Of, relating to, or like a cloister; secluded. **2.** Living in a cloister.

clomb (klōm) *v. Archaic.* A p.t. and p.part. of **climb.**

clomp (klŏmp) *intr.v.* **clomped, clomp•ing, clomps.** To walk heavily and noisily. [Imit.]

clone (klōn) *n.* **1.** A group of genetically identical cells descended from a single common ancestor. **2.** An organism descended asexually from a single ancestor, such as a plant produced by layering. **3.** A replica of a DNA sequence, such as a gene, produced by genetic engineering. **4.** One that copies or closely resembles another, as in appearance or function. *—v.* **cloned, clon•ing, clones.** *—tr.* **1.** To make multiple identical copies of (a DNA sequence). **2.a.** To establish and maintain pure lineages of (a cell) under laboratory conditions. **b.** To reproduce or propagate asexually: *clone a frog.* **3.** To produce a copy of; imitate. *—intr.* To grow as a clone. [Gk. *klōn*, twig.] **—clon′al** (klō′nəl) *adj.* **—clon′al•ly** *adv.* **—clon′er** *n.*

clo•nus (klō′nəs) *n., pl.* **-nus•es.** An abnormality in neuromuscular activity characterized by rapidly alternating muscular contraction and relaxation. [NLat. < Gk. *klonos*, turmoil.] **—clo′nic** (klō′nĭk, klŏn′ĭk) *adj.* **—clo•nic′i•ty** (klō-nĭs′ĭ-tē, klō-), **clo′nism** (klō′nĭz′əm, klŏn′ĭz′əm) *n.*

clop (klŏp) *n.* A sharp, hollow sound, as of a hoof on concrete. *—intr.v.* **clopped, clop•ping, clops.** To make or move with this sound. [Imit.]

clo•que also **clo•qué** (klō-kā′) *n.* A cotton, silk, or rayon fabric with a raised woven pattern and a puckered or quilted look. [Fr. *cloqué*, p.part. of *cloquer*, to become blistered < dial. *cloque*, blister < Med.Lat. *clocca*, bell. See CLOCK¹.]

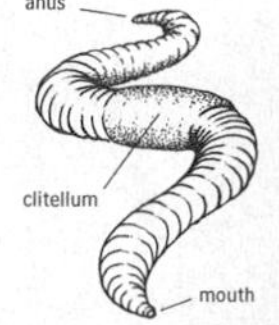

clitellum
Of an earthworm

cloche

cloister
Palermo University

ă pat	oi boy
ā pay	ou out
âr care	o͝o took
ä father	o͞o boot
ĕ pet	ŭ cut
ē be	ûr urge
ĭ pit	th thin
ī pie	*th* this
îr pier	hw which
ŏ pot	zh vision
ō toe	ə about, item
ô paw	

Stress marks:
′ (primary);
′ (secondary), as in
dictionary (dĭk′shə-nĕr′ē)

close (klōs) *adj.* **clos•er, clos•est. 1.** Being near in space or time. **2.** Being near in relationship. **3.** Bound by mutual interests, loyalties, or affections; intimate: *close friends.* **4.** Having little or no space between elements or parts; tight and compact: *a close weave.* **5.** Being near the surface; short: *a close haircut.* **6.** Being on the brink of: *close to tears.* **7.** Decided by a narrow margin; almost even: *a close election.* **8.** Faithful to the original. **9.** Rigorous; thorough: *close attention.* **10.** Shut; closed. **11.** Shut in; enclosed. **12.** Confining or narrow; crowded: *close quarters.* **13.** Fitting tightly. **14.** Lacking fresh air; stuffy: *a close room.* **15.** Confined to specific persons or groups: *a close secret.* **16.** Strictly confined or guarded. **17.** Hidden from view; secluded. **18.** Secretive; reticent. **19.** Giving or spending with reluctance; stingy. **20.** Not easily acquired; scarce: *Money was close.* **21.** *Ling.* Pronounced with the tongue near the palate, as the *ee* in *meet.* Used of vowels. **22.** Marked by more rather than less punctuation, esp. commas. — *v.* (klōz) **closed, clos•ing, clos•es.** — *tr.* **1.** To move (a door, for example) so that an opening or passage is covered or obstructed; shut. **2.** To bar access to. **3.** To fill or stop up: *closed the cracks.* **4.** To stop the operations of permanently or temporarily. **5.** To bring to an end; terminate: *close a letter.* **6.** To bring together all the elements or parts of: *closed ranks.* **7.** To join or unite; bring into contact: *close a circuit.* **8.** To draw or bind together the edges of: *close a wound.* **9.** To complete the final details or negotiations on: *close a deal.* **10.** *Archaic.* To enclose on all sides. — *intr.* **1.** To become shut. **2.** To come to an end; finish. **3.** To reach an agreement; come to terms. **4.** To cease operation. **5.a.** To engage at close quarters. **b.** To draw near. **6.** To come together. — *n.* (klōz). **1.** The act of closing. **2.** A conclusion; a finish. **3.** *Mus.* The concluding part of a phrase or theme; a cadence. **4.** (klōs). An enclosed place, esp. land surrounding or beside a cathedral or other building. **5.** (klōs). *Chiefly British.* A narrow way or alley. **6.** *Archaic.* A fight at close quarters. — *adv.* (klōs) **closer, closest.** In a close position or manner; closely: *close together.* — ***phrasal verbs.*** **close in. 1.** To seem to be gathering in on all sides. **2.** To advance on a target so as to block escape. **3.** To surround so as to make unusable. **close out. 1.** To dispose of (a line of merchandise) at reduced prices. **2.** To terminate, as by selling. — ***idioms.*** **close to home.** So as to affect one's feelings or interests. **close to the wind.** At a close angle into the direction from which the wind blows. [ME *clos,* closed < OFr. < Lat. *clausus,* p.part. of *claudere,* to close.] — **close′ly** *adv.* — **close′ness** *n.* — **clos′er** (klō′zər) *n.* — **clos′ing** (klō′zĭng) *n.*

Syns: *close, immediate, near, nearby, nigh, proximate.* The central meaning shared by these adjectives is "not far from another in space, time, or relationship": *an airport close to town; her immediate family; his nearest relative; a nearby library; the nighest route; a proximate town.* ***Ant:*** *far.*

Usage Note: Strictly speaking, the phrase *close proximity* says nothing that is not said by *proximity* itself. Like other common redundancies, however (*old adage, mental telepathy*), this usage is too widespread and too innocuous to be worth objecting to. See Usage Note at **redundancy.**

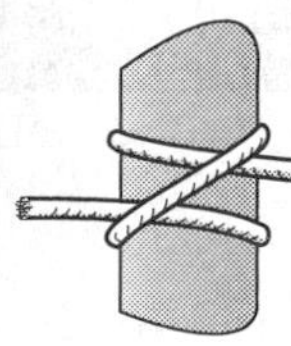
clove hitch

close call (klōs) *n. Informal.* A narrow escape.

close corporation (klōs) *n.* See **closed corporation.**

closed (klōzd) *adj.* **1.** Having boundaries; enclosed. **2.** Blocked or barred to passage or entry. **3.** Explicitly limited; restricted. **4.** Self-contained or self-sufficient. **5.** Barred to the public; conducted in secrecy. **6.** *Math.* **a.** Of or relating to a curve having no endpoints. **b.** Of or relating to a surface having no boundary curves. **c.** Of or relating to an interval containing both its endpoints. **d.** Characterized by or possessing the property by which an operation acting on an element in a set produces an element within the set. **7.** *Comp. Sci.* **a.** Of or relating to a file that cannot be accessed. **b.** Of or relating to a switch that is on. **8.** *Ling.* Ending in a consonant.

closed-cap•tioned (klōzd′kăp′shənd) *adj.* Broadcast with captions seen only on a specially equipped receiver.

closed chain *n. Chem.* See **ring**[1] 14.

closed circuit *n.* **1.** An electric circuit providing an uninterrupted, endless path for the flow of current. **2.** A television transmission circuit with a limited number of reception stations and no broadcast facilities. — **closed′-cir′cuit** (klōzd′sûr′kĭt) *adj.*

cloverleaf

closed corporation *n.* A corporation in which the stock is held by relatively few persons and is not publicly traded.

closed couplet *n.* A rhymed couplet forming a complete thought or syntactic unit, for example: *Should Humpty Dumpty chance to fall/Who next will prance atop the wall?*

closed-door (klōzd′dôr′, -dōr′) *adj.* Not open to the public.

closed-end investment company (klōzd′ĕnd′) *n.* A company with fixed capitalization whose shares are traded by investors and whose capital is invested in other companies.

closed interval *n. Math.* See **interval** 4.

close•down (klōz′doun′) *n.* A suspension or termination of operations: *a plant closedown.*

closed shop *n.* See **union shop.**

close-fist•ed (klōs′fĭs′tĭd) *adj.* Tightfisted; stingy.

close-grained (klōs′grānd′) *adj.* Dense or compact in structure or texture, as a wood composed of small-diameter cells.

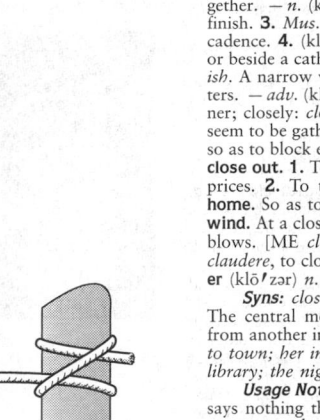

close-hauled (klōs′hôld′) *adv.* & *adj. Naut.* With sails trimmed flat for sailing as close to the wind as possible.

close-knit (klōs′nĭt′) *adj.* Held tightly together, as socially.

close-mind•ed (klōs′mīn′dĭd, klōz′-) or **closed-mind•ed** (klōzd′-) *adj.* Intolerant of the beliefs and opinions of others; unreceptive to new ideas. — **close′-mind′ed•ness** *n.*

close-mouthed (klōs′mouthd′, -moutht′) *adj.* Tightlipped.

close-or•der drill (klōs′ôr′dər) *n.* A military drill in marching, maneuvering, and formal handling of arms in which the participants perform at close intervals.

close•out (klōz′out′) *n.* A sale in which all remaining stock is disposed of, usu. at greatly reduced prices.

close shave (klōs) *n. Informal.* A narrow escape; a close call.

clos•et (klŏz′ĭt, klô′zĭt) *n.* **1.** A cabinet or enclosed recess for linens, household supplies, or clothing. **2.** A small private chamber, as for study or prayer. **3.** A water closet; a toilet. **4.** A state of secrecy or cautious privacy. — *tr.v.* **-et•ed, -et•ing, -ets.** To enclose or shut up in a private room, as for discussion. — *adj.* **1.** Private; confidential: *closet information.* **2.** Being so or engaging only in private; secret. **3.** Based on theory and speculation rather than practice. [ME, private room < OFr., dim. of *clos,* enclosure < Lat. *clausum* < neut. of *clausus,* enclosed. See CLOSE.] — **clos′et•ful′** *n.*

closet drama *n.* A play to be read rather than performed.

closet queen *n. Offensive.* Used as a disparaging term for a gay or homosexual man who chooses not to reveal his sexual orientation.

close-up (klōs′ŭp′) *n.* **1.** A close-range photograph, film, or television shot. **2.** An intimate view or description. — **close′-up′** *adj.*

clos•ing transaction (klō′zĭng) *n.* **1.** The last transaction for a security during a trading day. **2.** An option order that will eliminate or decrease the size of an existing option position.

clos•trid•i•um (klŏ-strĭd′ē-əm) *n., pl.* **-i•a** (-ē-ə). Any of various rod-shaped, spore-forming, chiefly anaerobic bacteria of the genus *Clostridium.* [NLat. *Clōstridium,* genus name < Gk. *klōstēr,* spindle < *klōthein,* to spin.]

clo•sure (klō′zhər) *n.* **1.** The act of closing or the state of being closed: *closure of an incision.* **2.** Something that closes or shuts. **3.** A bringing to an end; a conclusion. **4.** See **cloture. 5.** The property of being mathematically closed. — *tr.v.* **-sured, -sur•ing, -sures.** To cloture (a debate). [ME < OFr. < LLat. *clausūra,* lock < *clausus,* enclosed. See CLOSE.]

clot (klŏt) *n.* **1.** A thick, viscous, or coagulated mass or lump, as of blood. **2.** A clump, mass, or lump, as of clay. **3.** A compact group. — *v.* **clot•ted, clot•ting, clots.** — *intr.* To form into a clot or clots; coagulate. — *tr.* **1.** To cause to form into a clot or clots. **2.** To fill or cover with or as if with clots. [ME < OE *clott,* lump.]

cloth (klôth, klŏth) *n., pl.* **cloths** (klôths, klôthz, klŏths, klŏthz). **1.** Fabric or material formed by weaving, knitting, pressing, or felting natural or synthetic fibers. **2.** A piece of fabric or material used for a specific purpose. **3.** *Naut.* **a.** Canvas. **b.** A sail. **4.** The characteristic attire of a profession, esp. that of the clergy. **5.** The clergy. [ME < OE *clāth.*]

clothe (klōth) *tr.v.* **clothed** or **clad** (klăd), **cloth•ing, clothes. 1.** To put clothes on. **2.** To provide clothes for. **3.** To cover as with clothing. [ME *clothen* < OE *clāthian* < *clāth,* cloth.]

clothes (klōz, klōthz) *pl.n.* **1.** Articles of dress; wearing apparel. **2.** Bedclothes. [ME < OE *clāthas,* pl. of *clāth,* cloth.]

clothes•horse (klōz′hôrs′, klōthz′-) *n.* **1.** A frame for drying or airing clothes. **2.** A person overconcerned with dress.

clothes•line (klōz′līn′, klōthz′-) *n.* A cord, rope, or wire on which clothes may be hung to dry or air.

clothes moth *n.* Any of various moths of the family Tineidae, whose larvae feed on wool, hair, fur, and feathers.

clothes•pin (klōz′pĭn′, klōthz′-) *n.* A clip of wood or plastic for fastening clothes to a clothesline.

clothes•press also **clothes press** (klōz′prĕs′, klōthz′-) *n.* A chest, closet, or wardrobe in which clothes are kept.

clothes tree *n.* An upright pole or stand with hooks or pegs on which to hang clothing.

cloth•ier (klōth′yər, klō′thē-ər) *n.* One that makes or sells clothing or cloth.

cloth•ing (klō′thĭng) *n.* **1.** Clothes considered as a group; wearing apparel. **2.** A covering.

Clo•tho (klō′thō) *n. Gk. Myth.* One of the three Fates, the spinner of the thread of destiny.

cloth yard *n.* The standard unit of cloth measurement, equal to 36 inches (0.914 meter).

clot•ted cream (klŏt′ĭd) *n.* A thick cream made primarily in England by heating and cooling milk on which cream has already been allowed to rise, then skimming the cream.

clo•ture (klō′chər) *n.* A parliamentary procedure by which debate is ended and an immediate vote is taken on the matter under discussion. — *tr.v.* **-tured, -tur•ing, -tures.** To apply cloture to (a parliamentary debate). [Fr. *clôture* < OFr. *closture,* prob. alteration of *closure,* closure. See CLOSURE.]

cloud (kloud) *n.* **1.a.** A visible body of very fine water droplets or ice particles suspended in the atmosphere at altitudes ranging up to several miles above sea level. **b.** A mass, as of dust, suspended in the atmosphere or in outer space. **2.** A large moving body of things in the air or on the ground. **3.** Something that darkens or fills with gloom. **4.** A dark region or blemish, as on a polished stone. **5.** Something that obscures. **6.** Suspicion or a charge affecting a reputation. **7.** A collection of charged particles. — *v.* **cloud•ed, cloud•ing, clouds.** — *tr.* **1.** To cover with or as if with clouds. **2.** To make gloomy or troubled. **3.** To obscure. **4.** To cast aspersions on; sully. — *intr.* To become cloudy or overcast. — ***idiom.*** **in the clouds. 1.** Imaginary; unreal; fanciful. **2.** Impractical. [ME, hill, cloud < OE *clūd*, rock, hill.] — **cloud′less** *adj.*

cloud•ber•ry (kloud′bĕr′ē) *n.* A creeping perennial herb *(Rubus chamaemorus)* in the rose family, native to northern regions and having white flowers and edible yellowish fruit.

cloud•burst (kloud′bûrst′) *n.* A sudden heavy rainstorm.

cloud chamber *n.* A gas-filled device in which the path of charged subatomic particles can be detected by the formation of chains of droplets on ions generated by their passage.

cloud•land (kloud′lănd′) *n.* A realm of imagination or fantasy.

cloud•let (kloud′lĭt) *n.* A small cloud or something like one.

cloud nine *n. Informal.* A state of elation or great happiness.

cloud•y (klou′dē) *adj.* **-i•er, -i•est. 1.** Full of or covered with clouds; overcast. **2.** Of or like a cloud or clouds. **3.** Marked with indistinct masses or streaks: *cloudy marble.* **4.** Not transparent, as certain liquids. **5.a.** Open to more than one interpretation. **b.** Not clearly perceived or perceptible. **6.** Troubled; gloomy. — **cloud′i•ly** *adv.* — **cloud′i•ness** *n.*

clout (klout) *n.* **1.** A blow, esp. with the fist. **2.a.** *Baseball.* A long, powerful hit. **b.** *Sports.* An archery target. **3.** *Informal.* **a.** Influence; pull. **b.** Power; muscle. **4.** *Regional.* A piece of cloth, esp. a baby's diaper. — *tr.v.* **clout•ed, clout•ing, clouts.** To hit, esp. with the fist. [ME, prob. < OE *clūt*, cloth patch.]

clove[1] (klōv) *n.* **1.** An evergreen tree *(Syzygium aromaticum)* native to the Moluccas and widely cultivated for its aromatic dried flower buds. **2.** A flower bud of this plant, used as a spice. Often used in the plural. [ME < OFr. *clou (de girofle)*, nail (of the clove tree) < Lat. *clāvus*, nail.]

clove[2] (klōv) *n.* One of the small sections of a separable bulb, as that of garlic. [ME < OE *clufu*. See **gleubh-***.]

clove[3] (klōv) *v.* **1.** A p.t. of **cleave**[1]. **2.** *Archaic.* A p.part. of **cleave**[1].

clove[4] (klōv) *v. Archaic.* A p.t. of **cleave**[2].

clove hitch *n.* A knot used to secure a line to a spar, post, or other object, consisting of two half hitches made in opposite directions. [ME *clove*, split, p.part. of *cleven*, to split. See CLEAVE[1].]

clo•ven (klō′vən) *v.* A p.part. of **cleave**[1]. — *adj.* Split; divided.

cloven foot *n.* See **cloven hoof** 1. — **clo′ven-foot′ed** (klō′vən-fo͝ot′ĭd) *adj.*

cloven hoof *n.* **1.** A divided or cleft hoof, as in deer or cattle. **2.** Evil or Satan, often depicted as a figure with cleft hoofs. — **clo′ven-hoofed′** (klō′vən-ho͝oft′, -ho͞oft′, -ho͞ovd′, -ho͝ovd′) *adj.*

clove oil *n.* An aromatic oil obtained from the buds, stems, or leaves of the clove tree, used in flavoring and perfumery.

clove pink *n.* See **carnation** 1.

clo•ver (klō′vər) *n.* **1.** Any of various herbs of the genus *Trifolium* in the pea family, having trifoliolate leaves and dense heads of small flowers. **2.** Any of several other plants in the pea family, such as sweet clover. **3.** Any of several nonleguminous plants, such as water clover. — ***idiom.*** **in clover.** Living a carefree life. [ME < OE *clāfre*.]

clo•ver•leaf (klō′vər-lēf′) *n.* A highway interchange at which two highways have a series of entrance and exit ramps resembling the outline of a four-leaf clover and enabling vehicles to proceed in either direction on either highway. — *adj.* Resembling or shaped like a leaf of the clover plant.

Clo•vis[1] (klō′vĭs). **1.** A city of central CA in the foothills of the Sierra Nevada near Fresno. Pop. 50,323. **2.** A city of E NM near the TX border. Pop. 30,954.

Clo•vis[2] (klō′vĭs) *adj.* Of or relating to a culture widespread throughout North America from about 12,000 to 9,000 B.C., distinguished by sharp, fluted projectile points made of chalcedony or obsidian. [After CLOVIS[1] NM.]

Clovis I. A.D. 466?–511. King of the Franks (481–511) who unified Gaul as a single kingdom with Paris as its cap.

clown (kloun) *n.* **1.a.** A buffoon or jester who entertains by jokes, antics, and tricks, as in a circus or play. **b.** One who jokes and plays tricks. **2.** A coarse, rude, vulgar person; a boor. **3.** A peasant; a rustic. — *intr.v.* **clowned, clown•ing, clowns. 1.** To behave like a buffoon or jester. **2.** To perform as a buffoon or jester. [Of Scand. orig. (akin to Icel. *klunni*, clumsy person) or of LGer. orig.] — **clown′ish** *adj.* — **clown′ish•ly** *adv.* — **clown′ish•ness** *n.*

clown anemone *n.* See **anemone fish.**

clown fish *n.* See **anemone fish.**

cloy (kloi) *v.* **cloyed, cloy•ing, cloys.** — *tr.* To cause distaste or disgust by supplying with too much of something originally pleasant, esp. something rich or sweet; surfeit. — *intr.* To cause to feel surfeited. [Short for obsolete *accloy*, to clog < ME *acloien* < OFr. *encloer*, to drive a nail into < Med.Lat. *inclāvāre* : Lat. *in-*, in; see IN-[2] + Lat. *clāvāre*, to nail (< *clāvus*, nail).] — **cloy′ing•ly** *adv.* — **cloy′ing•ness** *n.*

cloze (klōz) *adj.* Based on or being a test of reading comprehension that asks one to supply words systematically deleted from a text. [Alteration of CLOSURE.]

CLU *abbr.* Chartered life underwriter.

club (klŭb) *n.* **1.** A stout heavy stick, usu. thicker at one end, suitable for use as a weapon. **2.** *Sports.* An implement used in some games to drive a ball, esp. a stick with a protruding head used in golf. **3.** *Games.* **a.** A black figure shaped like a trefoil or clover leaf on certain playing cards. **b.** A playing card with this figure. **c. clubs.** *(used with a sing. or pl. v.)* The suit of cards represented by this figure. **4.** A group of people organized for a common purpose, esp. a group that meets regularly: *a garden club.* **5.** The building, room, or other facility used for the meetings of an organized group. **6.** *Sports.* An athletic team or organization. **7.** A nightclub. — *v.* **clubbed, club•bing, clubs.** — *tr.* **1.** To strike or beat with or as if with a club. **2.** To gather or combine (hair, for example) into a club-like mass. **3.** To contribute to a joint or common purpose. — *intr.* To join or combine for a common purpose; form a club. [ME < ON *klubba*.]

club•ba•ble also **club•a•ble** (klŭb′ə-bəl) *adj. Informal.* Suited to membership in a social club; sociable.

clubbed (klŭbd) *adj.* Shaped like a club.

club•ber (klŭb′ər) *n.* **1.** One that wields a club. **2.** One who is active in a club.

club•by (klŭb′ē) *adj.* **-bi•er, -bi•est. 1.** Typical of a club or club members. **2.** Friendly; sociable. **3.** Clannish; exclusive. — **club′bi•ness** *n.*

club car *n.* A railroad passenger car equipped with lounge chairs, tables, a buffet or bar, and other comforts.

club chair *n.* An easy chair with arms and a low back.

club•foot (klŭb′fo͝ot′) *n.* **1.** A congenital deformity of the foot, usu. marked by a curled shape or twisted position of the ankle, heel, and toes. **2.** A foot so deformed. — **club′foot′ed** *adj.*

club•house (klŭb′hous′) *n.* **1.** A building occupied by a club. **2.** *Sports.* The locker room of an athletic team.

club moss or **club-moss** (klŭb′môs′, -mŏs′) *n.* Any of various vascular plants of the genus *Lycopodium*, often resembling mosses and reproducing by spores. [From the club-shaped strobiles on some species of this plant.]

club root *n.* A disease of cabbage and related plants, caused by a fungus *(Plasmodiophora brassicae)* and characterized by knobby or club-shaped swellings on the roots and wilting, yellowing, and stunted growth of aboveground parts.

club sandwich *n.* A sandwich composed of two or three slices of bread with various meats, tomato, lettuce, and dressing.

club soda *n.* See **soda water** 1a.

club steak *n.* See **Delmonico steak.**

cluck (klŭk) *n.* **1.a.** The characteristic sound made by a hen when brooding or calling its chicks. **b.** A sound similar to this. **2.** *Informal.* A stupid or foolish person. — *v.* **clucked, cluck•ing, clucks.** — *intr.* **1.** To utter a cluck. **2.** To make a cluck, as in coaxing a horse. — *tr.* **1.** To call by clucking. **2.** To express by clucking. [ME *clokken* < OE *cloccian*.]

clue[1] (klo͞o) *n.* Something that serves to guide or direct in the solution of a problem or mystery. — *tr.v.* **clued, clue•ing** or **clu•ing, clues.** To give (someone) guiding information. [Var. of CLEW[1] (< Theseus's use of a ball of thread as a guide through the Cretan labyrinth).]

clue[2] (klo͞o) *Naut.* — *n.* Var. of **clew**[1] 4. — *v.* Var. of **clew**[1] 2.

Cluj-Na•po•ca (klo͞ozh′nä-pô′kä). A city of W-central Romania NW of Bucharest; founded in the 12th cent. Pop. 301,244.

Clum•ber spaniel also **clum•ber spaniel** (klŭm′bər) *n.* A dog of a breed developed in England, having short legs, a stocky body, and a silky, predominantly white coat. [After *Clumber Park*, an estate in Nottinghamshire, England.]

Clumber spaniel

clump (klŭmp) *n.* **1.** A clustered mass; a lump: *clumps of soil.* **2.** A thick grouping, as of trees or bushes. **3.** A heavy dull sound; a thud. — *v.* **clumped, clump•ing, clumps.** — *intr.* **1.** To form clumps. **2.** To walk or move so as to make a clump. — *tr.* To gather into or form clumps of. [Prob. LGer. *klump* < MLGer. *klumpe*, cluster of trees.] — **clump′y** *adj.*

clum•sy (klŭm′zē) *adj.* **-si•er, -si•est. 1.** Lacking physical coordination, skill, or grace; awkward. **2.** Awkwardly constructed; unwieldy. **3.** Gauche; inept. [< obsolete *clumse*, to be numb with cold < ME *clomsen*, of Scand. orig.] — **clum′si•ly** *adv.* — **clum′si•ness** *n.*

clung (klŭng) *v.* P.t. and p.part. of **cling.**

clunk (klŭngk) *n.* **1.** A dull sound; a thump. **2.** A blow that produces a dull sound. **3.** *Informal.* A stupid, dull person. — *v.* **clunked, clunk•ing, clunks.** — *intr.* **1.** To make or move with a clunk. **2.** To strike something so as to make a dull sound. — *tr.* To strike so as to make a dull sound. [Imit.]

clunk•er (clŭng′kər) *n. Informal.* **1.** A decrepit machine, esp. an old car; a rattletrap. **2.** A failure; a flop.

clunk•y (klŭng′kē) *adj.* **-i•er, -i•est.** Clumsy; awkward.

Clu•ny (klo͞o′nē, klo͞o-nē′, klü-). A town of E-central France NNW of Lyons; site of an abbey founded in 910. Pop. 4,335.

ă pat	oi boy
ā pay	ou out
âr care	o͝o took
ä father	o͞o boot
ĕ pet	ŭ cut
ē be	ûr urge
ĭ pit	th thin
ī pie	*th* this
îr pier	hw which
ŏ pot	zh vision
ō toe	ə about, item
ô paw	

Stress marks:
′ (primary);
′ (secondary), as in **dictionary** (dĭk′shə-nĕr′ē)

clu•pe•id (klo͞o′pē-ĭd) *n.* Any of various soft-finned fishes of the family Clupeidae, as herrings. [< NLat. *Clupeidae*, family name < Lat. *clupea*, a small fish.] **—clu′pe•id** *adj.*
clus•ter (klŭs′tər) *n.* **1.** A group of the same or similar elements gathered or occurring closely together; a bunch. **2.** *Ling.* Two or more successive consonants in a word, as *cl* and *st* in the word *cluster.* *—v.* **-tered, -ter•ing, -ters.** *—intr.* To gather or grow into bunches. *—tr.* To cause to grow or form into bunches. [ME < OE *clyster.*]
cluster bean *n.* See **guar.**
clutch[1] (klŭch) *v.* **clutched, clutch•ing, clutch•es.** *—tr.* **1.** To grasp and hold tightly. **2.** To seize; snatch. *—intr.* **1.** To attempt to grasp or seize. **2.** To engage or disengage a motor vehicle's clutch. *—n.* **1.** A hand, claw, talon, or paw in the act of grasping. **2.** A tight grasp. **3.** Control or power. Often used in the plural. **4.** A device for gripping and holding. **5.a.** Any of various devices for engaging and disengaging two working parts of a shaft or of a shaft and a driving mechanism. **b.** The apparatus, such as a lever or pedal, that activates one of these devices. **6.** A tense, critical situation. **7.** A clutch bag. *—adj. Informal.* **1.** Being or occurring in a tense or critical situation. **2.** Tending to be successful in tense or critical situations. [ME *clucchen* < OE *clyccan.*]
clutch[2] (klŭch) *n.* **1.** The complete set of eggs produced or incubated at one time. **2.** A brood of chickens. **3.** A group; a bunch. *—tr.v.* **clutched, clutch•ing, clutch•es.** To hatch (chicks). [Var. of dial. *cletch*, to hatch < ME *clekken* < ON *klekja.*]
clutch bag *n.* A usu. strapless woman's purse.
clut•ter (klŭt′ər) *n.* **1.** A confused or disordered state or collection; a jumble. **2.** A confused noise; a clatter. *—v.* **-tered, -ter•ing, -ters.** *—tr.* To litter or pile in a disordered manner. *—intr.* **1.** To run or move with bustle and confusion. **2.** To make a clatter. [Prob. < ME *cloteren*, to clot < *clot*, lump < OE *clott.*]
Clyde (klīd). A river of SW Scotland flowing c. 171 km (106 mi) NW to the **Firth of Clyde,** an estuary of the North Channel.

Clydesdale

Clydes•dale (klīdz′dāl′) *n.* A large, powerful draft horse of a breed developed in the Clyde valley of Scotland.
clyp•e•us (klĭp′ē-əs) *n., pl.* **-e•i** (-ē-ī′). *Zool.* A shieldlike plate on the front of the head of an insect. [NLat. < Lat. *clipeus*, round shield.] **—clyp′e•al** (-ē-əl) *adj.*
clys•ter (klĭs′tər) *n.* An enema. [ME *clister*, ult. < Gk. *klustēr*, clyster pipe < *kluzein*, to wash out.]
Cly•tem•nes•tra also **Cly•taem•nes•tra** (klī′təm-nĕs′trə) *n. Gk. Myth.* The wife of Agamemnon who with her lover Aegisthus murdered him and was later murdered by Orestes and Electra.
cm *abbr.* Centimeter.
Cm The symbol for the element **curium.**
CM *abbr.* Common market.
c.m. *abbr.* **1.** Center of mass. **2.** Circular mil. **3.** Court-martial.
CMA also **C.M.A.** *abbr.* Certified medical assistant.
cmd. *abbr.* **1.** Command. **2. Cmd.** Commander.
cmdg. *abbr.* Commanding.
Cmdr *abbr.* Commander.
cml. *abbr.* Commercial.
CMSGT *abbr.* Chief master sergeant.
CMV *abbr.* Cytomegalovirus.
C/N *abbr.* Credit note.

coati
Nasua nasua

cni•do•blast (nī′də-blăst′) *n.* A cell in the epidermis of coelenterates in which a nematocyst is developed. [NLat. *cnīdā*, nematocyst (< Lat. *cnīdē*, nettle < Gk. *knidē*) + -BLAST.]
Cni•dus also **Cni•dos** (nī′dəs). An ancient Greek city of Asia Minor in present-day SW Turkey.
CNO *abbr.*, Chief of naval operations.
Cnos•sos or **Cnos•sus** (nŏs′əs). See **Knossos.**
CNS *abbr.* Central nervous system.
Cnut (kə-no͞ot′, -nyo͞ot′). See **Canute.**
Co[1] The symbol for the element **cobalt.**
Co[2] *abbr. Bible.* Corinthians.
CO *abbr.* **1.** Colorado. **2.** Or **C.O.** Commanding officer. **3.** Also **C.O.** Conscientious objector.
co. *abbr.* **1.** Or **co** also **Co.** Company. **2.** County.
c.o. *abbr.* **1.** *Accounting.* Carried over. **2.** Cash order.
c/o also **c.o.** *abbr.* Care of.
co– *pref.* **1.** Together; joint; jointly; mutually: *coeducation.* **2.a.** Partner or associate in an activity: *coauthor; cofounder.* **b.** Subordinate or assistant: *copilot.* **3.** To the same extent or degree: *coextensive.* **4.** Complement of an angle: *cotangent.* [ME < Lat., var. of *com–*, com-.]
CoA *abbr.* Coenzyme A.
co•ac•er•vate (kō-ăs′ər-vāt′) *n.* A cluster of droplets separated out of a lyophilic colloid. *—adj.* **1.** Of or relating to a cluster of droplets. **2.** *Biol.* Growing in clusters. *—tr.v.* **-vated, -vat•ing, -vates.** To cause to form a coacervate. [< Lat. *coacervātus*, p.part. of *coacervāre*, to heap together : *co-*, co- + *acervāre*, to heap (< *acervus*, a heap).] **—co•ac′er•vate** *adj.* **—co•ac′er•va′tion** *n.*

coat of arms
MacGregor family

coach (kōch) *n.* **1.a.** A motorbus. **b.** A railroad passenger car. **c.** A closed automobile, usu. with two doors. **d.** A large, closed, four-wheeled carriage with an exterior driver's seat; a stagecoach. **2.** An economical class of passenger accommodations on a commercial airplane or a train. **3.** *Sports.* A person who trains or directs athletes or athletic teams. **4.a.** A person who gives instruction, as in singing. **b.** A private tutor employed to prepare a student for an examination. *—tr. & intr.v.* **coached, coach•ing, coach•es. 1.** To train or tutor or to act as a trainer or tutor. **2.** To transport by or ride in a coach. [Fr. *coche* < obsolete Ger. *Kotsche* < Hung. *kocsi*, after *Kocs*, a town of NW Hungary (where such carriages were first made).] **—coach′a•ble** *adj.* **—coach′er** *n.*
coach dog *n.* See **Dalmatian** 2.
coach•man (kōch′mən) *n.* **1.** A man who drives a coach or carriage. **2.** An artificial fly used in angling.
co•ac•tion (kō-ăk′shən) *n.* **1.** An impelling or restraining force; a compulsion. **2.** Joint action. **3.** *Ecol.* Any of the reciprocal actions or effects, such as symbiosis, that can occur in a community. [ME *coaccioun* < Lat. *coāctiō*, *coāctiōn-*, a collecting < *coāctus*, p.part. of *cōgere*, to collect, condense. See COAGULUM. Senses 2 and 3 : co– + ACTION.] **—co•ac′tive** *adj.* **—co•ac′tive•ly** *adv.*
co•a•dapt•ed (kō′ə-dăp′tĭd) *adj. Ecol.* Of or relating to characteristics that have become established through mutually beneficial interaction between organisms in a community. **—co′ad•ap•ta′tion** (-ăd-ăp-tā′shən) *n.*
co•ad•ju•tant (kō-ăj′ə-tənt) *n.* A helper; an assistant.
co•ad•ju•tor (kō′ə-jo͞o′tər, kō-ăj′ə-tər) *n.* **1.** A coworker; an assistant. **2.** An assistant to a bishop. [ME *coadjutour*, assistant < Lat. *coadiūtor* : *co-*, co- + *adiūtor*, assistant (< *adiūtāre*, to aid; see ADJUTANT).]
co•ad•u•nate (kō-ăj′ə-nĭt, -nāt′) *adj.* Closely joined; grown together; united. [LLat. *coadūnātus*, p.part. of *coadūnāre*, to combine : Lat. *co-*, co- + Lat. *adūnāre*, to unite (*ad-*, ad- + *ūnus*, one; see **oi-no-***).] **—co•ad′u•na′tion** (-nā′shən) *n.* **—co•ad′u•na′tive** *adj.*
co•ag•u•lant (kō-ăg′yə-lənt) *n.* An agent that causes a liquid or sol to coagulate. **—co•ag′u•lant** *adj.*
co•ag•u•lase (kō-ăg′yə-lās′, -lāz′) *n.* An enzyme, such as thrombin, that induces coagulation. [COAGUL(ATE) + -ASE.]
co•ag•u•late (kō-ăg′yə-lāt′) *v.* **-lat•ed, -lat•ing, -lates.** *—tr.* To cause transformation of (a liquid or sol, for example) into or as if into a soft, semisolid, or solid mass. *—intr.* To become coagulated. [ME *coagulaten* < Lat. *coāgulāre*, *coāgulāt-* < *coāgulum*, coagulator. See COAGULUM.] **—co•ag′u•la•bil′i•ty** *n.* **—co•ag′u•la•ble** *adj.* **—co•ag′u•la′tion** *n.* **—co•ag′u•la′tor** *n.*
co•ag•u•lum (kō-ăg′yə-ləm) *n., pl.* **-la** (-lə). A coagulated mass, as of blood; a clot. [Lat., coagulator, rennet < *cōgere*, to condense : *co-*, co- + *agere*, to drive; see **ag-***.]
coal (kōl) *n.* **1.a.** A natural dark brown to black graphitelike material used as a fuel, formed from fossilized plants and consisting of at least 50 percent carbon by weight. **b.** A piece of this substance. **2.** A glowing or charred piece of solid fuel. **3.** Charcoal. *—v.* **coaled, coal•ing, coals.** *—tr.* **1.** To burn (a combustible solid) to a charcoal residue. **2.** To provide with coal. *—intr.* To take on coal. [ME *col* < OE.]
co•a•lesce (kō′ə-lĕs′) *intr.v.* **-lesced, -lesc•ing, -lesc•es. 1.** To grow together; fuse. **2.** To come together so as to form one whole; unite. [Lat. *coalēscere* : *co-*, co- + *alēscere*, to grow, inchoative of *alere*, to nourish; see **al-**[2]*****.] **—co′a•les′cence** *n.* **—co′a•les′cent** *adj.*
coal•fish (kōl′fĭsh′) *n.* Any of several black or dark-colored fishes, esp. the pollock or sablefish.
coal gas *n.* **1.** A gaseous mixture produced by the destructive distillation of bituminous coal and used as a commercial fuel. **2.** The gaseous mixture released by burning coal.
coal•i•fi•ca•tion (kō′lə-fĭ-kā′shən) *n.* Compression and hardening over long periods of time, by which coal is formed from plant materials.
co•a•li•tion (kō′ə-lĭsh′ən) *n.* **1.** An alliance, esp. a temporary one, of people, factions, parties, or nations. **2.** A combination into one body; a union. [Fr. < Med.Lat. *coalitiō*, *coalitiōn-* < Lat. *coalitus*, p.part. of *coalēscere*, to grow together. See COALESCE.] **—co′a•li′tion•ist** *n.*
coal measures *pl.n. Geol.* **1. Coal Measures.** A stratigraphic unit equivalent to the Pennsylvanian or Upper Carboniferous periods. **2.** Strata of the Carboniferous Period, usu. containing coal deposits.
coal oil *n.* See **kerosene.**
Coal•sack (kōl′săk′) *n.* **1.** A dark nebula that appears in the southern Milky Way. **2.** A similar dark nebula in the Northern Hemisphere near the constellation Cygnus.
coal tar *n.* A viscous black liquid containing numerous organic compounds that is obtained by the destructive distillation of coal and widely used, as in sealants or paints.
coam•ing (kō′mĭng) *n. Naut.* A raised rim or border around an opening designed to keep out water. [?]
co-an•chor or **co•an•chor** (kō-ăng′kər) *n.* Either of two news commentators coordinating a newscast. **—co-an′chor** *v.*
co•arc•tate (kō-ärk′tāt′) *adj. Zool.* **1.** Enclosed in an oval horny case. Used of an insect pupa. **2.** Constricted, narrowed, or compressed, as a segment of a blood vessel. [Lat. *coarctātus*, p.part. of *coarctāre*, to compress, alteration of *coartāre* :

co-, co- + *artāre*, to compress (< *artus*, tight, confined; see **ar-***).] — **co′arc·ta′tion** *n.*

coarse (kôrs, kōrs) *adj.* **coars·er, coars·est. 1.** Of low, common, or inferior quality. **2.a.** Lacking in delicacy or refinement. **b.** Vulgar or indecent. **3.** Consisting of large particles; not fine in texture. **4.** Rough, esp. to the touch: *a coarse tweed.* [ME *cors*, prob. < *course*, custom. See COURSE.] — **coarse′ly** *adv.* — **coars′en** *v.* — **coarse′ness** *n.*

coarse-grained (kôrs′grānd′, kōrs′-) *adj.* **1.** Having a rough, coarse texture. **2.** Not refined; indelicate and crude.

coast (kōst) *n.* **1.a.** Land next to the sea; the seashore. **b. Coast.** The Pacific Coast of the United States. **2.** A hill or other slope down which one may coast. **3.** The act of sliding or coasting; slide. **4.** *Obsolete.* The frontier or border of a country. — *v.* **coast·ed, coast·ing, coasts.** — *intr.* **1.a.** To slide down an incline through the effect of gravity. **b.** To move effortlessly and smoothly. See Syns at **slide. 2.** To move without further use of propelling power. **3.** To act or move aimlessly or with little effort. **4.** *Naut.* To sail near or along a coast. — *tr. Naut.* To sail or move along the coast or border of. [ME *coste* < OFr. < Lat. *costa*, side. See **kost-***.] — **coast′al** (kō′stəl) *adj.*

coast·er (kō′stər) *n.* **1.** One that coasts, as: **a.** One who acts in an aimless manner. **b.** A sled or toboggan. **c.** One who rides a sled or toboggan. **2.** *Naut.* A vessel engaged in coastal trade. **3.** A roller coaster. **4.a.** A disk, plate, or small mat placed under a bottle, pitcher, or drinking glass to protect the surface beneath. **b.** A small tray, often on wheels, for passing something around a table. **5.** A resident of a coastal region.

coaster brake *n.* A brake and clutch on the rear wheel and drive mechanism of a bicycle operated through reverse pressure on the pedals.

coast guard also **Coast Guard** *n.* **1.** The branch of a nation's armed forces responsible for coastal defense, protection of life and property at sea, and enforcement of customs, immigration, and navigation laws. **2.** A coast guard member.

coast·guards·man (kōst′gärdz′mən) *n.* A member of a coast guard.

coast·land (kōst′lănd′) *n.* The land along a coast.

coast·line (kōst′līn′) *n.* The shape or boundary of a coast.

Coast Mountains. A range of W British Columbia, Canada, and SE AK extending c. 1,609 km (1,000 mi) parallel to the Pacific coast and rising to 3,996.7 m (13,104 ft).

Coast Ranges. A series of mountain ranges of extreme W North America extending from SE AK to Baja California along the coastline of the Pacific Ocean.

Coast Salish *n.* The Salish-speaking Native American peoples inhabiting the northwest Pacific coast from the Strait of Georgia to southwest Washington.

coast-to-coast (kōst′tə-kōst′) *adj.* Reaching, airing, or traveling from one coast to another.

coast·ward (kōst′wərd) *adv. & adj.* Toward or directed toward a coast. — **coast′wards** (-wərdz) *adv.*

coast·wise (kōst′wīz′) *adv. & adj.* Along, by way of, or following a coast.

coat (kōt) *n.* **1.a.** A sleeved outer garment extending from the shoulders to the waist or below. **b.** A garment extending to just below the waist and usu. forming the top part of a suit. **2.** A natural outer covering; an integument. **3.** A layer of material covering something else; a coating. — *tr.v.* **coat·ed, coat·ing, coats. 1.** To provide or cover with a coat. **2.** To cover with a layer, as of paint. [ME *cote* < OFr., of Gmc. orig.] — **coat′ed** *adj.*

coat·dress (kōt′drĕs′) *n.* A dress that buttons up the front and is tailored somewhat like a coat.

co·a·ti (kō-ä′tē) *n.* Any of four species of mammals of the genera *Nasua* or *Nasuella* of South and Central America and the southwest United States, related to the raccoon but having a longer snout and tail. [Sp. and Port. *coatí* < Tupi : *cua*, belt + *tim*, nose.]

co·a·ti·mun·di also **co·a·ti·mon·di** (kō-ä′tē-mŭn′dē) *n.* A coati. [Poss. Tupi *coati* + *mundé*, animal trap.]

coat·ing (kō′tĭng) *n.* **1.** A layer of a substance spread over a surface for protection or decoration; a covering layer. **2.** Cloth for making coats.

coat of arms *n.*, *pl.* **coats of arms.** *Her.* **1.** A tabard or surcoat blazoned with bearings. **2.a.** An arrangement of bearings, usu. depicted on and around a shield, that indicates ancestry and distinctions. **b.** A representation of bearings.

coat of mail *n.*, *pl.* **coats of mail.** An armored coat made of chain mail, interlinked rings, or overlapping metal plates; a hauberk.

coat·room (kōt′ro͞om′, -ro͝om′) *n.* See **cloakroom** 1.

coat·tail (kōt′tāl′) *n.* **1.** The loose back part of a coat that hangs below the waist. **2. coattails.** The skirts of a formal or dress coat. — ***idioms.* on (someone's) coattails.** With the assistance of another. **on the coattails of. 1.** As a result of the success of another. **2.** Immediately following or as a direct result of.

coat tree *n.* See **clothes tree.**

co·au·thor or **co-au·thor** (kō-ô′thər) *n.* A collaborating or joint author. — **co·au′thor** *v.*

coax[1] (kōks) *v.* **coaxed, coax·ing, coax·es.** — *tr.* **1.** To persuade or try to persuade by pleading or flattery; cajole. **2.** To obtain by persistent persuasion. **3.** *Obsolete.* To caress; fondle. — *intr.* To use persuasion or inducement. [Obsolete *cokes*, to fool < *cokes*, fool.] — **coax′er** *n.*

co·ax[2] (kō′ăks, kō-ăks′) *n.* *Informal.* A coaxial cable.

co·ax·i·al (kō-ăk′sē-əl) *adj.* Having or mounted on a common axis.

coaxial cable *n.* A cable consisting of a conducting metal tube enclosing and insulated from a central conducting core, used for transmitting high-frequency signals.

cob (kŏb) *n.* **1.** A corncob. **2.** A male swan. **3.** A thickset, stocky, short-legged horse. **4.** A small lump or mass, as of coal. **5.** A mixture of clay and straw used as a building material. [Prob. < obsolete *cob*, round object, head, testicle.]

co·bal·a·min (kō-băl′ə-mĭn) also **co·bal·a·mine** (-mēn′) *n.* See **vitamin B_{12}.** [COBAL(T) + (VIT)AMIN.]

co·balt (kō′bôlt′) *n.* *Symbol* **Co** A metallic element, used chiefly for magnetic alloys and high-temperature alloys and in the form of its salts for blue glass and ceramic pigments. Atomic number 27; atomic weight 58.9332; melting point 1,495°C; boiling point 2,900°C; specific gravity 8.9; valence 2, 3. See table at **element.** [Ger. *Kobalt* < MHGer. *kobolt*, goblin (from the trouble it gave silver miners).]

cobalt 60 *n.* A radioactive isotope of cobalt with mass number 60, used in radiotherapy, metallurgy, and materials testing.

cobalt blue *n.* **1.** A blue to green pigment consisting of a variable mixture of cobalt oxide and alumina. **2.** *Color.* A moderate to deep vivid blue or strong greenish blue.

co·balt·ic (kō-bôl′tĭk) *adj.* Of or containing cobalt, esp. with valence 3.

co·balt·ite (kō′bôl-tīt′) also **co·balt·ine** (-tēn′) *n.* A rare mineral, cobalt sulfarsenide, CoAsS, that is a cobalt ore.

co·balt·ous (kō-bôl′təs) *adj.* Of or containing cobalt, esp. with valence 2.

Cobb (kŏb), **Tyrus ("Ty") Raymond.** 1886–1961. Amer. baseball player and manager who was the first player elected to the National Baseball Hall of Fame (1936).

Cob·bett (kŏb′ĭt), **William.** 1763?–1835. British journalist noted for his essays on the deterioration of rural life brought about by the Industrial Revolution.

cob·ble[1] (kŏb′əl) *n.* **1.** A cobblestone. **2.** *Geol.* A rock fragment between 64 and 256 millimeters in diameter, esp. a naturally rounded one. **3. cobbles.** See **cob coal.** — *tr.v.* **-bled, -bling, -bles.** To pave with cobblestones.

cob·ble[2] (kŏb′əl) *tr.v.* **-bled, -bling, -bles. 1.** To make or mend (boots or shoes). **2.** To put together clumsily; bungle.

cob·bler[1] (kŏb′lər) *n.* **1.** One that mends or makes boots and shoes. **2.** *Archaic.* One who is clumsy at work; a bungler. [ME *cobeler.*]

cob·bler[2] (kŏb′lər) *n.* **1.** A deep-dish fruit pie with a thick top crust. **2.** An iced drink made of wine or liqueur, sugar, and citrus fruit. [?]

cob·ble·stone (kŏb′əl-stōn′) *n.* A naturally rounded paving stone. [ME *cobelston* : obsolete *cobel*, prob. dim. of *cob*, round object; see COB + ME *ston, stone*, stone; see STONE.]

cob coal *n.* Coal in rounded lumps of various sizes.

Cob·den (kŏb′dən), **Richard.** 1804–65. British politician who was a leading supporter of free trade.

co·bel·lig·er·ent (kō′bə-lĭj′ər-ənt) *n.* One, such as a nation, that assists another or others in waging war.

Cobh (kōv). An urban district of S Ireland on Cork Harbor; called Queenstown from 1849 to 1922. Pop. 6,587.

co·bi·a (kō′bē-ə) *n.* A large food and game fish *(Rachycentron canadum)* of tropical and subtropical seas. [Origin unknown.]

Co·blenz (kō′blĕnts′). See **Koblenz.**

cob·nut (kŏb′nŭt′) *n.* **1.** The large edible nut of a cultivated variety of hazel. **2.** The plant bearing this fruit.

COBOL or **Co·bol** (kō′bôl′) *n.* *Comp. Sci.* A programming language based on English words and phrases, used for business applications. [*Co(mmon) B(usiness-)O(riented) L(anguage).*]

co·bra (kō′brə) *n.* **1.** Any of several venomous snakes, esp. of the genus *Naja*, that are native to Asia and Africa and capable of expanding the skin of the neck to form a flattened hood. **2.** Leather made from the skin of one of these snakes. [Short for Port. *cobra (de capello)*, snake (with a hood) < Lat. *colubra*, fem. of *coluber*.]

Co·burg (kō′bûrg′). A city of central Germany N of Nuremberg; first mentioned in the 11th cent. Pop. 44,239.

cob·web (kŏb′wĕb′) *n.* **1.a.** The web spun by a spider to catch its prey. **b.** A single thread of a cobweb. **2.** Something resembling a cobweb. **3.** An intricate plot; a snare. **4. cobwebs.** Confusion; disorder. — *tr.v.* **-webbed, -web·bing, -webs.** To cover with or as if with cobwebs. [ME *coppeweb* : *coppe*, spider (short for *attercoppe* < OE *āttercoppe* : *ātor*, poison + *copp*, head) + *web*, web; see WEB.]

co·ca (kō′kə) *n.* **1.** Any of certain Andean evergreen shrubs or small trees of the genus *Erythroxylum*, esp. *E. coca*, whose leaves contain cocaine and other alkaloids. **2.** The dried leaves of such a plant, used for extraction of cocaine and other alkaloids. [Sp. < Quechua *kúka*.]

cobblestone
Acorn Street on Beacon Hill, Boston

cobra
Indian cobra
Naja naja

ă pat	oi boy
ā pay	ou out
âr care	o͝o took
ä father	o͞o boot
ĕ pet	ŭ cut
ē be	ûr urge
ĭ pit	th thin
ī pie	*th* this
îr pier	hw which
ŏ pot	zh vision
ō toe	ə about, item
ô paw	

Stress marks:
′ (primary);
′ (secondary), as in
dictionary (dĭk′shə-nĕr′ē)

co•caine (kō-kān′, kō′kān′) *n.* A colorless or white crystalline alkaloid, $C_{17}H_{21}NO_4$, extracted from coca leaves, sometimes used in medicine as a local anesthetic and widely used as an illicit drug for its euphoric and stimulating effects. [Fr. *cocaïne* < *coca*, coca < Sp. See COCA.]

co•cain•ism (kō-kā′nĭz′əm) *n.* The habitual or excessive use of cocaine.

co•cain•ize (kō-kā′nīz′) *tr.v.* **-ized, -iz•ing, -iz•es.** To anesthetize (a body part) with cocaine. **—co•cain′i•za′tion** (-kā′nĭ-zā′shən) *n.*

co•car•cin•o•gen (kō′kär-sĭn′ə-jən, kō-kär′sĭn-ə-jĕn′) *n.* A substance or factor that will not promote cancer by itself but can potentiate cancer when acting with carcinogenic agents. **—co•car′cin•o•gen′ic** (-sə-nə-jĕn′ĭk) *adj.*

coc•cid (kŏk′sĭd) *n.* Any of various insects of the superfamily Coccoidea, such as the mealybugs. [< NLat. *Coccidae*, family name < *Coccus*, type genus < Gk. *kokkos*, grain.]

coc•cid•i•oi•do•my•co•sis (kŏk-sĭd′ē-oi′dō-mī-kō′sĭs) *n.* An infectious respiratory disease of human beings and other animals caused by inhaling the fungus *Coccidioides immitis.* [NLat. *Coccidioides*, genus name (< *Coccidium*, coccidium; see COCCIDIUM + *-oides* < Gk. *-oeidēs*, -oid) + MYCOSIS.]

coc•cid•i•o•sis (kŏk-sĭd′ē-ō′sĭs) *n.* A parasitic disease of many animals, including cattle and poultry, but rarely of human beings, resulting from infestation of the alimentary canal by protozoans of the order Coccidia. [NLat. *Coccidia*, order name, pl. of *coccidium*, coccidium; see COCCIDIUM + -OSIS.]

coc•cid•i•um (kŏk-sĭd′ē-əm) *n., pl.* **-i•a** (-ē-ə). Any of various parasitic protozoans belonging to the order Coccidia and responsible for coccidiosis. [NLat. *Coccidium*, originally a genus name : COCCUS + *-idium*, n. suff.]

coc•coid (kŏk′oid) *adj.* Shaped like or resembling a coccus; spherical. *—n.* A coccoid microorganism.

coc•co•lith (kŏk′ə-lĭth′) *n.* A microscopic calcite skeletal plate that protects certain marine phytoplankton and in a fossilized state forms chalk and limestone deposits. [cocc(us) (< its shape) + -LITH.]

coc•cus (kŏk′əs) *n., pl.* **coc•ci** (kŏk′sī, kŏk′ī). **1.** A bacterium having a spherical or spheroidal shape. **2.** *Bot.* A division containing a single seed that splits apart from a many-lobed fruit. [NLat. < Gk. *kokkos*, grain.] **—coc′cal** (kŏk′əl) *adj.*

-coccus *suff.* A microorganism of spherical or spheroidal shape: *streptococcus.* [< COCCUS.]

coc•cyg•e•al (kŏk-sĭj′ē-əl) *adj.* Of or relating to the coccyx. [< NLat. *coccyx, coccyg-*, coccyx. See COCCYX.]

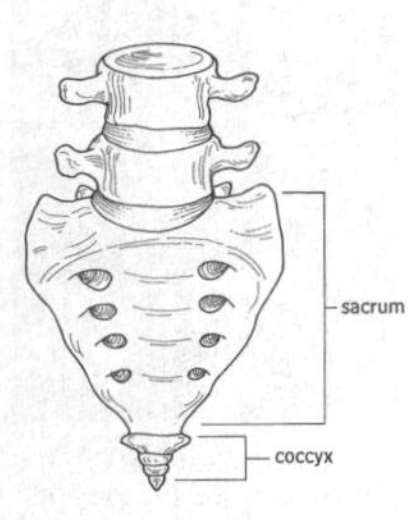

coccyx

coc•cyx (kŏk′sĭks) *n., pl.* **coc•cy•ges** (kŏk-sī′jēz, kŏk′sĭ-jēz′). A small triangular bone at the spinal column base in human beings and tailless apes, consisting of several fused rudimentary vertebrae. [NLat. < Gk. *kokkux*, cuckoo, coccyx.]

Co•cha•bam•ba (kō′chə-bäm′bə, kô′chä-bäm′bä). A city of W-central Bolivia NNW of Sucre; founded 1574. Pop. 317,251.

Co•chin[1] (kō′chĭn). A city of SW India on the Malabar Coast of the Arabian Sea; colonized by the Portuguese in 1503. Pop. 513,249.

Co•chin[2] (kō′chĭn, kŏch′ĭn) *n.* See **Cochin China[2]**.

Cochin Chi•na[1] (chī′nə). A region of S Indochina including the rich delta area of the Mekong R.

Cochin Chi•na[2] (chī′nə) *n.* A large domestic fowl of a breed developed in Asia, having thickly feathered legs. [After COCHIN CHINA[1].]

Jacqueline Cochran

coch•i•neal (kŏch′ə-nēl′, kŏch′ə-nēl′, kō′chə-, kō′chə-) *n.* **1.** A red dye made of the dried and pulverized bodies of female cochineal insects. **2.** *Color.* A vivid red. [Fr. *cochenille* < Sp. *cochinilla*, cochineal insect, prob. < VLat. **coccinella* < fem. dim. of Lat. *coccinus*, scarlet < Gk. *kokkinos* < *kokkos*, kermes berry.] **—coch′i•neal′** *adj.*

cochineal insect *n.* Any of several red scale insects of the family Dactylopiidae that feed on cacti and range from the southwest United States to Central America.

Co•chise (kō-chēs′, -chēz′). 1812?–74. Chiricahua Apache leader who directed Apache resistance to U.S. troops in AZ (1861–72).

coch•le•a (kŏk′lē-ə, kō′klē-ə) *n., pl.* **-le•ae** (-lē-ē′, -lē-ī′) also **-le•as.** A spiral-shaped cavity of the inner ear that contains nerve endings essential for hearing. [Lat., snail shell < Gk. *kokhlias*, snail < *kokhlos*, land snail.] **—coch′le•ar** *adj.*

cochlear nerve *n.* A division of the acoustic nerve that conducts auditory stimuli to the brain.

coch•le•ate (kŏk′lē-ĭt, -āt′, kō′klē-) also **coch•le•at•ed** (-ā′tĭd) *adj.* Shaped like a snail shell; spirally twisted. [Lat. *cochleātus* < *cochlea*, snail shell. See COCHLEA.]

Coch•ran (kŏk′rən), **Jacqueline.** 1910–80. Amer. aviator who held numerous national and international speed records.

cockatoo
Sulfur-crested cockatoo
Cacatua galerita

cock[1] (kŏk) *n.* **1.a.** An adult male chicken; a rooster. **b.** An adult male of various other birds. **2.** A weathervane shaped like a rooster; a weathercock. **3.** A leader or chief. **4.** A faucet or valve by which the flow of a liquid or gas can be regulated. **5.a.** The hammer of a firearm. **b.** The position of the hammer of a firearm when cocked. **6.** A tilting or jaunty turn upward. **7.** *Vulgar Slang.* The penis. **8.** *Archaic.* The characteristic cry of a rooster early in the morning. *—v.* **cocked, cock•ing, cocks.** *—tr.* **1.** To set the hammer of (a firearm) in a position ready for firing. **2.** To set (a device, such as a camera shutter) in a position ready for use. **3.** To tilt or turn up or to one side, usu. in a jaunty or alert manner. **4.** To raise in preparation to throw or hit. *—intr.* **1.** To cock the hammer of a firearm. **2.** To turn or stick up. **3.** To strut; swagger. **—*idioms.* cock a snoot (or snook).** *Slang.* To express scorn or derision by or as if by placing the thumb on the nose and wiggling the fingers; thumb one's nose. **cock of the walk.** An overbearing or domineering person. [ME *cok* < OE *cocc*, prob. < LLat. *coccus* < *coco*, a cackling, of imit. orig.]

cock[2] (kŏk) *n.* A cone-shaped pile of straw or hay. *—tr.v.* **cocked, cock•ing, cocks.** To arrange (straw or hay) into piles shaped like cones. [ME *cok.*]

cock•ade (kŏ-kād′) *n.* An ornament, such as a rosette, usu. worn on the hat as a badge. [Alteration of obsolete *cockard* < Fr. *cocarde* < OFr. *coquarde*, fem. of *coquard*, vain, cocky < *coq*, cock. See COCK[1].] **—cock•ad′ed** *adj.*

cock-a-hoop (kŏk′ə-ho͞op′, -ho͝op′) *adj.* **1.** Being in a state of boastful elation or exultation. **2.** Being askew. [< the phrase *to set cock on hoop*, to drink festively.] **—cock′-a-hoop′** *adv.*

Cock•aigne (kŏ-kān′) *n.* An imaginary land of easy and luxurious living. [ME *cokaigne* < OFr. < *(pais de) cokaigne*, (land of) plenty < MLGer. *kōkenje*, dim. of *kōke*, cake.]

cock-a-leek•ie also **cock•a•leek•ie** (kŏk′ə-lē′kē) *n.* A soup made with chicken broth and leeks. [Alteration of *cockie*, dim. of COCK[1] + *leekie*, dim. of LEEK.]

cock•a•lo•rum (kŏk′ə-lôr′əm, -lōr′-) *n.* **1.** A little man with an unduly high opinion of himself. **2.** Boastful talk; braggadocio. [Perh. alteration (influenced by Lat. *-ōrum*, nominal ending) of obsolete Flem. *kockeloeren*, to crow, of imit. orig.]

cock•a•ma•mie also **cock•a•ma•my** (kŏk′ə-mā′mē) *adj. Slang.* **1.** Trifling; nearly valueless. **2.** Ludicrous; nonsensical: *a cockamamie reason.* [Prob. alteration of DECALCOMANIA.]

cock-and-bull story (kŏk′ən-bo͝ol′) *n.* An absurd or highly improbable tale passed off as being true.

cock•a•tiel also **cock•a•teel** (kŏk′ə-tēl′) *n.* A small crested Australian parrot *(Nymphicus hollandicus)* having gray and yellow plumage. [Du. *kaketielje*, ult. < Malay *kakatua*, cockatoo. See COCKATOO.]

cock•a•too (kŏk′ə-to͞o′) *n., pl.* **-toos.** Any of various large parrots, esp. of the genus *Kakatoe* of Australia and adjacent areas, characterized by a long erectile crest. [Du. *kaketoe* < Malay *kakatua.*]

cock•a•trice (kŏk′ə-trĭs, -trīs′) *n. Myth.* A serpent hatched from a cock's egg and having the power to kill by its glance. [ME *cocatrice*, basilisk < OFr. *cocatris* < Med.Lat. *cocātrix, cocātric-*, poss. alteration of *calcātrix* < Lat. *calcāre*, to track < *calx, calc-*, heel.]

cock•boat (kŏk′bōt′) *n. Naut.* A small rowboat, esp. one used to ferry supplies from ship to shore. [ME *cokboot* : *cok*, cockboat (< AN *coque*, prob. ult. < Lat. *caudica* < *caudex, caudic-*, tree trunk) + *boot*, boat; see BOAT.]

cock•chaf•er (kŏk′chā′fər) *n.* Any of various European beetles of the family Scarabaeidae, esp. *Melolontha melolontha*, which is destructive to plants. [Poss. COCK[1] + CHAFER.]

Cock•croft (kŏk′krôft′, -krŏft′), Sir **John Douglas.** 1897–1967. British physicist who with Ernest Walton succeeded in splitting the atom (1931). They shared a 1951 Nobel Prize.

cock•crow (kŏk′krō′) *n.* The very beginning of the day; dawn.

cocked hat (kŏkt) *n.* A hat with the brim turned up in two or three places, esp. a three-cornered hat; a tricorn.

cock•er[1] (kŏk′ər) *n.* **1.** A cocker spaniel. **2.a.** A person who keeps or trains gamecocks. **b.** A person who promotes or attends cockfights.

cock•er[2] (kŏk′ər) *tr.v.* **-ered, -er•ing, -ers.** To pamper, spoil, or coddle. [ME *cokeren.*]

cock•er•el (kŏk′ər-əl) *n.* A young rooster. [ME *cokerel*, dim. of *cok*, cock. See COCK[1].]

cocker spaniel *n.* A dog of a breed originally developed in England, having long drooping ears and a variously colored silky coat. [From its original use in hunting woodcocks.]

cock•eye (kŏk′ī′) *n.* A squinting eye. [Poss. alteration (influenced by COCK[1]) of Ir.Gael. *caoch*, one-eyed, squinting (< OIr. *cáech*) + EYE.]

cock•eyed (kŏk′īd′) *adj. Informal.* **1.** Foolish; ridiculous; absurd. **2.** Askew; crooked. **3.** Intoxicated; drunk.

Cock•eys•ville (kŏk′ēz-vĭl′). A community of N MD, a suburb of Baltimore. Pop. 18,668.

cock•fight (kŏk′fīt′) *n.* A fight between gamecocks, often having metal spurs on their legs. **—cock′fight′ing** *adj. & n.*

cock•horse (kŏk′hôrs′) *n.* **1.** Something used as a toy horse, such as the knee of an adult. **2.** A horse added to a team of horses to assist a wagon, as through high water. [?]

cock•le[1] (kŏk′əl) *n.* **1.** Any of various bivalve mollusks of the family Cardiidae, having rounded or heart-shaped shells with radiating ribs. **2.** The shell of a cockle. **3.** A wrinkle; a pucker. **4.** *Naut.* A cockleshell. *—intr. & tr.v.* **-led, -ling, -les.** To become or cause to become wrinkled or puckered. **—*idiom.* cockles of (one's) heart.** One's innermost feelings. [ME *cokel* < OFr. *coquille*, shell < VLat. **cochillia* < Lat. *conchyllium* < Gk. *konkhulion*, dim. of *konkhē*, mussel.]

cock·le[2] (kŏk′əl) *n.* Any of several weedy plants, esp. the corn cockle. [ME *cokkel* < OE *coccel* < Med.Lat. **cocculus*, dim. of Lat. *coccus*, kermes berry < Gk. *kokkos*.]

cock·le·boat (kŏk′əl-bōt′) *n. Naut.* See **cockboat.**

cock·le·bur (kŏk′əl-bûr′) *n.* **1.** Any of several annual weeds of the genus *Xanthium* in the composite family, having fruits in a bur. **2.** A bur of this plant.

cock·le·shell (kŏk′əl-shĕl′) *n.* **1.a.** The shell of a cockle. **b.** A shell like that of a cockle. **2.** *Naut.* A small light boat.

cock·loft (kŏk′lôft′, -lŏft′) *n.* A small loft, garret, or attic.

cock·ney (kŏk′nē) or **Cockney** *n., pl.* **-neys** or **Cockney. 1.** A native of the East End of London. **2.** The dialect or accent of the natives of the East End of London. [ME *cokenei*, city dweller, pampered child, cock's egg : *coken*, cock + *ei*, egg (< OE *ǣg*; see **awi-***).] **— cock′ney** *adj.*

cock-of-the-rock (kŏk′əv-*thə*-rŏk′) *n., pl.* **cocks-of-the-rock.** Either of two South American birds *(Rupicola rupicola* or *R. peruviana)* having a distinctive crest and bright orange or reddish plumage in the male. [< its habit of nesting on rocks.]

cock·pit (kŏk′pĭt′) *n.* **1.a.** The space in the fuselage of a small airplane containing seats for the pilot, copilot, and sometimes passengers. **b.** The space set apart for the pilot and crew, as in a helicopter, large airliner, or transport aircraft. **2.** The driver's compartment in a racing car. **3.** An area for cockfights. **4.** A place where many battles have been fought. **5.** *Naut.* **a.** A compartment in an old warship below the water line, used as quarters and as a station for the wounded. **b.** An area in a small decked vessel, toward the stern and lower than the rest of the deck, from which the vessel is steered.

cock·roach (kŏk′rōch′) *n.* Any of numerous oval flat-bodied insects of the family Blattidae, including several species that are common household pests. [By folk ety. < obsolete *cacarootch* < Sp. *cucaracha* < *cuca*, caterpillar.]

cocks·comb (kŏks′kōm′) *n.* **1.** The comb of a rooster. **2.** The cap of a jester, decorated to resemble the comb of a rooster. **3.** An annual plant *(Celosia cristata)* cultivated for its fan-shaped or plumelike red or yellow flower clusters. **4.** *Obsolete.* Var. of **coxcomb** 1.

cocks·foot *n. Chiefly British.* Orchard grass.

cock·shy (kŏk′shī′) *n., pl.* **-shies.** *Chiefly British.* **1.** A mark aimed at in throwing contests. **2.** The throw in a throwing contest. [< a game in which sticks were shied at a cock.]

cock·spur hawthorn (kŏk′spûr′) *n.* A thorny North American tree *(Crataegus crus-galli)* having white flowers and small red fruit. [< the resemblance of its thorn to a cock's spur.]

cock·suck·er (kŏk′sŭk′ər) *n. Obscene.* **1.** One who performs fellatio. **2.** A mean or despicable person.

cock·sure (kŏk′sho͝or′) *adj.* **1.** Completely sure; certain. **2.** Too sure; overconfident. **— cock′sure′ly** *adv.* **— cock′sure′ness** *n.*

cock·tail (kŏk′tāl′) *n.* **1.** Any of various mixed alcoholic drinks consisting usu. of brandy, whiskey, vodka, or gin combined with fruit juices or other liquors and often served chilled. **2.** An appetizer, such as mixed fruit served with juice or seafood served with a sharp sauce: *shrimp cocktail.* — *adj.* **1.** Of or relating to cocktails: *a cocktail party.* **2.** Suitable for wear on semiformal occasions. [?]

cocktail table *n.* See **coffee table.**

cock·y (kŏk′ē) *adj.* **-i·er, -i·est.** Overly self-assertive or self-confident. **— cock′i·ly** *adv.* **— cock′i·ness** *n.*

Co·co (kō′kō). A river rising in N Nicaragua and flowing c. 483 km (300 mi) to the Caribbean Sea.

co·coa (kō′kō) *n.* **1.a.** A powder made from cacao seeds after they have been fermented, roasted, shelled, ground, and freed of most of their fat. **b.** A beverage made by mixing this powder with sugar in hot water or milk. **2.** *Color.* A moderate brown to reddish brown. [Alteration (influenced by *coco*, coconut palm; see COCONUT) of CACAO.] **— co′coa** *adj.*

Co·coa (kō′kō). A city of E-central Florida ESE of Orlando. Pop. 17,722.

cocoa bean *n.* See **cacao** 2.

cocoa butter *n.* A yellowish-white fatty solid obtained from cacao seeds and used in cosmetics, chocolate, and soap.

co·co·nut also **co·coa·nut** (kō′kə-nŭt′, -nət) *n.* **1.** The fruit of the coconut palm, consisting of a fibrous husk surrounding a large seed. **2.** The large, brown, hard-shelled seed of the coconut, containing white flesh surrounding a partially fluid-filled central cavity. **3.** The edible white flesh of the coconut. **4.** A coconut palm. [*coco* (< Port. *côco*, grinning skull, goblin, coconut, prob. < LLat. *coccum*, shell; see COCOON) + NUT.]

coconut milk *n.* **1.** A milky fluid extracted from the flesh of the coconut, used in foods or as a beverage. **2.** The watery fluid in the central cavity of the coconut, used chiefly as a beverage.

coconut oil *n.* An oil or semisolid fat obtained from the flesh of the coconut, used in foods, cosmetics, and soaps.

coconut palm *n.* A feather-leaved palm *(Cocos nucifera)* extensively cultivated in tropical regions for food, beverages, oil, thatching, fiber, utensils, and ornament.

co·coon (kə-ko͞on′) *n.* **1.a.** A protective case of silk or similar fibrous material spun by the larvae of moths and other insects that serves as a covering for their pupal stage. **b.** A similar natural protective covering or structure, such as the egg case of a spider. **2.** A protective plastic coating that is placed over stored military or naval equipment. **3.** Something suggestive of a cocoon in appearance or purpose. — *v.* **-cooned, -coon·ing, -coons.** — *tr.* To envelop in or as if in a cocoon. — *intr.* To retreat as if into a cocoon. [Fr. *cocon* < Prov. *coucoun*, dim. of *coco*, shell < LLat. *coccum* < Lat., berry, oak gall < Gk. *kokkos*, seed, berry.]

coco plum or **co·co·plum** (kō′kō-plŭm′) *n.* An evergreen shrub or small tree *(Chrysobalanus icaco)* native to the American and African tropics and having plumlike fruit. [Alteration of Sp. *icaco* < Arawak *ikaku*.]

Co·cos Islands (kō′kōs) also **Kee·ling Islands** (kē′lĭng). An Australian-administered island group in the E Indian Ocean SW of Sumatra.

co·cotte (kô-kôt′) *n.* A woman prostitute. [Fr., chicken, prostitute < fem. dim. of *coq*, cock < OFr. See COCK[1].]

co·co·yam (kō′kō-yăm′) *n.* See **taro.** [COCO(A) + YAM.]

Coc·teau (kŏk-tō′, kôk-), **Jean.** 1889–1963. French writer and filmmaker whose works include the novel *Les Enfants Terrible* (1929) and the film *Beauty and the Beast* (1945).

Co·cy·tus (kō-sī′təs, -sī′-) *n. Gk. Myth.* One of the five rivers of Hades.

cod[1] (kŏd) *n., pl.* **cod** or **cods.** Any of various marine fishes of the family Gadidae, esp. *Gadus morhua*, a food fish of northern Atlantic waters. [ME.]

cod[2] (kŏd) *n.* **1.** A husk or pod. **2.** *Archaic.* The scrotum. **3.** *Obsolete.* A bag. [ME < OE *codd*.]

Cod (kŏd), **Cape.** A hook-shaped peninsula of SE MA extending E and N into the Atlantic Ocean.

COD or **C.O.D.** *abbr.* **1.** Cash on delivery. **2.** Collect on delivery.

co·da (kō′də) *n. Mus.* A passage at the end of a movement or composition. [Ital. < Lat. *cauda*, tail.]

cod·dle (kŏd′l) *tr.v.* **-dled, -dling, -dles. 1.** To cook in water just below the boiling point. **2.** To treat indulgently; baby. [Poss. alteration of CAUDLE.] **— cod′dler** *n.*

code (kōd) *n.* **1.** A systematically arranged and comprehensive collection of laws. **2.** A systematic collection of regulations and rules of procedure or conduct. **3.a.** A system of signals used to represent letters or numbers in transmitting messages. **b.** A system of symbols, letters, or words given certain arbitrary meanings, used for messages requiring secrecy or brevity. **4.** A system of symbols and rules used to represent instructions to a computer. **5.** *Genet.* The genetic code. **6.** *Slang.* A patient whose heart has stopped beating, as in cardiac arrest. — *v.* **cod·ed, cod·ing, codes.** — *tr.* **1.** To systematize and arrange (laws and regulations) into a code. **2.** To convert (a message, for example) into code. — *intr.* **1.** *Genet.* To specify the genetic code for an amino acid or a polypeptide. **2.** *Slang.* To go into cardiac arrest. [ME < OFr. < Lat. *cōdex*, book. See CODEX.]

co·dec·li·na·tion (kō′dĕk-lə-nā′shən) *n. Astron.* The complement of the declination.

co·de·fen·dant (kō′dĭ-fĕn′dənt) *n. Law.* A joint defendant.

co·deine (kō′dēn′, -dē-ĭn) *n.* An alkaloid narcotic, $C_{18}H_{21}NO_3$, derived from opium or morphine and used as a cough suppressant, analgesic, and hypnotic. [Fr. *codéine* : Gk. *kōdeia*, poppy head (< *kōos*, cavity; see **keuə-***) + *-ine*, alkaloid; see -INE[2].]

code name *n.* A name assigned to conceal the identity or existence of something or someone.

co·de·ter·mi·na·tion (kō′dĭ-tûr′mə-nā′shən) *n.* Cooperation, esp. between labor and management, in policymaking.

code word *n.* **1.** A secret word or phrase used as a code name or password. **2.** A euphemism.

co·dex (kō′dĕks′) *n., pl.* **co·di·ces** (kō′dĭ-sēz′, kŏd′ĭ-). A manuscript volume, esp. of a classic work or of the Scriptures. [Lat. *cōdex*, *cōdic-*, tree trunk, wooden tablet, book, var. of *caudex*, stem, trunk.]

cod·fish (kŏd′fĭsh′) *n., pl.* **codfish** or **-fish·es.** See **cod**[1].

codg·er (kŏj′ər) *n. Informal.* A somewhat eccentric man, esp. an old one. [Perh. alteration of obsolete *cadger*, peddler. See CADGE.]

cod·i·cil (kŏd′ə-sĭl) *n.* **1.** *Law.* A supplement or an appendix to a will. **2.** A supplement or an appendix. [ME < OFr. *codicille* < Lat. *cōdicillus*, dim. of *cōdex*, *cōdic-*, codex. See CODEX.] **— cod′i·cil′la·ry** (kŏd′ə-sĭl′ə-rē) *adj.*

cod·i·fy (kŏd′ĭ-fī′, kō′də-) *tr.v.* **-fied, -fy·ing, -fies. 1.** To reduce to a code: *codify laws.* **2.** To arrange or systematize. **— cod′i·fi·ca′tion** (-fĭ-kā′shən) *n.* **— cod′i·fi′er** *n.*

cod·ling[1] (kŏd′lĭng) also **cod·lin** (-lĭn) *n.* **1.** A greenish, elongated English apple used for cooking. **2.** A small unripe apple. [Alteration of ME *querdlyng*, poss. < AN **querdelion*, lionheart : OFr. *cuer*, heart; see COURAGE + *de*, of (< Lat. *dē*; see DE–) + OFr. *lion*, lion; see LION.]

cod·ling[2] (kŏd′lĭng) *n., pl.* **-lings** or **codling.** A young cod.

codling moth also **codlin moth** *n.* A grayish moth *(Carpocapsa pomonella)* whose larvae are destructive to various fruits.

cod-liv·er oil (kŏd′lĭv′ər) *n.* An oil obtained from the liver of cod and related fishes, used as a source of vitamins A and D.

co·dom·i·nance (kō-dŏm′ə-nəns) *n. Genet.* A condition in which both alleles are codominant.

cock-of-the-rock

cockpit
Airplane

cockroach
American cockroach
Periplaneta americana

ă pat	oi boy
ā pay	ou out
âr care	o͝o took
ä father	o͞o boot
ĕ pet	ŭ cut
ē be	ûr urge
ĭ pit	th thin
ī pie	*th* this
îr pier	hw which
ŏ pot	zh vision
ō toe	ə about,
ô paw	item

Stress marks:
′ (primary);
′ (secondary), as in
dictionary (dĭk′shə-nĕr′ē)

co•dom•i•nant (kō-dŏm′ə-nənt) *adj.* **1.** *Genet.* Of or being two alleles of a gene pair in a heterozygote that are both fully expressed. **2.a.** *Ecol.* Being one of two or more of the most characteristic species in a biotic community. **b.** Influencing the presence and type of other species in the community. —*n.* *Ecol.* A codominant species in a biotic community.

co•don (kō′dŏn′) *n.* A sequence of three adjacent nucleotides constituting the genetic code that specifies the insertion of an amino acid in a specific structural position in a polypeptide chain during protein synthesis. [COD(E) + -ON[1].]

cod•piece (kŏd′pēs′) *n.* A pouch at the crotch of the tight-fitting breeches worn by men in the 15th and 16th centuries. [ME *codpece* : *cod*, bag, scrotum (< OE *codd*, bag) + *pece*, piece; see PIECE.]

cods•wal•lop (kŏdz′wŏl′əp) *n.* *Chiefly British.* Nonsense; rubbish. [?]

Co•dy (kō′dē), **William Frederick.** "Buffalo Bill." 1846–1917. Amer. frontier scout who after 1883 toured the U.S. and Europe with his Wild West Show.

William F. Cody
"Buffalo Bill"

co•ed or **co-ed** (kō′ĕd′) *Informal.* —*n.* A woman who attends a coeducational college or university. —*adj.* **1.** Coeducational. **2.** Open to both sexes. [Short for *coeducational.*]

co•ed•it (kō-ĕd′ĭt) *tr.v.* **-ed•it•ed, -ed•it•ing, -ed•its.** To edit (a print publication or a film) jointly with another or others. —**co•ed′i•tor** *n.*

co•ed•u•ca•tion (kō-ĕj′ə-kā′shən) *n.* The system of education in which both sexes attend the same institution or classes. —**co•ed′u•ca′tion•al** *adj.* —**co•ed′u•ca′tion•al•ly** *adv.*

co•ef•fi•cient (kō′ə-fĭsh′ənt) *n.* **1.** *Math.* A number or symbol multiplying a variable or an unknown quantity in an algebraic term, as 4 in the term $4x$ or x in the term $x(a+b)$. **2.** A numerical measure of a physical or chemical property that is constant for a system under specified conditions.

–coel or **–coele** or **–cele** *suff.* Chamber; cavity: *blastocoel.* [NLat. *-coela* < Gk. *koilos*, hollow. See **keuə-***.]

coe•la•canth (sē′lə-kănth′) *n.* Any of various mostly extinct fishes of the order Coelacanthiformes. [NLat. *Coelacanthus*, former genus name : *coel-*, hollow (< Gk. *koilos*; see -COEL) + *acanthus*, -spined (< Gk. *akantha*, spine).] —**coe′la•can′thine′** (-kăn′thīn′, -thĭn), **coe′la•can′thous** (-thəs) *adj.*

coe•len•ter•ate (sĭ-lĕn′tə-rāt′, -tər-ĭt) *n.* Any of various invertebrate animals of the phylum Coelenterata, marked by a radially symmetrical body with a saclike internal cavity and including the jellyfishes. [< NLat. *Coelenterata*, phylum name : *coel-*, hollow; see COELACANTH + ENTER(ON) + -ATE[1].] —**coe•len′ter•ate′, coe•len•ter′ic** (-tĕr′ĭk) *adj.*

coe•len•ter•on (sĭ-lĕn′tə-rŏn′, -tər-ən) *n., pl.* **-te•ra** (-tər-ə). The saclike cavity within the body of a coelenterate. [NLat. : *coel-*, hollow; see COELACANTH + ENTERON.]

coe•li•ac (sē′lē-ăk′) *adj.* Var. of **celiac.**

coe•lom also **ce•lom** or **coe•lome** (sē′ləm) *n.* The cavity within the body of all animals higher than the coelenterates and certain primitive worms, formed by the splitting of the embryonic mesoderm into two layers. [Ger. *Koelom* < Gk. *koilōma*, cavity < *koilos*, hollow. See **keuə-***.] —**coe•lom′ic** (sĭ-lŏm′ĭk, -lō′mĭk) *adj.*

coe•lo•mate (sē′lə-māt′) *adj.* Possessing a coelom: *a coelomate animal.* —**coe′lo•mate** *n.*

coeno– or **ceno–** *pref.* Common: *coenocyte.* [NLat. < Gk. *koino-* < *koinos.* See **kom***.]

coen•o•bite (sĕn′ə-bīt′, sē′nə-) *n.* Var. of **cenobite.**

coe•no•cyte (sē′nə-sīt′) *n.* A multinucleate cytoplasmic mass enclosed by a single cell wall, as in slime molds and certain fungi and algae. —**coe′no•cyt′ic** (-sĭt′ĭk) *adj.*

coelacanth

coe•nu•rus (sĭ-nŏŏr′əs, -nyŏŏr′-) *n., pl.* **-nu•ri** (-nŏŏr′ī′, -nyŏŏr′ī′). The parasitic larval stage of the tapeworm *Taenia multiceps*, consisting of a cyst in which the scolex develops and infecting the central nervous system of ruminants. [COEN(O)- + -UR(O)US.]

co•en•zyme (kō-ĕn′zīm′) *n.* A nonproteinaceous organic substance that usu. contains a vitamin or mineral and combines with the apoenzyme to form an active enzyme system. —**co′en•zy•mat′ic** (-zə-măt′ĭk) *adj.*

coenzyme A *n.* A coenzyme present in all living cells that functions as an acyl group carrier and is necessary for acetylation reactions.

coenzyme Q *n.* Ubiquinone.

co•e•qual (kō-ē′kwəl) *adj.* Equal with one another, as in rank or size. —*n.* An equal. —**co′e•qual′i•ty** (-kwŏl′ĭ-tē) *n.* —**co•e′qual•ly** *adv.*

coffee

co•erce (kō-ûrs′) *tr.v.* **-erced, -erc•ing, -erc•es. 1.** To force to act or think in a certain way by use of pressure, threats, or intimidation; compel. **2.** To dominate, restrain, or control forcibly: *coerced the strikers into compliance.* **3.** To bring about by force or threat: *efforts to coerce agreement.* [Lat. *coercēre*, to control, restrain : *co-*, co- + *arcēre*, to enclose, confine.] —**co•erc′er** *n.* —**co•erc′i•ble** *adj.*

co•er•cion (kō-ûr′zhən, -shən) *n.* **1.** The act or practice of coercing. **2.** Power or ability to coerce. —**co•er′cion•ar′y** (-zhə-nĕr′ē, -shə-) *adj.*

co•er•cive (kō-ûr′sĭv) *adj.* Characterized by or inclined to coercion. —**co•er′cive•ly** *adv.* —**co•er′cive•ness** *n.*

co•es•sen•tial (kō′ĭ-sĕn′shəl) *adj.* Having the same essence or nature. —**co′es•sen′ti•al′i•ty** (-shē-ăl′ĭ-tē), **co′es•sen′tial•ness** *n.* —**co′es•sen′tial•ly** *adv.*

co•e•ta•ne•ous (kō′ĭ-tā′nē-əs) *adj.* Of equal age, duration, or period; coeval. [< LLat. *coaetāneus*, a contemporary : Lat. *co-*, co- + Lat. *aetās*, age; see **aiw-***.] —**co′e•ta′ne•ous•ly** *adv.* —**co′e•ta′ne•ous•ness** *n.*

co•e•ter•nal (kō′ĭ-tûr′nəl) *adj.* Equally or jointly eternal. —**co′e•ter′nal•ly** *adv.*

co•e•ter•ni•ty (kō′ĭ-tûr′nĭ-tē) *n.* Existence for eternity with another or others.

Coeur d'A•lene (kôr′ də-lān′, kôrd′l-ān′, kûrd′-). A city of N ID on **Coeur D'Alene Lake** in the Panhandle E of Spokane WA. Pop. 24,563.

Coeur de Li•on (kûr′ də lē′ən, kœr də lyôN′). See **Richard I.**

co•e•val (kō-ē′vəl) *adj.* Originating or existing during the same period; lasting through the same era. [< LLat. *coaevus* : *co-*, co- + *aevum*, age; see **aiw-***.] —**co•e′val** *n.* —**co•e′val•ly** *adv.*

co•ev•o•lu•tion (kō′ĕv-ə-lōō′shən, -ē-və-) *n.* The evolution of two or more interdependent species, each adapting to changes in the other. —**co′ev•o•lu′tion•ar•y** *adj.* —**co′e•volve′** (-ĭ-vŏlv′) *v.*

co•ex•ist (kō′ĭg-zĭst′) *intr.v.* **-ist•ed, -ist•ing, -ists. 1.** To exist together, at the same time or in the same place. **2.** To live in peace with another or others despite differences, esp. as a matter of policy. —**co′ex•is′tence** *n.* —**co′ex•is′tent** *adj.*

co•ex•tend (kō′ĭk-stĕnd′) *intr. & tr.v.* **-tend•ed, -tend•ing, -tends.** To extend or cause to extend through the same space or duration. —**co′ex•ten′sion** *n.*

co•ex•ten•sive (kō′ĭk-stĕn′sĭv) *adj.* Having the same limits, boundaries, or scope. —**co′ex•ten′sive•ly** *adv.*

co•fac•tor (kō′făk′tər) *n.* A substance, such as a metallic iron or coenzyme, that must be associated with an enzyme for the enzyme to function.

C. of C. *abbr.* Chamber of commerce.

C. of E. *abbr.* Church of England.

cof•fee (kô′fē, kŏf′ē) *n.* **1.a.** Any of various tropical African shrubs or trees of the genus *Coffea*, esp. *C. arabica*, cultivated for their seeds that are dried, roasted, and ground to prepare a stimulating aromatic drink. **b.** The beanlike seeds of this plant, enclosed within a pulpy fruit. **c.** The beverage prepared from coffee seeds. **2.** *Color.* A moderate brown to dark brown or dark grayish brown. **3.** An informal social gathering at which coffee and other refreshments are served. [Alteration (influenced by Ital. *caffè* < Turk.) of Ottoman Turk. *qahveh* < Ar. *qahwah.*]

coffee break *n.* A short break from work during which coffee or other refreshments may be consumed.

cof•fee•cake (kô′fē-kāk′, kŏf′ē-) *n.* A cake or sweetened bread, often containing nuts or raisins.

cof•fee•house also **coffee house** (kô′fē-hous′, kŏf′ē-) *n.* A restaurant where coffee and other refreshments are served, esp. where people meet for conversation, games, or music.

coffee klatch or **coffee klatsch** (klăch, klăch) also **kaf•fee•klatsch** (kŏf′ē-klăch′, -klăch′, kô′fē-) *n.* A casual social gathering for coffee and conversation. [Partial transl. of Ger. *Kaffeeklatsch* : *Kaffee*, coffee + *Klatsch*, gossip.]

cof•fee•mak•er also **coffee maker** (kô′fē-mā′kər, kŏf′ē-) *n.* An apparatus used to brew coffee.

coffee mill *n.* A device for grinding roasted coffee beans.

cof•fee•pot (kô′fē-pŏt′, kŏf′ē-) *n.* A pot for brewing or serving coffee.

coffee shop *n.* A small restaurant in which coffee and light meals are served.

coffee table *n.* A long low table, often placed before a sofa.

cof•fee-ta•ble book (kô′fē-tā′bəl, kŏf′ē-) *n.* An oversize book of elaborate design used for display, as on a coffee table.

cof•fer (kô′fər, kŏf′ər) *n.* **1.** A strongbox. **2.a.** Financial resources; funds. Often used in the plural. **b.** A treasury. Often used in the plural. **3.** *Archit.* A decorative sunken panel in a ceiling, dome, soffit, or vault. **4.** The chamber formed by a canal lock. **5.** A cofferdam. **6.** A floating dock. —*tr.v.* **-fered, -fer•ing, -fers. 1.** To put in a coffer. **2.** *Archit.* To supply (a ceiling, for example) with decorative sunken panels. [ME *cofre* < OFr., alteration of **cofne* < Lat. *cophinus*, basket. See COFFIN.]

cof•fer•dam (kô′fər-dăm′, kŏf′ər-) *n.* **1.** A temporary watertight enclosure that is pumped dry so that construction, as of piers, may be undertaken. **2.** A watertight chamber attached to the side of a ship to facilitate repairs below the water line.

cof•fin (kô′fĭn, kŏf′ĭn) *n.* **1.** An oblong box in which a corpse is buried. **2.** The horny part of a horse's hoof. —*tr.v.* **-fined, -fin•ing, -fins.** To place in or as if in a coffin. [ME *cofin*, basket < OFr. < Lat. *cophinus* < Gk. *kophinos.*]

coffin bone *n.* The bone enclosed inside a horse's hoof.

coffin nail *n.* *Slang.* A cigarette.

cof•fle (kô′fəl, kŏf′əl) *n.* A group of animals, prisoners, or slaves chained together in a line. —*tr.v.* **-fled, -fling, -fles.** To fasten together in a coffle. [Ar. *qāfilah*, caravan.]

co•found (kō-found′) *tr.v.* **-found•ed, -found•ing, -founds.** To establish with another or others. —**co•found′er** *n.*

C. of S. *abbr.* Chief of staff.
co•func•tion (kō′fungk′shən) *n.* The trigonometric function of the complement of an angle: *Cotan θ is cofunction of tan θ.*
cog¹ (kŏg, kôg) *n.* **1.** One of a series of teeth, as on the rim of a wheel or gear, whose engagement transmits successive motive force to a corresponding wheel or gear. **2.** A cogwheel. **3.** A member of an organization who performs necessary but usu. minor or routine functions. [ME *cogge*, prob. of Scand. orig.; akin to Swed. *kugg, kugge*.] —**cogged** *adj.*
cog² (kŏg, kôg) *v.* **cogged, cog•ging, cogs.** —*tr.* To load or manipulate (dice) fraudulently. —*intr.* To cheat, esp. at dice. —*n.* An instance of cheating; a swindle. [?]
cog³ (kŏg, kôg) *n.* A tenon projecting from a wooden beam designed to fit into an opening in another beam to form a joint. —*tr.v.* **cogged, cog•ging, cogs.** To join with tenons. [Alteration (influenced by COG¹) of *cock*, to join with tenons.]
cog. *abbr.* Cognate.
co•gen•er•a•tion (kō-jĕn′ə-rā′shən) *n.* A process in which an industrial facility uses its waste energy to produce heat or electricity.
co•gent (kō′jənt) *adj.* Appealing to the intellect or powers of reasoning; convincing. See Syns at **valid.** [Lat. *cōgēns, cōgent-*, pr.part. of *cōgere*, to force : *co-*, co- + *agere*, to drive; see **ag-***.] —**co′gen•cy** (-jən-sē) *n.* —**co′gent•ly** *adv.*
cog•i•ta•ble (kŏj′ĭ-tə-bəl) *adj.* Thinkable; conceivable.
cog•i•tate (kŏj′ĭ-tāt′) *intr. & tr.v.* **-tat•ed, -tat•ing, -tates.** To take careful thought or think carefully about; ponder. [Lat. *cōgitāre, cōgitāt-* : *co-*, intensive pref.; see co- + *agitāre*, to consider; see AGITATE.] —**cog′i•ta′tor** *n.*
cog•i•ta•tion (kŏj′ĭ-tā′shən) *n.* **1.** Thoughtful consideration; meditation. **2.** A serious thought.
cog•i•ta•tive (kŏj′ĭ-tā′tĭv) *adj.* **1.** Of or relating to cogitation. **2.** Inclined to or capable of cogitation. —**cog′i•ta′tive•ly** *adv.* —**cog′i•ta′tive•ness** *n.*
co•gnac (kōn′yăk′, kŏn′-, kôn′-) *n.* A brandy distilled from white wine and produced in the vicinity of Cognac.
Co•gnac (kôn′yăk′, kŏn-, kô-nyăk′). A city of W France on the Charente R. NNE of Bordeaux; noted since the 18th cent. for its distilleries. Pop. 20,660.
cog•nate (kŏg′nāt′) *adj.* **1.** Related by blood; having a common ancestor. **2.** Related in origin, as certain words in genetically related languages descended from the same ancestral root. **3.** Related or analogous in nature, character, or function. —*n.* **1.** One related by blood or origin with another, esp. a person sharing an ancestor. **2.** A word related to one in another language. [Lat. *cognātus* : *co-*, co- + *gnātus*, born, p.part. of *nāscī*, to be born; see **genə-***.] —**cog•na′tion** *n.*
cog•ni•tion (kŏg-nĭsh′ən) *n.* **1.** The mental process or faculty of knowing, including aspects such as awareness, perception, reasoning, and judgment. **2.** That which comes to be known, as through reasoning or intuition; knowledge. [ME *cognicioun* < Lat. *cognitiō, cognitiōn-* < *cognitus*, p.part. of *cognōscere*, to learn : *co-*, intensive pref.; see co- + *gnōscere*, to know; see **gnō-***.] —**cog•ni′tion•al** *adj.*
cog•ni•tive (kŏg′nĭ-tĭv) *adj.* **1.** Of, characterized by, involving, or relating to cognition. **2.** Having a basis in or reducible to empirical factual knowledge. —**cog′ni•tive•ly** *adv.*
cognitive dissonance *n. Psychol.* A condition of conflict or anxiety resulting from inconsistency between belief and action, such as opposing animal slaughter and eating meat.
cognitive science *n.* The study of the nature of various mental tasks and the processes that enable them to be performed.
cog•ni•za•ble (kŏg′nĭ-zə-bəl, kŏg-nī′-) *adj.* **1.** Knowable or perceivable. **2.** *Law.* That can be tried before a particular court. —**cog′ni•za•bly** *adv.*
cog•ni•zance (kŏg′nĭ-zəns) *n.* **1.** Conscious knowledge or recognition; awareness. **2.** The range of what one can know or understand. **3.** Observance; notice: *We will take cognizance of your objections.* **4.** *Her.* A crest or badge worn to distinguish the bearer. [ME *conissaunce* < OFr. *conoissance* < *connoistre*, to know < Lat. *cognōscere*, to learn. See COGNITION.]
cog•ni•zant (kŏg′nĭ-zənt) *adj.* Fully informed; conscious. See Syns at **aware.** [< COGNIZANCE.]
cog•no•men (kŏg-nō′mən) *n., pl.* **-no•mens** or **-nom•i•na** (-nŏm′ə-nə). **1.a.** A family name; a surname. **b.** The third and usu. last name of a citizen of ancient Rome, as *Caesar* in *Gaius Julius Caesar.* **2.** A name, esp. a descriptive nickname or epithet. [Lat. *cognōmen* : *co-*, co- + *nōmen*, name; see **nŏ-men-***.] —**cog•nom′i•nal** (-nŏm′ə-nəl) *adj.*
co•gno•scen•te (kŏn′yə-shĕn′tē, kŏg′nə-) *n., pl.* **-ti** (-tē). A person with superior knowledge or highly refined taste; a connoisseur. [Obsolete Ital. < Lat. *cognōscēns, cognōscent-*, pr.part. of *cognōscere*, to know. See COGNITION.]
co•gon (kō-gōn′) *n.* An Old World perennial grass *(Imperata cylindrica)*, widespread as a weed in warm regions and used for thatching. [Sp. *cogón* < Tagalog *kúgon*.]
cog railway *n.* A railway designed to operate on steep slopes and having a locomotive with a center cogwheel that engages with a cogged center rail to provide traction.
Cogs•well chair (kŏgz′wĕl′, -wəl) *n.* An upholstered easy chair, open under the armrests, with a sloping back and cabriole front legs. [Prob. < the name *Cogswell*.]
cog•wheel (kŏg′hwēl′, -wēl′, kôg′-) *n.* **1.** A toothed wheel. **2.** One of a set of cogged wheels within a mechanism.
co•hab•it (kō-hăb′ĭt) *intr.v.* **-it•ed, -it•ing, -its. 1.** To live together as spouses. **2.** To live together in a sexual relationship when not legally married. [LLat. *cohabitāre* : Lat. *co-*, co- + Lat. *habitāre*, to dwell; see INHABIT.] —**co•hab′i•tant, co•hab′it•er** *n.* —**co•hab′i•ta′tion** *n.* —**co•hab′i•ta′tion•al** *adj.*
Co•han (kō′hăn′), **George Michael.** 1878–1942. Amer. singer, songwriter, and playwright whose songs include "I'm a Yankee Doodle Dandy."
co•heir (kō-âr′) *n.* A joint heir, as to an estate.
co•heir•ess (kō-âr′ĭs) *n.* A joint woman heir, as to an estate.
co•here (kō-hîr′) *v.* **-hered, -her•ing, -heres.** —*intr.* **1.** To stick or hold together in a mass that resists separation. **2.** To have internal elements or parts logically linked and aesthetically consistent. —*tr.* To cause to form a united, orderly, and aesthetically consistent whole. [Lat. *cohaerēre* : *co-*, co- + *haerēre*, to cling.]
co•her•ence (kō-hîr′əns, -hĕr′-) *n.* **1.** The quality or state of cohering, esp. a logical, orderly, and aesthetically consistent relationship of parts. **2.** *Phys.* The property of being coherent.
co•her•en•cy (kō-hîr′ən-sē) *n., pl.* **-cies.** Coherence.
co•her•ent (kō-hîr′ənt, -hĕr′-) *adj.* **1.** Sticking together; cohering. **2.** Marked by orderly, logical, and aesthetic consistency: *a coherent essay.* **3.** *Phys.* Of, relating to, or having waves with a constant phase relationship that are capable of exhibiting interference. **4.** Of or relating to a system of units of measurement in which a small number of base units are defined from which all others are derived by multiplication or division only. —**co•her′ent•ly** *adv.*
co•he•sion (kō-hē′zhən) *n.* **1.** The act, process, or condition of cohering. **2.** *Phys.* The intermolecular attraction by which the elements of a body are held together. **3.** *Bot.* The congenital union of parts of the same kind. [< Lat. *cohaesus*, p.part. of *cohaerēre*, to cling together. See COHERE.] —**co•he′sive** (-sĭv, -zĭv) *adj.* —**co•he′sive•ly** *adv.* —**co•he′sive•ness** *n.*
co•he•sion•less (kō-hē′zhən-lĭs) *adj.* Composed of particles that do not cohere. Used of soil.
Cohn (kōn), **Ferdinand Julius.** 1828–98. German botanist who is considered the founder of bacteriology.
co•ho (kō′hō) *n., pl.* **co•hos** or **coho.** The coho salmon.
Co•hoes (kə-hōz′). A city of E-central NY on the Hudson R. N of Albany; settled in 1665. Pop. 16,825.
co•hort (kō′hôrt′) *n.* **1.** A group or band of people. **2.** A companion or an associate. **3.** A generational group as defined in demographics, statistics, or market research. **4.a.** One of the 10 divisions of a Roman legion, consisting of 300 to 600 men. **b.** A group of soldiers. [ME < OFr. *cohorte* < Lat. *cohors, cohort-*. See **gher-¹***.]

Usage Note: The use of *cohort* to refer to an individual rather than a group has gained considerable currency in recent years and seems now to be the predominant usage. Seventy-one percent of the Usage Panel accepts the sentence *The cashiered dictator and his cohorts have all written their memoirs,* while only 43 percent accepts *The gangster walked into the room surrounded by his cohort.*

coho salmon *n.* A small silver edible fish *(Oncorhynchus kisutch)* native to North Pacific waters and introduced in the Great Lakes. [Alteration of *cohose* < Salish (Halkomelem) *k'ʷəxʷəθ*.]
co•hosh (kō′hŏsh′) *n.* Any of several North American plants, esp. blue cohosh, black cohosh, and baneberry. [< Eastern Abenaki *kkʷàhas*.]
co•host or **co-host** (kō′hōst′) —*n.* A joint host, as of a social event. —*tr.v.* **-host•ed, -host•ing, -hosts.** To serve as a joint host of. See Usage Note at **host¹.**
co•hune (kō-hōōn′) *n.* A feather-leaved Central American palm *(Orbignya cohune)* having hard-shelled fruits that yield a useful oil. [NLat., perh. < Am.Sp. < Mosquito *ókhún*.]
coif (koif) *n.* **1.** (*also* kwäf). A coiffure. **2.** A tight-fitting cap worn under a veil. **3.** A white skullcap once worn by English lawyers. **4.** A heavy skullcap of steel or leather, once worn under a helmet or mail hood. —*tr.v.* **coifed, coif•ing, coifs. 1.** (*also* kwäf). To arrange or dress (hair). **2.** To cover with or as if with a coif. [ME < OFr. *coife* < LLat. *cofea*, helmet, of Gmc. orig.]
coif•feur (kwä-fûr′) *n.* A male hairdresser. [Fr. < *coiffer*, to coif < OFr. *coife*, coif. See COIF.]
coif•feuse (kwä-fyōōz′, -fœz′) *n.* A woman hairdresser. [Fr., fem. of *coiffeur*, coiffeur. See COIFFEUR.]
coif•fure (kwä-fyŏŏr′) *n.* A hairstyle. —*tr.v.* **-fured, -fur•ing, -fures.** To arrange or dress (hair). [Fr. < *coiffer*, to coif. See COIFFEUR.]
coign (koin, kwoin) *n. & v.* Var. of **quoin.**
coil¹ (koil) *n.* **1.a.** A series of connected spirals or concentric rings formed by gathering or winding: *a coil of rope.* **b.** A single spiral or ring within such a series. **2.** A spiral pipe or series of spiral pipes, as in a radiator. **3.** *Elect.* **a.** A wound spiral of two or more turns of insulated wire, used to intro-

cog railway

ă pat	oi boy
ā pay	ou out
âr care	ŏŏ took
ä father	ōō boot
ĕ pet	ŭ cut
ē be	ûr urge
ĭ pit	th thin
ī pie	*th* this
îr pier	hw which
ŏ pot	zh vision
ō toe	ə about, item
ô paw	

Stress marks:
′ (primary);
′ (secondary), as in
dictionary (dĭk′shə-nĕr′ē)

duce inductance. **b.** Any of various devices that have such a spiral as the major component. **4.** A roll of postage stamps for use in a vending machine. — *v.* **coiled, coil•ing, coils.** — *tr.* **1.** To wind in concentric rings or spirals. **2.** To wind into a shape resembling a coil. — *intr.* **1.** To form concentric rings or spirals. **2.** To move in a spiral course. [Prob. < obsolete Fr. *coillir*, to gather < Lat. *colligere*. See COLLECT[1].] — **coil′er** *n.*

coil² (koil) *n.* A disturbance; a fuss. [?]

Coim•ba•tore (koim′bə-tôr′, -tôr′). A city of S India SSW of Bangalore. Pop. 704,514.

coin (koin) *n.* **1.** A small piece of metal, usu. flat and circular, authorized by a government for use as money. **2.** Metal money considered as a whole. **3.** A flat, circular object felt to resemble metal money: *coins of pepperoni.* **4.** *Archit.* A corner or cornerstone. — *tr.v.* **coined, coin•ing, coins. 1.** To make (pieces of money) from metal; mint or strike: *coined silver dollars.* **2.** To make pieces of money from (metal): *coin gold.* **3.** To devise (a new word or phrase). — *adj.* Requiring one or more pieces of metal money for operation. — ***idiom.* the other side of the coin.** One of two differing or opposing views or sides. [ME < OFr., die for stamping coins, wedge < Lat. *cuneus*, wedge.] — **coin′a•ble** *adj.* — **coin′er** *n.*

coin•age (koi′nĭj) *n.* **1.** The right or process of making coins. **2.a.** Metal currency. **b.** A system of metal currency. **3.a.** A new word or phrase. **b.** The invention of new words.

co•in•cide (kō′ĭn-sīd′) *intr.v.* **-cid•ed, -cid•ing, -cides. 1.** To occupy the same relative position or the same area in space. **2.** To happen at the same time or during the same period. **3.** To correspond exactly; be identical. **4.** To agree exactly, as in opinion; concur. [Med.Lat. *coincidere* : Lat. *co-*, co- + Lat. *incidere*, to occur; see INCIDENT.]

co•in•ci•dence (kō-ĭn′sĭ-dəns, -dĕns′) *n.* **1.** Occupation of the same relative position or area in space. **2.** A sequence of events that although accidental seems to have been planned.

co•in•ci•dent (kō-ĭn′sĭ-dənt) *adj.* **1.** Occupying the same area in space or happening at the same time. **2.** Being very similar to another, as in nature. **3.** Matching point for point; coinciding.

co•in•ci•den•tal (kō-ĭn′sĭ-dĕn′tl) *adj.* **1.** Occurring as or resulting from coincidence. **2.** Happening or existing at the same time. — **co•in′ci•den′tal•ly** *adv.*

co•in•sur•ance (kō′ĭn-sho͝or′əns) *n.* **1.** Insurance held by two or more insurers. **2.** A form of insurance in which one insures property for less than its value and is responsible for the difference.

co•in•sure (kō′ĭn-sho͝or′) *tr.v.* **-sured, -sur•ing, -sures. 1.** To insure jointly. **2.** To insure with coinsurance.

coir (koir) *n.* The fiber obtained from the husk of a coconut, used chiefly in making rope and matting. [Malayalam *kayar*, cord < *kayaru*, to be twisted.]

co•i•tus (kō′ĭ-təs, kō-ē′-) *n.* Heterosexual union involving insertion of the penis into the vagina. [Lat. < p.part. of *coīre*, to copulate : *co-*, co- + *īre*, to go, come; see **ei-***.] — **co′i•tal** *adj.* — **co′i•tal•ly** *adv.*

coitus in•ter•rup•tus (ĭn′tə-rŭp′təs) *n.* Coitus deliberately interrupted by withdrawal of the penis prior to ejaculation. [NLat. : Lat. *coitus*, coitus + Lat. *interruptus*, interrupted.]

coke¹ (kōk) *n.* The solid residue of impure carbon obtained from coal and other carbonaceous materials by destructive distillation, used as a fuel and in making steel. — *tr. & intr.v.* **coked, cok•ing, cokes.** To convert or be converted into coke. [Perh. < ME *colk*, core.]

coke² (kōk) *n. Slang.* Cocaine.

Coke (kōk). A trademark used for a soft drink. See Regional Note at **tonic.**

Coke (ko͝ok, kōk), Sir **Edward.** 1552–1634. English jurist who as chief justice of the Court of Common Pleas (1606–16) ruled that the common law is supreme law.

coliseum
Partial view of the Colosseum, Rome, Italy

col (kŏl) *n.* A pass between two mountain peaks or a gap in a ridge. [Fr. < OFr., neck < Lat. *collum*. See **kʷel-¹***.]

Col or **Col.** *abbr. Bible.* Colossians.

col. *abbr.* **1.** Collect; collected; collector. **2.** College; collegiate. **3.** Colonial; colony. **4.** Color. **5.** Column.

Col. *abbr.* **1.** Colombia. **2.** Colonel. **3.** Colorado.

col–¹ *pref.* Var. of **com–.**

col–² *pref.* Var. of **colo–.**

co•la¹ (kō′lə) *n.* A carbonated soft drink containing an extract of the cola nut and other flavorings. Also called regionally *dope.*

co•la² (kō′lə) *n.* Pl. of **colon¹** 2.

co•la³ (kō′lə) *n.* Pl. of **colon².**

co•la⁴ also **ko•la** (kō′lə) *n.* Either of two tropical African evergreen plants (*Cola acuminata* or *C. nitida*) having nutlike seeds yielding an extract that contains caffeine and theobromine and is used in carbonated beverages and pharmaceuticals. [Of West African orig.; akin to Temne *kōla*, kola nut.]

COLA (kō′lə) *n.* Cost-of-living adjustment.

col•an•der (kŭl′ən-dər, kŏl′-) *n.* A bowl-shaped kitchen utensil with perforations for draining off liquids and rinsing food. [ME *colyndore*, prob. alteration of OProv. *colador*, strainer < VLat. *cōlātōrium* < Lat. *cōlātus*, p.part. of *cōlāre*, to strain < *cōlum*, sieve.]

Col•bert (kôl-bĕr′, kōl-), **Jean Baptiste.** 1619–83. French politician who served as an adviser to Louis XIV.

col•can•non (kŏl-kăn′ən) *n.* An Irish dish of mashed potatoes and cabbage. [Ir.Gael. *cāl ceannan* : *cāl*, cabbage (< OIr. *cāl* < Lat. *caulis*) + *ceannan*, white-headed (*ceann*, head < OIr. *cenn* + *fionn*, white < OIr. *find*; see **weid-***).]

Col•ches•ter (kōl′chĕs′tər, -chĭ-stər). A municipal borough of SE England near the North Sea; site of the first Roman colony in Britain. Pop. 83,900.

col•chi•cine (kŏl′chĭ-sēn′, kŏl′kĭ-) *n.* A poisonous alkaloid, $C_{22}H_{25}NO_6$, obtained from the autumn crocus and used in plant breeding to induce chromosome doubling and in medicine to treat gout. [COLCHIC(UM) + -INE².]

col•chi•cum (kŏl′chĭ-kəm, kŏl′kĭ-) *n.* **1.** Any of various bulbous plants of the genus *Colchicum*, such as the autumn crocus. **2.** The dried ripe seeds or corms of the autumn crocus, both of which yield colchicine. [Lat., poisonous plant < Gk. *kolkhikon*, meadow saffron, after *Kolkhos*, Colchis.]

Col•chis (kŏl′kĭs). An ancient region on the Black Sea S of the Caucasus Mts.

col•co•thar (kŏl′kə-thər, -thär′) *n.* A ferric oxide obtained as a residue after heating ferrous sulfate, used in glass polishing and as a pigment. [Med.Lat. < Sp. *colcótar* < Ar. *qulquṭār*, poss. < Gk. *khalkanthos*, copper sulfate : *khalkos*, copper + *anthos*, flower.]

cold (kōld) *adj.* **cold•er, cold•est. 1.a.** Having a low temperature. **b.** Having a temperature lower than normal body temperature. **c.** Feeling no warmth; uncomfortably chilled. **2.a.** Marked by deficient heat: *a cold room.* **b.** Being at a temperature that is less than what is required: *cold oatmeal.* **c.** Chilled by refrigeration or ice. **3.** Lacking emotion; objective: *cold logic.* **4.** Having no appeal to the senses or feelings: *a cold decor.* **5.a.** Not affectionate or friendly; aloof. **b.** Exhibiting or feeling no enthusiasm: *a cold audience.* **c.** Devoid of sexual desire; frigid. **6.** *Color.* Being a tone or color that suggests little warmth. **7.** Having lost all freshness or vividness through passage of time: *a cold scent.* **8.a.** Marked by or sustaining a loss of body heat: *cold hands.* **b.** Appearing to be dead; unconscious. **c.** Dead: *cold in his grave.* **9.** Marked by unqualified certainty or sure familiarity. **10.** So intense as to be almost uncontrollable: *cold fury.* — *adv.* **1.** To an unqualified degree; totally: *cold sober.* **2.** With complete finality. **3.** Without advance preparation or introduction. — *n.* **1.a.** Relative lack of warmth. **b.** The sensation resulting from lack of warmth; chill. **2.** A condition of low air temperature; cold weather. **3.** A viral infection characterized by inflammation of the mucous membranes lining the upper respiratory passages and usu. accompanied by fever, chills, coughing, and sneezing. — ***idiom.* out in the cold.** Lacking benefits given to others; neglected. [ME < OE *ceald*. See **gel-***.] — **cold′ly** *adv.* — **cold′ness** *n.*

Syns: *cold, arctic, chilly, cool, frigid, frosty, gelid, glacial, icy.* The central meaning shared by these adjectives is "marked by a low temperature": *cold air; an arctic climate; a chilly day; cool water; a frigid room; a frosty morning; gelid seas; glacial winds; icy hands.* **Ant:** *hot.*

cold-blood•ed (kōld′blŭd′ĭd) *adj.* **1.a.** Lacking feeling or emotion. **b.** Executed without emotion. **2.** Ectothermic. — **cold′-blood′ed•ly** *adv.* — **cold′-blood′ed•ness** *n.*

cold chisel *n.* A chisel made of hardened, tempered steel and used for cutting cold metal.

cold•cock (kōld′kŏk′) *tr.v.* **-cocked, -cock•ing, -cocks.** *Slang.* To knock (another) unconscious.

cold cream *n.* An emulsion for softening and cleaning skin.

cold cut *n.* A slice of cold cooked meat. Often used in the plural.

cold drink *n.* **1.** A drink served or taken cold. **2.** *Chiefly Southern U.S.* See **soft drink.** See Regional Note at **tonic.**

cold duck *n.* A beverage made of sparkling Burgundy and champagne. [Transl. of Ger. *Kalte Ente*, a drink made from a mixture of wines.]

cold feet *pl.n. Slang.* Fearfulness or timidity preventing the completion of a course of action.

cold frame *n.* A structure consisting of a wooden or concrete frame and a top of glass or clear plastic, used for protecting and acclimatizing seedlings and plants.

cold front *n.* The leading portion of a cold atmospheric air mass moving against and replacing a warm air mass.

Cold Harbor (kōld). A locality in E VA ENE of Richmond; site of two Civil War battles (1862 and 1864).

cold-heart•ed (kōld′här′tĭd) *adj.* Devoid of sympathy or feeling. — **cold′-heart′ed•ly** *adv.* — **cold′-heart′ed•ness** *n.*

cold light *n.* **1.** Light producing little or no heat. **2.** Light emitted by a process other than incandescence.

cold pack *n.* **1.** A compress filled or moistened with a cold fluid and applied externally to swollen or injured body parts to relieve pain and swelling. **2.** A canning process in which uncooked food is packed in jars or cans, then sterilized by heat.

cold rubber *n.* A durable, strong synthetic rubber polymerized at low temperatures.

cold•shoul•der (kōld′shōl′dər) *tr.v.* **-dered, -der•ing, -ders.** *Informal.* To slight or snub (someone).

cold shoulder *n. Informal.* Deliberate coldness or disregard.
cold sore *n.* A small blister occurring on the lips and face and caused by herpes simplex.
cold storage *n.* **1.** Protective storage, as of foods or furs, in a refrigerated place. **2.** *Informal.* A state of abeyance.
cold sweat *n.* A reaction to nervousness, pain, or shock, marked by perspiration, chill, and cold moist skin.
cold turkey *n. Slang.* **1.** Immediate, complete withdrawal from something on which one has become dependent, such as an addictive drug. **2.** Blunt language or procedural method.
cold type *n.* Typesetting, such as photocomposition, done without the casting of metal.
cold war or **Cold War** *n.* **1.** A state of tension and military rivalry between nations that stops short of full-scale war. **2.** Such a state that existed from 1945 to 1990 between the United States and the former Soviet Union and their respective allies. — **cold warrior** *n.*
cold water *n. Informal.* Deprecation, as of a silly proposal.
cold-wa•ter (kōld′wô′tər, -wŏt′ər) *adj.* Lacking modern plumbing or heating facilities: *a cold-water flat.*
cold wave *n.* **1.** An onset of unusually cold weather within a 24-hour period. **2.** A chemically-set permanent wave.
cold-weld (kōld′wĕld′) *tr.v.* **-weld•ed, -weld•ing, -welds.** To weld under high pressure or vacuum without heat.
cold weld•ing (wĕl′dĭng) *n.* The welding of two materials under high pressure or vacuum without the use of heat.
cole (kōl) *n.* See **kale** 1. [ME *col* < OE *cāl* < Lat. *caulis*, cabbage.]
Cole (kōl), **Nat "King."** 1919–65. Amer. singer and pianist who recorded such popular ballads as "Mona Lisa."
Cole, Thomas. 1801–48. Amer. painter and leader of the Hudson River School.
co•lec•to•my (kə-lĕk′tə-mē) *n., pl.* **-mies.** Surgical removal of part or all of the colon.
cole•man•ite (kōl′mə-nīt′) *n.* A natural hydrated calcium borate, $Ca_2B_6O_{11}·5H_2O$, a source of borax. [After William Tell *Coleman* (1824–93), Amer. merchant in CA.]
co•le•op•ter•an (kō′lē-ŏp′tər-ən, kŏl′ē-) also **co•le•op•ter•on** (-tə-rŏn′) — *n.* Any of numerous insects of the order Coleoptera, having forewings modified to form protective covers for the hind wings and including the beetles and fireflies. — *adj.* Of, relating to, or belonging to the order Coleoptera. [< NLat. *Coleoptera*, order name < Gk. *koleopteros*, sheath-winged : *koleon*, sheath; see **kel-**[1]* + *pteron*, wing; see **pet-***.] — **co′le•op′ter•ous** (-tər-əs) *adj.*
co•le•op•tile (kō′lē-ŏp′tĭl, kŏl′ē-) *n.* A protective sheath enclosing the shoot tip and embryonic leaves of grasses. [< NLat. *coleoptilum* : Gk. *koleon*, sheath; see **kel-**[1]* + Gk. *ptilon*, plume; see **pet-***.]
co•le•o•rhi•za (kō′lē-ə-rī′zə, kŏl′ē-) *n., pl.* **-zae** (-zē). A protective sheath enclosing the embryonic root of grasses. [NLat. : Gk. *koleon*, sheath; see **kel-**[1]* + Gk. *rhiza*, root; see **wrād-***.]
Cole•ridge (kōl′rĭj, kō′lə-rĭj), **Samuel Taylor.** 1772–1834. British poet and critic whose works include "The Rime of the Ancient Mariner" (1798).
cole•slaw also **cole slaw** (kōl′slô′) *n.* A salad of finely shredded raw cabbage dressed with mayonnaise. [Du. *koolsla* : *kool*, cabbage (< MDu. *cōle* < Lat. *caulis*) + *sla*, salad (short for *salade* < Fr. < OFr.; see SALAD).]
Col•et (kŏl′ət), **John.** 1467?–1519. English scholar and theologian who founded St. Paul's School in London (1509).
Co•lette (kŏ-lĕt′, kô-), **(Sidonie Gabrielle Claudine).** 1873–1954. French writer whose works include *Gigi* (1945).
co•le•us (kō′lē-əs) *n.* Any of various Old World herbs of the genus *Coleus* in the mint family, having multicolored leaves. [NLat. *Coleus*, genus name < Gk. *koleos*, sheath (from the way its filaments are joined). See **kel-**[1]*.]
cole•wort (kōl′wûrt′, -wôrt′) *n.* See **kale** 1.
Col•fax (kōl′făks), **Schuyler.** 1823–85. Vice President of the U.S. (1869–73).
coli– *pref.* Var. of **colo–.**
col•ic (kŏl′ĭk) *n.* Severe abdominal pain caused by spasm, obstruction, or distention of any of the hollow viscera, such as the intestines. — *adj.* (kō′lĭk). Of, relating to, or affecting the colon. [ME *colik*, affecting the colon, colic < OFr. *colique* < Lat. *cōlica (passiō)*, (suffering) of the colon, fem. of *cōlicus* < Gk. *kōlikos* < *kolon*, colon.] — **col′ick•y** (kŏl′ĭ-kē) *adj.*
col•i•cin (kŏl′ĭ-sĭn, kō′lĭ-) *n.* Any of various antibacterial proteins produced by certain strains of the colon bacillus and lethal to related strains of bacteria. [COL(ON)[2] + -IC + -IN.]
col•ic•root (kŏl′ĭk-ro͞ot′, -ro͝ot′) *n.* **1.** Any of certain perennial herbs of the genus *Aletris* in the lily family, esp. *A. farinosa* of eastern North America, having racemes of white flowers and rootstocks formerly used to treat colic. **2.** Any of various other plants thought to relieve colic.
co•li•form (kō′lə-fôrm′, kŏl′ə-) *adj. Microbiol.* Of or relating to the bacilli that commonly inhabit the intestines of human beings and other vertebrates, esp. the colon bacillus. — **co′li•form′** *n.*
Co•li•gny or **Co•li•gni** (kô-lē-nyē′), **Gaspard de.** 1519–72. French general and Huguenot leader who was one of the first victims of the St. Bartholomew's Day Massacre (1572).
co•lin•e•ar (kō-lĭn′ē-ər) *adj.* **1.** Containing elements that correspond to one another and are arranged in the same linear sequence. **2.** Collinear. — **co•lin′e•ar′i•ty** (-ăr′ĭ-tē) *n.*
col•i•se•um also **col•os•se•um** (kŏl′ĭ-sē′əm) *n.* A large amphitheater for public sports events, entertainment, or assemblies. [Med.Lat. *Colisēum*, an amphitheater in Rome, Italy, var. of Lat. *Colossēum* < neut. of *colossēus*, gigantic < *colossus*, huge statue. See COLOSSUS.]
co•lis•tin (kə-lĭs′tĭn, kō-) *n. Microbiol.* An antibiotic produced by the bacterium *Bacillus polymyxa* or *B. colistinus* that is effective against a wide range of gram-negative bacteria. [< NLat. *Colistīnus*, species name < COLI–.]
co•li•tis (kə-lī′tĭs) *n.* Inflammation of the colon.
coll. *abbr.* **1.** Collateral. **2.** Collect; collection; collector. **3.** College; collegiate. **4.** Colloquial; colloquialism.
coll– *pref.* Var. of **collo–.**
col•lab•o•rate (kə-lăb′ə-rāt′) *intr.v.* **-rat•ed, -rat•ing, -rates. 1.** To work together, esp. in an intellectual effort. **2.** To cooperate treasonably, as with an enemy. [LLat. *collabōrāre*, *collabōrāt-* : Lat. *com-*, com- + Lat. *labōrāre*, to work (< *labor*, toil).] — **col•lab′o•ra′tion** *n.* — **col•lab′o•ra′tive** *adj.* — **col•lab′o•ra′tor** *n.*
col•lab•o•ra•tion•ist (kə-lăb′ə-rā′shə-nĭst) *n.* One that collaborates with an enemy occupation force. — **col•lab′o•ra′tion•ism** *n.*
col•lage (kō-läzh′, kə-) *n.* **1.a.** An artistic composition of materials and objects pasted over a surface. **b.** The art of creating such compositions. **2.** An assemblage of diverse elements: *a collage of memories.* — *v.* **-laged, -lag•ing, -lages.** — *tr.* To paste (diverse materials) over a surface, thereby creating an artistic product. — *intr.* To create such an artistic product. [Fr. < *coller*, to glue < *colle*, glue < VLat. **colla* < Gk. *kolla.*] — **col•lag′ist** *n.*
collage film *n.* A film with disparate scenes and no transition.
col•la•gen (kŏl′ə-jən) *n.* The fibrous protein constituent of bone, tendon, and other connective tissue. [Gk. *kolla*, glue + -GEN.] — **col′la•gen′ic** (-jĕn′ĭk), **col•lag′e•nous** (kə-lăj′ə-nəs) *adj.*
col•lag•e•nase (kə-lăj′ə-nās′, -nāz′, kŏl′ə-jə-) *n.* Any of various enzymes that catalyze the hydrolysis of collagen and gelatin.
col•lapse (kə-lăps′) *v.* **-lapsed, -laps•ing, -laps•es.** — *intr.* **1.** To fall down or inward suddenly; cave in. **2.** To break down suddenly in strength or health and cease to function. **3.** To fold compactly. — *tr.* To cause to fold, break down, or fall down or inward. — *n.* **1.** The act of falling down or inward, as from loss of supports. **2.** An abrupt failure of function, strength, or health; a breakdown. **3.** An abrupt loss of perceived value or of effect. [Lat. *collābī*, *collāps-*, to fall together : *com-*, com- + *lābī*, to fall.] — **col•laps′i•bil′i•ty** *n.* — **col•laps′i•ble, col•laps′a•ble** *adj.*
col•lar (kŏl′ər) *n.* **1.** The part of a garment that encircles the neck. **2.** A necklace. **3.a.** A restraining or identifying band put around the neck of an animal. **b.** The cushioned part of a harness that presses against the shoulders of a draft animal. **4.** *Biol.* An encircling structure or bandlike marking, as around an animal's neck, suggestive of a collar. **5.** Any of various ringlike devices used to limit, guide, or secure a machine part. **6.** *Slang.* An arrest, as of a criminal. — *tr.v.* **-lared, -lar•ing, -lars. 1.** To furnish with a collar. **2.** *Slang.* **a.** To seize or detain. **b.** To arrest (a criminal, for example). [ME *coler* < OFr. *colier* < Lat. *collāre* < *collum*, neck. See **kʷel-**[1]*.] — **col′lared** *adj.*
col•lar•bone (kŏl′ər-bōn′) *n.* See **clavicle** 1.
collar cell *n.* See **choanocyte.**
col•lard (kŏl′ərd) *n.* **1.** See **kale** 1. **2. collards.** The leaves of kale, used as a vegetable. [Var. of COLEWORT.]
collared peccary *n.* A small wild hog *(Tayassu tajacu)* with a range from the southwest United States to northern Argentina, having a gray and black coat with a white band.
collat. *abbr.* Collateral.
col•late (kə-lāt′, kŏl′āt′, kō′lāt′) *tr.v.* **-lat•ed, -lat•ing, -lates. 1.** To examine and compare carefully in order to note points of disagreement. **2.** To assemble in proper numerical or logical sequence. **3.** *Print.* **a.** To examine (gathered sheets) in order to arrange them in sequence before binding. **b.** To verify the order and completeness of (pages). **4.** *Eccles.* To admit (a cleric) to a benefice. [< Lat. *collātus*, p.part. of *cōnferre*, to bring together : *com-*, com- + *lātus*, brought; see **telə-***.] — **col•la′tor** *n.*
col•lat•er•al (kə-lăt′ər-əl) *adj.* **1.** Situated or running side by side; parallel. **2.** Coinciding in tendency or effect; accompanying. **3.** Serving to support or corroborate. **4.** Of a secondary nature; subordinate. **5.** Of, relating to, or guaranteed by a security pledged against the performance of an obligation: *a collateral loan.* **6.** Having an ancestor in common but descended from a different line. — *n.* **1.** Property acceptable as security for a loan or other obligation. **2.** A collateral relative. [ME < Med.Lat. *collāterālis* : Lat. *com-*, com- + Lat. *lātus*, *later-*, side.] — **col•lat′er•al•ly** *adv.*
col•lat•er•al•ize (kə-lăt′ər-ə-līz′) *tr.v.* **-ized, -iz•ing, -izes.**

collage
Merz 163, with Woman Spraying, 6⅛" × 4⅞", 1920 paper with cloth collage by Kurt Schwitters (1887–1948)

ă pat	oi boy
ā pay	ou out
âr care	o͝o took
ä father	o͞o boot
ĕ pet	ŭ cut
ē be	ûr urge
ĭ pit	th thin
ī pie	*th* this
îr pier	hw which
ŏ pot	zh vision
ō toe	ə about, item
ô paw	

Stress marks:
′ (primary);
′ (secondary), as in
dictionary (dĭk′shə-nĕr′ē)

[ME *colonie* < Lat. *colōnia* < *colōnus*, settler < *colere*, to cultivate. See **k^wel-1***.]

col•o•phon (kŏl′ə-fŏn′, -fən) *n.* **1.** An inscription, usu. at the end of a book, giving facts about its publication. **2.** A publisher's emblem or trademark, usu. on a title page. [LLat. *colophōn* < Gk. *kolophōn*, finishing touch. See **kel-2***.]

Col•o•phon (kŏl′ə-fŏn′). An ancient Greek city of Asia Minor NW of Ephesus.

col•or (kŭl′ər) *n.* **1.** That aspect of things that is caused by differing qualities of the light reflected or emitted by them, definable in terms of the observer or of the light, as: **a.** The appearance of objects or light sources as perceived by the individual and involving hue, lightness, and saturation for objects and hue, brightness, and saturation for light sources. **b.** The characteristics of light by which the individual is made aware of objects or light sources, described in terms of dominant wavelength, luminance, and purity. **2.** A substance, such as a dye or paint, that imparts a hue. **3.a.** The general appearance of the skin; complexion. **b.** A ruddy complexion. **c.** A reddening of the face; a blush. **4.** The skin pigmentation of a person not classed as white. **5. colors.** A flag or banner, as of a country. **6. colors.** The salute made during the ceremony of raising or lowering a flag. **7. colors.** A distinguishing symbol, badge, ribbon, mark, or combination of colors. **8. colors.** One's opinion or position. **9.** Character or nature. Often used in the plural. **10.a.** Outward appearance, often deceptive. **b.** Appearance of authenticity. **11.a.** Variety of expression. **b.** Vivid, picturesque detail. **12.** Traits of personality or behavior that attract interest. **13.** The use or effect of pigment in painting, as distinct from form. **14.** *Mus.* Tonal quality. **15.** *Law.* A mere semblance of legal right. **16.** A particle or bit of gold found in auriferous gravel or sand. **17.** *Phys.* A quantum characteristic of quarks that determines their role in the strong interaction. — *v.* **-ored, -or•ing, -ors.** — *tr.* **1.** To impart color to or change the color of. **2.a.** To give a distinctive character or quality to; modify. **b.** To exert an influence on; affect. **3.a.** To misrepresent. **b.** To gloss over; excuse. — *intr.* **1.a.** To take on color. **b.** To change color. **2.** To become red in the face; blush. [ME *colour* < OFr. < Lat. *color.* See **kel-1***.] — **col′or•er** *n.*

Usage Note: The terms *person of color* and *people of color* have been revived for use in formal contexts to refer to members or groups of non-European origin (e.g., Black people, Asians, Pacific Islanders, and Native Americans): *"These are profound tendencies which strike at . . . whites as well as people of color"* (Jesse Jackson). Many people prefer *people of color* as a rough substitute for *minorities* because these groups are not in fact in the minority in many parts of America. See Usage Note at **black.**

Colorado potato beetle
Leptinotarsa decemlineata

col•or•a•ble (kŭl′ər-ə-bəl) *adj.* **1.** Meant to deceive; not genuine. **2.** Seemingly true or genuine; plausible. See Syns at **plausible.** — **col′or•a•bil′i•ty, col′or•a•ble•ness** *n.* — **col′or•a•bly** *adv.*

Col•o•ra•do (kŏl′ə-răd′ō, -rä′dō). A state of the W-central U.S.; admitted as the 38th state in 1876. The region was added to the U.S. through the Louisiana Purchase (1803) and a cession by Mexico (1848). Cap. Denver. Pop. 3,307,912. — **Col′o•ra′dan** *adj.* & *n.*

Colorado blue spruce *n.* See **blue spruce.**

Colorado Desert. A region of SE CA W of the Colorado R.

Colorado potato beetle *n.* A small striped beetle *(Leptinotarsa decemlineata)* that is a major agricultural pest.

Colorado River. 1. A river of central Argentina rising in the Andes and flowing c. 853 km (530 mi) SE to the Atlantic Ocean. **2.** A river of the SW U.S. rising in the Rocky Mts. and flowing c. 2,333 km (1,450 mi) SW through the **Colorado Plateau** of W CO to the Gulf of California in NW Mexico. **3.** A river rising in NW TX and flowing c. 1,438 km (894 mi) SE to an inlet of the Gulf of Mexico.

colossus

Colorado Springs. A city of central CO S of Denver; site of the U.S. Air Force Academy (estab. 1958). Pop. 281,140.

col•or•ant (kŭl′ər-ənt) *n.* Something, esp. a dye, a pigment, an ink, or a paint, that colors or modifies the hue of something else. — *adj. Color.* Of or being a subtractive primary color.

col•or•a•tion (kŭl′ə-rā′shən) *n.* **1.** Arrangement of colors. **2.** The sum of the beliefs or principles of a person or a group.

col•or•a•tu•ra (kŭl′ər-ə-to͝or′ə, -tyo͝or′ə) *n. Mus.* **1.** Florid, ornamental vocal trills and runs. **2.** Music marked by coloratura. **3.** A singer, esp. a soprano, specializing in coloratura. [Obsolete Ital. < LLat. *colōrātūra*, coloring < Lat. *colōrātus*, p.part. of *colōrāre*, to color < *color*, color. See COLOR.]

color bar *n.* See **color line.**

col•or•blind or **col•or-blind** (kŭl′ər-blīnd′) *adj.* **1.** Partially or totally unable to distinguish certain colors. **2.a.** Not subject to racial prejudices. **b.** Not recognizing racial or class distinctions. — **col′or•blind′ness** *n.*

columbarium

col•or•breed (kŭl′ər-brēd′) *tr.v.* **-bred** (-brĕd′), **-breed•ing, -breeds.** To breed (plants or animals) selectively to produce new or desired colors.

col•or•cast (kŭl′ər-kăst′) *v.* **-cast** or **-cast•ed, -cast•ing, -casts.** — *tr.* To broadcast (a television program) in color. [COLOR + (BROAD)CAST.] — **col′or•cast′** *n.*

col•or-code (kŭl′ər-kōd′) *tr.v.* **-cod•ed, -cod•ing, -codes.** To color, as wires, according to a code for easy identification.

co•lo•rec•tal (kō′lə-rĕk′təl) *adj.* Associated with or involving both the colon and the rectum: *colorectal cancer.*

col•ored (kŭl′ərd) *adj.* **1.** Having color. **2.** Often **Colored.** *Offensive.* **a.** Of or belonging to a racial group not regarded as white. **b.** Of mixed racial strains. **3.** Distorted or biased. — *n.* also **Colored,** *pl.* **colored** or **coloreds** also **Colored** or **Coloreds.** *Offensive.* **1.** A person of a racial group not regarded as white. **2.** A person of mixed racial strains. See Usage Note at **black.**

col•or•fast (kŭl′ər-făst′) *adj.* Having color that will not run or fade with washing or wear. — **col′or•fast′ness** *n.*

color filter *n.* A photographic filter of colored glass that modifies light reaching film by selectively absorbing colors.

col•or•ful (kŭl′ər-fəl) *adj.* **1.** Full of color; abounding in colors. **2.** Characterized by rich variety; vividly distinctive: *colorful language.* — **col′or•ful•ly** *adv.* — **col′or•ful•ness** *n.*

color guard *n.* A ceremonial escort for a flag.

col•or•if•ic (kŭl′ə-rĭf′ĭk) *adj.* Producing or imparting color.

col•or•im•e•ter (kŭl′ə-rĭm′ĭ-tər) *n.* **1.** Any of various instruments used to determine or specify colors, as by comparison with spectroscopic or visual standards. **2.** An instrument that measures the concentration of a known constituent of a solution by comparison with colors of standard solutions of that constituent. — **col′or•i•met′ric** (-ər-ə-mĕt′rĭk) *adj.* — **col′or•i•met′ri•cal•ly** *adv.* — **col′or•im′e•try** *n.*

col•or•ing (kŭl′ər-ĭng) *n.* **1.** The art, manner, or process of applying color. **2.** A substance used to color something. **3.** Appearance with regard to color. **4.** Characteristic aspect, tone, or style. **5.** False or misleading appearance.

col•or•ist (kŭl′ər-ĭst) *n.* **1.** A painter skilled in achieving special effects with color. **2.** A hairdresser who specializes in dyeing hair. — **col′or•is′tic** *adj.*

col•or•ize (kŭl′ə-rīz′) *tr.v.* **-ized, -iz•ing, -iz•es.** To impart color to (black-and-white film) by means of a computer-assisted process. — **col′or•i•za′tion** (-ər-ĭ-zā′shən) *n.* — **col′or•iz•er** *n.*

col•or•less (kŭl′ər-lĭs) *adj.* **1.** Lacking color. **2.** Weak in color; pallid. **3.** Lacking animation, variety, or distinction; dull. — **col′or•less•ly** *adv.* — **col′or•less•ness** *n.*

color line *n.* A barrier, created by custom, law, or economic differences, separating nonwhite persons from whites.

co•lo•scope (kō′lə-skōp′) *n.* See **colonoscope.**

co•los•co•py (kə-lŏs′kə-pē) *n.* See **colonoscopy.**

Co•los•sae (kə-lŏs′ē). An ancient city of central Asia Minor. — **Co•los′sian** (-lŏsh′ən) *adj.* & *n.*

co•los•sal (kə-lŏs′əl) *adj.* Of a size, extent, or degree that elicits awe or taxes belief; immense. [Fr. < Lat. *colossus*, colossus. See COLOSSUS.] — **co•los′sal•ly** *adv.*

col•os•se•um (kŏl′ĭ-sē′əm) *n.* Var. of **coliseum.**

Co•los•sians (kə-lŏsh′ənz) *pl.n.* *(used with a sing. v.)* See table at **Bible.** [< Lat. *Colossēnses*, inhabitants of Colossae < *Colossae*, Colossae < Gk. *Kolossai.*]

co•los•sus (kə-lŏs′əs) *n., pl.* **-los•si** (-lŏs′ī′) or **-los•sus•es. 1.** A huge statue. **2.** Something likened to a huge statue, as in size or importance. [Lat. < Gk. *kolossos.*]

co•los•to•my (kə-lŏs′tə-mē) *n., pl.* **-mies. 1.** Surgical construction of an artificial excretory opening from the colon. **2.** The opening created by such a surgical procedure.

co•los•trum (kə-lŏs′trəm) *n.* The thin yellowish fluid secreted by the mammary glands at the time of parturition that is rich in antibodies and minerals and precedes the production of true milk. [Lat.] — **co•los′tral** (-trəl) *adj.*

col•our (kŭl′ər) *n.* & *v. Chiefly British.* Var. of **color.**

-colous *suff.* Having a specified kind of habitat: *rupicolous.* [< Lat. *-cola*, tiller, inhabitant. See **k^wel-1***.]

col•pi•tis (kŏl-pī′tĭs) *n.* See **vaginitis.** [Gk. *kolpos*, vagina + -ITIS.]

col•por•tage (kŏl′pôr′tĭj, -pōr′-) *n.* A colporteur work.

col•por•teur (kŏl′pôr′tər, -pōr′-) *n.* A peddler of devotional literature. [Fr., alteration of OFr. *comporteur* < *comporter*, to conduct, peddle. See COMPORT.]

col•po•scope (kŏl′pə-skōp′) *n.* A magnifying and photographic device used as an aid in the diagnostic examination of the vaginal and cervical epithelia. [Gk. *kolpos*, vagina, womb + -SCOPE.] — **col′po•scop′ic** (-skŏp′ĭk) *adj.*

col•pos•co•py (kŏl-pŏs′kə-pē) *n., pl.* **-pies.** Examination of the vaginal and cervical epithelia by means of a colposcope. [Gk. *kolpos*, vagina, womb + -SCOPY.]

colt (kōlt) *n.* **1.** A young male horse. **2.** A youthful or inexperienced person; a novice. [ME < OE.]

Colt (kōlt), **Samuel.** 1814–62. Amer. firearms inventor and manufacturer who developed the first revolver.

colt•ish (kōl′tĭsh) *adj.* **1.** Relating to or suggestive of a colt. **2.** Lively and frisky. — **colt′ish•ly** *adv.* — **colt′ish•ness** *n.*

Col•trane (kōl′trān), **John William.** 1926–67. Amer. jazz saxophonist and composer.

colts•foot (kōlts′fo͝ot′) *n., pl.* **-foots. 1.** A perennial Eurasian herb *(Tussilago farfara)* in the composite family, having yellow flower heads and hoof-shaped leaves. **2.** The dried leaves or flower heads of this plant. **3.** See **galax.**

col•u•brid (kŏl′ə-brĭd, kŏl′yə-) *n.* Any of numerous, widely distributed, chiefly nonvenomous snakes of the family Colubridae, which includes the garter snakes. [< NLat. *Colubridae*, family name < Lat. *coluber, colubr-*, snake.] — **col′u•brid** *adj.*

col•u•brine (kŏl′ə-brīn′, kŏl′yə-) *adj.* **1.** Of, relating to, or resembling a snake. **2.** Colubrid.

co•lu•go (kə-lo͞o′gō) *n., pl.* **-gos.** See **flying lemur.** [Of Malayan orig.]

Col•um (kŏl′əm), **Padraic.** 1881–1972. Irish-Amer. writer whose volumes of poetry include *Wild Earth* (1907).

Co•lum•ba (kə-lŭm′bə) *n.* A constellation in the Southern Hemisphere near Caelum and Puppis. [Lat. *columba*, dove.]

Columba also **Col•um** (kŭl′əm), Saint. 521–597. Irish missionary who Christianized N Scotland.

col•um•bar•i•um (kŏl′əm-bâr′ē-əm) also **col•um•bar•y** (kŏl′əm-bĕr′ē) *n., pl.* **-i•a** (-ē-ə) also **-ies. 1.a.** A vault with niches for urns containing ashes of the dead. **b.** A niche in such a vault. **2.a.** A dovecote. **b.** A pigeonhole in a dovecote. [Lat. *columbārium* < *columba*, dove.]

Co•lum•bi•a[1] (kə-lŭm′bē-ə). **1.** A community of N-central MD WSW of Baltimore. Pop. 75,883. **2.** A city of central MO NNW of Jefferson City; seat of the University of Missouri (estab. 1839). Pop. 69,101. **3.** The capital of SC in the central part. Pop. 98,052. **4.** A city of W-central TN SSW of Nashville; settled in 1807. Pop. 28,583.

Co•lum•bi•a[2] (kə-lŭm′bē-ə) *n.* The United States. [After Christopher COLUMBUS.]

Columbia Heights. A city of E MN, a suburb of Minneapolis. Pop. 18,910.

Co•lum•bi•an (kə-lŭm′bē-ən) *adj.* **1.** Of or relating to the United States. **2.** Of or relating to Christopher Columbus.

Columbia River. A river rising in SE British Columbia, Canada, and flowing c. 1,947 km (1,210 mi) S then W through the **Columbia Plateau** and along the WA–OR border to its outlet on the Pacific Ocean.

col•um•bine (kŏl′əm-bīn′) *n.* Any of various perennial herbs of the genus *Aquilegia*, native to north temperate regions and having showy flowers that have petals with long hollow spurs. [ME < Med.Lat. *columbīna* < fem. of Lat. *columbīnus*, dovelike (< the resemblance of the inverted flower to a cluster of doves) < *columba*, dove.]

co•lum•bite (kə-lŭm′bīt′) *n.* A black, red-brown, or colorless mineral, $(Fe, Mn)(Nb, Ta)_2O_6$, the principal ore of niobium. [COLUMB(IUM) + -ITE[1].]

co•lum•bi•um (kə-lŭm′bē-əm) *n.* Niobium. No longer in scientific use. [After COLUMBIA[2].]

Co•lum•bus (kə-lŭm′bəs). **1.** A city of W GA on the Chattahoochee R. SSW of Atlanta; settled in 1828. Pop. 179,278. **2.** A city of S-central IN SSE of Indianapolis. Pop. 31,802. **3.** A city of NE MS near the AL border. Pop. 23,799. **4.** A city of E-central NE at the confluence of the Loup and Platte rivers W of Omaha. Pop. 19,480. **5.** The cap. of OH, in the central part; laid out in 1812. Pop. 632,910.

Columbus, Christopher. 1451–1506. Italian explorer in the service of Spain who attempted to reach Asia by sailing W from Europe, thereby discovering America (1492).

Columbus Day *n.* October 12, observed in the United States in commemoration of the discovery in 1492 of the New World by Christopher Columbus.

col•u•mel•la (kŏl′yə-mĕl′ə, kŏl′ə-) *n., pl.* **-mel•lae** (-mĕl′ē). Any small columnlike structure in various plants and animals, often forming the central axis of development for the organism or an anatomical structure. [Lat., dim. of *columna*, column. See COLUMN.] — **col′u•mel′lar** (-mĕl′ər) *adj.* — **col′u•mel′late′** (-mĕl′āt′) *adj.*

col•umn (kŏl′əm) *n.* **1.** *Archit.* A supporting pillar consisting of a base, a cylindrical shaft, and a capital. **2.** Something resembling an architectural pillar. **3.a.** *Print.* One of two or more separated vertical sections of typed lines lying side by side on a page. **b.** A feature article that appears regularly in a publication. **4.** A formation, as of vehicles, in which all elements follow one behind the other. **5.** *Bot.* A columnlike structure, as one formed by the union of a stamen and the style in an orchid flower. **6.** *Anat.* Any of various tubular or pillarlike supporting structures in the body, usu. having a single tissue origin and function. [ME *columne* < Lat. *columna*. See **kel-**[2]*.] — **col′umned** (kŏl′əmd) *adj.*

co•lum•nar (kə-lŭm′nər) *adj.* **1.** Having the shape of a column. **2.** Constructed with or having columns.

columnar epithelium *n.* Epithelium consisting of one or more cell layers, the most superficial of which is composed of elongated cylindrical cells projecting toward the surface.

co•lum•ne•a (kə-lŭm′nē-ə) *n.* Any of various bushy or trailing tropical American plants of the genus *Columnea*, having colorful tubular flowers. [NLat. *Columnea*, genus name, after Fabius *Columna*, Latin name of Fabio Colonna (1567–1650?), Italian botanist.]

co•lum•ni•a•tion (kə-lŭm′nē-ā′shən) *n.* *Archit.* The use or arrangement of columns in a building.

col•um•nist (kŏl′əm-nĭst, -ə-mĭst) *n.* A writer of a column in a publication, such as a newspaper.

Col•ville (kōl′vĭl′, kŏl′-). A river rising in the Brooks Range of NW AK and flowing c. 603 km (375 mi) to the Arctic Ocean.

col•za (kŏl′zə, kōl′-) *n.* See **rape**[2]. [Fr. < Du. *koolzaad* : *kool*, cabbage (< MDu. *cōle* < Lat. *caulis*) + *zaad*, seed (< MDu. *saet*; see **sē-***).]

com. *abbr.* **1.** Combining. **2.** Combustion. **3.** Comedy; comic. **4.** Comma. **5.** Commentary. **6.** Commerce; commercial. **7.** Or **Com.** Commission; commissioner. **8.** Or **Com.** Committee. **9.** Common. **10.** Commune. **11.** Communication. **12.** Community.

Com. *abbr.* **1.** Also **com.** Commander. **2.** Commodore. **3.** Communist.

com– or **col–** or **con–** *pref.* Together; with; joint; jointly: *commingle*. [ME < Lat., together, intensive pref. < OLat. *com*. See **kom***.]

co•ma[1] (kō′mə) *n., pl.* **-mas.** A state of deep unconsciousness, usu. due to injury, disease, or poison, in which one can neither sense nor respond to stimuli or internal needs. [Gk. *kōma*, deep sleep.]

co•ma[2] (kō′mə) *n., pl.* **-mae** (-mē). **1.** *Astron.* The nebulous luminescent cloud containing the nucleus and constituting the major portion of the head of a comet. **2.** *Bot.* A usu. terminal tuft or cluster, esp. a tuft of hairs on a seed. **3.** *Phys.* A diffuse pear-shaped image of a point source. [Lat., hair < Gk. *komē*.] — **co′mal** *adj.*

Co•ma Ber•e•ni•ces (kō′mə bĕr′ə-nī′sēz′) *n.* A constellation in the northern sky near Boötes and Leo. [NLat. *Coma Berenicēs*, Berenice's hair : Lat. *coma*, hair + Lat. *Berenicēs*, genitive of *Berenicē*, Berenice (a queen of Egypt who promised her hair to Venus).]

Co•man•che (kə-măn′chē) *n., pl.* **Comanche** or **-ches. 1.** A member of a Native American people formerly ranging over the southern Great Plains from western Kansas to northern Texas and now located in Oklahoma. **2.** The Uto-Aztecan language of the Comanche. [Sp. < Ute *kɨmmanči*.] — **Co•man′che** *adj.*

co•mate[1] (kō′māt′) *adj.* Comose. [Lat. *comātus*, having long hair < *coma*, hair. See COMA[2].]

co•mate[2] (kō-māt′, kō′māt′) *n.* A mate; a companion.

co•ma•tose (kō′mə-tōs′, kŏm′ə-) *adj.* **1.** Of, relating to, or affected with coma; unconscious. **2.** Lethargic; torpid.

co•mat•u•lid (kə-măch′ə-lĭd) also **co•mat•u•la** (-lə) *n., pl.* **-lids** also **-lae** (-lē). Any of various marine invertebrates of the class Crinoidea that are attached to a surface by a stalk when young but may be free-swimming as adults. [< NLat. *Comātulidae*, former family name < LLat. *comātulus*, having neatly curled hair < Lat. *comātus*, having long hair. See COMATE[1].]

comb (kōm) *n.* **1.a.** A thin toothed strip used to smooth, arrange, or fasten the hair. **b.** An implement, such as a wool card, that resembles a hair comb in shape or use. **c.** A currycomb. **2.a.** The fleshy crest or ridge that grows on the crown of the head of certain birds and is most prominent in the male. **b.** Something resembling a fowl's comb. **3.** A honeycomb. — *v.* **combed, comb•ing, combs.** — *tr.* **1.** To dress or arrange with or as if with a comb. **2.** To card (wool or other fiber). **3.** To search thoroughly; look through. — *intr.* To roll and break. Used of waves. [ME < OE. See **gembh-***.]

comb. *abbr.* **1.** Combination. **2.** Combining. **3.** Combustion.

com•bat (kəm-băt′, kŏm′băt′) *v.* **-bat•ed, -bat•ing, -bats** or **-bat•ted, -bat•ting, -bats.** — *tr.* **1.** To oppose in battle; fight against. **2.** To oppose vigorously; struggle against. See Syns at **oppose.** — *intr.* To engage in fighting; contend or struggle. — *n.* (kŏm′băt′). Fighting, esp. armed battle; strife. See Syns at **conflict.** [Fr. *combattre* < OFr. < LLat. *combattere* : Lat. *com-*, com- + Lat. *battere*, to beat.] — **com′bat′** *adj.*

com•bat•ant (kəm-băt′nt, kŏm′bə-tnt) *n.* One that takes part in armed strife. — *adj.* Engaging in armed strife.

combat fatigue *n.* A nervous disorder brought on by the exhaustion and stress of combat or similar situations and characterized by anxiety, depression, and irritability.

com•bat•ive (kəm-băt′ĭv) *adj.* Eager or disposed to fight; belligerent. See Syns at **argumentative.** — **com•bat′ive•ly** *adv.* — **com•bat′ive•ness** *n.*

comb•er (kō′mər) *n.* **1.** One, such as a machine, that combs wool, for example. **2.** A long wave that has peaked or broken into foam; a breaker.

com•bi•na•tion (kŏm′bə-nā′shən) *n.* **1.** The act of combining or the state of being combined. **2.** The result of combining. **3.** An alliance for a common purpose; an association. **4.** A sequence of numbers or letters used to open a combination lock. **5.** *Math.* One or more elements selected from a set without regard to the order of selection. — **com′bi•na′tion•al** *adj.*

combination lock *n.* A lock that will open only when its dial is turned through a combination.

com•bi•na•tive (kŏm′bə-nā′tĭv, kəm-bī′nə-tĭv) *adj.* **1.** Of, relating to, or resulting from combination. **2.** Tending, serving, or able to combine.

com•bi•na•to•ri•al (kŏm′bə-nə-tôr′ē-əl, -tōr′-, kəm-bī′nə-) *adj.* **1.** Relating to or involving combinations. **2.** Relating to the arrangement and manipulation of mathematical elements in sets.

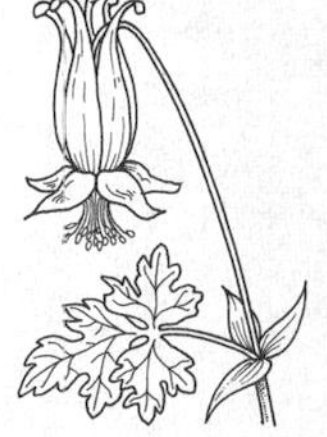
columbine

Christopher Columbus

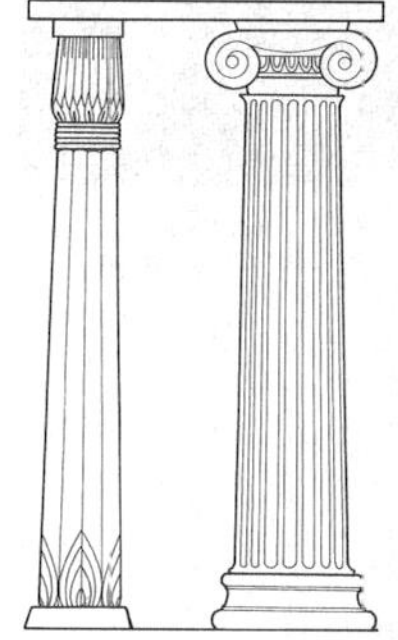
column
Left: Egyptian bundle-bud
Right: Greek Ionic

ă **pat**	oi **boy**
ā **pay**	ou **out**
âr **care**	o͝o **took**
ä **father**	o͞o **boot**
ĕ **pet**	ŭ **cut**
ē **be**	ûr **urge**
ĭ **pit**	th **thin**
ī **pie**	*th* **this**
îr **pier**	hw **which**
ŏ **pot**	zh **vision**
ō **toe**	ə **a**bout,
ô **paw**	it**e**m

Stress marks:
′ (primary);
′ (secondary), as in **dictionary** (dĭk′shə-nĕr′ē)

com•bi•na•tor•ics (kŏm′bə-nə-tôr′ĭks, -tŏr′-, kəm-bī′nə-) *n.* *(used with a sing. v.)* Combinatorial mathematics.

com•bine (kəm-bīn′) *v.* **-bined, -bin•ing, -bines.** —*tr.* **1.** To bring into a state of unity; merge. **2.** To join (two or more substances) to make a single substance; mix. **3.** To possess or exhibit in combination. **4.** (kŏm′bīn′). To harvest (a grain crop) using a combine. —*intr.* **1.** To become united; coalesce. **2.** To join forces for a common purpose. See Syns at **join. 3.** *Chem.* To form a compound. **4.** (kŏm′bīn′). To harvest a grain crop using a combine. —*n.* (kŏm′bīn′). **1.** A power-operated harvesting machine that cuts, threshes, and cleans grain. **2.** An association for the furtherance of political or commercial interests. **3.** A combination. [ME *combinen* < OFr. *combiner* < LLat. *combīnāre* : Lat. *com-*, com- + *bīnī*, two by two; see **dwo-***.] —**com•bin′er** *n.*

comb•ings (kō′mĭngz) *pl.n.* Small loose pieces of material, such as hairs or wool, removed with a comb.

com•bin•ing (kəm-bī′nĭng) *n.* **1.** The act or process of joining, merging, or mixing two or more things. **2.** (kŏm′bī-nĭng). The act or process of operating a combine.

combining form *n.* *Gram.* A modified form of an independent word in English or in a language such as Greek or Latin from which English has borrowed that occurs only in combination with other forms. It combines with words, affixes, or other combining forms to form compounds or derivatives, as *electro-* (from *electric*) in *electromagnet.*

comb jelly *n.* See **ctenophore.**

com•bo (kŏm′bō) *n., pl.* **-bos. 1.** *Mus.* A small jazz band. **2.** *Informal.* The product or result of combining.

com•bus•ti•ble (kəm-bŭs′tə-bəl) *adj.* **1.** Capable of igniting and burning. **2.** Easily aroused or excited. —*n.* A combustible substance. —**com•bus′ti•bil′i•ty** *n.* —**com•bus′ti•bly** *adv.*

com•bus•tion (kəm-bŭs′chən) *n.* **1.** The process of burning. **2.** A chemical change, esp. oxidation, accompanied by the production of heat and light. **3.** Violent anger or agitation. [ME < LLat. *combustiō*, *combustiōn-* < Lat. *combustus*, p.part. of *combūrere*, to burn up, blend of *com-*, com-, and *ambūrere*, to burn around (*ambi-*, ambi- + *ūrere*, to burn).] —**com•bus′tive** (-tĭv) *adj.*

combustion chamber *n.* An enclosure in which combustion, esp. of a fuel or propellant, is initiated and controlled.

com•bus•tor (kəm-bŭs′tər) *n.* A combustion chamber and its igniters, injectors, and other related apparatus in a jet engine or gas turbine.

comd. *abbr.* Command.

comdg. *abbr.* Commanding.

Comdr. *abbr.* Commander.

Comdt. *abbr.* Commandant.

come (kŭm) *intr.v.* **came** (kām), **come, com•ing, comes. 1.a.** To advance toward the speaker or toward a specified place; approach: *Come to me.* **b.** To advance in a specified manner: *The children came reluctantly.* **2.a.** To make progress; advance. **b.** To fare: *How are things coming?* **3.a.** To reach a particular point in a series or as a result of orderly progression. **b.** To arrive, as in due course: *Dawn comes at 5 A.M. in June.* **4.** To move into view; appear: *The moon came over the horizon.* **5.** To occur in time; take place: *come rain or shine.* **6.a.** To arrive at a particular result or end: *come to an understanding.* **b.** To arrive at or reach a particular state or condition: *Come to your senses!* **c.** To move or be brought to a particular position. **7.** To extend; reach: *water that came to my waist.* **8.** To have priority; rank. **9.a.** To reach a particular condition or to arrive at a specified viewpoint. **b.** To happen as a result. **10.** To fall to one: *No good can come of this.* **11.** To occur in the mind. **12.a.** To issue forth: *A cry came from the child.* **b.** To be derived; originate. **c.** To be descended: *They come from a good family.* **d.** To be within a given range or spectrum of reference or application. **13.** To be a native or resident of. **14.** To add up to a certain amount. **15.a.** To become: *The knot came loose.* **b.** To turn out to be. **16.** To be available or obtainable: *shoes that come in all sizes.* **17.** *Vulgar Slang.* To experience orgasm. —*n.* *Vulgar Slang.* Semen. —***phrasal verbs.*** **come about. 1.** To take place; happen. **2.** To turn around. **3.** *Naut.* To change tack. **come across. 1.** To meet or find by chance. **2.** *Slang.* **a.** To do what is wanted. **b.** To pay over money that is demanded. **3.** To give an impression. **come along. 1.** To make advances to a goal; progress. **2.** To go with someone else who takes the lead. **3.** To show up; appear. *the first offer that comes along.* **come around (**or **round). 1.** To recover; revive. **2.** To change one's opinion or position. **come at. 1.** To obtain; get. **2.** To rush at; attack. **come back. 1.** To return to or regain past success after a period of misfortune. **2.** To retort; reply. **3.** To recur to the memory. **come by. 1.** To gain possession of; acquire. **2.** To pay a visit. **come down. 1.** To lose wealth or position. **2.a.** To pass or be handed down by tradition. **b.** To be handed down from a higher authority. **3.** *Slang.* To happen; occur. **come in. 1.a.** To arrive. **b.** To become available for use. **c.** To start producing. Used of an oil well. **2.** To arrive among those who finish a contest or race. **3.** To perform or function in a particular way. **4.** To reply in a specified manner to a call or signal. **5.** To take on a specified role. **come into.** To acquire, esp. as an inheritance. **come off. 1.** To happen; occur. **2.** To acquit oneself. **3.** To turn out to be successful. **come on. 1.** To convey a particular personal image. **2.** *Slang.* To show sexual interest in someone. **3.a.** To progress or advance in increments. **b.** To begin in small increments or by degrees. **4.** To hurry up; move rapidly. Often used in the imperative: *Come on!* **5.** To stop an inappropriate behavior; abandon a position or an attitude; be obliging. Used chiefly in the imperative. **come out. 1.** To become known. **2.** To be issued or brought out. **3.** To make a formal social debut. **4.** To end up; result. **5.** To declare oneself publicly. **6.** To reveal that one is gay or homosexual. **come over. 1.** To change sides, as in a controversy. **2.** To pay a casual visit. **come through. 1.** To do what is required or anticipated. **2.a.** To become manifest. **b.** To be communicated in a specified manner. **come to.** To recover consciousness. **come up. 1.** To manifest itself; arise. **2.** To rise above the horizon. **3.** To rise, as in status or rank. **4.** To draw near; approach. **come upon.** To discover or meet by accident. —***idioms.*** **come a cropper.** To fail utterly. **come clean.** To confess all. **come down on.** To punish, oppose, or reprimand severely and often with force. **come down to. 1.** To confront or deal with forthrightly. **2.** To amount to in essence. **come down with.** To become sick with (an illness). **come in for.** To receive; be subjected to. **come into (one's) own. 1.** To get possession of what belongs to one. **2.** To obtain rightful recognition or prosperity. **come off it.** *Slang.* To stop acting or speaking foolishly or pretentiously. Often used in the imperative. **come out with. 1.** To put into words; say. **2.** To reveal publicly. **come to blows.** To begin a physical fight. **come to grief.** To meet with disaster; fail. **come to grips with.** To confront squarely and attempt to deal decisively with. **come to light (**or **hand).** To be clearly revealed or disclosed. **come to terms. 1.** To confront squarely and come to understand fully and objectively. **2.** To reach mutual agreement. **come true.** To happen as predicted. **come up against.** To encounter, esp. a difficulty or major problem. **come up with.** To bring forth or discover. [ME *comen* < OE *cuman.* See **gʷā-***.]

combine
Harvesting wheat

come•back (kŭm′băk′) *n.* **1.a.** A return to formerly enjoyed status or prosperity. **b.** A return to popularity. **2.** The act of making up a deficit, as in a contest. **3.** A reply; a retort.

co•me•di•an (kə-mē′dē-ən) *n.* **1.** A professional entertainer who tells jokes or performs various other comic acts. **2.** An actor in comedy. **3.** A writer of comedy. **4.** A person who amuses or tries to amuse. [Fr. *comédien*, player, comedian < *comédie*, comedy < Med.Lat. *cōmēdia.* See COMEDY.]

co•me•dic (kə-mē′dĭk) *adj.* Of or relating to comedy. —**co•me′di•cal•ly** *adv.*

co•me•di•enne (kə-mē′dē-ĕn′) *n.* A woman professional entertainer who tells jokes or performs various other comic acts. [Fr. *comédienne*, fem. of *comédien*, comedian. See COMEDIAN.]

com•e•do (kŏm′ĭ-dō′) *n., pl.* **-dos** or **-do•nes** (-dō′nēz). See **blackhead** 12. [Lat. *comedō*, glutton < *comedere*, to eat up : *com-*, intensive pref.; see COM- + *edere*, to eat; see **ed-***.]

com•e•do•gen•ic (kŏm′ĭ-dō-jĕn′ĭk) *adj.* Tending to produce or aggravate acne. [COMEDO + -GENIC.]

come•down (kŭm′doun′) *n.* **1.** A decline to a lower status or level. **2.a.** A feeling of disappointment or depression. **b.** A cause of disappointment or depression.

com•e•dy (kŏm′ĭ-dē) *n., pl.* **-dies. 1.a.** A dramatic work or film that is humorous or satirical and that usu. has a happy ending. **b.** The genre made up of such works. **2.** A literary work having humorous themes or characters. **3.** Popular entertainment composed of jokes, satire, or humorous performance. **4.** The art of composing or performing comedy. **5.** A humorous element of life or literature. **6.** A humorous occurrence. —***idiom.*** **comedy of errors.** A ludicrous event or sequence of events. [ME *comedie* < Med.Lat. *cōmēdia* < Lat. *cōmoedia* < Gk. *kōmōidia* < *kōmōidos*, comic actor : *kōmos*, revel + *aoidos*, singer (< *aeidein*, to sing; see **wed-**[2]*).]

comedy of manners *n., pl.* **comedies of manners.** A comedy satirizing the attitudes and behavior of a particular social group, often of fashionable society.

come-hith•er (kŭm-hĭth′ər) *adj.* Seductive; alluring.

come•ly (kŭm′lē) *adj.* **-li•er, -li•est. 1.** Pleasing and wholesome in appearance; attractive. **2.** Suitable; seemly. [ME *comli*, alteration of *cumli* < OE *cȳmlic*, lovely, delicate < *cȳme*, beautiful.] —**come′li•ness** *n.*

Co•me•ni•us (kə-mē′nē-əs), **John Amos.** 1592–1670. Czech theologian who held that science exalted divine majesty rather than threatened it.

come-on (kŭm′ŏn′, -ôn′) *n.* **1.** Something offered to allure or attract; an inducement, esp. to buy. **2.** *Slang.* A sexual or romantic approach or proposal.

com•er (kŭm′ər) *n.* **1.** One that arrives or comes. **2.** One showing promise of attaining success: *a political comer.*

co•mes•ti•ble (kə-mĕs′tə-bəl) *adj.* Fit to be eaten; edible. —*n.* Something that can be eaten as food. [Fr. < OFr. < LLat. *comēstibilis* < Lat. *comēstus*, alteration of *comēsus*, p.part. of *comedere*, to eat up : *com-*, com- + *edere*, to eat; see **ed-***.]

comet

com•et (kŏm′ĭt) *n.* A celestial body having a head consisting of a solid nucleus surrounded by a nebulous coma up to 2.4 million kilometers (1.5 million miles) in diameter and a vapor tail arising only in that part of its orbit that is sufficiently close to the sun. [ME *comete* < OE *comēta* < Lat. *comētēs* < Gk. *(astēr) komētēs*, long-haired (star) < *komē*, hair.] **— com′et·ar′y** (-ĭ-tĕr′ē), **co·met′ic** (kə-mĕt′ĭk) *adj.*

come·up·pance (kŭm′ŭp′əns) *n.* A punishment or retribution that one deserves; one's just deserts.

com·fit (kŭm′fĭt, kŏm′-) *n.* A confection that consists of a piece of fruit, a seed, or a nut coated with sugar. [ME *confit* < OFr. < Lat. *cōnfectum*, thing prepared, neut. p.part. of *cōnficere*, to prepare : *com-*, com- + *facere*, to make; see **dhē-***.]

com·fort (kŭm′fərt) *tr.v.* **-fort·ed, -fort·ing, -forts. 1.** To soothe in time of affliction or distress. **2.** To ease physically; relieve. *—n.* **1.** A condition or feeling of pleasurable ease, well-being, and contentment. **2.** Solace in time of grief or fear. **3.** Help; assistance. **4.** One that brings or provides comfort. **5.** The capacity to give physical ease and well-being. [ME *comforten* < OFr. *conforter*, to strengthen < LLat. *cōnfortāre* : Lat. *com-*, com- + Lat. *fortis*, strong; see **bhergh-**[2]*.] **— com′fort·ing·ly** *adv.*

com·fort·a·ble (kŭm′fər-tə-bəl, kŭmf′tə-bəl) *adj.* **1.** Providing physical comfort. **2.** Free from stress or anxiety; at ease. **3.** Sufficient to provide financial security: *comfortable earnings.* **— com′fort·a·ble·ness** *n.* **— com′fort·a·bly** *adv.*

com·fort·er (kŭm′fər-tər) *n.* **1.** One that comforts. **2. Comforter.** The Holy Spirit. **3.** A quilted bedcover. **4.** A narrow, long, typically woolen neck scarf.

comfort station *n.* A public restroom or toilet.

com·frey (kŭm′frē) *n., pl.* **-freys.** Any of various hairy perennial Eurasian herbs of the genus *Symphytum*, esp. *S. officinale* having flowers in coiled cymes and long used in herbal medicine. [ME *comferi* < OFr. *cumfirie* < VLat. **cōnfervia* < Lat. *cōnferva* < *cōnfervēre*, to boil together : *com-*, com- + *fervēre*, to boil; see FERVENT.]

com·fy (kŭm′fē) *adj.* **-fi·er, -fi·est.** *Informal.* Comfortable.

com·ic (kŏm′ĭk) *adj.* **1.** Characteristic of or having to do with comedy. **2.** Of or relating to comic strips. **3.** Amusing; humorous. *—n.* **1.a.** A comedian. **b.** A person whose behavior elicits laughter. **2.a. comics.** Comic strips. **b.** A comic book. **3.** A source of humor in art or life. [Lat. *cōmicus* < Gk. *kōmikos* < *kōmos*, revel.]

com·i·cal (kŏm′ĭ-kəl) *adj.* **1.** Provoking mirth or amusement; funny. **2.** Of or relating to comedy. **— com′i·cal′i·ty** (-kăl′ĭ-tē), **com′i·cal·ness** *n.* **— com′i·cal·ly** *adv.*

comic book *n.* A book of comic strips.

Co·mice (kō-mēs′, kə-) *n.* A cultivated variety of pear having blushed greenish-yellow skin and juicy flesh. [< Fr. *(Doyenne du) Comice*, (Dean of the) Show < *comice (agricole)*, (agricultural) show < OFr., convention < Lat. *comitia*. See COMITIA.]

comic opera *n. Mus.* An opera or operetta with a humorous plot, spoken dialogue, and usu. a happy ending.

com·ic-op·er·a (kŏm′ĭk-ŏp′ər-ə, -ŏp′rə) *adj.* Not to be taken seriously.

comic relief *n.* A humorous incident introduced into a serious literary work in order to relieve dramatic tension or heighten emotional impact.

comic strip *n.* A narrative series of cartoons.

Co·mines also **Com·mines** (kô-mēn′), **Philippe de.** 1447?–1511. French historian noted for his *Mémoires* (1524).

com·ing (kŭm′ĭng) *adj.* **1.** Approaching; forthcoming; next. **2.** Showing promise of fame or success. *—n.* Arrival; advent.

com·ing-out (kŭm′ĭng-out′) *n.* A social debut.

Com·in·tern (kŏm′ĭn-tûrn′) *n.* An association of Communist parties of the world, established in 1919 by Lenin and dissolved in 1943. [Russ. *komintern*, abbreviation of *Kommunisticheskiĭ Internatsional*, Communist International.]

co·mi·ti·a (kə-mĭsh′ē-ə, -mĭsh′ə) *n., pl.* **comitia.** A popular assembly in ancient Rome having legislative or electoral duties. [Lat. < pl. of *comitium*, assembly place : *com-*, com- + *itus*, p.part. of *īre*, to go; see **ei-***.] **— co·mi′tial** (-mĭsh′əl) *adj.*

com·i·ty (kŏm′ĭ-tē) *n., pl.* **-ties. 1.** An atmosphere of social harmony. **2.** See **comity of nations** 2. **3.** The principle by which the courts of one jurisdiction may accede or give effect to the laws or decisions of another. [Lat. *cōmitās* < *cōmis*, friendly. See **smei-***.]

comity of nations *n.* **1.** Courteous recognition accorded by one nation to the laws and institutions of another. **2.** The nations observing international comity.

com·ix (kŏm′ĭks) *pl.n.* Comic books and comic strips, esp. of the underground press. [Alteration of *comics*, pl. of COMIC.]

coml. *abbr.* Commercial.

comm. *abbr.* **1.** Commerce. **2.** Commission; commissioner. **3.** Also **Comm.** Committee. **4.** Commonwealth. **5.** Communication.

com·ma (kŏm′ə) *n.* **1.** *Gram.* A punctuation mark (,) used to indicate a separation of ideas or elements within the structure of a sentence. **2.** A pause or separation; a caesura. **3.** Any of several butterflies of the genus *Polygonia*, having brownish wings with irregularly notched edges. [Lat. < Gk. *komma*, piece cut off, short clause < *koptein*, to cut.]

comma fault *n.* Improper use of a comma to join two independent clauses.

com·mand (kə-mănd′) *v.* **-mand·ed, -mand·ing, -mands.** *—tr.* **1.** To direct with authority; give orders to. **2.** To have control or authority over; rule. **3.** To have at one's disposal. **4.** To deserve and receive as due; exact. **5.a.** To exercise dominating, authoritative influence over. **b.** To dominate by physical position; overlook. *—intr.* **1.** To give orders. **2.** To exercise authority or control as or as if one is a commander. *—n.* **1.** The act of commanding. **2.** An order given with authority. **3.** *Comp. Sci.* A signal that initiates an operation defined by an instruction. **4.a.** The authority to command. **b.** Possession and exercise of the authority to command. **5.** Ability to control or use; mastery. **6.** Dominance by location; extent of view. **7.a.** The jurisdiction of a commander. **b.** A military unit, post, district, or region under the control of one officer. **c.** A unit of the U.S. Air Force that is larger than an air force. *—adj.* **1.** Of, relating to, or constituting a command. **2.** Done or performed in response to a command. [ME *commaunden* < OFr. *comander* < LLat. *commandāre* : Lat. *com-*, com- + Lat. *mandāre*, to entrust; see **man-**[2]*.]

com·man·dant (kŏm′ən-dănt′, -dänt′) *n.* The commanding officer of a military organization. [Fr. < pr.part. of *commander*, to command < OFr. *comander*. See COMMAND.]

com·man·deer (kŏm′ən-dîr′) *tr.v.* **-deered, -deer·ing, -deers. 1.** To force into military service. **2.** To seize for military use; confiscate. **3.** To take arbitrarily or by force. [Afr. *kommandeer* < Fr. *commander*, to command < OFr. *comander*. See COMMAND.]

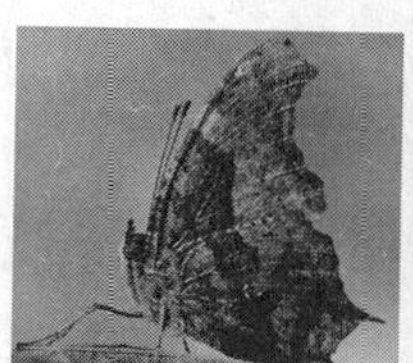

comma
Hop merchant
comma butterfly
Polygonia comma

com·mand·er (kə-măn′dər) *n.* **1.** A person who commands, esp. a commanding officer. **2.a.** A commissioned officer in the U.S. Navy or Coast Guard ranking above lieutenant commander and below captain. **b.** The chief commissioned officer of a military unit regardless of his or her rank. **3.** An officer in some knightly or fraternal orders.

commander in chief *n., pl.* **commanders in chief. 1.** Often **Commander in Chief.** The supreme commander of all the armed forces of a nation. **2.** The officer commanding a major armed force.

com·mand·ing (kə-măn′dĭng) *adj.* **1.** Having command; controlling. **2.** Dominating: *a commanding view of the ocean.* **— com·mand′ing·ly** *adv.* **— com·mand′ing·ness** *n.*

commanding officer *n.* A military officer in charge of a unit, post, camp, base, or station.

com·mand·ment (kə-mănd′mənt) *n.* **1.** A command; an edict. **2.** One of the Ten Commandments.

command module *n.* The portion of a spacecraft in which the astronauts live, communicate with a ground station, and operate controls during a flight.

command module
Apollo 15

com·man·do (kə-măn′dō) *n., pl.* **-dos** or **-does. 1.a.** A small fighting force specially trained for making quick, destructive raids against enemy-held areas. **b.** A member of such a force. **2.a.** An organized force of Boer troops in South Africa. **b.** A raid made by such a force. [Afr. *kommando* < Du. *commando*, unit of troops < Sp. *comando* < *comandar*, to command < LLat. *commandāre*. See COMMAND.]

command post *n.* **1.** The field headquarters used by the commander of a military unit. **2.** A headquarters used by a team or an organization.

comma splice *n.* See **comma fault.**

com·me·dia dell'ar·te (kə-mā′dē-ə dĕl-är′tē, -tĕ, -mĕd′ē-ə) *n.* A type of comedy developed in Italy in the 16th and 17th centuries and characterized by improvisation from a standard plot outline and the use of stock characters. [Ital. : *commedia*, comedy + *dell'arte*, of the guild, professional.]

comme il faut (kŭm′ ēl fō′) *adj.* In accord with conventions or standards. [Fr. : *comme*, as + *il faut*, proper.]

com·mem·o·rate (kə-mĕm′ə-rāt′) *tr.v.* **-rat·ed, -rat·ing, -rates. 1.** To honor the memory of with a ceremony. **2.** To serve as a memorial to. [Lat. *commemorāre, commemorāt-*, to remind : *com-*, com- + *memorāre* (< *memor*, mindful; see **(s)mer-**[1]*).] **— com·mem′o·ra′tor** *n.* **— com·mem′o·ra·to′ry** (-ər-ə-tôr′ē, -tōr′ē) *adj.*

com·mem·o·ra·tion (kə-mĕm′ə-rā′shən) *n.* **1.** The act of commemorating someone or something. **2.** Something that commemorates.

com·mem·o·ra·tive (kə-mĕm′ər-ə-tĭv, -ə-rā′-) *adj.* Commemorating someone or something. *—n.* Something commemorative.

com·mence (kə-mĕns′) *v.* **-menced, -menc·ing, -menc·es.** *—tr.* To begin; start. *—intr.* To enter upon or have a beginning; start. [ME *commencen* < OFr. *comencier* < VLat. **cominitiāre* : Lat. *com-*, com- + LLat. *initiāre*, to begin (< Lat. *initium*, beginning; see **ei-***).] **— com·menc′er** *n.*

com·mence·ment (kə-mĕns′mənt) *n.* **1.** A beginning; a start. **2.a.** A ceremony at which academic degrees or diplomas are conferred. **b.** The day on which such a ceremony occurs.

com·mend (kə-mĕnd′) *tr.v.* **-mend·ed, -mend·ing, -mends. 1.** To represent as worthy, qualified, or desirable; recommend. **2.** To express approval of; praise. See Syns at **praise.**

ă pat	oi boy
ā pay	ou out
âr care	ŏŏ took
ä father	ōō boot
ĕ pet	ŭ cut
ē be	ûr urge
ĭ pit	th thin
ī pie	*th* this
îr pier	hw which
ŏ pot	zh vision
ō toe	ə about, item
ô paw	

Stress marks:
′ (primary);
′ (secondary), as in
dictionary (dĭk′shə-nĕr′ē)

3. To commit to the care of another; entrust. [ME *commenden* < Lat. *commendāre* : *com-*, com- + *mandāre*, to entrust; see **man-**[2]*.] — **com•mend′a•ble** *adj.* — **com•mend′a•ble•ness** *n.* — **com•mend′a•bly** *adv.* — **com•men′da•to′ry** *adj.*

com•men•da•tion (kŏm′ən-dā′shən) *n.* **1.** The act of commending. **2.** Something, as an award, that commends.

com•men•sal (kə-mĕn′səl) *Biol.* — *adj.* Of, relating to, or characterized by commensalism. — *n.* An organism participating in a commensal relationship. [ME, sharing a meal < Med.Lat. *commēnsālis* : Lat. *com-*, com- + Lat. *mēnsa*, table.] — **com•men′sal•ly** *adv.*

com•men•sal•ism (kə-mĕn′sə-lĭz′əm) *n. Biol.* A symbiotic relationship between two organisms of different species in which one derives some benefit while the other is unaffected.

com•men•su•ra•ble (kə-mĕn′sər-ə-bəl, -shər-) *adj.* **1.** Measurable by a common standard. **2.** Commensurate; proportionate. **3.** *Math.* Exactly divisible by the same unit an integral number of times. Used of two quantities. [LLat. *commēnsūrābilis* : Lat. *com-*, com- + *mēnsūrābilis*, measurable (< *mēsūrāre*, to measure; see COMMENSURATE).] — **com•men′su•ra•bil′i•ty** *n.* — **com•men′su•ra•bly** *adv.*

com•men•su•rate (kə-mĕn′sər-ĭt, -shər-) *adj.* **1.** Of the same size, extent, or duration as another. **2.** Corresponding in size or degree; proportionate. **3.** Measurable by a common standard; commensurable. [LLat. *commēnsūrātus* : Lat. *com-*, com- + *mēnsūrātus* < p.part. of *mēnsūrāre*, to measure (< Lat. *mēnsūra*, measure; see MEASURE).] — **com•men′su•rate•ly** *adv.* — **com•men′su•ra′tion** *n.*

com•ment (kŏm′ĕnt) *n.* **1.a.** A written note intended as an explanation, an illustration, or a criticism of a passage in a book or other writing; an annotation. **b.** A series of annotations or explanations. **2.a.** A statement of fact or opinion, esp. one that expresses a personal reaction or attitude. **b.** An implied conclusion or judgment. **3.** Talk; gossip. **4.** *Comp. Sci.* Text in a program that does not function in the program itself but is used by the programmer to explain instructions. — *v.* **-ment•ed, -ment•ing, -ments.** — *intr.* **1.** To make a comment; remark. **2.** To serve as a judgmental commentary. — *tr.* To make comments on; annotate. [ME < LLat. *commentum*, interpretation < Lat., contrivance < neut. p.part. of *comminīscī*, to devise. See **men-**[1]*.]

Syns: *comment, observation, remark.* The central meaning shared by these nouns is "an expression of fact, opinion, or explanation": *an unpleasant comment about me; an observation about the movie; an offensive remark.*

com•men•tar•y (kŏm′ən-tĕr′ē) *n., pl.* **-ies. 1.** A series of explanations or interpretations. **2.** An expository treatise or series of annotations; an exegesis. Often used in the plural. **3.** An apt explanation or illustration. **4.** A personal narrative; a memoir. Often used in the plural. — **com′men•tar′i•al** (-târ′ē-əl) *adj.*

com•men•tate (kŏm′ən-tāt′) *v.* **-tat•ed, -tat•ing, -tates.** — *intr.* To serve as commentator. — *tr.* To make a running commentary on. [Back-formation < COMMENTATOR.]

com•men•ta•tor (kŏm′ən-tā′tər) *n.* **1.** A broadcaster or writer who reports and analyzes events in the news. **2.** One who writes or delivers a commentary or commentaries.

com•merce (kŏm′ərs) *n.* **1.** The buying and selling of goods, esp. on a large scale, as between cities or nations. See Syns at **business. 2.** Intellectual exchange or social interaction. **3.** Sexual intercourse. [Fr. < OFr. < Lat. *commercium* : *com-*, com- + *merx*, *merc-*, merchandise.]

Com•merce City (kŏm′ərs). A city of N-central CO, a suburb of Denver. Pop. 16,466.

com•mer•cial (kə-mûr′shəl) *adj.* **1.a.** Of or relating to commerce. **b.** Engaged in commerce. **c.** Involved in work that is intended for the mass market. **2.** Of, relating to, or being goods, often unrefined, produced and distributed in large quantities for use by industry. **3.** Having profit as a chief aim. **4.** Sponsored by an advertiser or supported by advertising. — *n.* An advertisement on television or radio. — **com•mer′cial•ly** *adv.*

commercial bank *n.* A bank whose principal functions are to receive demand deposits and make short-term loans.

com•mer•cial•ism (kə-mûr′shə-lĭz′əm) *n.* **1.** The practices, methods, aims, and spirit of commerce or business. **2.** An attitude that emphasizes tangible profit or success. — **com•mer′cial•ist** *n.* — **com•mer′cial•is′tic** *adj.*

com•mer•cial•ize (kə-mûr′shə-līz′) *tr.v.* **-ized, -iz•ing, -iz•es. 1.** To apply business methods to for profit. **2.a.** To do, exploit, or make chiefly for financial gain. **b.** To sacrifice the quality of for profit. — **com•mer′cial•i•za′tion** (-shə-lĭ-zā′shən) *n.*

commercial paper *n.* Short-term, unsecured, discounted, and negotiable notes sold by one company to another in order to satisfy immediate cash needs.

commercial traveler *n.* A traveling sales representative.

com•mie also **Com•mie** (kŏm′ē) *n. Informal.* A Communist. [Short for COMMUNIST.]

com•mi•na•tion (kŏm′ə-nā′shən) *n.* A formal denunciation. [ME *comminacioun* < Lat. *comminātiō*, *comminātiōn-* < *comminātus*, p.part. of *comminārī*, to threaten : *com-*, com- + *minārī*, to threaten; see MENACE.] — **com•min′a•to′ry** (kə-mĭn′ə-tôr′ē, -tōr′ē, kŏm′ĭ-nə-) *adj.*

Com•mines (kô-mēn′), **Philippe de.** See **Philippe de Comines.**

com•min•gle (kə-mĭng′gəl) *v.* **-gled, -gling, -gles.** — *intr.* To become blended. — *tr.* To cause to blend together; mix.

com•mi•nute (kŏm′ə-no͞ot′, -nyo͞ot′) *tr.v.* **-nut•ed, -nut•ing, -nutes.** To reduce to powder; pulverize. [Lat. *comminuere*, *comminūt-* : *com-*, com- + *minuere*, to lessen; see **mei-**[2]*.] — **com′mi•nu′tion** *n.*

com•mis•er•ate (kə-mĭz′ə-rāt′) *v.* **-at•ed, -at•ing, -ates.** — *tr.* To feel or express sorrow or pity for; sympathize with. — *intr.* To feel or express sympathy. [Lat. *commiserārī*, *commiserāt-* : *com-*, com- + *miserārī*, to pity (< *miser*, wretched).] — **com•mis′er•a′tive** *adj.* — **com•mis′er•a′tive•ly** *adv.* — **com•mis′er•a′tor** *n.*

com•mis•er•a•tion (kə-mĭz′ə-rā′shən) *n.* The feeling or expression of pity or sorrow.

com•mis•sar (kŏm′ĭ-sär′) *n.* **1.a.** An official of the Communist Party in charge of political indoctrination and the enforcement of party loyalty. **b.** The head of a commissariat in the Soviet Union until 1946. **2.** A person who tries to control public opinion. [Russ. *komissar* < Ger. *Kommissar*, deputy < Med.Lat. *commissārius*, agent. See COMMISSARY.]

com•mis•sar•i•at (kŏm′ĭ-sâr′ē-ĭt) *n.* **1.** A department of an army that provides supplies. **2.** A food supply. **3.** A major government department in the Soviet Union until 1946. [Fr. < Med.Lat. *commissārius*, agent. See COMMISSARY.]

com•mis•sar•y (kŏm′ĭ-sĕr′ē) *n., pl.* **-ies. 1.a.** A supermarket for military personnel and their dependents, usu. located on a military installation. **b.** A store where food and equipment are sold, as in a mining camp. **2.** A lunchroom or cafeteria, esp. one in a film or television studio. **3.** A person to whom a special duty is given by a higher authority; a deputy. [ME *commissarie*, agent < Med.Lat. *commissārius* < Lat. *commissus*, entrusted. See COMMISSION.]

com•mis•sion (kə-mĭsh′ən) *n.* **1.a.** The act of granting certain powers or the authority to carry out a particular task or duty. **b.** The authority so granted. **c.** The matter or task so authorized. **d.** A document conferring such authorization. **2.a.** A group of people officially authorized to perform certain duties or functions. **b.** Often **Commission.** A ruling council within the Mafia. **3.** The act of committing or perpetrating. **4.** A fee or percentage allowed to a sales representative or an agent for services rendered. **5.a.** An official document issued by a government, conferring on the recipient the rank of a commissioned officer in the armed forces. **b.** The rank and powers so conferred. — *tr.v.* **-sioned, -sion•ing, -sions. 1.** To grant a commission to. **2.** To place an order for. **3.** To put (a ship) into active service. — ***idioms.* in commission. 1.** In active service. Used of a ship. **2.** In use or in usable condition. **on commission.** With a sales commission serving as full or partial recompense for the work done. **out of commission. 1.** Not in active service. Used of a ship. **2.** Not in use or in working condition. [ME *commissioun* < Lat. *commissiō*, *commissiōn-* < *commissus*, p.part. of *committere*, to entrust. See COMMIT.] — **com•mis′sion•al** *adj.*

com•mis•sion•aire (kə-mĭsh′ə-nâr′) *n. Chiefly British.* A uniformed attendant. [Fr. < Med.Lat. *commissiōnārius* < Lat. *commissiō*, *commissiōn-*, commission. See COMMISSION.]

com•mis•sioned officer (kə-mĭsh′ənd) *n.* An officer who holds a commission and ranks as a second lieutenant or above in the U.S. Army, Air Force, or Marine Corps or as an ensign or above in the U.S. Navy or Coast Guard.

com•mis•sion•er (kə-mĭsh′ə-nər) *n.* **1.** A member of a commission. **2.** A person authorized by a commission to perform certain duties. **3.** A governmental official in charge of a department. **4.** *Sports.* An official selected by an athletic association or league to exercise administrative or regulatory powers over it. — **com•mis′sion•er•ship′** *n.*

commission merchant *n.* One that buys and sells goods for others on a commission basis.

commission plan *n.* Municipal government in which legislative and administrative functions and powers are vested in an elected commission rather than in a mayor and city council.

com•mis•sure (kŏm′ə-sho͝or′) *n.* **1.** A line or place at which two things join. **2.** *Anat.* **a.** A tract of nerve fibers passing from one side to the other of the spinal cord or brain. **b.** The point or surface where two parts, such as the eyelids, join or form a connection. [ME < Lat. *commissūra* < *commissus*, p.part. of *committere*, to join. See COMMIT.] — **com′mis•su′ral** *adj.*

com•mit (kə-mĭt′) *v.* **-mit•ted, -mit•ting, -mits.** — *tr.* **1.** To do, perform, or perpetrate. **2.** To put in trust or charge; entrust. **3.** To place officially in confinement or custody. **4.** To consign for future use or reference or for preservation. **5.** To put into a place to be kept safe or to be disposed of. **6.a.** To make known the views of (oneself) on an issue. **b.** To bind or obligate, as by a pledge. **7.** To refer (a legislative bill, for example) to a committee. — *intr.* To pledge or obligate one's own self. [ME *committen* < Lat. *committere* : *com-*, com- + *mittere*, to send.] — **com•mit′ta•ble** *adj.*

com•mit•ment (kə-mĭt**′**mənt) *n.* **1.** The act or an instance of committing, esp.: **a.** The act of referring a legislative bill to committee. **b.** Official consignment, as to a prison. **c.** A court order authorizing consignment to a prison. **2.a.** A pledge to do. **b.** Something pledged, esp. an engagement by contract involving financial obligation. **3.** The state of being bound emotionally or intellectually to someone or something.

com•mit•tal (kə-mĭt**′**l) *n.* **1.** The act of entrusting. **2.** The act or an instance of committing to confinement. **3.** The act of pledging oneself to a particular view or position.

com•mit•tee (kə-mĭt**′**ē) *n.* **1.** A group of people officially delegated to perform a function. See Usage Note at **collective noun. 2.** *Archaic.* A person to whom a trust or charge is committed. [< ME *committe,* trustee < AN *comité,* p.part. of *cometre,* to commit < Lat. *committere.* See COMMIT.]

com•mit•tee•man (kə-mĭt**′**ē-mən, -măn′) *n.* **1.** A man who is a member of a committee. **2.** A man who is a party leader of a ward or precinct.

committee of the whole *n.* The whole membership of a legislative body sitting as a committee to consider a proposal.

com•mit•tee•wom•an (kə-mĭt**′**ē-wo͝om′ən) *n.* **1.** A woman who is a member of a committee. **2.** A woman who is a party leader of a ward or precinct.

com•mix (kə-mĭks**′**, kŏ-) *v.* **-mixed, -mix•ing, -mix•es.** —*intr.* To be or become mixed. —*tr.* To cause to mix. [< ME *commixt,* mixed < Lat. *commixtus,* p.part. of *commiscēre,* to mix : *com-,* com- + *miscēre,* to mix; see **meik-*.**]

com•mix•ture (kə-mĭks**′**chər, kŏ-) *n.* **1.** The act or process of mixing. **2.** The result of mixing; a mixture.

com•mode (kə-mōd**′**) *n.* **1.** A low cabinet or chest of drawers, often elaborately decorated and usu. standing on legs or short feet. **2.a.** A movable stand or cupboard containing a washbowl. **b.** A chair enclosing a chamber pot. **c.** A toilet. **3.** A woman's ornate headdress, fashionable around 1700. [Fr. < *commode,* convenient < Lat. *commodus.* See COMMODIOUS.]

com•mo•di•ous (kə-mō**′**dē-əs) *adj.* **1.** Spacious; roomy. **2.** *Archaic.* Suitable; handy. [ME, convenient < Med.Lat. *commodiōsus* < Lat. *commodus* : *com-,* com- + *modus,* measure; see **med-*.**] —**com•mo′di•ous•ly** *adv.* —**com•mo′di•ous•ness** *n.*

com•mod•i•ty (kə-mŏd**′**ĭ-tē) *n., pl.* **-ties. 1.** Something useful that can be turned to commercial or other advantage. **2.** An article of trade or commerce, esp. an agricultural or mining product, that can be transported. **3.** Advantage; benefit. **4.** *Obsolete.* A quantity; lot. [ME *commodite* < OFr., convenience < Lat. *commoditās* < *commodus,* convenient. See COMMODIOUS.]

com•mo•dore (kŏm**′**ə-dôr′, -dōr′) *n.* **1.a.** A former commissioned rank in the U.S. Navy that is above captain and below rear admiral. **b.** One who holds this rank. **2.a.** The senior captain of a naval squadron or merchant fleet. **b.** The presiding officer of a yacht club. [Obsolete *commandore,* prob. < Du. *komandeur,* commander < Fr. *commandeur* < OFr. < *comander,* to command. See COMMAND.]

Com•mo•dus (kŏm**′**ə-dəs), **Lucius Aelius Aurelius.** A.D. 161–192. Emperor of Rome (180–192) who was murdered in a conspiracy led by his mistress.

com•mon (kŏm**′**ən) *adj.* **-er, -est. 1.a.** Belonging equally to or shared equally by two or more; joint. **b.** Of or relating to the community as a whole; public. See Syns at **general.** See Usage Note at **mutual. 2.** Widespread; prevalent. **3.a.** Occurring frequently or habitually; usual. **b.** Most widely known; ordinary. **4.** Having no special designation, status, or rank. **5.a.** Not distinguished by superior or noteworthy characteristics; average. **b.** Of no special quality; standard. **c.** Of mediocre or inferior quality; second-rate. **6.** Unrefined or coarse in manner; vulgar. **7.** *Gram.* **a.** Either masculine or feminine in gender. **b.** Representing one or all of the members of a class; not designating a unique entity. —*n.* **1. commons.** The common people; commonalty. **2. commons.** *(used with a sing. or pl. v.)* **a.** The political class composed of commoners. **b.** The parliamentary representatives of this class. **3.** See **House of Commons. 4.** A tract of land belonging to or used by a community as a whole. **5.** The legal right of a person to use the lands or waters of another, as for fishing. **6. commons.** *(used with a sing. v.)* A building or hall for dining, typically at a university or college. **7.** Common stock. **8.** *Eccles.* A service used for a particular class of festivals. —***idiom.* in common.** Equally with or by all. [ME *commune* < OFr. *commun* < Lat. *commūnis.* See **mei-**[1]***.**] —**com′mon•ly** *adv.* —**com′mon•ness** *n.*

com•mon•age (kŏm**′**ə-nĭj) *n.* **1.** The right to pasture animals on common land. **2.** The state of being held in common.

com•mon•al•i•ty (kŏm′ə-năl**′**ĭ-tē) *n., pl.* **-ties. 1.** The possession along with another or others of a certain attribute or set of attributes. **2.** See **commonalty** 1.

com•mon•al•ty (kŏm**′**ə-nəl-tē) *n., pl.* **-ties. 1.** The common people as opposed to the upper classes. **2.** A body corporate; a corporation. **3.** An entire group. [ME *communalte* < OFr. *comunalte* < Med.Lat. *commūnālitās* < LLat. *commūnālis,* of the community. See COMMUNAL.]

common bile duct *n.* The duct formed by the union of the cystic duct and the hepatic duct that carries bile from the liver and the gallbladder to the duodenum.

common carrier *n.* **1.** One that is in the business of transporting the public, goods, or messages for a fee. **2.** A company that provides telecommunications services to the public.

common cold *n.* See **cold** 3.

common denominator *n.* **1.** *Math.* A quantity into which all the denominators of a set of fractions may be divided without a remainder. **2.** A commonly shared theme or trait.

common divisor *n. Math.* A quantity that is a factor of two or more quantities.

com•mon•er (kŏm**′**ə-nər) *n.* **1.** One of the common people. **2.** A person without noble rank or title.

Com•mon Era (kŏm**′**ən) *n.* The period coinciding with the Christian era.

common fraction *n. Math.* A fraction having an integer as a numerator and an integer as a denominator.

common gender *n. Gram.* In Modern English, the gender of those nouns that apply to either sex, such as *spouse.*

common ground *n.* A foundation for mutual understanding.

common law *n. Law.* The system of laws originated and developed in England and based on court decisions, on the doctrines implicit in those decisions, and on customs and usages rather than on codified written laws.

com•mon-law marriage (kŏm**′**ən-lô′) *n.* A marriage existing by mutual agreement or the fact of cohabitation without a civil or religious ceremony.

common logarithm *n. Math.* A logarithm to the base 10, esp. as distinguished from a natural logarithm.

common market or **Common Market** *n.* An economic unit, typically formed of nations, intended to eliminate or markedly reduce trade barriers among its members.

Common Market. Officially **Eu•ro•pe•an Economic Community** (yo͝or′ə-pē**′**ən). An economic union orig. estab. in 1958 to promote trade and cooperation among the countries of Belgium, Luxembourg, the Netherlands, France, Italy, and West Germany. Ireland, Great Britain, and Denmark joined in 1973, Greece in 1981, and Spain and Portugal in 1986.

common measure *n.* **1.** *Mus.* See **common time. 2.** *Math.* See **common divisor. 3.** A ballad stanza form in iambic meter, often rhyming in alternating pairs, that is typical of many church hymns.

common multiple *n. Math.* A quantity into which each of two or more other quantities may be divided with zero remainder.

common noun *n. Gram.* A noun, such as *book* or *dog,* that can be preceded by the definite article and represents one or all of the members of a class.

com•mon•place (kŏm**′**ən-plās′) *adj.* Having no remarkable features, characteristics, or traits; ordinary. —*n.* **1.a.** A trite or obvious remark; a platitude. **b.** Something that is ordinary or common. **2.** *Archaic.* A passage marked for reference or entered in a commonplace book. [Transl. of Lat. *locus commūnis,* generally applicable literary passage, transl. of Gk. *koinos topos.*]

commonplace book *n.* A personal journal in which quotable passages, literary excerpts, and comments are written.

common pleas (plēz) *pl.n. (used with a sing. v.) Law.* In some states of the United States, a court of common pleas.

common room *n.* **1.** A faculty lounge in a college or university. **2.** A lounge for use by all members of a residential institution or community.

common salt *n.* **1.** See **salt** 1. **2.** Sodium chloride.

common school *n.* A public elementary school.

com•mon•sense (kŏm**′**ən-sĕns**′**) *adj.* Having or exhibiting native good judgment. —**com′mon•sen′si•ble** *adj.* —**com′mon•sen′si•bly** *adv.*

common sense *n.* Native good judgment. [Transl. of Lat. *sēnsus commūnis,* common feelings of humanity.]

com•mon-si•tus pick•et•ing (kŏm**′**ən-sī′təs pĭk**′**ĭ-tĭng) also **com•mon-site picketing** (kŏm**′**ən-sīt′) *n.* Picketing by a labor union of an entire construction project as a result of a grievance against a subcontractor. [Lat. *situs,* site. See SITE.]

common stock *n.* Ordinary capital shares of a corporation that have exclusive residual claim on the net assets and net income of the corporation after all prior claims are paid.

common time *n. Mus.* A meter with four quarter notes to the measure.

common touch *n.* The ability to appeal to the interests and sensibilities of the ordinary person.

com•mon•weal (kŏm**′**ən-wēl′) *n.* **1.** The public good or welfare. **2.** *Archaic.* A commonwealth or republic.

com•mon•wealth (kŏm**′**ən-wĕlth′) *n.* **1.** The people of a nation or state; the body politic. **2.** A nation or state governed by the people; a republic. **3. Commonwealth. a.** Used to refer to Kentucky, Massachusetts, Pennsylvania, and Virginia. **b.** Used to refer to a self-governing autonomous political unit voluntarily associated with the United States, namely, Puerto Rico and the Northern Mariana Islands. **4.** The English state and government from the death of Charles I in 1649 to the restoration of the monarchy in 1660, including the Protectorate of 1653 to 1659. **5.** *Archaic.* The public good.

Commonwealth of Independent States. A federation of self-

commode
18th-century German

ă pat	oi boy
ā pay	ou out
âr care	o͝o took
ä father	o͞o boot
ĕ pet	ŭ cut
ē be	ûr urge
ĭ pit	th thin
ī pie	*th* this
îr pier	hw which
ŏ pot	zh vision
ō toe	ə about, item
ô paw	

Stress marks:
′ (primary);
′ (secondary), as in
dictionary (dĭk**′**shə-nĕr′ē)

magnetic needles of a compass and marked with the 32 points of the compass and the 360 degrees of the circle.

com•pas•sion (kəm-păsh′ən) *n.* Deep awareness of the suffering of another coupled with the wish to relieve it. [ME *compassioun* < LLat. *compassiō, compassiōn-* < *compassus,* p.part. of *compatī,* to sympathize : Lat. *com-,* com- + Lat. *patī,* to suffer; see **pē(i)-***.]

com•pas•sion•ate (kəm-păsh′ə-nĭt) *adj.* Feeling or showing compassion; sympathetic. See Syns at **humane.** — *tr.v.* (-nāt′) **-at•ed, -at•ing, -ates.** To pity. — **com•pas′sion•ate•ly** *adv.* — **com•pas′sion•ate•ness** *n.*

compass plant *n.* A perennial herb *(Silphium laciniatum)* in the composite family, native to the Midwest United States and having yellow flowers and basal pinnate leaves.

com•pat•i•ble (kəm-păt′ə-bəl) *adj.* **1.** Capable of existing or performing in harmonious, agreeable, or congenial combination. **2.** Capable of integration and operation in a system with no modification or conversion required. **3.** Capable of forming a chemically or biochemically stable system. **4.** Of or relating to a television system in which color broadcasts can be received in black and white by sets incapable of color reception. **5.** *Medic.* Capable of being grafted, transfused, or transplanted from one individual to another without rejection. — *n.* A device that can be integrated into or used with another device or system of its type. [ME < Med.Lat. *compatībilis* < LLat. *compatī,* to sympathize. See COMPASSION.] — **com•pat′i•bil′i•ty, com•pat′i•ble•ness** *n.* — **com•pat′i•bly** *adv.*

com•pa•tri•ot (kəm-pā′trē-ət, -ŏt′) *n.* **1.** A person from one's own country. **2.** A colleague. [Fr. *compatriote* < LLat. *compatriōta* : Lat. *com-,* com- + LLat. *patriōta,* countryman; see PATRIOT.] — **com•pa′tri•ot′ic** (-ŏt′ĭk) *adj.*

compd. *abbr.* Compound.

com•peer (kŏm′pîr′, kəm-pîr′) *n.* **1.** A person of equal status or rank; a peer. **2.** A comrade, companion, or associate. [ME *comper* < OFr. < Lat. *compār,* equal. See COMPARE.]

com•pel (kəm-pĕl′) *tr.v.* **-pelled, -pel•ling, -pels. 1.** To force, drive, or constrain. **2.** To necessitate or pressure by force; exact. **3.** To exert a strong irresistible force on; sway. [ME *compellen* < Lat. *compellere* : *com-,* com- + *pellere,* to drive; see **pel-**[5]***.] — **com•pel′la•ble** *adj.* — **com•pel′la•bly** *adv.* — **com•pel′ler** *n.*

com•pel•la•tion (kŏm′pə-lā′shən) *n.* **1.** The act of addressing or designating someone by name. **2.** A name; an appellation. [Lat. *compellātiō, compellātiōn-* < *compellātus,* p.part. of *compellāre,* to address. See **pel-**[5]***.]

com•pel•ling (kəm-pĕl′ĭng) *adj.* **1.** Urgently requiring attention. **2.** Drivingly forceful: *compelling ambition.*

com•pend (kŏm′pĕnd′) *n.* A compendium.

com•pen•di•ous (kəm-pĕn′dē-əs) *adj.* Containing or stating briefly and concisely all the essentials. [ME < LLat. *compendiōsus* < Lat. *compendium,* a shortening. See COMPENDIUM.] — **com•pen′di•ous•ly** *adv.* — **com•pen′di•ous•ness** *n.*

com•pen•di•um (kəm-pĕn′dē-əm) *n., pl.* **-di•ums** or **-di•a** (-dē-ə). **1.** A short, complete summary; an abstract. **2.** A list or collection of various items. [Lat., a shortening < *compendere,* to weigh together : *com-,* com- + *pendere,* to weigh; see **(s)pen-***.]

com•pen•sa•ble (kəm-pĕn′sə-bəl) *adj.* Being such as to entitle or warrant compensation: *compensable injuries.*

com•pen•sate (kŏm′pən-sāt′) *v.* **-sat•ed, -sat•ing, -sates.** — *tr.* **1.** To offset; counterbalance. **2.** To make satisfactory payment or reparation to; recompense or reimburse. — *intr.* To serve as or provide a substitute or counterbalance. [Lat. *compēnsāre, compēnsāt-* : *com-,* com- + *pēnsāre,* to weigh; see **(s)pen-***.] — **com′pen•sa′tive** (kŏm′pən-sā′tĭv, kəm-pĕn′sə-tĭv) *adj.* — **com′pen•sa′tor** *n.* — **com•pen′sa•to′ry** (kəm-pĕn′sə-tôr′ē, -tōr′ē) *adj.*

com•pen•sa•tion (kŏm′pən-sā′shən) *n.* **1.** The act of compensating or the state of being compensated. **2.** Something given or received as payment or reparation. **3.** *Biol.* The increase in size or activity of one part of an organism or organ that makes up for the loss or dysfunction of another. **4.** *Psychol.* Behavior that develops to offset a real or imagined deficiency. — **com′pen•sa′tion•al** *adj.*

com•pere (kŏm′pâr′) *Chiefly British. n.* The master of ceremonies, as of a variety show. [Fr. *compère* < OFr., godfather, companion < Med.Lat. *compater* : Lat. *com-,* com- + Lat. *pater,* father; see PATER.] — **com′pere′** *v.*

com•pete (kəm-pēt′) *intr.v.* **-pet•ed, -pet•ing, -petes.** To strive with another or others to attain a goal. [LLat. *competere,* to strive together < Lat., to coincide, be suitable : *com-,* com- + *petere,* to seek; see **pet-***.]

com•pe•tence (kŏm′pĭ-təns) *n.* **1.a.** The state or quality of being adequately or well qualified; ability. **b.** A specific range of skill, knowledge, or ability. **2.** *Law.* The quality or condition of being legally qualified to perform an act. **3.** Sufficient means for a comfortable existence. **4.** *Microbiol.* The ability of bacteria to be genetically transformable. **5.** *Medic.* The ability to respond immunologically to antigenic agents.

com•pe•ten•cy (kŏm′pĭ-tən-se) *n., pl.* **-cies.** Competence.

com•pe•tent (kŏm′pĭ-tənt) *adj.* **1.** Properly or sufficiently qualified; capable. **2.** Adequate for the purpose. **3.** *Law.* Legally qualified or fit to perform an act. [ME, adequate < OFr. < Lat. *competēns, competent-,* pr.part. of *competere,* to be suitable. See COMPETE.] — **com′pe•tent•ly** *adv.*

com•pe•ti•tion (kŏm′pĭ-tĭsh′ən) *n.* **1.** The act of competing, as for profit or a prize; rivalry. **2.** A test of skill or ability; a contest. **3.** Rivalry between two or more businesses. **4.** A competitor. **5.** *Ecol.* The simultaneous demand by two or more organisms for limited environmental resources.

com•pet•i•tive (kəm-pĕt′ĭ-tĭv) *adj.* **1.** Of, involving, or determined by competition. **2.** Inclined to compete. — **com•pet′i•tive•ly** *adv.* — **com•pet′i•tive•ness** *n.*

com•pet•i•tor (kəm-pĕt′ĭ-tər) *n.* One that competes; a rival.

Com•piègne (kŏmp-yān′, kôN-pyĕn′yə). A city of N France on the Oise R. NE of Paris. The armistice ending World War I was signed nearby on Nov. 11, 1918. Pop. 40,384.

com•pi•la•tion (kŏm′pə-lā′shən) *n.* **1.** The act of compiling. **2.** Something, such as a report, that is compiled.

com•pile (kəm-pīl′) *tr.v.* **-piled, -pil•ing, -piles. 1.** To gather into a single book. **2.** To put together or compose from materials gathered from several sources. **3.** *Comp. Sci.* To translate (a program) into machine language. [ME *compilen* < OFr. *compiler,* prob. < Lat. *compīlāre,* to plunder : *com-,* com- + *pīla,* heap (of stones), pillar.]

com•pil•er (kəm-pī′lər) *n.* **1.** One that compiles. **2.** *Comp. Sci.* A program that compiles.

com•pla•cence (kəm-plā′səns) *n.* **1.** Contented self-satisfaction. **2.** Total lack of concern.

com•pla•cen•cy (kəm-plā′sən-sē) *n.* **1.** A feeling of contentment or self-satisfaction, esp. when coupled with an unawareness of danger or trouble. **2.** An instance of complacency.

com•pla•cent (kəm-plā′sənt) *adj.* **1.** Contented to a fault; self-satisfied and unconcerned. **2.** Eager to please; complaisant. [Lat. *complacēns, complacent-,* pr.part. of *complacēre,* to please : *com-,* com- + *placēre,* to please; see **plāk-**[1]***.] — **com•pla′cent•ly** *adv.*

com•plain (kəm-plān′) *intr.v.* **-plained, -plain•ing, -plains. 1.** To express feelings of pain, dissatisfaction, or resentment. **2.** To make a formal accusation or bring a formal charge. [ME *compleinen* < OFr. *complaindre, complaign-* < VLat. **complangere* : Lat. *com-,* com- + Lat. *plangere,* to lament; see **plāk-**[2]***.] — **com•plain′er** *n.*

com•plain•ant (kəm-plā′nənt) *n. Law.* A party that makes a complaint or files a formal charge; a plaintiff.

com•plaint (kəm-plānt′) *n.* **1.** An expression of pain, dissatisfaction, or resentment. **2.** A cause or reason for complaining; a grievance. **3.a.** A bodily disorder or disease; a malady or an ailment. **b.** The symptom or distress about which a patient seeks medical assistance. **4.** *Law.* **a.** A claim set forth by the plaintiff in a civil action. **b.** A formal charge, made under oath, of the commission of a crime or other such offense. [ME *compleinte* < OFr. *complainte* < fem. p.part. of *complaindre,* to complain. See COMPLAIN.]

com•plai•sance (kəm-plā′səns, -zəns) *n.* The inclination to comply willingly with the wishes of others; amiability.

com•plai•sant (kəm-plā′sənt, -zənt) *adj.* Exhibiting a desire or willingness to please; cheerfully obliging. [Fr. < OFr., pr.part. of *complaire,* to please < Lat. *complacēre.* See COMPLACENT.] — **com•plai′sant•ly** *adv.*

com•pleat (kəm-plēt′) *adj.* **1.** Of or characterized by a highly developed or wide-ranging skill or proficiency. **2.** Being an outstanding example of a kind; quintessential. [Var. of COMPLETE.]

com•plect (kəm-plĕkt′) *tr.v.* **-plect•ed, -plect•ing, -plects.** To join by weaving or twining together; interweave. [Lat. *complectī,* to entwine : *com-,* com- + *plectere,* to plait; see **plek-***.]

com•plect•ed (kəm-plĕk′tĭd) *adj. Informal.* Marked by or having a particular facial complexion. [Back-formation < *complection,* var. of COMPLEXION.]

com•ple•ment (kŏm′plə-mənt) *n.* **1.a.** Something that completes, makes up a whole, or brings to perfection. **b.** The quantity or number needed to make up a whole: *shelves with a full complement of books.* **c.** Either of two parts that complete the whole or mutually complete each other. **2.** An angle related to another so that the sum of their measures is 90°. **3.** *Gram.* A word or words used after a verb to complete a predicate construction. **4.** *Mus.* An interval that completes an octave when added to a given interval. **5.** The full crew of officers and enlisted personnel required to run a ship. **6.** *Biochem.* A complex system of proteins found in normal blood serum that combines with antibodies to destroy pathogenic bacteria and other foreign cells. **7.** *Math. & Logic.* For a universal set, the set of all elements in the set that are not in a specified subset. — *tr.v.* (-mĕnt′) **-ment•ed, -ment•ing, -ments.** To serve as a complement to. [ME < OFr. < Lat. *complēmentum* < *complēre,* to fill out. See COMPLETE.]

Usage Note: *Complement* means "something that completes or brings to perfection": *The antique silver was a complement to the beautifully set table. Compliment* means "an expression or act of courtesy or praise": *They gave us a compliment on our beautifully set table.*

com•ple•men•tal (kŏm′plə-mĕn′tl) *adj.* Having to do with or being a complement. — **com′ple•men′tal•ly** *adv.*

com•ple•men•tar•i•ty (kŏm′plə-mĕn-tăr′ĭ-tē) *n.* The state or quality of being complementary.

com•ple•men•ta•ry (kŏm′plə-mĕn′tə-rē, -trē) *adj.* **1.** Forming or serving as a complement; completing. **2.** Supplying mutual needs or offsetting mutual lacks. **3.** *Biochem.* Of or relating to the specific pairing of the purines and pyrimidines between strands of a DNA or an RNA molecule. — **com′ple•men′ta•ri•ly** (-tə-rə-lē, -trə-lē, -mĕn-târ′ə-lē) *adv.* — **com′ple•men′ta•ri•ness** *n.*

complementary angles *pl.n. Math.* Two angles whose sum is 90°.

complementary color *n.* Either one of two colors whose mixture in the right proportions produces white (in the case of light) or gray (in the case of pigment).

complement fixation *n.* The binding of active serum complement to a specific antigen-antibody pair used in various diagnostic tests.

com•plete (kəm-plēt′) *adj.* **-plet•er, -plet•est. 1.** Having all necessary or normal parts, components, or steps; entire. **2.** *Bot.* Having all principal parts, namely, the sepals, petals, stamens, and pistil or pistils. **3.** Having come to an end. **4.** Absolute; total. **5.a.** Skilled; accomplished. **b.** Thorough; consummate. — *tr.v.* **-plet•ed, -plet•ing, -pletes. 1.** To bring to a finish or an end. **2.** To make whole, with all necessary elements or parts. [ME *complet* < Lat. *complētus*, p.part. of *complēre*, to fill out : *com-*, com- + *plēre*, to fill; see **pelə-**[1]***.**] — **com•plete′ly** *adv.* — **com•plete′ness** *n.* — **com•ple′tive** *adj.*

Usage Note: *Complete* is sometimes held to be an absolute term like *perfect* or *chief.* Nonetheless, it can be qualified. A majority of the Usage Panel accepts the example *His book is the most complete treatment of the subject.*

complete blood count *n.* The determination of the quantity of each type of blood cell in a given sample of blood.

com•ple•tion (kəm-plē′shən) *n.* The act of completing or the state of being completed.

com•plex (kəm-plĕks′, kŏm′plĕks′) *adj.* **1.a.** Consisting of interconnected or interwoven parts; composite. **b.** Composed of two or more units: *a complex carbohydrate.* **2.** Involved or intricate; complicated. **3.** *Gram.* **a.** Consisting of at least one bound form. Used of a word. **b.** Consisting of an independent clause and at least one other independent or dependent clause. Used of a sentence. — *n.* (kŏm′plĕks′). **1.** A whole composed of interconnected or interwoven parts. **2.** *Psychiat.* A group of related, often repressed ideas and impulses that compel characteristic or habitual patterns of thought, feelings, and behavior. **3.** An exaggerated or obsessive concern or fear. **4.** *Medic.* The combination of factors, symptoms, or signs of a disease or disorder that forms a syndrome. [Lat. *complexus*, p.part. of *complectī*, to entwine. See COMPLECT.] — **com•plex′ly** *adv.* — **com•plex′ness** *n.*

Syns: *complex, complicated, intricate, involved, tangled, knotty.* These adjectives mean having parts so interconnected as to make the whole perplexing. *Complex* implies a combination of many associated parts: *a complex set of musical variations. Complicated* stresses elaborate relationship of parts: *complicated politics that thwart a cohesive policy. Intricate* refers to a pattern of intertwining parts that is difficult to follow or analyze: *"No one could soar into a more intricate labyrinth of refined phraseology"* (Anthony Trollope). *Involved* stresses confusion arising from the commingling of parts and the consequent difficulty of separating them: *a plot line criticized as being too involved. Tangled* strongly suggests the random twisting of many parts: *"Oh, what a tangled web we weave/When first we practice to deceive!"* (Sir Walter Scott). *Knotty* stresses intellectual complexity leading to difficulty of solution or comprehension: *a knotty problem.*

complex fraction *n. Math.* A fraction in which the numerator or the denominator or both contain fractions.

com•plex•ion (kəm-plĕk′shən) *n.* **1.** The natural color, texture, and appearance of the skin, esp. of the face. **2.** General character, aspect, or appearance. **3.** The combination of the four humors of cold, heat, moistness, and dryness in specific proportions, thought in ancient and medieval physiology to control the temperament and the constitution of the body. [ME *complexioun*, physical constitution < OFr. *complexion* < LLat. *complexiō, complexiōn-*, balance of the humors < Lat., combination < *complexus*, p.part. of *complectī*, to entwine. See COMPLECT.] — **com•plex′ion•al** *adj.*

com•plex•ioned (kəm-plĕk′shənd) *adj.* Of or having a specified complexion. Often used in combination: *fair-complexioned.*

com•plex•i•ty (kəm-plĕk′sĭ-tē) *n., pl.* **-ties. 1.** The quality or condition of being complex. **2.** Something complex.

complex number *n. Math.* Any number of the form $a + bi$, where a and b are real numbers and i^2 equals -1.

complex plane *n. Math.* A plane whose points have complex numbers as their coordinates.

com•pli•ance (kəm-plī′əns) *n.* **1.** The act of complying with a wish, request, or demand; acquiescence. **2.** A disposition or tendency to yield to the will of others. **3.a.** Extension or displacement of a loaded structure per unit load. **b.** Flexibility.

com•pli•an•cy (kəm-plī′ən-sē) *n.* Compliance.

com•pli•ant (kəm-plī′ənt) *adj.* Disposed or willing to comply; submissive. — **com•pli′ant•ly** *adv.*

com•pli•ca•cy (kəm-plĭk′ə-sē) *n., pl.* **-cies. 1.** The state of being complicated. **2.** A complication.

com•pli•cate (kŏm′plĭ-kāt′) *tr. & intr.v.* **-cat•ed, -cat•ing, -cates. 1.** To make or become complex or perplexing. **2.** To twist or become twisted together. — *adj.* (-kĭt). **1.** Complex, intricate, and involved. **2.** *Biol.* Folded longitudinally one or several times, as certain leaves. [Lat. *complicāre, complicāt-*, to fold together : *com-*, com- + *plicāre*, to fold; see **plek-*.**]

com•pli•cat•ed (kŏm′plĭ-kā′tĭd) *adj.* **1.** Containing intricately combined or involved parts. **2.** See Syns at **complex.** — **com′pli•cat′ed•ly** *adv.* — **com′pli•cat′ed•ness** *n.*

com•pli•ca•tion (kŏm′plĭ-kā′shən) *n.* **1.** The act of complicating. **2.** A confused or intricate relationship of parts. **3.** A factor, a condition, or an element that complicates. **4.** *Medic.* A secondary disease, an accident, or a negative reaction occurring during an illness and usu. aggravating it.

com•plice (kŏm′plĭs) *n. Archaic.* An associate; an accomplice. [ME < OFr. < LLat. *complex, complic-*, one closely connected with : Lat. *com-*, com- + Lat. *plicāre*, to fold; see **plek-*.**]

com•plic•it (kəm-plĭs′ĭt) *adj.* Having complicity.

com•plic•i•ty (kəm-plĭs′ĭ-tē) *n., pl.* **-ties.** Involvement as an accomplice in a questionable act or a crime.

com•pli•er (kəm-plī′ər) *n.* One that complies.

com•pli•ment (kŏm′plə-mənt) *n.* **1.** An expression of praise, admiration, or congratulation. **2.** A formal act of civility, courtesy, or respect. **3. compliments.** Good wishes; regards. See Usage Note at **complement.** — *tr.v.* **-ment•ed, -ment•ing, -ments. 1.** To pay a compliment to. **2.** To show fondness, regard, or respect for by giving a gift or performing a favor. [Fr. < Ital. *complimento* < Sp. *cumplimiento* < *cumplir*, to complete < Lat. *complēre*, to fill up : *com-*, com- + *plēre*, to fill; see **pelə-**[1]***.**]

com•pli•men•ta•ry (kŏm′plə-mĕn′tə-rē, -trē) *adj.* **1.** Expressing, using, or resembling a compliment. **2.** Given free to repay a favor or as an act of courtesy. — **com′pli•men′ta•ri•ly** *adv.*

complimentary close (klōz) *n.* A polite termination of a letter just before the writer's signature, such as *Yours truly.*

com•plin (kŏm′plĭn) or **com•pline** (-plĭn, -plīn′) *n. Eccles.* The last of the seven canonical hours recited or sung before retiring. [ME, alteration of *compli* < OFr. *complie* < Med. Lat. *(hōra) complēta*, final (hour) < Lat. *complētus*, p.part. of *complēre*, to complete. See COMPLETE.]

com•ply (kəm-plī′) *intr.v.* **-plied, -ply•ing, -plies. 1.** To act in accordance with another's command, request, rule, or wish. **2.** *Obsolete.* To be courteous or obedient. [ME *complien*, to carry out, fulfill < OFr. *complir* < Lat. *complēre.* See COMPLETE.]

com•po (kŏm′pō) *n., pl.* **-pos.** Any of various combined substances, such as mortar or plaster, formed by mixing ingredients. [Short for COMPOSITION.]

com•po•nent (kəm-pō′nənt) *n.* **1.** A constituent element, as of a system. See Syns at **element. 2.** A part of a mechanical or electrical complex. **3.** *Math.* One of a set of two or more vectors having a sum equal to a given vector. **4.** Any of the minimum number of substances required to specify completely the composition of all phases of a chemical system. — *adj.* Being or functioning as a constituent or an ingredient. [< Lat. *compōnēns, compōnent-*, pr.part. of *compōnere*, to put together : *com-*, com- + *pōnere*, to put; see **apo-*.**] — **com′po•nen′tial** (kŏm′pə-nĕn′shəl) *adj.*

com•port (kəm-pôrt′, -pōrt′) *v.* **-port•ed, -port•ing, -ports.** — *tr.* To conduct (oneself) in a particular manner. — *intr.* To agree, correspond, or harmonize. [ME *comporten* < OFr. *comporter*, to conduct < Lat. *comportāre*, to bring together : *com-*, com- + *portāre*, to carry; see **per-**[2]***.**]

com•port•ment (kəm-pôrt′mənt, -pōrt′-) *n.* Deportment.

com•pose (kəm-pōz′) *v.* **-posed, -pos•ing, -pos•es.** — *tr.* **1.** To make up the constituent parts of; constitute or form. See Usage Note at **comprise. 2.** To make or create by putting together parts or elements. **3.** To create or produce (a literary or musical piece). **4.** To make (oneself) calm or tranquil. **5.** To settle or adjust; reconcile: *They managed to compose their differences.* **6.** To arrange aesthetically or artistically. **7.** *Print.* To arrange or set (type or matter to be printed). — *intr.* **1.** To create a literary or a musical piece. **2.** *Print.* To set type. [ME *composen* < OFr. *composer*, alteration (influenced by *poser*, to put, place; see POSE[1]) of Lat. *compōnere.* See COMPONENT.]

com•posed (kəm-pōzd′) *adj.* Serenely self-possessed. — **com•pos′ed•ly** (-pō′zĭd-lē) *adv.* — **com•pos′ed•ness** *n.*

com•pos•er (kəm-pō′zər) *n.* One that composes, esp. music.

com•pos•ing room (kəm-pō′zĭng) *n. Print.* A room where typesetting is done.

composing stick *n. Print.* A small shallow tray, usu. metal and with an adjustable end, in which type is set by hand.

com•pos•ite (kəm-pŏz′ĭt) *adj.* **1.** Made up of distinct components; compound. **2.** *Math.* Having factors; factorable. **3.** *Bot.* Of, belonging to, or characteristic of the composite

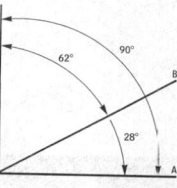

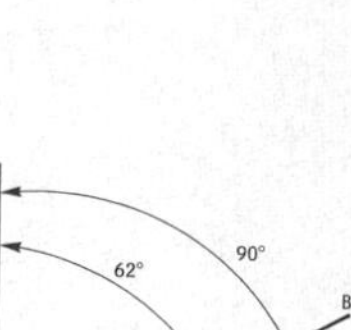

complementary angles

ă pat	oi boy
ā pay	ou out
âr care	ŏŏ took
ä father	ōō boot
ĕ pet	ŭ cut
ē be	ûr urge
ĭ pit	th thin
ī pie	*th* this
îr pier	hw which
ŏ pot	zh vision
ō toe	ə about, item
ô paw	

Stress marks:
′ (primary);
′ (secondary), as in
dictionary (dĭk′shə-nĕr′ē)

family. **4. Composite.** *Archit.* Of, relating to, or being in the Composite order. — *n.* **1.** A structure or an entity made up of distinct components. See Syns at **mixture. 2.** A complex material in which two or more distinct, structurally complementary substances combine to produce structural or functional properties not present in any individual component. **3.** *Bot.* A composite plant. [Fr. < OFr. < Lat. *compositus*, p.part. of *compōnere*, to put together. See COMPONENT.] — **com•pos′ite•ly** *adv.* — **com•pos′ite•ness** *n.*

composite family *n.* The largest family of flowering plants, the Compositae (Asteraceae), characterized by many small flowers arranged in a head looking like a single flower and subtended by an involucre of bracts.

composite number *n. Math.* An integer exactly divisible by at least one number other than itself or 1.

Composite order *n. Archit.* A Roman capital formed by superimposing Ionic volutes on a Corinthian capital.

com•po•si•tion (kŏm′pə-zĭsh′ən) *n.* **1.a.** The combining of distinct parts or elements to form a whole. **b.** The manner in which such parts are combined or related. **c.** General makeup: *the changing composition of the electorate.* **d.** The result or product of composing; a mixture or compound. **2.** Arrangement of artistic parts so as to form a unified whole. **3.a.** The art or act of composing a musical or literary work. **b.** A work of music, literature, or art, or its structure or organization. **4.** A short essay, esp. one written as an academic exercise. **5.** *Law.* A settlement whereby the creditors of a debtor about to enter bankruptcy agree to the discharge of their respective claims on receipt of a lesser amount than that actually owed. **6.** *Ling.* The formation of compounds from separate words. **7.** *Print.* Typesetting. [ME *composicioun* < OFr. *composition* < Lat. *compositiō*, *compositiōn-* < *compositus*, p.part. of *compōnere*, to put together. See COMPONENT.] — **com′po•si′tion•al** *adj.* — **com′po•si′tion•al•ly** *adv.*

com•pos•i•tive (kəm-pŏz′ĭ-tĭv) *adj.* Synthetic; compounded.

com•pos•i•tor (kəm-pŏz′ĭ-tər) *n. Print.* One that sets written material into type; a typesetter. [ME *compositur*, one who composes, settler of disputes < AN *compositour* < Lat., writer, compiler < *compōnere*, *composit-*, to put together. See COMPONENT.] — **com•pos′i•to′ri•al** (-tôr′ē-əl, -tōr′-) *adj.*

compos men•tis (mĕn′tĭs) *adj.* Of sound mind; sane. [Lat. : *compos*, having mastery of + *mentis*, genitive of *mēns*, mind.]

com•post (kŏm′pōst′) *n.* **1.** A mixture of decaying organic matter used to fertilize soil. **2.** A composition; a mixture. — *tr.v.* **-post•ed, -post•ing, -posts. 1.** To fertilize with a mixture of decaying organic matter. **2.** To convert (vegetable matter) to compost. [ME *composte* < OFr., mixture, compost < Lat. *compositum*, mixture < neut. p.part. of *compōnere*, to put together. See COMPONENT.]

com•po•sure (kəm-pō′zhər) *n.* A calm or tranquil state of mind; self-possession. [< COMPOSE.]

com•pote (kŏm′pōt) *n.* **1.** Fruit stewed or cooked in syrup. **2.** A long-stemmed dish used for holding fruit, nuts, or candy. [Fr. < OFr. *composte*, mixture < Lat. *composita*, fem. p.part. of *compōnere*, to put together. See COMPONENT.]

compote
Mid 19th-century American pressed glass compote made by the Boston and Sandwich Glass Company

com•pound¹ (kŏm-pound′, kəm-, kŏm′pound′) *v.* **-pound•ed, -pound•ing, -pounds.** — *tr.* **1.** To combine so as to form a whole; mix. **2.** To produce or create by combining two or more ingredients or parts. **3.** To settle (a debt, for example) by agreeing on an amount less than the claim; adjust. **4.** To compute (interest) on the principal and accrued interest. **5.** To add to; increase. — *intr.* **1.** To form a compound. **2.** To come to terms; agree. — *adj.* (kŏm′pound′, kŏm-pound′, kəm-). **1.** Consisting of two or more substances, ingredients, elements, or parts. **2.** *Bot.* Composed of more than one part. — *n.* (kŏm′pound′). **1.** A combination of two or more elements or parts. See Syns at **mixture. 2.** *Ling.* A word that consists either of two or more elements that are independent words, such as *loudspeaker,* or of specially modified combining forms of words, such as Greek *philosophia,* from *philo-,* "loving," and *sophia,* "wisdom." **3.** *Chem.* A substance consisting of atoms or ions of two or more different elements in definite proportions that cannot be separated by physical means. **4.** *Bot.* **a.** A leaf whose blade is divided into two or more distinct leaflets. **b.** A pistil composed of two or more united carpels. [Alteration of ME *compounen* < OFr. *compondre*, *compondre*, to put together < Lat. *compōnere*. See COMPONENT.] — **com•pound′a•ble** *adj.* — **com•pound′er** *n.*

com•pound² (kŏm′pound′) *n.* **1.** A building or buildings set off and enclosed by a barrier. **2.** An enclosed area used for prisoners of war. [Alteration of Malay *kampong*, village.]

com•pound-com•plex sentence (kŏm′pound-kŏm′plĕks) *n.* A sentence consisting of at least two coordinate independent clauses and one or more dependent clauses.

compound eye *n.* The eye of most insects and some crustaceans, which is composed of many light-sensitive elements, each forming a portion of an image.

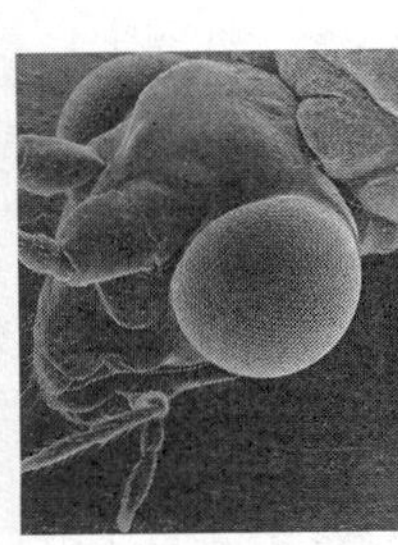

compound eye
Magnified compound eye of a green lacewing

compound fraction *n. Math.* See **complex fraction.**

compound fracture *n.* A fracture in which broken bone fragments lacerate soft tissue and protrude through an open wound in the skin.

compound interest *n.* Interest computed on the accumulated unpaid interest as well as on the original principal.

compound lens *n.* See **lens** 2.

compound microscope *n.* A microscope consisting of an objective and an eyepiece at opposite ends of an adjustable tube.

compound number *n. Math.* A quantity that is expressed in terms of two or more different units, such as 10 pounds 5 ounces or 3 feet 4 inches.

compound sentence *n.* A sentence of two or more coordinate independent clauses, often joined by a conjunction or conjunctions.

com•pra•dor also **com•pra•dore** (kŏm′prə-dôr′) *n.* **1.** A go-between; an intermediary. **2.** A native-born agent in China and certain other Asian countries formerly employed by a foreign business to help with commercial transactions. [Port. < LLat. *comparātor*, buyer < Lat. *comparāre*, to buy : *com-*, com- + *parāre*, to get; see **perə-¹*.**]

com•pre•hend (kŏm′prĭ-hĕnd′) *tr.v.* **-hend•ed, -hend•ing, -hends. 1.** To take in the meaning, nature, or importance of; grasp. See Syns at **apprehend. 2.** To take in as a part; include. [ME *comprehenden* < Lat. *comprehendere* : *com-*, com- + *prehendere*, to grasp; see **ghend-*.**] — **com′pre•hend′i•ble** *adj.* — **com′pre•hend′ing•ly** *adv.*

com•pre•hen•si•ble (kŏm′prĭ-hĕn′sə-bəl) *adj.* Readily comprehended or understood; intelligible. — **com′pre•hen′si•bil′i•ty, com′pre•hen′si•ble•ness** *n.* — **com′pre•hen′si•bly** *adv.*

com•pre•hen•sion (kŏm′prĭ-hĕn′shən) *n.* **1.a.** The act or fact of grasping the meaning, nature, or importance of; understanding. **b.** The knowledge that is acquired in this way. **2.** Capacity to include. **3.** *Logic.* The sum of meanings and corresponding implications inherent in a term. [ME *comprehensioun* < Lat. *comprehēnsiō*, *comprehēnsiōn-* < *comprehēnsus*, p.part. of *comprehendere*, to comprehend. See COMPREHEND.]

com•pre•hen•sive (kŏm′prĭ-hĕn′sĭv) *adj.* **1.** So large in scope or content as to include much: *a comprehensive history.* **2.** Marked by or showing extensive understanding. — **com′pre•hen′sive•ly** *adv.* — **com′pre•hen′sive•ness** *n.*

com•press (kəm-prĕs′) *tr.v.* **-pressed, -press•ing, -press•es. 1.** To press together. **2.** To make more compact by or as if by pressing. — *n.* (kŏm′prĕs′). **1.** *Medic.* A soft pad applied with pressure to a body part to control hemorrhage or supply heat, cold, moisture, or medication. **2.** A machine for compressing material. [ME *compressen* < OFr. *compresser* < LLat. *compressāre*, freq. of Lat. *comprimere* : *com-*, com- + *premere*, to press; see **per-⁴*.**]

com•pressed (kəm-prĕst′) *adj.* **1.** Pressed together or into less volume or space. **2.** *Biol.* Flattened, esp. laterally or lengthwise, as certain leafstalks or the bodies of many fishes.

compressed air *n.* Air under greater than atmospheric pressure, esp. when used to power a mechanical device or provide a portable supply of oxygen.

com•press•i•ble (kəm-prĕs′ə-bəl) *adj.* That can be compressed. — **com•press′i•bil′i•ty, com•press′i•ble•ness** *n.*

com•pres•sion (kəm-prĕsh′ən) *n.* **1.a.** The act or process of compressing. **b.** The state of being compressed. **2.a.** The process by which the working substance in a heat engine is compressed. **b.** The engine cycle during which this process occurs.

compression wave *n.* A wave propagated by means of the compression of a fluid, as a sound wave.

com•pres•sive (kəm-prĕs′ĭv) *adj.* Serving to or able to compress. — **com•pres′sive•ly** *adv.*

com•pres•sor (kəm-prĕs′ər) *n.* One that compresses, esp. a machine used to compress gases.

com•prise (kəm-prīz′) *tr.v.* **-prised, -pris•ing, -pris•es. 1.** To consist of; be composed of. **2.** To include; contain. **3.** *Usage Problem.* To compose; constitute. [ME *comprisen* < OFr. *compris*, p.part. of *comprendre*, to include < Lat. *comprehendere*. See COMPREHEND.] — **com•pris′a•ble** *adj.*

Usage Note: The whole *comprises* the parts; the parts *compose* the whole. In strict usage: *The Union comprises 50 states. Fifty states compose the Union.* While *comprise* is increasingly used in place of *compose,* in an earlier survey a majority of the Usage Panel found this use of *comprise* unacceptable. See Usage Note at **include.**

com•pro•mise (kŏm′prə-mīz′) *n.* **1.a.** A settlement of differences in which each side makes concessions. **b.** The result of such a settlement. **2.** Something that combines qualities or elements of different things. **3.** A concession to something detrimental or pejorative: *a moral compromise.* — *v.* **-mised, -mis•ing, -mis•es.** — *tr.* **1.** To settle by concessions. **2.** To expose or make liable to danger, suspicion, or disrepute. **3.** *Obsolete.* To pledge mutually. — *intr.* To make a compromise. [ME *compromis* < OFr. < Lat. *comprōmissum*, mutual promise < neut. p.part. of *comprōmittere*, to promise mutually : *com-*, com- + *prōmittere*, to promise; see PROMISE.] — **com′pro•mis′er** *n.*

compt. *abbr.* Compartment.

Comp•ton (kŏmp′tən). A city of S CA, a suburb between Los Angeles and Long Beach. Pop. 90,454.

Compton, Arthur Holly. 1892–1962. Amer. physicist who shared a 1927 Nobel Prize.

comp•trol•ler (kən-trō′lər) *n.* Var. of **controller** 2.

com•pul•sion (kəm-pŭl′shən) *n.* **1.a.** The act of compelling. **b.** The state of being compelled. **2.a.** An irresistible impulse to act, regardless of the rationality of the motivation. **b.** An act or acts performed in response to such an impulse. [ME < OFr. < LLat. *compulsiō, compulsiōn-* < Lat. *compulsus,* p.part. of *compellere,* to compel. See COMPEL.]

com•pul•sive (kəm-pŭl′sĭv) *adj.* **1.** Having the capacity to compel. **2.** *Psychol.* Caused or conditioned by compulsion or obsession. —*n.* A person with behavior patterns governed by a compulsion. —**com•pul′sive•ly** *adv.* —**com•pul′sive•ness, com′pul•siv′i•ty** (kŏm′pŭl-sĭv′ĭ-tē, kəm-) *n.*

com•pul•so•ry (kəm-pŭl′sə-rē) *adj.* **1.** Obligatory; required. **2.** Employing or exerting compulsion; coercive. —**com•pul′so•ri•ly** *adv.* —**com•pul′so•ri•ness** *n.*

com•punc•tion (kəm-pŭngk′shən) *n.* **1.** A strong uneasiness caused by a sense of guilt. **2.** A sting of conscience or a pang of doubt aroused by wrongdoing. [ME *compunccioun* < OFr. *componction* < LLat. *compūnctiō, compūnctiōn-,* sting of conscience, puncture < Lat. *compunctus,* p.part. of *compungere,* to sting : *com-,* com- + *pungere,* to prick; see **peuk-***.] —**com•punc′tious** (-shəs) *adj.* —**com•punc′tious•ly** *adv.*

com•pu•ta•tion (kŏm′pyo͞o-tā′shən) *n.* **1.a.** The act or process of computing. **b.** A method of computing. **2.** The result of computing. **3.** The act of operating a computer. —**com′pu•ta′tion•al** *adj.* —**com′pu•ta′tion•al•ly** *adv.*

com•pute (kəm-pyo͞ot′) *v.* **-put•ed, -put•ing, -putes.** —*tr.* **1.** To determine by mathematics, esp. by numerical methods. **2.** To determine by the use of a computer. —*intr.* **1.** To determine an amount or number. **2.** To use a computer. —*n.* Computation. [Lat. *computāre* : *com-,* com- + *putāre,* to reckon; see **peu-***.] —**com•put′a•bil′i•ty** *n.* —**com•put′a•ble** *adj.*

com•put•er (kəm-pyo͞o′tər) *n.* **1.** A device that computes, esp. a programmable electronic machine that performs high-speed operations or assembles, stores, correlates, or otherwise processes information. **2.** One who computes.

com•put•er•ist (kəm-pyo͞o′tər-ĭst) *n.* One who uses or operates a computer.

com•put•er•ize (kəm-pyo͞o′tə-rīz′) *tr.v.* **-ized, -iz•ing, -iz•es.** **1.** To furnish with a computer or computer system. **2.** To enter, process, or store (information) in a computer or system of computers. See Usage Note at **-ize.** —**com•put′er•iz′a•ble** *adj.* —**com•put′er•i•za′tion** (-pyo͞o′tər-ĭ-zā′shən) *n.*

com•put•er•ized axial tomography (kəm-pyo͞o′tə-rīzd′) *n.* Tomography in which computer analysis of a series of cross-sectional scans made along a single axis of a body structure or tissue is used to construct a three-dimensional image of that structure.

computer literacy *n.* The ability to use a computer and its software to accomplish practical tasks. —**computer literate** *adj.*

computer virus *n.* A computer program that copies itself into the other programs stored in a computer with either a benign or negative effect.

Comr. *abbr.* Commissioner.

com•rade (kŏm′răd′, -rəd) *n.* **1.** A person who shares one's interests or activities; a friend or companion. **2.** Often **Comrade.** A fellow member of a group, esp. a fellow member of the Communist Party. [Fr. *camarade* < OFr., roommate < OSp. *camarada,* barracks company, roommate < *camara,* room < LLat. *camera.* See CHAMBER.] —**com′rade•ship′** *n.*

Word History: A comrade can be socially or politically close, a closeness found at the etymological heart of the word *comrade.* Spanish preserved the Latin word *camara,* with its Late Latin meaning "chamber, room," and formed the derivative *camarada,* with the sense "roommates, especially barrack mates." *Camarada* then came to have the general sense "companion." English *comrade,* first recorded in the 16th century, came from Spanish and French, French having borrowed from Spanish. The political sense of *comrade,* now associated with Communism, had its origin in the late-19th-century use of the word as a title by socialists and communists in order to avoid such forms of address as *mister.* This usage, which originated in France during the French Revolution, is first recorded in English in 1884.

Com•stock (kŏm′stŏk′, kŭm′-), **Anthony.** 1844–1915. Amer. reformer notorious for his moral crusades against books and art that he considered obscene.

Com•stock•er•y (kŏm′stŏk′ə-rē, kŭm′-) *n.* Censorship of literature and other forms of expression because of perceived immorality or obscenity. [After Anthony COMSTOCK.]

Comstock Lode. A rich vein of gold and silver discovered in 1859 at Virginia City in W NV.

Comte (kôNt), **(Isidore) Auguste (Marie François).** 1798–1857. French philosopher and founder of positivism. —**Com′tism** (kŏm′tĭz′əm) *n.* —**Com′tist** (kŏm′tĭst) *n.*

con[1] (kŏn) *adv.* In opposition or disagreement; against. —*n.* **1.** An argument or opinion against something. **2.** One that holds an opposing opinion or view. [ME, short for *contra* < Lat. *contrā,* against. See CONTRA-.]

con[2] (kŏn) *tr.v.* **conned, con•ning, cons.** **1.** To study, peruse, or examine carefully. **2.** To learn or commit to memory. [ME *connen,* to know < OE *cunnan.* See **gnō-***.] —**con′ner** *n.*

con[3] or **conn** (kŏn) *Naut.* —*tr.v.* **conned, con•ning, cons** or **conns.** To direct the steering or course of (a vessel). —*n.* **1.** The station or post of the person who steers a vessel. **2.** The act or process of steering a vessel. [< *cond* < ME *conduen* < OFr. *conduire* < Lat. *condūcere,* to lead together. See CONDUCE.]

con[4] (kŏn) *Slang.* —*tr.v.* **conned, con•ning, cons.** To swindle (a victim) by first winning his or her confidence; dupe. —*n.* A swindle. —*adj.* Of, relating to, or involving a swindle or a fraud: *a con artist.* [Short for CONFIDENCE.]

con[5] (kŏn) *n. Slang.* A convict.

con. *abbr.* **1.** *Mus.* Concerto. **2.** *Lat.* Conjunx (wife). **3.** Connection. **4.** Consolidate; consolidated. **5.** Or **Con.** Consul. **6.** Continued.

con- *pref.* Var. of **com-.**

Con•a•kry (kŏn′ə-krē). The cap. of Guinea, in the SW on the Atlantic Ocean. Pop. 600,000.

con a•mo•re (kŏn′ ə-môr′ē, -mōr′ē, kôn′ ä-mô′rā) *adv.* **1.** *Mus.* Lovingly; tenderly. **2.** With devotion or zeal. [Ital. : *con,* with + *amore,* love.]

Co•nant (kō′nənt), **James Bryant.** 1893–1978. Amer. educator who was president of Harvard University (1933–53).

co•na•tion (kō-nā′shən) *n. Psychol.* The aspect of mental processes or behavior directed toward action or change. [Lat. *cōnātiō, cōnātiōn-,* effort < *cōnātus,* p.part. of *cōnārī,* to try.] —**co•na′tion•al, co′na•tive** (kō′nə-tĭv, kŏn′ə-) *adj.*

con bri•o (kŏn brē′ō, kôn) *adv. Mus.* With great energy; vigorously. [Ital. : *con,* with + *brio,* vigor.]

conc. *abbr.* **1.** Concentrate. **2.** Concrete.

con•cat•e•nate (kŏn-kăt′n-āt′, kən-) *tr.v.* **-nat•ed, -nat•ing, -nates.** **1.** To connect or link in a series or chain. **2.** *Comp. Sci.* To arrange (strings of characters) into a chained list. —*adj.* (-nĭt, -nāt′). Connected or linked in a series. [LLat. *concatēnāre, concatēnāt-* : *com-,* com- + *catēnāre,* to bind (< Lat. *catēna,* chain).] —**con•cat′e•na′tion** *n.*

computer
Personal computer with monitor, disk drive, and keyboard

con•cave (kŏn-kāv′, kŏn′kāv′) *adj.* Curved like the inner surface of a sphere. —*n.* A concave surface, structure, or line. —*tr.v.* **-caved, -cav•ing, -caves.** To make concave. [ME < Lat. *concavus* : *com-,* com- + *cavus,* hollow; see **keuə-***.] —**con•cave′ly** *adv.* —**con•cave′ness** *n.*

con•cav•i•ty (kŏn-kăv′ĭ-tē) *n., pl.* **-ties.** **1.** The state of being curved like the inner surface of a sphere. **2.** A surface or structure configured in such a curve.

con•ca•vo-con•cave (kŏn-kā′vō-kŏn-kāv′) *adj.* Concave on both surfaces; biconcave. Used of a lens.

con•ca•vo-con•vex (kŏn-kā′vō-kŏn-vĕks′) *adj.* **1.** Concave on one side and convex on the other. **2.** Having greater curvature on the concave side than on the convex side. Used of a lens.

con•ceal (kən-sēl′) *tr.v.* **-cealed, -ceal•ing, -ceals.** To keep from being seen, found, or observed; hide. See Syns at **hide**[1]. [ME *concelen* < OFr. *conceler* < Lat. *concēlāre* : *com-,* com- + *cēlāre,* to hide; see **kel-**[1]*.] —**con•ceal′a•ble** *adj.* —**con•ceal′er** *n.* —**con•ceal′ment** *n.*

con•cede (kən-sēd′) *v.* **-ced•ed, -ced•ing, -cedes.** —*tr.* **1.** To acknowledge, often reluctantly, as being true, just, or proper; admit. **2.** To yield or grant (a right, for example). —*intr.* To make a concession; yield. [Fr. *concéder* < Lat. *concēdere* : *com-,* com- + *cēdere,* to yield; see **ked-***.] —**con•ced′ed•ly** (-sē′dĭd-lē) *adv.* —**con•ced′er** *n.*

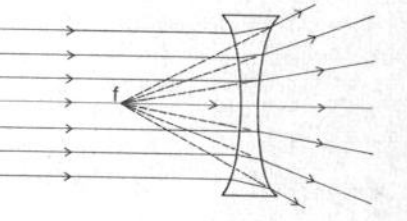

concave
Light passing through a double-concave lens, with f indicating the focus

con•ceit (kən-sēt′) *n.* **1.** A favorable and esp. unduly high opinion of one's own abilities or worth. **2.** An ingenious or witty turn of phrase or thought. **3.a.** An elaborate or exaggerated metaphor or simile. **b.** A poem or passage consisting of such a metaphor or simile. **4.a.** The result of intellectual activity; a thought or an opinion. **b.** A fanciful thought or idea. **5.a.** A fancy article; a knickknack. **b.** An extravagant, fanciful, and elaborate construction or structure. —*tr.v.* **-ceit•ed, -ceit•ing, -ceits.** **1.** *Chiefly British.* To take a fancy to. **2.** *Obsolete.* To understand; conceive. [ME, mind, conception < AN *conceite* < LLat. *conceptus.* See CONCEPT.]

con•ceit•ed (kən-sē′tĭd) *adj.* Holding or characterized by an unduly high opinion of oneself; vain. —**con•ceit′ed•ly** *adv.* —**con•ceit′ed•ness** *n.*

con•ceive (kən-sēv′) *v.* **-ceived, -ceiv•ing, -ceives.** —*tr.* **1.** To become pregnant with (offspring). **2.** To form or develop in the mind; devise. **3.** To apprehend mentally; understand. **4.** To be of the opinion that; think. —*intr.* **1.** To form or hold an idea. **2.** To become pregnant. [ME *conceiven* < OFr. *concevoir, conceiv-* < Lat. *concipere* : *com-,* com- + *capere,* to take; see **kap-***.] —**con•ceiv′a•bil′i•ty, con•ceiv′a•ble•ness** *n.* —**con•ceiv′a•ble** *adj.* —**con•ceiv′a•bly** *adv.* —**con•ceiv′er** *n.*

con•cel•e•brate (kən-sĕl′ə-brāt′) *v.* **-brat•ed, -brat•ing, -brates.** —*intr.* To take part in a concelebration of the Eucharist. —*tr.* To take part in (a Eucharist) as a joint celebrant. [Lat. *concelebrāre, concelebrāt-* : *com-,* com- + *celebrāre,* to celebrate; see CELEBRATE.] —**con•cel′e•brant** (-brənt) *n.*

con•cel•e•bra•tion (kən-sĕl′ə-brā′shən) *n.* Celebration of the Eucharist by two or more officiants.

ă pat	oi boy
ā pay	ou out
âr care	o͝o took
ä father	o͞o boot
ĕ pet	ŭ cut
ē be	ûr urge
ĭ pit	th thin
ī pie	*th* this
îr pier	hw which
ŏ pot	zh vision
ō toe	ə about, item
ô paw	

Stress marks:
′ (primary);
′ (secondary), as in
dictionary (dĭk′shə-nĕr′ē)

con•cen•ter (kən-sĕn′tər, kŏn-) *tr. & intr.v.* **-tered, -ter•ing, -ters.** To direct toward or come together at a common center. [Prob. Ital. *concentrare* or Fr. *concentrer* : both < Lat. *com-*, com- + Lat. *centrum*, center; see CENTER.]

con•cen•trate (kŏn′sən-trāt′) *v.* **-trat•ed, -trat•ing, -trates.** —*tr.* **1.a.** To direct or draw toward a common center; focus. **b.** To bring into one main body. **2.** To make (a solution or mixture) less dilute. —*intr.* **1.a.** To converge toward or meet in a common center. **b.** To increase by degree; gather. **2.** To direct one's thoughts or attention: *concentrated on the task.* —*n.* A product that has been concentrated, esp. a food that has been reduced in volume or bulk by the removal of liquid. [< CONCENTER.] —**con′cen•tra′tive** *adj.* —**con′cen•tra′tive•ly** *adv.* —**con′cen•tra′tor** *n.*

con•cen•tra•tion (kŏn′sən-trā′shən) *n.* **1.a.** The act or process of concentrating, esp. the fixing of close, undivided attention. **b.** The condition of being concentrated. **2.** Something that has been concentrated. **3.** *Chem.* The amount of a specified substance in a unit amount of another substance.

concentration camp *n.* A camp where prisoners of war, enemy aliens, and political prisoners are detained and confined, typically under harsh conditions.

con•cen•tric (kən-sĕn′trĭk) also **con•cen•tri•cal** (-trĭ-kəl) *adj.* Having a common center. [ME *concentrik* < Med.Lat. *concentricus* : Lat. *com-*, com- + Lat. *centrum*, center; see CENTER.] —**con•cen′tri•cal•ly** *adv.* —**con′cen•tric′i•ty** (kŏn′sĕn-trĭs′ĭ-tē) *n.*

Con•cep•ción (kən-sĕp′sē-ōn′, -sĕp′shən, kôn′sĕp-syôn′). A city of W-central Chile near the Pacific coast SSW of Santiago; founded 1550. Pop. 267,891.

con•cept (kŏn′sĕpt′) *n.* **1.** A general idea derived or inferred from specific instances or occurrences. **2.** Something formed in the mind; a thought or notion. See Syns at **idea. 3.** *Usage Problem.* A scheme; a plan. [LLat. *conceptus* < Lat., p.part. of *concipere*, to conceive. See CONCEIVE.]

Usage Note: In fields such as entertainment and advertising *concept* is often used loosely to mean "a scheme, plan," as in *The studio liked the concept for the new game show.* Perhaps this usage sounds most at home in these industries.

concession

con•cep•ta•cle (kən-sĕp′tə-kəl) *n.* A hollow chamber containing reproductive structures that appears on the surface of receptacles in certain algae and fungi. [Lat. *conceptāculum*, receptacle < *conceptus*, p.part. of *concipere*, to conceive. See CONCEIVE.]

con•cep•tion (kən-sĕp′shən) *n.* **1.a.** Formation of a viable zygote by the union of the sperm and the ovum; fertilization. **b.** The entity formed by the union of the sperm and the ovum; an embryo or a zygote. **2.a.** The ability to form or understand mental concepts and abstractions. **b.** Something conceived in the mind; a concept, plan, design, idea, or thought. See Syns at **idea. 3.** *Archaic.* A beginning; a start. [ME *concepcioun* < OFr. *conception* < Lat. *conceptiō*, *conceptiōn-* < *conceptus*. See CONCEPT.] —**con•cep′tion•al** *adj.* —**con•cep′tive** *adj.*

con•cep•tu•al (kən-sĕp′chōō-əl) *adj.* Of concepts or conception. [Med.Lat. *conceptuālis* < LLat. *conceptus*, a thought. See CONCEPT.] —**con•cep′tu•al•ly** *adv.*

conceptual art *n.* Art that is intended to convey an idea or a concept and that may not involve the creation or appreciation of a traditional art object. —**conceptual artist** *n.*

con•cep•tu•al•ism (kən-sĕp′chōō-ə-lĭz′əm) *n. Philos.* The doctrine that universals exist only within the mind and have no external or substantial reality. —**con•cep′tu•al•ist** *n.* —**con•cep′tu•al•is′tic** *adj.*

con•cep•tu•al•ize (kən-sĕp′chōō-ə-līz′) *v.* **-ized, -iz•ing, -iz•es.** —*tr.* To form a concept or concepts of, esp. to interpret in a conceptual way. —*intr.* To form concepts. —**con•cep′tu•al•i•za′tion** (-sĕp′chōō-ə-lĭ-zā′shən) *n.* —**con•cep′tu•al•iz′er** *n.*

con•cep•tus (kən-sĕp′təs) *n.* The product of conception at any point between fertilization and birth. [Lat., something conceived. See CONCEPT.]

con•cern (kən-sûrn′) *v.* **-cerned, -cern•ing, -cerns.** —*tr.* **1.** To have to do with or relate to. **2.** To be of interest or importance to: *This problem concerns all of us.* **3.** To engage the attention of; involve: *concerned ourselves with the task.* **4.** To cause anxiety or uneasiness in. —*intr. Obsolete.* To be of importance. —*n.* **1.** A matter that relates to or affects one. **2.** Regard for or interest in someone or something. **3.** A troubled or anxious state of mind arising from solicitude or interest. See Syns at **anxiety. 4.** A business establishment or enterprise; a firm. **5.** A contrivance; a gadget. [ME *concernen* < OFr. *concerner* < Med.Lat. *concernere* < LLat., to mingle together : Lat. *com-*, com- + Lat. *cernere*, to sift; see **krei-*.**]

conch

con•cerned (kən-sûrnd′) *adj.* **1.** Interested and involved. **2.** Anxious; troubled.

con•cern•ing (kən-sûr′nĭng) *prep.* In reference to. See Usage Note at **participle.**

con•cern•ment (kən-sûrn′mənt) *n.* **1.** A matter that is of concern. **2.** Reference, relation, or importance. **3.** Anxiety; worry.

con•cert (kŏn′sûrt′, -sərt) *n.* **1.** *Mus.* A performance given by one or more singers or instrumentalists or both. **2.a.** Agreement in purpose, feeling, or action. **b.** Unity achieved by mutual communication of views, ideas, and opinions: *acted in concert.* **c.** Concerted action. —*v.* (kən-sûrt′) **-cert•ed, -cert•ing, -certs.** —*tr.* **1.** To plan or arrange by mutual agreement. **2.** To adjust; settle. —*intr.* To act together in harmony. [Fr. < Ital. *concerto* < OItal., agreement, harmony, poss. < LLat. *concertus*, p.part. of *concernere*, to mingle together. See CONCERN.]

con•cert•ed (kən-sûr′tĭd) *adj.* **1.** Planned or accomplished together; combined: *a concerted effort.* **2.** *Mus.* Arranged in parts for voices or instruments. —**con•cert′ed•ly** *adv.*

concert grand *n. Mus.* The largest grand piano, being roughly 2.7 meters (9 feet) in length and having the volume, tone, and timbre appropriate for use in concerts.

con•cer•ti•na (kŏn′sər-tē′nə) *n. Mus.* A small hexagonal accordion with bellows and with buttons for keys. [CONCERT + Ital. *-ina*, fem. dim. suff.]

con•cer•ti•no (kŏn′chĕr-tē′nō) *n., pl.* **-nos.** *Mus.* **1.** A short concerto. **2.** The solo instrument group in a concerto grosso. [Ital., dim. of *concerto*, concert. See CONCERT.]

con•cer•tize (kŏn′sər-tīz′) *intr.v.* **-tized, -tiz•ing, -tiz•es.** *Mus.* To give concerts or perform in concerts.

con•cert•mas•ter (kŏn′sərt-măs′tər) *n. Mus.* The first violinist and assistant conductor in a symphony orchestra.

con•cert•mis•tress (kŏn′sərt-mĭs′trĭs) *n. Mus.* A woman first violinist and assistant conductor in a symphony orchestra.

con•cer•to (kən-chĕr′tō) *n., pl.* **-tos** or **-ti** (-tē). *Mus.* A composition for an orchestra and one or more solo instruments, typically in three movements. [Ital., concert. See CONCERT.]

concerto gros•so (grō′sō) *n., pl.* **concerti gros•si** (grō′sē). *Mus.* A composition for a small group of solo instruments and a full orchestra. [Ital. : *concerto*, concerto + *grosso*, large.]

concert pitch *n.* **1.** *Mus.* See **international pitch. 2.** The state of being ready and tensely alert.

con•ces•sion (kən-sĕsh′ən) *n.* **1.** The act of conceding. **2.a.** Something, such as a point previously claimed in argument, that is later conceded. **b.** An acknowledgment or admission. **3.** A grant of a tract of land, as by a government, in return for stipulated services or a promise that the land will be used for a specific purpose. **4.a.** The privilege of maintaining a subsidiary business within certain premises. **b.** The space allotted for such a business. **c.** The business itself. [ME < Lat. *concessiō*, *concessiōn-* < *concessus*, p.part. of *concēdere*, to concede. See CONCEDE.] —**con•ces′sion•al** *adj.* —**con•ces′sion•ar′y** (-sĕsh′ə-nĕr′ē) *adj.*

con•ces•sion•aire (kən-sĕsh′ə-nâr′) *n.* The holder or operator of a concession. [Fr. *concessionnaire* < *concession*, concession < Lat. *concessiō*. See CONCESSION.]

con•ces•sion•er (kən-sĕsh′ə-nər) *n.* A concessionaire.

con•ces•sive (kən-sĕs′ĭv) *adj.* **1.** Of the nature of or containing a concession. **2.** *Gram.* Expressing concession.

conch (kŏngk, kŏnch) *n., pl.* **conchs** (kŏngks) or **conch•es** (kŏn′chĭz). **1.** Any of various tropical marine gastropod mollusks, esp. of the genera *Strombus* and *Cassis*, having large, often brightly colored spiral shells and edible flesh. **2.** The shell of one of these gastropod mollusks, used as an ornament, in making cameos, or as a horn. **3.** *Anat.* See **concha** 1. [ME *conche* < OFr. < Lat. *concha*, mussel < Gk. *konkhē*.]

con•cha (kŏng′kə) *n., pl.* **-chae** (-kē′). **1.** *Anat.* Any of various structures that resemble a shell in shape. **2.** *Archit.* The half dome over an apse. [LLat., semidome < Lat., mussel shell. See CONCH.] —**con′chal** (-kəl) *adj.*

con•chif•er•ous (kŏng-kĭf′ər-əs) *adj.* Having or forming a shell.

con•chi•o•lin (kŏng-kī′ə-lĭn, kŏn-) *n.* A protein substance that is the organic basis of mollusk shells. [CONCH + -OL[1] + -IN.]

concho– or **conchi–** or **conch–** *pref.* Shell: *conchology.* [Gk. *konkho-* < *konkhos*, shell.]

Con•cho•bar (kŏn-kŭv′ər, -kōō′hŏŏr, kŏn′ər) *n. Myth.* The king of Ulster who abducted Deirdre.

con•choi•dal (kŏng-koid′l) *adj.* Of, relating to, or being a surface characterized by smooth shell-like convexities and concavities. [< Gk. *konkhoeidēs*, mussellike : *konkho-*, concho- + *-eidēs*, -oid.] —**con•choi′dal•ly** *adv.*

con•chol•o•gy (kŏng-kŏl′ə-jē) *n.* The branch of zoology that deals with the study of mollusks and shells. —**con′cho•log′i•cal** (-kə-lŏj′ĭ-kəl) *adj.* —**con•chol′o•gist** *n.*

con•cierge (kôɴ-syârzh′) *n.* **1.** A staff member of a hotel or apartment complex who assists guests or residents. **2.** A person, esp. in France, who lives in an apartment house, attends the entrance, and serves as a janitor. [Fr. < OFr. *cumcerges* < VLat. **cōnservius*, alteration of Lat. *cōnservus*, fellow slave : *com-*, com- + *servus*, slave.]

con•cil•i•ar (kən-sĭl′ē-ər) *adj.* Of, relating to, or generated by a council. [< Lat. *concilium*, council. See COUNCIL.]

con•cil•i•ate (kən-sĭl′ē-āt′) *v.* **-at•ed, -at•ing, -ates.** —*tr.* **1.** To overcome the distrust or animosity of; appease. **2.** To regain or try to regain (friendship or goodwill) by pleasant behavior. **3.** To make or try to make compatible; reconcile. —*intr.* To gain or try to gain friendship or goodwill. See Syns at **pacify.** [Lat. *conciliāre*, *conciliāt-* < *concilium*, meeting. See kelə-^{2}*.] **— con•cil′i•a•ble** (-ə-bəl) *adj.* **— con•cil′i•a′tion** *n.* **— con•cil′i•a′tor** *n.* **— con•cil′i•a•to′ry** (-ə-tôr′ē, -tōr′-ē) *adj.*

con•cin•ni•ty (kən-sĭn′ĭ-tē) *n., pl.* **-ties. 1.** Harmony in the arrangement or interarrangement of parts with respect to a whole. **2.** Studied elegance and facility in style of expression. **3.** An instance of harmonious arrangement or studied elegance and facility. [< Lat. *concinnitās* < *concinnāre*, to put in order < *concinnus*, deftly joined.]

con•cise (kən-sīs′) *adj.* Expressing much in few words; clear and succinct. [Lat. *concīsus*, p.part. of *concīdere*, to cut up : *com-*, com- + *caedere*, to cut; see **kaə-id-***.] **— con•cise′ly** *adv.* **— con•cise′ness** *n.*

con•ci•sion (kən-sĭzh′ən) *n.* **1.** The state or quality of being concise. **2.** *Archaic.* A cutting apart or off.

con•clave (kŏn′klāv′, kŏng′-) *n.* **1.** A secret or confidential meeting. **2.** *Rom. Cath. Ch.* **a.** The private rooms in which the cardinals meet to elect a new pope. **b.** The meeting held to elect a new pope. **3.** A meeting of family members or associates. [ME, private chamber, conclave of cardinals < Lat. *conclāve*, lockable room : *com-*, com- + *clāvis*, key.]

con•clude (kən-klo͞od′) *v.* **-clud•ed, -clud•ing, -cludes.** *— tr.* **1.** To bring to an end; close. **2.** To bring about (an agreement, for example). **3.** To reach a decision or form an opinion about. See Syns at **decide. 4.** To arrive at (a logical conclusion or end) by the process of reasoning; infer on the basis of convincing evidence. **5.** *Obsolete.* To confine; enclose. *— intr.* **1.** To come to an end; close. **2.** To come to a decision or an agreement. [ME *concluden* < Lat. *conclūdere* : *com-*, com- + *claudere*, to close.] **— con•clud′er** *n.*

con•clu•sion (kən-klo͞o′zhən) *n.* **1.** The close or last part; the end or finish. **2.** The result or outcome of an act or process. **3.** A judgment or decision reached after deliberation. **4.** A final arrangement or settlement, as of a treaty. **5.** *Law.* The close of a plea or deed. **6.a.** *Logic.* The proposition that must follow from the major and minor premises in a syllogism. **b.** The proposition concluded from one or more premises; a deduction. [ME *conclusioun* < OFr. *conclusion* < Lat. *conclūsiō, conclūsiōn-* < *conclūsus*, p.part. of *conclūdere*, to end. See CONCLUDE.]

con•clu•sive (kən-klo͞o′sĭv) *adj.* Serving to put an end to doubt, question, or uncertainty; decisive. **— con•clu′sive•ly** *adv.* **— con•clu′sive•ness** *n.*

con•clu•so•ry (kən-klo͞o′sə-rē) *adj.* **1.** Conclusive. **2.** *Law.* Convincing but not so that contradiction is impossible.

con•coct (kən-kŏkt′) *tr.v.* **-coct•ed, -coct•ing, -cocts. 1.** To prepare by mixing ingredients. **2.** To devise, using skill and intelligence; contrive. [Lat. *concoquere, concoct-*, to boil together : *com-*, com- + *coquere*, to cook; see **pek^{w}-***.] **— con•coct′er, con•coc′tor** *n.* **— con•coc′tion** *n.*

con•com•i•tance (kən-kŏm′ĭ-təns) *n.* **1.** Occurrence or existence together or in connection with one another. **2.** A concomitant.

con•com•i•tant (kən-kŏm′ĭ-tənt) *adj.* Occurring or existing concurrently; attendant. *— n.* One that is concomitant. [LLat. *concomitāns, concomitant-*, pr.part. of *concomitārī*, to accompany : Lat. *com-*, com- + Lat. *comitārī*, to accompany (< *comes, comit-*, companion; see **ei-***).] **— con•com′i•tant•ly** *adv.*

con•cord (kŏn′kôrd′, kŏng′-) *n.* **1.** Harmony or agreement of interests or feelings; accord. **2.** A treaty establishing peaceful relations. **3.** *Gram.* Agreement between words in person, number, gender, and case. [ME *concorde* < OFr. < Lat. *concordia* < *concors, concord-*, agreeing : *com-*, com- + *cor*, heart; see **kerd-***.]

Con•cord (kŏng′kərd). **1.** A city of W-central CA NE of Oakland. Pop. 111,348. **2.** A town of E MA on the **Concord River** WNW of Boston; site of an early battle of the Revolutionary War (Apr. 19, 1775). Pop. 17,076. **3.** A community of E-central MO, a suburb of St. Louis. Pop. 19,859. **4.** The cap. of NH, in the S-central part on the Merrimack R. Pop. 36,006. **5.** (kŏn′kôrd′). A city of S-central NC NE of Charlotte. Pop. 27,347.

con•cor•dance (kən-kôr′dns) *n.* **1.** Agreement; concord. **2.** An alphabetical index of all the words in a text or corpus of texts, showing every contextual occurrence of a word. **3.** *Genet.* The presence of a given trait in both members of a pair of twins.

con•cor•dant (kən-kôr′dnt) *adj.* Harmonious; agreeing. **— con•cor′dant•ly** *adv.*

con•cor•dat (kən-kôr′dăt′) *n.* **1.** A formal agreement; a compact. **2.** *Rom. Cath. Ch.* An agreement between the pope and a government for the regulation of church affairs. [Fr. < Med. Lat. *concordātum* < neut. p.part. of Lat. *concordāre*, to agree < *concors, concord-*, agreeing. See CONCORD.]

Con•cord grape (kŏng′kərd) *n.* A cultivated variety of the fox grape having dark blue to purple-black skin, used for making jelly, juice, and wine. [After CONCORD MA.]

con•course (kŏn′kôrs′, -kōrs′, kŏng′-) *n.* **1.** A large open space for the gathering or passage of crowds, as in an airport. **2.** A broad thoroughfare. **3.** A great crowd; a throng. **4.** The act of coming, moving, or flowing together. [ME *concours*, assembly < OFr. < Lat. *concursus* < p.part. of *concurrere*, to assemble : *com-*, com- + *currere*, to run; see **kers-***.]

con•cres•cence (kən-krĕs′əns) *n.* **1.** *Biol.* The growing together of related parts, tissues, or cells. **2.** The amassing of physical particles. [Lat. *concrēscentia* < *concrēscēns, concrēscent-*, pr.part. of *concrēscere*, to grow together. See CONCRETE.] **— con•cres′cent** *adj.*

con•crete (kŏn-krēt′, kŏng-, kŏn′krēt′, kŏng′-) *adj.* **1.** Of or relating to an actual, specific thing or instance; particular: *concrete evidence.* **2.** Existing in reality or in real experience; perceptible by the senses; real: *concrete objects.* **3.** Of or relating to a material thing or group of things as opposed to an abstraction. **4.** Formed by the coalescence of separate particles or parts into one mass; solid. **5.** Made of concrete. *— n.* (kŏn′krēt′, kŏng′-, kŏn-krēt′, kŏng-). **1.** A hard, strong construction material consisting of sand, conglomerate gravel, pebbles, broken stone, or slag in a mortar or cement matrix. **2.** A mass formed by the coalescence of particles. *— v.* (kŏn′-krēt′, kŏng′-, kŏn-krēt′, kŏng-) **-cret•ed, -cret•ing, -cretes.** *— tr.* **1.** To build, treat, or cover with concrete. **2.** To form into a mass by coalescence or cohesion of particles or parts. *— intr.* To harden; solidify. [ME *concret* < Lat. *concrētus*, p.part. of *concrēscere*, to grow together, harden : *com-*, com- + *crēscere*, to grow; see **ker-^{2}***.] **— con•crete′ly** *adv.* **— con•crete′ness** *n.*

concrete music *n.* Musique concrète.

concrete poetry *n.* Poetry that conveys meaning by graphic arrangement of letters, words, or symbols.

con•cre•tion (kən-krē′shən) *n.* **1.a.** The act or process of concreting into a mass; coalescence. **b.** The state of having been concreted. **2.** A solid hard mass. **3.** *Geol.* A rounded mass of mineral matter found in sedimentary rock. **4.** *Pathol.* A solid mass, usu. inorganic, formed in a cavity or tissue of the body; a calculus. **— con•cre′tion•ar′y** (-shə-nĕr′ē) *adj.*

con•cret•ism (kŏn-krē′tĭz′əm, kŏng-) *n.* The practice of representing abstract concepts or qualities in concrete form, as in concrete poetry. **— con•cret′ist** *n.*

con•cre•tize (kŏn′krĭ-tīz′, kŏng′-) *tr.v.* **-tized, -tiz•ing, -tiz•es.** To make real or specific. **— con′cre•ti•za′tion** (-tĭ-zā′-shən) *n.*

con•cu•bi•nage (kŏn-kyo͞o′bə-nĭj, kən-) *n.* **1.** *Law.* Cohabitation without legal marriage. **2.** The state of being a concubine.

con•cu•bine (kŏng′kyə-bīn′, kŏn′-) *n.* In certain societies, a woman contracted to a man as a secondary wife, often having few legal rights and low social status. [ME < OFr. < Lat. *concubīna* : *com-*, com- + *cubāre*, to lie down.]

con•cu•pis•cence (kŏn-kyo͞o′pĭ-səns) *n.* A strong desire, esp. sexual desire; lust. [ME < OFr. < LLat. *concupīscentia* < Lat. *concupīscēns, concupīscent-*, pr.part. of *concupīscere*, inchoative of *concupere*, to desire strongly : *com-*, com- + *cupere*, to desire.] **— con•cu′pis•cent** *adj.*

con•cur (kən-kûr′) *intr.v.* **-curred, -cur•ring, -curs. 1.** To be of the same opinion; agree. See Syns at **assent. 2.** To act together; cooperate. **3.** To occur at the same time; coincide. **4.** *Obsolete.* To converge. [ME *concurren* < Lat. *concurrere*, to meet : *com-*, com- + *currere*, to run; see **kers-***.]

con•cur•rence (kən-kûr′əns, -kŭr′-) *n.* **1.** Agreement in opinion. **2.** Cooperation, as of agents, circumstances, or events. **3.** Simultaneous occurrence. **— con•cur′ren•cy** *n.*

con•cur•rent (kən-kûr′ənt, -kŭr′-) *adj.* **1.** Happening at the same time as something else. **2.** Operating or acting in conjunction with another. **3.** Meeting or tending to meet at the same point; convergent. **4.** Being in accordance; harmonious. **— con•cur′rent** *n.* **— con•cur′rent•ly** *adv.*

concurrent resolution *n.* A resolution adopted by both houses of a bicameral legislature that does not have the force of law and does not require the signature of the chief executive.

con•cuss (kən-kŭs′) *tr.v.* **-cussed, -cuss•ing, -cuss•es.** To injure by concussion. [Lat. *concutere, concuss-*, to strike together : *com-*, com- + *quatere*, to strike; see **kwēt-***.]

con•cus•sion (kən-kŭsh′ən) *n.* **1.** A violent jarring; a shock. **2.** An injury to an organ, esp. the brain, produced by a violent blow and followed by a temporary or prolonged loss of function. [ME *concussioun*, bruise, contusion < Lat. *concussiō, concussiōn-*, concussion < *concussus*, p.part. of *concutere*, to strike together. See CONCUSS.] **— con•cus′sive** (-kŭs′ĭv) *adj.* **— con•cus′sive•ly** *adv.*

cond. *abbr.* **1.** Condition. **2.** Conductivity. **3.** Conductor.

Con•dé (kôN-dā′), Prince de. Louis II de Bourbon. 1621–86. French general during the Thirty Years' War.

con•demn (kən-dĕm′) *tr.v.* **-demned, -demn•ing, -demns. 1.** To express strong disapproval of. See Syns at **criticize. 2.** To pronounce judgment against; sentence. **3.** To judge or declare to be unfit for use or consumption, usu. by official order. **4.** *Law.* To appropriate (property) for public use. [ME *condemnen* < OFr. *condemner* < Lat. *condemnāre* : *com-*, com- + *damnāre*, to sentence (< *damnum*, penalty).] **— con•dem′na•ble** (-dĕm′nə-bəl) *adj.* **— con•dem′na•to′ry** (-nə-tôr′ē, -tōr′ē) *adj.* **— con•demn′er** *n.*

con•dem•na•tion (kŏn′dĕm-nā′shən) *n.* **1.a.** The act of condemning. **b.** The state of being condemned. **2.** Severe reproof;

ă pat	oi boy
ā pay	ou out
âr care	o͝o took
ä father	o͞o boot
ĕ pet	ŭ cut
ē be	ûr urge
ĭ pit	th thin
ī pie	*th* this
îr pier	hw which
ŏ pot	zh vision
ō toe	ə about, item
ô paw	

Stress marks:
′ (primary);
′ (secondary), as in dictionary (dĭk′shə-nĕr′ē)

condor
California condor
Gymnogyps californianus

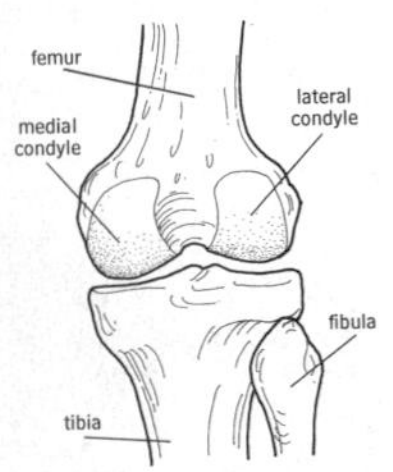

condyle
Posterior view of a right knee joint

ă pat oi boy
ā pay ou out
âr care o͝o took
ä father o͞o boot
ĕ pet ŭ cut
ē be ûr urge
ĭ pit th thin
ī pie *th* this
îr pier hw which
ŏ pot zh vision
ō toe ə about, item
ô paw

Stress marks:
ʹ (primary);
ʹ (secondary), as in dictionary (dĭkʹshə-nĕrʹē)

strong censure. **3.** A reason or occasion for condemning.

con•den•sate (kŏnʹdən-sātʹ, -dĕn-, kən-dĕnʹsātʹ) *n.* A product of condensation.

con•den•sa•tion (kŏnʹdĕn-sāʹshən, -dən-) *n.* **1.** The act of condensing. **2.** The state of being condensed. **3.** A condensate. **4.** *Phys.* **a.** The process by which a gas or vapor changes to a liquid. **b.** The liquid so formed. **5.** *Chem.* A chemical reaction in which water or another simple substance is released by the combination of two or more molecules. **6.** *Psychol.* The process by which a symbol or word is associated with the emotional content of a group of ideas, feelings, memories, or impulses. **—conʹden•saʹtion•al** *adj.*

con•dense (kən-dĕnsʹ) *v.* **-densed, -dens•ing, -dens•es.** *—tr.* **1.** To reduce the volume or compass of. **2.** To make more concise; abridge or shorten. **3.** *Phys.* **a.** To cause (a gas or vapor) to change to a liquid. **b.** To remove water from (milk, for example). *—intr.* **1.** To become more compact. **2.** To undergo condensation. [ME *condensen* < OFr. *condenser* < Lat. *condēnsāre* : *com-*, com- + *dēnsāre*, to thicken (< *dēnsus*, thick).] **—con•densʹa•bilʹi•ty** *n.* **—con•densʹa•ble, con•densʹi•ble** *adj.*

condensed milk (kən-dĕnstʹ) *n.* Cow's milk with sugar added, reduced by evaporation to a thick consistency.

con•dens•er (kən-dĕnʹsər) *n.* **1.** One that condenses, esp. an apparatus used to condense vapor. **2.** See **capacitor. 3.** A mirror, lens, or combination of lenses used to gather light and direct it upon an object or through a projection lens.

con•de•scend (kŏnʹdĭ-sĕndʹ) *intr.v.* **-scend•ed, -scend•ing, -scends. 1.** To descend to the level of one considered inferior. **2.** To deal with people in a patronizingly superior manner. [ME *condescenden* < OFr. *condescendre* < LLat. *condēscendere* : Lat. *com-*, com- + *dēscendere*, to descend; see DESCEND.] **—conʹde•scendʹer** *n.*

con•de•scen•dence (kŏnʹdĭ-sĕnʹdəns) *n.* Condescension.

con•de•scend•ing (kŏnʹdĭ-sĕnʹdĭng) *adj.* Displaying a patronizingly superior attitude. **—conʹde•scendʹing•ly** *adv.*

con•de•scen•sion (kŏnʹdĭ-sĕnʹshən) *n.* **1.** The act of condescending. **2.** Condescending behavior or attitude. [LLat. *condēscēnsiō*, *condēscēnsiōn-* < *condēscēnsus*, p.part. of *condēscendere*, to condescend. See CONDESCEND.]

con•dign (kən-dīnʹ) *adj.* Deserved; adequate. [ME *condigne* < OFr. < Lat. *condignus* : *com-*, com- + *dignus*, worthy; see **dek-***.] **—con•dignʹly** *adv.*

con•di•ment (kŏnʹdə-mənt) *n.* A sauce, relish, or spice used to season food. [ME < OFr. < Lat. *condīmentum* < *condīre*, to season. See **dhē-***.] **—conʹdi•menʹtal** (-mĕnʹtl) *adj.*

con•di•tion (kən-dĭshʹən) *n.* **1.** A mode or state of being. **2.a.** A state of health. **b.** A state of readiness or physical fitness. **3.** A disease or physical ailment: *a heart condition.* **4.** Social position; rank. **5.** One that is indispensable to the appearance or occurrence of another; prerequisite. **6.** One that restricts or modifies another; a qualification. **7. conditions.** Existing circumstances. **8.** *Gram.* The dependent clause of a conditional sentence. **9.** *Logic.* A proposition on which another proposition depends; the antecedent of a conditional proposition. **10.** *Law.* **a.** A provision making the effect of a legal instrument contingent on the occurrence of an uncertain future event. **b.** The event itself. **11.** An unsatisfactory grade given to a student, serving notice that deficiencies can be made up by the completion of additional work. **12.** *Obsolete.* Disposition; temperament. *—tr.v.* **-tioned, -tion•ing, -tions. 1.** To make dependent on a condition or conditions. **2.** To stipulate as a condition. **3.** To render fit for work or use. **4.** To accustom (oneself or another) to; adapt. **5.** To air-condition. **6.** To give the grade of condition to. **7.** *Psychol.* To cause an organism to respond in a specific manner to a conditioned stimulus in the absence of an unconditioned stimulus. **8.** To replace moisture or oils in (hair, for example) by use of a therapeutic product. [ME *condicioun* < OFr. *condicion* < LLat. *conditiō*, *conditiōn-*, alteration of Lat. *condiciō* < *condīcere*, to agree : *com-*, com- + *dīcere*, to talk; see **deik-***.]

con•di•tion•al (kən-dĭshʹə-nəl) *adj.* **1.** Imposing, depending on, or containing a condition. **2.** *Gram.* Stating, containing, or implying a condition. **3.** *Psychol.* Brought about by conditioning. *—n. Gram.* A mood, tense, clause, or word expressing a condition. **—con•diʹtion•alʹi•ty** (-dĭshʹə-nălʹĭ-tē) *n.* **—con•diʹtion•al•ly** *adv.*

conditional probability *n.* The probability that an event will occur, given that one or more other events have occurred.

con•di•tioned (kən-dĭshʹənd) *adj.* **1.** Subject to or dependent on a condition or conditions. **2.** Physically fit. **3.** Prepared for a specific action or process. **4.** *Psychol.* Exhibiting or trained to exhibit a conditioned response.

conditioned response *n. Psychol.* A new or modified response elicited by a stimulus after conditioning.

conditioned stimulus *n. Psychol.* A previously neutral stimulus that after repeated association with an unconditioned stimulus elicits the response effected by the unconditioned stimulus itself.

con•di•tion•er (kən-dĭshʹə-nər) *n.* One that conditions, esp. an additive or application that improves a substance.

con•di•tion•ing (kən-dĭshʹə-nĭng) *n. Psychol.* A process of behavior modification by which a subject comes to associate a desired behavior with a previously unrelated stimulus.

con•do (kŏnʹdō) *n., pl.* **-dos.** *Informal.* A condominium.

con•dole (kən-dōlʹ) *intr.v.* **-doled, -dol•ing, -doles.** To express sympathy or sorrow. [LLat. *condolēre*, to feel another's pain : Lat. *com-*, com- + Lat. *dolēre*, to grieve.] **—con•doʹla•toʹry** (-dōʹlə-tôrʹē, -tōrʹē) *adj.* **—con•dolʹer** *n.*

con•do•lence (kən-dōʹləns) *n.* **1.** Sympathy with a person who has experienced pain, grief, or misfortune. **2.** A formal declaration of condolence. **—con•doʹlent** *adj.*

con•dom (kŏnʹdəm, kŭnʹ-) *n.* A flexible sheath, usu. made of thin rubber or latex, designed to cover the penis during sexual intercourse for contraceptive purposes or as a means of preventing sexually transmitted diseases. [?]

con•do•min•i•um (kŏnʹdə-mĭnʹē-əm) *n., pl.* **-min•i•ums** also **-min•i•a** (-mĭnʹē-ə). **1.a.** Real estate, such as a unit in an apartment complex, that combines fee simple title to the unit and joint ownership in the common elements shared with other unit owners. **b.** A unit in such a complex. **2.a.** Joint sovereignty, esp. joint rule of territory by two or more nations, or a plan to achieve it. **b.** A politically dependent territory. **—conʹdo•minʹi•al** (-ē-əl) *adj.*

Con•don (kŏnʹdən), **Edward Uhler.** 1902–74. Amer. physicist who participated in the Manhattan Engineering District atomic bomb project (1943–45).

con•done (kən-dōnʹ) *tr.v.* **-doned, -don•ing, -dones.** To overlook, forgive, or disregard (an offense) without protest or censure. See Syns at **forgive.** [Lat. *condōnāre* : *com-*, com- + *dōnāre*, to give (< *dōnum*, gift; see **dō-***).] **—conʹdo•naʹtion** *n.* **—con•donʹer** *n.*

con•dor (kŏnʹdôrʹ, -dər) *n.* **1.** Either of two New World vultures, *Vultur gryphus* of the Andes or *Gymnogyps californianus,* having a bare head and neck and dull black plumage containing variable amounts of white. **2.** A gold coin of some South American countries bearing the figure of a condor. [Sp. *cóndor* < Quechua *cuntur.*]

Con•dor•cet (kôn-dôr-sĕʹ), Marquis de. Marie Jean Antoine Nicolas Caritat. 1743–94. French mathematician and philosopher known for his work on the theory of probability.

con•dot•tie•re (kŏnʹdə-tyârʹē, -tyârʹā) *n., pl.* **-tie•ri** (-tyârʹē). A leader of mercenary soldiers between the 14th and 16th centuries. [Ital. < *condotta*, troop of mercenaries < fem. p.part. of *condurre*, to conduct < Lat. *condūcere*, to lead together. See CONDUCE.]

con•duce (kən-do͞osʹ, -dyo͞osʹ) *intr.v.* **-duced, -duc•ing, -duc•es.** To contribute or lead to a specific result. [Lat. *condūcere* : *com-*, com- + *dūcere*, to lead; see **deuk-***.] **—con•ducʹer** *n.* **—con•ducʹing•ly** *adv.*

con•du•cive (kən-do͞oʹsĭv, -dyo͞oʹ-) *adj.* Tending to cause or bring about; contributive. See Syns at **favorable. —con•duʹcive•ness** *n.*

con•duct (kən-dŭktʹ) *v.* **-duct•ed, -duct•ing, -ducts.** *—tr.* **1.** To direct the course of; manage or control. **2.** To lead or guide. See Syns at **accompany. 3.** *Mus.* To lead (an orchestra, for example). **4.** To serve as a medium for conveying; transmit. **5.** To comport (oneself) in a specified way. *—intr.* **1.** To act as a conductor. **2.** To lead. *—n.* (kŏnʹdŭkt). **1.** The way a person acts, esp. morally or ethically. See Syns at **behavior. 2.** The act of directing or controlling; management. **3.** *Obsolete.* A guide; an escort. [ME *conducten* < Lat. *condūcere, conduct-*, to lead together. See CONDUCE.] **—con•ductʹi•bilʹi•ty** *n.* **—con•ductʹi•ble** *adj.*

con•duc•tance (kən-dŭkʹtəns) *n. Symbol* **G** A measure of a material's ability to conduct electric charge; the reciprocal of the resistance.

con•duc•tim•e•try (kŏnʹdŭk-tĭmʹĭ-trē) *n.* The scientific measurement of solution conductance. **—con•ducʹto•metʹric** *adj.*

con•duc•tion (kən-dŭkʹshən) *n.* The transmission or conveying of something through a medium or passage, esp. the transmission of electric charge or heat through a conducting medium without perceptible motion of the medium itself.

con•duc•tive (kən-dŭkʹtĭv) *adj.* Exhibiting conductivity.

con•duc•tiv•i•ty (kŏnʹdŭk-tĭvʹĭ-tē) *n., pl.* **-ties. 1.** The ability or power to conduct or transmit heat, electricity, or sound. **2.** The conductance of a material. **3.** *Physiol.* The conductibility of a structure, esp. the ability of a nerve to transmit a wave of excitation.

con•duc•tor (kən-dŭkʹtər) *n.* **1.** One who conducts, esp.: **a.** One who is in charge of a railroad train, bus, or streetcar. **b.** *Mus.* One who directs an orchestra or other such group. **2.** *Phys.* A substance or medium that conducts heat, light, sound, or esp. an electric charge. **3.** A lightning rod, as on a house or barn. **—conʹduc•toʹri•al** (kŏnʹdŭk-tôrʹē-əl, -tōrʹ-) *adj.* **—con•ducʹtor•shipʹ** *n*

con•duit (kŏnʹdo͞o-ĭt, -dĭt) *n.* **1.** A pipe or channel for conveying fluids. **2.** A tube or duct for enclosing electric wires or cable. **3.** A means by which something is transmitted. **4.** *Archaic.* A fountain. [ME < OFr. < Med.Lat. *conductus* < Lat., p.part. of *condūcere*, to lead together. See CONDUCE.]

con•du•pli•cate (kŏn-do͞oʹplĭ-kĭt, -dyo͞oʹ-) *adj.* Folded together lengthwise, as certain petals in a bud. [Lat. *condupli-*

cātus, p.part. of conduplicāre, to double : com-, com- + duplicāre, to double (< duplex, duplic-, double; see **dwo-***.)] **— con′du·pli·ca′tion** (-kā′shən) *n.*

con·dyle (kŏn′dīl′, -dl) *n.* A rounded prominence at the end of a bone, most often for articulation with another bone. [Lat. *condylus*, knuckle < Gk. *kondulos*.] **— con′dy·lar** (-də-lər) *adj.* **— con′dy·loid′** (-dl-oid′) *adj.*

con·dy·lo·ma (kŏn′dl-ō′mə) *n., pl.* **-mas** or **-ma·ta** (-mə-tə). A wartlike growth on the skin or mucous membrane, usu. in the area of the anus or external genitalia. [Gk. *kondulōma* < *kondulos*, knuckle.] **— con′dy·lo′ma·tous** (-mə-təs) *adj.*

cone (kōn) *n.* **1.** *Math.* **a.** The surface generated by a straight line, the generator, passing through a fixed point, the vertex, and moving along a fixed curve, the directrix. **b.** A right circular cone. **2.a.** The solid formed by a cone, bound by its vertex and a plane section taken anywhere above or below the vertex. **b.** Something cone-shaped. **3.** *Bot.* **a.** A unisexual reproductive structure of gymnospermous plants, typically consisting of a central axis around which there are scaly, overlapping, spirally arranged sporophylls that develop pollen-bearing sacs or naked ovules or seeds. **b.** A similar structure that produces spores on club mosses, horsetails, and spike mosses. **c.** Any reproductive structure resembling a cone. **4.** *Physiol.* One of the photoreceptors in the retina of the eye that is responsible for daylight and color vision. **5.** Any of various gastropod mollusks of the family Conidae of tropical and subtropical seas, having a conical shell and a poisonous, sometimes fatal sting. *— tr.v.* **coned, con·ing, cones.** To shape (something) like a cone or a segment of one. [Fr. *cône* and ME *cone*, angle of a quadrant, both < Lat. *cōnus* < Gk. *kōnos*. See **kō-***.]

cone·flow·er (kōn′flou′ər) *n.* Any of various North American plants of the genera *Rudbeckia, Ratibida,* and *Echinacea* in the composite family, having disk flowers on a cone-shaped central receptacle surrounded by colorful ray flowers.

cone·nose (kōn′nōz′) *n.* Any of various bloodsucking hemipterous insects of the family Reduviidae, esp. *Triatoma sanguisuga* having sucking mouthparts and a painful, toxic bite.

Con·es·to·ga (kŏn′ĭ-stō′gə) *n., pl.* **Conestoga** or **-gas.** See **Susquehannock** 1.

Conestoga wagon *n.* A heavy covered wagon with broad wheels, used by American pioneers for westward travel. [After *Conestoga*, a village of SE PA.]

co·ney[1] also **co·ny** (kō′nē, kŭn′ē) *n., pl.* **-neys** also **-nies.** **1.** A rabbit, esp. the European rabbit *(Oryctolagus cuniculus).* **2.** The fur of a rabbit. **3.** See **pika. 4.** See **hyrax. 5.a.** A grouper *(Epinephelus fulvus)* of the tropical Atlantic having dark brown or sharply bicolored skin and a few blue and black spots. **b.** *Chiefly Florida Keys & West Indies.* The red hind. **6.** *Archaic.* A dupe; a simpleton. [ME *coni* < OFr. *conis*, pl. of *conil* < Lat. *cunīculus*, poss. < *cunnus, cunus*, female pudenda.]

co·ney[2] (kō′nē) *n. Informal.* A Coney Island.

Co·ney Island[1] (kō′nē). A resort district of Brooklyn NY on the Atlantic Ocean, known for its amusement park.

Co·ney Island[2] (kō′nē) *n.* A hot dog with condiments.

conf. *abbr.* **1.** Conference. **2.** Confidential.

con·fab (kŏn′făb′) *Informal. — n.* A casual talk; confabulation. *— intr.v.* (kən-făb′, kŏn′făb′) **-fabbed, -fab·bing, -fabs.** To engage in casual talk.

con·fab·u·late (kən-făb′yə-lāt′) *intr.v.* **-lat·ed, -lat·ing, -lates. 1.** To talk casually; chat. **2.** *Psychol.* To replace fact with fantasy unconsciously in memory. [Lat. *cōnfābulārī, cōnfābulāt- : com-*, com- + *fābulārī*, to talk (< *fābula*, conversation; see FABLE).] **— con·fab′u·la′tion** *n.* **— con·fab′u·la′tor** *n.* **— con·fab′u·la·to′ry** (-lə-tôr′ē, -tōr′ē) *adj.*

con·fect (kən-fĕkt′) *tr.v.* **-fect·ed, -fect·ing, -fects. 1.** To make into a confection or preserve. **2.** To put together by combining materials. *— n.* (kŏn′fĕkt′). A sweet confection. [ME *confecten*, to prepare < Lat. *cōnficere, cōnfect- : com-*, com- + *facere*, to make; see **dhē-***.]

con·fec·tion (kən-fĕk′shən) *n.* **1.** The act or process of confecting or the result of it. **2.** A sweet preparation, such as candy. **3.** A sweetened medicinal compound; an electuary. **4.** A piece displaying splendid craft, skill, and work. *— tr.v.* **-tioned, -tion·ing, -tions.** To make into a confection.

con·fec·tion·ar·y (kən-fĕk′shə-nĕr′ē) *n., pl.* **-ies. 1.** A confectioner's shop. **2.** Sweet preparations; confections. **3.** *Obsolete.* A confectioner. **— con·fec′tion·ar′y** *adj.*

con·fec·tion·er (kən-fĕk′shə-nər) *n.* One that makes or sells confections.

con·fec·tion·ers' sugar (kən-fĕk′shə-nərz) *n.* Finely pulverized sugar with cornstarch added.

con·fec·tion·er·y (kən-fĕk′shə-nĕr′ē) *n., pl.* **-ies. 1.** Candies and other confections considered as a group. **2.** The skill or occupation of a confectioner. **3.** A confectioner's shop.

confed. *abbr.* Confederation.

con·fed·er·a·cy (kən-fĕd′ər-ə-sē) *n., pl.* **-cies. 1.a.** A union of persons, parties, or states; a league. **b.** The persons, parties, or states joined in such a union. **c. Confederacy.** The 11 Southern states that seceded from the United States in 1860 and 1861. **2.** A group of people united for unlawful practices; a conspiracy. [ME *confederacie* < AN < LLat. *cōnfoederātiō, cōnfoederātiōn-*, agreement < *cōnfoederātus*, p.part. of *cōnfoederāre*, to unite. See CONFEDERATE.]

con·fed·er·al (kən-fĕd′ər-əl, -fĕd′rəl) *adj.* **1.** Of confederation or a confederation. **2.** Of or involving the activities of two or more nations. **— con·fed′er·al·ist** *n.*

con·fed·er·ate (kən-fĕd′ər-ĭt) *n.* **1.** A member of a confederacy; an ally. **2.** One who assists in a plot; an accomplice. See Syns at **partner. 3. Confederate.** A supporter of the American Confederacy. *— adj.* **1.** United in a confederacy; allied. **2. Confederate.** Of or having to do with the American Confederacy. [< ME *confederat*, allied < LLat. *cōnfoederātus*, p.part. of *cōnfoederāre*, to unite : Lat. *com-*, com- + Lat. *foederāre*, to unite, (< *foedus, foeder-*, league; see **bheidh-***).] **— con·fed′er·ate′** (-ə-rāt′) *v.* **— con·fed′er·a′tive** *adj.*

con·fed·er·a·tion (kən-fĕd′ə-rā′shən) *n.* **1.a.** The act of forming into or becoming part of a confederacy. **b.** The state of being confederated. **2.** A group of confederates, esp. of states or nations, united for a common purpose; a league. **— con·fed′er·a′tion·ism** *n.* **— con·fed′er·a′tion·ist** *n.*

con·fer (kən-fûr′) *v.* **-ferred, -fer·ring, -fers.** *— tr.* **1.** To bestow (an honor, for example). **2.** To invest with (a characteristic, for example). *— intr.* To meet in order to deliberate together or compare views. [Lat. *cōnferre : com-*, com- + *ferre*, to bring; see **bher-**[1]*.] **— con·fer′ment, con·fer′ral** *n.* **— con·fer′ra·ble** *adj.* **— con·fer′rer** *n.*

con·fer·ee also **con·fer·ree** (kŏn′fə-rē′) *n.* **1.** A participant in a conference. **2.** One upon whom something is conferred.

con·fer·ence (kŏn′fər-əns, -frəns) *n.* **1.a.** A meeting for consultation or discussion. **b.** An exchange of views. **c.** A meeting of committees to settle differences between two legislative bodies. **2.** An assembly of clerical or of clerical and lay members from a particular district in Protestant churches. **3.** *Sports.* An association of teams. **4.** The act of conferring, as of an academic degree. [Med.Lat. *cōnferentia* < Lat. *cōnferēns, cōnferent-*, pr.part. of *cōnferre*, to bring together. See CONFER.] **— con′fer·en′tial** (-fə-rĕn′shəl) *adj.*

conference call *n.* A telephone call in which three or more people participate by means of a central switching unit.

con·fess (kən-fĕs′) *v.* **-fessed, -fess·ing, -fess·es.** *— tr.* **1.** To disclose (something damaging or inconvenient to oneself); admit. **2.** To acknowledge belief or faith in. **3.a.** To make known (one's sins), as to a priest. **b.** To hear the confession of (a penitent). *— intr.* **1.** To admit or acknowledge something damaging or inconvenient to oneself. **2.a.** To disclose one's sins, as to a priest. **b.** To listen to a confession. [ME *confessen* < OFr. *confesser* < VLat. **cōnfessāre* < Lat. *cōnfitērī, cōnfess- : com-*, com- + *fatērī*, to admit; see **bhā-**[2]*.] **— con·fess′a·ble** *adj.* **— con·fess′ed·ly** (-ĭd-lē) *adv.*

con·fes·sion (kən-fĕsh′ən) *n.* **1.** The act or process of confessing. **2.** Something confessed, esp. disclosure of one's sins to a priest. **3.** A statement acknowledging guilt, made by one accused or charged with an offense. **4.** An avowal of belief in a particular faith; a creed. **5.** A church or group of worshipers adhering to a specific creed.

con·fes·sion·al (kən-fĕsh′ə-nəl) *adj.* Of, relating to, or resembling confession. *— n.* A small enclosed stall in which a priest hears confessions.

con·fes·sor (kən-fĕs′ər) *n.* **1.** One who confesses. **2.** One who confesses faith in Christianity in the face of persecution but does not suffer martyrdom. **3.a.** A priest who hears confession and gives absolution. **b.** A priest who is one's spiritual mentor.

con·fet·ti (kən-fĕt′ē) *pl.n.* *(used with a sing. v.)* Small pieces or streamers of colored paper that are scattered around during the course of festive occasions. [Ital., pl. of *confetto*, candy < Med.Lat. *cōnfectum*, neut. of Lat. *cōnfectus*, p.part. of *cōnficere*, to prepare. See CONFECT.]

con·fi·dant (kŏn′fĭ-dănt′, -dänt′, kŏn′fĭ-dănt′, -dänt′) *n.* **1.** One to whom secrets or private matters are disclosed. **2.** A character in a drama or fiction, such as a friend, who is used to reveal the thoughts of a main character. [Fr. *confident* < Ital. *confidente* < Lat. *cōnfīdēns, cōnfīdent-*, pr.part. of *cōnfīdere*, to rely on. See CONFIDE.]

con·fi·dante (kŏn′fĭ-dănt′, -dänt′, kŏn′fĭ-dănt′, -dänt′) *n.* **1.** A woman to whom secrets or private matters are disclosed. **2.** A woman character in a drama or fiction, such as a friend, who is used to reveal the thoughts of a main character. [Fr. *confidente*, fem. of *confident*, confidant. See CONFIDANT.]

con·fide (kən-fīd′) *v.* **-fid·ed, -fid·ing, -fides.** *— tr.* **1.** To tell (something) in confidence. **2.** To put into another's keeping. *— intr.* To disclose private matters in confidence. [ME, to rely on < OFr. *confider* < Lat. *cōnfīdere : com-*, com- + *fīdere*, to trust; see **bheidh-***.] **— con·fid′er** *n.*

con·fi·dence (kŏn′fĭ-dəns) *n.* **1.** Trust or faith in a person or thing. **2.** A trusting relationship. **3.a.** That which is confided; a secret. **b.** A feeling of assurance that a confidant will keep a secret. **4.** A feeling of assurance, esp. of self-assurance. **5.** The state or quality of being certain. *— adj.* Of, relating to, or involving a swindle or fraud.

confidence game *n.* A swindle in which the victim is defrauded after his or her confidence has been won.

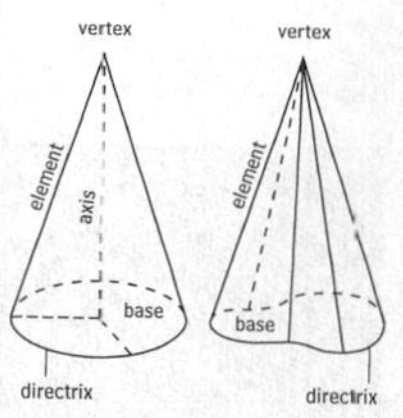

cone
Left: Right circular cone
Right: General cone

Conestoga wagon

confessional

confidence interval *n.* A statistical range with a specified probability that a given parameter lies within the range.

confidence man *n.* A man who swindles his victims by using a confidence game.

con•fi•dent (kŏn′fĭ-dənt) *adj.* **1.** Marked by assurance, as of success. **2.** Marked by confidence in oneself; self-assured. **3.** Very bold; presumptuous. **4.** *Obsolete.* Confiding; trustful. [Lat. *cōnfīdēns, cōnfīdent-*, pr.part. of *cōnfīdere*, to rely on. See CONFIDE.] **—con′fi•dent•ly** *adv.*

con•fi•den•tial (kŏn′fĭ-dĕn′shəl) *adj.* **1.** Done or communicated in confidence; secret. **2.** Entrusted with the confidence of another. **3.** Indicating confidence or intimacy. **4.** Containing secret information, the unauthorized disclosure of which poses a threat to national security. **—con′fi•den′ti•al′i•ty** (-shē-ăl′ĭ-tē), **con′fi•den′tial•ness** *n.* **—con′fi•den′tial•ly** *adv.*

confidential communication *n. Law.* A statement to someone, such as one's physician, attorney, priest, or spouse, who cannot be compelled to divulge the information.

con•fid•ing (kən-fī′dĭng) *adj.* Having a tendency to confide; trusting. **—con•fid′ing•ly** *adv.* **—con•fid′ing•ness** *n.*

con•fig•u•ra•tion (kən-fĭg′yə-rā′shən) *n.* **1.a.** Arrangement of parts or elements. **b.** The form, as of a figure, determined by the arrangement of its parts or elements. **2.** *Psychol.* Gestalt. **3.** *Chem.* The structural arrangement of atoms in a compound or molecule. **—con•fig′u•ra′tion•al•ly** *adv.* **—con•fig′u•ra′tive, con•fig′u•ra′tion•al** *adj.*

con•fig•ure (kən-fĭg′yər) *tr.v.* **-ured, -ur•ing, -ures.** To design, arrange, set up, or shape with a view to specific applications or uses. [Ult. < Lat. *cōnfigūrāre* : *com-*, com- + *figūrāre*, to form (< *figūra*, shape; see **dheigh-***).]

Confucius

con•fine (kən-fīn′) *v.* **-fined, -fin•ing, -fines.** *—tr.* **1.** To keep within bounds; restrict. **2.** To shut or keep in, esp. to imprison. **3.** To restrict in movement. *—intr. Archaic.* To border. *—n.* (kŏn′fīn′). **1. confines. a.** The limits of a space or an area; the borders. **b.** Restraining elements: *the confines of politics.* **c.** Purview; scope. **2.a.** *Archaic.* A restriction. **b.** *Obsolete.* A prison. [Fr. *confiner* < OFr. < *confins*, boundaries, ult. < Lat. *cōnfīne* < neut. of *cōnfīnis*, adjoining : *com-*, com- + *fīnis*, border.] **—con•fin′a•ble, con•fine′a•ble** *adj.* **—con•fin′er** *n.*

con•fine•ment (kən-fīn′mənt) *n.* **1.** The act of confining or the state of being confined. **2.** Lying-in.

con•firm (kən-fûrm′) *tr.v.* **-firmed, -firm•ing, -firms. 1.** To support or establish the certainty or validity of; verify. **2.** To make firmer; strengthen. **3.** To make valid or binding by a formal or legal act; ratify. **4.** To administer the religious rite of confirmation to. [ME *confirmen* < OFr. *confermer* < Lat. *cōnfirmāre* : *com-*, com- + *firmāre*, to strengthen (< *firmus*, strong; see **dher-***).] **—con•firm′a•bil′i•ty** *n.* **—con•firm′a•ble** *adj.* **—con•firm′a•to′ry** (-fûr′mə-tôr′ē, -tōr′ē) *adj.* **—con•firm′er** *n.*

con•fir•ma•tion (kŏn′fər-mā′shən) *n.* **1.a.** The act of confirming. **b.** Something that confirms; verification. **2.a.** A Christian rite admitting a baptized person to full membership in a church. **b.** A Jewish ceremony marking completion of a young person's religious training.

con•firmed (kən-fûrmd′) *adj.* **1.** Being firmly settled in habit; inveterate. **2.** Having been ratified; verified. **3.** Having received the rite of confirmation. **—con•firm′ed•ly** (-fûr′mĭd-lē) *adv.*

con•fis•ca•ble (kən-fĭs′kə-bəl) *adj.* Subject to confiscation.

con•fis•cate (kŏn′fĭ-skāt′) *tr.v.* **-cat•ed, -cat•ing, -cates. 1.** To seize (private property) for the public treasury. **2.** To seize by or as if by authority. *—adj.* (kŏn′fĭ-skāt′, kən-fĭs′kət). **1.** Seized by a government; appropriated. **2.** Having lost property through confiscation. [Lat. *cōnfiscāre, cōnfiscāt-* : *com-*, com- + *fiscus*, treasury.] **—con′fis•ca′tion** *n.* **—con′fis•ca′tor** *n.* **—con•fis′ca•to′ry** (kən-fĭs′kə-tôr′ē, -tōr′ē) *adj.*

Con•fi•te•or (kən-fē′tē-ər, -ôr′) *n.* A prayer in which sins are confessed. [Lat. *Cōnfiteor*, I confess, its first word, first pers. sing. pr.t. of *cōnfitērī*, to acknowledge. See CONFESS.]

con•fi•ture (kŏn′fĭ-chŏŏr′) *n.* A confection, preserve, or other sweetmeat. [Fr. < OFr. < *confit*, confection. See COMFIT.]

conga drum
A pair of conga drums

con•fla•grant (kən-flā′grənt) *adj.* Burning intensely; blazing. [Lat. *cōnflagrāns, cōnflagrant-*, pr.part. of *cōnflagrāre*, to burn up : *com-*, com- + *flagrāre*, to burn; see **bhel-¹***.]

con•fla•gra•tion (kŏn′flə-grā′shən) *n.* A large destructive fire. [Lat. *cōnflagrātiō, cōnflagrātiōn-* < *cōnflagrātus*, p.part. of *cōnflagrāre*, to burn up. See CONFLAGRANT.]

con•flate (kən-flāt′) *tr.v.* **-flat•ed, -flat•ing, -flates. 1.** To bring together; meld or fuse. **2.** To combine (two variant texts, for example) into one whole. [Lat. *cōnflāre, cōnflāt-* : *com-*, com- + *flāre*, to blow; see **bhlē-***.] **—con•fla′tion** *n.*

con•flict (kŏn′flĭkt′) *n.* **1.** A state of open, often prolonged fighting; a battle or war. **2.** A state of disharmony between incompatible or antithetical persons, ideas, or interests; a clash. **3.** *Psychol.* A psychic struggle resulting from the opposition or simultaneous functioning of mutually exclusive impulses, desires, or tendencies. **4.** Opposition between characters or forces in a work of drama or fiction, esp. opposition affecting the plot. *—intr.v.* (kən-flĭkt′) **-flict•ed, -flict•ing, -flicts. 1.** To be in or come into opposition; differ. **2.** *Archaic.* To engage in warfare. [ME < Lat. *cōnflīctus*, collision < p.part. of *cōnflīgere*, to strike together : *com-*, com- + *flīgere*, to strike.] **—con•flic′tion** *n.* **—con•flic′tive** *adj.* **—con•flic′tu•al** (kən-flĭk′chōō-əl) *adj.*

Syns: *conflict, contest, combat, fight, affray.* These nouns denote struggle between opposing forces for victory or supremacy. *Conflict* applies both to open fighting between hostile groups and to a struggle between antithetical forces: *"The kind of victory MacArthur had in mind . . . victory by expanding the conflict to all of China—would have been the wrong kind of victory"* (Harry S. Truman). *Contest* can refer either to friendly competition or to a hostile struggle to achieve an objective: *a spelling contest; the gubernatorial contest.* *Combat* most commonly implies an encounter between two armed persons or groups: *"Alexander had appeared to him, armed for combat"* (Connop Thirlwall). *Fight* usually refers to a clash involving individual adversaries: *A fight was scheduled between the world boxing champion and the challenger.* *Affray* suggests a public fight or brawl: *"Yet still the poachers came . . . for affrays in woods and on moors with liveried armies of keepers"* (Patricia Morison).

con•flict•ed (kən-flĭk′tĭd) *adj. Usage Problem.* Made uneasy by conflicting impulses.

Usage Note: Ninety-two percent of the Usage Panel rejected the use of *conflicted* in *Caught between loyalty to old employees and a recognition of the need to cut costs, many managers are conflicted about the reorganization plan.*

conflict of interest *n., pl.* **conflicts of interest.** A conflict between the private interests and the public obligations of a person in an official position.

con•flu•ence (kŏn′flōō-əns) *n.* **1.a.** A flowing together of two or more streams. **b.** The point of juncture of such streams. **c.** The combined stream formed by this juncture. **2.** A gathering, flowing, or meeting together at one juncture or point.

con•flu•ent (kŏn′flōō-ənt) *adj.* **1.** Flowing together; blended into one. **2.** *Pathol.* Merging or running together so as to form a mass, as sores in a rash. *—n.* **1.** One of two or more confluent streams. **2.** A tributary. [ME < Lat. *cōnfluēns, cōnfluent-*, pr.part. of *cōnfluere*, to flow together : *com-*, com- + *fluere*, to flow; see **bhleu-***.]

con•flux (kŏn′flŭks′) *n.* A confluence. [< Lat. *cōnfluxus*, p.part. of *cōnfluere*, to flow together. See CONFLUENT.]

con•fo•cal (kŏn-fō′kəl) *adj.* Having the same focus or foci. Used of a lens. **—con•fo′cal•ly** *adv.*

con•form (kən-fôrm′) *v.* **-formed, -form•ing, -forms.** *—intr.* **1.** To correspond in form or character; be similar. **2.** To act or be in accord or agreement; comply. **3.** To act in accordance with current customs or modes. See Syns at **adapt.** *—tr.* To bring into agreement or correspondence; make similar. [Ult. < Lat. *cōnformāre*, to shape after : *com-*, com- + *formāre*, to shape (< *forma*, shape).] **—con•form′er** *n.*

con•form•a•ble (kən-fôr′mə-bəl) *adj.* **1.** Corresponding; similar. **2.** Quick to comply; submissive. **3.** *Geol.* Of, relating to, or being strata that are parallel to each other without interruption. **—con•form′a•bil′i•ty, con•form′a•ble•ness** *n.* **—con•form′a•bly** *adv.*

con•for•mal (kən-fôr′məl) *adj.* **1.** *Math.* Of, relating to, or being a mapping in which all angles between intersecting curves remain unchanged. **2.** Of or relating to a map projection in which small areas are rendered with true shape. [LLat. *cōnformālis*, similar : Lat. *com-*, com- + Lat. *forma*, shape.]

con•for•mance (kən-fôr′məns) *n.* Conformity.

con•for•ma•tion (kŏn′fər-mā′shən) *n.* **1.** The act of conforming or the state of being conformed. **2.** The structure or outline of an item or entity, determined by the arrangement of its parts. **3.** A symmetrical arrangement of the parts of a thing. **4.** A spatial arrangement of atoms in a molecule brought about by free rotation of the atoms about a single chemical bond. **—con′for•ma′tion•al** *adj.* **—con′for•ma′tion•al•ly** *adv.*

con•form•ist (kən-fôr′mĭst) *n.* A person who uncritically or habitually conforms to the customs, rules, or styles of a group. *—adj.* Marked by conformity or convention.

con•form•i•ty (kən-fôr′mĭ-tē) *n., pl.* **-ties. 1.** Similarity in form or character; agreement. **2.** Action or behavior in correspondence with current customs, rules, or styles.

con•found (kən-found′, kŏn-) *tr.v.* **-found•ed, -found•ing, -founds. 1.** To cause to become confused or perplexed. **2.** To fail to distinguish; mix up. **3.** To make (something bad) worse. **4.** To cause to be ashamed; abash. **5.** To damn. **6.a.** To frustrate. **b.** *Archaic.* To bring to ruination. [ME *confounden* < AN *confundre* < Lat. *cōnfundere*, to mix together, confuse : *com-*, com- + *fundere*, to pour; see **gheu-***.]

con•found•ed (kən-foun′dĭd, kŏn-) *adj.* **1.** Confused; befuddled. **2.** Used as an intensive: *a confounded fool.* **—con•found′ed•ly** *adv.* **—con•found′ed•ness** *n.*

con•fra•ter•ni•ty (kŏn′frə-tûr′nĭ-tē) *n., pl.* **-ties.** An association of persons united in a common purpose or profession. [ME *confraternite* < OFr. < Med.Lat. *cōnfrāternitās* < *cōnfrāter*, colleague. See CONFRERE.]

con•frere (kŏn′frâr′) *n.* A fellow member of a fraternity or profession; a colleague. [ME < OFr. < Med.Lat. *cōnfrāter* : Lat. *com-*, com- + Lat. *frāter*, brother; see **bhrāter-***.]
con•front (kən-frŭnt′) *v.* **-front•ed, -front•ing, -fronts.** — *tr.* **1.** To come face to face with, esp. with defiance or hostility. **2.** To bring face to face with. **3.** To come up against; encounter. — *intr.* To engage in confrontation. [Fr. *confronter* < OFr., to adjoin < Med.Lat. *cōnfrontāre* : Lat. *com-*, com- + Lat. *frōns, front-*, front.] — **con′fron•ta′tive** *adj.* — **con•front′er** *n.* — **con•front′ment** *n.*
con•fron•ta•tion (kŏn′frŭn-tā′shən) *n.* **1.** The act of confronting or the state of being confronted, esp. a meeting face to face. **2.a.** A conflict involving armed forces: *a nuclear confrontation.* **b.** Discord or a clash of opinions and ideas: *ideological confrontation.* **3.** A focused comparison. — **con′fron•ta′tion•al** *adj.* — **con′fron•ta′tion•ist** *n.*
Con•fu•cius (kən-fyo͞o′shəs). c. 551–479 B.C. Chinese philosopher whose *Analects* contain a collection of his sayings. — **Con•fu′cian** (-shən) *adj. & n.* — **Con•fu′cian•ism** *n.*
con•fuse (kən-fyo͞oz′) *v.* **-fused, -fus•ing, -fus•es.** — *tr.* **1.a.** To cause to be unable to think with clarity or act with intelligence or understanding. **b.** To cause to feel embarrassment. **2.a.** To mistake for another. **b.** To make opaque; blur. **c.** To assemble without order or sense; jumble. **3.** *Archaic.* To bring to ruination. — *intr.* To make something unclear or incomprehensible. [ME *confusen* < OFr. *confus*, perplexed < Lat. *cōnfūsus*, p.part. of *cōnfundere*, to mix together. See CONFOUND.] — **con•fus′ing•ly** *adv.*
Syns: *confuse, addle, befuddle, discombobulate, fuddle, muddle, throw.* The central meaning shared by these verbs is "to cause to be unclear in mind or intent": *heavy traffic that confused the driver; problems that addle my brain; a question that befuddled even the professor; discombobulated by all the possibilities; a plot that fuddles one's comprehension; a head muddled by facts and figures; behavior that really threw me.*
con•fused (kən-fyo͞ozd′) *adj.* **1.** Being unable to think with clarity or act with understanding and intelligence. **2.a.** Lacking logical order or sense. **b.** Chaotic; jumbled. — **con•fus′ed•ly** (-fyo͞o′zĭd-lē) *adv.* — **con•fus′ed•ness** *n.*
con•fu•sion (kən-fyo͞o′zhən) *n.* **1.a.** The act of confusing or the state of being confused. **b.** An instance of being confused. **2.** *Psychol.* Impaired orientation with respect to time, place, or person; a disturbed mental state. — **con•fu′sion•al** *adj.*
con•fu•ta•tion (kŏn′fyo͞o-tā′shən) *n.* **1.** The act of confuting. **2.** Something that confutes.
con•fute (kən-fyo͞ot′) *tr.v.* **-fut•ed, -fut•ing, -futes. 1.** To prove to be wrong or in error; refute decisively. **2.** *Obsolete.* To confound. [Lat. *cōnfūtāre.* See **bhau-***.] — **con•fut′a•ble** *adj.* — **con•fu′ta•tive** (kən-fyo͞o′tə-tĭv) — **con•fut′er** *n.*
cong. *abbr. Pharm.* Congius (gallon).
Cong. *abbr.* **1.** Congregational. **2.** Congress. **3.** Congressional.
con•ga (kŏng′gə) *n.* **1.** A dance in which the dancers form a long winding line. **2.** Music for this dance. **3.** A conga drum. — *intr.v.* **-gaed, -ga•ing, -gas.** To perform this dance. [Am. Sp. *(danza) Conga*, Congo (dance) < Sp. *Congo*, of the Congo < Kongo *-kongo*, Kongo language and people.]
conga drum *n.* A tall, usu. tapering single-headed drum typically played by beating with the hands.
con game *n. Slang.* A confidence game.
con•gé (kŏn′zhā′, -jā′, kôN-zhā′) also **con•gee** (kŏn′jē) *n.* **1.** Formal or authoritative permission to depart. **2.** An abrupt dismissal. **3.** A leave-taking. **4.** A formal bow. **5.** *Archit.* A concave molding. [ME *conge* and Fr. *congé*, both < OFr. *congie* < Lat. *commeātus* < p.part. of *commeāre*, to come and go : *com-*, com- + *meāre*, to go; see **mei-**[1]*.]
con•geal (kən-jēl′) *v.* **-gealed, -geal•ing, -geals.** — *intr.* **1.** To solidify by or as if by freezing. **2.** To coagulate; jell. — *tr.* To cause to congeal. [ME *congelen* < OFr. *congeler* < Lat. *congelāre* : *com-*, com- + *gelāre*, to freeze; see **gel-***.] — **con•geal′a•ble** *adj.* — **con•geal′er** *n.* — **con•geal′ment** *n.*
con•gealed salad (kən-jēld′) *n. Chiefly Southern U.S.* A molded salad made of flavored gelatin, chopped fruits or vegetables, and sometimes other ingredients.
con•ge•la•tion (kŏn′jə-lā′shən) *n.* The process of congealing or the state of being congealed.
con•ge•ner (kŏn′jə-nər) *n.* **1.** A member of the same kind, class, or group. **2.** An organism belonging to the same taxonomic genus as another organism. [< Lat., of the same race : *com-*, com- + *genus, gener-*, race; see **genə-***.] — **con′ge•ner′ic** (-nĕr′ĭk), **con•gen′er•ous** (kən-jĕn′ər-əs, kŏn-) *adj.*
con•gen•ial (kən-jēn′yəl) *adj.* **1.** Having the same tastes, habits, or temperament; sympathetic. **2.** Of a pleasant disposition; friendly. **3.** Suited to one's needs or nature; agreeable. [Prob. < CON- + Lat. *genius*, the personification of one's natural inclinations; see GENIUS.] — **con•ge′ni•al′i•ty** (-jē′nē-ăl′ĭ-tē), **con•gen′ial•ness** *n.* — **con•gen′ial•ly** *adv.*
con•gen•i•tal (kən-jĕn′ĭ-tl) *adj.* **1.a.** Existing at or before birth. **b.** Acquired at birth or during uterine development, as a result of either hereditary or environmental influences. **2.** Being such as if by nature; inherent. [< Lat. *congenitus* : *com-*, com- + *genitus*, born, p.part. of *gignere*, to bear; see **genə-***.] — **con•gen′i•tal•ly** *adv.*
congenital anomaly *n.* See **birth defect.**
congenital myxedema *n.* See **cretinism.**
con•ger (kŏng′gər) *n.* Any of various large scaleless marine eels of the family Congridae, esp. *Conger oceanicus* native to Atlantic waters. [ME *congre* < OFr., prob. < LLat. *congrus* < Lat. *conger* < Gk. *gongros.*]
con•ge•ries (kən-jîr′ēz′, kŏn′jə-rēz′) *n. (used with a sing. v.)* A collection; an aggregation. [Lat. *congeriēs* < *congerere*, to heap up. See CONGEST.]
con•gest (kən-jĕst′) *v.* **-gest•ed, -gest•ing, -gests.** — *tr.* **1.** To overfill or overcrowd. **2.** *Pathol.* To cause the accumulation of excessive blood or tissue fluid in (a vessel or an organ). — *intr.* To become congested. [Lat. *congerere, congest-*, to heap up, crowd together : *com-*, com- + *gerere*, to carry.] — **con•ges′tion** *n.* — **con•ges′tive** *adj.*
congestive heart failure *n.* A condition marked by weakness, edema, and shortness of breath that is caused by inadequate blood circulation in the peripheral tissues and the lungs.
con•gi•us (kŏn′jē-əs) *n., pl.* **-gi•i** (-jē-ī′). **1.** *Pharm.* A gallon. **2.** An ancient Roman measure for liquids, equal to about seven eighths of a U.S. gallon (3.3 liters). [ME, a liquid measure < Lat. < Gk. *konkhion*, dim. of *konkhē, konkhos*, shellful.]
con•glo•bate (kŏn-glō′bāt′, kŏng′glō-) *tr.v.* **-bat•ed, -bat•ing, -bates.** To form into a globe or ball. [Lat. *conglobāre, conglobāt-* : *com-*, com- + *globus*, ball.] — **con•glo′bate** *adj.* — **con′glo•ba′tion** *n.*
con•globe (kən-glōb′) *tr.v.* **-globed, -glob•ing, -globes.** To conglobate.
con•glom•er•ate (kən-glŏm′ə-rāt′) *intr. & tr.v.* **-at•ed, -at•ing, -ates.** To form or cause to form into an adhering or rounded mass. — *n.* (-ər-ĭt). **1.** A corporation made up of a number of different companies that operate in diversified fields. **2.** A collected heterogeneous mass; a cluster: *a conglomerate of colors.* **3.** *Geol.* A rock consisting of pebbles and gravel embedded in cement. — *adj.* (-ər-ĭt). **1.** Gathered into a mass; clustered. **2.** *Geol.* Made up of loosely cemented heterogeneous material. [Lat. *conglomerāre, conglomerāt-* : *com-*, com- + *glomerāre*, to wind into a ball (< *glomus*, ball).] — **con•glom′er•at′ic** (-ə-răt′ĭk), **con•glom′er•it′ic** (-ə-rĭt′ĭk) *adj.* — **con•glom′er•a′tor** *n.*

Congo

con•glom•er•a•tion (kən-glŏm′ə-rā′shən) *n.* **1.a.** The act or process of conglomerating. **b.** The state of being conglomerated. **2.** An accumulation of miscellaneous things.
con•glu•ti•nate (kən-glo͞ot′n-āt′, kŏn-) *intr. & tr.v.* **-nat•ed, -nat•ing, -nates.** To become or cause to become stuck or glued together. [ME *conglutinaten* < Lat. *conglūtināre, conglūtināt-* : *com-*, com- + *glūtināre*, to glue (< *glūten*, glue).] — **con•glu′ti•nate′** *adj.* — **con•glu′ti•na′tion** *n.*
Con•go (kŏng′gō). **1.** A country of W-central Africa with a coastline on the Atlantic Ocean; achieved independence from France in 1960. Cap. Brazzaville. Pop. 1,912,429. **2.** See **Zaire.** — **Con′go•lese′** (-lēz′, -lēs′) *adj. & n.*
Congo eel *n.* An eellike amphibian *(Amphiuma means)* of the southeast United States having two pairs of tiny nonfunctioning legs.

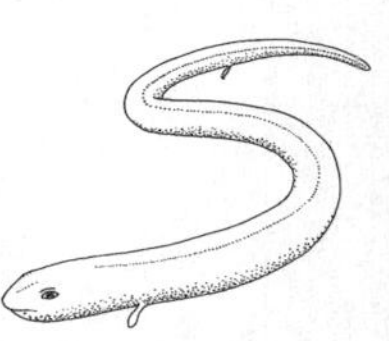
Congo eel
Amphiuma means

Congo Free State. See **Zaire.**
Congo red *n.* A brownish-red powder, $C_{32}H_{22}N_6Na_2O_6S_2$, used as a dye, an indicator, and a biological stain.
Congo River also **Zaire River** (zī′îr, zä-îr′). A river of central Africa flowing c. 4,666 km (2,900 mi) through Zaire to the Atlantic Ocean.
Congo snake *n.* See **Congo eel.**
con•gou (kŏng′gō, -go͞o) *n.* A grade of Chinese black tea. [Chin. (Amoy) *kong hu (te)*, elaborately prepared (tea).]
con•grat•u•late (kən-grăch′ə-lāt′, -grăj′-, kəng-) *tr.v.* **-lat•ed, -lat•ing, -lates.** To express joy or acknowledgment, as for the achievement or good fortune of (another). [Lat. *congrātulārī, congrātulāt-* : *com-*, com- + *grātulārī*, to rejoice (< *grātus*, pleasing; see **g^w^erə-**[2]*).] — **con•grat′u•la′tor** *n.* — **con•grat′u•la•to′ry** (-lə-tôr′ē, -tōr′ē) *adj.*
con•grat•u•la•tion (kən-grăch′ə-lā′shən, -grăj′-, kəng-) *n.* **1.** The act of congratulating. **2.** An expression of such joy or acknowledgment. Often used in the plural.
con•gre•gant (kŏng′grĭ-gənt) *n.* One who congregates, esp. a member of a group of people gathered for religious worship.
con•gre•gate (kŏng′grĭ-gāt′) *tr. & intr.v.* **-gat•ed, -gat•ing, -gates.** To bring or come together in a group, crowd, or assembly. See Syns at **gather.** — *adj.* (-gĭt). **1.** Gathered; assembled. **2.** Involving a group. [ME *congregaten* < Lat. *congregāre, congregāt-* : *com-*, com- + *gregāre*, to assemble (< *grex, greg-*, herd; see **ger-***).] — **con′gre•ga′tive** *adj.* — **con′gre•ga′tive•ness** *n.* — **con′gre•ga′tor** *n.*
con•gre•ga•tion (kŏng′grĭ-gā′shən) *n.* **1.** The act of assembling. **2.** A body of assembled people or things; a gathering. **3.a.** A group of people gathered for religious worship. **b.** Those who regularly worship at a specific church or synagogue. **4.** *Rom. Cath. Ch.* **a.** A religious institute in which only simple vows are taken. **b.** A division of the Curia.
con•gre•ga•tion•al (kŏng′grĭ-gā′shə-nəl) *adj.* **1.** Of or relating to a congregation. **2. Congregational.** Of or relating to Congregationalism or Congregationalists.

ă pat	oi boy
ā pay	ou out
âr care	o͝o took
ä father	o͞o boot
ĕ pet	ŭ cut
ē be	ûr urge
ĭ pit	th thin
ī pie	*th* this
îr pier	hw which
ŏ pot	zh vision
ō toe	ə about, item
ô paw	

Stress marks:
′ (primary);
′ (secondary), as in
dictionary (dĭk′shə-nĕr′ē)

con•gre•ga•tion•al•ism (kŏng′grĭ-gā′shə-nə-lĭz′əm) *n.* **1.** A church government in which each local congregation is self-governing. **2. Congregationalism.** The system of government and religious beliefs of a Protestant denomination in which each member church is self-governing. **— con′gre•ga′tion•al•ist** *n.*

con•gress (kŏng′grĭs) *n.* **1.** A formal assembly of representatives to discuss problems. **2.** The national legislative body of a nation, esp. a republic. **3. Congress. a.** The national legislative body of the United States, consisting of the Senate and the House of Representatives. **b.** The two-year session of this legislature between elections of the House of Representatives. **4.a.** The act of coming together or meeting. **b.** A single meeting, as of a political party. **5.** Sexual intercourse. [ME *congresse*, attendants < Lat. *congressus*, meeting < p.part. of *congredī*, to meet : *com-*, com- + *gradī*, to go; see **ghredh-*.**] **— con•gres′sion•al** (kən-grĕsh′ə-nəl, kəng-) *adj.* **— con•gres′sion•al•ly** *adv.*

Congress boot *n.* An ankle-high shoe with elastic material in the sides.

Congressional Medal of Honor *n.* The highest U.S. military decoration, awarded to members of the armed forces for gallantry and bravery beyond the call of duty.

con•gress•man (kŏng′grĭs-mən) *n.* A man who is a member of the U.S. Congress, esp. of the House of Representatives.

con•gress•peo•ple (kŏng′grĭs-pē′pəl) *n.* The members of the U.S. Congress considered as a group.

con•gress•per•son (kŏng′grĭs-pûr′sən) *n.* A congressman or congresswoman.

con•gress•wom•an (kŏng′grĭs-wo͝om′ən) *n.* A woman who is a member of the U.S. Congress, esp. of the House of Representatives.

Con•greve (kŏn′grēv′, kŏng′-), **William.** 1670–1729. English playwright known for *The Way of the World* (1700).

con•gru•ence (kŏng′gro͞o-əns, kən-gro͞o′-) *n., pl.* **-enc•es.** **1.** Agreement, harmony, conformity, or correspondence. **2.** *Math.* **a.** The state of being congruent. **b.** A statement that two quantities are congruent. **— con′gru•en•cy** *n.*

con•gru•ent (kŏng′gro͞o-ənt, kən-gro͞o′-) *adj.* **1.** Corresponding; congruous. **2.** *Math.* **a.** Coinciding exactly when superimposed. **b.** Having a difference divisible by a modulus: *congruent numbers.* [ME < Lat. *congruēns, congruent-*, pr.part. of *congruere*, to agree.] **— con′gru•ent•ly** *adv.*

con•gru•i•ty (kən-gro͞o′ĭ-tē, kŏn-) *n., pl.* **-ties. 1.** The quality or fact of being congruous. **2.** The quality or fact of being congruent. **3.** A point of agreement.

con•gru•ous (kŏng′gro͞o-əs) *adj.* **1.** Corresponding in character or kind; appropriate or harmonious. **2.** *Math.* Congruent. [< Lat. *congruus* < *congruere*, to agree.] **— con′gru•ous•ly** *adv.* **— con′gru•ous•ness** *n.*

con•ic (kŏn′ĭk) *adj.* Conical. *— n.* A conic section. [NLat. *cōnicus* < Gk. *kōnikos* < *kōnos*, cone. See **kō-*.**]

con•i•cal (kŏn′ĭ-kəl) *adj.* Of, relating to, or shaped like a cone.

conic projection or **conical projection** *n.* A method of projecting maps of parts of the earth's spherical surface on a surrounding cone, which is then flattened to a plane surface having concentric circles as parallels of latitude and radiating lines from the apex as meridians.

conic section *n.* **1.** A plane curve generated from the intersection of a right circular cone and a plane, including the circle, ellipse, hyperbola, and parabola. **2.** A graph of the general quadratic equation in two variables.

co•nid•i•o•phore (kə-nĭd′ē-ə-fôr′, -fōr′) *n.* A specialized fungal hypha that produces conidia. [CONIDI(UM) + -PHORE.] **— co•nid′i•oph′or•ous** (kə-nĭd′ē-ŏf′ər-əs) *adj.*

co•nid•i•um (kə-nĭd′ē-əm) *n., pl.* **-i•a** (-ē-ə). An asexually produced fungal spore, formed on a conidiophore. [NLat. < Gk. *konis*, dust.] **— co•nid′i•al** (-əl) *adj.*

con•i•fer (kŏn′ə-fər, kō′nə-) *n.* Any of various mostly needle-leaved or scale-leaved, chiefly evergreen, cone-bearing gymnospermous trees or shrubs, such as pines, spruces, and firs. [< NLat. *Cōniferae*, family name < Lat., fem. pl. of *cōnifer*, cone-bearing : *cōnus*, cone (< Gk. *kōnos*; see **kō-***) + *-fer*, -fer.] **— co•nif′er•ous** (kō-nĭf′ər-əs, kə-) *adj.*

co•ni•ine (kō′nē-ēn′) also **co•nin** (kō′nĭn) or **co•nine** (-nēn′) *n.* A poisonous, colorless liquid alkaloid, $C_5H_{10}NC_3H_7$, found in the poison hemlock. [LLat. *cōnium*, conium; see CONIUM + -INE[2].]

co•ni•um (kō′nē-əm) *n.* The poison hemlock. [LLat. *cōnium* < Gk. *kōneion*, prob. < *kōna*, liquid pitch.]

conj. *abbr.* **1.** Conjugation. **2.** Conjunction. **3.** Conjunctive.

con•jec•tur•al (kən-jĕk′chər-əl) *adj.* **1.** Based on or involving conjecture. **2.** Tending to conjecture. **— con•jec′tur•al•ly** *adv.*

con•jec•ture (kən-jĕk′chər) *n.* **1.** Inference or judgment based on incomplete evidence; guesswork. **2.** A statement, an opinion, or a conclusion based on guesswork. *— v.* **-tured, -tur•ing, -tures.** *— tr.* To infer from inconclusive evidence; guess. *— intr.* To make a conjecture. [ME < OFr. < Lat. *coniectūra* < *coniectus*, p.part. of *conicere*, to infer : *com-*, com- + *iacere*, to throw; see **yē-*.**] **— con•jec′tur•a•ble** *adj.* **— con•jec′tur•a•bly** *adv.* **— con•jec′tur•er** *n.*

con•join (kən-join′) *tr. & intr.v.* **-joined, -join•ing, -joins.** To join or become joined together; unite. [ME *conjoinen* < OFr. *conjoindre, conjoign-* < Lat. *coniungere* : *com-*, com- + *iungere*, to join; see **yeug-*.**] **— con•join′er** *n.*

con•joint (kən-joint′) *adj.* **1.** Joined together; combined. **2.** Of, consisting of, or involving two or more combined or associated entities; joint. [ME < OFr., p.part. of *conjoindre*, to conjoin. See CONJOIN.] **— con•joint′ly** *adv.*

con•ju•gal (kŏn′jə-gəl, kən-jo͞o′-) *adj.* Of or relating to marriage or the relationship of spouses. [Lat. *coniugālis* < *coniunx, coniug-*, spouse < *coniungere*, to marry. See CONJOIN.] **— con′ju•gal′i•ty** (-găl′ĭ-tē) *n.* **— con′ju•gal•ly** *adv.*

con•ju•gant (kŏn′jə-gənt) *n.* Either of a pair of organisms, cells, or gametes undergoing conjugation.

con•ju•gate (kŏn′jə-gāt′) *v.* **-gat•ed, -gat•ing, -gates.** *— tr.* **1.** *Gram.* To inflect (a verb) in its forms for distinctions such as number, person, voice, mood, and tense. **2.** To join together. *— intr.* **1.** *Biol.* To undergo conjugation. **2.** *Gram.* To be inflected. *— adj.* (-gĭt, -gāt′). **1.** Joined together, esp. in a pair or pairs; coupled. **2.** *Math. & Phys.* Inversely or oppositely related with respect to one of a group of otherwise identical properties. Used esp. of either or both of a pair of complex numbers differing only in the sign of the imaginary term. **3.** *Chem.* Relating to an acid and a base that are related by the difference of a proton. *— n.* (-gĭt, -gāt′). *Math. & Phys.* Either of a pair of conjugate quantities. [Lat. *coniugāre, coniugāt-*, to join together : *com-*, com- + *iugāre*, to join (< *iugum*, yoke; see **yeug-***).] **— con′ju•gate′ly** *adv.* **— con′ju•ga′tive** *adj.* **— con′ju•ga′tor** *n.*

con•ju•gat•ed protein (kŏn′jə-gā′tĭd) *n.* A compound, such as hemoglobin, made up of a protein molecule and a nonprotein prosthetic group.

con•ju•ga•tion (kŏn′jə-gā′shən) *n.* **1.a.** The act of conjugating. **b.** The state of being conjugated. **2.** *Gram.* **a.** The inflection of a particular verb. **b.** A presentation of the complete set of inflections of a verb. **c.** A class of verbs having similar inflected forms. **3.** *Biol.* **a.** The temporary union of two bacterial cells during which one cell transfers part or all of its genome to the other. **b.** A process of sexual reproduction in which ciliate protozoans of the same species temporarily couple and exchange genetic material. **c.** A process of sexual reproduction in certain algae and fungi in which temporary or permanent fusion occurs, resulting in the union of the male and female gametes. **— con′ju•ga′tion•al** *adj.* **— con′ju•ga′tion•al•ly** *adv.*

con•junct (kən-jŭngkt′, kŏn′jŭngkt′) *adj.* **1.** Joined together; united. **2.** Acting in association; combined. **3.** *Mus.* Of or relating to successive tones of the scale. *— n.* (kŏn′jŭngkt′). **1.** One that is in conjunction or association with another. **2.** *Logic.* One of the components of a conjunction. [ME < Lat. *coniūnctus*, p.part. of *coniungere*, to join together. See CONJOIN.] **— con•junct′ly** *adv.*

con•junc•tion (kən-jŭngk′shən) *n.* **1.a.** The act of joining. **b.** The state of being joined. **2.** A joint or simultaneous occurrence; concurrence. **3.** One resulting from or embodying a union; a combination. **4.** *Gram.* A part of speech such as *and* and *because* that connects words, phrases, clauses, or sentences. **5.** *Astron.* The position of two celestial bodies on the celestial sphere when they have the same celestial longitude. **6.** *Logic.* **a.** A compound proposition that has components joined by the word *and* or its symbol and is true only if all the components are true. **b.** The relationship between the components of a conjunction. **— con•junc′tion•al** *adj.*

con•junc•ti•va (kŏn′jŭngk-tī′və) *n., pl* **-vas** or **-vae** (-vē). The mucous membrane that lines the inner surface of the eyelid and the exposed surface of the eyeball. [ME < Med.Lat. *(membrāna) coniūnctīva*, connective (membrane), fem. of LLat. *coniūnctīvus* < Lat. *coniūnctus*, p.part. of *coniungere*, to join. See CONJOIN.] **— con′junc•ti′val** (-vəl) *adj.*

con•junc•tive (kən-jŭngk′tĭv) *adj.* **1.** Joining; connective. **2.** Joined together; combined. **3.** *Gram.* **a.** Of, relating to, or being a conjunction. **b.** Serving to connect elements of meaning and construction within sentences, as *and*, or between sentences, as *therefore.* *— n. Gram.* A connective word, esp. a conjunction or conjunctive adverb. **— con•junc′tive•ly** *adv.*

conjunctive adverb *n. Gram.* A function word that connects two sentences and provides adverbial emphasis, as *therefore* in *This intersection is dangerous; therefore drive slowly.*

con•junc•ti•vi•tis (kən-jŭngk′tə-vī′tĭs) *n. Pathol.* Inflammation of the conjunctiva, characterized by redness and often accompanied by a discharge.

con•junc•ture (kən-jŭngk′chər) *n.* **1.** A combination, as of events. **2.** A critical set of circumstances; a crisis.

con•ju•ra•tion (kŏn′jə-rā′shən) *n.* **1.** The act or art of conjuring. **2.** A magic spell or incantation. **3.** A magic trick or magical effect. **4.** *Archaic.* A solemn appeal; an entreaty.

con•jure (kŏn′jər, kən-jo͝or′) *v.* **-jured, -jur•ing, -jures.** *— tr.* **1.a.** To summon (a devil or spirit) by magical or supernatural power. **b.** To influence or effect by or as if by magic: *conjure away my doubts.* **2.a.** To call or bring to mind; evoke: *conjure up an image.* **b.** To imagine; picture. **3.** *Obsolete.* To call on or entreat solemnly, esp. by an oath. *— intr.* **1.** To perform magic tricks, esp. by sleight of hand. **2.a.** To summon a devil by magic or supernatural power. **b.** To practice black magic. **3.** *Obsolete.* To conspire. [Ult. < LLat. *coniūrāre*, to pray by something holy < Lat., to swear together : *com-*, com- + *iūrāre*, to swear; see **yewes-***.]

con•jur•er also **con•jur•or** (kŏn′jər-ər, kŭn′-) *n.* **1.** One that performs magic tricks; a magician. **2.** A sorcerer or sorceress.

conjure woman *n. Lower Southern U.S.* A Black woman who practices voodoo.

conk¹ (kŏngk) *n.* **1.** *Slang.* **a.** The head. **b.** A blow, esp. on the head. **2.** *Chiefly British.* The human nose. —*v.* **conked, conk•ing, conks.** —*tr.* To hit, esp. on the head. —*intr.* **1.** To stop functioning; fail: *The engine conked out.* **2.** To fall asleep, esp. suddenly or heavily: *I conked out.* **3.** To pass out; faint. **4.** To die. [?]

conk² (kŏngk) *n.* A hard, shelflike spore-bearing structure of certain wood-decaying fungi, found on stumps, logs, or trees. [Perh. alteration of CONCH.]

conk³ (kŏngk) *n.* A hairstyle in which the hair is straightened, usu. by chemical means. —*tr.v.* **conked, conk•ing, conks.** To straighten (tightly curled hair) usu. by chemical means. [Perh. alteration of *congolene*, substance for straightening hair.]

con man *n. Slang.* A confidence man.

conn (kŏn) *v.* & *n. Naut.* Var. of **con³**.

Conn. *abbr.* Connecticut.

Con•nacht (kŏn′ət, -əKHt) also **Con•naught** (-ôt′). A historical region of W-central Ireland.

con•nate (kŏn′āt′, kŏ-nāt′) *adj.* **1.** Existing at birth or from the beginning; inborn or inherent. **2.** Originating at the same time; related. **3.** Being in close accord or sympathy; congenial. **4.** *Biol.* United to a structure of the same kind, as one petal to another. [LLat. *connātus*, p.part. of *connāscī*, to be born with : Lat. *com-*, com- + Lat. *nāscī*, to be born; see **genə-***.] —**con′nate′ly** *adv.* —**con′nate′ness** *n.*

con•nat•u•ral (kə-năch′ər-əl, kŏ-) *adj.* **1.** Innate; inborn. **2.** Related or similar in nature; cognate. [Med.Lat. *connātūrālis* : Lat. *com-*, com- + Lat. *nātūrālis*, by birth; see NATURAL.] —**con•nat′u•ral′i•ty** (-ə-răl′ĭ-tē) *n.* —**con•nat′u•ral•ly** *adv.* —**con•nat′u•ral•ness** *n.*

con•nect (kə-nĕkt′) *v.* **-nect•ed, -nect•ing, -nects.** —*tr.* **1.** To join or fasten together. **2.** To associate or consider as related. See Syns at **join. 3.** To join to or by means of a communications circuit. **4.** To plug in (an electrical cord or device) to an outlet. —*intr.* **1.** To become joined or united. **2.** To be scheduled so as to provide continuing service, as between airplanes. **3.** To establish a rapport or relationship; relate. **4.** *Sports.* To hit or play a ball successfully. [ME *connecten* < Lat. *cōnectere* : *cō-*, co- + *nectere*, to bind; see **ned-***.] —**con•nect′i•ble, con•nect′a•ble** *adj.* —**con•nec′tor, con•nect′er** *n.*

con•nect•ed (kə-nĕk′tĭd) *adj.* **1.** Joined or fastened together. **2.** *Math.* Having a continuous path between any two points. Used of a curve, set, or surface. **3.** Related; associated. **4.** Logically or intelligibly ordered or presented; coherent. **5.** Associated with or related to persons of influence or position. —**con•nect′ed•ly** *adv.* —**con•nect′ed•ness** *n.*

Con•nect•i•cut (kə-nĕt′ĭ-kət). A state of the NE U.S.; admitted as one of the original Thirteen Colonies in 1788. The Fundamental Orders, a constitution based on the consent of the governed, was adopted by the colony in 1639. Cap. Hartford. Pop. 3,295,669.

Connecticut River. A river of the NE U.S. flowing c. 655 km (407 mi) from N NH to its outlet on Long Island Sound.

con•nect•ing rod (kə-nĕk′tĭng) *n.* A rod that transmits motion or power from one moving part to another, esp. the rod connecting the crankshaft of an automobile to a piston.

con•nec•tion (kə-nĕk′shən) *n.* **1.a.** The act of connecting. **b.** The state of being connected. **2.** One that connects; a link. **3.** An association or a relationship: *a connection between two crimes.* **4.** The logical or intelligible ordering of words or ideas; coherence. **5.** Reference or relation to something else; context. **6.** A person, esp. one of influence or position, with whom one is associated. **7.** A conveyance or scheduled run providing continuing service between means of transportation. **8.** A line of communication between two points in a telephone or similar wired system. **9.** *Slang.* **a.** A drug dealer. **b.** A purchase of illegal drugs. —**con•nec′tion•al** *adj.*

con•nec•tive (kə-nĕk′tĭv) *adj.* Serving or tending to connect. —*n.* **1.** One that connects. **2.** *Gram.* A word that connects words, phrases, clauses, and sentences. **3.** *Bot.* The portion of a stamen that connects the halves of an anther. —**con•nec′tive•ly** *adv.* —**con′nec•tiv′i•ty** (kŏn′ĕk-tĭv′ĭ-tē) *n.*

connective tissue *n.* Tissue arising chiefly from the embryonic mesoderm that is characterized by a highly vascular matrix and includes adipose tissue, cartilage, and bone.

Con•nel•ly (kŏn′ə-lē), **Marcus ("Marc") Cook.** 1890–1980. Amer. playwright, producer, and director whose works include *The Green Pastures* (1930).

con•nex•ion (kə-nĕk′shən) *n. Chiefly British.* Var. of **connection.**

con•ning tower (kŏn′ĭng) *n.* **1.** A raised, enclosed observation post in a submarine, often used as a means of entrance and exit. **2.** The armored pilothouse of a warship. [< CON³.]

con•nip•tion (kə-nĭp′shən) *n. Informal.* A fit of violent emotion, such as anger or panic. [?]

con•niv•ance also **con•niv•ence** (kə-nī′vəns) *n.* **1.** The act of conniving. **2.** *Law.* Knowledge of and tacit consent to the commission of an illegal act by another.

con•nive (kə-nīv′) *intr.v.* **-nived, -niv•ing, -nives. 1.** To cooperate secretly in an illegal or wrongful action; collude. **2.** To scheme; plot. **3.** To feign ignorance of or fail to act against a wrong, thus implying tacit consent: *conniving at the escape.* [Lat. *cōnīvēre, connīvēre*, to close the eyes.] —**con•niv′er** *n.* —**con•niv′er•y** *n.*

con•ni•vent (kə-nī′vənt) *adj. Biol.* Converging and touching but not fused, as an insect's wings. [Lat. *connīvēns, connīvent-*, pr.part. of *cōnīvēre*, to be tightly closed.]

con•nois•seur (kŏn′ə-sûr′, -so͝or′) *n.* **1.** A person with expert knowledge or training, esp. in the fine arts. **2.** A person of informed and discriminating taste. [Obsolete Fr. < OFr. *connoisseor* < *connoistre*, to know < Lat. *cognōscere*, to learn, know. See COGNITION.] —**con′nois•seur′ship′** *n.*

Con•nol•ly (kŏn′ə-lē), **Maureen.** "Little Mo." 1934–69. Amer. tennis player who was the first to win the grand slam of U.S., British, French, and Australian women's championships (1953).

Con•nors (kŏn′ərz), **James ("Jimmy") Scott.** b. 1952. Amer. tennis player who twice won both the U.S. and Wimbledon men's singles titles (1974 and 1982) and also won the U.S. title in 1976, 1978, and 1983.

Jimmy Connors
At the U.S. Open semifinals in 1991

con•no•ta•tion (kŏn′ə-tā′shən) *n.* **1.** The act or process of connoting. **2.a.** An idea or meaning suggested by or associated with a word or thing. **b.** The set of associative implications constituting the general sense of a word in addition to its literal sense. **3.** *Logic.* The set of attributes constituting the meaning of a term; intension. —**con′no•ta′tive** *adj.*

con•note (kə-nōt′) *tr.v.* **-not•ed, -not•ing, -notes. 1.** To suggest or imply in addition to literal meaning. See Usage Note at **denote. 2.** To have as a related or attendant condition. [Med.Lat. *connotāre*, to mark along with : Lat. *com-*, com- + Lat. *notāre*, to mark (< *nota*, mark; see **gnō-***).]

con•nu•bi•al (kə-no͞o′bē-əl, -nyo͞o′-) *adj.* Relating to marriage or the married state; conjugal. [Lat. *cōnūbiālis* < *cōnūbium*, marriage : *com-*, com- + *nūbere*, to marry.] —**con•nu′bi•al•ism, con•nu′bi•al′i•ty** (-ăl′ĭ-tē) *n.*

co•no•dont (kō′nə-dŏnt′, kŏn′ə-) *n. Paleont.* A Paleozoic microfossil usu. having a toothlike shape and considered to be the remains of an extinct marine organism. [Gk. *kōnos*, cone; see **kō-*** + -ODONT.]

co•noid (kō′noid′) also **co•noi•dal** (kō-noid′l) *adj.* Shaped like a cone. —**co′noid** *n.*

con•quer (kŏng′kər) *v.* **-quered, -quer•ing, -quers.** —*tr.* **1.** To defeat or subdue by force, esp. by force of arms. **2.** To gain or secure control of by or as if by force of arms: *conquering disease.* **3.** To overcome or surmount by physical, mental, or moral force: *conquered fear.* See Syns at **defeat.** —*intr.* To be victorious; win. [ME *conqueren* < OFr. *conquerre* < VLat. **conquaerere* < Lat. *conquīrere*, to procure : *com-*, com- + *quaerere*, to seek.] —**con′quer•a•ble** *adj.* —**con′quer•or, con′quer•er** *n.*

con•quest (kŏn′kwĕst′, kŏng′-) *n.* **1.** The act or process of conquering. **2.** Something acquired by conquering. **3.** One that has been captivated or overcome. [ME < OFr. < VLat. **conquaesīta*, fem. p.part. of **conquaerere*. See CONQUER.]

con•qui•an (kŏng′kē-ən) *n. Games.* Var. of **cooncan.**

con•quis•ta•dor (kŏn-kwĭs′tə-dôr′, kŏng-kē′stə-) *n., pl.* **-dors** or **-dor•es** (-dôr′ās, -ēz). A conqueror, esp. one of the 16th-century Spanish soldiers who defeated the civilizations of the New World. [Sp. < *conquistar*, to conquer < VLat. **conquīsītāre*, freq. of Lat. *conquīrere*, to procure. See CONQUER.]

Con•rad (kŏn′răd′), **Joseph.** 1857–1924. Polish-born British writer whose works include *Lord Jim* (1900).

Con•roe (kŏn′rō). A city of SE TX N of Houston. Pop. 27,610.

cons. *abbr.* **1.a.** Consigned. **b.** Consignment. **2.** Consonant. **3.** Also **Cons.** Constable. **4.** Constitution; constitutional. **5.** Construction. **6.** Also **Cons.** Consul.

con•san•guin•e•ous (kŏn′săn-gwĭn′ē-əs, -săng-) also **con•san•guine** (kŏn-săng′gwĭn, kən-) *adj.* Of the same lineage or origin. [< Lat. *cōnsanguineus* : *com-*, com- + *sanguineus*, of blood; see SANGUINE.] —**con′san•guin′e•ous•ly** *adv.*

con•san•guin•i•ty (kŏn′săn-gwĭn′ĭ-tē, -săng-) *n., pl.* **-ties. 1.** Relationship by blood or by a common ancestor. **2.** A close affinity or connection.

con•science (kŏn′shəns) *n.* **1.a.** The awareness of a moral or ethical aspect to one's conduct together with the urge to prefer right over wrong. **b.** A source of moral or ethical judgment or pronouncement. **c.** Conformity to one's own sense of right conduct. **2.** The part of the superego in psychoanalysis that judges the ethics of one's actions and thoughts and then transmits its judgments to the ego. **3.** *Obsolete.* Consciousness. —***idiom.* in (all good) conscience.** In all truth or fairness. [ME < OFr. < Lat. *cōnscientia* < *cōnsciēns, cōnscient-*, pr.part. of *cōnscīre*, to be conscious of : *com-*, com- + *scīre*,

ă pat	oi boy
ā pay	ou out
âr care	o͝o took
ä father	o͞o boot
ĕ pet	ŭ cut
ē be	ûr urge
ĭ pit	th thin
ī pie	*th* this
îr pier	hw which
ŏ pot	zh vision
ō toe	ə about, item
ô paw	

Stress marks:
′ (primary);
′ (secondary), as in
dictionary (dĭk′shə-nĕr′ē)

to know; see **skei-***.] **— con′science•less** *adj.*

conscience clause *n.* A clause in a law that relieves persons whose conscientious or religious scruples forbid compliance.

conscience money *n.* Money paid in compensation or atonement, as for a dishonest or morally objectionable act.

con•sci•en•tious (kŏn′shē-ĕn′shəs) *adj.* **1.** Guided by or in accordance with the dictates of conscience; principled. **2.** Thorough and assiduous: *conscientious work.* [Obsolete Fr. *conscientieux* < Med.Lat. *cōnscientiōsus* < Lat. *cōnscientia,* conscience. See CONSCIENCE.] **— con′sci•en′tious•ly** *adv.* **— con′sci•en′tious•ness** *n.*

conscientious objector *n.* One who on the basis of religion or principle refuses to bear arms or serve in the military.

con•scio•na•ble (kŏn′shə-nə-bəl) *adj.* **1.** Acceptable or permissible according to conscience. **2.** Conscientious; principled. [Obsolete *conscions* (var. of CONSCIENCE) + -ABLE.]

con•scious (kŏn′shəs) *adj.* **1.a.** Having an awareness of one's environment and one's own existence, sensations, and thoughts. See Syns at **aware. b.** Mentally perceptive or alert; awake. **2.** Capable of thought, will, or perception. **3.** Subjectively known or felt: *conscious remorse.* **4.** Intentionally conceived or done; deliberate: *a conscious insult.* **5.** Inwardly attentive or sensible; mindful: *conscious of being stared at.* **6.** Especially aware of or preoccupied with. Often used in combination: *a health-conscious diet.* — *n.* In psychoanalysis, the component of waking awareness perceptible by a person at any given instant; consciousness. [< Lat. *cōnscius* : *com-,* com- + *scīre,* to know; see **skei-***.] **— con′scious•ly** *adv.*

con•scious•ness (kŏn′shəs-nĭs) *n.* **1.** The state or condition of being conscious. **2.** A sense of identity, esp. the complex of attitudes, beliefs, and sensitivities held by or considered characteristic of an individual or a group. **3.a.** Special awareness or sensitivity: *class consciousness.* **b.** Alertness to or concern for a particular issue or situation. **4.** In psychoanalysis, the conscious.

con•scious•ness-rais•ing (kŏn′shəs-nĭs-rā′zĭng) *n.* **1.** A process of achieving greater awareness of one's needs in order to fulfill one's human potential. **2.** A method for making people aware of a political or social issue, esp. discrimination or injustice. **— con′scious•ness-rais′er** *n.*

con•script (kŏn′skrĭpt′) *n.* One compulsorily enrolled for service, esp. in the armed forces; a draftee. — *adj.* Enrolled compulsorily; drafted. — *tr.v.* (kən-skrĭpt′) **-script•ed, -script•ing, -scripts.** To enroll compulsorily into service; draft. [Lat. *cōnscriptus,* p.part. of *cōnscrībere,* to enroll : *com-,* com- + *scrībere,* to write; see **skrībh-***.]

con•scrip•tion (kən-skrĭp′shən) *n.* **1.** Compulsory enrollment, esp. for the armed forces; draft. **2.** A monetary payment exacted by a government in wartime.

con•se•crate (kŏn′sĭ-krāt′) *tr.v.* **-crat•ed, -crat•ing, -crates. 1.** To declare or set apart as sacred. **2.a.** To produce the ritual transformation of (the elements of the Eucharist) into the body and blood of Jesus. **b.** To sanctify (bread and wine) for use in Communion. **c.** To initiate (a priest) into the order of bishops. **3.** To dedicate solemnly to a service or goal. **4.** To make venerable; hallow: *consecrated by time.* — *adj.* Dedicated to a sacred purpose; sanctified. [ME *consecraten* < Lat. *cōnsecrāre, cōnsecrāt-* : *com-,* com- + *sacrāre,* to make sacred (< *sacer, sacr-,* sacred; see **sak-***).] **— con′se•cra′tive** *adj.* **— con′se•cra′tor** *n.* **— con′se•cra•to′ry** (-krə-tôr′ē, -tōr′ē) *adj.*

con•se•cra•tion (kŏn′sĭ-krā′shən) *n.* **1.** The act, process, or ceremony of consecrating. **2.** The state of being consecrated.

con•se•cu•tion (kŏn′sĭ-kyo͞o′shən) *n.* **1.** A sequence or succession. **2.** *Logic.* The relation of consequent to antecedent; deduction.

con•sec•u•tive (kən-sĕk′yə-tĭv) *adj.* **1.** Following one after another without interruption; successive. **2.** Marked by logical sequence. **3.** *Gram.* Expressing consequence or result. [Fr. *consécutif* < OFr. < Med.Lat. *cōnsecūtīvus* < *cōnsecūtus,* p.part. of Lat. *cōnsequī,* to follow closely. See CONSEQUENT.] **— con•sec′u•tive•ly** *adv.* **— con•sec′u•tive•ness** *n.*

con•sen•su•al (kən-sĕn′sho͞o-əl) *adj.* **1.** Of or expressing a consensus: *a consensual decision.* **2.a.** *Law.* Existing or entered into by mutual consent without formalization by document or ceremony: *a consensual marriage.* **b.** Involving the willing participation of both or all parties, esp. in an illegal practice. **3.** *Physiol.* **a.** Of or relating to a reflex of one body structure following stimulation of another. **b.** Of or relating to involuntary movement of a body part accompanying voluntary movement of another. **— con•sen′su•al•ly** *adv.*

con•sen•sus (kən-sĕn′səs) *n.* **1.** A view or stance reached by a group as a whole or by majority will. **2.** General agreement. [Lat. < p.part. of *cōnsentīre,* to agree. See CONSENT.]

con•sent (kən-sĕnt′) *intr.v.* **-sent•ed, -sent•ing, -sents. 1.** To give assent, as to the proposal of another; agree. See Syns at **assent. 2.** *Archaic.* To be of the same mind or opinion. — *n.* **1.** Acceptance or approval of what is planned or done by another; acquiescence. **2.** Agreement as to opinion or a course of action: *chosen by common consent.* [ME *consenten* < OFr. *consentir* < Lat. *cōnsentīre* : *com-,* com- + *sentīre,* to feel; see **sent-***.] **— con•sent′er** *n.*

con•sen•ta•ne•ous (kŏn′sĕn-tā′nē-əs) *adj.* **1.** Manifesting agreement; accordant. **2.** Unanimous. [< Lat. *cōnsentāneus* < *cōnsentīre,* to agree. See CONSENT.] **— con•sen′ta•ne′i•ty** (kən-sĕn′tə-nē′ĭ-tē), **con′sen•ta′ne•ous•ness** *n.* **— con′sen•ta′ne•ous•ly** *adv.*

consent decree *n. Law.* A judicial decree expressing a voluntary agreement between parties to a suit, esp. an agreement by a defendant to cease activities alleged by the government to be illegal in return for an end to the charges.

con•se•quence (kŏn′sĭ-kwĕns′, -kwəns) *n.* **1.** Something that logically or naturally follows from an action or condition. See Syns at **effect. 2.** The relation of a result to its cause. **3.** A logical conclusion or inference. **4.** Significance; importance. See Syns at **importance.** — *idiom.* **in consequence.** As a result; consequently.

con•se•quent (kŏn′sĭ-kwĕnt′, -kwənt) *adj.* **1.a.** Following as a natural effect, result, or conclusion. **b.** Following as a logical conclusion. **2.** Logically correct or consistent. **3.** *Geol.* Having a position or direction determined by the original form or slope of the earth's surface. — *n.* **1.** *Logic.* The conclusion, as of a syllogism or a conditional sentence. **2.** The second term of a ratio. [ME < OFr. < Lat. *cōnsequēns, cōnsequent-,* pr.part. of *cōnsequī,* to follow closely : *com-,* com- + *sequī,* to follow; see **sek**^{w}**-**^{1}*.]

con•se•quen•tial (kŏn′sĭ-kwĕn′shəl) *adj.* **1.** Following as an effect, result, or conclusion; consequent. **2.** Having important consequences; significant. **3.a.** Important; influential. **b.** Pompous; self-important. **— con′se•quen′ti•al′i•ty** (-shē-ăl′ĭ-tē), **con′se•quen′tial•ness** *n.* **— con′se•quen′tial•ly** *adv.*

con•se•quent•ly (kŏn′sĭ-kwĕnt′lē, -kwənt-lē) *adv.* As a result; therefore.

con•ser•van•cy (kən-sûr′vən-sē) *n., pl.* **-cies. 1.** Conservation, esp. of natural resources. **2.a.** An organization dedicated to the conservation of wildlife and wildlife habitats in the United States. **b.** *Chiefly British.* A commission supervising fisheries and navigation.

con•ser•va•tion (kŏn′sûr-vā′shən) *n.* **1.** The act or process of conserving. **2.a.** Preservation from loss, damage, or neglect. **b.** The controlled use and systematic protection of natural resources, such as forests. **3.** The maintenance of a physical quantity, such as mass, during a physical or chemical change. **— con′ser•va′tion•al** *adj.*

con•ser•va•tion•ist (kŏn′sûr-vā′shə-nĭst) *n.* One practicing or advocating conservation, esp. of natural resources.

conservation of charge *n.* A principle stating that the total electric charge of an isolated system remains constant regardless of changes within the system.

conservation of energy *n.* A principle stating that the total energy of an isolated system remains constant regardless of changes within the system.

conservation of mass *n.* A principle in classical physics stating that the total mass of an isolated system is unchanged by interaction of its parts.

conservation of momentum *n.* A principle stating that the total linear momentum of an isolated system remains constant regardless of changes within the system.

con•ser•va•tism (kən-sûr′və-tĭz′əm) *n.* **1.** The inclination, esp. in politics, to maintain the existing or traditional order. **2.** A political philosophy or attitude emphasizing respect for traditional institutions, distrust of government activism, and opposition to sudden change. **3. Conservatism.** The principles and policies of the Conservative Party or the Progressive Conservative Party. **4.** Caution; moderation.

con•ser•va•tive (kən-sûr′və-tĭv) *adj.* **1.** Favoring traditional views and values; tending to oppose change. **2.** Traditional or restrained in style: *a conservative suit.* **3.** Moderate; cautious. **4.a.** Of or relating to the political philosophy of conservatism. **b.** Belonging to a conservative party, group, or movement. **5. Conservative.** Of or belonging to the Conservative Party or the Progressive Conservative Party. **6. Conservative.** Of or adhering to Conservative Judaism. **7.** Tending to conserve; preservative. — *n.* **1.** One favoring traditional views and values. **2.** A supporter of political conservatism. **3. Conservative.** A member or supporter of the Conservative Party or the Progressive Conservative Party. **4.** *Archaic.* A preservative agent or principle. **— con•ser′va•tive•ly** *adv.* **— con•ser′va•tive•ness** *n.*

Conservative Judaism *n.* The branch of Judaism that allows for modifications in Jewish law when authorized by the Conservative rabbinate.

Conservative Party *n.* A major political party of the United Kingdom.

con•ser•va•tize (kən-sûr′və-tīz′) *tr.v.* **-tized, -tiz•ing, -tizes.** To make conservative or more conservative.

con•ser•va•tor (kən-sûr′və-tər, kŏn′sər-vā′tər) *n.* **1.** A person in charge of maintaining or restoring valuable items, as in a museum. **2.** One that conserves or preserves from injury, violation, or infraction. **3.** *Law.* One responsible for the person and property of an incompetent. **— con•ser′va•to′ri•al** (-tôr′ē-əl, -tōr′-) *adj.* **— con•ser′va•tor•ship′** *n.*

con•ser•va•to•ry (kən-sûr′və-tôr′ē, -tōr′ē) *n., pl.* **-ries. 1.** A greenhouse, esp. one in which plants are arranged aesthetically for display. **2.** A school of music or dramatic art.

con•serve (kən-sûrv′) *v.* **-served, -serv•ing, -serves.** —*tr.* **1.a.** To protect from loss or harm; preserve. **b.** To use carefully or sparingly, avoiding waste. **2.** To keep (a quantity) constant through physical or chemical reactions or evolutionary changes. **3.** To preserve (fruits) with sugar. —*intr.* To economize. —*n.* (kŏn′sûrv′). A jam made of fruits stewed in sugar. [ME *conserven* < OFr. *conserver* < Lat. *cōnservāre* : *com-*, com- + *servāre*, to preserve; see **ser-¹***.] —**con•serv′a•ble** *adj.* —**con•serv′er** *n.*

con•sid•er (kən-sĭd′ər) *v.* **-ered, -er•ing, -ers.** —*tr.* **1.** To think carefully about. **2.** To think or deem to be; regard as. See Usage Note at **as¹**. **3.** To form an opinion about; judge. **4.** To take into account; bear in mind. **5.** To show consideration for: *considered the feelings of others.* **6.** To esteem; regard. **7.** To look at thoughtfully. —*intr.* To think carefully; reflect. [ME *consideren* < OFr. < Lat. *cōnsīderāre* : *com-*, com- + *sīdus, sīder-*, star.] —**con•sid′er•er** *n.*

con•sid•er•a•ble (kən-sĭd′ər-ə-bəl) *adj.* **1.** Large in amount, extent, or degree. **2.** Worthy of consideration; significant. —*n. Informal.* A considerable amount, extent, or degree. —**con•sid′er•a•bly** *adv.*

con•sid•er•ate (kən-sĭd′ər-ĭt) *adj.* **1.** Having or marked by regard for the needs or feelings of others. See Syns at **thoughtful. 2.** Characterized by careful thought. —**con•sid′er•ate•ly** *adv.* —**con•sid′er•ate•ness** *n.*

con•sid•er•a•tion (kən-sĭd′ə-rā′shən) *n.* **1.a.** Careful thought; deliberation. **b.** A result of considering; an opinion or a judgment. **2.** A factor to be considered in forming a judgment or decision. **3.** A treatment or account. **4.** Thoughtful concern for others; solicitude. **5.** High regard; esteem. **6.** Payment given in exchange for a service rendered; recompense. **7.** *Law.* Something promised, given, or done that has the effect of making an agreement a legally enforceable contract. —***idiom.* in consideration of. 1.** In view of; on account of. **2.** In return for.

con•sid•ered (kən-sĭd′ərd) *adj.* **1.** Reached after or done with careful thought; deliberate. **2.** Highly regarded; esteemed.

con•sid•er•ing (kən-sĭd′ər-ĭng) *prep.* In view of; taking into consideration. See Usage Note at **participle.** —*adv. Informal.* All things considered.

con•sign (kən-sīn′) *v.* **-signed, -sign•ing, -signs.** —*tr.* **1.** To give over to the care of another; entrust. **2.** To turn over permanently to another's charge or to a lasting condition. **3.** To deliver (merchandise, for example) for custody or sale. **4.** To set apart, as for a special use or purpose; assign. —*intr. Obsolete.* To submit; consent. [ME *consignen*, to certify by seal < OFr. *consigner* < Lat. *cōnsignāre* : *com-*, com- + *signāre*, to mark (< *signum*, mark; see **sekʷ-¹***).] —**con•sign′a•ble** *adj.* —**con′sig•na′tion** (kŏn′sī-nā′shən, -sĭg-) *n.* —**con•sig′nor, con•sign′er** *n.*

con•sign•ee (kŏn′sī-nē′, kən-sī′nē′) *n.* The one to whom something, such as goods or merchandise, is consigned.

con•sign•ment (kən-sīn′mənt) *n.* **1.** The act of consigning. **2.** Something consigned. —***idiom.* on consignment.** With the provision that payment is expected only on completed sales and that unsold items may be returned.

con•sist (kən-sĭst′) *intr.v.* **-sist•ed, -sist•ing, -sists. 1.** To be made up or composed. See Usage Note at **include. 2.** To have a basis; reside or lie. **3.** To be compatible; accord. [Lat. *cōnsistere*, to stand still, to be composed of : *com-*, com- + *sistere*, to cause to stand; see **stā-***.]

con•sis•tence (kən-sĭs′təns) *n.* Consistency.

con•sis•ten•cy (kən-sĭs′tən-sē) *n., pl.* **-cies. 1.a.** Agreement or logical coherence among things or parts. **b.** Correspondence among related aspects; compatibility. **2.** Reliability or uniformity of successive results or events. **3.** Degree or texture of density, firmness, or viscosity.

con•sis•tent (kən-sĭs′tənt) *adj.* **1.** In agreement; compatible. **2.** Being in agreement with itself; coherent and uniform. **3.** Reliable; steady. **4.** *Math.* Having at least one common solution, as of two or more equations. [Lat. *cōnsistēns, cōnsistent-*, pr.part. of *cōnsistere*, to stand still. See CONSIST.] —**con•sis′tent•ly** *adv.*

con•sis•to•ry (kən-sĭs′tə-rē) *n., pl.* **-ries. 1.a.** *Rom. Cath. Ch.* An assembly of cardinals presided over by the pope for the solemn promulgation of papal acts. **b.** A governing body of a local congregation in certain Reformed churches. **c.** A regulatory court in Lutheran state churches. **d.** An Anglican diocesan court presided over by a bishop's chancellor or commissary. **2.** The meeting of a consistory. **3.** A council; a tribunal. [ME *consistorie* < OFr. < Lat. *cōnsistōrium*, place of assembly < *cōnsistere*, to stand together. See CONSIST.] —**con′sis•to′ri•al** (kŏn′sĭ-stôr′ē-əl, -stōr′-) *adj.*

con•so•ci•ate (kən-sō′shē-āt′) *tr. & intr.v.* **-at•ed, -at•ing, -ates.** To bring or come into friendly or cooperative association. —*adj.* (-ĭt). Associated; united. —*n.* (-ĭt). An associate or partner. [Lat. *cōnsociāre, cōnsociāt-*, to associate : *com-*, com- + *sociāre*, to associate (< *socius*, companion; see **sekʷ-¹***).]

con•so•ci•a•tion (kən-sō′shē-ā′shən) *n.* **1.** Friendly or cooperative association, as between groups. **2.** *Ecol.* A subdivision of an association having one dominant species of plant. **3.** A political arrangement in which various groups share power according to an agreed formula or mechanism. —**con•so′ci•a′tion•al** *adj.*

con•sol (kŏn′sŏl, kən-sŏl′) *n. Chiefly British.* A government bond in Great Britain, originally issued in 1751, that pays perpetual interest and has no date of maturity. Often used in the plural. [Short for *Consolidated Annuity.*]

consol. *abbr.* Consolidated.

con•so•la•tion (kŏn′sə-lā′shən) *n.* **1.a.** The act or an instance of consoling. **b.** The state of being consoled. **2.** One that consoles; a comfort: *Your kindness was a consolation.*

consolation prize *n.* A prize given to a competitor who loses or does not win the first prize.

con•sole¹ (kən-sōl′) *tr.v.* **-soled, -sol•ing, -soles.** To allay the sorrow or grief of. [Fr. *consoler* < OFr. < Lat. *cōnsōlārī* : *com-*, com- + *sōlārī*, to comfort.] —**con•sol′a•ble** *adj.* —**con•so′la•to′ry** (-sō′lə-tôr′ē, -tōr′ē, -sŏl′ə-) *adj.* —**con•sol′er** *n.* —**con•sol′ing•ly** *adv.*

con•sole² (kŏn′sōl′) *n.* **1.a.** A cabinet, as for a television set, designed to stand on the floor. **b.** A small freestanding storage cabinet. **2.** *Mus.* The desklike part of an organ that contains the keyboard, stops, and pedals. **3.a.** A central control panel for a mechanical, electrical, or electronic system. **b.** An instrument panel. **4.** The portion of a computer or peripheral that houses the apparatus used to operate the machine manually. **5.** A small storage compartment mounted between bucket seats in an automobile. **6.** An often scroll-shaped bracket used for decoration or for supporting a projecting member. **7.** A console table. [Fr., perh. short for *consolider*, to strengthen < Lat. *cōnsolidāre.* See CONSOLIDATE.]

console²

con•sole table (kŏn′sōl′) *n.* **1.** A table supported by decorative consoles fixed to a wall. **2.** A small table, often with curved legs resembling consoles, set against a wall.

con•sol•i•date (kən-sŏl′ĭ-dāt′) *v.* **-dat•ed, -dat•ing, -dates.** —*tr.* **1.** To unite into one system or whole; combine. **2.** To make strong or secure; strengthen. **3.** To make firm or coherent; form into a compact mass. —*intr.* **1.** To become solidified or united. **2.** To join in a merger or union. [Lat. *cōnsolidāre, cōnsolidāt-* : *com-*, com- + *solidāre*, to make firm (< *solidus*, firm; see **sol-***).] —**con•sol′i•da′tor** *n.*

con•sol•i•dat•ed school (kən-sŏl′ĭ-dā′tĭd) *n.* A public school serving pupils from several adjacent districts.

con•sol•i•da•tion (kən-sŏl′ĭ-dā′shən) *n.* **1.a.** The act or process of consolidating. **b.** The state of being consolidated. **2.** The merger of two or more commercial interests or corporations.

con•so•lute (kŏn′sə-lo͞ot′) *adj.* Of or relating to liquid substances that are capable of being mixed in all proportions. [LLat. *cōnsolūtus*, dissolved together : Lat. *com-*, com- + Lat. *solūtus*, p.part. of *solvere*, to loosen, dissolve; see **leu-***.]

con•som•mé (kŏn′sə-mā′, kŏn′sə-mā′) *n.* A clear soup made of strained meat or vegetable stock, served hot or as a cold jelly. [Fr. < p.part. of *consommer*, to use up < Lat. *cōnsummāre*, to finish. See CONSUMMATE.]

console table
Mid 18th-century French

con•so•nance (kŏn′sə-nəns) *n.* **1.** Agreement; harmony; accord. **2.a.** Close correspondence of sounds. **b.** The repetition of consonants or of a consonant pattern, esp. at the ends of words. **3.** *Mus.* A simultaneous combination of sounds conventionally regarded as pleasing and final in effect.

con•so•nant (kŏn′sə-nənt) *adj.* **1.** Being in agreement or accord. **2.** Corresponding or alike in sound, as words. **3.** Harmonious in sound or tone. **4.** Consonantal. —*n.* **1.** A speech sound produced by a partial or complete obstruction of the air stream by constriction of the speech organs. **2.** A letter or character representing such a speech sound. [ME < OFr. < Lat. *cōnsonāns, cōnsonant-*, pr.part. of *cōnsonāre*, to agree : *com-*, com- + *sonāre*, to sound; see **swen-***.] —**con′so•nant•ly** *adv.*

con•so•nan•tal (kŏn′sə-năn′tl) *adj.* **1.** Of, relating to, or having the nature of a consonant. **2.** Containing a consonant or consonants. —**con′so•nan′tal•ly** *adv.*

con•sort (kŏn′sôrt′) *n.* **1.** A husband or wife, esp. of a monarch. **2.** A companion or partner. **3.** A ship accompanying another in travel. **4.** Partnership; association. **5.** A group; a company. **6.** *Mus.* **a.** An ensemble of players. **b.** A group of instruments of the same family. —*v.* (kən-sôrt′) **-sort•ed, -sort•ing, -sorts.** —*intr.* **1.** To keep company; associate. **2.** To be in accord or agreement. —*tr.* **1.** To unite in company; associate. **2.** *Obsolete.* **a.** To escort; accompany. **b.** To espouse. [ME, colleague < OFr. < Lat. *cōnsors, cōnsort-* : *com-*, com- + *sors*, fate; see **ser-²***.]

con•sor•ti•um (kən-sôr′tē-əm, -shē-əm) *n., pl.* **-ti•a** (-tē-ə, -shē-ə). **1.a.** An association or a combination, as of businesses, in order to engage in a joint venture. **b.** A cooperative arrangement among groups or institutions. **2.** An association or a society. **3.** *Law.* A spouse's right to the company of, help of, affection of, and sexual relations with his or her mate. [Lat., fellowship < *cōnsors, cōnsort-*, partner. See CONSORT.] —**con•sor′ti•al** *adj.*

con•spe•cif•ic (kŏn′spĭ-sĭf′ĭk) *adj.* Of or belonging to the same species. —**con′spe•cif′ik** *n.*

ă pat	oi boy
ā pay	ou out
âr care	o͝o took
ä father	o͞o boot
ĕ pet	ŭ cut
ē be	ûr urge
ĭ pit	th thin
ī pie	*th* this
îr pier	hw which
ŏ pot	zh vision
ō toe	ə about, item
ô paw	

Stress marks:
′ (primary);
′ (secondary), as in
dictionary (dĭk′shə-nĕr′ē)

with. —*intr.* To be in or come into contact. —*adj.* **1.** Of, sustaining, or making contact. **2.** Caused or transmitted by touching. [Lat. *contāctus* < p.part. of *contingere*, to touch : *com-*, com- + *tangere*, to touch; see **tag-***.] —**con·tac′tu·al** (kən-tăk′cho͞o-əl) *adj.* —**con·tac′tu·al·ly** *adv.*

Usage Note: In 1969 only 34 percent of the Usage Panel accepted the use of *contact* as a verb, but in our most recent survey 65 percent of the Panel accepted the sentence *She immediately called an officer at the Naval Intelligence Service, who in turn contacted the FBI.* See Usage Note at **impact.**

contact dermatitis *n.* An acute or chronic skin inflammation resulting from contact with an irritating substance or allergen.

contact flight *n.* Aircraft navigation by visual observation of the horizon or of landmarks.

contact inhibition *n.* The cessation of cellular growth and division due to physical contact with other cells.

contact lens *n.* A thin plastic or glass lens that is fitted over the cornea of the eye to correct various vision defects.

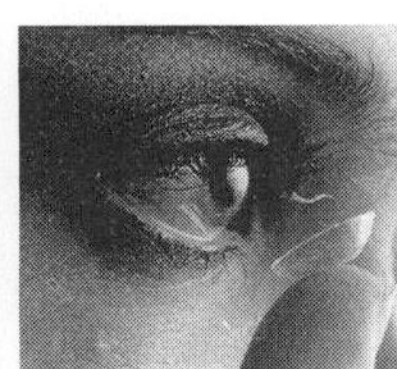

contact lens

con·tac·tor (kŏn′tăk′tər, kən-tăk′-) *n.* An electrical relay used to control the flow of power in a circuit.

contact print *n.* A print made by exposing a photosensitive surface in direct contact with a photographic negative.

contact sport *n. Sports.* A sport, such as hockey, that involves physical contact between players as part of normal play.

con·ta·gion (kən-tā′jən) *n.* **1.a.** Disease transmission by direct or indirect contact. **b.** A disease so transmitted; a contagious disease. **c.** See **contagium. 2.** A harmful, corrupting influence. **3.** The tendency to spread, as of a doctrine. [ME *contagioun* < Lat. *contāgiō, contāgiōn-* < *contingere, contāct-*, to touch. See CONTACT.]

con·ta·gious (kən-tā′jəs) *adj.* **1.** Of or relating to contagion. **2.** Transmissible by direct or indirect contact; communicable. **3.** Capable of transmitting disease. **4.** Spreading or tending to spread from one to another; infectious. —**con·ta′gious·ly** *adv.* —**con·ta′gious·ness** *n.*

contagious abortion *n. Veterinary Medic.* Brucellosis, esp. in cattle.

con·ta·gium (kən-tā′jəm) *n., pl.* **-gia** (-jə). The direct cause, such as a virus, of a communicable disease. [Lat. *contāgium*, contagion, contamination < *contāgiō*. See CONTAGION.]

con·tain (kən-tān′) *tr.v.* **-tained, -tain·ing, -tains. 1.a.** To have within; hold. **b.** To be capable of holding. **2.** To have as component parts; include or comprise. **3.a.** To hold or keep within limits; restrain. **b.** To halt the spread or development of; check: *a method of containing disease.* **4.** To check the expansion or influence of (a hostile power or ideology) by containment. **5.** *Math.* To be exactly divisible by. [ME *conteinen* < OFr. *contenir* < Lat. *continēre* : *com-*, com- + *tenēre*, to hold; see **ten-***.] —**con·tain′a·ble** *adj.*

Syns: *contain, hold, accommodate.* These verbs mean to have within or have a capacity. *Contain* means to have within or have as a part or constituent: *The book contains some amusing passages. Hold* primarily stresses capacity for containing: *The pitcher holds two pints but contains only one. Accommodate* refers to capacity for holding comfortably: *The restaurant accommodates 50 customers.*

con·tain·er (kən-tā′nər) *n.* **1.** A receptacle in which material is held or carried. **2.** A large reusable receptacle accommodating smaller cartons or cases in a single shipment.

con·tain·er·board (kən-tā′nər-bôrd′, -bōrd′) *n.* A corrugated or solid cardboard used to make containers.

con·tain·er·ize (kən-tā′nə-rīz′) *v.* **-ized, -iz·ing, -iz·es.** —*tr.* To package (cargo) in large standardized containers for efficient shipping and handling. —**con·tain′er·i·za′tion** (-tā′nər-ĭ-zā′shən) *n.*

container ship *n. Naut.* A ship fitted for transporting containerized cargo.

con·tain·ment (kən-tān′mənt) *n.* **1.** The act or condition of containing. **2.** A policy of checking the expansion or influence of a hostile power or ideology. **3.** A structure or system designed to prevent the accidental release of radioactive materials from a reactor.

con·tam·i·nant (kən-tăm′ə-nənt) *n.* One that contaminates.

con·tam·i·nate (kən-tăm′ə-nāt′) *tr.v.* **-nated, -nat·ing, -nates. 1.** To make impure or unclean by contact or mixture. **2.** To expose to or permeate with radioactivity. —*adj.* (-nĭt). *Archaic.* Contaminated. [ME *contaminaten* < Lat. *contāmināre, contāmināt-*. See **tag-***.] —**con·tam′i·na′tive** *adj.* —**con·tam′i·na′tor** *n.*

con·tam·i·na·tion (kən-tăm′ə-nā′shən) *n.* **1.a.** The act or process of contaminating. **b.** The state of being contaminated. **2.** One that contaminates.

contd. *abbr.* Continued.

conte (kônt) *n., pl.* **contes** (kônt). **1.** A short story or novella. **2.** A medieval narrative tale. [Fr. < OFr. *conter*, to relate, recount. See COUNT[1].]

con·temn (kən-tĕm′) *tr.v.* **-temned, -temn·ing, -temns.** To view with contempt; despise. See Syns at **despise.** [ME *contempnen*, to slight < Lat. *contemnere* : *com-*, com- + *temnere*, to despise.] —**con·temn′er** (-tĕm′ər, -tĕm′nər) *n.*

contemp. *abbr.* Contemporary.

con·tem·plate (kŏn′təm-plāt′) *v.* **-plat·ed, -plat·ing, -plates.** —*tr.* **1.** To look at attentively and thoughtfully. See Syns at **see[1]. 2.** To consider carefully and at length; meditate on or ponder. **3.** To have in mind as an intention or possibility. —*intr.* To ponder; meditate. [Lat. *contemplārī, contemplāt-* : *com-*, com- + *templum*, space for observing auguries; see **tem-***.] —**con′tem·pla′tor** *n.*

con·tem·pla·tion (kŏn′təm-plā′shən) *n.* **1.** The act or state of contemplating. **2.** Thoughtful observation or study. **3.** Meditation on spiritual matters, esp. as a form of devotion. **4.** Intention or expectation: *contemplation of a career change.*

con·tem·pla·tive (kən-tĕm′plə-tĭv, kŏn′təm-plā′-) *adj.* Disposed to or characterized by contemplation. See Syns at **pensive.** —*n.* **1.** A person given to contemplation. **2.** A member of a religious order emphasizing meditation. —**con·tem′pla·tive·ly** *adv.* —**con·tem′pla·tive·ness** *n.*

con·tem·po·ra·ne·ous (kən-tĕm′pə-rā′nē-əs) *adj.* Originating, existing, or happening during the same period of time. [Lat. *contemporāneus* : *com-*, com- + *tempus, tempor-*, time + *-āneus*, adj. suff.] —**con·tem′po·ra·ne′i·ty** (-pər-ə-nē′ĭ-tē, -nā′-), **con·tem′po·ra′ne·ous·ness** *n.* —**con·tem′po·ra·ne′ous·ly** *adv.*

con·tem·po·rar·y (kən-tĕm′pə-rĕr′ē) *adj.* **1.** Belonging to the same period of time: *a fact documented by two contemporary sources.* **2.** Of about the same age. **3.** Current; modern. —*n., pl.* **-ies. 1.** One of the same time or age. **2.** A person of the present age. [Med.Lat. *contemporārius* : Lat. *com-*, com- + Lat. *tempus, tempor-*, time + Lat. *-ārius*, -ary.] —**con·tem′po·rar′i·ly** (-tĕm′pə-râr′ə-lē) *adv.*

Usage Note: When *contemporary* is used in reference to something in the past, its meaning is not always clear. *Contemporary critics of Shakespeare* may mean critics in his time or critics in our time. Avoid misunderstanding by using phrases such as *critics in Shakespeare's time* or *modern critics.*

con·tem·po·rize (kən-tĕm′pə-rīz′) *v.* **-rized, -riz·ing, -riz·es.** —*tr.* To modernize. —*intr.* To be contemporary. —**con·tem′po·ri·za′tion** (-tĕm′pər-ĭ-zā′shən) *n.*

con·tempt (kən-tĕmpt′) *n.* **1.** Disparaging or haughty disdain; scorn. **2.** The state of being despised or dishonored; disgrace. **3.** Open disrespect or willful disobedience of the authority of a court of law or legislative body. [ME < Lat. *contemptus*, p.part. of *contemnere*, to despise. See CONTEMN.]

con·tempt·i·ble (kən-tĕmp′tə-bəl) *adj.* **1.** Deserving of contempt; despicable. **2.** *Obsolete.* Contemptuous. —**con·tempt′i·bil′i·ty, con·tempt′i·ble·ness** *n.* —**con·tempt′i·bly** *adv.*

con·temp·tu·ous (kən-tĕmp′cho͞o-əs) *adj.* Manifesting or feeling contempt; scornful. —**con·temp′tu·ous·ly** *adv.* —**con·temp′tu·ous·ness** *n.*

con·tend (kən-tĕnd′) *v.* **-tend·ed, -tend·ing, contends.** —*intr.* **1.** To strive in opposition or against difficulties; struggle. **2.** To compete, as in a race; vie. **3.** To strive in controversy or debate; dispute. —*tr.* To maintain or assert. [ME *contenden* < Lat. *contendere* : *com-*, com- + *tendere*, to stretch, strive; see **ten-***.] —**con·tend′er** *n.*

con·tent[1] (kŏn′tĕnt′) *n.* **1.** Something contained, as in a receptacle. Often used in the plural. **2.** The subject matter of a written work. Often used in the plural. **3.a.** The substantive or meaningful part. **b.** The meaning or significance of a literary or artistic work. **4.** The proportion of a specified substance: *a high protein content.* [ME < Med.Lat. *contentum*, neut. p.part. of Lat. *continēre*, to contain. See CONTAIN.]

con·tent[2] (kən-tĕnt′) *adj.* **1.** Desiring no more than what one has; satisfied. **2.** Ready to accept or acquiesce; willing. —*tr.v.* **-tent·ed, -tent·ing, -tents.** To make content or satisfied. —*n.* Contentment; satisfaction. [ME < OFr. < Lat. *contentus*, p.part. of *continēre*, to restrain. See CONTAIN.]

con·tent analysis (kŏn′tĕnt′) *n.* A systematic analysis of the content of a communication including themes and symbols to determine its objective or meaning.

con·tent·ed (kən-tĕn′tĭd) *adj.* Satisfied with things as they are; content. —**con·tent′ed·ly** *adv.* —**con·tent′ed·ness** *n.*

con·ten·tion (kən-tĕn′shən) *n.* **1.** The act or an instance of striving in controversy or debate. **2.** A striving to win in competition; rivalry. **3.** An assertion put forward in argument. [Ult. < Lat. *contentiō, contentiōn-* < *contentus*, p.part. of *contendere*, to contend. See CONTEND.]

con·ten·tious (kən-tĕn′shəs) *adj.* **1.** Given to contention; quarrelsome. See Syns at **argumentative. 2.** Involving or likely to cause contention; controversial. —**con·ten′tious·ly** *adv.* —**con·ten′tious·ness** *n.*

con·tent·ment (kən-tĕnt′mənt) *n.* **1.** The state of being contented; satisfaction. **2.** A source of satisfaction.

con·ter·mi·nous (kən-tûr′mə-nəs) also **co·ter·mi·nous** (kō-) *adj.* **1.** Sharing a boundary; contiguous. **2.** Contained in the same boundaries; coextensive. **3.** Sharing scope, range of meaning, or extent in time. [< Lat. *conterminus* : *com-*, com- + *terminus*, boundary.] —**con·ter′mi·nous·ly** *adv.* —**con·ter′mi·nous·ness** *n.*

contes (kônt) *n.* Pl. of **conte.**

con·tes·sa (kən-tĕs′ə, kōn-tĕs′sä) *n.* An Italian countess. [Ital., fem. of *conte*, count < LLat. *comes, comit-*. See COUNT[2].]

con•test (kŏn′tĕst′) *n.* **1.** A struggle for superiority or victory between rivals. **2.** A competition, esp. one in which entrants perform separately and are rated by judges. See Syns at **conflict.** —*v.* (kən-tĕst′, kŏn′tĕst′) **-test•ed, -test•ing, -tests.** —*tr.* **1.** To compete or strive for. **2.** To call into question and take an active stand against; dispute or challenge. See Syns at **oppose.** —*intr.* To struggle or compete; contend. [Prob. < Fr. *conteste* < *contester,* to dispute < OFr., to call to witness < Lat. *contestārī* : *com-*, com- + *testis,* witness; see **trei-***.] —**con•test′a•ble** *adj.* —**con′tes•ta′tion** (kŏn′tĕ-stā′shən) *n.* —**con•test′er** *n.*

con•tes•tant (kən-tĕs′tənt, kŏn′tĕs′tənt) *n.* **1.** One taking part in a contest; a competitor. **2.** One that contests or disputes something, such as an election or a will.

con•text (kŏn′tĕkst′) *n.* **1.** The part of a text or statement that surrounds a particular word or passage and determines its meaning. **2.** The circumstances in which an event occurs; a setting. [ME, composition < Lat. *contextus* < p.part. of *contexere,* to join together : *com-*, com- + *texere,* to weave; see **teks-***.]

con•tex•tu•al (kən-tĕks′cho͞o-əl, kŏn-) *adj.* Of, involving, or depending on a context. —**con•tex′tu•al•ly** *adv.*

con•tex•tu•al•ize (kən-tĕks′cho͞o-ə-līz′) *tr.v.* **-ized, -iz•ing, -iz•es.** To place (a word or idea, for example) in an appropriate context. —**con•tex′tu•al•i•za′tion** (-ə-lĭ-zā′shən) *n.*

con•tex•ture (kən-tĕks′chər, kŏn′tĕks′-) *n.* **1.** The act of weaving or assembling parts into a whole. **2.** An arrangement of interconnected parts; a structure. —**con•tex′tur•al** *adj.*

con•ti•gu•i•ty (kŏn′tĭ-gyo͞o′ĭ-tē) *n., pl.* **-ties. 1.** The state of being contiguous. **2.** A continuous mass or series.

con•tig•u•ous (kən-tĭg′yo͞o-əs) *adj.* **1.** Sharing an edge or boundary; touching. **2.** Neighboring; adjacent. **3.** Connected in time or space without a break: *the 48 contiguous states.* [< Lat. *contiguus* < *contingere, contig-*, to touch. See CONTACT.] —**con•tig′u•ous•ly** *adv.* —**con•tig′u•ous•ness** *n.*

con•ti•nence (kŏn′tə-nəns) *n.* **1.** Self-restraint; moderation. **2.** Voluntary control over urinary and fecal discharge. **3.** Partial or complete abstention from sexual activity.

con•ti•nent¹ (kŏn′tə-nənt) *n.* **1.** One of the principal land masses of the earth. **2. Continent.** The mainland of Europe. Used with *the.* [Lat. *(terra) continēns, continent-*, continuous (land), pr.part. of *continēre,* to hold together. See CONTAIN.]

con•ti•nent² (kŏn′tə-nənt) *adj.* Exercising continence. [ME < Lat. *continēns,* pr.part. of *continēre,* to restrain. See CONTAIN.] —**con′ti•nent•ly** *adv.*

con•ti•nen•tal (kŏn′tə-nĕn′tl) *adj.* **1.** Of, relating to, or characteristic of a continent. **2.** Often **Continental.** Of or relating to the mainland of Europe; European. **3. Continental.** Of or relating to the American colonies during and immediately after the Revolutionary War. —*n.* **1.** Often **Continental. a.** An inhabitant of a continent. **b.** An inhabitant of mainland Europe. **2.** A native of the continental United States living or working in Puerto Rico or the U.S. Virgin Islands. **3. Continental.** A soldier in the American army during the Revolutionary War. **4.** A piece of paper money issued by the Continental Congress during the Revolutionary War. —**con′ti•nen′tal•ism** *n.* —**con′ti•nen′tal•ist** *n.* —**con′ti•nen•tal′i•ty** (-nĕn-tăl′ĭ-tē) *n.* —**con′ti•nen′tal•ly** *adv.*

continental breakfast *n.* Breakfast consisting usu. of coffee or tea and a roll.

continental code *n.* A form of Morse code having no spaces between the dot and dash elements, commonly used in telegraphy outside the United States and Canada.

continental divide *n.* An extensive stretch of high ground from each side of which the river systems of a continent flow in opposite directions.

Continental Divide. A series of mountain ridges extending from AK to Mexico, mostly in the Rocky Mts.; often called the **Great Divide** in the U.S.

continental drift *n.* The movement, formation, or re-formation of continents described by the theory of plate tectonics.

continental shelf *n.* A submerged border of a continent that slopes gradually and extends to a point of steeper descent to the ocean bottom.

continental slope *n.* The descent from the continental shelf to the ocean bottom.

con•tin•gence (kən-tĭn′jəns) *n.* **1.** A joining or touching. **2.** Contingency.

con•tin•gen•cy (kən-tĭn′jən-sē) *n., pl.* **-cies. 1.a.** A possible but unlikely or unplanned event. **b.** A possibility that must be prepared for; a future emergency. **2.** The condition of dependence on chance; uncertainty. **3.** Something incidental to something else. —**con•tin′gen•cy** *adj.*

contingency fee *n.* A fee, as for an attorney, payable only in the event of a successful or satisfactory outcome.

contingency table *n.* A statistical table showing the observed frequencies of data elements classified in rows and columns according to two variables.

con•tin•gent (kən-tĭn′jənt) *adj.* **1.** Liable to occur but not certain; possible. **2.** Dependent on conditions or occurrences not yet established; conditional. **3.** Happening by chance or accident; fortuitous. **4.** *Logic.* True only under certain conditions; not necessarily or universally true. —*n.* **1.** An event or condition that is likely but not inevitable. **2.** A share or quota, as of troops, contributed to a general effort. **3.** A representative group forming part of an assemblage. [ME < Lat. *contingēns, contingent-*, pr.part. of *contingere,* to touch. See CONTACT.] —**con•tin′gent•ly** *adv.*

con•tin•u•a (kən-tĭn′yo͞o-ə) *n.* Pl. of **continuum.**

con•tin•u•al (kən-tĭn′yo͞o-əl) *adj.* **1.** Recurring regularly or frequently. **2.** Not interrupted. —**con•tin′u•al•ly** *adv.*

Syns: *continual, continuous, constant, ceaseless, incessant, perpetual, eternal, perennial, interminable.* These adjectives mean occurring repeatedly over a long period of time. *Continual* is chiefly restricted to what is intermittent or repeated at intervals: *the continual banging of the shutter in the wind. Continuous* implies lack of interruption: *a continuous line. Constant* stresses steadiness or persistence and unvarying nature: *constant chatter. Ceaseless* and *incessant* pertain to uninterrupted activity: *the ceaseless thunder of the surf; incessant questions. Perpetual* emphasizes both steadiness and duration: *a perpetual stream of visitors. Eternal* refers to what is everlasting, especially to what is seemingly without temporal beginning or end: *"That freedom can be retained only by the eternal vigilance which has always been its price"* (Elmer Davis). *Perennial* describes existence that goes on year after year, often with the suggestion of self-renewal: *perennial poverty. Interminable* refers to what is or seems to be endless and is often applied to something prolonged and wearisome: *an interminable argument.*

A	B	C	D
•–	–•••	–•–•	–••
E	F	G	H
•	••–•	––•	••••
I	J	K	L
••	•–––	–•–	•–••
M	N	O	P
––	–•	–––	•––•
Q	R	S	T
––•–	•–•	•••	–
U	V	W	X
••–	•••–	•––	–••–
Y	Z		
–•––	––••		

continental code

con•tin•u•ance (kən-tĭn′yo͞o-əns) *n.* **1.** The act or fact of continuing. **2.** The time during which something exists or lasts; duration. **3.** A continuation or sequel. **4.** *Law.* Postponement or adjournment to a future date.

Usage Note: *Continuance* is interchangeable with *continuation* in some of its senses. However, only *continuance* is used to refer to the duration of a state or condition, as in *his continuance in office. Continuation* applies especially to prolongation or resumption of action (*a continuation of the meeting*) or to physical extension (*the continuation of the street*).

con•tin•u•ant (kən-tĭn′yo͞o-ənt) *n. Ling.* A consonant that can be prolonged without change while breath lasts.

con•tin•u•a•tion (kən-tĭn′yo͞o-ā′shən) *n.* **1.a.** The act or fact of continuing. **b.** The state of being continued. **2.** An extension by which something is carried to a further point. **3.** A resumption after an interruption. See Usage Note at **continuance.**

continental shelf

con•tin•u•a•tive (kən-tĭn′yo͞o-ā′tĭv, -ə-tĭv) *adj.* Of, relating to, or serving to cause continuation. —*n.* Something that expresses or causes continuation. —**con•tin′u•a′tive•ly** *adv.*

con•tin•u•a•tor (kən-tĭn′yo͞o-ā′tər) *n.* One that continues, esp. a person who carries on the work of another.

con•tin•ue (kən-tĭn′yo͞o) *v.* **-ued, -u•ing, -ues.** —*intr.* **1.** To go on with a particular action or in a particular condition; persist. **2.** To exist over a prolonged period; last. **3.** To remain in the same state, capacity, or place. **4.** To go on after an interruption; resume. —*tr.* **1.** To carry forward; persist in. **2.** To carry further in time, space, or development; extend. **3.** To cause to remain or last; retain. **4.** To carry on after an interruption; resume. **5.** *Law.* To postpone or adjourn. [ME *continuen* < OFr. *continuer* < Lat. *continuāre* < *continuus,* continuous < *continēre,* to hold together. See CONTAIN.] —**con•tin′u•a•ble** *adj.* —**con•tin′u•er** *n.*

con•tin•ued fraction (kən-tĭn′yo͞od) *n.* A fraction whose numerator is a whole number and whose denominator is a whole number plus a fraction that has a denominator consisting of a whole number plus a fraction.

con•tin•u•ing education (kən-tĭn′yo͞o-ĭng) *n.* **1.** An instructional program featuring recent advances in a particular area. **2.** Instructional courses esp. for adult part-time students.

con•ti•nu•i•ty (kŏn′tə-no͞o′ĭ-tē, -nyo͞o′-) *n., pl.* **-ties. 1.** The state or quality of being continuous. **2.** An uninterrupted succession or flow; a coherent whole. **3.a.** A detailed script or scenario consulted to avoid discrepancies from shot to shot in a film. **b.** Spoken matter serving to link parts of a radio or television program so that no break occurs.

con•tin•u•o (kən-tĭn′yo͞o-ō′) *n., pl.* **-os.** *Mus.* A bass accompaniment, usu. on a keyboard instrument, in which numerals underneath the notes indicate the kinds of harmony to be played. [Ital. < Lat. *continuus,* continuous. See CONTINUE.]

con•tin•u•ous (kən-tĭn′yo͞o-əs) *adj.* **1.** Uninterrupted in time, sequence, substance, or extent. See Syns at **continual. 2.** Attached together in repeated units. **3.** *Math.* Of or relating to a line or curve that extends without a break or irregularity. —**con•tin′u•ous•ly** *adv.* —**con•tin′u•ous•ness** *n.*

continuous creation theory *n.* See **steady-state theory.**

continuous spectrum *n.* A spectrum without lines or bands, esp. one of radiation distributed over an uninterrupted range of wavelengths.

continuous variation *n. Genet.* Variation within a population in which a graded series of intermediate phenotypes falls between the extremes.

ă **pat**	oi **boy**
ā **pay**	ou **out**
âr **care**	o͝o **took**
ä **father**	o͞o **boot**
ĕ **pet**	ŭ **cut**
ē **be**	ûr **urge**
ĭ **pit**	th **thin**
ī **pie**	*th* **this**
îr **pier**	hw **which**
ŏ **pot**	zh **vision**
ō **toe**	ə **about,**
ô **paw**	**item**

Stress marks:
′ (primary);
′ (secondary), as in
dictionary (dĭk′shə-nĕr′ē)

continuous wave also **con•tin•u•ous-wave** (kən-tĭn′yo͞o-əs-wāv′) *adj.* Emitting or capable of emitting continuously; not pulsed: *a continuous wave laser.*

con•tin•u•um (kən-tĭn′yo͞o-əm) *n., pl.* **-tin•u•a** (-tĭn′yo͞o-ə) or **-tin•u•ums. 1.** A continuous extent, succession, or whole, no part of which can be distinguished from neighboring parts except by arbitrary division. **2.** *Math.* A set having the same number of points as all the real numbers in an interval. [Lat., neut. of *continuus*, continuous. See CONTINUE.]

con•tort (kən-tôrt′) *v.* **-tort•ed, -tort•ing, -torts.** —*tr.* To twist, wrench, or bend severely out of shape. —*intr.* To become twisted into a strained shape or expression. [Lat. *contorquēre, contort-*, to twist : *com-*, com- + *torquēre*, to twist; see **terkʷ-***.] —**con•tor′tion** *n.* —**con•tor′tive** *adj.*

con•tort•ed (kən-tôr′tĭd) *adj.* **1.** Twisted or strained out of shape. **2.** *Bot.* Twisted, bent, or partially rolled upon itself; convolute. —**con•tort′ed•ly** *adv.* —**con•tort′ed•ness** *n.*

con•tor•tion•ist (kən-tôr′shə-nĭst) *n.* One who contorts, esp. an acrobat. —**con•tor′tion•is′tic** *adj.*

con•tour (kŏn′to͝or′) *n.* **1.a.** The outline of a figure, body, or mass. **b.** A line that represents such an outline. See Syns at **outline. 2.** A surface, esp. of a curving form. Often used in the plural. **3.** A contour line. —*tr.v.* **-toured, -tour•ing, -tours. 1.** To make or shape the outline of; represent in contour. **2.** To build (a road, for example) to follow the contour of the land. —*adj.* **1.** Following the contour lines of uneven terrain to limit erosion of topsoil. **2.** Shaped to fit the outline or form of something. [Fr., alteration of Ital. *contorno* < *contornare*, to draw in outline : Lat. *com-*, com- + Lat. *tornāre*, to round off (< *tornus*, lathe < Gk. *tornos*; see **terə-¹***).]

contour feather *n.* Any of the outermost feathers of a bird, forming the visible body contour and plumage.

contour line *n.* A line on a map that joins points of equal elevation.

contour map *n.* A map showing elevations and surface configuration by means of contour lines.

contortionist

contr. *abbr.* **1.** Contract. **2.** Contraction. **3.** *Mus.* Contralto. **4.** Control.

contra– *pref.* **1.** Against; opposite; contrasting: *contraposition.* **2.** Lower in pitch: *contrabassoon.* [ME < Lat. *contrā-* < *contrā*, against. See **kom***.]

con•tra•band (kŏn′trə-bănd′) *n.* **1.** Goods prohibited by law or treaty from being imported or exported. **2.a.** Illegal traffic in contraband; smuggling. **b.** Smuggled goods. **3.** Goods that may be seized and confiscated by a belligerent if shipped to another belligerent by a neutral. **4.** During the Civil War, a slave who fled or was taken behind Union lines. —*adj.* Prohibited from being imported or exported. [Ital. *contrabbando* : *contra-*, against (< Lat. *contrā-*; see CONTRA–) + *bando*, legal proclamation (< LLat. *bannus*, of Gmc. orig.; see **bhā-²***).] —**con′tra•band′age** *n.* —**con′tra•band′ist** *n.*

con•tra•bass (kŏn′trə-bās′) *Mus.* —*n.* See **double bass.** —*adj.* Pitched an octave below the normal bass range. [Obsolete Ital. *contrabasso* : Ital. *contra-*, against (< Lat. *contrā-*; see CONTRA–) + Ital. *basso*, bass (< LLat. *bassus*, low).] —**con′tra•bass′ist** *n.*

con•tra•bas•soon (kŏn′trə-bə-so͞on′, -bă-) *n. Mus.* The largest and lowest pitched of the double-reed wind instruments, sounding an octave below the bassoon.

con•tra•cep•tion (kŏn′trə-sĕp′shən) *n.* Intentional prevention of conception or impregnation through the use of various devices, agents, drugs, sexual practices, or surgical procedures. [CONTRA– + (CON)CEPTION.]

con•tra•cep•tive (kŏn′trə-sĕp′tĭv) *adj.* Capable of preventing conception. —*n.* A device, drug, or chemical agent that prevents conception.

con•tract (kŏn′trăkt′) *n.* **1.a.** An agreement between two or more parties, esp. one written and enforceable by law. **b.** The writing or document containing such an agreement. **2.** The branch of law dealing with formal agreements between parties. **3.** Marriage as a formal agreement; betrothal. **4.** *Games.* **a.** The last and highest bid of a suit of one hand in bridge. **b.** The number of tricks thus bid. **5.** A paid assignment to murder someone. —*v.* (kən-trăkt′, kŏn′trăkt′) **-tract•ed, -tract•ing, -tracts.** —*tr.* **1.** To enter into by contract; establish or settle by formal agreement. **2.** To acquire or incur. **3.a.** To reduce in size by drawing together; shrink. **b.** To pull together; wrinkle. **4.** *Gram.* To shorten (a word or words) by omitting or combining letters or sounds. —*intr.* **1.** To enter into an agreement. **2.** To become reduced in size by or as if by being drawn together. [ME < Lat. *contrāctus*, p.part. of *contrahere*, to draw together : *com-*, com- + *trahere*, to draw.] —**con•tract′i•bil′i•ty, con•tract′i•ble•ness** *n.* —**con•tract′i•ble** *adj.*

contract bridge *n. Games.* Auction bridge in which tricks in excess of the contract may not count toward game bonuses.

con•trac•tile (kən-trăk′təl, -tīl′) *adj.* Capable of contracting or causing contraction. —**con′trac•til′i•ty** (kŏn′trăk-tĭl′ĭ-tē) *n.*

contractile vacuole *n.* A membrane-bound organelle in certain protists that maintains osmotic equilibrium by pumping fluid cyclically from within the cell to the outside, alternately filling and contracting to release its contents on the cell surface.

con•trac•tion (kən-trăk′shən) *n.* **1.** The act of contracting or the state of being contracted. **2.a.** A word or phrase formed by omitting or combining some sounds from a longer word or phrase. **b.** The formation of such a word. **3.** *Physiol.* The shortening and thickening of functioning muscle or muscle fiber. **4.** A period of decreased business activity.

con•trac•tor (kŏn′trăk′tər, kən-trăk′-) *n.* **1.** One that agrees to provide materials or services at a specified price, esp. for construction work. **2.** Something, esp. a muscle, that contracts.

con•trac•tu•al (kən-trăk′cho͞o-əl) *adj.* Of, relating to, or having the nature of a contract. —**con•trac′tu•al•ly** *adv.*

con•trac•ture (kən-trăk′chər) *n.* **1.** An abnormal, often permanent shortening, as of scar tissue, that results in distortion or deformity, esp. of a body joint. **2.** Such a deformity.

con•tra•cy•cli•cal (kŏn′trə-sī′klĭ-kəl, -sĭk′lĭ-) *adj.* Acting counter to an economic cycle.

con•tra•dance or **con•tra•danse** (kŏn′trə-dăns′) *n.* Var. of **contredanse.**

con•tra•dict (kŏn′trə-dĭkt′) *v.* **-dict•ed, -dict•ing, -dicts.** —*tr.* **1.** To assert or express the opposite of (a statement). **2.** To deny the statement of. **3.** To be contrary to; be inconsistent with. —*intr.* To utter a contradictory statement. [Lat. *contrādīcere, contrādict-*, to speak against : *contrā-*, contra- + *dīcere*, to speak; see **deik-***.] —**con′tra•dict′a•ble** *adj.* —**con′tra•dict′er, con′tra•dic′tor** *n.*

con•tra•dic•tion (kŏn′trə-dĭk′shən) *n.* **1.a.** The act of contradicting. **b.** The state of being contradicted. **2.** A denial. **3.** Inconsistency; discrepancy. **4.** Something that contains contradictory elements.

con•tra•dic•to•ry (kŏn′trə-dĭk′tə-rē) *adj.* **1.** Involving, of the nature of, or being a contradiction. **2.** Given to contradicting. —*n., pl.* **-ries.** *Logic.* Either of two propositions related in such a way that it is impossible for both to be true or both to be false. —**con′tra•dic′to•ri•ly** *adv.* —**con′tra•dic′to•ri•ness** *n.*

con•tra•dis•tinc•tion (kŏn′trə-dĭ-stĭngk′shən) *n.* Distinction by contrasting or opposing qualities. —**con′tra•dis•tinc′tive** *adj.* —**con′tra•dis•tinc′tive•ly** *adv.*

con•tra•dis•tin•guish (kŏn′trə-dĭ-stĭng′gwĭsh) *tr.v.* **-guished, -guish•ing, -guish•es.** To distinguish by contrasting qualities.

con•tra•ges•tive (kŏn′trə-jĕs′tĭv) *adj.* Capable of preventing gestation, either by preventing implantation or by causing the uterine lining to shed after implantation. —*n.* A contragestive drug or agent. —**con′tra•ges•ta′tion** (-jĕ-stā′shən)

con•trail (kŏn′trāl′) *n.* A visible trail of streaks of condensed water vapor or ice crystals sometimes forming in the wake of an aircraft. [CON(DENSATION) + TRAIL.]

con•tra•in•di•cate (kŏn′trə-ĭn′dĭ-kāt′) *tr.v.* **-cat•ed, -cat•ing, -cates.** To indicate the inadvisability of (a medical drug, for example). —**con′tra•in′di•ca′tion** *n.* —**con′tra•in•dic′a•tive** (-ĭn-dĭk′ə-tĭv) *adj.*

con•tra•lat•er•al (kŏn′trə-lăt′ər-əl) *adj.* Taking place or originating in a corresponding part on an opposite side.

con•tral•to (kən-trăl′tō) *n., pl.* **-tos.** *Mus.* **1.** The lowest female voice or voice part, intermediate in range between soprano and tenor. **2.** A woman with a contralto voice. [Ital. : *contra-*, below (< Lat. *contrā-*, contra-) + *alto*, alto; see ALTO.]

con•tra•po•si•tion (kŏn′trə-pə-zĭsh′ən) *n.* An opposite position; antithesis.

con•tra•pos•i•tive (kŏn′trə-pŏz′ĭ-tĭv) *n. Logic.* A proposition derived by negating and permuting the terms of another, equivalent proposition.

con•trap•pos•to (kōn′trə-pōs′tō) *n.* The position of a figure in painting or sculpture in which the hips and legs are turned in a different direction from that of the shoulders and head; the twisting of a figure on its own vertical axis. [Ital., p.part. of *contrapporre*, to set opposite, contrast < Lat. *contrāpōnere* : *contrā-*, contra- + *pōnere*, to place; see **apo-***.]

con•trap•tion (kən-trăp′shən) *n.* A mechanical device; a gadget. [Perh. blend of CONTRIVE and TRAP².]

con•tra•pun•tal (kŏn′trə-pŭn′tl) *adj. Mus.* Of, relating to, or incorporating counterpoint. [< obsolete Ital. *contrapunto*, counterpoint : Ital. *contra-*, against (< Lat. *contrā-*; see CONTRA–) + Ital. *punto*, point, note (< Lat. *punctum*; see PUNCTUAL).] —**con′tra•pun′tal•ly** *adv.*

con•tra•pun•tist (kŏn′trə-pŭn′tĭst) *n. Mus.* A specialist in counterpoint.

con•tra•ri•e•ty (kŏn′trə-rī′ĭ-tē) *n., pl.* **-ties. 1.** The quality or condition of being contrary. **2.** Something that is contrary.

con•trar•i•ous (kən-trâr′ē-əs) *adj.* Perverse; inimical. —**con•trar′i•ous•ly** *adv.*

con•trar•i•wise (kŏn′trĕr′ē-wīz′, kən-trâr′-) *adv.* **1.** From a contrasting point of view. **2.** In the opposite way or reverse order. **3.** In a perverse manner.

con•trar•y (kŏn′trĕr′ē) *adj.* **1.** Opposed, as in character or purpose. **2.** Opposite in direction or position. **3.** Adverse; unfavorable. **4.** (*also* kən-trâr′ē). Given to recalcitrant behavior; willful or perverse. —*n., pl.* **-ies. 1.** Something that is opposite or contrary. **2.** Either of two opposing or contrary things. **3.** *Logic.* A proposition related to another in such a way that if the latter is true, the former must be false, but if the latter is false, the former is not necessarily true. — *adv.* In an opposite direction or manner; counter. — ***idioms.* by contraries.** *Obsolete.* In opposition to what is expected. **on the contrary.** In opposition to what has been stated or what is expected. [ME *contrarie* < AN < Lat. *contrārius* : *contrā*, against; see **kom*** + *-ārius*, -ary.] — **con′trar′i•ly** *adv.* — **con′trar′i•ness** *n.*

con•trast (kən-trăst′, kŏn′trăst′) *v.* **-trast•ed, -trast•ing, -trasts.** — *tr.* To set in opposition in order to show or emphasize differences. — *intr.* To show differences when compared: *a color that contrasted with the dark background.* — *n.* (kŏn′trăst′). **1.a.** The act of contrasting; a setting off of dissimilar entities or objects. **b.** The state of being contrasted: *red berries standing in contrast against the snow.* **2.** A difference between entities or objects compared. **3.** One thing that is strikingly dissimilar to another. **4.** The use of opposing elements, such as colors or lines, in proximity to produce an intensified effect in a work of art. **5.** The difference in brightness between the light and dark areas of a picture, such as a photograph or video image. [Fr. *contraster* < Ital. *contrastare* < Med.Lat. *contrāstāre* : Lat. *contrā-*, contra- + Lat. *stāre*, to stand; see **stā-***.] — **con•trast′a•ble** *adj.* — **con•trast′ing•ly** *adv.*

Usage Note: The noun *contrast* may be followed by *between, with,* or *to*: *There is a sharp contrast between his earlier and later works. In contrast with* (or less frequently, *to*) *his early works, the later plays are less theatrical.* When *contrast* is used as a transitive verb, both *with* and *to* may follow, though *with* is more common.

contrast medium *n.* A substance, such as barium or air, used in radiography to increase the contrast of an image.

con•trast•y (kŏn′trăs′tē) *adj.* Having or producing sharp contrasts between light and dark areas in photography.

con•tra•vene (kŏn′trə-vēn′) *tr.v.* **-vened, -ven•ing, -venes.** **1.** To act or be counter to; violate. **2.** To oppose in argument; gainsay. [Fr. *contrevenir* < Med.Lat. *contrāvenīre*, to transgress < LLat., to oppose : Lat. *contrā-*, contra- + Lat. *venīre*, to come; see **gʷā-***.] — **con′tra•ven′er** *n.*

con•tra•ven•tion (kŏn′trə-vĕn′shən) *n.* The act of contravening; a violation.

con•tre•danse also **con•tre•dance** or **con•tra•dance** or **con•tra•danse** (kŏn′trə-dăns′) *n.* **1.** A folk dance performed in two lines with the partners facing each other. **2.** The music for a contredanse. [Fr., alteration (influenced by Fr. *contre-*, opposite < Lat. *contrā-*, contra-) of COUNTRY-DANCE.]

con•tre•temps (kŏn′trə-tän′, kôN′trə-täN′) *n., pl.* **contretemps** (-tänz′, -täNz′). An unforeseen event that disrupts the normal course of things; an inopportune occurrence. [Fr. : *contre-*, against (< Lat. *contrā-*; see CONTRA-) + *temps*, time (< Lat. *tempus*).]

contrib. *abbr.* **1.** Contribution. **2.** Contributor.

con•trib•ute (kən-trĭb′yo͞ot) *v.* **-ut•ed, -ut•ing, -utes.** — *tr.* **1.** To give or supply in common with others; give to a common fund or for a common purpose. **2.** To submit for publication. — *intr.* **1.** To make a contribution. **2.** To help bring about a result; act as a factor. **3.** To submit material for publication. [Lat. *contribuere, contribūt-*, to bring together : *com-*, com- + *tribuere*, to grant; see TRIBUTE.] — **con•trib′u•tive** *adj.* — **con•trib′u•tive•ly** *adv.* — **con•trib′u•tive•ness** *n.* — **con•trib′u•tor** *n.*

con•tri•bu•tion (kŏn′trĭ-byo͞o′shən) *n.* **1.** The act of contributing. **2.** Something contributed. **3.** A payment exacted for a special purpose; an impost or a levy.

con•trib•u•to•ry (kən-trĭb′yə-tôr′ē, -tōr′ē) *adj.* **1.** Of, relating to, or involving contribution. **2.** Helping to bring about a result. **3.** Subject to an impost or levy. — *n., pl.* **-ries.** One that contributes.

con•trite (kən-trīt′, kŏn′trīt′) *adj.* **1.** Feeling regret and sorrow for one's sins or offenses; penitent. **2.** Arising from or expressing contrition: *contrite words.* [ME *contrit* < Lat. *contrītus*, p.part. of *conterere*, to crush : *com-*, com- + *terere*, to grind; see **terə-¹***.] — **con•trite′ly** *adv.* — **con•trite′ness** *n.*

con•tri•tion (kən-trĭsh′ən) *n.* Sincere remorse for wrongdoing; repentance.

con•tri•vance (kən-trī′vəns) *n.* **1.a.** The act of contriving. **b.** The state of being contrived. **2.** Something contrived, as a mechanical device or a clever plan.

con•trive (kən-trīv′) *v.* **-trived, -triv•ing, -trives.** — *tr.* **1.** To plan with cleverness or ingenuity; devise. **2.** To invent or fabricate, esp. by improvisation. **3.** To plan with evil intent; scheme. **4.** To bring about, as by scheming; manage. — *intr.* To form plans or schemes. [ME *contreven* < OFr. *controver, contreuv-* < Med.Lat. *contropāre*, to compare : Lat. *com-*, com- + Lat. *tropus*, turn, manner, style (< Gk. *tropos*; see **trep-***).] — **con•triv′er** *n.*

con•trived (kən-trīvd′) *adj.* Obviously planned or calculated; not spontaneous; labored: *a novel with a contrived ending.* — **con•triv′ed•ly** (-trī′vĭd-lē, -trīvd′lē) *adv.*

con•trol (kən-trōl′) *tr.v.* **-trolled, -trol•ling, -trols.** **1.** To exercise authoritative or dominating influence over; direct. **2.** To hold in restraint; check: *controlled my temper.* **3.a.** To verify or regulate (a scientific experiment) by conducting a parallel experiment or by comparing with another standard. **b.** To verify (an account, for example) by using a duplicate register for comparison. — *n.* **1.** Authority or ability to manage or direct: *lost control of the skidding car.* **2.a.** A controlling agent, device, or organization. **b.** An instrument or set of instruments used to operate, regulate, or guide a machine or vehicle. Often used in the plural. **3.** A restraining device, measure, or limit; a curb: *price controls.* **4.a.** A standard of comparison for checking or verifying the results of an experiment. **b.** An individual or group used as a standard of comparison in a control experiment. **5.** An intelligence agent who supervises or instructs another agent. **6.** A spirit presumed to speak or act through a medium. [ME *controllen* < AN *contreroller* < Med.Lat. *contrārotulāre*, to check by duplicate register < *contrārotulus*, duplicate register : Lat. *contrā-*, contra- + Lat. *rotulus*, roll, dim. of *rota*, wheel; see **ret-***.] — **con•trol′la•bil′i•ty** *n.* — **con•trol′la•ble** *adj.*

control experiment *n.* An experiment that isolates the effect of one variable on a system by holding constant all variables but the one under observation.

con•trolled substance (kən-trōld′) *n.* A drug or chemical substance whose possession and use are regulated under the Controlled Substances Act.

con•trol•ler (kən-trō′lər) *n.* **1.** One that controls: *a controller of events.* **2.** Also **comp•trol•ler** (kən-trō′lər). An officer who audits accounts and supervises the financial affairs of a corporation or a governmental body. **3.** A regulating mechanism, as in a vehicle or an electric device. — **con•trol′ler•ship′** *n.*

con•trol•ling interest (kən-trō′lĭng) *n.* Ownership of a sufficient number of shares of stock in a company to control company policy.

control tower *n.* A tower at an airfield from which air traffic is controlled by radio and observed physically and by radar.

con•tro•ver•sial (kŏn′trə-vûr′shəl, -sē-əl) *adj.* **1.** Of, producing, or marked by controversy. **2.** Fond of controversy; disputatious. — **con′tro•ver′sial•ist** *n.* — **con′tro•ver′si•al′i•ty** (-shē-ăl′ĭ-tē, -sē-) *n.* — **con′tro•ver′sial•ly** *adv.*

con•tro•ver•sy (kŏn′trə-vûr′sē) *n., pl.* **-sies.** **1.** A dispute, esp. a public one, between sides holding opposing views. **2.** The act or practice of engaging in such disputes. [ME *controversie* < Lat. *contrōversia* < *contrōversus*, disputed : *contrā-*, contra- + *versus*, p.part. of *vertere*, to turn; see **wer-²***.]

con•tro•vert (kŏn′trə-vûrt′, kŏn′trə-vûrt′) *tr.v.* **-vert•ed, -vert•ing, -verts.** To raise arguments against; voice opposition to. [< CONTROVERSY.] — **con′tro•vert′i•ble** *adj.*

con•tu•ma•cious (kŏn′tə-mā′shəs, -tyə-) *adj.* Obstinately disobedient or rebellious; insubordinate. — **con′tu•ma′cious•ly** *adv.* — **con′tu•ma′cious•ness** *n.*

con•tu•ma•cy (kŏn′to͞o-mə-sē, -tyo͞o-) *n., pl.* **-cies.** Obstinate or contemptuous resistance to authority. [ME *contumacie* < Lat. *contumācia* < *contumāx*, insolent.]

con•tu•me•ly (kŏn′to͞o-mə-lē, -tyo͞o-, -təm-lē) *n., pl.* **-lies.** **1.** Rudeness or contempt arising from arrogance; insolence. **2.** An insolent or arrogant remark or act. [ME *contumelie* < OFr. < Lat. *contumēlia*; akin to *contumāx*, insolent.] — **con′tu•me′li•ous** (kŏn′tə-mē′lē-əs) *adj.* — **con′tu•me′li•ous•ly** *adv.*

con•tuse (kən-to͞oz′, -tyo͞oz′) *tr.v.* **-tused, -tus•ing, -tus•es.** To injure without breaking the skin; bruise. [ME *contusen* < Lat. *contundere, contūs-*, to beat : *com-*, com- + *tundere*, to beat.]

con•tu•sion (kən-to͞o′zhən, -tyo͞o′-) *n.* An injury in which the skin is not broken; a bruise.

co•nun•drum (kə-nŭn′drəm) *n.* **1.** A riddle in which a fanciful question is answered by a pun. **2.** A paradoxical, insoluble, or difficult problem; a dilemma. [?]

con•ur•ba•tion (kŏn′ər-bā′shən) *n.* A predominantly urban region including adjacent towns and suburbs; a metropolitan area. [CON- + Lat. *urbs*, city + -ATION.]

conv. *abbr.* **1.** Convention. **2.** Convertible. **3.** Convocation.

Conv. *abbr.* Conventual.

con•va•lesce (kŏn′və-lĕs′) *intr.v.* **-lesced, -lesc•ing, -lesc•es.** To return to health and strength after illness; recuperate. [Lat. *convalēscere* : *com-*, com- + *valēscere*, to grow strong, inchoative of *valēre*, to be strong; see **wal-***.]

con•va•les•cence (kŏn′və-lĕs′əns) *n.* **1.** Gradual return to health and strength after illness. **2.** The period needed for returning to health after illness. — **con′va•les′cent** *adj. & n.*

con•vect (kən-vĕkt′) *v.* **-vect•ed, -vect•ing, -vects.** — *tr.* To transfer (heat) by convection. — *intr.* To undergo convection. [Back-formation < CONVECTION.]

con•vec•tion (kən-vĕk′shən) *n.* **1.** The act or process of conveying; transmission. **2.** *Phys.* **a.** Heat transfer in a gas or liquid by the circulation of currents from one region to another. **b.** Fluid motion caused by an external force such as gravity. **3.** *Meteorol.* The transfer of heat or other atmospheric properties by massive motion within the atmosphere, esp.

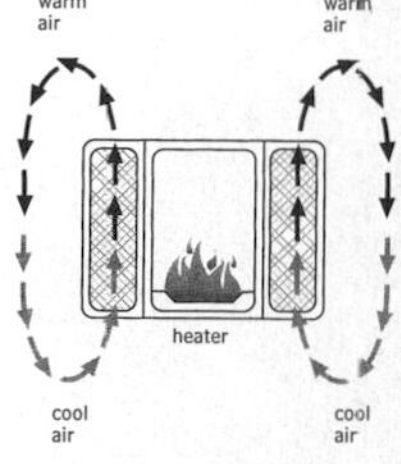

convection

ă pat | ā pay | âr care | ä father | ĕ pet | ē be | ĭ pit | ī pie | îr pier | ŏ pot | ō toe | ô paw
oi boy | ou out | o͝o took | o͞o boot | ŭ cut | ûr urge | th thin | *th* this | hw which | zh vision | ə about, item

Stress marks:
′ (primary);
′ (secondary), as in
dictionary (dĭk′shə-nĕr′ē)

by such motion directed upward. [LLat. *convectiō, convectiōn-* < *convectus*, p.part. of *convehere*, to carry together : Lat. *com-*, com- + Lat. *vehere*, to carry; see **wegh-***.] —**con·vec′tion·al** *adj.* —**con·vec′tive** *adj.* —**con·vec′tive·ly** *adv.*

con·vec·tor (kən-vĕk′tər) *n.* A partly enclosed, directly heated surface from which warm air circulates by convection.

con·vene (kən-vēn′) *v.* **-vened, -ven·ing, -venes.** —*intr.* To come together usu. for an official or public purpose; assemble formally. —*tr.* **1.** To cause to convene; convoke. **2.** To summon to appear, as before a tribunal. [ME *convenen* < OFr. *convenir* < Lat. *convenīre* : *com-*, com- + *venīre*, to come; see **gʷā-***.] —**con·ven′a·ble** *adj.* —**con·ven′er, con·ven′or** *n.*

con·ven·ience (kən-vēn′yəns) *n.* **1.** The quality of being suitable to one's comfort, purposes, or needs. **2.** Personal comfort or advantage. **3.** Something that increases comfort or saves work. **4.** *Chiefly British.* A lavatory.

convenience food *n.* A prepackaged food that can be prepared quickly and easily.

convenience store *n.* A small retail store that is open long hours and that typically sells staple groceries and snacks.

con·ven·ien·cy (kən-vēn′yən-sē) *n.*, *pl.* **-cies.** *Archaic.* Convenience.

con·ven·ient (kən-vēn′yənt) *adj.* **1.** Suited or favorable to one's comfort, purpose, or needs. **2.a.** Easy to reach; accessible. **b.** Close at hand; near: *convenient to transportation.* **3.** *Obsolete.* Fitting and proper; suitable. [ME < Lat. *conveniēns, convenient-*, pr.part. of *convenīre*, to be suitable, fit. See CONVENE.] —**con·ven′ient·ly** *adv.*

con·vent (kŏn′vənt, -vĕnt′) *n.* **1.** A community, esp. of nuns, bound by vows to a religious life under a superior. **2.** The building or buildings occupied by such a community. [ME *covent* < OFr. < Med.Lat. *conventus* < Lat., assembly < p.part. of *convenīre*, to assemble. See CONVENE.]

con·ven·ti·cle (kən-vĕn′tĭ-kəl) *n.* A religious meeting, esp. a secret or illegal one, such as those held by Dissenters in England and Scotland in the 16th and 17th centuries. [ME < Lat. *conventiculum*, meeting, dim. of *conventus*, assembly. See CONVENT.] —**con·ven′ti·cler** *n.*

con·ven·tion (kən-vĕn′shən) *n.* **1.a.** A formal meeting of members, representatives, or delegates, as of a political party or profession. **b.** The body of persons attending such an assembly. **2.** An agreement between states, sides, or military forces. **3.** General agreement on or acceptance of certain practices or attitudes. **4.** A practice or procedure widely observed in a group; a custom. **5.** A widely used device or technique, as in literature or painting. [ME *convencioun* < Lat. *conventiō, conventiōn-*, meeting < *conventus*, p.part. of *convenīre*, to assemble. See CONVENE.]

con·ven·tion·al (kən-vĕn′shə-nəl) *adj.* **1.** Based on or in accordance with general agreement, use, or practice; customary. **2.** Conforming to established practice or accepted standards; traditional. **3.a.** Devoted to or bound by conventions to the point of artificiality; ceremonious. **b.** Unimaginative; conformist. **4.** Represented, as in a work of art, in simplified or abstract form. **5.** Of, relating to, or resembling an assembly. **6.** Using means other than nuclear weapons or energy. —**con·ven′tion·al·ism** *n.* —**con·ven′tion·al·ist** *n.* —**con·ven′tion·al·ly** *adv.*

con·ven·tion·al·i·ty (kən-vĕn′shə-năl′ĭ-tē) *n.*, *pl.* **-ties.** **1.** The state, quality, or character of being conventional. **2.** A conventional act, idea, or practice. **3. conventionalities.** The rules of conventional social behavior.

con·ven·tion·al·ize (kən-vĕn′shə-nə-līz′) *tr.v.* **-ized, -iz·ing, -iz·es.** To make conventional. —**con·ven′tion·al·i·za′tion** (-vĕn′shə-nə-lĭ-zā′shən) *n.*

con·ven·tion·eer (kən-vĕn′shə-nîr′) *n.* One who attends a convention.

con·ven·tu·al (kən-vĕn′cho͞o-əl) *adj.* Of or relating to a convent. —*n.* **1.** A member of a convent. **2. Conventual.** A member of a branch of the Franciscan order that permits the accumulation and possession of common property. [ME < Med.Lat. *conventuālis* < *conventus*, convent. See CONVENT.]

con·verge (kən-vûrj′) *v.* **-verged, -verg·ing, -verg·es.** —*intr.* **1.a.** To tend toward or approach an intersecting point. **b.** To come together from different directions; meet. **2.** To tend toward or achieve union or a common conclusion or result. **3.** *Math.* To approach a limit. —*tr.* To cause to converge. [LLat. *convergere*, to incline together : Lat. *com-*, com- + Lat. *vergere*, to incline; see **wer-²***.]

con·ver·gence (kən-vûr′jəns) *n.* **1.** The act, condition, or fact of converging. **2.** *Math.* The property or manner of approaching a limit, such as a point, line, or value. **3.** The point of converging; a meeting place. **4.** *Physiol.* The coordinated turning of the eyes inward to focus on an object at close range. **5.** *Biol.* The adaptive evolution of superficially similar structures, such as bird wings, in unrelated species subjected to similar environments. —**con·ver′gen·cy** *n.* —**con·ver′gent** *adj.*

convertible
1989 Cadillac Allanté

convergent evolution *n.* See **convergence** 5.

con·ver·sant (kən-vûr′sənt, kŏn′vər-) *adj.* Familiar, as by study or experience. [ME *conversaunt*, associated with < OFr. *conversant*, pr.part. of *converser*, to associate with < Lat. *conversārī*. See CONVERSE¹.] —**con·ver′sance, con·ver′san·cy** *n.* —**con·ver′sant·ly** *adv.*

con·ver·sa·tion (kŏn′vər-sā′shən) *n.* **1.** A spoken exchange of thoughts, opinions, and feelings; a talk. **2.** An informal discussion of a matter by representatives of governments, institutions, or organizations. **3.** *Comp. Sci.* A real-time interaction with a computer. —**con′ver·sa′tion·al** *adj.* —**con′ver·sa′tion·al·ly** *adv.*

con·ver·sa·tion·al·ist (kŏn′vər-sā′shə-nə-lĭst) also **con·ver·sa·tion·ist** (-shə-nĭst) *n.* One given to or skilled at conversation.

conversation piece *n.* **1.** An unusual object that arouses comment or interest. **2.** A genre painting, popular esp. in the 18th century, depicting a group of fashionable people.

con·ver·sa·zi·o·ne (kŏn′vər-sät′sē-ō′nē, kôn′vĕr-sä-tsyô′nĕ) *n.*, *pl.* **-nes** or **-ni** (-nē). A meeting for conversation or discussion, esp. about art. [Ital. < Lat. *conversātiō, conversātiōn-*, dealings with persons < *conversātus*, p.part. of *conversārī*, to associate with. See CONVERSE¹.]

con·verse¹ (kən-vûrs′) *intr.v.* **-versed, -vers·ing, -vers·es.** **1.** To engage in a spoken exchange of thoughts, ideas, or feelings; talk. See Syns at **speak. 2.** *Comp. Sci.* To interact with a computer on-line. **3.** *Archaic.* To be familiar; associate. —*n.* (kŏn′vûrs′). **1.** Spoken interchange of thoughts and feelings; conversation. **2.** *Obsolete.* Social interaction. [ME *conversen*, to associate with < OFr. *converser* < Lat. *conversārī* : *com-*, com- + *versārī*, to occupy oneself; see **wer-²***.]

con·verse² (kən-vûrs′, kŏn′vûrs′) *adj.* Reversed, as in position, order, or action; contrary. —*n.* (kŏn′vûrs′). **1.** Something that has been reversed; an opposite. **2.** *Logic.* A proposition obtained by conversion. [Lat. *conversus*, p.part. of *convertere*, to turn around. See CONVERT.] —**con·verse′ly** *adv.*

con·ver·sion (kən-vûr′zhən, -shən) *n.* **1.a.** The act of converting. **b.** The state of being converted. **2.** A change in which one adopts a new religion, faith, or belief. **3.** Something that is changed from one use, function, or purpose to another. **4.** *Law.* **a.** The unlawful appropriation of another's property. **b.** The changing of real property to personal property or vice versa. **5.** The exchange of one type of security or currency for another. **6.** *Logic.* The interchange of the subject and predicate of a proposition. **7.** *Football.* A score made on a try for a point or points after a touchdown. **8.** *Psychiat.* A defense mechanism in which repressed ideas, conflicts, or impulses are manifested by bodily symptoms that have no physical cause. [ME *conversioun*, religious conversion < OFr. *conversion* < Lat. *conversiō, conversiōn-*, a turning around < *conversus*, p.part. of *convertere*, to turn around. See CONVERT.] —**con·ver′sion·al, con·ver′sion·ar′y** (-zhə-nĕr′ē, -shə-) *adj.*

conversion disorder *n.* See **conversion reaction.**

conversion factor *n.* A numerical factor used to multiply or divide a quantity expressed in one system of units in a conversion to another system.

conversion reaction *n.* A neurosis characterized by the presence of bodily symptoms having no discernible physical cause but for which there is evidence of a psychological conflict or need.

con·vert (kən-vûrt′) *v.* **-vert·ed, -vert·ing, -verts.** —*tr.* **1.** To change (something) into another form, substance, state, or product; transform. **2.** To change (something) from one use, function, or purpose to another. **3.** To persuade or induce to adopt a particular religion, faith, or belief. **4.** To exchange for something of equal value. **5.** To exchange (a security, for example) by substituting an equivalent of another form. **6.** To express in alternative units. **7.** *Logic.* To transform (a proposition) by conversion. **8.** *Law.* **a.** To appropriate (another's property) without right to one's own use. **b.** To change (property) from real to personal or from joint to separate or vice versa. —*intr.* **1.** To undergo a conversion: *converted to Islam.* **2.** To be converted: *a sofa that converts into a bed.* **3.** *Football.* To make a conversion. —*n.* (kŏn′vûrt′). One who has been converted, esp. from one religion or belief to another. [ME *converten* < OFr. *convertir* < Lat. *convertere*, to turn around : *com-*, com- + *vertere*, to turn; see **wer-²***.]

con·vert·ed rice (kən-vûr′tĭd) *n.* A white rice prepared from brown rice that has been soaked, steamed under pressure to force nutrients into the endosperm, and then dried and milled.

con·vert·er also **con·ver·tor** (kən-vûr′tər) *n.* **1.** A furnace in which pig iron is converted into steel by the Bessemer process. **2.** A machine that converts electric current from one kind to another. **3.** An electronic device that converts one frequency of a radio signal to another. **4.** A device that converts data from one code to another.

con·vert·i·ble (kən-vûr′tə-bəl) *adj.* **1.** That can be converted. **2.** Having a top that can be folded back or removed. **3.** Lawfully exchangeable for gold or another currency. —*n.* **1.** Something that can be converted. **2.** A convertible automobile. **3.** A convertible security. —**con·vert′i·bil′i·ty, con·vert′i·ble·ness** *n.* —**con·vert′i·bly** *adv.*

convertible security *n.* A security that at the holder's option may be exchanged for another asset.

con•vert•i•plane also **con•vert•a•plane** (kən-vûr′tə-plăn′) *n.* An airplane built to fly vertically as well as forward.

con•vex (kŏn′vĕks′, kən-vĕks′) *adj.* Having a surface or boundary that curves or bulges outward, as the exterior of a sphere. [Lat. *convexus.* See **wegh-***.] — **con′vex′ly** *adv.*

con•vex•i•ty (kən-vĕk′sĭ-tē) *n., pl.* **-ties. 1.** The state of being convex. **2.** A convex surface, body, part, or line.

con•vex•o-con•cave (kən-vĕk′sō-kən-kāv′) *adj.* **1.** Convex on one side and concave on the other. **2.** Having greater curvature on the convex side than on the concave side.

con•vex•o-con•vex (kən-vĕk′sō-kən-vĕks′) *adj.* Convex on both sides; biconvex. Used of a lens.

con•vey (kən-vā′) *tr.v.* **-veyed, -vey•ing, -veys. 1.** To take or carry from one place to another; transport. **2.** To serve as a medium of transmission for; transmit. **3.** To communicate or make known; impart. **4.** *Law.* To transfer ownership of or title to. **5.** *Archaic.* To steal. [ME *conveien* < OFr. *conveier* < Med.Lat. *conviāre,* to escort : Lat. *com-,* com- + *via,* way; see **wegh-***.] — **con•vey′a•ble** *adj.*

con•vey•ance (kən-vā′əns) *n.* **1.** The act of conveying. **2.** A means of conveying, esp. a vehicle for transportation. **3.** *Law.* **a.** Transfer of title to property from one person to another. **b.** The document by which a property transfer is effected. — **con•vey′anc•er** *n.*

con•vey•anc•ing (kən-vā′ən-sĭng) *n. Law.* The branch of legal practice dealing with the conveyance of property or real estate.

con•vey•er also **con•vey•or** (kən-vā′ər) *n.* One that conveys, esp. a mechanical apparatus, such as a moving belt, that transports materials or items from one place to another.

con•vict (kən-vĭkt′) *v.* **-vict•ed, -vict•ing, -victs.** — *tr.* **1.** *Law.* To find or prove (someone) guilty of an offense or crime, esp. by the verdict of a court. **2.** To show or declare to be blameworthy; condemn: *His remarks convicted him of insensitivity.* **3.** To make aware of one's sinfulness or guilt. — *intr.* To return a verdict of guilty in a court. — *n.* (kŏn′vĭkt′). *Law.* **1.** A person found or declared guilty of an offense or crime. **2.** A person serving a sentence of imprisonment. — *adj. Archaic.* Found guilty; convicted. [ME *convicten* < Lat. *convincere, convict-.* See CONVINCE.]

con•vic•tion (kən-vĭk′shən) *n.* **1.** *Law.* **a.** The judgment of a jury or judge that a person is guilty of a crime as charged. **b.** The state of being found or proved guilty. **2.a.** The act or process of convincing. **b.** The state of being convinced. See Syns at **certainty. 3.** A fixed or strong belief. — **con•vic′tion•al** *adj.*

con•vic•tive (kən-vĭk′tĭv) *adj.* Having power or serving to convince or convict. — **con•vic′tive•ly** *adv.*

con•vince (kən-vĭns′) *tr.v.* **-vinced, -vinc•ing, -vinc•es. 1.** To bring by the use of argument or evidence to firm belief or a course of action. **2.** *Obsolete.* To prove to be wrong or guilty. **3.** *Obsolete.* To conquer; overpower. [Lat. *convincere,* to prove wrong : *com-,* com- + *vincere,* to conquer; see **weik-³***.] — **con•vince′ment** *n.* — **con•vinc′er** *n.* — **con•vinc′i•ble** *adj.*

con•vinc•ing (kən-vĭn′sĭng) *adj.* **1.** Serving to convince: *a convincing argument.* **2.** Believable; plausible. See Syns at **valid.** — **con•vinc′ing•ly** *adv.* — **con•vinc′ing•ness** *n.*

con•viv•i•al (kən-vĭv′ē-əl) *adj.* **1.** Fond of feasting, drinking, and good company; sociable. **2.** Merry; festive: *a convivial atmosphere.* [LLat. *convīviālis* < Lat. *convīvium,* banquet : *com-,* com- + *vīvere,* to live; see **gʷei-***.] — **con•viv′i•al′i•ty** (-ăl′ĭ-tē) *n.* — **con•viv′i•al•ly** *adv.*

con•vo•ca•tion (kŏn′və-kā′shən) *n.* **1.a.** The act of convoking. **b.** A group of people convoked, esp. the members of a college or university community who are assembled for a ceremony. **2.** A clerical assembly of the Anglican Church similar to a synod but assembling only when called. **3.** An assembly of the clergy and representative laity of a section of a diocese of the Episcopal Church. — **con′vo•ca′tion•al** *adj.*

con•voke (kən-vōk′) *tr.v.* **-voked, -vok•ing, -vokes.** To cause to assemble in a meeting; convene. [Fr. *convoquer* < OFr. < Lat. *convocāre* : *com-,* com- + *vocāre,* to call; see **wekʷ-***.] — **con•vok′er** *n.*

con•vo•lute (kŏn′və-lo͞ot′) *adj.* Rolled or coiled together in overlapping whorls, as certain leaves or shells. — *intr. & tr.v.* **-lut•ed, -lut•ing, -lutes.** To coil or fold or cause to coil or fold in overlapping whorls. [Lat. *convolūtus,* p.part. of *convolvere,* to convolve. See CONVOLVE.] — **con′vo•lute′ly** *adv.*

con•vo•lut•ed (kŏn′və-lo͞o′tĭd) *adj.* **1.** Having numerous overlapping coils or folds. **2.** Intricate; complicated.

con•vo•lu•tion (kŏn′və-lo͞o′shən) *n.* **1.** A form or part that is folded or coiled. **2.** One of the convex folds of the surface of the brain. — **con′vo•lu′tion•al** *adj.*

con•volve (kən-vŏlv′) *v.* **-volved, -volv•ing, -volves.** — *tr.* To roll together; coil up. — *intr.* To form convolutions. [Lat. *convolvere* : *com-,* com- + *volvere,* to roll; see **wel-²***.]

con•vol•vu•lus (kən-vŏl′vyə-ləs) *n., pl.* **-lus•es** or **-li** (-lī′). Any of various mostly trailing or twining plants of the widespread genus *Convolvulus,* having funnel-shaped flowers. [Lat., bindweed < *convolvere,* to intertwine. See CONVOLVE.]

con•voy (kŏn′voi′) *n.* **1.** The act of accompanying or escorting, esp. for protective purposes. **2.** An accompanying and protecting force, as of ships or troops. **3.** A group, as of ships or motor vehicles, traveling together for safety or convenience. — *tr.v.* (kŏn′voi′, kən-voi′) **-voyed, -voy•ing, -voys.** To accompany, esp. for protection; escort. [< ME *convoyen,* to escort < OFr. *convoier,* var. of *conveier.* See CONVEY.]

con•vul•sant (kən-vŭl′sənt) *adj.* Causing or producing convulsions. — *n.* A convulsant agent, such as a drug.

con•vulse (kən-vŭls′) *tr.v.* **-vulsed, -vuls•ing, -vuls•es. 1.** To shake or agitate violently. **2.** To affect with muscular convulsions. **3.** To cause to shake with laughter or strong emotion. [Lat. *convellere, convuls-,* to pull violently : *com-,* com- + *vellere,* to pull.]

con•vul•sion (kən-vŭl′shən) *n.* **1.** An intense, paroxysmal, involuntary muscular contraction. **2.** An uncontrolled fit, as of laughter; a paroxysm. **3.** A violent disturbance.

con•vul•sive (kən-vŭl′sĭv) *adj.* **1.** Marked by or having the nature of convulsions. **2.** Having or producing convulsions. — **con•vul′sive•ly** *adv.* — **con•vul′sive•ness** *n.*

Con•way (kŏn′wā′). A city of central AR NNW of Little Rock. Pop. 26,481.

co•ny (kō′nē, kŭn′ē) *n.* Var. of **coney¹.**

coo (ko͞o) *v.* **cooed, coo•ing, coos.** — *intr.* **1.** To utter the murmuring sound of a dove or pigeon or a sound resembling it. **2.** To talk fondly or amorously in murmurs. — *tr.* To express or utter with soft murmuring sounds. [Imit.] — **coo′er** *n.*

Cooch Be•har (ko͞och′ bə-här′). A former princely state of NE India; came under British rule in 1772.

cook (ko͝ok) *v.* **cooked, cook•ing, cooks.** — *tr.* **1.** To prepare (food) for eating by applying heat. **2.** To prepare or treat by heating. **3.** *Slang.* To alter or falsify so as to make a more favorable impression; doctor. — *intr.* **1.** To prepare food for eating by applying heat. **2.** To undergo application of heat esp. for the purpose of later ingestion. **3.** *Slang.* To happen or develop. **4.** *Slang.* To proceed or perform very well. — *n.* A person who prepares food for eating. — ***phrasal verb.* cook up.** *Informal.* To fabricate; concoct. [ME *coken* < *coke,* cook < OE *cōc* < VLat. **cōcus* < Lat. *cocus, coquus* < *coquere,* to cook. See **pekʷ-***.]

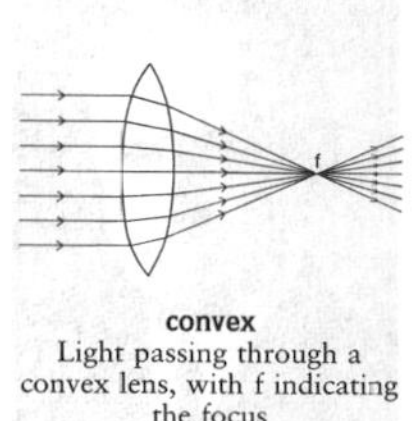
convex
Light passing through a convex lens, with f indicating the focus

Cook (ko͝ok), **James.** "Captain Cook." 1728–79. British navigator and explorer who commanded three major voyages of discovery, charting many islands of the Pacific Ocean.

Cook, Mount. Also **A•o•rang•i** (ä′ō-räng′gē). A mountain, 3,766.4 m (12,349 ft), of New Zealand on South I. in the Southern Alps.

cook•book (ko͝ok′bo͝ok′) *n.* A book containing recipes and other information about the preparation of food.

Cooke (ko͝ok), **Jay.** 1821–1905. Amer. financier whose bank collapse led to the Panic of 1873.

cook•er (ko͝ok′ər) *n.* **1.** One that cooks, esp. a utensil or an appliance for cooking. **2.** A person employed to operate cooking apparatuses in the commercial preparation of food and drink.

cook•er•y (ko͝ok′ə-rē) *n., pl.* **-ies. 1.** The art or practice of preparing food. **2.** A place for cooking.

Cooke•ville (ko͝ok′vĭl′). A city of central TN E of Nashville. Pop. 21,744.

cook•ie also **cook•y** (ko͝ok′ē) *n., pl.* **-ies. 1.** A small, usu. flat and crisp cake made from sweetened dough. **2.** *Slang.* A person. [Du. *koekje,* dim. of *koek,* cake < MDu. *koeke.*]

Cook Inlet. An inlet of the Gulf of Alaska in S AK W of the Kenai Peninsula.

Cook Islands. An island group of the S Pacific SE of Samoa; probably inhabited by Polynesians more than 1,500 years ago and first sighted by Capt. James Cook in 1773.

cook-off (ko͝ok′ôf′, -ŏf′) *n.* A cooking competition.

cook•out (ko͝ok′out′) *n.* A meal cooked and served outdoors.

Cook Strait. A narrow channel separating North I. and South I. in New Zealand.

conveyer

cook•ware (ko͝ok′wâr′) *n.* Cooking utensils.

cool (ko͞ol) *adj.* **cool•er, cool•est. 1.** Neither warm nor very cold; moderately cold. See Syns at **cold. 2.** Giving or suggesting relief from heat: *a cool blouse.* **3.** Marked by calm self-control: *a cool negotiator.* **4.** Marked by indifference, disdain, or dislike; unfriendly or unresponsive: *a cool greeting.* **5.** Of, relating to, or characteristic of colors, such as blue and green, that produce the impression of coolness. **6.** *Slang.* Excellent; first-rate: *a cool sports car.* **7.** *Slang.* Entire; full: *worth a cool million.* — *v.* **cooled, cool•ing, cools.** — *tr.* **1.** To make less warm. **2.** To make less ardent, intense, or zealous. — *intr.* **1.** To become less warm: *took a dip to cool off.* **2.** To become calmer. — *n.* **1.** A cool place, part, or time. **2.** The state or quality of being cool. **3.** *Slang.* Composure; poise. — ***idioms.* cool it.** *Slang.* To calm down; relax. **cool (one's) heels.** *Informal.* To wait or be kept waiting. [ME *cole* < OE *cōl.* See **gel-***.] — **cool′ish** *adj.* — **cool′ly** *adv.* — **cool′ness** *n.*

cool•ant (ko͞o′lənt) *n.* An agent that produces cooling, esp. a fluid that draws off heat by circulating through an engine.

cool•er (ko͞o′lər) *n.* **1.** A device, container, or room that cools or keeps cool. **2.** A cold drink, often a mixture of white wine and juice. **3.** *Slang.* A jail.

Coo•ley's anemia (ko͞o′lēz) *n.* A usu. fatal form of thalassemia

ă **pat**	oi **boy**
ā **pay**	ou **out**
âr **care**	o͝o **took**
ä **father**	o͞o **boot**
ĕ **pet**	ŭ **cut**
ē **be**	ûr **urge**
ĭ **pit**	th **thin**
ī **pie**	*th* **this**
îr **pier**	hw **which**
ŏ **pot**	zh **vision**
ō **toe**	ə **about,**
ô **paw**	**item**

Stress marks:
′ (primary);
′ (secondary), as in
dictionary (dĭk′shə-nĕr′ē)

soft, porous limestone, composed essentially of fragments of shells and coral and used as a building material. [Sp., cockle, prob. dim. of *concha*, shell < Lat., mussel. See CONCH.]

co•qui•to (kō-kē′tō) *n., pl.* **-tos.** A feather-leaved palm *(Jubaea chilensis)* native to Chile and having a sugary sap used for making wine and a kind of honey. [Sp., dim. of *coco*, coco palm < Port. *côco*. See COCONUT.]

cor. *abbr.* **1.** Corner. **2.** *Mus.* Cornet. **3.** Coroner. **4.** Corpus. **5.** Correction. **6.a.** Correspondence; correspondent. **b.** Corresponding.

Cor. *abbr. Bible.* Corinthians.

coral

cor•a•cle (kôr′ə-kəl, kŏr′-) *n. Naut.* A small rounded boat made of waterproof material stretched over a wicker or wooden frame. [Welsh *corwgl* < MIr. *curach* < OIr.]

cor•a•coid (kôr′ə-koid′, kŏr′-) *n.* **1.** A bony process projecting from the scapula toward the sternum in mammals. **2.** A beak-shaped bone articulating with the scapula and sternum in most lower vertebrates, such as birds and reptiles. [NLat. *coracoīdēs* < Gk. *korakoeidēs*, ravenlike : *korax*, *korak-*, raven + *-oeidēs*, -oid.] **— cor′a•coid** *adj.*

cor•al (kôr′əl, kŏr′-) *n.* **1.a.** A rocklike deposit consisting of the calcareous skeletons secreted by various anthozoans and often accumulating to form reefs or islands in warm seas. **b.** Any of numerous chiefly colonial marine polyps of the class Anthozoa that secrete such calcareous skeletons. **c.** The red-orange, pinkish, or white deposits secreted by corals of the genus *Corallium*. **d.** An object made of this material. **2.** *Color.* A deep or strong pink to moderate red or reddish orange. **3.** The unfertilized eggs of a female lobster, which turn reddish when cooked. *— adj. Color.* Of the color coral. [ME < OFr. < Lat. *corallium* < Gk. *korallion*.]

cor•al-bells (kôr′əl-bĕlz′, kŏr′-) *pl.n. (used with a sing. or pl. v.)* A species of alumroot *(Heuchera sanguinea)* native to the southwest United States and Mexico and cultivated for its clusters of bell-shaped flowers.

coral snake

cor•al•ber•ry (kôr′əl-bĕr′ē, kŏr′-) *n.* A North American deciduous shrub *(Symphoricarpos orbiculatus)* cultivated for its abundant clusters of coral-red berrylike fruits.

coral fungus *n.* Any of numerous fungi, esp. of the family Clavariaceae, whose spore-bearing structures resemble coral.

Cor•al Ga•bles (kôr′əl gā′bəlz, kŏr′-). A city of SE FL on Biscayne Bay SW of Miami. Pop. 40,091.

cor•al•line (kôr′ə-lĭn, -līn′, kŏr′-) *adj.* **1.** Of, consisting of, or producing coral. **2.** Resembling coral, esp. in color. *— n.* **1.** Any of various red algae of the family Corallinaceae whose fronds are covered with calcareous deposits. **2.** Any of various organisms that resemble coral. [Fr. *corallin* < LLat. *corallīnus* < Lat. *corallium*, coral. See CORAL.]

cor•al•loid (kôr′ə-loid′, kŏr′-) also **cor•al•loid•al** (-loid′l) *adj.* Resembling coral in appearance or form. [Lat. *corallium*, coral; see CORAL + -OID.]

coral pink *n. Color.* A moderate to deep yellowish pink.

coral reef *n.* An erosion-resistant marine ridge or mound consisting chiefly of compacted coral.

cor•al•root (kôr′əl-ro͞ot′, -ro͝ot′, kŏr′-) *n.* Any of several saprophytic, chiefly New World orchids of the genus *Corallorhiza*, having leafless stems and small flowers.

corbel

Coral Sea. An arm of the SW Pacific Ocean bounded by New Hebrides, NE Australia, and SE New Guinea.

coral snake *n.* Any of various venomous snakes of the genus *Micrurus*, native to tropical America and the southern United States and having red, yellow, and black bands.

Coral Springs. A city of SE FL, a suburb of Fort Lauderdale. Pop. 79,443.

coral vine *n.* A climbing woody vine *(Antigonon leptopus)* native to Mexico and cultivated for its red to white flowers.

Co•ran•tijn (kōr′ən-tīn′, kôr′-). See **Courantyne.**

cor•ban (kôr′bən, -băn′) *n.* A sacrifice made to God by the ancient Hebrews at the Temple in Jerusalem. [ME < LLat. < Gk. *korban* < Heb. *qurbān*.]

cor•beil also **cor•beille** (kôr′bəl, kôr-bā′) *n.* A sculptured basket of flowers or fruits used as an architectural ornament. [Fr. *corbeille* < LLat. *corbicula*, dim. of Lat. *corbis*, basket.]

cor•bel (kôr′bəl, -bĕl′) *n.* A bracket of stone, wood, or other building material, projecting from the face of a wall and generally used to support a cornice or an arch. *— tr.v.* **-beled, -bel•ing, -bels** also **-belled, -bel•ling, -bels.** To provide with or support by a corbel. [ME < OFr., dim. of *corp*, raven (being similar in shape to a raven's beak) < Lat. *corvus*.]

cor•bel•ing (kôr′bə-lĭng, -bĕl′-) *n.* An overlapping arrangement of bricks or stones in which each course extends farther out from the wall than the course below.

Cor•bett (kôr′bət), **James John.** "Gentleman Jim." 1866–1933. Amer. heavyweight boxing champion (1892–97).

cor•bie gable (kôr′bē) *n.* A gable roof with corbie-steps.

cor•bie-step also **cor•bie•step** (kôr′bē-stĕp′) *n.* One of a series of steps or steplike projections on the top of a gable wall. [ME *corbie*, raven < OFr. *corbin* < Lat. *corvīnus*, ravenlike. See CORBINA.]

cor•bi•na (kôr-bē′nə) also **cor•vi•na** (-vē′nə) *n.* **1.** A food and game fish *(Menticirrhus undulatus)* of North American Pacific waters. **2.** Any of several related marine fishes of the family Sciaenidae. [Sp. *corbina*, *corvina* < fem. of *corvino*, ravenlike (from its color) < Lat. *corvīnus* < *corvus*, raven.]

Cor•co•va•do (kôr′kə-vä′dō, kôr′kô-vä′do͞o). A mountain, 704.6 m (2,310 ft), of SE Brazil overlooking Rio de Janeiro; site of an enormous concrete statue of Christ the Redeemer.

Cor•cy•ra (kôr-sī′rə). See **Corfu.**

cord (kôrd) *n.* **1.** A slender rope usu. made of twisted strands or fibers. **2.** An insulated flexible electric wire fitted with a plug or plugs. **3.** A hangman's rope. **4.** An influence, feeling, or force that binds or restrains; a bond or tie. **5.** Also **chord** (*also* kōrd). *Anat.* A long ropelike structure, such as a nerve or tendon. **6.a.** A raised rib on the surface of cloth. **b.** A fabric or cloth with such ribs. **7. cords.** Trousers made of corduroy. **8.** A unit of quantity for cut fuel wood, equal to a stack measuring 4 × 4 × 8 feet or 128 cubic feet (3.62 cubic meters). *— tr.v.* **cord•ed, cord•ing, cords. 1.** To fasten or bind with a cord. **2.** To furnish with a cord. **3.** To pile (wood) in cords. [ME < OFr. *corde* < Lat. *chorda* < Gk. *khordē*. See **gherə-*.**] **— cord′er** *n.*

cord•age (kôr′dĭj) *n.* **1.** Cords or ropes, esp. the ropes in the rigging of a ship. **2.** The amount of wood in an area as measured in cords.

cor•date (kôr′dāt′) *adj.* Having a heart-shaped outline: *a cordate leaf.* [NLat. *cordātus* < Lat. *cor*, *cord-*, heart. See **kerd-*.**] **— cor′date′ly** *adv.*

Cor•day (kôr-dā′, kôr′dā), **Charlotte.** 1768–98. French Revolutionary heroine who was guillotined for the assassination of Jean Paul Marat in 1793.

cord•ed (kôr′dĭd) *adj.* **1.** Tied or bound with cords. **2.** Furnished with or made of cords. **3.** Ribbed or twilled: *a corded bedspread.* **4.** Stacked in cords: *corded firewood.*

cord grass *n.* Any of several perennial grasses of the genus *Spartina*, several of which form colonies in salt marshes.

cor•dial (kôr′jəl) *adj.* **1.** Warm and sincere; friendly: *a cordial greeting.* **2.** Strongly felt; fervent. **3.** Serving to invigorate; stimulating. *— n.* **1.** A stimulant; a tonic. **2.** A liqueur. [ME, of the heart < Med.Lat. *cordiālis* < Lat. *cor*, *cord-*, heart. See **kerd-*.**] **— cor•dial′i•ty** (-jăl′ĭ-tē, -jē-ăl′-, -dē-ăl′-), **cor′dial•ness** *n.* **— cor′dial•ly** *adv.*

cor•di•er•ite (kôr′dē-ə-rīt′) *n.* A dichroic violet-blue to gray mineral silicate of magnesium, aluminum, and sometimes iron. [Fr., after Pierre L. *Cordier* (1777–1861), French geologist.]

cor•di•form (kôr′də-fôrm′) *adj.* Heart-shaped. [Lat. *cor*, *cord-*, heart; see **kerd-*** + -FORM.]

cor•dil•le•ra (kôr′dl-yâr′ə, kôr-dĭl′ər-ə) *n.* A chain of mountains, esp. the principal mountain system of a continent. [Sp. < *cordilla*, dim. of *cuerda*, cord < Lat. *chorda*. See CORD.] **— cor′dil•le′ran** (-yâr′ən) *adj.*

Cor•dil•le•ra Cen•tral (kôr′dĭl-yĕr′ə sĕn-träl′, *-thē*-yĕ′rä). **1.** The central of three ranges of the Andes in W Colombia. **2.** A mountain range of central Dominican Republic. **3.** A range of the Andes extending NW and SE in N-central Peru. **4.** A range of S-central Puerto Rico.

Cordillera Mé•ri•da (mĕr′ĭ-də, mĕ′rē-*th*ä). A mountain range of W Venezuela extending NE and SW.

Cordillera Oc•ci•den•tal (ŏk′sĭ-dĕn-täl′, ôk′sē-*th*ĕn-). A range of the W Andes with branches in W Colombia and along the Pacific coast of Peru.

Cordillera O•rien•tal (ôr′ē-ĕn-täl′, ô′ryĕn-). A range of the E Andes with branches in central Bolivia, W Colombia, and SE Peru.

Cordillera Re•al (rā-äl′). A range of the Andes with branches in W Bolivia and central Ecuador.

Cor•dil•le•ras (kôr′dĭl-yĕr′əz, kôr′*th*ē-yĕ′räs). The complex of mountain ranges in W North America, Central America, and South America, extending from AK to Cape Horn.

cord•ite (kôr′dīt′) *n.* A smokeless explosive powder consisting of nitrocellulose, nitroglycerin, and petrolatum that has been dissolved in acetone, dried, and extruded in cords.

cord•less (kôrd′lĭs) *adj.* **1.** Having no cord. **2.** Using batteries as a source of power. **— cord′less•ly** *adv.*

cor•do•ba (kôr′də-bə, -və) *n.* See table at **currency.** [Am.Sp. *córdoba*, after Francisco Fernández de *Córdoba* (1475?–1526?), Spanish explorer.]

Cór•do•ba (kôr′də-bə, -və, *-th*ô-vä). **1.** A city of N-central Argentina NW of Buenos Aires; founded 1573. Pop. 993,055. **2.** A city of S Spain on the Guadalquivir R. ENE of Seville. Pop. 291,370. **— Cor′do•van** (-vən) *adj. & n.*

cor•don (kôr′dn) *n.* **1.** A line of people, military posts, or ships stationed around an area to enclose or guard it. **2.** A cord, braid, or ribbon worn as a fastening or an ornament. **3.** *Archit.* A stringcourse. **4.** *Bot.* A fruit tree pruned and trained to grow on a support as a ropelike stem. *— tr.v.* **-doned, -don•ing, -dons.** To form a cordon around (an area) so as to prevent movement in or out. [Fr. < OFr., dim. of *corde*, cord. See CORD.]

cor•don bleu (kôr′dôɴ blœ′) *n., pl.* **cor•dons bleus** (kôr′dôɴ blœ′). A person highly distinguished in a field, esp. a master chef. [Fr. : *cordon*, ribbon + *bleu*, blue.]

cor•don sa•ni•taire (kôr-dôɴ′ sä-nē-târ′) *n., pl.* **cor•dons sa•ni•taires** (kôr-dôɴ′ sä-nē-târ′). **1.** A barrier designed to

ă pat	oi boy
ā pay	ou out
âr care	o͝o took
ä father	o͞o boot
ĕ pet	ŭ cut
ē be	ûr urge
ĭ pit	th thin
ī pie	*th* this
îr pier	hw which
ŏ pot	zh vision
ō toe	ə about, item
ô paw	

Stress marks:
′ (primary);
′ (secondary), as in dictionary (dĭk′shə-nĕr′ē)

prevent a disease from spreading. **2.** A chain of states organized around a nation considered potentially hostile. [Fr., quarantine line : *cordon*, line + *sanitaire*, sanitary.]

cor•do•van (kôr′də-vən) *n.* A fine leather originally made of goatskin but now more frequently of split horsehide. [Sp. *cordován* < *Córdova*, Córdoba, Spain.]

cor•du•roy (kôr′də-roi′) *n.* **1.** A durable cut-pile fabric, usu. made of cotton, with vertical ribs. **2. corduroys.** Trousers made of corduroy. **3.** A road made of logs laid down crosswise. —*tr.v.* **-royed, -roy•ing, -roys.** To build (a corduroy). [Prob. < CORD + obsolete *duroy*, a coarse woolen fabric.] —**cor′du•roy′** *adj.*

cord•wood (kôrd′wo͝od′) *n.* **1.** Wood cut and piled in cords. **2.** Wood sold by the cord.

core (kôr, kōr) *n.* **1.** The hard or fibrous central part of certain fruits, containing the seeds. **2.** The central or innermost part. **3.** The basic or most important part; the essence. **4.** A set of subjects or courses that make up a required portion of a curriculum. **5.** *Elect.* A soft iron rod in a coil or transformer that provides a path for and intensifies the magnetic field produced by the windings. **6.a.** *Comp. Sci.* A memory, esp. one consisting of a series of tiny doughnut-shaped masses of magnetic material. **b.** One of the magnetic doughnut-shaped masses that make up such a memory. **7.** The central portion of Earth below the mantle, beginning at a depth of about 2,900 kilometers (1,800 miles) and probably consisting of iron and nickel. **8.** A mass of dry sand placed within a mold to provide openings or shape to a casting. **9.** The part of a nuclear reactor where fission occurs. **10.** A cylindrical mass drilled vertically into the earth and removed to determine composition or presence of oil or gas. **11.** The base to which veneer woods are glued. —*tr.v.* **cored, cor•ing, cores.** To remove the core of: *core apples.* [ME.]

CORE *abbr.* Congress of Racial Equality.

core dump *n. Comp. Sci.* A copy of the data stored in the core memory of a computer, usu. kept in external storage.

co•re•lig•ion•ist (kō′rĭ-lĭj′ə-nĭst) *n.* One having the same religion as another.

core memory *n. Comp. Sci.* See **core** 6a.

cor•e•op•sis (kôr′ē-ŏp′sĭs, kōr-) *n.* Any of various plants of the genus *Coreopsis* in the composite family, having showy radiate flower heads. [NLat. *Coreopsis*, genus name : Gk. *koris*, bedbug; see **sker-**[1]***** + -OPSIS.]

co•re•pres•sor (kō′rĭ-prĕs′ər) *n.* A substance that combines with and activates a genetic repressor, thus preventing gene transcription and inhibiting protein synthesis.

cor•er (kôr′ər, kōr′-) *n.* A device for coring apples.

co•re•spon•dent (kō′rĭ-spŏn′dənt) *n. Law.* A person charged with having committed adultery with the defendant in a divorce suit. —**co′re•spon′den•cy** *n.*

corf (kôrf) *n., pl.* **corves** (kôrvz). *Chiefly British.* A truck, tub, or basket used in a mine. [ME, basket < MDu. *corf* or MLGer. *korf*, both prob. < Lat. *corbis.*]

Cor•fu (kôr′fo͞o, -fyo͞o, kôr-fo͞o′) also **Kér•ki•ra** (kĕr′kē-rä′). Formerly **Cor•cy•ra** (kôr-sī′rə). An island of Greece in the Ionian Is. off the NW coast of the mainland; settled c. 700 B.C.

cor•gi (kôr′gē) *n.* A Welsh corgi. [Welsh : *cor*, dwarf + *ci*, dog; see **kwon-***.]

cor•i•a•ceous (kôr′ē-ā′shəs, kōr′-) *adj.* Of or like leather, esp. in texture. [< LLat. *coriāceus* < Lat. *corium*, leather. See **sker-**[1]*****.]

co•ri•an•der (kôr′ē-ăn′dər, kōr′-, kôr′ē-ăn′dər, kōr′-) *n.* **1.** An aromatic annual Eurasian herb *(Coriandrum sativum)* in the parsley family, cultivated for its edible fruits, leafy shoots, and roots. **2.** The young leafy plantlets of this herb, used in salads and as a flavoring and garnish. **3.** The seedlike fruit of this plant, used as a seasoning. [ME *coriandre* < OFr. < Lat. *coriandrum* < Gk. *koriandron.*]

Cor•inth (kôr′ĭnth, kŏr′-) also **Kó•rin•thos** (kô′rĭn-thôs′). A city of S Greece in the NE Peloponnesus on the Gulf of Corinth near the site of the ancient city of **Corinth**, a rich maritime power in the 7th and 6th cent. B.C. Pop. 22,658.

Corinth, Gulf of. Formerly **Gulf of Le•pan•to** (lĭ-păn′tō, lĕ′-pän-tô). An inlet of the Ionian Sea between the Peloponnesus and central Greece.

Corinth, Isthmus of. A narrow isthmus connecting central Greece with the Peloponnesus and crossed by the **Corinth Canal** (constructed 1881–93).

Co•rin•thi•an (kə-rĭn′thē-ən) *adj.* **1.** Of or relating to ancient Corinth or its people or culture. **2.** *Archit.* Of or relating to the Corinthian order. **3.** Elegantly or elaborately ornate. **4.** Given to licentious and profligate luxury. —*n.* **1.** A native or inhabitant of Corinth. **2.** A luxury-loving person; a bon vivant. **3.** A wealthy amateur sportsman, esp. an amateur yachtsman. **4. Corinthians.** *(used with a sing. v.)* See table at **Bible.**

Corinthian order *n. Archit.* The most ornate of the three classical orders, characterized by a column having a bell-shaped capital decorated with acanthus leaves.

Co•ri•o•lis force (kôr′ē-ō′lĭs, kōr′-) *n.* A fictitious force used mathematically to describe motion, as of aircraft or cloud formations, relative to a uniformly rotating frame of reference such as Earth. [After Gaspard G. de *Coriolis* (1792–1843), French mathematician.]

co•ri•um (kôr′ē-əm, kōr′-) *n., pl.* **-ri•a** (-ē-ə). *Anat.* See **dermis.** [Lat., skin. See **sker-**[1]*****.]

cork (kôrk) *n.* **1.** The lightweight elastic outer bark of the cork oak, used esp. for bottle closures, insulation, and floats. **2.a.** Something made of cork, esp. a bottle stopper. **b.** A bottle stopper made of other material, such as plastic. **3.** A small float used on a fishing line or net for buoyancy. **4.** *Bot.* A nonliving water-resistant tissue formed on the outside of the cork cambium in many seed plants. —*tr.v.* **corked, cork•ing, corks. 1.** To stop or seal with a cork. **2.** To restrain or check; hold back. **3.** To blacken with burnt cork. [ME < Du. *kurk* or LGer. *korck*, both < Sp. *alcorque*, cork-soled shoe, prob. < Ar. dial. *al-qūrq* < Lat. *quercus*, oak. See **perkʷu-***.]

Cork (kôrk). A city of S Ireland near the head of **Cork Harbor**, an inlet of the Atlantic Ocean. Pop. 136,344.

cork•age (kôr′kĭj) *n.* A charge at a restaurant for serving a bottle of liquor that was not bought on the premises.

cork•board (kôrk′bôrd′, -bōrd′) *n.* A construction and insulating material made of compressed and baked granules of cork.

cork cambium *n. Bot.* A lateral ring of meristematic tissue found in woody seed plants, producing cork on the outside of the ring and parenchyma on the inside of the ring.

corked (kôrkt) *adj.* **1.** Sealed with or as if with a cork. **2.** Tainted in flavor by an unsound cork. **3.** Blackened by burnt cork.

cork•er (kôr′kər) *n.* **1.** One that corks bottles, for example. **2.** *Slang.* A remarkable or astounding person or thing.

cork•ing (kôr′kĭng) *Slang.* —*adj.* Splendid; fine: *a corking party.* —*adv.* Used as an intensive. [< CORKER.]

cork oak *n.* A Mediterranean evergreen oak tree *(Quercus suber)* having thick bark that is periodically stripped, yielding commercial cork.

cork•screw (kôrk′skro͞o′) *n.* A device for drawing corks from bottles, consisting of a pointed metal spiral attached to a handle. —*adj.* Spiral in shape. —*intr. & tr.v.* **-screwed, -screw•ing, -screws.** To move or cause to move in a spiral or winding course.

cork•wood (kôrk′wo͝od′) *n.* **1.** A deciduous shrub or small tree *(Leitneria floridana)* native to the southeast United States and having lightweight wood. **2.** See **balsa.**

cork•y (kôr′kē) *adj.* **-i•er, -i•est. 1.** Of or resembling cork. **2.** *Informal.* Lively; buoyant. —**cork′i•ness** *n.*

corm (kôrm) *n.* A food-storing underground stem, sometimes bearing papery scale leaves, as in the crocus. [NLat. *cormus* < Gk. *kormos*, a trimmed tree trunk. See **sker-**[1]*****.]

cor•mel (kôr′məl, kôr-mĕl′) *n.* A small young corm produced by a mature corm. [CORM + *-el*, dim. suff. (< Lat. *-ellus*).]

cor•mo•rant (kôr′mər-ənt, -mə-rănt′) *n.* **1.** Any of several large marine diving birds of the genus *Phalacrocorax*, having webbed feet, a hooked bill, and a distensible pouch. **2.** A greedy, rapacious person. —*adj.* Greedy; rapacious. [ME *cormoraunt* < OFr. *cormorant* : *corp*, raven; see CORBEL + *marenc*, of the sea (< Lat. *marīnus*; see MARINE).]

corn[1] (kôrn) *n.* **1.a.** Any of numerous cultivated forms of a usu. tall annual cereal grass *(Zea mays)* bearing grains or kernels on large ears. **b.** The grains or kernels of this plant, used as food or fodder and yielding an edible oil or starch. **c.** An ear of this plant. **2.** *Chiefly British.* Any of various cereal plants or grains, esp. wheat or oats. **3.a.** A single grain of a cereal plant. **b.** A seed or fruit of various other plants, such as a peppercorn. **4.** Corn snow. **5.** *Informal.* Corn whiskey. **6.** *Slang.* Something considered trite, dated, melodramatic, or unduly sentimental. —*tr.v.* **corned, corn•ing, corns.** —*v.* —*tr.* **1.** To cause to form hard particles; granulate. **2.a.** To season and preserve with granulated salt. **b.** To preserve (beef, for example) in brine. **3.** To feed (animals) with corn or grain. [ME, grain < OE. See **grə-no-***.]

corn[2] (kôrn) *n.* A horny thickening of the skin, usu. on or near a toe, resulting from pressure or friction. [ME *corne* < OFr., horn < Lat. *cornū.* See **ker-**[1]*****.]

corn•ball (kôrn′bôl′) *Slang.* —*n.* One who behaves in a mawkish or unsophisticated manner. —*adj.* Mawkish or unsophisticated; corny: *cornball humor.* [< *corn ball*, a ball of popcorn and molasses.]

Corn Belt (kôrn). An agricultural region of the central U.S. primarily in IA and IL but also including parts of IN, MN, SD, NE, KS, MO, and OH.

corn borer *n.* **1.** The larva of a European moth *(Pyrausta nubilalis)*, now common in eastern North America, that feeds on and destroys corn and other plants. **2.** Any of various insect larvae similar to the corn borer that infest corn.

corn•braid (kôrn′brād′) *tr.v.* **-braid•ed, -braid•ing, -braids.** To style (hair) in rows of braids; cornrow. —**corn′braid′** *n.*

corn bread or **corn•bread** (kôrn′brĕd′) *n.* Bread made from cornmeal.

corn cake or **corn•cake** (kôrn′kāk′) *n. Chiefly Southern U.S.* See **johnnycake.** See Regional Note at **johnnycake.**

corn chip *n.* A thin, crisp piece of food made from cornmeal.

corn•cob (kôrn′kŏb′) *n.* **1.** The hard cylindrical core on which the kernels of an ear of corn grow. **2.** A corncob pipe.

corbie-step

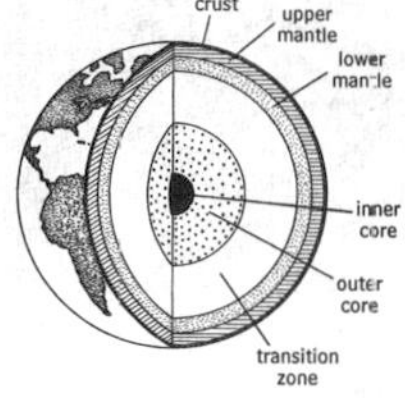

core
Cutaway view of Earth

Corinthian order

cormorant
Double-crested cormorant
Phalacrocorax auritus

corncob pipe *n.* A pipe with a bowl made of a dried corncob.

corn cockle *n.* A weedy annual Mediterranean plant *(Agrostemma githago)* having reddish flowers and opposite leaves.

corn•crake (kôrn′krāk′) *n.* A common Eurasian bird *(Crex crex)* with brownish-yellow plumage, found in grain fields and meadows.

corn•crib (kôrn′krĭb′) *n.* A structure for storing and drying ears of corn.

corn•dodg•er (kôrn′dŏj′ər) *n. Chiefly Southern U.S.* A small round ball of cornmeal, flour, milk, oil, and sugar that is fried in deep fat. Also called regionally *dodger.*

cor•ne•a (kôr′nē-ə) *n.* The transparent, convex anterior portion of the outer fibrous coat of the eyeball that covers the iris and the pupil. [Med.Lat. *cornea (tēla),* horny (tissue) < Lat. *corneus* < *cornū,* horn. See **ker-**[1]*.] **—cor′ne•al** (-əl) *adj.*

corn earworm *n.* The large, destructive larva of a moth *(Heliothis zea)* that feeds on corn and many other plants.

Cor•neille (kôr-nā′), **Pierre.** 1606–84. French playwright whose works include *Le Cid* (c. 1637) and *Horace* (1640).

cor•ne•i•tis (kôr′nē-ī′tĭs) *n.* Inflammation of the cornea.

cor•nel (kôr′nəl, -nĕl′) *n.* Any of various plants of the genus *Cornus,* which includes the bunchberry and dogwoods. [Short for Ger. *Kornelbaum* (< OHGer. *curnil-*) or < Fr. *cornouille,* both < Med.Lat. *corniola* < dim. of Lat. *cornus.*]

cor•nel•ian (kôr-nēl′yən) *n.* Var. of **carnelian.**

cornelian cherry *n.* **1.** A deciduous Eurasian shrub or small tree *(Cornus mas)* having small yellow flowers and cherrylike fruits. **2.** The fruit of this plant. [< CORNEL.]

Cor•nell (kôr-nĕl′), **Ezra.** 1807–74. Amer. businessman and philanthropist who cofounded Cornell University (1868).

Cornell, Katharine. 1893–1974. Amer. actress known for her performance in *A Bill of Divorcement* (1921).

cor•ne•ous (kôr′nē-əs) *adj.* Made of horn or a hornlike substance; horny. [< Lat. *corneus* < *cornū,* horn. See **ker-**[1]*.]

cor•ner (kôr′nər) *n.* **1.a.** The position at which two lines, surfaces, or edges meet and form an angle. **b.** The area enclosed or bounded by an angle formed in this manner: *the corner of one's eye.* **2.** The place where two roads or streets join or intersect. **3.a.** *Sports.* Any of the four angles of a boxing or wrestling ring where the ropes are joined. **b.** *Baseball.* Either side of home plate, toward or away from the batter. **4.** A threatening or embarrassing position from which escape is difficult. **5.** A remote, secluded, or secret place: *a beautiful corner of Paris.* **6.** A part or piece made to fit on a corner, as in mounting or for protection. **7.a.** A speculative monopoly of a stock or commodity created by purchasing all or most of the available supply in order to raise its price. **b.** Exclusive possession; monopoly. *—v.* **-nered, -ner•ing, -ners.** *—tr.* **1.** To furnish with corners. **2.** To place or drive into a corner. **3.** To form a corner in (a stock or commodity). *—intr.* **1.** To come together or be situated on or at a corner. **2.** To turn, as at a corner. *—adj.* **1.** Located at a street corner. **2.** Designed for use in a corner. [ME < AN < OFr. *corne,* corner, horn < VLat. **corna* < Lat. *cornua,* pl. of *cornū,* horn, point. See **ker-**[1]*.]

cor•ner•back also **corner back** (kôr′nər-băk′) *n. Football.* Either of two defensive halfbacks stationed a short distance behind the linebackers and relatively near the sidelines.

Cor•ner Brook (kôr′nər). A city of W-central Newfoundland, Canada, on the Gulf of St. Lawrence. Pop. 24,339.

cor•ner•stone also **corner stone** (kôr′nər-stōn′) *n.* **1.a.** A stone at the corner of a building uniting two intersecting walls; a quoin. **b.** Such a stone, often inscribed, laid at a ceremony marking the origin of a building. **2.** An indispensable and fundamental basis: *the cornerstone of an argument.*

cor•ner•wise (kôr′nər-wīz′) also **cor•ner•ways** (-wāz′) *adv.* **1.** With a corner toward the front. **2.** So as to form a corner. **3.** From corner to corner; diagonally.

cor•net (kôr-nĕt′) *n.* **1.** *Mus.* A wind instrument of the trumpet class, having three valves operated by pistons. **2.** (*also* kôr′nĭt). A piece of paper twisted into a cone and used to hold small wares such as candy or nuts. **3.** (*also* kôr′nĭt). A headdress, often cone-shaped, worn by women in the 12th and 13th centuries. [ME < OFr., dim. of *corn,* horn < Lat. *cornū.* See **ker-**[1]*.]

cor•net-à-pis•tons (kôr-nĕt′ə-pĭs′tənz) *n., pl.* **cor•nets-à-pis•tons** (kôr-nĕts′ə-pĭs′tənz). *Mus.* A cornet. [Fr. : *cornet,* horn, trumpet + *à,* with + *pistons,* valves.]

cor•net•ist also **cor•net•tist** (kôr-nĕt′ĭst) *n. Mus.* One who plays a cornet.

corn-fed (kôrn′fĕd′) *adj.* **1.** Fed on corn. **2.** *Slang.* Healthy and strong but unsophisticated.

corn flakes *pl.n.* A crisp, flaky, commercially prepared cold cereal made from coarse cornmeal.

corn•flow•er (kôrn′flou′ər) *n.* An annual Eurasian plant *(Centaurea cyanus)* in the composite family, having blue, purple, pink, or white flowers.

corn•husk (kôrn′hŭsk′) *n.* The leafy husk of an ear of corn.

corn•husk•ing (kôrn′hŭs′kĭng) *n.* **1.** The husking of corn. **2.** A social gathering for husking corn. **—corn′husk′er** *n.*

cor•nice (kôr′nĭs) *n.* **1.a.** A horizontal molded projection that crowns or completes a building or wall. **b.** The uppermost part of an entablature. **2.** The molding at the top of the walls of a room, between the walls and ceiling. **3.** An ornamental horizontal molding or frame used to conceal rods, picture hooks, or other devices. *—tr.v.* **-niced, -nic•ing, -nic•es.** To supply, decorate, or finish with or as if with a cornice. [Obsolete Fr. < Ital., poss. < Lat. *cornīx, cornīc-,* crow, from its resemblance to a crow's beak (influenced by Gk. *korōnis,* curved line, flourish < *korōnos,* curved; see CROWN).]

cor•nic•u•late (kôr-nĭk′yə-lāt′, -lĭt) *adj.* Having horns or hornlike projections. [Lat. *corniculātus* < *corniculum,* dim. of *cornū,* horn. See **ker-**[1]*.]

cor•ni•fi•ca•tion (kôr′nə-fĭ-kā′shən) *n.* The conversion of squamous epithelial cells into a horny material, such as hair, nails, or feathers. [Lat. *cornū,* horn; see **ker-**[1]* + -FICATION.]

Cor•nish (kôr′nĭsh) *adj.* Of or relating to Cornwall, its people, or the Cornish language. *—n.* **1.** The Brythonic language of Cornwall, which has been extinct since the late 18th century. **2.** Any of an English breed of domestic fowl often crossbred to produce roasters.

Cor•nish•man (kôr′nĭsh-mən) *n.* A man who is a native or inhabitant of Cornwall, England.

Cor•nish•wom•an (kôr′nĭsh-wŏŏm′ən) *n.* A woman who is a native or inhabitant of Cornwall, England.

Corn Law *n.* One of a series of British laws in force before 1846 that regulated the grain trade and restricted imports of grain.

corn lily *n.* Any of various bulbous herbs of the genus *Ixia,* native to southern Africa and widely cultivated as an ornamental for its showy colored flowers.

corn•meal also **corn meal** (kôrn′mēl′) *n.* Meal made from corn, used in a wide variety of foods.

corn oil *n.* A liquid obtained from the embryos of corn grains, used esp. as a cooking and salad oil and in margarines.

corn•pone or **corn pone** (kôrn′ pōn′) *—n. Chiefly Southern U.S.* See **johnnycake.** See Regional Notes at **johnnycake, pone.** *—adj. Informal.* Folksy and homespun, as in manner.

corn poppy *n.* An annual Eurasian plant *(Papaver rhoeas),* having usu. scarlet flowers.

corn•row (kôrn′rō′) *tr.v.* **-rowed, -row•ing, -rows.** To style (hair) by dividing into sections and braiding close to the scalp in rows. **—corn′row′** *n.*

corn salad *n.* Any of several plants of the genus *Valerianella,* esp. a Eurasian annual *(V. locusta* or *V. olitoria),* having small white to pale bluish flowers and edible young leaves.

corn silk *n.* The styles and stigmas that appear as a silky tuft or tassel at the tip of an ear of corn.

corn snow *n.* Snow that has melted and refrozen into a rough, granular surface.

corn•stalk also **corn stalk** (kôrn′stôk′) *n.* The stalk or stem of a corn plant.

corn•starch (kôrn′stärch′) *n.* Starch prepared from corn grains, used industrially and as a thickener in cooking.

corn sugar *n.* Dextrose obtained from cornstarch.

corn syrup *n.* A syrup prepared from cornstarch, used in industry and in numerous food products as a sweetener.

cor•nu (kôr′nōō, -nyōō) *n., pl.* **-nu•a** (-nōō-ə, -nyōō-ə). A part or structure, such as a bony protuberance, that resembles a horn. [Lat. *cornū,* horn. See **ker-**[1]*.] **—cor′nu•al** (-əl) *adj.*

cor•nu•co•pi•a (kôr′nə-kō′pē-ə, -nyə-) *n.* **1.** A goat's horn overflowing with fruit, flowers, and grain, signifying prosperity. **2.** *Gk. Myth.* The horn of the goat that suckled Zeus, which broke off and became filled with fruit. **3.** A cone-shaped ornament or receptacle. **4.** An overflowing store; an abundance. [LLat. *cornūcōpia* < Lat. *cornū cōpiae* : *cornū,* horn; see CORNU + *cōpiae,* genitive of *cōpia,* plenty; see **op-***.] **—cor′nu•co′pi•an** *adj.*

cor•nute (kôr-nōōt′, -nyōōt′) also **cor•nut•ed** (-nōō′tĭd, -nyōō′-) *adj.* **1.** Shaped like a horn. **2.** Having horns or horn-shaped processes. [Lat. *cornūtus* < *cornū,* horn. See CORNU.]

Corn•wall (kôrn′wôl′). **1.** A region of extreme SW England on a peninsula bounded by the Atlantic Ocean and English Channel. **2.** A city of SE Ontario, Canada, on the St. Lawrence R. and the NY border SE of Ottawa. Pop. 46,144.

Corn•wal•lis (kôrn-wŏl′ĭs, -wô′lĭs), **Charles.** 1st Marquis and 2nd Earl Cornwallis. 1738–1805. British military leader who surrendered at Yorktown (1781).

corn whiskey *n.* Whiskey distilled from corn.

corn•y (kôr′nē) *adj.* **-i•er, -i•est.** Trite, dated, melodramatic, or mawkishly sentimental. [< CORN[1].] **—corn′i•ly** *adv.* **—corn′i•ness** *n.*

co•rol•la (kə-rŏl′ə, -rō′lə) *n. Bot.* The petals of a flower considered as a group or unit. [Lat., small garland, dim. of *corōna,* garland. See CORONA.] **—co•rol′late′** (-rŏl′āt′) *adj.*

cor•ol•lar•y (kôr′ə-lĕr-ē, kŏr′-) *n., pl.* **-ies.** **1.** A proposition that follows with little or no proof required from one already proven. **2.** A deduction or an inference. **3.** A natural consequence or effect; a result. *—adj.* Consequent; resultant. [ME *corolarie* < Lat. *corollārium,* money paid for a garland, gratuity < *corolla,* small garland. See COROLLA.]

Cor•o•man•del Coast (kôr′ə-măn′dl). A region of SE India bounded by the Bay of Bengal and the Eastern Ghats.

co•ro•na (kə-rō′nə) *n., pl.* **-nas** or **-nae** (-nē). **1.** *Astron.* **a.** A

cornet
c. 1840 brass valve cornet

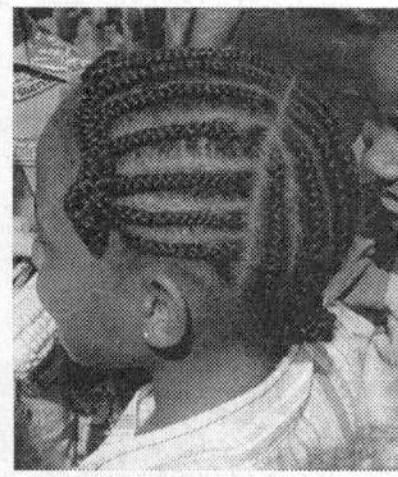

cornrow

cornucopia
Detail of a c. 1770–1780 wall painting at Marmion plantation in Virginia

faintly colored luminous ring appearing to surround a celestial body visible through a haze or thin cloud, caused by diffraction of light from suspended matter in the intervening medium. **b.** The luminous irregular envelope of highly ionized gas outside the chromosphere of the sun. **2.** *Archit.* The projecting top part of a cornice. **3.** A cigar with a long tapering body and blunt ends. **4.** *Anat.* The crownlike upper portion of a body part or structure. **5.** *Bot.* A crown-shaped, funnel-shaped, or trumpet-shaped outgrowth or appendage of the perianth of certain flowers, such as the daffodil. **6.** *Elect.* A faint glow enveloping the high-field electrode in a corona discharge. [Lat. *corōna.* See CROWN.]

Co•ro•na (kə-rō′nə). A city of S CA SW of Riverside. Pop. 76,095.

Corona Aus•tra•lis (ô-strā′lĭs) *n.* A constellation in the Southern Hemisphere near Telescopium and Sagittarius. [Lat. *Corōna austrālis* : *corōna*, crown + *austrālis*, southern.]

Corona Bo•re•al•is (bôr′ē-ăl′ĭs, -ā′lĭs, bōr′ē-) *n.* A constellation in the Northern Hemisphere between Hercules and Boötes. [Lat. *Corōna boreālis* : *corōna*, crown + *boreālis*, northern.]

corona discharge *n.* An electrical discharge characterized by a corona and occurring when one of two electrodes in a gas has a shape causing the electric field at its surface to be significantly greater than that between the electrodes.

Cor•o•na•do (kôr′ə-nä′dō, kŏr′-). A city of S CA on a narrow spit of land W of San Diego. Pop. 26,540.

Co•ro•na•do (kôr′ə-nä′dō, kŏr′-, kô′rô-nä′*th*ô), **Francisco Vásquez de.** 1510–54. Spanish explorer who was the first European to explore the American Southwest.

co•ro•na•graph also **co•ro•no•graph** (kə-rō′nə-grăf′) *n.* A telescope equipped with a disk that blacks out most of the sun, used to photograph the sun's corona.

cor•o•nal (kôr′ə-nəl, kŏr′-, kə-rō′nəl) *n.* A garland, wreath, or circlet for the head. —*adj.* **1.** Of or relating to a corona, esp. of the head. **2.** Of, relating to, or having the direction of the coronal suture or of the plane dividing the body into front and back portions.

coronal suture *n. Anat.* The suture extending across the skull between the two parietal bones and the frontal bone.

cor•o•nar•y (kôr′ə-nĕr′ē, kŏr′-) *adj.* **1.** Of, relating to, or being the coronary arteries or coronary veins. **2.** Of or relating to the heart. —*n.*, *pl.* **-ies.** A coronary thrombosis.

coronary artery *n.* Either of two arteries that originate in the aorta and supply blood to the muscular tissue of the heart.

coronary bypass surgery A surgical procedure performed to improve blood supply to the heart by removing a healthy blood vessel from another part of the body, such as the leg, and grafting it onto the heart to circumvent a blocked artery.

coronary care unit *n.* A hospital unit that is specially equipped to treat patients with serious heart conditions.

coronary occlusion *n.* The partial or complete obstruction of blood flow in a coronary artery, as by a thrombus.

coronary sinus *n.* A venous sinus that opens into the right atrium of the heart and serves to drain the coronary veins.

coronary thrombosis *n.* Obstruction of a coronary artery by a thrombus, often leading to destruction of heart muscle.

coronary vein *n.* Any of the veins that drains blood from the muscular tissue of the heart into the coronary sinus.

cor•o•na•tion (kôr′ə-nā′shən, kŏr′-) *n.* The act or ceremony of crowning a sovereign or the sovereign's consort. [ME *coronacioun* < Med.Lat. *corōnātiō*, *corōnātiōn-* < Lat. *corōnātus*, p.part. of *corōnāre*, to crown < *corōna*, crown. See CROWN.]

cor•o•ner (kôr′ə-nər, kŏr′-) *n.* A public officer who investigates by inquest any death thought to be of other than natural causes. [ME, officer of the crown < AN *corouner* < *coroune*, crown < Lat. *corōna*. See CROWN.] —**cor′o•ner•ship′** *n.*

cor•o•net (kôr′ə-nĕt′, kŏr′-) *n.* **1.** A small crown worn by nobles below the rank of sovereign. **2.** A chaplet or headband adorned with gold or jewels. **3.** The upper margin of a horse's hoof. [ME *coronette* < OFr., dim. of *corone*, crown < Lat. *corōna*. See CROWN.]

co•ro•no•graph (kə-rō′nə-grăf′) *n.* Var. of **coronagraph.**

Co•rot (kô-rō′, kə-), **Jean Baptiste Camille.** 1796–1875. French painter noted for his sketches of Italian landscapes.

co•ro•tate (kō-rō′tāt′) *intr.v.* **-tat•ed, -tat•ing, -tates.** To rotate in conjunction with another body. —**co′ro•ta′tion** *n.* —**co′ro•ta′tion•al** *adj.*

corp. *abbr.* Corporation.

cor•po•ra (kôr′pər-ə) *n.* Pl. of **corpus.**

corpora cal•lo•sa (kə-lō′-sə) *n. Anat.* Pl. of **corpus callosum.**

cor•po•ral[1] (kôr′pər-əl, kôr′prəl) *adj.* Of or relating to the body. See Syns at **bodily.** [ME < OFr. < Lat. *corporālis* < *corpus*, *corpor-*, body. See **kʷrep-*.**] —**cor′po•ral′i•ty** (-pə-răl′ĭ-tē) *n.* —**cor′po•ral•ly** *adv.*

cor•po•ral[2] (kôr′pər-əl, kôr′prəl) *n.* A noncommissioned officer in the U.S. Army ranking above private first class and below sergeant or in the U.S. Marine Corps ranking above lance corporal and below sergeant. [Obsolete Fr., alteration of *caporal* < OItal. *caporale* < *capo*, head < Lat. *caput.* See **kaput-*.**]

cor•po•ral[3] (kôr′pər-əl, kôr′prəl) *n. Eccles.* A white linen cloth on which the consecrated elements are placed during the Eucharist. [ME < OFr. and < Med.Lat. *corporāle*, both < Lat. *corporālis*, of the body < *corpus*, *corpor-*, body. See **kʷrep-*.**]

corpora lu•te•a (lo͞o′tē-ə) *n.* Pl. of **corpus luteum.**

corpora stri•a•ta (strī-ā′tə) *n. Anat.* Pl. of **corpus striatum.**

cor•po•rate (kôr′pər-ĭt, kôr′prĭt) *adj.* **1.** Formed into a corporation; incorporated. **2.** Of or relating to a corporation. **3.** United or combined into one body; collective. **4.** Corporative. [Lat. *corporātus*, p.part. of *corporāre*, to make into a body < *corpus*, body. See **kʷrep-*.**] —**cor′po•rate•ly** *adv.*

cor•po•ra•tion (kôr′pə-rā′shən) *n.* **1.** A body that is granted a charter legally recognizing it as a separate legal entity having its own rights, privileges, and liabilities distinct from those of its members. **2.** Such a body created for purposes of government. **3.** A group of people combined into one body.

cor•po•ra•tive (kôr′pər-ə-tĭv, -pə-rā′tĭv) *adj.* **1.** Of, relating to, or associated with a corporation. **2.** Of or relating to a government or political system in which the principal economic functions are organized as corporate entities.

cor•po•ra•tor (kôr′pə-rā′tər) *n.* A member of a corporation.

cor•po•re•al (kôr-pôr′ē-əl, -pōr′-) *adj.* **1.** Of, relating to, or characteristic of the body. See Syns at **bodily. 2.** Of a material nature; tangible. [< Lat. *corporeus* < *corpus*, *corpor-*, body. See **kʷrep-*.**] —**cor•po′re•al′i•ty** (-al′ĭ-tē), **cor•po′re•al•ness** *n.* —**cor•po′re•al•ly** *adv.*

cor•po•re•i•ty (kôr′pə-rē′ĭ-tē, -rā′-) *n.* The state of being material or corporeal; physical existence.

cor•po•sant (kôr′pə-zănt) *n.* See **Saint Elmo's fire.** [Port. and obsolete Sp. *corpo santo*, both < Lat. *corpus sanctum*, holy body : *corpus*, body; see **kʷrep-*** + *sanctus*, holy, p.part. of *sancīre*, to consecrate; see **sak-*.**]

corps (kôr, kōr) *n.*, *pl.* **corps** (kôrz, kōrz). **1.a.** A separate specialized branch or department of the armed forces. **b.** A tactical unit of ground combat forces between a division and an army under a lieutenant general. **2.** A body of persons acting together or associated under common direction. [Fr. < OFr. < Lat. *corpus*, body. See **kʷrep-*.**]

corps de bal•let (kôr′ də bă-lā′, kōr′) *n.* The dancers in a ballet company who perform as a group. [Fr. : *corps*, corps + *de*, of + *ballet*, ballet.]

corpse (kôrps) *n.* A dead body, esp. that of a human being. [ME *corps* < Lat. *corpus.* See **kʷrep-*.**]

corps•man (kôr′mən, kōr′-, kôrz′mən, kōrz′-) *n.* **1.** An enlisted person in the armed forces trained to give first aid and basic medical treatment. **2.** A member of a government-sponsored group designated as a corps.

cor•pu•lence (kôr′pyə-ləns) *n.* The condition of being excessively fat; obesity. [ME, corporality < Lat. *corpulentia*, corpulence < *corpulentus*, corpulent < *corpus*, body. See **kʷrep-*.**]

cor•pu•lent (kôr′pyə-lənt) *adj.* Excessively fat. See Syns at **fat.** —**cor′pu•lent•ly** *adv.*

cor•pus (kôr′pəs) *n.*, *pl.* **-po•ra** (-pər-ə). **1.** A large collection of writings of a specific kind or on a specific subject. **2.** The principal or capital as distinguished from the interest or income, as of a fund or estate. **3.** *Anat.* **a.** The main part of a body structure or organ. **b.** A distinct body mass or organ having a specific function. **4.** *Mus.* The overall length of a violin. [ME < Lat. See **kʷrep-*.**]

corpus cal•lo•sum (kə-lō′səm) *n.*, *pl.* **corpora cal•lo•sa** (kə-lō′sə). *Anat.* The arched bridge of nervous tissue that connects the two cerebral hemispheres, allowing communication between the right and left sides of the brain. [NLat. : Lat. *corpus*, body + Lat. *callōsum*, neut. of *callōsus*, callous.]

Cor•pus Chris•ti[1] (kôr′pəs krĭs′tē). A city of S TX on **Corpus Christi Bay,** an arm of the Gulf of Mexico. Pop. 257,453.

Cor•pus Chris•ti[2] (kôr′pəs krĭs′tē) *n. Rom. Cath. Ch.* A feast in honor of the Eucharist, traditionally observed on the first Thursday after Trinity Sunday. [ME < Med.Lat., body of Christ : Lat. *corpus*, body + Lat. *Christī*, genitive of *Christus*, Christ.]

cor•pus•cle (kôr′pə-səl, -pŭs′əl) *n.* **1.a.** An unattached body cell, such as a blood cell. **b.** A rounded globular mass of cells. **2.** A discrete particle, such as an electron. **3.** A minute globular particle. [Lat. *corpusculum*, dim. of *corpus*, body. See **kʷrep-*.**] —**cor•pus′cu•lar** (kôr-pŭs′kyə-lər) *adj.*

corpus de•lic•ti (dĭ-lĭk′tī′) *n.* **1.** *Law.* The material evidence in a homicide, such as the corpse, showing that a crime has been committed. **2.** A corpse. [NLat. : Lat. *corpus*, body + Lat. *delictī*, genitive of *delictum*, crime.]

corpus lu•te•um (lo͞o′tē-əm) *n.*, *pl.* **corpora lu•te•a** (lo͞o′tē-ə). A yellow progesterone-secreting mass of cells that forms from an ovarian follicle after the release of a mature egg. [NLat. : Lat. *corpus*, body + Lat. *lūteum*, yellow.]

corpus stri•a•tum (strī-ā′təm) *n.*, *pl.* **corpora stri•a•ta** (strī-ā′tə). *Anat.* Either of two gray and white striated bodies of nerve fibers in the lower lateral wall of each cerebral hemisphere. [NLat. : Lat. *corpus*, body + Lat. *striātum*, striated.]

corr. *abbr.* **1.** Correction. **2.** Correspondence; correspondent.

cor•rade (kə-rād′) *tr. & intr.v.* **-rad•ed, -rad•ing, -rades.** To erode or be eroded by abrasion. [Lat. *corrādere*, to scrape

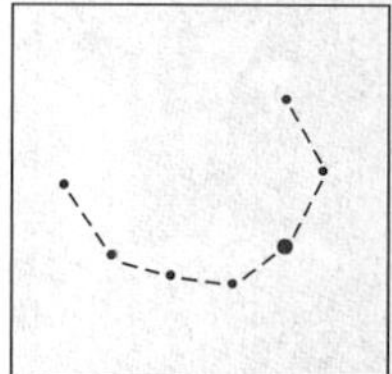
Corona Borealis

ă **pat**	oi **boy**
ā **pay**	ou **out**
âr **care**	o͝o **took**
ä **father**	o͞o **boot**
ĕ **pet**	ŭ **cut**
ē **be**	ûr **urge**
ĭ **pit**	th **thin**
ī **pie**	*th* **this**
îr **pier**	hw **which**
ŏ **pot**	zh **vision**
ō **toe**	ə **a**bout,
ô **paw**	item

Stress marks:
′ (primary);
′ (secondary), as in
dictionary (dĭk′shə-nĕr′ē)

together : *com-*, com- + *rādere*, to scrape; see **rēd-***.] **— cor•ra′sion** (-rā′zhən) *n.* **— cor•ra′sive** (-sĭv, -zĭv) *adj.*

cor•ral (kə-răl′) *n.* **1.** An enclosure for confining livestock. **2.** An enclosure formed by a circle of wagons for defense against attack during an encampment. *— tr.v.* **-ralled, -ral•ling, -rals. 1.** To drive into and hold in a corral. **2.** To arrange (wagons) in a corral. **3.** To take control or possession of. [Sp. < VLat. **currāle*, enclosure for carts < Lat. *currus*, cart < *currere*, to run. See **kers-***.]

cor•rect (kə-rĕkt′) *v.* **-rect•ed, -rect•ing, -rects.** *— tr.* **1.a.** To remove the errors from. **b.** To indicate the errors in. **2.** To punish for the purpose of improving or reforming. **3.** To remove, remedy, or counteract (a malfunction, for example). **4.** To adjust so as to meet a required standard or condition. *— intr.* **1.** To make corrections. **2.** To make adjustments; compensate. *— adj.* **1.** Free from error or fault; true or accurate. **2.** Conforming to standards; proper. [ME *correcten* < Lat. *corrigere, corrēct-*, to correct : *com-*, com- + *regere*, to rule; see **reg-***.] **— cor•rect′a•ble, cor•rect′i•ble** *adj.* **— cor•rect′ly** *adv.* **— cor•rect′ness** *n.* **— cor•rec′tor** *n.*

Syns: *correct, rectify, remedy, redress, reform, revise, amend.* These verbs mean to make right what is wrong. *Correct* refers to eliminating faults, errors, or defects: *correct spelling mistakes. Rectify* stresses the idea of bringing something into conformity with a standard of what is right: *The omission will be rectified. Remedy* involves removing or counteracting something considered a cause of harm or damage: *He took courses to remedy his ignorance. Redress* refers to setting right something considered immoral or unethical and usually involves making reparation: *the wrong to be redressed. Reform* implies broad change that alters form or character for the better: *"Let us reform our schools, and we shall find little reform needed in our prisons"* (John Ruskin). *Revise* suggests change that results from reconsideration: *revise a manuscript. Amend* implies improvement through alteration or correction: *"Whenever* [the people] *shall grow weary of the existing government, they can exercise their constitutional right of amending it"* (Abraham Lincoln).

corsage
Wrist corsage

cor•rec•tion (kə-rĕk′shən) *n.* **1.** The act or process of correcting. **2.** Something offered or substituted for a mistake or fault. **3.a.** Punishment intended to rehabilitate or improve. **b. corrections.** The treatment of offenders through a system of penal incarceration, rehabilitation, probation, and parole or the administrative system by which these are effectuated. **4.** An amount or quantity added or subtracted in order to correct. **5.** A decline in stock-market activity or prices following a period of increases. **— cor•rec′tion•al** *adj.*

cor•rec•ti•tude (kə-rĕk′tĭ-to͞od′, -tyo͞od′) *n.* Appropriate manners and behavior; propriety.

cor•rec•tive (kə-rĕk′tĭv) *adj.* Tending or intended to correct. *— n.* An agent that corrects. **— cor•rec′tive•ly** *adv.*

Cor•reg•gio (kə-rĕj′ō, -ē-ō′, kô-rĕd′jō), **Antonio Allegri da.** 1494–1534. Italian High Renaissance painter known for his use of chiaroscuro.

Cor•reg•i•dor (kə-rĕg′ĭ-dôr′, -dōr′, kôr-rĕ′hē-*th*ôr′). An island of the N Philippines at the entrance to Manila Bay.

correl. *abbr.* Correlative.

cor•re•late (kôr′ə-lāt′, kŏr′-) *v.* **-lat•ed, -lat•ing, -lates.** *— tr.* **1.** To put or bring into causal, complementary, parallel, or reciprocal relation. **2.** To establish or demonstrate as having a correlation. *— intr.* To be related by a correlation. *— adj.* (-lĭt, -lāt′). Related by a correlation, esp. having corresponding characteristics. *— n.* (-lĭt, -lāt′). Either of two correlate entities; a correlative. [Back-formation < CORRELATION.]

cor•re•la•tion (kôr′ə-lā′shən, kŏr′-) *n.* **1.** A causal, complementary, parallel, or reciprocal relationship, esp. a structural, functional, or qualitative correspondence between two comparable entities. **2.** *Statistics.* The simultaneous change in value of two numerically valued random variables: *the negative correlation between age and normal vision.* **3.** An act of correlating or the condition of being correlated. [Med.Lat. *correlātiō, correlātiōn-* : Lat. *com-*, com- + Lat. *relātiō*, relation, report (< *relātus*, p.part. of *referre*, to carry back; see RELATE).] **— cor′re•la′tion•al** *adj.*

correlation coefficient *n.* A measure of the interdependence of two random variables that ranges in value from −1 to +1, indicating perfect negative correlation at −1, absence of correlation at zero, and perfect positive correlation at +1.

cor•rel•a•tive (kə-rĕl′ə-tĭv) *adj.* **1.** Related; corresponding. **2.** *Gram.* Indicating a reciprocal or complementary relationship: *a correlative conjunction.* *— n.* **1.** Either of two correlative entities; a correlate. **2.** *Gram.* A correlative word or expression. **— cor•rel′a•tive•ly** *adv.*

Hernando Cortés

cor•re•spond (kôr′ĭ-spŏnd′, kŏr′-) *intr.v.* **-spond•ed, -spond•ing, -sponds. 1.** To be in agreement, harmony, or conformity; be consistent or compatible. **2.** To be similar, parallel, equivalent, or equal in character, quantity, origin, structure, or function: *English* navel *corresponds to Greek* omphalos. **3.** To communicate by letter, usu. over a period of time. [Fr. *correspondre* < Med.Lat. *correspondēre* : Lat. *com-*, com- + *respondēre*, to respond; see RESPOND.]

cor•re•spon•dence (kôr′ĭ-spŏn′dəns, kŏr′-) *n.* **1.** The act, fact, or state of agreeing or conforming. **2.** Similarity or analogy. **3.a.** Communication by the exchange of letters. **b.** The letters written or received. *— adj.* **1.** Of, relating to, or dealing with correspondence. **2.** Of, relating to, or constituting instruction by mail. **— cor′re•spon′den•cy** *n.*

correspondence principle *n.* The principle that predictions of quantum theory approach those of classical physics in the limit of large quantum numbers.

correspondence school *n.* A school that offers instruction by mail, sending lessons and examinations to a student.

cor•re•spon•dent (kôr′ĭ-spŏn′dənt, kŏr′-) *n.* **1.** One who communicates by means of letters. **2.** One employed by the print or broadcast media to supply news stories or articles. **3.** One that has regular business dealings with another, esp. at a distance. **4.** Something that corresponds; a correlative. *— adj.* Corresponding. **— cor′re•spon′dent•ly** *adv.*

cor•re•spond•ing (kôr′ĭ-spŏn′dĭng, kŏr′-) *adj.* **1.** Having the same or nearly the same relationship. **2.** Accompanying another. **3.a.** Having been assigned the responsibility of written communications. **b.** Participating at a distance from the rest of a group. **— cor′re•spond′ing•ly** *adv.*

cor•re•spon•sive (kôr′ĭ-spŏn′sĭv, kŏr′-) *adj.* Jointly responsive. **— cor′re•spon′sive•ly** *adv.*

cor•ri•da (kô-rē′də, -*th*ä) *n.* A bullfight. [Sp. < p.part. of *correr*, to run < Lat. *currere.* See **kers-***.]

cor•ri•dor (kôr′ĭ-dər, -dôr′, kŏr′-) *n.* **1.** A narrow hallway, passageway, or gallery, often with rooms or apartments opening onto it. **2.a.** A tract of land forming a passageway, such as one that allows an inland country access to the sea through another country. **b.** A restricted tract of land for the passage of trains. **c.** Restricted airspace for the passage of aircraft. **d.** The restricted path followed by a spacecraft on a particular mission. **3.** A thickly populated strip of land connecting two or more urban areas. *— **idiom.*** **corridors of power.** A place in which powerful leaders work and rule. [Fr. < Ital. *corridore* < *correre*, to run < Lat. *currere.* See **kers-***.]

cor•rie (kôr′ē, kŏr′ē) *n.* A round hollow in a hillside; a cirque. [Sc.Gael. *coire*, hollow, cauldron < OIr., cauldron.]

Cor•ri•en•tes (kôr′ē-ĕn′tĕs). A city of NE Argentina on the Paraná R.; founded 1588. Pop. 180,612.

Cor•ri•gan (kôr′ĭ-gən, kŏr′-), **Mairead.** b. 1944. Irish peace activist who shared the 1976 Nobel Peace Prize.

cor•ri•gen•dum (kôr′ə-jĕn′dəm, kŏr′-) *n., pl.* **-da** (-də). **1.** An error to be corrected, esp. a printer's error. **2. corrigenda.** A list of errors in a book along with their corrections. [Lat., neut. gerundive of *corrigere*, to correct. See CORRECT.]

cor•ri•gi•ble (kôr′ĭ-jə-bəl, kŏr′-) *adj.* Capable of being corrected, reformed, or improved. [ME < OFr. < Med.Lat. *corrigibilis* < Lat. *corrigere*, to correct. See CORRECT.] **— cor′ri•gi•bil′i•ty** *n.* **— cor′ri•gi•bly** *adv.*

cor•ri•val (kə-rī′vəl, kō-) *n.* A rival or an opponent. [Fr. < Lat. *corrīvālis* : *com-*, com- + *rīvālis*, rival; see RIVAL.] **— cor•ri′val** *adj.* **— cor•ri′val•ry** (-rē) *n.*

cor•rob•o•rant (kə-rŏb′ər-ənt) *adj. Archaic.* Producing or stimulating physical vigor. Used of a medicine.

cor•rob•o•rate (kə-rŏb′ə-rāt′) *tr.v.* **-rat•ed, -rat•ing, -rates.** To strengthen or support with other evidence; make more certain: *corroborated my story.* [Lat. *corrōborāre, corrōborāt-* : *com-*, com- + *rōborāre*, to strengthen (< *rōbur, rōbor-*, strength; see **reudh-***).] **— cor•rob′o•ra′tion** *n.* **— cor•rob′o•ra′tive** (-ə-rā′tĭv, -ər-ə-tĭv), **cor•rob′o•ra•to′ry** (-ər-ə-tôr′ē, -tōr′ē) *adj.* **— cor•rob′o•ra′tor** *n.*

cor•rob•o•ree (kə-rŏb′ə-rē) *n.* **1.** An Australian aboriginal dance festival held at night. **2.** *Australian.* **a.** A large, noisy celebration. **b.** A great tumult. [< Dharuk (Aboriginal language of SE Australia) *garaabara.*]

cor•rode (kə-rōd′) *v.* **-rod•ed, -rod•ing, -rodes.** *— tr.* **1.** To destroy a metal or alloy gradually, esp. by oxidation or chemical action. **2.** To impair steadily; deteriorate. *— intr.* To be eaten or worn away. [ME *corroden* < Lat. *corrōdere*, to gnaw away : *com-*, com- + *rōdere*, to gnaw; see **rēd-***.] **— cor•rod′i•ble, cor•ro′si•ble** (-rō′sə-bəl) *adj.*

cor•ro•sion (kə-rō′zhən) *n.* **1.a.** The act or process of corroding. **b.** The condition produced by corroding. **2.** A substance, such as rust, formed by corroding. [ME *corosioun*, corrosion of tissue < OFr. *corrosion* < Med.Lat. *corrōsiō, corrōsiōn-*, the act of gnawing < Lat. *corrōsus*, p.part. of *corrōdere*, to gnaw away. See CORRODE.]

cor•ro•sive (kə-rō′sĭv, -zĭv) *adj.* **1.** Having the capability or tendency to cause corrosion. **2.** Gradually destructive; steadily harmful: *corrosive anxiety.* **3.** Spitefully sarcastic: *corrosive wit.* *— n.* A substance having the capability to cause corrosion. **— cor•ro′sive•ly** *adv.* **— cor•ro′sive•ness** *n.*

corrosive sublimate *n.* See **mercuric chloride.**

cor•ru•gate (kôr′ə-gāt′, kŏr′-) *tr. & intr.v.* **-gat•ed, -gat•ing, -gates.** To shape or become shaped into folds or parallel and alternating ridges and grooves. [Lat. *corrūgāre, corrūgāt-*, to wrinkle up : *com-*, com- + *rūgāre*, to wrinkle (< *rūga*, wrinkle).] **— cor′ru•gat′ed** (-gā′tĭd), **cor′ru•gate′** *adj.*

corrugated iron *n.* A structural sheet iron, usu. galvanized, shaped in parallel furrows and ridges for rigidity.

cor•ru•ga•tion (kôr′ə-gā′shən, kŏr′-) *n* **1.a.** The act or process of corrugating. **b.** The state of being corrugated. **2.** A groove or ridge on a corrugated surface.

cor•rupt (kə-rŭpt′) *adj.* **1.** Marked by immorality and perversion; depraved. **2.** Venal; dishonest: *a corrupt mayor.* **3.** Containing errors or alterations, as a text. **4.** *Archaic.* Tainted; putrid. — *v.* **-rupt•ed, -rupt•ing, -rupts.** — *tr.* **1.** To destroy or subvert the honesty or integrity of. **2.** To ruin morally; pervert. **3.** To taint; contaminate. **4.** To cause to become rotten; spoil. **5.** To change the original form of (a text, for example). — *intr.* To become corrupt. [ME < Lat. *corruptus,* p.part. of *corrumpere,* to destroy : *com-,* com- + *rumpere,* to break; see **reup-***.] — **cor•rupt′er, cor•rup′tor** *n.* — **cor•rup′tive** *adj.* — **cor•rupt′ly** *adv.* — **cor•rupt′ness** *n.*

cor•rupt•i•ble (kə-rŭp′tə-bəl) *adj.* Capable of being corrupted: *corruptible judges.* — **cor•rupt′i•bil′i•ty, cor•rupt′i•ble•ness** *n.* — **cor•rupt′i•bly** *adv.*

cor•rup•tion (kə-rŭp′shən) *n.* **1.a.** The act or process of corrupting. **b.** The state of being corrupt. **2.** Decay; rot. **3.** *Archaic.* Something that corrupts.

cor•rup•tion•ist (kə-rŭp′shə-nĭst) *n.* One who defends or practices corruption, particularly in politics.

cor•sage (kôr-säzh′, -säj′) *n.* **1.** A small bouquet of flowers worn by a woman at the shoulder or waist or on the wrist. **2.** The bodice or waist of a dress. [ME, torso < OFr. < *cors,* body < Lat. *corpus.* See **kʷrep-***.]

cor•sair (kôr′sâr′) *n.* **1.** A pirate, esp. along the Barbary Coast. **2.** A swift pirate ship, often officially sanctioned. [Fr. *corsaire* < OProv. *corsari* < OItal. *corsaro* < Med.Lat. *cursārius* < *cursus,* plunder < Lat., run, course. See COURSE.]

corse (kôrs) *n. Archaic.* A corpse. [ME *cors* < OFr. < Lat. *corpus.* See **kʷrep-***.]

cor•se•let (kôr′slĭt) *n.* **1.** Also **cors•let.** Body armor, esp. a breastplate. **2.** Also **corse•lette** (kôr′sə-lĕt′). An undergarment combining a light corset and a brassiere. [Fr., dim. of OFr. *cors,* body. See CORSET.]

cor•set (kôr′sĭt) *n.* **1.** A close-fitting undergarment, often reinforced by stays, worn to support and shape the waistline, hips, and breasts. **2.** A medieval outer garment, esp. a laced jacket or bodice. — *tr.v.* **-set•ed, -set•ing, -sets.** To enclose in or as if in a corset. [ME, bodice < OFr., dim. of *cors,* body < Lat. *corpus.* See **kʷrep-***.]

Cor•si•ca (kôr′sĭ-kə). An Island of France in the Mediterranean N of Sardinia; ceded to France by Genoa in 1768. — **Cor′si•can** *adj. & n.*

Cor•si•ca•na (kôr′sĭ-kăn′ə). A city of NE TX SSE of Dallas. Pop. 22,911.

cor•tege also **cor•tège** (kôr-tĕzh′) *n.* **1.** A train of attendants, as of a distinguished person; a retinue. **2.a.** A ceremonial procession. **b.** A funeral procession. [Fr. *cortège* < OItal. *corteggio* < *corteggiare,* to pay honor < *corte,* court < Lat. *cohors, cohort-,* throng. See **gher-¹***.]

Cor•tés (kôr-tĕz′, -tĕs′), **Hernando** or **Hernán.** 1485–1547. Spanish conquistador who conquered Aztec Mexico.

cor•tex (kôr′tĕks′) *n., pl.* **-ti•ces** (-tĭ-sēz′) or **-tex•es. 1.** *Anat.* **a.** The outer layer of an internal organ or body structure, as of the kidney or adrenal gland. **b.** The outer layer of gray matter that covers the surface of the cerebral hemisphere. **2.** *Bot.* The region of tissue in a root or stem between the epidermis and the vascular tissue. **3.** An external layer, such as bark or rind. [Lat., bark. See **sker-¹***.]

cor•ti•cal (kôr′tĭ-kəl) *adj.* **1.** Of, relating to, derived from, or consisting of cortex. **2.** Of, relating to, associated with, or depending on the cerebral cortex. — **cor′ti•cal•ly** *adv.*

cortico– or **cortic–** *pref.* Cortex: *corticotropin.* [< Lat. *cortex, cortic-,* bark, rind. See CORTEX.]

cor•ti•coid (kôr′tĭ-koid′) *n.* A corticosteroid.

cor•ti•co•ste•roid (kôr′tĭ-kō-stîr′oid′,-stĕr′-) *n.* Any of the steroid hormones produced by the adrenal cortex or their synthetic equivalents, such as cortisol and aldesterone.

cor•ti•cos•ter•one (kôr′tĭ-kŏs′tə-rōn′) *n.* A corticosteroid, $C_{21}H_{30}O_4$, that functions in the metabolism of carbohydrates and proteins. [CORTICO– + STER(OL) + –ONE.]

cor•ti•co•tro•pin (kôr′tĭ-kō-trō′pən) also **cor•ti•co•tro•phin** (-trō′fĭn) *n.* See **ACTH.** [CORTICO– + –TROP(IC) + –IN.]

cor•tin (kôr′tn) *n.* An adrenal cortex extract that contains a mixture of hormones including cortisone. [CORT(EX) + –IN.]

cor•ti•sol (kôr′tĭ-sôl′, -zôl′, -sōl′, -zōl′) *n.* See **hydrocortisone** 1. [CORTIS(ONE) + –OL¹.]

cor•ti•sone (kôr′tĭ-sōn′, -zōn′) *n.* A naturally occurring corticosteroid, $C_{21}H_{28}O_5$, that functions primarily in carbohydrate metabolism and is used in the treatment of rheumatoid arthritis, adrenal insufficiency, certain allergies, and gout. [Alteration of CORTICOSTERONE.]

Cort•land¹ (kôrt′lənd). A city of central NY S of Syracuse; settled in 1792. Pop. 19,801.

Cort•land² (kôrt′lənd) *n.* A large red-skinned cultivated variety of apple. [After *Cortland,* a county of central NY.]

co•run•dum (kə-rŭn′dəm) *n.* An extremely hard mineral, aluminum oxide, Al_2O_3, that occurs in gem varieties such as ruby and sapphire and in a common form used chiefly in abrasives. [Tamil *kuruntam.*]

co•rus•cant (kə-rŭs′kənt) *adj.* Giving forth flashes of light.

cor•us•cate (kôr′ə-skāt′, kŏr′-) *intr.v.* **-cat•ed, -cat•ing, -cates. 1.** To give forth flashes of light; sparkle and glitter: *coruscating diamonds.* **2.** To exhibit sparkling virtuosity. [Lat. *coruscāre, coruscāt-,* to flash.] — **cor′us•ca′tion** *n.*

Cor•val•lis (kôr-văl′ĭs). A city of W OR on the Willamette R. SSW of Salem. Pop. 44,757.

cor•vée (kôr-vā′, kôr′vā′) *n.* **1.** Labor exacted by a local authority for little or no pay or instead of taxes and used esp. in the maintenance of roads. **2.** A day of unpaid work required of a vassal by a feudal lord. [Fr. *corvée* and ME *corve,* both < OFr. *corovee* < Med.Lat. *(opera) corrogāta,* (work) requested < Lat. *corrogāre,* to summon together : *com-,* com- + *rogāre,* to ask; see **reg-***.]

corves (kôrvz) *n.* Pl. of **corf.**

cor•vette (kôr-vĕt′) *n.* **1.** A fast, lightly armed warship, smaller than a destroyer, often armed for antisubmarine operations. **2.** An obsolete sailing warship, smaller than a frigate, usu. armed with one tier of guns. [Fr., a kind of warship, prob. < MDu. *corf,* basket, small ship. See CORF.]

cor•vi•na (kôr-vē′nə) *n.* Var. of **corbina.**

cor•vine (kôr′vīn′, -vĭn) *adj.* Of, resembling, or characteristic of crows. [Lat. *corvīnus* < *corvus,* raven.]

Cor•vus (kôr′vəs) *n.* A constellation in the Southern Hemisphere near Crater and Virgo. [Lat. *corvus,* raven.]

Cor•y•bant (kôr′ə-bănt′, kŏr′-) *n., pl.* **-bants** or **-ban•tes** (-băn′tēz′). *Gk. Myth.* A priest of Cybele whose rites were celebrated with ecstatic dances. — **Cor′y•ban′tic** *adj.*

co•ryd•a•lis (kə-rĭd′l-ĭs) *n.* Any of various herbs of the genus *Corydalis,* native chiefly to northern temperate regions and having finely divided leaves and spurred flowers. [NLat. *Corydalis,* genus name < Gk. *korudallis,* crested lark (< the shape of the flowers) < *korudos.* See **ker-¹***.]

cor•ymb (kôr′ĭmb, -ĭm, kŏr′-) *n.* A usu. flat-topped flower cluster in which the flower stalks grow upward from various points of the main stem to approximately the same height. [Fr. *corymbe* < Lat. *corymbus,* flower bunch < Gk. *korumbos,* head. See **ker-¹***.] — **cor′ym•bose′** (-ĭm-bōs′), **co•rym′bous** (kə-rĭm′bəs) *adj.* — **cor′ym•bose′ly** *adv.*

co•ry•ne•bac•te•ri•um (kôr′ə-nē-băk-tîr′ē-əm, kə-rĭn′ə-) *n.* Any of various gram-positive rod-shaped bacteria of the genus *Corynebacterium,* which includes many animal and plant pathogens. [NLat. *Corynēbacterium,* genus name : Gk. *korunē,* club; see **ker-¹*** + BACTERIUM.]

co•ryn•e•form (kə-rĭn′ə-fôrm′) *adj.* Having the shape of a corynebacterium. [CORYNE(BACTERIUM) + –FORM.]

cor•y•phae•us (kôr′ə-fē′əs, kŏr′-) *n., pl.* **-phae•i** (-fē′ī′). **1.** The leader of a Greek chorus. **2.** A leader or spokesperson. [Lat., leader < Gk. *koruphaios* < *koruphē,* head. See **ker-¹***.]

cor•y•phée (kôr′ə-fā′, kŏr′-) *n.* A ballet dancer ranking below a soloist and performing in small ensembles. [Fr. < Lat. *coryphaeus,* leader. See CORYPHAEUS.]

co•ry•za (kə-rī′zə) *n.* See **cold** 3. [LLat. *coryza* < Gk. *koruza,* catarrh.]

cos¹ (kôs, kŏs) *n.* See **romaine.** [After *Cos* (Kos).]

cos² *abbr.* Cosine.

Cos (kŏs, kôs). See **Kos.**

co•se•cant (kō-sē′kănt′, -kənt) *n. Math.* **1.** The reciprocal of the sine of an angle in a right triangle. **2.** The secant of the complement of a directed angle or arc.

co•seis•mal (kō-sīz′məl, -sīs′-) also **co•seis•mic** (-mĭk) — *adj.* Relating to or being a line connecting the points on a map that indicate the places simultaneously affected by an earthquake shock. — *n.* A coseismal line.

Co•sen•za (kō-zĕn′sə, kô-zĕn′tsä). A city of S Italy SE of Naples. Pop. 105,806.

cosh (kŏsh) *Chiefly British. n.* A weighted weapon similar to a blackjack. [Perh. < Romany *kosh,* stick.] — **cosh** *v.*

co•sign (kō-sīn′) *tr.v.* **-signed, -sign•ing, -signs. 1.** To sign (a document) jointly. **2.** To endorse (another's signature), as for a loan. — **co•sign′er** *n.*

co•sig•na•to•ry (kō-sĭg′nə-tôr′ē, -tōr′ē) *adj.* Signed jointly. — *n., pl.* **-ries.** One who cosigns.

co•sine (kō′sīn′) *n.* **1.** In a right triangle, the ratio of the length of the side adjacent to an acute angle to the length of the hypotenuse. **2.** The abscissa at the endpoint of an arc of a unit circle centered at the origin of a Cartesian coordinate system, the arc being of length *x* and subtending a positive or negative angle.

cos lettuce *n.* See **romaine.**

cos•met•ic (kŏz-mĕt′ĭk) *n.* **1.** A preparation designed to beautify the body by direct application. **2.** Something superficial used to cover a deficit or defect. — *adj.* **1.** Serving to beautify the body, esp. the face and hair. **2.** Serving to modify or improve the appearance of a physical feature, defect, or irregularity: *cosmetic surgery.* **3.a.** Decorative rather than functional. **b.** Lacking depth or significance; superficial: *cosmetic changes.* [Fr. *cosmétique* < Gk. *kosmētikos,* skilled in arranging < *kosmētos,* well-ordered < *kosmein,* to arrange < *kosmos,* order.] — **cos•met′i•cal•ly** *adv.*

cos•me•ti•cian (kŏz′mĭ-tĭsh′ən) *n.* One whose occupation is manufacturing, selling, or applying cosmetics.

cos•met•i•cize (kŏz-mĕt′ĭ-sīz′) *tr.v.* **-cized, -ciz•ing, -ciz•es.**

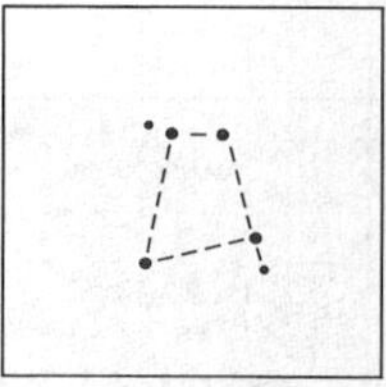

Corvus

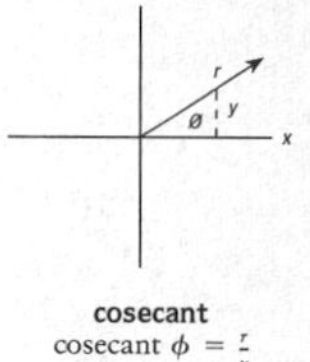

cosecant
cosecant $\phi = \frac{r}{y}$

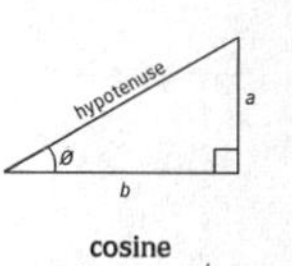

cosine
cosine $\phi = \frac{b}{Hyp}$

ă pat	oi boy
ā pay	ou out
âr care	ŏŏ took
ä father	ōō boot
ĕ pet	ŭ cut
ē be	ûr urge
ĭ pit	th thin
ī pie	*th* this
îr pier	hw which
ŏ pot	zh vision
ō toe	ə about, item
ô paw	

Stress marks:
′ (primary);
′ (secondary), as in **dictionary** (dĭk′shə-nĕr′ē)

To make superficially attractive or acceptable.

cos•me•tol•o•gy (kŏz′mĭ-tŏl′ə-jē) *n.* The study or art of cosmetics and their use. — **cos′me•tol′o•gist** *n.*

cos•mic (kŏz′mĭk) also **cos•mi•cal** (-mĭ-kəl) *adj.* **1.** Of or relating to the universe, esp. as distinct from Earth. **2.** Infinitely or inconceivably extended; vast. [Gk. *kosmikos* < *kosmos*, universe.] — **cos′mi•cal•ly** *adv.*

cosmic dust *n.* Clouds of fine solid particles of matter in interstellar space.

cosmic noise *n.* Radio-frequency radiation originating outside Earth's atmosphere, such as that originating from sunspots.

cosmic ray *n.* A stream of ionizing radiation of extraterrestrial origin, consisting chiefly of protons, alpha particles, and other atomic nuclei, that enters the atmosphere, collides with atomic nuclei, and produces secondary radiation.

cosmo– or **cosm–** *pref.* Universe; world: *cosmology.* [< Gk. *kosmos*, order, universe.]

cos•mo•chem•is•try (kŏz′mō-kĕm′ĭ-strē) *n.* The science of the chemical composition of the universe. — **cos′mo•chem′i•cal** (-ĭ-kəl) *adj.*

cos•mog•o•ny (kŏz-mŏg′ə-nē) *n., pl.* **-nies. 1.** The astrophysical study of the origin and evolution of the universe. **2.** A specific theory or model of the origin and evolution of the universe. — **cos′mo•gon′ic** (-mə-gŏn′ĭk), **cos′mo•gon′i•cal** *adj.* — **cos′mo•gon′i•cal•ly** *adv.* — **cos•mog′o•nist** *n.*

cos•mog•ra•phy (kŏz-mŏg′rə-fē) *n., pl.* **-phies. 1.** The study of the visible universe that includes geography and astronomy. **2.** A general description or depiction of the world or universe. — **cos•mog′ra•pher** *n.* — **cos′mo•graph′ic** (-mə-grăf′ĭk), **cos′mo•graph′i•cal** *adj.* — **cos′mo•graph′i•cal•ly** *adv.*

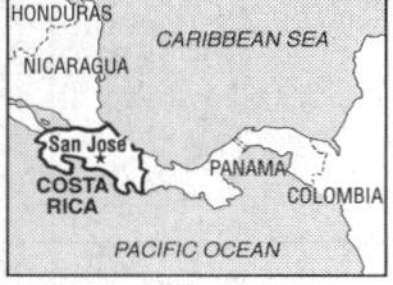

cos•mol•o•gy (kŏz-mŏl′ə-jē) *n., pl.* **-gies. 1.** The study of the physical universe considered as a totality of phenomena in time and space. **2.a.** The astrophysical study of the history, structure, and constituent dynamics of the universe. **b.** A specific theory or model of this structure and these dynamics. — **cos′mo•log′ic** (-mə-lŏj′ĭk), **cos′mo•log′i•cal** *adj.* — **cos′mo•log′i•cal•ly** *adv.* — **cos•mol′o•gist** *n.*

cos•mo•naut (kŏz′mə-nôt′) *n.* A Soviet astronaut. [Russ. *kosmonaut* : Gk. *kosmos*, universe + Gk. *nautēs*, sailor; see **nāu-***.]

cos•mop•o•lis (kŏz-mŏp′ə-lĭs) *n.* A large city inhabited by people from many different countries. [COSMO– + Gk. *polis*, city; see **pelə-³***.]

cos•mo•pol•i•tan (kŏz′mə-pŏl′ĭ-tn) *adj.* **1.** Pertinent or common to the whole world. **2.** Having constituent elements from all over the world or from many different parts of the world. **3.** So sophisticated as to be at home in all parts of the world or conversant with many spheres of interest. **4.** *Ecol.* Growing or occurring in many parts of the world; widely distributed. — *n.* A cosmopolitan person or organism; a cosmopolite. — **cos′mo•pol′i•tan•ism** *n.*

cos•mop•o•lite (kŏz-mŏp′ə-līt′) *n.* **1.** A cosmopolitan person. **2.** *Ecol.* An organism found in most parts of the world. **3.** See **painted lady.** [Gk. *kosmopolitēs* : *kosmos*, world + *politēs*, citizen (< *polis*, city; see **pelə-³***).] — **cos•mop′o•lit′ism** (-lī-tĭz′əm, -lĭ-tĭz′-) *n.*

cos•mos (kŏz′məs, -mŏs′, -mōs′) *n.* **1.** The universe regarded as an orderly, harmonious whole. **2.** An ordered, harmonious whole. **3.** Harmony and order as distinct from chaos. **4.** *pl.* **cos•mos•es** or **cosmos.** Any of various mostly Mexican herbs of the genus *Cosmos* in the composite family, having radiate flower heads. [Gk. *kosmos.*]

co•spon•sor (kō-spŏn′sər) *tr.v.* **-sored, -sor•ing, -sors.** To be a joint sponsor of. — *n.* A joint sponsor. — **co•spon′sor•ship′** *n.*

Cos•sack (kŏs′ăk) *n.* A member of a people of southern European Russia and adjacent parts of Asia, noted as cavalry soldiers esp. during czarist times. [Russ. *kazak* and Ukrainian *kozak*, both < South Turkic *qazaq*, adventurer. See KAZAKH.] — **Cos′sack′** *adj.*

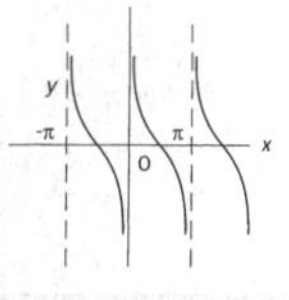

cos•set (kŏs′ĭt) *tr.v.* **-set•ed, -set•ing, -sets.** To pamper. — *n.* A pet, esp. a pet lamb. [Poss. < AN *coscet*, pet lamb < ME *cotsete*, cottage-dweller < OE *cotsǣta* : *cot*, cottage + *sǣta, -sǣte*, inhabitant; see **sed-***.]

cost (kôst) *n.* **1.** An amount paid or required in payment for a purchase; a price. **2.** The expenditure of something, such as time, necessary for the attainment of a goal. **3. costs.** *Law.* The charges fixed for litigation, often payable by the losing party. — *v.* **cost, cost•ing, costs.** — *intr.* To require a specified payment, expenditure, effort, or loss. — *tr.* **1.** To have as a price. **2.** To cause to lose, suffer, or sacrifice. **3.** *p.t. and p.part.* **costed.** To estimate or determine the cost of. [ME < OFr. < *coster*, to cost < Lat. *cōnstāre*, to be fixed, cost. See CONSTANT.]

cos•ta (kŏs′tə) *n., pl.* **-tae** (-tē). *Biol.* A rib or a riblike part, such as the midrib of a leaf. [Lat. See **kost-***.] — **cos′tal** *adj.*

Cos•ta Bra•va (kŏs′tə brä′və, kô′stə, kō′-, kôs′tä brä′vä). The Mediterranean coast of NE Spain from Barcelona to the French border.

cost accountant *n.* An accountant who keeps records of the costs of production and distribution. — **cost accounting** *n.*

Cos•ta del Sol (kŏs′tə dĕl sōl′, kô′stə, kô′stä *th*ĕl sôl′). The Mediterranean coast of S Spain NE of Gibraltar.

Cos•ta Me•sa (kŏs′tə mā′sə, kō′stə). A city of S CA SSW of Santa Ana. Pop. 96,537.

co•star also **co-star** (kō′stär′) *n.* A starring actor given equal status with another or others in a play or film. — **co′star** *v.*

cos•tard (kŏs′tərd) *n.* **1.** An English variety of large cooking apple. **2.** *Archaic.* The human head. [ME < ONFr., poss. < *coste*, rib < Lat. *costa.* See **kost-***.]

Cos•ta Ri•ca (kŏs′tə rē′kə, kô′stə, kō′-, kô′stä rē′kä). A country of Central America between Panama and Nicaragua; achieved independence from Spain in 1821. Cap. San José. Pop. 2,534,000. — **Cos′ta Ri′can** (rē′kən) *adj. & n.*

HONDURAS
CARIBBEAN SEA
NICARAGUA
San José
COSTA RICA
PANAMA
COLOMBIA
PACIFIC OCEAN

Costa Rica

cos•tate (kŏs′tət, kô′stāt′) *adj.* Having a costa or costae.

cost-ef•fec•tive (kôst′ĭ-fĕk′tĭv) *adj.* Economical in terms of the goods or services received for the money spent. — **cost′-ef•fec′tive•ly** *adv.* — **cost′-ef•fec′tive•ness** *n.*

Cos•tel•lo (kŏs-tĕl′ō), **John Aloysius.** 1891–1976. Irish politician and prime minister (1948–51 and 1954–57) who took Ireland out of the Commonwealth of Nations (1949).

Costello, Lou. 1908–59. Amer. comedian whose films with Bud Abbott include *Buck Privates* (1941).

cos•ter•mon•ger (kŏs′tər-mŭng′gər, -mŏng′-) *n. Chiefly British.* One who sells goods from a cart, barrow, or stand in the streets. [Obsolete *costard-monger* : COSTARD + MONGER.]

cos•tive (kŏs′tĭv) *adj.* **1.a.** Suffering from constipation. **b.** Causing constipation. **2.** Slow; sluggish. **3.** Stingy. [ME *costif* < OFr. *costeve*, p.part. of *costever*, to constipate < Lat. *cōnstīpāre.* See CONSTIPATE.] — **cos′tive•ly** *adv.* — **cos′tive•ness** *n.*

cost•ly (kôst′lē) *adj.* **-li•er, -li•est. 1.** Of high price or value; expensive. **2.** Entailing loss or sacrifice. — **cost′li•ness** *n.*

cost•mar•y (kôst′mâr′ē) *n., pl.* **-ies.** A Eurasian perennial herb *(Chrysanthemum balsamita)* in the composite family, having aromatic foliage used for potpourri, tea, or flavoring. [ME *costmarie* : *cost*, costmary (< OE < Lat. *costum* < Gk. *kostos* < Skt. *kuṣṭhaḥ*) + *marie*, Mary, the mother of Jesus.]

cost of living *n.* **1.** The average cost of the basic necessities of life, such as food, shelter, and clothing. **2.** The cost of basic necessities as defined by an accepted standard. — **cost′-of-liv′ing** (kôst′əv-lĭv′ĭng) *adj.*

cost-of-living index *n.* See **consumer price index.**

cost-plus (kôst′plŭs′) *n.* The cost of production plus a fixed rate of profit. — **cost′-plus′** *adj.*

cost-push (kôst′po͝osh′) *n.* Inflation in which increased production costs, as from higher wages, tend to drive prices up.

cos•trel (kŏs′trəl) *n.* A flat pear-shaped drinking vessel with loops for attachment to the belt of the user. [ME < OFr. *costerel*, poss. < *costier*, at the side < *coste*, rib < Lat. *costa.* See **kost-***.]

cos•tume (kŏs′to͞om′, -tyo͞om′) *n.* **1.** A prevalent fashion of dress, including garments, accessories, and hairstyle. **2.a.** A style of dress characteristic of a particular country, period, or people, often worn in a play or at a masquerade. **b.** An outfit or a disguise worn on Mardi Gras, Halloween, or similar occasions. **3.** A set of clothes appropriate for a particular occasion or season. — *tr.v.* (kŏ-sto͞om′, -styo͞om′, kŏs′to͞om′, -tyo͞om′) **-tumed, -tum•ing, -tumes. 1.** To put a costume on; dress. **2.** To design or furnish costumes for. [Fr. < Ital., style, dress < Lat. *cōnsuētūdō*, custom. See CUSTOM.]

cos•tum•er (kŏs′to͞o′mər, -tyo͞o′-, kŏ-sto͞o′mər, -styo͞o′-) also **cos•tum•i•er** (kŏ-sto͞o′mē-ər, -styo͞o′-, kôs′to͞om-yā′) *n.* One that makes or supplies costumes, as for plays.

co•sy (kō′zē) *adj., v., & n.* Var. of **cozy.**

cot¹ (kŏt) *n.* **1.** A narrow bed, esp. one made of canvas on a collapsible frame. **2.** *Chiefly British.* A crib. [Hindi *khāṭ* < Skt. *khaṭvā* < Tamil *kaṭṭu*, to bind, tie.]

cot² (kŏt) *n.* **1.** A small house. **2.** A protective covering or sheath. [ME < OE.]

co•tan•gent (kō-tăn′jənt) *n. Math.* **1.** The reciprocal of the tangent of an angle in a right triangle. **2.** The tangent of the complement of a directed angle or arc. — **co′tan•gen′tial** (-jĕn′shəl) *adj.*

y
-π
π
0
x

cotangent
Graph of cotangent function: $y = \cot x$

cote¹ (kōt) *n.* A small shed or shelter for sheep or birds. [ME < OE.]

cote² (kōt) *tr.v.* **cot•ed, cot•ing, cotes.** *Obsolete.* To go around by the side of; skirt. [Prob. < Fr. *côtoyer*, to skirt < *côté*, side < OFr. *coste*, rib. See COSTREL.]

Côte d'A•zur (kōt′ də-zo͞or′, dä-zür′). The Mediterranean coast of SE France.

co•ten•ant (kō-tĕn′ənt) *n.* One of two or more tenants sharing property. — **co•ten′an•cy** *n.*

Co•ten•tin (kō-tän-tăN′). A peninsula of NW France extending into the English Channel E of the Channel Is.

co•ter•ie (kō′tə-rē, kō′tə-rē′) *n.* A small, often select group who associate with one another frequently. [Fr. < OFr., peasant association < *cotier*, cottager, ult. poss. of Gmc. orig.]

co•ter•mi•nous (kō-tûr′mə-nəs) *adj.* Var. of **conterminous.**

Côte Saint Luc (sānt lo͞ok′, sənt, săN lük′). A city of S Quebec, Canada, a suburb of Montreal. Pop. 27,531.

co•thur•nus (kō-thûr′nəs) *n., pl.* **-ni** (-nī′). **1.** A buskin worn by actors of classical tragedy. **2.** The ancient style of classical tragedy. [Lat. < Gk. *kothornos.*]

co•tid•al (kō-tīd′l) *adj.* **1.** Indicating coincidence of high tides or low tides. **2.** Of or relating to a line that passes through each location on a coastal map where tides occur at the same time of day.

co•til•lion also **co•til•lon** (kō-tĭl′yən, kə-) *n.* **1.** A formal ball, esp. one at which girls are presented to society. **2.a.** A lively dance, originating in France in the 18th century, having intricate patterns and steps. **b.** A quadrille. **c.** Music for these dances. [Fr. *cotillon* < OFr., petticoat, dim. of *cote,* coat. See COAT.]

co•to•ne•as•ter (kə-tō′nē-ăs′tər) *n.* Any of various erect or creeping shrubs of the genus *Cotoneaster* in the rose family, native to Eurasia and having tiny red or black fruits. [NLat. *Cotoneaster,* genus name : Lat. *cotōneum,* quince; see QUINCE + Lat. *-aster,* partially resembling.]

Co•to•nou (kōt′n-o͞o′). A city of S Benin on the Gulf of Guinea. Pop. 215,000.

Co•to•pax•i (kō′tə-păk′sē, kô′tô-pä′hē). An active volcano, 5,900.8 m (19,347 ft), in the Andes of central Ecuador.

cot•quean (kŏt′kwēn′) *n. Archaic.* **1.** A coarse or scolding woman. **2.** A man concerned with domestic matters traditionally regarded as suitable for women. [COT[2] + QUEAN.]

Cots•wold (kŏt′swōld′) *n.* A sheep of a breed distinguished by its long wool, originally developed in the Cotswold Hills.

Cotswold Hills. A range of SW England extending c. 80 km (50 mi) NE from Bristol and rising to approx. 329 m (1,080 ft).

cot•ta (kŏt′ə) *n., pl.* **cot•tae** (kŏt′ē) or **cot•tas.** A short surplice. [Med.Lat., of Gmc. orig.]

cot•tage (kŏt′ĭj) *n.* **1.** A small single-storied house, esp. in the country. **2.** A small summer house. [ME *cotage* < AN < Med.Lat. *cotāgium,* of Gmc. orig.]

cottage cheese *n.* A soft white cheese made of strained and seasoned curds of skim milk. Also called regionally *smearcase.*

Cot•tage Grove (kŏt′ĭj). A city of E MN, a suburb of St. Paul. Pop. 22,935.

cottage industry *n.* **1.** A usu. small-scale industry carried on at home or out of the home by family members using their own equipment. **2.** A small, loosely organized industry.

cot•tag•er (kŏt′ĭ-jər) *n.* One who resides in a cottage.

cottage tulip *n.* A late-blooming type of garden tulip having long stems and egg-shaped, variously colored flowers.

Cott•bus also **Kott•bus** (kŏt′bəs, kôt′bo͝os′). A city of E-central Germany near the Polish border. Pop. 120,723.

cot•ter (kŏt′ər) *n.* **1.** A bolt, wedge, key, or pin inserted through a slot to hold parts together. **2.** A cotter pin. [?]

cotter pin *n.* A split cotter inserted through holes in two or more pieces and bent at the ends to fasten the pieces together.

Cot•ti•an Alps (kŏt′ē-ən). A range of the Alps between NW Italy and SE France rising to 3,843.6 m (12,602 ft).

cot•ton (kŏt′n) *n.* **1.a.** Any of various shrubby plants of the genus *Gossypium,* grown for the soft white downy fibers surrounding oil-rich seeds. **b.** The fiber of any of these plants, used in making textiles and other products. **c.** Thread or cloth manufactured from the fiber of these plants. **2.** The crop of these plants. **3.** Any of various soft downy substances produced by other plants. — *intr.v.* **-toned, -ton•ing, -tons.** *Informal.* **1.** To take a liking; attempt to be friendly: *a dog that didn't cotton to strangers.* **2.** To come to understand. Often used with *to* or *onto.* [ME *cotoun* < OFr. *coton* < OItal. *cotone* < Ar. dial. *qoṭon* < Ar. *quṭn.*]

Cot•ton (kŏt′n), **John.** 1584–1652. English-born Amer. cleric who fled religious persecution in England and settled in Boston, where he became a civil and religious leader.

Cotton Belt. An agricultural region of the SE U.S. extending through NC, SC, GA, AL, MS, TN, AR, LA, TX, and OK and including small sections of MO, KY, FL, and VA.

cotton candy *n.* A light, very sweet candy of threaded sugar.

cotton gin *n.* A machine that separates the seeds, seed hulls, and other small objects from the fibers of cotton.

cotton grass *n.* Any of various perennial grasslike plants of the genus *Eriophorum,* bearing at maturity one or more conspicuous tufts of cottony bristles.

cot•ton•mouth (kŏt′n-mouth′) *n.* See **water moccasin** 1.

cot•ton-pick•ing (kŏt′n-pĭk′ĭng) *adj. Informal.* Used as an intensive: *a cotton-picking fool.*

cot•ton•seed (kŏt′n-sēd′) *n.* The seed of the cotton plant.

cottonseed oil *n.* The usu. pale yellow oil obtained from cottonseed, used in manufacturing, industry, and cooking.

cotton stainer *n.* Any of various red and black bugs of the genus *Dysdercus* that pierce cotton bolls and stain the fibers.

cot•ton•tail (kŏt′n-tāl′) *n.* Any of several North American rabbits of the genus *Sylvilagus,* having grayish or brownish fur and a tail with a fluffy white underside.

cot•ton•weed (kŏt′n-wēd′) *n.* Any of various plants having cottony down, as some species of the genus *Froelichia.*

cot•ton•wood (kŏt′n-wo͝od′) *n.* Any of several North American poplar trees, esp. *Populus deltoides,* having triangular leaves and a tuft of cottony hairs on the seeds.

cotton wool *n.* Cotton in its natural or raw state.

cot•ton•y (kŏt′n-ē) *adj.* **1.** Of or resembling cotton; fluffy. **2.** Covered with fibers resembling cotton; nappy.

co•tur•nix (kə-tûr′nĭks) *n.* A small stub-tailed Eurasian quail *(Coturnix coturnix)* having sandy streaked plumage and commonly used in laboratory research. [Lat., quail.]

Co•ty (kō-tē′, kô-), **René.** 1882–1962. French politician and the last president (1953–59) of the Fourth Republic.

cot•y•le•don (kŏt′l-ēd′n) *n.* **1.** *Bot.* A leaf of the embryo of a seed plant, which upon germination either remains in the seed or emerges, enlarges, and becomes green. **2.** *Anat.* One of the lobules constituting the uterine side of the mammalian placenta, consisting mainly of a rounded mass of villi. [Lat., navelwort < Gk. *kotulēdōn* < *kotulē,* hollow object.] —**cot′y•le′don•al, cot′y•le′do•nous** (-ēd′n-əs) *adj.*

cot•y•loid (kŏt′l-oid′) also **cot•y•loid•al** (kŏt′l-oid′l) *adj.* Shaped like a cup. [Gk. *kotuloeidēs* : *kotulē,* hollow object + *-oeidēs,* -oid.]

couch (kouch) *n.* **1.a.** A sofa. **b.** A sofa on which a patient lies while undergoing psychoanalysis or psychiatric treatment. **2.a.** The frame or floor on which grain, usu. barley, is spread in malting. **b.** A layer of grain, usu. barley, spread to germinate. **3.** A priming coat of paint or varnish used in artistic painting. — *v.* **couched, couch•ing, couch•es.** — *tr.* **1.** To word in a certain manner; phrase. **2.** To cause (oneself) to lie down, as for rest. **3.** To embroider by laying thread flat on a surface and fastening it by stitches at regular intervals. **4.** To spread (grain) on a couch to germinate, as in malting. **5.** To lower (a spear, for example) to horizontal position, as for an attack. — *intr.* **1.** To lie down; recline, as for rest. **2.** To lie in ambush or concealment; lurk. **3.** To be in a heap or pile, as leaves for decomposition or fermentation. [ME *couche* < OFr. < *couchier,* to lay down, lie down < Lat. *collocāre.* See COLLOCATE.] —**couch′er** *n.*

couch•ant (kou′chənt) *adj. Her.* Lying down with the head raised. [ME < OFr., pr.part. of *couchier,* to lie down. See COUCH.]

cou•chette (ko͞o-shĕt′) *n.* **1.** A compartment on a European passenger train equipped with four to six berths for sleeping. **2.** A sleeping berth in one of these compartments. [Fr., dim. of *couche,* bed < OFr. See COUCH.]

couch grass *n.* A Eurasian grass *(Agropyron repens)* that has whitish-yellow root stocks and has become a troublesome weed in the New World. [Alteration of QUITCH GRASS.]

couch potato *n. Slang.* A person who spends much time sitting or lying down, usu. watching television.

cou•gar (ko͞o′gər) *n.* See **mountain lion.** [Fr. *couguar,* alteration of Port. *çuçuarana* < Tupi *suasuarana* : *suasú,* deer + *rana,* like (< its color).]

cough (kôf, kŏf) *v.* **coughed, cough•ing, coughs.** — *intr.* **1.** To expel air from the lungs suddenly and noisily, often to keep the respiratory passages free of irritating material. **2.** To make a noise similar to a cough. — *tr.* To expel by coughing. — *n.* **1.** The act of coughing. **2.** An illness marked by frequent coughing. —***phrasal verb.* cough up.** *Slang.* **1.** To hand over or relinquish (money or another possession), often reluctantly. **2.** To confess or disclose. [ME *coughen,* ult. of imit. orig.]

cough drop *n.* A small, often medicated and sweetened lozenge taken orally to ease coughing or soothe a sore throat.

Cough•lin (kŏg′lĭn), **Charles Edward.** 1891–1979. Canadian-born Amer. priest and political activist who gained a wide audience through radio broadcasts of his sermons.

cough syrup *n.* A sweetened medicated liquid taken orally to ease coughing.

could (ko͝od) *aux.v.* P.t. of **can[1]**. **1.** Used to indicate ability, possibility, or permission in the past: *I could run faster then. It could be no better. Only men could go to the club.* **2.** Used with hypothetical or conditional force: *If we could help, we would.* **3.** Used to indicate tentativeness or politeness: *I could be wrong. Could you come over here?*

could•est (ko͝od′ĭst) or **couldst** (ko͝odst) *aux.v. Archaic.* A second pers. sing. p.t. of **can[1]**.

could•n't (ko͝od′nt). Could not.

cou•lee (ko͞o′lē) *n.* **1.** *Western U.S.* A deep gulch or ravine with sloping sides, often dry in summer. **2.** *Louisiana & Southern Mississippi.* **a.** A streambed, often dry. **b.** A small stream, bayou, or canal. **3.** *Upper Midwest.* A valley with hills on either side. **4.a.** A stream of molten lava. **b.** A sheet of solidified lava. [Canadian Fr. *coulée* < Fr., flow < *couler,* to flow < Lat. *cōlāre,* to filter < *cōlum,* sieve.]

cou•lisse (ko͞o-lēs′) *n.* **1.** A grooved timber in which something slides. **2.a.** One of the side scenes of the stage in a theater. **b.** The space between the side scenes. **c.** A backstage area in a theater. [Fr. < OFr. *(porte) couleice,* sliding door. See PORTCULLIS.]

cou•loir (ko͞ol-wär′) *n.* A deep mountainside gorge or gully, esp. in the Swiss Alps. [Fr. < *couler,* to slide. See COULEE.]

cou•lomb[1] (ko͞o′lŏm′, -lōm′) *n.* The meter-kilogram-second unit of electrical charge equal to the quantity of charge transferred in one second by a steady current of one ampere. See table at **measurement.** [After Charles Augustin de COULOMB.]

cou•lomb[2] (ko͞o′lŏm′, -lōm′) or **cou•lom•bic** (ko͞o-lŏm′bĭk, -lōm′-) *adj.* Of or relating to the Coulomb force.

Cou•lomb (ko͞o′lŏm′, -lōm′, ko͞o-lŏm′, -lôN′), **Charles Augustin de.** 1736–1806. French physicist who pioneered research in magnetism and electricity.

cottonwood
Eastern cottonwood
Populus deltoides

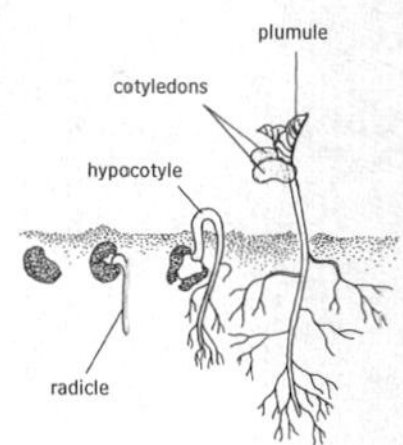

cotyledon

ă pat | oi boy
ā pay | ou out
âr care | o͝o took
ä father | o͞o boot
ĕ pet | ŭ cut
ē be | ûr urge
ĭ pit | th thin
ī pie | *th* this
îr pier | hw which
ŏ pot | zh vision
ō toe | ə about, item
ô paw |

Stress marks:
′ (primary);
′ (secondary), as in
dictionary (dĭk′shə-nĕr′ē)

Coulomb force *n.* An attractive or repulsive electrostatic force described by Coulomb's law.

Cou•lomb's law (ko͞o′lŏmz′, -lōmz′) *n.* The fundamental law of electrostatics stating that the force between two charged particles is directly proportional to the product of their charges and inversely proportional to the square of the distance between them. [After Charles Augustin de COULOMB.]

cou•lom•e•try (ko͞o-lŏm′ĭ-trē) *n.* An analytical method for determining the amount of a substance released during electrolysis in which the number of coulombs used is measured. [COULO(MB)[1] + -METRY.] — **cou′lo•met′ric** (-lə-mĕt′rĭk) *adj.*

coul•ter (kōl′tər) *n.* A blade or wheel attached to the beam of a plow that makes vertical cuts in the soil in advance of the plowshare. [ME *culter* < OE *culter* and < OFr. *coltre*, both < Lat. *culter*, knife, plowshare. See **skel-**[1]***.**]

Coul•ter pine (kōl′tər) *n.* A pine tree *(Pinus coulteri)* native to California having needles in bundles of three and heavy sharp-scaled cones. [After Thomas *Coulter* (1793–1843), Irish botanist.]

cou•ma•rin (ko͞o′mər-ĭn) *n.* A fragrant crystalline compound, $C_9H_6O_2$, extracted from several plants or produced synthetically and widely used in perfumes. [Fr. *coumarine* < *coumarou*, tonka bean tree < Sp. *coumarú* < Port. *cumaru* < Tupi *cumarú, commaru.*] — **cou′ma•ric** (-mər-ĭk) *adj.*

coun•cil (koun′səl) *n.* **1.a.** An assembly of persons called together for consultation, deliberation, or discussion. **b.** A body of people elected or appointed to serve in an administrative, legislative, or advisory capacity. **c.** An assembly of church officials and theologians convened for regulating matters of doctrine and discipline. **2.** The discussion or deliberation that takes place in such an assembly or body. [ME *counceil* < OFr. *concile* < Lat. *concilium.* See **kelə-**[2]***.**]

Usage Note: *Council* and *councilor* refer principally to a deliberative assembly, its work, and its membership. *Counsel* and *counselor* pertain chiefly to advice and guidance in general and to a person who provides it.

Coun•cil Bluffs (koun′səl). A city of SW IA on the Missouri R. opposite Omaha NE; settled in 1846. Pop. 54,315.

coun•cil•man (koun′səl-mən) *n.* A man who is a member of a council, esp. of the local governing body of a city or town.

council of ministers *n., pl.* **councils of ministers.** A body of advisers to a head of state.

coun•cil•or also **coun•cil•lor** (koun′sə-lər, -slər) *n.* A member of a council, as one convened to advise a governor. See Usage Note at **council.**

coun•cil•wom•an (koun′səl-wo͝om′ən) *n.* A woman who is a member of a council, esp. of the local governing body of a city or town.

coun•sel (koun′səl) *n.* **1.** The act of exchanging opinions and ideas; consultation. **2.** Advice or guidance, esp. as solicited from a knowledgeable person. See Syns at **advice. 3.** A plan of action. **4.** Private, guarded thoughts or opinions. **5.** A lawyer or group of lawyers giving legal advice and esp. conducting a case in court. — *v.* **-seled, -sel•ing, -sels** or **-selled, -sel•ling, -sels.** — *tr.* **1.** To give counsel to; advise. **2.** To recommend. — *intr.* To give or take advice. See Usage Note at **council.** [ME *counseil* < OFr. *conseil* < Lat. *cōnsilium*; akin to *cōnsulere*, to take counsel, consult.]

coun•sel•or also **coun•sel•lor** (koun′sə-lər, -slər) *n.* **1.** A person who counsels. **2.** An attorney, esp. a trial lawyer. **3.** A person who supervises young people at a summer camp. See Usage Note at **council.** — **coun′se•lor•ship′** *n.*

coun•sel•or-at-law (koun′sə-lər-ət-lô′, -slər-) *n., pl.* **coun•sel•ors-at-law.** An attorney; a counsel.

count[1] (kount) *v.* **count•ed, count•ing, counts.** — *tr.* **1.a.** To name or list (the units of a group or collection) one by one in order to determine a total; number. **b.** To recite numerals in ascending order up to and including. **c.** To include in a reckoning; take account of. **2.** *Informal.* **a.** To include by or as if by counting. **b.** To exclude by or as if by counting. **3.** To believe or consider to be; deem. — *intr.* **1.** To recite or list numbers in order or enumerate items by units or groups. **2.a.** To have importance. **b.** To have a specified importance or value. **3.** *Mus.* To keep time by counting beats. — *n.* **1.** The act of counting or calculating. **2.a.** A number reached by counting. **b.** The totality of specific items in a particular sample. **3.** *Law.* Any of the separate and distinct charges in an indictment. **4.** *Sports.* The counting from one to ten seconds, during which time a boxer who has been knocked down must rise or be declared the loser. **5.** *Baseball.* The number of balls and strikes called against a batter. — ***phrasal verb.*** **count on. 1.** To rely on; depend on. **2.** To be confident of. — ***idiom.*** **count heads** (or **noses**). To make a count of members, attendees, or participants by or as if by noting bodily presence. [ME *counten* < OFr. *conter* < Lat. *computāre*, to calculate : *com-*, com- + *putāre*, to think; see **peu-*.**]

Syns: *count, import, matter, signify, weigh.* The central meaning shared by these verbs is "to be of significance or importance": *an opinion that counts; actions that import little; decisions that really matter; thoughts that signify much; considerations that weigh with her.*

count[2] (kount) *n.* **1.** A nobleman in some European countries. **2.** Used as a title for such a nobleman. [ME *counte* < OFr. *conte* < LLat. *comes, comit-*, occupant of any state office < Lat., companion. See **ei-*.**]

count•a•ble (koun′tə-bəl) *adj.* **1.** That can be counted. **2.** *Math.* That can be put into a one-to-one correspondence with the positive integers. — **count′a•bil′i•ty** *n.* — **count′a•bly** *adv.*

count•down (kount′doun′) *n.* **1.** The counting backward aloud from an arbitrary starting number to indicate the time remaining before an event or operation. **2.** The checks and preparations carried out during this activity.

coun•te•nance (koun′tə-nəns) *n.* **1.** Appearance, esp. the expression of the face. **2.** The face or facial features. **3.a.** A look or expression indicative of encouragement or of moral support. **b.** Support or approval. **4.** *Obsolete.* Bearing; demeanor. — *tr.v.* **-nanced, -nanc•ing, -nanc•es.** To give or express approval to; condone. [ME *contenaunce* < OFr. < *contenir*, to behave. See CONTAIN.] — **coun′te•nanc•er** *n.*

coun•ter[1] (koun′tər) *adj.* Contrary; opposing. — *n.* **1.** One that is an opposite. **2.** *Sports.* A boxing blow given while receiving or parrying another. **3.** *Sports.* A fencing parry in which one foil follows the other in a circular fashion. **4.** A stiff piece of leather around the heel of a shoe. **5.** *Naut.* The portion of a ship's stern extending from the water line to the extreme outward swell. **6.** *Print.* The depression between the raised lines of a typeface. — *v.* **-tered, -ter•ing, -ters.** — *tr.* **1.** To meet or return (a blow) by another blow. **2.** To move or act in opposition to; oppose. **3.** To offer in response. — *intr.* To move, act, or respond so as to be in opposition. — *adv.* **1.** In a contrary manner or direction. **2.** To or toward an opposite or dissimilar course or outcome. [< COUNTER–.]

count•er[2] (koun′tər) *n.* **1.** A flat surface on which money is counted, business is transacted, or food is prepared or served. **2.** *Games.* A piece, as of wood, used for keeping a count or a place. **3.a.** An imitation coin; a token. **b.** A piece of money. [ME *countour* < AN *counteor* < Med.Lat. *computātōrium*, countinghouse < Lat. *computāre*, to calculate. See COUNT[1].]

count•er[3] (koun′tər) *n.* One that counts, esp. an electronic or mechanical device that automatically counts occurrences or repetitions of phenomena or events.

counter– *pref.* **1.** Contrary; opposite; opposing: *counterclaim.* **2.** Corresponding; complementary: *counterfoil.* [ME *countre-* < OFr. *contre-* < Lat. *contrā.* See **kom*.**]

coun•ter•act (koun′tər-ăkt′) *tr.v.* **-act•ed, -act•ing, -acts.** To oppose and mitigate the effects of by contrary action; check. — **coun′ter•ac′tion** *n.* — **coun′ter•ac′tive** *adj.*

coun•ter•ar•gu•ment (koun′tər-är′gyə-mənt) *n.* **1.** An argument in opposition to another. **2.** Something that undermines an argument or deters someone from action.

coun•ter•at•tack (koun′tər-ə-tăk′) *n.* A return attack. — *intr. & tr.v.* (koun′tər-ə-tăk′) **-tacked, -tack•ing, -tacks.** To deliver a return attack or make a return attack against.

coun•ter•bal•ance (koun′tər-băl′əns, koun′tər-băl′əns) *n.* **1.** A force or influence equally counteracting another. **2.** A weight that acts to balance another; a counterpoise. — *tr.v.* (koun′tər-băl′əns, koun′tər-băl′əns) **-anced, -anc•ing, -anc•es. 1.** To act as a counteracting force, influence, or weight to; counterpoise. **2.** To oppose with an equal force; offset.

coun•ter•change (koun′tər-chānj′) *tr v.* **-changed, -chang•ing, -chang•es. 1.** To cause to change places; transpose. **2.** To make checkered; variegate.

coun•ter•charge (koun′tər-chärj′) *n.* A charge in opposition to another charge. — *v.* (koun′tər-chärj′) **-charged, -charg•ing, -charg•es.** — *tr.* To bring a charge against (one's accuser). — *intr.* To make a countercharge.

coun•ter•check (koun′tər-chĕk′) *n.* **1.** Something that serves to check, restrict, or limit something else. **2.** Something that verifies a previous check. — *tr.v.* (koun′ter-chĕk′) **-checked, -check•ing, -checks. 1.** To oppose or check by a counteraction. **2.** To check again in order to verify.

counter check *n.* A bank check for the use of customers making a withdrawal.

coun•ter•claim (koun′tər-klām′) *n.* An opposing claim, esp. in a legal action. — *intr. & tr.v.* (koun′tər-klām′) **-claimed, -claim•ing, -claims.** To plead a counterclaim or make a counterclaim against. — **coun′ter•claim′ant** (-klā′mənt) *n.*

coun•ter•clock•wise (koun′tər-klŏk′wīz′) *adv. & adj.* In a direction opposite to the rotating hands of a clock.

coun•ter•con•di•tion•ing (koun′tər-kən-dĭsh′ə-nĭng) *n.* *Psychol.* Conditioning intended to replace a negative response to a stimulus with a positive response.

coun•ter•cul•ture (koun′tər-kŭl′chər) *n.* A culture with values or lifestyles in opposition to those of the established culture. — **coun′ter•cul′tur•al** *adj.* — **coun′ter•cul′tur•ist** *n.*

coun•ter•cur•rent (koun′tər-kûr′ənt, -kŭr′-) *n.* A current that flows opposite to the flow of another current. — **coun′ter•cur′rent** *adj.* — **coun′ter•cur′rent•ly** *adv.*

coun•ter•cy•cli•cal (koun′tər-sĭk′lĭ-kəl, -sī′klĭ-) *adj.* Intended to limit extreme developments in a business cycle.

coun•ter•dem•on•stra•tion (koun′tər-dĕm′ən-strā′shən) *n.* A demonstration held in opposition to another demonstration. — **coun′ter•dem′on•stra′tor** *n.*

coun•ter•es•pi•o•nage (koun′tər-ĕs′pē-ə-näzh′, -nĭj) *n.* Espionage to detect and counteract enemy espionage.

coun•ter•ex•am•ple (koun′tər-ĭg-zăm′pəl) *n.* An example that refutes or disproves a hypothesis, proposition, or theorem.

coun•ter•fac•tu•al (koun′tər-făk′cho͞o-əl) *adj.* Running contrary to the facts. —**coun′ter•fac′tu•al** *n.*

coun•ter•feit (koun′tər-fĭt′) *v.* **-feit•ed, -feit•ing, -feits.** —*tr.* **1.** To make a copy of, usu. with the intent to defraud; forge. **2.** To make a pretense of; feign. —*intr.* **1.** To carry on a deception; dissemble. **2.** To make fraudulent copies of something valuable. —*adj.* **1.** Made in imitation of what is genuine with the intent to defraud. **2.** Simulated; feigned. —*n.* A fraudulent imitation or facsimile. [ME *countrefeten* < *contrefet*, made in imitation < OFr. *contrefait*, p.part. of *contrefaire*, to counterfeit : *contre-*, counter- + *faire*, to make (< Lat. *facere*; see **dhē-***).] —**coun′ter•feit′er** *n.*

coun•ter•foil (koun′tər-foil′) *n.* The part of a check or other commercial paper retained by the issuer as a record.

coun•ter•force (koun′tər-fôrs′, -fōrs′) *n.* A contrary or opposing force.

coun•ter•glow (koun′tər-glō′) *n.* See **gegenschein.**

coun•ter•in•sur•gen•cy (koun′tər-ĭn-sûr′jən-sē) *n.* Political and military strategy or action intended to oppose and forcefully suppress insurgency. —**coun′ter•in•sur′gent** *n.*

coun•ter•in•tel•li•gence (koun′tər-ĭn-tĕl′ə-jəns) *n.* The branch of an intelligence service charged with keeping sensitive information from an enemy, preventing subversion and sabotage, and collecting political and military information.

coun•ter•ir•ri•tant (koun′tər-îr′ĭ-tənt) *n.* An agent that induces local inflammation to relieve inflammation in underlying or adjacent tissues. —*adj.* Of or producing the effect of such an agent. —**coun′ter•ir′ri•ta′tion** (-tā′shən) *n.*

coun•ter•man (koun′tər-măn′, -mən) *n.* A man who tends a counter, as in a diner.

coun•ter•mand (koun′tər-mănd′, koun′tər-mănd′) *tr.v.* **-mand•ed, -mand•ing, -mands. 1.** To cancel or reverse (a previously issued command or order). **2.** To recall by a contrary order. —*n.* (koun′tər-mănd′). **1.** An order or command reversing another one. **2.** Cancellation of an order or command. [ME *countremaunden* < OFr. *contremander* : *contre-*, counter- + *mander*, to command (< Lat. *mandāre*; see **man-²***).]

coun•ter•march (koun′tər-märch′) *n.* **1.** A march back or in a reverse direction. **2.** A complete reversal of method or conduct. —*intr. & tr.v.* (koun′tər-märch′) **-marched, -march•ing, -march•es.** To execute or cause to execute a countermarch.

coun•ter•mine (koun′tər-mīn′) *v.* **-mined, -min•ing, -mines.** —*tr.* **1.** To frustrate or defeat by secret and opposite measures. **2.** To make or use a countermine against. —*intr.* To make or lay down countermines. —*n.* (koun′tər-mīn′). **1.** A tunnel dug to intercept and destroy an enemy's mine. **2.** A plot to frustrate or defeat an attack.

coun•ter•move (koun′tər-mo͞ov′) *n.* A move made in opposition or retaliation to another. —*intr.v.* (koun′tər-mo͞ov′) **-moved, -mov•ing, -moves.** To make a move in retaliation or opposition. —**coun′ter•move′ment** *n.*

coun•ter•of•fen•sive (koun′tər-ə-fĕn′sĭv) *n.* A large-scale counterattack, intended to stop an enemy offensive.

coun•ter•of•fer (koun′tər-ô′fər, -ŏf′ər) *n.* An offer made in return by one who rejects an unsatisfactory offer.

coun•ter•pane (koun′tər-pān′) *n.* A cover for a bed; a bedspread. [Alteration of obsolete *counterpoint*, ult. < OFr. *coultepointe* < Med.Lat. *culcita puncta*, stitched quilt : Lat. *culcita*, quilt, mattress; see QUILT + Lat. *punctus*, stitched, pricked; see POINT.]

coun•ter•part (koun′tər-pärt′) *n.* **1.a.** One that closely resembles another. **b.** One that has the same functions and characteristics as another; an opposite number. **2.** A copy or duplicate of a legal paper. **3.a.** One of two parts that fit and complete each other. **b.** One that serves as a complement.

coun•ter•per•son (koun′tər-pûr′sən) *n.* A person who tends a counter, as in a diner.

coun•ter•plan (koun′tər-plăn′) *n.* **1.** A plan intended to counter or oppose another plan. **2.** An alternate plan.

coun•ter•plot (koun′tər-plŏt′) *n.* **1.** A plot or scheme intended to subvert another plot. **2.** See **subplot** 1. —*v.* **-plot•ted, -plot•ting, -plots.** —*intr.* To oppose or subvert one plot with another. —*tr.* To plot against; thwart with a counterplot.

coun•ter•point (koun′tər-point′) *n.* **1.** *Mus.* **a.** Melodic material that is added above or below an existing melody. **b.** The technique of combining two or more melodic lines in such a way that they establish a harmonic relationship while retaining their linear individuality. **c.** A composition or piece that incorporates or consists of contrapuntal writing. **2.a.** A contrasting but parallel element, item, or theme. **b.** Use of contrasting elements in a work of art. —*tr.v.* **-point•ed, -point•ing, -points. 1.** *Mus.* To write or arrange (music) in counterpoint. **2.** To set in contrast.

coun•ter•poise (koun′tər-poiz′) *n.* **1.** A counterbalancing weight. **2.** A force or influence that balances or equally counteracts another. **3.** The state of being in equilibrium. —*tr.v.* **-poised, -pois•ing, -pois•es. 1.** To oppose with an equal weight; counterbalance. **2.** To act against with an equal force or power; offset. [Alteration (influenced by POISE¹) of ME *countrepeis* < OFr. *contrepeis* : *contre-*, counter- + *peis*, weight; see AVOIRDUPOIS.]

coun•ter•pose (koun′tər-pōz′) *tr.v.* **-posed, -pos•ing, -pos•es.** To set in contrast, opposition, or balance.

coun•ter•pro•duc•tive (koun′tər-prə-dŭk′tĭv) *adj.* Tending to hinder rather than serve one's purpose. —**coun′ter•pro•duc′tive•ly** *adv.*

coun•ter•pro•pos•al (koun′tər-prə-pō′zəl) *n.* A proposal offered to nullify or substitute for a previous one.

coun•ter•punch (koun′tər-pŭnch′) *n.* A countering attack or blow, esp. one delivered by a boxer. —**coun′ter•punch′** *v.* —**coun′ter•punch′er** *n.*

coun•ter•ref•or•ma•tion (koun′tər-rĕf′ər-mā′shən) *n.* A reformation intended to counter the effects of a previous one.

Coun•ter Reformation (koun′tər) *n.* A reform movement within the Roman Catholic Church that arose in 16th-century Europe in response to the Protestant Reformation.

coun•ter•rev•o•lu•tion (koun′tər-rĕv′ə-lo͞o′shən) *n.* **1.** A revolution whose aim is the deposition and reversal of a political or social system set up by a previous revolution. **2.** A movement to oppose revolutionary tendencies and developments. —**coun′ter•rev′o•lu′tion•ar′y** (-shə-nĕr′ē) *adj. & n.* —**coun′ter•rev′o•lu′tion•ist** *n.*

coun•ter•shad•ing (koun′tər-shā′dĭng) *n.* Protective coloration in an animal or insect, marked by darker coloring of areas exposed to light and lighter coloring of shaded areas.

coun•ter•shaft (koun′tər-shăft′) *n.* An intermediate shaft between the powered and driven shafts in a belt drive.

coun•ter•sign (koun′tər-sīn′) *tr.v.* **-signed, -sign•ing, -signs.** To sign (a previously signed document), as for authentication. —*n.* **1.** A second or confirming signature. **2.a.** A secret sign or signal to be given to a sentry in order to pass; a password. **b.** A secret sign or signal given in answer to another.

coun•ter•sig•na•ture (koun′tər-sĭg′nə-chər) *n.* See **countersign** 1.

coun•ter•sink (koun′tər-sĭngk′) *n.* **1.** A hole with the top part enlarged so that the head of a screw or bolt will lie flush with or below the surface. **2.** A tool for making such a hole. —*tr.v.* **-sunk** (-sŭngk′), **-sink•ing, -sinks. 1.** To make a countersink on or in. **2.** To drive (a screw or bolt) into a countersink.

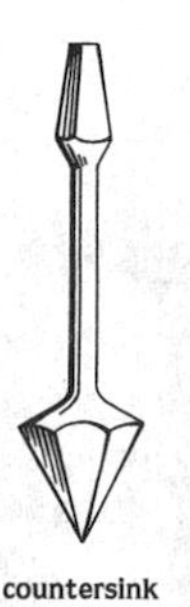
countersink

coun•ter•spy (koun′tər-spī′) *n., pl.* **-spies.** A spy working in opposition to enemy espionage.

coun•ter•stain (koun′tər-stān′) *n.* A stain used to color the components in a microscopic specimen that are not made visible by the principal stain. —**coun′ter•stain′** *v.*

coun•ter•sue (koun′tər-so͞o′) *tr.v.* **-sued, -su•ing, -sues.** *Law.* To bring proceedings against (a plaintiff) in opposition to a suit against oneself. —**coun′ter•suit′** (-so͞ot′) *n.*

coun•ter•ten•or (koun′tər-tĕn′ər) *n. Mus.* **1.** An adult male voice with a range above that of tenor. **2.** A singer having a voice that is within this range.

coun•ter•top (koun′tər-tŏp′) *n.* A level surface on a cabinet or display case, as in a kitchen or department store.

coun•ter•trans•fer•ence (koun′tər-trăns-fûr′əns, -trăns′fər-) *n.* The surfacing of a psychotherapist's own repressed feelings through identification with the emotions, experiences, or problems of a person undergoing treatment.

coun•ter•vail (koun′tər-vāl′, koun′tər-vāl′) *v.* **-vailed, -vail•ing, -vails.** —*tr.* **1.** To act against with equal force; counteract. **2.** To compensate for; offset. —*intr.* To act against an often detrimental influence or power. [ME *countrevaillen* < OFr. *contrevaloir, contrevail-* : *contre-*, counter- + *valoir*, to be worth (< Lat. *valēre*, to be strong; see **wal-***).]

coun•ter•weigh (koun′tər-wā′) *intr. & tr.v.* **-weighed, -weigh•ing, -weighs.** To counterbalance or cause to counterbalance.

coun•ter•weight (koun′tər-wāt′) *n.* **1.** A weight used as a counterbalance. **2.** A force or influence equally counteracting another. —**coun′ter•weight′ed** (-wā′tĭd) *adj.*

coun•ter•wom•an (koun′tər-wo͝om′ən) *n.* A woman who tends a counter, as in a diner.

count•ess (koun′tĭs) *n.* **1.** A woman holding the title of count or earl. **2.** The wife or widow of a count or an earl. **3.** Used as a title for such a noblewoman. [ME *countes* < OFr. *contesse*, fem. of *conte*, count. See COUNT².]

count•ing•house also **count•ing house** (koun′tĭng-hous′) *n.* A building, room, or office in which a business firm carries on operations such as accounting and correspondence.

count•less (kount′lĭs) *adj.* Incapable of being counted; innumerable. See Syns at **incalculable.** —**count′less•ly** *adv.*

count noun *n.* A noun that refers to a single entity and that can form a plural or occur in a noun phrase construction with an indefinite article, with numerals, or with such terms as *many.*

count palatine *n., pl.* **counts palatine. 1.a.** Any of various noblemen originally exercising certain royal powers within their own domains, esp. a count of the Holy Roman Empire. **b.** A feudal lord having sovereignty over his lands. **2.** The titled proprietor of a county palatine in England or Ireland.

ă pat	oi boy
ā pay	ou out
âr care	o͝o took
ä father	o͞o boot
ĕ pet	ŭ cut
ē be	ûr urge
ĭ pit	th thin
ī pie	*th* this
îr pier	hw which
ŏ pot	zh vision
ō toe	ə about, item
ô paw	

Stress marks:
′ (primary);
′ (secondary), as in
dictionary (dĭk′shə-nĕr′ē)

coun•tri•fied also **coun•try•fied** (kŭn′trĭ-fīd′) *adj.* **1.** Resembling or having the characteristics of country life; rural. **2.** Lacking sophistication.

coun•try (kŭn′trē) *n., pl.* **-tries. 1.a.** A nation or state. **b.** The territory of a nation or state; land. **c.** The people of a nation or state; populace. **2.** The land of a person's birth or citizenship. **3.** A region, territory, or large tract of land distinguishable by features of topography, biology, or culture. **4.** A district outside of cities and towns; a rural area. **5.** *Informal.* Country music. —*adj.* **1.** Of, relating to, or typical of the country. **2.** Of or relating to country music. [ME *countre* < OFr. *contree* < VLat. **(terra) contrāta,* (land) opposite, before < Lat. *contrā,* opposite. See **kom*.**]

country and western *n.* See **country music.**

country club *n.* A suburban club for social and sports activities, usu. featuring a golf course.

country cousin *n.* One whose ingenuousness or rustic ways may bemuse or entertain city dwellers.

coun•try-dance (kŭn′trē-dăns′) *n.* A folk dance of English origin in which two lines of dancers face each other.

country gentleman *n.* A man who owns a country estate.

coun•try•man (kŭn′trē-mən) *n.* **1.** A person from one's own country; a compatriot. **2.** A native or an inhabitant of a particular country. **3.** A man who lives in the country.

country mile *n. Informal.* A very great distance.

country music *n. Mus.* Popular music based on the folk style of the southern rural United States or on the music of cowboys in the American West.

coun•try•seat (kŭn′trē-sēt′) *n.* An estate or mansion in the country.

coun•try•side (kŭn′trē-sīd′) *n.* **1.** A rural region. **2.** The inhabitants of a rural region.

coun•try•wide (kŭn′trē-wīd′) *adv. & adj.* Throughout a whole country; nationwide: *a countrywide search.*

coun•try•wom•an (kŭn′trē-wo͝om′ən) *n.* **1.** A woman from one's own country; a compatriot. **2.** A woman from a particular country. **3.** A woman who lives in the country.

Gustave Courbet

coun•ty (koun′tē) *n., pl.* **-ties. 1.** An administrative subdivision of a state in the United States. **2.a.** A territorial division exercising administrative, judicial, and political functions in Great Britain and Ireland. **b.** The territory under the jurisdiction of a count or earl. **3.** The people living in a county. [ME *counte,* territorial division < OFr. *conte,* the territory of a count < Med.Lat. *comitātus* < LLat., the office of count < Lat., retinue < *comes, comit-,* companion. See **ei-*.**] —**coun′ty** *adj.*

county agent *n.* A government employee who serves as a consultant and adviser in a chiefly rural county on such matters as agriculture, education, and home economics.

county fair *n.* A fair usu. held every year in a county.

county palatine *n., pl.* **counties palatine.** The domain of a count palatine in England or Ireland.

county seat *n.* A town or city that is the administrative center of its county.

county town *n. Chiefly British.* A county seat.

coun•ty•wide (koun′tē-wīd′) *adv. & adj.* Throughout a whole county: *found at locations countywide.*

coup (ko͞o) *n., pl.* **coups** (ko͞oz). **1.** A brilliantly executed stratagem; a masterstroke. **2.** A coup d'état. [Fr., stroke < OFr. *colp* < LLat. *colpus.* See COPE[1].]

coup de grâce (ko͞o′ də gräs′) *n., pl.* **coups de grâce. 1.** A deathblow delivered to end the misery of a mortally wounded victim. **2.** A finishing stroke or decisive event. [Fr. : *coup,* stroke + *de,* of + *grâce,* mercy.]

coup de main (də măN′) *n., pl.* **coups de main.** A sudden action undertaken to surprise an enemy. [Fr. : *coup,* stroke, blow + *de,* of + *main,* hand.]

coup d'é•tat (dā-tä′) *n., pl.* **coups d'état** or **coup d'états** (dā-tä′). The sudden overthrow of a government by a usu. small group of persons in or previously in positions of authority. [Fr. : *coup,* blow, stroke + *de,* of + *état,* state.]

coup de thé•â•tre (də tā-ä′trə) *n., pl.* **coups de théâtre. 1.** A sudden, dramatic turn of events in a play. **2.** An unexpected and sensational event, esp. one that reverses or negates a situation. [Fr. : *coup,* stroke + *de,* of + *théâtre,* theater.]

coup d'oeil (dœ′yə) *n., pl.* **coups d'oeil.** A quick survey; a glance. [Fr. : *coup,* stroke + *de,* of + *oeil,* eye.]

coupe[1] (ko͞op) *n.* **1.a.** A dessert of ice cream or fruit-flavored ice, garnished and served in a special dessert glass. **b.** The stemmed glass in which a coupe is served. **2.** A shallow bowl-shaped dessert dish. [Fr., cup < LLat. *cuppa.*]

coupe[2] (ko͞op) *n.* Var. of **coupé** 2.

cou•pé (ko͞o-pā′) *n.* **1.** A closed four-wheel carriage with two seats inside and one outside. **2.** Also **coupe** (ko͞op). A closed two-door automobile. [Fr. < p.part. of *couper,* to cut < *coup,* blow. See COUP.]

Cou•pe•rin (ko͞o-pə-răN′, ko͞op-răN′), **François.** 1668–1733. French composer who was court organist to Louis XIV.

cou•ple (kŭp′əl) *n.* **1.** Two items of the same kind; a pair. **2.** Something that joins or connects two things together; a link. **3.** *(used with a sing. or pl. v.)* **a.** Two people united, as by marriage. **b.** Two people together. **4.** *Informal.* A few; several: *a couple of days.* **5.** *Phys.* A pair of forces of equal magnitude acting in parallel but opposite directions. —*v.* **-pled, -pling, -ples.** —*tr.* **1.** To link together; connect. **2.a.** To join as spouses; marry. **b.** To join in sexual union. **3.** *Elect.* To link (two circuits or currents) as by magnetic induction. —*intr.* **1.** To form pairs; join. **2.** To unite sexually; copulate. **3.** To join chemically. —*adj. Informal.* Two or few. [ME < OFr. < Lat. *cōpula,* bond, pair.]

Usage Note: When used to refer to two people who function socially as a unit, as in *a married couple,* the word *couple* may take either a singular or a plural verb, depending on whether the members are considered individually or collectively: *The couple were married last week. Only one couple was unaccounted for.* When a pronoun follows, *they* and *their* are more common than *it* and *its*: *The couple decided to spend their* (less commonly *its*) *vacation in Italy.* • Critics have sometimes maintained that *a couple of* is too inexact to be appropriate in formal writing. But the inexactitude of *a couple of* may usefully suggest that the writer is indifferent to the precise number of items involved. The usage should be considered unobjectionable on all levels of style.

cou•pler (kŭp′lər) *n.* **1.** One that couples, esp. a device for coupling two railroad cars. **2.** *Mus.* A device connecting two organ keyboards so that they may be played together.

cou•plet (kŭp′lĭt) *n.* **1.** A unit of verse consisting of two successive lines, usu. rhyming and having the same meter. **2.** Two similar things; a pair. [Fr. < OFr., dim. of *couple,* couple. See COUPLE.]

cou•pling (kŭp′lĭng) *n.* **1.** The act of forming couples. **2.** The act of uniting sexually. **3.** A device that links or connects. **4.** *Electron.* Transfer of energy from one circuit to another. **5.** The body part of a four-footed animal that connects the hindquarters to the forequarters.

cou•pon (ko͞o′pŏn′, kyo͞o′-) *n.* **1.** A negotiable certificate attached to a bond that represents a sum of interest due. **2.a.** One of a set of detachable certificates that may be torn off and redeemed as needed. **b.** A detachable part, as of an advertisement, that entitles the bearer to certain benefits, such as a refund. **c.** A certificate accompanying a product that may be redeemed for a cash discount. **d.** A printed form to be used as an order blank or for requesting information or obtaining a discount. **3.** A detachable slip calling for periodic payments, as for merchandise bought on an installment plan. [Fr. < OFr. *colpon,* piece cut off < *colper,* to cut < *colp,* blow. See COUP.]

cour•age (kûr′ĭj, kŭr′-) *n.* The state or quality of mind or spirit that enables one to face danger, fear, or vicissitudes with self-possession and resolution; bravery. [ME *corage* < OFr. < VLat. **corāticum* < Lat. *cor,* heart. See **kerd-*.**]

cou•ra•geous (kə-rā′jəs) *adj.* Having or characterized by courage; valiant. See Syns at **brave.** —**cou•ra′geous•ly** *adv.* —**cou•ra′geous•ness** *n.*

cou•rante (ko͞o-ränt′) *n.* **1.** A 17th-century French dance characterized by running and gliding steps to an accompaniment in triple time. **2.** *Mus.* The second movement of the classical baroque suite. [Fr. < fem. pr.part. of *courir,* to run < OFr. *courre* < Lat. *currere.* See **kers-*.**]

Cour•an•tyne also **Co•ran•tijn** (kōr′ən-tīn′, kôr′-). A river rising in SE Guyana and flowing c. 724 km (450 mi) to the Atlantic Ocean.

Cour•bet (ko͝or-bā′, -bĕ′), **Gustave.** 1819–77. French painter known for his realistic depiction of everyday scenes.

cour•gette (ko͝or-zhĕt′) *n. Chiefly British.* A zucchini. [Fr. dial., dim. of *courge,* gourd < OFr. *cohourde* < Lat. *cucurbita.*]

cou•ri•er (ko͝or′ē-ər, kûr′-, kŭr′-) *n.* **1.a.** A messenger, esp. one on official diplomatic business. **b.** A spy carrying secret information. **2.a.** A personal attendant hired to make arrangements for a journey. **b.** An employee of a travel agency serving as a guide for tourists. [Fr. *courrier* < OItal. *corriere* < *correre,* to run < Lat. *currere.* See **kers-*.**]

cour•lan (ko͝or′lən) *n.* See **limpkin.** [Fr., perh. alteration of *courliri* < Galibi *kurliri.*]

Cour•land also **Kur•land** (ko͝or′lənd). A historical region of S Latvia between the Baltic Sea and the Western Dvina R.

course (kôrs, kōrs) *n.* **1.** Onward movement in a particular direction; progress. **2.** The direction of continuing movement. **3.** The route or path taken by something, such as a stream, that moves. See Syns at **way. 4.** Movement in time; duration. **5.** *Sports.* A designated area of land or water on which a race is held or a sport played. **6.** A mode of action or behavior. **7.** A typical or natural manner of proceeding or developing; customary passage. **8.** A systematic or orderly succession; a sequence. **9.** A continuous layer of building material, such as brick on a wall or roof of a building. **10.a.** A complete body of prescribed studies constituting a curriculum. **b.** A unit of such a curriculum. **11.** A part of a meal served as a unit at one time. **12.** *Naut.* The lowest sail on a mast of a square-rigged ship. **13.** A point on the compass, esp. the one toward which a ship is sailing. —*v.* **coursed, cours•ing, cours•es.** —*tr.* **1.** To move swiftly through or over; traverse. **2.a.** To hunt (game) with hounds. **b.** To set (hounds) to chase game. —*intr.* **1.** To proceed or move swiftly along a specified course.

course
Slalom ski course

2. To hunt game with hounds. **—*idioms.* in due course.** At the proper or right time. **of course. 1.** In the natural or expected order of things; naturally. **2.** Without any doubt; certainly. [ME < OFr. *cours* < Lat. *cursus* < p.part. of *currere*, to run. See **kers-***.]

cours•er[1] (kôr′sər, kōr′-) *n.* **1.** A dog trained for coursing. **2.** A huntsman.

cours•er[2] (kôr′sər, kōr′-) *n.* A swift horse; a charger.

cours•ing (kôr′sĭng, kōr′-) *n.* Hunting with dogs trained to chase game by sight instead of scent.

court (kôrt, kōrt) *n.* **1.a.** An extent of open ground partially or completely enclosed by walls or buildings; a courtyard. **b.** A short street, esp. a wide alley walled by buildings on three sides. **c.** A large open section of a building, often with a glass roof or skylight. **d.** A large building standing in a courtyard. **2.a.** The place of residence of a sovereign or dignitary. **b.** The retinue of a sovereign. **c.** A sovereign's governing body, including the council of ministers and state advisers. **d.** A formal meeting or reception presided over by a sovereign. **3.** *Law.* **a.** A person or body of persons whose task is to hear and submit a decision on cases at law. **b.** The building, hall, or room in which such cases are heard and determined. **c.** The regular session of a judicial assembly. **d.** A similar authorized tribunal having military or ecclesiastical jurisdiction. **4.** *Sports.* An open level area marked with appropriate lines, upon which a game is played. **5.** The body of directors of an organization, esp. of a corporation. **6.** A legislative assembly. **—*v.* court•ed, court•ing, courts. —*tr.* 1.a.** To attempt to gain; seek. **b.** To behave so as to invite or incur. **2.** To try to gain the love or affections of, esp. to seek to marry. **3.** To attempt to gain the favor of by attention or flattery. **—*intr.*** To pursue a courtship; woo. **—*idiom.* pay court to. 1.** To flatter solicitously to obtain something or clear away antagonism. **2.** To seek someone's love; woo. [ME < OFr. *cort* < Lat. *cohors, cohort-*, courtyard, retinue. See **gher-[1]***.]

court bouillon (ko͝or, kôr, kōr) *n.* A poaching liquid for fish, usu. including water, vinegar or wine, vegetables, and seasonings. [Fr. : *court*, short + *bouillon*, broth.]

cour•te•ous (kûr′tē-əs) *adj.* Characterized by gracious consideration toward others. See Syns at **polite.** [ME *corteis*, courtly < OFr. < *cort*, court. See COURT.] **—cour′te•ous•ly** *adv.* **—cour′te•ous•ness** *n.*

cour•te•san (kôr′tĭ-zən, kōr′-) *n.* A woman who is a prostitute, esp. one whose clients are men of rank or wealth. [Fr. *courtisane* < OFr. < OItal. *cortigiana*, fem. of *cortigiano*, courtier < *corte*, court < Lat. *cohors, cohort-*. See **gher-[1]***.]

cour•te•sy (kûr′tĭ-sē) *n., pl.* **-sies. 1.a.** Polite behavior. **b.** A polite gesture or remark. **2.a.** Consent or agreement in spite of fact; indulgence. **b.** Willingness or generosity in providing something needed. **—*adj.* 1.** Given or done as a polite gesture. **2.** Free of charge. [ME *courtesie* < OFr. < *corteis*, courtly. See COURTEOUS.]

courtesy title *n.* **1.** A title of no legal validity that is assumed or granted by custom. **2.a.** In Great Britain, the title that the heir of a high-ranking peer customarily uses. **b.** In Great Britain, the prefixes *Lord* and *Lady* added to the given names of the younger children of dukes and marquises or *the Honourable* added to the children of viscounts and barons.

court•house (kôrt′hous′, kōrt′-) *n.* **1.** *Law.* A building housing judicial courts. **2.a.** A building housing the offices of a county government. **b.** A county seat.

court•i•er (kôr′tē-ər, -tyər, kōr′-) *n.* **1.** An attendant at a sovereign's court. **2.** One who seeks favor, esp. by insincere flattery or obsequious behavior. [ME *courteour* < AN < OFr. *cortoier*, to be at a royal court < *cort*, court. See COURT.]

court•ly (kôrt′lē, kōrt′-) *adj.* **-li•er, -li•est. 1.** Suitable for a royal court; stately. **2.** Elegant; refined: *courtly manners.* **3.** Flattering in an insincere way; obsequious. **—*adv.*** In a courtly manner; elegantly or politely. **—court′li•ness** *n.*

courtly love *n.* An idealized and often illicit form of love celebrated in the literature of the Middle Ages and the Renaissance in which a knight or courtier devotes himself to a noblewoman who is usu. married.

court-mar•tial (kôrt′mär′shəl, kōrt′-) *n., pl.* **courts-mar•tial** (kôrts′-, kōrts′-). **1.** A military or naval court of officers appointed by a commander to try persons for offenses under military law. **2.** A trial by such a military tribunal. **—*tr.v.* -tialed, -tial•ing, -tials** also **-tialled, -tial•ling, -tials.** To try by military tribunal. [< *martial court.*]

court of appeals *n., pl.* **courts of appeals.** *Law.* A court to which appeals are made on points of law resulting from the judgment of a lower court.

court of chancery *n., pl.* **courts of chancery.** *Law.* A court with jurisdiction in equity.

court of claims *n., pl.* **courts of claims.** *Law.* A U.S. federal court that determines claims brought by individuals against the government.

court of common pleas *n., pl.* **courts of common pleas.** *Law.* **1.** A court in some states of the United States having general jurisdiction. **2.** A court in Great Britain that formerly heard civil cases between commoners.

court of domestic relations *n., pl.* **courts of domestic relations.** *Law.* A court having the judicial authority to investigate and decide on cases involving marital and esp. parental rights and obligations.

Court of Exchequer (kôrt, kōrt) *n. Law.* A former superior court in Great Britain dealing with matters of revenue.

court of law *n., pl.* **courts of law.** *Law.* A court that hears cases and makes decisions based on statutes or the common law.

court of record *n., pl.* **courts of record.** *Law.* A court whose proceedings and decisions are retained on permanent record.

Court of Saint James's (sānt jāmz′, jām′zĭz) *n.* The British royal court.

court order *n. Law.* An order issued by a court that requires a person to do or refrain from doing something.

court plaster *n.* Cloth coated with an adhesive substance and used to cover cuts or scratches on the skin.

Cour•trai (ko͝or-trā′, ko͝or-). See **Kortrijk.**

court reporter *n. Law.* A stenographer who makes a verbatim record and transcription of proceedings, as in a court.

court•room (kôrt′ro͞om′, -ro͝om′, kōrt′-) *n. Law.* A room in which the proceedings of a court are held.

court•ship (kôrt′shĭp′, kōrt′-) *n.* The act, process, or period of courting.

court•side (kôrt′sīd′, kōrt′-) *n. Sports.* The area immediately bordering the official court of play, as in tennis or basketball.

courts-mar•tial (kôrts′mär′shəl, kōrts′-) *n.* Pl. of **court-martial.**

court tennis *n. Sports.* A form of tennis played in a large indoor court with a specially marked-out floor and high cement walls off which the ball may be played.

court•yard (kôrt′yärd′, kōrt′-) *n.* An open space surrounded by walls or buildings and adjoining or within a building.

cous•cous (ko͞os′ko͞os′) *n.* **1.** A pasta of North African origin made of crushed and steamed semolina. **2.** A North African dish consisting of pasta steamed with meat and vegetables. [Fr. < Ar. *kuskus* < *kaskasa*, to pulverize.]

cous•in (kŭz′ĭn) *n.* **1.** A child of one's aunt or uncle. **2.** A relative descended from a common ancestor by two or more steps in a diverging line. **3.** A relative by blood or marriage; a kinsman or kinswoman. **4.** A member of a kindred group or country: *our Canadian cousins.* **5.** Used as a form of address by a sovereign in addressing another sovereign or a high-ranking member of the nobility. [ME *cosin*, a relative < OFr. < Lat. *cōnsōbrīnus*, cousin : *com-*, com- + *sōbrīnus*, cousin on the mother's side; see **swesor-***.] **—cous′in•hood′** *n.* **—cous′in•ly** *adj.* **—cous′in•ship′** *n.*

Jacques Cousteau

cous•in-ger•man (kŭz′ĭn-jûr′mən) *n., pl.* **cous•ins-ger•man** (kŭz′ĭnz-). A child of one's aunt or uncle; a first cousin.

Cous•teau (ko͞o-stō′), **Jacques Yves.** b. 1910. French explorer and film producer who developed underwater laboratories.

couth (ko͞oth) *adj.* Marked by or possessing a high degree of sophistication; refined. **—*n.*** Refinement; sophistication. [Back-formation < UNCOUTH.]

cou•ture (ko͞o-to͝or′, -tür′) *n.* **1.** The business of designing, making, and selling high-fashion, usu. custom-made clothing. **2.** Dressmakers and fashion designers. **3.** The clothing created by designers. [Fr., sewing < OFr. *cousture* < VLat. **cōnsūtūra* < Lat. *cōnsuere, cōnsūt-*, to sew together : *com-*, com- + *suere*, to sew; see **syū-***.]

cou•tu•rier (ko͞o-to͝or′ē-ər, -ē-ā′, -tür-yā′) *n.* **1.** An establishment engaged in couture. **2.** One who designs for or owns such an establishment. [Fr., dressmaker < OFr. *cousturier* < *cousture*, sewing. See COUTURE.]

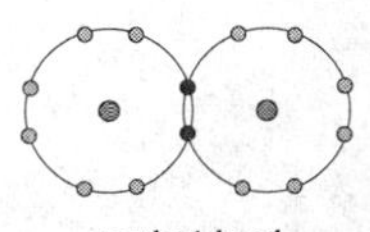

covalent bond

cou•tu•rière (ko͞o-to͝or′ē-ər, -ē-âr′, -tür-yĕr′) *n.* A woman who designs for or owns an establishment engaged in couture. [Fr., dressmaker, seamstress < OFr. *cousturiere*, fem. of *cousturier.* See COUTURIER.]

cou•vade (ko͞o-väd′) *n.* A practice in certain cultures in which the husband of a woman in labor takes to his bed as though he were bearing the child. [Fr. < OFr. < *couver*, to incubate, hatch < Lat. *cubāre*, to lie down on.]

co•va•lence (kō-vā′ləns) *n.* The number of electron pairs an atom can share with other atoms. **—co•va′len•cy** *n.* **—co•va′lent** *adj.* **—co•va′lent•ly** *adv.*

covalent bond *n.* A chemical bond formed by the sharing of electrons, esp. pairs of electrons, between atoms.

co•var•i•ance (kō-vâr′ē-əns) *n.* A statistical measure of the variance of two random variables that are observed or measured in the same mean time period.

co•var•i•ant (kō-vâr′ē-ənt) *adj.* **1.** *Phys.* Expressing or relating to the principle that physical laws have the same form regardless of the coordinate system in which they are expressed. **2.** *Statistics.* Varying with another quantity in a manner that leaves a specified relationship unchanged.

cove[1] (kōv) *n.* **1.** A small sheltered bay in the shoreline of a sea, river, or lake. **2.a.** A recess or small valley in the side of a mountain. **b.** A cave or cavern. **3.** A narrow gap or pass between hills or woods. **4.** *Archit.* **a.** A concave molding. **b.** A curved surface forming a junction between a ceiling and a wall. **—*tr.v.* coved, cov•ing, coves.** To make in an inward curving form. [ME, chamber, cave < OE *cofa.*]

cove[2] (kōv) *n. Chiefly British.* A fellow; a man. [Prob. < Romany *kova*, man.]

ă pat	oi boy
ā pay	ou out
âr care	o͝o took
ä father	o͞o boot
ĕ pet	ŭ cut
ē be	ûr urge
ĭ pit	th thin
ī pie	*th* this
îr pier	hw which
ŏ pot	zh vision
ō toe	ə about, item
ô paw	

Stress marks:
′ (primary);
′ (secondary), as in
dictionary (dĭk′shə-nĕr′ē)

co•vel•lite (kō-vĕl′īt′, kō′və-līt′) *n.* A lustrous indigo-blue mineral, CuS, a major copper ore. [After Nicolò *Covelli* (1790–1829), Italian mineralogist.]

cov•en (kŭv′ən, kō′vən) *n.* An assembly of 13 witches. [Perh. < ME *covent*, assembly, convent. See CONVENT.]

cov•e•nant (kŭv′ə-nənt) *n.* **1.** A binding agreement; a compact. **2.** *Law.* **a.** A formal sealed agreement or contract. **b.** A suit to recover damages for violation of such a contract. **3.** In the Bible, God's promise to the human race. — *v.* **-nant•ed, -nant•ing, -nants.** — *tr.* To promise by or as if by a covenant. — *intr.* To enter into a covenant. [ME < OFr. < pr.part. of *convenir*, to agree. See CONVENE.] — **cov′e•nant′al** (-năn′tl) *adj.* — **cov′e•nant′al•ly** *adv.*

cov•e•nant•ee (kŭv′ə-năn-tē′, -nən-) *n.* The party in a covenant to whom the promise is made.

cov•e•nant•er (kŭv′ə-năn′tər) *n.* **1.** One who makes a covenant. **2. Covenanter.** A Scottish Presbyterian who supported either the National Covenant of 1638 or the Solemn League and Covenant of 1643, intended to defend and extend Presbyterianism.

cov•e•nan•tor (kŭv′ə-năn′tər, -nən-, kŭv′ə-năn-tôr′) *n.* The party in a covenant by whom the promise is to be carried out.

Cov•ent Garden (kŭv′ənt, kŏv′-). An area in London long noted for its produce market (estab. 1671) and its royal theater (built 1731–32). The market was moved in 1974.

Cov•en•try[1] (kŭv′ĭn-trē). **1.** A city of central England ESE of Birmingham; famous as the home of Lady Godiva in the 11th cent. Pop. 318,600. **2.** A town of W-central RI SW of Providence; settled in 1643. Pop. 31,083.

covered wagon

Cov•en•try[2] (kŭv′ən-trē) *n.* A state of ostracism or exile. [After COVENTRY[1], England.]

cov•er (kŭv′ər) *v.* **-ered, -er•ing, -ers.** — *tr.* **1.** To place something upon or over, so as to protect or conceal. **2.** To overlay or spread with something. **3.a.** To put a cover or covering on. **b.** To wrap up; clothe. **4.** To invest (oneself) with a great deal of something. **5.a.** To spread over the surface of. **b.** To extend over. **6.a.** To copulate with (a female). Used esp. of horses. **b.** To sit on in order to hatch. **7.** To hide or screen from view or knowledge; conceal. **8.a.** To protect or shield from harm, loss, or danger. **b.** To protect by insurance. **c.** To compensate or make up for. **9.** To be sufficient to defray, meet, or offset the cost or charge of. **10.** To make provision for; take into account. **11.** To deal with; treat of. **12.** To travel or pass over; traverse. **13.a.** To have as one's territory or sphere of work. **b.** To be responsible for reporting the details of (an event or situation). **14.** To hold within the range and aim of a weapon, such as a firearm. **15.** To protect by occupying a strategic position. **16.** *Sports.* **a.** To be responsible for guarding (an opponent). **b.** To be responsible for defending (a position). **17.** To match (an opponent's stake) in a wager. **18.** To purchase (stock that one has shorted). **19.** *Games.* To play a higher-ranking card than (the one previously played). **20.** *Obsolete.* To pardon or remit. — *intr.* **1.** To spread over a surface to protect or conceal something. **2.** To act as a substitute or replacement during someone's absence. **3.** To hide something in order to save someone from censure or punishment: *cover up for a colleague.* **4.** *Games.* To play a higher card than the one previously played. — *n.* **1.** Something that covers or is laid, placed, or spread over or upon something else, as: **a.** A lid or top. **b.** A binding or enclosure for a book or magazine. **c.** A protective overlay, as for a mattress. **2.a.** Something that provides shelter. **b.** Strategic protection given by armed units during hostile action. **3.a.** Something, such as vegetation, covering the surface of the ground. **b.** Vegetation serving as protective concealment for wild animals. **4.a.** Something, such as darkness, that screens, conceals, or disguises. **b.** A false background and identity, esp. for a spy. **5.** A table setting for one person. **6.** A cover charge. **7.** An envelope or wrapper for mail. **8.** Funds sufficient to meet an obligation or secure against loss. **9.** One who substitutes for another. — ***idioms.*** **cover (one's) tracks.** To conceal traces so as to elude pursuers. **cover (the) ground. 1.** To traverse a given distance with satisfying speed. **2.** To deal with or accomplish something in a certain manner. **take cover.** To seek concealment or protection. **under cover. 1.** In an enclosure for mailing. **2.** Being hidden or protected, as by darkness. [ME *coveren* < OFr. *covrir* < Lat. *cooperīre*, to cover completely : *co-*, intensive pref.; see CO– + *operīre*, to cover; see **wer-[4]*.**] — **cov′er•a•ble** *adj.* — **cov′er•er** *n.* — **cov′er•less** *adj.*

cowcatcher

cov•er•age (kŭv′ər-ĭj) *n.* **1.** The extent or degree to which something is observed, analyzed, and reported. **2.a.** Inclusion in an insurance policy or protective plan. **b.** The extent of protection afforded by an insurance policy. **3.** The amount of funds reserved to meet liabilities. **4.** The percentage of persons reached by a medium of communication, such as television.

cov•er•alls (kŭv′ər-ôlz′) *pl.n.* A loose-fitting one-piece work garment worn to protect clothes.

cover boy *n.* An attractive young man whose picture is featured on a magazine cover.

cover charge *n.* A fixed amount added to the bill at a nightclub or restaurant for entertainment or services.

cover crop *n.* A crop planted between periods of regular crop production to prevent soil erosion and provide humus or nitrogen.

Cov•er•dale (kŭv′ər-dāl′), **Miles.** 1488–1568. English cleric who produced the first complete English Bible (1535).

cov•ered bridge (kŭv′ərd) *n.* A bridge whose roadway is protected by a roof and sides.

covered wagon *n.* A large wagon covered with an arched canvas top, used esp. by American pioneers for prairie travel.

cover girl *n.* An attractive young woman whose picture is featured on a magazine cover.

cover glass *n.* **1.** A small thin piece of glass used to cover a specimen on a microscope slide. **2.** A protective sheet of glass for a transparency.

cov•er•ing (kŭv′ər-ĭng) *n.* Something that covers so as to protect or conceal.

covering letter *n.* A letter sent with other documents to explain more fully or provide more information.

cov•er•let (kŭv′ər-lĭt) also **cov•er•lid** (-lĭd) *n.* A bedspread. [ME *coverlite* < AN *coverelyth* : OFr. *covrir*, to cover; see COVER + OFr. *lit*, bed (< Lat. *lectus*; see **legh-***).]

cover letter *n.* See **covering letter.**

covers *abbr. Math.* Versed cosine.

co•ver•sine (kō-vûr′sīn′) *n. Math.* See **versed cosine.**

cover slip *n.* See **cover glass** 1.

cover story *n.* **1.** A story in a magazine concerning the cover illustration. **2.** A false story intended to deceive.

cov•ert (kŭv′ərt, kō′vərt, kō-vûrt′) *adj.* **1.** Not openly practiced, avowed, engaged in, accumulated, or shown. **2.** Covered or covered over; sheltered. **3.** *Law.* Being married and therefore protected by one's husband. — *n.* **1.** A covering or cover. **2.a.** A covered place or shelter; a hiding place. **b.** Thick underbrush or woodland affording cover for game. **3.** *Zool.* One of the small feathers covering the bases of the longer feathers of a bird's wings or tail. **4.** A flock of coots. [ME < OFr. < p.part. of *covrir*, to cover. See COVER.] — **cov′ert•ly** *adv.* — **cov′ert•ness** *n.*

cov•er•ture (kŭv′ər-chər, -chŏŏr′) *n.* **1.a.** A covering; a shelter. **b.** The state of being concealed; disguise. **2.** *Law.* A married woman's status under common law. [ME < OFr. < *covert*, concealed. See COVERT.]

cov•er-up or **cov•er•up** (kŭv′ər-ŭp′) *n.* **1.** An effort or strategy of concealment, esp. a planned effort to prevent scandal. **2.** A loose garment for wear over other clothing.

cov•et (kŭv′ĭt) *v.* **-et•ed, -et•ing, -ets.** — *tr.* **1.** To feel blameworthy desire for (that which is another's). See Syns at **envy. 2.** To wish for longingly. See Syns at **desire.** — *intr.* To covet that which is another's. [ME *coveiten* < OFr. *coveitier* < *covitie*, desire < Lat. *cupiditās* < *cupidus*, desirous < *cupere*, to desire.] — **cov′et•a•ble** *adj.* — **cov′et•er** *n.* — **cov′et•ing•ly** *adv.*

cov•et•ous (kŭv′ĭ-təs) *adj.* **1.** Excessively and culpably desirous of the possessions of another. See Syns at **jealous. 2.** Marked by extreme desire to acquire or possess: *covetous of learning.* — **cov′et•ous•ly** *adv.* — **cov′et•ous•ness** *n.*

cov•ey (kŭv′ē) *n., pl.* **-eys. 1.** A family or small flock of birds, esp. partridge or quail. **2.** A small group, as of persons. [ME < OFr. *covee*, brood < fem. p.part. of *cover*, to incubate < Lat. *cubāre*, to lie down.]

Co•vi•na (kō-vē′nə). A city of S CA E of Los Angeles. Pop. 43,207.

cov•ing (kō′vĭng) *n.* See **cove[1]** 4.

Cov•ing•ton (kŭv′ĭng-tən). A city of extreme N KY on the Ohio R. opposite Cincinnati; settled in 1812. Pop. 43,264.

cow[1] (kou) *n.* **1.** The mature female of cattle of the genus *Bos.* **2.** The mature female of other large animals, such as whales or moose. **3.** A domesticated bovine of either sex or any age. — ***idiom.*** **till the cows come home.** *Informal.* For a long time. [ME *cou* < OE *cū*. See **g^wou-*.**] — **cow′y** *adj.*

cow[2] (kou) *tr.v.* **cowed, cow•ing, cows.** To frighten with threats or a show of force. [Prob. of Scand. orig.] — **cow′ed•ly** (-ĭd-lē) *adv.*

cow•ard (kou′ərd) *n.* One who shows cowardice. [ME < OFr. *couard* < *coue*, tail < Lat. *cauda.*] — **cow′ard** *adj.*

Cow•ard (kou′ərd), Sir **Noel Pierce.** 1899–1973. British actor, playwright, and composer noted esp. for his witty comedies, such as *Private Lives* (1930).

cow•ard•ice (kou′ər-dĭs) *n.* Ignoble fear in the face of danger or pain. [ME *cowardise* < OFr. *couardise*, alteration of *couardie* < *couard*, coward. See COWARD.]

cow•ard•ly (kou′ərd-lē) *adj.* Exhibiting the characteristics of a coward. — **cow′ard•li•ness** *n.* — **cow′ard•ly** *adv.*

cow•bane (kou′bān′) *n.* **1.** A perennial North American herb *(Oxypolis rigidior)* having pinnately compound leaves and umbels of small white flowers. **2.** Any of several related plants, such as the water hemlock.

cow•bell (kou′bĕl′) *n.* A bell on a cow's collar.

cow•ber•ry (kou′bĕr′ē) *n.* **1.** A low creeping evergreen shrub *(Vaccinium vitis-idaea)* native to northern parts of North America and Eurasia. **2.** The edible red berry of this plant.

cow•bird (kou′bûrd′) *n.* Any of various blackbirds of the genus *Molothrus*, esp. the common North American species *M. ater*, which lay their eggs in the nests of other birds.

cow•boy (kou′boi′) *n.* **1.** A hired man, esp. in the western United States, who tends cattle and works on horseback. Also called regionally *buckaroo, vaquero, waddy.* See Regional Note at **vaquero. 2.** An adventurous hero. **3.** *Slang.* A reckless person who ignores potential risks.

cowboy boot *n.* A high-arched boot with a high Cuban heel and usu. ornamental stitching.

cowboy hat *n.* A felt hat with a tall crown and wide brim.

cow•catch•er (kou′kăch′ər, -kĕch′-) *n.* The metal grille or frame projecting from the front of a locomotive and serving to clear the track of obstructions.

cow college *n. Informal.* **1.** An agricultural college. **2.** A college or university considered to be provincial.

cow•er (kou′ər) *intr.v.* **-ered, -er•ing, -ers.** To cringe in fear. [ME *couren,* of Scand. orig.]

Cowes (kouz). A town on the N coast of the Isle of Wight off S England; home of the Royal Yacht Club. Pop. 19,663.

cow•fish (kou′fĭsh′) *n., pl.* **cowfish** or **-fish•es. 1.** Any of various aquatic mammals, esp. a whale of the genus *Mesoplodon,* having a pointed snout. **2.** Any of various marine fishes of the family Ostraciidae, esp. *Lactophrys quadricornis,* having hornlike spines over each eye.

cow•girl (kou′gûrl′) *n.* A hired woman, esp. in the western United States, who tends cattle and works on horseback.

cow•hand (kou′hănd′) *n.* A cowboy or cowgirl.

cow•herd (kou′hûrd′) *n.* One who herds or tends cattle.

cow•hide (kou′hīd′) *n.* **1.a.** The hide of a cow. **b.** The leather made from this hide. **2.** A heavy flexible whip, usu. made of braided leather. —*tr.v.* **-hid•ed, -hid•ing, -hides.** To beat with a heavy flexible whip.

cowl (koul) *n.* **1.a.** The hood or hooded robe worn esp. by a monk. **b.** A draped neckline on a woman's garment. **2.** A hood-shaped covering used to increase the draft of a chimney. **3.** The top portion of the front part of an automobile body, supporting the windshield and dashboard. **4.** The cowling on an aircraft. —*tr.v.* **cowled, cowl•ing, cowls.** To cover with or as if with a cowl. [ME *coule* < OE *cugele* < LLat. *cuculla* < Lat. *cucullus,* hood.]

cowled (kould) *adj.* **1.** Wearing or supplied with a cowl; hooded. **2.** Having the shape of a hood.

Cow•ley (kou′lē), **Abraham.** 1618–67. English metaphysical poet whose works include *Davideis* (1656).

Cowley, Malcolm. 1898–1989. Amer. editor and critic noted for his studies of expatriate writers of the 1920's.

cow•lick (kou′lĭk′) *n.* A tuft of hair on the head that grows in a different direction from the rest and will not lie flat.

cowl•ing (kou′lĭng) *n.* A removable metal covering for an engine, esp. an aircraft engine.

cow•man (kou′mən, -măn′) *n.* **1.** An owner of cattle or a cattle ranch. **2.a.** See **cowboy** 1. **b.** A cowherd.

co•work•er or **co-work•er** (kō′wûr′kər) *n.* One that works with another; a fellow worker.

cow parsnip *n.* Any of several tall coarse herbs of the genus *Heracleum* in the parsley family, native chiefly to northern temperate regions and having compound umbels.

cow•pea (kou′pē′) *n.* **1.** An annual African plant *(Vigna unguiculata)* in the pea family, cultivated in warm regions for food, forage, and soil improvement. **2.** Its edible seed.

Cow•per (ko͞o′pər, kou′-, ko͝op′ər), **William.** 1731–1800. British poet considered a precursor of romanticism.

Cow•per's gland (kou′pərz, ko͞o′-) *n.* See **bulbourethral gland.** [After William *Cowper* (1666–1709), English surgeon.]

cow pilot *n.* See **sergeant major** 3.

cow•poke (kou′pōk′) *n.* See **cowboy** 1.

cow pony *n.* A small, agile horse used in herding cattle.

cow•pox (kou′pŏks′) *n.* A contagious skin disease of cattle, usu. characterized by postules on the udder, that is caused by a virus and when transmitted to humans confers immunity to smallpox.

cow•punch•er (kou′pŭn′chər) *n.* See **cowboy** 1.

cow•rie or **cow•ry** (kou′rē) *n., pl.* **-ries.** Any of various tropical marine gastropods of the family Cypraeidae, having glossy, often brightly marked shells, some of which are used as currency in the South Pacific and Africa. [Hindi *kauṛī* < Skt. *kapardikā,* dim. of *kapardaḥ,* shell, of Dravidian orig.]

co•write (kō-rīt′) *tr.v.* **-wrote** (-rōt′), **-writ•ten** (-rĭt′n), **-writ•ing, -writes.** To write jointly or in collaboration with another author. —**co′writ•er** *n.*

cow shark *n.* Any of several sharks of the family Hexanchidae of warm and temperate seas.

cow•shed (kou′shed′) *n.* A shed for housing cows.

cow•slip (kou′slĭp′) *n.* **1.** A Eurasian primrose *(Primula veris)* usu. having fragrant yellow flowers. **2.** See **marsh marigold. 3.** The Virginia cowslip. [ME *cowslyppe* < OE *cūslyppe* : *cū,* cow; see **g^{w}ou-*** + *slypa,* slime; see **sleubh-*.**]

cox (kŏks) *Naut. n.* A coxswain. —**cox** *v.*

cox•a (kŏk′sə) *n., pl.* **cox•ae** (kŏk′sē′). **1.** *Anat.* The hip or hip joint. **2.** *Zool.* The segment of the leg of an insect or other arthropod that adjoins the body. [Lat., hip.] —**cox′al** *adj.*

cox•al•gi•a (kŏk-săl′jē-ə, -jə) *n.* Pain in or disease of the hip or hip joint. [COX(A) + -ALGIA.] —**cox•al′gic** (-jĭk) *adj.*

cox•comb (kŏks′kōm′) *n.* **1.** A conceited dandy; a fop. **2.** *Obsolete.* A jester's cap; a cockscomb. [ME *cokkes comb,* crest of a cock : *cokkes,* genitive of *cok,* cock; see COCK[1] + *comb,* crest; see COMB.]

cox•comb•ry (kŏk′skōm′rē, -skəm-) *n., pl.* **-ries.** Behavior that is characteristic of a coxcomb; foppish conceit.

Cox•ey (kŏk′sē), **Jacob Sechler.** 1854–1951. Amer. businessman and reformer who led a march on Washington DC to protest unemployment (1894).

cox•i•tis (kŏk-sī′tĭs) *n.* Inflammation of the hip joint.

cox•sack•ie•vi•rus also **Cox•sack•ie virus** (ko͝ok-sä′kē-vī′rəs, kŏk-săk′ē-) *n.* Any of a group of enteroviruses that can cause a disease resembling poliomyelitis but without paralysis. [After *Coxsackie,* a village of E-central NY.]

cox•swain (kŏk′sən, -swān′) *Naut.* —*n.* **1.** A person who usu. steers a ship's boat and has charge of its crew. **2.** A person in a racing shell who usu. directs the rest of the crew. —*intr. & tr.v.* **-swained, -swain•ing, -swains.** To act as coxswain or serve as coxswain for. [ME *cokswaynne* : *cok,* cockboat; see COCKBOAT + *swain,* servant; see SWAIN.]

coy (koi) *adj.* **coy•er, coy•est. 1.** Tending to avoid people and social situations; reserved. **2.** Affectedly and usu. flirtatiously shy or modest. See Syns at **shy[1]. 3.** Annoyingly unwilling to make a commitment. [ME < OFr. *quei, coi,* quiet, still < VLat. **quētus* < Lat. *quiētus* < *quiēs,* quiet, stillness. See **k^{w}eiə-*.**] —**coy′ly** *adv.* —**coy′ness** *n.*

coy•dog (kī′dôg′, -dŏg′) *n.* The hybrid offspring of a coyote and a feral dog. [COY(OTE) + DOG.]

coy•o•te (kī-ō′tē, kī′ōt′) *n.* A small wolflike carnivorous animal *(Canis latrans)* native to western North America. [Am. Sp. < Nahuatl *cóyotl.*]

coy•o•til•lo (koi′ə-tĭl′ō, -tē′yō, kī′ə-) *n., pl.* **-los.** A poisonous shrub *(Karwinskia humboldtiana)* native to Texas and Mexico and having small greenish flowers and black fruits. [Am.Sp., dim. of *coyote,* coyote. See COYOTE.]

coy•pu (koi′po͞o) *n., pl.* **-pus.** A large aquatic South American rodent *(Myocastor coypus)* having webbed feet and a long tail. [Am.Sp. *coipú* < Araucanian *kóypu.*]

coz (kŭz) *n. Informal.* A cousin.

coz•en (kŭz′ən) *v.* **-ened, -en•ing, -ens.** —*tr.* **1.** To mislead by means of a petty trick or fraud; deceive. **2.** To persuade or induce to do something by cajoling or wheedling. **3.** To obtain by deceit or persuasion. —*intr.* To act deceitfully. [Perh. < ME *cosin,* fraud, trickery.] —**coz′en•er** *n.*

coz•en•age (kŭz′ə-nĭj) *n.* **1.** The art or practice of cozening. **2.** An act or example of cozening.

Co•zu•mel (kō′zə-mĕl′, so͞o-). An island off the coast of SE Mexico near Cancún.

co•zy also **co•sy** (kō′zē) —*adj.* **-zi•er, -zi•est** also **-si•er, -si•est. 1.** Snug, comfortable, and warm. **2.** Marked by friendly intimacy. **3.** *Informal.* Marked by close association for devious purposes. —*intr.v.* **-zied, -zy•ing, -zies** also **-sied, -sy•ing, -sies.** *Informal.* To try to get on friendly or intimate terms; ingratiate oneself. —*n., pl.* **-zies** also **-sies.** A padded or knitted covering placed esp. over a teapot to keep the tea hot. [Prob. of Scand. orig.] —**co′zi•ly** *adv.* —**co′zi•ness** *n.*

cp *abbr.* Candlepower.

cP *abbr.* Centipoise.

CP *abbr.* **1.** Chemically pure. **2.** Or **C.P.** Command post. **3.** Communist Party.

cp. *abbr.* **1.** Compare. **2.** Coupon.

C.P. *abbr.* Cape Province.

CPA also **C.P.A.** *abbr.* Certified public accountant.

cpd. *abbr.* Compound.

CPFF *abbr.* Cost plus fixed fee.

CPI *abbr.* Consumer price index.

cpl *abbr.* **1.** Complete. **2.** *Eccles.* Complin.

Cpl. *abbr.* Corporal.

cpm or **CPM** *abbr.* **1.** Cost per thousand. **2.** Cycles per minute.

CPO *abbr.* Chief petty officer.

CPR *abbr.* Cardiopulmonary resuscitation.

cps *abbr.* **1.** Characters per second. **2.** Cycles per second.

CPS also **C.P.S.** *abbr.* Certified professional secretary.

Cpt. or **CPT** *abbr.* Captain.

CPU *abbr. Comp. Sci.* Central processing unit.

CQ[1] (sē′kyo͞o′) *n.* Code letters used at the beginning of radio messages intended for all receivers. [?]

CQ[2] *abbr.* Call to quarters.

Cr The symbol for the element **chromium.**

CR *abbr. Psychol.* **1.** Conditioned reflex. **2.** Conditioned response.

cr. *abbr.* **1.** Credit; creditor. **2.** Creek. **3.** Crescendo. **4.** Crown.

C.R. *abbr.* Costa Rica.

crab[1] (krăb) *n.* **1.a.** Any of various predominantly marine crustaceans of the order Decapoda, characterized by a broad flattened cephalothorax covered by a hard carapace, short antennae, and five pairs of legs, of which the anterior pair are large and pincerlike. **b.** Any of various similar related crustaceans, such as the hermit crab. **c.** A horseshoe crab. **2.a.** A crab louse. **b. crabs.** *Slang.* Infestation by crab lice. **3.** The maneuvering of an aircraft partially into a crosswind to compensate for drift. **4.** A machine for handling or hoisting heavy

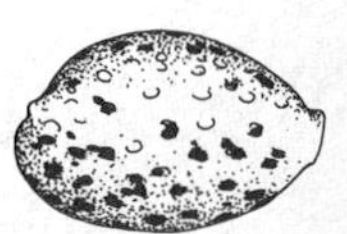

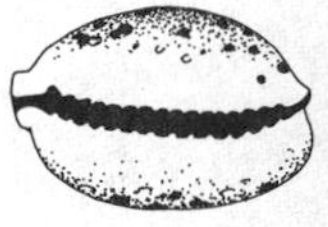

cowrie

coxswain
Coxswain and rower

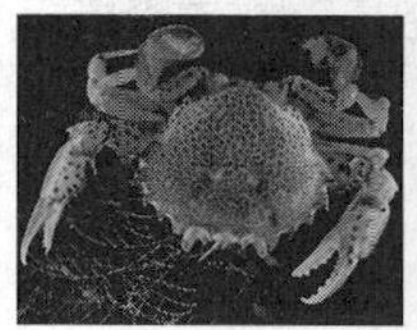

crab[1]
Lady crab
Ovalipes ocellatus

ă pat	oi boy
ā pay	ou out
âr care	o͝o took
ä father	o͞o boot
ĕ pet	ŭ cut
ē be	ûr urge
ĭ pit	th thin
ī pie	*th* this
îr pier	hw which
ŏ pot	zh vision
ō toe	ə about,
ô paw	item

Stress marks:
′ (primary);
′ (secondary), as in **dictionary** (dĭk′shə-nĕr′ē)

weights. — *v.* **crabbed, crab•bing, crabs.** — *intr.* **1.** To hunt or catch crabs. **2.** To scurry sideways in the manner of a crab. **3.** To drift diagonally or sideways. **4.** To direct an aircraft into a crosswind. — *tr.* **1.** To direct (an aircraft) partly into a crosswind to eliminate drift. **2.** To cause to move or scurry sideways. — ***idiom.*** **catch a crab.** To strike the water with an oar in recovering a stroke or miss it in making one. [ME *crabbe* < OE *crabba.* See **gerbh-*.**] — **crab•ber** *n.*

crab[2] (krăb) *n.* **1.** A crab apple tree or its fruit. **2.** A quarrelsome, ill-tempered person. — *v.* **crabbed, crab•bing, crabs.** — *intr. Informal.* To find fault; criticize someone or something. — *tr.* **1.** *Informal.* To interfere with and ruin; spoil. **2.** *Informal.* To find fault with; complain about. **3.** To make ill-tempered or sullen. [ME *crabbe,* poss. < *crabbe,* crab (shellfish). See CRAB[1].] — **crab′ber** *n.*

Crab (krăb) *n.* See **Cancer.**

crab apple also **crab•ap•ple** (krăb′ăp′əl) *n.* **1.** Any of several deciduous trees of the genus *Malus,* native to North America and Eurasia. **2.** The small tart fruit of such a tree.

crab•bed (krăb′ĭd) *adj.* **1.** Irritable and perverse in disposition; ill-tempered. **2.** Difficult to understand; complicated. **3.** Difficult to read. [ME < *crabbe,* crab (influenced by CRAB[2]). See CRAB[1].] — **crab′bed•ly** *adv.* — **crab′bed•ness** *n.*

crab•by (krăb′ē) *adj.* **-bi•er, -bi•est.** *Informal.* Grouchy; ill-tempered. — **crab′bi•ly** *adv.* — **crab′bi•ness** *n.*

crab•grass or **crab grass** (krăb′grăs′) *n.* Any of certain grasses of the genus *Digitaria,* esp. *D. sanguinalis* or *D. ischaemum,* widely naturalized in North America.

crab louse *n.* A sucking louse *(Phthirus pubis)* that generally infests the pubic region and causes severe itching.

crab•meat (krăb′mēt′) *n.* The edible flesh of a crab.

crab's eye (krăbz) *n.* See **rosary pea.**

crab•stick (krăb′stĭk′) *n.* **1.** A stick made of crab apple wood. **2.** A crabby, ill-tempered person.

crab•wise (krăb′wīz′) *adv.* **1.** Sideways. **2.** In a furtive or circumspect manner; indirectly.

crack (krăk) *v.* **cracked, crack•ing, cracks.** — *intr.* **1.** To break or snap apart. **2.** To make a sharp snapping sound. **3.** To break without complete separation of parts; fissure. **4.** To change sharply in pitch or timbre, as from hoarseness or emotion. Used of the voice. **5.** To break down; fail: *The defendant's composure began to crack.* **6.** To have a mental or physical breakdown. **7.** To move or go rapidly. **8.** *Chem.* To break into simpler molecules by means of heat. — *tr.* **1.** To cause to make a sharp snapping sound. **2.** To cause to break without complete separation of parts. **3.a.** To break with a sharp snapping sound. See Syns at **break. b.** To crush (wheat, for example) into small pieces. **4.** To strike with a sudden sharp sound. **5.** *Informal.* **a.** To break open or into: *crack a safe.* **b.** To open up for use or consumption: *crack a book.* **c.** To break through (an obstacle) in order to win acceptance or acknowledgment. **6.** To discover the solution to, esp. after considerable effort. **7.** To cause (the voice) to crack. **8.** *Informal.* To tell (a joke), esp. on impulse or in an effective manner. **9.** To cause to have a mental or physical breakdown. **10.** To impair or destroy. **11.** To reduce (petroleum) to simpler compounds by cracking. — *n.* **1.** A sharp snapping sound, such as the report of a firearm. **2.a.** A partial split or break; a fissure. **b.** A slight narrow space. **3.** A sharp resounding blow. **4.a.** A mental or physical impairment; a defect. **b.** A breaking, harshly dissonant vocal tone or sound, as in hoarseness. **5.** An attempt or try. **6.** A witty or sarcastic remark. **7.** A moment; an instant: *at the crack of dawn.* **8.** *Slang.* Purified potent cocaine that is smoked through a glass pipe and is considered highly addictive. — *adj.* Excelling in skill or achievement; first-rate: *a crack shot.* — ***phrasal verbs.*** **crack down.** To act more forcefully to regulate, repress, or restrain. **crack up.** *Informal.* **1.** To praise highly: *not the genius he was cracked up to be.* **2.a.** To damage or wreck (a vehicle or vessel). **b.** To wreck a vehicle in an accident. **3.** To have a mental or physical breakdown. **4.** To experience or cause to experience a great deal of amusement. — ***idiom.*** **crack the whip.** To behave in a domineering manner; demand hard work from those under one's control. [ME *craken* < OE *cracian.* See **gerə-[2]*.**]

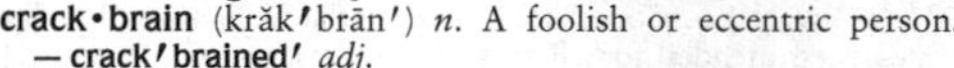

crack•brain (krăk′brān′) *n.* A foolish or eccentric person. — **crack′brained′** *adj.*

crack•down (krăk′doun′) *n.* An act or example of forceful regulation, repression, or restraint: *a crackdown on crime.*

cracked (krăkt) *adj.* **1.a.** Broken so that fissures appear on the surface: *a cracked mirror.* **b.** Broken into small or coarse pieces: *cracked corn.* **2.** Having a harsh or dissonant tone: *a cracked voice.* **3.** *Informal.* Mentally deranged; crazy.

crack•er (krăk′ər) *n.* **1.** A thin crisp wafer or biscuit, usu. made of unsweetened dough. **2.** One that cracks, esp.: **a.** A firecracker. **b.** A small cardboard cylinder covered with decorative paper that holds candy or a party favor and pops open. **c.** The apparatus used in the cracking of petroleum. **d.** One who makes unauthorized use of a computer, esp. to tamper with data or programs. **3.** *Offensive.* Used as a disparaging term for a poor white person of the rural, esp. southeast United States.

cradle
Top: 17th-century English oak cradle
Bottom: Supporting a boat

crag
Quoddy Head State Park, Maine

crack•er-bar•rel (krăk′ər-băr′əl) *adj.* Of or resembling the informal discussions carried on by persons at a country store: *cracker-barrel philosophy.*

crack•er•jack (krăk′ər-jăk′) also **crack•a•jack** (krăk′ə-) *adj. Slang.* Of excellent quality or ability; fine. [Prob. < CRACK, first-rate + JACK.] — **crack′er•jack′** *n.*

crack•ers (krăk′ərz) *adj. Chiefly British.* Insane; mad. [Prob. < CRACKER, breakdown.]

crack•ing (krăk′ĭng) *n. Chem.* Thermal decomposition of a complex substance, esp. the breaking of petroleum molecules into shorter molecules to extract low-boiling fractions such as gasoline. — *adj.* Excellent; great. — *adv.* Used as an intensive: *a cracking good show.*

crack•le (krăk′əl) *v.* **-led, -ling, -les.** — *intr.* **1.** To make a succession of slight sharp snapping noises. **2.** To show liveliness or brilliance. **3.** To craze. — *tr.* **1.** To crush (paper, for example) with sharp snapping sounds. **2.** To craze (china, for example). — *n.* **1.** The act or sound of crackling. **2.a.** A network of fine cracks on the surface of glazed pottery, china, or glassware. **b.** Crackleware. [Freq. of CRACK.]

crack•le•ware (krăk′əl-wâr′) *n.* Glazed pottery or glassware bearing a decorative surface network of fine cracks.

crack•ling (krăk′lĭng) *n.* **1.** A succession of slight sharp snapping noises. **2. cracklings.** The crisp bits that remain after rendering fat from meat or frying or roasting the skin, esp. of a pig or a goose. [Sense 2, Du. *krakeling* < obsolete Du. *kraeckelingh* < MDu. *krākelinc* < *krāken,* to crack. See CRACKNEL.]

crack•ly (krăk′lē) *adj.* **-li•er, -li•est.** Likely to crackle; crisp.

crack•nel (krăk′nəl) *n.* **1.** A hard crisp biscuit. **2. cracknels.** Crisp bits of fried pork fat; cracklings. [ME *crakenele,* alteration of OFr. *craquelin* < MDu. *krākelinc,* small cake < *krāken,* to crack. See **gerə-[2]*.**]

crack•pot (krăk′pŏt′) *n.* An eccentric person, esp. one with bizarre ideas. [CRACK(ED) + POT[1], skull (obsolete).]

crack•up or **crack-up** (krăk′ŭp′) *n. Informal.* **1.** A crash, as of an airplane. **2.** A mental or physical breakdown.

Crac•ow also **Kra•ków** (krăk′ou, krä′kou, -ko͞of). A city of S Poland on the Vistula R. SSE of Warsaw; national cap. from 1305 to 1595. Pop. 740,300.

–cracy *suff.* Government; rule: *meritocracy.* [Fr. *-cratie* < OFr. < LLat. *-cratia* < Gk. *-kratia* < *kratos,* strength, power. See **kar-*.**]

cra•dle (krăd′l) *n.* **1.** A small low bed for an infant, often furnished with rockers. **2.a.** The earliest period of life: *from the cradle to the grave.* **b.** A place of origin; a birthplace: *the cradle of civilization.* **3.a.** A framework of wood or metal used to support something. **b.** A framework used to protect an injured limb. **4.** A low flat framework that rolls on casters, used by a mechanic working beneath an automobile. **5.** The part of a telephone that contains the connecting switch upon which the receiver and mouthpiece unit is supported. **6.a.** A frame projecting above a scythe, used to catch grain as it is cut. **b.** A scythe equipped with such a frame. **7.** A boxlike device furnished with rockers, used for washing gold-bearing dirt. — *v.* **-dled, -dling, -dles.** — *tr.* **1.a.** To place or retain in or as if in a cradle. **b.** To care for or nurture in infancy. **c.** To hold or support protectively. **2.** To reap (grain) with a cradle. **3.** To place or support (a ship, for example) in a cradle. **4.** To wash (gold-bearing dirt) in a cradle. — *intr. Obsolete.* To lie in or as if in a cradle. [ME *cradel* < OE.] — **cra′dler** *n.*

cradle cap *n.* A form of dermatitis that occurs in infants and is characterized by heavy, yellow, crusted lesions on the scalp.

cra•dle•song (krăd′l-sông′, -sŏng′) *n.* A lullaby.

craft (krăft) *n.* **1.** Skill in doing or making something, as in the arts; proficiency. **2.** Skill in evasion or deception; guile. **3.a.** An occupation or trade requiring manual dexterity or skilled artistry. **b.** The membership of such an occupation or trade; guild. **4.** *pl.* **craft.** A boat, ship, or aircraft. — *tr.v.* **craft•ed, craft•ing, crafts. 1.** To make by hand. **2.** To make or construct (something) in a manner suggesting great care or ingenuity. [ME < OE *cræft.*] — **craft′er** *n.*

crafts•man (krăfts′mən) *n.* A man who practices a craft with great skill. — **crafts′man•like′** *adj.* — **crafts′man•ly** *adj.* — **crafts′man•ship′** *n.*

crafts•peo•ple (krăfts′pē′pəl) *n.* Artisans considered as a group.

crafts•per•son (krăfts′pûr′sən) *n.* A craftsman or a craftswoman.

crafts•wom•an (krăfts′wo͝om′ən) *n.* A woman who practices a craft with great skill.

craft union *n.* A labor union limited in membership to workers engaged in the same craft.

craft•work (krăft′wûrk′) *n.* Work made or done by craftspeople. — **craft′work′er** *n.*

craft•y (krăf′tē) *adj.* **-i•er, -i•est. 1.** Skilled in or marked by underhandedness, deviousness, or deception. **2.** *Chiefly British.* Skillful; dexterous. [ME < OE *cræftig,* strong, skillful < *cræft,* skill.] — **craft′i•ly** *adv.* — **craft′i•ness** *n.*

crag (krăg) *n.* A steeply projecting mass of rock forming part of a rugged cliff or headland. [ME < Welsh *craig* or Sc.Gael. *creagh.*] — **crag′ged** (krăg′ĭd) *adj.*

crag•gy (krăg′ē) *adj.* **-gi•er, -gi•est. 1.** Having crags. **2.** Rugged and uneven. **— crag′gi•ly** *adv.* **— crag′gi•ness** *n.*

Craig (krāg), **Edward Gordon.** 1872–1966. British theatrical producer, director, and designer known for his innovative productions and simplified stage designs.

Crai•gie (krā′gē), Sir **William Alexander.** 1876–1957. British lexicographer and philologist who was joint editor of the *Oxford English Dictionary* (1901–33).

Cra•io•va (krə-yō′və, krä-yô′vä). A city of SW Romania W of Bucharest; on the site of a Roman settlement. Pop. 260,422.

crake (krāk) *n.* Any of several short-billed birds of the family Rallidae, such as the corncrake. [ME, crow, prob. < ON *krāka.* See **gerə-[2]*.**]

cram (krăm) *v.* **crammed, cram•ming, crams.** *— tr.* **1.** To force, press, or squeeze into an insufficient space; stuff. **2.** To fill too tightly. **3.a.** To gorge with food. **b.** To eat quickly and greedily. **4.** *Informal.* To prepare (students) hastily for an impending examination. *— intr.* **1.** To gorge oneself with food. **2.** *Informal.* To study hastily for an impending examination. *— n.* **1.** A group that has been crammed together; a crush. **2.** *Informal.* Hasty study for an imminent examination. [ME *crammen* < OE *crammian.* See **ger-*.**] **— cram′mer** *n.*

Cram (krăm), **Ralph Adams.** 1863–1942. Amer. architect who designed part of the Cathedral of St. John the Divine in New York City.

cram•be (krăm′bē) *n.* Any of certain Old World annual plants of the genus *Crambe* in the mustard family, whose seeds yield a useful oil. [Lat. *crambē,* cabbage < Gk. *krambē.*]

cram•bo (krăm′bō) *n., pl.* **-boes** or **-bos. 1.** A word game in which a player or team must give a rhyme for a word or line presented by the opposing player or team. **2.** Doggerel. [Obsolete *crambe,* cabbage < Lat. *crambē (repetīta),* (warmed-over) cabbage, said of pedestrian writing < Gk. *krambē.*]

cramp[1] (krămp) *n.* **1.** A sudden, involuntary, spasmodic muscular contraction causing severe pain, often occurring as the result of strain or chill. **2.** A temporary partial paralysis of habitually or excessively used muscles. **3. cramps.** Spasmodic contractions of the uterus, such as those occurring during menstruation or labor, usu. causing pain in the abdomen. *— v.* **cramped, cramp•ing, cramps.** *— tr.* To affect with or as if with a cramp. *— intr.* To suffer from or experience cramps. [ME *crampe* < OFr., of Gmc. orig.]

cramp[2] (krămp) *n.* **1.** An adjustable frame to hold pieces together; a clamp. **2.** A cramp iron. **3.** A compressing or restraining force, influence, or thing. **4.** A confined position or part. *— tr.v.* **cramped, cramp•ing, cramps. 1.** To hold together with a cramp. **2.a.** To shut in so closely as to restrict the physical freedom of. **b.** To confine; restrict. **3.a.** To steer (the wheels of a vehicle) to make a turn. **b.** To jam (a wheel) by a short turn. *— adj.* **1.** Restricted; narrowed. **2.** Difficult to read or decipher. ***— idiom.*** **cramp (one's) style.** To restrict or prevent from free action or expression. [Prob. MDu. *crampe,* hook, cramp.]

cramp•fish (krămp′fĭsh′) *n., pl.* **crampfish** or **-fish•es.** See **electric ray.** [< CRAMP[1].]

cramp iron *n.* A bar, usu. of iron, with right-angle bends at both ends, used for holding together stones, timber, and other materials used in building.

cram•pon (krăm′pŏn′, -pən) *n.* **1.** A hinged pair of curved iron bars for raising heavy objects. Often used in the plural. **2.** A set of spikes attached to a shoe to prevent slipping when walking on ice or climbing. [ME < OFr., of Gmc. orig.]

Cra•nach (krä′näKH), **Lucas.** "the Elder." 1472–1553. German painter and engraver noted for his religious works.

cran•ber•ry (krăn′bĕr′ē) *n.* **1.** A mat-forming evergreen shrub *(Vaccinium macrocarpum)* of eastern North America. **2.** The tart red berries of this plant, used in sauces, jellies, relishes, and beverages. **3.** Any of several similar or related plants, esp. *V. oxycoccos.* [Partial transl. of LGer. *Kraanbere* : *Kraan,* crane (< MLGer. *kran;* see **gerə-[2]***) + *bere,* berry.]

cranberry bush *n.* A North American shrub *(Viburnum trilobum)* having white flower clusters and scarlet fruit.

crane (krān) *n.* **1.a.** Any of various large wading birds of the family Gruidae, having a long neck, long legs, and a long bill. **b.** A similar bird, such as a heron. **2.** A machine for hoisting and moving heavy objects by means of cables attached to a movable boom. **3.** Any of various devices with a swinging arm. *— v.* **craned, cran•ing, cranes.** *— tr.* **1.** To hoist or move with or as if with a crane. **2.** To strain and stretch (the neck, for example) in order to see better. *— intr.* **1.** To stretch one's neck toward something for a better view. **2.** To be irresolute; hesitate. [ME < OE *cran.* See **gerə-[2]*.**]

Crane (krān), **(Harold) Hart.** 1899–1932. Amer. poet whose works include *The Bridge* (1930).

Crane, Stephen. 1871–1900. Amer. writer best known for *The Red Badge of Courage* (1895).

crane fly *n.* Any of numerous long-legged slender-bodied flies of the family Tipulidae, resembling a large mosquito.

cranes•bill (krānz′bĭl′) *n.* See **geranium** 1.

Cran•ford (krăn′fərd). A community of NE NJ W of Elizabeth. Pop. 22,624.

cra•ni•a (krā′nē-ə) *n.* A pl. of **cranium.**

cra•ni•al (krā′nē-əl) *adj.* Of or relating to the skull or cranium. [< CRANIUM.] **— cra′ni•al•ly** *adv.*

cranial index *n.* The ratio of the maximum breadth to the maximum length of the skull, multiplied by 100.

cranial nerve *n.* Any of several nerves that arise in pairs from the brainstem and reach the periphery through openings in the skull.

cra•ni•ate (krā′nē-ĭt, -āt′) *adj.* Having a skull or cranium. *— n.* An animal or a human being having a skull or cranium.

cra•ni•ec•to•my (krā′nē-ĕk′tə-mē) *n., pl.* **-mies.** Surgical removal of a portion of the cranium.

cranio– or **crani–** *pref.* Cranium: *craniometer.* [< CRANIUM.]

cra•ni•o•cer•e•bral (krā′nē-ō-sĕr′ə-brəl, -sə-rē′brəl) *adj.* Of or relating to both the cranium and the cerebrum.

cra•ni•o•fa•cial (krā′nē-ō-fā′shəl) *adj.* Of or involving both the cranium and the face: *craniofacial surgery.*

cra•ni•ol•o•gy (krā′nē-ŏl′ə-jē) *n.* The scientific study of the skull, esp. in humans. **— cra′ni•o•log′i•cal** (-ə-lŏj′ĭ-kəl) *adj.* **— cra′ni•o•log′i•cal•ly** *adv.* **— cra′ni•ol′o•gist** *n.*

cra•ni•om•e•ter (krā′nē-ŏm′ĭ-tər) *n.* An instrument or device used to measure the skull. **— cra′ni•o•met′ric** (-ə-mĕt′rĭk), **cra′ni•o•met′ri•cal** *adj.*

cra•ni•om•e•try (krā′nē-ŏm′ĭ-trē) *n.* Measurement of the skull to determine its characteristics.

cra•ni•o•sac•ral (krā′nē-ō-săk′rəl, -sā′krəl) *adj.* **1.** Of or associated with both the cranium and the sacrum. **2.** Of or relating to the parasympathetic nervous system.

cra•ni•ot•o•my (krā′nē-ŏt′ə-mē) *n., pl.* **-mies. 1.** Surgical incision into the skull. **2.** The breaking of the fetal skull to reduce it for removal when normal delivery is not possible.

cra•ni•um (krā′nē-əm) *n., pl.* **-ni•ums** or **-ni•a** (-nē-ə). **1.** The skull of a vertebrate. **2.** The portion of the skull enclosing the brain; the braincase. [ME *craneum* < Med.Lat. *cranium* < Gk. *kranion.* See **ker-[1]*.**]

crank[1] (krăngk) *n.* **1.** A device for transmitting rotary motion, consisting of a handle or arm attached at right angles to a shaft. **2.** A clever turn of speech; a verbal conceit: *quips and cranks.* **3.** A peculiar or eccentric idea or action. **4.** *Informal.* **a.** A grouchy person. **b.** An eccentric person, esp. one who is unduly zealous. *— v.* **cranked, crank•ing, cranks.** *— tr.* **1.a.** To start or operate (an engine, for example) by turning a handle. **b.** To move or operate (a window, for example) by or as if by turning a handle. **2.** To make into the shape of a crank; bend. **3.** To provide with a handle that is used in turning. *— intr.* **1.** To turn a handle. **2.** To wind in a zigzagging course. *— adj.* Of, being, or produced by an eccentric person. ***— phrasal verbs.*** **crank out.** To produce, esp. mechanically and rapidly. **crank up. 1.** To cause to start or get started. **2.** To cause to intensify: *cranks up the sound.* [ME < OE *cranc-,* as in *crancstæf,* weaving implement.]

crank[2] (krăngk) *adj. Naut.* Liable to capsize; unstable. [?]

crank•case (krăngk′kās′) *n.* The metal case enclosing the crankshaft and associated parts in a reciprocating engine.

crank•pin also **crank pin** (krăngk′pĭn′) *n.* A bar or cylinder on a crank which attaches to a connecting rod.

crank•shaft (krăngk′shăft′) *n.* A shaft that turns or is turned by a crank.

crank•y[1] (krăng′kē) *adj.* **-i•er, -i•est. 1.** Having a bad disposition; peevish. **2.** Having eccentric ways; odd. **3.** Full of bends and turns; crooked. **4.** Working unpredictably; erratic. **5.** Rickety; loose. **— crank′i•ly** *adv.* **— crank′i•ness** *n.*

crank•y[2] (krăng′kē) *adj.* **-i•er, -i•est.** *Naut.* Liable to capsize.

Cran•mer (krăn′mər), **Thomas.** 1489–1556. English prelate who as archbishop of Canterbury (1533–53) revised the *Book of Common Prayer* (1552).

cran•ny (krăn′ē) *n., pl.* **-nies.** A small opening, as in a wall or rock face; a crevice. [ME *crani,* perh. alteration of OFr. *cren, cran,* notch < **crener,* to notch.] **— cran′nied** *adj.*

Cran•ston (krăn′stən). A city of E-central RI S of Providence; settled in 1636. Pop. 76,060.

crap[1] (krăp) *Vulgar Slang. — n.* **1.** Excrement. **2.** An act of defecating. **3.** Worthless nonsense; rubbish. *— intr.v.* **crapped, crap•ping, craps.** To defecate. [ME *crappe,* chaff < OFr. *crappe* < Med.Lat. *crappa,* perh. of Gmc. orig.]

crap[2] (krăp) *Games. — n.* See **craps.** *— v.* **crapped, crap•ping, craps.** To make a losing throw in the game of craps. [Back-formation < CRAPS.]

crape (krāp) *n.* **1.** See **crepe** 1. **2.** A black band worn in mourning. *— tr.v.* **craped, crap•ing, crapes.** To cover or drape with or as if with crape. [Alteration of Fr. *crêpe.* See CREPE.]

crape•hang•er (krāp′hăng′ər) *n.* A morose, gloomy, or pessimistic person.

crape jasmine *n.* An evergreen shrub *(Tabernaemontana divaricata)* native to India and having fragrant white flowers.

crape myrtle also **crepe myrtle** *n.* A deciduous shrub *(Lagerstroemia indica)* native to China and having variously colored flowers with crinkled petals.

crap•per (krăp′ər) *n. Vulgar Slang.* A toilet. [< CRAP[1].]

crap•pie (krăp′ē, krŏp′ē) *n., pl.* **-pies.** Either of two edible North American sunfishes, the black crappie *(Pomoxis nigromaculatus)* or the white crappie *(P. annularis).* [Canadian Fr. *crapet.*]

crampon

crane
Top: Black crowned crane *Balearica pavonina*
Bottom: Mechanical crane

ă pat	oi boy
ā pay	ou out
âr care	ŏŏ took
ä father	ōō boot
ĕ pet	ŭ cut
ē be	ûr urge
ĭ pit	th thin
ī pie	*th* this
îr pier	hw which
ŏ pot	zh vision
ō toe	ə about, item
ô paw	

Stress marks:
′ (primary);
′ (secondary), as in
dictionary (dĭk′shə-nĕr′ē)

craps (krăps) *pl.n. (used with a sing. or pl. v.)* **1.** A gambling game played with two dice in which a first throw of 7 or 11 wins. **2.** A losing throw in this game. [Louisiana Fr., game of hazard < E. *crabs*, lowest throw in hazard < CRAB[1] or CRAB[2].]

crap•shoot (krăp′sho͞ot′) *n. Slang.* A risky enterprise.

crap•shoot•er (krăp′sho͞o′tər) *n. Games.* A craps player.

crap•u•lence (krăp′yə-ləns) *n.* **1.** Sickness caused by excessive eating or drinking. **2.** Excessive indulgence; intemperance. [< CRAPULENT, sick from gluttony < LLat. *crāpulentus*, very drunk < Lat. *crāpula*, intoxication < Gk. *kraipalē*.] **—crap′u•lent** *adj.* **—crap′u•lous** *adj.*

crash[1] (krăsh) *v.* **crashed, crash•ing, crash•es.** *—intr.* **1.a.** To break violently or noisily; smash. **b.** To undergo sudden damage or destruction on impact. **2.** To make a sudden loud noise. **3.** To move noisily or so as to cause damage. **4.** To fail suddenly, as a market or an economy. **5.** *Slang.* To undergo a period esp. of depression after drug-taking. **6.** *Slang.* **a.** To find temporary lodging or shelter. **b.** To go to sleep. *—tr.* **1.** To cause to crash. **2.** To dash to pieces; smash. **3.** *Informal.* To join or enter (a party, for example) without invitation. *—n.* **1.** A sudden loud noise, as of an object breaking. **2.a.** A smashing to pieces. **b.** A collision, as between two automobiles. **3.** A sudden economic or fiscal failure. **4.** *Slang.* Mental depression after drug-taking. *—adj. Informal.* Of or characterized by an intensive effort to produce or accomplish: *a crash diet.* [ME *crasschen*; prob. akin to *crasen*, to shatter. See CRAZE.] **—crash′er** *n.*

crash[2] (krăsh) *n.* **1.** A coarse, light, unevenly woven fabric of cotton or linen, used for towels and curtains. **2.** Starched reinforced fabric used to strengthen the binding or the spine of a book. [< Russ. *krashenina*, colored linen < *krashenie*, coloring < *krasit′*, to color. See **ker-**[3]*.]

crater
Lunar crater Eratosthenes

Crash•aw (krăsh′ô), **Richard.** 1613?–49. English metaphysical poet whose works include *Steps to the Temple* (1646).

crash dive *n.* A rapid dive made by a submarine, esp. in an emergency. **—crash′-dive′** (krăsh′dīv′) *v.*

crash helmet *n.* A padded helmet worn to protect the head.

crash•ing (krăsh′ĭng) *adj.* Total; absolute: *a crashing bore.*

crash-land (krăsh′lănd′) *v.* **-land•ed, -land•ing, -lands.** *—tr.* To land (an aircraft or a spacecraft) under emergency conditions, usu. with damage to the craft. *—intr.* To crash-land an aircraft or a spacecraft. **—crash landing** *n.*

crash pad *n.* **1.** Padding inside vehicles for protecting occupants in the event of an accident or sudden stop. **2.** *Slang.* A place affording free and usu. temporary lodging.

crash•wor•thy (krăsh′wûr′*th*ē) *adj.* Capable of withstanding the effects of a crash. **—crash′wor′thi•ness** *n.*

crass (krăs) *adj.* **crass•er, crass•est.** So crude and unrefined as to be lacking in discrimination and sensibility. [Lat. *crassus*, dense.] **—crass′i•tude′** (-ĭ-to͞od′, -tyo͞od′), **crass′ness** *n.* **—crass′ly** *adv.*

Cras•sus (krăs′əs), **Marcus Licinius.** 115?–53 B.C. Roman politician and general who joined Julius Caesar and Pompey in the first triumvirate to challenge the senate's power (60).

-crat *suff.* A participant in or supporter of a specified form of government: *technocrat.* [Fr. *-crate* < Gk. *-kratēs*, ruler < *kratos*, strength, power. See -CRACY.]

crate (krāt) *n.* **1.** A container used for storing or shipping. **2.** *Slang.* An old rickety vehicle, esp. a decrepit automobile or aircraft. *—tr.v.* **crat•ed, crat•ing, crates.** To pack into a crate. [Lat. *crātis*, wickerwork.]

cra•ter (krā′tər) *n.* **1.** A bowl-shaped depression at the mouth of a volcano or geyser. **2.a.** A bowl-shaped depression in a surface made by an explosion or the impact of a body, such as a meteoroid. **b.** A pit; a hollow. **3.** Var. of **krater.** *—v.* **-tered, -ter•ing, -ters.** *—tr.* To make craters in. *—intr.* To form a crater or craters. [Lat. *crātēr* < Gk. *kratēr*, mixing vessel. See **kerə-***.]

Cra•ter (krā′tər) *n.* A constellation in the Southern Hemisphere near Hydra and Corvus. [Lat. *crātēr*, mixing bowl, crater. See CRATER.]

Crater Lake. A lake of SW OR in a volcanic crater of the Cascade Range.

cra•vat (krə-văt′) *n.* A scarf or band of fabric worn around the neck as a tie. [Fr. *cravate*, Croatian mercenary necktie < *Cravate*, a Croatian < Ger. dial. *Krabate* < Serbo-Croatian *Hrvāt*.]

crave (krāv) *v.* **craved, crav•ing, craves.** *—tr.* **1.** To have an intense desire for. See Syns at **desire. 2.** To need urgently; require. **3.** To beg earnestly for; implore. *—intr.* To have an eager or intense desire. [ME *craven* < OE *crafian*, to beg.] **—crav′er** *n.* **—crav′ing•ly** *adv.*

cra•ven (krā′vən) *adj.* Characterized by abject fear; cowardly. *—n.* A coward. [ME *cravant*, perh. < OFr. *crevant*, pr.part. of *crever*, to burst < Lat. *crepāre*, to break.] **—cra′ven•ly** *adv.* **—cra′ven•ness** *n.*

crav•ing (krā′vĭng) *n.* A consuming desire; a yearning.

craw (krô) *n.* **1.** The crop of a bird or insect. **2.** The stomach of an animal. **—*idiom.* stick in (one's) craw.** To cause abiding discontent and resentment in (one). [ME *crawe*.]

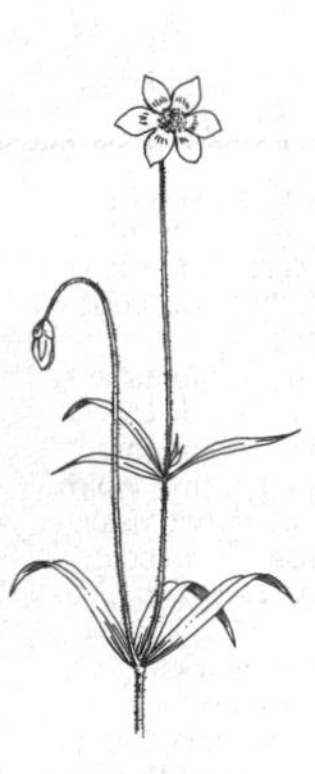

creamcups
Platystemon californicus

craw•dad (krô′dăd′) *n. Chiefly Southern U.S.* See **crayfish** 1. [Prob. alteration of CRAWFISH.]

craw•fish (krô′fĭsh′) *n.* Var. of **crayfish.** *—intr.v.* **-fished, -fish•ing, -fish•es.** *Informal.* To withdraw from an undertaking.

Craw•ford (krô′fərd), **Francis Marion.** 1854–1909. Amer. writer whose novels include *The Three Fates* (1892).

Crawford, Joan. 1908–77. Amer. actress noted for her performances in films such as *Mildred Pierce* (1945).

Crawford, Thomas. 1814–57. Amer. sculptor whose works include *Armed Freedom* atop the U.S. Capitol.

crawl[1] (krôl) *intr.v.* **crawled, crawl•ing, crawls. 1.** To move slowly on the hands and knees or by dragging the body along the ground; creep. **2.** To advance slowly, feebly, laboriously, or with frequent stops. **3.** To proceed or act servilely. **4.** To be or feel as if swarming or covered with moving things. See Syns at **teem**[1]. **5.** To swim the crawl. *—n.* **1.** The action of crawling. **2.** An extremely slow pace. **3.** *Sports.* A rapid swimming stroke consisting of alternating overarm strokes and a flutter kick. **4.** Words or figures that move across, up, or down a movie or television screen. [ME *craulen* < ON *krafla*. See **gerbh-***.] **—crawl′ing•ly** *adv.*

crawl[2] (krôl) *n.* A pen in shallow water, as for confining fish or turtles. [Afr. *kraal*, enclosure for animals. See KRAAL.]

crawl•er (krô′lər) *n.* **1.** One that crawls, esp. an early form of certain insect larvae. **2.** A vehicle, such as a bulldozer, that moves on continuous belts of metal plates.

crawl•space or **crawl space** (krôl′spās) *n.* A low or narrow space, such as one beneath the floor that gives workers access to plumbing or wiring equipment.

crawl•y (krô′lē) *adj.* **-i•er, -i•est.** *Informal.* **1.** Creepy. **2.** Feeling as if covered with moving things.

cray•fish (krā′fĭsh′) also **craw•fish** (krô′-) *n., pl.* **crayfish** or **-fish•es** also **crawfish** or **-fish•es. 1.** Any of various freshwater crustaceans of the genera *Cambarus* and *Astacus*, resembling a lobster but considerably smaller. Also called regionally *crawdad* **2.** See **spiny lobster.** [By folk ety. < ME *crevise* < OFr. *crevice*, perh. < OHGer. *krebiz*, edible crustacean. See **gerbh-***.]

cray•on (krā′ŏn′, -ən) *n.* **1.** A stick of colored wax, charcoal, or chalk, used for drawing. **2.** A drawing made with one of these sticks. *—tr.v.* **-oned, -on•ing, -ons.** To draw, color, or decorate with a crayon. [Fr., dim. of *craie*, chalk < Lat. *crēta*.] **—cray′on•ist** (-ə-nĭst) *n.*

craze (krāz) *v.* **crazed, craz•ing, craz•es.** *—tr.* **1.** To cause to become mentally deranged or obsessed **2.** To produce a network of fine cracks in the surface or glaze of. *—intr.* **1.** To become crazed. **2.** To become covered with fine cracks. *—n.* **1.** A short-lived popular fashion; a fad. **2.** A fine crack in a surface or glaze. [ME *crasen*, to shatter, of Scand. orig.]

cra•zy (krā′zē) *adj.* **-zi•er, -zi•est. 1.** Affected with madness; insane. **2.** *Informal.* Departing from proportion or moderation, esp.: **a.** Possessed by enthusiasm or excitement. **b.** Immoderately fond; infatuated. **c.** Intensely involved or preoccupied. **d.** Foolish or impractical; senseless. *—n., pl.* **-zies.** *Informal.* One who is or appears insane. **—*idiom.* like crazy.** *Informal.* To an exceeding degree. **—cra′zi•ly** *adv.* **—cra′zi•ness** *n.*

crazy bone *n. Informal.* The funny bone.

Cra•zy Horse (krā′zē hôrs′). 1849?–77. Sioux leader who resisted the encroachment of whites in the Black Hills and joined Sitting Bull at the Battle of Little Bighorn (1876).

crazy quilt *n.* **1.** A patchwork quilt of pieces of cloth of various shapes, colors, and sizes, arranged haphazardly. **2.** A disorderly mixture; a hodgepodge.

cra•zy•weed (krā′zē-wēd′) *n.* See **locoweed.**

C-re•ac•tive protein (sē′rē-ăk′tĭv) *n.* A globulin that appears in the blood in certain acute inflammatory conditions, such as rheumatic fever. [*C-(polysaccharide) reactive*.]

creak (krēk) *intr.v.* **creaked, creak•ing, creaks. 1.** To make a grating or squeaking sound. **2.** To move with a creaking sound. *—n.* A grating or squeaking sound. [ME *creken*, to croak, complain, of imit. orig.] **—creak′ing•ly** *adv.*

creak•y (krē′kē) *adj.* **-i•er, -i•est. 1.** Tending or likely to creak. **2.** Dilapidated; decrepit. **—creak′i•ly** *adv.* **—creak′i•ness** *n.*

cream (krēm) *n.* **1.a.** The yellowish fatty component of unhomogenized milk that tends to accumulate at the surface. **b.** Any of various substances resembling or containing cream: *hand cream.* **2.** *Color.* A pale yellow to yellowish white. **3.** The choicest part: *the cream of the crop.* *—v.* **creamed, cream•ing, creams.** *—intr.* **1.** To form cream. **2.** To form foam or froth at the top. *—tr.* **1.** To remove the cream from; skim. **2.** To select or remove the best part from: *cream off the highest achievers.* **3.** To beat into a creamy consistency. **4.** To prepare or cook in or with a cream sauce. **5.** To add cream to. **6.** *Slang.* To defeat overwhelmingly. [ME *creme* < OFr. *craime* (< LLat. *crāmum*, of Celt. orig.) and < OFr. *cresme* (< Lat. *chrīsma*, an anointing < Gk. *khrisma*, unguent < *khriein*, to anoint; see **ghrēi-***).] **—cream** *adj.*

cream cheese *n.* A soft white cheese made of cream and milk.

cream•cups (krēm′kŭps′) *pl.n. (used with a sing. or pl. v.)* An annual plant *(Platystemon californicus)* native to the southwest United States and Mexico and cultivated for its cream-colored to yellowish flowers.

cream•er (krē′mər) *n.* **1.** A small jug or pitcher for cream. **2.** A machine or device for separating cream from milk. **3.** A refrigerator in which milk is placed to form cream. **4.** A substitute for cream: *a nondairy coffee creamer.*

cream•er•y (krē′mə-rē) *n., pl.* **-ies.** An establishment where dairy products are prepared or sold.

cream of tartar *n.* See **potassium bitartrate.**

cream puff also **cream•puff** (krēm′pŭf′) *n.* **1.** A shell of light pastry filled with whipped cream, custard, or ice cream. **2.** *Slang.* A weakling. **3.** *Slang.* An old, esp. secondhand car in very good condition.

cream sauce *n.* A white sauce made by cooking together a mixture of flour and butter with milk or cream.

cream soda *n.* A sweet carbonated drink with a vanilla flavor.

cream•y (krē′mē) *adj.* **-i•er, -i•est.** Rich in or resembling cream. **—cream′i•ly** *adv.* **—cream′i•ness** *n.*

crease (krēs) *n.* **1.** A line made by pressing, folding, or wrinkling. **2.** *Sports.* **a.** An area marked off in front of the goal in hockey. **b.** One of the lines in cricket marking off the positions of the bowler and batter or the space between two of these lines. *—v.* **creased, creas•ing, creas•es.** *—tr.* **1.** To make a crease in. **2.** To graze or wound superficially with a bullet. *—intr.* To become wrinkled. [Alteration of *creaste,* perh. < ME *creste,* ridge. See CREST.] **—crease′less** *adj.* **—crease′proof′** *adj.* **—creas′er** *n.* **—creas′y** *adj.*

cre•ate (krē-āt′) *tr.v.* **-at•ed, -at•ing, -ates. 1.** To cause to exist; bring into being. See Syns at **found**[1]. **2.** To give rise to; produce: *created a stir.* **3.** To invest with an office or title; appoint. **4.** To produce through artistic or imaginative effort. *—adj. Archaic.* Created. [ME *createn* < Lat. *creāre, creāt-.* See **ker-**[2]*.]

cre•a•tine (krē′ə-tēn′, -tĭn) also **cre•a•tin** (-tĭn) *n.* A nitrogenous organic acid, $C_4H_9N_3O_2$, that supplies energy for muscle contraction. [Gk. *kreas,* **kreat-,* flesh; see **kreuə-*** + -INE[2].]

creatine phosphate *n.* See **phosphocreatine.**

cre•at•i•nine (krē-ăt′n-ēn′, -ĭn) *n.* A creatine anhydride, $C_4H_7N_3O$, formed by the metabolism of creatine, that is found in muscle tissue and blood. [CREATIN(E) + -INE[2].]

cre•a•tion (krē-ā′shən) *n.* **1.a.** The act of creating. **b.** The fact or state of having been created. **2.** The act of investing with a new office or title. **3.a.** The world and all things in it. **b.** All creatures or a class of creatures. **4. Creation.** *Theol.* The act of God by which the world was created. **5.** An original product of human invention or artistic imagination. **—cre•a′tion•al** *adj.*

cre•a•tion•ism (krē-ā′shə-nĭz′əm) *n.* The position that the account of the creation in Genesis is literally true. **—cre•a′tion•ist** *adj. & n.*

creation science *n.* An effort to give scientific proof for the account of the creation of the universe given in Genesis.

cre•a•tive (krē-ā′tĭv) *adj.* **1.** Having the ability or power to create. **2.** Productive; creating. **3.** Characterized by originality and expressiveness; imaginative. **—cre•a′tive•ly** *adv.* **—cre′a•tiv′i•ty** (-ĭ-tē), **cre•a′tive•ness** *n.*

cre•a•tor (krē-ā′tər) *n.* **1.** One that creates. **2. Creator.** God.

crea•ture (krē′chər) *n.* **1.** Something created. **2.a.** A living being, esp. an animal. **b.** A human being. **3.** One dependent on or subservient to another; a tool. **—crea′tur•al** *adj.* **—crea′ture•li•ness** *n.* **—crea′ture•ly** *adj.*

creature comfort *n.* Something that contributes to physical comfort.

crèche (krĕsh) *n.* **1.** A representation of the Nativity, usu. with statues or figurines. **2.** A foundling hospital. **3.** *Chiefly British.* A day nursery. [Fr. < OFr. *cresche,* crib, of Gmc. orig.]

Cré•cy (krĕs′ē, krā-sē′) or **Cré•cy-en-Pon•thieu** (-än-pôN-tyœ′). A town of N France NW of Amiens; site of the first decisive battle of the Hundred Years' War (Aug. 26, 1346).

cre•dence (krēd′ns) *n.* **1.** Acceptance as true or valid; belief. **2.** Claim to acceptance; trustworthiness. **3.** Recommendation; credentials. **4.** A small table or shelf for the bread, wine, and vessels of the Eucharist when not in use at the altar. [ME < OFr. < Med.Lat. *crēdentia* < Lat. *crēdēns, crēdent-,* pr.part. of *crēdere,* to believe. See **kerd-***.]

cre•den•tial (krĭ-dĕn′shəl) *n.* **1.** That which entitles one to confidence, credit, or authority. **2. credentials.** Evidence or testimonials concerning one's right to credit, confidence, or authority. *—tr.v.* **-tialed, -tial•ing, -tials.** *Usage Problem.* To supply with credentials. [< Med.Lat. *crēdentiālis,* giving authority < *crēdentia,* trust. See CREDENCE.]

Usage Note: The participle *credentialed* is well established in reference to certified teachers and some other professions, but its more general use to mean "possessing professional or expert credentials" is still widely considered jargon. The sentence *The board heard testimony from a number of credentialed witnesses* was unacceptable to 85 percent of the Usage Panel.

cre•den•za (krĭ-dĕn′zə) *n.* A buffet, sideboard, or bookcase, esp. one without legs. [Ital. < Med.Lat. *crēdentia,* trust (poss. < the precautionary tasting of food placed on a sideboard before being served. See CREDENCE.]

cred•i•bil•i•ty (krĕd′ə-bĭl′ĭ-tē) *n.* **1.** The quality, capability, or power to elicit belief. **2.** A capacity for belief.

credibility gap *n.* **1.** Public skepticism about the truth of statements, esp. official claims and pronouncements. **2.** A discrepancy or disparity, esp. between words and actions.

cred•i•ble (krĕd′ə-bəl) *adj.* **1.** Capable of being believed; plausible. See Syns at **plausible. 2.** Worthy of confidence; reliable. [ME < Lat. *crēdibilis* < *crēdere,* to believe. See **kerd-***.] **—cred′i•ble•ness** *n.* **—cred′i•bly** *adv.*

Usage Note: *Credible* is widely but incorrectly used where *credulous* would be appropriate, as in *He was credible* (should be *credulous*) *enough to believe the claims.*

cred•it (krĕd′ĭt) *n.* **1.** Belief or confidence in the truth of something. **2.** A reputation for sound character or quality; standing. **3.** A source of honor or distinction. **4.** Approval for an act, ability, or quality; praise. **5.** Influence based on the good opinion or confidence of others. **6.** An acknowledgment of work done. Often used in the plural. **7.a.** Official certification or recognition of successful completion of a course of study. **b.** A unit of study so certified. **8.** Reputation for solvency and integrity entitling a person to be trusted in buying or borrowing. **9.a.** An arrangement for deferred payment of a loan or purchase. **b.** The terms governing such an arrangement. **c.** The time allowed for deferred payment. **10.** *Accounting.* **a.** The deduction of a payment made by a debtor from an amount due. **b.** The right-hand side of an account on which such amounts are entered. **c.** An entry or the sum of the entries on this side. **d.** The positive balance or amount remaining in a person's account. **e.** A credit line. *—tr.v.* **-it•ed, -it•ing, -its. 1.** To believe in; trust. **2.a.** To regard as having performed an action or being endowed with a quality. **b.** To ascribe to a person; attribute. **3.** *Accounting.* **a.** To enter as a credit. **b.** To make a credit entry in: *credit an account.* **4.** To give or award an educational credit to. **5.** *Archaic.* To bring honor or distinction to. [Fr. < OFr. < OItal. *credito* < Lat. *crēditum,* loan < neut. p.part. of *crēdere,* to entrust. See **kerd-***.]

cred•it•a•ble (krĕd′ĭ-tə-bəl) *adj.* **1.** Deserving of often limited praise or commendation. **2.** Worthy of belief. **3.** Deserving of commercial credit. **4.** That can be assigned. **—cred′it•a•bil′i•ty, cred′it•a•ble•ness** *n.* **—cred′it•a•bly** *adv.*

credit bureau *n.* An organization that provides credit information on prospective customers.

credit card *n.* A card issued by a bank or business authorizing the holder to buy goods or services on credit.

credit hour *n.* A credit in a school or college, usu. representing one hour of class per week for one term.

credit line *n.* **1.** A line of copy acknowledging the source or origin of a news dispatch, published article, or other work. **2.** The maximum amount of credit given to a customer.

cred•i•tor (krĕd′ĭ-tər) *n.* One to whom money or its equivalent is owed.

credit rating *n.* An estimate of the amount of credit that can be extended to a company or person without undue risk.

credit union *n.* A cooperative organization that makes loans to its members at low interest rates.

cred•it•wor•thy (krĕd′ĭt-wûr′*th*ē) *adj.* Having an acceptable credit rating. **—cred′it•wor′thi•ness** *n.*

cre•do (krē′dō, krā′-) *n., pl.* **-dos. 1.** A creed. **2. Credo. a.** The Apostles' Creed or the Nicene Creed. **b.** The musical setting for the Apostles' Creed or the Nicene Creed, as in a choral Mass. [ME, the Apostles' Creed < Lat. *crēdō,* I believe (the first word of the Apostles' Creed or the Nicene Creed), first pers. sing. pr.t. of *crēdere,* to believe. See **kerd-***.]

cre•du•li•ty (krĭ-do͞o′lĭ-tē, -dyo͞o′-) *n.* A disposition to believe too readily. [ME *credulite* < OFr. < Lat. *crēdulitās* < *crēdulus,* credulous. See CREDULOUS.]

cred•u•lous (krĕj′ə-ləs) *adj.* **1.** Disposed to believe too readily; gullible. **2.** Arising from or characterized by credulity. See Usage Note at **credible.** [< Lat. *crēdulus* < *crēdere,* to believe. See **kerd-***.] **—cred′u•lous•ly** *adv.* **—cred′u•lous•ness** *n.*

Cree (krē) *n., pl.* **Cree** or **Crees. 1.** A member of a Native American people inhabiting a large area from eastern Canada west to Alberta and the Great Slave Lake. **2.** The Algonquian language of the Cree.

creed (krēd) *n.* **1.** A formal statement of religious belief; a confession of faith. **2.** A system of belief, principles, or opinions. [ME *crede* < OE *crēda* < Lat. *crēdō,* I believe. See CREDO.] **—creed′al** (krēd′l) *adj.*

creek (krēk, krĭk) *n.* **1.** A small stream, often a shallow or intermittent tributary to a river. Also called regionally *branch, kill, run.* **2.** A channel or stream running through a salt marsh. **3.** *Chiefly British.* A small inlet in a shoreline, extending farther inland than a cove. *—**idiom.*** **up the creek** (or **up the creek without a paddle).** *Informal.* In a difficult or inextricable position. [ME *creke,* prob. < ON *kriki,* bend.]

Creek (krēk) *n., pl.* **Creek** or **Creeks. 1.a.** A member of a Native American people formerly inhabiting eastern Alabama, southwest Georgia, and northwest Florida and now located in central Oklahoma and southern Alabama. **b.** The Muskogean language of the Creek. **2.** A member of a Native American confederacy made up of the Creek and various smaller southeast tribes.

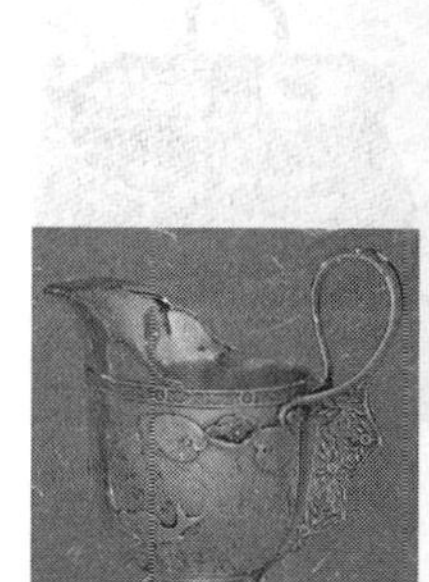

creamer
19th-century Tiffany silver creamer

ă pat	oi boy
ā pay	ou out
âr care	o͝o took
ä father	o͞o boot
ĕ pet	ŭ cut
ē be	ûr urge
ĭ pit	th thin
ī pie	*th* this
îr pier	hw which
ŏ pot	zh vision
ō toe	ə about, item
ô paw	

Stress marks:
′ (primary);
′ (secondary), as in **dictionary** (dĭk′shə-nĕr′ē)

crimp¹ (krĭmp) *tr.v.* **crimped, crimp•ing, crimps. 1.** To press or pinch into small regular folds or ridges. **2.** To bend or mold (leather) into shape. **3.** To cause (hair) to form tight curls or waves. **4.** To have a hampering or obstructive effect on. — *n.* **1.** The act of crimping. **2.** Something made by or as if by crimping, as: **a.** Hair that has been tightly curled or waved. **b.** A series of curls, as of wool fibers. **c.** A crease or bend. **3.** An obstructing or hampering agent or force. [Du. or LGer. *krimpen* < MDu. or MLGer.] — **crimp′er** *n.*

crimp² (krĭmp) *n.* A person who tricks or coerces men into service as sailors or soldiers. — *tr.v.* **crimped, crimp•ing, crimps.** To procure (sailors or soldiers) by trickery or coercion. [?]

crimp•y (krĭm′pē) *adj.* **-i•er, -i•est.** Full of crimps; wavy. — **crimp′i•ness** *n.*

crim•son (krĭm′zən) *n. Color.* A deep to vivid purplish red to vivid red. — *tr. & intr.v.* **-soned, -son•ing, -sons.** To make or become deeply or vividly red. [ME *cremesin*, ult. < Ar. *qirmizīy* < *qirmiz*, kermes insect. See KERMES.] — **crim′son** *adj.*

cringe (krĭnj) *intr.v.* **cringed, cring•ing, cring•es. 1.** To shrink back, as in fear; cower. **2.** To behave in a servile way; fawn. — *n.* An act or instance of cringing. [ME *crengen*, to bend haughtily, prob. ult. < OE *cringan*, to give way.]

crin•gle (krĭng′gəl) *n. Naut.* A small ring or grommet of rope or metal fastened to the edge of a sail. [LGer. *kringel*, dim. of *kring*, ring < MLGer.]

crin•kle (krĭng′kəl) *v.* **-kled, -kling, -kles.** — *intr.* **1.** To form wrinkles or ripples. **2.** To make a soft crackling sound; rustle. — *tr.* To cause to crinkle. — *n.* A wrinkle, ripple, or fold. [< ME *crinkled*, full of turnings.] — **crin′kly** *adj.*

crin•kle•root (krĭng′kəl-ro͞ot′, -ro͝ot′) *n.* A woodland plant *(Cardamine diphylla)* of eastern North America having fleshy rootstocks and trifoliolate leaves.

crinkleroot
Cardamine diphylla

cri•noid (krī′noid′) *n.* Any of various echinoderms of the class Crinoidea, characterized by a cup-shaped body, feathery radiating arms, and either a stalk or clawlike base. [< NLat. *Crinoidea*, class name : Gk. *krinon*, lily + Gk. *-oeidēs*, -oid.] — **cri′noid′** *adj.*

crin•o•line (krĭn′ə-lĭn) *n.* **1.** A coarse stiff fabric of cotton or horsehair used esp. to line and stiffen hats and garments. **2.** A petticoat made of this fabric. **3.** A hoop skirt. [Fr. < Ital. *crinolino* : *crino*, horsehair (< Lat. *crīnis*, hair; see **sker-²***) + *lino*, flax (< Lat. *līnum*; see **līno-***).] — **crin′o•line, crin′o•lined** (-lĭnd) *adj.*

cri•num (krī′nəm) *n.* Any of various bulbous plants of the genus *Crinum*, having strap-shaped leaves and showy flower umbels. [NLat. *Crinum*, genus name < Gk. *krinon*, lily.]

cri•ol•lo (krē-ō′lō, -ô′yô) *n., pl.* **-los** (-ō′lōz, -ô′yôs). A Spanish American of European, usu. Spanish descent. — *adj.* **1.** Of or relating to a criollo or criollos. **2.** Indigenous to or characteristic of a Spanish-American country. [Sp. See CREOLE.]

crip•ple (krĭp′əl) *n.* **1.** One that is partially disabled or unable to use a limb or limbs. **2.** A damaged or defective object or device. — *tr.v.* **-pled, -pling, -ples. 1.** To cause to lose the use of a limb or limbs. **2.** To disable, damage, or impair the functioning of. [ME *crepel* < OE *crypel.*] — **crip′pler** *n.*

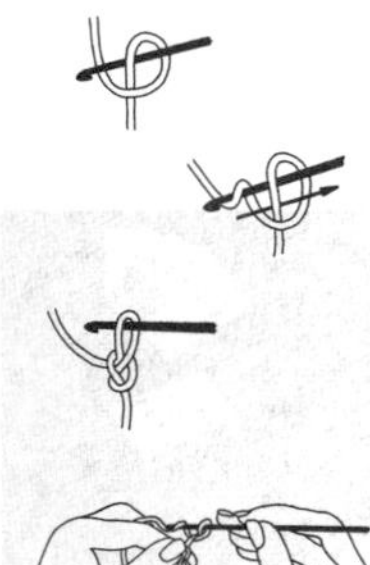
crochet

cri•sis (krī′sĭs) *n., pl.* **-ses** (-sēz). **1.a.** A crucial or decisive point or situation; a turning point. **b.** An unstable condition, as in political affairs, involving an impending abrupt or decisive change. **2.** A sudden change in the course of a disease or fever. **3.** An emotionally stressful event or a traumatic change in a person's life. **4.** A point in a story or drama when a conflict reaches its highest tension and must be resolved. [ME < Lat. < Gk. < *krinein*, to separate. See **krei-***.]

crisp (krĭsp) *adj.* **crisp•er, crisp•est. 1.** Firm but easily broken or crumbled; brittle. **2.** Pleasingly firm and fresh. **3.a.** Bracing; invigorating. **b.** Lively; sprightly. **4.** Conspicuously clean or new. **5.** Marked by clarity, conciseness, and briskness. **6.** Having small curls, waves, or ripples. — *tr. & intr.v.* **crisped, crisp•ing, crisps.** To make or become crisp. — *n.* **1.** Something crisp or easily crumbled. **2.** A dessert of fruit baked with a sweet crumbly topping. **3.** *Chiefly British.* A potato chip. [ME, curly < OE < Lat. *crispus*. See **sker-²***.] — **crisp′ly** *adv.* — **crisp′ness** *n.*

cris•pate (krĭs′pāt′) also **cris•pat•ed** (-pā′tĭd) *adj.* Curled or ruffled, as the margins of certain leaves. [Lat. *crispātus*, p.part. of *crispāre*, to curl < *crispus*, curly. See **sker-²***.]

cris•pa•tion (krĭs-pā′shən) *n.* **1.a.** The act of crisping or curling. **b.** The state of being crisped or curled. **2.** A slight involuntary muscular contraction, often producing a crawling sensation of the skin.

crisped (krĭspt) *adj. Bot.* Crispate.

crisp•er (krĭs′pər) *n.* One that crisps.

Cris•pin (krĭs′pĭn), Saint. 3rd cent. A.D. Roman shoemaker who with his brother Saint **Crispinian** sought to spread Christianity and was martyred.

Davy Crockett

crisp•y (krĭs′pē) *adj.* **-i•er, -i•est.** Crisp. — **crisp′i•ness** *n.*

criss•cross (krĭs′krôs′, -krŏs′) *v.* **-crossed, -cross•ing, -cross•es.** — *tr.* **1.** To mark with crossing lines. **2.** To move back and forth through or over. — *intr.* To move back and forth. — *n.* **1.** A mark or pattern made of crossing lines. **2.** A state of being at conflicting or contrary purposes. — *adj.* Crossing one another or marked by crossings. — *adv.* In a manner or direction that crosses or is marked by crossings. [Alteration of ME *Cristcrosse*, mark of a cross, short for *Crist-cross (me speed)*, may Christ's cross (give me success).]

cris•sum (krĭs′əm) *n., pl.* **cris•sa** (krĭs′ə). *Zool.* The feathers or area under the tail of a bird surrounding the cloacal opening. [NLat. < Lat. *crīsāre*, to move the buttocks during intercourse. See **sker-²***.] — **cris′sal** (-əl) *adj.*

cris•ta (krĭs′tə) *n., pl.* **-tae** (-tē). **1.** *Anat.* A crest or ridge. **2.** *Biol.* One of the inward projections or folds of the inner membrane of a mitochondrion. [Lat. See **sker-²***.]

cris•tate (krĭs′tāt′) also **cris•tat•ed** (-tā′tĭd) *adj.* Having or forming a crest or crista. [Lat. *cristātus* < *crista*, tuft. See **sker-²***.]

crit. *abbr.* Critic; critical; criticism.

cri•te•ri•on (krī-tîr′ē-ən) *n., pl.* **-te•ri•a** (-tîr′ē-ə) or **-te•ri•ons.** A standard, rule, or test on which a judgment or decision can be based. [Gk. *kritērion* < *kritēs*, judge < *krinein*, to separate, judge. See **krei-***.] — **cri•te′ri•al** (-əl) *adj.*

Usage Note: Like the analogous etymological plurals *agenda* and *data, criteria* is widely used as a singular form. Unlike them, however, it is not yet acceptable in that use.

crit•ic (krĭt′ĭk) *n.* **1.** One who forms and expresses judgments of the merits, faults, value, or truth of a matter. **2.** One who analyzes, classifies, interprets, or evaluates literary or other artistic works. **3.** One who tends to make harsh or carping judgments. [Lat. *criticus* < Gk. *kritikos*, able to discern < *kritēs*, judge < *krinein*, to separate, judge. See **krei-***.]

crit•i•cal (krĭt′ĭ-kəl) *adj.* **1.** Inclined to judge severely and find fault. **2.** Characterized by careful, exact evaluation and judgment. **3.** Of, relating to, or characteristic of critics or criticism. **4.** Forming or having the nature of a turning point. **5.a.** Of or relating to a medical crisis. **b.** Being or relating to a grave physical condition. **6.** Indispensable; essential. **7.** Being in or verging on a state of crisis or emergency. **8.** Fraught with danger or risk. **9.** *Math.* Of or relating to a point at which a curve has a maximum, minimum, or point of inflection. **10.** *Chem. & Phys.* Of or relating to the value of a measurement, such as temperature, at which an abrupt change in a quality, property, or state occurs. **11.** *Phys.* Capable of sustaining a nuclear chain reaction. — **crit′i•cal•ly** *adv.* — **crit′i•cal•ness** *n.*

critical angle *n.* **1.** *Phys.* The smallest angle of incidence at which a light ray can be completely reflected from the boundary between two media. **2.** The angle of attack of an airfoil at which airflow abruptly changes, causing changes in the lift and drag of an aircraft.

crit•i•cal•i•ty (krĭt′ĭ-kăl′ĭ-tē) *n.* **1.** The quality, state, or degree of being of the highest importance. **2.** *Phys.* The point at which a nuclear reaction is self-sustaining.

critical mass *n.* **1.** The smallest mass of a fissionable material that will sustain a nuclear chain reaction. **2.** A very important or crucial stage.

critical point *n.* **1.** *Phys.* The temperature and pressure at which the liquid and gaseous phases of a pure stable substance become identical. **2.** *Math.* A maximum, minimum, or point of inflection of a curve.

critical state *n.* See **critical point** 1.

crit•ic•as•ter (krĭt′ĭ-kăs′tər) *n.* A petty or inferior critic. [CRITIC + Lat. *-aster*, pejorative suff.]

crit•i•cism (krĭt′ĭ-sĭz′əm) *n.* **1.** The act of criticizing, esp. adversely. **2.** A critical comment or judgment. **3.a.** The practice of analyzing, classifying, interpreting, or evaluating literary or other artistic works. **b.** A critical article or essay; a critique. **c.** The investigation of the origin and history of literary documents; textual criticism.

crit•i•cize (krĭt′ĭ-sīz′) *v.* **-cized, -ciz•ing, -ciz•es.** — *tr.* **1.** To find fault with. See Usage Note at **critique. 2.** To judge the merits and faults of; analyze and evaluate. — *intr.* To act as a critic. — **crit′i•ciz′a•ble** *adj.* — **crit′i•ciz′er** *n.*

Syns: *criticize, blame, reprehend, censure, condemn, denounce.* These verbs mean to express an unfavorable judgment. *Criticize* can mean merely to evaluate without necessarily finding fault; however, the word usually implies the expression of disapproval: *The review criticized the novel. Blame* emphasizes the finding of fault and the fixing of responsibility: *"People are always blaming their circumstances for what they are"* (George Bernard Shaw). *Reprehend* implies sharp disapproval: *"reprehends students who have protested apartheid"* (New York Times). *Censure* refers to open and strong expression of criticism; often it implies a formal reprimand: *"No man can justly censure or condemn another, because indeed no man truly knows another"* (Thomas Browne). *Condemn* denotes the pronouncement of harshly adverse judgment: *"The wrongs which we seek to condemn and punish have been so calculated, so malignant and so devastating that civilization cannot tolerate their being ignored"* (Robert H. Jackson). *Denounce* implies public proclamation of condemnation or repudiation: *The press denounced him.*

cri•tique (krĭ-tēk′) *n.* **1.** A critical review or commentary, esp. one dealing with works of art or literature. **2.** A critical discussion of a specified topic. **3.** The art of criticism. — *tr.v.* **-tiqued, -tiqu•ing, -tiques.** *Usage Problem.* To review or discuss critically. [Fr. < Gk. *kritikē (tekhnē),* (art) of criticism < fem. of *kritikos,* critical. See CRITIC.]

Usage Note: *Critique* has been used as a verb meaning "to review or discuss critically" since the 18th century, but lately this usage has gained much wider currency, in part because the verb *criticize,* once neutral between praise and censure, is now mainly used in a negative sense. However, 69 percent of the Usage Panel rejects the sentence *As mock inquisitors grill him, top aides take notes and critique the answers with the President afterward.* In most contexts one can usually substitute *go over, review,* or *analyze.*

crit•ter (krĭt′ər) *n. Regional.* **1.** A living creature. **2.** A domestic animal, esp. a cow, horse, or mule. **3.** A person. [Alteration of CREATURE.]

Regional Note: *Critter,* a pronunciation spelling of *creature,* actually reflects a pronunciation that would have been very familiar to Shakespeare: 16th- and 17th-century English had not yet begun to pronounce the *-ture* suffix with its modern (ch) sound. This archaic pronunciation still exists in regional American *critter.* The most common meaning of *critter* is "a living creature," whether wild or domestic. In old-fashioned regional speech *critter* and *beast* denoted a large domestic animal. The more restricted senses "a cow," "a horse," or "a mule" are still regionally specific. The use of *critter* among younger speakers is almost always somewhat jocular or informal.

croak (krōk) *n.* A low, hoarse sound, as that characteristic of frogs and crows. — *v.* **croaked, croak•ing, croaks.** — *tr.* **1.** To utter in a croak. **2.** *Slang.* To kill. — *intr.* **1.a.** To utter a croak. **b.** To speak with a low, hoarse voice. **2.** To mutter discontentedly; grumble. **3.** *Slang.* To die. [< ME *croken,* to croak, prob. of imit. orig.] — **croak′i•ly** *adv.* — **croak′y** *adj.*

croak•er (krō′kər) *n.* **1.a.** A croaking animal, esp. a frog. **b.** A person who grumbles or habitually predicts evil. **2.** Any of various fishes, chiefly of the family Sciaenidae, that make croaking or grunting sounds.

Croat (krōt, krō′ăt′) *n.* **1.** A native or inhabitant of Croatia. **2.** Serbo-Croatian as used in Croatia. [NLat. *Croata* < Serbo-Croatian *Hrvāt.*]

Cro•a•tia (krō-ā′shə, -shē-ə). A region of S Europe along the NE Adriatic coast; settled by Croats in the 7th cent. and later part of the Austro-Hungarian Empire and a constituent republic of Yugoslavia (after 1946). Croatia declared its independence in Jun. 1991. Cap. Zagreb.Pop. 4,396,397.

Cro•a•tian (krō-ā′shən) *n.* See **Croat.** — *adj.* Of or relating to Croatia or its people, language, or culture.

croc (krŏk) *n. Informal.* A crocodile.

Cro•ce (krō′chĕ), **Benedetto.** 1866–1952. Italian philosopher noted for his *Philosophy of the Spirit* (1902–17).

cro•chet (krō-shā′) *v.* **-cheted** (-shād′), **-chet•ing** (-shā′ĭng), **-chets** (-shāz′). — *tr.* To make by looping thread with a hooked needle. — *intr.* To crochet a piece of needlework. — *n.* Needlework made by crocheting. [< Fr. *crocheter* < OFr. *crochet,* hook, dim. of *croche,* fem. of *croc,* of Gmc. orig.]

cro•ci (krō′sī, -kī) *n.* Pl. of **crocus.**

cro•cid•o•lite (krō-sĭd′l-īt′) *n.* A fibrous lavender-blue or greenish mineral, a sodium iron silicate used as a commercial form of asbestos. [Gk. *krokus, krokis, krokud-, krokid-,* nap on woolen cloth + -LITE.]

crock[1] (krŏk) *n.* **1.a.** An earthenware vessel. **b.** A broken piece of earthenware. **2.** *Slang.* Foolish talk; nonsense. [ME *crokke* < OE *crocc.*]

crock[2] (krŏk) *Regional.* — *n.* Soot. — *v.* **crocked, crock•ing, crocks.** — *tr.* To soil with or as if with crock. — *intr.* To give off soot or color. [?]

crock[3] (krŏk) *Chiefly British.* — *n.* One that is worn-out, decrepit, or impaired; a wreck. — *v.* **crocked, crock•ing, crocks.** — *intr.* To become weak or disabled. Often used with *up.* — *tr.* To disable; wreck. Often used with *up.* [?]

crocked (krŏkt) *adj. Slang.* Drunk. [Poss. < CROCK[3].]

crock•er•y (krŏk′ə-rē) *n.* Earthenware.

crock•et (krŏk′ĭt) *n. Archit.* A projecting ornament, usu. in the form of a cusp or curling leaf, placed along outer angles of pinnacles and gables. [ME *croket,* ornamental curl of hair, hook < ONFr. *croquet,* shepherd's crook, dim. of *croque,* var. of OFr. *croche.* See CROCHET.]

Crock•ett (krŏk′ĭt), **David ("Davy").** 1786–1836. Amer. frontiersman and politician who joined the Texas revolutionaries fighting against Mexico and died at the siege of the Alamo.

Crock-Pot (krŏk′pŏt′). A trademark used for an electric cooker that maintains a low temperature.

croc•o•dile (krŏk′ə-dīl′) *n.* **1.** Any of various large aquatic reptiles, chiefly of the genus *Crocodylus,* native to tropical and subtropical regions and having thick armorlike skin and long tapering jaws. **2.** A crocodilian reptile. **3.** Leather made from crocodile skin. [ME *cocodril* < OFr. < Lat. *cocodrillus,* var. of *crocodīlus* < Gk. *krokodilos* : *krokē,* pebble + *drilos,* circumcised man, worm.]

Word History: The crocodile may owe its name to its resemblance to a lizard that lived in the stone walls of Ionia. This lizard's name, *krokodilos,* is thought to be a compound of *krokē,* "pebble, gravel," and *drilos,* which is only attested as meaning "circumcised man" but is assumed to mean "worm" as well. According to Herodotus, Ionians in Egypt noted the resemblance, probably humorously, between basking crocodiles and their own "worm of the stones."

crocodile bird *n.* A black and white African bird *(Pluvianus aegyptius)* that is related to the plover and feeds on insects that parasitize crocodiles.

Croc•o•dile River (krŏk′ə-dīl′). See **Limpopo.**

crocodile tears *pl.n.* An insincere display of grief; false tears. [From the belief that crocodiles weep either to attract a victim or when eating one.]

croc•o•dil•i•an (krŏk′ə-dĭl′ē-ən, -dĭl′yən) *n.* Any of various reptiles of the order Crocodylia, which includes the alligators, crocodiles, caimans, and gavials. — *adj.* **1.** Of, relating to, or resembling a crocodile. **2.** Belonging to the order Crocodylia.

croc•o•ite (krŏk′ō-īt′, krō′kō-) also **croc•oi•site** (krŏk′wə-zīt′) *n.* A rare lead chromate mineral, $PbCrO_4$, that forms brilliant orange crystals. [Alteration of Fr. *crocoise* < Gk. *krokoeis,* saffron-colored < *krokos,* saffron. See CROCUS.]

cro•cus (krō′kəs) *n., pl.* **-cus•es** or **-ci** (-sī, -kī). **1.a.** Any of various perennial Eurasian herbs of the genus *Crocus,* having grasslike leaves and showy, variously colored flowers. **b.** Any of several other plants, such as the autumn crocus. **2.** *Color.* A grayish to light reddish purple. **3.** A dark red powdered variety of iron oxide, Fe_2O_3, used as an abrasive for polishing. **4.** A coarse, loosely woven material like burlap. See Regional Note at **gunnysack.** [ME < OFr. < Lat. < Gk. *krokos,* of Semitic orig.]

crocus sack *n. South Atlantic U.S.* See **gunnysack.** See Regional Note at **gunnysack.**

Croe•sus[1] (krē′səs). d. c. 546 B.C. Last king of Lydia (560–546), whose kingdom fell to the Persians under Cyrus.

Croe•sus[2] (krē′səs) *n.* A very wealthy man. [After CROESUS[1].]

croft (krôft, krŏft) *n. Chiefly British.* **1.** A small enclosed field or pasture near a house. **2.** A small farm, esp. a tenant farm. [ME < OE.]

croft•er (krôf′tər, krŏf′-) *n. Chiefly British.* One who rents and cultivates a croft; a tenant farmer.

crois•sant (krwä-säN′, krə-sänt′) *n.* A rich crescent-shaped roll of leavened dough or puff pastry. [Fr. < OFr. *creissant, croissant,* crescent. See CRESCENT.]

Croix de Guerre (krwä′ də gâr′) *n., pl.* **Croix de Guerre.** A French military decoration for bravery in combat. [Fr. : *croix,* cross + *de,* of + *guerre,* war.]

cro•ker sack (krō′kər) *n. Lower Southern U.S.* See **gunnysack.** See Regional Note at **gunnysack.** [Alteration of CROCUS SACK.]

Cro-Mag•non (krō-măg′nən, -măn′yən) *n.* An early form of modern human being *(Homo sapiens)* inhabiting Europe in the late Paleolithic Era and characterized by a broad face and tall stature, known from skeletal remains found in the Cro-Magnon cave in southern France. — **Cro-Mag′non** *adj.*

crom•lech (krŏm′lĕk′) *n.* **1.** A prehistoric monument consisting of monoliths encircling a mound. **2.** A dolmen. [Welsh : *crom,* fem. of *crwm,* arched + *llech,* stone.]

Cromp•ton (krŏmp′tən), **Samuel.** 1753–1827. British inventor of the spinning mule (1779).

Crom•well (krŏm′wĕl′, -wəl, krŭm′-), **Oliver.** 1599–1658. English military, political, and religious figure who led the Parliamentarian victory in the English Civil War (1642–49) and ruled as lord protector (1653–58). His son **Richard** (1626–1712) succeeded him briefly (1658–59) before the restoration of the monarchy. — **Crom•well′i•an** *adj.*

Cromwell, Thomas. Earl of Essex. 1485?–1540. English politician who proposed the legislation that established the monarch as head of the established church (1534).

crone (krōn) *n.* An ugly, withered old woman; a hag. [ME < ONFr. *carogne,* carrion, cantankerous woman < VLat. **carōnia,* carrion < Lat. *carō, carn-,* flesh. See **sker-**[1]*.]

Cro•nus (krō′nəs) *n. Gk. Myth.* A Titan who ruled the universe until dethroned by his son Zeus.

cro•ny (krō′nē) *n., pl.* **-nies.** A long-time close friend or companion. [Poss. < Gk. *khronios,* long lasting < *khronos,* time.]

cro•ny•ism (krō′nē-ĭz′əm) *n.* Favoritism shown to old friends without regard for their qualifications.

crook[1] (kro͝ok) *n.* **1.** An implement or tool, such as a bishop's crosier with a bent or curved part. **2.** A part that is curved or bent like a hook. **3.** A curve or bend; a turn. **4.** *Informal.* One who makes a living by dishonest methods. — *v.* **crooked, crook•ing, crooks.** — *tr.* To make a crook in; bend. — *intr.* To bend or curve. See Syns at **bend**[1]. [ME *crok* < ON *krōkr.*]

crook[2] (kro͝ok) *adj. Australian.* **1.** Out of order; faulty. **2.** Not well; ill. **3.** Of poor quality; inferior. **4.** Not honest; crooked. [< CROOKED or CROOK[1].]

crook•back (kro͝ok′băk′) *n. Obsolete.* See **hunchback** 1. — **crook′backed′** *adj.*

crook•ed (kro͝ok′ĭd) *adj.* **1.** Having or marked by bends, curves, or angles. **2.** *Informal.* Dishonest or unscrupulous; fraudulent. — **crook′ed•ly** *adv.* — **crook′ed•ness** *n.*

crocodile

Oliver Cromwell

ă **pat**	oi **boy**
ā **pay**	ou **out**
âr **care**	o͝o **took**
ä **father**	o͞o **boot**
ĕ **pet**	ŭ **cut**
ē **be**	ûr **urge**
ĭ **pit**	th **thin**
ī **pie**	*th* **this**
îr **pier**	hw **which**
ŏ **pot**	zh **vision**
ō **toe**	ə **about,**
ô **paw**	**item**

Stress marks:
′ (primary);
′ (secondary), as in
dictionary (dĭk′shə-nĕr′ē)

and a hoarse cough. [< dialectal *croup*, to croak.] — **croup′·ous** (kro͞o′pəs), **croup′y** *adj.*

croup² (kro͞op) *n.* The rump of a beast of burden, esp. a horse. [ME *croupe* < OFr., of Gmc. orig.]

crou·pi·er (kro͞o′pē-ər, -pē-ā′) *n.* An attendant at a gaming table who collects and pays bets. [Fr., one behind another on a horse, croupier < *croupe*, rump < OFr. See CROUP².]

crouse (kro͞os) *adj. Scots.* Lively; vivacious. [ME *crous*, fierce, bold, perh. < MFlem. *cruus*, curly, bold.]

crous·tade (kro͞o-städ′) *n.* A molded or hollowed bowllike crust, as of pastry, filled with another food. [Fr. < Prov. *croustado* < Lat. *crustātus*, p.part. of *crustāre*, to encrust < *crusta*, crust. See CRUST.]

crou·ton (kro͞o′tŏn′, kro͞o-tŏn′) *n.* A small crisp piece of toasted or fried bread. [Fr. *croûton*, dim. of *croûte*, crust < OFr. *crouste* < Lat. *crusta*. See **kreus-***.]

crow¹ (krō) *n.* **1.** Any of several large glossy black birds of the genus *Corvus*, having a characteristic raucous call, esp. *C. brachyrhynchos* of North America. **2.** A crowbar. — ***idiom.* as the crow flies.** In a straight line. [ME *croue* < OE *crāwe*. See **gerə-²***.]

crow² (krō) *intr.v.* **crowed, crow·ing, crows. 1.** To utter the shrill cry characteristic of a cock. **2.** To exult loudly, as over another's defeat; boast. **3.** To make a sound expressive of pleasure or well-being, characteristic of an infant. — *n.* **1.** The shrill cry of a cock. **2.** A crowing sound. [ME *crouen* < OE *crāwan*. See **gerə-²***.]

Crow¹ (krō) *n.*, *pl.* **Crow** or **Crows. 1.** A member of a Native American people formerly inhabiting the northern Great Plains between the Platte and Yellowstone rivers and now in southeast Montana. **2.** The Siouan language of the Crow.

Crow² (krō) *n.* See **Corvus.**

crow's-nest

crow·bar (krō′bär′) *n.* A straight bar of iron or steel, with the working end shaped like a chisel and often slightly bent and forked, used as a lever. — *tr.v.* **-barred, -bar·ring, -bars.** To extract, remove, or insert forcibly. [< the resemblance of its forked end to a crow's foot or beak.]

crow·ber·ry (krō′bĕr′ē) *n.* **1.** A low-growing evergreen shrub *(Empetrum nigrum)* native to cool regions of the Northern Hemisphere and having tiny leaves, small pinkish or purplish flowers, and black berrylike fruits. **2.** The fruit of this plant.

crow blackbird *n.* See **grackle** 1.

crowd¹ (kroud) *n.* **1.** A large number of persons gathered together; a throng. **2.** The common people; the populace. **3.** A group of people united by a common characteristic, as age. **4.** A group of people attending a public function. **5.** A large number of things positioned or considered together. — *v.* **crowd·ed, crowd·ing, crowds.** — *intr.* **1.** To congregate in a restricted area; throng. **2.** To advance by pressing or shoving. — *tr.* **1.** To force by or as if by pressing or shoving. **2.** To draw or stand near to. **3.** To press, cram, or force tightly together. **4.** To fill or occupy to overflowing. **5.** *Informal.* To put pressure on, as to pay a debt. — ***idiom.* crowd (on) sail.** *Naut.* To spread a large amount of sail to increase speed. [< ME *crowden*, to crowd < OE *crūdan*, to hasten.] — **crowd′er** *n.*

crowd² (kroud, kro͝od) *n.* **1.** *Mus.* An ancient Celtic stringed instrument that was bowed or plucked. **2.** *Chiefly British.* A fiddle. [ME *croud* < Welsh *crwth*, hump, crowd.]

crow·foot (krō′fo͝ot′) *n.* **1.** *pl.* **-foots. a.** Any of numerous plants of the genus *Ranunculus* that have palmately cleft or divided leaves, such as the buttercups. **b.** Any of several other plants having leaves or other parts somewhat resembling a bird's foot. **2.** *pl.* **-feet** (-fēt′). A caltrop used to delay the advance of mounted troops and infantry.

crown (kroun) *n.* **1.** An ornamental circlet or head covering, often made of precious metal set with jewels and worn as a symbol of sovereignty. **2.** Often **Crown. a.** The power, position, or empire of a monarch or of a state governed by constitutional monarchy. **b.** The monarch as head of state. **3.** A distinction or reward for achievement, esp. a title signifying championship in a sport. **4.** Something resembling a diadem in shape. **5.a.** A coin stamped with a crown or crowned head. **b.** A silver coin formerly used in Great Britain and worth five shillings. **c.** Any one of several coins, such as the koruna, having a name that means "crown." **d.** See table at **currency. 6.a.** The top or highest part of the head. **b.** The head itself. **7.** The top or upper part of a hat. **8.** The highest point or summit. **9.** The highest, primary, or most valuable part, attribute, or state. **10.** *Dentistry.* **a.** The part of a tooth that is covered by enamel and projects beyond the gum line. **b.** An artificial substitute for the natural crown of a tooth. **11.** *Naut.* The lowest part of an anchor, where the arms are joined to the shank. **12.** *Bot.* **a.** The upper part of a tree, which includes the branches and leaves. **b.** The part of a plant where the stem and roots merge. **c.** The persistent, mostly underground base of a perennial herb. **d.** See **corona** 5. **13.** The crest of an animal, esp. of a bird. **14.** The portion of a cut gem above the girdle. — *v.* **crowned, crown·ing, crowns.** — *tr.* **1.** To put a crown or garland on the head of. **2.** To invest with regal power; enthrone. **3.** To confer honor, dignity, or reward upon. **4.** To surmount or be the highest part of. **5.** To form the crown, top, or chief ornament of. **6.** To bring to completion or successful conclusion; consummate. **7.** *Dentistry.* To put a crown on (a tooth). **8.** *Games.* To make (a piece in checkers that has reached the last row) into a king by placing another piece upon it. **9.** *Informal.* To hit on the head. — *intr.* To reach a stage in labor when a large segment of the fetal scalp is visible at the vaginal orifice. [ME *crowne* < AN *coroune* < Lat. *corōna* < Gk. *korōnē, korōna* < *korōnos*, curved. See **sker-²***.]

Crucifixion
The Crucifixion
by Nathaniel Currier

crown canopy *n.* See **canopy** 5.

crown colony *n.* A British colony in which the government in London has some control of legislation, usu. administered by an appointed governor.

crown daisy *n.* See **garland chrysanthemum.**

crown glass *n.* **1.** A soda-lime optical glass that is exceptionally hard and clear, with low refraction and low dispersion. **2.** A form of window glass made by whirling a glass bubble to make a flat circular disk with a lump left in the center.

crown jewel *n.* **1.a.** A precious stone that is part of a sovereign's regalia. **b. crown jewels.** The jewels used ceremonially by a sovereign. **2.** Something resembling such jewels.

crown lens *n.* The crown-glass element in an achromatic lens.

crown-of-thorns (kroun′əv-thôrnz′) *n.* **1.** A trailing or climbing spiny shrub *(Euphorbia milii)* native to Madagascar and having showy flower clusters with usu. red petallike bracts. **2.** The Christ's thorn.

Crown Point. 1. A city of NW IN, a suburb of Gary. Pop. 17,728. **2.** A village of NE NY on the W shore of Lake Champlain; site of major battles during the French and Indian War and the American Revolution.

crown prince *n.* The male heir apparent to a throne.

crown princess *n.* **1.** The female heir apparent or heir presumptive to a throne. **2.** The wife of a crown prince.

crown roast *n.* A roast consisting of the rib sections of two loins placed upright and fastened together in a circle.

crown saw *n.* A cylindrical saw with teeth on the bottom edge of the cylinder, used for cutting round holes.

crown vetch *n.* A perennial European herb *(Coronilla varia)* in the pea family, grown for forage and erosion control and having small flower clusters and pinnately compound leaves.

crow's-foot (krōz′fo͝ot′) *n.*, *pl.* **-feet** (-fēt′). **1.** A lasting wrinkle or wrinkles formed at the outer corner of the eye. Often used in the plural. **2.** A three-pointed embroidery stitch.

crow's-nest (krōz′nĕst′) *n.* **1.** *Naut.* A small lookout platform with a railing and windscreen, located near the top of a ship's mast or superstructure. **2.** A similar platform on shore.

croze (krōz) *n.* A groove inside the end of a barrel or cask into which the head is set. [Fr. *creux* < OFr. *crues*, groove < VLat. **crosus*, perh. of Celt. orig.]

cro·zier (krō′zhər) *n.* Var. of **crosier.**

CRP *abbr.* C-reactive protein.

CRT *abbr.* Cathode-ray tube.

cru (kro͞o) *n.*, *pl.* **crus. 1.** A vineyard or wine-producing region in France. **2.** A grade or class of wine. [Fr. < p.part. of *croître*, to grow < OFr. *creistre*. See CRESCENT.]

cru·ces (kro͞o′sēz) *n.* Pl. of **crux.**

cru·cial (kro͞o′shəl) *adj.* **1.a.** Extremely significant or important. **b.** Vital to the resolution of a crisis; decisive. **2.** *Archaic.* Having the form of a cross. [< NLat. *(instantia) crucis, (experimentum) crucis*, crossroads (case), crossroads (experiment) < Lat. *crux, cruc-*, cross.] — **cru′cial·ly** *adv.*

cru·ci·ate (kro͞o′shē-āt′) *adj.* **1.** Arranged in or forming a cross; cruciform. **2.a.** Overlapping or crossing, as the wings of some insects when at rest. **b.** Shaped like a cross. [NLat. *cruciātus* < Lat. *crux, cruc-*, cross.] — **cru′ci·ate′ly** *adv.*

cru·ci·ble (kro͞o′sə-bəl) *n.* **1.** A vessel made of a refractory substance such as graphite or porcelain, used for melting and calcining materials at high temperatures. **2.** A severe test, as of belief. [ME *crusible* < Med.Lat. *crūcibulum*, night-light, crucible, poss. < OFr. *croisuel*, cresset. See CRESSET.]

crucible steel *n.* See **drill steel.**

cru·ci·fer (kro͞o′sə-fər) *n.* **1.** One who bears a cross in a religious procession. **2.** *Bot.* Any of various plants in the mustard family (Cruciferae or Brassicaceae), which includes the alyssum, cabbage, and many weeds. [LLat. : Lat. *crux, cruc-*, cross + Lat. *-fer*, -fer.] — **cru·cif′er·ous** (-sĭf′ər-əs) *adj.*

cru·ci·fix (kro͞o′sə-fĭks′) *n.* **1.** An image or figure of Jesus on the cross. **2.** A cross as a symbol of the Crucifixion. [ME < OFr. < LLat. *crucifixus* < Lat., p.part. of *crucifigere*, crucify. See CRUCIFY.]

cru·ci·fix·ion (kro͞o′sə-fĭk′shən) *n.* **1.a.** The act of crucifying; execution on a cross. **b. Crucifixion.** The crucifying of Jesus on Calvary. **c.** A representation of Jesus on the cross. **2.** An extremely difficult, painful trial; torturous suffering.

cru·ci·form (kro͞o′sə-fôrm′) *adj.* Shaped like a cross; cruciate. [Lat. *crux, cruc-*, cross + -FORM.] — **cru′ci·form′** *n.* — **cru′ci·form′ly** *adv.*

cru·ci·fy (kro͞o′sə-fī′) *tr.v.* **-fied, -fy·ing, -fies. 1.** To put (a person) to death by nailing or binding to a cross. **2.** To mortify or subdue (the flesh). **3.** To treat cruelly. [ME *crucifien* < OFr. *crucifier*, alteration of Lat. *crucifigere* : *crux, cruc-*, cross + *figere*, to attach; see **dhīgʷ-***.] — **cru′ci·fi′er** *n.*

crud (krŭd) *n.* **1.** *Slang.* **a.** A coating or an incrustation of filth or refuse. **b.** Something loathsome, despicable, or worthless. **c.** One who is contemptible or disgusting. **2.** A disease or ailment, imaginary or real, esp. of the skin. [ME *crudde*, poss. < OE **cruden*, p.part. of *crūdan*, to press.]

crud·dy (krŭd′ē) *adj.* **-di·er, -di·est.** *Slang.* Worthless, loathsome, or disgusting. **— crud·di·ness** *n.*

crude (kro͞od) *adj.* **crud·er, crud·est. 1.** Being in an unrefined or natural state; raw. **2.** Lacking tact, refinement, or taste. **3.a.** Not carefully or completely made; rough. **b.** *Statistics.* In an unanalyzed form; not adjusted to allow for related circumstances or data. **4.** Displaying a lack of knowledge or skill. **5.** Undisguised or unadorned; blunt. **6.** *Archaic.* Unripe or immature. *— n.* A substance, esp. petroleum, in its unrefined state. [ME < Lat. *crūdus.* See **kreuə-*.**] **— crude′ly** *adv.* **— cru′di·ty** (kro͞o′dĭ-tē), **crude′ness** *n.*

crude oil *n.* Unrefined petroleum.

cru·di·tés (kro͞o′dĭ-tā′) *pl.n.* Cut raw vegetables, such as carrot sticks, often served with a dip as an appetizer. [Fr., pl. of *crudité*, indigestibility < OFr. *crudite* < Lat. *crūditās*, indigestion, undigested food < *crūdus*, raw. See CRUDE.]

cru·el (kro͞o′əl) *adj.* **-el·er, -el·est** or **-el·ler, -el·lest. 1.** Disposed to inflict pain or suffering. **2.** Causing suffering. [ME < OFr. < Lat. *crūdēlis.* See **kreuə-*.**] **— cru′el·ly** *adv.*

Syns: *cruel, fierce, ferocious, barbarous, inhuman, savage, vicious.* These adjectives mean inclined to inflict violence, pain, or hardship or to find satisfaction in the suffering of others. *Cruel* implies both disposition to harm and satisfaction in or indifference to suffering: *a cruel tyrant. Fierce* suggests the fearless aggression of a wild animal: *fierce anger. Ferocious* adds to *fierce* connotations of rabid fury and rampant brutality: *a ferocious attack dog. Barbarous* suggests harshness and cruelty that befit only primitive human beings: *a barbarous crime. Inhuman* means markedly deficient in those qualities such as kindness and sympathy: *cruel and inhuman behavior. Savage* implies wild or uncivilized behavior: *a savage outburst of temper. Vicious* suggests malicious, violent, or destructive behavior: *a vicious kick.*

cru·el·ty (kro͞o′əl-tē) *n., pl.* **-ties. 1.** The quality or condition of being cruel. **2.** Something that causes pain or suffering. **3.** *Law.* The infliction of physical or mental distress, esp. when considered a determinant in granting a divorce.

cru·et (kro͞o′ĭt) *n.* **1.** A small glass bottle for holding a condiment at the table. **2.** A small vessel for holy water or for water or wine used in the consecration of the Eucharist. [ME < OFr., dim. of *crue*, flask, of Gmc. orig.]

Cruik·shank (kro͝ok′shăngk′), **George.** 1792–1878. British caricaturist and illustrator of works by Charles Dickens.

cruise (kro͞oz) *v.* **cruised, cruis·ing, cruis·es.** *— intr.* **1.a.** To sail or travel about, as for pleasure. **b.** To go or move along, esp. in an unhurried or unconcerned fashion. **2.** To travel at a constant speed or at a speed providing maximum operating efficiency for a sustained period. **3.a.** *Informal.* To move leisurely about an area in the hope of discovering something. **b.** *Slang.* To look for a sexual partner, as in a public place. **4.** To inspect a wooded area to determine its lumber yield. *— tr.* **1.** To travel about or journey over. **2.** To inspect in order to determine lumber yield. *— n.* The act or an instance of cruising, esp. a sea voyage for pleasure. [Du. *kruisen*, to cross < *kruis*, cross < MDu. *cruce* < Lat. *crux, cruc-*, cross.]

cruise control *n.* **1.** A system in a motor vehicle for maintaining a constant speed. **2.** Maintenance of a constant speed in such a vehicle.

cruise missile *n.* An aircraft without a crew that serves as a self-contained bomb.

cruis·er (kro͞o′zər) *n.* **1.** One of a class of fast warships of medium tonnage with a long cruising radius and less armor and firepower than a battleship. **2.** *Naut.* A cabin cruiser. **3.** See **squad car.**

crul·ler (krŭl′ər) *n.* **1.** A small, usu. ring-shaped or twisted cake of sweet dough fried in deep fat. **2.** *Chiefly New England & Pennsylvania.* An unraised doughnut, usu. twisted but also shaped into rings or oblongs. [< obsolete Du. *krulle-koken*, rolled-up cake < MDu. *crulle-koken* < *crulle*, curly.]

crumb (krŭm) *n.* **1.** A very small piece broken from a baked item, such as cake or bread. **2.** A small fragment, scrap, or portion: *eraser crumbs.* **3.** The soft inner portion of bread. **4.** *Slang.* A contemptible, untrustworthy, or loathsome person. *— v.* **crumbed, crumb·ing, crumbs.** *— tr.* **1.** To break into very small pieces; crumble. **2.** To cover or prepare with very small pieces of bread. **3.** To brush (a table or cloth) clear of small scraps or fragments of food. *— intr.* To break apart in very small pieces. [ME *crome* < OE *cruma.*]

crum·ble (krŭm′bəl) *v.* **-bled, -bling, -bles.** *— tr.* To break into small fragments or particles. *— intr.* **1.** To fall into small fragments or particles; disintegrate. **2.** To give way; collapse. [Alteration of ME *cremelen* < OE **crymelen*, freq. of *gecrymman*, to break into crumbs < *cruma*, crumb.]

crum·bly (krŭm′blē) *adj.* **-bli·er, -bli·est.** Easily crumbled; friable. **— crum′bli·ness** *n.*

crum·horn (krŭm′hôrn′) *n. Mus.* Var. of **krummhorn.**

crum·my also **crumb·y** (krŭm′ē) *adj.* **-mi·er, -mi·est** also **-i·er, -i·est.** *Slang.* **1.** Miserable or wretched. **2.** Shabby or cheap: *a crummy little rowboat.* [Prob. < CRUMB.]

crump (krŭmp) *v.* **crumped, crump·ing, crumps.** *— tr.* **1.** To crush or crunch with the teeth. **2.** To strike heavily with a crunching sound. *— intr.* To make a crunching sound, esp. in walking over snow. *— n.* **1.a.** A crunching sound. **b.** The sound of an exploding shell. **2.** A heavy blow. [Imit.]

crum·pet (krŭm′pĭt) *n.* A small flat round of bread, baked on a griddle and usu. served toasted. [Poss. < ME *crompid (cake)*, curled (cake), prob. p.part. of *crumpen*, to curl up, prob. < *crumb, crump*, crooked < OE.]

crum·ple (krŭm′pəl) *v.* **-pled, -pling, -ples.** *— tr.* **1.** To crush together or press into wrinkles; rumple. **2.** To cause to fall apart. *— intr.* **1.** To become wrinkled. **2.** To fall apart; collapse. *— n.* An irregular fold, crease, or wrinkle. [ME *crumplen*, prob. freq. of *crumpen*, to curl up. See CRUMPET.] **— crum′ply** *adj.*

crunch (krŭnch) *v.* **crunched, crunch·ing, crunch·es.** *— tr.* **1.** To chew with a noisy crackling sound. **2.** To crush, grind, or tread noisily. **3.** *Slang.* To perform operations on; manipulate or process (numerical or mathematical data). *— intr.* **1.** To chew noisily with a crackling sound. **2.** To move with a crushing sound. **3.** To produce or emit a crushing sound. *— n.* **1.** The act or sound of crunching. **2.a.** A decisive confrontation. **b.** A critical moment or situation. [Alteration of *craunch*, poss. of imit. orig.] **— crunch′a·ble** *adj.*

crunch·er (crŭnch′ər) *n. Slang.* A finishing or decisive blow.

crunch·y (krŭn′chē) *adj.* **-i·er, -i·est.** Making a crunching or cracking sound, as when chewed; crisp.

crup·per (krŭp′ər) *n.* **1.** A leather strap looped under a horse's tail and attached to a harness or saddle to keep it from slipping forward. **2.** The rump of a horse; the croup. [ME *crouper* < OFr. *cropiere* < *croupe*, rump. See CROUP[2].]

cru·ral (kro͝or′əl) *adj.* Of or relating to the leg, shank, or thigh. [Lat. *crūrālis* < *crūs, crūr-*, leg.]

crus (kro͞os, krŭs) *n., pl.* **cru·ra** (kro͝or′ə). **1.** The section of the leg or hind limb between the knee and foot; shank. **2.a.** A leglike part. **b.** A body part consisting of elongated masses or diverging bands that resemble legs or roots. [Lat. *crūs, crūr-*, leg.]

cru·sade (kro͞o-sād′) *n.* **1.** Often **Crusade.** Any of the military expeditions undertaken by European Christians in the 11th, 12th, and 13th centuries to recover the Holy Land from the Muslims. **2.** A holy war undertaken with papal sanction. **3.** A vigorous concerted movement for a cause or against an abuse. [Fr. *croisade* and Sp. *cruzada*, both ult. < Lat. *crux, cruc-*, cross.] **— cru·sade′** *v.* **— cru·sad′er** *n.*

cru·sa·do (kro͞o-sä′dō) also **cru·za·do** (-zä′-) *n., pl.* **-does** or **-dos.** An old Portuguese coin of gold or silver having a cross pictured on the reverse. [Port. < p.part. of *cruzar*, to mark with a cross < *cruz*, cross < Lat. *crux, cruc-*.]

cruse (kro͞oz, kro͞os) *n.* A small earthenware container for holding liquids. [ME *crouse*, perh. < MDu. *cruyse*, pot.]

crush (krŭsh) *v.* **crushed, crush·ing, crush·es.** *— tr.* **1.** To press between opposing bodies so as to break or injure. **2.** To break, pound, or grind (stone or ore, for example) into small fragments or powder. **3.** To put down; subdue. **4.** To overwhelm or oppress severely. **5.** To crumple or rumple. **6.** To hug, esp. with great force. **7.** To press upon, shove, or crowd. **8.** To extract or obtain by pressing or squeezing. **9.** *Archaic.* To drink; quaff. *— intr.* **1.** To be or become crushed. **2.** To proceed or move by crowding or pressing. *— n.* **1.** The act of crushing; extreme pressure. **2.** The state of being crushed. **3.** A great crowd. **4.** A substance prepared by or as if by crushing, esp. a fruit drink. **5.** *Informal.* **a.** A usu. temporary infatuation. **b.** The object of such an infatuation. **6.** A decisive or critical moment or situation. **7.** The process of stamping or crushing grapes for wine. [ME *crushen* < OFr. *croissir*, of Gmc. orig.] **— crush′a·ble** *adj.* **— crush′er** *n.* **— crush′-proof′** (-pro͞of′) *adj.*

crushed (krŭsht) *adj.* Treated so as to have a permanently crinkled or rumpled appearance. Used of a fabric.

crust (krŭst) *n.* **1.a.** The hard outer portion or surface area of bread. **b.** A piece of bread consisting mostly of the crust. **c.** A hard and dry piece of bread. **2.** A pastry shell, as of a pie. **3.** A hard, crisp covering or surface. **4.** A hard deposit formed on the interior of a wine bottle as the wine matures. **5.** *Geol.* **a.** The exterior portion of the earth that lies above the Mohorovičić discontinuity. **b.** The outermost solid layer of a planet or moon. **6.** The hard outer covering of certain plants and animals. **7.** *Pathol.* An outer layer formed by the drying of a bodily exudate such as blood; a scab. **8.** *Informal.* Insolence; audacity; gall. *— v.* **crust·ed, crust·ing, crusts.** *— tr.* **1.** To cover with a crust. **2.** To form into a crust. *— intr.* **1.** To become covered with a crust. **2.** To harden into a crust. [ME *cruste* < OFr. *crouste* < Lat. *crusta.* See **kreus-*.**] **— crust′less** *adj.*

crus·ta·cean (krŭ-stā′shən) *n.* Any of various predominantly aquatic arthropods of the class Crustacea, including lobsters and crabs, characteristically having a segmented body, a chitinous exoskeleton, and paired jointed limbs. [< NLat. *Crustācea*, class name, neut. pl. of *crustāceus*, hard-shelled < Lat.

cruet
c. 1817 French cruet holder by Jean Baptiste Claude Odiot (1763–1850)

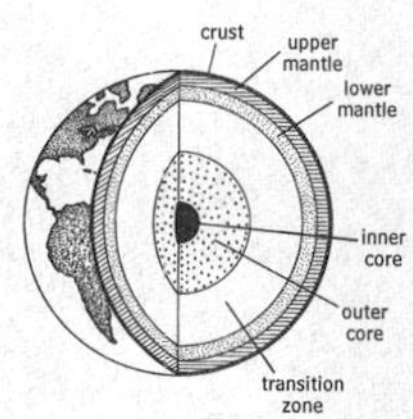

crust
Cutaway view of Earth

ă pat	oi boy
ā pay	ou out
âr care	o͝o took
ä father	o͞o boot
ĕ pet	ŭ cut
ē be	ûr urge
ĭ pit	th thin
ī pie	*th* this
îr pier	hw which
ŏ pot	zh vision
ō toe	ə about, item
ô paw	

Stress marks:
′ (primary);
′ (secondary), as in
dictionary (dĭk′shə-nĕr′ē)

crusta, shell. See **kreus-***.] — **crus•ta′cean** *n.*

crus•ta•ceous (krŭ-stā′shəs) *adj.* **1.** Having, resembling, or constituting a hard crust or shell. **2.** Crustacean. [Lat. *crusta*, shell; see **kreus-*** + -ACEOUS.]

crus•tose (krŭs′tōs′) *adj.* Of or relating to a lichen whose thallus is thin, crusty, and closely adherent to or embedded in the surface on which it grows. [Lat. *crustōsus*, crusted < *crusta*, crust. See **kreus-***.]

crust•y (krŭs′tē) *adj.* **-i•er, -i•est. 1.** Having, resembling, or being a crust. **2.** Seemingly rough and surly in manner. — **crust′i•ly** *adv.* — **crust′i•ness** *n.*

crutch (krŭch) *n.* **1.** A staff or support used as an aid in walking, usu. designed to fit under the armpit and often used in pairs. **2.** A forked leg rest on a sidesaddle. **3.** A device used for assistance or support; a prop: *a mnemonic crutch.* **4.** The crotch of a person or an animal. **5.** A forked device or part. — *tr.v.* **crutched, crutch•ing, crutch•es.** To support on or as if on crutches; prop up. [ME *crucche* < OE *crycc.*]

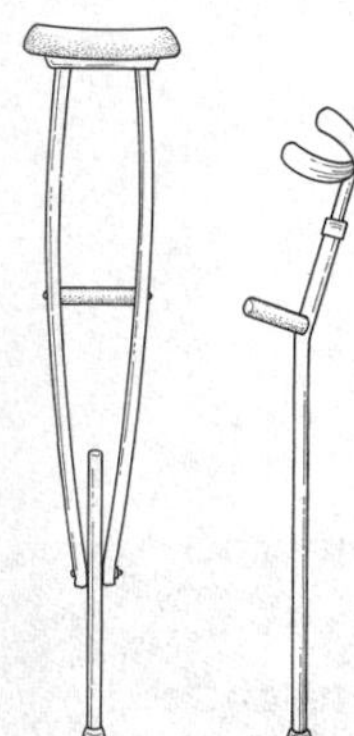

crutch
Left: Full-length crutch
Right: Elbow crutch

crux (krŭks, kro͝oks) *n., pl.* **crux•es** or **cru•ces** (kro͞o′sēz). **1.** The basic, central, or critical point or feature: *the crux of the matter.* **2.** A puzzling or apparently insoluble problem. [Prob. short for Med.Lat. *crux (interpretum)*, torment (of interpreters) < Lat. *crux*, cross.]

Crux (krŭks, kro͝oks) *n.* See **Southern Cross.**

cru•za•do (kro͞o-zä′dō) *n.* Var. of **crusado.**

Cru•zan (kro͞o-zăn′, kro͞o′zăn) *n.* A native or inhabitant of St. Croix in the U.S. Virgin Islands. [< Am.Sp. *Santa Cruz*, St. Croix.] — **Cru′zan** *adj.*

cru•zei•ro (kro͞o-zâr′ō, -zā′ro͞o) *n., pl.* **-ros.** See table at **currency.** [Port. < *cruz*, cross < Lat. *crux, cruc-.*]

crwth (kro͞oth) *n. Mus.* See **crowd**[2] 1. [Welsh.]

cry (krī) *v.* **cried** (krīd), **cry•ing, cries** (krīz). — *intr.* **1.** To sob or shed tears because of grief, sorrow, or pain; weep. **2.** To call loudly; shout. **3.** To utter a characteristic sound or call. Used of an animal. **4.** To demand or require immediate action or remedy: *cried out for change.* — *tr.* **1.** To utter loudly; call out. **2.** To proclaim or announce in public. **3.** To bring into a particular condition by weeping. **4.** *Archaic.* To beg for; implore. — *n., pl.* **cries** (krīz). **1.** A loud utterance of an emotion, such as fear or despair. **2.** A loud exclamation; a shout or call. **3.** A fit of weeping. **4.** An urgent entreaty or appeal. **5.** A public or general demand or complaint. **6.** A common view or general report. **7.** An advertising of wares by calling out. **8.** A rallying call or signal. **9.** A slogan, esp. a political one. **10.** The characteristic call or utterance of an animal. **11.a.** The baying of hounds during the chase. **b.** A pack of hounds. **12.** *Obsolete.* Clamor; outcry. **13.** *Obsolete.* A public announcement; a proclamation. — ***phrasal verbs.*** **cry down.** To belittle or disparage. **cry off.** To break or withdraw from a promise, agreement, or undertaking. **cry up.** To praise highly; extol. — ***idioms.*** **cry havoc.** To sound an alarm; warn. **cry (one's) eyes (**or **heart) out.** To weep inconsolably for a long time. **cry on (someone's) shoulder.** To tell one's problems to gain sympathy. **cry over spilled milk.** To regret in vain what cannot be undone. **cry wolf.** To raise a false alarm. **in full cry.** In hot pursuit, as hounds hunting. [ME *crien* < OFr. *crier* < VLat. **critāre* < Lat. *quirītāre*, to cry out.]

Syns: *cry, weep, wail, keen, whimper, sob, blubber.* These verbs mean to make inarticulate sounds of grief, unhappiness, or pain. *Cry* and *weep* both involve the shedding of tears; *cry* more strongly implies accompanying sound: *"And when he* [William of Orange] *died the little children cried in the streets"* (John Lothrop Motley). *"I weep for what I'm like when I'm alone"* (Theodore Roethke). *Wail* refers primarily to sustained, inarticulate mournful sound: *"The women . . . began to wail together"* (Joseph Conrad). *Keen* suggests wailing and lamentation for the dead: *"It is the wild Irish women keening over their dead"* (George A. Lawrence). *Whimper* refers to low, plaintive broken or repressed cries: *The prisoner whimpered for clemency. Sob* is marked by convulsive breathing or gasping: *"sobbing and crying . . . as if her heart would break"* (Laurence Sterne). *Blubber* refers to noisy shedding of tears with broken or inarticulate speech: *He blubbered like a child.*

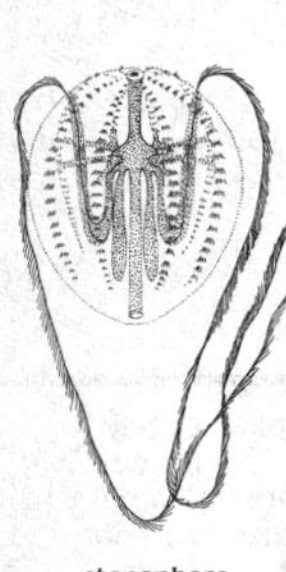

ctenophore

cry•ba•by (krī′bā′bē) *n.* A person who cries or complains frequently with little cause.

cry•ing (krī′ĭng) *adj.* Requiring action or attention.

cryo– *pref.* Cold; freezing: *cryoscopy.* [< Gk. *kruos*, icy cold. See **kreus-***.]

cry•o•bank (krī′ə-băngk′) *n.* A cryogenic place of storage for semen or transplantable tissues.

cry•o•bi•ol•o•gy (krī′ō-bī-ŏl′ə-jē) *n.* The study of the effects of very low temperatures on living organisms. — **cry′o•bi′o•log′i•cal** (-bī′ə-lŏj′ĭ-kəl) *adj.* — **cry′o•bi′o•log′i•cal•ly** *adv.* — **cry′o•bi•ol′o•gist** *n.*

cry•o•gen (krī′ə-jən) *n.* A liquid, such as liquid nitrogen, that boils at a temperature below about 110°K (−160°C) and is used to obtain very low temperatures; a refrigerant.

cry•o•gen•ic (krī′ə-jĕn′ĭk) *adj.* **1.** Of or relating to low temperatures. **2.** Requiring or suitable to cryogenic storage. — **cry′o•gen′i•cal•ly** *adv.*

cry•o•gen•ics (krī′ə-jĕn′ĭks) *n.* *(used with a sing. or pl. v.)* The production of low temperatures or the study of low-temperature phenomena.

cry•og•e•ny (krī-ŏj′ə-nē) *n.* See **cryogenics.**

cry•o•lite (krī′ə-līt′) *n.* A vitreous natural fluoride of aluminum and sodium, Na_3AlF_6, used chiefly in the electrolytic recovery of aluminum.

cry•om•e•ter (krī-ŏm′ĭ-tər) *n.* A thermometer capable of measuring very low temperatures.

cry•on•ics (krī-ŏn′ĭks) *n.* *(used with a sing. v.)* The process of freezing and storing dead bodies under the assumption that they may be reanimated. [CRY(O)– + *-onics*, as in BIONICS.] — **cry•on′ic** *adj.*

cry•o•phil•ic (krī′ə-fĭl′ĭk) also **cry•oph•i•lous** (krī-ŏf′ə-ləs) *adj.* Having an affinity for or thriving at low temperatures.

cry•o•probe (krī′ə-prōb′) *n.* A surgical instrument used to apply extreme cold to tissues during cryosurgery.

cry•o•scope (krī′ə-skōp′) *n.* An instrument used to measure the freezing point of a liquid.

cry•os•co•py (krī-ŏs′kə-pē) *n.* A technique for determining the molecular weight of a solute by dissolving a known quantity of it in a solvent and recording the amount by which the freezing point of the solvent drops. — **cry′o•scop′ic** (-ə-skŏp′ĭk) *adj.*

cry•o•stat (krī′ə-stăt′) *n.* An apparatus used to maintain constant low temperature. — **cry′o•stat′ic** *adj.*

cry•o•sur•ger•y (krī′ō-sûr′jə-rē) *n.* The selective exposure of tissues to extreme cold, often by applying a probe containing liquid nitrogen, to bring about the destruction or elimination of abnormal cells. — **cry′o•sur′geon** (-jən) *n.* — **cry′o•sur′gi•cal** (-jĭ-kəl) *adj.*

cry•o•ther•a•py (krī′ō-thĕr′ə-pē) *n.* The local or general use of low temperatures in medical therapy.

crypt (krĭpt) *n.* **1.** An underground vault or chamber, esp. one used as a burial place. **2.** *Anat.* A small pit, recess, or glandular cavity in the body. [Lat. *crypta* < Gk. *kruptē* < fem. of *kruptos*, hidden < *kruptein*, to hide.]

crypt– *pref.* Var. of **crypto–.**

crypt•a•nal•y•sis (krĭp′tə-năl′ĭ-sĭs) *n.* **1.** The analysis and deciphering of cryptographic writings or systems. **2.** Also **crypt•an•a•lyt•ics** (krĭp′tăn-ə-lĭt′ĭks). *(used with a sing. v.)* The study of techniques for cryptanalysis. [CRYPT(OGRAM) + ANALYSIS.] — **crypt•an′a•lyst** (krĭp-tăn′ə-lĭst) *n.* — **crypt•an′a•lyt′ic** (-lĭt′ĭk) *adj.* — **crypt•an′a•lyze′** *v.*

cryp•tic (krĭp′tĭk) also **cryp•ti•cal** (-tĭ-kəl) *adj.* **1.** Having hidden meaning; mystifying. See Syns at **ambiguous. 2.** Secret or occult. **3.** Using code or cipher. **4.** *Biol.* Tending to conceal or camouflage: *cryptic coloring.* [LLat. *crypticus* < Gk. *kruptikos* < *kruptos*, hidden < *kruptein*, to hide.] — **cryp′ti•cal•ly** *adv.* — **cryp′tic•ness** *n.*

cryp•to (krĭp′tō) *n., pl.* **-tos.** One who covertly supports a certain doctrine, group, or party. — *adj.* **1.** Secret; covert. **2.** Of, relating to, or employing cryptography. [< CRYPTO–.]

crypto– or **crypt–** *pref.* Hidden; secret: *cryptoclastic.* [< Gk. *kruptos*, hidden < *kruptein*, to hide.]

cryp•to•clas•tic (krĭp′tō-klăs′tĭk) *adj.* Composed of microscopic rock fragments.

cryp•to•coc•co•sis (krĭp′tə-kŏ-kō′sĭs) *n.* A systemic infection caused by the fungus *Cryptococcus neoformans* that most often occurs in the central nervous system.

cryp•to•coc•cus (krĭp′tə-kŏk′əs) *n.* Any of various yeastlike fungi of the genus *Cryptococcus*, commonly occurring in the soil and including certain pathogenic species. — **cryp′to•coc′cal** *adj.*

cryp•to•crys•tal•line (krĭp′tō-krĭs′tə-lĭn, -līn′) *adj.* Having a microscopic crystalline structure.

cryp•to•gam (krĭp′tə-găm′) *n. Bot.* A member of a formerly recognized taxonomic group that included all seedless plants, such as mosses. [< NLat. *Cryptogamia*, genus name : CRYPTO– + *-gamia*, -gamy.] — **cryp′to•gam′ic, cryp•tog′a•mous** (-tŏg′ə-məs) *adj.*

cryp•to•gen•ic (krĭp′tə-jĕn′ĭk) also **cryp•tog•e•nous** (krĭp-tŏj′ə-nəs) *adj.* Of obscure or unknown origin.

cryp•to•gram (krĭp′tə-grăm′) *n.* **1.** A piece of writing in code or cipher. **2.** A figure or representation having a secret or occult significance. — **cryp′to•gram′mic** *adj.*

cryp•to•graph (krĭp′tə-grăf′) *n.* **1.** See **cryptogram** 1. **2.** A system of secret or cipher writing; a cipher. **3.a.** A device for translating plain text into cipher. **b.** A device for deciphering codes and ciphers. — *tr.v.* **-graphed, -graph•ing, -graphs.** To write (a message, for example) in code or cipher.

cryp•tog•ra•pher (krĭp-tŏg′rə-fər) *n.* One who uses, studies, or develops cryptographic systems and writings.

cryp•tog•ra•phy (krĭp-tŏg′rə-fē) *n.* **1.** The process or skill of communicating in or deciphering secret writings or ciphers. **2.** Secret writing. — **cryp′to•graph′ic** (-tə-grăf′ĭk) *adj.* — **cryp′to•graph′i•cal•ly** *adv.*

cryp•tol•o•gy (krĭp-tŏl′ə-jē) *n.* The study of cryptanalysis or cryptography. — **cryp′to•log′ic** (-tə-lŏj′ĭk), **cryp′to•log′i•cal** (-ĭ-kəl) *adj.* — **cryp•tol′o•gist** *n.*

cryp•to•me•ri•a (krĭp′tə-mîr′ē-ə) *n.* See **Japanese cedar.** [NLat. *Cryptomeria*, genus name : CRYPTO– + Gk. *meros*, part.]

crypt•or•chism (krĭp-tôr′kĭz′əm) also **crypt•or•chi•dism** (-kĭ-dĭz′əm) *n.* A developmental defect marked by the failure of the testes to descend into the scrotum. [< NLat. *cryptorchidismus* : CRYPT(O)- + *orchis*, testicle (< Gk. *orkhis*).] — **crypt•or′chid** *n.*

cryp•to•zo•ite (krĭp′tə-zō′īt′) *n.* A malarial parasite at the stage of development in which it inhabits bodily tissue before invading the red blood cells. [CRYPTO- + ZO(O)- + -ITE[1].]

crys•tal (krĭs′təl) *n.* **1.a.** A homogenous solid formed by a repeating three-dimensional pattern of atoms, ions, or molecules and having fixed distances between constituent parts. **b.** The unit cell of such a pattern. **2.** A mineral, esp. a transparent form of quartz, having a crystalline structure and often characterized by external planar faces. **3.a.** A natural or synthetic crystalline material having piezoelectric or semiconducting properties. **b.** An electronic device, such as a detector, using such a material. **4.a.** A high-quality clear, colorless glass. **b.** An object, esp. a vessel or an ornament, made of such glass. **c.** Such objects considered as a group. **5.** A clear glass or plastic protective cover for the face of a watch or clock. **6.** *Slang.* A stimulant drug, usu. methamphetamine, in its powdered form. — *adj.* Clear or transparent. [ME *cristal* < OFr. < Lat. *crystallum* < Gk. *krustallos*. See **kreus-***.]

Crys•tal (krĭs′təl). A city of E MN, a suburb of Minneapolis. Pop. 23,788.

crystal ball *n.* **1.** A globe of quartz crystal or glass in which images are supposedly visible to fortune tellers. **2.** A vehicle or technique for making predictions.

crystal detector *n.* A rectifying detector used esp. in early radio receivers and consisting of a semiconducting crystal in point contact with a fine metal wire.

crystal gaz•ing (gā′zĭng) *n.* **1.** Divination by gazing into a crystal ball. **2.** The making of determinations or predictions using questionable or unscientific means. — **crystal gazer** *n.*

Crystal Lake. A city of NE IL N of Elgin. Pop. 24,512.

crystal lattice *n.* A geometric arrangement of the points in space at which the atoms, molecules, or ions of a crystal occur.

crys•tal•lif•er•ous (krĭs′tə-lĭf′ər-əs) also **crys•tal•lig•er•ous** (-lĭj′-) *adj.* Producing or containing crystals.

crys•tal•line (krĭs′tə-lĭn, -līn′, -lēn′) *adj.* **1.** Being, relating to, or composed of crystal or crystals. **2.** Resembling crystal, as in transparency or structure. [ME *cristallin* < OFr. < Lat. *crystallinus* < Gk. *krustallinos* < *krustallos*, crystal. See **kreus-***.] — **crys′tal•lin′i•ty** (-lĭn′ĭ-tē) *n.*

crystalline lens *n.* The lens of an eye.

crys•tal•lite (krĭs′tə-līt′) *n.* Any of numerous minute rudimentary crystalline bodies of unknown composition found in glassy igneous rocks. — **crys′tal•lit′ic** (-lĭt′ĭk) *adj.*

crys•tal•lize also **crys•tal•ize** (krĭs′tə-līz′) — *v.* **-lized, -liz•ing, -liz•es** also **-ized, -iz•ing, -iz•es.** — *tr.* **1.** To cause to form crystals or assume a crystalline structure. **2.** To give a definite and usu. permanent form to. **3.** To coat with crystals, as of sugar. — *intr.* **1.** To assume a crystalline form. **2.** To take on a definite and usu. permanent form. — **crys′tal•liz′a•ble** *adj.* — **crys′tal•li•za′tion** (-lĭ-zā′shən) *n.* — **crys′tal•liz′er** *n.*

crystallo– or **crystall–** *pref.* Crystal: *crystallize.* [< Gk. *krustallo-* < *krustallos*, crystal. See **kreus-***.]

crys•tal•log•ra•phy (krĭs′tə-lŏg′rə-fē) *n.* The science of crystal structure and phenomena. — **crys′tal•log′ra•pher** *n.* — **crys′tal•lo•graph′ic** (-lə-grăf′ĭk), **crys′tal•lo•graph′i•cal** *adj.* — **crys′tal•lo•graph′i•cal•ly** *adv.*

crys•tal•loid (krĭs′tə-loid′) *n.* **1.** *Chem.* A substance that can be crystallized. **2.** *Bot.* Any of various minute crystallike particles consisting of protein and found in certain plant cells. — **crys′tal•loid′, crys′tal•loi′dal** (-loid′l) *adj.*

crystal pleat *n.* One of a series of very narrow pleats creased in the same direction.

crystal set *n.* An early radio receiver using a crystal detector.

crystal violet *n.* A dye derived from gentian violet that is used as a general biological stain and an acid-base indicator.

Cs The symbol for the element **cesium.**

CS *abbr.* **1.** Capital stock. **2.** Chief of staff. **3.a.** Christian Science. **b.** Christian Scientist. **4.** Civil service.

cs. *abbr.* Case.

C.S.A. *abbr.* Confederate States of America.

csc *abbr. Math.* Cosecant.

CSC *abbr.* Civil Service Commission.

C-sec•tion (sē′sĕk′shən) *n.* A cesarean section.

CSF *abbr.* Cerebrospinal fluid.

csk. *abbr.* **1.** Cask. **2.** Countersink.

CST *abbr.* Or **C.S.T.** Central Standard Time.

c-store or **C-store** (sē′stôr′, -stōr′) *n.* A convenience store.

CT *abbr.* Connecticut.

ct. *abbr.* **1.** Cent. **2.** Certificate. **3.** Court.

Ct. *abbr.* **1.** Connecticut. **2.** Count (title).

cten•oid (tĕn′oid′, tē′noid′) *adj. Biol.* **1.** Comblike. **2.** Having marginal projections that resemble the teeth of a comb. [Gk. *ktenoeidēs* : *kteis*, *kten-*, comb + *-oeidēs*, -oid.]

cten•o•phore (tĕn′ə-fôr′, -fōr′) *n.* Any of various marine animals of the phylum Ctenophora, having transparent gelatinous bodies bearing eight rows of comblike cilia used for swimming. [< NLat. *Ctenophora*, phylum name : Gk. *kteis*, *kten-*, comb + NLat. *-phora* < neut. pl. of Gk. *-phoros*, -phore.] — **cte•noph′o•ran** (tĭ-nŏf′ər-ən) *adj.*

Ctes•i•phon (tĕs′ə-fŏn′, tē′sə-). An ancient city of central Iraq on the Tigris R. SE of Baghdad.

ctf. *abbr.* Certificate.

ctg. *abbr.* Cartage.

ctge. *abbr.* Cartage.

ctn *abbr. Math.* Cotangent.

ctn. *abbr.* Carton.

ctr. *abbr.* **1.** Center. **2.** Counter.

CT scan (sē′tē′) *n.* See **CAT scan.**

CT scanner *n.* See **CAT scanner.**

Cu The symbol for the element **copper**[1] 1. [Lat. *cuprum.*]

cu. or **cu** *abbr.* Cubic.

cua•dril•la (kwä-drē′yə, -drēl′yə) *n.*, *pl.* **-las.** The group of assistants to the matador in a bullfight. [Sp., dim. of *cuadra*, square < Lat. *quadra.* See QUADRILLE[1].]

Cuan•za also **Kwan•za** (kwän′zə). A river rising in central Angola and flowing c. 965 km (600 mi) to the Atlantic Ocean.

cuat•ro (kwä′trō) *n.*, *pl.* **-ros.** *Mus.* A small guitarlike instrument of Latin America, usu. having four or five pairs of strings. [Sp. < Lat. *quattuor*, four. See QUATRAIN.]

cub (kŭb) *n.* **1.** The young of certain carnivorous animals, such as the bear. **2.** A youth, esp. one who is inexperienced, awkward, or ill-mannered. **3.** A novice or learner, esp. in newspaper reporting. **4. Cub.** A Cub Scout. [?]

Cu•ba (kyo͞o′bə). An island country in the Caribbean Sea S of FL; a Spanish colony until 1898. Cap. Havana. Pop. 9,723,605. — **Cu′ban** *adj. & n.*

cub•age (kyo͞o′bĭj) *n.* Cubic content, volume, or displacement.

Cuban heel *n.* A broad heel of moderate height with a slightly tapered back and straight front, used in shoes and boots.

Cuban sandwich *n. Florida.* See **submarine** 2. See Regional Note at **submarine.**

cu•ba•ture (kyo͞o′bə-cho͝or′, -chər) *n.* **1.** The determination of the cubic contents of a solid. **2.** Cubage. [CUB(E) + (QUADR)ATURE.]

cub•by (kŭb′ē) *n.*, *pl.* **-bies.** A small room; a cubbyhole.

cub•by•hole (kŭb′ē-hōl′) *n.* **1.** A snug or cramped space or room. **2.** A small compartment. **3.** A category, esp. an over-restrictive one. [< *cub*, pen, hutch (perh. < Flem. *cubbe* < MFlem.) + HOLE.]

cube (kyo͞ob) *n.* **1.** *Math.* A regular solid having six congruent square faces. **2.a.** Something having the general shape of a cube: *a cube of sugar.* **b.** A cubicle used for work or study. **3.** *Math.* The third power of a number or quantity. **4. cubes.** *Slang.* Cubic inches. Used esp. of an internal combustion engine. — *tr.v.* **cubed, cub•ing, cubes. 1.** *Math.* To raise (a quantity or number) to the third power. **2.** To determine the cubic contents of. **3.** To form or cut into cubes; dice. **4.** To tenderize (meat) by breaking the fibers with superficial cuts in a pattern of squares. [Lat. *cubus* < Gk. *kubos.*] — **cub′er** *n.*

cu•bé also **cu•be** (kyo͞o′bā′, kyo͞o-bā′) *n.* Any of several tropical American woody plants of the genus *Lonchocarpus* in the pea family, whose roots are a source of rotenone. [Am.Sp.]

cu•beb (kyo͞o′bĕb′) *n.* **1.** A tropical southeast Asian shrubby vine *(Piper cubeba)* having spicy berrylike fruits and heart-shaped leaves. **2.** The dried unripe berrylike fruit of this plant, used in perfumery, pharmaceuticals, and flavorings. [ME *cubebe* < OFr. < Med.Lat. *cubēba* < Ar. *kabābah.*]

cube root *n. Math.* A number whose cube is equal to a given number.

cube steak *n.* A thin slice of beef tenderized by cubing.

cu•bic (kyo͞o′bĭk) *adj.* **1.a.** Having the shape of a cube. **b.** Shaped similar to a cube. **2.a.** Having three dimensions. **b.** Having a volume equal to a cube whose edge is of a stated length. **3.** *Math.* Of the third power, order, or degree. **4.** Of or relating to a crystalline form that has three equal axes at right angles to each other; isometric. — *n. Math.* A cubic expression, curve, or equation. — **cu′bic•ly** *adv.*

cu•bi•cal (kyo͞o′bĭ-kəl) *adj.* **1.** Cubic. **2.** Of or relating to volume. — **cu′bi•cal•ly** *adv.* — **cu′bi•cal•ness** *n.*

cu•bi•cle (kyo͞o′bĭ-kəl) *n.* A small compartment, as for work, sleep, or study. [ME < Lat. *cubiculum*, bed chamber < *cubāre*, to lie down.]

cubic measure *n.* A unit, such as a cubic foot, or a system of units used to measure volume or capacity.

cubic zirconia *n.* A synthetic gemstone, ZrO_2, used in jewelry as an artificial diamond.

cu•bi•form (kyo͞o′bə-fôrm′) *adj.* Having the shape of a cube.

cub•ism also **Cub•ism** (kyo͞o′bĭz′əm) *n.* A nonobjective school of painting and sculpture, marked by reduction and fragmentation of natural forms into abstract, often geometric structures. — **cub′ist** *n.* — **cu•bis′tic** *adj.* — **cu•bis′ti•cal•ly** *adv.*

cu•bit (kyo͞o′bĭt) *n.* An ancient unit of linear measure, originally equal to the length of the forearm from the tip of the middle finger to the elbow, or about 17 to 22 inches (43 to 56 centimeters). [ME *cubite* < Lat. *cubitum*, cubit, elbow.]

cu•boid (kyo͞o′boid′) *adj.* Having the approximate shape of a cube. — *n.* **1.** *Anat.* A tarsal bone on the outer side of the foot

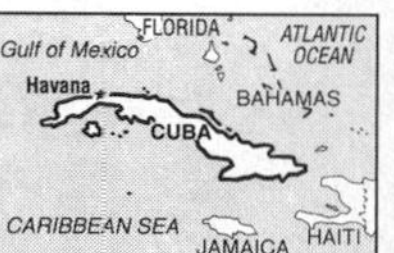

Cuba

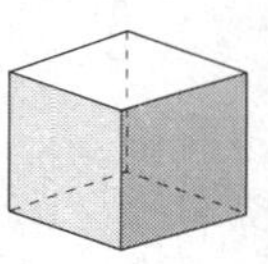
cube

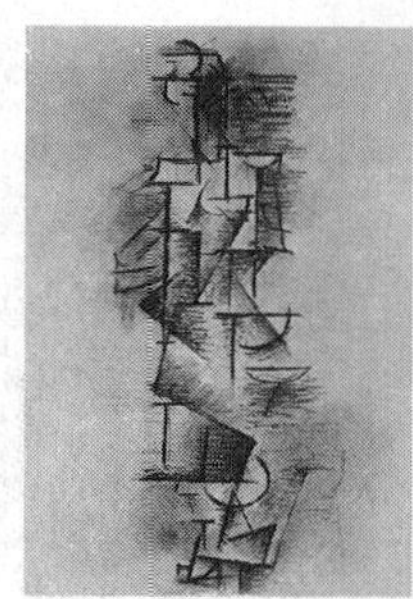
cubism
1910 drawing *Nude Woman* by Pablo Picasso

ă pat	oi boy
ā pay	ou out
âr care	o͝o took
ä father	o͞o boot
ĕ pet	ŭ cut
ē be	ûr urge
ĭ pit	th thin
ī pie	*th* this
îr pier	hw which
ŏ pot	zh vision
ō toe	ə about, item
ô paw	

Stress marks:
′ (primary);
′ (secondary), as in
dictionary (dĭk′shə-nĕr′ē)

in front of the calcaneus and behind the fourth and fifth metatarsal bones. **2.** *Math.* A rectangular parallelepiped. —**cu•boi′dal** (kyo͞o-boid′l) *adj.*

Cub Scout *n.* A member of the junior division of the Boy Scouts, for boys of ages eight through ten.

cu•chi•fri•to (ko͞o′chĭ-frē′tō) *n.* **-tos.** A small deep-fried cube of pork. [Am.Sp. : *cuchí*, pig (alteration of Sp. *cochino*, dim. of *coch*, interj. used to call pigs) + Sp. *frito*, p.part. of *freír*, to fry (< Lat. *frīgere*).]

Cu•chul•ain (ko͞o-kŭl′ĭn, -KHŭl′-) *n. Myth.* A hero of ancient Ulster who defended it against the rest of Ireland.

cuck•ing stool (kŭk′ĭng) *n.* An instrument of punishment, consisting of a chair in which the offender was tied and exposed to public derision or ducked in water. [ME *cukking stol* < *cukken*, to defecate, of Scand. orig. See **kakka-***.]

cuck•old (kŭk′əld, ko͝ok′-) *n.* A man married to an unfaithful wife. —*tr.v.* **-old•ed, -old•ing, -olds.** To make a cuckold of. [ME *cokewald* < AN **cucuald* < *cucu*, the cuckoo < VLat. **cuccūlus* < Lat. *cucūlus*.]

cuck•old•ry (kŭk′əl-drē, ko͝ok′-) *n.* **1.** The state of being a cuckold. **2.** The act of making someone a cuckold.

cuck•oo (ko͞o′ko͞o, ko͝ok′o͞o) *n., pl.* **-oos. 1.a.** A grayish European bird *(Cuculus canorus)* that has a characteristic two-note call and lays its eggs in the nests of birds of other species. **b.** Any of various related birds of the family Cuculidae, having grayish-brown plumage. **2.** The cuckoo's call or cry. **3.** *Slang.* A foolish or crazy person. —*tr.v.* **-ooed, -oo•ing, -oos.** To repeat incessantly. —*adj. Slang.* Lacking in sense; foolish or crazy. [ME *cuccu*, of imit. orig.]

cuckoo clock

cuckoo clock *n.* A wall or shelf clock that announces intervals of time with a sound imitative of a cuckoo's call and often with the emergence of a mechanical bird from a small door.

cuck•oo•flow•er (ko͞o′ko͞o-flou′ər, ko͝ok′o͞o-) *n.* **1.** A perennial herb *(Cardamine pratensis)* in the mustard family, native to the northern temperate regions and having pink, purple, or white flowers. **2.** See **ragged robin.**

cuck•oo•pint (ko͞o′ko͞o-pīnt′, ko͝ok′o͞o-) *n.* A European plant *(Arum maculatum)* having arrow-shaped leaves and a yellow-green spathe. [< obsolete *cuckoopintle* < ME *cokkupintel* : *cokku*, *cuccu*, cuckoo; see CUCKOO + *pintel*, penis (< OE).]

cuckoo spit *n.* A frothy mass of liquid secreted on plant stems as a protective covering by nymphs of the spittlebug.

cu•cul•late (kyo͞o′kə-lāt′, kyo͞o-kŭl′āt′) *adj. Bot.* Having the shape of a cowl or hood; hooded. [Med.Lat. *cucullātus* < Lat. *cucullus*, hood.] —**cu′cul•late′ly** *adv.*

cu•cum•ber (kyo͞o′kŭm′bər) *n.* **1.a.** A tendril-bearing, climbing or sprawling annual plant *(Cucumis sativus)* having edible cylindrical fruit with a green rind and crisp white flesh. **b.** The edible fruit of this plant. **2.** Any of several related or similar plants, such as the bur cucumber. [ME *cucomer* < OFr. *coucombre* < Lat. *cucumis*, *cucumer-*.]

cucumber tree *n.* Any of certain magnolias, esp. *Magnolia acuminata*, a deciduous tree of eastern North America, having greenish-yellow flowers and a cucumber-shaped fruit.

cu•cur•bit (kyo͞o-kûr′bĭt) *n.* **1.** Any of various mostly climbing or trailing plants of the family Cucurbitaceae, which includes the squash, pumpkin, and cucumber. **2.** A gourd-shaped flask forming the body of an alembic, formerly used in distillation. [ME *cucurbite* < OFr. < Lat. *cucurbita*, gourd.]

Cú•cu•ta (ko͞o′kə-tə, -ko͞o-tä′). A city of NE Colombia near the Venezuelan border. Pop. 355,828.

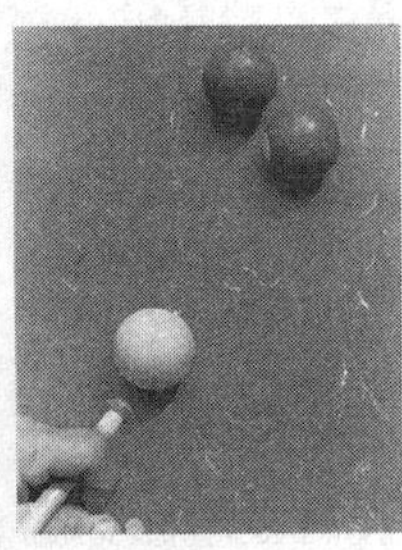

cue ball

cud (kŭd) *n.* **1.** Food regurgitated from the first stomach to the mouth of a ruminant and chewed again. **2.** Something held in the mouth and chewed. [ME < OE *cudu*.]

Cud•a•hy (kŭd′ə-hē). **1.** A city of S CA SE of Los Angeles. Pop. 22,817. **2.** A city of SE WI, a suburb of Milwaukee. Pop. 18,659.

cud•bear (kŭd′bâr′) *n.* A purplish-red dye derived from certain lichens. [After *Cuthbert* Gordon, 18th-cent. Scottish chemist.]

cud•dle (kŭd′l) *v.* **-dled, -dling, -dles.** —*tr.* To fondle in the arms; hug tenderly. —*intr.* To nestle; snuggle. —*n.* The act of cuddling. [?] —**cud′dle•some, cud′dly** *adj.*

cud•dy¹ (kŭd′ē) *n., pl.* **-dies. 1.** *Naut.* A small cabin or the galley on a ship. **2.** A small room, cupboard, or closet. [?]

cud•dy² (kŭd′ē) *n., pl.* **-dies.** *Scots.* **1.** A donkey. **2.** A fool; a dolt. [Perh. < *Cuddy*, nickname for *Cuthbert*.]

cudg•el (kŭj′əl) *n.* A short, heavy stick; a club. —*tr.v.* **-eled, -el•ing, -els** or **-elled, -el•ling, -els.** To beat or strike with or as if with a cudgel. [ME *cuggel* < OE *cycgel*.]

cud•weed (kŭd′wēd′) *n.* **1.** Any of various woolly plants of the genus *Gnaphalium* in the composite family, having small whitish or yellowish flower heads. **2.** Any of several similar and related plants in the genus *Filago*.

cue¹ (kyo͞o) *n.* **1.** *Games.* A long tapered rod with a leather tip, used in billiards and pool. **2.** *Games.* A long stick with a concave attachment at one end for shoving disks in shuffleboard. **3.** A queue of hair. **4.** A line of waiting people or vehicles; a queue. —*v.* **cued, cu•ing, cues.** —*tr.* **1.** *Games.* To strike with a cue. **2.** To braid or twist (hair) into a queue. —*intr.* To form a line or queue. [Var. of QUEUE.]

cue² (kyo͞o) *n.* **1.** A signal, such as a word, used to prompt another event in a performance, such as an actor's speech. **2.a.** A reminder or a prompting. **b.** A hint or suggestion. **3.** *Psychol.* A stimulus that elicits or signals a type of behavior. **4.** *Archaic.* One's assigned role or function. **5.** *Archaic.* A mood; a disposition. —*tr.v.* **cued, cu•ing, cues. 1.** To give a cue to; signal or prompt. **2.** To insert or cause to be inserted into the sequence of a performance. —***phrasal verb.* cue (someone) in.** To give information or instructions to (a latecomer, for example). [Perh. < *q*, *qu*, abbreviation of Lat. *quandō*, when, used for actors' copies of plays. See **kʷo-***.]

cue³ (kyo͞o) *n.* The letter *q*.

cue ball *n. Games.* The white ball in billiards and pool.

Cuen•ca (kwĕng′kə, -kä). A city of S-central Ecuador SE of Guayaquil; founded 1557. Pop. 157,213.

Cuer•na•va•ca (kwĕr-nə-vä′kə, -nä-vä′kä). A city of S-central Mexico in the **Cuernavaca Valley** near Mexico City. Pop. 192,770.

cues•ta (kwĕs′tə) *n.* A ridge with a gentle slope on one side and a cliff on the other. [Sp. < Lat. *costa*, side. See **kost-***.]

cuff¹ (kŭf) *n.* **1.a.** A fold used as trimming at the bottom of a sleeve. **b.** A band, often open with a button closure, at the bottom of a sleeve. **2.** The turned-up fold at the bottom of a trouser leg. **3.** The band at the top of a sock. **4.** The part of a glove over the wrist. **5.** A handcuff. **6.** *Medic.* An inflatable band used with a sphygmomanometer in measuring arterial blood pressure. —*tr.v.* **cuffed, cuff•ing, cuffs. 1.** To form a cuff on. **2.** To put handcuffs on. —***idioms.* off the cuff.** In an extemporaneous or informal manner. **on the cuff.** On credit. [ME *cuffe*, mitten.]

cuff² (kŭf) *tr.v.* **cuffed, cuff•ing, cuffs.** To strike with or as if with the open hand; slap. —*n.* Such a blow or slap. [?]

cuff link or **cuff•link** (kŭf′lĭngk′) *n.* A fastening for a shirt cuff, usu. of two buttons or buttonlike parts connected with a chain or shank that passes through two slits in the cuff.

Cu•fic (ko͞o′fĭk, kyo͞o′-) *adj.* Var. of **Kufic.**

Cu•ia•bá (ko͞o′yə-bä′). A city of W-central Brazil W of Brasília on the **Cuiabá River**, c. 483 km (300 mi). Pop. 167,880.

cui bo•no (kwē′ bō′nō) *n.* Utility, advantage, or self-interest considered as the determinant of value or motivation. [Lat. : *cui*, to whose, dative of *quī* + *bonō*, dative of *bonum*, advantage.]

cui•rass (kwĭ-răs′) *n.* **1.a.** A piece of armor for protecting the breast and back. **b.** The breastplate alone. **2.** A defense or protection. **3.** *Zool.* A protective covering of bony plates or scales. —*tr.v.* **-rassed, -rass•ing, -rass•es.** To protect with a cuirass. [ME *curas* < OFr. *cuirace*, *cuirasse*, prob. alteration of OProv. *coirassa* < LLat. *coriācea (vestis)*, leather (garment), fem. of *coriāceus* < Lat. *corium*, hide. See **sker-¹***.]

cui•ras•sier (kwîr′ə-sîr′) *n.* A horse soldier wearing a cuirass. [Fr. < *cuirasse*, cuirass < OFr. See CUIRASS.]

Cui•si•nart (kwē′zə-närt′, kwē′zə-närt′). A trademark used for a kind of food processor and its attachments.

cui•sine (kwĭ-zēn′) *n.* **1.** A characteristic manner or style of preparing food: *Spanish cuisine.* **2.** Food; fare. [Fr. < OFr. < VLat. **cocīna*, var. of Lat. *coquīna*, kitchen, cookery < *coquere*, to cook. See **pekʷ-***.]

cuisse (kwĭs) also **cuish** (kwĭsh) *n.* Plate armor worn to protect the front of the thigh. [ME *quisse*, prob. back-formation < *quisseues*, pl. of *quisseu*, cuisse < OFr. *quisseuz*, pl. of *quissel* < *quisse*, thigh < Lat. *coxa*, hip.]

cuke (kyo͞ok) *n. Informal.* A cucumber.

Cul•bert•son (kŭl′bərt-sən), **Ely.** 1891–1955. Amer. contract bridge authority whose books include *The Contract Bridge Blue Book* (1930).

culch or **cultch** (kŭlch) *n.* **1.** A natural bed for oysters, consisting of gravel or crushed shells to which the oyster spawn may adhere. **2.** The spawn of the oyster. **3.** Also **scultch** or **sculch** (skŭlch). *New England.* Clean trash or rubbish, such as string, paper, and cloth. **4.** A person or thing not highly regarded. [Perh. ult. < OFr. *culche*, *couche*, couch. See COUCH.]

cul-de-sac (kŭl′dĭ-săk′, ko͝ol′-) *n., pl.* **culs-de-sac** (kŭlz′-, ko͝olz′-) or **cul-de-sacs** (kŭl′-). **1.a.** A dead-end street. **b.** An impasse. **2.** *Anat.* A saclike cavity or tube open only at one end. [Fr. : *cul*, bottom + *de*, of + *sac*, sack.]

Cu•le•bra Cut (ko͞o-lā′brə). See **Gaillard Cut.**

Culebra Peak. A mountain, 4,284.3 m (14,047 ft), in the Sangre de Cristo Mts. of extreme S-central CO.

cu•let (kyo͞o′lĭt, kŭl′ĭt) *n.* **1.** The small flat face at the bottom of a gem cut as a brilliant. **2.** Armor consisting of overlapping plates used to protect the buttocks. [Obsolete Fr., dim. of *cul*, rump < Lat. *cūlus*. See **(s)keu-***.]

cu•lex (kyo͞o′lĕks′) *n., pl.* **-li•ces** (-lĭ-sēz′). Any of various mosquitoes of the genus *Culex*, which includes the common house mosquito *(C. pipiens)*. [Lat., gnat.]

Cu•lia•cán (ko͞ol′yə-kän′). A city of W Mexico WNW of Durango on the **Culiacán River**, c. 282 km (175 mi); founded 1531. Pop. 304,826.

cu•li•nar•y (kyo͞o′lə-nĕr′ē, kŭl′ə-) *adj.* Of or relating to a kitchen or to cookery. [Lat. *culīnārius* < *culīna*, kitchen. See **pekʷ-***.]

cull (kŭl) *tr.v.* **culled, cull•ing, culls. 1.** To pick out from others; select. **2.** To gather; collect. **3.** To remove rejected members or parts from (a herd, for example). —*n.* Something picked out from others, esp. because inferior. [ME *cullen* < OFr. *cuillir* < Lat. *colligere*. See COLLECT[1].] —**cull′er** *n.*

Cul•len (kŭl′ən), **Countée.** 1903–46. Amer. poet whose works include *Colors* (1926) and *Copper Sun* (1927).

cul•let (kŭl′ĭt) *n.* Scraps of broken or waste glass gathered for remelting, esp. with new material. [Prob. alteration of *collet*, neck of glass left on the blowing iron < Fr., collar, dim. of *col*, neck < OFr. < Lat. *collum*. See **kʷel-**[1]*.]

cul•lion (kŭl′yən) *n. Archaic.* A contemptible fellow; a rascal. [ME *coilon*, testicle < OFr. *coillon* < Lat. *culleus*, bag.]

cul•lis (kŭl′ĭs) *n.* A gutter or groove in a roof. [ME *colis* < OFr. *coleis*, channel < *coler*, to pour < Lat. *cōlāre*, to filter < *cōlum*, sieve.]

Cul•lo•den Moor (kə-lŏd′n, -lôd′n). A moor in N Scotland E of Inverness; site of the final defeat of the Highland Jacobites (1746).

cul•ly (kŭl′ē) *Archaic.* —*n., pl.* **-lies.** A fool or dupe. —*tr.v.* **-lied, -ly•ing, -lies.** To fool; cheat. [Perh. < CULLION.]

culm[1] (kŭlm) *n.* The stem of a grass or similar plant. [Lat. *culmus*, stalk.]

culm[2] (kŭlm) *n.* **1.** Waste from anthracite coal mines, consisting of fine coal, coal dust, and dirt. **2.a.** Carboniferous shale. **b.** Inferior anthracite coal. [ME *colme*, coal dust, perh. < OE *col*, coal.]

cul•mi•nant (kŭl′mə-nənt) *adj.* **1.** Being at the highest altitude. **2.** Reaching the highest point or degree; highest.

cul•mi•nate (kŭl′mə-nāt′) *v.* **-nat•ed, -nat•ing, -nates.** —*intr.* **1.a.** To reach the highest point or degree; climax. **b.** To come to completion; end. **2.** *Astron.* To reach the highest point above an observer's horizon. Used of stars and other celestial bodies. —*tr.* To bring to the point of greatest intensity or to completion. [LLat. *culmināre, culmināt-* < Lat. *culmen, culmin-*, summit. See **kel-**[2]*.] —**cul′mi•na′tion** *n.*

cu•lotte (ko͞o-lŏt′, kyo͞o-, ko͞o′lŏt′, kyo͞o′-) *n.* A woman's full trousers cut to resemble a skirt. Often used in the plural. [Fr., breeches, dim. of *cul*, rump < Lat. *cūlus*. See **(s)keu-***.]

cul•pa•ble (kŭl′pə-bəl) *adj.* Deserving of blame or censure as being wrong, evil, improper, or injurious. [ME *coupable* < OFr. < Lat. *culpābilis* < *culpāre*, to blame < *culpa*, fault.] —**cul′pa•bil′i•ty** *n.* —**cul′pa•bly** *adv.*

Cul•pep•er (kŭl′pĕp′ər), Lord **Thomas.** 1635–89. English colonial administrator who governed Virginia (1677–83).

cul•prit (kŭl′prĭt) *n.* **1.** One charged with an offense or crime. **2.** One guilty of a fault or crime. [Prob. < *cul. prit*, abbreviation for AN **culpable: prit d'averrer nostre bille*, guilty: (I am) ready to aver our indictment.]

culs-de-sac (kŭlz′dĭ-săk′, ko͝olz′-) *n.* Pl. of **cul-de-sac.**

cult (kŭlt) *n.* **1.a.** A religion or religious sect generally considered to be extremist or false, with its followers often living communally under an authoritarian charismatic leader. **b.** The followers of such a religion or sect. **2.** A system or community of religious worship and ritual. **3.** The formal means of expressing religious reverence. **4.** A usu. nonscientific method claimed by its originator to cure a particular disease. **5.a.** Obsessive, esp. faddish devotion to or veneration for a person, principle, or thing. **b.** The object of such devotion. **6.** An exclusive group of persons sharing an esoteric, usu. artistic or intellectual interest. [Lat. *cultus*, worship < p.part. of *colere*, to cultivate. See **kʷel-**[1]*.] —**cul′tic, cult′ish** *adj.* —**cult′ism** *n.* —**cult′ist** *n.*

cultch (kŭlch) *n.* Var. of **culch.**

cul•ti (kŭl′tī) *n.* Pl. of **cultus.**

cul•ti•gen (kŭl′tə-jən) *n.* An organism, esp. a cultivated plant, not known to have a wild or uncultivated counterpart. [CULTI(VATED) + -GEN.]

cul•ti•va•ble (kŭl′tə-və-bəl) *adj.* Capable of undergoing cultivation: *cultivable land.* —**cul′ti•va•bil′i•ty** *n.*

cul•ti•var (kŭl′tə-vär′, -vâr′) *n.* A horticultural race or variety of a plant that has originated and persisted only under cultivation. [CULTI(VATED) + VAR(IETY).]

cul•ti•vate (kŭl′tə-vāt′) *tr.v.* **-vat•ed, -vat•ing, -vates. 1.a.** To improve and prepare (land), as by plowing, for raising crops; till. **b.** To loosen or dig soil around (growing plants). **2.** To grow or tend (a plant or crop). **3.** To promote the growth of (a biological culture). **4.** To nurture; foster. See Syns at **nurture. 5.** To form and refine, as by education. **6.** To seek the acquaintance or goodwill of. [Med.Lat. *cultivāre, cultivāt-* < *cultīvus*, tilled < Lat. *cultus*, p.part. of *colere*, to till. See **kʷel-**[1]*.] —**cul′ti•vat′a•ble** *adj.*

cul•ti•vat•ed (kŭl′tə-vā′tĭd) *adj.* **1.** Of or relating to cultivation; produced in cultivation. **2.** Educated; polished; refined.

cul•ti•va•tion (kŭl′tə-vā′shən) *n.* **1.a.** The act of cultivating. **b.** The state of being cultivated. **2.** Refinement; culture.

cul•ti•va•tor (kŭl′tə-vā′tər) *n.* **1.** One who cultivates. **2.** An implement or a machine for loosening the soil and destroying weeds around growing plants.

cul•trate (kŭl′trāt′) also **cul•trat•ed** (-trā′tĭd) *adj.* Sharp-edged and pointed; knifelike: *cultrate leaves.* [Lat. *cultrātus* < *culter, cultr-*, knife. See **skel-**[1]*.]

cul•tur•al (kŭl′chər-əl) *adj.* Of or relating to culture or cultivation. —**cul′tur•al•ly** *adv.*

cultural anthropology *n.* The scientific study of the development of human cultures based on archaeological, ethnologic, ethnographic, linguistic, social, and psychological data and methods of analysis.

cul•ture (kŭl′chər) *n.* **1.a.** The totality of socially transmitted behavior patterns, arts, beliefs, institutions, and all other products of human work and thought. **b.** These products considered as the expression of a particular period, class, community, or population. **c.** These products considered with respect to a particular category, such as a field, subject, or mode of expression: *oral culture.* **2.** Intellectual and artistic activity and the works produced by it. **3.a.** Development of the intellect through training or education. **b.** Enlightenment resulting from such training or education. **4.** A high degree of taste and refinement formed by aesthetic and intellectual training. **5.** Special training and development. **6.** The cultivation of soil; tillage. **7.** The breeding of animals or growing of plants, esp. to produce improved stock. **8.** *Biol.* **a.** The culturing of microorganisms or other living matter. **b.** Such a growth or colony. —*tr.v.* **-tured, -tur•ing, -tures. 1.** To cultivate. **2.a.** To grow (microorganisms, for example) in a culture medium. **b.** To use (a substance) as a culture medium. [ME, cultivation < OFr. < Lat. *cultūra* < *cultus*, p.part. of *colere*. See CULTIVATE.]

cul•tured (kŭl′chərd) *adj.* **1.** Educated, polished, and refined. **2.** Produced under artificial and controlled conditions.

culture medium *n.* A liquid or gelatinous substance containing nutrients in which microorganisms or tissues are cultivated for scientific purposes.

culture shock *n.* A condition of confusion and anxiety affecting a person suddenly exposed to an alien culture or milieu.

cul•tus (kŭl′təs) *n., pl.* **-tus•es** or **-ti** (-tī). A cult, esp. a religious one. [Lat., veneration. See CULT.]

cul•ver (kŭl′vər) *n.* A dove or a pigeon. [ME < OE *culufre* < VLat. **columbra* < Lat. *columbula*, dim. of *columba*, dove.]

Cul•ver City (kŭl′vər). A city of S CA, a suburb of Los Angeles. Pop. 38,793.

cul•ver•in (kŭl′vər-ĭn) *n.* **1.** An early, crudely made musket. **2.** A long heavy cannon used in the 16th and 17th centuries. [ME < OFr. *coulevrine* < *couleuvre*, snake < Lat. *colubra*, fem. of *coluber*.]

cul•vert (kŭl′vərt) *n.* **1.** A sewer or drain crossing under a road or embankment. **2.a.** The part of a road or embankment over a culvert. **b.** The channel or conduit for a culvert. [?]

cum (ko͝om, kŭm) *prep.* Together with; plus. Often used in combination: *our attic-cum-studio.* [Lat. See **kom***.]

cum. *abbr.* Cumulative.

Cu•mae (kyo͞o′mē). An ancient city and Greek colony of S-central Italy near present-day Naples; adopted Roman culture after the 2nd cent. B.C.

Cu•ma•ná (ko͞o′mä-nä′). A city of NE Venezuela on the Caribbean Sea E of Caracas; founded 1521. Pop. 173,000.

cum•ber (kŭm′bər) *tr.v.* **-bered, -ber•ing, -bers. 1.** To weigh down; burden: *cumbered with duties.* **2.** To hamper or hinder, as by being in the way. **3.** To litter; clutter up. **4.** *Archaic.* To bother; distress. —*n.* A hindrance; an encumbrance. [ME *cumbren*, to annoy < OFr. *combrer* < *combre*, hindrance < VLat. **comboros*, of Celt. orig.] —**cum′ber•er** *n.*

Cum•ber•land (kŭm′bər-lənd). A city of NW MD in the Panhandle on the Potomac R. and the WV border. Pop. 23,706.

Cumberland Gap. A natural passage through the Cumberland Plateau near the junction of the KY, VA, and TN borders.

Cumberland Plateau or **Cumberland Mountains.** The SW section of the Appalachian Mts., extending NE to SW from S WV through VA, KY, and TN into N AL.

Cumberland River. A river rising in SE KY and flowing c. 1,105 km (687 mi) SW into N TN then NW to the Ohio R. in SW KY.

cum•ber•some (kŭm′bər-səm) *adj.* **1.** Difficult to handle because of weight or bulk. **2.** Troublesome or onerous. —**cum′ber•some•ly** *adv.*

Cum•bri•a (kŭm′brē-ə). A Celtic kingdom of NW England. The S part came under Anglo-Saxon control c. 944; the N portion passed to Scotland in 1018. —**Cum′bri•an** *adj. & n.*

cum•brous (kŭm′brəs) *adj.* Cumbersome. [ME < *cumbren*, to annoy. See CUMBER.] —**cum′brous•ly** *adv.* —**cum′brous•ness** *n.*

cum•in (kŭm′ĭn, ko͞o′mĭn, kyo͞o′-) *n.* **1.a.** An annual Mediterranean herb *(Cuminum cyminum)* in the parsley family, having finely divided leaves and clusters of small white or pink flowers. **b.** The seedlike fruit of this plant used for seasoning. **2.** Black cumin. [ME < OFr. < Lat. *cumīnum* < Gk. *kuminon*, prob. of Semitic orig.]

cum lau•de (ko͝om lou′də, lou′dē, kŭm lô′dē) *adv. & adj.* With honor. Used to express academic distinction: *graduated cum laude.* [Prob. Med.Lat. *cum laudē* : Lat. *cum*, with + Lat. *laudē*, ablative of *laus*, praise.]

cum•mer•bund (kŭm′ər-bŭnd′) *n.* A broad sash, esp. one worn as an article of formal dress, as with a dinner jacket. [Hindi *kamarband* < Pers. : *kamar*, waist + *band*, band; see BUND[1].]

Cum•mings (kŭm′ĭngz), **Edward Estlin.** e.e. cummings.

ă pat	oi boy
ā pay	ou out
âr care	o͝o took
ä father	o͞o boot
ĕ pet	ŭ cut
ē be	ûr urge
ĭ pit	th thin
ī pie	*th* this
îr pier	hw which
ŏ pot	zh vision
ō toe	ə about, item
ô paw	

Stress marks:
′ (primary);
′ (secondary), as in
dictionary (dĭk′shə-nĕr′ē)

1894–1962. Amer. writer best known for his lyrical and typographically eccentric poetry.

cum•quat (kŭm′kwŏt′) *n.* Var. of **kumquat.**

cum•shaw (kŭm′shô′) *n.* A tip; a gratuity. [Pidgin E. < Chin. (Amoy) *gamsia*, an expression of thanks.]

cu•mu•late (kyo͞om′yə-lāt′) *v.* **-lat•ed, -lat•ing, -lates.** —*tr.* **1.** To gather in a heap; accumulate. **2.** To combine into one unit; merge. —*intr.* To become massed. —*adj.* Having cumulated or been cumulated. [Lat. *cumulāre, cumulāt-* < *cumulus*, heap. See **keuə-*.**] —**cu′mu•la′tion** *n.*

cu•mu•la•tive (kyo͞om′yə-lā′tĭv, -yə-lə-tĭv) *adj.* **1.** Increasing or enlarging by successive addition. **2.** Acquired by or resulting from accumulation. **3.** Of or relating to interest or a dividend added to the next payment if not paid when due. **4.** *Law.* **a.** Supporting the same point as earlier evidence. **b.** Imposed more severely upon a repeat offender. **c.** Following successively. **5.** *Statistics.* **a.** Of or relating to the sum of the frequencies of experimentally determined values of a random variable that are less than or equal to a specified value. **b.** Of or relating to experimental error that increases in magnitude with each successive measurement. —**cu′mu•la′tive•ly** *adv.* —**cu′mu•la′tive•ness** *n.*

cumulative voting *n.* A system of voting in which each voter is given as many votes as there are positions to be filled and allowed to cast those votes for one candidate or distribute them in any way among the candidates.

cu•mu•li•form (kyo͞om′yə-lə-fôrm′) *adj.* Having the shape of a cumulus.

cumulo– or **cumuli–** or **cumul–** *pref.* Cumulus: *cumulonimbus.* [< CUMULUS.]

cumulonimbus

cu•mu•lo•nim•bus (kyo͞om′yə-lō-nĭm′bəs) *n., pl.* **-bus•es** or **-bi** (-bī). An extremely dense, vertically developed cumulus with a glaciated top extending to great heights, usu. producing heavy rains, thunderstorms, or hailstorms.

cu•mu•lous (kyo͞o′myə-ləs) *adj.* Resembling a pile or mound.

cu•mu•lus (kyo͞om′yə-ləs) *n., pl.* **-li** (-lī′). **1.** A dense white, fluffy flat-based cloud with a multiple rounded top, usu. formed by the ascent of thermally unstable air masses. **2.** A pile, mound, or heap. [Lat., heap. See **keuə-*.**]

Cu•nax•a (kyo͞o-năk′sə). An ancient town of Babylonia NW of Babylon; site of a battle (401 B.C.) in which Artaxerxes II of Persia defeated his brother Cyrus the Younger.

cunc•ta•tion (kŭngk-tā′shən) *n.* Procrastination; delay. [Lat. *cūnctātiō, cūnctātiōn-* < *cūnctātus*, p.part. of *cūnctārī*, to delay. See **konk-*.**] —**cunc′ta′tive** (kŭngk′tā′tĭv, -tə-tĭv) *adj.* —**cunc′ta′tor** *n.*

cu•ne•al (kyo͞o′nē-əl) *adj.* Wedge-shaped. [NLat. *cuneālis* < Lat. *cuneus*, wedge.]

cu•ne•ate (kyo͞o′nē-ĭt, -āt′) *adj. Bot.* Wedge-shaped. [Lat. *cuneātus*, p.part. of *cuneāre*, to make wedge-shaped < *cuneus*, wedge.] —**cu′ne•ate′ly** *adv.*

cumulus

cu•ne•i•form (kyo͞o′nē-ə-fôrm′, kyo͞o-nē′-) *adj.* **1.** Wedge-shaped. **2.a.** Being a character or characters formed by the arrangement of small wedge-shaped elements and used in ancient Sumerian, Akkadian, Assyrian, Babylonian, and Persian writing. **b.** Relating to, composed in, or using such characters. **3.** *Anat.* Of, relating to, or being a wedge-shaped bone or cartilage. —*n.* **1.** Writing typified by the use of cuneiform characters. **2.** *Anat.* A wedge-shaped bone, esp. one in the tarsus of the foot. [Prob. < Fr. *cunéiforme* < Lat. *cuneus*, wedge.]

Cu•ne•ne also **Ku•ne•ne** (ko͞o-nā′nə). A river rising in W-central Angola and flowing c. 1,207 km (750 mi) S and W to the Atlantic Ocean.

cun•ner (kŭn′ər) *n.* A small fish *(Tautogolabrus adspersus)* of North American Atlantic waters. [?]

cun•ni•lin•gus (kŭn′ə-lĭng′gəs) *n.* Oral stimulation of the clitoris or vulva. [NLat. < Lat., he who licks the vulva : *cunnus*, vulva; see **(s)keu-*** + *lingere*, to lick; see **leigh-*.**] —**cun′ni•lin′gual** *adj.*

cun•ning (kŭn′ĭng) *adj.* **1.** Marked by or given to artful subtlety and deceptiveness. **2.** Executed with or exhibiting ingenuity. **3.** Delicately pleasing; pretty or cute. —*n.* **1.** Skill in deception; guile. **2.** Skill or adeptness in execution or performance; dexterity. [ME, pr.part. of *connen*, to know < OE *cunnan*. See **gnō-*.**] —**cun′ning•ly** *adv.* —**cun′ning•ness** *n.*

Cunningham (kŭn′ĭng-hăm′), **Merce.** b. c. 1922. Amer. dancer and choreographer whose works include *Squaregame* (1976).

cunt (kŭnt) *n. Obscene.* **1.** The female genitals. **2.a.** Used as a disparaging term for a woman. **b.** Used as a disparaging term for a disagreeable person. [ME *cunte.*]

cup (kŭp) *n.* **1.a.** A small open container, usu. with a flat bottom and a handle, used for drinking. **b.** Such a container and its contents. **2.** A unit of capacity or volume equal to 16 tablespoons or 8 fluid ounces (237 milliliters). See table at **measurement. 3.** The bowl of a drinking vessel. **4.** The chalice or the wine used in the Eucharist. **5.** A decorative cup-shaped vessel awarded as a prize or trophy. **6.** *Sports.* A golf hole or the metal container inside a hole. **7.** Either of the two parts of a brassiere that fit over the breasts. **8.** An athletic supporter having a reinforcement of plastic or metal. **9.** A sweetened, flavored, usu. chilled beverage, esp. one made with wine. **10.** A dish served in a cup-shaped vessel. **11.a.** A cuplike object. **b.** *Biol.* A cuplike structure or organ. **12.** A lot or portion to be suffered or enjoyed. —*tr.v.* **cupped, cup•ping, cups. 1.** To place in or as in a cup. **2.** To shape like a cup. **3.** To subject to cupping. —***idioms.* cup of tea. 1.** Something that one excels in or enjoys. **2.** A matter to be reckoned or dealt with. **in (one's) cups.** Intoxicated; drunk. [ME *cuppe* < OE < LLat. *cuppa*, drinking vessel, perh. var. of Lat. *cūpa*, tub, cask.]

cup•bear•er (kŭp′bâr′ər) *n.* One who fills and distributes cups of wine, as in a royal household.

cup•board (kŭb′ərd) *n.* A closet or cabinet, usu. with shelves for storing food, crockery, and utensils.

cup•cake (kŭp′kāk′) *n.* A small cake baked in a cup-shaped container.

cu•pel (kyo͞o′pəl, kyo͞o-pĕl′) *n.* **1.** A porous cup, often made of bone ash, used in assaying to separate precious metals from base elements. **2.** The bottom or receptacle in a silver-refining furnace. —*tr.v.* **-peled, -pel•ing, -pels** or **-pelled, -pel•ling, -pels.** To assay or separate from base metals in a cupel. [Fr. *coupelle* < OFr., dim. of *coupe*, cup < LLat. *cuppa*, drinking vessel.] —**cu′pel•ler, cu′pel•er** *n.*

cu•pel•la•tion (kyo͞o′pə-lā′shən) *n.* A refining process for nonoxidizing metals, such as gold, in which a metallic mixture is oxidized at high temperatures and base metals are separated by absorption into the walls of a cupel.

Cu•per•ti•no (ko͞o′pər-tē′nō, kyo͞o′-). A city of W CA W of San Jose. Pop. 40,263.

cup•ful (kŭp′fo͝ol′) *n., pl.* **-fuls. 1.** The amount that a cup can hold. **2.** A measure of capacity equal to one cup.

cup fungus *n.* Any of various ascomycetous fungi, esp. of the family Pezizaceae, characterized by a spore-bearing structure that is often stalkless and cup-shaped or disk-shaped.

Cu•pid (kyo͞o′pĭd) *n.* **1.** *Rom. Myth.* The god of love; the son of Venus. **2. cupid.** A representation of Cupid as a naked cherubic boy usu. having wings and holding a bow and arrow, used as a symbol of love. [Middle English *Cupide* < OFr. < Lat. *cupīdō*, desire, Cupid < *cupere*, to desire.]

cu•pid•i•ty (kyo͞o-pĭd′ĭ-tē) *n.* Excessive desire, esp. for wealth; covetousness or avarice. [ME *cupidite* < OFr. < Lat. *cupiditās* < *cupidus*, desiring < *cupere*, to desire.]

Cu•pid's bow (kyo͞o′pĭdz bō′) *n., pl.* **Cupid's bows.** An archery bow that curves inward at the center and usu. outward at the ends.

cu•po•la (kyo͞o′pə-lə) *n.* **1.** *Archit.* **a.** A domed roof or ceiling. **b.** A small structure surmounting a roof. **2.** A cylindrical shaft type of blast furnace used for remelting metals before casting. **3.** A small rounded and domed structure on a tracked armored vehicle. [Ital. < LLat. *cūpula*, dim. of Lat. *cūpa*, tub.]

cup•pa (kŭp′ə) *n. Chiefly British.* A cup of tea.

cup•ping (kŭp′ĭng) *n.* A treatment in which evacuated glass cups are applied to skin to draw blood to the surface.

cu•pre•ous (ko͞o′prē-əs, kyo͞o′-) *adj.* Of, resembling, or containing copper; coppery. [< LLat. *cūpreus* < *cūprum*, copper. See COPPER[1].]

cu•pric (ko͞o′prĭk, kyo͞o′-) *adj.* Of or containing divalent copper.

cu•prif•er•ous (ko͞o-prĭf′ər-əs, kyo͞o-) *adj.* Containing copper.

cu•prite (ko͞o′prīt′, kyo͞o′-) *n.* A natural red secondary ore of copper, essentially Cu_2O, that forms as a result of weathering.

cupro– or **cupri–** or **cupr–** *pref.* Copper: *cupriferous.* [< LLat. *cūprum*, copper. See COPPER[1].]

cu•pro•nick•el (ko͞o′prō-nĭk′əl, kyo͞o′-) *n.* An alloy of copper that contains 10 to 30 percent nickel.

cu•prous (ko͞o′prəs, kyo͞o′-) *adj.* Of, relating to, or containing univalent copper.

cu•pu•late (kyo͞o′pyə-lāt′, -lĭt) also **cu•pu•lar** (-lər) *adj.* **1.** Resembling a small cup. **2.** Having or bearing a cupule.

cu•pule (kyo͞o′pyo͞ol) *n. Biol.* A small cup-shaped structure or organ, such as the cup at the base of an acorn. [LLat. *cūpula*, little cask, dim. of Lat. *cūpa*, tub.]

cur (kûr) *n.* **1.** A dog considered to be inferior or undesirable; a mongrel. **2.** A base or cowardly person. [ME *curre*, perh. of Scand. orig. See **gerə-[2]*.**]

cur. *abbr.* **1.** Currency. **2.** Current.

cur•a•ble (kyo͝or′ə-bəl) *adj.* Being such that curing or healing is possible: *curable diseases.* —**cur′a•bil′i•ty, cur′a•ble•ness** *n.* —**cur′a•bly** *adv.*

cu•ra•çao (kyo͝or′ə-sō′, -sou′, ko͝or′-) also **cu•ra•çoa** (-sō′ə) *n.* A liqueur flavored with the peel of the sour orange. [After CURAÇAO.]

Cu•ra•çao (ko͝or′ə-sou′, -sō′, kyo͝or′-, ko͝or′ə-sou′, -sō′, kyo͝or′-). An island of the Netherlands Antilles in the S Caribbean Sea off the NW coast of Venezuela; settled by the Spanish in 1527 and under Dutch control after 1634.

cu•ra•cy (kyo͝or′ə-sē) *n., pl.* **-cies.** The office, duties, or term of office of a curate. [CURA(TE)[1] + -CY.]

cu•ra•re also **cu•ra•ri** (ko͞o-rä′rē, kyo͞o-) *n.* **1.** A dark resinous extract obtained from several tropical American woody plants, esp. *Chondrodendron tomentosum* or certain species of *Strychnos,* used as an arrow poison by some Indian peoples

ă pat	oi boy
ā pay	ou out
âr care	o͝o took
ä father	o͞o boot
ĕ pet	ŭ cut
ē be	ûr urge
ĭ pit	th thin
ī pie	*th* this
îr pier	hw which
ŏ pot	zh vision
ō toe	ə about,
ô paw	item

Stress marks:
′ (primary);
′ (secondary), as in
dictionary (dĭk′shə-nĕr′ē)

of South America. **2.** A purified preparation or alkaloid obtained from *Chondrodendron tomentosum,* used in medicine and surgery to relax skeletal muscles. **3.** A plant yielding curare. [Port. or Sp. *curaré,* both of Cariban and Tupian orig.]

cu•ra•rize (ko͝o-rä′rīz′, kyo͞o-) *tr.v.* **-rized, -riz•ing, -riz•es. 1.** To poison with curare. **2.** To treat with curare. **—cu•ra′ri•za′tion** (-rĭ-zā′shən) *n.*

cu•ras•sow (ko͝or′ə-sō′, kyo͝or′-) *n.* Any of several long-tailed crested South and Central American game birds of the family Cracidae. [Alteration of CURAÇAO.]

cu•rate[1] (kyo͝or′ĭt) *n.* **1.** A cleric, esp. one in charge of a parish. **2.** A cleric who assists a rector or vicar. [ME *curat* < Med.Lat. *cūrātus* < LLat. *cūra,* spiritual charge < Lat., care. See CURE.]

cu•rate[2] (kyo͝or′āt′) *tr.v. Usage Problem.* To act as curator of; organize and oversee. [Back-formation < CURATOR.]

Usage Note: The verb *curate* is widely used in art circles to mean "arrange or supervise (an exhibition of art)," as in *She has curated two exhibitions for the Modern Museum.* This usage is rejected by 81 percent of the Usage Panel.

cu•ra•tive (kyo͝or′ə-tĭv) *adj.* **1.** Serving or tending to cure. **2.** Of or relating to the cure of disease. **—***n.* Something that cures; a remedy. [ME < OFr. *curatif* < Med.Lat. *cūrātīvus* < Lat. *cūrātus,* p.part. of *cūrāre,* to cure < *cūra,* care. See CURE.] **—cu′ra•tive•ly** *adv.* **—cu′ra•tive•ness** *n.*

cu•ra•tor (kyo͞o-rā′tər, kyo͝or′ə-tər) *n.* One that manages or oversees, as the administrative director of a museum collection. [ME *curatour,* legal guardian < OFr. *curateur* < Lat. *cūrātor,* overseer < *cūrāre,* to take care of. See CURATIVE.] **—cu′ra•to′ri•al** (kyo͝or′ə-tôr′ē-əl, -tōr′-) *adj.* **—cu•ra′tor•ship′** *n.*

curb (kûrb) *n.* **1.** A concrete border or row of joined stones forming part of a gutter along the edge of a street. **2.** An enclosing framework, such as that around a skylight. **3.** A raised margin along an edge used to confine or strengthen. **4.** Something that checks or restrains. **5.** A chain or strap that passes under a horse's lower jaw and helps restrain the horse. **—***tr.v.* **curbed, curb•ing, curbs. 1.** To check, restrain, or control as if with a curb; rein in. **2.** To lead (a dog) off the sidewalk into the gutter so that it can defecate. **3.** To furnish with a curb. [Blend of ME, curved piece of wood (< OFr. *corbe,* curved object < *corbe,* curved < Lat. *curvus*) and ME *corbe,* horse strap (< *corben,* to bow down, halt < OFr. *corber,* to bow down < Lat. *curvāre* < *curvus,* curved, bent; see **sker-[2]***).]

curb•ing (kûr′bĭng) *n.* **1.** The material used to construct a curb. **2.** A row of curbstones; a curb.

curb roof *n.* A roof having two slopes on each side, as a gambrel roof or a mansard roof.

curb service *n.* Service or attendance, esp. from a restaurant, provided to customers remaining in their parked vehicles.

curb•side (kûrb′sīd′) *n.* **1.** The side of a pavement or street bordered by a curb. **2.** A sidewalk. **—curb′side′** *adj.*

curb•stone (kûrb′stōn′) *n.* A stone or row of stones that constitutes a curb. **—***adj.* Untrained or unsophisticated.

cur•cu•li•o (kər-kyo͞o′lē-ō′) *n., pl.* **-os.** See **snout beetle.** [Lat. *curculiō,* a kind of weevil.]

cur•cu•ma (kûr′kyə-mə) *n.* Any of various tropical Asian plants of the genus *Curcuma,* which includes turmeric. [NLat. *Curcuma,* genus name < Ar. *kurkum,* saffron.]

curd (kûrd) *n.* **1.** The part of milk that coagulates and is used to make cheese. **2.** A coagulated liquid that resembles milk curd. **—***intr. & tr.v.* **curd•ed, curd•ing, curds.** To form or cause to form into curd. [ME, var. of *crud.*] **—curd′y** *adj.*

curd cheese *n. Chiefly British.* Cottage cheese.

cur•dle (kûr′dl) *v.* **-dled, -dling, -dles. —***intr.* **1.a.** To change into curd. **b.** To become congealed as if by having changed into curd. **2.** To go bad or become spoiled. **—***tr.* To cause to change into or as if into curd. [Freq. of CURD.]

cure (kyo͝or) *n.* **1.** Restoration of health; recovery from disease. **2.** A method or course of medical treatment used to restore health. **3.** An agent, that restores health; a remedy. **4.** Something that corrects or relieves a harmful or disturbing situation. **5.** *Eccles.* Spiritual charge or care, as of a priest for a congregation. **6.** The office or duties of a curate. **7.** The act or process of preserving a product. **—***v.* **cured, cur•ing, cures. —***tr.* **1.** To restore to health. **2.** To effect a recovery from. **3.** To remove or remedy (something harmful or disturbing). **4.** To preserve (meat, for example), as by salting, smoking, or aging. **5.** To prepare, preserve, or finish (a substance) by a chemical or physical process. **6.** To vulcanize (rubber). **—***intr.* **1.** To effect a cure or recovery. **2.** To be prepared, preserved, or finished by a chemical or physical process. [ME < OFr., medical treatment < Lat. *cūra* < OLat. *coisa-.*] **—cur′er** *n.*

Syns: *cure, heal, remedy.* The central meaning shared by these verbs is "to set right an undesirable or unhealthy condition": *cure an ailing economy; heal a wounded spirit; remedy a structural defect.*

cu•ré (kyo͞o-rā′, kyo͝or′ā′) *n.* A parish priest. [Fr. < OFr. < Med.Lat. *cūrātus.* See CURATE[1].]

cure-all (kyo͝or′ôl′) *n.* A remedy that cures all diseases or evils.

cu•ret•tage (kyo͝or′ĭ-täzh′) *n.* The removal of tissue or growths from a body cavity by scraping with a curette.

cu•rette also **cu•ret** (kyo͞o-rĕt′) *n.* A surgical instrument shaped like a scoop or spoon, used to remove tissue or growths from a body cavity. [Fr. < OFr. < *curer,* to cure < Lat. *cūrāre,* to take care of < *cūra,* care. See CURE.]

cu•rette•ment (kyo͞o-rĕt′mənt) *n.* See **curettage.**

cur•few (kûr′fyo͞o) *n.* **1.** A regulation requiring certain or all people to leave the streets or be home at a prescribed hour. **2.a.** The time at which a curfew begins. **b.** The signal for a curfew. [ME *curfeu* < OFr. *cuevrefeu* : *covrir,* to cover; see COVER + *feu,* fire (< Lat. *focus,* hearth).]

cu•ri•a (ko͝or′ē-ə, kyo͝or′-) *n., pl.* **cu•ri•ae** (ko͝or′ē-ē′, kyo͝or′-). **1.a.** One of the ten subdivisions of a tribe in early Rome. **b.** The assembly place of such a subdivision. **2.** The Roman senate or any of the various buildings in which it met in republican Rome. **3.** The ensemble of central administrative and governmental services in imperial Rome. **4.** Often **Curia.** *Rom. Cath. Ch.* The central administration governing the Church. **5.a.** A medieval assembly or council. **b.** A medieval royal court of justice. [Lat. *cūria,* council, curia. See **wī-ro-***.] **—cu′ri•al** *adj.*

cu•rie (kyo͝or′ē, kyo͞o-rē′) *n.* A unit of radioactivity, equal to the amount of a radioactive isotope that decays at the rate of 3.7×10^{10} disintegrations per second. [After Marie CURIE.]

Cu•rie also **Cu•rie-Jo•liot** (kyo͝or′ē, -zhô-lyō′, kyo͞o-rē′, kü-), **Irène.** See Irène **Joliot-Curie.**

Curie, Marie. 1867–1934. Polish-born French chemist who shared a 1903 Nobel Prize with her husband, **Pierre Curie** (1859–1906), and Henri Becquerel for research on radioactivity. In 1911 she won a second Nobel Prize for her discovery of radium and polonium.

Curie point *n.* A transition temperature marking a change in the magnetic or ferroelectric properties of a substance. [After Pierre CURIE.]

cu•ri•o (kyo͝or′ē-ō′) *n., pl.* **-os.** A curious or unusual object of art or piece of bric-a-brac. [Short for CURIOSITY.]

cu•ri•o•sa (kyo͝or′ē-ō′sə, -zə) *pl.n.* Books or other writings dealing with unusual, esp. pornographic, topics. [NLat. *cūriōsa,* neut. pl. of Lat. *cūriōsus,* inquisitive. See CURIOUS.]

cu•ri•os•i•ty (kyo͝or′ē-ŏs′ĭ-tē) *n., pl.* **-ties. 1.** A desire to know or learn. **2.** A desire to know about what does not concern one; nosiness. **3.** An object that arouses interest, as by being extraordinary. **4.** A strange or odd aspect. **5.** *Archaic.* Fastidiousness. [ME *curiosite* < OFr. < Lat. *cūriōsitās* < *cūriōsus,* inquisitive. See CURIOUS.]

cu•ri•ous (kyo͝or′ē-əs) *adj.* **1.** Eager to learn more. **2.** Unduly inquisitive; prying. **3.** Arousing interest because of novelty or strangeness. **4.** *Archaic.* **a.** Accomplished with skill or ingenuity. **b.** Extremely careful; scrupulous. [ME < OFr. *curios* < Lat. *cūriōsus,* careful, inquisitive < *cūra,* care. See CURE.] **—cu′ri•ous•ly** *adv.* **—cu′ri•ous•ness** *n.*

Syns: *curious, inquisitive, snoopy, nosy.* These adjectives apply to persons who show a marked desire for information or knowledge. *Curious* most often implies an avid desire to know or learn, though it can suggest prying: *a curious child. Inquisitive* frequently suggests excessive curiosity and the asking of many questions: *"Remember, no revolvers. The police are, I believe, proverbially inquisitive"* (Lord Dunsany). *Snoopy* suggests underhanded prying: *a snoopy neighbor. Nosy* implies impertinent curiosity likened to that of an animal using its nose to examine or probe: *He went through my mail in his nosy way.* See also Syns at **strange.**

Cu•ri•ti•ba (ko͝or′ĭ-tē′bə). A city of SE Brazil SW of São Paulo; founded 1654. Pop. 1,024,975.

cu•ri•um (kyo͝or′ē-əm) *n. Symbol* **Cm** A metallic synthetic radioactive transuranic element. Atomic number 96; longest-lived isotope Cm 247; melting point (estimated) 1,350°C; valence 3. See table at **element.** [After Marie CURIE and Pierre CURIE.]

curl (kûrl) *v.* **curled, curl•ing, curls. —***tr.* **1.** To twist (the hair, for example) into ringlets or coils. **2.** To form into a coiled or spiral shape: *curled the ribbon.* **3.** To decorate with coiled or spiral shapes. **4.** To raise and turn under (the upper lip), as in snarling. **—***intr.* **1.** To form ringlets or coils. **2.** To assume a spiral or curved shape. **3.** To move in a curve or spiral. **4.** *Sports.* To engage in curling. **—***n.* **1.** Something with a spiral or coiled shape. **2.** A coil or ringlet of hair. **3.** A treatment in which the hair is curled. **4.a.** The act of curling. **b.** The state of being curled. **5.** *Sports.* A weightlifting exercise in which a barbell is raised to the chest or shoulder and lowered without moving the upper arms, shoulders, or back. **6.** Any of various plant diseases in which leaves roll up. **—*phrasal verb.* curl up.** To assume a position with legs drawn up. [ME *curlen* < *crulle,* curly, perh. of MLGer. orig.]

curl•er (kûr′lər) *n.* **1.** One that curls, as a device on which hair is wound for curling. **2.** *Sports.* A player of curling.

cur•lew (kûrl′yo͞o, kûr′lo͞o) *n.* Any of several brownish long-legged shore birds of the genus *Numenius,* having long, slender, downward-curving bills. [ME *curleu* < OFr. *courlieu,* perh. of imit. orig.]

Cur•ley (kûr′lē), **James Michael.** 1874–1958. Amer. politi-

cuneiform

cupola

Marie Curie

Pierre Curie

cian who was mayor of Boston four times between 1914 and 1950 and governor of MA (1935–37).

curl•i•cue also **curl•y•cue** (kûr′lĭ-kyo͞o′) *n.* A fancy twist or curl, such as a flourish made with a pen. [CURLY + CUE[1], tail, and poss. CUE[3].] — **curl′i•cued** *adj.*

curl•ing (kûr′lĭng) *n. Sports.* A game originating in Scotland in which two four-person teams slide heavy oblate stones toward the center of a circle at either end of a length of ice.

curling iron *n.* A rod-shaped metal implement used when heated to curl the hair.

curl paper *n.* A piece of soft paper on which a lock of hair is rolled up for curling.

curl•y (kûr′lē) *adj.* **-i•er, -i•est. 1.** Having curls. **2.** Tending to curl. **3.** Having a wavy grain. — **curl′i•ly** *adv.* — **curl′i•ness** *n.*

curly top *n.* A viral disease of many plants characterized by curled leaves and stunted growth.

cur•mudg•eon (kər-mŭj′ən) *n.* An ill-tempered person full of resentment and stubborn notions. [?] — **cur•mudg′eon•ly** *adj.* — **cur•mudg′eon•ry** *n.*

cur•rach also **cur•ragh** (kûr′əKH, kûr′ə) *n. Scots & Irish.* A coracle. [ME *currok* < Ir.Gael. *curach* < OIr.]

cur•rant (kûr′ənt, kŭr′-) *n.* **1.** Any of various deciduous shrubs of the genus *Ribes,* native chiefly to the Northern Hemisphere and having edible, variously colored berries. **2.** The fruits of any of these plants. **3.** A small seedless raisin of the Mediterranean region, used chiefly in baking. [< ME *(raysons of) coraunte,* (raisins of) Corinth, currants < AN *(raisins de) Corauntz* < Lat. *Corinthus,* Corinth < Gk. *Korinthos.*]

cur•ren•cy (kûr′ən-sē, kŭr′-) *n., pl.* **-cies. 1.** Money in any form when in actual use as a medium of exchange, esp. paper money. **2.** Transmission from person to person as a medium of exchange. **3.** General acceptance or use. [< ME *curraunt,* in circulation. See CURRENT.]

cur•rent (kûr′ənt, kŭr′-) *adj.* **1.a.** Belonging to the present time. **b.** Being in progress now. **2.** Passing from one to another; circulating. **3.** Prevalent, esp. at the present time. **4.** Running; flowing. — *n.* **1.** A steady, smooth onward movement. **2.** The part of a body of liquid or gas that has a continuous onward movement. **3.** A general tendency, movement, or course. **4.** *Symbol* **i, I** *Elect.* **a.** A flow of electric charge. **b.** The amount of electric charge flowing past a specified circuit point per unit time. [ME *curraunt* < OFr. *corant,* pr.part. of *courre,* to run < Lat. *currere.* See **kers-***.] — **cur′rent•ly** *adv.* — **cur′rent•ness** *n.*

current assets *pl.n.* Cash or assets convertible into cash at short notice.

current density *n. Phys.* **1.** *Symbol* **j, J** The ratio of the magnitude of current flowing in a conductor or in a beam of subatomic particles to the cross-sectional area perpendicular to the flow. **2.** The number of subatomic particles per unit time crossing a unit area in a designated plane perpendicular to the direction of particle movement.

cur•ri•cle (kûr′ĭ-kəl) *n.* A light, open two-wheeled carriage, drawn by two horses abreast. [< Lat. *curriculum,* course, racing chariot < *currere,* to run. See CURRENT.]

cur•ric•u•lum (kə-rĭk′yə-ləm) *n., pl.* **-la** (-lə) or **-lums. 1.** All the courses of study offered by an educational institution. **2.** A group of related courses, often in a special field of study. [Lat., course < *currere,* to run. See CURRENT.] — **cur•ric′u•lar** (-lər) *adj.*

cur•ric•u•lum vi•tae (kə-rĭk′yə-ləm vī′tē, vē′tī, kə-rĭk′o͞o-lo͝om wē′tī′) *n., pl.* **cur•ric•u•la vi•tae** (-lə). A summary of one's education, professional history, and job qualifications. [Lat. *curriculum vītae,* the race of life : *curriculum,* course + *vītae,* genitive of *vīta,* life.]

cur•ri•er (kûr′ē-ər, kŭr′-) *n.* One that prepares tanned hides for use. [ME *curreiour* < OFr. < Lat. *coriārius* < *corium,* leather. See **sker-**[1]*.]

Cur•ri•er (kûr′ē-ər, kŭr′-), **Nathaniel.** 1813–88. Amer. lithographer who with his partner James Merritt Ives produced more than 7,000 prints.

cur•ri•er•y (kûr′ē-ə-rē, kŭr′-) *n., pl.* **-ies.** The trade, work, or shop of a currier.

cur•rish (kûr′ĭsh) *adj.* Snarling and bad-tempered. — **cur′rish•ly** *adv.*

cur•ry[1] (kûr′ē, kŭr′ē) *tr.v.* **-ried, -ry•ing, -ries. 1.** To groom (a horse) with a currycomb. **2.** To prepare (tanned hides) for use, as by soaking. — ***idiom.*** **curry favor.** To seek or gain favor by fawning. [ME *curreien* < AN *curreier,* to arrange, curry < VLat. **conrēdāre* : Lat. *com-,* com- + VLat. **-rēdāre,* to ready (of Gmc. orig.; see **reidh-***).]

cur•ry[2] also **cur•rie** (kûr′ē, kŭr′ē) — *n., pl.* **-ries. 1.** Curry powder. **2.** A heavily spiced sauce or relish made with curry powder. **3.** A dish seasoned with curry powder. — *tr.v.* **-ried, -ry•ing, -ries.** To season (food) with curry. [Tamil *kaṟi.*]

Cur•ry (kûr′ē, kŭr′ē), **John Steuart.** 1897–1946. Amer. painter noted for his scenes of rural America.

cur•ry•comb (kûr′ē-kōm′, kŭr′-) *n.* A comb with metal teeth, used for grooming horses. — *tr.v.* **-combed, -comb•ing, -combs.** To groom with a currycomb.

currycomb

curry powder *n.* A pungent blended condiment prepared from cumin, coriander, turmeric, and other spices.

curse (kûrs) *n.* **1.a.** An appeal or prayer for evil or misfortune to befall someone or something. **b.** The evil or misfortune that comes in or as if in response to such an appeal. **2.** One that is accursed. **3.** A source or cause of evil; a scourge. **4.** A profane word or phrase; a swearword. **5.** *Eccles.* A censure, ban, or anathema. **6.** *Slang.* Menstruation. Used with *the.* — *v.* **cursed** or **curst** (kûrst), **curs•ing, curs•es.** — *tr.* **1.** To invoke evil or misfortune upon; damn. **2.** To swear at. **3.** To bring evil upon; afflict. **4.** *Eccles.* To put under a ban or an anathema; excommunicate. — *intr.* To utter curses; swear. [ME < OE *curs.*] — **curs′er** *n.*

curs•ed (kûr′sĭd, kûrst) also **curst** (kûrst) *adj.* So wicked and detestable as to deserve to be cursed. — **curs′ed•ly** *adv.* — **curs′ed•ness** *n.*

cur•sive (kûr′sĭv) *adj.* Having the successive letters joined together: *cursive writing.* — *n.* **1.** A cursive character or letter. **2.** A manuscript written in cursive characters. **3.** *Print.* A type style that imitates handwriting. [Fr. *(écriture) cursive,* cursive (handwriting) < Med.Lat. *(scripta) cursīva* < Lat. *cursus,* p.part. of *currere,* to run. See **kers-***.] — **cur′sive•ly** *adv.* — **cur′sive•ness** *n.*

cur•sor (kûr′sər) *n. Comp. Sci.* A movable indicator on a display, marking the position at which a character can be entered, corrected, or deleted. [ME, runner < Lat. < *cursus,* p.part. of *currere,* to run. See **kers-***.]

cur•so•ri•al (kûr-sôr′ē-əl, -sōr′-) *adj.* Adapted to or specialized for running. [< LLat. *cursōrius,* of running. See CURSORY.]

cur•so•ry (kûr′sə-rē) *adj.* Performed with haste and scant attention to detail. [LLat. *cursōrius,* of running < Lat. *cursor, cursōr-,* runner. See CURSOR.] — **cur′so•ri•ly** *adv.* — **cur′so•ri•ness** *n.*

curt (kûrt) *adj.* **curt•er, curt•est. 1.** Rudely brief or abrupt, as in speech or manner. **2.** Using few words; terse. **3.** Having been shortened. [ME, short, brief < AN < Lat. *curtus.* See **sker-**[1]*.] — **curt′ly** *adv.* — **curt′ness** *n.*

cur•tail (kər-tāl′) *tr.v.* **-tailed, -tail•ing, -tails.** To cut short; abbreviate. [ME *curtailen,* to restrict, prob. blend of OFr. *courtauld,* docked; see CURTAL, and ME *taillen,* to cut (< OFr. *tailler;* see TAILOR).] — **cur•tail′er** *n.* — **cur•tail′ment** *n.*

cur•tain (kûr′tn) *n.* **1.** Material that hangs over an opening as a decoration, shade, or screen. **2.** Something that functions as or resembles a screen, cover, or barrier: *a curtain of mist.* **3.a.** The movable screen or drape that separates a stage from an auditorium or serves as a backdrop. **b.** The rising or opening of a theater curtain at the beginning of a performance or an act. **c.** The fall or closing of a theater curtain at the end of a performance or an act. **d.** The concluding line, speech, or scene of a play or an act. **4.** The part of a rampart or parapet connecting two bastions or gates. **5.** *Archit.* An enclosing wall connecting two towers or similar structures. **6. curtains.** *Slang.* **a.** The end. **b.** Absolute ruin. **c.** Death. — *tr.v.* **-tained, -tain•ing, -tains. 1.** To provide (something) with or as if with a curtain. **2.** To shut off (something) with or as if with a curtain. [ME *cortine* < OFr. < LLat. *cōrtīna* < Lat. *cōrs, cōrt-,* var. of *cohors,* court. See COURT.]

curtain call *n.* The appearance of performers or a performer at the end of a performance in response to applause.

curtain lecture *n.* A private reprimand given to a husband by his wife.

curtain rais•er (rā′zər) *n.* **1.** A short play or skit presented before the principal production. **2.** A preliminary event.

cur•tal (kûr′tl) *n. Archaic.* **1.** An animal with a docked tail. **2.** Something cut short or docked. — *adj. Obsolete.* Cut short or docked. [Obsolete Fr. *courtault* < OFr. < *court,* short < Lat. *curtus.* See **sker-**[1]*.]

curtal ax *n. Archaic.* A cutlass. [By folk ety. < earlier *coutelace, curtelace,* cutlass < OFr. *coutelas.* See CUTLASS.]

cur•tate (kûr′tāt′) *adj.* Abbreviated. [Lat. *curtātus,* p.part. of *curtāre,* to shorten < *curtus,* cut short. See CURT.]

cur•te•sy (kûr′tĭ-sē) *n., pl.* **-sies.** *Law.* The life tenure that by common law is held by a man over the property of his deceased wife if children with rights of inheritance were born during the marriage. [ME *courtesie, curtesie.* See COURTESY.]

cur•ti•lage (kûr′tl-ĭj) *n. Law.* The enclosed area immediately surrounding a house or dwelling. [ME < OFr. *courtillage* < *courtil,* dim. of *cort,* court. See COURT.]

Cur•tis (kûr′tĭs), **Benjamin Robbins.** 1809–74. Amer. jurist; associate justice of the U.S. Supreme Court (1851–57).

Curtis, Charles. 1860–1936. Vice President of the U.S. (1929–33).

Cur•tiss (kûr′tĭs), **Glenn Hammond.** 1878–1930. Amer. aviation pioneer who developed the first seaplane (1911).

curt•sy or **curt•sey** (kûrt′sē) — *n., pl.* **-sies** or **-seys.** A gesture of respect or reverence made chiefly by women by bending the knees with one foot forward and lowering the body. — *intr.v.* **-sied, -sy•ing, -sies** or **-seyed, -sey•ing, -seys.** To make a curtsy. [Var. of COURTESY.]

cu•rule (kyo͝or′o͞ol′) *adj.* Privileged to sit in a curule chair; of superior rank. [Lat. *curūlis,* of a curule chair < *currus,* chariot < *currere,* to run. See **kers-***.]

curule chair *n.* A seat with heavy curved legs and no back, reserved for the use of the highest officials in ancient Rome.

cur•va•ceous (kûr-vā′shəs) *adj.* Having the curves of a full or voluptuous figure. — **cur•va′ceous•ness** *n.*

cur•va•ture (kûr′və-cho͝or′, -chər) *n.* **1.** The act of curving or the state of being curved. **2.** *Math.* **a.** The rate of change in the angle of a tangent that moves over a given arc with respect to the length of the arc. **b.** The reciprocal of the radius of a circle. **3.** *Medic.* A curving or bending, esp. an abnormal one: *curvature of the spine.* [ME < Lat. *curvātūra* < *curvātus,* p.part. of *curvāre,* to bend < *curvus,* curved. See **sker-[2]*.**]

curve (kûrv) *n.* **1.a.** A line that bends in a smooth continuous fashion. **b.** A surface that bends in a smooth continuous fashion. **c.** Something characterized by such a line or surface, esp. a contour of the human body. **2.** A relatively smooth bend in a road or other course. **3.a.** A line representing data on a graph. **b.** A trend derived from or as if from such a graph. **4.** A method of grading students based on relative performance. **5.** *Math.* **a.** The graph of a function on a coordinate plane. **b.** The intersection of two surfaces in three dimensions. **6.** *Baseball.* A curve ball. **7.** *Slang.* A trick or deception. — *v.* **curved, curv•ing, curves.** — *intr.* To move in or take the shape of a curve. — *tr.* **1.** To cause to curve. See Syns at **bend[1]**. **2.** *Baseball.* To pitch a curve ball to. **3.** To grade (students, for example) on a curve. [< ME, curved < Lat. *curvus.* See **sker-[2]*.**] — **curv′ed•ness** *n.* — **curv′y** *adj.*

curve ball or **curve•ball** (kûrv′bôl′) *n. Baseball.* A pitched ball that veers or breaks to the left when thrown with the right hand and to the right when thrown with the left hand. — ***idiom.*** **pitch (**or **throw) (someone) a curve ball.** *Slang.* **1.** To mislead; deceive. **2.** To cause to be surprised, esp. unpleasantly so.

cur•vet (kûr-vĕt′) *n.* A light leap by a horse, in which both hind legs leave the ground just before the forelegs are set down. — *v.* **-vet•ted, -vet•ting, -vets** or **-vet•ed, -vet•ing, -vets.** — *intr.* **1.** To leap in a curvet. **2.** To prance; frolic. — *tr.* To cause to leap in a curvet. [Ital. *corvetta* < OItal. < OFr. *courbette* < *courber,* to curve < Lat. *curvāre* < *curvus,* curved. See **sker-[2]*.**]

cur•vi•lin•e•ar (kûr′və-lĭn′ē-ər) also **cur•vi•lin•e•al** (-əl) *adj.* Formed, bounded, or characterized by curved lines. [Lat. *curvus,* curved; see CURVE + LINEAR.] — **cur′vi•lin′e•ar′i•ty** (-ē-ăr′ĭ-tē) *n.* — **cur′vi•lin′e•ar•ly** *adv.*

Cur•zon (kûr′zən), **George Nathaniel.** 1859–1925. British politician who served as viceroy of India (1898–1905) and secretary of state for foreign affairs (1919–24).

Cus•co (ko͞o′skō). See **Cuzco.**

cu•sec (kyo͞o′sĕk′) *n.* A volumetric unit for measuring the flow of liquids, equal to one cubic foot per second.

Cush[1] (kŭsh, ko͝osh). In the Bible, the oldest son of Ham.

Cush[2] also **Kush** (kŭsh, ko͝osh). **1.** An ancient region of NE Africa where the biblical descendants of Cush settled; often identified with Ethiopia. **2.** An ancient kingdom of Nubia in N Sudan; flourished from the 11th cent. B.C. to the 4th cent. A.D. — **Cush′ite′** *adj. & n.*

cu•shaw (kə-shô′, ko͞o′shô′) *n.* Any of several kinds of winter squash *(Cucurbita mixta)* having a curved neck. [?]

Cush•ing (ko͝osh′ĭng), **Caleb.** 1800–79. Amer. politician and diplomat who negotiated the treaty (1844) that opened five Chinese ports to U.S. trade.

Cushing, Harvey Williams. 1869–1939. Amer. neurologist noted for his study of the brain and the pituitary gland.

Cushing, William. 1732–1810. Amer. jurist; associate justice of the U.S. Supreme Court (1789–1810).

Cush•ing's disease (ko͝osh′ĭngz) *n.* The form of Cushing's syndrome involving the pituitary gland.

Cushing's syndrome *n.* A syndrome caused by an increased production of ACTH or by excessive intake of glucocorticoids, characterized by obesity and weakening of the muscles. [After Harvey Williams CUSHING.]

cush•ion (ko͝osh′ən) *n.* **1.** A pad or pillow with a soft filling, used for resting, reclining, or kneeling. **2.** Something resilient used as a rest, support, or shock absorber. **3.** A padlike body part. **4.** *Games.* The rim bordering the playing surface of a billiard table. **5.** A pillow used in lacemaking. **6.** Something that mitigates or relieves an adverse effect. — *tr.v.* **-ioned, -ion•ing, -ions. 1.** To provide with a cushion. **2.** To place or seat on a cushion. **3.** To cover or hide (something) with or as if with a cushion. **4.** To protect as if with cushions. **5.** To mitigate the effects of. [ME *cushin* < OFr. *coussin* < VLat. **coxīnum* < Lat. *coxa,* hip.] — **cush′ion•y** *adj.*

Cush•it•ic (ko͝o-shĭt′ĭk) *n.* A branch of the Afro-Asiatic language family spoken in Somalia, Ethiopia, and northern Kenya and including Beja, Orono, and Somali. — **Cush•it′ic** *adj.*

cush•y (ko͝osh′ē) *adj.* **-i•er, -i•est.** *Informal.* Making few demands; comfortable: *a cushy job.* [?] — **cush′i•ly** *adv.* — **cush′i•ness** *n.*

cusk (kŭsk) *n., pl.* **cusk** or **cusks. 1.** A food fish *(Brosme brosme)* of North Atlantic coastal waters that is related to the cod. **2.** See **burbot.** [Prob. alteration of *tusk,* codfish, perh. < Norw. dial., var. of Norw. *tosk* < ON *thorskr.* See **ters-*.**]

cusp (kŭsp) *n.* **1.** A point or pointed end. **2.** *Anat.* **a.** A pointed or rounded projection on the chewing surface of a tooth. **b.** A triangular fold or flap of a heart valve. **3.** *Math.* A point at which a curve crosses itself and at which the two tangents to the curve coincide. **4.** *Archit.* The point of intersection of two ornamental arcs or curves. **5.** *Astron.* Either point of a crescent moon. **6.** A transitional point or time, as between two astrological signs. [Lat. *cuspis,* point.]

cus•pate (kŭs′pāt′) also **cus•pat•ed** (-pā′tĭd) *adj.* **1.** Having a cusp. **2.** Shaped like a cusp.

cus•pid (kŭs′pĭd) *n.* A canine tooth. [< Lat. *cuspis, cuspid-,* point.]

cus•pi•date (kŭs′pĭ-dāt′) also **cus•pi•dat•ed** (-dā′tĭd) *adj.* **1.** Having a cusp. **2.** *Biol.* Terminating in or tipped with a sharp firm point. [Lat. *cuspidātus,* p.part. of *cuspidāre,* to make pointed < *cuspis, cuspid-,* point.]

cus•pi•da•tion (kŭs′pĭ-dā′shən) *n. Archit.* Decoration with cusps.

cus•pi•dor (kŭs′pĭ-dôr′, -dōr′) *n.* A spittoon. [Port. < *cuspir,* to spit < Lat. *cōnspuere,* to spit upon : *com-,* com- + *spuere,* to spit.]

cuss (kŭs) *Informal.* — *intr. & tr.v.* **cussed, cuss•ing, cuss•es.** To curse or curse at. — *n.* **1.** A curse. **2.** An odd or perverse creature. [Alteration of CURSE.]

cuss•ed (kŭs′ĭd) *adj. Informal.* **1.** Perverse; stubborn. **2.** Cursed. — **cuss′ed•ly** *adv.* — **cuss′ed•ness** *n.*

cus•tard (kŭs′tərd) *n.* A dish consisting of milk, eggs, flavoring, and sometimes sugar, boiled or baked until set. [ME *crustade, custard,* a pie with a crust, prob. < OProv. *croustado.* See CROUSTADE.] — **cus′tard•y** *adj.*

custard apple *n.* **1.** Any of several tropical American trees of the genus *Annona,* esp. *A. reticulata,* having large, nearly heart-shaped edible fruits. **2.** The fruit of any of these trees.

Cus•ter (kŭs′tər), **George Armstrong.** 1839–76. Amer. soldier who was killed and his troops annihilated by Sioux and Cheyenne warriors at Little Bighorn.

cus•to•di•al (kŭ-stō′dē-əl) *adj.* **1.** Of or relating to the work of guarding or maintaining. **2.a.** Having custody, esp. of a child. **b.** Of or relating to child custody. **3.** Marked by care and supervision rather than efforts to cure.

cus•to•di•an (kŭ-stō′dē-ən) *n.* **1.** One in charge of something; a caretaker. **2.** A janitor. — **cus•to′di•an•ship′** *n.*

cus•to•dy (kŭs′tə-dē) *n., pl.* **-dies. 1.** The act or right of guarding, esp. such a right granted by a court. **2.** Care, supervision, and control exerted by one in charge. See Syns at **care. 3.** The state of being detained or held under guard, esp. by the police: *took the suspect into custody.* [ME *custodie* < Lat. *custōdia* < *custōs, custōd-,* guard.]

cus•tom (kŭs′təm) *n.* **1.** A practice followed by people of a particular group or region. **2.** A habitual practice of a person. See Syns at **habit. 3.** *Law.* A common tradition or usage so long established that it has the force or validity of law. **4.a.** Habitual patronage. **b.** Habitual customers; patrons. **5. customs.** *(used with a sing. v.)* **a.** A duty or tax imposed on imported and, less commonly, exported goods. **b.** The governmental agency authorized to collect these duties. **c.** The procedure for inspecting goods and baggage entering a country. **6.** Tribute, service, or rent paid by a feudal tenant to a lord. — *adj.* **1.** Made to order. **2.** Specializing in the making or selling of made-to-order goods. [ME *custume* < OFr. *costume* < Lat. *cōnsuētūdō, cōnsuētūdin-* < *cōnsuētus,* p.part. of *cōnsuēscere,* to accustom : *com-,* com- + *suēscere,* to become accustomed; see **s(w)e-*.**]

cus•tom•a•ble (kŭs′tə-mə-bəl) *adj.* Subject to tariffs.

cus•tom•ar•y (kŭs′tə-mĕr′ē) *adj.* **1.** Commonly practiced, used, or encountered; usual. See Syns at **usual. 2.** Based on custom or tradition rather than written law or contract. — **cus′tom•ar′i•ly** (-mâr′ə-lē) *adv.* — **cus′tom•ar′i•ness** *n.*

cus•tom-built (kŭs′təm-bĭlt′) *adj.* Built according to the specifications of the buyer.

cus•tom•er (kŭs′tə-mər) *n.* **1.** One that buys goods or services. **2.** *Informal.* An individual with whom one must deal.

cus•tom•house (kŭs′təm-hous′) also **cus•toms•house** (-təmz-) *n.* A governmental building or office where customs are collected and ships are cleared for entering or leaving the country.

cus•tom•ize (kŭs′tə-mīz′) *tr.v.* **-ized, -iz•ing, -iz•es.** To make or alter to individual or personal specifications. — **cus′tom•i•za′tion** (-ĭ-zā′shən) *n.* — **cus′tom•iz′er** *n.*

cus•tom-made (kŭs′təm-mād′) *adj.* Made according to the specifications of an individual purchaser.

customs union *n.* An international association organized to eliminate customs restrictions between member nations and establish a uniform tariff policy toward nonmember nations.

cut (kŭt) *v.* **cut, cut•ting, cuts.** — *tr.* **1.** To penetrate with a sharp edge; strike a narrow opening in. **2.** To separate into parts with or as if with a sharp-edged instrument; sever. **3.** To sever the edges or ends of; shorten: *cut one's hair.* **4.** To reap; harvest: *cut grain.* **5.** To fell by sawing; hew. **6.** To have (a new tooth) grow through the gums. **7.** To form or shape by severing or incising. **8.a.** To form by penetrating, probing, or digging: *cut a trench.* **b.** To exhibit the appearance or give the impression of: *cuts a fine figure.* **9.** To separate from a main

ă pat	oi boy
ā pay	ou out
âr care	o͝o took
ä father	o͞o boot
ĕ pet	ŭ cut
ē be	ûr urge
ĭ pit	th thin
ī pie	*th* this
îr pier	hw which
ŏ pot	zh vision
ō toe	ə about,
ô paw	item

Stress marks:
′ (primary);
′ (secondary), as in
dictionary (dĭk′shə-nĕr′ē)

CURRENCY TABLE: LISTED BY COUNTRY

COUNTRY	BASIC UNIT	SUBUNIT
Afghanistan	afghani	100 puls
Albania	lek	100 qindarka
Algeria	dinar	100 centimes
Andorra	peseta	100 centimos
Angola	kwanza	100 lwei
Argentina	austral	100 centavos
Australia	dollar	100 cents
Austria	schilling	100 groschen
Bahamas	dollar	100 cents
Bahrain	dinar	1000 fils
Bangladesh	taka	100 paisas
Barbados	dollar	100 cents
Belgium	franc	100 centimes
Belize	dollar	100 cents
Benin	franc	100 centimes
Bhutan	ngultrum	100 chetrums
Bolivia	boliviano	100 centavos
Botswana	pula	100 thebe
Brazil	cruzeiro	100 centavos
Brunei	dollar	100 cents
Bulgaria	lev	100 stotinki
Burkina Faso	franc	100 centimes
Burma	kyat	100 pyas
Burundi	franc	100 centimes
Cambodia	riel	100 sen
Cameroon	franc	100 centimes
Canada	dollar	100 cents
Cape Verde	escudo	100 centavos
Cayman Islands	dollar	100 cents
Central African Republic	franc	100 centimes
Chad	franc	100 centimes
Chile	peso	100 centesimos
China	yuan	10 jiao
Colombia	peso	100 centavos
Comoros	franc	100 centimes
Congo	franc	100 centimes
Costa Rica	colon	100 centimos
Cuba	peso	100 centavos
Cyprus	pound	100 cents
Czechoslovakia	koruna	100 halers
Denmark	krone	100 öre
Djibouti	franc	100 centimes
Dominica	dollar	100 cents
Dominican Republic	peso	100 centavos
Ecuador	sucre	100 centavos
Egypt	pound	100 piasters
El Salvador	colon	100 centavos
Equatorial Guinea	ekpwele	
Ethiopia	birr	100 cents
Fiji	dollar	100 cents
Finland	markka	100 penni
France	franc	100 centimes
Gabon	franc	100 centimes
Gambia	dalasi	100 butut
Germany	deutsche mark	100 pfennigs
Ghana	cedi	100 pesewa
Greece	drachma	100 lepta
Grenada	dollar	100 cents
Guatemala	quetzal	100 centavos
Guinea	franc	100 centimes
Guinea-Bissau	peso	100 centavos
Guyana	dollar	100 cents
Haiti	gourde	100 centimes
Honduras	lempira	100 centavos
Hong Kong	dollar	100 cents
Hungary	forint	100 fillér
Iceland	krona	100 aurar
India	rupee	100 paise
Indonesia	rupiah	100 sen
Iran	rial	100 dinars
Iraq	dinar	1000 fils
Ireland	pound	100 pence
Israel	shekel	100 agorot
Italy	lira	100 centesimi
Ivory Coast	franc	100 centimes
Jamaica	dollar	100 cents
Japan	yen	100 sen
Jordan	dinar	1000 fils
Kenya	shilling	100 cents
Kiribati	dollar	100 cents
Kuwait	dinar	1000 fils
Laos	kip	100 at
Lebanon	pound	100 piasters
Lesotho	loti	100 lisente
Liberia	dollar	100 cents
Libya	dinar	100 dirhams
Liechtenstein	franc	100 centimes
Luxembourg	franc	100 centimes
Macao	pataca	100 avos
Madagascar	franc	100 centimes
Malawi	kwacha	100 tambala
Malaysia	ringgit	100 sen
Maldives	rufiyaa	100 larees
Mali	franc	100 centimes
Malta	lira	100 cents
Mauritania	ouguiya	5 khoums
Mauritius	rupee	100 cents
Mexico	peso	100 centavos
Monaco	franc	100 centimes
Mongolia	tugrik	100 mongo
Morocco	dirham	100 centimes
Mozambique	metical	100 centavos
Namibia	rand	100 cents
Nauru	dollar	100 cents
Nepal	rupee	100 paisas
Netherlands	guilder	100 cents
Netherlands Antilles	guilder	100 cents
New Zealand	dollar	100 cents
Nicaragua	cordoba	100 centavos
Niger	franc	100 centimes
Nigeria	naira	100 kobos
North Korea	won	100 chon
Norway	krone	100 öre
Oman	riyal-omani	1000 baiza
Pakistan	rupee	100 paisas
Panama	balboa	100 centesimos
Papua New Guinea	kina	100 toea
Paraguay	guarani	100 centimos
Peru	inti	
Philippines	peso	100 centavos
Poland	zloty	100 groszy
Portugal	escudo	100 centavos
Qatar	riyal	100 dirhams
Romania	leu	100 bani
Rwanda	franc	100 centimes
Saint Lucia	dollar	100 cents
Saint Vincent and the Grenadines	dollar	100 cents
San Marino	lira	100 centesimi
São Tomé and Príncipe	dobra	100 centavos
Saudi Arabia	riyal	100 halala
Senegal	franc	100 centimes
Seychelles	rupee	100 cents
Sierra Leone	leone	100 cents
Singapore	dollar	100 cents
Solomon Islands	dollar	100 cents
Somalia	shilling	100 cents
South Africa	rand	100 cents
South Korea	won	100 chon
Spain	peseta	100 centimos
Sri Lanka	rupee	100 cents
Sudan	pound	100 piasters
Suriname	guilder	100 cents
Swaziland	lilangeni	100 cents
Sweden	krona	100 öre
Switzerland	franc	100 centimes
Syria	pound	100 piasters
Taiwan	dollar	100 cents
Tanzania	shilling	100 cents
Thailand	baht	100 satang
Togo	franc	100 centimes
Tonga	pa'anga	100 seniti
Trinidad and Tobago	dollar	100 cents
Tunisia	dinar	1000 millimes
Turkey	lira	100 kurus
Tuvalu	dollar	100 cents
Uganda	shilling	100 cents
Union of Soviet Socialist Republics	ruble	100 kopecks
United Arab Emirates	dirham	1000 fils
United Kingdom	pound	100 pence
United States	dollar	100 cents
Uruguay	peso	100 centesimos
Vanuatu	vatu	100 centimes
Vatican City	lira	100 centesimi
Venezuela	bolivar	100 centimos
Vietnam	dong	10 hao
Western Samoa	tala	100 sene
Yemen	dinar	100 fils
Yugoslavia	dinar	100 para
Zaire	zaire	100 makuta
Zambia	kwacha	100 ngwee
Zimbabwe	dollar	100 cents

CURRENCY TABLE: LISTED BY BASIC UNIT (BOLD) AND SUBUNIT

UNIT	COUNTRY
afghani	Afghanistan
agora	Israel
at	Laos
aurar	(pl. of *eyrir*)
austral	Argentina
avo	Macao
baht	Thailand
baiza	Oman
balboa	Panama
ban	Romania
birr	Ethiopia
bolivar	Venezuela
boliviano	Bolivia
butut	Gambia
cedi	Ghana
cent	Australia
	Bahamas
	Barbados
	Belize
	Brunei
	Canada
	Cayman Islands
	Cyprus
	Dominica
	Ethiopia
	Fiji
	Grenada
	Guyana
	Hong Kong
	Jamaica
	Kenya
	Kiribati
	Liberia
	Malta
	Mauritius
	Namibia
	Nauru
	Netherlands
	Netherlands Antilles
	New Zealand
	Saint Lucia
	Saint Vincent and the Grenadines
	Seychelles
	Sierra Leone
	Singapore
	Solomon Islands
	Somalia
	South Africa
	Sri Lanka
	Suriname
	Swaziland
	Taiwan
	Tanzania
	Trinidad and Tobago
	Tuvalu
	Uganda
	United States
	Zimbabwe
centavo	Argentina
	Bolivia
	Brazil
	Cape Verde
	Colombia
	Cuba
	Dominican Republic
	Ecuador
	El Salvador
	Guatemala
	Guinea-Bissau
	Honduras
	Mexico
	Mozambique
	Nicaragua
	Philippines
	Portugal
	São Tomé and Príncipe
centesimo	Chile
	Italy
	Panama
	San Marino
	Vatican City
centime	Algeria
	Belgium
	Benin
	Burkina Faso
	Burundi
	Cameroon
	Central African Republic
	Chad
	Comoros
	Congo
	Djibouti
	France
	Gabon
	Guinea
	Haiti
	Ivory Coast
	Liechtenstein
	Luxembourg
	Madagascar
	Mali
	Monaco
	Morocco
	Niger
	Rwanda
	Senegal
	Switzerland
	Togo
	Vanuatu
centimo	Andorra
	Costa Rica
	Paraguay
	Spain
	Venezuela
chetrum	Bhutan
chon	North Korea
	South Korea
colon	Costa Rica
	El Salvador
cordoba	Nicaragua
cruzeiro	Brazil
dalasi	Gambia
deutsche mark	Germany
dinar	Algeria
	Bahrain
	Iraq
	Jordan
	Kuwait
	Libya
	Tunisia
	Yemen
	Yugoslavia
dinar	Iran
dirham	Morocco
	United Arab Emirates
dirham	Libya
	Qatar
dobra	São Tomé and Príncipe
dollar	Australia
	Bahamas
	Barbados
	Belize
	Brunei
	Canada
	Cayman Islands
	Dominica
	Fiji
	Grenada
	Guyana
	Hong Kong
	Jamaica
	Kiribati
	Liberia
	Nauru
	New Zealand
	Saint Lucia
	Saint Vincent and the Grenadines
	Singapore
	Solomon Islands
	Taiwan
	Trinidad and Tobago
	Tuvalu
	United States
	Zimbabwe
dong	Vietnam
drachma	Greece
ekpwele	Equatorial Guinea
escudo	Cape Verde
	Portugal
eyrir	Iceland
fillér	Hungary
fils	Bahrain
	Iraq
	Jordan
	Kuwait
	United Arab Emirates
	Yemen
forint	Hungary
franc	Belgium
	Benin
	Burkina Faso
	Burundi
	Cameroon
	Central African Republic
	Chad
	Comoros
	Congo
	Djibouti
	France
	Gabon
	Guinea
	Ivory Coast
	Liechtenstein
	Luxembourg
	Madagascar
	Mali
	Monaco
	Niger
	Rwanda
	Senegal
	Switzerland
	Togo
gourde	Haiti
groschen	Austria
grosz	Poland
guarani	Paraguay
guilder	Netherlands
	Netherlands Antilles
	Suriname
halala	Saudi Arabia
haler	Czechoslovakia
hao	Vietnam
inti	Peru
jiao	China
khoum	Mauritania
kina	Papua New Guinea
kip	Laos
kobo	Nigeria
kopeck	U.S.S.R.
koruna	Czechoslovakia
krona	Iceland
	Sweden
krone	Denmark
	Norway
kurus	Turkey
kwacha	Malawi
	Zambia
kwanza	Angola
kyat	Burma
laree	Maldives
lek	Albania
lempira	Honduras
leone	Sierra Leone
lepton	Greece
leu	Romania
lev	Bulgaria
likuta	Zaire
lilangeni	Swaziland
lira	Italy
	Malta
	San Marino
	Turkey
	Vatican City
lisente	(pl. of *sente*)
loti	Lesotho
lwei	Angola
makuta	(pl. of *likuta*)
markka	Finland
metical	Mozambique
millime	Tunisia
mongo	Mongolia
naira	Nigeria
ngultrum	Bhutan
ngwee	Zambia
öre	Denmark
	Norway
	Sweden
ouguiya	Mauritania
pa'anga	Tonga
paisa	Bangladesh
	India
	Nepal
	Pakistan
para	Yugoslavia
pataca	Macao
penni	Finland
penny	Ireland
	United Kingdom
peseta	Andorra
	Spain
pesewa	Ghana
peso	Chile
	Colombia
	Cuba
	Dominican Republic
	Guinea-Bissau
	Mexico
	Philippines
	Uruguay
pfennig	Germany
piaster	Egypt
	Lebanon
	Sudan
	Syria
pound	Cyprus
	Egypt
	Ireland
	Lebanon
	Sudan
	Syria
	United Kingdom
pul	Afghanistan
pula	Botswana
pya	Burma
qindarka	Albania
quetzal	Guatemala
rand	Namibia
	South Africa
rial	Iran
riel	Cambodia
ringgit	Malaysia
riyal	Qatar
	Saudi Arabia
riyal-omani	Oman
ruble	U.S.S.R.
rufiyaa	Maldives
rupee	India
	Mauritius
	Nepal
	Pakistan
	Seychelles
	Sri Lanka
rupiah	Indonesia
satang	Thailand
schilling	Austria
sen	Cambodia
	Indonesia
	Japan
	Malaysia
sene	Western Samoa
seniti	Tonga
sente	Lesotho
shekel	Israel
shilling	Kenya
	Somalia
	Tanzania
	Uganda
stotinka	Bulgaria
sucre	Ecuador
taka	Bangladesh
tala	Western Samoa
tambala	Malawi
thebe	Botswana
toea	Papua New Guinea
tugrik	Mongolia
vatu	Vanuatu
won	North Korea
	South Korea
yen	Japan
yuan	China
zaire	Zaire
zloty	Poland

body; detach. **10.** To discharge from a group or number. **11.** To pass through or across; cross: *a sailboat cutting the water.* **12.** *Games.* To divide (a deck of cards) into two parts. **13.** To reduce the size, extent, or duration of; curtail or shorten: *cut a budget.* **14.** To lessen the strength of; dilute: *cut whiskey with water.* **15.** To dissolve by breaking down the fat of: *Soap cuts grease.* **16.** To injure the feelings of; hurt keenly. **17.** To refuse to speak to or recognize; snub. **18.** To fail to attend purposely: *cut a class.* **19.** *Informal.* To cease; stop: *cut an engine.* **20.** *Sports.* To strike (a ball) so that it spins in a reverse direction. **21.a.** To perform: *cut a caper.* **b.** To make out and issue: *cut a check.* **22.** *Slang.* To be able to manage; handle successfully. **23.** To stop filming (a movie scene). **24.a.** To record a performance on (a phonograph record or other medium). **b.** To make a recording of. **25.** To edit (film or recording tape). — *intr.* **1.** To make an incision or a separation. **2.** To allow incision or severing: *Butter cuts easily.* **3.** To function as a sharp-edged instrument. **4.** To grow through the gums. Used of teeth. **5.** To penetrate injuriously. **6.** To change direction abruptly: *Cut to the left.* **7.** To go directly and often hastily: *cut across a field.* **8.** *Games.* To cut a deck of cards. **9.** To make an abrupt change of image or sound, as in filming. — *n.* **1.** The act of cutting. **2.** The result of cutting, esp. an opening or wound made by a sharp edge. **3.** A part that has been cut from a main body: *a cut of cloth.* **4.** A passage made by digging or probing. **5.** The elimination or removal of a part. **6.** A reduction. **7.** The style in which a garment is cut. **8.** *Informal.* A portion of profits or earnings; a share. **9.** A wounding remark; an insult. **10.** An unexcused absence, as from school. **11.** A step in a scale of value or quality; degree. **12.** *Print.* **a.** An engraved block or plate. **b.** A print made from such a block. **13.** *Sports.* A stroke that causes a ball to spin in a reverse direction. **14.** *Baseball.* A swing of a bat. **15.** *Games.* The act of cutting a deck of cards. **16.** One of the objects used in drawing lots. **17.** An abrupt change of image or sound, as between shots in a film. **18.** A movie at a given stage in its editing. **19.** A single selection of music from a recording, esp. a phonograph recording. — ***phrasal verbs.*** **cut back. 1.** To shorten by cutting; prune. **2.** To reduce or decrease. **cut down. 1.** To kill or strike down. **2.** To alter by removing extra or additional fittings. **3.** To reduce the amount taken or used. **cut in. 1.** To move into a line of people or things out of turn. **2.** To interrupt. **3.** To interrupt a dancing couple in order to dance with one of them. **4.** To connect or become connected into an electrical circuit. **5.** To mix in with or as if with cutting motions. **6.** To include, esp. among those profiting. **cut off. 1.** To separate from others; isolate. **2.** To stop suddenly; discontinue. **3.** To shut off; bar. **4.** To interrupt the course or passage of. **5.** To interrupt or break the line of communication of. **6.** To disinherit. **cut out. 1.** To remove by or as if by cutting. **2.** To form or shape by or as if by cutting. **3.** To take the place of; supplant. **4.** To suit or fit by nature. **5.** To assign beforehand or by necessity; predetermine. **6.** To deprive. **7.** To stop; cease. **8.** *Informal.* To depart hastily. **9.** *Chiefly Southern U.S.* To turn off (a light or television set). **cut up.** *Informal.* **1.** To behave in a playful, comic, or boisterous way; clown. **2.** To criticize severely. — ***idioms.*** **cut a fat hog.** *Texas.* To take on more than one is able to accomplish. **cut corners.** To do something in the easiest or most inexpensive way. **cut down to size.** To deflate the self-importance of. **cut loose.** To speak or act without restraint. **cut no ice.** To make no effect or impression. **cut (one's) losses.** To withdraw from a losing situation. **cut (one's) teeth on.** To learn or do as a beginner. **cut short.** To stop before the end; abbreviate. [ME *cutten.*] — **cut′ta•ble** *adj.*

cutaway

cut-and-dried (kŭt′n-drīd′) also **cut-and-dry** (-drī′) *adj.* **1.** Prepared and arranged in advance; settled. **2.** Ordinary.

cu•ta•ne•ous (kyo͞o-tā′nē-əs) *adj.* Of, relating to, or affecting the skin. [< NLat. *cutāneus,* ult. < Lat. *cutis,* skin. See **(s)keu-***.] — **cu•ta′ne•ous•ly** *adv.*

cut•a•way (kŭt′ə-wā′) *n.* **1.** A man's formal daytime coat, with front edges sloping diagonally from the waist and forming tails at the back. **2.** A brief shot that interrupts the visual continuity of the main action of a film, often to depict related matter or supposedly concurrent action. **3.** A model or diagram of an object with part of the outer layer removed so as to reveal the interior.

cut•back (kŭt′băk′) *n.* **1.** A decrease; a curtailment. **2.** A sharp reversal of direction, as of a ball carrier in football.

cutch (kŭch) *n.* See **catechu** 1. [Malay *kachu,* of Dravidian orig.]

cute (kyo͞ot) *adj.* **cut•er, cut•est. 1.** Delightfully pretty or dainty. **2.** Obviously contrived to charm; precious. **3.** Shrewd; clever. [Short for ACUTE.] — **cute′ly** *adv.* — **cute′ness** *n.*

Word History: *Cute* was originally a shortened form of *acute* in the sense "keenly perceptive or discerning, shrewd." In this sense *cute* is first recorded in a dictionary published in 1731. Probably *cute* came to be used as a term of approbation for things demonstrating acuteness, and so it went on to develop its own sense of "attractive, fetching."

cute•sy (kyo͞ot′sē) *adj.* **-si•er, -si•est.** *Informal.* Deliberately or affectedly cute; precious. — **cute′si•ness** *n.*

cut flower *n.* Any of various showy flowers used in fresh arrangements.

cut glass *n.* Glassware shaped or decorated by cutting instruments or abrasive wheels. — **cut′-glass′** (kŭt′glăs′) *adj.*

cut•grass also **cut grass** (kŭt′grăs′) *n.* **1.** Any of several grasses of the genus *Leersia,* having leaves with very rough margins. **2.** Any of several other grasses with rough margins.

cu•ti•cle (kyo͞o′tĭ-kəl) *n.* **1.** The outermost layer of the skin of vertebrates; epidermis. **2.** The strip of hardened skin at the base and sides of a fingernail or toenail. **3.** Dead or hardened epidermis. **4.** *Zool.* The noncellular, hardened or membranous protective covering of many invertebrates. **5.** *Bot.* The layer of cutin covering the epidermis of the aerial parts of plants. [Lat. *cutīcula,* dim. of *cutis,* skin. See **(s)keu-***.] — **cu•tic′u•lar** (-tĭk′yə-lər) *adj.*

cut•ie also **cut•ey** (kyo͞o′tē) *n., pl.* **-ies** also **-eys.** *Informal.* A cute person.

cu•tin (kyo͞ot′n) *n. Bot.* A waxlike water-repellent material present in the walls of some plant cells and forming the cuticle. [Lat. *cutis,* skin; see **(s)keu-*** + -IN.]

cu•tin•ize (kyo͞ot′n-īz′) *v.* **-ized, -iz•ing, -iz•es.** — *tr.* To coat or impregnate with cutin. — *intr.* To become coated or impregnated with cutin. — **cu′tin•i•za′tion** (-ĭ-zā′shən) *n.*

cu•tis (kyo͞o′tĭs) *n., pl.* **-tes** (-tēz) or **-tis•es.** *Anat.* See **dermis.** [Lat., skin. See **(s)keu-***.]

cut•lass also **cut•las** (kŭt′ləs) *n.* **1.** A short heavy sword with a curved single-edged blade, once used as a weapon by sailors. **2.** *Caribbean.* A machete. [Fr. *coutelas* < OFr. *coutelasse,* prob. aug. of *coutel,* knife < Lat. *cultellus,* dim. of *culter,* knife. See **skel-[1]*.**]

cutlass fish *n.* Any of several marine fishes of the genus *Trichiurus,* having a ribbonlike body and a pointed tail.

cut•ler (kŭt′lər) *n.* One who makes, repairs, or sells knives or other cutting instruments. [ME *cuteler* < OFr. *coutelier* < *coutel,* knife. See CUTLASS.]

Cut•ler Ridge (kŭt′lər). A community of SE FL on Biscayne Bay SSW of Miami. Pop. 21,268.

cut•ler•y (kŭt′lə-rē) *n.* **1.** Cutting instruments and tools. **2.** Utensils such as knives, forks, and spoons used as tableware. **3.** The occupation of a cutler. [Middle English *cutellerie* < OFr. *coutelerie* < *coutel,* knife. See CUTLASS.]

cut•let (kŭt′lĭt) *n.* **1.** A thin slice of meat, usu. veal or lamb, cut from the leg or ribs. **2.** A patty of chopped meat or fish, usu. coated with bread crumbs and fried; a flat croquette. [Fr. *côtelette* < OFr. *costelette,* dim. of *coste,* rib < Lat. *costa.* See **kost-***.]

cut•off also **cut-off** (kŭt′ôf′, -ŏf′) — *n.* **1.** A designated limit or point of termination. **2.** A shortcut or bypass. **3.** A new channel cut by a river across the neck of an oxbow. **4.** The act or an instance of cutting off. **5.** *Baseball.* The interception by an infielder of a throw to home plate from the outfield. **6.** A device that cuts off a flow of fluid. **7.** *Mus.* A conductor's signal for a stop or break. **8. cutoffs.** Pants made into shorts by cutting off part of the legs. — *adj.* Being a limit or point of termination.

cut•out (kŭt′out′) *n.* **1.** Something cut out or intended to be cut out from something else. **2.** *Elect.* A device that interrupts, bypasses, or disconnects a circuit or circuit element.

cut•o•ver (kŭt′ō′vər) *adj.* Cleared of trees, esp. those that bear valuable lumber.

cut•purse (kŭt′pûrs′) *n.* A pickpocket.

cut-rate (kŭt′rāt′) *adj.* Sold or on sale at a reduced price.

Cut•tack (kŭt′ək). A city of E India SW of Calcutta; long noted for its gold and silver filigree work. Pop. 269,950.

cut•ter (kŭt′ər) *n.* **1.** One that cuts, esp. in tailoring. **2.** A device or machine that cuts. **3.** *Naut.* **a.** A single-masted sailing vessel with two or more headsails and a mast set somewhat farther aft than that of a sloop. **b.** A ship's boat used for transporting stores or passengers. **4.** A small, lightly armed boat used by the Coast Guard. **5.** A small sleigh, usu. seating one person and drawn by a single horse.

cut•throat (kŭt′thrōt′) *n.* **1.** A murderer, esp. one who cuts throats. **2.** An unprincipled, ruthless person. — *adj.* **1.** Cruel; murderous. **2.** Relentless or merciless in competition. **3.** *Sports & Games.* Being a form of a game in which each of three or more players acts and scores individually.

cutthroat trout *n.* A large trout *(Salmo clarkii)* found in western North American waters similar to the rainbow trout, but with red or orange markings on the lower jaw.

cut time *n. Mus.* Duple or quadruple meter with the half note being the unit of time.

cut•ting (kŭt′ĭng) *adj.* **1.** Capable of or designed for incising, shearing, or severing. **2.** Sharply penetrating; piercing. **3.** Injuring or capable of injuring the feelings of others. — *n.* **1.** A part cut off from a main body. **2.** A part removed from a plant to propagate a new plant. **3.** An excavation made through high ground in a construction project. **4.** The editing of film or recording tape. **5.** *Chiefly British.* A clipping, as from a newspaper. — **cut′ting•ly** *adv.*

cutting edge *n.* **1.** An effective quality or element. **2.** The position of greatest advancement or importance; the forefront.

cut•tle•bone (kŭt′l-bōn′) *n.* The calcareous internal shell of a cuttlefish, used as a dietary supplement for cage birds or ground into powder for use as a polishing agent. [ME : *codel, cutil*, cuttlefish; see CUTTLEFISH + BONE.]

cut•tle•fish (kŭt′l-fĭsh′) *n., pl.* **cuttlefish** or **-fish•es.** Any of various squidlike cephalopod marine mollusks of the genus *Sepia*, having a calcareous internal shell. [Prob. ME *codel, cutil*, cuttlefish (< OE *cudele*) + FISH.]

cut•up (kŭt′ŭp′) *n. Informal.* A mischievous person.

cut•wa•ter (kŭt′wô′tər, -wŏt′ər) *n.* **1.** *Naut.* The forward part of a ship's prow. **2.** The wedge-shaped end of a bridge pier, designed to divide the current and break up ice floes.

cut•work (kŭt′wûrk′) *n.* Openwork embroidery in which the ground fabric is cut away from the design.

cut•worm (kŭt′wûrm′) *n.* The larva of various moths of the family Noctuidae that feed on and destroy many plants.

cu•vette (kyo͞o-vĕt′) *n.* A small, transparent, often tubular laboratory vessel. [Fr., dim. of *cuve*, tub < Lat. *cūpa*.]

Cu•vier (kyo͞o′vē-ā′, ko͞ov-yā′, kü-vyā′), Baron **Georges Léopold Chrétien Frédéric Dagobert.** 1769–1832. French naturalist considered the founder of comparative anatomy.

Cuy•a•ho•ga Falls (kī′ə-hō′gə, kə-hō′-, -hô′-, -hä′-). A city of NE OH, a suburb of Akron on the **Cuyahoga River**, c. 129 km (80 mi). Pop. 48,950.

Cuz•co also **Cus•co** (ko͞o′skō). A city of S Peru in the Andes ESE of Lima; built on the site of an ancient Incan city supposedly founded in the 11th cent. Pop. 89,563.

CV *abbr.* **1.** Cardiovascular. **2.** Curriculum vitae.

cv. *abbr.* Cultivar.

C.V. *abbr.* Cape Verde.

CVA *abbr.* Cerebrovascular accident.

cvt. *abbr.* Convertible.

cw or **CW** *abbr.* Continuous wave.

cw. *abbr.* Clockwise.

cwm (ko͞om) *n.* See **cirque.** [Welsh, valley.]

CWO *abbr.* Chief warrant officer.

c.w.o. *abbr.* Cash with order.

cwt. or **cwt** *abbr.* Hundredweight.

CY *abbr.* Calendar year.

–cy *suff.* **1.** State; condition; quality: *bankruptcy.* **2.** Rank; office: *baronetcy.* [ME *-cie* < OFr. *-cie, -tie* < Lat. *-cia, -tia* and Gk. *-kia, -keia, -tia, -teia.*]

cy•an (sī′ăn′, -ən) *n. Color.* A greenish blue, considered a primary color in printing and photography. [Gk. *kuanos*, dark blue.]

cyan– *pref.* Var. of **cyano–.**

cy•an•am•ide also **cy•an•am•id** (sī-ăn′ə-mĭd) *n.* **1.** A caustic acidic crystalline compound, NHCNH, prepared by treating calcium cyanamide with sulfuric acid. **2.** Calcium cyanamide.

cy•a•nate (sī′ə-nāt′, -nət) *n.* A salt or ester of cyanic acid.

cy•an•ic (sī-ăn′ĭk) *adj.* **1.** Relating to or containing cyanogen. **2.** *Color.* Of a blue or bluish hue.

cyanic acid *n.* A poisonous, unstable, highly volatile organic acid, HOCN, used to prepare cyanates.

cy•a•nide (sī′ə-nīd′) *n.* also **cy•a•nid** (-nĭd). Any of various salts or esters of hydrogen cyanide containing a CN group, esp. the extremely poisonous compounds potassium cyanide and sodium cyanide. — *tr.v.* **-nid•ed, -nid•ing, -nides. 1.** To treat (a metal surface) with cyanide to produce a hard surface. **2.** To treat (an ore) with cyanide to extract gold or silver.

cyanide process *n.* A process of extracting gold or silver from ores by treating them with a solution of sodium cyanide or calcium cyanide.

cy•a•nine (sī′ə-nēn′, -nĭn) *n.* Any of various blue dyes, used to sensitize photographic emulsions to a greater range of light.

cy•a•nite (sī′ə-nīt′) *n.* Var. of **kyanite.**

cyano– or **cyan–** *pref.* **1.** Blue: *cyanotype.* **2.a.** Cyanogen: *cyanic.* **b.** Cyanide: *cyanogenesis.* [Gk. *kuano-* < *kuanos*, dark blue.]

cy•a•no•ac•ry•late (sī′ə-nō-ăk′rə-lāt′, sī-ăn′ō-) *n.* A strongly adhesive substance that is used in industry and medicine.

cy•a•no•bac•te•ri•um (sī′ə-nō-băk-tîr′ē-əm, sī-ăn′ō-) *n.* A photosynthetic bacterium of the class Coccogoneae or Hormogoneae, generally blue-green in color.

cy•a•no•co•bal•a•min (sī′ə-nō′kō-băl′ə-mĭn, sī-ăn′ō-) *n.* See **vitamin B_{12}.**

cy•an•o•gen (sī-ăn′ə-jən) *n.* **1.** A colorless, flammable, pungent, highly poisonous gas, C_2N_2, used as a rocket propellant, insecticide, and chemical weapon. **2.** A univalent radical, CN.

cy•a•no•hy•drin (sī′ə-nō-hī′drĭn, sī-ăn′ō-) *n.* Any of several compounds that contain both the CN and OH radicals. [CYANO– + HYDR(O)– + –IN.]

cy•a•no•sis (sī′ə-nō′sĭs) *n.* A bluish discoloration of the skin and mucous membranes resulting from inadequate oxygenation of the blood. —**cy′a•not′ic** (-nŏt′ĭk) *adj.*

cy•an•o•type (sī-ăn′ə-tīp′) *n.* See **blueprint** 1.

Cyb•e•le (sĭb′ə-lē) *n. Gk. Myth.* The Phrygian goddess of nature.

cy•ber•nate (sī′bər-nāt′) *tr.v.* **-nat•ed, -nat•ing, -nates.** To control (an industrial process) by computer. [CYBERN(ETICS) + -ATE[1].] —**cy′ber•na′tion** *n.*

cy•ber•net•ics (sī′bər-nĕt′ĭks) *n.* (*used with a sing. v.*) The theoretical study of communication and control processes in biological, mechanical, and electronic systems, esp. the comparison of these processes in biological and artificial systems. [< Gk. *kubernētēs*, governor < *kubernan*, to govern.] —**cy′ber•net′ic** *adj.* —**cy′ber•net′i•cal•ly** *adv.* —**cy′ber•net′i•cist, cy′ber•ne•ti′cian** (-nĭ-tĭsh′ən) *n.*

cy•ber•punk (sī′bər-pŭngk′) *n.* Fast-paced science fiction involving futuristic computer-based societies. [CYBER(NETICS) + PUNK.] —**cy′ber•punk′** *adj.*

cy•borg (sī′bôrg′) *n.* A human being who has certain physiological processes aided or controlled by mechanical or electronic devices. [CYB(ERNETIC) + ORG(ANISM).]

cy•cad (sī′kăd′, -kəd) *n.* Any of various palmlike gymnospermous cone-bearing evergreen plants of the division Cycadophyta, native to warm regions and having large pinnately compound leaves. [NLat. *Cycas, Cycad-*, genus name < Gk. *kukas*, erroneous reading of *koïkas*, accusative pl. of *koïx*, a kind of palm tree, perh. of Egypt. orig.]

cycl– *pref.* Var. of **cyclo–.**

Cyc•la•des (sĭk′lə-dēz′) also **Ki•klá•dhes** (kē-klä′*th*ĕs). A group of islands of SE Greece in the S Aegean Sea. The name was used in ancient times for the islands surrounding Delos.

cy•cla•mate (sī′klə-māt′, sĭk′lə-) *n.* A salt of cyclamic acid formerly used as an artificial sweetener, esp. sodium cyclamate or calcium cyclamate. [CYCLAM(IC ACID) + –ATE[2].]

cy•cla•men (sī′klə-mən, sĭk′lə-) *n.* Any of various plants of the genus *Cyclamen*, having decorative leaves and showy flowers with reflexed petals. [NLat., genus name < Lat. *cyclamīnos* < Gk. *kuklaminos*, prob. < *kuklos*, circle, wheel (perh. from its bulbous roots). See CYCLE.]

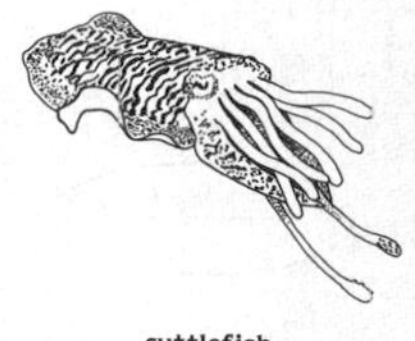

cuttlefish

cyc•la•mic acid (sĭk′lə-mĭk′, sī′klə-) *n.* A crystalline acid, $C_6H_{13}NO_3S$, used to produce cyclamates. [Short for *cycl(ohexylsulf)amic acid.*]

cy•clase (sī′klās′, -klāz′) *n.* An enzyme that acts as a catalyst in the cyclization of a compound. [CYCL(IC) + –ASE.]

cy•cle (sī′kəl) *n.* **1.** An interval of time during which a characteristic, often regularly repeated event or sequence of events occurs. **2.a.** A single complete execution of a periodically repeated phenomenon. **b.** A periodically repeated sequence of events. **3.** The orbit of a celestial body. **4.** A long period of time; an age. **5.a.** The aggregate of traditional poems or stories organized around a central theme or hero: *the Arthurian cycle.* **b.** A series of poems or songs on the same theme: *Schubert's song cycles.* **6.** A bicycle, motorcycle, or similar vehicle. **7.** *Bot.* A circular or whorled arrangement of flower parts. — *v.* **-cled, -cling, -cles.** — *intr.* **1.** To occur in or pass through a cycle. **2.** To move in or as if in a cycle. **3.** To ride a bicycle, motorcycle, or similar vehicle. — *tr.* To use in or put through a cycle. [ME < LLat. *cyclus* < Gk. *kuklos*, circle. See **k^{w}el-[1]*.**] —**cy′cler** *n.*

cy•clic (sī′klĭk, sĭk′lĭk) or **cy•cli•cal** (sī′klĭ-kəl, sĭk′lĭ-kəl) *adj.* **1.a.** Of, relating to, or characterized by cycles. **b.** Recurring or moving in cycles. **2.** *Chem.* Of or relating to compounds having atoms arranged in a ring or closed-chain structure. **3.** *Bot.* **a.** Having parts arranged in a whorl. **b.** Forming a whorl. —**cy′cli•cal′i•ty** (sĭk′lə-kăl′ĭ-tē, sī′klə-) *n.* —**cy′cli•cal•ly** *adv.*

cyclic AMP *n.* A cyclic nucleotide of adenosine that acts at the cellular level as a regulator of various metabolic processes.

cyclic GMP *n.* A cyclic nucleotide of guanosine thought to act at the cellular level as a regulator of various metabolic processes.

cy•clist (sī′klĭst) *n.* One who rides or races a bicycle, motorcycle, or similar vehicle.

cy•cli•za•tion (sī′klĭ-zā′shən, sĭk′lĭ-) *n.* The formation of one or more rings in a hydrocarbon.

cyclo– or **cycl–** *pref.* **1.** Circle; cycle: *cyclorama.* **2.** A cyclic compound: *cyclohexane.* [Gk. *kuklo-* < *kuklos*, circle. See **k^{w}el-[1]*.**]

cy•clo•al•kane (sī′klō-ăl′kān) *n.* An alicyclic hydrocarbon with a saturated ring.

cy•clo•hex•ane (sī′klō-hĕk′sān′) *n.* An extremely flammable, colorless mobile liquid, C_6H_{12}, obtained from petroleum and benzene and used in the manufacture of nylon and as a solvent.

cy•clo•hex•i•mide (sī′klō-hĕk′sə-mīd′, -mĭd) *n.* A colorless crystalline compound, $C_{15}H_{23}NO_4$, used as a fungicide.

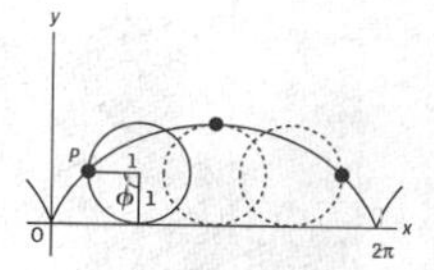

cycloid
Coordinates of *P*:
$x = \phi - \sin\phi$
$y = 1 - \cos\phi$

cy•cloid (sī′kloid′) *adj.* **1.** Resembling a circle. **2.** *Zool.* **a.** Thin, rounded, and smooth-edged; disklike. Used of fish scales. **b.** Having or composed of such scales. **3.** *Psychiat.* Afflicted with or relating to cyclothymia. — *n.* **1.** *Math.* The curve traced by a point on the circumference of a circle that rolls on a straight line. **2.** *Zool.* A cycloid fish. [Fr. *cycloïde* < Gk. *kukloeidēs*, circular : *kuklos*, circle; see **k^{w}el-[1]*** + *-oeidēs*, -oid.] —**cy•cloi′dal** (-kloid′l) *adj.*

cy•clom•e•ter (sī-klŏm′ĭ-tər) *n.* **1.** An instrument that records the revolutions of a wheel to indicate distance traveled. **2.** An instrument that measures circular arcs. —**cy′clo•met′ric** (-klə-mĕt′rĭk) *adj.* —**cy•clom′e•try** *n.*

cy•clone (sī′klōn′) *n.* **1.** *Meteorol.* An atmospheric system characterized by the rapid spiraling movement of air masses toward a low-pressure center, circulating counterclockwise in

ă pat	oi boy
ā pay	ou out
âr care	o͝o took
ä father	o͞o boot
ĕ pet	ŭ cut
ē be	ûr urge
ĭ pit	th thin
ī pie	*th* this
îr pier	hw which
ŏ pot	zh vision
ō toe	ə about, item
ô paw	

Stress marks:
′ (primary);
′ (secondary), as in **dictionary** (dĭk′shə-nĕr′ē)

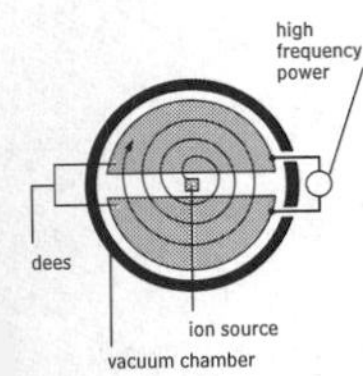

cyclotron

the Northern Hemisphere and clockwise in the Southern Hemisphere. **2.** A violent rotating windstorm. **3.** Any of various devices using centrifugal force to separate materials. [< Gk. *kuklōn*, pr.part. of *kukloun*, to rotate < *kuklos*, circle. See **kʷel-¹***.] **— cy•clon′ic** (-klŏn′ĭk), **cy•clon′i•cal** *adj.*

cyclone cellar *n.* An underground shelter in or adjacent to a house, used for protection from severe windstorms.

cy•clo•par•af•fin (sī′klō-păr′ə-fĭn) *n.* See **cycloalkane.**

cy•clo•pe•an (sī′klə-pē′ən, sī-klō′pē-) *adj.* **1.** Often **Cyclopean.** Relating to or suggestive of a Cyclops. **2.** Of or constituting a primitive style of masonry characterized by the use of massive stones of irregular shape and size.

cy•clo•pe•di•a also **cy•clo•pae•di•a** (sī′klə-pē′dē-ə) *n.* An encyclopedia. [Short for ENCYCLOPEDIA.] **— cy′clo•pe′dic** (-dĭk) *adj.* **— cy′clo•pe′dist** (-dĭst) *n.*

cy•clo•phos•pha•mide (sī′klə-fŏs′fə-mīd′) *n.* An immunosuppressive antineoplastic drug, $C_7H_{15}Cl_2N_2P$, used to treat Hodgkin's disease, lymphoma, and certain leukemias.

cy•clo•ple•gia (sī′klə-plē′jə) *n.* Paralysis of the ciliary muscles of the eye, resulting in the loss of visual accomodation.

cy•clo•pro•pane (sī′klə-prō′pān′) *n.* A highly flammable explosive colorless gas, C_3H_6, sometimes used as an anesthetic.

Cy•clops (sī′klŏps) *n., pl.* **Cy•clo•pes** (sī-klō′pēz). *Gk. Myth.* **1.** Any of the three one-eyed Titans who forged thunderbolts for Zeus. **2.** Any of a race of one-eyed giants, reputedly descended from these Titans, inhabiting Sicily. [Lat. < Gk. *Kuklōps* : *kuklos*, circle; see CYCLE + *ōps*, eye; see MYOPIA.]

cy•clo•ram•a (sī′klə-răm′ə, -rä′mə) *n.* **1.** A large composite picture placed on the walls of a cylindrical room so as to appear in natural perspective to a spectator standing in the center of the room. **2.** A large curtain or wall, usu. concave, at the rear of a stage. [CYCL(O)– + (PAN)ORAMA.]

cy•clo•sis (sī-klō′sĭs) *n., pl.* **-ses** (-sēz). The streaming rotary motion of protoplasm within a cell. [NLat. < Gk. *kuklōsis*, a surrounding < *kukloun*, to surround < *kuklos*, circle. See **kʷel-¹***.]

cy•clo•spor•ine (sī′klə-spôr′ēn, -ĭn, -spōr′-) also **cy•clo•spor•in** (-ĭn) *n.* An immunosuppressive drug obtained from certain soil fungi, used mainly to prevent the rejection of transplanted organs.

cy•clo•stome (sī′klə-stōm′) *n.* Any of various primitive eel-like vertebrates of the class Agnatha, lacking jaws and true teeth and with a circular, sucking mouth. [< NLat. *Cyclostomī* and *Cyclostomata*, class names : CYCLO– + Gk. *stoma, stomat-*, mouth.] **— cy•clos′to•mate′** (sī-klŏs′tə-māt′, -mĭt), **cy′clo•stom′a•tous** (sī′klə-stŏm′ə-təs, -stō′mə-) *adj.*

cy•clo•thy•mi•a (sī′klə-thī′mē-ə) *n. Psychiat.* A mild affective disorder characterized by alternating periods of elation and depression. **— cy′clo•thy′mic** (-mĭk) *adj. & n.*

cy•clo•tron (sī′klə-trŏn′) *n.* A circular particle accelerator in which charged subatomic particles generated at a central source are accelerated spirally outward in a plane perpendicular to a fixed magnetic field by an alternating electric field.

cy•der (sī′dər) *n. Chiefly British.* Var. of **cider.**

cyg•net (sĭg′nĭt) *n.* A young swan. [ME *cignet* < AN, dim. of OFr. *cygne*, swan < Lat. *cygnus* < Gk. *kuknos*.]

Cyg•nus (sĭg′nəs) *n.* A constellation in the Northern Hemisphere near Lacerta and Lyra. [Lat. *cygnus*, swan. See CYGNET.]

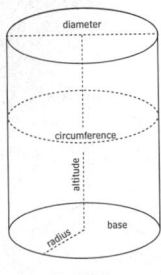

diameter
circumference
altitude
radius
base

cylinder

cyl•in•der (sĭl′ən-dər) *n.* **1.** *Math.* **a.** The surface generated by a straight line intersecting and moving along a closed plane curve, the directrix, while remaining parallel to a fixed straight line that is not on or parallel to the plane of the directrix. **b.** The portion of such a surface bounded by two parallel planes and the regions of the planes bounded by the surface. **c.** A solid bounded by two parallel planes and such a surface, esp. such a surface having a circle as its directrix. **2.** A cylindrical container or object. **3.** *Engineering.* **a.** The chamber in which a piston of a reciprocating engine moves. **b.** The chamber of a pump from which fluid is expelled by a piston. **4.** The rotating chamber of a revolver that holds the cartridges. **5.** Any of several rotating parts in a printing press, esp. one that carries the paper. **6.** *Archaeol.* A cylindrical stone or clay object with an engraved design or inscription. [Lat. *cylindrus* < Gk. *kulindros* < *kulindein*, to roll.]

cylinder head *n.* The closed, often detachable end of a cylinder in an internal-combustion engine.

cy•lin•dri•cal (sə-lĭn′drĭ-kəl) also **cy•lin•dric** (-drĭk) *adj.* **1.** Of or having the shape of a cylinder, esp. of a circular one. **2.** *Math.* Of or relating to the coordinate system formed by two polar coordinates in a plane and a rectangular coordinate measured from the plane. **— cy•lin′dri•cal′i•ty** (-kăl′ĭ-tē) *n.* **— cy•lin′dri•cal•ly** *adv.*

cyl•in•droid (sĭl′ən-droid′) *n. Math.* A cylindrical surface or solid all of whose sections perpendicular to the elements are elliptical. *— adj.* Resembling a cylinder.

cy•ma (sī′mə) *n.* A molding having a partly concave and partly convex curve in profile, used esp. in classical architecture. [Gk. *kuma*, wave, cyma < *kuein*, to swell. See **keuə-***.]

cy•ma•tium (sī-mā′shəm, -shē-əm) *n., pl.* **-tia** (-shə, -shē-ə). *Archit.* **1.** See **cyma. 2.** The upper molding of a classical cornice. [Lat. < Gk. *kumation*, dim. of *kuma*, cyma. See CYMA.]

cymbal
Pair of cymbals

cym•bal (sĭm′bəl) *n. Mus.* A percussion instrument consisting of a concave brass plate that makes a loud clashing tone when hit with a drumstick or when used in pairs. [ME < OE and < OFr. *cymbale*, both < Lat. *cymbalum* < Gk. *kumbalon* < *kumbē*, bowl.] **— cym′bal•eer′** (sĭm′bə-lîr′), **cym′bal•er, cym′bal•ist** *n.*

cym•bid•i•um (sĭm-bĭd′ē-əm) *n.* Any of various epiphytic orchids of the genus *Cymbidium,* native to tropical Asia and Australia and having elongate clusters of showy blooms. [NLat. *Cymbidium*, genus name < Lat. *cymba*, boat < Gk. *kumbē*.]

cyme (sīm) *n. Bot.* A usu. flat-topped or convex flower cluster in which the main axis and each branch end in a flower. [Lat. *cȳma*, young cabbage sprout < Gk. *kuma*. See CYMA.] **— cy•mif′er•ous** (sī-mĭf′ər-əs) *adj.*

cy•mene (sī′mēn′) *n.* Any of three isomeric liquid hydrocarbons, $C_{10}H_{14}$, obtained chiefly from the essential oils of cumin and thyme and used to manufacture synthetic resins. [Fr. *cymène* < Gk. *kuminon*, cumin, prob. of Semitic orig.]

cym•ling (sĭm′lĭng) also **cym•lin** (-lĭn) *n.* A greenish-white, flat round squash with a scalloped edge. [Alteration of SIMNEL.]

cy•mo•gene (sī′mə-jēn′) *n.* A flammable gaseous fraction of petroleum, consisting chiefly of butane. [CYM(ENE) + -GENE.]

cy•moid (sī′moid′) *adj.* **1.** *Archit.* Resembling a cyma. **2.** *Bot.* Resembling a cyme.

cy•mo•phane (sī′mə-fān′) *n.* An opalescent variety of chrysoberyl having a shimmering luster. [Fr. : Gk. *kuma*, wave, cyma; see CYMA + Gk. *-phanēs*, appearing; see -PHANE.]

cy•mose (sī′mōs′) also **cy•mous** (-məs) *adj.* **1.** Relating to or resembling a cyme; determinate. **2.** Bearing a cyme or cymes. [CYM(E) + -OSE¹.] **— cy′mose′ly** *adv.*

Cym•ric (kĭm′rĭk, sĭm′-) *adj.* Of or relating to the Cymry. *— n.* See **Welsh** 2.

Cym•ry (kĭm′rē, sĭm′-) *n. (used with a pl. v.)* **1.** The Brythonic Celts of Wales, Cornwall, and Brittany. **2.** The Welsh. [Welsh, pl. of *Cymro*, the Welsh people, Wales < British Celt. **kombrogos*, fellow countryman. See **merg-***.]

Cyn•e•wulf (kĭn′ə-wo͝olf′) or **Cyn•wulf** (kĭn′wo͝olf′). fl. c. 900. Anglo-Saxon poet whose works include *Juliana.*

cyn•ic (sĭn′ĭk) *n.* **1.** A person who believes all people are motivated by selfishness. **2. Cynic.** A member of a sect of ancient Greek philosophers who believed virtue to be the only good and self-control to be the only means of achieving virtue. *— adj.* **1.** Cynical. **2. Cynic.** Of or relating to the Cynics or their beliefs. [Lat. *cynicus*, Cynic philosopher < Gk. *kunikos* < *kuōn, kun-*, dog. See **kwon-***.]

Word History: A cynic may be pardoned for thinking that this is a dog's life. The Greek word *kunikos*, from which *cynic* comes, was originally an adjective meaning "doglike," from *kuōn*, "dog." The word was most likely applied to the Cynic philosophers because of the nickname *kuōn* given to Diogenes of Sinope, the prototypical Cynic. He is said to have barked in public and urinated on the leg of a table. The first use of the word recorded in English, in a work published from 1547 to 1564, is in the plural for members of this philosophical sect.

cyn•i•cal (sĭn′ĭ-kəl) *adj.* **1.** Scornful of the motives, virtue, or integrity of others. **2.** Expressing or exhibiting scorn and bitter mockery. **— cyn′i•cal•ly** *adv.* **— cyn′i•cal•ness** *n.*

cyn•i•cism (sĭn′ĭ-sĭz′əm) *n.* **1.** A cynical attitude or quality. **2.** A cynical comment or act. **3. Cynicism.** The beliefs of the ancient Cynics.

cy•no•sure (sī′nə-sho͝or′, sĭn′ə-) *n.* **1.** An object that serves as a focal point of attention and admiration. **2.** Something that serves to guide. [Fr., Ursa Minor (which contains the guiding star Polaris) < Lat. *cynosūra* < Gk. *kunosoura*, dog's tail, Ursa Minor : *kuōn, kun-*, dog; see **kwon-*** + *oura*, tail; see **ors-***.] **— cy′no•sur′al** *adj.*

CYO *abbr.* Catholic Youth Organization.

cy•pher (sī′fər) *n. & v.* Var. of **cipher.**

cy pres (sē′ prā′) *n.* The legal doctrine that allows a court freedom in interpreting the terms of a will or gift if carrying out the terms literally would be impracticable or illegal and as long as the general intent of the testator or donor is observed. [ME < AN : *cy*, thus + *pres*, nearly.]

cy•press (sī′prĭs) *n.* **1.a.** Any of various Eurasian and North American evergreen trees or shrubs of the genus *Cupressus,* having scalelike leaves and globose woody cones. **b.** Any of several similar or related coniferous trees. **c.** The wood of any of these trees. **2.** Cypress branches used as a symbol of mourning. [ME *cipres* < OFr. < LLat. *cypressus*, prob. blend of Lat. *cupressus* and *cyparissus* (< Gk. *kuparissos*).]

cypress

Cy•press (sī′prĭs). A city of S CA, a suburb of Long Beach. Pop. 42,655.

cypress vine *n.* An annual twining tropical American vine *(Ipomoea quamoclit)* having pinnately cut leaves and showy, usu. scarlet flowers.

Cyp•ri•an (sĭp′rē-ən) *adj.* **1.** Of or relating to Cyprus; Cypriot. **2.a.** Of or relating to the ancient worship of Aphrodite on Cyprus. **b.** Licentious; wanton. *— n.* **1.** See **Cypriot** 1. **2.** Also **cyprian. a.** A wanton person. **b.** A prostitute.

Cyprian, Saint. d. A.D. 258. Christian prelate and martyr in North Africa.

cyp•ri•nid (sĭp′rə-nĭd) *n.* Any of the freshwater fishes of the family Cyprinidae, which includes the minnows, carps, and shiners. [< NLat. *Cyprinidae*, family name < *Cyprīnus*, type genus < Lat. *cyprīnus*, carp < Gk. *kuprinos*.] —**cyp′ri•nid** *adj.*

cy•prin•o•dont (sĭ-prĭn′ə-dŏnt′, -prī′nə-) *n.* Any of various small soft-finned fishes of the family Cyprinodontidae, which includes the killifishes and topminnows. [Lat. *cyprīnus*, carp (< Gk. *kuprinos*) + -ODONT.] —**cy•prin′o•dont′** *adj.*

cyp•ri•noid (sĭp′rə-noid′, sĭ-prī′-) *adj.* Of, relating to, or resembling a carp or other cyprinid fish. —*n.* A cyprinoid fish. [< NLat. *Cyprīnoidēa*, suborder name < *Cyprīnus*, type genus. See CYPRINID.]

Cyp•ri•ot (sĭp′rē-ət, -ŏt′) also **Cyp•ri•ote** (-ōt′, -ət) —*n.* **1.** A native or inhabitant of Cyprus. **2.** The ancient or modern Greek dialect of Cyprus. —*adj.* Of or relating to Cyprus or its people or culture. [Fr. *cypriote* < Gk. *Kupriōtēs* < *Kupros*, Cyprus.]

cyp•ri•pe•di•um (sĭp′rĭ-pē′dē-əm) *n.* Any of various orchids of the genus *Cypripedium,* such as the lady's slipper. [NLat. *Cypripedium*, genus name : LLat. *Cypris*, Venus (< Gk. *Kupris*, Aphrodite < *Kupros*, Cyprus, legendary birthplace of Aphrodite) + NLat. *-pedium* (alteration of Gk. *pedilon*, sandal; see **ped-***).]

Cy•prus (sī′prəs). An island country in the E Mediterranean Sea S of Turkey; site of an ancient Neolithic culture and settled by Phoenicians c. 800 B.C. It achieved independence from Great Britain in 1960. Cap. Nicosia. Pop. 642,731.

cyp•se•la (sĭp′sə-lə) *n., pl.* **-lae** (-lē′). An achene fruit derived from an inferior ovary, characteristic of plants in the composite family. [NLat. < Gk. *kupselē*, hollow vessel.]

Cy•ra•no de Ber•ge•rac (sîr′ə-nō də bûr′zhə-răk′, bĕr′-), **Savinien de.** 1619–55. French satirist and duelist whose works include the drama *The Pedant Imitated* (1654).

Cyr•e•na•ic (sîr′ə-nā′ĭk, sī′rə-) *adj.* **1.** Of or relating to Cyrenaica or Cyrene. **2.** Of or advocating the doctrines of Aristippus of Cyrene, who argued that pleasure is the only good in life. —**Cyr′e•na′ic** *n.*

Cyr•e•na•i•ca (sîr′ə-nā′ĭ-kə, sī′rə-). An ancient region of NE Libya bordering on the Mediterranean Sea; colonized by Greeks in the 7th cent. B.C.

Cy•re•ne (sī-rē′nē). An ancient Greek city of Cyrenaica; founded c. 630 B.C. and noted as an intellectual center.

Cyr•il (sîr′əl), Saint. 827–869. Christian missionary and theologian who with his brother St. Methodius (826–885) worked in Moravia, translating the Scriptures into Old Church Slavonic.

Cy•ril•lic (sə-rĭl′ĭk) *adj.* Of, relating to, or being any of the alphabets based on Glagolitic and used for certain Slavic languages, such as Russian.

Cy•rus (sī′rəs). "the Younger." 424?–401 B.C. Persian prince who led a mammoth force of Greeks against his brother Artaxerxes II. The retreat that followed his defeat and death are described in Xenophon's *Anabasis.*

Cyrus II. "Cyrus the Great." 600?–529? B.C. King of Persia (550–529) and founder of the Persian Empire.

cyst (sĭst) *n.* **1.** *Pathol.* An abnormal membranous sac containing a gaseous, liquid, or semisolid substance. **2.** *Anat.* A sac or vesicle in the body. **3.** *Biol.* A small capsulelike sac that encloses certain organisms in their dormant or larval stage. **4.** *Bot.* A thick-walled resting spore, as in certain algae or fungi. [NLat. *cystis* < Gk. *kustis*, bladder. See **kwes-***.]

cyst– *pref.* Var. of **cysto–.**

cys•tec•to•my (sĭ-stĕk′tə-mē) *n., pl.* **-mies. 1.** Surgical removal of a cyst. **2.a.** Surgical removal of the gallbladder. **b.** Surgical removal of all or part of the urinary bladder.

cys•te•ine (sĭs′tə-ēn′, -ĭn, -tē-) *n.* An amino acid, $C_3H_7O_2NS$, derived from cystine and found in most proteins. [CYST(INE) + -EIN.]

cys•tic (sĭs′tĭk) *adj.* **1.** Of, relating to, or having the characteristic of a cyst. **2.** Having or containing cysts or a cyst. **3.** Enclosed in a cyst. **4.** *Anat.* Of, relating to, or involving the gallbladder or urinary bladder.

cystic duct *n.* The duct that conveys bile from the gallbladder to the common bile duct.

cys•ti•cer•coid (sĭs′tĭ-sûr′koid) *n.* The larval stage of certain tapeworms, resembling a cysticercus but having the scolex completely filling the enclosing cyst. [CYSTICERC(US) + -OID.]

cys•ti•cer•co•sis (sĭs′tĭ-sər-kō′sĭs) *n.* The condition of being infested with cysticerci. [CYSTICERC(US) + -OSIS.]

cys•ti•cer•cus (sĭs′tĭ-sûr′kəs) *n., pl.* **-ci** (-sī′). The larval stage of many tapeworms, consisting of a single invaginated scolex enclosed in a fluid-filled cyst. [NLat. : Gk. *kustis*, cyst; see CYST + Gk. *kerkos*, tail.]

cystic fibrosis *n.* A hereditary disease of the exocrine glands, affecting mainly the pancreas, respiratory system, and sweat glands and characterized by the production of abnormally viscous mucus, usu. resulting in chronic respiratory infections and impaired pancreatic function.

cys•tine (sĭs′tēn′) *n.* A white crystalline amino acid, $C_6H_{12}N_2O_4S_2$, found in many proteins, esp. keratin. [From its discovery in bladder stones.]

cys•ti•tis (sĭ-stī′tĭs) *n.* Inflammation of the urinary bladder.

cysto– or **cyst–** *pref.* Bladder; cyst; sac: *cystocele.* [< NLat. *cystis*, bladder < Gk. *kustis*. See **kwes-***.]

cys•to•cele (sĭs′tə-sēl′) *n.* Herniation of the urinary bladder through the wall of the vagina.

cys•toid (sĭs′toid′) *adj.* Formed like or resembling a cyst. —*n.* A cystoid structure.

cys•to•lith (sĭs′tə-lĭth′) *n.* **1.** *Bot.* A mineral concretion, usu. of calcium carbonate, occurring in the epidermal cells of certain plants, such as figs. **2.** See **urinary calculus.**

cys•to•scope (sĭs′tə-skōp′) *n.* A tubular instrument used to examine the interior of the urinary bladder and ureter. —**cys′to•scop′ic** (-skŏp′ĭk) *adj.* —**cys•tos′co•py** (sĭ-stŏs′kə-pē) *n.*

cys•tos•to•my (sĭ-stŏs′tə-mē) *n., pl.* **-mies.** The surgical formation of an opening into the urinary bladder.

cyt– *pref.* Var. of **cyto–.**

–cyte *suff.* Cell: *leukocyte.* [NLat. *-cyta* < Gk. *kutos*, hollow vessel. See **(s)keu-***.]

Cy•the•ra (sĭ-thîr′ə, sĭth′ər-ə) also **Kí•thi•ra** (kē′thē-rä′). An island of S Greece in the Mediterranean Sea S of the Peloponnesus; chief center for the worship of Aphrodite.

Cyth•e•re•a (sĭth′ə-rē′ə) *n. Gk. Myth.* See **Aphrodite.**

cy•ti•dine (sī′tĭ-dēn′) *n.* A nucleoside, $C_9H_{13}N_3O_5$, composed of cytosine and ribose. [CYT(O)- + -ID(E) + -INE[2].]

cyto– or **cyt–** *pref.* Cell: *cytoplasm.* [< Gk. *kutos*, hollow vessel. See **(s)keu-***.]

cy•to•chem•is•try (sī′tō-kĕm′ĭ-strē) *n.* The branch of biochemistry that studies the chemical composition and activity of cells. —**cy′to•chem′i•cal** (-kĕm′ĭ-kəl) *adj.*

cy•to•chrome (sī′tə-krōm′) *n.* Any of a class of iron-containing proteins important in cell respiration as catalysts of oxidation-reduction reactions.

cy•to•gen•e•sis (sī′tō-jĕn′ĭ-sĭs) *n.* The formation, development, and variation of cells.

cy•to•ge•net•ics (sī′tō-jə-nĕt′ĭks) *n.* (*used with a sing. v.*) The branch of biology that deals with heredity and the cellular components associated with heredity. —**cy′to•ge•net′ic, cy′to•ge•net′i•cal** *adj.* —**cy′to•ge•net′i•cal•ly** *adv.* —**cy′to•ge•net′i•cist** (-sĭst) *n.*

cy•tog•e•ny (sī-tŏj′ə-nē) *n.* See **cytogenesis.**

cy•to•ki•ne•sis (sī′tō-kĭ-nē′sĭs, -kī-) *n.* The division of the cytoplasm of a cell following the division of the nucleus. —**cy′to•ki•net′ic** (-nĕt′ĭk) *adj.*

cy•to•ki•nin (sī′tə-kī′nĭn) *n.* Any of a class of plant hormones that promote cell division and growth and delay the senescence of leaves.

cy•tol•o•gy (sī-tŏl′ə-jē) *n.* The branch of biology that deals with cell formation, structure, and function. —**cy′to•log′ic** (-tə-lŏj′ĭk), **cy′to•log′i•cal** *adj.* —**cy•tol′o•gist** *n.*

cy•tol•y•sin (sī-tŏl′ĭ-sĭn) *n.* A substance, such as an antibody, capable of dissolving or destroying cells. [CYTOLYS(IS) + -IN.]

cy•tol•y•sis (sī-tŏl′ĭ-sĭs) *n.* The dissolution or destruction of a cell. —**cy′to•lyt′ic** (sī′tə-lĭt′ĭk) *adj.*

cy•to•me•gal•ic (sī′tō-mĭ-găl′ĭk) *adj.* Of, relating to, or characterized by greatly enlarged cells.

cy•to•meg•a•lo•vi•rus (sī′tə-mĕg′ə-lō-vī′rəs) *n.* Any of a group of herpes viruses that attack and enlarge epithelial cells.

cy•to•mem•brane (sī′tə-mĕm′brān) *n.* See **cell membrane.**

cy•to•path•ic (sī′tə-păth′ĭk) *adj.* Of or relating to degeneration or disease of cells.

cy•to•path•o•gen•ic (sī′tə-păth′ə-jĕn′ĭk) *adj.* Of, relating to, or producing pathological changes in cells. —**cy′to•path′o•ge•nic′i•ty** (-jə-nĭs′ĭ-tē) *n.*

cy•to•phil•ic (sī′tə-fĭl′ĭk) *adj.* Having an affinity for cells.

cy•to•pho•tom•e•ter (sī′tō-fō-tŏm′ĭ-tər) *n.* An instrument used to identify and locate the chemical compounds within a cell by measuring the intensity of light passing through stained sections of the cytoplasm. —**cy′to•pho′to•met′ric** (-tə-mĕt′rĭk) *adj.* —**cy′to•pho′to•met′ri•cal•ly** *adv.* —**cy′to•pho•tom′e•try** *n.*

cy•to•plasm (sī′tə-plăz′əm) *n.* The protoplasm outside the nucleus of a cell. —**cy′to•plas′mic** (-plăz′mĭk) *adj.* —**cy′to•plas′mi•cal•ly** *adv.*

cy•to•plast (sī′tə-plăst′) *n.* The intact cytoplasm of a single cell. —**cy′to•plas′tic** (-plăs′tĭk) *adj.*

cy•to•sine (sī′tə-sēn′) *n.* A pyrimidine base, $C_4H_5N_3O$, that is an essential constituent of RNA and DNA. [CYT(O)- + (RIB)OS(E) + -INE[2].]

cy•to•skel•e•ton (sī′tə-skĕl′ĭ-tn) *n.* The internal framework of a cell, composed largely of actin filaments and microtubules.

cy•to•sol (sī′tə-sôl′, -sŏl′) *n.* The fluid component of cytoplasm, excluding organelles and the insoluble, usu. suspended cytoplasmic components. [CYTO- + SOL(UTION).]

cy•to•sta•sis (sī′tə-stā′sĭs, -stăs′ĭs) *n.* Arrest of cellular growth and multiplication.

cy•to•sta•tic (sī′tə-stăt′ĭk) *adj.* Inhibiting or suppressing cellular growth and multiplication. —*n.* A cytostatic agent. —**cy′to•stat′i•cal•ly** *adv.*

cy•to•tax•on•o•my (sī′tō-tăk-sŏn′ə-mē) *n.* The classification of organisms based on cellular structure and function,

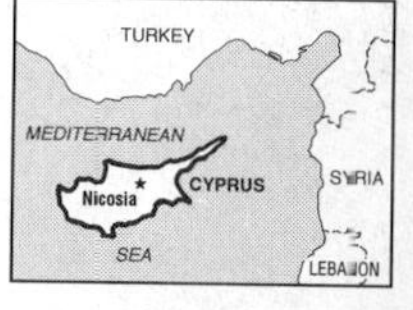

Cyprus

FORMS	SOUND
А а	a
Б б	b
В в	v
Г г	g
Д д	d
Е е Ё ё	e, ë
Ж ж	zh
З з	z
И и Й й	i, ĭ
К к	k
Л л	l
М м	m
Н н	n
О о	o
П п	p
Р р	r
С с	s
Т т	t
У у	u
Ф ф	f
Х х	kh
Ц ц	ts
Ч ч	ch
Ш ш	sh
Щ щ	shch
Ъ ъ	"
Ы ы	y
Ь ь	'
Э э	e
Ю ю	yu
Я я	ya

Cyrillic

ă pat	oi boy
ā pay	ou out
âr care	o͝o to͝ok
ä father	o͞o bo͞ot
ĕ pet	ŭ cut
ē be	ûr urge
ĭ pit	th thin
ī pie	*th* this
îr pier	hw which
ŏ pot	zh vision
ō toe	ə about,
ô paw	item

Stress marks:
′ (primary);
′ (secondary), as in
dictionary (dĭk′shə-nĕr′ē)

esp. on the structure and number of chromosomes. —**cy′to·tax′o·nom′ic** (-tăk′sə-nŏm′ĭk) *adj.* —**cy′to·tax·on′o·mist** *n.*

cy·to·tech·nol·o·gist (sī′tə-tĕk-nŏl′ə-jĭst) *n.* A technician trained in medical examination and identification of cellular abnormalities. —**cy′to·tech·nol′o·gy** *n.*

cy·to·tox·ic (sī′tə-tŏk′sĭk) *adj.* Of, relating to, or producing a toxic effect on cells. —**cy′to·tox·ic′i·ty** (-tŏk-sĭs′ĭ-tē) *n.*

cytotoxic T cell *n.* See **killer cell.**

cy·to·tox·in (sī′tə-tŏk′sĭn) *n.* A substance having a specific toxic effect on certain cells.

CZ or **C.Z.** *abbr.* Canal Zone.

czar (zär, tsär) *n.* **1.** Also **tsar** or **tzar** (zär, tsär). A male monarch or emperor, esp. one of the emperors who ruled Russia before the revolution of 1917. **2.** A person having great power; an autocrat. **3.** *Informal.* An appointed official having special powers to regulate or supervise an activity. [Russ. *tsar′* < ORuss. *tsĭsarĭ*, emperor, king < Old Church Slavonic *tsěsarĭ* < Goth. *kaisar* < Gk. < Lat. *Caesar*, emperor. See CAESAR.] —**czar′dom** *n.*

Usage Note: The word *czar* can also be spelled *tsar*. *Czar* is the most common form in American usage and virtually the only one employed in the extended senses "any tyrant" or informally, "one in authority." But *tsar* more accurately transliterates the Russian and appears more often in scholarly writing with reference to one of the Russian emperors.

czar·das (chär′däsh′) *n.* **1.** An intricate Hungarian dance characterized by variations in tempo. **2.** Music for this dance. [Hung. *csárdás* < *csárda*, wayside tavern < Serbo-Croatian *čardāk*, watchtower < Turk. *çardak*, hut, trellis < Pers. *chār ṭāq* < *chahār ṭāq*, four-cornered vault : *chahār*, four (< OIran. *cathwārō*; see **kʷetwer-***) + *ṭāq*, vault.]

czar·e·vitch (zär′ə-vĭch′, tsär′-) *n.* The eldest son of a Russian czar. [Russ. *tsarevich* : *tsar′*, czar; see CZAR + *-evich*, masc. patronymic suff.]

cza·rev·na (zä-rĕv′nə, tsä-) *n.* **1.** The daughter of a Russian czar. **2.** The wife of a czarevitch. [Russ. *tsarevna* : *tsar′*, czar; see CZAR + *-evna*, fem. patronymic suff.]

cza·ri·na (zä-rē′nə, tsä-) *n.* The wife of a Russian czar. [Alteration (perh. influenced by Lat. *rēgīna*, queen) of Russ. *tsaritsa* : *tsar′*, czar; see CZAR + *-itza*, fem. suff.]

czar·ism (zär′ĭz′əm, tsär′-) *n.* The system of government in Russia under the czars. —**czar′ist** *adj. & n.*

cza·rit·za (zä-rĭt′sə, tsä-rēt′-) *n.* An empress of Russia. [Russ. *tsaritsa* : *tsar′*, czar; see CZAR + *-itza*, fem. suff.]

Czech (chĕk) *n.* **1.** A native or inhabitant of Czech Republic or of Czechoslovakia. **2.** The Slavic language of the Czechs. [Pol. < Czech *Čech.*] —**Czech** *adj.*

Czech·o·slo·va·ki·a (chĕk′ə-slə-vä′kē-ə, -ō-slō-). A former country of central Europe; formed in 1918 and divided in Jan. 1993 into Czech Republic and Slovakia. —**Czech′o·slo′vak, Czech′o·slo·va′ki·an** *adj. & n.*

Czech Republic. A country of central Europe; part of Czechoslovakia until Jan. 1993. Cap. Prague. Pop. 10,291,927.

Czer·ny (chĕr′nē), **Karl.** 1791–1857. Austrian pianist and composer whose works include *School of the Left Hand.*

Czę·sto·cho·wa (chĕn′stə-kō′və, chĕɴ′stô-hô′vä). A city of S Poland N of Katowice. Pop. 246,600.

Dd

d[1] or **D** (dē) *n., pl.* **d's** or **D's. 1.** The fourth letter of the modern English alphabet. **2.** Any of the speech sounds represented by the letter *d.* **3.** The fourth in a series. **4.** *Mus.* **a.** The second tone in the scale of C major or the fourth tone in the relative minor scale. **b.** A key or scale in which D is the tonic. **5. D.** The lowest passing grade given to a student in a school or college. **6.** Something shaped like the letter D.

d[2] *abbr.* **1.** Day. **2.** Deuteron. **3.** *Phys.* Down quark.

dachshund
Shorthaired dachshund

D[1] **1.** The symbol for the isotope deuterium. **2.** Also **d.** The symbol for the Roman numeral 500.

D[2] also **D.** *abbr.* Democrat; democratic.

d. *abbr.* **1.** Dam (zoology). **2.** Date. **3.** Daughter. **4.** Also **D.** Deputy. **5.** Died. **6.** Also **D.** Dose. **7.** Also **D.** Drachma. **8.** *Chiefly British.* Penny (1/12 of a shilling).

D. *abbr.* **1.** Department. **2.** Diopter. **3.** Doctor (in academic degrees). **4.** Don (title). **5.** Duchess. **6.** Duke.

'd 1. Had. **2.** Would; should. **3.** Did.

DA[1] (dē′ā′) *n.* See **ducktail.** [Abbreviation of *duck's ass.*]

DA[2] *abbr.* **1.** Delayed action. **2.** Deposit account.

Da. *abbr.* Danish.

D.A. *abbr.* **1.** Also **DA.** *Law.* District attorney. **2.** Doctor of Arts.

dab[1] (dăb) *v.* **dabbed, dab·bing, dabs.** —*tr.* **1.** To apply with short poking strokes: *dabbed paint on the spot.* **2.** To cover lightly with or as if with a moist substance. **3.** To strike or hit lightly. —*intr.* To tap gently; pat. —*n.* **1.** A small amount: *a dab of jelly.* **2.** A quick light pat. [ME *dabben*, to strike.]

dab[2] (dăb) *n.* Any of various flatfishes, chiefly of the genera *Limanda* and *Hippoglossoides.* [ME *dabbe.*]

dab[3] (dăb) *n. Chiefly British.* A dab hand. [?]

dab·ber (dăb′ər) *n.* A cushioned pad used by printers and engravers to apply ink.

dab·ble (dăb′əl) *v.* **-bled, -bling, -bles.** —*tr.* To splash or spatter with or as if with a liquid. —*intr.* **1.** To splash liquid gently and playfully. **2.** To undertake something without serious intent. **3.** To bob forward and under in shallow water to feed off the bottom. [Poss. < Du. *dabbelen*, freq. of *dabben*, to strike, tap.]

dab·bler (dăb′lər) *n.* One who engages in an activity superficially or without serious intent.

dab·bling duck (dăb′lĭng) *n.* Any of various ducks, chiefly of the genus *Anas,* including the mallards and teals, that feed by dabbling in shallow water.

dab·chick (dăb′chĭk′) *n.* Any of various small grebes of the genus *Podiceps.* [Alteration of *dobchick* : ME *doppe*, diving bird (< OE *-doppe*; see DIDAPPER) + CHICK.]

dab hand *n.* A person skilled in a particular activity.

Dą·bro·wa Gór·ni·cza (dôm-brô′və gŏŏr-nē′chə). A city of S Poland NE of Katowice. Pop. 136,800.

da ca·po (dä kä′pō) *adv. Mus.* From the beginning. [Ital. : *da*, from + *capo*, head.]

Dac·ca also **Dha·ka** (dăk′ə, dä′kə). The cap. of Bangladesh, in the E-central part; under British rule 1765–1947. Pop. 1,850,000.

dace (dās) *n., pl.* **dace** or **dac·es.** Any of various small freshwater fishes of the family Cyprinidae, which also includes carps and minnows. [ME *dace, darce* < OFr. *dars* < LLat. *darsus*, poss. of Celt. orig.]

da·cha (dä′chə) *n.* A Russian country house or villa. [Russ., gift, land, country house. See **dō-***.]

Da·chau (dä′kou′, -ᴋʜou′). A city of SE Germany NNW of Munich; site of a Nazi concentration camp. Pop. 33,141.

dachs·hund (däks′hŏŏnt′, dăk′sənt) *n.* A small dog of a breed developed in Germany, having a long body, a usu. shorthaired dark coat, and very short legs. [Ger. : *Dachs*, badger (< MHGer. *dahs* < OHGer.; see **teks-***) + *Hund*, dog (< MHGer. *hunt* < OHGer.; see **kwon-***.]

Da·ci·a (dā′shē-ə, -shə). An ancient region and Roman province corresponding roughly to present-day Romania; abandoned to the Goths after A.D. 270. —**Da′ci·an** *adj. & n.*

da·coit also **da·koit** (də-koit′) *n.* **1.** A member of the robber bands of India and Burma who lived in the hills and attacked in armed gangs. **2.** A member of a robber gang in modern India and Burma. [Hindi *ḍakait.*]

da·coit·y (də-koi′tē) *n.* Robbery by a band or gang of dacoits. [Hindi *ḍakaitī* < *ḍakait*, dacoit.]

dac·quoise (dă-kwŏz′) *n.* A cake made of meringue layers with fruit or cream fillings between the layers. [Fr. < fem. of *dacquois*, of Dax, a town of SW France.]

Da·cron (dā′krŏn′, dăk′rŏn′). A trademark used for a synthetic polyester fabric or the fiber from which it is made.

dac·tyl (dăk′təl) *n.* **1.** A metrical foot consisting of one accented syllable followed by two unaccented or of one long syllable followed by two short, as in *flattery.* **2.** A finger, toe, or similar part or structure; a digit. [ME *dactil* < Lat. *dactylus* < Gk. *daktulos*, finger, dactyl.] —**dac·tyl′ic** (-tĭl′ĭk) *adj. & n.* —**dac·tyl′i·cal·ly** *adv.*

dactylo– or **dactyl–** *pref.* Finger; toe; digit: *dactylogram.* [< Gk. *daktulos*, finger.]

dac·tyl·o·gram (dăk-tĭl′ə-grăm′) *n.* A fingerprint.

dac·ty·log·ra·phy (dăk′tə-lŏg′rə-fē) *n.* The study of fingerprints as a method of identification. —**dac′ty·lo·graph′ic** (-lō-grăf′ĭk) *adj.*

dac·ty·lol·o·gy (dăk′tə-lŏl′ə-jē) *n.* The use of the fingers to communicate, as in the manual alphabet.

dad (dăd) *n. Informal.* A father. [Prob. of baby-talk orig.]

Da·da or **da·da** (dä′dä) *n.* A European artistic and literary movement (1916–1923) that flouted conventional values by producing works marked by nonsense and travesty. [Fr. *dada*, hobbyhorse, Dada, of baby-talk orig.] —**Da′da·ism** *n.* —**Da′da·ist** *adj. & n.* —**Da′da·is′tic** *adj.*

dad·dy (dăd′ē) *n., pl.* **-dies.** *Informal.* A father. —**dad′dy·ish** *adj.*

daddy long•legs (lông′lĕgz′, lŏng′-) *n., pl.* **daddy longlegs.** **1.** Any of various arachnids of the order Phalangida, with a small rounded body and long slender legs. **2.** See **crane fly.**

dad•gum (dăd′gŭm′) *adj. Chiefly Southern U.S.* Used as an intensive to express mild annoyance. See Regional Note at **damned.** [Alteration of GODDAMN.]

da•do (dā′dō) *n., pl.* **-does. 1.** *Archit.* The section of a pedestal between base and surbase. **2.** The lower portion of the wall of a room, decorated differently from the upper section. **3.a.** A rectangular groove cut into a board so that a like piece may be fitted into it. **b.** The board so cut. — *tr.v.* **-doed, -do•ing, -does. 1.** To furnish with a dado. **2.** To cut a dado in. [Ital. < Lat. *datum,* neut. p.part. of *dare,* to give. See **dō-*.**]

dae•dal (dēd′l) *adj.* **1.** Intricate in design or function. **2.** Finely or skillfully made or employed; artistic. [Lat. *daedalus* < Gk. *daidalos.*]

Dae•da•lus (dĕd′l-əs) *n. Gk. Myth.* A legendary artist and inventor, builder of the Labyrinth. — **Dae•da′li•an, Dae•da′le•an** (dĭ-dā′lē-ən, -dāl′yən) *adj.*

dae•mon (dē′mən) *n.* Var. of **demon** 4, 5.

dae•mon•ic (dĭ-mŏn′ĭk) *adj.* Var. of **demonic.**

daf•fo•dil (dăf′ə-dĭl) *n.* **1.a.** A bulbous plant *(Narcissus pseudonarcissus)* having usu. yellow flowers with a trumpet-shaped central crown. **b.** The flower of this plant. **2.** *Color.* A brilliant to vivid yellow. [Alteration of ME *affodil* < Lat. *asphodelus,* asphodel. See ASPHODEL.]

daf•fy (dăf′ē) *adj.* **-fi•er, -fi•est.** *Informal.* **1.** Silly; foolish. **2.** Crazy. [< obsolete *daff,* fool < ME *daffe;* prob. akin to *dafte,* foolish. See DAFT.] — **daf′fi•ly** *adv.* — **daf′fi•ness** *n.*

daft (dăft) *adj.* **daft•er, daft•est. 1.** Mad; crazy. **2.** Foolish; stupid. **3.** *Scots.* Frolicsome. [ME *dafte,* foolish < OE *gedæfte,* meek.] — **daft′ly** *adv.* — **daft′ness** *n.*

dag¹ (dăg) *n.* **1.** A lock of matted or dung-coated wool. **2.** A hanging end or shred. [ME *dagge,* shred.]

dag² *abbr.* Decagram.

Da•gan (dä′gän′) *n. Myth.* The Babylonian god of the earth.

Da•ges•tan (dä′gĭ-stän, də-gyĭ-). A region of SW Russia on the Caspian Sea; settled in the 1st millennium B.C.

dag•ger (dăg′ər) *n.* **1.** A short pointed weapon with sharp edges. **2.** Something that agonizes, torments, or wounds. **3.** *Print.* **a.** See **obelisk** 2. **b.** A double dagger. — *idiom.* **look daggers at.** To glare at angrily or hatefully. [ME *daggere,* alteration of OFr. *dague,* ult. perh. < VLat. **dāca (ēnsis),* Dacian (knife) < fem. of Lat. *Dācus.*]

da•go also **Da•go** (dā′gō) *n., pl.* **-gos** or **-goes.** *Offensive Slang.* Used as a disparaging term for an Italian, a Spaniard, or a Portuguese. [Alteration of Sp. *Diego,* a given name < Lat. *Jacōbus,* Jacob.]

Da•gon (dā′gŏn′) *n. Myth.* The chief god of the ancient Philistines and later the Phoenicians, represented as half-man and half-fish.

Da•guerre (də-gâr′, dä-gĕr′), **Louis Jacques Mandé.** 1789–1851. French artist who invented the daguerreotype process.

da•guerre•o•type (də-gâr′ə-tīp′) *n.* **1.** An early photographic process with the image made on a light-sensitive silver-coated metallic plate. **2.** A photograph made by this process. — *tr.v.* **-typed, -typ•ing, -types.** To make a daguerreotype of. [Fr., after Louis Jacques Mandé DAGUERRE.] — **da•guerre′o•typ′er** *n.* — **da•guerre′o•typ′y** *n.*

dag•wood also **Dag•wood** (dăg′wo͝od′) *n.* A multilayered sandwich. [After *Dagwood* Bumstead in the comic strip *Blondie.*]

dah (dä) *n.* A dash in Morse code. [Imit.]

dahl (däl) *n.* **1.** See **cajan pea. 2.** An East Indian stew made with lentils, onions, and various spices. [Hindi *dāl,* dahl seed < Skt. *dalaḥ, dalam,* piece split off < *dalati,* he splits.]

dahl•ia (dăl′yə, däl′-, dāl′-) *n.* Any of several plants of the genus *Dahlia,* native to Mexico, Colombia, and Central America and having tuberous roots and showy rayed flower heads. [NLat. *Dahlia,* genus name, after Anders *Dahl* (1751–87), Swedish botanist.]

Da•ho•mey (də-hō′mē, dä-ô-mā′). See **Benin** 2. — **Da•ho′me•an** (də-hō′mē-ən), **Da•ho′man** (-mən) *adj. & n.*

da•hoon (də-ho͞on′) *n.* A small tree *(Ilex cassine)* of the southeast United States having red or orange to yellow fruit and leathery dark green leaves. [?]

dai•kon (dī′kŏn′, -kən) *n.* A white radish *(Raphanus sativus* var. *longipinnatus)* of Japan having a long edible root. [J. : *dai,* big + *kon,* root.]

dai•ly (dā′lē) *adj.* **1.** Of or occurring during the day. **2.** Happening or done every day. **3.** Computed or assessed for each day: *a daily record.* **4.** Everyday: *clothes for daily use.* — *adv.* **1.** Every day. **2.** Once a day. — *n., pl.* **-lies. 1.** A newspaper published every day or every weekday. **2. dailies.** The first unedited print of all the alternative shots or takes of a motion picture, usu. viewed after a day's shooting; the rushes. [ME *dayly* < OE *dæglīc* < *dæg,* day. See DAY.] — **dai′li•ness, dai′ly•ness** *n.*

daily double *n. Sports & Games.* A bet won by choosing both winners of two specified races on one day, as in horse racing.

dai•mi•o or **dai•my•o** (dī′mē-ō′, dīm′yō′) *n., pl.* **daimio** or **-mi•os** also **daimyo** or **-my•os.** A feudal lord of Japan. [J. *daimyō* : *dai,* great (< Chin. *dà*) + *myō,* name (< Chin. *míng*).]

dai•mon (dī′mōn′) *n.* Var. of **demon** 4, 5.

dain•ty (dān′tē) *adj.* **-ti•er, -ti•est. 1.** Delicately beautiful or charming; exquisite. **2.** Delicious or choice. See Syns at **delicate. 3.** Of refined taste; discriminating. **4.** Overfastidious; squeamish. — *n., pl.* **-ties.** Something delicious; a delicacy. [ME *deinte,* excellence, excellent < OFr. *deintie* < Lat. *dignitās* < *dignus,* worthy. See **dek-*.**] — **dain′ti•ly** *adv.* — **dain′ti•ness** *n.*

dai•qui•ri (dī′kə-rē, dăk′ə-) *n., pl.* **-ris.** A cocktail of rum, lime or lemon juice, and sugar. [After *Daiquirí,* a village of E Cuba.]

Dai•ren (dī′rĕn′). See **Dalian.**

dair•y (dâr′ē) *n., pl.* **-ies. 1.** A commercial establishment for processing or selling milk and milk products. **2.** A place where milk and cream are stored and processed. **3.** A dairy farm. **4.** The dairy business; dairying. — *adj.* **1.** Of, for, or relating to milk or milk products. **2.** Of or relating to dairying. **3.** *Judaism.* Containing or intended for use with dairy products exclusively, in accordance with kashrut. [ME *daierie* < AN : ME *daie,* dairymaid (< OE *dǣge,* bread kneader; see **dheigh-*)** + *-erie,* place (< OFr.; see -ERY).]

dairy cattle *pl.n.* Cows raised for milk rather than meat.

dairy farm *n.* A farm for producing milk and milk products.

dair•y•ing (dâr′ē-ĭng) *n.* The business of operating a dairy.

dair•y•maid (dâr′ē-mād′) *n.* A woman or girl who works in a dairy.

dair•y•man (dâr′ē-mən) *n.* **1.** A man who owns or manages a dairy. **2.** A man who works in a dairy.

dair•y•wom•an (dâr′ē-wo͝om′ən) *n.* **1.** A woman who owns or manages a dairy. **2.** A woman who works in a dairy.

da•is (dā′ĭs, dī′-, dās) *n.* A raised platform for speakers or guests. [ME *deis* < AN, platform < LLat. *discus,* table < Lat., discus, quoit. See DISK.]

dai•shi•ki (dī-shē′kē) *n.* Var. of **dashiki.**

dai•sy (dā′zē) *n., pl.* **-sies. 1.** Any of several plants of the composite family, esp. a Eurasian plant *(Chrysanthemum leucanthemum)* having flower heads with a yellow center and white rays. **2.** A European plant *(Bellis perennis)* having flower heads with pink or white rays. **3.** *Slang.* One deemed excellent. [ME *daisie* < OE *dæges ēage* : *dæges,* genitive of *dæg,* day; see **agh-*** + *ēage,* eye; see **okʷ-*.**]

daisy chain *n.* **1.** A garland of daisies joined together in a long chain. **2.** Something likened to a garland.

daisy wheel *n.* A printing device used esp. in the printers attached to computers and word processors and consisting of characters fixed at the ends of spokes on a wheel.

Da•kar (də-kär′, dăk′är′). The cap. of Senegal, in the W part on the Atlantic Ocean; former cap. of French West Africa (1904–59). Pop. 1,341,000.

da•koit (də-koit′) *n.* Var. of **dacoit.**

Da•ko•ta (də-kō′tə) *n., pl.* **Dakota** or **-tas. 1.** A member of any of the Sioux peoples, esp. any of the peoples of the Santee branch. **2.** The Siouan language of the Dakota. — **Da•ko′tan** *adj. & n.*

Da•ko•tas (də-kō′təz). The Dakota Terr. or (after 1889) the states of ND and SD.

Dakota Territory. A territory of the N-central U.S. organized in 1861 and divided into the states of ND and SD in 1889.

dal *abbr.* Decaliter.

Da•la•dier (də-lä′dē-ā′, dä-lä-dyā′), **Édouard.** 1884–1970. French public official who signed the Munich Pact with Adolf Hitler in Sep. 1938.

Da•lai La•ma (dä′lī lä′mə) *n.* The traditional ruler and highest priest of the Lamaist religion in Tibet and Mongolia. [Tibetan : Mongolian *dalai,* ocean + Tibetan *bla-ma,* monk.]

da•la•si (dä-lä′sē) *n., pl.* **dalasi.** See table at **currency.** [Mandingo, poss. ult. < E. *dollars.* See DOLLAR.]

dale (dāl) *n.* A valley. [ME < OE *dæl.*]

Dale (dāl), Sir **Henry Hallett.** 1875–1968. British physiologist who shared a 1936 Nobel Prize.

Dale, Sir **Thomas.** d. 1619. English-born colonial administrator noted for his strict rule of Virginia (1611–16).

Dale City. A community of NE VA SW of Alexandria. Pop. 47,170.

da•leth (dä′lĭd, -lĕt, -lĕth) *n.* The fourth letter of the Hebrew alphabet. [Heb. *dāleth* < *dālt,* door.]

Da•ley (dā′lē), **Richard Joseph.** 1902–76. Amer. politician who was mayor of Chicago (1955–76).

Dal•hou•sie (dăl-ho͞o′zē, -hou′-), 10th Earl and 1st Marquis of. James Andrew Broun Ramsay. 1812–60. British colonial administrator who served as governor-general in India (1847–56).

Da•li (dä′lē), **Salvador.** 1904–89. Spanish surrealist artist whose works include *Persistence of Memory* (1931). — **Da′li•esque′** (-ĕsk′) *adj.*

Dal•ian (däl′yän′) also **Ta•lien** (tä′lyĕn′). Formerly **Dai•ren** (dī′rĕn′). A city of NE China on the Bo Hai; opened to foreign commerce in 1901. Pop. 1,380,000.

Dal•las (dăl′əs). A city of NE TX on the Trinity R. E of Fort Worth; founded by French settlers in 1841. Pop. 1,006,877.

daffodil
Narcissus pseudonarcissus

Salvador Dali
Photographed in 1936

ă pat	oi boy
ā pay	ou out
âr care	o͝o took
ä father	o͞o boot
ĕ pet	ŭ cut
ē be	ûr urge
ĭ pit	th thin
ī pie	*th* this
îr pier	hw which
ŏ pot	zh vision
ō toe	ə about,
ô paw	item

Stress marks:
′ (primary);
′ (secondary), as in
dictionary (dĭk′shə-nĕr′ē)

Dallas, George Mifflin. 1792–1864. Vice President of the U.S. (1845–49).

dalles (dălz) *pl.n.* The rapids of a river between the precipices of a gorge or narrow valley. [Fr., pl. of *dalle,* gutter < OFr. < ON *dæla.*]

Dalles (dălz), **The.** A city of N OR on the Columbia R. E of Portland. Pop. 11,060.

dal•li•ance (dăl′ē-əns) *n.* **1.** Frivolous spending of time; dawdling. **2.** Playful flirtation.

Dal•lis grass (dăl′ĭs) *n.* A tall South American perennial grass *(Paspalum dilatatum)* grown for pasturage in the southern United States. [Prob. alteration of DALLAS TX.]

Dall sheep (dôl) or **Dall's sheep** (dôlz) *n.* A wild sheep *(Ovis dalli)* of the mountains of northwest North America having curved yellowish horns. [After William Healey *Dall* (1845–1927), Amer. naturalist.]

dal•ly (dăl′ē) *v.* **-lied, -ly•ing, -lies.** —*intr.* **1.** To play amorously; flirt. **2.** To trifle; toy. **3.** To waste time; dawdle. —*tr.* To waste (time). [ME *dalien* < OFr. *dalier.*] —**dal′li•er** *n.* —**dal′ly•ing•ly** *adv.*

Dal•ma•ti•a (dăl-mā′shə). A historical region of SE Europe on the Adriatic Sea; divided between Serbia and Croatia in the 10th cent. and held by numerous powers after the 15th cent.

Dal•ma•tian (dăl-mā′shən) *n.* **1.** A native or inhabitant of Dalmatia. **2.** Also **dalmatian.** A dog of a breed believed to have originated in Dalmatia, having a short, smooth white coat covered with dark spots. —*adj.* Of or relating to Dalmatia or its inhabitants or culture.

Dalmatian

dal•mat•ic (dăl-măt′ĭk) *n.* **1.** A wide-sleeved garment worn over the alb by a deacon or bishop at Mass. **2.** A wide-sleeved garment worn by an English monarch at coronation. [ME *dalmatik* < OFr. *dalmatique* < Med.Lat. *dalmatica (vestis),* Dalmatian (garment) < Lat. *dalmaticus,* Dalmatian.]

dal se•gno (däl sān′yō) *adv. Mus.* From a place marked by the sign § to a designated point. Used as a direction to repeat a passage. [Ital. : *da,* from + *il,* the + *segno,* sign.]

dal•ton (dôl′tən) *n.* See **atomic mass unit.** [After John DALTON.]

Dal•ton (dôl′tən). A city of NW GA SE of Chattanooga TN. Pop. 21,761.

Dalton, John. 1766–1844. British chemist who formulated the atomic theory and studied colorblindness.

Dalton, Robert. 1867–92. Amer. outlaw noted for his exploits as a horse thief, train robber, and leader of the Dalton gang.

dal•ton•ism also **Dal•ton•ism** (dôl′tə-nĭz′əm) *n.* An inherited defect in perception of red and green. [After John DALTON.] —**dal•to′ni•an** (-tō′nē-ən), **dal•ton′ic** (-tŏn′ĭk) *adj.*

Da•ly (dā′lē), **(John) Augustin.** 1839–99. Amer. playwright best known for *Under the Gaslight* (1867).

Daly City. A city of W CA, a suburb of San Francisco; settled in 1906. Pop. 92,311.

dam¹ (dăm) *n.* **1.a.** A barrier built across a waterway to control the flow or raise the level of water. **b.** A body of water controlled by such a barrier. **2.** A barrier against the passage of liquid or loose material, as a rubber sheet used in dentistry to isolate a tooth. **3.** An obstruction; a hindrance. —*tr.v.* **dammed, dam•ming, dams. 1.** To hold back by a dam. **2.** To close up; obstruct. [ME, prob. < OE *damm.]

dalmatic
1570 Dutch clerical dalmatic

dam² (dăm) *n.* **1.** A female parent. Used of a four-legged animal. **2.** *Archaic.* A mother. [ME *dam, dame,* lady, mother. See DAME.]

dam³ *abbr.* Decameter.

dam•age (dăm′ĭj) *n.* **1.** Impairment of the usefulness or value of person or property; harm. **2. damages.** *Law.* Money ordered to be paid as compensation for injury or loss. **3.** *Informal.* Cost; price. —*v.* **-aged, -ag•ing, -ag•es.** —*tr.* To cause damage to. See Syns at **spoil.** —*intr.* To suffer or be susceptible to damage. [ME < OFr. : *dam,* loss (< Lat. *damnum*) + *-age,* -age.] —**dam′age•a•bil′i•ty** *n.* —**dam′age•a•ble** *adj.* —**dam′ag•ing•ly** *adv.*

damage control *n.* An effort to minimize damage or loss.

Da•man (də-män′). A region of NW India on the E shore of the Gulf of Cambay; annexed by India in 1961.

Da•man•hur (dăm′ən-ho͝or′, dä′män-ho͝or′). A city of NE Egypt on the Nile delta NW of Cairo. Pop. 221,500.

dam•ar (dăm′ər) *n.* Var. of **dammar.**

dam•as•cene (dăm′ə-sēn′, dăm′ə-sēn′) *tr.v.* **-cened, -cen•ing, -cenes.** To decorate (metal) with wavy patterns of inlay or etching. —*n.* Metalwork that is damascened. —*adj.* **1.** Of or relating to damascening. **2.** Of or relating to damask. [Fr. *damasquiner* < *damasquin,* of Damascus < Lat. *Damascēnus* < Gk. *Damaskēnos* < *Damaskos,* Damascus.]

Father Damien

Da•mas•cus (də-măs′kəs). Cap. of Syria, in the SW part; inhabited since prehistoric times. Pop. 1,259,000. —**Dam′a•scene′** (dăm′ə-sēn′) *adj. & n.*

Damascus steel *n.* An early form of steel having wavy markings, developed in Near Eastern countries and used chiefly in sword blades.

dam•ask (dăm′əsk) *n.* **1.** A rich patterned fabric of cotton, linen, silk, or wool. **2.** A fine twilled table linen. **3.** Damascus steel. **4.** The wavy pattern on Damascus steel. —*tr.v.* **-asked, -ask•ing, -asks. 1.** To damascene. **2.** To decorate or weave with rich patterns. [ME, Damascus, damask < Lat. *Damascus* < Gk. *Damaskos.*] —**dam′ask** *adj.*

damask rose *n.* A rose *(Rosa damascena)* native to Asia that has fragrant red or pink flowers and is used as a source of attar. [< ME *Damask,* Damascus. See DAMASK.]

damask steel *n.* Damascus steel.

dame (dām) *n.* **1.** Used formerly as a courtesy title for a woman in authority or a mistress of a household. **2.a.** A married woman; a matron. **b.** An elderly woman. **3.** *Slang.* A woman. **4.** *Chiefly British.* **a.** A woman holding a nonhereditary title conferred by a sovereign. **b.** The wife or widow of a knight. **c.** Used as the title for such a woman. [ME < OFr. < Lat. *domina,* fem. of *dominus,* lord, master. See **dem-*.**]

dame's rocket (dāmz) *n., pl.* **dame's rockets.** A European plant *(Hesperis matronalis)* having clusters of fragrant flowers.

Da•mien de Veus•ter (dā′mē-ən də vyo͞o′stər, dä-myăN′ də vœ-stĕr′), **Joseph.** "Father Damien." 1840–89. Belgian Roman Catholic missionary who ministered to the leper colony on Molokai (1873–89).

Dam•i•et•ta (dăm′ē-ĕt′ə) also **Dum•yat** (do͝om-yät′). A city of NE Egypt on the Nile delta NNE of Cairo; conquered by Crusaders in 1219. Pop. 118,100.

dam•mar or **dam•ar** also **dam•mer** (dăm′ər) *n.* Any of various hard resins obtained from trees of the genera *Shorea, Balanocarpus,* and *Hopea,* native to southeast Asia and used in varnishes and lacquers. [Malay *damar,* resin.]

dam•mit (dăm′ĭt) *interj.* Used to express anger, irritation, contempt, or disappointment. [Alteration of *damn it.*]

damn (dăm) *v.* **damned, damn•ing, damns.** —*tr.* **1.** To pronounce an adverse judgment upon. **2.** To cause the failure of; ruin. **3.** To condemn as harmful, illegal, or immoral. **4.** *Theol.* To condemn to everlasting punishment. **5.** To swear at. —*intr.* To swear; curse. —*interj.* Used to express anger, irritation, contempt, or disappointment. —*n.* **1.** The saying of "damn" as a curse. **2.** *Informal.* The least bit; a jot. —*adv. & adj.* Damned. —***idiom.* damn it.** Used as an intensive: *We must finish, damn it.* [ME *dampnen* < OFr. *dampner* < Lat. *damnāre,* to condemn, inflict loss upon < *damnum,* loss.] —**damn′ing•ly** *adv.*

dam•na•ble (dăm′nə-bəl) *adj.* Deserving condemnation; odious. —**dam′na•ble•ness** *n.* —**dam′na•bly** *adv.*

dam•na•tion (dăm-nā′shən) *n.* **1.** The act of damning or the condition of being damned. **2.** *Theol.* **a.** Condemnation to everlasting punishment. **b.** Everlasting punishment. **3.** Ruin caused by adverse criticism. —*interj.* Used to express anger or annoyance. See Regional Note at **tarnation.**

dam•na•to•ry (dăm′nə-tôr′ē, -tōr′ē) *adj.* Threatening with or expressing condemnation; damning.

damned (dămd) *adj.* **damned•er** (dăm′dər), **damned•est** (dăm′dĭst). **1.** Condemned, esp. to eternal punishment. **2.** *Informal.* Detestable. **3.** Used as an intensive. —*adv.* **damneder, damnedest.** Used as an intensive. —*n. Theol.* Souls doomed to eternal punishment.

Regional Note: There are many regional variants, mostly euphemisms, for *damned,* both as an oath and as a mild intensive. Southern exclamations and intensives tend to begin with *dad–,* a euphemism for "god"; hence *dadblamed, dadblasted, dadburn,* and *dadgum.* Another such euphemism is the better known *doggone,* probably originally Southern but now widespread. Like *dadgum, doggone* is used as a mild intensive: *"The best doggone deals in Alabama"* (billboard in Montgomery). A common regional variant of *damned* is *durn,* also euphemistic and relatively mild.

damned•est (dăm′dĭst) *adj.* Superl. of **damned.** —*n.* All that is possible; the utmost: *did my damnedest.*

Dam•o•cles (dăm′ə-klēz′). fl. 4th cent. B.C. Greek courtier to Dionysius the Elder who according to legend was forced to sit under a sword suspended by a single hair to demonstrate the precariousness of a king's fortunes.

Da•mon (dā′mən) *n.* A legendary Greek who pledged his life so his condemned friend Pythias could arrange his affairs.

dam•o•sel also **dam•oi•selle** or **dam•o•zel** (dăm′ə-zĕl′) *n. Archaic.* A young woman; a damsel. [ME *damoisele* < OFr. *damoiselle,* damsel. See DAMSEL.]

damp (dămp) *adj.* **damp•er, damp•est. 1.** Slightly wet. See Syns at **wet. 2.** *Archaic.* Dejected. —*n.* **1.** Moisture in the air; humidity. **2.** Foul or poisonous gas in the air in coal mines. **3.** Lowness of spirits; depression. **4.** A restraint or check; a discouragement. —*tr.v.* **damped, damp•ing, damps. 1.** To make damp or moist; moisten. **2.** To extinguish (a fire, for example) by cutting off air. **3.** To restrain or check; discourage. **4.** *Mus.* To provide (the strings of a keyboard instrument) with dampers to reduce the dynamic level. **5.** *Phys.* To decrease the amplitude of (a wave). —***phrasal verb.* damp off.** *Bot.* To be affected by damping off. [ME, poison gas, perh. < MDu., vapor.] —**damp′ish** *adj.* —**damp′ly** *adv.* —**damp′ness** *n.*

damp•en (dăm′pən) *v.* **-ened, -en•ing, -ens.** —*tr.* **1.** To make damp. **2.** To deaden, restrain, or depress. **3.** To soundproof. —*intr.* To become damp. —**damp′en•er** *n.*

damp•er (dăm′pər) *n.* **1.** One that deadens or restrains. **2.** An adjustable plate, as in a furnace flue, for controlling the draft.

3. *Mus.* **a.** A device in keyboard instruments for deadening the vibrations of the strings. **b.** A mute for various brass instruments. **4.** A device that eliminates or diminishes vibrations or oscillations.

Dam•pi•er (dăm′pē-ər), **William.** 1652–1715. English buccaneer who described his circumnavigation of the globe in *A New Voyage Round the World* (1697).

damp•ing (dăm′pĭng) *n.* The capacity built into a mechanical or electrical device to prevent excessive correction and the resulting instability or oscillatory conditions.

damping off *n. Bot.* A disease of seedlings that is caused by fungi and results in wilting and death.

Dam•rosch (dăm′rŏsh), **Walter Johannes.** 1862-1950. Amer. musician who introduced Wagner's works in the U.S.

dam•sel (dăm′zəl) *n.* A young woman or girl; a maiden. [ME *damisele* < OFr. *dameisele, damoiselle* < VLat. **dominicella*, dim. of *domina*, lady. See DAME.]

dam•sel•fish (dăm′zəl-fĭsh′) *n., pl.* **damselfish** or **-fish•es.** Any of various small, usu. brightly colored tropical marine fishes of the family Pomacentridae.

dam•sel•fly (dăm′zəl-flī′) *n.* Any of various often brightly colored predatory insects having a long slender body and elongated wings that fold together when the insect is at rest.

dam•son (dăm′zən, -sən) *n.* **1.** A Eurasian plum tree *(Prunus insititia)* having edible fruit. **2.** The oval, bluish-black, juicy plum of this tree. [ME *damson, damacene* < Lat. *(prūnum) Damascēnum*, (plum) of Damascus < *Damascēnus.* See DAMASCENE.]

dan also **Dan** (dän, dăn) *n.* **1.** *Sports.* **a.** Any of 12 levels of proficiency at the grade of black belt in martial arts such as judo and karate. **b.** One at such a level. **2.** *Games.* An expert or expert level in shogi and other such games. [J.]

Dan[1] (dăn). In the Bible, a son of Jacob and the forebear of one of the tribes of Israel.

Dan[2] (dăn) *n. Archaic.* Used formerly as a title of honor for respected men, such as clerics and poets. [ME < OFr. < Med. Lat. *Domnus* < Lat. *dominus*, master, lord. See **dem-***.]

Dan. *abbr.* **1.** *Bible.* Daniel. **2.** Danish.

Da•na (dā′nə), **Charles Anderson.** 1819–97. Amer. newspaper editor who owned the *New York Sun.*

Dana, Richard Henry. 1815–82. Amer. lawyer and writer best known for his *Two Years Before the Mast* (1840).

Dan•a•e also **Dan•a•ë** (dăn′ə-ē′) *n. Gk. Myth.* The daughter of Eurydice and Acrisius and mother of Perseus who was imprisoned by her father in a bronze chamber.

Da•na•i•des also **Da•na•ï•des** (də-nā′ĭ-dēz′) *pl.n. Gk. Myth.* The daughters of Danaus who at their father's command murdered their bridegrooms and were condemned in Hades to pour water eternally into a leaky vessel.

Dan•a•kil (dăn′ə-kĭl′, də-nä′kēl). A desert region of NE Ethiopia and N Djibouti bordering on the Red Sea.

Da Nang or **Da•nang** (də năng′, dä′ näng′). Formerly **Tou•rane** (to͞o-rän′). A city of central Vietnam on the South China Sea; site of a U.S. military base during the Vietnam War. Pop. 318,655.

Dan•a•us also **Dan•a•üs** (dăn′ē-əs) *n. Gk. Myth.* A king of Argos and father of the Danaides.

Dan•bur•y (dăn′bĕr′ē, -bə-rē). A city of SW CT NW of Bridgeport; settled in 1685. Pop. 65,585.

dance (dăns) *v.* **danced, danc•ing, danc•es.** *—intr.* **1.** To move rhythmically, usu. to music, using prescribed or improvised steps and gestures. **2.a.** To leap or skip about excitedly. **b.** To appear to flash or twinkle. **c.** *Informal.* To appear to skip about; vacillate. **3.** To bob up and down. *—tr.* **1.** To perform (a dance). **2.** To cause to dance. **3.** To bring to a particular condition by dancing. *—n.* **1.** A series of rhythmical motions and steps, usu. to music. **2.** The art of dancing. **3.** A party of people for dancing; a ball. **4.** One round or turn of dancing: *May I have this dance?* **5.** A musical or rhythmical accompaniment composed or played for dancing. **6.** The act or an instance of dancing. [ME *dauncen* < OFr. *danser*, perh. of Gmc. orig.] **—dance′a•ble** *adj.* **—danc′er** *n.* **—danc′ing•ly** *adv.*

D and C *n.* Dilation and curettage.

dan•de•li•on (dăn′dl-ī′ən) *n.* **1.** A Eurasian plant *(Taraxacum officinale)* of the composite family, having yellow flower heads and deeply notched leaves. **2.** Any of several related plants. **3.** *Color.* A brilliant to vivid yellow. [ME *dent-de-lioun* < OFr. *dentdelion* < Med.Lat. *dēns leōnis*, lion's tooth : Lat. *dēns, dent-*, tooth; see **dent-*** + Lat. *leōnis*, genitive of *leō*, lion; see LION.]

dan•der[1] (dăn′dər) *n. Informal.* Temper or anger: *What got their dander up?* [Perh. alteration of *dunder*, fermented cane juice used in rum-making, fermentation, poss. alteration of Sp. *redundar*, to overflow < Lat. *redundāre.* See REDUNDANT.]

dan•der[2] (dăn′dər) *n.* Scurf from the coat or feathers of animals, often of an allergenic nature. [Alteration of DANDRUFF.]

Dan•die Din•mont (dăn′dē dĭn′mŏnt′) *n.* A small terrier having a rough grayish or brownish coat and drooping ears. [After *Dandie Dinmont*, the owner of two such dogs in *Guy Mannering*, a novel by Sir Walter Scott.]

dan•di•fy (dăn′də-fī′) *tr.v.* **-fied, -fy•ing, -fies.** To dress as or cause to resemble a dandy. **—dan′di•fi•ca′tion** (-fĭ-kā′-shən) *n.*

dan•dle (dăn′dl) *tr.v.* **-dled, -dling, -dles. 1.** To move (a small child) up and down on the knees or in the arms in a playful way. **2.** To pamper or pet. *—n. Narragansett Bay.* See **seesaw** 1. See Regional Note at **teeter-totter.** [?] **—dan′dler** *n.*

dandle board *n. Narragansett Bay.* See **seesaw** 1. See Regional Note at **teeter-totter.**

Dan•dong (dän′dông′) also **Tan•tung** (tän′to͝ong′) or **An•tung** (än′to͝ong′). A city of NE China on the Yalu R. opposite North Korea. Pop. 400,000.

dan•druff (dăn′drəf) *n.* A scaly scurf formed on the scalp, sometimes caused by seborrhea. [*dand-*, of unknown orig. + dial. *hurf*, scurf (< ON *hrufa*, crust, scab).] **—dan′druff•y** *adj.*

dan•dy (dăn′dē) *n., pl.* **-dies. 1.** A man who affects extreme elegance in clothes and manners; a fop. **2.** *Informal.* Something very agreeable. *—adj.* **-di•er, -di•est. 1.** Suggestive of a dandy; foppish. **2.** *Informal.* Fine; good. [Perh. short for *jack-a-dandy*, fop.] **—dan′dy•ish** *adj.* **—dan′dy•ish•ly** *adv.* **—dan′dy•ism** *n.*

Dane (dān) *n.* **1.** A native or inhabitant of Denmark. **2.** A person of Danish ancestry. [ME *Dan* < ON *Danr.*]

Dane•geld (dān′gĕld′) also **Dane•gelt** (-gĕlt′) *n.* A tax levied in England from the 10th to the 12th century to finance protection against Danish invasion. [ME : *Dane*, genitive pl. of *Dan*, Dane; see DANE + *geld*, tribute (< OE *geld, gield*, payment).]

Dane•law also **Dane•lagh** (dān′lô′) *n.* **1.** The body of law established by the Danish invaders in northeast England in the ninth and tenth centuries. **2.** The sections of England under this law. [ME *Denelage* < OE *Dena lagu* : *Dena*, genitive of *Dene*, the Danes + *lagu*, law; see LAW.]

dang (dăng) *n., adv., & adj.* Damn. [Alteration of DAMN.]

dan•ger (dān′jər) *n.* **1.** Exposure or vulnerability to harm or risk. **2.** A source or an instance of risk or peril. **3.** *Obsolete.* Power, esp. power to harm. [ME *daunger*, power, peril < OFr. *dangier* < VLat. **dominiārium*, power < Lat. *dominium*, sovereignty < *dominus*, lord, master. See **dem-***.]

dan•ger•ous (dān′jər-əs) *adj.* **1.** Involving or filled with danger; perilous. **2.** Being able or likely to do harm. **—dan′ger•ous•ly** *adv.* **—dan′ger•ous•ness** *n.*

dan•gle (dăng′gəl) *v.* **-gled, -gling, -gles.** *—intr.* **1.** To hang loosely and swing to and fro. **2.** To be a hanger-on. *—tr.* **1.** To cause to hang loosely or swing. **2.** To cause (one's hopes) to hang uncertainly. *—n.* **1.** The act or an instance of dangling. **2.** Something dangled. [Perh. < Dan. *dangle* or Swed. *dangla.*] **—dan′gler** *n.* **—dan′gly** *adj.*

dan•gle•ber•ry (dăng′gəl-bĕr′ē) *n.* A deciduous shrub *(Gaylussacia frondosa)* of the eastern United States having dark blue fruits. [Prob. alteration of *tangleberry.*]

dan•gling participle (dăng′glĭng) *n. Gram.* A participle, usu. in a subordinate clause, that lacks a clear grammatical relation with the subject of the sentence, such as *approaching* in *Approaching New York, the skyline came into view.*

Dan•iel (dăn′yəl) *n. Bible.* **1.** A Hebrew prophet of the 6th cent. B.C. **2.** See table at **Bible.** [Heb. *Dānī'ēl*, God is my judge.]

Daniel, Peter Vivian. 1784–1860. Amer. jurist; associate justice of the U.S. Supreme Court (1841–60).

Dan•iels (dăn′yəlz), **Josephus.** 1862–1948. Amer. journalist who served as secretary of the navy (1913–21).

da•ni•o (dā′nē-ō′) *n., pl.* **-os.** Any of various small, often brightly colored freshwater fishes of the genera *Danio* and *Brachydanio*, popular as aquarium fish. [NLat. *Danio*, genus name.]

Dan•ish (dā′nĭsh) *adj.* Of or relating to Denmark, the Danes, their language, or their culture. *—n.* **1.** The North Germanic language of the Danes. **2.** *pl.* **Danish** or **-ish•es.** A Danish pastry. [ME, alteration (influenced by ON *Danr*, Dane) of *Denish* < OE *Denisc* < *Dene*, the Danes.]

Danish pastry *n.* A sweet pastry made with raised dough.

Dan•ite (dăn′īt′) *n. Bible.* A descendant of Dan. *—adj.* Of or relating to the Hebrew tribe descended from Dan.

dank (dăngk) *adj.* **dank•er, dank•est.** Disagreeably damp or humid. See Syns at **wet.** [ME, prob. of Scand. orig.] **—dank′ly** *adv.* **—dank′ness** *n.*

D'An•nun•zio (dän-no͞on′tsyō), **Gabriele.** 1863–1938. Italian writer who supported Benito Mussolini's fascist regime.

Da•no-Nor•we•gian (dā′-nō-nôr-wē′jən) *n.* An official literary form of Norwegian based on written Danish.

dan•seur (dän-sœr′) *n., pl.* **-seurs** (-sœr′). A man who dances. [Fr. < OFr. < *danser*, to dance. See DANCE.]

dan•seuse (dän-sœz′) *n., pl.* **-seuses** (-sœz′). A woman who dances. [Fr., fem. of *danseur*, danseur. See DANSEUR.]

Dan•te A•li•ghie•ri (dän′tā ä′lē-gyĕ′rē, dăn′tē). 1265–1321. Italian poet renowned for *The Divine Comedy* (completed 1321). **—Dan′te•an** *adj. & n.* **—Dan•tesque′** (dän-tĕsk′, dăn-) *adj.*

Dan•ton (dän-tôn′), **Georges Jacques.** 1759–94. French Revolutionary leader who was guillotined for his opposition to the excesses of the Reign of Terror.

dandelion
Taraxacum officinale

ă pat	oi boy
ā pay	ou out
âr care	o͝o took
ä father	o͞o boot
ĕ pet	ŭ cut
ē be	ûr urge
ĭ pit	th thin
ī pie	*th* this
îr pier	hw which
ŏ pot	zh vision
ō toe	ə about, item
ô paw	

Stress marks:
′ (primary);
′ (secondary), as in **dictionary** (dĭk′shə-nĕr′ē)

Dan•ube (dăn′yo͞ob). A river of S-central Europe rising in SW Germany and flowing c. 2,848 km (1,770 mi) SE to the Black Sea. — **Dan•u′bi•an** *adj.*

Dan•vers (dăn′vərz). A town of NE MA NNE of Boston; settled in the 1630's. Pop. 24,174.

Dan•ville (dăn′vĭl′). **1.** A city of W CA, a suburb of Oakland. Pop. 31,306. **2.** A city of E IL ENE of Decatur. Pop. 33,828. **3.** An independent city of S VA near the NC border; founded 1793. Pop. 53,056.

Dan•zig (dăn′sĭg, dän′tsĭk). See **Gdańsk.**

Danzig Free City. A former state (1919–39) on the Gulf of Gdańsk surrounding and including the city of Gdańsk.

dap (dăp) *intr.v.* **dapped, dap•ping, daps. 1.** To fish by letting a baited hook fall onto the water. **2.** To dip quickly into water, as a bird does. **3.** To skip or bounce, esp. over water. [Prob. alteration of DAB[1].]

daph•ne (dăf′nē) *n.* Any of several Eurasian shrubs of the genus *Daphne,* often cultivated for their glossy evergreen foliage and small bell-shaped flowers. [Lat. *daphnē,* laurel < Gk.]

Daph•ne (dăf′nē) *n. Gk. Myth.* A nymph who metamorphosed into a laurel tree as a means of escaping from Apollo.

daph•ni•a (dăf′nē-ə) *n., pl.* **daphnia.** Any of various water fleas of the genus *Daphnia,* some species of which are used as food for aquarium fish. [NLat. *Daphnia,* genus name, perh. < Lat. *Daphnē,* Daphne.]

Daph•nis (daf′nĭs) *n. Gk. Myth.* A Sicilian shepherd famed as a musician and the inventor of pastoral poetry.

Da Pon•te (də pŏn′tē, dä pôn′tĕ), **Lorenzo.** 1749–1838. Italian-born Amer. educator who wrote the libretto for Mozart's *Marriage of Figaro* (1786).

dap•per (dăp′ər) *adj.* **1.a.** Neatly dressed; trim. **b.** Very stylish in dress. **2.** Lively and alert. [ME *daper,* elegant, prob. < MDu. *dapper,* quick, strong.] — **dap′per•ly** *adv.* — **dap′per•ness** *n.*

dapple-gray

dap•ple (dăp′əl) *n.* **1.a.** Mottled or spotted marking, as on a horse's coat. **b.** An individual spot. **2.** An animal with a dappled skin or coat. — *tr.v.* **-pled, -pling, -ples.** To mark or mottle with spots. — **dap′ple** *adj.*

dap•pled (dăp′əld) *adj.* Spotted; mottled. [ME, prob. < ON *depill,* spot, splash, dim. of *dapi,* pool.]

dap•ple-gray (dăp′əl-grā′) *adj.* Gray with a mottled pattern of darker gray. — *n.* A horse having a coat of mottled gray. [ME *dappel-grai,* prob. alteration (influenced by DAPPLED) of **appel-grai,* apple-gray < ON *apalgrār* : *apall-,* apple + *grār,* gray.]

dap•sone (dăp′sōn′, -zōn′) *n.* An antibacterial drug, $C_{12}H_{12}N_2O_2S$, used to treat leprosy and some forms of dermatitis. [D(I)-[1] + A(MINO)- + (DI)P(HENYL) + S(ULF)ONE.]

DAR *abbr.* Daughters of the American Revolution.

Dar•by and Joan (där′bē; jōn) *n.* An elderly, happily married couple who are seldom seen apart. [Prob. after *Darby and Joan,* a couple in an 18th-cent. English ballad.]

Dard (därd) also **Dar•dic** (där′dĭk) *n.* A group of Indic languages spoken in the upper Indus River valley.

Dar•dan (där′dn) or **Dar•da•ni•an** (där-dā′nē-ən) *n. Archaic.* A Trojan. [After *Dardanus,* the mythical founder of Troy.] — **Dar′dan** *adj.*

Dar•da•nelles (där′dn-ĕlz′). Formerly **Hel•les•pont** (hĕl′ĭ-spŏnt′). A strait connecting the Aegean Sea with the Sea of Marmara; scene of the exploits of Hero and Leander.

Dar•da•nus (där′dn-əs) *n. Gk. Myth.* The founder of Troy.

dare (dâr) *v.* **dared, dar•ing, dares.** — *tr.* **1.** To have the courage for. **2.** To challenge (someone) to do something requiring boldness. **3.** To confront boldly; defy. — *intr.* To be bold enough to do or try something: *Dive if you dare.* — *aux.* To be courageous or bold enough to: *I dare not say.* — *n.* An act of daring; a challenge. [ME *daren* < OE *dearr,* first and third pers. sing. pr. indic. of *durran,* to venture, dare. See **dhers-*.**] — **dar′er** *n.*

Darius I
Fifth-century B.C. low relief from Persepolis, widely recognized as Darius the Great

Dare (dâr), **Virginia.** 1587–87? The first child of English parents born in America; disappeared with other members of the Lost Colony of Roanoke I.

dare•dev•il (dâr′dĕv′əl) *n.* One who is recklessly bold. — **dare′dev′il** *adj.* — **dare′dev′il•ry, dare′dev′il•try** *n.*

dare•say (dâr′sā′) *intr. & tr.v.* To think very likely or almost certain; suppose. Used in the first pers. sing. pr.t.

Dar es Sa•laam (där′ ĕs sə-läm′). The de facto cap. of Tanzania, in the E part on an arm of the Indian Ocean; founded 1862. Pop. 757,346.

Dar•fur (där-fo͝or′). A region and former sultanate of W Sudan; occupied since prehistoric times.

Dar•i•en (dăr′ē-ĕn′, dâr′-, dăr′ē-ən, dâr′-). A town of SW CT NW of Stamford; settled c. 1641. Pop. 18,196.

Da•ri•én (dâr′ē-ĕn′, där-yĕn′). A region of E Panama on the **Gulf of Darién,** a wide bay of the Caribbean between E Panama and NW Colombia. In 1513 Vasco Núñez de Balboa led an expedition across the **Isthmus of Darién** (now the Isthmus of Panama) and became the first European to view the Pacific Ocean from the New World.

dar•ing (dâr′ĭng) *adj.* Willing to take risks; bold and venturesome. — *n.* Audacious bravery; boldness. — **dar′ing•ly** *adv.* — **dar′ing•ness** *n.*

Da•rí•o (dä-rē′ō), **Rubén.** 1867–1916. Nicaraguan poet whose works include *Cantos de Vida y Esperanza* (1905).

Da•ri•us I (də-rī′əs). "Darius the Great." 550?–486 B.C. King of Persia (521–486) who expanded the empire, organized a highly efficient administrative system, and invaded Greece.

Dar•jee•ling[1] (där-jē′lĭng). A town of NE India in the Himalaya Mts. at an altitude of 2,287.5 m (7,500 ft). Pop. 57,603.

Dar•jee•ling[2] (där-jē′lĭng) *n.* A fine variety of black tea grown esp. in the northern part of India.

dark (därk) *adj.* **dark•er, dark•est. 1.a.** Lacking or having very little light: *a dark corner.* **b.** Lacking brightness: *a dark day.* **2.** Reflecting only a small fraction of incident light. **3.** Of a shade tending toward black in comparison with other shades. Used of a color. **4.** Having a swarthy complexion. **5.** Gloomy; dismal. **6.** Sullen or threatening: *a dark scowl.* **7.** Difficult to understand; obscure. **8.** Concealed or secret; mysterious. **9.** Lacking enlightenment or culture: *a dark age in history.* **10.** Exhibiting or stemming from evil characteristics; sinister. **11.** Having richness or depth: *a dark vocal tone.* **12.** Not giving performances; closed. — *n.* **1.** Absence of light. **2.** A place having little or no light. **3.** Night; nightfall: *home before dark.* **4.** A deep hue or color. — *idiom.* **in the dark. 1.** In a state of ignorance; uninformed. **2.** In secret. [ME *derk* < OE *deorc.*] — **dark′ish** *adj.* — **dark′ly** *adv.* — **dark′ness** *n.*

Syns: dark, dim, murky, dusky, obscure. These adjectives indicate the absence of light or clarity. *Dark,* the most widely applicable, can refer to insufficiency of illumination for seeing: *a dark evening.* The word can also denote deepness of shade or color (*dark brown*), absence of cheer (*a dark, somber mood*), or lack of rectitude (a dark past). *Dim* suggests lack of clarity of outline: *"life and the memory of it cramped/dim, on a piece of Bristol board"* (Elizabeth Bishop); it can also apply to a source of light to indicate insufficiency: *"storied Windows richly dight/Casting a dim religious light"* (John Milton). *Murky* implies darkness, often extreme, such as that produced by smoke or fog: *"The path was altogether indiscernible in the murky darkness which surrounded them"* (Sir Walter Scott). *Dusky* applies principally to the dimness that is characteristic of diminishing light, as at twilight: *"The dusky night rides down the sky/And ushers in the morn"* (Henry Fielding); it often refers to deepness of shade of a color: *"A dusky blush rose to her cheek"* (Edith Wharton). *Obscure* usually means unclear to the mind or senses but it can also refer to physical darkness: *the obscure rooms of a shuttered mansion.*

dark adaptation *n.* The adjustments of the eye, including increased activity of rods in the retina, that make vision possible in relative darkness. — **dark′-a•dapt′** (därk′ə-dăpt′) *v.* — **dark′-a•dapt′ed** (därk′ə-dăp′tĭd) *adj.*

Dark Age *n.* **1.** An era of repression and unenlightenment. **2. Dark Ages. a.** The period from about A.D. 476 to about the year 1000. **b.** The period from the end of classical civilization to the revival of learning in the West; the Middle Ages.

dark•en (där′kən) *v.* **-ened, -en•ing, -ens.** — *tr.* **1.a.** To make dark or darker. **b.** To give a darker hue to. **2.** To fill with sadness. **3.** To render vague or uncertain. **4.** To tarnish or stain. — *intr.* To become dark or darker. — **dark′en•er** *n.*

dark-field microscope (därk′fēld′) *n.* A microscope in which an object is illuminated only from the sides so that it appears bright against a dark background.

dark horse *n.* **1.** One who achieves unexpected political success, typically as a nominee at a party's convention. **2.** A little-known, unexpectedly successful entrant.

dark lantern *n.* A lantern whose light can be blocked, as by a sliding panel.

dar•kle (där′kəl) *v.* **-kled, -kling, -kles.** — *intr.* **1.** To appear darkly or indistinctly. **2.a.** To grow dark. **b.** To become gloomy. — *tr.* To make dark or indistinct.

dar•kling (där′klĭng) *adv.* In the dark. — *adj.* **1.** Occurring in the dark. **2.** Dark; dim. — *n.* The dark.

darkling beetle *n.* A beetle of the family Tenebrionidae, having a brown or black body and feeding on decaying vegetation, living plants, or stored grain.

dark•room (därk′ro͞om′, -ro͝om′) *n.* A room in which photographic materials are processed, either in complete darkness or with a safelight.

dark•some (därk′səm) *adj.* Dark and somber.

dark star *n.* A star normally obscure or too faint for visual observation, esp. the component of an eclipsing binary star detectable by spectral analysis or in the eclipse of the bright component.

Dar•lan (där-läɴ′), **Jean Louis Xavier François.** 1881–1942. French admiral who helped persuade French territories in N and W Africa to side with the Allies after 1942.

dar•ling (där′lĭng) *n.* **1.** A dearly beloved person. **2.** One that is greatly liked or preferred; a favorite. — *adj.* **1.** Dearly beloved. **2.** Regarded with special favor; favorite. **3.** *Informal.* Charming or amusing: *a darling hat.* [ME *dereling* < OE *dēorling* : *dēore,* dear + *-ling,* dim. suff.; see -LING[1].]

Dar•ling Range (där′lĭng). An upland region of SW Australia extending along the Pacific coast N and S of Perth.

Darling River. A river rising in SE Australia and flowing c. 2,739 km (1,702 mi) to the Murray R.

Dar•ling•ton (där′lĭng-tən). A borough of NE England S of Newcastle. Pop. 97,800.

Darm•stadt (därm′stăt, -shtät′). A city of SW Germany SE of Frankfurt; chartered 1330. Pop. 134,718.

darn¹ (därn) *v.* **darned, darn•ing, darns.** *—tr.* To mend (a garment, for example) by weaving thread or yarn across a gap or hole. *—intr.* To repair a hole, as in a garment, by weaving thread or yarn across it. *—n.* A hole so repaired. [Fr. dial. *darner*, perh. < Norman Fr. *darne*, piece < Breton *darn.*] **—darn′er** *n.*

darn² (därn) *interj.* Used to express dissatisfaction or annoyance. *—adv. & adj.* Damn. *—tr. & intr.v.* **darned, darn•ing, darns.** To damn. [Alteration of DAMN.]

dar•na•tion (där-nā′shən) *n. & interj.* Damnation. See Regional Note at **tarnation.**

darned (därnd) *adj.* Damned.

darned•est or **darnd•est** (därn′dĭst) *n.* The most possible.

dar•nel (där′nəl) *n.* Any of several Eurasian grasses of the genus *Lolium,* esp. *L. temulentum* or *L. perenne.* [ME.]

darn•ing needle (där′nĭng) *n.* **1.** A long large-eyed needle used in darning. **2.** *Upper Northern U.S.* See **dragonfly.** See Regional Note at **dragonfly.**

Darn•ley (därn′lē), Lord. Henry Stewart or Stuart. 1545–67. Scottish nobleman and second husband (1565–67) of Mary Queen of Scots.

Dar•row (dăr′ō), **Clarence Seward.** 1857–1938. Amer. lawyer known for his highly publicized defense of so-called lost causes, such as the Scopes evolution trial (1925).

dart (därt) *n.* **1.a.** A slender, pointed missile, often having tail fins, thrown by hand, shot from a blowgun, or expelled by an exploding bomb. **b.** An object like a dart in shape, use, or effect. **2.** The stinger of an insect. **3. darts.** *(used with a sing. or pl. v.) Games.* A game in which darts are thrown at a target. **4.** A sudden, rapid movement. **5.** A tapered tuck sewn to adjust the fit of a garment. *—v.* **dart•ed, dart•ing, darts.** *—intr.* To move suddenly and rapidly. *—tr.* **1.** To thrust or throw suddenly and rapidly. **2.** To cause to move swiftly and abruptly. [ME < OFr., of Gmc. orig.]

dart•er (där′tər) *n.* **1.** One that moves suddenly and rapidly. **2.** See **anhinga. 3.** Any of various small, often brilliantly colored eastern North American freshwater fishes of the family Percidae, closely related to the perches.

Dart•ford (därt′fərd). A municipal borough of SE England ESE of London. Pop. 77,900.

Dart•moor (därt′mo͝or′, -môr′, -mōr′). An upland region of SW England noted for its bare granite tors.

Dart•mouth (därt′məth). **1.** A city of S Nova Scotia, Canada, on an inlet of the Atlantic opposite Halifax; founded by the British in the 1750's. Pop. 62,277. **2.** A town of SE MA on Buzzards Bay SW of New Bedford. Pop. 27,244.

Dar•von (där′vŏn). A trademark used for propoxyphene hydrochloride.

Dar•win (där′wĭn), **Charles Robert.** 1809–82. British naturalist who developed a theory of evolution based on natural selection in works such as *Origin of Species* (1859). **—Dar•win′i•an** *adj. & n.*

Darwin, Erasmus. 1731–1802. British physician, scientist, reformer, and poet who wrote *Zoonomia* (1794–96).

Dar•win•ism (där′wĭ-nĭz′əm) *n.* A theory of biological evolution developed by Charles Darwin and others, stating that all species of organisms arise and develop through the natural selection of inherited variations that increase the individual's ability to survive and reproduce. **—Dar′win•ist** *n.* **—Dar′win•is′tic** *adj.*

dash¹ (dăsh) *v.* **dashed, dash•ing, dash•es.** *—tr.* **1.** To break or smash by striking violently. **2.** To hurl, knock, or thrust with sudden violence. **3.** To splash; bespatter. **4.** To perform or complete hastily: *dash off a letter.* **5.a.** To add an enlivening or altering element to. **b.** To affect by adding an element to. **6.a.** To destroy or wreck. **b.** To confound; abash. *—intr.* **1.** To strike violently; smash. **2.** To move with haste; rush. *—n.* **1.** A swift, violent blow or stroke. **2.a.** A splash. **b.** A small amount of an added ingredient. **3.** A quick stroke, as with a pencil or brush. **4.** A sudden movement; a rush. **5.** *Sports.* A short footrace run at top speed. **6.** A spirited quality; verve. **7.** A punctuation mark (—) used in writing. **8.** In Morse code, the long sound or signal used with the dot and silent intervals to represent letters or numbers. **9.** A dashboard. [ME *dashen*, prob. of Scand. orig.; akin to Dan. *daske*, to beat.]

dash² (dăsh) *tr.v.* **dashed, dash•ing, dash•es.** To damn. [Alteration of DAMN.]

dash•board (dăsh′bôrd′, -bōrd′) *n.* A panel under the windshield of a vehicle, containing indicator dials, compartments, and sometimes controls.

da•sheen (dă-shēn′) *n.* See **taro.** [?]

dash•er (dăsh′ər) *n.* One that dashes, esp. the plunger of an ice-cream freezer.

da•shi (dä′shē) *n.* A clear soup stock, usu. with a fish or vegetable base. [J., broth.]

da•shi•ki (də-shē′kē) also **dai•shi•ki** (dī-) *n., pl.* **-kis.** A loose, brightly colored African garment. [Yoruba *danşiki.*]

dash•ing (dăsh′ĭng) *adj.* **1.** Audacious and gallant; spirited. **2.** Marked by showy elegance; splendid. **—dash′ing•ly** *adv.*

Dasht-e-Ka•vir (dăsht′ē-kə-vîr′, däsht′ē-kä-vîr′). A salt desert of N-central Iran SE of the Elburz Mts.

Dasht-e-Lut (däsht′ē-lo͞ot′). A sand and stone desert of E Iran extending S from the Dasht-e-Kavir.

das•sie (dăs′ē) *n.* See **hyrax.** [Afr., dim. of *das*, badger < MDu. See **teks-*.**]

das•tard (dăs′tərd) *n.* A sneaking, malicious coward. [ME, prob. alteration of ON *dæstr*, exhausted < p.part. of *dæsa*, to languish, decay.]

das•tard•ly (dăs′tərd-lē) *adj.* Cowardly and malicious; base. **—das′tard•li•ness** *n.*

das•y•ure (dăs′ē-yo͝or′) *n.* Any of various often carnivorous marsupials of the family Dasyuridae of Australia, Tasmania, and adjacent islands. [NLat. *Dasyurus*, genus name : Gk. *dasus*, hairy + *oura*, tail; see **ors-*.**]

dat. *abbr.* Dative.

da•ta (dā′tə, dăt′ə, dä′tə) *pl.n. (used with a sing. or pl. v.)* **1.** Factual information, esp. information organized for analysis. **2.** *Comp. Sci.* Numerical or other information represented in a form suitable for processing by computer. **3.** Values derived from scientific experiments. **4.** Pl. of **datum** 1. [Lat., pl. of *datum.* See DATUM.]

Usage Note: *Data* originated as the plural of Latin *datum,* "something given," and many maintain that it must still be treated as a plural form. The practice of treating *data* as a plural in English, however, often does not correspond to its meaning, given an understanding of what counts as data in modern research. Since scientists and researchers think of data as a singular mass entity like information, it is entirely natural that they should have come to talk about it as such and that others should defer to their practice. Sixty percent of the Usage Panel accepts the use of *data* with a singular verb and pronoun in the sentence *Once the data is in, we can begin to analyze it.*

data bank or **da•ta•bank** (dā′tə-băngk′, dăt′ə-) *n. Comp. Sci.* **1.** See **database. 2.** An organization chiefly concerned with building, maintaining, and using a database.

da•ta•base (dā′tə-bās′, dăt′ə-) *Comp. Sci.* *—n.* also **data base.** A collection of data arranged for ease of retrieval. *—tr.v.* **-based, -bas•ing, -bas•es.** To put (data) into a database.

data carrier *n. Comp. Sci.* A medium, such as magnetic tape, that records or communicates data.

data processing *n. Comp. Sci.* **1.** Conversion of data into a form that can be processed by computer. **2.** The storing or processing of data by a computer. **—da′ta-pro′cess′ing** (dā′tə-prŏs′ĕs′ĭng, -prō′sĕs′-, dăt′ə-) *adj.*

data processor *n.* **1.** *Comp. Sci.* A device, such as a calculator or computer, that performs operations on data. **2.** A person who processes data.

data set *n. Comp. Sci.* **1.** An electronic device that provides an interface in the transmission of data to a remote station. **2.** A collection of related data records on a computer-readable medium, such as a disk. **3.** See **modem.**

date¹ (dāt) *n.* **1.a.** Time stated in terms of the day, month, and year. **b.** A statement of calendar time, as on a document. **2.** A specified day of a month. **3.** A particular point or period of time at which something happened or is expected to happen. **4.** The time during which something lasts; duration. **5.** The time or historical period to which something belongs. **6.a.** An appointment, esp. to go out socially. See Syns at **engagement. b.** A person's companion on such an outing. **7.** An engagement for a performance. *—v.* **dat•ed, dat•ing, dates.** *—tr.* **1.** To mark or supply with a date. **2.** To determine the date of. **3.** To betray the age of: *Pictures of old cars date the book.* **4.** To go on a date with. *—intr.* **1.** To have origin in a particular time in the past: *This statue dates from 500 B.C.* **2.** To become old-fashioned. **3.** To go on dates. [ME < OFr. < Med.Lat. *data* < Lat. *data (Romae)*, issued (at Rome) (on a certain day), fem. p.part. of *dare*, to give. See **dō-*.**] **—dat′a•ble, date′a•ble** *adj.* **—dat′er** *n.*

date² (dāt) *n.* **1.** The edible fruit of the date palm, containing a thin hard seed. **2.** A date palm. [ME < OFr. < OProv. *datil* < Lat. *dactylus* < Gk. *daktulos*, finger, date (< its shape).]

dat•ed (dā′tĭd) *adj.* **1.** Displaying a date. **2.** Old-fashioned; out-of-date. **—dat′ed•ly** *adv.* **—dat′ed•ness** *n.*

date•less (dāt′lĭs) *adj.* **1.** Having no date. **2.** So ancient that no date can be determined. **3.** Having no limits in time.

date•line (dāt′līn′) *n.* A phrase at the head of a newspaper or magazine article giving the date and place of origin. **—date′line′** *v.*

date line *n.* The International Date Line.

date palm *n.* A palm tree *(Phoenix dactylifera)* of western Asia and northern Africa having featherlike leaves and bearing clusters of dates.

date rape *n.* Rape perpetrated by the victim's social escort.

da•tive (dā′tĭv) *Gram.* *—adj.* Of, relating to, or being the grammatical case that marks the recipient of action or the object of certain prepositions. *—n.* **1.** The dative case. **2.** A word or form in the dative case. [ME *datif* < Lat. *(cāsus)*

Charles Darwin

ă pat	oi boy
ā pay	ou out
âr care	o͝o took
ä father	o͞o boot
ĕ pet	ŭ cut
ē be	ûr urge
ĭ pit	th thin
ī pie	*th* this
îr pier	hw which
ŏ pot	zh vision
ō toe	ə about,
ô paw	item

Stress marks:
′ (primary);
′ (secondary), as in
dictionary (dĭk′shə-nĕr′ē)

datīvus, (case) of giving (transl. of Gk. *dotikē (ptōsis)*) < *datus,* p.part. of *dare,* to give. See **dō-***.] **—da′tive·ly** *adv.*

Da·tong (dä′tông′) also **Ta·tung** (tä′to͝ong′). A city of NE China W of Beijing. Pop. 688,200.

da·tum (dā′təm, dăt′əm, dä′təm) *n.* **1.** *pl.* **-ta** (-tə). A fact or proposition used to draw a conclusion or make a decision. See Usage Note at **data**. **2.** *pl.* **-tums**. A point, line, or surface used as a reference, as in surveying. [Lat., something given < neut. p.part. of *dare,* to give. See **dō-***.]

da·tu·ra (də-to͝or′ə, -tyo͝or′ə) *n.* Any of several plants of the genus *Datura,* having large trumpet-shaped flowers, prickly fruits, and leaves and seeds that yield narcotic alkaloids. [NLat. *Datura,* genus name < Hindi *dhatūrā* < Skt. *dhattūrā,* thorn apple.]

datura

daub (dôb) *v.* **daubed, daub·ing, daubs.** *—tr.* **1.** To cover or smear with a soft adhesive substance, such as plaster or grease. **2.** To apply paint to with crude strokes. *—intr.* To paint with crude strokes. *—n.* **1.** The act or a stroke of daubing. **2.** A soft adhesive coating material, such as plaster or grease. **3.** Matter daubed on; a smear. **4.** A crude painting or picture. [ME *dauben* < OFr. *dauber* < Lat. *dēalbāre,* to whitewash : *dē-,* intensive pref.; see DE- + *albus,* white; see **albho-***.] **—daub′er** *n.* **—daub′er·y** (dô′bə-rē) *n.*

Dau·bi·gny (dō-bē-nyē′), **Charles François.** 1817–78. French painter known for his sensitive portrayal of light.

Dau·det (dō-dā′), **Alphonse.** 1840–97. French writer whose naturalistic stories include *Lettres de mon Moulin* (1869).

Dau·gav·pils (dou′gəf-pĭlz′, -găf-pēlz′). A city of SE Latvia SE of Riga; founded in the 13th cent. Pop. 124,000.

daugh·ter (dô′tər) *n.* **1.** One's female child. **2.** A female descendant. **3.** A woman considered as if in a relationship of child to parent. **4.** One personified or regarded as a female descendant. **5.** *Phys.* The immediate product of the radioactive decay of an element. *—adj.* Possessing the characteristics or relationship of a daughter. [ME *doughter* < OE *dohtor.* See **dhughəter-***.] **—daugh′ter·ly** *adj.*

daughter cell *n. Biol.* Either of the two identical cells that form when a cell divides.

daugh·ter-in-law (dô′tər-ĭn-lô′) *n., pl.* **daugh·ters-in-law** (dô′tərz-). The wife of one's son.

Dau·mier (dō-myā′), **Honoré.** 1808–1879. French artist best known for his bitterly satirical lithographs.

daunt (dônt, dänt) *tr.v.* **daunt·ed, daunt·ing, daunts.** To abate the courage of; discourage. See Syns at **dismay**. [ME *daunten* < OFr. *danter* < Lat. *domitāre,* freq. of *domāre,* to tame. See **demə-***.] **—daunt′er** *n.* **—daunt′ing·ly** *adv.*

daunt·less (dônt′lĭs, dänt′-) *adj.* Incapable of being intimidated or discouraged; fearless. **—daunt′less·ness** *n.*

dau·phin (dô′fĭn) *n.* **1.** The eldest son of the king of France from 1349 to 1830. **2.** Used as a title for such a nobleman. [ME < OFr., title of the lords of Dauphiné < *Dalphin, Dalfin,* a surname < *dalfin,* dolphin (< the device on the family's coat of arms). See DOLPHIN.]

davit

dau·phine (dô-fēn′) *n.* The wife of a dauphin. [Fr., fem. of *dauphin.* See DAUPHIN.]

Dau·phi·né (dō-fē-nā′). A historical region and former province of SE France bordering on Italy.

DAV *abbr.* Disabled American Veterans.

Da·vao (dä′vou′). A city of SE Mindanao, Philippines, on **Davao Gulf**, an inlet of the Pacific. Pop. 270,600.

Dav·e·nant or **D'Av·e·nant** (dăv′ə-nənt, dăv′nənt), Sir **William.** 1606–68. English playwright whose works include *The Siege of Rhodes* (1656).

dav·en·port (dăv′ən-pôrt′, -pōrt′) *n.* **1.** A large sofa, often convertible into a bed. **2.** A small desk. [< *davenport,* a small writing desk (obsolete), prob. < manufacturer's name.]

Dav·en·port (dăv′ĭn-pôrt′, -pōrt′). A city of E IA on the Mississippi R. opposite Rock Island IL. Pop. 95,333.

Da·vid (dā′vĭd). d. c. 962 B.C. The second king of Judah and Israel; reputed author of many of the Psalms.

David, Saint. c. 520–600. Patron saint of Wales, whose shrine was a pilgrimage site during the Middle Ages.

David I. 1082?–1153. King of Scotland (1124–53) who transformed his realm into a feudalistic society.

Da·vid (dä′vət), **Gerard.** 1460?–1523. Dutch painter of religious subjects; one of the most important Flemish primitives.

Da·vid (dä-vēd′), **Jacques Louis.** 1748–1825. French painter whose works include *The Death of Marat* (1793).

Da·vid·son (dā′vĭd-sən), **Jo(seph).** 1883–1952. Amer. sculptor known for his portrait busts.

Da·vie (dā′vē). A town of SE FL SW of Fort Lauderdale. Pop. 47,217.

Da·vies (dā′vēz), **Arthur Bowen.** 1862–1928. Amer. painter and organizer of the revolutionary Armory Show in 1913.

Dá·vi·la y Pa·di·lla (dä′və-lə ē pä-dē′ə, dä′vē-lä ē pä-thē′-yä), **Agustín.** 1562–1604. Mexican prelate who wrote a noted study of the Spanish colonial era.

da Vin·ci (də vĭn′chē, dä), **Leonardo.** See **Leonardo da Vinci.**

Da·vis (dā′vĭs). A city of central CA W of Sacramento. Pop. 46,209.

Davis, Alexander Jackson. 1803–92. Amer. architect noted for his Greek revival buildings.

Moshe Dayan

Davis, Benjamin Oliver. 1877–1970. Amer. cavalry officer who was the first Black general in the U.S. Army (1940–48). His son **Benjamin Oliver Davis, Jr.** (b. 1912), was the first Black general in the U.S. Air Force (1954–70).

Davis, Bette. 1908–89. Amer. actress whose films include *Dangerous* (1935) and *Jezebel* (1938).

Davis, David. 1815–86. Amer. jurist; associate justice of the U.S. Supreme Court (1862–77).

Davis, Jefferson. 1808–89. Amer. soldier and president of the Confederacy (1861–65); indicted for treason (1866) but never prosecuted.

Davis, Miles Dewey, Jr. 1926–91. Amer. jazz musician acclaimed for his warm, often muted trumpet style.

Davis, Rebecca Blaine Harding. 1831–1910. Amer. writer whose works include *Margaret Howth* (1862).

Davis, Richard Harding. 1864–1916. Amer. writer known as the leading correspondent of his day.

Davis, Sammy, Jr. 1925–90. Amer. entertainer famous for his exuberant dancing, singing, and acting.

Davis, Stuart. 1894–1964. Amer. artist who often incorporated jazz tempos into his canvases.

Davis Strait. A strait of the N Alantic between SE Baffin I. and SW Greenland.

dav·it (dăv′ĭt, dā′vĭt) *n. Naut.* Any of various small cranes that project over the side of a ship and are used for hoisting. [ME *daviot* < Norman Fr. *daviot,* dim. of *Davi,* David.]

Da·vy (dā′vē), Sir **Humphry.** 1778–1829. British chemist who was a pioneer of electrochemistry.

Davy Jones (jōnz′) *n.* The bottom of the sea, as personified in songs and stories. [?]

Davy Jones's locker (jōn′zĭz, jōnz) *n.* The bottom of the sea, esp. as the grave of all who perish at sea.

daw (dô) *n.* A jackdaw. [ME *dawe* < OE **dāwe.*]

daw·dle (dôd′l) *v.* **-dled, -dling, -dles.** *—intr.* **1.** To take more time than necessary. **2.** To move aimlessly or lackadaisically. *—tr.* To waste (time) by idling. [Perh. alteration of dial. *daddle,* to diddle.] **—daw′dler** *n.* **—daw′dling·ly** *adv.*

Dawes (dôz), **Charles Gates.** 1865–1951. Vice President of the U.S. (1925–29) who shared the 1925 Nobel Peace Prize.

Dawes, William. 1745–99. Amer. patriot who rode with Paul Revere on Apr. 18, 1775, to warn of the British advance on Lexington and Concord.

dawn (dôn) *n.* **1.** The time at which daylight first begins. **2.** A first appearance; a beginning. See Syns at **beginning**. *—intr.v.* **dawned, dawn·ing, dawns. 1.** To begin to become daylight. **2.** To begin to appear or develop; emerge. **3.** To begin to be perceived. [< ME *daunen,* to dawn, prob. ult. < OE *dagung* < *dagian,* to dawn. See **agh-***.]

dawn redwood *n.* A cone-bearing Chinese tree *(Metasequoia glyptostroboides)* related to the redwood.

Daw·son (dô′sən). A town of W Yukon Terr., Canada, at the confluence of the Yukon and Klondike rivers; a boom town during the Klondike gold rush of the late 1890's. Pop. 697.

Dawson, Sir **John William.** 1820–99. Canadian geologist and anti-Darwinist who was an authority on fossils.

Dawson Creek. A city of NE British Columbia, Canada; S terminus of the Alaska Highway. Pop. 11,373.

day (dā) *n.* **1.** The period of light between dawn and nightfall; the interval from sunrise to sunset. **2.a.** The 24-hour period during which Earth completes one rotation on its axis. **b.** The period during which a celestial body makes a similar rotation. **3.** One of the numbered 24-hour periods into which a week, month, or year is divided. **4.** The portion of a 24-hour period that is devoted to work, school, or business: *an eight-hour day.* **5.** A 24-hour period or a portion of it reserved for a certain activity: *a day of rest.* **6.a.** A period, as of vigor or success, in one's lifetime. **b.** A period of opportunity. **7.** A period of time in history; an era. *—adj.* **1.** Of or relating to the day. **2.** Working during the day. **3.** Occurring before nightfall: *a day hike.* **—*idioms.*** **day after day.** For many days; continuously. **day in, day out.** Every day without fail; continuously. [ME *dai, day* < OE *dæg.* See **agh-***.]

Day (dā), **Clarence Shepard, Jr.** 1874–1935. Amer. writer best known for his autobiographical *Life with Father* (1935).

Day, Dorothy. 1897–1980. Amer. journalist and reformer who cofounded the *Catholic Worker* in 1933.

Day or **Daye** (dā), **Stephen.** 1594?–1668. English-born colonist who printed the *Bay Psalm Book* in 1640.

Day, William Rufus. 1849–1923. Amer. jurist; associate justice of the U.S. Supreme Court (1903–22).

Day·ak (dā′ăk′) or **Dy·ak** (dī′-) *n., pl.* **Dayak** or **-aks** also **Dyak** or **-aks. 1.** A member of any of various Indonesian peoples inhabiting Borneo. **2.** The language of the Dayak.

Da·yan (dä-yän′), **Moshe.** 1915–81. Israeli military leader who directed the 1967 Six-Day War.

day bed or **day·bed** (dā′bĕd′) *n.* A couch or sofa that is convertible into a bed.

day·book (dā′bo͝ok′) *n.* **1.** A book in which daily transactions are recorded. **2.** A diary.

day·break (dā′brāk′) *n.* The beginning of day; dawn.

day camp *n.* A children's camp providing recreation and meals during the day but no overnight facilities.

day•care or **day care** (dā′kâr′) *n.* Provision of daytime training, supervision, and recreation for children, the disabled, or the elderly.

day•dream (dā′drēm′) *n.* A dreamlike musing while awake, esp. of the fulfillment of wishes. —*intr.v.* **-dreamed** or **-dreamt** (-drĕmt′), **-dream•ing, -dreams.** To have dreamlike musings while awake. —**day′dream′er** *n.*

day•flow•er (dā′flou′ər) *n.* Any of various plants of the genus *Commelina,* having blue or purplish flowers that wilt quickly.

day•fly (dā′flī′) *n.* See **mayfly.**

Day-Glo (dā′glō′). A trademark used for fluorescent coloring agents and materials.

day labor *n.* Labor paid by the day. —**day laborer** *n.*

day letter *n.* A telegram sent during the day.

Day Lew•is (lo͞o′ĭs), **Cecil.** 1904–72. Irish-born poet and critic who became poet laureate in 1968.

day•light (dā′līt′) *n.* **1.** The light of day; sunlight. **2.a.** Daybreak. **b.** Daytime. **3.** Exposure to public notice. **4.** Understanding of what had been obscure. **5. daylights.** *Slang.* One's wits.

day•light-sav•ing time (dā′līt-sā′vĭng) *n.* Time during which clocks are set one hour or more ahead of standard time to provide more daylight at the end of the working day during late spring, summer, and early fall.

day lily or **day•lil•y** (dā′lĭl′ē) *n.* Any of several perennial Eurasian herbs of the genus *Hemerocallis* in the lily family, having lilylike flowers.

day•long (dā′lông′, -lŏng′) *adj.* Lasting through the whole day. —*adv.* Through the day; all day.

day nursery *n.* A facility for the supervision of preschool children, esp. during the hours that their parents are at work.

Day of Atonement *n.* See **Yom Kippur.** [Transl. of Heb. *yôm kippûr.*]

Day of Judgment *n.* See **Judgment Day** 1.

day one *n. Informal.* The very beginning; the first day.

day room *n.* A recreation room, as in a barracks.

day school *n.* **1.** A private school for pupils living at home. **2.** A school that holds classes during the day.

day•side (dā′sīd′) *n.* **1.** Office personnel who work days. **2.** The side of a planet facing the sun. —**day′side′** *adj.*

days of grace (dāz) *pl.n.* Extra days allowed for payment of a note or bill after it has come due. [Transl. of Lat. *diēs gratiae.*]

day•star (dā′stär′) *n.* **1.** The morning star. **2.** The sun.

day student *n.* A student at a school who does not reside in the facilities provided by the institution.

day•time (dā′tīm′) *n.* The time between sunrise and sunset. —*adj.* Occurring in or appropriate for use during the day.

day-to-day (dā′tə-dā′) *adj.* **1.** Occurring on a routine or daily basis. **2.** Subsisting one day at a time.

Day•ton (dāt′n). A city of SW OH NNE of Cincinnati; home of Orville and Wilbur Wright. Pop. 182,044.

Day•to•na Beach (dā-tō′nə). A city of NE FL on the Atlantic coast NNE of Orlando; site of automobile speed trials and races since the early 1900's. Pop. 54,176.

day-trip•per (dā′trĭp′ər) *n.* One who takes a trip during the day without an overnight stop.

daze (dāz) *tr.v.* **dazed, daz•ing, daz•es. 1.** To stun, as with a heavy blow or shock; stupefy. **2.** To dazzle, as with strong light. —*n.* A stunned or bewildered condition. [ME *dasen,* of Scand. orig.; akin to ON *dasask,* to become weary.]

daz•zle (dăz′əl) *v.* **-zled, -zling, -zles.** —*tr.* **1.** To dim the vision of, esp. by intense light. **2.** To amaze or bewilder with spectacular display: *a skater who dazzled the audience.* —*intr.* **1.** To become blinded. **2.** To inspire admiration or wonder. —*n.* The act of dazzling or the state of being dazzled. [Freq. of DAZE.] —**daz′zler** *n.* —**daz′zling•ly** *adv.*

dB *abbr.* Decibel.

DB or **D.B.** *abbr.* Daybook.

d.b.a. *abbr.* Doing business as.

D.B.A. *abbr.* Doctor of Business Administration.

D.B.E. *abbr.* Dame Commander of the British Empire.

d.b.h. *abbr.* Diameter at breast height.

D.Bib. *abbr.* Douay Bible.

dble. *abbr.* Double.

dc or **DC** *abbr.* Direct current.

DC or **D.C.** *abbr.* District of Columbia.

D.C. *abbr.* **1.** *Mus.* Da capo. **2.** Doctor of Chiropractic.

D.C.L. *abbr.* **1.** Doctor of Canon Law. **2.** Doctor of Civil Law.

DCM or **D.C.M.** *abbr.* Distinguished Conduct Medal.

dd. *abbr.* Delivered.

D.D. *abbr.* **1.** Dishonorable discharge. **2.** *Lat.* Divinitatis Doctor (Doctor of Divinity).

D-day (dē′dā′) *n.* The unnamed day for launching an operation, esp. June 6, 1944, the day the Allies invaded France during World War II. [*D* (abbr. of DESIGNATED) + DAY.]

D.D.S. *abbr.* **1.** Doctor of Dental Science. **2.** Doctor of Dental Surgery.

DDT (dē′dē-tē′) *n.* A colorless contact insecticide, $C_{14}H_9Cl_5$, banned in the United States for most uses since 1972. [D(I-CHLORO)D(IPHENYL)T(RICHLOROETHANE).]

DE *abbr.* Delaware.

de– *pref.* **1.** Do or make the opposite of; reverse: *decriminalize.* **2.** Remove or remove from: *delouse.* **3.** Out of: *deplane.* **4.** Reduce; degrade: *declass.* **5.** Derived from: *deverbative.* [ME *de-* < OFr. *de-* or *des-;*, OFr. *de-* < Lat. *dē-,* from, off, apart, away, down, out, completely (< *dē;* see **de-***) or < OFr. *des-,* out, off, apart, away, completely (< Lat. *dis-,* dis-, and Lat. *dē-*).]

de•ac•ces•sion (dē′ăk-sĕsh′ən) *v.* **-sioned, -sion•ing, -sions.** —*tr.* To remove and sell (a work of art) from a museum collection, esp. to purchase other works of art. —*intr.* To deaccession a work of art. —**de′ac•ces′sion** *n.*

dea•con (dē′kən) *n.* **1.** A cleric ranking below a priest in the Anglican, Eastern Orthodox, and Roman Catholic churches. **2.** A Protestant layperson who assists the minister. **3.** Used as a title prefixed to the surname of such a person: *Deacon Brown.* [ME *deken* < OE *dīacon* < LLat. *diāconus* < Gk. *diakonos,* attendant.]

dea•con•ess (dē′kə-nĭs) *n.* **1.** A Protestant woman who assists the minister. **2.** Used as a title prefixed to the surname of such a woman: *Deaconess Brown.*

dea•con•ry (dē′kən-rē) *n., pl.* **-ries. 1.** The office or position of a deacon. **2.** Deacons considered as a group.

de•ac•ti•vate (dē-ăk′tə-vāt′) *tr.v.* **-vat•ed, -vat•ing, -vates. 1.** To render inactive or ineffective. **2.** To inhibit, block, or disrupt the action of (a biological agent). **3.** To remove from active military status. —**de•ac′ti•va′tion** *n.* —**de•ac′ti•va′tor** *n.*

dead (dĕd) *adj.* **dead•er, dead•est. 1.** Having lost life; no longer alive. **2.** Marked for death; doomed. **3.a.** Having the physical appearance of death: *a dead pallor.* **b.** Lacking feeling or sensitivity; unresponsive. **c.** Weary and worn-out; exhausted. **4.a.** Not having the capacity to live; inanimate or inert. **b.** Not having the capacity to produce or sustain life; barren: *dead soil.* **5.a.** No longer in existence, use, or operation. **b.** No longer having significance or relevance. **c.** Physically inactive; dormant: *a dead volcano.* **6.a.** Not commercially productive; idle: *dead capital.* **b.** Not circulating or running; stagnant: *dead air.* **7.a.** Devoid of activity; quiet: *a dead town.* **b.** Lacking animation or excitement; dull. **8.** Having no resonance. Used of sounds. **9.** Having grown cold; extinguished: *dead coals.* **10.** Lacking elasticity or bounce. **11.** Out of operation because of a fault or breakdown. **12.a.** Sudden; abrupt: *a dead stop.* **b.** Complete; utter: *dead silence.* **c.** Exact; unerring. **13.** *Sports.* Out of play. Used of a ball. **14.a.** Lacking connection to electric current. **b.** Drained of electric charge; discharged: *a dead battery.* —*n.* **1.** One who has died: *respect for the dead.* **2.** The period of greatest intensity: *the dead of winter.* —*adv.* **1.** Absolutely; altogether. **2.** Directly; exactly. **3.** Suddenly. —***idioms.* dead and buried.** No longer relevant. **dead in the water.** Unable to function or move. **dead to rights.** In the very act of making an error or committing a crime. [ME *ded* < OE *dēad.* See **dheu-²*.**] —**dead′ness** *n.*

dead air *n.* An unintended interruption in a broadcast during which there is no sound.

dead•beat¹ (dĕd′bēt′) *n. Slang.* **1.** One who does not pay debts. **2.** A lazy person; a loafer.

dead•beat² (dĕd′bēt′) *adj.* Having an indicator that stops without oscillation.

dead bolt also **dead•bolt** (dĕd′bōlt′) *n.* A bolt on a lock that is moved by turning the key or knob without activation of a spring.

dead center *n.* The point at the end of each stroke of a moving crank and connecting rod at which the two lie in the same straight line and the turning force applied by the connecting rod is zero.

dead duck *n. Slang.* One doomed to failure or to death.

dead•en (dĕd′n) *v.* **-ened, -en•ing, -ens.** —*tr.* **1.** To render less intense or vigorous: *deaden the pain.* **2.** To make soundproof. **3.** To make less colorful or brilliant. —*intr.* **1.** To become dead. **2.** To lose vigor, brilliance, or liveliness. —**dead′en•er** *n.*

dead end *n.* **1.** An end of a passage, such as a street, that affords no exit. **2.** A point beyond which no movement or progress can be made; an impasse.

dead-end (dĕd′ĕnd′) *adj.* **1.** Having no exit. **2.** Permitting no advancement: *a dead-end job.* **3.** *Informal.* Tough and rowdy: *a dead-end gang.* —*intr.v.* **-end•ed, -end•ing, -ends.** To terminate with no exit or possibility of advancement.

dead•en•ing (dĕd′n-ĭng) *n.* Material used for soundproofing.

dead•eye (dĕd′ī′) *n.* **1.** *Naut.* A flat disk with a grooved perimeter, pierced by holes through which the lanyards are passed to fasten the shrouds. **2.** *Slang.* An expert shooter.

dead•fall (dĕd′fôl′) *n.* **1.** A trap for large animals in which a heavy weight falls on the prey. **2.** A mass of fallen timber and brush.

dead hand *n.* **1.** The ever-present, oppressive influence of past events. **2.** Mortmain. [ME *dede hond,* transl. of OFr. *mortemain* or Med.Lat. *manus mortua,* mortmain.]

dead•head (dĕd′hĕd′) *Informal.* —*n.* **1.** A person who uses a free ticket for admittance or entertainment. **2.** A vehicle carrying no passengers or freight. **3.** A sluggish or dull-witted person. **4.** A partially submerged log or trunk. —*v.* **-head•**

day lily

dead bolt
Lock and extended bolt

ă pat	oi boy
ā pay	ou out
âr care	o͝o took
ä father	o͞o boot
ĕ pet	ŭ cut
ē be	ûr urge
ĭ pit	th thin
ī pie	*th* this
îr pier	hw which
ŏ pot	zh vision
ō toe	ə about, item
ô paw	

Stress marks:
′ (primary);
′ (secondary), as in **dictionary** (dĭk′shə-nĕr′ē)

ed, **-head•ing, -heads.** — *tr.* **1.** To pilot or drive (a vehicle) carrying no passengers or freight. **2.** To pull (dead or dying blossoms) off a flower. — *adv.* Without passengers or freight.

dead heat *n. Sports.* A race in which two or more contestants compete evenly or finish at the same time.

dead letter *n.* **1.** An unclaimed or undelivered letter that after a time is destroyed or returned to the sender by the postal service. **2.** A law, directive, or factor formally in effect but no longer valid or enforced.

dead lift *n. Sports.* A weightlifting event in which the weight is lifted from the floor to the level of the hips and then lowered by controlled effort to the floor.

dead•light (dĕd′līt′) *n.* **1.** *Naut.* **a.** A strong shutter fastened over a porthole in stormy weather. **b.** A thick window in a ship's side or deck. **2.** A skylight that cannot be opened.

dead•line (dĕd′līn′) *n.* **1.** A time limit, as for payment of a debt. **2.** A line in a prison that prisoners can cross only at the risk of being shot. — *tr.v.* **-lined, -lin•ing, -lines.** To govern by setting a time limit.

dead load *n.* The fixed weight of a structure or piece of equipment, such as a bridge on its supports.

dead•lock (dĕd′lŏk′) *n.* A standstill resulting from the opposition of two unrelenting forces. — *tr. & intr.v.* **-locked, -lock•ing, -locks.** To bring or come to a standstill.

dead•ly (dĕd′lē) *adj.* **-li•er, -li•est. 1.** Causing or tending to cause death. **2.** Suggestive of death. **3.** Wanting to kill; implacable. **4.a.** Destructive in effect: *a deadly critique.* **b.** Tending to take away vitality, effectiveness, or force. **5.** Absolute; utter: *deadly concentration.* **6.** Extreme or terrible. **7.** Extremely accurate; unerring. **8.** Dull, tedious, and boring. — *adv.* **1.** So as to suggest death. **2.** To an extreme. — **dead′li•ness** *n.*

deadly nightshade *n.* **1.** See **belladonna** 1. **2.** See **bittersweet nightshade.**

deadly sin *n.* One of the seven sins — anger, covetousness, envy, gluttony, lust, pride, and sloth — that are regarded as fatal to one's soul.

dead-man's float (dĕd′mănz′) *n. Sports.* A prone floating position in which the swimmer's arms are extended straight forward above the head and the legs are held together.

dead march *n. Mus.* A slow, solemn funeral march.

dead nettle *n.* Any of several weedy plants of the genus *Lamium,* having clusters of small, usu. purplish flowers.

dead-on (dĕd′ôn′, -ŏn′) *adj. Informal.* Precisely accurate and to the point.

dead•pan (dĕd′păn′) *n.* **1.** An expressionless face. **2.** A person, esp. a performer, who has or assumes a blank expression. — *adj.* Impassively matter-of-fact, as in style or expression: *deadpan humor.* — *adv.* With a deadpan face. — *tr. & intr.v.* **-panned, -pan•ning, -pans.** To express or express oneself in a deadpan way.

James Dean

dead point *n.* See **dead center.**

dead reckoning *n.* **1.** A method of estimating the position of an aircraft or a ship without astronomical observations, as by applying to a known position the course and distance traveled since. **2.** Prediction based on inference; guesswork. [Poss. alteration of *ded.,* abbr. of *deduced* < *deduce,* to trace from the beginning. See DEDUCE.]

Dead Sea (dĕd). A salt lake, c. 397 m (1,300 ft) below sea level, between Israel and Jordan; the lowest point on the earth.

dead weight *n.* **1.** The weight of a heavy motionless mass. **2.** An oppressive burden or difficulty. **3.** See **dead load.**

dead•wood (dĕd′wo͝od′) *n.* **1.** Dead branches or wood on a tree. **2.** One that is burdensome or superfluous. **3.** *Naut.* The vertical planking between the keel of a vessel and the sternpost.

deaf (dĕf) *adj.* **deaf•er, deaf•est. 1.** Partially or completely lacking in the sense of hearing. **2. Deaf.** Of or relating to the Deaf or their culture. **3.** Refusing to listen. — *n.* **1.** Deaf people considered as a group. **2. Deaf.** The community of deaf people who use American Sign Language. [ME *def, deef* < OE *dēaf.*] — **deaf′ly** *adv.* — **deaf′ness** *n.*

Usage Note: Some writers have lately introduced a distinction between the lowercase noun *deaf,* which is used to refer simply to people with extensive hearing disorders, and the capitalized noun *Deaf,* which refers to the community that uses American Sign Language as a primary means of communication.

deaf•en (dĕf′ən) *v.* **-ened, -en•ing, -ens.** — *tr.* **1.** To make deaf, esp. momentarily by a loud noise. **2.** To make soundproof. — *intr.* To cause deafness. — **deaf′en•ing•ly** *adv.*

deaf-mute also **deaf mute** (dĕf′myo͞ot′) *Offensive.* — *n.* A person who can neither hear nor speak. — *adj.* (dĕf-myo͞ot′). Unable to speak or hear.

deal¹ (dēl) *v.* **dealt** (dĕlt), **deal•ing, deals.** — *tr.* **1.** To give out as a share or portion; apportion. **2.** To distribute among several recipients. See Syns at **distribute. 3.** To sell: *deal cocaine.* **4.** To administer; deliver: *dealt him a blow.* **5.** *Games.* **a.** To distribute (playing cards) among players. **b.** To give (a specific card) to a player while so distributing. — *intr.* **1.** To be occupied; treat: *deals with the Middle Ages.* **2.** To behave in a specified way toward another or others; have transactions: *deals honestly with me.* **3.** To take action with respect to someone or something: *dealing with complaints.* See Syns at **treat. 4.** To do business; trade: *dealing in diamonds.* **5.** *Games.* To distribute playing cards. — *n.* **1.** The act or a round of apportioning or distributing. **2.** *Games.* **a.** Distribution of playing cards. **b.** The cards so distributed; a hand. **c.** The right or turn of a player to distribute the cards. **3.** An indefinite quantity or degree. **4.** An agreement often arranged secretly, as in politics. **5.a.** A business transaction. **b.** An agreement, esp. one that is mutually beneficial. **6.** *Informal.* A sale favorable esp. to the buyer; a bargain. **7.** *Informal.* Treatment received: *a raw deal.* [ME *delen* < OE *dǣlan,* to divide, share. See **dail-***.]

deal² (dēl) *n.* **1.** A fir or pine board cut to standard dimensions. **2.** Fir or pine wood. [ME *dele* < MDu. and MLGer. *dele,* plank.]

de•a•late (dē-ā′lāt′) or **de•a•lat•ed** (-lā′tĭd) — *adj.* Having lost the wings. Used of insects that shed their wings after a mating flight. — *n.* A dealate insect. — **de′a•la′tion** *n.*

deal•er (dē′lər) *n.* **1.** One engaged in buying and selling: *a drug dealer.* **2.** *Games.* The one who distributes cards.

deal•er•ship (dē′lər-shĭp′) *n.* A franchise to sell specified items in a certain area.

deal•fish (dēl′fĭsh′) *n., pl.* **dealfish** or **-fish•es.** An Atlantic ribbonfish *(Trachipterus arcticus)* having a compressed, tapering silvery body. [< DEAL².]

deal•ing (dē′lĭng) *n.* **1. dealings.** Transactions or relations with others, usu. in business. **2.** Method or manner of conduct in relation to others; treatment: *honest dealing.*

de•am•i•nate (dē-ăm′ə-nāt′) *tr.v.* **-nat•ed, -nat•ing, -nates.** To remove an amino group, NH_2, from (an organic compound). — **de•am′i•na′tion** *n.*

de•am•i•nize (dē-ăm′ə-nīz′) *tr.v.* **-nized, -niz•ing, -niz•es.** To deaminate. — **de•am′i•ni•za′tion** (-nĭ-zā′shən) *n.*

dean (dēn) *n.* **1.a.** An administrative officer in charge of a college, faculty, or division in a university. **b.** An officer of a college or high school who counsels students and supervises the enforcement of rules. **2.** *Eccles.* The head of the chapter of canons governing a cathedral or collegiate church. **3.** *Rom. Cath. Ch.* A priest appointed to oversee a group of parishes within a diocese. **4.** The senior member of a body or group. [ME *deen* < OFr. *deien* < LLat. *decānus,* chief of ten < Gk. *dekanos* < *deka,* ten. See **dekm̥***.] — **dean′ship′** *n.*

Dean (dēn), **James Byron.** 1931–55. Amer. actor whose films include *East of Eden* and *Rebel Without a Cause* (both 1955).

Deane (dēn), **Silas.** 1737–89. Amer. diplomat who persuaded France to supply aid to the Revolutionary cause.

dean•er•y (dē′nə-rē) *n., pl.* **-ies.** The office, jurisdiction, or official residence of an ecclesiastical dean.

dean's list (dēnz) *n., pl.* **deans' lists.** A list of students, esp. in a college, who have attained high academic rank.

dear¹ (dîr) *adj.* **dear•er, dear•est. 1.a.** Loved and cherished: *my dearest friend.* **b.** Greatly valued; precious: *lost everything dear to them.* **2.** Highly esteemed or regarded. Used in direct address, esp. in salutations. **3.a.** High-priced; expensive. **b.** Charging high prices. **4.** Earnest; ardent. **5.** *Obsolete.* Noble; worthy. — *n.* **1.** One that is greatly loved. **2.** An endearing, lovable, or kind person. — *adv.* **1.** With fondness; affectionately. **2.** At a high cost: *sold their wares dear.* — *interj.* Used as a polite exclamation, chiefly of surprise or distress. [ME *dere* < OE *dēore.*] — **dear′ly** *adv.* — **dear′ness** *n.*

dear² (dîr) *adj.* Severe; grievous. [ME *dere* < OE *dēor.*]

Dear•born (dîr′bôrn′, -bərn). A city of SE MI W of Detroit. Pop. 89,286.

Dearborn, Henry. 1751–1829. Amer. soldier and politician who fought in the American Revolution.

Dearborn Heights. A city of SE MI, a suburb of Detroit. Pop. 60,838.

Dear John (dîr) *n.* A letter, as to a serviceman, requesting a divorce or ending a personal relationship.

dearth (dûrth) *n.* **1.** A scarce supply; a lack. **2.** Shortage of food; famine. [ME *derthe* < OE **dēorthu,* costliness < *dēore,* costly. See DEAR¹.]

death (dĕth) *n.* **1.** The act of dying; termination of life. **2.** The state of being dead. **3.** The cause of dying. **4.** A manner of dying: *a heroine's death.* **5.** Often **Death.** A personification of the destroyer of life, usu. represented as a skeleton holding a scythe. **6.a.** Bloodshed; murder. **b.** Execution. **7.** *Law.* Civil death. **8.** The termination or extinction of something. — ***idioms.*** **at death's door.** Near to death; gravely ill or injured. **be the death of (someone).** To distress or irritate (someone) to an intolerable degree. **put to death.** To execute. **to death.** To an intolerable degree; extremely. [ME *deeth* < OE *dēath.* See **dheu-²***.]

death angel *n. Bot.* See **death cup.**

death•bed (dĕth′bĕd′) *n.* **1.** The bed on which a person dies. **2.** The last hours before death.

death benefit *n.* Insurance money payable to a deceased person's stipulated beneficiary.

death•blow (dĕth′blō′) *n.* **1.** A stroke or blow that causes death. **2.** A destructive event or occurrence.

death camas also **death camass** *n.* Any of several plants of the genus *Zigadenus* of western North America that have clusters of greenish flowers and are poisonous to livestock.

death cup *n.* A poisonous, usu. white mushroom *(Amanita phalloides)* having a prominent cup-shaped base.

death duty *n. Chiefly British.* A tax on inherited property; an inheritance tax.

death house *n.* See **death row.**

death instinct *n. Psychiat.* **1.** A primitive impulse for destruction, decay, and death, manifested by a turning away from pleasure, postulated by Sigmund Freud as coexisting with and opposing the life instinct. **2.** Death wish.

death•less (dĕth′lĭs) *adj.* Not subject to termination or death; immortal. —**death′less•ly** *adv.* —**death′less•ness** *n.*

death•ly (dĕth′lē) *adj.* **1.** Of, resembling, or characteristic of death: *a deathly silence.* **2.** Causing death; fatal. —*adv.* **1.** In the manner of death. **2.** Extremely; very: *deathly cold.*

death mask *n.* A cast of a person's face taken after death.

death penalty *n.* A sentence of punishment by execution.

death rate *n.* The ratio of total deaths to total population in a specified community or area over a specified period of time.

death rattle *n.* A gurgling or rattling sound sometimes made in the throat of a dying person, caused by breath passing through mucus.

death row (rō) *n.* The part of a prison for housing inmates who have received the death penalty.

death's-head (dĕths′hĕd′) *n.* The human skull as a symbol of mortality or death.

deaths•man (dĕths′mən) *n. Archaic.* An executioner.

death tax *n.* **1.** See **inheritance tax. 2.** See **estate tax.**

death•trap (dĕth′trăp′) *n.* **1.** An unsafe building or other structure. **2.** A perilous circumstance or situation.

Death Valley. An arid desert basin of E CA and W NV.

death warrant *n.* **1.** *Law.* An official order authorizing a person's execution. **2.** Something that destroys hope or expectation; a deathblow.

death•watch (dĕth′wŏch′) *n.* **1.** A vigil kept beside a dying or dead person. **2.** One who guards a condemned person before execution. **3.** A deathwatch beetle.

deathwatch beetle *n.* Any of several wood-burrowing beetles of the family Anobiidae, esp. *Xestobium rufovillosum,* whose head makes a clicking sound that was superstitiously regarded as a portent of death.

death wish *n.* **1.** *Psychiat.* A desire for self-destruction, often accompanied by feelings of depression, hopelessness, and self-reproach. **2.** The desire for the death of another person toward whom one has unconscious hostility.

Deau•ville (dō′vĭl, dō-vēl′). A resort city of NW France on the English Channel. Pop. 4,682.

deb (dĕb) *n. Informal.* A debutante.

deb. *abbr.* Debenture.

de•ba•cle (dĭ-bä′kəl, -băk′əl) *n.* **1.** A sudden collapse, downfall, or defeat; a rout. **2.** A total, often ludicrous failure. **3.** The breaking up of ice in a river. **4.** A violent flood. [Fr. *débâcle* < *débâcler,* to unbar < OFr. *desbacler* : *des-,* de- + *bacler,* to bar, ult. < Lat. *baculum,* rod. See **bak-*.**]

De Ba•key (də bā′kē), **Michael Ellis.** b. 1908. Amer. surgeon who implanted the first totally artificial heart in a human being (1966).

de•bar (dē-bär′) *tr.v.* **-barred, -bar•ring, -bars. 1.** To exclude or shut out; bar. **2.** To forbid, hinder, or prevent. [ME *debarren* < OFr. *desbarer,* to unbar : *des-,* de- + *barer,* to bar (< *barre,* bar; see BAR[1]).] —**de•bar′ment** *n.*

de•bark (dĭ-bärk′) *v.* **-barked, -bark•ing, -barks.** —*tr.* To unload, as from a ship or an airplane. —*intr.* To disembark. [Fr. *débarquer* : *dé-,* from (< OFr. *de-*; see DE-) + *barque,* ship (< OFr.; see BARK[3]).] —**de′bar•ka′tion** (dē′bär-kā′shən) *n.*

de•base (dĭ-bās′) *tr.v.* **-based, -bas•ing, -bas•es.** To lower in character, quality, or value; degrade. See Syns at **degrade.** [DE- + BASE[2].] —**de•base′ment** *n.* —**de•bas′er** *n.*

de•bat•a•ble (dĭ-bā′tə-bəl) *adj.* **1.** That can be argued or discussed. **2.** Open to dispute. —**de•bat′a•bly** *adv.*

de•bate (dĭ-bāt′) *v.* **-bat•ed, -bat•ing, -bates.** —*intr.* **1.** To consider something; deliberate. **2.** To engage in argument by discussing opposing points. **3.** To engage in a formal discussion or argument. **4.** *Obsolete.* To fight or quarrel. —*tr.* **1.** To deliberate on; consider. **2.** To dispute or argue about. **3.** To discuss or argue (a question, for example) formally. **4.** *Obsolete.* To fight or argue for or over. —*n.* **1.** A discussion involving opposing points; an argument. **2.** Deliberation; consideration. **3.** A formal contest of argumentation in which two opposing teams defend and attack a given proposition. **4.** *Obsolete.* Conflict; strife. [ME *debaten* < OFr. *debatre* : *de-,* de- + *battre,* to beat; see BATTER[1].] —**de•bate′ment** *n.* —**de•bat′er** *n.*

de•bauch (dĭ-bôch′) *v.* **-bauched, -bauch•ing, -bauch•es.** —*tr.* **1.a.** To corrupt morally. **b.** To lead away from excellence or virtue. **2.** To reduce the value or quality of; debase. **3.** *Archaic.* To cause to forsake allegiance. —*intr.* To indulge in dissipation. —*n.* **1.** The act or a period of debauchery. **2.** An orgy. [Fr. *débaucher* < OFr. *desbauchier,* to lead astray, rough-hew timber : *des-,* de- + *bauch,* beam, of Gmc. orig.] —**de•bauch′ed•ly** (-bô′chĭd-lē) *adv.* —**de•bauch′er** *n.*

de•bauch•ee (dĭ-bô′chē′, dĕb′ə-shē′, -shā′) *n.* A person who habitually indulges in debauchery or dissipation; a libertine.

de•bauch•er•y (dĭ-bô′chə-rē) *n., pl.* **-ies. 1.a.** Extreme indulgence in sensual pleasures; dissipation. **b. debaucheries.** Orgies. **2.** *Archaic.* Seduction from morality, allegiance, or duty.

de•ben•ture (dĭ-bĕn′chər) *n.* **1.** A certificate or voucher acknowledging a debt. **2.** An unsecured bond issued by a corporation or governmental agency and backed only by the credit standing of the issuer. **3.** A customhouse certificate providing for the payment of a drawback. [ME *debentur* < Lat. *dēbentur,* they are due, third pers. pl. passive of *dēbēre,* to owe. See **ghabh-*.**]

de•bil•i•tate (dĭ-bĭl′ĭ-tāt′) *tr.v.* **-tat•ed, -tat•ing, -tates.** To sap the strength or energy of; enervate. [Lat. *dēbilitāre, dēbilitāt-* < *dēbilis,* weak. See **bel-*.**] —**de•bil′i•ta′tion** *n.* —**de•bil′i•ta′tive** *adj.*

de•bil•i•tat•ed (dĭ-bĭl′ĭ-tā′tĭd) *adj.* Showing impairment of energy or strength; enfeebled.

de•bil•i•ty (dĭ-bĭl′ĭ-tē) *n., pl.* **-ties.** The state of being weak or feeble; infirmity. [ME *debilite* < OFr. < Lat. *dēbilitās* < *dēbilis,* weak. See **bel-*.**]

deb•it (dĕb′ĭt) *n.* **1.** An item of debt as recorded in an account. **2.a.** An entry of a sum in the debit or left-hand side of an account. **b.** The sum of such entries. **3.** The left-hand side of an account where bookkeeping entries are made. **4.** A drawback; a detriment. —*tr.v.* **-it•ed, -it•ing, -its. 1.** To enter (a sum) on the left-hand side of an account. **2.** To charge with a debit. [ME *debite* < Lat. *dēbitum,* debt. See DEBT.]

deb•o•nair also **deb•o•naire** (dĕb′ə-nâr′) *adj.* **1.** Suave; urbane. **2.** Affable; genial. **3.** Carefree and gay; jaunty. [ME *debonaire,* gracious, kindly < OFr. < *de bon aire,* of good lineage or disposition : *de,* of (< Lat. *dē*; see DE-) + *bon, bonne,* good (< Lat. *bonus*; see **deu-[2]***) + *aire,* nest, family; see AERIE.] —**deb′o•nair′ly** *adv.* —**deb′o•nair′ness** *n.*

de•bone (dē-bōn′) *tr.v.* **-boned, -bon•ing, -bones.** To remove the bones from: *debone a chicken breast.*

Deb•o•rah (dĕb′ər-ə, dĕb′rə). In the Bible, a judge who aided the Israelites in their victory over the Canaanites.

de•bouch (dĭ-bouch′, -bo͞osh′) *v.* **-bouched, -bouch•ing, -bouch•es.** —*intr.* **1.** To march from a narrow or confined area into the open. **2.** To emerge; issue. —*tr.* To cause to emerge or issue. [Fr. *déboucher* : *dé-,* out of (< OFr. *des-*; see DE-) + *bouche,* mouth (< Lat. *bucca*).]

de•bouch•ment (dĭ-bouch′mənt, -bo͞osh′-) *n.* **1.** The act or an instance of marching from a narrow confined area into the open. **2.** A debouchure.

de•bou•chure (dĭ-bo͞o′sho͝or′) *n.* An opening or mouth, as of a river or stream.

De•bre•cen (dĕb′rĭt-sĕn′, -rĕ-tsĕn′). A city of E Hungary near the Romanian border E of Budapest. Pop. 208,891.

dé•bride•ment (dā′brēd-mäN′, dĭ-brēd′mənt) *n.* Surgical removal of dead or contaminated tissue and foreign matter from a wound. [Fr. < *débrider,* to unbridle, open up < OFr. *desbrider* : *des-,* de- + *bride,* bridle (prob. < MHGer. *brīdel,* rein).] —**dé•bride′** *v.*

de•brief (dē-brēf′) *tr.v.* **-briefed, -brief•ing, -briefs. 1.** To question to obtain knowledge or intelligence gathered esp. on a military mission. **2.** To instruct not to reveal classified information after leaving employment.

de•bris also **dé•bris** (də-brē′, dā-, dā′brē′) *n.* **1.a.** The scattered remains of something broken or destroyed; rubble or wreckage. **b.** Carelessly discarded refuse; litter. **2.** *Geol.* An accumulation of relatively large rock fragments: *glacial debris.* [Fr. *débris* < OFr. *debrisier,* to break to pieces : *de-,* intensive pref.; see DE- + *brisier,* to break (< VLat. **brīsāre,* to press grapes, prob. of Celt. orig.).]

Debs (dĕbz), **Eugene Victor.** 1855–1926. Amer. labor organizer and socialist leader who ran unsuccessfully for President five times between 1900 and 1920.

debt (dĕt) *n.* **1.** Something owed, such as money, goods, or services. **2.a.** An obligation or liability to pay or render something to someone else. **b.** The condition of owing. **3.** An offense requiring forgiveness or reparation; a trespass. [ME *dette* < OFr. < VLat. **dēbita,* pl. of Lat. *dēbitum,* debt, neut. p.part. of *dēbēre,* to owe. See **ghabh-*.**] —**debt′less** *adj.*

debt•or (dĕt′ər) *n.* **1.** One that owes something to another. **2.** One who is guilty of a trespass or sin. [ME *dettour* < OFr. *dettor* < Lat. *dēbitor* < *dēbitus,* p.part. of *dēbēre,* to owe. See DEBT.]

de•bug (dē-bŭg′) *tr.v.* **-bugged, -bug•ging, -bugs. 1.** To remove a hidden electronic device, such as a microphone, from. **2.** To search for and correct malfunctioning elements or errors in: *debug a computer program.* **3.** To remove insects from, as with a pesticide. —**de•bug′ger** *n.*

de•bunk (dē-bŭngk′) *tr.v.* **-bunked, -bunk•ing, -bunks.** To expose or ridicule the falseness or exaggerated claims of: *debunk a supposed miracle drug.* —**de•bunk′er** *n.*

De•bus•sy (də-byo͞o′sē, dĕb′yo͞o-sē′, də-bü-sē′), **Claude Achille.** 1862–1918. French composer considered the first exponent of musical impressionism.

de•but also **dé•but** (dā-byo͞o′, dā′byo͞o′) —*n.* **1.** A first public appearance, as of a performer. **2.** The formal presentation

death cup
Amanita phalloides

ă pat	oi boy
ā pay	ou out
âr care	o͝o took
ä father	o͞o boot
ĕ pet	ŭ cut
ē be	ûr urge
ĭ pit	th thin
ī pie	*th* this
îr pier	hw which
ŏ pot	zh vision
ō toe	ə about, item
ô paw	

Stress marks:
′ (primary);
′ (secondary), as in
dictionary (dĭk′shə-nĕr′ē)

of playing cards. **4.** A tape deck. **5.** *Slang.* A packet of narcotics. — *tr.v.* **decked, deck•ing, decks. 1.** To furnish with or as if with a deck. **2.** *Slang.* To knock down with force. — *idioms.* **clear the deck.** *Informal.* To prepare for action. **hit the deck.** *Slang.* **1.** To get out of bed. **2.** To fall or drop to a prone position. **3.** To prepare for action. **on deck. 1.** On hand; present. **2.** *Sports.* Waiting to take one's turn. [ME *dekke* < MDu. *dec,* roof, covering. See **(s)teg-*.**]

deck² (dĕk) *tr.v.* **decked, deck•ing, decks. 1.** To clothe with finery; adorn. Often used with *out.* **2.** To decorate. [Du. *dekken,* to cover < MDu. *decken.* See **(s)teg-*.**]

deck chair *n.* A folding chair usu. with arms and a leg rest.

deck•er (dĕk′ər) *n.* Something having a deck or an indicated number of levels. Often used in combination: *double-decker buses.*

deck hand *n. Naut.* A member of a ship's crew who performs manual labor.

deck•house (dĕk′hous′) *n. Naut.* A superstructure on the upper deck of a ship.

deck•le (dĕk′əl) *n.* **1.** A frame used in making paper by hand to form paper pulp into sheets of a desired size. **2.** A deckle edge. [Ger. *Deckel* < *Decke,* cover < *decken,* to cover < MHGer. < OHGer. *decchen.* See **(s)teg-*.**]

deckle edge *n.* The rough edge of handmade paper formed in a deckle. — **deck′le-edged′** (dĕk′əl-ĕjd′) *adj.*

deck tennis *n. Sports.* A game in which a small ring is tossed back and forth over a net.

decl. *abbr.* Declension.

de•claim (dĭ-klām′) *v.* **-claimed, -claim•ing, -claims.** — *intr.* **1.** To deliver a formal recitation, esp. as an exercise in rhetoric or elocution. **2.** To speak loudly and vehemently; inveigh. — *tr.* To utter or recite with rhetorical effect. [ME *declamen* < Lat. *dēclāmāre* : *dē-,* intensive pref.; see DE- + *clāmāre,* to cry out; see **kelə-²*.**] — **de•claim′er** *n.*

dec•la•ma•tion (dĕk′lə-mā′shən) *n.* **1.** A recitation delivered as an exercise in rhetoric or elocution. **2.a.** Vehement oratory. **b.** A speech marked by strong feeling; a tirade. [ME *declamacioun* < Lat. *dēclāmātiō, dēclāmātiōn-* < *dēclāmātus,* p.part. of *dēclāmāre,* to declaim. See DECLAIM.]

de•clam•a•to•ry (dĭ-klăm′ə-tôr′ē, -tōr′ē) *adj.* **1.** Characteristic of a declamation. **2.** Pompously rhetorical; bombastic.

de•clar•ant (dĭ-klâr′ənt) *n.* One that makes a declaration, esp. a person who has signed a declaration of intent to become a U.S. citizen.

dec•la•ra•tion (dĕk′lə-rā′shən) *n.* **1.** An explicit formal announcement, either oral or written. **2.** The act or process of declaring. **3.** A statement of taxable goods or of properties subject to duty. **4.** *Games.* A bid, esp. the final bid of a hand in certain card games.

de•clar•a•tive (dĭ-klâr′ə-tĭv, -klăr′-) *adj.* Serving to declare or state. — **de•clar′a•tive•ly** *adv.*

de•clar•a•to•ry (dĭ-klâr′ə-tôr′ē, -tōr′ē) *adj.* Declarative.

de•clare (dĭ-klâr′) *v.* **-clared, -clar•ing, -clares.** — *tr.* **1.** To make known formally or officially. **2.** To state emphatically or authoritatively; affirm. **3.** To reveal or make manifest; show. **4.** To make a full statement of (dutiable goods, for example). — *intr.* **1.** To make a declaration. **2.** To proclaim one's support, choice, opinion, or resolution. **3.** To choose the order in which cards are to be played from the dummy as well as from one's own hand in games such as bridge. [ME *declaren* < OFr. *declarer* < Lat. *dēclārāre* : *dē-,* intensive pref.; see DE- + *clārāre,* to make clear (< *clārus,* clear; see **kelə-²***).] — **de•clar′a•ble** *adj.* — **de•clar′er** *n.*

de•class (dē-klăs′) *tr.v.* **-classed, -class•ing, -class•es.** To lower in class or status.

dé•clas•sé (dā′klä-sā′) *adj.* **1.** Lowered in class, rank, or social position. **2.** Lacking high station or birth; of inferior social status. [Fr., p.part. of *déclasser,* to lower in class : *dé-,* down (< Lat. *dē-*; see DE-) + *classe,* class; see CLASS.]

de•clas•si•fy (dē-klăs′ə-fī′) *tr.v.* **-fied, -fy•ing, -fies.** To remove security classification from (a document). — **de•clas′si•fi′a•ble** *adj.* — **de•clas′si•fi•ca′tion** (-fĭ-kā′shən) *n.*

de•claw (dē-klô′) *tr.v.* **-clawed, -claw•ing, -claws.** To remove the claws from: *declaw a cat.*

de•clen•sion (dĭ-klĕn′shən) *n.* **1.** *Ling.* **a.** In certain languages, the inflection of nouns, pronouns, and adjectives in categories such as case, number, and gender. **b.** A class of words of one language with the same or a similar system of inflections. **2.** A descending slope; a descent. **3.** A decline or decrease; deterioration. **4.** A deviation, as from a standard or practice. [ME *declenson* < OFr. *declinaison* < Lat. *dēclīnātiō, dēclīnātiōn-,* grammatical declension, declination. See DECLINATION.] — **de•clen′sion•al** *adj.*

dec•li•na•tion (dĕk′lə-nā′shən) *n.* **1.** A sloping or bending downward. **2.** A falling off, esp. from prosperity or vigor. **3.** A deviation, as from a specific direction or standard. **4.** A refusal to accept. **5.** Magnetic declination. **6.** *Astron.* The angular distance to a point on a celestial object, measured north or south from the celestial equator. [ME *declinacioun* < OFr. *declination* < Lat. *dēclīnātiō, dēclīnātiōn-* < *dēclīnātus,* p.part. of *dēclīnāre,* to turn away. See DECLINE.] — **dec′li•na′tion•al** *adj.*

de•cline (dĭ-klīn′) *v.* **-clined, -clin•ing, -clines.** — *intr.* **1.** To express polite refusal. **2.a.** To slope downward; descend. **b.** To bend downward; droop. **3.** To degrade or lower oneself; condescend. **4.** To deteriorate gradually; fail. **5.a.** To sink, as the setting sun. **b.** To draw to a gradual close; wane. — *tr.* **1.** To refuse politely. See Syns at **refuse¹. 2.** To cause to slope or bend downward. **3.** *Gram.* To inflect (a noun, a pronoun, or an adjective) for number and case. — *n.* **1.** The process or result of declining. **2.** A downward movement. **3.** The period when something approaches an end. **4.** A downward slope; a declivity. **5.** A disease that gradually weakens or wastes the body. [ME *declinen* < OFr. *decliner* < Lat. *dēclīnāre,* to turn away, bend downward, change the form of a word : *dē-,* de- + *-clīnāre,* to lean, bend; see **klei-*.**] — **de•clin′a•ble** *adj.* — **de•clin′er** *n.*

de•cliv•i•tous (dĭ-klĭv′ĭ-təs) *adj.* Rather steep.

de•cliv•i•ty (dĭ-klĭv′ĭ-tē) *n., pl.* **-ties.** A downward slope. [Lat. *dēclīvitās* < *dēclīvis,* sloping down : *dē-,* de- + *clīvus,* slope; see **klei-*.**]

dec•o (dĕk′ō) *n.* Art deco.

de•coct (dĭ-kŏkt′) *tr.v.* **-coct•ed, -coct•ing, -cocts. 1.** To extract the flavor of by boiling. **2.** To make concentrated; boil down. [ME *decocten,* to boil < Lat. *dēcoquere, dēcoct-,* to boil down or away : *dē-,* de- + *coquere,* to boil, to cook; see **pekʷ-*.**] — **de•coc′tion** *n.*

de•code (dē-kōd′) *tr.v.* **-cod•ed, -cod•ing, -codes.** To convert from code into plain text. — **de•cod′er** *n.*

de•col•late¹ (dĭ-kŏl′āt′) *tr.v.* **-lat•ed, -lat•ing, -lates.** To behead. [Lat. *dēcollāre, dēcollāt-* : *dē-,* de- + *collum,* neck; see **kʷel-¹*.**] — **de′col•la′tion** *n.*

de•col•late² (dĕk′ə-lāt′, dē-kō′-) *tr.v.* **-lat•ed, -lat•ing, -lates.** To separate the copies of (a computer printout, for example). — **de′col•la′tor** *n.*

dé•colle•tage (dā′kôl-täzh′) *n.* **1.** A low neckline on a woman's garment. **2.** A dress with a low neckline in front. [Fr. < *décolleté,* having a low neckline. See DÉCOLLETÉ.]

dé•colle•té (dā′kôl-tā′) *adj.* **1.** Cut low at the neckline: *a décolleté dress.* **2.** Wearing a garment that is low-cut or strapless. [Fr., p.part. of *décolleter,* to lower a neckline, uncover the neck : *dé-,* off (< Lat. *dē-*; see DE-) + *collet,* collar (< OFr., dim. of *col,* neck, collar < Lat. *collum,* neck; see **kʷel-¹***).]

de•col•o•nize (dē-kŏl′ə-nīz′) *tr.v.* **-nized, -niz•ing, -niz•es.** To free (a colony) from dependent status. — **de•col′o•ni•za′tion** (-nĭ-zā′shən) *n.*

de•col•or•ant (dē-kŭl′ər-ənt) *n.* A bleaching agent.

de•col•or•ize (dē-kŭl′ə-rīz′) *tr.v.* **-ized, -iz•ing, -iz•es.** To remove the color from. — **de•col′or•i•za′tion** (-kŭl′ər-ĭ-zā′shən) *n.* — **de•col′or•iz′er** *n.*

de•com•mis•sion (dē′kə-mĭsh′ən) *tr.v.* **-sioned, -sion•ing, -sions.** To withdraw (a ship, for example) from active service.

de•com•pen•sa•tion (dē′kŏm-pən-sā′shən) *n.* Failure of the heart to maintain adequate blood circulation. — **de•com′pen•sate′** *v.*

de•com•pose (dē′kəm-pōz′) *v.* **-posed, -pos•ing, -pos•es.** — *tr.* **1.** To separate into components or basic elements. **2.** To cause to rot. — *intr.* **1.** To become broken down into components; disintegrate. **2.** To decay; putrefy. — **de′com•pos′a•bil′i•ty** *n.* — **de′com•pos′a•ble** *adj.*

de•com•pos•er (dē′kəm-pō′zər) *n. Ecol.* An organism, often a bacterium or fungus, that feeds on and breaks down dead plant or animal matter.

de•com•po•si•tion (dē-kŏm′pə-zĭsh′ən) *n.* **1.** The act or result of decomposing; disintegration. **2.a.** *Chem.* Separation into constituents by chemical reaction. **b.** *Biol.* Breakdown or decay of organic materials. — **de•com′po•si′tion•al** *adj.*

de•com•pound¹ (dē-kŏm′pound′, dē′kəm-pound′) *adj.* **1.** Compounded or consisting of things or parts that are already compound. **2.** *Bot.* Having or consisting of compound divisions; bipinnate: *a decompound leaf.*

de•com•pound² (dē′kəm-pound′) *tr.v.* **-pound•ed, -pound•ing, -pounds.** To decompose.

de•com•press (dē′kəm-prĕs′) *v.* **-pressed, -press•ing, -press•es.** — *tr.* **1.** To relieve of pressure or compression. **2.** To bring (a person exposed to conditions of increased pressure) gradually back to normal atmospheric pressure. — *intr.* **1.** To adjust to normal atmospheric conditions after being exposed to increased pressure. **2.** *Informal.* To relax.

de•com•pres•sion (dē′kəm-prĕsh′ən) *n* **1.** The act or process of decompressing. **2.** A surgical procedure used to relieve pressure on an organ or part, such as the abdomen.

decompression chamber *n.* A compartment in which atmospheric pressure can be gradually raised or lowered, used esp. in readjusting divers to normal atmospheric pressure.

decompression sickness *n.* A disorder, seen esp. in deep-sea divers or in caisson workers, caused by the formation of nitrogen bubbles in the blood following a rapid drop in pressure and characterized by severe pains in the joints and chest, skin irritation, cramps, and paralysis.

de•con•di•tion (dē′kən-dĭsh′ən) *v.* **-tioned, -tion•ing, -tions.** — *tr.* **1.** *Psychol.* To cause (a conditioned response, such as a phobia) to become extinct. **2.** To cause to decline from a condition of physical fitness. — *intr.* To lose physical fitness.

de•con•gest (dē′kən-jĕst′) *tr.v.* **-gest•ed, -gest•ing, -gests.** To relieve the congestion of (sinuses, for example). —**de′con•ges′tion** (-jĕs′chən) *n.* —**de′con•ges′tive** *adj.*

de•con•ges•tant (dē′kən-jĕs′tənt) *n.* A medication or treatment that breaks up congestion, as of the sinuses, by reducing swelling. — *adj.* Capable of relieving congestion.

de•con•struct (dē′kən-strŭkt′) *tr.v.* **-struct•ed, -struct•ing, -structs.** To write about or analyze (a literary text, for example), following the tenets of deconstruction.

de•con•struc•tion (dē′kən-strŭk′shən) *n.* A philosophical movement and theory of literary criticism that asserts that words can only refer to other words, and attempts to demonstrate how statements about any text subvert their own meanings. —**de′con•struc′tion•ism** *n.* —**de′con•struc′tion•ist** *n.* & *adj.*

de•con•tam•i•nate (dē′kən-tăm′ə-nāt′) *tr.v.* **-nat•ed, -nat•ing, -nates. 1.** To eliminate contamination in. **2.** To make safe by eliminating harmful substances, such as noxious chemicals or radioactive material. —**de′con•tam′i•nant** (-nənt) *n.* —**de′con•tam′i•na′tion** *n.* —**de′con•tam′i•na′tor** *n.*

de•con•trol (dē′kən-trōl′) *tr.v.* **-trolled, -trol•ling, -trols.** To stop control of, esp. by the government. —**de′con•trol′** *n.*

dé•cor or **de•cor** (dā′kôr′, dā-kôr′) *n.* **1.a.** Decoration. **b.** A decorative style or scheme, as of a room. **2.** A stage setting; scenery. [Fr. < *décorer*, to decorate < Lat. *decorāre*, to beautify. See DECORATE.]

dec•o•rate (dĕk′ə-rāt′) *tr.v.* **-rat•ed, -rat•ing, -rates. 1.** To furnish or adorn with something ornamental; embellish. **2.** To confer a medal or other honor on. [< ME *decorat*, made beautiful < Lat. *decorātus*, p.part. of *decorāre*, to beautify < *decus, decor-*, honor, ornament. See **dek-***.]

dec•o•ra•tion (dĕk′ə-rā′shən) *n.* **1.** The act, process, or art of decorating. **2.** Something used to decorate. **3.** An emblem of honor, such as a medal or badge.

Dec•o•ra•tion Day (dĕk′ə-rā′shən) *n.* See **Memorial Day.**

dec•o•ra•tive (dĕk′ər-ə-tĭv, -ə-rā′-) *adj.* Serving to decorate or embellish; ornamental. —**dec′o•ra•tive•ly** *adv.* —**dec′o•ra•tive•ness** *n.*

dec•o•ra•tor (dĕk′ə-rā′tər) *n.* One that decorates, esp. an interior decorator.

dec•o•rous (dĕk′ər-əs, dĭ-kôr′əs, -kōr′-) *adj.* Characterized by or exhibiting decorum; proper: *decorous behavior.* [< Lat. *decōrus*, becoming, handsome < *decor*, seemliness, beauty. See **dek-***.] —**dec′o•rous•ly** *adv.* —**dec′o•rous•ness** *n.*

de•cor•ti•cate (dē-kôr′tĭ-kāt′) *tr.v.* **-cat•ed, -cat•ing, -cates. 1.** To remove the bark, husk, or outer layer from; peel. **2.** To remove the surface layer, membrane, or fibrous cover of. [Lat. *dēcorticāre, dēcorticāt-* : *dē-*, de- + *cortex, cortic-*, bark, rind; see **sker-**[1]*.] —**de•cor′ti•ca′tion** *n.* —**de•cor′ti•ca′tor** *n.*

de•co•rum (dĭ-kôr′əm, -kōr′-) *n.* **1.** Appropriateness of behavior or conduct; propriety. **2.** The conventions of polite behavior. **3.** The appropriateness of an element of an artistic or literary work, such as style or tone, to other elements, such as subject matter and character. [Lat. *decōrum* < *decōrus*, becoming, handsome. See DECOROUS.]

de•cou•page also **dé•cou•page** (dā′ko͞o-päzh′) *n.* **1.** The technique of decorating a surface with cutouts, as of paper. **2.** A creation produced by this technique. [Fr. *découpage* < *découper*, to cut up or out < OFr. *descolper* : *des-*, de- + *colper*, to cut (< *colp*, stroke; see COUP).]

de•cou•ple (dē-kŭp′əl) *tr.v.* **-pled, -pling, -ples. 1.** *Electron.* To reduce or eliminate the coupling of (one circuit or part to another). **2.** To separate or detach. —**de•cou′pler** *n.*

de•coy (dē′koi′, dĭ-koi′) *n.* **1.a.** A living or artificial bird or other animal used to entice game into a trap or within shooting range. **b.** An enclosed place into which wildfowl are lured for capture. **2.** A means used to mislead or lead into danger. — *tr.v.* (dĭ-koi′) **-coyed, -coy•ing, -coys.** To lure or entrap by or as if by a decoy. [Poss. < Du. *de kooi*, the cage : *de*, the (< MDu.; see **to-***) + *kooi*, cage (< MDu. *côie* < Lat. *cavea*).] —**de•coy′er** *n.*

de•crease (dĭ-krēs′) *intr.* & *tr.v.* **-creased, -creas•ing, -creas•es.** To grow or cause to grow gradually less or smaller, as in number, amount, or intensity. — *n.* (dē′krēs′). **1.** The act or process of decreasing. **2.** The amount by which something decreases. [ME *decresen* < OFr. *decreistre, decreiss-* < Lat. *dēcrēscere* : *dē-*, de- + *crēscere*, to grow; see **ker-**[2]*.] —**de•creas′ing•ly** *adv.*

Syns: *decrease, lessen, reduce, dwindle, abate, diminish, subside.* These verbs mean to become or cause to become smaller or less. *Decrease* and *lessen* refer to steady or gradual diminution: *Lack of success decreases confidence. His appetite lessens as his illness progresses. Reduce* emphasizes bringing down in size, degree, or intensity: *The workers reduced their wage demands. Dwindle* suggests decreasing bit by bit to a vanishing point: *Their savings dwindled away. Abate* stresses a decrease in amount or intensity and suggests a reduction of excess: *Toward evening the fire began to abate. Diminish* implies taking away or removal: *The warden's authority diminished after the revolt. Subside* implies a falling away to a more normal level: *Our wild enthusiasm did not subside.*

de•cree (dĭ-krē′) *n.* **1.** An authoritative order having the force of law. **2.** *Law.* The judgment of a court of equity, admiralty, probate, or divorce. — *v.* **-creed, -cree•ing, -crees.** — *tr.* To ordain, establish, or decide by decree. See Syns at **dictate.** — *intr.* To issue a decree. [ME *decre* < OFr. *decret* < Lat. *dēcrētum*, principle, decision < neut. p.part. of *dēcernere*, to decide : *dē-*, de- + *cernere*, to sift; see **krei-***.] —**de•cree′a•ble** *adj.* —**de•cre′er** *n.*

dec•re•ment (dĕk′rə-mənt) *n.* **1.** The act or process of decreasing or becoming gradually less. **2.** The amount lost by gradual diminution or waste. **3.** *Math.* The amount by which a variable is decreased; a negative increment. [Lat. *dēcrēmentum* < *dēcrēscere*, to decrease. See DECREASE.] —**dec′re•men′tal** (-mĕn′tl) *adj.*

de•crep•it (dĭ-krĕp′ĭt) *adj.* Weakened, worn out, impaired, or broken down by old age, illness, or hard use. [ME < OFr. < Lat. *dēcrepitus*, worn out : *dē-*, de- + *crepitus*, p.part. of *crepāre*, to burst.] —**de•crep′it•ly** *adv.*

de•crep•i•tate (dĭ-krĕp′ĭ-tāt′) *v.* **-tat•ed, -tat•ing, -tates.** — *tr.* To roast or calcine (crystals or salts) until they emit a crackling sound or until crackling stops. — *intr.* To make a crackling sound when roasted. [NLat. *dēcrepitāre, dēcrepitāt-* : Lat. *dē-*, de- + Lat. *crepitāre*, to crackle, freq. of *crepāre*, to burst, crack.] —**de•crep′i•ta′tion** *n.*

de•crep•i•tude (dĭ-krĕp′ĭ-to͞od′, -tyo͞od′) *n.* The quality or condition of being weakened, worn out, impaired, or broken down by old age, illness, or hard use.

de•cre•scen•do (dā′krə-shĕn′dō, dē′-) *Mus.* — *adv.* & *adj.* With gradually diminishing force or loudness. — *n., pl.* **-dos. 1.** A gradual decrease in force or loudness. **2.** A decrescendo passage. [Ital., gerund of *decrescere*, to decrease < Lat. *dēcrēscere*. See DECREASE.]

de•cres•cent (dĭ-krĕs′ənt) *adj.* Becoming gradually less; waning. [Lat. *dēcrēscēns, dēcrēscent-*, pr.part. of *dēcrēscere*, to decrease. See DECREASE.]

de•cre•tal (dĭ-krēt′l) *n. Rom. Cath. Ch.* A decree, esp. a papal letter giving a decision on a point of canon law. [ME < OFr. *decretale* < LLat. *dēcrētālis*, fixed by decree < Lat. *dēcrētum*, principle, decision. See DECREE.]

de•cre•tive (dĭ-krē′tĭv) *adj.* Decretory.

dec•re•to•ry (dĕk′rĭ-tôr′ē, -tōr′ē, dĭ-krē′tə-rē) *adj.* Of, relating to, or having the force of a decree.

de•crim•i•nal•ize (dē-krĭm′ə-nə-līz′) *tr.v.* **-ized, -iz•ing, -iz•es.** To reduce or abolish criminal penalties for. —**de•crim′i•nal•i•za′tion** (-nə-lĭ-zā′shən) *n.*

de•cry (dĭ-krī′) *tr.v.* **-cried, -cry•ing, -cries. 1.** To condemn openly. **2.** To depreciate (currency, for example) by official proclamation or by rumor. [Fr. *décrier* < OFr. *descrier* : *des-*, de- + *crier*, to cry; see CRY.] —**de•cri′er** *n.*

de•crypt (dē-krĭpt′) *tr.v.* **-crypt•ed, -crypt•ing, -crypts. 1.** To decipher. **2.** To decode. — *n.* (dē′krĭpt′). A deciphered or decoded message. [DE- + *-crypt* (< CRYPTOGRAM).] —**de•cryp′tion** *n.*

de•cu•bi•tus ulcer (dĭ-kyo͞o′bĭ-təs) *n.* See **bedsore.** [Med.Lat. *dēcubitus*, lying down, being bedridden < p.part. of Lat. *dēcumbere*, to lie down. See DECUMBENT.]

de•cum•bent (dĭ-kŭm′bənt) *adj.* **1.** Lying down; reclining. **2.** *Bot.* Lying or growing on the ground but with erect or rising tips. [Lat. *dēcumbēns, dēcumbent-*, pr.part. of *dēcumbere*, to lie down : *dē-*, de- + *-cumbere*, to lie down.] —**de•cum′bence** (-bəns), **de•cum′ben•cy** (-bən-sē) *n.*

dec•u•ple (dĕk′yə-pəl) *adj.* **1.** Ten times as great; tenfold. **2.** In groups of ten. [ME < OFr. < LLat. *decuplus* : Lat. *decem*, ten; see **dekm̥*** + Lat. *-plus*, -fold; see **pel-**[2]*.]

de•cur•rent (dĭ-kûr′ənt, -kŭr′-) *adj. Bot.* Having the leaf base extending down the stem below the insertion. [ME < Lat. *dēcurrēns, dēcurrent-*, pr.part. of *dēcurrere*, to run down : *dē-*, de- + *currere*, to run; see **kers-***.] —**de•cur′rent•ly** *adv.*

de•cus•sate (dĭ-kŭs′āt′, dĕk′ə-sāt′) *tr.* & *intr.v.* **-sat•ed, -sat•ing, -sates.** To cross or become crossed so as to form an X; intersect. — *adj.* **1.** Intersected or crossed in the form of an X. **2.** *Bot.* Arranged on a stem in opposite pairs at right angles to those above or below. [Lat. *decussāre, decussāt-* < *decussis*, the number ten, intersection of two lines (from the Romans' use of X for the numeral 10), a ten as coin : *decem*, ten; see **dekm̥*** + *assis*, as (coin).] —**de•cus′sate′ly** *adv.*

dec•us•sa•tion (dĕk′ə-sā′shən, dē′kə-) *n.* **1.** A crossing in the shape of an X. **2.** *Anat.* An X-shaped crossing, esp. of nerves or bands of nerve fibers, connecting corresponding parts on opposite sides of the brain or spinal cord.

D.Ed. *abbr.* Doctor of Education.

de•dans (də-dän′) *n., pl.* **dedans** (-dän′, -dänz′). *Sports.* **1.** A screened gallery for spectators at the service end of a court tennis court. **2.** The spectators at a court tennis match. [Fr. < *dedans*, inside < OFr. *dedenz* : *de*, of, from (< Lat. *dē*; see DE-) + *denz*, within (< LLat. *deintus*, from within : Lat. *dē* + Lat. *intus*, within; see **en***).]

Ded•ham (dĕd′əm). A town of E MA, a suburb of Boston on the Charles R. Pop. 23,782.

ded•i•cate (dĕd′ĭ-kāt′) *tr.v.* **-cat•ed, -cat•ing, -cates. 1.** To set apart for a deity or for religious purposes; consecrate.

decoy

ă pat	oi boy
ā pay	ou out
âr care	o͝o took
ä father	o͞o boot
ĕ pet	ŭ cut
ē be	ûr urge
ĭ pit	th thin
ī pie	*th* this
îr pier	hw which
ŏ pot	zh vision
ō toe	ə about, item
ô paw	

Stress marks:
′ (primary);
′ (secondary), as in
dictionary (dĭk′shə-nĕr′ē)

2. A lack or shortage, esp. of something essential to health.

deficiency disease *n.* A disease, such as rickets or scurvy, that is caused by a dietary deficiency of specific nutrients, esp. a vitamin or mineral.

de•fi•cient (dĭ-fĭsh′ənt) *adj.* **1.** Lacking an essential quality or element. **2.** Inadequate in amount or degree; insufficient. [Lat. *dēficiēns, dēficient-*, pr.part. of *dēficere*, to fail, be wanting. See DEFECT.] **—de•fi′cient** *n.* **—de•fi′cient•ly** *adv.*

def•i•cit (dĕf′ĭ-sĭt) *n.* **1.a.** Inadequacy or insufficiency. **b.** A deficiency or impairment in mental or physical functioning. **c.** An unfavorable condition or position; a disadvantage. **2.a.** The amount by which a sum of money falls short of the required or expected amount; a shortage. **b.** A business loss. [Fr. *déficit* < Lat. *dēficit*, it is lacking, third pers. sing. pr.t. of *dēficere*, to fail, be lacking. See DEFECT.]

deficit spending *n.* The spending of public funds obtained by borrowing rather than by taxation.

de•fi•er (dĭ-fī′ər) *n.* One that defies: *a defier of tradition.*

def•i•lade (dĕf′ə-lād′, -läd′) *tr.v.* **-lad•ed, -lad•ing, -lades.** To arrange (fortifications) in such a way as to give protection from enfilading and other fire. **—** *n.* **1.** The act or procedure of defilading. **2.** A fortified position offering protection from enfilading and other fire. [DE- + (EN)FILADE.]

de•file[1] (dĭ-fīl′) *tr.v.* **-filed, -fil•ing, -files. 1.** To make filthy or dirty; pollute. **2.** To debase the pureness or excellence of; corrupt. **3.** To profane or sully (a good name, for example). **4.** To make unclean or unfit for ceremonial use; desecrate. **5.** To violate the chastity of. [ME *defilen*, alteration (influenced by *filen* < OE *fȳlan*; see **pū-***) of *defoulen*, to trample on, abuse, pollute < OFr. *defouler*, to trample, full cloth : *de-*, de- + *fouler*, to trample, beat down; see FULL[2].] **—de•file′ment** *n.* **—de•fil′er** *n.* **—de•fil′ing•ly** *adv.*

de•file[2] (dĭ-fīl′) *intr.v.* **-filed, -fil•ing, -files.** To march in single file or in files or columns. **—** *n.* **1.** A narrow gorge or pass that restricts lateral movement, as of troops. **2.** A march in a line. [Fr. *défiler* : *dé-*, away, off (< OFr. *de-*; see DE-) + *file*, line, file (< OFr. *filer*, march in line; see FILE[1]).]

de•fine (dĭ-fīn′) *v.* **-fined, -fin•ing, -fines. —** *tr.* **1.a.** To state the precise meaning of (a word, for example). **b.** To describe the nature or basic qualities of; explain. **2.a.** To delineate the outline or form of. **b.** To specify distinctly. **3.** To serve to distinguish; characterize. **—** *intr.* To make or write a definition. [ME *definen, diffinen* < OFr. *definir, diffiner* < Lat. *dēfīnīre*, to limit, determine : *dē-*, intensive pref.; see DE- + *fīnis*, boundary, limit.] **—de•fin′a•bil′i•ty** *n.* **—de•fin′a•ble** *adj.* **—de•fin′a•bly** *adv.* **—de•fine′ment** *n.* **—de•fin′er** *n.*

de•fin•i•en•dum (dĭ-fĭn′ē-ĕn′dəm) *n., pl.* **-da** (-də). A word or expression that is being defined. [Lat. *dēfīniendum*, neut. gerundive of *dēfīnīre*, to define. See DEFINE.]

de•fin•i•ens (dĭ-fĭn′ē-ĕnz′) *n., pl.* **-en•ti•a** (-ĕn′shē-ə, -shə). The word or words serving to define another word or expression, as in a dictionary entry. [Lat. *dēfīniēns*, pr.part. of *dēfīnīre*, to define. See DEFINE.]

def•i•nite (dĕf′ə-nĭt) *adj.* **1.** Having distinct limits: *definite restrictions on smoking.* **2.** Indisputable; certain: *a definite victory.* **3.** Clearly defined; explicitly precise. **4.** *Gram.* Limiting or particularizing. **5.** *Bot.* **a.** Of a specified number not exceeding 20, as certain floral organs, esp. stamens. **b.** Cymose; determinate. [ME *diffinite*, defined < Lat. *dēfīnītus*, p.part. of *dēfīnīre*, to define. See DEFINE.] **—def′i•nite•ly** *adv.* **—def′i•nite•ness** *n.*

Usage Note: *Definite* and *definitive* both apply to what is precisely defined or explicitly set forth. But *definitive* generally refers specifically to a judgment or description that serves as a standard or reference point for others, as in *the definitive decision of the court* (which sets forth a final resolution of a judicial matter).

definite article *n. Gram.* A member of the class of determiners that restrict or particularize a noun, as *the* in English.

definite integral *n. Math.* An integral between two specified limits, usu. expressed as $\int_b^a f(x)dx$, whose value is the area bounded by the curve $f(x)$, the limits a and b, and the x-axis.

def•i•ni•tion (dĕf′ə-nĭsh′ən) *n.* **1.a.** A statement conveying fundamental character. **b.** A statement of the meaning of a word, phrase, or term. **2.** The act or process of stating a precise meaning or significance; formulation of a meaning. **3.a.** The act of making clear and distinct. **b.** The state of being closely outlined or determined. **4.a.** The clarity of detail in an optically produced image, such as a photograph, effected by a combination of resolution and contrast. **b.** The degree of clarity with which a televised image or broadcast signal is received. [ME *diffinicioun* < OFr. *definition* < Lat. *dēfīnītiō-, dēfīnītiōn-* < *dēfīnītus*, p.part. of *dēfīnīre*, to define. See DEFINE.] **—def′i•ni′tion•al** *adj.*

de•fin•i•tive (dĭ-fĭn′ĭ-tĭv) *adj.* **1.** Precisely defined or explicit. **2.** Supplying or being a final settlement or decision; conclusive. **3.** Authoritative and complete: *a definitive biography.* See Usage Note at **definite. 4.** *Biol.* Fully formed or developed, as an organ or structure. **—** *n. Gram.* A word that defines or limits, such as the definite article. **—de•fin′i•tive•ly** *adv.* **—de•fin′i•tive•ness** *n.*

definitive host *n.* The host organism in or on which a parasite reaches reproductive maturity.

de•fin•i•tude (dĭ-fĭn′ĭ-to͞od′, -tyo͞od′) *n.* The quality of being definite or exact; precision.

def•la•grate (dĕf′lə-grāt′) *intr. & tr.v.* **-grat•ed, -grat•ing, -grates.** To burn or cause to burn with great heat and intense light. [Lat. *dēflagrāre, dēflagrāt-* : *dē-*, intensive pref.; see DE- + *flagrāre*, to blaze; see **bhel-**[1]*****.] **—def′la•gra′tion** *n.*

de•flate (dĭ-flāt′) *v.* **-flat•ed, -flat•ing, -flates. —** *tr.* **1.a.** To release contained air or gas from. **b.** To collapse by releasing contained air or gas. **2.** To reduce the size or importance of. **3.** *Econ.* **a.** To reduce the amount or availability of (currency or credit), effecting a decline in prices. **b.** To produce deflation in (an economy). **—** *intr.* To be or become deflated. [DE- + (IN)FLATE.] **—de•fla′tor** *n.*

de•fla•tion (dĭ-flā′shən) *n.* **1.** The act of deflating or the condition of being deflated. **2.** *Econ.* A persistent decrease in the level of consumer prices or a persistent increase in the purchasing power of money because of a reduction in available currency and credit. **—de•fla′tion•ar′y** (-shə-nĕr′ē) *adj.* **—de•fla′tion•ist** *n.*

de•flect (dĭ-flĕkt′) *intr. & tr.v.* **-flect•ed, -flect•ing, -flects.** To turn aside or cause to turn aside; bend or deviate. [Lat. *dēflectere* : *dē-*, de- + *flectere*, to bend.] **—de•flect′a•ble** *adj.* **—de•flec′tive** *adj.* **—de•flec′tor** *n.*

de•flec•tion (dĭ-flĕk′shən) *n.* **1.** The act of deflecting or the condition of being deflected. **2.** Deviation or a specified amount of deviation. **3.** The deviation of an indicator of a measuring instrument from zero or from its normal position.

de•flexed (dĭ-flĕkst′, dē′flĕkst′) *adj. Bot.* Bent or turned downward at a sharp angle: *deflexed petals.* [< Lat. *dēflexus*, p.part. of *dēflectere*, to bend. See DEFLECT.]

de•flex•ion (dĭ-flĕk′shən) *n. Chiefly British.* Var. of **deflection.**

def•lo•ra•tion (dĕf′lə-rā′shən) *n.* **1.** The act of deflowering. **2.** Rupture of the hymen, typically in sexual intercourse. [ME *defloracioun* < LLat. *dēflōrātiō, dēflōrātiōn-* < *dēflōrātus*, p.part. of *dēflōrāre*, to deflower. See DEFLOWER.]

de•flow•er (dē-flou′ər) *tr.v.* **-ered, -er•ing, -ers. 1.** To take away the virginity of (a woman). **2.** To destroy the innocence, integrity, or beauty of; ravage. [ME *deflouren* < OFr. *desflourer* < LLat. *dēflōrāre* : Lat. *dē-*, ce- + Lat. *flōs, flōr-*, flower; see **bhel-**[3]*****.] **—de•flow′er•er** *n.*

de•fo•cus (dē-fō′kəs) *tr.v.* **-cused, -cus•ing, -cus•es** or **-cussed, -cus•sing, -cus•ses.** To cause (a beam or a lens) to deviate from accurate focus. **—** *n.* The act or result of defocusing a lens.

De•foe (dĭ-fō′), **Daniel.** 1660–1731. British writer whose works include *Robinson Crusoe* (1719).

de•fog (dē-fôg′, -fŏg′) *tr.v.* **-fogged, -fog•ging, -fogs.** To remove condensed water vapor from. **—de•fog′ger** *n.*

de•fo•li•ant (dē-fō′lē-ənt) *n.* A chemical sprayed or dusted on plants to cause the leaves to fall off.

de•fo•li•ate (dē-fō′lē-āt′) *v.* **-at•ed, -at•ing, -ates. —** *tr.* **1.** To deprive of foliage. **2.** To cause the leaves to fall off of, esp. by the use of chemicals. **—** *intr.* To lose foliage. [LLat. *dēfoliāre, dēfoliāt-* : Lat. *dē-*, de- + Lat. *folium*, leaf; see **bhel-**[3]*****.] **—de•fo′li•ate** (-ĭt) *adj.* **—de•fo′li•a′tion** *n.* **—de•fo′li•a′tor** *n.*

de•force (dē-fôrs′, -fōrs′) *tr.v.* **-forced, -forc•ing, -forc•es.** *Law.* To withhold (something) by force from the rightful owner. [ME *deforcen* < AN *deforcer* < OFr. *desforcier* : *des-*, de- + *forcier*, to force (< VLat. **fortiāre* < Lat. *fortis*, strong; see **bhergh-**[2]*****).] **—de•force′ment** *n.*

de•for•est (dē-fôr′ĭst, -fŏr′-) *tr.v.* **-est•ed, -est•ing, -ests.** To cut down and clear away the trees or forests from. **—de•for′es•ta′tion** (-ĭ-stā′shən) *n.* **—de•for′est•er** *n.*

De For•est (dĭ fôr′ĭst, fŏr′-), **Lee.** 1873–1961. Amer. electrical engineer and originator of radio news broadcasts (1916).

de•form (dĭ-fôrm′) *v.* **-formed, -form•ing, -forms. —** *tr.* **1.** To spoil the natural form of; misshape. **2.** To spoil the beauty or appearance of; disfigure. **3.** *Phys.* To alter the shape of by pressure or stress. **—** *intr.* To become deformed. [ME *deformen* < OFr. *deformer* < Lat. *dēformāre* : *dē-*, de- + *forma*, form.] **—de•form′a•bil′i•ty** *n.* **—de•form′a•ble** *adj.*

de•for•ma•tion (dē′fôr-mā′shən, dĕf′ər-) *n.* **1.a.** The act or process of deforming. **b.** The condition of being deformed. **2.** An alteration of form for the worse. **3.** *Phys.* **a.** An alteration of shape by pressure or stress. **b.** The resultant shape.

de•formed (dĭ-fôrmd′) *adj.* Distorted in form; misshapen.

de•for•mi•ty (dĭ-fôr′mĭ-tē) *n., pl.* **-ties. 1.** The state of being deformed. **2.** A bodily malformation, distortion, or disfigurement. **3.** One that is deformed. **4.** Gross ugliness or distortion.

de•fraud (dĭ-frôd′) *tr.v.* **-fraud•ed, -fraud•ing, -frauds.** To take something from by fraud; swindle. [ME *defrauden* < OFr. *defrauder* < Lat. *dēfraudāre* : *dē-*, de- + *fraudāre*, to cheat (< *fraus, fraud-*, fraud).] **—de′fraud•a′tion** (dē′frô-dā′shən) *n.* **—de•fraud′er** *n.*

de•fray (dĭ-frā′) *tr.v.* **-frayed, -fray•ing, -frays.** To undertake the payment of (costs or expenses); pay. [Fr. *défrayer* < OFr. *desfrayer* : *des-*, de- + **frai*, expense (< Lat. *frāctum* < neut.

p.part. of *frangere*, to break; see **bhreg-***).] —**de•fray′a•ble** *adj.* —**de•fray′al** *n.*

de•frock (dē-frŏk′) *tr.v.* **-frocked, -frock•ing, -frocks.** To unfrock.

de•frost (dē-frôst′, -frŏst′) *v.* **-frost•ed, -frost•ing, -frosts.** —*tr.* **1.** To remove ice or frost from. **2.** To cause to thaw. —*intr.* To become thawed.

de•frost•er (dē-frô′stər, -frŏs′tər) *n.* **1.** A device to remove or prevent frost. **2.** A device that thaws frozen goods.

deft (dĕft) *adj.* **deft•er, deft•est.** Quick and skillful; adroit. See Syns at **dexterous.** [ME, gentle, humble, var. of *dafte*, foolish. See DAFT.] —**deft′ly** *adv.* —**deft′ness** *n.*

de•fu•el (dē-fyo͞o′əl) *tr.v.* **-eled, -el•ing, -els** also **-elled, -el•ling, -els.** To remove the fuel from: *defuel a rocket.*

de•funct (dĭ-fŭngkt′) *adj.* Having ceased to exist or live. [Lat. *dēfūnctus*, p.part. of *dēfungī*, to finish : *dē-*, de- + *fungī*, to perform.] —**de•func′tive** *adj.* —**de•funct′ness** *n.*

de•fund (dē-fŭnd′) *tr.v.* **-fund•ed, -fund•ing, -funds.** To stop the flow of funds to: *defund a federal program.*

de•fuse (dē-fyo͞oz′) *tr.v.* **-fused, -fus•ing, -fus•es. 1.** To remove the fuse from (an explosive device). **2.** To make less dangerous, tense, or hostile.

de•fy (dĭ-fī′) *tr.v.* **-fied, -fy•ing, -fies. 1.a.** To oppose or resist with boldness and assurance. **b.** To refuse to submit to or cooperate with. **2.** To be unaffected by; resist or withstand. **3.** To challenge or dare (someone) to do something. [ME *defien* < OFr. *desfier* < VLat. **disfīdāre* : Lat. *dis-*, dis- + Lat. *fīdus*, faithful; see **bheidh-***.]

deg or **deg.** *abbr.* Degree.

dé•ga•gé (dā′gä-zhā′) *adj.* Free and relaxed in manner; casual. [Fr., p.part. of *dégager*, to disengage < OFr. *desgagier* : *des-*, de- + *gage*, pledge (of Gmc. orig.).]

De•gas (də-gä′), **(Hilaire Germain) Edgar.** 1834–1917. French painter and sculptor noted for his studies of ballet dancers.

de Gaulle (də gōl′, gôl′), **Charles André Joseph Marie.** 1890–1970. French general and politician who was the first president (1959–69) of the Fifth Republic.

de•gauss (dē-gous′) *tr.v.* **-gaussed, -gauss•ing, -gauss•es. 1.** To neutralize the magnetic field of (a ship, for example). **2.** To erase information from (a magnetic disk or other storage device). [DE- + GAUSS.] —**de•gauss′er** *n.*

de•gen•er•a•cy (dĭ-jĕn′ər-ə-sē) *n., pl.* **-cies. 1.** The process of degenerating. **2.** The state of being degenerate. **3.** Corrupt, vulgar, vicious behavior, esp. sexual. **4.** *Genet.* The presence in a genetic code of multiple codons for the same amino acid.

de•gen•er•ate (dĭ-jĕn′ər-ĭt) *adj.* **1.** Having declined, as in function or nature, from a former or original state. **2.** Having fallen to an inferior or undesirable state, esp. mentally or morally. **3.** *Phys.* Taking on several discrete values or existing in two or more quantum states: *degenerate energy levels.* **4.** *Phys.* Characterized by great density and consisting of atoms stripped of electrons: *degenerate matter.* **5.** *Medic.* Characterized by degeneration, as of tissue. **6.** *Biol.* Having lost one or more highly developed functions, characteristics, or structures through evolution. **7.** *Genet.* **a.** Coding for the same amino acid as another codon. **b.** Having more than one codon specify the same amino acid. Used of a genetic code. —*n.* **1.** A depraved, corrupt, or vicious person. **2.** A person lacking or having progressively lost normative biological or psychological characteristics. —*intr.v.* (-ə-rāt′) **-at•ed, -at•ing, -ates. 1.** To fall below a normal or desirable state, esp. functionally or morally; deteriorate. **2.** To decline in quality. **3.** To undergo degeneration. [Lat. *dēgenerātus*, p.part. of *dēgenerāre*, to depart from one's own kind, deteriorate : *dē-*, de- + *genus*, *gener-*, race; see **genə-***.] —**de•gen′er•ate•ly** *adv.* —**de•gen′er•ate•ness** *n.*

de•gen•er•a•tion (dĭ-jĕn′ə-rā′shən) *n.* **1.** The process of degenerating. **2.** The state of being degenerate. **3.** *Medic.* Gradual deterioration of specific tissues, cells, or organs with corresponding impairment or loss of function. **4.** *Biol.* The evolutionary decline or loss of a function, characteristic, or structure in an organism or a species. **5.** *Electron.* Loss of or gain in power in an amplifier caused by unintentional negative feedback.

de•gen•er•a•tive (dĭ-jĕn′ər-ə-tĭv) *adj.* Of, relating to, causing, or characterized by degeneration: *a degenerative disease.*

degenerative joint disease *n.* See **osteoarthritis.**

de•glam•or•ize (dē-glăm′ə-rīz′) *tr.v.* **-ized, -iz•ing, -iz•es.** To make less glamorous.

de•glaze (dē-glāz′) *tr.v.* **-glazed, -glaz•ing, -glaz•es. 1.** To remove glaze from (pottery, for example). **2.** To dissolve what remains of a sautée or roast in (a pan or pot) by heating with liquid.

de•glu•ti•nate (dĭ-glo͞ot′n-āt′) *tr.v.* **-nat•ed, -nat•ing, -nates.** To extract the gluten from (wheat flour, for example). [Lat. *dēglūtināre*, *dēglūtināt-* : *dē-*, de- + *glūten*, *glutin-*, glue.] —**de•glu′ti•na′tion** *n.*

de•glu•ti•tion (dē′glo͞o-tĭsh′ən) *n.* The act or process of swallowing. [Fr. *déglutition* < *déglutir*, to swallow < Lat. *dēglūtīre* : *dē-*, de- + *glūtīre*, to gulp.] —**de•glu′ti•to′ry** (-tĭ-tôr′ē, -tōr′ē) *adj.*

de•grad•a•ble (dĭ-grā′də-bəl) *adj.* That can be chemically degraded: *degradable paper products.* —**de•grad′a•bil′i•ty** *n.*

deg•ra•da•tion (dĕg′rə-dā′shən) *n.* **1.** The act or process of degrading. **2.** The state of being degraded; degeneration. **3.** A decline to a lower condition, quality, or level. **4.** *Geol.* A general lowering of the earth's surface by erosion or weathering. **5.** *Chem.* Decomposition of a compound by stages, exhibiting well-defined intermediate products.

de•grade (dĭ-grād′) *tr.v.* **-grad•ed, -grad•ing, -grades. 1.** To reduce in grade, rank, or status; demote. **2.** To lower in dignity; dishonor or disgrace. **3.** To lower in moral or intellectual character; debase. **4.** To reduce in worth or value: *degrade a currency.* **5.** To impair in physical structure or function. **6.** *Geol.* To lower or wear by erosion or weathering. **7.** To cause (an organic compound) to undergo degradation. [ME *degraden* < OFr. *degrader* < LLat. *dēgradāre* : Lat. *dē-*, de- + Lat. *gradus*, step; see **ghredh-***.] —**de•grad′er** *n.*

Syns: *degrade, abase, debase, demean, humble, humiliate.* These verbs mean to deprive of self-esteem or self-worth. *Degrade* implies reduction to a state of shame or disgrace: *"Charity degrades those who receive it and hardens those who dispense it"* (George Sand). *Abase* refers principally to loss of rank or prestige: *refused to abase herself by pleading. Debase* implies reduction in quality or value: *"debasing the moral currency"* (George Eliot). *Demean* suggests lowering in social position: *"It puts him where he can make the advances without demeaning himself"* (William Dean Howells). *Humble* refers to lowering in rank or to driving out undue pride: *Loss humbled him.* To *humiliate* is to subject to loss of self-respect or dignity: *a humiliating defeat.*

de•grad•ed (dĭ-grā′dĭd) *adj.* **1.** Reduced in rank, dignity, or esteem. **2.** Having been corrupted or depraved. **3.** Having been reduced in quality or value. —**de•grad′ed•ly** *adv.* —**de•grad′ed•ness** *n.*

de•grad•ing (dĭ-grā′dĭng) *adj.* Tending or intended to degrade. —**de•grad′ing•ly** *adv.*

de•gran•u•la•tion (dē-grăn′yə-lā′shən) *n.* The process of losing granules.

de•grease (dē-grēs′, -grēz′) *tr.v.* **-greased, -greas•ing, -greas•es.** To remove grease from. —**de•greas′er** *n.*

de•gree (dĭ-grē′) *n.* **1.** One of a series of steps in a process, course, or progression; a stage. **2.** A step in a direct hereditary line of descent or ascent. **3.** Relative social or official rank, dignity, or position. **4.** Relative intensity or amount, as of a quality or an attribute: *degree of accuracy.* **5.** The extent or measure of a state of being, an action, or a relation. **6.** A unit division of a temperature scale. **7.** *Math.* A planar unit of angular measure equal in magnitude to 1/360 of a complete revolution. **8.** A unit of latitude or longitude, equal to 1/360 of a great circle. **9.** *Math.* **a.** The greatest sum of the exponents of the variables in a term of a polynomial or polynomial equation. **b.** The exponent of the derivative of highest order in a differential equation in standard form. **10.a.** An academic title given by a college or university to a student who has completed a course of study. **b.** A similar title conferred as an honorary distinction. **11.** *Law.* A division or classification of a specific crime according to its seriousness: *second-degree murder.* **12.** A classification of the severity of an injury, esp. a burn: *a third-degree burn.* **13.** *Gram.* One of the forms used in the comparison of adjectives and adverbs. **14.** *Mus.* **a.** One of the seven notes of a diatonic scale. **b.** A space or line of the staff. —***idioms.*** **by degrees.** Little by little; gradually. **to a degree.** To a small extent; in a limited way. [ME *degre* < OFr. < VLat. **dēgradus* : Lat. *dē-*, de- + Lat. *gradus*, step; see **ghredh-***.]

de•greed (dĭ-grēd′) *adj.* Having or requiring an academic degree.

de•gree-day (dĭ-grē′dā′) *n.* A unit of measurement equal to a difference of one degree between the mean outdoor temperature on a certain day and a reference temperature.

degree of freedom *n., pl.* **degrees of freedom. 1.** *Statistics.* Any of the unrestricted independent random variables that constitute a statistic. **2.** *Phys.* **a.** Any of the minimum number of coordinates required to specify completely the motion of a mechanical system. **b.** Any of the independent thermodynamic variables, such as pressure, required to specify a system with a given number of phases and components.

de•gres•sion (dĭ-grĕsh′ən, dē-) *n.* A descent by stages or steps. [ME < Med.Lat. *dēgressiō*, *dēgressiōn-*, descent < Lat. *dēgressus*, p.part. of *dēgredī*, to step down : *dē-*, de- + *gradī*, to step; see **ghredh-***.] —**de•gres′sive** *adj.*

de•gust (dĭ-gŭst′, dē-) *tr.v.* **-gust•ed, -gust•ing, -gusts.** To taste with relish; savor. [Lat. *dēgustāre* : *dē-*, de- + *gustāre*, to taste; see **geus-***.] —**de′gus•ta′tion** (dē′gŭ-stā′shən) *n.*

de•hisce (dĭ-hĭs′) *intr.v.* **-hisced, -hisc•ing, -hisc•es. 1.** *Bot.* To open at definite places, discharging seeds or other contents. **2.** *Medic.* To rupture or break open. [Lat. *dehīscere* : *dē-*, de- + *hīscere*, to split, inchoative of *hiāre*, to be open.]

de•his•cence (dē-hĭs′əns) *n.* **1.** *Bot.* An opening at definite places at maturity to release or expose the contents, such as seeds from a fruit. **2.** *Medic.* A splitting open or a rupture, as of a surgical wound. —**de•his′cent** *adj.*

de•horn (dē-hôrn′) *tr.v.* **-horned, -horn•ing, -horns. 1.** To re-

Charles de Gaulle

ă pat	oi boy
ā pay	ou out
âr care	o͝o took
ä father	o͞o boot
ĕ pet	ŭ cut
ē be	ûr urge
ĭ pit	th thin
ī pie	*th* this
îr pier	hw which
ŏ pot	zh vision
ō toe	ə about, item
ô paw	

Stress marks:
′ (primary);
′ (secondary), as in
dictionary (dĭk′shə-nĕr′ē)

move the horns from. **2.** To prevent growth in the horns of (cattle, for example), as by cauterization.

Deh•ra Dun (dā′rə do͞on′). A city of N India NNE of Delhi. Pop. 211,416.

de•hu•man•ize (dē-hyo͞o′mə-nīz′) *tr.v.* **-ized, -iz•ing, -iz•es. 1.** To deprive of human qualities such as compassion. **2.** To render mechanical and routine. **—de•hu′man•i•za′tion** (-mə-nĭ-zā′shən) *n.*

de•hu•mid•i•fy (dē′hyo͞o-mĭd′ə-fī′) *tr.v.* **-fied, -fy•ing, -fies.** To remove atmospheric moisture from. **—de′hu•mid′i•fi•ca′tion** (-fĭ-kā′shən) *n.* **—de′hu•mid′i•fi′er** *n.*

de•hy•dra•tase (dē-hī′drə-tās′, -tāz′) *n. Biochem.* An enzyme that catalyzes the removal of oxygen and hydrogen from organic compounds in the form of water.

de•hy•drate (dē-hī′drāt′) *v.* **-drat•ed, -drat•ing, -drates.** —*tr.* **1.** To remove water from; make anhydrous. **2.** To preserve by removing water from (vegetables, for example). —*intr.* To lose water or moisture. **—de•hy′dra′tor** *n.*

de•hy•dra•tion (dē′hī-drā′shən) *n.* **1.** The process of removing water from a substance or compound. **2.** Excessive loss of water from the body, an organ, or a body part.

de•hy•dra•tor (dē-hī′drā′tər) *n.* **1.** A substance that removes water. **2.** A container or an engineered system for removing water from substances such as absorbents or food.

de•hy•dro•chlo•rin•ase (dē-hī′drə-klôr′ə-nās′, -nāz′, -klōr′-) *n. Biochem.* An enzyme that catalyzes the removal of hydrogen and chlorine from a chlorinated hydrocarbon.

de•hy•dro•chlo•rin•ate (dē-hī′drə-klôr′ə-nāt′, -klōr′-) *tr.v.* **-at•ed, -at•ing, -ates.** *Biochem.* To remove hydrogen and chlorine or hydrogen chloride from (a compound). **—de•hy′dro•chlo′ri•na′tion** *n.*

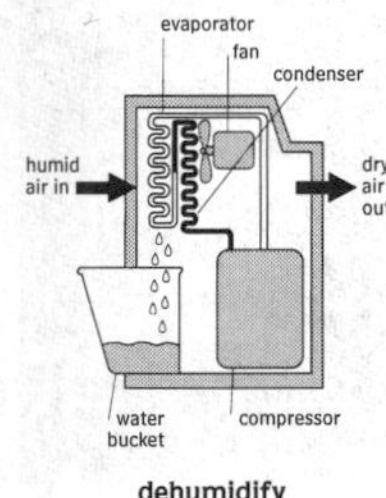

dehumidify

de•hy•dro•gen•ase (dē′hī-drŏj′ə-nās′, -nāz′, dē-hī′drə-jə-) *n. Biochem.* An enzyme that catalyzes the removal and transfer of hydrogen from a substrate in an oxidation-reduction reaction.

de•hy•dro•gen•ate (dē′hī-drŏj′ə-nāt′, dē-hī′drə-jə-) *tr.v.* **-at•ed, -at•ing, -ates.** *Chem.* To remove hydrogen from. **—de•hy′dro•gen•a′tion** *n.*

de•hy•dro•gen•ize (dē′hī-drŏj′ə-nīz′, dē-hī′drə-jə-) *tr.v.* **-ized, -iz•ing, -iz•es.** *Chem.* To dehydrogenate. **—de•hy′dro•gen•i•za′tion** (-ə-nĭ-zā′shən) *n.*

de•hyp•no•tize (dē-hĭp′nə-tīz′) *tr.v.* **-tized, -tiz•ing, -tiz•es.** To arouse from a hypnotic state.

de•ice (dē-īs′) *tr.v.* **-iced, -ic•ing, -ic•es.** To make or keep free of ice; melt ice from: *deiced the plane's wings.*

de•ic•er (dē-ī′sər) *n.* **1.** A device used on an aircraft to keep or remove ice from the wings and propeller. **2.** A compound used to prevent the formation of ice.

deic•tic (dīk′tĭk) *adj.* **1.** *Logic.* Directly proving by argument. **2.** *Ling.* Serving to point out or specify, as the demonstrative pronoun *this.* [Gk. *deiktikos* < *deiktos*, able to show directly < *deiknunai*, to show. See **deik-***.] **—deic′ti•cal•ly** *adv.*

de•if•ic (dē-ĭf′ĭk) *adj.* **1.** Making or tending to make divine. **2.** Of or characterized by divine or godlike nature. [LLat. *deificus* : Lat. *deus*, god; see **deiw-*** + Lat. *-ficus*, -fic.]

de•i•fi•ca•tion (dē′ə-fĭ-kā′shən) *n.* **1.a.** The act or process of deifying. **b.** The condition of being deified. **2.** One that embodies the qualities of a god.

Eugène Delacroix

de•i•fy (dē′ə-fī′) *tr.v.* **-fied, -fy•ing, -fies. 1.** To make a god of; raise to the condition of a god. **2.** To worship or revere as a god: *deify a leader.* **3.** To idealize; exalt: *deifying success.* [ME *deifien* < OFr. *deifier* < LLat. *deificāre* < *deificus*, deific. See DEIFIC.] **—de′i•fi′er** *n.*

deign (dān) *v.* **deigned, deign•ing, deigns.** —*intr.* To think it appropriate to one's dignity; condescend. —*tr.* To condescend to give; vouchsafe. [ME *deinen* < OFr. *deignier*, to regard as worthy < Lat. *dignārī* < *dignus*, worthy. See **dek-***.]

deil (dēl) *n. Scots.* **1.** The devil; Satan. **2.** A mischievous person; an imp. [Sc. < ME *dele*, var. of *devel.* See DEVIL.]

Dei•mos (dē′mōs, dā′-, dī′mŏs) *n.* A satellite of Mars. [Gk., one of the sons of Ares < *deimos*, fear, terror.]

de•in•dus•tri•al•ize (dē′ĭn-dŭs′trē-ə-līz′) *v.* **-ized, -iz•ing, -iz•es.** —*tr.* **1.** To cause (a nation or an area) to lose industrial capability or strength. **2.** To deprive (a defeated country) of its industrial infrastructure and potential. —*intr.* To undergo or suffer loss of industrial infrastructure and potential. **—de′in•dus′tri•al•i•za′tion** (-ə-lĭ-zā′shən) *n.*

de•in•sti•tu•tion•al•ize (dē-ĭn′stĭ-to͞o′shə-nə-līz′, -tyo͞o′-) *tr.v.* **-ized, -iz•ing, -iz•es. 1.** To remove the institutional status of. **2.** To release (a mental health patient, for example) from an institution for placement and care in the community. **—de•in′sti•tu′tion•al•i•za′tion** (-shə-nə-lĭ-zā′shən) *n.*

de•i•on•ize (dē-ī′ə-nīz′) *tr.v.* **-ized, -iz•ing, -iz•es.** To remove ions from (a solution) using an ion-exchange process. **—de•i′on•iz′er** *n.*

Deir•dre (dîr′drə, -drē) *n.* A legendary princess of Ulster who killed herself after King Conchobar murdered her lover.

de•ism (dē′ĭz′əm) *n.* The belief, based on reason, in a God who created the universe and has since assumed no control over life, exerted no influence on nature, and given no supernatural revelation. [Fr. *déisme* < Lat. *deus*, god. See **deiw-***.] **—de′ist** *n.* **—de•is′tic** *adj.* **—de•is′ti•cal•ly** *adv.*

de•i•ty (dē′ĭ-tē) *n., pl.* **-ties. 1.** A god or goddess. **2.a.** The essential nature or condition of being a god; divinity. **b. Deity.** God. Used with *the.* [ME *deite* < OFr. < LLat. *deitās*, divine nature < Lat. *deus*, god. See **deiw-***.]

dé•jà vu (dā′zhä vü′) *n.* **1.** *Psychol.* The illusion of having already experienced something actually being experienced for the first time. **2.a.** An impression of having seen or experienced something before. **b.** Dull familiarity; monotony. [Fr. : *déjà*, already + *vu*, seen.]

de•ject (dĭ-jĕkt′) *tr.v.* **-ject•ed, -ject•ing, -jects.** To lower the spirits of; dishearten. [ME *dejecten* < Lat. *dēicere, dēiect-*, to cast down : *dē-*, de- + *iacere*, to throw; see **yē-***.]

de•ject•ed (dĭ-jĕk′tĭd) *adj.* Being in low spirits; depressed. **—de•ject′ed•ly** *adv.* **—de•ject′ed•ness** *n.*

de•jec•tion (dĭ-jĕk′shən) *n.* **1.** The state of being dejected; low spirits. **2.** *Medic.* **a.** Evacuation of the bowels; defecation. **b.** Excrement.

de ju•re (dē jo͝or′ē, dā yo͝or′ā) *adv. & adj. Law.* According to law; by right. [Lat. *dē iūre* : *dē*, from + *iūre*, ablative of *iūs*, law.]

dek– or **deka–** *pref.* Var. of **deca–**.

De Kalb (dĭ kălb′). A city of N IL SSE of Rockford. Pop. 34,925.

Dek•ker (dĕk′ər), **Thomas.** 1572–1632. English playwright noted for his comedy *The Shoemaker's Holiday* (1600).

de Koo•ning (dĭ ko͞o′nĭng), **Willem.** b. 1904. Dutch-born Amer. painter and leader of the abstract expressionist school. His wife, **Elaine Fried de Kooning** (1920–89), painted in a variety of styles.

del. *abbr.* **1.** Delegate; delegation. **2.** Delete.

Del. *abbr.* Delaware.

De•la•croix (də-lä-krwä′), **(Ferdinand Victor) Eugène.** 1798–1863. French romantic painter known for his vast, dramatic canvases, such as *Liberty Leading the People* (1830).

Del•a•go•a Bay (dĕl′ə-gō′ə). An inlet of the Indian Ocean in S Mozambique; first explored by the Portuguese after 1544.

de la Mare (də lə mâr′, dĕl′ə-mâr′), **Walter John.** 1873–1956. British writer whose works include *Early One Morning* (1935) and *O Lovely England* (1953).

de•lam•i•nate (dē-lăm′ə-nāt′) *intr.v.* **-nat•ed, -nat•ing, -nates.** To split into thin layers.

de•lam•i•na•tion (dē-lăm′ə-nā′shən) *n.* **1.** The act of splitting or separating a laminate into layers. **2.** *Embryol.* The splitting of the blastoderm into two cell layers to form a gastrula.

De•land (də-lănd′), **Margaret.** 1857–1945. Amer. writer whose works include *The Awakening of Helen Richie* (1906).

De•la•ney (də-lā′nē), **Shelagh.** b. 1930. British playwright best known for *A Taste of Honey* (1958).

De•la•no (də-lā′nō). A city of S-central CA in the San Joaquin Valley NNW of Bakersfield. Pop. 22,762.

De•lan•y (də-lā′nē), **Martin Robinson.** 1812–85. Amer. physician who cofounded and edited the *North Star* (1847–49).

de la Roche (də lə rōch′, rôsh′), **Mazo.** 1885–1961. Canadian writer known for her series of novels, including *Jalna* (1927), that feature the Whiteoak family of Ontario.

De•la•roche (də-lä-rōsh′, -rôsh′), **Hippolyte Paul.** 1797–1856. French portrait and mural painter whose eclectic works combine elements of the classical and romantic schools.

De•la•vigne (də-lä-vēn′yə), **(Jean François) Casimir.** 1793–1843. French writer known for his satiric elegies *Les Messéniennes* (1818).

Del•a•ware¹ (dĕl′ə-wâr′) *n., pl.* **Delaware** or **-wares. 1.** A member of a group of closely related Native American peoples formerly inhabiting the Delaware and Hudson river valleys and the area between and now living in Oklahoma, Kansas, Wisconsin, and Ontario. **2.** One or both of the Algonquian languages of the Delaware. **—Del′a•war′e•an** *adj.*

Del•a•ware² (dĕl′ə-wâr′). **1.** A state of the E U.S. on the Atlantic Ocean; admitted as the first of the original Thirteen Colonies in 1787. The region was settled by the Dutch in 1631 and by Swedes in 1638. Cap. Dover. Pop. 668,696. **2.** A city of central OH N of Columbus. Pop. 20,030.

Del•a•ware³ (dĕl′ə-wâr′) *n.* A variety of grape having sweet, light red fruit. [After DELAWARE².]

Delaware Bay. An estuary of the Delaware R. emptying into the Atlantic between E DE and S NJ.

Delaware River. A river rising in SE NY and flowing c. 451 km (280 mi) to N DE, where it enters Delaware Bay.

De La Warr (dĕl′ə wâr′, wər), Baron. Thomas West. 1577–1618. English-born Amer. colonial administrator chosen as the first governor of the Virginia Company colony.

de•lay (dĭ-lā′) *v.* **-layed, -lay•ing, -lays.** —*tr.* **1.** To postpone until a later time; defer. **2.** To cause to be later or slower than expected or desired: *Traffic delayed us.* —*intr.* To act or move slowly; put off an action or a decision. —*n.* **1.** The act of delaying; postponement. **2.** The condition of being delayed; detainment. **3.** The period of time during which one is delayed. **4.** The interval of time between two events. [ME *delaien* < AN *delaier* < OFr. *deslaier* : *des-*, de- + *laier*, to leave, of Gmc. orig. See **leip-***.] **—de•lay′er** *n.*

Del•brück (dĕl′bro͝ok′, -brük′), **Max.** 1906–81. German-born Amer. biologist who shared a 1969 Nobel Prize.

Del City (dĕl). A city of central OK, a suburb of Oklahoma City. Pop. 23,928.

de•le (dē′lē) *Print.* — *n.* A sign indicating that something is to be removed from typeset matter. — *tr.v.* **-led, -le•ing, -les. 1.** To remove, esp. from written or typeset matter; delete. **2.** To mark with a sign indicating deletion. [Lat. *dēle*, third pers. sing. imper. of *dēlēre*, to delete.]

de•lec•ta•ble (dĭ-lĕk′tə-bəl) *adj.* **1.** Greatly pleasing; delightful. **2.** Greatly pleasing to the taste; delicious. — *n.* Something delectable. [ME < OFr. < Lat. *dēlectābilis* < *dēlectāre*, to please. See DELIGHT.] — **de•lec′ta•bil′i•ty, de•lec′ta•ble•ness** *n.* — **de•lec′ta•bly** *adv.*

de•lec•ta•tion (dē′lĕk-tā′shən) *n.* **1.** Delight. **2.** Enjoyment; pleasure. [ME *delectacioun* < OFr. < Lat. *dēlectātiō*, *dēlectātiōn-* < *dēlectus*, p.part. of *dēlectāre*, to please. See DELIGHT.]

De•led•da (dĕ-lĕd′dä), **Grazia.** 1875–1936. Italian writer who won the 1926 Nobel Prize for literature.

del•e•ga•cy (dĕl′ĭ-gə-sē) *n.*, *pl.* **-cies. 1.** The act of delegating or state of being delegated. **2.** The authority, office, or position of a delegate. **3.** A body of delegates; a delegation.

de•le•gal•ize (dē-lē′gə-līz′) *tr.v.* **-ized, -iz•ing, -iz•es.** To make illegal. — **de•le′gal•i•za′tion** (-gə-lĭ-zā′shən) *n.*

del•e•gate (dĕl′ĭ-gāt′, -gĭt) *n.* **1.** A person authorized to act as another's representative; a deputy or an agent. **2.** A representative to a conference or convention. **3.** A member of a House of Delegates, the lower house of the Maryland, Virginia, or West Virginia legislature. **4.** A representative of a U.S. territory in the House of Representatives who is entitled to speak but not vote. — *tr.v.* (-gāt′) **-gat•ed, -gat•ing, -gates. 1.** To authorize and send (another person) as one's representative. **2.** To commit or entrust (a task or power) to another. **3.** *Law.* To appoint (one's debtor) as a debtor to one's creditor in place of oneself. [ME *delegat* < Med.Lat. *dēlēgātus* < p.part. of *dēlēgāre*, to dispatch : Lat. *dē-*, de- + Lat. *lēgāre*, to send; see **leg-***.] — **del′e•ga′tor** *n.*

del•e•ga•tion (dĕl′ĭ-gā′shən) *n.* **1.a.** The act of delegating. **b.** The condition of being delegated. **2.** A person or group of persons officially elected or appointed as representatives.

de•le•git•i•mize (dē′lə-jĭt′ə-mīz′) *tr.v.* **-mized, -miz•ing, -miz•es.** To revoke the legal or legitimate status of. — **de′le•git′i•mi•za′tion** (-mĭ-zā′shən) *n.*

de Les•seps (də lĕs′əps, lĕ-sĕps′), Vicomte **Ferdinand Marie.** See Ferdinand Marie de **Lesseps.**

de•lete (dĭ-lēt′) *tr.v.* **-let•ed, -let•ing, -letes.** To remove by striking out or canceling. See Syns at **erase.** [Lat. *dēlēre*, *dēlēt-*, to wipe out.]

del•e•te•ri•ous (dĕl′ĭ-tîr′ē-əs) *adj.* Having a harmful effect; injurious. [< Gk. *dēlētērios* < *dēlētēr*, destroyer < *dēleisthai*, to harm.] — **del′e•te′ri•ous•ly** *adv.* — **del′e•te′ri•ous•ness** *n.*

de•le•tion (dĭ-lē′shən) *n.* **1.** The act of deleting; removal by striking out. **2.** Material that has been removed from a written text. **3.** *Genet.* The loss, as through mutation, of one or more nucleotides from a chromosome.

delft (dĕlft) *n.* **1.** A style of glazed earthenware, usu. blue and white, originally made in Delft, Netherlands. **2.** Such pottery.

Delft (dĕlft). A city of SW Netherlands SE of The Hague; noted for its pottery since the 16th cent. Pop. 86,733.

Del•hi (dĕl′ē). A city of N-central India on the Jumna R. The new section of Delhi is the cap. of India. Pop. 4,884,234.

del•i (dĕl′ē) *n.*, *pl.* **-is.** *Informal.* A delicatessen.

de•lib•er•ate (dĭ-lĭb′ər-ĭt) *adj.* **1.** Done with or marked by full consciousness of the nature and effects; intentional: *a deliberate insult.* **2.** Arising from or marked by careful consideration: *a deliberate decision.* See Syns at **voluntary. 3.** Unhurried in action, movement, or manner, as if trying to avoid error. — *v.* (-ə-rāt′) **-at•ed, -at•ing, -ates.** — *intr.* **1.** To think carefully and often slowly, as about a choice to be made. **2.** To consult with another or others in a process of reaching a decision. — *tr.* To consider (a matter) carefully and often slowly, as by weighing alternatives. [Lat. *dēlīberātus*, p.part. of *dēlīberāre*, to consider, weigh : *dē-*, de- + *lībrāre*, to balance (< *lībra*, a balance, scales).] — **de•lib′er•ate•ly** *adv.* — **de•lib′er•ate•ness** *n.*

de•lib•er•a•tion (dĭ-lĭb′ə-rā′shən) *n.* **1.** The act or process of deliberating. **2. deliberations.** Discussion and consideration of all sides of an issue. **3.** Thoughtfulness in decision or action. **4.** Leisureliness in motion or manner.

de•lib•er•a•tive (dĭ-lĭb′ə-rā′tĭv, -ər-ə-tĭv) *adj.* **1.** Assembled or organized for deliberation or debate. **2.** Characterized by or for use in deliberation or debate. — **de•lib′er•a′tive•ly** *adv.* — **de•lib′er•a′tive•ness** *n.*

De•libes (də-lēb′), **(Clément Philibert) Léo.** 1836–91. French composer whose melodic works include *Coppélia* (1870).

del•i•ca•cy (dĕl′ĭ-kə-sē) *n.*, *pl.* **-cies. 1.** The quality of being delicate. **2.** Something pleasing and appealing, esp. a choice food. **3.** Fineness of appearance, construction, or execution; elegance. **4.** Frailty of bodily constitution or health. **5.** Sensitivity of perception, discrimination, or taste; refinement. **6.a.** Sensitivity to the feelings of others; tact. **b.** Sensitivity to what is proper; propriety. **c.** Undue sensitivity to or concern with what may be considered offensive or improper; squeamishness. **7.** The need for tact in treatment or handling: *a topic of some delicacy.* **8.** Sensitivity to very small changes; precision. [ME *delicacie* < *delicat*, delicate. See DELICATE.]

del•i•cate (dĕl′ĭ-kĭt) *adj.* **1.** Pleasing to the senses, esp. in a subtle way: *a delicate violin passage.* **2.** Exquisitely fine or dainty. **3.** Frail in constitution or health. **4.** Easily broken or damaged. **5.** Marked by sensitivity of discrimination: *a critic's delicate ear.* **6.a.** Considerate of the feelings of others. **b.** Concerned with propriety. **c.** Squeamish or fastidious. **7.** Requiring tactful treatment. **8.** Fine or soft in touch or skill. **9.** Measuring, indicating, or responding to very small changes; precise. **10.** Very subtle in difference or distinction. [ME *delicat* and Fr. *délicat*, both < Lat. *dēlicātus*, pleasing.] — **del′i•cate•ly** *adv.* — **del′i•cate•ness** *n.*

Syns: *delicate, choice, dainty, elegant, exquisite, fine.* The central meaning shared by these adjectives is "appealing to refined taste": *a delicate flavor; choice exotic flowers; a dainty dish; elegant handwriting; an exquisite wine; the finest embroidery.* See also Syns at **fragile.**

del•i•ca•tes•sen (dĕl′ĭ-kə-tĕs′ən) *n.* **1.** A shop that sells foods ready for serving. **2.** Ready-to-serve foods such as cheeses and salads. [Ger. *Delikatessen* < pl. of *Delikatesse*, delicacy < Fr. *délicatesse* < Ital. *delicatezza* < *delicato*, delicate, dainty < Lat. *dēlicātus*, pleasing.]

de•li•cious (dĭ-lĭsh′əs) *adj.* **1.** Highly pleasing or agreeable to the senses, esp. of taste or smell. **2.** Very pleasant; delightful: *a delicious revenge.* [ME < AN < LLat. *dēliciōsus*, pleasing < Lat. *dēlicia*, pleasure < *dēlicere*, to allure. See DELIGHT.] — **de•li′cious•ly** *adv.* — **de•li′cious•ness** *n.*

De•li•cious (dĭ-lĭsh′əs) *n.* A variety of sweet apple whose flesh is often streaked with yellow and red.

de•lict (dĭ-lĭkt′) *n.* *Law.* A legal offense; a misdemeanor. [Lat. *dēlictum* < neut. p.part. of *dēlinquere*, to offend. See DELINQUENT.]

de•light (dĭ-līt′) *n.* **1.** Great pleasure; joy. **2.** Something giving great pleasure or enjoyment. — *v.* **-light•ed, -light•ing, -lights.** — *intr.* **1.** To take great pleasure or joy: *delights in dogs.* **2.** To give great pleasure or joy: *a vista that delights.* — *tr.* To please greatly. See Syns at **please.** [ME *delit* < OFr., a pleasure < *delitier*, to please, charm < Lat. *dēlectāre*, freq. of *dēlicere*, to allure : *dē-*, de- + *lacere*, to entice.]

de•light•ed (dĭ-lī′tĭd) *adj.* **1.** Filled with delight. **2.** *Obsolete.* Delightful. — **de•light′ed•ly** *adv.* — **de•light′ed•ness** *n.*

de•light•ful (dĭ-līt′fəl) *adj.* Greatly pleasing. — **de•light′ful•ly** *adv.* — **de•light′ful•ness** *n.*

de•light•some (dĭ-līt′səm) *adj.* Delightful. — **de•light′some•ly** *adv.* — **de•light′some•ness** *n.*

De•li•lah (də-lī′lə). In the Bible, a lover of Samson who betrayed him to the Philistines.

de•lim•it (dĭ-lĭm′ĭt) also **de•lim•i•tate** (-ĭ-tāt′) *tr.v.* **-it•ed, -it•ing, -its** also **-tat•ed, -tat•ing, -tates.** To establish the limits or boundaries of. [Fr. *délimiter* < Lat. *dēlīmitāre* : *dē-*, de- + *līmitāre*, to limit (< *līmes*, *līmit-*, boundary line).] — **de•lim′i•ta′tion** *n.* — **de•lim′i•ta′tive** *adj.*

de•lim•it•er (dĭ-lĭm′ĭ-tər) *n.* *Comp. Sci.* A character marking the beginning or end of a unit of data.

de•lin•e•ate (dĭ-lĭn′ē-āt′) *tr.v.* **-at•ed, -at•ing, -ates. 1.** To draw or trace the outline of; sketch out. **2.** To represent pictorially; depict. **3.** To depict in words or gestures; describe. [Lat. *dēlīneāre*, *dēlīneāt-* : *dē-*, de- + *līnea*, line, thread; see LINE[1].] — **de•lin′e•a′tion** *n.* — **de•lin′e•a′tive** *adj.* — **de•lin′e•a′tor** *n.*

de•lin•quen•cy (dĭ-lĭng′kwən-sē, -lĭn′-) *n.*, *pl.* **-cies. 1.** Juvenile delinquency. **2.** Failure to do what law or duty requires. **3.** An offense or a misdemeanor; a misdeed. **4.** A debt or other financial obligation on which payment is overdue. — *adj.* Of or relating to juvenile delinquency.

de•lin•quent (dĭ-lĭng′kwənt, -lĭn′-) *adj.* **1.** Failing to do what law or duty requires. **2.** Overdue in payment. — *n.* **1.** A juvenile delinquent. **2.** A person who neglects or fails to do what law or duty requires. [Lat. *dēlinquēns*, *dēlinquent-*, pr.part. of *dēlinquere*, to offend : *dē-*, de- + *linquere*, to leave, abandon; see **leikʷ-***.] — **de•lin′quent•ly** *adv.*

del•i•quesce (dĕl′ĭ-kwĕs′) *intr.v.* **-quesced, -quesc•ing, -quesc•es. 1.a.** To melt away. **b.** To disappear as if by melting. **2.** *Chem.* To dissolve and become liquid by absorbing moisture from the air. **3.** *Bot.* **a.** To branch out into numerous subdivisions that lack a main axis. **b.** To become fluid or soft on maturing, as certain fungi. [Lat. *dēliquēscere* : *dē-*, de- + *liquēscere*, to melt, inchoative of *liquēre*, to be liquid.] — **del′i•ques′cence** *n.* — **del′i•ques′cent** *adj.*

de•lir•i•ous (dĭ-lîr′ē-əs) *adj.* **1.** Of, suffering from, or characteristic of delirium. **2.** Marked by uncontrolled excitement or emotion; ecstatic. — **de•lir′i•ous•ly** *adv.* — **de•lir′i•ous•ness** *n.*

de•lir•i•um (dĭ-lîr′ē-əm) *n.*, *pl.* **-i•ums** or **-i•a** (-ē-ə). **1.** A temporary state of mental confusion and clouded consciousness, characterized by anxiety, hallucinations, trembling, and incoherent speech. **2.** A state of uncontrolled excitement or emotion. [Lat. *dēlīrium* < *dēlīrāre*, to be deranged : *dē-*, de-

delft
Early 18th-century Rosh Hashanah plate

ă pat	oi boy
ā pay	ou out
âr care	ŏŏ took
ä father	ōō boot
ĕ pet	ŭ cut
ē be	ûr urge
ĭ pit	th thin
ī pie	*th* this
îr pier	hw which
ŏ pot	zh vision
ō toe	ə about, item
ô paw	

Stress marks:
′ (primary);
′ (secondary), as in
dictionary (dĭk′shə-nĕr′ē)

+ *līra,* furrow; see **leis-**[1]***.**] **— de•lir′i•ant** *adj.*

delirium tre•mens (trē′mənz) *n.* An acute, sometimes fatal episode of delirium usu. caused either by withdrawal from alcohol following habitual excessive drinking or by an episode of heavy alcohol consumption. [NLat. *dēlīrium tremēns* : Lat. *dēlīrium,* delirium + Lat. *tremēns,* trembling.]

de•list (dē-lĭst′) *tr.v.* **-list•ed, -list•ing, -lists.** To remove from a list, esp. from a list of securities that may be traded on a stock exchange.

De•lius (dē′lē-əs, dēl′yəs), **Frederick.** 1862–1934. British composer of romantic, impressionistic works.

de•liv•er (dĭ-lĭv′ər) *v.* **-ered, -er•ing, -ers.** *—tr.* **1.** To bring or transport to the proper place or recipient; distribute. **2.** To surrender (someone or something) to another; hand over. **3.** To secure (something promised or desired), as for a candidate or political party. **4.** To throw or hurl. **5.** To strike (a blow). **6.** To express in words; declare or utter. **7.a.** To give birth to. **b.** To assist (a woman) in giving birth. **c.** To assist or aid in the birth of. **8.** To give forth or produce. **9.** To set free, as from misery, peril, or evil. *—intr.* **1.** To produce or achieve what is desired or expected; make good. **2.** To give birth. ***—idiom.* deliver (oneself) of.** To pronounce; utter. [ME *deliveren* < OFr. *delivrer* < LLat. *dēlīberāre* : Lat. *dē-,* de- + *līberāre,* to free (< *līber,* free; see **leudh-***).] **— de•liv′er•a•bil′i•ty** *n.* **— de•liv′er•a•ble** *adj.* **— de•liv′er•er** *n.*

de•liv•er•ance (dĭ-lĭv′ər-əns, -lĭv′rəns) *n.* **1.** The act of delivering or the condition of being delivered. **2.** Rescue from bondage or danger. **3.** A publicly expressed opinion or judgment, such as the verdict of a jury.

de•liv•er•y (dĭ-lĭv′ə-rē, -lĭv′rē) *n., pl.* **-ies. 1.a.** The act of conveying or delivering. **b.** Something delivered, as a shipment. **2.a.** The act of transferring to another. **b.** *Law.* A formal act of transferring ownership of property to another. **3.** The act of giving up; surrender. **4.** The act or manner of throwing or discharging. **5.** The act of giving birth; parturition. **6.a.** Utterance or enunciation. **b.** The act or manner of speaking or singing. **7.** The act of releasing or rescuing.

delivery room *n.* **1.** A room or an area in a hospital that is equipped for delivering babies. **2.** A room or an area set aside for making or receiving deliveries.

dell (dĕl) *n.* A small wooded valley. [ME *del* < OE *dell.*]

del•la Rob•bia (dĕl′ə rō′bē-ə, dĕl′lä rôb′byä), **Luca.** 1400?–82. Italian sculptor noted for his terra-cotta works.

dells (dĕlz) *pl.n.* The rapids of a river. [Alteration of DALLES.]

Del•mar•va Peninsula (dĕl-mär′və). A peninsula of the E U.S. separating Chesapeake Bay from Delaware Bay and the Atlantic Ocean and including DE and parts of E MD and VA.

Del•mon•i•co (dĕl-mŏn′ĭ-kō′), **Lorenzo.** 1813–81. Swiss-born Amer. restaurateur who popularized European cuisine in New York City.

Delmonico steak *n.* A small, often boned steak from the front section of the short loin of beef. [After Lorenzo DELMONICO.]

de•lo•cal•ize (dē-lō′kə-līz′) *tr.v.* **-ized, -iz•ing, -iz•es. 1.** To remove from a native or usual locality. **2.** To broaden the range or scope of. **— de•lo′cal•i•za′tion** (-kə-lĭ-zā′shən) *n.*

De•lorme or **de l'Orme** (də-lôrm′), **Philibert.** 1515?–70. French architect who built the Tuileries in Paris.

De•los (dē′lŏs′, dĕl′ōs). An island of SE Greece in the Cyclades Is. of the S Aegean; traditionally sacred to Apollo.

de•louse (dē-lous′) *tr.v.* **-loused, -lous•ing, -lous•es.** To rid (a person or an animal) of lice by physical or chemical means.

Del•phi (dĕl′fī′). An ancient town of central Greece near Mt. Parnassus; seat of a famous oracle of Apollo.

Del•phic (dĕl′fĭk) also **Del•phi•an** (-fē-ən) *adj.* **1.** *Gk. Myth.* Of or relating to Delphi or to the oracle of Apollo at Delphi. **2.** Obscurely prophetic; oracular. **— Del′phi•cal•ly** *adv.*

del•phin•i•um (dĕl-fĭn′ē-əm) *n.* A plant of the genus *Delphinium,* esp. any of several tall cultivated varieties with palmate leaves and long racemes of spurred flowers. [NLat. *Delphinium,* genus name < Gk. *delphinion,* larkspur, dim. of *delphis, delphin-,* dolphin (from the shape of the nectary).]

Del•phi•nus (dĕl-fī′nəs) *n.* A constellation in the Northern Hemisphere near Pegasus and Aquila. [Lat. *delphīnus,* dolphin. See DOLPHIN.]

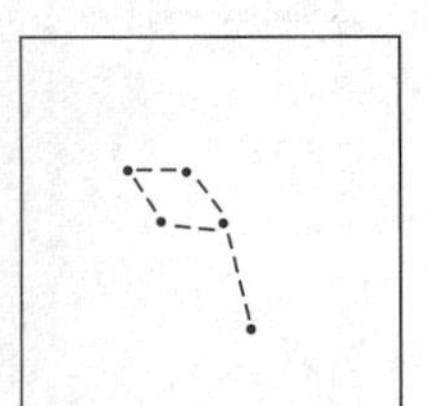

Delphinus

Del•ray Beach (dĕl′rā′). A city of SE FL on the Atlantic Ocean N of Boca Raton; settled in 1901. Pop. 47,181.

Del Ri•o (dĕl rē′ō). A city of SW TX on the Rio Grande W of San Antonio; founded 1868. Pop. 30,705.

del•ta (dĕl′tə) *n.* **1.** The fourth letter of the Greek alphabet. **2.** An object shaped like a triangle. **3.a.** A usu. triangular alluvial deposit at the mouth of a river. **b.** A similar deposit at the mouth of a tidal inlet, caused by tidal currents. **4.** *Math.* A finite increment in a variable. [ME < Lat. < Gk.; akin to Heb. *delet,* door < Phoenician *dalt.*] **— del•ta′ic** (-tā′ĭk), **del′tic** (-tĭk) *adj.*

delta ray *n.* An electron ejected from matter by ionizing radiation.

delta wave *n.* A brain wave with a frequency of one to three hertz that is associated with deep sleep in normal adults.

delta wing *n.* An aircraft with swept-back wings that give it the appearance of an isosceles triangle.

del•ti•ol•o•gy (dĕl′tē-ŏl′ə-jē) *n.* The collection and study of post cards. [< Gk. *deltion,* dim. of *deltos,* letter.]

del•toid (dĕl′toid′) *n.* A thick triangular muscle covering the shoulder joint, used to raise the arm from the side. *—adj.* **1.** Triangular. **2.** Of or relating to the deltoid. [NLat. *deltoidēs* < Gk. *deltoeidēs,* triangular : *delta,* delta; see DELTA + *-oeidēs,* -oid.]

de•lude (dĭ-lo͞od′) *tr.v.* **-lud•ed, -lud•ing, -ludes. 1.** To deceive the mind or judgment of: *deluding consumers.* See Syns at **deceive. 2.** *Obsolete.* To elude or evade. **3.** *Obsolete.* To frustrate the hopes or plans of. [ME *deluden* < Lat. *dēlūdere* : *dē-,* de- + *lūdere,* to play; see **leid-***.] **— de•lud′er** *n.* **— de•lud′ing•ly** *adv.*

del•uge (dĕl′yo͞oj) *n.* **1.a.** A great flood. **b.** A heavy downpour. **2.** Something that overwhelms as if by a great flood: *a deluge of mail.* **3. Deluge.** In the Bible, the great flood that occurred in the time of Noah. *—tr.v.* **-uged, -ug•ing, -ug•es. 1.** To overrun with water; inundate. **2.** To overwhelm with a large number or amount; swamp. [< ME, flood < OFr. < Lat. *dīluvium* < *dīluere,* to wash away : *dis-,* apart; see DIS- + *-luere,* to wash; see **leu(ə)-***.]

de•lu•sion (dĭ-lo͞o′zhən) *n.* **1.a.** The act or process of deluding. **b.** The state of being deluded. **2.** A false belief or opinion. **3.** *Psychiat.* A false belief strongly held in spite of invalidating evidence, esp. as a symptom of mental illness. [ME *delusioun* < Lat. *dēlūsiō, dēlūsiōn-* < *dēlūsus,* p.part. of *dēlūdere,* to delude. See DELUDE.] **— de•lu′sion•al** *adj.*

de•lu•sive (dĭ-lo͞o′sĭv) *adj.* **1.** Tending to delude. **2.** Having the nature of a delusion; false. **— de•lu′sive•ly** *adv.* **— de•lu′sive•ness** *n.*

de•lu•so•ry (dĭ-lo͞o′sə-rē, -zə-) *adj.* Tending to deceive.

de luxe also **de•luxe** (dĭ-lŭks′, -lo͝oks′) *—adj.* Particularly elegant and luxurious; sumptuous. *—adv.* In an elegant and luxurious manner; sumptuously. [Fr. : *de,* of + *luxe,* luxury.]

delve (dĕlv) *v.* **delved, delv•ing, delves.** *—intr.* **1.** To search deeply and laboriously: *delved into archives.* **2.** To dig the ground, as with a spade. *—tr. Archaic.* To dig (ground) with a spade. [ME *delven,* to dig < OE *delfan.*] **— delv′er** *n.*

dely. *abbr.* Delivery.

dem. *abbr.* **1.** *Gram.* Demonstrative. **2.** Demurrage.

Dem. *abbr.* Democrat; Democratic.

de•mag•net•ize (dē-măg′nĭ-tīz′) *tr.v.* **-ized, -iz•ing, -iz•es. 1.** To remove magnetic properties from. **2.** To erase (a magnetic storage device). **— de•mag′net•i•za′tion** (-nĭ-tĭ-zā′shən) *n.* **— de•mag′net•iz′er** *n.*

dem•a•gog•ic (dĕm′ə-gŏj′ĭk, -gŏg′-, -gō′jĭk) also **dem•a•gog•i•cal** (-gŏj′ĭ-kəl, -gŏg′-, -gō′jĭ-kəl) *adj.* Of or relating to a demagogue. **— dem′a•gog′i•cal•ly** *adv.*

dem•a•gog•ism (dĕm′ə-gô′gĭz-əm, -gŏg′ĭz-) *n.* Demagoguery.

dem•a•gogue (dĕm′ə-gôg′, -gŏg′) *n.* **1.** A leader who obtains power by means of impassioned appeals to emotions and prejudices. **2.** A leader of the common people in ancient times. [Gk. *dēmagōgos,* popular leader : *dēmos,* people; see **dā-*** + *agōgos,* leading (< *agein,* to lead; see **ag-***).]

dem•a•gogu•er•y (dĕm′ə-gô′gə-rē, -gŏg′ə-) *n.* The practices or rhetoric of a demagogue.

dem•a•gog•y (dĕm′ə-gŏj′ē, -gô′jē, -gŏg′ē, -gō′jē) *n.* The character or practices of a demagogue; demagoguery.

de•mand (dĭ-mănd′) *v.* **-mand•ed, -mand•ing, -mands.** *—tr.* **1.** To ask for urgently or peremptorily. **2.** To claim as just or due: *demand payment.* **3.** To ask to be informed of. **4.** To require as useful, just, proper, or necessary; call for. **5.** *Law.* To claim formally; lay legal claim to. *—intr.* To make a demand. *—n.* **1.** The act of demanding. **2.** Something demanded. **3.** An urgent requirement or need. **4.** The state of being sought after: *in demand as a speaker.* **5.** *Econ.* **a.** The desire to possess a commodity or make use of a service, combined with the ability to purchase it. **b.** The amount of a commodity or service that people are ready to buy for a given price: *supply and demand.* **6.** *Comp. Sci.* A coding technique in which a command to read or write is initiated as the need for a new block of data occurs, thus eliminating the need to store data. **7.** *Law.* A formal claim. **8.** *Archaic.* An emphatic question or inquiry. ***—idiom.* on demand. 1.** When presented for payment. **2.** When needed or asked for. [ME *demanden* < OFr. *demander,* to charge with doing, and < Med.Lat. *dēmandāre,* to demand, both < Lat., to entrust : *dē-,* de- + *mandāre,* to entrust; see **man-**[2]***.**] **— de•mand′a•ble** *adj.*

Syns: *demand, claim, exact, require.* The central meaning shared by these verbs is "to ask for urgently or insistently": *demanding work; claiming repayment of a debt; exacted obedience; tax payments required by law.*

de•mand•ant (dĭ-măn′dənt) *n. Archaic.* A plaintiff.

demand deposit *n.* A bank deposit that can be withdrawn without advance notice.

de•mand•ing (dĭ-măn′dĭng) *adj.* Requiring much effort or attention. **— de•mand′ing•ly** *adv.*

demand loan *n.* See **call loan.**

demand note *n.* A bill or draft payable on demand.

de•mand-pull (dĭ-mănd′po͝ol′) *n.* Increased demand for a limited supply of goods and services, tending to cause consumer prices to increase. **— de•mand′-pull′** *adj.*

de·man·toid (dĭ-măn′toid′) *n.* A transparent green variety of garnet used as a gem. [Ger. < *Demant*, diamond < MHGer. *diemant* < OFr. *diamant*. See DIAMOND.]

de·mar·cate (dĭ-mär′kāt′, dē′mär-kāt′) *tr.v.* **-cat·ed, -cat·ing, -cates. 1.** To set the boundaries of; delimit. **2.** To separate clearly as if by boundaries; distinguish. [Back-formation < DEMARCATION.] **— de·mar′ca′tor** *n.*

de·mar·ca·tion also **de·mar·ka·tion** (dē′mär-kā′shən) *n.* **1.** The setting or marking of boundaries or limits. **2.** A separation; a distinction. [Sp. *demarcación* < *demarcar*, to mark boundaries : *de-*, off (< Lat. *dē-*; see DE–) + *marcar*, to mark (< Ital. *marcare* < OItal., of Gmc. orig.; see **merg-***).]

dé·marche (dā-märsh′) *n.* **1.** A course of action; a maneuver. **2.** A diplomatic representation or protest. **3.** A statement or protest addressed by citizens to public authorities. [Fr. < OFr. *demarche*, gait < *demarchier*, to march : *de-*, de- + *marchier*, to march (prob. of Gmc. orig.; see MARCH[1]).]

de·ma·te·ri·al·ize (dē′mə-tîr′ē-ə-līz′) *tr. & intr.v.* **-ized, -iz·ing, -iz·es.** To deprive of or lose apparent physical substance; make or become immaterial. **— de′ma·te′ri·al·i·za′tion** (-ə-lĭ-zā′shən) *n.*

deme (dēm) *n.* **1.** One of the townships of ancient Attica. **2.** *Ecol.* A local, usu. stable population of interbreeding organisms of the same kind. [Gk. *dēmos*, people. See **dā-***.]

de·mean[1] (dĭ-mēn′) *tr.v.* **-meaned, -mean·ing, -means.** To conduct or behave (oneself) in a particular manner. [ME *demeinen*, to govern < OFr. *demener* : *de-*, de- + *mener*, to conduct (< Lat. *mināre*, to drive (animals) < *minārī*, to threaten < *minae*, threats; see **men-[2]***).]

de·mean[2] (dĭ-mēn′) *tr.v.* **-meaned, -mean·ing, -means. 1.** To debase, as in dignity. **2.** To humble (oneself). See Syns at **degrade.** [DE– + MEAN[2].] **— de·mean′ing·ly** *adv.*

de·mean·or (dĭ-mē′nər) *n.* The way in which a person behaves; deportment.

de·ment (dĭ-mĕnt′) *tr.v.* **-ment·ed, -ment·ing, -ments.** To make insane. [LLat. *dēmentāre* < Lat. *dēmēns*, *dēment-*, senseless : *dē-*, de- + *mēns*, mind; see **men-[1]***.]

de·ment·ed (dĭ-mĕn′tĭd) *adj.* **1.** Mentally ill; insane. **2.** Suffering from dementia. **— de·ment′ed·ly** *adv.* **— de·ment′ed·ness** *n.*

de·men·tia (dĭ-mĕn′shə) *n.* **1.** Deterioration of intellectual faculties resulting from a disorder of the brain and often accompanied by emotional disturbance. **2.** Madness; insanity. See Syns at **insanity.** [Lat. *dēmentia*, madness < *dēmēns*, *dēment-*, senseless. See DEMENT.] **— de·men′tial** *adj.*

de·mer·it (dĭ-mĕr′ĭt) *n.* **1.a.** A quality or characteristic deserving of blame or censure; a fault. **b.** Absence of merit. **2.** A mark made against one's record for a fault or for misconduct. [ME *demerite*, offense < OFr. *desmerite* < Lat. *dēmeritum* < neut. p.part. of *dēmerēre*, to deserve : *dē-*, de- + *merēre*, to earn; see MERIT.] **— de·mer′i·to′ri·ous** (-tôr′ē-əs, -tōr′-) *adj.* **— de·mer′i·to′ri·ous·ly** *adv.*

Dem·er·ol (dĕm′ə-rôl′, -rŏl′, -rōl′). A trademark used for a medicinal preparation of meperidine.

de·mer·sal (dĭ-mûr′səl) *adj.* Dwelling at or near, sinking to, or deposited near the bottom of a body of water. [< Lat. *dēmersus*, p.part. of *dēmergere*, to sink : *dē-*, de- + *mergere*, to sink.]

de·mesne (dĭ-mān′, -mēn′) *n.* **1.** Manorial land retained for the private use of a feudal lord. **2.** The grounds belonging to a mansion or country house. **3.** An extensive piece of landed property; an estate. **4.** A district; a territory. **5.** A realm; a domain. [ME *demeine*, **demesne* < AN < OFr. *demaine*. See DOMAIN.]

De·me·ter (dĭ-mē′tər) *n. Gk. Myth.* The goddess of the harvest, daughter of Rhea and Cronus and mother of Persephone. [Gk. *Dēmētēr*. See **māter-***.]

demi– *pref.* **1.** Half: *demirelief*. **2.** To some degree; part; partly: *demigod*. [ME *demi*, a half of a measure or unit < OFr. < Med.Lat. *dīmedius* < Lat. *dīmidius*, divided in half : *dis-*, dis- + *medius*, half; see MEDIUM.]

dem·i·god (dĕm′ē-gŏd′) *n.* **1.** *Myth.* **a.** A male being, often the offspring of a deity and a mortal, who has some divine powers. **b.** An inferior deity; a minor god. **c.** A deified man. **2.** A person who is highly honored or revered.

dem·i·god·dess (dĕm′ē-gŏd′ĭs) *n.* **1.** A female being, often the offspring of a deity and a mortal, who has some divine powers. **2.** A deified woman.

dem·i·john (dĕm′ē-jŏn′) *n.* A large narrow-necked bottle made of glass or earthenware, usu. encased in wickerwork. [Prob. alteration of Fr. *dame-jeanne* : *dame*, lady; see DAME + *Jeanne*, personal name.]

de·mil·i·ta·rize (dē-mĭl′ĭ-tə-rīz′) *tr.v.* **-rized, -riz·ing, -riz·es. 1.** To eliminate the military nature of. **2.** To forbid military presence in. **3.** To replace military with civilian control of. **— de·mil′i·ta·ri·za′tion** (-tər-ĭ-zā′shən) *n.*

De Mille (də mĭl′), **Agnes George.** b. 1905. Amer. choreographer whose works include innovative dances for musicals such as *Oklahoma!* (1943) and *Carousel* (1945).

De Mille, Cecil Blount. 1881–1959. Amer. filmmaker known for his spectacular epic productions, including *The Ten Commandments* (1923 and 1956).

dem·i·mon·daine (dĕm′ē-mŏn-dān′, -mŏn′dān′) *n.* A woman belonging to the demimonde. [Fr. < *demi-monde*, demimonde. See DEMIMONDE.]

dem·i·monde (dĕm′ē-mŏnd′) *n.* **1.a.** A class of women financially supported by lovers or protectors. **b.** Women prostitutes considered as a group. **2.** A group whose respectability is dubious or whose success is marginal. [Fr. : *demi-*, demi- + *monde*, world (< Lat. *mundus*).]

de·min·er·al·i·za·tion (dē-mĭn′ər-ə-lĭ-zā′shən) *n.* **1.** The act or process of removing minerals or mineral salts from a liquid. **2.** The loss, deprivation, or removal of minerals or mineral salts from the body, esp. through disease.

de·min·er·al·ize (dē-mĭn′ər-ə-līz′) *tr.v.* **-ized, -iz·ing, -iz·es.** To remove minerals or mineral salts from (a liquid). **— de·min′er·al·i′zer** *n.*

dem·i·re·lief (dĕm′ē-rĭ-lēf′) *n.* See **half relief.**

dem·i·rep (dĕm′ē-rĕp′) *n.* A person of doubtful reputation or respectability. [DEMI– + REP(UTATION).]

de·mise (dĭ-mīz′) *n.* **1.a.** Death. **b.** The end of existence or activity; termination: *the demise of the streetcar.* **2.** *Law.* Transfer of an estate by lease or will. **3.** The transfer of a ruler's authority by death or abdication. *— v.* **-mised, -mis·ing, -mis·es.** *— tr.* **1.** *Law.* To transfer (an estate) by will or lease. **2.** To transfer (sovereignty) by abdication or will. *— intr.* **1.** *Law.* To be transferred by will or descent. **2.** To die. [ME, transfer of property < OFr. *dimis*, p.part. of *demettre*, to release. See DEMIT.] **— de·mis′a·ble** *adj.*

dem·i·sem·i·qua·ver (dĕm′ē-sĕm′ē-kwā′vər) *n. Chiefly British.* A thirty-second note.

de·mis·sion (dĭ-mĭsh′ən) *n.* Relinquishment of an office or function. [Ult. < Lat. *dīmissiō*, *dīmissiōn-*, dismissal < *dīmissus*, p.part. of *dīmittere*, to release. See DEMIT.]

de·mit (dĭ-mĭt′) *v.* **-mit·ted, -mit·ting, -mits.** *— tr.* **1.** To relinquish (an office or function). **2.** *Archaic.* To dismiss. *— intr.* To give up an office or position; resign. [ME *dimitten*, to release < OFr. *demettre* < Lat. *dīmittere* : *dis-*, away; see DIS– + *mittere*, to send.]

dem·i·tasse (dĕm′ē-tăs′, -täs′) *n.* **1.** A small cup of strong black coffee or espresso. **2.** The small cup used to serve this drink. [Fr. : *demi-*, demi- + *tasse*, cup (< OFr. < Ar. *ṭašt*, basin < Pers.).]

dem·i·urge (dĕm′ē-ûrj′) *n.* **1.** A powerful creative force or personality. **2.** A public magistrate in some ancient Greek states. **3. Demiurge.** A deity in Gnosticism, Manichaeism, and other religions who creates the material world and is sometimes viewed as the originator of evil. **4. Demiurge.** A Platonic deity who orders or fashions the material world out of chaos. [LLat. *dēmiurgus* < Gk. *dēmiourgos*, artisan : *dēmios*, public (< *dēmos*, people; see **dā-***) + *ergos*, worker (< *ergon*, work; see **werg-***).] **— dem′i·ur′geous** (-ûr′jəs), **dem′i·ur′gic** (-jĭk), **dem′i·ur′gi·cal** (-jĭ-kəl) *adj.* **— dem′i·ur′gi·cal·ly** *adv.*

dem·i·world (dĕm′ē-wûrld′) *n.* See **demimonde** 2.

dem·o (dĕm′ō) *n.*, *pl.* **-os.** *Informal.* **1.a.** A demonstration, as of a product. **b.** A brief recording used to illustrate the qualities of a musician or other performer. **2.** A product used for demonstration and often sold later at a discount. **— dem′o** *v.*

de·mob (dē-mŏb′) *Chiefly British. tr.v.* **-mobbed, -mob·bing, -mobs.** To demobilize (armed forces). **— de·mob′** *n.*

de·mo·bil·ize (dē-mō′bə-līz′) *tr.v.* **-ized, -iz·ing, -iz·es. 1.** To discharge from military service or use. **2.** To disband (troops). **— de·mo′bil·i·za′tion** (-bə-lĭ-zā′shən) *n.*

de·moc·ra·cy (dĭ-mŏk′rə-sē) *n.*, *pl.* **-cies. 1.** Government by the people, exercised either directly or through elected representatives. **2.** A society with such a government. **3.** The common people, considered as the primary source of political power. **4.** Majority rule. **5.** The principles of social equality and individual rights. [Fr. *démocratie* < LLat. *dēmocratia* < Gk. *dēmokratia* : *dēmos*, people; see **dā-*** + *-kratia*, -cracy.]

dem·o·crat (dĕm′ə-krăt′) *n.* **1.** An advocate of democracy. **2. Democrat.** A Democratic Party member. [Fr. *démocrate*, back-formation < *démocratie*, democracy. See DEMOCRACY.]

Democrat, Mount. A peak, 4,315.1 m (14,148 ft), of central CO in the Park Range of the Rocky Mts.

dem·o·crat·ic (dĕm′ə-krăt′ĭk) *adj.* **1.** Of, characterized by, or advocating democracy. **2.** Of or for the people in general; popular. **3.** Believing in or practicing social equality. **4. Democratic.** Of, relating to, or characteristic of the Democratic Party. **— dem′o·crat′i·cal·ly** *adv.*

Democratic Party *n.* One of the two major U.S. political parties, owing its origin to a split in the Democratic-Republican Party under Andrew Jackson in 1828.

Dem·o·crat·ic-Re·pub·li·can Party (dĕm′ə-krăt′ĭk-rĭ-pŭb′lĭ-kən) *n.* A U.S. political party founded by Thomas Jefferson in 1792 in opposition to the Federalist Party.

de·moc·ra·tize (dĭ-mŏk′rə-tīz′) *tr.v.* **-tized, -tiz·ing, -tiz·es.** To make democratic. **— de·moc′ra·ti·za′tion** (-tĭ-zā′shən) *n.*

De·moc·ri·tus (dĭ-mŏk′rĭ-təs). "the Laughing Philosopher." 460?–370? B.C. Greek philosopher who believed that pleasure, along with self-control, is the goal of human life.

dé·mo·dé (dā-mō-dā′) *adj.* No longer in fashion; outmoded.

demijohn

ă pat	oi **boy**
ā pay	ou **out**
âr care	ŏŏ **took**
ä father	ōō **boot**
ĕ pet	ŭ cut
ē be	ûr **urge**
ĭ pit	th **thin**
ī pie	*th* this
îr pier	hw **which**
ŏ pot	zh vision
ō toe	ə about, item
ô paw	

Stress marks:
′ (primary);
′ (secondary), as in
dictionary (dĭk′shə-nĕr′ē)

[Fr., p.part. of *démoder*, to outmode : *dé-*, out (< OFr. *de-*; see DE–) + *mode*, fashion; see MODE.]

de•mod•u•late (dē-mŏj′ə-lāt′, -mŏd′yə-) *tr.v.* **-lat•ed, -lat•ing, -lates.** To extract (information) from a modulated carrier wave. —**de•mod′u•la′tor** *n.*

de•mod•u•la•tion (dē-mŏj′ə-lā′shən) *n.* The conversion of a modulated carrier wave into a current equivalent to the original signal.

De•mo•gor•gon (dē′mə-gôr′gən, dē′mə-gôr′-) *n. Myth.* A terrifying ancient deity or demon of the underworld.

dem•o•graph•ic (dĕm′ə-grăf′ĭk, dē′mə-) also **dem•o•graph•i•cal** (-ĭ-kəl) *adj.* Of or relating to demography. —**dem′o•graph′i•cal•ly** *adv.*

dem•o•graph•ics (dĕm′ə-grăf′ĭks, dē′mə-) *n. (used with a pl. v.)* The characteristics of human populations and population segments, esp. when used to identify consumer markets.

de•mog•ra•phy (dĭ-mŏg′rə-fē) *n.* The study of the characteristics of human populations. [Fr. *démographie* : Gk. *dēmos*, people; see **dā-*** + Fr. *-graphie*, writing (< Gk. *-graphia*, -graphy).] —**de•mog′ra•pher** *n.*

dem•oi•selle (dĕm′wə-zĕl′) *n.* **1.** A young woman. **2.** A demoiselle crane. **3.** See **damselfly. 4.** See **damselfish.** [Fr., damsel < OFr. *dameisele.* See DAMSEL.]

demoiselle crane *n.* A small crane *(Anthropoides virgo)* of Asia, northern Africa, and Europe having gray and black plumage and white plumes at the side of the head.

demoiselle crane
Anthropoides virgo

de•mol•ish (dĭ-mŏl′ĭsh) *tr.v.* **-ished, -ish•ing, -ish•es. 1.** To tear down completely; raze. **2.** To do away with completely; put an end to. **3.** To damage (someone's reputation, for example) severely. See Syns at **ruin.** [Fr. *démolir, démoliss-* < Lat. *dēmōlīrī* : *dē-*, de- + *mōlīrī*, to build (< *mōlēs*, mass).]

dem•o•li•tion (dĕm′ə-lĭsh′ən, dē′mə-) *n.* **1.** The act or process of wrecking or destroying, esp. by explosives. **2. demolitions.** Explosives, esp. when designed or used as weapons. [Fr. *démolition* < Lat. *dēmōlītiō, dēmōlītiōn-* < *dēmōlīrī*, to demolish. See DEMOLISH.] —**dem′o•li′tion•ist** *n.*

demolition derby *n. Sports.* A contest in which drivers crash old cars into each other until only one is left running.

de•mon (dē′mən) *n.* **1.** An evil supernatural being; a devil. **2.** A persistently tormenting person, force, or passion. **3.** One who is extremely zealous, skillful, or diligent. **4.** Also **dae•mon** or **dai•mon** (dī′mōn′). *Gk. Myth.* An inferior deity. **5.** Also **dae•mon** or **dai•mon** (dī′mōn′). An attendant spirit; a genius. [ME < LLat. *daemōn* < Lat., spirit < Gk. *daimōn*, divine power. See **dā-*.**]

demon. *abbr. Gram.* Demonstrative.

de•mon•e•tize (dē-mŏn′ĭ-tīz′, -mŭn′-) *tr.v.* **-tized, -tiz•ing, -tiz•es. 1.** To divest (a coin, for example) of monetary value. **2.** To stop using (a metal) as a monetary standard. [Fr. *démonétiser* : *dé-*, away from (< OFr. *de-*; see DE–) + Lat. *monēta*, coin; see MONEY.] —**de•mon′e•ti•za′tion** (-tĭ-zā′shən) *n.*

de•mo•ni•ac (dĭ-mō′nē-ăk′) also **de•mo•ni•a•cal** (dē′mə-nī′ə-kəl) —*adj.* **1.** Possessed, produced, or influenced by a demon. **2.** Of, resembling, or suggestive of a devil; fiendish. —*n.* One who is or seems to be possessed by a demon. [ME *demoniak* < LLat. *daemoniacus* < Gk. **daimoniakos* < *daimonios*, of a spirit < *daimōn*, divine power. See DEMON.] —**de′mo•ni′a•cal•ly** *adv.*

demolition
Scollay Square, Boston, in the early 1960's

de•mon•ic also **dae•mon•ic** (dĭ-mŏn′ĭk) *adj.* **1.** Befitting a demon; fiendish. **2.** Motivated by a spiritual force or genius; inspired. —**de•mon′i•cal•ly** *adv.*

de•mon•ize (dē′mə-nīz′) *tr.v.* **-ized, -iz•ing, -iz•es. 1.** To turn into or as if into a demon. **2.** To possess by or as if by a demon. **3.** To represent as evil or diabolic: *demonized the enemy.* —**de′mon•i•za′tion** (-mə-nĭ-zā′shən) *n.*

de•mon•ol•o•gy (dē′mə-nŏl′ə-jē) *n.* **1.** The study of demons. **2.** Belief in or worship of demons. **3.** A list or catalog of one's enemies. —**de′mon•o•log′ic** (-ə-lŏj′ĭk), **de′mon•o•log′i•cal** (-ĭ-kəl) *adj.* —**de′mon•ol′o•gist** *n.*

de•mon•stra•ble (dĭ-mŏn′strə-bəl) *adj.* **1.** Capable of being demonstrated or proved. **2.** Obvious; apparent. —**de•mon′stra•bil′i•ty, de•mon′stra•ble•ness** *n.* —**de•mon′stra•bly** *adv.*

dem•on•strate (dĕm′ən-strāt′) *v.* **-strat•ed, -strat•ing, -strates.** —*tr.* **1.** To show clearly and deliberately; manifest. **2.** To show to be true by reasoning or adducing evidence; prove. **3.** To present by experiments, examples, or practical application; explain and illustrate. **4.** To show the use of (an article) to a prospective buyer. —*intr.* **1.** To give a demonstration. **2.** To participate in a public display of opinion, as by marching. [Lat. *dēmōnstrāre, dēmōnstrāt-* : *dē-*, completely; see DE– + *mōnstrāre*, to show (< *mōnstrum*, divine portent < *monēre*, to warn; see **men-**[1]***).]

dem•on•stra•tion (dĕm′ən-strā′shən) *n.* **1.** The act of showing or making clear. **2.** Conclusive evidence; proof. **3.** An illustration or explanation by exemplification or practical application. **4.** A manifestation, as of one's feelings. **5.** A public display of group opinion.

de•mon•stra•tive (dĭ-mŏn′strə-tĭv) *adj.* **1.** Serving to manifest or prove. **2.** Involving or characterized by demonstration. **3.** Given to or marked by the open expression of emotion. **4.** *Gram.* Specifying or singling out the person or thing referred to. —*n. Gram.* A demonstrative pronoun or adjective. —**de•mon′stra•tive•ly** *adv.* —**de•mon′stra•tive•ness** *n.*

dem•on•stra•tor (dĕm′ən-strā′tər) *n.* **1.** One that demonstrates, as at a rally. **2.** An article used in a demonstration.

de•mor•al•ize (dĭ-môr′ə-līz′, -mŏr′-) *tr.v.* **-ized, -iz•ing, -iz•es. 1.** To undermine the confidence or morale of. **2.** To disorder; confuse. **3.** To debase the morals of; corrupt. —**de•mor′al•i•za′tion** (-ə-lĭ-zā′shən) *n.* —**de•mor′al•iz′er** *n.*

De Mor•gan (dĭ môr′gən), **Augustus.** 1806–71. British mathematician who with George Boole laid the foundation for modern symbolic logic.

de•mos (dē′mŏs′) *n.* **1.** The common people; the populace. **2.** The common people of an ancient Greek state. [Gk. *dēmos*, district, people. See **dā-*.**]

De•mos•the•nes (dĭ-mŏs′thə-nēz′). 384–322 B.C. Greek orator whose reputation is based mainly on his *Philippics.*

de•mote (dĭ-mōt′) *tr.v.* **-mot•ed, -mot•ing, -motes.** To reduce in grade, rank, or status. [DE– + (PRO)MOTE.] —**de•mo′tion** *n.*

de•mot•ic (dĭ-mŏt′ĭk) *adj.* **1.** Of or relating to the common people; popular. **2.** Of, relating to, or written in the simplified form of ancient Egyptian hieratic writing. **3. Demotic.** Of or relating to a form of modern Greek based on colloquial use. —*n.* **Demotic.** Demotic Greek. [Gk. *dēmotikos* < *dēmotēs*, a commoner < *dēmos*, people. See **dā-*.**]

de•mount (dē-mount′) *tr.v.* **-mount•ed, -mount•ing, -mounts.** To remove (a motor, for example) from a position on a mounting or other support. —**de•mount′a•ble** *adj.*

Demp•sey (dĕmp′sē), **William Harrison ("Jack").** "the Manassa Mauler." 1895–1983. Amer. prizefighter who won the world heavyweight title in 1919.

de•mul•cent (dĭ-mŭl′sənt) *adj.* Serving to soothe or soften. —*n.* A usu. mucilaginous or oily substance used esp. to soothe pain in mucuous membranes. [Lat. *dēmulcēns, dēmulcent-*, pr.part. of *dēmulcēre*, to soften : *dē-*, de- + *mulcēre*, to stroke.]

de•mur (dĭ-mûr′) *intr.v.* **-murred, -mur•ring, -murs. 1.** To voice opposition; object. See Syns at **object. 2.** *Law.* To enter a demurrer. **3.** To delay. —*n.* **1.** The act of demurring. **2.** An objection. **3.** A delay. [ME *demuren*, to delay < AN *demurer* < Lat. *dēmorārī* : *dē-*, de- + *morārī*, to delay (< *mora*, delay).] —**de•mur′ra•ble** *adj.*

de•mure (dĭ-myo͝or′) *adj.* **-mur•er, -mur•est. 1.** Modest and reserved in manner or behavior. **2.** Affectedly shy, modest, or reserved. See Syns at **shy**[1]. [ME, prob. < AN (influenced by OFr. *mur, meur*, mature, serious < Lat. *mātūrus*; see MATURE), p.part. of *demurer*, to delay, wait. See DEMUR.] —**de•mure′ly** *adv.* —**de•mure′ness** *n.*

de•mur•rage (dĭ-mûr′ĭj, -mŭr′-) *n.* **1.** Detention of a ship or other cargo conveyance during loading or unloading beyond the scheduled time of departure. **2.** Compensation paid for such detention.

de•mur•ral (dĭ-mûr′əl, -mŭr′-) *n.* The act of demurring, esp. a mild, polite, or considered expression of opposition.

de•mur•rer (dĭ-mûr′ər, -mŭr′-) *n.* **1.** One that demurs; an objector. **2.** An objection. **3.** *Law.* A method of objecting that admits the facts of the opponent's argument but denies that they sustain the pleading based upon them.

de•my (dĭ-mī′) *n., pl.* **-mies.** Any of several standard sizes of paper, esp. paper measuring 16 by 21 inches. [Alteration of DEMI–.]

de•my•e•lin•ate (dē-mī′ə-lə-nāt′) *tr.v.* **-at•ed, -at•ing, -ates.** To destroy or remove the myelin sheath of (a nerve fiber), as through disease. —**de•my′e•lin•a′tion** *n.*

de•mys•ti•fy (dē-mĭs′tə-fī′) *tr.v.* **-fied, -fy•ing, -fies.** To make less mysterious; clarify. —**de•mys′ti•fi•ca′tion** (-fĭ-kā′shən) *n.* —**de•mys′ti•fi′er** *n.*

de•my•thol•o•gize (dē′mĭ-thŏl′ə-jīz′) *tr.v.* **-gized, -giz•ing, -giz•es. 1.** To rid of mythological elements in order to discover the underlying meaning. **2.** To remove the mysterious or mythical aspects from. —**de′my•thol′o•gi•za′tion** (-jĭ-zā′shən) *n.* —**de′my•thol′o•giz′er** *n.*

den (dĕn) *n.* **1.** The shelter or retreat of a wild animal; a lair. **2.** A cave or hollow used as a refuge or hiding place. **3.** A hidden or squalid dwelling place: *a den of thieves.* **4.** A secluded room for study or relaxation. **5.** A unit of about eight to ten Cub Scouts. —*intr.v.* **denned, den•ning, dens.** To inhabit or hide in a den. [ME < OE *denn.*]

Den. *abbr.* Denmark.

De•na•li (də-nä′lē). See Mount **McKinley.**

de•nar•i•us (dĭ-nâr′ē-əs) *n., pl.* **-i•i** (-ē-ī′). **1.** An ancient Roman silver coin. **2.** An ancient Roman gold coin valued at 25 silver denarii. [ME < Lat. *dēnārius.* See DENARY.]

den•a•ry (dĕn′ə-rē) *adj.* **1.** Tenfold. **2.** Divided or counted by tens; decimal. [Lat. *dēnārius* < *dēnī*, by tens. See **dekm̥*.**]

de•na•tion•al•ize (dē-năsh′ə-nə-līz′) *tr.v.* **-ized, -iz•ing, -iz•es. 1.** To deprive of national rights or characteristics. **2.** To transfer (an industry, for example) from governmental to private ownership. —**de•na′tion•al•i•za′tion** (-shə-nə-lĭ-zā′shən) *n.*

de•nat•u•ral•ize (dē-năch′ər-ə-līz′) *tr.v.* **-ized, -iz•ing, -iz•**

es. **1.** To make unnatural. **2.** To deprive of the rights of citizenship. **—de·nat′u·ral·i·za′tion** (-ər-ə-lĭ-zā′shən) *n.*

de·na·ture (dē-nā′chər) *tr.v.* **-tured, -tur·ing, -tures. 1.** To change the nature or natural qualities of. **2.** To render unfit to eat or drink without destroying other uses, esp. to add methanol to (ethyl alcohol). **3.** *Biochem.* To alter (a protein) structurally, as with heat, so that its original properties, esp. its biological activity, are diminished or eliminated. **4.** *Phys.* To add nonfissionable matter to (fissionable material) so as to prevent use in an atomic weapon. **—de·na′tur·ant** *n.* **—de·na′tur·a′tion** *n.*

den·dri·form (dĕn′drə-fôrm′) *adj.* Shaped like or having the form of a tree.

den·drite (dĕn′drīt′) *n.* **1.a.** A mineral crystallizing in another mineral in the form of a branching or treelike mark. **b.** A rock or mineral bearing such a mark or marks. **2.** A branched protoplasmic extension of a nerve cell that conducts impulses from adjacent cells inward toward the cell body.

den·drit·ic (dĕn-drĭt′ĭk) also **den·drit·i·cal** (-ĭ-kəl) *adj.* **1.** Of, relating to, or resembling a dendrite. **2.** Dendriform. **—den·drit′i·cal·ly** *adv.*

dendro– or **dendri–** or **dendr–** *pref.* Tree; treelike: *dendrochronology.* [< Gk. *dendron*, tree. See **deru-*.**]

den·dro·chro·nol·o·gy (dĕn′drō-krə-nŏl′ə-jē) *n.* The study of climate changes and past events by comparing the successive annual growth rings of trees or old timber. **—den′dro·chron′o·log′i·cal** (-krŏn′ə-lŏj′ĭ-kəl) *adj.* **—den′dro·chron′o·log′i·cal·ly** *adv.* **—den′dro·chro·nol′o·gist** *n.*

den·droid (dĕn′droid′) also **den·droid·al** (dĕn-droid′l) *adj.* Shaped like a tree.

den·drol·o·gy (dĕn-drŏl′ə-jē) *n.* The botanical study of trees and other woody plants. **—den′dro·log′ic** (-drə-lŏj′ĭk), **den′dro·log′i·cal** *adj.* **—den·drol′o·gist** *n.*

den·dron (dĕn′drŏn′) *n.* See **dendrite** 2. [Gk., tree. See **deru-*.**]

dene (dēn) *n. Chiefly British.* A sandy tract or dune by the seashore. [Poss. East Frisian *düne*, a sand dune; akin to DUNE.]

De·neb (dĕn′ĕb′) *n.* The brightest star in the constellation Cygnus. [Ar. *ḏanab*, tail.]

De·neb·o·la (də-nĕb′ə-lə) *n.* A star in the constellation Leo. [< Ar. *ḏanab al-'asad*, tail of the lion.]

den·e·ga·tion (dĕn′ĭ-gā′shən) *n.* A denial. [Ult. < Lat. *dēnegāre, dēnegāt-*, to deny. See DENY.]

de·ner·vate (dē-nûr′vāt) *tr.v.* **-vat·ed, -vat·ing, -vates.** *Medic.* To deprive (an organ or body part) of a nerve supply, as by surgery or with drugs. **—de′ner·va′tion** *n.*

den·gue (dĕng′gē, -gā) *n.* An acute, infectious tropical disease caused by an arbovirus transmitted by mosquitoes and marked by high fever, rash, headache, and severe muscle and joint pain. [Sp., alteration (influenced by *dengue*, affectation) of Swahili *ki-dinga*.]

Deng Xiao·ping (dŭng′ shou′pĭng′, dœng′ shyou′pĭng′) also **Teng Hsiao-ping** (tŭng′ shyou′pĭng′, dœng′). b. 1904. Chinese Communist leader who officially retired as head of state in Nov. 1989.

de·ni·a·ble (dĭ-nī′ə-bəl) *adj.* **1.** Possible to contradict or declare untrue. **2.** Being such that plausible disavowal is possible. **—de·ni′a·bil′i·ty** *n.* **—de·ni′a·bly** *adv.*

de·ni·al (dĭ-nī′əl) *n.* **1.** A refusal to comply with or satisfy a request. **2.a.** A refusal to grant the truth of a statement or allegation; a contradiction. **b.** *Law.* The opposing by a defendant of an allegation of the plaintiff. **3.a.** A refusal to accept or believe something, such as a belief. **b.** *Psychol.* An unconscious defense mechanism marked by refusal to acknowledge painful realities, thoughts, or feelings. **4.** The act of disowning or disavowing; repudiation. **5.** Self-denial.

de·ni·er¹ (dĭ-nī′ər) *n.* One that denies.

den·ier² (dən-yā′) *n.* **1.** (*also* dĕn′yər). A unit of fineness for rayon, nylon, and silk, based on a standard mass per length of 1 gram per 9,000 meters of yarn. **2.** (*also* də-nîr′).**a.** A small coin of varying composition and value current in western Europe from the eighth century until the French Revolution. **b.** *Archaic.* A small trifling sum. [ME *denere*, a coin < OFr. *dener* < Lat. *dēnārius*. See DENARIUS.]

den·i·grate (dĕn′ĭ-grāt′) *tr.v.* **-grat·ed, -grat·ing, -grates. 1.** To attack the character or reputation of; speak ill of; defame. **2.** To disparage; belittle. [Lat. *dēnigrāre, dēnigrāt-*, to blacken, defame : *dē-*, de- + *niger, nigr-*, black.] **—den′i·gra′tion** *n.* **—den′i·gra′tor** *n.*

den·im (dĕn′ĭm) *n.* **1.a.** A coarse twilled cloth, usu. cotton, used for jeans, overalls, and work uniforms. **b. denims.** Trousers or another garment made of this cloth. **2.** A similar but finer fabric used in draperies and upholstery. [Fr. *(serge) de Nîmes*, (serge) of Nîmes, after NÎMES, France.]

De·nis or **De·nys** (dĕn′ĭs, də-nē′), Saint. 3rd cent. A.D. First bishop of Paris and patron saint of France.

Den·i·son (dĕn′ĭ-sən). A city of N TX near the OK border NNE of Dallas. Pop. 21,505.

de·ni·tri·fy (dē-nī′trə-fī′) *tr.v.* **-fied, -fy·ing, -fies. 1.** To remove nitrogen or nitrogen groups from (a compound). **2.** To reduce (nitrates or nitrites) to nitrogen-containing gases. **—de·ni′tri·fi·ca′tion** (-fĭ-kā′shən) *n.*

den·i·zen (dĕn′ĭ-zən) *n.* **1.** An inhabitant; a resident. **2.** One that frequents a particular place. **3.** *Ecol.* An animal or a plant naturalized in a region. **4.** *Chiefly British.* A foreigner who is granted rights of residence and sometimes of citizenship. *—tr.v.* **-zened, -zen·ing, -zens.** *Chiefly British.* To make a denizen of. [ME *denisein* < AN *denzein* < *deinz*, within < LLat. *dēintus*, from within. See DEDANS.] **—den′i·zen·a′tion** *n.*

Den·mark (dĕn′märk′). A country of N Europe on Jutland and adjacent islands; united with Sweden until 1523 and with Norway until 1814. Cap. Copenhagen. Pop. 5,112,130.

Denmark Strait. A channel between Greenland and Iceland connecting the Arctic Ocean with the N Atlantic Ocean.

den mother *n.* A woman who supervises a den of Cub Scouts.

denom. *abbr.* Denomination.

de·nom·i·nate (dĭ-nŏm′ə-nāt′) *tr.v.* **-nat·ed, -nat·ing, -nates. 1.** To issue or express in terms of a given monetary unit. **2.** To give a name to; designate. *—adj.* (-ə-nĭt). Of or relating to a quantity as a multiple of a unit: 12 *in* 12 pounds *is denominate.* [Lat. *dēnōmināre, dēnōmināt-* : *dē-*, de- + *nōmināre*, to name (< *nōmen*, name; see **nō-men-***).] **—de·nom′i·na·ble** (-nə-bəl) *adj.*

de·nom·i·na·tion (dĭ-nŏm′ə-nā′shən) *n.* **1.** A large group of religious congregations united under a common faith and name and administratively organized. **2.** One of a series of kinds, values, or sizes, as of currency or weights. **3.** A name or designation, esp. for a class or group. **—de·nom′i·na′tion·al** *adj.* **—de·nom′i·na′tion·al·ly** *adv.*

de·nom·i·na·tion·al·ism (dĭ-nŏm′ə-nā′shə-nə-lĭz′əm) *n.* **1.** The tendency to divide into religious denominations. **2.** Support of such division. **3.** Strict denominational adherence; sectarianism. **—de·nom′i·na′tion·al·ist** *n.*

de·nom·i·na·tive (dĭ-nŏm′ə-nā′tĭv, -nə-tĭv) *adj.* **1.** Giving or constituting a name; naming. **2.** Formed from a noun or an adjective. *—n.* A word, esp. a verb, that derives from a noun or an adjective.

de·nom·i·na·tor (dĭ-nŏm′ə-nā′tər) *n.* **1.** *Math.* The expression written below the line in a common fraction that indicates the number of parts into which one whole is divided. **2.** A common trait or characteristic. **3.** An average level or standard.

de·no·ta·tion (dē′nō-tā′shən) *n.* **1.** The act of denoting; indication. **2.** Something, such as a sign, that denotes. **3.** Something signified or referred to; a particular meaning of a symbol. **4.** The most specific or direct meaning of a word, in contrast to its figurative or associated meanings.

de·no·ta·tive (dĭ-nō′tə-tĭv, dē′nō-tā′-) *adj.* **1.** Denoting or naming; designative. **2.** Specific; direct. **—de·no′ta·tive·ly** *adv.*

de·note (dĭ-nōt′) *tr.v.* **-not·ed, -not·ing, -notes. 1.** To mark; indicate. **2.** To serve as a symbol or name for the meaning of; signify. **3.** To signify directly; refer to specifically. [Fr. *dénoter* < Lat. *dēnotāre* : *dē-*, de- + *notāre*, to mark; see CONNOTE.] **—de·not′a·ble** *adj.* **—de·no′tive** *adj.*

Usage Note: In speaking of words or expressions *denote* describes the relation between the expression and the thing it conventionally names, whereas *connote* describes the relation between the word and the images or associations it evokes. Thus the word *Christmas* denotes a holiday and connotes turkey and mistletoe.

de·noue·ment also **dé·noue·ment** (dā′no͞o-mäɴ′) *n.* **1.a.** The final resolution of a dramatic or narrative plot. **b.** The events following the climax of a drama or novel in which such a resolution takes place. **2.** The outcome of a sequence of events; the end result. [Fr. *dénouement* < OFr. *desnouement*, an untying < *desnouer*, to undo : *des-*, de- + *nouer*, to tie (< Lat. *nōdāre* < *nōdus*, knot; see **ned-***).]

de·nounce (dĭ-nouns′) *tr.v.* **-nounced, -nounc·ing, -nounc·es. 1.** To condemn openly as being evil or reprehensible. See Syns at **criticize. 2.** To accuse formally. **3.** To give formal announcement of the ending of (a treaty). [ME *denouncen*, to proclaim < AN *denuncier* and Med.Lat. *dēnūntiāre*, both < Lat. : *dē-*, de- + *nūntiāre*, to announce (< *nūntius*, messenger; see **neu-***).] **—de·nounce′ment** *n.* **—de·nounc′er** *n.*

dense (dĕns) *adj.* **dens·er, dens·est. 1.a.** Having a high concentration of parts or mass per unit. **b.** Crowded closely together; compact. **2.** Hard to penetrate; thick: *a dense jungle.* **3.a.** Permitting little light to pass through, because of compactness of matter: *a dense fog.* **b.** Opaque, with good contrast between light and dark. Used of a photographic negative. **4.** Difficult to understand because of complexity or obscurity. **5.** Slow to apprehend; thickheaded. [Lat. *dēnsus*.] **—dense′ly** *adv.* **—dense′ness** *n.*

den·sim·e·ter (dĕn-sĭm′ĭ-tər) *n.* An instrument used to measure density or specific gravity. [Lat. *dēnsus*, dense + -METER.] **—den′si·met′ric** (-sə-mĕt′rĭk) *adj.*

den·si·tom·e·ter (dĕn′sĭ-tŏm′ĭ-tər) *n.* **1.** An apparatus for measuring the optical density of a material. **2.** See **densimeter.** [DENSIT(Y) + -METER.] **—den′si·tom′e·try** (-ĭ-trē) *n.*

den·si·ty (dĕn′sĭ-tē) *n., pl.* **-ties. 1.** The quality or condition of being dense. **2.a.** The quantity of something per unit measure, esp. per unit length, area, or volume. **b.** The mass per unit

Deng Xiaoping

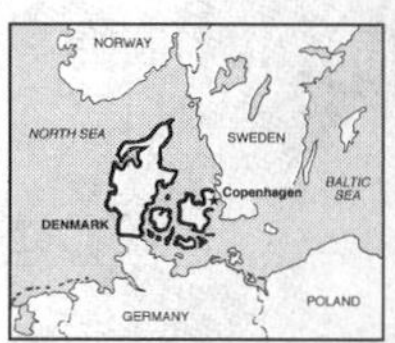

Denmark

ă pat oi boy
ā pay ou out
âr care o͝o took
ä father o͞o boot
ĕ pet ŭ cut
ē be ûr urge
ĭ pit th thin
ī pie *th* this
îr pier hw which
ŏ pot zh vision
ō toe ə about, item
ô paw

Stress marks:
′ (primary);
′ (secondary), as in
dictionary (dĭk′shə-nĕr′ē)

volume of a substance under specified conditions of pressure and temperature. **3.** *Comp. Sci.* The number of units of useful information contained within a linear dimension. **4.** The number of beings or objects per unit of area. **5.** The degree of optical opacity of a medium or material, as of a photographic negative. **6.** Thickness of consistency; impenetrability. **7.** Complexity of structure or content. **8.** Stupidity; dullness.

dent[1] (dĕnt) *n.* **1.** A depression in a surface made by pressure or a blow. **2.** *Informal.* A significant, usu. diminishing effect. **3.** *Informal.* Meaningful progress; headway. — *v.* **dent•ed, dent•ing, dents.** — *tr.* To make a dent in. — *intr.* To become dented. [ME *dent,* var. of *dint,* blow < OE *dynt.*]

dent[2] (dĕnt) *n.* See **tooth** 3. [Fr. See DENTIST.]

dent. *abbr.* Dental; dentist; dentistry.

dent– *pref.* Var. of **denti–**.

den•tal (dĕn′tl) *adj.* **1.** Of, relating to, or for the teeth. **2.** Of, relating to, or intended for dentistry. **3.** *Ling.* Articulated with the tip of the tongue near or against the upper front teeth, as English *t* and *d.* — *n. Ling.* A dental consonant. [NLat. *dentālis* < Lat. *dēns, dent-,* tooth. See **dent-***.]

dental caries *n.* The formation of cavities in the teeth by the action of bacteria; tooth decay.

dental floss *n.* A waxed or unwaxed thread used to remove food particles and plaque from the teeth.

dental hygienist *n.* A person trained and licensed to provide preventive dental services, usu. in conjunction with a dentist.

dental implant *n.* A tooth, usu. artificial, anchored in the gums or jawbone to replace a missing tooth.

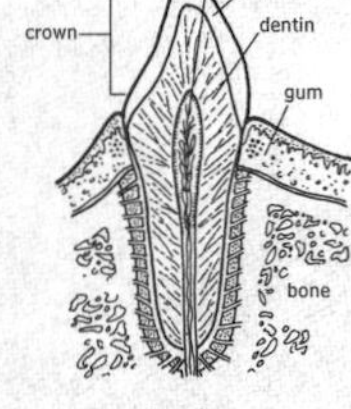

dentin

den•ta•li•um (dĕn-tā′lē-əm) *n., pl.* **-li•a** (-lē-ə) or **-li•ums.** Any of various tooth shells of the genus *Dentalium.* [NLat. *Dentālium,* genus name < *dentālis,* toothy. See DENTAL.]

dental plate *n.* See **denture** 1.

dental technician *n.* One who makes dental devices, such as bridges, to the specifications of a dentist.

den•tate (dĕn′tāt′) *adj.* Edged with toothlike projections; toothed: *dentate leaves.* [Lat. *dentātus* < *dēns, dent-,* tooth. See **dent-***.] — **den′tate′ly** *adv.*

den•ta•tion (dĕn-tā′shən) *n.* **1.** The condition of being dentate. **2.** A toothlike part or projection.

dent corn *n.* A tall-growing variety of corn *(Zea mays* var. *indentata)* having yellow or white kernels indented at the tip.

denti– or **dent–** *pref.* **1.** Tooth: *dentoid.* **2.** Dental: *dentilabial.* [< Lat. *dēns, dent-,* tooth. See **dent-***.]

den•ti•cle (dĕn′tĭ-kəl) *n.* A small tooth or toothlike projection. [ME < Lat. *denticulus,* dim. of *dēns, dent-,* tooth. See **dent-***.] — **den•tic′u•lar** *adj.*

den•tic•u•late (dĕn-tĭk′yə-lĭt) also **den•tic•u•lat•ed** (-lā′tĭd) *adj.* **1.** Finely toothed or notched; minutely dentate. **2.** *Archit.* Having dentils. [Lat. *denticulātus* < *denticulus,* denticle. See DENTICLE.] — **den•tic′u•late•ly** *adv.* — **den•tic′u•la′tion** *n.*

den•ti•form (dĕn′tə-fôrm′) *adj.* Shaped like a tooth.

den•ti•frice (dĕn′tə-frĭs′) *n.* A substance, such as a paste or powder, for cleaning the teeth. [Fr. < OFr. < Lat. *dentifricium* : *denti-,* denti- + *fricāre,* to rub.]

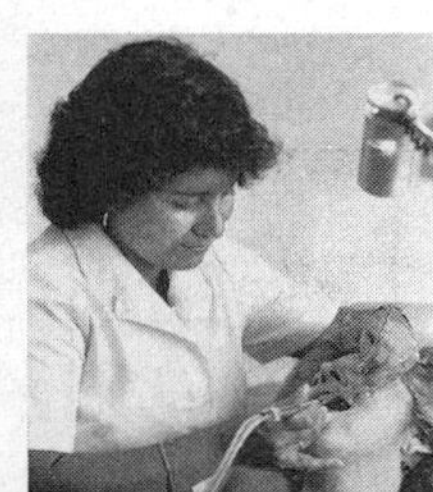
dentist

den•tig•er•ous (dĕn-tĭj′ər-əs) *adj.* Having or furnished with teeth. [DENTI– + Lat. *gerere,* to bear.]

den•til (dĕn′tĭl) *n. Archit.* One of a series of small rectangular blocks forming a molding or projecting beneath a cornice. [Obsolete Fr. *dentille* < OFr., dim. of *dent,* tooth. See DENTIST.]

den•tin (dĕn′tĭn) or **den•tine** (-tēn′) *n.* The main calcareous part of a tooth beneath the enamel, surrounding the pulp chamber and root canals. — **den•tin′al** (dĕn-tē′nəl, dĕn′tə-) *adj.*

den•tist (dĕn′tĭst) *n.* A person who is trained and licensed to practice dentistry. [Fr. *dentiste* < *dent,* tooth < OFr. < Lat. *dēns, dent-.* See **dent-***.]

den•tist•ry (dĕn′tĭ-strē) *n.* The medical science concerned with diseases of the teeth, gums, and related oral structures, including the restoration of defective teeth.

den•ti•tion (dĕn-tĭsh′ən) *n.* **1.** *Zool.* The type, number, and arrangement of teeth. **2.** The process of growing new teeth; teething. [Lat. *dentītiō, dentītiōn-* < *dentītus,* p.part. of *dentīre,* to teethe < *dēns, dent-,* tooth. See DENTIST.]

den•toid (dĕn′toid′) *adj.* Tooth-shaped; toothlike.

Den•ton (dĕn′tən). A city of NE TX NNW of Dallas. Pop. 66,270.

den•tu•lous (dĕn′chə-ləs) *adj.* Possessing teeth; toothed. [Back-formation < EDENTULOUS, toothless.]

den•ture (dĕn′chər) *n.* **1.** A partial or complete set of artificial teeth for either jaw. **2.** A complete set of removable artificial teeth for both jaws. Often used in the plural. [Fr. < OFr. < *dent,* tooth. See DENTIST.]

de•nu•cle•ar•ize (dē-no͞o′klē-ə-rīz′, -nyo͞o′-) *v.* **-ized, -iz•ing, -iz•es.** — *tr.* To remove or ban nuclear weapons from. — *intr.* To reduce or eliminate a store of nuclear weapons. — **de•nu′cle•ar•i•za′tion** (-ər-ĭ-zā′shən) *n.*

de•nu•date (dĭ-no͞o′dāt′, -nyo͞o′-) *tr.v.* **-dat•ed, -dat•ing, -dates.** To denude. — *adj.* Bare; denuded. [Lat. *dēnūdāre, dēnūdāt-.* See DENUDE.]

Denver boot

de•nude (dĭ-no͞od′, -nyo͞od′) *tr.v.* **-nud•ed, -nud•ing, -nudes.** **1.** To divest of covering; make bare. **2.** *Geol.* To expose (rock strata) by erosion. [Lat. *dēnūdāre* : *dē-,* de- + *nūdāre,* to make bare (< *nūdus,* nude; see **nog^{w}-***).] — **de′nu•da′tion** (dē′no͞o-dā′shən, -nyo͞o-, dĕn′yo͞o-) *n.*

de•nu•mer•a•ble (dĭ-no͞o′mər-ə-bəl, -nyo͞o′-) *adj.* Countable. [< *denumerate,* to count < LLat. *dēnumerāre, dēnumerāt-,* alteration of Lat. *dīnumerāre* : *dī-, dis-,* dis- + *numerāre,* to number; see NUMERATE.] — **de•nu′mer•a•bil′i•ty** *n.* — **de•nu′mer•a•bly** *adv.*

de•nun•ci•a•tion (dĭ-nŭn′sē-ā′shən, -shē-) *n.* **1.** The act or an instance of denouncing, esp. publically. **2.** The act of accusing another of a crime before a public prosecutor. [ME *denunciacioun* < Lat. *dēnuntiātiō, dēnuntiātiōn-* < *dēnuntiātus,* p.part. of *dēnuntiāre,* to announce. See DENOUNCE.] — **de•nun′ci•a′tive** (-ā′tĭv, -ə-tĭv), **de•nun′ci•a•to′ry** (-ə-tôr′ē, -tōr′ē) *adj.*

Den•ver (dĕn′vər). The cap. of CO, in the N-central part on the South Platte R.; settled in 1858. Pop. 467,610.

Denver boot *n.* A device locked to the wheel of a vehicle to keep it from being driven, used esp. to force settlement of traffic violations.

de•ny (dĭ-nī′) *tr.v.* **-nied, -ny•ing, -nies. 1.** To declare untrue; contradict. **2.** To refuse to believe; reject. **3.** To refuse to recognize or acknowledge; disavow. **4.a.** To decline to grant or allow; refuse. **b.** To give a refusal to; turn down or away. **c.** To restrain (oneself) esp. from indulgence in pleasures. [ME *denien* < OFr. *denier* < Lat. *dēnegāre* : *dē-,* de- + *negāre,* to say no; see **ne***.]

De•nys (dĕn′ĭs, də-nē′), Saint. See Saint **Denis.**

de•o•dar (dē′ə-där′) or **de•o•dar•a** (-där′ə) *n.* A tall cedar *(Cedrus deodara)* that is an important timber tree in India. [Hindi *deodār* < Skt. *devadāru* : *deva-,* divine; see **deiw-*** + *dāru,* wood; see **deru-***.]

de•o•dor•ant (dē-ō′dər-ənt) *n.* A substance used to mask or suppress unwanted odors. — *adj.* Capable of masking or neutralizing odors.

de•o•dor•ize (dē-ō′də-rīz′) *tr.v.* **-ized, -iz•ing, -iz•es. 1.** To mask or neutralize the odor of. **2.** To make more acceptable, as by elimination or suppression of an offensive aspect. — **de•o′dor•i•za′tion** (-dər-ĭ-zā′shən) *n.* — **de•o′dor•iz′er** *n.*

de•on•tol•o•gy (dē′ŏn-tŏl′ə-jē) *n.* The theory or study of moral obligation; ethics. [Gk. *deon, deont-,* obligation, necessity (< neut. pr.part. of *dein,* to need, lack; see **deu-**[1]*) + -LOGY.] — **de•on′to•log′i•cal** (-tə-lŏj′ĭ-kəl) *adj.* — **de′on•tol′o•gist** *n.*

de•ox•i•dize (dē-ŏk′sĭ-dīz′) *tr.v.* **-dized, -diz•ing, -diz•es.** To remove oxygen from (a compound); reduce. — **de•ox′i•di•za′tion** (-dĭ-zā′shən) *n.* — **de•ox′i•diz′er** *n.*

deoxy– *pref.* Being a molecule containing less oxygen than another to which it is closely related: *deoxycorticosterone.*

de•ox•y•cor•ti•cos•ter•one (dē-ŏk′sē-kôr′tĭ-kŏs′tə-rōn′) *n.* A steroid hormone, $C_{21}H_{30}O_3$, secreted by the adrenal cortex or synthesized and used to treat adrenal insufficiency.

de•ox•y•gen•ate (dē-ŏk′sə-jə-nāt′) *tr.v.* **-at•ed, -at•ing, -ates.** To remove dissolved oxygen from (a liquid, such as water). — **de•ox′y•gen•a′tion** *n.*

de•ox•y•ri•bo•nu•cle•ase (dē-ok′sē-rī′bō-no͞o′klē-ās′, -āz′, -nyo͞o′-) *n.* DNase.

de•ox•y•ri•bo•nu•cle•ic acid (dē-ŏk′sē-rī′bō-no͞o-klē′ĭk, -klā′-, -nyo͞o-) *n.* DNA.

de•ox•y•ri•bo•nu•cle•o•tide (dē-ŏk′sē-rī′bō-no͞o′klē-ə-tīd′, -nyo͞o′-) *n.* A nucleotide containing deoxyribose.

de•ox•y•ri•bose (dē-ŏk′sē-rī′bōs′) *n.* A sugar, $C_5H_{10}O_4$, that is a constituent of DNA.

dep. *abbr.* **1.** Department. **2.** Departure. **3.** Dependency. **4.** Deponent. **5.** Deposed. **6.** Deposit. **7.** Depot. **8.** Deputy.

de•part (dĭ-pärt′) *v.* **-part•ed, -part•ing, -parts.** — *intr.* **1.** To go away; leave. **2.** To die. **3.** To vary, as from a regular course; deviate. See Syns at **swerve.** — *tr.* To go away from; leave. [ME *departen* < OFr. *departir,* to split, divide : *de-,* de- + *partir,* to divide (< Lat. *partīre* < *pars, part-,* part; see PART).]

de•part•ed (dĭ-pär′tĭd) *adj.* **1.** Bygone; past. **2.** Dead. — *n.* A dead person, esp. one who has died recently.

de•part•ment (dĭ-pärt′mənt) *n.* **1.** A distinct, usu. specialized division of a large organization, esp.: **a.** A principal administrative division of a government: *the fire department.* **b.** A specialized division of a business: *the personnel department.* **c.** A division of a school or college dealing with a particular subject: *the physics department.* **2. Department.** One of the principal executive divisions of the U.S. government, headed by a cabinet officer. **3.** A section of a department store selling a particular line of merchandise. **4.** An administrative district in France. **5.** *Informal.* An area of particular knowledge or responsibility; a specialty. [Fr. *département* < OFr., separation < *departir,* to divide. See DEPART.] — **de′part•men′tal** (dē′pärt-mĕn′tl) *adj.* — **de′part•men′tal•ly** *adv.*

de•part•men•tal•ize (dē′pärt-mĕn′tl-īz′) *tr.v.* **-ized, -iz•ing, -iz•es.** To organize into departments. — **de′part•men′tal•i•za′tion** (-ĭ-zā′shən) *n.*

department store *n.* A large retail store offering a variety of merchandise and services in separate departments.

de•par•ture (dĭ-pär′chər) *n.* **1.** The act of leaving. **2.** A starting out, as on a trip or a course of action. **3.** A divergence or deviation, as from an established rule or procedure.

de•pau•pe•rate (də-pô′pər-ĭt) *adj.* **1.** Arrested in growth or development; stunted. **2.** Severely diminished; impoverished. **—de•pau′pe•ra′tion** (-pə-rā′shən) *n.*

de•pend (dĭ-pĕnd′) *intr.v.* **-pend•ed, -pend•ing, -pends. 1.** To rely, esp. for support or maintenance. **2.** To place trust or confidence. **3.** To be determined, conditioned, or contingent. **4.** To have a dependence or addiction. **5.** To be pending or undecided, as in a court. **6.** To hang down. [ME *dependen,* to hang down < OFr. *dependre* < Lat. *dēpendēre* : *dē-,* de- + *pendēre,* to hang; see **(s)pen-***.]

Usage Note: *Depend,* indicating condition or contingency, is always followed by *on* or *upon,* as in *It depends on who is in charge.*

de•pend•a•ble (dĭ-pĕn′də-bəl) *adj.* Trustworthy. **—de•pend′a•bil′i•ty, de•pend′a•ble•ness** *n.* **—de•pend′a•bly** *adv.*

de•pend•ence also **de•pend•ance** (dĭ-pĕn′dəns) *n.* **1.** The state of being dependent, as for support. **2.a.** Subordination to someone or something needed or greatly desired. **b.** Trust; reliance. **3.** The state of being determined, influenced, or controlled by something else. **4.** A compulsive or chronic need; an addiction: *an alcohol dependence.*

de•pend•en•cy also **de•pend•an•cy** (dĭ-pĕn′dən-sē) *n., pl.* **-cies. 1.** Dependence. **2.** Something dependent or subordinate. **3.** A territory under the jurisdiction of a state of which it does not form an integral part.

de•pend•ent (dĭ-pĕn′dənt) *adj.* **1.** Contingent on another. **2.** Subordinate. **3.** Relying on or requiring the aid of another for support. **4.** Hanging down. *—n.* also **de•pend•ant** (dĭ-pĕn′dənt). One who relies on another esp. for financial support. **—de•pend′ent•ly** *adv.*

dependent clause *n. Gram.* A clause that cannot stand alone as a full sentence and functions as a noun, adjective, or adverb within a sentence.

dependent variable *n.* **1.** *Math.* A variable whose value is determined by the value assumed by an independent variable. **2.** *Statistics.* The observed variable in an experiment whose changes are determined by one or more independent variables.

de•per•son•al•i•za•tion (dē-pûr′sə-nə-lĭ-zā′shən) *n.* **1.a.** The act of depersonalizing. **b.** The state of being depersonalized. **2.** *Psychol.* A state in which the normal sense of personal identity and reality is lost.

de•per•son•al•ize (dē-pûr′sə-nə-līz′) *tr.v.* **-ized, -iz•ing, -iz•es. 1.** To deprive of individual character or a sense of personal identity. **2.** To render impersonal.

De•pew (dĭ-pyo͞o′). A village of W New York, a suburb of Buffalo. Pop. 17,673.

de•pict (dĭ-pĭkt′) *tr.v.* **-pict•ed, -pict•ing, -picts. 1.** To represent in a picture or sculpture. **2.** To represent in words; describe. [ME *depicten* < Lat. *dēpingere, dēpict-* : *dē-,* de- + *pingere,* to picture; see **peig-***.] **—de•pic′tion** *n.*

de•pig•men•ta•tion (dē-pĭg′mən-tā′shən, -mĕn-) *n.* Loss or removal of normal pigmentation.

dep•i•late (dĕp′ə-lāt′) *tr.v.* **-lat•ed, -lat•ing, -lates.** To remove hair from (the body). [Lat. *dēpilāre, dēpilāt-* : *dē-,* de- + *pilāre,* to deprive of hair (< *pilus,* hair).] **—dep′i•la′tion** *n.* **—dep′i•la′tor** *n.*

de•pil•a•to•ry (dĭ-pĭl′ə-tôr′ē, -tōr′ē) *adj.* Having the capability to remove hair. *—n., pl.* **-ries.** A preparation that is used to remove unwanted hair from the body.

de•plane (dē-plān′) *intr.v.* **-planed, -plan•ing, -planes.** To disembark from an airplane.

de•plete (dĭ-plēt′) *tr.v.* **-plet•ed, -plet•ing, -pletes.** To decrease the fullness of; use up or empty out. [Lat. *dēplēre, dēplēt-,* to empty : *dē-,* de- + *plēre,* to fill; see **pelə-¹***.] **—de•plet′a•ble** *adj.*

Syns: *deplete, drain, exhaust, impoverish, enervate.* These verbs all mean to weaken severely by removing something essential. *Deplete* refers to using up gradually and only hints at harmful consequences: *depleted my food supply. Drain* suggests gradual drawing off and implies more harm: *War drains a nation's economy. Exhaust* stresses reduction to a point of no further usefulness: *"The resources of civilization are not yet exhausted"* (William Ewart Gladstone). *Impoverish* refers to severe reduction of essential resources or qualities: *"His death has eclipsed the gaiety of nations, and impoverished the public stock of harmless pleasure"* (Samuel Johnson). *Enervate* refers to weakening or destruction of vitality or strength: *Idleness enervates the will to succeed.*

de•ple•tion (dĭ-plē′shən) *n.* **1.** The act or process of depleting. **2.** The state of being depleted; exhaustion. **3.** The use or consumption of a resource faster than it is replenished.

de•plor•a•ble (dĭ-plôr′ə-bəl, -plōr′-) *adj.* **1.** Worthy of severe condemnation or reproach. **2.** Lamentable; woeful. **3.** Wretched; bad. **—de•plor′a•ble•ness, de•plor′a•bil′i•ty** *n.* **—de•plor′a•bly** *adv.*

de•plore (dĭ-plôr′, -plōr′) *tr.v.* **-plored, -plor•ing, -plores. 1.** To feel or express strong disapproval of; condemn. **2.** To express sorrow or grief over. **3.** To regret; bemoan. [Fr. *déplorer,* lament, regret < Lat. *dēplōrāre* : *dē-,* de- + *plōrāre,* to wail.]

de•ploy (dĭ-ploi′) *v.* **-ployed, -ploy•ing, -ploys.** *—tr.* **1.a.** To position (troops) in readiness for combat. **b.** To bring (forces or material) into action. **c.** To base (a weapons system) in the field. **2.** To distribute (persons or forces) systematically or strategically. **3.** To put into use or action. *—intr.* To be or become deployed. [Fr. *déployer* < OFr. *despleier* < Lat. *displicāre,* to scatter : *dis-,* dis- + *plicāre,* to fold; see **plek-***.] **—de•ploy′a•bil′i•ty** *n.* **—de•ploy′a•ble** *adj.* **—de•ploy′er** *n.* **—de•ploy′ment** *n.*

de•plume (dē-plo͞om′) *tr.v.* **-plumed, -plum•ing, -plumes.** To pluck the feathers from. **—de′plu•ma′tion** *n.*

de•po•lar•ize (dē-pō′lə-rīz′) *tr.v.* **-ized, -iz•ing, -iz•es. 1.** To eliminate or counteract the polarization of. **2.** To demagnetize. **—de•po′lar•i•za′tion** (-lər-ĭ-zā′shən) *n.*

de•po•lit•i•cize (dē′pə-lĭt′ĭ-sīz′) *tr.v.* **-cized, -ciz•ing, -ciz•es.** To remove the political aspect from. **—de′po•lit′i•ci•za′tion** (-sĭ-zā′shən) *n.*

de•pone (dĭ-pōn′) *v.* **-poned, -pon•ing, -pones.** *—tr.* To testify or declare under oath. *—intr.* To give testimony. [ME *deponen* < Med.Lat. *dēpōnere* < Lat., to put down : *dē-,* de- + *pōnere,* to put; see **apo-***.]

de•po•nent (dĭ-pō′nənt) *adj. Gram.* Being a verb of active meaning but passive or middle form, as certain Latin and Greek verbs. *—n.* **1.** *Gram.* A deponent verb. **2.** *Law.* One who testifies under oath, esp. in writing. [ME < Lat. *dēpōnēns, dēpōnent-,* pr.part. of *dēpōnere,* to put down. See DEPONE.]

de•pop•u•late (dē-pŏp′yə-lāt′) *tr.v.* **-lat•ed, -lat•ing, -lates.** To reduce sharply the population of, as by disease, war, or forcible relocation. [Lat. *dēpopulāri, dēpopulāt-,* to lay waste : *dē-,* de- + *populārī,* to ravage (< *populus,* people, throng).] **—de•pop′u•la′tion** *n.* **—de•pop′u•la′tor** *n.*

de•port (dĭ-pôrt′, -pōrt′) *tr.v.* **-port•ed, -port•ing, -ports. 1.** To expel from a country. See Syns at **banish. 2.** To behave or conduct (oneself) in a given manner; comport. [Fr. *déporter,* to banish < Lat. *dēportāre,* to carry away : *dē-,* de- + *portāre,* to carry; see **per-²***. Sense 2, ME < OFr. *deporter,* to behave < Lat. *dēportāre.*]

de•port•a•ble (dĭ-pôr′tə-bəl, -pōr′-) *adj.* **1.** Subject to deportation: *a deportable alien.* **2.** Punishable by deportation.

de•por•ta•tion (dē′pôr-tā′shən, -pōr-) *n.* **1.** The act or an instance of deporting. **2.** Expulsion of an undesirable alien from a country.

de•port•ee (dē′pôr-tē′, -pōr-) *n.* A deported person.

de•port•ment (dĭ-pôrt′mənt, -pōrt′-) *n.* A manner of personal conduct; behavior. See Syns at **behavior.**

de•pos•al (dĭ-pō′zəl) *n.* The act or an instance of deposing from office.

de•pose (dĭ-pōz′) *v.* **-posed, -pos•ing, -pos•es.** *—tr.* **1.a.** To remove from office or power. **b.** To dethrone. **2.** *Law.* **a.** To state or affirm in a deposition or by affidavit. **b.** To take a deposition from. **3.** To put or lay down; deposit. *—intr. Law.* To give a deposition; testify. [ME *deposen* < OFr. *deposer,* alteration (influenced by *poser,* to put; see POSE¹) of Lat. *dēpōnere,* to put down. See DEPONE.] **—de•pos′a•ble** *adj.*

de•pos•it (dĭ-pŏz′ĭt) *v.* **-it•ed, -it•ing, -its.** *—tr.* **1.** To put or set down; place. **2.** To lay down or leave behind by a natural process. **3.a.** To give over or entrust for safekeeping. **b.** To put (money) in a bank or financial account. **4.** To give as partial payment or security. *—intr.* To become deposited; settle. *—n.* **1.** Something that is entrusted for safekeeping. **2.** The condition of being deposited. **3.** A partial or initial payment of a cost or debt. **4.** A sum of money given as security for an item acquired for temporary use. **5.** A depository. **6.** Something deposited, esp. by a natural process, as: **a.** *Geol.* A concentration of mineral matter or sediment in a layer, vein, or pocket. **b.** *Physiol.* An accumulation of organic or inorganic material in a body tissue, structure, or fluid. **c.** A sediment or precipitate that has settled out of a solution. **7.** A coating or crust left on a surface, as by evaporation. [Lat. *dēpōnere, dēpōsit-* : *dē-,* de- + *pōnere,* to put; see **apo-***.] **—de•pos′i•tor** *n.*

de•pos•i•tar•y (dĭ-pŏz′ĭ-tĕr′ē) *n.* **-ies. 1.** One entrusted with something for preservation or safekeeping. **2.** A depository.

dep•o•si•tion (dĕp′ə-zĭsh′ən) *n.* **1.** The act of deposing, as from high office. **2.** The act of depositing, esp. the laying down of matter by a natural process. **3.** Something deposited; a deposit. **4.** *Law.* Testimony under oath, esp. a statement by a witness that is written down or recorded for use in court. **5. Deposition.** The removal of Jesus from the cross. **—dep′o•si′tion•al** *adj.*

de•pos•i•to•ry (dĭ-pŏz′ĭ-tôr′ē, -tōr′ē) *n., pl.* **-ries. 1.** A place where something is deposited, as for storage or safekeeping; a repository. **2.** A trustee; a depositary.

de•pot (dē′pō, dĕp′ō) *n.* **1.** A railroad or bus station. **2.** A warehouse or storehouse. **3.a.** A storage installation for military equipment and supplies. **b.** A station for assembling military recruits and forwarding them to active units. [Fr. *dépôt* < OFr. *depost* < Lat. *dēpositum,* something deposited < neut. p.part. of *dēpōnere,* to put down, deposit. See DEPOSIT.]

de•prave (dĭ-prāv′) *tr.v.* **-praved, -prav•ing, -praves.** To de-

deodar
Cedrus deodara

ă pat	oi boy
ā pay	ou out
âr care	o͝o took
ä father	o͞o boot
ĕ pet	ŭ cut
ē be	ûr urge
ĭ pit	th thin
ī pie	*th* this
îr pier	hw which
ŏ pot	zh vision
ō toe	ə about, item
ô paw	

Stress marks:
′ (primary);
′ (secondary), as in
dictionary (dĭk′shə-nĕr′ē)

base, esp. morally. [ME *depraven*, to corrupt < OFr. *depraver* < Lat. *dēprāvāre* : *dē-*, de- + *prāvus*, crooked.] —**dep′ra•va′tion** (dĕp′rə-vā′shən) *n.* —**de•prav′er** *n.*

de•praved (dĭ-prāvd′) *adj.* Morally corrupt; perverted. —**de•prav′ed•ly** (-prā′vĭd-lē, -prāvd′lē) *adv.*

de•prav•i•ty (dĭ-prăv′ĭ-tē) *n.*, *pl.* **-ties. 1.** Moral corruption or degradation. **2.** A depraved act or condition.

dep•re•cate (dĕp′rĭ-kāt′) *tr.v.* **-cat•ed, -cat•ing, -cates. 1.** To express disapproval of; deplore. **2.** To belittle; depreciate. [Lat. *dēprecārī*, *dēprecāt-*, to ward off by prayer : *dē-*, de- + *precārī*, to pray; see **prek-***.] —**dep′re•cat′ing•ly** *adv.* —**dep′re•ca′tion** *n.* —**dep′re•ca′tor** *n.*

Usage Note: The first and fully accepted meaning of *deprecate* is "to express disapproval of." But the word is now used, almost to the exclusion of *depreciate*, in the sense "to belittle or mildly disparage," as in *He deprecated his own contribution.* In an earlier survey this newer sense was approved by a majority of the Usage Panel.

dep•re•ca•to•ry (dĕp′rĭ-kə-tôr′ē, -tōr′ē) also **dep•re•ca•tive** (-kā′tĭv) *adj.* **1.** Expressing disapproval or criticism. **2.** Mildly disparaging or uncomplimentary, esp. of oneself. —**dep′re•ca•to′ri•ly** *adv.*

de•pre•cia•ble (dĭ-prē′shə-bəl) *adj.* That can be depreciated in value: *depreciable assets.*

de•pre•ci•ate (dĭ-prē′shē-āt′) *v.* **-at•ed, -at•ing, -ates.** —*tr.* **1.** To lessen the price or value of. **2.** To think or speak of as being of little worth; belittle. See Usage Note at **deprecate.** —*intr.* To diminish in price or value. [Med.Lat. *dēpreciāre*, *dēpreciāt-*, alteration of Lat. *dēpretiāre* : *dē-*, de- + *pretium*, price; see **per-[5]***.] —**de•pre′ci•a′tor** *n.*

de•pre•ci•a•tion (dĭ-prē′shē-ā′shən) *n.* **1.** A loss in value, as because of wear. **2.** *Accounting.* An allowance made for a loss in value of property. **3.** Reduction in the purchasing value of money. **4.** An instance of disparaging or belittlement.

de•pre•cia•to•ry (dĭ-prē′shə-tôr′ē, -tōr′ē) also **de•pre•cia•tive** (-shə-tĭv, -shē-ā′tĭv) *adj.* **1.** Diminishing in value. **2.** Disparaging; belittling.

dep•re•date (dĕp′rĭ-dāt′) *v.* **-dat•ed, -dat•ing, -dates.** —*tr.* To ransack; plunder. —*intr.* To engage in plundering. [LLat. *dēpraedārī*, *dēpraedāt-* : Lat. *dē-*, de- + Lat. *praedārī*, to plunder (< *praeda*, booty; see **ghend-***).] —**dep′re•da′tor** *n.* —**de•pred′a•to′ry** (dĭ-prĕd′ə-tôr′ē, -tōr′ē, dĕp′rĭ-də-) *adj.*

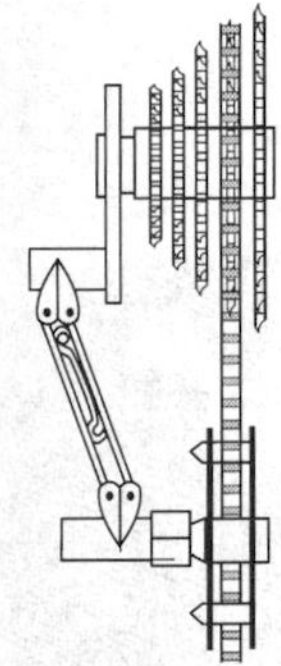
derailleur

dep•re•da•tion (dĕp′rĭ-dā′shən) *n.* **1.** A predatory attack; a raid. **2.** Damage or loss; ravage: *the depredations of time.*

de•press (dĭ-prĕs′) *tr.v.* **-pressed, -press•ing, -press•es. 1.** To lower in spirits; deject. **2.a.** To cause to drop or sink; lower. **b.** To press down: *Depress the typewriter key.* **3.** To lessen the activity or force of; weaken. **4.** To lower prices in (a financial market). [ME *depressen*, to push down < OFr. *depresser* < Lat. *dēprimere*, *dēpress-* : *dē-*, de- + *premere*, to press; see **per-[4]***.] —**de•press′i•ble** *adj.*

de•pres•sant (dĭ-prĕs′ənt) *adj.* Tending to lower the rate of vital physiological activities. —*n.* A depressant agent, esp. a drug.

de•pressed (dĭ-prĕst′) *adj.* **1.** Low in spirits; dejected. **2.** Suffering from psychological depression. **3.** Sunk below the surrounding region. **4.** Lower in amount, degree, or position. **5.a.** Sluggish in growth or activity. **b.** Suffering from social and economic hardship: *a depressed region.*

de•press•ing (dĭ-prĕs′ĭng) *adj.* **1.** Causing esp. emotional depression. **2.** Dismal; dreary. —**de•press′ing•ly** *adv.*

de•pres•sion (dĭ-prĕsh′ən) *n.* **1.a.** The act of depressing. **b.** The condition of being depressed. **2.** An area that is sunk below its surroundings; a hollow. **3.** The condition of feeling sad or despondent. **4.** *Psychol.* A psychotic or neurotic condition characterized by an inability to concentrate, insomnia, and feelings of sadness, dejection, and hopelessness. **5.a.** A reduction in activity or force. **b.** A reduction in physiological vigor or activity. **c.** A lowering in amount, degree, or position. **6.** *Econ.* A period of drastic decline in an economy, characterized by decreasing business activity, falling prices, and unemployment. **7.** *Meteorol.* A region of low barometric pressure. **8.** The angular distance below the horizontal plane through the point of observation.

derby

de•pres•sive (dĭ-prĕs′ĭv) *adj.* **1.** Tending to depress or lower. **2.** Depressing; gloomy. **3.** Of or relating to psychological depression. —*n.* A person suffering from psychological depression. —**de•pres′sive•ly** *adv.* —**de•pres′sive•ness** *n.*

de•pres•sor (dĭ-prĕs′ər) *n.* **1.** Something that depresses or is used to depress: *a tongue depressor.* **2.** A muscle that draws down a part of the body.

de•pres•sur•ize (dē-prĕsh′ə-rīz′) *tr.v.* **-ized, -iz•ing, -iz•es.** To reduce the air or gas pressure within (a chamber, for example). —**de•pres′sur•i•za′tion** (-prĕsh′ər-ĭ-zā′shən) *n.*

de•priv•al (dĭ-prī′vəl) *n.* Deprivation.

dep•ri•va•tion (dĕp′rə-vā′shən) *n.* **1.a.** The act or an instance of depriving; loss. **b.** The condition of being deprived; privation. **2.** A removal of rank or office.

de•prive (dĭ-prīv′) *tr.v.* **-prived, -priv•ing, -prives. 1.** To take something away from: *deprived me of the inheritance.* **2.** To keep from possessing or enjoying; deny. **3.** To remove from office. [ME *depriven* < OFr. *depriver* < Med.Lat. *dēprīvāre* : Lat. *dē-*, de- + Lat. *prīvāre*, to rob (< *prīvus*, alone, without; see **per[1]***).] —**de•priv′a•ble** *adj.*

de•prived (dĭ-prīvd′) *adj.* **1.** Marked by deprivation, esp. of economic or social necessities. **2.** Lacking in advantage, opportunity, or experience.

de•pro•gram (dē-prō′grăm′, -grəm) *tr.v.* **-grammed, -gram•ming, -grams** or **-gramed, -gram•ing, -grams.** To counteract or try to counteract the effect of an indoctrination, esp. of a religion or cult. —**de•pro′gram′mer** *n.*

dept. *abbr.* **1.** Department. **2.** Deputy.

depth (dĕpth) *n.* **1.** The condition or quality of being deep. **2.a.** The extent, measurement, or dimension downward, backward, or inward. **b.** The measurement or sense of distance from an observation point, such as linear perspective in painting. **3.** A deep part or place. Often used in the plural. **4.a.** The most profound or intense part or stage. **b.** Intensity; force: *the depth of their feelings.* **5.** The severest or worst part. **6.** A low point, level, or degree. **7.** Intellectual complexity or penetration; profundity. **8.** The range of one's understanding or competence. **9.** Strength held in reserve, esp. a supply of capable replacements. **10.** The degree of richness or intensity: *depth of color.* **11.** Lowness in pitch. **12.** Complete detail; thoroughness. [ME *depthe* < *dep*, deep. See DEEP.]

depth charge *n.* A charge designed for detonation at a preset depth under water, used esp. against submarines.

depth perception *n.* The ability to perceive spatial relationships, esp. distances between objects, in three dimensions.

depth psychology *n.* **1.** Psychology of the unconscious mind. **2.** Psychoanalysis.

depth sounder *n.* An ultrasonic instrument used to measure the depth of water under a ship.

dep•u•rate (dĕp′yə-rāt′) *tr. & intr.v.* **-rat•ed, -rat•ing, -rates.** To cleanse or purify or become cleansed or purified. [Med.Lat. *dēpūrāre*, *dēpūrāt-* : Lat. *dē-*, de- + *pūrus*, pure; see **peuə-***.] —**dep′u•ra′tion** *n.* —**dep′u•ra′tor** *n.*

dep•u•ta•tion (dĕp′yə-tā′shən) *n.* **1.** A person or group appointed to represent another or others; a delegation. **2.a.** The act of deputing. **b.** The state of being deputed.

de•pute (dĭ-pyo͞ot′) *tr.v.* **-put•ed, -put•ing, -putes. 1.** To appoint or authorize as an agent or a representative. **2.** To assign (authority or duties) to another; delegate. [ME *deputen* < OFr. *deputer* < LLat. *dēputāre*, to allot < Lat., to consider : *dē-*, de- + *putāre*, to ponder; see **peu-***.]

dep•u•tize (dĕp′yə-tīz′) *tr. & intr.v.* **-tized, -tiz•ing, -tiz•es.** To appoint or serve as a deputy. —**dep′u•ti•za′tion** (-tĭ-zā′shən) *n.*

dep•u•ty (dĕp′yə-tē) *n.*, *pl.* **-ties. 1.** A person appointed or empowered to act for another. **2.** An assistant exercising full authority in the absence of a superior and equal authority in emergencies. **3.** A representative in a legislative body in certain countries. [ME *depute* < OFr. < p.part. of *deputer*, to depute. See DEPUTE.]

De Quin•cey (dĭ kwĭn′sē, -zē), **Thomas.** 1785–1859. British writer of *Confessions of an English Opium Eater* (1821).

der. *abbr.* **1.** Derivation. **2.** Derivative.

de•rac•i•nate (də-răs′ə-nāt′) *tr.v.* **-nat•ed, -nat•ing, -nates. 1.** To pull out by the roots; uproot. **2.** To displace from one's native or accustomed environment. [< Fr. *déraciner* < OFr. *desraciner* : *des-*, de- + *racine*, root (< LLat. *rādīcīna* < Lat. *rādīx*; see **wrād-***).] —**de•rac′i•na′tion** *n.*

de•rail (dē-rāl′) *intr. & tr.v.* **-railed, -rail•ing, -rails. 1.** To run or cause to run off the rails. **2.** To come or bring to a sudden halt. [Fr. *dérailler* : *dé-*, off (< OFr. *de-*; see DE–) + *rail*, rail (< E.; see RAIL[1]).] —**de•rail′ment** *n.*

de•rail•leur (dĭ-rā′lər) *n.* A device for shifting gears on a bicycle by moving the chain between sprocket wheels of different sizes. [Fr. *dérailleur* < *dérailler*, to derail. See DERAIL.]

De•rain (də-răN′), **André.** 1880–1954. French artist who was orig. a fauvist and later adopted a more conservative style.

de•range (dĭ-rānj′) *tr.v.* **-ranged, -rang•ing, -rang•es. 1.** To disturb the order or arrangement of. **2.** To upset the normal condition or functioning of. **3.** To disturb mentally; make insane. [Fr. *déranger* < OFr. *desrengier* : *des-*, de- + *reng*, line (of Gmc. orig.; see **sker-[2]***).] —**de•range′ment** *n.*

der•by (dûr′bē; *British* där′bē) *n.*, *pl.* **-bies. 1.** *Sports.* Any of various annual horseraces, esp. for three-year-olds. **2.** *Sports.* A formal race usu. having an open field of contestants: *a motorcycle derby.* **3.** A stiff felt hat with a round crown and a narrow, curved brim. [After Edward Stanley, 12th Earl of *Derby* (1752–1834), founder of the English Derby.]

Der•by (där′bē). A city of central England W of Nottingham; settled by the Romans. Pop. 216,500.

de•reg•u•late (dē-rĕg′yə-lāt′) *tr.v.* **-lat•ed, -lat•ing, -lates.** To free from regulation, esp. government regulation: *deregulate the airline industry.* —**de•reg′u•la′tion** *n.* —**de•reg′u•la′tor** *n.* —**de•reg′u•la•to′ry** (-lə-tôr′ē, -tōr′ē) *adj.*

der•e•lict (dĕr′ə-lĭkt′) *adj.* **1.** Deserted by an owner or keeper; abandoned. **2.** Run-down; dilapidated. **3.** Neglectful of duty or obligation; remiss. —*n.* **1.** Abandoned property, esp. a ship abandoned at sea. **2.** A homeless or jobless person; a vagrant. [Lat. *dērelictus*, p.part. of *dērelinquere*, to abandon : *dē-*, de- + *relinquere*, to leave behind; see RELINQUISH.]

der•e•lic•tion (dĕr′ə-lĭk′shən) *n.* **1.** Willful neglect, as of duty or principle. **2.a.** The act of abandoning; abandonment. **b.** A state of abandonment or neglect.

de•ride (dĭ-rīd′) *tr.v.* **-rid•ed, -rid•ing, -rides.** To speak of or treat with contemptuous mirth. See Syns at **ridicule.** [Lat. *dērīdēre* : *dē-*, de- + *rīdēre*, to laugh at.] **—de•rid′er** *n.* **—de•rid′ing•ly** *adv.*

de ri•gueur (də rē-gœr′) *adj.* Required by the current fashion or custom. [Fr. : *de*, of + *rigueur*, rigor, strictness.]

de•ri•sion (dĭ-rĭzh′ən) *n.* **1.a.** Contemptuous or jeering laughter; ridicule. **b.** A state of being derided. **2.** An object of ridicule. [ME *derisioun* < AN < LLat. *dērīsiō, dērīsiōn-* < Lat. *dērīsus*, p.part. of *dērīdēre*, to deride. See DERIDE.]

de•ri•sive (dĭ-rī′sĭv, -zĭv, -rĭs′ĭv, -rĭz′-) *adj.* Mocking; jeering. **—de•ri′sive•ly** *adv.* **—de•ri′sive•ness** *n.*

de•ri•so•ry (dĭ-rī′sə-rē, -zə-) *adj.* **1.** Expressing derision; derisive. **2.** Laughable; ridiculous.

deriv. *abbr.* **1.** Derivation. **2.** Derivative.

der•i•vate (dĕr′ə-vāt′) *adj.* Derivative.

der•i•va•tion (dĕr′ə-vā′shən) *n.* **1.** The act or process of deriving. **2.** The state or fact of being derived; originating. **3.** Something derived; a derivative. **4.** The form or source from which something is derived; an origin. **5.** The historical origin and development of a word; an etymology. **6.** *Ling.* **a.** The process by which words are formed from existing words or bases by adding affixes, as *singer* from *sing*, by changing the shape of the word or base, as *song* from *sing*, or by adding an affix and changing the pronunciation of the word or base, as *electricity* from *electric*. **b.** A linguistic description of word formation. **7.** *Logic & Math.* A process indicating through a sequence of statements that a result necessarily follows from the initial assumptions. **—der′i•va′tion•al** *adj.*

de•riv•a•tive (dĭ-rĭv′ə-tĭv) *adj.* **1.** Resulting from or employing derivation. **2.** Copied or adapted from others. —*n.* **1.** Something derived. **2.** *Ling.* A word formed from another by derivation. **3.** *Math.* **a.** The limiting value of the ratio of the change in a function to the corresponding change in its independent variable. **b.** The instantaneous rate of change of a function with respect to its variable. **c.** The slope of a curve at a given point. **4.** *Chem.* A compound derived or obtained from another and containing essential elements of the parent substance. **—de•riv′a•tive•ly** *adv.* **—de•riv′a•tive•ness** *n.*

de•rive (dĭ-rīv′) *v.* **-rived, -riv•ing, -rives.** —*tr.* **1.** To obtain or receive from a source. **2.** To arrive at by reasoning; deduce or infer. **3.** To trace the origin or development of (a word). **4.** *Chem.* To produce or obtain (a compound) from another substance by chemical reaction. —*intr.* To issue from a source; originate. See Syns at **stem**[1]. [ME *deriven*, to be derived from < OFr. *deriver* < Lat. *dērīvāre*, to derive, draw off : *dē-*, de- + *rīvus*, stream; see **rei-***.] **—de•riv′a•ble** *adj.* **—de•riv′er** *n.*

-derm *suff.* Skin; covering: *blastoderm.* [< Gk. *derma*, skin (poss. influenced by Fr. *-derme*). See **der-***.]

der•ma[1] (dûr′mə) *n.* See **dermis.** [Gk., skin. See **der-***.]

der•ma[2] (dûr′mə) *n.* Beef casing stuffed with a seasoned mixture of matzo meal or flour, onion, and suet. [Poss. Yiddish *gederem*, intestines < MHGer. *darm*, intestine < OHGer. See **terə-**[1]***.]

derma- or **derm-** or **dermo-** *pref.* Skin: *dermal.* [< Gk. *derma*, skin. See DERMA[1].]

-derma *suff.* Skin; skin disease: *scleroderma.* [NLat. < Gk. *derma*, skin. See **der-***.]

der•ma•bra•sion (dûr′mə-brā′zhən) *n.* A surgical procedure to remove skin imperfections, such as scars, by abrading the surface of the skin with fine sandpaper or wire brushes.

der•mal (dûr′məl) also **der•mic** (-mĭk) *adj.* Of or relating to the skin or dermis.

der•map•ter•an (dər-măp′tər-ən) *n.* Any of various insects of the order Dermaptera, having an elongated body with pincerlike appendages at the posterior end. [< NLat. *Dermaptera*, order name : Gk. *derma-*, derma- + Gk. *ptera*, pl. of *pteron*, wing; see -PTER.] **—der•map′ter•an** *adj.*

der•ma•ti•tis (dûr′mə-tī′tĭs) *n.* Inflammation of the skin.

dermato- or **dermat-** *pref.* Skin: *dermatophyte.* [Gk. *derma, dermat-*, skin. See **der-***.]

der•mat•o•gen (dûr-măt′ə-jən) *n. Bot.* The outer layer of apical meristem, from which the epidermis is formed.

der•ma•toid (dûr′mə-toid′) also **der•moid** (-moid′) *adj.* Resembling skin; skinlike.

der•ma•tol•o•gy (dûr′mə-tŏl′ə-jē) *n.* The branch of medicine that is concerned with the physiology and pathology of the skin. **—der′ma•to•log′i•cal** (-tə-lŏj′ĭ-kəl), **der′ma•to•log′ic** *adj.* **—der′ma•tol′o•gist** *n.*

der•ma•tome (dûr′mə-tōm′) *n.* **1.** *Anat.* An area of skin innervated by sensory fibers from a single spinal nerve. **2.** *Medic.* An instrument used in cutting thin slices of the skin, as for skin grafts. **3.** *Embryol.* The part of a mesodermal somite from which the dermis develops. [DERMA[1] + -TOME.]

der•mat•o•phyte (dûr-măt′ə-fīt′, dûr′mə-tə-) *n.* Any of various fungi that can cause parasitic skin infections. **—der•mat′o•phyt′ic** (-fĭt′ĭk) *adj.*

der•ma•to•phy•to•sis (dûr′mə-tō′fī-tō′sĭs) *n.* A fungal infection of the skin, esp. athlete's foot.

der•ma•to•plas•ty (dûr′mə-tō-plăs′tē) *n.* The use of skin grafts in plastic surgery to correct defects or replace skin.

der•ma•to•sis (dûr′mə-tō′sĭs) *n., pl.* **-ses** (-sēz). *Pathol.* A skin disease, esp. one without inflammation.

-dermatous *suff.* Having a specified kind of skin: *sclerodermatous.* [Gk. *derma, dermat-*, skin; see DERMATO- + -OUS.]

der•mic (dûr′mĭk) *adj.* Var. of **dermal.**

der•mis (dûr′mĭs) *n.* The sensitive connective tissue layer of the skin located below the epidermis, containing nerve endings, sweat and sebaceous glands, and blood and lymph vessels. [NLat., back-formation < *epidermis*. See EPIDERMIS.]

dermo- *pref.* Var. of **derma-.**

der•moid (dûr′moid′) *adj.* Var. of **dermatoid.**

der•nier cri (dĕr′nyā krē′) *n.* The latest thing; the newest fashion. [Fr. : *dernier*, last, latest + *cri*, cry.]

der•o•gate (dĕr′ə-gāt′) *v.* **-gat•ed, -gat•ing, -gates.** —*intr.* **1.** To take away; detract. **2.** To deviate from a standard or expectation; go astray. —*tr.* To disparage; belittle. [ME *derogaten* < Lat. *dērogāre, dērogāt-* : *dē-*, de- + *rogāre*, to ask; see **reg-***.] **—der′o•ga′tion** *n.*

de•rog•a•tive (dĭ-rŏg′ə-tĭv, dĕr′ə-gā′-) *adj.* **1.** Tending to derogate; detractive. **2.** Disparaging; derogatory. **—de•rog′a•tive•ly** *adv.*

de•rog•a•to•ry (dĭ-rŏg′ə-tôr′ē, -tōr′ē) *adj.* **1.** Disparaging; belittling. **2.** Tending to detract or diminish. **—de•rog′a•to′ri•ly** *adv.* **—de•rog′a•to′ri•ness** *n.*

der•rick (dĕr′ĭk) *n.* **1.** A machine for hoisting and moving heavy objects, consisting of a movable boom equipped with cables and pulleys and connected to the base of an upright stationary beam. **2.** A tall framework over a drilled hole, esp. an oil well, used to support boring equipment. [Obsolete *derrick*, hangman, gallows, after *Derick*, 16th-cent. English hangman.]

derrick
For hole-boring equipment

der•ri•ère also **der•ri•ere** (dĕr′ē-âr′) *n.* The buttocks; the rear. [Fr., behind < OFr. *deriere*, in back of < VLat. **dē retrō* : Lat. *dē*, from, of; see DE- + Lat. *retrō*, back; see RETRO-.]

der•ring-do (dĕr′ĭng-do͞o′) *n.* Daring or reckless action. [ME < *durring don*, daring to do : *durring*, pr.part. of *durren*, to dare (< OE *durran*; see DARE) + *don*, to do; see DO[1].]

der•rin•ger (dĕr′ĭn-jər) *n.* A short-barreled pistol that has a large bore and is small enough to be carried in a pocket. [After Henry *Deringer* (1786–1868), Amer. gunsmith.]

der•ris (dĕr′ĭs) *n.* Any of various usu. woody vines of the genus *Derris* of tropical Asia, whose roots yield the insecticide rotenone. [NLat., genus name < Gk., covering. See **der-***.]

Der•ry (dĕr′ē). See **Londonderry.**

der•vish (dûr′vĭsh) *n.* **1.** A member of any of various Muslim mystical or ascetic orders, many of which are known for acts of ecstatic devotion. **2.** One that possesses abundant, often frenzied energy. [Turk. *derviş*, mendicant < Pers. *darvēsh*.]

dervish

DES (dē′ē-ĕs′) *n.* A synthetic compound, $C_{18}H_{20}O_2$, having estrogenic properties and no longer prescribed during pregnancy because of the incidence of certain vaginal cancers in the daughters of women so treated. [D(I)E(THYL)S(TILBESTROL).]

de•sa•cral•ize (dē-sā′krə-līz′, -săk′rə-) *tr.v.* **-ized, -iz•ing, -iz•es.** To divest of sacred or religious significance.

de•sal•i•nate (dē-săl′ə-nāt′) *tr.v.* **-nat•ed, -nat•ing, -nates.** To desalinize. **—de•sal′i•na′tion** *n.* **—de•sal′i•na′tor** *n.*

de•sal•i•nize (dē-săl′ə-nīz′) *tr.v.* **-nized, -niz•ing, -niz•es.** To remove salts and other chemicals from (sea water or soil, for example). **—de•sal′i•ni•za′tion** (-nĭ-zā′shən) *n.*

de•salt (dē-sôlt′) *tr.v.* **-salt•ed, -salt•ing, -salts.** To desalinize.

De•sargues (dā-zärg′), **Gérard.** 1591–1661. French army officer regarded as one of the founders of modern geometry.

des•cant (dĕs′kănt′) *n.* **1.** Also **dis•cant** (dĭs′-). *Mus.* **a.** An ornamental melody or counterpoint sung or played above a theme. **b.** The highest part sung in part music. **2.** A discussion or discourse on a theme. —*intr.v.* (dĕs′kănt′, dĕ-skănt′) **-cant•ed, -cant•ing, -cants. 1.** To comment at length; discourse. **2.** Also **dis•cant** (dĭs′kănt′, dĭ-skănt′). *Mus.* **a.** To sing or play a descant. **b.** To sing melodiously. [ME < AN *descaunt* < Med.Lat. *discantus*, a refrain : Lat. *dis-*, dis- + Lat. *cantus*, song < p.part. of *canere*, to sing; see **kan-***.] **—des′cant′er** *n.*

Des•cartes (dā-kärt′), **René.** 1596–1650. French mathematician and philosopher who founded analytic geometry and is known for his rationalistic premise "I think, therefore I am."

de•scend (dĭ-sĕnd′) *v.* **-scend•ed, -scend•ing, -scends.** —*intr.* **1.** To move from a higher to a lower place; come or go down. **2.** To slope, extend, or incline downward. **3.a.** To come from an ancestor or ancestry. **b.** To come down from a source; derive. **c.** To pass by inheritance. **4.** To lower oneself; stoop. **5.** To proceed or progress downward, as in rank. **6.** To arrive or attack in a sudden or an overwhelming manner. —*tr.* **1.a.** To move from a higher to a lower part of; go down. **b.** To get down from. **2.** To extend or proceed downward along. [ME *descenden* < OFr. *descendre* < Lat. *dēscendere* : *dē-*, de- + *scandere*, to climb; see **skand-***.] **—de•scend′i•ble, de•scend′a•ble** *adj.*

de•scen•dant (dĭ-sĕn′dənt) *n.* **1.** A person, an animal, or a

ă pat	oi boy
ā pay	ou out
âr care	o͝o took
ä father	o͞o boot
ĕ pet	ŭ cut
ē be	ûr urge
ĭ pit	th thin
ī pie	*th* this
îr pier	hw which
ŏ pot	zh vision
ō toe	ə about,
ô paw	item

Stress marks:
′ (primary);
′ (secondary), as in
dictionary (dĭk′shə-nĕr′ē)

plant whose descent can be traced to a particular individual or group. **2.** Something derived from a prototype or earlier form.

de•scen•dent also **de•scen•dant** (dĭ-sĕn**′**dənt) *adj.* **1.** Moving downward; descending. **2.** Proceeding by descent from an ancestor.

de•scend•er (dĭ-sĕn**′**dər) *n.* **1.** One that descends. **2.** *Print.* **a.** The part of the lowercase letters, such as *q,* that extends below the other lowercase letters. **b.** A letter with such a part.

de•scent (dĭ-sĕnt**′**) *n.* **1.** The act or an instance of descending. **2.** A way down. **3.** A downward incline or passage. **4.a.** Hereditary derivation; lineage. **b.** One generation of a specific lineage. **5.a.** The fact or process of coming down or being derived from a source. **b.** Development in form or structure during transmission from an original source. **6.** *Law.* Transference of property by inheritance. **7.** A lowering or decline, as in level. **8.** A sudden visit or attack; an onslaught. [ME < OFr. < *descendre,* to descend. See DESCEND.]

Des•chutes (dā-sho͞ot**′**, də-sho͞ots**′**). A river rising in the Cascade Range of W-central OR and flowing c. 402 km (250 mi) to the Columbia R. near The Dalles.

de•scram•ble (dē-skrăm**′**bəl) *tr.v.* **-bled, -bling, -bles.** To unscramble (a coded message or signal, for example).

de•scribe (dĭ-skrīb**′**) *tr.v.* **-scribed, -scrib•ing, -scribes. 1.** To give an account of in speech or writing. **2.** To convey an idea or impression of; characterize. **3.** To represent pictorially; depict. **4.** To trace the form or outline of: *describe a circle with a compass.* [ME *describen* < Lat. *dēscrībere,* to write down : *dē-,* de- + *scrībere,* to write; see **skrībh-***.] **—de•scrib′a•ble** *adj.* **—de•scrib′er** *n.*

de•scrip•tion (dĭ-skrĭp**′**shən) *n.* **1.** The act, process, or technique of describing. **2.** A statement or an account describing something. **3.** A pictorial representation. **4.** A kind. [ME *descripcioun* < AN < Lat. *dēscrīptiō, dēscrīptiōn-* < *dēscrīptus,* p.part. of *dēscrībere,* to write down. See DESCRIBE.]

ascender

hq

descender

descender

de•scrip•tive (dĭ-skrĭp**′**tĭv) *adj.* **1.** Involving or characterized by description; serving to describe. **2.** Concerned with classification or description: *a descriptive science.* **3.** *Gram.* **a.** Expressing an attribute of the modified noun, as *green* in *green grass.* Used of an adjective or adjectival clause. **b.** Nonrestrictive. **—de•scrip′tive•ly** *adv.* **—de•scrip′tive•ness** *n.*

descriptive clause *n. Gram.* A nonrestrictive clause.

descriptive linguistics *n.* The study of a language or languages at a specific stage of development, with emphasis on constructing a complete grammar rather than on historical development or comparison with other languages.

de•scrip•tor (dĭ-skrĭp**′**tər) *n. Comp. Sci.* Information used to identify an item in a data storage and retrieval system. [LLat., describer < Lat. *dēscrībere, dēscript-,* to describe. See DESCRIBE.]

de•scry (dĭ-skrī**′**) *tr.v.* **-scried, -scry•ing, -scries. 1.** To catch sight of (something difficult to discern). See Syns at **see[1]**. **2.** To discover by careful observation or scrutiny; detect. [ME *descrien* < OFr. *descrier,* to call, cry out. See DECRY.] **—de•scri′er** *n.*

des•e•crate (dĕs**′**ĭ-krāt′) *tr.v.* **-crat•ed, -crat•ing, -crates.** To violate the sacredness of; profane. [DE- + (CON)SECRATE.] **—des′e•crat′er, des′e•cra′tor** *n.* **—des′e•cra′tion** *n.*

de•seg•re•gate (dē-sĕg**′**rĭ-gāt′) *v.* **-gat•ed, -gat•ing, -gates.** *—tr.* **1.** To abolish or eliminate segregation in. **2.** To open (a school or workplace, for example) to members of all races or ethnic groups, esp. by force of law. *—intr.* To become open to members of all races or ethnic groups. **—de•seg′re•ga′tion** *n.* **—de•seg′re•ga′tion•ist** *n.*

de•sen•si•tize (dē-sĕn**′**sĭ-tīz′) *tr.v.* **-tized, -tiz•ing, -tiz•es. 1.** To render insensitive or less sensitive. **2.** *Immunol.* To make (an individual) nonreactive or insensitive to an antigen. **3.** To make emotionally insensitive or unresponsive, as by long exposure or repeated shocks. **4.** To make (a photographic film or substance) less sensitive to light. **—de•sen′si•ti•za′tion** (-tĭ-zā**′**shən) *n.* **—de•sen′si•tiz′er** *n.*

Des•er•et (dĕz′ə-rĕt**′**). An area in the SW U.S. proposed by the Mormons in 1849 as an independent state or a U.S. state.

desert[1]

des•ert[1] (dĕz**′**ərt) *n.* **1.** A barren or desolate area, esp.: **a.** A dry, often sandy region of little rainfall, extreme temperatures, and sparse vegetation. **b.** A region of permanent cold that is largely or entirely devoid of life. **2.** An empty or forsaken place; a wasteland. **3.** *Archaic.* A wild, uncultivated, and uninhabited region. *—adj.* **1.** Of, relating to, characteristic of, or inhabiting a desert: *desert fauna.* **2.** Barren and uninhabited; desolate. [ME < OFr. < LLat. *dēsertum* < neut. p.part. of *dēserere,* to desert. See DESERT[3].]

de•sert[2] (dĭ-zûrt**′**) *n.* **1.** Something that is deserved or merited, esp. a punishment. Often used in the plural. **2.** The state or fact of deserving reward or punishment. [ME < OFr. *deserte* < fem. p.part. of *deservir,* to deserve. See DESERVE.]

Word History: When Shakespeare says in Sonnet 72, "Unless you would devise some virtuous lie/To do more for me than mine own desert," he is using the word *desert* in the sense of "worthiness; deserving," a word that is most familiar to us in the phrase *just deserts.* This word goes back to the Latin word *dēservīre,* "to devote oneself to the service of," which in Vulgar Latin came to mean "to merit by service." *Dēservīre* is made up of *dē-,* meaning "thoroughly," and *servīre,* "to serve." Knowing this, we can distinguish this *desert* from *desert,* "a wasteland," and *desert,* "to abandon," both of which go back to Latin *dēserere,* "to forsake, leave uninhabited," which is made up of *dē-*, expressing the notion of undoing, and the verb *serere,* "to link together."

de•sert[3] (dĭ-zûrt**′**) *v.* **-sert•ed, -sert•ing, -serts.** *—tr.* **1.** To leave empty or alone; abandon. **2.** To withdraw from, esp. in spite of a responsibility or duty; forsake. **3.** To abandon (a military post, for example) in violation of orders or an oath. *—intr.* To forsake one's duty or post, esp. to be absent without leave from the armed forces with no intention of returning. [Fr. *déserter* < LLat. *dēsertāre* < Lat. *dēserere, dēsert-* : *dē-,* de- + *serere,* to join; see **ser-[2]***.] **—de•sert′er** *n.*

de•sert•i•fi•ca•tion (dĭ-zûr′tə-fĭ-kā**′**shən) *n.* The transformation of arable or habitable land to desert.

de•ser•tion (dĭ-zûr**′**shən) *n.* **1.a.** The act or an instance of deserting. **b.** The state of being deserted. **2.** *Law.* Willful abandonment of one's spouse or children or both without their consent and with the intention of forsaking all legal obligations to them.

de•serve (dĭ-zûrv**′**) *v.* **-served, -serv•ing, -serves.** *—tr.* To be worthy of; merit. See Syns at **earn[1]**. *—intr.* To be worthy or deserving. [ME *deserven* < OFr. *deservir* < Lat. *dēservīre,* to serve zealously : *dē-,* intensive pref.; see DE- + *servīre,* to serve; see SERVE.]

de•served (dĭ-zûrvd**′**) *adj.* Merited or earned. **—de•serv′ed•ly** (-zûr′vĭd-lē) *adv.* **—de•serv′ed•ness** *n.*

de•serv•ing (dĭ-zûr**′**vĭng) *adj.* Worthy, as of reward, praise, or aid. *—n.* Merit; worthiness. **—de•serv′ing•ly** *adv.*

de Se•ver•sky (də sə-vĕr**′**skē), **Alexander Procofieff.** 1894–1974. Russian-born Amer. aeronautical engineer.

de•sex (dē-sĕks**′**) *tr.v.* **-sexed, -sex•ing, -sex•es.** To remove part or all of the reproductive organs of; neuter.

de•sex•u•al•ize (dē-sĕk**′**sho͞o-ə-līz′) *tr.v.* **-ized, -iz•ing, -iz•es. 1.** To take away the sexual quality of. **2.** To desex. **—de•sex′u•al•i•za′tion** (-ə-lĭ-zā**′**shən) *n.*

des•ha•bille (dĕs′ə-bēl**′**, -bē**′**) *n.* Var. of **dishabille.**

De Si•ca (də sē**′**kə), **Vittorio.** 1901–74. Italian filmmaker whose works include *The Bicycle Thief* (1948).

des•ic•cant (dĕs**′**ĭ-kənt) *n.* A substance, such as calcium oxide or silica gel, that has a high affinity for water and is used as a drying agent. [< Lat. *dēsiccāns, dēsiccant-,* pr.part. of *dēsiccāre,* to desiccate. See DESICCATE.] **—des′ic•cant** *adj.*

des•ic•cate (dĕs**′**ĭ-kāt′) *v.* **-cat•ed, -cat•ing, -cates.** *—tr.* **1.** To dry out thoroughly. **2.** To preserve (foods) by removing the moisture. **3.** To make dry, dull, or lifeless. *—intr.* To become dry; dry out. *—adj.* (*also* -kĭt). Lacking spirit or animation; arid. [Lat. *dēsiccāre, dēsiccāt-* : *dē-,* de- + *siccāre,* to dry up (< *siccus,* dry).] **—des′ic•ca′tion** *n.* **—des′ic•ca′tive** *adj.* **—des′ic•ca′tor** *n.*

de•sid•er•ate (dĭ-sĭd**′**ə-rāt′) *tr.v.* **-at•ed, -at•ing, -ates.** To wish to have or see happen. [Lat. *dēsīderāre, dēsīderāt-,* to desire. See DESIRE.] **—de•sid′er•a′tion** *n.*

de•sid•er•a•tive (dĭ-sĭd**′**ər-ə-tĭv, -ə-rā′-, -zĭd**′**-) *adj.* **1.** Of, relating to, or expressing desire. **2.** *Gram.* Being a clause, a sentence, or in some languages an inflected verb form that expresses desire.

de•sid•er•a•tum (dĭ-sĭd′ə-rā**′**təm, -rä**′**-) *n., pl.* **-ta** (-tə). Something considered necessary or highly desirable. [Lat. *dēsīderātum* < neut. p.part. of *dēsīderāre,* to desire. See DESIRE.]

de•sign (dĭ-zīn**′**) *v.* **-signed, -sign•ing, -signs.** *—tr.* **1.a.** To conceive or fashion in the mind; invent. **b.** To formulate a plan for; devise. **2.** To plan out in systematic, usu. graphic form. **3.** To create or contrive for a particular purpose or effect. **4.** To have as a goal or purpose; intend. **5.** To create or execute in an artistic or highly skilled manner. *—intr.* **1.** To make or execute plans. **2.** To have a goal or purpose in mind. **3.** To create designs. *—n.* **1.a.** A drawing or sketch. **b.** A graphic representation, esp. a detailed plan for construction or manufacture. **2.** The purposeful or inventive arrangement of parts or details. **3.** The art or practice of designing or making designs. **4.** Something designed, esp. a decorative or an artistic work. **5.** An ornamental pattern. **6.** A basic scheme or pattern that affects and controls function or development. **7.** A plan; a project. See Syns at **plan. 8.a.** A reasoned purpose; an intent. **b.** Deliberate intention. **9.** A secretive plot or scheme. Often used in the plural. [ME *designen* < Lat. *dēsignāre,* to designate. See DESIGNATE.] **—de•sign′a•ble** *adj.*

des•ig•nate (dĕz**′**ĭg-nāt′) *tr.v.* **-nat•ed, -nat•ing, -nates. 1.** To indicate or specify; point out. **2.** To give a name or title to; characterize. **3.** To select and set aside for a duty, an office, or a purpose. See Syns at **allocate.** *—adj.* (-nĭt). Appointed but not yet installed in office. [Lat. *dēsignāre, dēsignāt-* : *dē-,* de- + *signāre,* to mark (< *signum,* sign; see **sek[w-1]***).] **—des′ig•na′tive, des′ig•na•to′ry** (-nə-tôr′ē, -tōr′ē) *adj.* **—des′ig•na′tor** *n.*

des•ig•nat•ed hitter (dĕz′ĭg-nā**′**tĭd) *n. Baseball.* A player designated at the start of a game to bat instead of the pitcher.

des•ig•na•tion (dĕz′ĭg-nā**′**shən) *n.* **1.** The act of designating; a marking or pointing out. **2.** Nomination or appointment. **3.** A distinguishing name or title.

des•ig•nee (dĕz′ĭg-nē′) *n.* A person who has been designated.

de•sign•er (dĭ-zī′nər) *n.* One that produces designs. —*adj.* **1.** Bearing the name, signature, or identifying pattern of a specific designer. **2.** Conceived or created by a designer.

designer drug *n.* A drug with properties and effects similar to a known drug but slightly altered, esp. in order to evade legal restrictions.

de•sign•ing (dĭ-zī′nĭng) *adj.* **1.** Conniving; crafty. **2.** Showing or exercising forethought. —**de•sign′ing•ly** *adv.*

de•sir•a•ble (dĭ-zīr′ə-bəl) *adj.* **1.** Worth having or seeking, as by being useful, advantageous, or pleasing. **2.** Worth doing or achieving; advisable. **3.** Arousing desire, esp. sexual desire. —*n.* A desirable person or thing. —**de•sir′a•bil′i•ty, de•sir′a•ble•ness** *n.* —**de•sir′a•bly** *adv.*

de•sire (dĭ-zīr′) *tr.v.* **-sired, -sir•ing, -sires. 1.** To wish or long for; want. **2.** To express a wish for; request. —*n.* **1.** A wish or longing. **2.** A request or petition. **3.** The object of longing. **4.** Sexual appetite; passion. [ME *desiren* < OFr. *desirer* < Lat. *dēsīderāre* : *dē-*, de- + *sīdus, sīder-*, star.] —**de•sir′er** *n.*

Syns: *desire, covet, crave, want, wish.* The central meaning shared by these verbs is "to have a strong longing for": *desire peace; coveted the new convertible; craving fame and fortune; wanted a drink of water; got all she wished.*

de•sir•ous (dĭ-zīr′əs) *adj.* Having or expressing desire; desiring. —**de•sir′ous•ly** *adv.* —**de•sir′ous•ness** *n.*

de•sist (dĭ-sĭst′, -zĭst′) *intr.v.* **-sist•ed, -sist•ing, -sists.** To cease doing something; forbear. See Syns at **stop.** [ME *desisten* < OFr. *desister* < Lat. *dēsistere* : *dē-*, de- + *sistere*, to bring to a standstill; see **stā-*.**]

desk (dĕsk) *n.* **1.** A piece of furniture typically having a flat or sloping top for writing and often drawers or compartments. **2.** A table, counter, or booth at which specified functions are performed. **3.** A department of a large organization in charge of a specified operation. **4.** A lectern. **5.** *Mus.* A music stand in an orchestra. [ME *deske* < Med.Lat. *desca*, table < OItal. *desco* < Lat. *discus*, quoit. See DISK.]

desk•man (dĕsk′măn′, -mən) *n.* A man who works at a desk, esp. a newspaper writer.

desk•top (dĕsk′tŏp′) *n.* The top of a desk. —*adj.* Designed for use on a desk or table: *a desktop telephone.*

desktop publishing *n. Comp. Sci.* The design and production of publications, such as newsletters, using microcomputers with graphics capability.

des•man (dĕs′mən) *n., pl.* **-mans.** Either of two aquatic, insectivorous molelike mammals, *Desmana moschata* of eastern Europe and western Asia or *Galemys pyrenaicus* of southwest Europe, having a long snout and a flattened scaly tail. [Short for Swed. *desmanråtta*, muskrat : *desman*, musk (< MLGer. *desem* < Med.Lat. *bisamum*, of Semitic orig.; akin to Heb. *beśem*, odor) + *råtta*, rat (akin to OE *ræt*).]

des•mid (dĕs′mĭd) *n.* Any of various green unicellular freshwater algae of the family Desmidiaceae, often forming colonies. [< NLat. *Desmidiaceae*, family name < *Desmidium*, type genus < Gk. *desmos*, bond < *dein*, to bind.]

Des Moines (dĭ moin′). The cap. of IA, in the S-central part on the Des Moines R. Pop. 193,187.

Des Moines River. A river rising in SW MN and flowing c. 861 km (535 mi) across IA to the Mississippi R.

Des•mou•lins (dā-mo͞o-lăɴ′), **(Lucie Simplice) Camille (Benoît).** 1760–94. French journalist who was guillotined for urging moderation during the Reign of Terror.

Des•na (də-snä′, dyə-). A river rising in W Russia and flowing c. 885 km (550 mi) to the Dnieper R. in the Ukraine.

des•o•late (dĕs′ə-lĭt, dĕz′-) *adj.* **1.a.** Devoid of inhabitants; deserted. **b.** Barren; lifeless. **2.** Rendered unfit for habitation or use. **3.** Dreary; dismal. **4.** Bereft of friends or hope; sad and forlorn. See Syns at **sad.** —*tr.v.* (-lāt′) **-lat•ed, -lat•ing, -lates. 1.** To rid or deprive of inhabitants. **2.** To lay waste; devastate. **3.** To forsake; abandon. **4.** To make lonely, forlorn, or wretched. [ME < Lat. *dēsōlātus*, p.part. of *dēsōlāre*, to abandon : *dē-*, de- + *sōlus*, alone; see **s(w)e-*.**] —**des′o•late•ly** *adv.* —**des′o•late•ness** *n.* —**des′o•lat′er, des′o•la′tor** *n.*

des•o•la•tion (dĕs′ə-lā′shən, dĕz′-) *n.* **1.** The act or an instance of desolating. **2.** The state of being desolate. **3.** Devastation; ruin. **4.a.** The state of being abandoned or forsaken; loneliness. **b.** Wretchedness; misery.

de•sorb (dē-sôrb′, -zôrb′) *tr.v.* **-sorbed, -sorb•ing, -sorbs.** To remove (an absorbed or adsorbed substance) from. —**de•sorp′tion** (-sôrp′shən, -zôrp′-) *n.*

de So•to (dĭ sō′tō, dē sô′tô), **Hernando** or **Fernando.** 1496?–1542. Spanish explorer who explored much of S North America, crossing the Mississippi R. in 1541.

de•spair (dĭ-spâr′) *intr.v.* **-spaired, -spair•ing, -spairs. 1.** To lose all hope. **2.** To be overcome by a sense of futility or defeat. —*n.* **1.** Complete loss of hope. **2.** One despaired of or causing despair. [ME *despeiren* < OFr. *desperer* < Lat. *dēspērāre* : *dē-*, de- + *spērāre*, to hope; see **spē-*.**]

de•spair•ing (dĭ-spâr′ĭng) *adj.* Characterized by or resulting from despair; hopeless. —**de•spair′ing•ly** *adv.*

des•patch (dĭ-spăch′) *v. & n.* Var. of **dispatch.**

des•per•a•do (dĕs′pə-rä′dō, -rā′-) *n., pl.* **-does** or **-dos.** A bold or desperate outlaw, esp. of the American frontier. [Prob. < Sp. *desperado, desesperado*, desperate one < p.part. of *desesperar*, to despair < Lat. *dēspērāre*. See DESPAIR.]

des•per•ate (dĕs′pər-ĭt) *adj.* **1.** Having lost all hope; despairing. **2.** Marked by, arising from, or showing despair. **3.** Reckless or violent because of despair. **4.** Undertaken out of extreme urgency or as a last resort. **5.** Nearly hopeless; critical. **6.** Suffering or driven by great need or distress. **7.** Extremely intense. [ME *desperat* < Lat. *dēspērātus*, p.part. of *dēspērāre*, to despair. See DESPAIR.] —**des′per•ate•ly** *adv.*

des•per•a•tion (dĕs′pə-rā′shən) *n.* **1.** The condition of being desperate. **2.** Recklessness arising from despair.

des•pi•ca•ble (dĕs′pĭ-kə-bəl, dĭ-spĭk′ə-) *adj.* Deserving of contempt or scorn; vile. [LLat. *dēspicābilis* < Lat. *dēspicārī*, to despise. See **spek-*.**] —**des′pi•ca•ble•ness** *n.* —**des′pi•ca•bly** *adv.*

de•spise (dĭ-spīz′) *tr.v.* **-spised, -spis•ing, -spis•es. 1.** To regard with contempt or scorn. **2.** To dislike intensely; loathe. **3.** To regard as unworthy of one's interest or concern: *despised any thought of their own safety.* [ME *despisen* < OFr. *despire, despis-* < Lat. *dēspicere* : *dē-*, de- + *specere*, to look; see **spek-*.**] —**de•spis′al** (-spī′zəl) *n.* —**de•spis′er** *n.*

Syns: *despise, contemn, disdain, scorn, scout.* The central meaning shared by these verbs is "to regard with utter contempt": *despises incompetence; contemned the actions of the dictator; disdained my suggestion; scorns sentimentality; scouted simplistic explanations.* ***Ant:*** *esteem.*

de•spite (dĭ-spīt′) *prep.* In spite of; notwithstanding. —*n.* **1.** Contemptuous defiance or disregard. **2.** Spite; malice. [Short for *in despite of* < ME *despit*, spite < OFr. < Lat. *dēspectus* < p.part. of *dēspicere*, to despise. See DESPISE.]

de•spite•ful (dĭ-spīt′fəl) *adj.* Full of malice; spiteful. —**de•spite′ful•ly** *adv.* —**de•spite′ful•ness** *n.*

de•spit•e•ous (dĭ-spĭt′ē-əs) *adj. Archaic.* Despiteful. —**de•spit′e•ous•ly** *adv.*

Des Plaines (dĕs plānz′). A city of NE IL, a suburb of Chicago. Pop. 53,223.

de•spoil (dĭ-spoil′) *tr.v.* **-spoiled, -spoil•ing, -spoils. 1.** To sack; plunder. **2.** To deprive of something valuable by force; rob. [ME *despoilen* < OFr. *despoillier* < Lat. *dēspoliāre* : *dē-*, de- + *spoliāre*, to plunder (< *spolium*, booty).] —**de•spoil′er** *n.* —**de•spoil′ment** *n.*

de•spo•li•a•tion (dĭ-spō′lē-ā′shən) *n.* The act of despoiling or the condition of being despoiled. [LLat. *dēspoliātiō*, *dēspoliātiōn-* < Lat. *dēspoliātus*, p.part. of *dēspoliāre*, to despoil. See DESPOIL.]

de•spond (dĭ-spŏnd′) *intr.v.* **-spond•ed, -spond•ing, -sponds.** To become disheartened or discouraged. —*n.* Despondency. [Lat. *dēspondēre*, to give up : *dē-*, de- + *spondēre*, to promise; see **spend-*.**] —**de•spond′ing•ly** *adv.*

de•spon•dence (dĭ-spŏn′dəns) *n.* Despondency.

de•spon•den•cy (dĭ-spŏn′dən-sē) *n.* Depression of spirits from loss of hope, confidence, or courage; dejection.

de•spon•dent (dĭ-spŏn′dənt) *adj.* Feeling or expressing despondency; dejected. —**de•spon′dent•ly** *adv.*

des•pot (dĕs′pət) *n.* **1.** A ruler with absolute power. **2.** A person who wields power oppressively; a tyrant. **3.a.** A Byzantine emperor or prince. **b.** An Eastern Orthodox bishop or patriarch. [Fr. *despote* < Med.Lat. *despota* < Gk. *despotēs*, master. See **dem-*.**] —**des•pot′ic** (dĭ-spŏt′ĭk) *adj.* —**des•pot′i•cal•ly** *adv.*

des•pot•ism (dĕs′pə-tĭz′əm) *n.* **1.** Rule by or as if by a despot; absolute power or authority. **2.** The actions of a despot; tyranny. **3.a.** A government or political system in which the ruler exercises absolute power. **b.** A state so ruled.

des•qua•mate (dĕs′kwə-māt′) *intr.v.* **-mat•ed, -mat•ing, -mates.** To shed, peel, or come off in scales. Used of skin. [Lat. *dēsquāmāre*, *dēsquāmāt-* : *dē-*, de- + *squāma*, scale.] —**des′qua•ma′tion** *n.*

Des•sa•lines (dĕ-sä-lēn′), **Jean Jacques.** 1758?–1806. African-born emperor of Haiti (1804–06) who defeated the French (1803) to gain the island's independence.

Des•sau (dĕs′ou). A city of E-central Germany N of Leipzig; site of the Bauhaus school (1925–32). Pop. 103,738.

des•sert (dĭ-zûrt′) *n.* **1.** A usu. sweet course or dish served at the end of a meal. **2.** *Chiefly British.* Fresh fruit, nuts, or sweetmeats served after the sweet course of a dinner. [Fr. < OFr. *desservir*, to clear the table : *des-*, de- + *servir*, to serve; see SERVE.]

des•sert•spoon (dĭ-zûrt′spo͞on′) *n.* A spoon intermediate between a tablespoon and a teaspoon, used for dessert.

dessert wine *n.* A usu. sweet wine, such as Sauternes, served with or after dessert.

de•sta•bi•lize (dē-stā′bə-līz′) *tr.v.* **-lized, -liz•ing, -liz•es. 1.** To upset the stability or smooth functioning of. **2.** To undermine the power of (a government or leader) by subversive or terrorist acts. —**de•sta′bi•li•za′tion** (-lĭ-zā′shən) *n.*

de•stain (dē-stān′) *tr.v.* **-stained, -stain•ing, -stains.** To remove stain from (a specimen) to aid in microscopic study.

de•ster•i•lize (dē-stĕr′ə-līz′) *tr.v.* **-lized, -liz•ing, -liz•es.** To release (gold) from an inactive status and return it to use as a backing for credit and new currency.

Hernando de Soto

ă pat	oi boy
ā pay	ou out
âr care	o͝o took
ä father	o͞o boot
ĕ pet	ŭ cut
ē be	ûr urge
ĭ pit	th thin
ī pie	*th* this
îr pier	hw which
ŏ pot	zh vision
ō toe	ə about,
ô paw	item

Stress marks:
′ (primary);
′ (secondary), as in
dictionary (dĭk′shə-nĕr′ē)

1. In Greek and Roman drama, a god lowered by stage machinery to resolve a plot. **2.** An unexpected, artificial, or improbable character, device, or event introduced in a work of fiction or drama to resolve a situation. [NLat. *deus ex machinā* : *deus*, god + *ex*, from + *machina*, machine.]

Deut. *abbr. Bible.* Deuteronomy.

deu•ter•ag•o•nist (do͞o′tə-răg′ə-nĭst, dyo͞o-) *n.* The character second in importance to the protagonist in classical Greek drama. [Gk. *deuteragōnistēs*, an actor of second-class parts : *deuteros*, second; see **deu-**[1*] + *agōnistēs*, actor; see PROTAGONIST.]

deu•ter•a•no•pi•a (do͞o′tər-ə-nō′pē-ə, dyo͞o′-) *n.* A form of colorblindness characterized by insensitivity to green. [DEUTER(O)- + AN- + -OPIA, so called because green is considered the second primary color.] **—deu′ter•a•nope′** (-nōp′) *n.* **—deu′ter•a•nop′ic** (-nŏp′ĭk, -nō′pĭk) *adj.*

deu•ter•ate (do͞o′tə-rāt′, dyo͞o′-) *tr.v.* **-at•ed, -at•ing, -ates.** To introduce deuterium into (a chemical compound). [DEUTER(IUM) + -ATE[1].] **—deu′te•ra′tion** *n.*

deu•te•ri•um (do͞o-tîr′ē-əm, dyo͞o-) *n. Symbol* **D** An isotope of hydrogen with one proton and one neutron in the nucleus having an atomic weight of 2.014. [DEUTER(O)- + -IUM.]

deuterium oxide *n.* An isotopic form of water with composition D_2O, used as a moderator in nuclear reactors.

deutero- or **deuter-** *pref.* Second; secondary: *deuterocanonical.* [Gk. *deuteros*, second, secondary. See **deu-**[1*].]

deu•ter•o•ca•non•i•cal (do͞o′tə-rō′kə-nŏn′ĭ-kəl, dyo͞o′-) *adj. Bible.* Of, relating to, or being a second canon, esp. that consisting of sections of the Bible not included in the original Roman Catholic canon but accepted by theologians in 1548 at the Council of Trent.

deu•ter•og•a•my (do͞o′tə-rŏg′ə-mē, dyo͞o′-) *n.* See **digamy.**

deu•ter•on (do͞o′tə-rŏn′, dyo͞o′-) *n.* The nucleus of a deuterium atom, consisting of a bound proton and neutron. [DEUTER(IUM) + -ON[1].]

Deu•ter•on•o•my (do͞o′tə-rŏn′ə-mē, dyo͞o′-) *n.* See table at **Bible.** [LLat. *deuteronomium* < Gk. *deuteronomion*, a second law (< *(to) deuteronomion (touto)*, Septuagint, mistransl. of Heb. *mišnê hattôrâ hazzō't*, a copy of this law) : *deuteros*, second; see **deu-**[1*] + *nomos*, law; see **nem-***.] **—Deu′ter•o•nom′ic** (-tər-ə-nŏm′ĭk) *adj.*

deuto- or **deut-** *pref.* Second; secondary: *deutoplasm.* [Alteration of DEUTERO-.]

deu•to•plasm (do͞o′tə-plăz′əm, dyo͞o′-) *n.* The nutritive substances or yolk in the cytoplasm of an ovum or other cell. **—deu′to•plas′mic** *adj.*

deut•sche mark also **deut•sche•mark** (doi′chə-märk′) *n.* See table at **currency.** [Ger. : *deutsch*, German + *Mark*, mark.]

deut•zi•a (do͞ot′sē-ə, dyo͞ot′-) *n.* Any of various shrubs of the genus *Deutzia*, cultivated for their white or pinkish flowers. [After Jan van der *Deutz*, 18th-cent. Dutch patron of botany.]

dev. *abbr.* Deviation.

De Va•le•ra (dĕv′ə-lĕr′ə, -lîr′ə), **Eamon.** 1882–1975. Irish political leader and first president of the Republic of Ireland (1959–73).

de•val•ue (dē-văl′yo͞o) also **de•val•u•ate** (-văl′yo͞o-āt′) *—v.* **-ued, -u•ing, -ues** also **-at•ed, -at•ing, -ates.** *—tr.* **1.** To lessen or cancel the value of. **2.** To lower the exchange value of (a currency) by lowering its gold equivalency. *—intr.* To devalue a currency. **—de•val′u•a′tion** *n.*

De•va•na•ga•ri (dā′və-nä′gə-rē) *n.* The alphabet in which Sanskrit and many modern Indian languages are written. [Skt. *devanāgarī* : *deva-*, divine; see **deiw-*** + *nāgarī*, fem. of *nāgara-*, of a town (< *nagaram*, town, prob. of Dravidian orig.).]

dev•as•tate (dĕv′ə-stāt′) *tr.v.* **-tat•ed, -tat•ing, -tates. 1.** To lay waste; destroy. **2.** To overwhelm; confound; stun. [Lat. *dēvāstāre, dēvāstāt-* : *dē-*, de- + *vāstāre*, to lay waste (< *vāstus*, empty, desolate; see **eu-**[2*]).] **—dev′as•tat′ing•ly** *adv.* **—dev′as•ta′tion** *n.* **—dev′as•ta′tor** *n.*

de•vel•op (dĭ-vĕl′əp) *v.* **-oped, -op•ing, -ops.** *—tr.* **1.** To bring from latency to or toward fulfillment. **2.a.** To expand or enlarge. **b.** To aid in the growth of; strengthen. **c.** To improve the quality of; refine: *developing my piano technique.* **3.a.** To cause to become more complex; elaborate. **b.** *Mus.* To elaborate (a theme) with rhythmic and harmonic variations. **4.a.** To bring into being gradually: *develop a new industry.* **b.** To set forth or clarify by degrees. **5.a.** To come to have gradually; acquire: *develop a taste for opera.* **b.** To become affected with; contract; *developed a rash.* **6.** To cause gradually to acquire a specific role, function, or form, as: **a.** To influence the behavior of. **b.** To cause (a tract of land) to serve a particular purpose. **c.** To make available and effective to fulfill a particular end. **d.** To convert or transform: *developed the play into a movie.* **7.** *Games.* To move (a chess piece) to or toward a more strategic position. **8.a.** To process (a photosensitive material), esp. with chemicals, in order to render a recorded image visible. **b.** To render (an image) visible by this means. *—intr.* **1.a.** To grow by degrees into a more advanced, evolved, or mature state. See Syns at **mature. b.** To increase or expand. **2.** To come gradually into existence or activity. **3.** To come gradually to light; be disclosed. [Fr. *développer* < OFr. *desveloper* : *des-*, dis- + *voloper*, to wrap (poss. of Celt. orig.).] **—de•vel′op•a•ble** *adj.*

de•vel•oped (dĭ-vĕl′əpt) *adj.* Advanced in industrial capability, technological sophistication, and economic productivity.

de•vel•op•er (dĭ-vĕl′ə-pər) *n.* **1.** One that develops: *a developer of hidden talent.* **2.** A person who develops real estate, esp. for residential or commercial use. **3.** A chemical used to render visible the image recorded on a photosensitive surface.

de•vel•op•ing (dĭ-vĕl′ə-pĭng) *adj.* Having a relatively low level of industrial capability, technological sophistication, and economic productivity.

de•vel•op•ment (dĭ-vĕl′əp-mənt) *n.* **1.** The act of developing. **2.** The state of being developed. **3.** A significant event, occurrence, or change. **4.** A group of dwellings built by the same contractor. **5.** Determination of the best techniques for applying a new device or process to production of goods or services. **6.** *Mus.* **a.** Elaboration of a theme with rhythmic and harmonic variations. **b.** The part of a movement in sonata form in which the theme is elaborated and explored. **—de•vel′op•men′tal** (-mĕn′tl) *adj.* **—de•vel′op•men′tal•ly** *adv.*

Syns: *development, evolution, progress.* The central meaning shared by these nouns is "a progression from a simpler or lower to a more advanced, mature, or complex form or stage": *the development of an idea into reality; the evolution of a plant; attempts made to foster social progress.*

dé•vel•op•pé (də-vĕl′ə-pā′) *n.* A ballet movement in which one leg is raised to the knee of the other leg and fully extended. [Fr. < p.part. of *développer*, to develop. See DEVELOP.]

De•ven•ter (dā′vən-tər). A city of E-central Netherlands on the Ijssel R. ENE of Utrecht. Pop. 64,823.

de•ver•bal *n.* See **deverbative.**

de•verb•a•tive (dē-vûr′bə-tĭv) *Gram. —adj.* **1.** Formed from a verb, such as the noun *worker* derived from the verb *work.* **2.** Used in derivation from a verb, such as the suffix *-er* in *teacher.* *—n.* A deverbative word or element.

Dev•er•eux (dĕv′ə-ro͞o′), **Robert.** 2nd Earl of Essex. 1566–1601. English noble and favorite of Elizabeth I.

de•vest (dĭ-vĕst′) *tr.v.* **-vest•ed, -vest•ing, -vests. 1.** *Law.* To take away (a right or possession, for example). **2.** *Archaic.* **a.** To remove the clothing or covering of. **b.** To deprive of a title, right, or item of property. [Obsolete Fr. *desvestir*, to undress < Med.Lat. *disvestīre* : Lat. *dis-*, dis- + Lat. *vestis*, garment; see **wes-**[2*].]

De•vi (dā′vē) *n. Hinduism.* A mother goddess having various manifestations and roles, esp. that of consort to Shiva. [Skt. *devī*, fem. of *devaḥ*, god. See **deiw-***.]

de•vi•ant (dē′vē-ənt) *adj.* Differing from a norm or from the accepted standards of a society. *—n.* One that differs from a norm, esp. a person whose behavior is deviant. [ME *deviaunt* < LLat. *dēviāns, dēviant-*, pr.part. of *dēviāre*, to deviate. See DEVIATE.] **—de′vi•ance, de′vi•an•cy** *n.*

de•vi•ate (dē′vē-āt′) *v.* **-at•ed, -at•ing, -ates.** *—intr.* **1.** To turn aside from a course or way. **2.** To depart, as from a norm or a purpose; stray. See Syns at **swerve.** *—tr.* To cause to turn aside or differ. *—n.* (-ĭt). A deviant. [LLat. *dēviāre, dēviāt-* : Lat. *dē-*, de- + Lat. *via*, road; see **wegh-***.] **—de′vi•a′tor** *n.* **—de′vi•a•to′ry** (-ə-tôr′ē, -tōr′ē) *adj.*

de•vi•a•tion (dē′vē-ā′shən) *n.* **1.** The act of deviating or turning aside. **2.** An abnormality; a departure. **3.** Deviant behavior or attitudes. **4.** Divergence from an accepted political policy or party line. **5.** Deflection of a compass needle caused by local magnetic influence. **6.** *Statistics.* The difference, esp. the absolute difference, between one number in a set and the mean of the set. **—de′vi•a′tion•ism** *n.* **—de′vi•a′tion•ist** *adj. & n.*

de•vice (dĭ-vīs′) *n.* **1.** A contrivance or an invention serving a particular purpose. **2.a.** A technique or means. **b.** A plan or scheme, esp. a malign one. **3.** A literary contrivance, such as parallelism or personification, used to achieve a particular effect. **4.** A decorative design or pattern, as one used in embroidery. **5.** A graphic symbol or motto, esp. in heraldry. **6.** *Archaic.* The act, state, or power of devising. ***—idiom.*** **leave to (one's) own devices.** To allow to do as one pleases. [ME < OFr. *devis*, division, wish and OFr. *devise*, design, both < Lat. *dīvīsus, dīvīsa*, p.part. of *dīvidere*, to divide.]

dev•il (dĕv′əl) *n.* **1.** Often **Devil.** *Theol.* In many religions, the major personified spirit of evil, ruler of Hell, and foe of God. Used with *the.* **2.** A subordinate evil spirit; a demon. **3.** A wicked or malevolent person. **4.** A person: *the poor devil.* **5.** An energetic, mischievous, daring, or clever person. **6.** *Print.* A printer's devil. **7.** A device or machine, esp. one having teeth or spikes and used for tearing. **8.** An outstanding example, esp. of something difficult or bad. **9.** A severe reprimand or expression of anger. **10.** *Informal.* Used as an intensive: *Who the devil do you think you are?* *—tr.v.* **-iled, -il•ing, -ils** or **-illed, -il•ling, -ils. 1.** To season (food) heavily. **2.** To annoy, torment, or harass. **3.** To tear up (cloth or rags) in a toothed machine. ***—idioms.*** **between the devil and the deep blue sea.** Between two equally unacceptable choices. **give the devil his due.** To give credit to a disagreeable or malevolent person. **go to the devil. 1.** To be unsuccessful; fail.

2. To become depraved. **3.** Used in the imperative to express anger or impatience. [ME *devel* < OE *dēofol* < Lat. *diabolus* < LGk. *diabolos* < Gk., slanderer < *diaballein*, to slander : *dia-*, dia- + *ballein*, to hurl; see **gʷelə-***.]

dev•il•fish (dĕv′əl-fĭsh′) *n., pl.* **devilfish** or **-fish•es. 1.** See **manta** 2. **2.** See **octopus** 1. **3.** See **gray whale.**

dev•il•ish (dĕv′ə-lĭsh) *adj.* **1.** Of, resembling, or characteristic of a devil, as: **a.** Malicious; evil. **b.** Mischievous, teasing, or annoying. **2.** Excessive; extreme: *devilish heat.* —*adv.* Extremely; very. —**dev′il•ish•ly** *adv.* —**dev′il•ish•ness** *n.*

dev•il•kin (dĕv′əl-kĭn) *n.* A little devil; an imp.

dev•il-may-care (dĕv′əl-mā-kâr′) *adj.* **1.** Heedless of caution; reckless. **2.** Jovial and rakish in manner.

dev•il•ment (dĕv′əl-mənt) *n.* Devilish behavior; mischief.

dev•il's advocate (dĕv′əlz) *n.* **1.** One who argues against a cause or position simply for the sake of argument or to determine the validity of the cause or position. **2.** *Rom. Cath. Ch.* An official appointed to present arguments against a proposed canonization or beatification.

devil's bit *n.* See **blazing star** 1.

devil's darning needle *n.* **1.** *Upper Northern U.S.* See **dragonfly.** See Regional Note at **dragonfly. 2.** See **damselfly.**

devil's food cake *n.* A rich chocolate cake.

Dev•il's Island (dĕv′ĭlz). An island in the Caribbean off French Guiana; a French penal colony after the 1850's.

devil's paintbrush *n.* See **orange hawkweed.**

devil's walking stick *n.* See **Hercules' club** 1.

dev•il•try (dĕv′əl-trē) or **dev•il•ry** (-əl-rē) *n., pl.* **-tries** or **-ries. 1.** Reckless mischief. **2.** Extreme cruelty; wickedness. **3.** Evil magic; witchcraft. **4.** An act of mischief, cruelty, or witchcraft. [Alteration of DEVILRY.]

dev•il•wood (dĕv′əl-wo͝od′) *n.* A tree *(Osmanthus americanus)* of the southeast United States having fragrant greenish flowers, hard wood, and whitish bark.

De Vin•ne (də vĭn′ē), **Theodore Low.** 1828–1914. Amer. printer who wrote *The Practice of Typography* (1900–04).

de•vi•ous (dē′vē-əs) *adj.* **1.** Not straightforward; shifty. **2.** Departing from the correct or accepted way; erring. **3.** Deviating from the straight or direct course; roundabout. **4.** Away from a main road or course; distant or removed. [< Lat. *dēvius*, out-of-the-way : *dē-*, de- + *via*, road; see **wegh-***.] —**de′vi•ous•ly** *adv.* —**de′vi•ous•ness** *n.*

de•vise (dĭ-vīz′) *tr.v.* **-vised, -vis•ing, -vis•es. 1.** To form, plan, or arrange in the mind; design or contrive. **2.** *Law.* To transmit or give (real property) by will. **3.** *Archaic.* To suppose; imagine. —*n. Law.* **1.a.** The act of transmitting or giving real property by will. **b.** The property or lands so transmitted or given. **2.** A will or clause in a will transmitting or giving real property. [ME *devisen* < OFr. *deviser* < VLat. **dēvīsāre* < Lat. **dīvīsāre*, freq. of *dīvidere*, to divide.] —**de•vis′a•ble** *adj.* —**de•vis′er** *n.*

de•vi•see (dĭ-vī′zē′, dĕv′ĭ-zē′) *n. Law.* One to whom a devise is made.

de•vi•sor (dĭ-vī′zər, dĕv′ĭ-zôr′) *n. Law.* One that makes a devise.

de•vi•tal•ize (dē-vīt′l-īz′) *tr.v.* **-ized, -iz•ing, -iz•es.** To diminish or destroy the strength or vitality of. —**de•vit′al•i•za′tion** (-ĭ-zā′shən) *n.*

de•vit•ri•fy (dē-vĭt′rə-fī′) *tr.v.* **-fied, -fy•ing, -fies.** To cause (a glassy material) to become crystalline and brittle. —**de•vit′ri•fi′a•ble** *adj.* —**de•vit′ri•fi•ca′tion** (-fĭ-kā′shən) *n.*

de•vo•cal•ize (dē-vō′kə-līz′) *tr.v.* **-ized, -iz•ing, -iz•es.** *Ling.* To devoice. —**de•vo′cal•i•za′tion** (-kə-lĭ-zā′shən) *n.*

de•voice (dē-vois′) *tr.v.* **-voiced, -voic•ing, -voic•es.** *Ling.* To pronounce (a normally voiced sound) without vibration of the vocal chords so as to make it wholly or partly voiceless.

de•void (dĭ-void′) *adj.* Completely lacking. [ME, p.part. of *devoiden*, to remove, eliminate < OFr. *desvoidier* : *des-*, de- + *voidier*, to empty (< *voide*, empty; see VOID).]

de•voir (dəv-wär′, dĕv′wär′) *n.* **1.** An act or expression of respect or courtesy; civility. Often used in the plural. **2.** Duty or responsibility. [ME, duty < OFr. < *devoir*, to owe < Lat. *dēbēre*. See **ghabh-***.]

de•vol•a•til•ize (dē-vŏl′ə-tl-īz′) *tr.v.* **-ized, -iz•ing, -iz•es.** To remove volatile material from: *devolatilize coal.* —**de•vol′a•til•i•za′tion** (-ĭ-zā′shən) *n.*

dev•o•lu•tion (dĕv′ə-lo͞o′shən, dē′və-) *n.* **1.** A passing down or descent through successive stages of time or a process. **2.** Transference, as of rights or qualities, to a successor. **3.** Delegation of duties to a subordinate or substitute. **4.** A transfer of powers from a central government to local units. **5.** *Biol.* Degeneration. [LLat. *dēvolūtiō*, *dēvolūtiōn-* < Lat. *dēvolūtus*, p.part. of *dēvolvere*, to roll down, fall to. See DEVOLVE.] —**dev′o•lu′tion•ar′y** (-shə-nĕr′ē) *adj.* —**dev′o•lu′tion•ist** *n.*

de•volve (dĭ-vŏlv′) *v.* **-volved, -volv•ing, -volves.** —*tr.* **1.** To pass on or delegate to another. **2.** *Archaic.* To cause to roll onward or downward. —*intr.* **1.** To be passed on or transferred to another. **2.** *Archaic.* To roll onward or downward. [ME *devolven*, to transfer < OFr. *devolver*, to confer, ascribe < Lat. *dēvolvere*, to roll down, fall to : *dē-*, de- + *volvere*, to roll; see **wel-**[2]*.] —**de•volve′ment** *n.*

Dev•on[1] (dĕv′ən). A region of SW England on the English Channel; part of Wessex after the 8th cent.

Dev•on[2] (dĕv′ən) *n.* Any of a breed of reddish cattle developed in the English county of Devon and raised primarily for beef.

De•vo•ni•an (dĭ-vō′nē-ən) *adj.* Of or belonging to the fourth period of the Paleozoic Era, characterized by the appearance of forests and amphibians. See table at **geologic time.** —*n.* The Devonian Period or its deposits. [After *Devon*, a county of SW England.]

Devon Island. An island of NE Northwest Terrs., Canada, between Baffin and Ellesmere islands.

Dev•on•shire cream (dĕv′ən-shîr′, -shər) *n.* See **clotted cream.** [After *Devonshire*, or Devon, a county of SW England.]

de•vote (dĭ-vōt′) *tr.v.* **-vot•ed, -vot•ing, -votes. 1.** To give or apply (one's time, attention, or self) to an activity, cause, or person. **2.** To set apart for a purpose or use. **3.** To set apart by or as if by a vow or solemn act; consecrate: *a temple devoted to Apollo.* [Lat. *dēvovēre*, *dēvōt-*, to vow : *dē-*, de- + *vovēre*, to vow.] —**de•vote′ment** *n.*

de•vot•ed (dĭ-vō′tĭd) *adj.* **1.** Feeling or displaying strong affection or attachment; ardent. **2.** Having been consecrated; dedicated. —**de•vot′ed•ly** *adv.* —**de•vot′ed•ness** *n.*

dev•o•tee (dĕv′ə-tē′, -tā′) *n.* **1.** One who is ardently devoted to something; an enthusiast or advocate: *a devotee of sports.* **2.** An ardent or fanatical adherent of a religion.

de•vo•tion (dĭ-vō′shən) *n.* **1.** Ardent affection and dedication, as to a person. See Syns at **love. 2.** Religious ardor or zeal; piety. **3.a.** An act of religious observance or prayer. Often used in the plural. **b. devotions.** Prayers or religious texts. **4.** The act of devoting or the state of being devoted.

de•vo•tion•al (dĭ-vō′shə-nəl) *adj.* Of, relating to, expressive of, or used in devotion, esp. of a religious nature. —*n.* A short religious service. —**de•vo′tion•al•ly** *adv.*

de•vour (dĭ-vour′) *tr.v.* **-voured, -vour•ing, -vours. 1.** To eat up greedily. **2.** To destroy, consume, or waste: *Flames devoured the house.* **3.** To take in eagerly: *devour a novel.* **4.** To prey upon voraciously: *devoured by jealousy.* [ME *devouren* < OFr. *devourer* < Lat. *dēvorāre* : *dē-*, de- + *vorāre*, to swallow.] —**de•vour′er** *n.* —**de•vour′ing•ly** *adv.*

de•vout (dĭ-vout′) *adj.* **-er, -est. 1.** Devoted to religion or religious obligations. **2.** Displaying reverence or piety. **3.** Sincere; earnest: *devout wishes for their success.* [ME < OFr. < Lat. *dēvōtus*, p.part. of *dēvovēre*, to vow. See DEVOTE.] —**de•vout′ly** *adv.* —**de•vout′ness** *n.*

De Vries (də vrēs′), **Hugo.** 1848–1935. Dutch botanist who studied evolution by observing mutations.

dew (do͞o, dyo͞o) *n.* **1.** Water droplets condensed from the air, usu. at night, onto cool surfaces. **2.** Something moist, fresh, pure, or renewing. **3.** Moisture, as in the form of tears, that appears in small drops. —*tr.v.* **dewed, dew•ing, dews.** To wet with or as if with dew. [ME *deu* < OE *dēaw*. See **dheu-**[1]*.]

de•wan (dĭ-wän′) *n.* Any of various government officials in India. [Hindi *dīvān* < Pers., account book.]

Dew•ar (do͞o′ər, dyo͞o′-), Sir **James.** 1842–1923. Scottish-born chemist who invented cordite (1889) with Sir Frederick Abel.

Dewar flask *n.* A container used esp. to store liquefied gases, having a double wall with a vacuum between the walls and silvered surfaces facing the vacuum. [After Sir James DEWAR.]

de•wat•er (dē-wô′tər, -wŏt′ər) *tr.v.* **-ered, -er•ing, -ers.** To remove water from (a waste product, for example).

dew•ber•ry (do͞o′bĕr′ē, dyo͞o′-) *n.* **1.** Any of several trailing forms of the blackberry, such as *Rubus hispidus* of North America. **2.** The fruit of any of these plants.

dew•claw (do͞o′klô′, dyo͞o′-) *n.* A digit or claw not reaching the ground and found on the feet of certain mammals. [Perh. < alteration of TOE.] —**dew′clawed′** *adj.*

dew•drop (do͞o′drŏp′, dyo͞o′-) *n.* A drop of dew.

Dew•ey (do͞o′ē, dyo͞o′ē), **George.** 1837–1917. Amer. naval officer active in the Spanish-American War.

Dewey, John. 1859–1952. Amer. philosopher and educator who was a leading exponent of philosophical pragmatism.

Dewey, Melvil. 1851–1931. Amer. librarian and founder of the decimal system of classification (1876).

Dewey, Thomas Edmund. 1902–71. Amer. politician who was the Republican nominee for President in 1944 and 1948.

Dewey decimal classification *n.* A system used in libraries for organizing publications into subject categories corresponding to three-digit numerals, with further specification expressed by numerals following a decimal point. [After Melvil DEWEY.]

dew•fall (do͞o′fôl′, dyo͞o′-) *n.* **1.** The formation of dew. **2.** The time of evening when dew begins to form.

dew•lap (do͞o′lăp′, dyo͞o′-) *n.* **1.** A fold of loose skin hanging from the neck of certain animals. **2.** A pendulous part similar to this, such as the wattle of a bird. [ME *dewlappe* : *dew*, orig. unknown + *lappe*, fold; see LAP[2].]

DEW line (do͞o, dyo͞o) *n.* A line of radar stations near the 70th parallel across North America, maintained by the United States and Canada to give advance warning of enemy aircraft and missiles. [*D(istant) E(arly) W(arning).*]

devilwood
Osmanthus americanus

Thomas Dewey

ă pat	oi boy
ā pay	ou out
âr care	o͝o to͝ok
ä father	o͞o bo͞ot
ĕ pet	ŭ cut
ē be	ûr urge
ĭ pit	th thin
ī pie	*th* this
îr pier	hw which
ŏ pot	zh vision
ō toe	ə about, item
ô paw	

Stress marks:
′ (primary);
′ (secondary), as in
dictionary (dĭk′shə-nĕr′ē)

diam. *abbr.* Diameter.

di•a•mag•net (dī′ə-măg′nĭt) *n.* A diamagnetic substance.

di•a•mag•net•ic (dī′ə-măg-nĕt′ĭk) *adj.* Of or relating to a substance that is repelled by a magnet. —**di′a•mag′ne•tism** (-nĭ-tĭz′əm) *n.*

di•a•man•te or **di•a•man•té** (dē′ə-män-tā′) *n.* **1.** A small glittering ornament, such as a sequin, applied to fabric. **2.** Fabric covered with many of these ornaments. [Fr. *diamanté,* decorated with diamonds < *diamant,* diamond. See DIAMOND.]

di•am•e•ter (dī-ăm′ĭ-tər) *n.* **1.** *Math.* **a.** A straight line segment passing through the center of a figure, esp. of a circle or sphere, and terminating at the periphery. **b.** The length of such a segment. **2.** Thickness or width. [ME *diametre* < OFr. < Lat. *diametrus* < Gk. *diametros* : *dia-,* dia- + *metron,* measure; see **mē-²***.] —**di•am′e•tral** (-trəl) *adj.*

di•a•met•ri•cal (dī′ə-mĕt′rĭ-kəl) also **di•a•met•ric** (-rĭk) *adj.* **1.** Of, relating to, or along a diameter. **2.** Exactly opposite; contrary. —**di′a•met′ri•cal•ly** *adv.*

di•am•ine (dī-ăm′ēn′, -ĭn, dī′ə-mēn′, -mĭn) *n.* Any of various chemical compounds containing two amino groups.

di•a•mond (dī′ə-mənd, dī′mənd) *n.* **1.** An extremely hard crystalline form of carbon that is usu. colorless and is used as a gemstone and in abrasives, cutting tools, and other applications. **2.** A figure with four equal sides forming two inner obtuse angles and two inner acute angles; a rhombus or lozenge. **3.** *Games.* **a.** A red lozenge-shaped figure on certain playing cards. **b.** A playing card with this figure. **c. diamonds.** *(used with a sing. or pl. v.)* The suit of cards represented by this figure. **4.** *Baseball.* **a.** An infield. **b.** The whole playing field. —*tr.v.* **-mond•ed, -mond•ing, -monds.** To adorn with or as if with diamonds. [ME *diamaunt* < OFr. *diamant* < Med.Lat. *diamas, diamant-,* alteration of Lat. *adamas.* See ADAMANT.]

Diana
Greek bell krater showing Actaeon being killed by his own dogs

di•a•mond•back moth (dī′ə-mənd-băk′, dī′mənd-) *n.* One of several small moths of the family Plutellidae, having front wings that reveal diamond-shaped spots when folded.

diamondback rattlesnake *n.* Either of two large venomous rattlesnakes *(Crotalus adamanteus* or *C. atrox)* found in the southern and western United States and in Mexico and having diamond-shaped markings on the back.

diamondback terrapin *n.* One of several edible turtles of the genus *Malaclemys* of the southern Atlantic and Gulf coasts of the United States, having a carapace with diamond-shaped markings.

Di•a•mond Head (dī′ə-mənd, dī′mənd). A promontory, 232.1 m (761 ft), on the SE coast of Oahu HI.

di•a•mond•if•er•ous (dī′ə-mən-dĭf′ər-əs, dī′mən-) *adj.* Bearing or yielding diamonds.

diamond in the rough *n., pl.* **diamonds in the rough.** One having exceptionally good qualities but lacking polish and refinement.

Di•an•a (dī-ăn′ə) *n. Rom. Myth.* The virgin goddess of hunting and childbirth, traditionally associated with the moon. [ME < Lat. *Diāna.* See **deiw-***.]

Diana, Princess of Wales. Lady Diana Frances Spencer. b. 1961. Consort (since 1981) of Charles, Prince of Wales, heir to the British throne.

Diana
Princess of Wales

di•an•drous (dī-ăn′drəs) *adj. Bot.* Having two stamens.

Di•ane de Poi•tiers (dē-än′ də pwä-tyā′). 1499–1566. French lover of Henry II.

di•an•thus (dī-ăn′thəs) *n.* A plant of the genus *Dianthus,* which includes carnations and pinks. [NLat. *Dianthus,* genus name, prob. alteration (influenced by DI-¹) of Gk. *diosanthos,* carnation : *Dios-,* of Zeus; see DIOSCURI + *anthos,* flower.]

di•a•pa•son (dī′ə-pā′zən, -sən) *n. Mus.* **1.** A rich outpouring of harmonious sound. **2.** The entire range of an instrument or voice. **3.** Either of the two principal stops on a pipe organ that form the tonal basis for the entire scale of the instrument. **4.** The interval and the consonance of an octave. **5.** A standard indication of pitch. **6.** A tuning fork. [ME *diapasoun* < Lat. *diapāsōn,* the whole octave < Gk. *(dia) pasōn (khordōn),* (through) all (the notes), fem. genitive pl. of *pas.* See **pant-***.]

di•a•pause (dī′ə-pôz′) *n. Zool.* A period of suspended development and diminished physiological activity, as in certain insects. [Gk. *diapausis,* pause < *diapauein,* to pause : *dia-,* between; see DIA- + *pauein,* to stop.]

di•a•pe•de•sis (dī′ə-pĭ-dē′sĭs) *n., pl.* **-ses** (-sēz). The movement of blood cells, esp. white blood cells, through capillary walls into body tissue. [Gk. *diapēdēsis,* transudation < *diapēdan,* to ooze through : *dia-,* dia- + *pēdan,* to leap, throb; see **ped-***.] —**di′a•pe•det′ic** (-dĕt′ĭk) *adj.*

di•a•per (dī′ə-pər, dī′pər) *n.* **1.a.** A folded piece of absorbent material, such as cloth, that is placed between a baby's legs and fastened at the waist to contain excretions. **b.** A similar piece of material, worn by incontinent adults. **2.a.** A white cotton or linen fabric patterned with small diamond-shaped figures. **b.** A piece of such cloth. **c.** Such a pattern. —*tr.v.* **-pered, -per•ing, -pers. 1.** To put a diaper on. **2.** To weave or decorate in a diamond-shaped pattern. [ME, a patterned fabric < OFr. *diapre, diaspre* < Med.Lat. *diasprum,* a white silken material < Med.Gk. *diaspros,* pure white : *dia-,* intensive pref.; see DIA- + *aspros,* white (prob. < Lat. *asper,* rough).]

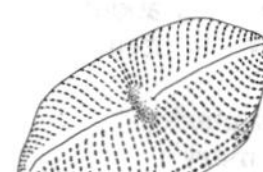

diatom

di•aph•a•nous (dī-ăf′ə-nəs) *adj.* **1.** Of such fine texture as to be transparent or translucent. **2.** Characterized by delicacy of form. See Syns at **airy. 3.** Vague or insubstantial. [< Med.Lat. *diaphanus,* transparent < Gk. *diaphanēs* < *diaphainein,* to be transparent : *dia-,* dia- + *phainein, phan-,* to show; see **bhā-¹***.] —**di′a•pha•ne′i•ty** (dī′ə-fə-nē′ĭ-tē), **di•aph′a•nous•ness** *n.* —**di•aph′a•nous•ly** *adv.*

di•a•pho•re•sis (dī′ə-fə-rē′sĭs, dī-ăf′ə-) *n.* Perspiration, esp. when copious and medically induced. [LLat. *diaphorēsis* < Gk. < *diaphorein,* to disperse : *dia-,* dia- + *phorein,* to convey, freq. of *pherein,* to carry; see **bher-¹***.]

di•a•pho•ret•ic (dī′ə-fə-rĕt′ĭk, dī-ăf′ə-) *adj.* Producing or increasing perspiration. —*n.* A diaphoretic medicine or other agent. [DIAPHOR(ESIS) + -ETIC.]

di•a•phragm (dī′ə-frăm′) *n.* **1.** *Anat.* A muscular membranous partition separating the abdominal and thoracic cavities and functioning in respiration. **2.** A membranous part that divides or separates. **3.** A thin disk, as in a telephone receiver, that vibrates in response to sound waves to produce electric signals or vibrates in response to electric signals to produce sound waves. **4.** A contraceptive device consisting of a thin flexible disk, usu. made of rubber, that covers the uterine cervix to prevent the entry of sperm during sexual intercourse. **5.** A disk having a fixed or variable opening used to restrict the amount of light traversing a lens or optical system. [ME *diafragma* < LLat. *diaphragma,* midriff < Gk., partition < *diaphrassein,* to barricade : *dia-,* intensive pref.; see DIA- + *phrassein, phrag-,* to enclose.] —**di′a•phrag•mat′ic** (-frăg-măt′ĭk) *adj.* —**di′a•phrag•mat′i•cal•ly** *adv.*

di•aph•y•sis (dī-ăf′ĭ-sĭs) *n., pl.* **-ses** (-sēz′). *Anat.* The shaft of a long bone. [Gk. *diaphusis,* spinous process of the tibia < *diaphuesthai,* to grow between : *dia-,* dia- + *phuesthai,* to grow, middle voice of *phuein;* see **bheuə-***.] —**di′a•phys′i•al, di′a•phys′e•al** (dī′ə-fĭz′ē-əl) *adj.*

di•a•pir (dī′ə-pîr′) *n.* An anticlinal fold in which a mobile core, such as gypsum, has pierced through the more brittle overlying rock. [Fr. < Gk. *diapeirein,* to push through : *dia-,* dia- + *peirein,* to pierce; see **per-²***.] —**di′a•pir′ic** *adj.*

di•a•poph•y•sis (dī′ə-pŏf′ĭ-sĭs) *n., pl.* **-ses** (-sēz′). *Anat.* The superior or articular surface of the transverse process of a vertebra. [DI(A)- + APOPHYSIS.]

di•ar•chy also **dy•ar•chy** (dī′är′kē) *n., pl.* **-chies.** Government by two joint rulers.

di•a•rist (dī′ə-rĭst) *n.* A person who keeps a diary.

di•ar•rhe•a also **di•ar•rhoe•a** (dī′ə-rē′ə) *n.* Excessive and frequent evacuation of watery feces, usu. indicating gastrointestinal disorder. [ME *diaria* < Med.Lat. < LLat. *diarrhoea* < Gk. *diarrhoia* < *diarrhein,* to flow through : *dia-,* dia- + *rhein,* to flow, run; see **sreu-***.] —**di′ar•rhe′al, di′ar•rhe′ic** (-ĭk), **di′ar•rhet′ic** (-rĕt′ĭk) *adj.*

di•ar•thro•sis (dī′är-thrō′sĭs) *n., pl.* **-ses** (-sēz). Any of several types of bone articulation permitting free motion in a joint, as that of the shoulder or hip. [Gk. *diarthrōsis* < *diarthroun,* to articulate : *dia-,* between; see DIA- + *arthroun,* to fasten by a joint (< *arthron,* joint; see **ar-***).] —**di′ar•thro′di•al** (-dē-əl) *adj.*

di•a•ry (dī′ə-rē) *n., pl.* **-ries. 1.** A daily record, esp. a personal record of events, experiences, and observations. **2.** A book for use in keeping a diary. [Lat. *diārium,* daily allowance, daily journal < *diēs,* day. See **deiw-***.]

Di•as (dē′əs, -əsh), **Bartolomeu.** 1450?–1500. Portuguese navigator; the first to round the Cape of Good Hope (1488).

Di•as•po•ra (dī-ăs′pər-ə) *n.* **1.** The dispersion of Jews outside Israel from the sixth century B.C., when the Jews were exiled to Babylonia, until the present time. **2.** Often **diaspora.** The body of Jews or Jewish communities outside Palestine or modern Israel. **3. diaspora.** A dispersion of an originally homogeneous people. **4. diaspora.** A dispersion of an originally homogeneous entity, such as a language or a culture. [Gk. *diaspora,* dispersion < *diaspeirein,* to spread about : *dia-,* apart; see DIA- + *speirein,* to sow, scatter; see **sper-***.]

di•a•spore (dī′ə-spôr′, -spōr′) *n.* **1.** A pearly hydrous aluminum oxide, AlO(OH), found in bauxite and corundum and used as a refractory and abrasive. **2.** *Bot.* See **disseminule.** [< Gk. *diaspora,* dispersion, scattering. See DIASPORA.]

di•a•stase (dī′ə-stās′, -stāz′) *n.* An amylase or a mixture of amylases that converts starch to maltose, found in certain germinating grains such as malt. [Fr. < Gk. *diastasis,* separation < *diistanai,* to separate : *dia-,* apart; see DIA- + *histanai,* to cause to stand; see **stā-***.] —**di′a•sta′sic** (-stā′sĭk, -zĭk) *adj.*

di•a•ste•ma (dī′ə-stē′mə) *n., pl.* **-ma•ta** (-mə-tə). A gap or space between two teeth. [LLat. *diastēma,* interval < Gk. < *diastēnai,* to separate, second aorist of *diistanai.* See DIASTASE.] —**di′a•ste•mat′ic** (-stə-măt′ĭk) *adj.*

di•as•to•le (dī-ăs′tə-lē) *n.* **1.** *Physiol.* The normal rhythmically occurring relaxation and dilatation of the heart chambers, during which they fill with blood. **2.** The lengthening of a short syllable in Greek and Latin verse. [Gk. *diastolē,* dilation < *diastellein,* to expand : *dia-,* apart; see DIA- + *stellein,* to place; see **stel-***.] —**di′a•stol′ic** (dī′ə-stŏl′ĭk) *adj.*

di•as•tro•phism (dī-ăs′trə-fĭz′əm) *n.* The process of deformation by which the major features of the earth's crust are formed. [< Gk. *diastrophē*, distortion < *diastrephein*, to distort : *dia-*, apart; see DIA- + *strephein*, to twist; see **streb(h)-***.] — **di′a•stroph′ic** (dī′ə-strŏf′ĭk, -strō′fĭk) *adj.*

di•a•tes•sa•ron (dī′ə-tĕs′ər-ən) *n.* The four Gospels combined into a single narrative. [ME, interval of a fourth < Lat. *diatessarōn*, made of four (ingredients) < Gk. *dia tessarōn*, out of four : *dia-*, according to; see DIA- + *tessarōn*, genitive of *tessares*, four; see **kʷetwer-***.]

di•a•ther•my (dī′ə-thûr′mē) *n.* The therapeutic generation of local heat in body tissues by high-frequency electromagnetic currents. — **di′a•ther′mic** (-mĭk) *adj.*

di•ath•e•sis (dī-ăth′ĭ-sĭs) *n., pl.* **-ses** (-sēz′). A hereditary predisposition of the body to a disease, an allergy, or another disorder. [Gk., disposition, condition < *diatithenai*, to dispose : *dia-*, dia- + *tithenai*, to place, set; see **dhē-***.] — **di′a•thet′ic** (dī′ə-thĕt′ĭk) *adj.*

di•a•tom (dī′ə-tŏm′) *n. Bot.* Any of various microscopic one-celled or colonial algae of the class Bacillariophyceae, having cell walls of silica consisting of two interlocking symmetrical valves. [NLat. *diatoma* < Gk. *diatomos*, cut in half < *diatemnein*, to cut in half : *dia-*, dia- + *temnein*, to cut; see **tem-***.]

di•a•to•ma•ceous (dī′ə-tə-mā′shəs, dī-ăt′ə-) *adj.* Consisting of diatoms or their skeletons.

diatomaceous earth *n.* A light-colored porous rock composed of the shells of diatoms.

di•a•tom•ic (dī′ə-tŏm′ĭk) *adj.* Made up of two atoms.

di•at•o•mite (dī-ăt′ə-mīt′) *n.* Powdered diatomaceous earth used as a filler, a filtering agent, and an absorbent.

di•a•ton•ic (dī′ə-tŏn′ĭk) *adj. Mus.* Of or using only the eight tones of a standard major or minor scale without chromatic deviations. [LLat. *diatonicus* < Gk. *diatonikos* : *dia-*, dia- + *tonos*, tone; see TONE.] — **di′a•ton′i•cal•ly** *adv.* — **di′a•ton′i•cism** (-ĭ-sĭz′əm) *n.*

di•a•tribe (dī′ə-trīb′) *n.* A bitter, abusive denunciation. [Lat. *diatriba*, learned discourse < Gk. *diatribē*, pastime, lecture < *diatribein*, to consume, wear away : *dia-*, intensive pref.; see DIA- + *tribein*, to rub; see **terə-¹***.]

di•at•ro•pism (dī-ăt′rə-pĭz′əm) *n.* The tendency of certain plants or their parts to arrange themselves at right angles to a stimulus. — **di′a•trop′ic** (dī′ə-trŏp′ĭk, -trō′pĭk) *adj.*

Dí•az (dē′äs, -äz), **(José de la Cruz) Porfirio.** 1830–1915. Mexican soldier and politician who served as president (1877–80 and 1884–1911).

Dí•az del Cas•til•lo (dē′äth *th*ĕl kä-stēl′yô), **Bernal.** 1492?–1581. Spanish soldier and historian noted for his eyewitness account of the conquest of Mexico (1519–21).

Dí•az de Vi•var (dē′äth *th*ĕ vē-vär′), **Rodrigo.** See the **Cid.**

di•az•e•pam (dī-ăz′ə-păm′) *n.* A tranquilizer, $C_{16}H_{13}ClN_2O$, used in the treatment of anxiety and as a muscle relaxant and anticonvulsant. [DIAZ(O) + EP(OXIDE) + AM(MONIA).]

di•a•zine (dī′ə-zēn′, dī-ăz′ĭn) *n.* A heterocyclic compound with four carbon atoms and two nitrogen atoms, esp. any of three isomers of $C_4H_4N_2$. [DI-¹ + AZ(O)- + -INE².]

di•az•i•non (dī-ăz′ə-nŏn′) *n.* A liquid, $C_{12}H_{21}N_2O_3PS$, used as an insecticide. [DIAZ(O) + -IN(E)² + -ON³.]

di•az•o (dī-ăz′ō) *adj.* Relating to or containing a pair of bonded nitrogen atoms.

di•a•zo•ni•um (dī′ə-zō′nē-əm) *n.* The univalent cation RN_2, in which R is an aromatic hydrocarbon. [DIAZ(O) + (AMM)ONIUM.]

di•ba•sic (dī-bā′sĭk) *adj.* **1.** Containing two replaceable hydrogen atoms. **2.** Of or relating to salts or acids forming salts with two atoms of a univalent metal.

dib•ber (dĭb′ər) *n.* A dibble. [Alteration of DIBBLE.]

dib•ble (dĭb′əl) *n.* A pointed gardening implement used to make holes in soil. — *tr.v.* **-bled, -bling, -bles. 1.** To make holes in (soil) with a dibble. **2.** To plant by means of a dibble. [ME *dibbel.*] — **dib′bler** *n.*

di•bro•mide (dī-brō′mīd′, -mĭd) *n.* A chemical compound containing two bromine atoms.

dibs (dĭbz) *pl.n. Slang.* **1.** A claim; rights: *I have dibs on that piece of pie.* **2.** Money, esp. in small amounts. [Short for *dibstones*, counters used in a game, prob. < obsolete *dib*, to tap.]

di•car•box•yl•ic (dī-kär′bŏk-sĭl′ĭk) *adj.* Containing two carboxyl groups per molecule.

di•cast (dī′kăst′, dĭk′ăst′) *n.* One of 6,000 citizens chosen yearly in ancient Athens to sit in the law courts and act as judge and juror. [Gk. *dikastēs*, judge < *dikazein*, to judge < *dikē*, right, custom. See **deik-***.] — **di•cas′tic** *adj.*

dice (dīs) *n.* **1.** *Games.* Pl. of **die²** 3. **2.** *pl.* **dice** also **dices.** A small cube, as of food. — *v.* **diced, dic•ing, dic•es.** — *intr. Games.* To play or gamble with dice. — *tr.* **1.** *Games.* To win or lose (money) by gambling with dice. **2.** To cut (food) into small cubes. **3.** To decorate with dicelike figures. [Pl. of DIE².]

di•cen•tra (dī-sĕn′trə) *n.* A plant of the genus *Dicentra*, which includes the bleeding heart. [NLat. *Dicentra*, genus name : DI-¹ + Greek *kentron*, point (< *kentein*, to prick; see **kent-***).]

di•ceph•a•lous (dī-sĕf′ə-ləs) *adj.* Having two heads.

dic•er (dī′sər) *n.* A device used for dicing food.

dic•ey (dī′sē) *adj.* **-i•er, -i•est.** Involving or fraught with danger or risk. [< DICE.]

di•cha•si•um (dī-kā′zē-əm, -zhē-əm, -zhəm) *n., pl.* **-si•a** (-zē-ə, -zhē-ə, -zhə). *Bot.* A cyme having two lateral flowers or branches originating from opposite points beneath a terminal flower. [NLat. < Gk. *dikhasis*, division < *dikhazein*, to divide in two < *dikha*, in two. See **dwo-***.] — **di•cha′si•al** (-zē-əl, -zhē-əl, -zhəl) *adj.* — **di•cha′si•al•ly** *adv.*

di•chlo•ride (dī-klôr′īd′, -klōr′-) *n.* A chemical compound containing two chlorine atoms.

di•chlo•ro•di•phen•yl•tri•chlo•ro•eth•ane (dī-klôr′ō-dī-fĕn′əl-trī-klôr′ō-ĕth′ān′, -klōr′-, -fē′nəl-, dī-klōr′-) *n.* DDT.

dicho– or **dich–** *pref.* In two; into two parts: *dichogamous.* [Gk. *dikho-* < *dikha*, in two. See **dwo-***.]

di•chog•a•mous (dī-kŏg′ə-məs) *adj. Bot.* Having pistils and stamens that mature at different times, thus promoting cross-pollination. — **di•chog′a•my** (-mē) *n.*

di•chon•dra (dī-kŏn′drə) *n.* A small creeping herb *(Dichondra micrantha)* cultivated as a substitute for lawn grass. [NLat., genus name : DI-¹ + Gk. *khondros*, granule; see CHONDRO-.]

di•chot•o•mize (dī-kŏt′ə-mīz′) *v.* **-mized, -miz•ing, -miz•es.** — *tr.* To separate into two parts or classifications. — *intr.* To be or become divided into parts or branches; fork. — **di•chot′o•mist** (-mĭst) *n.* — **di•chot′o•mi•za′tion** (-mĭ-zā′shən) *n.*

di•chot•o•mous (dī-kŏt′ə-məs) *adj.* **1.** Divided or dividing into two parts or classifications. **2.** Marked by dichotomy. — **di•chot′o•mous•ly** *adv.* — **di•chot′o•mous•ness** *n.*

di•chot•o•my (dī-kŏt′ə-mē) *n., pl.* **-mies. 1.** Division into two usu. contradictory parts or opinions. **2.** *Astron.* The phase of the moon, Mercury, or Venus when half of the disk is illuminated. **3.** *Bot.* Branching characterized by successive forking into two approximately equal divisions. [Gk. *dikhotomia* < *dikhotomos*, divided in two : *dikho-*, dicho- + *temnein*, to cut; see **tem-***.]

di•chro•ic (dī-krō′ĭk) *adj.* **1.** Manifesting dichroism. **2.** *Pathol.* Dichromatic. [< Gk. *dikhroos*, bicolored : *di-*, two; see DI-¹ + *khrōs*, color, skin.]

di•chro•ism (dī′krō-ĭz′əm) *n. Chem.* **1.** The property possessed by some solutions of showing different colors at different concentrations. **2.** The property possessed by some crystals of exhibiting two different colors when viewed along different axes.

di•chro•ite (dī-krō′īt′) *n.* See **cordierite.** [DICHRO(IC) + -ITE¹.]

di•chro•mate (dī-krō′māt′, dī′krō-) *n.* A compound containing the divalent negative ion, Cr_2O_7, usu. having a characteristic orange-red color.

di•chro•mat•ic (dī′krō-măt′ĭk) *adj.* **1.** Possessing or exhibiting two colors. **2.** *Zool.* Having two distinct color phases not associated with season, sex, or age, as certain species of birds. **3.** *Pathol.* Of or relating to dichromatism.

di•chro•ma•tism (dī-krō′mə-tĭz′əm) also **di•chro•mism** (-mĭz′əm) *n.* **1.** The quality or condition of being dichromatic. **2.** *Pathol.* A form of colorblindness in which only two of the three fundamental colors can be distinguished because of a lack of one of the cone pigments.

di•chro•mic (dī-krō′mĭk) *adj.* **1.** *Pathol.* Dichromatic. **2.** *Chem.* Containing two chromium atoms per molecule.

dichromic acid *n.* An acid, $H_2Cr_2O_7$, known only in solution.

dick¹ (dĭk) *n. Slang.* A detective. [Shortening and alteration of DETECTIVE.]

dick² (dĭk) *n.* **1.** *Chiefly British.* A fellow; a guy. **2.** *Vulgar Slang.* A penis. [< *Dick*, nickname for *Richard.*]

Dick (dĭk), **George Frederick.** 1881–1967. Amer. medical researcher who teamed with his wife, **Gladys Henry Dick** (1881–1963), to isolate the germ that causes scarlet fever.

dick•cis•sel (dĭk-sĭs′əl, dĭk′sĭs′-) *n.* A sparrowlike bird *(Spiza americana)* native to southern Ontario and the central United States, the male of which has a yellow breast marked with a small black bib on the throat. [Imit. of its song.]

dick•ens (dĭk′ənz) *n. Informal.* **1.** A severe reprimand or expression of anger: *gave me the dickens for being late.* **2.** Used as an intensive: *What in the dickens is that?* [Perh. < the name *Dickens* < dim. of *Dick.* See DICK².]

Dick•ens (dĭk′ĭnz), **Charles John Huffam.** "Boz." 1812–70. British writer known for his tales of Victorian life, including *David Copperfield* (1849–50). — **Dick•en′si•an** (dĭ-kĕn′zē-ən) *adj.*

dick•er (dĭk′ər) *intr.v.* **-ered, -er•ing, -ers.** To bargain; barter. — *n.* The act or process of bargaining. [Prob. < *dicker*, a quantity of ten, ten hides < ME *diker*, perh. < OE **dicor* < Lat. *decuria*, set of ten < *decem*, ten. See **dekm̥***.]

dick•ey also **dick•ie** or **dick•y** (dĭk′ē) *n., pl.* **-eys** also **-ies. 1.a.** A woman's blouse front worn under a suit jacket or low-necked garment. **b.** A detachable shirt front or collar. **c.** A child's bib or pinafore. **2.** A donkey. **3.** A small bird. **4.a.** The driver's seat on a carriage. **b.** A rear seat for servants on a carriage. [< dim. of *Dick*, nickname for *Richard.*]

Dick•in•son (dĭk′ĭn-sən), **Emily Elizabeth.** 1830–86. Amer. poet who wrote more than a thousand verses.

Dickinson, John. 1732–1808. Amer. Revolutionary politician

dibble

Charles Dickens

Emily Dickinson
Only known extant photograph, taken at age 16

ă pat	oi boy
ā pay	ou out
âr care	o͝o took
ä father	o͞o boot
ĕ pet	ŭ cut
ē be	ûr urge
ĭ pit	th thin
ī pie	*th* this
îr pier	hw which
ŏ pot	zh vision
ō toe	ə about, item
ô paw	

Stress marks:
′ (primary);
′ (secondary), as in dictionary (dĭk′shə-nĕr′ē)

who wrote *Letters from a Farmer in Pennsylvania* (1767–68).

Dick test *n.* A skin test used to determine immunity or susceptibility to scarlet fever. [After George Frederick DICK and Gladys Henry DICK.]

dick•y[1] (dĭk′ē) *n.* Var. of **dickey.**

dick•y[2] (dĭk′ē) *adj. Informal.* Impaired; faulty; weak. [?]

di•cli•nous (dī-klī′nəs) *adj. Bot.* Having stamens and pistils in separate flowers. [DI-[1] + Gk. *klinē*, bed, couch; see **klei-*** + -OUS.] **—di′cli′ny** (dī′klī′nē) *n.*

di•cot•y•le•don (dī′kŏt′l-ēd′n) also **di•cot** (dī′kŏt′) *n.* A flowering plant having two embryonic seed leaves or cotyledons that usu. appear at germination. **—di′cot′y•le′don•ous** *adj.*

di•cro•tism (dī′krə-tĭz′əm) *n.* A condition in which the pulse is felt as two beats per single heartbeat. [< Gk. *dikrotos*, double-beating : *di-*, two; see DI-[1] + *krotos*, rattling noise.] **—di•crot′ic** (-krŏt′ĭk) *adj.*

dict. *abbr.* **1.** Dictation. **2.** Dictionary.

Dic•ta•phone (dĭk′tə-fōn′). A trademark used for an apparatus that records and reproduces dictation for transcription.

dic•tate (dĭk′tāt′, dĭk-tāt′) *v.* **-tat•ed, -tat•ing, -tates.** *—tr.* **1.** To say or read aloud to be recorded or written by another. **2.a.** To prescribe with authority; impose. **b.** To control or command. *—intr.* **1.** To dictate material. **2.** To issue orders or commands. *—n.* (dĭk′tāt′). **1.** A directive; a command. **2.** A guiding principle. [Lat. *dictāre, dictāt-*, freq. of *dīcere*, to say. See **deik-*.**]

Syns: *dictate, decree, impose, ordain, prescribe.* The central meaning shared by these verbs is "to set forth expressly and authoritatively": *victors dictating the terms of surrender; budget cuts decreed by the legislature; impose obedience; a separation ordained by fate; taxes prescribed by law.*

dic•ta•tion (dĭk-tā′shən) *n.* **1.a.** The act or process of dictating material to another for transcription. **b.** The material so dictated. **2.** An authoritative command or order.

dic•ta•tor (dĭk′tā′tər, dĭk-tā′-) *n.* **1.a.** An absolute ruler. **b.** A tyrant; a despot. **2.** An ancient Roman magistrate appointed temporarily to deal with an immediate crisis or emergency. **3.** One who dictates: *the dictator of the letter.*

dic•ta•to•ri•al (dĭk′tə-tôr′ē-əl, -tōr′-) *adj.* **1.** Tending to dictate; domineering. **2.** Of, relating to, or characteristic of a dictator or dictatorship; autocratic. **—dic′ta•to′ri•al•ly** *adv.* **—dic′ta•to′ri•al•ness** *n.*

dic•ta•tor•ship (dĭk-tā′tər-shĭp′, dĭk′tā′-) *n.* **1.** The office or tenure of a dictator. **2.** A state or government under dictatorial rule. **3.** Absolute or despotic control or power.

dic•tion (dĭk′shən) *n.* **1.** Choice and use of words in speech or writing. **2.** Distinctness of pronunciation in speech or singing. [ME *diccion*, a saying, word < OFr. < Lat. *dictiō, dictiōn-*, rhetorical delivery < *dictus*, p.part. of *dīcere*, to say. See **deik-*.**] **—dic′tion•al** *adj.* **—dic′tion•al•ly** *adv.*

Babe Didrikson

dic•tion•ar•y (dĭk′shə-nĕr′ē) *n., pl.* **-ies. 1.** A reference book containing an alphabetical list of words, with information given for each word, usu. including meaning, pronunciation, and etymology. **2.** A book listing the words of a language with translations into another language. **3.** A book listing words or other linguistic items in a particular category or subject with information about them: *a medical dictionary.* **4.** *Comp. Sci.* A list of words stored in machine-readable form for reference, as by spelling-checking software. [Med.Lat. *dictiōnārium* < Lat. *dictiō, dictiōn-*, diction. See DICTION.]

dic•tum (dĭk′təm) *n., pl.* **-ta** (-tə) or **-tums. 1.** An authoritative, often formal pronouncement. **2.** *Law.* See **obiter dictum** 1. [Lat. < neut. p.part. of *dīcere*, to say. See **deik-*.**]

dic•ty•o•some (dĭk′tē-ə-sōm′) *n. Bot.* The Golgi apparatus in plant cells. [Gk. *diktuon*, net (< *dikein*, to throw; see **deik-***) + -SOME[3].]

did (dĭd) *v.* P.t. of **do**[1].

di•dact (dī′dăkt′) *n.* A didactic person. [Back-formation < DIDACTIC.]

di•dac•tic (dī-dăk′tĭk) also **di•dac•ti•cal** (-tĭ-kəl) *adj.* **1.** Intended to instruct. **2.** Morally instructive. **3.** Inclined to teach or moralize excessively. [Gk. *didaktikos*, skillful in teaching < *didaktos*, taught < *didaskein, didak-*, to teach, educate.] **—di•dac′ti•cal•ly** *adv.* **—di•dac′ti•cism** (-tĭ-sĭz′əm) *n.*

di•dac•tics (dī-dăk′tĭks) *n.* *(used with a sing. or pl. v.)* Instruction; teaching; pedagogy.

di•dap•per (dī′dăp′ər) *n.* A small grebe, such as the dabchick. [ME *didopper*, alteration of *divedap* : < OE *dūfedoppa*, pelican : *dūfan*, to dive; see DIVE[1] + *-doppa*, a kind of bird.]

did•dle[1] (dĭd′l) *v.* **-dled, -dling, -dles.** *tr.v.* **1.** *Slang.* To cheat; swindle. **2.** *Comp. Sci.* To fabricate, change, or otherwise manipulate (data) illegally. [Perh. akin to OE *dydrian*, to deceive, or < var. of dial. *doodle*, fool, simpleton; akin to LGer. *dudeldopp*.] **—did′dler** *n.*

did•dle[2] (dĭd′l) *v.* **-dled, -dling, -dles.** *—tr.* **1.** To jerk up and down or back and forth. **2.** *Vulgar Slang.* **a.** To have intercourse with (a woman). **b.** To practice masturbation upon. *—intr.* **1.** To shake rapidly; jiggle. **2.** *Slang.* To play; fiddle. **3.** *Slang.* To waste time: *diddled around all morning.* [Prob. alteration of dial. *didder*, to quiver, tremble < ME *dideren*, var. of *daderen, doderen*, perh. < LGer.]

did•dly (dĭd′lē) *n. Slang.* A small or worthless amount. [Short for *diddlyshit.* See DIDDLYSQUAT.]

did•dly•squat (dĭd′lē-skwŏt′) *n. Slang.* Diddly. [Alteration of *diddlyshit* : *diddly* (alteration of DOODLE) + SHIT.]

Di•de•rot (dē′də-rō′, dē-drō′), **Denis.** 1713–84. French philosopher and writer whose supreme accomplishment was his work on the *Encyclopédie* (1751–72).

did•n't (dĭd′nt). Did not.

di•do (dī′dō) *n., pl.* **-dos** or **-does.** A mischievous prank or antic; a caper. [?]

Di•do (dī′dō) *n. Rom. Myth.* The founder and queen of Carthage, who fell in love with Aeneas and killed herself when he abandoned her.

Did•rik•son (dĭd′rĭk-sən), **Mildred Ella ("Babe").** Married name Zaharias. 1914–56. Amer. athlete who excelled in golf and track and won two gold medals at the 1932 Olympics.

didst (dĭdst) *v. Archaic.* Second pers. sing. p.t. of **do**[1].

di•dym•i•um (dī-dĭm′ē-əm) *n.* **1.** *Symbol* **Di** A metallic mixture, once considered an element, composed of neodymium and praseodymium. **2.** A mixture of rare-earth elements and oxides used chiefly in manufacturing and coloring various forms of glass. [< Gk. *didumos*, twin, double. See **dwo-*.**]

did•y•mous (dĭd′ə-məs) *adj.* Arranged or occurring in pairs; twin. [< Gk. *didumos*, twin. See **dwo-*.**]

di•dyn•a•mous (dī-dĭn′ə-məs) *adj. Bot.* Having four stamens in two pairs of unequal length. [< NLat. *Didynamia*, former class name : DI-[1] + Gk. *dunamis*, power; see DYNAMIC.]

die[1] (dī) *intr.v.* **died, dy•ing** (dī′ĭng), **dies. 1.** To cease living; become dead; expire. **2.** To cease existing, esp. by degrees; fade. **3.** To experience an agony or suffering suggestive of that of death. **4.** *Informal.* To desire something greatly. **5.a.** To cease operation; stop. **b.** To be destroyed, as in combat. ***—phrasal verbs.*** **die back.** *Bot.* To be affected by dieback. **die down.** To lose strength; subside. **die off.** To undergo a sudden sharp decline in population. **die out.** To cease living completely; become extinct. ***—idiom.*** **die hard.** To take a long time in passing out of existence. [ME *dien*, prob. < ON *deyja.* See **dheu-**[2]*****.]

die[2] (dī) *n., pl.* **dies** or **dice** (dīs). **1.** *pl.* **dies.** A device used for cutting out, forming, or stamping material, esp.: **a.** An engraved metal piece used for impressing a design onto a softer metal, as in coining money. **b.** One of several component pieces that are fitted into a diestock to cut threads on screws or bolts. **c.** A part on a machine that punches shaped holes in, cuts, or forms sheet metal, cardboard, or other stock. **d.** A metal block containing small conical holes through which plastic, metal, or other ductile material is extruded or drawn. **2.** *pl.* **dies.** *Archit.* The dado of a pedestal, esp. when cube-shaped. **3.** *pl.* **dice.** *Games.* **a.** A small cube marked on each side with from one to six dots, usu. used in pairs in gambling and in various other games. **b. dice.** *(used with a sing. v.)* A game of chance using dice. *—tr.v.* **died, die•ing, dies.** To cut, form, or stamp with or as if with a die. ***—idioms.*** **load the dice. 1.** To make an outcome highly probable; predetermine a result. **2.** To put another at a distinct disadvantage, as through prior maneuver. **the die is cast.** The decision has been made and is irrevocable. [ME *de*, gaming die < OFr. < Lat. *datum* < neut. p.part. of *dare*, to give. See **dō-*.**]

die•back (dī′băk′) *n. Bot.* The gradual dying of plant shoots, starting at the tips, caused by disease or climate.

di•e•cious (dī-ē′shəs) *adj. Bot.* Var. of **dioecious.**

Die•fen•ba•ker (dē′fən-bā′kər), **John George.** 1895–1979. Canadian politician who served as prime minister (1957–63).

dief•fen•bach•i•a (dē′fən-bä′kē-ə, -băk′ē-ə) *n.* Any of several plants of the genus *Dieffenbachia* native to tropical America and having jointed stems and variegated leaves. [NLat., genus name, after Ernst *Dieffenbach* (1811–55), German naturalist.]

die-hard also **die•hard** (dī′härd′) *—adj.* Stubbornly resisting change or clinging to a seemingly hopeless or dated cause. *—n.* A diehard person. **—die′-hard′ism** *n.*

diel•drin (dēl′drĭn) *n.* A chlorinated hydrocarbon, $C_{12}H_8Cl_6O$, used as an insecticide and in mothproofing. [< *Diel(s-A)ld(e)r (reaction)*, after Otto Paul Hermann DIELS and Kurt ALDER.]

di•e•lec•tric (dī′ĭ-lĕk′trĭk) *n.* A nonconductor of electricity, esp. a substance with electrical conductivity less than a millionth (10^{-6}) of a siemens. [DI(A)- + ELECTRIC.] **—di′e•lec′tric** *adj.* **—di′e•lec′tri•cal•ly** *adv.*

dielectric constant *n. Phys.* See **permittivity.**

dielectric heating *n.* The heating of electrically nonconducting materials by a rapidly varying electromagnetic field.

Diels (dēlz, dēls), **Otto Paul Hermann.** 1876–1954. German chemist who shared a 1950 Nobel Prize.

Di•em (dē-ĕm′, dyĕm), **Ngo Dinh.** 1901–63. Vietnamese politician who was president of South Vietnam (1954–63).

Dien Bien Phu (dyĕn′ byĕn′ fo͞o′). A town of NW Vietnam near the Laos border; site of a French military base that fell to Vietminh troops on May 7, 1954, after a 56-day siege.

di•en•ceph•a•lon (dī′ĕn-sĕf′ə-lŏn′, -lən) *n.* The posterior part of the forebrain that connects the mesencephalon with the cerebral hemispheres, encloses the third ventricle, and contains the thalamus and hypothalamus. [DI(A)- + ENCEPHALON.] **— di•en•ce•phal′ic** (-sə-făl′ĭk) *adj.*

die-off (dī′ôf′, -ŏf′) *n.* The elimination of a species, population, or community of plants or animals as a result of natural causes.

Di•eppe (dē-ĕp′, dyĕp). A city of NE France on the English Channel N of Rouen; site of a disastrous Allied commando raid (Aug. 19, 1942). Pop. 35,957.

di•er•e•sis or **di•aer•e•sis** (dī-ĕr′ĭ-sĭs) *n., pl.* **-ses** (-sēz′). **1.** *Ling.* **a.** A mark (¨) placed over the second of two adjacent vowels to indicate that they are to be pronounced as separate sounds rather than a dipthong, as in *naïve.* **b.** A mark (¨) placed over a vowel, such as the final vowel in *Brontë,* to indicate that the vowel is not silent. **2.** *Poetry.* A break or pause in a line of verse when the end of a word and the end of a metric foot coincide. [LLat. *diaeresis* < Gk. *diairesis* < *diairein,* to divide : *dia-,* apart; see DIA- + *hairein,* to take.]

die•sel (dē′zəl, -səl) *n.* **1.** A diesel engine. **2.** A vehicle powered by a diesel engine.

Die•sel (dē′zəl), **Rudolf.** 1858–1913. German engineer who devised and patented (1892) an internal-combustion engine.

diesel engine *n.* An internal-combustion engine that uses the heat of highly compressed air to ignite a spray of fuel introduced after the compression stroke starts. [After Rudolf DIESEL.]

die•sink•er (dī′sĭng′kər) *n.* One that makes or engraves metal dies for stamping or shaping. **— die′sink′ing** *n.*

Di•es I•rae (dē′ās îr′ā′) *n.* A medieval Latin hymn describing Judgment Day, used in some masses for the dead. [Med.Lat. *Diēs īrae,* day of wrath (the first words of the hymn) : Lat. *diēs,* day + Lat. *īrae,* genitive of *īra,* wrath.]

di•e•sis (dī′ĭ-sĭs) *n., pl.* **-ses** (-sēz′). *Print.* See **double dagger.** [Med.Lat., semitone (shown by a double dagger) < Lat., quarter tone < Gk. *diesis,* letting through < *diienai,* to send through : *dia-,* dia- + *hienai,* to send; see **yē-*.**]

die•stock (dī′stŏk′) *n.* An apparatus for holding the dies that cut threads on screws, bolts, pipes, or rods.

di•es•trus (dī-ĕs′trəs) also **di•es•trum** (-trəm) *n.* The sexually inactive period of the estrous cycle. [DI(A)- + ESTRUS.] **— di•es′trous** *adj.*

di•et¹ (dī′ĭt) *n.* **1.** The usual food and drink of a person or animal. **2.** A regulated selection of foods, esp. as medically prescribed. **3.** Something used, enjoyed, or provided regularly: *a diet of detective novels.* — *v.* **-et•ed, -et•ing, -ets.** — *intr.* To eat and drink according to a regulated system, esp. so as to lose weight or control a medical condition. — *tr.* To regulate or prescribe food and drink for. [ME *diete* < OFr. < Lat. *diaeta,* way of living, diet < Gk. *diaita.*] **— di′et•er** *n.*

di•et² (dī′ĭt) *n.* **1.** A national or local legislative assembly in certain countries, such as Japan. **2.** A formal general assembly of the princes or estates of the Holy Roman Empire. [ME *diete,* day's journey, day for meeting, assembly < Med.Lat. *diēta,* alteration (influenced by Lat. *diēs,* day; see **deiw-***) of Lat. *diaeta,* daily routine. See DIET¹.]

di•e•tar•y (dī′ĭ-tĕr′ē) *adj.* Of or relating to diet. — *n., pl.* **-ies.** **1.** A system or regimen of dieting. **2.** A regulated daily food allowance. **— di′e•tar′i•ly** (-târ′ə-lē) *adv.*

dietary law *n. Judaism.* The body of regulations prescribing the kinds and combinations of food that may be eaten.

di•e•tet•ic (dī′ĭ-tĕt′ĭk) *adj.* **1.** Of or relating to diet or its regulation. **2.** Specially prepared or processed for restrictive diets. [LLat. *diaetēticus* < Gk. *diaitētikos* < *diaita,* diet. See DIET¹.] **— di′e•tet′i•cal•ly** *adv.*

di•e•tet•ics (dī′ĭ-tĕt′ĭks) *n. (used with a sing. v.)* The study of nutrition as it relates to health.

di•eth•yl•car•bam•a•zine citrate (dī-ĕth′əl-kär-băm′ə-zēn′) *n.* An anthelmintic agent, $C_{16}H_{29}O_8N_3$, used esp. in the treatment of ascariasis and filariasis. [DI-¹ + ETHYL + CARBAM(IC ACID) + (PIPER)AZINE.]

di•eth•yl ether (dī-ĕth′əl) *n.* See **ether** 2.

di•eth•yl•stil•bes•trol (dī-ĕth′əl-stĭl-bĕs′trôl′, -trōl′, -trŏl′) *n.* DES.

diethyl tol•u•am•ide (tŏl′yo͞o-ăm′īd′, -ĭd) *n.* Deet. [DI-¹ + ETHYL + TOLU(ENE) + AMIDE.]

di•e•ti•tian or **di•e•ti•cian** (dī′ĭ-tĭsh′ən) *n.* A person specializing in dietetics. [DIET¹ + *-itian* (alteration of -ICIAN).]

Die•trich (dē′trĭk, -trĭKH), **Marlene.** 1901–92. German-born Amer. actress and singer whose films include *The Blue Angel* (1930) and *Destry Rides Again* (1939).

dif. *abbr.* Difference.

diff. *abbr.* Difference.

dif•fer (dĭf′ər) *intr.v.* **-fered, -fer•ing, -fers.** **1.** To be dissimilar or unlike in nature, quality, amount, or form. **2.** To be of a different opinion; disagree. **3.** *Obsolete.* To quarrel; dispute. [ME *differren* < OFr. *differer* < Lat. *differre,* to differ, delay : *dis-,* apart; see DIS- + *ferre,* to carry; see **bher-¹*.**]

dif•fer•ence (dĭf′ər-əns, dĭf′rəns) *n.* **1.** The quality or condition of being unlike or dissimilar. **2.a.** An instance of disparity or unlikeness. **b.** A degree or amount by which things differ. **c.** A specific point distinguishing one thing from another. **3.** A noticeable change or effect. **4.a.** A disagreement or controversy. **b.** A cause of a disagreement or controversy. **5.** Discrimination in taste or choice; distinction. **6.** *Math.* **a.** The amount by which one quantity is greater or less than another. **b.** The amount that remains after one quantity is subtracted from another. **7.** *Archaic.* A distinct mark or peculiarity. — *tr.v.* **-enced, -enc•ing, -enc•es.** To distinguish.

Syns: *difference, dissimilarity, unlikeness, divergence, variation, distinction, discrepancy.* These nouns refer to a lack of correspondence or agreement. *Difference* is the most general: *differences in color and size; a difference of opinion. Dissimilarity* is difference between things otherwise alike or comparable: *a dissimilarity between the sisters' personalities. Unlikeness* usually implies greater and more obvious difference: *an unlikeness among their teaching styles. Divergence* suggests an increasing difference: *points of divergence between British and American English. Variation* occurs between things of the same class or species; often it refers to modification of something original, prescribed, or typical: *variations in temperature; a variation in shape. Distinction* often means a difference in detail, determinable only by close inspection: *the distinction between "good" and "excellent." A discrepancy* is a difference between things that should correspond or match: *a discrepancy between words and actions.*

dif•fer•ent (dĭf′ər-ənt, dĭf′rənt) *adj.* **1.** Unlike in form, quality, amount, or nature; dissimilar. **2.** Distinct or separate: *That's a different issue.* **3.** Various or assorted: *interviewed different people.* **4.** Differing from all others; unusual. [ME < OFr. < Lat. *differēns, different-,* pr.part. of *differre,* to differ. See DIFFER.] **— dif′fer•ent•ly** *adv.* **— dif′fer•ent•ness** *n.*

Usage Note: *Different from* and *different than* are both common in British and American English. Critics since the 18th century have singled out *different than* as incorrect, though it is well attested in the works of reputable writers. Where the comparison is drawn directly between two persons or things, *from* is usually the safer choice: *My book is different from* (not *than*) *yours.* But *different than* is more acceptably used, particularly in American usage, where the object of comparison is expressed by a full clause: *The campus is different than it was 20 years ago* (or *The campus is different from how it was 20 years ago*). • The construction *different to* is chiefly British.

dif•fer•en•ti•a (dĭf′ə-rĕn′shē-ə, -shə) *n., pl.* **-ti•ae** (-shē-ē′). An attribute that distinguishes one entity from another, esp. one species from others of the same genus. [Lat., difference < *differēns, different-,* pr.part. of *differre,* to differ. See DIFFER.]

dif•fer•en•tia•ble (dĭf′ə-rĕn′shə-bəl, -shē-ə-) *adj.* **1.** That can be differentiated: *differentiable species.* **2.** *Math.* Possessing a derivative. **— dif′fer•en′tia•bil′i•ty** *n.*

dif•fer•en•tial (dĭf′ə-rĕn′shəl) *adj.* **1.** Of, relating to, or showing a difference. **2.** Being or making a difference; distinctive. **3.** Dependent on or using a specific difference or distinction. **4.** *Math.* Of or relating to differentiation. **5.** Involving differences in speed or direction of motion. — *n.* **1.** *Math.* **a.** An infinitesimal increment in a variable. **b.** The product of the derivative of a function containing one variable multiplied by the increment of the independent variable. **2.** Differential gear. **3.** A difference in wage rate or in price. **— dif′fer•en′tial•ly** *adv.*

differential calculus *n. Math.* **1.** The mathematics of the variation of a function with respect to changes in independent variables. **2.** The study of slopes of curves, accelerations, maxima, and minima by means of derivatives and differentials.

differential coefficient *n. Math.* See **derivative** 3.

differential equation *n. Math.* An equation that expresses a relationship between functions and their derivatives.

differential gear *n.* An arrangement of gears in an epicyclic train permitting the rotation of two shafts at different speeds, used on the rear axle of automotive vehicles to allow different rates of wheel rotation on curves.

differential windlass *n.* A hoisting device that has two drums of different sizes on the same axis and a line wound on the larger and unwound from the smaller for extra lifting power.

dif•fer•en•ti•ate (dĭf′ə-rĕn′shē-āt′) *v.* **-at•ed, -at•ing, -ates.** — *tr.* **1.** To constitute the distinction between. **2.** To perceive or show the difference in or between; discriminate. **3.** To make different by alteration or modification. **4.** *Math.* To calculate the derivative or differential of (a function). — *intr.* **1.** To become distinct or specialized. **2.** To make distinctions; discriminate. **3.** *Biol.* To undergo a progressive developmental change to a more specialized form or function. Used esp. of embryonic cells or tissues. **— dif′fer•en′ti•a′tion** *n.*

dif•fi•cult (dĭf′ĭ-kŭlt′, -kəlt) *adj.* **1.** Hard to do or accomplish; demanding considerable effort or skill; arduous. **2.** Hard to endure; trying. **3.** Hard to comprehend or solve. **4.** Hard to please, satisfy, or manage. **5.** Hard to persuade or convince; stubborn. [ME, back-formation < *difficulte,* difficulty. See DIFFICULTY.] **— dif′fi•cult′ly** *adv.*

dif•fi•cul•ty (dĭf′ĭ-kŭl′tē, -kəl-) *n., pl.* **-ties.** **1.** The condition or quality of being difficult. **2.** Something not easily done, comprehended, or solved. **3.** A troublesome or embarrassing state of affairs, esp. of financial affairs. Often used in the plural. **4.** A laborious effort; a struggle; trouble. **5.** A disa-

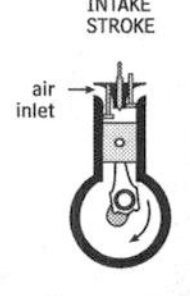

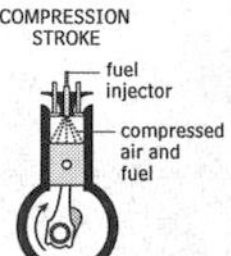

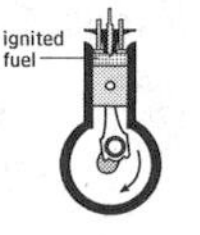

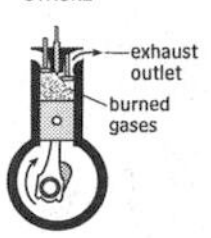

diesel engine

ă pat	oi boy
ā pay	ou out
âr care	o͝o to͝ok
ä father	o͞o bo͞ot
ĕ pet	ŭ cut
ē be	ûr urge
ĭ pit	th thin
ī pie	*th* this
îr pier	hw which
ŏ pot	zh vision
ō toe	ə about, item
ô paw	

Stress marks:
′ (primary);
′ (secondary), as in **dictionary** (dĭk′shə-nĕr′ē)

greement or dispute. **6.** Reluctance or an objection; unwillingness. [ME *difficulte* < OFr. *dificulte* < Lat. *difficultās* < *difficilis,* difficult : *dis-,* dis- + *facilis,* easy; see **dhē-***.]

Syns: *difficulty, hardship, rigor, vicissitude.* The central meaning shared by these nouns is "something that requires great effort to overcome": *grappling with financial difficulties; a life of hardship; undergoing the rigors of prison; withstood the vicissitudes of an army career.*

dif•fi•dence (dĭf′ĭ-dəns, -dĕns′) *n.* The quality or state of being diffident; timidity or shyness.

dif•fi•dent (dĭf′ĭ-dənt, -dĕnt′) *adj.* **1.** Lacking or marked by a lack of self-confidence; shy and timid. See Syns at **shy**[1]. **2.** Reserved in manner. [ME < Lat. *diffīdēns, diffīdent-,* pr.part. of *diffīdere,* to mistrust : *dis-,* dis- + *fīdere,* to trust; see **bheidh-***.] **—dif′fi•dent•ly** *adv.*

dif•fract (dĭ-frăkt′) *intr. & tr.v.* **-fract•ed, -fract•ing, -fracts.** To undergo or cause to undergo diffraction. [Back-formation < DIFFRACTION.] **—dif•frac′tive** *adj.* **—dif•frac′tive•ly** *adv.* **—dif•frac′tive•ness** *n.*

dif•frac•tion (dĭ-frăk′shən) *n.* Change in the directions and intensities of a group of waves after passing by an obstacle or through an aperture. [NLat. *diffrāctiō, diffrāctiōn-* < Lat. *diffrāctus,* p.part. of *diffringere* : *dis-,* apart; see DIS- + *frangere,* to break; see **bhreg-***.]

diffraction grating *n.* A usu. glass or polished metal surface having a large number of very fine parallel grooves or slits cut in the surface in order to diffract light.

dif•fuse (dĭ-fyo͞oz′) *v.* **-fused, -fus•ing, -fus•es.** *—tr.* **1.** To pour out and cause to spread freely. **2.** To spread about or scatter; disseminate. **3.** To make less brilliant; soften. *—intr.* **1.** To become widely dispersed; spread out. **2.** *Phys.* To undergo diffusion. *—adj.* (dĭ-fyo͞os′). **1.** Widely spread or scattered; not concentrated. **2.** Characterized by verbosity; wordy. [< ME, dispersed < AN *diffus* < Lat. *diffūsus,* p.part. of *diffundere,* to spread : *dis-,* out, apart; see DIS- + *fundere,* to pour; see **gheu-***.] **—dif•fuse′ly** (-fyo͞os′lē) *adv.* **—dif•fuse′ness** (-fyo͞os′nĭs) *n.*

dif•fus•er (dĭ-fyo͞o′zər) *n.* **1.** One that diffuses, as: **a.** A light fixture that spreads light evenly. **b.** A medium that scatters light, used in photography to soften shadows. **c.** A device placed in front of a loudspeaker diaphragm to diffuse the sound waves. **2.** A flow passage in a wind tunnel that decelerates a stream of gas or liquid from a high to a low velocity.

dif•fus•i•ble (dĭ-fyo͞o′zə-bəl) *adj.* Capable of diffusing or of undergoing diffusion: *diffusible dyes.* **—dif•fus′i•bly** *adv.*

dif•fu•sion (dĭ-fyo͞o′zhən) *n.* **1.** The process of diffusing or the condition of being diffused. **2.** Needless profusion of words; prolixity. **3.** *Phys.* **a.** The scattering of incident light by reflection from a rough surface. **b.** The transmission of light through a translucent material. **c.** The spontaneous intermingling of the particles of two or more substances as a result of random thermal motion. **—dif•fu′sion•al** *adj.*

dif•fu•sive (dĭ-fyo͞o′sĭv, -zĭv) *adj.* Characterized by diffusion. **—dif•fu′sive•ly** *adv.* **—dif•fu′sive•ness** *n.*

dig (dĭg) *v.* **dug** (dŭg), **dig•ging, digs.** *—tr.* **1.** To break up, turn over, or remove (earth, for example), as with a shovel. **2.** To make or form by removing earth or other material: *dug my way out of the snow.* **3.** To obtain by digging: *dig coal.* **4.** To learn or discover by careful research or investigation: *dug out the real facts.* **5.** To force down and into something; thrust. **6.** To poke or prod. **7.** *Slang.* **a.** To understand fully: *Do you dig me?* **b.** To like, enjoy, or appreciate. **c.** To take notice of. *—intr.* **1.** To loosen, turn over, or remove earth or other material. **2.** To make one's way by or as if by pushing aside or removing material. **3.** *Slang.* To have understanding. *—n.* **1.** A poke or thrust. **2.** A sarcastic, taunting remark; a gibe. **3.** An archaeological excavation. **4. digs.** *Chiefly British.* Lodgings. ***—phrasal verb.*** **dig in. 1.** To dig trenches for protection. **2.** To hold on stubbornly, as to a position; entrench oneself. **3.a.** To begin to work intensively. **b.** To begin to eat heartily. [ME *diggen;* perh. akin to OFr. *digue,* dike, trench. See **dhīgʷ-***.]

dig. *abbr.* Digest.

di•gam•ma (dī-găm′ə) *n.* A letter occurring in certain early forms of Greek and transliterated in English as *w.* [Lat. < Gk. : *di-,* two; see DI-[1] + *gamma,* gamma; see GAMMA.]

dig•a•my (dĭg′ə-mē) *n.* Remarriage after the death or divorce of one's first husband or wife. **—dig′a•mous** (-məs) *adj.*

di•gas•tric (dī-găs′trĭk) *Anat.* *—adj.* Having two fleshy ends connected by a thinner tendinous portion. Used of certain muscles. *—n.* A muscle of the lower jaw that elevates the hyoid bone and assists in lowering the jaw.

di•gest (dī-jĕst′, dĭ-) *v.* **-gest•ed, -gest•ing, -gests.** *—tr.* **1.** *Physiol.* To convert (food) into simpler chemical compounds that can be absorbed and assimilated by the body, as by chemical and muscular action in the alimentary canal. **2.** To absorb or assimilate mentally. **3.a.** To organize into a systematic arrangement, usu. by summarizing or classifying. **b.** To condense or abridge (a written work). **4.** To endure or bear patiently. **5.** *Chem.* To soften or disintegrate by means of chemical action, heat, or moisture. *—intr.* **1.** *Physiol.* **a.** To become assimilated into the body. **b.** To assimilate food substances. **2.** *Chem.* To undergo exposure to heat, liquids, or chemical agents. *—n.* (dī′jĕst′). **1.** A collection of previously published material, such as articles, usu. edited or condensed. **2.** *Law.* A systematic arrangement of statutes or court decisions. **3.** A periodical containing literary abridgments or other condensed works. **4. Digest.** See **pandect** 3. [ME *digesten* < Lat. *dīgerere, dīgest-,* to separate, arrange : *dī-, dis-,* apart; see DIS- + *gerere,* to carry.]

dig
Archaeological dig in Iraq

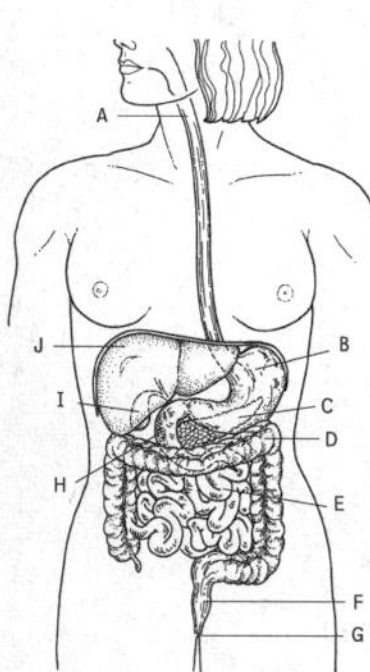

digestive system
A. Esophagus
B. Stomach
C. Pancreas
D. Large intestine
E. Small intestine
F. Rectum
G. Anus
H. Duodenum
I. Gallbladder
J. Liver

di•gest•er (dī-jĕs′tər, dĭ-) *n.* **1.** One that makes a digest. **2.** *Chem.* A vessel in which substances are softened or decomposed, usu. for further processing.

di•gest•i•ble (dī-jĕs′tə-bəl, dĭ-) *adj.* Easy to digest. **—di•gest′i•bil′i•ty, di•gest′i•ble•ness** *n.* **—di•gest′i•bly** *adv.*

di•ges•tion (dī-jĕs′chən, dĭ-) *n.* **1.** *Physiol.* **a.** The process by which food is converted into substances that can be absorbed and assimilated by the body. **b.** The result of this process. **c.** The ability to digest food. **2.** The process of decomposing organic matter in sewage by bacteria. **3.** Assimilation of ideas or information; understanding.

di•ges•tive (dī-jĕs′tĭv, dĭ-) *adj.* **1.** Relating to or aiding digestion. **2.** Serving to digest food. *—n.* A substance that aids digestion. **—di•ges′tive•ly** *adv.* **—di•ges′tive•ness** *n.*

digestive gland *n.* A gland, such as the pancreas, that secretes into the alimentary canal substances necessary for digestion.

digestive system *n.* The alimentary canal and digestive glands regarded as an integrated system responsible for the ingestion, digestion, and absorption of food.

digestive tract *n.* See **alimentary canal**.

dig•ger (dĭg′ər) *n.* **1.a.** One that digs. **b.** A tool or machine used for digging or excavating. **2.** *Informal.* A soldier from New Zealand or Australia in World War I.

digger wasp *n.* Any of various wasps of the family Sphecidae that burrow into the ground to build their nests.

dig•gings (dĭg′ĭngz) *pl.n.* **1.** An excavation site, as of ore. **2.** Excavated materials. **3.** *Chiefly British.* Rooms; lodgings.

dight (dīt) *tr.v.* **dight** or **dight•ed, dight•ing, dights.** *Archaic.* To dress; adorn. [ME *dighten* < OE *dihtan,* to arrange < Lat. *dictāre,* to dictate. See DICTATE.]

dig•it (dĭj′ĭt) *n.* **1.a.** A human finger or toe. **b.** A corresponding part in other vertebrates. **2.** A unit of length derived from the breadth of a finger and equal to about ¾ of an inch (2.0 centimeters). **3.a.** One of the ten Arabic number symbols, 0 through 9. **b.** Such a symbol used in a system of numeration. [ME < Lat. *digitus,* finger, toe. See **deik-***.]

dig•i•tal (dĭj′ĭ-tl) *adj.* **1.** Of, relating to, or resembling a digit, esp. a finger. **2.** Operated or done with the fingers. **3.** Having digits. **4.** Expressed in digits, esp. for use by a computer. **5.** Using or giving a reading in digits: *a digital clock.* *—n.* A key played with the finger, as on a piano. **—dig′i•tal•ly** *adv.*

digital computer *n.* *Comp. Sci.* A computer that performs calculations and logical operations with quantities represented as digits, usu. in the binary number system.

dig•i•tal•in (dĭj′ĭ-tăl′ĭn) *n.* **1.** A white crystalline glycoside, $C_{36}H_{56}O_{14}$, obtained from the seeds of the common foxglove. **2.** One of several mixtures of digitalis glycosides extracted from common foxglove leaves or seeds. [DIGITAL(IS) + -IN.]

dig•i•tal•is (dĭj′ĭ-tăl′ĭs) *n.* **1.** A plant of the genus *Digitalis,* which includes the foxgloves. **2.** A drug prepared from the seeds and dried leaves of this plant, used in medicine as a cardiac stimulant. [Lat. *digitālis,* of a finger (from the finger-shaped corollas of foxglove) < *digitus,* finger. See DIGIT.]

dig•i•tal•ize (dĭj′ĭ-tl-īz′) *tr.v.* **-ized, -iz•ing, -iz•es. 1.** To administer digitalis in a dosage sufficient to achieve the maximum therapeutic effect without producing toxic symptoms. **2.** To digitize. **—dig′i•tal•i•za′tion** (-ĭ-zā′shən) *n.*

digital recording *n.* **1.** A method of recording in which portions of sound waves are converted into numbers and stored for later reproduction. **2.** A record, tape, or disk that is recorded using this process.

dig•i•tate (dĭj′ĭ-tāt′) also **dig•i•tat•ed** (-tā′tĭd) *adj.* **1.** Having digits or fingerlike projections. **2.** *Bot.* Having parts arising from a common point; palmate. **—dig′i•tate′ly** *adv.*

dig•i•ta•tion (dĭj′ĭ-tā′shən) *n.* **1.** Division into fingerlike parts. **2.** A fingerlike part or process.

dig•i•ti•grade (dĭj′ĭ-tĭ-grād′) *adj.* Relating to an animal, such as a horse or dog, whose weight is borne on the toes. [Fr. : Lat. *digitus,* toe; see DIGIT + Lat. *gradus,* step; see GRADE.]

dig•i•tize (dĭj′ĭ-tīz′) *tr.v.* **-tized, -tiz•ing, -tiz•es.** To put (data, for example) into digital form. **—dig′i•ti•za′tion** (-tĭ-zā′shən) *n.* **—dig′i•tiz′er** *n.*

dig•i•tox•in (dĭj′ĭ-tŏk′sĭn) *n.* A highly active glycoside, $C_{41}H_{64}O_{13}$, derived from digitalis and prescribed in the treatment of certain cardiac conditions. [DIGI(TALIS) + TOXIN.]

di•glos•si•a (dī-glŏs′ē-ə, glô′sē-ə) *n.* A situation in which complementary social functions are distributed between two varieties of a language, a prestigious, formal variety and a common, colloquial variety. [< Gk. *diglōssos,* speaking two languages : *di-,* two; see DI-[1] + *glōssa,* language.]

di•glyc•er•ide (dī-glĭs′ə-rīd′) *n.* An ester of two fatty acids and glycerol.

dig•ni•fied (dĭg′nə-fīd′) *adj.* Having or expressing dignity. **—dig′ni•fied′ly** (-fīd′lē, -fī′ĭd-lē) *adv.*

dig•ni•fy (dĭg′nə-fī′) *tr.v.* **-fied, -fy•ing, -fies. 1.** To confer dignity or honor on; give distinction to. **2.** To raise the status of (something unworthy or lowly); make honorable. [ME *dignifien* < OFr. *dignifier* < LLat. *dignificāre* : Lat. *dignus*, worthy; see **dek-*** + Lat. *-ficāre*, -fy.]

dig•ni•tar•y (dĭg′nĭ-tĕr′ē) *n.*, *pl.* **-ies.** A person of high rank or position.

dig•ni•ty (dĭg′nĭ-tē) *n.*, *pl.* **-ties. 1.** The quality or state of deserving esteem or respect. **2.** Inherent nobility and worth. **3.a.** Poise and self-respect. **b.** Stateliness and formality in manner and appearance. **4.** The respect and honor associated with an important position. **5.** A high office or rank. **6. dignities.** The ceremonial symbols and observances attached to high office. **7.** *Archaic.* A dignitary. [ME *dignite* < OFr. < Lat. *dignitās* < *dignus*, worthy. See **dek-***.]

dig•ox•in (dĭj-ŏk′sĭn) *n.* A cardiac glycoside, $C_{41}H_{64}O_{14}$, obtained from the leaves of a foxglove, *Digitalis lanata*, with pharmacological effects similar to digitalis. [DIG(ITALIS) + (T)OXIN.]

di•graph (dī′grăf′) *n.* **1.** A pair of letters representing a single speech sound, such as the *ph* in *pheasant.* **2.** A single character consisting of two letters run together and representing a single sound, such as Old English *æ.* **—di•graph′ic** (dī-grăf′ĭk) *adj.*

di•gress (dī-grĕs′, dĭ-) *intr.v.* **-gressed, -gress•ing, -gress•es.** To turn aside, esp. from the main subject in writing or speaking; stray. See Syns at **swerve.** [Lat. *digredī, dīgress-* : *dī-, dis-*, apart; see DIS- + *gradī*, to go; see **ghredh-***.]

di•gres•sion (dī-grĕsh′ən, dĭ-) *n.* **1.** The act of digressing. **2.** An instance of digressing, esp. a written or spoken passage with no bearing on the main topic. **—di•gres′sion•al** *adj.*

di•gres•sive (dī-grĕs′ĭv, dĭ-) *adj.* Marked by digressions; rambling. **—di•gres′sive•ly** *adv.* **—di•gres′sive•ness** *n.*

di•he•dral (dī-hē′drəl) *adj. Math.* **1.** Formed by or having two plane faces; two-sided. **2.** Relating to, having, or forming a dihedral angle. —*n.* **1.** *Math.* A dihedral angle. **2.** *Aeronautics.* The upward or downward inclination of an aircraft wing from true horizontal.

dihedral angle *n.* **1.** *Math.* The angle formed by two intersecting planes. **2.** *Aeronautics.* The dihedral of an aircraft wing.

di•hy•brid (dī-hī′brĭd) *n. Genet.* The hybrid of parents that differ at only two gene loci, for which each parent is homozygous with different alleles.

di•hy•dric (dī-hī′drĭk) *adj.* Containing two hydroxyl radicals.

di•hy•drox•y•phen•yl•al•a•nine (dī′hī-drŏk′sē-fĕn′əl-ăl′ə-nēn′, -fē′nəl-) *n.* Dopa.

Di•jon (dē-zhôN′). A city of E France N of Lyons; noted for its foodstuffs. Pop. 140,942.

dik-dik (dĭk′dĭk′) *n.* Any of several very small African antelopes of the genus *Madoqua.* [Perh. of East African orig.]

dike[1] also **dyke** (dīk) —*n.* **1.a.** An embankment of earth and rock built to prevent floods. **b.** *Chiefly British.* A low wall, often of sod, dividing or enclosing lands. **2.** A barrier blocking a passage, esp. for protection. **3.** A raised causeway. **4.** A ditch; a channel. **5.** *Geol.* A long mass of igneous rock that cuts across the structure of adjacent rock. —*tr.v.* **diked, dik•ing, dikes** also **dyked, dyk•ing, dykes. 1.** To protect, enclose, or provide with a dike. **2.** To drain with dikes or ditches. [ME < OE *dīc*, trench; see **dhīgʷ-*** and < ON *dīki*, ditch.] **—dik′er** *n.*

dike[2] (dīk) *n. Offensive Slang.* Var. of **dyke[2]**.

dik•tat (dĭk-tät′) *n.* **1.** A harsh, unilaterally imposed settlement with a defeated party. **2.** An authoritative or dogmatic statement or decree. [Ger. < Lat. *dictātum* < neut. p.part. of *dictāre*, to dictate. See DICTATE.]

dil. *abbr.* Dilute.

Di•lan•tin (dī-lăn′tĭn). A trademark used for phenytoin.

di•lap•i•date (dĭ-lăp′ĭ-dāt′) *tr. & intr.v.* **-dat•ed, -dat•ing, -dates. 1.** To bring or fall into a state of partial ruin, decay, or disrepair. **2.** *Archaic.* To squander; waste. [Lat. *dīlapidāre, dīlapidāt-*, to demolish, destroy : *dī-, dis-*, apart; see DIS- + *lapidāre*, to throw stones (< *lapis, lapid-*, stone; see LAPIDARIAN).] **—di•lap′i•da′tion** *n.*

di•lap•i•dat•ed (dĭ-lăp′ĭ-dā′tĭd) *adj.* Having fallen into a state of disrepair or deterioration; broken-down and shabby.

di•la•tan•cy (dī-lāt′n-sē, dĭ-) *n.*, *pl.* **-cies. 1.** The increase in volume of a granular substance when its shape is changed, caused by greater distance between its component particles. **2.** The phenomenon whereby a viscous substance solidifies under pressure.

di•la•tant (dī-lāt′nt, dĭ-) *adj.* **1.** Tending to dilate; dilating. **2.** Exhibiting dilatancy. —*n.* A dilator.

dil•a•ta•tion (dĭl′ə-tā′shən, dī′lə-) *n.* **1.a.** The act or process of expanding; dilation. **b.** The condition of being expanded or stretched. **c.** A dilated formation or part. **2.** *Medic.* The condition of being abnormally enlarged or dilated, as of an organ or a tubular structure. **3.** Lengthy explanation or elaboration of a subject in writing or speech. **—dil′a•ta′tion•al** *adj.*

dilatation and curettage *n.* Dilation and curettage.

dil•a•ta•tor (dĭl′ə-tā′tər, dī′lə-) *n.* A dilator.

di•late (dī-lāt′, dī′lāt′) *v.* **-lat•ed, -lat•ing, -lates.** —*tr.* To make wider or larger. —*intr.* **1.** To become wider or larger. **2.** To speak or write at great length; expatiate. [ME *dilaten* < OFr. *dilater* < Lat. *dīlātāre*, to enlarge : *dī-, dis-*, apart; see DIS- + *lātus*, wide.] **—di•lat′a•bil′i•ty** *n.* **—di•lat′a•ble** *adj.* **—di•lat′a•bly** *adv.* **—di•la′tive** *adj.*

di•lat•ed (dī-lā′tĭd, dī′lā′-) *adj.* **1.** Having been widened; expanded. **2.** Distended. **—di•lat′ed•ness** *n.*

di•la•tion (dī-lā′shən, dĭ-) *n.* **1.** The act of expanding or the state of being expanded. **2.** *Medic.* See **dilatation** 2.

dilation and curettage *n.* A surgical procedure in which the cervix is expanded with a dilator and the uterine lining scraped with a curette, performed to diagnose and treat certain uterine conditions.

dil•a•tom•e•ter (dĭl′ə-tŏm′ĭ-tər, dī′lə-) *n.* An instrument used to measure thermal expansion and dilation in solids and liquids. [DILATE + -METER.] **—dil′a•to•met′ric** (-tə-mĕt′rĭk) *adj.* **—dil′a•tom′e•try** *n.*

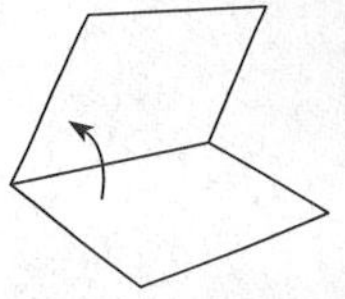
dihedral angle

di•la•tor (dī-lā′tər, dī′lā′-, dĭ-lā′-) *n.* **1.** A muscle that dilates a body part, such as a blood vessel. **2.** An instrument that dilates a body part, such as a cavity, canal, or orifice.

dil•a•to•ry (dĭl′ə-tôr′ē, -tōr′ē) *adj.* **1.** Intended to delay. **2.** Tending to postpone or delay. [ME *dilatorie* < Lat. *dīlātōrius* < *dīlātor*, delayer < *dīlātus*, p.part. of *differre*, to delay : *dī-, dis-*, apart; see DIS- + *lātus*, carried; see **telə-***.] **—dil′a•to′ri•ly** *adv.* **—dil′a•to′ri•ness** *n.*

dil•do also **dil•doe** (dĭl′dō) *n.*, *pl.* **-dos** also **-does.** An object used as a substitute for an erect penis. [?]

di•lem•ma (dĭ-lĕm′ə) *n.* **1.** A situation that requires a choice between equally unfavorable or mutually exclusive options. **2.** *Usage Problem.* A problem that seems to defy a satisfactory solution. **3.** *Logic.* An argument that presents a choice of two or more alternatives, each of which contradicts the original contention and is conclusive. [LLat. < Gk. *dilēmma*, ambiguous proposition : *di-*, two; see DI-[1] + *lēmma*, proposition; see LEMMA[1].] **—dil′em•mat′ic** (dĭl′ə-măt′ĭk) *adj.*

Usage Note: In its primary sense *dilemma* denotes a situation in which a choice must be made between alternative courses of action or argument. Although citational evidence attests to widespread use of the term meaning simply "problem" or "predicament" and involving no issue of choice, 74 percent of the Usage Panel rejected the sentence *Juvenile drug abuse is the great dilemma of the 1980's.*

dik-dik

dil•et•tante (dĭl′ĭ-tänt′, dĭl′ĭ-tänt′, -tän′tē, -tănt′, -tăn′tē) *n.*, *pl.* **-tantes** also **-tan•ti** (-tän′tē, -tăn′-). **1.** A dabbler in an art or a field of knowledge. **2.** A lover of the fine arts; a connoisseur. —*adj.* Superficial; amateurish. [Ital., arts lover < pr.part. of *dilettare*, to delight < Lat. *dēlectāre.* See DELIGHT.] **—dil′et•tan′tish** *adj.* **—dil′et•tan′tism** *n.*

dil•i•gence[1] (dĭl′ə-jəns) *n.* **1.** Earnest, persistent application to an undertaking; assiduity. **2.** Attentive care; heedfulness.

dil•i•gence[2] (dĭl′ə-jəns, dē′lē-zhäns′) *n.* A large stagecoach. [Fr. < *carrosse de) diligence*, speed (coach) < OFr., dispatch < Lat. *dīligentia* < *dīligēns, dīligent-*, diligent. See DILIGENT.]

dil•i•gent (dĭl′ə-jənt) *adj.* Marked by persevering, painstaking effort. [ME < OFr. < Lat. *dīligēns, dīligent-*, pr.part. of *dīligere*, to esteem, love : *dī-, dis-*, apart; see DIS- + *legere*, to choose; see **leg-***.] **—dil′i•gent•ly** *adv.*

dill (dĭl) *n.* **1.** An aromatic herb *(Anethum graveolens)* native to Eurasia and having finely dissected leaves and small yellow flowers clustered in umbels. **2.** The leaves or seeds of this plant, used as a seasoning. [ME *dile* < OE.]

dill
Anethum graveolens

dill pickle *n.* A pickled cucumber flavored with dill.

dil•ly (dĭl′ē) *n.*, *pl.* **-lies.** *Slang.* One that is remarkable or extraordinary, as in size or quality: *had a dilly of a fight.* [Obsolete *dilly*, delightful, alteration of DELIGHTFUL.]

dil•ly-dal•ly (dĭl′ē-dăl′ē) *intr.v.* **-lied, -lying, -lies.** To waste time, esp. in indecision; dawdle or vacillate. [Redup. of DALLY.] **—dil′ly-dal′li•er** *n.*

dil•u•ent (dĭl′yo͞o-ənt) *adj.* Serving to dilute. —*n. Chem.* An inert substance used to dilute. [Lat. *dīluēns, dīluent-*, pr.part. of *dīluere*, to dilute. See DILUTE.]

di•lute (dī-lo͞ot′, dĭ-) *tr.v.* **-lut•ed, -lut•ing, -lutes. 1.** To make thinner or less concentrated by adding a liquid. **2.** To lessen the force, strength, purity, or brilliance of, esp. by admixture. —*adj.* Weakened; diluted. [Lat. *dīluere, dīlūt-* : *dī-, dis-*, apart, away; see DIS- + *-luere*, to wash (< *lavere*; see **leu(ə)-***).] **—di•lut′er, di•lut′or** *n.* **—di•lu′tive** *adj.*

di•lu•tion (dī-lo͞o′shən, dĭ-) *n.* **1.a.** The process of making weaker or less concentrated. **b.** A dilute or weakened condition. **2.** A diluted substance. **3.** A decrease in the equity position of a share of stock because of the issuance of additional shares.

di•lu•vi•al (dĭ-lo͞o′vē-əl) also **di•lu•vi•an** (-ən) *adj.* Of, relating to, or produced by a flood. [LLat. *dīluviālis* < Lat. *dīluvium*, flood < *dīluere*, to wash away. See DILUTE.]

dim (dĭm) *adj.* **dim•mer, dim•mest. 1.a.** Lacking in brightness: *a dim room.* **b.** Emitting only a small amount of light; faint. **2.** Lacking luster; dull and subdued. **3.a.** Faintly outlined; indistinct. **b.** Obscure to the mind or the senses: *a dim recollection.* See Syns at **dark. 4.** Lacking sharpness or clarity of understanding or perception. **5.** Lacking keenness or vigor. **6.** Negative, unfavorable, or disapproving. —*tr. & intr.v.* **dimmed, dim•ming, dims.** To make or become dim. —*n.*

ă **pat**	oi **boy**
ā **pay**	ou **out**
âr **care**	o͝o **took**
ä **father**	o͞o **boot**
ĕ **pet**	ŭ **cut**
ē **be**	ûr **urge**
ĭ **pit**	th **thin**
ī **pie**	*th* **this**
îr **pier**	hw **which**
ŏ **pot**	zh **vision**
ō **toe**	ə **about,**
ô **paw**	**item**

Stress marks:
′ (primary);
′ (secondary), as in
dictionary (dĭk′shə-nĕr′ē)

1.a. A parking light on a motor vehicle. **b.** Low beam. **2.** *Archaic.* Dusk. [ME < OE.] — **dim′ly** *adv.* — **dim′ness** *n.*

dim. *abbr.* **1.** Dimension. **2.** Diminished. **3.** *Mus.* Diminuendo. **4.** Diminutive.

Di•Mag•gio (də-mä′zhē-ō, -măj′ē-ō), **Joseph Paul.** "Jolting Joe." b. 1914. Amer. baseball player considered the best all-around player ever at center field.

dime (dīm) *n.* **1.** A coin of the United States or Canada worth ten cents. **2.** *Slang.* A dime bag. — ***idioms.* a dime a dozen.** Overabundant; commonplace. **on a dime.** At a precise point; within a narrowly defined area: *a sports car that stops on a dime.* [ME, tenth part < OFr. *disme* < Lat. *decima (pars),* tenth (part) < *decem,* ten. See **dekm̥***.]

dime bag *n. Slang.* A specified amount of an unlawful drug, packaged and sold for a fixed price, usu. about ten dollars.

di•men•hy•dri•nate (dī′mĕn-hī′drə-nāt′) *n.* An antihistamine, $C_{24}H_{28}ClN_5O_3$, used to treat motion sickness and allergies. [DIME(THYL) + (AMI)N(E) + *hydrinate* (HYDR(O)- + (AM)IN(E) + ATE[2]).]

dime novel *n.* A melodramatic novel of romance or adventure, usu. in paperback. [After the *Dime Book Series,* pub. by Erastus Flavel Beadle.] — **dime novelist** *n.*

di•men•sion (dĭ-mĕn′shən, dī-) *n.* **1.** A measure of spatial extent, esp. width, height, or length. **2.** Extent or magnitude; scope. Often used in the plural. **3.** Aspect; element. **4.** *Math.* **a.** One of the least number of independent coordinates required to specify uniquely a point in space or in space and time. **b.** The range of such a coordinate. **5.** *Phys.* A physical property, such as mass, length, time, or a combination thereof, regarded as a fundamental measure or as one of a set of fundamental measures of a physical quantity. — *tr.v.* **-sioned, -sion•ing, -sions. 1.** To cut or shape to specified dimensions. **2.** To mark with specified dimensions. [ME *dimensioun* < Lat. *dīmēnsiō, dīmēnsiōn-,* extent < *dīmēnsus,* p.part. of *dīmētīrī,* to measure out : *dī-, dis-,* dis- + *mētīrī,* to measure; see **mē-**[2]*.] — **di•men′sion•al** *adj.* — **di•men′sion•al′i•ty** (-shə-năl′ĭ-tē) *n.* — **di•men′sion•al•ly** *adv.*

Joe DiMaggio

di•mer (dī′mər) *n.* **1.** A molecule consisting of two identical simpler molecules. **2.** A chemical compound consisting of dimers. [DI-[1] + (POLY)MER.] — **di•mer′ic** (dī-mĕr′ĭk) *adj.*

di•mer•cap•rol (dī′mər-kăp′rôl, -rōl, -rŏl) *n.* An oily viscous liquid, $C_3H_8OS_2$, used as an antidote for poisoning caused by lewisite, organic arsenic compounds, and heavy metals including gold. [DI-[1] + MERCAP(TAN) + (P)R(OPANE) + -OL(E).]

dim•er•ous (dĭm′ər-əs) *adj.* **1.** Consisting of two parts or segments, as the tarsus in certain insects. **2.** *Bot.* Having flower parts in sets of two. — **dim′er•ism** *n.*

dime store *n.* See **five-and-ten.**

dim•e•ter (dĭm′ĭ-tər) *n.* A line of verse consisting of two metrical feet. [LLat. < Gk. *dimetros,* having two meters : *di-,* two; see DI-[1] + *metron,* meter; see METER[1].]

di•meth•yl (dī-mĕth′əl) *n.* An organic compound, esp. ethane, containing two methyl groups.

di•meth•yl•ni•tros•a•mine (dī-mĕth′əl-nī-trō′sə-mēn′, -nī′trō-săm′ĭn) *n.* A carcinogenic nitrosamine, $C_2H_6N_2O$, that occurs in tobacco smoke and certain foods.

di•meth•yl•sulf•ox•ide (dī-mĕth′əl-sŭl-fŏk′sīd′) *n.* DMSO.

dimin. *abbr.* **1.** *Mus.* Diminuendo. **2.** Diminutive.

di•min•ish (dĭ-mĭn′ĭsh) *v.* **-ished, -ish•ing, -ish•es.** — *tr.* **1.a.** To make smaller or less or to cause to appear so. **b.** To detract from the authority, reputation, or prestige of. **2.** To cause to taper. **3.** *Mus.* To reduce (a perfect or minor interval) by a semitone. — *intr.* **1.** To become smaller or less. See Syns at **decrease. 2.** To taper. [ME *diminishen,* blend of *diminuen,* to lessen (< OFr. *diminuer* < Lat. *dīminuere,* var. of *dēminuere* : *dē-,* de- + *minuere,* to lessen) and *minishen,* to reduce (< OFr. *minuiser* < VLat. **minūtiāre* < Lat. *minūtia,* smallness < *minūtus,* small < p.part. of *minuere,* to lessen; see **mei-**[2]*).] — **di•min′ish•a•ble** *adj.* — **di•min′ish•ment** *n.*

di•min•ished capacity (dĭ-mĭn′ĭsht) *n. Law.* Lack of ability to achieve the state of mind necessary for the commission of a particular crime.

di•min•ish•ing returns (dĭ-mĭn′ĭ-shĭng) *pl.n.* A yield rate that after a certain point fails to increase proportionately to additional outlays of capital or investments of time and labor.

dingo
Canis dingo

di•min•u•en•do (dĭ-mĭn′yo͞o-ĕn′dō) *n., adv., & adj. Mus.* Decrescendo. [Ital., pr.part. of *diminuire,* to diminish < Lat. *dīminuere.* See DIMINISH.]

dim•i•nu•tion (dĭm′ə-no͞o′shən, -nyo͞o′-) *n.* **1.a.** The act or process of diminishing. **b.** The resulting reduction; decrease. **2.** *Mus.* Repetition of a theme in notes one-quarter or one-half the duration of the original. [ME *diminucioun* < OFr. *diminution* < Lat. *dīminūtiō, dīminūtiōn-* < *dīminūtus,* p.part. of *dīminuere.* See DIMINISH.] — **dim′i•nu′tion•al** *adj.*

di•min•u•tive (dĭ-mĭn′yə-tĭv) *adj.* **1.** Extremely small in size; tiny. See Syns at **small. 2.** *Gram.* Of or being a suffix that indicates smallness, youth, familiarity, affection, or contempt, as *-kin* in *lambkin.* — *n.* **1.** *Gram.* A diminutive suffix, word, or name. **2.** A very small person or thing. [ME *diminutif* < OFr. < Lat. *dīminūtīvus* < *dīminūtus,* p.part. of *dīminuere.* See DIMINISH.] — **di•min′u•tive•ly** *adv.* — **di•min′u•tive•ness** *n.*

dim•i•ty (dĭm′ĭ-tē) *n., pl.* **-ties.** A sheer crisp cotton fabric with raised woven stripes or checks. [ME *demyt* < Med.Lat. *dimitum* < Gk. *dimiton* < neut. of *dimitos,* double-threaded : *di-,* two; see DI-[1] + *mitos,* thread.]

dim•mer (dĭm′ər) *n.* **1.** A rheostat or other device used to vary the intensity of an electric light. **2.a.** A parking light on a motor vehicle. **b.** Low beam.

di•mor•phic (dī-môr′fĭk) also **di•mor•phous** (-fəs) *adj.* Existing or occurring in two distinct forms; exhibiting dimorphism.

di•mor•phism (dī-môr′fĭz′əm) *n.* **1.** *Biol.* The existence within a species of two distinct forms that differ in one or more characteristics, such as shape. **2.** *Bot.* The occurrence of two distinct forms of the same parts in one plant. **3.** *Chem. & Phys.* Dimorphic crystallization.

dim-out (dĭm′out′) *n.* **1.** Restricted use of lights at night, as to make a city less visible from the air in wartime. **2.** The semidarkness resulting from restricted use of lights at night.

dim•ple (dĭm′pəl) *n.* **1.** A small natural indentation in the flesh on a part of the human body, as in the cheek. **2.** A slight depression or indentation in a surface. — *v.* **-pled, -pling, -ples.** — *intr.* To form dimples by smiling. — *tr.* To produce dimples in. [ME *dimpel* < OE **dympel.*] — **dim′ply** *adj.*

dim sum (dĭm′ so͝om′, sŭm′) *n.* A traditional Chinese meal in which small portions of a variety of foods, including dumplings, are served in succession. [Chin. (Cantonese) *dim sem* < Chin. (Mandarin) *diǎn xīn,* light refreshments : *diǎn,* spot, drop + *xīn,* heart, center.]

dim•wit (dĭm′wĭt′) *n. Slang.* A stupid person. — **dim′wit′ted** *adj.* — **dim′wit′ted•ly** *adv.* — **dim′wit′ted•ness** *n.*

din (dĭn) *n.* A jumble of loud, usu. discordant sounds. See Syns at **noise.** — *v.* **dinned, din•ning, dins.** — *tr.* **1.** To stun with deafening noise. **2.** To instill by wearying repetition. — *intr.* To make a loud noise. [ME *dine* < OE *dyne.*]

di•nar (dĭ-när′, dē′när′) *n.* **1.** See table at **currency. 2.** Any of several units of gold and silver currency formerly used in the Middle East. [Ar. *dīnār* < LGk. *dēnarion* < Lat. *dēnārius.* See DENARIUS.]

Di•nar•ic Alps (dĭ-năr′ĭk). A range of the Balkan Peninsula extending c. 644 km (400 mi) along the E coast of the Adriatic Sea.

dine (dīn) *v.* **dined, din•ing, dines.** — *intr.* To have dinner. — *tr.* To give dinner to; entertain at dinner. [ME *dinen* < OFr. *diner, disner* < VLat. **disiūnāre* < **disiēiūnāre* : Lat. *dis-,* dis- + Lat. *iēiūnium,* fast.]

din•er (dī′nər) *n.* **1.** One that dines. **2.** See **dining car. 3.** A small, usu. inexpensive restaurant with a long counter and booths housed in a building resembling a dining car.

Di•ne•sen (dē′nĭ-sən, dĭn′ĭ-), **Isak.** Baroness Karen Blixen. 1885–1962. Danish writer who is best known for her memoir *Out of Africa* (1937).

di•nette (dī-nĕt′) *n.* **1.** A nook or alcove located in or near a kitchen and used for informal meals. **2.** The table and chairs used to furnish such an area. [DINE + -ETTE.]

ding[1] (dĭng) *v.* **dinged, ding•ing, dings.** — *intr.* **1.** To ring; clang. **2.** To speak persistently and repetitiously. — *tr.* **1.** To cause to clang. **2.** To instill with constant repetition. — *n.* A ringing sound. [Partly imit. and partly alteration of DIN.]

ding[2] (dĭng) *n. Informal.* A small dent or nick, as in a car. [< *ding,* to strike, beat on (< ME *dingen;* akin to ON *dengja*) and < DING[1].] — **ding** *v.*

ding-a-ling (dĭng′ə-lĭng) *n. Slang.* A scatterbrained or eccentric person.

ding•bat (dĭng′băt′) *n.* **1.** *Slang.* A stupid or silly person. **2.** An object, such as a brick, used as a missile. **3.** *Slang.* An unspecified gadget or other small article. **4.** *Print.* A typographical ornament or symbol. [?]

ding-dong (dĭng′dông′, -dŏng′) *n.* **1.** The peal of a bell. **2.** *Slang.* An empty-headed person; a fool. — *intr.v.* **-donged, -dong•ing, -dongs.** To ring; jingle. — *adj.* Characterized by a hammering exchange, as of blows. [Imit.]

din•ghy (dĭng′ē) *n., pl.* **-ghies.** *Naut.* **1.** A small open boat carried as a tender, lifeboat, or pleasure craft on a larger boat. **2.** A small rowboat. **3.** An inflatable rubber life raft. [Hindi *ḍiṅgī,* dim. of *ḍeṅgā,* boat.]

din•gle (dĭng′gəl) *n.* A small wooded valley; a dell. [ME, dell, hollow.]

Ding Ling (dĭng′ lĭng′). 1904–86. Chinese writer whose works explore the role of women in Communist China.

din•go (dĭng′gō) *n., pl.* **-goes.** A wild dog *(Canis dingo)* of Australia having a reddish-brown or yellowish-brown coat. [Dharuk (Aboriginal language of SE Australia) *diŋgu.*]

din•gus (dĭng′əs) *n. Slang.* An article whose name is unknown or forgotten. [Du. *dinges,* prob. < Ger., genitive of *Ding,* thing < OHGer.]

din•gy (dĭn′jē) *adj.* **-gi•er, -gi•est. 1.** Darkened with smoke and grime; dirty or discolored. **2.** Shabby, drab, or squalid. [Poss. < ME *dinge,* dung, var. of *dung.* See DUNG.] — **din′gi•ly** *adv.* — **din′gi•ness** *n.*

din•ing car (dī′nĭng) *n.* A railroad car in which meals are served.

dining room *n.* A room in which meals are eaten.

di•ni•tro•ben•zene (dī-nī′trō-bĕn′zēn′, -bĕn-zēn′) *n.* Any of three isomeric compounds, $C_6H_4(NO_2)_2$, made from a mixture of nitric acid, sulfuric acid, and heated benzene and used in celluloid manufacture, in dyes, and in organic synthesis.

dink (dĭngk) *n. Sports.* A drop shot. [Perh. alteration of DINKY.]

DINK or **dink** (dĭnk) *n.* A two-income couple with no children. [*D(ual) I(ncome) N(o) K(ids).*]

din•key also **din•ky** (dĭng′kē) *n., pl.* **-keys** also **-kies.** A small locomotive used in a railroad yard, as for shunting. [< DINKY.]

din•kum (dĭn′kəm) *Australian. —adj.* Genuine; real. *—adv.* Honestly; truly. [< E. dial. and Australian, work.]

din•ky (dĭng′kē) *adj.* **-ki•er, -ki•est.** *Informal.* **1.** Of small size or consequence; insignificant. **2.** Of poor quality; shabby. [Prob. < Sc. *dink,* neat, trim.]

din•ner (dĭn′ər) *n.* **1.a.** The chief meal of the day, eaten in the evening or at midday. **b.** A banquet or formal meal in honor of a person or an event. **c.** The food prepared for either of these meals. **2.** A full-course meal served at a fixed price. [ME *diner,* morning meal < OFr. *disner, diner,* to dine, morning meal. See DINE.]

Word History: In Middle English *dinner* meant "breakfast," as did the Old French word *disner,* or *diner,* which was the source of our word. The Old French word came from the Vulgar Latin word **disiūnāre,* meaning "to break one's fast; that is, to eat one's first meal," a notion also contained in our word *breakfast.* The Vulgar Latin word was derived from an earlier word, **disiēiūnāre,* the Latin elements of which are *dis–,* denoting reversal, and *iēiūnium,* "fast." Middle English *diner* not only meant "breakfast" but, echoing usage of the Old French word *diner,* more commonly meant "the first big meal of the day, usually eaten between 9 A.M. and noon." Customs change, however, and over the years we have let the chief meal become the last meal of the day.

dinner jacket *n.* See **tuxedo** 1.

dinner theater *n.* A restaurant that presents a play during or after dinner.

din•ner•ware (dĭn′ər-wâr′) *n.* **1.** The tableware used in serving a meal. **2.** A set of dishes.

di•no•flag•el•late (dī′nō-flăj′ə-lĭt, -lāt′, -flə-jĕl′ĭt) *n.* Any of numerous minute, chiefly marine protozoans of the order Dinoflagellata, having two flagella and a cellulose covering and forming a chief constituent of plankton. [< NLat. *Dinoflagellata,* class name : Gk. *dinos,* eddy (< *dinein,* to whirl) + Lat. *flagellum,* flagellum; see FLAGELLUM.]

di•no•saur (dī′nə-sôr′) *n.* **1.** Any of various extinct, often gigantic, chiefly terrestrial reptiles of the orders Saurischia and Ornithischia that lived in the Mesozoic Era. **2.** A relic of the past. **3.** One hopelessly outmoded or unwieldy. [Gk. *deinos,* monstrous + Gk. *sauros,* lizard.] **—di′no•sau′ri•an** (-sôr′-ē-ən) *adj. & n.* **—di′no•sau′ric** *adj.*

di•no•there (dī′nə-thîr′) *n.* Any of various extinct elephantlike mammals of the genus *Dinotherium* that existed during the Miocene, Pliocene, and Pleistocene epochs. [< NLat. *Dinotherium,* genus name : Gk. *deinos,* monstrous + Gk. *thērion,* dim. of *thēr,* beast; see **ghwer-*.**]

dint (dĭnt) *n.* **1.** Force or effort; power: *by dint of hard work.* **2.** A dent. *—tr.v.* **dint•ed, dint•ing, dints. 1.** To put a dent in. **2.** To impress or drive in forcibly. [ME. See DENT[1].]

di•nu•cle•o•tide (dī-no͞o′klē-ə-tīd′, -nyo͞o′-) *n.* A nucleotide molecule that consists of two nucleotide units.

Din•wid•die (dĭn-wĭd′ē, dĭn′wĭd-ē), **Robert.** 1693–1770. British colonial administrator in Virginia (1751–58).

di•oc•e•san (dī-ŏs′ĭ-sən) *adj.* Of or relating to a diocese. *—n.* The bishop of a diocese.

di•o•cese (dī′ə-sĭs, -sēs′, -sēz′) *n.* The district under the jurisdiction of a bishop. [ME *diocise* < OFr. < LLat. *diocēsis* < Lat. *dioecēsis,* jurisdiction < Gk. *dioikēsis,* administration < *dioikein,* to keep house, administer : *dia-,* intensive pref.; see DIA– + *oikein, oikē-,* to inhabit (< *oikos,* house; see **weik-[1]***).]

Di•o•cle•tian (dī′ə-klē′shən). A.D. 245?–313? Emperor of Rome (284–305) who divided the empire into east and west (286) and led the last persecution of the Christians (303).

di•ode (dī′ōd′) *n.* **1.** An electronic device that restricts current flow chiefly to one direction. **2.** An electron tube having a cathode and an anode. **3.** A two-terminal semiconductor device used chiefly as a rectifier.

di•oe•cious also **di•e•cious** (dī-ē′shəs) *adj. Bot.* Having the male and female reproductive organs on separate individuals of the same species. [< NLat. *Dioecia,* former class name : DI–[1] + Gk. *oikia,* a dwelling; see **weik-[1]*.**] **—di•oe′cious•ly** *adv.* **—di•oe′cism** (-sĭz′əm) *n.*

Di•og•e•nes (dī-ŏj′ə-nēz′). d. c. 320 B.C. Greek philosopher who founded the Cynic school of philosophy.

di•oi•cous (dī-oi′kəs) *adj. Bot.* Having sex organs on separate plants; unisexual. Used of mosses and related plants. [< NLat. *dioecus* : DI–[1] + Gk. *oikos,* house; see **weik-[1]*.**]

Di•o•mede Islands (dī′ə-mēd′). Two rocky islands in the Bering Strait between AK and Siberia. **Little Diomede** belongs to the U.S.; **Big Diomede,** to Russia.

Di•o•me•des (dī′ə-mē′dēz) *n. Gk. Myth.* One of the Greek heroes of the Trojan War.

Di•o•ne (dī-ō′nē) *n.* **1.** *Gk. Myth.* The mother of Aphrodite by Zeus. **2.** A satellite of Saturn. [Gk. *Diōnē* < *Dios,* genitive of *Zeus,* Zeus. See **deiw-*.**]

Di•o•nys•i•a (dī′ə-nĭz′ē-ə, -nĭzh′ē-ə, -nĭs′ē-ə) *pl.n.* Ancient Greek festivals held chiefly at Athens in honor of Dionysus, esp. fall festivals related to the development of Greek drama. [Lat. *Dionȳsia* < Gk. *(ta) Dionusia (hiera),* (festivities) of Dionysus, neut. pl. of *Dionusios.* See DIONYSIAN.]

Di•o•nys•i•ac (dī′ə-nĭs′ē-ăk′) *adj.* **1.a.** *Gk. Myth.* Of or relating to Dionysus. **b.** Of or relating to the Dionysia. **2.** Often **dionysiac.** Ecstatic or wild; Dionysian. [Lat. *Dionȳsiacus* < Gk. *Dionusiakos* < *Dionusios.* See DIONYSIAN.]

Di•o•nys•i•an (dī′ə-nĭsh′ən, -nĭzh′ən, -nĭs′ē-ən) *adj.* **1.** *Gk. Myth.* **a.** Of or relating to Dionysus. **b.** Of or devoted to the worship of Dionysus. **2.** Often **dionysian.** Of an ecstatic, orgiastic, or irrational nature; frenzied or undisciplined. **3.** Often **dionysian.** In the philosophy of Nietzsche, of or displaying creative-intuitive power as opposed to critical-rational power. [< Lat. *Dionȳsius* < Gk. *Dionusios* < *Dionusos,* Dionysus.]

Di•o•ny•si•us (dī-ə-nĭsh′ē-əs, -nĭsh′əs, -nī′sē-əs). "the Elder." 430?–367 B.C. Tyrant of Syracuse (405–367) noted for his campaigns against the Carthaginians in Sicily. His son **Dionysius** (395?–343?), "the Younger," succeeded him as tyrant in 367 and was exiled in 343 for his despotic rule.

Dionysius Ex•ig•u•us (ĕg-zĭg′yo͞o-əs, ĕk-sĭg′-). A.D. 500?–560? Scythian monk and scholar who introduced the method of reckoning the Christian era from the birth of Jesus.

Dionysius of Hal•i•car•nas•sus (hăl′ĭ-kär-năs′əs). 1st cent. B.C. Greek historian who wrote a 20-volume history of Rome, of which 10 volumes are extant.

Di•o•ny•sus (dī′ə-nī′səs, -nē′-) *n. Gk. & Rom. Myth.* The god of wine and of an orgiastic religion celebrating the power and fertility of nature. [Lat. *Dionȳsus* < Gk. *Dionusos.*]

di•o•phan•tine analysis (dī′ə-făn′tīn′, -tĭn) *n.* A method for determining integral solutions of certain algebraic equations. [After *Diophantus,* 3rd-cent. A.D. Greek mathematician.]

di•op•side (dī-ŏp′sīd′) *n.* A light green monoclinic pyroxene mineral, $CaMgSi_2O_6$, used as a gemstone and refractory. [Fr. : *di-,* two (< Gk.; see DI–[1]) + Gk. *opsis,* –opsis.]

Dionysus
Detail from a Roman sarcophagus

di•op•ter (dī-ŏp′tər) *n.* A unit of measurement of the refractive power of lenses equal to the reciprocal of the focal length measured in meters. [Obsolete *diopter,* an instrument for measuring angles < Lat. *dioptra* < Gk. : *dia-,* dia- + *optos,* visible; see **okʷ-*.**] **—di•op′tral** (-trəl) *adj.*

di•op•tom•e•ter (dī′ŏp-tŏm′ĭ-tər) *n.* An instrument used for measuring ocular refraction. [DI(A)– + OPT(IC) + –METER.] **—di′op•tom′e•try** *n.*

di•op•tric (dī-ŏp′trĭk) also **di•op•tri•cal** (-trĭ-kəl) *adj.* **1.** Of or relating to dioptrics. **2.** Relating to optical refraction; refractive. [< Gk. *dioptrikos,* of a diopter < *dioptra,* diopter. See DIOPTER.]

di•op•trics (dī-ŏp′trĭks) *n. (used with a sing. v.)* The study of the refraction of light. [< DIOPTRIC.]

Di•or (dē-ôr′), **Christian.** 1905–57. French fashion designer best known for his New Look of 1947.

di•o•ram•a (dī′ə-răm′ə, -rä′mə) *n.* **1.** A three-dimensional scene in which figures, stuffed wildlife, or other objects are arranged naturalistically against a painted background. **2.** A scene reproduced on cloth transparencies with lights shining through the cloths to produce changes in effect, intended for viewing at a distance through an aperture. [Fr., blend of *dia-,* through (< Gk.; see DIA–) and *panorama,* panorama (< E.; see PANORAMA).] **—di′o•ram′ic** (-răm′ĭk) *adj.*

di•o•rite (dī′ə-rīt′) *n.* Any of various dark granite-textured crystalline rocks rich in plagioclase. [Fr. < Gk. *diorizein,* to distinguish : *dia-,* apart, between; see DIA– + *horizein,* to divide, limit; see HORIZON.] **—di′o•rit′ic** (-rĭt′ĭk) *adj.*

Di•os•cu•ri (dī-ŏs′kyə-rī′, dī′ə-skyo͝or′ī) *pl.n. Gk. Myth.* Castor and Pollux, the twin sons of Leda, who were transformed by Zeus into the constellation Gemini. [Gk. *Dioskouroi* : *Dios,* genitive of *Zeus,* Zeus; see **deiw-*** + *kouroi,* of *kouros,* boy; see **ker-[2]*.**]

di•ox•ane (dī-ŏk′sān′) *n.* A flammable, potentially explosive liquid, $C_4H_8O_2$, used as a solvent for fats, greases, and resins.

di•ox•ide (dī-ŏk′sīd) *n.* A compound with two oxygen atoms per molecule.

di•ox•in (dī-ŏk′sĭn) *n.* Any of several carcinogenic or teratogenic heterocyclic hydrocarbons that occur as impurities in petroleum-derived herbicides. [DI–[1] + ox(o)– + –IN.]

dip (dĭp) *v.* **dipped, dip•ping, dips.** *—tr.* **1.** To plunge briefly into a liquid, as in order to wet, coat, or saturate. **2.** To color or dye by immersing. **3.** To immerse (an animal) in a disinfectant solution. **4.** To form (a candle) by repeatedly immersing a wick in melted wax or tallow. **5.** To galvanize or plate (metal) by immersion. **6.** To scoop up by plunging the hand or a receptacle below the surface, as of a liquid; ladle. **7.** To lower and raise (a flag) in salute. **8.** To lower or drop (something) suddenly. *—intr.* **1.** To plunge into water or other liquid and come out quickly. **2.** To plunge the hand or a receptacle into liquid or a container, esp. so as to take something up or out. **3.** To make inroads into funds. **4.** To drop down or sink out of sight suddenly. **5.** To drop suddenly before

ă pat	oi boy
ā pay	ou out
âr care	o͝o took
ä father	o͞o boot
ĕ pet	ŭ cut
ē be	ûr urge
ĭ pit	th thin
ī pie	*th* this
îr pier	hw which
ŏ pot	zh vision
ō toe	ə about, item
ô paw	

Stress marks:
′ (primary);
′ (secondary), as in
dictionary (dĭk′shə-nĕr′ē)

climbing. Used of an aircraft. **6.** To slope downward; decline: *The road dipped.* **7.** To decline slightly and usu. temporarily. **8.** *Geol.* To lie at an angle to the horizontal plane, as a rock stratum or vein. **9.a.** To read here and there at random; browse. **b.** To investigate a subject superficially; dabble. —*n.* **1.** A brief plunge or immersion, esp. a quick swim. **2.** A liquid into which something is dipped, as for dyeing or disinfecting. **3.** A savory creamy mixture into which food may be dipped. **4.** An amount taken up by dipping. **5.** A container for dipping. **6.** A candle made by repeated dipping in tallow or wax. **7.** A downward slope; a decline. **8.** A sharp downward course; a drop. **9.** *Geol.* The downward inclination of a rock stratum or vein in reference to the plane of the horizon. **10.** Magnetic dip. **11.** A hollow or depression. **12.** *Sports.* A gymnastic exercise on the parallel bars in which the body is lowered by bending the elbows until the chin approaches the bars and then is raised by straightening the arms. **13.** *Slang.* A pickpocket. **14.** *Slang.* A foolish or stupid person. [ME *dippen* < OE *dyppan.* See **dheub-***.]

dip. *abbr.* Diploma.

di•pep•ti•dase (dī-pĕp′tĭ-dās′, -dāz′) *n.* An enzyme that hydrolyzes dipeptides into their constituent amino acids.

di•pep•tide (dī-pĕp′tīd′) *n.* A peptide that on hydrolysis yields two amino acid molecules.

di•pet•al•ous (dī-pĕt′l-əs) *adj.* Having two petals.

di•phase (dī′fāz′) also **di•pha•sic** (dī-fā′zĭk) *adj.* Having two phases.

di•phen•yl (dī-fĕn′əl, -fē′nəl) *n.* See **biphenyl.**

di•phen•yl•a•mine (dī-fĕn′əl-ə-mēn′, -ăm′ĭn, -fē′nəl-) *n.* A crystalline compound, $(C_6H_5)_2NH$, used as a stabilizer for plastics and in the manufacture of dyes and explosives.

di•phen•yl•hy•dan•to•in (dī-fĕn′əl-hī-dăn′tō-ĭn, -fē′nəl-) *n.* See **phenytoin.** [DIPHENYL + *hydantoin* (HYD(ROGEN) + (ALL)ANTO(IS) + -IN).]

di•phos•gene (dī-fŏz′jēn′) *n.* A liquid, $ClCO_2CCl_3$, used in organic synthesis, yielding a poison gas used in World War I.

di•phos•phate (dī-fŏs′fāt′) *n.* An ester of phosphoric acid containing two phosphate groups.

di•phos•pho•gly•cer•ic acid (dī-fŏs′fō-glĭ-sĕr′ĭk) *n.* A diphosphate of glyceric acid that is an important intermediate in various metabolic processes, such as photosynthesis.

diph•the•ri•a (dĭf-thîr′ē-ə, dĭp-) *n.* An acute infectious disease caused by the bacillus *Corynebacterium diphtheriae,* characterized by the production of a systemic toxin and the formation of a false membrane in the throat and causing difficulty in breathing, high fever, and weakness. [NLat. *diphthēria* < Fr. *diphthérie* < Gk. *diphthera*, piece of hide, leather.] —**diph′the•rit′ic** (-thə-rĭt′ĭk), **diph•ther•′ic** (-thĕr′ĭk), **diph•the′ri•al** *adj.*

diph•thong (dĭf′thông′, -thŏng′, dĭp′-) *n. Ling.* A complex speech sound or glide that begins with one vowel and gradually changes to another vowel within the same syllable, as (oi) in *boil.* [ME *diptonge* < OFr. *diptongue* < LLat. *dipthongus* < Gk. *diphthongos* : *di-*, two; see DI-[1] + *phthongos*, sound.] —**diph•thon′gal** *adj.*

diph•thong•ize (dĭf′thông-īz′, -thŏng-, dĭp′-) *tr. & intr.v.* **-ized, -iz•ing, -iz•es.** *Ling.* To pronounce as or become a diphthong. —**diph′thong•i•za′tion** (-ĭ-zā′shən) *n.*

di•phy•let•ic (dī′fī-lĕt′ĭk) *adj.* Descended from two ancestral lines or individuals.

di•phyl•lous (dī-fĭl′əs) *adj. Bot.* Having two leaves.

di•phy•o•dont (dī-fī′ə-dŏnt′) *adj.* Having two successive sets of teeth, deciduous and permanent. [< Gk. *diphuēs*, double (*di-*, two; see DI-[1]) + *phuein*, to grow; see **bheuə-***.]

dipl. *abbr.* Diplomat; diplomatic.

di•ple•gia (dī-plē′jə, -jē-ə) *n.* Paralysis of corresponding parts on both sides of the body.

di•plex (dī′plĕks′) *adj.* Capable of simultaneous transmission or reception of two messages in the same radio channel. [DI-[1] + (DU)PLEX.]

di•plex•er (dī′plĕk-sər) *n.* A coupling device that permits two radio transmitters to share the same antenna.

diplo– or **dipl–** *pref.* **1.** Double: *diplococcus.* **2.** Having double the basic number of chromosomes; diploid: *diplont.* [< Gk. < *diploos*, double. See **dwo-***.]

dip•lo•blas•tic (dĭp′lō-blăs′tĭk) *adj.* Derived from the ectoderm and the endoderm. Used of lower invertebrates.

dip•lo•coc•cus (dĭp′lō-kŏk′əs) *n., pl.* **-coc•ci** (-kŏk′sī′, -kŏk′ī′). Any of various paired spherical bacteria, including those of the genus *Diplococcus,* some of which are pathogenic. —**dip′lo•coc′cal** (-kŏk′əl), **dip′lo•coc′cic** (-kŏk′sĭk, -kŏk′ĭk) *adj.*

di•plod•o•cus (dĭ-plŏd′ə-kəs, dī-) *n.* A very large herbivorous dinosaur of the genus *Diplodocus* that existed during the Jurassic Period. [NLat. *Diplodocus*, genus name : Gk. *diplo-*, diplo- + Gk. *dokos*, beam; see **dek-***.]

dip•lo•e (dĭp′lō-ē′) *n.* The spongy, porous bony tissue between the hard outer and inner bone layers of the cranium. [NLat. *diploē* < Gk., a fold, doubling < fem. of *diploos*, twofold. See **dwo-***.] —**dip′lo•ic** (-lō-ĭk) *adj.*

dip•loid (dĭp′loid′) *adj.* **1.** Double or twofold. **2.** *Genet.* Having two sets of chromosomes. —*n. Genet.* An organism having diploid cells. [Gk. *diplous*, double; see **dwo-*** + -OID.] —**dip′loi′dy** (-loi′dē) *n.*

di•plo•ma (dĭ-plō′mə) *n.* **1.** A document issued by an educational institution to testify that the recipient has earned a degree or successfully completed a particular course of study. **2.** A certificate conferring a privilege or honor. **3.** An official document or charter. [Lat. *diplōma*, letter of introduction < Gk., document, folded paper < *diploos*, double. See **dwo-***.]

di•plo•ma•cy (dĭ-plō′mə-sē) *n.* **1.** The art or practice of conducting international relations, as in negotiating alliances. **2.** Tact and skill in dealing with people.

dip•lo•mat (dĭp′lə-măt′) *n.* **1.** One appointed to represent a government in its relations with other governments. **2.** One who uses skill and tact in dealing with others. [Fr. *diplomate*, back-formation < *diplomatique*, diplomatic. See DIPLOMATIC.]

dip•lo•mate (dĭp′lə-māt′) *n.* One granted a diploma, esp. a physician certified as a specialist by a board of examiners.

dip•lo•mat•ic (dĭp′lə-măt′ĭk) *adj.* **1.** Of or involving diplomacy or diplomats. **2.** Using or marked by tact and sensitivity in dealing with others. **3.a.** Of or relating to diplomatics. **b.** Being an exact copy of the original. [Fr. *diplomatique* < NLat. *diplōmaticus* < Lat. *diplōma*, *diplōmat-*, letter of introduction. See DIPLOMA.] —**dip′lo•mat′i•cal•ly** *adv.*

diplomatic corps *n.* The body of diplomatic personnel in residence at a nation's capital.

diplomatic immunity *n.* The exemption from taxation and ordinary processes of law afforded to diplomatic personnel in a foreign country.

dip•lo•mat•ics (dĭp′lə-măt′ĭks) *n. (used with a sing. v.)* The branch of paleography that deals with the study of ancient official documents and determines their age and authenticity.

di•plo•ma•tist (dĭ-plō′mə-tĭst) *n.* A diplomat.

dip•lont (dĭp′lŏnt′) *n.* An organism having somatic cells with the diploid number of chromosomes. —**dip•lont′ic** (-lŏn′tĭk) *adj.*

dip•lo•pi•a (dĭ-plō′pē-ə) *n.* See **double vision.** —**dip•lo′pic** (-plō′pĭk, dĭ-plŏp′ĭk) *adj.*

dip•lo•pod (dĭp′lə-pŏd′) *n.* See **millipede.** —**dip•lop′o•dous** (-lŏp′ə-dəs) *adj.*

dip•lo•sis (dĭ-plō′sĭs) *n.* The formation during fertilization of the diploid number of chromosomes by the fusion of the nuclei of two haploid gametes. [NLat. *diplōsis* < Gk., a doubling < *diploun*, to double < *diploos*, double. See DIPLO-.]

dip•no•an (dĭp′nō-ən) *n.* Any of various fishes of the group Dipnoi, marked by modified lungs that enable them to breathe atmospheric air. [< NLat. *Dipnoi*, order name < Gk., pl. of *dipnoos*, having two apertures for breathing : *di-*, two; see DI-[1] + *-pnoos*, breathing (< *pnoē*, breath < *pnein*, to breathe; see **pneu-***).] —**dip′no•an** *adj.*

dip•o•dy (dĭp′ə-dē) *n., pl.* **-dies.** A prosodic unit consisting of two feet. [LLat. *dipodia* < Gk. < *dipous*, two-footed : *di-*, two; see DI-[1] + *pous*, *pod-*, foot; see -POD.]

di•pole (dī′pōl′) *n.* **1.** *Phys.* A pair of equal and opposite electric charges or magnetic poles, separated by a small distance. **2.** *Electron.* An antenna, usu. fed from the center, consisting of two equal horizontal rods. —**di•pol′ar** *adj.*

dipole moment *n.* **1.** The product of either charge in an electric dipole with the distance separating them. **2.** Magnetic moment.

dip•per (dĭp′ər) *n.* **1.** One that dips, esp. a container for taking up water. **2.** One of several small birds of the genus *Cinclus* that dive into swift streams and feed along the bottom.

Dip•per (dĭp′ər) *n.* **1.** The Big Dipper. **2.** The Little Dipper.

dip•py (dĭp′ē) *adj.* **-pi•er, -pi•est.** *Slang.* Foolish. [?]

di•pro•pel•lant (dī′prə-pĕl′ənt) *n.* See **bipropellant.**

di•prot•ic (dī-prŏt′ĭk) *adj.* Having two hydrogen ions to donate to bases in an acid-base reaction. [DI-[1] + PROT(ON) + -IC.]

dip•so•ma•ni•a (dĭp′sə-mā′nē-ə, -mān′yə) *n.* An insatiable, often periodic craving for alcoholic beverages. [Gk. *dipsa*, thirst + -MANIA.] —**dip′so•ma′ni•ac** (-āk′) *adj. & n.* —**dip′so•ma•ni′a•cal** (-mə-nī′ə-kəl) *adj.*

dip•stick (dĭp′stĭk′) *n.* A graduated rod for measuring the depth or amount of liquid in a container.

dip•ter•an (dĭp′tər-ən) also **dip•ter•on** (-tə-rŏn′) *n.* A dipterous insect. —**dip′ter•an** *adj.*

dip•ter•ous (dĭp′tər-əs) *adj.* **1.** Of, relating to, or belonging to the Diptera, a large order of insects that includes the true flies and mosquitoes and is characterized by a single pair of membranous wings and a pair of club-shaped balancing organs. **2.** Having two wings, as certain insects, or winglike appendages, as certain fruits and seeds. [< NLat. *Diptera*, order name < Gk. *dipteros*, having two wings : *di-*, two; see DI-[1] + *pteron*, wing; see -PTER.]

dip•tych (dĭp′tĭk) *n.* **1.** An ancient writing tablet having two leaves hinged together. **2.** A work consisting of two painted or carved panels that are hinged together. [LLat. *diptycha* < Gk. *diptukha* < neut. pl. of *diptukhos*, folded double : *di-*, two; see DI-[1] + *ptukhē*, fold (< *ptussein*, *ptukh-*, to fold).]

di•pyr•id•a•mole (dī-pĭr′ĭ-də-mōl′, -pə-rĭd′ə-) *n.* A drug, $C_{24}H_{40}N_8O_4$, that acts as a coronary vasodilator. [DI-[1] + PYRID(INE) + -AM(INE) + -OLE.]

di•quat (dī′kwăt′) *n.* A strong yellow crystalline herbicide, $C_{12}H_{12}Br_2N_2$, used to control water weeds. [DI-[1] + QUAT(ERNARY).]
dir. *abbr.* Director.
Di•rac (dĭ-răk′), **Paul Adrien Maurice.** 1902–84. British mathematician and physicist who shared a 1933 Nobel Prize.
dire (dīr) *adj.* **dir•er, dir•est. 1.** Warning of or having dreadful consequences; calamitous. **2.** Urgent; desperate: *dire poverty.* [Lat. *dīrus*, fearsome, terrible; akin to Gk. *deinos*.] **—dire′ly** *adv.* **—dire′ness** *n.*
di•rect (dĭ-rĕkt′, dī-) *v.* **-rect•ed, -rect•ing, -rects.** *—tr.* **1.** To manage or conduct the affairs of; regulate. **2.** To have or take charge of; control. **3.** To give authoritative instructions to: *directed them to answer.* **4.** To cause to move toward a goal; aim. **5.** To show or indicate the way for. **6.** To cause to move in or follow a straight course. **7.** To indicate the intended recipient on (a letter, for example). **8.** To address or adapt (remarks, for example) to a specific person, audience, or purpose. **9.a.** To give guidance and instruction to (musicians, for example) in the performance of a work. **b.** To supervise the performance of. *—intr.* **1.** To give commands or directions. **2.** To conduct a performance or rehearsal. *—adj.* **1.** Proceeding without interruption in a straight course or line; not deviating or swerving. **2.** Straightforward and candid; frank. **3.** Having no intervening persons, conditions, or agencies; immediate. **4.** Effected by action of the voters rather than through elected representatives or delegates. **5.** Being of unbroken descent; lineal: *a direct descendant.* **6.** Consisting of the exact words of the writer or speaker. **7.** Lacking compromising or mitigating elements; absolute. **8.** *Math.* Varying in the same manner as another quantity, esp. increasing if another quantity increases or decreasing if it decreases. **9.** *Astron.* Moving west to east in the same direction as the sun's movement against the stars. Used of a planet. *—adv.* Straight; directly. [ME *directen* < Lat. *dīrigere, dīrēct-*, to give direction to : *dī-, dis-*, apart; see DIS- + *regere*, to guide; see **reg-*.**]
direct action *n.* The strategic use of immediately effective acts, such as strikes or sabotage, to achieve a political or social end.
direct current *n.* An electric current flowing in one direction only.
di•rect•ed (dĭ-rĕk′tĭd) *adj. Math.* Having an indicated positive sense.
di•rec•tion (dĭ-rĕk′shən, dī-) *n.* **1.** The act or function of directing. **2.** Management, supervision, or guidance of an action or operation. **3.** The art or action of musical or theatrical directing. **4.** *Mus.* A word or phrase in a score indicating how a passage is to be played or sung. **5.** An instruction or series of instructions for doing or finding something. Often used in the plural. **6.** An authoritative indication; an order or a command. **7.a.** The distance-independent relationship between two points in space that specifies the angular position of either with respect to the other; the relationship by which the alignment or orientation of any position with respect to any other position is established. **b.** A position to which motion or another position is referred. **c.** A line leading to a place or point. **d.** The line or course along which a person or thing moves. **8.** The statement in degrees of the angle measured between due north and a given line or course on a compass. **9.** A course or area of development; a tendency toward a particular end or goal. [ME, arrangement < Lat. *dīrēctiō, dīrēctiōn-* < *dīrēctus*, p.part. of *dīrigere*, to direct. See DIRECT.] **—di•rec′tion•less** *adj.*
di•rec•tion•al (dĭ-rĕk′shə-nəl, dī-) *adj.* **1.** Of or indicating direction. **2.** *Electron.* Capable of receiving or sending signals in one direction only. **3.** Relating to guidance in effort, behavior, or thought. **4.** Serving to point the future direction, as of fashion. *—n.* A directional signal. **—di•rec′tion•al′i•ty** (-shə-năl′ĭ-tē) *n.*
directional antenna *n.* An antenna that receives or sends signals most effectively in a particular direction.
directional signal *n.* One of two lights on the front and rear of an automotive vehicle that indicate the direction of a turn.
direction finder *n.* A device for determining the source of a transmitted signal, consisting mainly of a radio receiver and a coiled rotating antenna.
di•rec•tive (dĭ-rĕk′tĭv, dī-) *n.* An order or instruction, esp. one from a central authority. *—adj.* Serving to direct.
di•rect•ly (dĭ-rĕkt′lē, dī-) *adv.* **1.** In a direct line or manner; straight. **2.** Without anyone or anything intervening. **3.** Exactly or totally. **4.** At once; instantly. **5.** Candidly; frankly. **6.** *Chiefly Southern U.S.* In a little while; shortly. *—conj. Chiefly British.* As soon as.
direct mail *n.* Advertisements or other printed matter mailed directly to prospective customers or contributors. **—di•rect′-mail′** (dĭ-rĕkt′māl′, dī-) *adj.* **—direct mailer** *n.*
direct object *n. Gram.* The word or phrase in a sentence referring to the one receiving the action of a transitive verb. For example, in *mail the letter, letter* is the direct object.
di•rec•tor (dĭ-rĕk′tər, dī-) *n.* **1.** One that supervises, controls, or manages. **2.** A member of a group of persons chosen to govern the affairs of an institution or a corporation. **3.** A person who supervises the creative aspects of a dramatic production or film and instructs the actors and crew. **4.** *Mus.* The conductor of an orchestra or a chorus. **—di•rec′tor•ship′** *n.*
di•rec•tor•ate (dĭ-rĕk′tər-ĭt, dī-) *n.* **1.** The office or position of a director. **2.** A board of directors, as of a corporation. **3.** The entire staff of a bureau or department.
di•rec•to•ri•al (dĭ-rĕk′tôr′ē-əl, -tōr′-, dī-) *adj.* **1.** Of or relating to a director or directorate. **2.** Serving to direct; directive. **—di•rec′to′ri•al•ly** *adv.*
di•rec•tor's chair (dĭ-rĕk′tərz, dī-) *n.* A folding armchair with a usu. canvas back and seat.
di•rec•to•ry (dĭ-rĕk′tə-rē, dī-) *n., pl.* **-ries. 1.** A book containing an alphabetical or classified listing of names, addresses, and other data. **2.** *Comp. Sci.* **a.** A listing of the files contained in a storage device, such as a magnetic disk. **b.** A description of the various characteristics of a file, such as the layout of the fields in it. **3.** A book of rules or directions. **4.** A group or body of directors. *—adj.* Serving to direct.
direct primary *n.* A primary in which a party's candidates for public office are nominated by direct vote of the people.
di•rec•trix (dĭ-rĕk′trĭks, dī-) *n., pl.* **di•rec•trix•es** or **di•rec•tri•ces** (dī′rĕk-trī′sēz). **1.** *Math.* The fixed curve traversed by a generatrix in generating a conic section or a cylinder. **2.** The median line in the trajectory of fire of an artillery piece.
direct tax *n.* A tax levied directly on the taxpayer.
dire•ful (dīr′fəl) *adj.* **1.** Inspiring dread; terrible. **2.** Foreshadowing evil or disaster; ominous. **—dire′ful•ly** *adv.* **—dire′ful•ness** *n.*
dire wolf *n.* A large wolflike mammal *(Canis dirus)* that inhabited North America during the Pleistocene Epoch.
dirge (dûrj) *n.* **1.** *Mus.* **a.** A funeral hymn or lament. **b.** A slow, mournful musical composition. **2.** A mournful or elegiac poem or other literary work. [ME, an antiphon at Matins in the Office for the Dead < Med.Lat. *dīrige Domine*, direct, Lord, imper. of *dīrigere*, to direct. See DIRECT.]
dir•ham (də-răm′) *n.* See table at **currency.** [Ar. < Gk. *drakhmē*, drachma.]
dir•i•gi•ble (dĭr′ə-jə-bəl, də-rĭj′ə-bəl) *n.* See **airship.** [Lat. *dīrigere*, to direct; see DIRECT + -IBLE.]
dirk (dûrk) *n.* A dagger. *—tr.v.* **dirked, dirk•ing, dirks.** To stab with a dirk. [Sc. *durk*.]
dirn•dl (dûrn′dl) *n.* **1.** A full-skirted dress with a tight bodice, low neck, and short full sleeves. **2.** A full skirt with a gathered waistband. [Ger., short for *Dirndlkleid* : Ger. dial. *Dirndl*, dim. of *Dirne*, girl (< OHGer. *diorna*) + *Kleid*, dress.]

dirndl

dirt (dûrt) *n.* **1.** Earth or soil. **2.a.** A filthy or soiling substance, such as mud. **b.** Excrement. **3.** A squalid or filthy condition. **4.** One that is mean or vile. **5.a.** Obscene language or subject matter. **b.** Malicious or scandalous gossip. **c.** Information that embarrasses or accuses. **6.** Unethical behavior; corruption. **7.** Material, such as gravel, from which metal is extracted in mining. [ME, var. of *drit*, excrement, filth, mud < ON.]
dirt bike *n.* A motorbike or bicycle designed for use on rough surfaces, such as dirt roads or trails.

dirt bike

dirt-cheap (dûrt′chēp′) *adv. & adj.* Very cheap.
dirt dauber *n. Chiefly Southern U.S.* See **potter wasp.**
dirt farmer *n. Informal.* A farmer who does all the work on his or her property. **—dirt farming** *n.*
dirt-poor (dûrt′pŏŏr′) *adj.* Lacking most of life's necessities.
dirt•y (dûr′tē) *adj.* **-i•er, -i•est. 1.a.** Soiled, as with dirt; unclean. **b.** Spreading dirt; polluting. **c.** Apt to soil with dirt or grime. **2.** Squalid or filthy; run-down. **3.a.** Obscene or indecent. **b.** Malicious or scandalous: *a dirty lie.* **4.a.** Unethical or sordid: *dirty politics.* **b.** Not sportsmanlike: *a dirty fighter.* **c.** Acquired by illicit or improper means: *dirty money.* **d.** *Slang.* Possessing or using illegal drugs. **5.a.** Unpleasant or distasteful; thankless. **b.** Very unfortunate or regrettable: *a dirty shame.* **6.** Expressing disapproval or hostility: *a dirty look.* **7.** Not bright and clear in color; somewhat drab. Often used in combination: *dirty-blonde hair.* **8.** Producing a great amount of long-lived radioactive fallout. Used of nuclear weapons. **9.** Stormy; rough: *dirty weather.* *—v.* **-ied, -y•ing, -ies.** *—tr.* **1.** To make soiled. **2.** To stain or tarnish with dishonor. *—intr.* To become soiled. **—dirt′i•ly** *adv.* **—dirt′i•ness** *n.*
dirty linen *n. Informal.* Personal affairs that could cause embarrassment or distress if made public.
dirty old man *n. Informal.* A middle-aged or elderly man with lewd or lecherous inclinations.
dirty pool *n. Slang.* Unjust or dishonest conduct. [< POOL[2].]
dirty rice *n. Southern Louisiana.* White rice cooked with chicken livers and gizzards and seasoned with herbs and spices.
dirty tricks *pl.n. Informal.* **1.** Covert intelligence operations that disrupt the economy or the political situation in another country. **2.** Unethical behavior in politics, esp. acts that destroy the credibility of an opponent. **3.** Commercial espionage. **—dirty trickster** *n.*
dirty word *n.* A word, an expression, or a concept that is inappropriate or offensive from a particular point of view.
Dis (dĭs) *n. Rom. Myth.* **1.** The god of the underworld; Pluto. **2.** The underworld.
dis. *abbr.* **1.** Discharge. **2.** Discount. **3.** Distance. **4.** Distant.

ă pat	oi boy
ā pay	ou out
âr care	ŏŏ took
ä father	ōō boot
ĕ pet	ŭ cut
ē be	ûr urge
ĭ pit	th thin
ī pie	*th* this
îr pier	hw which
ŏ pot	zh vision
ō toe	ə about,
ô paw	item

Stress marks:
′ (primary);
′ (secondary), as in
dictionary (dĭk′shə-nĕr′ē)

dis– *pref.* **1.** Not: *dissimilar.* **2.a.** Absence of: *disinterest.* **b.** Opposite of: *disfavor.* **3.** Undo; do the opposite of: *disarrange.* **4.a.** Deprive of: *disfranchise.* **b.** Remove: *disbud.* **5.a.** Free from: *disintoxicate.* **6.** Used as an intensive: *disannul.* [ME < OFr. *des-* < Lat. *dis-*, *dī-* < *dis*, apart, asunder.]

dis•a•bil•i•ty (dĭs′ə-bĭl′ĭ-tē) *n.*, *pl.* **-ties. 1.a.** The condition of being disabled; incapacity. **b.** The period of such a condition. **2.** A disadvantage or deficiency, esp. a physical or mental impairment that impedes normal achievement. **3.** Something that hinders or incapacitates. **4.** *Law.* A legal incapacity or disqualification.

dis•a•ble (dĭs-ā′bəl) *tr.v.* **-bled, -bling, -bles. 1.** To deprive of capability or effectiveness, esp. to impair the physical abilities of. **2.** *Law.* To render legally disqualified. **3.** *Comp. Sci.* To suppress (an interrupt feature). **—dis•a′ble•ment** *n.* **—dis•a′bling** *adj.* **—dis•a′bling•ly** *adv.*

dis•a•bled (dĭs-ā′bəld) *adj.* **1.** Inoperative: *a disabled vehicle.* **2.** Impaired, as in physical functioning: *a disabled veteran.* —*n.* Physically impaired people considered as a group. See Usage Note at **handicapped.**

dis•a•buse (dĭs′ə-byo͞oz′) *tr.v.* **-bused, -bus•ing, -bus•es.** To free from a falsehood or misconception. [Fr. *désabuser* : *dés-*, dis- + *abuser*, to delude (< OFr., to misuse; see ABUSE).]

di•sac•cha•ri•dase (dī-săk′ər-ĭ-dās′, -dāz′) *n.* An enzyme, such as invertase or lactase, that catalyzes the hydrolysis of disaccharides to monosaccharides.

di•sac•cha•ride (dī-săk′ə-rīd′) *n.* Any of a class of carbohydrates that yield two monosaccharides upon hydrolysis.

dis•ac•cord (dĭs′ə-kôrd′) *n.* Lack of harmony; disagreement. —*intr.v.* **-cord•ed, -cord•ing, -cords.** To disagree. [< ME *disaccorden*, to disagree < OFr. *desacorder* : *des-*, dis- + *acorder*, to agree; see ACCORD.]

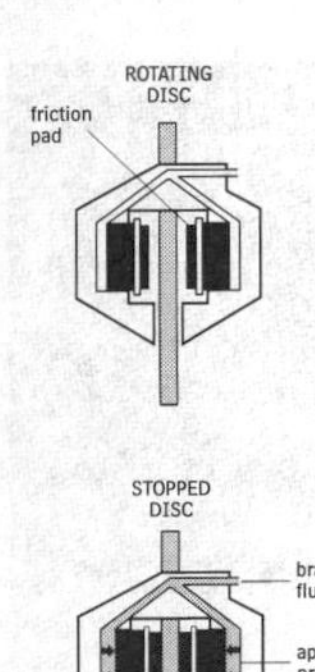

disc brake

dis•ac•cus•tom (dĭs′ə-kŭs′təm) *tr.v.* **-tomed, -tom•ing, -toms.** To render (a person) unaccustomed to something to which the person had been accustomed. [ME *disacustome* < OFr. *desacostumer* : *des-*, dis- + *acostumer*, to accustom; see ACCUSTOM.]

dis•ad•van•tage (dĭs′əd-văn′tĭj) *n.* **1.** An unfavorable condition. **2.** Something that places one in an unfavorable condition. **3.** Damage or loss, esp. to reputation or finances; detriment. —*tr.v.* **-taged, -tag•ing, -tag•es.** To put at a disadvantage; hinder or harm. [ME *disavauntage* < OFr. *desavantage* : *des-*, dis- + *avantage*, advantage; see ADVANTAGE.]

Syns: *disadvantage, detriment, drawback, handicap.* The central meaning shared by these nouns is "a condition, circumstance, or characteristic unfavorable to success": *poor health, a disadvantage in a job; acted freely without detriment; a job with drawbacks; illiteracy, a real handicap.*

dis•ad•van•taged (dĭs′əd-văn′tĭjd) *adj.* **1.** Deprived of some necessities or advantages of life, such as adequate housing or medical care. **2.** Being at a disadvantage, esp. with respect to competitive or opposing elements or forces. —*n.* Deprived people considered as a group. **—dis′ad•van′taged•ness** *n.*

dis•ad•van•ta•geous (dĭs-ăd′vən-tā′jəs, dĭs′ăd-vən-) *adj.* Detrimental; unfavorable. **—dis•ad′van•ta′geous•ly** *adv.* **—dis•ad′van•ta′geous•ness** *n.*

dis•af•fect (dĭs′ə-fĕkt′) *tr.v.* **-fect•ed, -fect•ing, -fects.** To cause to lose affection or loyalty. **—dis′af•fec′tion** *n.*

dis•af•fect•ed (dĭs′ə-fĕk′tĭd) *adj.* Resentful and rebellious, esp. against authority. **—dis′af•fect′ed•ly** *adv.*

dis•af•fil•i•ate (dĭs′ə-fĭl′ē-āt′) *v.* **-at•ed, -at•ing, -ates.** —*tr.* To remove from association. —*intr.* To end an affiliation. **—dis′af•fil′i•a′tion** *n.*

dis•af•firm (dĭs′ə-fûrm′) *tr.v.* **-firmed, -firm•ing, -firms.** To deny or contradict. **—dis′af•fir′mance** (dĭs′ə-fûr′məns), **dis•af′fir•ma′tion** (dĭs-ăf′ər-mā′shən) *n.*

dis•ag•gre•gate (dĭs-ăg′rĭ-gāt′) *v.* **-gat•ed, -gat•ing, -gates.** —*tr.* To divide into parts. —*intr.* To break up or apart. **—dis•ag′gre•ga′tion** (-grə-gā′shən) *n.* **—dis•ag′gre•ga′tive** *adj.*

dis•a•gree (dĭs′ə-grē′) *intr.v.* **-greed, -gree•ing, -grees. 1.** To fail to correspond. **2.a.** To have a differing opinion. **b.** To dispute or quarrel. **3.** To cause adverse effects. [ME *disagreen* < OFr. *desagreer* : *des-*, dis- + *agreer*, to agree; see AGREE.]

dis•a•gree•a•ble (dĭs′ə-grē′ə-bəl) *adj.* **1.** Not to one's liking; unpleasant or offensive. **2.** Having a quarrelsome, bad-tempered manner. **—dis′a•gree′a•ble•ness** *n.* **—dis′a•gree′a•bly** *adv.*

dis•a•gree•ment (dĭs′ə-grē′mənt) *n.* **1.** A failure or refusal to agree. **2.** A disparity; an inconsistency. **3.a.** A conflict or difference of opinion. **b.** A quarrel.

dis•al•low (dĭs′ə-lou′) *tr.v.* **-lowed, -low•ing, -lows. 1.** To refuse to allow. **2.** To reject as invalid, untrue, or improper. [ME *disallowen* < OFr. *desalouer*, to reprimand : *des-*, dis- + *alouer*, to approve; see ALLOW.] **—dis′al•low′a•ble** *adj.* **—dis′al•low′ance** *n.*

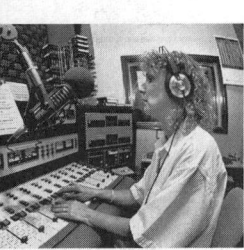

disc jockey

dis•am•big•u•ate (dĭs′ăm-bĭg′yo͞o-āt′) *tr.v.* **-at•ed, -at•ing, -ates.** To establish a single grammatical or semantic interpretation for. **—dis′am•big′u•a′tion** *n.*

dis•an•nul (dĭs′ə-nŭl′) *tr.v.* **-nulled, -null•ing, -nuls.** To annul or cancel. **—dis′an•nul′ment** *n.*

dis•ap•pear (dĭs′ə-pîr′) *intr.v.* **-peared, -pear•ing, -pears. 1.** To pass out of sight; vanish. **2.** To cease to exist. **—dis′ap•pear′ance** *n.*

Syns: *disappear, evanesce, evaporate, fade, vanish.* The central meaning shared by these verbs is "to pass out of sight or existence": *a skyscraper disappearing in the fog; time seeming to evanesce; courage evaporating; memories fading away; hope slowly vanishing.* ***Ant:*** *appear.*

dis•ap•point (dĭs′ə-point′) *v.* **-point•ed, -point•ing, -points.** —*tr.* **1.** To fail to satisfy the hope, desire, or expectation of. **2.** To frustrate or thwart. —*intr.* To cause disappointment. [ME *disappointen* < OFr. *desapointier*, to remove from office : *des-*, dis- + *apointer*, to appoint; see APPOINT.]

dis•ap•point•ed (dĭs′ə-poin′tĭd) *adj.* Thwarted in hope, desire, or expectation. **—dis′ap•point′ed•ly** *adv.*

dis•ap•point•ing (dĭs′ə-poin′tĭng) *adj.* Not up to expectations. **—dis′ap•point′ing•ly** *adv.*

dis•ap•point•ment (dĭs′ə-point′mənt) *n.* **1.a.** The act of disappointing. **b.** The condition or feeling of being disappointed. **2.** One that disappoints.

dis•ap•pro•ba•tion (dĭs-ăp′rə-bā′shən) *n.* Moral disapproval; condemnation.

dis•ap•prov•al (dĭs′ə-pro͞o′vəl) *n.* The act of disapproving; condemnation or censure.

dis•ap•prove (dĭs′ə-pro͞ov′) *v.* **-proved, -prov•ing, -proves.** —*tr.* **1.** To have an unfavorable opinion of; condemn. **2.** To refuse to approve; reject. —*intr.* To have an unfavorable opinion. **—dis′ap•prov′er** *n.* **—dis′ap•prov′ing•ly** *adv.*

dis•arm (dĭs-ärm′) *v.* **-armed, -arm•ing, -arms.** —*tr.* **1.a.** To divest of weapons. **b.** To deprive of the means of attack or defense; render harmless. **2.a.** To overcome or allay the suspicion, hostility, or antagonism of. **b.** To win the confidence of. —*intr.* **1.** To lay down arms. **2.** To reduce or abolish armed forces. [ME *disarmen* < OFr. *desarmer* : *des-*, dis- + *armer*, to arm (< Lat. *armāre* < *arma*, weapons; see **ar-***).] **—dis•arm′er** *n.*

dis•ar•ma•ment (dĭs-är′mə-mənt) *n.* **1.** The act of laying down arms, esp. the reduction or abolition of a nation's military forces and armaments. **2.** The condition of being disarmed.

dis•arm•ing (dĭs-är′mĭng) *adj.* Tending to allay suspicion or hostility; winning favor. **—dis•arm′ing•ly** *adv.*

dis•ar•range (dĭs′ə-rānj′) *tr.v.* **-ranged, -rang•ing, -rang•es.** To upset the proper order of. **—dis′ar•range′ment** *n.*

dis•ar•ray (dĭs′ə-rā′) *n.* **1.** A state of disorder; confusion. **2.** Disorderly dress. —*tr.v.* **-rayed, -ray•ing, -rays. 1.** To throw into confusion; upset. **2.** To undress.

dis•ar•tic•u•late (dĭs′är-tĭk′yə-lāt′) *v.* **-lat•ed, -lat•ing, -lates.** —*tr.* To separate at the joints. —*intr.* To become disjointed. **—dis′ar•tic′u•la′tion** *n.* **—dis′ar•tic′u•la′tor** *n.*

dis•as•sem•ble (dĭs′ə-sĕm′bəl) *v.* **-bled, -bling, -bles.** —*tr.* To take apart. —*intr.* **1.** To come apart. **2.** To break up in random fashion. **—dis′as•sem′bly** *n.*

dis•as•so•ci•ate (dĭs′ə-sō′shē-āt′, -sē-) *tr.v.* **-at•ed, -at•ing, -ates.** To remove from association; dissociate. **—dis′as•so′ci•a′tion** *n.*

dis•as•ter (dĭ-zăs′tər, -săs′-) *n.* **1.a.** An occurrence causing widespread destruction and distress; a catastrophe. **b.** A grave misfortune. **2.** *Informal.* A total failure. **3.** *Obsolete.* An evil influence of a star or planet. [Fr. *désastre* < Ital. *disastro* : *dis-*, pejorative pref. (< Lat. *dis-*; see DIS–) + *astro*, star (< Lat. *astrum* < Gk. *astron*; see **ster-³***).]

disaster area *n.* An area that officially qualifies for emergency governmental aid as a result of a catastrophe.

dis•as•trous (dĭ-zăs′trəs, -săs′-) *adj.* **1.** Accompanied by or causing distress or disaster; calamitous. **2.** Extremely bad; terrible. **—dis•as′trous•ly** *adv.* **—dis•as′trous•ness** *n.*

dis•a•vow (dĭs′ə-vou′) *tr.v.* **-vowed, -vow•ing, -vows.** To disclaim knowledge of, responsibility for, or association with. [ME *disavowen* < OFr. *desavouer* : *des-*, dis- + *avouer*, to avow; see AVOW.] **—dis′a•vow′a•ble** *adj.* **—dis′a•vow′al** *n.*

dis•band (dĭs-bănd′) *v.* **-band•ed, -band•ing, -bands.** —*tr.* To dissolve the organization of (a corporation, for example). —*intr.* To cease to function as an organization; disperse. [Obsolete Fr. *desbander*, to separate someone from a troop : *des-*, dis- + OFr. *band*, troop; see BAND².] **—dis•band′ment** *n.*

dis•bar (dĭs-bär′) *tr.v.* **-barred, -bar•ring, -bars.** *Law.* To expel (an attorney) from the practice of law by official action or procedure. **—dis•bar′ment** *n.*

dis•be•lief (dĭs′bĭ-lēf′) *n.* Refusal or reluctance to believe.

dis•be•lieve (dĭs′bĭ-lēv′) *v.* **-lieved, -liev•ing, -lieves.** —*tr.* To refuse to believe in; reject. —*intr.* To withhold or reject belief. **—dis′be•liev′er** *n.* **—dis′be•liev′ing•ly** *adv.*

dis•branch (dĭs-brănch′) *tr.v.* **-branched, -branch•ing, -branch•es. 1.** To cut or break a branch from (a tree). **2.** To remove (a limb or branch) from a tree.

dis•bud (dĭs-bŭd′) *tr.v.* **-bud•ded, -bud•ding, -buds. 1.** To remove buds from (a plant) to promote better blooms or control its shape. **2.a.** To prevent the growth of developing horns on (livestock). **b.** To remove such horns from (livestock).

dis•bur•den (dĭs-bûr′dn) *v.* **-dened, -den•ing, -dens.** —*tr.* **1.a.** To relieve (a pack animal, for example) of a burden.

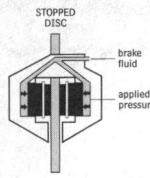

b. To free of a burden or trouble. **2.** To unload. — *intr.* To unload a burden. — **dis•bur′den•ment** *n.*

dis•bur•sal (dĭs-bûr′səl) *n.* Disbursement.

dis•burse (dĭs-bûrs′) *tr.v.* **-bursed, -burs•ing, -burs•es.** To pay out; expend. See Syns at **spend.** [Obsolete Fr. *desbourser* < OFr. *desborser* : *des-*, dis- + *borse*, purse (< LLat. *bursa*, purse; see BURSA).] — **dis•burs′a•ble** *adj.* — **dis•burs′er** *n.*

dis•burse•ment (dĭs-bûrs′mənt) *n.* **1.** The act or process of disbursing. **2.** Money paid out; expenditure.

disc (dĭsk) *n. & v.* Var. of **disk.**

disc. *abbr.* Discount.

disc– *pref.* Var. of **disco–.**

dis•calced (dĭs-kălst′) *adj.* Barefoot or wearing sandals. Used of certain religious orders. [< Lat. *discalceātus* : *dis-*, dis- + *calceātus*, shod (< *calceus*, shoe < *calx*, *calc-*, heel).]

dis•cant (dĭs′kănt′) *Mus.* — *n.* Var. of **descant** 1. — *v.* (dĭs′-kănt′, dĭ-skănt′). Var. of **descant** 2.

dis•card (dĭ-skärd′) *v.* **-card•ed, -card•ing, -cards.** — *tr.* **1.** To throw away; reject. **2.** *Games.* **a.** To throw out (a playing card) from a hand. **b.** To play (a card other than a trump) from a suit different from that of the card led. — *intr. Games.* To discard a playing card. — *n.* (dĭs′kärd′). **1.** *Games.* **a.** The act of discarding in a card game. **b.** A discarded playing card. **2.** One that is discarded. — **dis•card′a•ble** *adj.* — **dis•card′er** *n.*

dis•car•nate (dĭs-kär′nĭt, -nāt′) *adj.* Having no material body or form. [DIS– + (IN)CARNATE.] — **dis•car′nate** *n.*

disc brake also **disk brake** *n.* A brake in which the friction is caused by a set of pads that press against a rotating disk.

dis•cern (dĭ-sûrn′, -zûrn′) *v.* **-cerned, -cern•ing, -cerns.** — *tr.* **1.** To perceive with the eyes or intellect; detect. **2.** To recognize or comprehend mentally. **3.** To perceive or recognize as distinct; distinguish. See Syns at **see**[1]. — *intr.* To perceive differences. [ME *discernen* < OFr. *discerner* < Lat. *discernere*, to separate : *dis-*, apart; see DIS– + *cernere*, to perceive; see **krei-***.] — **dis•cern′er** *n.*

dis•cern•i•ble (dĭ-sûr′nə-bəl, -zûr′-) *adj.* Perceptible, as by vision or the intellect. See Syns at **perceptible.** — **dis•cern′i•bly** *adv.*

dis•cern•ing (dĭ-sûr′nĭng, -zûr′-) *adj.* Exhibiting keen insight and good judgment; perceptive. — **dis•cern′ing•ly** *adv.*

dis•cern•ment (dĭ-sûrn′mənt, -zûrn′-) *n.* **1.** The act or process of exhibiting keen insight and good judgment. **2.** Keenness of insight and judgment.

dis•charge (dĭs-chärj′) *v.* **-charged, -charg•ing, -charg•es.** — *tr.* **1.a.** To relieve of a burden or of contents; unload. **b.** To unload or empty (contents). **2.a.** To release, as from confinement or duty. **b.** To let go; empty out. **c.** To pour forth; emit. **d.** To shoot. **3.** To remove from office or employment; dismiss. **4.** To perform the obligations or demands of (an office, duty, or task). **5.** To comply with the terms of (a promise, for example). **6.** *Law.* **a.** To acquit completely. **b.** To set aside; annul. **7.** To remove (color) from cloth, as by chemical bleaching. **8.** To cause the release of stored energy or electric charge from (a battery, for example). **9.** *Archit.* **a.** To apportion (weight) evenly, as over a door. **b.** To relieve (a part) of excess weight by distribution of pressure. — *intr.* **1.** To get rid of a burden or weight. **2.a.** To go off; fire. **b.** To pour forth, emit, or release contents. **c.** To become blurred, as a dye; run. **3.** To undergo the release of stored energy or electric charge. — *n.* (dĭs′chärj′, dĭs-chärj′). **1.** The act of removing a load or burden. **2.** The act of shooting or firing a projectile or weapon. **3.a.** A flowing out or pouring forth; emission; secretion. **b.** The amount or rate of emission or ejection. **c.** Something discharged, released, emitted, or excreted. **4.** The act or an instance of removing an obligation, a burden, or a responsibility. **5.a.** Fulfillment of the terms of something, such as a debt. **b.** Performance, as of an office. **6.a.** Dismissal or release from employment, service, care, or confinement. **b.** An official document certifying such release, esp. from military service. **7.** *Law.* An annulment or acquittal; dismissal, as of a court order. **8.** *Elect.* **a.** Release of stored energy in a capacitor. **b.** Conversion of chemical energy to electric energy in a storage battery. **c.** A flow of electricity in a dielectric, esp. in a rarefied gas. **d.** Elimination of net electric charge from a charged body. [ME *dischargen* < OFr. *deschargier* < LLat. *discarricāre* : Lat. *dis-*, dis- + LLat. *carricāre*, to load; see CHARGE.] — **dis•charge′a•ble** *adj.* — **dis′charg•ee′** *n.* — **dis•charg′er** *n.*

discharge lamp *n.* A lamp that generates light by means of an internal electrical discharge between electrodes in a gas.

discharge tube *n.* A closed insulating vessel containing a gas at low pressure through which an electric current flows when sufficient voltage is applied to its electrodes.

disc harrow *n.* Var. of **disk harrow.**

disci– *pref.* Var. of **disco–.**

dis•ci•form (dĭs′ə-fôrm′, dĭs′kə-) *adj.* Flat and rounded in shape; discoid: *disciform fungi.*

dis•ci•ple (dĭ-sī′pəl) *n.* **1.a.** One who assists in spreading the teachings of another. **b.** An active adherent, as of a movement. **2.** Often **Disciple.** One of the original followers of Jesus. **3. Disciple.** A member of the Disciples of Christ. [ME < OE *discipul* and < OFr. *desciple*, both < Lat. *discipulus*, pupil < *discere*, to learn. See **dek-***.] — **dis•ci′ple•ship′** *n.*

Dis•ci•ples of Christ (dĭ-sī′pəlz) *pl.n.* *(used with a sing. or pl. v.)* A Christian denomination founded in 1809 that accepts the Bible as the only rule of Christian faith and practice.

dis•ci•plin•a•ble (dĭs′ə-plĭn′ə-bəl, dĭs′ə-plĭn′-) *adj.* **1.** Deserving of or subject to discipline. **2.** Easily taught.

dis•ci•pli•nar•i•an (dĭs′ə-plə-nâr′ē-ən) *n.* One that enforces or believes in strict discipline. — *adj.* Disciplinary.

dis•ci•pli•nar•y (dĭs′ə-plə-nĕr′ē) *adj.* **1.** Of, relating to, or used for discipline: *disciplinary measures.* **2.** Of or relating to a specific field of academic study. — **dis′ci•pli•nar′i•ly** (-nâr′ə-lē) *adv.* — **dis′ci•pli•nar′i•ty** (-nâr′ĭ-tē, -năr′-) *n.*

dis•ci•pline (dĭs′ə-plĭn) *n.* **1.** Training expected to produce a specific character or pattern of behavior, esp. training that produces moral or mental improvement. **2.** Controlled behavior resulting from disciplinary training; self-control. **3.a.** Control obtained by enforcing compliance or order. **b.** A systematic method to obtain obedience. **c.** Order based on submission to authority. **4.** Punishment to correct or train. **5.** A set of rules or methods, as those regulating the practice of a church or monastic order. **6.** A branch of knowledge or teaching. — *tr.v.* **-plined, -plin•ing, -plines.** **1.** To train by instruction and practice, esp. to teach self-control to. **2.** To teach to accept authority. **3.** To punish to gain control or enforce obedience. **4.** To impose order on. [ME < OFr. *descepline* < Lat. *disciplīna* < *discipulus*, pupil. See DISCIPLE.] — **dis′ci•pli•nal** (-plə-nəl) *adj.* — **dis′ci•plin′er** *n.*

dis•ci•plined (dĭs′ə-plĭnd) *adj.* Possessing or indicative of discipline.

disc jockey also **disk jockey** *n.* An announcer who presents popular recorded music, esp. on the radio.

dis•claim (dĭs-klām′) *v.* **-claimed, -claim•ing, -claims.** — *tr.* **1.** To deny or renounce claim to or connection with; disown. **2.** To deny the validity of; repudiate. **3.** *Law.* To renounce one's right or claim to. — *intr. Law.* To renounce a right or claim. [ME *disclaimen* < AN *desclaimer* : *des-*, dis- + *claimer*, to claim (< Lat. *clāmāre*, to cry out; see CLAIM).]

dis•claim•er (dĭs-klā′mər) *n.* **1.** A repudiation or denial of responsibility or connection. **2.** *Law.* A renunciation of one's right or claim. [ME, denial of a feudal claim < AN *desclaimer*, to disclaim, denial of a feudal claim. See DISCLAIM.]

dis•cla•ma•tion (dĭs′klə-mā′shən) *n.* The act or an instance of disavowing; renunciation. [Prob. < AN *desclaimer, disclamer*, to disclaim. See DISCLAIM.]

dis•cli•max (dĭs-klī′măks′) *n. Ecol.* A climax community disturbed by various influences, esp. by human beings and domestic animals.

dis•close (dĭ-sklōz′) *tr.v.* **-closed, -clos•ing, -clos•es.** **1.** To expose to view, as by removing a cover. **2.** To make known (something secret). [ME *disclosen* < OFr. *desclore, desclos-* : *des-*, dis- + *clore*, to close (< Lat. *claudere*).] — **dis•clos′a•ble** *adj.* — **dis•clos′er** *n.*

dis•clos•ing agent (dĭ-sklō′zĭng) *n.* A dye used in dentistry to reveal the presence of dental plaque.

dis•clo•sure (dĭ-sklō′zhər) *n.* **1.** The act or process of revealing or uncovering. **2.** Something uncovered; a revelation.

dis•co (dĭs′kō) *n., pl.* **-cos.** **1.** A discotheque. **2.a.** *Mus.* Popular dance music characterized by strong repetitive bass rhythms. **b.** A style of dancing done esp. to disco music. [Short for DISCOTHEQUE.] — **dis′co** *adj. & v.*

disco– or **disc–** also **disci–** *pref.* **1.** Disk: *discoid.* **2.** Phonograph record: *discophile.* [Lat. < Gk. *disko-* < *diskos*, disk. See DISK.]

dis•cog•ra•phy (dĭ-skŏg′rə-fē) *n., pl.* **-phies.** **1.** The study and cataloging of phonograph records. **2.** A comprehensive list of the recordings made by a performer or of a composer's works. — **dis•cog′ra•pher** *n.* — **dis′co•graph′i•cal** (dĭs′kə-grăf′ĭ-kəl), **dis′co•graph′ic** (-grăf′ĭk) *adj.*

dis•coid (dĭs′koid′) also **dis•coi•dal** (dĭ-skoid′l) *adj.* **1.** Disk-shaped. **2.** Relating to or having a disk. **3.** *Bot.* Having disk flowers only. Used of a composite flower head. — **dis′coid′** *n.*

dis•col•or (dĭs-kŭl′ər) *v.* **-ored, -or•ing, -ors.** — *tr.* To alter or spoil the color of; stain. — *intr.* To become altered or spoiled in color. [ME *discolouren* < OFr. *discolerer* : *des-*, dis- + *colourer*, to color (< Lat. *colōrāre* < *color*, color; see COLOR).]

dis•col•or•a•tion (dĭs-kŭl′ə-rā′shən) *n.* **1.a.** The act of discoloring. **b.** The condition of being discolored. **2.** A discolored spot, smudge, or area; a stain.

dis•com•bob•u•late (dĭs′kəm-bŏb′yə-lāt′) *tr.v.* **-lat•ed, -lat•ing, -lates.** To throw into confusion. See Syns at **confuse.** [Perh. alteration of DISCOMPOSE.] — **dis′com•bob′u•la′tion** *n.*

dis•com•fit (dĭs-kŭm′fĭt) *tr.v.* **-fit•ed, -fit•ing, -fits.** **1.** To make uneasy or perplexed; disconcert. **2.** To thwart the plans of; frustrate. **3.** *Archaic.* To defeat in battle. — *n.* Discomfiture. [ME *discomfiten* < OFr. *desconfit*, p.part. of *desconfire, descumfire*, to defeat : *des-*, dis- + *confire*, to make (< Lat. *cōnficere*, to prepare; see COMFIT).]

Usage Note: *Discomfit* originally meant "to defeat, frustrate," and its newer meaning "to embarrass, disconcert,"

ă pat	oi boy
ā pay	ou out
âr care	o͝o to͝ok
ä father	o͞o bo͞ot
ĕ pet	ŭ cut
ē be	ûr urge
ĭ pit	th thin
ī pie	*th* this
îr pier	hw which
ŏ pot	zh vision
ō toe	ə about, item
ô paw	

Stress marks:
′ (primary);
′ (secondary), as in
dictionary (dĭk′shə-nĕr′ē)

olently; spew. **3.** To surrender (stolen money, for example) unwillingly. — *intr.* To discharge or pour forth contents. [ME *disgorgen* < OFr. *desgorger* : *des-*, dis- + *gorger*, to pack (< *gorge*, throat; see GORGE).] — **dis•gorge′ment** *n.*

dis•grace (dĭs-grās′) *n.* **1.** Loss of honor or reputation; shame. **2.** The condition of being strongly and generally disapproved. **3.** One that brings disfavor or discredit. — *tr.v.* **-graced, -grac•ing, -grac•es. 1.** To bring shame or dishonor on. **2.** To deprive of favor or good repute; treat with disfavor. [Fr. *disgrâce* < Ital. *disgrazia* : *dis-*, not (< Lat.; see DIS-) + *grazia*, favor (< Lat. *grātia* < *grātus*, pleasing; see **gʷerə-²***).] — **dis•grac′er** *n.*

dis•grace•ful (dĭs-grās′fəl) *adj.* Bringing or warranting disgrace. — **dis•grace′ful•ly** *adv.* — **dis•grace′ful•ness** *n.*

dis•grun•tle (dĭs-grŭn′tl) *tr.v.* **-tled, -tling, -tles.** To discontent. [DIS- + *gruntle*, to grumble (< ME *gruntelen*, freq. of *grunten*, to grunt; see GRUNT).] — **dis•grun′tle•ment** *n.*

dis•guise (dĭs-gīz′) *tr.v.* **-guised, -guis•ing, -guis•es. 1.a.** To modify the manner or appearance of to prevent recognition. **b.** To furnish with a disguise. **2.** To conceal or obscure by dissemblance; misrepresent. — *n.* **1.a.** The act or an instance of disguising. **b.** The condition of being disguised. **2.** Clothes or accessories concealing one's identity. **3.a.** Appearance that misrepresents the character of something. **b.** A pretense or misrepresentation. [ME *disguisen* < OFr. *desguiser* : *des-*, dis- + *guise*, manner; see GUISE.] — **dis•guis′ed•ly** (-gī′zĭd-lē) *adv.* — **dis•guise′ment** *n.* — **dis•guis′er** *n.*

dis•gust (dĭs-gŭst′) *tr.v.* **-gust•ed, -gust•ing, -gusts. 1.** To excite nausea or loathing in; sicken. **2.** To offend the taste or moral sense of; repel. — *n.* Profound repugnance excited by something offensive. [Fr. *dégoûter* < OFr. *desgouster*, to lose one's appetite : *des-*, dis- + *gouster*, to eat, taste (< Lat. *gustāre*; see **geus-***).]

Syns: disgust, nauseate, repel, revolt, sicken. The central meaning shared by these verbs is "to offend the senses or feelings of": *a disgusting stench; nauseating hypocrisy; repelled by arrogance; revolting brutality; a sickening odor.*

dis•gust•ed (dĭs-gŭs′tĭd) *adj.* Filled with disgust or irritated impatience. — **dis•gust′ed•ly** *adv.*

dis•gust•ful (dĭs-gŭst′fəl) *adj.* **1.** Causing disgust; repugnant. **2.** Full of or marked by disgust. — **dis•gust′ful•ly** *adv.*

dis•gust•ing (dĭs-gŭs′tĭng) *adj.* Arousing disgust; repugnant. — **dis•gust′ing•ly** *adv.*

dish (dĭsh) *n.* **1.a.** An open, usu. shallow concave container for holding or serving food. **b. dishes.** The containers and often the utensils used when eating. **c.** A shallow concave container. **2.** The amount a dish can hold. **3.a.** The food contained in a dish. **b.** A particular variety or preparation of food: *a tasty dish.* **4.a.** A depression similar to that in a food dish. **b.** The degree of concavity in such a depression. **5.** *Electron.* A dish antenna. **6.** *Slang.* A good-looking person, esp. a woman. — *v.* **dished, dish•ing, dish•es.** — *tr.* **1.** To serve (food) in or as if in a dish. **2.** To present: *dished up the entertainment.* **3.** To hollow out; make concave. **4.** *Chiefly British.* To foil or cheat; ruin. — *intr. Informal.* To talk idly, esp. to gossip. — ***phrasal verb.* dish out.** To give out; dispense freely. [ME < OE *disc* < Lat. *discus.* See DISK.]

dish antenna

dis•ha•bille (dĭs′ə-bēl′, -bē′) also **des•ha•bille** (dĕs′-) *n.* **1.** The state of being partially or very casually dressed. **2.** Casual or lounging attire. **3.** An intentionally careless manner. [Fr. *déshabillé* < p.part. of *déshabiller*, to undress : *des-*, dis- + *habiller*, to clothe; see HABILIMENT.]

dish antenna *n. Electron.* A microwave transmitter or receiver consisting of a concave parabolic reflector.

dis•har•mo•ni•ous (dĭs′här-mō′nē-əs) *adj.* Lacking in harmony. — **dis′har•mo′ni•ous•ly** *adv.*

dis•har•mo•nize (dĭs-här′mə-nīz′) *tr.v.* **-nized, -niz•ing, -niz•es.** To make disharmonious.

dis•har•mo•ny (dĭs-här′mə-nē) *n.* Lack of harmony; discord.

dish•cloth (dĭsh′klôth′, -klŏth′) *n.* A cloth for washing dishes.

dishcloth gourd *n.* See **loofa** 2.

dis•heart•en (dĭs-här′tn) *tr.v.* **-ened, -en•ing, -ens.** To shake or destroy the courage or resolution of; dispirit. — **dis•heart′en•ing•ly** *adv.* — **dis•heart′en•ment** *n.*

dished (dĭsht) *adj.* **1.** Concave. **2.** Slanting toward one another at the bottom. Used of a pair of wheels.

di•shev•el (dĭ-shĕv′əl) *tr.v.* **-eled, -el•ing, -els** or **-elled, -el•ling, -els. 1.a.** To let fall (hair or clothing) in disarray. **b.** To disarrange the hair or clothing of. **2.** To throw into disorder. [Back-formation < DISHEVELED.] — **di•shev′el•ment** *n.*

di•shev•eled or **di•shev•elled** (dĭ-shĕv′əld) *adj.* **1.** Being in loose disarray; unkempt, as hair. **2.** Marked by disorder; untidy. [ME *discheveled* < OFr. *deschevele*, p.part. of *descheveler*, to disarrange the hair : *des-*, apart; see DIS- + *chevel*, hair (< Lat. *capillus*).]

dis•hon•est (dĭs-ŏn′ĭst) *adj.* **1.** Disposed to lie, cheat, defraud, or deceive. **2.** Resulting from or marked by a lack of honesty. [ME *dishoneste*, dishonorable < OFr. *deshoneste*, prob. < Med.Lat. **dishonestus* : Lat. *dis-*, dis- + Lat. *honestus*, honorable; see HONEST.] — **dis•hon′est•ly** *adv.*

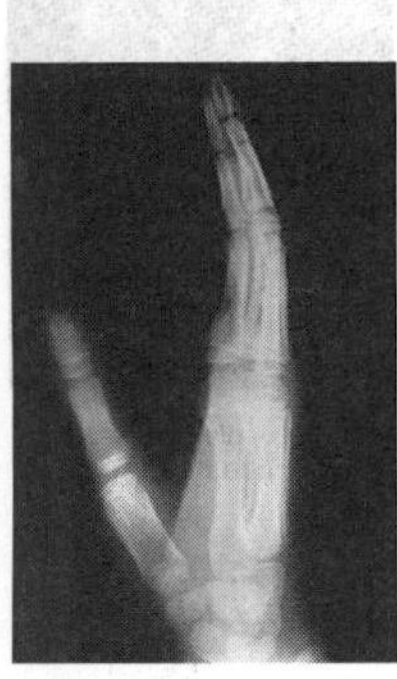

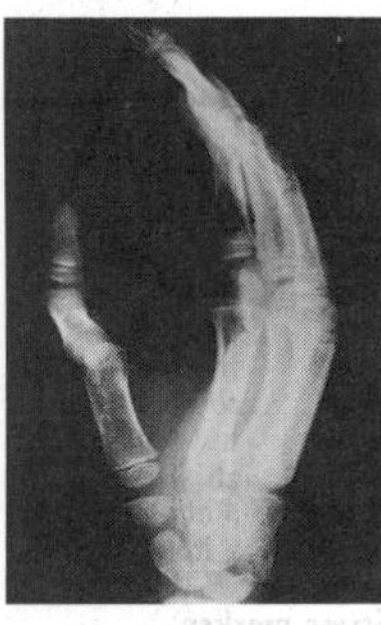

dislocate
Top: X-ray of a normal hand
Bottom: X-ray showing dislocated thumb

dis•hon•es•ty (dĭs-ŏn′ĭ-stē) *n.* **-ties. 1.** Lack of honesty or integrity; improbity. **2.** A dishonest act or statement.

dis•hon•or (dĭs-ŏn′ər) *n.* **1.** Loss of honor or reputation. **2.** The condition of having lost honor or good repute. **3.** A cause of loss of honor: *had become a dishonor to the club.* **4.** Failure to pay or refusal to accept a commercial obligation. — *tr.v.* **-ored, -or•ing, -ors. 1.** To bring disgrace upon. **2.** To treat in a disrespectful manner. **3.** To fail or refuse to accept or pay (a bill, for example). [ME *dishonour* < OFr. *deshonor* : *des-*, dis- + *honor*, honor; see HONOR.] — **dis•hon′or•er** *n.*

dis•hon•or•a•ble (dĭs-ŏn′ər-ə-bəl) *adj.* **1.** Marked by or causing dishonor or discredit. **2.** Lacking integrity; unprincipled. — **dis•hon′or•a•ble•ness** *n.* — **dis•hon′or•a•bly** *adv.*

dishonorable discharge *n.* Discharge from the armed forces for a grave offense, such as cowardice or murder.

dish•pan (dĭsh′păn′) *n.* A flat-bottomed basin for washing dishes.

dish•rag (dĭsh′răg′) *n.* A dishcloth.

dish•tow•el (dĭsh′tou′əl) *n.* A towel for drying dishes.

dish•wash•er (dĭsh′wŏsh′ər, -wô′shər) *n.* **1.** A person who washes dishes. **2.** A machine for washing dishes.

dish•wa•ter (dĭsh′wô′tər, -wŏt′ər) *n.* Water in which dishes are washed.

dish•y (dĭsh′ē) *adj.* **-i•er, -i•est.** *Chiefly British.* Good-looking; attractive.

dis•il•lu•sion (dĭs′ĭ-lo͞o′zhən) *tr.v.* **-sioned, -sion•ing, -sions.** To free or deprive of illusion. — *n.* **1.** The act of disenchanting. **2.** The condition or fact of being disenchanted. — **dis′il•lu′sion•ment** *n.* — **dis′il•lu′sive** (-sĭv, -zĭv) *adj.*

dis•in•cen•tive (dĭs′ĭn-sĕn′tĭv) *n.* Something that prevents or discourages action; a deterrent.

dis•in•cli•na•tion (dĭs-ĭn′klə-nā′shən) *n.* A lack of inclination; a mild aversion or reluctance.

dis•in•cline (dĭs′ĭn-klīn′) *v.* **-clined, -clin•ing, -clines.** — *tr.* To make reluctant or averse. — *intr.* To be unwilling.

dis•in•clined (dĭs′ĭn-klīnd′) *adj.* Unwilling or reluctant.

dis•in•fect (dĭs′ĭn-fĕkt′) *tr.v.* **-fect•ed, -fect•ing, -fects.** To cleanse so as to destroy or prevent the growth of disease-carrying microorganisms. — **dis′in•fec′tion** *n.*

dis•in•fec•tant (dĭs′ĭn-fĕk′tənt) *n.* An agent, such as heat, that disinfects by destroying, neutralizing, or inhibiting the growth of disease-carrying microorganisms. — *adj.* Serving to disinfect.

dis•in•fest (dĭs′ĭn-fĕst′) *tr.v.* **-fest•ed, -fest•ing, -fests.** To rid of vermin. — **dis•in′fes•ta′tion** (-fĕ-stā′shən) *n.*

dis•in•fes•tant (dĭs′ĭn-fĕs′tənt) *n.* An agent that eradicates an infestation, as of vermin.

dis•in•fla•tion (dĭs′ĭn-flā′shən) *n.* Downward movement of inflated prices to a more normal level. — **dis′in•fla′tion•ar′y** (-shə-nĕr′ē) *adj.*

dis•in•form (dĭs′ĭn-fôrm′) *tr.v.* **-formed, -form•ing, -forms.** To give disinformation to. [Back-formation < DISINFORMATION.] — **dis′in•form′er, dis′in•form′ant** *n.*

dis•in•for•ma•tion (dĭs-ĭn′fər-mā′shən) *n.* **1.** Deliberately misleading information announced or leaked by a government to influence another nation. **2.** Dissemination of disinformation. [Poss. transl. of Russ. *dezinformatsiya.*]

dis•in•gen•u•ous (dĭs′ĭn-jĕn′yo͞o-əs) *adj.* Not straightforward or candid; crafty. — **dis′in•gen′u•ous•ly** *adv.* — **dis′in•gen′u•ous•ness** *n.*

dis•in•her•it (dĭs′ĭn-hĕr′ĭt) *tr.v.* **-it•ed, -it•ing, -its. 1.** To exclude from inheritance. **2.** To deprive of a right or privilege. — **dis′in•her′i•tance** *n.*

dis•in•hi•bi•tion (dĭs′ĭn-hə-bĭsh′ən, -ĭn-ə-, dĭs-ĭn′-) *n.* A loss of inhibition, as through the influence of drugs or alcohol.

dis•in•te•grate (dĭs-ĭn′tĭ-grāt′) *v.* **-grat•ed, -grat•ing, -grates.** — *intr.* **1.** To become reduced to components, fragments, or particles. **2.** *Phys. & Chem.* To decay or undergo a transformation from a more massive to a less massive nucleus by the emission of particles or radiation. — *tr.* To cause to disintegrate. — **dis•in′te•gra′tion** *n.* — **dis•in′te•gra′tive** *adj.* — **dis•in′te•gra′tor** *n.*

dis•in•ter (dĭs′ĭn-tûr′) *tr.v.* **-terred, -ter•ring, -ters. 1.** To dig up or remove from a grave or tomb; exhume. **2.** To bring to public notice; disclose. — **dis′in•ter′ment** *n.*

dis•in•ter•est (dĭs-ĭn′tər-ĭst, -ĭn′trĭst) *n.* **1.** Freedom from selfish bias or self-interest. **2.** Lack of interest; indifference. — *tr.v.* **-est•ed, -est•ing, -ests.** To divest of interest.

dis•in•ter•est•ed (dĭs-ĭn′trĭ-stĭd, -ĭn′tə-rĕs′tĭd) *adj.* **1.** Free of bias and self-interest; impartial. **2.a.** Not interested; indifferent. **b.** Having lost interest. — **dis•in′ter•est•ed•ly** *adv.* — **dis•in′ter•est•ed•ness** *n.*

Usage Note: Many maintain that the word *disinterested* can legitimately be used only in its sense of "having no stake in (an outcome or issue)," as in *Since the judge stands to profit from the sale of the company, she cannot be considered a disinterested party in the dispute.* In our most recent survey 89 percent of the Usage Panel rejected the sentence *His unwillingness to give five minutes of his time proves that he is disinterested* [uninterested] *in finding a solution to the problem,* a proportion that is not significantly different from the 93 percent who disapproved in an earlier survey.

dis•in•tox•i•cate (dĭs′ĭn-tŏk′sĭ-kāt′) *tr.v.* **-cat•ed, -cat•ing, -cates.** To free from the effects of intoxication or from dependence on intoxicating agents. **—dis′in•tox′i•ca′tion** *n.*

dis•in•vest•ment (dĭs′ĭn-vĕst′mənt) *n.* Withdrawal of capital investment from a company or country.

dis•join (dĭs-join′) *v.* **-joined, -join•ing, -joins.** *—tr.* To undo the joining of; separate. *—intr.* To become separated. [ME *disjoinen* < OFr. *desjoindre* < Lat. *disiungere* : *dis-*, dis- + *iungere*, to join; see JOIN.]

dis•joint (dĭs-joint′) *v.* **-joint•ed, -joint•ing, -joints.** *—tr.* **1.** To put out of joint; dislocate. **2.** To take apart at the joints. **3.** To destroy the coherence or connections of. **4.** To separate; disjoin. *—intr.* **1.** To come apart at the joints. **2.** To become dislocated. *—adj. Math.* Having no elements in common. Used of sets. [ME *disjointen*, to destroy, ult. < OFr. *desjoint*, p.part. of *desjoindre*, to disjoin. See DISJOIN.]

dis•joint•ed (dĭs-join′tĭd) *adj.* **1.** Separated at the joints. **2.** Out of joint; dislocated. **3.** Lacking order or coherence. **—dis•joint′ed•ly** *adv.* **—dis•joint′ed•ness** *n.*

dis•junct (dĭs-jŭngkt′) *adj.* **1.** Characterized by separation. **2.** *Mus.* Relating to progression by intervals larger than major seconds. [ME *disjuncte* < Lat. *disiūnctus*, p.part. of *disiungere*, to disjoin. See DISJOIN.]

dis•junc•tion (dĭs-jŭngk′shən) *n.* **1.** The act of disjoining or the condition of being disjointed. **2.** *Logic.* A proposition that presents two or more alternative terms, with the assertion that only one is true. **3.** *Genet.* The separation of homologous chromosomes during meiosis.

dis•junc•tive (dĭs-jŭngk′tĭv) *adj.* **1.** Serving to separate or divide. **2.** *Gram.* Serving to establish a relationship of contrast or opposition, as the conjunction *but* in *rich but unhappy.* **3.** *Logic.* **a.** Of a proposition that presents two or more alternative terms. **b.** Of a syllogism that contains a disjunction as one premise. *—n. Gram.* A disjunctive conjunction. **—dis•junc′tive•ly** *adv.*

dis•junc•ture (dĭs-jŭngk′chər) *n.* Disjunction; separation.

disk also **disc** (dĭsk) *—n.* **1.** A thin, flat, circular object or plate. **2.** Something resembling such an object. **3.a.** The disk used in a disc brake. **b.** A disk used on a disk harrow. **4.** A round flattened structure in an animal, such as an intervertebral disk. **5.** *Bot.* The flower head of composite plants, such as the daisy. **6.a.** A phonograph record. **b.** An optical disk, esp. a compact disk. **c.** *Comp. Sci.* A magnetic disk. **7.** A circular grid in a phototypesetting machine. *—tr.v.* **disked, disk•ing, disks** also **disced, disc•ing, discs.** To work (soil) with a disk harrow. [Lat. *discus*, quoit < Gk. *diskos* < *dikein*, to throw. See **deik-***.]

disk brake *n.* Var. of **disc brake.**

disk drive *n. Comp. Sci.* A device that reads data stored on a magnetic or optical disk and writes data onto the disk for storage.

disk•ette (dĭ-skĕt′) *n. Comp. Sci.* See **floppy disk.**

disk flower *n.* Any of the tiny tubular flowers in the center of the flower head of certain composite plants, such as the daisy.

disk harrow or **disc harrow** *n.* A harrow equipped with a series of disks set on edge or at an angle on one or more axles.

disk jockey *n.* Var. of **disc jockey.**

disk wheel *n.* A spokeless wheel in which a disk joins the hub to the rim.

dis•like (dĭs-līk′) *tr.v.* **-liked, -lik•ing, -likes.** To regard with distaste or aversion. *—n.* An attitude or a feeling of distaste or aversion. **—dis•lik′a•ble** *adj.*

dis•lo•cate (dĭs′lō-kāt′, dĭs-lō′kāt) *tr.v.* **-cat•ed, -cat•ing, -cates. 1.** To put out of usual or proper position or relationship. **2.** To displace (a body part), esp. to displace a bone from its normal position. **3.** To throw into confusion; disrupt. [Med. Lat. *dislocāre*, *dislocāt-* : *dis-*, dis- + Lat. *locāre*, to place (< *locus*, place).]

dis•lo•ca•tion (dĭs′lō-kā′shən) *n.* **1.** The act or process of dislocating or the state of having been dislocated. **2.** Displacement of a body part, esp. the temporary displacement of a bone from its normal position. **3.** *Chem.* An imperfection in a crystal structure resulting from an absence of an atom or atoms in one or more layers. **4.** *Geol.* See **displacement** 3.

dis•lodge (dĭs-lŏj′) *v.* **-lodged, -lodg•ing, -lodg•es.** *—tr.* To remove or force out from a position or dwelling previously occupied. *—intr.* To move or go from a dwelling or former position. [ME *disloggen* < OFr. *deslogier* : *des-*, dis- + *logier*, to lodge (< *loge*, shed, of Gmc. orig.).] **—dis•lodge′ment, dis•lodg′ment** *n.*

dis•loy•al (dĭs-loi′əl) *adj.* Lacking loyalty. [ME **disloial* < OFr. *desloial* : *des-*, dis- + *loial*, loyal; see LOYAL.] **—dis•loy′al•ly** *adv.*

dis•loy•al•ty (dĭs-loi′əl-tē) *n., pl.* **-ties. 1.** The quality of being disloyal; faithlessness. **2.** A disloyal act.

dis•mal (dĭz′məl) *adj.* **1.** Causing gloom or depression; dreary: *dismal weather.* **2.** Characterized by ineptitude, dullness, or a lack of merit. **3.** *Obsolete.* Dreadful; disastrous. *—n. Chiefly South Atlantic U.S.* See **pocosin.** [ME, unlucky days, unlucky < AN, unlucky days < Med.Lat. *diēs malī* : Lat. *diēs*, day; see **deiw-*** + Lat. *malī*, pl. of *malus*, evil; see **mel-³***.] **—dis′mal•ly** *adv.* **—dis′mal•ness** *n.*

Dis•mal Swamp (dĭz′məl). A swampy region of SE VA and NE NC.

dis•man•tle (dĭs-măn′tl) *tr.v.* **-tled, -tling, -tles. 1.a.** To take apart; disassemble. **b.** To put an end to in a gradual systematic way. **2.** To strip of furnishings or equipment. **3.** To strip of covering or clothing. [Obsolete Fr. *desmanteler*, to raze fortifications round a town < OFr. : *des-*, dis- + *emmanteler*, to cover with a coat, shelter (ult. < *mantel*, cloak; see MANTLE).] **—dis•man′tle•ment** *n.*

dis•mast (dĭs-măst′) *tr.v.* **-mast•ed, -mast•ing, -masts.** *Naut.* To remove or break off the mast of.

dis•may (dĭs-mā′) *tr.v.* **-mayed, -may•ing, -mays. 1.** To destroy the courage or resolution of by exciting dread or apprehension. **2.** To cause to lose enthusiasm; disillusion. **3.** To upset or alarm. *—n.* A sudden or complete loss of courage in the face of trouble or danger. [ME *dismaien* < AN **desmaiier* : prob. *de-*, intensive pref.; see DE- + OFr. *esmaier*, to frighten (< VLat. **exmagāre*, to deprive of power : Lat. *ex-*, ex- + Gmc. **magan*, to be able to; see **magh-***).] **—dis•may′ing•ly** *adv.*

Syns: *dismay, appall, daunt, horrify, shake.* These verbs mean to deprive a person of courage or the power to act as a result of fear or anxiety. *Dismay* is the least specific: *Plummeting stock prices dismayed speculators. Appall* implies helplessness caused by an awareness of the enormity of something: *"for as this appalling ocean surrounds the verdant land"* (Herman Melville). *Daunt* suggests abated courage: *"captains courageous, whom death could not daunt"* (Anonymous ballad). *Horrify* implies dread, shock, or revulsion: *horrified by the prospect of war.* To *shake* is to dismay profoundly: *"A little swift brutality shook him to the very soul"* (John Galsworthy). See also Syns at **fear.**

dis•mem•ber (dĭs-mĕm′bər) *tr.v.* **-bered, -ber•ing, -bers. 1.** To cut, tear, or pull off the limbs of. **2.** To divide into pieces. [ME *dismembren* < OFr. *desmembrer* < VLat. **dismembrāre* : Lat. *dis-*, dis- + Lat. *membrum*, limb; see MEMBER.] **—dis•mem′ber•ment** *n.*

dis•miss (dĭs-mĭs′) *tr.v.* **-missed, -miss•ing, -miss•es. 1.** To end the employment or service of; discharge. **2.** To direct or allow to leave. **3.a.** To stop considering; rid one's mind of; dispel. See Syns at **eject. b.** To refuse to accept or recognize; reject. **4.** *Law.* To put (a claim or action) out of court without further hearing. [ME *dismissen* < Med.Lat. *dismittere*, *dismiss-*, var. of Lat. *dīmittere* : *dī-*, *dis-*, apart; see DIS- + *mittere*, to send.] **—dis•miss′i•ble** *adj.* **—dis•mis′sion** (-mĭsh′ən) *n.*

dis•miss•al (dĭs-mĭs′əl) *n.* **1.a.** The act of dismissing. **b.** The condition of being dismissed. **2.** An order or notice of discharge.

dis•mis•sive (dĭs-mĭs′ĭv) *adj.* **1.** Serving to dismiss. **2.** Showing indifference or disregard: *a dismissive shrug.*

dis•mount (dĭs-mount′) *v.* **-mount•ed, -mount•ing, -mounts.** *—intr.* To get off or down, as from a horse. *—tr.* **1.** To remove from a support, setting, or mounting. **2.** To unseat or throw off, as from a horse. **3.** To disassemble (a mechanism, for example). *—n.* (dĭs′mount′). The act or manner of dismounting, esp. from a horse. [Prob. alteration of obsolete Fr. *desmonter*, to unseat : *des-*, dis- + *monter*, to mount; see MOUNT¹.] **—dis•mount′a•ble** *adj.*

Walt Disney

Dis•ney (dĭz′nē), **Walter ("Walt") Elias.** 1901–66. Amer. animator and motion picture executive whose full-length animated features include *Snow White* (1938).

dis•o•be•di•ence (dĭs′ə-bē′dē-əns) *n.* Refusal or failure to obey. **—dis′o•be′di•ent** *adj.* **—dis′o•be′di•ent•ly** *adv.*

dis•o•bey (dĭs′ə-bā′) *v.* **-beyed, -bey•ing, -beys.** *—intr.* To refuse or fail to follow an order or a rule. *—tr.* To refuse or fail to obey (an order, for example). [ME *disobeien* < OFr. *desobeir* < VLat. **disobedīre* : Lat. *dis-*, dis- + Lat. *oboedīre*, to obey; see OBEY.] **—dis′o•bey′er** *n.*

dis•o•blige (dĭs′ə-blīj′) *tr.v.* **-bliged, -blig•ing, -blig•es. 1.** To refuse or neglect to act in accord with the wishes of. **2.** To inconvenience. **3.** To give offense to; affront. **—dis′o•blig′ing•ly** *adv.*

dis•or•der (dĭs-ôr′dər) *n.* **1.** A lack of order or regular arrangement; confusion. **2.** A breach of civic order; a public disturbance. **3.** An ailment that affects the mind or body. *—tr.v.* **-dered, -der•ing, -ders. 1.** To throw into confusion or disarray. **2.** To disturb the normal physical or mental health of; derange.

dis•or•dered (dĭs-ôr′dərd) *adj.* **1.** Being in a condition of confusion or disarray. **2.** Physically or mentally ill. **—dis•or′dered•ly** *adv.* **—dis•or′dered•ness** *n.*

dis•or•der•ly (dĭs-ôr′dər-lē) *adj.* **1.** Lacking regular or logical order or arrangement. **2.** Undisciplined. **3.** *Law.* Disturbing the public peace or decorum. **—dis•or′der•li•ness** *n.*

disorderly conduct *n. Law.* An offense involving disturbance of the public peace and decency.

dis•or•gan•ize (dĭs-ôr′gə-nīz′) *tr.v.* **-ized, -iz•ing, -iz•es.** To destroy the organization, systematic arrangement, or unity of. **—dis•or′gan•i•za′tion** (-gə-nĭ-zā′shən) *n.*

dis•o•ri•ent (dĭs-ôr′ē-ĕnt′, -ōr′-) *tr.v.* **-ent•ed, -ent•ing, -ents.** To cause (a person, for example) to experience disorientation.

dis•o•ri•en•ta•tion (dĭs-ôr′ē-ĕn-tā′shən) *n.* **1.** Loss of one's

ă pat	oi boy
ā pay	ou out
âr care	ŏŏ took
ä father	ōō boot
ĕ pet	ŭ cut
ē be	ûr urge
ĭ pit	th thin
ī pie	*th* this
îr pier	hw which
ŏ pot	zh vision
ō toe	ə about, item
ô paw	

Stress marks:
′ (primary);
′ (secondary), as in
dictionary (dĭk′shə-nĕr′ē)

sense of direction, position, or relationship with one's surroundings. **2.** Intellectual or moral confusion. **3.** *Psychol.* A state of confusion regarding place, time, or personal identity.

dis•own (dĭs-ōn′) *tr.v.* **-owned, -own•ing, -owns.** To refuse to acknowledge or accept as one's own; repudiate.

disp. *abbr.* Dispensary.

dis•par•age (dĭ-spăr′ĭj) *tr.v.* **-aged, -ag•ing, -ag•es. 1.** To speak of in a slighting way; belittle. **2.** To reduce in esteem or rank. [ME *disparagen,* to degrade < OFr. *desparager* : *des-,* dis- + *parage,* high birth (< *per,* peer; see PEER[2]).] **—dis•par′age•ment** *n.* **—dis•par′ag•er** *n.* **—dis•par′ag•ing•ly** *adv.*

dis•pa•rate (dĭs′pər-ĭt, dĭ-spăr′ĭt) *adj.* Fundamentally distinct or different; entirely dissimilar. [Lat. *disparātus,* p.part. of *disparāre,* to separate : *dis-,* apart; see DIS– + *parāre,* to prepare; see **perə-[1]*.**] **—dis′pa•rate•ly** *adv.* **—dis′pa•rate•ness** *n.*

dis•par•i•ty (dĭ-spăr′ĭ-tē) *n., pl.* **-ties. 1.** The condition or fact of being unequal, as in age; difference. **2.** Unlikeness; incongruity. [Fr. *disparité* < OFr. *desparite* < LLat. *disparitās* : Lat. *dis-,* dis- + LLat. *paritās,* equality; see PARITY[1].]

dis•pas•sion (dĭs-păsh′ən) *n.* Freedom from passion, bias, or emotion; objectivity.

dis•pas•sion•ate (dĭs-păsh′ə-nĭt) *adj.* Devoid of or unaffected by passion, emotion, or bias. See Syns at **fair[1]. —dis•pas′sion•ate•ly** *adv.* **—dis•pas′sion•ate•ness** *n.*

dis•patch also **des•patch** (dĭ-spăch′) **—***tr.v.* **-patched, -patch•ing, -patch•es. 1.** To relegate to a specific destination or send on specific business. **2.a.** To complete, transact, or dispose of promptly. **b.** To eat up (food); finish off (a dish or meal). **3.** To put to death summarily. **—***n.* **1.** The act of sending off, as to a specific destination. **2.** The act of putting to death. **3.** Speed in performance or movement. See Syns at **haste. 4.** (*also* dĭs′păch′). A written message, esp. an official communication, sent with speed. **5.** (*also* dĭs′păch′). A news item sent to a news organization, as by a correspondent. [Sp. *despachar* or Ital. *dispacciare,* both prob. ult. < OProv. *empachar,* to impede < VLat. **impāctāre,* freq. of Lat. *impingere,* to dash against. See IMPINGE.]

dis•patch•er (dĭs-păch′ər) *n.* One that dispatches, as: **a.** One that sends out trains, buses, trucks, or cars according to a schedule. **b.** *Comp. Sci.* A routine that controls the access of input and output devices to the processing system.

dis•pel (dĭ-spĕl′) *tr.v.* **-pelled, -pel•ling, -pels. 1.** To rid one's mind of: *managed to dispel my doubts.* **2.** To drive away or off by or as if by scattering. [ME *dispellen* < Lat. *dispellere* : *dis-,* apart; see DIS– + *pellere,* to drive; see **pel-[5]*.**]

dis•pen•sa•ble (dĭ-spĕn′sə-bəl) *adj.* **1.** Not essential; unimportant. **2.** Capable of being dispensed, administered, or distributed. **3.** Subject to dispensation, as a vow or church law. **—dis•pen′sa•bil′i•ty, dis•pen′sa•ble•ness** *n.*

dis•pen•sa•ry (dĭ-spĕn′sə-rē) *n., pl.* **-ries. 1.** An office in a hospital, school, or other institution from which medical supplies, preparations, and treatments are dispensed. **2.** A public institution that dispenses medicines or medical aid.

dis•pen•sa•tion (dĭs′pən-sā′shən, -pĕn-) *n.* **1.a.** The act of dispensing. **b.** Something dispensed. **c.** A specific arrangement or system by which something is dispensed. **2.** An exemption or a release from an obligation or a rule, granted by or as if by an authority. **3.a.** An exemption from a church law or a vow granted by an ecclesiastical authority. **b.** The document containing this exemption. **4.** *Theol.* **a.** The divine ordering of worldly affairs. **b.** A religious system considered to have been divinely revealed or appointed. **—dis′pen•sa′tion•al** *adj.*

dis•pen•sa•to•ry (dĭ-spĕn′sə-tôr′ē, -tōr′ē) *n., pl.* **-ries.** A book in which the contents, preparation, and uses of medicines are described; a pharmacopoeia.

dis•pense (dĭ-spĕns′) *v.* **-pensed, -pens•ing, -pens•es. —***tr.* **1.** To deal out in parts or portions; distribute. See Syns at **distribute. 2.** To prepare and give out (medicines). **3.** To administer (laws, for example). **4.** To exempt or release, as from a religious obligation. **—***intr.* To grant a dispensation or an exemption. ***—phrasal verb.*** **dispense with. 1.** To manage without; forgo: *Let's dispense with the formalities.* **2.** To get rid of; do away with. [ME *dispensen* < OFr. *dispenser* < Lat. *dispēnsāre,* to distribute, freq. of *dispendere,* to weigh out : *dis-,* out; see DIS– + *pendere,* to weigh; see **(s)pen-*.**]**dis•pens•er** (dĭ-spĕn′sər) *n.* One that dispenses or gives out, esp. a machine or container that allows the contents to be removed and used in convenient or prescribed amounts.

dis•peo•ple (dĭs-pē′pəl) *tr.v.* **-pled, -pling, -ples.** To depopulate.

dis•per•sal (dĭ-spûr′səl) *n.* The act or process of dispersing or the condition of being dispersed; distribution.

dis•perse (dĭ-spûrs′) *v.* **-persed, -pers•ing, -pers•es. —***tr.* **1.a.** To drive off or scatter in different directions: *The police dispersed the crowd.* **b.** To strew or distribute widely. **2.** To cause to vanish or disappear. **3.** To disseminate (knowledge, for example). **4.** To separate (light) into spectral rays. **5.** To distribute (particles) evenly throughout a medium. **—***intr.* **1.** To move in different directions; scatter. **2.** To vanish; dissipate. [ME *dispersen* < OFr. *disperser* < Lat. *dispergere, dispers-,* to disperse : *dis-,* apart; see DIS– + *spargere,* to scatter.] **—dis•per′sant** *n.* **—dis•pers′ed•ly** (-spûr′sĭd-lē) *adv.* **—dis•pers′er** *n.* **—dis•pers′i•ble** *adj.*

disperse phase *n.* The particles or droplets in a disperse system that are dispersed throughout a medium.

disperse system *n. Chem.* A system, such as a colloid, consisting of a disperse phase in a dispersion medium.

dis•per•sion (dĭ-spûr′zhən, -shən) *n.* **1.a.** The act or process of dispersing. **b.** The state of being dispersed. **2.** *Statistics.* The degree of scatter of data, usu. about an average value, such as the median. **3.** *Phys.* **a.** Separation of a complex wave into its component parts according to a given characteristic, such as wavelength. **b.** Separation of visible light into colors by refraction or diffraction. **4.** *Chem.* See **disperse system.**

dispersion medium *n.* The continuous medium, such as a gas, liquid, or solid, in which a disperse phase is distributed.

dis•per•sive (dĭ-spûr′sĭv, -zĭv) *adj.* **1.** Tending to become dispersed. **2.** Tending to produce dispersion. **—dis•per′sive•ly** *adv.* **—dis•per′sive•ness** *n.*

dis•pir•it (dĭ-spĭr′ĭt) *tr.v.* **-it•ed, -it•ing, -its.** To lower in or deprive of spirit; dishearten. [DI(S)– + SPIRIT.]

dis•pir•it•ed (dĭ-spĭr′ĭ-tĭd) *adj.* Marked by low spirits; dejected. **—dis•pir′it•ed•ly** *adv.*

dis•place (dĭs-plās′) *tr.v.* **-placed, -plac•ing, -plac•es. 1.** To move from the usual place or position, esp. to force to leave a homeland. **2.** To take the place of; supplant. **3.** To discharge from an office or position. **—dis•place′a•ble** *adj.* **—dis•plac′er** *n.*

displaced person *n.* One who has been driven from one's homeland by war or internal upheaval.

dis•place•ment (dĭs-plās′mənt) *n.* **1.a.** The act of displacing. **b.** The condition of having been displaced. **2.** *Phys.* **a.** The weight or volume of a fluid displaced by a floating body, used esp. as a measurement of the weight or bulk of ships. **b.** A vector or the magnitude of a vector from the initial position to a subsequent position assumed by a body. **3.** *Geol.* **a.** The relative movement between the two sides of a fault. **b.** The distance between the two sides of a fault. **4.** *Psychiat.* A defense mechanism in which emotion, affect, or desires shift from the original object to a more acceptable or immediate substitute.

displacement ton *n. Naut.* A unit for measuring the displacement of a ship afloat, equivalent to one long ton or about one cubic meter of salt water.

dis•play (dĭ-splā′) *v.* **-played, -play•ing, -plays. —***tr.* **1.a.** To present or hold up to view. **b.** *Comp. Sci.* To provide (information or graphics) on a screen. **2.** To give evidence of; manifest. **3.** To exhibit ostentatiously; show off. **4.** To be endowed with an identifiable form or character. **5.** To express, as by gestures or bodily posture. **6.** To spread out; unfurl. **—***intr. Comp. Sci.* To provide information or graphics on a screen. **—***n.* **1.a.** The act of displaying. **b.** A public exhibition. **c.** Objects or merchandise set out for viewing by the public. **2.** A demonstration or manifestation. **3.a.** *Biol.* A specialized pattern of visually communicative behavior such as the presentation of colors or plumage by male birds as part of courtship. **b.** An instance of such behavior. **4.** Ostentatious exhibition. **5.** An advertisement or headline designed to catch the eye. **6.a.** *Comp. Sci.* A device that gives information in a visual form, as on a screen. **b.** A visual representation of information. [ME *displayen* < AN *despleier* < Med.Lat. *displicāre,* to unfold < Lat., to scatter : *dis-,* apart; see DIS– + *plicāre,* to fold; see **plek-*.**]

dis•please (dĭs-plēz′) *v.* **-pleased, -pleas•ing, -pleas•es. —***tr.* To cause annoyance or vexation to. **—***intr.* To cause annoyance or displeasure. [ME *displesen* < OFr. *desplaire, desplais-* < VLat. **displacēre* < Lat. *displicēre* : Lat. *dis-,* dis- + Lat. *placēre,* to please; see PLEASE.] **—dis•pleas′ing•ly** *adv.*

dis•pleas•ure (dĭs-plĕzh′ər) *n.* **1.** The condition or fact of being displeased; dissatisfaction. **2.** Discomfort, uneasiness, or pain. **3.** *Archaic.* An injurious offense. [ME *displesure* < OFr. *desplaisir* : *des-,* dis- + *plaisir,* pleasure; see PLEASURE.]

dis•plode (dĭ-splōd′) *tr. & intr.v.* **-plod•ed, -plod•ing, -plodes.** *Archaic.* To explode. [Lat. *displōdere* : *dis-,* dis- + *plaudere,* to clap, beat.]

dis•port (dĭ-spôrt′, -spōrt′) *v.* **-port•ed, -port•ing, -ports. —***intr.* To amuse oneself in a light frolicsome manner. **—***tr.* **1.** To amuse (oneself) in a light frolicsome manner. **2.** To display. **—***n.* Frolicsome diversion. [ME *disporten* < OFr. *desporter,* to divert : *des-,* apart; see DIS– + *porter,* to carry (< Lat. *portāre;* see PORT[5]).]

dis•pos•a•ble (dĭ-spō′zə-bəl) *adj.* **1.** Designed to be disposed of after use: *disposable razors.* **2.a.** Remaining to a person after taxes have been deducted: *disposable income.* **b.** Free for use; available. **—***n.* An article, such as a paper diaper, that can be disposed of after one use. **—dis•pos′a•bil′i•ty** *n.*

dis•pos•al (dĭ-spō′zəl) *n.* **1.** A particular order, distribution, or placement. **2.** A particular method of attending to or settling matters. **3.** Transference by gift or sale. **4.** The act or process of getting rid of something. **5.** An electric device installed below a sink that grinds garbage so it can be flushed away. **6.** The liberty or power to dispose of.

dis•pose (dĭ-spōz′) *v.* **-posed, -pos•ing, -pos•es.** —*tr.* **1.** To place or set in a particular order; arrange. **2.** To put (business affairs, for example) into correct, definitive, or conclusive form. **3.** To put into a willing or receptive frame of mind; incline. See Syns at **incline.** —*intr.* To settle or decide a matter. —*n. Obsolete.* **1.** Disposal. **2.** Disposition; demeanor. —***phrasal verb.* dispose of. 1.** To attend to; settle: *disposed of the problem quickly.* **2.** To transfer or part with. **3.** To get rid of; throw out. **4.** To kill or destroy. [ME *disposen* < OFr. *disposer,* alteration (influenced by *poser,* to put, place; see POSE[1]) : of Lat. *dispōnere,* to arrange : *dis-,* apart; see DIS- + *pōnere,* to put; see **apo-***.] —**dis•pos′er** *n.*

dis•po•si•tion (dĭs′pə-zĭsh′ən) *n.* **1.** One's usual mood; temperament. **2.a.** A habitual inclination; a tendency. **b.** A physical property or tendency. **3.** Arrangement, positioning, or distribution. **4.** A final settlement. **5.** An act of disposing of; a bestowal or transfer to another. **6.a.** The power or liberty to control, direct, or dispose. **b.** Management; control. [ME *disposicioun* < OFr. *disposition* < Lat. *dispositiō, dispositiōn-* < *dispositus,* p.part. of *dispōnere,* to dispose. See DISPOSE.]

dis•pos•sess (dĭs′pə-zĕs′) *tr.v.* **-sessed, -sess•ing, -sess•es.** To deprive (another) of the possession or occupancy of something. —**dis′pos•ses′sion** (-zĕsh′ən) *n.* —**dis′pos•ses′sor** *n.* —**dis′pos•ses′so•ry** (-zĕs′ə-rē) *adj.*

dis•pos•sessed (dĭs′pə-zĕst′) *adj.* **1.** Deprived of possession. **2.** Spiritually impoverished or alienated. —**dis′pos•sessed′** *n.*

dis•praise (dĭs-prāz′) *tr.v.* **-praised, -prais•ing, -prais•es.** To express disapproval of; censure. —*n.* Disapproval; censure. [ME *dispreisen* < OFr. *despreiser,* var. of *desprisier* < LLat. *dēpretiāre.* See DEPRECIATE.] —**dis•prais′er** *n.* —**dis•prais′ing•ly** *adv.*

dis•prize (dĭs-prīz′) *tr.v.* **-prized, -priz•ing, -priz•es.** *Archaic.* To disdain or undervalue; scorn. [ME *disprisen* < OFr. *desprisier.* See DISPRAISE.]

dis•proof (dĭs-pro͞of′) *n.* **1.** The act of refuting or disproving. **2.** Evidence that refutes or disproves.

dis•pro•por•tion (dĭs′prə-pôr′shən, -pōr′-) *n.* **1.** Absence of proportion, symmetry, or proper relation. **2.** An instance of a disproportionate relation. —*tr.v.* **-tioned, -tion•ing, -tions.** To make disproportionate.

dis•pro•por•tion•al (dĭs′prə-pôr′shə-nəl, -pōr′-) *adj.* Disproportionate. —**dis′pro•por′tion•al•ly** *adv.*

dis•pro•por•tion•ate (dĭs′prə-pôr′shə-nĭt, -pōr′-) *adj.* Out of proportion, as in size, shape, or amount. —**dis′pro•por′tion•ate•ly** *adv.* —**dis′pro•por′tion•ate•ness** *n.*

dis•prove (dĭs-pro͞ov′) *tr.v.* **-proved, -prov•ing, -proves.** To prove to be false, invalid, or in error; refute. [ME *disproven* < OFr. *desprover* : *des-,* dis- + *prover,* to prove; see PROVE.] —**dis•prov′a•ble** *adj.* —**dis•prov′al** *n.*

dis•put•a•ble (dĭ-spyo͞o′tə-bəl, dĭs′pyə-) *adj.* Open to dispute; debatable. —**dis•put′a•bil′i•ty** *n.* —**dis•put′a•bly** *adv.*

dis•pu•tant (dĭ-spyo͞ot′nt, dĭs′pyə-tənt) *adj.* Engaged in dispute or argument. —*n.* One engaged in a dispute.

dis•pu•ta•tion (dĭs′pyə-tā′shən) *n.* **1.** The act of disputing; debate. **2.** An academic exercise consisting of a formal debate or an oral defense of a thesis.

dis•pu•ta•tious (dĭs′pyə-tā′shəs) *adj.* Inclined to dispute. See Syns at **argumentative.** —**dis′pu•ta′tious•ly** *adv.* —**dis′pu•ta′tious•ness** *n.*

dis•pute (dĭ-spyo͞ot′) *v.* **-put•ed, -put•ing, -putes.** —*tr.* **1.** To argue about; debate. **2.** To question the truth or validity of; doubt. **3.** To strive to win (a prize, for example); contest for. **4.** To strive against; resist. —*intr.* **1.** To engage in discussion or argument; debate. **2.** To quarrel angrily. —*n.* **1.** A verbal controversy; a debate. **2.** An angry altercation; a quarrel. [ME *disputen* < OFr. *desputer* < Lat. *disputāre,* to examine : *dis-,* apart; see DIS- + *putāre,* to reckon; see **peu-***.] —**dis•put′er** *n.*

dis•qual•i•fi•ca•tion (dĭs-kwŏl′ə-fĭ-kā′shən) *n.* **1.** The act of disqualifying or the condition of having been disqualified. **2.** Something that disqualifies.

dis•qual•i•fy (dĭs-kwŏl′ə-fī′) *tr.v.* **-fied, -fy•ing, -fies. 1.a.** To render unqualified or unfit. **b.** To declare unqualified or ineligible. **2.** To deprive of legal rights, powers, or privileges.

dis•qui•et (dĭs-kwī′ĭt) *tr.v.* **-et•ed, -et•ing, -ets.** To deprive of peace or rest; trouble. —*n.* Absence of peace or rest; anxiety. —*adj. Archaic.* Uneasy; restless. —**dis•qui′et•ing•ly** *adv.* —**dis•qui′et•ly** *adv.* —**dis•qui′et•ness** *n.*

dis•qui•e•tude (dĭs-kwī′ĭ-to͞od′, -tyo͞od′) *n.* Worried unease.

dis•qui•si•tion (dĭs′kwĭ-zĭsh′ən) *n.* A formal discourse on a subject, often in writing. [Lat. *disquīsītiō, disquīsītiōn-,* investigation < *disquīsītus,* p.part. of *disquīrere,* to investigate : *dis-,* dis- + *quaerere,* to search for.]

Dis•rae•li (dĭz-rā′lē), **Benjamin.** 1st Earl of Beaconsfield. 1804–81. British politician who served as prime minister (1868 and 1874–80).

Benjamin Disraeli

dis•rate (dĭs-rāt′) *tr.v.* **-rat•ed, -rat•ing, -rates.** To reduce in rank or rating; demote.

dis•re•gard (dĭs′rĭ-gärd′) *tr.v.* **-gard•ed, -gard•ing, -gards. 1.** To pay no attention or heed to. **2.** To treat without proper respect or attentiveness. —*n.* Lack of thoughtful attention or regard. —**dis′re•gard′er** *n.* —**dis′re•gard′ful** *adj.*

dis•rel•ish (dĭs-rĕl′ĭsh) *tr.v.* **-ished, -ish•ing, -ish•es.** To have distaste for; dislike. —*n.* Distaste; aversion.

dis•re•mem•ber (dĭs′rĭ-mĕm′bər) *v.* **-bered, -ber•ing, -bers.** —*tr.* To fail to remember. —*intr.* To forget.

dis•re•pair (dĭs′rĭ-pâr′) *n.* The condition of needing repair.

dis•rep•u•ta•ble (dĭs-rĕp′yə-tə-bəl) *adj.* Lacking respectability, as in character or appearance. —**dis•rep′u•ta•bil′i•ty, dis•rep′u•ta•ble•ness** *n.* —**dis•rep′u•ta•bly** *adv.*

dis•re•pute (dĭs′rĭ-pyo͞ot′) *n.* Damage to or loss of reputation.

dis•re•spect (dĭs′rĭ-spĕkt′) *n.* Lack of respect, esteem, or courteous regard. —*tr.v.* **-spect•ed, -spect•ing, -spects.** To show a lack of respect for: *disrespected her elders.*

dis•re•spect•a•ble (dĭs′rĭ-spĕk′tə-bəl) *adj.* Unworthy of respect. —**dis′re•spect′a•bil′i•ty** *n.*

dis•re•spect•ful (dĭs′rĭ-spĕkt′fəl) *adj.* Having or exhibiting a lack of respect; rude and discourteous. —**dis′re•spect′ful•ly** *adv.* —**dis′re•spect′ful•ness** *n.*

dis•robe (dĭs-rōb′) *v.* **-robed, -rob•ing, -robes.** —*tr.* To remove the clothing or covering from. —*intr.* To undress oneself. —**dis•rob′er** *n.*

dis•rupt (dĭs-rŭpt′) *tr.v.* **-rupt•ed, -rupt•ing, -rupts. 1.** To throw into confusion or disorder. **2.** To interrupt or impede the progress, movement, or procedure of. **3.** To break or burst; rupture. [Lat. *disrumpere, disrupt-,* to break apart : *dis-,* dis- + *rumpere,* to break apart; see **reup-***.] —**dis•rupt′er, dis•rup′tor** *n.* —**dis•rup′tion** *n.*

dis•rup•tive (dĭs-rŭp′tĭv) *adj.* Relating to, causing, or produced by disruption. —**dis•rup′tive•ly** *adv.*

diss. *abbr.* Dissertation.

dis•sat•is•fac•tion (dĭs-săt′ĭs-făk′shən) *n.* **1.** The condition or feeling of being displeased or unsatisfied; discontent. **2.** A cause of discontent.

dis•sat•is•fac•to•ry (dĭs-săt′ĭs-făk′tə-rē) *adj.* Unsatisfactory.

dis•sat•is•fied (dĭs-săt′ĭs-fīd′) *adj.* Feeling or exhibiting a lack of satisfaction. —**dis•sat′is•fied′ly** *adv.*

dis•sat•is•fy (dĭs-săt′ĭs-fī′) *tr.v.* **-fied, -fy•ing, -fies.** To fail to satisfy; disappoint.

dissd. *abbr.* Dissolved.

dis•seat (dĭs-sēt′) *tr.v.* **-seat•ed, -seat•ing, -seats.** *Archaic.* To unseat.

dis•sect (dĭ-sĕkt′, dī-, dī′sĕkt′) *tr.v.* **-sect•ed, -sect•ing, -sects. 1.** To cut apart or separate (tissue), esp. for anatomical study. **2.** To examine, analyze, or criticize in minute detail. See Syns at **analyze.** [Lat. *dissecāre, dissect-,* to cut apart : *dis-,* dis- + *secāre,* to cut up; see **sek-***.] —**dis•sec′ti•ble** *adj.* —**dis•sec′tor** *n.*

dis•sect•ed (dĭ-sĕk′tĭd, dī-) *adj.* **1.** *Bot.* Divided into many deep, narrow segments: *dissected leaves.* **2.** *Geol.* Cut by irregular valleys and hills.

dis•sec•tion (dĭ-sĕk′shən, dī-) *n.* **1.** The act or an instance of dissecting. **2.** Something that has been dissected, such as a tissue specimen under study. **3.** A detailed examination or analysis.

dis•seize also **dis•seise** (dĭs-sēz′) *tr.v.* **-seized, -seiz•ing, -seiz•es** also **-seised, -seis•ing, -seis•es.** *Law.* To dispossess unlawfully of real property; oust. [ME *disseisen* < AN *disseisir,* var. of OFr. *dessaisir* : *des-,* dis- + *saisir,* to seize; see SEIZE.]

dis•sei•zin also **dis•sei•sin** (dĭs-sē′zĭn) *n. Law.* Wrongful dispossession of one in the possession of real property. [ME *disseisine* < AN, var. of OFr. *dessaisine* : *des-,* dis- + *seisine,* seisin; see SEISIN.]

dis•sem•ble (dĭ-sĕm′bəl) *v.* **-bled, -bling, -bles.** —*tr.* **1.** To disguise or conceal behind a false appearance. **2.** To make a false show of; feign. —*intr.* To dissemble one's real nature, motives, or feelings. [ME *dissemblen* < OFr. *dessembler,* to be different : *des-,* dis- + *sembler,* to appear, seem; see SEMBLABLE.] —**dis•sem′blance** *n.* —**dis•sem′bler** *n.* —**dis•sem′bling•ly** *adv.*

dis•sem•i•nate (dĭ-sĕm′ə-nāt′) *v.* **-nat•ed, -nat•ing, -nates.** —*tr.* **1.** To scatter widely, as in sowing seed. **2.** To spread abroad; promulgate: *disseminate information.* —*intr.* To become diffused; spread. [Lat. *dissēmināre, dissēmināt-* : *dis-,* dis- + *sēmināre,* to sow (< *sēmen, sēmin-,* seed; see **sē-***).] —**dis•sem′i•na′tion** *n.* —**dis•sem′i•na′tor** *n.*

dis•sem•i•nat•ed (dĭ-sĕm′ə-nā′tĭd) *adj.* Spread over a large area of a body, a tissue, or an organ.

dis•sem•i•nule (dĭ-sĕm′ə-nyo͞ol′) *n.* A reproductive plant part, such as a seed, fruit, or spore, that is modified for dispersal. [DISSEMIN(ATE) + -ULE.]

dis•sen•sion (dĭ-sĕn′shən) *n.* Difference of opinion. [ME *dissencioun* < OFr. *dissension* < Lat. *dissēnsiō, dissēnsiōn-* < *dissēnsus,* p.part. of *dissentīre,* to dissent. See DISSENT.]

dis•sent (dĭ-sĕnt′) *intr.v.* **-sent•ed, -sent•ing, -sents. 1.** To differ in opinion or feeling; disagree. **2.** To withhold assent or approval. —*n.* **1.** Difference of opinion or feeling; disagreement. **2.** The refusal to conform to the authority or doctrine of an established church; nonconformity. **3.** *Law.* A justice's

ă pat	oi boy
ā pay	ou out
âr care	o͝o took
ä father	o͞o boot
ĕ pet	ŭ cut
ē be	ûr urge
ĭ pit	th thin
ī pie	*th* this
îr pier	hw which
ŏ pot	zh vision
ō toe	ə about, item
ô paw	

Stress marks:
′ (primary);
′ (secondary), as in
dictionary (dĭk′shə-nĕr′ē)

refusal to concur with the opinion of a majority. [ME *dissenten* < Lat. *dissentīre* : *dis-*, dis- + *sentīre*, to feel; see **sent-***.] —**dis•sent′ing•ly** *adv.*

dis•sent•er (dĭ-sĕn′tər) *n.* **1.** One who dissents. **2.** Often **Dissenter.** One who refuses to accept the doctrines of an established church, esp. the Church of England.

dis•sen•tient (dĭ-sĕn′shənt) *adj.* Dissenting, esp. from the sentiment or policies of a majority. —*n.* A dissenter. —**dis•sen′tience** *n.*

dis•sent•ing opinion (dĭ-sĕn′tĭng) *n. Law.* See **dissent** 3.

dis•sep•i•ment (dĭ-sĕp′ə-mənt) *n. Bot.* A partition dividing an organ into chambers. [Lat. *dissaepīmentum*, partition < *dissaepīre*, to divide : *dis-*, dis- + *saepīre*, hedge off (< *saepēs*, hedge).] —**dis•sep′i•men′tal** (-mĕn′tl) *adj.*

dis•ser•tate (dĭs′ər-tāt′) also **dis•sert** (dĭ-sûrt′) *intr.v.* **-tat•ed, -tat•ing, -tates** also **-sert•ed, -sert•ing, -serts.** To discourse formally. [Lat. *dissertāre*, *dissertāt-*, freq. of *disserere*, to discuss : *dis-*, dis- + *serere*, to connect; see **ser-**^{2}***.**] —**dis′ser•ta′tor** *n.*

dis•ser•ta•tion (dĭs′ər-tā′shən) *n.* A lengthy formal treatise, esp. one written by a candidate for the doctoral degree at a university; a thesis.

dis•serve (dĭs-sûrv′) *tr.v.* **-served, -serv•ing, -serves.** To treat badly; harm.

dis•serv•ice (dĭs-sûr′vĭs) *n.* A harmful action; an injury.

dis•sev•er (dĭ-sĕv′ər) *v.* **-ered, -er•ing, -ers.** —*tr.* **1.** To separate; sever. **2.** To divide into parts; break up. —*intr.* To become separated or disunited. [ME *disseveren* < OFr. *dessevrer* < LLat. *dissēparāre* : Lat. *dis-*, dis- + Lat. *sēparāre*; see SEPARATE.] —**dis•sev′er•ance, dis•sev′er•ment** *n.*

dis•si•dence (dĭs′ĭ-dəns) *n.* Disagreement, as of opinion or belief; dissent.

dis•si•dent (dĭs′ĭ-dənt) *adj.* Disagreeing, as in opinion or belief. —*n.* One who disagrees; a dissenter. [Lat. *dissidēns*, *dissident-*, pr.part. of *dissidēre*, to disagree : *dis-*, apart; see DIS- + *sedēre*, to sit; see **sed-***.]

dis•sim•i•lar (dĭ-sĭm′ə-lər) *adj.* Unlike; different. —**dis•sim′i•lar•ly** *adv.*

dis•sim•i•lar•i•ty (dĭ-sĭm′ə-lăr′ĭ-tē) *n., pl.* **-ties. 1.** The quality of being distinct or unlike; difference. **2.** A point of distinction or difference. See Syns at **difference.**

dis•sim•i•late (dĭ-sĭm′ə-lāt′) *v.* **-lat•ed, -lat•ing, -lates.** —*tr.* **1.** To make unlike or dissimilar. **2.** *Ling.* To cause to undergo dissimilation. —*intr.* **1.** To become unlike or dissimilar. **2.** *Ling.* To undergo dissimilation. [DIS- + (AS)SIMILATE.]

dis•sim•i•la•tion (dĭ-sĭm′ə-lā′shən) *n.* **1.** The act or process of making or becoming dissimilar. **2.** *Ling.* The process by which one of two similar or identical sounds in a word becomes less like the other, such as the *l* in English *marble* (from French *marbre*).

dis•si•mil•i•tude (dĭs′ə-mĭl′ĭ-to͞od′, -tyo͞od′) *n.* Lack of resemblance; dissimilarity. [ME < Lat. *dissimilitūdō* < *dissimilis*, different : *dis-*, dis- + *similis*, like; see SIMILAR.]

dis•sim•u•late (dĭ-sĭm′yə-lāt′) *v.* **-lat•ed, -lat•ing, -lates.** —*tr.* To disguise (one's intentions, for example) under a feigned appearance. —*intr.* To conceal one's feelings or intentions. [ME *dissimulaten* < Lat. *dissimulāre*, *dissimulāt-* : *dis-*, dis- + *simulāre*, to simulate; see SIMULATE.] —**dis•sim′u•la′tion** *n.* —**dis•sim′u•la′tive** *adj.* —**dis•sim′u•la′tor** *n.*

distaff
Distaff highlighted in oval

dis•si•pate (dĭs′ə-pāt′) *v.* **-pat•ed, -pat•ing, -pates.** —*tr.* **1.** To drive away; disperse. **2.** To attenuate to or almost to the point of disappearing. **3.a.** To spend or expend intemperately or wastefully; squander. **b.** To use up, esp. recklessly; exhaust: *dissipated their energy.* **4.** To cause to lose (energy, such as heat) irreversibly. —*intr.* **1.** To vanish by dispersion. **2.** To indulge in the intemperate pursuit of pleasure. [ME *dissipaten* < Lat. *dissipāre*, *dissipāt-*.] —**dis′si•pat′er, dis′si•pa′tor** *n.* —**dis′si•pa′tive** *adj.*

dis•si•pat•ed (dĭs′ə-pā′tĭd) *adj.* **1.** Intemperate in the pursuit of pleasure; dissolute. **2.** Wasted or squandered. **3.** Irreversibly lost. Used of energy. —**dis′si•pat′ed•ly** *adv.* —**dis′si•pat′ed•ness** *n.*

dis•si•pa•tion (dĭs′ə-pā′shən) *n.* **1.** The act of dissipating or the condition of having been dissipated. **2.** Wasteful expenditure or consumption. **3.** Dissolute indulgence in sensual pleasure; intemperance. **4.** An amusement; a diversion.

dis•so•cia•ble (dĭ-sō′shə-bəl, -shē-ə-bəl) *adj.* That can be dissociated; separable. —**dis•so′cia•bil′i•ty, dis•so′cia•ble•ness** *n.* —**dis•so′cia•bly** *adv.*

dis•so•ci•ate (dĭ-sō′shē-āt′, -sē-) *v.* **-at•ed, -at•ing, -ates.** —*tr.* **1.** To remove from association; separate. **2.** *Chem.* To cause to undergo dissociation. —*intr.* **1.** To cease associating; part. **2.** *Biol.* To mutate or change morphologically, often reversibly. **3.** *Chem.* To undergo dissociation. [Lat. *dissociāre*, *dissociāt-* : *dis-*, dis- + *sociāre*, to unite (< *socius*, companion; see **sek**^{w}**-**^{1}***).**] —**dis•so′ci•a′tive** *adj.*

dis•so•ci•a•tion (dĭ-sō′sē-ā′shən, -shē-) *n.* **1.** The act of dissociating or the condition of having been dissociated. **2.** *Chem.* The process by means of which a physical change, as in pressure or temperature, or the action of a solvent causes a molecule to split into simpler groups of atoms, single atoms, or ions. **3.** *Psychiat.* Separation of a group of related psychological activities into autonomously functioning units, as in the generation of multiple personalities.

dis•sol•u•ble (dĭ-sŏl′yə-bəl) *adj.* That can be dissolved. [Lat. *dissolūbilis* < *dissolūtus*, p.part. of *dissolvere*, to dissolve. See DISSOLVE.] —**dis′sol•u•bil′i•ty, dis•sol′u•ble•ness** *n.*

dis•so•lute (dĭs′ə-lo͞ot′) *adj.* Lacking moral restraint; indulging in sensual pleasures or vices. [ME < Lat. *dissolūtus*, p.part. of *dissolvere*, to dissolve. See DISSOLVE.] —**dis′so•lute′ly** *adv.* —**dis′so•lute′ness** *n.*

dis•so•lu•tion (dĭs′ə-lo͞o′shən) *n.* **1.** Decomposition into fragments or parts; disintegration. **2.** Indulgence in sensual pleasures; debauchery. **3.** Termination or extinction by disintegration or dispersion. **4.** Extinction of life; death. **5.** Annulment or termination of a formal or legal bond, or contract. **6.** Formal dismissal of an assembly or legislature. **7.** Reduction to a liquid form; liquefaction. —**dis′so•lu′tive** *adj.*

dis•solve (dĭ-zŏlv′) *v.* **-solved, -solv•ing, -solves.** —*tr.* **1.** To cause to pass into solution. **2.** To reduce (solid matter) to liquid form; melt. **3.** To cause to disappear or vanish; dispel. **4.** To break into component parts; disintegrate. **5.** To bring to an end by or as if by breaking up; terminate. **6.** To dismiss (a legislative body, for example). **7.** To cause to break down emotionally or psychologically; upset. **8.** To cause to lose definition; blur; confuse. **9.** *Law.* To annul; abrogate. —*intr.* **1.** To pass into solution. **2.** To become liquid; melt. **3.** To break up or disperse. **4.** To become disintegrated; disappear. **5.** To be overcome emotionally or psychologically. **6.** To lose clarity or definition; fade away. **7.** To shift scenes in a film or videotape by having one scene fade out while the next scene simultaneously grows clearer. —*n.* A transition in a film or videotape made by fading out one scene while the next scene grows clearer. [ME *dissolven* < Lat. *dissolvere* : *dis-*, dis- + *solvere*, to release; see **leu-***.] —**dis•solv′a•ble** *adj.* —**dis•solv′er** *n.*

dis•sol•vent (dĭ-zŏl′vənt) *adj.* Capable of dissolving a substance; solvent. —*n.* A solvent.

dis•so•nance (dĭs′ə-nəns) *n.* **1.** A harsh disagreeable combination of sounds; discord. **2.** Lack of agreement, consistency, or harmony; conflict. **3.** *Mus.* A combination of tones considered to suggest unrelieved tension and require resolution.

dis•so•nan•cy (dĭs′ə-nən-sē) *n., pl.* **-cies.** Dissonance.

dis•so•nant (dĭs′ə-nənt) *adj.* **1.** Harsh and inharmonious in sound; discordant. **2.** Being at variance; disagreeing. **3.** *Mus.* Constituting or producing a dissonance. [ME *dissonaunt* < OFr. *dissonant* < Lat. *dissonāns*, *dissonant-*, pr.part. of *dissonāre*, to be dissonant : *dis-*, apart; see DIS- + *sonāre*, to sound; see **swen-***.] —**dis′so•nant•ly** *adv.*

dis•suade (dĭ-swād′) *tr.v.* **-suad•ed, -suad•ing, -suades.** To deter (a person) from a course of action or a purpose by persuasion or exhortation. [Lat. *dissuādēre* : *dis-*, dis- + *suādēre*, to advise; see **swād-***.] —**dis•suad′er** *n.*

dis•sua•sion (dĭ-swā′zhən) *n.* The act or an instance of dissuading. [Ult. < Lat. *dissuāsiō*, *dissuāsiōn-* < *dissuāsus*, p.part. of *dissuādēre*, to dissuade. See DISSUADE.] —**dis•sua′sive** *adj.* —**dis•sua′sive•ly** *adv.* —**dis•sua′sive•ness** *n.*

dis•syl•la•ble (dĭ′sĭl′ə-bəl, dĭ-sĭl′-, dĭ-) *n.* Var. of **disyllable.**

dis•sym•me•try (dĭs-sĭm′ĭ-trē) *n., pl.* **-tries.** Lack of symmetry. —**dis′sym•met′ric** (dĭs′sĭ-mĕt′rĭk), **dis′sym•met′ri•cal** (-rĭ-kəl) *adj.* —**dis′sym•met′ri•cal•ly** *adv.*

dist. *abbr.* **1.** Distance; distant. **2.** District.

dis•taff (dĭs′tăf′) *n.* **1.a.** A staff that holds the unspun flax, wool, or tow from which thread is drawn in spinning by hand. **b.** An attachment for a spinning wheel that serves this purpose. **2.** Work and concerns traditionally considered important to women. **3.** Women considered as a group. [ME *distaf* < OE *distæf* : *dis-*, bunch of flax + *stæf*, staff.]

distaff side *n.* The female line or maternal branch of a family.

dis•tal (dĭs′təl) *adj.* **1.** Anatomically located far from a point of reference. **2.** Situated farthest from the middle and front of the jaw, as a tooth. [DIST(ANT) + -AL^{1}.] —**dis′tal•ly** *adv.*

dis•tance (dĭs′təns) *n.* **1.** The extent of space between two objects or places; an intervening space. **2.** The fact or condition of being apart in space; remoteness. **3.** *Math.* The length or numerical value of a straight line or curve. **4.a.** The extent of space between points on a measured course. **b.** The length of a race, esp. of a horserace. **5.a.** A point or an area that is far away. **b.** A depiction of a point or an area that is far away. **6.** A stretch of space without designation of limit; an expanse. **7.** The extent of time between two events; an intervening period. **8.** A point removed in time. **9.** The period or length of a contest. **10.** An amount of progress. **11.** Difference or disagreement. **12.** Chillness of manner; aloofness. —*tr.v.* **-tanced, -tanc•ing, -tanc•es. 1.** To place or keep at or as if at a distance. **2.** To cause to appear at a distance. **3.** To leave far behind; outrun.

dis•tant (dĭs′tənt) *adj.* **1.a.** Separate or apart in space. **b.** Far removed; remote. **2.** Coming from or going to a distance: *a distant sound.* **3.** Far removed or apart in time: *the distant past.* **4.** Far apart in relationship: *a distant cousin.* **5.** Minimally similar: *a distant likeness.* **6.** Far removed mentally.

7. Aloof or chilly. [ME *distaunt* < OFr. < Lat. *distāns, distant-*, pr.part. of *distāre*, to be remote : *dī-, dis-*, apart; see DIS- + *stāre*, to stand; see **stā-***.] **—dis′tant•ly** *adv.*

dis•taste (dĭs-tāst′) *n.* Dislike or aversion. —*tr.v.* **-tast•ed, -tast•ing, -tastes.** *Archaic.* **1.** To feel repugnance for; dislike. **2.** To offend; displease.

dis•taste•ful (dĭs-tāst′fəl) *adj.* **1.a.** Unpleasant; disagreeable. **b.** Objectionable; offensive. **2.** Expressing aversion or dislike. **—dis•taste′ful•ly** *adv.* **—dis•taste′ful•ness** *n.*

Dist. Atty. *abbr. Law.* District attorney.

dis•tem•per[1] (dĭs-tĕm′pər) *n.* **1.a.** An infectious viral disease occurring in dogs, characterized by catarrh, vomiting, fever, lethargy, partial paralysis, and sometimes death. **b.** A similar viral disease of cats characterized by fever, vomiting, diarrhea leading to dehydration, and sometimes death. **c.** Any of various similar mammalian diseases. **2.** An illness or a disease; an ailment. **3.** Ill humor; testiness. **4.** Disorder or disturbance, esp. of a social or political nature. —*tr.v.* **-pered, -per•ing, -pers. 1.** To put out of order. **2.** *Archaic.* To unsettle; derange. [< ME *distemperen*, to upset the balance of the humors < OFr. *destemprer*, to disturb < LLat. *distemperāre* : Lat. *dis-*, dis- + Lat. *temperāre*, to mix properly.]

dis•tem•per[2] (dĭs-tĕm′pər) *n.* **1.a.** A process of painting in which pigments are mixed with water and a glue-size or casein binder, used esp. for flat wall decoration. **b.** The paint used in this process. **2.** A painting made by this process. —*tr.v.* **-pered, -per•ing, -pers. 1.** To mix (powdered pigments or colors) with water and size. **2.** To paint (a work) in distemper. [ME *distemperen*, to dilute. See DISTEMPER[1].]

dis•tend (dĭ-stĕnd′) *v.* **-tend•ed, -tend•ing, -tends.** —*intr.* To swell out or expand from or as if from internal pressure. —*tr.* **1.** To cause to distend; dilate. **2.** To extend. [ME *distenden* < Lat. *distendere* : *dis-*, dis- + *tendere*, to stretch; see **ten-***.]

dis•ten•si•ble (dĭ-stĕn′sə-bəl) *adj.* That can be distended: *a fish with a distensible stomach.* **—dis•ten′si•bil′i•ty** *n.*

dis•ten•tion also **dis•ten•sion** (dĭ-stĕn′shən) *n.* The act of distending or the state of being distended. [ME *distensioun* < OFr. < Lat. *distēnsiō, distēnsiōn-*, alteration of *distentiō* < *distentus*, p.part. of *distendere*, to distend. See DISTEND.]

dis•tich (dĭs′tĭk) *n., pl.* **-tichs. 1.** A unit of verse consisting of two lines, esp. as used in Greek and Latin elegiac poetry. **2.** A rhyming couplet. [Lat. *distichon* < Gk. *distikhon* < neut. of *distikhos*, having two rows or verses : *di-*, two; see DI-[1] + *stikhos*, line of verse; see **steigh-***.]

dis•ti•chous (dĭs′tĭ-kəs) *adj. Bot.* Arranged in two vertical rows on opposite sides of an axis: *distichous leaves.* [< Lat. *distichus*, having two rows < Gk. *distikhos*. See DISTICH.] **—dis′ti•chous•ly** *adv.*

dis•till also **dis•til** (dĭ-stĭl′) —*v.* **-tilled, -till•ing, -tills** also **-tilled, -til•ling, -tils.** —*tr.* **1.** To subject (a substance) to distillation. **2.** To separate (a distillate) by distillation. **3.** To increase the concentration of, separate, or purify by or as if by distillation. **4.** To separate or extract the essential elements of. **5.** To exude or give off (matter) in drops or small quantities. —*intr.* **1.** To undergo or be produced by distillation. **2.** To fall or exude in drops or small quantities. [ME *distillen* < OFr. *distiller* < Lat. *dīstillāre*, var. of *dēstillāre*, to trickle : *dē-*, de- + *stillāre*, to drip (< *stilla*, drop).] **—dis•till′a•ble** *adj.*

dis•til•late (dĭs′tə-lāt′, -lĭt, dĭ-stĭl′ĭt) *n.* **1.** A liquid condensed from vapor in distillation. **2.** A purified form; an essence.

dis•til•la•tion (dĭs′tə-lā′shən) *n.* **1.** The evaporation and subsequent collection of a liquid by condensation as a means of purification. **2.** The extraction of the volatile components of a mixture by the condensation and collection of the vapors that are produced as the mixture is heated. **3.** A distillate.

dis•till•er (dĭ-stĭl′ər) *n.* **1.** One that distills, as a condenser. **2.** One that makes alcoholic liquors by the process of distillation.

dis•till•er•y (dĭ-stĭl′ə-rē) *n., pl.* **-ies.** An establishment for distilling, esp. for distilling alcoholic liquors.

dis•tinct (dĭ-stĭngkt′) *adj.* **1.** Readily distinguishable from all others; discrete. **2.** Easily perceived by the senses or intellect; clear. See Syns at **apparent. 3.** Clearly defined; unquestionable. **4.** Very likely; probable. **5.** Notable: *a distinct honor.* [ME, p.part. of *distincten*, to discern < OFr. *destincter* < Lat. *dīstīnctus*, p.part. of *dīstinguere*, to distinguish. See DISTINGUISH.] **—dis•tinct′ly** *adv.* **—dis•tinct′ness** *n.*

dis•tinc•tion (dĭ-stĭngk′shən) *n.* **1.** The act of distinguishing; differentiation. **2.** The condition or fact of being dissimilar or distinct; difference. See Syns at **difference. 3.** A distinguishing factor, attribute, or characteristic. **4.a.** Excellence or eminence, as of performance, character, or reputation. **b.** A special feature or quality conferring superiority. **5.** Recognition of achievement or superiority; honor.

dis•tinc•tive (dĭ-stĭngk′tĭv) *adj.* **1.** Serving to identify; distinguishing. **2.** Characteristic or typical. **3.** *Ling.* Phonemically relevant and capable of conveying a difference in meaning, as nasalization in the initial sound of *mat* versus *bat.* **—dis•tinc′tive•ly** *adv.* **—dis•tinc′tive•ness** *n.*

dis•tin•gué (dēs′tăng-gā′, dĭs′-, dĭ-stăng′gā) *adj.* Distinguished in appearance, manner, or bearing. [Fr., p.part. of *distinguer*, to distinguish < OFr. See DISTINGUISH.]

dis•tin•guish (dĭ-stĭng′gwĭsh) *v.* **-guished, -guish•ing, -guish•es.** —*tr.* **1.** To perceive as being different or distinct. **2.** To perceive distinctly; discern. **3.** To make noticeable or different; set apart. **4.** To cause (oneself) to be eminent or recognized. —*intr.* To perceive or indicate differences; discriminate. [Alteration of obsolete *distingue* < ME *distinguen* < OFr. *distinguer* < Lat. *dīstinguere*, to separate. See **steig-***.] **—dis•tin′guish•a•ble** *adj.* **—dis•tin′guish•a•bly** *adv.*

dis•tin•guished (dĭ-stĭng′gwĭsht) *adj.* **1.** Characterized by excellence or distinction; eminent. **2.** Dignified in conduct or appearance.

Dis•tin•guished Conduct Medal (dĭ-stĭng′gwĭsht) *n.* A British military decoration for distinguished conduct in the field.

Distinguished Flying Cross *n.* **1.** A U.S. military decoration awarded for heroism or extraordinary achievement in aerial combat. **2.** A British military decoration awarded to officers of the Royal Air Force for extraordinary achievement.

Distinguished Service Cross *n.* **1.** A U.S. Army decoration awarded for exceptional heroism in combat. **2.** A British military decoration awarded to officers of the Royal Navy for gallantry in action.

Distinguished Service Medal *n.* **1.** A U.S. military decoration awarded for distinguished performance in a duty of great responsibility. **2.** A British military decoration awarded to noncommissioned officers and members of the Royal Navy and Royal Marines for distinguished conduct in war.

Distinguished Service Order *n.* A British military decoration for gallantry in action.

dis•tort (dĭ-stôrt′) *tr.v.* **-tort•ed, -tort•ing, -torts. 1.** To twist out of a proper or natural relation of parts; misshape. **2.** To give a false or misleading account of; misrepresent. **3.** To cause to work in a twisted or disorderly manner; pervert. [Lat. *distorquēre, distort-* : *dis-*, apart; see DIS- + *torquēre*, to twist; see **terkʷ-***.] **—dis•tort′er** *n.* **—dis•tor′tive** (-stôr′tĭv) *adj.*

dis•tor•tion (dĭ-stôr′shən) *n.* **1.a.** The act or an instance of distorting. **b.** The condition of being distorted. **2.** A statement that twists fact; a misrepresentation. **3.** A change in the shape of an image resulting from imperfections in an optical system, such as a lens. **4.** *Electron.* **a.** An undesired change in the waveform of a signal. **b.** A consequence of such a change, esp. a lack of fidelity in reception or reproduction. **5.** *Psychol.* The modification of unconscious impulses into forms acceptable by conscious or dreaming perception. **—dis•tor′tion•al, dis•tor′tion•ar′y** *adj.*

distr. *abbr.* **1.** Distribution. **2.** Distributor.

dis•tract (dĭ-străkt′) *tr.v.* **-tract•ed, -tract•ing, -tracts. 1.** To cause to turn away from the original focus of attention or interest; divert. **2.** To pull in conflicting emotional directions; unsettle. [ME *distracten* < Lat. *distrahere, distrāct-*, to pull away : *dis-*, apart; see DIS- + *trahere*, to draw.] **—dis•tract′ing•ly** *adv.* **—dis•trac′tive** *adj.*

dis•tract•ed (dĭ-străk′tĭd) *adj.* **1.** Having the attention diverted. **2.** Suffering conflicting emotions; distraught. **—dis•tract′ed•ly** *adv.*

dis•tract•er also **dis•trac•tor** (dĭ-străk′tər) *n.* One of the incorrect answers presented as a choice in a multiple-choice test.

dis•trac•tion (dĭ-străk′shən) *n.* **1.** The act of distracting or the condition of being distracted. **2.** Something, esp. an amusement, that distracts. **3.** Extreme mental or emotional disturbance; obsession: *loved the puppy to distraction.*

dis•train (dĭ-strān′) *v.* **-trained, -train•ing, -trains.** —*tr.* **1.** To seize and hold (property) to compel payment or reparation. **2.** To seize the property of (a person) in order to compel payment of debts. —*intr.* To levy a distress. [ME *distreinen* < OFr. *destreindre, destreign-* < Med.Lat. *dīstringere, dīstrinct-* < Lat., to hinder : *dī-, dis-*, apart; see DIS- + *stringere*, to draw tight; see **streig-***.] **—dis•train′a•ble** *adj.* **—dis•train′ment** *n.* **—dis•trai′nor, dis•train′er** *n.*

dis•train•ee (dĭs′trā-nē′) *n. Law.* One that has been distrained.

dis•traint (dĭ-strānt′) *n. Law.* The act or process of distraining; distress. [< DISTRAIN.]

dis•trait (dĭ-strā′) *adj.* Inattentive or preoccupied, esp. because of anxiety. [ME < OFr., p.part. of *distraire*, to distract < Lat. *distrahere*. See DISTRACT.]

dis•traught (dĭ-strôt′) *adj.* **1.** Deeply agitated, as from emotional conflict. **2.** Mad; insane. [ME, alteration of *distract*, p.part. of *distracten*, to distract. See DISTRACT.]

dis•tress (dĭ-strĕs′) *tr.v.* **-tressed, -tress•ing, -tress•es. 1.** To cause strain, anxiety, or suffering to. See Syns at **trouble. 2.** To mar or otherwise treat (a fabric, for example) to give the appearance of an antique or of heavy use. **3.** *Archaic.* To constrain or overcome by harassment. —*n.* **1.** Anxiety or mental suffering. **2.a.** Severe strain resulting from exhaustion or an accident. **b.** Acute physical discomfort. **c.** Physical deterioration caused by hard use over time. **3.** The condition of being in need of immediate assistance: *a motorist in distress.* [ME *distressen* < OFr. *destresser* < *destresse*, constraint < VLat. **districtia* < Lat. *dīstrictus*, p.part. of *dīstringere*, to hinder. See DISTRAIN.] **—dis•tress′ing•ly** *adv.*

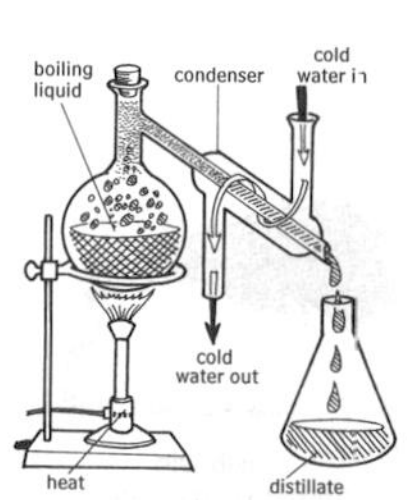

distillation
Simple distillation

ă pat	oi boy
ā pay	ou out
âr care	ŏŏ took
ä father	ōō boot
ĕ pet	ŭ cut
ē be	ûr urge
ĭ pit	th thin
ī pie	*th* this
îr pier	hw which
ŏ pot	zh vision
ō toe	ə about,
ô paw	item

Stress marks:
′ (primary);
′ (secondary), as in
dictionary (dĭk′shə-nĕr′ē)

nation. **2.a.** To know by inspiration, intuition, or reflection. **b.** To guess. **3.** To locate (underground water or minerals) with a divining rod; douse. *— intr.* **1.** To practice divination. **2.** To guess. [ME < OFr. *devine* < Lat. *dīvīnus*, divine, foreseeing < *dīvus*, god. See **deiw-***. V., ME *divinen* < OFr. *deviner* < Lat. *dīvīnāre* < *dīvīnus*, foreseeing.] **— di•vine′ly** *adv.* **— di•vine′ness** *n.* **— di•vin′er** *n.*

Di•vine Liturgy (dĭ-vīn′) *n.* The Eastern Orthodox Eucharistic rite.

Divine Office *n.* The office of the breviary.

divine right *n.* The doctrine that monarchs derive their right to rule directly from God and are accountable only to God.

diving bell *n.* A large vessel for underwater work, open on the bottom and supplied with air under pressure.

diving board *n. Sports.* A flexible board projecting over water from which a dive may be executed.

diving suit *n.* A heavy waterproof garment with a detachable air-fed helmet, used for underwater work.

di•vin•ing rod (dĭ-vī′nĭng) *n.* A forked branch or stick that is believed to indicate subterranean water or minerals by bending downward when held over a source.

di•vin•i•ty (dĭ-vĭn′ĭ-tē) *n., pl.* **-ties. 1.** The state or quality of being divine. **2.a. Divinity.** The godhead; God. Used with *the.* **b.** A deity, such as a god or goddess. **3.** Godlike character. **4.** Theology. **5.** A soft white candy, usu. containing nuts.

di•vis•i•ble (dĭ-vĭz′ə-bəl) *adj.* Capable of being divided, esp. with no remainder. **— di•vis′i•bil′i•ty, di•vis′i•ble•ness** *n.* **— di•vis′i•bly** *adv.*

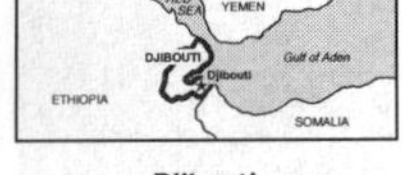

Djibouti

di•vi•sion (dĭ-vĭzh′ən) *n.* **1.a.** The act or process of dividing. **b.** The state of having been divided. **2.** The proportional distribution of a quantity or entity. **3.** Something, such as a partition, that serves to divide. **4.** One of the parts, sections, or groups into which something is divided. **5.a.** An administrative or functional unit of government or corporate activity. **b.** A territorial section marked off for political or governmental purposes. **6.a.** A self-contained administrative and tactical military unit that is smaller than a corps. **b.** A group of several ships of similar type forming a tactical unit in the U.S. Navy. **c.** A unit of the U.S. Air Force larger than a wing and smaller than an air force. **7.** *Bot.* The highest taxonomic category corresponding approximately to a phylum in zoological classification. See table at **taxonomy. 8.** A category created for purposes of competition, as in boxing. **9.a.** Variance of opinion; disagreement. **b.** A splitting into factions; disunion. **10.** The separation of members of a parliament according to their stand on an issue put to vote. **11.** *Math.* The operation of determining how many times one quantity is contained in another; the inverse of multiplication. **12.** *Biol.* Cell division. **13.** A type of propagation in which plants grow from parts of a parent plant such as bulbs, suckers, or rhizomes. [ME *divisioun* < OFr. *division* < Lat. *dīvīsiō, dīvīsiōn-* < *dīvīsus*, p.part. of *dīvidere*, to divide. See DIVIDE.] **— di•vi′sion•al** *adj.*

DNA

di•vi•sion•ism (də-vĭzh′ə-nĭz′əm) *n.* A branch of neoimpressionism in which colors are divided into their components and arranged so that the eye organizes the shape.

division sign *n. Math.* **1.** The symbol (÷) placed between two quantities written on a single line to indicate the division of the first by the second. **2.** The symbol (/) placed between two quantities written horizontally, as in ⅔, or the symbol (—) placed between two quantities written vertically, as in $\frac{2}{3}$, to indicate a fraction.

di•vi•sive (dĭ-vī′sĭv) *adj.* Creating dissension or discord. **— di•vi′sive•ly** *adv.* **— di•vi′sive•ness** *n.*

di•vi•sor (dĭ-vī′zər) *n. Math.* The quantity by which another quantity, the dividend, is to be divided.

di•vorce (dĭ-vôrs′, -vōrs′) *n.* **1.** The legal dissolution of a marriage. **2.** A complete or radical severance of closely connected things. *— v.* **-vorced, -vorc•ing, -vorc•es.** *— tr.* **1.** To dissolve the marriage between. **2.** To end marriage with (one's spouse) by divorce. **3.** To cut off or separate. See Syns at **separate.** *— intr.* To obtain a divorce. [ME < OFr. < Lat. *dīvortium* < *dīvortere*, to divert, var. of *dīvertere*. See DIVERT.]

di•vor•cé (dĭ-vôr-sā′, -sē′, -vōr-, -vôr′sā′, -sē′, -vōr′-) *n.* A divorced man. [Fr., masc. p.part. of *divorcer*, to divorce < OFr. < *divorce*, divorce. See DIVORCE.]

di•vor•cée (dĭ-vôr-sā′, -sē′, -vōr-, -vôr′sā′, -sē′, -vōr′-) *n.* A divorced woman. [Fr., fem. p.part. of *divorcer*, to divorce < OFr. < *divorce*, divorce. See DIVORCE.]

di•vorce•ment (dĭ-vôrs′mənt, -vōrs′-) *n.* Complete separation.

Doberman pinscher

div•ot (dĭv′ət) *n.* **1.** *Sports.* A piece of turf torn up by a golf club in striking a ball. **2.** *Scots.* A thin square of turf or sod used for roofing. [Sc., a turf.]

di•vulge (dĭ-vŭlj′) *tr.v.* **-vulged, -vulg•ing, -vulg•es.** To make known (something private or secret). [ME *divulgen* < OFr. *divulguer* < Lat. *dīvulgāre*, to publish : *dī-, dis-*, among; see DIS- + *vulgāre*, to spread among the multitude (< *vulgus*, common people).] **— di•vul′gence** *n.* **— di•vulg′er** *n.*

div•vy (dĭv′ē) *Slang. — tr.v.* **-vied, -vy•ing, -vies.** To divide: *divvied up the loot.* *— n., pl.* **-vies.** A share or portion. [Shortening and alteration of DIVIDEND.]

Dix (dĭks), **Dorothea Lynde.** 1802–87. Amer. educator who worked to improve treatment of the mentally ill.

Dix, Dorothy. See Elizabeth Meriwether **Gilmer.**

Dix•ie¹ (dĭk′sē). A region of the S and E U.S., usu. comprising the states that joined the Confederacy during the Civil War. The term was popularized in the song "Dixie's Land" (1859) by Daniel D. Emmett (1815–1904).

Dix•ie² (dĭk′sē) *n.* Any one of several songs of this name, popular as Confederate war songs. **— *idiom.* whistle Dixie.** *Slang.* To engage in unrealistically rosy fantasizing.

Dix•ie•crat (dĭk′sē-krăt′) *n.* A member of a dissenting group of Democrats in the South who formed the States' Rights Party in 1948. [DIXIE¹ + (DEMO)CRAT.] **— Dix′ie•crat′ic** *adj.*

Dix•ie•land (dĭk′sē-lănd′) *n. Mus.* A style of instrumental jazz associated with New Orleans and characterized by a relatively fast two-beat rhythm and by group and solo improvisations.

Di•yar•ba•kir (dĭ-yär′bə-kîr′, dē-yär′bŏŏk-ər). A city of SE Turkey on the Tigris R.; captured by the Ottoman Turks in 1515. Pop. 235,617.

di•zen (dī′zən, dĭz′ən) *tr.v.* **-zened, -zen•ing, -zens.** *Archaic.* To deck out in fine clothes and ornaments; bedizen. [Poss. MDu. *disen*, to prepare a distaff with flax for spinning < MLGer. *dise, disene*, bunch of flax.] **— di′zen•ment** *n.*

di•zy•got•ic (dī′zī-gŏt′ĭk) or **di•zy•gous** (dī-zī′gəs) *adj.* Derived from two separately fertilized eggs. Used esp. of fraternal twins.

diz•zy (dĭz′ē) *adj.* **-zi•er, -zi•est. 1.** Having a whirling sensation and a tendency to fall. **2.** Bewildered or confused. **3.a.** Producing or tending to produce giddiness: *a dizzy height.* **b.** Caused by giddiness; reeling. **4.** Characterized by impulsive haste; very rapid. **5.** *Slang.* Scatterbrained or silly. *— tr.v.* **-zied, -zy•ing, -zies. 1.** To make dizzy. **2.** To confuse or bewilder. [ME *dusie, disi* < OE *dysig*, foolish.] **— diz′zi•ly** *adv.* **— diz′zi•ness** *n.* **— diz′zy•ing•ly** *adv.*

DJ *abbr.* Disc jockey.

D.J. *abbr.* **1.** *Law.* District judge. **2.** *Lat.* Doctor Juris (Doctor of Law).

Dja•kar•ta (jə-kär′tə). See **Jakarta.**

djel•la•ba or **djel•la•bah** also **jel•la•ba** (jə-lä′bə) or **ga•la•bi•a** (-bē-ə) *n.* A long, loose, hooded garment with full sleeves, worn esp. in Muslim countries. [Fr. < Ar. *jallābīyah* < *jallāb*, attractive.]

Dji•bou•ti (jĭ-bōō′tē). **1.** Formerly **A•fars and Is•sas** (ə-färs′; ī′səs). A country of E Africa on the Gulf of Aden; gained independence from France in 1977. Pop. 226,000. **2.** The cap. of Djibouti, in the SE part on an inlet of the Gulf of Aden; founded by the French in 1888. Pop. 120,000.

Dji•las (jĭl′äs), **Milovan.** b. 1911. Montenegrin writer and politician who was dismissed in 1954 for criticizing the Communist regime.

djin•ni or **djin•ny** (jĭn′ē, jĭ-nē′) *n.* Var. of **jinni.**

Djok•ja•kar•ta (jŏk′yə-kär′tə). See **Jogjakarta.**

dk. *abbr.* **1.** Dark. **2.** Deck. **3.** Dock.

dl *abbr.* Deciliter.

D layer *n.* The lowest layer of the ionosphere, existing only during the day.

D.Lit. or **D.Litt.** *abbr. Lat.* Doctor Litterarum (Doctor of Letters; Doctor of Literature).

dlr. *abbr.* Dealer.

D.L.S. *abbr.* Doctor of Library Science.

dm *abbr.* Decimeter.

DM *abbr.* **1.** Data management. **2.** Deutsche mark.

D.M.A. *abbr.* Doctor of Musical Arts.

D.M.D. *abbr. Lat.* Dentariae Medicinae Doctor (Doctor of Dental Medicine).

D.M.L. *abbr.* Doctor of Modern Languages.

DMSO (dē′ĕm-ĕs-ō′) *n.* A colorless hygroscopic liquid, $(CH_3)_2SO$, used as an industrial solvent and as a penetrant to convey medications into the tissues. [D(I)M(ETHYL)S(ULF)O(XIDE).]

Dn *abbr. Bible.* Daniel.

dn. *abbr.* Down.

DNA (dē′ĕn-ā′) *n.* A nucleic acid that carries the genetic information in the cell and is capable of self-replication and synthesis of RNA, consisting of two long chains of nucleotides twisted into a double helix and joined by hydrogen bonds, the sequence of nucleotides determining individual hereditary characteristics. [D(EOXYRIBO)N(UCLEIC) A(CID).]

DNA fingerprint *n.* The distinctive patterns of an individual's DNA, used as a means of identification. **— DNA fingerprinting** *n.*

DNA polymerase *n.* An enzyme that catalyzes the replication and repair of DNA by using single-stranded DNA as a template.

DNase also **DNAse** (dē-ĕn′ās) or **DNAase** (dē′ĕn-ā′ās) *n.* An enzyme that catalyzes the hydrolysis of DNA.

DNA virus *n.* A virus having a genome composed of DNA.

Dne•pro•dzer•zhinsk (nĕp′rō-dər-zhĭnsk′, dnyĭ′prə-dzĭr-zhĭnsk′). A city of E-central Ukraine on the Dnieper R. SSW of Kharkov. Pop. 271,000.

Dne•pro•pe•trovsk (nĕp′rō-pə-trôfsk′, dnyĭ′prə-pyĭ-trôfsk′). A city of E-central Ukraine on the Dnieper R. SSW of Kharkov; founded 1787. Pop. 1,153,000.

Dnie•per (nē′pər, dnyĕ′pər). A river rising in W-central Russia near Smolensk and flowing c. 2,285 km (1,420 mi) S through Belorussia and the Ukraine to the Black Sea.

Dnies•ter (nē′stər, dnyĕ′stər). A river rising in W Ukraine and flowing c. 1,368 km (850 mi) generally SE to the Black Sea.

do¹ (do͞o) *v.* **did** (dĭd), **done** (dŭn), **do•ing, does** (dŭz). *— tr.* **1.a.** To perform or execute: *doing your assigned task.* **b.** To fulfill the requirements of: *did my duty.* **c.** To carry out; commit: *a crime done on purpose.* **2.a.** To produce, esp. by creative effort. **b.** To play the part or role of in a creative production. **c.** To mimic. **3.a.** To bring about; effect: *Crying won't do any good.* **b.** To render; give: *Do honor to your family.* **4.** To put forth; exert: *Do your best.* **5.a.** To take care of or put in order: *did the bedrooms.* **b.** To prepare for further use esp. by washing: *did the dishes.* **6.a.** To set or style (the hair). **b.** To apply cosmetics to. **7.** To have as an occupation or a profession. **8.** To work out by studying: *doing a homework assignment.* **9.** *Informal.* **a.** To travel (a specified distance): *do a mile a minute.* **b.** To make a tour of; visit. **10.a.** To be sufficient for; serve: *This room will do us nicely.* **b.** *Informal.* To serve (a prison term). **11.** *Slang.* To cheat; swindle. **12.** *Slang.* To take (drugs) illegally. *— intr.* **1.** To behave or conduct oneself; act: *Do as I say.* **2.a.** To get along; fare. **b.** To carry on; manage: *We can do without you.* **c.** To make good use of something out of need: *I could do with a hot bath.* **3.a.** To serve a purpose. **b.** To be proper or fitting. **4.** To take place; happen. **5.** Used as a substitute for an antecedent verb: *worked as hard as we did.* **6.** Used after another verb for emphasis: *Run quickly, do! — aux.* **1.** Used with the infinitive without *to* in questions, negative statements, and inverted phrases: *Do you understand? I did not sleep well. Little did we know!* **2.** Used as a means of emphasis: *I do want to be sure. — n., pl.* **do's** or **dos. 1.** A statement of what should be done. **2.** *Informal.* An entertainment; a party. **3.** *Regional.* A commotion. **4.** *Chiefly British.* A swindle; a cheat. **5.** *Archaic.* Duty; deed. ***— phrasal verbs.*** **do by.** To behave with respect to; deal with. **do for.** To care or provide for; take care of. **do in.** *Slang.* **1.** To tire completely; exhaust. **2.** To kill. **3.** To ruin utterly. **do up. 1.** To adorn or dress lavishly. **2.** To wrap and tie (a package). **3.** To fasten: *do up the buttons.* **do without.** To manage in spite of a lack or absence. ***— idioms.*** **do a disappearing act.** *Informal.* To vanish. **do away with. 1.** To make an end of; eliminate. **2.** To destroy; kill. **do (one) proud.** To act or perform in a way that gives cause for pride. **do (one's) bit.** To contribute toward an overall effort. **do (one's) own thing.** *Slang.* To do what one does or likes best. **do or die.** To exert supreme effort. [ME *don* < OE *dōn.* See **dhē-*.**]

do² (dō) *n. Mus.* The first tone of the diatonic scale in solfeggio. [Ital., more singable replacement of *ut.* See GAMUT.]

D.O. *abbr.* **1.** Doctor of Optometry. **2.** Doctor of Osteopathy.

DOA *abbr.* Dead on arrival.

do•a•ble (do͞o′ə-bəl) *adj.* Possible to do.

DOB *abbr.* Date of birth.

dob•bin (dŏb′ĭn) *n.* A horse, esp. a working farm horse. [< *Dobbin,* alteration of *Robin,* nickname for *Robert.*]

dob•by (dŏb′ē) *n., pl.* **-bies. 1.** A part in a loom that controls the harnesses to permit the weaving of small geometric figures. **2.a.** Such a woven figure. **b.** A fabric with dobbies. [Perh. < *Dobbie,* dim. of *Dob,* alteration of *Rob,* nickname for *Robert.*]

Do•ber•man pin•scher (dō′bər-mən pĭn′shər) *n.* A medium-sized to large dog of a breed originating in Germany, having short hair and a smooth, usu. dark coat. [Ger. *Dobermann* (after Ludwig *Dobermann,* 19th-cent. German dog breeder) + Ger. *Pinscher,* terrier (prob. < PINCH, from the cropping of its ears and tail).]

Do•bie (dō′bē), **James Frank.** 1888–1964. Amer. historian best known for his works on the history of the Southwest.

do•bra (dō′brə) *n.* See table at **currency.** [Port., ult. < Lat. *duplus,* double. See DUPLE.]

dob•son (dŏb′sən) *n.* See **hellgrammite.** [Prob. < the name *Dobson.*]

dob•son•fly (dŏb′sən-flī′) *n.* An insect *(Corydalus cornutus)* having four large many-veined wings and in the male long pincerlike mandibles.

doc (dŏk) *n. Informal.* A physician, dentist, or veterinarian. [Short for DOCTOR.]

doc. *abbr.* Document.

do•cent (dō′sənt, dō-sĕnt′) *n.* **1.** A teacher or lecturer at a university who is not a regular faculty member. **2.** A lecturer or tour guide in a museum or cathedral. [Obsolete Ger. < Lat. *docēns, docent-,* pr.part. of *docēre,* to teach. See **dek-*.**]

Do•ce•tism (dō-sē′tĭz′əm, dō′sə-tĭz′əm) *n.* An opinion esp. associated with the Gnostics that Jesus had no human body and only appeared to have died on the cross. [Prob. < LGk. *Dokētai,* espousers of Docetism < Gk. *dokein,* to seem. See **dek-*.**] **— Do•ce′tist** *n.*

doc•ile (dŏs′əl, -īl′) *adj.* **1.** Ready and willing to be taught; teachable. **2.** Yielding to supervision or direction; tractable. [Lat. *docilis* < *docēre,* to teach. See **dek-*.**] **— doc′ile•ly** *adv.* **— do•cil′i•ty** (dŏ-sĭl′ĭ-tē, dō-) *n.*

dock¹ (dŏk) *n.* **1.** The area of water between two piers or alongside a pier that receives a ship for loading, unloading, or repairs. **2.** A pier; a wharf. **3.** A group of piers on a commercial waterfront that serve as a landing area for ships or boats. Often used in the plural. **4.** A platform at which trucks or trains load or unload cargo. *— v.* **docked, dock•ing, docks.** *— tr.* **1.** To maneuver (a vessel or vehicle) into or next to a dock. **2.** *Aerospace.* To couple (two or more spacecraft, for example) in space. *— intr.* To move or come into a dock. [Du. *dok* < MDu. *doc* < *dūken,* to go under water, dive.]

dock² (dŏk) *n.* **1.** The solid or fleshy part of an animal's tail. **2.** The tail of an animal after it has been bobbed or clipped. *— tr.v.* **docked, dock•ing, docks. 1.** To clip short or cut off (an animal's tail, for example). **2.** To deprive of a benefit or a part of one's wages, esp. as a punishment. **3.** To withhold or deduct a part from (one's salary or wages). [ME *dok.*]

dock³ (dŏk) *n.* An enclosed place where the defendant stands or sits in a court of law. ***— idiom.*** **in the dock.** On trial or under intense scrutiny. [Obsolete Flem. *docke,* cage.]

dock⁴ (dŏk) *n.* See **sorrel¹** 1. [ME < OE *docce.*]

dock•age (dŏk′ĭj) *n.* **1.** A charge for docking privileges. **2.** Facilities for docking vessels. **3.** The docking of ships.

dock•er¹ (dŏk′ər) *n.* A dockhand.

dock•er² (dŏk′ər) *n.* One that docks something, such as an animal's tail.

dock•et (dŏk′ĭt) *n.* **1.** *Law.* **a.** A calendar of the cases awaiting action in a court. **b.** A brief entry of the court proceedings in a legal case. **c.** The book containing such entries. **2.** A summary or other brief statement of the contents of a document; an abstract. **3.** A list of things to be done. **4.** A label or ticket on a package listing the contents or directions for assembling or operating. *— tr.v.* **-et•ed, -et•ing, -ets. 1.** *Law.* To enter in a court calendar or a record of court proceedings. **2.** To provide with a brief identifying statement. **3.** To label or ticket (a parcel). [ME *doggett,* summary, digest.]

dobsonfly
Corydalus cornutus

dock•hand (dŏk′hănd′) *n.* A longshoreman.

dock•mack•ie (dŏk′măk′ē) *n.* A shrub *(Viburnum acerifolium)* of eastern North America having clusters of white flowers. [Prob. < American Du., perh. of Mahican orig.]

dock•side (dŏk′sīd′) *n.* The area adjacent to a boating dock.

dock•work•er (dŏk′wûr′kər) *n.* A dockhand.

dock•yard (dŏk′yärd′) *n.* **1.** An area, often bordering a body of water, with facilities for dry-docking ships. **2.** *Chiefly British.* A navy yard.

doc•tor (dŏk′tər) *n.* **1.** A person, esp. a physician, dentist, or veterinarian, trained in the healing arts and licensed to practice. **2.a.** A person who has earned the highest academic degree awarded by a college or university in a specified discipline. **b.** A person awarded an honorary degree by a college or university. **3.** Used as a title and form of address for a person holding the degree of doctor. **4.** *Rom. Cath. Ch.* An eminent theologian. **5.** A rig or device contrived for a special use, as in an emergency. *— v.* **-tored, -tor•ing, -tors.** *— tr.* **1.** *Informal.* To give medical treatment to. **2.** To repair, esp. in a makeshift manner; rig. **3.a.** To falsify or change in such a way as to make favorable to oneself. **b.** To add ingredients to improve or conceal the taste, appearance, or quality of. **c.** To alter or modify for a specific end. *— intr. Informal.* To practice medicine. [ME, an expert, authority < OFr. *docteur* < Lat. *doctor,* teacher < *docēre,* to teach. See **dek-*.**] **— doc′tor•al** *adj.* **— doc′tor•ly** *adj.*

dock¹

doc•tor•ate (dŏk′tər-ĭt) *n.* The degree or status of a doctor as conferred by a university.

doc•tri•naire (dŏk′trə-nâr′) *n.* A doctrinaire person. *— adj.* Of or characteristic of a person inflexibly attached to a practice or theory without regard to its practicality. [Fr. < *doctrine,* doctrine < OFr. See DOCTRINE.] **— doc′tri•nair′ism** *n.* **— doc′tri•nar′i•an** *n.*

doc•tri•nal (dŏk′trə-nəl) *adj.* Characterized by, belonging to, or concerning doctrine. **— doc′tri•nal•ly** *adv.*

doc•trine (dŏk′trĭn) *n.* **1.** A principle or system presented for acceptance or belief, as by a religious or philosophic group; dogma. **2.** A rule or principle of law, esp. established by precedent. **3.** A statement of government policy, esp. in foreign affairs and military strategy. **4.** *Archaic.* Something taught; a teaching. [ME < OFr. < Lat. *doctrīna* < *doctor,* teacher < *docēre,* to teach. See **dek-*.**]

doc•u•ment (dŏk′yə-mənt) *n.* **1.a.** A written or printed paper that bears the original, official, or legal form of something and can furnish evidence or information. **b.** Something, such as a recording or photograph, that can furnish evidence or information. **c.** A writing that contains information. **2.** Something, esp. a material substance such as a coin bearing a symbol or mark, that serves as evidence. *— tr.v.* (-mĕnt′) **-ment•ed, -ment•ing, -ments. 1.** To furnish with a document or documents. **2.** To support (a claim, for example) with evidence or information. **3.** To support (statements in a book, for example) with written references or citations; annotate. [ME, precept < OFr. < Lat. *documentum,* example, proof < *docēre,* to teach. See **dek-*.**] **— doc′u•ment′a•ble** *adj.* **— doc′u•ment′al** (-mĕn′tl) *adj.* **— doc′u•ment′er** *n.*

doc•u•ment•al•ist (dŏk′yə-mĕn′tl-ĭst′) *n.* A specialist in documentation.

ă pat	oi boy
ā pay	ou out
âr care	o͝o took
ä father	o͞o boot
ĕ pet	ŭ cut
ē be	ûr urge
ĭ pit	th thin
ī pie	*th* this
îr pier	hw which
ŏ pot	zh vision
ō toe	ə about,
ô paw	item

Stress marks:
′ (primary);
′ (secondary), as in
dictionary (dĭk′shə-nĕr′ē)

doc•u•men•tar•i•an (-mĕn-târ′ē-ən, -mən-) also **doc•u•men•ta•rist** (dŏk′yə-mĕn′tər-ĭst) *n.* One that makes documentaries or a documentary.

doc•u•men•ta•ry (dŏk′yə-mĕn′tə-rē) *adj.* **1.** Consisting of, concerning, or based on documents. **2.** Presenting facts objectively without editorializing or fictional matter. *—n., pl.* **-ries.** A work, such as a film, presenting its subject matter factually, often with news films, interviews, and narration.

doc•u•men•ta•tion (dŏk′yə-mĕn-tā′shən) *n.* **1.a.** The act or an instance of supplying documents, references, or records. **b.** The documents or references supplied. **2.** The collation, synopsizing, and coding of printed material for reference. **3.** *Comp. Sci.* The organized collection of material that describes a computer program or system.

DOD *abbr.* Department of Defense.

dod•der[1] (dŏd′ər) *intr.v.* **-dered, -der•ing, -ders. 1.** To shake or tremble, as from age; totter. **2.** To progress feebly and unsteadily. [Alteration of ME *daderen.*] **—dod′der•er** *n.*

dod•der[2] (dŏd′ər) *n.* Any of various leafless annual parasitic herbs of the genus *Cuscuta,* having slender twining stems and small whitish flowers. [ME *doder,* poss. < MDu., yolk of an egg.]

dod•dered (dŏd′ərd) *adj.* **1.** *Bot.* Lacking the top branches because of age or decay. **2.** Infirm; feeble. [Prob. alteration of *dodded,* p.part. of dialectal *dod,* to lop off < ME *dodden,* perh. < *dodde,* a measure of grain.]

dod•der•ing (dŏd′ər-ĭng) *adj.* Infirm, feeble, and often senile.

do•dec•a•gon (dō-dĕk′ə-gŏn′) *n.* A polygon with 12 sides. [Gk. *dōdekagōnon* : *dōdeka,* twelve (*duo,* two; see **dwo-*** + *deka,* ten; see **dekm̥***) + *-gōnon,* -gon.] **—do′de•cag′o•nal** (dō′dĕ-kăg′ə-nəl) *adj.*

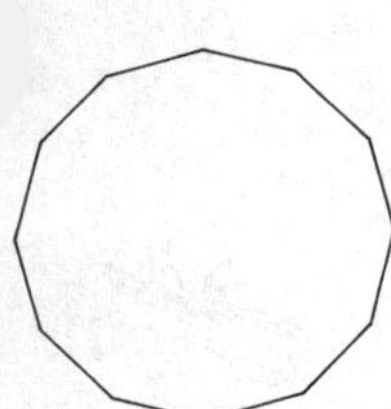

dodecagon

do•dec•a•he•dron (dō′dĕk-ə-hē′drən) *n., pl.* **-drons** or **-dra** (-drə). A polyhedron with 12 faces. [Gk. *dōdekaedron* : *dōdeka,* twelve; see DODECAGON + *-edron,* -hedron.] **—do′dec•a•he′dral** *adj.*

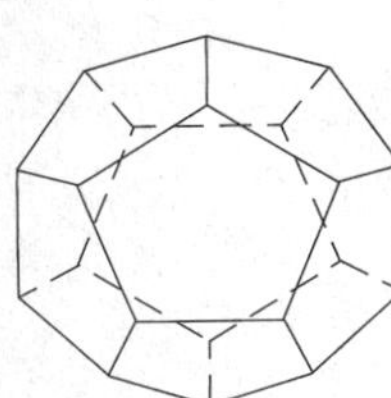

dodecahedron

Do•dec•a•nese (dō-dĕk′ə-nēz′, -nēs′). An island group of SE Greece in the Aegean Sea between Turkey and Crete; held by Turkey from 1522 until 1912.

do•dec•a•phon•ic (dō′dĕk-ə-fŏn′ĭk) *adj. Mus.* Relating to, composed in, or consisting of twelve-tone music. [Gk. *dōdeka,* twelve; see DODECAGON + PHON(O)–, tone, pitch + –IC.] **—do•dec′a•phon•ist** (dō-dĕk′ə-fə-nĭst, dō′də-kăf′ə-) *n.* **—do•dec′a•phon′y** (dō-dĕk′ə-fō′nē, dō′də-kăf′ə-), **do•dec′a•phon•ism** *n.*

dodge (dŏj) *v.* **dodged, dodg•ing, dodg•es.** *—tr.* **1.** To avoid (a blow, for example) by moving or shifting quickly aside. **2.** To evade (an obligation, for example) by cunning or deceit. **3.** To blunt or reduce the intensity of (a section of a photograph) by shading during the printing process. *—intr.* **1.** To move aside or in a given direction by shifting or twisting suddenly. **2.** To practice trickery or cunning; prevaricate. *—n.* **1.** The act of dodging. **2.** An ingenious expedient intended to evade or trick. [?]

Dodge (dŏj), **Mary Elizabeth Mapes.** 1831–1905. Amer. writer best known for *Hans Brinker, or the Silver Skates* (1865).

dodge ball *n. Games.* A game in which players outside a circle try to eliminate players inside by hitting them with a ball.

Dodge City. A city of SW KS on the Arkansas R. W of Wichita; laid out on the Santa Fe Trail in 1872. Pop. 21,129.

dodg•er (dŏj′ər) *n.* **1.** One that dodges or evades. **2.** A shifty, dishonest person; a trickster. **3.** A small printed handbill. **4.** *Chiefly Southern U.S.* See **corndodger.**

Dodg•son (dŏj′sən), **Charles Lutwidge.** Lewis Carroll. 1832–98. British mathematician and writer renowned for the classics *Alice's Adventures in Wonderland* (1865) and *Through the Looking-Glass* (1872).

Charles Dodgson
"Lewis Carroll"

dodg•y (dŏj′ē) *adj.* **-i•er, -i•est.** *Chiefly British.* **1.** Evasive; shifty. **2.** Unsound, unstable, and unreliable. **3.** So risky as to require very deft handling.

do•do (dō′dō) *n., pl.* **-does** or **-dos. 1.** A large clumsy flightless bird *(Raphus cucullatus)* formerly of the island of Mauritius in the Indian Ocean and extinct since the late 17th century. **2.** *Informal.* One who is hopelessly passé. **3.** *Informal.* A stupid person; an idiot. [Port. *dodó,* alteration of obsolete Du. *dodors* : Du. *dot,* tuft of feathers + obsolete Du. *ors,* tail (< MDu. *ærs;* see **ors-***).]

dodo
Raphus cucullatus

Do•do•ma (dō′də-mä, -dō-). The official cap. of Tanzania, in the central part. Pop. 46,000.

doe (dō) *n., pl.* **doe** or **does. 1.** The female of a deer or related animal. **2.** The female of various mammals, such as the hare, goat, or kangaroo. [ME *do* < OE *dā.*]

Doe•nitz also **Dö•nitz** (dœ′nĭts), **Karl.** 1891–1980. German officer who was chief naval commander during World War II.

do•er (do͞o′ər) *n.* **1.** One who does something. **2.** A particularly active, energetic person: *a real doer in party politics.*

does (dŭz) *v.* Third pers. sing. pr.t. of **do**[1].

doe•skin (dō′skĭn′) *n.* **1.a.** The skin of a doe, deer, or goat. **b.** Leather made from this skin, used esp. for gloves. **2.** A fine woolen fabric. **3.** A densely napped finish for certain woolen fabrics.

does•n't (dŭz′ənt). Does not.

do•est (do͞o′ĭst) *v. Archaic.* A second pers. sing. pr.t. of **do**[1].

do•eth (do͞o′əth) *v. Archaic.* A third pers. sing. pr.t. of **do**[1].

doff (dôf, dŏf) *tr.v.* **doffed, doff•ing, doffs. 1.** To take off; remove. **2.** To tip or remove (one's hat) in salutation. **3.** To put aside; discard. [ME *doffen* < *don off,* to do off : *don,* to do; see DO[1] + *off,* off; see OFF.]

dog (dôg, dŏg) *n.* **1.** A domesticated canid *(Canis familiaris)* related to foxes and wolves and raised in many breeds. **2.** Any of various members of the family Canidae, such as the dingo. **3.** A male animal of the family Canidae, esp. of the fox or a domesticated breed. **4.** Any of various other animals, such as the prairie dog. **5.** *Informal.* **a.** A person: *you lucky dog!* **b.** A contemptible person: *You stole my watch, you dog.* **6.** *Slang.* **a.** An unattractive or uninteresting person. **b.** An inferior product or creation. **7. dogs.** *Slang.* The feet. **8.** See **andiron. 9.** *Slang.* A hot dog; a wiener. **10.** Any of various hooked or U-shaped metallic devices used for gripping or holding heavy objects. **11.** *Astron.* A sun dog. *—adv.* Totally; completely. Often used in combination: *dog-tired.* *—tr.v.* **dogged, dog•ging, dogs. 1.** To track or trail persistently. **2.** To hold or fasten with a dog. ***—idioms.* dog it.** *Slang.* To fail to expend the effort to accomplish something. **go to the dogs.** To go to ruin; degenerate. **put on the dog.** *Informal.* To make an ostentatious display. [ME *dogge* < OE *docga.*]

dog-and-po•ny show (dôg′ən-pō′nē, dŏg′-) *n. Slang.* An elaborate presentation orchestrated to gain approval, as for a policy. [From the razzle-dazzle of animal acts at circuses.]

dog•bane (dôg′bān′, dŏg′-) *n.* Any of several plants of the genus *Apocynum,* having milky juice and bell-shaped flowers.

dog•ber•ry (dôg′bĕr′ē, dŏg′-) *n.* **1.** A wild gooseberry *(Ribes cynosbati)* of eastern North America bearing large prickly berries. **2.** A wild mountain ash *(Pyrus decora)* of eastern North America. **3.** The fruit of either of these plants.

dog biscuit *n.* A hard cracker for dogs.

dog•cart (dôg′kärt′, dŏg′-) *n.* **1.** A vehicle for two persons seated back to back and drawn by one horse. **2.** A cart pulled by dogs.

dog•catch•er (dôg′kăch′ər, dŏg′-) *n.* A dog officer.

dog collar *n.* **1.** A collar for a dog. **2.** *Informal.* A clerical collar. **3.** A choker.

dog days *pl.n.* **1.** The sultry period of summer between early July and early September. **2.** A period of stagnation. [Transl. of LLat. *diēs canīculārēs,* Dog Star days (so called because the Dog Star (Sirius) rises and sets with the sun during this time) : Lat. *diēs,* days + LLat. *canīculāris,* of the Dog Star.]

doge (dōj) *n.* The elected chief magistrate of the former republics of Venice and Genoa. [Ital. dial. < Lat. *dux, duc-,* leader < *dūcere,* to lead. See **deuk-***.]

dog-ear (dôg′îr′, dŏg′-) *n.* A turned-down corner of a page in a book. *—tr.v.* **-eared, -ear•ing, -ears. 1.** To turn down the corner of (a page of a book). **2.** To make worn or shabby from overuse. **—dog′-eared′** *adj.*

dog-eat-dog (dôg′ēt-dôg′, dŏg′ēt-dŏg′) *adj.* Ruthlessly acquisitive or competitive: *a dog-eat-dog society.*

dog•face (dôg′fās′, dŏg′-) *n. Slang.* A U.S. Army foot soldier, esp. in World War II.

dog fennel *n.* **1.** A strong-smelling European weed *(Anthemis cotula)* naturalized in North America. **2.** A weedy plant *(Eupatorium capillifolium)* of the southeast United States having pinnately divided leaves and long clusters of greenish flowers.

dog•fight (dôg′fīt′, dŏg′-) *n.* **1.a.** A violent fight between or as if between dogs. **b.** An illegal organized fight between dogs. **2.** An aerial battle between fighter planes. **—dog′fight′er** *n.*

dog•fish (dôg′fĭsh′, dŏg′-) *n., pl.* **dogfish** or **-fish•es. 1.** Any of various small sharks, chiefly of the family Squalidae, of Atlantic and Pacific coastal waters. **2.** See **bowfin.**

dog•ged (dô′gĭd, dŏg′ĭd) *adj.* Stubbornly persevering; tenacious. See Syns at **obstinate. —dog′ged•ly** *adv.* **—dog′ged•ness** *n.*

Dog•ger Bank (dô′gər, dŏg′ər). An extensive sandbank of the central North Sea between Great Britain and Denmark.

dog•ger•el (dô′gər-əl, dŏg′ər-) also **dog•grel** (dôg′rəl, dŏg′-) *n.* Clumsy verse, often having an irregular form and monotonous rhymes. [< ME, poor, worthless < *dogge,* dog. See DOG.] **—dog′ger•el** *adj.*

dog•gish (dô′gĭsh, dŏg′ĭsh) *adj.* **1.** Relating to or suggestive of a dog. **2.** Surly; gruff. **3.** *Informal.* Showily stylish. **—dog′gish•ly** *adv.* **—dog′gish•ness** *n.*

dog•go (dô′gō, dŏg′ō) *adv. Informal.* In concealment. [Prob. < DOG.]

dog•gone (dôg′gôn′, -gŏn′, dŏg′-) *Informal.* *—tr. & intr.v.* To damn. *—interj., n., adv., & adj.* Damn. See Regional Note at **damned.** [Alteration of Sc. *dagone* < *dag on (it)* : *dag,* confound (prob. alteration of *goddamn*) + ON.]

dog•gy or **dog•gie** (dô′gē, dŏg′ē) *—n., pl.* **-gies.** A dog, esp. a small one. *—adj.* **-gi•er, -gi•est.** Of or suggestive of a dog; doggish.

doggy bag or **doggie bag** *n.* A bag for leftover food that a customer of a restaurant may take home after a meal.

dog•hanged (dôg′hăngd, dŏg′-) *adj. Chiefly Southern U.S.* Hangdog. See Regional Note at **everwhere.**

dog•house (dôg′hous′, dŏg′-) *n.* A small shelter for a dog. ***—idiom.* in the doghouse.** *Slang.* In great disfavor or trouble.

do•gie also **do•gy** (dō′gē) *n., pl.* **-gies.** *Western U.S.* A stray or motherless calf. [?]

dog iron *n. Upper Southern U.S.* See **andiron.** [(FIRE)DOG + (AND)IRON.]

dog•leg (dôg′lĕg′, dŏg′-) *n.* **1.a.** Something that has a sharp bend, esp. a road or route that bends abruptly. **b.** A sharp bend or turn. **2.** *Sports.* A golf hole in which the fairway is abruptly angled. —*intr.v.* **-legged, -leg•ging, -legs.** To make a sharp bend or turn. —**dog′leg′ged** (-lĕg′ĭd, -lĕgd′) *adj.*

dog•ma (dôg′mə, dŏg′-) *n., pl.* **-mas** or **-ma•ta** (-mə-tə). **1.** *Theol.* A doctrine or a system relating to matters such as morality and faith, set forth authoritatively by a church. **2.** An authoritative principle, belief, or statement of ideas or opinion, esp. one considered to be absolutely true. **3.** A principle or belief or a group of them. [Lat. < Gk., opinion, belief < *dokein*, to seem, think. See **dek-***.]

dog•mat•ic (dôg-măt′ĭk, dŏg-) *adj.* **1.** Relating to, characteristic of, or resulting from dogma. **2.** Characterized by an authoritative, arrogant assertion of unproved or unprovable principles. [LLat. *dogmaticus* < Gk. *dogmatikos* < *dogma, dogmat-*, belief. See DOGMA.] —**dog•mat′i•cal•ly** *adv.*

dog•mat•ics (dôg-măt′ĭks, dŏg-) *n. (used with a sing. v.)* The study of religious dogmas, esp. of a Christian church.

dog•ma•tism (dôg′mə-tĭz′əm, dŏg′-) *n.* Arrogant, stubborn assertion of opinion or belief.

dog•ma•tist (dôg′mə-tĭst, dŏg′-) *n.* **1.** An arrogantly assertive person. **2.** One who expresses or sets forth dogma.

dog•ma•tize (dôg′mə-tīz′, dŏg′-) *v.* **-tized, -tiz•ing, -tiz•es.** —*intr.* To express oneself dogmatically. —*tr.* To proclaim as dogma. —**dog′ma•ti•za′tion** (-tĭ-zā′shən) *n.*

dog officer *n.* One appointed or elected to impound stray dogs.

do-good•er (do͞o′go͝od′ər) *n.* A naive idealist who supports philanthropic or humanitarian causes or reforms. —**do′-good′** *adj.* —**do′-good′ing** *adj. & n.* —**do′-good′ism** *n.*

dog paddle *n. Sports.* A prone swimming stroke in which the arms and legs remain submerged and each limb paddles in alternation.

Dog•rib (dôg′rĭb′, dŏg′-) *n., pl.* **Dogrib** or **-ribs. 1.** A member of a Native American people inhabiting an area between the Great Bear and Great Slave lakes in the Northwest Territories of Canada. **2.** The Athabaskan language of this people. [Transl. of Cree *atimospikay*.]

dog rose *n.* A prickly wild rose *(Rosa canina)* native to Europe and having fragrant pink or white flowers.

dogs•bod•y (dôgz′bŏd′ē, dŏgz′-) *n. Chiefly British.* One who does menial work; a drudge. [British slang, naval rations (obsolete), midshipman.]

dog's chance (dôgz, dŏgz) *n. Slang.* A very slim chance.

dog•sled or **dog sled** (dôg′slĕd′, dŏg′-) *n.* A sled pulled by one or more dogs. —**dog′sled′** *v.* —**dog′sled′der** *n.* —**dog′sled′ding** *n.*

dog's life *n. Slang.* A miserably unhappy existence.

dog's mercury *n.* A creeping ill-smelling Old World weed *(Mercurialis perennis)* having small greenish flowers.

Dog Star (dôg, dŏg) *n.* **1.** See **Sirius. 2.** See **Procyon.** [The brightest star in the constellation Canis Major, the Big Dog.]

dog tag *n.* **1.** A metal identification disk attached to a dog's collar. **2.** A metal identification tag worn on a chain around the neck by members of the armed forces.

dog•tooth (dôg′to͞oth′, dŏg′-) *n.* **1.** A canine tooth; an eyetooth. **2.** *Archit.* A medieval ornament consisting of four leaflike projections radiating from a raised center.

dogtooth violet *n.* Any of several plants of the genus *Erythronium,* having leaves with reddish blotches and lilylike flowers on leafless stems.

dog•trot (dôg′trŏt′, dŏg′-) *n.* **1.** A steady trot like that of a dog. **2.** *Chiefly Southern U.S.* A roofed passage between two parts of a structure. —**dog′trot′** *v.*

dog•watch (dôg′wŏch′, dŏg′-) *n.* **1.** *Naut.* Either of two periods of watch duty, from 4 to 6 P.M. or 6 to 8 P.M. **2.** A late night shift. [Prob. < *dog-sleep*, a light or interrupted sleep.]

dog•wood (dôg′wo͝od′, dŏg′-) *n.* **1.** A tree *(Cornus florida)* of eastern North America having small greenish flowers surrounded by four large showy white or pink bracts that resemble petals. **2.** Any of several trees or shrubs of the genus *Cornus.*

do•gy (dō′gē) *n. Western U.S.* Var. of **dogie.**

Do•ha (dō′hə, -hä). The cap. of Qatar, on the Persian Gulf. Pop. 190,000.

doi•ly (doi′lē) *n., pl.* **-lies. 1.** A small ornamental mat, usu. of lace or linen. **2.** A small table napkin. [After *Doily* or *Doyly*, 18th-cent. London draper.]

do•ing (do͞o′ĭng) *n.* **1.** Performance of an act. **2. doings. a.** Daily activities. **b.** Social events and activities.

do-it-your•self (do͞o′ĭt-yər-sĕlf′) *adj.* Of, relating to, or designed to be done by an amateur. —**do′-it-your•self′er** *n.*

do•jo (dō′jō) *n.* A school for training in Japanese arts of self-defense, such as judo and karate. [J. *dōjō*.]

dol. *abbr.* **1.** Dollar. **2.** *Mus.* Dolce.

do•lab•ri•form (dō-lăb′rə-fôrm′) also **do•lab•rate** (-rāt′) *adj. Biol.* Having the shape of the head of an ax. [Lat. *dolābra*, pickax (< *dolāre*, to hew) + -FORM.]

Dol•by (dōl′bē). A trademark used for an electronic device that eliminates noise from recorded sound and audio signals.

dol•ce (dōl′chā′) *Mus. adv. & adj.* Gently and sweetly. [< Ital., sweet < Lat. *dulcis*.]

dolce vi•ta (vē′tə, -tä) *n.* A luxurious self-indulgent way of life. [Ital. : *dolce*, sweet + *vita*, life.]

dol•drums (dōl′drəmz′, dôl′-, dŏl′-) *pl.n. (used with a sing. or pl. v.)* **1.a.** A period of stagnation or slump. **b.** A period of depression or unhappy listlessness. **2.a.** A region of the ocean near the equator, characterized by calms, light winds, or squalls. **b.** The weather conditions of these regions. [Alteration (influenced by TANTRUM) of obsolete *doldrum*, dullard < ME *dold*, p.part. of *dullen*, to dull < *dul*, dull. See DULL.]

dole¹ (dōl) *n.* **1.** Charitable dispensation of goods, esp. money, food, or clothing. **2.** A share of money, food, or clothing charitably given. **3.** *Chiefly British.* The distribution of government relief payments to the unemployed; welfare. **4.** *Archaic.* One's fate. —*tr.v.* **doled, dol•ing, doles. 1.** To dispense as charity. **2.** To give out in small portions. See Syns at **distribute.** —***idiom.* on the dole.** Receiving regular relief payments. [ME *dol*, part, share < OE *dāl*. See **dail-***.]

dole² (dōl) *n. Archaic.* Sorrow; grief; dolor. [ME *dol* < OFr. *dol, deul* < LLat. *dolus* < Lat. *dolēre*, to feel pain, grieve.]

dole•ful (dōl′fəl) *adj.* **1.** Filled with or expressing grief; mournful. See Syns at **sad. 2.** Causing grief. —**dole′ful•ly** *adv.* —**dole′ful•ness** *n.*

dol•er•ite (dŏl′ə-rīt′) *n. Chiefly British.* A dark fine-grained igneous rock; diabase. [Fr. *dolérite* < Gk. *doleros*, deceitful (from its easily being mistaken for diorite) < *dolos*, trick. See **del-²***.] —**dol′er•it′ic** (ə-rĭt′ĭk) *adj.*

dol•i•cho•ce•phal•ic (dŏl′ĭ-kō-sə-făl′ĭk) also **dol•i•cho•ceph•a•lous** (-sĕf′ə-ləs) *adj.* Having a relatively long head with a cephalic index below 76. [Gk. *dolikhos*, long; see **del-¹*** + -CEPHALIC.] —**dol′i•cho•ceph′a•lism** (-sĕf′ə-lĭz′-əm), **dol′i•cho•ceph′a•ly** (-sĕf′ə-lē) *n.*

dol•i•cho•cra•ni•al (dŏl′ə-kō-krā′nē-əl) also **dol•i•cho•cra•nic** (-nĭk) *adj.* Having a relatively long skull with a cranial index of 74.9 or less. [Gk. *dolikhos*, long; see **del-¹*** + CRANIAL.] —**dol′i•cho•cra′ny** *n.*

do-lit•tle (do͞o′lĭt′l) *n. Informal.* A lazy person.

doll (dŏl) *n.* **1.** A child's usu. small toy representing a human being. **2.** A pretty child. **3.** *Slang.* **a.** An attractive person. **b.** A woman. **c.** A sweetheart or darling. **d.** A helpful or obliging person. —***phrasal verb.* doll up.** *Slang.* **1.** To dress oneself smartly and often ostentatiously, esp. for a special occasion. **2.** To embellish to make much more attractive. [< *Doll*, nickname for *Dorothy*.]

dol•lar (dŏl′ər) *n.* **1.** See table at **currency. 2.** A coin or note worth one dollar. [LGer. *Daler*, taler < Ger. *Taler*, short for *Joachimstaler*, after *Joachimstal* (Jáchymov), a town of NE Czechoslovakia where similar coins were first minted.]

dollar cost averaging *n.* Periodic investment of a fixed dollar amount.

Dol•lard des Or•meaux or **Dol•lard-des-Or•meaux** (dō-yär′-dā-zôr-mō′). A town of S Quebec, Canada, a suburb of Montreal. Pop. 39,940.

dollar diplomacy *n.* **1.** A policy aimed at furthering U.S. interests abroad by encouraging the investment of capital in foreign countries. **2.** A policy intended to safeguard a nation's foreign investments.

dol•lar•fish (dŏl′ər-fĭsh′) *n., pl.* **dollarfish** or **-fish•es.** See **moonfish** 1.

dollar sign *n.* The symbol ($) for a dollar when placed before a numeral.

Doll•fuss (dôl′fo͞os′), **Engelbert.** 1892–1934. Austrian politician who as chancellor (1932–34) established an authoritarian one-party state.

doll•house (dŏl′hous′) *n.* **1.** A small model house used as a children's toy or to display miniature dolls and furniture. **2.** A house so small that it is likened to a toy house.

dol•lop (dŏl′əp) *n.* **1.** A large lump or portion of a solid matter. **2.** A small quantity or splash of a liquid. **3.** A modicum; a bit. [Earlier tuft, clump; perh. akin to Norw. *dolp*, lump.]

dol•ly (dŏl′ē) *n., pl.* **-lies. 1.** *Informal.* A child's doll. **2.a.** A hand truck or low mobile platform for transporting heavy loads. **b.** Such a platform used for work underneath a motor vehicle. **3.** A wheeled apparatus used to transport a movie or television camera about a set. **4.** A small locomotive, as for use on a construction site. **5.** A tool used to hold one end of a rivet while the other end is hammered to form a head. **6.** A small piece of wood or metal placed on the head of a pile to prevent damage while it is being driven.

Dol•ly Var•den (dŏl′ē vär′dn) *n.* A colorfully spotted trout *(Salvelinus malma)* of northwest North America and eastern Asia. [After *Dolly Varden*, a character known for her colorful costume in the novel *Barnaby Rudge* by Charles Dickens.]

dol•ma (dôl′mə, -mä) *n., pl.* **dol•mas** or **dol•ma•des** (dôl-mä′dĕs). A grape leaf stuffed usu. with rice, minced lamb, and herbs and served as an appetizer. [Turk., filling.]

dol•man (dŏl′mən) *n.* A woman's garment having capelike arm pieces. [Fr. < Ger. < Magyar *dolmany* < Turk. *dōlāmān*, robe < *dolamak*, to wind.]

dogtooth

dogwood
Cornus florida

ă pat	oi boy
ā pay	ou out
âr care	o͝o took
ä father	o͞o boot
ĕ pet	ŭ cut
ē be	ûr urge
ĭ pit	th thin
ī pie	*th* this
îr pier	hw which
ŏ pot	zh vision
ō toe	ə about, item
ô paw	

Stress marks:
′ (primary);
′ (secondary), as in
dictionary (dĭk′shə-nĕr′ē)

dolman sleeve *n.* A full sleeve that is very wide at the armhole and narrow at the wrist.

dol•men (dōl′mən, dŏl′-) *n.* A prehistoric megalithic structure consisting of upright stones with a capstone, typically forming a chamber. [Fr. < Breton **taolvean* : **taol*, alteration of *tol*, key + *men*, stone; see MENHIR.]

dol•o•mite (dō′lə-mīt′, dŏl′ə-) *n.* **1.** A mineral, $CaMg(CO_3)_2$, used in fertilizer and in construction. **2.** A magnesia-rich sedimentary rock resembling limestone. [Fr., after Déodat de *Dolomieu* (1750–1801), French geologist.] **—dol′o•mit′ic** (-mĭt′ĭk) *adj.* **—dol′o•mit′i•za′tion** (-mĭt′ĭ-zā′-shən) *n.* **—dol′o•mit•ize′** (-mĭ-tīz′) *v.*

Do•lo•mite Alps (dō′lə-mīt′, dŏl′ə-). A range of the E Alps in NE Italy rising to 3,344.3 m (10,965 ft).

do•lor (dō′lər) *n.* Sorrow; grief. [ME *dolour* < OFr. < Lat. *dolor*, pain < *dolēre*, to suffer, feel pain.]

do•lo•ro•so (dō′lə-rō′sō) *Mus.* —*adv.* With a mournful or plaintive tempo or quality. —*adj.* Mournful; plaintive. [Ital. < Lat. *dolōrōsus*, dolorous. See DOLOROUS.]

do•lor•ous (dō′lər-əs, dŏl′ər-) *adj.* Marked by or exhibiting sorrow, grief, or pain. [ME < OFr. *doloros* < LLat. *dolōrōsus* < *dolor*, dolor. See DOLOR.] **—do′lor•ous•ly** *adv.* **—do′lor•ous•ness** *n.*

dol•phin (dŏl′fĭn, dôl′-) *n.* **1.** Any of various cetaceans of the family Delphinidae, related to whales but usu. smaller and having a beaklike snout. **2.** Either of two marine game fishes *(Coryphaena hippurus* or *C. equisetis)* having iridescent coloring. [ME < OFr. *daulfin*, blend of *daufin* and OProv. *dalfin*, both < Med.Lat. **dalfinus* < Lat. *delphinus* < Gk. *delphis, delfin-* < *delphus*, womb (from its shape).]

dolphin

dolphin kick *n.* A swimming kick in which the legs are moved up and down with the feet held together.

dolphin striker *n. Naut.* A small vertical spar under the bowsprit of a sailboat that extends the martingale.

dolt (dōlt) *n.* A person regarded as stupid. [ME *dulte* < p.part. of *dullen*, to dull < *dul*, dull. See DULL.] **—dolt′ish** *adj.* **—dolt′ish•ly** *adv.* **—dolt′ish•ness** *n.*

Dol•ton (dōl′tən). A village of N IL S of Chicago. Pop. 23,930.

Dom (dŏm; *Portuguese* dõN) *n.* **1.** Used formerly as a title for men of the Portuguese and Brazilian royalty, aristocracy, and hierarchy, preceding the given name. **2.** *Rom. Cath. Ch.* Used as a title before the names of Benedictine and Carthusian monks in orders. [Port. < Lat. *dominus*, lord, master. See **dem-***.]

dom. *abbr.* **1.** Domestic. **2.** Dominant. **3.** Dominion.

-dom *suff.* **1.** State; condition: *stardom.* **2.a.** Domain; position; rank: *dukedom.* **b.** Those that collectively have a specified position, office, or character: *officialdom.* [ME < OE *-dōm.* See **dhē-***.]

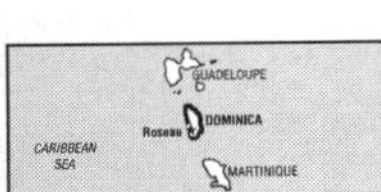

Dominica

do•main (dō-mān′) *n.* **1.** A territory over which rule or control is exercised. **2.** A sphere of activity, concern, or function; a field. **3.** *Phys.* A region in a ferromagnetic material in which the direction of spontaneous magnetization is uniform and different from that in neighboring regions. **4.** *Law.* Public domain. **5.** *Math.* **a.** The set of all possible values of an independent variable of a function. **b.** An open connected set that contains at least one point. [Fr. *domaine*, blend of OFr. *demaine* (< LLat. *dominicum*) and Lat. *dominium*, property, both < *dominus*, lord. See **dem-***.]

dome (dōm) *n.* **1.a.** A hemispherical roof or vault. **b.** A structure or other object resembling a dome. **2.** *Slang.* The human head. **3.** *Chem.* A form of crystal with two similarly inclined faces that meet at an edge parallel to the horizontal axis. **4.** *Archaic.* A large stately building. —*v.* **domed, dom•ing, domes.** —*tr.* **1.** To cover with or as if with a dome. **2.** To shape like a dome. —*intr.* To rise or swell into the shape of a dome. [< Fr. *dôme*, dome, cathedral (< Ital. *duomo*, cathedral < Lat. *domus*, house; see **dem-***) and < Fr. *dôme*, roof (< Prov. *doma* < Gk. *dōma*, house; see **dem-***).]

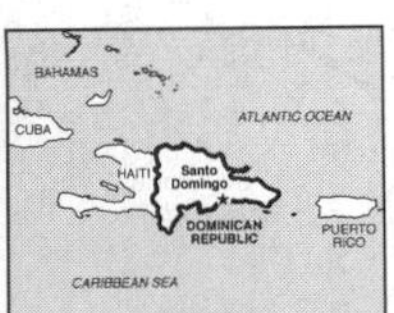

Dominican Republic

Domes•day Book (do͞omz′dā′, dōmz′-) also **Dooms•day Book** (do͞omz′-) *n.* The written census and survey of English landowners made by order of William the Conqueror in 1085–1086. [< ME *domesday*, doomsday. See DOOMSDAY.]

do•mes•tic (də-mĕs′tĭk) *adj.* **1.** Of or relating to the family or household: *domestic chores.* **2.** Fond of home life and household affairs. **3.** Tame or domesticated. Used of animals. **4.** Of or relating to a country's internal affairs. **5.** Produced in or indigenous to a particular country. *domestic wine.* —*n.* **1.** A household servant. **2.a.** Cotton cloth. **b.** Household linens. Often used in the plural. **3.** A product or substance of domestic origin. [ME < OFr. *domestique* < Lat. *domesticus* < *domus*, house. See **dem-***.] **—do•mes′ti•cal•ly** *adv.*

do•mes•ti•cate (də-mĕs′tĭ-kāt′) *tr.v.* **-cat•ed, -cat•ing, -cates. 1.** To make comfortable at home; make domestic. **2.** To adopt or fit for domestic use or life. **3.a.** To train or adapt (an animal or a plant) to live with and be of use to human beings. **b.** To introduce and accustom (an animal or a plant) into another region; naturalize. **4.** To bring down to an ordinary person's level. **—do•mes′ti•ca′tion** *n.*

domino[1]

do•mes•tic•i•ty (dō′mĕ-stĭs′ĭ-tē) *n., pl.* **-ties. 1.** The quality or condition of being domestic. **2.** Home life or devotion to it. **3. domesticities.** Household affairs.

do•mes•ti•cize (də-mĕs′tĭ-sīz′) *tr.v.* **-cized, -ciz•ing, -ciz•es.** To domesticate.

domestic prelate *n. Rom. Cath. Ch.* A priest who is an honorary member of the papal household.

domestic relations court *n. Law.* In certain U.S. states, a court with jurisdiction over family disputes, esp. involving the welfare of children.

do•mi•cal (dō′mĭ-kəl, dŏm′ĭ-) *adj.* Shaped like or having a dome. [DOM(E) + (CON)ICAL.] **—do′mi•cal•ly** *adv.*

dom•i•cile (dŏm′ĭ-sīl′, -səl, dō′mĭ-) *n.* **1.** A residence; a home. **2.** One's legal residence. —*v.* **-ciled, -cil•ing, -ciles.** —*tr.* **1.** To establish (one) in a residence. **2.** To provide with often temporary lodging. —*intr.* To dwell. [ME *domicilie* < OFr. *domicile* < Lat. *domicilium* < *domus*, house. See **dem-***.] **—dom′i•cil′i•ar′y** (-sĭl′ē-ĕr′ē) *adj.*

dom•i•nance (dŏm′ə-nəns) *n.* The condition or fact of being dominant.

dom•i•nant (dŏm′ə-nənt) *adj.* **1.** Exercising the most influence or control. **2.** Most prominent, as in position; ascendant. **3.** *Genet.* Of, relating to, or being an allele that produces the same phenotypic effect whether inherited with a homozygous or heterozygous allele. **4.** *Ecol.* Of, relating to, or being a species that is most characteristic of an ecological community, usu. determining the presence, abundance, and type of other species. **5.** *Mus.* Relating to or based on the dominant. —*n.* **1.** *Genet.* A dominant allele or trait. **2.** *Ecol.* A dominant species. **3.** *Mus.* The fifth tone of a diatonic scale. [ME *dominaunt* < OFr. < Lat. *dominans, dominant-*, pr.part. of *dominārī*, to dominate. See DOMINATE.] **—dom′i•nant•ly** *adv.*

dom•i•nate (dŏm′ə-nāt′) *v.* **-nat•ed, -nat•ing, -nates.** —*tr.* **1.** To control or govern by superior authority or power. **2.** To exert a supreme, guiding influence on or over. **3.** To enjoy a commanding or controlling position in: *dominating the market.* **4.** To overlook from a height. —*intr.* **1.** To have or exert strong authority or mastery. **2.** To be situated in or occupy a position more elevated or decidedly superior to others. [Lat. *dominārī, domināt-*, to rule < *dominus*, lord. See **dem-***.] **—dom′i•na′tive** *adj.* **—dom′i•na′tor** *n.*

dom•i•na•tion (dŏm′ə-nā′shən) *n.* **1.a.** Mastery or supremacy over another or others. **b.** The exercise of such mastery or supremacy. **2. dominations.** *Theol.* The fourth of the nine orders of angels.

dom•i•na•trix (dŏm′ə-nā′trĭks) *n., pl.* **-na•trix•es** or **-na•tri•ces** (-nā′trĭ-sēz′, -nə-trī′sēz). **1.** A woman who is the dominating partner in a sadomasochistic relationship. **2.** A woman regarded as overbearing. [DOMINA(TE) + -TRIX.]

dom•i•neer (dŏm′ə-nîr′) *v.* **-neered, -neer•ing, -neers.** —*tr.* To rule or control arbitrarily or arrogantly; tyrannize. —*intr.* To rule or control in such a way. [Du. *domineren* < Fr. *dominer* < Lat. *dominārī*, to dominate. See DOMINATE.]

dom•i•neer•ing (dŏm′ə-nîr′ĭng) *adj.* Tending to domineer; overbearing. **—dom′i•neer′ing•ly** *adv.*

Dom•i•nic (dŏm′ə-nĭk), Saint. 1170?–1221. Spanish-born priest who founded the Dominican order (1216).

Dom•i•ni•ca (dŏm′ə-nē′kə, də-mĭn′ĭ-kə). An island country of the E Caribbean between Guadeloupe and Martinique; gained its independence from Great Britain in 1978. Cap. Roseau. Pop. 77,000. **—Dom′i•ni′can** *adj. & n.*

do•min•i•cal (də-mĭn′ĭ-kəl) *adj. Eccles.* **1.** Of or associated with Jesus as the Lord. **2.** Relating to Sunday as the Lord's day. [LLat. *dominicālis* < Lat. *dominicus*, of a lord < *dominus*, lord. See **dem-***.]

Do•min•i•can[1] (də-mĭn′ĭ-kən) *adj.* Of or relating to the Dominican Republic or its people or culture. —*n.* **1.** A native or inhabitant of the Dominican Republic. **2.** A person of Dominican ancestry.

Do•min•i•can[2] (də-mĭn′ĭ-kən) *n. Rom. Cath. Ch.* A member of an order of preaching friars established in 1216 by Saint Dominic. **—Do•min′i•can** *adj.*

Dominican Republic. A country of the West Indies on the E part of Hispaniola; became independent from Haiti in 1844. Cap. Santo Domingo. Pop. 5,674,977.

dom•i•nie (dŏm′ə-nē′, dō′mə-) *n. Scots.* **1.** A cleric. **2.** A schoolmaster. [Obsolete *domine*, clergyman < Lat., vocative of *dominus*, lord. See **dem-***.]

do•min•ion (də-mĭn′yən) *n.* **1.** Control or the exercise of control; sovereignty. **2.** A territory or sphere of influence or control; a realm. **3.** Often **Dominion.** One of the self-governing nations in the British Commonwealth. **4. dominions.** *Theol.* See **domination** 2. [ME *dominioun* < OFr. *dominion* < Med. Lat. *dominiō, dominion-* < Lat. *dominium*, property < *dominus*, lord. See **dem-***.]

Dominion Day *n.* See **Canada Day.**

Dom•i•nique (dŏm′ə-nēk′, dŏm′ə-nĭk) also **Dom•i•nick** (dŏm′ə-nĭk) *n.* One of a breed of American domestic fowl having gray barred plumage, yellow legs, and a rose-colored comb. [After DOMINICA.]

dom•i•no[1] (dŏm′ə-nō′) *n., pl.* **-noes** or **-nos. 1.** *Games.* A small rectangular block, the face of which is divided into halves, each half being blank or marked by dots. **2. dominoes.** *(used with a sing. or pl. v.)* A game played with these small blocks. [Fr., prob. < *domino*, mask, perh. because of the resemblance between the eyeholes and the spots on some of the tiles. See DOMINO[2].]

dom•i•no[2] (dŏm′ə-nō′) *n., pl.* **-noes** or **-nos. 1.a.** A costume consisting of a hooded robe worn with an eye mask at a masquerade. **b.** The mask so worn. **2.** One wearing this costume. [Fr., prob. < Lat. *(benedīcāmus) dominō*, (let us praise) the Lord < *dominus*, lord. See **dem-***.]

Dom•i•no (dŏm′ə-nō′), **Fats.** b. 1928. Amer. singer whose songs of the early 1950's include *Blue Monday.*

domino effect *n.* A cumulative effect produced when one event sets off a chain of similar events.

domino theory *n.* A theory that one event will set off a train of similar events.

Do•mi•tian (də-mĭsh′ən). A.D. 51–96. Emperor of Rome (81–96) who completed the conquest of Britain.

don[1] (dŏn) *n.* **1. Don.** Used as a courtesy title before the name of a man in a Spanish-speaking area. **2.** *Chiefly British.* **a.** A head, tutor, or fellow at a college of Oxford or Cambridge. **b.** A college or university professor. **3.** The leader of an organized-crime family. **4.** *Archaic.* An important personage. [Sp. dial. and Ital., both < Lat. *dominus*, lord. See **dem-***.]

don[2] (dŏn) *tr.v.* **donned, don•ning, dons. 1.** To put on (clothing). **2.** To assume or take on: *donned the air of the injured party.* [ME, contraction of *do on*, to put on. See DO[1].]

Do•ña (dō′nyä) *n.* Used as a courtesy title before the name of a woman in a Spanish-speaking area. [Sp. < Lat. *domina*, fem. of *dominus*, lord. See DON[1].]

do•nate (dō′nāt′, dō-nāt′) *tr.v.* **-nat•ed, -nat•ing, -nates.** To present as a gift to a fund or cause; contribute. [Back-formation < DONATION.] **—do′na•tor** *n.*

Don•a•tel•lo (dŏn′ə-tĕl′ō, dô′nä-tĕl′lô). 1386?–1466. Italian sculptor renowned for his lifelike statues, such as the bronze *David.*

do•na•tion (dō-nā′shən) *n.* **1.** The act of giving to a fund or cause. **2.** A gift or grant; a contribution. [ME *donacioun*, gift, benefice < OFr. < Lat. *dōnātiō, dōnātiōn-* < *dōnātus*, p.part. of *dōnāre*, to give < *dōnum*, gift. See **dō-***.]

Don•a•tist (dŏn′ə-tĭst, dō′nə-) *n.* A member of a rigorist, schismatic Christian sect that arose in North Africa in the fourth century A.D. [Med.Lat. *Donatista*, after *Donatus*, 4th-cent. A.D. ecclesiastic.] **—Don′a•tism** *n.*

don•a•tive (dō′nə-tĭv, dŏn′ə-) *n.* A special donation; a gift. —*adj.* Characterized by, constituting, or subject to donation. [Lat. *dōnātīvum* < neut. of *dōnātīvus*, of a donation < *dōnātus*, p.part. of *dōnāre*, to give. See DONATION.]

Don•cas•ter (dŏng′kə-stər). A borough of N-central England NE of Sheffield. Pop. 81,900.

done (dŭn) *v.* P.part. of **do[1]**. —*adj.* **1.** Carried out or accomplished; finished. **2.** Cooked adequately. **3.** Socially acceptable. **4.** *Informal.* Worn out; exhausted. **—*idiom.* done for.** *Informal.* Doomed to death or destruction. **—done′ness** *n.*

do•nee (dō-nē′) *n.* The recipient of a gift. [DON(OR) + -EE[1].]

Do•nets (də-nĕts′, dŭ-nyĕts′). A river rising in W Russia and flowing c. 1,046 km (650 mi) through E Ukraine to join the Don R.

Donets Basin also **Don•bas** (dŏn′bäs). A major industrial region of E Ukraine and SW Russia N of the Sea of Azov and W of the Donets R.; developed after the 1870's.

Do•netsk (də-nĕtsk′, dŭ-nyĕtsk′). A city of E Ukraine ESE of Kiev; founded c. 1870. Pop. 1,073,000.

dong[1] (dông, dŏng) *n.* See table at **currency.** [Vietnamese < Chin. *tóng*, copper coin.]

dong[2] (dông, dŏng) *n.* *Vulgar Slang.* A penis. [?]

Dö•nitz (dœ′nĭts), **Karl.** See Karl **Doenitz.**

Don•i•zet•ti (dŏn′ĭ-zĕt′ē, dô′nē-dzĕt′tē), **Gaetano.** 1797–1848. Italian composer whose operas include *Lucia di Lammermoor* (1835).

don•jon (dŏn′jən, dŭn′-) *n.* The fortified main tower of a castle; a keep. [Var. of DUNGEON.]

Don Juan (dŏn wŏn′, hwŏn′, jo͞o′ən) *n.* **1.** A libertine; a profligate. **2.** A man who obsessively seduces women. [After *Don Juan*, legendary 14th-cent. Spanish nobleman.]

don•key (dŏng′kē, dŭng′-, dông′-) *n., pl.* **-keys. 1.** The domesticated ass *(Equus asinus).* **2.** *Slang.* An obstinate or stupid person. [Perh. < the name *Duncan* or of imit. orig.]

donkey engine *n.* **1.** A small auxiliary steam engine used for hoisting or pumping, esp. on a ship. **2.** A small locomotive.

don•key•work (dŏng′kē-wûrk′, dŭng′-, dông′-) *n. Slang.* Hard physical labor.

Don•na (dŏn′ə, dôn′nä) *n.* Used as a courtesy title before the name of a woman in an Italian-speaking area. [Ital. < Lat. *domina.* See DOÑA.]

Donne (dŭn), **John.** 1572–1631. English cleric and metaphysical poet whose works include *Divine Poems* (1607).

don•née (dŏ-nā′, dô-) *n.* A set of literary or artistic principles or assumptions on which a creative work is based. [Fr. < fem. p.part. of *donner*, to give < OFr. < Lat. *dōnāre.* See DONATE.]

Don•ner Pass (dŏn′ər). A pass, 2,162.1 m (7,089 ft), in the Sierra Nevada of E CA near Lake Tahoe; named after the Donner Party, trapped here in Oct. 1846.

don•nish (dŏn′ĭsh) *adj.* Of, relating to, or held to be characteristic of a university don; bookish or pedantic.

don•ny•brook (dŏn′ē-bro͝ok′) *n.* An uproar; a free-for-all. [After *Donnybrook* fair, held in Donnybrook, a suburb of Dublin, Ireland, and noted for its brawls.]

do•nor (dō′nər) *n.* **1.** One that contributes something to a cause or fund. **2.** *Medic.* One from whom blood, tissue, or an organ is taken for use in a transfusion or transplant. **3.** *Electron.* An element introduced into a semiconductor with a negative valence greater than that of the pure semiconductor. [ME < AN *donour* < Lat. *dōnātor* < *dōnāre*, to give. See DONATION.]

do-no•thing (do͞o′nŭth′ĭng) *Informal.* —*adj.* Offering no initiative for change, esp. in politics. —*n.* An idle or lazy person. **—do′-no′thing•ism** *n.*

Don Qui•xo•te (dŏn′ kē-hō′tē, kwĭk′sət) *n.* An impractical idealist bent on righting incorrigible wrongs. [After *Don Quixote*, hero of a satiric romance by Miguel de Cervantes.]

Don River (dŏn). A river of W Russia flowing c. 1,963 km (1,220 mi) to the Sea of Azov.

don't (dōnt). **1.** Do not. **2.** *Non-Standard.* Does not. —*n., pl.* **don'ts** (dōnts). A statement of what should not be done.

do•nut (dō′nŭt′, -nət) *n.* Var. of **doughnut.**

doo•dad (do͞o′dăd′) *n.* *Informal.* An unnamed or nameless gadget or trinket.

doo•dle (do͞od′l) *v.* **-dled, -dling, -dles.** —*intr.* **1.** To scribble aimlessly, esp. when preoccupied. **2.** To kill time. —*tr.* To draw (figures) while preoccupied. —*n.* A figure, design, or scribble drawn or written absent-mindedly. [E. dial., to fritter away time, perh. < *doodle*, fool. See DOODLEBUG.]

doo•dle•bug (do͞od′l-bŭg′) *n.* **1.** See **ant lion** 2. **2.** A divining rod. [Perh. dial. *doodle*, fool, simpleton (< LGer. *dudel-*) + BUG.]

doo-doo (do͞o′do͞o′) *n. Slang.* Fecal matter or something likened to it. [Of baby-talk orig.]

doo•hick•ey (do͞o′hĭk′ē) *n., pl.* **-eys.** *Informal.* An unnamed gadget or trinket. [Perh. DOO(DAD) + HICKEY.]

Doo•lit•tle (do͞o′lĭt′l), **Hilda.** H.D. 1886–1961. Amer. poet known for works such as *Sea Garden* (1916).

Doolittle, James ("Jimmy") Harold. b. 1896. Amer. army aviator who commanded daring bombing raids of Tokyo and other Japanese cities in Apr. 1942.

doom (do͞om) *n.* **1.** A decision or judgment, esp. an official condemnation to a severe penalty. **2.** Fate, esp. a tragic or ruinous one. **3.** Inevitable destruction or ruin. **4.** Judgment Day. **5.** A statute or ordinance, esp. in Anglo-Saxon England. —*tr.v.* **doomed, doom•ing, dooms. 1.** To condemn to ruination or death. **2.** To destine to an unhappy end. [ME *dom* < OE *dōm*, judgment. See **dhē-***.]

doom palm *n.* A palm *(Hyphaene thebaica)* native to the Nile Valley and having fruits the size of an orange with a distinctive aroma and taste. [Prob. < Ar. dial. *dōm.*]

doom•say•er (do͞om′sā′ər) *n.* One who predicts calamity at every opportunity.

dooms•day (do͞omz′dā′) *n.* Judgment Day. [ME *domesday* < OE *dōmes dæg* : *dōmes*, genitive of *dōm*, judgment; see DOOM + *dæg*, day; see DAY.]

Dooms•day Book (do͞omz′dā′) *n.* Var. of **Domesday Book.**

door (dôr, dōr) *n.* **1.a.** A movable structure used to close off an entrance, typically consisting of a panel that swings on hinges or that slides or rotates. **b.** A similar part on a piece of furniture or a vehicle. **2.** A doorway. **3.** The room or building to which a door belongs. **4.** A means of approach or access. **—*idioms.* at (one's) door.** Within one's sphere of accountability. **close** (or **shut**) **the door on.** To refuse to allow for the possibility of. **leave the door open.** To allow for the possibility of: *Leave the door open for changes.* **show (someone) the door.** *Informal.* **1.** To eject (someone) from the premises. **2.** To terminate the employment of; fire. [ME *dor* < OE *duru, dor.* See **dhwer-***.] **—door′less** *adj.*

door•bell (dôr′bĕl′, dōr′-) *n.* A bell, chime, or buzzer outside a door that is rung to announce the presence of a visitor.

door•jamb (dôr′jăm′, dōr′-) *n.* Either of the two vertical pieces framing a doorway and supporting the lintel.

door•keep•er (dôr′kē′pər, dōr′-) *n.* One who is employed to guard an entrance or gateway.

door•knob (dôr′nŏb′, dōr′-) *n.* A knob-shaped handle for opening and closing a door.

door•man (dôr′măn′, -mən, dōr′-) *n.* A man employed to attend the entrance of a building.

door•mat (dôr′măt′, dōr′-) *n.* **1.** A mat placed before a doorway for wiping the shoes. **2.** *Slang.* One who submits meekly to domination or mistreatment by others.

door•nail (dôr′nāl′, dōr′-) *n.* A large-headed nail. **—*idiom.* dead as a doornail.** Undoubtedly dead.

Door Peninsula (dôr). A peninsula of E WI between Green Bay and Lake Michigan.

door•post (dôr′pōst′, dōr′-) *n.* See **doorjamb.**

door prize *n.* A prize awarded by lottery to the holder of a ticket purchased at or before a function.

door•sill (dôr′sĭl′, dōr′-) *n.* The threshold of a doorway.

door•step (dôr′stĕp′, dōr′-) *n.* A step leading to a door.

door•stop (dôr′stŏp′, dōr′-) *n.* **1.** A wedge inserted under a door to hold it open. **2.** A weight or spring that prevents a

donkey
Equus asinus

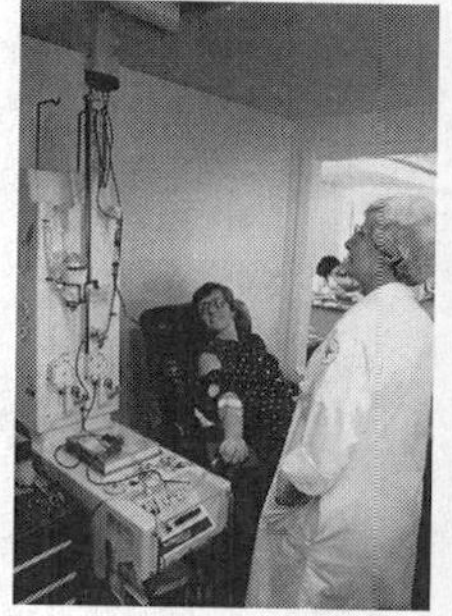

donor
An apheresis donor

ă **pat**	oi **boy**
ā **pay**	ou **out**
âr **care**	o͝o **took**
ä **father**	o͞o **boot**
ĕ **pet**	ŭ **cut**
ē **be**	ûr **urge**
ĭ **pit**	th **thin**
ī **pie**	*th* **this**
îr **pier**	hw **which**
ŏ **pot**	zh **vision**
ō **toe**	ə **about,**
ô **paw**	**item**

Stress marks:
′ (primary);
′ (secondary), as in
dictionary (dĭk′shə-nĕr′ē)

door from slamming. **3.** A rubber-tipped projection on a wall to protect it from the impact of an opening door.

door•way (dôr′wā′, dōr′-) *n.* The entranceway to a room, building, or passage.

door•wom•an (dôr′wo͝om′ən, dōr′-) *n.* A woman employed to attend the entrance of a building.

door•yard (dôr′yärd′, dōr′-) *n.* The yard in front of the door of a house.

doo-wop or **doo•wop** (do͞o′wŏp′) *n. Mus.* A style of music of the 1950's, characterized by words and nonsense syllables sung in harmony by small groups against a stylized rhythmic melody. [Imit.] **—doo′-wop′** *adj.*

doo•zy or **doo•zie** (do͞o′zē) *n., pl.* **-zies.** *Slang.* Something extraordinary or bizarre. [Poss. blend of DAISY and *Duesenberg,* a luxury car of the late twenties and thirties.]

do•pa (dō′pə) *n.* An amino acid, $C_9H_{11}NO_4$, formed in the liver from tyrosine and converted to dopamine in the brain. [*d(ihydr)o(xy)p(henyl)a(lanine).*]

do•pa•mine (dō′pə-mēn′) *n.* A monoamine neurotransmitter formed in the brain by the decarboxylation of dopa and essential to the normal functioning of the central nervous system. [DOP(A) + AMINE.]

dop•ant (dō′pənt) *n. Electron.* An impurity added to a pure semiconductor material to alter its conductive properties for use in transistors and diodes. [DOP(E) + -ANT.]

dope (dōp) *n.* **1.** *Informal.* **a.** A narcotic, esp. an addictive one. **b.** Narcotics considered as a group. **c.** An illicit drug, esp. marijuana. **2.** A narcotic preparation used to stimulate a racehorse. **3.** *Informal.* A person regarded as stupid. **4.** *Informal.* Factual information, esp. of a private nature. **5.** *Chem.* An absorbent or adsorbent material used in manufacturing, such as nitroglycerin used in dynamite. **6.** A lacquer formerly used to protect, waterproof, and tauten the cloth surfaces of airplane wings. **7.** *Chiefly Southern U.S.* See **cola**[1]. **8.** *Lower Northern U.S.* Syrup or sweet sauce poured on ice cream. —*v.* **doped, dop•ing, dopes.** —*tr.* **1.** *Informal.* **a.** To administer a narcotic to. **b.** To add a narcotic to. **2.** *Informal.* To figure out (a puzzle, for example). **3.** *Informal.* To make a rough plan of: *doped out a plan.* **4.** *Electron.* To treat (a semiconductor) with a dopant. —*intr. Informal.* To take narcotics. [Du. *doop,* sauce < *doopen,* to dip.] **—dop′er** *n.*

Regional Note: *Dope,* which commonly means "a narcotic or narcotics," came into English from the Dutch word *doop,* "sauce." Throughout the 19th century it meant "gravy." In the lower northern United States, from Pennsylvania westward to Missouri, *dope* is now the term for an ice-cream topping, such as syrup. In the South *dope* means "a cola-flavored soft drink." The term might be related to the northern usage as a reference to the syrup base of a cola drink. However, folk wisdom has it that *dope* recalls the minute amounts of cocaine in the original Atlanta recipe for Coca-Cola, which was named after this exotic ingredient.

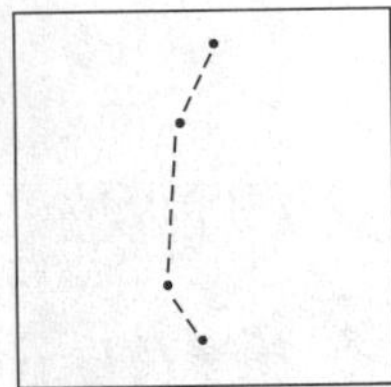
Dorado

dope sheet *n. Slang.* A scratch sheet.

dope•ster (dōp′stər) *n.* One that analyzes and forecasts future events, as in sports or politics.

dop•ey also **dop•y** (dō′pē) *adj.* **dop•i•er, dop•i•est.** *Slang.* **1.** Dazed or lethargic, as if drugged. **2.** Stupid; doltish: *a dopey kid.* **3.** Silly; foolish: *a dopey answer.*

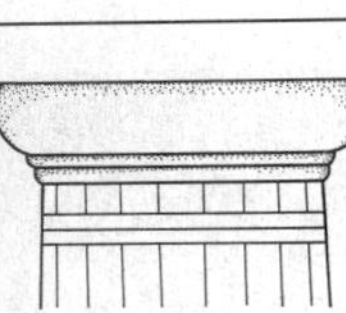
Doric order

dop•pel•gäng•er or **dop•pel•gang•er** (dŏp′əl-găng′ər, dôp′əl-gĕng′ər) *n.* A ghostly double of a living person, esp. one that haunts its living counterpart. [Ger., a double : *doppel,* double (< Fr. *double;* see DOUBLE) + *Gänger,* goer (< *Gang,* a going < MHGer. *ganc* < OHGer.).]

Dop•pler (dŏp′lər) *adj.* Of, relating to, or using the Doppler effect or Doppler radar.

Doppler effect *n. Phys.* An apparent change in the frequency of waves, as of sound or light, when the source and observer are in motion relative to each other, the frequency increasing as the source and observer approach each other and decreasing as they move apart. [After Christian Johann *Doppler* (1803–53), Austrian physicist and mathematician.]

dormer

Doppler radar *n.* Radar that uses the Doppler effect to measure velocity.

Dor. *abbr.* Doric.

Do•ra•do (də-rä′dō) *n.* A constellation of the Southern Hemisphere near Reticulum and Pictor. [Sp., dolphin (fish) < LLat. *deaurātus,* p.part. of *deaurāre,* to gild. See DORY[2].]

dor•bee•tle (dôr′bēt′l) *n.* A European dung beetle *(Geotrupes stercorarius)* that flies with a droning sound. [Obsolete *dor,* a buzzing bee or beetle (< ME *dorre* < OE *dora*) + BEETLE[1].]

Dor•ches•ter (dôr′chĕs′tər, -chĭ-stər). A municipal borough of S England W of Poole; the model for Casterbridge in Thomas Hardy's novels. Pop. 14,049.

Dor•dogne (dôr-dōn′, -dôn′yə). A river rising in the Auvergne Mts. of S-central France and flowing c. 483 km (300 mi) SW to join the Garonne R. N of Bordeaux.

dory[1]
Oil painting of a Cape Ann dory by Albert S. Bigelow

Dor•drecht (dôr′drĕkt′, -drĕKHt′) also **Dort** (dôrt). A city of SW Netherlands on the Meuse R. SE of Rotterdam; founded in the 11th cent. Pop. 107,475.

Do•ré (dô-rā′), **(Paul) Gustave.** 1832–83. French artist best known for his imaginative drawings and lithographs.

Do•ri•an (dôr′ē-ən, dōr′-) *n.* One of a Hellenic people that invaded Greece around 1100 B.C. [Lat. *Dōriānus* < *Dōrius* < Gk. *Dōrios* < *Dōris,* Doris.] **—Do′ri•an** *adj.*

Dor•ic (dôr′ĭk, dŏr′-) *n.* A dialect of ancient Greek spoken in the Peloponnesus, Crete, certain Aegean Islands, Sicily, and Italy. —*adj.* **1.** Of, relating to, or being Doric. **2.** In the style of or being the Doric order. [Lat. *Dōricus* < Gk. *Dōrikos* < *Dōris,* Doris.]

Doric order *n.* The oldest and simplest of the three orders of classical Greek architecture, characterized by heavy columns with plain saucer-shaped capitals and no base.

Dor•is (dôr′ĭs, dōr′-, dŏr′-). An ancient region of central Greece; traditional homeland of the Dorians.

Dor•king (dôr′kĭng) *n.* A heavy-bodied domestic fowl having five toes on each foot and raised chiefly for food. [After *Dorking,* an urban district of S England.]

dorm (dôrm) *n. Informal.* A dormitory.

dor•mant (dôr′mənt) *adj.* **1.** Lying asleep or as if asleep; inactive. **2.** Latent but capable of being activated. **3.** Temporarily quiescent. See Syns at **inactive. 4.** In a condition of biological rest or inactivity. [ME < OFr. < pr.part. of *dormir,* to sleep < Lat. *dormīre.*] **—dor′man•cy** *n.*

dor•mer (dôr′mər) *n.* **1.** A window set vertically into a small gable projecting from a sloping roof. **2.** The gable holding such a window. [Obsolete Fr. *dormeor,* sleeping room < *dormir,* to sleep. See DORMANT.]

dor•min (dôr′mĭn) *n.* Abscisic acid. [DORM(ANCY) + -IN.]

dor•mi•to•ry (dôr′mĭ-tôr′ē, -tōr′ē) *n., pl.* **-ries. 1.** A room providing sleeping quarters for a number of persons. **2.** A building for housing a number of persons, as at a school or resort. [Lat. *dormītōrium* < *dormītōrius,* of sleep < *dormītus,* p.part. of *dormīre,* to sleep.]

dor•mouse (dôr′mous′) *n.* Any of various squirrellike Old World rodents of the family Gliridae. [ME, prob. alteration (influenced by *mouse;* see MOUSE) of AN *dormeus,* inclined to sleep, hibernating < OFr. *dormir,* to sleep. See DORMANT.]

dor•my also **dor•mie** (dôr′mē) *adj. Sports.* Ahead of an opponent in a golf match by as many strokes as there are holes remaining to be played. [?]

dor•nick[1] (dôr′nĭk) *n.* A coarse damask. [ME, after *Doornik* (Tournai), a city of SW Belgium.]

dor•nick[2] (dôr′nĭk) *n. Lower Northern U.S.* A stone small enough to throw from a field being cleared. [Prob. < Ir.Gael. *dornóg,* a small round stone.]

do•ron•i•cum (də-rŏn′ĭ-kəm) *n.* A plant of the genus *Doronicum,* which includes the leopard's bane. [NLat. < Ar. *dorūnaj* < Pers. *darūnak.*]

dors– *pref.* Var. of **dorso–.**

dor•sa (dôr′sə) *n. Anat.* Pl. of **dorsum.**

dor•sad (dôr′săd′) *adv. Anat.* In the direction of the back; dorsally.

dor•sal (dôr′səl) *adj.* **1.** *Anat.* Of, toward, on, in, or near the back or upper surface of an organ, a part, or an organism. **2.** *Bot.* Of or on the outer surface, underside, or back of an organ. [ME < LLat. *dorsālis* < Lat. *dorsuālis* < *dorsum,* back.] **—dor′sal•ly** *adv.*

dorsal fin *n.* The main fin located on the back of fishes and certain marine mammals.

dorsal root *n.* The more posterior of the two nerve fiber bundles of a spinal nerve that carries sensory information to the central nervous system.

Dor•set (dôr′sĭt). A region of SW England on the English Channel; part of the Anglo-Saxon kingdom of Wessex.

Dorset Horn *n.* A domestic sheep of a breed having large horns and medium-length, fine-textured wool. [After DORSET.]

Dor•sey (dôr′sē), **Tommy.** 1905–56. Amer. band leader who with his brother **Jimmy** (1904–57) established swing bands popular in the 1930's and 1940's.

dorsi– *pref.* Var. of **dorso–.**

dor•si•ven•tral (dôr′sĭ-vĕn′trəl) or **dor•so•ven•tral** (-sō-) *adj.* **1.** *Bot.* Flattened and having distinct upper and lower surfaces, as most leaves do. **2.** *Biol.* Extending from a dorsal to a ventral surface. **—dor′si•ven′tral•ly** *adv.*

dorso– or **dorsi–** or **dors–** *pref.* **1.** Back: *dorsad.* **2.** Dorsal: *dorsoventral.* [< Lat. *dorsum,* back.]

dor•so•lat•er•al (dôr′sō-lăt′ər-əl) *adj.* Of or involving both the back and the side. **—dor′so•lat′er•al•ly** *adv.*

dor•sum (dôr′səm) *n., pl.* **-sa** (-sə). *Anat.* **1.** The back. **2.** The upper outer surface, as of an organ or part. [Lat., back.]

Dort (dôrt). See **Dordrecht.**

Dort•mund (dôrt′mənd, -mo͝ont′). A city of W-central Germany NNE of Cologne; first mentioned c. 885. Pop. 579,697.

Dor•val (dôr-văl′). A town of S Quebec, Canada, a suburb of Montreal on Montreal I. Pop. 17,722.

do•ry[1] (dôr′ē, dōr′ē) *n., pl.* **-ries.** A small, narrow, flatbottom boat with high sides and a sharp prow. [?]

do•ry[2] (dôr′ē, dōr′ē) *n., pl.* **-ries. 1.** John Dory. **2.** See **walleye** 3. [ME *dorre* < OFr. *doree* < fem. p.part. of *dorer,* to gild < LLat. *deaurāre* : Lat. *de-,* de- + Lat. *aurum,* gold.]

DOS (dŏs, dôs) *n. Comp. Sci.* An operating system that resides on a disk. [*d(isk) o(perating) s(ystem).*]

dos•age (dō′sĭj) *n.* **1.a.** Administration of a therapeutic agent in prescribed amounts. **b.** Determination of that amount.

c. The amount so administered. **2.** Addition of an ingredient to a substance in a specific amount, esp. to wine.

dose (dōs) *n.* **1.** *Medic.* **a.** A specified quantity of a therapeutic agent prescribed to be taken at one time or at stated intervals. **b.** The amount of radiation administered as therapy to a given site. **2.** An ingredient added, esp. to wine, to impart flavor or strength. **3.** *Informal.* An amount, esp. of something unpleasant, to which one is subjected. **4.** *Slang.* A venereal infection. —*tr.v.* **dosed, dos•ing, dos•es. 1.** To give (someone) a dose, as of medicine. **2.** To give or prescribe (medicine) in specified amounts. [Fr. < LLat. *dosis* < Gk. *dosis*, something given < *didonai*, to give. See **dō-***.] —**dos′er** *n.*

do-si-do (dō′sē-dō′) *n., pl.* **-dos. 1.** A movement in square dancing in which two dancers approach each other and circle back to back, then return to their original positions. **2.** The call given to signal such a movement. [Alteration of Fr. *dos à dos*, back to back < *dos*, back < OFr. See DOSSIER.]

do•sim•e•ter (dō-sĭm′ĭ-tər) *n.* An instrument that measures the amount of radiation absorbed in a given period.

do•sim•e•try (dō-sĭm′ĭ-trē) *n. Medic.* The accurate measurement of doses, esp. of radiation. —**do•si•met′ric** (-sə-mĕt′rĭk) *adj.*

Dos Pas•sos (dōs păs′ōs), **John Roderigo.** 1896–1970. Amer. writer best known for the trilogy *U.S.A.* (1930–36).

doss (dŏs) *Chiefly British.* —*n.* A crude or makeshift bed. —*intr.v.* **dossed, doss•ing, doss•es.** To go to bed; sleep. [Perh. alteration of *dorse*, back < Lat. *dorsum*.]

dos•sal also **dos•sel** (dŏs′əl) *n.* An ornamental hanging of rich fabric, as behind an altar. [Med.Lat. *dossāle* < neut. of *dossālis*, dorsal < LLat. *dorsālis*. See DORSAL.]

dos•si•er (dŏs′ē-ā′, dô′sē-ā′) *n.* A collection of papers giving detailed information about a person or subject. [Fr. < OFr., papers labeled on the back < *dos*, back < Lat. *dorsum*.]

dost (dŭst) *v. Archaic.* A second pers. sing. pr.t. of **do[1]**.

Dos•to•yev•sky or **Dos•to•ev•ski** (dŏs′tə-yef′skē, -toi-, dŭs-), **Feodor Mikhailovich.** 1821–81. Russian writer whose works include *Crime and Punishment* (1866) and *The Brothers Karamazov* (1879–80). —**Dos′to•yev′ski•an** *adj.*

dot[1] (dŏt) *n.* **1.a.** A tiny round mark made by or as if by a pointed instrument; a spot. **b.** Such a mark used in orthography, as above an *i*. **2.** A tiny amount. **3.** In Morse and similar codes, the short sound or signal used in combination with the dash and silent intervals to represent letters, numbers, or punctuation. **4.** *Math.* **a.** A decimal point. **b.** A symbol of multiplication. **5.** *Mus.* A mark after a note indicating an increase in time value by half. —*v.* **dot•ted, dot•ting, dots.** —*tr.* **1.** To mark with a dot. **2.** To form or make with dots. **3.** To cover with or as if with dots. —*intr.* To make a dot. —***idiom.* on (or at) the dot.** Punctual or punctually. [ME **dot* < OE *dott*, head of a boil.] —**dot′ter** *n.*

dot[2] (dŏt, dō) *n.* A woman's marriage portion; a dowry. [Fr. < Lat. *dōs, dōt-*, dowry. See **dō-***.]

dot•age (dō′tĭj) *n.* A deterioration of mental faculties; senility. [ME < *doten*, to dote.]

dot•ard (dō′tərd) *n.* A person who is in his or her dotage. [ME < *doten*, to dote.]

dote (dōt) *intr.v.* **dot•ed, dot•ing, dotes.** To show excessive love or fondness. [ME *doten*.]

doth (dŭth) *v. Archaic.* A third pers. sing. pr.t. of **do[1]**.

Do•than (dō′thən). A city of SE AL near the FL border; settled in 1885. Pop. 53,589.

dot matrix *n. Comp. Sci.* A dense grid of dots or pins used to form alphanumeric characters or designs.

dot product *n. Math.* See **scalar product.** [From the use of a dot to indicate the function, as in *x·y*.]

dot•ted swiss (dŏt′ĭd) *n.* A crisp cotton fabric with dots.

dot•tle (dŏt′l) *n.* The plug of tobacco ash left in the bowl of a pipe after it has been smoked. [< DOT[1], lump (obsolete).]

dot•ty (dŏt′ē) *adj.* **-ti•er, -ti•est. 1.a.** Mentally unbalanced; crazy. **b.** Amusingly eccentric or unconventional. **c.** Ridiculous or absurd. **2.** Having a feeble or unsteady gait; shaky. **3.** Obsessively infatuated or enamored. [Prob. alteration of Sc. *dottle*, silly < ME *doten*, to dote.] —**dot′ti•ly** *adv.* —**dot′ti•ness** *n.*

Dou or **Douw** (dou), **Gerard** or **Gerrit.** 1613–75. Dutch genre painter whose works include *Woman with Dropsy*.

Dou•ai (do͞o-ā′). Formerly **Dou•ay** (do͞o-ā′). A town of N France NE of Amiens; site of a Roman Catholic college for English priests founded by Philip II of Spain. Pop. 42,576.

Dou•a•la also **Du•a•la** (do͞o-ä′lä). A city of SW Cameroon on the Bight of Biafra. Pop. 841,000.

Dou•ay Bible (do͞o′ā, do͞o-ā′) *n.* A 16th-century English translation of the Vulgate Bible by Roman Catholic scholars. [After DOUAI.]

dou•ble (dŭb′əl) *adj.* **1.** Twice as much in size, strength, number, or amount. **2.** Composed of two like parts: *double doors.* **3.** Composed of two unlike parts; dual: *a double meaning.* **4.** Accommodating or designed for two: *a double bed.* **5.** Characterized by duplicity; deceitful. **6.** *Bot.* Having many more than the usual number of petals, usu. in a crowded or an overlapping arrangement. —*n.* **1.** Something increased twofold. **2.** One that closely resembles another; a duplicate. **3.a.** An actor's understudy. **b.** An actor who takes the place of another actor in scenes requiring special skills or preparations. **4.** An apparition; a wraith. **5.a.** A sharp turn in a direction of movement; a reversal. **b.** A sharp, often devious change in position or argument; a shift. **6. doubles.** *Sports.* A form of a game having two players on each side. **7.** *Baseball.* See **two-base hit. 8.** *Games.* A bid doubling one's opponent's bid in bridge, indicating the ability to take tricks and increasing the penalties and bonuses in scoring. —*v.* **-bled, -bling, -bles.** —*tr.* **1.** To make twice as great. **2.** To be twice as much as. **3.** To fold in two. **4.** To clench (one's fist). **5.** To duplicate; repeat. **6.** *Games.* To challenge (an opponent's bid) with a double in bridge. **7.** *Mus.* To duplicate (another part or voice) an octave higher or lower or in unison. **8.** *Naut.* To sail around. —*intr.* **1.** To be increased twofold. **2.** To turn sharply or all the way around; reverse one's course: *doubled back.* **3.** To serve in an additional capacity. **4.** To replace an actor in the actor's absence or in a certain scene. **5.** *Baseball.* To hit a two-base hit. **6.** *Games.* To announce a double in bridge. —*adv.* **1.** To twice the amount or extent; doubly. **2.** Two together; in pairs. **3.** In two: *bent double.* —***phrasal verb.* double up. 1.** To bend suddenly, as in pain. **2.** To share accommodations meant for one. —***idiom.* on (or at) the double. 1.** Immediately. **2.** In double time. [ME < OFr. < Lat. *duplus*. See **dwo-***.] —**dou′ble•ness** *n.*

double agent *n.* A person pretending to spy for one government while actually spying for another.

double bar *n. Mus.* A double vertical or heavy black line through a staff marking the end of a main section of a composition.

dou•ble-bar•reled (dŭb′əl-băr′əld) *adj.* **1.** Having two barrels mounted side by side. **2.** Serving two purposes; twofold.

double bass (bās) *n. Mus.* The largest bowed stringed instrument in the modern orchestra, also used in jazz, having a deep range beginning about three octaves below middle C.

double bass

double bassoon *n.* See **contrabassoon.**

double bind *n.* **1.** A psychological impasse created by contradictory demands. **2.** A situation in which one must choose between equally unsatisfactory alternatives.

double blind *n.* A testing procedure, designed to eliminate bias, in which the identity of those receiving a test treatment is concealed from both administrators and subjects until the study ends. —**dou′ble-blind′** (dŭb′əl-blīnd′) *adj.*

double boiler *n.* A cooking utensil consisting of two nested pans, designed to allow slow, even cooking or heating of food in the upper pan by the action of water boiling in the lower.

double bond *n.* A covalent bond in which two electron pairs are shared between two atoms.

dou•ble-breast•ed (dŭb′əl-brĕs′tĭd) *adj.* **1.** Fastened by lapping one front edge of a garment over the other and usu. having a double row of buttons with a single row of buttonholes. Used esp. of a coat or jacket. **2.** Having a double-breasted coat.

double-decker
Tour bus in Victoria, Canada

double check *n.* A careful reinspection or reexamination to assure accuracy or proper condition; verification.

dou•ble-check (dŭb′əl-chĕk′) *v.* **-checked, -check•ing, -checks.** —*tr.* To inspect or examine again; verify. —*intr.* To make a double check.

double chin *n.* A fold of fatty flesh beneath the chin.

dou•ble-cross (dŭb′əl-krôs′, -krŏs′) *tr.v.* **-crossed, -cross•ing, -cross•es.** To betray by violating a prior agreement. —*n.* **1.** Often **double cross.** An act of betrayal. **2. double cross.** *Genet.* A cross in which each parent is the product of a single cross. —**dou′ble-cross′er** *n.*

double dagger *n. Print.* A reference mark (‡) used in printing and writing.

double date *n.* A date in which two couples participate. —**dou′ble-date′** (dŭb′əl-dāt′) *v.*

Dou•ble•day (dŭb′əl-dā′), **Abner.** 1819–93. Amer. army officer traditionally considered the inventor of baseball.

double dutch

dou•ble-deal•ing (dŭb′əl-dē′lĭng) *adj.* Duplicitous or deceitful; treacherous. —*n.* Duplicity or deceit; treachery. —**dou′ble-deal′er** *n.*

dou•ble-deck•er (dŭb′əl-dĕk′ər) *n.* Something, such as a structure or sandwich, that has two decks, floors, or layers.

double decomposition *n.* A chemical reaction between two compounds in which the first and second parts of one reactant are united, respectively, with the second and first parts of the other.

dou•ble-dig•it (dŭb′əl-dĭj′ĭt) *adj.* Being between 10 and 99 percent.

double dip•ping (dĭp′ĭng) *n.* The practice of drawing two incomes from the government, usu. by holding a government job and receiving a pension. —**double dipper** *n.*

double dribble *n. Basketball.* An illegal dribble in which a player uses both hands simultaneously to dribble the ball or begins to dribble the ball a second time after a complete stop.

double dutch also **double Dutch** (dŭch) *n.* A jump rope game in which two ropes are swung crisscross by two turners.

dou•ble-edged (dŭb′əl-ĕjd′) *adj.* **1.** Having two cutting edges: *a double-edged blade.* **2.a.** Effective or capable of being interpreted in two ways. **b.** Having a dual purpose.

ă pat	oi boy
ā pay	ou out
âr care	o͝o took
ä father	o͞o boot
ĕ pet	ŭ cut
ē be	ûr urge
ĭ pit	th thin
ī pie	*th* this
îr pier	hw which
ŏ pot	zh vision
ō toe	ə about, item
ô paw	

Stress marks:
′ (primary);
′ (secondary), as in
dictionary (dĭk′shə-nĕr′ē)

dou•ble-en•ten•dre (dŭb′əl-än-tän′drə, do͞o-bläN-täN′drə) *n.* **1.** A word or phrase having a double meaning, esp. when the second meaning is risqué. **2.** The use of such a word or phrase; ambiguity. [Obsolete Fr. : *double*, double + *entendre*, meaning, interpretation.]

double entry *n.* A method of bookkeeping in which a transaction is entered as a debit to one account and a credit to another, so that the totals of debits and credits are equal.

dou•ble-faced (dŭb′əl-fāst′) *adj.* **1.** Having two faces or aspects. **2.** Usable on both sides. **3.** Duplicitous; hypocritical.

double feature *n.* A movie program consisting of two full-length films.

double fertilization *n.* The union in flowering plants of one sperm nucleus with an egg, forming a diploid zygote, and another with two polar nuclei, forming an endosperm.

dou•ble-head•er also **dou•ble•head•er** (dŭb′əl-hĕd′ər) *n.* **1.** *Sports.* Two events held in succession on the same program, esp. in baseball. **2.** A train pulled by two locomotives.

double helix *n.* The coiled structure of double-stranded DNA in which strands linked by hydrogen bonds form a spiral configuration.

double indemnity *n.* A clause in an insurance policy that provides for payment of double the face value of the contract in case of accidental death.

double jeopardy *n. Law.* The act of putting one already tried or convicted through a second trial for the same offense.

dou•ble-joint•ed (dŭb′əl-join′tĭd) *adj.* Having unusually flexible joints, esp. of the limbs or fingers.

double knit also **dou•ble-knit** (dŭb′əl-nĭt′) *n.* A jerseylike knit fabric of two interlocked sides. **— dou′ble-knit′** *adj.*

double negative *n. Gram.* A construction that employs two negatives, esp. to express a single negation.

Usage Note: Double or multiple negatives are acceptably used when they combine to form an affirmative: *He cannot just do nothing* (that is, "he must do something"). An affirmative meaning is also assigned when *not* is used together with an adjective or adverb that begins with a negative prefix such as *in–* or *un–*, conveying a weaker affirmative than does the positive adjective or adverb by itself; for example, *a not infrequent visitor* may visit less frequently than *a frequent visitor.* • A double (or more accurately, multiple) negative is considered unacceptable when it is used to convey or reinforce a negative meaning, as in *He didn't say nothing* (meaning in Standard English "he didn't say anything"). Such constructions were once wholly acceptable in English. But in the 18th century the view was advanced that "two Negatives in English destroy one another, or are equivalent to an Affirmative"; and today this view is generally accepted. • The restriction on multiple negatives extends to the combination of negatives with adverbs such as *hardly* and *scarcely*; therefore it is regarded as incorrect to say *I couldn't hardly do it.* Multiple negatives continue to be widely used in a number of nonstandard varieties of English and are often used by speakers of all backgrounds when they want to strike a colloquial or popular note, as in *You don't go nowhere 'til you clean up that room!* But constructions like these are considered marks of ignorance or illiteracy when they appear in formal speech or in writing. See Usage Notes at **hardly, scarcely.**

dou•ble-park (dŭb′əl-pärk′) *tr. & intr.v.* **-parked, -park•ing, -parks.** To park alongside another vehicle already parked parallel to the curb. **— dou′ble-park′er** *n.*

double play *n. Baseball.* A play in which two players are put out.

double pneumonia *n.* Pneumonia affecting both lungs.

dou•ble-quick (dŭb′əl-kwĭk′) *adj.* Very quick; rapid. *— n.* A marching cadence; double time. *— intr. & tr.v.* **-quicked, -quick•ing, -quicks.** To double-time.

dou•bler (dŭb′lər) *n.* A device that doubles the frequency or voltage of an input signal.

double reed *n. Mus.* **1.** A pair of joined reeds that vibrate together to produce sound in certain wind instruments. **2.** An instrument using a double reed. **— dou′ble-reed′** *adj.*

double refraction *n.* See **birefringence.**

double salt *n.* A salt that ionizes in solution as if it were two salts but forms a single substance upon crystallization.

dou•ble-space (dŭb′əl-spās′) *intr. & tr.v.* **-spaced, -spac•ing, -spac•es.** To type so that there is a full space between lines.

dou•ble•speak (dŭb′əl-spēk′) *n.* See **double talk** 2.

double standard *n.* A set of principles permitting greater opportunity or liberty to one than to another, esp. the granting of greater sexual freedom to men than to women.

double star *n.* See **binary star.**

dou•blet (dŭb′lĭt) *n.* **1.** A close-fitting jacket worn by European men between the 15th and 17th centuries. **2.a.** A pair of similar or identical things. **b.** A member of such a pair. **c.** *Phys.* A multiplet with two members. **3.** *Ling.* One of two words derived from the same historical source by different routes of transmission. **4. doublets.** *Games.* A throw of two dice such that the same face of each lands on top. [ME < OFr., dim. of *double*, double. See DOUBLE.]

doublet
c. 1565 portrait of Robert Dudley, First Earl of Leicester, by Steven van der Meulen (fl. 1543–1563)

double take *n.* A delayed reaction to an unusual remark or circumstance, often used as a comic device.

double talk *n.* **1.** Meaningless speech that consists of nonsense syllables mixed with intelligible words; gibberish. **2.** Deliberately ambiguous or evasive language.

dou•ble-team (dŭb′əl-tēm′) *tr.v.* **-teamed, -team•ing, -teams.** *Sports.* To guard or cover (an offensive player) with two defensive players simultaneously.

dou•ble•think (dŭb′əl-thĭngk′) *n.* Thought marked by the acceptance of gross contradictions and falsehoods, esp. when used as a technique of self-indoctrination.

double time *n.* **1.** A marching pace of 180 three-foot steps per minute. **2.** *Mus.* Duple time. **3.** A rate of pay that is twice the regular rate. **— dou′ble-time′** (dŭb′əl-tīm′) *v.*

dou•ble•ton (dŭb′əl-tən) *n. Games.* A pair of cards that are the only ones of their suit in a hand dealt to a player. [DOUBLE + SINGLE(TON).]

dou•ble-tongue (dŭb′əl-tŭng′) *intr.v.* **-tongued, -tongu•ing, -tongues.** *Mus.* To play a rapidly repeated series of notes on a wind instrument by placing the tongue alternately between the positions for *t* and *k*.

dou•ble•tree (dŭb′əl-trē′) *n.* A crossbar on a wagon or carriage to which two whiffletrees are attached for harnessing two animals abreast.

dou•ble-u (dŭb′əl-yo͞o′) *n.* The letter *w*.

double vision *n.* A disorder of vision in which a single object appears double.

dou•bloon (dŭ-blo͞on′) *n.* A gold coin formerly used in Spain and Spanish America. [Sp. *doblón*, aug. of *dobla*, Spanish coin < Lat. *dupla*, fem. of *duplus*, double. See **dwo-*.**]

dou•bly (dŭb′lē) *adv.* **1.** To a double degree; twice: *doubly protected; made doubly certain.* **2.** In a twofold manner.

Doubs (do͞o). A river rising in the Jura Mts. of E France and flowing c. 434 km (270 mi) to the Saône R.

doubt (dout) *v.* **doubt•ed, doubt•ing, doubts.** *— tr.* **1.** To be undecided or skeptical about. **2.** To tend to disbelieve; distrust. **3.** To regard as unlikely. **4.** *Archaic.* To suspect; fear. *— intr.* To be undecided or skeptical. *— n.* **1.** A lack of certainty that often leads to irresolution. See Syns at **uncertainty. 2.** A lack of trust. **3.** A point about which one is uncertain or skeptical. **4.** The condition of being unsettled or unresolved. **— *idioms.* beyond (**or **without) doubt.** Without question; certainly; definitely. **no doubt. 1.** Certainly. **2.** Probably. [ME *douten* < OFr. *douter* < Lat. *dubitāre*, to waver. See **dwo-*.**] **— doubt′er** *n.*

doubt•ful (dout′fəl) *adj.* **1.** Subject to or causing doubt: *doubtful prospects.* **2.** Experiencing or showing doubt. **3.** Of uncertain outcome; undecided. **4.** Raising doubts as to legitimacy, honesty, or respectability; suspicious: *the candidate's doubtful past.* **— doubt′ful•ly** *adv.* **— doubt′ful•ness** *n.*

doubt•ing Thom•as (dou′tĭng tŏm′əs) *n.* One who is habitually doubtful. [After St. THOMAS, who doubted Jesus's resurrection until he had proof of it.]

doubt•less (dout′lĭs) *adv.* **1.** Certainly. **2.** Presumably; probably. *— adj.* Certain; assured. **— doubt′less•ly** *adv.*

dou•ceur (do͞o-sûr′, -sœr′) *n.* Money given as a tip, gratuity, or bribe. [Fr. < LLat. *dulcor*, sweetness < Lat. *dulcis*, sweet.]

douche (do͞osh) *n.* **1.a.** A stream of water often containing medicinal or cleansing agents and applied to a body part or cavity. **b.** A stream of air applied similarly. **2.** The application of a douche. **3.** An instrument for applying a douche. *— v.* **douched, douch•ing, douch•es.** *— tr.* To cleanse or treat by means of a douche. *— intr.* To apply a douche to oneself. [Fr., shower < Ital. *doccia*, conduit, back-formation < *doccione*, pipe < Lat. *ductiō*, *ductiōn-*, act of leading < *ductus*, p.part. of *dūcere*, to lead. See **deuk-*.**]

dough (dō) *n.* **1.a.** A soft thick mixture of dry ingredients, such as flour, and liquid that is kneaded, shaped, and baked, esp. as bread or pastry. **b.** A pasty mass similar to this mixture. **2.** *Slang.* Money. [ME *dogh* < OE *dāg.* See **dheigh-*.**]

dough•boy (dō′boi′) *n.* **1.** A piece of bread dough rolled thin and fried in deep fat. **2.** An American World War I infantryman.

dough•face (dō′fās) *n.* A Northerner who sided with the South in the U.S. Civil War, esp. a proslavery member of Congress.

dough•nut also **do•nut** (dō′nŭt′, -nət) *n.* **1.** A small ring-shaped cake made of rich light dough fried in deep fat. Also called regionally *olicook.* **2.** Something whose form is reminiscent of a doughnut. **3.** A fast, tight 360° turn made in a motor vehicle or motorized boat.

dough•ty (dou′tē) *adj.* **-ti•er, -ti•est.** Marked by stouthearted courage. [ME < OE *dohtig.* See **dheugh-*.**] **— dough′ti•ly** *adv.* **— dough′ti•ness** *n.*

Dough•ty (dou′tē), **Charles Montagu.** 1843–1926. British traveler noted for *Travels in Arabia Deserta* (1888).

dough•y (dō′ē) *adj.* **-i•er, -i•est.** Having the consistency or appearance of dough. **— dough′i•ness** *n.*

Doug•las (dŭg′ləs). A municipal borough of SE I. of Man, England, on the Irish Sea. Pop. 20,368.

Douglas, Stephen Arnold. "the Little Giant." 1813–61. Amer. politician who served as U.S. representative (1843–47) and senator (1847–61) from IL; engaged Abraham Lincoln in a famous series of debates (1858).

Douglas, William Orville. 1898–1980. Amer. jurist; associate justice of the U.S. Supreme Court (1939–75).

Douglas fir *n.* A tall evergreen timber tree *(Pseudotsuga menziesii* formerly *P. taxifolia)* of northwest North America having short needles and egg-shaped cones. [After David *Douglas* (1798–1834), Scottish botanist.]

Doug•las-Home (dŭg′ləs-hyo͞om′), Sir **Alexander Frederick.** b. 1903. British prime minister (1963–64).

Doug•lass (dŭg′ləs), **Frederick.** 1817–95. Amer. abolitionist and journalist who escaped from slavery (1838) and wrote *Narrative of the Life of Frederick Douglass* (1845).

Dou•kho•bor (do͞o′kə-bôr′) *n.* Var. of **Dukhobor.**

doum (do͞om) *n.* See **doom palm.** [Fr., prob. < Ar. dial. *dūm.*]

dour (do͝or, dour) *adj.* **dour•er, dour•est. 1.** Marked by sternness or harshness; forbidding. **2.** Silently ill-humored; gloomy. **3.** Sternly obstinate; unyielding. [ME, poss. < MIr. *dúr*, prob. < Lat. *dūrus*, hard. See **deru-*.**] **— dour′ly** *adv.* **— dour′ness** *n.*

dou•ra or **dou•rah** (do͝or′ə) *n.* Var. of **durra.**

dou•rine (do͞o-rēn′) *n.* A contagious venereal disease of mules, horses, and asses, caused by the protozoan parasite *Trypanosoma equiperdum.* [French < Ar. *darina*, to be dirty.]

Dou•ro (dôr′o͞o, dō′ro͞o) also **Due•ro** (dwĕr′ō). A river rising in N-central Spain and flowing c. 772 km (480 mi) along the Spanish-Portuguese border to the Atlantic Ocean.

douse[1] also **dowse** (dous) *— v.* **doused, dous•ing, dous•es** also **dowsed, dows•ing, dows•es.** *— tr.* **1.** To plunge into liquid; immerse. **2.** To wet thoroughly; drench. **3.** To put out (a light or fire); extinguish. *— intr.* To become thoroughly wet. *— n.* A thorough drenching. [< obsolete *douse*, to strike.] **— dous′er** *n.*

douse[2] (douz) *v.* Var. of **dowse**[1].

Douw (dou), **Gerard.** See Gerard **Dou.**

dove[1] (dŭv) *n.* **1.** Any of various birds of the family Columbidae, having a small head and a characteristic cooing call. **2.** A gentle innocent person. **3.** A person who advocates peace, conciliation, or negotiation. [ME *douve* < OE **dūfe.*] **— dov′ish** *adj.* **— dov′ish•ness** *n.*

dove[2] (dōv) *v.* See Regional Note at **wake**[1].

Dove (dŭv) *n.* See **Columba.**

dove•cote (dŭv′kōt′, -kŏt′) also **dove•cot** (-kŏt′) *n.* A compartmental structure, often raised on a pole, for housing domesticated pigeons.

dove•kie also **dove•key** (dŭv′kē) *n.* A small black-and-white sea bird *(Alle alle)* of the Arctic and northern Atlantic oceans having a short bill and a stout body. [Dim. of DOVE[1].]

Do•ver (dō′vər). **1.** A municipal borough of SE England on the Strait of Dover opposite Calais, France; a strategic port since medieval times. Pop. 33,700. **2.** The cap. of DE in the central part; founded 1683. Pop. 27,630. **3.** A city of SE NH NW of Portsmouth; settled c. 1623. Pop. 25,042.

Dover, Strait of. A narrow channel at the E end of the English Channel between SE England and N France.

dove•tail (dŭv′tāl′) *n.* **1.** A fan-shaped tenon that forms a tight interlocking joint when fitted into a corresponding mortise. **2.** A joint formed by interlocking one or more such tenons and mortises. *— v.* **-tailed, -tail•ing, -tails.** *— tr.* **1.** To cut into or join by means of dovetails. **2.** To connect or combine precisely or harmoniously. *— intr.* **1.** To be joined together by means of dovetails. **2.** To combine or interlock into a unified whole.

dow•a•ger (dou′ə-jər) *n.* **1.** A widow who holds a title or property derived from her deceased husband. **2.** An elderly woman of high social station. [Obsolete Fr. *douagière* < *douage*, dower < *douer*, to endow < Lat. *dōtāre* < *dōs*, *dōt-*, dowry. See **dō-*.**]

dow•a•ger's hump (dou′ə-jərz) *n.* An abnormal curvature of the spine that is primarily manifested as a rounded hump in the upper back and typically affects older women.

Dow•den (doud′n), **Edward.** 1843–1913. Irish editor, writer, and critic noted for his works on Shakespeare.

dow•dy (dou′dē) *adj.* **-di•er, -di•est. 1.** Lacking stylishness or neatness; shabby. **2.** Old-fashioned; antiquated. *— n., pl.* **-dies.** A dowdy person; a frump. [< ME *doude*, immoral, unattractive, or shabbily dressed woman.] **— dow′di•ly** *adv.* **— dow′di•ness** *n.* **— dow′dy•ish** *adj.*

dow•el (dou′əl) *n.* **1.** A usu. round pin that fits tightly into a corresponding hole to fasten or align two adjacent pieces. **2.** A piece of wood driven into a wall to act as an anchor for nails. *— tr.v.* **-eled, -el•ing, -els** also **-elled, -el•ling, -els. 1.** To fasten or align with dowels. **2.** To equip with dowels. [ME *doule*, part of a wheel, perh. < MLGer. *dovel*, plug, or < OFr. *doele*, barrel stave (dim. of *douve* < LLat. *doga*, vessel < Gk. *dokhē*, receptacle; see SYNECDOCHE).]

dow•er (dou′ər) *n.* **1.** The part or interest of a deceased man's real estate allotted by law to his widow for her lifetime. **2.** See **dowry** 1. **3.** A natural endowment or gift; a dowry. *— tr.v.* **-ered, -er•ing, -ers.** To give a dower to; endow. [ME *douere* < OFr. *douaire* < Med.Lat. *dōtārium* < Lat. *dōs*, *dōt-*, dowry. See **dō-*.**]

dow•itch•er (dou′ĭ-chər) *n.* Either of two shore birds *(Limnodromus griseus* or *L. scolopaceus)* of northern regions having brownish plumage and a long straight bill. [Perh. < Mohawk *tawístawis*, snipe.]

Dow Jones Averages. A trademark used for an index of the relative price of selected stocks based on a formula developed and periodically revised by Dow Jones & Company, Inc.

down[1] (doun) *adv.* **1.a.** From a higher to a lower place or position. **b.** Toward, to, or on the ground, floor, or bottom: *tripped and fell down.* **2.** In or into a sitting, kneeling, or reclining position. **3.** Toward or in the south; southward. **4.a.** Away from a place considered central or a center of activity, such as a city or town. **b.** Away from the present place. **5.** To a specific location or source: *tracking a rumor down.* **6.** Toward or at a low or lower point on a scale. **7.a.** To or in a quiescent or subdued state: *calmed down.* **b.** In or into an inactive or inoperative state. **8.** To or at a lower intensity. **9.** To or into a lower or inferior condition, as of subjection, defeat, or disgrace. **10.** To an extreme degree; heavily: *worn down.* **11.** Seriously or vigorously: *get down to work.* **12.** From earlier times or people. **13.** To a reduced or concentrated form. **14.** In writing; on paper: *wrote it down.* **15.** In partial payment at the time of purchase. **16.** Into or toward a secure position: *nailed down the boards.* *— adj.* **1.a.** Moving or directed downward. **b.** Low or lower: *prices were down.* **c.** Reduced; diminished. **2.** Afflicted; sick: *down with a cold.* **3.** Malfunctioning or not operating, esp. temporarily. **4.** Low in spirits; depressed. **5.a.** *Sports & Games.* Trailing an opponent: *down 20 points.* **b.** *Football.* Not in play. **c.** *Baseball.* Retired; out. **6.** Completed; done: *three down, two to go.* **7.** Learned or known perfectly: *had algebra down.* *— prep.* **1.** In a descending direction along, upon, into, or through. **2.** Along the course of: *walking down the street.* **3.** In or at. *— n.* **1.** A downward movement; descent. **2.** *Football.* Any of a series of four plays during which a team must advance at least ten yards to keep the ball. *— v.* **downed, down•ing, downs.** *— tr.* **1.** To bring, put, strike, or throw down. **2.** To swallow hastily; gulp. **3.** *Football.* To put (the ball) out of play by touching it to the ground. *— intr.* To go or come down; descend. **— *idioms.* down on.** *Informal.* Hostile or negative toward; ill-disposed to. **down on (one's) luck.** Afflicted by misfortune. [ME *doun* < OE *-dūne*, as in *ofdūne*, downward < *dūne*, dative of *dūn*, hill. See **dhū-no-*.**]

Frederick Douglass

down[2] (doun) *n.* **1.** Fine, soft, fluffy feathers forming the first plumage of a young bird and underlying the contour feathers in certain adult birds. **2.** *Bot.* A covering of soft short hairs, as on some leaves or fruit. **3.** A soft, silky, or feathery substance. [ME *doun* < ON *dūnn.*]

down[3] (doun) *n.* **1.** An expanse of rolling, grassy, treeless upland used for grazing. Often used in the plural. **2.** Often **Down.** Any of several breeds of sheep having short wool, originally bred in the Downs of southern England. [ME *doune* < OE *dūn.* See **dhū-no-*.**]

down-and-out or **down and out** (doun′ənd-out′, -ən-) *adj.* **1.** Lacking funds, resources, or prospects. **2.** Incapacitated; prostrate. **— down′-and-out′, down′-and-out′er** *n.*

down-at-heel (doun′ət-hēl′) or **down-at-the-heel** (-ət-thə-) *adj.* **1.** Worn out from long use or neglect; dilapidated. **2.** Shabbily dressed because of poverty; seedy.

down•beat (doun′bēt′) *n.* **1.** *Mus.* The downward stroke made by a conductor to indicate the first beat of a measure. **2.** *Informal.* A period of stagnation or inactivity. *— adj.* Cheerless; pessimistic.

down-bow or **down•bow** (doun′bō′) *n. Mus.* A stroke made by drawing a bow from handle to tip across the strings of a violin or other bowed instrument.

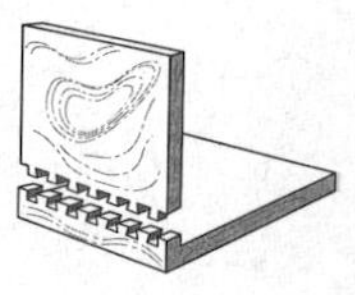
dovetail

down•burst (doun′bûrst′) *n.* An extremely powerful downward air current from a cumulonimbus cloud, typically associated with thunderstorm activity.

down•cast (doun′kăst′) *adj.* **1.** Directed downward. **2.** Low in spirits; depressed.

down•court (doun-kôrt′, -kōrt′) *Sports. adv. & adj.* To, into, or in the far end of the court, esp. in basketball.

down•draft (doun′drăft′) *n.* **1.** A strong downward current of air. **2.** A downward trend; downturn.

Down East Also **down East** (doun ēst′). New England, esp. Maine. **— Down East′er, down-East′er** (down-ē′stər) *n.* **— Down East′ern** *adj.*

down•er (dou′nər) *n. Slang.* **1.** A depressant or sedative drug. **2.** A depressing experience or predicament.

Dow•ners Grove (dou′nərz). A village of NE IL, a manufacturing suburb of Chicago. Pop. 46,858.

Dow•ney (dou′nē). A city of S CA, a suburb of Los Angeles. Pop. 91,444.

down•fall (doun′fôl′) *n.* **1.a.** A sudden loss of wealth, rank, reputation, or happiness; ruin. **b.** A cause of sudden ruin. **2.** A fall of rain or snow, esp. a heavy or unexpected one.

down•fall•en (doun′fô′lən) *adj.* Fallen, as from high position; ruined.

down•field (doun′-fēld′) *adv. & adj. Sports.* To, into, or in the defensive team's end of the field.

down•grade (doun′grād′) *n.* **1.** A descending slope, as in a road. **2.** A turn or trend downward. **3.** A decline, as in fortune. *— tr.v.* **-grad•ed, -grad•ing, -grades. 1.** To lower the

ă pat	oi boy
ā pay	ou out
âr care	o͝o took
ä father	o͞o boot
ĕ pet	ŭ cut
ē be	ûr urge
ĭ pit	th thin
ī pie	*th* this
îr pier	hw which
ŏ pot	zh vision
ō toe	ə about, item
ô paw	

Stress marks:
′ (primary);
′ (secondary), as in
dictionary (dĭk′shə-nĕr′ē)

status or salary of. **2.** To minimize the importance, value, or reputation of.

down·haul (doun′hôl′) *n. Naut.* A rope or set of ropes for hauling down or securing a sail or spar.

down·heart·ed (doun′här′tĭd) *adj.* Low in spirits; depressed. **—down′heart′ed·ly** *adv.* **—down′heart′ed·ness** *n.*

down·hill (doun′hĭl′) *adv.* **1.** Down the slope of a hill. **2.** Toward a lower or worse condition. *—adj.* (doun′hĭl′). **1.** Sloping downward; descending. **2.** *Sports.* Of, relating to, or constituting skiing down a slope. *—n.* **1.** A downhill skiing race. **2.** A downward gradient; a descending slope.

down-home (doun′hōm′) *adj.* Of, relating to, or reminiscent of a simple, wholesome, unpretentious lifestyle, esp. that associated with the rural southern United States.

Down·ing (dou′nĭng), **Andrew Jackson.** 1815–52. Amer. landscape architect who designed the grounds of the U.S. Capitol.

Downing Street[1]. A thoroughfare in London, England, off Whitehall. No. 10 Downing Street is the official residence of the first lord of the Treasury, who is usu. the prime minister of Great Britain.

Downing Street[2] *n.* The British government.

down·link (doun′lĭngk′) *n.* A transmission path by which radio or other signals are sent to the earth from an aircraft or communications satellite.

down·load (doun′lōd′) *v.* **-load·ed, -load·ing, -loads.** *—tr.* **1.** To unload. **2.** *Comp. Sci.* To transfer (data or programs) from a central computer to a peripheral computer or device. *—intr. Comp. Sci.* To download data or programs.

downspout

down-mar·ket also **down·mar·ket** (doun′mär′kĭt) *adj.* Appealing to or designed for low-income consumers; downscale.

down payment *n.* A partial payment made at the time of purchase with the balance to be paid later.

down·play (doun′plā′) *tr.v.* **-played, -play·ing, -plays.** To minimize the significance of; play down.

down·pour (doun′pôr′, -pōr′) *n.* A heavy fall of rain.

down quark *n.* A quark, with a charge of −⅓ and a mass about 607 times that of the electron, that is a component of protons and neutrons. See table at **subatomic particle.**

down·range (doun′rānj′) *adv. & adj.* Away from the launch site and along the flight line of a missile test range.

down·rig·ger (doun′rĭg′ər) *n. Naut.* A trolling rig that consists of a weighted cable attached below the boat to a fishing line, used to troll live bait at or near the floor.

down·right (doun′rīt′) *adj.* **1.** Thoroughgoing; unequivocal. **2.** Forthright; candid. *—adv.* Thoroughly; absolutely.

down·riv·er (doun′rĭv′ər) *adv. & adj.* Toward or near the mouth of a river; in the direction of the current.

Downs (dounz). Two roughly parallel ranges of chalk hills in SE England: the **North Downs** extending c. 161 km (100 mi) from W to E; the **South Downs,** c. 105 km (65 mi).

down·scale (doun′skāl′) *adj.* Of, for, or relating to low-income consumers. *—tr. & intr.v.* **-scaled, -scal·ing, -scales.** To reduce in scale; scale down.

down·shift (doun′shĭft′) *intr.v.* **-shift·ed, -shift·ing, -shifts.** To shift a motor vehicle into a lower gear. **—down′shift′** *n.*

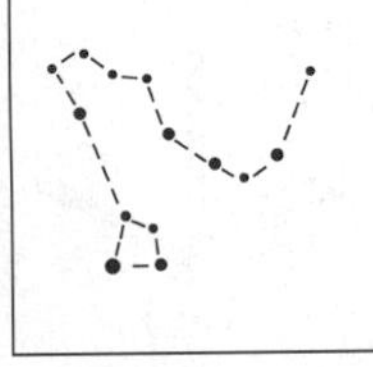
Draco[2]

down·side (doun′sīd′) *n.* **1.** The lower side or portion. **2.** A disadvantageous aspect. **3.** A downward tendency.

down·size (doun′sīz′) *tr.v.* **-sized, -siz·ing, -siz·es.** To make in a smaller size.

down·slide (doun′slīd′) *n.* A downward course; a decline.

down·spout (doun′spout′) *n.* A vertical pipe for carrying rainwater down from a roof gutter.

down·stage (doun′stāj′) *adv.* Toward, at, or on the front part of a stage. **—down′stage′** *adj. & n.*

down·stairs (doun′stârz′) *adv.* **1.** Down the stairs. **2.** To or on a lower floor. *—adj.* (doun′stârz′) also **down·stair** (-stâr′). Located on a lower or main floor. *—n.* (doun′stârz′) *(used with a sing. v.)* The lower or main floor.

down·state (doun′stāt′) *n.* The southerly section of a state in the United States. *—adv. & adj.* To, from, or in the southerly section of a state. **—down′stat′er** *n.*

down·stream (doun′strēm′) *adj.* In the direction of a stream's current. *—adv.* (doun′strēm′). Down a stream.

down·swing (doun′swĭng′) *n.* **1.** A swing downward, as of a golf club. **2.** A decline, as of a business.

Down syndrome (doun) or **Down's syndrome** (dounz) *n.* A congenital disorder, caused by the presence of an extra 21st chromosome, in which the affected person has mild to moderate mental retardation, short stature, and a flattened facial profile. [After John L.H. *Down* (1828–96), British physician.]

down·tick (doun′tĭk′) *n.* **1.** A decrease, esp. a small or incremental one. **2.** A transaction in a stock market security below the price of the previous transaction.

down·time (doun′tīm′) *n.* The period of time when something is not in operation, esp. as the result of a malfunction.

down-to-earth (doun′to͞o-ûrth′, -tə-) *adj.* Realistic; sensible.

down·town (doun′toun′) *n.* The lower part or the business center of a city or town. *—adv.* (doun′toun′). To, toward, or in the downtown area. *—adj.* (doun′toun′). Of, relating to, or located downtown.

down·trend (doun′trĕnd′) *n.* A downward trend; a downturn. **—down′trend′** *v.*

down·trod·den (doun′trŏd′n) *adj.* Oppressed; tyrannized.

down·turn (doun′tûrn′) *n.* A tendency downward, esp. in business or economic activity.

down under *adv. Informal.* To or in Australia or New Zealand.

down·ward (doun′wərd) *adv. & adj.* **1.** From a higher to a lower place, point, level, or state. **2.** From a prior source or earlier time. **—down′ward·ly** *adv.* **—down′wards** *adv.*

down·wind (doun′wĭnd′) *adv.* In the direction in which the wind blows. **—down′wind′** *adj.*

down·y (dou′nē) *adj.* **-i·er, -i·est. 1.** Made of or covered with down. **2.a.** Resembling down. **b.** Quietly soothing; soft.

downy mildew *n.* A disease of plants caused by fungi of the order Peronosporales and characterized by gray, velvety patches of spores on the lower surfaces of leaves.

downy woodpecker *n.* A North American woodpecker *(Picoides pubescens)* having a solid white back and a small bill.

dow·ry (dou′rē) *n., pl.* **-ries. 1.** Money or property brought by a bride to her husband at marriage. **2.** A sum of money required of a postulant at a convent. **3.** A natural endowment or gift; a talent. **4.** *Archaic.* See **dower** 1. [ME *douerie* < AN *douarie* < Med.Lat. *dōtārium, dōāria,* dower. See DOWER.]

dowse[1] also **douse** (douz) *intr.v.* **dowsed, dows·ing, dows·es** also **doused, dous·ing, dous·es.** To use a divining rod to search for underground water or minerals. [?]

dowse[2] (dous) *v. & n.* Var. of **douse**[1].

dows·er (dou′zər) *n.* **1.** A person who uses a divining rod to search for underground water or minerals. **2.** A divining rod.

Dow·son (dou′sən), **Ernest Christopher.** 1867–1900. British poet best known for his refrain "I have been faithful to thee, Cynara, in my fashion."

dox·ol·o·gy (dŏk-sŏl′ə-jē) *n., pl.* **-gies.** An expression of praise to God, esp. a short hymn sung as part of a Christian worship service. [Med.Lat. *doxologia* < Gk., praise : *doxa,* glory, honor (< *dokein,* to seem; see **dek-***) + *-logia,* -logy.] **—dox′o·log′i·cal** (dŏk′sə-lŏj′ĭ-kəl) *adj.* **—dox′o·log′i·cal·ly** *adv.*

dox·y (dŏk′sē) *n., pl.* **-ies.** *Slang.* **1.** A prostitute. **2.** A paramour. [Perh. < obsolete Du. *docke,* doll.]

doy·en (doi-ĕn′, doi′ən, dwä-yăN′) *n.* A man who is the eldest or senior member of a group. [Prob. Fr. < OFr. *doien* < LLat. *decānus,* chief of ten. See DEAN.]

doy·enne (doi-ĕn′, dwä-yĕn′) *n.* A woman who is the eldest or senior member of a group. [Fr., fem. of *doyen,* senior member. See DOYEN.]

Doyle (doil), Sir **Arthur Conan.** 1859–1930. British writer known chiefly for his stories featuring Sherlock Holmes.

D'Oy·ly Carte (doi′lē kärt′), **Richard.** See Richard D'Oyly **Carte.**

doz. *abbr.* Dozen.

doze (dōz) *v.* **dozed, doz·ing, doz·es.** *—intr.* To sleep lightly and intermittently. *—tr.* To spend (time) dozing or as if dozing. *—n.* A short light sleep. ***—phrasal verb.* doze off.** To fall into a doze. [Prob. of Scand. orig.] **—doz′er** *n.*

doz·en (dŭz′ən) *n.* **1.** *pl.* **dozen.** A set of 12. **2. dozens.** An indefinite large number. *—adj.* Twelve. [ME *dozeine* < OFr. *dozaine* < *doze,* twelve, ult. < Lat. *duodecim* : *duo,* two; see **dwo-*** + *decem,* ten; see **dekm̥***.] **—doz′enth** (-ənth) *adj.*

do·zy (dō′zē) *adj.* **-zi·er, -zi·est.** Half asleep; drowsy. **—doz′i·ly** *adv.* **—do′zi·ness** *n.*

DP *abbr.* **1.** *Comp. Sci.* Data processing. **2.** Dew point. **3.** Also **D.P.** Displaced person. **4.** *Baseball.* Double play.

D.Ph. *abbr.* Doctor of Philosophy.

D.Phil. *abbr.* Doctor of Philosophy.

DPT *abbr.* Diphtheria, pertussis, tetanus.

dpt. *abbr.* **1.** Department. **2.** Deponent.

dr *abbr.* Dram.

DR *abbr.* **1.** Dead reckoning. **2.** Dining room.

dr. *abbr.* Debtor.

Dr. *abbr.* **1.** Doctor. **2.** Drive.

drab[1] (drăb) *adj.* **drab·ber, drab·best. 1.** *Color.* **a.** Of a dull light brown. **b.** Of a light olive brown or khaki color. **2.** Faded and dull in appearance. **3.** Dull or commonplace in character; dreary. *—n.* **1.** *Color.* A moderate to grayish yellowish brown or light olive brown. **2.** Cloth of a light or grayish brown or unbleached natural color, esp. a heavy woolen or cotton fabric. [Alteration of obsolete Fr. *drap,* cloth < OFr. See DRAPE.] **—drab′ly** *adv.* **—drab′ness** *n.*

drab[2] (drăb) *n.* **1.** A slattern. **2.** A prostitute. *—intr.v.* **drabbed, drab·bing, drabs.** To consort with prostitutes. [Poss. of Celt. orig. (akin to Sc.Gael. *dràbag,* Ir.Gael. *drabóg,* slattern) or < Du. *drab,* dregs.]

drab[3] (drăb) *n.* A negligible amount: *finished the work in dribs and drabs.* [Prob. alteration of DRIB.]

drab·ble (drăb′əl) *tr. & intr.v.* **-bled, -bling, -bles.** To make or become wet and soiled by dragging; draggle. [ME *drabelen.*]

dra·cae·na (drə-sē′nə) *n.* Any of several tropical plants of the genera *Dracaena* and *Cordyline,* having decorative foliage. [LLat., female dragon < Gk. *drakaina,* fem. of *drakōn,* serpent. See DRAGON.]

drachm (drăm) *n.* **1.** A dram. **2.** A drachma.

ă pat	oi boy
ā pay	ou out
âr care	o͝o took
ä father	o͞o boot
ĕ pet	ŭ cut
ē be	ûr urge
ĭ pit	th thin
ī pie	*th* this
îr pier	hw which
ŏ pot	zh vision
ō toe	ə about, item
ô paw	

Stress marks:
′ (primary);
′ (secondary), as in **dictionary** (dĭk′shə-nĕr′ē)

drach•ma (drăk′mə) *n., pl.* **-mas** or **-mae** (-mē). **1.** See table at **currency. 2.** An ancient Greek silver coin. **3.** One of several modern units of weight, esp. the dram. [Lat. < Gk. *drakhmē* < *drassesthai, drakh-*, to grasp.]

Dra•co[1] (drā′kō). 7th cent. B.C. Athenian politician whose legal code (c. 621) was noted for its severity. **— Dra•co′ni•an** *adj.*

Dra•co[2] (drā′kō) *n.* A constellation in the polar region of the Northern Hemisphere near Cepheus and Ursa Major. [Lat. *dracō*, dragon. See DRAGON.]

dra•co•ni•an (drā-kō′nē-ən, drə-) *adj.* Exceedingly harsh; very severe: *draconian budget cuts.* [After DRACO[1].]

dra•con•ic[1] (drā-kŏn′ĭk) *adj.* Of or suggestive of a dragon. [< Lat. *dracō, dracōn-*, dragon. See DRAGON.]

dra•con•ic[2] (drā-kŏn′ĭk, drə-) *adj.* Draconian. **— dra•con′i•cal•ly** *adv.*

Dra•cut (drā′kət). A town of NE MA on the Merrimack R. near the NH border; settled in 1664. Pop. 25,594.

draft (drăft) *n.* **1.** A current of air in an enclosed area. **2.** A device that regulates the flow or circulation of air. **3.a.** The act of pulling loads; traction. **b.** Something that is pulled or drawn; a load. **c.** A team of animals used to pull loads. **4.** *Naut.* The depth of a vessel's keel below the water line, esp. when loaded. **5.** A heavy demand on resources. **6.** A written order directing the payment of money from an account or fund. **7.a.** A gulp, a swallow, or an inhalation. **b.** The amount taken in by a single act of drinking or inhaling. **c.** A measured portion; a dose. **8.a.** The drawing of a liquid, as from a keg. **b.** An amount drawn. **9.a.** The process or method of selecting one or more individuals from a group, as for a duty. **b.** Compulsory enrollment in the armed forces; conscription. **c.** A body of people selected or conscripted. **10.** *Sports.* A system in which the exclusive rights to new players are distributed among professional teams. **11.a.** The act of drawing in a fishnet. **b.** The quantity of fish caught. **12.a.** A preliminary version of a plan, document, or picture. **b.** A representation of something to be constructed. **13.** A narrow line chiseled on a stone to guide a stonecutter in leveling its surface. **14.** A slight taper given a die to facilitate the removal of a casting. **15.** An allowance made for loss in weight of merchandise. *— v.* **draft•ed, draft•ing, drafts.** *— tr.* **1.** To select from a group for some usu. compulsory service. **2.** To draw up a preliminary version of or plan for. **3.** To create by thinking and writing; compose. *— intr.* To drive close behind another vehicle to take advantage of the reduced air pressure in its wake. *— adj.* **1.** Suited for or used for drawing heavy loads. **2.** Drawn from a cask or tap. **— *idiom.* on draft.** Drawn from a large container, such as a keg. [ME *draught*, act of drawing < OE **dreaht*; akin to *dragan*, to draw.]

draft board *n.* A local board of civilians in charge of the selection of persons for compulsory military service.

draft•ee (drăf-tē′) *n.* One who is drafted, esp. for military service.

draft•er (drăf′tər) *n.* One that drafts, esp. a person who drafts plans or designs or composes a document.

draft•ing (drăf′tĭng) *n.* The systematic representation and dimensional specification of mechanical and architectural structures.

drafts•man (drăfts′mən) *n.* **1.** A man who draws plans or designs, as of structures to be built. **2.** A man who draws, esp. an artist. **— drafts′man•ship′** *n.*

drafts•per•son (drăfts′pûr′sən) *n.* A drafter.

drafts•wom•an (drăfts′wo͝om′ən) *n.* **1.** A woman who draws plans or designs, as of structures to be built. **2.** A woman who draws, esp. an artist.

draft•y (drăf′tē) *adj.* **-i•er, -i•est.** Having or exposed to drafts of air. **— draft′i•ly** *adv.* **— draft′i•ness** *n.*

drag (drăg) *v.* **dragged, drag•ging, drags.** *— tr.* **1.** To pull along with difficulty or effort; haul. See Syns at **pull. 2.** To cause to trail along a surface, esp. the ground. **3.** To move or bring by force or with great effort. **4.a.** To search or sweep the bottom of (a body of water), as with a dragnet. **b.** To bring up or catch by such means. **5.** To prolong tediously: *dragged the story out.* **6.** *Baseball.* To hit (a bunt) while taking the first steps toward first base. *— intr.* **1.** To trail along the ground. **2.** To move slowly or with effort. **3.** To lag behind. **4.** To pass or proceed slowly, tediously, or laboriously. **5.** To search or dredge the bottom of a body of water. **6.** To take part in or as if in a drag race. **7.** To draw on a cigarette, pipe, or cigar. *— n.* **1.** The act of dragging. **2.** Something, such as a harrow, that is dragged along the ground. **3.** A device, such as a grappling hook, that is used for dragging under water. **4.** A heavy sledge or cart for hauling loads. **5.** A large four-horse coach with seats inside and on top. **6.** Something, such as a sea anchor, that retards motion. **7.** One that impedes or slows progress; a drawback or burden. **8.** The degree of resistance involved in dragging or hauling. **9.** The retarding force exerted on a moving body by a fluid medium such as air. **10.** A slow laborious motion or movement. **11.a.** The scent or trail of an animal. **b.** Something that provides an artificial scent. **12.** *Slang.* One that is obnoxiously tiresome. **13.** A puff on a cigarette, pipe, or cigar. **14.** *Slang.* A street or road. **15.** The clothing characteristic of one sex when worn by a member of the opposite sex. **— *idiom.* drag (one's) feet** (or **heels**). To act or work with intentional slowness; delay. [ME *draggen* < ON *draga* or var. of ME *drawen*; see DRAW.]

drag bunt *n.* *Baseball.* A bunt executed while taking the first steps toward first base.

dra•gée (drä-zhā′) *n.* A small, often medicated candy. [Fr. < OFr. *dragie.* See DREDGE[2].]

drag•ger (drăg′ər) *n.* One that drags, esp. a vessel using nets dragged along the bottom to catch fish.

drag•gle (drăg′əl) *v.* **-gled, -gling, -gles.** *— tr.* To make wet and dirty by dragging on the ground. *— intr.* **1.** To become wet and muddy by being dragged. **2.** To follow slowly; straggle. [Prob. freq. of DRAG.]

drag•gy (drăg′ē) *adj.* **-gi•er, -gi•est. 1.** Dull and listless. **2.** *Slang.* Very tiresome.

drag•line (drăg′līn′) *n.* **1.** A line used for dragging. **2.** A kind of dredging machine.

drag link *n.* A link for transmitting rotary motion between cranks on two parallel but slightly offset shafts.

drag•net (drăg′nĕt′) *n.* **1.** A system of coordinated procedures to catch wanted persons such as criminals. **2.a.** A net for trawling; a trawl. **b.** A net for catching small game.

drag•o•man (drăg′ə-mən) *n., pl.* **-mans** or **-men.** An interpreter or guide in countries where Arabic, Turkish, or Persian is spoken. [ME *dragman* < OFr. *drugeman* < Med.Lat. *dragumannus* < Med.Gk. *dragoumanos* < Ar. *tarjumān* < Aram. *tūrgemānā* < Akkadian *targumānu*, interpreter.]

drag•on (drăg′ən) *n.* **1.** A mythical monster traditionally represented as a gigantic reptile with a lion's claws, a serpent's tail, wings, and a scaly skin. **2.a.** A fiercely vigilant or intractable person. **b.** Something very formidable or dangerous. **3.** Any of various lizards, such as the Komodo dragon. **4.** *Archaic.* A large snake or serpent. [ME < OFr. < Lat. *dracō, dracōn-*, large serpent < Gk. *drakōn*, perh. < *derkesthai*, to look.]

Drag•on (drăg′ən) *n.* See **Draco[2].**

drag•on•et (drăg′ə-nĭt) *n.* Any of various small, often brightly colored marine fishes of the family Callionymidae, having a slender body and a flattened head. [ME, young dragon < OFr., dim. of *dragon*, dragon. See DRAGON.]

drag•on•fly (drăg′ən-flī′) *n., pl.* **-flies.** Any of various insects of the order Odonata or suborder Anisoptera, having a long slender body and two pairs of net-veined wings. Also called regionally *darning needle, devil's darning needle, ear sewer, mosquito hawk, skeeter hawk, snake doctor, snake feeder, spindle.*

Regional Note: Regional terms for the dragonfly are numerous, providing good evidence for dialect boundaries in the United States. The greatest variety of terms is to be found in the South, where the most widespread term is *snake doctor* (from a folk belief that dragonflies take care of snakes). The Midland equivalent is *snake feeder*. In the Lower South one hears *mosquito hawk* or, in the South Atlantic states, *skeeter hawk*. The imagery outside the South alludes to the insect's shape: Upper Northern speakers call it a *darning needle* or a *devil's darning needle*; those in Coastal New Jersey, a *spindle*; and Northern Californians, an *ear sewer*.

drag•on•head (drăg′ən-hĕd′) *n.* Any of several plants of the genera *Dracocephalum* and *Physostegia,* having terminal spikes of rose-pink or purplish flowers.

drag•on•root (drăg′ən-ro͞ot′, -ro͝ot′) *n.* See **green dragon.**

drag•on's blood (drăg′ənz) *n.* **1.** A red, resinous substance obtained from the fruit of a climbing palm *(Daemonorops draco)* of tropical Asia. **2.** Any of several resins similar to this substance.

dragon's mouth *n.* See **swamp pink.**

dragon tree *n.* A tree *(Dracaena draco)* of the Canary Islands having a thick trunk, sword-shaped leaves, and orange fruit.

dra•goon (drə-go͞on′, dră-) *n.* A heavily armed trooper in some European armies of the 17th and 18th centuries. *— tr.v.* **-gooned, -goon•ing, -goons. 1.** To subjugate or persecute by the imposition of troops. **2.** To compel by violent measures or threats; coerce. [Fr. *dragon*, carbine, dragoon < OFr., dragon. See DRAGON.]

drag queen *n.* *Offensive Slang.* A man, esp. a gay or homosexual man, who dresses as a woman.

drag race *n.* A race between two cars to determine which can accelerate faster from a standstill. [< DRAG, an automobile (slang).] **— drag racer** *n.* **— drag racing** *n.*

drag•ster (drăg′stər) *n.* **1.** An automobile specially built or modified for drag racing. **2.** One who races a dragster.

drag strip *n.* A short straight course or track for drag racing.

drain (drān) *v.* **drained, drain•ing, drains.** *— tr.* **1.** To draw off (a liquid) by a gradual process. **2.a.** To cause liquid to go out from; empty. **b.** To draw off the surface water of. **3.** To drink all the contents of. **4.a.** To deplete gradually, esp. to the point of complete exhaustion. See Syns at **deplete. b.** To fatigue or spend emotionally or physically. *— intr.* **1.** To flow off or out. **2.** To become empty by the drawing off of liquid. **3.** To discharge surface or excess water. **4.** To become gradually depleted; dwindle. *— n.* **1.** A pipe or channel by which liquid is

draft
Top: Hauling logs
Bottom: Draft beer

dragonfly

dragon tree
Dracaena draco

drawn off. **2.** *Medic.* A device, such as a tube, inserted into the opening of a wound or body cavity to facilitate discharge of fluid or purulent material. **3.** The act or process of draining. **4.a.** A gradual outflow or loss; consumption or depletion. **b.** Something that causes a gradual loss. — ***idiom.* down the drain.** To or into the condition of being wasted or lost. [ME *dreinen*, to strain, drain < OE *drēahnian*.] — **drain′a•ble** *adj.* — **drain′er** *n.*

drain•age (drā′nĭj) *n.* **1.** The action or a method of draining. **2.** A system of drains. **3.** Something drained off. **4.** *Medic.* The removal of fluid or purulent material from a wound or body cavity.

drainage basin *n.* An area drained by a river system.

drain•pipe (drān′pīp′) *n.* A pipe for carrying off water or sewage.

drake[1] (drāk) *n.* A male duck. [ME.]

drake[2] (drāk) *n.* A mayfly used as fishing bait. [ME, dragon < OE *draca* < West Gmc. **drako* < Lat. *dracō.* See DRAGON.]

Drake (drāk), Sir **Francis.** 1540?–96. English explorer who was the first Englishman to circumnavigate the world (1577–80).

Dra•kens•burg Mountains (drä′kənz-bûrg′). A range of E South Africa, Lesotho, and Swaziland rising to 3,164.6 m (11,425 ft).

Drake Passage. A strait between Cape Horn and Antarctica that connects the S Atlantic and Pacific oceans.

dram (drăm) *n.* **1.a.** A unit of weight in the U.S. Customary System equal to 1/16 of an ounce or 27.34 grains (1.77 grams). **b.** A unit of apothecary weight equal to 1/8 of an ounce or 60 grains (3.89 grams). See table at **measurement. 2.a.** A small draft: *took a dram of brandy.* **b.** A small amount; a bit. [ME *dragme*, a drachma, a unit of weight < OFr. < LLat. *dragma* < Lat. *drachma.* See DRACHMA.]

Sir Francis Drake

dram. *abbr.* Dramatic; dramatist.

dra•ma (drä′mə, drăm′ə) *n.* **1.a.** A prose or verse composition, esp. one telling a serious story, that is intended for representation by actors impersonating the characters and performing the dialogue and action. **b.** A serious narrative work or program for television, radio, or the cinema. **2.** Theatrical plays of a particular kind or period: *Elizabethan drama.* **3.** The art or practice of writing or producing dramatic works. **4.** A situation or succession of events in real life having the dramatic progression or emotional effect characteristic of a play. **5.** The quality or condition of being dramatic. [LLat. *drāma, drāmat-* < Gk. < *dran*, to do, perform.]

Dram•a•mine (drăm′ə-mēn′). A trademark used for dimenhydrinate.

dra•mat•ic (drə-măt′ĭk) *adj.* **1.** Of or relating to drama or the theater. **2.** Marked by or expressive of the action or emotion associated with drama or the theatre. **3.** Arresting or forceful in appearance or effect. **4.** *Mus.* Having a powerful, expressive singing voice. [LLat. *drāmaticus* < Gk. *dramatikos* < *drama, dramat-*, drama. See DRAMA.] — **dra•mat′i•cal•ly** *adv.*

dramatic irony *n.* The dramatic effect achieved by a speech that shows an incongruity of which the characters in the play remain unaware.

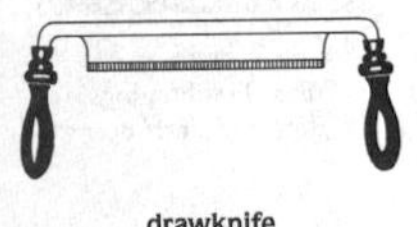
drawknife

dramatic monologue *n.* A literary, usu. verse composition revealing a speaker's character in a monologue addressed to the reader or to a presumed listener.

dra•mat•ics (drə-măt′ĭks) *n.* *(used with a sing. or pl. v.)* **1.** The art or practice of acting and stagecraft. **2.** Dramatic or stagy behavior: *Cut the dramatics.*

dram•a•tis per•so•nae (drăm′ə-tĭs pər-sō′nē, drä′mə-tĭs pər-sō′nī′) *pl.n.* **1.** The characters in a play or story. **2.** A list of the characters in a play or story. [Lat. *drāmatis*, genitive of *drāma*, drama + *persōnae*, pl. of *persona*, character.]

dram•a•tist (drăm′ə-tĭst, drä′mə-) *n.* One who writes plays.

dram•a•ti•za•tion (drăm′ə-tĭ-zā′shən, drä′mə-) *n.* **1.** The act or art of dramatizing, as of a literary work. **2.** A work adapted for dramatic presentation.

dram•a•tize (drăm′ə-tīz′, drä′mə-) *v.* **-tized, -tiz•ing, -tiz•es.** — *tr.* **1.** To adapt (a literary work) for performance. **2.** To present or view in a dramatic or melodramatic way. — *intr.* **1.** To be adaptable to dramatic form. **2.** To self-dramatize.

dram•a•turge (drăm′ə-tûrj′, drä′mə-) *n.* A writer or adapter of plays; a playwright. [Fr. < Gk. *dramatourgos* : *drama, dramat-*, drama; see DRAMA + *ergon*, work; see **werg-***.]

dram•a•tur•gy (drăm′ə-tûr′jē, drä′mə-) *n.* The art of the theater, esp. the writing of plays. — **dram′a•tur′gic, dram′a•tur′gi•cal** *adj.*

drank (drăngk) *v.* P.t. of **drink.**

dr ap *abbr.* Apothecaries' dram.

drape (drāp) *v.* **draped, drap•ing, drapes.** — *tr.* **1.** To cover, dress, or hang with or as if with cloth in loose folds. **2.** To arrange or let fall in loose folds. **3.** To hang or rest limply: *draped my legs over the chair.* — *intr.* To fall or hang in loose folds. — *n.* **1.** A drapery; a curtain. **2.** The way in which cloth falls or hangs. [ME *drapen*, to weave < OFr. *draper* < *drap*, cloth < LLat. *drappus.*]

dreadnought
U.S.S. *Alabama*

drap•er (drā′pər) *n.* *Chiefly British.* A dealer in cloth or clothing and dry goods. [ME, weaver or seller of cloth < OFr. *drapier* < *drap*, cloth. See DRAPE.]

Dra•per (drā′pər), **Henry.** 1837–82. Amer. astronomer who was the first to photograph a stellar spectrum (1872).

drap•er•y (drā′pə-rē) *n.*, *pl.* **-ies. 1.** Cloth or clothing gracefully arranged in loose folds. **2.** A piece or pieces of heavy fabric hanging straight in loose folds, used as a curtain. **3.** Cloth; fabric. **4.** *Chiefly British.* The business of a draper.

dras•tic (drăs′tĭk) *adj.* **1.** Severe or radical in nature; extreme. **2.** Taking violent or rapid effect. [Gk. *drastikos*, active < *drastos*, to be done < *dran*, to do.] — **dras′ti•cal•ly** *adv.*

drat (drăt) *interj.* Used to express annoyance. [Short for *God rot.*]

drat•ted (drăt′ĭd) *adj.* Damned; confounded.

draught (drăft) *n., v., & adj.* *Chiefly British.* Var. of **draft.**

draughts (drăfts, dräfts) *n.* *(used with a sing. or pl. v.) Chiefly British.* The game of checkers. [ME *draughtes*, pl. of *draught*, act of pulling, move at chess. See DRAFT.]

Dra•va or **Dra•ve** (drä′və) also **Drau** (drou). A river rising in the Carnic Alps of S Austria and flowing c. 724 km (450 mi) through NE Slovenia and N Croatia to the Danube R.

dr avdp *abbr.* Avoirdupois dram.

Dra•vid•i•an (drə-vĭd′ē-ən) *n.* **1.** A large family of languages spoken esp. in southern India and northern Sri Lanka that includes Tamil, Telugu, Malayalam, and Kannada. **2.** A member of any Dravidian-speaking people, esp. the pre-Indo-European ones of southern India. [< Sanksrit *drāviḍaḥ*, a Dravidian.] — **Dra•vid′i•an, Dra•vid′ic** (-vĭd′ĭk) *adj.*

draw (drô) *v.* **drew** (dro͞o), **drawn** (drôn), **draw•ing, draws.** — *tr.* **1.a.** To cause to move after or toward one by applying continuous force; drag. See Syns at **pull. b.** To cause to move in a given direction or to a given position, as by leading: *drew the children with him.* **c.** To move or pull so as to cover or uncover something: *draw the curtains.* **2.** To cause to flow forth: *drew blood.* **3.** To suck or take in (air, for example); inhale. **4.** To require (a specified depth of water) for floating. **5.** To take or pull out: *drew out a wallet.* **6.** To extract or take for one's own use: *drew strength from faith.* **7.** To eviscerate; disembowel. **8.a.** To cause to come by attracting; attract. **b.** To select or take in from a given group, type, or region. **9.** To bring to a certain condition or action; lead. **10.** To bring on oneself as a result; provoke: *drew enemy fire.* **11.** To evoke as a response; elicit. **12.** To earn; gain: *drew interest.* **13.a.** To withdraw (money). **b.** To use (a check, for example) when paying. **c.** To receive on a regular basis or at a specified time: *draw a pension.* **14.** To take or receive by chance: *draw lots.* **15.** *Games.* **a.** To take (cards) from a dealer or central stack. **b.** To force (a card) to be played. **16.** To end or leave (a contest) tied or undecided. **17.** To hit or strike (a ball) so as to give it backspin. **18.** To pull back the string of (a bow). **19.** To distort the shape of. **20.** To stretch taut. **21.a.** To flatten, stretch, or mold (metal) by hammering or die stamping. **b.** To shape or elongate (a wire, for example) by pulling through dies. **22.a.** To inscribe (a line or lines) with a pencil or other marking implement. **b.** To make a likeness of on a surface, using mostly lines; depict with lines. **c.** To portray in writing or speech; depict with words. **23.** To formulate or devise from evidence or data at hand: *drew a comparison.* **24.** To compose or write out in legal format. — *intr.* **1.** To proceed or move steadily. **2.** To attract customers or spectators. **3.** To pour forth liquid. **4.** To cause suppuration. **5.** To take in a draft of air. **6.** To steep in or as if in the manner of tea. **7.** To pull out a weapon for use. **8.** To use or call upon part of a fund or supply. **9.** To contract or tighten. **10.** To conclude a contest without either side winning; tie. **11.** To make a likeness with lines on a surface; sketch. — *n.* **1.a.** An act of drawing. **b.** The result of drawing. **2.** Something drawn, esp. a lot, card, or cards drawn at random. **3.** An inhalation, esp. through a pipe or other smoking implement. **4.** One that attracts interest, customers, or spectators. **5.** The movable part of a drawbridge. **6.** A special advantage; an edge. **7.** A contest ending without either side winning. **8.** A small natural depression that water drains into; a shallow gully. — ***phrasal verbs.* draw away.** To move ahead of competitors. **draw back.** To retreat. **draw down.** To deplete by consuming or spending. **draw on.** To approach. **draw out. 1.** To prolong; protract. **2.** To induce to speak freely. **draw up. 1.** To compose or write in a set form; write out. **2.** To bring (troops, for example) into order. **3.** To bring or come to a halt. **4.** To bring (oneself) into an erect posture, often as an expression of dignity or indignation. **5.** *Chiefly Southern U.S.* To shrink when washed. Used of clothes. — ***idioms.* draw a blank.** To fail to find or remember something. **draw and quarter. 1.** To execute (a prisoner) by tying each limb to a horse and driving the horses in different directions. **2.** To disembowel and dismember after hanging. **draw straws.** To decide by a lottery with straws of unequal lengths. [ME *drauen* < OE *dragan.*]

draw•back (drô′băk′) *n.* **1.** A disadvantage or inconvenience. See Syns at **disadvantage. 2.** A refund or remittance.

draw•bar (drô′bär′) *n.* **1.** A bar across the rear of a tractor for hitching machinery. **2.** A railroad coupler.

draw•bridge (drô′brĭj′) *n.* A bridge that can be raised or drawn aside either to prevent access or to permit passage.

draw•down (drô′doun′) *n.* **1.** The act, process, or result of

depleting: *the drawdown of oil supplies.* **2.** A lowering of the water level in a reservoir or other body of water.
draw•ee (drô'ē') *n.* The party on which an order for the payment of money is drawn.
draw•er (drô'ər) *n.* **1.** One that draws, esp. one that draws an order for the payment of money. **2.** (*also* drôr). A boxlike compartment in furniture that can be pulled out and pushed in. **3. drawers** (drôrz). Underpants.
draw•ing (drô'ĭng) *n.* **1.** The act or an instance of drawing. **2.a.** The art of representing objects or forms on a surface chiefly by means of lines. **b.** A work produced by this art.
drawing card *n.* An attraction drawing large audiences.
drawing pin *n. Chiefly British.* A thumbtack.
drawing room *n.* **1.** A large room in which guests are entertained. **2.** A ceremonial reception. **3.** A large private room on a railroad sleeping car. [Akin to *withdrawing room.*]
draw•knife (drô'nīf') *n.* A knife with a handle at each end of the blade, used with a drawing motion to shave a surface.
drawl (drôl) *v.* **drawled, drawl•ing, drawls.** —*intr.* To speak with lengthened or drawn-out vowels. —*tr.* To utter with lengthened or drawn-out vowels. —*n.* The speech or manner of speaking of one who drawls. [Prob. < LGer. *drauelen*, to loiter, delay.] —**drawl'er** *n.*
drawn (drôn) *v.* P.part. of **draw.** —*adj.* Haggard, as from fatigue or ill health.
drawn butter *n.* Melted butter, often seasoned and used as a sauce. [*drawn*, p.part. of DRAW, to bring to a proper consistency (obsolete).]
draw poker *n. Games.* Poker in which each player is dealt five cards and may replace some after the first round of betting.
draw•shave (drô'shāv') *n.* See **drawknife.**
draw•string (drô'strĭng') *n.* A cord or ribbon run through a hem or casing and pulled to tighten or close an opening.
draw•tube (drô'to͞ob', -tyo͞ob') *n.* A tube that slides within another tube, as in a small hand telescope.
dray (drā) *n.* A low heavy cart without sides, used for haulage. —*tr.v.* **drayed, dray•ing, drays.** To haul by means of a dray. [ME *draie*, sledge, cart < OE *dragan*, to draw.]
dray•age (drā'ĭj) *n.* **1.** Transport by dray. **2.** A charge for transport by dray.
dray•man (drā'mən) *n.* A driver of a dray.
Dray•ton (drāt'n), **Michael.** 1563–1631. English poet whose works include *Idea, The Shepherd's Garland* (1593).
dread (drĕd) *v.* **dread•ed, dread•ing, dreads.** —*tr.* **1.** To be in terror of. **2.** To anticipate with alarm, distaste, or reluctance. **3.** *Archaic.* To hold in awe or reverence. —*intr.* To be very afraid. —*n.* **1.** Profound fear; terror. **2.** Fearful or distasteful anticipation. See Syns at **fear. 3.** An object of fear, awe, or reverence. **4.** *Archaic.* Awe; reverence. —*adj.* **1.** Causing terror or fear. **2.** Inspiring awe. [ME *dreden*, short for *adreden* < OE *adrǣdan* < *ondrǣdan*, to advise against, fear : *ond-, and-*, against; see UN-² + *rǣdan*, to advise; see REDE.]
dread•ful (drĕd'fəl) *adj.* **1.** Inspiring dread; terrible. **2.** Extremely unpleasant; distasteful or shocking: *dreadful heat.* —**dread'ful•ly** *adv.* —**dread'ful•ness** *n.*
dread•locks (drĕd'lŏks') *pl.n.* Long thin braids or natural locks of hair densely radiating from the scalp, in a style popularized by Rastafarians. —**dread'locked'** *adj.*
dread•nought (drĕd'nôt') *n.* A heavily armed battleship.
dream (drēm) *n.* **1.** A series of images, ideas, emotions, and sensations occurring involuntarily in the mind during certain stages of sleep. **2.** A daydream; a reverie. **3.** A state of abstraction; a trance. **4.** A wild fancy or hope. **5.** A condition or achievement that is longed for; an aspiration. **6.** One exceptionally gratifying, excellent, or beautiful. —*v.* **dreamed** or **dreamt** (drĕmt), **dream•ing, dreams.** —*intr.* **1.** To experience a dream in sleep. **2.** To daydream. **3.** To have a deep aspiration: *dreaming of peace.* **4.** To regard something as feasible or practical: *wouldn't dream of going.* —*tr.* **1.** To experience a dream of while asleep. **2.** To conceive of; imagine. **3.** To pass (time) idly or in reverie. —***phrasal verb.* dream up.** To invent; concoct. [ME *drem* < OE *drēam*, joy, music; akin to Old Saxon *drōm*, mirth, dream.]
dream•er (drē'mər) *n.* **1.** One that dreams. **2.a.** A visionary. **b.** An idealist. **3.** A habitually impractical person.
dream•land (drēm'lănd') *n.* **1.** An ideal or imaginary land. **2.** A state of sleep.
dream•scape (drēm'skāp') *n.* A dreamlike scene or picture having surreal qualities.
dream vision *n.* A narrative poem, esp. in medieval literature, in which the main character falls asleep and experiences events having allegorical, didactic, or moral significance.
dream•y (drē'mē) *adj.* **-i•er, -i•est. 1.** Resembling a dream; ethereal or vague. **2.** Given to daydreams or reverie. **3.** Soothing and serene. **4.** *Informal.* Inspiring delight; wonderful. —**dream'i•ly** *adv.* —**dream'i•ness** *n.*
drear (drîr) *adj.* Dreary.
drea•ry (drîr'ē) *adj.* **-ri•er, -ri•est. 1.** Dismal; bleak. **2.** Boring; dull: *dreary tasks.* [ME *dreri*, bloody, frightened, sad < OE *drēorig*, bloody, sad < *drēor*, gore. See **dhreu-*.**] —**drea'ri•ly** *adv.* —**drea'ri•ness** *n.*
dreck (drĕk) *n. Slang.* Trash, esp. inferior merchandise. [Ger. *Dreck* and Yiddish *drek*, both < MHGer. *drëc.* See **sker-³*.**] —**dreck'y** *adj.*
dredge¹ (drĕj) *n.* **1.** Any of various machines equipped with scooping or suction devices and used to deepen harbors and waterways and in underwater mining. **2.** *Naut.* A boat or barge equipped with a dredge. **3.** An implement consisting of a net on a frame, used for gathering shellfish. —*v.* **dredged, dredg•ing, dredg•es.** —*tr.* **1.** To clean, deepen, or widen with a dredge. **2.** To bring up with a dredge: *dredged up the silt.* **3.** To come up with; unearth: *dredged up bitter memories.* —*intr.* To use a dredge. [ME *dreg-*, in *dreg-boat*, boat for dredging; akin to OE *dragan*, to draw.]
dredge² (drĕj) *tr.v.* **dredged, dredg•ing, dredg•es.** To coat (food) by sprinkling with a powder, such as sugar. [< obsolete *dredge*, a sweetmeat < ME *dragge* < OFr. *dragie*, alteration of Lat. *tragēmata*, confectionary < Gk., pl. of *tragēma*, sweetmeat. See **terə-¹*.**]
dredg•er¹ (drĕj'ər) *n.* **1.** A dredging machine. **2.** *Naut.* A barge or boat equipped with a dredge.
dredg•er² (drĕj'ər) *n.* A container with a perforated lid used for coating food with a powder, such as flour or sugar.
D region *n.* The region of the ionosphere about 40 to 65 kilometers (25 to 40 miles) above the earth.
dreg (drĕg) *n.* **1.** The sediment in a liquid; lees. Often used in the plural. **2.** The basest or least desirable portion. Often used in the plural. **3.** A small amount; a residue. [ME *dreg* < ON *dregg.*]
drei•del also **drei•dl** (drād'l) *n.* A spinning top commemorating the rededication of the Temple in Jerusalem and used in Hanukkah games. [Yiddish *dreydl* < *dreyen*, to turn < MHGer. *drǣjen* < OHGer. *drāen.*]
Drei•ser (drī'sər, -zər), **Theodore Herman Albert.** 1871–1945. Amer. writer and editor whose novels include *Sister Carrie* (1900) and *An American Tragedy* (1925).
drench (drĕnch) *tr.v.* **drenched, drench•ing, drench•es. 1.** To wet through and through; soak. **2.** To administer a drench to (an animal). **3.** To provide with something in great abundance; surfeit. —*n.* **1.** The act of wetting or becoming wet through and through. **2.** A large dose of liquid medicine, esp. one administered to an animal by pouring down the throat. [ME *drenchen*, to drown < OE *drencan*, to give to drink, drown. See **dhreg-*.**] —**drench'er** *n.*
Dres•den (drĕz'dən). A city of E-central Germany ESE of Leipzig; long noted for its china industry. Pop. 522,532.
Dresden china *n.* Meissen porcelain. [After DRESDEN.]
dress (drĕs) *v.* **dressed, dress•ing, dress•es.** —*tr.* **1.a.** To put clothes on; clothe. **b.** To furnish with clothing. **2.** To decorate or adorn. **3.** To arrange a display in. **4.** To arrange (troops) in ranks; align. **5.** To apply medication, bandages, or other therapeutic materials to (a wound). **6.** To arrange and groom (the hair), as by styling, combing, or washing. **7.** To groom (an animal); curry. **8.** To cultivate (land or plants). **9.** To clean (fish or fowl) for cooking or sale. **10.** To trim and finish the surface of. —*intr.* **1.** To put on clothes. **2.** To wear clothes of a certain kind or style. **3.** To wear formal clothes. **4.** To get into proper alignment with others. —*n.* **1.** Clothing; apparel. **2.** A style of clothing. **3.** A one-piece outer garment for women or girls. **4.** Outer covering or appearance; guise. —*adj.* **1.** Suitable for formal occasions. **2.** Requiring formal clothes. —***phrasal verbs.* dress down. 1.** To scold; reprimand. **2.** To wear informal clothes, befitting an occasion or location. **dress up.** To wear formal or fancy clothes. —***idiom.* dress ship.** *Naut.* To display the ensign, signal flags, and bunting on a ship. [ME *dressen* < OFr. *drecier*, to arrange < VLat. **dīrectiāre* < Lat. *dīrectus*, p.part. of *dīrigere*, to direct. See DIRECT.]
dres•sage (drə-säzh', drĕ-) *n. Sports.* The guiding of a horse through a series of complex maneuvers by slight movements of the rider's hands, legs, and weight. [Fr., preparation, training, dressage < *dresser*, to set up, arrange, train < OFr. *drecier*, to set up, arrange. See DRESS.]
dress circle *n.* A section of seats in a theater or opera house, usu. the first tier above the orchestra.
dress code *n.* A set of rules, as in a school, indicating the approved manner of dress.
dress•er¹ (drĕs'ər) *n.* **1.** One that dresses: *a careful dresser.* **2.** A wardrobe assistant, as for an actor.
dress•er² (drĕs'ər) *n.* **1.** A low chest of drawers often supporting a mirror and typically used for holding clothes and personal items. **2.** A cupboard or set of shelves for dishes or kitchen utensils. [ME *dressour*, table for preparing food < OFr. *dreceur* < *drecier*, to set up, arrange. See DRESS.]
dress•ing (drĕs'ĭng) *n.* **1.** A therapeutic or protective material applied to a wound. **2.** A sauce for certain dishes, such as salads. **3.** A stuffing, as for fish. **4.** Fertilizing material for soil.
dressing gown *n.* A robe worn for lounging or before dressing.
dressing room *n.* A room, as in a theater, for changing costumes or clothes and applying makeup.
dressing table *n.* A low table with a mirror at which one sits while applying makeup.
dress•mak•er (drĕs'mā'kər) *n.* One that makes women's clothing, esp. dresses. —**dress'mak'ing** *n.*

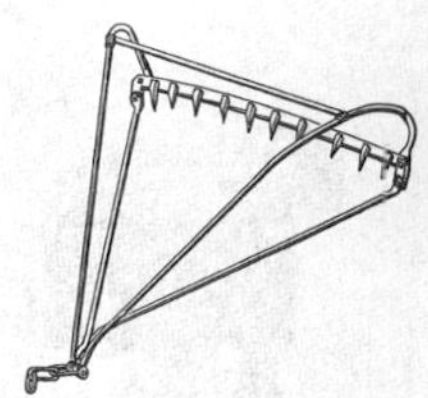
dredge¹
Oyster dredge without net

dreidel

ă **pat**	oi **boy**
ā **pay**	ou **out**
âr **care**	o͝o **took**
ä **father**	o͞o **boot**
ĕ **pet**	ŭ **cut**
ē **be**	ûr **urge**
ĭ **pit**	th **thin**
ī **pie**	*th* **this**
îr **pier**	hw **which**
ŏ **pot**	zh **vision**
ō **toe**	ə **about,**
ô **paw**	**item**

Stress marks:
' (primary);
' (secondary), as in
dictionary (dĭk'shə-nĕr'ē)

dress rehearsal *n.* A full uninterrupted rehearsal of a play with costumes and stage properties.
dress•y (drĕs′ē) *adj.* **-i•er, -i•est. 1.** Showy or elegant in dress or appearance. **2.** Smart; stylish. **—dress′i•ness** *n.*
drew (dro͞o) *v.* P.t. of **draw.**
Drew (dro͞o). Family of Amer. actors, including **John** (1827–62), his wife, **Louisa** (1820–97), and their son **John** (1853–1927).
Drew, Daniel. 1797–1879. Amer. financier who as a director of the Erie Railroad manipulated stock prices.
Drex•el Hill (drĕk′səl). A community of SE PA, a suburb of Philadelphia. Pop. 29,744.
Drey•fus (drī′fəs, drā-), **Alfred.** 1859–1935. French army officer who was convicted of treason (1894) but later acquitted when the evidence against him was shown to have been forged by anti-Semites.
drib (drĭb) *n.* A negligible amount. [Perh. < DRIBLET.]
drib•ble (drĭb′əl) *v.* **-bled, -bling, -bles.** *—intr.* **1.** To flow or fall in drops or an unsteady stream; trickle. **2.** To let saliva drip from the mouth; drool. **3.** *Sports.* **a.** To dribble a ball or puck. **b.** To advance by dribbling. *—tr.* **1.** To let flow or fall in drops or an unsteady stream. **2.** *Sports.* **a.** To move (a ball or puck) by repeated light bounces or kicks, as in basketball or soccer. **b.** To hit (a baseball, for example) so that it bounces slowly. *—n.* **1.** A weak, unsteady stream; a trickle. **2.** A small quantity; a bit. **3.** *Sports.* The act of dribbling a ball. [Freq. of obsolete *drib*, alteration of DRIP.] **—drib′bler** *n.*
drib•let (drĭb′lĭt) *n.* **1.** A tiny falling drop of liquid. **2.** A small amount or portion. [< obsolete *drib*, to fall in drops, alteration of DRIP.]
dried (drīd) *v.* P.t. and p.part. of **dry.**
dri•er¹ also **dry•er** (drī′ər) *n.* **1.** One that dries. **2.** A substance added to paint, varnish, or ink to speed drying.
dri•er² (drī′ər) *adj.* A comp. of **dry.**
dries (drīz) *v.* Third pers. sing. pr.t. of **dry.**
dri•est (drī′ĭst) *adj.* A superl. of **dry.**
drift (drĭft) *v.* **drift•ed, drift•ing, drifts.** *—intr.* **1.** To be carried along by currents of air or water. **2.** To proceed or move unhurriedly and smoothly. **3.** To move leisurely or sporadically from place to place, esp. without purpose or regular employment. **4.a.** To wander from a set course or point of attention; stray. **b.** To vary from or oscillate randomly about a fixed setting, position, or mode of operation. **5.** To be piled up in banks or heaps by the force of a current. *—tr.* **1.** To cause to be carried in a current. **2.** To pile up in banks or heaps. **3.** *Western U.S.* To drive (livestock) slowly or far afield, esp. for grazing. *—n.* **1.** The act or condition of drifting. **2.** Something moving along in a current of air or water. **3.** A bank or pile, as of sand or snow, heaped up by currents of air or water. **4.** *Geol.* Rock debris transported and deposited by or from ice, esp. by or from a glacier. **5.a.** A general trend or tendency, as of opinion. **b.** General meaning or purport; tenor: *caught my drift.* **6.a.** A gradual change in position. **b.** A gradual deviation from an original course, model, method, or intention. **c.** Variation or random oscillation about a fixed setting, position, or mode of behavior. **7.** A gradual change in the output of a circuit or amplifier. **8.** The rate of flow of a water current. **9.a.** A tool for ramming or driving something down. **b.** A tapered steel pin for enlarging and aligning holes. **10.a.** A horizontal or nearly horizontal passageway in a mine running through or parallel to a vein. **b.** A secondary mine passageway between two main shafts or tunnels. **11.** A drove or herd, esp. of swine. [< ME, drove, herd, act of driving. See **dhreibh-***.] **—drift′y** *adj.*

drill press

drift•age (drĭf′tĭj) *n.* Matter borne or deposited by air or water.
drift•er (drĭf′tər) *n.* One that drifts, esp. a person who moves aimlessly from place to place or from job to job.
drift net *n.* A large fishing net buoyed up by floats that is carried along with the current or tide.
drift•wood (drĭft′wo͝od′) *n.* Wood floating in or washed up by the water.
drill¹ (drĭl) *n.* **1.a.** An implement with cutting edges or a pointed end for boring holes in hard materials, usu. by a rotating abrasion or repeated blows; a bit. **b.** The hand-operated or hand-powered holder for this implement. **c.** A harsh loud noise made by or as if by a powered tool of this kind. **2.a.** Disciplined repetitious exercise as a means of teaching and perfecting a skill or procedure. **b.** A task or exercise of this kind. **3.** The training of soldiers in marching and the manual of arms. **4.** Any of various marine gastropod mollusks, chiefly of the genus *Urosalpinx,* that bore holes into the shells of bivalve mollusks. *—v.* **drilled, drill•ing, drills.** *—tr.* **1.a.** To make a hole in (a hard material) with a drill. **b.** To make (a hole) with or as if with a drill. **2.** To strike or hit sharply. **3.a.** To instruct thoroughly by repetition in a skill or procedure. **b.** To infuse knowledge of or skill in by repetitious instruction. See Syns at **practice. 4.** To train (soldiers) in marching and the manual of arms. *—intr.* **1.** To make a hole with or as if with a drill. **2.** To perform a training exercise. [Obsolete Du. *dril* < *drillen,* to bore < MDu. *drillen.* See **terə-¹***.] **—drill′er** *n.*
drill² (drĭl) *n.* **1.** A shallow trench or furrow in which seeds are planted. **2.** A row of planted seeds. **3.** A machine or implement for planting seeds in holes or furrows. *—tr.v.* **drilled, drill•ing, drills. 1.** To sow (seeds) in rows. **2.** To plant (a field) in drills. [Perh. < *drill,* rill < ME *drille,* sip.]
drill³ (drĭl) *n.* Durable cotton or linen twill of varying weights, generally used for work clothes. [Short for *drilling,* alteration of Ger. *Drillich* < MHGer. *drilich* < OHGer. *drilīh,* alteration of Lat. *trilīx, trilīc-,* triple-twilled. See TRELLIS.]
drill⁴ (drĭl) *n.* A baboon *(Papio leucophaeus)* of western Africa. [Poss. of West African orig.]
drill instructor *n.* A noncommissioned officer who instructs recruits in military drill and discipline.
drill•mas•ter (drĭl′măs′tər) *n.* **1.** A drill instructor. **2.** An instructor given to extremely rigorous training.
drill press *n.* A powered vertical drilling machine in which the drill is pressed to the work automatically or by a hand lever.
drill steel *n.* A high-grade steel used in tools and dies that is made by fusing low-carbon steel with charcoal or cast iron.
drill•stock (drĭl′stŏk′) *n.* The part of a drilling tool or machine that holds the shank of a drill or bit.
Drin (drēn). A river of Albania flowing c. 282 km (175 mi) to the Adriatic Sea.
Dri•na (drē′nə, -nä). A river rising in E Bosnia-Herzegovina and flowing c. 459 km (285 mi) to the Sava R.
drink (drĭngk) *v.* **drank** (drăngk), **drunk** (drŭngk), **drink•ing, drinks.** *—tr.* **1.** To take into the mouth and swallow (a liquid). **2.** To swallow the liquid contents of (a vessel). **3.** To take in or soak up; absorb. **4.** To take in eagerly through the senses or intellect: *drank in its beauty.* **5.a.** To give or make (a toast). **b.** To toast (a person or an occasion, for example). **6.** To bring to a specific state by drinking alcoholic liquors: *drank our sorrows away.* *—intr.* **1.** To swallow liquid: *drank noisily.* **2.** To imbibe alcoholic liquors: *drink socially.* **3.** To salute a person or an occasion with a toast: *drank to you.* *—n.* **1.** A liquid for drinking; a beverage. **2.** An amount of liquid swallowed. **3.** An alcoholic beverage. **4.** Excessive or habitual indulgence in alcoholic liquor. **5.** *Slang.* A body of water; the sea. [ME *drinken* < OE *drincan.* See **dhreg-***.]
drink•a•ble (drĭng′kə-bəl) *adj.* Suitable or fit for drinking; potable. *—n.* A beverage. **—drink′a•bil′i•ty** *n.*
drink•er (drĭng′kər) *n.* **1.** One that drinks. **2.** One who drinks alcoholic liquors, esp. habitually or excessively.
drink•ing fountain (drĭng′kĭng) *n.* A device with a nozzle that when activated provides a stream of drinking water.
drip (drĭp) *v.* **dripped, drip•ping, drips.** *—intr.* **1.** To fall in drops. **2.** To shed drops. **3.** To ooze or be saturated with or as if with liquid. *—tr.* To let fall in or as if in drops. *—n.* **1.** The process of forming and falling in drops. **2.a.** Liquid or moisture that falls in drops. **b.** A slight intermittent flow or leak. **3.** The sound made by liquid falling in drops. **4.** A projection on a cornice or sill that protects the area below from rainwater. **5.** *Slang.* A tiresome or annoying person. [ME *drippen.* See **dhreu-***.]
drip coffee *n.* Coffee made by pouring boiling water through a perforated container holding ground coffee into a pot.
drip-dry (drĭp′drī′) *adj.* Made of a fabric that will not wrinkle when hung dripping wet for drying. *—intr.v.* **-dried, -dry•ing, -dries.** To dry with no wrinkles when hung dripping wet.
drip•less (drĭp′lĭs) *adj.* Designed to prevent dripping.
drip pan *n.* A pan for catching the drippings from roasting meat. Also called regionally *bakersheet.*
drip•ping (drĭp′ĭng) *n.* **1.** The act or sound of something falling in drops. **2.** The fat and juices exuded from roasting meat, often used in making gravy. Often used in the plural.
drip•py (drĭp′ē) *adj.* **-pi•er, -pi•est. 1.** Characterized by dripping; drizzly. **2.** *Slang.* **a.** Tiresome or annoying. **b.** Mawkishly sentimental. **—drip′pi•ly** *adv.* **—drip′pi•ness** *n.*
drip•stone (drĭp′stōn′) *n.* **1.** A protective drip made of stone, as on a cornice over a door. **2.** Calcium carbonate in the form of stalactites or stalagmites.
drive (drīv) *v.* **drove** (drōv), **driv•en** (drĭv′ən), **driv•ing, drives.** *—tr.* **1.** To push, propel, or press onward forcibly; urge forward. **2.** To repulse forcefully; put to flight. **3.** To guide, control, or direct (a vehicle). **4.a.** To convey or transport in a vehicle. **b.** To traverse in a vehicle. **5.** To supply the motive force or power to and cause to function. **6.** To compel or force to work, often excessively. **7.** To force into or from a particular act or state: *drove me crazy.* **8.** To force to go through or penetrate. **9.** To create or produce by penetrating forcibly: *drove a hole in the tire.* **10.** To carry through vigorously to a conclusion. **11.a.** *Sports.* To throw, strike, or cast (a ball, for example) hard or rapidly. **b.** *Baseball.* To cause (a run) to be scored. **12.a.** To chase (game) into the open or into traps or nets. **b.** To search (an area) for game in such a manner. *—intr.* **1.** To move along or advance quickly as if pushed by an impelling force. **2.** To rush, dash, or advance violently against an obstruction. **3.** To operate a vehicle, such as a car. **4.** To go or be transported in a vehicle. **5.a.** *Sports.* To hit, throw, or impel a ball or other missile forcibly. **b.** *Basketball.* To move directly to the basket with the ball. **6.** To make an effort to reach or achieve an objective; aim. *—n.* **1.** The act

of driving. **2.** A trip or journey in a vehicle. **3.** A road for automobiles and other vehicles. **4.a.** The means or apparatus for transmitting motion or power to a machine or from one machine part to another. **b.** The means by which automotive power is applied to a roadway: *four-wheel drive.* **5.** *Comp. Sci.* A device that reads data from and writes data onto a storage medium, such as a floppy disk. **6.** A strong organized effort to accomplish a purpose. **7.** Energy, push, or aggressiveness. **8.** *Psychol.* A strong motivating tendency or instinct, esp. of sexual or aggressive origin, that prompts activity toward a particular end. **9.** A massive sustained military offensive. **10.a.** *Sports.* The act of hitting, knocking, or thrusting a ball very swiftly. **b.** *Sports.* The stroke or thrust by which a ball is driven. **c.** *Basketball.* The act of driving. **11.a.** A rounding up and driving of cattle to new pastures or to market. **b.** A gathering and driving of logs down a river. **c.** The cattle or logs thus driven. **—*phrasal verb.* drive at.** To mean to do or say. [ME *driven* < OE *drīfan.* See **dhreibh-*.**] **—driv′a•bil′i•ty** *n.* **—driv′a•ble** *adj.*

drive-in (drīv′ĭn′) *n.* An establishment designed to serve customers in their motor vehicles. **—drive′-in′** *adj.*

driv•el (drĭv′əl) *v.* **-eled, -el•ing, -els** or **-elled, -el•ling, -els.** —*intr.* **1.** To slobber; drool. **2.** To flow like spittle or saliva. **3.** To talk stupidly or childishly. —*tr.* **1.** To allow to flow from the mouth. **2.** To say (something) stupidly. —*n.* **1.** Saliva flowing from the mouth. **2.** Stupid or senseless talk. [ME *drevelen* < OE *dreflian.*] **—driv′el•er** *n.*

drive•line (drīv′līn′) *n.* The components of an automotive vehicle that connect the transmission with the driving axles.

driv•en (drĭv′ən) *v.* P.part. of **drive.** —*adj.* **1.** Piled up or carried along by a current: *driven snow.* **2.** Motivated by or having a compulsive quality or need: *a driven person.*

driv•er (drī′vər) *n.* **1.** One that drives, as the operator of a motor vehicle. **2.** A tool, such as a hammer, used to impart forceful pressure. **3.** A machine part that transmits motion or power to another part. **4.** *Sports.* A golf club with a wide head and a long shaft, used for long shots. **5.** *Naut.* A jib-headed spanker.

driver ant *n.* See **army ant.**

driv•er's seat (drī′vərz) *n.* A position of control or authority.

drive shaft also **drive•shaft** (drīv′shăft′) *n.* A rotating shaft that transmits mechanical power from a motor or an engine to a point or region of application.

drive train *n.* See **driveline.**

drive-up (drīv′ŭp′) *adj.* Designed to serve customers in their motor vehicles. **—drive′-up′** *n.*

drive•way (drīv′wā′) *n.* A private road that connects a house, a garage, or another building with the street.

driv•ing (drī′vĭng) *adj.* **1.** Transmitting power or motion. **2.** Violent, intense, or forceful: *a driving rain.* **3.** Energetic or active: *a driving personality.* **—driv′ing•ly** *adv.*

driz•zle (drĭz′əl) *v.* **-zled, -zling, -zles.** —*intr.* To rain gently in fine mistlike drops. —*tr.* **1.** To let fall in fine drops or particles. **2.** To moisten with fine drops. —*n.* A fine, gentle, misty rain. [Perh. < ME *drisning,* fall of dew < OE *-drysnian,* in *gedrysnian,* to pass away, vanish. See **dhreu-*.**] **—driz′zly** *adj.*

Dro•ghe•da (drô′ĭ-də, drŏ′hĭ-). A municipal borough of E Ireland on the Boyne R.; overrun by Oliver Cromwell (1649). Pop. 23,247.

drogue (drōg) *n.* **1.** *Naut.* See **sea anchor. 2.** A drogue parachute. **3.** A funnel-shaped device towed behind an aircraft as a target. **4.** A funnel-shaped device at the end of the hose of a tanker aircraft, used as a receptacle for the probe of a receiving aircraft. [Perh. alteration of DRAG.]

drogue parachute *n.* **1.** A parachute used to stabilize or decelerate a fast-moving object, esp. a small parachute used to slow down a reentering spacecraft. **2.** A small parachute used to pull a main parachute from its storage pack.

droit (droit, drwä) *n. Law.* **1.** A legal right. **2.** Something to which one has legal right. [ME, a fee allowed by law < OFr., right < LLat. *dīrectum* < neut. of Lat. *dīrectus,* straight. See DIRECT.]

droll (drōl) *adj.* **droll•er, droll•est.** Amusingly odd or whimsically comical. —*n. Archaic.* A buffoon. [Fr. *drôle,* buffoon, droll < OFr. *drolle,* bon vivant, poss. < MDu. *drol,* goblin.] **—droll′ness** *n.* **—drol′ly** *adv.*

droll•er•y (drō′lə-rē) *n., pl.* **-ies. 1.** A comical or whimsical quality. **2.** A comical or whimsical way of acting or talking. **3.a.** The act of joking. **b.** Something comical or whimsical.

-drome *suff.* **1.** Racecourse: *hippodrome.* **2.** Field; arena: *airdrome.* **3.** Running: *palindrome.* [Lat. *-dromos* < Gk. *dromos,* racecourse.]

drom•e•dar•y (drŏm′ĭ-dĕr′ē, drŭm′-) *n., pl.* **-ies.** The one-humped domesticated camel *(Camelus dromedarius)* of northern Africa and western Asia. [ME *dromedarie* < OFr. *dromedaire* < LLat. *dromedārius* < Lat. *dromas, dromad-* < Gk., running.]

drom•ond (drŏm′ənd, drŭm′-) *n. Naut.* A large medieval sailing galley. [ME < AN *dromund* < LLat. *dromō, dromōn-,* a kind of ship < LGk. *dromōn* < Gk. *dromos,* race.]

-dromous *suff.* Running; moving: *catadromous.* [< NLat. *-dromus* < Gk. *-dromos* < *dromos,* act of running.]

drone¹ (drōn) *n.* **1.** A male bee, esp. a honeybee, that has no sting, performs no work, and has the sole function of mating with the queen bee. **2.** An idle person who lives off others. **3.** A pilotless, remote-controlled aircraft. [ME < OE *drān.*]

drone² (drōn) *v.* **droned, dron•ing, drones.** —*intr.* **1.** To make a continuous low dull humming sound. **2.** To speak in a monotonous tone. **3.** To pass or act in a monotonous way. —*tr.* To utter in a monotonous low tone. —*n.* **1.** A continuous low humming or buzzing sound. **2.** *Mus.* **a.** Any of the pipes of a bagpipe tuned to produce a single tone. **b.** A single sustained tone. [Prob. < DRONE¹ (< the bee's humming sound).]

drool (dro͞ol) *v.* **drooled, drool•ing, drools.** —*intr.* **1.** To let saliva run from the mouth; drivel. **2.** *Informal.* To show extravagant appreciation or desire. **3.** *Informal.* To talk nonsense. —*tr.* To let run from the mouth. —*n.* **1.** Saliva. **2.** *Informal.* Senseless talk; drivel. [Perh. alteration of DRIVEL.]

droop (dro͞op) *v.* **drooped, droop•ing, droops.** —*intr.* **1.** To bend or hang downward. **2.** To bend or sag gradually. **3.** To sag in dejection or exhaustion. —*tr.* To let bend or hang down. —*n.* The act or condition of drooping. [ME *droupen* < ON *drūpa.* See **dhreu-*.**] **—droop′i•ly, droop′ing•ly** *adv.* **—droop′y** *adj.*

drop (drŏp) *n.* **1.** The smallest quantity of liquid heavy enough to fall in a spherical mass. See table at **measurement. 2.** A small quantity of a substance. **3. drops.** Liquid medicine administered in drops. **4.** A trace or hint: *not a drop of pity.* **5.a.** Something shaped or hanging like a drop. **b.** A small globular piece of hard candy. **6.** The act of falling; descent. **7.** A swift decline or decrease, as in quality, quantity, or intensity. **8.a.** The vertical distance from a higher to a lower level. **b.** The distance through which something falls or drops. **9.** A sheer incline, such as the face of a cliff. **10.a.** A descent by parachute. **b.** Personnel and equipment landed by means of parachute. **11.** Something that is arranged to fall or be lowered. **12.** A drop curtain. **13.** A slot through which something is deposited in a receptacle. **14.** A central place or establishment where something, such as mail, is brought and subsequently distributed. **15.a.** A predetermined location for the deposit and subsequent removal of secret communications or illicit goods. **b.** The act of depositing such communications or materials. **16.** *Electron.* A connection made available for an input or output unit on a transmission line. —*v.* **dropped, drop•ping, drops.** —*intr.* **1.** To fall in drops. **2.** To fall from a higher to a lower place or position. **3.** To become less, as in number, intensity, or volume. **4.** To descend from one level to another. **5.** To fall or sink into a state of exhaustion or death. **6.** To pass or slip into a specified state or condition. —*tr.* **1.** To let fall by releasing hold of. **2.** To let fall in drops. **3.** To cause to become less; reduce. **4.** To cause to fall, as by hitting or shooting. **5.** To give birth to. Used of animals. **6.** To say or offer casually: *drop a hint.* **7.** To write at one's leisure: *drop me a note.* **8.** To cease consideration or treatment of. **9.** To terminate an association or a relationship with. **10.** To leave unfinished. **11.** To leave out (a letter, for example) in speaking or writing. **12.** To leave or set down at a particular place; unload. **13.** To parachute. **14.** To lower the level of (the voice). **15.** To lose (a game or contest, for example). **16.** *Slang.* To take, as a drug, by mouth. **17.** *New England.* To poach (an egg). **—*phrasal verbs.* drop behind.** To fall behind; fail to keep up. **drop by.** To stop in for a short visit. **drop off. 1.** To fall asleep. **2.** To decrease: *Sales dropped off last month.* **drop out. 1.** To withdraw from participation, as in a school. **2.** To withdraw from established society, esp. because of disillusion with conventional values. **—*idiom.* get (or have) the drop on.** To achieve a distinct advantage over. [ME *droppe* < OE *dropa.* See **dhreu-*.**]

drop cloth *n.* A sheet, as of cloth or plastic, for protection against spills or dripping, used esp. by painters.

drop curtain *n.* **1.** An unframed curtain that is lowered to a stage from the flies, often serving as background scenery. **2.** A theater curtain that is lowered or raised vertically rather than drawn to the side.

drop•forge (drŏp′fôrj′, -fōrj′) *tr.v.* **-forged, -forg•ing, -forg•es.** To forge or stamp (a metal) between dies by the force of a falling weight such as a drop hammer.

drop hammer *n.* A machine consisting of an anvil aligned with a hammer that is dropped to forge or stamp molten metal.

drop-in (drŏp′ĭn′) *n.* **1.** One who casually drops in, as to visit or obtain an appointment. **2.** An informal social event.

drop kick *n. Football.* A kick made by dropping the ball to the ground and kicking it just as it starts to rebound. **—drop′-kick′** (drŏp′kĭk′) *v.*

drop leaf *n.* A hinged wing on a table that can be folded down when not in use.

drop•let (drŏp′lĭt) *n.* A tiny drop.

droplet infection *n.* An infection transmitted by droplets of moisture expelled from the upper respiratory tract, as through coughing.

drop•light (drŏp′līt′) *n.* A hanging lamp that can be lowered and raised on its cord.

drop-off (drŏp′ôf′, -ŏf′) *n.* **1.** A steep or abrupt downward

dromedary
Camelus dromedarius

drop leaf
Mid to late 18th-century American drop leaf table

ă **pat**	oi **boy**
ā **pay**	ou **out**
âr **care**	o͝o **took**
ä **father**	o͞o **boot**
ĕ **pet**	ŭ **cut**
ē **be**	ûr **urge**
ĭ **pit**	th **thin**
ī **pie**	*th* **this**
îr **pier**	hw **which**
ŏ **pot**	zh **vision**
ō **toe**	ə **about,**
ô **paw**	**item**

Stress marks:
′ (primary);
′ (secondary), as in
dictionary (dĭk′shə-nĕr′ē)

slope. **2.** A noticeable decrease: *a drop-off in attendance.*

drop•out (drŏp′out′) *n.* **1.a.** One who quits school. **b.** One who has withdrawn from a given social group. **2.** *Comp. Sci.* **a.** A segment of magnetic tape lacking expected information. **b.** The failure to read a bit of stored information.

drop•per (drŏp′ər) *n.* One that drops, esp. a small tube with a suction bulb at one end for drawing in a liquid and releasing it in drops.

drop•ping (drŏp′ĭng) *n.* **1.** Something dropped. **2. droppings.** The excrement of animals.

drop shot *n. Sports.* A shot in various racquet games in which a ball or shuttlecock drops quickly after crossing the net or hitting the wall.

drop•sy (drŏp′sē) *n.* Edema. No longer in scientific use. [ME *dropesie,* short for *idropesie* < OFr. *ydropisie* < Med.Lat. *ydrōpisia* < Lat. *hydrōpisis* < Gk. *hudrōpiasis* < *hudrōps,* dropsy, a dropsical person < *hudōr,* water. See **wed-¹*.**] **— drop′si•cal** (-sĭ-kəl) *adj.* **— drop′si•cal•ly** *adv.*

drop•wort (drŏp′wôrt′, -wûrt′) *n.* A Eurasian plant *(Filipendula vulgaris)* having finely divided leaflets and small white flowers.

dros•er•a (drŏs′ər-ə) *n.* See **sundew.** [Gk., fem. of *droseros,* dewy < *drosos,* dew.]

drosh•ky (drŏsh′kē) also **dros•ky** (drŏs′-) *n., pl.* **-kies** also **-kys.** An open four-wheeled horse-drawn carriage formerly used in Russia and Poland. [Russ. *drozhki,* dim. of *drogi,* wagon, pl. of *droga,* shaft of a wagon.]

dro•soph•i•la (drō-sŏf′ə-lə, drə-) *n.* Any of various small fruit flies of the genus *Drosophila,* esp. *D. melanogaster* used in genetic research. [NLat. *Drosophila,* genus name : Gk. *drosos,* dew + NLat. *-phila,* pl. of *-philus,* -phile.]

dross (drŏs, drôs) *n.* **1.** A waste product or an impurity, esp. an oxide, formed on the surface of molten metal. **2.** Worthless, commonplace, or trivial matter. [ME *dros* < OE *drōs,* dregs.] **— dross′y** *adj.*

drought (drout) also **drouth** (drouth) *n.* **1.** A long period of abnormally low rainfall. **2.** A prolonged dearth or shortage. [ME < OE *drūgoth.*] **— drought′y** *adj.*

drove¹ (drōv) *v.* P.t. of **drive.**

drove² (drōv) *n.* **1.** A flock or herd being driven in a body. **2.a.** A large mass of people moving or acting as a body. **b.** A large body of like things. **3.a.** A stonemason's broad-edged chisel used for rough hewing. **b.** A stone surface dressed with such a chisel. [ME < OE *drāf* < *drīfan,* to drive. See **dhreibh-*.**]

drov•er (drō′vər) *n.* One that drives cattle or sheep.

drown (droun) *v.* **drowned, drown•ing, drowns.** *— tr.* **1.** To kill by submerging and suffocating in water or another liquid. **2.** To drench thoroughly or cover with or as if with a liquid. **3.** To deaden one's awareness of; blot out. **4.** To muffle or mask (a sound) by a louder sound. *— intr.* To die by suffocating in water or another liquid. [ME *drounen,* prob. of Scand. orig. See **dhreg-*.**]

drowse (drouz) *v.* **drowsed, drows•ing, drows•es.** *— intr.* To be half-asleep. *— tr.* **1.** To make drowsy. **2.** To pass (time) by drowsing. *— n.* The condition of being sleepy. [Perh. ult. < OE *drūsian,* to sink, be sluggish. See **dhreu-*.**]

drows•y (drou′zē) *adj.* **-i•er, -i•est. 1.** Dull with sleepiness; sluggish. **2.** Produced or marked by sleepiness. **3.** Inducing sleepiness. **— drows′i•ly** *adv.* **— drows′i•ness** *n.*

dr t *abbr.* Troy dram.

drub (drŭb) *v.* **drubbed, drub•bing, drubs.** *— tr.* **1.** To thrash with a stick. **2.** To instill forcefully. **3.a.** To defeat emphatically. **b.** To berate harshly. **4.** To stamp (the feet). *— intr.* **1.** To beat the ground; stamp. **2.** To pound; throb. *— n.* A blow with a heavy instrument. [Perh. Ar. *ḍaraba,* to beat.] **— drub′ber** *n.*

drub•bing (drŭb′ĭng) *n.* **1.** A thrashing. **2.** A total defeat.

drudge¹ (drŭj) *n.* A person who performs drudgery. *— intr.v.* **drudged, drudg•ing, drudg•es.** To perform drudgery. [< ME *druggen,* to labor; akin to OE *drēogan,* to work, suffer.] **— drudg′er** *n.* **— drudg′ing•ly** *adv.*

drudge² (drŭj) *n. & v. Chesapeake Bay.* Var. of **dredge¹.**

drudg•er•y (drŭj′ə-rē) *n., pl.* **-ies.** Tedious, menial, or unpleasant work.

drudge•work (drŭj′wûrk′) *n.* Drudgery.

drug (drŭg) *n.* **1.a.** A substance used in the diagnosis, treatment, or prevention of a disease or as a component of a medication. **b.** Such a substance as recognized or defined by the U.S. Food, Drug, and Cosmetic Act. **2.** A chemical substance, such as a narcotic, that affects the central nervous system, causing changes in behavior and often addiction. **3.** *Obsolete.* A chemical or dye. *— tr.v.* **drugged, drug•ging, drugs. 1.** To administer a drug to. **2.** To poison or mix (food or drink) with a drug. **3.** To stupefy or dull with or as if with a drug. [ME *drogge* < OFr. *drogue,* drug, perh. < MDu. *droge (vate),* dry (cases), pl. of *drog,* dry.]

drug•get (drŭg′ĭt) *n.* **1.a.** A heavy felted fabric of wool or wool and cotton, used as a floor covering. **b.** A coarse rug of this fabric, made in India. **2.** A fabric woven wholly or partly of wool, formerly used for clothing. [Fr. *droguet,* prob. < *drogue,* drug, worthless object. See DRUG.]

drug•gie also **drug•gy** (drŭg′ē) *n., pl.* **-gies.** *Slang.* One that takes or is addicted to drugs.

drug•gist (drŭg′ĭst) *n.* **1.** A pharmacist. **2.** One who sells drugs.

drug•gy¹ (drŭg′ē) *Slang. adj.* **-gi•er, -gi•est.** Of or relating to drugs or drug use.

drug•gy² (drŭg′ē) *n.* Var. of **druggie.**

drug•store also **drug store** (drŭg′stôr′, -stōr′) *n.* A store where prescriptions are filled and drugs and other items are sold.

dru•id also **Dru•id** (drōō′ĭd) *n.* A member of an order of priests in ancient Gaul and Britain who appear in Welsh and Irish legend as prophets and sorcerers. [< Lat. *druidēs,* druids, of Celt. orig. See **deru-*.**] **— dru•id′ic** (drōō-ĭd′ĭk), **dru•id′i•cal** (-ĭ-kəl) *adj.* **— dru•id′i•cal•ly** *adv.* **— dru′id•ism** *n.*

drum (drŭm) *n.* **1.** *Mus.* **a.** A percussion instrument consisting of a hollow cylinder or hemisphere with a membrane stretched tightly over one or both ends, played by beating with the hands or sticks. **b.** A sound produced by this instrument. **2.** Something resembling a drum in shape or structure, esp. a barrellike metal container or a metal cylinder wound with cable, wire, or heavy rope. **3.** Any of various marine and freshwater fishes of the family Sciaenidae that make a drumming sound. **4.** *Anat.* The eardrum. *— v.* **drummed, drum•ming, drums.** *— intr.* **1.** To play a drum or drums. **2.** To thump or tap rhythmically or continually. **3.** To produce a booming reverberating sound by beating the wings, as certain birds do. *— tr.* **1.** To perform (a piece or tune) on or as if on a drum. **2.** To summon by or as if by beating a drum. **3.** To make known to or force upon (a person) by constant repetition. **4.** To expel or dismiss in disgrace: *was drummed out of the army.* **— *phrasal verb.* drum up. 1.** To bring about by continuous, persistent effort. **2.** To devise; invent: *drummed up an alibi.* [ME *drom* < MDu. *tromme,* prob. of imit. orig.]

drum•beat (drŭm′bēt′) *n.* **1.** The sound produced by beating a drum. **2.** A cause supported ardently and vehemently.

drum•beat•er (drŭm′bē′tər) *n.* One that supports a cause, esp. vehemently. **— drum′beat′ing** *n.*

drum•fire (drŭm′fīr′) *n.* **1.** Heavy continuous gunfire. **2.** Something likened to continuous gunfire.

drum•head (drŭm′hĕd′) *n.* **1.** *Mus.* The membrane stretched over the open end of a drum. **2.** *Naut.* The circular top part of a capstan, used to hold bars for turning.

drum•lin (drŭm′lĭn) *n.* An elongated hill or ridge of glacial drift. [< *drum,* ridge < Ir.Gael. *druim,* back, ridge < OIr.]

drum major *n.* A man who leads a marching band or drum corps, often twirling a baton.

drum majorette *n.* A woman who leads a marching band or drum corps, often twirling a baton. See Usage Note at **-ette.**

drum memory *n. Comp. Sci.* A memory device consisting of a rotating metal cylinder with a magnetizable coating on its outer surface, usu. used as random-access memory.

drum•mer (drŭm′ər) *n. Mus.* One who plays a drum.

Drum•mond•ville (drŭm′ənd-vĭl′). A city of S Quebec, Canada, NE of Montreal. Pop. 27,374.

drum printer *n.* A line printer in which a revolving cylinder acts as the printing element.

drum•stick (drŭm′stĭk′) *n.* **1.** *Mus.* A stick for beating a drum. **2.** The lower part of the leg of a cooked fowl.

drunk (drŭngk) *v.* P.part. of **drink.** *— adj. Usage Problem.* **1.a.** Intoxicated with alcoholic liquor to the point of impairment of physical and mental faculties. **b.** Caused or influenced by intoxication. **2.** Overcome by strong feeling or emotion: *drunk with power.* *— n.* **1.** A drunkard. **2.** A bout of drinking.

Usage Note: As an adjective the form *drunk* is used predicatively while the form *drunken* is now used only attributively: *He was drunk last night. A drunken man sat at the table beside us.* The attributive use of *drunk* is generally unacceptable in formal style. But the phrases *drunk driver* and *drunk driving* are supported not only by common usage but also, in many jurisdictions, by a legal distinction between *drunk driver* (a driver whose alcohol level exceeds the legal limit) and *drunken driver* (a driver who is inebriated).

drunk•ard (drŭng′kərd) *n.* One who is habitually drunk.

drunk•en (drŭng′kən) *adj. Usage Problem.* **1.** Delirious with or as if with strong drink; intoxicated. **2.** Habitually drunk. **3.** Of, involving, or occurring during intoxication. See Usage Note at **drunk. — drunk′en•ly** *adv.* **— drunk′en•ness** *n.*

dru•pa•ceous (drōō-pā′shəs) *adj.* **1.** Resembling, relating to, or consisting of a drupe. **2.** Producing drupes.

drupe (drōōp) *n.* A fleshy fruit, such as a peach, usu. having a single hard stone that encloses a seed. [Lat. *drūpa, druppa,* overripe olive < Gk., olive, poss. an alteration of *drupepēs,* ripened on the tree : *dru-,* tree; see **deru-*** + *peptein, pep-,* ripe; see **pekʷ-*.**]

drupe•let (drōōp′lĭt) *n.* A small drupe, such as one of the many subdivisions of a raspberry or blackberry.

druse (drōōz) *n.* A crust of tiny crystals lining a rock cavity, usu. composed of the same minerals that occur in the rock. [Ger., weathered ore, prob. < MHGer. *druos,* gland, tumor.]

druth•ers (drŭth′ərz) *pl.n. Informal.* A choice or preference.

[Alteration of the phrase *'d rather* < *would rather.*]

Druze also **Druse** (dro͞oz) *n.* A member of a Syrian people following a religion marked by monotheism and a belief in al-Hakim (985–1021), an Ismaili caliph, as the embodiment of God. [Ar. *Durūz,* pl. of *durzī,* a Druse, after Ismail al-*Darazi* (d. c. 1019), Muslim religious leader.]

dry (drī) *adj.* **dri•er** (drī′ər) , **dri•est** (drī′ĭst) or **dry•er** or **dry•est. 1.** Free from liquid or moisture: *dry clothes.* **2.** Having or characterized by little or no rain. **3.** Marked by the absence of natural or normal moisture. **4.** Not under water. **5.** Having all the water or liquid drained away, evaporated, or exhausted: *a dry river.* **6.** No longer yielding liquid, esp. milk. **7.** Lacking a mucous or watery discharge: *a dry cough.* **8.** Not shedding tears. **9.** Needing or desiring drink; thirsty. **10.** No longer wet: *The paint is dry.* **11.** Of or relating to solid rather than liquid substances or commodities: *dry weight.* **12.** Not sweet as a result of the decomposition of sugar during fermentation. Used of wines. **13.** Having a large proportion of strong liquor to other ingredients: *a dry martini.* **14.** Eaten or served without butter, gravy, or other garnish. **15.** Having no adornment or coloration; plain. **16.** Devoid of bias or personal concern. **17.a.** Lacking tenderness, warmth, or involvement; severe. **b.** Matter-of-fact or indifferent in manner. **18.** Wearisome; dull. **19.** Humorous or sarcastic in a shrewd, impersonal way: *dry wit.* **20.** Prohibiting or opposed to the sale or consumption of alcoholic beverages: *a dry law.* **21.** Unproductive of the expected results. **22.** Constructed without mortar or cement: *dry masonry.* —*v.* **dried** (drīd), **dry•ing, dries** (drīz). —*tr.* **1.** To remove the moisture from; make dry. **2.** To preserve (food, for example) by extracting the moisture. —*intr.* To become dry. —*n., pl.* **drys.** *Informal.* A prohibitionist. —***phrasal verbs.*** **dry out.** *Informal.* To undergo a cure for alcoholism. **dry up. 1.** To make or become unproductive, esp. to do so gradually. **2.** *Informal.* To stop talking. [ME *drie* < OE *drȳge.*] —**dry′ly, dri′ly** *adv.* —**dry′ness** *n.*

dry•ad (drī′əd, -ăd′) *n. Gk. Myth.* A divinity presiding over forests and trees; a wood nymph. [ME *Driad* < Lat. *Dryas, Dryad-* < Gk. *Druas* < *drus,* tree. See **deru-***.] —**dry•ad′ic** (-ăd′ĭk) *adj.*

dry•as•dust (drī′əz-dŭst′) *n.* A dull pedant. [After Dr. Jonas *Dryasdust,* a fictitious character to whom Sir Walter Scott dedicated some of his novels.] —**dry′as•dust′** *adj.*

dry cell *n.* A voltage-generating cell having an electrolyte in the form of moist paste.

dry-clean (drī′klēn′) *tr.v.* **-cleaned, -clean•ing, -cleans.** To clean (clothing or fabrics) with chemical solvents that have little or no water. —**dry cleaner** *n.* —**dry clean′ing** *n.*

Dry•den (drīd′n), **John.** 1631–1700. English writer whose works include critical essays, dramas, and poems.

dry dock *n. Naut.* A large dock in the form of a basin from which the water can be emptied, used for building or repairing a ship below its water line.

dry-dock (drī′dŏk′) *tr. & intr.v.* **-docked, -dock•ing, -docks.** *Naut.* To place in or go into a dry dock.

dry•er (drī′ər) *n.* **1.** An appliance that removes moisture by heating or another process: *a hair dryer.* **2.** Var. of **drier**[1].

dry farm•ing (fär′mĭng) *n.* A type of farming practiced in arid areas without irrigation by planting drought-resistant crops and mulching or tilling to protect the soil moisture from evaporation. —**dry farm** *n.* —**dry′-farm′** (drī′färm′) *v.* —**dry farmer** *n.*

dry fly *n.* An artificial fly used in fishing that floats on the surface of the water when cast.

dry gangrene *n.* Gangrene that develops as a result of arterial obstruction and is characterized by mummification of the dead tissue and absence of bacterial decomposition.

dry goods *pl.n.* Textiles, clothing, and related articles of trade.

dry ice *n.* Solid carbon dioxide that sublimates at −78.5°C (−110°F) and is used as a coolant. [Originally a trademark.]

dry•ing oil (drī′ĭng) *n.* An organic oil used as a binder in paints and varnishes.

dry kiln *n.* An oven for drying and seasoning cut lumber.

dry measure *n.* A system of units for measuring dry commodities such as grains, fruits, and vegetables.

dry mop *n.* See **dust mop.**

dry nurse *n.* A nurse employed to care for but not breast-feed an infant. —**dry′-nurse′** (drī′nûrs′) *v.*

dry•o•pith•e•cine (drī′ō-pĭth′ĭ-sēn′) *n.* An extinct ape of the genus *Dryopithecus,* known from Old World Miocene and Pliocene fossils and considered an ancestor of the anthropoid apes and human beings. [< NLat. *Dryopithēcus,* genus name : Gk. *drus,* oak; see **deru-*** + Gk. *pithēkos,* ape.] —**dry′o•pith′e•cine′** *adj.*

dry point *n.* **1.** A technique of intaglio engraving in which a hard steel needle is used to incise lines in a metal plate, with the rough burr at the sides of the incised lines often retained. **2.** An engraving or print made using this technique.

dry rot *n.* **1.** A fungous disease that causes timber to become brittle and crumble into powder. **2.** A plant disease in which the plant tissue remains dry while bulbs, fruits, or woody tissues decay.

dry run *n.* **1.** A trial exercise; a rehearsal. **2.** A test exercise in combat skills without the use of live ammunition.

dry-salt•er (drī′sôl′tər) *n. Chiefly British.* A dealer in chemical products and dyes. —**dry′salt′er•y** *n.*

dry socket *n.* A painful inflamed condition at the site of extraction of a tooth that occurs when a blood clot fails to form properly or is dislodged.

Dry Tor•tu•gas (drī tôr-to͞o′gəz). An island group of S FL W of Key West; named *Tortugas* ("turtles") by Ponce de León.

dry wall or **dry•wall** (drī′wôl′) *n.* **1.a.** Plasterboard. **b.** A wall or ceiling constructed of a prefabricated material, such as plasterboard or paneling. **2.** A wall constructed from rocks that are not cemented together.

dry wash *n.* Cleaned but not ironed laundry.

dry well also **dry•well** (drī′wĕl′) *n.* A subterranean chamber near a building, with stones or gravel inside, used to collect rainwater from the roof to prevent soil erosion.

d.s. *abbr.* Also **D.S.** *Mus.* Dal segno.

DSC or **D.S.C.** *abbr.* Distinguished Service Cross.

DSM or **D.S.M.** *abbr.* Distinguished Service Medal.

DSO or **D.S.O.** *abbr.* Distinguished Service Order.

DST or **D.S.T.** *abbr.* Daylight-saving time.

Dt. *abbr. Bible.* Deuteronomy.

D.T. *abbr.* Doctor of Theology.

D.T.'s or **d.t.'s** (dē′tēz′) *n. (used with a sing. or pl. v.)* Delirium tremens.

Du. *abbr.* **1.** Duke. **2.** Dutch.

du•ad (do͞o′ăd′, dyo͞o′-) *n.* A unit of two objects; a pair. [Gk. *duas, duad-,* two < *duo.* See **dwo-***.]

du•al (do͞o′əl, dyo͞o′-) *adj.* **1.** Composed of two usu. like or complementary parts; double. **2.** Having a double character or purpose. **3.** *Gram.* Of, relating to, or being a number category that indicates two persons or things. —*n. Gram.* **1.** The dual number. **2.** An inflected form of a noun, adjective, pronoun, or verb used with two items or people. [Lat. *duālis* < *duo,* two. See **dwo-***.] —**du′al•ly** *adv.*

Du•a•la (do͞o-ä′lä). See **Douala.**

du•al•ism (do͞o′ə-lĭz′əm, dyo͞o′-) *n.* **1.** The state of being double; duality. **2.** *Philos.* The view that the world consists of or is explicable as two basic entities, such as mind and matter. **3.** *Psychol.* The view that the mind and body function separately, without interchange. **4.** *Theol.* **a.** The view that the world is ruled by the antagonistic forces of good and evil. **b.** The view that human beings have two basic natures, the physical and the spiritual. —**du′al•ist** *n.* —**du′al•is′tic** *adj.* —**du′al•is′ti•cal•ly** *adv.*

du•al•i•ty (do͞o-ăl′ĭ-tē, dyo͞o-) *n.* The quality or character of being twofold; dichotomy.

du•al-pur•pose (do͞o′əl-pûr′pəs, dyo͞o′-) *adj.* Designed for or serving two purposes.

Duar•te (dwär′tē). A city of S CA E of Pasadena. Pop. 20,688.

dub[1] (dŭb) *tr.v.* **dubbed, dub•bing, dubs. 1.** To tap lightly on the shoulder to confer knighthood. **2.** To honor with a new title or description. **3.** To give a name to facetiously or playfully; nickname. **4.** To strike, cut, or rub (timber, for example) so as to make even or smooth. **5.** To dress (a fowl). **6.** To execute (a golf stroke, for example) poorly. —*n.* An awkward person or player; a bungler. [ME *dubben* < OE *dubbian,* perh. < OFr. *aduber.*]

dub[2] (dŭb) *v.* **dubbed, dub•bing, dubs.** —*tr.* **1.** To thrust at; poke. **2.** To beat (a drum). —*intr.* **1.** To make a thrust. **2.** To beat on a drum. —*n.* **1.** The act of dubbing. **2.** A drumbeat. [Perh. < LGer. *dubben,* to hit, strike.]

dub[3] (dŭb) *tr.v.* **dubbed, dub•bing, dubs. 1.a.** To transfer (recorded material) onto a new recording medium. **b.** To copy (a record or tape). **2.** To insert a new soundtrack, esp. a synchronized translation of the original dialogue, into (a film). **3.** To add (sound) into a film or tape. —*n.* **1.** The new sounds added by dubbing. **2.** A dubbed tape or record. [Short for DOUBLE.] —**dub′ber** *n.*

dub[4] (dŭb) *n. Scots.* A puddle or small pool. [?]

Du•bai (do͞o-bī′). A city and sheikdom of E United Arab Emirates on the Persian Gulf. Pop. 265,702.

Du Bar•ry (do͞o băr′ē, dyo͞o-, dü bä-rē′), Comtesse. Marie Jeanne Bécu. "Madame Du Barry." 1743–93. French courtier and influential lover of Louis XV.

Du•bawnt (do͞o-bônt′). A river, c. 933 km (580 mi), of SE Northwest Terrs., Canada, flowing through **Dubawnt Lake.**

dub•bin (dŭb′ĭn) also **dub•bing** (-ĭng) *n.* An application of tallow and oil for dressing leather. [< DUB[1].]

Dub•ček (do͝ob′chĕk, do͝op′-), **Alexander.** 1921–92. Czechoslovakian politician who became head of a democratically elected parliament in 1990.

du Bel•lay (do͞o bə-lā′, dü bĕ-lā′), **Joachim.** See Joachim du **Bellay.**

du•bi•e•ty (do͞o-bī′ĭ-tē, dyo͞o-) *n., pl.* **-ties. 1.** A feeling of doubt that often results in wavering. See Syns at **uncertainty. 2.** A matter of doubt. [LLat. *dubietās* < Lat. *dubius,* doubtful. See DUBIOUS.]

Du•bin•sky (do͞o-bĭn′skē), **David.** 1892–1982. Russian-born Amer. labor leader who was president of the International Ladies' Garment Workers Union (1932–66).

ă pat	oi boy
ā pay	ou out
âr care	o͝o took
ä father	o͞o boot
ĕ pet	ŭ cut
ē be	ûr urge
ĭ pit	th thin
ī pie	*th* this
îr pier	hw which
ŏ pot	zh vision
ō toe	ə about, item
ô paw	

Stress marks:
′ (primary);
′ (secondary), as in
dictionary (dĭk′shə-nĕr′ē)

du•bi•ous (do͞o′bē-əs, dyo͞o′-) *adj.* **1.** Fraught with uncertainty or doubt; undecided. **2.** Arousing doubt; doubtful. **3.** Of questionable character. [< Lat. *dubius.* See **dwo-*.**] —**du′bi•ous•ly** *adv.* —**du′bi•ous•ness** *n.*

du•bi•ta•ble (do͞o′bĭ-tə-bəl, dyo͞o′-) *adj.* Subject to doubt or question; uncertain. [Lat. *dubitābilis* < *dubitāre,* to doubt. See DOUBT.] —**du′bi•ta•bly** *adv.*

Dub•lin (dŭb′lĭn). **1.** The cap. of Ireland, in the E-central part on the Irish Sea; scene of the Easter Rebellion of Apr. 24, 1916. Pop. 525,882. **2.** A city of central GA ESE of Macon. Pop. 16,312. —**Dub′lin•er** *n.*

Du Bois (do͞o bois′), **William Edward Burghardt.** 1868–1963. Amer. civil rights leader who cofounded the NAACP.

W.E.B. Du Bois

Du•bon•net (do͞o′bə-nā′, dyo͞o′-). A trademark used for apéritif wines.

Du•bos (do͞o-bôs′, -bō′, dü-), **René Jules.** 1901–82. French-born Amer. bacteriologist noted for his research on natural antibiotics.

Du•brov•nik (do͞o′brôv-nĭk′). Formerly **Ra•gu•sa** (rə-go͞o′zə, rä-go͞o′zä). A city of extreme S Croatia on the Adriatic Sea; medieval center of Serbo-Croatian culture and literature. Pop. 31,106.

Du•buf•fet (do͞o-bə-fā′, dü-bü-fĕ′), **Jean.** b. 1901. French artist known for his *art brut,* or "raw art."

Du•buque (də-byo͞ok′). A city of E IA on the Mississippi R. opposite the IL-WI border; settled in 1833. Pop. 57,546.

du•cal (do͞o′kəl, dyo͞o′-) *adj.* Of or relating to a duke or dukedom. [ME < OFr. < LLat. *ducālis* < Lat. *dux, duc-,* leader. See DUKE.] —**du′cal•ly** *adv.*

duc•at (dŭk′ət) *n.* **1.** Any of various gold coins formerly used in certain European countries. **2.** *Slang.* **a.** A piece of money. **b.** An admission ticket. [ME < OFr. < OItal. *ducato* < Med.Lat. *ducātus,* duchy. See DUCHY.]

du•ce (do͞o′chā) *n.* A leader or commander; a chief. [Ital. < Lat. *dux, duc-.* See DUKE.]

Du•champ (do͞o-shäɴ′, dü), **Marcel.** 1887–1968. French-born artist known for *Nude Descending a Staircase* (1912).

Du•chenne's muscular dystrophy (do͞o-shĕnz′) *n.* The most common form of muscular dystrophy, affecting almost exclusively males, beginning in early childhood and usu. causing death before adulthood. [After Guillaume B.A. *Duchenne* (1806–75), French physician.]

duch•ess (dŭch′ĭs) *n.* **1.** A noblewoman of the highest rank, esp. in British peerage. **2.** A woman holding title to a duchy in her own right. **3.** The wife or widow of a duke. **4.** Used as the title for such a noblewoman. [ME *duchesse* < OFr. < Med.Lat. *ducissa* < Lat. *dux, duc-,* leader. See DUKE.]

duch•y (dŭch′ē) *n., pl.* **-ies.** The territory ruled by a duke or duchess; a dukedom. [ME *duchie* < OFr. *duche* < Med.Lat. *ducātus* < Lat. *dux, duc-,* leader. See DUKE.]

duck¹ (dŭk) *n.* **1.** Any of various wild or domesticated swimming birds of the family Anatidae, characteristically having a broad flat bill, short legs, and webbed feet. **2.** A female duck. **3.** The flesh of a duck used as food. **4.** *Slang.* A person, esp. one thought of as peculiar. **5.** *Chiefly British.* A dear. Often used in the plural with a singular verb. [ME *doke* < OE *dūce,* poss. < **dūcan,* to dive. See DUCK².]

ducking stool

duck² (dŭk) *v.* **ducked, duck•ing, ducks.** —*tr.* **1.** To lower quickly, esp. so as to avoid something. **2.** To evade; dodge: *duck responsibility.* **3.** To push suddenly under water. **4.** *Games.* To deliberately play a card that is lower than (an opponent's card). —*intr.* **1.** To lower the head or body. **2.** To move swiftly, esp. so as to escape being seen. **3.** To submerge the head or body briefly in water. **4.** To evade a responsibility or obligation. Often used with *out.* **5.** *Games.* To lose a trick by deliberately playing lower than one's opponent. —*n.* **1.** A quick lowering of the head or body. **2.** A plunge into water. [ME *douken,* to dive, poss. < OE **dūcan*; akin to MLGer. and MDu. *dūken.*] —**duck′er** *n.*

duck³ (dŭk) *n.* **1.** A durable, closely woven heavy cotton or linen fabric. **2. ducks.** Clothing made of duck, esp. white trousers. [Du. *doek,* cloth < MDu. *doec.*]

duck⁴ (dŭk) *n.* **1.** An amphibious military truck used during World War II. **2.** An amphibious truck used in emergencies, as to evacuate flood victims. [Alteration (influenced by DUCK¹) of *DUKW,* its code designation.]

duck•bill (dŭk′bĭl′) *n.* See **platypus.**

duck-billed platypus (dŭk′bĭld′) *n.* See **platypus.**

duck•board (dŭk′bôrd′, -bōrd′) *n.* A board or boardwalk laid across wet or muddy ground or flooring.

duck hawk *n.* See **peregrine falcon.**

duck•ing stool (dŭk′ĭng) *n.* A device formerly used in Europe and New England for punishment, consisting of a chair in which an offender was tied and ducked into water.

duck•ling (dŭk′lĭng) *n.* A young duck.

duck•pin (dŭk′pĭn′) *n. Sports.* **1.** A bowling pin that is shorter and squatter than a tenpin. **2. duckpins.** *(used with a sing. v.)* A bowling game played with such pins and a small ball.

ducks and drakes (dŭks) *n. Games.* The game of skipping flat stones along the surface of water. —***idiom.*** **make ducks and drakes of** (or **play ducks and drakes with**). To squander; waste.

Daphne du Maurier

duck soup *n. Slang.* An easily accomplished task.

duck•tail (dŭk′tāl′) *n.* A hairstyle in which the hair is swept back at the sides to meet in an upturned point in back.

duck•weed (dŭk′wēd′) *n.* Any of various small, free-floating, stemless aquatic flowering plants of the genus *Lemna.*

duck•y (dŭk′ē) *adj.* **-i•er, -i•est.** *Slang.* Excellent; fine.

Du•com•mun (dü-kô-mœɴ′), **Elie.** 1833–1906. Swiss journalist who shared the 1902 Nobel Peace Prize.

duct (dŭkt) *n.* **1.** An often enclosed passage or channel for conveying a substance, esp. a liquid or gas. **2.** *Anat.* A tubular body canal or passage, esp. one for carrying a glandular secretion: *a tear duct.* **3.** A tube or pipe for enclosing electrical cables or wires. —*tr.v.* **duct•ed, duct•ing, ducts. 1.** To channel through a duct: *duct the moist air away.* **2.** To supply with ducts. [Lat. *ductus,* act of leading < p.part. of *dūcere,* to lead. See **deuk-*.**] —**duct′al** *adj.* —**duct′less** *adj.*

duc•tile (dŭk′təl, -tīl′) *adj.* **1.** Easily drawn into wire or hammered thin. **2.** Easily molded or shaped. **3.** Capable of being readily persuaded or influenced. [ME *ductil* < OFr. < Lat. *ductilis* < *ductus,* p.part. of *dūcere,* to lead. See **deuk-*.**] —**duc•til′i•ty** (-tĭl′ĭ-tē), **duc′ti•li•bil′i•ty** (-lə-bĭl′ĭ-tē) *n.*

duct•ing (dŭk′tĭng) *n.* **1.** A duct or system of ducts. **2.** Material for making ducts.

duct•less gland (dŭkt′lĭs) *n.* See **endocrine gland.**

duct•ule (dŭk′to͞ol′) *n.* A small duct.

duct•work (dŭkt′wûrk′) *n.* A group or system of ducts.

dud (dŭd) *n.* **1.** A bomb, shell, or explosive round that fails to detonate. **2.** *Informal.* One that is disappointingly ineffective or unsuccessful. **3. duds.** *Informal.* **a.** Clothing. **b.** Personal belongings. [ME *dudde,* a cloak.]

dude (do͞od, dyo͞od) *n.* **1.** *Informal.* An Easterner or city person who vacations on a ranch in the West. **2.** *Informal.* A man who is very fancy or sharp in dress and demeanor. **3.** *Slang.* A person, esp. a man or boy. —*tr.v.* **dud•ed, dud•ing, dudes.** *Slang.* To dress elaborately or flamboyantly. [?]

du•deen (do͞o-dēn′) *n.* A short-stemmed clay pipe. [Ir.Gael. *dúidín,* dim. of *dúd,* stump, pipe.]

dude ranch *n.* A resort patterned after a Western ranch, with outdoor activities such as horseback riding.

dudg•eon¹ (dŭj′ən) *n.* A sullen, angry, or indignant humor. [?]

dudg•eon² (dŭj′ən) *n.* **1.** *Obsolete.* A wood used to make knife handles. **2.** *Archaic.* **a.** A dagger with a hilt of this wood. **b.** The hilt of a dagger. [ME *dogeon,* poss. < AN.]

Dud•ley (dŭd′lē). A borough of W-central England WNW of Birmingham. Pop. 300,700.

Dudley, Robert. 1st Earl of Leicester. 1532?–88. English courtier, politician, and favorite of Elizabeth I.

Dudley, Thomas. 1576–1653. English colonial administrator who served as governor of Massachusetts Bay Colony (1634, 1640, 1645, and 1650).

due (do͞o, dyo͞o) *adj.* **1.** Payable immediately or on demand. **2.** Owed as a debt; owing. **3.** In accord with right, convention, or courtesy; appropriate. **4.** Meeting special requirements; sufficient: *due cause.* **5.** Expected or scheduled, esp. appointed to arrive. **6.a.** Anticipated; looked for. **b.** Expecting or ready for something as part of a normal course or sequence. **7.** *Usage Problem.* Capable of being attributed. See Usage Note at **due to.** —*n.* **1.** Something owed or deserved: *received your due.* **2. dues.** A charge or fee for membership, as in a club. —*adv.* **1.** Straight; directly: *Go due west.* **2.** *Archaic.* Duly. [ME < OFr. *deu,* p.part. of *devoir,* to owe < Lat. *dēbēre.* See **ghabh-*.**]

due bill *n.* A written acknowledgment of indebtedness to a given party but not payable to order or transferable by endorsement.

du•el (do͞o′əl, dyo͞o′-) *n.* **1.** A prearranged formal combat between two persons, usu. over a point of honor. **2.** A struggle for domination between two contending persons, groups, or ideas. —*v.* **-eled, -el•ing, -els** or **-elled, -el•ling, -els.** —*tr.* **1.** To engage (another) in or as if in formal combat. **2.** To oppose actively and forcefully. —*intr.* To engage in or as if in formal combat. [ME *duelle* < Med.Lat. *duellum* < Lat., war, var. of *bellum.*] —**du′el•er, du′el•ist** *n.*

du•en•de (do͞o-ĕn′dā′) *n.* The ability to attract others by personal magnetism and charm. [Sp. dial. < Sp., ghost.]

due process *n. Law.* A set course for judicial or other government activities designed to protect the individual's legal rights.

Due•ro (dwĕr′ō). See **Douro.**

du•et (do͞o-ĕt′, dyo͞o-) *n.* **1.** *Mus.* **a.** A composition for two voices or instruments. **b.** The two performers of a duet. **2.** A pair. [Ital. *duetto,* dim. of *duo* < Lat., two. See **dwo-*.**]

due to *prep.* Because of.

Usage Note: *Due to* has been widely used for many years as a compound preposition like *owing to,* but some critics have insisted that the adjectival status of *due* must be retained. According to this view, it is incorrect to say *The concert was canceled due to the rain,* as opposed to the acceptable *The cancellation of the concert was due to the rain.*

Du•fay (do͞o-fā′, dü-), **Guillaume.** 1400?–74. Flemish composer particularly known for his Mass compositions.

duff¹ (dŭf) *n.* A stiff flour pudding boiled in a cloth bag or steamed. [Dialectal variation of DOUGH.]

duff[2] (dŭf) *n.* **1.** Decaying leaves and branches covering a forest floor. **2.** Fine coal; slack. [?]

duff[3] (dŭf) *n. Slang.* The buttocks. [?]

duf•fel or **duf•fle** (dŭf′əl) *n.* **1.** A blanket fabric made of low-grade woolen cloth with a nap on both sides. **2.** Clothing and other personal gear carried by a camper. [Du., after *Duffel*, a town of N Belgium.]

duff•er (dŭf′ər) *n.* **1.** *Informal.* **a.** An incompetent or dull-witted person. **b.** A casual or mediocre player of a sport, esp. golf. **2.** *Slang.* A peddler of cheap merchandise. **3.** *Slang.* Something worthless or useless. [?]

duffle bag or **duffel bag** *n.* A large cylindrical cloth bag of canvas or duck for carrying personal belongings.

duffle coat or **duffel coat** *n.* A warm, usu. hooded coat made of duffel or a similar material and fastened with toggles.

Du•fy (do͞o-fē′, dü-), **Raoul.** 1877–1953. French painter noted for his brightly colored scenes of racing and the seaside.

dug[1] (dŭg) *n.* An udder, breast, or teat of a female animal. [?]

dug[2] (dŭg) *v.* P.t. and p.part. of **dig.**

du•gong (do͞o′gŏng′, -gông′) *n.* A herbivorous marine mammal *(Dugong dugon)* of the Indian Ocean having flipperlike forelimbs and a deeply notched tail fin. [NLat. *Dugong*, genus name, poss. < Malay *duyong.*]

dug•out (dŭg′out′) *n.* **1.** A boat or canoe made of a hollowed-out log. **2.** A pit dug into the ground or on a hillside and used as a shelter. **3.** *Baseball.* Either of two shelters at the side of a field where the players stay while not on the field.

Du•ha•mel (do͞o′ə-mĕl′, dyo͞o′-, dü-ä-), **Georges.** 1884–1966. French writer and physician whose romans-fleuves include *Life and Adventures of Salavin* (1920–32).

dui•ker (dī′kər) *n.* Any of various small African antelopes of the genera *Cephalopus* or *Sylvicapra.* [Afr. < Du. *duiken*, to dive < MDu. *dūken.*]

Duis•burg (do͞os′bûrg′, do͞oz′-, düs′bo͝ork′). A city of W-central Germany at the confluence of the Rhine and Ruhr rivers. Pop. 522,829.

duke (do͞ok, dyo͞ok) *n.* **1.** A nobleman of the highest rank, esp. in British peerage. **2.** A sovereign prince who rules an independent duchy in some European countries. **3.** Used as the title for such a nobleman. **4.** *Slang.* A fist. Often used in the plural: *Put up your dukes!* **5.** *Bot.* A type of cherry intermediate between a sweet and a sour cherry. *—intr.v.* **duked, duk•ing, dukes.** To fight, esp. with fists. [ME < OFr. *duc* < Lat. *dux, duc-*, leader < *dūcere*, to lead. See **deuk-*.**]

duke•dom (do͞ok′dəm, dyo͞ok′-) *n.* **1.** A duchy. **2.** The office, rank, or title of a duke.

Du•kho•bor also **Dou•kho•bor** (do͞o′kə-bôr′) *n.* A member of a Russian Christian movement founded in the 18th century and marked by rejection of ecclesiastical and state authority. [Russ. *Dukhobor* : *dukh*, spirit, Holy Ghost + *-bor*, fighter (< *borot'sya*, to fight).]

Dul•bec•co (dŭl-bĕk′ō), **Renato.** b. 1914. Italian-born Amer. virologist who shared a 1975 Nobel Prize.

dul•cet (dŭl′sĭt) *adj.* **1.a.** Pleasing to the ear; melodious. **b.** Having a soothing agreeable quality. **2.** *Archaic.* Sweet to the taste. [Alteration of ME *doucet* < OFr., dim. of *douce*, fem. of *doux*, sweet < Lat. *dulcis.*] **—dul′cet•ly** *adv.*

dul•ci•fy (dŭl′sə-fī′) *tr.v.* **-fied, -fy•ing, -fies. 1.** To make agreeable or gentle; mollify. **2.** To sweeten. [LLat. *dulcificāre*, to sweeten : Lat. *dulcis*, sweet + *-ficāre*, -fy.] **—dul′ci•fi•ca′tion** (-fĭ-kā′shən) *n.*

dul•ci•mer (dŭl′sə-mər) *n. Mus.* An instrument with wire strings stretched over a sound box, played by striking with two padded hammers or by plucking. [Alteration (influenced by Lat. *dulcis*, sweet) of ME *doucemer* < OFr. *doulcemer, doulcemele*, prob. < Lat. *dulce melos*, sweet song : *dulce*, neut. of *dulcis*, sweet + *melos*, song (< Gk. *melos*).]

dull (dŭl) *adj.* **dull•er, dull•est. 1.** Intellectually weak or obtuse; stupid. **2.** Lacking responsiveness or alertness; insensitive. **3.** Dispirited; depressed. **4.** Not brisk or rapid; sluggish. **5.** Not having a sharp edge or point; blunt. **6.** Not intensely or keenly felt. **7.** Arousing no interest or curiosity; boring. **8.** Not bright or vivid. Used of a color. **9.** Cloudy or overcast. **10.** Not clear or resonant: *a dull thud.* *—tr. & intr.v.* **dulled, dull•ing, dulls.** To make or become dull. [ME *dul*; akin to OE *dol.*] **—dull′ish** *adj.* **—dull′ness, dul′ness** *n.* **—dul′ly** *adv.*

dull•ard (dŭl′ərd) *n.* One regarded as mentally dull; a dolt.

Dul•les (dŭl′ĭs), **John Foster.** 1888–1959. Amer. diplomat who served as U.S. secretary of state (1953–59).

dulls•ville (dŭlz′vĭl) *n. Slang.* A dull place, thing, or state.

dulse (dŭls) *n.* An edible red alga *(Palmaria palmata)* that grows on rocky shores on both sides of the northern Atlantic Ocean. [Sc.Gael. *duileasg* < OIr. *duilesc.*]

Du•luth (də-lo͞oth′). A city of NE MN on Lake Superior opposite Superior WI; settled in the 1850's. Pop. 85,493.

du•ly (do͞o′lē, dyo͞o′-) *adv.* **1.** In a proper manner. **2.** At the expected time. [ME *duely* < *due*, due. See DUE.]

du•ma (do͞o′mə) *n.* A Russian national parliament during czarist times. [Russ., of Gmc. orig. See **dhē-*.**]

Du•mas (do͞o-mä′, dyo͞o-, dü-), **Alexandre.** "Dumas *père.*" 1802–70. French writer of historical romances, such as *The Count of Monte Cristo* and *The Three Musketeers* (both 1844). His son **Alexandre** (1824–95), "Dumas *fils,*" was a dramatist whose works include *La Dame aux Camélias* (1852).

du Mau•ri•er (do͞o môr′ē-ā′, dyo͞o, dü mô-ryā′), Dame **Daphne.** 1907–89. British writer best known for *Rebecca* (1938).

du Maurier, George Louis Palmella Busson. 1834–96. British illustrator and writer noted for his caricatures in *Punch* and his novel *Trilby* (1894).

dumb (dŭm) *adj.* **dumb•er, dumb•est. 1.a.** Lacking the power of speech. Used of animals and inanimate objects. **b.** *Offensive.* Incapable of using speech; mute. Used of human beings. **2.** Temporarily speechless, as with shock or fear: *dumb with disbelief.* **3.** Unwilling to speak; taciturn. **4.** Not expressed or articulated in sounds or words. **5.** Conspicuously unintelligent; stupid. **6.** Unintentional; haphazard: *dumb luck.* **7.** *Comp. Sci.* Incapable of processing data. *—tr.v.* **dumbed, dumb•ing, dumbs.** To make silent or dumb. [ME < OE.] **—dumb′ly** *adv.* **—dumb′ness** *n.*

Syns: *dumb, inarticulate, mute, speechless.* The central meaning shared by these adjectives is "lacking the faculty of speech or the power to speak": *was struck dumb with stage fright; inarticulate with rage; mute with astonishment; speechless with horror.*

dumb•bell (dŭm′bĕl′) *n.* **1.** A weight consisting of a short bar with a metal ball or disk at each end that is lifted for muscular exercise. **2.** *Slang.* One regarded as stupid. [< an apparatus like that used to ring a church bell but without the bell.]

dumb cane *n.* See **dieffenbachia.** [So called because its leaves contain a substance that swells the throat when eaten.]

dumb•found also **dum•found** (dŭm′found′) *tr.v.* **-found•ed, -found•ing, -founds.** To fill with astonishment and perplexity; confound. [DUMB + (CON)FOUND.]

dum•bo (dŭm′bō) *n., pl.* **-bos.** *Slang.* A stupid person.

dumb plant *n.* See **dieffenbachia.** [See DUMB CANE.]

dumb show *n.* **1.** A part of a play, esp. in medieval and Renaissance drama, enacted silently. **2.** Communication or acting by expressive gestures; pantomine.

dumb•struck (dŭm′strŭk′) *adj.* So shocked or astonished as to be rendered speechless.

dumb•wait•er (dŭm′wā′tər) *n.* **1.** A small elevator used to convey food or other goods from one floor of a building to another. **2.** A portable serving stand or table.

dumbwaiter

dum•dum bullet (dum′dum′) *n.* A hollow-point small-arms bullet designed to expand upon impact, inflicting a gaping wound. [After *Dum Dum*, a town of NE India.]

dumm•kopf (do͝om′kôf′, -kôpf′, dŭm′-) *n.* A person regarded as stupid. [Ger. : *dumm*, dumb (< MHGer. *tump, tumb* < OHGer. *tumb*) + *kopf*, head (< MHGer., cup, cranium < OHGer., cup < LLat. *cuppa*).]

dum•my (dŭm′ē) *n., pl.* **-mies. 1.** An imitation of a real or original object, intended as a practical substitute. **2.a.** A mannequin for displaying clothes. **b.** A figure manipulated by a ventriloquist. **c.** A stuffed or pasteboard figure used as a target. **d.** *Football.* A heavy stuffed cylindrical bag used for blocking and tackling practice. **3.** A person regarded as stupid. **4.** A silent or taciturn person. **5.** A person or an agency secretly in the service of another. **6.** *Print.* **a.** One of a set of model pages with text and illustrations pasted into place to direct the printer. **b.** A set of bound blank pages used as a model to show the size and general appearance of a book being published. **7.** *Games.* **a.** The partner in bridge whose exposed hand is played by the declarer. **b.** The hand thus exposed. **8.** *Comp. Sci.* A character or other piece of information entered into a computer only to meet prescribed conditions, such as word length, and not affecting operations. *—adj.* **1.** Simulating or replacing something but lacking its function. **2.** Serving as a front or cover for another: *a dummy corporation.* **3.** *Comp. Sci.* Entered or provided only to meet prescribed conditions: *a dummy variable.* *—tr.v.* **-mied, -my•ing, -mies.** *Print.* To make a model of (a publication or page). **—*phrasal verb.*** **dummy up.** *Slang.* To keep silence; clam up. [< DUMB.]

dummy
Young performer with a ventriloquist's dummy

Du•mont (do͞o′mŏnt′, dyo͞o′-). A borough of NE NJ, a suburb of Hackensack; settled in 1677. Pop. 17,187.

dump (dŭmp) *v.* **dumped, dump•ing, dumps.** *—tr.* **1.** To release or throw down in a large mass. **2.a.** To empty (material) out of a container or vehicle. **b.** To empty out (a container or vehicle), as by overturning or tilting. **3.a.** To get rid of; discard. **b.** *Informal.* To discard or reject unceremoniously. **4.** To place (goods or stock, for example) on the market in large quantities and at a low price. **5.** *Comp. Sci.* To transfer (data stored internally in a computer) from one place to another without processing. **6.** *Slang.* To knock down; beat. *—intr.* **1.** To fall or drop abruptly. **2.** To discharge cargo or contents; unload. **3.** *Slang.* To criticize another severely. *—n.* **1.** A place where refuse is dumped. **2.** A storage place for goods or supplies; a depot. **3.** An unordered accumulation; a pile. **4.** *Comp. Sci.* An instance or the result of dumping stored data. **5.** *Slang.* A poorly maintained or disreputable place. [ME *dumpen*, to fall suddenly, drop, of Scand. orig.] **—dump′er** *n.*

dump•ling (dŭmp′lĭng) *n.* **1.** A small ball of dough cooked

ă pat	oi boy
ā pay	ou out
âr care	o͝o took
ä father	o͞o boot
ĕ pet	ŭ cut
ē be	ûr urge
ĭ pit	th thin
ī pie	*th* this
îr pier	hw which
ŏ pot	zh vision
ō toe	ə about,
ô paw	item

Stress marks:
′ (primary);
′ (secondary), as in
dictionary (dĭk′shə-nĕr′ē)

with stew or soup. **2.** Sweetened dough wrapped around fruit, baked and served as a dessert. **3.** *Informal.* A short chubby creature. [?]

dumps (dŭmps) *pl.n.* A gloomy, melancholy state of mind; depression. Often used with *the.* [Prob. < Du. *domp,* haze < MDu. *damp,* vapor.]

dump•site (dŭmp′sīt′) *n.* The location of a dump, esp. a garbage dump.

Dump•ster (dŭmp′stər). A trademark used for containers designed for receiving, transporting, and dumping waste materials.

dump truck *n.* A heavy-duty truck having a bed that tilts backward to dump loose material.

Isadora Duncan

dump•y^{1} (dŭm′pē) *adj.* **-i•er, -i•est.** Short and stout. [Prob. < *dump,* lump.] **—dump′i•ly** *adv.* **—dump′i•ness** *n.*

dum•py^{2} (dŭm′pē) *adj.* **-i•er, -i•est.** Resembling a dump, as in shabbiness; disreputable.

dumpy level *n.* A surveyor's instrument having a short telescope fixed rigidly to a horizontally rotating table.

Dum•yat (do͝om-yät′). See **Damietta.**

dun^{1} (dŭn) *tr.v.* **dunned, dun•ning, duns.** To importune (a debtor) for payment. —*n.* **1.** One that duns. **2.** An importunate demand for payment. [?]

dun^{2} (dŭn) *n.* **1.** *Color.* An almost neutral brownish gray to dull grayish brown. **2.** A fishing fly having this color. **3.** A horse of this color. [ME < OE *dunn,* perh. of Celt. orig.]

Du•nant (do͞o-näɴ′, dü-), **Jean Henri.** 1828–1910. Swiss philanthropist who founded the International Red Cross (1864) and shared the 1901 Nobel Peace Prize.

Dun•bar (dŭn′bär), **Paul Laurence.** 1872–1906. Amer. writer noted for his poetry, as in *Lyrics of Lowly Life* (1896).

Dun•bar (dŭn-bär′), **William.** 1460?–1520? Scottish poet whose works include *The Thrissill and the Rois* (1503).

Dun•can (dŭng′kən). A city of S OK SSW of Oklahoma City. Pop. 21,732.

Duncan, Isadora. 1878–1927. Amer. dancer whose simple costumes and free movement greatly influenced modern dance.

Dun•can•ville (dŭng′kən-vĭl′). A city of NE TX, a suburb of Dallas. Pop. 35,748.

dunce (dŭns) *n.* A person regarded as stupid. [After John Duns Scotus, whose writings were ridiculed in the 16th century.]

dunce cap also **dunce's cap** (dŭn′sĭz) *n.* A cone-shaped paper cap, formerly placed on the head of a slow or lazy pupil.

Dun•das (dŭn′dəs). A town of SE Ontario, Canada, a suburb of Hamilton. Pop. 19,586.

Dun•dee (dŭn-dē′). A burgh of E-central Scotland on the N bank of the Firth of Tay; a stronghold of the Covenanters in the Scottish Reformation. Pop. 185,616.

dun•der•head (dŭn′dər-hĕd′) *n.* A dunce. [Perh. Du. *donder,* thunder (< MDu. *doner;* see **(s)tenə-***) + head.]

dun•drear•ies (dŭn-drîr′ēz) *pl.n.* Long sideburns worn with a clean-shaven chin. [After Lord *Dundreary,* a character in the play *Our American Cousin* by Tom Taylor (1817–80).]

dune (do͞on, dyo͞on) *n.* A hill or ridge of wind-blown sand. [Fr. < OFr. < MDu. *dūne.* See **dhū-no-*.**]

dune buggy *n.* A recreational vehicle having oversize tires designed for use on sand dunes or beaches.

dune buggy

Dun•e•din (dŭn-ēd′n). **1.** A city of SE South I., New Zealand; settled in 1848. Pop. 74,500. **2.** A city of W-central FL on the Gulf of Mexico W of Tampa. Pop. 34,012.

Dun•ferm•line (dŭn-fûrm′lĭn). A burgh of E-central Scotland NW of Edinburgh; long a royal residence. Pop. 53,800.

dung (dŭng) *n.* **1.a.** Animal excrement. **b.** Manure. **2.** Something foul or abhorrent. —*tr.v.* **dunged, dung•ing, dungs.** To fertilize (land) with manure. [ME < OE.] **—dung′y** *adj.*

dun•ga•ree (dŭng′gə-rē′) *n.* **1.** A sturdy, often blue denim fabric. **2. dungarees.** Pants or overalls made of this. [Hindi *dungrī.*]

dung beetle *n.* Any of various beetles of the family Scarabaeidae that form balls of dung on which they feed and in which they lay their eggs.

Dun•ge•ness crab (dŭn′jə-nĕs′, -nĭs) *n.* An edible crab *(Cancer magister)* common along the Pacific coast from Alaska to northern California. [After *Dungeness,* a town of NW WA.]

dun•geon (dŭn′jən) *n.* **1.** A dark, often underground chamber or cell used to confine prisoners. **2.** A donjon. [ME *donjon,* castle keep, dungeon < OFr., keep, prob. < Med.Lat. *domniō,* the lord's tower < Lat. *dominus,* master. See **dem-*.**]

dung•hill (dŭng′hĭl′) *n.* **1.** A heap of animal excrement. **2.** A foul degraded condition or place.

du•nite (do͞o′nīt′, dŭn′īt′) *n.* A dense igneous rock that consists mainly of olivine and is a source of magnesium. [After Mt. *Dun* in N S I., New Zealand.] **—du•nit′ic** (do͞o-nĭt′ĭk, də-) *adj.*

dunk (dŭngk) *v.* **dunked, dunk•ing, dunks.** —*tr.* **1.** To plunge into liquid; immerse. **2.** To dip (food) into a liquid before eating it. **3.** *Basketball.* To slam (a ball) through the basket from above. —*intr.* **1.** To submerge oneself briefly in water. **2.** *Basketball.* To make a dunk shot. —*n.* **1.** The act or an instance of dunking. **2.** *Basketball.* A dunk shot. [Penn.Du. *dunke* < MHGer. *dunken* < OHGer. *dunkōn.*] **—dunk′er** *n.*

dunk shot

Dunk•er (dŭng′kər) also **Dun•kard** (-kərd) *n.* A member of the German Baptist Brethren, a group opposed to military service and the taking of legal oaths. [Penn.Du. < *dunke,* to dunk (< baptism by immersion). See dunk.]

Dun•kirk^{1} (dŭn′kûrk′). Also **Dun•kerque** (dœɴ-kĕrk′). A city of N France on the North Sea. In World War II more than 330,000 Allied troops were evacuated from its beaches in the face of enemy fire (May–Jun. 1940). Pop. 73,120.

Dun•kirk^{2} (dŭn′kûrk′) *n.* **1.** A desperate retreat. **2.** A condition in which a desperate last effort is the only alternative to total defeat. [After Dunkirk^{1}.]

dunk shot *n. Basketball.* A shot made by jumping and slamming the ball down through the basket.

Dun Laoghai•re (dŭn lâr′ə). A borough of E-central Ireland on the Irish Sea SE of Dublin. Pop. 54,496.

dun•lin (dŭn′lĭn) *n.* A rust-brown and white sandpiper *(Calidris alpina)* native to northern regions of North America, Europe, and Asia. [dun^{2} + -lin(g)^{1}.]

Dun•more (dŭn-môr′, -mōr′), 4th Earl of. John Murray. 1732–1809. British colonial governor of Virginia (1771–76) who opposed the independence of the colonies.

dun•nage (dŭn′ĭj) *n.* **1.** Loose packing material used to protect a ship's cargo from damage during transport. **2.** Personal baggage. [ME *dennage* < MDu. *denne,* flooring of a ship.]

Dunne (dŭn), **Finley Peter.** 1867–1936. Amer. humorist known for his books featuring Mr. Dooley, a satiric Irish saloonkeeper.

Duns Sco•tus (dŭnz skō′təs), **John.** "the Subtle Doctor." 1265?–1308. Scottish Franciscan monk and theologian who wrote *On the First Principal.*

Dun•stan (dŭn′stən), Saint. 924–988. English prelate who as archbishop of Canterbury (959–978) attempted to integrate the Danes and the English as a nation.

du•o (do͞o′ō, dyo͞o′ō) *n., pl.* **-os. 1.** *Mus.* **a.** A duet. **b.** Two performers singing or playing together. **2.** Two people in close association. [Ital. < Lat., two. See **dwo-*.**]

duo– *pref.* Two: *duopoly.* [Lat. < *duo,* two. See **dwo-*.**]

du•o•dec•i•mal (do͞o′ə-dĕs′ə-məl, dyo͞o′-) *adj.* **1.** Of, relating to, or based on the number 12. **2.** Of or relating to twelfths. —*n.* A twelfth. [< Lat. *duodecimus,* twelfth < *duodecim,* twelve : *duo,* two; see **dwo-*** + *decem,* ten; see **dekm̥*.**]

du•o•dec•i•mo (do͞o′ə-dĕs′ə-mō′, dyo͞o′-) *n., pl.* **-mos.** *Print.* **1.** The size (5 by 7¾ inches) of book pages formed by folding single sheets from a printing press into 12 leaves each. **2.** A book composed of pages of this size. [Lat. *(in) duodecimō,* (in) a twelfth, ablative of *duodecimus,* twelfth. See duodecimal.]

du•o•de•num (do͞o′ə-dē′nəm, dyo͞o′-, do͞o-ŏd′n-əm, dyo͞o-) *n., pl.* **du•od•e•na** (do͞o′ə-dē′nə, dyo͞o′-, do͞o-ŏd′n-ə, dyo͞o-) or **du•o•de•nums.** The beginning portion of the small intestine, starting at the lower end of the stomach and extending to the jejunum. [ME < Med.Lat., short for *intestinum duodēnum digitōrum,* intestine of twelve fingers (in length) < Lat. *duodēnum,* genitive pl. of *duodēnī,* twelve each < *duodecim,* twelve. See duodecimal.] **—du′o•de′nal** (do͞o′ə-dē′nəl, dyo͞o′-, do͞o-ŏd′n-əl, dyo͞o-) *adj.*

du•o•logue (do͞o′ə-lôg′, -lŏg′, dyo͞o′-) *n.* A dialogue or conversation between two persons.

duo•mo (dwō′mō) *n., pl.* **-mos.** A cathedral, esp. one in Italy. [Ital. See dome.]

du•op•o•ly (do͞o-ŏp′ə-lē, dyo͞o-) *n.* An economic or political condition in which power is concentrated in two persons or groups. [duo- + (mono)poly.]

dup. *abbr.* Duplicate.

dupe (do͞op, dyo͞op) *n.* **1.** An easily deceived person. **2.** A person who functions as the tool of another person or power. —*tr.v.* **duped, dup•ing, dupes.** To deceive (an unwary person). See Syns at **deceive.** [Fr. < OFr., prob. alteration of *huppe,* hoopoe (< the bird's stupid appearance). See hoopoe.] **—dup′a•bil′i•ty** *n.* **—dup′a•ble** *adj.* **—dup′er** *n.*

dup•er•y (do͞o′pə-rē, dyo͞o′-) *n., pl.* **-ies.** The act of duping or the condition of having been duped.

du•ple (do͞o′pəl, dyo͞o′-) *adj.* **1.** Consisting of two; double. **2.** *Mus.* Consisting of two or a multiple of two beats to the measure. [Lat. *duplus.* See **dwo-*.**]

du•plex (do͞o′plĕks′, dyo͞o′-) *adj.* **1.** Twofold; double. **2.** Relating to or being a single assembly of machinery having two identical units capable of operating simultaneously or independently. **3.** *Electron.* Of or relating to a communications mode that provides simultaneous transmission and reception in both directions. —*n.* **1.** A house divided into two living units or residences. **2.** A duplex apartment. [Lat. See **dwo-*.**] **—du•plex′i•ty** (-plĕk′sĭ-tē) *n.*

duplex apartment *n.* An apartment having rooms on two adjoining floors connected by an inner staircase.

du•pli•cate (do͞o′plĭ-kĭt, dyo͞o′-) *adj.* **1.** Identically copied from an original. **2.** Existing or growing in two corresponding parts; double. **3.** *Games.* Of or being a manner of play in cards in which several different partnerships or teams play the same deals and compare scores at the end. —*n.* **1.** An identical copy; a facsimile. **2.** One that corresponds exactly to another, esp. an original. **3.** *Games.* A duplicate card game.

—*v.* (-kāt′) **-cat•ed, -cat•ing, -cates.** —*tr.* **1.** To make an exact copy of. **2.** To make twofold; double. **3.** To make or perform again; repeat. —*intr.* To become duplicate. [ME < Lat. *duplicātus*, p.part. of *duplicāre*, to double < *duplex*, *duplic-*, twofold. See **dwo-**.**] —**du′pli•ca•ble, du′pli•cat′a•ble** (-kā′tə-bəl) *adj.* —**du′pli•cate•ly** *adv.* —**du′pli•ca′tive** *adj.* —**du′pli•ca•to′ry** (-kĭ-tôr′ē, -tōr′ē) *adj.*

du•pli•ca•tion (do͞o′plĭ-kā′shən, dyo͞o′-) *n.* **1.a.** The act or procedure of duplicating. **b.** The condition of being duplicated. **2.** A duplicate; a replica. **3.** *Genet.* **a.** The occurrence of a repeated section of genetic material in a chromosome. **b.** The formation of such a duplication.

du•pli•ca•tor (do͞o′plĭ-kā′tər, dyo͞o′-) *n.* A machine, such as a mimeograph, that reproduces printed or written material.

du•plic•i•tous (do͞o-plĭs′ĭ-təs, dyo͞o-) *adj.* Given to or marked by deliberate deceptiveness in behavior or speech. —**du•plic′i•tous•ly** *adv.* —**du•plic′i•tous•ness** *n.*

du•plic•i•ty (do͞o-plĭs′ĭ-tē, dyo͞o-) *n., pl.* **-ties. 1.a.** Deliberate deceptiveness in behavior or speech. **b.** An instance of duplicity; double-dealing. **2.** The quality or state of being twofold or double. [ME *duplicite* < OFr. < LLat. *duplicitās*, doubleness < Lat. *duplex*, *duplic-*, twofold. See **dwo-**.**]

Du Pont de Ne•mours (do͞o pŏnt′ də nə-mo͝or′, dü pôɴ′), **Pierre Samuel.** 1739–1817. French-born economist and politician who helped negotiate the Louisiana Purchase (1803). His son **Eleuthère Irénée** (1771–1834) is best known for founding a gunpowder works (1802) in Delaware.

du Pré (do͞o prā′, dyo͞o), **Jacqueline.** 1945–87. British cellist noted for her performance of Elgar's *Concerto.*

Du•que de Ca•xi•as (do͞o′kē də kə-shē′əs, do͞o′kĭ dĭ kä-shē′äs). A city of SE Brazil, a suburb of Rio de Janeiro. Pop. 306,243.

du•ra•ble (do͝or′ə-bəl, dyo͝or′-) *adj.* **1.** Capable of withstanding wear and tear or decay. **2.** Lasting; stable: *a durable friendship.* **3.** *Econ.* Not depleted or consumed by use. —*n.* *Econ.* A durable manufactured product, such as an automobile. [ME < OFr. < Lat. *dūrābilis* < *dūrāre*, to last. See **deuə-**.**] —**du′ra•bil′i•ty, du′ra•ble•ness** *n.* —**du′ra•bly** *adv.*

durable press *n.* See **permanent press.**

du•ral (do͝or′əl, dyo͝or′-) *adj.* Of or relating to the dura mater.

du•ra ma•ter (do͝or′ə mā′tər, mä′-, dyo͝or′ə) *n.* The outermost tough fibrous membrane covering the brain and the spinal cord and lining the inner surface of the skull. [ME < Med.Lat. *dūra mater (cerebri)*, hard mother (of the brain), dura mater : Lat. *dūra*, fem. of *dūrus*, hard; see DURAMEN + Lat. *mater*, mother; see MATER.]

du•ra•men (do͞o-rā′mən, dyo͞o-) *n. Bot.* See **heartwood.** [Lat. *dūrāmen*, hard growth of a vine < *dūrāre*, to harden < *dūrus*, hard. See **deru-**.**]

du•rance (do͝or′əns, dyo͝or′-) *n.* Confinement or restraint by force; imprisonment. [ME *duraunce*, duration < OFr. *durance* < *durer*, to last < Lat. *dūrāre*. See **deuə-**.**]

Du•rand (də-rănd′), **Asher Brown.** 1796–1886. Amer. artist known for his paintings of the Hudson R. valley.

Du•ran•go (do͞o-răng′gō). A city of N-central Mexico NNW of Guadalajara; founded c. 1560. Pop. 257,915.

Du•rant (də-rănt′), **William James.** 1885–1981. Amer. historian who with his wife **Ariel** (1898–1981) wrote *The Story of Civilization* (11 volumes, 1935–75).

Du•ran•te (də-răn′tē), **Jimmy.** 1893–1980. Amer. comedian remembered for his work on television and in films and Broadway shows, including *Red, Hot, and Blue* (1936).

du•ra•tion (do͞o-rā′shən, dyo͞o-) *n.* **1.** Continuance or persistence in time. **2.** A period of existence or persistence. [ME *duracioun* < OFr. *duration* < Med.Lat. *dūrātiō*, *dūrātiōn-* < Lat. *dūrātus*, p.part. of *dūrāre*, to last. See **deuə-**.**]

Dur•ban (dûr′bən). A city of E South Africa on **Durban Bay,** an inlet of the Indian Ocean; settled in 1824. Pop. 677,760.

dur•bar (dûr′bär′) *n.* **1.** A state reception formerly given by Indian princes for a British sovereign or one given for an Indian prince by his subjects. **2.** The court of an Indian prince. [Urdu *darbār*, audience hall, court < Pers. : *dar*, indoors (< MPers., door < OPers. *duvara-*); see **dhwer-*** + *bār*, audience hall (< East Iran. **dwāra-*, courtyard; see **dhwer-***).]

Dü•ren (do͝or′ən, dür′-). A city of W-central Germany SW of Cologne; once a center of Carolingian culture. Pop. 84,631.

Dü•rer (do͝or′ər, dyo͝or′-, dü′rər), **Albrecht.** 1471–1528. German painter and engraver who incorporated the classicism of the Italian Renaissance into N European art.

du•ress (do͞o-rĕs′, dyo͞o-) *n.* **1.** Constraint by threat; coercion. **2.** *Law.* **a.** Illegal coercion. **b.** Forcible confinement. [ME *duresse*, harshness, compulsion < OFr. *durece*, hardness < Lat. *dūritia* < *dūrus*, hard. See **deru-**.**]

Dur•ga•pur (do͝or′gə-po͝or′, -gä-). A city of NE India NW of Calcutta. Pop. 311,798.

Dur•ham¹ (dûr′əm). A city of N-central NC E of Greensboro; settled c. 1750. Pop. 136,611.

Dur•ham² (dûr′əm) *n.* See **shorthorn.** [After *Durham*, a county of N England.]

du•ri•an (do͝or′ē-ən, -än′, dyo͝or′-) *n.* **1.** A southeast Asian tree *(Durio zibethinus).* **2.** The edible fruit of this plant, having a hard prickly rind and soft pulp. [Malay *dūrian* < *dūri*, thorn.]

dur•ing (do͝or′ĭng, dyo͝or′-) *prep.* **1.** Throughout the course or duration of. **2.** At some time in. [ME < pr.part. of *duren*, to last < OFr. *durer* < Lat. *dūrāre*. See **deuə-**.**]

Durk•heim (dûrk′hīm, dür-kĕm′), **Émile.** 1858–1917. French social scientist and a founder of sociology.

dur•mast (dûr′măst′) *n.* A European oak *(Quercus petraea)* having tough elastic wood. [Perh. alteration of *dun mast* : DUN² + MAST².]

durn (dûrn) *Chiefly Southern U.S. interj., adv., adj., & v.* Var. of **darn².** See Regional Note at **damned.**

du•roc also **Du•roc** (do͝or′ŏk′, dyo͝or′-) *n.* A large red hog of a breed developed in the 19th century in the United States. [After *Duroc*, a horse of the breed's developer.]

Du•ro•cher (də-rō′chər, -shər), **Leo Ernest.** 1906–91. Amer. baseball player and manager remembered for his pithy sayings, such as "Nice guys finish last."

Du•roc-Jer•sey (do͝or′ŏk-jûr′zē, dyo͝or′-) *n.* See **duroc.**

dur•ra also **dou•ra** or **dou•rah** (do͝or′ə) *n.* An Asian and northern African cereal grain *(Sorghum bicolor).* [Ar. *dura*, grain.]

Dur•rell (dûr′əl), **Lawrence George.** 1912–90. British writer best known for *The Alexandria Quartet* (1957–60).

Dür•ren•matt (do͝or′ən-mät′, dyo͝or′-, dür′-), **Friedrich.** b. 1921. Swiss writer known for his absurdist novels and plays, such as *The Visit* (1956).

Dur•rës (do͝or′əs). A city of W Albania on the Adriatic Sea; founded as a Greek colony c. 625 B.C. Pop. 72,400.

durst (dûrst) *v. Archaic.* A p.t. and p.part. of **dare.**

du•rum (do͝or′əm, dyo͝or′-, dûr′-, dŭr′-) *n.* A hardy wheat *(Triticum turgidum,* formerly *T. durum)* used chiefly in making pasta. [< Lat. *dūrum*, neut. of *dūrus*, hard. See **deru-**.**]

Du•se (do͞o′zĕ), **Eleonora.** 1859?–1924. Italian actress who was highly acclaimed for her roles in the plays of Gabriele D'Annunzio and Henrik Ibsen.

Du•shan•be (do͞o-shăm′bə, -shäm′-, -shŭn-byĕ′). The cap. of Tadzhikistan, in the W part of the republic. Pop. 552,000.

dusk (dŭsk) *n.* The darker stage of twilight, esp. in the evening. —*adj.* Tending to darkness; dusky. —*intr. & tr.v.* **dusked, dusk•ing, dusks.** To become or make dark or dusky. [< ME, dark, alteration of OE *dox.*]

dusk•y (dŭs′kē) *adj.* **-i•er, -i•est. 1.** Characterized by little or inadequate light; shadowy. **2.** Rather dark in color. See Syns at **dark.** —**dusk′i•ly** *adv.* —**dusk′i•ness** *n.*

dusky grouse *n.* See **blue grouse.**

Düs•sel•dorf (do͞os′əl-dôrf′, düs′-). A city of W-central Germany on the Rhine R. NNW of Cologne; chartered 1288. Pop. 565,843.

dust (dŭst) *n.* **1.** Fine dry particles of matter. **2.** A cloud of fine dry particles. **3.** Particles of matter regarded as the result of disintegration. **4.a.** Earth, esp. when regarded as the substance of the grave. **b.** The surface of the ground. **5.** A debased or despised condition. **6.** Something of no worth. **7.** *Chiefly British.* Rubbish readied for disposal. **8.** Confusion; agitation; commotion. —*v.* **dust•ed, dust•ing, dusts.** —*tr.* **1.** To remove dust from by wiping, brushing, or beating. **2.** To sprinkle with a powdery substance. **3.** To apply or strew in fine particles. —*intr.* **1.** To clean by removing dust. **2.** To cover itself with dust. Used of a bird. —***phrasal verb.* dust off.** To restore to use. [ME < OE *dūst.*]

dust•bin (dŭst′bĭn′) *n. Chiefly British.* A trash can.

dust bowl *n.* A region left arid by drought and dust storms.

dust cover *n.* **1.** A removable or hinged plastic cover used to protect a piece of equipment. **2.** See **dust jacket** 1.

dust devil *n.* A small whirlwind, usu. of short duration, that swirls dust, debris, and sand to great heights.

dust•er (dŭs′tər) *n.* **1.** One that dusts, esp.: **a.** A cloth or brush used to remove dust. **b.** A device for sifting or scattering a powdered substance. **2.** A smock worn to protect one's clothing from dust. **3.** A woman's loose dress-length housecoat.

dust•ing (dŭs′tĭng) *n.* **1.** A light sprinkling: *a dusting of new snow.* **2.** *Slang.* A beating or defeat.

dusting powder *n.* A fine powder used on the skin.

dust jacket *n.* **1.** A removable paper cover used to protect a book. **2.** A cardboard sleeve for a phonograph record.

dust mop *n.* A mop used dry to remove dust from floors.

dust•pan (dŭst′păn′) *n.* A short-handled pan or scoop into which dust is swept.

dust ruffle *n.* A gathered or pleated strip of cloth reaching from the bottom of a mattress or box spring to the floor.

dust storm *n.* A severe windstorm that sweeps clouds of dust across an extensive area, esp. in an arid region.

dust•up (dŭst′ŭp′) *n. Slang.* A row; a dispute.

dust•y (dŭs′tē) *adj.* **-i•er, -i•est. 1.** Covered or filled with dust. **2.** Consisting of or resembling dust; powdery. **3.** Tinged with gray. **4.** Timeworn; stale. —**dust′i•ly** *adv.* —**dust′i•ness** *n.*

dusty miller *n.* Any of various plants of the genera *Artemisia, Centaurea, Chrysanthemum, Lychnis,* and *Senecio,* having leaves and stems covered with dustlike down.

Dutch (dŭch) *adj.* **1.a.** Of or relating to the Netherlands or its

Jimmy Durante

Albrecht Dürer
1500 self-portrait

ă pat	oi boy
ā pay	ou out
âr care	o͝o took
ä father	o͞o boot
ĕ pet	ŭ cut
ē be	ûr urge
ĭ pit	th thin
ī pie	*th* this
îr pier	hw which
ŏ pot	zh vision
ō toe	ə about, item
ô paw	

Stress marks:
′ (primary);
′ (secondary), as in
dictionary (dĭk′shə-nĕr′ē)

E e

e[1] or **E** (ē) *n., pl.* **e's** or **E's.** **1.** The fifth letter of the modern English alphabet. **2.** Any of the speech sounds represented by the letter *e.* **3.** The fifth in a series. **4.** *Mus.* **a.** The third tone in the scale of C major or the fifth tone in the relative minor scale. **b.** A key or scale in which E is the tonic. **5. E. a.** A grade that indicates below average work or failing status. **b.** A grade that indicates excellence in achievement or quality. **6. e.** *Math.* The base of the natural system of logarithms, having a numerical value of approx. 2.7183.

e[2] *abbr.* **1.** Electron. **2.** Or **e.** *Baseball.* Error.

E *abbr.* **1.** Or **E.** also **e** or **e.** East. **2.** Or **E.** English.

e. or **E.** *abbr.* Engineer; engineering.

E. *abbr.* Earl.

ea. *abbr.* Each.

each (ēch) *adj.* Being one of two or more considered individually; every: *Each person voted.* —*pron.* Every one of a group considered individually; each one. —*adv.* For or to each one; apiece. [ME *ech* < OE *ǣlc.* See **līk-*.**]

Usage Note: The traditional rule holds that when the subject of a sentence begins with *each,* it is grammatically singular, and the verb and following pronouns must be singular as well: *Each of the suites has its own bath.* When *each* follows a plural subject, however, the verb and subsequent pronouns remain in the plural: *The suites each have their own baths.* See Usage Notes at **every, he[1].**

each other *pron.* Each the other. Used to indicate that a relationship or an action is reciprocal: *The boys like each other.*

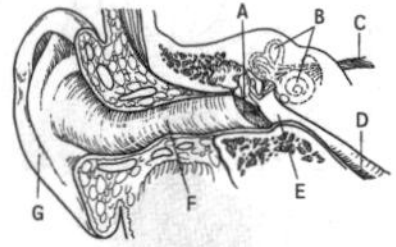

ear
A. Eardrum
B. Inner ear
C. Auditory nerve
D. Eustachian tube
E. Middle ear
F. Ear canal
G. Auricle

Eads (ēdz), **James Buchanan.** 1820–87. Amer. engineer who bridged the Mississippi R. at St. Louis (1874).

Ea•gan (ē′gən). A city of E MN, a suburb of Minneapolis–St. Paul. Pop. 47,409.

ea•ger[1] (ē′gər) *adj.* **-ger•er, -ger•est. 1.** Having or exhibiting keen interest, intense desire, or impatient expectancy. See Usage Note at **anxious. 2.** *Obsolete.* Tart; sharp; cutting. [ME *eger,* sour, sharp, impetuous < AN *egre* < Lat. *ācer.* See **ak-*.**] —**ea′ger•ly** *adv.* —**ea′ger•ness** *n.*

ea•ger[2] (ē′gər, ā′-) *n.* Var. of **eagre.**

eager beaver *n. Informal.* One that is exceptionally industrious or zealous. —**ea′ger-bea′ver** (ē′gər-bē′vər) *adj.*

ea•gle (ē′gəl) *n.* **1.** Any of various large birds of prey of the family Accipitridae, characterized by a hooked bill, keen vision, and long broad wings. **2.** A representation of an eagle used as an emblem or insignia. **3.** A gold coin formerly used in the United States, stamped with an eagle on the reverse side and worth ten dollars. **4.** *Sports.* A golf score of two strokes under par on a hole. —*v.* **-gled, -gling, -gles.** —*tr.* To shoot (a hole in golf) in two strokes under par. —*intr.* To score an eagle in golf. [ME *egle* < AN < OProv. *aigla* < Lat. *aquila.*]

ea•gle-eyed (ē′gəl-īd′) *adj.* **1.** Having keen eyesight. **2.** Showing close attention to detail; perceptive.

Ea•gle Pass (ē′gəl). A city of SW TX on the Rio Grande WSW of San Antonio. Pop. 20,651.

eagle ray *n.* Any of numerous rays of the family Myliobatididae, having massive jaws and winglike pectoral fins.

Eagle Scout *n.* One holding the highest rank in the Boy Scouts.

ea•glet (ē′glĭt) *n.* A young eagle.

ea•gre also **ea•ger** (ē′gər, ā′gər) *n.* See **bore[3].** [?]

Ea•kins (ā′kĭnz), **Thomas.** 1844–1916. Amer. painter whose works include *Max Schmitt in a Single Scull* (1871).

eal•dor•man (ôl′dər-mən) *n.* The chief magistrate of a district in Anglo-Saxon England. [OE. See ALDERMAN.]

Amelia Earhart

Eames (ēmz), **Charles.** 1907–78. Amer. designer noted for his chairs made of aluminum tubing and molded plywood.

Eames chair A trademark for a functional chair with seat and back shaped to the contours of the human body.

ear[1] (îr) *n.* **1.** *Anat.* **a.** The vertebrate organ of hearing, which maintains equilibrium as well as senses sound. **b.** The part of this organ that is externally visible. **2.** An invertebrate organ analogous to the mammalian ear. **3.** The sense of hearing. **4.** Sensitivity or receptiveness to sound, esp.: **a.** Sharpness or refinement of hearing: *a good ear for harmony.* **b.** The ability to retain and reproduce a passage of music: *plays the piano by ear.* **c.** Responsiveness to the sounds or forms of spoken language. **5.** Sympathetic or favorable attention. **6.** Something resembling the external ear in position or shape, esp.: **a.** A flexible tuft of feathers located above the eyes of certain birds that functions only in visual communication. **b.** A projecting handle, as on a vase. **7.** A small box in the upper corner of the page in a newspaper or periodical that contains a printed notice. **8. ears.** *Informal.* Headphones. —***idioms.*** **all ears.** *Informal.* Acutely attentive. **give (or lend) an ear.** To pay close attention; listen attentively. **have (or keep) an ear to the ground.** To be on the watch for new trends or information. **in one ear and out the other.** Without any influence or effect; unheeded. **on its (or someone's) ear.** In a state of amazement, excitement, or uproar. **play it by ear.** *Informal.* To act according to the circumstances; improvise. [ME *ere* < OE *ēare.* See **ous-*.**]

ear[2] (îr) *n.* The seed-bearing spike of a cereal plant, such as corn. —*intr.v.* **eared, ear•ing, ears.** To form or grow ears. [ME *ere* < OE *ēar.* See **ak-*.**]

ear•ache (îr′āk′) *n.* Pain in the ear; otalgia.

ear•bob (îr′bŏb′) *n. Chiefly Southern U.S.* See **earring.**

ear canal *n.* The narrow tubelike passage through which sound enters the ear.

ear•drop (îr′drŏp′) *n.* **1.** An earring, esp. one with a pendant. **2. eardrops.** Liquid medicine administered into the ear.

ear•drum (îr′drŭm′) *n. Anat.* The thin oval-shaped membrane that separates the middle ear from the external ear.

eared (îrd) *adj.* **1.** Having ears or earlike projections. **2.** Having a specified kind or number of ears.

eared seal *n.* Any of various seals of the family Otariidae, which includes the fur seals, characterized by external ears, oarlike front flippers, and hind flippers for walking on land.

ear•flap (îr′flăp′) *n.* A flap on a cap that may be turned down to cover the ears.

ear•ful (îr′fo͝ol′) *n.* **1.** An abundant or excessive amount of something heard. **2.** Gossip, esp. of an intimate or scandalous nature. **3.** A scolding or reprimand.

Ear•hart (âr′härt′), **Amelia.** 1897?–1937. Amer. aviator who was the first woman to fly solo across the Atlantic Ocean (1932). She crashed and disappeared in the Pacific Ocean while attempting to fly around the world.

ear•ing (îr′ĭng) *n. Naut.* A short line attaching an upper corner of a sail to the yard. [Perh. < EAR[1].]

earl (ûrl) *n.* **1.** A British nobleman next in rank above a viscount and below a marquis. **2.** Used as a title for such a nobleman. [ME *erl,* nobleman of high rank < OE *eorl.*]

ear•lap (îr′lăp′) *n.* See **earflap.**

earl•dom (ûrl′dəm) *n.* The rank, title, or territory of an earl.

ear•less seal (îr′lĭs) *n.* Any of various seals of the family Phocidae, marked by short fore flippers, reduced hind flippers for swimming, and the absence of external ears.

ear•lobe also **ear lobe** (îr′lōb′) *n.* The soft, fleshy, pendulous lower part of the external ear.

ear•ly (ûr′lē) *adj.* **-li•er, -li•est. 1.** Of or occurring near the beginning of a given series, period of time, or course of events. **2.a.** Of or belonging to a previous or remote period of time. **b.** Of or belonging to an initial stage of development. **3.** Occurring, developing, or appearing before the expected or usual time. **4.** Maturing or developing relatively soon. **5.** Occurring in the near future. —*adv.* **-lier, -liest. 1.** Near the beginning of a given series, period of time, or course of events. **2.** At or during a remote or initial period. **3.** Before the expected or usual time: *arrived early.* **4.** Soon in relation to others of its kind. [ME *erli* < OE *ǣrlīce* : *ǣr,* before; see **ayer-*** + *-līce,* adv. suff.; see -LY[2].] —**ear′li•ness** *n.*

Ear•ly (ûr′lē), **Jubal Anderson.** 1816–94. Amer. Confederate general whose forces threatened Washington DC (1864) but were ultimately defeated by Union troops.

early bird *n. Informal.* **1.** A person who arises early in the morning. **2.** One that arrives or takes place early or before others. —**ear′ly-bird′** (ûr′lē-bûrd′) *adj.*

early on *adv.* At an early stage or point.

ear•mark (îr′märk′) *n.* **1.** An identifying feature or characteristic. **2.** An identifying mark on the ear of a domestic animal. —*tr.v.* **-marked, -mark•ing, -marks. 1.** To reserve or set aside for a particular purpose. See Syns at **allocate. 2.** To place an identifying or distinctive mark on. **3.** To mark the ear of (a domestic animal) for identification.

ear•muff (îr′mŭf′) *n.* Either of a pair of ear coverings often attached to a headband and worn to protect the ears.

earn[1] (ûrn) *tr.v.* **earned, earn•ing, earns. 1.** To gain esp. for the performance of service, labor, or work. **2.** To acquire or deserve as a result of effort or action. **3.** To yield as return or profit. —***idiom.*** **earn (one's) spurs.** To gain a position through hard work, often in the face of difficulties. [ME *ernen* < OE *earnian.*] —**earn′er** *n.*

Syns: *earn, deserve, merit, rate, win.* The central meaning shared by these verbs is "to gain as a result of one's behavior or effort": *earns a large salary; deserves our congratulations; a suggestion that merits consideration; an event that rates a mention in the news; a candidate who won wide support.*

earn[2] (ûrn) *intr.v.* **earned, earn•ing, earns.** *Obsolete.* To yearn. [ME *ernen,* var. of *yernen.* See YEARN.]

earned run (ûrnd) *n. Baseball.* A run scored without the aid of an error, used in computing earned run averages.

earned run average *n. Baseball.* A measure of a pitcher's performance obtained by dividing the total of earned runs by the total of innings pitched and multiplying by nine.

ear•nest¹ (ûr′nĭst) *adj.* **1.** Marked by or showing deep sincerity or seriousness: *an earnest gesture of goodwill.* **2.** Of an important or weighty nature; grave. See Syns at **serious.** —*idiom.* **in earnest. 1.** With a purposeful or sincere intent: *study in earnest.* **2.** Serious; determined. [ME *ernest* < OE *eornoste.* See **er-¹*.**] —**ear′nest•ly** *adv.* —**ear′nest•ness** *n.*

ear•nest² (ûr′nĭst) *n.* **1.** Money paid in advance as part payment to bind a contract or bargain. **2.** A token of something to come; a promise or an assurance. [ME *ernest*, var. of *ernes*, alteration of OFr. *erres*, pl. of *erre*, pledge < Lat. *arra*, alteration of *arrabō* < Gk. *arrabōn*, earnest-money < Heb. *'ērābôn* < *'ārab*, to pledge.]

earn•ings (ûr′nĭngz) *pl.n.* **1.** Salary or wages. **2.a.** Business profits. **b.** Gains from investments.

Earp (ûrp), **Wyatt.** 1848–1929. Amer. law officer involved in the gunfight at the O.K. Corral in Tombstone AZ (1881).

ear•phone (îr′fōn′) *n.* A device that converts electric signals to audible sound and fits over or in the ear.

ear•piece (îr′pēs′) *n.* **1.** A part, as of a hearing aid, that fits in or is held next to the ear. **2.** See **earphone. 3.** Either of the two parts of an eyeglasses frame that fit on the ear.

ear•plug (îr′plŭg′) *n.* **1.** An object made of a soft pliable material and fitted into the ear canal to block the entry of water or sound. **2.** An earphone, esp. one that fits into the ear.

ear•ring (îr′rĭng, îr′ĭng) *n.* An ornament worn on or pendent from the ear, esp. the earlobe. Also called regionally *earbob.*

ear rot *n.* Any of various fungus diseases of corn characterized by decay and molding of the ears.

ear sew•er (sō′ər) *n. Northern California.* See **dragonfly.** See Regional Note at **dragonfly.**

ear shell *n.* **1.** See **abalone. 2.** The shell of the abalone.

ear•shot (îr′shŏt′) *n.* The range within which sound can be heard by the unaided ear; hearing distance.

ear•split•ting (îr′splĭt′ĭng) *adj.* Loud and shrill enough to hurt the ears.

earth (ûrth) *n.* **1.a.** The land surface of the world. **b.** The softer friable part of land; soil, esp. productive soil. **2.** Often **Earth.** The third planet from the sun, having a sidereal period of revolution about the sun of 365.26 days at a mean distance of approx. 149 million kilometers (92.96 million miles) and an average radius of 6,374 kilometers (3,959 miles). **3.** The realm of mortal existence; the temporal world. **4.** The human inhabitants of the world. **5.a.** Worldly affairs and pursuits. **b.** Everyday life; reality. **6.** The substance of the human body; clay. **7.** The lair of a burrowing animal. **8.** *Chiefly British.* The ground of an electrical circuit. **9.** *Chem.* Any of several metallic oxides, such as alumina, that are difficult to reduce. —*v.* **earthed, earth•ing, earths.** —*tr.* **1.** To cover or heap (plants) with soil for protection. **2.** To chase (an animal) into an underground hiding place. —*intr.* To burrow or hide in the ground. Used of a hunted animal. —*idiom.* **on earth.** Among all the possibilities: *Why on earth did you go?* [ME *erthe* < OE *eorthe.* See **er-²*.**]

earth•born (ûrth′bôrn′) *adj.* **1.** Springing from or born on the earth. **2.** Human; mortal: *earthborn existence.*

earth•bound also **earth-bound** (ûrth′bound′) *adj.* **1.** Fastened in or to the soil. **2.a.** Attached or confined to the earth or to earthly concerns. **b.** Unimaginative; ordinary.

earth•en (ûr′thən, *-thən*) *adj.* **1.** Made of earth or clay: *an earthen fortification; an earthen pot.* **2.** Earthly; worldly.

earth•en•ware (ûr′thən-wâr′, *-thən-*) *n.* Pottery made from a porous clay that is fired at relatively low temperatures.

earth•light (ûrth′līt′) *n.* See **earthshine.**

earth•ling (ûrth′lĭng) *n.* **1.** One, esp. a human being, that inhabits the planet Earth. **2.** A person devoted to the world.

earth•ly (ûrth′lē) *adj.* **1.** Of, relating to, or characteristic of this earth. **2.a.** Terrestrial; not heavenly or divine. **b.** Worldly. **3.** Conceivable; possible. —**earth′li•ness** *n.*

earth•man (ûrth′măn′) *n.* A human inhabitant of the planet Earth; an earthling.

earth mother *n.* **1.** A goddess or female spirit representing the earth as the giver of life. **2.** A woman combining maternal and sensual qualities.

earth•mov•er (ûrth′mo͞o′vər) *n.* A machine, such as a backhoe, used for digging or pushing earth. —**earth′mov′ing** *adj.*

earth•nut (ûrth′nŭt′) *n.* **1.a.** A Eurasian and northern African plant *(Conopodium denudatum)* having tuberous roots that are edible when roasted. **b.** The tuber of this plant. **2.** Any of various other similar plants, such as the peanut.

earth•quake (ûrth′kwāk′) *n.* A sudden movement of the earth's crust caused by the release of stress accumulated along geologic faults or by volcanic activity.

earth•rise (ûrth′rīz′) *n.* The rising of the earth above the horizon as seen from the moon.

earth science *n.* Any of several sciences concerned with the origin, structure, and physical phenomena of the earth.

earth•shak•ing (ûrth′shā′kĭng) *adj.* Very important.

earth•shine (ûrth′shīn′) *n.* The sunlight reflected from the earth's surface that illuminates part of the moon.

earth smoke *n. Bot.* See **fumitory.**

earth station *n.* An on-ground terminal linked to a spacecraft or satellite by an antenna and associated electronic equipment for transmitting or receiving messages, tracking, or control.

earth tone *n.* Any of various rich warm tones of brown.

earth•ward (ûrth′wərd) *adv. & adj.* To or toward the earth. —**earth′wards** *adv.*

earth•work (ûrth′wûrk′) *n.* **1.** An earthen embankment, esp. one used as a fortification. **2.** *Engineering.* Excavation and embankment of earth. **3.** A work of art made by altering an area of land or a natural geographic feature.

earth•worm (ûrth′wûrm′) *n.* Any of various terrestrial annelid worms of the class Oligochaeta, esp. those of the family Lumbricidae, that help aerate and enrich soil.

earth•y (ûr′thē) *adj.* **-i•er, -i•est. 1.** Of, relating to, consisting of, or resembling earth: *an earthy smell.* **2.** Relating to or characteristic of this world; worldly. **3.** Crude or off-color; indecent. **4.** Hearty or uninhibited; natural: *an earthy enjoyment of life.* —**earth′i•ly** *adv.* —**earth′i•ness** *n.*

ear trumpet *n.* A horn-shaped device formerly used to direct sound into the ear of a hearing-impaired person.

ear tuft *n.* See **ear¹** 6a.

ear•wax (îr′wăks′) *n.* The yellowish waxlike secretion of certain glands lining the canal of the external ear.

ear•wig (îr′wĭg′) *n.* Any of various elongate insects of the order Dermaptera, having a pair of pincerlike appendages protruding from the rear of the abdomen. —*tr.v.* **-wigged, -wig•ging, -wigs.** To attempt to influence by persistent confidential argument or talk. [ME *erwig* < OE *ēarwicga* : *ēare*, ear; see EAR¹ + *wicga*, insect; see **wegh-*.**]

earwig

ear•worm (îr′wûrm′) *n.* See **corn earworm.**

ease (ēz) *n.* **1.** The condition of being comfortable or relieved. **2.a.** Freedom from pain, worry, or agitation. **b.** Freedom from constraint or embarrassment; naturalness. **3.a.** Freedom from difficulty, hardship, or effort. **b.** Readiness or dexterity in performance; facility. **4.** Freedom from financial difficulty; affluence: *a life of ease.* **5.** A state of rest, relaxation, or leisure. —*v.* **eased, eas•ing, eas•es.** —*tr.* **1.** To free from pain, worry, or agitation. **2.a.** To lessen the discomfort or pain of. **b.** To alleviate; assuage: *a drug to ease the pain.* **3.** To give respite from: *eased the burden on her staff.* **4.** To slacken the strain, pressure, or tension of; loosen: *ease off a cable.* **5.** To reduce the difficulty or trouble of: *ease credit terms.* **6.** To move or maneuver slowly and carefully. —*intr.* **1.** To lessen, as in discomfort, pressure, or stress. **2.** To move or proceed with little effort. —*idiom.* **at ease. 1.** In a relaxed position, esp. standing silently at rest with the right foot stationary. **2.** Used as a command for troops to assume a relaxed position. [ME *ese* < OFr. *aise*, perh. < Lat. *adiacēns*, lying near. See ADJACENT.]

ease•ful (ēz′fəl) *adj.* Affording or characterized by comfort and peace; restful. —**ease′ful•ly** *adv.* —**ease′ful•ness** *n.*

ea•sel (ē′zəl) *n.* An upright frame for displaying or supporting something, such as an artist's canvas. [Du. *ezel*, ass, easel < MDu. *esel* < Lat. *asellus*, dim. of *asinus.*]

easel

ease•ment (ēz′mənt) *n.* **1.** The act of easing or the condition of being eased. **2.** Something that affords ease or comfort. **3.** *Law.* A right, such as a right of way, afforded a person to make limited use of another's real property.

eas•i•ly (ē′zə-lē) *adv.* **1.** In an easy manner; with ease. **2.** Without question; certainly. **3.** In all likelihood; well.

east (ēst) *n.* **1.a.** The cardinal point on the compass 90° clockwise from due north and directly opposite west. **b.** The direction of the earth's axial rotation. **2.** An area or a region lying in the east. **3.** Often **East. a.** The eastern part of the earth, esp. eastern Asia. **b.** The eastern part of a region or country. **4.** Often **East. a.** The region of the United States east of the Allegheny Mountains and north of the Mason-Dixon Line. **b.** The former Communist bloc of countries in Asia and Eastern Europe. —*adj.* **1.** To, toward, of, facing, or in the east. **2.** Originating in or coming from the east: *a cool east wind.* —*adv.* In, from, or toward the east. [ME *est* < OE *ēast.* See **aus-*.**]

East An•gli•a (ăng′glē-ə). A region and Anglo-Saxon kingdom of E England; settled by Angles in the late 5th cent. A.D.

East A•sia (ā′zhə, ā′shə). A region of Asia coextensive with the Far East. —**East A′sian** *adj. & n.*

East Ber•lin (bûr-lĭn′). See **Berlin.** —**East Ber•lin′er** *n.*

East Bes•kids (bĕs′kĭdz, bĕs-kēdz′). See **Beskids.**

east•bound (ēst′bound′) *adj.* Going toward the east.

East•bourne (ēst′bôrn′, -bōrn′). A borough of SE England on the English Channel SSE of London. Pop. 77,300.

East Bruns•wick (brŭnz′wĭk). A community of central NJ S of New Brunswick. Pop. 43,548.

east by north *n.* The direction or compass point halfway between due east and east-northeast, or 78°45′ east of due north. —*adv. & adj.* Toward or from east by north.

east by south *n.* The direction or compass point halfway between due east and east-southeast, or 101°15′ east of due north. —*adv. & adj.* Toward or from east by south.

East Cape. See Cape **Dezhnev.**

East•ches•ter (ēst′chĕs′tər). A community of SE NY, a suburb of New York City. Pop. 18,537.

ă pat	oi boy
ā pay	ou out
âr care	o͝o took
ä father	o͞o boot
ĕ pet	ŭ cut
ē be	ûr urge
ĭ pit	th thin
ī pie	*th* this
îr pier	hw which
ŏ pot	zh vision
ō toe	ə about, item
ô paw	

Stress marks:
′ (primary);
′ (secondary), as in dictionary (dĭk′shə-nĕr′ē)

East Chi•ca•go (shĭ-kä′gō, -kô′-). A city of NW IN on Lake Michigan SSE of Chicago IL. Pop. 33,892.

East Chi•na Sea (chī′nə). An arm of the W Pacific bounded by China, South Korea, Taiwan, and the Ryukyu and Kyushu islands.

East Cleve•land (klēv′lənd). A city of NE OH, a suburb of Cleveland. Pop. 33,096.

East Coast. A region of the E U.S. along the Atlantic coastline, esp. the urban corridor from Boston to Washington DC

East De•troit (dĭ-troit′). A city of SE MI, a suburb of Detroit. Pop. 35,283.

East End. A section of E London N of the Thames R.; long a densely populated working-class and immigrant area centered around the docks and warehouses.

Eas•ter (ē′stər) *n.* **1.** A Christian feast commemorating the Resurrection of Jesus, traditionally observed on the first Sunday following the full moon that occurs on or next after March 21. **2.** Eastertide. [ME *ester* < OE *ēastre.* See **aus-*.**]

Easter egg *n.* A dyed or decorated egg associated with Easter.

Easter Island. Locally **Ra•pa Nu•i** (rä′pə no͞o′ē). An island of Chile in the S Pacific Ocean W of the mainland; famous for its colossal heads carved from volcanic rock.

Easter lily *n.* Any of various lilies, esp. *Lilium longiflorum* var. *eximium,* having large white trumpet-shaped flowers that are displayed during the Easter season.

east•er•ly (ē′stər-lē) *adj.* **1.** Situated toward the east. **2.** Coming or being from the east: *easterly winds.* —*n., pl.* **-lies.** A storm or wind coming from the east. —**east′er•ly** *adv.*

Easter Island
Massive carved figures on Easter Island

Easter Monday *n.* The Monday following Easter, observed as a holiday in some countries and in North Carolina.

east•ern (ē′stərn) *adj.* **1.** Situated in, toward, or facing the east. **2.** Coming from the east: *eastern breezes.* **3.** Native to or growing in the east. **4.** Often **Eastern.** Of, relating to, or characteristic of eastern regions or the East. **5. Eastern. a.** Of or relating to the Eastern Church. **b.** Of or relating to the Eastern Orthodox Church. [ME *estern* < OE *ēasterne.* See **aus-*.**] —**east′ern•ness′** *n.*

Eastern Church *n.* **1.** The church of the Byzantine Empire. **2.** The Eastern Orthodox Church. **3.** Often **Eastern church.** A Uniat church.

Eastern Empire. The Byzantine Empire.

east•ern•er also **East•ern•er** (ē′stər-nər) *n.* A native or inhabitant of the east, esp. the eastern United States.

Eastern Eu•rope (yo͝or′əp). The countries of E Europe, esp. those allied with the U.S.S.R. in the Warsaw Pact (1955–91).

Eastern Ghats (gôts). See **Ghats.**

Eastern Hemisphere. The half of the earth comprising Europe, Africa, Asia, and Australia.

east•ern•most (ē′stərn-mōst′) *adj.* Farthest east.

Eastern Orthodox Church *n.* The body of modern churches, including the Greek and Russian Orthodox, that is derived from the church of the Byzantine Empire, adheres to the Byzantine rite, and acknowledges the honorary primacy of the patriarch of Constantinople.

Eastern Shore. A region of MD and VA E of Chesapeake Bay.

Eastern Shoshone *n.* See **Shoshone** 1c.

Eastern Sioux *n.* See **Santee**[1].

George Eastman

Eastern Standard Time *n.* Standard time in the fifth time zone west of Greenwich, England, reckoned at 75° west and used, for example, in the eastern part of North America.

Eas•ter•tide (ē′stər-tīd′) *n.* The Easter season.

East Fri•sian Islands (frĭzh′ən, frē′zhən). See **Frisian Islands.**

East Germanic *n.* The subdivision of the Germanic languages that includes Gothic.

East Ger•ma•ny (jûr′mə-nē). A former country of N Europe on the Baltic Sea; formed in 1949 from the zone occupied by Soviet troops after World War II and reunified with West Germany in Oct. 1990. —**East Ger′man** *adj. & n.*

East Hart•ford (härt′fərd). A town of N-central CT on the Connecticut R.; settled c. 1640. Pop. 50,452.

East Ha•ven (hā′vən). A town of S CT on Long Island Sound E of New Haven. Pop. 26,144.

East In•dies (ĭn′dēz). Indonesia. The term is sometimes used to refer to all of Southeast Asia. —**East In′di•an** *adj. & n.*

east•ing (ē′stĭng) *n.* **1.** The difference in longitude between two positions as a result of movement to the east. **2.** Progress toward the east.

East•lake (ēst′lāk′). A city of NE OH, a suburb of Cleveland on Lake Erie. Pop. 21,161.

East Lan•sing (lăn′sĭng). A city of S-central MI, a suburb of Lansing. Pop. 50,677.

East•leigh (ēst′lē). A municipal borough of S England NNE of Southampton. Pop. 92,400.

East•main (ēst′mān′). A river rising in central Quebec, Canada, and flowing c. 821 km (510 mi) E to James Bay.

East•man (ēst′mən), **George.** 1854–1932. Amer. industrialist who invented a dry-plate process of photographic film development, flexible film, and a process for color photography.

eaves

East Mo•line (mō-lēn′). A city of NW IL, a suburb of Moline on the Mississippi R. Pop. 20,147.

east-north•east (ēst′nôrth′ēst′) *n.* The direction or compass point halfway between due east and northeast, or 67°30′ east of due north. —*adj.* To, toward, of, facing, or in the east-northeast. —*adv.* In, from, or toward the east-northeast.

East•on (ē′stən). **1.** A town of SE MA SW of Brockton; settled in 1694. Pop. 19,807. **2.** A city of E PA N of Philadelphia; founded 1751. Pop. 26,276.

East Or•ange (ôr′ĭnj, ŏr′-). A city of NE NJ, a suburb of Newark. Pop. 73,552.

East Pak•i•stan (păk′ĭ-stăn′, pä′kĭ-stän′). A former region of S Asia on the Bay of Bengal; held by Pakistan from 1947 to 1971, when it achieved independence as Bangladesh.

East Pe•or•i•a (pē-ôr′ē-ə, -ōr′-). A city of N-central IL, a suburb of Peoria on the Illinois R. Pop. 21,378.

East Point. A city of NW GA, a suburb of Atlanta. Pop. 34,402.

East Prov•i•dence (prŏv′ĭ-dəns). A city of E RI, a suburb of Providence. Pop. 50,380.

East Prus•sia (prŭsh′ə). A historical region and former province of Prussia on the Baltic Sea; separated from Germany by the Polish Corridor from 1919 to 1939 and divided between Poland and the U.S.S.R. in 1945.

East Ridge. A city of SE TN, a suburb of Chattanooga on the GA border. Pop. 21,101.

East River. A narrow tidal strait connecting Upper New York Bay with Long Island Sound and separating the boroughs of Manhattan and the Bronx from Brooklyn and Queens.

East Saint Lou•is (sānt lo͞o′ĭs). A city of SW IL on the Mississippi R. opposite St. Louis MO. Pop. 40,944.

East Si•ber•i•an Sea (sī-bîr′ē-ən). An arm of the Arctic Ocean from Wrangel I. to the New Siberian Is.

east-south•east (ēst′south′ēst′) *n.* The direction or compass point halfway between due east and southeast, or 112°30′ east of due north. —*adj.* To, toward, of, facing, or in the east-southeast. —*adv.* In, from, or toward the east-southeast.

east•ward (ēst′wərd) *adv. & adj.* Toward, to, or in the east. —*n.* An eastward direction, point, or region. —**east′ward•ly** *adv. & adj.* —**east′wards** *adv.*

eas•y (ē′zē) *adj.* **-i•er, -i•est. 1.** Capable of being accomplished or acquired with ease; posing no difficulty. **2.** Requiring or exhibiting little effort or endeavor; undemanding. **3.** Free from worry, anxiety, trouble, or pain. **4.a.** Affording comfort or relief; soothing. **b.** Prosperous; well-off. **5.** Causing little hardship or distress. **6.** Socially at ease. **7.a.** Relaxed in attitude; easygoing. **b.** Not strict or severe; lenient. **8.** Readily exploited, imposed on, or tricked. **9.a.** Not hurried or forced; moderate: *an easy pace.* **b.** Light; gentle. **10.** Not steep or abrupt; gradual. **11.** *Econ.* **a.** Less in demand and therefore readily obtainable. **b.** Plentiful and therefore at low interest rates. **12.** Promiscuous; loose. —*adv.* **1.** Without haste or agitation. **2.** With little effort; easily. **3.** In a restrained or moderate manner. **4.** Without much hardship or cost. —***idiom.*** **easy as pie.** *Informal.* Capable of being accomplished or done with no difficulty. [ME *esi* < OFr. *aaisie,* p.part. of *aaisier,* to put at ease : *a-,* to (< Lat. *ad-,* ad- + *aise,* ease; see EASE).] —**eas′i•ness** *n.*

Syns: easy, simple, facile, effortless, smooth, light. These adjectives mean requiring little effort or posing little if any difficulty. *Easy* applies to tasks that require little effort: *"The diagnosis of disease is often easy, often difficult, and often impossible"* (Peter M. Latham). *Simple* implies lack of complexity that facilitates understanding or performance: *"the faculty . . . of reducing his thought on any subject to the simplest and plainest terms possible"* (Baron Charnwood). *Facile* stresses readiness and fluency (*a facile speaker*); often, though, the word implies glibness, insincerity, superficiality, or lack of care: *a facile explanation for a complex phenomenon. Effortless* refers to performance in which the application of great strength or skill makes the execution seem easy: *wrote effortless prose. Smooth* suggests freedom from hindrances or difficulties that impede progress: *a smooth path to success. Light* refers to tasks or responsibilites that are not taxing or burdensome: *light duties; light taxes.*

easy chair *n.* A large, comfortable, well-upholstered chair.

eas•y•go•ing also **eas•y-go•ing** (ē′zē-gō′ĭng) *adj.* **1.a.** Living without undue worry or concern; calm. **b.** Lax or negligent; careless. **c.** Relaxed in attitude or standards. **2.** Not rigorous, demanding, or stressful. **3.** Leisurely; unhurried.

easy street *n.* *Informal.* A condition of financial security.

eat (ēt) *v.* **ate** (āt), **eat•en** (ēt′n), **eat•ing, eats.** —*tr.* **1.a.** To take into the body by the mouth for digestion or absorption. **b.** To include habitually or by preference in one's diet. **2.** To consume, ravage, or destroy by or as if by ingesting. **3.** To erode or corrode: *Waves ate away the beach.* **4.** To produce by or as if by eating. **5.** *Slang.* To absorb the cost or expense of. **6.** *Informal.* To bother or annoy. —*intr.* **1.a.** To consume food. **b.** To have or take a meal. **2.** To exercise a consuming or eroding effect. **3.** To cause persistent annoyance or distress. —***phrasal verb.*** **eat up.** *Slang.* To receive or enjoy enthusiastically or avidly. —***idioms.*** **eat crow.** To be forced to accept a humiliating defeat. **eat (one's) heart out. 1.** To feel bitter anguish or grief. **2.** To be consumed by jealousy. **eat (one's) words.** To retract something that one has said. **eat out of (someone's) hand.** To be manipulated or dominated by another. **eat (someone) alive.** *Slang.* To overwhelm or defeat thoroughly. [ME *eten* < OE *etan.* See **ed-***.] **—eat′er** *n.*

eat•a•ble (ē′tə-bəl) *adj.* Fit to be eaten; edible: *an eatable meal.* —*n.* **1.** Something fit to be eaten. **2. eatables** Food.

eat•er•y (ē′tə-rē) *n., pl.* **-ies.** *Informal.* A restaurant.

eat•ing (ē′tĭng) *adj.* **1.** Suitable for being eaten, esp. without cooking. **2.** Used in the ingestion of food, as at the table.

eating disorder *n.* A potentially life-threatening neurotic condition, such as anorexia nervosa or bulimia.

eats (ēts) *pl.n. Slang.* Food, esp. snacks.

Eau Claire (ō klâr′). A city of W-central WI at the mouth of the **Eau Clair River,** c. 113 km (70 mi). Pop. 56,856.

eau de co•logne (ō′ də kə-lōn′) *n., pl.* **eaux de cologne** (ō′, ōz′). See **cologne.** [Fr. *eau-de-cologne.* See COLOGNE.]

eau de vie (ō′ də vē′) *n., pl.* **eaux de vie** (ō′, ōz′). Brandy. [Fr. *eau-de-vie* : *eau,* water + *de,* of + *vie,* life.]

eaves (ēvz) *pl.n.* The projecting overhang at the lower edge of a roof. [ME *eves* < OE *efes.* See **upo***.]

eaves•drop (ēvz′drŏp′) *intr.v.* **-dropped, -drop•ping, -drops.** To listen secretly to the private conversation of others. [Prob. back-formation < *eavesdropper,* one who eavesdrops < ME *evesdropper* < *evesdrop,* place where water falls from the eaves < OE *yfes drype.* See **upo***.] **—eaves′drop′per** *n.*

eaves spout *n. New England & Northern U.S.* See **gutter** 2. See Regional Note at **gutter.**

eaves trough *n. Northern U.S.* See **gutter** 2. See Regional Note at **gutter.**

E•ban (ē′bən), **Abba.** b. 1915. South African-born Israeli politician who served as ambassador to the U.S. (1950–59) and foreign minister (1966–74).

ebb (ĕb) *n.* **1.** Ebb tide. **2.** A period of decline or diminution. —*intr.v.* **ebbed, ebb•ing, ebbs. 1.** To fall back from the flood stage. **2.** To fall away or back; decline or recede. [ME *ebbe* < OE *ebba.* See **apo-***.]

ebb tide *n.* The receding or outgoing tide; the period between high water and the succeeding low water.

EBCDIC (ĕb′sē-dĭk) *n. Comp. Sci.* A standard code that uses 8 bits to represent each of up to 256 alphanumeric characters. [*E(xtended) B(inary) C(oded) D(ecimal) I(nterchange) C(ode).*]

Eb•la (ĕb′lə, ē′blə). An ancient city of SW Asia near the site of Aleppo, Syria. The cuneiform Ebla Tablets (discovered 1974–75) describe a thriving 3rd-millennium B.C. civilization centered around the city.

Eb•la•ite (ĕb′lə-īt′, ē′blə-) *n.* The Semitic language of Ebla.

EbN *abbr.* East by north.

eb•on (ĕb′ən) *adj.* **1.** Made of ebony. **2.** Black in color. —*n.* Ebony. [ME *eban,* ebony wood < OFr. < Lat. *ebenus,* ebony tree < Gk. *ebenos.* See EBONY.]

eb•on•ite (ĕb′ə-nīt′) *n.* A relatively inelastic rubber, made by vulcanization and used as an electrical insulating material.

eb•on•ize (ĕb′ə-nīz′) *tr.v.* **-ized, -iz•ing, -iz•es.** To stain black like ebony.

eb•on•y (ĕb′ə-nē) *n., pl.* **-ies. 1.** A tropical tree *(Diospyros ebenum)* of southern Asia having hard dark-colored heartwood. **2.** The wood of this tree, used in cabinetwork and for piano keys. **3.** The color black; ebon. —*adj.* **1.** Made of or suggesting ebony. **2.** Black in color. [Prob. < ME *hebenyf,* ebony wood < alteration of LLat. *ebeninus,* of ebony < Gk. *ebeninos* < *ebenos,* ebony tree < Egypt. *h-b-ny.*]

Eb•ro (ē′brō, ĕb′rō, ĕ′vrô). A river rising in N Spain and flowing c. 925 km (575 mi) to the Mediterranean Sea.

EbS *abbr.* East by south.

e•bul•lience (ĭ-bo͝ol′yəns, ĭ-bŭl′-) *n.* Zestful enthusiasm.

e•bul•lien•cy (ĭ-bo͝ol′yən-sē, ĭ-bŭl′-) *n.* Ebullience.

e•bul•lient (ĭ-bo͝ol′yənt, ĭ-bŭl′-) *adj.* **1.** Zestfully enthusiastic. **2.** Boiling or seeming to boil; bubbling. [Lat. *ēbulliēns, ēbullient-,* pr.part. of *ēbullīre,* to bubble up : *ē-, ex-,* up, out; see EX- + *bullīre,* to bubble, boil.] **—e•bul′lient•ly** *adv.*

eb•ul•li•tion (ĕb′ə-lĭsh′ən) *n.* **1.** The state or process of boiling. **2.** A sudden violent outpouring, as of emotion. [ME *ebullitiun* < LLat. *ēbullītiō, ēbullītiōn-* < Lat. *ēbullītus,* p.part. of *ēbullīre,* to bubble up. See EBULLIENT.]

e•bur•na•tion (ē′bər-nā′shən, ĕb′ər-) *n.* Degeneration of bone into a hard ivorylike mass. [< Lat. *eburnus,* ivory < *ebur.* See IVORY.]

EBV *abbr.* Epstein-Barr virus.

Ec. *abbr.* Ecuador.

E•ca•te•pec de Mo•re•los (ā-kä′tə-pĕk′ də mô-rĕl′əs, ĕ-kä′tä-pĕk′ dĕ mô-rĕ′lôs). A city of central Mexico near Mexico City; on the site of an Aztec kingdom estab. in the 12th cent. Pop. 741,821.

Ec•ba•ta•na (ĕk-băt′n-ə). A city of ancient Media on the site of present-day Hamadan in W Iran; captured by Cyrus the Great in 549 B.C.

ec•ce ho•mo (ĕk′sē hō′mō, ĕk′ē) *n.* A depiction of Jesus wearing the crown of thorns. [LLat. *ecce homō,* behold the man : Lat. *ecce,* behold + Lat. *homō,* man.]

ec•cen•tric (ĭk-sĕn′trĭk, ĕk-) *adj.* **1.** Departing from a recognized, conventional, or established norm or pattern. See Syns at **strange. 2.** Deviating from a circular form or path, as in an ellipse. **3.a.** Not situated at or in the geometric center. **b.** Having the axis located elsewhere than at the geometric center. —*n.* **1.** One that deviates markedly from an established norm, esp. a person of odd or unconventional behavior. **2.** *Phys.* A disk or wheel having an eccentric axis of revolution so that it can impart reciprocating motion. [ME *eccentrik,* planetary orbit of which the earth is not at the center < Med.Lat. *eccentricus,* not having the same center < Gk. *ekkentros* : *ek-,* out of; see ECTO- + *kentron,* center (< *kentein,* to prick; see **kent-***).] **—ec•cen′tri•cal•ly** *adv.*

ec•cen•tric•i•ty (ĕk′sĕn-trĭs′ĭ-tē) *n., pl.* **-ties. 1.a.** The quality of being eccentric. **b.** Deviation from the normal, expected, or established. **2.** An example or instance of eccentric behavior. **3.** *Phys.* The distance between the center of an eccentric and its axis. **4.** *Math.* The ratio of the distance of any point on a conic section from a focus to its distance from the corresponding directrix.

ec•chy•mo•sis (ĕk′ĭ-mō′sĭs) *n.* The passage of blood from ruptured blood vessels into subcutaneous tissue, marked by a purple discoloration of the skin. [NLat. < Gk. *ekkhumōsis,* extravasation < *ekkhumousthai,* to extravasate : *ek-,* out; see ECTO- + *khumos,* juice; see **gheu-***.] **—ec′chy•mot′ic** (-mŏt′ĭk) *adj.*

eccl. *abbr.* Ecclesiastic; ecclesiastical.

Ec•cles (ĕk′əlz), Sir **John Carew.** b. 1903. Australian physiologist who shared a 1963 Nobel Prize.

Eccles. *abbr.* **1.** *Bible.* Ecclesiastes. **2. eccles.** Ecclesiastic; ecclesiastical.

ec•cle•si•a (ĭ-klē′zhē-ə, -zē-ə) *n., pl.* **-si•ae** (-zhē-ē′, -zē-ē′). **1.** The political assembly of citizens of an ancient Greek state. **2.** A church or congregation. [Lat. *ecclēsia* < Gk. *ekklēsia* < *ekkalein,* to summon forth : *ek-,* out; see ECTO- + *kalein, klē-,* to call; see **kelə-**[2]*.]

Ec•cle•si•as•tes (ĭ-klē′zē-ăs′tēz′) *n. (used with a sing. v.)* See table at **Bible.** [LLat. *Ecclēsiastēs* < Gk. *Ekklēsiastēs,* preacher (transl. of Heb. *Qoholeth*) < *ekklēsiastēs,* a member of the ecclesia < *ekklēsia,* ecclesia. See ECCLESIA.]

ec•cle•si•as•tic (ĭ-klē′zē-ăs′tĭk) *adj.* Ecclesiastical. —*n.* A minister or priest; a cleric. [LLat. *ecclēsiasticus* < Gk. *ekklēsiastikos* < *ekklēsiastēs,* a member of the ecclesia. See ECCLESIASTES.]

ec•cle•si•as•ti•cal (ĭ-klē′zē-ăs′tĭ-kəl) *adj.* **1.** Of or relating to a church, esp. as an organized institution. **2.** Appropriate to a church. **—ec•cle′si•as′ti•cal•ly** *adv.*

ec•cle•si•as•ti•cism (ĭ-klē′zē-ăs′tə-sĭz′əm) *n.* **1.** Ecclesiastical principles, practices, and activities. **2.** Excessive adherence to ecclesiastical principles and forms.

Ec•cle•si•as•ti•cus (ĭ-klē′zē-ăs′tĭ-kəs) *n.* See table at **Bible.**

ec•cle•si•ol•o•gy (ĭ-klē′zē-ŏl′ə-jē) *n.* **1.** The branch of theology concerned with the nature, constitution, and functions of a church. **2.** The study of ecclesiastical architecture and ornamentation. [ECCLESI(A) + -LOGY.] **—ec•cle′si•o•log′i•cal** (-ə-lŏj′ĭ-kəl) *adj.*

ec•crine (ĕk′rĭn, -rīn′, -rēn′) *adj.* **1.** Relating to an eccrine gland or its secretion, esp. sweat. **2.** Exocrine. [< Gk. *ekkrinein,* to secrete : *ek-,* out; see ECTO- + *krinein,* to separate; see **krei-***.]

eccrine gland *n.* A sweat gland.

ec•dys•i•ast (ĕk-dĭz′ē-ăst′, -əst) *n.* A striptease artist.

ec•dy•sis (ĕk′dĭ-sĭs) *n., pl.* **-ses** (-sēz′). The shedding of an outer integument or layer of skin, as by insects or snakes; molting. [Gk. *ekdusis,* a stripping off < *ekduein,* to take off : *ek-,* out, off; see ECTO- + *duein,* to put on.]

ec•dy•sone (ĕk′də-sōn′) *n.* A steroid hormone produced by insects and crustaceans that promotes growth and controls molting. [ECDYS(IS) + (HORM)ONE.]

e•ce•sis (ĭ-sē′sĭs) *n.* The successful establishment of a plant or animal species in a habitat. [< Gk. *oikēsis,* inhabitation < *oikein,* to dwell < *oikos,* house. See **weik-**[1]*.]

ECG *abbr.* **1.** Electrocardiogram. **2.** Electrocardiograph.

E•che•ga•ray y Ei•za•guir•re (ā′chə-gə-rī′ ē ā′sə-gîr′ā, -gwîr′ā, ĕ′chĕ-gä-rī′ ē ā′thä-gē′rĕ), **José.** 1832–1916. Spanish playwright who shared the 1904 Nobel Prize for literature.

ech•e•lon (ĕsh′ə-lŏn′) *n.* **1.a.** A formation of troops in which each unit is positioned successively to the left or right of the rear unit to form an oblique or steplike line. **b.** A flight formation or arrangement of craft in this manner. **c.** A similar formation of groups, units, or individuals. **2.** A subdivision of a military or naval force. **3.** A level of responsibility or authority in a hierarchy; a rank. —*tr. & intr.v.* **-loned, -lon•ing, -lons.** To arrange or take place in an echelon. [Fr. *échelon* < OFr. *eschelon,* rung of a ladder < *eschiele,* ladder < LLat. *scāla* < Lat. *scālae,* steps. See **skand-***.]

ech•e•ve•ri•a (ĕch′ə-və-rē′ə) *n.* Any of numerous tropical American plants of the genus *Echeveria,* having thick leaves often clustered in a rosette. [NLat. *Echeveria,* genus name, after Atanasio *Echeverría,* 19th-cent. Mexican illustrator.]

e•chid•na (ĭ-kĭd′nə) *n.* Any of several nocturnal, burrowing, egg-laying mammals of the genera *Tachyglossus* and *Zaglossus* of Australia, Tasmania, and New Guinea, having a spiny coat, slender snout, and an extensible sticky tongue used for catching insects. [Lat., adder, viper < Gk. *ekhidna* < *ekhis.*]

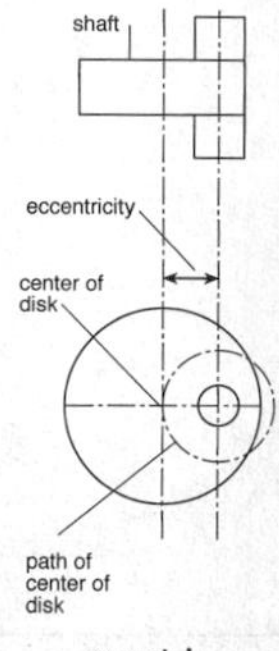

eccentric

echeveria
Echeveria pulvinata

echidna
Tachyglossus aculeatus

ă pat	oi boy
ā pay	ou out
âr care	o͝o took
ä father	o͞o boot
ĕ pet	ŭ cut
ē be	ûr urge
ĭ pit	th thin
ī pie	*th* this
îr pier	hw which
ŏ pot	zh vision
ō toe	ə about, item
ô paw	

Stress marks:
′ (primary);
′ (secondary), as in
dictionary (dĭk′shə-nĕr′ē)

ech•i•nate (ĕk′ə-nāt′) *adj.* Bearing or covered with spines or bristles; prickly.

echino– or **echin–** *pref.* **1.** Spiny; prickly: *echinate.* **2.** Echinoderm: *echinoid.* [< Lat. *echīnus*, sea urchin. See ECHINUS.]

e•chi•no•coc•cus (ĭ-kī′nə-kŏk′əs) *n., pl.* **-coc•ci** (-kŏk′sī′, -kŏk′ī′). Any of several parasitic tapeworms of the genus *Echinococcus,* the larvae of which infect mammals, causing serious or fatal disease. [NLat. *Echinococcus*, genus name : ECHINO– + –COCCUS.]

e•chi•no•derm (ĭ-kī′nə-dûrm′) *n.* Any of numerous radially symmetrical marine invertebrates of the phylum Echinodermata, which includes the starfishes, having an internal calcareous skeleton and often covered with spines. **—e•chi′no•der′mal, e•chi′no•der′ma•tous** (-dûr′mə-təs) *adj.*

e•chi•noid (ĭ-kī′noid′) *n.* An echinoderm of the class Echinoidea, which includes the sand dollars and sea urchins.

e•chi•nus (ĭ-kī′nəs) *n., pl.* **-ni** (-nī′). **1.** A sea urchin of the genus *Echinus.* **2.** *Archit.* A convex molding just below the abacus of a Doric capital. [Lat. *echīnus*, sea urchin < Gk. *ekhinos*, sea urchin, hedgehog < *ekhis*, adder, viper.]

ech•o (ĕk′ō) *n., pl.* **-oes. 1.a.** Repetition of a sound by reflection of sound waves from a surface. **b.** The sound produced in this manner. **2.** A repetition or an imitation. **3.** A remnant or vestige. **4.** One who imitates another, as in opinions or dress. **5.** A sympathetic response. **6.** A consequence or repercussion. **7.** Repetition of certain sounds or syllables in poetry, as in echo verse. **8.** *Mus.* Soft repetition of a note or phrase. **9.** *Electron.* A reflected wave received by a radio or radar. —*v.* **-oed, -o•ing, -oes.** —*tr.* **1.** To repeat (a sound) by the reflection of sound waves from a surface. **2.** To repeat or imitate. —*intr.* **1.** To be repeated by or as if by an echo. **2.** To resound with or as if with an echo; reverberate. [ME < OFr. < Lat. *ēchō* < Gk. *ēkhō*.] **—ech′o•er** *n.* **—ech′o•ey** *adj.*

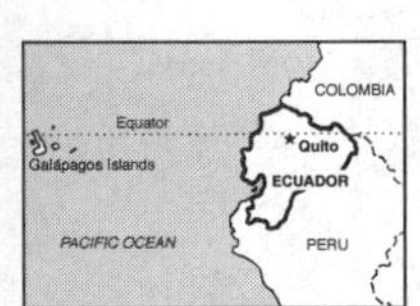

Ecuador

Ech•o (ĕk′ō) *n. Gk. Myth.* A nymph who pined away out of love for Narcissus until nothing but her voice remained.

ech•o•car•di•o•gram (ĕk′ō-kär′dē-ə-grăm′) *n.* A visual record produced by an echocardiograph.

ech•o•car•di•o•graph (ĕk′ō-kär′dē-ə-grăf′) *n.* An instrument that employs the differential transmission and reflection of ultrasonic waves to visualize structural and functional abnormalities of the heart. **—ech′o•car′di•o•graph′ic** *adj.* **—ech′o•car′di•og′ra•phy** (-ŏg′rə-fē) *n.*

echo chamber *n.* A room or enclosure with acoustically reflective walls that produce echoes or similar sound effects.

ech•o•en•ceph•a•lo•gram (ĕk′ō-ĕn-sĕf′ə-lə-grăm′, -ə-lō-) *n.* A visual record produced by an echoencephalograph.

ech•o•en•ceph•a•lo•graph (ĕk′ō-ĕn-sĕf′ə-lə-grăf′, -ə-lō-) *n.* An instrument that uses the differential transmission and reflection of ultrasonic waves to create a detailed visual image of the brain. **—ech′o•en•ceph′a•lo•graph′ic** *adj.* **—ech′o•en•ceph′a•log′ra•phy** (-lŏg′rə-fē) *n.*

ech•o•gram (ĕk′ō-grăm′) *n.* See **sonogram.**

e•chog•ra•phy (ĕ-kŏg′rə-fē) *n.* See **ultrasonography.**

e•cho•ic (ĕ-kō′ĭk) *adj.* **1.** Of or resembling an echo. **2.** Imitative of natural sounds; onomatopoeic: *an echoic word.*

ech•o•la•li•a (ĕk′ō-lā′lē-ə) *n.* **1.** *Psychiat.* The immediate and involuntary repetition of words or phrases just spoken by others. **2.** An infant's repetition of the sounds made by others. [ECHO + Gk. *lalia*, talk (< *lalos*, talkative).]

ech•o•lo•ca•tion (ĕk′ō-lō-kā′shən) *n.* **1.** A sensory system in certain animals, such as bats and dolphins, in which usu. high-pitched sounds are emitted and their echoes interpreted to determine the direction and distance of objects. **2.** *Electron.* A process for determining the location of objects by emitting sound waves and analyzing the waves reflected back to the sender by the object. **—ech′o•lo•cate′** *v.*

Mary Baker Eddy

echo sounder *n.* A device for measuring depth of water by sending pressure waves down from the surface and recording the time until the echo returns from the bottom.

ech•o•vi•rus (ĕk′ō-vī′rəs) *n., pl.* **-rus•es.** *Microbiol.* Any of a number of retroviruses of the family Picornaviridae, inhabiting the gastrointestinal tract and associated with various diseases. [*e(nteric) c(ytopathogenic) h(uman) o(rphan) virus.*]

Eck (ĕk), **Johann.** 1486–1543. German Roman Catholic theologian and opponent of the reforms of Martin Luther.

Eck•hart also **Eck•art** or **Eck•ardt** (ĕk′härt′, -ärt′), **Johannes.** "Meister Eckhart." 1260?–1327? German theologian regarded as the founder of mysticism in Germany.

é•clair (ā-klâr′, ā′klâr′) *n.* An elongated pastry filled with custard or whipped cream and usu. iced with chocolate. [Fr. < OFr. *esclair*, lightning < *esclairier*, to light up < VLat. **exclāriāre* < Lat. *exclārāre* : *ex-*, intensive pref.; see EX– + *clārus*, clear; see **kelə-**[2]*.]

é•clair•cisse•ment (ā-klâr-sēs-mäɴ′) *n.* A clarification; an enlightenment. [Fr. < OFr. *esclarcir, esclarciss-*, to clarify < VLat. **exclāricīre*, var. of **exclāriāre.* See ÉCLAIR.]

e•clamp•si•a (ĭ-klămp′sē-ə) *n.* Coma and convulsions during or immediately after pregnancy, accompanied by edema, hypertension, and proteinuria. [NLat. < Gk. *eklampsis*, a shining forth < *eklampein*, to shine forth : *ek-*, out; see ECTO– + *lampein*, to shine.] **—e•clamp′tic** (-tĭk) *adj.*

é•clat (ā-klä′, ā′klä′) *n.* **1.** Great brilliance, as of performance or achievement. **2.** Conspicuous success. **3.** Great acclamation or applause. **4.** *Archaic.* Notoriety; scandal. [Fr., brilliance < OFr. *esclat*, splinter < *esclater*, to burst out, splinter, prob. of Gmc. orig.]

e•clec•tic (ĭ-klĕk′tĭk) *adj.* **1.** Selecting or employing individual elements from a variety of sources. **2.** Made up of or combining elements from a variety of sources. —*n.* One that follows an eclectic method. [Gk. *eklektikos*, selective < *eklektos*, selected < *eklegein*, to select : *ek-*, out; see ECTO– + *legein*, to gather; see **leg-***.] **—e•clec′ti•cal•ly** *adv.*

e•clec•ti•cism (ĭ-klĕk′tə-sĭz′əm) *n.* An eclectic system.

e•clipse (ĭ-klĭps′) *n.* **1.a.** The partial or complete obscuring of one celestial body by another. **b.** The period of time during which an eclipse occurs. **2.** A temporary or permanent dimming or cutting off of light. **3.a.** A fall into obscurity or disuse; a decline. **b.** A disgraceful or humiliating end; a downfall: *the eclipse of the governor's career.* —*tr.v.* **e•clipsed, e•clips•ing, e•clips•es. 1.a.** To cause an eclipse of. **b.** To obscure; darken. **2.a.** To obscure or diminish in importance, fame, or reputation. **b.** To surpass; outshine. [ME < OFr. < Lat. *eclīpsis* < Gk. *ekleipsis* < *ekleipein*, to fail to appear : *ek-*, out; see ECTO– + *leipein*, to leave; see **leik**^{w}**-***.]

e•clip•tic (ĭ-klĭp′tĭk) *n.* **1.** The intersection plane of the earth's orbit with the celestial sphere, along which the sun appears to move as viewed from the earth. **2.** A great circle inscribed on a terrestrial globe inclined at an approx. angle of 23°27′ to the equator and representing the apparent path of the sun during a year. [ME *ecliptik* < Med.Lat. *(līnea) eclīptica*, ecliptic (line) < Lat. *eclīpticus*, of an eclipse < Gk. *ekleiptikos* < *ekleipein*, to fail to appear. See ECLIPSE.]

ec•logue (ĕk′lôg′, -lŏg′) *n.* A pastoral poem, usu. in the form of a dialogue between shepherds. [ME *eclog* < Lat. *ecloga* < Gk. *eklogē*, selection < *eklegein*, to select. See ECLECTIC.]

e•clo•sion (ĭ-klō′zhən) *n.* The emergence of an adult insect from a pupal case or an insect larva from an egg. [Fr. *éclosion* < *éclore*, to open < OFr. < VLat. **exclaudere*, to shut out : Lat. *ex-*, ex- + Lat. *claudere*, to shut.]

eco– *pref.* Ecology; ecological: *ecosystem.* [< ECOLOGY.]

ec•o•ca•tas•tro•phe (ĕk′ō-kə-tăs′trə-fē, ē′kō-) *n.* A large-scale disruption of nature, usu. due to human intervention.

ec•o•cide (ĕk′ō-sīd′, ē′kō-) *n.* Heedless or deliberate destruction of the natural environment, as by pollutants.

ecol. *abbr.* **1.** Ecology. **2.** Ecological.

E. co•li (ē kō′lī) *n.* A bacillus *(Escherichia coli)* normally found in the human gastrointestinal tract and existing as numerous strains. [NLat. *Escherichia coli* : after Theodor *Escherich* (1857–1911), German physician, + Lat. *colī*, genitive of *colon*; see COLON[2].]

e•col•o•gy (ĭ-kŏl′ə-jē) *n., pl.* **-gies. 1.a.** The science of the relationships between organisms and their environments. **b.** The relationship between organisms and their environment. **2.** The branch of sociology that studies the relationships between human groups and their physical and social environments. **3.** The study of the detrimental effects of modern civilization on the environment. [Ger. *Ökologie* : Gk. *oikos*, house; see **weik-**[1]* + Ger. *-logie*, study (< Gk. *-logia*, -logy).] **—ec′o•log′i•cal** (ĕk′ə-lŏj′ĭ-kəl, ē′kə-), **ec′o•log′ic** (-ĭk) *adj.* **—ec′o•log′i•cal•ly** *adv.* **—e•col′o•gist** *n.*

econ. *abbr.* Economics; economist; economy.

e•con•o•met•rics (ĭ-kŏn′ə-mĕt′rĭks) *n. (used with a sing. v.)* Application of mathematical and statistical techniques to economics in the study of problems, theories, and models and in the analysis of data. **—e•con′o•met′ric, e•con′o•met′ri•cal** *adj.* **—e•con′o•met′ri•cal•ly** *adv.* **—e•con′o•me•tri′cian** (-mĭ-trĭsh′ən), **e•con′o•met′rist** *n.*

ec•o•nom•ic (ĕk′ə-nŏm′ĭk, ē′kə-) *adj.* **1.a.** Of or relating to the production, development, and management of material wealth, as of a country or household. **b.** Of or relating to an economy. **2.** Of or relating to the science of economics. **3.** Of or relating to the practical necessities of life; material. **4.a.** Financially rewarding; economical. **b.** Efficient; economical.

ec•o•nom•i•cal (ĕk′ə-nŏm′ĭ-kəl, ē′kə-) *adj.* **1.** Prudent and thrifty in management. See Syns at **sparing. 2.** Intended to save money, as by efficient operation; economic. **—ec′o•nom′i•cal•ly** *adv.*

economic rent *n.* See **rent**[1] 3.

ec•o•nom•ics (ĕk′ə-nŏm′ĭks, ē′kə-) *n.* **1.** *(used with a sing. v.)* The social science that deals with the production, distribution, and consumption of goods and services and with the theory and management of economies or economic systems. **2.** *(used with a sing. or pl. v.)* Economic matters, esp. relevant financial considerations.

e•con•o•mist (ĭ-kŏn′ə-mĭst) *n.* **1.** A specialist in economics. **2.** *Archaic.* An economical person.

e•con•o•mize (ĭ-kŏn′ə-mīz′) *v.* **-mized, -miz•ing, -miz•es.** —*intr.* **1.** To practice economy, as by reducing expenditures. **2.** To make economical use of something. —*tr.* To use or manage with thrift. **—e•con′o•miz′er** *n.*

e•con•o•my (ĭ-kŏn′ə-mē) *n., pl.* **-mies. 1.a.** Careful, thrifty management of resources, such as money, materials, or labor. **b.** An example or result of such management; a saving.

2.a. The system or range of economic activity in a country, region, or community. **b.** A specific type of economic system. **3.** An orderly functional arrangement of parts; an organized system. **4.** Efficient, sparing, or conservative use. **5.** Economy class. **6.** *Theol.* The method of God's government of and activity within the world. — *adj.* Economical or inexpensive to buy or use. [ME *yconomye*, management of a household < Lat. *oeconomia* < Gk. *oikonomia* < *oikonomos*, one who manages a household : *oikos*, house; see **weik-**[1]* + *nemein*, to allot, manage; see **nem-***.]

economy class *n.* The least expensive class of accommodations, esp. on an airplane.

ec•o•spe•cies (ĕk′ō-spē′shēz, -sēz, ē′kō-) *n.*, *pl.* **ecospecies.** A taxonomic species considered in terms of its ecological characteristics and usu. including several interbreeding ecotypes.

ec•o•sphere (ĕk′ō-sfîr′, ē′kō-) *n.* The regions of the universe, esp. on the earth, that are capable of supporting life.

ec•o•sys•tem (ĕk′ō-sĭs′təm, ē′kō-) *n.* An ecological community together with its environment, functioning as a unit.

ec•o•type (ĕk′ə-tīp′, ē′kə-) *n.* The smallest taxonomic subdivision of an ecospecies, consisting of populations adapted to a particular set of environmental conditions. — **ec′o•typ′ic** (-tĭp′ĭk) *adj.*

ec•ru (ĕk′ro͞o, ā′kro͞o) *n. Color.* A grayish to pale yellow or light grayish-yellowish brown. [Fr. *écru*, raw, unbleached < OFr. *escru* : *es-*, intensive pref. (< Lat. *ex-*; see EX–) + *cru*, raw (< Lat. *crūdus*; see **kreuə-***).]

ec•sta•sy (ĕk′stə-sē) *n.*, *pl.* **-sies. 1.** Intense joy or delight. **2.** A state of emotion so intense that one is carried beyond rational thought and self-control: *an ecstasy of rage.* **3.** The trance, frenzy, or rapture associated with mystic or prophetic exaltation. [ME *extasie* < OFr. < LLat. *extasis*, terror < Gk. *ekstasis*, astonishment, distraction < *existanai*, to displace, derange : *ex-*, out of; see EXO– + *histanai*, to place; see **stā-***.]

ec•stat•ic (ĕk-stăt′ĭk) *adj.* **1.** Marked by or expressing ecstasy. **2.** Being in a state of ecstasy; enraptured. [Fr. *extatique* < Gk. *ekstatikos* < *ekstasis*, distraction. See ECSTASY.] — **ec•stat′i•cal•ly** *adv.*

ECT *abbr.* Electroconvulsive therapy.

ecto– *pref.* Outer; external: *ectoparasite.* [Gk. *ekto-* < *ektos*, outside < *ek*, *ek-*, out. See **eghs***.]

ec•to•derm (ĕk′tə-dûrm′) *n.* **1.** The outermost of the three primary germ layers of an embryo, from which the epidermis, nervous tissue, and, in vertebrates, sense organs develop. **2.** The outer layer of a diploblastic animal, such as a jellyfish. — **ec′to•der′mal, ec′to•der′mic** *adj.*

ec•tog•e•nous (ĕk-tŏj′ə-nəs) also **ec•to•gen•ic** (ĕk′tə-jĕn′ĭk) *adj. Biol.* Able to live and develop outside a host.

ec•to•morph (ĕk′tə-môrf′) *n.* An individual having a lean, slightly muscular body build in which tissues derived from the embryonic ectoderm predominate. [ECTO(DERM) + –MORPH.] — **ec′to•mor′phic** *adj.*

–ectomy *suff.* Surgical removal: *tonsillectomy.* [NLat. *-ectomia* : Gk. *ek-*, out; see ECTO– + *-tomia*, -tomy.]

ec•to•par•a•site (ĕk′tə-păr′ə-sīt′) *n.* A parasite, such as a flea, that lives on the exterior of another organism. — **ec′to•par′a•sit′ic** (-sĭt′ĭk) *adj.* — **ec′to•par′a•sit′ism** *n.*

ec•to•pi•a (ĕk-tō′pē-ə) *n.* An abnormal location or position of an organ or a body part, occurring congenitally or as the result of injury. [NLat. < Gk. *ektopos*, away from a place : *ek-*, away from, out of; see ECTO– + *topos*, place.] — **ec•top′ic** (-tŏp′ĭk) *adj.*

ectopic pregnancy *n.* Implantation and subsequent development of a fertilized ovum outside the uterus.

ec•to•plasm (ĕk′tə-plăz′əm) *n.* **1.** *Biol.* The outer portion of the cytoplasm of a cell, sometimes distinguishable as a somewhat rigid gelled layer beneath the cell membrane. **2.a.** The visible substance believed to emanate from the body of a spiritualistic medium during communication with the dead. **b.** An immaterial or ethereal substance, esp. the transparent corporeal presence of a spirit or ghost. **3.** *Informal.* An image projected onto a movie screen. — **ec′to•plas′mic** *adj.*

ec•to•therm (ĕk′tə-thûrm′) *n.* An organism that regulates its body temperature largely by exchanging heat with its surroundings; a poikilotherm.

ec•to•ther•mic (ĕk′tə-thûr′mĭk) also **ec•to•ther•mal** (ĕk′tə-thûr′məl) or **ec•to•ther•mous** (-məs) *adj.* Of or relating to an ectotherm; cold-blooded.

é•cu (ā-kyo͞o′) *n.*, *pl.* **é•cus** (ā-kyo͞o′). Any of various old French coins, esp. a silver five-franc piece. [Fr. < OFr. *escu* < Lat. *scūtum*, shield. See **skei-***.]

Ecua. *abbr.* Ecuador.

Ec•ua•dor (ĕk′wə-dôr′). A country of NW South America on the Pacific Ocean; gained independence from Spain in 1830. Cap. Quito. Pop. 8,050,630. — **Ec′ua•dor′i•an** *adj. & n.*

ec•u•men•i•cal (ĕk′yə-mĕn′ĭ-kəl) also **ec•u•men•ic** (-mĕn′ĭk) *adj.* **1.** Of worldwide scope or applicability; universal. **2.a.** Of or relating to the worldwide Christian church. **b.** Concerned with establishing or promoting unity among churches or religions. [< LLat. *oecūmenicus* < Gk. *oikoumenikos* < *(hē) oikoumenē (gē)*, (the) inhabited (world), fem. pr. passive part. of *oikein*, to inhabit < *oikos*, house. See **weik-**[1]*.] — **ec′u•men′i•cal** *n.* — **ec′u•men′i•cal•ism** *n.* — **ec′u•men′i•cal•ly** *adv.*

ecumenical patriarch *n.* The patriarch of Constantinople, the highest ecclesiastical official of the Eastern Orthodox Church.

ec•u•men•i•cism (ĕk′yə-mĕn′ĭ-sĭz′əm) *n.* Ecumenism. — **ec′u•men′i•cist** *n.*

ec•u•me•nism (ĕk′yə-mə-nĭz′əm, ĭ-kyo͞o′-) *n.* **1.** A movement promoting unity among Christian churches or denominations. **2.** A movement promoting unity among religions through cooperation and understanding. — **ec′u•men′ist** *n.*

ec•ze•ma (ĕk′sə-mə, ĕg′zə-, ĭg-zē′-) *n.* A noncontagious skin inflammation, marked chiefly by redness, itching, and the outbreak of lesions. [NLat. < Gk. *ekzema* < *ekzein*, to boil over : *ek-*, out; see ECTO– + *zein*, to boil; see **yes-***.] — **ec•zem′a•tous** (ĕg-zĕm′ə-təs, -zē′mə-təs, ĭg-) *adj.*

ed. *abbr.* **1.** Edition; editor. **2.** Education.

E.D. *abbr.* Election district.

–ed[1] *suff.* Used to form the past tense of regular verbs: *tasted.* [ME *-ede* < OE *-ade, -ede, -ode.*]

–ed[2] *suff.* Used to form the past participle of regular verbs: *absorbed.* [ME < OE *-ad, -ed, -od.*]

–ed[3] *suff.* Having; characterized by; resembling: *blackhearted.* [ME *-ede, -de* < OE *-ed, -od.*]

e•da•cious (ĭ-dā′shəs) *adj.* Characterized by voracity; devouring. [< Lat. *edāx, edāc-* < *edere*, to eat. See **ed-***.] — **e•dac′i•ty** (ĭ-dăs′ĭ-tē) *n.*

E•dam[1] (ē′dəm, ē′dăm′, ā-däm′). A town of W Netherlands on the Ijsselmeer; chartered 1357. Pop. 24,019.

E•dam[2] (ē′dəm, ē′dăm′) *n.* A mild yellow Dutch cheese, usu. covered with red wax. [After EDAM[1].]

e•daph•ic (ĭ-dăf′ĭk) *adj.* **1.** Of or relating to soil, esp. as it affects living organisms. **2.** Influenced by the soil rather than by the climate. [< Gk. *edaphos*, ground, soil. See **sed-***.]

Ed•da (ĕd′ə) *n.* **1.** A collection of Old Norse poems, called the Elder or Poetic Edda, assembled in the early 13th century. **2.** A manual of Icelandic poetry, called the Younger or Prose Edda, written by Snorri Sturluson. [ON.] — **Ed′dic** *adj.*

Ed•ding•ton (ĕd′ĭng-tən), Sir **Arthur Stanley.** 1882–1944. British mathematician, astronomer, and physicist who was an early exponent of the theory of relativity.

ed•do (ĕd′ō) *n.*, *pl.* **-does.** See **taro.** [Of Niger-Congo orig.; akin to Akan (Fante) *edwo*, yam.]

ed•dy (ĕd′ē) *n.*, *pl.* **-dies. 1.** A current, as of water or air, moving contrary to the main current, esp. in a circular motion. **2.** A drift or tendency counter to or separate from a main current, as of history. — *v.* **-died, -dy•ing, -dies.** — *intr.* To move in or as if in an eddy. — *tr.* To cause to eddy. [ME *ydy*, prob. of Scand. orig.; akin to ON *idha.*]

Ed•dy (ĕd′ē), **Mary (Morse) Baker.** 1821–1910. Amer. religious leader who founded Christian Science (1879).

Ed•dy•stone Rocks (ĕd′ĭ-stən). A rocky islet of SW England in the English Channel S of Plymouth.

E•de. 1. (ā′də). A city of central Netherlands NW of Arnhem. Pop. 71,952. **2.** (ā′dā, ā-dā′). A city of W Nigeria NE of Ibadan; a former center of Yoruba culture. Pop. 216,400.

e•del•weiss (ā′dəl-vīs′, -wīs′) *n.* An alpine plant *(Leontopodium alpinum)* native to Europe and having leaves covered with whitish down and small flower heads surrounded by whitish bracts. [Ger. : *edel*, noble (< MHGer. *edele* < OHGer. *edili*) + *weiss*, white (< MHGer. *wīz* < OHGer. *wīz, hwīz*; see **kweit-***).]

e•de•ma also **oe•de•ma** (ĭ-dē′mə) *n.*, *pl.* **-mas** or **-ma•ta** (-mə-tə). **1.** *Pathol.* An excessive accumulation of serous fluid in tissue spaces or a body cavity. **2.** *Bot.* Extended swelling in plant organs caused primarily by an excessive accumulation of water. [ME *ydema* < Gk. *oidēma*, a swelling < *oidein*, to swell.] — **e•dem′a•tous** (ĭ-dĕm′ə-təs) *adj.*

E•den[1] (ēd′n) *n.* **1.** *Bible.* The garden that was the first home of Adam and Eve. **2.** A delightful place; a paradise. **3.** A state of innocence or ultimate happiness. [ME < LLat. < Gk. *Ēdēn* < Heb. *'Ēden* < *'ēden*, delight.] — **E•den′ic** (ē-dĕn′ĭk) *adj.*

E•den[2] (ēd′n). A city of N NC near the VA border N of Greensboro. Pop. 15,238.

Eden, Sir **(Robert) Anthony.** 1st Earl of Avon. 1897–1977. British politician who served as prime minister (1955–57).

Eden Prairie. A city of E MN, a suburb of Minneapolis. Pop. 39,311.

e•den•tate (ē-dĕn′tāt′) *Biol. adj.* **1.** Lacking teeth. **2.** Of or belonging to the order Edentata, which includes mammals having few or no teeth, such as anteaters and sloths. [Lat. *ēdentātus*, p.part. of *ēdentāre*, to knock out the teeth : *ē-, ex-*, ex- + *dēns, dent-*, tooth; see **dent-***.] — **e•den′tate′** *n.*

e•den•tu•lous (ē-dĕn′chə-ləs) *adj. Biol.* Toothless. [< Lat. *ēdentulus* : *ē-, ex-*, ex- + *dēns, dent-*, tooth; see **dent-***.]

E•der (ā′dər). A river rising in central Germany and flowing c. 177 km (110 mi) E to the Fulda R.

E•der•le (ā′dər-lē), **Gertrude Caroline.** b. 1906. Amer. swimmer who in 1926 became the first woman to swim the English Channel.

E•des•sa (ĭ-dĕs′ə). An ancient city of Mesopotamia on the site of Urfa in SE Turkey; captured by Crusaders in 1097.

edelweiss
Leontopodium alpinum

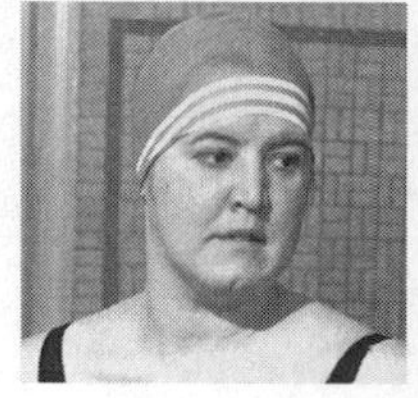
Gertrude Ederle

ă pat	oi boy
ā pay	ou out
âr care	o͝o took
ä father	o͞o boot
ĕ pet	ŭ cut
ē be	ûr urge
ĭ pit	th thin
ī pie	*th* this
îr pier	hw which
ŏ pot	zh vision
ō toe	ə about, item
ô paw	

Stress marks:
′ (primary);
′ (secondary), as in dictionary (dĭk′shə-nĕr′ē)

edge (ĕj) *n.* **1.a.** A thin sharpened side, as of the blade of a cutting instrument. **b.** The degree of sharpness of a cutting blade. **c.** A penetrating, incisive quality. **2.** Keenness, as of desire; zest. **3.a.** The line of intersection of two surfaces. **b.** A rim or brink. **4.a.** The area or part away from the middle; an extremity. **b.** A dividing line; a border. See Syns at **border.** **c.** A point of transition. **5.** A margin of superiority; an advantage. — *v.* **edged, edg•ing, edg•es.** — *tr.* **1.a.** To give an edge to (a blade); sharpen. **b.** *Sports.* To tilt (a ski or both skis) in such a way that an edge or both edges bite into the snow. **2.a.** To put a border or edge on. **b.** To act as or be an edge of. **3.** To advance or push slightly or gradually. **4.** To trim or shape the edge of. — *intr.* To move gradually or hesitantly. — ***phrasal verb.*** **edge out.** To surpass or beat by a small margin: *edged out her opponent in the final seconds.* — ***idioms.*** **on edge.** Highly tense or nervous; irritable. **on the edge. 1.** In a precarious position. **2.** In a state of keen excitement, as from risk. [ME *egge* < OE *ecg.* See **ak-*.**]

edg•er (ĕj′ər) *n.* One that edges.

edge tool *n.* A tool, such as a chisel, that has a cutting edge.

edge•wise (ĕj′wīz′) also **edge•ways** (-wāz′) *adv.* **1.** With the edge foremost. **2.** On, by, with, or toward the edge.

Edge•wood (ĕj′wo͝od′). A community of NE MD on an inlet of Chesapeake Bay NE of Baltimore. Pop. 23,903.

Edge•worth (ĕj′wûrth′), **Maria.** 1767–1849. British writer noted for her realistic novels, such as *Castle Rackrent* (1800).

edg•ing (ĕj′ĭng) *n.* Something that forms or serves as an edge or a border.

edg•y (ĕj′ē) *adj.* **-i•er, -i•est. 1.** Nervous or irritable. **2.** Having a sharp or biting edge. — **edg′i•ly** *adv.* — **edg′i•ness** *n.*

edh also **eth** (ĕ*th*) *n.* **1.** A letter (ð) appearing in Old English, Old Saxon, Old Norse, and modern Icelandic to represent an interdental fricative. **2.** The symbol in the International Phonetic Alphabet for the interdental voiced fricative. [Icel. *edh.*]

ed•i•ble (ĕd′ə-bəl) *adj.* Fit to be eaten. — *n.* Something fit to be eaten; food. [LLat. *edibilis* < Lat. *edere,* to eat. See **ed-*.**] — **ed′i•bil′i•ty, ed′i•ble•ness** *n.*

e•dict (ē′dĭkt′) *n.* **1.** A decree or proclamation issued by an authority and having the force of law. **2.** A formal pronouncement or command. [Lat. *ēdictum* < neut. p.part. of *ēdīcere,* to declare : *ē-, ex-,* ex- + *dīcere,* to speak; see **deik-*.**]

ed•i•fi•ca•tion (ĕd′ə-fĭ-kā′shən) *n.* Intellectual, moral, or spiritual improvement; enlightenment.

Thomas Edison
Photographed in 1893

ed•i•fice (ĕd′ə-fĭs) *n.* **1.** A building, esp. one of imposing appearance or size. **2.** An elaborate conceptual structure. [ME < OFr. < Lat. *aedificium* < *aedificāre,* to build : *aedis,* a building + *-ficāre,* -fy.]

ed•i•fy (ĕd′ə-fī′) *tr.v.* **-fied, -fy•ing, -fies.** To instruct esp. so as to encourage intellectual, moral, or spiritual improvement. [ME *edifien* < OFr. *edifier* < LLat. *aedificāre,* to instruct spiritually < Lat., to build. See EDIFICE.] — **ed′i•fi′er** *n.*

E•di•na (ĭ-dī′nə). A city of E MN, a suburb of Minneapolis. Pop. 46,070.

Ed•in•burg (ĕd′n-bûrg′). A city of S TX near the Mexican border WNW of Brownsville. Pop. 29,885.

Ed•in•burgh (ĕd′n-bûr′ə, -bŭr′ə, -brə). The cap. of Scotland, in the E part on the Firth of Forth. Pop. 446,361.

Edinburgh, Duke of. See Prince **Philip.**

E•dir•ne (ĕ-dîr′nĕ). Formerly **A•dri•a•no•ple** (ā′drē-ə-nō′pəl). A city of NW Turkey NW of Istanbul; founded c. A.D. 125 by the Roman emperor Hadrian. Pop. 71,914.

Ed•i•son (ĕd′ĭ-sən). A community of central NJ NE of New Brunswick. Pop. 88,680.

Edison, Thomas Alva. 1847–1931. Amer. inventor who patented over a thousand inventions, among them the phonograph (1878) and an incandescent lamp (1879).

ed•it (ĕd′ĭt) *tr.v.* **-it•ed, -it•ing, -its. 1.a.** To prepare (written material) for publication or presentation, as by correcting, revising, or adapting. **b.** To prepare an edition of. **c.** To modify or adapt so as to make suitable or acceptable. **2.** To supervise the publication of (a magazine, for example). **3.** To assemble the components of (a soundtrack, for example), as by cutting and splicing. **4.** To eliminate; delete: *edited the best scene out.* — *n.* An act or instance of editing. [Partly backformation < EDITOR and partly < Fr. *éditer,* to publish (< Lat. *ēditus,* p.part. of *ēdere;* see EDITION).]

edit. *abbr.* Edition; editor.

e•di•tion (ĭ-dĭsh′ən) *n.* **1.a.** The entire number of copies of a publication issued at one time or from a single set of type. **b.** A single copy from this group. **c.** The form in which a publication is issued: *a paperback edition.* **d.** A version of an earlier publication having substantial changes or additions. **2.** All the copies of a specified issue of a newspaper. **3.** A broadcast of a radio or television news program. **4.a.** The entire number of like or identical items issued or produced as a set. **b.** Any of the various or successive forms in which something is offered or presented. **5.** One that closely resembles an original; a version. [ME *edicion,* version < Lat. *ēditiō, ēditiōn-,* publication, production < *ēditus,* p.part. of *ēdere,* to publish, produce : *ē-, ex-,* ex- + *dare,* to give; see **dō-*.**]

ed•i•tor (ĕd′ĭ-tər) *n.* **1.** One who edits, esp. as an occupation. **2.** One who writes editorials. **3.** A device for editing film, consisting basically of a splicer and viewer. **4.** *Comp. Sci.* A program or set of instructions used to edit text or data files. [LLat. *ēditor,* publisher < Lat. *ēditus,* p.part. of *ēdere,* to publish. See EDITION.]

ed•i•to•ri•al (ĕd′ĭ-tôr′ē-əl, -tōr′-) *n.* **1.** An article in a publication expressing the opinion of its editors or publishers. **2.** A commentary on television or radio expressing the opinion of the station or network. — *adj.* **1.** Of or relating to an editor or editing. **2.** Of or resembling an editorial, esp. in expressing an opinion. — **ed′i•to′ri•al•ly** *adv.*

ed•i•to•ri•al•ist (ĕd′ĭ-tôr′ē-ə-lĭst, -tōr′-) *n.* One who writes or presents editorials.

ed•i•to•ri•al•ize (ĕd′ĭ-tôr′ē-ə-līz′, -tōr′-) *intr.v.* **-ized, -iz•ing, -iz•es. 1.** To express an opinion in or as if in an editorial. **2.** To present an opinion as an objective report. — **ed′i•to′ri•al•i•za′tion** (-ə-lĭ-zā′shən) *n.* — **ed′i•to′ri•al•i′zer** *n.*

editor in chief *n., pl.* **editors in chief.** The editor having final responsibility for the operations and policies of a publication.

ed•i•tor•ship (ĕd′ĭ-tər-shĭp′) *n.* The position, functions, or guidance of an editor.

Ed.M. *abbr. Lat.* Educationis Magister (Master of Education).

Ed•mond (ĕd′mənd). A city of central OK N of Oklahoma City. Pop. 52,315.

Ed•monds (ĕd′məndz). A city of NW WA on Puget Sound N of Seattle; settled in 1866. Pop. 30,744.

Ed•mon•ton (ĕd′mən-tən). The cap. of Alberta, Canada, in the central part N of Calgary; founded 1795 as a fort and trading post of the Hudson's Bay Company. Pop. 532,246.

Ed•mund II (ĕd′mənd). "Edmund Ironside." 993?–1016. King of the English (1016) who partitioned the kingdom in a settlement with Canute.

E•do (ĕd′ō). See **Tokyo.**

E•dom (ē′dəm). An ancient country of Palestine between the Dead Sea and the Gulf of Aqaba. According to the Bible, the original inhabitants were descendants of Esau.

E•dom•ite (ē′də-mīt′) *n.* A member of a Semitic people inhabiting Edom in ancient times. — **E′dom•it′ish** *adj.*

EDP *abbr. Comp. Sci.* Electronic data processing.

EDT or **E.D.T.** *abbr.* Eastern Daylight Time.

EDTA (ē′dē-tē-ā′) *n.* A crystalline acid, $C_{10}H_{16}N_2O_8$, that is a strong chelating agent and whose sodium salt is used as an antidote for metal poisoning and as an anticoagulant. [*e(thylene)d(iamine)t(etraacetic) a(cid).*]

educ. *abbr.* Education; educational.

ed•u•ca•ble (ĕj′ə-kə-bəl) *adj.* Capable of being educated or taught: *educable youngsters.* — **ed′u•ca•bil′i•ty** *n.*

ed•u•cate (ĕj′ə-kāt′) *v.* **-cat•ed, -cat•ing, -cates.** — *tr.* **1.** To develop the innate capacities of, esp. by schooling or instruction. See Syns at **teach. 2.** To provide with knowledge or training in a particular area or for a particular purpose. **3.a.** To provide with information; inform. **b.** To bring to an understanding or acceptance. **4.** To stimulate or develop the mental or moral growth of. **5.** To develop or refine (one's taste or appreciation, for example). — *intr.* To teach or instruct a person or group. [ME *educaten* < Lat. *ēducāre, ēducātus.* See **deuk-*.**]

ed•u•cat•ed (ĕj′ə-kā′tĭd) *adj.* **1.** Having an education, esp. one above the average. **2.a.** Showing evidence of schooling, training, or experience. **b.** Having or exhibiting cultivation; cultured. **3.** Based on experience or factual knowledge.

ed•u•ca•tion (ĕj′ə-kā′shən) *n.* **1.** The act or process of educating or being educated. **2.** The knowledge or skill obtained or developed by a learning process. **3.** A program of instruction of a specified kind or level: *driver education.* **4.** The field of study concerned with the pedagogy of teaching and learning. **5.** An instructive or enlightening experience.

ed•u•ca•tion•al (ĕj′ə-kā′shə-nəl) *adj.* **1.** Of or relating to education. **2.** Serving to educate; instructive. — **ed′u•ca′tion•al•ly** *adv.*

educational television *n.* **1.** See **public television. 2.** An often closed-circuit video system that provides education.

ed•u•ca•tion•ist (ĕj′ə-kā′shə-nĭst) also **ed•u•ca•tion•al•ist** (-shə-nə-lĭst) *n.* A specialist in the theory of education.

ed•u•ca•tive (ĕj′ə-kā′tĭv) *adj.* Educational.

ed•u•ca•tor (ĕj′ə-kā′tər) *n.* **1.** One trained in teaching; a teacher. **2.a.** A specialist in the theory and practice of education. **b.** An administrator of a school or an educational institution.

e•duce (ĭ-do͞os′, ĭ-dyo͞os′) *tr.v.* **e•duced, e•duc•ing, e•duc•es. 1.** To draw or bring out; elicit. **2.** To assume or work out from given facts; deduce. [ME *educen,* to direct the flow of < Lat. *ēdūcere* : *ē-, ex-,* ex- + *dūcere,* to lead; see **deuk-*.**] — **e•duc′i•ble** *adj.* — **e•duc′tion** (ĭ-dŭk′shən) *n.*

Ed•ward¹ (ĕd′wərd). "the Confessor." 1003?–66. King of the English (1042–66) whose reign was marked by political conflict between Norman and English groups.

Edward². Prince of Wales. "the Black Prince." 1330–76. English soldier during the Hundred Years' War who fought at Crécy (1346) and Poitiers (1356).

Edward I. 1239–1307. King of England (1272–1307) whose Model Parliament of 1295 is sometimes considered England's first full parliament.

Edward II. 1284–1327. King of England (1307–27) who was defeated at Bannockburn by the Scots (1314).

Edward III. 1312–77. King of England (1327–77) who reigned during the beginning of the Hundred Years' War.

Edward IV. 1442–83. King of England (1461–70 and 1471–83) who was crowned after the Yorkist victory in the Wars of the Roses, dethroned in 1470, and recrowned in 1471.

Edward V. 1470–83. King of England (1483) who was crowned at the age of 13 on the death of his father, Edward IV, and was immediately confined in the Tower of London, where he and his younger brother were murdered.

Edward VI. 1537–53. King of England and Ireland (1547–53) who was the son of Henry VIII and Jane Seymour.

Edward VII. 1841–1910. King of Great Britain and Ireland (1901–10) who was known for his elegant, sporting style. **—Ed•ward′i•an** (ĕd-wôr′dē-ən, -wär′-) *adj. & n.*

Edward VIII. Later Duke of Windsor. 1894–1972. King of Great Britain and Ireland (1936) who abdicated in order to marry (1937) Wallis Warfield Simpson, an Amer. divorcée.

Edward, Lake. A lake in the Great Rift Valley of central Africa on the Zaire-Uganda border.

Ed•wards (ĕd′wərdz), **Jonathan.** 1703–58. Amer. theologian whose works stimulated the Great Awakening.

Ed•win (ĕd′wĭn). 585?–633. King of Northumbria (617–633) who was converted to Christianity (627).

E.E. *abbr.* **1.** Electrical engineer. **2.** Electrical engineering.

-ee[1] *suff.* **1.a.** One that receives or benefits from a specified action: *addressee.* **b.** One that possesses a specified thing: *mortgagee.* **2.** One that performs a specified action: *absentee.* [ME < AN *-e, -ee,* p.part. suff. < Lat. *-ātus.* See -ATE[1].]

Usage Note: The suffix *-ee* was first used in English to refer to indirect objects and then direct objects of transitive verbs, as in *donee* or *draftee.* Beginning around the mid-19th century, primarily in American English, it was often extended to denote the agent or subject of an intransitive verb; for example, *standee.* Although the pattern is very common, in general such words retain an informal character as jocular nonce words.

-ee[2] *suff.* **1.a.** One resembling: *goatee.* **b.** A particular, esp. a diminutive kind of: *bootee.* **2.** One connected with: *bargee.* [Var. of -Y[1].]

EEC *abbr.* European Economic Community.

EEG *abbr.* **1.** Electroencephalogram. **2.** Electroencephalograph.

eel (ēl) *n., pl.* **eel** or **eels. 1.** Any of various long, snakelike, scaleless marine or freshwater fishes of the order Anguilliformes or Apodes that characteristically migrate from fresh to salt water to spawn. **2.** Any of several similar fishes, such as the lamprey. [ME *ele* < OE *ǣl.*]

eel•grass (ēl′grăs′) *n.* Any of several submersed aquatic plants of the genus *Vallisneria.*

eel•pout (ēl′pout′) *n., pl.* **eelpout** or **-pouts. 1.** Any of various bottom-dwelling marine fishes of the family Zoarcidae, having an elongated body and a large head. **2.** See **burbot.**

eel•worm (ēl′wûrm′) *n.* Any of various often parasitic nematode worms, such as the vinegar eel.

e'en[1] (ēn) *n.* Evening.

e'en[2] (ēn) *adv.* Even.

EEO *abbr.* Equal employment opportunity.

-eer *suff.* One associated with, concerned with, or engaged in: *balladeer.* [Fr. *-ier* < OFr. < Lat. *-ārius,* -ary.]

e'er (âr) *adv.* Ever.

ee•rie or **ee•ry** (îr′ē) *adj.* **-ri•er, -ri•est. 1.a.** Inspiring inexplicable fear, dread, or uneasiness. **b.** Suggestive of the supernatural; mysterious. **2.** *Scots.* Frightened or intimidated by superstition. [ME *eri,* fearful < OE *earg,* cowardly.] **—ee′ri•ly** *adv.* **—ee′ri•ness** *n.*

ef (ĕf) *n.* The letter *f.*

eff. *abbr.* Efficiency.

ef•face (ĭ-fās′) *tr.v.* **-faced, -fac•ing, -fac•es. 1.** To rub or wipe out; erase. **2.** To make indistinct as if by rubbing. See Syns at **erase. 3.** To conduct (oneself) inconspicuously. [ME *effacen* < Fr. *effacer* < OFr. *esfacier* : *es-,* out (< Lat. *ex-,* ex-) + *face,* face (< Lat. *faciēs;* see **dhē-***).] **—ef•face′a•ble** *adj.* **—ef•face′ment** *n.* **—ef•fac′er** *n.*

ef•fect (ĭ-fĕkt′) *n.* **1.** Something brought about by a cause or an agent; a result. **2.** The power to produce an outcome or achieve a result; influence. **3.** A scientific law, hypothesis, or phenomenon. **4.** Advantage; avail. **5.** The condition of being in full force or execution. **6.a.** Something that produces a specific impression or supports a general design or intention. **b.** A particular impression. **c.** Production of a desired impression. **7.** The basic or general meaning; import. **8. effects.** Movable belongings; goods. *—tr.v.* **-fect•ed, -fect•ing, -fects. 1.** To bring into existence. **2.** To produce as a result. **3.** To bring about. See Usage Note at **affect[1]**. *—idiom.* **in effect.** In essence; to all purposes. [ME < OFr. < Lat. *effectus,* p.part. of *efficere,* to accomplish : *ex-,* ex- + *facere,* to make; see **dhē-***.] **—ef•fect′er** *n.* **—ef•fect′i•ble** *adj.*

Syns: *effect, consequence, result, outcome, upshot, sequel.* These nouns denote something, such as an occurrence, a situation, or a condition, that is caused by an antecedent. An *effect* is produced by the action of an agent or a cause and follows it in time: *"Every cause produces more than one effect"* (Herbert Spencer). A *consequence* has a less sharply definable relationship to its cause: *"Servitude is at once the consequence of his crime and the punishment of his guilt"* (John P. Curran). A *result* is viewed as the end product of the operation of the cause: *"Judging from the results I have seen . . . I cannot say . . . that I agree with you"* (William H. Mallock). An *outcome* implies finality and may suggest the operation of a cause over a relatively long period: *an unlikely outcome for the story.* An *upshot* is a decisive result, often climactic: *"The upshot of the matter . . . was that she showed both of them the door"* (Robert Louis Stevenson). A *sequel* is a consequence that ensues after a lapse of time: *"Our dreams are the sequel of our waking knowledge"* (Ralph Waldo Emerson).

ef•fec•tive (ĭ-fĕk′tĭv) *adj.* **1.a.** Having an intended or expected effect. **b.** Producing a strong impression or response; striking. **2.** Operative; in effect. **3.** Existing in fact; actual: *a decline in the effective demand.* **4.** Prepared for use or action, esp. in warfare. *—n.* A soldier or a piece of military equipment that is ready for combat. **—ef•fec′tive•ness, ef′fec•tiv′i•ty** *n.*

ef•fec•tive•ly (ĭ-fĕk′tĭv-lē) *adv.* **1.** In an effective way. **2.** For all practical purposes; in effect.

ef•fec•tor (ĭ-fĕk′tər) *n.* **1.** A muscle, a gland, or an organ capable of responding to a stimulus, esp. a nerve impulse. **2.** A nerve ending that carries impulses to an effector. **3.** *Biochem.* A molecule that when bound to the allosteric site of an enzyme causes either a decrease or an increase in the activity of the enzyme. **4.** *Comp. Sci.* A device used to produce a desired change in an object in response to input.

ef•fec•tu•al (ĭ-fĕk′cho͞o-əl) *adj.* Producing or sufficient to produce a desired effect; fully adequate. [ME *effectuel* < OFr. < LLat. *effectuālis* < Lat. *effectus,* accomplishment. See EFFECT.] **—ef•fec′tu•al′i•ty** (-ăl′ĭ-tē), **ef•fec′tu•al•ness** *n.* **—ef•fec′tu•al•ly** *adv.*

ef•fec•tu•ate (ĭ-fĕk′cho͞o-āt′) *tr.v.* **-at•ed, -at•ing, -ates.** To bring about; effect. [Med.Lat. *effectuāre, effectuāt-* < Lat. *effectus,* an effect. See EFFECT.] **—ef•fec′tu•a′tion** *n.*

ef•fem•i•na•cy (ĭ-fĕm′ə-nə-sē) *n.* The quality or condition of being effeminate.

ef•fem•i•nate (ĭ-fĕm′ə-nĭt) *adj.* **1.** Having qualities or characteristics more often associated with women than men. **2.** Marked by weakness and excessive refinement. [ME *effeminat* < Lat. *effēminātus,* p.part. of *effēmināre,* to make feminine : *ex-,* ex- + *fēmina,* woman; see **dhē(i)-***.] **—ef•fem′i•nate** *n.* **—ef•fem′i•nate•ly** *adv.* **—ef•fem′i•nate•ness** *n.*

ef•fen•di (ĭ-fĕn′dē) *n., pl.* **-dis.** Used as a title of respect for men in Turkey. [Turk. *efendi* < Med.Gk. *aphentēs,* master, alteration of Gk. *authentēs.* See AUTHENTIC.]

ef•fer•ent (ĕf′ər-ənt) *adj.* **1.** Directed away from a central organ or section. **2.** Carrying impulses from the central nervous system to an effector. *—n.* An efferent organ or body part, such as a blood vessel. [< Lat. *efferēns, efferent-,* pr.part. of *efferre,* to carry off : *ex-,* ex- + *ferre,* to carry; see **bher-[1]***.] **—ef′fer•ent•ly** *adv.*

ef•fer•vesce (ĕf′ər-vĕs′) *intr.v.* **-vesced, -vesc•ing, -vesc•es. 1.** To emit small bubbles of gas, as a carbonated or fermenting liquid. **2.** To escape from a liquid as bubbles; bubble up. **3.** To show high spirits or excitement. [Lat. *effervēscere* : *ex-,* up, out; see EX- + *fervēscere,* to start boiling, inchoative of *fervēre,* to boil; see **bhreu-***.] **—ef′fer•ves′cence, ef′fer•ves′cen•cy** *n.* **—ef′fer•ves′cent** *adj.* **—ef′fer•ves′cent•ly** *adv.*

ef•fete (ĭ-fēt′) *adj.* **1.** Depleted of vitality, force, or effectiveness; exhausted. **2.** Marked by self-indulgence, triviality, or decadence: *an effete intellectual.* **3.** Overrefined; effeminate. **4.** No longer productive; infertile. [Lat. *effētus,* worn out, exhausted : *ex-,* ex- + *fētus,* bearing young, pregnant; see **dhē(i)-***.] **—ef•fete′ly** *adv.* **—ef•fete′ness** *n.*

ef•fi•ca•cious (ĕf′ĭ-kā′shəs) *adj.* Producing or capable of producing a desired effect. [< Lat. *efficāx, efficāc-* < *efficere,* to effect. See EFFECT.] **—ef′fi•ca′cious•ly** *adv.* **—ef′fi•ca′cious•ness** *n.*

ef•fi•ca•cy (ĕf′ĭ-kə-sē) *n.* Power or capacity to produce a desired effect; effectiveness. [Lat. *efficācia* < *efficāx, efficāc-,* efficacious. See EFFICACIOUS.]

ef•fi•cien•cy (ĭ-fĭsh′ən-sē) *n., pl.* **-cies. 1.a.** The quality or property of being efficient. **b.** The degree to which this quality is exercised. **2.a.** The ratio of the effective or useful output to the total input in any system. **b.** The ratio of the energy delivered by a machine to the energy supplied for its operation. **3.** An efficiency apartment.

efficiency apartment *n.* A small, usu. furnished apartment with a private bathroom and kitchenette.

ef•fi•cient (ĭ-fĭsh′ənt) *adj.* **1.** Acting directly to produce an effect: *an efficient cause.* **2.a.** Acting or producing effectively with a minimum of waste, expense, or unnecessary effort. **b.** Exhibiting a high ratio of output to input. [ME < OFr. < Lat. *efficiēns, efficient-,* pr.part. of *efficere,* to effect. See EFFECT.] **—ef•fi′cient•ly** *adv.*

ef•fi•gy (ĕf′ə-jē) *n., pl.* **-gies. 1.** A crude figure or dummy representing a hated person or group. **2.** A likeness or image,

Edward VIII
Photographed while Duke of Windsor

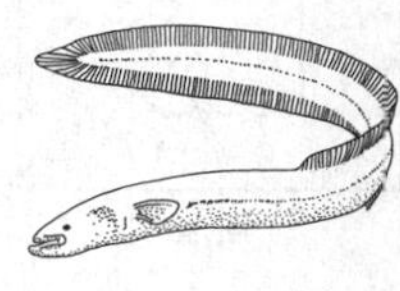

eel

ă pat	oi boy
ā pay	ou out
âr care	o͝o took
ä father	o͞o boot
ĕ pet	ŭ cut
ē be	ûr urge
ĭ pit	th thin
ī pie	*th* this
îr pier	hw which
ŏ pot	zh vision
ō toe	ə about, item
ô paw	

Stress marks:
′ (primary);
′ (secondary), as in **dictionary** (dĭk′shə-nĕr′ē)

esp. of a person. — ***idiom.* in effigy.** Symbolically, esp. in the form of an effigy. [Fr. *effigie* < Lat. *effigiēs*, likeness < *effingere*, to portray : *ex-*, ex- + *fingere*, to shape; see **dheigh-***.]

ef•flo•resce (ĕf′lə-rĕs′) *intr.v.* **-resced, -resc•ing, -resc•es. 1.** To blossom; bloom. **2.** *Chem.* **a.** To become a powder by losing water of crystallization, as when a hydrated crystal is exposed to air. **b.** To become covered with a powdery deposit. [Lat. *efflōrēscere* : *ex-*, ex- + *flōrēscere*, inchoative of *flōrēre*, to blossom (< *flōs*, *flōr-*, flower; see **bhel-[3]***).]

ef•flo•res•cence (ĕf′lə-rĕs′əns) *n.* **1.** *Bot.* A state or time of flowering; anthesis. **2.a.** A gradual process of unfolding or developing. **b.** The highest point; the culmination. **3.** *Chem.* **a.** The deposit that results from the process of efflorescing. **b.** The process of efflorescing. **c.** A growth of salt crystals on a surface caused by evaporation of salt-laden water. **4.** *Pathol.* Redness, a rash, or an eruption on the skin. — **ef′flo•res′cent** *adj.*

egg-and-dart

ef•flu•ence (ĕf′lo͞o-əns) *n.* **1.** The act or an instance of flowing out. **2.** Something that flows out or forth; an emanation.

ef•flu•ent (ĕf′lo͞o-ənt) *adj.* Flowing out or forth. —*n.* Something that flows out or forth, esp.: **a.** A stream flowing out of a body of water. **b.** An outflow from a sewer or sewage system. **c.** A discharge of liquid waste, as from a factory or nuclear plant. [ME < Lat. *effluēns*, *effluent-*, pr.part. of *effluere*, to flow out : *ex-*, ex- + *fluere*, to flow; see **bhleu-***.]

ef•flu•vi•um (ĭ-flo͞o′vē-əm) *n., pl.* **-vi•a** (-vē-ə) or **-vi•ums. 1.** A usu. invisible emanation or exhalation. **2.a.** A byproduct or residue; waste. **b.** The fumes given off by waste or decaying matter. **3.** An impalpable emanation; an aura. [Lat. < *effluere*, to flow out. See EFFLUENT.] — **ef•flu′vi•al** *adj.*

ef•flux (ĕf′lŭks′) *n.* **1.** A flowing outward. **2.** Something that flows out or forth; an effluence. **3.** A passing or an expiration, as of time. [< Lat. *effluxus*, p.part. of *effluere*, to flow out. See EFFLUENT.] — **ef•flux′ion** (ĭ-flŭk′shən) *n.*

eggplant
Solanum melongena var. *esculenta*

ef•fort (ĕf′ərt) *n.* **1.** The use of physical or mental energy to do something. **2.** A difficult exertion of the strength or will. **3.** A usu. earnest attempt. **4.** Something done or produced through exertion; an achievement. **5.** *Phys.* Force applied against inertia. [ME < OFr. *esfort* < *esforcier*, to force, exert < Med. Lat. *exfortiāre* : Lat. *ex-*, ex- + Lat. *fortis*, strong; see **bhergh-[2]***.] — **ef′fort•ful** *adj.* — **ef′fort•ful•ly** *adv.*

ef•fort•less (ĕf′ərt-lĭs) *adj.* Calling for, requiring, or showing little or no effort. See Syns at **easy.** — **ef′fort•less•ly** *adv.* — **ef′fort•less•ness** *n.*

ef•front•er•y (ĭ-frŭn′tə-rē) *n., pl.* **-ies.** Brazen boldness; presumptuousness. [Fr. *effronterie* < *effronté*, shameless < OFr. *esfronte*, poss. < LLat. *effrōns*, *effront-* : *ex-*, ex- + *frōns*, *front-*, front, forehead.]

ef•ful•gence (ĭ-fo͝ol′jəns, ĭ-fŭl′-) *n.* A brilliant radiance.

ef•ful•gent (ĭ-fo͝ol′jənt, ĭ-fŭl′-) *adj.* Shining brilliantly; resplendent. See Syns at **bright.** [Lat. *effulgēns*, *effulgent-*, pr.part. of *effulgēre*, to shine out : *ex-*, ex- + *fulgēre*, to shine; see **bhel-[1]***.]

ef•fuse (ĭ-fyo͞os′) *adj. Bot.* Spreading out loosely. —*v.* (ĭ-fyo͞oz′) **-fused, -fus•ing, -fus•es.** —*tr.* **1.** To pour out (a liquid). **2.** To radiate; diffuse. —*intr.* **1.** To spread or flow out. **2.** To ooze forth; exude. [Lat. *effūsus*, p.part. of *effundere*, to pour out : *ex-*, ex- + *fundere*, to pour; see **gheu-***.]

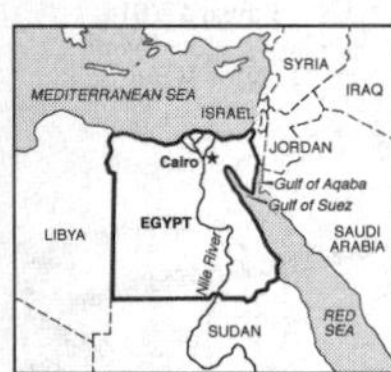

Egypt

ef•fu•sion (ĭ-fyo͞o′zhən) *n.* **1.a.** The act or an instance of effusing. **b.** Liquid or other matter poured forth. **2.** An unrestrained outpouring of feeling, as in speech or writing. **3.** *Pathol.* **a.** The seeping of serous, purulent, or bloody fluid into a body cavity or tissue. **b.** The effused fluid.

ef•fu•sive (ĭ-fyo͞o′sĭv) *adj.* **1.** Unrestrained or excessive in emotional expression; gushy. **2.** Profuse; overflowing: *effusive praise.* — **ef•fu′sive•ly** *adv.* — **ef•fu′sive•ness** *n.*

Ef•ik (ĕf′ĭk) *n., pl.* **Efik** or **-iks. 1.** A member of a people inhabiting southern Nigeria. **2.** The Niger-Congo language of the Efik people, closely related to Ibibio. — **Ef′ik** *adj.*

eft (ĕft) *n.* An immature newt. [ME *evete* < OE *efeta.*]

EFTS *abbr.* Electronic funds transfer system.

eft•soons (ĕft-so͞onz′) *adv. Archaic.* **1.** Soon afterward; presently. **2.** Once again. [< ME *eftsone* < OE *eftsōna* : *eft*, again; see **apo-*** + *sōna*, soon.]

e.g. *abbr.* Exempli gratia.

e•gad (ĭ-găd′) or **e•gads** (ĭ-gădz′) *interj.* Used as a mild exclamation. [Alteration of *oh God.*]

Eg•a•di Islands (ĕg′ə-dē) also **Ae•ga•de•an Isles** (ē-gā′dē-ən) or **Ae•ga•tes** (-tēz). An island group of SW Italy in the Mediterranean Sea W of Sicily.

e•gal•i•tar•i•an (ĭ-găl′ĭ-târ′ē-ən-) *adj.* Affirming, promoting, or characterized by belief in equal political, economic, and social rights for all people. [< Fr. *égalitaire* < *égalité*, equality < Lat. *aequālitās* < *aequālis*, equal. See EQUAL.] — **e•gal′i•tar′i•an** *n.* — **e•gal′i•tar′i•an•ism** *n.*

Albert Einstein

Eg•bert (ĕg′bərt). d. 839. West Saxon king (802–839) who became the first overlord of all the English peoples (829).

EGD *abbr.* Electrogasdynamics.

E•ge•ri•a (ĭ-jîr′ē-ə) *n.* A woman adviser or counselor. [After *Egeria*, Roman adviser to Numa Pompilius, a legendary king.]

e•gest (ē-jĕst′) *tr.v.* **e•gest•ed, e•gest•ing, e•gests.** To discharge or excrete from the body. [Lat. *ēgerere*, *ēgest-*, to carry out : *ē-*, *ex-*, ex- + *gerere*, to carry.] — **e•ges′tion** *n.* — **e•ges′tive** *adj.*

e•ges•ta (ē-jĕs′tə) *pl.n.* Egested matter. [Lat., neut. pl. of *ēgestus*, p.part. of *ēgerere*, to carry out. See EGEST.]

EGF *abbr.* Epidermal Growth Factor.

egg[1] (ĕg) *n.* **1.a.** A female gamete; an ovum. **b.** The round or oval reproductive body of various animals, consisting usu. of an embryo surrounded by nutrient material and a protective covering. **c.** A bird egg, esp. that of a hen, used as food. **2.** Something that is egg-shaped. **3.** *Slang.* A fellow; a person: *a good egg.* —*tr.v.* **egged, egg•ing, eggs. 1.** To cover with beaten egg, as in cooking. **2.** *Slang.* To throw eggs at. — ***idioms.* put** (or **have**) **all (one's) eggs in one basket.** *Informal.* To risk everything on a single venture. **egg on (one's) face.** *Informal.* Embarrassment; humiliation. [ME *egge*, bird's egg < ON *egg.* See **awi-***.] — **egg′y** *adj.*

egg[2] (ĕg) *tr.v.* **egged, egg•ing, eggs.** To encourage or incite to action: *eggs me on.* [ME *eggen* < ON *eggja.* See **ak-***.]

egg-and-dart (ĕg′ən-därt′) *n.* A decorative molding consisting of a series of egg-shaped figures alternating with dart-shaped, anchor-shaped, or tongue-shaped figures.

egg•beat•er (ĕg′bē′tər) *n.* A hand-held kitchen utensil with rotating blades for beating, whipping, or mixing.

egg case *n.* An ootheca.

egg cell *n.* See **egg[1]** 1a.

egg cream *n.* A drink made of milk, syrup, and soda water.

egg•cup (ĕg′kŭp′) *n.* A cup for holding a usu. soft-boiled egg.

eg•ger also **eg•gar** (ĕg′ər) *n.* Any of various moths of the family Lasiocampidae, whose larvae often construct tentlike webs among the branches of trees.

egg•fruit (ĕg′fro͞ot′) *n. Bot.* See **canistel.**

egg•head (ĕg′hĕd′) *n. Informal.* An intellectual; a highbrow.

egg•head•ed (ĕg′hĕd′ĭd) *adj. Informal.* Befitting or having the qualities of an intellectual. — **egg′head′ed•ness** *n.*

Eg•gle•ston (ĕg′əl-stən), **Edward.** 1837–1902. Amer. writer whose novels include *The Hoosier Schoolmaster* (1871).

egg•nog (ĕg′nŏg′) *n.* A drink consisting of milk or cream, sugar, and eggs beaten together and often mixed with an alcoholic liquor such as rum or brandy. [EGG[1] + *nog*, ale.]

egg•plant (ĕg′plănt′) *n.* **1.a.** An Indian plant *(Solanum melongena* var. *esculenta)* cultivated for its large edible, ovoid, usu. purple-skinned fruit. **b.** The fruit of this plant. **2.** *Color.* A blackish purple.

egg roll *n.* A usu. deep-fried cylindrical casing of thin egg dough around minced vegetables and often seafood or meat.

eggs Ben•e•dict (ĕgz′ bĕn′ĭ-dĭkt′) *pl.n. (used with a sing. or pl. v.)* A dish consisting of toasted halves of English muffin topped with broiled ham, poached eggs, and hollandaise sauce. [Prob. < the name *Benedict.*]

egg•shell (ĕg′shĕl′) *n.* **1.** The thin brittle exterior covering of the egg of a bird or reptile. **2.** *Color.* A pale yellow to yellowish white. — **egg′shell′** *adj.*

egg timer *n.* A small hourglass running three to five minutes, used for timing the boiling of eggs.

egg tooth *n.* A toothlike projection from the beak of embryonic birds or the upper jaw of embryonic reptiles, used to cut the egg membrane and shell upon hatching.

egg white *n.* The albumen of an egg.

e•gis (ē′jĭs) *n.* Var. of **aegis.**

eg•lan•tine (ĕg′lən-tīn′, -tēn′) *n.* See **sweetbrier.** [ME *eglentin* < OFr. *eglantine*, dim. of *aiglent* < VLat. **aculentum* < neut. of **aculentus*, spiny < Lat. *aculeus*, spine < *acus*, needle. See **ak-***.]

e•go (ē′gō, ĕg′ō) *n., pl.* **e•gos. 1.** The self, esp. as distinct from the world and other selves. **2.** In psychoanalysis, the part of the psyche that is conscious, most directly controls thought and behavior, and is most aware of external reality. **3.a.** An exaggerated sense of self-importance. **b.** Appropriate pride in oneself. [NLat. < Lat., I. See **eg***.]

e•go•cen•tric (ē′gō-sĕn′trĭk, ĕg′ō-) *adj.* **1.** Holding the view that the ego is the center, object, and norm of all experience. **2.a.** Confined in attitude or interest to one's own needs or affairs. **b.** Caring only about oneself; selfish. **3.** *Philos.* **a.** Viewed or perceived from one's own mind as a center. **b.** Taking one's own self as the starting point in a philosophical system. — **e′go•cen′tric** *n.* — **e′go•cen′tric•al•ly** *adv.* — **e′go•cen•tric′i•ty** (-trĭs′ĭ-tē), **e′go•cen′trism** *n.*

ego ideal *n.* In psychoanalysis, the part of one's ego containing an idealized self based on people one wishes to emulate.

e•go•ism (ē′gō-ĭz′əm, ĕg′ō-) *n.* **1.a.** The ethical doctrine that morality is based on self-interest. **b.** The ethical belief that self-interest justly and properly motivates all conduct. **2.** Excessive preoccupation with one's own well-being and interests, usu. accompanied by conceit. **3.** Egotism; conceit.

e•go•ist (ē′gō-ĭst, ĕg′ō-) *n.* **1.** One devoted to one's own interests and advancement; an egocentric person. **2.** An egotist. **3.** An adherent of egoism. — **e′go•is′tic, e′go•is′ti•cal** *adj.* — **e′go•is′ti•cal•ly** *adv.*

e•go•ma•ni•a (ē′gō-mā′nē-ə, -mān′yə, ĕg′ō-) *n.* Obsessive egoism. — **e′go•ma′ni•ac′** (-nē-ăk′) *n.* — **e′•go•ma•ni′a•cal** (-mə-nī′ə-kəl) *adj.* — **e′go•ma•ni′a•cal•ly** *adv.*

e•go•tism (ē′gə-tĭz′əm, ĕg′ə-) *n.* **1.** The tendency to speak or

write of oneself excessively and boastfully. **2.** An inflated sense of one's own importance; conceit. [EGO + *-tism*, as in NEPOTISM.]
e•go•tist (ē′gə-tĭst, ĕg′ə-) *n.* **1.** A conceited, boastful person. **2.** A selfish, self-centered person. — **e′go•tis′tic, e′go•tis′ti•cal** *adj.* — **e′go•tis′ti•cal•ly** *adv.*
ego trip *n. Slang.* An act or experience that gratifies the ego.
e•go-trip (ē′gō-trĭp′, ĕg′ō-) *intr.v.* **-tripped, -trip•ping, -trips.** *Slang.* To act egotistically. — **e′go-trip′per** *n.*
e•gre•gious (ĭ-grē′jəs, -jē-əs) *adj.* Conspicuously bad or offensive. [< Lat. *ēgregius*, outstanding : *ē-*, *ex-*, ex- + *grex*, *greg-*, herd; see **ger-***.] — **e•gre′gious•ly** *adv.* — **e•gre′gious•ness** *n.*
e•gress (ē′grĕs′) *n.* **1.** The act of coming or going out; emergence. **2.** The right of going out. **3.** A path or opening for going out; an exit. **4.** *Astron.* The emergence of a celestial body from eclipse or occultation. — *intr.v.* **e•gressed, e•gress•ing, e•gress•es.** To go out; emerge. [Lat. *ēgressus* < p.part. of *ēgredī*, to go out : *ē-*, *ex-*, ex- + *gradī*, to go; see **ghredh-***.]
e•gres•sion (ĭ-grĕsh′ən) *n.* The act or process of emerging; egress.
e•gret (ē′grĭt, ĕg′rĭt) *n.* Any of several usu. white herons of the genera *Bubulcus, Casmerodius, Egretta,* and related genera, characteristically having long showy drooping plumes during the breeding season. [ME < OFr. *aigrette* < OProv. *aigreta* < *aigron*, heron, of Gmc. orig.]
E•gypt (ē′jĭpt). Formerly (1958–61) **United Ar•ab Republic** (ăr′əb). A country of NE Africa on the Mediterranean Sea. A flourishing ancient kingdom and one of the earliest known civilizations, it became an independent state in 1922. Cap. Cairo. Pop. 48,503,000.
E•gyp•tian (ĭ-jĭp′shən) *n.* **1.** A native or inhabitant of Egypt. **2.** The now extinct Afro-Asiatic language of the ancient Egyptians. — *adj.* **1.** Of or relating to Egypt or its people or culture. **2.** Of the language of the ancient Egyptians.
Egyptian clover *n.* See **berseem.**
Egyptian corn *n.* See **durra.**
Egyptian cotton *n.* A fine long-staple cotton grown chiefly in northern Africa.
Egyptian millet *n.* See **Johnson grass.**
Egyptian mongoose *n.* See **ichneumon** 1.
Egyptian paper rush *n.* See **papyrus** 1.
E•gyp•tol•o•gy (ē′jĭp-tŏl′ə-jē) *n.* The study of the culture and artifacts of the ancient Egyptian civilization. — **E•gyp′to•log′i•cal** (ĭ-jĭp′tə-lŏj′ĭ-kəl) *adj.* — **E′gyp•tol′o•gist** *n.*
eh (ā, ĕ) *interj.* Used in asking a question or in seeking repetition or confirmation of a statement.
EHF *abbr.* Extremely high frequency.
EHP *abbr.* **1.** Effective horsepower. **2.** Electric horsepower.
Eh•ren•burg (ĕr′ən-bo͝org′, ĕr′yĭn-bo͝ork′), **Ilya Grigorievich.** 1891–1967. Russian writer whose novels include *The Storm* (1948) and *The Thaw* (1954).
Ehr•lich (âr′lĭkн), **Paul.** 1854–1915. German bacteriologist who shared a 1908 Nobel Prize.
EHV *abbr.* Extra-high voltage.
Eich•mann (īk′mən, īкн′-, īкн-män′), **Adolf.** 1906–62. German Nazi official who was head of the Gestapo's Jewish section (1939–45). Captured by the Israeli secret service (1960), he was tried and executed in Israel.
ei•der (ī′dər) *n.* Any of several large sea ducks, esp. of the genus *Somateria* of northern regions having predominantly black and white plumage in the male. [Ult. < ON *æðhar*, genitive of *æðr.*]
ei•der•down also **eider down** (ī′dər-doun′) *n.* **1.** The down of the eider duck. **2.** A quilt stuffed with the down of the eider duck. **3.** A warm, napped fabric.
eider duck *n.* The eider.
ei•det•ic (ī-dĕt′ĭk) *adj.* Of, relating to, or marked by detailed and vivid recall of visual images. [Ger. *eidetisch* < Gk. *eidos*, form. See **weid-***.] — **ei•det′i•cal•ly** *adv.*
ei•do•lon (ī-dō′lən) *n., pl.* **-lons** or **-la** (-lə). **1.** A phantom; an apparition. **2.** An image of an ideal. [Gk. *eidōlon* < *eidos*, form. See **weid-***.]
Eif•fel (ī′fəl, ī-fĕl′), **Alexandre Gustave.** 1832–1923. French engineer who designed the Eiffel Tower, 300 m (984 ft) high, for the Paris Exhibition of 1889.
Ei•gen (ī′gən), **Manfred.** b. 1927. German chemist who shared a 1967 Nobel Prize.
eight (āt) *n.* **1.** The cardinal number equal to 7 + 1. **2.** The eighth in a set or sequence. **3.** Something having eight parts, units, or members. [ME *eighte* < OE *eahta*. See **oktō(u)***.] — **eight** *adj. & pron.*
eight ball *n. Games.* A black pool ball that bears the number eight. — ***idiom.* behind the eight ball.** *Slang.* In an unfavorable or uncomfortable position.
eight•een (ā-tēn′) *n.* **1.** The cardinal number equal to 17 + 1. **2.** The 18th in a set or sequence. [ME *eightetene* < OE *eahtatēne*. See **oktō(u)***.] — **eight•een′** *adj. & pron.*
eight•een•mo (ā-tēn′mō) *n., pl.* **-mos.** *Print.* See **octodecimo.** [< *18mo*, abbr. of OCTODECIMO.]
eight•eenth (ā-tēnth′) *n.* **1.** The ordinal number matching the number 18 in a series. **2.** One of 18 equal parts. — **eight•eenth′** *adv. & adj.*
eight•een-wheel•er (ā′tēn-hwē′lər, -wē′-) or **18-wheel•er** *n. Informal.* A combination of a tractor and a semitrailer.
eighth (ātth, āth) *n.* **1.** The ordinal number matching the number eight in a series. **2.** One of eight equal parts. [ME *eighthe* < OE *eahtotha* < *eahta*, eight. See **oktō(u)***.] — **eighth** *adv. & adj.*
eighth note *n. Mus.* A note having one-eighth the time value of a whole note.
eight•i•eth (ā′tē-ĭth) *n.* **1.** The ordinal number matching the number 80 in a series. **2.** One of 80 equal parts. — **eight′i•eth** *adv. & adj.*
eight•pen•ny nail (āt′pĕn′ē) *n.* A nail 2½ inches (6.4 centimeters) long. [From the former price per hundred.]
eight•vo (āt′vō′) *n., pl.* **-vos.** *Print.* See **octavo.** [< *8vo*, abbr. of OCTAVO.]
eight•y (ā′tē) *n., pl.* **-ies. 1.** The cardinal number equal to 8 × 10. **2. eighties. a.** Often **Eighties.** The decade from 80 to 89 in a century. **b.** A decade or the numbers from 80 to 89. [ME *eighti* < OE *eahtatig*. See **oktō(u)***.] — **eight′y** *adj. & pron.*
eight•y-six or **86** (ā′tē-sĭks′) *tr.v.* **eight•y-sixed, eight•y-six•ing, eight•y-six•es** or **86•ed, 86•ing, 86•es.** *Slang.* **1.** To refuse to serve (an unwelcome customer) at a bar or restaurant. **2.a.** To throw out; eject. **b.** To throw away; discard.
-ein *suff.* A chemical compound related to a specified compound with a similar name ending in *-in* or *-ine*: *phthalein.* [Alteration of -IN.]
Eind•ho•ven (īnt′hō′vən). A city of S Netherlands SE of Rotterdam; chartered 1232. Pop. 192,854.
ein•korn (īn′kôrn′) *n.* A one-seeded wheat *(Triticum monococcum)* grown in arid regions. [Ger. : *ein*, one (< MHGer. < OHGer.; see **oi-no-***) + *Korn*, grain (< MHGer. < OHGer.; see **gr̥ə-no-***).]
Ein•stein (īn′stīn′), **Albert.** 1879–1955. German-born Amer. theoretical physicist whose theories of relativity revolutionized modern thought. He won a 1921 Nobel Prize.
ein•stein•i•um (īn-stī′nē-əm) *n. Symbol* **Es** A radioactive transuranic element synthesized by neutron irradiation of plutonium or other elements. Its longest-lived isotope is Es 254 with a half-life of 276 days. Atomic number 99; melting point 860°C. See table at **element.** [After Albert EINSTEIN.]
Eir•e (âr′ə, ī′rə, âr′ē, ī′rē). See **Ireland²**.
Ei•sen•how•er (ī′zən-hou′ər), **Dwight David.** "Ike." 1890–1969. Amer. general and the 34th President of the U.S. (1953–61). As supreme commander of the Allies (1943–45) he launched the invasion of Normandy (Jun. 6, 1944).
Eisenhower, Mamie Geneva Doud. b. 1896. First Lady of the U.S. (1953–61).
Ei•sen•staedt (ī′zən-stăt′), **Alfred.** b. 1898. German-born Amer. photographer who pioneered photojournalism.
Ei•sen•stein (ī′zən-stīn′, ā′zyĭn-shtān′), **Sergei Mikhailovich.** 1898–1948. Soviet filmmaker whose influential works include *Potemkin* (1925) and *Alexander Nevsky* (1938).
eis•tedd•fod (ā-stĕth′vŏd, ī-stĕth′-) *n., pl.* **eis•tedd•fods** or **eis•tedd•fod•au** (ā′stĕth-vŏd′ī, ī′stĕth-). An annual competitive festival of Welsh poets and musicians. [Welsh : *eistedd*, sitting; see **sed-*** + *bod*, to be; see **bheuə-***.]
ei•ther (ē′thər, ī′thər) *pron.* The one or the other: *Either will be fine.* — *conj.* Used before the first of two or more coordinates or clauses linked by *or*: *Either we go or we stay.* — *adj.* **1.** Any one of two; one or the other: *Wear either coat.* **2.** One and the other; each: *rings on either hand.* — *adv.* Likewise; also. Used as an intensive following negative statements: *If you don't order a dessert, I won't either.* [ME < OE *ǣther*, *ǣghwæther*. See **kʷo-***.]

Usage Note: The traditional rule holds that *either* as a pronoun or an adjective should be used only to refer to one of two items and that *any* is required when more than two items are involved: *Any* (not *either*) *of the three candidates would be good.* But reputable writers have often violated this rule. • In *either . . . or* constructions the two conjunctions should be followed by parallel elements. The following is regarded as correct: *You may have either the ring or the bracelet.* • When used as a pronoun, *either* is singular and takes a singular verb: *The two left-wing parties disagree with each other more than either does with the right.* When followed by *of* and a plural noun, *either* is often used with a plural verb: *Either of the parties have enough support to form a government.* But this usage is widely regarded as incorrect; in an earlier survey it was rejected by 92 percent of the Usage Panel. • When all the elements in an *either . . . or* construction (or a *neither . . . nor* construction) used as the subject of a sentence are singular, the verb is singular; when the elements are plural, the verb is plural. When the construction mixes singular and plural elements, it has sometimes been suggested that the verb should agree with whichever noun phrase is closest to it; thus one would write *Either Eve or the Kays* have been *invited*, but *Either the Kays or Eve* has been *invited*. This pattern is accepted by 54 percent of the Usage Panel. Others have maintained that such sentences should be rewritten. See Usage Notes at **every, neither, or¹**.

Dwight D. Eisenhower
Photographed in 1956

Mamie Eisenhower

ă pat	oi boy
ā pay	ou out
âr care	o͝o took
ä father	o͞o boot
ĕ pet	ŭ cut
ē be	ûr urge
ĭ pit	th thin
ī pie	*th* this
îr pier	hw which
ŏ pot	zh vision
ō toe	ə about, item
ô paw	

Stress marks:
′ (primary);
′ (secondary), as in
dictionary (dĭk′shə-nĕr′ē)

ei•ther-or (ē′thər-ôr′, ī′thər-) *n.* A strictly limited choice or division between two options. — **ei′ther-or′** *adj.*

e•jac•u•late (ĭ-jăk′yə-lāt′) *v.* **-lat•ed, -lat•ing, -lates.** — *tr.* **1.** To eject or discharge abruptly, esp. to discharge (semen) in orgasm. **2.** To utter suddenly and passionately; exclaim. — *intr.* To eject semen. — *n.* (ĭ-jăk′yə-lĭt). Semen ejaculated in orgasm. [Lat. *ēiaculārī, ēiaculāt-* : *ē-, ex-*, ex- + *iaculārī*, to throw (< *iaculum*, dart; see **yē-***).] — **e•jac′u•la′tor** *n.*

e•jac•u•la•tion (ĭ-jăk′yə-lā′shən) *n.* **1.a.** The act of ejaculating. **b.** An abrupt discharge of fluid, esp. of seminal fluid. **2.** A sudden short exclamation, esp. a brief pious utterance or prayer. — **e•jac′u•la•to′ry** (-yə-lə-tôr′ē, -tōr′ē)

e•ject (ĭ-jĕkt′) *v.* **e•ject•ed, e•ject•ing, e•jects.** — *tr.* **1.** To throw out forcefully; expel. **2.a.** To compel to leave. **b.** To evict. — *intr.* To make an emergency exit from an aircraft by deployment of an ejection seat or capsule. [ME *ejecten* < Lat. *ēicere, ēiect-* : *ē-, ex-*, ex- + *iacere*, to throw; see **yē-***.] — **e•ject′a•ble** *adj.* — **e•jec′tive** *adj.*

Syns: *eject, expel, evict, dismiss, oust.* These verbs mean to put out by force. To *eject* is to throw or cast out from within: *The fire ejected yellow flames into the night sky. Expel* means to drive out or away and implies permanent removal: *expelled a student from a university. Evict* most commonly refers to the expulsion of persons from property by legal process: *evicted the noisy tenants. Dismiss* refers to putting someone or something out of one's mind: *trying to dismiss his fears. Oust* is applied chiefly to the removal of a person from a position lawfully or otherwise: *ousting the prime minister.*

e•jec•ta (ĭ-jĕk′tə) *pl.n.* Ejected matter, as that from an erupting volcano. [NLat. *eiecta*, neut. pl. of Lat. *ēiectus*, p.part. of *ēicere*, to throw out. See EJECT.]

e•jec•tion (ĭ-jĕk′shən) *n.* **1.** The act of ejecting or the condition of being ejected. **2.** Ejected matter.

ejection seat *n.* A seat designed to eject the occupant clear of an aircraft during an in-flight emergency.

e•ject•ment (ĭ-jĕkt′mənt) *n.* **1.** The act or an instance of ejecting; dispossession. **2.** *Law.* An action to regain possession of real estate held by another.

e•jec•tor (ĭ-jĕk′tər) *n.* **1.** One that ejects, esp. a device in a gun that ejects the empty shell after each firing. **2.** A pump using a jet of water, air, or steam to withdraw a fluid from a space.

eland
Common eland
Taurotragus oryx

eke¹ (ēk) *tr.v.* **eked, ek•ing, ekes. 1.** To supplement with great effort. Used with *out.* **2.** To get with great effort or strain. Used with *out.* **3.** To make (a supply) last by practicing strict economy. Used with *out.* [ME *eken*, to increase < OE *ēcan.* See **aug-***.]

eke² (ēk) *adv. Archaic.* Also. [ME < OE *ēc.*]

EKG *abbr.* **1.** Electrocardiogram. **2.** Electrocardiograph.

e•kis•tics (ĭ-kĭs′tĭks) *n.* *(used with a sing. v.)* The science of human settlements, including city or community design. [Ult. < Gk. *oikistikos*, of settlements < *oikistēs*, founder < *oikizein*, to settle < *oikos*, house. See ECONOMY.] — **e•kis′tic, e•kis′ti•cal** *adj.* — **ek′is•ti′cian** (ĕk′ĭ-stĭsh′ən) *n.*

ek•pwe•le (ĕk-pwā′lē, -lā) *n.* See table at **currency.**

el¹ also **ell** (ĕl) *n.* The letter *l.*

el² (ĕl) *n. Informal.* An elevated railway.

el. *abbr.* Elevation.

e•lab•o•rate (ĭ-lăb′ər-ĭt) *adj.* **1.** Planned or executed with painstaking attention to numerous parts or details. **2.** Intricate and rich in detail. — *v.* (ĭ-lăb′ə-rāt′) **-rat•ed, -rat•ing, -rates.** — *tr.* **1.** To work out with care and detail; develop thoroughly. **2.** To produce by effort; create. — *intr.* **1.** To become elaborate. **2.** To express at greater length or in greater detail. [Lat. *ēlabōrātus*, p.part. of *ēlabōrāre*, to work out : *ē-, ex-*, intensive pref.; see EX- + *labōrāre*, to work (< *labōr*, work).] — **e•lab′o•rate•ly** *adv.* — **e•lab′o•rate•ness** *n.* — **e•lab′o•ra′tion** *n.* — **e•lab′o•ra′tor** *n.*

Eleanor of Aquitaine
The Embarkation for the Second Crusade, early 15th-century miniature from *Grandes Chroniques de France*

El•a•gab•a•lus (ĕl′ə-găb′ə-ləs). See **Heliogabalus.**

E•laine (ĭ-lān′) *n.* **1.** In Arthurian legend, a woman who died of unrequited love of Lancelot. **2.** In Arthurian legend, the mother of Galahad by Lancelot.

El Al•a•mein (ĕl ăl′ə-mān′, ä′lə-). A town of N Egypt on the Mediterranean Sea; site of a decisive Allied victory in World War II (Nov. 1942).

E•lam (ē′ləm) also **Su•si•a•na** (so͞o′zē-ä′nə, -ăn′ə). An ancient country of SW Asia; estab. E of the Tigris R. before 3000 B.C. and known for its warlike people, traditionally thought to be descended from Noah's son Shem.

E•la•mite (ē′lə-mīt′) *n.* **1.** A native or inhabitant of Elam. **2.** The language of the ancient Elamites.

é•lan (ā-läN′, ā-län′) *n.* **1.** Enthusiastic vigor and liveliness. **2.** Distinctive style or flair. [Fr. < OFr. *eslan*, rush < *eslancer*, to hurl : *es-*, out (< Lat. *ex-*; see EX-) + *lancer*, to throw (< LLat. *lanceāre*, to throw a lance < Lat. *lancea*, lance).]

e•land (ē′lənd) *n., pl.* **eland** also **e•lands.** Either of two large African antelopes *(Taurotragus oryx* or *T. derbianus)* having a light brown or grayish coat and spirally twisted horns. [Afr. < Du., elk < obsolete Ger. *Elend*, of Baltic origin.]

electric guitar

élan vi•tal (vē-tăl′) *n.* The vital force hypothesized by Henri Bergson as a source of efficient causation and evolution in nature. [Fr. : *élan*, ardor + *vital*, vital.]

el•a•pid (ĕl′ə-pĭd) *n.* Any of several venomous snakes of the family Elapidae, which includes the cobras, mambas, and coral snakes. [< NLat. *Elapidae*, family name < Med.Gk. *elaps, elap-*, fish, var. of Gk. *ellops.*] — **el′a•pid** *adj.*

e•lapse (ĭ-lăps′) *intr.v.* **e•lapsed, e•laps•ing, e•laps•es.** To slip by; pass. — *n.* Passage; lapse. [Lat. *ēlābī, ēlāps-* : *ē, ex-*, ex- + *lābī*, to slip.]

E•la•ra (ē′lər-ə) *n.* A moon of Jupiter. [Gk., mother by Zeus of the giant Tityus.]

e•las•mo•branch (ĭ-lăz′mə-brăngk′) *n.* Any of numerous fishes of the class Chondrichthyes, characterized by a cartilaginous skeleton and placoid scales and including the sharks, rays, and skates. [< NLat. *Elasmobranchii*, former subclass name : Gk. *elasmos*, metal beaten out (< *elaunein, elas-*, to beat) + LLat. *branchia*, gill (< Lat. *branchiae*, gills < Gk. *brankhia*).] — **e•las′mo•branch′** *adj.*

e•las•tase (ĭ-lăs′tās, -tāz) *n.* An enzyme found esp. in pancreatic juice that catalyzes the hydrolysis of elastin.

e•las•tic (ĭ-lăs′tĭk) *adj.* **1.a.** Easily resuming original shape after being stretched or expanded; flexible. **b.** Springy; rebounding. **2.** *Phys.* Returning to or capable of returning to an initial form or state after deformation. **3.** Quick to recover: *an elastic spirit.* **4.** Capable of adapting to change or a variety of circumstances. — *n.* **1.a.** A flexible stretchable fabric made with interwoven strands of rubber or an imitative synthetic fiber. **b.** An object made of this fabric. **2.** A rubber band. [NLat. *elasticus* < LGk. *elastos*, beaten, ductile, var. of Gk. *elatos* < *elaunein*, to beat out.] — **e•las′ti•cal•ly** *adv.*

elastic collision *n. Phys.* A collision of particles in which the total kinetic energy of the particles is conserved.

elastic fiber *n.* A thick yellow connective-tissue fiber composed principally of elastin and characterized by great elasticity.

e•las•tic•i•ty (ĭ-lă-stĭs′ĭ-tē, ē′lă-) *n.* **1.** The condition or property of being elastic; flexibility. **2.** *Phys.* **a.** The property of being elastic. **b.** The degree of elasticity.

e•las•ti•cized (ĭ-lăs′tĭ-sīzd′) *adj.* Made with strands or inserts of elastic.

elastic tissue *n.* A type of connective tissue consisting mainly of elastic fibers.

e•las•tin (ĭ-lăs′tĭn) *n.* A protein that is the principal structural component of elastic fibers. [ELAST(IC) + -IN.]

e•las•to•mer (ĭ-lăs′tə-mər) *n.* Any of various polymers having the elastic properties of natural rubber. [ELAST(IC) + -MER(E).] — **e•las′to•mer′ic** (-mĕr′ĭk) *adj.*

e•late (ĭ-lāt′) *tr.v.* **e•lat•ed, e•lat•ing, e•lates.** To make proud or joyful. — *adj.* Elated. [< Lat. *ēlātus*, p.part. of *efferre*, to bring out, exalt : *ē-, ex-*, ex- + *lātus*, brought; see **telə-***.] — **e•la′tion** *n.*

e•lat•ed (ĭ-lā′tĭd) *adj.* Exultantly proud and joyful. — **e•lat′ed•ly** *adv.* — **e•lat′ed•ness** *n.*

el•a•ter (ĕl′ə-tər) *n.* **1.** An elaterid beetle. **2.** *Bot.* A tiny elongated structure that forces the dispersal of spores. [Gk. *elatēr*, driver < *elaunein*, to drive.]

e•lat•er•id (ĭ-lăt′ər-ĭd) *n.* Any of numerous beetles of the family Elateridae, which includes the click beetles. [< NLat. *Elatēridae*, family name < Gk. *elatēr*, driver. See ELATER.] — **e•lat′er•id** *adj.*

e•lat•er•ite (ĭ-lăt′ə-rīt′) *n.* A brown-to-black, soft, elastic hydrocarbon resin. [ELATER, elasticity (obsolete) + -ITE¹.]

E layer *n.* A region of the ionosphere, occurring from about 90 to 150 kilometers (55 to 95 miles) above Earth that strongly reflects radio waves in the range from one to three megahertz.

El•ba (ĕl′bə). An island of Italy in the Tyrrhenian Sea between Corsica and the mainland; site of Napoleon Bonaparte's first exile (May 1814–Feb. 1815).

El•be (ĕl′bə, ĕlb). A river of Czech Republic and Germany flowing c. 1,167 km (725 mi) to the North Sea.

El•bert (ĕl′bərt), **Mount.** A peak, 4,402.1 m (14,433 ft), in the Sawatch Range of central CO.

el•bow (ĕl′bō′) *n.* **1.a.** The joint or bend of the arm between the forearm and the upper arm. **b.** The bony outer projection of this joint. **2.** A joint, as of a bird, corresponding to the human elbow. **3.** Something having a bend or an angle similar to an elbow, esp.: **a.** A length of pipe with a sharp bend in it. **b.** A sharp bend in a river or road. — *v.* **-bowed, -bow•ing, -bows.** — *tr.* **1.a.** To push or jostle (another or others) with the elbow. **b.** To shove (another or others) aside with the elbow. **2.** To open up (a means of passage, for example) by or as if by use of the elbow. — *intr.* **1.** To make one's way by pushing with the elbow. **2.** To turn at an angle; bend. — ***idioms.*** **at (one's) elbow.** Close at hand; nearby. **out at the elbows. 1.** Poorly dressed. **2.** Lacking money. [ME *elbowe* < OE *elnboga.* See **el-***.]

elbow grease *n. Informal.* Strenuous physical effort.

el•bow•room (ĕl′bō-ro͞om′, -ro͝om′) *n.* **1.** Room to move around or work freely. **2.** Ample scope.

El•brus (ĕl-bro͞os′), **Mount.** A peak, 5,645.6 m (18,510 ft), in the Caucasus Mts. of NW Georgia.

El•burz Mountains (ĕl-bo͝orz′). A range of N Iran rising to 5,774.9 m (18,934 ft).

El Ca•jon (kə-hōn′). A city of S CA, a suburb of San Diego. Pop. 88,693.

El Cap•i•tan (kăp′ĭ-tăn′). A peak, 2,308.5 m (7,569 ft), in the Sierra Nevada of central CA.

El Cen•tro (sĕn′trō). A city of S CA in the Imperial Valley near the Mexican border. Pop. 31,384.

El Cer•ri•to (sə-rē′tō). A city of W CA on San Francisco Bay N of Oakland. Pop. 22,731.

El•che (ĕl′chĕ). A city of SE Spain SW of Alicante; held by the Moors from the 8th to the 13th cent. Pop. 144,600.

eld•er¹ (ĕl′dər) *adj.* **1.** Greater than another in age or seniority. **2.** Superior to another or others, as in rank. —*n.* **1.** An older person. **2.** An older, influential member of a family, tribe, or community. **3.** One of the governing officers of a church, often having pastoral or teaching functions. [ME *eldre* < OE *eldra.* See **al-²*.**] —**el′der•ship′** *n.*

Usage Note: *Elder* and *eldest* generally apply to persons, unlike *older* and *oldest,* which also apply to things. *Elder* and *eldest* are used principally with reference to seniority.

el•der² (ĕl′dər) *n.* Any of various shrubs or small trees of the genus *Sambucus,* having clusters of small white flowers and red or purplish-black berrylike fruit. [ME *eldre* < OE *ellærn.*]

el•der•ber•ry (ĕl′dər-bĕr′ē) *n.* **1.** The small edible purplish-black fruit of the common American elder *(Sambucus canadensis).* **2.** A shrub or tree that bears elderberries.

eld•er•care (ĕl′dər-kâr′) *n.* Social and medical programs and facilities intended for the care of the aged.

eld•er•ly (ĕl′dər-lē) *adj.* **1.** Being past middle age and approaching old age; rather old. **2.** Of, relating to, or characteristic of older persons or life in later years. —*n.* **1.** *pl.* **-lies.** An elderly person. **2.** Older people considered as a group. —**el′der•li•ness** *n.*

elder statesman *n.* A prominent experienced older person.

eld•est (ĕl′dĭst) *adj.* Greatest in age or seniority. See Usage Note at **elder¹.** [ME < OE *eldesta.* See **al-²*.**]

El Di•en•te Peak (dē-ĕn′tē). A mountain, 4,318.5 m (14,159 ft) high, in the Rocky Mts. of SW CO.

El Do•ra•do¹ (də-rä′dō). **1.** A vaguely defined historical region and city of the New World, often thought to be in N South America; fabled for its great wealth. **2.** A city of S AR near the LA border SSW of Little Rock. Pop. 23,146.

El Do•ra•do² (də-rä′dō) *n.* A place of fabulous wealth or inordinately great opportunity. [After El Dorado¹.]

el•dritch (ĕl′drĭch) *adj.* Strange or unearthly; eerie. [Perh. ME **elriche* : OE *el-,* strange, other; see **al-¹*** + OE *rīce,* realm; see **reg-*.**]

E•le•a (ē′lē-ə) also **Ve•li•a** (vē′lē-ə). An ancient Greek colony of S Italy; center of the Eleatic school of philosophy.

El•ea•nor of Aq•ui•taine (ĕl′ə-nər, -nôr′; ăk′wĭ-tān′). 1122?–1204. Queen of France (1137–52) and England (1152–1204). Her marriage to Louis VII of France was annulled in 1152, and she then married Henry II of England.

El•e•at•ic (ĕl′ē-ăt′ĭk) *adj. Philos.* Of or characteristic of the school of philosophy founded by Xenophanes and Parmenides and holding that immutable being is the only knowable reality and that change is an illusion. [Lat. *Eleāticus* < Gk. *Eleatikos* < Elea.] —**El′e•a′tic** *n.* —**El′e•at′i•cism** (-ĭ-sĭz′əm) *n.*

elec. *abbr.* **1.** Electric; electrical. **2.** Electrician. **3.** Electricity.

el•e•cam•pane (ĕl′ĭ-kăm-pān′) *n.* A tall plant *(Inula helenium)* native to central Asia and having rayed yellow flower heads. [ME *elecampana* : OE *elene* (ult. < Gk. *helenion;* see **wel-²***) + Med.Lat. *campāna,* of the field (< Lat. *campānea,* fem. of *campāneus* < *campus,* field).]

e•lect (ĭ-lĕkt′) *v.* **e•lect•ed, e•lect•ing, e•lects.** —*tr.* **1.** To select by vote for an office or for membership. **2.** To pick out; select. **3.** To decide, esp. by preference. **4.** *Theol.* To select by divine will for salvation. —*intr.* To make a choice or selection. —*adj.* **1.** Chosen deliberately; singled out. **2.a.** Elected but not yet installed. Often used in combination: *the governor-elect.* **b.** Chosen for marriage. Often used in combination: *the bride-elect.* **3.** *Theol.* Selected by divine will for salvation. —*n.* **1.** One that is chosen or selected. **2.** *Theol.* One selected by divine will for salvation. **3.** *(used with a pl. v.)* An exclusive group of people. [ME *electen* < Lat. *ēligere, ēlēct-,* to select : *ē-, ex-,* ex- + *legere,* to choose; see **leg-*.**] —**e•lect′a•bil′i•ty** *n.* —**e•lect′a•ble** *adj.*

e•lec•tion (ĭ-lĕk′shən) *n.* **1.a.** The act or power of electing. **b.** The fact of being elected. **2.** The right or ability to make a choice. See Syns at **choice.** **3.** *Theol.* Predestined salvation, esp. as conceived by Calvinists.

E•lec•tion Day (ĭ-lĕk′shən) *n.* A day set by law for the election of public officials.

e•lec•tion•eer (ĭ-lĕk′shə-nîr′) *intr.v.* **-eered, -eer•ing, -eers.** To work actively for a candidate or political party. —**e•lec′tion•eer′er** *n.*

e•lec•tive (ĭ-lĕk′tĭv) *adj.* **1.** Of or relating to a selection by vote. **2.** Filled or obtained by election. **3.** Having the power or authority to elect; electoral. **4.** Permitting or involving a choice; optional: *elective surgery.* —*n.* An optional academic course or subject. —**e•lec′tive•ly** *adv.* —**e•lec′tive•ness** *n.*

e•lec•tor (ĭ-lĕk′tər) *n.* **1.** A qualified voter in an election. **2.** A member of the Electoral College. **3.** One of the German princes of the Holy Roman Empire entitled to elect the emperor.

e•lec•tor•al (ĭ-lĕk′tər-əl) *adj.* **1.** Of, relating to, or composed of electors. **2.** Relating to election. —**e•lec′tor•al•ly** *adv.*

E•lec•tor•al College (ĭ-lĕk′tər-əl) *n.* An electoral body chosen to elect the U.S. President and Vice President.

e•lec•tor•ate (ĭ-lĕk′tər-ĭt) *n.* **1.** A body of qualified voters. **2.** The dignity or territory of an elector of the Holy Roman Empire.

electr– *pref.* Var. of **electro–.**

E•lec•tra (ĭ-lĕk′trə) *n. Gk. Myth.* A daughter of Clytemnestra and Agamemnon who with her brother Orestes avenged their father by killing their mother and her lover Aegisthus.

Electra complex *n.* In psychoanalysis, a daughter's unconscious libidinal desire for her father.

e•lec•tret (ĭ-lĕk′trĭt) *n.* A solid dielectric that exhibits persistent dielectric polarization. [electr(icity) + (magn)et.]

e•lec•tric (ĭ-lĕk′trĭk) *adj.* **1.** Of, relating to, or operated by electricity. **2.a.** Emotionally exciting; thrilling. **b.** Exceptionally tense; highly charged with emotion. —*n.* An electrically powered machine or vehicle. [NLat. *ēlectricus,* deriving from amber, as by rubbing < Lat. *ēlectrum,* amber < Gk. *ēlektron.*] —**e•lec′tri•cal•ly** *adv.*

electrical engineering *n.* The branch of engineering that deals with the technology of electricity, esp. the design and application of circuitry and equipment for power generation and distribution, machine control, and communications. —**electrical engineer** *n.*

electrical storm *n.* A thunderstorm.

electric arc *n. Elect.* An arc.

electric chair *n.* **1.** A chair used in the electrocution of a prisoner sentenced to death by law. **2.** Execution by means of electrocution. **3.** The sentence of death by electrocution.

electric eel *n.* A long eellike freshwater fish *(Electrophorus electricus)* of northern South America having organs capable of producing a powerful electric discharge.

electric eye *n.* See **photoelectric cell.**

electric field *n.* A region of space characterized by the existence of a force generated by electric charge.

electric guitar *n. Mus.* A guitar with one or more electronic pickups that transmit sound to an amplifier.

e•lec•tri•cian (ĭ-lĕk-trĭsh′ən, ē′lĕk-) *n.* One whose occupation is the installation, maintenance, repair, or operation of electric equipment and circuitry.

e•lec•tric•i•ty (ĭ-lĕk-trĭs′ĭ-tē, ē′lĕk-) *n.* **1.a.** The physical phenomena arising from the behavior of electrons and protons caused by attraction of particles with opposite charges and repulsion of particles with the same charge. **b.** The physical science of such phenomena. **2.** Electric current as a source of power. **3.** Intense, contagious emotional excitement.

electric ray *n.* Any of various tropical or subtropical marine fishes of the family Torpedinidae, capable of producing an electric discharge that is used to stun or kill prey.

e•lec•tri•fy (ĭ-lĕk′trə-fī′) *tr.v.* **-fied, -fy•ing, -fies.** **1.** To produce electric charge on or in (a conductor). **2.a.** To wire or equip (a building, for example) for the use of electric power. **b.** To provide with electric power. **c.** *Mus.* To amplify (music) by electronic means. **3.** To thrill, startle greatly, or shock. —**e•lec′tri•fi′a•ble** *adj.* —**e•lec′tri•fi•ca′tion** (-fĭ-kā′shən) *n.* —**e•lec′tri•fi′er** *n.* —**e•lec′tri•fy′ing•ly** *adv.*

electro– or **electr–** *pref.* **1.a.** Electricity: *electromagnet* **b.** Electric; electrically: *electrocute.* **2.** Electrolysis: *electrodeposit.* **3.** Electron: *electronegative.* [NLat. *ēlectro-* < Lat. *ēlectrum,* amber < Gk. *ēlektron.*]

e•lec•tro•a•cous•tics (ĭ-lĕk′trō-ə-ko͞o′stĭks) *n. (used with a sing. v.)* The science that deals with the interaction or interconversion of electric and acoustic phenomena. —**e•lec′tro•a•cous′tic** *adj.* —**e•lec′tro•a•cous′tic•al•ly** *adv.*

e•lec•tro•car•di•o•gram (ĭ-lĕk′trō-kär′dē-ə-grăm′) *n.* The curve traced by an electrocardiograph.

e•lec•tro•car•di•o•graph (ĭ-lĕk′trō-kär′dē-ə-grăf′) *n.* An instrument used in the detection and diagnosis of heart abnormalities that generates a record of the electrical currents associated with heart muscle activity. —**e•lec′tro•car′di•o•graph′ic** (-grăf′ĭk) *adj.* —**e•lec′tro•car′di•o•graph′i•cal•ly** *adv.* —**e•lec′tro•car′di•og′ra•phy** (-kär′dē-ŏg′rə-fē) *n.*

e•lec•tro•chem•i•cal cell (ĭ-lĕk′trō-kĕm′ĭ-kəl) *n.* See **cell** 5a.

e•lec•tro•chem•is•try (ĭ-lĕk′trō-kĕm′ĭ-strē) *n.* The science of the interaction or interconversion of electric and chemical phenomena. —**e•lec′tro•chem′i•cal•ly** *adv.* —**e•lec′tro•chem′ist** *n.*

e•lec•tro•con•vul•sive therapy (ĭ-lĕk′trō-kən-vŭl′sĭv) *n.* Administration of electric current to the brain through electrodes on the head to induce unconsciousness and brief convulsions, used esp. to treat acute depression.

e•lec•tro•cute (ĭ-lĕk′trə-kyo͞ot′) *tr.v.* **-cut•ed, -cut•ing, -cutes.** **1.** To kill with electricity. **2.** To execute (a condemned prisoner) by means of electricity. [electro– + (exe)cute.] —**e•lec′tro•cu′tion** (-kyo͞o′shən) *n.*

e•lec•trode (ĭ-lĕk′trōd′) *n.* **1.** A solid electric conductor through which an electric current enters or leaves an electrolytic cell or other medium. **2.** A collector or emitter of electric charge or of electric-charge carriers, as in a semiconducting device.

e•lec•tro•de•pos•it (ĭ-lĕk′trō-dĭ-pŏz′ĭt) *tr.v.* **-it•ed, -it•ing,**

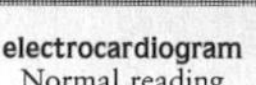

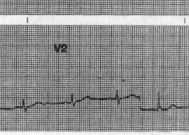

electrocardiogram
Normal reading

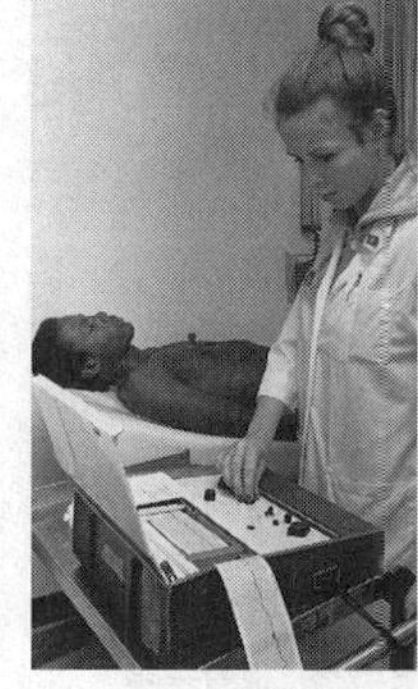

electrocardiograph
Nurse monitoring an electrocardiograph

ă pat, ā pay, âr care, ä father, ĕ pet, ē be, ĭ pit, ī pie, îr pier, ŏ pot, ō toe, ô paw, oi boy, ou out, o͝o took, o͞o boot, ŭ cut, ûr urge, th thin, *th* this, hw which, zh vision, ə about, item

Stress marks:
′ (primary);
′ (secondary), as in **dictionary** (dĭk′shə-nĕr′ē)

-its. To deposit (a dissolved or suspended substance) on an electrode by electrolysis. — *n.* The substance so deposited. — **e•lec'tro•dep'o•si'tion** (-dĕp'ə-zĭsh'ən, -dē'pə-) *n.*

e•lec•tro•di•al•y•sis (ĭ-lĕk'trō-dī-ăl'ĭ-sĭs) *n., pl.* **-ses** (-sēz'). Dialysis at a rate increased by the application of an electric potential across the dialysis membrane.

e•lec•tro•dy•nam•ics (ĭ-lĕk'trō-dī-năm'ĭks) *n. (used with a sing. v.)* The physics of the relationship between electric current and magnetic or mechanical phenomena. — **e•lec'tro•dy•nam'ic** *adj.*

e•lec•tro•dy•na•mom•e•ter (ĭ-lĕk'trō-dī'nə-mŏm'ĭ-tər) *n.* An instrument that measures current by indicating the level of magnetic attraction or repulsion between a fixed and a movable coil, one of which carries the unknown current.

e•lec•tro•en•ceph•a•lo•gram (ĭ-lĕk'trō-ĕn-sĕf'ə-lə-grăm') *n.* A graphic record of the electrical activity of the brain as recorded by an electroencephalograph.

e•lec•tro•en•ceph•a•lo•graph (ĭ-lĕk'trō-ĕn-sĕf'ə-lə-grăf') *n.* An instrument that generates a record of the electrical activity of the brain. — **e•lec'tro•en•ceph'a•lo•graph'ic** *adj.* — **e•lec'tro•en•ceph'a•log'ra•phy** (-lŏg'rə-fē) *n.*

e•lec•tro•form (ĭ-lĕk'trə-fôrm') *tr.v.* **-formed, -form•ing, -forms.** To produce or reproduce (an object) by electrodeposition on a mold.

e•lec•tro•gas•dy•nam•ics (ĭ-lĕk'trə-găs'dī-năm'ĭks) *n. (used with a sing. v.)* Generation of electrical energy from the kinetic energy contained in a high-pressure, ionized, moving combustion gas. — **e•lec'tro•gas'dy•nam'ic** *adj.*

e•lec•tro•gen•e•sis (ĭ-lĕk'trə-jĕn'ĭ-sĭs) *n.* Production of electrical impulses in living organisms or tissues. — **e•lec'tro•gen'ic** *adj.*

e•lec•tro•graph (ĭ-lĕk'trə-grăf') *n.* **1.** An electrically produced graph or tracing. **2.** Equipment used to produce such a graph or tracing in facsimile transmission.

e•lec•tro•hy•drau•lic (ĭ-lĕk'trō-hī-drô'lĭk) *adj.* Of, relating to, or involving a combination of electric and hydraulic mechanisms. — **e•lec'tro•hy•drau'li•cal•ly** *adv.*

e•lec•tro•kin•et•ics (ĭ-lĕk'trō-kĭ-nĕt'ĭks) *n. (used with a sing. v.)* The electrodynamics of heating effects and current distribution in electric networks.

e•lec•trol•o•gist (ĭ-lĕk-trŏl'ə-jĭst, ē'lĕk-) *n.* One who removes body hair by means of an electric current.

e•lec•tro•lu•mi•nes•cence (ĭ-lĕk'trō-lo͞o'mə-nĕs'əns) *n.* **1.** Direct conversion of electric energy to light by a solid phosphor subjected to an alternating electric field. **2.** Emission of light caused by electric discharge in a gas. — **e•lec'tro•lu'mi•nes'cent** *adj.*

e•lec•trol•y•sis (ĭ-lĕk-trŏl'ĭ-sĭs, ē'lĕk-) *n.* **1.** Chemical decomposition, produced in an electrolyte by an electric current. **2.** Destruction of living tissue, esp. of hair roots, by means of an electric current applied with a needle-shaped electrode.

e•lec•tro•lyte (ĭ-lĕk'trə-līt') *n.* **1.** A chemical compound that ionizes when dissolved or molten to produce an electrically conductive medium. **2.** *Physiol.* Any of various ions required by cells to regulate the electric charge and flow of water molecules across the cell membrane.

e•lec•tro•lyt•ic (ĭ-lĕk'trə-lĭt'ĭk) *adj.* **1.a.** Of or relating to electrolysis. **b.** Produced by electrolysis. **2.** Of or relating to electrolytes. — **e•lec'tro•lyt'i•cal•ly** *adv.*

e•lec•tro•lyze (ĭ-lĕk'trə-līz') *tr.v.* **-lyzed, -lyz•ing, -lyz•es.** To cause to decompose by electrolysis.

e•lec•tro•mag•net (ĭ-lĕk'trō-măg'nĭt) *n.* A magnet consisting essentially of a coil of insulated wire around a soft iron core, magnetized only when current flows through the wire.

e•lec•tro•mag•net•ic (ĭ-lĕk'trō-măg-nĕt'ĭk) *adj.* Of or exhibiting electromagnetism. — **e•lec'tro•mag•net'i•cal•ly** *adv.*

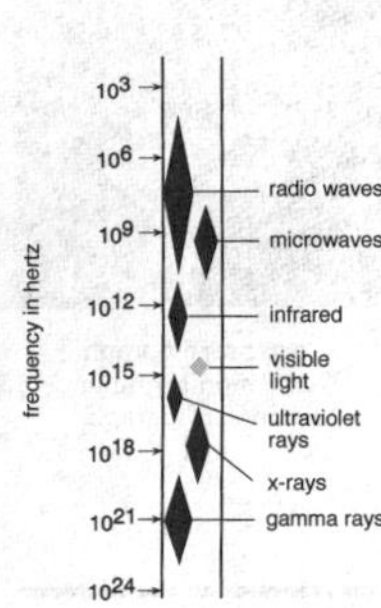

electromagnetic spectrum

electromagnetic field *n.* The field associated with electric charge in motion, having both electric and magnetic components.

electromagnetic pulse *n.* The pulse of intense electromagnetic radiation generated by a nuclear explosion.

electromagnetic spectrum *n.* The entire range of radiation extending in frequency from approx. 10^{23} hertz to 0 hertz or, in wavelengths, from 10^{-13} centimeter to infinity.

electromagnetic unit *n.* Any of various systems of units for electricity and magnetism in which the permeability of free space is taken as unity and the abampere is the fundamental unit of current.

electromagnetic wave *n.* A wave propagated as a periodic disturbance of the electromagnetic field when an electric charge oscillates or accelerates.

e•lec•tro•mag•net•ism (ĭ-lĕk'trō-măg'nĭ-tĭz'əm) *n.* **1.** Magnetism produced by electric charge in motion. **2.** The physics of electricity and magnetism.

e•lec•tro•mech•an•i•cal (ĭ-lĕk'trō-mə-kăn'ĭ-kəl) *adj.* Relating to a mechanical device or system that is actuated or controlled by electricity.

e•lec•tro•met•al•lur•gy (ĭ-lĕk'trō-mĕt'l-ûr'jē) *n.* The use of electric and electrolytic processes to purify metals or reduce metallic compounds to metals. — **e•lec'tro•met'al•lur'gi•cal** *adj.*

e•lec•trom•e•ter (ĭ-lĕk'trŏm'ĭ-tər, ē'lĕk-) *n.* An instrument for measuring voltage.

e•lec•tro•mo•tive (ĭ-lĕk'trō-mō'tĭv) *adj.* Of, relating to, or producing electric current.

electromotive force *n.* The energy per unit charge that is converted from chemical, mechanical, or other forms of energy into electrical energy in a battery or dynamo.

e•lec•tro•my•o•gram (ĕ-lĕk'trō-mī'ō-grăm') *n.* A graphic record of the electrical activity of a muscle as recorded by an electromyograph.

e•lec•tro•my•o•graph (ĭ-lĕk-trō-mī'ə-graf') *n.* An instrument that produces an audio or visual record of the electrical activity of a skeletal muscle. — **e•lec'tro•my'o•graph'ic** *adj.* — **e•lec'tro•my'o•graph'i•cal•ly** *adv.* — **e•lec'tro•my•og'ra•phy** (-mī-ŏg'rə-fē) *n.*

e•lec•tron (ĭ-lĕk'trŏn') *n.* A stable subatomic particle in the lepton family having a rest mass of 9.1066×10^{-28} gram and a unit negative electric charge of approx. 1.602×10^{-19} coulomb. See table at **subatomic particle.** [ELECTR(IC) + -ON[1].]

e•lec•tro•neg•a•tive (ĭ-lĕk'trō-nĕg'ə-tĭv) *adj.* **1.** Having a negative electric charge. **2.** Tending to attract electrons to form a chemical bond. **3.** Capable of acting as a negative electrode.

electron gun *n.* The electrode, esp. in a cathode-ray tube, that produces a beam of accelerated electrons.

electron hole *n. Phys.* See **hole** 9.

e•lec•tron•ic (ĭ-lĕk-trŏn'ĭk, ē'lĕk-) *adj.* **1.** Of or relating to electrons. **2.** Of, relating to, or involving the controlled conduction of electrons or other charge carriers, esp. in a vacuum, gas, or semiconducting material. **3.** Of or relating to electronics. — **e•lec'tron'i•cal•ly** *adv.*

electronic flash *n.* A portable flash lamp for photography that uses a capacitor as a power source.

electronic mail *n. Comp. Sci.* **1.** Messages transmitted electronically via telecommunication links, as between terminals. **2.** The process of sending such messages.

electronic music *n. Mus.* Music produced or altered by electronic means, as by a tape recorder or synthesizer.

e•lec•tron•ics (ĭ-lĕk'trŏn'ĭks, ē'lĕk-) *n.* **1.** *(used with a sing. v.)* The science and technology of electronic phenomena. **2.** *(used with a pl. v.)* Electronic devices and systems.

electron lens *n.* Any of various devices that use an electric or a magnetic field to focus a beam of electrons.

electron microscope *n.* Any of a class of microscopes that use electrons rather than visible light to produce images with linear magnification approaching or exceeding a million (10^6).

electron multiplier *n.* A vacuum tube in which current amplification occurs through repeated collisions of secondary electrons with a series of anodes.

electron neutrino *n.* A stable elementary particle in the lepton family having a mass very close to zero and no charge. See table at **subatomic particle.**

electron optics *n. (used with a sing. v.)* The science of the control of electron motion by electron lenses in systems or under conditions analogous to those involving or affecting visible light.

electron pair *n.* Two electrons functioning or regarded as functioning in concert, esp. two electrons that form a nonpolar covalent bond between atoms.

electron transport *n. Biochem.* The successive passage of electrons from one cytochrome or flavoprotein to another by a series of oxidation-reduction reactions during the aerobic production of ATP.

electron tube *n.* A sealed enclosure, either highly evacuated or containing a controlled quantity of gas, in which electrons can be made sufficiently mobile to act as the principal carriers of current between at least one pair of electrodes.

electron volt *n.* A unit of energy equal to the energy acquired by an electron falling through a potential difference of one volt, approx. 1.602×10^{-19} joule. See table at **measurement.**

e•lec•tro•phile (ĭ-lĕk'trə-fīl') *n.* A chemical compound or group attracted to electrons and tending to accept them.

e•lec•tro•pho•re•sis (ĭ-lĕk'trō-fə-rē'sĭs) *n.* **1.** The migration of charged colloidal particles or molecules through a solution in an electric field. **2.** A method of analyzing substances based on the rate of movement of each component in a colloidal suspension while in an electric field. — **e•lec'tro•pho•ret'ic** (-rĕt'ĭk) *adj.*

e•lec•tro•pho•ret•o•gram (ĭ-lĕk'trō-fə-rĕt'ə-grăm') *n.* A record of the results of an electrophoresis.

e•lec•troph•o•rus (ĭ-lĕk'trŏf'ər-əs, ē'lĕk-) *n., pl.* **-o•ri** (-ə-rī', -ə-rē'). An apparatus for generating static electricity, consisting of a hard rubber disk and a metal plate. [NLat. : ELECTRO- + Gk. *-phoros*, -phorous.]

e•lec•tro•phys•i•ol•o•gy (ĭ-lĕk'trō-fĭz'ē-ŏl'ə-jē) *n.* **1.** The branch of physiology that studies the relationship between electric phenomena and bodily processes. **2.** The electric activity associated with a bodily part or function. — **e•lec'tro•phys'i•o•log'ic** (-ə-lŏj'ĭk), **e•lec'tro•phys'i•o•log'i•cal** (-ĭ-kəl) *adj.* — **e•lec'tro•phys'i•o•log'i•cal•ly** *adv.* — **e•lec'tro•phys'i•ol'o•gist** *n.*

e•lec•tro•plate (ĭ-lĕk′trə-plāt′) *tr.v.* **-plat•ed, -plat•ing, -plates.** To coat or cover with a thin layer of metal by electrodeposition.

e•lec•tro•pos•i•tive (ĭ-lĕk′trō-pŏz′ĭ-tĭv) *adj.* **1.** Having a positive electric charge. **2.** Capable of acting as a positive electrode. **3.** Tending to release electrons to form a chemical bond.

e•lec•tro•re•cep•tor (ĭ-lĕk′trō-rĭ-sĕp′tər) *n.* Any of a series of sensory organs in certain fish that detect electric fields.

e•lec•tro•scope (ĭ-lĕk′trə-skōp′) *n.* An instrument used to detect the presence, sign, and in some configurations the magnitude of an electric charge by the mutual attraction or repulsion of metal foils or pith balls. **—e•lec′tro•scop′ic** (-skŏp′ĭk) *adj.*

e•lec•tro•shock (ĭ-lĕk′trō-shŏk′) *n.* See **electroconvulsive therapy.** —*tr.v.* **-shocked, -shock•ing, -shocks.** To administer electroconvulsive therapy to.

electroshock therapy *n.* See **electroconvulsive therapy.**

e•lec•tro•stat•ic (ĭ-lĕk′trō-stăt′ĭk) *adj.* **1.a.** Of or relating to electric charges at rest. **b.** Produced or caused by such charges. **2.** Of or relating to electrostatics. **—e•lec′tro•stat′i•cal•ly** *adv.*

electrostatic generator *n.* Any of various devices, such as the Van de Graaff generator, that generate high voltages by accumulating large quantities of electric charge.

electrostatic precipitation *n.* The removal of very fine particles suspended in a gas by electrostatic charging and subsequent precipitation onto a collector in a strong electric field.

electrostatic printing *n.* A process for printing or copying in which electrostatic charges are used to form the image in powder or ink on the surface to be printed.

e•lec•tro•stat•ics (ĭ-lĕk′trō-stăt′ĭks) *n.* (*used with a sing. v.*) The physics of electrostatic phenomena.

electrostatic unit *n.* Any unit of electricity or magnetism in the centimeter-gram-second system based on the forces of interaction between electric charges.

e•lec•tro•sur•ger•y (ĭ-lĕk′trō-sûr′jə-rē) *n.* The surgical use of high-frequency electric current. **—e•lec′tro•sur′gi•cal** (-jĭ-kəl) *adj.* **—e•lec′tro•sur′gi•cal•ly** *adv.*

e•lec•tro•ther•a•peu•tics (ĭ-lĕk′trō-thĕr′ə-pyo͞o′tĭks) *n.* (*used with a sing. v.*) See **electrotherapy.**

e•lec•tro•ther•a•py (ĭ-lĕk′trō-thĕr′ə-pē) *n., pl.* **-pies.** Medical therapy using electric currents.

e•lec•tro•ther•mal (ĭ-lĕk′trō-thûr′məl) *adj.* **1.** Of, relating to, or involving both electricity and heat. **2.** Of or relating to the production of heat by electricity.

e•lec•trot•o•nus (ĭ-lĕk′trŏt′n-əs, ē′lĕk-) *n.* Alteration in nerve or muscle excitability and conductivity while a constant electric current passes through. **—e•lec′tro•ton′ic** (-trə-tŏn′ĭk) *adj.*

e•lec•tro•type (ĭ-lĕk′trə-tīp′) *n.* **1.** A metal plate used in letterpress printing, made by electroplating a lead or plastic mold of the page to be printed. **2.** The process of making an electrotype. **—e•lec′tro•type′** *v.* **—e•lec′tro•typ′er** *n.* **—e•lec′tro•typ′ic** (-trō-tĭp′ĭk) *adj.*

e•lec•tro•va•lence (ĭ-lĕk′trō-vā′ləns) *n.* **1.** Valence characterized by the transfer of electrons from atoms of one element to atoms of another during the formation of an ionic bond between the atoms. **2.** The number of electric charges lost or gained by an atom in such a transfer. **—e•lec′tro•va′lent** *adj.*

e•lec•tro•va•len•cy (ĭ-lĕk′tro-vā′lən-sē) *n.* Electrovalence.

electrovalent bond *n.* See **ionic bond.**

e•lec•trum (ĭ-lĕk′trəm) *n.* An alloy of silver and gold. [ME < Lat. *ēlectrum*, amber < Gk. *ēlektron*.]

e•lec•tu•ar•y (ĭ-lĕk′cho͞o-ĕr′ē) *n., pl.* **-ies.** A drug mixed with sugar and water or honey into a pasty mass suitable for oral administration. [ME *electuarie* < LLat. *ēlēctuārium*, prob. alteration of Gk. *ekleikton* < *ekleikhein*, to lick up : *ek-*, out; see **eghs*** + *leikhein*, to lick; see **leigh-*.**]

el•ee•mos•y•nar•y (ĕl′ə-mŏs′ə-nĕr′ē, ĕl′ē-ə-) *adj.* **1.** Of, relating to, or dependent on charity. **2.** Contributed as an act of charity; gratuitous. [Med.Lat. *eleēmosynārius* < LLat. *eleēmosyna*, alms. See ALMS.]

el•e•gance (ĕl′ĭ-gəns) *n.* **1.a.** Refinement, grace, and beauty in movement, appearance, or manners. **b.** Tasteful opulence in form, decoration, or presentation. **2.a.** Restraint and grace of style. **b.** Scientific precision. **3.** Something elegant.

el•e•gan•cy (ĕl′ĭ-gən-sē) *n., pl.* **-cies.** Elegance.

el•e•gant (ĕl′ĭ-gənt) *adj.* Characterized by or exhibiting refined, tasteful beauty of manner, form, or style. See Syns at **delicate.** [ME < OFr. < Lat. *ēlegāns*, *ēlegant-*, ult. < *ēligere*, to select. See ELECT.] **—el′e•gant•ly** *adv.*

el•e•gi•ac (ĕl′ə-jī′ək, ĭ-lē′jē-ăk′) *adj.* **1.** Of, relating to, or involving elegy or mourning or expressing sorrow for that which is irrecoverably past. **2.** Of or composed in elegiac couplets. [LLat. *elegīacus* < Gk. *elegeiakos* < *elegeia*, elegy. See ELEGY.] **—el′e•gi′ac** *n.* **—el′e•gi′a•cal** *adj.* **—el′e•gi′a•cal•ly** *adv.*

elegiac couplet *n.* A unit of verse in Greek and Roman prosody consisting of a line of dactylic hexameter followed by a line of dactylic pentameter.

elegiac stanza *n.* A four-line stanza in iambic pentameter that rhymes on alternate lines.

el•e•gist (ĕl′ə-jĭst) *n.* The creator of an elegy.

el•e•gize (ĕl′ə-jīz′) *v.* **-gized, -giz•ing, -giz•es.** —*intr.* To compose an elegy. —*tr.* To compose an elegy upon or for.

el•e•gy (ĕl′ə-jē) *n., pl.* **-gies. 1.** A poem composed in elegiac couplets. **2.a.** A poem or song composed esp. as a lament for a deceased person. **b.** Something resembling such a poem or song. **3.** *Mus.* A composition that is melancholy or pensive in tone. [Fr. *élégie* < Lat. *elegīa* < Gk. *elegeia* < pl. of *elegeion*, elegiac distich < *elegos*, song, mournful song.]

elem. *abbr.* Elementary.

el•e•ment (ĕl′ə-mənt) *n.* **1.** A fundamental, essential, or irreducible constituent of a composite entity. **2. elements.** The basic assumptions or principles of a subject. **3.** *Math.* **a.** A member of a set. **b.** A point, line, or plane. **c.** A part of a geometric configuration, such as an angle in a triangle. **d.** The generatrix of a geometric figure. **e.** Any of the terms in the rectangular array of terms that constitute a matrix or determinant. **4.** *Chem. & Phys.* A substance composed of atoms having an identical number of protons in each nucleus. **5.** One of four substances, earth, air, fire, or water, formerly regarded as a fundamental constituent of the universe. **6.** *Elect.* The resistance wire in an electrical appliance such as a heater or an oven. **7. elements.** The forces that constitute the weather, esp. severe or inclement weather. **8.** An environment naturally suited to or associated with an individual. **9.** A distinct group within a larger community. **10. elements.** The bread and wine of the Eucharist. [ME < OFr. < Lat. *elementum*.]

Syns: *element, component, constituent, factor, ingredient.* The central meaning shared by these nouns is "one of the individual parts of which a composite entity is made up": *the grammatical elements of a sentence; jealousy, a component of his character; melody and harmony, two of the constituents of a musical composition; ambition as a key factor in her success; humor, an effective ingredient of a speech.*

element 104 *n.* An artificially produced radioactive element with atomic number 104 whose most stable isotope has a half-life of approx. 70 seconds.

element 105 *n.* An artificially produced radioactive element with atomic number 105 whose most stable isotope has a half-life of approx. 40 seconds.

el•e•men•tal (ĕl′ə-mĕn′tl) *adj.* **1.** Of, relating to, or being an element. **2.a.** Fundamental or essential; basic. **b.** Of or relating to fundamentals; elementary. **c.** Constituting an integral part; inborn. **3.** Of such character as to resemble a force of nature in power or effect. **—el′e•men′tal** *n.* **—el′e•men′tal•ly** *adv.*

el•e•men•ta•ry (ĕl′ə-mĕn′tə-rē, -trē) *adj.* **1.** Of, relating to, or constituting the basic, essential, or fundamental part. **2.** Of, relating to, or involving the fundamental or simplest aspects of a subject. **3.** Of or relating to an elementary school or elementary education. **—el′e•men•ta′ri•ly** (-tĕr′ə-lē) *adv.* **—el′e•men′ta•ri•ness** *n.*

elementary particle *n.* Any of the subatomic particles that compose matter and energy, esp. one hypothesized or regarded as an irreducible constituent of matter. See table at **subatomic particle.**

elementary school *n.* **1.** A school usu. for the first six or eight grades. **2.** The first six to eight years of formal education.

el•e•mi (el′ə-mē) *n., pl.* **-mis.** Any of various oily resins derived from certain tropical trees, esp. *Canarium luzonicum*, and used in making varnishes and inks. [< NLat. *elimi*, prob. < Ar. *elemī*, var. of *al-lamīy*, the elemi.]

el•e•phant (ĕl′ə-fənt) *n.* **1.** Either of two very large herbivorous mammals, *Elephas maximus* of south-central Asia or *Loxodonta africana* of Africa, having thick skin, a long prehensile trunk, and long curved tusks of ivory. **2.** Any of various extinct or living animals related to either of these two animals. [ME *elefaunt* < OFr. *olifant* < VLat. **olifantus* < Lat. *elephantus* < Gk. *elephas*, *elephant-*.]

elephant folio *n.* *Print.* A book or publication of the largest size, often about 60 centimeters (2 feet) in height.

el•e•phan•ti•a•sis (ĕl′ə-fən-tī′ə-sĭs) *n.* Chronic, often extreme enlargement and hardening of cutaneous and subcutaneous tissue, esp. of the legs and external genitals, usu. caused by infestation of the lymph glands and vessels with a filarial worm. [Lat. < Gk. : *elephas*, *elephant-*, elephant + *-iasis*, -iasis.]

el•e•phan•tine (ĕl′ə-făn′tēn′, -tīn′, ĕl′ə-fən-) *adj.* **1.** Of or relating to an elephant. **2.a.** Enormous in size or strength. **b.** Ponderously clumsy.

elephant seal *n.* Either of two large seals, *Mirounga angustirostris* mainly of Pacific coastal waters of California or *M. leonina* of coastal waters of the Southern Hemisphere, the males of which have an inflatable trunklike proboscis.

el•e•phant's foot (ĕl′ə-fənts) *n., pl.* **elephant's foots. 1.** An African species of yam (*Dioscorea elephantipes*) with clusters of tubers that grow above the ground. **2.** Any of several plants of the genus *Elephantopus* in the composite family, having purplish flowers grouped in discoid flower heads.

Eleusinian mysteries *pl.n.* The ancient religious rites celebrat-

elephant
Top: African elephant
Loxodonta africana
Bottom: Indian elephant
Elephas maximus

ă pat	oi boy
ā pay	ou out
âr care	o͝o took
ä father	o͞o boot
ĕ pet	ŭ cut
ē be	ûr urge
ĭ pit	th thin
ī pie	*th* this
îr pier	hw which
ŏ pot	zh vision
ō toe	ə about, item
ô paw	

Stress marks:
′ (primary);
′ (secondary), as in
dictionary (dĭk′shə-nĕr′ē)

PERIODIC TABLE OF THE ELEMENTS

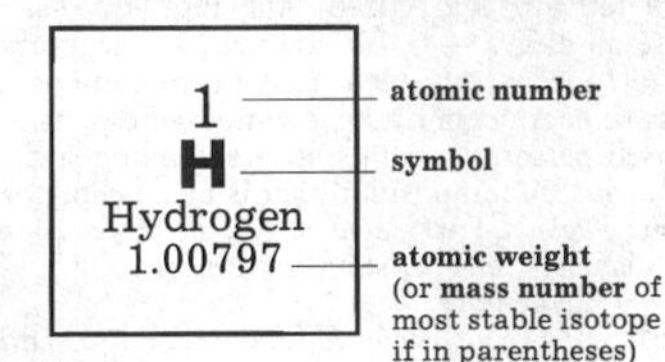

The periodic table arranges the chemical elements in two ways. The first is by **atomic number**, starting with hydrogen (atomic number = 1) in the upper left-hand corner and continuing in ascending order from left to right. The second is by the number of electrons in the outermost **shell**. Elements having the same number of electrons in the outermost shell are placed in the same column. Since the number of electrons in the outermost shell in large part determines the chemical nature of an element, elements in the same column have similar chemical properties.

This arrangement of the elements was devised by **Dmitri Mendeleev** in 1869, before all the elements were yet known. To maintain the overall logic of the table, Mendeleev allowed space for undiscovered elements whose existence he predicted.

The table has since been filled in, most recently by the addition of Element 104 and Element 105. The solid lines around these elements indicate that they have been isolated experimentally although not officially named. Broken lines around elements 106–109 indicate that these elements, though not yet isolated, are known to exist.

The **lanthanide** series (elements 57–71) and the **actinide** series (elements 89–103) do not conform to the **periodic law** and are therefore placed below the main body of the table.

	GROUP 1a	GROUP 2a	GROUP 3b	GROUP 4b	GROUP 5b	GROUP 6b	GROUP 7b	GROUP 8	GROUP 8
PERIOD 1	1 **H** Hydrogen 1.00797								
PERIOD 2	3 **Li** Lithium 6.939	4 **Be** Beryllium 9.0122							
PERIOD 3	11 **Na** Sodium 22.9898	12 **Mg** Magnesium 24.312							
PERIOD 4	19 **K** Potassium 39.102	20 **Ca** Calcium 40.08	21 **Sc** Scandium 44.956	22 **Ti** Titanium 47.90	23 **V** Vanadium 50.942	24 **Cr** Chromium 51.996	25 **Mn** Manganese 54.9380	26 **Fe** Iron 55.847	27 **Co** Cobalt 58.9332
PERIOD 5	37 **Rb** Rubidium 85.47	38 **Sr** Strontium 87.62	39 **Y** Yttrium 88.905	40 **Zr** Zirconium 91.22	41 **Nb** Niobium 92.906	42 **Mo** Molyb- denum 95.94	43 **Tc** Technetium (99)	44 **Ru** Ruthenium 101.07	45 **Rh** Rhodium 102.905
PERIOD 6	55 **Cs** Cesium 132.905	56 **Ba** Barium 137.34	57-71* Lanthanides	72 **Hf** Hafnium 178.49	73 **Ta** Tantalum 180.948	74 **W** Tungsten 183.85	75 **Re** Rhenium 186.2	76 **Os** Osmium 190.2	77 **Ir** Iridium 192.2
PERIOD 7	87 **Fr** Francium (223)	88 **Ra** Radium (226)	89-103** Actinides	104	105	106	107	108	109

*LANTHANIDES	57 **La** Lanthanum 138.91	58 **Ce** Cerium 140.12	59 **Pr** Praseo- dymium 140.907	60 **Nd** Neodym- ium 144.24	61 **Pm** Prome- thium (145)	62 **Sm** Samarium 150.35	63 **Eu** Europium 151.96
**ACTINIDES	89 **Ac** Actinium (227)	90 **Th** Thorium 232.038	91 **Pa** Protac- tinium (231)	92 **U** Uranium 238.03	93 **Np** Neptunium (237)	94 **Pu** Plutonium (244)	95 **Am** Americium (243)

TABLE OF THE ELEMENTS

ELEMENT	SYMBOL	ATOMIC NUMBER	ELEMENT	SYMBOL	ATOMIC NUMBER	ELEMENT	SYMBOL	ATOMIC NUMBER	ELEMENT	SYMBOL	ATOMIC NUMBER
Actinium	Ac	89	Cadmium	Cd	48	Element 104	–	104	Holmium	Ho	67
Aluminum	Al	13	Calcium	Ca	20	Element 105	–	105	Hydrogen	H	1
Americium	Am	95	Californium	Cf	98	Erbium	Er	68	Indium	In	49
Antimony	Sb	51	Carbon	C	6	Europium	Eu	63	Iodine	I	53
Argon	Ar	18	Cerium	Ce	58	Fermium	Fm	100	Iridium	Ir	77
Arsenic	As	33	Cesium	Cs	55	Fluorine	F	9	Iron	Fe	26
Astatine	At	85	Chlorine	Cl	17	Francium	Fr	87	Krypton	Kr	36
Barium	Ba	56	Chromium	Cr	24	Gadolinium	Gd	64	Lanthanum	La	57
Berkelium	Bk	97	Cobalt	Co	27	Gallium	Ga	31	Lawrencium	Lr	103
Beryllium	Be	4	Copper	Cu	29	Germanium	Ge	32	Lead	Pb	82
Bismuth	Bi	83	Curium	Cm	96	Gold	Au	79	Lithium	Li	3
Boron	B	5	Dysprosium	Dy	66	Hafnium	Hf	72	Lutetium	Lu	71
Bromine	Br	35	Einsteinium	Es	99	Helium	He	2	Magnesium	Mg	12

GROUP 8	GROUP 1b	GROUP 2b	GROUP 3a	GROUP 4a	GROUP 5a	GROUP 6a	GROUP 7a	GROUP 0
								2 **He** Helium 4.0026
			5 **B** Boron 10.811	6 **C** Carbon 12.01115	7 **N** Nitrogen 14.0067	8 **O** Oxygen 15.9994	9 **F** Fluorine 18.9984	10 **Ne** Neon 20.183
			13 **Al** Aluminum 26.9815	14 **Si** Silicon 28.086	15 **P** Phos-phorus 30.9738	16 **S** Sulfur 32.064	17 **Cl** Chlorine 35.453	18 **Ar** Argon 39.948
28 **Ni** Nickel 58.71	29 **Cu** Copper 63.546	30 **Zn** Zinc 65.37	31 **Ga** Gallium 69.72	32 **Ge** Germanium 72.59	33 **As** Arsenic 74.9216	34 **Se** Selenium 78.96	35 **Br** Bromine 79.904	36 **Kr** Krypton 83.80
46 **Pd** Palladium 106.4	47 **Ag** Silver 107.868	48 **Cd** Cadmium 112.40	49 **In** Indium 114.82	50 **Sn** Tin 118.69	51 **Sb** Antimony 121.75	52 **Te** Tellurium 127.60	53 **I** Iodine 126.9044	54 **Xe** Xenon 131.30
78 **Pt** Platinum 195.09	79 **Au** Gold 196.967	80 **Hg** Mercury 200.59	81 **Tl** Thallium 204.37	82 **Pb** Lead 207.19	83 **Bi** Bismuth 208.980	84 **Po** Polonium (210)	85 **At** Astatine (210)	86 **Rn** Radon (222)

64 **Gd** Gadolinium 157.25	65 **Tb** Terbium 158.924	66 **Dy** Dysprosium 162.50	67 **Ho** Holmium 164.930	68 **Er** Erbium 167.26	69 **Tm** Thulium 168.934	70 **Yb** Ytterbium 173.04	71 **Lu** Lutetium 174.97
96 **Cm** Curium (247)	97 **Bk** Berkelium (247)	98 **Cf** Californium (251)	99 **Es** Einsteinium (254)	100 **Fm** Fermium (257)	101 **Md** Mende-levium (256)	102 **No** Nobelium (255)	103 **Lr** Lawren-cium (257)

ELEMENT	SYMBOL	ATOMIC NUMBER	ELEMENT	SYMBOL	ATOMIC NUMBER	ELEMENT	SYMBOL	ATOMIC NUMBER	ELEMENT	SYMBOL	ATOMIC NUMBER
Manganese	Mn	25	Palladium	Pd	46	Rubidium	Rb	37	Terbium	Tb	65
Medelevium	Md	101	Phosphorus	P	15	Ruthenium	Ru	44	Thallium	Tl	81
Mercury	Hg	80	Platinum	Pt	78	Samarium	Sm	62	Thorium	Th	90
Molybdenum	Mo	42	Plutonium	Pu	94	Scandium	Sc	21	Thulium	Tm	69
Neodymium	Nd	60	Polonium	Po	84	Selenium	Se	34	Tin	Sn	50
Neon	Ne	10	Potassium	K	19	Silicon	Si	14	Titanium	Ti	22
Neptunium	Np	93	Praseodymium	Pr	59	Silver	Ag	47	Tungsten	W	74
Nickel	Ni	28	Promethium	Pm	61	Sodium	Na	11	Uranium	U	92
Niobium	Nb	41	Protactinium	Pa	91	Strontium	Sr	38	Vanadium	V	23
Nitrogen	N	7	Radium	Ra	88	Sulfur	S	16	Xenon	Xe	54
Nobelium	No	102	Radon	Rn	86	Tantalum	Ta	73	Ytterbium	Yb	70
Osmium	Os	76	Rhenium	Re	75	Technetium	Tc	43	Yttrium	Y	39
Oxygen	O	8	Rhodium	Rh	45	Tellurium	Te	52	Zinc	Zn	30
									Zirconium	Zr	40

ed at Eleusis in honor of Demeter. [< Lat. *Eleusīnius*, of Eleusis < Gk. *Eleusinios* < *Eleusis*, *Eleusin-*, Eleusis.]

E•leu•sis (ĭ-lo͞o′sĭs). An ancient city of E Greece near Athens. — **El′eu•sin′i•an** (ĕl′yo͝o-sĭn′ē-ən) *adj. & n.*

elev. *abbr.* Elevation.

el•e•vate (ĕl′ə-vāt′) *tr.v.* **-vat•ed, -vat•ing, -vates. 1.** To move (something) to a higher place or position from a lower one; lift. **2.** To increase the amplitude, intensity, or volume of. **3.** To promote to a higher rank. **4.** To raise to a higher moral, cultural, or intellectual level. **5.** To lift the spirits of; elate. See Syns at **lift.** [ME *elevaten* < Lat. *ēlevāre*, *ēlevāt-* : *ē-*, *ex-*, up; see EX- + *levāre*, to raise; see **legʷh-*.**]

el•e•vat•ed (ĕl′ə-vā′tĭd) *adj.* **1.a.** Raised esp. above the ground. **b.** Increased in amount or degree. **2.a.** Morally or intellectually superior. **b.** Formal; lofty. **3.** Elated in feeling or mood; high-spirited. —*n.* An elevated railway.

elevated railway *n.* A railway that operates on a raised structure in order to permit passage beneath it.

el•e•va•tion (ĕl′ə-vā′shən) *n.* **1.a.** The act or an instance of elevating. **b.** The condition of being elevated. **2.** An elevated place or position. **3.** The height to which something is elevated above a point of reference. **4.** Loftiness of thought or feeling. **5.** A scale drawing of the side, front, or rear of a structure. **6.** The height of a thing above a reference level; altitude. **7.a.** The ability to achieve height in a jump. **b.** The degree of height reached by such a jump.

el•e•va•tor (ĕl′ə-vā′tər) *n.* **1.a.** A platform or an enclosure raised and lowered in a vertical shaft to transport people or freight. **b.** The enclosure or platform with its operating equipment, motor, cables, and accessories. **2.** A movable control surface, usu. attached to the horizontal stabilizer of an aircraft, that is used to produce motion up or down. **3.** A mechanism, often with buckets or scoops attached to a conveyor, used for hoisting materials. **4.** A granary equipped with devices for hoisting and discharging grain.

e•lev•en (ĭ-lĕv′ən) *n.* **1.** The cardinal number equal to 10 + 1. **2.** The 11th in a set or sequence. **3.** Something with 11 parts or members, esp. a football team. [ME *elleven* < OE *endleofan.* See **oi-no-*.**] — **e•lev′en** *adj. & pron.*

e•lev•ens•es (ĭ-lĕv′ən-zəs) *pl.n. Chiefly British.* Tea or coffee taken at midmorning and often accompanied by a snack.

e•lev•enth (ĭ-lĕv′ənth) *n.* **1.** The ordinal number matching the number 11 in a series. **2.** One of 11 equal parts. — **e•lev′enth** *adv. & adj.*

eleventh hour *n.* The latest possible time.

el•e•von (ĕl′ə-vŏn′) *n.* A control surface on an airplane that combines the functions of an elevator and an aileron.

elf (ĕlf) *n., pl.* **elves** (ĕlvz). **1.** A small, often mischievous creature considered to have magical powers. **2.a.** A lively mischievous child. **b.** A usu. sprightly or mischievous or sometimes spiteful person. [ME < OE *ælf.* See **albho-*.**]

George Eliot

ELF *abbr.* Extremely low frequency.

El Fer•rol (fə-rôl′, fĕ-) also **El Ferrol del Cau•dil•lo** (dĕl′ kou-dē′ō, -*thē*′ô). A city of NW Spain on the Atlantic Ocean; an important naval station since the 18th cent. Pop. 90,410.

elf•in (ĕl′fĭn) *adj.* **1.a.** Relating to or suggestive of an elf. **b.** Made, done, or produced by an elf. **2.** Small and sprightly; mischievous. **3.** Having a magical quality or charm; fairylike. [Prob. < ME *elvene*, pl. of *elve*, elf < OE *-elfen*, as in *wuduelfen*, dryad. See **albho-*.**]

elf•ish (ĕl′fĭsh) also **elv•ish** (ĕl′vĭsh) *adj.* **1.** Of or relating to elves. **2.** Prankish; mischievous. — **elf′ish•ly** *adv.* — **elf′ish•ness** *n.*

elf•lock (ĕlf′lŏk′) *n.* A lock of hair tangled as if by elves. Often used in the plural.

El•gar (ĕl′gär′, -gər), Sir **Edward.** 1857–1934. British composer whose works include *Enigma Variations* (1896).

El•gin (ĕl′jĭn). A city of NE IL on the Fox R. WNW of Chicago. Pop. 77,010.

El Grec•o (grĕk′ō). See El **Greco.**

el•hi (ĕl′hī′) *adj. Informal.* Of, relating to, involving, or designed for use in grades 1 to 12.

E•li (ē′lī). In the Bible, a judge of Israel who was the teacher of Samuel.

Elizabeth II
1957 photograph by
Antony Armstrong Jones
(Lord Snowdon)

e•lic•it (ĭ-lĭs′ĭt) *tr.v.* **-it•ed, -it•ing, -its. 1.a.** To bring or draw out (something latent); educe. **b.** To arrive at (a truth, for example) by logic. **2.** To call forth (a reaction, for example). [Lat. *ēlicere*, *ēlicit-* : *ē-*, *ex-*, ex- + *lacere*, to entice.] — **e•lic′i•ta′tion** *n.* — **e•lic′i•tor** *n.*

e•lide (ĭ-līd′) *tr.v.* **e•lid•ed, e•lid•ing, e•lides. 1.a.** To omit or slur over (a syllable, for example) in pronunciation. **b.** To strike out (something written). **2.a.** To eliminate or leave out of consideration. **b.** To cut short; abridge. [Lat. *ēlīdere*, to strike out : *ē-*, *ex-*, ex- + *laedere*, to strike.]

el•i•gi•ble (ĕl′ĭ-jə-bəl) *adj.* **1.** Qualified or entitled to be chosen. **2.** Desirable and worthy of choice, esp. for marriage. **3.** *Football.* Allowed under the rules to catch a forward pass. [ME < OFr. < LLat. *ēligibilis* < Lat. *ēligere*, to select. See ELECT.] — **el′i•gi•bil′i•ty** *n.* — **el′•i•gi•ble** *n.* — **el′i•gi•bly** *adv.*

E•li•jah (ĭ-lī′jə). 9th cent. B.C. A Hebrew prophet who according to the Bible was carried skyward in a chariot of fire.

e•lim•i•nate (ĭ-lĭm′ə-nāt′) *tr.v.* **-nat•ed, -nat•ing, -nates. 1.** To get rid of; remove. **2.a.** To leave out or omit from consideration; reject. **b.** To remove from consideration by defeating, as in a contest. **3.** *Math.* To remove (an unknown quantity) by combining equations. **4.** *Physiol.* To excrete (bodily wastes). [Lat. *ēlīmināre*, *ēlīmināt-*, to banish : *ē-*, *ex-*, ex- + *līmen*, *līmin-*, threshold.] — **e•lim′i•na′tion** *n.* — **e•lim′i•na′tive, e•lim′i•na•to′ry** (-nə-tôr′ē, -tōr′ē) *adj.* — **e•lim′i•na′tor** *n.*

El•i•ot (ĕl′ē-ət), **Charles William.** 1834–1926. Amer. educator who was president of Harvard University (1869–1909).

Eliot, George. Mary Ann Evans. 1819–80. British writer whose novels include *Middlemarch* (1871–72).

Eliot, John. 1604–90. English missionary who contributed to *The Bay Psalm Book* (1640), the first book printed in New England.

Eliot, T(homas) S(tearns). 1888–1965. Amer.-born British critic and writer whose works include "The Love Song of J. Alfred Prufrock" (1915) and *The Waste Land* (1922). He won the 1948 Nobel Prize for literature.

E•lis (ē′lĭs). A region and city of ancient Greece in the W Peloponnesus; site of the original Olympic games.

ELISA (ĭ-lī′zə, -sə) *n.* A sensitive immunoassay that uses an enzyme linked to an antibody or antigen as a marker for the detection of a specific protein, esp. an antigen or antibody. [*e(nzyme)-l(inked) i(mmunoad)s(orbent) a(ssay).*]

E•lis•a•beth•ville (ĭ-lĭz′ə-bəth-vĭl′). See **Lubumbashi.**

E•li•sha (ĭ-lī′shə). 9th cent. B.C. A Hebrew prophet who was chosen by Elijah to be his successor.

e•li•sion (ĭ-lĭzh′ən) *n.* **1.a.** *Ling.* Omission of a final or initial sound in pronunciation. **b.** Omission of an unstressed vowel or syllable, as in scanning a verse. **2.** The act or an instance of omitting something. [Lat. *ēlīsiō*, *ēlīsiōn-* < *ēlīsus*, p.part. of *ēlīdere*, to strike out. See ELIDE.]

e•lite or **é•lite** (ĭ-lēt′, ā-lēt′) *n., pl.* **elite** or **e•lites. 1.a.** A group or class of persons or a member of such a group or class, enjoying superior intellectual, social, or economic status. **b.** The best or most skilled members of a group. **2.** A size of type on a typewriter, equal to 12 characters per linear inch. [Fr. *élite* < OFr. *eslite* < fem. p.part. of *eslire*, to choose < Lat. *ēligere.* See ELECT.] — **e•lite′** *adj.*

e•lit•ism or **é•lit•ism** (ĭ-lē′tĭz′əm, ā-lē′-) *n.* **1.** The belief that certain persons or members of certain groups deserve favored treatment by virtue of their perceived superiority. **2.a.** The sense of entitlement enjoyed by such a group. **b.** Control, rule, or domination by such a group. — **e•lit′ist** *adj. & n.*

e•lix•ir (ĭ-lĭk′sər) *n.* **1.** A sweetened aromatic solution of alcohol and water, serving as a vehicle for medicine. **2.a.** See **philosophers' stone. b.** A substance believed to maintain life indefinitely. **c.** A substance or medicine believed to have the power to cure all ills. **3.** An underlying principle. [ME, a substance of transmutative properties < OFr. *elissir* < Med.Lat. *elixir* < Ar. *al-'iksīr* : *al*, the + *iksīr*, elixir (prob. < Gk. *xērion*, desiccative powder < *xēros*, dry).]

E•liz•a•beth¹ (ĭ-lĭz′ə-bəth). The mother of John the Baptist and a kinswoman of Mary.

Elizabeth². 1843–1916. Queen of Romania (1881–1916) and poet who wrote as Carmen Sylva.

Elizabeth³. b. 1900. Queen of Great Britain and Northern Ireland (1936–52) as the wife of George VI.

Elizabeth⁴. A city of NE NJ S of Newark; settled in 1664. Pop. 110,002.

Elizabeth I. 1533–1603. Queen of England and Ireland (1558–1603) who reestablished Protestantism in England. Her reign was marked by the execution of Mary Queen of Scots (1587) and the defeat of the Spanish Armada (1588). — **E•liz′a•be′than** (ĭ-lĭz′ə-bē′thən, -bĕth′ən) *adj. & n.*

Elizabeth II. b. 1926. Queen of Great Britain and Northern Ireland (since 1952).

Elizabethan sonnet *n.* See **Shakespearean sonnet.**

Elizabeth Pe•trov•na (pə-trôv′nə). 1709–62. Empress of Russia (1741–62) during the War of the Austrian Succession (1740–48) and the Seven Years' War (1756–63).

elk (ĕlk) *n., pl.* **elk** or **elks. 1.** See **wapiti. 2.** The moose. **3.** A light pliant leather of horsehide or calfskin, tanned and finished to resemble elk hide. [ME, prob. alteration of OE *eolh.*]

Elk Grove Village (ĕlk). A village of NE IL, a suburb of Chicago. Pop. 33,429.

Elk•hart (ĕl′kärt′, ĕlk′härt′). A city of N IN E of South Bend; settled in 1824. Pop. 43,627.

elk•hound (ĕlk′hound′) *n.* The Norwegian elkhound.

Elk Mountains. A range of the Rocky Mts. in W-central CO rising to 4,350.8 m (14,265 ft).

ell¹ (ĕl) *n.* **1.** A wing of a building at right angles to the main structure. **2.** A right-angled bend in a pipe or conduit; an elbow. [< its L shape, or short for ELBOW.]

ell² (ĕl) *n.* An English linear measure equal to 45 inches (114 centimeters). [ME < OE *eln*, the length from the elbow to the middle finger's tip, ell. See **el-*.**]

ell³ (ĕl) *n.* Var. of **el¹.**

el•lag•ic acid (ĭ-lăj′ĭk) *n.* A yellow crystalline compound, $C_{14}H_6O_8$, that is obtained from tannins and used as a hemostatic. [Fr. *ellagique* < *ellag*, backward spelling of *galle*, plant gall < Lat. *galla*.]

Elles•mere Island (ĕlz′mîr′). An island of N Northwest Terrs., Canada, in the Arctic Ocean near Greenland.

Ellesmere Port. A municipal borough of NW England on the Mersey R. SSE of Liverpool. Pop. 82,500.

El•lice Islands (ĕl′ĭs). See **Tuvalu.**

El•ling•ton (ĕl′ĭng-tən), **Edward Kennedy.** "Duke." 1899–1974. Amer. composer, pianist, and bandleader whose compositions include "Mood Indigo" (1930).

El•li•ot Lake (ĕl′ē-ət). A community of S-central Ontario, Canada, WSW of Sudbury. Pop. 16,723.

el•lipse (ĭ-lĭps′) *n.* **1.** A plane curve, esp.: **a.** A conic section whose plane is not parallel to the axis, base, or generatrix of the intersected cone. **b.** The locus of points for which the sum of the distances from each point to two fixed points is equal. **2.** Ellipsis. [Fr. < Lat. *ellīpsis* < Gk. *elleipsis* < *elleipein*, to fall short (from the relationship between the line joining the vertices of a conic and the line through the focus and parallel to the directrix of a conic). See ELLIPSIS.]

el•lip•sis (ĭ-lĭp′sĭs) *n., pl.* **-ses** (-sēz). **1.a.** The omission of a word or phrase necessary for a complete syntactical construction but not necessary for understanding. **b.** An example of such omission. **2.** A mark or series of marks (. . . or * * * , for example) used in writing or printing to indicate an omission. [Lat. *ellīpsis* < Gk. *elleipsis* < *elleipein*, to fall short : *en-*, in; see EN-[2] + *leipein*, to leave; see **leikʷ-*.**]

el•lip•soid (ĭ-lĭp′soid′) *n.* A geometric surface, all of whose plane sections are either ellipses or circles. **— el•lip′soid′, el′lip•soid′al** (-soid′l) *adj.*

el•lip•tic (ĭ-lĭp′tĭk) or **el•lip•ti•cal** (-tĭ-kəl) *adj.* **1.** Of, relating to, or having the shape of an ellipse. **2.** Containing or characterized by ellipsis. **3.a.** Of or relating to extreme economy of oral or written expression. **b.** Marked by deliberate obscurity of style or expression. [NLat. *ellīpticus* < Gk. *elleiptikos*, defective < *elleipsis*, a falling short, ellipsis < *elleipein*, to fall short. See ELLIPSIS.] **— el•lip′ti•cal•ly** *adv.*

el•lip•tic•i•ty (ĭ-lĭp′-tĭs′ĭ-tē) *n.* **1.** Deviation from perfect circular or spherical form toward elliptic or ellipsoidal form. **2.** The degree of this deviation.

El•lis (ĕl′ĭs), **(Henry) Havelock.** 1859–1939. British psychologist and writer known for his pioneering works on sexuality.

Ellis Island. An island of Upper New York Bay SW of Manhattan; chief immigration station of the U.S. (1892–1943).

El•li•son (ĕl′ĭ-sən), **Ralph Waldo.** b. 1914. Amer. writer whose works include *Invisible Man* (1952).

[illegible]•worth (ĕlz′wûrth′), **Lincoln.** 1880–1951. Amer. explorer [illegible]o took part in several polar expeditions.

[illegible]orth, Oliver. 1745–1807. Amer. jurist; chief justice of the [illegible] Supreme Court (1796–1800).

[illegible]th Land. A high plateau of W Antarctica S of the Ant[illegible]eninsula that includes the **Ellsworth Mountains,** rising [illegible].3 m (16,860 ft).

elm (ĕlm) *n.* Any of various deciduous trees of the genus *Ulmus*, characteristically having arching or curving branches and serrate leaves with asymmetrical bases. [ME < OE.]

El•man (ĕl′mən), **Mischa.** 1891–1967. Russian-born Amer. violinist regarded as one of the foremost violinists of his time.

El Man•su•ra (măn-so͝or′ə). A city of N Egypt on a branch of the Nile R. Pop. 328,700.

elm bark beetle *n.* Either of two bark beetles *(Scolytus multistriatus* or *Hylurgopinus rufipes)* that transmit the fungus causing Dutch elm disease.

Elm•hurst (ĕlm′hûrst′). A city of NE IL, a suburb of Chicago. Pop. 42,029.

El•mi•ra (ĕl-mī′rə). A city of S NY near the PA border W of Binghamton. Pop. 33,724.

El Mis•ti (mē′stē). A dormant volcano, 5,825.8 m (19,101 ft), in the Cordillera Occidental of S Peru.

El Mon•te (mŏn′tē). A city of S CA E of Los Angeles. Pop. 106,209.

Elm•wood Park (ĕlm′wo͝od′). **1.** A village of NE IL, a suburb of Chicago. Pop. 23,206. **2.** A borough of NE NJ SE of Paterson. Pop. 17,623.

El Ni•ño (nēn′yō) *n. Oceanography.* A warming of the ocean surface off the western coast of South America, occurring every 4 to 12 years when upwelling of cold nutrient-rich water does not occur and affecting weather over much of the Pacific Ocean. [Am.Sp. < Sp., the Christ child (the onset of the warming being at Christmastide) : *el*, the (< Lat. *ille*; see **al-[1]***) + *niño*, child (< OSp. *ninno* < VLat. **ninnus*).]

El O•beid (ō-bād′). See **Al Ubayyid.**

el•o•cu•tion (ĕl′ə-kyo͞o′shən) *n.* **1.** The art of public speaking. **2.** A style or manner of speaking, esp. in public. [ME *elocucion* < Lat. *ēlocūtiō*, *ēlocūtiōn-* < *ēlocūtus*, p.part. of *ēloquī*, to speak out : *ē-*, *ex-*, ex- + *loquī*, to speak; see **tolkʷ-*.**] **— el′o•cu′tion•ar′y** (-shə-nĕr′ē) *adj.* **— el′o•cu′tion•ist** *n.*

e•lo•de•a (ĭ-lō′dē-ə) *n.* Any of various small submersed herbs of the genus *Elodea*, having grasslike leaves. [NLat. *Elodea*, genus name < Gk. *helōdēs*, marshy < *helos*, marsh.]

e•loign (ĭ-loin′) *tr.v.* **e•loigned, e•loign•ing, e•loigns.** *Archaic.* **1.** To remove or carry away to a distance, esp. so as to conceal. **2.** To take (oneself) to a distance. [ME *elongen* < OFr. *esloigner* : *es-*, from (< Lat. *ex-*; see EX-) + *loing*, far (< Lat. *longē*, distant < *longus*, long; see **del-[1]***).]

e•lon•gate (ĭ-lông′gāt′, ĭ-lŏng′-) *tr. & intr.v.* **-gat•ed, -gat•ing, -gates.** To make or grow longer. *— adj.* or **elongated. 1.** Made longer; extended. **2.** Having more length than width; slender. [LLat. *ēlongāre*, *ēlongāt-* : Lat. *ē-*, *ex-*, ex- + Lat. *longē*, distant; see ELOIGN.]

e•lon•ga•tion (ĭ-lông′-gā′shən, ĭ-lŏng′-, ē′lông-, ē′lŏng-) *n.* **1.** The act of elongating or the condition of being elongated. **2.** Something that elongates; an extension. **3.** The angular distance between two celestial bodies as seen from Earth.

e•lope (ĭ-lōp′) *intr.v.* **e•loped, e•lop•ing, e•lopes. 1.** To run away with a lover, esp. with the intention of getting married. **2.** To run away; abscond. [Perh. AN *aloper*, to run away from one's husband with a lover < MDu. *ontlopen*, to run away : *ont-*, away from, along; see **ant-*** + *lopen*, to run.] **— e•lope′ment** *n.* **— e•lop′er** *n.*

el•o•quence (ĕl′ə-kwəns) *n.* **1.a.** Persuasive powerful discourse. **b.** The skill or power of using such discourse. **2.** The quality of persuasive powerful expression.

el•o•quent (ĕl′ə-kwənt) *adj.* **1.** Characterized by eloquence. **2.** Vividly or movingly expressive. See Syns at **expressive.** [ME < OFr. < Lat. *ēloquēns*, *ēloquent-*, pr.part. of *ēloquī*, to speak out. See ELOCUTION.] **— el′o•quent•ly** *adv.* **— el′o•quent•ness** *n.*

El Pas•o (păs′ō). A city of extreme W TX on the Rio Grande opposite Ciudad Juárez, Mexico. Pop. 515,342.

El Sal•va•dor (săl′və-dôr′, säl′vä-*th*ôr′). A country of Central America on the Pacific; achieved independence from Spain in 1821. Cap. San Salvador. Pop. 4,949,000. **— El Sal′va•dor′i•an** (săl′və-dôr′ē-ən, -dōr′-) *adj. & n.*

else (ĕls) *adj.* **1.** Other; different: *Ask somebody else.* **2.** Additional; more: *anything else.* *— adv.* **1.** In a different or an additional time, place, or manner: *Where else did he go?* **2.** If not; otherwise: *Be careful, or else you will fall.* **— *idiom.* or else.** Regardless of any extenuating circumstances: *Be there or else!* [ME *elles* < OE. See **al-[1]***.]

Usage Note: *Else* is often used redundantly in combination with prepositions such as *but, except,* and *besides*: *No one else but Sam knew* (omit *else*). • When a pronoun is followed by *else,* the possessive form is generally written thus: *someone else's* (not *someone's else*). Both *who else's* and *whose else* are in use but not *whose else's.* See Usage Notes at **who, whose.**

else•where (ĕls′hwâr′, -wâr′) *adv.* In or to a different or another place: *has property at the shore and elsewhere.*

El•si•nore (ĕl′sə-nôr′, -nōr′). See **Helsingør.**

El To•ro (tôr′ō). A community of S CA SE of Santa Ana. Pop. 62,685.

el•u•ant (ĕl′yo͞o-ənt) *n.* A substance used as a solvent in the process of elution. [< Lat. *ēluēns*, *ēluent-*, pr.part. of *ēluere*, to wash out. See ELUTE.]

el•u•ate (ĕl′yo͞o-ĭt, -āt′) *n.* The solution of solvent and dissolved matter resulting from elution. [Lat. *ēluere*, to wash out; see ELUTE + -ATE[1].]

e•lu•ci•date (ĭ-lo͞o′sĭ-dāt′) *v.* **-dat•ed, -dat•ing, -dates.** *— tr.* To make clear or plain, esp. by explanation. *— intr.* To give an explanation that clarifies. [LLat. *ēlūcidāre*, *ēlūcidāt-* : Lat. *ē-*, *ex-*, intensive pref.; see EX- + Lat. *lūcidus*, bright (< *lūcēre*, to shine; see **leuk-***).] **— e•lu′ci•da′tion** *n.* **— e•lu′ci•da′tive** *adj.* **— e•lu′ci•da′tor** *n.*

e•lude (ĭ-lo͞od′) *tr.v.* **e•lud•ed, e•lud•ing, e•ludes. 1.** To evade or escape from, as by daring, cleverness, or skill. **2.** To escape the understanding or grasp of. [Lat. *ēlūdere* : *ē-*, *ex-*, ex- + *lūdere*, to play (< *lūdus*, play; see **leid-***).]

E•lul (ĕl′o͝ol, ĕ-lo͞ol′) *n.* The 12th month of the year in the Jewish calendar. [Heb. *'Elūl* < Akkadian *ulūlu*, *elūlu*, the month Ululu (August/September).]

e•lu•sive (ĭ-lo͞o′sĭv, -zĭv) *adj.* **1.** Tending to elude capture, perception, comprehension, or memory. **2.** Difficult to define or describe. [< Lat. *ēlūsus*, p.part. of *ēlūdere*, to elude. See ELUDE.] **— e•lu′sive•ly** *adv.* **— e•lu′sive•ness** *n.*

e•lute (ĭ-lo͞ot′) *tr.v.* **e•lut•ed, e•lut•ing, e•lutes.** To extract (one material) from another, usu. by means of a solvent. [< Lat. *ēluere*, *ēlūt-*, to wash out : *ē-*, *ex-*, ex- + *-luere*, to wash; see **leu(ə)-*.**] **— e•lu′tion** *n.*

e•lu•tri•ate (ĭ-lo͞o′trē-āt′) *tr.v.* **-at•ed, -at•ing, -ates. 1.** To purify, separate, or remove (ore, for example) by washing, decanting, and settling. **2.** To wash away the lighter or finer particles of (soil, for example). [Lat. *elutriāre*, *elutriāt-* (< **elutrium*, vat, bath < Gk. **elutrion*, dim. of *elutron*, tank; see ELYTRON) or *ēlūtriāre* (< **ēlūtor*, one who washes < *ēluere*, to wash out; see ELUTE).] **— e•lu′tri•a′tion** *n.*

e•lu•vi•ate (ĭ-lo͞o′vē-āt′) *intr.v.* **-at•ed, -at•ing, -ates.** To undergo eluviation.

e•lu•vi•a•tion (ĭ-lo͞o′vē-ā′shən) *n.* The lateral or downward movement of dissolved or suspended material within soil when rainfall exceeds evaporation. [ELUVI(UM) + -ATION.]

e•lu•vi•um (ĭ-lo͞o′vē-əm) *n.* Residual deposits of soil, dust, and rock particles produced by the wind. [NLat. *ēluvium* <

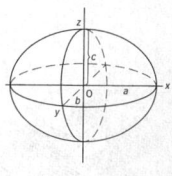

ellipsoid

$$\frac{x^2}{a^2} + \frac{y^2}{b^2} - \frac{z^2}{c^2} = 1$$

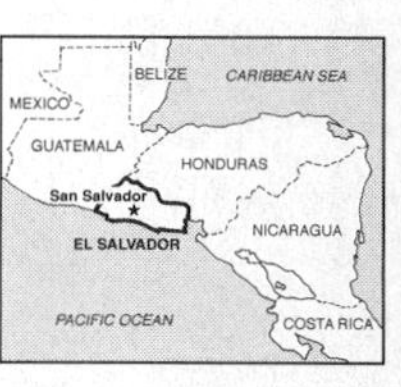

El Salvador

ă pat
ā pay
âr care
ä father
ĕ pet
ē be
ĭ pit
ī pie
îr pier
ŏ pot
ō toe
ô paw
oi boy
ou out
o͝o took
o͞o boot
ŭ cut
ûr urge
th thin
th this
hw which
zh vision
ə about, item

Stress marks:
′ (primary);
′ (secondary), as in
dictionary (dĭk′shə-nĕr′ē)

Lat. *ēluere*, to wash out. See ELUTE.] —**e•lu′vi•al** (-əl) *adj.*
el•ver (ĕl′vər) *n.* See **glass eel.** [Alteration of *eelfare*, a brood of young eels : EEL + FARE, journey (obsolete).]
elves (ĕlvz) *n.* Pl. of **elf.**
elv•ish (ĕl′vĭsh) *adj.* Var. of **elfish.**
E•ly (ē′lē), **Isle of.** A region of E-central England with extensive drained fens. The city of **Ely** (pop. 10,268) is noted for its cathedral, dating from the 11th cent.
E•ly•ri•a (ĭ-lîr′ē-ə). A city of N OH WSW of Cleveland; settled in 1817. Pop. 56,746.
E•ly•sian (ĭ-lĭzh′ən) *adj.* **1.** *Gk. Myth.* Of or relating to Elysium. **2.** Blissful; delightful.
Elysian Fields *pl.n. Gk. Myth.* The abode of the blessed dead.
E•ly•si•um (ĭ-lĭz′ē-əm, ĭ-lĭzh′-) *n.* **1.** *Gk. Myth.* The Elysian Fields. **2.** A place or condition of ideal happiness. [Lat. *Ēlysium* < Gk. *Ēlusion (pedion)*, Elysian (fields).]
El•y•tis (ĕl′ē-tēs′), **Odysseus.** b. 1911. Greek poet who won the 1979 Nobel Prize for literature.
el•y•tron (ĕl′ĭ-trŏn′) *n., pl.* **-tra** (-trə). Either of the leathery or chitinous forewings of a beetle or a related insect, serving to encase the thin hind wings used in flight. [NLat. < Gk. *elutron*, sheath. See **wel-²***.] —**el′y•troid′** (-troid′) *adj.*
em (ĕm) *n.* **1.** The letter *m.* **2.** *Print.* **a.** The width of a square piece of type, used as a unit of measure for matter set in that size of type. **b.** Such a measure for 12-point type; a pica.
EM *abbr.* **1.** Electromagnetic. **2.** Electron microscope. **3.** Enlisted man.
E.M. *abbr.* Engineer of Mines.
em–¹ *pref.* Var. of **en–¹.**
em–² *pref.* Var. of **en–².**
'em (əm) *pron. Informal.* Them. [< ME *hem* < OE *him, heom*, dative and accusative pl. of *hē*, he. See HE¹.]
e•ma•ci•ate (ĭ-mā′shē-āt′) *tr. & intr.v.* **-at•ed, -at•ing, -ates.** To make or become extremely thin, as by starvation. [Lat. *ēmaciāre, ēmaciāt-* : *ē-, ex-*, intensive pref.; see EX- + *maciāre*, to make thin (< *macer*, thin; see **māk-***).] —**e•ma′ci•a′tion** *n.*
E-mail (ē′māl′) *n.* or **e-mail** *Comp. Sci.* See **electronic mail.** —*v.* **E-mailed, E-mail•ing, E-mails** or **e-mailed** or **e-mail•ing** or **e-mails.** —*tr.* To write and send by electronic mail. —*intr.* To write and send electronic mail.
em•a•lan•ge•ni (ĕm′ə-läng-gĕn′ē) *n.* Pl. of **lilangeni.**
em•a•nate (ĕm′ə-nāt′) *intr. & tr.v.* **-nat•ed, -nat•ing, -nates.** To come or send forth, as from a source. See Syns at **stem¹.** [Lat. *ēmānāre, ēmānāt-*, to flow out : *ē-, ex-*, ex- + *mānāre*, to flow.] —**em′a•na′tive** *adj.*
em•a•na•tion (ĕm′ə-nā′shən) *n.* **1.** The act or an instance of emanating. **2.a.** Something that issues from a source; an emission. **b.** *Chem.* An isotope of radon. No longer in scientific use. —**em′a•na′tion•al** *adj.*

emblem
International medical alert emblem

e•man•ci•pate (ĭ-măn′sə-pāt′) *tr.v.* **-pat•ed, -pat•ing, -pates.** **1.** To free from bondage, oppression, or restraint; liberate. **2.** *Law.* To release (a child) from the control of parents or a guardian. [Lat. *ēmancipāre, ēmancipāt-* : *ē-, ex-*, ex- + *mancipium*, ownership (< *manceps*, purchaser; see **man-²***).] —**e•man′ci•pa′tion** *n.* —**e•man′ci•pa′tive, e•man′ci•pa•to′ry** (-pə-tôr′ē, -tōr′ē) *adj.* —**e•man′ci•pa′tor** *n.*
e•mar•gi•nate (ĭ-mär′jə-nĭt, -nāt′) *adj. Bot.* Having a shallow notch at the tip. [Lat. *ēmarginātus*, p.part. of *ēmargināre*, to take the edge away : *ē-, ex-*, ex- + *margō, margin-*, margin; see **merg-***.] —**e•mar′gi•na′tion** (-nā′shən) *n.*
e•mas•cu•late (ĭ-măs′kyə-lāt′) *tr.v.* **-lat•ed, -lat•ing, -lates.** **1.** To castrate. **2.** To deprive of strength or vigor; weaken. —*adj.* (-lĭt). Deprived of virility, strength, or vigor. [Lat. *ēmasculāre, ēmasculāt-* : *ē-, ex-*, ex- + *masculus*, male, dim. of *mās*, male, man.] —**e•mas′cu•la′tion** *n.* —**e•mas′cu•la′tive, e•mas′cu•la•to′ry** (-lə-tôr′ē, -tōr′ē) *adj.* —**e•mas′cu•la′tor** *n.*
em•balm (ĕm-bäm′) *tr.v.* **-balmed, -balm•ing, -balms.** **1.** To treat (a corpse) with preservatives in order to prevent decay. **2.** To protect from change or oblivion; preserve or fix. **3.** To impart fragrance to; perfume. [ME *embaumen* < OFr. *embasmer* : *en-*, in; see EN-¹ + *basme*, balm; see BALM.] —**em•balm′er** *n.* —**em•balm′ment** *n.*
em•bank (ĕm-băngk′) *tr.v.* **-banked, -bank•ing, -banks.** To confine, support, or protect with an embankment.
em•bank•ment (ĕm-băngk′mənt) *n.* **1.** The act of embanking. **2.** A mound of earth or stone built to hold back water or support a roadway.
em•bar•go (ĕm-bär′gō) *n., pl.* **-goes.** **1.** A government order prohibiting the movement of merchant ships into or out of its ports. **2.** A prohibition by a government on certain or all trade with a foreign nation. **3.** A prohibition; a ban. —*tr.v.* **-goed, -go•ing, -goes.** To impose an embargo on. [Sp. < *embargar*, to impede < VLat. **imbarricāre*, to barricade : Lat. *in-*, in; see EN-¹ + VLat. **barricāre*, to barricade (< **barrīca*, barrel, barrier < **barra*, bar, barrier).]
em•bark (ĕm-bärk′) *v.* **-barked, -bark•ing, -barks.** —*tr.* **1.** To cause to board a vessel or aircraft. **2.** To enlist (a person or persons) or invest (capital) in an enterprise. —*intr.* **1.** To go aboard a vessel or aircraft. **2.** To set out on a venture; commence. [Fr. *embarquer* : *en-*, in; see EN-¹ + *barque*, ship; see BARK³.] —**em′bar•ka′tion, em•bark′ment** *n.*
em•bar•rass (ĕm-băr′əs) *tr.v.* **-rassed, -rass•ing, -rass•es.** **1.** To cause to feel self-conscious or ill at ease; disconcert. **2.** To involve in or hamper with financial difficulties. **3.** To hinder with obstacles or difficulties; impede. **4.** To complicate. [Fr. *embarrasser*, to encumber, hamper < Sp. *embarazar* < Ital. *imbarazzare* < *imbarazzo*, obstacle, obstruction < *imbarrare*, to block, bar : *in-*, in (< Lat.; see EN-¹) + VLat. **barra*, bar.] —**em•bar′rassed•ly** *adv.* —**em•bar′rass•ing•ly** *adv.*
em•bar•rass•ment (ĕm-băr′əs-mənt) *n.* **1.** The act or an instance of embarrassing. **2.** The state of being embarrassed. **3.** A source of embarrassment. **4.** An overabundance.
em•bas•sage (ĕm′bə-sĭj) *n. Archaic.* An embassy. [ME *ambassage*, office or function of an ambassador, poss. var. of *ambassade* < OFr., ult. < Med.Lat. *ambactiāta* < *ambactia* < Lat. *ambactus*, servant. See **ag-***.]
em•bas•sy (ĕm′bə-sē) *n., pl.* **-sies.** **1.** A building containing the offices of an ambassador and staff. **2.** The position, function, or assignment of an ambassador. **3.** A mission to a foreign government headed by an ambassador. **4.** A staff of diplomatic representatives headed by an ambassador. [Var. of *ambassy*, office or function of an ambassador < obsolete Fr. *ambassée* < Med.Lat. *ambactiāta*. See EMBASSAGE.]
em•bat•tle (ĕm-băt′l) *tr.v.* **-tled, -tling, -tles.** **1.** To prepare for battle; array. **2.** To furnish with battlements for defense. [ME *embataillen* < OFr. *embataillier* : *en-*, in; see EN-¹ + *batailler*, to battle (< *bataille*, battle; see BATTLE).]
em•bat•tled (ĕm-băt′ld) *adj.* **1.** Prepared or fortified for battle or engaged in battle. **2.** Beset, as with criticism.
em•bat•tle•ment (ĕm-băt′l-mənt, ĭm-) *n.* See **battlement.**
em•bay (ĕm-bā′) *tr.v.* **-bayed, -bay•ing, -bays.** To put, shelter, or detain in a bay.
em•bay•ment (ĕm-bā′mənt) *n.* **1.** A bay or baylike shape. **2.** The formation of a bay.
em•bed (ĕm-bĕd′) also **im•bed** (ĭm-) —*v.* **-bed•ded, -bed•ding, -beds.** —*tr.* **1.** To fix firmly in a surrounding mass: *embed a post in concrete.* **2.** To enclose snugly or firmly. **3.** To cause to be an integral part of a surrounding whole. —*intr.* To become embedded. —**em•bed′ment** *n.*
em•bel•lish (ĕm-bĕl′ĭsh) *tr.v.* **-lished, -lish•ing, -lish•es.** **1.** To make beautiful, as by ornamentation; decorate. **2.** To add ornamental or fictitious details to (a story, for example). [ME *embelishen* < OFr. *embellir, embelliss-* : *en-*, causative pref.; see EN-¹ + *bel*, beautiful (< Lat. *bellus*; see **deu-²***).] —**em•bel′lish•er** *n.*
em•bel•lish•ment (ĕm-bĕl′ĭsh-mənt) *n.* **1.** The act of embellishing or the state of being embellished. **2.** Something that embellishes. **3.** *Mus.* A note that embellishes a melody.
em•ber (ĕm′bər) *n.* **1.** A small glowing piece of coal or wood, as in a dying fire. **2. embers.** The smoldering coal or ash of a dying fire. [ME *embre* < OE *ǣmerge.*]
Em•ber Day (ĕm′bər) *n.* A day for prayer and fasting in some Christian churches, observed on the Wednesday, Friday, and Saturday after the first Sunday of Lent, after Whitsunday, after September 14, and after December 13. [ME *ymber daye* < OE *ymbrendæg* : *ymbryne*, recurrence, course of time (*ymbe*, around; see **ambhi*** + *ryne*, a running; see **rei-***) + *dæg*, day; see DAY.]
em•bez•zle (ĕm-bĕz′əl) *tr.v.* **-zled, -zling, -zles.** To take (money, for example) for one's own use in violation of a trust. [ME *embesilen* < AN *enbesiler* : OFr. *en-*, intensive pref.; see EN-¹ + OFr. *besillier*, to ravage.] —**em•bez′zle•ment** *n.* —**em•bez′zler** *n.*
em•bit•ter (ĕm-bĭt′ər) *tr.v.* **-tered, -ter•ing, -ters.** **1.** To make bitter in flavor. **2.** To arouse bitter feelings in: *was embittered by years of unrewarded labor.* —**em•bit′ter•ment** *n.*
em•blaze¹ (ĕm-blāz′) *tr.v.* **-blazed, -blaz•ing, -blaz•es.** **1.** To set on fire. **2.** To cause to glow; light up.
em•blaze² (ĕm-blāz′) *tr.v.* **-blazed, -blaz•ing, -blaz•es.** *Archaic.* **1.** To emblazon. **2.** To decorate lavishly.
em•bla•zon (ĕm-blā′zən) *tr.v.* **-zoned, -zon•ing, -zons.** **1.a.** To adorn (a surface) richly with prominent markings. **b.** To inscribe (a prominent marking) on a surface: *emblazon a cross on a banner.* **2.** To make resplendent with brilliant colors. **3.** To make illustrious; celebrate. —**em•bla′zon•er** *n.* —**em•bla′zon•ment** *n.*
em•bla•zon•ry (ĕm-blā′zən-rē) *n., pl.* **-ries.** **1.** The act or art of emblazoning. **2.** Colorful or prominent decoration.
em•blem (ĕm′bləm) *n.* **1.** An object or a representation that functions as a symbol. **2.** A distinctive badge, design, or device. **3.** An allegorical picture usu. inscribed with a verse or motto presenting a moral lesson. [ME, pictorial fable < Lat. *emblēma, emblēmat-*, raised ornament < Gk., embossed design < *emballein*, to insert, set in : *en-*, in; see EN-² + *ballein*, to throw; see **gʷelə-***.]
em•blem•at•ic (ĕm′blə-măt′ĭk) or **em•blem•at•i•cal** (-ĭ-kəl) *adj.* Of, relating to, or serving as an emblem; symbolic. —**em′blem•at′i•cal•ly** *adv.*
em•blem•a•tize (ĕm-blĕm′ə-tīz′) also **em•blem•ize** (ĕm′blə-mīz′) *tr.v.* **-tized, -tiz•ing, -tiz•es** also **-ized, -iz•ing, -iz•**

es. To represent with or as if with an emblem; symbolize.

em•ble•ments (ĕm′blə-mənts) *pl.n. Law.* The crops or products of the land legally belonging to a tenant. [< ME *emblaiment* < OFr. *emblaement* < *emblaer*, to sow with grain < Med.Lat. *imblādāre* : Lat. *in-*, in; see EN-[1] + Med.Lat. *blādum, blādium*, grain (of Gmc. orig.; see **bhel-**[3*]).]

em•bod•i•ment (ĕm-bŏd′ē-mənt, ĭm-) *n.* **1.** The act of embodying or the state of being embodied. **2.** One that embodies: *The painting is the embodiment of harmony.*

em•bod•y (ĕm-bŏd′ē) *tr.v.* **-bod•ied, -bod•y•ing, -bod•ies. 1.** To give a bodily form to; incarnate. **2.** To represent in bodily or material form: *The manager embodied archaic thinking.* **3.** To make part of a system or whole; incorporate.

em•bold•en (ĕm-bōl′dən) *tr.v.* **-ened, -en•ing, -ens.** To foster boldness or courage in; encourage.

em•bo•lec•to•my (ĕm′bə-lĕk′tə-mē) *n., pl.* **-mies.** Surgical removal of an embolus. [EMBOL(US) + -ECTOMY.]

em•bol•ic (ĕm-bŏl′ĭk) *adj.* **1.** *Pathol.* Of or caused by an embolus or an embolism. **2.** *Embryol.* Of or relating to emboly.

em•bo•lism (ĕm′bə-lĭz′əm) *n.* **1.** Obstruction or occlusion of a blood vessel by an embolus. **2.** An embolus. [ME *embolisme*, insertion < LLat. *embolismus* < Gk. *embolismos* < *emballein*, to insert. See EMBLEM.] **— em′bo•lis′mic** *adj.*

em•bo•lus (ĕm′bə-ləs) *n., pl.* **-li** (-lī′). A mass, such as an air bubble or a blood clot, that travels through the bloodstream and lodges so as to obstruct or occlude a blood vessel. [Lat., piston of a pump < Gk. *embolos*, stopper, plug < *emballein*, to insert. See EMBLEM.]

em•bo•ly (ĕm′bə-lē) *n., pl.* **-lies.** *Embryol.* The formation of a gastrula from a blastula by invagination. [Gk. *embolē*, insertion < *emballein*, to insert. See EMBLEM.]

em•bon•point (äɴ′bôɴ-pwăɴ′) *n.* The condition of being plump; stoutness. [Fr. < *en bon point*, in good condition : *en*, in + *bon*, good + *point*, condition.]

em•bos•om (ĕm-bo͝oz′əm, -bo͞o′zəm) *tr.v.* **-omed, -om•ing, -oms. 1.** To enclose protectively; envelop. **2.** *Archaic.* To clasp to or hold in the bosom.

em•boss (ĕm-bôs′, -bŏs′) *tr.v.* **-bossed, -boss•ing, -boss•es. 1.** To mold or carve in relief: *emboss a design on a coin.* **2.** To decorate with or as if with a raised design: *emboss leather.* **3.** To adorn; decorate. [ME *embosen* < OFr. *embocer* : *en-*, in; see EN-[1] + *boce*, knob.] **— em•boss′er** *n.*

em•boss•ment (ĕm-bôs′mənt, -bŏs′-) *n.* **1.** The act or process of embossing or the condition of being embossed. **2.** Embossed ornamentation. **3.** The distance between the nondeformed part of a document surface and a specified point on a printed character in optical character recognition.

em•bou•chure (äm′bo͞o-sho͝or′) *n.* **1.** The mouth of a river. **2.** *Mus.* **a.** The mouthpiece of a wind instrument. **b.** The manner in which the lips and tongue are applied to such a mouthpiece. [Fr. < *emboucher*, to put or go into the mouth < OFr. : *en-*, in; see EN-[1] + *bouche*, mouth (< Lat. *bucca*, cheek).]

em•bowed (ĕm-bōd′) *adj.* **1.** Bent or curved like a bow. **2.** *Archit.* Having an arch or arches.

em•bow•el (ĕm-bou′əl) *tr.v.* **-eled, -el•ing, -els** or **-elled, -el•ling, -els. 1.** To disembowel. **2.** *Obsolete.* To enclose. [Obsolete Fr. *emboueler* : *en-*, intensive pref.; see EN-[1] + OFr. *boeler* (< *boel, bouele*, entrails; see BOWEL).]

em•bow•er (ĕm-bou′ər) *tr.v.* **-ered, -er•ing, -ers.** To enclose in or as if in a bower.

em•brace (ĕm-brās′) *v.* **-braced, -brac•ing, -brac•es.** *— tr.* **1.** To clasp or hold close with the arms, usu. as an expression of affection. **2.a.** To surround; enclose. **b.** To twine around. **3.** To include as part of something broader. **4.** To take up willingly or eagerly. **5.** To avail oneself of. *— intr.* To join in an embrace. *— n.* **1.** An act of embracing; a hug. **2.** An enclosure or encirclement. **3.** Eager acceptance. [ME *embracen* < OFr. *embracer* : *en-*, in; see EN-[1] + *brace*, the two arms; see BRACE.] **— em•brace′a•ble** *adj.* **— em•brace′ment** *n.* **— em•brac′er** *n.*

em•branch•ment (ĕm-brănch′mənt) *n.* **1.** A branching out, as of a mountain range or river. **2.** A branch or ramification.

em•bran•gle (ĕm-brăng′gəl) *tr.v.* **-gled, -gling, -gles.** To entangle; embroil. [EN-[1] + dial. *brangle*, to shake, waver, confuse (var. of *branle* < Fr. *branler* < OFr. *brandeler*, perh. < *brand*, sword; see BRANDISH).] **— em•bran′gle•ment** *n.*

em•bra•sure (ĕm-brā′zhər) *n.* **1.** An opening in a thick wall for a door or window, esp. one with sides angled so that the opening is larger on the inside than on the outside. **2.** A flared opening for a gun in a wall or parapet. [Fr. < *embraser*, to widen an opening.] **— em•bra′sured** *adj.*

em•brit•tle (ĕm-brĭt′l) *tr. & intr.v.* **-tled, -tling, -tles.** To make or become brittle. **— em•brit′tle•ment** *n.*

em•bro•cate (ĕm′brə-kāt′) *tr.v.* **-cat•ed, -cat•ing, -cates.** To moisten and rub (a part of the body) with a liniment or lotion. [Med.Lat. *embrocāre, embrocāt-* < LLat. *embrocha*, lotion < Gk. *embrokhē* < *embrekhein*, to foment : *en-*, in; see EN-[2] + *brekhein*, to wet.]

em•bro•ca•tion (ĕm′brə-kā′shən) *n.* **1.** The act or process of moistening and rubbing a part of the body with a liniment or lotion. **2.** A liniment or lotion.

em•broi•der (ĕm-broi′dər) *v.* **-dered, -der•ing, -ders.** *— tr.* **1.** To ornament with needlework. **2.** To make by means of needlework: *embroider a design.* **3.** To add embellishments to: *embroider the truth.* *— intr.* **1.** To make needlework. **2.** To add embellishments. [ME *embrouderen*, partly < *embrouden* (< *brouden, broiden*, braided, embroidered < OE *brogden*, p.part. of *bregdan*, to weave; see BRAID) and partly < OFr. *embroder* (*en-*, intensive pref.; see EN-[1] + *broder, brosder*, to embroider, of Gmc. orig.).] **— em•broi′der•er** *n.*

em•broi•der•y (ĕm-broi′də-rē) *n., pl.* **-ies. 1.** The act or art of embroidering. **2.** Ornamentation of fabric with needlework. **3.** A piece of embroidered fabric. **4.** Embellishment with fanciful details.

em•broil (ĕm-broil′) *tr.v.* **-broiled, -broil•ing, -broils. 1.** To involve in argument, contention, or hostile actions. **2.** To throw into confusion or disorder; entangle. [Fr. *embrouiller* : *en-*, intensive pref.; see EN-[1] + *brouiller*, to confuse (< OFr.; see BROIL[2]).] **— em•broil′ment** *n.*

em•brown (ĕm-broun′) *tr.v.* **-browned, -brown•ing, -browns. 1.** To make brown or dusky. **2.** To darken.

em•brue (ĕm-bro͞o′) *v.* Var. of **imbrue.**

em•bry•o (ĕm′brē-ō′) *n., pl.* **-os. 1.a.** An organism in its early stages of development, esp. before it has reached a recognizable form. **b.** An organism at any time before full development, birth, or hatching. **2.a.** The fertilized egg of a vertebrate animal following cleavage. **b.** In human beings, the product of conception from implantation through the eighth week of development. **3.** *Bot.* The rudimentary plant contained within a seed or an archegonium. **4.** A rudimentary or beginning stage. [Med.Lat. *embryō* < Gk. *embruon* : *en-*, in; see EN-[2] + *bruein*, to be full to bursting.]

em•bry•o•gen•e•sis (ĕm′brē-ō-jĕn′ĭ-sĭs) also **em•bry•og•e•ny** (-ŏj′ə-nē) *n.* The development and growth of an embryo. **— em′bry•o•gen′ic** (-jĕn′ĭk), **em′bry•o•ge•net′ic** (-ō-jə-nĕt′ĭk) *adj.*

em•bry•ol•o•gy (ĕm′brē-ŏl′ə-jē) *n.* **1.** The branch of biology that deals with the formation, early growth, and development of living organisms. **2.** The embryonic structure or development of a particular organism. **— em′bry•o•log′ic** (-ə-lŏj′ĭk), **em′bry•o•log′i•cal** *adj.* **— em′bry•o•log′i•cal•ly** *adv.* **— em′bry•ol′o•gist** *n.*

em•bry•on•ic (ĕm′brē-ŏn′ĭk) also **em•bry•on•al** (ĕm′brē-ə-nəl) *adj.* **1.** Of, relating to, or being an embryo. **2.** Also **em•bry•ot•ic** (-ŏt′ĭk). Rudimentary; incipient: *an embryonic nation.* **— em′bry•on′ic•al•ly** *adv.*

embryonic disk *n.* **1.** A platelike mass of cells in the blastocyst from which a mammalian embryo develops. **2.** See **germinal disk.**

embryonic membrane *n.* Any of the membranous structures closely associated with or surrounding a vertebrate embryo, including the amnion, chorion, allantois, and yolk sac.

embryonic shield *n.* See **embryonic disk** 1.

embryo sac *n.* The female gametophyte of a seed plant, within which the embryo develops.

em•cee (ĕm′sē′) *n.* A master of ceremonies. **— em′cee′** *v.*

-eme *suff.* A distinctive unit of linguistic structure: *semanteme.* [Fr. *-ème* < *phonème*, phoneme. See PHONEME.]

e•mend (ĭ-mĕnd′) *tr.v.* **e•mend•ed, e•mend•ing, e•mends.** To improve by critical editing. [ME *emenden* < Lat. *ēmendāre* : *ē-, ex-*, ex- + *mendum*, defect, fault.] **— e•mend′er** *n.*

e•men•date (ē′mĕn-dāt′, ĭ-mĕn′-) *tr.v.* **-dat•ed, -dat•ing, -dates.** To make textual corrections in. [Lat. *ēmendāre, ēmendāt-*, to emend. See EMEND.] **— e′men•da′tor** (-dā′tər) *n.* **— e•men′da•to′ry** (ĭ-mĕn′də-tôr′ē, -tōr′ē) *adj.*

e•men•da•tion (ĭ-mĕn′dā′shən, ē′mĕn-) *n.* **1.** The act of emending. **2.** An alteration intended to improve.

em•er•ald (ĕm′ər-əld, ĕm′rəld) *n.* **1.** A brilliant green to grass-green transparent variety of beryl, used as a gemstone. **2.** *Color.* A strong yellowish green. *— adj. Color.* Of a strong yellowish green. [ME *emeraude* < OFr. < Med.Lat. *esmeralda, esmeraldus* < Lat. *smaragdus* < Gk. *smaragdos.*]

e•merge (ĭ-mûrj′) *intr.v.* **e•merged, e•merg•ing, e•merg•es. 1.** To rise from or as if from a surrounding fluid. **2.** To come forth from obscurity: *new leaders who may emerge.* **3.** To become evident. **4.** To come into existence. [Lat. *ēmergere* : *ē-, ex-*, ex- + *mergere*, to immerse.]

e•mer•gence (ĭ-mûr′jəns) *n.* **1.** The act or process of emerging. **2.** *Bot.* A superficial outgrowth of plant tissue.

e•mer•gen•cy (ĭ-mûr′jən-sē) *n., pl.* **-cies. 1.** A serious situation or occurrence that happens unexpectedly and demands immediate action. **2.** A condition of urgent need for action or assistance. *— adj.* For use during emergencies.

emergency brake *n.* An additional brake system in a vehicle, commonly used as a parking brake.

emergency room *n.* The section of a health care facility intended to provide rapid treatment for victims of sudden illness or trauma.

e•mer•gent (ĭ-mûr′jənt) *adj.* **1.a.** Coming into view, existence, or notice. **b.** Emerging: *emergent nations.* **2.** Rising above a surrounding medium, esp. a fluid. **3.** Demanding prompt action; urgent. **4.** Occurring as a consequence; resultant. *— n.* One that is coming into view or existence.

embroidery
Crewelwork

ă pat	oi boy
ā pay	ou out
âr care	o͝o took
ä father	o͞o boot
ĕ pet	ŭ cut
ē be	ûr urge
ĭ pit	th thin
ī pie	*th* this
îr pier	hw which
ŏ pot	zh vision
ō toe	ə about, item
ô paw	

Stress marks:
′ (primary);
′ (secondary), as in
dictionary (dĭk′shə-nĕr′ē)

emergent evolution *n.* A theory holding that new types of organisms and characteristics appear at certain stages of evolution, usu. as a result of a rearrangement of the preexisting elements.

e•merg•ing (ĭ-mûr′jĭng) *adj.* Newly formed or just coming into prominence; emergent: *emerging markets.*

e•mer•i•ta (ĭ-mĕr′ĭ-tə) *adj.* Retired but retaining an honorary title corresponding to that held immediately before retirement. Used of a woman. — *n., pl.* **-tae** (-tē′) or **-tas.** A woman who holds emerita status. [Lat. *ēmerita*, fem. of *ēmeritus.* See EMERITUS.]

e•mer•i•tus (ĭ-mĕr′ĭ-təs) *adj.* Retired but retaining an honorary title corresponding to that held immediately before retirement. — *n., pl.* **-ti** (-tī′). One who holds emeritus status. [Lat. *ēmeritus*, p.part. of *ēmerērī*, to earn by service : *ē-*, *ex-*, from; see EX- + *merērī*, to deserve, earn; see **(s)mer-**[2]*.]

e•mersed (ĭ-mûrst′) *adj. Bot.* Rising above the surface of water: *emersed plants.* [< Lat. *ēmersus.* See EMERSION.]

e•mer•sion (ĭ-mûr′zhən, -shən) *n.* The act of emerging; emergence. [< Lat. *ēmersus*, p.part. of *ēmergere*, to emerge. See EMERGE.]

Em•er•son (ĕm′ər-sən), **Ralph Waldo.** 1803–82. Amer. writer and philosopher whose works include *Nature* (1836). — **Em′er•so′ni•an** (-sō′nē-ən) *adj.*

em•er•y (ĕm′ə-rē, ĕm′rē) *n.* A fine-grained impure corundum used for grinding and polishing. [ME < OFr. *emeri, emeril* < LLat. *smericulum* < Gk. *smiris.*]

emery board *n.* A nail file consisting of a strip of cardboard coated with powdered emery.

em•e•sis (ĕm′ĭ-sĭs) *n., pl.* **-ses** (-sēz′). The act of vomiting. [Gk. < *emein*, to vomit. See **wemə-***.]

e•met•ic (ĭ-mĕt′ĭk) *adj.* Causing vomiting. — *n.* An agent that causes vomiting. [Lat. *emetica*, fem. of *emeticus*, provoking vomiting < Gk. *emetikos* < *emetos*, vomiting < *emein*, to vomit. See **wemə-***.] — **e•met′i•cal•ly** *adv.*

em•e•tine (ĕm′ĭ-tēn′) *n.* A bitter-tasting crystalline alkaloid, $C_{29}H_{40}N_2O_4$, derived from ipecac root and used in the treatment of amebiasis and as an emetic. [Fr. *émétine* < *émétique*, emetic < Lat. *emeticus.* See EMETIC.]

emf or **EMF** *abbr.* Electromotive force.

EMG *abbr.* Electromyogram.

-emia or **-hemia** also **-aemia** or **-haemia** *suff.* Blood: *leukemia.* [NLat. < Gk. *-aimia* < *haima*, blood. See HEMO-.]

em•i•grant (ĕm′ĭ-grənt) *n.* One that emigrates. — *adj.* Of or relating to emigrants or the act of emigrating.

em•i•grate (ĕm′ĭ-grāt′) *intr.v.* **-grat•ed, -grat•ing, -grates.** To leave one country or region to settle in another. See Usage Note at **migrate.** [Lat. *ēmigrāre, ēmigrāt-* : *ē-*, *ex-*, ex- + *migrāre*, to move; see **mei-**[1]*.] — **em′i•gra′tion** (ĕm′ĭ-grā′shən) *n.*

é•mi•gré (ĕm′ĭ-grā′) *n.* One who has left a native country, esp. for political reasons. [Fr. < p.part. of *émigrer*, to emigrate < Lat. *ēmigrāre.* See EMIGRATE.]

E•mi•lia-Ro•ma•gna (ĕ-mēl′yə-rō-mä′nyä). A region of N Italy bordering on the Adriatic Sea; part of the kingdom of Italy after 1861.

em•i•nence (ĕm′ə-nəns) *n.* **1.** A position of great distinction or superiority: *rose to eminence as a surgeon.* **2.** A rise of ground; a hill. **3.a.** A person of high station or great achievements. **b.** Also **Eminence.** *Rom. Cath. Ch.* Used with *His* or *Your* as a title and form of address for a cardinal.

ém•i•nence grise (ā-mē-näNs grēz′) *n., pl.* **ém•i•nence grises** (ā-mē-näNs grēz′). A powerful adviser or decision-maker who operates secretly or unofficially. [Fr., the power behind the throne : *éminence*, power + *gris*, gray, shadowy.]

em•i•nen•cy (ĕm′ə-nən-sē) *n., pl.* **-cies.** Eminence.

em•i•nent (ĕm′ə-nənt) *adj.* **1.** Towering or standing out above others; prominent. **2.** Of high rank, station, or quality; noteworthy. **3.** Outstanding, as in character or performance; distinguished. See Syns at **noted.** [ME < Lat. *ēminēns, ēminent-*, pr.part. of *ēminēre*, to stand out : *ē-*, *ex-*, ex- + *-minēre*, to jut out; see **men-**[2]*.] — **em′i•nent•ly** *adv.*

eminent domain *n. Law.* The right of a government to appropriate private property for public use, usu. with compensation to the owner.

e•mir (ĭ-mîr′, ā-mîr′) also **a•mir** (ə-mîr′, ā-mîr′) *n.* A prince, chieftain, or governor, esp. in the Middle East. [Fr. *émir* < Ar. *'amīr*, commander < *'amara*, to command.]

e•mir•ate (ĭ-mîr′ĭt, -āt′) *n.* **1.** The office of an emir. **2.** The nation or territory ruled by an emir.

em•is•sar•y (ĕm′ĭ-sĕr′ē) *n., pl.* **-ies.** An agent sent on a mission to represent or advance the interests of another.

e•mis•sion (ĭ-mĭsh′ən) *n.* **1.** The act or an instance of emitting. **2.** Something emitted. **3.** A substance discharged into the air, esp. a pollutant. [Lat. *ēmissiō, ēmissiōn-*, a sending out < *ēmissus*, p.part. of *ēmittere*, to send out. See EMIT.]

emission spectrum *n.* The characteristic spectrum of radiation directly emitted by a substance subjected to a specific excitation.

e•mis•sive (ĭ-mĭs′ĭv) *adj.* Having the power or tendency to emit matter or energy; emitting.

em•is•siv•i•ty (ĕm′ĭ-sĭv′ĭ-tē) *n.* The ratio of the radiation emitted by a surface to the radiation emitted by a blackbody at the same temperature.

e•mit (ĭ-mĭt′) *tr.v.* **e•mit•ted, e•mit•ting, e•mits. 1.** To give or send out matter or energy. **2.a.** To give out as sound; utter. **b.** To voice; express. **3.** To issue with authority, esp. to put (currency) into circulation. [Lat. *ēmittere*, to send out : *ē-*, *ex-*, ex- + *mittere*, to send.] — **e•mit′ter** *n.*

em•men•a•gogue (ĭ-mĕn′ə-gôg′, -gŏg′) *n.* A drug or an agent that induces or hastens menstrual flow. [Gk. *emmēna*, the menses (< neut. pl. of *emmēnos*, monthly : *en-*, in; see EN-[2] + *mēn*, month; see **mē-**[2]*) + -AGOGUE.]

em•mer (ĕm′ər) *n.* A Eurasian wheat *(Triticum dicoccum)* first cultivated by the Babylonians and now widely grown as a cereal grain and livestock feed. [Ger. < OHGer. *amaro.*]

em•met (ĕm′ĭt) *n. Archaic.* An ant. [ME *emete* < OE *ǣmete.*]

em•me•tro•pi•a (ĕm′ĭ-trō′pē-ə) *n.* The condition of the normal eye when parallel rays are focused exactly on the retina and vision is perfect. [Gk. *emmetros*, well-proportioned, fitting (*en*, in; see EN-[2] + *metron*, measure; see METER[2]) + -OPIA.] — **em′me•trop′ic** (-trŏp′ĭk, -trō′pĭk) *adj.*

Em•my (ĕm′ē) *n., pl.* **-mys.** A statuette awarded annually by the Academy of Television Arts and Sciences for outstanding achievement in television. [Poss. alteration of *immy*, alteration of *image orthicon.*]

e•mol•lient (ĭ-mŏl′yənt) *adj.* **1.** Softening and soothing, esp. to the skin. **2.** Making less harsh or abrasive; mollifying. — *n.* **1.** An agent that softens or soothes the skin. **2.** An agent that assuages or mollifies. [Lat. *ēmolliēns, ēmollient-*, pr.part. of *ēmollīre*, to soften : *ē-*, *ex-*, intensive pref.; see EX- + *mollīre*, to soften (< *mollis*, soft; see **mel-**[1]*).]

e•mol•u•ment (ĭ-mŏl′yə-mənt) *n.* Payment for an office or employment; compensation. [ME < Lat. *ēmolumentum*, gain, originally a miller's fee for grinding grain < *ēmolere*, to grind out : *ē-*, *ex-*, ex- + *molere*, to grind; see **melə-***.]

e•mote (ĭ-mōt′) *intr.v.* **e•mot•ed, e•mot•ing, e•motes.** To express emotion, esp. in an excessive or theatrical manner. [Back-formation < EMOTION.] — **e•mot′er** *n.*

e•mo•tion (ĭ-mō′shən) *n.* **1.** An intense mental state that arises subjectively rather than through conscious effort; a strong feeling. **2.** A state of mental agitation or disturbance: *a quavering voice that betrayed emotion.* See Syns at **feeling. 3.** The part of the consciousness that involves feeling; sensibility. [Fr. *émotion* < OFr. *esmovoir*, to excite < VLat. **exmovēre* : Lat. *ex-*, ex- + Lat. *movēre*, to move; see **meuə-***.]

e•mo•tion•al (ĭ-mō′shə-nəl) *adj.* **1.** Of or relating to emotion. **2.** Readily affected with or stirred by emotion. **3.** Arousing or intended to arouse the emotions: *an emotional appeal.* **4.** Marked by or exhibiting emotion. — **e•mo′tion•al′i•ty** (-shə-năl′ĭ-tē) *n.* — **e•mo′tion•al•ly** *adv.*

e•mo•tion•al•ism (ĭ-mō′shə-nə-lĭz′əm) *n.* **1.** An inclination to rely on or place too much value on emotion. **2.** Undue display of emotion.

e•mo•tion•al•ist (ĭ-mō′shə-nə-lĭst) *n.* **1.** One whose conduct, thought, or rhetoric is governed by emotion rather than reason. **2.** A very emotional person. — **e•mo′tion•al•is′tic** *adj.*

e•mo•tion•al•ize (ĭ-mō′shə-nə-līz′) *tr.v.* **-ized, -iz•ing, -iz•es.** To impart an emotional quality to.

e•mo•tive (ĭ-mō′tĭv) *adj.* **1.** Of or relating to emotion. **2.** Characterized by, expressing, or exciting emotion: *an emotive trial lawyer.* — **e•mo′tive•ly** *adv.* — **e•mo′tive•ness, e′mo•tiv′i•ty** (ē′mō-tĭv′ĭ-tē) *n.*

emp. *abbr.* Emperor; empire; empress.

em•pale (ĕm-pāl′) *v.* Var. of **impale.**

em•pa•na•da (ĕm′pə-nä′də, -pä-nä′thä) *n.* A Spanish or Latin-American turnover with a flaky crust and a spicy or sweet filling. [Sp. < p.part. of *empanar*, to coat with breadcrumbs : *en-*, in (< Lat. *in-*; see EN-[1]) + *pan*, bread; see PANADA.]

em•pan•el (ĕm-păn′əl) *v. Law.* Var. of **impanel.**

em•pa•thet•ic (ĕm′pə-thĕt′ĭk) *adj.* Empathic. — **em′pa•thet′i•cal•ly** *adv.*

em•path•ic (ĕm-păth′ĭk) *adj.* Of, relating to, or characterized by empathy.

em•pa•thize (ĕm′pə-thīz′) *intr.v.* **-thized, -thiz•ing, -thiz•es.** To feel or experience empathy. — **em′pa•thiz′er** *n.*

em•pa•thy (ĕm′pə-thē) *n.* **1.** Identification with and understanding of another's situation, feelings, and motives. **2.** The attribution of one's feelings to an object. [EN-[2] + -PATHY.]

Em•ped•o•cles (ĕm-pĕd′ə-klēz′). 5th cent. B.C. Greek philosopher who believed that matter is composed of elemental particles of fire, water, earth, and air and that change is caused by motion.

em•pen•nage (ĕm′pə-nĭj) *n.* The tail of an airplane. [Fr. < *empenner*, to feather an arrow : *en-*, in; see EN-[1] + *penne*, feather (< Lat. *penna*; see **pet-***).]

em•per•or (ĕm′pər-ər) *n.* **1.** The male ruler of an empire. **2.a.** The emperor butterfly. **b.** The emperor moth. [ME *emperour* < OFr. *empereor* < Lat. *imperātor* < *imperāre*, to command : *in-*, in; see EN-[1] + *parāre*, to prepare; see **perə-**[1]*.] — **em′per•or•ship′** *n.*

emperor butterfly *n.* Any of several butterflies of the family Nymphalidae, having orange wings with dark markings.

emperor moth *n.* Any of several moths of the family Saturnidae, esp. *Saturnia pavonia* of Eurasia, having distinctively patterned wings.
emperor penguin *n.* A large penguin *(Aptenodytes forsteri)* of Antarctic regions having yellow-orange patches on the neck.
em•per•y (ĕm′pə-rē) *n., pl.* **-ies** Absolute dominion or jurisdiction; sovereignty. [ME *emperie* < OFr. < Lat. *imperium.* See EMPIRE.]
em•pha•sis (ĕm′fə-sĭs) *n., pl.* **-ses** (-sēz′). **1.** Special forcefulness of expression that gives importance to something singled out; stress. **2.** Special attention or effort directed toward something. **3.** Prominence given to a syllable, word, or words, as by raising the voice or printing in italic type. [Lat. < Gk. < *emphainein*, to exhibit, display : *en-*, in; see EN-[2] + *phainein*, to show; see **bhā-**[1]*.]
Syns: *emphasis, accent, stress.* The central meaning shared by these nouns is "special weight placed on something considered important": *emphasis on science; the accent on jazz; stress on law and order.*
em•pha•size (ĕm′fə-sīz′) *tr.v.* **-sized, -siz•ing, -siz•es.** To give emphasis to; stress. [< EMPHASIS.]
em•phat•ic (ĕm-făt′ĭk) *adj.* **1.** Expressed or performed with emphasis: *an emphatic "no."* **2.** Forceful and definite in expression or action. **3.** Standing out in a striking way. [Med. Lat. *emphaticus* < Gk. *emphatikos* < *emphainein*, to exhibit, display. See EMPHASIS.] **—em•phat′i•cal•ly** *adv.*
em•phy•se•ma (ĕm′fĭ-sē′mə, -zē′-) *n.* **1.** A pathological condition of the lungs marked by an abnormal increase in the size of the air spaces, resulting in labored breathing and an increased susceptibility to infection. **2.** An abnormal distention of body tissues caused by retention of air. [Gk. *emphusēma*, inflation < *emphusan*, to blow in : *en-*, in; see EN-[2] + *phūsān*, to blow (< *phusa*, bellows, bladder).] **—em′phy•sem′a•tous** (-sĕm′ə-təs, -sē′mə-, -zĕm′ə-, -zē′mə-) *adj.* **—em′phy•se′mic** *adj. & n.*
em•pire (ĕm′pīr′) *n.* **1.a.** A political unit comprising a number of territories or nations and ruled by a single supreme authority. **b.** The territory included in such a unit. **2.** An extensive enterprise under a unified authority: *a publishing empire.* **3.** Imperial or imperialistic sovereignty or domination. [ME < OFr. < Lat. *imperium* < *imperāre*, to command. See EMPEROR.]
Em•pire (ŏm-pîr′, ĕm′pīr′) *adj.* Of, relating to, or characteristic of a neoclassic style, as in clothing or furniture, prevalent in France during the first part of the 19th century. [After the First *Empire* of France (1804–15).]
em•pir•ic (ĕm-pîr′ĭk) *n.* **1.** One who is guided by practical experience rather than precepts or theory. **2.** An unqualified or dishonest practitioner; a charlatan. [Lat. *empiricus* < Gk. *empeirikos*, experienced < *empeiros*, skilled : *en-*, in; see EN-[2] + *peiran*, to try (< *peira*, try, attempt; see **per-**[3]*).]
em•pir•i•cal (ĕm-pîr′ĭ-kəl) *adj.* **1.a.** Relying on or derived from observation or experiment. **b.** Verifiable or provable by means of observation or experiment: *empirical laws.* **2.** Guided by practical experience and not theory, esp. in medicine. **—em•pir′i•cal•ly** *adv.*
empirical formula *n.* A chemical formula that indicates the relative proportions of the elements in a molecule rather than the actual number of atoms of the elements.
em•pir•i•cism (ĕm-pîr′ĭ-sĭz′əm) *n.* **1.** The view that experience, esp. of the senses, is the only source of knowledge. **2.a.** Employment of empirical methods, as in science. **b.** An empirical conclusion. **3.** The practice of medicine that disregards theory and relies solely on practical experience. **—em•pir′i•cist** *n.*
em•place (ĕm-plās′) *tr.v.* **-placed, -plac•ing, -plac•es.** To put into place or position: *emplace a fortification on the hilltop.*
em•place•ment (ĕm-plās′mənt) *n.* **1.** A prepared position, such as a mounting or silo, for a military weapon. **2.** The act of putting into a certain position; placement. **3.** Position; location. [Fr. < obsolete *emplacer*, to place in position : *en-*, in; see EN-[1] + OFr. *place*, open space; see PLACE.]
em•plane (ĕm-plān′) *v.* Var. of **enplane.**
em•ploy (ĕm-ploi′) *tr.v.* **-ployed, -ploy•ing, -ploys. 1.a.** To engage the services of; put to work. **b.** To provide with gainful work. **2.** To put to use or service. **3.** To devote (time, for example) to an activity or purpose. **—*n.* 1.** The state of being employed. **2.** *Archaic.* Occupation. [ME *emploien* < OFr. *emploier* < Lat. *implicāre*, to involve : *in-*, in; see EN-[1] + *plicāre*, to fold; see **plek-***.] **—em•ploy′a•bil′i•ty** *n.* **—em•ploy′a•ble** *adj.* **—em•ploy′er** *n.*
em•ploy•ee also **em•ploy•e** (ĕm-ploi′ē, ĭm-, ĕm′ploi-ē′) *n.* A person who works for another in return for compensation.
em•ploy•ment (ĕm-ploi′mənt) *n.* **1.a.** The act of employing. **b.** The state of being employed. **2.** The work in which one is engaged; occupation. **3.** An activity to which one devotes time. **4.** The percentage or number of people employed.
employment agency *n.* An agency that finds jobs for people seeking them and finds people to fill particular jobs.
em•poi•son (ĕm-poi′zən) *tr.v.* **-soned, -son•ing, -sons. 1.** To fill with venom; embitter. **2.** *Archaic.* To poison.
Em•po•ri•a (ĕm-pôr′ē-ə, -pōr′-). A city of E-central KS SW of Topeka; founded 1856. Pop. 25,512.
em•po•ri•um (ĕm-pôr′ē-əm, -pōr′-) *n., pl.* **-po•ri•ums** or **-po•ri•a** (-pôr′ē-ə, -pōr′-). **1.** A place where various goods are bought and sold; a marketplace. **2.** A large retail store or place of business. [Lat. < Gk. *emporion* < *emporos*, traveler, merchant : *en-*, in; see EN-[2] + *poros*, journey; see **per-**[2]*.]
em•pow•er (ĕm-pou′ər) *tr.v.* **-ered, -er•ing, -ers.** To invest with power, esp. legal power or official authority. **—em•pow′er•ment** *n.*
em•press (ĕm′prĭs) *n.* **1.** The woman ruler of an empire. **2.** The wife or widow of an emperor. [ME *emperesse* < OFr., fem. of *empereor*, emperor. See EMPEROR.]
em•presse•ment (äɴ′prĕs-mäɴ′) *n.* Effusive cordiality. [Fr. < *s'empresser*, to be eager : *en-*, in; see EN-[1] + *presser*, to press (< OFr.; see PRESS[1]).]
em•prise (ĕm-prīz′) *n.* **1.** A chivalrous or adventurous undertaking. **2.** Chivalrous daring or prowess. [ME < OFr. < fem. p.part. of *emprendre*, to undertake < VLat. **imprendere* : Lat. *in-*, in; see EN-[1] + Lat. *prendere*, to take, grasp; see **ghend-***.]
emp•ty (ĕmp′tē) *adj.* **-ti•er, -ti•est. 1.a.** Holding or containing nothing. **b.** *Math.* Having no elements or members; null. **2.** Having no occupants or inhabitants; vacant. **3.** Lacking force or power. **4.** Lacking purpose or substance; meaningless. **5.** Not put to use; idle. **6.** Needing nourishment; hungry. **7.** Devoid; destitute. **—*v.* -tied, -ty•ing, -ties. —*tr.* 1.** To remove the contents of. **2.** To transfer or pour off completely. **3.** To unburden; relieve. **—*intr.* 1.** To become empty. **2.** To discharge its contents. **—*n., pl.* -ties.** *Informal.* An empty container. [ME < OE *ǣmtig*, vacant, unoccupied < *ǣmetta*, leisure. See **med-***.] **—emp′ti•ly** *adv.* **—emp′ti•ness** *n.*
emp•ty-hand•ed (ĕmp′tē-hăn′dĭd) *adj.* **1.** Bearing nothing. **2.** Having received or gained nothing.
emp•ty-head•ed (ĕmp′tē-hĕd′ĭd) *adj.* Lacking sense or discretion; scatterbrained.
Emp•ty Quarter (ĕmp′tē). See **Rub al Khali.**
em•pur•ple (ĕm-pûr′pəl) *tr. & intr.v.* **-pled, -pling, -ples.** To make or become purple.
em•py•e•ma (ĕm′pī-ē′mə) *n., pl.* **-ma•ta** (-mə-tə). The presence of pus in a body cavity, esp. the pleural cavity. [Med.Lat. *empyēma* < Gk. *empuēma* < *empuein*, to suppurate. See **pū̆-***.] **—em′py•e′mic** *adj.*
em•py•re•al (ĕm′pī-rē′əl, ĕm-pîr′ē-əl) *adj.* **1.** Empyrean. **2.** Of the sky; celestial. **3.** Elevated; sublime. [ME *emperiall* < Med.Lat. *empȳreus* < Gk. *empurios*, fiery : *en-*, in; see EN-[2] + *pur*, fire; see **pūr-***.]
em•py•re•an (ĕm′pī-rē′ən, ĕm-pîr′ē-ən) *n.* **1.a.** The highest reaches of heaven, believed by the ancients to be a realm of pure fire or light. **b.** The abode of God and the angels; paradise. **2.** The sky. [< Med.Lat. *empȳreum* < *empȳreus*, empyreal. See EMPYREAL.] **—em′py•re′an** *adj.*
Ems (ĕmz, ĕms). A river of NW Germany flowing c. 335 km (208 mi) to the North Sea at the Netherlands border.
EMS *abbr.* Electrical muscle stimulation.
EMT *abbr.* Emergency medical technician.
e•mu[1] (ē′myo͞o) *n.* A large flightless Australian bird *(Dromiceius novaehollandiae)* related to and resembling the ostrich and the cassowary. [Port. *ema*, rhea.]
emu[2] *abbr.* Electromagnetic unit.
em•u•late (ĕm′yə-lāt′) *tr.v.* **-lat•ed, -lat•ing, -lates. 1.** To strive to equal or excel, esp. through imitation. **2.** To compete with successfully; approach or attain equality with. **3.** *Comp. Sci.* To imitate the function of (another system), as by modifications to hardware or software. **—*adj.*** (-lĭt). *Obsolete.* Ambitious; emulous. [Lat. *aemulārī*, *aemulāt-* < *aemulus*, emulous.] **—em′u•la′tive** *adj.* **—em′u•la′tive•ly** *adv.* **—em′u•la′tor** *n.*
em•u•la•tion (ĕm′yə-lā′shən) *n.* **1.** Effort or ambition to equal or surpass another. **2.** Imitation of another. **3.** *Comp. Sci.* The process or technique of emulating. **4.** *Obsolete.* Jealous rivalry.
em•u•lous (ĕm′yə-ləs) *adj.* **1.** Eager or ambitious to equal or surpass another. **2.** Characterized or prompted by a spirit of rivalry. **3.** *Obsolete.* Covetous of power or honor; envious. [< Lat. *aemulus.*] **—em′u•lous•ly** *adv.* **—em′u•lous•ness** *n.*
e•mul•si•ble (ĭ-mŭl′sə-bəl) *adj.* That can be emulsified.
e•mul•si•fy (ĭ-mŭl′sə-fī′) *tr.v.* **-fied, -fy•ing, -fies.** To make into an emulsion. [EMULSI(ON) + -FY.] **—e•mul′si•fi•ca′tion** (-fĭ-kā′shən) *n.* **—e•mul′si•fi′er** *n.*
e•mul•sion (ĭ-mŭl′shən) *n.* **1.** A suspension of small globules of one liquid in a second liquid with which the first will not mix: *an emulsion of oil in vinegar.* **2.** A photosensitive coating, usu. of silver halide grains in a thin gelatin layer, on photographic film, paper, or glass. [NLat. *ēmulsiō*, *ēmulsiōn-* < Lat. *ēmulsus*, p.part. of *ēmulgēre*, to milk out : *ē-*, *ex-*, ex- + *mulgēre*, to milk; see **melg-***.] **—e•mul′sive** *adj.*
e•munc•to•ry (ĭ-mŭngk′tə-rē) *adj.* Serving to carry waste out of the body; excretory. **—*n., pl.* -ries.** An emunctory organ. [ME *emunctorie* < Med.Lat. *ēmunctōrius* < Lat. *ēmunctus*, p.part. of *ēmungere*, to blow one's nose : *ē-*, *ex-*, intensive pref.; see EX- + *mungere*, to blow one's nose.]
en (ĕn) *n.* **1.** The letter *n.* **2.** *Print.* A space equal to half the width of an em.

Empire
Top: Detail of *Comtesse Daru*, 1810, by Jacques Louis David
Bottom: c. 1810 American couch by Samuel McIntire (1757–1811)

ă pat | oi boy
ā pay | ou out
âr care | o͝o took
ä father | o͞o boot
ĕ pet | ŭ cut
ē be | ûr urge
ĭ pit | th thin
ī pie | *th* this
îr pier | hw which
ŏ pot | zh vision
ō toe | ə about, item
ô paw

Stress marks:
′ (primary);
′ (secondary), as in **dictionary** (dĭk′shə-nĕr′ē)

en–[1] or **em–** or **in–** *pref.* **1.a.** To put into or onto: *encapsulate.* **b.** To go into or onto: *enplane.* **2.** To cover or provide with: *enrobe.* **3.** To cause to be: *endear.* **4.** Thoroughly. Used often as an intensive: *entangle.* [ME < OFr. < Lat. *in-*, in. See **en***.]

en–[2] or **em–** *pref.* In; into; within: *enzootic.* [ME < Lat. < Gk. See **en***.]

–en[1] *suff.* **1.a.** To cause to be: *cheapen.* **b.** To become: *redden.* **2.a.** To cause to have: *hearten.* **b.** To come to have: *lengthen.* [ME *-enen, -nen* < OE *-nian.*]

–en[2] *suff.* Made of; resembling: *earthen.* [ME < OE.]

en•a•ble (ĕ-nā′bəl) *tr.v.* **-bled, -bling, -bles. 1.a.** To supply with the means, knowledge, or opportunity; make able. **b.** To make feasible or possible. **2.** To give legal power, capacity, or sanction to. **3.** To make operational; activate. **— en•a′bler** *n.*

en•act (ĕn-ăkt′) *tr.v.* **-act•ed, -act•ing, -acts. 1.** To make into law: *Congress enacted a tax reform bill.* **2.** To act (something) out, as on a stage. **— en•act′a•ble** *adj.* **— en•ac′tor** *n.*

en•act•ment (ĕn-ăkt′mənt) *n.* **1.a.** The act of enacting. **b.** The state of being enacted. **2.** Something that has been enacted.

e•nam•el (ĭ-năm′əl) *n.* **1.** A vitreous, usu. opaque protective or decorative coating baked on metal, glass, or ceramic ware. **2.** An object having such a coating, as in a piece of cloisonné. **3.** A coating that dries to a hard glossy finish. **4.** A paint that dries to a hard glossy finish. **5.** *Anat.* The hard calcareous substance covering a tooth. *— tr.v.* **-eled, -el•ing, -els** or **-elled, -el•ling, -els. 1.** To coat, inlay, or decorate with enamel. **2.** To give a glossy or brilliant surface to. **3.** To adorn with a brightly colored surface. [< ME *enamelen*, to put on enamel < AN *enamailler* : *en-*, on (< OFr.; see EN–[1]) + *amail*, enamel (< OFr. *esmail*, of Gmc. orig.; see **mel-**[1]*.)] **— e•nam′el•er, e•nam′el•ist** *n.*

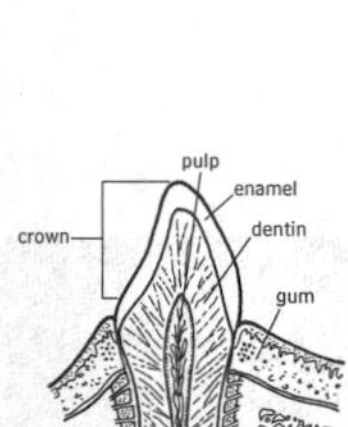

enamel
Cross section of an incisor

e•nam•el•ware (ĭ-năm′əl-wâr′) *n.* Ware coated with enamel.

en•am•or (ĭ-năm′ər) *tr.v.* **-ored, -or•ing, -ors.** To inspire with love; captivate. [ME *enamouren* < OFr. *enamourer* : *en-*, causative pref.; see EN–[1] + *amour*, love; see AMOUR.]

en•am•our (ĭ-năm′ər) *v. Chiefly British.* Var. of **enamor.**

en•an•ti•o•mer (ĭ-năn′tē-ə-mər) *n.* See **enantiomorph.** [Gk. *enantios*, opposite; see **ant-*** + –MER(E).] **— en•an′ti•o•mer′ic** (-mĕr′ĭk) *adj.*

en•an•ti•o•morph (ĕ-năn′tē-ə-môrf′) *n.* Either of a pair of crystals, molecules, or compounds that are mirror images of each other but are not identical. [Gk. *enantios*, opposite; see **ant-*** + –MORPH.] **— en•an′ti•o•mor′phic, en•an′ti•o•mor′phous** *adj.* **— en•an′ti•o•morph′ism** *n.*

en•ar•thro•sis (ĕn′är-thrō′sĭs) *n., pl.* **-ses** (-sēz). *Anat.* See **ball-and-socket joint** 1. [Gk. *enarthrōsis* < *enarthros*, jointed : *en-*, in; see EN–[2] + *arthron*, joint; see **ar-***.]

e•nate (ĭ-nāt′, ē′nāt′) *adj.* **1.** Growing outward. **2.** Also **e•nat•ic** (ĭ-năt′ĭk). Related on the mother's side. *— n.* A relative on one's mother's side. [Lat. *ēnātus*, p.part. of *ēnāscī*, to issue forth : *ē-, ex-*, ex- + *nāscī*, to be born; see **genə-***.]

e•na•tion (ē-nā′shən) *n. Bot.* An outgrowth on the surface of an organ.

en bloc (äN blôk′, ĕn blŏk′) *adv.* As a unit; all together. [Fr. : *en*, in + *bloc*, lump, bloc.]

en bro•chette (äN′ brô-shĕt′) *adv.* On a skewer: *lamb en brochette.* [Fr. : *en*, on + *brochette*, stick, skewer.]

enc. *abbr.* **1.** Enclosed. **2.** Enclosure.

en•cage (ĕn-kāj′) *tr.v.* **-caged, -cag•ing, -cag•es.** To confine in or as if in a cage.

en•camp (ĕn-kămp′) *v.* **-camped, -camp•ing, -camps.** *— intr.* To set up camp or live in a camp. *— tr.* To provide quarters for in a camp.

en•camp•ment (ĕn-kămp′mənt) *n.* **1.a.** The act of encamping. **b.** The state of being encamped. **2.** A camp; a campsite.

en•cap•su•late (ĕn-kăp′sə-lāt′) also **in•cap•su•late** (ĭn-) *— v.* **-lat•ed, -lat•ing, -lates.** *— tr.* **1.** To encase in or as if in a capsule. **2.** To express in a brief summary; epitomize: *headlines that encapsulate the news.* *— intr.* To become encapsulated. **— en•cap′su•la′tion** *n.* **— en•cap′su•la′tor** *n.*

en•cap•su•lat•ed (ĕn-kăp′sə-lā′tĭd) *adj.* Enclosed by a protective coating or membrane: *an encapsulated bacterium.*

en•cap•sule (ĕn-kăp′səl, -so͞ol) *tr.v.* **-suled, -sul•ing, -sules.** To encapsulate.

en•case (ĕn-kās′) also **in•case** (ĭn-) *tr.v.* **-cased, -cas•ing, -cas•es.** To enclose in or as if in a case. **— en•case′ment** *n.*

en•caus•tic (ĕn-kô′stĭk) *n.* **1.** A paint consisting of pigment mixed with beeswax and fixed with heat after application. **2.** The art of painting with this substance. **3.** A painting produced with this substance. [Lat. *encausticus* < Gk. *enkaustikos* < *enkaiein*, to paint in encaustic : *en-*, in; see EN–[2] + *kaiein*, to burn.]

encaustic
Late third- to early fourth-century Egyptian encaustic on wood panel portrait

–ence *suff.* **1.** State or condition: *dependence.* **2.** Action: *emergence.* [ME < Lat. *-entia* (< *-ēns*, -ent) and < OFr. *-ance*, -ance.]

en•ceinte[1] (ĕn-sānt′, än-sănt′) *adj.* Carrying an unborn child; pregnant. [Fr. < OFr., poss. < Med.Lat. *incincta*, without a girdle (*in-*, not; see IN–[1] + Lat. *cincta*, fem. p.part. of *cingere*, to gird; see **kenk-***), by folk ety. < Lat. *inciēns*, pregnant. See **keuə-***.]

en•ceinte[2] (ĕn-sānt′, än-sănt′, äN-săNt′) *n.* **1.** An encircling fortification around a fort, castle, or town. **2.** A structure or an area protected by an encircling fortification. [Fr. < LLat. *incincta* < fem. p.part. of *incingere*, to surround closely : Lat. *in-*, in; see IN–[2] + Lat. *cingere*, to gird; see **kenk-***.]

En•cel•a•dus (ĕn-sĕl′ə-dəs) *n.* **1.** *Gk. Myth.* A giant who was defeated in battle and buried under Mount Etna by Athena. **2.** A satellite of Saturn. [Lat. < Gk. *Enkelados.*]

en•ce•phal•ic (ĕn′sə-făl′ĭk) *adj.* **1.** Of or relating to the brain. **2.** Located within the cranial cavity.

en•ceph•a•li•tis (ĕn-sĕf′ə-lī′tĭs) *n.* Inflammation of the brain. **— en•ceph′a•lit′ic** (-lĭt′ĭk) *adj.*

encephalitis le•thar•gi•ca (lə-thär′jĭ-kə) *n.* A viral epidemic encephalitis marked by apathy, paralysis of the extrinsic eye muscle, and extreme muscular weakness. [NLat. *encephalitis lēthargica* : ENCEPHALITIS + Lat. *lēthargicus*, sleepy.]

encephalo– or **encephal–** *pref.* Brain: *encephalitis.* [NLat. < Gk. *(muelos) enkephalos*, (marrow) in the head : *en-*, in; see EN–[2] + *kephalē*, head; see **ghebh-el-***.]

en•ceph•a•lo•gram (ĕn-sĕf′ə-lə-grăm′, -ə-lō-) *n.* **1.** An x-ray picture of the brain taken by encephalography. **2.** See **electroencephalogram.**

en•ceph•a•lo•graph (ĕn-sĕf′ə-lə-grăf′, -ə-lō-) *n.* **1.** See **encephalogram** 1. **2.** See **electroencephalograph.**

en•ceph•a•log•ra•phy (ĕn-sĕf′ə-lŏg′rə-fē) *n., pl.* **-phies.** Radiographic examination of the brain in which some of the cerebrospinal fluid is replaced with air or another gas that acts as a contrasting medium. **— en•ceph′a•lo•graph′ic** (-ə-lə-grăf′ĭk, -ə-lō-) *adj.* **— en•ceph′a•lo•graph′i•cal•ly** *adv.*

en•ceph•a•lo•my•e•li•tis (ĕn-sĕf′ə-lō-mī′ə-lī′tĭs) *n.* Inflammation of the brain and spinal cord.

en•ceph•a•lon (ĕn-sĕf′ə-lŏn′) *n., pl.* **-la** (-lə). The brain of a vertebrate. [Gk. *enkephalon*, neut. of *enkephalos*, in the head. See ENCEPHALO–.] **— en•ceph′a•lous** *adj.*

en•ceph•a•lop•a•thy (ĕn-sĕf′ə-lŏp′ə-thē) *n., pl.* **-thies.** Any of various diseases of the brain. **— en•ceph′a•lo•path′ic** (-lə-păth′ĭk) *adj.*

en•chain (ĕn-chān′) *tr.v.* **-chained, -chain•ing, -chains.** To bind with or as if with chains. **— en•chain′ment** *n.*

en•chant (ĕn-chănt′) *tr.v.* **-chant•ed, -chant•ing, -chants. 1.** To cast a spell over; bewitch. **2.** To attract and delight; entrance. See Syns at **charm.** [ME *enchanten* < OFr. *enchanter* < Lat. *incantāre*, to cast a spell : *in-*, against; see EN–[1] + *cantāre*, to sing, freq. of *canere*; see **kan-***.]

en•chant•er (ĕn-chăn′tər) *n.* **1.** One that delights or fascinates. **2.** A sorcerer or magician.

en•chant•ing (ĕn-chăn′tĭng) *adj.* Having the power to enchant; charming: *enchanting music.* **— en•chant′ing•ly** *adv.*

en•chant•ment (ĕn-chănt′mənt) *n.* **1.a.** The act of enchanting. **b.** The state of being enchanted. **2.** Something that enchants.

en•chant•ress (ĕn-chăn′trĭs) *n.* **1.** A woman of great charm or fascination. **2.** A woman who practices magic; a sorceress.

en•chase (ĕn-chās′) *tr.v.* **-chased, -chas•ing, -chas•es. 1.** To set (a gem, for example). **2.** To set with or as if with gems: *enchase a brooch.* **3.** To decorate or ornament by inlaying or engraving. [ME, to engrave < OFr. *enchasser*, to set gems : *en-*, in; see EN–[1] + *chasse*, case (< Lat. *capsa*, box).]

en•chi•la•da (ĕn′chə-lä′də) *n.* A tortilla rolled and stuffed, as with meat, and served with a chili sauce. [Am.Sp. : *en-*, in (< Lat. *in-*; see EN–[1]) + *chile*, chili pepper; see CHILI.]

en•chi•rid•i•on (ĕn′kī-rĭd′ē-ən) *n., pl.* **-i•ons** or **-i•a** (-ē-ə). A handbook; a manual. [LLat. *enchīridion* < Gk. *enkheiridion* : *en-*, in; see EN–[2] + *kheir*, hand; see **ghesor-*** + *-idion*, dim. suff.]

–enchyma *suff.* Cellular tissue: *chlorenchyma.* [< PARENCHYMA.]

en•ci•na (ĕn-sē′nə) *n.* See **live oak.** [Sp., holm oak < LLat. *īlicīna* < Lat. *īlex, īlic-*.]

en•ci•pher (ĕn-sī′fər) *tr.v.* **-phered, -pher•ing, -phers.** To put (a message, for example) into cipher. **— en•ci′pher•er** *n.* **— en•ci′pher•ment** *n.*

en•cir•cle (ĕn-sûr′kəl) *tr.v.* **-cled, -cling, -cles. 1.** To form a circle around; surround. **2.** To move or go around completely; make a circuit of. **— en•cir′cle•ment** *n.*

encl. *abbr.* **1.** Enclosed. **2.** Enclosure.

en•clasp (ĕn-klăsp′) also **in•clasp** (ĭn-) *tr.v.* **-clasped, -clasp•ing, -clasps.** To hold in a clasp; embrace.

en•clave (ĕn′klāv′, ŏn′-) *n.* **1.** A country or part of a country lying wholly within the boundaries of another. **2.** A distinctly bounded area enclosed within a larger unit: *ethnic enclaves in a city.* [Fr. < OFr. *enclaver*, to enclose < VLat. **inclāvāre* : Lat. *in-*, in; see EN–[1] + Lat. *clāvis*, key.]

en•clit•ic (ĕn-klĭt′ĭk) *Ling.* *— n.* A word or particle that has no independent accent and forms a unit with the preceding word, as *'em* in *Give 'em the works.* *— adj.* Forming an enclitic. [LLat. *encliticus* < Gk. *enklitikos* < *enklinein*, to lean on : *en-*, on, in; see EN–[2] + *klinein*, to lean; see **klei-***.]

en•close (ĕn-klōz′) also **in•close** (ĭn-) *tr.v.* **-closed, -clos•ing, -clos•es. 1.** To surround on all sides; close in. **2.** To fence in. **3.** To contain, esp. so as to envelop or shelter. **4.** To insert into the same envelope or package. [ME *enclosen* < OFr. *enclos*, p.part. of *enclore* < Lat. *inclūdere.* See INCLUDE.]

en•clo•sure (ĕn-klō′zhər) *n.* **1.a.** The act of enclosing. **b.** The state of being enclosed. **2.** Something enclosed: *a letter with a supplemental enclosure.* **3.** Something that encloses.

en•code (ĕn-kōd′) *tr.v.* **-cod•ed, -cod•ing, -codes. 1.** To put into code. **2.** *Comp. Sci.* To convert (a program, for example) into machine language. **— en•cod′er** *n.*

en•co•mi•ast (ĕn-kō′mē-ăst′, -əst) *n.* One who delivers or writes an encomium; a eulogist. [Gk. *enkōmiastēs* < *enkōmiazein*, to praise < *enkōmion*, encomium. See ENCOMIUM.] **— en•co′mi•as′tic** (-ăs′tĭk), **en•co′mi•as′ti•cal** (-tĭ-kəl) *adj.*

en•co•mi•um (ĕn-kō′mē-əm) *n., pl.* **-mi•ums** or **-mi•a** (-mē-ə). **1.** Warm, glowing praise. **2.** A formal expression of praise; a tribute. [Lat. *encōmium* < Gk. *enkōmion (epos)*, (speech) praising a victor < *enkōmios*, of the victory procession : *en-*, in; see EN–² + *kōmos*, celebration.]

en•com•pass (ĕn-kŭm′pəs) *tr.v.* **-passed, -pass•ing, -pass•es. 1.** To form a circle or ring around; surround. **2.** To enclose; envelop. **3.** To constitute or include. **4.** To accomplish; achieve. **— en•com′pass•ment** *n.*

en•core (ŏn′kôr′, -kōr′) *n.* **1.** A demand by an audience for an additional performance, usu. expressed by applause. **2.** An additional performance in response to the demand of an audience. *— tr.v.* **-cored, -cor•ing, -cores.** To demand an encore of. *— interj.* Used to demand an additional performance. [Fr., still, yet, again, prob. < VLat. **hinc ad hōram*, from that to this hour : Lat. *hinc*, from here (< *hic*, this) + Lat. *ad*, to; see AD– + Lat. *hōram*, accusative of *hōra*, hour; see HOUR.]

en•coun•ter (ĕn-koun′tər) *n.* **1.** A meeting, esp. one that is unexpected or brief. **2.** A hostile or adversarial confrontation or meeting. *— v.* **-tered, -ter•ing, -ters.** *— tr.* **1.** To meet, esp. unexpectedly; come upon. **2.** To confront in battle or contention. **3.** To come up against: *encounter obstacles.* *— intr.* To meet, esp. unexpectedly. [ME *encountre* < OFr. < *encontrer*, to meet < LLat. *incontrāre* : Lat. *in-*, in; see EN–¹ + Lat. *contrā*, against; see **kom*.**]

encounter group *n.* A psychotherapy group designed to enhance sensitivity and self-awareness.

en•cour•age (ĕn-kûr′ĭj, -kŭr′-) *tr.v.* **-aged, -ag•ing, -ag•es. 1.** To inspire with hope, courage, or confidence. **2.** To give support to; foster. **3.** To stimulate; spur. [ME *encouragen* < OFr. *encoragier* : *en-*, causative pref.; see EN–¹ + *corage*, courage; see COURAGE.] **— en•cour′ag•er** *n.*

en•cour•age•ment (ĕn-kûr′ĭj-mənt, -kŭr′-) *n.* **1.** The act of encouraging. **2.** The state of being encouraged. **3.** One that encourages.

en•cour•ag•ing (ĕn-kûr′ə-jĭng, -kŭr′-) *adj.* Giving courage, confidence, or hope. **— en•cour′ag•ing•ly** *adv.*

en•croach (ĕn-krōch′) *intr.v.* **-croached, -croach•ing, -croach•es. 1.** To take another's possessions or rights gradually or stealthily. **2.** To advance beyond proper or former limits. [ME *encrochen*, to seize illegally < OFr. *encrochier*, to seize : *en-*, in; see EN–¹ + *croc*, hook (of Gmc. orig.).] **— en•croach′er** *n.* **— en•croach′ment** *n.*

en•crust (ĕn-krŭst′) also **in•crust** (ĭn-) *tr.v.* **-crust•ed, -crust•ing, -crusts.** To cover or surmount with or as if with a crust. [Poss. < Fr. *incruster* < Lat. *incrustāre* : *in-*, on; see EN–¹ + *crusta*, crust; see **kreus-*.**]

en•crust•a•tion (ĕn′krŭs-tā′shən) *n.* Var. of **incrustation.**

en•crypt (ĕn-krĭpt) *tr.v.* **-crypt•ed, -crypt•ing, -crypts. 1.** To put into code or cipher. **2.** *Comp. Sci.* To scramble access codes to (computerized information) so as to prevent unauthorized access. [EN–¹ + (DE)CRYPT.] **— en•cryp′tion** *n.*

en•cum•ber (ĕn-kŭm′bər) *tr.v.* **-bered, -ber•ing, -bers. 1.** To put a heavy load on; burden. **2.** To hinder or impede the action or performance of. **3.** To burden with legal or financial obligations. [ME *encombren* < OFr. *encombrer*, to block up : *en-*, in; see EN–¹ + *combre*, hindrance (< Gaulish **comboros*).]

en•cum•brance (ĕn-kŭm′brəns) *n.* **1.** One that encumbers; a burden or impediment. **2.** *Law.* A lien or claim on property.

en•cum•branc•er (ĕn-kŭm′brən-sər) *n.* *Law.* One that holds an encumbrance.

ency. *abbr.* Encyclopedia.

–ency *suff.* Condition or quality: *complacency.* [ME, var. of *-ence*, -ence.]

encyc. *abbr.* Encyclopedia.

encycl. *abbr.* Encyclopedia.

en•cyc•li•cal (ĕn-sĭk′lĭ-kəl) *adj.* Intended for general or wide circulation. *— n. Rom. Cath. Ch.* A papal letter addressed to the bishops of the Church or the hierarchy of a particular country. [< LLat. *encyclicus*, circular < Gk. *enkuklios* : *en-*, in; see EN–² + *kuklos*, circle; see **kʷel-¹*.**]

en•cy•clo•pe•di•a (ĕn-sī′klə-pē′dē-ə) *n.* A reference work containing articles on a wide range of subjects or on numerous aspects of a field, usu. arranged alphabetically. [Med.Lat. *encyclopaedia*, general education course < alteration of Gk. *enkuklios paideia*, general education : *enkuklios*, circular, general; see ENCYCLICAL + *paideia*, education (< *pais, paid-*, child; see **pau-***).]

en•cy•clo•pe•dic (ĕn-sī′klə-pē′dĭk) *adj.* **1.** Of, relating to, or characteristic of an encyclopedia. **2.** Embracing many subjects; comprehensive. **— en•cy′clo•pe′di•cal•ly** *adv.*

en•cy•clo•pe•dism (ĕn-sī′klə-pē′dĭz′əm) *n.* Encyclopedic learning.

en•cy•clo•pe•dist (ĕn-sī′klə-pē′dĭst) *n.* **1.** A person who writes for or compiles an encyclopedia. **2. Encyclopedist.** One of the writers of the French *Encyclopédie* (1751–1772), including its editors, Diderot and d'Alembert.

en•cyst (ĕn-sĭst′) *v.* **-cyst•ed, -cyst•ing, -cysts.** *— tr.* To enclose in a cyst. *— intr.* To take the form of or become enclosed in a cyst. **— en•cyst′ment, en′cys•ta′tion** *n.*

end (ĕnd) *n.* **1.** Either extremity of something that has length. **2.** The outside or extreme edge or physical limit; a boundary. **3.** The point in time when an action, an event, or a phenomenon ceases or is completed; the conclusion. **4.** A result; an outcome. **5.** Something toward which one strives; a goal. See Syns at **intention. 6.** The termination of life or existence; death. **7.** The ultimate extent; the very limit. **8.** *Slang.* The very best; the ultimate. **9.** A remainder; a remnant. **10.a.** A share of a responsibility or obligation. **b.** A particular area of responsibility. **11.** *Football.* **a.** Either of the players in the outermost position on the line of scrimmage. **b.** The position played by such a player. *— v.* **end•ed, end•ing, ends.** *— tr.* **1.** To bring to a conclusion. **2.** To form the last or concluding part of. **3.** To destroy: *ended our hopes.* *— intr.* **1.** To come to a finish; cease. **2.** To die. ***— idioms.* in the end.** Eventually; ultimately. **no end.** A great deal. [ME *ende* < OE. See **ant-*.**]

end– *pref.* Var. of **endo–.**

en•da•moe•ba or **en•da•me•ba** (ĕn′də-mē′bə) *n.* Var. of **entamoeba.**

en•dan•ger (ĕn-dān′jər) *tr.v.* **-gered, -ger•ing, -gers.** To expose to harm or danger; imperil. **— en•dan′ger•ment** *n.*

***Syns:** endanger, hazard, imperil, jeopardize, risk.* The central meaning shared by these verbs is "to subject to danger, loss, or destruction": *driving that endangers lives; hazarded his health; a forest imperiled by acid rain; strikes that jeopardized profits; was reluctant to risk her money.*

en•dan•gered (ĕn-dān′jərd) *adj.* Faced with extinction.

end•arch (ĕn′därk′) *adj. Bot.* Of or relating to a xylem whose early development is from the center outward. [END(O)– + Gk. *arkhē*, beginning (< *arkhein*, to begin, rule).]

end•ar•te•rec•to•my (ĕn′där-tə-rĕk′tə-mē) *n., pl.* **-mies.** Surgical excision of the inner lining of an artery that is clogged with plaque. [NLat. *endartērium*, inner lining of an artery (ENDO– + *artērium*, artery < Lat. *artēria*; see ARTERY) + –ECTOMY.]

end•ar•te•ri•tis (ĕn′där-tə-rī′tĭs) *n.* Inflammation of the inner lining of an artery. [NLat. *endartērium*, inner lining of an artery; see ENDARTERECTOMY + –ITIS.]

end•brain (ĕnd′brān′) *n.* See **telencephalon.**

en•dear (ĕn-dîr′) *tr.v.* **-deared, -dear•ing, -dears.** To make beloved or sympathetic.

en•dear•ing (ĕn-dîr′ĭng) *adj.* Inspiring affection or warm sympathy: *an endearing smile.* **— en•dear′ing•ly** *adv.*

en•dear•ment (ĕn-dîr′mənt) *n.* **1.** The act of endearing. **2.** An expression of affection, such as a caress.

en•deav•or (ĕn-dĕv′ər) *n.* **1.** A conscientious or concerted effort toward an end; an earnest attempt. **2.** Purposeful or industrious activity; enterprise. *— v.* **-ored, -or•ing, -ors.** *— tr.* To attempt (fulfillment of a responsibility, for example) by employment or expenditure of effort. *— intr.* To work with a set or specified goal or purpose. [ME *endevour* < *endeveren*, to make an effort < *(putten) in dever*, (to put oneself) in duty : *in*, in; see IN¹ + *dever*, duty (< OFr. *deveir, devoir*; see DEVOIR).] **— en•deav′or•er** *n.*

en•deav•our (ĕn-dĕv′ər) *n. & v. Chiefly British.* Var. of **endeavor.**

En•de•cott also **En•di•cott** (ĕn′dĭ-kət, -kŏt′), **John.** 1588?–1665. English-born Amer. colonial administrator who was a founder and governor of the Massachusetts Bay Colony.

en•dem•ic (ĕn-dĕm′ĭk) *adj.* **1.** Prevalent in or peculiar to a particular locality, region, or people. **2.** *Ecol.* Native to or confined to a certain region. *— n. Ecol.* An endemic plant or animal. [< Gk. *endēmos* : *en-*, in; see EN–² + *dēmos*, people; see **dā-*.**] **— en•dem′i•cal•ly** *adv.* **— en•dem′ism** *n.*

En•der•by Land (ĕn′dər-bē). A region of Antarctica between Queen Maud Land and Wilkes Land; claimed by Australia.

end•er•gon•ic (ĕn′dər-gŏn′ĭk) *adj.* Requiring energy. [END(O)– + Gk. *ergon*, work; see **werg-*** + –IC.]

en•der•mic (ĕn-dûr′mĭk) *adj.* Acting medicinally by absorption through the skin. **— en•der′mi•cal•ly** *adv.*

En•ders (ĕn′dərz), **John Franklin.** 1897–1985. Amer. bacteriologist who shared a 1954 Nobel Prize.

end•game also **end game** (ĕnd′gām′) *n.* **1.** *Games.* The final stage of a chess game after most of the pieces have been removed from the board. **2.** The final stage of an extended process or course of events.

end•ing (ĕn′dĭng) *n.* **1.** A conclusion or termination. **2.** A concluding part; a finale. **3.** *Gram.* The final morpheme added to a word base to make an inflectional form.

en•dive (ĕn′dīv′, ŏn′dēv′) *n.* **1.** An Indian plant *(Cichorium endivia)* cultivated for its leaves used in salads. **2.** A variety of the common chicory *(Cichorium intybus)* cultivated for its

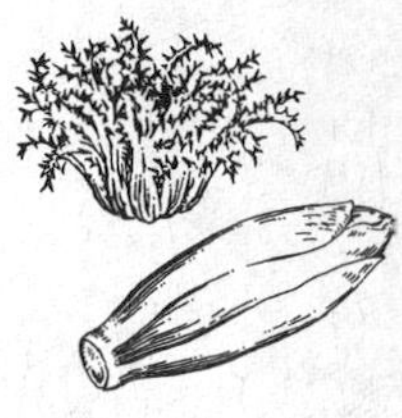

endive
Top: Curly endive
Bottom: Belgian endive

ă pat	oi boy
ā pay	ou out
âr care	ŏŏ took
ä father	ōō boot
ĕ pet	ŭ cut
ē be	ûr urge
ĭ pit	th thin
ī pie	*th* this
îr pier	hw which
ŏ pot	zh vision
ō toe	ə about, item
ô paw	

Stress marks:
′ (primary);
′ (secondary), as in
dictionary (dĭk′shə-nĕr′ē)

whitish leaves used in salads. [ME < OFr. < Med.Lat. *endivia* < Med.Gk. *entubia*, pl. dim. of Gk. *entubon*, perh. < Egypt. *tybi*, January (because the plant grows in this month).]

end leaf *n.* See **endpaper.**

end•less (ĕnd′lĭs) *adj.* **1.** Being or seeming to be without an end or a limit; boundless. **2.** Formed with the ends joined; continuous. — **end′less•ly** *adv.* — **end′less•ness** *n.*

end line *n. Sports.* A line perpendicular to the sidelines that marks an end boundary of a playing field or court.

end•long (ĕnd′lông′, -lŏng′) *adv. Archaic.* Lengthwise.

end man *n.* The person at the end of a line or row.

end•most (ĕnd′mōst′) *adj.* Being at or closest to the end; last.

end•note (ĕnd′nōt′) *n.* A note placed at the end of an article, a chapter, or a book that comments on or cites a reference for a designated part of the text.

endo– or **end–** *pref.* Inside; within: *endometrium.* [Gk. < *endo*, within. See **en*.**]

en•do•bi•ot•ic (ĕn′də-bī-ŏt′ĭk) *adj.* Living as a parasite or symbiont within the tissues of a host.

en•do•car•di•tis (ĕn′dō-kär-dī′tĭs) *n.* Inflammation of the endocardium. [ENDOCARD(IUM) + -ITIS.] — **en′do•car•dit′ic** (-dĭt′ĭk) *adj.*

en•do•car•di•um (ĕn′dō-kär′dē-əm) *n., pl.* **-di•a** (-dē-ə). The thin serous membrane, composed of endothelial tissue, that lines the interior of the heart. [NLat. : ENDO– + Gk. *kardia*, heart; see **kerd-*.**] — **en′do•car′di•al** *adj.*

en•do•carp (ĕn′də-kärp′) *n.* The hard inner layer of the pericarp of many fruits, as a peach pit. — **en′do•car′pal** *adj.*

en•do•cra•ni•um (ĕn′dō-krā′nē-əm) *n., pl.* **-ni•a** (-nē-ə). **1.** The outermost layer of the dura mater. **2.** The inner surface of the skull.

en•do•crine (ĕn′də-krĭn, -krēn′, -krīn′) *adj.* **1.** Secreting internally. **2.** Of or relating to endocrine glands or the hormones secreted by them. —*n.* **1.** The secretion of an endocrine gland; a hormone. **2.** An endocrine gland. [Fr. : Gk. *endo-*, endo- + Gk. *krinein*, to separate; see **krei-*.**]

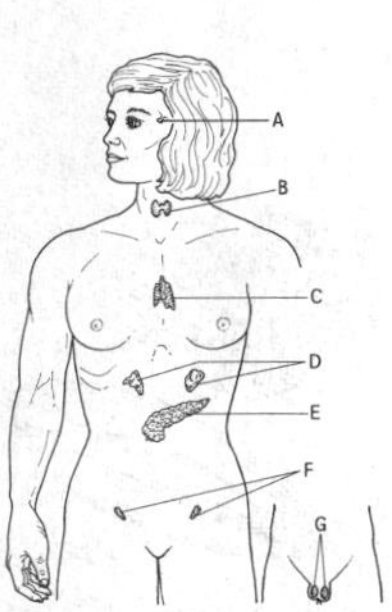

endocrine gland *n.* Any of various glands, such as the thyroid, adrenal, or pituitary, having hormonal secretions that pass directly into the bloodstream.

endocrine gland
A. Pituitary gland
B. Thyroid
C. Thymus
D. Adrenal glands
E. Pancreas
F. Ovaries
G. Testes

en•do•cri•nol•o•gy (ĕn′də-krə-nŏl′ə-jē) *n.* The study of the glands and hormones of the body and their related disorders. — **en′do•cri′no•log′ic** (-krĭn′ə-lŏj′ĭk), **en′do•crin′o•log′i•cal** *adj.* — **en′do•cri•nol′o•gist** *n.*

en•do•cy•to•sis (ĕn′dō-sī-tō′sĭs) *n.* A process of cellular ingestion by which the plasma membrane folds inward to bring substances into the cell. — **en′do•cyt′ic** (-sĭt′ĭk), **en′do•cy•tot′ic** (-sī-tŏt′ĭk) *adj.* — **en′do•cy•tose′** (-tōs′) *v.*

en•do•derm (ĕn′də-dûrm′) also **en•to•derm** (ĕn′tə-) *n.* The innermost of the three primary germ layers of an animal embryo, developing into the gastrointestinal tract, the lungs, and associated structures. — **en′do•der′mal** *adj.*

en•do•der•mis (ĕn′də-dûr′mĭs) *n. Bot.* The innermost layer of the cortex that forms a sheath around the vascular tissue of roots and some stems. [ENDO– + (EPI)DERMIS.]

en•do•don•tia (ĕn′dō-dŏn′shə, -shē-ə) *n.* Endodontics.

en•do•don•tics (ĕn′dō-dŏn′tĭks) *n.* (*used with a sing. v.*) The branch of dentistry that deals with diseases of the tooth root, dental pulp, and surrounding tissue. [ENDO– + (ORTHO)DONTICS.] — **en′do•don′tic** *adj.* — **en′do•don′tist** *n.*

en•do•en•zyme (ĕn′dō-ĕn′zīm′) *n.* An enzyme that acts on or is retained within the cell producing it.

en•do•er•gic (ĕn′dō-ûr′jĭk) *adj. Chem.* Endothermic. [ENDO– + Gk. *ergon*, work; see **werg-*** + -IC.]

en•dog•a•my (ĕn-dŏg′ə-mē) *n.* **1.** *Anthro.* Marriage within a particular group in accordance with custom or law. **2.** *Bot.* Fertilization resulting from pollination among flowers of the same plant. **3.** *Biol.* Reproduction by the fusion of gametes of similar ancestry. — **en•dog′a•mous** *adj.*

en•dog•e•nous (ĕn-dŏj′ə-nəs) *adj.* **1.** Produced or growing from within. **2.** *Biol.* Originating or produced within an organism, a tissue, or a cell: *endogenous secretions.* — **en•dog′e•nous•ly** *adv.* — **en•dog′e•ny** *n.*

en•do•lymph (ĕn′də-lĭmf′) *n.* The fluid in the labyrinth of the inner ear. — **en′do•lym•phat′ic** (-lĭm-făt′ĭk) *adj.*

en•do•me•tri•o•sis (ĕn′dō-mē′trē-ō′sĭs) *n.* A condition, usu. resulting in pain and dysmenorrhea, characterized by the abnormal occurrence of endometrial tissue outside the uterus.

en•do•me•tri•um (ĕn′dō-mē′trē-əm) *n., pl.* **-tri•a** (-trē-ə). The membrane that lines the uterus. [NLat. : ENDO– + Gk. *mētra*, uterus; see METRO–.] — **en′do•me′tri•al** *adj.*

en•do•mi•to•sis (ĕn′dō-mī-tō′sĭs) *n.* A process by which chromosomes replicate without the division of the cell nucleus. — **en′do•mi•tot′ic** (-tŏt′ĭk) *adj.*

en•do•morph (ĕn′də-môrf′) *n.* **1.** A mineral enclosed within another mineral, such as tourmaline in quartz. **2.** *Physiol.* An individual characterized by prominence of the abdomen and other soft body parts developed from the embryonic endodermal layer. [ENDO(DERM) + -MORPH.]

en•do•mor•phic (ĕn′də-môr′fĭk) *adj.* **a.** Of or relating to an endomorph. **b.** Created through endomorphism.

en•do•morph•ism (ĕn′də-môr′fĭz′əm) *n.* **1.** *Geol.* A change within an intrusive igneous rock caused by the assimilation of portions of the surrounding rock. **2.** *Math.* A homomorphism that maps a set onto itself.

en•do•nu•cle•ase (ĕn′dō-nōō′klē-ās′, -āz′, -nyōō′-) *n.* Any of a group of enzymes that catalyze the hydrolysis of bonds between nucleic acids in the interior of a DNA or an RNA sequence.

en•do•par•a•site (ĕn′dō-păr′ə-sīt′) *n.* A parasite, such as a tapeworm, that lives within another organism. — **en′do•par•a•sit′ic** (-sĭt′ĭk) *adj.* — **en′do•par′a•sit•ism** (-sĭ-tĭz′əm) *n.*

en•do•pep•ti•dase (ĕn′dō-pĕp′tĭ-dās′, -dāz′) *n.* Any of a large group of enzymes that catalyze the hydrolysis of peptide bonds in the interior of a polypeptide chain or protein molecule.

en•do•phyte (ĕn′də-fīt′) *n.* A plant, such as a fungus, growing within another plant. — **en′do•phyt′ic** (-dō-fĭt′ĭk) *adj.*

en•do•plasm (ĕn′də-plăz′əm) *n.* A central, less viscous portion of the cytoplasm that is distinguishable in certain cells, esp. motile cells. — **en′do•plas′mic** *adj.*

endoplasmic reticulum *n.* A membrane network within the cytoplasm of cells involved in the synthesis, modification, and transport of cellular materials.

end organ *n.* The encapsulated termination of a sensory nerve.

en•dor•phin (ĕn-dôr′fĭn) *n.* Any of a group of peptide hormones that are found mainly in the brain and reduce the sensation of pain. [ENDO(GENOUS) + (MO)RPHIN(E).]

en•dorse (ĕn-dôrs′) also **in•dorse** (ĭn-) *tr.v.* **-dorsed, -dors•ing, -dors•es. 1.** To write one's signature on the back of (a check, for example) as evidence of the legal transfer of its ownership, esp. in return for the cash or credit indicated on its face. **2.** To place (one's signature), as on a contract, to indicate approval of its contents or terms. **3.** To acknowledge (receipt of payment) by signing a bill or other instrument. **4.** To give approval of or support to, esp. publicly; sanction. See Syns at **approve.** [ME *endosen* < AN *endosser* < Med.Lat. *indorsāre* : Lat. *in-*, upon, in; see EN–[1] + Lat. *dorsum*, back.] — **en•dors′a•ble** *adj.* — **en•dors′er, en•dor′sor** *n.*

en•dor•see (ĕn′dôr-sē′) *n.* One to whom ownership of a negotiable document is transferred by endorsement.

en•dorse•ment (ĕn-dôrs′mənt) *n.* **1.** The act of endorsing. **2.** Something, such as a signature, that endorses or validates. **3.** Approbation; sanction; support: *sought the union's endorsement.* **4.** An amendment to a contract, such as an insurance policy, by which the original terms are changed.

en•do•scope (ĕn′də-skōp′) *n.* An instrument for viewing the interior of a body canal or a hollow organ such as the colon. — **en′do•scop′ic** (-skŏp′ĭk) *adj.* — **en′do•scop′i•cal•ly** *adv.* — **en•dos′co•py** (ĕn-dŏs′kə-pē) *n.*

en•do•skel•e•ton (ĕn′dō-skĕl′ĭ-tn) *n.* An internal supporting skeleton, derived from the mesoderm, characteristic of vertebrates and certain invertebrates. — **en′do•skel′e•tal** (-ĭ-tl) *adj.*

en•dos•mo•sis (ĕn′dŏz-mō′sĭs, -dŏs-) *n.* The inward flow of a fluid through a permeable membrane toward a fluid of greater concentration. — **en′dos•mot′ic** (-mŏt′ĭk) *adj.* — **en′dos•mot′i•cal•ly** *adv.*

en•do•sperm (ĕn′də-spûrm′) *n.* The nutritive tissue within seeds of flowering plants, surrounding the embryo.

en•do•spore (ĕn′də-spôr′, -spōr′) *n.* **1.** A small asexual spore, as that formed by some bacteria. **2.** The inner layer of the wall of a spore.

en•dos•te•um (ĕn-dŏs′tē-əm) *n., pl.* **-te•a** (-tē-ə). The thin layer of cells lining the medullary cavity of a bone. [NLat. : END(O)– + Gk. *osteon*, bone; see **ost-*.**] — **en•dos′te•al** *adj.*

en•do•the•ci•um (ĕn′dō-thē′sē-əm, -shē-əm) *n., pl.* **-ci•a** (-sē-ə, -shē-ə). *Bot.* The inner tissue of an anther or a moss capsule. [NLat. : ENDO– + Gk. *thēkion*, dim. of *thēkē*, chest, receptacle; see **dhē-*.**]

en•do•the•li•o•ma (ĕn′dō-thē′lē-ō′mə) *n., pl.* **-ma•ta** (-mə-tə) or **-mas.** Any of various neoplasms derived from endothelium.

en•do•the•li•um (ĕn′dō-thē′lē-əm) *n., pl.* **-li•a** (-lē-ə). A layer of epithelial cells that lines serous cavities, lymph vessels, and blood vessels. [NLat. : ENDO– + Gk. *thēlē*, nipple; see **dhē(i)-*.**] — **en′do•the′li•al, en′do•the′li•oid′** *adj.*

en•do•therm (ĕn′də-thûrm′) *n.* An organism that generates heat to maintain its body temperature, typically above the temperature of its surroundings; a homeotherm.

en•do•ther•mic (ĕn′dō-thûr′mĭk) also **en•do•ther•mal** (-məl) *adj.* **1.** *Chem.* Characterized by or causing the absorption of heat; endoergic. **2.** *Biol.* Of or relating to an endotherm; warm-blooded. — **en′do•ther′my** *n.*

en•do•tox•in (ĕn′dō-tŏk′sən) *n.* A toxin produced by certain bacteria and released upon destruction of the bacterial cell. — **en′do•tox′ic** *adj.*

en•do•tra•che•al (ĕn′də-trā′kē-əl) *adj.* Within or passing through the trachea: *an endotracheal tube.*

en•dow (ĕn-dou′) *tr.v.* **-dowed, -dow•ing, -dows. 1.** To provide with property or income. **2.a.** To equip or supply with a talent or quality. **b.** To imagine as having a usu. favorable trait: *endowed the dog with human intelligence.* **3.** *Obsolete.* To provide with a dower. [ME *endowen* < AN *endouer* : OFr. *en–*, intensive pref.; see EN–[1] + OFr. *douer*, to give a dowry to (< Lat. *dōtāre* < *dōs, dōt-*, dowry; see **dō-***).]

en•dow•ment (ĕn-dou′mənt) *n.* **1.** The act of endowing. **2.** Funds or property donated to an institution, an individual, or a group. **3.** A natural gift, ability, or quality.

end•pa•per also **end paper** (ĕnd′pā′pər) *n.* Either of two folded sheets of heavy paper having one half pasted to the inside front or back cover of a book and the other half pasted to the base of the first or last page.

end plate *n. Physiol.* The area of synaptic contact between a motor nerve and a muscle fiber.

end•play (ĕnd′plā′) *Games.* — *n.* A play in bridge that forces an opponent to lead and results in the opponents' losing one or more tricks that they would have won had they not been leading. — *tr.v.* **-played, -play•ing, -plays.** To force (a bridge opponent) to lead disadvantageously.

end•point or **end point** also **end-point** (ĕnd′point′) *n.* **1.** Either of two points marking the end of a line segment. **2.** *Chem.* The point in a titration at which no more titrant should be added. **3.** A tip or point of termination.

end product *n.* The result of a completed series of processes or changes.

end run *n.* **1.** *Football.* A play in which the ball carrier attempts to run around one end of the defensive line. **2.** *Informal.* A maneuver in which impediments are bypassed, often by deceit or trickery.

end-run (ĕnd′rŭn′) *tr.v.* **-ran** (-răn′), **-run•ning, -runs.** *Informal.* To bypass (an impediment) often by deceit or trickery.

end-stopped (ĕnd′stŏpt′) *adj.* Ending in a syntactic and rhythmic pause. Used of a line of verse or a couplet.

end table *n.* A small table, usu. placed at either end of a couch or beside a chair.

en•due (ĕn-do͞o′, -dyo͞o′) also **in•due** (ĭn-) *tr.v.* **-dued, -du•ing, -dues. 1.** To provide with a quality or trait; endow. **2.** To put on (a piece of clothing). [ME *enduen* < OFr. *enduire*, to lead in, induct < Lat. *indūcere*. See INDUCE. Sense 2, ME *induen*, to clothe < Lat. *induere*, to put on. See **eu-^{1}***.]

en•dur•a•ble (ĕn-do͝or′ə-bəl, -dyo͝or′-) *adj.* Possible to be endured; tolerable or bearable. — **en•dur′a•bly** *adv.*

en•dur•ance (ĕn-do͝or′əns, -dyo͝or′-) *n.* **1.** The act, quality, or power of withstanding hardship or stress. **2.** The state or fact of persevering. **3.** Continuing existence; duration.

en•dure (ĕn-do͝or′, -dyo͝or′) *v.* **-dured, -dur•ing, -dures.** — *tr.* **1.** To carry on through despite hardships; undergo. **2.** To bear with tolerance: *endure the consequences.* See Syns at **bear^{1}**. — *intr.* **1.** To continue in existence; last: *endured for centuries.* **2.** To suffer patiently without yielding. [ME *enduren* < OFr. *endurer* < Lat. *indūrāre*, to make hard : *in-*, against, into; see EN-^{1} + *dūrus*, hard; see **deru-***.]

en•dur•ing (ĕn-do͝or′ĭng, -dyo͝or′-) *adj.* **1.** Lasting; continuing; durable: *a novel of enduring interest.* **2.** Long-suffering; patient. — **en•dur′ing•ly** *adv.* — **en•dur′ing•ness** *n.*

en•dur•o (ĕn-do͝or′ō, -dyo͝or′ō) *n.*, *pl.* **-os.** *Sports.* A race, as of motorcycles or runners, that tests endurance.

end user also **end-us•er** (ĕnd′yo͞o′zər) *n.* The final consumer of a product, esp. the one for whom the product is designed.

end•wise (ĕnd′wīz′) also **end•ways** (-wāz′) *adv.* **1.** On end; upright. **2.** With the end foremost. **3.** Lengthwise. **4.** End to end.

En•dym•i•on (ĕn-dĭm′ē-ən) *n. Gk. Myth.* A handsome young man who was loved by Selene and whose youth was preserved by eternal sleep.

end zone *n. Football.* The area at either end of the playing field between the goal line and the end line.

ENE *abbr.* East-northeast.

-ene *suff.* An unsaturated organic compound, esp. one containing a double bond between carbon atoms: *ethylene.* [< Gk. *-ēnē*, fem. adj. suff.]

en•e•ma (ĕn′ə-mə) *n.*, *pl.* **-mas. 1.** The injection of liquid into the rectum through the anus for therapeutic or diagnostic purposes, such as stimulating evacuation of the bowels. **2.** The fluid so injected. [LLat. < Gk. < *enienai*, to send in, inject : *en-*, in; see EN-^{2} + *hienai*, to send; see **yē-***.]

en•e•my (ĕn′ə-mē) *n.*, *pl.* **-mies. 1.** One who feels hatred toward, intends injury to, or opposes another; a foe. **2.a.** A hostile power or force, such as a nation. **b.** A member or unit of such a force. **3.** A group of foes or hostile forces. See Usage Note at **collective noun. 4.** Something destructive or injurious in its effects. — *adj.* Of, relating to, or being a hostile power or force. [ME *enemi* < OFr. < Lat. *inimīcus* : *in-*, not; see IN-^{1} + *amīcus*, friend.]

Syns: *enemy, foe, opponent.* The central meaning shared by these nouns is "one who is hostile to or opposes the purposes or interests of another": *betrayed by enemies; a foe of fascism; a political opponent.*

en•er•get•ic (ĕn′ər-jĕt′ĭk) *adj.* **1.** Possessing, exerting, or displaying energy. **2.** Of or relating to energy. [Gk. *energētikos* < *energein*, to be active < *energos*, active. See ENERGY.] — **en′er•get′i•cal•ly** *adv.*

en•er•get•ics (ĕn′ər-jĕt′ĭks) *n.* (*used with a sing. v.*) **1.** The study of the flow and transformation of energy. **2.** The flow and transformation of energy within a particular system.

en•er•gize (ĕn′ər-jīz′) *v.* **-gized, -giz•ing, -giz•es.** — *tr.* **1.** To give energy to; activate or invigorate. **2.** To supply with an electric current; connect to a source of electricity. — *intr.* To release or put out energy. — **en′er•giz′er** *n.*

en•er•gy (ĕn′ər-jē) *n.*, *pl.* **-gies. 1.** The capacity for work or vigorous activity; vigor; power. See Syns at **strength. 2.a.** Exertion of vigor or power. **b.** Vitality and intensity of expression. **3.a.** Usable heat or power. **b.** A source of usable power, such as petroleum or coal. **4.** *Phys.* The capacity of a physical system to do work. [Fr. *énergie* < LLat. *energīa* < Gk. *energeia* < *energos*, active : *en-*, in, at; see EN-^{2} + *ergon*, work; see **werg-***.]

energy audit *n.* An evaluation of energy consumption, as in a home or business, to determine how energy can be conserved.

energy density *n.* The energy per unit volume of a region of space.

energy efficiency ratio *n.* A measure of the efficiency of a heating or cooling unit, equal to the unit's output in BTU's per hour divided by its consumption of energy in watts.

energy level *n.* **1.** The energy characteristic of a stationary state of a physical system, esp. a quantum mechanical system. **2.** The stationary state of a quantum mechanical system.

en•er•vate (ĕn′ər-vāt′) *tr.v.* **-vat•ed, -vat•ing, -vates. 1.** To weaken or destroy the strength or vitality of. See Syns at **deplete. 2.** *Medic.* To remove a nerve or part of a nerve. — *adj.* (ĭ-nûr′vĭt). Deprived of strength; debilitated. [Lat. *ēnervāre*, *ēnervāt-* : *ē-*, *ex-*, ex- + *nervus*, sinew; see **(s)neəu-***.] — **en′er•va′tion** *n.* — **en′er•va′tive** *adj.* — **en′er•va′tor** *n.*

E•nes•co (ə-nĕs′kō, ĕ-nĕs′-), **Georges.** 1881–1955. Romanian-born violinist and composer whose works include the opera *Oedipus* (1936).

en•face (ĕn-fās′) *tr.v.* **-faced, -fac•ing, -fac•es.** To write on the face of (a check, for example). — **en•face′ment** *n.*

en•fant ter•ri•ble (äN-fäN′ tĕ-rē′blə) *n.* **en•fants ter•ri•bles** (äN-fäN′ tĕ-rē′blə). One whose unconventional behavior, work, or ideas are a source of embarrassment or dismay to others. [Fr. : *enfant*, child + *terrible*, frightful.]

en•fee•ble (ĕn-fē′bəl) *tr.v.* **-bled, -bling, -bles.** To make feeble; weaken. — **en•fee′ble•ment** *n.* — **en•fee′bler** *n.*

en•feoff (ĕn-fĕf′, -fēf′) *tr.v.* **-feoffed, -feoff•ing, -feoffs.** To invest with a feudal estate or fee. [ME *enfeffen* < AN *enfeoffer* : OFr. *en-*, causative pref.; see EN-^{1} + OFr. *fief*, fief; see FEE.] — **en•feoff′ment** *n.*

en•fet•ter (ĕn-fĕt′ər, ĭn-) *tr.v.* **-tered, -ter•ing, -ters.** To bind in fetters; enchain.

En•field (ĕn′fēld′). A town of N CT near the MA border; settled c. 1680. Pop. 45,532.

Enfield rifle *n.* Any of several rifles formerly used by British and American troops, esp. the .30 or .303 caliber bolt-action breechloading model. [After *Enfield*, a borough of London in SE England.]

en•fi•lade (ĕn′fə-lād′, -läd′) *n.* **1.** Gunfire directed along the length of a target, such as a column of troops. **2.** A target vulnerable to sweeping gunfire. — *tr.v.* **-lad•ed, -lad•ing, -lades.** To rake with gunfire. [Fr., series, string, row < *enfiler*, to string together, run through < OFr. : *en-*, in, on; see EN-^{1} + *fil*, thread (< Lat. *fīlum*; see **gʷhī-***).]

en•fleu•rage (ŏn′flə-räzh′, -räj′) *n.* A process in making perfume in which odorless fats or oils absorb the fragrance of fresh flowers. [Fr. < *enfleurer*, to saturate with the perfume of flowers : *en-*, causative pref.; see EN-^{1} + *fleur*, flower (< OFr. *flour* < Lat. *flōs*, *flōr-*; see **bhel-^{3}***).]

en•fold (ĕn-fōld′) *tr.v.* **-fold•ed, -fold•ing, -folds. 1.** To cover with or as if with folds; envelop. **2.** To hold within limits; enclose. **3.** To embrace. — **en•fold′er** *n.*

en•force (ĕn-fôrs′, -fōrs′) *tr.v.* **-forced, -forc•ing, -forc•es. 1.** To compel observance of or obedience to. **2.** To impose (a kind of behavior, for example); compel. **3.** To give force to; reinforce. [ME *enforcen* < OFr. *enforcier*, to exert force, compel, and < *enforcir*, to strengthen : *en-*, causative pref.; see EN-^{1} + *force*, strength; see FORCE.] — **en•force′a•bil′i•ty** *n.* — **en•force′a•ble** *adj.* — **en•force′ment** *n.* — **en•forc′er** *n.*

en•fran•chise (ĕn-frăn′chīz′) *tr.v.* **-chised, -chis•ing, -chis•es. 1.** To bestow a franchise on. **2.** To endow with the rights of citizenship, esp. the right to vote. **3.** To free, as from bondage. [ME *enfraunchisen* < OFr. *enfranchir*, *enfranchiss-*, to set free : *en-*, intensive pref.; see EN-^{1} + *franchir* (< *franc*, free; see FRANK^{1}).] — **en•fran′chise′ment** *n.*

eng. *abbr.* **1.** Engine. **2.** Engineer. **3.** Engineering.

Eng. *abbr.* **1.** England. **2.** English.

En•ga•dine (ĕng′gə-dēn′). A valley of the Inn R. in E Switzerland, divided into the **Upper Engadine** in the SW and the **Lower Engadine** in the NE.

en•gage (ĕn-gāj′) *v.* **-gaged, -gag•ing, -gag•es.** — *tr.* **1.** To obtain the services of; employ. **2.** To arrange for the use of; reserve. **3.** To pledge or promise, esp. to marry. **4.** To attract and hold the attention of; engross. **5.** To win over or attract. **6.** To draw into; involve. **7.** To require the use of; occupy. **8.** To enter or bring into conflict with. **9.** To interlock or cause to interlock; mesh: *engage the clutch.* **10.** To give or take as security. — *intr.* **1.** To involve oneself or become occupied; participate. **2.** To assume an obligation; agree. **3.** To enter into conflict or battle. **4.** To become meshed or inter-

ă **pat**	oi **boy**
ā **pay**	ou **out**
âr **care**	o͝o **took**
ä **father**	o͞o **boot**
ĕ **pet**	ŭ **cut**
ē **be**	ûr **urge**
ĭ **pit**	th **thin**
ī **pie**	*th* **this**
îr **pier**	hw **which**
ŏ **pot**	zh **vision**
ō **toe**	ə **a**bout,
ô **paw**	item

Stress marks:
′ (primary);
′ (secondary), as in
dictionary (dĭk′shə-nĕr′ē)

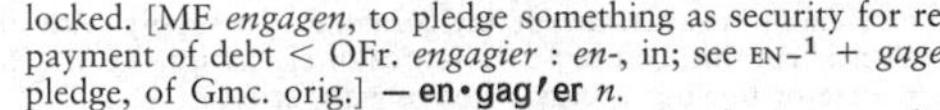

locked. [ME *engagen,* to pledge something as security for repayment of debt < OFr. *engagier* : *en-,* in; see EN-[1] + *gage,* pledge, of Gmc. orig.] — **en•gag′er** *n.*

en•ga•gé (ĕn′gä-zhā′) *adj.* Actively committed, as to a political cause. [Fr., p.part. of *engager,* to engage < OFr. *engagier,* to pledge. See ENGAGE.]

en•gaged (ĕn-gājd′) *adj.* **1.** Employed, occupied, or busy. **2.** Committed, as to a cause. **3.** Pledged to marry; betrothed. **4.** Involved in conflict or battle. **5.** Being in gear; meshed. **6.** Partly imbedded in or attached to another part.

en•gage•ment (ĕn-gāj′mənt) *n.* **1.** The act of engaging or the state of being engaged. **2.** Betrothal. **3.** Something that serves to engage; a pledge. **4.** A promise or agreement to be at a particular place at a particular time. **5.a.** Employment, esp. for a specified time. **b.** A specific period of employment. **6.** A hostile encounter; a battle. **7.** The condition of being in gear.

Syns: engagement, appointment, assignation, date, rendezvous, tryst. The central meaning shared by these nouns is "a commitment to appear at a certain time and place": *a business engagement; a dental appointment; a secret assignation; a date for tennis; a rendezvous of agents at the border; a lovers' tryst.*

Friedrich Engels

en•gag•ing (ĕn-gā′jĭng) *adj.* Charming; attractive: *an engaging smile.* — **en•gag′ing•ly** *adv.*

en garde (äN gärd′) *interj.* Used to warn a fencer to assume the position preparatory to a match. [Fr. : *en,* on + *garde,* guard.]

en•gar•land (ĕn-gär′lənd) *tr.v.* **-land•ed, -land•ing, -lands.** To encircle or deck with or as if with a garland.

En•gels (ĕng′gəlz, -əls), **Friedrich.** 1820–95. German socialist theorist and writer who collaborated with Karl Marx on *The Communist Manifesto* (1848).

en•gen•der (ĕn-jĕn′dər) *v.* **-dered, -der•ing, -ders.** — *tr.* **1.** To bring into existence; give rise to. **2.** To procreate; propagate. — *intr.* To come into existence; originate. [ME *engendren* < OFr. *engendrer* < Lat. *ingenerāre* : *in-,* in; see EN-[1] + *generāre,* to produce; see GENERATE.] — **en•gen′der•er** *n.*

en•gine (ĕn′jĭn) *n.* **1.a.** A machine that converts energy into mechanical force or motion. **b.** Such a machine distinguished from an electric, spring-driven, or hydraulic motor by use of a fuel. **2.a.** A mechanical appliance, instrument, or tool. **b.** An agent, an instrument, or a means of accomplishment. **3.** A locomotive. **4.** A fire engine. — *tr.v.* **-gined, -gin•ing, -gines.** To equip with an engine or engines. [ME *engin,* skill, machine < OFr., innate ability < Lat. *ingenium.* See **genə-*.**]

engine block *n.* The cast metal block containing the cylinders of an internal-combustion engine.

en•gi•neer (ĕn′jə-nîr′) *n.* **1.** One who is trained or professionally engaged in a branch of engineering. **2.** One who operates an engine. **3.** One who skillfully or shrewdly manages an enterprise. — *tr.v.* **-neered, -neer•ing, -neers. 1.** To plan, construct, or manage as an engineer. **2.** To alter or produce by methods of genetic engineering. **3.** To plan, manage, and put through by skillful acts or contrivance; maneuver. [ME *enginour* < OFr. *engigneor* < Med.Lat. *ingeniātor,* contriver < *ingeniāre,* to contrive < Lat. *ingenium,* ability. See ENGINE.]

en•gi•neer•ing (ĕn′jə-nîr′ĭng) *n.* **1.a.** The application of science to practical ends such as the design, manufacture, and operation of structures, machines, and systems. **b.** The profession of or the work performed by an engineer. **2.** Skillful maneuvering or direction: *social engineering.*

en•gird (ĕn-gûrd′) *tr.v.* **-girt** (-gûrt′), **-gird•ing, -girds.** *Archaic.* To encircle.

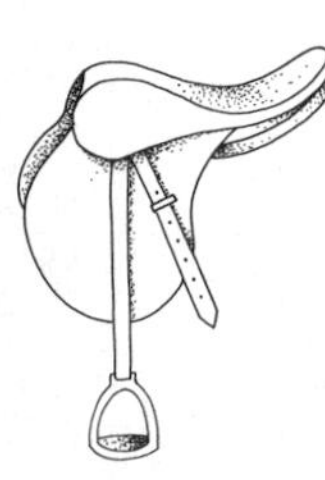

English saddle

en•gir•dle (ĕn-gûr′dl) *tr.v.* **-dled, -dling, -dles.** To encircle or surround with or as if with a girdle.

en•gla•cial (ĕn-glā′shəl) *adj.* Located or occurring within a glacier.

Eng•land (ĭng′glənd). A division of the United Kingdom, the S part of the island of Great Britain. Acts of union joined England with Wales (1536) and Scotland (1707) to create the political entity of Great Britain and with Ireland (1801) to form the United Kingdom. Cap. London. Pop. 46,220,955.

En•gle•wood (ĕng′gəl-wo͝od′). **1.** A city of N-central CO, a suburb of Denver. Pop. 29,387. **2.** A city of NE NJ E of Paterson; settled by the Dutch in the 17th cent. Pop. 24,850.

Eng•lish (ĭng′glĭsh) *adj.* **1.** Of, relating to, or characteristic of England or its people or culture. **2.** Of or relating to the English language. — *n.* **1.** The people of England. **2.a.** The West Germanic language of England, the United States, and other countries that are or have been under English influence. **b.** The English language of a particular time, region, person, or group of persons: *American English.* **3.** A translation into or an equivalent in the English language. **4.** A course or class in the study of English language, literature, or composition. **5.** Often **english.** *Sports & Games.* The spin given to a ball by striking it on one side or releasing it with a sharp twist. — *tr.v.* **-lished, -lish•ing, -lish•es. 1.** To translate into English. **2.** To adapt into English; Anglicize. [ME < OE *Englisc* < *Engle,* the Angles.] — **Eng′lish•ness** *n.*

English setter

English bulldog *n.* A shorthaired stocky dog; a bulldog.

English Channel. An arm of the Atlantic Ocean between W France and S England opening into the North Sea.

English daisy *n.* See **daisy** 2.

English foxhound *n.* Any of a breed of medium-sized hunting dog originating in England and having straight legs and a smooth black and white or tan and white coat.

English horn *n. Mus.* A double-reed woodwind instrument similar to but larger than the oboe and pitched lower by a fifth.

Eng•lish•man (ĭng′glĭsh-mən) *n.* **1.** A man who is a native or inhabitant of England. **2.** A man of English descent.

English muffin *n.* A flat round muffin made from yeast dough, baked on a griddle and usu. split and toasted.

English plantain *n.* See **ribgrass.**

English saddle *n.* A light hornless saddle with a steel cantle and pommel, a padded seat, and full side flaps.

English setter *n.* Any of a breed of medium-sized dog developed in England and having a long silky white coat usu. with black or brownish markings.

English sheepdog *n.* An Old English sheepdog.

English sonnet *n.* See **Shakespearean sonnet.**

English sparrow *n.* See **house sparrow.**

English springer spaniel *n.* Any of a breed of medium-sized hunting dog originating in England and having a silky liver and white or black and white coat.

English toy spaniel *n.* Any of a breed of spaniel having a short turned-up nose, a thick wavy coat, and a mane.

English walnut *n.* **1.** A Eurasian tree *(Juglans regia)* cultivated in southern Europe and California for its valuable wood and its large edible nuts. **2.** The nut of this tree.

Eng•lish•wom•an (ĭng′glĭsh-wo͝om′ən) *n.* **1.** A woman who is a native or inhabitant of England. **2.** A woman of English descent.

en•glut (ĕn-glŭt′) *tr.v.* **-glut•ted, -glut•ting, -gluts.** To gulp down; swallow greedily. [AN *englutir* < LLat. *inglūtīre* : Lat. *in-,* intensive pref.; see IN-[2] + Lat. *gluttīre,* to swallow.]

en•gorge (ĕn-gôrj′) *v.* **-gorged, -gorg•ing, -gorg•es.** — *tr.* **1.** To devour greedily. **2.** To gorge; glut. **3.** To fill to excess, as with blood or other fluid. — *intr.* To feed ravenously. [Fr. *engorger* < OFr. *engorgier* : *en-,* in; see EN-[1] + *gorge,* throat; see GORGE.] — **en•gorge′ment** *n.*

engr. *abbr.* **1.** Engineer. **2.a.** Engraved. **b.** Engraver. **c.** Engraving.

en•graft (ĕn-grăft′) *tr.v.* **-graft•ed, -graft•ing, -grafts. 1.** To graft (a scion) onto or into another plant. **2.** To plant firmly; establish. — **en•graft′ment** *n.*

en•grailed (ĕn-grāld′) *adj.* **1.** Indented along the edge with small curves. **2.** Having an edge or a margin formed by a series of raised dots. [ME *engreled* < OFr. *engresle,* p.part. of *engresler,* to engrail : *en-,* causative pref.; see EN-[1] + *gresle,* slender, tapered (< Lat. *gracilis*).]

en•grain (ĕn-grān′) *tr.v.* **-grained, -grain•ing, -grains.** To ingrain. [ME *engreinen,* to dye with cochineal or kermes < OFr. *engrainer* : *en-,* causative pref.; see EN-[1] + *graine,* grain; see GRAIN.]

en•gram (ĕn′grăm′) *n.* A physical alteration thought to occur in living neural tissue in response to stimuli, posited as an explanation for memory.

en•grave (ĕn-grāv′) *tr.v.* **-graved, -grav•ing, -graves. 1.** To carve, cut, or etch into a material. **2.** To carve, cut, or etch a design or letters into. **3.a.** To carve, cut, or etch into a block or surface used for printing. **b.** To print from a block or plate made by such a process. **4.** To impress deeply as if by carving or etching. — **en•grav′er** *n.*

en•grav•ing (ĕn-grā′vĭng) *n.* **1.** The art or technique of one that engraves. **2.** A design or text engraved on a surface. **3.** An engraved surface for printing. **4.** A print made from an engraved plate or block.

en•gross (ĕn-grōs′) *tr.v.* **-grossed, -gross•ing, -gross•es. 1.** To occupy exclusively; absorb. **2.** To acquire most or all of (a commodity); monopolize (a market). **3.a.** To write or transcribe in a large clear hand. **b.** To write or print the final draft of (an official document). [ME *engrossen,* to collect in large quantity, monopolize < OFr. *engrossier* < *en gros,* in large quantity : *en,* in (< Lat. *in;* see IN-[2]) + *gros,* large; see GROSS.] — **en•gross′er** *n.*

en•gross•ing (ĕn-grō′sĭng) *adj.* Occupying one's complete attention; wholly absorbing. — **en•gross′ing•ly** *adv.*

en•gross•ment (ĕn-grōs′mənt) *n.* The act of engrossing or the state of being engrossed.

en•gulf (ĕn-gŭlf′) *tr.v.* **-gulfed, -gulf•ing, -gulfs.** To swallow up or overwhelm by or as if by overflowing and enclosing. — **en•gulf′ment** *n.*

en•hance (ĕn-hăns′) *tr.v.* **-hanced, -hanc•ing, -hanc•es.** To make greater, as in value, beauty, or reputation; augment. [ME *enhauncen* < AN *enhauncer,* var. of OFr. *enhaucier* < VLat. **inaltiāre* < LLat. *inaltāre* : Lat. *in-,* causative pref.; see EN-[1] + Lat. *altus,* high; see **al-[2]*.**] — **en•hance′ment** *n.* — **en•hanc′er** *n.* — **en•hanc′ive** *adj.*

en•har•mon•ic (ĕn′här-mŏn′ĭk) *adj. Mus.* Of, relating to, or involving tones that are identical in pitch but are written differently according to the key in which they occur. [LLat. *enharmonicus* < Gk. *enarmonios* : *en-,* in; see EN-[2] + *harmonia,* harmony; see HARMONY.] — **en′har•mon′i•cal•ly** *adv.*

E•nid (ĕ′nĭd). A city of N-central OK NNW of Oklahoma City. Pop. 45,309.

e•nig•ma (ĭ-nĭg′mə) *n.* **1.** One that is puzzling or inexplicable. **2.** A perplexing speech or text; a riddle. [Lat. *aenigma* < Gk. *ainigma* < *ainissesthai*, *ainig-*, to riddle < *ainos*, fable.]

en•ig•mat•ic (ĕn′ĭg-măt′ĭk) or **en•ig•mat•i•cal** (-ĭ-kəl) *adj.* Of or resembling an enigma; puzzling. See Syns at **ambiguous.** [Gk. *ainigmatikos* < *ainigma*, *ainigmat-*, riddle. See ENIGMA.] — **en′ig•mat′i•cal•ly** *adv.*

en•isle (ĕn-īl′) *tr.v.* **-isled, -isl•ing, -isles. 1.** To make into an island. **2.** To set apart from others; isolate.

En•i•we•tok (ĕn′ə-wē′tŏk′, ə-nē′wĭ-). An atoll in the Ralik Chain of the Marshall Is. in the W-central Pacific; site of U.S. atomic tests (1948–54).

en•jamb•ment or **en•jambe•ment** (ĕn-jăm′mənt, -jămb′) *n.* The continuation of a syntactic unit from one line or couplet of a poem to the next with no pause. [Fr. *enjambement* < OFr. *enjamber*, to straddle : *en-*, causative pref.; see EN-[1] + *jambe*, leg; see JAMB.]

en•join (ĕn-join′) *tr.v.* **-joined, -join•ing, -joins. 1.** To direct or impose with authority and emphasis. **2.** To prohibit or forbid. See Syns at **forbid.** [ME *enjoinen* < OFr. *enjoindre* < Lat. *iniungere* : *in-*, causative pref.; see EN-[1] + *iungere*, to join; see **yeug-***.] — **en•join′er** *n.* — **en•join′ment** *n.*

en•joy (ĕn-joi′) *v.* **-joyed, -joy•ing, -joys.** —*tr.* **1.** To receive pleasure or satisfaction from. **2.** To have the use or benefit of. —*intr.* To have a pleasurable or satisfactory time. [ME *enjoien* < OFr. *enjoir* : *en-*, intensive pref.; see EN-[1] + *joir*, to rejoice (< Lat. *gaudēre*; see **gāu-***).] — **en•joy′a•ble** *adj.* — **en•joy′a•bly** *adv.* — **en•joy′er** *n.*

en•joy•ment (ĕn-joi′mənt) *n.* **1.** The act or state of enjoying. **2.** Use or possession of something beneficial or pleasurable. **3.** Something that gives pleasure.

en•keph•a•lin (ĕn-kĕf′ə-lĭn) *n.* Either of two polypeptides having opiate qualities that are produced in the brain. [Gk. *enkephalos*, in the head (*en-*, in; see **en*** + *kephalē*, head; see **ghebh-el-***) + -IN.]

en•kin•dle (ĕn-kĭn′dl) *v.* **-dled, -dling, -dles.** —*tr.* **1.** To set afire; light. **2.** To incite; arouse. **3.** To make luminous and glowing. —*intr.* To catch fire. — **en•kin′dler** *n.*

enl. *abbr.* **1.** Enlarged. **2.** Enlisted.

en•lace (ĕn-lās′) also **in•lace** (ĭn-) *tr.v.* **-laced, -lac•ing, -lac•es. 1.** To wrap or wind about with or as if with a lace or laces; encircle. **2.** To interlace; entwine. — **en•lace′ment** *n.*

en•large (ĕn-lärj′) *v.* **-larged, -larg•ing, -larg•es.** —*tr.* **1.** To make larger; add to. **2.** To give greater scope to; expand. See Syns at **increase.** —*intr.* **1.** To become larger; grow. **2.** To speak or write at greater length or in greater detail; elaborate. [ME *enlargen* < OFr. *enlargier* : *en-*, causative pref.; see EN-[1] + *large*, large; see LARGE.] — **en•larg′er** *n.*

en•large•ment (ĕn-lärj′mənt) *n.* **1.** An act of enlarging or the state of being enlarged. **2.** Something that enlarges; an addition. **3.** Something that has been enlarged.

en•light•en (ĕn-līt′n) *tr.v.* **-ened, -en•ing, -ens. 1.** To give spiritual or intellectual insight to. **2.** To give information to; inform or instruct. — **en•light′en•er** *n.*

en•light•en•ment (ĕn-līt′n-mənt) *n.* **1.a.** The act or a means of enlightening. **b.** The state of being enlightened. **2. Enlightenment.** A philosophical movement of the 18th century that emphasized the use of reason to examine accepted doctrines and traditions and brought about many humanitarian reforms. Used with *the.* **3.** *Buddhism.* A state in which the individual transcends desire and suffering and attains Nirvana.

en•list (ĕn-lĭst′) *v.* **-list•ed, -list•ing, -lists.** —*tr.* **1.** To engage (persons or a person) for service in the armed forces. **2.** To engage the support of. —*intr.* **1.** To enter the armed forces. **2.** To participate actively in a cause. — **en•list′ment** *n.*

en•list•ed man (ĕn-lĭs′tĭd) *n.* A man in the armed forces who ranks below a commissioned officer or warrant officer.

enlisted person *n.* A member of the armed forces who ranks below a commissioned officer or warrant officer.

enlisted woman *n.* A woman in the armed forces who ranks below a commissioned officer or warrant officer.

en•list•ee (ĕn-lĭs′tē′) *n.* A person who enlists or is enlisted for service in the armed forces.

en•liv•en (ĕn-lī′vən) *tr.v.* **-ened, -en•ing, -ens.** To make lively; animate. — **en•liv′en•er** *n.* — **en•liv′en•ment** *n.*

en masse (ŏn măs′) *adv.* In one group or body; all together: *marched en masse to the capitol.* [Fr. : *en*, in + *masse*, mass.]

en•mesh (ĕn-mĕsh′) also **im•mesh** (ĭm-) *tr.v.* **-meshed, -mesh•ing, -mesh•es.** To entangle, involve, or catch in or as if in a mesh. See Syns at **catch.** — **en•mesh′ment** *n.*

en•mi•ty (ĕn′mĭ-tē) *n., pl.* **-ties.** Deep-seated, often mutual hatred. [ME *enemite* < OFr. *enemistie* < VLat. **inimīcitās* < Lat. *inimīcus*, enemy. See ENEMY.]

en•ne•ad (ĕn′ē-ăd′) *n.* A group or set of nine. [Gk. *enneas*, *ennead-* < *ennea*, nine. See **newn̥***.]

en•no•ble (ĕn-nō′bəl) *tr.v.* **-bled, -bling, -bles. 1.** To make noble; dignify. **2.** To confer nobility upon. [ME **ennoblen* < OFr. *ennoblir* : *en-*, causative pref.; see EN-[1] + *noble*, noble; see NOBLE.] — **en•no′ble•ment** *n.* — **en•no′bler** *n.*

en•nui (ŏn-wē′, ŏn′wē) *n.* Listlessness and dissatisfaction resulting from lack of interest; boredom. [Fr. < OFr. *enui* < *ennuier*, to annoy, bore < VLat. **inodiāre* < Lat. *in odiō (esse)*, (to be) odious : *in*, in; see IN-[2] + *odiō*, ablative of *odium*, hate; see **od-***.]

Word History: Ennui is an odious feeling, and the word *ennui* comes from an odious phrase. The Latin phrase *mihi in odiō est* (literally translated as "to me in a condition of dislike or hatred is"), meaning "I hate or dislike," gave rise to the Vulgar Latin verb **inodiāre,* "to make odious," the source of Modern French *ennuyer,* "to annoy, bore." In Old French a noun meaning "worry, boredom," came from the verb *ennuier.* This noun in its Modern French form *ennui* was borrowed into English in the sense "boredom," the English word being first recorded in 1732.

e•no•ki (ē-nŏk′ē) *n.* Enokidake.

e•no•ki•da•ke (ĭ-nō′kē-dä′kē) *n.* A widely cultivated mushroom *(Flammulina velutipes)* native to North America and eastern Asia and superficially resembling the bean sprout. [J. : *enoki*, Chinese nettle tree + *take*, bamboo, mushroom.]

e•nol (ē′nôl′, ē′nōl′) *n.* An organic compound containing a hydroxyl group attached to a doubly bonded carbon atom. [< -EN(E) + -OL[1].] — **e•nol′ic** (ē-nŏl′ĭk) *adj.*

e•no•lase (ē′nə-lās′, -lāz′) *n.* An enzyme present in muscle tissue that acts in carbohydrate metabolism.

e•nol•o•gy also **oe•nol•o•gy** (ē-nŏl′ə-jē) *n.* The study of wine and the making of wine. [Gk. *oinos*, wine + -LOGY.] — **e′no•log′i•cal** (ē′nə-lŏj′ĭ-kəl) *adj.* — **e•nol′o•gist** *n.*

e•nor•mi•ty (ĭ-nôr′mĭ-tē) *n., pl.* **-ties. 1.** The quality of passing all moral bounds; excessive wickedness or outrageousness. **2.** A monstrous offense or evil; an outrage. **3.** *Usage Problem.* Great size; immensity. [Fr. *énormité* < OFr. < Lat. *ēnormitās* < *ēnormis*, unusual, enormous. See ENORMOUS.]

Usage Note: *Enormity* is frequently used to refer simply to the property of being enormous, but many would prefer that *enormity* be reserved for a property that evokes a negative moral judgment. Fifty-nine percent of the Usage Panel rejects the use of *enormity* in the sentence *At that point the engineers sat down to design an entirely new viaduct, apparently undaunted by the enormity of their task.*

e•nor•mous (ĭ-nôr′məs) *adj.* **1.** Very great in size, extent, number, or degree. **2.** *Archaic.* Very wicked; heinous. [< Lat. *ēnormis*, unusual, huge : *ē-*, *ex-*, ex- + *norma*, norm; see **gnō-***.] — **e•nor′mous•ly** *adv.* — **e•nor′mous•ness** *n.*

e•nough (ĭ-nŭf′) *adj.* Sufficient to satisfy a need or a desire; adequate. —*pron.* An adequate number or quantity. —*adv.* **1.** To a satisfactory amount or degree; sufficiently: *cooked enough.* **2.** Very; fully; quite: *glad enough to leave.* **3.** Tolerably; rather: *sang well enough.* —*interj.* Used to express impatience or exasperation. [ME *enogh* < OE *genōg.* See **nek-[2]***.]

e•nounce (ĭ-nouns′) *tr.v.* **e•nounced, e•nounc•ing, e•nounc•es. 1.** To declare formally; state. **2.** To pronounce clearly; enunciate. [< Fr. *énoncer* < Lat. *ēnūntiāre*, to speak out. See ENUNCIATE.] — **e•nounce′ment** *n.*

e•now (ĭ-nou′) *adj. & adv. Archaic.* Enough. [ME, var. of *enogh.* See ENOUGH.]

en pas•sant (äN′ pä-säN′) *adv.* **1.** In passing; by the way; incidentally. **2.** *Games.* Used in reference to a move in chess in which a pawn that has just completed an initial advance to its fourth rank is captured by an opponent pawn as if it had only moved to its third rank. [Fr. : *en*, in + *passant*, passing.]

en•phy•tot•ic (ĕn′fī-tŏt′ĭk) *adj.* Of or relating to a plant disease that causes a relatively constant amount of damage each year. [EN-[2] + -PHYT(E) + -OTIC.] — **en′phy•tot′ic** *n.*

en•plane (ĕn-plān′) also **em•plane** (ĕm-) *intr.v.* **-planed, -plan•ing, -planes.** To board an airplane.

en prise (än′ prēz′, äN) *adj. Games.* Exposed to possible capture. Used of a chess piece. [Fr. : *en*, in + *prise*, grip, grasp.]

en•quire (ĕn-kwīr′) *v.* Var. of **inquire.**

en•quir•y (ĕn-kwīr′ē, ĕn′kwə-rē) *n., pl.* **-ies.** Var. of **inquiry.**

en•rage (ĕn-rāj′) *tr.v.* **-raged, -rag•ing, -rag•es.** To put into a rage; infuriate. [ME **enragen* < OFr. *enrager* : *en-*, causative pref.; see EN-[1] + *rage*, rage; see RAGE.] — **en•rage′ment** *n.*

en rap•port (äN′ rə-pôr′, -pōr′, rä-) *adj.* Being in agreement; harmonious. [Fr. : *en*, in + *rapport*, agreement.]

en•rapt (ĕn-răpt′) *adj.* Filled with or transported by delight.

en•rap•ture (ĕn-răp′chər) *tr.v.* **-tured, -tur•ing, -tures.** To fill with rapture or delight. — **en•rap′ture•ment** *n.*

en•rich (ĕn-rĭch′) *tr.v.* **-riched, -rich•ing, -rich•es. 1.** To make rich or richer. **2.** To make fuller, more meaningful, or more rewarding. **3.** To add fertilizer to. **4.** To add nutrients to. **5.** To add to the beauty or character of; adorn. **6.** *Phys.* To increase the amount of one or more radioactive isotopes in (a material, esp. a nuclear fuel). [ME *enrichen* < OFr. *enrichier* : *en-*, causative pref.; see EN-[1] + *riche*, rich; see RICH.] — **en•rich′er** *n.*

en•rich•ment (ĕn-rĭch′mənt) *n.* **1.** The act of enriching or the state of being enriched. **2.** Something that enriches.

en•robe (ĕn-rōb′) *tr.v.* **-robed, -rob•ing, -robes.** To dress in or as if in a robe.

en•roll also **en•rol** (ĕn-rōl′) —*v.* **-rolled, -roll•ing, -rolls** also **-rols.** —*tr.* **1.** To enter or register in a roll, list, or record.

ă **pat**	oi **boy**
ā **pay**	ou **out**
âr **care**	ŏŏ **took**
ä **father**	ōō **boot**
ĕ **pet**	ŭ **cut**
ē **be**	ûr **urge**
ĭ **pit**	th **thin**
ī **pie**	*th* **this**
îr **pier**	hw **which**
ŏ **pot**	zh **vision**
ō **toe**	ə **about, item**
ô **paw**	

Stress marks:
′ (primary);
′ (secondary), as in **dictionary** (dĭk′shə-nĕr′ē)

2. To roll or wrap up. **3.** To write or print a final copy of; engross. — *intr.* To place one's name on a roll or register. [ME *enrollen* < OFr. *enroller* : *en-*, in; see EN–[1] + *rolle*, roll (< Lat. *rotula*, little wheel; see ROLL).] — **en•roll•ee'** *n.*

en•roll•ment also **en•rol•ment** (ĕn-rōl'mənt) *n.* **1.a.** The act or process of enrolling. **b.** The state of being enrolled. **2.** The number enrolled. **3.** A record or an entry.

en•root (ĕn-ro͞ot', -ro͝ot') *tr.v.* **-root•ed, -root•ing, -roots.** To establish firmly by or as if by roots; implant.

en route (ŏn ro͞ot', ĕn) *adv. & adj.* On or along the way. [Fr. : *en*, on + *route*, route.]

ENS or **Ens.** *abbr.* Ensign.

en•san•guine (ĕn-săng'gwĭn) *tr.v.* **-guined, -guin•ing, -guines.** To cover or stain with or as if with blood.

En•sche•da (ĕn'skə-dā', -SKHə-). A city of E Netherlands near the German border. Pop. 144,938.

en•sconce (ĕn-skŏns') *tr.v.* **-sconced, -sconc•ing, -sconc•es. 1.** To settle (oneself) securely or comfortably. **2.** To place or conceal in a secure place. [EN–[1] + SCONCE[1].]

en•sem•ble (ŏn-sŏm'bəl) *n.* **1.** A unit or group of parts that contribute to a single effect, esp.: **a.** A coordinated outfit or costume. **b.** A group of supporting artists who perform together. **2.** *Mus.* **a.** A work for two or more vocalists or instrumentalists. **b.** Those who perform it. [Fr. < OFr., together < LLat. *insimul*, at the same time : *in-*, intensive pref.; see IN–[2] + *simul*, at the same time; see **sem-[1]***.]

En•se•na•da (ĕn'sə-nä'də). A city of NW Mexico on the Pacific Ocean. Pop. 120,483.

en•shrine (ĕn-shrīn') also **in•shrine** (ĭn-) *tr.v.* **-shrined, -shrin•ing, -shrines. 1.** To enclose in or as if in a shrine. **2.** To cherish as sacred. — **en•shrine'ment** *n.*

en•shroud (ĕn-shroud') *tr.v.* **-shroud•ed, -shroud•ing, -shrouds.** To cover with or as if with a shroud.

en•si•form (ĕn'sə-fôrm') *adj.* Shaped like a sword, as the leaf of an iris. [Lat. *ēnsis*, sword + -FORM.]

en•sign (ĕn'sən, -sīn') *n.* **1.** A national flag displayed on ships and aircraft. **2.** A standard or banner, as of a military unit. **3.** *Archaic.* A standard-bearer. **4.** (ĕn'sən). A commissioned officer in the U.S. Navy or Coast Guard, ranking below lieutenant junior grade. **5.a.** A badge of office or power; an emblem. **b.** A sign; a token. [ME *ensigne* < OFr. *enseigne* < Lat. *īnsignia*, insignia. See INSIGNIA.]

en•si•lage (ĕn'sə-lĭj) *n.* **1.** The process of storing and fermenting green fodder in a silo. **2.** Fodder preserved in a silo; silage. — *tr.v.* **-laged, -lag•ing, -lag•es.** To ensile. [Fr. < *ensiler*, to ensile. See ENSILE.]

en•sile (ĕn-sīl') *tr.v.* **-siled, -sil•ing, -siles.** To store (fodder) in a silo for preservation. [Fr. *ensiler* < Sp. *ensilar* : *en-*, in (< Lat. *in-*); see EN–[1] + *silo*, silo; see SILO.]

en•slave (ĕn-slāv') *tr.v.* **-slaved, -slav•ing, -slaves.** To make into a slave. — **en•slave'ment** *n.* — **en•slav'er** *n.*

en•snare (ĕn-snâr') also **in•snare** (ĭn-) *tr.v.* **-snared, -snar•ing, -snares.** To take or catch in or as if in a snare. See Syns at **catch.** — **en•snare'ment** *n.* — **en•snar'er** *n.*

en•snarl (ĕn-snärl') *tr.v.* **-snarled, -snarl•ing, -snarls.** To entangle in or as if in a snarl.

En•sor (ĕn'sôr), **James.** 1860–1949. Belgian painter whose works include *Entry of Christ into Brussels* (1888).

en•soul (ĕn-sōl') also **in•soul** (ĭn-) *tr.v.* **-souled, -soul•ing, -souls. 1.** To endow with a soul. **2.** To place, receive, or cherish in the soul.

en•sphere (ĕn-sfîr') also **in•sphere** (ĭn-) *tr.v.* **-sphered, -spher•ing, -spheres.** To enclose in or as if in a sphere.

en•sta•tite (ĕn'stə-tīt') *n.* A variety of orthorhombic pyroxene having a magnesium silicate base, mainly $MgSiO_3$, usu. found embedded in igneous rocks and meteorites. [Gk. *enstatēs*, adversary (because of its refractory quality) : *en-*, in, at, near; see EN–[2] + *-statēs*, one that stands; see **stā-*** + -ITE[1].]

en•sue (ĕn-so͞o') *intr.v.* **-sued, -su•ing, -sues. 1.** To follow as a result. See Syns at **follow. 2.** To take place subsequently. [ME *ensuen* < OFr. *ensuivre*, *ensu-* < VLat. **īnsequere* < Lat. *īnsequī*, to follow closely : *in-*, intensive pref.; see EN–[1] + *sequī*, to follow; see **sekʷ-[1]***.]

en suite (äN swēt') *adv. & adj.* In or as part of a series or set. [Fr. : *en*, in + *suite*, a following, sequence.]

en•sure (ĕn-sho͝or') *tr.v.* **-sured, -sur•ing, -sures.** To make sure or certain; insure. See Usage Note at **assure.** [ME *ensuren* < AN *enseurer* : OFr. *en-*, causative pref.; see EN–[1] + OFr. *seur*, secure, var. of *sur*; see SURE.]

ENT *abbr. Medic.* Ear, nose, and throat.

ent– *pref.* Var. of **ento–.**

–ent *suff.* **1.a.** Performing, promoting, or causing a specified action: *absorbent.* **b.** Being in a specified state or condition: *bivalent.* **2.** One that performs, promotes, or causes a specified action: *referent.* [ME < OFr. < Lat. *-ēns*, *-ent-*, pr.part. suff.]

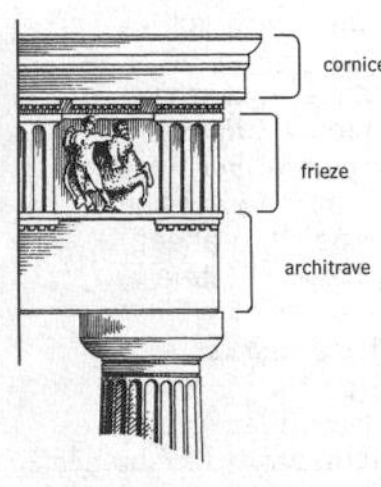

entablature

en•tab•la•ture (ĕn-tăb'lə-cho͝or') *n.* The upper section of a classical building, resting on the columns and constituting the architrave, frieze, and cornice. [Obsolete Fr. < Ital. *intavolatura* < *intavolare*, to put on a table : *in-*, in, on (< Lat.; see EN–[1]) + *tavola*, table (< Lat. *tabula*, board).]

en•tail (ĕn-tāl', ĭn-) *tr.v.* **-tailed, -tail•ing, -tails. 1.** To have, impose, or require as a necessary accompaniment or consequence. **2.** To limit the inheritance of (property) to a specified succession of heirs. **3.** To bestow or impose on a person or a specified succession of heirs. — *n.* **1.a.** The act of entailing, esp. property. **b.** The state of being entailed. **2.** An entailed estate. **3.** A predetermined order of succession, as to an estate or an office. **4.** Something transmitted as if by unalterable inheritance. [ME *entaillen*, to limit inheritance to specific heirs : *en-*, intensive pref.; see EN–[1] + *taille*, tail; see TAIL[2].] — **en•tail'ment** *n.*

en•ta•moe•ba or **en•ta•me•ba** (ĕn'tə-mē'bə) also **en•da•moe•ba** or **en•da•me•ba** (ĕn'də-) *n., pl.* **-bas** or **-bae** (-bē). Any of several parasitic amoebas of the genus *Entamoeba*, esp. *E. histolytica*, which causes amebic dysentery. [NLat. *Entamoeba*, genus name : ENT(O)– + AMOEBA.]

en•tan•gle (ĕn-tăng'gəl) *tr.v.* **-gled, -gling, -gles. 1.** To twist together or entwine into a confusing mass; snarl. **2.** To complicate; confuse. **3.** To involve in or as if in a tangle. See Syns at **catch.** — **en•tan'gle•ment** *n.* — **en•tan'gler** *n.*

En•teb•be (ĕn-tĕb'ə, -tĕb'ē). A town of S Uganda on Lake Victoria; cap. of Uganda (1894–1962). Pop. 21,289.

en•tel•e•chy (ĕn-tĕl'ĭ-kē) *n., pl.* **-chies. 1.** In the philosophy of Aristotle, the condition of a thing whose essence is fully realized; actuality. **2.** In some philosophical systems, a vital force that directs an organism toward self-fulfillment. [LLat. *entelechīa* < Gk. *entelekheia* : *entelēs*, complete (*en-*, in; see EN–[2] + *telos*, completion; see **kʷel-[1]***) + *ekhein*, to have; see **segh-***.]

en•tente (ŏn-tŏnt') *n.* **1.** An agreement between two or more governments or powers for cooperative action or policy. **2.** The parties to such an agreement. [Fr. < OFr., intent < fem. p.part. of *entendre*, to understand, intend. See INTEND.]

en•ter (ĕn'tər) *v.* **-tered, -ter•ing, -ters.** — *tr.* **1.** To come or go into. **2.** To penetrate; pierce. **3.** To introduce; insert. **4.a.** To become a participant, member, or part of; join. **b.** To gain admission to (a school, for example). **5.** To cause to become a participant, member, or part of; enroll. **6.** To embark on; begin. **7.** To make a beginning in; take up: *entered medicine.* **8.** To write or put in. **9.** To place formally on record; submit. **10.** To go to or occupy in order to claim possession of (land). **11.** To report (a ship or cargo) to customs. — *intr.* **1.** To come or go in; make an entry. **2.** To effect penetration. **3.** To become a member or participant. — ***phrasal verbs.*** **enter into. 1.** To participate in; take an active role or interest in. **2.** To become party to (a contract). **3.** To become a component of; form a part of. **4.** To consider; investigate. **enter on** (or **upon**). **1.** To set out on; begin. **2.** To begin considering; take up. **3.** To take possession of. [ME *entren* < OFr. *entrer* < Lat. *intrāre* < *intrā*, inside. See **en***.] — **en'ter•a•ble** *adj.*

en•ter•ic (ĕn-tĕr'ĭk) also **en•ter•al** (ĕn'tər-əl) *adj.* Of, relating to, or being within the intestine.

enteric fever *n.* See **typhoid fever.**

en•ter•i•tis (ĕn'tə-rī'tĭs) *n.* Inflammation of the intestinal tract, esp. of the small intestine.

entero– or **enter–** *pref.* Intestine: *enteritis.* [NLat. < Gk. *enteron*, intestine. See **en***.]

en•ter•o•bac•ter•i•um (ĕn'tə-rō-băk-tîr'ē-əm) *n., pl.* **-i•a** (-ē-ə). Any of various gram-negative rod-shaped bacteria of the family Enterobacteriaceae that includes some pathogens of plants and animals, such as the colon bacillus and salmonella.

en•ter•o•bi•a•sis (ĕn'tə-rō-bī'ə-sĭs) *n.* Infestation of the intestine with pinworms. [NLat. *Enterobius*, pinworm genus (ENTERO– + Gk. *bios*, life; see BIO–) + -IASIS.]

en•ter•o•coele (ĕn'tə-rō-sēl') *n. Embryol.* The coelom formed from a pocketlike outgrowth of the wall of the archenteron, esp. in echinoderms and chordates.

en•ter•o•gas•trone (ĕn'tə-rō-găs'trōn') *n.* A hormone released by the upper intestinal mucosa that inhibits gastric motility and secretion. [ENTERO– + GASTR(O)– + (HORM)ONE.]

en•ter•o•hep•a•ti•tis (ĕn'tə-rō-hĕp'ə-tī'tĭs) *n.* See **blackhead** 2.

en•ter•o•ki•nase (ĕn'tə-rō-kī'nās', -nāz', -kĭn'ās', -āz') *n.* An enzyme secreted by the upper intestinal mucosa that converts the inactive trypsinogen to the digestive enzyme trypsin.

en•ter•on (ĕn'tə-rŏn') *n.* The alimentary canal; the intestines. [Gk. See **en***.]

en•ter•o•tox•in (ĕn'tə-rō-tŏk'sĭn) *n.* A toxin produced by bacteria that is specific for intestinal cells and causes the vomiting and diarrhea associated with food poisoning.

en•ter•o•vi•rus (ĕn'tə-rō-vī'rəs) *n., pl.* **-rus•es.** Any of a subgroup of picornaviruses, including polioviruses, that infect the gastrointestinal tract and often spread to other areas of the body, esp. the nervous system. — **en'ter•o•vi'ral** *adj.*

en•ter•prise (ĕn'tər-prīz') *n.* **1.** An undertaking, esp. one of some scope, complication, and risk. **2.** A business organization. **3.** Industrious systematic activity, esp. when directed toward profit. **4.** Willingness to undertake new ventures; initiative. [ME < OFr. *entreprise* < p.part. of *entreprendre*, to undertake : *entre-*, between (< Lat. *inter-*; see INTER–) + *prendre*, to take (< Lat. *prendere*; see **ghend-***).] — **en'ter•pris'er** *n.*

En•ter•prise (ĕn′tər-prīz′). A city of SE AL SSE of Montgomery. Pop. 20,123.

en•ter•pris•ing (ĕn′tər-prī′zĭng) *adj.* Showing initiative and enterprise. **—en′ter•pris′ing•ly** *adv.*

en•ter•tain (ĕn′tər-tān′) *v.* **-tained, -tain•ing, -tains.** *—tr.* **1.** To hold the attention of with something amusing or diverting. **2.** To extend hospitality toward. **3.a.** To consider; contemplate. **b.** To hold in mind; harbor. **4.** *Archaic.* To continue with; maintain. **5.** *Obsolete.* To take into service; hire. **6.** To give admittance to; receive. *—intr.* **1.** To show hospitality to guests. **2.** To provide entertainment. [ME *entertinen*, to maintain < OFr. *entretenir* < Med.Lat. *intertenēre* : Lat. *inter*, among; see INTER- + Lat. *tenēre*, to hold; see **ten-***.] **—en′ter•tain′er** *n.*

en•ter•tain•ing (ĕn′tər-tā′nĭng) *adj.* Agreeably diverting; amusing. **—en′ter•tain′ing•ly** *adv.*

en•ter•tain•ment (ĕn′tər-tān′mənt) *n.* **1.** The act of entertaining. **2.** The art or field of entertaining. **3.** Something that amuses, pleases, or diverts, esp. a performance or show. **4.** The pleasure afforded by being entertained; amusement. **5.** *Archaic.* Maintenance; support. **6.** *Obsolete.* Employment.

en•thal•py (ĕn′thăl′pē, ĕn-thăl′-) *n., pl.* **-pies.** *Symbol* **H** A thermodynamic function of a system, equal to its internal energy plus the product of its volume and pressure. [< Gk. *enthalpein*, to heat in (*en-*, in; see EN-^{2} + *thalpein*, to heat) + -Y^{2}.]

en•thrall (ĕn-thrôl′) also **in•thrall** (ĭn-) *tr.v.* **-thralled, -thrall•ing, -thralls. 1.** To hold spellbound; captivate. **2.** To enslave. [ME, to put in bondage : *en-*, causative pref.; see EN-^{1} + *thrall*, slave; see THRALL.] **—en•thrall′ing•ly** *adv.* **—en•thrall′ment** *n.*

en•throne (ĕn-thrōn′) also **in•throne** (ĭn-) *tr.v.* **-throned, -thron•ing, -thrones. 1.a.** To seat on a throne. **b.** To invest with sovereign power or with the authority of high office. **2.** To raise to a lofty position; exalt. **—en•throne′ment** *n.*

en•thuse (ĕn-thōōz′) *v.* **-thused, -thus•ing, -thus•es.** *—tr.* To make enthusiastic. *—intr.* To show or express enthusiasm.

en•thu•si•asm (ĕn-thōō′zē-ăz′əm) *n.* **1.** Great excitement for or interest in a subject or cause. **2.** A source or cause of great excitement or interest. **3.** *Archaic.* **a.** Ecstasy arising from supposed possession by a god. **b.** Religious fanaticism. [LLat. *enthūsiasmus* < Gk. *enthousiasmos* < *enthousiazein*, to be inspired by a god < *entheos*, possessed : *en-*, in; see EN-^{2} + *theos*, god; see **dhēs-***.]

en•thu•si•ast (ĕn-thōō′zē-ăst′) *n.* **1.** One who is filled with enthusiasm; one who is ardently absorbed in an interest or pursuit. **2.** A zealot; a fanatic. [Gk. *enthousiastēs*, possessed person < *enthousiazein*, to be inspired. See ENTHUSIASM.]

en•thu•si•as•tic (ĕn-thōō′zē-ăs′tĭk) *adj.* Having or demonstrating enthusiasm. **—en•thu′si•as′ti•cal•ly** *adv.*

en•thy•meme (ĕn′thə-mēm′) *n. Logic.* A syllogism in which one of the premises or the conclusion is not stated explicitly. [Lat. *enthȳmēma* < Gk. *enthumēma*, a rhetorical argument < *enthumeisthai*, to consider : *en-*, in; see EN-^{2} + *thumos*, mind.]

en•tice (ĕn-tīs′) *tr.v.* **-ticed, -tic•ing, -tic•es.** To attract by arousing hope or desire; lure. [ME *enticen* < OFr. *enticier*, to instigate, poss. < VLat. **intītiāre*, to set afire : Lat. *in-*, in; see EN-^{1} + Lat. *tītiō*, firebrand.] **—en•tice′ment** *n.* **—en•tic′er** *n.* **—en•tic′ing•ly** *adv.*

en•tire (ĕn-tīr′) *adj.* **1.** Having no part excluded or left out; whole. See Syns at **whole. 2.** With no reservations or limitations; complete. **3.** All in one piece; intact. **4.** Of one piece; continuous. **5.** Not castrated. **6.** *Bot.* Not having an indented margin: *an entire leaf.* **7.** Unmixed or unalloyed; pure or homogenous. *—n.* **1.** The whole; the entirety. **2.** An uncastrated horse; a stallion. [ME < OFr. *entier* < Lat. *integrum*, neut. of *integer.* See **tag-***.] **—en•tire′ness** *n.*

en•tire•ly (ĕn-tīr′lē) *adv.* **1.** Wholly; completely: *entirely satisfied.* **2.** Solely or exclusively: *He was entirely to blame.*

en•tire•ty (ĕn-tī′rĭ-tē, -tīr′tē) *n., pl.* **-ties. 1.** The state of being entire or complete; wholeness. **2.** The entire amount or extent; the whole.

en•ti•tle (ĕn-tīt′l) *tr.v.* **-tled, -tling, -tles. 1.** To give a name or title to. **2.** To furnish with a right or claim to something. [ME *entitlen* < OFr. *entiteler* < Med.Lat. *intitulāre* : Lat. *in-*, provide with; see EN-^{1} + Lat. *titulus*, title.] **—en•ti′tle•ment** *n.*

entitlement program *n.* A government program that guarantees and provides benefits to a particular group.

en•ti•ty (ĕn′tĭ-tē) *n., pl.* **-ties. 1.** Something that exists as a discrete unit. **2.** The fact of existence; being. **3.** The existence of something considered apart from its properties. [Med.Lat. *entitās* < Lat. *ēns*, *ent-*, pr.part. of *esse*, to be. See **es-***.]

ento– or **ent–** *pref.* Inside; within: *entozoan.* [NLat. < Gk. *entos*, within. See **en***.]

en•to•blast (ĕn′tə-blăst′) *n.* Any of the blastomeres of an embryo from which the endoderm develops.

en•to•derm (ĕn′tə-dûrm′) *n.* Var. of **endoderm.**

en•toil (ĕn-toil′) *tr.v.* **-toiled, -toil•ing, -toils.** *Archaic.* To ensnare; entrap.

entom. *abbr.* Entomology.

en•tomb (ĕn-tōōm′) *tr.v.* **-tombed, -tomb•ing, -tombs. 1.** To place in or as if in a tomb or grave. **2.** To serve as a tomb for. **—en•tomb′ment** *n.*

entomo– *pref.* Insect: *entomology.* [Fr. < Gk. *entomon* < neut. of *entomos*, cut (< its segmented body) < *entemnein*, to cut up : *en-*, in; see EN-^{2} + *temnein*, to cut; see **tem-***.]

en•to•mol•o•gy (ĕn′tə-mŏl′ə-jē) *n.* The scientific study of insects. **—en′to•mo•log′ic** (-mə-lŏj′ĭk), **en′to•mo•log′i•cal** (-ĭ-kəl) *adj.* **—en′to•mo•log′i•cal•ly** *adv.* **—en′to•mol′o•gist** *n.*

en•to•moph•a•gous (ĕn′tə-mŏf′ə-gəs) *adj.* Feeding on insects; insectivorous.

en•to•moph•i•lous (ĕn′tə-mŏf′ə-ləs) *adj. Bot.* Pollinated by insects. **—en′to•moph′i•ly** *n.*

en•tou•rage (ŏn′tōō-räzh′) *n.* **1.** A group of attendants or associates; a retinue. **2.** One's environment or surroundings. [Fr. < *entourer*, to surround < OFr. *entour*, surroundings : *en-*, in; see EN-^{1} + *tour*, circuit; see TOUR.]

en•to•zo•an (ĕn′tə-zō′ən) *n., pl.* **-zo•a** (-zō′ə). Any of various animals, such as tapeworms, that live within other animals, usu. as parasites. **—en′to•zo′ic** *adj.*

en•tr'acte (ŏn′trăkt′, äN-träkt′) *n.* **1.a.** The interval between two acts of a theatrical performance. **b.** Another performance, as of music or dance, provided between two acts of a theatrical performance. **2.** An interval likened to the one occurring between two acts of a drama. [Fr. : *entre*, between (< Lat. *inter*; see INTER-) + *acte*, act (< OFr.; see ACT).]

en•trails (ĕn′trālz′, -trəlz) *pl.n.* **1.** The internal organs, esp. the intestines. **2.** Internal parts. [< ME *entraille* < OFr. < Med.Lat. *intrālia*, alteration of Lat. *interānea* < neut. pl. of *interāneus*, internal < *inter*, within. See **en***.]

en•train^{1} (ĕn-trān′) *tr.v.* **-trained, -train•ing, -trains. 1.** To pull or draw along after itself. **2.** *Chem.* To carry (suspended particles, for example) along in a current. [Fr. *entrainer* < OFr. : *en-*, in; see EN-^{1} + *trainer*, to drag; see TRAIN.] **—en•train′er** *n.* **—en•train′ment** *n.*

en•train^{2} (ĕn-trān′) *v.* **-trained, -train•ing, -trains.** *—intr.* To go aboard a train. *—tr.* To put aboard a train.

en•trance^{1} (ĕn′trəns) *n.* **1.** The act or an instance of entering. **2.** A means or point by which to enter. **3.** Permission or power to enter; admission. **4.** The point, as in a musical score, at which a performer is to begin. **5.** The first entry of an actor into a scene. [ME *entraunce*, right to enter < OFr. < *entrer*, to enter. See ENTER.]

en•trance^{2} (ĕn-trăns′) *tr.v.* **-tranced, -tranc•ing, -tranc•es. 1.** To put into a trance. **2.** To fill with delight, wonder, or enchantment. See Syns at **charm. —en•trance′ment** *n.* **—en•tranc′ing•ly** *adv.*

en•trance•way (ĕn′trəns-wā′) *n.* An entryway.

en•trant (ĕn′trənt) *n.* One that enters, esp. a competition. [Fr. < pr.part. of *entrer*, to enter < OFr. See ENTER.]

en•trap (ĕn-trăp′) *tr.v.* **-trapped, -trap•ping, -traps. 1.** To catch in or as if in a trap. **2.a.** To lure into danger, difficulty, or a compromising situation. See Syns at **catch. b.** To lure into performing an illegal act. [Fr. *entraper* < OFr. : *en-*, in; see EN-^{1} + *trape*, trap (of Gmc. orig.).] **—en•trap′ment** *n.*

en•treat (ĕn-trēt′) also **in•treat** (ĭn-) *—v.* **-treat•ed, -treat•ing, -treats.** *—tr.* **1.** To make an earnest request of. **2.** To ask for earnestly; petition for. **3.** *Archaic.* To deal with; treat. *—intr.* To make an earnest request or petition; plead. [ME *entreten* < AN *entreter* : *en-*, causative pref.; see EN-^{1} + *treter*, to treat; see TREAT.] **—en•treat′ing•ly** *adv.* **—en•treat′ment** *n.*

en•treat•y (ĕn-trē′tē) *n., pl.* **-ies.** An earnest request or petition; a plea.

en•tre•chat (ŏn′trə-shä′) *n.* A jump in ballet during which the dancer crosses the legs a number of times, alternately back and forth. [Fr., earlier *entrechas*, alteration of Ital. *(capriola) intrecciata*, intricate (caper), fem. p.part. of *intrecciare*, to intertwine : *in-*, in (< Lat.; see IN-^{2}) + *treccia*, tress; see TRESS.]

en•tre•côte (äN′trə-kōt′) *n.* A cut of steak taken from between the ribs. [Fr. : *entre*, between (< Lat. *inter*; see INTER-) + *côte*, rib (< Lat. *costa*; see COSTA).]

en•trée or **en•tree** (ŏn′trā, ŏn-trā′) *n.* **1.a.** The main dish of a meal. **b.** A dish served in formal dining immediately before the main course or between two principal courses. **2.a.** The act of entering. **b.** The power, permission, or liberty to enter; admittance. [Fr. < OFr. See ENTRY.]

en•tre•mets (ŏn′trə-mā′, -mĕ′) *n., pl.* **-mets** (-māz′, -mĕ′). A side dish served in addition to the principal course. [ME *entremetes* < OFr. *entremes, entremets* : *entre*, between (< Lat. *inter*; see INTER-) + *mes, mets*, dish; see MESS.]

en•trench (ĕn-trĕnch′) also **in•trench** (ĭn-) *—v.* **-trenched, -trench•ing, -trench•es.** *—tr.* **1.** To provide with a trench, esp. for fortifying or defending. **2.** To fix firmly or securely. *—intr.* **1.** To dig or occupy a trench. **2.** To encroach, infringe, or trespass. **—en•trench′ment** *n.*

en•tre•pôt (ŏn′trə-pō′) *n.* **1.** A place where goods are stored and from which they are distributed. **2.** A trading or market center. [Fr. < *entreposer*, to store : *entre*, in, among (< Lat. *inter-*; see INTER-) + *poser*, to place (< OFr.; see POSE^{1}).]

en•tre•pre•neur (ŏn′trə-prə-nûr′, -nōōr′) *n.* A person who organizes, operates, and assumes the risk for a business ven-

ă **pat**	oi **boy**
ā **pay**	ou **out**
âr **care**	ŏŏ **took**
ä **father**	ōō **boot**
ĕ **pet**	ŭ **cut**
ē **be**	ûr **urge**
ĭ **pit**	th **thin**
ī **pie**	*th* **this**
îr **pier**	hw **which**
ŏ **pot**	zh **vision**
ō **toe**	ə **about, item**
ô **paw**	

Stress marks:
′ (primary);
′ (secondary), as in **dictionary** (dĭk′shə-nĕr′ē)

ture. [Fr. < OFr. < *entreprendre*, to undertake. See ENTERPRISE.] **—en′tre·pre·neur′i·al** *adj.* **—en′tre·pre·neur′i·al·ism, en′tre·pre·neur′ism, en′tre·pre·neur′ship′** *n.*

en·tre·sol (ĕn′tər-sŏl′, ĕn′trə-, ŏn-trə-sôl′) *n.* The floor just above the ground floor of a building; a mezzanine. [Fr. : *entre-*, between (< Lat. *inter-*; see INTER–) + *sol*, floor (< Lat. *solum*).]

en·tro·py (ĕn′trə-pē) *n.*, *pl.* **-pies. 1.** *Symbol* **S** For a closed thermodynamic system, a measure of the thermal energy unavailable to do work. **2.** A measure of the disorder or randomness in a closed system. **3.** A measure of the loss of information in a transmitted message. **4.** A hypothetical tendency for all matter and energy in the universe toward a state of inert uniformity. **5.** Inevitable and steady deterioration of a system or society. [Ger. *Entropie* : Gk. *en-*, in; see EN–[2] + Gk. *tropē*, transformation; see **trep-***.] **—en·tro′pic** (ĕn-trō′pĭk, -trŏp′ĭk) *adj.* **—en·tro′pi·cal·ly** *adv.*

en·trust (ĕn-trŭst′) also **in·trust** (ĭn-) *tr.v.* **-trust·ed, -trust·ing, -trusts. 1.** To give over (something) to another for care, protection, or performance. **2.** To give as a trust to (someone).

en·try (ĕn′trē) *n.*, *pl.* **-tries. 1.a.** The act or an instance of entering. **b.** The privilege or right of entering. **2.** A means or place by which to enter. **3.a.** The inclusion or insertion of an item, as in a record. **b.** An item entered in this way. **4.a.** An entry word, as in a dictionary; a headword. **b.** A headword along with its text. **5.** One in a competition. [ME *entre* < OFr. *entree* < fem. p.part. of *entrer*, to enter. See ENTER.]

en·try·way (ĕn′trē-wā′) *n.* A passage by which to enter.

entry word *n.* See **headword** 1.

en·twine (ĕn-twīn′) also **in·twine** (ĭn-) *—v.* **-twined, -twin·ing, -twines.** *—tr.* To twine around or together. *—intr.* To twine or twist together. **—en·twine′ment** *n.*

en·twist (ĕn-twĭst′) also **in·twist** (ĭn-) *tr.v.* **-twist·ed, -twist·ing, -twists.** To twist together; entwine.

e·nu·cle·ate (ĭ-no͞o′klē-āt′, ĭ-nyo͞o′-) *tr.v.* **-at·ed, -at·ing, -ates. 1.** *Medic.* To remove (a tumor, for example) whole from an enveloping cover or sac. **2.** *Biol.* To remove the nucleus of. **3.** *Archaic.* To explain; elucidate. *—adj.* (-ĭt, -āt′). *Biol.* Lacking a nucleus. [Lat. *ēnucleāre, ēnucleāt-*, to take out the kernel : *ē-, ex-*, ex- + *nucleus*, kernel; see NUCLEUS.] **—e·nu′cle·a′tion** *n.* **—e·nu′cle·a′tor** *n.*

e·nu·mer·a·ble (ĭ-no͞o′mər-ə-bəl, ĭ-nyo͞o′-) *adj.* Denumerable.

e·nu·mer·ate (ĭ-no͞o′mə-rāt′, ĭ-nyo͞o′-) *tr.v.* **-at·ed, -at·ing, -ates. 1.** To count off or name one by one; list. **2.** To determine the number of; count. [Lat. *ēnumerāre, ēnumerāt-*, to count out : *ē-, ex-*, ex- + *numerus*, number; see **nem-***.] **—e·nu′mer·a′tion** *n.* **—e·nu′mer·a′tive** (-mə-rā′tĭv, -mər-ə-) *adj.* **—e·nu′mer·a′tor** *n.*

e·nun·ci·ate (ĭ-nŭn′sē-āt′) *v.* **-at·ed, -at·ing, -ates.** *—tr.* **1.** To pronounce; articulate. **2.** To state or set forth precisely or systematically. **3.** To announce; proclaim. *—intr.* To make articulate sounds. [Lat. *ēnūntiāre, ēnūntiāt-* : *ē-, ex-*, ex- + *nūntiāre*, to announce (< *nūntius*, messenger; see **neu-***).] **—e·nun′ci·a·ble** (-ə-bəl) *adj.* **—e·nun′ci·a′tion** *n.* **—e·nun′ci·a′tive** (-sē-ā′tĭv, -sē-ə-tĭv) *adj.* **—e·nun′ci·a′tive·ly** *adv.* **—e·nun′ci·a′tor** *n.*

en·ure (ĭn-yo͝or′) *v.* Var. of **inure.**

en·u·re·sis (ĕn′yə-rē′sĭs) *n.* The involuntary discharge of urine. [NLat. < Gk. *enourein*, to urinate in : *en-*, in; see EN–[2] + *ourein*, to urinate.] **—en′u·ret′ic** (-rĕt′ĭk) *adj.*

en·vel·op (ĕn-vĕl′əp) *tr.v.* **-oped, -op·ing, -ops. 1.** To enclose or encase completely with or as if with a covering. **2.** To attack (an enemy's flank). [ME *envolupen*, to be involved in < OFr. *envoluper, envoloper* : *en-*, in; see EN–[1] + *voloper*, to wrap up.] **—en·vel′op·er** *n.* **—en·vel′op·ment** *n.*

en·ve·lope (ĕn′və-lōp′, ŏn′-) *n.* **1.** A flat folded paper container, esp. for a letter. **2.** Something that envelops; a wrapping. **3.** *Biol.* An enclosing structure or cover, such as a membrane or the outer coat of a virus. **4.** The bag containing the gas in a balloon or an airship. **5.** The set of limitations within which a technological system, esp. an aircraft, can perform safely and effectively. **6.** The coma of a comet. **7.** *Math.* A curve or surface that is tangent to every one of a family of curves or surfaces. [Fr. *enveloppe* < *envelopper*, to envelop < OFr. *envoloper*. See ENVELOP.]

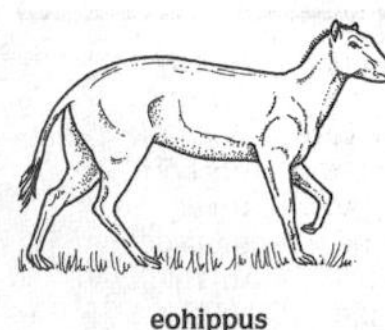
eohippus

en·ven·om (ĕn-vĕn′əm) *tr.v.* **-omed, -om·ing, -oms. 1.** To make poisonous or noxious. **2.** To embitter. [ME *envenimen*, to poison < OFr. *envenimer* : *en-*, cover with; see EN–[1] + *venim*, venom; see VENOM.]

en·vi·a·ble (ĕn′vē-ə-bəl) *adj.* So desirable as to arouse envy. **—en′vi·a·bly** *adv.*

en·vi·ous (ĕn′vē-əs) *adj.* **1.** Feeling, expressing, or characterized by envy. See Syns at **jealous. 2.** *Archaic.* Eager to emulate; emulous. **—en′vi·ous·ly** *adv.* **—en′vi·ous·ness** *n.*

en·vi·ron (ĕn-vī′rən, -vī′ərn) *tr.v.* **-roned, -ron·ing, -rons.** To encircle; surround. [ME *envirounen* < OFr. *environner* < *environ*, round about : *en-*, in; see EN–[1] + *viron*, circle (< *virer*, to turn; see VEER[1]).]

en·vi·ron·ment (ĕn-vī′rən-mənt, -vī′ərn-) *n.* **1.** The conditions that surround one; surroundings. **2.** The totality of circumstances around an organism or a group of organisms, esp.: **a.** The combination of external conditions that affect organisms. **b.** The social and cultural conditions affecting an individual or a community.

en·vi·ron·men·tal (ĕn-vī′rən-mĕn′tl, -vī′ərn-) *adj.* **1.** Of or relating to the environment. **2.** Relating to or concerned with the ecological impact of altering the environment. **3.** *Medic.* Of or relating to potentially harmful factors originating in the environment. **—en·vi′ron·men′tal·ly** *adv.*

en·vi·ron·men·tal·ism (ĕn-vī′rən-mĕn′tl-ĭz′əm, -vī′ərn-) *n.* **1.** Advocacy for or work toward protecting the natural environment. **2.** The theory that environment rather than heredity is the primary influence on intellectual growth and cultural development. **—en·vi′ron·men′tal·ist** *n.*

en·vi·rons (ĕn-vī′rənz, -vī′ərnz) *pl.n.* **1.** A surrounding area, esp. of a city. **2.** Surroundings; environment. [Fr. < OFr., pl. of *environ*, circuit < *environ*, round about. See ENVIRON.]

en·vis·age (ĕn-vĭz′ĭj) *tr.v.* **-aged, -ag·ing, -ag·es. 1.** To conceive an image of, esp. as a future possibility. **2.** To consider or regard in a certain way. [Fr. *envisager* : OFr. *en-*, in; see EN–[1] + OFr. *visage*, face; see VISAGE.]

en·vi·sion (ĕn-vĭzh′ən) *tr.v.* **-sioned, -sion·ing, -sions.** To picture in the mind; imagine.

en·voy[1] (ĕn′voi′, ŏn′-) *n.* **1.** A representative of a government sent on a diplomatic mission. **2.** A minister plenipotentiary assigned to a foreign embassy, ranking below the ambassador. **3.** A messenger; an agent. [Fr. *envoyé*, messenger < p.part. of *envoyer*, to send < OFr. *envoier* < LLat. *inviāre*, to be on the way : Lat. *in-*, in, on; see EN–[1] + Lat. *via*, way; see **wegh-***.]

en·voy[2] also **en·voi** (ĕn′voi′, ŏn′-) *n.* **1.** A short closing stanza in certain verse forms, such as the ballade or sestina. **2.** The concluding portion of a prose work or a play. [ME *envoie* < OFr. < *envoier*, to send. See ENVOY[1].]

en·vy (ĕn′vē) *n.*, *pl.* **-vies. 1.a.** A feeling of discontent and resentment aroused by desire for the possessions or qualities of another. **b.** The object of such feeling. **2.** *Obsolete.* Malevolence. *—tr.v.* **-vied, -vy·ing, -vies. 1.** To feel envy toward. **2.** To regard with envy. [ME *envie* < OFr. < Lat. *invidia* < *invidus*, envious < *invidēre*, to envy : *in-*, in, on; see EN–[1] + *vidēre*, to see; see **weid-***.] **—en′vi·er** *n.*

Syns: *envy, begrudge, covet.* These verbs mean to feel resentful or painful desire for another's advantages or possessions. *Envy*, the most general, combines discontent, resentment, and desire: "*When I peruse . . . the victories of mighty generals, I do not envy the generals*" (Walt Whitman). *Begrudge* stresses ill will and reluctance to acknowledge another's right or claim: *begrudged him success. Covet* stresses a secret or culpable longing for something to which one has no right: *coveted my award.*

en·wind (ĕn-wīnd′) also **in·wind** (ĭn-) *tr.v.* **-wound** (-wound′), **-wind·ing, -winds.** To wind around or about.

en·womb (ĕn-wo͞om′) *tr.v.* **-wombed, -womb·ing, -wombs.** To enclose in or as if in a womb.

en·wrap (ĕn-răp′) also **in·wrap** (ĭn-) *tr.v.* **-wrapped, -wrap·ping, -wraps. 1.a.** To wrap up; enclose. **b.** To envelop. **2.** To absorb completely; engross.

en·wreathe (ĕn-rēth′) also **in·wreathe** (ĭn-) *tr.v.* **-wreathed, -wreath·ing, -wreathes.** To surround with or as if with a wreath.

en·zo·ot·ic (ĕn′zō-ŏt′ĭk) *adj.* Affecting or peculiar to animals of a specific geographic area. Used of a disease. *—n.* An enzootic disease. [EN–[2] + ZO(O)– + –OTIC.]

en·zyme (ĕn′zīm) *n.* Any of numerous proteins or conjugated proteins produced by living organisms and functioning as biochemical catalysts. [Ger. *Enzym* < Med.Gk. *enzumos*, leavened : Gk. *en-*, in; see EN–[2] + Gk *zumē*, leaven, yeast.] **—en′zy·mat′ic** (-zə-măt′ĭk), **en·zy′mic** (-zī′mĭk, -zĭm′ĭk) *adj.* **—en′zy·mat′i·cal·ly, en·zy′mi·cal·ly** *adv.*

en·zy·mol·o·gy (ĕn′zə-mŏl′ə-jē) *n.* The branch of science that deals with enzymes. **—en′zy·mol′o·gist** *n.*

EO *abbr.* Executive order.

e.o. *abbr. Lat.* Ex officio (by virtue of office).

eo– *pref.* Most primitive; earliest: *eohippus.* [< Gk. *ēōs*, dawn. See **aus-***.]

E·o·cene (ē′ə-sēn′) *adj.* Of or relating to the second oldest of the five major epochs of the Tertiary Period, characterized by the rise of mammals. See table at **geologic time.** *—n.* The Eocene Epoch or its deposits.

e·o·hip·pus (ē′ō-hĭp′əs) *n.* A small herbivorous extinct mammal of the genus *Hyracotherium* (or *Eohippus*) from the Eocene Epoch of the western United States, related ancestrally to the horse. [NLat. : EO– + Gk. *hippos*, horse; see **ekwo-***.]

e·o·li·an also **ae·o·li·an** (ē-ō′lē-ən, ē-ōl′yən) *adj.* Relating to, caused by, or carried by the wind. [< AEOLUS.]

e·o·lith (ē′ə-lĭth′) *n.* A crude stone artifact, such as a flint.

E·o·lith·ic (ē′ə-lĭth′ĭk) *adj.* Of or relating to the postulated earliest period of human culture preceding the Lower Paleolithic.

E·o·lus (ē-ō′ləs), **Mount.** A peak, 4,295.3 m (14,083 ft), in the San Juan Mts. of SW CO.

e.o.m. *abbr.* End of month.

e·on also **ae·on** (ē′ŏn′, ē′ən) *n.* **1.** An indefinitely long period of time; an age. **2.** The longest division of geologic time, containing two or more eras. [LLat. *aeōn* < Gk. *aiōn*. See **aiw-***.]

e•o•ni•an also **ae•o•ni•an** (ē-ō′nē-ən) *adj.* Of, relating to, or constituting an eon.

E•os (ē′ŏs′) *n. Gk. Myth.* The goddess of the dawn. [Gk. *Ēōs* < *ēōs*, dawn. See **aus-***.]

e•o•sin (ē′ə-sən) *n.* **1.** A red crystalline powder, $C_{20}H_8O_5Br_4$, used in textile dyeing and ink manufacturing. **2.** The red sodium or potassium salt of this powder, used in biology to stain cells. [Gk. *ēōs*, dawn (from its color); see **aus-*** + -IN.]

e•o•sin•o•phil (ē′ə-sĭn′ə-fĭl′) also **e•o•sin•o•phile** (-fīl′) *n.* **1.** A type of white blood cell containing cytoplasmic granules easily stained by eosin or other acid dyes. **2.** A microorganism, cell, or histological element easily stained by eosin or other acid dyes. —**e′o•sin′o•phil′**, **e′o•sin′o•phil′ic**, **e′o•si•noph′i•lous** (ē′ō-sĭ-nŏf′ə-ləs) *adj.*

e•o•sin•o•phil•i•a (ē′ə-sĭn′ə-fĭl′ē-ə) *n.* An increase in the number of eosinophils in the blood.

–eous *suff.* Having the nature of; resembling: *gaseous.* [ME < OFr. *-eux, -eus* (< Lat. *-ōsus*) and < Lat. *-eus*.]

Ep *abbr. Bible.* Ephesians.

EP *abbr.* **1.** European plan. **2.** Extended play.

ep– *pref.* Var. of **epi–**.

EPA *abbr.* Environmental Protection Agency.

e•pact (ē′păkt′) *n.* The period of time necessary to bring the solar calendar into harmony with the lunar calendar. [Fr. *épacte* < LLat. *epacta* < Gk. *epaktē (hēmera)*, intercalary (day), fem. of *epaktos*, brought in, inserted < *epagein*, to bring in, introduce : *ep-, epi-*, epi- + *agein*, to lead; see **ag-***.]

E•pam•i•non•das (ĭ-păm′ə-nŏn′dəs). 418?–362 B.C. Theban general who defeated Spartan forces at Leuctra (371).

ep•ar•chy (ĕp′är′kē) *n., pl.* **-chies.** A diocese of an Eastern Orthodox Church. [Gk. *eparkhia*, provincial government < *eparkhein*, to rule over : *ep-, epi-*, epi- + *arkhein*, to rule.]

ep•au•let also **ep•au•lette** (ĕp′ə-lĕt′, ĕp′ə-lĕt′) *n.* A shoulder ornament, esp. a fringed strap worn on military uniforms. [Fr. *épaulette*, dim. of *épaule*, shoulder < OFr. *espaule* < LLat. *spatula*, shoulder blade. See ESPALIER.]

é•pée also **e•pee** (ā-pā′, ĕp′ā) *n.* **1.** A fencing sword with a bowl-shaped guard and a long narrow fluted blade with no cutting edge and a blunted point. **2.** The art or sport of fencing with an épée. [Fr. < OFr. *espee* < Lat. *spatha*, broad double-edged sword. See SPATULA.] —**é•pée′ist** *n.*

ep•ei•rog•e•ny (ĕp′ī-rŏj′ə-nē) *n., pl.* **-nies.** Uplift or depression of the earth's crust, affecting large areas of land or ocean bottom. [Gk. *ēpeiros*, continent + -GENY.] —**e•pei′ro•gen′ic** (ĭ-pī′rō-jĕn′ĭk) *adj.* —**e•pei′ro•gen′i•cal•ly** *adv.*

e•pen•the•sis (ĭ-pĕn′thĭ-sĭs) *n., pl.* **-ses** (-sēz′). The insertion of a sound in the middle of a word. [LLat. < Gk. < *epentithenai*, to insert : *ep-, epi-*, epi- + *en-*, in; see EN–² + *tithenai*, to place; see **dhē-***.] —**ep′en•thet′ic** (ĕp′ĭn-thĕt′ĭk) *adj.*

e•pergne (ĭ-pûrn′, ā-pârn′) *n.* A large table centerpiece consisting of a frame with extended arms or branches supporting holders, as for flowers. [Perh. alteration of Fr. *épargne*, a saving < *épargner*, to save < OFr. *espargnier*, of Gmc. orig.]

ep•ex•e•ge•sis (ĕp-ĕk′sə-jē′sĭs) *n.* Additional explanation or explanatory material. [Gk. *epexēgēsis* < *epexēgeisthai*, to explain in detail : *ep-, epi-*, epi- + *exēgeisthai*, to explain; see EXEGESIS.] —**ep•ex′e•get′ic** (-jĕt′ĭk), **ep•ex′e•get′i•cal** *adj.* —**ep•ex′e•get′i•cal•ly** *adv.*

Eph. *abbr. Bible.* Ephesians.

e•phah also **e•pha** (ē′fə, ĕf′ä) *n.* An ancient Hebrew unit of dry measure, equal to 1⁄10 homer or about one bushel (35 liters). [Heb. *'êpâ*, prob. < Egypt. *'pt.*]

e•phebe (ĕf′ēb′, ĭ-fēb′) also **e•phe•bus** (ĭ-fē′bəs) *n., pl.* **e•phebes** also **e•phe•bi** (ĭ-fē′bī). A youth between 18 and 20 in ancient Greece. [Lat. *ephēbus* < Gk. *ephēbos* : *ep-, epi-*, epi- + *hēbē*, early manhood.] —**e•phe′bic** *adj.*

e•phed•rine (ĭ-fĕd′rĭn, ĕf′ĭ-drēn′) *n.* An odorless powdered or crystalline alkaloid, $C_{10}H_{15}NO$, used to treat allergies and asthma. [Lat. *ephedra*, horsetail (< Gk. *ephedros*, sitting upon : *ep-, epi-*, epi- + *hedra*, seat; see **sed-***) + -INE².]

e•phem•er•al (ĭ-fĕm′ər-əl) *adj.* **1.** Lasting for a markedly brief time. **2.** Living or lasting only for a day. —*n.* A markedly short-lived thing. [< Gk. *ephēmeros* : *ep-, epi-*, epi- + *hēmera*, day.] —**e•phem′er•al′i•ty**, **e•phem′er•al•ness** *n.* —**e•phem′er•al•ly** *adv.*

e•phem•er•id (ĭ-fĕm′ər-ĭd) *n.* An insect of the order Ephemeroptera; a mayfly. [< NLat. *Ephemeridae*, former order name < Gk. *ephēmeron*, mayfly. See EPHEMERON.]

e•phem•er•is (ĭ-fĕm′ər-ĭs) *n., pl.* **eph•e•mer•i•des** (ĕf′ə-mĕr′ə-dēz′). A table giving the coordinates of a celestial body at a number of specific times during a given period. [LLat. *ephēmeris* < Gk., diary < *ephēmeros*, daily. See EPHEMERAL.]

ephemeris time *n.* A system for the measurement of time based on the orbital positions of the earth, moon, and planets.

e•phem•er•on (ĭ-fĕm′ə-rŏn′) *n., pl.* **-er•a** (-ər-ə) or **-er•ons.** **1.** A short-lived thing. **2. ephemera** Printed matter of passing interest. [Gk. *ephēmeron*, mayfly < neut. of *ephēmeros*, daily, short-lived. See EPHEMERAL.]

E•phe•sian (ĭ-fē′zhən) *n.* **1.** A native or inhabitant of Ephesus. **2. Ephesians.** *(used with a sing. v.)* See table at **Bible.** [< Lat. *Ephesiī*, inhabitants of Ephesus < Gk. *Ephesioi* < *Ephesos*, Ephesus.] —**E•phe′sian** *adj.*

Eph•e•sus (ĕf′ĭ-səs). An ancient city of Greek Asia Minor in W Turkey. Its temple, dedicated to Artemis, or in Roman times Diana, was one of the Seven Wonders of the World.

eph•od (ĕf′ŏd′, ē′fŏd′) *n.* An upper garment of the ancient Hebrew high priest. [ME < LLat. < Heb. *'ēpôd.*]

eph•or (ĕf′ôr′, -ər) *n., pl.* **-ors** or **-o•ri** (-ə-rī′). One of a body of five elected magistrates exercising supervisory power over the kings of Sparta. [Lat. *ephorus* < Gk. *ephoros* < *ephoran*, to oversee : *ep-, epi-*, epi- + *horan*, to see; see **wer-³***.]

epi– or **ep–** *pref.* **1.** On; upon: *epiphyte.* **2.** Over; above: *epicenter.* **3.** Around: *epicarp.* **4.** Close to; near: *epicalyx.* **5.** Besides: *epiphenomenon.* **6.** After: *epilogue.* [Gk. < *epi*, upon. See **epi***.]

ep•i•blast (ĕp′ə-blăst′) *n. Embryol.* The outer layer of a blastula that gives rise to the ectoderm after gastrulation. —**ep′i•blast′ic** *adj.*

e•pib•o•ly (ĭ-pĭb′ə-lē) *n. Embryol.* The growth of a rapidly dividing group of cells around a more slowly dividing group of cells, as in the formation of a gastrula. [Gk. *epibolē*, a laying on < *epiballein*, to throw on : *epi-*, epi- + *ballein*, to throw; see **gʷelə-***.] —**ep′i•bol′ic** (ĕp′ə-bŏl′ĭk) *adj.*

ep•ic (ĕp′ĭk) *n.* **1.** An extended narrative poem in elevated or dignified language, celebrating the feats of a legendary or traditional hero. **2.** A literary or dramatic composition resembling an epic. **3.** A series of events considered appropriate to an epic. —*adj.* **1.** Of, constituting, or suggestive of a literary epic. **2.** Surpassing the usual or ordinary, esp. in scope or size. **3.** Heroic and impressive in quality. [< Lat. *epicus*, epic < Gk. *epikos* < *epos*, song. See **wekʷ-***.]

ep•i•ca•lyx (ĕp′ĭ-kā′lĭks, -kăl′ĭks) *n., pl.* **-ca•lyx•es** or **-ca•ly•ces** (-kā′lĭ-sēz′, -kăl′ĭ-). A series of bracts subtending and resembling a calyx, as in the carnation.

ep•i•can•thic fold (ĕp′ĭ-kăn′thĭk) *n.* A fold of skin of the upper eyelid that partially covers the inner corner of the eye.

ep•i•can•thus (ĕp′ĭ-kăn′thəs) *n., pl.* **-thi** (-thī, -thē). See **epicanthic fold.** [NLat. : EPI– + CANTHUS.]

ep•i•car•di•um (ĕp′ĭ-kär′dē-əm) *n., pl.* **-di•a** (-dē-ə). The inner layer of the pericardium that is in actual contact with the surface of the heart. [NLat. : EPI– + Gk. *kardia*, heart; see **kerd-***.] —**ep′i•car′di•al** *adj.*

ep•i•carp (ĕp′ĭ-kärp′) *n. Bot.* See **exocarp.**

ep•i•cene (ĕp′ĭ-sēn′) *adj.* **1.** Belonging to or resembling both the male and the female. **2.** Effeminate; unmanly. **3.** Sexless; neuter. **4.** *Ling.* Having a single noun form for both the male and the female. —*n.* **1.** One that is epicene. **2.** *Ling.* An epicene word. [ME, having one noun form for either gender < Lat. *epicoenus* < Gk. *epikoinos*, in common : *epi-*, epi- + *koinos*, common; see **kom***.] —**ep′i•cen′ism** *n.*

ep•i•cen•ter (ĕp′ĭ-sĕn′tər) *n.* **1.** The point of the earth's surface directly above the focus of an earthquake. **2.** A focal point: *at the epicenter of the crisis.* —**ep′i•cen′tral** *adj.*

ep•i•chlo•ro•hy•drin (ĕp′ĭ-klôr′ə-hī′drĭn, -klōr′-) *n.* A colorless liquid, C_3H_5OCl, used as a solvent in making resins.

ep•i•con•dyle (ĕp′ĭ-kŏn′dīl, -dl) *n.* A rounded projection at the end of a bone, located on or above a condyle and usu. serving as a place of attachment for ligaments and tendons.

ep•i•cot•yl (ĕp′ĭ-kŏt′l) *n.* The stem of a seedling or an embryo located between the cotyledons and the first true leaves.

ep•i•crit•ic (ĕp′ĭ-krĭt′ĭk) *adj.* Of or relating to sensory nerve fibers that enable the perception of slight differences in the intensity of stimuli, esp. touch or temperature. [Gk. *epikritikos*, decisive < *epikritēs*, decider < *epikrinein*, to decide : *epi-*, epi- + *krinein*, to judge; see **krei-***.]

epic simile *n.* An extended simile elaborated in great detail.

Ep•ic•te•tus (ĕp′ĭk-tē′təs). A.D. 55?–135? Greek Stoic philosopher who believed that one should act in life as one would at a banquet, by taking a polite portion of all that is offered.

ep•i•cure (ĕp′ĭ-kyo͝or′) *n.* **1.** A person with refined taste, esp. in food and wine. **2.** A person devoted to sensuous pleasure and luxurious living. See Usage Note at **gourmet.** [ME, an Epicurean < Med.Lat. *epicūrus* < Lat. *Epicūrus*, Epicurus < Gk. *Epikouros.*]

ep•i•cu•re•an (ĕp′ĭ-kyo͝o-rē′ən, -kyo͝or′ē-) *adj.* **1.** Devoted to the pursuit of pleasure. **2.** Suited to an epicure's tastes. **3. Epicurean.** Of or relating to Epicurus or Epicureanism. —*n.* **1.** A devotee of epicurean living; an epicure. **2. Epicurean.** A follower of Epicurus. [ME *Epicurien* < *Epicure*. See EPICURE.]

Ep•i•cu•re•an•ism (ĕp′ĭ-kyo͝o-rē′ə-nĭz′əm, -kyo͝or′ē-) *n.* The philosophy of Epicurus that considered happiness, or the avoidance of pain, to be the highest good.

ep•i•cur•ism (ĕp′ĭ-kyo͝o-rĭz′əm, ĕp′ĭ-kyo͝or′ĭz-əm) *n.* The beliefs, tastes, or lifestyle of an epicure.

Ep•i•cu•rus (ĕp′ĭ-kyo͝or′əs). 341?–270 B.C. Greek philosopher who founded the school of Epicureanism in c. 306.

ep•i•cu•ti•cle (ĕp′ĭ-kyo͞o′tĭ-kəl) *n.* The outermost layer of cuticle of an arthropod exoskeleton, composed mostly of wax.

ep•i•cy•cle (ĕp′ĭ-sī′kəl) *n.* **1.** In Ptolemaic cosmology, a small circle, the center of which moves on the circumference of a larger circle at whose center is Earth and the circumference of which describes the orbit of a planet. **2.** *Math.* A circle whose

epaulet

ă pat	oi boy
ā pay	ou out
âr care	o͝o took
ä father	o͞o boot
ĕ pet	ŭ cut
ē be	ûr urge
ĭ pit	th thin
ī pie	*th* this
îr pier	hw which
ŏ pot	zh vision
ō toe	ə about, item
ô paw	

Stress marks:
′ (primary);
′ (secondary), as in
dictionary (dĭk′shə-nĕr′ē)

Jacob Epstein

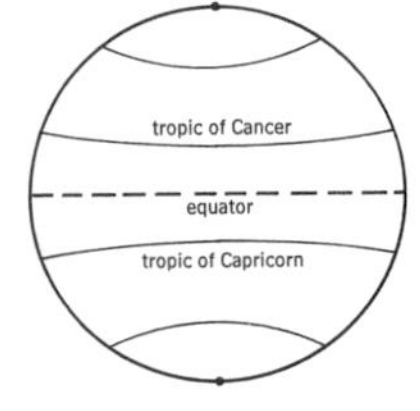

equator

Equatorial Guinea

low shrinkage, used esp. in surface coatings and adhesives. **2.** See **epoxide.** — *tr.v.* **-ied, -y•ing, -ies.** To fasten together with epoxy. [EP(I)- + OXY(GEN).]

Ep•ping Forest (ĕp′ĭng). A former royal hunting preserve of SE England NE of London, now a public park.

EPROM (ē′prŏm′) *n. Comp. Sci.* A programmable read-only memory erasable by exposure to ultraviolet light and reprogrammable. [*e(rasable-)p(rogrammable) r(ead-)o(nly) m(emory).*]

ep•si•lon (ĕp′sə-lŏn′, -lən) *n.* The fifth letter of the Greek alphabet. [Gk. *e psilon*, simple e < *psilos*, simple.]

Ep•som and Ew•ell (ĕp′səm; yo͞o′əl). A municipal borough of SE England near London. The Derby is run annually at Epsom Downs racetrack. Pop. 69,000.

Epsom salts *pl.n.* *(used with a sing. v.)* Hydrated magnesium sulfate, $MgSO_4 \cdot 7H_2O$, used as a cathartic and as an agent to reduce inflammation. [After *Epsom*, former name of Epsom and Ewell, England.]

Ep•stein (ĕp′stīn′), Sir **Jacob.** 1880–1959. Amer.-born British sculptor who is particularly noted for his busts.

Ep•stein-Barr virus (ĕp′stīn-bär′) *n.* A herpes virus that causes infectious mononucleosis and is also associated with various types of human cancers. [After Michael A. *Epstein* and Y.M. *Barr*, 20th-cent. British virologists.]

eq. *abbr.* **1.** Equal. **2.** Equation. **3.** Equivalent.

E.Q. *abbr.* Educational quotient.

eq•ua•ble (ĕk′wə-bəl, ē′kwə-) *adj.* **1.a.** Unvarying; steady. **b.** Free from extremes. **2.** Not easily disturbed; serene. [Lat. *aequābilis* < *aequāre*, to make even < *aequus*, even.] — **eq′ua•bil′i•ty, eq′ua•ble•ness** *n.* — **eq′ua•bly** *adv.*

e•qual (ē′kwəl) *adj.* **1.** Having the same quantity, measure, or value as another. **2.** *Math.* Being the same or identical to in value. **3.a.** Having the same privileges, status, or rights. **b.** Being the same for all members of a group. **4.a.** Having the requisite qualities for a task or situation. **b.** Adequate in extent, amount, or degree. **5.** Impartial; just; equitable. **6.** Tranquil; equable. **7.** Showing or having no variance in proportion, structure, or appearance. — *n.* One that is equal to another. — *tr.v.* **e•qualed, e•qual•ing, e•quals** or **e•qualled, e•qual•ling, e•quals. 1.** To be equal to, esp. in value. **2.** To do, make, or produce something equal to. [ME < Lat. *aequālis* < *aequus*, even, level.] — **e′qual•ly** *adv.*

e•qual•i•tar•i•an (ĭ-kwŏl′ĭ-târ′ē-ən) *adj.* Egalitarian. — **e•qual′i•tar′i•an•ism** *n.*

e•qual•i•ty (ĭ-kwŏl′ĭ-tē) *n., pl.* **-ties. 1.** The state or quality of being equal. **2.** *Math.* A statement, usu. an equation, that one thing equals another. [ME *equalite* < OFr. < Lat. *aequālitās* < *aequālis*, equal. See EQUAL.]

e•qual•ize (ē′kwə-līz′) *v.* **-ized, -iz•ing, -iz•es.** — *tr.* **1.** To make equal: *equalized responsibilities.* **2.** To make uniform. — *intr.* To constitute or induce equality, equilibrium, or balance. — **e′qual•i•za′tion** (ē′kwə-lĭ-zā′shən) *n.*

e•qual•iz•er (ē′kwə-lī′zər) *n.* **1.** One that equalizes, as: **a.** A device for equalizing pressure or strain. **b.** A tone control system designed to compensate for frequency distortion in audio systems. **2.** *Slang.* A deadly weapon, such as a firearm.

equal opportunity *n.* Absence of discrimination, as in the workplace, based on race, color, age, gender, national origin, religion, or mental or physical disability.

equal sign *n.* The symbol (=) used to indicate logical or mathematical equality.

equal temperament *n. Mus.* Modification of the intervals of just intonation in the tuning of instruments of fixed intonation to permit the modulation of harmony.

e•qua•nim•i•ty (ē′kwə-nĭm′ĭ-tē, ĕk′wə-) *n.* The quality of being calm and even-tempered; composure. [Lat. *aequanimitās* < *aequanimus*, even-tempered, impartial : *aequus*, even + *animus*, mind; see **anə-***.]

e•quate (ĭ-kwāt′) *v.* **e•quat•ed, e•quat•ing, e•quates.** — *tr.* **1.** To make equal or equivalent. **2.** To reduce to a standard or average; equalize. **3.** To consider, treat, or depict as equal or equivalent. — *intr.* To be or seem to be equal; correspond. [ME *equaten* < Lat. *aequāre, aequāt-* < *aequus*, even.]

e•qua•tion (ĭ-kwā′zhən, -shən) *n.* **1.** The act or process of equating or of being equated. **2.** The state of being equal. **3.** *Math.* A statement asserting the equality of two expressions, usu. written as a linear array of symbols that are separated into left and right sides and joined by an equal sign. **4.** *Chem.* A representation of a chemical reaction, usu. written as a linear array in which the symbols and quantities of the reactants are separated from those of the products by an equal sign, an arrow, or a set of opposing arrows. **5.** A complex of variable elements or factors. — **e•qua′tion•al** *adj.* — **e•qua′tion•al•ly** *adv.*

e•qua•tor (ĭ-kwā′tər) *n.* **1.a.** The imaginary great circle around the earth's surface, equidistant from the poles and perpendicular to the earth's axis of rotation, dividing the earth into the Northern Hemisphere and the Southern Hemisphere. **b.** A similar great circle drawn on the surface of a celestial body at right angles to the axis of rotation. **2.** The celestial equator. **3.** A circle that divides a sphere or other surface into congruent parts. [ME < Med.Lat. *aequātor (diēī et noctis)*, equalizer (of day and night) < Lat. *aequāre*, to equalize. See EQUATE.]

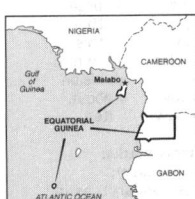

e•qua•to•ri•al (ē′kwə-tôr′ē-əl, -tōr′-, ĕk′wə-) *adj.* **1.a.** Of, relating to, or resembling the earth's equator. **b.** Relating to conditions that exist at the earth's equator. **2.** Having or constituting a telescope mounting with two perpendicular axes, one of which is parallel to the earth's rotational axis. — **e′qua•to′ri•al•ly** *adv.*

E•qua•to•ri•al Guin•ea (ē′kwə-tôr′ē-əl gĭn′ē, -tōr′-, ĕk′wə-). A country of W-central Africa including islands in the Gulf of Guinea; gained independence from Spain in 1968. Cap. Malabo. Pop. 300,000.

equatorial plate *n.* The plane located midway between the poles of a dividing cell during the metaphase stage of mitosis or meiosis and formed from the migration of the chromosomes to the center of the spindle.

eq•uer•ry (ĕk′wə-rē) *n., pl.* **-ries. 1.** A personal attendant to the British royal household. **2.** An officer who supervises the horses belonging to a royal or noble household. [Fr. *écurie*, stable < OFr. *escurie* < *escuier*, squire. See SQUIRE.]

e•ques•tri•an (ĭ-kwĕs′trē-ən) *adj.* **1.** Of or relating to horseback riding or horseback riders. **2.** Depicted or represented on horseback. — *n.* One who rides or performs on horseback. [< Lat. *equester, equestr-* < *eques*, horseman < *equus*, horse. See **ekwo-***.] — **e•ques′tri•an•ism, e•ques′tri•an•ship** *n.*

e•ques•tri•enne (ĭ-kwĕs′trē-ĕn′) *n.* A woman who rides or performs on horseback. [EQUESTR(IAN) + *-ienne*, one pertaining to (< Fr., fem. of *-ien*, -ian).]

equi– *pref.* Equal; equally: *equiangular.* [ME < Lat. *aequi-* < *aequus*, equal.]

e•qui•an•gu•lar (ē′kwē-ăng′gyə-lər, ĕk′wē-) *adj.* Having all angles equal.

e•qui•dis•tant (ē′kwĭ-dĭs′tənt, ĕk′wĭ-) *adj.* Equally distant. — **e′qui•dis′tance** (-təns) *n.* — **e′qui•dis′tant•ly** *adv.*

e•qui•lat•er•al (ē′kwə-lăt′ər-əl, ĕk′wə-) *adj.* Having all sides or faces equal. — *n.* **1.** A side exactly equal to others. **2.** An equilateral geometric figure. — **e′qui•lat′er•al•ly** *adv.*

e•quil•i•brate (ĭ-kwĭl′ə-brāt′) *v.* **-brat•ed, -brat•ing, -brates.** — *intr.* To be in or bring about equilibrium. — *tr.* To maintain in or bring into equilibrium. — **e•quil′i•bra′tion** *n.* — **e•quil′i•bra•to′ry** (-brə-tôr′ē, -tōr′ē) *adj.*

e•quil•i•bra•tor (ĭ-kwĭl′ə-brā′tər) *n.* A device that brings about and helps maintain equilibrium.

e•quil•i•brist (ĭ-kwĭl′ə-brĭst) *n.* A person who performs feats of balance. [Fr. *équilibriste* < *équilibre*, equilibrium < Lat. *aequilībrium.* See EQUILIBRIUM.] — **e•quil′i•bris′tic** *adj.*

e•qui•lib•ri•um (ē′kwə-lĭb′rē-əm, ĕk′wə-) *n., pl.* **-ri•ums** or **-ri•a** (-rē-ə). **1.** A condition in which all acting influences are canceled by others, resulting in a stable, balanced, or unchanging system. **2.** Mental or emotional balance; poise. **3.** *Phys.* The state of a body or physical system at rest or in unaccelerated motion in which the resultant of all forces acting on it is zero and the sum of all torques about any axis is zero. **4.** *Chem.* The state of a chemical reaction in which its forward and reverse reactions occur at equal rates so that the concentration of the reactants and products does not change with time. [Lat. *aequilībrium* : *aequi-*, equi- + *lībra*, balance.]

e•qui•mo•lar (ē′kwə-mō′lər, ĕk′wə-) *adj. Chem.* Having an equal number of moles.

e•quine (ē′kwīn′, ĕk′wīn′) *adj.* **1.** Of, relating to, or characteristic of a horse. **2.** Of or belonging to the family Equidae, which includes horses and zebras. [Lat. *equinus* < *equus*, horse. See **ekwo-***.] — **e′quine′** *n.*

e•qui•noc•tial (ē′kwə-nŏk′shəl, ĕk′wə-) *adj.* **1.** Relating to an equinox. **2.** Relating to the celestial equator. — *n.* **1.** A violent wind and rain storm at or near the time of the equinox. **2.** See **celestial equator.** [ME *equinoxial* < OFr. < Lat. *aequinoctiālis* < *aequinoctium*, equinox. See EQUINOX.]

equinoctial circle *n.* See **celestial equator.**

e•qui•nox (ē′kwə-nŏks′, ĕk′wə-) *n.* **1.** Either of two points on the celestial sphere at which the ecliptic intersects the celestial equator. **2.** Either of the two times during a year when the sun crosses the celestial equator and when day and night are of approximately equal length. [ME < OFr. *equinoxe* < Med.Lat. *aequinoxium* < Lat. *aequinoctium* : *aequi-*, equi- + *nox, noct-*, night; see **nekʷ-t-***.]

e•quip (ĭ-kwĭp′) *tr.v.* **e•quipped, e•quip•ping, e•quips. 1.a.** To supply with necessities such as provisions. **b.** To furnish with the qualities necessary for performance. **2.** To dress up. [Fr. *équiper* < OFr. *esquiper*, of Gmc. orig.]

equip. *abbr.* Equipment.

eq•ui•page (ĕk′wə-pĭj) *n.* **1.** Equipment or furnishings. **2.a.** A horse-drawn carriage with attendants. **b.** The carriage itself. **3.** *Archaic.* A retinue, as of a royal personage. **4.** *Archaic.* **a.** A set of small household articles, such as a tea service. **b.** A collection of small articles for personal use. [Fr. *équipage* < *équiper*, to equip. See EQUIP.]

e•quip•ment (ĭ-kwĭp′mənt) *n.* **1.** The act of equipping or the state of being equipped. **2.** Something with which a person, an organization, or a thing is equipped. **3.** The rolling stock esp. of a transportation system. **4.** The qualities or traits that make up the mental and emotional resources of an individual.

e•qui•poise (ē′kwə-poiz′, ĕk′wə-) *n.* **1.** Equality in distribution, as of weight or emotional forces; equilibrium. **2.** A counterpoise; a counterbalance.

e•qui•pol•lent (ē′kwə-pŏl′ənt, ĕk′wə-) *adj.* **1.** Equal in force, power, effectiveness, or significance. **2.** *Logic.* Validly derived from each other; deducible. **3.** Equivalent. —*n.* An equivalent. [ME < OFr. < Lat. *aequipollēns, aequipollent-* : *aequi-*, equi- + *pollēns*, pr.part. of *pollēre*, to be powerful.] —**e′qui•pol′lence** *n.* —**e′qui•pol′lent•ly** *adv.*

e•qui•pon•der•ance (ē′kwə-pŏn′dər-əns, ĕk′wə-) *n.* Equality of weight; equipoise. —**e′qui•pon′der•ant** *adj.*

e•qui•pon•der•ate (ē′kwə-pŏn′də-rāt′, ĕk′wə-) *tr.v.* **-at•ed, -at•ing, -ates. 1.** To counterbalance. **2.** To give equal balance or weight to. [Med.Lat. *aequiponderāre, aequiponderāt-* : Lat. *aequi-*, equi- + Lat. *ponderāre*, to weigh; see **(s)pen-***.]

e•qui•po•ten•tial (ē′kwə-pə-tĕn′shəl, ĕk′wə-) *adj.* **1.** Having equal potential. **2.** *Phys.* Having the same electric potential at every point.

e•qui•prob•a•ble (ē′kwə-prŏb′ə-bəl, ĕk′wə-) *adj.* Having equal mathematical or logical probability.

eq•ui•se•tum (ĕk′wə-sē′təm) *n., pl.* **-tums** or **-ta** (-tə). See **horsetail.** [Lat. *equisaetum*, horsetail : *equus*, horse; see **ekwo-*** + *saeta*, bristle, stiff hair.]

eq•ui•ta•ble (ĕk′wĭ-tə-bəl) *adj.* Marked by or having equity; just and impartial. See Syns at **fair[1]**. [Fr. *équitable* < OFr. < *equite*, equity. See EQUITY.] —**eq′ui•ta•ble•ness** *n.* —**eq′ui•ta•bly** *adv.*

eq•ui•tant (ĕk′wĭ-tənt) *adj.* Overlapping at the base to form a flat fanlike arrangement in two ranks, as the leaves of some irises. [Lat. *equitāns, equitant-*, pr.part. of *equitāre*, to ride horseback < *eques, equit-*, horseman < *equus*, horse. See **ekwo-***.]

eq•ui•ta•tion (ĕk′wĭ-tā′shən) *n.* The art and practice of riding a horse. [Lat. *equitātiō, equitātiōn-* < *equitāre*, to ride horseback. See EQUITANT.]

eq•ui•ty (ĕk′wĭ-tē) *n., pl.* **-ties. 1.** The state, quality, or ideal of being just, impartial, and fair. **2.** Something that is just, impartial, and fair. **3.** *Law.* **a.** Justice applied in circumstances covered by law yet influenced by principles of ethics and fairness. **b.** A system of jurisprudence supplementing and serving to modify the rigor of common law. **c.** An equitable right or claim. **d.** Equity of redemption. **4.** The residual value of a business or property beyond any mortgage thereon and liability therein. **5.a.** The market value of securities less any debt incurred. **b.** Common stock and preferred stock. **6.** Funds provided to a business by the sale of stock. [ME *equite* < OFr. < Lat. *aequitās* < *aequus*, even, fair.]

equity of redemption *n. Law.* The right of one who has mortgaged property to redeem that property upon payment of the sum due within a reasonable time after the due date.

equity stock *n.* Common stock and preferred stock.

equiv. *abbr.* Equivalence; equivalency; equivalent.

e•quiv•a•lence (ĭ-kwĭv′ə-ləns) *n.* The state or condition of being equivalent; equality.

equivalence relation *n. Math.* A reflexive, symmetrical, and transitive relationship between elements of a set that establishes any two of them as equivalent or nonequivalent.

e•quiv•a•len•cy (ĭ-kwĭv′ə-lən-sē) *n., pl.* **-cies.** Equivalence.

e•quiv•a•lent (ĭ-kwĭv′ə-lənt) *adj.* **1.a.** Equal, as in value, force, or meaning. **b.** Having similar or identical effects. **2.** Being essentially equal, all things considered. **3.** *Math.* **a.** Capable of being put into a one-to-one relationship. Used of two sets. **b.** Having similar, corresponding, or congruent parts. **4.** *Chem.* Having the same ability to combine. —*n.* **1.** Something essentially equal to another. **2.** *Chem.* Equivalent weight. [ME < LLat. *aequivalēns, aequivalent-*, pr.part. of *aequivalēre*, to have equal force : Lat. *aequi-*, equi- + Lat. *valēre*, to be strong; see **wal-***.] —**e•quiv′a•lent•ly** *adv.*

equivalent weight *n. Chem.* The weight of a substance that will combine with or replace one mole of hydrogen or one-half mole of oxygen, equal to the atomic weight divided by the valence.

e•quiv•o•cal (ĭ-kwĭv′ə-kəl) *adj.* **1.** Open to two or more interpretations and often intended to mislead; ambiguous. See Syns at **ambiguous. 2.** Of uncertain significance. **3.** Of a doubtful or uncertain nature. [< LLat. *aequivocus* : Lat. *aequi-*, equi- + Lat. *vōx, vōc-*, voice; see **wekʷ-***.] —**e•quiv′o•cal′i•ty** (-kăl′ĭ-tē), **e•quiv′o•cal•ness** *n.* —**e•quiv′o•cal•ly** *adv.*

e•quiv•o•cate (ĭ-kwĭv′ə-kāt′) *intr.v.* **-cat•ed, -cat•ing, -cates. 1.** To use equivocal language intentionally. **2.** To avoid making an explicit statement. [ME *equivocaten* < Med.Lat. *aequivocāre, aequivocāt-* < LLat. *aequivocus*, equivocal. See EQUIVOCAL.] —**e•quiv′o•ca′tor** *n.*

e•quiv•o•ca•tion (ĭ-kwĭv′ə-kā′shən) *n.* **1.** The use of equivocal language. **2.** An equivocal statement or expression.

eq•ui•voque also **eq•ui•voke** (ĕk′wə-vōk′, ē′kwə-) *n.* **1.** An equivocal word, phrase, or expression. **2.** A pun. **3.** A double meaning. [Fr. *équivoque* < LLat. *aequivocus*, ambiguous. See EQUIVOCAL.]

Er The symbol for the element **erbium.**

ER *abbr.* Emergency room.

-er[1] *suff.* **1.a.** One that performs a specified action: *swimmer.* **b.** One that undergoes or is capable of undergoing a specified action: *broiler.* **c.** One that has: *ten-pounder.* **d.** One associated or involved with: *banker.* **2.a.** Native or resident of: *New Yorker.* **b.** One that is: *foreigner.* [ME, partly < OE *-ere* (< Gmc. **-ārjaz*), partly < Anglo-Fr. *-er* (< OFr. *-ier* < Lat. *-ārius*, -ary), and partly < OFr. *-ere, -eor*; see -OR[1].]

-er[2] *suff.* Used to form the comparative degree of adjectives and adverbs: *darker; faster.* [ME < OE *-re, -ra.*]

e•ra (îr′ə, ĕr′ə) *n.* **1.** A period of time as reckoned from a specific point in history. **2.a.** A period of time characterized by particular circumstances, events, or personages. **b.** A point that marks the beginning of such a period of time. **3.** The longest division of geologic time, made up of one or more periods. [LLat. *aera* < Lat., counters, pl. of *aes, aer-*, bronze coin. See **ayes-***.]

ERA *abbr.* **1.** *Baseball.* Earned run average. **2.** Equal Rights Amendment.

e•rad•i•cate (ĭ-răd′ĭ-kāt′) *tr.v.* **-cat•ed, -cat•ing, -cates. 1.** To tear up by the roots. **2.** To get rid of as if by tearing up by the roots: *eradicating poverty.* [ME *eradicaten* < Lat. *ērādīcāre, ērādīcāt-* : *ē-, ex-*, ex- + *rādīx, rādīc-*, root; see **wrād-***.] —**e•rad′i•ca•ble** (-kə-bəl) *adj.* —**e•rad′i•ca′tion** *n.* —**e•rad′i•ca′tive** *adj.* —**e•rad′i•ca′tor** *n.*

equestrian

e•rase (ĭ-rās′) *tr.v.* **e•rased, e•ras•ing, e•ras•es. 1.a.** To remove (something written, for example) by rubbing, wiping, or scraping. **b.** To remove (recorded material) from a magnetic tape or other storage medium. **c.** To remove recorded material from (a magnetic tape, for example). **2.** To remove all traces of. **3.** To remove or destroy as if by wiping out. [Lat. *ērādere, ērās-*, to scratch out : *ē-, ex-*, ex- + *rādere*, to scrape; see **rēd-***.] —**e•ras′a•bil′i•ty** *n.* —**e•ras′a•ble** *adj.*

Syns: *erase, expunge, efface, delete, cancel.* These verbs mean to remove or invalidate something, especially something recorded. To *erase* is to wipe or rub out, literally or figuratively: *erased the equation from the blackboard. Expunge* implies complete removal: *expunged their names from the list. Efface* also refers to the removal of every trace: *tried to efface prejudice from his mind. Delete* is used principally in the sense of removing matter from a manuscript: *deleted expletives from the transcript. Cancel* refers to invalidating by or as if by crossing something out: *cancel a debt.*

e•ras•er (ĭ-rā′sər) *n.* An implement, such as a piece of rubber, used for erasing.

E•ras•mus (ĭ-răz′məs), **Desiderius.** 1466?–1536. Dutch Renaissance scholar and Roman Catholic theologian whose works include *The Praise of Folly* (1509).

E•ras•tus (ĭ-răs′təs), **Thomas.** 1524–83. Swiss Protestant theologian who opposed Calvinism.

e•ra•sure (ĭ-rā′shər) *n.* **1.** The act or an instance of erasing. **2.** The state of being erased.

Er•a•to (ĕr′ə-tō′) *n. Gk. Myth.* The Muse of lyric poetry and mime.

E•ra•tos•the•nes (ĕr′ə-tŏs′thə-nēz′). 3rd cent. B.C. Greek astronomer and geographer who devised a map of the world and estimated the circumference of the earth.

Erasmus

Er•bil (îr′bĭl, ĕr′-). See **Irbil.**

er•bi•um (ûr′bē-əm) *n. Symbol* **Er** A soft rare-earth element, used in metallurgy and nuclear research. Atomic number 68; atomic weight 167.26; melting point 1,497°C; boiling point 2,900°C; specific gravity 9.051; valence 3. See table at **element.** [After *Ytterby*, a town in Sweden.]

ere (âr) *prep.* Previous to; before. —*conj.* Rather than; before. [ME *er* < OE *ǣr.* See **ayer-***.]

Er•e•bus (ĕr′ə-bəs) *n. Gk. Myth.* The region of the underworld through which the dead pass before reaching Hades.

e•rect (ĭ-rĕkt′) *adj.* **1.** Being in an upright position: *an erect posture.* **2.** Vertical, as a straight line or plane. **3.** Being in a stiff, rigid physiological condition. **4.** *Archaic.* Wide-awake; alert. —*tr.v.* **e•rect•ed, e•rect•ing, e•rects. 1.** To construct by assembling. **2.** To raise to a rigid or upright condition. **3.** To fix in an upright position. **4.** To set up; establish. **5.** *Math.* To construct (a perpendicular, for example) from or on a given base. [ME < Lat. *ērēctus*, p.part. of *ērigere*, to set up : *ē-, ex-*, ex- + *regere*, to guide; see **reg-***.] —**e•rect′a•ble** *adj.* —**e•rect′ly** *adv.* —**e•rect′ness** *n.*

e•rec•tile (ĭ-rĕk′təl, -tīl′) *adj.* **1.** Capable of being raised to an upright position. **2.** *Anat.* Of or relating to tissue that is capable of filling with blood and becoming rigid. —**e•rec•til′i•ty** (-tĭl′ĭ-tē) *n.*

e•rec•tion (ĭ-rĕk′shən) *n.* **1.** The act of erecting. **2.** Something erected; a construction. **3.** *Physiol.* **a.** The firm and enlarged condition of a body part or organ when the erectile tissue surrounding it becomes filled with blood, esp. of the penis or clitoris. **b.** The process of filling with blood.

e•rec•tor (ĭ-rĕk′tər) *n.* **1.** One that erects. **2.** *Anat.* A muscle that causes or maintains the erection of a body part.

E region *n.* See **E layer.**

ere•long (âr-lông′, -lŏng′) *adv.* Before long; soon.

er•e•mite (âr′ə-mīt′) *n.* A recluse or hermit, esp. a religious recluse. [ME < LLat. *erēmīta.* See HERMIT.] —**er′e•mit′ic** (-mĭt′ĭk), **er′e•mit′i•cal** *adj.*

ă pat	oi boy
ā pay	ou out
âr care	o͝o took
ä father	o͞o boot
ĕ pet	ŭ cut
ē be	ûr urge
ĭ pit	th thin
ī pie	*th* this
îr pier	hw which
ŏ pot	zh vision
ō toe	ə about, item
ô paw	

Stress marks:
′ (primary);
′ (secondary), as in
dictionary (dĭk′shə-nĕr′ē)

escapement

escritoire
Late 18th-century French

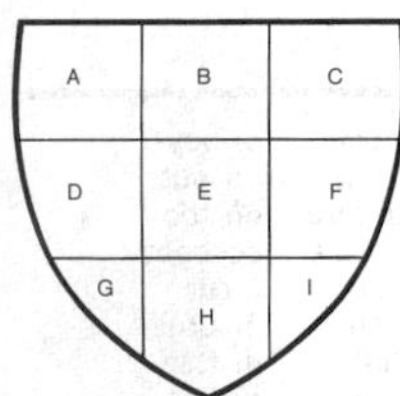

escutcheon
A. Dexter chief
B. Center chief
C. Sinister chief
D. Dexter flank
E. Fess point
F. Sinister flank
G. Dexter base
H. Center base
I. Sinister base

es•cap•ee (ĭ-skā′pē′, ĕs′kā-) *n.* One that has escaped, esp. an escaped prisoner. See Usage Note at **–ee**[1].

es•cape•ment (ĭ-skāp′mənt) *n.* **1.** A mechanism consisting in general of an escape wheel and an anchor, used esp. in timepieces to control movement of the wheel and provide periodic energy impulses to a pendulum or balance. **2.** A mechanism, as in a typewriter, that controls the lateral movement of the carriage. **3.a.** An escape. **b.** A means or way of escape.

escape velocity *n.* The minimum velocity that a body must have to overcome the gravitational attraction of another.

escape wheel *n.* The rotating notched wheel periodically engaged and disengaged by the anchor in an escapement.

es•cap•ism (ĭ-skā′pĭz′əm) *n.* The tendency to escape from daily reality or routine by indulging in daydreaming, fantasy, or entertainment. **—es•cap′ist** *adj.* **—es•cap′ist** *n.*

es•cap•ol•o•gy (ĕs′kā-pŏl′ə-jē) *n.* The art, skill, or practice of escaping. **—es′cap•ol′o•gist** *n.*

es•car•got (ĕs′kär-gō′) *n., pl.* **-gots** (-gō′). An edible snail, esp. one prepared as an appetizer or entrée. [Fr. < OFr. < OProv. *escaragol.*]

es•ca•role (ĕs′kə-rōl′) *n.* A variety of endive *(Cichorium endivia)* having leaves with irregular frilled edges and often used in salads. [Fr. < OFr. *scariole* < LLat. *ēscāriola*, chicory < Lat. *ēscārius*, of food < *ēsca*, food < *edere*, to eat. See **ed-***.]

es•carp (ĭ-skärp′) *n.* **1.** A steep slope or cliff; an escarpment. **2.** The inner wall of a ditch or trench dug around a fortification. —*tr.v.* **-carped, -carp•ing, -carps. 1.** To cause to form a steep slope. **2.** To furnish with an escarp. [Fr. *escarpe* < Ital. *scarpa*. See SCARP.]

es•carp•ment (ĭ-skärp′mənt) *n.* **1.** A steep slope or long cliff caused by erosion or faulting separating two level areas of differing heights. **2.** A steep slope before a fortification.

–escence *suff.* State; process. Used to form nouns from adjectives in *-escent* or verbs in *-esce*: *fluorescence*. [Fr. < OFr. < Lat. *-ēscentia* < *-ēscēns*, *-ēscent-*, -escent.]

–escent *suff.* **1.** Beginning to be; becoming: *juvenescent*. **2.** Characterized by; resembling: *opalescent*. [Fr. < OFr. < Lat. *-ēscēns*, *-ēscent-*, pr.part. suff. of inchoative verbs in *-ēscere*.]

esch•a•lot (ĕsh′ə-lŏt′) *n.* See **shallot.** [Obsolete Fr. *eschallotte*. See SHALLOT.]

es•char (ĕs′kär′) *n.* A dry scab or slough formed on the skin as a result of a burn or by the action of a corrosive or caustic substance. [ME *escare* < OFr. See SCAR[1].]

es•cha•rot•ic (ĕs′kə-rŏt′ĭk) *adj.* Producing an eschar. —*n.* A caustic or corrosive substance or drug.

es•cha•tol•o•gy (ĕs′kə-tŏl′ə-jē) *n.* **1.** The branch of theology dealing with the end of the world or of humanity. **2.** A belief or doctrine concerning the last things, such as death, the destiny of humanity, the Second Coming, or the Last Judgment. [Gk. *eskhatos*, last; see **eghs*** + -LOGY.] **—es•chat′o•log′i•cal** (ĭ-skăt′l-ŏj′ĭ-kəl, ĕs′kə-tə-lŏj′-) *adj.* **—es•chat′o•log′i•cal•ly** *adv.* **—es′cha•tol′o•gist** *n.*

es•cheat (ĭs-chēt′) *n.* **1.** Reversion of land held under feudal tenure to the manor in the absence of legal heirs or claimants. **2.** *Law.* **a.** Reversion of property to the state in the absence of legal heirs or claimants. **b.** Property that has reverted to the state when no legal heirs or claimants exist. —*intr. & tr.v.* **-cheat•ed, -cheat•ing, -cheats.** *Law.* To revert or cause to revert by escheat. [ME *eschete* < OFr. (< *escheoir*, to fall out) and < Med.Lat. *escheta*, both < VLat. **excadēre*, to fall out : Lat. *ex-*, ex- + Lat. *cadere*, to fall; see **kad-***.] **—es•cheat′a•ble** *adj.*

es•cheat•age (ĭs-chē′tĭj) *n.* *Law.* The right of the state to acquire property by escheat.

es•chew (ĕs-cho͞o′) *tr.v.* **-chewed, -chew•ing, -chews.** To avoid; shun. [ME *escheuen* < OFr. *eschivir*, of Gmc. orig.; akin to SHY[1].] **—es•chew′al** (-əl) *n.*

Es•cof•fier (ĕs-kô-fyā′), **Auguste.** 1846–1935. French chef whose cookery books include *Le Guide Culinaire* (1903).

es•co•lar (ĕs′kə-lär′) *n., pl.* **escolar** or **-lars.** Any of several slender fishes of the family Gempylidae, esp. *Lepidocybium flavobrunneum* of warm marine waters. [Sp., student < LLat. *scholāris*, of a school. See SCHOLAR.]

Es•con•di•do (ĕs′kən-dē′dō). A city of S CA N of San Diego. Pop. 108,635.

Es•co•ri•al (ĕ-skôr′ē-əl, ĕ-skōr′-, ĕs′kô-rē-äl′). A monastery and palace of central Spain near Madrid (built 1563–84).

es•cort (ĕs′kôrt′) *n.* **1.a.** One or more persons accompanying another to guide, protect, or show honor. **b.** A man who is the companion of a woman, esp. on a social occasion. **2.a.** One or more vehicles accompanying another vehicle to guide, protect, or honor its passengers. **b.** One or more warships or planes used to defend or protect other craft from attack. **3.** The state of being escorted. —*tr.v.* (ĭ-skôrt′, ĕ-skôrt′, ĕs′kôrt′) **-cort•ed, -cort•ing, -corts.** To accompany as an escort. See Syns at **accompany.** [Fr. *escorte* < Ital. *scorta* < *scorgere*, to guide < VLat. **excorrigere* : Lat. *ex-*, ex- + Lat. *corrigere*, to set right; see CORRECT.]

es•cri•toire (ĕs′krĭ-twär′) *n.* **1.** A writing table; a desk. **2.** A desk with a top section for books. [Obsolete Fr. < OFr. *escriptoire*, study < Med.Lat. *scriptōrium*. See SCRIPTORIUM.]

es•crow (ĕs′krō′, ĕ-skrō′) *n.* Money, property, a deed, or a bond put into the custody of a third party for delivery to a grantee only after the fulfillment of the conditions specified. —*tr.v.* **-crowed, -crow•ing, -crows.** To place in escrow. **—*idiom.* in escrow.** In trust as an escrow. [AN *escrowe*, var. of OFr. *escroe*, scroll. See SCROLL.]

es•cu•do (ĭ-sko͞o′dō) *n., pl.* **-dos.** See table at **currency.** [Port. and Sp., shield, escudo < Lat. *scūtum*, shield. See **skei-***.]

es•cu•lent (ĕs′kyə-lənt) *adj.* Suitable for eating; edible. [Lat. *ēsculentus* < *ēsca*, food < *edere*, to eat. See **ed-***.] **—es′cu•lent** *n.*

es•cutch•eon (ĭ-skŭch′ən) *n.* **1.** *Her.* A shield or shield-shaped emblem bearing a coat of arms. **2.** An ornamental or protective plate, as for a keyhole. **3.** *Naut.* The plate on the stern of a ship inscribed with the ship's name. **—*idiom.* a blot on (one's) escutcheon.** Dishonor to one's reputation. [ME *escochon* < AN *escuchon* < VLat. **scūtiō*, *scūtiōn-* < Lat. *scūtum*, shield. See **skei-***.] **—es•cutch′eoned** *adj.*

Es•dra•e•lon (ĕs′drā-ē′lŏn, -drə-, ĕz′-), **Plain of.** A fertile plain of N Israel extending from the coastal lowlands near Mt. Carmel to the Jordan R. valley.

Es•dras (ĕz′drəs) *n.* *Bible.* Either of two books of the Septuagint corresponding to the Hebrew books of Ezra and Nehemiah.

ESE *abbr.* East-southeast.

–ese *suff.* **1.** Of, relating to, characteristic of, or originating in a specified place: *Vietnamese*. **2.** Native or inhabitant of: *Taiwanese*. **3.a.** Language or dialect of: *Chinese*. **b.** Literary style or diction of: *journalese*. [ME < Ital. < Lat. *-ēnsis*, originating in.]

es•er•ine (ĕs′ə-rēn′) *n.* See **physostigmine.** [NLat. : Efik *esere*, Calabar bean + -INE[2].]

Es•fa•han (ĕs′fə-hän′). See **Isfahan.**

Esk. *abbr.* Eskimo.

es•ker (ĕs′kər) *n.* A long narrow ridge of coarse gravel deposited by a stream flowing in or under a decaying glacial ice sheet. [Ir.Gael. *eiscir* < OIr. *escir*.]

Es•kils•tu•na (ĕs′kĭl-styo͞o′nə, -nä). A city of SE Sweden W of Stockholm; chartered 1659. Pop. 88,664.

Es•ki•mo (ĕs′kə-mō′) *n., pl.* **Eskimo** or **-mos. 1.** A member of a group of peoples inhabiting the Arctic coastal regions of North America and parts of Greenland and northeast Siberia and generally considered Native Americans in Alaska and Canada. See Usage Note at **Native American. 2.** Any of the languages of the Eskimo peoples. [Fr. *Esquimaux*, poss. < Sp. *esquimao, esquimal* < Montagnais *ayashkimew*, Micmac.] **—Es′ki•mo′an** *adj.*

Eskimo dog *n.* A large dog of a breed used in Arctic regions for pulling sleds and having a thick coat and a plumed tail.

Es•ki•şe•hir (ĕs′kĭ-shə-hîr′). A city of W-central Turkey W of Ankara. Pop. 309,341.

ESL *abbr.* English as a second language.

ESOP (ē′sŏp) *n.* A plan under which the employees of a company or corporation acquire its capital stock. [*E(mployee) S(tock-)O(wnership) P(lan).*]

e•soph•a•gus also **oe•soph•a•gus** (ĭ-sŏf′ə-gəs) *n., pl.* **-gi** (-jī′, -gī′). The muscular tube for the passage of food from the pharynx to the stomach; the gullet. [ME *isophagus* < Med. Lat. < Gk. *oisophagos*.] **—e•soph′a•ge′al** (-jē′əl) *adj.*

es•o•ter•ic (ĕs′ə-tĕr′ĭk) *adj.* **1.a.** Meant for or understood by only a specific group. See Syns at **mysterious. b.** Of or relating to what is known by a restricted number of people. **2.a.** Confined to a small group. **b.** Not publicly disclosed; confidential. [Gk. *esōterikos* < *esōterō*, comp. of *esō*, within. See **en***.] **—es′o•ter′i•cal•ly** *adv.*

es•o•ter•i•ca (ĕs′ə-tĕr′ĭ-kə) *pl.n.* *(used with a sing. or pl. v.)* Esoteric matters or items. [Gk. < neut. pl. of *esōterikos*, esoteric. See ESOTERIC.]

es•o•ter•i•cism (ĕs′ə-tĕr′ĭ-sĭz′əm) *n.* **1.** Esoteric teachings or practices. **2.** The quality or condition of being esoteric.

ESP (ē′ĕs-pē′) *n.* Communication or perception by means other than the physical senses. [*e(xtra)s(ensory) p(erception).*]

esp. *abbr.* Especially.

es•pa•drille (ĕs′pə-drĭl′) *n.* A shoe usu. having a fabric upper and a flexible sole, as of rope. [Fr. < Prov. *espardilho*, dim. of *espart*, esparto < Lat. *spartum*. See ESPARTO.]

es•pal•ier (ĭ-spăl′yər, -yā′) *n.* **1.** A tree or shrub trained to grow in a flat plane against a wall, often in a symmetrical pattern. **2.** A trellis or other framework on which an espalier is grown. —*tr.v.* **-iered, -ier•ing, -iers. 1.** To train as or on an espalier. **2.** To provide with an espalier. [Fr. < Ital. *spalliera*, shoulder support < *spalla*, shoulder < LLat. *spatula*, shoulder blade < Lat. See SPATULA.]

es•par•to (ĭ-spär′tō) *n., pl.* **-tos.** A tough wiry grass *(Stipa tenacissima)* of northern Africa, used in making paper and cordage. [Sp. < Lat. *spartum* < Gk. *sparton*, rope.]

es•pe•cial (ĭ-spĕsh′əl) *adj.* **1.** Of special importance or significance; exceptional. **2.** Relating to or directed toward a particular person, group, or purpose. **3.** Peculiar to the individual; characteristic. [ME < OFr. < Lat. *speciālis*, of a kind < *speciēs*, species. See **spek-***.]

es•pe•cial•ly (ĕ-spĕsh′ə-lē, ĭ-spĕsh′-) *adv.* To an extent or degree deserving of special emphasis; particularly.

es•per•ance (ĕs′pər-əns) *n. Obsolete.* Hope. [ME *esperaunce* < OFr. < VLat. **spērantia* < Lat. *spērāns, spērant-*, pr.part. of *spērāre*, to hope. See **spē-***.]

Es•pe•ran•to (ĕs′pə-răn′tō, -rän′-) *n.* An artificial international language with vocabulary based on words common to many European languages and regularized inflections. [After Dr. *Esperanto*, "one who hopes," pseudonym of Ludwik Lejzer Zamenhof (1859–1917), Polish philologist.] **—Es′pe•ran′tist** *adj. & n.*

es•pi•al (ĭ-spī′əl) *n.* **1.** The act of watching or observing; observation. **2.** A taking notice of something; a discovery. **3.** The fact of being seen or noticed. [ME *espiaille* < OFr. < *espier*, to watch. See ESPY.]

es•pi•o•nage (ĕs′pē-ə-näzh′, -nĭj) *n.* The act or practice of spying or of using spies to obtain secret information. [Fr. *espionnage* < *espionner*, to spy < OFr. *espion*, spy < OItal. *spione*, of Gmc. orig. See **spek-***.]

Es•pí•ri•tu San•to (ĕ-spîr′ĭ-to͞o sän′tō). An island of the New Hebrides in the S Pacific Ocean.

es•pla•nade (ĕs′plə-näd′, -nād′) *n.* A flat open stretch of pavement or grass, esp. one designed as a promenade along a shore. [Fr. < Ital. *spianata* < *spianare*, to level < Lat. *explānāre*, to make plain. See EXPLAIN.]

Es•poo (ĕs′pō, -pô). A town of S Finland, a suburb of Helsinki. Pop. 152,929.

es•pous•al (ĭ-spou′zəl, -səl) *n.* **1.a.** A betrothal. **b.** A wedding ceremony. **2.** Adoption of an idea or a cause. [ME *espousaille* < sing. of OFr. *espousailles*, betrothal < Lat. *spōnsālia* < neut. pl. of *spōnsālis*, of a betrothal < *spōnsus*, spouse. See SPOUSE.]

es•pouse (ĭ-spouz′) *tr.v.* **-poused, -pous•ing, -pous•es. 1.a.** To take in marriage; marry. **b.** To give (a woman) in marriage. **2.** To give one's loyalty or support to (a cause, for example); adopt. [ME *espousen* < OFr. *espouser* < Lat. *spōnsāre* < *spondēre, spōns-*, to betroth. See **spend-***.] **—es•pous′er** *n.*

es•pres•so (ĭ-sprĕs′ō, ĕ-sprĕs′ō) also **ex•pres•so** (ĭk-sprĕs′ō, ĕk-) *n., pl.* **-sos.** A strong coffee brewed by forcing steam under pressure through darkly roasted powdered coffee beans. [Ital. *(caffè) espresso*, espresso (coffee), p.part. of *esprimere*, to press out < Lat. *exprimere* : *ex-*, ex- + *premere*, to press; see PRESS[1].]

es•prit (ĕ-sprē′) *n.* **1.** Liveliness of mind or spirit. **2.** Esprit de corps. [Fr. < Lat. *spīritus*, spirit. See SPIRIT.]

esprit de corps (də kôr′) *n.* A common spirit of comradeship, enthusiasm, and devotion to a cause among the members of a group. [Fr. : *esprit*, spirit + *de*, of + *corps*, group.]

es•py (ĭ-spī′) *tr.v.* **-pied, -py•ing, -pies.** To catch sight of (something distant, partially hidden, or obscure); glimpse. See Syns at **see**[1]. [ME *espien* < OFr. *espier*, to watch, of Gmc. orig. See **spek-***.]

Esq. *abbr.* Esquire (title).

-esque *suff.* In the manner of; resembling: *Lincolnesque.* [Fr. < Ital. *-esco* < VLat. **-iscus*, of Gmc. orig.]

Es•qui•line (ĕs′kwə-līn′, -lĭn). One of the seven hills of ancient Rome; site of Nero's Golden House and Trajan's *Thermae*, or hot baths. **—Es′qui•line′** *adj.*

Es•qui•mau (ĕs′kə-mō′) *n., pl.* **Esquimau** or **-maux** (-mōz′). An Eskimo. [Fr., sing. of *Esquimaux*, Eskimo. See ESKIMO.]

es•quire (ĕs′kwīr′, ĭ-skwīr′) *n.* **1.** A man of the English gentry ranking directly below a knight. **2. Esquire.** Used as an honorific usu. in its abbreviated form, esp. after the name of an attorney or a consular officer: *Jane Doe, Esq.* **3.** In medieval times, a candidate for knighthood who served a knight as an attendant and a shield bearer. **4.** *Archaic.* An English country gentleman; a squire. [ME *esquier* < OFr. *escuier* < LLat. *scūtārius*, shield bearer < Lat. *scūtum*, shield. See **skei-***.]

ess (ĕs) *n.* The letter *s.*

-ess *suff.* Female: *lioness.* [ME *-esse* < OFr. < LLat. *-issa* < Gk.]

Usage Note: Critics argue that sexist connotations are implicit in the feminine suffix *-ess* in words such as *ambassadress, sculptress, waitress, stewardess, hostess, actress,* and many others, in that the suffix implies that the denoted roles differ as performed by women and men. Thus 65 percent of the Usage Panel rejects *sculptress* in the sentence *Georgia O'Keeffe is not as well known as a sculptress as she is as a painter.* With certain occupations, however, differentiation based on gender may be legitimate: acting, for example, is an occupation in which the parts one plays may in fact depend on one's sex. Thus 92 percent accepts *actress* in *There are not very many good parts available for older actresses,* though it should be noted that many women prefer to be called *actors.* For most social roles gender is felt to make a legitimate difference, and the suffix is accepted. Thus 87 percent of the Panel accepts *hostess* in the sentence *Mary Ann is such a charming hostess that her parties always go off smoothly.* See Usage Note at **man.**

es•say (ĕs′ā′, ĕ-sā′) *n.* **1.** (ĕs′ā′).**a.** A short literary composition on a single subject, usu. presenting the personal view of the author. **b.** Something resembling such a composition. **2.** A testing or trial of the value or nature of a thing: *an essay of my capabilities.* **3.** An initial attempt or endeavor, esp. a tentative attempt. —*tr.v.* (ĕ-sā′, ĕs′ā′) **-sayed, -say•ing, -says. 1.** To make an attempt at; try. **2.** To subject to a test. [< ME *essayen*, to try < OFr. *essaier* < VLat. **exagiāre*, to weigh out < LLat. *exagium*, a weighing : Lat. *ex-*, ex- + Lat. *agere*, to drive; see **ag-***.] **—es•say′er** *n.*

es•say•ist (ĕs′ā′ĭst) *n.* A writer of essays.

es•say•is•tic (ĕs′ā-ĭs′tĭk) *adj.* **1.** Of or relating to an essay or a writer of essays. **2.** Resembling an essay in nature or quality.

Es•sen (ĕs′ən). A city of W-central Germany N of Cologne; founded in the 9th cent. Pop. 625,705.

es•sence (ĕs′əns) *n.* **1.** The intrinsic or indispensable properties that characterize or identify something. **2.** The most important ingredient; the crucial element. **3.** The inherent unchanging nature of a thing or class of things. **4.a.** An extract that has the fundamental properties of a substance in concentrated form. **b.** Such an extract in a solution of alcohol. **c.** A perfume or scent. **5.** One that has or shows an abundance of a quality as if highly concentrated. **6.** Something that exists, esp. a spiritual or incorporeal entity. **—*idioms.* in essence.** By nature; essentially. **of the essence.** Of the greatest importance; crucial. [ME *essencia* and Fr. *essence*, both < Lat. *essentia* < **essēns*, **essent-*, pr.part. of *esse*, to be. See **es-***.]

Es•sene (ĕs′ēn′, ĭ-sēn′) *n.* A member of an ascetic Jewish sect that existed in ancient Palestine from the second century B.C. to the second century A.D. **—Es•se′ni•an** (ĕ-sē′nē-ən), **Es•sen′ic** (ĕ-sĕn′ĭk) *adj.* **—Es•se′nism** *n.*

es•sen•tial (ĭ-sĕn′shəl) *adj.* **1.** Constituting or being part of the essence of something; inherent. **2.** Basic or indispensable; necessary. See Syns at **indispensable. 3.** *Medic.* Of, relating to, or being a dysfunction or a disease of an unknown cause. **4.** *Biochem.* Being a substance that is required for normal functioning but cannot be synthesized by the body and therefore must be included in the diet. —*n.* **1.** Something fundamental. **2.** Something necessary or indispensable. **—es•sen′ti•al′i•ty** (-shē-ăl′ĭ-tē), **es•sen′tial•ness** *n.* **—es•sen′tial•ly** *adv.*

essential oil *n.* A volatile oil, usu. having the odor or flavor of the plant it is from, used in perfumes and flavorings.

Es•se•qui•bo (ĕs′ĭ-kwē′bō). A river rising on the Brazilian border of S Guyana and flowing c. 965 km (600 mi) generally N to the Atlantic Ocean.

Es•sex (ĕs′ĭks). **1.** A historical region and Anglo-Saxon kingdom of SE England. **2.** A community of NE MD, a suburb of Baltimore. Pop. 40,872.

Essex, 2nd Earl of. See Robert **Devereux.**

Ess•ling•en (ĕs′lĭng-ən). A city of SW Germany on the Neckar R. SE of Stuttgart; founded in the 8th cent. Pop. 86,996.

es•so•nite (ĕs′ə-nīt′) also **hes•so•nite** (hĕs′-) *n.* A brown or yellowish-brown variety of garnet. [Fr. < Gk. *hēssōn*, inferior, comp. of *ēka, hēka*, slightly.]

EST or **E.S.T.** *abbr.* Eastern Standard Time.

est. *abbr.* **1.** Established. **2.** *Law.* Estate. **3.** Estimate.

Est. *abbr. Bible.* Esther.

-est[1] *suff.* Used to form the superlative degree of adjectives and adverbs: *greatest; earliest.* [ME < OE *-est, -ast, -ost.*]

-est[2] or **-st** *suff.* Used to form the archaic second person singular of English verbs: *comest.* [ME < OE *-est, -ast.*]

es•tab•lish (ĭ-stăb′lĭsh) *tr.v.* **-lished, -lish•ing, -lish•es. 1.a.** To set up; found. See Syns at **found**[1]. **b.** To bring about; generate. **2.a.** To place in a secure position or condition; install. **b.** To make firm or secure. **3.** To cause to be recognized and accepted. **4.** To introduce and put (a law, for example) into force. **5.** To prove the validity or truth of. **6.** To make a state institution of (a church). [ME *establishen* < OFr. *establir, establiss-* < Lat. *stabilīre* < *stabilis*, firm. See **stā-***.] **—es•tab′lish•er** *n.*

es•tab•lished church (ĭ-stăb′lĭsht) *n.* A church that a government recognizes and supports as a national institution.

es•tab•lish•ment (ĭ-stăb′lĭsh-mənt) *n.* **1.a.** The act of establishing. **b.** The condition or fact of being established. **2.** Something established, as: **a.** An arranged order or system, esp. a legal code. **b.** A permanent civil, political, or military organization. **c.** An established church. **d.** A place of residence or business with its possessions and staff. **e.** A public or private institution, such as a hospital or school. **3.** Often **Establishment.** An established social order, as: **a.** A group of influential, powerful people in a government or society. **b.** A controlling group in a given field of activity.

es•tab•lish•men•tar•i•an (ĭ-stăb′lĭsh-mən-târ′ē-ən) *adj.* Of, relating to, or supporting a political or social establishment. **—es•tab′lish•men•tar′i•an** *n.* **—es•tab′lish•men•tar′i•an•ism** *n.*

es•ta•mi•net (ĕ-stä′mē-nā′) *n.* A small café. [Fr., prob. < Walloon *staminé*, cowshed < *stamō*, hitching post.]

es•tan•cia (ĕ-stän′syä) *n.* A large estate or cattle ranch in Spanish America. [Sp., room, enclosure, country estate < VLat. **stantia*, something standing < Lat. *stāns, stant-*, pr.part. of *stāre*, to stand. See **stā-***.]

es•tate (ĭ-stāt′) *n.* **1.** A landed property, usu. large in size.

ă pat	oi boy
ā pay	ou out
âr care	o͝o took
ä father	o͞o boot
ĕ pet	ŭ cut
ē be	ûr urge
ĭ pit	th thin
ī pie	*th* this
îr pier	hw which
ŏ pot	zh vision
ō toe	ə about, item
ô paw	

Stress marks:
′ (primary);
′ (secondary), as in
dictionary (dĭk′shə-nĕr′ē)

2. All of one's possessions, esp. the property and debts left at death. **3.** *Law.* The nature and extent of an owner's rights to land or other property. **4.** *Chiefly British.* A housing development. **5.** The situation or circumstances of one's life. **6.** Social position or rank, esp. of high order. **7.** A major social class, such as the nobility, formerly possessing distinct political rights. **8.** *Archaic.* Display of wealth or power; pomp. [ME *estat,* condition < OFr. See STATE.]

Es•tates-Gen•er•al (ĭ-stāts′jĕn′ər-əl) *pl.n.* See **States-General.** [Transl. of Fr. *états généraux.*]

estate tax *n.* A tax imposed on the right to transfer property by inheritance and assessed on the net value of a decedent's estate before distribution to the heirs.

Es•te (ĕs′tā). Italian noble family that prospered from the late 10th to the early 19th cent.

es•teem (ĭ-stēm′) *tr.v.* **-teemed, -teem•ing, -teems. 1.** To regard with respect; prize. See Syns at **appreciate. 2.** To regard as; consider. —*n.* **1.** Favorable regard. **2.** *Archaic.* Judgment; opinion. [ME *estemen,* to appraise < OFr. *estimer* < Lat. *aestimāre.*]

es•ter (ĕs′tər) *n.* Any of a class of organic compounds corresponding to the inorganic salts and formed from an organic acid and an alcohol. [Ger., short for *Essigäther* : *Essig,* vinegar (< MHGer. *ezzich* < OHGer. *ezzih* < Lat. *acētum;* see **ak-***) + *Äther,* ether (< Lat. *aethēr;* see ETHER).]

es•ter•ase (ĕs′tə-rās′, -rāz′) *n.* Any of various enzymes that catalyze the hydrolysis of an ester.

Es•ter•ha•zy (ĕs′tər-hä′zē), **(Marie Charles) Ferdinand Walsin.** 1847–1923. French army officer who confessed (1899) to forging the evidence against Alfred Dreyfus.

es•ter•i•fi•ca•tion (ĕ-stĕr′ə-fĭ-kā′shən) *n.* A chemical reaction resulting in the formation of at least one ester product.

es•ter•i•fy (ĕ-stĕr′ə-fī′) *intr. & tr.v.* **-fied, -fy•ing, -fies.** To change or cause to change to an ester.

Es•ther (ĕs′tər) *n. Bible.* **1.** The Jewish queen of Persia who saved her people from massacre. **2.** See table at **Bible.** [Heb. *Estēr* < Pers. *sitareh,* star. See **ster-**[3]*.]

es•the•sia (ĕs-thē′zhə) *n.* Var. of **aesthesia.**

es•the•si•om•e•ter (ĕs-thē′zē-ŏm′ĭ-tər) *n.* An instrument used to measure tactile sensitivity. [ESTHESI(A) + -METER.]

es•thete (ĕs′thēt) *n.* Var. of **aesthete.**

es•thet•ic (ĕs-thĕt′ĭk) *adj. & n.* Var. of **aesthetic.**

es•the•ti•cian (ĕs′thĭ-tĭsh′ən) *n.* Var. of **aesthetician.**

es•thet•i•cism (ĕs-thĕt′ĭ-sĭz′əm) *n.* Var. of **aestheticism.**

es•thet•ics (ĕs-thĕt′ĭks) *n.* Var. of **aesthetics.**

Estonia

Es•tienne (ĕs-tyĕn′) or **É•tienne** (ĕ-tyĕn′). French family of printers, including **Henri** (1460?–1520), who established the business in Paris (c. 1505); his son **Robert** (1503–59), who published Latin (1523) and Greek (1550) New Testaments; and his grandson **Henri** (1528–98), who published his own Greek dictionary (1572).

es•ti•ma•ble (ĕs′tə-mə-bəl) *adj.* **1.** Possible to estimate. **2.** Deserving of esteem; admirable: *an estimable book.* [ME < OFr. < Lat. *aestimābilis* < *aestimāre,* to value.] —**es′ti•ma•ble•ness** *n.* —**es′ti•ma•bly** *adv.*

es•ti•mate (ĕs′tə-māt′) *tr.v.* **-mat•ed, -mat•ing, -mates. 1.** To calculate approximately (the amount, extent, magnitude, position, or value of something). **2.** To form an opinion about; evaluate. —*n.* (-mĭt). **1.** The act of evaluating or appraising. **2.** A rough calculation, as of size. **3.** A statement of the approximate cost of work to be done. **4.** A judgment based on one's impressions; an opinion. [Lat. *aestimāre, aestimāt-.*] —**es′ti•ma′tive** *adj.* —**es′ti•ma′tor** *n.*

Syns: *estimate, appraise, assess, assay, evaluate, rate.* These verbs mean to form a judgment of worth or significance. *Estimate* usually implies a subjective and somewhat inexact judgment: *difficult to estimate results in advance. Appraise* stresses expert judgment: *appraised works of art. Assess* implies authoritative judgment in setting a monetary value on something as a basis for taxation: *assessing real estate. Assay* refers to careful examination, esp. to chemical analysis of an ore: *will assay the substance.* In extended senses *appraise, assess,* and *assay* can refer to any critical analysis. *Evaluate* implies considered judgment in ascertaining value: *evaluating a student's thesis. Rate* involves determining the rank or grade of someone or something in relation to others: *rated in the top ten.*

étagère
Mid 19th-century American

es•ti•ma•tion (ĕs′tə-mā′shən) *n.* **1.a.** The act or an instance of estimating. **b.** The amount, extent, position, size, or value reached in an estimate. **2.** An opinion or a judgment. **3.** Favorable regard; esteem.

es•ti•val also **aes•ti•val** (ĕs′tə-vəl) *adj.* Of, relating to, or appearing in summer. [ME < OFr. < Lat. *aestīvālis* < *aestīvus* < *aestās,* summer.]

es•ti•vate also **aes•ti•vate** (ĕs′tə-vāt′) *intr.v.* **-vat•ed, -vat•ing, -vates. 1.** To spend the summer, as at a special place. **2.** *Zool.* To pass the summer in a dormant or torpid state. [Lat. *aestīvāre, aestīvāt-* < *aestīvus,* estival. See ESTIVAL.]

es•ti•va•tion also **aes•ti•va•tion** (ĕs′tə-vā′shən) *n.* **1.** The act of spending or passing the summer. **2.** *Zool.* A state of dormancy or torpor during the summer. **3.** *Bot.* The arrangement of flower parts in the bud.

Es•to•ni•a (ĕ-stō′nē-ə). A country of NE Europe on the Baltic Sea. Settled before the 1st cent. A.D., it declared its independence in Feb. 1917 but was incorp. into the U.S.S.R. as a constituent republic in 1940. It gained full independence in 1991. Cap. Tallinn. Pop. 1,530,000.

Es•to•ni•an (ĕ-stō′nē-ən) *adj.* Of or relating to Estonia or its people, language, or culture. —*n.* **1.** A native or inhabitant of Estonia. **2.** The Finno-Ugric language of Estonia.

es•top (ĕ-stŏp′) *tr.v.* **-topped, -top•ping, -tops. 1.** *Law.* To impede or prohibit by estoppel. **2.** *Archaic.* To stop up. [ME *estoppen* < AN *estopper* < VLat. **stuppāre,* to stop up. See STOP.] —**es•top′page** (ĕ-stŏp′ĭj) *n.*

es•top•pel (ĕ-stŏp′əl) *n. Law.* A bar preventing one from contradicting what one has previously stated as the truth. [Obsolete Fr. *estouppail* < OFr. *estouper,* to stop up < VLat. **stuppāre.* See STOP.]

Es•tour•nelles de Con•stant (ĕ-sto͝or-nĕl′ də kôN-stäN′), Baron **Constant de Rebecque d'.** 1852–1924. French diplomat who shared the 1908 Nobel Peace Prize.

es•tra•di•ol (ĕs′trə-dī′ôl′, -ōl′, -ŏl′) *n.* An estrogenic hormone, $C_{18}H_{24}O_2$, produced by the ovaries and used in treating estrogen deficiency. [ESTR(US) + DI-[1] + -OL[1].]

es•tra•gon (ĕs′trə-gŏn′) *n.* Tarragon. [Fr., prob. alteration of *targon* < Med.Lat. *tragonia, tarchon.* See TARRAGON.]

es•trange (ĭ-strānj′) *tr.v.* **-tranged, -trang•ing, -trang•es. 1.** To make hostile, unsympathetic, or indifferent; alienate. **2.** To remove from an accustomed place or set of associations. [ME *estraungen* < OFr. *estrangier* < Lat. *extrāneāre,* to treat as a stranger, disown < *extrāneus,* foreign. See STRANGE.] —**es•trange′ment** *n.* —**es•trang′er** *n.*

es•tray (ĭ-strā′) *Archaic.* —*n.* A stray. —*intr.v.* **-trayed, -tray•ing, -trays.** To stray. [ME *astrai* < AN *estray* < *estraier,* to stray < OFr. See STRAY.]

Es•tre•ma•du•ra (ĕs′trə-mə-do͝or′ə, ĕs′trä-mä-*tho͞o*′rä). **1.** A historical region and former province of W Portugal surrounding Lisbon. **2.** A historical region of W-central Spain bordering on Portugal; reconquered from the Moors in the 12th and 13th cent. —**Es′tre•ma•du′ran** *adj. & n.*

es•tri•ol (ĕs′trī-ôl′, -ōl′, -ŏl′, ĕ-strī′-) *n.* An estrogenic hormone, $C_{18}H_{24}O_3$, found in the urine during pregnancy. [ES-(TRUS) + TRI- + -OL[1].]

es•tro•gen also **oes•tro•gen** (ĕs′trə-jən) *n.* Any of several steroid hormones produced chiefly by the ovaries and responsible for promoting estrus and the development and maintenance of female secondary sex characteristics. —**es′tro•gen′ic** (-jĕn′ĭk) *adj.* —**es′tro•gen′i•cal•ly** *adv.*

es•trone (ĕs′trōn′) *n.* An estrogenic hormone, $C_{18}H_{22}O_2$, used in the treatment of estrogen deficiency.

es•trous (ĕs′trəs) *adj.* Of, relating to, or being in estrus.

estrous cycle *n.* The recurrent set of physiological and behavioral changes that take place from one period of estrus to another.

es•trus also **oes•trus** (ĕs′trəs) *n.* The periodic state of sexual excitement in most female mammals, excluding humans, preceding ovulation and during which the female is most receptive to mating; heat. [NLat. < Lat. *oestrus,* frenzy, gadfly < Gk. *oistros.* See **eis-***.]

es•tu•a•rine (ĕs′cho͞o-ə-rīn′, -rēn′) *adj.* Of, relating to, or found in an estuary.

es•tu•ar•y (ĕs′cho͞o-ĕr′ē) *n., pl.* **-ies. 1.** The part of the wide lower course of a river where its current is met by the tides. **2.** An arm of the sea that meets the mouth of a river. [Lat. *aestuārium* < *aestus,* tide, surge, heat.] —**es′tu•ar′i•al** (-âr′ē-əl) *adj.*

esu *abbr.* Electrostatic unit.

e•su•ri•ent (ĭ-so͝or′ē-ənt, ĭ-zo͝or′-) *adj.* Hungry; greedy. [Lat. *ēsuriēns, ēsurient-,* pr.part. of *ēsurīre,* desiderative of *edere,* to eat. See **ed-***.] —**e•su′ri•ence** (-əns), **e•su′ri•en•cy** (-ən-sē) *n.* —**e•su′ri•ent•ly** *adv.*

-et *suff.* **1.** Small: *falconet.* **2.** Something worn on: *labret.* [ME < OFr. < VLat. *-*ittum.*]

e•ta (ā′tə, ē′tə) *n.* The seventh letter of the Greek alphabet. [Gk. *ēta,* of Phoenician orig.; akin to Heb. *ḥēt,* heth.]

ETA or **e.t.a.** *abbr.* Estimated time of arrival.

é•ta•gère also **e•ta•gere** (ā′tä-zhâr′) *n.* A piece of furniture with open shelves for small ornaments. [Fr. < OFr. *estagiere,* scaffold < *estage,* floor. See STAGE.]

et al. *abbr. Lat.* Et alii (and others).

et•a•mine (ĕt′ə-mēn′) *n.* A soft, light, loosely woven cotton or worsted. [Fr. < OFr. *estamine* < Lat. *stāminea* < fem. of *stāmineus,* made of threads < *stāmen,* thread. See **stā-***.]

eta particle *n.* A neutral elementary particle that has a mass 1,074 times that of an electron.

et cet•er•a (ĕt sĕt′ər-ə, sĕt′rə). And other things of the same class; and so forth. —*n.* **et•cet•er•a. 1.** A number of persons or things. **2. etceteras.** Additional odds and ends; extras. [Lat. : *et,* and + *cētera,* the rest, neut. pl. of *cēterus;* see **ko-***.]

etch (ĕch) *v.* **etched, etch•ing, etch•es.** —*tr.* **1.a.** To cut into the surface of (glass, for example) by the action of acid. **b.** To make or create by this method. **2.** To impress, delineate, or imprint clearly. —*intr.* To engage in etching. [Du. *etsen* <

Ger. *ätzen* < MHGer. *etzen* < OHGer. *ezzen*, to eat. See **ed-***.] — **etch′er** *n.*

etch•ing (ĕch′ĭng) *n.* **1.** The art of preparing etched plates for printing designs and pictures. **2.** A design etched on a plate. **3.** An impression made from an etched plate.

ETD or **e.t.d.** *abbr.* Estimated time of departure.

e•ter•nal (ĭ-tûr′nəl) *adj.* **1.** Having no beginning or end; existing outside time. See Syns at **infinite. 2.** Continuing without interruption; perpetual. See Syns at **continual. 3.** Forever true or changeless. **4.** Seemingly endless; interminable. **5.** Of or relating to spiritual communion with God, esp. in the afterlife. — *n.* **1.** Something timeless, uninterrupted, or endless. **2. Eternal.** God. [ME < OFr. < LLat. *aeternālis* < Lat. *aeternus*. See **aiw-***.] — **e′ter•nal′i•ty** (ē′tər-năl′ĭ-tē), **e•ter′nal•ness** *n.* — **e•ter′nal•ly** *adv.*

e•ter•nal•ize (ĭ-tûr′nə-līz′) *tr.v.* **-ized, -iz•ing, -iz•es.** To eternize.

e•terne (ĭ-tûrn′) *adj. Archaic.* Eternal. [ME < OFr. < Lat. *aeternus*. See ETERNAL.]

e•ter•ni•ty (ĭ-tûr′nĭ-tē) *n., pl.* **-ties. 1.** Time without beginning or end; infinite time. **2.** The state or quality of being eternal. **3.a.** The timeless state following death. **b.** The afterlife; immortality. **4.** A very long or seemingly endless time: *waited for an eternity.* [ME *eternite* < OFr. < Lat. *aeternitās* < *aeternus*, eternal. See ETERNAL.]

e•ter•nize (ĭ-tûr′nīz′) *tr.v.* **-nized, -niz•ing, -niz•es. 1.a.** To make eternal. **b.** To protract for an indefinite period. **2.** To make perpetually famous. [Fr. *éterniser* < OFr. *eterne*, eternal. See ETERNE.] — **e•ter′ni•za′tion** (-nĭ-zā′shən) *n.*

e•te•sian (ĭ-tē′zhən) *adj.* Occurring annually. Used of the northerly summer winds of the Mediterranean. [< Lat. *etēsius* < Gk. *etēsios* < *etos*, year. See **wet-²***.] — **e•te′sian** *n.*

eth (*ĕth*) *n.* Var. of **edh.**

Eth. *abbr.* Ethiopia.

-eth¹ or **-th** *suff.* Used to form the archaic third person singular present indicative of verbs: *leadeth.* [ME < OE *-eth, -ath.*]

-eth² *suff.* Var. of **-th³.**

eth•ane (ĕth′ān′) *n.* A colorless odorless gaseous alkane, C_2H_6, that occurs as a constituent of natural gas and is used as a fuel and a refrigerant. [ETH(YL) + -ANE.]

eth•a•nol (ĕth′ə-nôl′, -nōl′, -nŏl′) *n.* See **alcohol** 1. [ETHAN(E) + -OL¹.]

eth•a•nol•a•mine (ĕth′ə-nŏl′ə-mēn′, -nō′lə-) *n.* A colorless liquid, $NH_2(CH_2)_2ON$, used in the purification of petroleum, in dry cleaning, and in paints and pharmaceuticals.

Eth•el•bert (ĕth′əl-bûrt′). 552?–616. Anglo-Saxon king who ruled Britain S of the Humber and codified English law (604).

Eth•el•red II also **Aeth•el•red II** (ĕth′əl-rĕd′). "Ethelred the Unready." 968?–1016. King of the English (978–1016) whose kingdom was ultimately conquered by the Danes.

eth•ene (ĕth′ēn′) *n.* See **ethylene.** [ETH(YL) + -ENE.]

e•ther (ē′thər) *n.* **1.** Any of a class of organic compounds in which two hydrocarbon groups are linked by an oxygen atom. **2.** A volatile, highly flammable liquid, $C_2H_5OC_2H_5$, derived from the distillation of ethyl alcohol with sulfuric acid and widely used as a reagent, a solvent, and an anesthetic. **3.** The regions of space beyond the earth's atmosphere; the heavens. **4.** The element once believed to fill all space above the sphere of the moon and compose the stars and planets. **5.** *Phys.* An all-pervading, infinitely elastic, massless medium formerly postulated as the medium of propagation of electromagnetic waves. [ME, upper air < Lat. *aethēr* < Gk. *aithēr*.] — **e•ther′ic** (ĭ-thĕr′ĭk, ĭ-thîr′-) *adj.*

e•the•re•al (ĭ-thîr′ē-əl) *adj.* **1.** Light and insubstantial; intangible. See Syns at **airy. 2.** Highly refined; delicate. **3.a.** Of the celestial spheres; heavenly. **b.** Not of this world; spiritual. **4.** *Chem.* Of or relating to ether. [< Lat. *aetherius* < Gk. *aitherios* < *aithēr*, upper air.] — **e•the′re•al′i•ty** (-ăl′ĭ-tē), **e•the′re•al•ness** *n.* — **e•the′re•al•ly** *adv.*

e•the•re•al•ize (ĭ-thîr′ē-ə-līz′) *tr. & intr.v.* **-ized, -iz•ing, -iz•es.** To make or become ethereal. — **e•the′re•al•i•za′tion** (-ə-lĭ-zā′shən) *n.*

Eth•er•ege (ĕth′ər-ĭj, ĕth′rĭj), Sir **George.** 1635?–92? English playwright known for *She Would if She Could* (1668).

e•ther•i•fy (ĭ-thĕr′ə-fī′) *tr.v.* **-fied, -fy•ing, -fies.** To convert (an alcohol) into an ether. — **e•ther′i•fi•ca′tion** (-fĭ-kā′shən) *n.*

e•ther•ize (ē′thə-rīz′) *tr.v.* **-ized, -iz•ing, -iz•es. 1.** To subject to the fumes of ether; anesthetize. **2.** To etherify. — **e′ther•i•za′tion** (ē′thər-ĭ-zā′shən) *n.* — **e′ther•iz′er** *n.*

eth•ic (ĕth′ĭk) *n.* **1.a.** A set of principles of right conduct. **b.** A theory or a system of moral values. **2. ethics.** *(used with a sing. v.)* The study of the general nature of morals and of specific moral choices; moral philosophy. **3. ethics.** *(used with a sing. or pl. v.)* The rules or standards governing the conduct of a person or the members of a profession. [ME *ethik* < OFr. *ethique* (< LLat. *ēthica* < Gk. *ēthika*, ethics) and < Lat. *ēthicē* (< Gk. *ēthikē*), both < Gk. *ēthikos*, ethical < *ēthos*, character. See **s(w)e-***.]

eth•i•cal (ĕth′ĭ-kəl) *adj.* **1.** Of, relating to, or dealing with ethics. **2.** Being in accordance with the accepted principles that govern the conduct of a profession. See Syns at **moral. 3.** Of or relating to a drug dispensed solely on the prescription of a physician. — *n.* An ethical drug. — **eth′i•cal•ly** *adv.* — **eth′i•cal•ness, eth′i•cal′i•ty** (-kăl′ĭ-tē) *n.*

eth•i•cist (ĕth′ĭ-sĭst) also **e•thi•cian** (ĕ-thĭsh′ən) *n.* A specialist in ethics.

E•thi•o•pi•a (ē′thē-ō′pē-ə). Formerly **Ab•ys•sin•i•a** (ăb′ĭ-sĭn′ē-ə) A country of NE Africa. An ancient kingdom converted to Christianity in the 4th cent. A.D., it became independent in 1896 but was held by Italy from 1935 to 1941. Cap. Addis Ababa. Pop. 32,775,000.

E•thi•o•pi•an (ē′thē-ō′pē-ən) *adj.* **1.** Of or relating to Ethiopia or its peoples or cultures. **2.** Of or relating to the zoogeographic region that includes Africa and most of Arabia. — *n.* A native or inhabitant of Ethiopia.

E•thi•op•ic (ē′thē-ŏp′ĭk, -ō′pĭk) *n.* The Afro-Asiatic language of ancient Ethiopia that is still used as a liturgical language in the Christian Church in Ethiopia. — *adj.* **1.** Of or relating to Ethiopic. **2.** Ethiopian.

eth•moid (ĕth′moid′) also **eth•moid•al** (ĕth-moid′l) — *adj.* Of, relating to, or being a light spongy bone forming part of the walls and septum of the superior nasal cavity and containing numerous perforations for the passage of the olfactory nerve fibers. — *n.* The ethmoid bone. [Fr. *ethmoïde* < Gk. *ēthmoeidēs*, sievelike : *ēthmos*, strainer (< *ēthein*, to sift) + *-eidēs, -oeidēs*, -oid.]

eth•narch (ĕth′närk′) *n.* The ruler of a province or a people. [Gk. *ethnarkhēs* : *ethnos*, nation; see ETHNIC + *-arkhēs*, -arch.] — **eth′nar′chy** *n.*

eth•nic (ĕth′nĭk) *adj.* **1.a.** Of or relating to sizable groups of people with a common, distinctive racial, national, religious, linguistic, or cultural heritage. **b.** Being a member of a particular ethnic group. **c.** Of, relating to, or distinctive of members of such a group. **2.** Relating to a people not Christian or Jewish. — *n.* A member of a particular ethnic group, esp. one with the language or customs of the group. [ME, heathen < LLat. *ethnicus* < Gk. *ethnikos* < *ethnos*, people. See **s(w)e-***.]

eth•ni•cal (ĕth′nĭ-kəl) *adj.* **1.** Ethnic. **2.** Of or relating to ethnology. — **eth′ni•cal•ly** *adv.*

eth•nic•i•ty (ĕth-nĭs′ĭ-tē) *n.* Ethnic character, background, or affiliation.

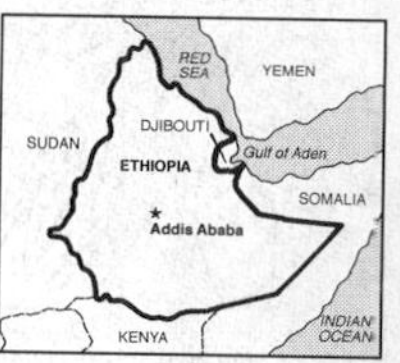

Ethiopia

ethno– *pref.* Race; people: *ethnology.* [Gk. < *ethnos*, people. See **s(w)e-***.]

eth•no•cen•trism (ĕth′nō-sĕn′trĭz′əm) *n.* **1.** Belief in the superiority of one's own ethnic group. **2.** Overriding concern with race. — **eth′no•cen′tric** (-trĭk) *adj.* — **eth′no•cen′tri•cal•ly** *adv.* — **eth′no•cen•tric′i•ty** (-sĕn-trĭs′ĭ-tē) *n.*

eth•nog•ra•phy (ĕth-nŏg′rə-fē) *n.* **1.** The branch of anthropology that deals with the scientific description of specific human cultures. **2.** Ethnology. — **eth•nog′ra•pher** *n.* — **eth′no•graph′ic** (ĕth′nə-grăf′ĭk), **eth′no•graph′i•cal** *adj.* — **eth′no•graph′i•cal•ly** *adv.*

eth•no•his•to•ry (ĕth′nō-hĭs′tə-rē) *n.* The scientific study of the development of human cultures. — **eth′no•his•to′ri•an** (-hĭ-stôr′ē-ən, -stōr′-, stŏr′-) *n.* — **eth′no•his•to′ric** (-hĭ-stôr′ĭk, -stŏr′-), **eth′no•his•to′ri•cal** *adj.*

eth•nol•o•gy (ĕth-nŏl′ə-jē) *n.* **1.** The science that analyzes and compares human cultures; cultural anthropology. **2.** The branch of anthropology that deals with the origin, distribution, and characteristics of the human races. — **eth′no•log′ic** (ĕth′nə-lŏj′ĭk), **eth′no•log′i•cal** *adj.* — **eth′no•log′i•cal•ly** *adv.* — **eth•nol′o•gist** *n.*

eth•no•mu•si•col•o•gy (ĕth′nō-myōō′zĭ-kŏl′ə-jē) *n.* **1.** The study of music that is distinct from the European classical tradition. **2.** The comparative study of music of different cultures. — **eth′no•mu′si•co•log′i•cal** (-kə-lŏj′ĭ-kəl) *adj.* — **eth′no•mu′si•col′o•gist** *n.*

e•tho•gram (ē′thə-grăm′) *n.* A pictorial catalog of the behavioral patterns of an organism or a species.

e•thol•o•gy (ĭ-thŏl′ə-jē, ē-thŏl′-) *n.* **1.** The scientific study of animal behavior, esp. in nature. **2.** The study of human ethos and its formation. [Fr. *éthologie* < Lat. *ēthologia*, art of depicting character < Gk. : *ēthos*, character; see ETHOS + *-logia*, -logy.] — **eth′o•log′i•cal** (ĕth′ə-lŏj′ĭ-kəl) *adj.* — **e•thol′o•gist** *n.*

e•thos (ē′thŏs′) *n.* The disposition, character, or fundamental values peculiar to a specific person, people, culture, or movement. [Gk. *ēthos*, character. See **s(w)e-***.]

eth•ox•yl (ĭ-thŏk′səl) also **eth•ox•y** (ĭ-thŏk′sē) *n.* The univalent radical C_2H_5O. [ETH(YL) + OX(O)- + -YL.]

eth•yl (ĕth′əl) *n.* A univalent organic radical, C_2H_5. [ETH(ER) + -YL.] — **eth•yl′ic** (ĕ-thĭl′ĭk) *adj.*

ethyl acetate *n.* A colorless volatile flammable liquid, $CH_3COOC_2H_5$, used in perfumes, flavorings, lacquers, pharmaceuticals, and rayon and as a general solvent.

ethyl alcohol *n.* See **alcohol** 1.

eth•yl•a•mine (ĕth′ə-lə-mēn′, -lăm′ən) *n.* A colorless volatile liquid, $C_2H_5NH_2$, used in petroleum refining and detergents and in organic synthesis.

eth•yl•ate (ĕth′ə-lāt′) *tr.v.* **-at•ed, -at•ing, -ates.** To introduce the ethyl group into (a compound). — **eth′yl•a′tion** *n.*

ethyl chloride *n.* A chemical compound, C_2H_5Cl, a gas at or-

ă pat	oi boy
ā pay	ou out
âr care	ŏŏ took
ä father	ōō boot
ĕ pet	ŭ cut
ē be	ûr urge
ĭ pit	th thin
ī pie	*th* this
îr pier	hw which
ŏ pot	zh vision
ō toe	ə about, item
ô paw	

Stress marks:
′ (primary);
′ (secondary), as in
dictionary (dĭk′shə-nĕr′ē)

dinary temperatures and a colorless volatile flammable liquid when compressed, used as a solvent and refrigerant.

eth•yl•ene (ĕth′ə-lēn′) *n.* A colorless flammable gas, C_2H_4, used as a source of organic compounds, in welding metals, to color citrus fruits, and as an anesthetic. **—eth′yl•e′nic** (-ə-lē′nĭk, -lĕn′ĭk) *adj.*

ethylene glycol *n.* A colorless syrupy poisonous alcohol, $HOCH_2CH_2OH$, used as an antifreeze.

ethyl ether *n.* See **ether** 2.

-etic *suff.* Used to form adjectives usu. from nouns ending in *-esis,* as in *aphaeretic* from *aphaeresis.* [Lat. *-ēticus* < Gk. *-ētikos* < *-etos,* verbal adj. ending.]

É•tienne (ĕ-tyĕn′). See **Estienne.**

e•ti•o•late (ē′tē-ə-lāt′) *v.* **-lat•ed, -lat•ing, -lates.** *—tr.* **1.** *Bot.* To cause (a plant) to develop without chlorophyll by preventing exposure to sunlight. **2.a.** To cause to appear pale and sickly. **b.** To make weak by stunting the growth or development of. *—intr. Bot.* To become blanched or whitened, as when grown without sunlight. [Fr. *étioler* < Norman Fr. *étieuler,* to grow into haulm < *éteule,* stalk < OFr. *esteule* < VLat. **stupula* < Lat. *stipula.*] **—e′ti•o•la′tion** *n.*

e•ti•ol•o•gy also **ae•ti•ol•o•gy** (ē′tē-ŏl′ə-jē) *n., pl.* **-gies. 1.a.** The study of causes or origins. **b.** The branch of medicine that deals with the causes or origins of disease. **2.a.** Assignment of a cause, an origin, or a reason for something. **b.** The cause or origin of a disease or disorder as determined by medical diagnosis. [LLat. *aetiologia* < Gk. *aitiologia* : *aitia,* cause + *-logia,* -logy.] **—e′ti•o•log′ic** (-ə-lŏj′ĭk), **e′ti•o•log′i•cal** *adj.* **—e′ti•o•log′i•cal•ly** *adv.* **—e′ti•ol′o•gist** *n.*

et•i•quette (ĕt′ĭ-kĕt′, -kĭt) *n.* The practices and forms prescribed by social convention or by authority. [Fr. < OFr. *estiquet,* label. See TICKET.]

Et•na also **Aet•na** (ĕt′nə), **Mount.** An active volcano, 3,325.1 m (10,902 ft), of E Sicily; first known eruption 475 B.C.

ETO *abbr.* European theater of operations.

E•ton (ēt′n). An urban district of SE-central England on the Thames R. opposite Windsor; site of the largest of England's public schools (founded 1440). Pop. 3,523.

Eton collar *n.* A broad white collar worn over the lapels of a jacket. [After *Eton* College, England.]

Eton jacket *n.* A waist-length black jacket that has wide lapels and is cut square at the hips. [After *Eton* College, England.]

E•tru•ri•a (ĭ-trŏŏr′ē-ə). An ancient country of W-central Italy in Tuscany and parts of Umbria; center of the Etruscan civilization until the 3rd cent. B.C. **—E•tru′ri•an** *adj. & n.*

E•trus•can (ĭ-trŭs′kən) *adj.* Of or relating to ancient Etruria or its people, language, or culture. *—n.* **1.** A native or inhabitant of ancient Etruria. **2.** The extinct language of the Etruscans, of unknown linguistic affiliation.

eucalyptus

et seq. *abbr. Lat.* Et sequens (and the following one or ones).

-ette *suff.* **1.** Small; diminutive: *kitchenette.* **2.** Female: *usherette.* **3.** An imitation or inferior kind of cloth: *leatherette.* [ME < OFr., fem. of *-et,* -et.]

Usage Note: The French diminutive suffix *-ette* in its use to form nouns denoting women is most likely derived from the French use of *-ette* to form feminine versions of masculine personal names, as in *Paulette.* In this sense the suffix was first applied to an English common noun in *suffragette,* which served as the model for a number of words that referred to women who occupied positions once reserved for men. Among these only *usherette* and *drum majorette* have survived, but the pattern is still widely used to coin the names of women's social groups and auxiliaries, as well as in formations such as *bachelorette.* In each case the use of what is essentially a diminutive or pet name suffix to refer to women betrays a patronizing attitude. See Usage Note at **brunette.**

e•tude (ā′to͞od′, -tyo͞od′) *n. Mus.* **1.** A piece composed for the development of a specific point of technique. **2.** A composition featuring a point of technique but performed because of its artistic merit. [Fr. *étude* < OFr. *estudie,* study. See STUDY.]

é•tui (ā-twē′) *n., pl.* **é•tuis** (ā-twēz′). A small, usu. ornamental case for holding articles such as needles. [Fr. < OFr. *estui,* prison < *estuier,* to guard < VLat. **estudiāre,* to treat carefully < Lat. *studium,* study. See STUDY.]

Eugénie
After a portrait by Franz Winterhalter (1805–1873)

et ux. *abbr. Lat.* Et uxor (and wife).

ETV *abbr.* Educational television.

etym. *abbr.* Etymological; etymology.

et•y•mo•log•i•cal (ĕt′ə-mə-lŏj′ĭ-kəl) also **et•y•mo•log•ic** (-lŏj′ĭk) *adj.* Of or relating to etymology or based on the principles of etymology. **—et′y•mo•log′i•cal•ly** *adv.*

et•y•mol•o•gist (ĕt′ə-mŏl′ə-jĭst) *n.* A specialist in etymology.

et•y•mol•o•gize (ĕt′ə-mŏl′ə-jīz′) *v.* **-gized, -giz•ing, -giz•es.** *—tr.* To trace and state the etymology of. *—intr.* To give or suggest the etymology of a word.

et•y•mol•o•gy (ĕt′ə-mŏl′ə-jē) *n., pl.* **-gies. 1.** The origin and historical development of a linguistic form as shown by determining its basic elements, earliest known use, and changes in form and meaning, tracing its transmission from one language to another, identifying its cognates in other languages, and reconstructing its ancestral form where possible. **2.** The branch of linguistics that deals with etymologies. [ME *etimologie* < OFr. *ethimologie* < Med.Lat. *ethimologia* < Lat. *etymologia* < Gk. *etumologia* : *etumon,* true sense of a word; see ETYMON + *-logia,* -logy.]

et•y•mon (ĕt′ə-mŏn′) *n., pl.* **-mons** or **-ma** (-mə). **1.** An earlier form of a word in the same language or in an ancestor language. **2.** A word or morpheme from which compounds and derivatives are formed. **3.** A foreign word from which a particular loan word is derived. [Lat. < Gk. *etumon,* true sense of a word < *etumos,* true.]

Eu The symbol for the element **europium.**

eu- *pref.* **1.** Good; well; true: *euplastic.* **2.** A derivative of a specified substance: *eucaine.* [ME < Lat. < Gk. See **(e)su-*.**]

Eu•boe•a (yo͞o-bē′ə) also **Ev•voia** (ĕv′yä). An island of central Greece in the Aegean Sea E of the mainland.

eu•caine (yo͞o′kān′) *n.* A crystalline substance, $C_{15}H_{21}NO_2$, used as a local anesthetic in veterinary medicine.

eu•ca•lyp•tol (yo͞o′kə-lĭp′tôl′, -tōl′, -tŏl′) also **eu•ca•lyp•tole** (-tōl′) *n.* A colorless oily liquid, $C_{10}H_{18}O$, derived from eucalyptus and used in pharmaceuticals and flavoring.

eu•ca•lyp•tus (yo͞o′kə-lĭp′təs) *n., pl.* **-tus•es** or **-ti** (-tī′). Any of numerous trees of the genus *Eucalyptus,* native to Australia and having aromatic leaves that yield an oil used medicinally and wood valued as timber. [NLat. *Eucalyptus,* genus name : Gk. *eu-,* eu- + Gk. *kaluptos,* covered (< *kaluptein,* to cover; see **kel-[1]***).]

eu•car•y•ote (yo͞o-kăr′ē-ōt′, -ē-ət) *n.* Var. of **eukaryote.**

Eu•cha•rist (yo͞o′kər-ĭst) *n.* **1.** A sacrament and the central act of worship in many Christian churches, in which bread and wine are consecrated and consumed in remembrance of Jesus's death; Communion. **2.** The consecrated elements of this rite; Communion. [ME *eukarist* < OFr. *eucariste* < LLat. *eucharistia* < Gk. *eukharistia* < *eukharistos,* grateful, thankful : *eu-,* eu- + *kharizesthai,* to show favor (< *kharis,* grace; see **gher-[2]***).] **—Eu′cha•ris′tic, Eu′cha•ris′ti•cal** *adj.*

eu•chre (yo͞o′kər) *n. Games.* **1.** A card game played usu. with the highest 32 cards, in which each player is dealt 5 cards and the player making the trump is required to take at least 3 tricks to win. **2.** The act of euchring an opponent. *—tr.v.* **-chred, -chring, -chres. 1.** *Games.* To prevent (an opponent) from taking 3 tricks in euchre. **2.** To deceive by sly or underhand means; cheat: *euchred us out of our savings.* [?]

eu•chro•ma•tin (yo͞o-krō′mə-tĭn′) *n.* Chromosomal material that is genetically active and stains lightly with basic dyes. **—eu′chro•mat′ic** (yo͞o′krō-măt′ĭk) *adj.*

Euck•en (oi′kən), **Rudolf Christoph.** 1846–1926. German philosopher who won the 1908 Nobel Prize for literature.

Eu•clid[1] (yo͞o′klĭd). 3rd cent. B.C. Greek mathematician who applied the deductive principles of logic to geometry. **—Eu•clid′e•an, Eu•clid′i•an** *adj.*

Eu•clid[2] (yo͞o′klĭd). A city of NE OH. Pop. 54,875.

eu•de•mon also **eu•dae•mon** (yo͞o-dē′mən) *n.* A good or benevolent spirit.

eu•de•mon•ism also **eu•dae•mon•ism** (yo͞o-dē′mə-nĭz′əm) *n.* A system of ethics that evaluates actions in terms of their capacity to produce happiness. **—eu•de′mo•nist** *n.* **—eu•de′mon•is′tic, eu•de′mon•is′ti•cal** *adj.*

Eu•gene (yo͞o-jēn′). A city of W OR on the Willamette R. S of Salem. Pop. 112,669.

Eu•gene (yo͞o-jēn′, yo͞o′jēn′, œ-zhĕn′). Prince of Savoy. 1663–1736. Austrian general in service to the Holy Roman Empire during the War of the Spanish Succession (1701–14).

eu•gen•ic (yo͞o-jĕn′ĭk) *adj.* **1.** Of or relating to eugenics. **2.** Relating or adapted to the production of good or improved offspring. **—eu•gen′i•cal•ly** *adv.*

eu•gen•i•cist (yo͞o-jĕn′ĭ-sĭst) also **eu•gen•ist** (yo͞o′jə-nĭst) *n.* An advocate of or a specialist in eugenics.

eu•gen•ics (yo͞o-jĕn′ĭks) *n. (used with a sing. v.)* The study of hereditary improvement of the human race by controlled selective breeding.

Eu•gé•nie (yo͞o-jē′nē, œ-zhā-nē′). 1826–1920. Empress of France (1853–71) as the wife of Napoleon III who acted as regent during the emperor's absences.

eu•ge•nol (yo͞o′jə-nôl′, -nōl′, -nŏl′) *n.* A colorless aromatic liquid $C_{10}H_{12}O_2$, made from clove oil and used as a dental analgesic and in perfumery. [NLat. *Eugenia,* genus of the clove plant (after EUGENE, Prince of Savoy) + -OL(E).]

eu•gle•na (yo͞o-glē′nə) *n.* Any of various single-celled freshwater organisms of the genus *Euglena,* marked by the presence of chlorophyll, a reddish eyespot, and one anterior flagellum. [NLat. : Gk. *eu-,* eu- + Gk. *glēnē,* eyeball.]

eu•he•mer•ism (yo͞o-hē′mə-rĭz′əm, -hĕm′ə-) *n.* A theory attributing the origin of the gods to the deification of historical heroes. [After *Euhemerus,* 4th-cent. B.C. Greek philosopher.] **—eu•he′mer•ist** *n.* **—eu•he′mer•is′tic** *adj.* **—eu•he′mer•is′ti•cal•ly** *adv.* **—eu•he′mer•ize** *v.*

eu•kar•y•ote also **eu•car•y•ote** (yo͞o-kăr′ē-ōt, -ē-ət) *n.* An organism whose cells contain a distinct membrane-bound nucleus. [EU- + Gk. *karuōtos,* having nuts (< *karuon,* nut; see **kar-***).] **—eu•kar′y•ot′ic** (-ŏt′ĭk) *adj.*

eu•la•chon (yo͞o′lə-kŏn′) *n., pl.* **eulachon** or **-chons.** See **candlefish.** [Chinook Jargon *vlâkân.*]

Eu•ler (oi′lər), **Leonhard.** 1707–83. Swiss mathematician noted for his development of integral calculus.

Eu·less (yo͞o′lĭs). A city of NE TX, a suburb of Fort Worth. Pop. 38,149.

eu·lo·gize (yo͞o′lə-jīz′) *tr.v.* **-gized, -giz·ing, -giz·es.** To praise highly in speech or writing. **— eu′lo·gist** (-jĭst), **eu′lo·giz′er** *n.*

eu·lo·gy (yo͞o′lə-jē) *n., pl.* **-gies. 1.** A laudatory speech or piece of writing, esp. for someone who has died. **2.** High praise or commendation. [ME *euloge* < Med.Lat. *eulogium* < Gk. *eulogia*, praise : *eu-*, eu- + *-logia*, -logy.] **— eu′lo·gis′tic** (-jĭs′tĭk) *adj.* **— eu′lo·gis′ti·cal·ly** *adv.*

Eu·men·i·des (yo͞o-mĕn′ĭ-dēz′) *pl.n. Gk. Myth.* The Furies.

eu·nuch (yo͞o′nək) *n.* **1.** A castrated man employed as a harem attendant or as a functionary in certain Asian courts. **2.** A man or boy whose testes are nonfunctioning or have been removed. [ME *eunuk* < Lat. *eunūchus* < Gk. *eunoukhos* : *eunē*, bed + *-okhos*, keeping (< *ekhein*, to keep; see **segh-***).] **— eu′nuch·ism** *n.*

eu·on·y·mus (yo͞o-ŏn′ə-məs) *n.* Any of various plants of the genus *Euonymus*, having decorated foliage or fruits. [Lat. *euōnymus*, a tree of Lesbos < Gk. *euōnumos*, of good name : *eu-*, eu- + *onuma*, name; see **nō-men-***.]

eu·pat·rid (yo͞o-păt′rĭd, yo͞o′pə-trĭd) *n., pl.* **-ri·dae** (-rĭ-dē′) or **-rids.** A member of the hereditary aristocracy of ancient Athens. [Gk. *eupatridēs* : *eu-*, eu- + *patēr, patr-*, father; see **pəter-*** + *-idēs*, patronymic suff.] **— eu·pat′rid** *adj.*

eu·pep·si·a (yo͞o-pĕp′sē-ə, -shə) *n.* Good digestion. [Gk. < *eupeptos*, eupeptic. See EUPEPTIC.]

eu·pep·tic (yo͞o-pĕp′tĭk) *adj.* **1.a.** Relating to or having good digestion. **b.** Conducive to digestion. **2.** Cheerful; happy. [< Gk. *eupeptos* : *eu-*, eu- + *peptein*, to digest; see **pekʷ-***.] **— eu·pep′ti·cal·ly** *adv.*

eu·phe·mism (yo͞o′fə-mĭz′əm) *n.* The act or an example of substituting a mild, indirect, or vague term for a harsh, blunt, or offensive one. [Gk. *euphēmismos* < *euphēmizein*, to use auspicious words < *euphēmia*, such use : *eu-*, eu- + *phēmē*, speech; see **bhā-²***.] **— eu′phe·mist** *n.* **— eu′phe·mis′tic** (-mĭs′tĭk) *adj.* **— eu′phe·mis′ti·cal·ly** *adv.*

eu·phe·mize (yo͞o′fə-mīz′) *v.* **-mized, -miz·ing, -miz·es.** *— tr.* To speak of or refer to by means of a euphemism. *— intr.* To use euphemisms. **— eu′phe·miz′er** *n.*

eu·phen·ics (yo͞o-fĕn′ĭks) *n.* *(used with a sing. v.)* The study or practice of phenotypic improvement of humans after birth. [Blend of EU(GEN)ICS and PHEN(OTYPE).] **— eu·phen′ic** *adj.*

eu·pho·ni·ous (yo͞o-fō′nē-əs) *adj.* Pleasing or agreeable to the ear. **— eu·pho′ni·ous·ly** *adv.* **— eu·pho′ni·ous·ness** *n.*

eu·pho·ni·um (yo͞o-fō′nē-əm) *n. Mus.* A brass wind instrument similar to the tuba but having a somewhat higher pitch and a mellower sound. [< Gk. *euphōnos*, sweet-voiced. See EUPHONY.]

eu·pho·ny (yo͞o′fə-nē) *n., pl.* **-nies.** Agreeable sound, esp. in the phonetic quality of words. [Fr. *euphonie* < LLat. *euphōnia* < Gk. < *euphōnos*, sweet-voiced : *eu-*, eu- + *phōnē*, sound; see **bhā-²***.] **— eu·phon′ic** (yo͞o-fŏn′ĭk) *adj.* **— eu·phon′i·cal·ly** *adv.* **— eu′pho·nize** *v.*

eu·phor·bi·a (yo͞o-fôr′bē-ə) *n.* A plant of the genus *Euphorbia*, which includes the spurges. [ME *euforbia* < Lat. *euphorbea*, after *Euphorbus*, 1st-cent. A.D. Greek physician.]

eu·pho·ri·a (yo͞o-fôr′ē-ə, -fōr′-) *n.* A feeling of great happiness or well-being. [NLat. < Gk. < *euphoros*, healthy : *eu-*, eu- + *pherein*, to bear; see **bher-¹***.] **— eu·phor′ic** (-fôr′ĭk, -fŏr′-) *adj.* **— eu·phor′i·cal·ly** *adv.*

eu·phor·i·ant (yo͞o-fôr′ē-ənt, -fōr′-) *n.* A drug that tends to produce euphoria. **— eu·phor′i·ant** *adj.*

eu·phot·ic (yo͞o-fōt′ĭk) *adj.* Of, relating to, or being the uppermost layer of a body of water that receives sufficient light for photosynthesis and the growth of green plants.

Eu·phra·tes (yo͞o-frā′tēz). A river of SW Asia flowing c. 2,735 km (1,700 mi) from central Turkey through Syria and into Iraq, where it joins the Tigris R.

Eu·phros·y·ne (yo͞o-frŏs′ə-nē) *n. Gk. Myth.* One of the three Graces.

eu·phu·ism (yo͞o′fyo͞o-ĭz′əm) *n.* **1.** A literary style of the late 16th and early 17th centuries, characterized by elaborate alliteration, antitheses, and similes. **2.** Affected elegance of language. [After *Euphues*, a character created by John Lyly < Gk. *euphuēs*, shapely : *eu-*, eu- + *phuein*, to grow, bring forth; see **bheuə-***.] **— eu′phu·ist** *n.* **— eu′phu·is′tic, eu′phu·is′ti·cal** *adj.* **— eu′phu·is′ti·cal·ly** *adv.*

eu·plas·tic (yo͞o-plăs′tĭk) *adj.* Readily transformed into tissue, as in the healing of a wound.

eu·ploid (yo͞o′ploid′) *adj.* Having a chromosome number that is an exact multiple of the haploid number. *— n.* A euploid cell or organism. **— eu′ploi′dy** *n.*

eup·ne·a (yo͞op-nē′ə) *n.* Normal breathing. [NLat. < Gk. *eupnoia* < *eupnoos*, breathing well : *eu-*, eu- + *pnein*, to breathe; see **pneu-***.] **— eup·ne′ic** *adj.*

Eur. *abbr.* Europe; European.

Eur·a·sia (yo͞o-rā′zhə). The land mass comprising the continents of Europe and Asia.

Eur·a·sian (yo͞o-rā′zhən) *adj.* **1.** Of or relating to Eurasia. **2.** Of mixed European and Asian descent. *— n.* A person of mixed European and Asian descent.

EURATOM *abbr.* European Atomic Energy Community.

eu·re·ka (yo͞o-rē′kə) *interj.* Used to express triumph upon finding or discovering something. [Gk. *heurēka*, I have found (it), first pers. perfect of *heuriskein*, to find.]

Eu·re·ka (yo͞o-rē′kə). A city of NW CA on Humboldt Bay, an arm of the Pacific. Pop. 27,025.

eu·rhyth·mics (yo͞o-rĭth′mĭks) *n.* Var. of **eurythmics.**

eu·rhyth·my (yo͞o-rĭth′mē) *n.* Var. of **eurythmy.**

Eu·rip·i·des (yo͞o-rĭp′ĭ-dēz′). 480?–406 B.C. Greek dramatist whose surviving works include *Medea* and *The Trojan Women.* **— Eu·rip′i·de′an** *adj.*

eu·ri·pus (yo͞o-rī′pəs) *n., pl.* **-pi** (-pī′). A sea channel characterized by turbulent and unpredictable currents. [Lat. < Gk. *euripos* : *eu-*, eu- + *rhipē*, rush (< *riptein*, to throw).]

Euro– *pref.* Europe; European: *Eurocrat.*

Eu·ro·cen·tric (yo͝or′ō-sĕn′trĭk) also **Eu·ro·po·cen·tric** (yo͞o-rō′pə-) *adj.* Centered or focused on Europe and the Europeans. **— Eu·ro·cen′trism** *n.*

Eu·ro·crat (yo͝or′ə-krăt′) *n.* An administrative official at the headquarters of the Common Market. **— Eu′ro·crat′ic** *adj.*

Eu·ro·cur·ren·cy (yo͝or′ō-kûr′ən-sē, -kŭr′-) *n., pl.* **-cies.** Funds deposited in a bank when those funds are denominated in a currency differing from the bank's domestic currency.

Eu·ro·dol·lar (yo͝or′ō-dŏl′ər) *n.* A U.S. dollar on deposit with a bank abroad, esp. in Europe.

Eu·ro·pa (yo͞o-rō′pə) *n.* **1.** *Gk. Myth.* A Phoenician princess abducted to Crete by Zeus in the form of a bull and the mother of Minos, Rhadamanthus, and Sarpedon. **2.** A satellite of Jupiter. [Lat. *Eurōpa* < Gk. *Eurōpē.*]

Eu·rope (yo͝or′əp). The sixth-largest continent, extending W from the Dardanelles, Black Sea, and Ural Mts.

Eu·ro·pe·an (yo͝or′ə-pē′ən) *n.* **1.** A native or inhabitant of Europe. **2.** A person of European descent. *— adj.* Of or relating to Europe or its peoples, languages, or cultures.

European corn borer *n.* See **corn borer** 1.

European Economic Community. See **Common Market.**

Eu·ro·pe·an·ize (yo͝or′ə-pē′ə-nīz′) *tr.v.* **-ized, -iz·ing, -iz·es.** To make European. **— Eu′ro·pe′an·i·za′tion** *n.*

European plan *n.* A hotel plan in which the rates include only the charges for a room and not for meals.

European U.S.S.R. A historical region of the U.S.S.R. W of the Ural Mts. and the Caspian Sea.

eu·ro·pi·um (yo͞o-rō′pē-əm) *n. Symbol* **Eu** A rare-earth element occurring in monazite and bastnaesite and used as a neutron absorber in nuclear research. Atomic number 63; atomic weight 151.96; melting point 826°C; boiling point 1,439°C; specific gravity 5.259; valence 2, 3. See table at **element.** [After EUROPE.]

Eu·ro·po·cen·tric (yo͞o-rō′pə-sĕn′trĭk) *adj.* Var. of **Eurocentric.**

Eu·rus (yo͝or′əs) *n. Gk. Myth.* The god of the east or southeast wind.

eury– *pref.* Wide; broad: *eurythermal.* [< Gk. *eurus*, wide.]

eu·ry·bath·ic (yo͝or′ə-băth′ĭk) *adj.* Capable of living in a wide range of water depths. Used of an aquatic organism. **— eu′ry·bath′** *n.*

Eu·ryd·i·ce (yo͞o-rĭd′ĭ-sē) *n. Gk. Myth.* The wife of Orpheus, whom he failed to rescue from the underworld when he looked back at her and so violated the command of Hades.

eu·ry·ha·line (yo͝or′ə-hā′līn′, -hăl′-īn′) *adj.* Capable of tolerating a wide range of salt water concentrations. Used of an aquatic organism.

eu·ryp·ter·id (yo͞o-rĭp′tər-ĭd) *n.* Any of various large segmented aquatic arthropods of the order Eurypterida that existed from the Ordovician Period to the Permian Period. [< NLat. *Eurypterida*, order name < pl. of *Eurypterus*, genus name : EURY– + Gk. *pteron*, wing; see –PTER.]

eu·ry·ther·mal (yo͝or′ə-thûr′məl) also **eu·ry·ther·mic** (-mĭk) or **eu·ry·ther·mous** (-məs) *adj.* Adaptable to a wide range of temperatures. Used of an organism. **— eu′ry·therm′** *n.*

eu·ryth·mics also **eu·rhyth·mics** (yo͞o-rĭth′mĭks) *n.* *(used with a sing. v.)* The art of interpreting music by rhythmical free-style bodily movement. **— eu·ryth′mic** *adj.*

eu·ryth·my also **eu·rhyth·my** (yo͞o-rĭth′mē) *n.* **1.** Harmony of proportion in architecture. **2.** A system of rhythmical bodily movements performed to a recitation of verse or prose. [Lat. *eurythmia* < Gk. *euruthmia* < *euruthmos*, rhythmic, well-proportioned : *eu-*, eu- + *rhuthmos*, proportion; see RHYTHM.]

eu·ry·top·ic (yo͝or′ĭ-tŏp′ĭk) *adj.* Able to adapt to a wide range of environmental conditions; widely distributed. Used of a plant or an animal. [Gk. *eurus*, wide + Gk. *topos*, place + –IC.] **— eu′ry·to·pic′i·ty** (-tō-pĭs′ĭ-tē) *n.*

Eu·se·bi·us of Cae·sa·re·a (yo͞o-sē′bē-əs; sē′zə-rē′ə, sĕs′-ə-, sĕz′ə-). A.D. 260?–340? Palestinian theologian who wrote a history of the Christian church until the year 324.

eu·sta·chian tube or **Eu·sta·chian tube** (yo͞o-stā′shən, -shē-ən, -kē-ən) *n. Anat.* A slender tube that connects the tympanic cavity with the nasal part of the pharynx and serves to equalize air pressure on either side of the eardrum. [After Bartolommeo EUSTACHIO.]

ă pat	oi boy
ā pay	ou out
âr care	o͝o took
ä father	o͞o boot
ĕ pet	ŭ cut
ē be	ûr urge
ĭ pit	th thin
ī pie	*th* this
îr pier	hw which
ŏ pot	zh vision
ō toe	ə about, item
ô paw	

Stress marks:
′ (primary);
′ (secondary), as in **dictionary** (dĭk′shə-nĕr′ē)

Eu•sta•chi•o (yo͞o-stä′kē-ō, ĕ′o͞o-stä′kyô), **Bartolommeo.** 1520–74. Italian anatomist noted for his descriptions of the human ear and heart.

eu•sta•sy (yo͞o′stə-sē) *n., pl.* **-sies.** A worldwide change in sea level. [< *eustatic*, of eustasy : EU– + STAT(O)– + –IC.] — **eu•stat′ic** (-stăt′ĭk) *adj.*

eu•stele (yo͞o′stēl, yo͞o-stē′lē) *n. Bot.* The central cylinder in which the primary vascular tissue is arranged around a pith.

eu•tec•tic (yo͞o-tĕk′tĭk) *adj.* **1.** Of, relating to, or formed at the lowest possible temperature of solidification for any mixture of specified constituents. **2.** Exhibiting the constitution or properties of such a solid. —*n.* **1.** A eutectic mixture, solution, or alloy. **2.** The eutectic temperature. [< Gk. *eutēktos*, easily melted : *eu-*, eu- + *tēktos*, melted (< *tēkein*, to melt).]

Eu•ter•pe (yo͞o-tûr′pē) *n. Gk. Myth.* The Muse of lyric poetry and music.

eu•tha•na•sia (yo͞o′thə-nā′zhə, -zhē-ə) *n.* The act or practice of ending the life of an individual suffering from a terminal illness or an incurable condition. [Gk., a good death : *eu-*, eu- + *thanatos*, death.]

eu•than•ize (yo͞o′thə-nīz′) also **eu•than•a•tize** (yo͞o-thăn′-ə-tīz′) *tr.v.* **-ized, -iz•ing, -iz•es** also **-a•tized, -a•tiz•ing, -a•tiz•es.** To subject to euthanasia.

eu•then•ics (yo͞o-thĕn′ĭks) *n. (used with a sing. v.)* The study of the improvement of human functioning and well-being by improvement of living conditions. [< Gk. *euthenein*, to flourish.] — **eu•then′ist** *n.*

eu•ther•i•an (yo͞o-thîr′ē-ən) *adj.* Of or belonging to the infraclass Eutheria, including the placental mammals. [< NLat. *Eutheria*, infraclass name : Gk. *eu-*, eu- + Gk. *thēria*, pl. of *thērion*, wild animal; see TREACLE.] — **eu•ther′i•an** *n.*

eu•troph•ic (yo͞o-trŏf′ĭk, -trō′fĭk) *adj. Ecol.* Having waters rich in mineral and organic nutrients, causing plant life, esp. algae, to proliferate, thereby reducing the dissolved oxygen content and often killing off other organisms. [< Gk. *eutrophos*, well-nourished : *eu-*, eu- + *trephein*, to nourish.] — **eu•troph′i•ca′tion** *n.* — **eu′tro•phy** (yo͞o′trə-fē) *n.*

eV *abbr.* Electron volt.

EVA *abbr.* Extravehicular activity.

e•vac•u•ant (ĭ-văk′yo͞o-ənt) *adj.* Causing evacuation, esp. of the bowels; purgative. —*n.* A purgative.

e•vac•u•ate (ĭ-văk′yo͞o-āt′) *v.* **-at•ed, -at•ing, -ates.** —*tr.* **1.a.** To empty or remove the contents of. **b.** To create a vacuum in. **2.** To discharge (waste matter), esp. from the bowels. **3.a.** To relinquish military possession or occupation of (a town, for example). **b.** To withdraw or send away (troops or inhabitants) from a threatened area. **4.** To withdraw or depart from; vacate. —*intr.* **1.** To evacuate a place or area, esp. as a protective measure. **2.** To excrete waste matter from the body. [ME *evacuaten* < Lat. *ēvacuāre, ēvacuāt-*, to empty out : *ē-*, *ex-*, ex- + *vacuus*, empty (< *vacāre*, to be empty; see **eu-²***).] — **e•vac′u•a′tive** *adj.* — **e•vac′u•a′tor** *n.*

e•vac•u•a•tion (ĭ-văk′yo͞o-ā′shən) *n.* **1.** The act of evacuating or the condition of being evacuated. **2.** *Physiol.* **a.** Discharge of waste materials from the excretory passages of the body, esp. from the bowels. **b.** The material so discharged.

e•vac•u•ee (ĭ-văk′yo͞o-ē′) *n.* A person evacuated from a dangerous area.

e•vade (ĭ-vād′) *v.* **e•vad•ed, e•vad•ing, e•vades.** —*tr.* **1.** To escape or avoid by cleverness or deceit: *evade arrest.* **2.a.** To avoid fulfilling, answering, or performing: *evade responsibility.* **b.** To fail to make payment of (taxes). **3.** To avoid giving a direct answer to. **4.** To baffle or elude. —*intr.* **1.** To practice evasion. **2.** To use cleverness or deceit in avoiding or escaping. [Fr. *évader* < Lat. *ēvādere* : *ē-*, *ex-*, ex- + *vādere*, to go.] — **e•vad′a•ble, e•vad′i•ble** *adj.* — **e•vad′er** *n.*

e•vag•i•nate (ĭ-văj′ə-nāt′) *tr.v.* **-nat•ed, -nat•ing, -nates.** To cause (a body part) to turn inside out by eversion of an inner surface. [Lat. *ēvāgīnāre, ēvāgīnāt-*, to unsheath : *ē-*, *ex-*, ex- + *vāgīna*, sheath.] — **e•vag′i•na′tion** *n.*

e•val•u•ate (ĭ-văl′yo͞o-āt′) *tr.v.* **-at•ed, -at•ing, -ates. 1.** To ascertain or fix the value or worth of. **2.** To examine and judge carefully; appraise. See Syns at **estimate. 3.** *Math.* To calculate the numerical value of; express numerically. [Ult. < Fr. *évaluation* < OFr. < *evaluer*, to evaluate : *e-*, out (< Lat. *ē-*, *ex-*; see EX–) + *value*, value; see VALUE.] — **e•val′u•a′tion** *n.* — **e•val′u•a•tive** *adj.* — **e•val′u•a•tor** *n.*

ev•a•nesce (ĕv′ə-nĕs′) *intr.v.* **-nesced, -nesc•ing, -nesc•es.** To dissipate or disappear like vapor. See Syns at **disappear.** [Lat. *ēvānēscere*, to vanish : *ē-*, *ex-*, ex- + *vānēscere*, to disappear (< *vānus*, empty; see **eu-²***).] — **ev′a•nes′cence** *n.*

ev•a•nes•cent (ĕv′ə-nĕs′ənt) *adj.* Vanishing or likely to vanish like vapor. — **ev′a•nes′cent•ly** *adv.*

e•van•gel (ĭ-văn′jəl) *n.* **1.** The Christian gospel. **2.** An evangelist. [ME *evaungel* < LLat. *ēvangelium* < Gk. *euangelion*, good news < *euangelos*, bringing good news : *eu-*, eu- + *angelos*, messenger.]

e•van•gel•i•cal (ē′văn-jĕl′ĭ-kəl, ĕv′ən-) also **e•van•gel•ic** (-jĕl′ĭk) —*adj.* **1.** Of, relating to, or in accordance with the Christian gospel, esp. one of the four gospel books of the New Testament. **2. Evangelical.** Of, relating to, or being a Protestant church that founds its teaching on the gospel. **3. Evangelical.** Of, relating to, or being a Christian church believing in the authority of the Bible, in salvation through regeneration, and in a transformed personal life. **4.** Of or relating to the group in the Church of England that stresses personal conversion and salvation by faith. **5.** Marked by ardent or crusading enthusiasm. —*n.* **Evangelical.** A member of an evangelical church or party. — **e′van•gel′i•cal•ly** *adv.*

e•van•gel•i•cal•ism (ē′văn-jĕl′ĭ-kə-lĭz′əm, ĕv′ən-) *n.* **1.** Often **Evangelicalism.** Evangelical beliefs or doctrines. **2.** Adherence to a church or party professing evangelicalism.

e•van•gel•ism (ĭ-văn′jə-lĭz′əm) *n.* **1.** Zealous preaching and dissemination of the gospel, as through missionary work. **2.** Militant zeal for a cause. — **e•van′gel•is′tic** (-jə-lĭs′tĭk) *adj.* — **e•van′gel•is′ti•cal•ly** *adv.*

e•van•gel•ist (ĭ-văn′jə-lĭst) *n.* **1.** Often **Evangelist.** Any one of the authors of the four New Testament gospel books. **2.** One who practices evangelism.

e•van•gel•ize (ĭ-văn′jə-līz′) *v.* **-ized, -iz•ing, -iz•es.** —*tr.* **1.** To preach the gospel to. **2.** To convert to Christianity. —*intr.* To preach the gospel. — **e•van′gel•i•za′tion** (-jə-lĭ-zā′shən) *n.* — **e•van′gel•iz′er** *n.*

Ev•ans (ĕv′ənz), Sir **Arthur John.** 1851–1941. British archaeologist who unearthed remnants of the Bronze Age Minoan civilization in Crete.

Evans, Herbert McLean. 1882–1971. Amer. anatomist who discovered vitamin E (1922).

Evans, Mary Ann. See George **Eliot.**

Evans, Mount. A peak, 4,350.5 m (14,264 ft), of N-central CO in the Front Range of the Rocky Mts.

Evans, Walker. 1903–75. Amer. photographer noted for his images of the rural South during the 1930's.

Ev•ans•ton (ĕv′ən-stən). A city of NE IL on Lake Michigan N of Chicago. Pop. 73,233.

Ev•ans•ville (ĕv′ənz-vĭl′). A city of extreme SW IN on the Ohio R. and the KY border. Pop. 126,272.

e•vap•o•ra•ble (ĭ-văp′ər-ə-bəl) *adj.* That can evaporate or undergo evaporation. — **e•vap′o•ra•bil′i•ty** *n.*

e•vap•o•rate (ĭ-văp′ə-rāt′) *v.* **-rat•ed, -rat•ing, -rates.** —*tr.* **1.a.** To convert or change into a vapor. **b.** To draw off in the form of vapor. **2.** To draw moisture from, as by heating, leaving only the dry solid portion. **3.** To deposit (a metal) on a substrate by vacuum sublimation. —*intr.* **1.a.** To change into vapor. **b.** To pass off in or as vapor. **2.** To produce vapor. **3.** To disappear; vanish. See Syns at **disappear.** [ME *evaporaten* < Lat. *ēvapōrāre, ēvapōrāt-* : *ē-*, *ex-*, ex- + *vapor*, steam.] — **e•vap′o•ra′tion** *n.* — **e•vap′o•ra′tive** *adj.* — **e•vap′o•ra′tive•ly** *adv.* — **e•vap′o•ra•tiv′i•ty** (-ərə-tĭv′ĭ-tē) *n.* — **e•vap′o•ra′tor** *n.*

e•vap•o•rat•ed milk (ĭ-văp′ə-rā′tĭd) *n.* Concentrated milk made by evaporating some of the water from whole milk.

e•vap•o•rite (ĭ-văp′ə-rīt′) *n.* A sedimentary deposit that results from the evaporation of seawater. [EVAPOR(ATION) + –ITE¹.] — **e•vap′o•rit′ic** (-rĭt′ĭk) *adj.*

e•va•sion (ĭ-vā′zhən) *n.* **1.** The act or an instance of evading. **2.** A means of evading; a subterfuge. [ME *evasioun* < OFr. *evasion* < LLat. *ēvāsiō, ēvāsiōn-* < Lat. *ēvāsus*, p.part. of *ēvādere*, to evade. See EVADE.]

e•va•sive (ĭ-vā′sĭv) *adj.* **1.** Inclined or intended to evade. **2.** Intentionally vague or ambiguous; equivocal: *an evasive statement.* — **e•va′sive•ly** *adv.* — **e•va′sive•ness** *n.*

eve (ēv) *n.* **1.** The evening or day preceding a special day. **2.** The period immediately preceding a certain event: *the eve of war.* **3.** Evening. [ME, var. of *even*. See EVEN².]

Eve (ēv). In the Bible, the first woman and the wife of Adam.

e•vec•tion (ĭ-vĕk′shən) *n.* Solar perturbation of the lunar orbit. [Lat. *ēvectiō, ēvectiōn-*, a going up < *ēvectus*, p.part. of *ēvehere*, to raise up : *ē-*, *ex-*, up from; see EX– + *vehere*, to carry; see **wegh-***.] — **e•vec′tion•al** *adj.*

Eve•lyn (ēv′lĭn, ĕv′-), **John.** 1620–1706. English writer noted for his *Diary* (published 1818).

e•ven¹ (ē′vən) *adj.* **1.a.** Having a horizontal surface; flat. **b.** Having no irregularities, roughness, or indentations; smooth. **c.** Being in the same plane or line; parallel. **2.a.** Having no variations or fluctuations; uniform. **b.** Of uniform distribution. **c.** Placid; calm. **3.a.** Equal or identical in degree, extent, or amount. **b.** Equally matched or balanced. **c.** Just; fair. **d.** Having nothing due on either side; square. **e.** Having exacted full revenge. **4.** Having equal probability; as likely as not. **5.** *Sports.* **a.** Having an equal score. **b.** Being equal for each opponent. Used of a score. **6.** *Math.* **a.** Exactly divisible by 2. **b.** Characterized or indicated by a number exactly divisible by 2. **7.a.** Having an even number in a series. **b.** Having an even number of members. **8.** Having an exact amount, extent, or number; precise. —*adv.* **1.a.** To a greater degree or extent. Used as an intensive with comparative adjectives and adverbs: *looked sick and felt even worse.* **b.** Indeed; moreover. Used as an intensive: *Even I know better.* **c.** Used as an intensive to indicate something that is unexpected: *declined even to consider the idea.* **2.** At the same time; already; just. **3.** To a degree that extends; fully: *loyal even unto death.* **4.** Exactly; precisely. —*tr. & intr.v.* **e•vened, e•ven•ing, e•vens.** To make or become even. —***idiom.*** **on an even keel.**

In a stable or unimpaired state. [ME < OE *efen.*] — **e′ven•er** *n.* — **e′ven•ly** *adv.* — **e′ven•ness** *n.*

e•ven² (ē′vən) *n. Archaic.* Evening. [ME < OE *ǣfen.*]

e•ven•fall (ē′vən-fôl′) *n.* The beginning of evening; twilight.

e•ven•hand•ed (ē′vən-hăn′dĭd) *adj.* Showing no partiality; fair. — **e′ven•hand′ed•ly** *adv.* — **e′ven•hand′ed•ness** *n.*

eve•ning (ēv′nĭng) *n.* **1.** The period of decreasing daylight between afternoon and night. **2.** The period between sunset or the evening meal and bedtime. **3.** A later period or time. **4.** *Chiefly Southern U.S.* Middle to late afternoon. [ME < OE *ǣfnung* < *ǣfnian,* to become evening < *ǣfen,* evening.]

evening clothes *pl.n.* See **evening dress** 1.

evening dress *n.* **1.** Clothing worn for evening social events. **2.** See **evening gown.**

evening gown *n.* A woman's formal dress.

Eve•ning Prayer (ēv′nĭng prâr) *n.* A daily evening service in the Anglican Church.

evening primrose *n.* Any of various North American plants of the genus *Oenothera,* characteristically having four-petaled yellow flowers that open in the evening.

evening star *n.* A planet, esp. Venus or Mercury, that is prominent in the west shortly after sunset.

E•ven•ki (ĭ-wĕng′kē, ĭ-vĕng′-) also **E•wen•ki** (ĭ-wĕng′kē) *n., pl.* **Evenki** or **-kis** also **Ewenki** or **-kis. 1.** A member of a people inhabiting a large area of eastern Siberia and northern Nei Monggol (Inner Mongolia). **2.** The Tungusic language of the Evenki. [Russ., Evenki people < Evenki *əwənki.*]

e•ven-pin•nate (ē′vən-pĭn′āt) *adj. Bot.* Of or relating to a compound leaf not terminating in a leaflet.

e•ven•song (ē′vən-sông′, -sŏng′) *n.* **1.** See **Evening Prayer. 2.** *Rom. Cath. Ch.* A service that includes the office of Vespers. **3.** A song sung in the evening. **4.** *Archaic.* Evening.

e•ven-ste•ven (ē′vən-stē′vən) *adj. Informal.* **1.** Having nothing due or owed on either side: *an even-steven transaction.* **2.** Having an equal score, as in a game or contest.

e•vent (ĭ-vĕnt′) *n.* **1.a.** Something that takes place; an occurrence. **b.** A significant occurrence or happening. See Syns at **occurrence. c.** A social gathering or activity. **2.** The final result; the outcome. **3.** *Sports.* A contest or an item in a sports program. **4.** *Phys.* A point in space-time. — ***idioms.* at all events.** In any case. **in any event.** In any case. **in the event.** If it should happen; in case. [Lat. *ēventus* < p.part. of *ēvenīre,* to happen : *ē-, ex-,* ex- + *venīre,* to come; see **gʷā-*.**]

e•ven-tem•pered (ē′vən-tĕm′pərd) *adj.* Easygoing; calm.

e•vent•ful (ĭ-vĕnt′fəl) *adj.* **1.** Full of events. **2.** Important; momentous. — **e•vent′ful•ly** *adv.* — **e•vent′ful•ness** *n.*

e•ven•tide (ē′vən-tīd′) *n.* Evening. [ME < OE *ǣfentīd* : *ǣfen,* evening + *tīd,* time; see **dā-*.**]

e•ven•tu•al (ĭ-vĕn′cho͞o-əl) *adj.* **1.** Occurring at some future time; ultimate: *his eventual failure.* See Syns at **last¹. 2.** *Archaic.* Dependent on circumstance; contingent. [Fr. *éventuel* < Lat. *ēventus,* outcome. See EVENT.]

e•ven•tu•al•i•ty (ĭ-vĕn′cho͞o-ăl′ĭ-tē) *n., pl.* **-ties.** Something that may occur; a possibility.

e•ven•tu•al•ly (ĭ-vĕn′cho͞o-ə-lē) *adv.* At an unspecified future time.

e•ven•tu•ate (ĭ-vĕn′cho͞o-āt′) *intr.v.* **-at•ed, -at•ing, -ates.** To result ultimately.

ev•er (ĕv′ər) *adv.* **1.** At all times; always: *ever hoping to strike it rich.* **2.a.** At any time. **b.** In any way; at all: *How did they ever manage?* See Usage Note at **rarely. 3.** To a great extent or degree. Used for emphasis often with *so: He was ever so sorry.* — ***idioms.* ever and again (**or **anon).** Now and then; occasionally. **for ever and a day.** Always; forever. [ME < OE *ǣfre.* See **aiw-*.**]

ev•er•bloom•ing (ĕv′ər-blo͞o′mĭng) *adj.* Blooming throughout the growing season.

Ev•er•est (ĕv′ər-ĭst, ĕv′rĭst), **Mount.** A mountain, 8,853.5 m (29,028 ft), of the central Himalaya Mts. on the border of Tibet and Nepal; first scaled in 1953.

Ev•er•ett (ĕv′ər-ĭt, ĕv′rĭt). **1.** A city of E MA, a suburb of Boston. Pop. 35,701. **2.** A city of NW WA on Puget Sound N of Seattle. Pop. 69,961.

Everett, Edward. 1794–1865. Amer. cleric, educator, and diplomat who served as U.S. secretary of state (1852–53).

ev•er•glade (ĕv′ər-glād′) *n.* A tract of marshland, usu. under water and with patches of tall grass. [After the EVERGLADES.]

Ev•er•glades (ĕv′ər-glādz′). A subtropical swamp area of S FL including **Everglades National Park.**

ev•er•green (ĕv′ər-grēn′) *adj.* **1.** Having foliage that persists and remains green through the year. **2.** Perennially fresh or interesting; enduring. — *n.* **1.** An evergreen tree, shrub, or plant. **2. evergreens.** Twigs or branches of evergreen plants used as decoration.

Ev•er•green Park (ĕv′ər-grēn′). A village of NE IL, a suburb of Chicago. Pop. 20,874.

ev•er•last•ing (ĕv′ər-lăs′tĭng) *adj.* **1.** Lasting forever; eternal. **2.a.** Continuing indefinitely or for a long period of time. **b.** Persisting too long; tedious. — *n.* **1. Everlasting.** God. **2.** Eternal duration; eternity. **3.** Any of various plants that retain form and color long after they are dry. — **ev′er•last′ing•ly** *adv.* — **ev′er•last′ing•ness** *n.*

ev•er•more (ĕv′ər-môr′, -mōr′) *adv.* **1.** Forever; always. **2.** In a future time.

Ev•ers (ĕv′ərz), **Medgar Wiley.** 1925–63. Amer. civil rights worker in MS who was killed by a sniper. His work was continued by his brother **Charles** (b. 1923).

e•ver•sion (ĭ-vûr′zhən, -shən) *n.* **1.a.** The act of turning inside out. **b.** The condition of being turned inside out. **2.** The condition of being turned outward. [ME *eversioun* < OFr. *eversion* < Lat. *ēversiō, ēversiōn-* < *ēversus,* p.part. of *ēvertere,* to overturn. See EVERT.] — **e•ver′si•ble** (-sə-bəl) *adj.*

e•vert (ĭ-vûrt′) *tr.v.* **e•vert•ed, e•vert•ing, e•verts.** To turn inside out or outward. [Back-formation < ME *everted,* turned upside down < Lat. *ēvertus,* p.part. of *ēvertere,* to overturn : *ē-, ex-,* ex- + *vertere,* to turn; see **wer-²*.**]

Ev•ert (ĕv′ərt), **Christine ("Chris") Marie.** b. 1954. Amer. tennis player who won women's singles titles at the U.S. Open (1975–78, 1980, and 1982) and Wimbledon (1974, 1976, and 1981).

ev•er•where (ĕv′ər-hwâr′, -wâr′) *adv. Chiefly Southern U.S.* **1.** Everywhere. **2.** Wherever.

Regional Note: Inversion — the reversal of the two halves of a compound word — is a common process in Southern dialects. The commonly occurring *everwhere* is an example of inversion when it means "wherever." Other examples of Southern inversion cited by Craig M. Carver in *American Regional Dialects* are *peckerwood, hoppergrass, doll-baby, tie-tongued, doghanged* (meaning "hangdog"), and *right-out* ("outright").

ev•er•which (ĕv′ər-hwĭch′, -wĭch′) *pron. Chiefly Southern U.S.* Whichever. See Regional Note at **everwhere.**

eve•ry (ĕv′rē) *adj.* **1.a.** Constituting each and all members of a group without exception. **b.** Being all possible: *every chance of winning.* **2.** Being each of a specified succession of objects or intervals: *every two hours.* **3.** Being the highest degree or expression of: *had every hope of succeeding.* — ***idioms.* every bit.** *Informal.* In all ways; equally. **every now and then (**or **again).** From time to time; occasionally. **every once in a while.** From time to time. **every other.** Each alternate: *every other week.* **every so often.** At intervals; occasionally. **every which way.** *Informal.* **1.** In every direction. **2.** In complete disorder. [ME *everi, everich* < OE *ǣfre ǣlc* : *ǣfre,* ever; see **aiw-*** + *ǣlc,* each; see **līk-*.**]

Usage Note: *Every* is representative of a large class of English words and expressions that are singular in form but felt to be plural in sense. The class includes, for example, noun phrases introduced by *every, any,* and certain uses of *some.* These expressions invariably take a singular verb; we say *Every car has been tested.* But when a sentence contains a pronoun whose antecedent is introduced by *every,* people persist in using the plural pronoun, as in *Every car must have their brakes tested.* This pattern is still widely regarded as grammatically incorrect in writing. See Usage Notes at **any, either, he¹, neither, none.**

eve•ry•bod•y (ĕv′rē-bŏd′ē, -bŭd′ē) *pron.* Every person; everyone.

eve•ry•day (ĕv′rē-dā′) *adj.* **1.** Appropriate for ordinary days or routine occasions: *everyday wear.* **2.** Commonplace; ordinary: *everyday worries.* — *n.* The ordinary or routine day or occasion. — **eve′ry•day′ness** *n.*

Eve•ry•man or **eve•ry•man** (ĕv′rē-măn′) *n.* **1.** An ordinary person, representative of humanity and usu. perceived as male. **2.** An ordinary man, representative of all men.

eve•ry•one (ĕv′rē-wŭn′) *pron.* Every person; everybody. See Usage Notes at **every, he¹.**

eve•ry•place (ĕv′rē-plās′) *adv. Informal.* Everywhere.

Usage Note: The terms *everyplace* (or *every place*), *anyplace* (or *any place*), *someplace* (or *some place*), and *no place* are widely used in speech and informal writing as equivalents for *everywhere, anywhere, somewhere,* and *nowhere.* Though these usages are not incorrect, they should be avoided in formal writing. But when the two-word expressions *every place, any place, some place,* and *no place* are used to mean "every (any, some, no) spot or location," they are entirely appropriate at all levels of style. Acceptability can often be gauged by seeing whether an expression with *-where* can be substituted.

eve•ry•thing (ĕv′rē-thĭng′) *pron.* **1.a.** All things or all of a group of things. **b.** All relevant matters: *told me everything.* **2.** The most important fact or consideration.

eve•ry•where (ĕv′rē-hwâr′, -wâr′) *adv.* In any or every place; in all places. See Usage Note at **everyplace.**

Eve•ry•wom•an or **eve•ry•wom•an** (ĕv′rē-wo͝om′ən) *n.* An ordinary woman, representative of all women.

evg. *abbr.* Evening.

e•vict (ĭ-vĭkt′) *tr.v.* **e•vict•ed, e•vict•ing, e•victs. 1.** To put out (a tenant, for example) by legal process; expel. **2.** To force out; eject. See Syns at **eject. 3.** *Law.* To recover (property, for example) by a superior claim or legal process. [ME *evicten* < Lat. *ēvincere, ēvict-,* to vanquish : *ē-, ex-,* intensive pref.; see EX- + *vincere,* to defeat; see **weik-³*.**] — **e•vict•ee′** (ĭ-vĭk-tē′, ĭ-vĭk′tē) *n.* — **e•vic′tion** *n.* — **e•vic′tor** *n.*

ev•i•dence (ĕv′ĭ-dəns) *n.* **1.** A thing or things helpful in forming a conclusion or judgment: *evidence of a burglary.*

Chris Evert
Playing at the French Open tournament, 1986

ă pat	oi boy
ā pay	ou out
âr care	o͝o took
ä father	o͞o boot
ĕ pet	ŭ cut
ē be	ûr urge
ĭ pit	th thin
ī pie	*th* this
îr pier	hw which
ŏ pot	zh vision
ō toe	ə about, item
ô paw	

Stress marks:
′ (primary);
′ (secondary), as in **dictionary** (dĭk′shə-nĕr′ē)

2. Something indicative; an outward sign: *evidence of grief.* **3.** *Law.* The documentary or oral statements and the material objects admissible as testimony in a court of law. — *tr.v.* **-denced, -denc•ing, -denc•es. 1.** To indicate clearly; exemplify or prove. **2.** To support by testimony; attest. — ***idiom.*** **in evidence. 1.** Plainly visible; to be seen. **2.** *Law.* As legal evidence. [ME < OFr. < LLat. *ēvidentia* < Lat. *ēvidēns, ēvident-*, obvious. See EVIDENT.]

ev•i•dent (ĕv′ĭ-dənt) *adj.* Easily seen or understood; obvious. See Syns at **apparent.** [ME < OFr. < Lat. *ēvidēns, ēvident-* : *ē-, ex-*, ex- + *vidēns*, pr.part. of *vidēre*, to see; see **weid-***.]

ev•i•den•tial (ĕv′ĭ-dĕn′shəl) *adj. Law.* Of, providing, or constituting evidence. — **ev′i•den′tial•ly** *adv.*

ev•i•den•tia•ry (ĕv′ĭ-dĕn′shə-rē, -shē-ĕr′ē) *adj. Law.* **1.** Of evidence; evidential. **2.** For the presentation or determination of evidence: *an evidentiary hearing.*

ev•i•dent•ly (ĕv′ĭ-dənt-lē, ĕv′ĭ-dĕnt′lē) *adv.* **1.** Obviously; clearly. **2.** According to the evidence available.

e•vil (ē′vəl) *adj.* **e•vil•er, e•vil•est. 1.** Morally bad or wrong; wicked. See Syns at **bad[1]**. **2.** Causing ruin, injury, or pain; harmful. **3.** Characterized by or indicating future misfortune; ominous. **4.** Bad or blameworthy by report; infamous. **5.** Marked by anger or spite; malicious. — *n.* **1.** The quality of being morally bad or wrong; wickedness. **2.** That which causes harm, misfortune, or destruction. **3.** An evil force, power, or personification. **4.** Something causing suffering, injury, or destruction. — *adv. Archaic.* In an evil manner. [ME < OE *yfel.* See **wep-***.] — **e′vil•ly** *adv.* — **e′vil•ness** *n.*

e•vil•do•er (ē′vəl-dōō′ər) *n.* One that performs evil acts. — **e′vil•do′ing** *n.*

evil eye *n.* **1.** A look or stare believed to harm others. **2.** The presumed power to harm others by magic or supernatural means.

e•vil-mind•ed (ē′vəl-mīn′dĭd) *adj.* Having evil thoughts, opinions, or intentions. — **e′vil-mind′ed•ly** *adv.* — **e′vil-mind′ed•ness** *n.*

ewer
Mid 13th-century Persian engraved brass ewer

e•vince (ĭ-vĭns′) *tr.v.* **e•vinced, e•vinc•ing, e•vinc•es.** To show or demonstrate clearly; manifest. [Lat. *ēvincere*, to prevail, prove. See EVICT.] — **e•vinc′i•ble** *adj.*

e•vis•cer•ate (ĭ-vĭs′ə-rāt′) *v.* **-at•ed, -at•ing, -ates.** — *tr.* **1.** To remove the entrails of; disembowel. **2.** To take away a vital or essential part of. **3.** *Medic.* **a.** To remove the contents of (an organ). **b.** To remove an organ, such as an eye, from (a patient). — *intr. Medic.* To protrude through a wound or surgical incision. [Lat. *ēviscerāre, ēviscerāt-* : *ē-, ex-*, ex- + *viscera*, internal organs; see VISCERA.] — **e•vis′cer•a′tion** *n.*

ev•i•ta•ble (ĕv′ĭ-tə-bəl) *adj.* Avoidable. [Lat. *ēvītābilis* < *ēvītāre*, to shun : *ex-*, ex- + *vītāre*, to avoid.]

ev•o•ca•tion (ĕv′ə-kā′shən, ē′və-) *n.* **1.** The act of evoking. **2.** Creation anew through memory or imagination. — **ev′o•ca′tor** *n.*

e•voc•a•tive (ĭ-vŏk′ə-tĭv) *adj.* Tending or having the power to evoke. — **e•voc′a•tive•ly** *adv.* — **e•voc′a•tive•ness** *n.*

e•voke (ĭ-vōk′) *tr.v.* **e•voked, e•vok•ing, e•vokes. 1.** To summon or call forth. **2.** To call to mind by naming, citing, or suggesting. **3.** To re-create, esp. through imagination. [Lat. *ēvocāre* : *ē-, ex-*, ex- + *vocāre*, to call; see **wek^w-***.] — **ev′o•ca•ble** (ĕv′ə-kə-bəl, ĭ-vō′kə-) *adj.*

ev•o•lute (ĕv′ə-lōōt′, ē′və-) *n. Math.* The locus of the centers of curvature of a given curve. [< Lat. *ēvolūtus*, p.part. of *ēvolvere*, to unroll. See EVOLVE.]

ev•o•lu•tion (ĕv′ə-lōō′shən, ē′və-) *n.* **1.** A gradual process in which something changes into a different and usu. more complex or better form. See Syns at **development. 2.a.** The process of developing. **b.** Gradual development. **3.** *Biol.* **a.** The theory that groups of organisms change morphologically and physiologically with time, mainly as a result of natural selection. **b.** The historical development of a related group of organisms; phylogeny. **4.** A movement that is part of a set of ordered movements. **5.** *Math.* The extraction of a root of a quantity. [Lat. *ēvolūtiō, ēvolūtiōn-* < *ēvolūtus*, p.part. of *ēvolvere*, to unroll. See EVOLVE.] — **ev′o•lu′tion•al, ev′o•lu′tion•ar′y** (-shə-nĕr′ē) *adj.* — **ev′o•lu′tion•ar′i•ly** *adv.*

ev•o•lu•tion•ism (ĕv′ə-lōō′shə-nĭz′əm, ē′və-) *n.* **1.** A theory of biological evolution, esp. that of Darwin. **2.** Advocacy of or belief in biological evolution. — **ev′o•lu′tion•ist** *n.*

e•volve (ĭ-vŏlv′) *v.* **e•volved, e•volv•ing, e•volves.** — *tr.* **1.a.** To develop or achieve gradually: *evolve a style of one's own.* **b.** To work (something) out; devise. **2.** *Biol.* To develop (a characteristic) by evolutionary processes. **3.** To give off; emit. — *intr.* **1.** To undergo gradual change; develop. **2.** *Biol.* To develop or arise through evolutionary processes. [Lat. *ēvolvere*, to unroll : *ē-, ex-*, ex- + *volvere*, to roll; see **wel-[2]***.] — **e•volv′a•ble** *adj.* — **e•volve′ment** *n.*

e•vul•sion (ĭ-vŭl′shən) *n.* A forcible extraction. [Lat. *ēvolsiō, ēvolsiōn-* < *ēvulsus*, p.part. of *ēvellere*, to pull out : *ē-, ex-*, ex- + *vellere*, to pull.]

Ev•voia (ĕv′yä). See **Euboea.**

ev•zone (ev′zōn′) *n.* An infantryman of a special corps of the Greek army. [Mod.Gk. *euzōnos* < Gk., well-girded, dressed for exercise : *eu-*, well; see EU- + *zōnē*, girdle.]

EW *abbr.* Enlisted woman.

ewe (yōō) *n.* A female sheep, esp. when full grown. [ME < OE *ēwe, eōwu.* See **owi-***.]

E•we (ā′wā′, ā′vā′) *n., pl.* **Ewe** or **E•wes. 1.** A member of a people inhabiting southeast Ghana, southern Togo, and southern Benin. **2.** The Gbe language of the Ewe people.

Ew•ell (yōō′əl), **Richard Stoddert.** 1817–72. Amer. Confederate general in the U.S. Civil War.

ewe-neck (yōō′nĕk′) *n.* A defect in a horse or dog in which the neck is thin and has a concave arch. — **ewe′-necked′** *adj.*

E•wen•ki (ĭ-wĕng′kē) *n.* Var. of **Evenki.**

ew•er (yōō′ər) *n.* A pitcher, esp. a decorative one with a base, an oval body, and a flaring spout. [ME *euer* < AN < VLat. **aquāria* < Lat. *aquārius*, of water < *aqua*, water. See **ak^w-ā-***.]

Ew•ing (yōō′ĭng). A community of W-central NJ NNW of Trenton. Pop. 34,185.

ex[1] (ĕks) *prep.* **1.** Not including; without: *a stock price ex dividend.* **2.** *Bus.* Free of any transport or handling charges incurred before removal from a given location. **3.** From, but not having graduated with, the class of. [Lat. See **eghs***.]

ex[2] (ĕks) *n.* The letter *x.*

ex[3] (ĕks) *n. Slang.* A former spouse or partner. [< EX–.]

Ex or **Ex.** *abbr. Bible.* Exodus.

ex. *abbr.* **1.** Examination. **2.** Example. **3.** Except; exception. **4.** Exchange. **5.** Executive. **6.** Express. **7.** Extra.

ex– *pref.* **1.** Outside; out of; away from: *exodontia.* **2.** Not; without: *excaudate.* **3.** Former: *ex-president.* [ME (< OFr. < Lat.) and Gk.; see **eghs***.]

ex•ac•er•bate (ĭg-zăs′ər-bāt′) *tr.v.* **-bat•ed, -bat•ing, -bates.** To increase the severity, violence, or bitterness of; aggravate. [Lat. *exacerbāre, exacerbāt-* : *ex-*, intensive pref.; see EX– + *acerbāre*, to make harsh (< *acerbus*, harsh; see **ak-***).] — **ex•ac′er•ba′tion** *n.*

ex•act (ĭg-zăkt′) *adj.* **1.** Strictly and completely in accord with fact; not deviating from truth or reality. **2.** Marked by accurate measurements or inferences with small margins of error. **3.** Marked by strict adherence to standards or rules. — *tr.v.* **-act•ed, -act•ing, -acts. 1.** To force the payment or yielding of; extort. **2.** To demand and obtain by or as if by force or authority. See Syns at **demand.** [Lat. *exāctus*, p.part. of *exigere*, to weigh out, demand : *ex-*, ex- + *agere*, to weigh; see **ag-***.] — **ex•act′a•ble** *adj.* — **ex•act′ness** *n.* — **ex•ac′tor, ex•act′er** *n.*

ex•act•a (ĭg-zăk′tə) *n. Sports & Games.* A method of betting in which the bettor must correctly pick those finishing in the first and second places in that sequence. [< Am.Sp. *quiniela exacta*, exact quiniela (a game of chance) < Sp. *exacta*, fem. of *exacto* < Lat. *exāctus.* See EXACT.]

ex•act•ing (ĭg-zăk′tĭng) *adj.* **1.** Making severe demands; rigorous. **2.** Requiring great care, effort, or attention. — **ex•act′ing•ly** *adv.* — **ex•act′ing•ness** *n.*

ex•ac•tion (ĭg-zăk′shən) *n.* **1.a.** The act of exacting. **b.** Excessive or unjust demand; extortion. **2.** Something exacted.

ex•ac•ti•tude (ĭg-zăk′tĭ-tōōd′, -tyōōd′) *n.* The state or quality of being exact.

ex•act•ly (ĭg-zăkt′lē) *adv.* **1.** In an exact manner; accurately. **2.** In all respects; just. **3.** As you say.

ex•ag•ger•ate (ĭg-zăj′ə-rāt′) *v.* **-at•ed, -at•ing, -ates.** — *tr.* **1.** To represent as greater than is actually the case; overstate. **2.** To enlarge or increase to an abnormal degree. — *intr.* To make overstatements. [Lat. *exaggerāre, exaggerāt-*, to heap up, magnify : *ex-*, intensive pref.; see EX– + *aggerāre*, to pile up (< *agger*, pile < *aggerere*, to bring to : *ad-*, ad- + *gerere*, to bring).] — **ex•ag′ger•at′ed•ly** *adv.* — **ex•ag′ger•a′tion** *n.* — **ex•ag′ger•a′tive, ex•ag′ger•a•to′ry** (-ə-tôr′ē, -tōr′ē) *adj.* — **ex•ag′ger•a′tor** *n.*

Syns: *exaggerate, inflate, magnify, overstate.* The central meaning shared by these verbs is "to represent something as being larger or greater than it actually is": *exaggerated the size of the fish; inflated her own importance; magnifying his success; overstated their income.* ***Ant:*** *minimize.*

ex•alt (ĭg-zôlt′) *tr.v.* **-alt•ed, -alt•ing, -alts. 1.** To raise in rank, character, or status; elevate. **2.** To glorify, praise, or honor. **3.** To increase the effect or intensity of; heighten. **4.** *Obsolete.* To fill with sublime emotion; elate. [ME *exalten* < Lat. *exaltāre* : *ex-*, up, away; see EX– + *altus*, high; see **al-[2]***.] — **ex•alt′er** *n.*

ex•al•ta•tion (ĕg′zôl-tā′shən) *n.* **1.** The act of exalting or the condition of being exalted. **2.** A state or feeling of intense, often excessive exhilaration or well-being.

ex•alt•ed (ĭg-zôl′tĭd) *adj.* **1.** Elevated in rank, character, or status. **2.** Lofty; sublime; noble. **3.** Exaggerated; inflated. — **ex•alt′ed•ly** *adv.* — **ex•alt′ed•ness** *n.*

ex•am (ĭg-zăm′) *n.* An examination; a test.

ex•a•men (ĭg-zā′mən) *n.* An examination; an investigation. [Lat. *exāmen*, a weighing out. See EXAMINE.]

ex•am•i•nant (ĭg-zăm′ə-nənt) *n.* **1.** One who examines. **2.** One who is examined; an examinee.

ex•am•i•na•tion (ĭg-zăm′ə-nā′shən) *n.* **1.** The act of examining or the state of being examined. **2.** A set of questions or exercises testing knowledge or skill. **3.** A formal interrogation: *examination of the witness.* — **ex•am′i•na′tion•al** *adj.*

ex•am•ine (ĭg-zăm′ĭn) *tr.v.* **-ined, -in•ing, -ines. 1.a.** To observe carefully or critically; inspect. **b.** To study or analyze. **2.** To test or check the condition or health of. **3.** To determine the qualifications, aptitude, or skills of by means of questions or exercises. **4.** To question formally, as to elicit information. See Syns at **ask.** [ME *examinen* < OFr. *examiner* < Lat. *exāmināre* < *exāmen*, a weighing out < *exigere*, to weigh out. See EXACT.] **— ex•am′in•a•ble** *adj.* **— ex•am′in•er** *n.*

ex•am•in•ee (ĭg-zăm′ə-nē′) *n.* One that is examined.

ex•am•ple (ĭg-zăm′pəl) *n.* **1.** One that is representative of a group as a whole. **2.** One serving as a pattern of a specific kind. **3.** A similar case that constitutes a model or precedent. **4.a.** A punishment given as a warning or deterrent. **b.** One that has been given such a punishment. **5.** A problem or exercise used to illustrate a principle or method. **— *idiom.* for example.** As an illustrative instance. [ME < OFr. *example, essaumple* < Lat. *exemplum* < *eximere*, to take out : *ex-*, ex- + *emere*, to take; see **em-***.]

ex•an•the•ma (ĕg′zăn-thē′mə) also **ex•an•them** (ĭg-zăn′-thəm) *n., pl.* **-them•a•ta** (-thĕm′ə-tə) or **-the•mas** also **-thems.** *Medic.* **1.** A skin eruption accompanying certain infectious diseases. **2.** A disease, such as measles or scarlet fever, accompanied by a skin eruption. [LLat. *exanthēma* < Gk., eruption < *exanthein*, to burst forth : *ex-*, ex- + *anthein*, to blossom (< *anthos*, flower).] **— ex•an′the•mat′ic** (ĭg-zăn′-thə-măt′ĭk), **ex′an•them′a•tous** (ĕg′zăn-thĕm′ə-təs) *adj.*

ex•arch[1] (ĕk′särk′) *n.* **1.** A bishop in the Eastern Orthodox Church ranking immediately below a patriarch. **2.** The ruler of a province in the Byzantine Empire. [LLat. *exarchus*, an overseer < Gk. *exarkhos* < *exarkhein*, to lead : *ex-*, ex- + *arkhein*, to rule.] **— ex•arch′al** *adj.* **— ex′ar′chate** (ĕk′sär′-kāt), **ex′ar′chy** (-kē) *n.*

ex•arch[2] (ĕk′särk′) *adj. Bot.* Of or relating to a xylem whose early development is away from the center and toward the periphery. [EX(O)- + Gk. *arkhē*, beginning (< *arkhein*, to rule, begin).] **— ex′arch′** *n.*

ex•as•per•ate (ĭg-zăs′pə-rāt′) *tr.v.* **-at•ed, -at•ing, -ates. 1.** To make very angry or impatient; annoy greatly. **2.** To increase the gravity or intensity of. [Lat. *exasperāre, exasperāt-* : *ex-*, intensive pref.; see EX- + *asperāre*, to make rough (< *asper*, rough).] **— ex•as′per•at′ed•ly** *adv.* **— ex•as′per•at′er** *n.* **— ex•as′per•at′ing•ly** *adv.*

ex•as•per•a•tion (ĭg-zăs′pə-rā′shən) *n.* **1.** The act or an instance of exasperating. **2.** The state of being exasperated; frustrated annoyance.

exc. *abbr.* **1.** Excellent. **2.** Except; exception.

Exc. *abbr.* Excellency.

Ex•cal•i•bur (ĕk-skăl′ə-bər) *n.* In Arthurian legend, the sword belonging to King Arthur. [ME, alteration (perh. influenced by Lat. *chalybs*, steel) of Med.Lat. *Caliburnus* < Middle Welsh *Caletuwlch* or MIr. *Caladbolg*, a legendary sword.]

ex ca•the•dra (ĕks′ kə-thē′drə) *adv. & adj.* With the authority derived from one's office or position. [Lat. *ex cathedrā* : *ex*, from + *cathedrā*, ablative of *cathedra*, chair.]

ex•cau•date (ĕk-skô′dāt′) *adj.* Without a tail; tailless.

ex•ca•vate (ĕk′skə-vāt′) *v.* **-vat•ed, -vat•ing, -vates.** *— tr.* **1.** To make a hole in; hollow out. **2.** To form by hollowing out. **3.** To remove by digging or scooping out. **4.** To expose or uncover by or as if by digging. *— intr.* To engage in excavation. [Lat. *excavāre, excavāt-*, to hollow out : *ex-*, ex- + *cavāre*, to hollow (< *cavus*, hollow; see **keuə-***).]

ex•ca•va•tion (ĕk′skə-vā′shən) *n.* **1.** The act or process of excavating. **2.** A hole formed by excavating.

ex•ca•va•tor (ĕk′skə-vā′tər) *n.* One that excavates, esp. a backhoe.

ex•ceed (ĭk-sēd′) *tr.v.* **-ceed•ed, -ceed•ing, -ceeds. 1.** To be greater than; surpass. **2.** To go beyond the limits of: *exceeded their authority.* [ME *exceden* < OFr. *exceder* < Lat. *excēdere* : *ex-*, ex- + *cēdere*, to go; see **ked-***.]

ex•ceed•ing (ĭk-sē′dĭng) *adj.* Extreme; extraordinary: *exceeding darkness.* *— adv. Archaic.* Exceedingly.

ex•ceed•ing•ly (ĭk-sē′dĭng-lē) *adv.* To an advanced or unusual degree; extremely.

ex•cel (ĭk-sĕl′) *v.* **-celled, -cel•ling, -cels.** *— tr.* To do or be better than; surpass. *— intr.* To show superiority; surpass others. [ME *excellen* < Lat. *excellere.* See **kel-**[2]***.**]

ex•cel•lence (ĕk′sə-ləns) *n.* **1.** The state, quality, or condition of excelling; superiority. **2.** Something in which one excels. **3. Excellence.** Excellency.

Ex•cel•len•cy (ĕk′sə-lən-sē) *n., pl.* **-cies.** Used with *His, Her,* or *Your* as a title and form of address for certain high officials.

ex•cel•lent (ĕk′sə-lənt) *adj.* **1.** Of the highest or finest quality; exceptionally good of its kind. **2.** *Archaic.* Superior. [ME < OFr. < Lat. *excellēns, excellent-*, pr.part. of *excellere*, to excel. See EXCEL.] **— ex′cel•lent•ly** *adv.*

ex•cel•si•or (ĭk-sĕl′sē-ər) *n.* Slender curved wood shavings used esp. for packing. [Originally a trade name.]

ex•cept (ĭk-sĕpt′) *prep.* With the exclusion of; other than; but. *— conj.* **1.** If it were not for the fact that; only: *I would buy the suit, except that it costs too much.* **2.** Otherwise than: *They didn't open their mouths except to complain.* **3.** Unless. *— v.* **-cept•ed, -cept•ing, -cepts.** *— tr.* To leave out; exclude. *— intr.* To object. [ME < Lat. *exceptus*, p.part. of *excipere*, to exclude : *ex-*, ex- + *capere*, to take; see **kap-***.]

Usage Note: *Except* in the sense of "with the exclusion of" or "other than" is generally construed as a preposition, not a conjunction. A personal pronoun that follows *except* is therefore in the objective case: *No one except me knew it.*

ex•cept•ing (ĭk-sĕp′tĭng) *prep.* With the exception of. *— conj.* Except.

ex•cep•tion (ĭk-sĕp′shən) *n.* **1.** The act of excepting or the condition of being excepted; exclusion. **2.** One that is excepted, esp. a case that does not conform to a rule or generalization. **3.** An objection or a criticism. **4.** *Law.* A formal objection taken in the course of an action or a proceeding.

ex•cep•tion•a•ble (ĭk-sĕp′shə-nə-bəl) *adj.* Open or liable to objection or debate; objectionable or debatable. **— ex•cep′tion•a•bil′i•ty** *n.* **— ex•cep′tion•a•bly** *adv.*

Usage Note: *Exceptionable* and *exceptional* are not interchangeable. Only *exceptionable* is equivalent to "objectionable" or "debatable"; *exceptional* is equivalent to "uncommon" or "extraordinary."

ex•cep•tion•al (ĭk-sĕp′shə-nəl) *adj.* **1.** Being an exception; uncommon. **2.** Well above average; extraordinary. See Usage Note at **exceptionable. 3.** Deviating widely from a norm, as of physical or mental ability. **— ex•cep′tion•al′i•ty, ex•cep′tion•al•ness** *n.* **— ex•cep′tion•al•ly** (-shə-năl′ĭ-tē) *adv.*

ex•cep•tive (ĭk-sĕp′tĭv) *adj.* **1.** Of, being, or containing an exception. **2.** *Archaic.* Captious; faultfinding.

ex•cerpt (ĕk′sûrpt′) *n.* A passage or segment taken from a longer work, such as a literary composition. *— tr.v.* (ĭk-sûrpt′) **-cerpt•ed, -cerpt•ing, -cerpts. 1.** To select or use (an excerpt). **2.** To select or use material from (a longer work). [< ME, excerpted < Lat. *excerptus*, p.part. of *excerpere*, to pick out : *ex-*, ex- + *carpere*, to pluck; see **kerp-***.]

ex•cess (ĭk-sĕs′, ĕk′sĕs′) *n.* **1.** The state of exceeding what is normal or sufficient. **2.** An amount or quantity beyond what is normal or sufficient; a surplus. **3.** The amount or degree by which one quantity exceeds another: *the excess of sales over costs.* **4.** Intemperance; overindulgence. **5.** A behavior or an action that exceeds proper or lawful bounds. *— adj.* Being more than is usual, required, or permitted. See Syns at **superfluous.** *— tr.v.* **-cessed, -cess•ing, -cess•es.** To eliminate the job or position of. **— *idiom.* in excess of.** Greater than; more than. [ME < OFr. < Lat. *excessus*, p.part. of *excēdere*, to exceed. See EXCEED.]

ex•ces•sive (ĭk-sĕs′ĭv) *adj.* Exceeding a normal, usual, reasonable, or proper limit. **— ex•ces′sive•ly** *adv.* **— ex•ces′sive•ness** *n.*

Syns: *excessive, exorbitant, extravagant, immoderate, inordinate, extreme, unreasonable.* These adjectives mean exceeding a normal, usual, reasonable, or proper limit. *Excessive* describes a quantity, an amount, or a degree that is more than what is justifiable, tolerable, or desirable: *excessive drinking. Exorbitant* usually refers to a quantity or degree that far exceeds what is customary or fair: *an exorbitant price. Extravagant* sometimes specifies lavish or unwise expenditure (*extravagant gifts*); often it implies unbridled divergence from the bounds of reason or sound judgment (*extravagant claims*). *Immoderate* denotes lack of due moderation: *immoderate enthusiasm. Inordinate* implies an overstepping of bounds imposed by authority or dictated by good sense: *inordinate demands. Extreme* suggests the utmost degree of excessiveness: *extreme joy. Unreasonable* applies to what exceeds reasonable limits: *charged an unreasonable rent.*

exch. *abbr.* **1.** Exchange. **2.** Also **Exch.** Exchequer.

ex•change (ĭks-chānj′) *v.* **-changed, -chang•ing, -chang•es.** *— tr.* **1.** To give in return for something received; trade. **2.** To give and receive reciprocally; interchange. **3.** To give up for a substitute. **4.** To turn in for replacement. *— intr.* **1.** To give something in return for something received; make an exchange. **2.** To be received in exchange: *The British pound once exchanged for $2.80.* *— n.* **1.** The act or an instance of exchanging. **2.** One that is exchanged. **3.** A place where things are exchanged, esp. a center where securities or commodities are bought and sold. **4.** A telephone exchange. **5.a.** A system of payments using instruments, such as negotiable drafts, instead of money. **b.** The fee or percentage charged for participating in such a system of payment. **6.** A bill of exchange. **7.** A rate of exchange. **8.** The amount of difference in the actual value of two or more currencies or between values of the same currency at two or more places. [ME *eschaungen* < AN *eschaungier* < VLat. **excambiāre* : Lat. *ex-*, ex- + LLat. *cambīre*, to exchange, barter; see CHANGE.] **— ex•change′a•ble** *adj.*

exchange rate *n.* A rate of exchange.

ex•cheq•uer (ĕks′chĕk′ər, ĭks-chĕk′ər) *n.* **1. Exchequer.** The British governmental department charged with the collection and management of the national revenue. **2. Exchequer.** In Great Britain, the Court of Exchequer. **3.** A treasury, as of a nation or an organization. **4.** Financial resources; funds. [Alteration of ME *escheker* < OFr. *eschequier*, counting table, chessboard < *eschec*, check. See CHECK.]

ă pat	oi boy
ā pay	ou out
âr care	o͝o took
ä father	o͞o boot
ĕ pet	ŭ cut
ē be	ûr urge
ĭ pit	th thin
ī pie	*th* this
îr pier	hw which
ŏ pot	zh vision
ō toe	ə about, item
ô paw	

Stress marks:
′ (primary);
′ (secondary), as in **dictionary** (dĭk′shə-nĕr′ē)

ex•ci•mer (ĕk′sə-mər) *n.* A diatomic molecule existing in an energy level above the ground state. [EXC(ITED) + (D)IMER.]

ex•cip•i•ent (ĭk-sĭp′ē-ənt) *n.* An inert substance used as a diluent or vehicle for a drug. [Lat. *excipiēns, excipient-*, pr.part. of *excipere*, to take out, exclude. See EXCEPT.]

ex•cise[1] (ĕk′sīz′) *n.* **1.** An internal tax imposed on the production, sale, or consumption of a commodity or the use of a service within a country. **2.** A licensing charge or a fee levied for certain privileges. — *tr.v.* **-cised, -cis•ing, -cis•es.** To levy an excise on. [MDu. *excijs*, alteration of *accijs*, tax, prob. < OFr. *acceis*, partly < VLat. **accēnsum* (Lat. *ad-*, ad- + Lat. *cēnsus*, tax; see CENSUS) and partly < OFr. *assise*, legislative ordinance; see ASSIZE.] — **ex•cis′a•ble** *adj.*

ex•cise[2] (ĭk-sīz′) *tr.v.* **-cised, -cis•ing, -cis•es.** To remove by or as if by cutting. [Lat. *excīdere, excīs-* : *ex-*, ex- + *caedere*, to cut; see **kaə-id-***.] — **ex•ci′sion** (-sĭzh′ən) *n.*

ex•cit•a•ble (ĭk-sī′tə-bəl) *adj.* **1.** Easily excited. **2.** Capable of responding to stimuli. — **ex•cit′a•bil′i•ty, ex•cit′a•ble•ness** *n.* — **ex•cit′a•bly** *adv.*

ex•ci•tant (ĭk-sīt′nt) *adj.* Tending to excite; stimulating. — *n.* An agent or stimulus that excites; a stimulant.

ex•ci•ta•tion (ĕk′sī-tā′shən) *n.* **1.** The act or process of exciting or an instance of it. **2.** The state or condition of being excited. **3.** *Physiol.* The activity produced in an organ, a tissue, or a part, such as a nerve cell, as a result of stimulation.

ex•ci•ta•tive (ĭk-sī′tə-tĭv) or **ex•ci•ta•to•ry** (-sī′tə-tôr′ē, -tōr′ē) *adj.* Causing or tending to cause excitation.

ex•cite (ĭk-sīt′) *tr.v.* **-cit•ed, -cit•ing, -cites. 1.** To stir to activity. **2.** To call forth (a reaction, for example); elicit. **3.** To arouse strong feeling in: *excited the crowd.* **4.** *Physiol.* To produce increased activity or response in (an organ, a tissue, or a part); stimulate. **5.** *Phys.* **a.** To increase the energy of. **b.** To raise (an atom, for example) to a higher energy level. [ME *exciten* < Lat. *excitāre*, freq. of *exciēre* : *ex-*, ex- + *ciēre*, to set in motion; see **kei-[2]***.]

ex•cit•ed (ĭk-sī′tĭd) *adj.* **1.** Being in a state of excitement; emotionally aroused; stirred. **2.** *Phys.* Being at an energy level higher than the ground state. — **ex•cit′ed•ly** *adv.*

ex•cite•ment (ĭk-sīt′mənt) *n.* **1.a.** The act or an instance of exciting. **b.** The condition of being excited. **2.** Something that excites.

ex•cit•er (ĭk-sī′tər) *n.* **1.** One that excites: *an exciter of animosity.* **2.** An auxiliary generator used to provide field current for a larger generator or alternator. **3.** *Electron.* An oscillator for generating the carrier frequency of a transmitter.

ex•cit•ing (ĭk-sī′tĭng) *adj.* Creating or producing excitement: *an exciting story.* — **ex•cit′ing•ly** *adv.*

ex•ci•ton (ĕk′sĭ-tŏn′, -sī-) *n. Phys.* An electrically neutral excited state of an insulator or semiconductor, often regarded as a bound state of an electron and a hole. [EXCIT(ATION) + -ON[1].]

ex•ci•ton•ics (ĕk′sĭ-tŏn′ĭks, -sī-) *n.* *(used with a sing. v.) Phys.* The study of excitons and their behavior in semiconductors and dielectrics.

ex•ci•tor (ĭk-sī′tər) *n.* A nerve whose stimulation induces an increase in activity of the part it supplies.

excl. *abbr.* **1.** Exclamation. **2.** Exclusive.

ex•claim (ĭk-sklām′) *v.* **-claimed, -claim•ing, -claims.** — *intr.* To cry out suddenly or vehemently, as from surprise. — *tr.* To express or utter (something) suddenly or vehemently. [Fr. *exclamer* < Lat. *exclāmāre* : *ex-*, ex- + *clāmāre*, to call; see **kelə-[2]***.] — **ex•claim′er** *n.*

ex•cla•ma•tion (ĕk′sklə-mā′shən) *n.* **1.** A forceful utterance. **2.** An outcry, as of protest. **3.** *Gram.* An interjection.

exclamation mark *n.* See **exclamation point.**

exclamation point *n.* A punctuation mark (!) used after an exclamation.

ex•clam•a•tory (ĭk-sklăm′ə-tôr′ē, -tōr′ē) *adj.* Constituting, containing, relating to, or using exclamation.

ex•clave (ĕk′sklāv′) *n.* A part of a country that is isolated from the main part and surrounded by foreign territory. [EX- + (EN)CLAVE.]

ex•clude (ĭk-sklōōd′) *tr.v.* **-clud•ed, -clud•ing, -cludes. 1.** To prevent from entering; keep out; bar. **2.** To prevent from being included, considered, or accepted; reject. **3.** To put out; expel. [ME *excluden* < Lat. *exclūdere* : *ex-*, ex- + *claudere*, to shut.] — **ex•clud′a•bil′i•ty** *n.* — **ex•clud′a•ble, ex•clud′i•ble** *adj. & n.* — **ex•clud′er** *n.*

ex•clu•sion (ĭk-sklōō′zhən) *n.* **1.** The act or practice of excluding. **2.** The condition or fact of being excluded. [ME *exclusioun* < Lat. *exclūsiō, exclūsiōn-* < *exclūsus*, p.part. of *exclūdere*, to shut. See EXCLUDE.] — **ex•clu′sion•ar′y** *adj.*

exclusionary rule *n. Law.* A rule that forbids the use of illegally obtained evidence in a criminal trial.

ex•clu•sion•ist (ĭk-sklōō′zhə-nĭst) *n.* One that advocates the exclusion of another or others, as from exercising a right. — **ex•clu′sion•ism** *n.* — **ex•clu′sion•ist, ex•clu′sion•is′tic** *adj.*

exclusion principle *n.* The principle that two particles of a given type, such as electrons, cannot simultaneously occupy a particular quantum state.

ex•clu•sive (ĭk-sklōō′sĭv) *adj.* **1.** Excluding or tending to exclude. **2.** Not divided or shared with others. **3.** Not accompanied by others; single or sole. **4.** Complete; undivided. **5.** Excluding some or most, as from membership. **6.** Catering to a wealthy clientele; expensive. — *n.* **1.** A news item initially released to only one publication or broadcaster. **2.** An exclusive right or privilege. — **ex•clu′sive•ly** *adv.* — **ex•clu′sive•ness, ex′clu•siv′i•ty** (ĕk′sklōō-sĭv′ĭ-tē) *n.*

exclusive of *prep.* Not including or considering.

ex•cog•i•tate (ĭk-skŏj′ĭ-tāt′) *tr.v.* **-tat•ed, -tat•ing, -tates.** To consider or think (something) out carefully and thoroughly. [Lat. *excōgitāre, excōgitāt-*, to find out by thinking : *ex-*, ex- + *cōgitāre*, to think; see COGITATE.] — **ex•cog′i•ta′tion** *n.* — **ex•cog′i•ta′tive** *adj.*

ex•com•mu•ni•ca•ble (ĕks′kə-myōō′nĭ-kə-bəl) *adj.* Meriting, liable to, or punishable by excommunication.

ex•com•mu•ni•cate (ĕks′kə-myōō′nĭ-kāt′) *tr.v.* **-cat•ed, -cat•ing, -cates. 1.** To deprive of the right of church membership by ecclesiastical authority. **2.** To exclude by or as if by decree from membership or participation in a group. — *n.* (-kĭt). A person who has been excommunicated. — *adj.* (-kĭt, -kāt′). Having been excommunicated. [ME *excommunicaten* < LLat. *excommūnicāre, excommūnicāt-* : Lat. *ex-*, ex- + Lat. *commūnicāre*, to share (< *commūnis*, common; see COMMON).] — **ex′com•mu′ni•ca′tive** (-kā′tĭv, -kə-), **ex′com•mu′ni•ca•to′ry** (-kə-tôr′ē, -tōr′ē) *adj.* — **ex′com•mu′ni•ca′tor** *n.*

ex•com•mu•ni•ca•tion (ĕks′kə-myōō′nĭ-kā′shən) *n.* **1.** The act of excommunicating. **2.** The state of being excommunicated. **3.** An excommunicative ecclesiastical censure.

ex•co•ri•ate (ĭk-skôr′ē-āt′, -skōr′-) *tr.v.* **-at•ed, -at•ing, -ates. 1.** To tear or wear off the skin of; abrade. **2.** To censure strongly; denounce. [ME *excoriaten* < Lat. *excoriāre, excoriāt-* : *ex-*, ex- + *corium*, skin; see **sker-[1]***.] — **ex•co′ri•a′tion** *n.* — **ex•co′ri•a′tor** *n.*

ex•cre•ment (ĕk′skrə-mənt) *n.* Waste material, esp. fecal matter, expelled after digestion. [Lat. *excrēmentum* < *excrētus*, p.part. of *excernere*, to excrete. See EXCRETE.] — **ex′cre•men′tal, ex′cre•men•ti′tious** (-mĕn-tĭsh′əs) *adj.*

ex•cres•cence (ĭk-skrĕs′əns) *n.* **1.** An abnormal outgrowth or enlargement, such as a wart. **2.** A normal outgrowth, such as a fingernail or a beard. **3.** A usu. unwanted or unncessary accretion. [ME < Lat. *excrēscentia* < neut. pl. of *excrēscēns, excrēscent-*, pr.part. of *excrēscere*, to grow out : *ex-*, ex- + *crēscere*, to grow; see **ker-[2]***.]

ex•cres•cen•cy (ĭk-skrĕs′ən-sē) *n., pl.* **-cies. 1.** The state or condition of being excrescent. **2.** An excrescence.

ex•cres•cent (ĭk-skrĕs′ənt) *adj.* **1.** Growing out abnormally, excessively, or superfluously. **2.** *Ling.* Of or relating to epenthesis; epenthetic. — **ex•cres′cent•ly** *adv.*

ex•cre•ta (ĭk-skrē′tə) *pl.n.* Waste matter, such as sweat, urine, or feces, discharged from the body. [Lat. *excrēta* < neut. pl. p.part. of *excernere*, to excrete. See EXCRETE.] — **ex•cre′tal** *adj.*

ex•crete (ĭk-skrēt′) *tr.v.* **-cret•ed, -cret•ing, -cretes.** To separate and discharge (waste) from blood, tissues, or organs. [Lat. *excernere, excrēt-* : *ex-*, ex- + *cernere*, to separate; see **krei-***.]

ex•cre•tion (ĭk-skrē′shən) *n.* **1.** The act or process of excreting. **2.** The excreted matter.

ex•cre•to•ry (ĕk′skrĭ-tôr′ē, -tōr′ē) *adj.* Of, relating to, or used in excretion: *excretory organs.*

ex•cru•ci•ate (ĭk-skrōō′shē-āt′) *tr.v.* **-at•ed, -at•ing, -ates. 1.** To inflict severe pain on; torture. **2.** To inflict great mental distress on. [Lat. *excruciāre, excruciāt-* : *ex-*, intensive pref.; see EX- + *cruciāre*, to crucify, torture (< *crux, cruc-*, cross; see CROSS).] — **ex•cru′ci•a′tion** *n.*

ex•cru•ci•at•ing (ĭk-skrōō′shē-ā′tĭng) *adj.* **1.** Intensely painful; agonizing. **2.** Very intense or extreme. — **ex•cru′ci•at′ing•ly** *adv.*

ex•cul•pate (ĕk′skəl-pāt′, ĭk-skŭl′-) *tr.v.* **-pat•ed, -pat•ing, -pates.** To clear of guilt or blame. [Med.Lat. *exculpāre, exculpāt-* : Lat. *ex-*, ex- + Lat. *culpa*, guilt.] — **ex•cul′pa•ble** (ĭk-skŭl′pə-bəl) *adj.* — **ex′cul•pa′tion** *n.*

ex•cul•pa•to•ry (ĭk-skŭl′pə-tôr′ē, -tōr′ē) *adj.* Acting or tending to exculpate.

ex•cur•rent (ĭk-skûr′ənt, -skŭr′-) *adj.* **1.a.** Running or flowing outwardly. **b.** Marked by an outward flow of current. **2.** *Bot.* **a.** Having a single undivided trunk with lateral branches. **b.** Extending beyond the apex of a leaf. [Lat. *excurrēns, excurrent-*, pr.part. of *excurrere*, to run out. See EXCURSION.]

ex•cur•sion (ĭk-skûr′zhən) *n.* **1.** A usu. short journey made for pleasure; an outing. **2.** A roundtrip on a passenger vehicle at a special low fare. **3.** A group taking a short pleasure trip together. **4.** A diversion or deviation from a main topic; a digression. **5.** *Phys.* **a.** A movement from and back to a mean position or axis in an oscillating or alternating motion. **b.** The distance traversed in such a movement. [Lat. *excursiō, excursiōn-* < *excursus*, p.part. of *excurrere*, to run out : *ex-*, ex- + *currere*, to run; see **kers-***.]

ex•cur•sion•ist (ĭk-skûr′zhə-nĭst) *n.* A person who goes on an excursion.

ex•cur•sive (ĭk-skûr′sĭv) *adj.* Of, given to, or characterized by digression. — **ex•cur′sive•ly** *adv.* — **ex•cur′sive•ness** *n.*
ex•cur•sus (ĭk-skûr′səs) *n., pl.* **-sus•es. 1.** A lengthy appended exposition of a topic or point. **2.** A digression. [Lat. < p.part. of *excurrere,* to run out. See EXCURSION.]
ex•cus•a•to•ry (ĭk-skyo͞o′zə-tôr′ē, -tōr′ē) *adj.* Tending or serving to excuse.
ex•cuse (ĭk-skyo͞oz′) *tr.v.* **-cused, -cus•ing, -cus•es. 1.a.** To explain (a fault or an offense) in the hope of being forgiven or understood. **b.** To seek to remove the blame from. **2.a.** To grant pardon to; forgive. **b.** To make allowance for; overlook. See Syns at **forgive. 3.** To serve as justification for. **4.** To free, as from an obligation or duty; exempt. **5.** To give permission to leave; release. — *n.* (ĭk-skyo͞os′). **1.** An explanation offered to justify or obtain forgiveness. **2.** A reason or grounds for excusing. **3.** The act of excusing. **4.** A note explaining an absence. **5.** *Informal.* An inferior example. [ME *excusen* < OFr. *excuser* < Lat. *excūsāre* : *ex-,* ex- + *causa,* accusation; see CAUSE.] — **ex•cus′a•ble** *adj.* — **ex•cus′a•ble•ness** *n.* — **ex•cus′a•bly** *adv.* — **ex•cus′er** *n.*
ex•ec (ĭg-zĕk′) *n. Informal.* **1.** An executive. **2.** The executive officer of a unit of the armed forces.
exec. *abbr.* Executor.
ex•e•cra•ble (ĕk′sĭ-krə-bəl) *adj.* **1.** Deserving of execration; hateful. **2.** Extremely inferior; very bad. [ME < Lat. *execrābilis* < *execrārī, exsecrārī,* to execrate. See EXECRATE.] — **ex′e•cra•ble•ness** *n.* — **ex′e•cra•bly** *adv.*
ex•e•crate (ĕk′sĭ-krāt′) *tr.v.* **-crat•ed, -crat•ing, -crates. 1.** To declare to be hateful or abhorrent; denounce. **2.** To feel loathing for; abhor. **3.** *Archaic.* To invoke a curse on. [Lat. *execrārī, execrāt-* : *ex-,* ex- + *sacrāre,* to consecrate (< *sacer,* sacred; see **sak-***).] — **ex′e•cra′tive, ex′e•cra•to′ry** (-krə-tôr′ē, -tōr′ē) *adj.* — **ex′e•cra′tor** *n.*
ex•e•cra•tion (ĕk′sĭ-krā′shən) *n.* **1.** The act of cursing. **2.** A curse. **3.** Something that is cursed or loathed.
ex•ec•u•tant (ĭg-zĕk′yə-tənt) *n.* One who performs or carries out, esp. a skilled performer.
ex•e•cute (ĕk′sĭ-kyo͞ot′) *tr.v.* **-cut•ed, -cut•ing, -cutes. 1.** To put into effect; carry out. **2.** To perform; do. **3.** To create (a work of art, for example) in accordance with a prescribed design. **4.** To make valid, as by signing. **5.** To perform or carry out what is required by: *executed the terms of a will.* **6.** To put to death, esp. by carrying out a lawful sentence. **7.** *Comp. Sci.* To run (a program or an instruction). [ME *executen* < OFr. *executer* < Med.Lat. *execūtāre* < Lat. *execūtor,* executor < *execūtus,* p.part. of *exequī, exsequī,* to pursue, accomplish : *ex-,* ex- + *sequī,* to follow; see **sekʷ-1***.] — **ex′e•cut′a•ble** *adj.* — **ex′e•cut′er** *n.*
ex•e•cu•tion (ĕk′sĭ-kyo͞o′shən) *n.* **1.a.** The act of executing something. **b.** The state of being executed. **2.** The manner, style, or result of performance. **3.** The act or an instance of execution or being executed as a lawful penalty. **4.** *Law.* **a.** The carrying into effect of a court judgment. **b.** A writ empowering an officer to enforce a judgment. **c.** Validation of a legal document by the performance of all necessary formalities. **5.** *Archaic.* Effective, punitive, or destructive action.
ex•e•cu•tion•er (ĕk′sĭ-kyo͞o′shə-nər) *n.* One who executes, esp. one who puts a condemned person to death.
ex•ec•u•tive (ĭg-zĕk′yə-tĭv) *n.* **1.** A person or group having administrative or managerial authority in an organization. **2.** The chief officer of a government, state, or political division. **3.** The executive branch of government. **4.** *Comp. Sci.* A set of coded instructions designed to process and control other coded instructions. — *adj.* **1.** Of, relating to, capable of, or suited for carrying out or executing. **2.** Having, characterized by, or relating to administrative or managerial authority: *executive skills.* **3.** Of or relating to the branch of government charged with the execution of a country's laws and the administration of its functions. [ME, to be carried out < OFr. *exécutif* < *executer,* to carry out. See EXECUTE.]
executive agreement *n.* An agreement made between the executive branch of the U.S. government and a foreign government without ratification by the Senate.
executive council *n.* **1.** A council that advises or assists a political executive. **2.** A council having the highest executive power or authority.
executive officer *n.* **1.a.** The officer second in command of a military unit smaller than a division. **b.** The officer second in command of a naval unit. **2.** A person with executive power in an organization.
executive order *n.* See **regulation** 3.
executive privilege *n.* The principle that members of the executive branch of government cannot legally be forced to disclose confidential communications when such disclosure would adversely affect executive operations or procedures.
executive secretary *n.* A secretary having administrative duties and responsibilities.
executive session *n.* A session, as of a committee, often closed to the public, in which executive business is transacted.
ex•ec•u•tor (ĭg-zĕk′yə-tər, ĕk′sĭ-kyo͞o′tər) *n.* **1.** One who carries out or performs something. **2.** *Law.* One appointed by a testator to execute the testator's will. — **ex•ec′u•to′ri•al** (-tôr′ē-əl, -tōr′-) *adj.* — **ex•ec′u•tor•ship′** *n.*
ex•ec•u•to•ry (ĭg-zĕk′yə-tôr′ē, -tōr′ē) *adj.* **1.** Of or relating to execution or administration; executive. **2.** In effect; operative. **3.** *Law.* Intended to go into effect or having the potential of becoming effective at a future time; contingent.
ex•ec•u•trix (ĭg-zĕk′yə-trĭks′) *n., pl.* **-trix•es** or **-tri•ces** (-trī′sēz′). *Law.* A woman who is appointed by a testator to execute the testator's will.
ex•e•dra (ĕk′sĭ-drə, ĭk-sē′-) *n.* **1.** A usu. curved outdoor bench with a high back. **2.** An often semicircular portico with seats that was used in ancient Greece and Rome as a place for discussions. [Lat. < Gk. : *ex-,* ex- + *hedra,* seat; see **sed-***.]
ex•e•ge•sis (ĕk′sə-jē′sĭs) *n., pl.* **-ses** (-sēz). Critical interpretation or explanation, esp. textual. [Gk. *exēgēsis* < *exēgeisthai,* to interpret : *ex-,* ex- + *hēgeisthai,* to lead; see **sāg-***.]
ex•e•gete (ĕk′sə-jēt′) also **ex•e•ge•tist** (ĕk′sə-jĕt′ĭst) *n.* A person skilled in exegesis. [Gk. *exēgētēs* < *exēgeisthai,* to interpret. See EXEGESIS.]
ex•e•get•ic (ĕk′sə-jĕt′ĭk) also **ex•e•get•i•cal** (-ĭ-kəl) *adj.* Of or relating to exegesis. — **ex′e•get′i•cal•ly** *adv.*
ex•em•plar (ĭg-zĕm′plär′, -plər) *n.* **1.** One that is worthy of imitation; a model. **2.** One that is typical or representative; an example. **3.** An ideal that serves as a pattern; an archetype. **4.** A copy, as of a book. [ME *exemplere* < LLat. *exemplārium* < Lat. *exemplum,* example. See EXAMPLE.]
ex•em•pla•ry (ĭg-zĕm′plə-rē) *adj.* **1.** Worthy of imitation; commendable. **2.** Serving as a model. **3.** Serving as an illustration; typical. **4.** Serving as a warning; admonitory. [< ME *exaumplarie, exemplere,* an exemplar. See EXEMPLAR.] — **ex′em•plar′i•ly** (ĕg′zəm-plâr′ə-lē) *adv.* — **ex•em′pla•ri•ness, ex′em•plar′i•ty** (ĕg′zəm-plăr′ĭ-tē) *n.*
ex•em•pli•fi•ca•tion (ĭg-zĕm′plə-fĭ-kā′shən) *n.* **1.** The act of exemplifying. **2.** One that exemplifies; an example.
ex•em•pli•fy (ĭg-zĕm′plə-fī′) *tr.v.* **-fied, -fy•ing, -fies. 1.** To illustrate by example. **2.** To serve as an example of. [ME *exemplifien* < OFr. *exemplifier* < Med.Lat. *exemplificāre* : Lat. *exemplum,* example; see EXAMPLE + Lat. *-ficāre,* -fy.] — **ex•em′pli•fi′a•ble** *adj.* — **ex•em′pli•fi′er** *n.*
ex•em•pli gra•ti•a (ĭg-zĕm′plē grā′shē-ə, ĕk-sĕm′plē grä′tē-ä′) *adv.* For example. [Lat. *exemplī grātiā,* for the sake of example.]
ex•em•plum (ĭg-zĕm′pləm) *n., pl.* **-pla** (-plə). **1.** An example. **2.** A brief story used to make a point in an argument or illustrate a moral truth. [Lat. See EXAMPLE.]
ex•empt (ĭg-zĕmpt′) *tr.v.* **-empt•ed, -empt•ing, -empts. 1.** To make exempt. **2.** *Obsolete.* To set apart; isolate. — *adj.* **1.** Freed from an obligation, a duty, or a liability to which others are subject; excused. **2.** *Obsolete.* Set apart; isolated. — *n.* One who is exempt. [ME *exempten* < OFr. *exempter* < *exempt,* exempt < Lat. *exemptus,* p.part. of *eximere,* to take out. See EXAMPLE.] — **ex•empt′i•ble** *adj.*
ex•emp•tion (ĭg-zĕmp′shən) *n.* **1.** The act or an instance of exempting. **2.** The state of being exempt; immunity. **3.** One that is exempted, esp. an amount of income that is exempted from taxation.
ex•en•ter•ate (ĭg-zĕn′tə-rāt′) *tr.v.* **-at•ed, -at•ing, -ates. 1.** To disembowel; eviscerate. **2.** *Medic.* To remove the contents of (an organ). [Lat. *exenterāre, exenterāt-,* to disembowel : *ex-,* ex- + Gk. *enteron,* entrails; see **en***.] — **ex•en′ter•a′tion** *n.*
ex•er•cise (ĕk′sər-sīz′) *n.* **1.** An act of employing or putting into play; use. **2.** The discharge of a duty, function, or office. **3.** Activity that requires physical or mental exertion, esp. when performed to develop or maintain fitness. **4.** A task, problem, or other effort performed to develop or maintain fitness or increase skill. **5. exercises.** A program that includes speeches, presentations, and other ceremonial activities performed before an audience. — *v.* **-cised, -cis•ing, -cis•es.** — *tr.* **1.** To put into play or operation; employ. **2.** To bring to bear; exert. **3.a.** To subject to practice or exertion in order to train, strengthen, or develop. **b.** To put through exercises. See Syns at **practice. 4.** To carry out the functions of; execute. **5.a.** To absorb the attentions of, esp. by worry or anxiety. **b.** To stir to anger or alarm; upset. — *intr.* To take exercise. [ME < OFr. *exercice* < Lat. *exercitium* < *exercitus,* p.part. of *exercēre,* to exercise : *ex-,* ex- + *arcēre,* to restrain.] — **ex′er•cis′a•ble** *adj.*
exercise bicycle *n.* A stationary piece of fitness equipment having a saddle seat, handlebars, and pedals, used chiefly to strengthen the cardiovascular system.
exercise book *n.* A booklet for students, usu. containing problems or exercises and space for answers or practice.
ex•er•cis•er (ĕk′sər-sī′zər) *n.* **1.** One that exercises: *an exerciser of racehorses.* **2.** A device for exercising the body.
ex•er•ci•ta•tion (ĭg-zûr′sĭ-tā′shən) *n.* The act or an instance of exercising. [ME *exercitacioun* < Lat. *exercitātiō, exercitātiōn-* < *exercitāre,* freq. of *exercēre,* to exercise. See EXERCISE.]
ex•er•gon•ic (ĕk′sər-gŏn′ĭk) *adj.* Releasing energy. [EX(O)- + Gk. *ergon,* work; see **werg-*** + -IC.]
ex•ergue (ĕk′sûrg′, ĕg′zûrg′) *n.* A space on the reverse of a coin or medal, usu. below the central design and often giving

ă pat	oi boy
ā pay	ou out
âr care	o͝o took
ä father	o͞o boot
ĕ pet	ŭ cut
ē be	ûr urge
ĭ pit	th thin
ī pie	*th* this
îr pier	hw which
ŏ pot	zh vision
ō toe	ə about, item
ô paw	

Stress marks:
′ (primary);
′ (secondary), as in
dictionary (dĭk′shə-nĕr′ē)

the date and place of engraving. [Fr. < NLat. *exergum* : Gk. *ex-*, ex- + Gk. *ergon*, work; see **werg-***.]

ex•ert (ĭg-zûrt′) *tr.v.* **-ert•ed, -ert•ing, -erts. 1.** To put to use or effect; put forth. **2.** To bring to bear; exercise. **3.** To put (oneself) to strenuous effort. [Lat. *exserere, exsert-*, to put forth, stretch out : *ex-*, ex- + *serere*, to join; see **ser-**[2]*.]

ex•er•tion (ĭg-zûr′shən) *n.* The act or an instance of exerting, esp. a strenuous effort.

Ex•e•ter (ĕk′sĭ-tər). A borough of SW England NE of Plymouth; strategically important since Roman times. Pop. 99,200.

ex•e•unt (ĕk′sē-ənt, -o͝ont′). Used as a stage direction to indicate that two or more performers leave the stage. [Lat., third pers. pl. of *exīre*, to go out. See EXIT.]

ex•fo•li•ate (ĕks-fō′lē-āt′) *v.* **-at•ed, -at•ing, -ates.** —*tr.* **1.** To remove (a layer of bark, for example) in flakes or scales; peel. **2.** To cast off in scales, flakes, or splinters. —*intr.* To come off or separate into flakes, scales, or layers. [Lat. *exfoliāre, exfoliāt-*, to strip of leaves : *ex-*, ex- + *folium*, leaf; see **bhel-**[3]*.] —**ex•fo′li•a′tion** *n.* —**ex•fo′li•a′tive** *adj.* —**ex•fo′li•a′tor** *n.*

ex•ha•lant also **ex•ha•lent** (ĕks-hā′lənt, ĕk-sā′-) —*adj.* Functioning in exhalation. —*n.* An organ, such as the siphon of a clam, that is used for exhalation.

ex•ha•la•tion (ĕks′hə-lā′shən, ĕk′sə-) *n.* **1.** The act or an instance of exhaling. **2.** Something, such as air, that is exhaled.

ex•hale (ĕks-hāl′, ĕk-sāl′) *v.* **-haled, -hal•ing, -hales.** —*intr.* **1.a.** To breathe out. **b.** To emit air or vapor. **2.** To be given off or emitted. —*tr.* **1.** To blow (something) forth or breathe (something) out. **2.** To give off; emit. [ME *exalen* < Lat. *exhālāre* : *ex-*, ex- + *hālāre*, to breathe.]

ex•haust (ĭg-zôst′) *v.* **-haust•ed, -haust•ing, -hausts.** —*tr.* **1.** To wear out completely. **2.** To drain of resources or properties; deplete. See Syns at **deplete. 3.** To use up completely. **4.** To treat completely; cover thoroughly: *exhaust a topic.* **5.** To draw out the contents of; drain. **6.** To let out or draw off. —*intr.* To escape or pass out. —*n.* **1.a.** The escape or release of vaporous waste material, as from an engine. **b.** The fumes or gases so released. **2.** A duct or pipe through which waste material is emitted. **3.** An apparatus for drawing out noxious air or waste material by means of a partial vacuum. [Lat. *exhaurīre, exhaust-* : *ex-*, ex- + *haurīre*, to draw.] —**ex•haust′ed•ly** *adv.* —**ex•haust′er** *n.* —**ex•haust′i•bil′i•ty** *n.* —**ex•haust′i•ble** *adj.* —**ex•haust′ing•ly** *adv.*

ex•haus•tion (ĭg-zôs′chən) *n.* **1.** The act or an instance of exhausting. **2.** The state of being exhausted; extreme fatigue.

ex•haus•tive (ĭg-zô′stĭv) *adj.* **1.** Treating all parts or aspects without omission; thorough. **2.** Tending to exhaust. —**ex•haus′tive•ly** *adv.* —**ex•haus′tive•ness** *n.* —**ex′haus•tiv′i•ty** *n.*

ex•haust•less (ĭg-zôst′lĭs) *adj.* Impossible to exhaust; inexhaustible. —**ex•haust′less•ly** *adv.* —**ex•haust′less•ness** *n.*

exhaust pipe *n.* See **tailpipe.**

ex•hib•it (ĭg-zĭb′ĭt, ĕg-) *v.* **-it•ed, -it•ing, -its.** —*tr.* **1.** To show outwardly; display. **2.a.** To present for others to see. **b.** To present in a public exhibition or contest. **3.** To give evidence or an instance of; demonstrate. **4.** *Law.* **a.** To submit (evidence or documents) in a court. **b.** To present or introduce officially. —*intr.* To put something on public display. —*n.* **1.** The act or an instance of exhibiting. **2.** Something exhibited. **3.** A public showing; an exhibition. **4.** *Law.* Something, such as a document, formally introduced as evidence in court. [ME *exhibiten* < Lat. *exhibēre, exhibit-* : *ex-*, ex- + *habēre*, to hold; see **ghabh-***.] —**ex•hib′i•tor, ex•hib′it•er** *n.* —**ex•hib′i•to′ry** (-ĭ-tôr′ē, -tōr′ē) *adj.*

ex•hi•bi•tion (ĕk′sə-bĭsh′ən) *n.* **1.** The act or an instance of exhibiting. **2.** Something exhibited; an exhibit. **3.** A large-scale public showing, as of art. **4.** *Chiefly British.* A grant given to a scholar by a school or university.

ex•hi•bi•tion•ism (ĕk′sə-bĭsh′ə-nĭz′əm) *n.* **1.** The act or practice of deliberately behaving so as to attract attention. **2.** *Psychiat.* A psychosexual disorder marked by the compulsive exposure of the genitalia in public. —**ex′hi•bi′tion•ist** *n.* —**ex′hi•bi′tion•is′tic** *adj.*

ex•hib•i•tive (ĭg-zĭb′ĭ-tĭv) *adj.* Tending to exhibit: *behavior exhibitive of certain instincts.* —**ex•hib′i•tive•ly** *adv.*

ex•hil•a•rant (ĭg-zĭl′ər-ənt) *adj.* Serving to exhilarate; exhilarating. —*n.* Something that exhilarates or stimulates.

ex•hil•a•rate (ĭg-zĭl′ə-rāt′) *tr.v.* **-rat•ed, -rat•ing, -rates. 1.** To cause to feel happily refreshed and energetic; elate. **2.** To invigorate; stimulate. [Lat. *exhilarāre, exhilarāt-* : *ex-*, intensive pref.; see EX– + *hilarāre*, to make cheerful (< *hilaris, hilarus*, cheerful < Gk. *hilaros*).] —**ex•hil′a•ra′ting** *adj.* —**ex•hil′a•rat′ing•ly** *adv.* —**ex•hil′a•ra′tion** *n.* —**ex•hil′a•ra′tive** *adj.* —**ex•hil′a•ra′tor** *n.*

ex•hort (ĭg-zôrt′) *v.* **-hort•ed, -hort•ing, -horts.** —*tr.* To urge by strong, often stirring argument, admonition, advice, or appeal. —*intr.* To make urgent appeal. [ME *exhorten* < Lat. *exhortārī* : *ex-*, intensive pref.; see EX– + *hortārī*, to encourage; see **gher-**[2]*.] —**ex•hort′er** *n.*

ex•hor•ta•tion (ĕg′zôr-tā′shən, ĕk′sôr-) *n.* **1.** The act or an instance of exhorting. **2.** A speech or discourse that exhorts.

ex•hor•ta•tive (ĭg-zôr′tə-tĭv) also **ex•hor•ta•to•ry** (-tôr′ē, -tōr′ē) *adj.* Acting or intended to exhort.

ex•hume (ĭg-zo͞om′, -zyo͞om′, ĭk-syo͞om′, ĕks-hyo͞om′) *tr.v.* **-humed, -hum•ing, -humes. 1.** To remove from a grave; disinter. **2.** To bring to light, esp. after a period of obscurity. [Fr. *exhumer* < Med.Lat. *exhumāre* : Lat. *ex-*, ex- + Lat. *humus*, ground; see **dhghem-***.] —**ex′hu•ma′tion** (ĕg′zyo͞o-mā′shən, ĕks′hyo͞o-) *n.* —**ex•hum′er** *n.*

ex•i•gence (ĕk′sə-jəns) *n.* Exigency.

ex•i•gen•cy (ĕk′sə-jən-sē, ĭg-zĭj′ən-) *n., pl.* **-cies. 1.** The state or quality of requiring much effort or immediate action. **2.** A pressing or urgent situation. **3.** A requirement or need. Often used in the plural.

ex•i•gent (ĕk′sə-jənt) *adj.* **1.** Requiring immediate action or remedy. See Syns at **urgent. 2.** Requiring much effort or expense; demanding. [Lat. *exigēns, exigent-*, pr.part. of *exigere*, to demand. See EXACT.] —**ex′i•gent•ly** *adv.*

ex•i•gu•i•ty (ĕk′sĭ-gyo͞o′ĭ-tē) *n.* The quality or condition of being scanty or meager.

ex•ig•u•ous (ĭg-zĭg′yo͞o-əs, ĭk-sĭg′-) *adj.* Quite scanty; meager. [< Lat. *exiguus* < *exigere*, to measure out, demand. See EXACT.] —**ex•ig′u•ous•ly** *adv.* —**ex•ig′u•ous•ness** *n.*

ex•ile (ĕg′zīl′, ĕk′sīl′) *n.* **1.a.** Enforced removal from one's native country. **b.** Self-imposed absence from one's country. **2.** The condition or a period of living away from one's native country. **3.** One who lives in exile, whether forced or voluntary. —*tr.v.* **-iled, -il•ing, -iles.** To send into exile; banish. See Syns at **banish.** [ME *exil* < OFr. < Lat. *exilium* < *exul, exsul*, exiled person, wanderer.] —**ex•il′ic** (ĭg-zĭl′ĭk, ĭk-sĭl′-), **ex•il′ian** (ĭg-zĭl′yən, -zĭl′ē-ən, ĭk-sĭl′yən, -sĭl′ē-ən) *adj.*

ex•ine (ĕk′sēn′, -sīn′) *n. Bot.* The outer layer of the wall of a spore or pollen grain. [EX(O)– + Gk. *is, in-*, tendon; see **wei-***.]

ex•ist (ĭg-zĭst′) *intr.v.* **-ist•ed, -ist•ing, -ists. 1.** To have actual being; be real. **2.** To have life; live. **3.** To live at a minimal level; subsist. **4.** To continue to be; persist. **5.** To be present under certain circumstances or in a specified place; occur. [Lat. *existere, exsistere*, to come forth, be manifest : *ex-*, ex- + *sistere*, to stand; see **stā-***.]

ex•is•tence (ĭg-zĭs′təns) *n.* **1.** The fact or state of existing; being. **2.** The fact or state of continued being; life. **3.a.** All that exists. **b.** A thing that exists; an entity. **4.** A mode or manner of existing. **5.** Specific presence; occurrence.

ex•is•tent (ĭg-zĭs′tənt) *adj.* **1.** Having life or being; existing. **2.** Occurring or present at the moment; current. —*n.* One that exists.

ex•is•ten•tial (ĕg′zĭ-stĕn′shəl, ĕk′sĭ-) *adj.* **1.** Of or relating to existence. **2.** Based on experience; empirical. **3.** Of or as conceived by existentialism. —**ex′is•ten′tial•ly** *adv.*

ex•is•ten•tial•ism (ĕg′zĭ-stĕn′shə-lĭz′əm, ĕk′sĭ-) *n. Philos.* A philosophy that emphasizes the uniqueness and isolation of the individual in a hostile or indifferent universe, regards existence as unexplainable, and stresses free choice and responsibility for one's actions. —**ex′is•ten′tial•ist** *adj. & n.*

ex•it (ĕg′zĭt, ĕk′sĭt). Used as a stage direction for a specified actor to leave the stage. —*n.* **1.** The act of going away or out. **2.** A passage or way out. **3.** The departure of a performer from the stage. **4.** Death. **5.** *Comp. Sci.* A computer programming technique for ending a repeated cycle of operations. —*v.* **-it•ed, -it•ing, -its.** —*intr.* To make one's exit; depart. —*tr.* To go out of; leave. [< Lat., third pers. sing. of *exīre*, to go out : *ex-*, ex- + *īre*, to go; see **ei-***.]

exit poll *n.* A poll taken of a sample of voters as they leave a polling place, used esp. to predict the outcome of an election.

ex li•bris (ĕks lī′brĭs, lē′-) *n., pl.* **ex libris.** See **bookplate.** [Lat. *ex librīs*, from the books.]

ex ni•hi•lo (ĕks nē′ə-lō′, nī′-, nĭ′-) *adv. & adj.* Out of nothing. [Lat. *ex nihilō*.]

exo– *pref.* Outside; external: *exoskeleton.* [< Gk. *exō*, outside < *ex*, out of. See **eghs***.]

ex•o•bi•ol•o•gy (ĕk′sō-bī-ŏl′ə-jē) *n.* The branch of biology that deals with the search for extraterrestrial life and the effects of extraterrestrial surroundings on living organisms. —**ex′o•bi′o•log′i•cal** (-ə-lŏj′ĭ-kəl) *adj.*

ex•o•carp (ĕk′sō-kärp′) *n. Bot.* The outermost layer of the fruit wall.

ex•o•crine (ĕk′sə-krĭn, -krēn, -krīn′) *adj.* **1.** Secreting externally, directly or through a duct: *exocrine cells.* **2.** Of, relating to, or produced by an exocrine gland. [EXO– + Gk. *krinein*, to separate; see **krei-***.]

exocrine gland *n. Physiol.* An externally secreting gland, such as a salivary gland or sweat gland.

ex•o•cy•clic (ĕk′sō-sī′klĭk, -sĭk′lĭk) *adj.* External to a chemical ring structure: *an exocyclic double bond.*

ex•o•cy•to•sis (ĕk′sō-sī-tō′sĭs) *n., pl.* **-ses** (-sēz′). *Biol.* A process of cellular secretion or excretion in which substances contained in vesicles are discharged from the cell by fusion of the vesicular membrane with the outer cell membrane. —**ex′o•cy•tose′** (-tōs′) *v.* —**ex′o•cy•tot′ic** (-tŏt′ĭk) *adj.*

Exod. *abbr. Bible.* Exodus.

ex•o•don•tia (ĕk′sə-dŏn′shə, -shē-ə) *n.* Exodontics.

ex•o•don•tics (ĕk′sə-dŏn′tĭks) *n. (used with a sing. v.)* The dental specialty that deals with extraction of teeth. — **ex′o·don′tist** *n.*

ex·o·dus (ĕk′sə-dəs) *n.* **1.** A departure of a large number of people. **2. Exodus. a.** The departure of the Israelites from Egypt. **b.** See table at **Bible.** [LLat. < Gk. *exodos* : *ex-*, out; see EXO- + *hodos*, way, journey.]

ex·o·en·zyme (ĕk′sō-ĕn′zīm′) *n.* An enzyme that functions outside the cell from which it originates.

ex·o·er·gic (ĕk′sō-ûr′jĭk) *adj.* Exothermic. [EXO- + Gk. *ergon*, work; see **werg-*** + -IC.]

ex of·fi·ci·o (ĕks′ ə-fĭsh′ē-ō′) *adv. & adj.* By virtue of office or position. [Lat. *ex officiō*.]

ex·og·a·my (ĕk-sŏg′ə-mē) *n., pl* **-mies. 1.** The custom of marrying outside a social unit, such as a tribe. **2.** *Biol.* The fusion of two gametes that are not closely related. — **ex′o·gam′ic** (ĕk′sə-găm′ĭk), **ex·og′a·mous** (ĕk-sŏg′ə-məs) *adj.*

ex·og·e·nous (ĕk-sŏj′ə-nəs) *adj.* **1.** *Biol.* Derived or developed from outside the body; originating externally. **2.** *Bot.* Characterized by the addition of layers of woody tissue. **3.** *Medic.* Having a cause external to the body. Used of diseases. [Fr. *exogène* : Gk. *exō-*, outside; see EXO- + Fr. *-gène*, -gen.] — **ex·og′e·nous·ly** *adv.*

ex·on (ĕk′sŏn) *n. Genet.* A nucleotide sequence in DNA that carries the code for the final messenger RNA molecule and thus defines the amino acid sequence during protein synthesis. [*ex(pressed)* + -ON[1].] — **ex·on′ic** *adj.*

ex·on·er·ate (ĭg-zŏn′ə-rāt′) *tr.v.* **-at·ed, -at·ing, -ates. 1.** To free from blame. **2.** To free from a responsibility, obligation, or task. [ME *exoneraten* < Lat. *exonerāre*, *exonerāt-*, to free from a burden : *ex-*, ex- + *onus*, *oner-*, burden.] — **ex·on′er·a′tion** *n.* — **ex·on′er·a′tive** *adj.*

ex·o·nu·cle·ase (ĕk′sō-no͞o′klē-ās′, -āz′, -nyo͞o′-) *n.* Any of a group of enzymes that catalyze the hydrolysis of single nucleotides from the end of a DNA or RNA chain.

ex·o·pep·ti·dase (ĕk′sō-pĕp′tĭ-dās′, -dāz′) *n.* Any of a group of enzymes that catalyze the hydrolysis of single amino acids from the end of a polypeptide chain.

ex·oph·thal·mic goiter (ĕk′səf-thăl′mĭk) *n.* See **Graves' disease.**

ex·oph·thal·mos also **ex·oph·thal·mus** (ĕk′səf-thăl′məs) *n.* Abnormal protrusion of the eyeball. [NLat. *exophthalmus* < Gk. *exophthalmos*, with prominent eyes : *ex-*, ex- + *ophthalmos*, eye; see **okʷ-*.**] — **ex′oph·thal′mic** *adj.*

ex·or·bi·tance (ĭg-zôr′bĭ-təns) *n.* **1.** Excessiveness, as of price. **2.** Behavior or an action exceeding what is right or proper.

ex·or·bi·tant (ĭg-zôr′bĭ-tənt) *adj.* Exceeding all bounds, as of custom or fairness. See Syns at **excessive.** [ME, aberrant, flagrant < OFr., excessive, extreme < LLat. *exorbitāns*, *exorbitant-*, pr.part. of *exorbitāre*, to deviate : Lat. *ex-*, ex- + Lat. *orbita*, path, track; see ORBIT.] — **ex·or′bi·tant·ly** *adv.*

ex·or·cise (ĕk′sôr-sīz′, -sər-) *tr.v.* **-cised, -cis·ing, -cis·es. 1.** To expel (an evil spirit) by or as if by incantation, command, or prayer. **2.** To free from evil spirits or malign influences. [ME *exorcisen* < LLat. *exorcizāre* < Gk. *exorkizein* : *ex-*, ex- + *horkizein*, to make one swear (< *horkos*, oath).] — **ex′or·cis′er** *n.*

ex·or·cism (ĕk′sôr-sĭz′əm, -sər-) *n.* **1.** The act, practice, or ceremony of exorcising. **2.** A formula used in exorcising. — **ex′or·cist** *n.*

ex·or·di·um (ĭg-zôr′dē-əm, ĭk-sôr′-) *n., pl.* **-di·ums** or **-di·a** (-dē-ə). A beginning or introductory part, esp. of a speech or treatise. [Lat. < *exōrdīrī*, to begin : *ex-*, intensive pref.; see EX- + *ōrdīrī*, to begin; see **ar-*.**] — **ex·or′di·al** *adj.*

ex·o·skel·e·ton (ĕk′sō-skĕl′ĭ-tn) *n.* A hard outer structure, such as the shell of a crustacean, that provides protection or support for an organism. — **ex′o·skel′e·tal** (-ĭ-tl) *adj*

ex·os·mo·sis (ĕk′sŏz-mō′sĭs, -sŏs-) *n.* The passage of a fluid through a semipermeable membrane toward a solution of lower concentration, esp. the passage of water through a cell membrane into the surrounding medium. [EX(O)- + OSMOSIS.] — **ex′os·mot′ic** (-mŏt′ĭk) *adj.*

ex·o·sphere (ĕk′sō-sfîr′) *n.* **1.** The outermost region of a planet's atmosphere. **2.** The outermost layer of Earth's atmosphere, lying above the thermosphere and extending far into space. — **ex′o·spher′ic** (-sfîr′ĭk, -sfĕr′-) *adj.*

ex·o·spore (ĕk′sō-spôr′, -spōr′) *n. Bot.* The outermost layer of a spore in some algae and fungi.

ex·o·spor·i·um (ĕk′sō-spôr′ē-əm, -spōr′-) *n., pl.* **-i·a** (-ē-ə). *Bot.* See **exine.** [NLat. : EXO- + *spora*, spore; see SPORE.]

ex·os·to·sis (ĕk′sŏ-stō′sĭs) *n., pl.* **-ses** (-sēz). A bony growth on the surface of a bone or tooth. [Gk. *exostōsis* : *ex-*, out of; see EXO- + *osteon*, bone; see **ost-*** + *-ōsis*, -osis.]

ex·o·ter·ic (ĕk′sə-tĕr′ĭk) *adj.* **1.** Not confined to an inner circle of disciples or initiates. **2.** Comprehensible to or suited to the public; popular. **3.** Of or relating to the outside; external. [Lat. *exōtericus*, external < Gk. *exōterikos* < *exōterō*, comp. of *exō*, outside < *ex*, out. See **eghs*.**] — **ex′o·ter′i·cal·ly** *adv.*

ex·o·ther·mic (ĕk′sō-thûr′mĭk) also **ex·o·ther·mal** (-məl) *adj.* Releasing heat. — **ex′o·ther′mi·cal·ly** *adv.*

ex·ot·ic (ĭg-zŏt′ĭk) *adj.* **1.** From another part of the world. **2.** Intriguingly unusual or different. See Syns at **fantastic. 3.** Of or involving striptease. — *n.* **1.** One that is exotic. **2.** A striptease performer. [Lat. *exōticus* < Gk. *exōtikos* < *exō*, outside < *ex*, out. See **eghs*.**] — **ex·ot′i·cal·ly** *adv.* — **ex·ot′i·cism** (-ĭ-sĭz′əm), **ex·ot′ic·ness** *n.*

ex·ot·i·ca (ĭg-zŏt′ĭ-kə) *pl.n.* Things that are curiously unusual or excitingly strange. [Lat. *exōtica* < neut. pl. of *exōticus*, exotic. See EXOTIC.]

ex·o·tox·in (ĕk′sō-tŏk′sĭn) *n.* A poisonous substance secreted by a microorganism and released externally.

exp *abbr. Math.* Exponent; exponential.

exp. *abbr.* **1.** Expenses. **2.** Experiment; experimental. **3.** Expiration. **4.** Export. **5.** Express.

ex·pand (ĭk-spănd′) *v.* **-pand·ed, -pand·ing, -pands.** — *tr.* **1.** To increase the size, volume, quantity, or scope of; enlarge. See Syns at **increase. 2.** To express at length or in detail. **3.** To open (something) up or out; spread out. **4.** *Math.* To write (a quantity) as a sum of terms in an extended form. — *intr.* **1.** To become greater in size, volume, quantity, or scope. **2.** To speak or write at length or in detail. **3.** To open up or out; unfold. **4.** To feel expansive. [ME *expanden*, to spread out < Lat. *expandere* : *ex-*, ex- + *pandere*, to spread; see **petə-*.**] — **ex·pand′a·ble** *adj.* — **ex·pand′er** *n.*

ex·pand·ing universe theory (ĭk-spăn′dĭng) *n.* **1.** The cosmological theory holding that the universe is expanding, based on the interpretation of the red shift as indicating that all galaxies are moving away from one another. **2.** The cosmogonical theory holding that all matter and energy in the universe originated from the big bang.

ex·panse (ĭk-spăns′) *n.* **1.** A wide and open extent, as of surface, land, or sky. **2.a.** Expansion. **b.** The distance or amount of expansion. [Lat. *expānsum* < neut. p.part. of *expandere*, to spread out. See EXPAND.]

ex·pan·si·ble (ĭk-spăn′sə-bəl) *adj.* That can expand or be expanded: *an expansible antenna.* — **ex·pan′si·bil′i·ty** *n.*

ex·pan·sile (ĭk-spăn′səl, -sīl′) *adj.* Of, relating to, or capable of expansion.

ex·pan·sion (ĭk-spăn′shən) *n.* **1.a.** The act or process of expanding. **b.** The state of being expanded. **2.a.** An expanded part. **b.** A product of expanding: *The book is an expansion of a Ph.D. thesis.* **3.** The extent or amount by which something has expanded. **4.** *Math.* **a.** A quantity written in an extended form. **b.** The process of obtaining this form. **5.** An expanse. **6.** A period of increased economic or business activity.

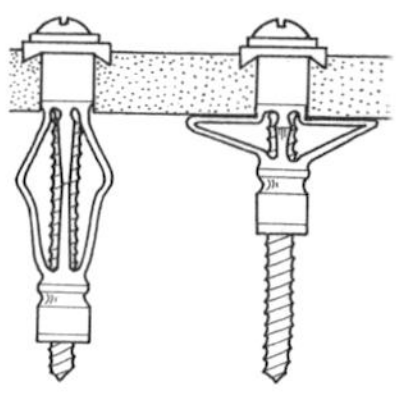
expansion bolt

ex·pan·sion·ar·y (ĭk-spăn′shə-nĕr′ē) *adj.* Tending toward or causing expansion or expansionism.

expansion bolt *n.* A bolt having an attachment that expands as the bolt is driven into a surface.

ex·pan·sion·ism (ĭk-spăn′shə-nĭz′əm) *n.* A nation's practice or policy of territorial or economic expansion. — **ex·pan′sion·ist** *adj. & n.*

ex·pan·sive (ĭk-spăn′sĭv) *adj.* **1.** Capable of expanding or tending to expand. **2.** Broad in size or extent; comprehensive. **3.** Disposed to be open, communicative, and generous; outgoing. **4.** Grand in scale. **5.** *Psychiat.* Marked by euphoria and delusions of grandeur. — **ex·pan′sive·ly** *adv.* — **ex·pan′sive·ness, ex′pan·siv′i·ty** (ĕk′spăn-sĭv′ĭ-tē) *n.*

ex par·te (ĕks pär′tē) *adv. & adj.* **1.** *Law.* From or on one side only, with the other side absent or unrepresented. **2.** From a one-sided or strongly biased point of view. [Lat.]

ex·pa·ti·ate (ĭk-spā′shē-āt′) *intr.v.* **-at·ed, -at·ing, -ates. 1.** To speak or write at length. **2.** To wander freely. [Lat. *expatiārī*, *expatiāt-* : *ex-*, ex- + *spatiārī*, to spread (< *spatium*, space).] — **ex·pa′ti·a′tion** *n.*

ex·pa·tri·ate (ĕk-spā′trē-āt′) *v.* **-at·ed, -at·ing, -ates.** — *tr.* **1.** To send into exile. See Syns at **banish. 2.** To remove (oneself) from residence in one's native land. — *intr.* **1.** To give up residence in one's homeland. **2.** To renounce allegiance to one's homeland. — *n.* (-ĭt, -āt′). **1.** One who has taken up residence in a foreign country. **2.** One who has renounced one's native land. — *adj.* (-ĭt, -āt′). Residing in a foreign country; expatriated. [Med.Lat. *expatriāre*, *expatriāt-* : Lat. *ex-*, ex- + Lat. *patria*, native land (< *patrius*, paternal < *pater*, father; see **pəter-***).] — **ex·pa′tri·a′tion** *n.*

ex·pect (ĭk-spĕkt′) *v.* **-pect·ed, -pect·ing, -pects.** — *tr.* **1.a.** To look forward to the probable occurrence or appearance of. **b.** To consider likely or certain; anticipate. **2.** To consider reasonable or due. **3.** To consider obligatory; require. **4.** *Informal.* To presume; suppose. — *intr.* **1.** To look forward to the birth of one's child. Used in progressive tenses: *She is expecting in May.* **2.** To be pregnant. Used in progressive tenses. [Lat. *exspectāre* : *ex-*, ex- + *spectāre*, to look at, freq. of *specere*, to see; see **spek-*.**] — **ex·pect′a·ble** *adj.* — **ex·pect′a·bly** *adv.* — **ex·pect′ed·ly** *adv.* — **ex·pect′ed·ness** *n.*

Syns: *expect, anticipate, hope, await.* These verbs relate to the idea of looking ahead to something in the future. To *expect* is to look forward to the likely occurrence or appearance of someone or something: *"We should not expect something for nothing — but we all do and call it Hope"* (Edgar W. Howe). *Anticipate* sometimes refers to taking advance action: *anticipated the attack and locked the gates.* The term can also

ă pat	oi boy
ā pay	ou out
âr care	o͝o took
ä father	o͞o boot
ĕ pet	ŭ cut
ē be	ûr urge
ĭ pit	th thin
ī pie	*th* this
îr pier	hw which
ŏ pot	zh vision
ō toe	ə about, item
ô paw	

Stress marks:
′ (primary);
′ (secondary), as in
dictionary (dĭk′shə-nĕr′ē)

delivery or transport. —*n.* **1.a.** A rapid, efficient system for the delivery of goods and mail. **b.** Goods and mail conveyed by such a system. **2.** A means of transport, such as a train, that travels rapidly and makes few or no stops before its destination. **3.** *Chiefly British.* **a.** A special messenger. **b.** A message delivered by special courier. [ME *expressen* < OFr. *expresser* < Med.Lat. *expressāre,* freq. of Lat. *exprimere* : *ex-,* ex- + *premere,* to press; see **per-**4*.] —**ex•press′er** *n.* —**ex•press′i•ble** *adj.*

ex•pres•sion (ĭk-sprĕsh′ən) *n.* **1.** The act of expressing, conveying, or representing in words, art, music, or movement; a manifestation. **2.** Something that expresses or communicates. **3.** *Math.* An operation or a quantity stated in symbolic form, such as $\sqrt{x}$, y^2, or $x + y$. **4.** The manner in which one expresses oneself, esp. in speaking, depicting, or performing. **5.** A particular word or phrase. **6.** The outward manifestation of a mood or a disposition. **7.** A facial aspect or a look that conveys a special feeling. **8.** The act of pressing or squeezing out. **9.** *Genet.* The act or process of expressing a gene.

ex•pres•sion•ism (ĭk-sprĕsh′ə-nĭz′əm) *n.* A movement in the arts during the early part of the 20th century that emphasized subjective expression of the artist's inner experiences. —**ex•pres′sion•ist** *n.* —**ex•pres′sion•is′tic** *adj.* —**ex•pres′sion•is′ti•cal•ly** *adv.*

ex•pres•sion•less (ĭk-sprĕsh′ən-lĭs) *adj.* Lacking expression.

ex•pres•sive (ĭk-sprĕs′ĭv) *adj.* **1.** Of, relating to, or characterized by expression. **2.** Serving to express or indicate. **3.** Full of expression; significant: *an expressive glance.* —**ex•pres′sive•ly** *adv.* —**ex•pres′sive•ness** *n.*

Syns: expressive, eloquent, meaningful, significant. The central meaning shared by these adjectives is "effectively conveying a feeling, an idea, or a mood": *an expressive gesture; an eloquent speech; a meaningful look; a significant smile.*

ex•pres•siv•i•ty (ĕk′sprĕ-sĭv′ĭ-tē) *n., pl.* **-ties. 1.** The quality of being expressive. **2.** *Genet.* The degree to which an expressed gene produces its effects in an organism.

ex•press•ly (ĭk-sprĕs′lē) *adv.* **1.** In an express or a definite manner; explicitly. **2.** Especially; particularly.

ex•pres•so (ĭk-sprĕs′ō, ĕk-) *n.* Var. of **espresso.**

ex•press•way (ĭk-sprĕs′wā′) *n.* A major divided highway designed for high-speed travel.

ex•pro•pri•ate (ĕk-sprō′prē-āt′) *tr.v.* **-at•ed, -at•ing, -ates. 1.** To deprive of possession. **2.** To transfer (another's property) to oneself. [Med.Lat. *expropriāre, expropriāt-* : Lat. *ex-,* ex- + Lat. *propriāre,* to appropriate (< *proprius,* one's own; see PROPER).] —**ex•pro′pri•a′tion** *n.* —**ex•pro′pri•a′tor** *n.* —**ex•pro′pri•a•to′ry** (-ə-tôr′ē, -tōr′ē) *adj.*

expt. *abbr.* Experiment.

exptl. *abbr.* Experimental.

ex•pul•sion (ĭk-spŭl′shən) *n.* The act of expelling or the state of being expelled. [ME *expulsioun* < OFr. *expulsion* < Lat. *expulsiō, expulsiōn-* < *expulsus,* p.part. of *expellere,* to expel. See EXPEL.]

expressionism
No More War!
by Käthe Kollwitz

ex•punc•tion (ĭk-spŭngk′shən, -spŭng′shən) *n.* The act of expunging or the condition of being expunged. [LLat. *expunctiō, expunctiōn-,* execution < Lat. *expunctus,* p.part. of *expungere,* to strike out. See EXPUNGE.]

ex•punge (ĭk-spŭnj′) *tr.v.* **-punged, -pung•ing, -pung•es. 1.** To erase or strike out. **2.** To eliminate completely; annihilate. See Syns at **erase.** [Lat. *expungere* : *ex-,* ex- + *pungere,* to prick; see **peuk-***.] —**ex•pung′er** *n.*

ex•pur•gate (ĕk′spər-gāt′) *tr.v.* **-gat•ed, -gat•ing, -gates.** To remove erroneous, vulgar, obscene, or otherwise objectionable material from (a book, for example) before publication. [Lat. *expūrgāre, expūrgāt-,* to purify : *ex-,* intensive pref.; see EX- + *pūrgāre,* to cleanse; see **peuə-***.] —**ex′pur•ga′tion** *n.* —**ex′pur•ga′tor** *n.*

ex•pur•ga•to•ry (ĭk-spûr′gə-tôr′ē, -tōr′ē) also **ex•pur•ga•to•ri•al** (-tôr′ē-əl, -tōr′-) *adj.* Of or relating to expurgation or an expurgator.

expy *abbr.* Expressway.

ex•qui•site (ĕk′skwĭ-zĭt, ĭk-skwĭz′ĭt) *adj.* **1.** Marked by intricate and beautiful design or execution. **2.** Of such beauty or delicacy as to arouse delight. See Syns at **delicate. 3.** Excellent; flawless. **4.** Acutely perceptive or discriminating. **5.** Intense; keen. **6.** *Obsolete.* Ingeniously devised or thought out. —*n.* One excessively fastidious in dress, manners, or taste. [ME *exquisit,* carefully chosen < Lat. *exquīsītus,* p.part. of *exquīrere,* to search out : *ex-,* ex- + *quaerere,* to seek.] —**ex′qui•site•ly** *adv.* —**ex′qui•site•ness** *n.*

exr. *abbr.* Executor.

exrx. *abbr.* Executrix.

ex•san•gui•nate (ĕks-săng′gwə-nāt′) *tr.v.* **-nat•ed, -nat•ing, -nates.** To drain of blood. [< Lat. *exsanguinātus,* drained of blood : *ex-,* ex- + *sanguis, sanguin-,* blood.] —**ex•san′gui•na′tion** *n.*

ex•san•guine (ĕks-săng′gwĭn) *adj.* Lacking blood; anemic. [Lat. *exsanguis, exsanguin-* : *ex-,* ex- + *sanguis,* blood.]

ex•scind (ĭk-sĭnd′) *tr.v.* **-scind•ed, -scind•ing, -scinds.** To cut out; excise. [Lat. *exscindere* : *ex-,* ex- + *scindere,* to cut; see **skei-***.]

ex•sert (ĭk-sûrt′) *tr.v.* **-sert•ed, -sert•ing, -serts.** To thrust (something) out or forth; cause to protrude. —*adj.* Also **ex•sert•ed** (-sûr′tĭd). Thrust outward or protruding. [Lat. *exserere, exsert-.* See EXERT.] —**ex•ser′tion** *n.*

ex•sic•cate (ĕk′sĭ-kāt′) *intr. & tr.v.* **-cat•ed, -cat•ing, -cates.** To dry up or cause to dry up. [Ult. < Lat. *exsiccāre, exsiccāt-* : *ex-,* ex- + *siccāre,* to dry (< *siccus,* dry).] —**ex′sic•ca′tion** *n.* —**ex′sic•ca′tive** *adj.* —**ex′sic•ca′tor** *n.*

ex•stip•u•late (ĕks-stĭp′yə-lĭt) *adj. Bot.* Lacking stipules.

ext. *abbr.* **1.** Extension. **2.a.** External. **b.** Externally. **3.** Extinct. **4.** Extra. **5.** Extract.

ex•tant (ĕk′stənt, ĕk-stănt′) *adj.* **1.** Still in existence; not destroyed, lost, or extinct. **2.** *Archaic.* Standing out; projecting. [Lat. *exstāns, exstant-,* pr.part. of *exstāre,* to stand out : *ex-,* ex- + *stāre,* to stand; see **stā-***.]

ex•tem•po•ral (ĭk-stĕm′pər-əl) *adj. Archaic.* Extemporaneous. [Lat. *extemporālis* < *ex tempore.* See EXTEMPORE.]

ex•tem•po•ra•ne•ous (ĭk-stĕm′pə-rā′nē-əs) *adj.* **1.** Carried out or performed with little or no preparation; impromptu. **2.** Prepared in advance but delivered without notes or text. **3.** Skilled at or given to unrehearsed speech or performance. **4.** Provided, made, or adapted as an expedient; makeshift. [< LLat. *extemporāneus* < Lat. *ex tempore.* See EXTEMPORE.] —**ex•tem′po•ra•ne′i•ty** (-pər-ə-nē′ĭ-tē), **ex•tem′po•ra′ne•ous•ness** *n.* —**ex•tem′po•ra′ne•ous•ly** *adv.*

ex•tem•po•rar•y (ĭk-stĕm′pə-rĕr′ē) *adj.* Spoken, done, or composed with little or no preparation or forethought. [< EXTEMPORE.] —**ex•tem′po•rar′i•ly** (-râr′ə-lē) *adv.*

ex•tem•po•re (ĭk-stĕm′pə-rē) *adj.* Extemporary. —*adv.* In an extemporaneous manner. [Lat. *ex tempore* : *ex,* of; see EX- + *tempore,* ablative of *tempus,* time.]

ex•tem•po•rize (ĭk-stĕm′pə-rīz′) *v.* **-rized, -riz•ing, -riz•es.** —*tr.* To do or perform (something) without prior preparation or practice. —*intr.* To perform an act or utter something in an impromptu manner; improvise. —**ex•tem′po•ri•za′tion** (-pər-ĭ-zā′shən) *n.* —**ex•tem′po•riz′er** *n.*

ex•tend (ĭk-stĕnd′) *v.* **-tend•ed, -tend•ing, -tends.** —*tr.* **1.** To open or straighten (something) out; unbend. **2.** To stretch or spread (something) out to greater or fullest length. **3.a.** To exert (oneself) vigorously or to full capacity. **b.** To cause to move at full gallop. Used of a horse. **4.a.** To increase in quantity or bulk by adding a cheaper substance. **b.** To adulterate. **5.a.** To enlarge the area, scope, or range of. **b.** To expand the influence of. **c.** To make more comprehensive or inclusive. See Syns at **increase. 6.a.** To offer. **b.** To make available; provide. **7.a.** To cause (something) to be or last longer. **b.** To prolong the time allowed for payment of. **8.** *Chiefly British.* **a.** To appraise or assess; value. **b.** To seize or make a levy on for the purpose of settling a debt. —*intr.* To be or become long, large, or comprehensive. [ME *extenden* < OFr. *extendre* < Lat. *extendere* : *ex-,* ex- + *tendere,* to stretch; see **ten-***.] —**ex•tend′i•bil′i•ty** *n.* —**ex•tend′a•ble, ex•tend′i•ble** *adj.*

ex•tend•ed (ĭk-stĕn′dĭd) *adj.* **1.** Stretched or pulled out: *an extended telescope.* **2.** Continued for a long period of time; protracted. **3.** Enlarged or broad in meaning, scope, or influence. —**ex•tend′ed•ly** *adv.*

extended family *n.* A family group that consists of parents, children, and other close relatives, often in close proximity.

ex•tend•er (ĭk-stĕn′dər) *n.* A substance added to another substance to modify, dilute, or adulterate it.

ex•ten•si•ble (ĭk-stĕn′sə-bəl) *adj.* **1.** Capable of being extended or protruded. **2.** *Comp. Sci.* Of or relating to a programming language or a system that can be modified by changing or adding features. —**ex•ten′si•bil′i•ty** *n.*

ex•ten•sile (ĭk-stĕn′sĭl) *adj.* Extensible.

ex•ten•sion (ĭk-stĕn′shən) *n.* **1.** The act of extending or the condition of being extended. **2.** The amount, degree, or range to which something extends or can extend. **3.a.** The act of straightening or extending a limb. **b.** The position assumed by an extended limb. **4.** *Medic.* The application of traction to a fractured or dislocated limb to restore the normal position. **5.a.** An addition that increases the area, influence, operation, or contents of something. **b.** An additional telephone connected to a main line. **6.a.** An allowance of extra time, esp. for the repayment of a debt. **b.** The period of this extra time. **7.** The property of an object by which it occupies space. **8.** A program in a university, college, or school for students unable to attend at the usual time or in the usual place. **9.** *Logic.* The class of objects designated by a specific term or concept; denotation. **10.** *Math.* A set that includes a given and similar set as a subset. [ME *extensioun* < OFr. *extension* < Lat. *extēnsiō, extēnsiōn-* < *extēnsus,* p.part. of *extendere,* to extend. See EXTEND.] —**ex•ten′sion•al** *adj.*

ex•ten•si•ty (ĭk-stĕn′sĭ-tē) *n., pl.* **-ties. 1.a.** The quality of having extension or being extensive. **b.** A specific degree or range of extension. **2.** The attribute of sensation that enables one to perceive space or size.

ex•ten•sive (ĭk-stĕn′sĭv) *adj.* **1.** Large in extent, range, or amount. **2.** Of or relating to the cultivation of vast areas of land with a minimum of labor or expense. —**ex•ten′sive•ly** *adv.* —**ex•ten′sive•ness** *n.*

ex•ten•som•e•ter (ĕk′stĕn-sŏm′ĭ-tər) *n.* An instrument used to measure minute deformations in a test specimen of a material. [EXTENS(ION) + -METER.]

ex•ten•sor (ĭk-stĕn′sər) *n.* A muscle that extends or straightens a limb or body part. [NLat. < Lat. *extēnsus,* p.part. of *extendere,* to stretch out. See EXTEND.]

ex•tent (ĭk-stĕnt′) *n.* **1.a.** The range, magnitude, or distance over which a thing extends. **b.** The degree to which a thing extends. **2.** An extensive space or area. **3.** *Archaic.* An assessment or a valuation, esp. for taxation. [ME *extente,* assessment on land < AN < fem. p.part. of *extendre,* to extend < Lat. *extendere.* See EXTEND.]

ex•ten•u•ate (ĭk-stĕn′yo͞o-āt′) *tr.v.* **-at•ed, -at•ing, -ates. 1.** To lessen or attempt to lessen the magnitude or seriousness of, esp. by providing partial excuses. **2.** *Archaic.* **a.** To make thin or emaciated. **b.** To reduce the strength of. **3.** *Obsolete.* To belittle; disparage. [Lat. *extenuāre, extenuāt-* : *ex-,* ex- + *tenuāre,* to make thin (< *tenuis,* thin; see **ten-***).] **— ex•ten′u•a′tive** *adj. & n.* **— ex•ten′u•a′tor** *n.* **— ex•ten′u•a•to′ry** (-ə-tôr′ē, -tōr′ē) *adj.*

ex•ten•u•a•tion (ĭk-stĕn′yo͞o-ā′shən) *n.* **1.** The act of extenuating or the condition of being extenuated; partial justification. **2.** A partial excuse.

ex•te•ri•or (ĭk-stîr′ē-ər) *adj.* **1.** Outer; external. **2.** Originating or acting from the outside. **3.** Suitable for use outside: *an exterior paint.* **—** *n.* **1.** A part or a surface that is outside. **2.** An external or outward appearance. **3.** A representation in visual art of the outdoors. [Lat., comp. of *exter,* outward. See **eghs***.] **— ex•te′ri•or•ly** *adv.*

exterior angle *n. Math.* **1.** The angle between any side of a polygon and an extended adjacent side. **2.** Any of the four angles that do not include a region of the space between two lines intersected by a transversal.

ex•te•ri•or•i•ty (ĭk-stîr′ē-ôr′ĭ-tē, -ŏr′-) *n.* Outwardness; externality.

ex•te•ri•or•ize (ĭk-stîr′ē-ə-rīz′) *tr.v.* **-ized, -iz•ing, -iz•es.** To turn outward; externalize.

ex•ter•mi•nate (ĭk-stûr′mə-nāt′) *tr.v.* **-nat•ed, -nat•ing, -nates.** To get rid of by destroying completely; extirpate. [Lat. *extermināre, extermināt-,* to drive out : *ex-,* ex- + *termināre,* to mark boundaries (< *terminus,* boundary marker).] **— ex•ter′mi•na′tion** *n.* **— ex•ter′mi•na′tive, ex•ter′mi•na•to′ry** (-nə-tôr′ē, -tōr′ē) *adj.*

ex•ter•mi•na•tor (ĭk-stûr′mə-nā′tər) *n.* One that exterminates, esp. one whose occupation is the killing of vermin.

ex•tern or **ex•terne** (ĕk′stûrn′) *n.* A person associated with but not officially residing in an institution, esp. a nonresident physician on a hospital staff. [Lat. *externus,* external. See EXTERNAL.] **— ex′tern•ship′** *n.*

ex•ter•nal (ĭk-stûr′nəl) *adj.* **1.** Relating to, existing on, or connected with the outside or an outer part; exterior. **2.** Suitable for application to the outside. **3.** Existing independently of the mind. **4.** Acting or coming from the outside: *external pressures.* **5.** Of or relating chiefly to outward appearance; superficial. **6.** Of or relating to foreign affairs or foreign countries. **—** *n.* **1.** An exterior part or surface. **2. externals. a.** Outer circumstances. **b.** Outward appearances. [ME < Lat. *externus,* outward < *exter.* See **eghs***.] **— ex•ter′nal•ly** *adv.*

external auditory canal *n.* See **ear canal.**

ex•ter•nal-com•bus•tion engine (ĭk-stûr′nəl-kəm-bŭs′chən) *n.* An engine, such as a steam engine, in which the fuel is burned outside the engine cylinder.

external ear *n.* The outer portion of the ear including the auricle and the passage leading to the eardrum.

ex•ter•nal•ism (ĭk-stûr′nə-lĭz′əm) *n.* Excessive concern with outer circumstances or appearances. **— ex•ter′nal•ist** *n.*

ex•ter•nal•i•ty (ĕk′stər-năl′ĭ-tē) *n., pl.* **-ties. 1.** The state or quality of being external or externalized. **2.** Something that is external.

ex•ter•nal•ize (ĭk-stûr′nə-līz′) *tr.v.* **-ized, -iz•ing, -iz•es. 1.a.** To make external. **b.** To manifest externally. **2.** To attribute to outside causes. **3.** To project or attribute (inner conflicts or feelings) to external circumstances or causes. **— ex•ter′nal•i•za′tion** (-nə-lĭ-zā′shən) *n.*

external respiration *n.* The exchange of oxygen and carbon dioxide between the environment and respiratory organs.

ex•ter•o•cep•tor (ĕk′stə-rō-sĕp′tər) *n.* A sense organ, such as the ear, that receives and responds to stimuli originating from outside the body. [Lat. *exter,* outside; see EXTERIOR + (RE)CEPTOR.] **— ex′ter•o•cep′tive** *adj.*

ex•ter•ri•to•ri•al (ĕks′tĕr-ĭ-tôr′ē-əl, -tōr′-) *adj.* Extraterritorial. **— ex′ter•ri•to′ri•al′i•ty** (-ăl′ĭ-tē) *n.* **— ex′ter•ri•to′ri•al•ly** *adv.*

ex•tinct (ĭk-stĭngkt′) *adj.* **1.** No longer existing or living. **2.** No longer burning or active. **3.** No longer in use. **4.** *Law.* Lacking a claimant; void. [ME < Lat. *exstīnctus,* p.part. of *exstinguere,* to extinguish. See EXTINGUISH.]

ex•tinc•tion (ĭk-stĭngk′shən) *n.* **1.a.** The act of extinguishing. **b.** The condition of being extinguished. **2.** The fact of being extinct or the process of becoming extinct. **3.** *Psychol.* A reduction or a loss in the strength or rate of a conditioned response when the unconditioned stimulus or reinforcement is withheld.

ex•tinc•tive (ĭk-stĭngk′tĭv) *adj.* Tending to extinguish or make extinct.

ex•tin•guish (ĭk-stĭng′gwĭsh) *tr.v.* **-guished, -guish•ing, -guish•es. 1.** To put out (a fire, for example); quench. **2.** To put an end to (hopes, for example); destroy. **3.** To obscure; eclipse. **4.** *Law.* **a.** To settle or discharge (a debt). **b.** To nullify. **5.** *Psychol.* To bring about the extinction of (a conditioned response). [Lat. *exstinguere* : *ex-,* intensive pref.; see EX- + *stinguere,* to quench; see **steig-***.] **— ex•tin′guish•a•ble** *adj.* **— ex•tin′guish•ment** *n.*

ex•tin•guish•er (ĭk-stĭng′gwĭ-shər) *n.* One that extinguishes, esp.: **a.** Any of various portable mechanical devices for spraying a fire with chemicals. **b.** A small metal cone or cup on a long handle, used to snuff out candles; a snuffer.

ex•tir•pate (ĕk′stər-pāt′) *tr.v.* **-pat•ed, -pat•ing, -pates. 1.** To pull up by the roots. **2.** To destroy totally; exterminate. **3.** To remove by surgery. [Lat. *exstirpāre, exstirpāt-* : *ex-,* ex- + *stirps,* root.] **— ex′tir•pa′tion** *n.* **— ex′tir•pa′tive** *adj.* **— ex′tir•pa′tor** *n.*

ex•tol also **ex•toll** (ĭk-stōl′) *tr.v.* **-tolled, -tol•ling, -tols** also **-tolled, -toll•ing, -tolls.** To praise highly; exalt. See Syns at **praise.** [ME *extollen* < Lat. *extollere,* to lift up, praise : *ex-,* up from; see EX- + *tollere,* to lift; see **telə-***.] **— ex•tol′ler** *n.* **— ex•tol′ment** *n.*

ex•tort (ĭk-stôrt′) *tr.v.* **-tort•ed, -tort•ing, -torts.** To obtain from another by coercion or intimidation. [Lat. *extorquēre, extort-,* to wrench out, extort : *ex-,* ex- + *torquēre,* to twist; see **terkʷ-***.] **— ex•tort′er** *n.* **— ex•tor′tive** *adj.*

ex•tor•tion (ĭk-stôr′shən) *n.* **1.** The act or an instance of extorting. **2.** Illegal use of one's official position or powers to obtain property, funds, or patronage. **3.** An excessive or exorbitant charge. **4.** Something extorted. **— ex•tor′tion•ar′y** (-shə-nĕr′ē) *adj.* **— ex•tor′tion•ist, ex•tor′tion•er** *n.*

ex•tor•tion•ate (ĭk-stôr′shə-nĭt) *adj.* **1.** Marked by extortion. **2.** Exorbitant; immoderate. **— ex•tor′tion•ate•ly** *adv.*

ex•tra (ĕk′strə) *adj.* **1.** More than or beyond what is usual, normal, expected, or necessary. See Syns at **superfluous. 2.** Better than ordinary; superior. **3.** Subject to an additional charge. **—** *n.* **1.** Something more than is usual or necessary. **2.** Something for which an additional charge is made. **3.** A special edition of a newspaper. **4.a.** An additional or alternate worker. **b.** A performer hired to play a minor part, as in a crowd scene. **5.** Something of exceptional quality. **—** *adv.* To an exceptional extent or degree; unusually. [Prob. short for EXTRAORDINARY.]

extra– or **extro–** *pref.* Outside; beyond: *extraterritorial.* [LLat. < Lat. *extrā.* See **eghs***.]

ex•tra-base hit (ĕk′strə-bās′) *n. Baseball.* A double, a triple, or a home run.

ex•tra•cel•lu•lar (ĕk′strə-sĕl′yə-lər) *adj.* Located or occurring outside a cell or cells. **— ex′tra•cel′lu•lar•ly** *adv.*

ex•tra•cor•po•re•al (ĕk′strə-kôr-pôr′ē-əl, -pōr′-) *adj.* Situated or occurring outside the body. **— ex′tra•cor•po′re•al•ly** *adv.*

ex•tract (ĭk-străkt′) *tr.v.* **-tract•ed, -tract•ing, -tracts. 1.** To draw or pull out, using great force or effort. **2.** To obtain despite resistance. **3.** To obtain from a substance by chemical or mechanical action, as by pressure, distillation, or evaporation. **4.** To remove for separate consideration or publication; excerpt. **5.a.** To derive or obtain (information, for example) from a source. **b.** To deduce (a principle or doctrine); construe (a meaning). **c.** To derive (pleasure or comfort) from an experience. **6.** *Math.* To determine or calculate (the root of a number). **—** *n.* (ĕk′străkt′). **1.** A passage from a literary work; an excerpt. **2.** A concentrated preparation of the essential constituents of a food, a flavoring, or another substance; a concentrate. [ME *extracten* < Lat. *extrahere, extract-* : *ex-,* ex- + *trahere,* to draw.] **— ex•tract′a•ble, ex•tract′i•ble** *adj.* **— ex•trac′tor** *n.*

ex•trac•tion (ĭk-străk′shən) *n.* **1.** The act of extracting or the condition of being extracted. **2.** Something obtained by extracting; an extract. **3.** Origin; lineage.

ex•trac•tive (ĭk-străk′tĭv) *adj.* **1.** Used in or obtained by extraction. **2.** Possible to extract. **—** *n.* **1.** Something that may be extracted. **2.** The insoluble portion of an extract. **— ex•trac′tive•ly** *adv.*

ex•tra•cur•ric•u•lar (ĕk′strə-kə-rĭk′yə-lər) *adj.* **1.** Being outside the regular curriculum of a school or college. **2.** Being outside one's usual duties. **3.** *Informal.* Extramarital.

ex•tra•dit•a•ble (ĕk′strə-dī′tə-bəl) *adj.* **1.** Subject to extradition: *extraditable fugitives.* **2.** Making liable to extradition.

ex•tra•dite (ĕk′strə-dīt′) *Law.* **—** *v.* **-dit•ed, -dit•ing, -dites. —** *tr.* **1.** To give up or deliver (a fugitive, for example) to the legal jurisdiction of another government or authority. **2.** To obtain the extradition of. See Syns at **banish. —** *intr.* To perform or engage in the process of extradition.

ex•tra•di•tion (ĕk′strə-dĭsh′ən) *n. Law.* Legal surrender of a fugitive to the jurisdiction of another state, country, or government for trial. [Fr. : Lat. *ex-,* ex- + Lat. *trāditiō, trāditiōn-,* a handing over; see TRADITION.]

ex•tra•dos (ĕk′strə-dŏs′, -dōs′) *n., pl.* **-dos** (-dōz′) or **-dos•es.** *Archit.* The upper or exterior curve of an arch. [Fr. : Lat.

exterior angle
Left: Exterior angles on the same side
Right: Exterior opposite angles

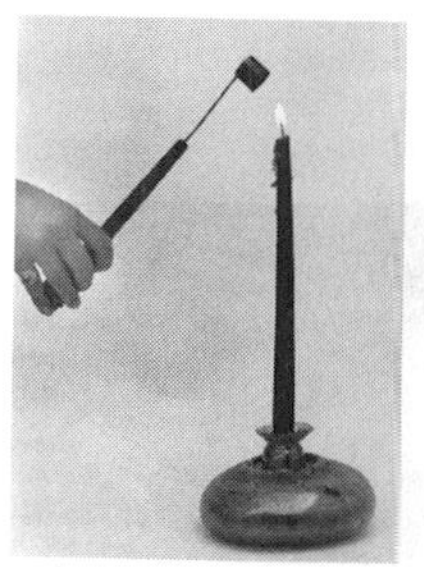

extinguisher
Candle snuffer

ă **pat**	oi **boy**
ā **pay**	ou **out**
âr **care**	o͝o **took**
ä **father**	o͞o **boot**
ĕ **pet**	ŭ **cut**
ē **be**	ûr **urge**
ĭ **pit**	th **thin**
ī **pie**	*th* **this**
îr **pier**	hw **which**
ŏ **pot**	zh **vision**
ō **toe**	ə **about, item**
ô **paw**	

Stress marks:
′ (primary);
′ (secondary), as in
dictionary (dĭk′shə-nĕr′ē)

F f

f¹ or **F** (ĕf) *n., pl.* **f's** or **F's. 1.** The sixth letter of the modern English alphabet. **2.** Any of the speech sounds represented by the letter *f.* **3.** The sixth in a series. **4. F** A failing grade in schoolwork. **5.** Something shaped like the letter F. **6.** Or **F** *Mus.* **a.** The fourth tone in the scale of C major or the sixth tone in the relative minor scale. **b.** A key or scale in which F is the tonic.
f² *abbr.* **1.** Focal length. **2.** Or **F** *Mus.* Forte. **3.** *Math.* Function.
F¹ The symbol for the element **fluorine.**
F² *abbr.* **1.** Fahrenheit. **2.** Farad. **3.** Or **F.** Fellow (of a university or another institution). **4.** Filial generation.
f. *abbr.* **1.** Farthing. **2.** Or **F.** Female. **3.** Or **F.** *Gram.* Feminine. **4.** Or **F.** *Metall.* Fine. **5.** Or **F.** Folio. **6.** Following. **7.** *Sports.* Foul. **8.** Franc.
F. *abbr.* **1.** French. **2.** Friday.
f/ *abbr.* Relative aperture of a lens.
fa (fä) *n. Mus.* The fourth tone of the diatonic scale in solfeggio. [ME < Med.Lat. See GAMUT.]
FA *abbr.* **1.** Or **F.A.** Fine art. **2.** *Sports.* Football Association.
f.a. *abbr.* Fire alarm.
FAA *abbr.* Federal Aviation Administration.
fab¹ (făb) *n. Informal.* Fabrication: *a shed of metal fab.*
fab² (făb) *adj. Slang.* Fabulous; wonderful.
Fa•ber•gé (făb′ər-zhā′), **Peter Carl.** 1846–1920. Russian goldsmith and jeweler whose works include jeweled and enameled Easter eggs for European royalty.
Fa•bi•an (fā′bē-ən) *adj.* **1.a.** Of or relating to the caution and avoidance of direct confrontation typical of Quintus Fabius Maximus. **b.** Cautious or dilatory, as in taking action. **2.** Of, relating to, or being a member of the Fabian Society, which was committed to gradual means for spreading socialist principles. [Lat. *Fabiānus*, after Quintus FABIUS MAXIMUS VERRUCOSUS.] **—Fa′bi•an** *n.* **—Fa′bi•an•ism** *n.* **—Fa′bi•an•ist** *n.*
Fa•bi•us Max•i•mus Ver•ru•co•sus (fā′bē-əs măk′sə-məs vĕr-yo͞o-kō′səs, -o͞o-), **Quintus.** d. 203 B.C. Roman general who defeated Hannibal (209) by delaying tactics.
fa•ble (fā′bəl) *n.* **1.** A usu. short narrative making an edifying or cautionary point and often employing animal characters that act like human beings. **2.** A story about legendary persons and exploits. **3.** A falsehood; a lie. **—***v.* **-bled, -bling, -bles.** **—***tr.* To recount as if true. **—***intr. Archaic.* To compose fables. [ME < OFr. < Lat. *fābula* < *fārī*, to speak. See **bhā-²*.**] **—fa′bler** *n.*
fa•bled (fā′bəld) *adj.* **1.** Made known or famous by fables; legendary. **2.** Existing only in fables; fictitious.
fab•li•au (făb′lē-ō′) *n., pl.* **-li•aux** (-lē-ō′, -ōz′). A medieval verse tale characterized by comic ribald treatment of themes drawn from life. [Fr. < ONFr. < OFr. *fablel*, dim. of *fable*, fable. See FABLE.]
fab•ric (făb′rĭk) *n.* **1.a.** A cloth produced esp. by knitting, weaving, or felting fibers. **b.** The texture or quality of such cloth. **2.** A complex underlying structure. **3.a.** A method or style of construction. **b.** A structural material, such as masonry. **c.** A physical structure; a building. [ME *fabryke*, something constructed < OFr. *fabrique* < Lat. *fabrica*, craft, workshop < *faber, fabr-*, workman, artificer.]
fab•ric•a•ble (făb′rĭ-kə-bəl) *adj.* Capable of being shaped or formed: *a fabricable alloy.* **—fab′ric•a•bil′i•ty** *n.*
fab•ri•cate (făb′rĭ-kāt′) *tr.v.* **-cat•ed, -cat•ing, -cates. 1.** To make; create. **2.** To construct by combining or assembling diverse, typically standardized parts. **3.** To concoct in order to deceive: *fabricated an excuse.* [ME *fabricaten* < Lat. *fabricārī, fabricāt-*, to make < *fabrica*, craft. See FABRIC.] **—fab′ri•ca′tion** *n.* **—fab′ri•ca′tor** *n.*
fab•u•late (făb′yə-lāt′) *intr.v.* **-lat•ed, -lat•ing, -lates.** To compose fables or stories, esp. employing fantasy. [Lat. *fābulārī, fābulāt-*, to talk < *fābula*, tale, talk. See FABLE.] **—fab′u•la′tion** *n.* **—fab′u•la′tor** *n.*
fab•u•list (făb′yə-lĭst) *n.* **1.** A composer of fables. **2.** An inventor or teller of falsehoods; a liar. [Fr. *fabuliste* < Lat. *fābula*, fable. See FABLE.]
fab•u•lous (făb′yə-ləs) *adj.* **1.** Barely credible; astonishing. **2.** Extremely pleasing or successful: *a fabulous vacation.* **3.a.** Of the nature of a fable or myth; legendary. **b.** Told of or celebrated in fables or legends. [ME, mythical < OFr. *fabuleux* < Lat. *fābulōsus* < *fābula*, fable. See FABLE.] **—fab′u•lous•ly** *adv.* **—fab′u•lous•ness** *n.*
fac. *abbr.* **1.** Facsimile. **2.** Faculty.
fa•çade also **fa•cade** (fə-säd′) *n.* **1.** *Archit.* The face of a building, esp. the principal face. **2.** An artificial or deceptive front. [Fr. < Ital. *facciata* < *faccia*, face < VLat. **facia* < Lat. *faciēs.* See **dhē-*.**]
face (fās) *n.* **1.a.** The front of the head from the top of the forehead to the base of the chin and from ear to ear. **b.** A person. **2.** A person's countenance. **3.** A contorted facial expression; a grimace. **4.** Outward appearance. **5.a.** Value or standing in the eyes of others; prestige: *lose face.* **b.** Self-assurance; confidence. **6.** Effrontery; impudence. **7.** The most significant or prominent surface of an object, esp.: **a.** The surface presented to view; the front. **b.** A façade. **c.** Outer surface: *the face of the earth.* **d.** A marked side: *the face of a clock.* **e.** The right side, as of fabric. **8.** *Geometry.* A planar surface of a geometric solid. **9.** Any of the surfaces of a rock or crystal. **10.** The end, as of a mine or tunnel, at which work is advancing. **11.** The appearance and geologic surface features of an area of land; topography. **12.** *Print.* A typeface or range of typefaces. **—***v.* **faced, fac•ing, fac•es. —***tr.* **1.** To occupy a position with the face toward. **2.** To front on. **3.a.** To confront with complete awareness. **b.** To overcome by confronting boldly or bravely. **c.** To confront with impudence. **4.a.** To be certain to encounter; have in store: *faced a long ordeal.* **b.** To bring or to be brought face to face with. **5.** To cause (troops) to change direction by giving a command. **6.** *Games.* To turn (a playing card) so that the face is up. **7.** To furnish with a surface or cover of a different material. **8.** To line or trim the edge of, esp. with contrasting material. **9.** To treat the surface of so as to smooth. **—***intr.* **1.** To be turned or placed with the front toward a specified direction. **2.** To turn the face in a specified direction. **—*phrasal verbs.*** **face down.** To attain mastery over or overcome by confronting in a determined manner. **face off.** *Sports.* To start play in ice hockey, lacrosse, and other games by releasing the puck or ball between two opposing players. **face up.** To confront, an unpleasant situation, for example, with resolution. **—*idioms.*** **face the music.** To accept the unpleasant consequences, esp. of one's own actions. **face to face. 1.** In each other's presence; in direct communication: *spoke face to face.* **2.** Directly confronting: *We were face to face with death.* **in (the) face of.** Despite the opposition of; notwithstanding. **on the face of it.** From appearances alone; apparently. **show (one's) face.** To make an appearance. **to (one's) face.** In the view or hearing of. [ME < OFr. < VLat. **facia* < Lat. *faciēs.* See **dhē-*.**] **—face′a•ble** *adj.*
face angle *n. Math.* The angle formed between two edges of a polyhedral angle.
face card *n. Games.* A king, queen, or jack of a deck of cards.
face•cloth also **face cloth** (fās′klôth′, -klŏth′) *n.* See **washcloth.**
face•down (fās′doun′) *n.* A confrontation with an opponent or enemy. **—***adv.* (fās′doun′). In a position so that the face is down: *floating facedown in the water.*
face-hard•en (fās′här′dn) *tr.v.* **-hard•ened, -hard•en•ing, -hard•ens.** To harden the surface of (a metal).
face-lift (fās′lĭft′) also **face•lift•ing** (-lĭf′tĭng) *n.* **1.** Plastic surgery to remove wrinkles or other visible signs of aging for cosmetic purposes. **2.** A restyling or modernization, as of a building.
face•mask (fās′măsk′) *n.* A protective or disguising cover for the face, often enveloping the entire head.

facemask
Field hockey goalie's mask

face-off (fās′ôf′, -ŏf′) *n.* **1.** *Sports.* A method of starting play in ice hockey, lacrosse, and other games in which an official drops the puck or ball between two opposing players who contend for its control. **2.** A confrontation.
face•plate (fās′plāt′) *n.* **1.** A disk attached to the mandrel of a lathe to hold the work to be turned. **2.** The glass front of a cathode-ray tube upon which the image is displayed. **3.** A protective plate covering the human face, as of a welder.
fac•er (fā′sər) *n.* **1.** One that faces, esp. a device used in smoothing or dressing a surface. **2.** An unexpected stunning blow or defeat.
face-sav•er (fās′sā′vər) *n.* Something that prevents loss of dignity or self-esteem. **—face′-sav′ing** *n.*
fac•et (făs′ĭt) *n.* **1.** One of the flat polished surfaces cut on a gemstone or occurring naturally on a crystal. **2.** *Anat.* A small smooth flat surface, as on a bone or tooth. **3.** *Biol.* One of the lenslike visual units of a compound eye, as of an insect. **4.** One of numerous aspects, as of a subject; a phase. [Fr. *facette* < OFr., dim. of *face*, face. See FACE.] **—fac′et•ed, fac′et•ted** *adj.*
fa•cete (fə-sēt′) *adj. Archaic.* Witty; facetious. [Lat. *facētus.*]
fa•ce•ti•ae (fə-sē′shē-ē′) *pl.n.* Witty or humorous writings and sayings. [Lat., pl. of *facētia*, jest. See FACETIOUS.]
fa•ce•tious (fə-sē′shəs) *adj.* Playfully jocular; humorous. [Fr. *facétieux* < *facétie*, jest < Lat. *facētia* < *facētus*, witty.] **—fa•ce′tious•ly** *adv.* **—fa•ce′tious•ness** *n.*
face•up (fās′ŭp′) *adv.* In a position so that the face is up.
face value *n.* **1.** The value printed or written on the face, as of a bill or bond. **2.** Apparent significance or value.

fa•cial (fā′shəl) *adj.* Of or concerning the face: *facial hair.* —*n.* A treatment for the face, usu. consisting of a massage and the application of cosmetic creams. —**fa′cial•ly** *adv.*

facial index *n.* The ratio of facial length to facial width multiplied by 100.

facial nerve *n.* Either of the seventh pair of cranial nerves that control facial muscles and relay sensation from the taste buds of the front part of the tongue.

-facient *suff.* **1.** Causing; bringing about: *somnifacient.* **2.** Something that causes or brings about: *abortifacient.* [< Lat. *faciēns, facient-*, pr.part. of *facere*, to do. See **dhē-***.]

fa•ci•es (fā′shē-ēz′, -shēz) *n., pl.* **facies. 1.** *Biol.* The general aspect or outward appearance, as of a given growth of flora. **2.** *Medic.* The appearance or expression of the face, esp. when typical of a disorder or disease. **3.** *Geol.* A rock or stratified body distinguished from others by its appearance or composition. [Lat. *faciēs.* See **dhē-***.]

fac•ile (făs′əl) *adj.* **1.** Done or achieved with little effort or difficulty; easy. See Syns at **easy. 2.** Working, acting, or speaking with effortless ease and fluency. **3.** Arrived at without due care, effort, or examination; superficial. **4.** Readily manifested, together with an aura of insincerity and lack of depth: *a facile slogan.* **5.** *Archaic.* Pleasingly mild, as in disposition or manner. [ME < OFr. < Lat. *facilis.* See **dhē-***.] —**fac′ile•ly** *adv.* —**fac′ile•ness** *n.*

fa•cil•i•tate (fə-sĭl′ĭ-tāt′) *tr.v.* **-tat•ed, -tat•ing, -tates.** To make easy or easier. [< Fr. *faciliter* < OFr. < Ital. *facilitare* < *facile*, facile < Lat. *facilis.* See FACILE.] —**fa•cil′i•ta′tive** (-tā′tĭv) *adj.* —**fa•cil′i•ta′tor** *n.*

fa•cil•i•ta•tion (fə-sĭl′ĭ-tā′shən) *n.* **1.a.** The act of making easy or easier. **b.** The state of being made easy or easier. **2.** *Physiol.* The lowering of the threshold for propagation of an action potential of a neuron.

fa•cil•i•ty (fə-sĭl′ĭ-tē) *n., pl.* **-ties. 1.** Ease in moving, acting, or doing; aptitude. **2.** Readiness to be persuaded; pliability. **3.** Something that facilitates an action or a process. Often used in the plural. **4.** Something created to serve a particular function: *health care facilities.*

fac•ing (fā′sĭng) *n.* **1.** A piece of material sewn to the edge of a garment, such as a dress or coat, as lining or decoration. **2.** An outer layer or coating applied to a surface for protection or decoration.

fac•sim•i•le (făk-sĭm′ə-lē) *n.* **1.** An exact copy or reproduction, as of a document. **2.a.** A method of transmitting images or printed matter by electronic means. **b.** An image so transmitted. —*adj.* **1.** Of or used to produce exact reproductions, as of documents. **2.** Exactly reproduced; duplicate. [Lat. *fac simile*, make similar : *fac*, imper. of *facere*, to make; see **dhē-*** + *simile*, neut. of *similis*, similar; see SIMILAR.]

fact (făkt) *n.* **1.** Information presented as objectively real. **2.** A real occurrence; an event: *the facts of the accident.* **3.a.** Something having real, demonstrable existence. **b.** The quality of being real or actual. **4.** A thing that has been done, esp. a crime: *an accessory before the fact.* **5.** *Law.* The aspect of a case at law comprising events determined by evidence. —***idiom.* in (point of) fact.** In reality or in truth; actually. [Lat. *factum*, deed < neut. p.part. of *facere*, to do. See **dhē-***.]

Usage Note: *Fact* has a long history of usage in the sense "allegation of fact," as in *"This tract was distributed to thousands of American teachers, but the facts and the reasoning are wrong"* (Albert Shanker). This practice has led inevitably to the introduction of the phrases *true facts* and *real facts*, as in *The true facts of the case may never be known.* These usages may occasion qualms among critics who hold that facts cannot be other than true, but they are often useful.

fact-find•ing (făkt′fīn′dĭng) *n.* Discovery or determination of facts or accurate information. —*adj.* Of, relating to, or used in the discovery or determination of facts. —**fact′-find′er** *n.*

fac•tic•i•ty (făk-tĭs′ĭ-tē) *n.* The quality or condition of being a fact: *historical facticity.*

fac•tion¹ (făk′shən) *n.* **1.** A group of persons forming a cohesive, usu. contentious minority within a larger group. **2.** Conflict within an organization or nation; internal dissension. [Fr. < Lat. *factiō, factiōn-* < *factus*, p.part. of *facere*, to do. See **dhē-***.] —**fac′tion•al** *adj.* —**fac′tion•al•ism** *n.* —**fac′tion•al•ly** *adv.*

fac•tion² (făk′shən) *n.* A form of fiction incorporating real people or events as essential elements. [Blend of FACT and FICTION.]

-faction *suff.* Production; making: *petrifaction.* [ME *-faccioun* < OFr. *-faction* < Lat. *-factiō, -factiōn-* < *factus*, p.part. of *facere*, to make. See **dhē-***.]

fac•tion•al•ize (făk′shə-nə-līz′) *tr.v.* **-ized, -iz•ing, -iz•es.** To split (a group, for example) into disputatious factions.

fac•tious (făk′shəs) *adj.* **1.** Of, relating to, produced by, or characterized by internal dissension. **2.** Given to or promoting internal dissension. —**fac′tious•ly** *adv.* —**fac′tious•ness** *n.*

fac•ti•tious (făk-tĭsh′əs) *adj.* **1.** Produced artificially rather than by a natural process. **2.** Lacking authenticity or genuineness; sham. [< Lat. *facticius* < *factus*, p.part. of *facere*, to make. See **dhē-***.] —**fac•ti′tious•ly** *adv.* —**fac•ti′tious•ness** *n.*

fac•ti•tive (făk′tĭ-tĭv) *adj.* Of or constituting a transitive verb, such as *elect*, that in some constructions takes an objective complement to modify its direct object. [NLat. *factitīvus* < Lat. *factitāre*, to do, practice, freq. of *facere*, to do. See **dhē-***.] —**fac′ti•tive•ly** *adv.*

fact of life *n., pl.* **facts of life. 1.** Something unavoidable that must be faced or dealt with. **2. facts of life.** The basic physiological functions involved in sex and reproduction.

fac•toid (făk′toid) *n.* Unverified or inaccurate information that is presented in the press as factual and is then accepted as true because of constant repetition. —**fac•toid′al** *adj.*

fac•tor (făk′tər) *n.* **1.** One that actively contributes to an accomplishment, a result, or a process. See Syns at **element. 2.a.** One who acts for someone else; an agent. **b.** A person or firm that accepts accounts receivable as security for short-term loans. **3.** *Math.* One of two or more quantities that divides a given quantity without a remainder: *2 and 3 are factors of 6.* **4.** A quantity by which a stated quantity is multiplied or divided, so as to indicate an increase or decrease in a measurement. **5.** A gene. No longer in technical usage. **6.** *Physiol.* A substance that functions in a specific biochemical reaction or bodily process, such as blood coagulation. —*tr.v.* **-tored, -tor•ing, -tors.** To determine or indicate explicitly the factors of. —***phrasal verb.* factor in.** To figure in. [ME *factour*, perpetrator, agent < OFr. *facteur* < Lat. *factor*, maker < *facere*, to make. See **dhē-***.] —**fac′tor•a•ble** *adj.* —**fac′tor•ship′** *n.*

factor VIII *n.* See **antihemophilic factor.**

factor IX *n.* A protein substance in blood plasma that participates in and is essential for the blood-clotting process.

fac•tor•age (făk′tər-ĭj) *n.* **1.** The business of a factor. **2.** The commission or fee paid to a factor.

fac•to•ri•al (făk-tôr′ē-əl, -tōr′-) *n.* The product of all the positive integers from 1 to a given number. For example, 4 factorial, usu. written 4!, is equal to 24 (1 × 2 × 3 × 4 = 24). —*adj.* Of or relating to a factor or factorial.

fac•tor•ize (făk′tə-rīz′) *tr.v.* **-ized, -iz•ing, -iz•es.** *Math.* To factor. —**fac′tor•i•za′tion** (-tər-ĭ-zā′shən) *n.*

fac•to•ry (făk′tə-rē) *n., pl.* **-ries. 1.a.** A building or group of buildings in which goods are manufactured; a plant. **b.** A vessel in which newly caught seafood is prepared for shipment and sale. **2.** A business establishment for commercial agents or factors in a foreign country. **3.** The source of prolific production. [LLat. *factōria*, mill, and Med.Lat. *factōria*, establishment for factors, both < Lat. *factor*, factor. See FACTOR.]

fac•to•tum (făk-tō′təm) *n.* An employee or assistant who serves in a wide range of capacities. [Med.Lat. *factōtum* : Lat. *fac*, imper. of *facere*, to do; see **dhē-*** + Lat. *tōtum*, everything < neut. of *tōtus*, all; see **teutā-***.]

fac•tu•al (făk′cho͞o-əl) *adj.* **1.** Of the nature of fact; real. **2.** Of or containing facts. —**fac′tu•al′i•ty** (-ăl′ĭ-tē) *n.* —**fac′tu•al•ly** *adv.* —**fac′tu•al•ness** *n.*

fac•tu•al•ism (făk′cho͞o-ə-lĭz′əm) *n.* Devotion or adherence to fact. —**fac′tu•al•ist** *n.*

fac•u•la (făk′yə-lə) *n., pl.* **-lae** (-lē′). Any of various large bright spots or veined patches on the sun's photosphere, usu. near sunspots. [Lat., small torch, dim. of *fax, fac-*, torch.]

fac•ul•ta•tive (făk′əl-tā′tĭv) *adj.* **1.** Of or relating to a mental faculty. **2.a.** Capable of occurring or not occurring; contingent. **b.** Not required or compulsory; optional. **3.** Granting permission or authority. **4.** *Biol.* Capable of functioning under varying environmental conditions. —**fac′ul•ta′tive•ly** *adv.*

fac•ul•ty (făk′əl-tē) *n., pl.* **-ties. 1.** An inherent power or ability. **2.** Any of the powers or capacities possessed by the human mind. **3.** The ability to perform or act. **4.a.** Any of the divisions or comprehensive branches of learning at a college or university. **b.** The teachers and instructors within such a division. **c.** A body of teachers. **5.** All of the members of a learned profession. **6.** Authorization granted by authority; conferred power. **7.** *Archaic.* An occupation; a trade. [ME *faculte* < OFr. < Lat. *facultās*, power, ability < *facilis*, easy. See **dhē-***.]

fad (făd) *n.* A fashion taken up enthusiastically for a brief period of time; a craze. [Poss. < *fidfad*, fussy person, fussy < FIDDLE-FADDLE.] —**fad′dism** *n.* —**fad′dist** *n.* —**fad′dy** *adj.*

fad•dish (făd′ĭsh) *adj.* **1.** Having the nature of a fad. **2.** Given to fads. —**fad′dish•ly** *adv.* —**fad′dish•ness** *n.*

fade (fād) *v.* **fad•ed, fad•ing, fades.** —*intr.* **1.** To lose brightness, loudness, or brilliance gradually; dim. **2.** To lose freshness; wither. **3.** To lose strength or vitality; wane. **4.** To disappear gradually; vanish. See Syns at **disappear.** —*tr.* **1.** To cause to lose brightness, freshness, or strength. **2.** *Football.* To move back from the scrimmage line. Used of a quarterback. **3.** *Games.* To meet the bet of (an opposing player) in dice. —*n.* **1.** A gradual diminution in the brightness of an image in cinema or television. **2.** A periodic reduction in the received strength of a radio transmission. —***phrasal verbs.* fade in. 1.** To appear gradually. **2.** To cause to appear or be heard gradually. **fade out.** To disappear or cause to disappear gradually. [ME *faden* < OFr. *fader* < *fade*, faded, prob. < VLat. **fatidus*, alteration of Lat. *fatuus*, insipid.]

fade•a•way (fād′ə-wā′) *n.* The act or an instance of gradually

ă **pat**	oi **boy**
ā **pay**	ou **out**
âr **care**	o͝o **took**
ä **father**	o͞o **boot**
ĕ **pet**	ŭ **cut**
ē **be**	ûr **urge**
ĭ **pit**	th **thin**
ī **pie**	*th* **this**
îr **pier**	hw **which**
ŏ **pot**	zh **vision**
ō **toe**	ə **about, item**
ô **paw**	

Stress marks:
′ (primary);
′ (secondary), as in
dictionary (dĭk′shə-nĕr′ē)

fal•con•er (făl′kə-nər, fôl′-, fô′kə-) *n.* **1.** One that breeds and trains falcons. **2.** One that hunts with falcons.

fal•con•et (făl′kə-nĕt′, fôl′-, fô′kə-) *n.* **1.** A small or young falcon. **2.** Any of several small falcons, esp. of the genus *Microhierax* native to tropical Asia.

fal•con-gen•tle (făl′kən-jĕn′tl, fôl′-, fô′kən-) *n.* A female falcon, esp. a peregrine falcon. [ME *faucon gentil* < OFr. *faucon gentil*, noble falcon.]

fal•con•ry (făl′kən-rē, fôl′-, fô′kən-) *n. Sports.* **1.** Hunting of game with falcons. **2.** The art of training falcons for hunting.

fal•de•ral (făl′də-răl′) *n.* Var. of **folderol.**

fald•stool (fôld′sto͞ol′) *n.* **1.** A folding or small desk stool at which worshipers kneel to pray. **2.** A folding chair or stool, esp. one used by a bishop. **3.** A desk at which the litany is recited. [Partial transl. of Med.Lat. *faldistolium*, folding stool, of Gmc. orig. See **pel-**[2]*.]

Fa•lis•can (fə-lĭs′kən) *n.* **1.** A member of an ancient Italic people of southern Etruria. **2.** The language of this people, closely related to Latin. — *adj.* Of or relating to the Faliscans or their language or culture. [< Lat. *Faliscus* < *Falerii*, a city of ancient Etruria.]

Fal•kirk (fôl′kûrk′). A burgh of central Scotland W of Edinburgh; site of Edward I's defeat of the Scots (1298). Pop. 37,800.

Falk•land Islands (fôk′lənd, fôlk′-). A group of islands in the S Atlantic E of the Strait of Magellan; controlled by Great Britain since the 1830's but also claimed by Argentina.

fall (fôl) *v.* **fell** (fĕl), **fall•en** (fô′lən), **fall•ing, falls.** — *intr.* **1.** To drop or come down freely under the influence of gravity. **2.** To drop oneself to a lower or less erect position: *fell back in my chair.* **3.a.** To lose an upright or erect position suddenly. **b.** To drop wounded or dead, esp. in battle. **4.** To go or come as if by falling: *Night fell quickly.* **5.** To come to rest; settle: *The light fell on my book.* **6.** To hang down: *The hair fell in ringlets.* **7.** To be cast down: *Her eyes fell.* **8.** To assume an expression of consternation or disappointment: *His face fell.* **9.** To undergo conquest or capture, esp. as the result of an armed attack. **10.a.** To experience defeat or ruin. **b.** To lose office. **11.** To slope downward. **12.a.** To lessen in amount or degree: *The air pressure is falling.* **b.** To decline in financial value. **c.** To lose weight: *The child fell off to 60 pounds.* **13.** To diminish in pitch or volume. **14.a.** To give in to temptation; sin. **b.** To lose one's chastity. **15.** To pass into a particular state, condition, or situation: *fall in love.* **16.** To occur at a specified time. **17.** To occur at a specified place: *The stress falls on the last syllable.* **18.** To come, as by chance. **19.a.** To be given by assignment or distribution: *The task fell to me.* **b.** To be given by right or inheritance. **20.** To be included within the range or scope of something. **21.** To come into contact; strike: *My gaze fell on him.* **22.** To come out; issue: *Compliments fell from their lips.* **23.** To begin vigorously: *fell to work.* **24.** To be born. Used chiefly of lambs. — *tr.* To cut down (a tree); fell. — *n.* **1.** The act or an instance of falling. **2.** A sudden drop from a relatively erect to a less erect position. **3.** Something that has fallen: *a fall of hail.* **4.a.** An amount that has fallen. **b.** The distance that something falls. **5.** Autumn. **6. falls.** *(used with a sing. or pl. v.)* A waterfall. **7.** A downward movement or slope. **8.** Any of several pendent articles of dress, esp.: **a.** A veil hung from a woman's hat and down the back. **b.** An ornamental cascade of lace or trimming attached to a dress, usu. at the collar. **c.** A woman's hairpiece with long free-hanging hair. **9.a.** An overthrow; a collapse. **b.** Armed capture of a place under siege. **10.** A reduction in value, amount, or degree. **11.** A marked, often sudden decline in status, rank, or importance. **12.a.** A moral lapse. **b.** A loss of chastity. **13.** Often **Fall.** *Theol.* The loss of innocence and grace resulting from Adam's eating the forbidden fruit in the Garden of Eden. **14.** *Sports.* **a.** The act of throwing or forcing a wrestling opponent down on his or her back. **b.** Any of various wrestling maneuvers so used. **15. falls.** *Naut.* The apparatus used to hoist and transfer cargo or lifeboats. **16.** The end of a cable, rope, or chain that is pulled by the power source in hoisting. **17.a.** The birth of an animal, esp. a lamb. **b.** All the animals born at one birth; a litter. **18.** A family of woodcock in flight. **19.** *Bot.* The outer series of perianth in the irises and related plants. — ***phrasal verbs.*** **fall apart.** To break down; collapse. **fall away. 1.** To withdraw one's friendship and support. **2.** To become gradually diminished in size. **3.** To drift off an established course. **fall back. 1.** To give ground; retreat. **2.** To recede. **fall behind. 1.** To fail to keep up a pace; lag behind. **2.** To be financially in arrears. **fall down.** To fail to meet expectations; lag in performance. **fall for. 1.** To become infatuated with; start to love. **2.** To be deceived or swindled by. **fall in. 1.** To take one's place in a military formation. **2.** To sink inward; cave in. **fall off. 1.** To become less; decrease. **2.** *Naut.* To change course to leeward. **fall on (or upon). 1.** To attack suddenly and viciously. **2.** To meet with; encounter. **fall out. 1.a.** To leave a barracks, for example, in order to take one's place in a military formation. **b.** To leave a military formation. **2.** To quarrel. **3.** To happen; occur. **fall through.** To fail; miscarry. **fall to.** To begin an activity energetically.

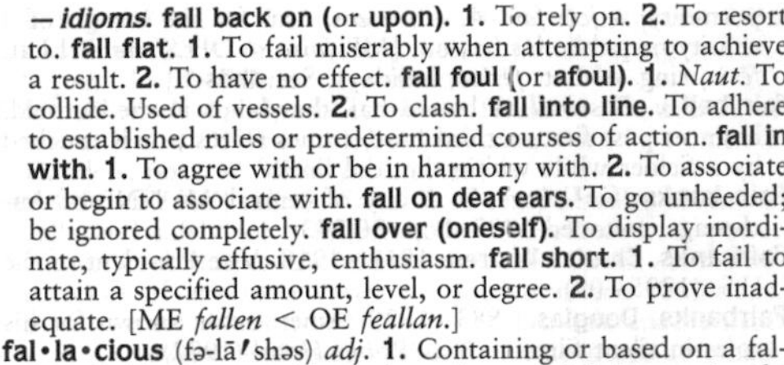
— ***idioms.*** **fall back on (or upon). 1.** To rely on. **2.** To resort to. **fall flat. 1.** To fail miserably when attempting to achieve a result. **2.** To have no effect. **fall foul (or afoul). 1.** *Naut.* To collide. Used of vessels. **2.** To clash. **fall into line.** To adhere to established rules or predetermined courses of action. **fall in with. 1.** To agree with or be in harmony with. **2.** To associate or begin to associate with. **fall on deaf ears.** To go unheeded; be ignored completely. **fall over (oneself).** To display inordinate, typically effusive, enthusiasm. **fall short. 1.** To fail to attain a specified amount, level, or degree. **2.** To prove inadequate. [ME *fallen* < OE *feallan.*]

fal•la•cious (fə-lā′shəs) *adj.* **1.** Containing or based on a fallacy. **2.** Tending to mislead; deceptive. — **fal•la′cious•ly** *adv.*

fal•la•cy (făl′ə-sē) *n., pl.* **-cies. 1.** A false notion. **2.** A statement or argument based on a false or invalid inference. **3.** Incorrectness of reasoning or belief; erroneousness. **4.** The quality of being deceptive. [Alteration of ME *fallace* < OFr. < Lat. *fallācia*, deceit < *fallāx, fallāc-*, deceitful < *fallere*, to deceive.]

fal•lal (fă-lăl′, făl′ăl′) *n.* A showy article of dress. [?] — **fal•lal′er•y** *n.*

fall•back (fôl′băk′) *n.* **1.a.** Something to which one can resort or retreat. **b.** A retreat. **2.** Something that falls back. — *adj.* Of, relating to, or constituting a resort or place of retreat.

fall•board (fôl′bôrd′, -bōrd′) *n. Mus.* The hinged cover protecting the keyboard of a piano.

fall•fish (fôl′fĭsh′) *n., pl.* **fallfish** or **-fish•es.** A small silvery freshwater fish *(Semotilus corporalis)* of streams and rivers in eastern North America.

fall guy *n. Slang.* **1.** A scapegoat. **2.** A gullible victim; a dupe.

fal•li•ble (făl′ə-bəl) *adj.* **1.** Capable of making an error. **2.** Tending or likely to be erroneous: *fallible hypotheses.* [ME < Med.Lat. *fallibilis* < Lat. *fallere*, to deceive.] — **fal′li•bil′i•ty, fal′li•ble•ness** *n.* — **fal′li•bly** *adv.*

fall•ing-out (fô′lĭng-out′) *n., pl.* **fall•ings-out** or **fall•ing-outs.** A disagreement; a quarrel.

falling rhythm *n.* A rhythmic pattern in which the stress regularly occurs on the first syllable of each foot, as in *Jack and Jill went up the hill.*

falling star *n.* See **meteor.**

fall line *n.* **1.** A line connecting the waterfalls of nearly parallel rivers that marks a drop in land level. **2.** The natural line of descent, as for skiing, between two points on a slope.

fall•off (fôl′ôf′, -ŏf′) *n.* A reduction or decrease.

fal•lo•pi•an tube also **Fal•lo•pi•an tube** (fə-lō′pē-ən) *n.* Either of a pair of slender ducts through which ova pass from the ovaries to the uterus in human beings and higher mammals. [After Gabriele *Fallopio* (1523–62), Italian anatomist.]

fall•out (fôl′out′) *n.* **1.a.** The slow descent of minute particles of debris in the atmosphere following an explosion, esp. the descent of radioactive debris after a nuclear explosion. **b.** Such particles. **2.** An incidental result or side effect.

fal•low (făl′ō) *adj.* **1.** Plowed but left unseeded during a growing season: *fallow farmland.* **2.** Characterized by inactivity. — *n.* **1.** Fallow land. **2.** The act of plowing land and leaving it unseeded. **3.** The condition or period of being unseeded. — *tr.v.* **-lowed, -low•ing, -lows. 1.** To plow (land) without seeding it afterward. **2.** To plow and till (land), esp. to eradicate or reduce weeds. [ME *falow* < OE *fealh*, fallow land.]

fallow deer *n.* A small Eurasian deer *(Dama dama)* having a yellowish-red coat spotted with white in summer and broad flattened antlers in the male. [Obsolete *fallow*, reddish-yellow < ME *falow, falwe* < OE *fealu.* See **pel-**[1]*.]

fallow deer
Dama dama

Fall River. A city of SE MA on the RI border WNW of New Bedford. Pop. 92,703.

Fal•mouth (făl′məth). A town of SE MA on SW Cape Cod; site of Woods Hole Oceanographic Institution. Pop. 27,960.

false (fôls) *adj.* **fals•er, fals•est. 1.** Contrary to fact or truth. **2.** Deliberately untrue. **3.** Arising from mistaken ideas. **4.** Intentionally deceptive. **5.** Not keeping faith; treacherous. **6.** Not genuine or real. **7.** Erected temporarily, as for support during construction. **8.** Resembling but not accurately or properly designated as such: *a false thaw in January.* **9.** *Mus.* Of incorrect pitch. **10.** Unwise; imprudent. — *adv.* In a treacherous or faithless manner. [ME *fals* < OFr. < Lat. *falsus* < p.part. of *fallere*, to deceive.] — **false′ly** *adv.* — **false′ness** *n.*

false alarm *n.* **1.** An emergency alarm that is set off unnecessarily. **2.** A signal or warning that is groundless.

false arrest *n. Law.* Unlawful or unjustifiable arrest.

false fruit *n.* **1.** See **accessory fruit. 2.** See **pome.**

false-heart•ed (fôls′här′tĭd) *adj.* Of a deceitful nature; treacherous. — **false′-heart′ed•ness** *n.*

false•hood (fôls′ho͝od′) *n.* **1.** An untrue statement; a lie. **2.** The practice of lying. **3.** Lack of conformity to truth.

false imprisonment *n. Law.* Detention or imprisonment of a person contrary to the provisions of law.

false indigo *n.* **1.** A shrub *(Amorpha fruticosa)* of eastern North America having compound leaves and purplish flowers. **2.** A plant *(Baptisia australis)* of the southeast United States having compound leaves and deep blue or purplish flowers.

false miterwort *n.* See **foamflower.**

false pretense *n. Law.* False representation of fact or circumstance, calculated to mislead.
false rib *n.* Any of the lower ribs that do not unite directly with the sternum.
false Sol•o•mon's seal (sŏl′ə-mənz) *n.* Any of several plants of the genus *Smilacina,* native to North America and Asia and having a plumelike cluster of small greenish-white flowers.
fal•set•to (fôl-sĕt′ō) *n., pl.* **-tos.** *Mus.* **1.** A male singing voice marked by artificially produced tones in an upper register beyond the normal range esp. of a tenor. **2.** One that sings in this way. [Ital., dim. of *falso,* false < Lat. *falsus.* See FALSE.] **—fal•set′to** *adv.*
fals•ie (fôl′sē) *n. Informal.* Padding or a pad worn inside a brassiere to make the breasts appear larger. Often used in the plural.
fal•si•fy (fôl′sə-fī′) *v.* **-fied, -fy•ing, -fies.** *—tr.* **1.** To state untruthfully; misrepresent. **2.a.** To make false by altering or adding to. **b.** To counterfeit; forge: *falsify a visa.* **3.** To declare or prove to be false. *—intr.* To make untrue statements; lie. [ME *falsifien* < OFr. *falsifier* < LLat. *falsificāre* : Lat. *falsus,* false; see FALSE + Lat. *-ficāre,* -fy.] **—fal′si•fi•ca′tion** (-fĭ-kā′shən) *n.* **—fal′si•fi′er** *n.*
fal•si•ty (fôl′sĭ-tē) *n., pl.* **-ties. 1.** The quality or condition of being false. **2.** Something false; a lie.
Fal•staff•i•an (fôl-stăf′ē-ən) *adj.* Characterized by joviality and conviviality. [After Sir John *Falstaff,* a character in *Henry IV* and *The Merry Wives of Windsor* by Shakespeare.]
Fal•ster (făl′stər, fôl′-). An island of SE Denmark in the Baltic Sea off the S tip of Sjaelland.
falt•boat (fält′bōt′, fôlt′-) *n. Naut.* See **foldboat.** [Partial transl. of Ger. *Faltboot,* folding boat : *falten,* to fold (< MHGer. *valten* < OHGer. *faldan;* see **pel-**[2]*) + *Boot,* boat.]
fal•ter (fôl′tər) *intr.v.* **-tered, -ter•ing, -ters. 1.** To be unsteady in purpose or action, as from loss of courage or confidence; waver. **2.** To speak hesitatingly; stammer. **3.a.** To move ineptly or haltingly; stumble. **b.** To operate or perform unsteadily or with a loss of effectiveness: *The engine faltered.* *—n.* **1.** Unsteadiness in speech or action. **2.** A faltering sound. [ME *falteren,* to stagger, poss. < ON *faltrask,* to be puzzled, hesitate.] **—fal′ter•er** *n.* **—fal′ter•ing•ly** *adv.*
FAM *abbr.* Free and Accepted Masons.
fam. *abbr.* **1.** Familiar. **2.** Family.
fame (fām) *n.* **1.a.** Great renown. **b.** Public estimation; reputation. **2.** *Archaic.* Rumor. *—tr.v.* **famed, fam•ing, fames. 1.** To make renowned or famous. **2.** *Archaic.* To report to be. [ME < OFr. < Lat. *fāma.* See **bhā-**[2]*.]
famed (fāmd) *adj.* Having great fame. See Syns at **noted.**
fa•mil•ial (fə-mĭl′yəl) *adj.* **1.** Of or relating to a family. **2.** Occurring or tending to occur among members of a family, usu. by heredity: *familial traits; familial disease.*
fa•mil•iar (fə-mĭl′yər) *adj.* **1.** Often encountered or seen; common. **2.** Having fair knowledge; acquainted. **3.** Of established friendship; intimate. **4.** Natural and unstudied; informal. **5.** Taking undue liberties; presumptuous. **6.** Familial. **7.** Domesticated; tame. Used of animals. *—n.* **1.** A close friend or associate. **2.** An attendant spirit, often taking animal form. **3.** One who performs domestic service in the household of a high official. **4.** A person who frequents a place. [ME < OFr. *familier* < Lat. *familiāris,* domestic < *familia,* family. See FAMILY.] **—fa•mil′iar•ly** *adv.*
fa•mil•iar•i•ty (fə-mĭl′yăr′ĭ-tē, -mĭl′ē-ăr′-) *n., pl.* **-ties. 1.** Considerable acquaintance with. **2.** Established friendship. **3.a.** An excessively familiar or informal act; an impropriety. **b.** A sexual advance. **4.** The quality or condition of being familiar.
fa•mil•iar•ize (fə-mĭl′yə-rīz′) *tr.v.* **-ized, -iz•ing, -iz•es. 1.** To make known, recognized, or familiar. **2.** To make acquainted with. **—fa•mil′iar•i•za′tion** (-yər-ĭ-zā′shən) *n.* **—fa•mil′iar•iz′er** *n.*
fam•i•ly (făm′ə-lē, făm′lē) *n., pl.* **-lies. 1.a.** A fundamental social group in society typically consisting of parents and their offspring. **b.** Two or more people who share goals and values, have commitments to one another, and reside usu. in the same place. **2.** All the members of a household under one roof. **3.** A group of persons sharing common ancestry. See Usage Note at **collective noun. 4.** Lineage, esp. distinguished lineage. **5.** A locally independent organized crime unit. **6.a.** A group of like things; a class. **b.** A group of individuals derived from a common stock. **7.** *Biol.* A taxonomic category of related organisms ranking below an order and above a genus. See table at **taxonomy. 8.** *Ling.* A group of languages descended from the same parent language. **9.** *Math.* A set of functions or surfaces that can be generated by varying the parameters of a general equation. **10.** *Chem.* A group of elements with similar chemical properties. **11.** *Chem.* A vertical column in the periodic table of elements. *—adj.* **1.** Of or relating to a family. **2.** Being suitable for a family. [ME *familie* < Lat. *familia,* household < *famulus,* servant.]
family Bible *n.* A Bible with special pages to record births, deaths, and marriages.
family circle *n.* A section of theater seats that are less expensive than some others.
family doctor *n.* **1.** A physician who practices the specialty of family medicine. **2.** See **general practitioner.**
family man *n.* **1.** A man having a wife and children. **2.** A man devoted to his family.
family medicine *n.* The branch of medicine that deals with provision of comprehensive health care to people regardless of age or sex, placing particular emphasis on the family unit.
family name *n.* See **surname** 1.
family physician *n.* See **family doctor** 1.
family plan•ning (plăn′ĭng) *n.* Birth control.
family practice *n.* See **family medicine.**
family practitioner *n.* See **family doctor** 1.
family room *n.* A recreation room esp. for family use.
family style *adv. & adj.* Having food placed on the table at a sit-down meal so that participants serve themselves.
family tree *n.* **1.** A genealogical diagram of a family's ancestry. **2.** The ancestors and descendants of a family.
fam•ine (făm′ĭn) *n.* **1.** A drastic wide-reaching food shortage. **2.** A drastic shortage; a dearth. **3.** Severe hunger; starvation. **4.** *Archaic.* Extreme appetite. [ME < OFr. < *faim,* hunger < Lat. *famēs.*]
fam•ish (făm′ĭsh) *v.* **-ished, -ish•ing, -ish•es.** *—tr.* **1.** To cause to endure severe hunger. **2.** To cause to starve to death. *—intr.* **1.** To endure severe deprivation, esp. of food. **2.** To undergo starvation and die. [ME *famishen,* alteration of *famen* < OFr. *afamer* < VLat. **affamāre* : Lat. *ad-,* ad- + Lat. *famēs,* hunger.] **—fam′ish•ment** *n.*
fa•mous (fā′məs) *adj.* **1.** Well or widely known. See Syns at **noted. 2.** *Informal.* First-rate; excellent. [ME < AN < Lat. *fāmōsus* < *fāma,* fame. See **bhā-**[2]*.] **—fa′mous•ly** *adv.* **—fa′mous•ness** *n.*
fam•u•lus (făm′yə-ləs) *n., pl.* **-li** (-lī′). A private secretary or other close attendant. [Ger. < Lat.]
fan[1] (făn) *n.* **1.** A device for creating a current of air or a breeze, esp.: **a.** A machine using an electric motor to rotate thin rigid vanes to move air, as for cooling. **b.** A collapsible, usu. wedge-shaped device made of a light material. **2.** A machine for winnowing. **3.** Something resembling an open fan in shape: *a peacock's fan.* *—v.* **fanned, fan•ning, fans.** *—tr.* **1.** To move or cause a current of (air) with or as if with a fan. **2.** To direct a current of air or a breeze upon, esp. to cool. **3.** To stir (something) up by or as if by fanning: *fanned resentment.* **4.** To open (something) out into the shape of a fan. **5.a.** To fire (an automatic gun) in a continuous sweep by keeping one's finger on the trigger. **b.** To fire (a nonautomatic gun) rapidly by chopping the hammer with the palm. **6.** To winnow. **7.** *Baseball.* To strike out (a batter). *—intr.* **1.** To spread out like a fan. **2.** *Baseball.* To strike out. [ME, winnowing fan < OE *fann* < Lat. *vannus.* See **wet-**[1]*.]
fan[2] (făn) *n. Informal.* An ardent devotee; an enthusiast. [Short for FANATIC.]
fa•nat•ic (fə-năt′ĭk) *n.* A person marked or motivated by an extreme unreasoning enthusiasm, as for a cause. *—adj.* Fanatical. [Lat. *fānāticus,* inspired by orgiastic rites, relating to a temple < *fānum,* temple. See **dhēs-***.]
fa•nat•i•cal (fə-năt′ĭ-kəl) *adj.* Possessed with or motivated by excessive, irrational zeal. **—fa•nat′i•cal•ly** *adv.* **—fa•nat′i•cal•ness** *n.*
fa•nat•i•cism (fə-năt′ĭ-sĭz′əm) *n.* Excessive, irrational zeal.
fa•nat•i•cize (fə-năt′ĭ-sīz′) *v.* **-cized, -ciz•ing, -ciz•es.** *—tr.* To make fanatical. *—intr.* To behave as a fanatic.
fan belt *n.* A taut rubber belt that transfers torque from the crankshaft to the shaft of the cooling fan on an engine.
fan•ci•er (făn′sē-ər) *n.* **1.** One who has a special enthusiasm for or interest in something. **2.** One who breeds a plant or an animal for those features held to be desirable.
fan•ci•ful (făn′sĭ-fəl) *adj.* **1.** Created in the fancy; unreal: *a fanciful story.* **2.** Tending to indulge in fancy: *a fanciful mind.* **3.** Showing invention or whimsy in design; imaginative. See Syns at **fantastic. —fan′ci•ful•ly** *adv.* **—fan′ci•ful•ness** *n.*
fan•cy (făn′sē) *n., pl.* **-cies. 1.** The mental faculty through which whims, visions, and fantasies are summoned up; imagination, esp. of a whimsical or fantastic nature. **2.** An image or a fantastic invention created by the mind. **3.** A capricious notion; a whim. **4.** A capricious liking or inclination. **5.** Critical sensibility; taste. **6.** Amorous or romantic attachment; love. **7.a.** The enthusiasts of a sport or pursuit considered as a group. **b.** The sport or pursuit, such as boxing, engaging the interest of such a group. *—adj.* **-ci•er, -ci•est. 1.** Highly decorated. **2.** Arising in the fancy; capricious. **3.** Executed with skill; complex or intricate. **4.** Of superior grade; fine. **5.** Excessive or exorbitant. **6.** Bred for unusual qualities or special points. *—tr.v.* **-cied, -cy•ing, -cies. 1.** To visualize; imagine. **2.** To take a fancy to; like. **3.** To suppose; guess. [< ME *fantsy,* imagination, fantasy < *fantasie.* See FANTASY.] **—fan′ci•ly** *adv.* **—fan′ci•ness** *n.*
fancy dress *n.* A masquerade costume.
fan•cy-free (făn′sē-frē′) *adj.* **1.** Having no commitments or restrictions; carefree. **2.** Not in love or married; unattached.
fan•cy•work (făn′sē-wûrk′) *n.* Decorative needlework, such as embroidery.
fan•dan•go (făn-dăng′gō) *n., pl.* **-gos. 1.** An animated Span-

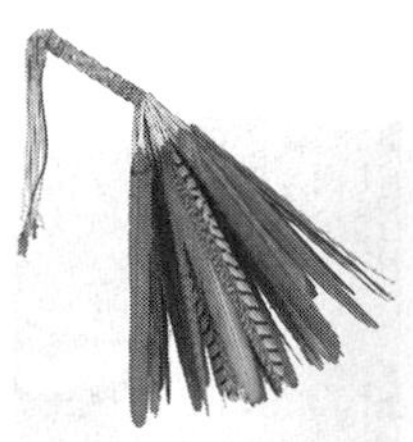

fan[1]
Comanche peyote fan with beaded handle and macaw and pheasant feathers

ă pat	oi boy
ā pay	ou out
âr care	ŏŏ took
ä father	ōō boot
ĕ pet	ŭ cut
ē be	ûr urge
ĭ pit	th thin
ī pie	*th* this
îr pier	hw which
ŏ pot	zh vision
ō toe	ə about,
ô paw	item

Stress marks:
′ (primary);
′ (secondary), as in
dictionary (dĭk′shə-nĕr′ē)

waist, used by European women in the 16th and 17th centuries. [Alteration of obsolete *verdynggale* < OFr. *verdugale* < OSp. *verdugado* < *verdugo*, stick, shoot of a tree < *verde*, green < Lat. *viridis* < *virēre*, to be green.]

Fa•ruk I (fə-ro͞ok′). See **Farouk I.**

Far West. A region of the U.S. orig. comprising all territories W of the Mississippi R.; now generally restricted to the area W of the Great Plains. —**Far′ West′ern** *adj.*

f.a.s. also **F.A.S.** *abbr.* Free alongside ship.

fas•ces (făs′ēz′) *pl.n.* A bundle of rods bound around an ax with the blade projecting, carried before ancient Roman magistrates as an emblem of authority. [Lat., pl. of *fascis*, bundle.]

fas•ci•a (făsh′ē-ə) *n., pl.* **fas•ci•ae** (făsh′-ē-ē′, fā′shē-ē). **1.** *Anat.* A sheet or band of fibrous tissue that envelops, separates, or binds together muscles, organs, and other soft structures of the body. **2.** A broad and distinct band of color. **3.** (*also* fā′shē-ə). *Archit.* A flat horizontal band or member between moldings, esp. in a classical entablature. **4.** (fā′shə). *Chiefly British.* The dashboard of a motor vehicle. [Lat., band.] —**fas′ci•al** *adj.*

fas•ci•ate (făsh′ē-āt′) also **fas•ci•at•ed** (-ā′tĭd) *adj.* **1.** *Bot.* Abnormally flattened or coalesced, as certain stems. **2.** *Zool.* Marked by broad bands of color, as certain insects. [Lat. *fasciātus* < *fascia*, band.]

fas•ci•a•tion (făs′ē-ā′shən, făsh′ē-) *n.* **1.** The act of binding up or fastening, as with bandages. **2.** The manner in which something is bound up or fastened. **3.** *Bot.* An abnormal flattening or coalescence of stems, as in broccoli.

fas•ci•cle (făs′ĭ-kəl) *n.* **1.** A small bundle. **2.** One of the parts of a book published in separate sections. **3.** *Bot.* A bundle or cluster of stems, flowers, or leaves. **4.** See **fasciculus.** [Lat. *fasciculus*, dim. of *fascis*, bundle.] —**fas′ci•cled** *adj.*

fas•cic•u•lar (fə-sĭk′yə-lər) *adj.* Of, relating to, or composed of fascicles. —**fas•cic′u•lar•ly** *adv.*

fas•cic•u•late (fə-sĭk′yə-lĭt) also **fas•cic•u•lat•ed** (-lā′tĭd) *adj.* Arranged in or formed of fascicles; fascicular. —**fas•cic′u•late•ly** *adv.* —**fas•cic′u•la′tion** *n.*

fas•ci•cule (făs′ĭ-kyo͞ol′) *n.* See **fascicle** 2.

fas•cic•u•lus (fə-sĭk′yə-ləs) *n., pl.* **-li** (-lī′). A bundle of anatomical fibers, as of muscle. [Lat., fascicle. See FASCICLE.]

fas•ci•nate (făs′ə-nāt′) *v.* **-nat•ed, -nat•ing, -nates.** —*tr.* **1.** To hold an intense interest or attraction for. See Syns at **charm. 2.** To hold motionless; spellbind. **3.** *Obsolete.* To bewitch. —*intr.* To be irresistibly charming or attractive. [Lat. *fascināre, fascināt-*, to cast a spell on < *fascinum*, an evil spell, a phallic-shaped amulet.]

fas•ci•nat•ing (făs′ə-nā′tĭng) *adj.* Possessing the power to charm or allure; captivating. —**fas′ci•nat′ing•ly** *adv.*

fas•ci•na•tion (făs′ə-nā′shən) *n.* **1.** The capability of eliciting intense interest or of being very attractive. **2.** The state of being intensely interested or attracted: *listened in fascination.* **3.** An attractive, intensely interesting quality or trait.

fas•ci•na•tor (făs′ə-nā′tər) *n.* **1.** One that fascinates. **2.** A woman's head scarf.

fas•cine (fă-sēn′, fə-) *n.* A cylindrical bundle of sticks bound together for use in construction, as of fortresses, earthworks, sea walls, or dams. [Fr. < Lat. *fascīna* < *fascis*, bundle.]

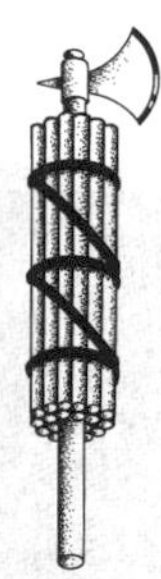

fasces

fas•cism (făsh′ĭz′əm) *n.* **1.** Often **Fascism. a.** A system of government marked by a totalitarian dictator, socioeconomic controls, suppression of the opposition, and usu. a policy of belligerent nationalism and racism. **b.** A political philosophy or movement based on or advocating such a system. **2.** Oppressive dictatorial control. [Ital. *fascismo* < *fascio*, group < LLat. *fascium*, neut. of Lat. *fascis*, bundle.] —**fas•cis′tic** (fə-shĭs′tĭk) *adj.*

fas•cist (făsh′ĭst) *n.* **1.** Often **Fascist.** An advocate or adherent of fascism. **2.** A reactionary or dictatorial person. —*adj.* **1.** Often **Fascist.** Of, advocating, or practicing fascism. **2. Fascist.** Of or relating to the Fascisti. [Ital. *fascista* < *fascio*, group. See FASCISM.]

Fa•scis•ti (fă-shē′stē) *pl.n.* The members of a political party that controlled Italy under Benito Mussolini from 1922 to 1943. [Ital., pl. of *fascista*, fascist. See FASCIST.]

fash•ion (făsh′ən) *n.* **1.** The prevailing style or custom, as in dress. **2.** Something, such as a garment, that is in the current mode. **3.** The style of the social elite. **4.a.** Manner or mode; way. **b.** A personal, often idiosyncratic manner. See Syns at **method. 5.** Kind or variety; sort. **6.** Shape or form; configuration. —*tr.v.* **-ioned, -ion•ing, -ions. 1.** To give shape or form to; make. **2.** To train or influence into a particular state or character. **3.** To adapt, as to a purpose or an occasion; accommodate. **4.** *Obsolete.* To contrive. —***idiom.* after** (or **in) a fashion.** In some way or other, esp. to a limited extent. [ME *facioun* < OFr. *façon*, appearance, manner < Lat. *factiō, factiōn-*, a making < *factus*, p.part. of *facere*, to make, do. See **dhē-*.**] —**fash′ion•er** *n.*

fash•ion•a•ble (făsh′ə-nə-bəl) *adj.* **1.** Conforming to the current style; stylish. **2.** Associated with or frequented by persons of fashion. —*n.* A stylish person. —**fash′ion•a•bil′i•ty, fash′ion•a•ble•ness** *n.* —**fash′ion•a•bly** *adv.*

fashion plate *n.* **1.** A person who consistently wears the latest fashions. **2.** An illustration of current styles in dress.

fast[1] (făst) *adj.* **fast•er, fast•est. 1.** Acting, moving, or capable of acting or moving quickly; swift. **2.** Accomplished in relatively little time: *a fast visit.* **3.** Indicating a time somewhat ahead of the actual time: *The clock is fast.* **4.** Adapted to or suitable for rapid movement. **5.** Designed for or compatible with a short exposure time: *fast film.* **6.a.** Dissipated; wild: *a fast crowd.* **b.** Flouting moral standards; sexually promiscuous. **7.** Resistant, as to destruction or fading: *fast colors.* **8.** Firmly fixed or fastened. **9.** Fixed firmly in place; secure. **10.** Firm in loyalty. **11.** Lasting; permanent. **12.** Deep; sound: *in a fast sleep.* —*adv.* **1.** In a secure manner; tightly. **2.** To a sound degree; deeply. **3.** In a rapid manner; quickly. **4.** In quick succession. **5.** Ahead of the correct or expected time. **6.** In a dissipated, immoderate way. **7.** *Archaic.* Close by; near. [ME < OE *fæst*, firm, fixed. See **past-*.**]

Syns: *fast, rapid, swift, fleet, speedy, quick, hasty, expeditious.* These adjectives refer to something marked by great speed. *Fast* and *rapid* are often used interchangeably, though *fast* is more often applied to the person or thing in motion, and *rapid*, to the activity or movement involved: *a fast runner; rapid strides. Swift* suggests smoothness and sureness of movement (*a swift current*), and *fleet,* lightness of movement (*The cheetah is the fleetest of animals*). *Speedy* refers to velocity (*a speedy train*) or to promptness or hurry (*a speedy resolution to the problem*). *Quick* most often applies to what takes little time or to what is prompt: *a quick snack; her quick reaction. Hasty* implies hurried action (*a hasty visit*) and often a lack of care or thought (*regretted the hasty decision*). *Expeditious* suggests rapid efficiency: *sent the package by the most expeditious means.* See also Syns at **faithful.**

fast[2] (făst) *intr.v.* **fast•ed, fast•ing, fasts. 1.** To abstain from food. **2.** To eat very little or abstain from certain foods, esp. as a religious discipline. —*n.* **1.** The act or practice of fasting. **2.** A period of fasting. [ME *fasten* < OE *fæstan*. See **past-*.**]

fast•back (făst′băk′) *n.* An automobile designed with a curving downward slope from roof to rear.

fast•ball (făst′bôl′) *n. Baseball.* A pitch thrown at the pitcher's maximum speed.

fast break *n. Sports.* A rush by the offense toward the goal before the defense is ready.

fas•ten (făs′ən) *v.* **-tened, -ten•ing, -tens.** —*tr.* **1.** To attach firmly to something else, as by pinning or nailing. **2.a.** To make fast or secure. **b.** To close, as by fixing firmly in place. **3.** To fix or direct steadily: *fastened her gaze on me.* **4.** To place; attribute. **5.** To impose (oneself) without welcome. —*intr.* **1.** To become attached, fixed, or joined. **2.** To take firm hold; cling fast. **3.** To focus steadily; concentrate. [ME *fastnen* < OE *fæstnian*. See **past-*.**] —**fas′ten•er** *n.*

fas•ten•ing (făs′ə-nĭng) *n.* Something, such as a hook, used to attach one thing to another firmly.

fast food *n.* Inexpensive food, such as hamburgers, prepared and served quickly. —**fast′-food′** (făst′fo͞od′) *adj.*

fast-for•ward or **fast forward** (făst-fôr′wərd) *n.* **1.a.** A function on a recording device, such as a videocassette player, that permits rapid advancement of the tape. **b.** The mechanism, such as a button, that activates this function. **2.** *Informal.* A rapidly changing situation. —**fast•for′ward** *v.*

fas•tid•i•ous (fă-stĭd′ē-əs, fə-) *adj.* **1.** Possessing or displaying meticulous attention to detail. **2.** Difficult to please; exacting. **3.** Excessively scrupulous or sensitive, esp. in matters of taste or propriety. [ME, squeamish, particular, haughty < OFr. *fastidieux* < Lat. *fastīdiōsus* < *fastīdium*, squeamishness, haughtiness, prob. < *fastus*, disdain.] —**fas•tid′i•ous•ly** *adv.* —**fas•tid′i•ous•ness** *n.*

fas•tig•i•ate (fă-stĭj′ē-ĭt) also **fas•tig•i•at•ed** (-ē-ā′tĭd) *adj. Bot.* Having erect branches tapering toward the top, as in the Lombardy poplar. [Med.Lat. *fastīgiātus*, high < Lat. *fastīgium*, apex, height.] —**fas•tig′i•ate•ly** *adv.*

fas•tig•i•um (fă-stĭj′ē-əm) *n.* The period of maximum severity of a disease or fever. [Lat. *fastīgium*, apex, height.]

fast lane *n. Informal.* A reckless, self-indulgent, and free-spending sphere of activity. —**fast′-lane′** (făst′lān′) *adj.*

fast•ness (făst′nĭs) *n.* **1.** The condition or quality of being fast, esp.: **a.** Firmness; security. **b.** Rapidity; swiftness. **2.** The quality or condition of color retention; colorfastness. **3.a.** A secure or fortified place. **b.** A remote, secret place.

fast one *n. Informal.* A shrewd trick or swindle; a deceitful or treacherous act.

fast-talk (făst′tôk′) *tr.v.* **-talked, -talk•ing, -talks.** *Informal.* To persuade, mislead, or obtain with a smooth line of talk: *fast-talked him out of his money.* —**fast′-talk′er** *n.*

fast track *n. Informal.* The quickest and most direct route to achieve a goal, as in professional advancement. —**fast′-track′** (făst′trăk′) *adj.* —**fast track′er** *n.*

fat (făt) *n.* **1.a.** The ester of glycerol and fatty acids. **b.** Any of various organic compounds constituting the esters of glycerol and fatty acids. **c.** A mixture of such compounds occurring in organic tissue, esp. in the adipose tissue of animals and in the seeds, nuts, and fruits of plants. **d.** Animal tissue containing such substances. **e.** A solidified animal or vegetable oil. **2.** Obesity; corpulence. **3.** The best or richest part. **4.** Unnecessary excess. —*adj.* **fat•ter, fat•test. 1.** Having much or too much fat or flesh; plump or obese. **2.** Full of fat or oil; greasy. **3.** Abounding in desirable elements. **4.** Fertile or productive; rich. **5.** Having an abundance or amplitude; well-stocked. **6.a.** Yielding profit or plenty; lucrative or rewarding. **b.** Prosperous; wealthy. **7.a.** Thick; large. **b.** Puffed up; swollen. *—tr. & intr.v.* **fat•ted, fat•ting, fats.** To make or become fat; fatten. *—idiom.* **fat chance.** *Slang.* Very little or no chance. [ME < OE *fǣtt,* fatted. See **peiə-*.**] **—fat′ly** *adv.* **—fat′ness** *n.*

Syns: *fat, obese, corpulent, fleshy, portly, stout, pudgy, rotund, plump, chubby.* These adjectives mean having an abundance and often an excess of flesh. *Fat* implies excessive weight and generally has negative connotations: *felt fat and sloppy. Obese* and *corpulent* imply gross overweight: *"a woman of robust frame . . . though stout, not obese"* (Charlotte Brontë). *He was corpulent but surprisingly graceful. Fleshy* implies a not necessarily excessive abundance of flesh: *firm fleshy arms. Portly* refers to bulk combined with a stately or imposing bearing, and *stout,* to a thickset, bulky figure: *"a portly, rubicund man of middle age"* (Winston Churchill). *Millet is known for his paintings of stout peasants. Pudgy* means short and fat: *pudgy fingers. Rotund* suggests roundness of figure, often in a squat person: *"this pink-faced rotund specimen of prosperity"* (George Eliot). *Plump* and *chubby* apply to a pleasing fullness: *a plump lad; chubby cheeks.*

fa•tal (fāt′l) *adj.* **1.** Causing or capable of causing death. **2.** Causing ruin or destruction; disastrous. **3.** Of decisive importance; fateful. **4.** Concerned with or determining destiny. **5.** *Obsolete.* Having been destined; fated. [ME, fateful < OFr. < Lat. *fātālis* < *fātum,* prophecy, doom. See FATE.]

fa•tal•ism (fāt′l-ĭz′əm) *n.* **1.** The doctrine that all events are predetermined and unalterable. **2.** Acceptance of this belief. **—fa′tal•ist** *n.* **—fa′tal•is′tic** *adj.* **—fa′tal•is′ti•cal•ly** *adv.*

fa•tal•i•ty (fā-tăl′ĭ-tē, fə-) *n., pl.* **-ties. 1.a.** A death resulting from an accident or a disaster. **b.** One killed in such an occurrence. **2.** The ability to cause death or disaster. **3.** The quality of being determined by fate. **4.** A decree made by fate; destiny. **5.** The quality of being doomed to disaster.

fatality rate *n.* See **death rate.**

fa•tal•ly (fāt′l-ē) *adv.* **1.** So as to cause death; mortally: *fatally injured.* **2.** So as to result in disaster or ruin. **3.** According to the decree of fate; inevitably.

fa•ta mor•ga•na (fä′tə môr-gä′nə) *n.* See **mirage** 1. [Ital., mirage, Morgan le Fay (< the belief that her witchcraft caused it) : *fata,* fairy (< VLat. *fāta,* goddess of fate; see FAIRY) + *Morgana,* Morgan (prob. < OIr. *Morrigain*).]

fat•back (făt′băk′) *n.* The strip of fat from the upper part of a side of pork, usu. dried and salt-cured.

fat body *n.* **1.** A food reserve of fatty tissue in the larval stages of certain insects. **2.** A mass of fatty tissue located near the genital glands in some amphibians, including the frogs.

fat cat *n. Slang.* **1.** A wealthy and highly privileged person. **2.** A wealthy contributor to a political campaign.

fat cell *n.* Any of various cells found in adipose tissue that are specialized for the storage of fat.

Fat City or **fat city** *n. Slang.* A condition or set of circumstances characterized by great prosperity.

fate (fāt) *n.* **1.a.** The supposed force, principle, or power that predetermines events. **b.** The inevitable events predestined by this force. **2.** A final result or consequence; an outcome. **3.** Unfavorable destiny; doom. **4. Fates.** *Gk. & Rom. Myth.* The three goddesses who control human destiny. Used with *the.* [ME < OFr. *fat* < Lat. *fātum,* prophecy, doom, neut. p.part. of *fārī,* to speak. See **bhā-²*.**]

fat•ed (fā′tĭd) *adj.* **1.** Governed by fate; predetermined. **2.** Condemned to death or destruction; doomed.

fate•ful (fāt′fəl) *adj.* **1.** Vitally affecting subsequent events; being of great consequence; momentous: *a fateful decision.* **2.** Controlled by or as if by fate; predetermined. **3.** Bringing death or disaster; fatal. **4.** Ominously prophetic; portentous: *a fateful sign.* **—fate′ful•ly** *adv.* **—fate′ful•ness** *n.*

fath or **fath.** *abbr.* Fathom.

fat•head (făt′hĕd′) *n. Slang.* A stupid person. **—fat′head′ed** *adj.* **—fat′head′ed•ly** *adv.* **—fat′head′ed•ness** *n.*

fa•ther (fä′*th*ər) *n.* **1.** A man who begets or raises a child. **2.** A male parent of an animal. **3.** A male ancestor. **4.** A man who creates, originates, or founds something. **5.** An early form; a prototype. **6. Father. a.** God. **b.** The first person of the Christian Trinity. **7.** An elderly or venerable man. Used as a title of respect. **8.** One of the leading men, as of a city. **9.** Or **Father.** A church father. **10.a.** A Christian priest. **b.** Used as a title and form of address. *—v.* **-thered, -ther•ing, -thers.** *—tr.* **1.** To procreate (offspring) as the male parent. **2.** To act or serve as a father to (a child). **3.** To create, found, or originate. **4.** To acknowledge responsibility for. **5.a.** To attribute the paternity, creation, or origin of. **b.** To assign falsely or unjustly; foist. *—intr.* To act or serve as a father. [ME *fader* < OE *fæder.* See **pəter-*.**]

Father Christmas *n. Chiefly British.* Santa Claus.

father confessor *n.* **1.** A priest who hears confessions. **2.** A person in whom one confides.

father figure *n.* An older man, often in a position of power or influence, who elicits the emotions usu. reserved for a father.

fa•ther•hood (fä′*th*ər-ho͝od′) *n.* **1.** The state of being a father. **2.** The qualities of a father. **3.** Fathers considered as a group.

fa•ther-in-law (fä′*th*ər-ĭn-lô′) *n., pl.* **fa•thers-in-law** (fä′*th*ərz-). **1.** The father of one's husband or wife. **2.** *Archaic.* A stepfather.

fa•ther•land (fä′*th*ər-lănd′) *n.* **1.** One's native land. **2.** The land of one's ancestors.

fa•ther•less (fä′*th*ər-lĭs) *adj.* **1.** Having no living father. **2.** Having no known father. **—fa′ther•less•ness** *n.*

fa•ther•ly (fä′*th*ər-lē) *adj.* **1.** Of, like, or appropriate to a father. **2.** Showing the affection of a father. *—adv.* In a manner befitting a father. **—fa′ther•li•ness** *n.*

Fa•ther's Day (fä′*th*ərz) *n.* The third Sunday in June, observed in honor of fathers.

fath•om (fă*th*′əm) *n., pl.* **fathom** or **fath•oms.** A unit of length equal to 6 feet (1.83 meters), used principally in the measurement and specification of marine depths. *—tr.v.* **-omed, -om•ing, -oms. 1.** To determine the depth of; sound. **2.** To penetrate to the meaning or nature of; comprehend. [ME *fathme* < OE *fæthm,* outstretched arms. See **petə-*.**] **—fath′om•a•ble** *adj.*

Fa•thom•e•ter (fă-*th*ŏm′ĭ-tər). A trademark used for a sonic depth finder.

fath•om•less (fă*th*′əm-lĭs) *adj.* **1.** Too deep to be fathomed or measured. **2.** Too obscure or complicated to be understood. **—fath′om•less•ly** *adv.* **—fath′om•less•ness** *n.*

fa•tid•ic (fə-tĭd′ĭk) also **fa•tid•i•cal** (-ĭ-kəl) *adj.* Relating to or characterized by prophecy; prophetic. [Lat. *fātidicus* : *fātum,* prophecy, doom; see FATE + *dīcere,* to say; see **deik-*.**]

fat•i•ga•ble (făt′ĭ-gə-bəl) *adj.* Subject to fatigue. [Fr. < OFr. < LLat. *fatīgābilis* < Lat. *fatīgāre,* to fatigue.] **—fat′i•ga•bil′i•ty** *n.*

fa•tigue (fə-tēg′) *n.* **1.** Physical or mental weariness due to exertion. **2.** Something, such as an effort or activity, that causes weariness. **3.** The weakening or failure of a material, such as metal or wood, from prolonged stress. **4.a.** Manual or menial labor, such as barracks cleaning, assigned to soldiers. **b. fatigues.** A military uniform for labor or field duty. *—v.* **-tigued, -tigu•ing, -tigues.** *—tr.* **1.** To tire with physical or mental exertion; weary. **2.** To create fatigue in (a metal or other material). *—intr.* To be or become fatigued. [Fr. < OFr. < *fatiguer,* to fatigue < Lat. *fatīgāre.*]

Fat•i•ma also **Fat•i•mah** (făt′ə-mə). 616?–633. Daughter of the Islamic prophet Muhammad; considered by Muslims to be one of the Four Perfect Women.

Fá•ti•ma (făt′ə-mə). A village of W-central Portugal NNE of Lisbon; a Christian pilgrimage site after the reported appearance of the Virgin Mary in 1917.

Fat•i•mid (făt′ə-mĭd′) also **Fat•i•mite** (-mīt′). A Muslim dynasty that ruled North Africa and parts of Egypt (909–1171).

fat•ling (făt′lĭng) *n.* A young animal, such as a lamb or calf, fattened for slaughter.

fat pine *n. Chiefly Southern U.S.* Easily ignited resin-rich kindling. Also called regionally *fatwood.* See Regional Note at **lightwood.**

fat•so (făt′sō) *n., pl.* **-soes.** *Slang.* A fat person.

fat-sol•u•ble (făt′sŏl′yə-bəl) *adj.* Soluble in fats or fat compounds.

fat•ten (făt′n) *v.* **-tened, -ten•ing, -tens.** *—tr.* **1.** To make plump or fat. **2.** To fertilize (land). **3.** To increase the amount or substance of; swell. *—intr.* To grow fat or fatter. **—fat′ten•er** *n.*

fat•tish (făt′ĭsh) *adj.* Somewhat fat. **—fat′tish•ness** *n.*

fat•ty (făt′ē) *adj.* **-ti•er, -ti•est. 1.** Containing or composed of fat: *fatty food.* **2.** Characteristic of fat; greasy. **3.** Derived from or chemically related to fat. *—n., pl.* **-ties.** *Informal.* A fat person. **—fat′ti•ly** *adv.* **—fat′ti•ness** *n.*

fatty acid *n.* Any of a large group of monobasic acids, esp. those found in animal and vegetable fats and oils, having the general formula $C_nH_{2n+1}COOH$.

fa•tu•i•ty (fə-to͞o′ĭ-tē, -tyo͞o′-, fă-) *n., pl.* **-ties. 1.** Smug stupidity; utter foolishness. **2.** Something that is utterly stupid or silly. [Lat. *fatuitās* < *fatuus,* silly, foolish.]

fat•u•ous (făch′o͞o-əs) *adj.* **1.** Vacuously, smugly, and unconsciously foolish. **2.** Delusive; unreal. [< Lat. *fatuus.*] **—fat′u•ous•ly** *adv.* **—fat′u•ous•ness** *n.*

fat•wood (făt′wo͝od′) *n. Chiefly Southern U.S.* See **fat pine.** See Regional Note at **lightwood.**

fau•bourg (fō′bo͝or′, -bo͝org′) *n. New Orleans.* A district of metropolitan New Orleans lying outside the original city limits. See Regional Note at **beignet.** [ME *faubourgh* < OFr. *faubourg,* alteration of *forsborc* : *fors,* outside (< Lat. *forīs*; see **dhwer-*)** + *borc,* town (< LLat. *burgus,* fort, of Gmc. orig.; see **bhergh-²*).**]

Regional Note: In contemporary American English the word *fauborg,* a synonym for *suburb* borrowed from French, is virtually confined to the city of New Orleans with its French background. Even there it is used not as a common noun like *suburb* but in combination in the names of various quarters of the city, for example, *Faubourg Sainte Marie.*

ă pat	oi boy
ā pay	ou out
âr care	o͝o took
ä father	o͞o boot
ĕ pet	ŭ cut
ē be	ûr urge
ĭ pit	th thin
ī pie	*th* this
îr pier	hw which
ŏ pot	zh vision
ō toe	ə about, item
ô paw	

Stress marks:
′ (primary);
′ (secondary), as in **dictionary** (dĭk′shə-nĕr′ē)

fe•cund (fē′kənd, fĕk′ənd) *adj.* **1.** Productive of offspring or vegetation; fruitful. **2.** Intellectually productive. [ME < OFr. *fecond* < Lat. *fēcundus.* See **dhē(i)-*.**] —**fe•cun′di•ty** (fĭ-kŭn′dĭ-tē) *n.*

fe•cun•date (fē′kən-dāt′, fĕk′ən-) *tr.v.* **-dat•ed, -dat•ing, -dates. 1.** To make fecund or fruitful. **2.** To impregnate; fertilize. [Lat. *fēcundāre, fēcundāt-* < *fēcundus,* fruitful. See FECUND.] —**fe′cun•da′tion** *n.*

fed (fĕd) *v.* P.t. and p.part. of **feed.**

Fed (fĕd) *n. Informal.* **1.a.** The Federal Reserve System. **b.** The Federal Reserve Board. **2.** Often **fed.** A federal agent or official.

fed. *abbr.* **1.** Federal. **2.** Federated. **3.** Federation.

fe•da•yee (fĕ-dä′yē′, -dä′ē′, -dă′-) *n., pl.* **-yeen** (-yēn′, -ēn′). A commando or guerrilla, esp. an Arab commando operating in the Middle East. [Ar. *fedā'yūn,* commandos < *fidā'iy,* one who sacrifices himself for his country < *fidā',* sacrifice.]

fed•er•a•cy (fĕd′ər-ə-sē) *n., pl.* **-cies.** *Archaic.* An alliance; a confederacy. [Short for CONFEDERACY.]

fed•er•al (fĕd′ər-əl, fĕd′rəl) *adj.* **1.** Of, relating to, or being a form of government in which individual states recognize the sovereignty of a central authority but retain certain powers. **2.** Of or constituting a form of government in which sovereign power is divided between a central authority and a number of constituent political units. **3.** Of or relating to the central government of a federation as distinct from the governments of its member units. **4.** Favorable to or advocating federation. **5.** Relating to or formed by a treaty or compact between constituent political units. **6. Federal. a.** Of, relating to, or supporting Federalism or the Federalist Party. **b.** Of, relating to, or loyal to the Union cause during the American Civil War. **7.** Often **Federal.** Of, relating to, or being the central government of the United States. **8. Federal.** Relating to or characteristic of a style of architecture, furniture, and decoration produced in the United States esp. in the late 18th and early 19th centuries and characterized by adaptations of classical forms. —*n.* **1. Federal. a.** A supporter of the Union during the American Civil War, esp. a Union soldier. **b.** A Federalist. **2.** Often **Federal.** A federal agent or official. [< Lat. *foedus, foeder-,* league, treaty. See **bheidh-*.**] —**fed′er•al•ly** *adv.*

federal district also **Federal District** *n.* An area that is reserved as the site of the national capital of a federation.

fed•er•al•ism (fĕd′ər-ə-lĭz′əm, fĕd′rə-) *n.* **1.a.** A system of government in which power is divided between a central authority and constituent political units. **b.** Advocacy of such a system of government. **2. Federalism.** The doctrine of the Federalist Party.

fed•er•al•ist (fĕd′ər-ə-lĭst, fĕd′rə-) *n.* **1.** An advocate of federalism. **2. Federalist.** A member or supporter of the Federalist Party. —**fed′er•a•list** *adj.*

Federalist Party *n.* A U.S. political party founded in 1787 to advocate the establishment of a strong federal government and the adoption by the states of the Constitution.

fed•er•al•ize (fĕd′ər-ə-līz′, fĕd′rə-) *tr.v.* **-ized, -iz•ing, -iz•es. 1.** To unite in a federal union. **2.** To subject to the authority of a federal government; put under federal control. —**fed′er•al•i•za′tion** (-lĭ-zā′shən) *n.*

Federal Reserve System *n.* A U.S. banking system that consists of 12 federal reserve banks, each one serving member banks within its own district.

fed•er•ate (fĕd′ə-rāt′) *v.* **-at•ed, -at•ing, -ates.** —*tr.* To cause to join into a league, federal union, or similar association. —*intr.* To become united in such a union. —*adj.* (fĕd′ər-ĭt, fĕd′rĭt). United in a federation. [Lat. *foederāre, foederāt-,* to ratify an agreement < *foedus, foeder-,* league, treaty. See **bheidh-*.**]

fed•er•a•tion (fĕd′ə-rā′shən) *n.* **1.** The act of federating, esp. of states into a league or federal union. **2.** A league or association formed by federating, esp. a government or political body.

fed•er•a•tive (fĕd′ə-rā′tĭv, fĕd′ər-ə-, fĕd′rə-) *adj.* Forming, belonging to, or of the nature of a federation; federal. —**fed′er•a′tive•ly** *adv.*

fe•do•ra (fĭ-dôr′ə, -dōr′ə) *n.* A soft felt hat with a fairly low crown creased lengthwise and a brim that can be turned up or down. [After *Fédora,* a play by Victorien Sardou.]

fed up *adj.* Unable or unwilling to put up with something any longer.

fee (fē) *n.* **1.** A fixed sum charged, as by an institution or by law, for a privilege: *tuition fees.* **2.** A charge for professional services: *a surgeon's fee.* **3.** A tip; a gratuity. **4.** *Law.* An inherited or heritable estate in land. **5.a.** In feudal law, an estate in land granted by a lord to his vassal on condition of homage and service. **b.** The land so held. —*tr.v.* **feed, fee•ing, fees. 1.** To give a tip to. **2.** *Scots.* To hire. —*idiom.* **in fee.** *Law.* In absolute and legal possession. [ME *fe* < AN *fee,* fief < OFr. *fie, fief,* of Gmc. orig. See **peku-*.**]

fee•ble (fē′bəl) *adj.* **-bler, -blest. 1.a.** Lacking strength; weak. **b.** Indicating weakness. **2.** Lacking vigor, force, or effectiveness; inadequate. [ME *feble* < OFr. < Lat. *flēbilis,* lamentable < *flēre,* to weep.] —**fee′ble•ness** *n.* —**fee′bly** *adv.*

Federal
Early 19th-century sewing table attributed to Nehemiah Adams (fl. 1790–1840)

fedora
Worn by Humphrey Bogart

fee•ble-mind•ed (fē′bəl-mīn′dĭd) *adj.* **1.** *Offensive.* Deficient in intelligence. **2.** Lacking intelligent consideration and forethought. **3.** *Obsolete.* Irresolute and weak-willed. —**fee′ble-mind′ed•ly** *adv.* —**fee′ble-mind′ed•ness** *n.*

feed (fēd) *v.* **fed** (fĕd), **feed•ing, feeds.** —*tr.* **1.a.** To give food or nourishment to. **b.** To provide as food or nourishment. **2.a.** To be food for: *enough to feed a dozen.* **b.** To produce food for. **3.a.** To provide for consumption, utilization, or operation: *feed data into a computer.* **b.** To supply with something essential for growth, maintenance, or operation: *rain feeding reservoirs.* **c.** To distribute (a local broadcast) to a larger audience or group of receivers by network or satellite. **4.a.** To minister to; gratify. **b.** To support or promote; encourage. **5.** To supply as a cue. **6.** *Sports.* To pass a ball or puck to (a teammate). —*intr.* **1.** To eat. **2.** To be nourished or supported. **3.a.** To move steadily, as into a machine for processing. **b.** To be channeled; flow: *This road feeds into the freeway.* —*n.* **1.a.** Food for animals or birds. **b.** The amount of such food given at one time. **2.** *Informal.* A meal, esp. a large one. **3.** The act of eating. **4.a.** Material or an amount of material supplied, as to a machine or furnace. **b.** The act of supplying such material. **5.a.** An apparatus that supplies material to a machine. **b.** The aperture through which such material enters a machine. **6.** Distribution of a local broadcast by network or satellite to a larger audience. —*idiom.* **off (one's) feed.** Suffering a lack of appetite; sick. [ME *feden* < OE *fēdan.* See **pā-*.**]

feed•back (fēd′băk′) *n.* **1.a.** The return of a portion of the output of a process or system to the input, esp. when used to maintain performance or to control a system or process. **b.** The portion of the output so returned. **2.** The return of information about the result of a process or activity; an evaluative response.

feed•bag (fēd′băg′) *n.* A bag that fits over a horse's muzzle and holds feed.

feed•er (fē′dər) *n.* **1.** One that supplies food. **2.** One that is fed, esp. an animal being fattened for market. **3.** One that feeds materials into a machine for further processing. **4.** Something that contributes to the operation, maintenance, or supply of something else, esp.: **a.** A tributary stream. **b.** A branch line of a transport system, as of an airline or a railroad. **5.** Any of the medium-voltage lines used to distribute electric power from a substation to consumers or to smaller substations. **6.** A transmission line between an antenna and a transmitter.

feed•lot (fēd′lŏt′) *n.* A plot of ground on which livestock are fattened for market.

feed•stock (fēd′stŏk′) *n.* Raw material required for an industrial process.

feed•stuff (fēd′stŭf′) *n.* Food for livestock; fodder.

feel (fēl) *v.* **felt** (fĕlt), **feel•ing, feels.** —*tr.* **1.a.** To perceive through the sense of touch: *feel a peach.* **b.** To perceive as a physical sensation: *feel the cold.* **2.a.** To touch. **b.** To examine by touching. **3.** To test or explore with caution: *feel one's way in a new job.* **4.a.** To undergo the experience of. **b.** To be aware of; sense. **c.** To be emotionally affected by. **5.a.** To be persuaded of (something) on the basis of intuition, emotion, or other indefinite grounds. **b.** To believe; think. —*intr.* **1.** To experience sensations of touch. **2.a.** To produce a particular sensation, esp. through the sense of touch. **b.** To produce a particular impression; appear to be; seem: *It feels good to be home.* See Usage Note at **well²**. **3.** To be conscious of a specified kind or quality of physical, mental, or emotional state: *felt content.* **4.** To seek or explore something by the sense of touch: *felt for the switch.* **5.** To have compassion. —*n.* **1.** Perception by or as if by touch; sensation. **2.** The sense of touch. **3.** The nature or quality of something as perceived by or as if by the sense of touch. **4.** Overall impression or effect; atmosphere. **5.** Intuitive awareness or natural ability. —*phrasal verbs.* **feel out.** To try cautiously or indirectly to ascertain the viewpoint or nature of. **feel up.** *Vulgar Slang.* To touch or fondle (someone) sexually. —*idioms.* **feel in (one's) bones.** To have an intuition of. **feel like.** *Informal.* To have an inclination or desire for. **feel like (oneself).** To sense oneself as being in one's normal state. [ME *felen* < OE *fēlan.* See **pōl-*.**]

feel•er (fē′lər) *n.* **1.** Something, such as a hint or question, designed to elicit the attitudes or intentions of others. **2.** *Zool.* A sensory or tactile organ, such as an antenna.

feel•ing (fē′lĭng) *n.* **1.a.** The sensation involving perception by touch. **b.** A sensation experienced through touch. **c.** A physical sensation: *a feeling of warmth.* **2.** An affective state, such as that resulting from emotions or desires: *a feeling of excitement.* **3.** An awareness or impression: *had the feeling he was being followed.* **4.a.** An emotional state or disposition; an emotion: *expressed deep feeling.* **b.** A tender emotion; a fondness. **5.a.** Capacity to experience the higher emotions; sensibility: *a man of feeling.* **b. feelings.** Susceptibility to emotional response; sensibilities: *His feelings are easily hurt.* **6.** Opinion based more on emotion than on reason; sentiment. **7.** A general impression conveyed by a person, place, or thing. **8.a.** Appreciative regard or understanding. **b.** Intuitive awareness or aptitude; a feel. —*adj.* **1.** Having the ability to feel emotionally; sentient; sensitive. **2.** Easily moved emotionally; sympathetic. **3.** Expressive of sensibility or emotion: *a feeling glance.* —**feel′ing•ly** *adv.*

Syns: *feeling, emotion, passion, sentiment.* These nouns refer to complex and usually strong subjective human response. Although *feeling* and *emotion* are sometimes interchangeable, *feeling* is the more general and neutral: *"Poetry is the spontaneous overflow of powerful feelings: it takes its origin from emotion recollected in tranquillity"* (William Wordsworth). *Emotion* often implies the presence of excitement or agitation: *"Poetry is not a turning loose of emotion, but an escape from emotion"* (T.S. Eliot). *Passion* is intense compelling emotion: *"They seemed like ungoverned children inflamed with the fiercest passions of men"* (Francis Parkman). *Sentiment* often applies to a thought or opinion arising from or influenced by emotion. The word can also refer to delicate, sensitive, or higher feelings: *"The mystic reverence, the religious allegiance, which are essential to a true monarchy, are imaginative sentiments that no legislature can manufacture in any people"* (Walter Bagehot).

fee simple *n., pl.* **fees simple.** *Law.* **1.** An estate in land of which the inheritor has unqualified ownership and power of disposition. **2.** Private ownership of real estate in which the owner has the right to control, use, and transfer the property at will.

fee splitting *n.* The practice of sharing fees with professional colleagues, such as physicians, for patient or client referrals.

feet (fēt) *n.* Pl. of **foot.**

fee tail *n., pl.* **fees tail.** *Law.* An estate in land limited in inheritance to a particular class of heirs.

feign (fān) *v.* **feigned, feign•ing, feigns.** —*tr.* **1.a.** To give a false appearance of: *feign sleep.* **b.** To represent falsely; pretend to. **2.** To imitate so as to deceive: *feign another's voice.* **3.** To fabricate: *feigned an excuse.* **4.** *Archaic.* To invent or imagine. —*intr.* To pretend; dissemble. [ME *feinen* < OFr. *feindre* < Lat. *fingere,* to shape, form. See **dheigh-***.]

feigned (fānd) *adj.* **1.** Not real; pretended: *feigned modesty.* **2.** Made-up; fictitious.

Fei•ning•er (fī′nĭng-ər), **Lyonel Charles Adrian.** 1871–1956. Amer.-born artist who developed a delicate geometric style with intersecting planes of translucent colors.

feint (fānt) *n.* **1.** A feigned attack designed to draw defensive action away from a target. **2.** A deceptive action to divert attention from one's real purpose. —*v.* **feint•ed, feint•ing, feints.** —*intr.* To make a feint. —*tr.* **1.** To deceive with a feint. **2.** To make a deceptive show of. [Fr. *feinte* < OFr. < p.part. of *feindre,* to feign. See FEIGN.]

Fei•sal (fī′səl). See **Faisal.**

feist (fīst) also **fice** (fīs) *n. Chiefly Southern U.S.* A small mongrel dog. [Var. of obsolete *fist,* short for *fisting dog* < ME *fisten,* to break wind. See **pezd-***.]

feist•y (fī′stē) *adj.* **-i•er, -i•est. 1.** Touchy; quarrelsome. **2.** Full of spirit or pluck; spunky. [< FEIST.] —**feist′i•ness** *n.*

Fei•sul (fī′səl). See **Faisal.**

fe•la•fel (fə-lä′fəl) *n.* Var. of **falafel.**

feld•spar (fĕld′spär′, fĕl′-) also **fel•spar** (fĕl′-) *n.* Any of a group of abundant rock-forming minerals occurring in igneous, sedimentary, and metamorphic rocks and consisting of silicates of aluminum with potassium, sodium, and calcium. [Partial transl. of obsolete Ger. *Feldspath* : *Feld,* field (< MHGer. *veld* < OHGer. *feld*; see **pelə-**[2]*) + *Spath,* spar.]

feld•spath•ic (fĕld-spăth′ĭk, fĕl-) *adj.* Of, relating to, or containing feldspar. [< obsolete Ger. *Feldspath,* feldspar. See FELDSPAR.]

fe•li•cif•ic (fē′lĭ-sĭf′ĭk) *adj.* Producing or intended to produce happiness. [Lat. *fēlix, fēlīc-,* fortunate; see **dhē(i)-*** + -FIC.]

fe•lic•i•tate (fĭ-lĭs′ĭ-tāt′) *tr.v.* **-tat•ed, -tat•ing, -tates. 1.** To offer congratulations to. **2.** *Archaic.* To make happy. —*adj. Obsolete.* Made happy. [LLat. *fēlīcitāre, fēlīcitāt-,* to make happy < *fēlīx, fēlīc-,* fortunate. See **dhē(i)-***.] —**fe•lic′i•ta′tor** *n.*

fe•lic•i•ta•tion (fĭ-lĭs′ĭ-tā′shən) *n.* Congratulations. Often used in the plural.

fe•lic•i•tous (fĭ-lĭs′ĭ-təs) *adj.* **1.** Admirably suited; apt: *a felicitous comparison.* **2.** Agreeably appropriate in manner or style: *a felicitous writer.* **3.** Happy or fortunate: *a felicitous life.* —**fe•lic′i•tous•ly** *adv.* —**fe•lic′i•tous•ness** *n.*

fe•lic•i•ty (fĭ-lĭs′ĭ-tē) *n., pl.* **-ties. 1.a.** Great happiness; bliss. **b.** An instance of this. **2.** A cause or source of happiness. **3.a.** An appropriate and pleasing manner or style: *felicity of expression.* **b.** An instance of this. **4.** *Archaic.* Good fortune. [ME *felicite* < OFr. *felicite* < Lat. *fēlīcitās* < *fēlīx, fēlīc-,* fortunate. See **dhē(i)-***.]

fe•lid (fē′lĭd) *adj.* Feline. [< NLat. *Fēlidae,* family name < *Fēlis,* type genus < Lat. *fēlēs,* cat.] —**fe′lid** *n.*

fe•line (fē′līn′) *adj.* **1.** Of or belonging to the family Felidae, which includes the lions, tigers, jaguars, and cats; felid. **2.** Suggestive of a cat, as in suppleness or stealthiness. —*n.* An animal of the family Felidae. [Lat. *fēlīnus* or LLat. *fēlīneus,* both < Lat. *fēlēs,* cat.] —**fe′line′ly** *adv.* —**fe′line′ness, fe•lin′i•ty** (fĭ-lĭn′ĭ-tē) *n.*

feline distemper *n.* See **distemper**[1] 1b.

fell[1] (fĕl) *tr.v.* **felled, fell•ing, fells. 1.a.** To make fall by striking; cut or knock down: *fell a tree.* **b.** To kill: *was felled by a bullet.* **2.** To sew or finish (a seam) with the raw edges flattened, turned under, and stitched down. —*n.* **1.** The timber cut down in one season. **2.** A felled seam. [ME *fellen* < OE *fellan, fyllan.*] —**fell′a•ble** *adj.*

fell[2] (fĕl) *adj.* **1.** Inhumanly cruel; fierce. **2.** Capable of destroying; lethal. **3.** Dire; sinister. **4.** *Scots.* Sharp and biting. —***idiom.* at** (or **in**) **one fell swoop.** All at once. [ME *fel* < OFr., nominative of *felon.* See FELON[1].] —**fell′ness** *n.*

fell[3] (fĕl) *n.* **1.** The hide of an animal; a pelt. **2.** A thin membrane beneath the hide. [ME *fel* < OE *fell.* See **pel-**[3]*.]

fell[4] (fĕl) *n. Chiefly British.* **1.** An upland stretch of open country; a moor. **2.** A barren or stony hill. [ME *fel* < ON *fell, fjall,* mountain, hill.]

fell[5] (fĕl) *v.* P.t. of **fall.**

fel•la (fĕl′ə) *n. Informal.* A man or boy; a fellow.

fel•lah (fĕl′ə, fə-lä′) *n., pl.* **fel•la•hin** or **fel•la•heen** (fĕl′ə-hēn′, fə-lä-hēn′). A peasant or an agricultural laborer in an Arab country. [Ar. *fallāḥ,* dialectal var. of *fallāḥ* < *falaḥa,* to cultivate, till.]

fel•late (fə-lāt′) *v.* **-lat•ed, -lat•ing, -lates.** —*tr.* To perform fellatio on. —*intr.* To engage in fellatio. [Lat. *fellāre, fellāt-,* to suck. See FELLATIO.] —**fel•la′tion** (-lā′shən) *n.* —**fel•la′tor** *n.*

fel•la•ti•o (fə-lā′shē-ō′, -lä′tē-ō′, fĕ-) *n.* Oral stimulation of the penis. [NLat. < Lat. *fellātus,* p.part. of *fellāre,* to suck. See **dhē(i)-***.]

fell•er[1] (fĕl′ər) *n.* **1.** A lumberjack. **2.** One that fells seams.

fel•ler[2] (fĕl′ər) *n. Informal.* A man or boy; a fellow.

Fel•li•ni (fə-lē′nē, fĕl-), **Federico.** b. 1920. Italian filmmaker whose works include *La Dolce Vita* (1960).

fel•low (fĕl′ō) *n.* **1.a.** A man or boy. **b.** *Informal.* A boyfriend. **2.** A comrade or an associate. **3.a.** A person of equal rank or background; a peer. **b.** One of a pair; a mate. **4.** A member of a learned society. **5.** A graduate student receiving support for further study. **6.** *Chiefly British.* **a.** An incorporated senior member of a college or university. **b.** A member of the governing body of a college or university. **7.** *Obsolete.* A person of a lower social class. —*adj.* Being of the same kind, group, occupation, society, or locality; sharing certain characteristics or interests. [ME *felau* < OE *fēolaga* < ON *fēlagi,* business partner, fellow < *fēlag,* partnership : *fē,* property, money; see **peku-*** + *lag,* a laying down; see **legh-***.]

Word History: The word *fellow,* borrowed into English from Old Norse, is related to the Old Icelandic word *fēlagi,* meaning "a partner or shareholder of any kind." Old Icelandic *fēlagi* is derived from *fēlag,* "partnership," a compound made up of *fē,* "livestock, property, money," and *lag,* "a laying in order" and "fellowship." The notion of putting one's property together lies behind the senses of *fēlagi* meaning "partner" and "consort." In Old Icelandic *fēlagi* also had the general sense "fellow, mate, comrade," as does *fellow.*

fellow feeling *n.* **1.** Sympathetic awareness of others; rapport. **2.** Community of interest.

fellow man also **fel•low•man** (fĕl′ō-măn′) *n.* Another human being.

fellow servant *n. Law.* One of a group of employees working under such circumstances that the employer is not liable for injury to one worker resulting from the negligence of another.

fel•low•ship (fĕl′ō-shĭp′) *n.* **1.a.** The condition of sharing similar interests, ideals, or experiences, as by reason of profession, religion, or nationality. **b.** The companionship of peers in a congenial atmosphere. **2.** A close association of friends or equals sharing similar interests. **3.** Friendship; comradeship. **4.a.** The financial grant made to a fellow in a college or university. **b.** The status of having been awarded such a grant. **c.** A foundation established for the awarding of such a grant.

fellow traveler *n.* One who sympathizes with or supports the tenets and program of an organized group, such as the Communist Party, without being a member.

fel•ly (fĕl′ē) also **fel•loe** (fĕl′ō) *n., pl.* **-lies** also **-loes.** The rim or a section of the rim of a wheel supported by spokes. [ME *felie, felwe* < OE *felg.*]

fel•on[1] (fĕl′ən) *n.* **1.** *Law.* One who has committed a felony. **2.** *Archaic.* An evil person. —*adj. Archaic.* Evil; cruel. [ME *feloun* < OFr. *felon,* wicked, a wicked person < Med.Lat. *fellō, fellōn-,* poss. of Gmc. orig.]

fel•on[2] (fĕl′ən) *n.* A painful purulent infection at the end of a finger or toe in the area surrounding the nail. [ME *feloun,* prob. < Lat. *fel,* gall, bile. See **ghel-**[2]*.]

fe•lo•ni•ous (fə-lō′nē-əs) *adj.* **1.** *Law.* Having the nature of, relating to, or concerning a felony. **2.** *Archaic.* Evil; wicked. —**fe•lo′ni•ous•ly** *adv.* —**fe•lo′ni•ous•ness** *n.*

fel•o•ny (fĕl′ə-nē) *n., pl.* **-nies.** *Law.* **1.** One of several crimes, such as murder, rape, or burglary, punishable by a more stringent sentence than that given for a misdemeanor. **2.** Any of several crimes in early English law punishable by forfeiture of land or goods and by possible loss of life or a bodily part.

fel•sic (fĕl′sĭk) *n.* Relating to or containing a group of light-

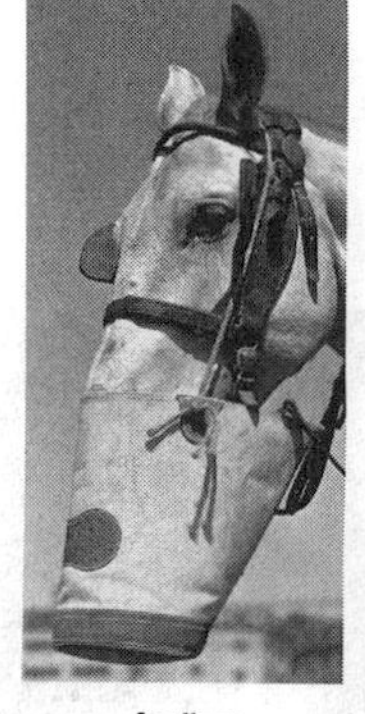
feedbag

ă pat	oi boy
ā pay	ou out
âr care	o͝o took
ä father	o͞o boot
ĕ pet	ŭ cut
ē be	ûr urge
ĭ pit	th thin
ī pie	*th* this
îr pier	hw which
ŏ pot	zh vision
ō toe	ə about, item
ô paw	

Stress marks:
′ (primary);
′ (secondary), as in
dictionary (dĭk′shə-nĕr′ē)

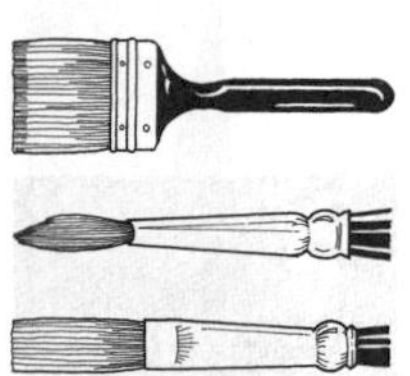

ferrule
Top: Household brush
Center: Round brush
Bottom: Flat-edged brush

fer•rule (fĕr′əl) *n.* **1.** A metal ring or cap placed around a pole or shaft for reinforcement. **2.** A bushing used to secure a pipe joint. [Alteration of ME *verrele* < OFr. *virole* < Lat. *viriola,* dim. of *viriae,* bracelets. See **wei-***.] — **fer′rule** *v.*

fer•ry (fĕr′ē) *v.* **-ried, -ry•ing, -ries.** — *tr.* **1.** *Naut.* **a.** To transport (people, vehicles, or goods) by boat across a body of water. **b.** To cross (a body of water) by a ferry. **2.a.** To deliver (a vehicle, esp. an aircraft) under its own power to its eventual user. **b.** To transport (people or goods) esp. by aircraft. — *intr.* To cross a body of water on or as if on a ferry. — *n., pl.* **-ries. 1.** *Naut.* **a.** A ferryboat. **b.** A place where passengers or goods are ferried. **2.** A franchise or legal right to operate a ferrying service for a fee. **3.** A service and route for ferrying an aircraft. [ME *ferien* < OE *ferian.* See **per-[2]***.]

fer•ry•boat (fĕr′ē-bōt′) *n. Naut.* A boat used to ferry passengers, vehicles, or goods.

fer•tile (fûr′tl) *adj.* **1.** *Biol.* **a.** Capable of initiating, sustaining, or supporting reproduction. **b.** Capable of growing and developing; able to mature. **2.** *Bot.* Bearing functional reproductive structures. **3.** Bearing or producing crops or vegetation abundantly; fruitful. **4.** Rich in material needed to sustain plant growth: *fertile soil.* **5.** Highly or continuously productive; prolific. **6.** *Phys.* Capable of producing fissionable material. [ME *fertil* < OFr. *fertile* < Lat. *fertilis* < *ferre,* to bear. See **bher-[1]***.] — **fer′tile•ly** *adv.* — **fer′tile•ness** *n.*

Fer•tile Cres•cent (fûr′tl krĕs′ənt). A region of the Middle East across the N part of the Syrian Desert extending from the Nile Valley to the Tigris and Euphrates rivers.

fer•til•i•ty (fər-tĭl′ĭ-tē) *n.* **1.** The condition, quality, or degree of being fertile. **2.** The birthrate of a population.

fer•til•i•za•tion (fûr′tl-ĭ-zā′shən) *n.* **1.** The act or process of initiating biological reproduction by insemination or pollination. **2.** The union of male and female gametes to form a zygote. **3.** The act or process of applying a fertilizer. — **fer′til•i•za′tion•al** *adj.*

fer•til•ize (fûr′tl-īz′) *v.* **-ized, -iz•ing, -iz•es.** — *tr.* **1.** To cause the fertilization of (an ovum, for example). **2.** To make (soil, for example) fertile. **3.** To spread fertilizer on. — *intr.* To spread fertilizer. — **fer′til•iz′a•ble** *adj.*

fer•til•iz•er (fûr′tl-ī′zər) *n.* Any of a large number of natural and synthetic materials, including manure and nitrogen, phosphorus, and potassium compounds, spread on or worked into soil to increase its capacity to support plant growth.

fer•ule (fĕr′əl) *n.* An instrument, such as a cane, used in punishing children. — *tr.v.* **-uled, -ul•ing, -ules.** To punish with a ferule. [ME *ferul,* fennel stalk < Lat. *ferula,* rod.]

fe•ru•lic acid (fə-rōō′lĭk) *n.* A compound, $C_{10}H_{10}O_4$, related to vanillin and obtained from certain plants. [< NLat. *Ferula,* plant genus < Lat. *ferula,* giant fennel.]

fer•ven•cy (fûr′vən-sē) *n., pl.* **-cies.** The condition or quality of being fervent.

fer•vent (fûr′vənt) *adj.* **1.** Having or showing great emotion or zeal; ardent: *fervent protests.* **2.** Extremely hot; glowing. [ME < OFr. < Lat. *fervēns, fervent-,* pr.part. of *fervēre,* to boil. See **bhreu-***.] — **fer′vent•ly** *adv.* — **fer′vent•ness** *n.*

fer•vid (fûr′vĭd) *adj.* **1.** Marked by great passion or zeal. **2.** Extremely hot; burning. [Lat. *fervidus* < *fervēre,* to boil. See **bhreu-***.] — **fer′vid•ly** *adv.* — **fer′vid•ness** *n.*

fer•vor (fûr′vər) *n.* **1.** Great warmth and intensity of emotion. **2.** Intense heat. [ME *fervour* < OFr. < Lat. *fervor* < *fervēre,* to boil. See **bhreu-***.]

fer•vour (fûr′vər) *n. Chiefly British.* Var. of **fervor.**

Fès (fĕs). See **Fez.**

fes•cen•nine (fĕs′ə-nīn′, -nēn′) *adj.* Licentious; obscene. [Lat. *Fescennīnus,* of Fescennia, a town of ancient Etruria known for its licentious poetry.]

fes•cue (fĕs′kyōō) *n.* Any of various grasses of the genus *Festuca,* often cultivated as pasturage. [Alteration of ME *festu,* straw < OFr. < LLat. *festūcum* < Lat. *festūca.*]

fess[1]

fess[1] also **fesse** (fĕs) *n. Her.* A wide horizontal band forming the middle section of an escutcheon. [ME *fesse* < OFr. < Lat. *fascia,* band.]

fess[2] (fĕs) *intr.v.* **fessed, fess•ing, fess•es.** *Informal.* To admit to something; confess. [Short for CONFESS.]

fesse (fĕs) *n. Her.* Var. of **fess[1]**.

fess point *n. Her.* The center point of an escutcheon.

fest (fĕst) *n.* A gathering or an occasion characterized by a specified activity. Often used in combination: *a music fest.* [< Ger. *Fest,* festival < MHGer. *vëst* < Lat. *fēstum.* See FEAST.]

festoon

fes•tal (fĕs′təl) *adj.* Of, relating to, or of the nature of a feast or festival; festive. [ME < OFr. < LLat. *fēstālis* < Lat. *fēstum,* feast. See FEAST.] — **fes′tal•ly** *adv.*

fes•ter (fĕs′tər) *v.* **-tered, -ter•ing, -ters.** — *intr.* **1.** To generate pus; suppurate. **2.** To form an ulcer. **3.** To undergo decay; rot. **4.a.** To be or become an increasing source of irritation or poisoning; rankle. **b.** To be subject to or exist in a condition of decline. — *tr.* To infect, inflame, or corrupt. — *n.* A small festering sore or ulcer; a pustule. [ME *festren* < *festre,* fistula < OFr. < Lat. *fistula.*]

fes•ti•nate (fĕs′tə-nĭt) *adj.* Hasty. — *intr.v.* (-nāt′) **-nat•ed, -nat•ing, -nates.** To hasten. [Lat. *festīnātus,* p.part. of *festīnāre,* to hasten.] — **fes′ti•nate•ly** *adv.*

fes•ti•val (fĕs′tə-vəl) *n.* **1.** An occasion for feasting or celebration, esp. a day or time of religious significance that recurs at regular intervals. **2.** An often regularly recurring program of cultural performances, exhibitions, or competitions: *a film festival.* **3.** Revelry; conviviality. — *adj.* Of, relating to, or suitable for a feast or festival; festive. [< ME, festive < OFr. < Med.Lat. *fēstivālis* < Lat. *fēstīvus* < *fēstus.* See **dhēs-***.]

fes•ti•val•go•er (fĕs′tə-vəl-gō′ər) *n.* One who attends a festival.

fes•tive (fĕs′tĭv) *adj.* **1.** Of, relating to, or appropriate for a feast or festival. **2.** Merry; joyous. [Lat. *fēstīvus* < *fēstus.* See **dhēs-***.] — **fes′tive•ly** *adv.* — **fes′tive•ness** *n.*

fes•tiv•i•ty (fĕ-stĭv′ĭ-tē) *n., pl.* **-ties. 1.** A joyous feast, holiday, or celebration; a festival. **2.** The pleasure, joy, and gaiety of a festival or celebration. **3. festivities.** The proceedings or events of a festival.

fes•toon (fĕ-stōōn′) *n.* **1.** A string or garland, as of flowers, suspended in a loop or curve between two points. **2.** A representation of such a string or garland, as in painting or sculpture. — *tr.v.* **-tooned, -toon•ing, -toons. 1.** To decorate with or as if with festoons; hang festoons on. **2.** To form or make into festoons. [Fr. *feston* < Ital. *festone* < *festa,* feast < VLat. **fēsta.* See FEAST.]

fes•toon•er•y (fĕ-stōō′nə-rē) *n., pl.* **-ies. 1.** An arrangement of festoons. **2.** Festoons considered as a group.

fest•schrift (fĕst′shrĭft′) *n., pl.* **-schrif•ten** (-shrĭf′tən) or **-schrifts.** A volume of learned articles or essays by colleagues and admirers, serving as a tribute or memorial esp. to a scholar. [Ger. : *Fest,* festival; see FEST + *Schrift,* writing (ult. < Lat. *scrībere,* to write; see **skrībh-***).]

FET *abbr.* **1.** Federal estate tax. **2.** Also **F.E.T.** Federal Excise Tax. **3.** Field-effect transistor.

fet– *pref.* Var. of **feto–.**

fet•a (fĕt′ə, fē′tə) *n.* A white semisoft Greek cheese made usu. of goat's or ewe's milk and preserved in brine. [Mod.Gk. *(turi) pheta,* (cheese) slice < Ital. *fetta,* slice < **offetta,* dim. of **offa* < Lat. *offa,* morsel of food.]

fe•tal also **foe•tal** (fēt′l) *adj.* Of, relating to, characteristic of, or being a fetus.

fetal alcohol syndrome *n.* A complex of birth defects including cardiac or neural abnormalities and physical and mental growth retardation, occurring in an infant as a result of excess alcohol consumption by the mother during pregnancy.

fetal position *n.* A position of the body at rest in which the spine is curved, the head is bowed forward, and the arms and legs are drawn in toward the chest.

fetch[1] (fĕch) *v.* **fetched, fetch•ing, fetch•es.** — *tr.* **1.** To come or go after and take or bring back. **2.a.** To cause to come. **b.** To bring in as a price. **c.** To interest or attract. **3.a.** To draw in (breath); inhale. **b.** To bring forth (a sigh, for example) with obvious effort. **4.** *Informal.* To deliver (a blow) by striking; deal. **5.** *Naut.* To arrive at; reach. — *intr.* **1.a.** To go after something and return with it. **b.** To retrieve killed game. Used of a hunting dog. **2.** To take an indirect route. — *n.* **1.** The act or an instance of fetching. **2.** *Comp. Sci.* A program routine that brings a module of a program from storage into main memory for immediate use. **3.** A stratagem or trick. **4.a.** The distance over which a wind blows. **b.** The distance traveled by waves with no obstruction. — ***phrasal verb.* fetch up. 1.** To reach a stopping place or goal; end up. **2.** To make up (lost time, for example). **3.** To bring forth; produce. **4.** To bring to a halt; stop. [ME *fecchen* < OE *feccean.* See **ped-***.] — **fetch′er** *n.*

fetch[2] (fĕch) *n. Chiefly British.* **1.** A ghost; an apparition. **2.** A doppelgänger. [?]

fetch•ing (fĕch′ĭng) *adj.* Very attractive; charming: *a fetching new hairstyle.* — **fetch′ing•ly** *adv.*

fete also **fête** (fāt, fĕt) — *n.* **1.** A festival or feast. **2.a.** An elaborate, often outdoor entertainment. **b.** An elaborate party. — *tr.v.* **fet•ed, fet•ing, fetes** also **fêt•ed, fêt•ing, fêtes. 1.** To celebrate or honor with a fete. **2.** To pay honor to. [Fr. *fête* < OFr. *feste.* See FEAST.]

feti– *pref.* Var. of **feto–.**

fe•ti•cide (fē′tĭ-sīd′) *n.* Intentional destruction of a human fetus. — **fe′ti•cid′al** (-sīd′l) *adj.*

fet•id (fĕt′ĭd, fē′tĭd) also **foe•tid** (fē′tĭd) *adj.* Having an offensive odor. [ME < Lat. *fētidus* < *fētēre,* to stink.] — **fet′id•ly** *adv.* — **fet′id•ness** *n.*

fet•ish also **fet•ich** (fĕt′ĭsh, fē′tĭsh) *n.* **1.** An object that is believed to have magical or spiritual powers, esp. such an object associated with animistic or shamanistic religious practices. **2.** An object of unreasonably excessive attention or reverence. **3.** Something, such as a nonsexual part of the body, that arouses sexual desire and may become necessary for sexual gratification. **4.** An abnormally obsessive preoccupation or attachment; a fixation. [Fr. *fétiche* < Port. *feitiço,* artificial, charm < Lat. *factīcius,* artificial. See FACTITIOUS.]

fet•ish•ism also **fet•ich•ism** (fĕt′ĭ-shĭz′əm, fē′tĭ-) *n.* **1.** Worship of or belief in magical fetishes. **2.** Excessive attachment or regard. **3.** The displacement of sexual arousal or gratification to a fetish. — **fet′ish•ist** *n.* — **fet′ish•is′tic** *adj.* — **fet′ish•is′ti•cal•ly** *adv.*

fet•ish•ize (fĕt**′**ĭ-shīz′) *tr.v.* **-ized, -iz•ing, -iz•es.** To make a fetish of.

fet•lock (fĕt**′**lŏk′) *n.* **1.a.** A projection on the lower part of the leg of a horse or related animal, above and behind the hoof. **b.** A tuft of hair on such a projection. **2.** The joint marked by such a projection. [ME *fitlok.* See **ped-***.]

feto– or **feti–** or **fet–** *pref.* Fetus; fetal: *fetology.* [< FETUS.]

fe•tol•o•gy (fē-tŏl**′**ə-jē) *n.* The medical study and treatment of the fetus, esp. within the uterus. **— fe•tol′o•gist** *n.*

fe•tor (fē**′**tər, -tôr′) also **foe•tor** (fē**′**tər) *n.* An offensive odor; a stench. [ME *fetoure* < Lat. *fētor* < *fētēre,* to stink.]

fe•to•scope (fē**′**tə-skōp′) *n.* A flexible fiberoptic device used to view a fetus in utero. **— fe•tos′co•py** (fē-tŏs**′**kə-pē) *n.*

fet•ter (fĕt**′**ər) *n.* **1.** A chain or shackle for the ankles or feet. **2.** Something that restricts; a restraint. **—** *tr.v.* **-tered, -ter•ing, -ters. 1.** To put fetters on; shackle. **2.** To restrict the freedom of. [ME *feter* < OE. See **ped-***.]

fet•tle (fĕt**′**l) *n.* **1.a.** Proper or sound condition. **b.** Mental or emotional state; spirits: *in fine fettle.* **2.** *Metall.* Loose sand or ore used to line the hearth of a reverberatory furnace in preparation for pouring molten metal. **—** *tr.v.* **-tled, -tling, -tles.** *Metall.* To line the hearth of (a reverberatory furnace) with fettle. [< ME *fetlen,* to make ready, poss. < OE *fetel,* girdle.]

fet•tling (fĕt**′**lĭng) *n.* *Metall.* Fettle.

fet•tuc•ci•ne (fĕt′ə-chē**′**nē) *n.* Pasta in narrow flat strips. [Ital., pl. dim. of *fettucia,* ribbon, poss. dim. of *fetta,* slice. See FETA.]

fettuccine Al•fre•do (ăl-frā**′**dō, äl-) *n.* A dish consisting of fettuccine in a rich cream sauce with Parmesan cheese. [After *Alfredo all'Augusteo,* a restaurant in Rome.]

fe•tus also **foe•tus** (fē**′**təs) *n., pl.* **-tus•es. 1.** The unborn young of a viviparous vertebrate having a basic structural resemblance to the adult animal. **2.** In human beings, the unborn young from the end of the eighth week after conception to the moment of birth, as distinguished from the earlier embryo. [ME < Lat. *fētus,* offspring. See **dhē(i)-***.]

feud[1] (fyōōd) *n.* A bitter, often prolonged quarrel or state of enmity, esp. such a state of hostilities between two families or clans. **—** *intr.v.* **feud•ed, feud•ing, feuds.** To carry on or perpetuate a feud. [Alteration (prob. influenced by FEUD[2]) of ME *fede* < OFr. *faide,* of Gmc. orig.]

feud[2] (fyōōd) *n.* See **fee** 5a. [Med.Lat. *feudum,* of Gmc. orig. See **peku-***.]

feud. *abbr.* Feudal; feudalism.

feu•dal (fyōōd**′**l) *adj.* **1.** Of, relating to, or characteristic of feudalism. **2.** Of or relating to lands held in fee or to the holding of such lands. **— feu′dal•ly** *adv.*

feu•dal•ism (fyōōd**′**l-ĭz′əm) *n.* **1.** A political and economic system of Europe from the 9th to about the 15th century, based on the holding of all land in fief or fee and the resulting relation of lord to vassal and characterized by homage, legal and military service of tenants, and forfeiture. **2.** A political, economic, or social order resembling this medieval system. **— feu′dal•ist** *n.* **— feu′dal•is′tic** *adj.*

feu•dal•i•ty (fyōō-dăl**′**ĭ-tē) *n., pl.* **-ties. 1.** The quality or state of being feudal. **2.** A feudal holding, system, or regime.

feu•dal•ize (fyōōd**′**l-īz′) *tr.v.* **-ized, -iz•ing, -iz•es.** To make feudal. **— feu′dal•i•za′tion** (-ĭ-zā**′**shən) *n.*

feu•da•to•ry (fyōō**′**də-tôr′ē, -tōr′ē) *n., pl.* **-ries. 1.** A person holding land by feudal fee; a vassal. **2.** A feudal fee. **—** *adj.* **1.** Of, relating to, or characteristic of the feudal relationship between vassal and lord. **2.** Owing feudal homage or allegiance. [Med.Lat. *feudatōrius* < *feudātus,* p.part. of *feudāre,* to enfeoff < *feudum,* fee, fief. See FEUD[2].]

feud•ist[1] (fyōō**′**dĭst) *n.* A participant in a feud.

feud•ist[2] (fyōō**′**dĭst) *n.* A specialist in feudal law.

feuil•le•ton (fœ′yə-tôN**′**) *n.* **1.a.** The part of a European newspaper given to light fiction, reviews, and articles of general entertainment. **b.** An article appearing in such a section. **2.a.** A novel published in installments. **b.** A light popular work of fiction. **3.** A short literary essay or sketch. [Fr. < *feuillet,* sheet of paper, little leaf, dim. of *feuille,* leaf < OFr. *foille* < Lat. *folium.* See **bhel-**[3]*.] **— feuil′le•ton′ism** (-tôn**′**ĭz′əm, -tôN′nĭz′-) *n.* **— feuil′le•ton′ist** *n.* **— feuil′le•ton•is′tic** *adj.*

fe•ver (fē**′**vər) *n.* **1.a.** Abnormally high body temperature. **b.** Any of various diseases characterized by fever. **2.a.** A condition of heightened activity or excitement. **b.** A contagious, usu. short-lived enthusiasm or craze: *disco fever.* **—** *v.* **-vered, -ver•ing, -vers. —** *tr.* To effect fever in. **—** *intr.* To be or become feverish. [ME < OE *fefor* and < OFr. *fievre,* both < Lat. *febris.*]

fever blister *n.* See **cold sore.**

fe•ver•few (fē**′**vər-fyōō′) *n.* A Eurasian aromatic plant *(Chrysanthemum parthenium)* having buttonlike white-rayed flower heads. [ME *feverfu* < OE *feferfuge* and < AN **fevrefue,* both < LLat. *febrifugia* : *febris,* fever + *fuga,* flight.]

fe•ver•ish (fē**′**vər-ĭsh) *adj.* **1.a.** Of, relating to, or resembling a fever. **b.** Having a fever or fever symptoms. **c.** Causing or tending to cause fever. **2.** Marked by intense agitation, emotion, or activity. **— fe′ver•ish•ly** *adv.* **— fe′ver•ish•ness** *n.*

fever pitch *n.* A state of extreme agitation or excitement.

fever tree *n.* Any of several trees of the southeast United States having leaves or bark used to allay fever.

fe•ver•weed (fē**′**vər-wēd′) *n.* Any of various plants considered to have medicinal properties.

fe•ver•wort (fē**′**vər-wûrt′, -wôrt′) *n.* See **horse gentian.**

few (fyōō) *adj.* **few•er, few•est. 1.** Amounting to or consisting of a small number. **2.** Being more than one but indefinitely small in number. **—** *n. (used with a pl. v.)* **1.** An indefinitely small number of persons or things: *a few of the books.* **2.** An exclusive or limited number: *the discerning few.* **—** *pron. (used with a pl. v.)* A small number of persons or things: *"For many are called, but few are chosen"* (Matthew 22:14). [ME *fewe* < OE *fēawe.* See **pau-***.] **— few′ness** *n.*

Usage Note: The traditional rule holds that *fewer* is used with expressions denoting things that can be counted (*fewer than four*), while *less* is used with mass terms denoting things of measurable extent (*less paper*). However, *less than* is used before a plural noun that denotes a measure of time, amount, or distance: *less than three weeks. Less* is sometimes used with plural nouns in the expressions *no less than* (as in *No less than 30 of his colleagues attended*) and *or less* (as in *25 words or less*).

fey (fā) *adj.* **1.a.** Having or displaying an otherworldly, magical, or fairylike aspect or quality. **b.** Having visionary power; clairvoyant. **c.** Appearing touched or crazy, as if under a spell. **2.** *Scots.* **a.** Fated to die soon. **b.** Full of the sense of approaching death. [ME *feie,* fated to die < OE *fǣge.*] **— fey′ly** *adv.* **— fey′ness** *n.*

Feyn•man (fīn**′**mən), **Richard Phillips.** 1918–88. Amer. physicist who shared a 1965 Nobel Prize.

fez (fĕz) *n., pl.* **fez•zes.** A man's felt cap in the shape of a flat-topped cone, usu. red with a black tassel hanging from the crown. [Fr. < Turk. *fes* < FEZ.]

Fez (fĕz) also **Fès** (fĕs). A city of N-central Morocco NE of Casablanca; orig. founded in the 9th cent. Pop. 448,823.

Fez•zan (fə-zăn**′**). A region of SW Libya; under Turkish control from the 16th cent. until 1912.

ff *abbr. Mus.* Fortissimo.

ff. *abbr.* **1.** Folios. **2.** Following.

FFA *abbr.* Future Farmers of America.

F.F.A. or **f.f.a.** *abbr. Bus.* Free from alongside.

FG *abbr.* **1.** *Football & Basketball.* Field goal. **2.** Fine grain.

FHA *abbr.* **1.** Federal Housing Administration. **2.** Future Homemakers of America.

FHLBB *abbr.* Federal Home Loan Bank Board.

fhp or **f.hp.** *abbr.* Friction horsepower.

fi•a•cre (fē-ä**′**krə) *n.* A small hackney carriage. [Fr., after the Hôtel de St. *Fiacre* in Paris.]

fi•an•cé (fē′än-sā**′**, fē-än**′**sā′) *n.* A man engaged to be married. [Fr. < p.part. of *fiancer,* to betroth < OFr. *fiancier* < *fiance,* trust < *fier,* to trust < VLat. **fidāre* < Lat. *fidere.* See **bheidh-***.]

fi•an•cée (fē′än-sā**′**, fē-än**′**sā′) *n.* A woman engaged to be married. [Fr., fem. of *fiancé,* fiancé. See FIANCÉ.]

fi•an•chet•to (fē′ən-kĕt**′**ō, -chĕt**′**ō) *Games.* **—** *n., pl.* **-chet•ti** (-kĕt**′**ē, -chĕt**′**ē). The development in chess of a bishop from its original position to the second square of the adjacent knight's file. **—** *tr. & intr.v.* **-chet•toed, -chet•to•ing, -chet•tos.** To develop as or set up a fianchetto. [Ital., dim. of *fianco,* flank < OItal. < OFr. *flanc.* See FLANK.]

fi•as•co (fē-ăs**′**kō, -ä**′**skō) *n., pl.* **-coes** or **-cos.** A complete failure. [Fr. < Ital. *fare fiasco,* to make a bottle, fail < *fiasco,* bottle (transl. of Fr. *bouteille,* bottle, error) < LLat. *flascō.* See FLASK.]

fi•at (fē**′**ət, -ăt′, -ät′, fī**′**ăt′, -ət) *n.* **1.** An arbitrary order or decree. **2.** Authorization or sanction: *government fiat.* [Med. Lat. < Lat., let it be done, third pers. sing. pr. subjunctive of *fierī,* to become, to be done. See **bheuə-***.]

fiat money *n.* Legal tender, esp. paper currency, authorized by a government but not based on or convertible into gold or silver.

fib (fĭb) *n.* An insignificant or childish lie. **—** *intr.v.* **fibbed, fib•bing, fibs.** To tell a fib. [Perh. < obsolete and dial. *fible-fable,* nonsense, redup. of FABLE.] **— fib′ber** *n.*

fi•ber (fī**′**bər) *n.* **1.** A threadlike object or structure. **2.** *Bot.* One of the elongated thick-walled cells that give strength and support to plant tissue. **3.** *Anat.* **a.** Any of the filaments constituting the extracellular matrix of connective tissue. **b.** Any of various elongated cells or threadlike structures, esp. a muscle fiber or a nerve fiber. **4.a.** A natural or synthetic filament capable of being spun into yarn. **b.** Material made of such filaments. **5.a.** Something that provides substance or texture. **b.** Essential character or structure. **c.** Basic strength or toughness; fortitude. **6.** Coarse indigestible plant matter, consisting primarily of polysaccharides such as cellulose, that when eaten stimulates intestinal peristalsis. [Fr. *fibre* < OFr. < Lat. *fibra.*] **— fi′bered** *adj.*

fi•ber•board (fī**′**bər-bôrd′, -bōrd′) *n.* A building material composed of wood chips or plant fibers bonded together and compressed into rigid sheets.

fi•ber•fill (fī**′**bər-fĭl′) *n.* Lightweight synthetic fiber used as filling or insulation, as in comforters, pillows, and outerwear.

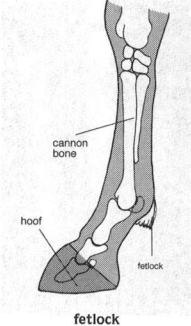

cannon bone

hoof

fetlock

fetlock

ă **pat**	oi **boy**
ā **pay**	ou **out**
âr **care**	ŏŏ **took**
ä **father**	ōō **boot**
ĕ **pet**	ŭ **cut**
ē **be**	ûr **urge**
ĭ **pit**	th **thin**
ī **pie**	*th* **this**
îr **pier**	hw **which**
ŏ **pot**	zh **vision**
ō **toe**	ə **about,**
ô **paw**	**item**

Stress marks:
′ (primary);
′ (secondary), as in
dictionary (dĭk**′**shə-nĕr′ē)

ance. [ME *fiers* < OFr. < Lat. *ferus*. See **ghwer-***.] **— fierce′ly** *adv.* **— fierce′ness** *n.*

fier•y (fīr′ē, fī′ə-rē) *adj.* **-i•er, -i•est. 1.a.** Consisting of or containing fire. **b.** Burning or glowing. **c.** Using or effected with fire. **d.** Easily ignited; flammable. **2.** Having the color of fire; brightly red. **3.a.** Torridly hot. **b.** Feverishly hot and flushed. **c.** Being in an inflamed, usu. painful condition: *a fiery boil.* **4.a.** Easily excited or emotionally volatile; tempestuous. **b.** Charged with emotion; spirited. [ME < *fier*, fire. See FIRE.] **— fier′i•ly** *adv.* **— fier′i•ness** *n.* **— fier′y** *adv.*

fig[1]

Fie•so•le (fē-ā′zə-lē, fyĕ′zô-lĕ). A town of central Italy overlooking the Arno R. and the city of Florence. Pop. 14,774.

Fie•so•le (fyĕ′zō-lā, -zô-lĕ), **Giovanni Angelica da.** See Fra **Angelico.**

fi•es•ta (fē-ĕs′tə) *n.* A festival or religious holiday, esp. a saint's day celebrated in Spanish-speaking countries. [Sp. < VLat. **fēsta*. See FEAST.]

fife (fīf) *n. Mus.* A small high-pitched transverse flute used primarily to accompany drums in a military or marching band. [Prob. Ger. *Pfeife* < MHGer. *pfīfe* < OHGer. *pfīffa* < VLat. **pīpa* < Lat. *pīpāre*, to chirp.] **— fif′er** *n.*

Fife (fīf). A region of E Scotland between the Firths of Forth and Tay; once a Pict kingdom.

fife rail *n. Naut.* A rail around the lower part of a ship's mast to which the belaying pins for the rigging are secured.

FIFO (fī′fō) *n. Accounting.* See **first-in, first-out.**

fif•teen (fĭf-tēn′) *n.* **1.** The cardinal number equal to 14 + 1. **2.** The 15th in a set or sequence. [ME *fiftene* < OE *fīftēne*. See **penk^{w}e***.] **— fif•teen′** *adj. & pron.*

fif•teenth (fĭf-tēnth′) *n.* **1.** The ordinal number matching the number 15 in a series. **2.** One of 15 equal parts. **— fif•teenth′** *adv. & adj.*

fifth (fĭfth) *n.* **1.** The ordinal number matching the number five in a series. **2.** One of five equal parts. **3.** One fifth of a gallon or four fifths of a quart of liquor. **4.** *Mus.* **a.** An interval encompassing five diatonic tones, such as C, D, E, F, and G. **b.** The harmonic combination of the two tones constituting the extremities of such an interval. **c.** The dominant in a given key or tonality. **5. Fifth.** The Fifth Amendment. Used with *the.* [ME < OE *fīfta*. See **penk^{w}e***.] **— fifth** *adv. & adj.* **— fifth′ly** *adv.*

Fifth Amendment *n.* An amendment to the Constitution of the United States, ratified in 1791, that deals with the rights of accused criminals by providing for due process of law, forbidding double jeopardy, and stating that no person may be forced to testify as a witness against himself or herself.

figurehead

fifth column *n.* A clandestine subversive organization within a country furthering an invading enemy's aims. [Applied (1936) to rebel sympathizers in Madrid when it was being attacked by four columns of rebel troops.] **— fifth col′um•nism** (kŏl′əm-nĭz′əm) *n.* **— fifth columnist** *n.*

fifth estate *n.* A class or group in society other than the nobility, the clergy, the middle class, and the press.

fifth wheel *n.* **1.a.** A wheel or portion of a wheel placed horizontally over the forward axle of a carriage to provide support and stability during turns. **b.** A similar device over the rear axle or axles of a tractor or pickup truck, serving as a coupling for a semitrailer. **2.** An additional wheel carried on a four-wheeled vehicle as a spare. **3.** An extra and unnecessary person or thing.

fif•ti•eth (fĭf′tē-ĭth) *n.* **1.** The ordinal number matching the number 50 in a series. **2.** One of 50 equal parts. **— fif′ti•eth** *adv. & adj.*

fif•ty (fĭf′tē) *n.* **1.** The cardinal number equal to 5 × 10. **2. fifties. a.** Often **Fifties.** The decade from 50 to 59 in a century. **b.** A decade or the numbers from 50 to 59. [ME *fifti* < OE *fīftig*. See **penk^{w}e***.] **— fif′ty** *adj. & pron.*

fif•ty-fif•ty (fĭf′tē-fĭf′tē) *adj.* **1.** Divided or shared in two equal portions. **2.** Being equally likely and unlikely or favorable and unfavorable. **— fif′ty-fif′ty** *adv.*

fig[1] (fĭg) *n.* **1.a.** Any of several Mediterranean trees or shrubs of the genus *Ficus*, widely cultivated for their edible fruit. **b.** The sweet pear-shaped fruit of this plant, having numerous tiny seedlike fruits. **2.a.** Any of several plants bearing similar fruit. **b.** The fruit of such a plant. **3.** A trivial or contemptible amount: *didn't care a fig.* [ME < OFr. *figue* < OProv. *figa* < VLat. **fīca* < Lat. *fīcus*.]

figure skating
Scott Hamilton,
photographed in 1983

fig[2] (fĭg) *n.* **1.** Dress; array. **2.** Physical condition; shape. [Perh. < *fig*, dress up, var. of *feague*, to make a horse lively, prob. < Du. *vegen*, to brush < MDu. *vēghen*.]

fig. *abbr.* **1.** Figurative. **2.** Figure.

fight (fīt) *v.* **fought** (fôt), **fight•ing, fights.** *— intr.* **1.a.** To attempt to harm or gain power over an adversary by blows or with weapons. **b.** *Sports.* To engage in boxing or wrestling. **2.** To engage in a quarrel; argue. **3.** To strive vigorously and resolutely. *— tr.* **1.a.** To contend with physically or in battle. **b.** To wage or carry on (a battle). **c.** To contend for, by or as if by combat. **2.a.** *Sports.* To box or wrestle against in a ring. **b.** To participate in (a boxing match, for example). **3.** To set (a boxer, for example) in combat with another. **4.** To contend with or struggle against. See Syns at **oppose. 5.** To try to prevent the development or success of. **6.** To gain by struggle or striving. *— n.* **1.** A confrontation between opposing groups in which each attempts to harm or gain power over the other, as with weapons. **2.** A quarrel or conflict. **3.a.** A physical conflict between two or more individuals. **b.** *Sports.* A boxing or wrestling match. **4.** A struggle to achieve an objective. See Syns at **conflict. 5.** The power or inclination to fight; pugnacity. **— *phrasal verb.* fight off.** To defend against or drive back (a hostile force, for example). **— *idioms.* fight fire with fire.** To combat one evil or one set of negative circumstances by reacting in kind. **fight shy of.** To avoid meeting or confronting. [ME *fighten* < OE *feohtan, fihtan*.] **— fight′a•bil′i•ty** *n.* **— fight′a•ble** *adj.* **— fight′ing•ly** *adv.*

fight•er (fī′tər) *n.* **1.** One that fights, as: **a.** A soldier; a warrior. **b.** *Sports.* A boxer; a pugilist. **c.** A fast, maneuverable combat aircraft used to engage enemy aircraft. **2.** A pugnacious, unyielding, or determined person.

fight•er-bomb•er (fī′tər-bŏm′ər) *n.* A versatile aircraft capable of functioning as a fighter and a bomber chiefly in tactical and defensive operations.

fight•ing chance *n.* A chance to win but only with a struggle.

fight-or-flight reaction (fīt′ôr-flīt′) *n.* A set of physiological changes, such as elevated heart rate, initiated by the sympathetic nervous system in response to stress.

fig leaf *n.* **1.** A stylized representation of the leaf of a fig, used esp. to conceal genitalia on statues of men and boys. **2.** Something that serves as a usu. insufficient concealment.

fig marigold *n.* Any of various plants of the genus *Mesembryanthemum*, native to southern Africa and having thick, fleshy leaves and variously colored flowers.

fig•ment (fĭg′mənt) *n.* Something invented, made up, or fabricated: *just a figment of the imagination.* [ME < Lat. *figmentum* < *fingere*, to form. See **dheigh-***.]

fig•ur•al (fĭg′yər-əl) *adj.* Of, relating to, consisting of, or forming a pictorial composition or design of human or animal figures.

fig•u•rant (fĭg′yə-ränt′, -rănt′, -räɴ′) *n.* **1.** A member of a corps de ballet who does not perform solos. **2.** A stage performer having no speaking part; a supernumerary. [Fr. < pr.part. of *figurer*, to represent < OFr. < Lat. *figūrāre*, to form < *figūra*, figure. See FIGURE.]

fig•u•ra•tion (fĭg′yə-rā′shən) *n.* **1.** The act of forming something into a particular shape. **2.** A shape, a form, or an outline. **3.** The act of representing with figures. **4.** A figurative representation. **5.** *Mus.* Ornamentation of a passage by the use of embellishing and often repeating figures.

fig•u•ra•tive (fĭg′yər-ə-tĭv) *adj.* **1.a.** Based on or making use of figures of speech; metaphorical. **b.** Containing many figures of speech; ornate. **2.** Represented by a figure or resemblance; symbolic or emblematic. **3.** Of or relating to artistic representation by means of animal or human figures. **— fig′u•ra•tive•ly** *adv.* **— fig′u•ra•tive•ness** *n.*

fig•ure (fĭg′yər) *n.* **1.a.** A written or printed symbol representing something other than a letter, esp. a number. **b. figures.** Mathematical calculations. **c.** An amount represented in numbers. **2.a.** *Math.* A geometric form consisting of any combination of points, lines, or planes. **b.** The outline, form, or silhouette of a thing. **c.** The shape or form of a human body. **d.** An indistinct object or shape. **3.a.** A person, esp. a well-known one. **b.** A person's public image or presence. **4.** Impression or appearance made. **5.** A person, an animal, or an object that symbolizes something. **6.** A pictorial or sculptural representation, esp. of the human body. **7.a.** A diagram. **b.** A design or pattern, as in a textile. **8.** An illustration printed from an engraved plate or block. **9.a.** A configuration or distinct group of steps in a dance. **b.** A pattern traced by a series of movements, as in ice skating. **10.** *Mus.* A brief melodic or harmonic unit often constituting the base for a larger phrase or structure. **11.** *Logic.* Any one of the forms that a syllogism can take, depending on the position of the middle term. *— v.* **-ured, -ur•ing, -ures.** *— tr.* **1.** *Math.* To calculate with numbers. **2.** To make a likeness of; depict. **3.** To adorn with a design or figures. **4.** *Mus.* To indicate the chordal structure of (a bass line of single notes) with a sequence of conventionalized numbers. **5.** *Informal.* **a.** To conclude, believe, or predict: *I never figured that you'd go.* **b.** To consider or regard. *— intr.* **1.** *Math.* To calculate; compute. **2.a.** To be or seem important or prominent. **b.** To be pertinent or involved. **3.** *Informal.* To seem reasonable or expected: *It figures.* **— *phrasal verbs.* figure in.** To include, as in making an account. **figure on.** *Informal.* **1.** To depend on. **2.** To take into consideration; expect. **3.** To plan. **figure out.** *Informal.* **1.** To discover or decide. **2.** To solve or decipher. [ME < OFr. < Lat. *figūra*. See **dheigh-***.] **— fig′ur•er** *n.*

fig•ured (fĭg′yərd) *adj.* **1.** Shaped or fashioned in a particular way. **2.** Decorated with a design; patterned. **3.** Represented, as in graphic art or sculpture; depicted.

figured bass (bās) *n. Mus.* See **continuo.**

figure eight *n.* A form or representation, such as a knot or an ice-skating maneuver, that has the shape of the numeral 8.

fig•ure•head (fĭg′yər-hĕd′) *n.* **1.** A person given a position of nominal leadership but having no actual authority. **2.** *Naut.* A carved figure on the prow of a ship.

figure of speech *n.*, *pl.* **figures of speech.** An expression, such as a metaphor or hyperbole, in which words are used in a nonliteral way or a device, such as anaphora or chiasmus, in which normal word patterns are repeated or altered, as a means of heightening rhetorical effect.

figure skat•ing (skā′tĭng) *n. Sports.* Ice skating involving defined, usu. elaborate figures. **—figure skater** *n.*

fig•u•rine (fĭg′yə-rēn′) *n.* A small molded or sculptured figure; a statuette. [Fr. < Ital. *figurina*, dim. of *figura*, figure < Lat. *figūra*. See FIGURE.]

fig•wort (fĭg′wûrt′, -wôrt′) *n.* Any of various plants of the genus *Scrophularia*, having loose branching clusters of small greenish or purple flowers. [< FIG[1], piles (obsolete).]

Fi•ji (fē′jē). An island country of the SW Pacific comprising c. 320 islands; annexed by Great Britain in 1874 and gained independence in 1970. Cap. Suva. Pop. 686,000.

Fi•ji•an (fē′jē-ən) *n.* **1.** A native or inhabitant of Fiji. **2.** The Austronesian language of Fiji. *—adj.* Of or relating to Fiji or its people, language, or culture.

fi•la (fī′lə) *n.* Pl. of **filum.**

fil•a•ment (fĭl′ə-mənt) *n.* **1.** A fine or thinly spun thread, fiber, or wire. **2.** *Bot.* **a.** The stalk that bears the anther in a stamen. **b.** A chainlike series of cells, as in many algae. **3.a.** A fine wire heated electrically to incandescence in an electric lamp. **b.** *Electron.* A high-resistance wire or ribbon forming the cathode in some thermionic tubes. [NLat. *fīlāmentum* < LLat. *fīlāre*, to spin < Lat. *fīlum*, thread. See **gʷhī-*.**] **—fil′a•men′tous** (-mĕn′təs), **fil′a•men′ta•ry** (-mĕn′tə-rē, -mĕn′trē) *adj.*

fi•lar (fī′lər) *adj.* **1.** Of or relating to a thread. **2.** Having fine threads across the field of view for measuring small distances, as in a telescope eyepiece. [< Lat. *fīlum*, thread. See **gʷhī-*.**]

fil•a•ree (fĭl′ə-rē′) *n.* See **alfilaria.** [Alteration of ALFILARIA.]

fi•lar•i•a (fə-lâr′ē-ə) *n.*, *pl.* **-i•ae** (-ē-ē′). Any of various threadlike parasitic nematodes of the superfamily Filarioidea that live in the blood and lymphatic tissues and usu. develop as larvae in mosquitos and other biting insects. [NLat. *Filāria*, former genus name < Lat. *fīlum*, thread. See **gʷhī-*.**] **—fi•lar′i•al** (-ē-əl), **fi•lar′i•an** (-ē-ən) *adj.*

fil•a•ri•a•sis (fĭl′ə-rī′ə-sĭs) *n.*, *pl.* **-ses** (-sēz′). Disease caused by infestation of tissue with filariae. [FILAR(IA) + -IASIS.]

fil•a•ture (fĭl′ə-cho͝or′, -chər) *n.* **1.** The act or process of spinning, drawing, or twisting into threads. **2.** The act or process of reeling raw silk from cocoons. **3.** A reel used in drawing silk from cocoons. **4.** An establishment where silk is reeled. [Fr. < LLat. *fīlātus*, p.part. of *fīlāre*, to spin. See FILAMENT.]

fil•bert (fĭl′bərt) *n.* **1.** See **hazel** 1. **2.** See **hazelnut.** [ME < AN *philber*, after St. *Philibert* (d. 684), whose feast day in late August coincides with the ripening of the nut.]

filch (fĭlch) *tr.v.* **filched, filch•ing, filch•es.** To take (something, esp. something of little value) in a furtive manner; snitch. [ME *filchen*.] **—filch′er** *n.*

Filch•ner Ice Shelf (fĭlk′nər). An area of Antarctica at the head of Weddell Sea; first explored in 1912.

file[1] (fīl) *n.* **1.** A container, such as a cabinet or folder, for keeping papers in order. **2.a.** A collection of papers or published materials kept or arranged in convenient order. **b.** *Comp. Sci.* A collection of related data or program records. **3.a.** A line of persons, animals, or things positioned one behind the other. **b.** A line of troops or military vehicles so positioned. **4.** *Games.* Any of the rows of squares that run vertically or between players on a chessboard or checkerboard. **5.** *Archaic.* A list or roll. *—v.* **filed, fil•ing, files.** *—tr.* **1.** To put or keep (papers, for example) in useful order for storage or reference. **2.** To enter (a legal document) on public official record. **3.** To send or submit (copy) to a newspaper. **4.** To carry out the first stage of (a lawsuit, for example): *filed charges.* *—intr.* **1.** To march or walk in a line. **2.** To put items in a file. **3.** To make application; apply: *file for a divorce.* **4.** To enter one's name in a political contest. ***—idiom.* on file.** In or as if in a file for easy reference. [< ME *filen*, to put documents on file < OFr. *filer*, to spin thread, to put documents on a thread < LLat. *fīlāre*, to spin, draw out in a long line < Lat. *fīlum*, thread. See **gʷhī-*.**]

file[2] (fīl) *n.* **1.** Any of several hardened steel tools with cutting ridges for forming, smoothing, or reducing esp. metallic surfaces. **2.** A nail file. **3.** *Chiefly British.* A crafty or artful person. *—tr.v.* **filed, fil•ing, files.** To smooth, reduce, or remove with or as if with a file. [ME < OE *fīl*. See **peig-*.**]

file[3] (fīl) *tr.v.* **filed, fil•ing, files.** *Archaic.* To make sullied or corrupt; defile. [ME *filien* < OE *fȳlan*. See **pū̆-*.**]

fi•lé (fē′lā, fĭ-lā′) *n.* Powdered sassafras leaves used to thicken and season soups, stews, and gumbos. [Louisiana Fr. < Fr., p.part. of *filer*, to spin thread < OFr. See FILE[1].]

file•fish (fīl′fĭsh′) *n.*, *pl.* **filefish** or **-fish•es.** Any of various chiefly tropical marine fishes of the family Balistidae with a flat body and rough spiny scales.

fi•let[1] (fĭ-lā′, fĭl′ā′) *n.* A net or lace with a simple pattern of squares. [Fr. < OFr., dim. of *fil*, thread < Lat. *fīlum.* See FILE[1].]

fi•let[2] (fĭ-lā′, fĭl′ā′) *n.* Var. of **fillet** 2. *—v.* Var. of **fillet** 2.

fi•let mi•gnon (fĭ-lā′ mēn-yôN′, fĭl′ā) *n.*, *pl.* **fi•lets mi•gnons** (fĭ-lā′ mēn-yôN′, fĭl′ā). A small, round, very choice cut of beef from the loin. [Fr. : *filet*, fillet + *mignon*, dainty.]

fil•i•al (fĭl′ē-əl) *adj.* **1.** Of, relating to, or befitting a son or daughter. **2.** Having or assuming the relationship of child or offspring to parent. **3.** *Genet.* Of or relating to a generation or the sequence of generations following the parental generation. [ME < OFr. < LLat. *fīliālis* < Lat. *fīlius*, son. See **dhē(i)-*.**] **—fil′i•al•ly** *adv.*

fil•i•a•tion (fĭl′ē-ā′shən) *n.* **1.** The condition or fact of being the child of a certain parent. **2.** A line of descent; derivation. **3.a.** The act or fact of forming a new branch, as of a society or language group. **b.** The branch thus formed.

fil•i•bus•ter (fĭl′ə-bŭs′tər) *n.* **1.a.** The use of obstructionist tactics, esp. prolonged speechmaking, in order to delay legislative action. **b.** An instance of the use of this delaying tactic. **2.** An adventurer who engages in a private military action in a foreign country. *—v.* **-tered, -ter•ing, -ters.** *—intr.* **1.** To use obstructionist tactics in a legislative body. **2.** To take part in a private military action in a foreign country. *—tr.* To use obstructionist tactics against (a legislative measure, for example). [< Sp. *filibustero*, freebooter < Fr. *flibustier* < Du. *vrijbuiter*, pirate. See FREEBOOTER.] **—fil′i•bus′ter•er** *n.*

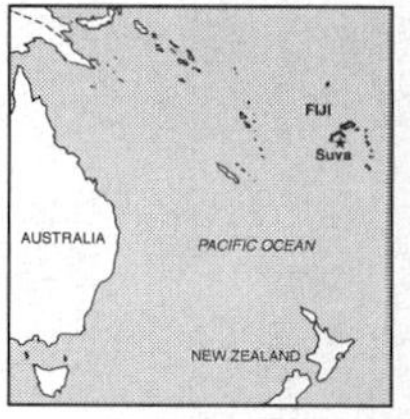

Fiji

fil•i•form (fĭl′ə-fôrm′, fī′lə-) *adj.* Having the form of or resembling a thread or filament. [Lat. *fīlum*, thread; see **gʷhī-*** + -FORM.]

fil•i•gree (fĭl′ĭ-grē′) *n.* **1.** Delicate and intricate ornamental work made of gold, silver, or other fine twisted wire. **2.a.** An intricate, delicate, or fanciful ornamentation. **b.** A design resembling such ornamentation. *—tr.v.* **-greed, -gree•ing, -grees.** To decorate with or as if with filigree. [Alteration of Fr. *filigrane* < Ital. *filigrana* : Lat. *fīlum*, thread; see **gʷhī-*** + Lat. *grānum*, grain; see **gr̥ə-no-*.**]

fil•ing (fī′lĭng) *n.* **1.** A particle or shaving removed by a file. **2.** The act or an instance of using a file.

fil•i•o•pi•e•tis•tic (fĭl′ē-ō-pī′ĭ-tĭs′tĭk) *adj.* Of or relating to an often immoderate reverence for forebears or tradition. [Lat. *fīlius*, son; see FILIAL + PIETISTIC.]

Fil•i•pi•no (fĭl′ə-pē′nō) *n.*, *pl.* **-nos. 1.** A native or inhabitant of the Philippines. **2.** The Austronesian language based on Tagalog that draws its lexicon from other Philippine languages and is the official language of the Philippines. *—adj.* Of or relating to the Philippines or its peoples, languages, or cultures. [Sp. < *(Islas) Filipinas*, Philippine (Islands).]

fill (fĭl) *v.* **filled, fill•ing, fills.** *—tr.* **1.a.** To put into as much as can be held. **b.** To supply to the fullest extent. **c.** To build up the level of (low-lying land) with material such as earth or gravel. **d.** To stop or plug up (an opening, for example). **e.** To repair a cavity in (a tooth). **f.** To add a foreign substance to (cloth or wood, for example). **2.a.** To satiate, as with food and drink. **b.** To satisfy or meet; fulfill. See Syns at **satisfy. c.** To complete (something) by insertion or addition: *fill in the blanks.* **d.** To supply with material, such as writing. **3.** To supply as required: *fill a prescription.* **4.a.** To place a person in: *fill a job vacancy.* **b.** To possess and discharge the duties of; hold. **5.a.** To occupy the whole of; pervade. **b.** To spread throughout. **c.** To engage or occupy completely; make full: *our hearts filled with joy.* **6.** To cover the surface of (an inexpensive metal) with a layer of precious metal. **7.** *Naut.* To cause (a sail) to swell. *—intr.* **1.** To become full. **2.** To swell. Used of a sail. *—n.* **1.** An amount needed to make full, complete, or satisfied. **2.** Material for filling a container, cavity, or passage. **3.a.** A built-up piece of land; an embankment. **b.** The material, such as gravel, used for this. ***—phrasal verbs.* fill in. 1.** *Informal.* To provide with information that is essential or newly acquired. **2.** To act as a substitute; stand in. **fill out. 1.** To complete (a form, for example) by providing required information. **2.** To become or make more fleshy. ***—idioms.* fill (someone's) shoes.** To assume someone's position or duties. **fill the bill.** *Informal.* To serve a particular purpose. [ME *fillen* < OE *fyllan.* See **pelə-[1]*.**]

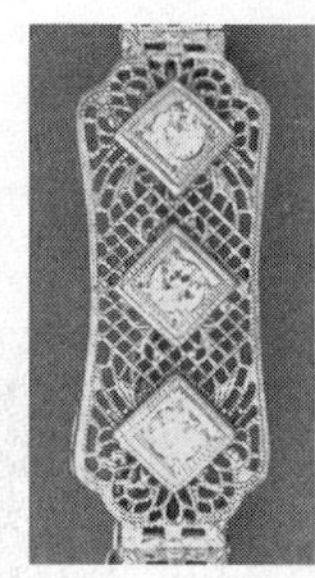
filigree
Detail of a bracelet

filled gold (fĭld) *n.* A relatively inexpensive metal such as brass with a surface layer of bonded gold.

filled milk *n.* Skim milk with vegetable oils added to substitute for butterfat.

fill•er (fĭl′ər) *n.* One that fills, as: **a.** Something added in order to augment weight or size or fill space. **b.** A composition, esp. a semisolid that hardens on drying, used to fill pores, cracks, or holes in construction surfaces before finishing. **c.** Tobacco used to form the body of a cigar. **d.** A short item used to fill space in a publication. **e.** Something used to fill time on radio or television. **f.** A sheaf of loose papers used to fill a notebook or binder. **g.** *Archit.* An element, such as a plate, used to fill the space between two supporting members.

fil•lér (fĭl′âr′) *n.*, *pl.* **fillér** or **-lérs.** See table at **currency.** [Hung.]

fil•let (fĭl′ĭt) *n.* **1.** A narrow strip of ribbon or similar material, often worn as a headband. **2.** Also **fi•let** (fĭ-lā′, fĭl′ā′). **a.** A strip or compact piece of boneless meat or fish, esp. the beef tenderloin. **b.** A boneless strip of meat rolled and tied, as for roasting. **3.** *Archit.* **a.** A thin flat molding used as separation between or ornamentation for larger moldings. **b.** A ridge between the indentations of a fluted column. **4.** A narrow

ă pat	oi boy
ā pay	ou out
âr care	o͝o took
ä father	o͞o boot
ĕ pet	ŭ cut
ē be	ûr urge
ĭ pit	th thin
ī pie	*th* this
îr pier	hw which
ŏ pot	zh vision
ō toe	ə about, item
ô paw	

Stress marks:
′ (primary);
′ (secondary), as in
dictionary (dĭk′shə-nĕr′ē)

decorative line impressed onto the cover of a book. **5.** *Her.* A narrow horizontal band placed in the lower fourth area of the chief. **6.** *Anat.* A loop-shaped band of fibers, such as the lemniscus. — *tr.v.* **-let•ed, -let•ing, -lets. 1.** To bind or decorate with or as if with a fillet. **2.** Also **fi•let** (fĭ-lā′, fĭl′ā′). To slice, bone, or make into fillets. [ME *filet* < OFr., dim. of *fil,* thread < Lat. *fīlum.* See **gʷhī-***.]

fill-in (fĭl′ĭn′) *n. Informal.* **1.** One that serves as a substitute for another. **2.** A short informative summary.

fill•ing (fĭl′ĭng) *n.* **1.** An act or instance of filling. **2.** Something used to fill a space, cavity, or container. **3.** An edible mixture used to fill pastries, sandwiches, or cakes. **4.** The horizontal threads that cross the warp in weaving; weft.

filling station *n.* See **service station** 1.

fil•lip (fĭl′əp) *n.* **1.** A snap or light blow made by pressing a fingertip against the thumb and suddenly releasing it. **2.** A slight goad or incentive; a small stimulus. — *tr.v.* **-liped, -lip•ing, -lips.** To strike, propel, arouse, or stimulate. [Imit.]

Fill•more (fĭl′môr′, -mōr′), **Millard.** 1800–74. The 13th President of the U.S. (1850–53), who succeeded to office after the death of Zachary Taylor.

fil•ly (fĭl′ē) *n., pl.* **-lies. 1.** A young female horse. **2.** *Informal.* A lively high-spirited girl. [ME *filli* < ON *fylja.* See **pau-***.]

film (fĭlm) *n.* **1.** A thin skin or membrane. **2.** A thin opaque abnormal coating on the cornea of the eye. **3.** A thin covering or coating: *a film of dust.* **4.** A thin flexible transparent sheet, as of plastic, used in wrapping or packaging. **5.a.** A thin sheet or strip of flexible material, such as a cellulose derivative, coated with a photosensitive emulsion and used to make photographic negatives or transparencies. **b.** A sheet or strip of developed photographic negatives or transparencies. **6.a.** A movie. **b.** Movies considered as a group. **7.** A coating of magnetic alloys on glass used in manufacturing computer storage devices. — *v.* **filmed, film•ing, films.** — *tr.* **1.** To cover with or as if with a film. **2.** To make a movie of or based on: *film a rocket launch.* — *intr.* **1.** To become coated or obscured with or as if with a film. **2.** To make or shoot scenes for a movie. [ME < OE *filmen.* See **pel-³***.]

film•card (fĭlm′kärd′) *n.* A microfiche.

film•dom (fĭlm′dəm) *n.* **1.** The movie industry. **2.** The people employed in the movie industry.

film•go•er (fĭlm′gō′ər) *n.* One who frequently goes to see movies. — **film′go′ing** *adj.*

film•ic (fĭl′mĭk) *adj.* Of, relating to, or characteristic of movies; cinematic. — **film′i•cal•ly** *adv.*

film•mak•er (fĭlm′mā′kər) *n.* One who directs or produces movies.

film•mak•ing (fĭlm′mā′kĭng) *n.* The making of movies.

film•og•ra•phy (fĭl-mŏg′rə-fē) *n., pl.* **-phies.** A list of movies, as of a given director or actor. — **film•og′ra•pher** *n.*

film•set•ting (fĭlm′sĕt′ĭng) *n.* Photocomposition.

film•strip (fĭlm′strĭp′) *n.* A length of film containing photographs or other graphic matter prepared for still projection.

film•y (fĭl′mē) *adj.* **-i•er, -i•est. 1.** Of, resembling, or consisting of film; gauzy. See Syns at **airy. 2.** Covered by or as if by a film; hazy. — **film′i•ly** *adv.* — **film′i•ness** *n.*

fil•o•plume (fĭl′ə-plo͞om′, fī′lə-) *n.* A hairlike feather having few or no barbs, usu. located between contour feathers. [Lat. *fīlum,* thread; see **gʷhī-*** + PLUME.]

fi•lose (fī′lōs′) *adj.* **1.** Threadlike. **2.** Having or ending in a threadlike part or process. [Lat. *fīlum,* thread; see **gʷhī-*** + -OSE¹.]

fils¹ (fēs) *n.* Used to distinguish a son from his father when they have the same given name. [Fr. < Lat. *fīlius,* son. See **dhē(i)-***.]

fils² (fĭls) *n., pl.* **fils.** See table at **currency.** [Ar. *fals, fils* < Lat. *follis,* bellows, purse, piece of money. See **bhel-²***.]

fil•ter (fĭl′tər) *n.* **1.a.** A porous material through which a liquid or gas is passed to separate the fluid from suspended particles. **b.** A device containing such a substance. **2.** Any of various electric, electronic, acoustic, or optical devices that reject signals, vibrations, or radiations of certain frequencies but pass others. — *v.* **-tered, -ter•ing, -ters.** — *tr.* **1.** To pass (a liquid or gas) through a filter. **2.** To remove by passing through a filter: *filters out sand.* — *intr.* **1.** To pass through or as if through a filter. **2.** To come or go gradually and in small groups. [ME *filtre* < OFr. < Med.Lat. *filtrum,* of Gmc. orig. See **pel-⁵***.] — **fil′ter•er** *n.* — **fil′ter•less** *adj.*

fil•ter•a•ble (fĭl′tər-ə-bəl, fĭl′trə-) also **fil•tra•ble** (-trə-bəl) *adj.* **1.** That can be filtered or separated by filtering. **2.** That can pass through a given pore size. — **fil′ter•a•bil′i•ty** *n.*

filterable virus *n.* A virus that is small enough to pass through a fine-pored filter, as of diatomite or porcelain.

filter bed *n.* A layer of sand or gravel on the bottom of a reservoir or tank, used to filter water or sewage.

filter feeder *n.* An aquatic animal, such as a clam or sponge, that feeds by filtering particulate organic material from water.

filter paper *n.* Porous paper suitable for use as a filter.

filth (fĭlth) *n.* **1.a.** Foul or dirty matter. **b.** Disgusting garbage or refuse. **2.** A dirty or corrupt condition; foulness. **3.** Something, such as language, considered obscene, prurient, or immoral. [ME < OE *fȳlth.* See **pū̆-***.]

Millard Fillmore

filth•y (fĭl′thē) *adj.* **-i•er, -i•est. 1.** Covered or smeared with filth; disgustingly dirty. **2.** Obscene; scatological. **3.** Vile; nasty: *a filthy traitor.* — **filth′i•ly** *adv.* — **filth′i•ness** *n.*

fil•trate (fĭl′trāt′) *tr. & intr.v.* **-trat•ed, -trat•ing, -trates.** To put or go through a filter. — *n.* Material, esp. liquid, passed through a filter. [NLat. *filtrāre, filtrāt-,* to filter < Med.Lat. *filtrum,* filter. See FILTER.]

fil•tra•tion (fĭl-trā′shən) *n.* The act or process of filtering.

fi•lum (fī′ləm) *n., pl.* **-la** (-lə). A threadlike anatomical structure; a filament. [Lat. *fīlum,* thread. See **gʷhī-***.]

fim•bri•a (fĭm′brē-ə) *n., pl.* **-bri•ae** (-brē-ē′). A fringelike part or structure, as at the opening of the fallopian tubes. [LLat. *fimbria,* fringe, fem. sing. of Lat. *fimbriae,* threads, fringe.] — **fim′bri•al** *adj.*

fim•bri•ate (fĭm′brē-ĭt, -āt′) also **fim•bri•at•ed** (-ā′tĭd) *adj.* Having fimbriae; fringed, as the edge of a petal. [Lat. *fimbriātus* < *fimbriae,* fringe.] — **fim′bri•a′tion** *n.*

fin¹ (fĭn) *n.* **1.** A membranous appendage extending from the body of a fish or other aquatic animal, for propelling, steering, or balancing the body in the water. **2.** Something resembling a fin, as: **a.** An airfoil used to stabilize an aircraft, a missile, or a projectile in flight. **b.** A projecting vane for cooling, as on a radiator or an engine cylinder. **c.** See **tail fin** 2. **3.** See **flipper** 2. — *v.* **finned, fin•ning, fins.** — *tr.* To equip with fins. — *intr.* **1.** To emerge with the fins above water. **2.** To swim, as a fish. **3.** To lash the water with the fins. Used of a dying whale. [ME < OE *finn.*]

fin² (fĭn) *n. Slang.* A five-dollar bill. [Yiddish *finf,* five < OHGer. *funf, finf.* See **penkʷe***.]

fin. *abbr.* **1.** Finance; financial. **2.** Finish.

Fin. *abbr.* Finland; Finnish.

fi•na•gle (fə-nā′gəl) *v.* **-gled, -gling, -gles.** — *tr.* **1.** To obtain or achieve by indirect, usu. deceitful methods: *finagle a day off.* **2.** To cheat; swindle. — *intr.* To use crafty, deceitful methods. [Prob. < dial. *fainaigue,* to cheat.] — **fi•na′gler** *n.*

fi•nal (fī′nəl) *adj.* **1.** Forming or occurring at the end; last. **2.** Of or constituting the end result of a succession or process; ultimate. **3.** Not to be changed or reconsidered; unalterable. See Syns at **last¹.** — *n.* Something that comes at or forms the end, esp.: **a.** The last or one of the last of a series of contests. **b.** The last examination of an academic course. [ME < OFr. < Lat. *fīnālis* < *fīnis,* end.] — **fi′nal•ly** *adv.*

fi•nal•e (fə-năl′ē, -nä′lē) *n.* The concluding part, esp. of a musical composition. [Ital. < Lat. *fīnālis,* final. See FINAL.]

fi•nal•ist (fī′nə-lĭst) *n.* A contestant in the final session of a competition.

fi•nal•i•ty (fī-năl′ĭ-tē, fə-) *n., pl.* **-ties. 1.** The condition or fact of being final. **2.** A final, conclusive, or decisive act.

fi•nal•ize (fī′nə-līz′) *tr.v.* **-ized, -iz•ing, -iz•es.** *Usage Problem.* To put into final form; complete or conclude. — **fi′nal•i•za′tion** (-nə-lĭ-zā′shən) *n.* — **fi′nal•iz′er** *n.*

Usage Note: *Finalize* is frequently associated with the language of bureaucracy and so is objected to by many writers. The sentence *We will finalize plans for a class reunion* was unacceptable to 71 percent of the Usage Panel. A substitute can always be found from among *complete, conclude, make final,* and *put into final form.* See Usage Note at **-ize.**

fi•nance (fə-năns′, fī-, fī′năns′) *n.* **1.** The science of the management of money and other assets. **2.** The management of money, banking, investments, and credit. **3. finances.** Monetary resources; funds, esp. those of a government or corporate body. **4.** The supplying of funds or capital. — *tr.v.* **-nanced, -nanc•ing, -nanc•es. 1.** To provide or raise the funds or capital for. **2.** To supply funds to: *financing her through law school.* **3.** To furnish credit to. [ME *finaunce,* settlement, money supply < OFr. *finance,* payment < *finer,* to pay ransom < *fin,* end < Lat. *fīnis.*] — **fi•nance′a•ble** *adj.*

finance company *n.* A company that makes loans to clients.

fi•nan•cial (fə-năn′shəl, fī-) *adj.* Of, relating to, or involving finance, finances, or financiers. — **fi•nan′cial•ly** *adv.*

Syns: *financial, pecuniary, fiscal, monetary.* These adjectives mean of or relating to money. *Financial* frequently refers to transactions involving money on a large scale: *corporations with financial reverses. Pecuniary* is more appropriate to the private small-scale dealings of individuals: *pecuniary compensation. Fiscal* applies especially to a nation's financial practices and policies: *chief fiscal officer of our government. Monetary* has special reference to the coinage, printing, or circulation of currency: *The dollar is a monetary unit.*

fin•an•cier (fĭn′ən-sîr′, fə-năn′-, fī′nən-) *n.* One who is occupied with or expert in large-scale financial affairs. [Fr. < OFr. < *finance,* payment. See FINANCE.]

fin•back (fĭn′băk′) *n.* A rorqual, esp. *Balaenoptera physalus* of the Atlantic and Pacific coasts, that attains a length of about 21 meters (70 feet).

fin•ca (fĭng′kə, fĕng′kä) *n.* A rural property, esp. a large farm or ranch, in Spanish America. [Am.Sp. < Sp., real estate < OSp. *fincar,* to pitch tents, reside < VLat. **fingicāre* < Lat. *figere,* to fasten. See **dhīgʷ-***.]

finch (fĭnch) *n.* Any of various small birds of the family Fringillidae, including the goldfinches, sparrows, and canaries, having a short stout bill for cracking seeds. [ME < OE *finc.*]

find (fīnd) *v.* **found** (found), **find•ing, finds.** —*tr.* **1.** To come upon, often by accident; meet with. **2.** To come upon after a search. **3.** To discover or ascertain through observation, experience, or study. **4.a.** To perceive to be, after experience or consideration. **b.** To experience or feel: *found comfort.* **5.** To recover (something lost). **6.** To recover the use of; regain. **7.** To succeed in reaching; arrive at. **8.** To obtain or acquire by effort. **9.** To decide on and make a declaration about: *The jurors found him guilty.* **10.** To furnish; supply. **11.a.** To bring (oneself) to an awareness of what one truly wishes to be and do in life. **b.** To perceive (oneself) to be in a specific place or condition. —*intr.* To come to a legal decision or verdict. —*n.* **1.** The act of finding. **2.** Something that is found, esp. an unexpectedly valuable discovery. —***phrasal verb.* find out. 1.** To ascertain (something), as by examination or inquiry. **2.** To detect the true nature or character of; expose. **3.** To detect and apprehend; catch. [ME *finden* < OE *findan.* See **pent-*.**] —**find′a•ble** *adj.*

find•er (fīn′dər) *n.* **1.** One that finds. **2.** A viewfinder. **3.** A low-power wide-angle telescope fixed to one more powerful and pointed the same way for initially locating an object.

fin-de-siè•cle (făN′də-sē-ĕk′lə) *adj.* Of or characteristic of the last part of the 19th century, esp. regarding its artistic, effete sophistication. [Fr. : *fin,* end + *de,* of + *siècle,* century.]

find•ing (fīn′dĭng) *n.* **1.** Something found. **2.a.** A conclusion reached after examination or investigation: *a coroner's findings.* **b.** A statement or document containing an authoritative decision or conclusion. **3. findings.** Small tools and materials used by an artisan.

Find•lay (fĭnd′lē). A city of NW OH S of Toledo. Pop. 35,703.

fine[1] (fīn) *adj.* **fin•er, fin•est. 1.** Of superior quality, skill, or appearance. **2.** Very small in size, weight, or thickness. **3.a.** Free from impurities. **b.** *Metall.* Containing pure metal in a specified proportion or amount: *gold 21 carats fine.* **4.** Very sharp; keen: *a blade with a fine edge.* **5.** Thin; slender: *fine hairs.* **6.** Exhibiting careful and delicate artistry: *fine china.* See Syns at **delicate. 7.** Consisting of very small particles; not coarse: *fine dust.* **8.a.** Subtle or precise. **b.** Able to make or detect effects of great subtlety or precision; sensitive. **9.** Trained to the highest degree of physical efficiency: *a fine racehorse.* **10.** Characterized by refinement or elegance. **11.** Being in a state of satisfactory health; quite well: *I'm fine. And you?* **12.** Used as an intensive: *a fine mess.* —*adv.* **1.** Finely. **2.** *Informal.* Very well. —*tr. & intr.v.* **fined, fin•ing, fines.** To make or become finer, purer, or cleaner. [ME *fin* < OFr. < Lat. *fīnis,* end.] —**fine′ness** *n.*

fine[2] (fīn) *n.* **1.** A sum of money to be paid as a penalty for an offense. **2.** *Law.* **a.** A forfeiture or penalty to be paid to the offended party in a civil action. **b.** An amicable settlement of a suit over land ownership. **3.** *Obsolete.* An end; a termination. —*tr.v.* **fined, fin•ing, fines.** To require the payment of a fine from; impose a fine on. —***idiom.* in fine. 1.** In conclusion; finally. **2.** In summation; in brief. [ME *fin* < OFr., settlement, compensation < Med.Lat. *fīnis* < Lat. *fīnis,* end.] —**fin′a•ble, fine′a•ble** *adj.*

fi•ne[3] (fē′nā) *n. Mus.* The end. [Ital. < Lat. *fīnis,* end.]

fine art (fīn) *n.* **1.a.** Art produced or intended for beauty, not utility. **b.** Any of the art forms, such as music, used to create this art. Often used in the plural. **2.** Something requiring highly developed technique and skill: *the fine art of teaching.*

fine-drawn (fīn′drôn′) *adj.* **1.** Drawn out to a slender threadlike state. **2.** Subtly or precisely fashioned: *a fine-drawn theory.* **3.** Delicately formed: *fine-drawn features.*

fine-grained (fīn′grānd′) *adj.* Having a fine, smooth, even grain: *fine-grained wood.*

fine•ly (fīn′lē) *adv.* **1.** In a fine manner; splendidly. **2.** To a fine point; discriminatingly. **3.** In small pieces or parts; minutely.

fine print (fīn) *n.* **1.** The part of a document, esp. a contract, containing qualifications or restrictions in small type or obscure language. **2.** Something presented so as to be ambiguous or obscure.

fin•er•y (fī′nə-rē) *n., pl.* **-ies.** Elaborate adornment, esp. fine clothing and accessories.

fines herbes (fēn zĕrb′, fēn ĕrb′) *pl.n.* Finely chopped herbs, esp. parsley, chives, tarragon, and thyme, used together as a seasoning. [Fr. : *fines,* fem. pl. of *fin,* fine + *herbes,* pl. of *herbe,* herb.]

fine-spun (fīn′spŭn′) *adj.* **1.** Developed to extreme fineness or subtlety; elaborate. **2.** Excessively fine or subtle; overwrought.

fi•nesse (fə-nĕs′) *n.* **1.** Refinement and delicacy of performance, execution, or artisanship. **2.** Skillful subtle handling of a situation; tactful diplomatic maneuvering. **3.** *Games.* A method of leading up to a tenace to prevent an opponent from winning the trick with an intermediate card. **4.** A stratagem in which one appears to decline an advantage. —*v.* **-nessed, -ness•ing, -ness•es.** —*tr.* **1.** To accomplish by the use of finesse. **2.** To handle with a deceptive or evasive strategy. **3.** *Games.* To play (a card) in a finesse. —*intr.* **1.** To use finesse. **2.** *Games.* To make use of a finesse in cards. [Fr., fineness, subtlety < *fin,* fine. See FINE[1].]

fine structure (fīn) *n.* **1.** *Phys.* The splitting of spectral lines caused by the magnetic moments of orbiting electrons in the atomic nucleus. **2.** *Biol.* See **ultrastructure.**

fine-toothed comb (fīn′tōōtht′, -tōōthd′) *n.* **1.** A comb with teeth set close together. **2.** A thorough method of searching or investigating in minute detail.

fine-tune (fīn′tōōn′, -tyōōn′) *tr.v.* **-tuned, -tun•ing, -tunes.** To adjust minutely for optimal performance or effectiveness.

fin•fish (fĭn′fĭsh′) *n.* A true fish, as opposed to a shellfish.

Fin•gal's Cave (fĭng′gəlz). A cavern of W Scotland on Staffa I. in the Inner Hebrides.

fin•ger (fĭng′gər) *n.* **1.** One of the five digits of the hand, esp. one other than the thumb. **2.** The part of a glove designed to cover a finger. **3.** Something, such as an oblong peninsula, that resembles a digit of the hand. **4.** The length or width of a finger. **5.** A degree of participation; a share. **6.** An obscene gesture of defiance or derision made by pointing or jabbing the middle finger upward. Often used with *the.* —*v.* **-gered, -ger•ing, -gers.** —*tr.* **1.** To touch with the fingers; handle. **2.** *Mus.* **a.** To mark (a score) with indications of which fingers are to play the notes. **b.** To play (an instrument) by using the fingers in a particular order or way. **3.** *Slang.* **a.** To inform on. **b.** To designate, esp. as an intended victim. —*intr.* **1.** To handle something with the fingers. **2.** *Mus.* To use the fingers in playing an instrument. —***idioms.* have** (or **keep**) **(one's) fingers crossed.** To hope for a successful or advantageous outcome. **twist** (or **wrap**) **around (one's) little finger.** To dominate utterly and effortlessly. [ME < OE. See **penkʷe*.**] —**fin′ger•er** *n.* —**fin′ger•less** *adj.*

fin•ger•board (fĭng′gər-bôrd′, -bōrd′) *n. Mus.* A strip of wood on the neck of a stringed instrument against which the strings are pressed in playing.

finger bowl *n.* A bowl with water for rinsing the fingers at the table.

fin•ger•breadth (fĭng′gər-brĕdth′) *n.* The breadth of one finger.

fin•gered (fĭng′gərd) *adj.* Having a finger or fingers, esp. of a specific number or kind. Often used in combination.

finger hole *n.* **1.** *Mus.* Any of the holes on a wind instrument that cause a change in pitch when covered by a finger. **2.** A hole or an opening for a finger, as in a bowling ball.

fin•ger•ing (fĭng′gər-ĭng) *n. Mus.* **1.** The technique used in playing an instrument with the fingers. **2.** The indication on a score of which fingers are to be used in playing.

Fin•ger Lakes (fĭng′gər). A group of 11 elongated glacial lakes in W-central NY.

fin•ger•ling (fĭng′gər-lĭng) *n.* A young or small fish, esp. a young salmon or trout.

finger millet *n.* An annual plant *(Eleusine coracana)* in the grass family, native to the Old World tropics.

fin•ger•nail (fĭng′gər-nāl′) *n.* The nail on a finger.

fin•ger-paint (fĭng′gər-pānt′) *tr. & intr.v.* **-paint•ed, -paint•ing, -paints.** To make by or engage in finger painting.

finger painting *n.* **1.** The technique of painting by applying color to moistened paper with the fingers. **2.** A picture so made.

fin•ger•pick (fĭng′gər-pĭk′) *v.* **-picked, -pick•ing, -picks.** —*intr.* To play a stringed instrument, such as the guitar, by plucking individual strings with the fingers. —*tr.* To play (a stringed instrument) in this manner. —**fin′ger•pick′er** *n.*

finger pick *n.* A pointed, slightly curved plectrum worn on the fingertip, used in playing the guitar, for example.

finger post *n.* A guidepost in the shape of a pointing hand.

fin•ger•print (fĭng′gər-prĭnt′) *n.* **1.** An impression on a surface of the curves formed by the ridges on a fingertip, esp. when made in ink and used as a means of identification. **2.** A distinctive or identifying mark or characteristic. —*tr.v.* **-print•ed, -print•ing, -prints. 1.** To take the fingerprints of. **2.** To identify by means of a distinctive mark or characteristic.

fingerprint

fin•ger•spell•ing (fĭng′gər-spĕl′ĭng) *n.* Communication by means of a manual alphabet. —**fin′ger•spell′** *v.*

fin•ger•tip (fĭng′gər-tĭp′) *n.* The extreme end or tip of a finger. —***idiom.* at (one's) fingertips.** Readily available.

finger wave *n.* A wave set into dampened hair using only the fingers and a comb.

fin•i•al (fĭn′ē-əl) *n.* **1.** *Archit.* An ornament fixed to the peak of an arch or arched structure. **2.** An ornamental terminating part, such as the screw on top of a lampshade. [ME, last, finial, var. of *final.* See FINAL.]

fin•i•cal (fĭn′ĭ-kəl) *adj.* Finicky. [Prob. < FINE[1].] —**fin′i•cal•ly** *adv.* —**fin′i•cal•ness** *n.*

fin•ick•y (fĭn′ĭ-kē) *adj.* **-i•er, -i•est.** Insisting capriciously on getting just what one wants; hard to please: *a finicky eater.* [< *finick,* a finical person < FINICAL.] —**fin′ick•i•ness** *n.*

fin•is (fĭn′ĭs, fī′nĭs, fē-nē′) *n.* The end; the conclusion. [ME < Lat. *fīnis.*]

fin•ish (fĭn′ĭsh) *v.* **-ished, -ish•ing, -ish•es.** —*tr.* **1.** To arrive at or attain the end of. **2.** To bring to an end; terminate. **3.** To consume all of; use up. **4.** To bring to a desired or required state: *finish a painting.* **5.** To give (wood, for example) a desired or particular surface texture. **6.** To destroy; kill. **7.** To bring about the ruin of. —*intr.* **1.** To come to an end; stop. **2.** To reach the end of a task, course, or relationship.

ă **pat**	oi **boy**
ā **pay**	ou **out**
âr **care**	ŏŏ **took**
ä **father**	ōō **boot**
ĕ **pet**	ŭ **cut**
ē **be**	ûr **urge**
ĭ **pit**	th **thin**
ī **pie**	*th* **this**
îr **pier**	hw **which**
ŏ **pot**	zh **vision**
ō **toe**	ə **about, item**
ô **paw**	

Stress marks:
′ (primary);
′ (secondary), as in
dictionary (dĭk′shə-nĕr′ē)

— *n.* **1.** The final part; the conclusion. **2.** The reason for one's ruin; downfall. **3.** Something that completes, concludes, or perfects, esp.: **a.** The last treatment or coating of a surface. **b.** The surface texture produced by such a treatment or coating. **c.** A material used in surfacing or finishing. **4.** Completeness, thoroughness, refinement, or smoothness of execution; polish. [ME *finishen* < OFr. *finir, finiss-*, to complete < Lat. *fīnīre* < *fīnis*, end.] —**fin′ish·er** *n.*

fin·ished (fĭn′ĭsht) *adj.* **1.** Accomplished; expert; polished: *a finished artist.* **2.** Exhibiting much skill or polish.

fin·ish·ing school (fĭn′ĭ-shĭng) *n.* A private girls' school that stresses training in cultural subjects and social activities.

finishing touch *n.* A small change or addition that serves to complete something.

finish line *n. Sports.* A line that marks the end of a course for racing.

fi·nite (fī′nīt′) *adj.* **1.a.** Having bounds; limited: *finite fuel reserves.* **b.** Existing, persisting, or enduring for a limited time only; impermanent. **2.** *Math.* **a.** Being neither infinite nor infinitesimal. **b.** Having a positive or negative numerical value; not zero. **c.** Having a limited number of elements. Used of a set. **3.** *Gram.* Limited, as by person and number. Used of a verb that can serve as or in a predicate. —*n.* A finite thing. [ME *finit* < Lat. *fīnītus*, p.part. of *fīnīre*, to limit < *fīnis*, end.] —**fi′nite′ly** *adv.* —**fi′nite′ness** *n.*

Finland

fin·i·tude (fĭn′ĭ-to͞od′, -tyo͞od′, fī′nĭ-) *n.* The quality or condition of being finite.

fink (fĭngk) *Slang.* —*n.* **1.** A contemptible person. **2.** An informer. **3.** A hired strikebreaker. —*intr.v.* **finked, fink·ing, finks. 1.** To inform against another person. **2.** To withhold promised support or participation; back down. [?]

Fin·land (fĭn′lənd). A country of N Europe on the Gulf of Bothnia; gained independence from Russia in 1919. Cap. Helsinki. Pop. 4,893,748. —**Fin′land·er** *n.*

Finland, Gulf of. An arm of the Baltic Sea bordering on Finland, Russia, and Estonia.

Fin·land·ize (fĭn′lən-dīz′) *tr.v.* **-ized, -iz·ing, -iz·es.** To cause (a country or other political unit) to adopt a neutral or conciliatory posture and policy in its relations with a great power. —**Fin′land·i·za′tion** *n.*

Fin·lay River (fĭn′lē). A river of N British Columbia, Canada, flowing c. 402 km (250 mi) to the Peace R.

Finn (fĭn) *n.* **1.** A native or inhabitant of Finland. **2.** One who speaks Finnish or a Finnic language. [< Swed. *Finne.*]

fin·nan had·die (fĭn′ən hăd′ē) *n.* Smoked haddock. [< alteration of *Findon* or *Findhorn*, villages of NE Scotland.]

Finn·bog·a·dót·tir (fĭn′bō-gə-dô′tər, -gä-dō′tĭr), **Vigdís.** b. 1930. President of Iceland (since 1980) and the first democratically elected woman head of state.

Vigdís Finnbogadóttir
Photographed in 1987

finned (fĭnd) *adj.* Having a fin, fins, or finlike parts. Often used in combination: *single-finned.*

Fin·nic (fĭn′ĭk) *adj.* Of or relating to Finland or the Finns. —*n.* A branch of Finno-Ugric that includes Finnish, Estonian, and Lapp.

Finn·ish (fĭn′ĭsh) *adj.* Of or relating to Finland or its people, language, or culture. —*n.* The Finno-Ugric language of the Finns.

Fin·no-U·gric (fĭn′ō-o͞o′grĭk, -yo͞o′-) also **Fin·no-U·gri·an** (-o͞o′grē-ən, -yo͞o′-) —*n.* A subfamily of the Uralic language family that includes Finnish, Hungarian, and Estonian. —*adj.* **1.** Of or relating to the Finns and the Ugrians. **2.** Of or relating to Finno-Ugric.

fin·ny (fĭn′ē) *adj.* **-ni·er, -ni·est. 1.** Having a fin or fins. **2.** Resembling a fin; finlike. **3.** Of, relating to, or full of fish.

fi·noc·chi·o also **fi·no·chi·o** (fə-nō′kē-ō′) *n.* A variety of fennel *(Foeniculum vulgare* var. *dulce)* whose blanched aromatic stalks are eaten as a vegetable. [Ital. < Lat. *fēniculum*, fennel, dim. of *fēnum*, hay. See **dhē(i)-***.]

Fin·ster·aar·horn (fĭn′stər-är′hôrn′). A peak, 4,276.7 m (14,022 ft), of the Bernese Alps in S-central Switzerland.

fin whale *n.* See **finback.**

fiord (fyôrd, fyōrd) *n.* Var. of **fjord.**

fip·ple (fĭp′əl) *n. Mus.* **1.** A mouthpiece for certain wind instruments, such as a recorder, that channels the breath toward the sounding edge of a side opening. **2.** A similar object in an organ pipe. [?]

fipple flute *n. Mus.* A flute, such as a recorder, with a fipple.

fir (fûr) *n.* **1.a.** Any of several evergreen trees of the genus *Abies*, having single flattened needles and erect cones with deciduous scales. **b.** Any of several similar or related trees, such as the Douglas fir. **2.** The wood of these trees. [ME *firre*, prob. of Scand. orig. See **perkʷu-***.] —**fir′ry** *adj.*

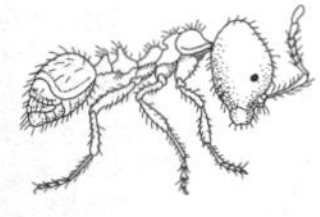

fire ant

Fir·dau·si (fĭr-dou′sē) also **Fir·du·si** (fər-do͞o′-). Abul Kasim Mansur. 940?–1020? Persian epic poet who wrote *Book of Kings* (1010), a history of Persia.

fire (fīr) *n.* **1.a.** A chemical change that releases heat and light and is accompanied by flame, esp. the exothermic oxidation of a combustible substance. **b.** Burning fuel or other material. **2.a.** Burning intensity of feeling; ardor. **b.** Enthusiasm. **3.** Luminosity or brilliance, as of a cut and polished gemstone. **4.** Liveliness and vivacity of imagination; brilliance. **5.** A severe test; a trial or torment. **6.** A fever or bodily inflammation. **7.a.** The discharge of firearms or artillery. **b.** The launching of a missile, rocket, or similar ballistic body. **c.** Discharged bullets or other projectiles. **8.** Intense, repeated attack or criticism. —*v.* **fired, fir·ing, fires.** —*tr.* **1.a.** To cause to burn; ignite. **b.** To light (something) up as if by fire. **2.a.** To add fuel to (something burning). **b.** To maintain or fuel a fire in. **3.a.** To bake in a kiln. **b.** To dry by heating. **4.** To arouse the emotions of; make enthusiastic or ardent. **5.a.** To discharge (a firearm, for example). **b.** To detonate (an explosive). **6.a.** To propel (a projectile); launch (a missile). **b.** *Informal.* To throw with force and speed; hurl. **c.** To utter or direct with insistence: *fired questions back.* **7.** *Games.* To score (a number) in a game or contest. **8.** *Informal.* To discharge from a position; dismiss. —*intr.* **1.** To become ignited; flame up. **2.a.** To become excited or ardent. **b.** To become angry or annoyed. **3.** To tend a fire. **4.a.** To shoot a weapon. **b.** To detonate an explosive. **c.** To ignite fuel, as in an engine. **5.** *Informal.* To project or hurl a missile: *The pitcher wound up and fired.* **6.** *Physiol.* To generate an electrical impulse. Used of a neuron. **7.** To become yellowed or brown before reaching maturity, as grain. —***phrasal verbs.* fire away.** *Informal.* To start to talk or ask questions. **fire off. 1.** To utter or ask rapidly. **2.** To write and send (a letter, for example) in haste. —***idioms.* on fire. 1.** Ignited; ablaze. **2.** Filled with enthusiasm or excitement. **start** (or **light** or **build) a fire under.** *Slang.* To urge or goad to action. **under fire. 1.** Exposed or subjected to enemy attack. **2.** Exposed or subjected to critical attack or censure. [ME *fir* < OE *fȳr.* See **pūr-***.] —**fire′a·ble** *adj.* —**fir′er** *n.*

fire alarm *n.* **1.** A device, such as a siren, used in announcing a fire. **2.** The signal, esp. the noise, produced by such a device.

fire ant *n.* Any of several ants of the genus *Solenopsis* of the southern United States and tropical America that cause painful stings.

fire·arm (fīr′ärm′) *n.* A weapon, esp. a pistol or rifle, capable of firing a projectile and using an explosive as a propellant.

fire·ball (fīr′bôl′) *n.* **1.** A brilliantly burning sphere. **2.** An intensely luminous, hot spherical cloud of dust, gas, and vapor from a nuclear explosion. **3.** A meteor as bright or brighter than any planet. **4.** An energetic dynamic person.

fire·bird (fīr′bûrd′) *n.* Any of various birds, such as the Baltimore oriole, having bright scarlet or orange plumage.

fire blight *n.* A destructive disease of apple and pear trees, caused by a bacterium *(Erwinia amylovora)* that blackens the leaves and kills the branches.

fire·board (fīr′bôrd′, -bōrd′) *n. Upper Southern U.S.* See **mantel** 2.

fire·boat (fīr′bōt′) *n. Naut.* A boat equipped to fight fires along waterfronts and on ships.

fire·bomb (fīr′bŏm′) *n.* A bomb used to start a fire; an incendiary bomb. —**fire′bomb′** *v.* —**fire′bomb′er** *n.*

fire·box (fīr′bŏks′) *n.* **1.** A chamber in which fuel is burned. **2.** A box containing a fire alarm.

fire·brand (fīr′brănd′) *n.* **1.** A person who stirs up trouble or kindles a revolt. **2.** A piece of burning wood.

fire·brat (fīr′brăt′) *n.* A small wingless insect *(Thermobia domestica)* inhabiting warm areas of buildings.

fire·break (fīr′brāk′) *n.* A strip of cleared or plowed land used to stop the spread of a fire.

fire·brick (fīr′brĭk′) *n.* A refractory brick, usu. made of fire clay, used to line furnaces, fireboxes, chimneys, or fireplaces.

fire brigade *n.* An organized body of firefighters.

fire·bug (fīr′bŭg′) *n. Informal.* An arsonist; a pyromaniac.

fire clay also **fire·clay** (fīr′klā′) *n.* A type of clay able to withstand intense heat, used to make firebricks, crucibles, and other objects that are exposed to high temperatures.

fire control *n.* The control of gunfire delivery on military targets.

fire·crack·er (fīr′krăk′ər) *n.* A small explosive charge and a fuse in a heavy paper casing, exploded to make noise.

fire·damp (fīr′dămp′) *n.* **1.** A combustible gas, chiefly methane, occurring naturally in mines from the decomposition of coal. **2.** The explosive mixture of firedamp and air.

fire department *n.* A department, esp. of a municipal government, whose purpose is preventing and putting out fires.

fire·dog (fīr′dôg′, -dŏg′) *n. Chiefly South Atlantic U.S.* See **andiron.**

fire door *n.* A door made of fire-resistant material that can be closed to prevent the spread of fire.

fire·drake (fīr′drāk′) *n.* A fiery dragon of Germanic mythology. [ME *firdrake* < OE *fȳrdraca* : *fȳr*, fire; see FIRE + *draca*, dragon; see DRAKE².]

fire drill *n.* An exercise in the use of firefighting equipment or the evacuation of a building in case of a fire.

fire-eat·er (fīr′ē′tər) *n.* **1.** A performer who pretends to swallow fire. **2.** A belligerent person or a militant partisan. —**fire′-eat′ing** *adj.*

fire engine *n.* Any of various large motor vehicles that carry firefighters and equipment to a fire and support extinguishing operations, as by pumping water.

fire escape *n.* A structure or device, such as an outside stairway, erected for emergency exit in the event of fire.

fire extinguisher *n.* A portable apparatus containing chemicals that can be discharged in a jet to extinguish a small fire.
fire•fight (fīr′fīt′) *n.* An exchange of gunfire.
fire•fight•er also **fire fighter** (fīr′fī′tər) *n.* A member of a fire department who fights fires. —**fire′fight′ing** *adj. & n.*
fire•flood (fīr′flŭd′) or **fire•flood•ing** (-flŭd′ĭng) *n.* A procedure for extracting additional oil from a well by injecting compressed air into the petroleum reservoir and burning some of the oil to increase the flow.
fire•fly (fīr′flī′) *n.* Any of various nocturnal beetles of the family Lampyridae, producing a flashing light in its abdomen.
fire•guard (fīr′gärd′) *n.* **1.** A metal screen placed in front of an open fireplace to catch sparks. **2.** See **firebreak.**
fire•house (fīr′hous′) *n.* See **fire station.**
fire hydrant *n.* An upright pipe with a nozzle or spout for drawing water from a water main.
fire irons *pl.n.* Implements, such as tongs, a shovel, and a poker, used to tend a fireplace.
Fire Island (fīr). A narrow barrier island off the S shore of Long I. in SE NY.
fire•light (fīr′līt′) *n.* The light from a fire, as in a fireplace.
fire•lock (fīr′lŏk′) *n.* See **flintlock** 2.
fire•man (fīr′mən) *n.* **1.** A firefighter. **2.** A man who tends fires; a stoker. **3.** An enlisted person in the U.S. Navy engaged in the operation of engineering machinery.
Fi•ren•ze (fē-rĕn′dzĕ). See **Florence** 1.
fire opal *n.* An opal with brilliant flamelike colors.
fire•place (fīr′plās′) *n.* **1.** An open recess for holding a fire at the base of a chimney; a hearth. **2.** A structure, usu. of stone or brick, for holding an outdoor fire.
fire•plug (fīr′plŭg′) *n.* See **fire hydrant.**
fire•pow•er (fīr′pou′ər) *n.* The capacity, as of a weapon, for delivering fire.
fire•proof (fīr′pro͞of′) *adj.* Impervious or resistant to fire. —*tr.v.* **-proofed, -proof•ing, -proofs.** To make fireproof.
fire sale *n.* A sale of merchandise damaged by fire.
fire screen *n.* See **fireguard** 1.
fire ship *n.* A military vessel loaded with explosives and combustibles and set adrift among enemy ships or fortifications.
fire•side (fīr′sīd′) *n.* **1.** The area immediately surrounding a fireplace or hearth. **2.** A home. —*adj.* At or as if at a fireside.
fire station *n.* A building for fire equipment and firefighters.
fire•stone (fīr′stōn′) *n.* **1.** A flint or pyrite used to strike a fire. **2.** A fire-resistant stone, such as certain sandstones.
fire•storm (fīr′stôrm′) *n.* **1.** A vast intense fire that generates and is fed by strong inrushing winds from all sides. **2.** An intense violent outburst from many sources.
fire thorn *n.* Any of various thorny evergreen shrubs of the genus *Pyracantha,* native to Asia and having red or orange berries.
fire tower *n.* A tower in which a lookout for fires is posted.
fire•trap (fīr′trăp′) *n.* A building that can catch fire easily or is difficult to escape from in the event of fire.
fire•wall (fīr′wôl) *n.* A fireproof wall used as a barrier to prevent the spread of fire. —*intr.v.* **-walled, -wall•ing, -walls.** *Slang.* To apply maximum acceleration or thrust. Used of motor vehicles or aircraft.
fire•wa•ter (fīr′wô′tər, -wŏt′ər) *n. Slang.* Strong liquor, esp. whiskey. [Transl. of Ojibwa *ishkodewaaboo,* whiskey.]
fire•weed (fīr′wēd′) *n.* **1.** Any of various plants of the genus *Epilobium,* esp. *E. angustifolium,* having long terminal spikelike flower clusters. **2.** Any of several weedy North American plants of the genus *Erechtites,* having small flowers grouped in discoid heads.
fire•wood (fīr′wo͝od′) *n.* Wood used as fuel.
fire•work (fīr′wûrk′) *n.* **1.a.** A device consisting of explosives and combustibles, set off to generate colored lights, smoke, and noise for amusement. **b. fireworks.** A display of such devices. **2. fireworks. a.** An exciting or spectacular display, as of musical virtuosity. **b.** A display of rage or fierce contention.
fir•ing (fīr′ĭng) *n.* **1.** The process of applying fire or heat, as in the hardening or glazing of ceramics. **2.** Fuel for fires.
firing line *n.* **1.** The line of positions from which fire is directed at a target. **2.** The forefront of an activity; the vanguard.
firing pin *n.* The part of the bolt or breech of a firearm that strikes the primer and detonates the charge of a projectile.
firing squad *n.* **1.** A detachment assigned to shoot persons condemned to death. **2.** A detachment of soldiers chosen to fire a salute at a military funeral.
fir•kin (fûr′kĭn) *n.* **1.** A small wooden barrel or covered vessel. **2.** Any of several British units of capacity, usu. equal to about ¼ of a barrel or 9 gallons (34 liters). [ME *ferken, ferdekin,* prob. < MDu. **verdelkijn,* dim. of *veerdel,* one fourth : *veerde,* fourth; see **k**ʷ**etwer-*** + *deel,* part; see **dail-*.**]
firm¹ (fûrm) *adj.* **firm•er, firm•est. 1.** Resistant to externally applied pressure. **2.** Marked by or indicating the tone and resiliency of healthy tissue. **3.** Securely fixed in place. **4.** Indicating or possessed of determination or resolution. **5.** Constant; steadfast. **6.a.** Not subject to change; fixed and definite: *a firm offer.* **b.** Unfluctuating; steady. **7.** Strong and sure. —*tr. & intr.v.* **firmed, firm•ing, firms.** To make or become firm. —*adv.* **firmer, firmest.** Without wavering; resolutely: *stand firm.* [ME *ferm* < OFr. < Lat. *firmus.* See **dher-*.**] —**firm′ly** *adv.* —**firm′ness** *n.*
Syns: *firm, hard, solid.* The central meaning shared by these adjectives is "tending not to yield to external pressure, touch, or force": *a firm mattress; hard as granite; solid ice.* ***Ant:*** *soft.*
firm² (fûrm) *n.* **1.** A commercial partnership of two or more persons, esp. when unincorporated. **2.** The name or designation under which a company transacts business. [Ital. *firma* < *firmare,* to ratify by signature < Med.Lat. *firmāre* < Lat., to confirm < *firmus,* firm. See **dher-*.**]
fir•ma•ment (fûr′mə-mənt) *n.* The vault or expanse of the heavens; the sky. [ME < OFr. < LLat. *firmāmentum* < Lat., support < *firmāre,* to strengthen. See FIRM².] —**fir′ma•ment′al** (-mĕn′tl) *adj.*
fir•mer chisel (fûr′mər) *n.* A chisel or gouge with a thin blade, used to shape and finish wood by hand. [Fr. *fermoir* < OFr., alteration of *formoir* < *former,* to form < Lat. *formāre* < *forma,* form.]
firm•ware (fûrm′wâr′) *n. Comp. Sci.* Programming instructions that are stored in a read-only memory unit rather than being implemented through software.
firn (fîrn) *n.* Granular, partially consolidated snow that has passed through one summer melt season but is not yet glacial ice. [Ger. < Ger. dial., of last year < OHGer. *firni,* old.]
first (fûrst) *n.* **1.** The ordinal number matching the number one in a series. **2.** The one coming, occurring, or ranking before or above all others. **3.** The beginning; the outset: *at first.* **4.** *Mus.* The voice or instrument highest in pitch or carrying the principal part. **5.** The transmission gear or corresponding gear ratio used to produce the range of lowest drive speeds in a motor vehicle. **6.** The winning position in a contest. **7.** *Baseball.* **a.** First base. **b.** A first baseman. —*adj.* **1.** Corresponding in order to the number one. **2.** Coming before all others in order or location. **3.** Occurring or acting before all others in time; earliest. **4.** Ranking above all others, as in importance or quality; foremost. **5.** *Mus.* Being highest in pitch or carrying the principal part. **6.** Of, relating to, or being the transmission gear or corresponding gear ratio used to produce the range of lowest drive speeds in a motor vehicle. —*adv.* **1.** Before or above all others in time, order, rank, or importance. **2.** For the first time. **3.** Rather; preferably: *would die first.* **4.** In the first place; to begin with. See Usage Note at **firstly.** [ME < OE *fyrst.* See **per¹*.**]
first aid *n.* Emergency treatment administered to an injured or sick person before professional medical care is available. —**first′-aid′** (fûrst′ād′) *adj.*
first base *n.* **1.** *Baseball.* **a.** The first of the bases in the infield, counterclockwise from home plate. **b.** The fielding position occupied by the first baseman. **2.** *Slang.* The first stage or step toward completion or success.
first baseman *n. Baseball.* The infielder near first base.
first-born (fûrst′bôrn′) *adj.* First in order of birth; born first. —*n.* The first-born child.
first class *n.* **1.** The first, highest, or best group in a system of classification. **2.** The most luxurious and expensive class of accommodations on a train or other conveyance. **3.** A class of mail including sealed letters, post cards, and packages.
first-class (fûrst′klăs′) *adj.* **1.** Being or belonging to the first, highest, or best group in a system of classification. **2.** Of the utmost excellence or highest quality; first-rate. —**first′class′** *adv.*
first cousin *n.* See **cousin** 1.
first-de•gree burn (fûrst′dĭ-grē′) *n.* A mild burn that produces redness of the skin but no blistering.
first down *n. Football.* **1.** The first in the series of four downs in which an offensive team must advance ten yards to retain possession of the ball. **2.** A gain of ten or more yards entitling the offensive team to a new series of downs.
first edition *n.* **1.a.** The first published copies of a literary work printed from the same type and distributed at the same time. **b.** One such copy. **2.** The day's first press run of a newspaper.
first family also **First Family** *n.* **1.** A family having high social status, often because of descent. **2.** The family of the chief executive of a city, state, or country.
first finger *n.* See **index finger.**
first floor *n.* **1.** The ground floor of a building. **2.** *Chiefly British.* The floor immediately above the ground floor.
first fruits also **first•fruits** (fûrst′fro͞ots′) *pl.n.* **1.** The first gathered fruits of a harvest, offered to God in gratitude. **2.** The first results of an undertaking.
first generation *n.* **1.** Persons who have left one country and settled in another. **2.** Persons whose parents are immigrants. **3.** *Comp. Sci.* The period of computer technology during the late 1940's and early 1950's, when computers were built with vacuum tubes. —**first′-gen′er•a′tion** *adj.*
first•hand (fûrst′hănd′) *adj.* Received from the original source: *firsthand information.* —**first′hand′** *adv.*
first-in, first-out (fûrst′ĭn′ fûrst′out′) *n. Accounting.* A method of inventory accounting in which the oldest remaining items are assumed to have been the first sold.

fire tower

firkin
Mid 19th-century American Shaker firkin

ă pat	oi boy
ā pay	ou out
âr care	o͝o took
ä father	o͞o boot
ĕ pet	ŭ cut
ē be	ûr urge
ĭ pit	th thin
ī pie	*th* this
îr pier	hw which
ŏ pot	zh vision
ō toe	ə about, item
ô paw	

Stress marks:
′ (primary);
′ (secondary), as in **dictionary** (dĭk′shə-nĕr′ē)

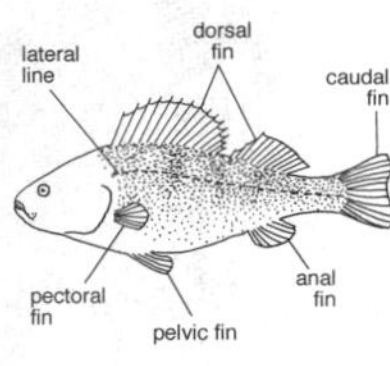

fish

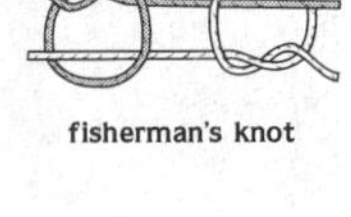
fisherman's knot

fish ladder
At Bonneville Dam on the Columbia River

first lady *n.* **1.** Often **First Lady.** The wife or hostess of the chief executive of a country, state, or city. **2.** The foremost woman of a specified profession or art.

first lieutenant *n.* A commissioned officer in the U.S. Army, Air Force, and Marines ranking above second lieutenant and below captain.

first•ling (fûrst′lĭng) *n.* **1.** The first of a kind or category. **2.** A first-born offspring.

first•ly (fûrst′lē) *adv.* In the first place; to begin with.
Usage Note: There is ample reputable precedent for using both *first* and *firstly* to begin an enumeration: *Our objectives are, first* (or *firstly*), *to recover from last year's slump.* Consistency is best served if any succeeding items are introduced by a parallel form, as in *first . . . second . . . third* or *firstly . . . secondly . . . thirdly.*

first mate *n.* An officer on a merchant ship ranking immediately below the captain.

first name *n.* The name that occurs first in a person's full name.

first night *n.* **1.** The opening performance of a theatrical production. **2.** The performance presented on such a night.

first night•er (nī′tər) *n.* One in the audience at a first night.

first offender *n.* One convicted of a legal offense for the first time.

first papers *pl.n.* The documents first filed by one applying for U.S. citizenship.

first person *n.* **1.a.** A category of linguistic forms, such as verbs and pronouns, designating the speaker or writer of the sentence in which they appear. **b.** One of these forms. **2.** A style of writing in which first person forms are used.

first-rate (fûrst′rāt′) *adj.* Foremost in quality, rank, or importance. — *adv. Informal.* Very well; excellently.

first sergeant *n.* The senior noncommissioned officer of a U.S. Army or Marine Corps unit, who is equivalent in rank to a master sergeant and performs administrative duties.

first strike *n.* The initial use of strategic nuclear weapons against a nuclear-armed adversary, with the goal of destroying retaliatory capacity. **— first′-strike′** (fûrst′strīk′) *adj.*

first-string (fûrst′strĭng′) *adj.* **1.** *Sports.* Of, relating to, or being a regular member, as of a football team, rather than a substitute. **2.** First-rate. **— first′-string′er** *n.*

first water *n.* **1.** The highest degree of quality or purity in diamonds or pearls. **2.** The foremost rank or quality. [Prob. transl. of Ar. *mā'*, water, water luster.]

First World also **first world** (fûrst) *n.* During the Cold War, the industrialized capitalist countries of the world. **— first′-world′** (fûrst′wûrld′) *adj.*

First World War *n.* World War I.

firth (fûrth) *n. Scots.* A long narrow inlet of the sea. [ME *furth* < ON *fjördhr.* See **per-**[2]***.**]

fisc (fĭsk) *n.* The treasury of a kingdom or state. [Fr. < Lat. *fiscus*, money basket, treasury.]

fis•cal (fĭs′kəl) *adj.* **1.** Of or relating to government expenditures, revenues, and debt. **2.** Of or relating to finance or finances. See Syns at **financial.** [Fr. < Lat. *fiscālis* < *fiscus*, money basket, treasury.] **— fis′cal•ly** *adv.*

fiscal year *n.* A 12-month period for which an organization plans the use of its funds.

Fi•scher (fĭsh′ər), **Emil Hermann.** 1852–1919. German chemist who won a 1902 Nobel Prize.

Fischer, Hans. 1881–1945. German chemist who won a 1930 Nobel Prize.

Fischer, Robert ("Bobby") James. b. 1943. Amer. chess player who was world champion (1972–74).

fish (fĭsh) *n., pl.* **fish** or **fish•es. 1.** Any of numerous cold-blooded aquatic vertebrates of the superclass Pisces, characteristically having fins, gills, and a streamlined body and including specifically: **a.** Any of the class Osteichthyes, having a bony skeleton. **b.** Any of the class Chondrichthyes, having a cartilaginous skeleton and including the sharks. **2.** The flesh of such animals used as food. **3.** Any of various primitive aquatic vertebrates of the class Cyclostomata, lacking jaws and including the lampreys and hagfishes. **4.** Any of various unrelated aquatic animals, such as a jellyfish, cuttlefish, or crayfish. **5.** *Informal.* A person who is deficient in something. — *v.* **fished, fish•ing, fish•es.** — *intr.* **1.** To catch or try to catch fish. **2.** To look for something by feeling one's way; grope. **3.** To seek something in a sly or indirect way. — *tr.* **1.a.** To catch or try to catch (fish). **b.** To catch or try to catch fish in. **2.** To catch or pull as if fishing. **— *phrasal verb.* fish out.** To deplete (a lake, for example) of fish by fishing. **— *idioms.* fish in troubled waters.** To try to take advantage of a confused situation. **fish or cut bait.** *Informal.* To proceed with an activity or abandon it altogether. **like a fish out of water.** Completely unfamiliar with one's surroundings or activity. **neither fish nor fowl.** Having no specific characteristics; indefinite. **other fish to fry.** *Informal.* Other matters to attend to. [ME < OE *fisc.*]

Fish (fĭsh), **Hamilton.** 1808–93. Amer. politician who served as U.S. secretary of state (1869–77).

fish and chips *pl.n.* Fried fillets of fish and French-fried potatoes.

fish•bowl also **fish bowl** (fĭsh′bōl′) *n.* **1.** A transparent bowl for keeping live fish. **2.** *Informal.* A place lacking in privacy.

fish cake *n.* A fried cake or patty of chopped fish, often mixed with potato, bread crumbs, or rice.

fish•er (fĭsh′ər) *n.* **1.** One that fishes, as a person or ship. **2.a.** A carnivorous mammal *(Martes pennanti)* of northern North America having thick dark-brown fur. **b.** This fur.

fish•er•man (fĭsh′ər-mən) *n.* **1.** One who fishes as an occupation or for sport. **2.** A commercial fishing vessel.

fish•er•man's bend (fĭsh′ər-mənz) *n.* A knot used to secure the end of a line to a ring or spar, made by two turns with the end passed back under both.

fisherman's knot *n.* A knot used to join two lines, made by securing either end to the opposite standing part by an overhand knot.

fish•er•y (fĭsh′ə-rē) *n., pl.* **-ies. 1.** The industry or activity of catching, processing, or selling fish or other aquatic animals. **2.** A place where fish or other aquatic animals are caught. **3.** A fishing business. **4.** A fish hatchery. **5.** The legal right to fish in specified areas.

Fish•es (fĭsh′ĭz) *pl.n. (used with a sing. v.)* See **Pisces** 1, 2a.

fish•eye (fĭsh′ī′) *adj.* **1.** Of, relating to, or being a photographic lens that covers about 180°, producing a circular image with exaggerated foreshortening in the center and increasing distortion toward the periphery. **2.** *Slang.* A suspicious unfriendly look.

fish farm *n.* A commercial facility consisting of tanks or ponds in which fish are raised for food.

fish flour *n.* A flour made of dried and powdered fish.

fish fry *n.* **1.** A cookout or other meal at which fried fish is the main course. **2.** A piece of fried fish.

fish•gig (fĭsh′gĭg′) *n.* A pronged instrument for spearing fish. [Alteration (influenced by FISH) of obsolete *fisgig* < Sp. *fisga*, ult. < Lat. *fixus*, fixed. See FIX.]

fish hawk *n.* See **osprey** 1.

fish•hook (fĭsh′ho͝ok′) *n.* A barbed metal hook used for catching fish.

fish•ing (fĭsh′ĭng) *n.* **1.** The act, occupation, or sport of catching fish. **2.** A place for catching fish.

fishing rod *n.* A rod of wood, steel, or fiberglass used with a line for catching fish.

fish joint *n.* A joint formed by bolting a fishplate to each side of two abutting rails, timbers, or beams. [< FISH(PLATE).]

fish ladder *n.* A series of pools arranged like ascending steps at the side of a stream, enabling migrating fish to swim upstream around a dam or other obstruction.

fish•meal (fĭsh′mēl′) *n.* A nutritive mealy substance produced from fish or fish parts and used as animal feed and fertilizer.

fish•mon•ger (fĭsh′mŭng′gər, -mŏng′-) *n. Chiefly British.* One that sells fish.

fish•net (fĭsh′nĕt′) *n.* **1.** Netting used to catch fish. **2.** A mesh fabric resembling such netting.

fish•plate (fĭsh′plāt′) *n.* A metal or wooden plate bolted to the sides of two abutting rails or beams, used esp. in the laying of railroad track. [Prob. < Fr. *fiche*, peg (< OFr.; see MICROFICHE) + PLATE.]

fish•pond (fĭsh′pŏnd′) *n.* A pond containing edible fish.

fish protein concentrate *n.* A protein-rich flour or paste prepared from ground fish and added to foods as a supplement.

fish•skin disease (fĭsh′skĭn′) *n.* See **ichthyosis.**

fish stick *n.* An oblong piece of breaded fish fillet.

fish story *n. Informal.* An implausible boastful story.

fish•tail (fĭsh′tāl′) *adj.* Resembling or suggestive of the tail of a fish in shape or movement. — *intr.v.* **-tailed, -tail•ing, -tails. 1.** To have the rear end of a forward-moving vehicle swerve from side to side out of control. **2.** To swing the tail of an airplane from side to side in order to reduce speed.

fish•wife (fĭsh′wīf′) *n.* **1.** A woman who sells fish. **2.** A woman regarded as coarse and abusive.

fish•y (fĭsh′ē) *adj.* **-i•er, -i•est. 1.** Resembling or suggestive of fish, as in odor. **2.** Cold or expressionless. **3.** *Informal.* Inspiring doubt or suspicion. **— fish′i•ly** *adv.* **— fish′i•ness** *n.*

Fisk (fĭsk), **James.** 1834–72. Amer. speculator who attempted to corner the gold market with Jay Gould (1869).

Fiske (fĭsk), **John.** 1842–1901. Amer. historian and philosopher known for his writings on religion and science.

fissi– *pref.* **1.** Fission: *fissiparous.* **2.** Split; cleft: *fissipalmate.* [< Lat. *fissus*, p.part. of *findere*, to split. See **bheid-*.**]

fis•sile (fĭs′əl, -īl′) *adj.* **1.** Possible to split. **2.** *Phys.* Fissionable, esp. by neutrons. **3.** *Geol.* Easily split along close parallel planes. [Lat. *fissilis* < *fissus*, split. See FISSI–.] **— fis•sil′i•ty** (fĭ-sĭl′ĭ-tē) *n.*

fis•sion (fĭsh′ən) *n.* **1.** The act or process of splitting into parts. **2.** A nuclear reaction in which an atomic nucleus, esp. a heavy nucleus, splits into fragments, usu. two fragments of comparable mass, with the release of energy. **3.** *Biol.* An asexual reproductive process in which a unicellular organism divides into two or more independently maturing daughter cells. [Lat. *fissiō, fissiōn-*, a cleaving < *fissus*, split. See FISSI–.] **— fis′sion•a•ble** *adj.* **— fis′sion•a•bil′i•ty** *n.*

fission bomb *n.* See **atom bomb** 1.

fis•si•pal•mate (fĭs′ə-păl′māt′) *adj.* Having lobed or partially webbed separated toes, as the feet of certain birds.

fis•sip•a•rous (fĭ-sĭp′ər-əs) *adj.* **1.** Reproducing by biological fission. **2.** Tending to break up into parts or break away from a main body; factious. — **fis•sip′a•rous•ly** *adv.* — **fis•sip′a•rous•ness** *n.*

fis•si•ped (fĭs′ə-pĕd′) *adj.* Having the toes separated from one another. — *n.* A fissiped mammal.

fis•sure (fĭsh′ər) *n.* **1.** A long narrow opening; a crack or cleft. **2.** The process of splitting or separating; division. **3.** A separation into subgroups or factions; a schism. **4.** *Anat.* A normal groove or furrow, as in the brain, that divides an organ into lobes or separates it into parts. **5.** *Medic.* A break in a tissue, usu. where it joins a mucous membrane. — *intr. & tr.v.* **-sured, -sur•ing, -sures.** To form a crack or cleft or cause a crack or cleft in. [ME, cut < OFr. < Lat. *fissūra* < *fissus,* split. See FISSI-.]

fist (fĭst) *n.* **1.** The hand closed tightly with the fingers bent against the palm. **2.** *Informal.* A grasp; a clutch: *had a fortune in their fists.* **3.** *Print.* See **index** 3. — *tr.v.* **fist•ed, fist•ing, fists. 1.** To clench into a fist. **2.** To grasp with the fist. [ME < OE *fȳst.* See **penkʷe*.**]

fist•fight (fĭst′fīt′) *n.* A fight with the bare fists.

fist•ful (fĭst′fo͝ol′) *n., pl.* **-fuls.** The amount held by a fist.

fist•ic (fĭs′tĭk) *adj. Sports.* Of or relating to boxing; pugilistic.

fist•i•cuffs (fĭs′tĭ-kŭfs′) *pl.n.* **1.** A fistfight. **2.** *Sports.* Boxing. [< *fisty cuffs* : *fisty,* with the fists (< FIST) + CUFF².] — **fist′i•cuff′er** *n.*

fis•tu•la (fĭs′chə-lə) *n., pl.* **-las** or **-lae** (-lē′). An abnormal duct or passage resulting from injury, disease, or a congenital disorder that connects an abscess or a hollow organ to the body surface or to another hollow organ. [ME < Lat.]

fis•tu•lous (fĭs′chə-ləs) or **fis•tu•lar** (-lər) *adj.* **1.** Of or resembling a fistula. **2.** Tubular and hollow, as the leaves of a scallion. **3.** Made of or containing tubular parts.

fit¹ (fĭt) *v.* **fit•ted** or **fit, fit•ted, fit•ting, fits.** — *tr.* **1.a.** To be the proper size and shape for. **b.** To cause to be the proper size and shape. **c.** To measure for proper size. **2.** To be appropriate to; suit. **3.** To conform or agree with. **4.** To make suitable; adapt. See Syns at **adapt. 5.** To make ready; prepare. **6.** To equip; outfit: *fit out a ship.* **7.** To provide a place or time for: *fit it in the box.* **8.** To insert or adjust so as to be properly in place. — *intr.* **1.** To be the proper size and shape. **2.** To be suited; belong: *fit in with us.* **3.** To be in harmony; agree. — *adj.* **fit•ter, fit•test. 1.** Suited, adapted, or acceptable for a given circumstance or purpose. **2.** Appropriate; proper: *as seems fit.* **3.** Physically sound; healthy. — *n.* **1.** The state, quality, or way of being fitted. **2.** The manner in which clothing fits. **3.** The degree of precision with which surfaces are adjusted or adapted to each other in a machine or collection of parts. — ***idioms.*** **fit to be tied.** Roused to great anger or indignation; outraged. **fit to kill.** *Slang.* To an extreme or elaborate degree. [ME *fitten,* to be suitable, marshal troops.] — **fit′ly** *adv.* — **fit′ter** *n.*

fit² (fĭt) *n.* **1.** *Medic.* **a.** A seizure or a convulsion, esp. one caused by epilepsy. **b.** The sudden appearance of a symptom such as coughing. **2.** A sudden outburst of emotion. **3.** A sudden period of vigorous activity. — ***idiom.*** **by (or in) fits and starts.** With irregular intervals of action and inaction; intermittently. [ME, hardship, prob. < OE *fitt,* struggle.]

fit³ (fĭt) *n. Archaic.* A section of a poem or ballad. [ME < OE.]

fitch (fĭch) *n.* **1.** See **polecat** 1a. **2.** The fur of this animal. [ME *fiche* < MDu. *vitsche, visse.*]

Fitch (fĭch), **John.** 1743–98. Amer. steamboat pioneer whose early designs (1787–90) received insufficient financial backing for large-scale production.

Fitch, (William) Clyde. 1865–1909. Amer. playwright whose works include *Beau Brummel* (1890).

Fitch•burg (fĭch′bûrg′). A city of N-central MA N of Worcester; settled in 1740. Pop. 41,194.

fitch•ew (fĭch′o͞o) also **fitch•et** (-ĭt) *n. Archaic.* The Old World polecat or its fur. [ME *ficheux,* poss. < Walloon *ficheau,* dim. of MDu. *vitsche, visse.*]

fit•ful (fĭt′fəl) *adj.* Occurring in or characterized by intermittent bursts, as of activity; irregular. See Syns at **periodic.** — **fit′ful•ly** *adv.* — **fit′ful•ness** *n.*

fit•ness (fĭt′nĭs) *n.* The state or condition of being physically fit, esp. as the result of exercise and proper nutrition.

fit•ting (fĭt′ĭng) *adj.* Suiting a situation; appropriate. — *n.* **1.** The trying on of clothes whose fit is being adjusted. **2.** A small detachable part, as for a machine. **3. fittings.** *Chiefly British.* Furnishings or fixtures. — **fit′ting•ly** *adv.* — **fit′ting•ness** *n.*

Fitz•ger•ald (fĭts-jĕr′əld), **Ella.** b. 1918. Amer. jazz singer best known for her scat singing.

Fitzgerald, F(rancis) Scott (Key). 1896–1940. Amer. writer whose works include *The Great Gatsby* (1925).

Fitz•Ger•ald (fĭts-jĕr′əld), **Edward.** 1809–83. British poet and translator of *The Rubáiyát of Omar Khayyám* (1859).

FitzGerald, George Francis. 1851–1901. Irish physicist noted for discoveries in the field of electromagnetic radiation.

Fiu•me (fyo͞o′mā, -mĕ). See **Rijeka.**

five (fīv) *n.* **1.** The cardinal number equal to 4 + 1. **2.** The fifth in a set or sequence. **3.** Something that has five parts, units, or members. **4.** A five-dollar bill. **5. fives.** *(used with a sing. v.) Sports.* One of several forms of handball originating in England, in which only the receiving side can score points. [ME < OE *fīf.* See **penkʷe*.**] — **five** *adj. & pron.*

five-and-dime (fīv′ən-dīm′) *n.* See **five-and-ten.**

five-and-ten (fīv′ən-tĕn′) *n.* A retail store selling a wide variety of inexpensive articles. [Short for *five-and-ten-cent store.*]

Five Civilized Nations (fīv) *pl.n.* The Cherokee, Chickasaw, Choctaw, Creek, and Seminole peoples.

five-fin•ger (fīv′fĭng′gər) *n.* Any of several plants having palmately compound leaves with five leaflets.

Five Forks. A crossroads in SE VA SW of Petersburg where the last important Civil War battle was fought on Apr. 1, 1865.

Five Nations *pl.n.* The original Iroquois confederacy of the Mohawk, Oneida, Onondaga, Cayuga, and Seneca peoples.

fiv•er (fī′vər) *n.* **1.** *Informal.* A five-dollar bill. **2.** *Chiefly British.* A five-pound note.

five-way chili (fīv′wā′) *n. Cincinnati.* A main dish consisting of noodles, chili con carne, kidney beans, onions, and cheese.

fix (fĭks) *v.* **fixed, fix•ing, fix•es.** — *tr.* **1.a.** To place securely; make stable or firm. **b.** To secure to another; attach. **2.a.** To put into a stable or unalterable form. **b.** To make (a chemical) nonvolatile or stable. **c.** *Biol.* To convert (nitrogen) into stable, biologically assimilable compounds. **d.** To kill and preserve (a specimen) intact for microscopic study. **e.** To prevent discoloration of (a photographic image) by washing or coating with a chemical preservative. **3.** To direct steadily: *fixed her eyes on the road.* **4.** To capture or hold: *fixed our attention.* **5.a.** To set or place definitely; establish: *fixed her residence here.* **b.** To determine with accuracy; ascertain. **c.** To agree on; arrange. **6.** To assign; attribute: *fixing the blame.* **7.a.** To correct or set right; adjust. **b.** To restore to proper condition or working order; repair. **8.** To make ready; prepare. **9.** To spay or castrate (an animal). **10.** *Informal.* To take revenge upon; get even with. **11.** To influence the outcome or actions of by improper or unlawful means: *fix a jury.* — *intr.* **1.** To direct one's efforts or attention; concentrate: *fixed on the goal.* **2.** To become stable or firm; harden: *The plaster is fixing.* **3.** *Chiefly Southern U.S.* To be on the verge of; to be making preparations for. Used in progressive tenses with the infinitive: *It's fixing to rain.* — *n.* **1.a.** The act of adjusting, correcting, or repairing. **b.** *Informal.* Something that repairs or restores; a solution: *no easy fix.* **2.** The position, as of a ship or aircraft, determined by visual observations with the aid of equipment. **3.** A clear determination or understanding. **4.** An instance of arranging a special consideration, such as an exemption, or an illegal outcome, esp. by means of bribery. **5.** A difficult or embarrassing situation; a predicament. **6.** *Slang.* An intravenous injection of a narcotic. — ***phrasal verb.*** **fix up. 1.** To improve the appearance or condition of; refurbish. **2.** To provide; equip. **3.** *Informal.* To provide a companion on a date for. [ME *fixen* < *fix,* fixed in position < Lat. *fixus,* p.part. of *fīgere,* to fasten. See **dhīgʷ-*.**] — **fix′a•ble** *adj.* — **fix′er** *n.*

Regional Note: *Fixing to* means "to be on the verge of or in preparation for (doing a given thing)," but like the modal auxiliaries, it has only a single invariant form, the present participle followed by the infinitive marker *to*: *They were fixing to leave without me.* Semantically, *fixing to* can refer only to events that immediately follow the speaker's point of reference.

fix•ate (fĭk′sāt′) *v.* **-at•ed, -at•ing, -ates.** — *tr.* **1.** To make stable or stationary. **2.** To focus one's eyes or attention on. **3.** To command the exclusive or repeated attention of; preoccupy obsessively. **4.** *Psychol.* **a.** To attach (oneself) immaturely or neurotically to a person or thing. **b.** To cause (the libido) to be arrested at an early stage of psychosexual development. — *intr.* **1.** To focus the eyes or attention. **2.** *Psychol.* **a.** To form a fixation. **b.** To be arrested at an early stage of psychosexual development.

fix•a•tion (fĭk-sā′shən) *n.* **1.** The act or process of fixing or fixating. **2.** An obsession. **3.** *Psychol.* A strong attachment to a person or thing, esp. formed in childhood or infancy and manifested in immature or neurotic behavior throughout life.

fix•a•tive (fĭk′sə-tĭv) *n.* Something that fixes, protects, or preserves, esp.: **a.** A liquid preservative applied to artwork, such as charcoal drawings. **b.** A solution used to preserve and harden fresh tissue for microscopic examination. **c.** A liquid mixed with perfume to prevent rapid evaporation. — **fix′a•tive** *adj.*

fixed (fĭkst) *adj.* **1.** Firmly in position; stationary. **2.** Determined; established; set. **3.** Not subject to change or variation; constant: *a fixed income.* **4.** *Chem.* **a.** Not readily evaporating; nonvolatile. **b.** Being in a stable, combined form. **5.** Firmly, often dogmatically held. **6.** Supplied, esp. with funds or needs. Often used in combination: *a well-fixed bachelor.* **7.** Illegally prearranged as to outcome. — **fix′ed•ly** (fĭk′sĭd-lē) *adv.* — **fix′ed•ness** *n.*

fixed head *n.* A stationary device, such as a tape-recording head, that reads and imprints information on a single track of magnetic tape.

Ella Fitzgerald

F. Scott Fitzgerald

ă pat	oi boy
ā pay	ou out
âr care	o͝o took
ä father	o͞o boot
ĕ pet	ŭ cut
ē be	ûr urge
ĭ pit	th thin
ī pie	*th* this
îr pier	hw which
ŏ pot	zh vision
ō toe	ə about, item
ô paw	

Stress marks:
′ (primary);
′ (secondary), as in
dictionary (dĭk′shə-nĕr′ē)

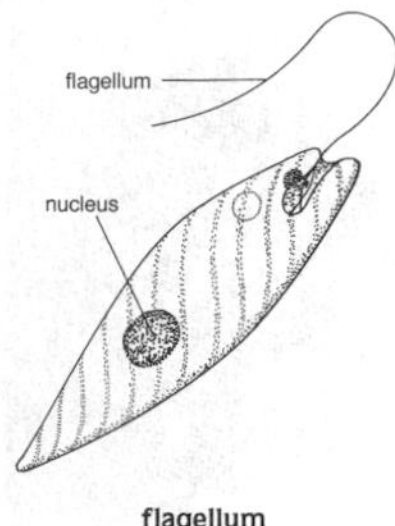

flagellum

flagon
c. 1780 pewter flagon attributed to Thomas Carpenter

fixed oil *n.* A nonvolatile oil, esp. a fatty oil of vegetable origin.
fixed-point (fĭkst′point′) *adj.* Of, relating to, or being a method of writing numbers with the decimal point located at a single unchanging position.
fixed star *n.* A star so distant from Earth that its position relative to other stars appears unchanging and its movements can be measured only over long periods of time.
fix•ings (fĭk′sĭngz) *pl.n. Informal.* Accessories; trimmings.
fix•i•ty (fĭk′sĭ-tē) *n., pl.* **-ties. 1.** The quality or condition of being fixed. **2.** Something fixed or immovable.
fix•ture (fĭks′chər) *n.* **1.** Something securely fixed in place. **2.** Something attached as a permanent appendage, apparatus, or appliance: *plumbing fixtures.* **3.** *Law.* A chattel bound to realty. **4.** One invariably present in and long associated with a place. **5.a.** The act or process of fixing. **b.** The condition of being fixed. [Var. of obsolete *fixure* < LLat. *fīxūra* < Lat. *fīxus*, fixed. See FIX.]
fizz (fĭz) *intr.v.* **fizzed, fizz•ing, fizz•es.** To make a hissing or bubbling sound. —*n.* **1.** A fizzling sound. **2.** Effervescence. **3.** An effervescent beverage. [Imit.] —**fizz′y** *adj.*
fiz•zle (fĭz′əl) *intr.v.* **-zled, -zling, -zles. 1.** To make a hissing or sputtering sound. **2.** *Informal.* To fail or end weakly, esp. after a hopeful beginning. —*n. Informal.* A failure; a fiasco. [Prob. < obsolete *fist*, to break wind < ME *fisten.* See **pezd-***.]
fjeld (fyĕld) *n.* A high, barren plateau in the Scandinavian countries. [Dan. < ON *fjall.*]
fjord or **fiord** (fyôrd, fyōrd) *n.* A long, narrow, deep inlet of the sea between steep slopes. [Norw. < ON *fjördhr.* See **per-²***.]
fl or **fl.** *abbr.* Fluid.
fL *abbr.* Foot-lambert.
FL *abbr.* **1.** Florida. **2.** Focal length. **3.** Foreign languages.
fl. *abbr.* **1.** *Football.* Flankerback. **2.** Floor. **3.** Florin. **4.** Floruit. **5.** Flute.
Fla. *abbr.* Florida.
flab (flăb) *n.* Soft fatty body tissue. [Back-formation < FLABBY.]
flab•ber•gast (flăb′ər-găst′) *tr.v.* **-gast•ed, -gast•ing, -gasts.** To cause to be overcome with astonishment. [?]
flab•by (flăb′ē) *adj.* **-bi•er, -bi•est. 1.** Lacking firmness; flaccid: *a flabby waist.* **2.** Lacking force or vitality; ineffectual: *flabby self-pity.* [Alteration of *flappy*, tending to flap < FLAP.] —**flab′bi•ly** *adv.* —**flab′bi•ness** *n.*
fla•bel•late (flə-bĕl′ĭt, flăb′ə-lāt′) also **fla•bel•li•form** (flə-bĕl′ə-fôrm′) *adj.* Fan-shaped. [Lat. *flābellum*, fan; see FLABELLUM + -ATE¹.]
fla•bel•lum (flə-bĕl′əm) *n., pl.* **-bel•la** (-bĕl′ə). A fan-shaped anatomical structure. [Lat. *flābellum*, fan, dim. of *flābra*, breeze < *flāre*, to blow. See **bhlē-***.]
flac•cid (flăk′sĭd, flăs′ĭd) *adj.* **1.** Lacking firmness, resilience, or muscle tone. **2.** Lacking vigor or energy: *flaccid management.* [Lat. *flaccidus* < *flaccus*, flabby.] —**flac•cid′i•ty** (-sĭd′ĭ-tē), **flac′cid•ness** *n.* —**flac′cid•ly** *adv.*
flack¹ (flăk) *Informal.* —*n.* A press agent; a publicist. —*v.* **flacked, flack•ing, flacks.** —*intr.* To act as a press agent. —*tr.* To act as a press agent for. [?] —**flack′er•y** *n.*
flack² (flăk) *n.* Var. of **flak.**
flac•on (flăk′ən, -ŏn′) *n.* A small, often decorative bottle with a tight-fitting stopper or cap. [Fr. < OFr. See FLAGON.]
flag¹ (flăg) *n.* **1.** A piece of cloth, usu. rectangular, of distinctive color and design, used as a symbol, a standard, a signal, or an emblem. **2.** National or other allegiance, as symbolized by a flag: *ships of the same flag.* **3.** A ship carrying the flag of an admiral; a flagship. **4.** A marking device attached to an object to attract attention or ease identification; a tab. **5.** The masthead of a newspaper. **6.** *Mus.* A cross stroke added to a note that is less than a quarter note in value. **7.** A distinctively shaped or marked tail, as of a dog. **8.** *Comp. Sci.* A bit or series of bits with two stable states, used in software to indicate a single piece of information. —*tr.v.* **flagged, flag•ging, flags. 1.** To mark with a flag or flags for identification or ornamentation: *flag a page.* **2.a.** To signal with or as if with a flag. **b.** To signal to stop: *flag a cab.* [?] —**flag′ger** *n.*
flag² (flăg) *n.* A plant, such as an iris, that has long sword-shaped leaves. [ME *flagge*, reed, of Scand. orig.]
flag³ (flăg) *intr.v.* **flagged, flag•ging, flags. 1.** To hang limply; droop. **2.** To decline in vigor or strength. **3.** To decline in interest: *The conversation flagged.* [Poss. of Scand. orig.]
flag⁴ (flăg) *n.* A flagstone. —*tr.v.* **flagged, flag•ging, flags.** To pave with slabs of flagstone. [ME *flagge*, piece of turf < ON *flaga*, slab of stone. See **plāk-¹***.]
Flag Day (flăg) *n.* June 14, observed in commemoration of the adoption in 1777 of the official U.S. flag.
flag•el•lant (flăj′ə-lənt, flə-jĕl′ənt) *n.* **1.** One who whips, esp. one who scourges oneself for religious discipline or public penance. **2.** One who seeks sexual gratification in beating or being beaten by another person. [Lat. *flagellāns*, *flagellant-* < pr.part. of *flagellāre*, to whip. See FLAGELLATE.] —**flag′el•lant** *adj.* —**flag′el•lant•ism** *n.*
fla•gel•lar (flə-jĕl′ər) *adj.* Of or relating to a flagellum.
flag•el•late (flăj′ə-lāt′) *tr.v.* **-lat•ed, -lat•ing, -lates. 1.** To whip or flog; scourge. **2.** To punish or impel as if by whipping. —*adj.* (-lĭt, -lāt′, flə-jĕl′ĭt). **1.** *Biol.* Flagellated. **2.** Resembling a flagellum; whiplike. **3.** Relating to or caused by a flagellate organism. —*n.* (-lĭt, -lāt′, flə-jĕl′ĭt). An organism, such as a euglena, having a flagellum. [Lat. *flagellāre*, *flagellāt-*, to whip < *flagellum*, dim. of *flagrum*, whip.]
flag•el•lat•ed (flăj′ə-lā′tĭd) *adj. Biol.* Having a flagellum or flagella.
flag•el•la•tion (flăj′ə-lā′shən) *n.* **1.** The act or practice of flagellating. **2.** *Biol.* The flagellar arrangement on an organism.
fla•gel•li•form (flə-jĕl′ə-fôrm′) *adj.* Long, thin, and tapering; whip-shaped: *flagelliform appendages.* [Lat. *flagellum*, little whip; see FLAGELLUM + -FORM.]
fla•gel•lin (flə-jĕl′ĭn) *n.* The chief protein component of bacterial flagella.
fla•gel•lum (flə-jĕl′əm) *n., pl.* **-gel•la** (-jĕl′ə). **1.** *Biol.* A long threadlike appendage, esp. a whiplike extension of certain cells or unicellular organisms used for locomotion. **2.** A whip. [Lat., dim. of *flagrum*, whip.]
flag•eo•let (flăj′ə-lĕt′, -lā′) *n. Mus.* A small flutelike instrument with a cylindrical mouthpiece, four finger holes, and two thumbholes. [Fr., dim. of OFr. *flajol*, flute < VLat. **flābeolum*, poss. alteration of Lat. *flābellum*, dim. of *flābrum*, gust of wind < *flāre*, to blow. See INFLATE.]
Flagg (flăg), **James Montgomery.** 1877–1960. Amer. artist and writer best known for his World War I recruiting poster of Uncle Sam saying "I Want You."
flag•ging¹ (flăg′ĭng) *adj.* **1.** Declining; weakening: *flagging strength.* **2.** Languid; drooping. —**flag′ging•ly** *adv.*
flag•ging² (flăg′ĭng) *n.* A pavement laid with flagstones.
fla•gi•tious (flə-jĭsh′əs) *adj.* **1.** Characterized by extremely brutal or cruel crimes; vicious. **2.** Infamous; scandalous. [ME *flagicious*, wicked < Lat. *flāgitiōsus* < *flāgitium*, shameful act, protest < *flāgitāre*, to importune, to demand vehemently.] —**fla•gi′tious•ly** *adv.* —**fla•gi′tious•ness** *n.*
flag•man (flăg′mən) *n.* One who signals with or carries a flag.
flag of convenience *n., pl.* **flags of convenience.** A foreign flag under which a merchant vessel is registered for purposes of reducing operating costs or avoiding government regulations.
flag officer *n.* An officer in the navy or coast guard holding a rank higher than captain, such as rear admiral.
flag of truce *n., pl.* **flags of truce.** A white flag shown to an enemy to request a conference or signal surrender.
flag•on (flăg′ən) *n.* **1.** A large vessel with a handle, spout, and often a lid, used for holding wine or other liquors. **2.** The quantity that a flagon can hold. [ME < OFr. *flacon* < LLat. *flascō*, *flascōn-*, bottle. See FLASK.]
flag•pole (flăg′pōl′) *n.* A pole on which a flag is raised. —***idiom.*** **run (something) up the flagpole.** *Slang.* To test (a plan, for example) and then measure the response to it.
fla•grant (flā′grənt) *adj.* **1.** Conspicuously bad, offensive, or reprehensible: *a flagrant miscarriage of justice.* See Usage Note at **blatant. 2.** *Obsolete.* Flaming; blazing. [Lat. *flagrāns*, *flagrant-*, pr.part. of *flagrāre*, to burn. See **bhel-¹***.] —**fla′gran•cy, fla′grance** *n.* —**fla′grant•ly** *adv.*
fla•gran•te de•lic•to (flə-grăn′tē dĭ-lĭk′tō) *adv.* In the very act; red-handed. [Med.Lat. *flagrante dēlictō*, while the crime is blazing : *flagrante*, ablative of *flagrāns*, blazing + *dēlictō*, ablative of *dēlictum*, offense.]
flag•ship (flăg′shĭp′) *n.* **1.** A ship that carries a fleet or squadron commander and bears the commander's flag. **2.** The chief one of a related group: *the flagship of a newspaper chain.*
Flag•stad (flăg′stăd′, flăg′stä′), **Kirsten Marie.** 1895–1962. Norwegian soprano known for her performances in Wagnerian roles.
flag•staff (flăg′stăf′) *n.* See **flagpole.**
Flag•staff (flăg′stăf′). A city of N-central AZ NE of Prescott; site of Lowell Observatory (founded 1894). Pop. 45,857.
flag•stick (flăg′stĭk′) *n. Sports.* A removable pole with a flag marking each hole on the putting greens of a golf course.
flag•stone (flăg′stōn′) *n.* **1.** A flat slab of stone used as a paving material. **2.** An evenly layered sedimentary rock that can be split into paving stones.
flag-wav•ing (flăg′wā′vĭng) *n.* Excessive or fanatical patriotism; chauvinism. —**flag′-wav′er** *n.*
Fla•her•ty (flă′ər-tē, flä′-), **Robert Joseph.** 1884–1951. Amer. explorer and documentary filmmaker whose works include *Nanook of the North* (1922).
flail (flāl) *n.* A manual threshing device consisting of a wooden handle or staff and a shorter free-swinging stick attached to its end. —*v.* **flailed, flail•ing, flails.** —*tr.* **1.** To beat or strike with or as if with a flail. **2.** To wave or swing vigorously; thrash: *flailed my arms to get their attention.* **3.** To thresh using a flail. —*intr.* **1.** To move vigorously or erratically; thrash about. **2.** To strike or lash out violently. **3.** To thresh grain. [ME < OE *flegil* and < OFr. *flaiel*, both < LLat. *flagellum*, threshing tool < Lat. *flagrum*, whip.]
flair (flâr) *n.* **1.** A natural talent or aptitude. **2.** Instinctive discernment; keenness. **3.** Distinctive elegance or style. [ME, fragrance < OFr. < *flairer*, to scent < LLat. *flāgrāre*, alteration of Lat. *frāgrāre*, to emit an odor.]
flak also **flack** (flăk) *n.* **1.a.** Antiaircraft artillery. **b.** The bursting shells fired from such artillery. **2.** *Informal.* **a.** Excessive or

abusive criticism. **b.** Dissension; opposition. [Ger. < *Fl(ieger)a(bwehr)k(anone),* aircraft-defense gun.]

flake[1] (flāk) *n.* **1.** A flat thin piece or layer; a chip. **2.** A small piece; a bit. **3.** A small crystalline bit of snow. **4.** *Slang.* A somewhat eccentric person; an oddball. **5.** *Slang.* Cocaine. —*v.* **flaked, flak•ing, flakes.** —*tr.* **1.** To break flat, thin pieces or layers from; chip. **2.** To cover, mark, or overlay with or as if with flakes. —*intr.* To come off in flat thin pieces or layers; chip off. —***phrasal verb.*** **flake out.** *Slang.* **1.** To fall asleep or collapse from fatigue or exhaustion. **2.** To act in an odd or eccentric manner. [ME. See **plāk-[1]*.**] —**flak′er** *n.*

flake[2] (flāk) *n.* A frame or platform for drying fish or produce. [ME *fleke* < ON *fleki,* hurdle, battle shield. See **plāk-[1]*.**]

flak jacket *n.* A bulletproof jacket or vest.

flak•y also **flak•ey** (flā′kē) *adj.* **-i•er, -i•est. 1.** Made of or resembling flakes. **2.** Forming or tending to form flakes or thin crisp fragments: *flaky pastry.* **3.** *Slang.* Somewhat eccentric; odd. —**flak′i•ly** *adv.* —**flak′i•ness** *n.*

flam[1] (flăm) *n. Informal.* **1.** A lie or hoax; a deception. **2.** Nonsense; drivel. [Short for FLIMFLAM.]

flam[2] (flăm) *n. Mus.* A drumbeat consisting of two almost simultaneous strokes. [Prob. of imit. orig.]

flam•bé (fläm-bā′, flăN-) *tr.v.* **-béed, -bé•ing, -bés.** To drench with a liquor and ignite. —*adj.* Served flaming in ignited liquor: *steak flambé.* [< Fr., p.part. of *flamber,* to flame < OFr. < *flambe,* flame. See FLAME.]

flam•beau (flăm′bō′) *n., pl.* **-beaux** (-bōz′) or **-beaus. 1.** A lighted torch. **2.** A large ornamental candlestick. [Fr. < OFr. < *flambe,* flame. See FLAME.]

flam•boy•ant (flăm-boi′ənt) *adj.* **1.** Highly elaborate; ornate. **2.** Richly colored; resplendent. **3.** *Archit.* Of or having the wavy lines and flamelike forms of 15th- and 16th-century French Gothic architecture. **4.** Marked by striking audacity or verve. **5.** Given to ostentatious display; showy. See Syns at **showy.** —*n.* See **royal poinciana.** [Fr. < OFr., pr.part. of *flamboyer,* to blaze < *flambe,* flame. See FLAME.] —**flam•boy′ance, flam•boy′an•cy** *n.* —**flam•boy′ant•ly** *adv.*

flame (flām) *n.* **1.** The hot glowing mixture of burning gases and fine suspended matter associated with rapid combustion. **2.** The condition of active blazing combustion: *burst into flame.* **3.** Something resembling a flame. **4.** A violent or intense passion. **5.** *Informal.* A sweetheart. —*v.* **flamed, flam•ing, flames.** —*intr.* **1.** To burn brightly; blaze. **2.** To color or flash suddenly. —*tr.* **1.** To burn, ignite, or scorch (something) with a flame. **2.** *Obsolete.* To foment; incite. [ME < AN *flaumbe,* var. of OFr. *flambe* < *flamble* < Lat. *flammula,* dim. of *flamma.* See **bhel-[1]*.**] —**flam′er** *n.*

flame cell *n.* A hollow cell in the excretory system of certain invertebrates, including flatworms and rotifers, containing cilia that propel waste products into excretory tubules.

fla•men (flā′mən) *n., pl.* **fla•mens** or **flam•i•nes** (flăm′ə-nēz′). A priest, esp. of an ancient Roman deity. [ME *flamin* < Lat. *flāmen.*]

fla•men•co (flə-mĕng′kō) *n., pl.* **-cos. 1.a.** A dance style of the Andalusian Gypsies characterized by forceful, often improvised rhythms. **b.** A dance in this style. **2.** The guitar music that usu. accompanies a flamenco. [Sp., Flemish < MDu. *Vlāming,* Fleming.]

flame nettle *n.* See **coleus.**

flame•out (flām′out′) *n.* Failure of a jet aircraft engine due to the extinction of the flame in the combustion chamber.

flame•proof (flām′pro͞of′) *adj.* Resistant to catching fire; flame-retardant. —*tr.v.* **-proofed, -proof•ing, -proofs.** To make flameproof. —**flame′proof′er** *n.*

flame-re•tard•ant (flām′rĭ-tär′dnt) *adj.* Resistant to catching fire. —**flame′-re•tard′ant** *n.*

flame•throw•er (flām′thrō′ər) *n.* A weapon that projects ignited incendiary fuel, such as napalm, in a steady stream.

flam•ing (flā′mĭng) *adj.* **1.** On fire; ablaze. **2.** Resembling a flame. **3.** Intense; ardent. **4.** *Informal.* Used as an intensive: *a flaming fanatic.* —**flam′ing•ly** *adv.*

fla•min•go (flə-mĭng′gō) *n., pl.* **-gos** or **-goes. 1.** Any of several large tropical wading birds of the family Phoenicopteridae, having reddish or pinkish plumage, long legs, and a long flexible neck. **2.** *Color.* A moderate reddish orange. [Port. *flamengo* or Sp. *flamenco,* both prob. < OProv. *flamenc* < *flama,* flame < Lat. *flamma.* See **bhel-[1]*.**]

Fla•min•i•an Way (flə-mĭn′ē-ən). An ancient Roman road, the principal artery between Rome and Cisalpine Gaul.

flam•ma•ble (flăm′ə-bəl) *adj.* Easily ignited and capable of burning rapidly; inflammable. [< Lat. *flammāre,* to set fire to < *flamma,* flame. See **bhel-[1]*.**] —**flam′ma•bil′i•ty** *n.* —**flam′ma•ble** *n.*

Usage Note: Historically, *flammable* and *inflammable* mean the same thing. However, the presence of the prefix *in–* has misled many people into assuming that *inflammable* means "not flammable" or "noncombustible." Use *flammable* in contexts imparting warnings or on product labels.

Flam•ma•rion (flə-mâr′ē-ōN′), **Camille.** 1842–1925. French astronomer who founded the French Astronomical Society (1887).

flam•y (flā′mē) *adj.* **-i•er, -i•est.** Resembling a flame; flaming.

flan (flăn, flän, fläN) *n.* **1.** A tart filled with custard, fruit, or cheese. **2.** A custard topped with caramel syrup. **3.** A metal disk to be stamped as a coin; a blank. [Fr. < OFr. *flaon* < LLat. *fladō, fladōn-,* flat cake, of Gmc. orig. See **plat-*.**]

Flan•a•gan (flăn′ə-gən), **Edward Joseph.** 1886–1948. Amer. priest who founded Boys Town (1917), a community for underprivileged children.

Flan•ders (flăn′dərz). A historical region of NW Europe including parts of N France, W Belgium, and SW Netherlands along the North Sea.

flâ•ne•rie (flän-rē′, flä′nə-rē′) *n.* Aimless idling; dawdling. [Fr. < *flâner,* to idle about, stroll. See FLÂNEUR.]

flâ•neur (flä-nûr′) *n.* An aimless idler; a loafer. [Fr. < *flâner,* to idle about, stroll, of Gmc. orig. See **pelə-[2]*.**]

flange (flănj) *n.* A protruding rim, edge, rib, or collar, as on a pipe shaft, used to strengthen an object, hold it in place, or attach it to another object. [Poss. var. of *flanch,* device at the side of an escutcheon, perh. < Fr. *flanche,* fem. of *flanc,* side. See FLANK.] —**flange** *v.*

flank (flăngk) *n.* **1.** The part of the body of a person or an animal between the last rib and the hip; the side. **2.** A cut of meat from the flank of an animal. **3.** A lateral part or side. **4.a.** The right or left side of a military formation. **b.** The right or left side of a bastion. —*tr.v.* **flanked, flank•ing, flanks. 1.** To protect or guard the flank of. **2.** To menace or attack the flank of. **3.** To be placed or situated at the flank or side of. **4.** To put (something) on each side of. [ME < OE *flanc* < OFr. *flanc,* of Gmc. orig.]

flan•ken (flăng′kən) *n.* **1.** A cut of meat taken from the short ribs of beef. **2.** A dish prepared from this cut of beef by boiling or stewing, often served with horseradish. [Yiddish < Ger., pl. of *Flanke,* flank, side < Fr. *flanc.* See FLANK.]

flank•er (flăng′kər) *n.* **1.** One that flanks, esp. a soldier positioned to protect the flank of a column of troops. **2.** *Football.* A flankerback.

flank•er•back (flăng′kər-băk′) *n. Football.* An offensive halfback stationed just behind the line of scrimmage and slightly wide of the formation, used chiefly as a pass receiver.

flan•nel (flăn′əl) *n.* **1.** A soft woven cloth of wool or a blend of wool and cotton or synthetics. **2. flannels. a.** Outer clothing, esp. trousers, made of this cloth. **b.** Underclothing made of this cloth. [ME, a woolen cloth or garment, perh. var. of *flanyn,* sackcloth, prob. < OFr. *flaine,* a coarse wool.]

flannel cake *n.* See **pancake.**

flan•nel•ette (flăn′ə-lĕt′) *n.* A soft cotton cloth with a nap.

flannel leaf *n.* See **mullein.**

Flan•ner (flăn′ər), **Janet.** Genêt. 1892–1978. Amer. journalist who was Paris correspondent for the *New Yorker* (1925–75).

flap (flăp) *n.* **1.** A flat, usu. thin piece attached at one side. **2.** A projecting or hanging piece usu. intended to double over and protect or cover: *the flap of an envelope.* **3.a.** The act of waving or fluttering. **b.** The sound produced by this motion. **4.** A blow given with something flat; a slap. **5.** A control surface on the trailing edge of an aircraft wing, used primarily to increase lift or drag. **6.** Either of the folded ends of a book jacket that fit inside the front and back covers. **7.** *Medic.* Partially detached tissue used in surgical grafting or in covering the end of a bone after amputation. **8.** *Informal.* A commotion or disturbance. —*v.* **flapped, flap•ping, flaps.** —*tr.* **1.** To wave (the arms, for example) up and down. **2.** To cause to move or sway with a fluttering or waving motion. **3.** To hit with something broad and flat; slap. **4.** *Informal.* To fling down; toss. —*intr.* **1.** To move or sway while fixed at one edge or corner; flutter. **2.** To wave arms or wings up and down. **3.** To fly by beating the air with the wings. **4.** *Informal.* To become upset or flustered. [ME *flappe,* slap.]

flap•doo•dle also **flap-doo•dle** (flăp′do͞od′l) *n. Slang.* Foolish talk; nonsense. [?]

flap•jack (flăp′jăk′) *n.* See **pancake.**

flap•pa•ble (flăp′ə-bəl) *adj. Informal.* Easily excited or upset.

flap•per (flăp′ər) *n.* **1.** A broad flexible part, such as a flipper. **2.** A young woman, esp. one in the 1920's who showed disdain for convention. [Sense 2, British slang, very young female prostitute, flapper, poss. < *flapper,* fledgling partridge or duck (< FLAP) or < dial. *flap,* loose or flighty girl.]

flare (flâr) *v.* **flared, flar•ing, flares.** —*intr.* **1.** To flame up with a bright wavering light. **2.** To burst into intense sudden flame. **3.a.** To erupt or intensify suddenly: *Tempers flared.* **b.** To become suddenly angry. **4.** To expand or open outward in shape: *with nostrils flaring.* —*tr.* **1.** To cause to flame up. **2.** To signal with a blaze of light. —*n.* **1.** A brief wavering blaze of light. **2.** A device that produces a bright light for signaling, illumination, or identification. **3.** An outbreak, as of emotion or activity. **4.** An expanding or opening outward. **5.** An unwanted reflection within an optical system or the resultant fogging of the image. **6.** A solar flare. **7.** *Football.* A quick pass to a back running toward the sideline. **8.** *Medic.* An area of redness on the skin surrounding the primary site of infection or irritation. [?]

flare•back (flâr′băk′) *n.* **1.** A flame produced in the breech of a gun by ignition of residual gases. **2.** A burst of something aimed back at its origin; a backfire.

flamenco

flamingo

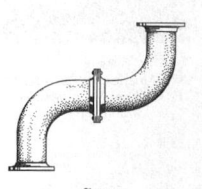

flange

ă pat	oi boy
ā pay	ou out
âr care	o͝o took
ä father	o͞o boot
ĕ pet	ŭ cut
ē be	ûr urge
ĭ pit	th thin
ī pie	*th* this
îr pier	hw which
ŏ pot	zh vision
ō toe	ə about,
ô paw	item

Stress marks:
′ (primary);
′ (secondary), as in
dictionary (dĭk′shə-nĕr′ē)

flare-up (flâr′ŭp′) *n.* **1.** A sudden outbreak of flame or light. **2.** An outburst or eruption: *a flare-up of anger.* **3.** A recurrence or an intensification: *a flare-up of rheumatism.*

flash (flăsh) *v.* **flashed, flash•ing, flash•es.** — *intr.* **1.** To burst forth into or as if into flame. **2.** To give off light or be lighted in sudden or intermittent bursts. **3.** To appear or occur suddenly. **4.** To move or proceed rapidly. **5.** *Slang.* To think of or remember something suddenly. **6.** *Slang.* To expose oneself in an indecent manner. — *tr.* **1.a.** To cause (light) to appear suddenly or in intermittent bursts. **b.** To cause to burst into flame. **c.** To reflect (light). **d.** To cause to reflect light from (a surface). **2.** To make known or signal by flashing lights. **3.** To communicate or display at great speed. **4.** To exhibit briefly. **5.** To display ostentatiously; flaunt. **6.** To fill suddenly with water. **7.** To cover with a thin protective layer. — *n.* **1.** A sudden, brief, intense display of light. **2.** A sudden perception. **3.** A split second; an instant. **4.** A brief news dispatch or transmission. **5.** *Slang.* Gaudy or ostentatious display. **6.** A flashlight. **7.a.** Instantaneous illumination for photography. **b.** A device, such as a flashgun, used to produce such illumination. **8.** *Slang.* The pleasurable sensation that accompanies the use of a drug; a rush. **9.** *Obsolete.* The language or cant of thieves, tramps, or underworld figures. — *adj.* **1.** Happening suddenly or very quickly: *flash freezing.* **2.** *Slang.* Ostentatious; showy. **3.** Of or relating to figures of quarterly economic growth released by the government and subject to later revision. **4.** Of or relating to photography using instantaneous illumination. **5.** Of or relating to thieves, swindlers, and underworld figures. — ***idiom.* flash in the pan.** One that promises great success but fails. [ME *flashen,* to splash, var. of *flasken,* of imit. orig.]

flash•back (flăsh′băk′) *n.* **1.a.** A literary or cinematic device in which an earlier event is inserted into a narrative. **b.** The episode or scene depicted by means of this device. **2.** An unexpected recurrence of the effects of a hallucinogenic drug after its original use. **3.** *Psychol.* A recurring, intensely vivid mental image of a past traumatic experience.

flash•board (flăsh′bôrd′, -bōrd′) *n.* A board or structure of boards extending above a dam to increase its capacity.

flash•bulb or **flash bulb** (flăsh′bŭlb′) *n.* A glass bulb filled with aluminum or magnesium foil that is ignited to produce a short-duration high-intensity light flash for photography.

flash burn *n.* A burn resulting from brief exposure to intense radiation.

flash butt weld•ing (wĕl′dĭng) *n.* A technique for joining metal rail or pipe in which an electric current melts and welds the ends of the metal, yielding a strong smooth joint.

flash card also **flash•card** (flăsh′kärd′) *n.* A card printed with words or numbers and briefly displayed in a learning drill.

flash•cube (flăsh′kyo͞ob′) *n.* A cube with four flashbulbs that attaches to a camera and rotates to an unused bulb when a picture is taken.

flash•er (flăsh′ər) *n.* **1.** A device that automatically switches an electric lamp off and on, as in a commercial display sign. **2.** *Slang.* One who engages in indecent exposure.

flash flood also **flash•flood** (flăsh′flŭd′) *n.* A sudden flood of great volume, usu. caused by a heavy rain.

flash-for•ward (flăsh′fôr′wərd) *n.* **1.** A literary or cinematic device in which a future event is inserted into the narrative. **2.** The episode or scene depicted by means of this device.

flash•gun (flăsh′gŭn′) *n.* A dry-cell powered photographic apparatus that holds and electrically triggers a flashbulb.

flash•ing (flăsh′ĭng) *n.* Sheet metal used to reinforce and weatherproof the joints and angles of a roof.

flash lamp *n.* An electric lamp for producing a high-intensity light of very short duration for use in photography.

flash•light (flăsh′līt′) *n.* **1.** A small portable lamp usu. powered by batteries. **2.** A brief brilliant flood of light from a photographic lamp. **3.** A bright light that flashes regularly.

flash•o•ver (flăsh′ō′vər) *n.* **1.** An unintended electric arc, as between two conductors. **2.** The temperature at which all flammable material in an area will ignite simultaneously.

flash point also **flash•point** (flăsh′point′) *n.* **1.** The lowest temperature at which the vapor of a combustible liquid can be made to ignite momentarily. **2.** The point at which eruption into significant action, creation, or violence occurs.

flash•tube also **flash tube** (flăsh′to͞ob′) *n.* A gas discharge tube that emits a brief intense flash of light.

flash unit *n.* **1.** An electronic flash system containing both a power supply and a flashtube in a single compact unit. **2.a.** See **flashgun. b.** A flashgun and reflector.

flash weld•ing (wĕl′dĭng) *n.* See **flash butt welding.**

flash•y (flăsh′ē) *adj.* **-i•er, -i•est. 1.** Cheap and showy; gaudy. **2.** Giving a momentary or superficial impression of brilliance. — **flash′i•ly** *adv.* — **flash′i•ness** *n.*

flask (flăsk) *n.* **1.** A small container having a narrow neck and usu. a cap, esp.: **a.** A flat, relatively thin container for liquor. **b.** A container for carrying gunpowder or shot. **c.** A vial or round long-necked vessel for laboratory use. **2.** A frame for holding a sand mold in a foundry. [ME, cask, keg < OFr. *flasque* < LLat. *flascō,* of Gmc. orig.]

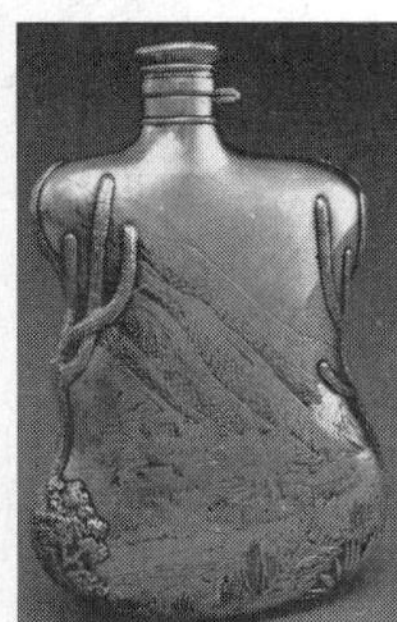

flask
1888 American silver flask by the Gorham Manufacturing Company

flatboat
1870 print by Currier and Ives

flat[1] (flăt) *adj.* **flat•ter, flat•test. 1.** Having a horizontal surface without a slope, tilt, or curvature. **2.** Having a smooth, even, level surface: *flat seams in the skirt.* **3.** Having a relatively broad surface in relation to thickness or depth. **4.** Stretched out or lying at full length along the ground; prone. **5.** Free of qualification; absolute. **6.** Fixed; unvarying: *a flat rate.* **7.** Lacking interest or excitement; dull. **8.a.** Lacking in flavor. **b.** Having lost effervescence or sparkle. **9.a.** Deflated. Used of a tire. **b.** Electrically discharged. Used of a storage battery. **10.** Of or relating to a horizontal line that displays no ups or downs and signifies the absence of physiological activity. **11.** Commercially inactive; sluggish. **12.** Unmodulated; monotonous: *a flat voice.* **13.** Lacking variety in tint or shading; uniform. **14.** Not glossy; mat: *flat paint.* **15.** *Mus.* **a.** Being below the correct pitch. **b.** Being one half step lower than the corresponding natural key: *the key of B flat.* **16.** Being the vowel *a* as pronounced in *bad* or *cat.* **17.** *Naut.* Having the edges pulled tight. Used of a sail. — *adv.* **1.a.** Level with the ground; horizontally. **b.** On or up against a flat surface; at full length. **2.** So as to be flat. **3.a.** Directly; completely: *flat broke.* **b.** Exactly; precisely: *six minutes flat.* **4.** *Mus.* Below the intended pitch. **5.** *Bus.* Without interest charge. — *n.* **1.** A flat surface or part. **2.** A stretch of level ground. Often used in the plural. **3.** A shallow frame or box for seeds or seedlings. **4.** Stage scenery on a movable wooden frame. **5.** A flatcar. **6.** A deflated tire. **7.** A shoe with a flat heel. **8.** A large flat piece of mail. **9.** A horse that competes in a flat race. **10.** *Mus.* **a.** A sign (♭) affixed to a note to indicate that it is to be lowered by a half step. **b.** A note that is lowered a half step. **11.** *Football.* The area of the field to either side of an offensive formation. — *v.* **flat•ted, flat•ting, flats.** — *tr.* **1.** To make flat; flatten. **2.** *Mus.* To lower (a note) a semitone. — *intr. Mus.* To sing or play below the proper pitch. [ME < ON *flatr.* See **plat-***.] — **flat′ly** *adv.* — **flat′ness** *n.*

flat[2] (flăt) *n.* **1.** An apartment on one floor of a building. **2.** *Archaic.* A story in a house. [Alteration of Sc. *flet,* inner part of a house < ME < OE, floor, dwelling. See **plat-***.]

flat•bed (flăt′bĕd′) *n.* **1.** An open truck bed or trailer with no sides, used to carry large objects. **2.** A railroad flatcar.

flat-bed press (flăt′bĕd′) *n. Print.* A press in which the type, locked into a chase, is supported by a flat surface or bed and the paper is applied to the type either by a flat platen or by a cylinder against which the bed moves.

flat•boat (flăt′bōt′) *n. Naut.* A boat with a flat bottom and square ends used to transport freight on inland waterways.

flat•bot•tom (flăt′bŏt′əm) or **flat•bot•tomed** (-bŏt′əmd) *adj.* Having a flat bottom: *a flatbottom boat.*

flat•bread (flăt′brĕd′) *n.* Any of various breads made from usu. unleavened dough and baked in flat, often round loaves.

flat•car (flăt′kär′) *n.* A railroad freight car without sides or a roof.

flat-coat•ed retriever (flăt′kō′tĭd) *n.* A medium-sized sporting dog of a breed originally developed in England, having a thick smooth coat that is black or deep reddish brown.

flat•fish (flăt′fĭsh′) *n., pl.* **flatfish** or **-fish•es.** Any of numerous chiefly marine fishes of the order Pleuronectiformes, including the flounders, soles, and halibuts, having a laterally compressed body with both eyes on the upper side.

flat•foot (flăt′fo͝ot′) *n.* **1.** *pl.* **-feet** (-fēt′). A condition in which the arch of the foot is abnormally flat so that the entire sole makes contact with the ground. **2.** *pl.* **-foots. a.** *Informal.* A person with flat feet. **b.** *Slang.* A police officer. — *intr.v.* **-foot•ed, -foot•ing, -foots.** To walk in a flat-footed manner.

flat-foot•ed (flăt′fo͝ot′ĭd) *adj.* **1.** Of or having flatfoot. **2.a.** Steady on the feet. **b.** *Informal.* Without reservation; forthright. **3.** Unable to react quickly; unprepared. — **flat′-foot′ed•ly** *adv.* — **flat′-foot′ed•ness** *n.*

Flat•head (flăt′hĕd′) *n., pl.* **Flathead** or **-heads. 1.a.** A member of a Native American people of western Montana and northern Idaho, now principally on Flathead Lake. **b.** The Salishan language of the Flathead. **2.** See **Interior Salish.**

flat•head catfish (flăt′hĕd′) *n.* A large yellow and brown catfish *(Pylodictis olivaris)* that is common in streams of the Mississippi Valley and southeast United States.

Flathead River. A river rising in SE British Columbia, Canada, and flowing c. 386 km (240 mi) across the MT border to **Flathead Lake** and the Clark Fork R.

flat•i•ron (flăt′ī′ərn) *n.* An iron for pressing clothes, esp. one that is heated externally, as on a hearth or stove.

flat•land (flăt′lănd′, -lənd) *n.* **1.** Land that varies little in elevation. **2. flatlands.** A geographic area composed chiefly of land that varies little in elevation. — **flat′land′er** *n.*

flat•let (flăt′lĭt) *n. Chiefly British.* An efficiency apartment.

flat•ling (flăt′lĭng) also **flat•lings** (-lĭngs) *adv. Chiefly British.* With the flat side or edge of a sword.

flat out *adv. Informal.* **1.** In a direct manner; bluntly: *told me the truth flat out.* **2.** At top speed: *running flat out.*

flat-out (flăt′out′) *adj. Informal.* Thoroughgoing; out-and-out: *a flat-out deception.*

flat pick *n. Mus.* A flat, often triangular plectrum, used in picking and strumming a guitar or similar instrument. — **flat′-pick′** (flăt′pĭk′) *v.* — **flat′-pick′er** *n.*

flat silver *n.* Utensils made of silver or silver plate.

flat•ten (flăt′n) *v.* **-tened, -ten•ing, -tens.** —*tr.* **1.** To make flat or flatter. **2.** To knock down; lay low. —*intr.* To become flat or flatter. —**flat′ten•er** *n.*

flat•ter¹ (flăt′ər) *v.* **-tered, -ter•ing, -ters.** —*tr.* **1.** To compliment excessively and often insincerely, esp. in order to win favor. **2.** To please or gratify the vanity of. **3.a.** To portray favorably: *a photograph that flatters its subject.* **b.** To show off becomingly or advantageously. —*intr.* To practice flattery. [ME *flateren* < OFr. *flater*, of Gmc. orig. See **plat-***.] —**flat′ter•er** *n.* —**flat′ter•ing•ly** *adv.*

flat•ter² (flăt′ər) *n.* **1.** A flat-faced swage or hammer used by blacksmiths. **2.** A die plate for flattening metal into strips.

flat•ter•y (flăt′ə-rē) *n., pl.* **-ies. 1.** The act or practice of flattering. **2.** Excessive or insincere praise.

flat•tish (flăt′ĭsh) *adj.* Somewhat flat.

flat•top (flăt′tŏp′) *n. Informal.* **1.** An aircraft carrier. **2.** A short haircut in which the hair is brushed straight up and cropped flat across the top.

flat•u•lence (flăch′ə-ləns) *n.* **1.** The presence of excessive gas in the digestive tract. **2.** Self-importance; pomposity.

flat•u•len•cy (flăch′ə-lən-sē) *n.* Flatulence.

flat•u•lent (flăch′ə-lənt) *adj.* **1.** Of, afflicted with, or caused by flatulence. **2.** Inducing or generating flatulence. **3.** Pompous; bloated. [Fr. < Lat. *flātus*, fart. See FLATUS.] —**flat′u•lent•ly** *adv.*

fla•tus (flā′təs) *n.* Gas generated in or expelled from the digestive tract, esp. the stomach or intestines. [Lat. *flātus*, wind, fart < *flāre*, to blow. See **bhlē-***.]

flat•ware (flăt′wâr′) *n.* **1.** Tableware that is fairly flat and fashioned usu. of a single piece, as plates. **2.** Table utensils such as knives, forks, and spoons.

flat•wise (flăt′wīz′) also **flat•ways** (-wāz′) *adv.* With the flat side down or in contact with a surface.

flat•work (flăt′wûrk′) *n.* Laundry, such as sheets and linens, that can be ironed by a mangle rather than by hand.

flat•worm (flăt′wûrm′) *n.* Any of various parasitic and nonparasitic worms of the phylum Platyhelminthes, such as a tapeworm, having a flat, bilaterally symmetrical body.

Flau•bert (flō-bâr′), **Gustave.** 1821–80. French writer considered a forerunner of naturalism whose works include *Madame Bovary* (1857). —**Flau•ber′tian** (-shən, -tē-ən) *adj.*

flaunt (flônt) *v.* **flaunt•ed, flaunt•ing, flaunts.** —*tr.* **1.** To exhibit ostentatiously or shamelessly. **2.** *Usage Problem.* To show contempt for; scorn. —*intr.* **1.** To parade oneself ostentatiously; show oneself off. **2.** To wave grandly. [?] —**flaunt′er** *n.* —**flaunt′ing•ly** *adv.*

Usage Note: *Flaunt* as a transitive verb means "to exhibit ostentatiously": *She flaunted her diamonds.* To *flout* is "to show contempt for": *She flouted the proprieties.* For some time now *flaunt* has been used in the sense "to show contempt for," even by educated users of English. This usage is still widely seen as erroneous and is best avoided.

flaunt•y (flôn′tē) *adj.* **-i•er, -i•est.** Inclined to flaunt; ostentatious. —**flaunt′i•ly** *adv.* —**flaunt′i•ness** *n.*

flau•ta (flou′tä) *n.* A tortilla rolled around a filling such as beef or cheese into a flutelike shape and usu. deep-fried. [Sp., flute, prob. < OProv. *flaüt.* See FLUTE.]

flau•tist (flô′tĭst, flou′-) *n. Mus.* A flutist. [Ital. *flautista* < *flauto*, flute < OProv. *flaüt.* See FLUTE.]

fla•va•none (flā′və-nōn′) *n.* A crystalline compound, $C_{15}H_{12}O_2$, derived from flavone. [FLAV(O)– + –AN(E) + –ONE.]

fla•ves•cent (flə-vĕs′ənt) *adj.* Turning yellow; yellowish. [Lat. *flāvēscēns, flāvēscent-*, pr.part. of *flāvēscere*, to turn yellow, inchoative of *flāvēre*, to be yellow < *flāvus*, yellow. See **bhel-¹***.]

fla•vin (flā′vĭn) also **fla•vine** (-vēn′) *n.* **1.** Any of various water-soluble yellow pigments, including riboflavin, found in plant and animal tissue as coenzymes of flavoprotein. **2.** A ketone, $C_{10}H_6N_4O_2$, found in various natural yellow pigments.

flavin adenine dinucleotide *n.* A coenzyme, $C_{27}H_{33}N_9O_{15}P_2$, that is a derivative of riboflavin and functions in certain oxidation-reduction reactions in the body.

fla•vine (flā′vēn′) *n.* A brownish-red crystalline powder, $C_{14}H_{15}N_3Cl_2$, used as an antiseptic.

flavin mononucleotide *n.* A derivative of riboflavin, $C_{17}H_{21}N_4O_9P$, that functions as a coenzyme of various flavoproteins in some bodily oxidation-reduction reactions.

flavo– or **flav–** *pref.* **1.** Yellow: *flavin.* **2.** Flavin: *flavoprotein.* [Lat. *flāvus*, yellow. See **bhel-¹***.]

fla•vone (flā′vōn′) *n.* A crystalline compound, $C_{15}H_{10}O_2$, the parent substance of a number of yellow pigments, occurring in primrose leaves, seed capsules, and stems.

fla•vo•noid (flā′və-noid′) *n.* Any of a large group of plant substances that includes the anthocyanins.

fla•vo•pro•tein (flā′vō-prō′tēn′, -tē-ĭn) *n.* Any of a group of enzymes containing flavin bound to protein and acting as dehydrogenation catalysts in biological reactions.

fla•vor (flā′vər) *n.* **1.** Distinctive taste; savor. **2.** A distinctive yet intangible quality felt to be characteristic of a given thing. **3.** A flavoring: *artificial flavors.* **4.** *Phys.* The property that distinguishes the six quark varieties: up, down, strange, charmed, top, and bottom. **5.** *Archaic.* Aroma; fragrance. —*tr.v.* **-vored, -vor•ing, -vors.** To give flavor to. [ME *flavour*, aroma < OFr. *flaor* < VLat. **flātor* < Lat. *flāre*, to blow. See **bhlē-***.] —**fla′vor•er** *n.* —**fla′vor•less** *adj.* —**fla′vor•ous** (-əs), **fla′vor•some** (-səm), **fla′vor•y** *adj.*

fla•vor•ful (flā′vər-fəl) *adj.* Full of flavor; savory.

fla•vor•ing (flā′vər-ĭng) *n.* A substance that imparts flavor.

fla•vor•ist (flā′vər-ĭst) *n.* One who blends artificially isolated chemicals to create the taste and smell of a particular food.

fla•vour (flā′vər) *n. & v. Chiefly British.* Var. of **flavor.**

flaw¹ (flô) *n.* **1.** An imperfection, often concealed, that impairs soundness: *a flaw in the crystal.* **2.** A defect or shortcoming in something intangible: *a character flaw.* **3.** A defect in a legal document that can render it invalid. —*tr. & intr.v.* **flawed, flaw•ing, flaws.** To make or become defective. [ME *flaue*, splinter, perh. < ON *flaga*, slab of stone. See **plāk-¹***.]

flaw² (flô) *n.* **1.a.** A brief gust or blast of wind. **b.** A passing storm; a squall. **2.** *Obsolete.* A burst of passion. [Prob. of Scand. orig.; akin to Swed. *flaga*, gust of wind.] —**flaw′y** *adj.*

flaw•less (flô′lĭs) *adj.* Being entirely without flaw or imperfection; perfect. See Syns at **perfect.** —**flaw′less•ly** *adv.* —**flaw′less•ness** *n.*

flax (flăks) *n.* **1.a.** Any of several plants of the genus *Linum*, esp. the widely cultivated *L. usitatissimum* having blue flowers, seeds that yield linseed oil, and slender stems. **b.** The fine light-colored textile fiber obtained from the stems of this plant. **c.** Any of several similar plants. **2.** *Color.* A pale grayish yellow. [ME < OE *fleax.* See **plek-***.]

flax•en (flăk′sən) *adj.* **1.** Made of or resembling flax. **2.** Having the pale grayish-yellow color of flax fiber: *flaxen braids.*

flax•seed (flăks′sēd′) *n.* The seed of flax, the source of linseed oil and emollient medicinal preparations.

flax•y (flăk′sē) *adj.* **-i•er, -i•est.** Resembling flax.

flay (flā) *tr.v.* **flayed, flay•ing, flays. 1.** To strip off the skin or outer covering of. **2.** To strip of money or goods; fleece. **3.** To whip or lash. **4.** To assail with stinging criticism; excoriate. [ME *flen* < OE *flēan.*] —**flay′er** *n.*

F layer *n.* **1.** The highest zone of the ionosphere, extending at night from about 190 to 400 kilometers (120 to 250 miles) and during the day from about 145 to 400 kilometers (90 to 250 miles) above the earth's surface. **2.** Either of two layers, the lower designated F_1 and the higher F_2, into which the F layer is divided during the day.

fld. *abbr.* Field.

fl dr *abbr.* Fluid dram.

flea (flē) *n.* **1.** Any of various small wingless bloodsucking insects of the order Siphonaptera that have legs adapted for jumping and are parasitic on warm-blooded animals. **2.** Any of various small crustaceans that resemble or move like fleas, such as the water flea. —***idiom.*** **a flea in (one's) ear.** An annoying hint or a stinging rebuke. [ME *fle* < OE *flēah.*]

flea•bag (flē′băg′) *n. Informal.* A seedy run-down hotel or other lodging place.

flea•bane (flē′bān′) *n.* Any of various plants of the genus *Erigeron*, having many-rayed daisylike flower heads.

flea beetle *n.* Any of various small herbivorous beetles of the subfamily Alticinae that have hind legs adapted for jumping.

flea•bite (flē′bīt′) *n.* **1.a.** The bite of a flea. **b.** The small red mark of a flea's bite. **2.** A trifling loss, inconvenience, or annoyance.

flea-bit•ten (flē′bĭt′n) *adj.* **1.** Covered with fleas or fleabites. **2.** *Informal.* Seedy; delapidated: *a flea-bitten couch.* **3.** Having a pale coat with reddish-brown flecks. Used of horses.

flea collar *n.* A collar, as for a cat or dog, containing a substance that repels or kills fleas.

flea market *n.* A market, usu. held outdoors, where antiques, used household goods, and curios are sold.

flea•pit (flē′pĭt′) *n. Chiefly British.* A cheap or squalid theater.

flèche (flĕsh, flāsh) *n.* A slender spire, esp. one on a church above the intersection of the nave and transepts. [Fr., arrow, flèche < OFr., arrow, of Gmc. orig. See **pleu-***.]

flé•chette (flā-shĕt′, flĕ-) *n.* A steel missile or dart dropped from an aircraft. [Fr., dim. of *flèche*, arrow. See FLÈCHE.]

fleck (flĕk) *n.* **1.** A tiny mark or spot. **2.** A small bit or flake. —*tr.v.* **flecked, fleck•ing, flecks.** To spot or streak. [Prob. < ME *flekked*, spotted; akin to ON *flekkr*, spot.]

flec•tion (flĕk′shən) *n. Anat.* Var. of **flexion** 1.

fledge (flĕj) *v.* **fledged, fledg•ing, fledg•es.** —*tr.* **1.** To take care of (a young bird) until it can fly. **2.** To cover with or as if with feathers. **3.** To provide (an arrow) with feathers. —*intr.* To grow the plumage necessary for flight. [Prob. < obsolete *fledge*, feathered < ME *flegge* < OE **flycge.* See **pleu-***.]

fledg•ling also **fledge•ling** (flĕj′lĭng) —*n.* **1.** A young bird that has recently fledged. **2.** A young or inexperienced person. —*adj.* New and untried or inexperienced.

flee (flē) *v.* **fled** (flĕd), **flee•ing, flees.** —*intr.* **1.** To run away, as from trouble or danger. **2.** To pass swiftly away; vanish: *"of time fleeing beneath him"* (William Faulkner). —*tr.* To

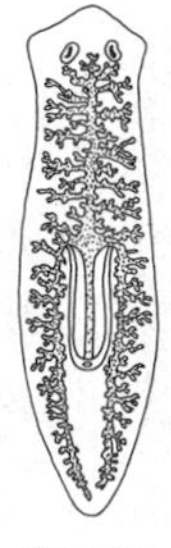
flatworm

flax

flèche
Amiens Cathedral, France

ă pat	oi boy
ā pay	ou out
âr care	ŏŏ took
ä father	ōō boot
ĕ pet	ŭ cut
ē be	ûr urge
ĭ pit	th thin
ī pie	*th* this
îr pier	hw which
ŏ pot	zh vision
ō toe	ə about, item
ô paw	

Stress marks:
′ (primary);
′ (secondary), as in **dictionary** (dĭk′shə-nĕr′ē)

flee from. [ME *flen* < OE *flēon.* See **pleu-***.] **—fle′er** *n.*

fleece (flēs) *n.* **1.a.** The coat of wool of a sheep or similar animal. **b.** The wool shorn from a sheep at one time. **2.** A soft woolly covering or mass. **3.** Fabric with a soft deep pile. *—tr.v.* **fleeced, fleec•ing, fleec•es. 1.** To defraud of money or property; swindle. **2.** To shear the fleece from. **3.** To cover with or as if with fleece. [ME *fles* < OE *flēos.*] **—fleec′er** *n.*

fleec•y (flē′sē) *adj.* **-i•er, -i•est.** Of, resembling, or covered with fleece: *fleecy clouds.* **—fleec′i•ly** *adv.* **—fleec′i•ness** *n.*

fleer (flîr) *intr.v.* **fleered, fleer•ing, fleers.** To smirk or laugh in contempt or derision. *—n.* A taunting, scoffing, or derisive look or gibe. [ME *flerien,* of Scand. orig.] **—fleer′ing•ly** *adv.*

fleet[1] (flēt) *n.* **1.** A number of warships operating together under one command. **2.** A group of vessels or vehicles, such as taxicabs, owned or operated as a unit. [ME *flete* < OE *flēot* < *flēotan,* to float. See **pleu-***.]

fleet[2] (flēt) *adj.* **fleet•er, fleet•est. 1.** Moving swiftly; rapid or nimble. See Syns at **fast[1]**. **2.** Fleeting; evanescent. *—v.* **fleet•ed, fleet•ing, fleets.** *—intr.* **1.** To move or pass swiftly. **2.** To fade out; vanish. **3.** *Archaic.* To flow. **4.** *Obsolete.* To drift. *—tr.* **1.** To cause (time) to pass quickly. **2.** *Naut.* To alter the position of (tackle or rope, for example). [Prob. < ON *fljōtr.* V. < ME *fleten,* to drift, float < OE *flēotan.* See **pleu-***.] **—fleet′ly** *adv.* **—fleet′ness** *n.*

Fleet Admiral (flēt) *n.* See **Admiral of the Fleet.**

fleet•ing (flē′tĭng) *adj.* Passing quickly; ephemeral. **—fleet′ing•ly** *adv.* **—fleet′ing•ness** *n.*

Fleet Street *n.* British journalism. [After *Fleet Street* in central London, long the headquarters of many British newspapers.]

flei•shig (flā′shĭk) *adj.* Consisting of, prepared with, or relating to meat or meat products. [Yiddish *fleyshik* < *fleysh,* meat < MHGer. *vleisch,* meat < OHGer. *fleisk,* flesh.]

Flem. *abbr.* Flemish.

Flem•ing (flĕm′ĭng) *n.* **1.** A native or inhabitant of Flanders. **2.** A Belgian who speaks Flemish. [ME < MDu. *Vlāming.*]

Fleming, Sir **Alexander.** 1881–1955. British bacteriologist who discovered penicillin in 1928 and shared a 1945 Nobel Prize.

Fleming, Ian Lancaster. 1908–64. British writer noted for his spy novels featuring the secret agent James Bond.

Fleming, Peggy Gale. b. 1948. Amer. figure skater who won the women's title at the 1968 Olympics.

Flem•ish (flĕm′ĭsh) *adj.* Of or relating to Flanders, the Flemings, or their language or culture. *—n.* **1.** The West Germanic language of the Flemings. **2.** The Flemings.

Flens•burg (flĕnz′bûrg, flĕns′bo͝ork′). A city of N Germany on **Flensburg Fjord,** an arm of the Baltic Sea. Pop. 86,873.

flense (flĕns) *tr.v.* **flensed, flens•ing, flens•es.** To strip the blubber or skin from (a whale, for example). [Dan.] **—flens′er** *n.*

flesh (flĕsh) *n.* **1.a.** The soft tissue of the body of a vertebrate, consisting mainly of skeletal muscle and fat. **b.** The surface or skin of the human body. **2.** The meat of animals as distinguished from the edible tissue of fish or fowl. **3.** *Bot.* The pulpy, usu. edible part of a fruit or vegetable. **4.** Excess fatty tissue; plumpness. **5.a.** The body as opposed to the mind or soul. **b.** The physical or carnal nature of humankind. **c.** Sensual appetites. **6.** Humankind in general; humanity. **7.** One's family; kin. **8.** Substance; reality. *—v.* **fleshed, flesh•ing, flesh•es.** *—tr.* **1.** To give substance or detail to; fill out: *fleshed out the story.* **2.** To clean (a hide) of adhering flesh. **3.** To encourage (a falcon, for example) to participate in the chase by feeding it flesh from a kill. **4.** To inure to battle or bloodshed. **5.** To plunge or thrust (a weapon) into flesh. *—intr.* To become plump or fleshy; gain weight. **—*idiom.* in the flesh. 1.** Alive. **2.** In person; present. [ME < OE *flǣsc.*] **—flesh′less** *adj.*

fleur-de-lis
On a gold florin

flesh and blood *n.* **1.** Human nature or physical existence, together with its weaknesses. **2.** A person's blood relatives; kin. **3.** Substance and depth in artistic portrayal; lifelikeness.

flesh fly *n.* Any of various flies of the family Sarcophagidae whose larvae are parasitic in animal tissue or feed on carrion.

flesh•ly (flĕsh′lē) *adj.* **-li•er, -li•est. 1.** Of or relating to the body; corporeal. See Syns at **bodily. 2.** Of, relating to, or inclined to carnality; sensual. **3.** Not spiritual; worldly. **4.** Tending to plumpness; fleshy. **—flesh′li•ness** *n.*

flesh•pot (flĕsh′pŏt′) *n.* **1.** A district or an establishment offering sensual pleasures or entertainment. Often used in the plural. **2.** Physical or sensual gratification.

flesh wound (wo͞ond) *n.* A wound that penetrates the flesh but does not damage underlying bones or vital organs.

flesh•y (flĕsh′ē) *adj.* **-i•er, -i•est. 1.a.** Relating to, consisting of, or resembling flesh. **b.** Having abundant flesh; plump. See Syns at **fat. 2.** Having a juicy or pulpy texture. **3.** Fleshly; carnal. **—flesh′i•ness** *n.*

fleshy fruit *n.* A fruit that has a soft, pulpy wall.

fletch (flĕch) *tr.v.* **fletched, fletch•ing, fletch•es.** To feather (an arrow). [Prob. back-formation < FLETCHER.]

fletch•er (flĕch′ər) *n.* One who makes arrows. [ME *fleccher* < OFr. *flechier* < *fleche,* arrow, of Gmc. orig. See **pleu-***.]

Fletch•er (flĕch′ər), **John.** 1579–1625. English playwright who collaborated with Francis Beaumont on romantic tragicomedies, including *The Maid's Tragedy* (1611).

fleur-de-lis or **fleur-de-lys** (flûr′də-lē′, flo͝or′-) *n., pl.* **fleurs-de-lis** or **fleurs-de-lys** (flûr′də-lēz′, flo͝or′-). **1.** An iris, esp. a white-flowered form of *Iris germanica.* **2.** *Her.* A device consisting of a stylized three-petaled iris flower, used as the armorial emblem of the kings of France. [ME *flour de lice* < OFr. *flor de lis* : *flor,* flower + *de,* of + *lis,* lily.]

Fleu•ry (flœ-rē′), **André Hercule de.** 1653–1743. French prelate who served as prime minister (1726–43) to Louis XV.

flew (flo͞o) *v.* P.t. of **fly[1]**.

flews (flo͞oz) *pl.n.* The pendulous corners of the upper lip of certain dogs, such as the bloodhound. [?]

flex (flĕks) *v.* **flexed, flex•ing, flex•es.** *—tr.* **1.** To bend (something pliant or elastic). **2.a.** To bend (a joint). **b.** To bend (a joint) repeatedly. **3.a.** To contract (a muscle, for example). **b.** To move by muscular control: *flexes his brow.* **4.** To exhibit or show off the strength of. *—intr.* To bend. *—n.* **1.** *Chiefly British.* Flexible insulated electric cord. **2.** The act or an instance of flexing; a bending. **3.** Pliancy; flexibility. **—*idiom.* flex (one's) muscles.** *Informal.* To exhibit or show off one's strength. [Lat. *flectere, flex-,* to bend.]

flex•a•gon (flĕk′sə-gŏn′) *n.* A paper construction that can be flexed along its folds to reveal and conceal its faces.

flexi– or **flex–** *pref.* Flexible: *flexitime.* [< FLEXIBLE.]

flex•i•ble (flĕk′sə-bəl) *adj.* **1.a.** Capable of being bent or flexed; pliable. **b.** Capable of being bent repeatedly without injury or damage. **2.** Susceptible to influence or persuasion; tractable. **3.** Responsive to change; adaptable. [< Lat. *flexibilis* < *flexus,* p.part. of *flectere,* to bend.] **—flex′i•bil′i•ty, flex′i•ble•ness** *n.* **—flex′i•bly** *adv.*

flex•ile (flĕk′səl, -sīl′) *adj.* Flexible.

flex•ion (flĕk′shən) *n.* **1.** Also **flec•tion.** *Anat.* **a.** The bending of a joint or limb by the action of flexors. **b.** The resulting condition of being bent. **2.** A part that is bent. [Lat. *flexiō, flexiōn-,* a bending < *flexus,* p.part. of *flectere,* to bend.]

flex•i•time (flĕk′sĭ-tīm′) *n.* See **flextime.**

flex•og•ra•phy (flĕk-sŏg′rə-fē) *n.* A system of printing on a rotary press employing water-based ink, used esp. for printing on plastic or cardboard. **—flex•og′ra•pher** *n.* **—flex′o•graph′ic** (-sə-grăf′ĭk) *adj.* **—flex′o•graph′i•cal•ly** *adv.*

flex•or (flĕk′sər) *n.* A muscle that when contracted acts to bend a joint or limb in the body. [NLat. < Lat. *flexus,* p.part. of *flectere,* to bend.]

flex•time (flĕks′tīm′) *n.* A system by which employees may schedule their work, esp. their starting and finishing hours.

flex•u•ous (flĕk′sho͞o-əs) *adj.* Bending or winding alternately from side to side; sinuous. [< Lat. *flexuōsus* < *flexus,* a bending, a turning < *flectere,* to bend.] **—flex′u•os′i•ty** (-ŏs′ĭ-tē) *n.* **—flex′u•ous•ly** *adv.*

flex•ure (flĕk′shər) *n.* **1.** A curve, turn, or fold. **2.** The act or an instance of bending or flexing; flexion. **—flex′ur•al** *adj.*

fley (flā) *tr.v.* **fleyed, fley•ing, fleys.** *Scots.* To frighten. [ME *fleien* < OE *flȳgan, flēgan.* See **pleu-***.]

flib•ber•ti•gib•bet (flĭb′ər-tē-jĭb′ĭt) *n.* A silly, scatterbrained, or garrulous person. [ME *flipergebet.*]

flic (flĭk) *n. Slang.* A police officer, esp. in France. [Fr.]

flick[1] (flĭk) *n.* **1.a.** A light quick blow, jerk, or touch. **b.** The sound accompanying this motion. **2.** A light splash, dash, or daub. *—v.* **flicked, flick•ing, flicks.** *—tr.* **1.** To touch or hit with a light quick blow. **2.** To cause to move with a light blow; snap. **3.** To remove with a light quick blow. *—intr.* To twitch or flutter. [Imit.] **—flick′a•ble** *adj.*

flick[2] (flĭk) *n. Slang.* A movie. [Short for FLICKER[1].]

flick•er[1] (flĭk′ər) *v.* **-ered, -er•ing, -ers.** *—intr.* **1.** To move waveringly; flutter. **2.** To burn unsteadily. *—tr.* To cause to move waveringly. *—n.* **1.** A brief movement; a tremor. **2.** An inconstant or wavering light. **3.** A brief or slight sensation. **4.** *Slang.* A movie. [ME *flikeren,* to flutter < OE *flicerian.*]

flick•er[2] (flĭk′ər) *n.* Any of various large North American woodpeckers of the genus *Colaptes,* esp. *C. auratus,* the common flicker, which has a brown back, spotted breast, and white rump. [Perh. < FLICK[1].]

flied (flīd) *intr.v.* P.t. and p.part. of **fly[1]** 7.

fli•er also **fly•er** (flī′ər) *n.* **1.** One, such as an insect or a bird, that flies with wings. **2.** The pilot of an aircraft. **3.** A passenger in an aircraft. **4.** A pamphlet or circular for mass distribution. **5.** A step in a straight stairway. **6.** *Informal.* A daring venture.

flies (flīz) *v.* Third pers. sing. pr.t. of **fly[1]**.

flight[1] (flīt) *n.* **1.a.** The motion of an object in or through a medium, esp. through the earth's atmosphere or through space. **b.** An instance of such motion. **c.** The distance covered in such motion. **2.a.** The act or process of flying through the air by means of wings. **b.** The ability to fly. **3.** A swift passage or movement. **4.** A scheduled airline run or trip. **5.** A group, esp. of birds or aircraft, flying together. **6.** A number of aircraft in the U.S. Air Force forming a subdivision of a squadron. **7.** An exuberant or transcendent effort or display: *flights of oratory.* **8.** A series of stairs rising from one landing to another. *—intr.v.* **flight•ed, flight•ing, flights.** To migrate or fly in flocks. [ME < OE *flyht.* See **pleu-***.]

flight[2] (flīt) *n.* The act or an instance of running away; an escape. [ME < OE **flyht.* See **pleu-***.]

flight attendant *n.* One who assists aircraft passengers.
flight bag *n.* A lightweight flexible piece of luggage with zippered outside pockets.
flight deck *n.* **1.** The upper deck of an aircraft carrier, used as a runway. **2.** An elevated compartment in certain aircraft, used by the pilot, copilot, and flight engineer.
flight engineer *n.* The crew member responsible for the mechanical performance of an aircraft in flight.
flight feather *n.* Any of the comparatively large stiff feathers of a bird's wing or tail that are necessary for flight.
flight•less (flīt′lĭs) *adj.* Incapable of flying. Used of certain birds, such as the penguin.
flight line *n.* The area of an airfield where aircraft are onloaded, offloaded, and serviced.
flight recorder *n.* A device, as on an aircraft, that documents preflight checks, in-flight procedures, and the landing.
flight surgeon *n.* An air force physician who specializes in aeromedicine.
flight-test (flīt′tĕst′) *tr.v.* **-test•ed, -test•ing, -tests.** To test (an aircraft, for example) during flight.
flight•wor•thy (flīt′wûr′thē) *adj.* Of, relating to, or being an aircraft that is fit to fly. **— flight′wor′thi•ness** *n.*
flight•y (flī′tē) *adj.* **-i•er, -i•est. 1.a.** Given to capricious or unstable behavior. **b.** Irresponsible or silly. **2.** Easily excited; skittish. **— flight′i•ly** *adv.* **— flight′i•ness** *n.*
flim•flam (flĭm′flăm′) *Informal.* *— n.* **1.** Nonsense; humbug. **2.** A deception; a swindle. *— tr.v.* **-flammed, -flam•ming, -flams.** To swindle; cheat. [Prob. of Scand. orig.] **— flim′-flam′mer** *n.* **— flim′flam′mer•y** *n.*
flim•sy (flĭm′zē) *adj.* **-si•er, -si•est. 1.** Light, thin, and insubstantial. **2.** Lacking solidity or strength. **3.** Lacking plausibility; unconvincing. *— n., pl.* **-sies. 1.** Thin paper usu. used to make multiple copies. **2.** Something written on this thin paper. [?] **— flim′si•ly** *adv.* **— flim′si•ness** *n.*
flinch (flĭnch) *intr.v.* **flinched, flinch•ing, flinch•es. 1.** To start or wince involuntarily, as from surprise or pain. **2.** To recoil, as from something unpleasant or difficult; shrink. *— n.* An act or instance of flinching. [Obsolete Fr. *flenchir*, of Gmc. orig.] **— flinch′er** *n.* **— flinch′ing•ly** *adv.*
flin•ders (flĭn′dərz) *pl.n.* Bits, fragments, or splinters. [ME *flendris*, poss. of Scand. orig.; akin to Norw. *flindra*, splinter.]
Flin•ders Range (flĭn′dərz). A mountain range of S-central Australia E of Lake Torrens rising to 1,189.5 m (3,900 ft).
Flinders River. An intermittent river of NE Australia flowing c. 837 km (520 mi) to the Gulf of Carpentaria.
fling (flĭng) *v.* **flung** (flŭng), **fling•ing, flings.** *— tr.* **1.** To throw with violence. See Syns at **throw. 2.** To put or send suddenly or unexpectedly. **3.** To throw (oneself) into an activity with abandon and energy. **4.** To cast aside; discard. *— intr.* To move quickly, violently, or impulsively. *— n.* **1.** The act of flinging. **2.** A brief period of indulging one's impulses. See Syns at **binge. 3.** *Informal.* A usu. brief attempt or effort. [ME *flingen*, of Scand. orig. See **plak-²***.]
flint (flĭnt) *n.* **1.** A hard fine-grained quartz that sparks when struck with steel. **2.a.** A piece of flint used to produce a spark. **b.** A cylinder of a spark-producing alloy, used in lighters to ignite the fuel. **3.** A piece of flint used as a tool by early humans. **4.** Something hard like flint. [ME < OE.]
Flint (flĭnt). A city of SE-central MI NNW of Detroit; founded on the site of a fur-trading post estab. in 1819. Pop. 140,761.
flint corn *n.* A variety of corn *(Zea mays* var. *indurata)* having small hard grains.
flint glass *n.* A soft, fusible, lustrous, brilliant lead-oxide optical glass with high refraction and low dispersion.
flint•head (flĭnt′hĕd′) *n.* See **wood ibis.**
flint•lock (flĭnt′lŏk′) *n.* **1.** An obsolete gunlock in which a flint embedded in the hammer produces a spark that ignites the charge. **2.** A firearm having this type of gunlock.
Flint River. A river of W GA flowing c. 531 km (330 mi) to join the Chattahoochee R. and form the Apalachicola R.
flint•y (flĭn′tē) *adj.* **-i•er, -i•est. 1.** Containing or composed of flint. **2.** Unyielding; stern. **— flint′i•ly** *adv.* **— flint′i•ness** *n.*
flip (flĭp) *v.* **flipped, flip•ping, flips.** *— tr.* **1.** To throw or toss with a light, brisk motion. **2.** To toss in the air, imparting a spin. **3.a.** To turn over or around, esp. with a light, quick motion. **b.** To turn through; leaf. **4.** To strike quickly or lightly; flick. **5.** To move or act on with a quick motion. *— intr.* **1.** To turn over: *The canoe flipped over.* **2.** To turn a somersault in the air. **3.** To move in twists and turns. **4.** To move quickly and lightly; snap: *The lid flipped open.* **5.** To leaf; browse. **6.** *Slang.* **a.** To go crazy. Often used with *out.* **b.** To react strongly and esp. enthusiastically. *— n.* **1.** The act of flipping, esp.: **a.** A flick or tap. **b.** A short, quick movement. **c.** A somersault. **2.** *Informal.* A reversal; a flipflop. **3.** A mixed drink made with any of various alcoholic beverages and often beaten eggs. *— adj.* **flip•per, flip•pest.** *Informal.* Marked by casual disrespect; impertinent. ***— idiom.* flip (one's) lid.** *Slang.* **1.** To react strongly, as with anger or enthusiasm. **2.** To go crazy. [Perh. imit.]
flip•book (flĭp′bo͝ok′) *n.* A small book consisting of a series of images that give the illusion of continuous movement when the edges of the pages are flipped quickly.
flip-flop (flĭp′flŏp′) *n.* **1.** The movement or sound of repeated flapping. **2.** A backward somersault or handspring. **3.** *Informal.* A reversal, as of a stand or position. **4.** A backless, often foam rubber sandal held to the foot at the big toe by means of a thong. **5.** *Electron.* An electronic circuit or mechanical device capable of assuming either of two stable states, esp. a computer circuit used to store a single bit. **— flip′-flop′** *v.*
flip•pant (flĭp′ənt) *adj.* **1.** Marked by disrespectful levity or casualness; pert. **2.** *Archaic.* Talkative; voluble. [Prob. < FLIP.] **— flip′pan•cy** *n.* **— flip′pant•ly** *adv.*
flip•per (flĭp′ər) *n.* **1.** A wide flat limb, as of a seal or whale, adapted for swimming. **2.** A rubber foot covering with a flat flexible part that extends forward from the toes, used in swimming.
flip side *n.* *Informal.* **1.** The reverse side, as of a phonograph record. **2.** The opposite side.
flirt (flûrt) *v.* **flirt•ed, flirt•ing, flirts.** *— intr.* **1.** To make playfully romantic or sexual overtures. **2.** To deal playfully, triflingly, or superficially with. **3.** To move abruptly or jerkily. *— tr.* **1.** To toss or flip suddenly. **2.** To move quickly. *— n.* **1.** One given to flirting. **2.** An abrupt jerking movement. [?]
flir•ta•tion (flûr-tā′shən) *n.* **1.** The practice of flirting. **2.** A superficial, usu. temporary romance. **3.** A brief involvement.
flir•ta•tious (flûr-tā′shəs) *adj.* **1.** Given to flirting. **2.** Full of playful allure. **— flir•ta′tious•ly** *adv.* **— flir•ta′tious•ness** *n.*
flit (flĭt) *intr.v.* **flit•ted, flit•ting, flits. 1.** To move about rapidly and nimbly. **2.** To move quickly from one condition or location to another. *— n.* **1.** A fluttering or darting movement. **2.** *Informal.* An empty-headed, silly, often erratic person. [ME *flitten* < ON *flytja*, convey. See **pleu-***.] **— flit′ter** *n.*
flitch (flĭch) *n.* **1.** A salted and cured side of bacon. **2.** A longitudinal cut from a tree trunk. **3.** One of several planks secured together to form a single beam. [ME *flicche* < OE *flicce.*]
flit•ter (flĭt′ər) *intr.v.* **-tered, -ter•ing, -ters.** To flutter. [Freq. of FLIT.]
float (flōt) *v.* **float•ed, float•ing, floats.** *— intr.* **1.a.** To remain suspended within or on the surface of a fluid without sinking. **b.** To be suspended in or move through space as if supported by a liquid. **2.** To move from place to place, esp. at random. **3.** To move easily or lightly. **4.** *Econ.* To find a value relative to other currencies solely in response to supply and demand. *— tr.* **1.** To cause to remain suspended without sinking or falling. **2.a.** To put into the water; launch: *float a ship.* **b.** To start or establish (a business enterprise, for example). **3.** To flood (land), as for irrigation. **4.** *Econ.* To allow (the exchange value of a currency) to float. **5.** To release (a security) for sale. **6.** To arrange for (a loan). **7.** To make the surface of (plaster, for example) level or smooth. **8.** *Comp. Sci.* To convert (data) from fixed-point to floating-point notation. *— n.* **1.** Something that floats, as: **a.** A raft. **b.** A buoy. **c.** A life preserver. **d.** A buoyant object, such as a cork, used to hold a net or fishing line afloat. **e.** A landing platform attached to a wharf and floating on the water. **f.** A floating ball attached to a lever to regulate the water level in a tank. **2.** *Biol.* An air-filled sac or structure that aids in the flotation of an aquatic organism. **3.** A decorated exhibit or scene mounted on a mobile platform and pulled or driven in a parade. **4.** A sum of money representing checks that are outstanding. **5.** A tool for smoothing the surface of plaster or cement. **6.** A soft drink with ice cream floating in it. See Regional Note at **milk shake.** [ME *floten* < OE *flotian.* See **pleu-***.] **— float′a•ble** *adj.*
float•age (flō′tĭj) *n.* Var. of **flotage.**
float•a•tion (flō-tā′shən) *n.* Var. of **flotation.**
float•er (flō′tər) *n.* **1.** One that floats or is capable of floating. **2.** One who wanders; a drifter. **3.** An employee who is reassigned from job to job or shift to shift. **4.** One who votes illegally in different polling places. **5.** An insurance policy that protects property in transit or regularly subject to use in varying places. **6.** *Slang.* A corpse recovered from a body of water, esp. after some time. **7.** A speck in the visual field, usu. perceived to be moving, due to minute clumps of cells or proteins in the vitreous humor.
float•ing (flō′tĭng) *adj.* **1.** Buoyed on or suspended in or as if in a fluid. **2.** Not secured in place; unattached. **3.** Inclined to move or be moved about. **4.** *Econ.* **a.** Available for use; in circulation. Used of capital. **b.** Short-term and usu. unfunded. Used of a debt. **5.** Designed or constructed to operate smoothly and without vibration. **6.** Of or relating to an organ of the body that is movable or out of normal position.
floating dock *n.* **1.** A structure that can be submerged to dock a ship and then raised to lift the ship from the water for repairs. **2.** A dock that can move up and down with the rise and fall of the water level.
float•ing-point (flō′tĭng-point′) *adj.* Of, relating to, or being a method of writing numbers with a mantissa representing the value of the digits and a characteristic indicating the power of the number base, such as 3×10^{-5}.
floating rib *n.* A false rib whose anterior end is unattached.

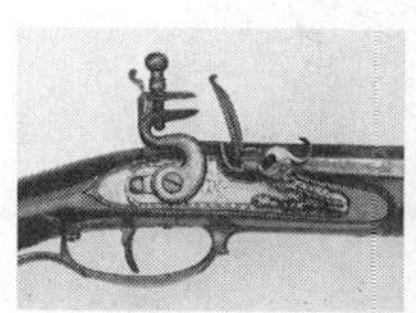

flintlock
Late 18th-century American Kentucky rifle

ă **pat**	oi **boy**
ā **pay**	ou **out**
âr **care**	o͝o **took**
ä **father**	o͞o **boot**
ĕ **pet**	ŭ **cut**
ē **be**	ûr **urge**
ĭ **pit**	th **thin**
ī **pie**	*th* **this**
îr **pier**	hw **which**
ŏ **pot**	zh **vision**
ō **toe**	ə **about,**
ô **paw**	**item**

Stress marks:
′ (primary);
′ (secondary), as in
dictionary (dĭk′shə-nĕr′ē)

float•plane (flōt′plān′) *n.* An aircraft equipped with one or more floats for landing on or taking off from a body of water.
floc (flŏk) *n.* A flocculent mass formed in a fluid through precipitation or aggregation of suspended particles.
floc•cose (flŏk′ōs) *adj. Bot.* Covered with tufts of soft hair. [LLat. *floccōsus* < Lat. *floccus*, tuft of wool.]
floc•cu•late (flŏk′yə-lāt′) *v.* **-lat•ed, -lat•ing, -lates.** —*tr.* **1.** To cause (soil) to form lumps or masses. **2.** To cause (clouds) to form fluffy masses. —*intr.* To form lumpy or fluffy masses. —*n.* Something that has flocculated. —**floc′cu•la′tion** *n.*
floc•cule (flŏk′yōōl) *n.* A flocculus suspended in or precipitated from a solution. [NLat. *flocculus.* See FLOCCULUS.]

floe
In Antarctica

floc•cu•lent (flŏk′yə-lənt) *adj.* **1.** Having a fluffy or woolly appearance. **2.** *Chem.* Made up of or containing woolly masses. **3.** *Zool.* Having a soft, waxy, and woollike covering, as certain insects. —**floc′cu•lence** *n.* —**floc′cu•lent•ly** *adv.*
floc•cu•lus (flŏk′yə-ləs) *n., pl.* **-li** (-lī′). **1.** A small fluffy mass or tuft. **2.** *Anat.* Either of two small lobes on the lower posterior border of the cerebellum. **3.** *Astron.* Any of various cloudlike masses of gases appearing as patches on the surface of the sun. [NLat., dim. of Lat. *floccus*, tuft of wool.]
flock[1] (flŏk) *n.* **1.** A group of animals that live, travel, or feed together. **2.** A group of people under the leadership of one person, esp. the members of a church. **3.** A large crowd or number. See Usage Note at **collective noun.** —*intr.v.* **flocked, flock•ing, flocks.** To congregate or travel in a flock or crowd. [ME *flok* < OE *floc.*]
flock[2] (flŏk) *n.* **1.** A tuft, as of fiber or hair. **2.** Waste wool or cotton used for stuffing furniture and mattresses. **3.** An inferior grade of wool added to cloth for extra weight. **4.** Pulverized wool or felt that is applied to paper, cloth, or metal to produce a texture or pattern. **5.** See **floccule.** —*tr.v.* **flocked, flock•ing, flocks. 1.** To stuff with flock. **2.** To texture or pattern with flock. [ME *flok* < OFr. *floc* < Lat. *floccus*, tuft of wool.]
Flod•den (flŏd′n). A hill of N England near the Scottish border; site of the Battle of Flodden Field (Sep. 9, 1513) in which the English defeated the Scots under James IV.
floe (flō) *n.* **1.** An ice floe. **2.** A segment that has separated from an ice floe. [Prob. < Norw. *flo*, layer < ON *flō.* See **plāk-**[1]***.]
flog (flŏg, flôg) *tr.v.* **flogged, flog•ging, flogs. 1.** To beat severely with a whip or rod. **2.** *Informal.* To publicize aggressively. [Perh. < alteration of Lat. *flagellāre.* See FLAGELLATE.] —**flog′ger** *n.*
flood (flŭd) *n.* **1.** An overflowing of water onto land that is normally dry. **2.** A flood tide. **3.** An abundant flow or outpouring. **4.** A floodlight. **5. Flood.** The biblical universal deluge during the life of Noah. —*v.* **flood•ed, flood•ing, floods.** —*tr.* **1.** To cover or submerge with or as if with a flood; inundate. **2.** To fill with an abundance or an excess. —*intr.* **1.** To become inundated or submerged. **2.** To pour forth; overflow. [ME *flod* < OE *flōd.* See **pleu-***.]

floppy disk

flood•gate (flŭd′gāt′) *n.* **1.** A gate used to control the flow of a body of water. **2.** Something that restrains a flood.
flood•light (flŭd′līt′) *n.* **1.** Artificial light in an intensely bright and broad beam. **2.** A unit that produces a beam of intense light; a flood. —*tr.v.* **-light•ed** or **-lit** (-lĭt′), **-light•ing, -lights.** To illuminate with a floodlight.
flood•plain also **flood plain** (flŭd′plān′) *n.* A plain bordering a river and subject to flooding.
flood tide also **flood•tide** (flŭd′tīd′) *n.* **1.** The incoming or rising tide; the period between low water and the succeeding high water. **2.** A climax or high point: *a flood tide of fears.*
flood•wall (flŭd′wôl′) *n.* A wall built along a shore or bank to protect an area from floods.
flood•wat•er (flŭd′wô′tər, -wŏt′ər) *n.* The water of a flood. Often used in the plural.
floor (flôr, flōr) *n.* **1.a.** The surface of a room on which one stands. **b.** The lower or supporting surface of a structure. **2.a.** A story or level of a building. **b.** The occupants of such a story. **3.** A level surface or area used for a specified purpose. **4.** The surface of a structure on which vehicles travel. **5.a.** The part of a legislative chamber or meeting hall where members are seated and from which they speak. **b.** The right to address an assembly, as granted under parliamentary procedure. **c.** The body of assembly members. **6.** The part of a room or building where the principal business or work takes place, esp.: **a.** The area of an exchange where securities are traded. **b.** The part of a retail store in which merchandise is displayed and sales are made. **c.** The area of a factory where the product is manufactured or assembled. **7.** The ground or lowermost surface, as of an ocean. **8.** A lower limit or base: *a pricing floor.* —*tr.v.* **floored, floor•ing, floors. 1.** To provide with a floor. **2.** *Informal.* To press (the accelerator of a motor vehicle) to the floor. **3.a.** To knock down. **b.** To stun; overwhelm. [ME *flor* < OE *flōr.* See **pelə-**[2]***.] —**floor′er** *n.*
floor•age (flôr′ĭj, flōr′-) *n.* Floor space.
floor•board (flôr′bôrd′, flōr′bōrd′) *n.* **1.** A board in a floor. **2.** The floor of a motor vehicle.
floor exercise *n. Sports.* An event in competitive gymnastics that consists of various tumbling maneuvers on a mat.
floor•ing (flôr′ĭng, flōr′-) *n.* **1.** A floor. **2.** Material, such as lumber or tile, used in making floors.
floor lamp *n.* A tall lamp with a base that stands on the floor.
floor leader *n.* The member of a legislature chosen by fellow party members to direct the party's activities on the floor.
floor manager *n.* **1.** See **floorwalker. 2.** A person who directs from the floor, as at a political convention.
floor plan *n.* A scale diagram of a room or building drawn as if seen from above.
floor sample *n.* Merchandise sold at a reduced price because it has been a display or demonstration model.
floor•show (flôr′shō′, flōr′-) *n.* A series of entertainments presented in a nightclub.
floor•walk•er (flôr′wô′kər, flōr′-) *n.* A department store employee who supervises sales personnel and assists customers.
floo•zy also **floo•zie** (flōō′zē) *n., pl.* **-zies.** *Slang.* A woman regarded as gaudy or tawdry. [?]
flop (flŏp) *v.* **flopped, flop•ping, flops.** —*intr.* **1.** To fall or lie down heavily and noisily. **2.** To move about loosely or limply. **3.** *Informal.* To fail utterly. **4.** *Slang.* **a.** To rest idly; lounge. **b.** To go to bed. —*tr.* To drop or lay (something) down heavily and noisily. —*n.* **1.** The act of flopping. **2.** The sound made when flopping. **3.** *Informal.* An utter failure. [Alteration of FLAP.] —**flop′per** *n.*
flop•house (flŏp′hous′) *n.* A cheap run-down hotel or boarding house.
flop•py (flŏp′ē) *adj.* **-pi•er, -pi•est.** Tending to flop; loose and flexible. —*n., pl.* **-pies.** *Comp. Sci.* A floppy disk. —**flop′pi•ly** *adv.* —**flop′pi•ness** *n.*
floppy disk *n. Comp. Sci.* A flexible plastic disk coated with magnetic material and covered by a protective jacket, used in microcomputers and minicomputers to store data.
flo•ra (flôr′ə, flōr′ə) *n., pl.* **flo•ras** or **flo•rae** (flôr′ē′, flōr′ē′). **1.** Plants considered as a group, esp. the plants of a particular country, region, or time. **2.** A treatise describing the plants of a region or time. **3.** The bacteria and other microorganisms that normally inhabit a body organ or part. [< FLORA.]
Flo•ra (flôr′ə, flōr′ə) *n. Rom. Myth.* The goddess of flowers. [Lat. *Flōra* < *flōs, flōr-*, flower. See **bhel-**[3]***.]
flo•ral (flôr′əl, flōr′-) *adj.* Of, relating to, or suggestive of a flower: *a fabric with a floral pattern.* —**flo′ral•ly** *adv.*
floral cup *n.* A tubular or cup-shaped structure of a flower, bearing on its rim the sepals, petals, and stamens.
floral envelope *n.* The perianth of a flower.
floral tube *n.* A tube usu. formed by the basal fusion of the perianth and stamens, as in the flowers of the daffodil.
Flor•ence (flôr′əns, flŏr′-). **1.** Also **Fi•ren•ze** (fē-rĕn′dzĕ). A city of central Italy on the Arno R. E of Pisa; a powerful city-state during the Renaissance. Pop. 453,293. **2.** A city of NW AL WNW of Decatur; founded 1818. Pop. 36,426. **3.** A city of NE SC ENE of Columbia. Pop. 29,813.
Florence fennel *n.* See **finocchio.**
Flor•en•tine (flôr′ən-tēn′, -tīn′, flŏr′-) *adj.* **1.** Of or relating to Florence, Italy. **2.** Of or relating to the style of art and architecture that flourished in Florence, Italy, during the Renaissance. **3.** Often **florentine.** Having or characterizing a dull chased or rubbed finish. Used of gold. **4.** Prepared, cooked, or served with spinach. —*n.* A native or inhabitant of Florence, Italy. [Lat. *Flōrentīnus* < *Flōrentia*, Florence, Italy.]
Flo•res (flôr′ĭs, -ēz, flōr′-). An island of E Indonesia in the Lesser Sundas on the **Flores Sea,** between the E end of the Java Sea and the W end of the Banda Sea S of Sulawesi.
flo•res•cence (flô-rĕs′əns, flə-) *n.* A condition, time, or period of flowering. [NLat. *flōrēscentia* < Lat. *flōrēscēns, flōrēscent-*, pr.part. of *flōrēscere*, inchoative of *flōrēre*, to flower, bloom. See FLOURISH.] —**flo•res′cent** *adj.*
flo•ret (flôr′ĭt, flōr′-) *n.* A small or reduced flower, esp. one of the grasses and composite plants. [ME *flouret* < OFr. *florete*, dim. of *flor*, flower. See FLOWER.]
Flo•rey (flôr′ē, flōr′ē), Sir **Howard Walter.** 1898–1968. Australian-born pathologist who shared a 1945 Nobel Prize.
Flo•ri•a•nó•po•lis (flôr′ē-ə-nŏp′ə-lĭs, flōr-, flô′ryə-nô′pōō-lēs′). A city of SE Brazil on an island just off the coast; linked to the mainland by a suspension bridge. Pop. 153,652.
flo•ri•at•ed also **flo•re•at•ed** (flôr′ē-ā′tĭd, flōr′-) *adj.* Decorated with floral designs. [< Lat. *flōs, flōr-*, flower. See **bhel-**[3]***.]
flo•ri•bun•da (flôr′ə-bŭn′də, flōr′-) *n.* Any of several hybrid roses bearing numerous single or double flowers. [NLat., fem. of *floribundus*, blossoming freely < Lat. *flōs, flōr-*, flower. See FLOWER.]
flo•ri•cane (flôr′ĭ-kān′, flōr′-) *n.* The flowering and fruiting stem of a biennial plant, esp. of a bramble. [Lat. *flōs, flōr-*, flower; see FLOWER + CANE.]
flo•ri•cul•ture (flôr′ĭ-kŭl′chər, flōr′-) *n.* The cultivation of flowering and ornamental plants. [Lat. *flōs, flōr-*, flower; see FLOWER + CULTURE.] —**flo′ri•cul′tur•al** *adj.* —**flo′ri•cul′tur•al•ly** *adv.* —**flo′ri•cul′tur•ist** *n.*
flor•id (flôr′ĭd, flŏr′-) *adj.* **1.** Flushed with rosy color; ruddy. **2.** Very ornate; flowery. **3.** *Archaic.* Healthy. **4.** *Obsolete.* Abounding in or covered with flowers. [Fr. *floride* < Lat.

flōridus < *flōs, flōr-*, flower. See **bhel-³***.] —**flo·rid′i·ty** (flə-rĭd′ĭ-tē, flô-), **flor′id·ness** *n.* —**flor′id·ly** *adv.*

Flor·i·da (flôr′ĭ-də, flŏr′-). A state of the SE U.S. bordering on the Atlantic Ocean and the Gulf of Mexico; admitted as the 27th state in 1845. The region was ceded to the U.S. by Spain in 1819. Cap. Tallahassee. Pop. 13,003,362. —**Flo·rid′i·an** (flə-rĭd′ē-ən), **Flor′i·dan** (-ĭd-n) *adj. & n.*

Florida, Straits of. Also **Florida Strait.** A sea passage between Cuba and the Florida Keys, linking the Gulf of Mexico with the Atlantic Ocean.

Florida arrowroot *n.* Coontie.

Florida Keys. A chain of coral and limestone islands and reefs extending c. 241 km (150 mi) from S of Miami to Key West.

flo·rif·er·ous (flô-rĭf′ər-əs) *adj.* Bearing flowers. [< Lat. *flōrifer*, bearing flowers : *flōs, flōr-*, flower; see FLOWER + *-fer*, -fer.] —**flo·rif′er·ous·ly** *adv.* —**flo·rif′er·ous·ness** *n.*

flor·i·gen (flôr′ə-jən, flŏr′-) *n.* A plant hormone that promotes flowering. [Lat. *flōs, flōr-*, flower; see **bhel-³*** + -GEN.] —**flor′i·gen′ic** (-jĕn′ĭk) *adj.*

flor·in (flôr′ĭn, flŏr′-) *n.* **1.** A guilder. **2.** A British coin worth two shillings. **3.a.** A gold coin first issued at Florence, Italy, in 1252. **b.** Any of several gold coins similar to the Florentine florin, formerly used in Europe. [ME < OFr. < OItal. *fiorino* < *fiore*, flower < Lat. *flōs, flōr-*, flower. See **bhel-³***.]

Flo·ri·o (flôr′ē-ō′, flōr′-), **John.** 1553?–1625. English lexicographer noted for his Italian-English dictionary (1598).

Flor·is·sant (flôr′ĭ-sənt, flŏr′-). A city of E MO, a suburb of St. Louis; settled by the French in the 1760's. Pop. 51,206.

flo·rist (flôr′ĭst, flōr′-, flŏr′-) *n.* One in the business of raising or selling flowers and ornamental plants. [Lat. *flōs, flōr-*, flower; see **bhel-³*** + -IST.] —**flo′rist·ry** *n.*

flo·rist·ics (flô-rĭs′tĭks, flō-) *n.* (*used with a sing. v.*) The study of the number, distribution, and relationships of plant species in one or more areas.

-florous *suff.* Having a specified kind or number of flowers: *tubuliflorous.* [< LLat. *-flōrus* < Lat. *flōs, flōr-*, flower. See **bhel-³***.]

flo·ru·it (flôr′yo͞o-ĭt, -o͞o-, flōr′-, flŏr′-) *n.* The period during which a person, school, or movement was most active or flourishing. [Lat. *flōruit*, third pers. sing. perfect t. of *flōrēre*, to flourish. See FLOURISH.]

Flo·ry (flôr′ē, flōr′ē), **Paul John.** 1910–1985. Amer. chemist who won a 1974 Nobel Prize.

floss (flôs, flŏs) *n.* **1.** Dental floss. **2.** Short or waste silk fibers, esp. from a silkworm cocoon. **3.** Soft, loosely twisted thread, as of silk, used in embroidery. **4.** A downy or silky fibrous substance, such as corn silk. —*v.* **flossed, floss·ing, floss·es.** —*tr.* To clean between (teeth) with dental floss. —*intr.* To use dental floss. [Perh. alteration of Fr. *floche*, tuft of wool < OFr. *floc, floche* < Lat. *floccus*.] —**floss′er** *n.*

floss·y (flô′sē, flŏs′ē) *adj.* **-i·er, -i·est. 1.** Superficially stylish; slick: *flossy articles.* **2.** Of, relating to, or resembling floss. —**floss′i·ly** *adv.* —**floss′i·ness** *n.*

flo·tage also **float·age** (flō′tĭj) *n.* **1.** See **flotation** 1. **2.** Floating objects or material; flotsam.

flo·ta·tion also **float·a·tion** (flō-tā′shən) *n.* **1.** The act, process, or condition of floating. **2.** The act or an instance of launching or initiating, esp. one involving the floating of stocks or bonds. **3.** The process of separating different materials, esp. minerals, by agitating a pulverized mixture of the materials with water, oil, or chemicals. **4.** The capability, esp. of a vehicle tread or tire, to remain on top of a soft surface.

flotation device *n.* A life preserver.

flo·til·la (flō-tĭl′ə) *n.* **1.a.** A small fleet. **b.** A fleet of small craft. **2.** A U.S. Navy organizational unit of two or more squadrons of small warships. **3.** *Informal.* A group of vehicles owned or operated as a unit. [Sp., dim. of *flota*, fleet < OFr. *flote* < ON *floti*. See **pleu-***.]

flot·sam (flŏt′səm) *n.* **1.a.** Wreckage or cargo afloat after a shipwreck. **b.** Floating refuse or debris. **2.** Discarded odds and ends. **3.** Vagrant, usu. destitute people. [AN *floteson* < OFr. *floter*, to float, of Gmc. orig. See **pleu-***.]

Usage Note: *Flotsam*, in maritime law, applies to wreckage or cargo left floating on the sea after a shipwreck. *Jetsam* applies to cargo or equipment thrown overboard (jettisoned) from a ship in distress and either sunk or washed ashore. The common phrase *flotsam and jetsam* is now used loosely to describe any objects found floating or washed ashore.

flounce¹ (flouns) *n.* A strip of decorative, usu. gathered or pleated material attached by one edge, as on a garment. —*tr.v.* **flounced, flounc·ing, flounc·es.** To trim with a flounce. [Alteration of *frounce* < ME, pleat < OFr. *fronce*, of Gmc. orig. See **sker-²***.]

flounce² (flouns) *intr.v.* **flounced, flounc·ing, flounc·es. 1.a.** To move in a lively or bouncy manner. **b.** To move with exaggerated or affected motions. **2.** To move clumsily; flounder. —*n.* The act of flouncing. [Poss. of Scand. orig.]

flounc·ing (floun′sĭng) *n.* **1.** Material used to make flounces. **2.** A flounce or an arrangement of flounces, as on a curtain.

floun·der¹ (floun′dər) *intr.v.* **-dered, -der·ing, -ders. 1.** To make clumsy attempts to move or regain one's balance. **2.** To move or act clumsily and in confusion. See Syns at **blunder.** See Usage Note at **founder¹.** —*n.* The act of floundering. [Prob. alteration of FOUNDER¹.]

floun·der² (floun′dər) *n., pl.* **flounder** or **-ders.** Any of various marine flatfishes of the families Bothidae and Pleuronectidae, which include important food fishes. [ME < AN *floundre*, of Scand. orig. See **plat-***.]

flour (flour) *n.* **1.** A fine powdery foodstuff obtained by grinding and sifting the meal of a grain, esp. wheat, used chiefly in baking. **2.** Any of various similar finely ground or powdered foodstuffs, as of cassava, fish, or bananas. **3.** A soft fine powder. —*tr.v.* **floured, flour·ing, flours. 1.** To cover or coat with flour. **2.** To make into flour. [ME. See FLOWER.] —**flour′y** *adj.*

flour·ish (flûr′ĭsh, flŭr′-) *v.* **-ished, -ish·ing, -ish·es.** —*intr.* **1.** To grow well or luxuriantly; thrive. **2.** To do or fare well; prosper. **3.** To be in a period of highest productivity, excellence, or influence. **4.** To make bold, sweeping movements. —*tr.* To wield, wave, or exhibit dramatically. —*n.* **1.** A dramatic or stylish movement, as of waving or brandishing. **2.** An embellishment or ornamentation: *many rhetorical flourishes.* **3.** An ostentatious act or gesture. **4.** *Mus.* A showy or ceremonious passage, such as a fanfare. [ME *florishen* < OFr. *florir, floriss-* < VLat. **flōrīre* < Lat. *flōrēre* < *flōs, flōr-*, flower. See **bhel-³***.] —**flour′ish·er** *n.*

Syns: *flourish, brandish, wave.* The central meaning shared by these verbs is "to swing back and forth boldly and dramatically": *flourished her newly signed contract; brandishing a sword; waving a baton.*

flout (flout) *v.* **flout·ed, flout·ing, flouts.** —*tr.* To show contempt for; scorn: *flouted convention.* See Usage Note at **flaunt.** —*intr.* To be scornful. —*n.* A contemptuous action or remark; an insult. [Perh. < ME *flouten*, to play the flute < OFr. *flauter* < *flaute*, flute. See FLUTE.] —**flout′er** *n.* —**flout′ing·ly** *adv.*

flow (flō) *v.* **flowed, flow·ing, flows.** —*intr.* **1.a.** To move or run smoothly with unbroken continuity, as a fluid. **b.** To issue in a stream; pour forth. **2.** To circulate, as the blood in the body. **3.** To move with a continual shifting of the component particles: *Wheat flowed into the bin.* **4.** To proceed steadily and easily. **5.** To exhibit a smooth or graceful continuity. **6.** To hang loosely and gracefully. **7.** To rise. Used of the tide. **8.** To arise; derive. See Syns at **stem¹. 9.a.** To abound or teem. **b.** To stream copiously; flood: *Contributions flowed in.* **10.** To menstruate. **11.** To undergo plastic deformation without cracking or breaking. Used of rocks, metals, or minerals. —*tr.* **1.** To release as a flow. **2.** To cause to flow. —*n.* **1.a.** The act of flowing. **b.** The smooth motion characteristic of fluids. **2.a.** A stream or current. **b.** A flood or an overflow. **c.** A residual mass that has stopped flowing: *a hardened lava flow.* **3.a.** A continuous output or outpouring. **b.** A continuous movement or circulation: *a flow of paperwork.* **4.** The amount that flows in a given period of time. **5.** The rising of the tide. **6.** Continuity and smoothness of appearance. **7.** A general movement or tendency. **8.** The sequence in which operations are performed. **9.** An apparent ease or effortlessness of performance. **10.** Menstrual discharge. [ME *flouen* < OE *flōwan*. See **pleu-***.] —**flow′ing·ly** *adv.*

flow·age (flō′ĭj) *n.* **1.** The act of flowing or overflowing. **2.a.** The state of being flooded. **b.** A body of water formed by usu. deliberate flooding. **3.** An outflow or overflow. **4.** The gradual plastic deformation of a solid body, as by heat.

flow chart also **flow·chart** (flō′chärt′) *n.* A schematic representation of a sequence of operations.

flow·er (flou′ər) *n.* **1.a.** The reproductive structure of some seed-bearing plants, characteristically having either specialized male or female organs or both male and female organs enclosed in an outer envelope of petals and sepals. **b.** Such a structure having showy or colorful parts; a blossom. **2.** A plant that is cultivated or appreciated for its blossoms. **3.** The condition or a time of having developed flowers. **4.** Something, such as an ornament, that resembles a flower in shape, fineness, or attractiveness. **5.** The period of highest development; the peak. **6.** The highest example or best representative. **7.** A natural development or outgrowth. **8. flowers.** *Chem.* A fine powder produced by condensation or sublimation of a compound. —*v.* **-ered, -er·ing, -ers.** —*intr.* **1.** To produce a flower or flowers; blossom. **2.** To develop naturally or fully; mature. —*tr.* To decorate with flowers or a floral pattern. [ME *flour*, flower, best of anything, flour < OFr. *flor* < Lat. *flōs, flōr-*. See **bhel-³***.] —**flow′er·er** *n.* —**flow′er·less** *adj.*

flow·er·age (flou′ər-ĭj) *n.* **1.** Flowers considered as a group. **2.** The process or state of flowering.

flower bug *n.* Any of a group of bugs in the family Anthocoridae, which feed on insects that infest flowers.

flower child *n.* *Informal.* A hippie, esp. one advocating universal peace and love. —**flow′er-child′** (flou′ər-chīld′) *adj.*

flow·er·et (flou′ər-ĭt) *n.* A small flower; a floret.

flower girl *n.* A young girl who carries flowers in a procession.

flower head *n.* **1.** *Bot.* A dense short compact cluster of sessile flowers, as of composite plants or clover. **2.** A very dense grouping of flower buds, as in broccoli and cauliflower.

flow·er·ing dogwood (flou′ər-ĭng) *n.* See **dogwood.**

flotilla
On the Indian Ocean

ă pat	oi boy
ā pay	ou out
âr care	o͝o took
ä father	o͞o boot
ĕ pet	ŭ cut
ē be	ûr urge
ĭ pit	th thin
ī pie	*th* this
îr pier	hw which
ŏ pot	zh vision
ō toe	ə about, item
ô paw	

Stress marks:
′ (primary);
′ (secondary), as in
dictionary (dĭk′shə-nĕr′ē)

flowering maple *n.* Any of various tropical plants of the genus *Abutilon,* having lobed leaves like those of the maple.

flowering plant *n.* A plant that produces flowers and fruit; an angiosperm.

flowering quince *n.* Any of several shrubs of the genus *Chaenomeles,* native to Asia and having spiny branches and red or pink flowers.

flower people *n. Informal.* Flower children.

flow•er•pot (flou′ər-pŏt′) *n.* A pot in which plants are grown.

flower power *n. Informal.* A movement in the 1960's and 1970's, expressing countercultural beliefs and ideals.

flow•er•y (flou′ə-rē) *adj.* **-i•er, -i•est. 1.** Of, relating to, or suggestive of flowers. **2.** Abounding in or covered with flowers. **3.** Full of ornate or grandiloquent expressions; highly embellished: *a flowery speech.* **—flow′er•i•ness** *n.*

flow meter *n.* An instrument for monitoring, measuring, or recording the rate of flow, pressure, or discharge of a fluid.

flown[1] (flōn) *v.* P.part. of **fly[1]**.

flown[2] (flōn) *adj. Archaic.* Filled to excess. [Obsolete, p.part. of FLOW.]

flow•stone (flō′stōn′) *n.* A layered deposit of calcium carbonate on rock where water has flowed or dripped.

fl oz or **fl. oz.** *abbr.* Fluid ounce.

flu (flo͞o) *n. Informal.* Influenza. [Short for INFLUENZA.]

flub (flŭb) *Informal.* **—*tr.v.*** **flubbed, flub•bing, flubs.** To botch; bungle. **—*n.*** The act or an instance of botching or bungling. [?] **—flub′ber** *n.*

flub•dub (flŭb′dŭb′) *n. Informal.* Pretentious nonsense; bunkum. [?]

fluc•tu•ate (flŭk′cho͞o-āt′) *v.* **-at•ed, -at•ing, -ates. —*intr.* 1.** To vary irregularly. **2.** To rise and fall in or as if in waves; undulate. **—*tr.*** To cause to fluctuate. [Lat. *flūctuāre, flūctuāt-* < *flūctus,* a flowing < p.part. of *fluere, flūct-,* to flow. See **bhleu-*.**] **—fluc′tu•ant** (-ənt) *adj.* **—fluc′tu•a′tion** *n.*

flue[1] (flo͞o) *n.* **1.** A pipe, tube, or channel for conveying hot air, gas, steam, or smoke, as from a furnace or fireplace to a chimney. **2.** *Mus.* **a.** An organ pipe sounded by means of an air current striking a lip in the side of the pipe and causing the air within to vibrate. **b.** The lipped opening in such a pipe. [?]

flue[2] (flo͞o) *n.* A fishing net. [ME < MDu. *vlūwe.* See **pleu-*.**]

flu•ent (flo͞o′ənt) *adj.* **1.a.** Able to express oneself readily and effortlessly. **b.** Flowing effortlessly; polished: *fluent Russian.* **2.** Flowing or moving smoothly; graceful. **3.** Flowing or capable of flowing; fluid. [Lat. *fluēns, fluent-,* pr.part. of *fluere,* to flow. See **bhleu-*.**] **—flu′en•cy** *n.* **—flu′ent•ly** *adv.*

flue pipe *n. Mus.* An organ pipe with a lipped opening; a flue.

flu•er•ic (flo͞o-ĕr′ĭk) *adj.* Fluidic. [Lat. *fluere,* to flow; see **bhleu-*** + -IC.]

flu•er•ics (flo͞o-ĕr′ĭks) *n.* *(used with a sing. v.)* Fluidics.

flue stop *n. Mus.* An organ stop controlling a set of flue pipes.

fluff (flŭf) *n.* **1.** Light down or fuzz, as on a young bird. **2.** Something having a very light, soft, or frothy consistency or appearance. **3.** Something of little substance or consequence, esp.: **a.** Light or superficial entertainment. **b.** Inflated or padded material. **4.** *Informal.* An error, esp. in the delivery of lines, as by an actor. **—*v.*** **fluffed, fluff•ing, fluffs. —*tr.* 1.** To make fluffy. **2.** *Informal.* **a.** To ruin or mar by a mistake or blunder. **b.** To forget or botch (one's lines). **—*intr.* 1.** To become fluffy. **2.** *Informal.* To make an error, esp. in the delivery of lines. [?]

fluff•y (flŭf′ē) *adj.* **-i•er, -i•est. 1.a.** Of, relating to, or resembling fluff. **b.** Covered with fluff. **2.** Light and airy; soft: *a fluffy soufflé.* **3.a.** Light or frivolous. **b.** Lacking depth or precision; fuzzy. **—fluff′i•ly** *adv.* **—fluff′i•ness** *n.*

flü•gel•horn or **flue•gel•horn** (flo͞o′gəl-hôrn′, flü′-) *n. Mus.* A bugle with valves, similar to the cornet but having a wider bore. [Ger. : *Flügel,* flank (used to summon flanks in battle) (< MHGer. *vlügel,* wing, flank; see **pleu-***) + *Horn,* horn (< MHGer. < OHGer.; see **ker-[1]***).] **—flü′gel•horn′ist** *n.*

flu•id (flo͞o′ĭd) *n.* A continuous amorphous substance whose molecules move freely past one another and that assumes the shape of its container; a liquid or gas. **—*adj.* 1.** Of, relating to, or characteristic of a fluid. **2.** Readily reshaped; pliable. **3.** Smooth and flowing; graceful. **4.a.** Changing or tending to change; variable. **b.** Characterized by or allowing social mobility. **5.** Convertible into cash: *fluid assets.* [< ME, flowing < OFr. *fluide* < Lat. *fluidus* < *fluere,* to flow. See **bhleu-*.**] **—flu•id′i•ty** (-ĭd′ĭ-tē), **flu′id•ness** *n.* **—flu′id•ly** *adv.*

fluid dram *n.* A unit of volume or capacity in the apothecary system, equal to ⅛ of a fluid ounce (3.70 milliliters).

fluid drive *n.* An automotive transmission coupling that provides a smooth start, consisting of two separate turbines that rotate on the same axis in a surrounding liquid.

fluid dynamics *n.* *(used with a sing. v.)* The branch of science concerned with gases and liquids in motion.

flu•id•ex•tract (flo͞o′ĭd-ĕk′străkt′) *n.* A concentrated alcohol solution of a drug of such strength that each milliliter is the equivalent of one gram of the dry form of the drug.

flu•id•ic (flo͞o-ĭd′ĭk) *adj.* **1.** Of, relating to, or characteristic of a fluid. **2.** Relating to or controlled by fluidics.

flu•id•ics (flo͞o-ĭd′ĭks) *n.* *(used with a sing. v.)* The technology of using the flows and pressures of fluids in sensing, control, and information-processing systems with no moving parts.

flu•id•ize (flo͞o′ĭ-dīz′) *tr.v.* **-ized, -iz•ing, -iz•es. 1.** To make fluid. **2.** To pulverize (a solid) so finely that it takes on most of the properties of a fluid. **—flu′id•i•za′tion** (-ĭ-dĭ-zā′shən) *n.*

fluid mechanics *n.* *(used with a sing. v.)* The branch of mechanics concerned with the properties of gases and liquids.

fluid ounce *n.* **1.** A unit of volume or capacity in the U.S. Customary System, used in liquid measure, equal to 29.57 milliliters (1.804 cubic inches). **2.** A unit of volume or capacity in the British Imperial System, used in liquid and dry measure, equal to 28.41 milliliters (1.734 cubic inches).

fluke[1] (flo͝ok) *n.* **1.** Any of various flatfishes, esp. a flounder of the genus *Paralichthys.* **2.** See **trematode.** [ME < OE *flōc.* See **plāk-[1]*.**]

fluke[2] (flo͝ok) *n.* **1.** *Naut.* The triangular blade at the end of an arm of an anchor, designed to catch in the ground. **2.** A barb or barbed head, as on an arrow. **3.** Either of the two horizontally flattened divisions of a whale's tail. [Poss. < FLUKE[1].]

fluke[3] (flo͝ok) *n.* **1.** A stroke of good luck. **2.** A chance occurrence; an accident. **3.** *Games.* An accidentally good or successful stroke in billiards or pool. [?]

fluk•y also **fluk•ey** (flo͞o′kē) *adj.* **-i•er, -i•est. 1.** Resulting from or depending on mere chance. **2.** Constantly shifting; uncertain. [< FLUKE[3].] **—fluk′i•ly** *adv.* **—fluk′i•ness** *n.*

flume (flo͞om) *n.* **1.** A narrow gorge, usu. with a stream flowing through it. **2.** An open artificial channel or chute carrying a stream of water, as for conveying logs. [ME *flum,* river < OFr. < Lat. *flūmen* < *fluere,* to flow. See **bhleu-*.**]

flum•mer•y (flŭm′ə-rē) *n., pl.* **-ies. 1.** Meaningless or deceptive language; humbug. **2.a.** Any of several soft, sweet, bland foods, such as custard. **b.** A sweet gelatinous pudding made by straining boiled oatmeal or flour. [Welsh *llymru,* soft jelly from sour oatmeal.]

flum•mox (flŭm′əks) *tr.v.* **-moxed, -mox•ing, -mox•es.** *Informal.* To confuse; perplex. [Prob. of E. dial. orig.]

flung (flŭng) *v.* P.t. and p.part. of **fling.**

flunk (flŭngk) *Informal.* **—*v.*** **flunked, flunk•ing, flunks. —*intr.*** To fail, esp. in a course or an examination. **—*tr.* 1.** To fail (an examination or course). **2.** To give a failing grade to. **—*n.* 1.** The act or an instance of flunking. **2.** A failing grade. **—*phrasal verb.*** **flunk out.** To expel or be expelled from a school or course because of work below standard. [?]

flun•ky also **flun•key** (flŭng′kē) *n., pl.* **-kies** also **-keys. 1.** A person of slavish or unquestioning obedience; a lackey. **2.** One who does menial or trivial work; a drudge. **3.** A liveried manservant. [Sc., perh. < FLANKER, an attendant at one's flank.] **—flun′ky•ism** *n.*

flu•or (flo͞o′ôr′, -ər) *n.* See **fluorite.** [NLat., mineral belonging to a group used as fluxes < Lat., a flowing < *fluere,* to flow. See **bhleu-*.**]

fluor– *pref.* Var. of **fluoro–.**

fluo•resce (flo͝o-rĕs′, flô-, flō-) *intr.v.* **-resced, -resc•ing, -resc•es.** To undergo, produce, or show fluorescence. [Back-formation < FLUORESCENCE.] **—fluo•resc′er** *n.*

fluo•res•ce•in (flo͝o-rĕs′ē-ĭn, flô-, flō-) *n.* A compound, $C_{20}H_{12}O_5$, that exhibits intense fluorescence in alkaline solution and is used in medicine and to trace water flow.

fluo•res•cence (flo͝o-rĕs′əns, flô-, flō-) *n.* **1.** The emission of electromagnetic radiation, esp. of visible light, stimulated in a substance by the absorption of incident radiation and persisting only as long as the stimulating radiation is continued. **2.** The property of emitting such radiation. **3.** The radiation so emitted. [FLUOR(SPAR) + -ESCENCE.]

fluo•res•cent (flo͝o-rĕs′ənt, flô-, flō-) *adj.* **1.a.** Of or relating to fluorescence. **b.** Exhibiting or produced by fluorescence: *fluorescent plankton.* **2.** Glowing as if with fluorescence; vivid: *fluorescent colors.* **—*n.*** A fluorescent lamp.

fluorescent lamp *n.* A lamp that produces visible light by fluorescence, esp. a glass tube whose inner wall is coated with a material that fluoresces when an electrical current causes a vapor within the tube to discharge electrons.

fluor•i•date (flo͝or′ĭ-dāt′, flôr′-, flōr′-) *tr.v.* **-dat•ed, -dat•ing, -dates.** To add a fluorine compound to (a drinking water supply, for example) for the purpose of reducing tooth decay. **—fluor′i•da′tion** *n.*

fluor•ide (flo͝or′īd′, flôr′-, flōr′-) *n.* A binary compound of fluorine with another element. [FLUOR(INE) + -IDE.]

fluor•i•na•tion (flo͝or′ĭ-nā′shən, flôr′-, flōr′-) *n.* A chemical reaction that introduces fluorine into a compound.

fluor•ine (flo͝or′ēn′, -ĭn, flôr′-, flōr′-) *n. Symbol* **F** A highly corrosive poisonous gaseous halogen element, the most reactive of all the elements, used in a wide variety of industrially important compounds. Atomic number 9; atomic weight 18.9984; freezing point −219.62°C; melting point −223°C; boiling point −188.14°C; specific gravity of liquid 1.108 (at boiling point); valence 1. See table at **element.**

fluor•ite (flo͝or′īt′, flôr′-, flōr′-) *n.* A mineral, CaF_2, that is often fluorescent in ultraviolet light.

fluoro– or **fluor–** *pref.* **1.** Fluorine: *fluorosis.* **2.** Fluorescence: *fluoroscope.* [< FLUORINE and < FLUOR.]

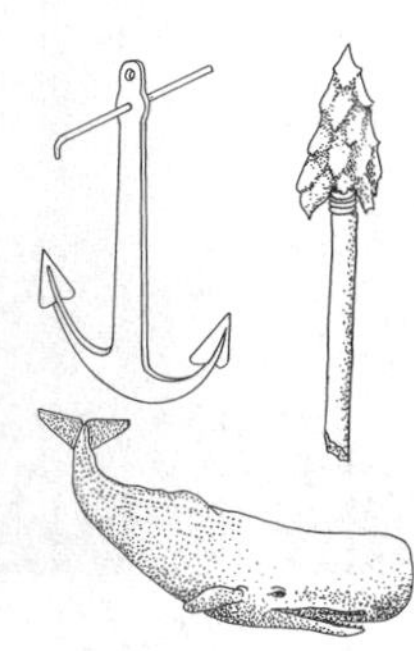

fluke[2]
Of an admiralty anchor (*top left*), an arrowhead (*top right*), and a sperm whale (*bottom*)

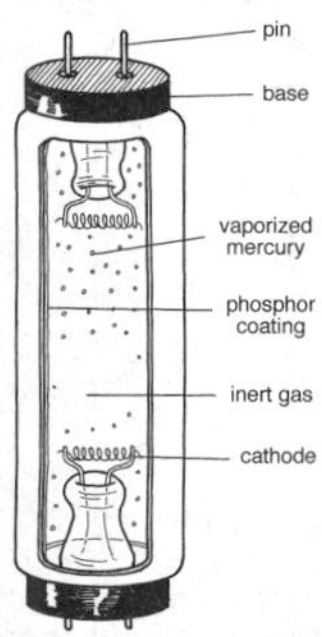

fluorescent lamp

fluor•o•car•bon (flo͝or′ō-kär′bən, flôr′-, flōr′-) *n.* An inert liquid or gaseous halocarbon compound in which fluorine replaces some or all hydrogen molecules, used in aerosol propellants and refrigerants and in making plastics and resins.

fluor•o•chem•i•cal (flo͝or′ō-kĕm′ĭ-kəl, flôr′-, flōr′-) *n.* A chemical compound containing fluorine, esp. a fluorocarbon.

fluor•o•chrome (flo͝or′ə-krōm′, flôr′-, flōr′-) *n.* Any of a group of fluorescent dyes used to stain biological specimens.

fluo•rog•ra•phy (flo͞o-rŏg′rə-fē, flô-, flō-) *n.* See **photofluorography.**

fluo•rom•e•ter (flo͞o-rŏm′ĭ-tər, flô-, flō-) *n.* An instrument to detect and measure fluorescence. **—fluo•rom′e•try** *n.*

fluor•o•scope (flo͝or′ə-skōp′, flôr′-, flōr′-) *n.* An x-ray device equipped with a fluorescent screen on which the internal structures of an optically opaque object may be continuously viewed as shadowy images. *—tr.v.* **-scoped, -scop•ing, -scopes.** To examine the interior of (an object) with a fluoroscope. **—fluor′o•scop′ic** (-skŏp′ĭk) *adj.*

fluo•ros•co•py (flo͞o-rŏs′kə-pē, flô-, flō-) *n., pl.* **-pies.** Examination by means of a fluoroscope. **—fluo•ros′co•pist** *n.*

fluo•ro•sis (flo͞o-rō′sĭs, flô-, flō-) *n.* An abnormal condition caused by excessive intake of fluorine, characterized chiefly by mottling of the teeth. **—fluo•rot′ic** (-rŏt′ĭk) *adj.*

fluor•o•u•ra•cil (flo͝or′ō-yo͝or′ə-sĭl, flôr′-, flōr′-) *n.* An antineoplastic agent, $C_4H_3FN_2O_2$, used esp. in the treatment of cancers of the skin, breast, and digestive system.

flu•or•spar (flo͞o′ər-spär′, flo͝or′spär′) *n.* See **fluorite.**

flur•ry (flûr′ē, flŭr′ē) *n., pl.* **-ries. 1.** A brief light snowfall. **2.a.** A sudden gust of wind. **b.** A stirring mass, as of dust; a shower. **3.** A sudden burst or commotion; a stir. **4.** A short period of active trading, as on a stock exchange. *—v.* **-ried, -ry•ing, -ries.** *—tr.* To agitate, stir, or confuse. *—intr.* To move or come down in a flurry. [Perh. < *flurr,* to scatter.]

flush¹ (flŭsh) *v.* **flushed, flush•ing, flush•es.** *—intr.* **1.** To turn red, as from fever, embarrassment, or strong emotion; blush. **2.** To glow, esp. with a reddish color. **3.** To flow suddenly and abundantly, as from containment; flood. **4.** To be emptied or cleaned by a rapid flow of water, as a toilet. *—tr.* **1.** To cause to redden or glow. **2.** To excite or elate. **3.a.** To clean, rinse, or empty with a rapid flow of a liquid, esp. water. **b.** To remove or eliminate by or as if by flushing. *—n.* **1.a.** A flooding flow or rush, as of water. **b.** The act of cleaning or rinsing by or as if by flushing. **2.** A blush or glow. **3.a.** A reddening of the skin, as with fever or exertion. **b.** A brief sensation of heat over all or part of the body. **4.** A rush of strong feeling. **5.** A state of freshness or vigor. *—adj.* **flush•er, flush•est. 1.** Having a healthy reddish color; flushed. **2.** Having an abundant supply of money; affluent. **3.** Marked by abundance; plentiful. **4.** Swelling; overflowing. **5.a.** Having surfaces in the same plane; even. **b.** Arranged with adjacent sides, surfaces, or edges close together. **c.** *Print.* Aligned evenly with a margin, as along an edge of a typeset page; not indented. **6.** Direct, straightforward, or solid. **7.** Designed to be emptied or cleaned by flushing. *—adv.* **1.** So as to be even, in one plane, or aligned with a margin. **2.** Squarely or solidly. [Prob. < FLUSH³, to dart out.] **—flush′er** *n.* **—flush′ness** *n.*

flush² (flŭsh) *n. Games.* A hand in which all the cards are of the same suit but not in numerical sequence. [Fr. *flux, flus* < OFr. *flux* < Lat. *flūxus,* flux. See FLUX.]

flush³ (flŭsh) *v.* **flushed, flush•ing, flush•es.** *—tr.* **1.** To frighten (a game bird, for example) from cover. **2.** To drive or force into the open. *—intr.* To dart out or fly from cover. *—n.* A bird or flock of birds that has been frightened from cover. [ME *flusshen.*]

Flush•ing (flŭsh′ĭng). **1.** A section of New York City in N Queens on W Long I.; site of two world's fairs (1939–40 and 1964–65). **2.** See **Vlissingen.**

flus•ter (flŭs′tər) *tr. & intr.v.* **-tered, -ter•ing, -ters.** To make or become nervous or upset. *—n.* A state of agitation, confusion, or excitement. [< ME *flostring,* agitation, prob. of Scand. orig. See **pleu-*.**]

flute (flo͞ot) *n.* **1.** *Mus.* **a.** A high-pitched woodwind instrument consisting of a slender tube closed at one end with keys and finger holes on the side and an opening near the closed end across which the breath is blown. **b.** Any of various similar reedless woodwind instruments, such as the recorder. **2.a.** *Archit.* A long, usu. rounded groove incised as a decorative motif on the shaft of a column, for example. **b.** A similar groove or furrow, as on a piece of furniture. **3.** A tall narrow wineglass. *—v.* **flut•ed, flut•ing, flutes.** *—tr.* **1.** *Mus.* To play (a tune) on a flute. **2.** To produce in a flutelike tone. **3.** To make flutes in (a column, for example). *—intr.* **1.** *Mus.* To play a flute. **2.** To sing, whistle, or speak with a flutelike tone. [ME *floute* < OFr. *flaute* and < MDu. *flute* (MDu. < OFr.) < OProv., perh. a blend of *flaujol,* flageolet (< VLat. **flābeolum;* see FLAGEOLET) and *laut,* lute; see LUTE¹.] **—flut′er** *n.* **—flut′ey, flut′y** *adj.*

flut•ing (flo͞o′tĭng) *n.* **1.a.** *Archit.* A decorative motif consisting of a series of uniform, usu. vertical flutes. **b.** The act of incising or making grooves. **2.** The grooves formed by narrow pleats in cloth.

flut•ist (flo͞o′tĭst) *n. Mus.* One who plays the flute.

flut•ter (flŭt′ər) *v.* **-tered, -ter•ing, -ters.** *—intr.* **1.** To wave or flap rapidly in an irregular manner. **2.a.** To fly by a quick light flapping of the wings. **b.** To flap the wings without flying. **3.** To move or fall in a manner suggestive of tremulous flight. **4.** To vibrate or beat rapidly or erratically. **5.** To move quickly in a nervous, restless, or excited fashion; flit. *—tr.* To cause to flutter. *—n.* **1.** The act of fluttering. **2.** A condition of nervous excitement or agitation. **3.** A commotion; a stir. **4.** *Pathol.* Abnormally rapid pulsation, esp. of the atria or ventricles of the heart. **5.** Rapid fluctuation in the pitch of a sound reproduction resulting from variations in the speed of the recording or reproducing equipment. **6.** *Chiefly British.* A small bet; a gamble. [ME *floteren* < OE *floterian.* See **pleu-*.**] **—flut′ter•er** *n.* **—flut′ter•y** *adj.*

flutter kick *n. Sports.* A swimming kick in which the legs are held horizontally and alternately moved up and down in rapid strokes without bending the knees.

flu•vi•al (flo͞o′vē-əl) *adj.* **1.** Of, relating to, or inhabiting a river or stream. **2.** Produced by the action of a river or stream. [ME < Lat. *fluviālis* < *fluvius,* river < *fluere,* to flow. See **bhleu-*.**]

flu•vi•a•tile (flo͞o′vē-ə-tīl′) *adj.* Fluvial. [Fr. < Lat. *fluviātilis* < *fluvius,* river. See FLUVIAL.]

flux (flŭks) *n.* **1.a.** A flow or flowing. **b.** A continued flow; a flood. **2.** The flowing in of the tide. **3.** *Medic.* The discharge of large quantities of fluid material from the body, esp. the discharge of watery feces from the intestines. **4.a.** The rate of flow of fluid, particles, or energy through a given surface. **b.** See **flux density. c.** The lines of force of a magnetic field. **5.** Constant or frequent change; fluctuation. **6.** *Chem. & Metall.* A substance that aids, induces, or otherwise actively participates in fusing or flowing, as: **a.** A substance applied to a surface to be joined by welding, soldering, or brazing. **b.** A mineral added to the metals in a furnace to promote fusing. **c.** An additive that improves the flow of plastics during fabrication. **d.** A readily fusible glass or enamel used as a base in ceramic work. *—v.* **fluxed, flux•ing, flux•es.** *—tr.* **1.** To melt; fuse. **2.** To apply a flux to. *—intr.* **1.** To become fluid. **2.** To flow; stream. [ME < OFr. < Lat. *flūxus* < p.part. of *fluere,* to flow. See **bhleu-*.**]

flux density *n. Phys.* The rate of flux per unit area.

flux gate *n. Phys.* A detector used to indicate the direction of the earth's magnetic field.

flux•ion (flŭk′shən) *n.* **1.a.** A flow or flowing. **b.** Continual change. **2.** *Archaic.* **a.** See **derivative** 3. **b. fluxions.** Differential calculus. [Fr. < LLat. *flūxiō, flūxiōn-* < Lat. *flūxus,* flux. See FLUX.] **—flux′ion•al, flux′ion•ar′y** (flŭk′shə-nĕr′ē) *adj.* **—flux′ion•al•ly** *adv.*

fly¹ (flī) *v.* **flew** (flo͞o), **flown** (flōn), **fly•ing, flies** (flīz). *—intr.* **1.** To engage in flight, esp.: **a.** To move through the air by means of wings or winglike parts. **b.** To travel by air. **c.** To operate an aircraft or spacecraft. **2.a.** To rise in or be carried through the air by the wind. **b.** To float or flap in the air. **3.** To move or be sent through the air with great speed. **4.a.** To move with great speed; rush or dart. **b.** To flee; escape. **c.** To hasten; spring. **5.** To pass by swiftly. **6.** To be dissipated; vanish. **7.** *p.t. and p.part.* **flied** (flīd). *Baseball.* To hit a fly ball. **8.** To undergo an explosive reaction; burst: *The dropped dish flew into pieces.* **9.** *Informal.* To gain acceptance or approval; go over. *—tr.* **1.a.** To cause to fly or float in the air. **b.** *Naut.* To operate under (a particular flag). **2.a.** To pilot (an aircraft or a spacecraft). **b.** To carry or transport in an aircraft or a spacecraft. **c.** To pass over or through in flight. **d.** To perform in a spacecraft or an aircraft. **3.a.** To flee or run from. **b.** To avoid; shun. *—n., pl.* **flies. 1.** The act of flying; flight. **2.a.** A fold of cloth that covers a fastening of a garment, esp. one on the front of trousers. **b.** The fastening or opening covered by such a fold. **3.** A flap that covers an entrance or forms a rooflike extension for a tent or the canopy of a vehicle. **4.** A flyleaf. **5.** *Baseball.* A fly ball. **6.a.** The span of a flag from the staff to the outer edge. **b.** The outer edge of a flag. **7.** A flywheel. **8. flies.** The area directly over the stage of a theater, containing overhead lights, drop curtains, and equipment for raising and lowering sets. **9.** *Chiefly British.* A one-horse carriage, esp. one for hire. ***—phrasal verb.* fly at.** To attack fiercely; assault. ***—idioms.* fly high.** To be elated. **fly off the handle.** *Informal.* To become suddenly enraged. **let fly. 1.** To shoot, hurl, or release. **2.** To lash out; assault. **on the fly. 1.** On the run; in a hurry. **2.** While in the air; in flight. [ME *flien* < OE *flēogan.* See **pleu-*.**] **—fly′a•ble** *adj.*

fly² (flī) *n., pl.* **flies. 1.a.** Any of numerous two-winged insects of the order Diptera, esp. any of the family Muscidae, which includes the housefly. **b.** Any of various other flying insects, such as the caddis fly. **2.** A fishing lure simulating a fly. ***—idiom.* fly in the ointment.** A detrimental circumstance or detail; a drawback. [ME *flie* < OE *flēoge.* See **pleu-*.**]

fly³ (flī) *adj.* **1.** *Chiefly British.* Mentally alert; sharp. **2.** *Slang.* Stylish and hip; cool. [Prob. < FLY¹.]

fly agaric *n.* A poisonous mushroom *(Amanita muscaria)* usu. having a red or orange cap with white gills and patches.

flute

fluting

ă pat	oi boy
ā pay	ou out
âr care	o͝o took
ä father	o͞o boot
ĕ pet	ŭ cut
ē be	ûr urge
ĭ pit	th thin
ī pie	*th* this
îr pier	hw which
ŏ pot	zh vision
ō toe	ə about, item
ô paw	

Stress marks:
′ (primary);
′ (secondary), as in
dictionary (dĭk′shə-nĕr′ē)

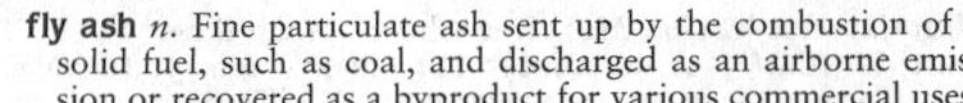

fly ash *n.* Fine particulate ash sent up by the combustion of a solid fuel, such as coal, and discharged as an airborne emission or recovered as a byproduct for various commercial uses.

fly•a•way (flī′ə-wā′) *adj.* **1.** Made or worn loose or draped, as to allow or suggest fluttering in the wind. **2.a.** Prepared for immediate flight. **b.** Designed for air travel. **3.** Given to frivolity; flighty.

fly ball *n. Baseball.* A ball that is batted in a high arc.

fly•blow (flī′blō′) *n.* The egg or larva of a blowfly, usu. deposited on meat. —*tr.v.* **-blew** (-blo͞o′), **-blown** (-blōn′), **-blow•ing, -blows. 1.** To deposit flyblows on. **2.** To contaminate; taint.

flycatcher
Acadian flycatcher
Empidonax virescens

fly•blown (flī′blōn′) *adj.* **1.** Contaminated with flyblows. **2.a.** Tainted; corrupt. **b.** Dirty or rundown; squalid.

fly book *n.* A case for carrying flies for fishing.

fly•boy or **fly-boy** (flī′boi′) *n. Slang.* A member of an air force, esp. a pilot.

fly bridge *n. Naut.* See **flying bridge.**

fly•by also **fly-by** (flī′bī′) *n., pl.* **-bys.** A flight passing close to a specified target or position.

fly-by-night (flī′bī-nīt′) *Informal.* —*adj.* **1.** Unreliable or unscrupulous, esp. with regard to business dealings. **2.** Of an impermanent or insubstantial nature. —*n.* also **fly-by-night•er** (-nī′tər). **1.** An unscrupulous or undependable person, esp. one who leaves secretly without paying creditors. **2.** Something shaky or impermanent.

fly-cast (flī′kăst′) *intr.v.* **-cast, -cast•ing, -casts.** To cast artificial flies with a fly rod, as in fishing. —**fly′-cast′er** *n.* —**fly′-cast′ing** *n.*

fly•catch•er (flī′kăch′ər, -kĕch′-) *n.* **1.** Any of various Eurasian birds of the family Muscicapidae that feed on insects, usu. catching them in flight. **2.** Any of various similar American birds of the family Tyrannidae.

fly•er (flī′ər) *n.* Var. of **flier.**

fly-fish•ing (flī′fĭsh′ĭng) *n.* The art or sport of angling with artificial flies for bait.

fly gallery *n.* A narrow elevated platform at the side of the stage in a theater, from which a stagehand works the ropes controlling equipment in the flies.

fly•ing (flī′ĭng) *adj.* **1.** Of or relating to aviation. **2.** Capable of or engaged in flight: *a flying mammal.* **3.** Situated, extending, or functioning in the air. **4.a.** Swiftly moving; fleet. **b.** Done or performed swiftly in or as if in the air. **5.** Brief; hurried. **6.** Capable of swift deployment or response. **7.** *Naut.* Not secured by spars or stays. Used of a sail. —*n.* **1.** Flight in an aircraft or a spacecraft. **2.** The piloting or navigation of an aircraft or a spacecraft. —***idiom.*** **with flying colors.** With complete or outstanding success.

flying boat *n.* A large seaplane that floats on its hull.

flying bomb *n.* See **robot bomb.**

flying bridge *n. Naut.* A small, usu. open platform located above the main bridge, as on a powerboat, equipped with a secondary set of navigational controls.

flying bridge

flying buttress *n. Archit.* A masonry support consisting usu. of a pier or buttress connected to the main structure by an arch along which the thrust is borne.

flying dragon *n.* See **flying lizard.**

Fly•ing Dutchman (flī′ĭng) *n.* **1.** A spectral ship said to appear in storms near the Cape of Good Hope. **2.** The captain of this ship, condemned to sail the seas until Judgment Day.

flying field *n.* A graded field on which airplanes may land and take off.

flying fish *n.* Any of various marine fishes of the family Exocoetidae, having enlarged winglike pectoral fins capable of sustaining them in brief gliding flight over the water.

flying fox *n.* Any of various fruit-eating bats of the suborder Megachiroptera, chiefly inhabiting tropical Africa, Asia, and Australia and having a foxlike muzzle and small pointed ears.

flying frog *n.* Either of two arboreal frogs *(Rhacophorus reinwardtii* or *R. nigropalmatus)* of southeast Asia, having toes connected by webbing and capable of making long leaps.

flying gurnard *n.* Any of various chiefly tropical marine fishes of the family Dactylopteridae, having greatly enlarged winglike pectoral fins that facilitate gliding through the water.

flying jib *n. Naut.* A light sail set forward of the outermost jib and attached to an extension of the jib boom.

flying lemur *n.* Either of two arboreal mammals, *Cynocephalus volans* of the Philippines or *C. variegatus* of southeast Asia, that are sustained in gliding leaps by a wide fur-covered membrane extending from each side of the body.

flying lizard *n.* Any of various small tropical Asian lizards of the genus *Draco,* having winglike membranes on each side of the body that enable it to glide through the air.

flying machine *n.* A machine designed for flight, esp. an early experimental type of aircraft.

flying mare *n. Sports.* A wrestling throw in which one grabs one's opponent's wrist, turns one's back to the opponent, and flips the opponent over one's shoulder onto the ground.

flying buttress
Amiens Cathedral, France

flying phalanger *n.* Any of several marsupials of the family Petauridae, esp. one of the genus *Petaurus,* of Australia, New Guinea, and Tasmania, having folds of skin between the forelegs and hind legs that enable it to glide through the air.

flying saucer *n.* Any of various unidentified flying objects of presumed extraterrestrial origin, typically described as luminous moving disks.

flying squad *n. Chiefly British.* A small mobile unit, esp. of motorized police, capable of moving quickly into action.

flying squirrel *n.* Any of various nocturnal squirrels of the genera *Pteromys, Petaurista, Glaucomys,* and related genera, having membranes along each side of the body between the forelegs and hind legs that enable it to glide between trees.

flying start *n.* **1.** *Sports.* A racing start in which the contestants are already moving when they cross the starting line. **2.** A quick or auspicious beginning.

flying wedge *n.* A moving wedge-shaped formation, as of police, used esp. for penetrating crowds.

fly•leaf (flī′lēf′) *n.* A blank or specially printed leaf at the beginning or end of a book.

fly-o•ver (flī′ō′vər) *n.* **1.** A flight over a specific location, usu. at low altitude, as by a formation of military aircraft. **2.** *Chiefly British.* An overpass, as on a highway.

fly•pa•per (flī′pā′pər) *n.* Paper coated with a sticky, sometimes poisonous substance, used to catch flies.

Fly River (flī). A river, c. 1,046 km (650 mi), rising in W Papua New Guinea and flowing SE to the Gulf of Papua.

fly rod *n.* A long flexible fishing rod used in fly-fishing.

fly•sheet (flī′shēt′) *n.* A printed sheet or pamphlet; a handbill.

fly•speck (flī′spĕk′) *n.* **1.** A small dark speck or stain made by the excrement of a fly. **2.** A minute or insignificant spot. —*tr.v.* **-specked, -speck•ing, -specks. 1.** To mark or foul with flyspecks. **2.** *Slang.* To examine closely.

fly swat *n. Chiefly Southern U.S.* See **fly swatter.**

fly swatter *n.* An implement used to kill insects, usu. consisting of a piece of plastic or wire mesh attached to a long handle. Also called regionally *fly swat.*

fly•trap (flī′trăp′) *n.* **1.** A trap for catching flies. **2.** An insectivorous plant, such as the Venus's-flytrap.

fly-ty•ing (flī′tī′ĭng) *n.* The art or hobby of making artificial fishing flies. —**fly′-ti′er** (-tī′ər) *n.*

fly•way (flī′wā′) *n.* A seasonal route followed by birds migrating to and from their breeding areas.

fly•weight (flī′wāt′) *n.* **1.** *Sports.* **a.** A professional boxer weighing no more than 112 pounds (approx. 51 kilograms), lighter than a bantamweight. **b.** A contestant in various other sports in the lightest weight class. **2.** Something that is particularly small, light, or inconsequential.

fly•wheel (flī′hwēl′, -wēl′) *n.* **1.** A heavy-rimmed rotating wheel used to minimize variations in angular velocity and revolutions per minute, as in a machine subject to fluctuation in drive and load. **2.** An analogous device, esp. one used to regulate the speed of clockwork.

Fm The symbol for the element **fermium.**

FM *abbr.* **1.** Field manual. **2.** Also **F.M.** Field marshal. **3.** Also **fm.** Frequency modulation.

fm. *abbr.* **1.** Fathom. **2.** From.

FMB *abbr.* Federal Maritime Board.

FMCS *abbr.* Federal Mediation and Conciliation Service.

FN *abbr.* Foreign national.

fn. *abbr.* Footnote.

FNMA *abbr.* Federal National Mortgage Association.

f-num•ber (ĕf′nŭm′bər) *n.* The ratio of the focal length of a lens or lens system to the effective diameter of its aperture. [F(OCAL LENGTH) + NUMBER.]

FO *abbr.* **1.** Also **F.O.** Field-grade officer. **2.** Field order. **3.** Finance officer. **4.** Also **F/O.** Flight officer. **5.** Also **F.O.** Foreign office.

foal (fōl) *n.* The young offspring of a horse or other equine animal, esp. one under a year old. —*intr.v.* **foaled, foal•ing, foals.** To give birth to a foal. [ME *fole* < OE *fola.* See **pau-*.**]

foam (fōm) *n.* **1.a.** A mass of bubbles of air or gas in a matrix of liquid film, esp. an accumulation of fine frothy bubbles formed in or on the surface of a liquid, as from agitation or fermentation. **b.** A thick chemical froth, such as shaving cream. **2.a.** Frothy saliva produced esp. as a result of physical exertion or a pathological condition. **b.** The frothy sweat of a horse or other equine animal. **3.** The sea. **4.** Any of various light porous semirigid or spongy materials used for thermal insulation or shock absorption. —*v.* **foamed, foam•ing, foams.** —*intr.* **1.** To produce or issue as foam; froth. **2.** To produce foam from the mouth, as from exertion or a pathological condition. —*tr.* **1.** To cause to produce foam. **2.** To cause to become foam. [ME *fom* < OE *fām.*]

foam•flow•er (fōm′flou′ər) *n.* A plant *(Tiarella cordifolia)* of eastern North America with small white flowers.

foam rubber *n.* A light firm spongy rubber made by beating air into latex and then curing it, used in upholstery and insulation.

foam•y (fō′mē) *adj.* **-i•er, -i•est. 1.** Of, relating to, or resembling foam. **2.** Consisting of or covered with foam. —**foam′i•ly** *adv.* —**foam′i•ness** *n.*

fob[1] (fŏb) *n.* **1.** A small pocket at the front waistline of a man's trousers or in the front of a vest, used esp. to hold a watch. **2.a.** A short chain or ribbon attached to a pocket watch and worn hanging in front of the vest or waist. **b.** An ornament or seal attached to such a chain or ribbon. [Prob. of Gmc. orig.]

fob[2] (fŏb) *tr.v.* **fobbed, fob•bing, fobs.** *Archaic.* To cheat or deceive (another). —*phrasal verb.* **fob off. 1.** To dispose of (goods) by fraud or deception; palm off. **2.** To put off or appease by deceitful or evasive means: *was fobbed off with promises.* [ME *fobben*, prob. < *fob*, trickster.]

f.o.b. also **F.O.B.** *abbr.* Free on board.

fo•cal (fō′kəl) *adj.* **1.** Of or relating to a focus. **2.** Placed at or measured from a focus. —**fo′cal•ly** *adv.*

focal distance *n.* See **focal length.**

focal infection *n.* A bacterial infection localized in a specific part of the body that may spread to another part of the body.

fo•cal•ize (fō′kə-līz′) *tr. & intr.v.* **-ized, -iz•ing, -iz•es. 1.** To adjust or come to a focus. **2.** To bring or be brought to a focus; sharpen. **3.** To concentrate or be concentrated; localize. —**fo′cal•i•za′tion** (-kə-lĭ-zā′shən) *n.*

focal length *n.* The distance from the surface of a lens or mirror to its focal point.

focal point *n.* See **focus** 1a.

Foch (fôsh, fŏsh), **Ferdinand.** 1851–1929. French marshal and commander in chief of Allied forces during World War I.

fo'c's'le (fōk′səl) *n. Naut.* Var. of **forecastle.**

fo•cus (fō′kəs) *n., pl.* **-cus•es** or **-ci** (-sī′, -kī′). **1.a.** A point at which rays of light or other radiation converge or from which they appear to diverge, as after refraction or reflection in an optical system. **b.** See **focal length. 2.a.** The distinctness or clarity of an image rendered by an optical system. **b.** The state of maximum distinctness or clarity of such an image: *in focus.* **c.** An apparatus used to adjust the focal length of an optical system in order to make an image distinct or clear. **3.** A center of interest or activity. See Syns at **center. 4.** Close or narrow attention; concentration. **5.** A condition in which something can be clearly apprehended or perceived. **6.** *Pathol.* The region of a localized bodily infection or disease. **7.** *Geol.* The point of origin of an earthquake. **8.** *Math.* A fixed point whose relationship with a directrix determines a conic section. —*v.* **-cused, -cus•ing, -cus•es** or **-cussed, -cus•sing, -cus•ses.** —*tr.* **1.** To cause (light rays, for example) to converge on or toward a central point; concentrate. **2.a.** To render (an object or image) in clear outline or sharp detail by adjustment of one's vision or an optical device; bring into focus. **b.** To adjust (a lens, for example) to produce a clear image. **3.** To direct toward a particular point or purpose. —*intr.* **1.** To converge on or toward a central point of focus; be focused. **2.** To adjust one's vision or an optical device so as to render a clear, distinct image. **3.** To concentrate attention or energy. [Lat., hearth.] —**fo′cus•er** *n.*

fod•der (fŏd′ər) *n.* **1.** Feed for livestock, esp. coarsely chopped hay or straw. **2.** Raw material, as for artistic creation. **3.** A consumable, often inferior item or resource that is in demand and usu. abundant supply. —*tr.v.* **-dered, -der•ing, -ders.** To feed with fodder. [ME < OE *fōdor.* See **pā-***.]

foe (fō) *n.* **1.** A personal enemy. **2.** An enemy in war. **3.** An adversary; an opponent: *a foe of tax reform.* See Syns at **enemy. 4.** Something that serves to oppose, injure, or impede. [ME *fo* < OE *gefā* < *fāh*, hostile.]

foehn also **föhn** (fœn, fān) *n.* A warm dry wind coming off the lee slopes of a mountain range, esp. off the northern slopes of the Alps. [Ger. *Föhn* < MHGer. *fœnne* < OHGer. *phōno* < VLat. **faōnius* < Lat. *favōnius*, the west wind < *favēre*, to be favorable.]

foe•man (fō′mən) *n.* A foe in battle; an enemy.

foe•tal (fēt′l) *adj.* Var. of **fetal.**

foe•tid (fĕ′tĭd) *adj.* Var. of **fetid.**

foe•tor (fē′tər) *n.* Var. of **fetor.**

foe•tus (fē′təs) *n.* Var. of **fetus.**

fog[1] (fôg, fŏg) *n.* **1.** Condensed water vapor in cloudlike masses lying close to the ground and limiting visibility. **2.a.** An obscuring haze, as of atmospheric dust. **b.** A mist or film clouding a surface, as of a window or lens. **3.** A cloud of vaporized liquid, esp. a chemical spray used in fighting fires. **4.a.** A state of mental vagueness or bewilderment. **b.** Something that obscures or conceals; a haze. **5.** A blur on a developed photographic image. —*v.* **fogged, fog•ging, fogs.** —*tr.* **1.** To cover or envelop with or as if with fog. **2.** To cause to be obscured; cloud. **3.** To make vague, hazy, or confused. **4.** To obscure or dim (a photographic image). —*intr.* **1.** To be covered with or as if with fog. **2.** To be blurred, clouded, or obscured. **3.** To be dimmed or obscured. Used of a photographic image. [Perh. of Scand. orig.] —**fog′ger** *n.*

fog[2] (fôg, fŏg) *n.* **1.** A new growth of grass on a mowed or grazed field. **2.** Tall decaying grass left standing after the cutting or grazing season. [ME *fogge*, tall grass. See **pŭ-***.]

fog bank *n.* A dense mass of fog defined against clearer surrounding air, often as viewed from a distance at sea.

fog•bound (fôg′bound′, fŏg′-) *adj.* **1.** Immobilized by heavy fog. **2.** Enveloped or obscured by fog: *fogbound cliffs.*

fog•bow (fôg′bō′, fŏg′-) *n.* A faint arc-shaped light, similar to a rainbow, that sometimes appears in fog opposite the sun.

Fog•gia (fô′jə). A city of S Italy NE of Naples. Pop. 157,126.

fog•gy (fô′gē, fŏg′ē) *adj.* **-gi•er, -gi•est. 1.a.** Full of or surrounded by fog. **b.** Resembling or suggestive of fog. **2.** Clouded or blurred by or as if by fog; vague: *a foggy memory.* —**fog′gi•ly** *adv.* —**fog′gi•ness** *n.*

Fog•gy Bottom (fŏg′ē) *n.* The U.S. Department of State. [< its location in a low-lying area of Washington DC near the Potomac R.]

fog•horn (fôg′hôrn′, fŏg′-) *n.* **1.** *Naut.* A horn for sounding warning signals in fog or darkness, used esp. on ships, buoys, and coastal installations. **2.** A booming insistent voice.

fo•gy also **fo•gey** (fō′gē) *n., pl.* **-gies** also **-geys.** A person of stodgy or old-fashioned habits and attitudes. [Sc. *fogey.*] —**fo′gy•ish** *adj.* —**fo′gy•ism** *n.*

föhn (fœn, fān) *n.* Var. of **foehn.**

foi•ble (foi′bəl) *n.* **1.** A minor weakness or failing of character. **2.** The weaker section of a sword blade, from the middle to the tip. [Obsolete Fr. *foible*, weak point of a sword, weak < OFr. *feble*, weak. See FEEBLE.]

foil[1] (foil) *tr.v.* **foiled, foil•ing, foils. 1.** To prevent from being successful; thwart. **2.** To obscure or confuse (a trail or scent) so as to evade pursuers. —*n. Archaic.* **1.** A repulse; a setback. **2.** The trail or scent of an animal. [ME *foilen*, to trample, defile, var. of *filen*, to defile. See FILE[3].]

foil[2] (foil) *n.* **1.** A thin flexible leaf or sheet of metal: *aluminum foil.* **2.** A thin layer of polished metal placed under a displayed gem to lend it brilliance. **3.** One that by contrast underscores or enhances the distinctive characteristics of another. **4.** The reflective metal coating on the back of a glass mirror. **5.** *Archit.* A curvilinear, often lobelike figure or space formed between the cusps of intersecting arcs, found esp. in Gothic tracery and Moorish ornament. **6.a.** An airfoil. **b.** *Naut.* A hydrofoil. —*tr.v.* **foiled, foil•ing, foils. 1.** To cover or back with foil. **2.** To set off by contrast. [ME < OFr. *foille* < Lat. *folia*, pl. of *folium*, leaf. See **bhel-**[3]*.]

foil[3] (foil) *n.* **1.** A fencing sword having a usu. circular guard and a thin flexible four-sided blade with a button on the tip to prevent injury. **2.** The act or sport of fencing with such a sword. Often used in the plural. [?]

foin (foin) *Archaic.* —*intr.v.* **foined, foin•ing, foins.** To thrust with a pointed weapon. —*n.* A thrust with a pointed weapon. [ME *foinen*, ult. < Lat. *fuscina*, three-pronged spear.]

foi•son (foi′zən) *n.* **1.** *Scots.* Physical strength or power. **2.** *Archaic.* A plentiful harvest; abundance. **3. foisons.** *Obsolete.* Reserves of power; resources. [ME *foisoun* < OFr. *foison* < Lat. *fūsiō, fūsiōn-*, a pouring < *fūsus*, p.part. of *fundere*, to pour. See **gheu-***.]

foist (foist) *tr.v.* **foist•ed, foist•ing, foists. 1.** To pass off as genuine, valuable, or worthy. **2.** To impose (something or someone unwanted) upon another by coercion or trickery. **3.** To insert fraudulently or deceitfully. [Prob. Du. dial. *vuisten*, to take in hand < MDu. < *vuist*, fist. See **penkʷe-***.]

Fo•kine (fô-kēn′, fō-), **Michel.** 1880–1942. Russian-born choreographer whose works include *Petrouchka* (1916).

Fok•ker (fŏk′ər, fô′kər), **Anthony Herman Gerard.** 1890–1939. Dutch-born Amer. aircraft designer.

fol. *abbr.* **1.** Folio. **2.** Following.

fol•a•cin (fŏl′ə-sĭn) *n.* See **folic acid.** [FOL(IC) AC(ID) + -IN.]

fo•late (fō′lāt′) *n.* **1.** A salt or ester of folic acid. **2.** See **folic acid.** [FOL(IC ACID) + -ATE[2].]

fold[1] (fōld) *v.* **fold•ed, fold•ing, folds.** —*tr.* **1.** To bend over or double up so that one part lies on another part. **2.** To make compact by doubling or bending over parts. **3.** To bring from an extended to a closed position. **4.** To bring from a compact to an extended position; unfold. **5.** To place together and intertwine. **6.** To envelop or clasp; enfold. **7.** To blend in (a cooking ingredient) by gently turning a mixture on top of it. **8.a.** *Informal.* To discontinue operating; close. **b.** *Games.* To withdraw (one's hand) in defeat, as by laying cards face down on a table. **9.** *Geol.* To form bends in (a stratum of rock). —*intr.* **1.a.** To become folded. **b.** To be capable of being folded. **2.** *Informal.* To close, esp. for lack of financial success; fail. **3.** *Games.* To withdraw from a game in defeat. **4.** *Informal.* **a.** To give in; buckle. **b.** To weaken or collapse from exertion. —*n.* **1.** The act or an instance of folding. **2.** A part that has been folded over or against another. **3.** A line or mark made by folding; a crease. **4.** A coil or bend, as of rope. **5.** *Chiefly British.* A hill or dale in undulating country. **6.** *Geol.* A bend in a stratum of rock. **7.** *Anat.* A crease or ridge apparently formed by folding, as of a membrane; a plica. [ME *folden* < OE *fealdan, faldan.* See **pel-**[2]*.] —**fold′a•ble** *adj.*

fold[2] (fōld) *n.* **1.** A fenced enclosure for domestic animals, esp. sheep. **2.** A flock of sheep. **3.a.** A group of people or institutions with common beliefs and aims. **b.** A religious congregation. —*tr.v.* **fold•ed, fold•ing, folds.** To place or keep (sheep, for example) in a fenced enclosure. [ME < OE *fald.*]

-fold *suff.* **1.** Divided into a specified number of parts: *fivefold.* **2.** Multiplied by a specified number: *fiftyfold.* [ME < OE *-feald, -fald.* See **pel-**[2]*.]

fold•a•way (fōld′ə-wā′) *adj.* Designed to be folded up for easy storage: *a foldaway bed.* —**fold′a•way′** *n.*

fold•boat (fōld′bōt′) *n. Naut.* A small boat resembling a kayak, consisting of rubberized canvas stretched over a collapsible frame. [Transl. of Ger. *Faltboot.*]

flying squirrel

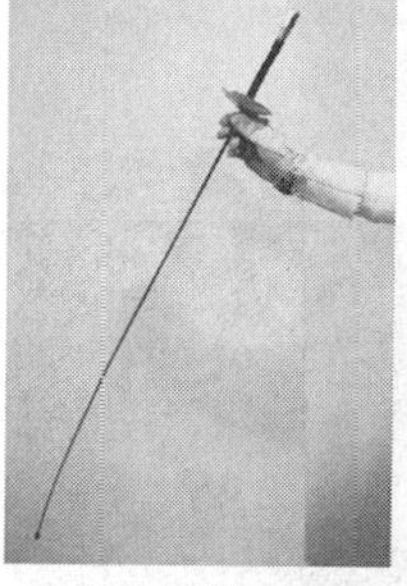

foil[3]

ă pat	oi boy
ā pay	ou out
âr care	ŏŏ took
ä father	ōō boot
ĕ pet	ŭ cut
ē be	ûr urge
ĭ pit	th thin
ī pie	*th* this
îr pier	hw which
ŏ pot	zh vision
ō toe	ə about, item
ô paw	

Stress marks:
′ (primary);
′ (secondary), as in
dictionary (dĭk′shə-nĕr′ē)

fold•er (fōl′dər) *n.* **1.** One that folds or is folded, such as a booklet of one or more folded sheets of paper. **2.** A flexible cover folded in the center, used to hold loose paper.

fol•de•rol (fŏl′də-rŏl′) also **fal•de•ral** (făl′də-răl′) *n.* **1.** Foolishness; nonsense. **2.** A trifle; a gewgaw. [From a nonsense refrain in some old songs.]

fold•ing door (fōl′dĭng) *n.* A door with hinged or pleated sections that fold together when the door is opened.

folding door

folding money *n.* Paper money.

fold•out (fōld′out′) *n.* **1.** *Print.* A folded insert or section, as of a cover, whose full size exceeds that of the regular page. **2.** A piece or part, as of furniture, that folds out or down from a closed position. **—fold′out′** *adj.*

fold•up (fōld′ŭp′) *adj.* Designed to fold up, as for storage or carrying; collapsible. *—n.* **1.** An object that folds up. **2.** *Informal.* A complete failure or breakdown; a collapse.

fo•li•a (fō′lē-ə) *n. Geol. & Math.* Pl. of **folium.**

fo•li•a•ceous (fō′lē-ā′shəs) *adj.* **1.** Of, relating to, or resembling the leaf of a plant. **2.** Having leaves or leaflike structures. **3.** *Geol.* Consisting of thin, leaflike layers, as of minerals. [< Lat. *foliāceus* < *folium*, leaf. See FOLIUM.]

fo•li•age (fō′lē-ĭj, fō′lĭj) *n.* **1.a.** Plant leaves, esp. tree leaves, considered as a group. **b.** A cluster of leaves. **2.** An ornamental representation of leaves, stems, and flowers, esp. in architecture. [Alteration of ME *foilage* < OFr. *foillage* < *foille*, leaf. See FOIL[2].] **—fo′li•aged** *adj.*

fo•li•ar (fō′lē-ər) *adj.* Of or relating to a leaf or leaves. [NLat. *foliāris* < Lat. *folium*, leaf. See FOLIUM.]

fo•li•ate (fō′lē-ĭt, -āt′) *adj.* **1.** Of or relating to leaves. **2.** Shaped like a leaf. **3.** *Geol.* Foliated. *—v.* (-āt′) **-at•ed, -at•ing, -ates.** *—tr.* **1.** To hammer or cut (metal) into thin leaf or foil. **2.a.** To coat (glass, for example) with metal foil. **b.** To furnish or adorn with metal foil. **3.** To separate into thin layers or laminae. **4.** To decorate with foliage or foils. **5.** To number the leaves of (a manuscript, for example). *—intr.* **1.** To produce foliage. **2.** To split into thin leaflike layers or folia. [Lat. *foliātus*, bearing foliage < *folium*, leaf. See FOLIUM.]

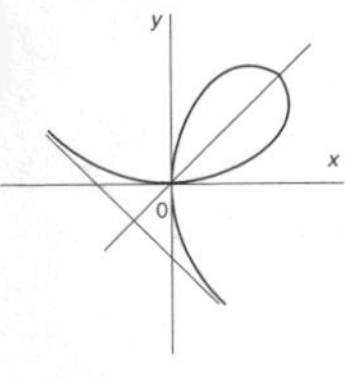

folium
Folium of Descartes
$x^3 + y^3 = 3axy$

-foliate *suff.* Having a specified kind or number of leaves: *trifoliate.* [< FOLIATE.]

fo•li•at•ed (fō′lē-ā′tĭd) *adj. Geol.* Of or relating to rock that exhibits a layered structure.

fo•li•a•tion (fō′lē-ā′shən) *n.* **1.** The state of being in leaf. **2.** Decoration with sculpted or painted foliage. **3.** *Archit.* Decoration of an opening with cusps and foils, as in Gothic tracery. **4.a.** The act, process, or product of forming metal into thin leaf or foil. **b.** The act or process of coating glass with metal foil. **5.a.** The process of numbering consecutively the leaves of a book or manuscript. **b.** The leaves so numbered. **6.** *Geol.* The layered structure common to metamorphic rocks.

fo•lic acid (fō′lĭk, fŏl′ĭk) *n.* A compound, $C_{19}H_{19}N_7O_6$, of the vitamin B complex group, occurring in green plants, fresh fruit, liver, and yeast. [Lat. *folium*, leaf; see FOLIUM + -IC.]

Henry Fonda
Holding his American Film Institute's Life Achievement Award; photographed with daughter Jane in 1978

fo•lie à deux (fô-lē′ ä dœ′, fŏl′ē) *n.* A condition in which symptoms of a mental disorder occur simultaneously in two people who share a close association. [Fr. : *folie*, madness + *à*, between + *deux*, two.]

fo•li•o (fō′lē-ō′) *n., pl.* **-os. 1.a.** A large sheet of paper folded once in the middle, making two leaves or four pages of a book or manuscript. **b.** A book or manuscript of the largest common size, usu. about 38 centimeters (15 inches) in height, consisting of such folded sheets. **2.a.** A leaf of a book numbered only on the front side. **b.** A number on such a leaf. **c.** A page number. **3.** *Accounting.* A page in a ledger or two facing pages that are assigned a single number. *—tr.v.* **-oed, -o•ing, -os.** To number consecutively the pages or leaves of (a book, for example). [ME < LLat. *foliō*, ablative of *folium*, leaf of paper < Lat., leaf. See **bhel-**[3]*.]

-foliolate *suff.* Having a specified kind or number of leaflets: *bifoliolate.* [New Latin *foliolātus* < Fr. *foliole*, leaflet < LLat. *foliolum*, dim. of Lat. *folium*, leaf. See FOLIUM.]

fo•li•ose (fō′lē-ōs′) *adj.* **1.** Bearing numerous leaves; leafy. **2.** Of, relating to, or resembling a leaf. **3.** Of or relating to a lichen whose thallus is flat and leafy. [Lat. *foliōsus* < *folium*, leaf. See FOLIUM.]

fo•li•um (fō′lē-əm) *n., pl.* **-li•a** (-lē-ə). **1.** *Geol.* A thin leaflike layer or stratum occurring esp. in metamorphic rock. **2.** *Math.* A plane cubic curve having a single loop, a node, and two ends asymptotic to the same line. [Lat., leaf. See **bhel-**[3]*.]

fondue

folk (fōk) *n., pl.* **folk** or **folks. 1.a.** The common people of a society or region considered esp. as the originators or carriers of the customs, beliefs, and arts that make up a distinctive culture. **b.** *Archaic.* A nation; a people. **2. folks.** *Informal.* People in general. **3.** People of a specified group or kind. Often used in the plural. **4. folks.** *Informal.* **a.** The members of one's family or childhood household; one's relatives. **b.** One's parents. *—adj.* Of, occurring in, or originating among the common people or folk. ***—idiom.* just folks.** *Informal.* Down-to-earth, open-hearted. [ME < OE *folc.* See **pelə-**[1]*.]

folk art also **folk-art** (fōk′ärt′) *n.* Art usu. reflecting the traditional culture of a nation or region, esp. everyday or festive items produced or decorated by unschooled artists. **—folk′-art′** *adj.* **—folk artist** *n.*

folk dance or **folk-dance** also **folk•dance** (fōk′dăns′) *n.* **1.a.** A traditional dance originating among the common people of a nation or region. **b.** The music accompanying such a dance. **2.** A social gathering at which folk dances are performed. **—folk′-dance′** *adj.* **—folk dancer** *n.* **—folk danc′ing** (dăn′sĭng) *n.*

folk etymology also **folk-et•y•mol•o•gy** (fōk′ĕt-ə-mŏl′ə-jē) *n.* A change in the form of a word or phrase resulting from a mistaken assumption about its composition or meaning, as in *shamefaced* for earlier *shamfast*, "bound by shame."

folk•ie also **folk•y** (fō′kē) *Mus. —n., pl.* **-ies.** A folk singer or musician. *—adj.* **-i•er, -i•est.** Of, relating to, or in the style of folk music.

folk•ish (fō′kĭsh) *adj.* **1.** Of or characteristic of folk music, art, or literature. **2.** Simple or natural; folksy. **—folk′ish•ly** *adv.* **—folk′ish•ness** *n.*

folk•lore (fōk′lôr′, -lōr′) *n.* **1.** The traditional beliefs, myths, tales, and practices of a people, transmitted orally. **2.** The comparative study of folk knowledge and culture. **3.a.** A body of widely accepted but usu. specious notions about a place, a group, or an institution. **b.** A popular but unfounded belief. **—folk′lor′ic** *adj.* **—folk′lor′ish** *adj.* **—folk′lor′ist** *n.* **—folk′lor•is′tic** *adj.*

folk•lor•is•tics (fōk′lô-rĭs′tĭks, -lō-) *n.* (*used with a sing. v.*) See **folklore** 2.

folk medicine *n.* Traditional medicine as practiced by nonprofessional healers or embodied in local custom or lore, generally involving the use of natural and esp. herbal remedies.

folk•moot (fōk′mo͞ot′) or **folk•mote** (-mōt′) *n.* A general assembly of the people of a town, district, or shire in medieval England. [ME < OE *folcmōt* : *folc*, folk; see FOLK + *mōt*, meeting.]

folk music *n. Mus.* **1.** Music originating among the common people of a nation or region and spread about or passed down orally. **2.** Contemporary music in the style of traditional folk music. **—folk′-mu′sic** (fōk′myo͞o′zĭk) *adj.*

folk-rock or **folk rock** (fōk′rŏk′) *n. Mus.* A variety of music combining rock 'n' roll and folk music. **—folk′-rock′** *adj.*

folk•sing•er or **folk-sing•er** also **folk sing•er** (fōk′sĭng′ər) *n. Mus.* A singer of folksongs. **—folk sing′ing** (sĭng′ĭng) *n.*

folk•song or **folk-song** also **folk song** (fōk′sông′, -sŏng′) *n. Mus.* **1.** A song of the folk music of a people or area. **2.** A song composed in the style of traditional folk music.

folk•sy (fōk′sē) *adj.* **-si•er, -si•est.** *Informal.* **1.** Simple and unpretentious in behavior. **2.** Characterized by informality and affability: *a friendly, folksy town.* **3.** Modest; low-key: *folksy humor.* **—folk′si•ly** *adv.* **—folk′si•ness** *n.*

folk•tale or **folk-tale** also **folk tale** (fōk′tāl′) *n.* A story or legend forming part of an oral tradition.

folk•way (fōk′wā′) *n.* A practice, custom, or belief shared by the members of a group as part of their common culture. Often used in the plural.

folk•y (fō′kē) *n. & adj. Mus.* Var. of **folkie.**

fol•li•cle (fŏl′ĭ-kəl) *n.* **1.** *Anat.* **a.** A small body cavity or sac. **b.** A cavity in the ovary containing a maturing ovum in its encasing cells. **2.** *Bot.* A dry single-chambered fruit that splits along only one seam to release its seeds, as in larkspur. [Lat. *folliculus*, little bag, dim. of *follis*, bellows. See **bhel-**[2]*.]

follicle mite *n.* Any of various tiny mites of the genus *Demodex* that infest the hair follicles of mammals.

fol•li•cle-stim•u•lat•ing hormone (fŏl′ĭ-kəl-stĭm′yə-lā′tĭng) *n.* A gonadotropic hormone of the anterior pituitary gland that stimulates the growth of follicles in the ovary and induces the formation of sperm in the testis.

fol•lic•u•lar (fə-lĭk′yə-lər) *adj.* **1.** Relating to, having, or resembling a follicle or follicles. **2.** Affecting or growing out of a follicle or follicles.

fol•lic•u•late (fə-lĭk′yə-lĭt) also **fol•lic•u•lat•ed** (-lā′tĭd) *adj.* Having or consisting of a follicle or follicles.

fol•low (fŏl′ō) *v.* **-lowed, -low•ing, -lows.** *—tr.* **1.** To come or go after; proceed behind. **2.a.** To go after in or as if in pursuit. **b.** To keep under surveillance. **3.a.** To move along the course of; take. **b.** To go in the direction of; be guided by. **4.** To accept the guidance, command, or leadership of. **5.** To adhere to; practice. **6.** To take as a model or precedent; imitate. **7.a.** To act in agreement or compliance with; obey. **b.** To keep to or stick to: *followed the recipe.* **8.** To engage in (a trade or occupation); work at. **9.** To come after in order, time, or position. **10.** To bring something about at a later time than or as a consequence of. **11.** To occur or be evident as a consequence of. **12.a.** To watch or observe closely. **b.** To be attentive to; pay close heed to. **c.** To keep oneself informed of the course, progress, or fortunes of. **13.** To grasp the meaning or logic of; understand. *—intr.* **1.** To come, move, or take place after another person or thing in order or time. **2.** To occur or be evident as a consequence; result. **3.** To grasp the meaning or reasoning of something; understand. *—n.* **1.** The act or an instance of following. **2.** *Games.* A billiards shot in which the cue ball is struck above center so that it follows the path of the object ball after impact. — ***phrasal verbs.*** **follow along.** To move or proceed in unison or in accord with an example. **follow through. 1.** *Sports.* To carry a stroke to natural completion after hitting or releasing a ball or other object. **2.** To carry an act, a project, or an intention to completion; pursue fully. **follow up. 1.** To carry to completion; follow through on. **2.** To increase the effectiveness or enhance the success of by further action. — ***idioms.*** **as follows.** As will be stated next. Used to introduce a specified enumeration, explanation, or command. **follow (one's) nose. 1.** To move straight ahead or in a direct path. **2.** *Informal.* To be guided by instinct. **follow suit. 1.** *Games.* To play a card of the same suit as the one led. **2.** To do as another has done; follow an example. [ME *folowen* < OE *folgian.*]

Syns: *follow, succeed, ensue, result, supervene.* These verbs mean to come after something or someone. *Follow,* which has the widest application, can refer to coming after in time or order, as a consequence or result, or by the operation of logic: *Night follows day.* To *succeed* is to come next after another, especially in planned order determined by considerations such as rank, inheritance, or election: *"The son of a mandarin has no prescriptive right to succeed his father"* (H.G. Wells). *Ensue* usually applies to what follows as a consequence or by way of logical development: *Rioting ensued after the demonstration. Result* implies that what follows is caused by what has preceded: *Failure to file an income tax return can result in a fine. Supervene,* in contrast, refers to something that has little relation to what has preceded and is often unexpected: *"A bad harvest supervened"* (Charlotte Brontë).

Usage Note: *As follows* (not *as follow*) is the established form of the idiom, no matter whether the noun that precedes it is singular or plural: *The regulations are as follows.*

fol•low•er (fŏl′ō-ər) *n.* **1.** One who subscribes to the teachings or methods of another; an adherent: *a follower of Gandhi.* **2.** A servant; a subordinate. **3.** A fan; an enthusiast. **4.** One that imitates or copies another. **5.** A machine element moved by another machine element.

fol•low•er•ship (fŏl′ō-ər-shĭp′) *n.* **1.** The act or condition of following a leader. **2.** A group of followers; a following.

fol•low•ing (fŏl′ō-ĭng) *adj.* **1.** Coming next in time or order. **2.** Now to be enumerated: *The following may come.* **3.** Blowing in the same direction as the course of a ship or an aircraft. Used of wind or seas. — *n.* A group or gathering of admirers, adherents, or disciples. — *prep.* Subsequent to; after.

fol•low-on (fŏl′ō-ŏn′, -ôn′) *adj.* Following as a related or consequent aspect or development. — **fol′low-on′** *n.*

follow shot *n.* **1.** A shot in a movie in which the camera moves to follow a moving subject. **2.** *Games.* A follow in billiards.

fol•low-through or **fol•low•through** (fŏl′ō-thrōō′) *n.* **1.** The act or an instance of following through. **2.** *Sports.* The concluding part of a stroke, as after a ball has been hit.

fol•low-up or **fol•low•up** (fŏl′ō-ŭp′) — *n.* **1.** The act or an instance of following up, as to review new developments. **2.** One that follows up, as to further an end. **3.** A news article or report adding information on a previously reported item. — *adj.* Intended to follow up, as to reinforce or evaluate previous action.

fol•ly (fŏl′ē) *n., pl.* **-lies. 1.** A lack of good sense, understanding, or foresight. **2.a.** An act or instance of foolishness. **b.** A costly undertaking having an absurd or ruinous outcome. **3. follies.** *(used with a sing. or pl. v.)* An elaborate theatrical revue consisting of music, dance, and skits. **4.** *Obsolete.* **a.** Perilously or criminally foolish action. **b.** Evil; wickedness. **c.** Lewdness; lasciviousness. [ME *folie* < OFr. < *fol,* foolish < LLat. *follis,* windbag, fool. See FOOL.]

Fol•som (fōl′səm) *adj.* Of or relating to a western North American culture flourishing east of the Rocky Mountains in the late Pleistocene Period and notable for its leaf-shaped flint projectile points. [After *Folsom,* a town of NE NM.]

Fo•mal•haut (fō′məl-hôt′) *n.* The brightest star in the constellation Piscis Austrinus. [Ar. *fum al-ḥūt,* mouth of the fish, Fomalhaut.]

fo•ment (fō-mĕnt′) *tr.v.* **-ment•ed, -ment•ing, -ments. 1.** To promote the growth of; incite. **2.** To treat (the skin, for example) by fomentation. [ME *fomenten,* to apply warm liquids to the skin, ult. < Lat. *fōmentum,* poultice < **fovementum* < *fovēre,* to warm.] — **fo•ment′er** *n.*

fo•men•ta•tion (fō′mən-tā′shən, -mĕn-) *n.* **1.** The act of fomenting; incitement. **2.a.** A substance or material used as a warm moist medicinal compress; a poultice. **b.** The therapeutic application of warmth and moisture, as to relieve pain.

Fon (fŏn) *n., pl.* **Fon** or **Fons. 1.** A people of Benin and neighboring parts of Nigeria. **2.** The Gbe language of the Fon.

fond¹ (fŏnd) *adj.* **fond•er, fond•est. 1.** Having a strong liking, inclination, or affection. **2.** Affectionate; tender: *a fond embrace.* **3.** Immoderately affectionate or indulgent; doting. **4.** Cherished; dear: *my fondest hopes.* **5.** *Archaic.* Naively credulous or foolish. [ME *fonned,* foolish, prob. < p.part. of *fonnen,* to be foolish, prob. < *fonne,* fool.] — **fond′ly** *adv.*

fond² (fŏnd) *n.* The background of a design in lace. [Fr. < OFr. *fonds, fond* < Lat. *fundus,* bottom.]

Fon•da (fŏn′də), **Henry.** 1905–82. Amer. actor noted for films such as *The Grapes of Wrath* (1940) and *On Golden Pond* (1981). His daughter **Jane** (b. 1937) won Academy Awards for *Klute* (1971) and *Coming Home* (1978).

fon•dant (fŏn′dənt) *n.* **1.** A sweet creamy sugar paste used in candies and icings. **2.** A candy containing this paste. [Fr. < pr.part. of *fondre,* to melt < Lat. *fundere.* See **gheu-*.**]

Fond du Lac (fŏn′ də lăk′, dyə). A city of E WI at the S end of Lake Winnebago SSE of Oshkosh. Pop. 37,757.

fon•dle (fŏn′dl) *v.* **-dled, -dling, -dles.** — *tr.* **1.** To handle, stroke, or caress, usu. lovingly. **2.** *Obsolete.* To treat with indulgence and solicitude; pamper. — *intr.* To show fondness or affection by caressing. [Freq. of FOND¹, to show fondness for (obsolete).] — **fon′dler** *n.*

fond•ness (fŏnd′nĭs) *n.* **1.** Warm affection or liking. See Syns at **love. 2.** A strong inclination or preference; a taste: *a fondness for sweets.* **3.** *Archaic.* Naive trustfulness; credulity.

fon•due also **fon•du** (fŏn-dōō′, -dyōō′) *n.* **1.a.** A hot dish made of melted cheese and wine and eaten with bread. **b.** A similar dish, esp. one consisting of a melted sauce in which pieces of food, such as bread or meat, are dipped or cooked. **2.** A soufflé usu. made with cheese and bread crumbs. [Fr. < fem. p.part. of *fondre,* to melt. See FONDANT.] — **fon•due′** *v.*

Fon•se•ca (fôn-sā′kə, -sĕ′kä), **Gulf of.** An inlet of the Pacific Ocean in W Central America.

font¹ (fŏnt) *n.* **1.** A basin for holding baptismal water in a church. **2.** A receptacle for holy water; a stoup. **3.** The oil reservoir in an oil-burning lamp. **4.** An abundant source; a fount: *She was a font of wisdom.* [ME < OE < LLat. *fōns, font-* < Lat., fountain.] — **font′al** (fŏn′tl) *adj.*

font² (fŏnt) *n. Print.* A set of type of one size and face. [Fr. *fonte,* casting < OFr., ult. < Lat. *fundere,* to pour forth.]

Fon•taine•bleau (fŏn′tĭn-blō′, fôN-tĕn-blō′). A town of N France SE of Paris; site of the signing of the revocation of the Edict of Nantes (1685). Pop. 15,679.

Fon•tan•a (fŏn-tăn′ə). A city of S CA W of San Bernardino. Pop. 87,535.

fon•ta•nel also **fon•ta•nelle** (fŏn′tə-nĕl′) *n.* Any of the soft membranous gaps between the incompletely formed cranial bones of a fetus or an infant. [ME *fontinel* < OFr. *fontanele,* dim. of *fontaine,* fountain. See FOUNTAIN.]

Fon•tanne (fŏn-tăn′), **Lynn.** 1887?–1983. British-born Amer. actress who often performed with her husband Alfred Lunt.

Fon•teyn (fŏn-tān′), Dame **Margot.** 1919–91. British ballerina noted for her portrayal of Aurora in *Sleeping Beauty.*

fon•ti•na (fŏn-tē′nə) *n.* A ripened cheese of variable texture and flavor, originally produced in Italy. [Ital.]

Foo•chow (fōō′jō′, -chou′). See **Fuzhou.**

food (fōōd) *n.* **1.** Material, usu. of plant or animal origin, that contains or consists of essential body nutrients, such as carbohydrates, fats, proteins, vitamins, or minerals, and is ingested and assimilated by an organism to produce energy, stimulate growth, and maintain life. **2.** A specified kind of nourishment. **3.** Nourishment eaten in solid form. **4.** Something that nourishes or sustains in a way suggestive of physical nourishment. [ME *fode* < OE *fōda.* See **pā-*.**]

food chain *n.* A succession of organisms in an ecological community that constitutes a continuation of food energy from one organism to another as each consumes a lower member and in turn is preyed upon by a higher member.

food cycle *n.* See **food web.**

food•ie (fōō′dē) *n. Slang.* A person who has an ardent or refined interest in food; a gourmet.

food poi•son•ing (poi′zə-nĭng) *n.* **1.** An acute, often severe gastrointestinal disorder characterized by vomiting and diarrhea and caused by eating food contaminated with bacteria, esp. bacteria of the genus *Salmonella.* **2.** Poisoning caused by ingesting substances that contain natural toxins.

food processor *n.* An appliance consisting of a container housing interchangeable rotating blades and used for preparing foods, as by shredding, slicing, chopping, or blending.

food pyramid *n. Ecol.* A graphic representation of the structure of a food chain, depicted as a broad-based pyramid formed by producers tapering to a point formed by end consumers.

food stamp *n.* A stamp or coupon, issued by the government to people with low incomes, redeemable for food at stores.

food•stuff (fōōd′stŭf′) *n.* A substance that can be used or prepared for use as food.

food vacuole *n. Biol.* A vacuole in which phagocytized food is digested.

food web *n.* A complex of interrelated food chains in an ecological community.

foo•fa•raw (fōō′fə-rô′) *n.* **1.** Excessive or flashy ornamentation. **2.** A fuss over a trifling matter. [Prob. < Sp. *fanfarrón,* boaster, and < Fr. *frou-frou,* rustling, both of imit. orig.]

fool (fōōl) *n.* **1.** One who is regarded as deficient in judgment, sense, or understanding. **2.** One who acts unwisely on a given occasion. **3.** One who has been tricked or made to appear ridiculous; a dupe. **4.** *Informal.* A person with a talent or an enthusiasm for a certain activity. **5.** A member of a royal or noble household who provided entertainment, as with jokes or antics; a jester. **6.** A dessert made of stewed or puréed fruit

font¹
Baptismal font

food processor

ă pat	oi boy
ā pay	ou out
âr care	ŏŏ took
ä father	ōō boot
ĕ pet	ŭ cut
ē be	ûr urge
ĭ pit	th thin
ī pie	*th* this
îr pier	hw which
ŏ pot	zh vision
ō toe	ə about,
ô paw	item

Stress marks:
′ (primary);
′ (secondary), as in
dictionary (dĭk′shə-nĕr′ē)

fool's cap

footbridge
McMinnville's Airport Park, Oregon

footpath

mixed with cream or custard and served cold. **7.** *Archaic.* A mentally deficient person. — *v.* **fooled, fool•ing, fools.** — *tr.* **1.** To deceive or trick; dupe. **2.** To confound or prove wrong; surprise, esp. pleasantly. — *intr.* **1.** *Informal.* **a.** To speak or act facetiously or in jest; joke. **b.** To behave comically; clown. **c.** To feign; pretend. **2.** To engage in idle or frivolous activity. **3.** To toy, tinker, or mess. — *adj. Informal.* Foolish; stupid. — ***phrasal verbs.*** **fool around.** *Informal.* **1.** To engage in idle or casual activity; putter. **2.** To engage in frivolous activity; make fun. **3.** To engage in casual, often promiscuous sexual acts. **fool away.** To waste (time or money) foolishly; squander. — ***idiom.*** **play (**or **act) the fool. 1.** To act in an irresponsible or foolish manner. **2.** To behave in a playful or comical manner. [ME *fol* < OFr. < LLat. *follis*, windbag, fool < Lat. *follis*, bellows. See **bhel-²*.**]

fool•er•y (fo͞o′lə-rē) *n., pl.* **-ies. 1.** Foolish behavior or speech. **2.** An instance of foolish behavior or speech; a jest.

fool•har•dy (fo͞ol′här′dē) *adj.* **-di•er, -di•est.** Unwisely bold or venturesome; rash. [ME *folhardi* < OFr. *fol hardi* : *fol*, fool; see FOOL + *hardi*, bold; see HARDY¹.] — **fool′har′di•ly** *adv.* — **fool′har′di•ness** *n.*

fool•ish (fo͞o′lĭsh) *adj.* **1.** Lacking or exhibiting a lack of good sense or judgment; silly. **2.** Resulting from stupidity or misinformation; unwise. **3.** Arousing laughter; absurd or ridiculous. **4.** Immoderate or stubborn; unreasonable. **5.** Embarrassed; abashed. **6.** Insignificant; trivial. — **fool′ish•ly** *adv.* — **fool′ish•ness** *n.*

fool•proof (fo͞ol′pro͞of′) *adj.* **1.** Designed so as to be impervious to human incompetence, error, or misuse: *a foolproof safety lock.* **2.** Effective; infallible: *a foolproof scheme.*

fools•cap (fo͞olz′kăp′) *n.* **1.** *Chiefly British.* A sheet of writing or printing paper measuring approx. 13 by 16 inches. **2.** A fool's cap. [From the original watermark of a fool's cap.]

fool's cap (fo͞olz) *n.* **1.** A gaily decorated cap, usu. with a number of loose peaks tipped with bells, formerly worn by court jesters and clowns. **2.** See **dunce cap.**

fool's errand *n., pl.* **fools' errands.** A fruitless mission or undertaking.

fool's gold *n.* See **pyrite.**

fool's paradise *n.* A state of delusive contentment or false hope.

fool's-pars•ley (fo͞olz′pär′slē) *n.* A poisonous European weed *(Aethusa cynapium)* having finely divided leaves, umbels of small white flowers, and an unpleasant odor.

foot (fo͝ot) *n., pl.* **feet** (fēt). **1.** The lower extremity of the vertebrate leg that is in direct contact with the ground in standing or walking. **2.** A structure used for locomotion or attachment in an invertebrate animal, such as the muscular organ extending from the ventral side of a mollusk. **3.** Something suggestive of a foot in position or function, esp.: **a.** The lowest part; the bottom: *the foot of a page.* **b.** The end opposite the head, top, or front: *the foot of a bed.* **c.** The termination of the leg of a piece of furniture, esp. when shaped or modeled. **d.** The part of a sewing machine that holds down and guides the cloth. **e.** *Naut.* The lower edge of a sail. **f.** *Bot.* The base of the sporophyte in mosses and liverworts. **4.** The inferior part or rank. **5.** The part of a stocking or high-topped boot that encloses the foot. **6.a.** A manner of moving; a step. **b.** Speed or momentum, as in a race. **7.** *(used with a pl. v.)* Foot soldiers; infantry. **8.** A unit of poetic meter consisting of stressed and unstressed syllables, or of long and short syllables, in any of various set combinations. **9.** A unit of length in the U.S. Customary and British Imperial systems equal to 12 inches (0.3048 meter). See table at **measurement. 10. foots.** Sediment that forms during the refining of oil and other liquids; dregs. — *v.* **foot•ed, foot•ing, foots.** — *intr.* **1.** To go on foot; walk. Often used with *it*: *had to foot it to the store.* **2.** To dance. Often used with *it.* **3.** *Naut.* To make headway; sail. — *tr.* **1.** To go by foot over, on, or through; tread. **2.** To execute the steps of (a dance). **3.** To add up (a column of numbers) and write the sum at the bottom; total: *footed up the bill.* **4.** To pay; defray. **5.** To provide (a stocking, for example) with a foot. — ***idioms.*** **at (someone's) feet.** Enchanted or fascinated by. **best foot forward.** A favorable initial impression. **feet of clay.** An underlying weakness or fault. **foot in the door.** *Slang.* **1.** An initial point of or opportunity for entry. **2.** A first step in working toward a goal. **have one foot in the grave.** *Informal.* To be on the verge of death. **on (one's) feet. 1.** Standing up. **2.** Fully recovered, as after an illness. **3.** In a sound or stable operating condition. **4.** In an impromptu situation; extemporaneously. **on the right foot.** In an auspicious manner. **on the wrong foot.** In an inauspicious manner. [ME *fot* < OE *fōt.* See **ped-*.**]

Usage Note: Used in combination with numbers to form expressions denoting units of measure, *foot* and *feet* are used typically in the following: *a four-foot plank; a plank four feet* (less frequently, *four foot*) *long.*. When *foot* is combined with greater numbers than one to refer to simple distance, however, only the plural *feet* is used: *a ledge 20 feet* (not *foot*) *away.*

foot•age (fo͝ot′ĭj) *n.* **1.** Length, extent, or amount based on measurement in feet. **2.a.** An amount or length of film or videotape. **b.** A shot or series of shots of a specified nature or subject: *news footage.*

foot-and-mouth disease (fo͝ot′n-mouth′) *n.* An acute, highly contagious degenerative but usu. nonfatal viral disease of cattle and other cloven-hoofed animals, characterized by fever and the eruption of vesicles around the mouth and hoofs.

foot•ball (fo͝ot′bôl′) *n.* **1.** *Sports.* **a.** A game played by two teams of 11 players each on a rectangular 100-yard-long field with goal lines and goal posts at either end, the object being to gain the ball and advance it in running or passing plays across the opponent's goal line or kick it between the opponent's goal posts. **b.** The inflated oval ball used in this game. **2.** *Chiefly British.* **a.** Rugby. **b.** Soccer. **c.** The ball used in Rugby or soccer. **3.** *Informal.* A problem or issue that is discussed but not settled. — **foot′ball′er** *n.*

foot•bath (fo͝ot′băth′, -bäth′) *n.* A small bath, such as a basin or shallow pool, for washing or disinfecting the feet.

foot•board (fo͝ot′bôrd′, -bōrd′) *n.* **1.** An upright board across the foot of a bedstead. **2.** A board or small raised platform on which to support or rest the feet, as in a carriage.

foot•boy (fo͝ot′boi′) *n.* A boy employed as a servant or page.

foot brake *n.* A brake operated by pressure of the foot on a pedal, as in an automobile or on a bicycle.

foot•bridge (fo͝ot′brĭj′) *n.* A bridge designed for pedestrians.

foot-can•dle (fo͝ot′kăn′dl) *n.* A unit of measure of the intensity of light falling on a surface, equal to one lumen per square foot and originally defined with reference to a standardized candle burning at one foot from a given surface.

foot•cloth (fo͝ot′klôth′, -klŏth′) *n.* *Archaic.* A richly ornamented cloth draped over the back of a horse.

foot-drag•ging (fo͝ot′drăg′ĭng) *n.* Failure to take prompt or required action. — **foot′-drag′ger** *n.*

foot•ed (fo͝ot′ĭd) *adj.* Having feet or a foot: *a footed sofa.* Often used in combination: *web-footed; four-footed.*

foot•er (fo͝ot′ər) *n.* **1.** One that is an indicated number of feet in height or length. Often used in combination: *a six-footer.* **2.** Printed matter positioned in the bottom margin of a page, esp. a title, page number, or date repeated throughout a document created on a word-processing system. **3.** See **footing** 4.

foot•fall (fo͝ot′fôl′) *n.* See **footstep** 1.

foot fault *n. Sports.* A fault against the server, as in tennis, called for failure to keep both feet behind the base line.

foot•gear (fo͝ot′gîr′) *n.* Sturdy footwear, such as boots.

foot•hill (fo͝ot′hĭl′) *n.* A hill near the base of a mountain or mountain range.

foot•hold (fo͝ot′hōld′) *n.* **1.** A place providing support for the foot in climbing or standing. **2.** A firm or secure position that provides a base for further advancement.

foot•ing (fo͝ot′ĭng) *n.* **1.** Secure placement of the feet in standing or moving. **2.a.** A surface or its condition with respect to its suitability for walking or running, esp. the condition of a racetrack. **b.** A secure place for the feet; a foothold. **3.** The act of moving on foot. **4.** *Archit.* The supporting base or groundwork of a structure, as for a wall. **5.** A basis or foundation. **6.a.** Position or rank in relation to others; standing. **b.** Terms of social interaction. **7.** The act of making a foot, as for a stocking. **8.** The sum of a column of figures.

foot-lam•bert (fo͝ot′lăm′bərt) *n.* A unit of luminance equal to $1/\pi$ candela per square foot.

foo•tle (fo͝ot′l) *Informal.* — *intr.v.* **-tled, -tling, -tles. 1.** To waste time; trifle. **2.** To talk nonsense. — *n.* Nonsense; foolishness. [Prob. var. of *footer*, to screw around < obsolete *fouter*, a fuck < Fr. *foutre*, to fuck < Lat. *futuere.* See **bhau-*.**] — **foo′tler** *n.*

foot•less (fo͝ot′lĭs) *adj.* **1.** Having no feet. **2.** Lacking a firm support or basis; unsubstantial. **3.** *Informal.* Not competent or skillful; inept. — **foot′less•ly** *adv.* — **foot′less•ness** *n.*

foot•lights (fo͝ot′līts′) *pl.n.* **1.** Lights placed in a row along the front of a stage floor. **2.** The theater as a profession.

foo•tling (fo͝ot′lĭng) *adj. Informal.* **1.** Lacking importance or significance. **2.** Stupid; inept. [Pr.part. of FOOTLE.]

foot•lock•er (fo͝ot′lŏk′ər) *n.* A trunk for storing personal belongings, esp. one kept at the foot of a bed, as in a barracks.

foot•loose (fo͝ot′lo͞os′) *adj.* Having no attachments or ties; free to do as one pleases.

foot•man (fo͝ot′mən) *n.* **1.** A man employed as a servant to wait at table, attend the door, and run various errands, as in a palace. **2.** *Archaic.* A foot soldier; an infantryman.

foot•mark (fo͝ot′märk′) *n.* See **footprint** 1.

foot•note (fo͝ot′nōt′) *n.* **1.** A note at the bottom of a page of a book or manuscript that comments on or cites a reference for a designated part of the text. **2.** Something related to but of lesser importance than a larger work or occurrence. — *tr.v.* **-not•ed, -not•ing, -notes.** To furnish with or comment on in footnotes.

foot•pace (fo͝ot′pās′) *n.* **1.** A walking pace. **2.** A raised platform in a room, as for a lecturer; a dais.

foot•pad¹ (fo͝ot′păd′) *n.* A thief who preys on pedestrians. [FOOT + obsolete *pad*, highwayman (prob. < MDu. *pad*, path; see **pent-***).]

foot•pad² (fo͝ot′păd′) *n.* A plate or similar structure on the leg of a spacecraft that distributes weight and helps prevent sinking after landing.

foot•path (fo͝ot′păth′, -päth′) *n.* A path for pedestrians.

foot-pound (fo͝ot′pound′) *n.* A unit of work equal to the work required to raise a mass of one pound a distance of one foot.
foot-pound•al (fo͝ot′poun′dl) *n.* A unit of work equal to the work done by a force of one poundal acting through a distance of one foot.
foot-pound-sec•ond (fo͝ot′pound′sĕk′ənd) *adj.* Of or relating to the British, Canadian, or U.S. system of measurement with base units of the foot, the pound, and the second.
foot•print (fo͝ot′prĭnt′) *n.* **1.** An outline or indentation left by a foot on a surface. **2.** An area within which a spacecraft is supposed to land. **3.** A designated area affected or covered by a device or phenomenon.
foot•race or **foot race** (fo͝ot′rās′) *n. Sports.* A race run by contestants on foot. **— foot′rac′ing** *n.*
foot•rest (fo͝ot′rĕst′) *n.* A support on which to rest the feet.
foot•rope (fo͝ot′rōp′) *n. Naut.* **1.** A rope attached to the lower border of a sail. **2.** A rope, rigged beneath a yard, for sailors to stand on during the reefing or furling of a sail.
foot rot *n.* **1.** A bacterial infection of the feet in certain hoofed animals often resulting in loss of the hoof. **2.** A disease of plants in which the stem or trunk rots at its base.
foot•sie also **foot•sy** (fo͝ot′sē) *n. Informal.* The flirtatious act of secretly touching the feet or legs of another with one's own, as under a table. ***— idiom.*** **play footsie with. 1.** To flirt with, esp. in secret. **2.** To cooperate or curry favor with in a sly or devious way. [< dim. of FOOT.]
foot•slog (fo͝ot′slŏg′) *intr.v.* **-slogged, -slog•ging, -slogs.** To march or trudge through or as if through mud. **— foot′slog′ger** *n.*
foot soldier *n.* A soldier who fights on foot; an infantryman.
foot•sore (fo͝ot′sôr′, -sōr′) *adj.* Having sore or tired feet, as from too much walking. **— foot′sore′ness** *n.*
foot•stalk (fo͝ot′stôk′) *n.* A supporting stalk, such as a peduncle or pedicel.
foot•stall (fo͝ot′stôl′) *n.* The pedestal, plinth, or base of a pillar, column, or statue.
foot•step (fo͝ot′stĕp′) *n.* **1.a.** A step with the foot. **b.** The sound of a foot stepping. **2.** The distance covered by a step: *a footstep away.* **3.** See **footprint** 1. **4.** A step on which to go up or down. ***— idiom.*** **follow in (someone's) footsteps.** To carry on the behavior, work, or tradition of.
foot•stone (fo͝ot′stōn′) *n.* A marking stone placed at the foot of a grave.
foot•stool (fo͝ot′sto͞ol′) *n.* A low stool for supporting the feet.
foot•wall (fo͝ot′wôl′) *n.* The mass of rock underlying a mineral deposit in a mine.
foot•way (fo͝ot′wā′) *n.* A walk or path for pedestrians.
foot•wear (fo͝ot′wâr′) *n.* Attire, such as shoes, for the feet.
foot•work (fo͝ot′wûrk′) *n.* **1.** *Sports.* The manner in which the feet are used or maneuvered, as in figure skating. **2.** Work that involves moving around on foot; legwork. **3.** *Informal.* Skillful dealing or maneuvering; tactics.
foo•zle (fo͞o′zəl) *tr.v.* **-zled, -zling, -zles.** To manage clumsily; bungle. *— n.* The act of bungling, esp. a poor stroke in golf. [Perh. < Ger. dial. *fuseln*, to work poorly or slowly.]
fop (fŏp) *n.* A man who is preoccupied with and often vain about his clothes and manners; a dandy. [ME, fool; prob. akin to ME *fob*, trickster, cheat. See FOB[2].]
fop•per•y (fŏp′ə-rē) *n., pl.* **-ies. 1.** Foolishness. **2.** The dress or manner of a fop.
fop•pish (fŏp′ĭsh) *adj.* Of, relating to, or characteristic of a fop; dandified. **— fop′pish•ly** *adv.* **— fop′pish•ness** *n.*
for (fôr; fər *when unstressed*) *prep.* **1.a.** Used to indicate the object, aim, or purpose of an action or activity: *for sale.* **b.** Used to indicate a destination: *headed for town.* **2.** Used to indicate the object of a desire, an intention, or a perception: *a nose for news.* **3.a.** Used to indicate the recipient or beneficiary of an action: *lunch for us.* **b.** On behalf of: *spoke for the members.* **c.** In favor of: *Were they for the proposal?* **d.** In place of: *a substitute for eggs.* **4.a.** Used to indicate equivalence or equality: *ten dollars for a ticket.* **b.** Used to indicate correlation or correspondence: *two steps back for every step forward.* **5.a.** Used to indicate amount, extent, or duration: *walked for miles.* **b.** Used to indicate a specific time: *a date for two o'clock.* **6.a.** As being: *take for granted.* **b.** Used to indicate an actual or implied listing or choosing: *For one thing, we can't afford it.* **7.** As a result of; because of: *jumped for joy.* **8.** Used to indicate appropriateness or suitability: *It is for the judge to decide.* **9.** Notwithstanding; despite. **10.a.** As regards; concerning: *a stickler for neatness.* **b.** Considering the nature or usual character of: *spry for his age.* **c.** In honor of: *named for her grandmother.* *— conj.* Because; since. [ME < OE. See **per**[1]*.]
FOR *abbr.* Free on rail.
for. *abbr.* **1.** Foreign. **2.** Forest; forestry.
for– *pref.* Completely; excessively, esp. with destructive or detrimental effect: *forworn.* [ME < OE. See **per**[1]*.]
fo•ra (fôr′ə, fōr′ə) *n.* Pl. of **forum.**
for•age (fôr′ĭj, fŏr′-) *n.* **1.** Food for domestic animals; fodder. **2.** The act of looking or searching for food or provisions. *— v.* **-aged, -ag•ing, -ag•es.** *— intr.* **1.** To wander in search of food or provisions. **2.** To make a raid, as for food. **3.** To conduct a search; rummage. *— tr.* **1.** To collect forage from; strip of food or supplies. **2.** *Informal.* To obtain by foraging: *foraged a snack.* [ME < OFr. *fourrage* < *forrer*, to forage < *feurre*, fodder, of Gmc. orig. See **pā-***.] **— for′ag•er** *n.*
For•a•ker (fôr′ə-kər, fŏr′-), **Mount.** A peak, 5,307 m (17,400 ft), in the Alaska Range of S-central AK.
for•am (fôr′əm, fŏr′-) *n.* A foraminifer.
fo•ra•men (fə-rā′mən) *n., pl.* **-ram•i•na** (-răm′ə-nə) or **-ra•mens.** An opening or orifice, as in a bone. [Lat. *forāmen*, an opening < *forāre*, to bore.] **— fo•ram′i•nal** (-răm′ə-nəl), **fo•ram′i•nous** (-nəs) *adj.*
foramen magnum *n.* The large orifice in the base of the skull through which the spinal cord passes to become the medulla oblongata. [NLat. *forāmen magnum* : Lat. *forāmen*, opening + Lat. *magnus*, large.]
foramen o•val•e (ō-văl′ē, -vā′lē, -vä′-) *n.* An opening in the septum between the atria of the heart, usu. present only in the fetus. [NLat. *forāmen ōvāle* : Lat. *forāmen*, opening + Med. Lat. *ōvālis*, oval.]
for•a•min•i•fer (fôr′ə-mĭn′ə-fər, fŏr′-) also **for•a•min•i•fer•an** (-mĭn′ə-fər-ən) *n., pl.* **fo•ram•i•nif•er•a** (fə-răm′ə-nĭf′ər-ə) or **for•a•min•i•fers.** Any of the chiefly marine protozoans of the order Foraminifera, having a calcareous shell with perforations through which numerous pseudopods protrude. [< NLat. *Forāminifera*, order name : Lat. *forāmen*, *forāmin-*, an opening + Lat. *-fer*, -fer.] **— fo•ram′i•nif′er•ous** (fə-răm′ə-nĭf′ər-əs), **fo•ram′i•nif′er•al** *adj.*
for•as•much as (fôr′əz-mŭch′ əz) *conj.* Inasmuch as; since.
for•ay (fôr′ā′, fŏr′ā′, fŏr′ā′) *n.* **1.** A sudden raid or military advance. **2.** A venture or an initial attempt, esp. outside one's usual area. *— v.* **-ayed, -ay•ing, -ays.** *— intr.* **1.** To make a raid. **2.** To make inroads, as for profit or adventure. *— tr. Archaic.* To pillage for spoils. [ME *forrai* < *forraien*, to plunder, prob. back-formation < *forreour*, raider, plunderer < OFr. *forrier* < *forrer*, to forage. See FORAGE.]
forb (fôrb) *n.* A broad-leaved herb other than a grass, esp. one growing in a field, prairie, or meadow. [< Gk. *phorbē*, fodder < *pherbein*, to graze.]
for•bear[1] (fôr-bâr′) *v.* **-bore** (-bôr′, -bōr′), **-borne** (-bôrn′, -bōrn′), **-bear•ing, -bears.** *— tr.* **1.** To refrain from; resist: *forbear replying.* **2.** To desist from; cease. **3.** *Obsolete.* To avoid or shun. *— intr.* **1.** To hold back; refrain. **2.** To be tolerant or patient in the face of provocation. [ME *forberen* < OE *forberan*, to endure. See **bher-**[1]*.] **— for•bear′er** *n.*
for•bear[2] (fôr′bâr′, fōr′-) *n.* Var. of **forebear.**
for•bear•ance (fôr-bâr′əns) *n.* **1.** The act of forbearing. **2.** Tolerance and restraint in the face of provocation; patience. See Syns at **patience. 3.** The quality of being forbearing. **4.** *Law.* The act of a creditor who refrains from enforcing a debt when it falls due.
for•bid (fər-bĭd′, fôr-) *tr.v.* **-bade** (-băd′, -bād′) or **-bad** (-băd′), **-bid•den** (-bĭd′n) or **-bid, -bid•ding, -bids. 1.** To command (someone) not to do something. **2.** To command against the doing or use of (something); prohibit. **3.** To have the effect of preventing; preclude: *Discretion forbids a reply.* [ME *forbidden, forbeden* < OE *forbēodan*. See **bheudh-***.] **— for•bid′dance** *n.* **— for•bid′der** *n.*

Syns: *forbid, ban, enjoin, interdict, prohibit, proscribe.* The central meaning shared by these verbs is "to refuse to allow": *laws that forbid speeding; banned smoking; was enjoined from broadcasting; interdict trafficking in drugs; rules that prohibit swimming; proscribed the importation of certain fruits.* ***Ant:*** *permit.*

for•bid•den (fər-bĭd′n, fôr-) *adj. Phys.* Having a low probability of occurrence. Used of quantum phenomena.
For•bid•den City (fər-bĭd′n, fôr-). A walled enclosure of central Beijing, China, containing the palaces of former rulers.
forbidden fruit *n.* An indulgence or a pleasure that is illegal or is believed immoral. [From the story of the fruit forbidden to Adam and Eve in Genesis 2:16–3:19.]
for•bid•ding (fər-bĭd′ĭng, fôr-) *adj.* **1.** Tending or threatening to impede progress. **2.** Unpleasant; disagreeable. **3.** Having a menacing aspect. **— for•bid′ding•ly** *adv.*
force (fôrs, fōrs) *n.* **1.** The capacity to do work or cause physical change; energy, strength, or active power. **2.a.** Power made operative against resistance; exertion. See Syns at **strength. b.** The use of physical power or violence to compel or restrain. **3.a.** Intellectual power or vigor, esp. as conveyed in writing or speech. **b.** Moral strength. **c.** A capacity for affecting the mind or behavior; efficacy. **d.** One that possesses such capacity: *the forces of evil.* **4.a.** A body of persons or other resources organized or available for a certain purpose. **b.** A person or group capable of influential action. **5.a.** Military strength. **b.** The entire military strength, as of a nation. Often used in the plural. **c.** A unit of a nation's military personnel, esp. one deployed into combat. **6.** *Law.* Legal validity. **7.** *Phys.* A vector quantity that tends to produce an acceleration of a body in the direction of its application. *— tr.v.* **forced, forc•ing, forc•es. 1.** To compel through pressure or necessity. **2.a.** To gain by force or coercion. **b.** To move or effect against resistance or inertia. **c.** To inflict or impose relentlessly. **3.a.** To put undue strain on. **b.** To increase or ac-

footrope

ă pat	oi boy
ā pay	ou out
âr care	o͝o took
ä father	o͞o boot
ĕ pet	ŭ cut
ē be	ûr urge
ĭ pit	th thin
ī pie	*th* this
îr pier	hw which
ŏ pot	zh vision
ō toe	ə about, item
ô paw	

Stress marks:
′ (primary);
′ (secondary), as in
dictionary (dĭk′shə-nĕr′ē)

celerate (a pace, for example) to the maximum. **c.** To produce with effort and against one's will: *force a smile.* **d.** To use (language) clumsily. **4.a.** To move, open, or clear by force. **b.** To break down or open by force: *force a lock.* **5.** To rape. **6.** *Bot.* To cause to grow or mature by artificially accelerating normal processes. **7.** *Baseball.* **a.** To put (a runner) out on a force play. **b.** To allow (a run) to be scored by walking a batter with the bases loaded. **8.** *Games.* To cause an opponent to play (a particular card). *—idioms.* **force (someone's) hand.** To force to act or speak prematurely or unwillingly. **in force. 1.** In full strength; in large numbers. **2.** In effect; operative. [ME < OFr. < Med.Lat. *fortia* < neut. pl. of Lat. *fortis,* strong. See **bhergh-²*.**] **—force′a•ble** *adj.* **—forc′er** *n.*

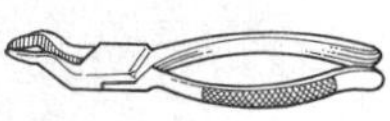

forceps
Top: Obstetrical
Bottom: Dental

forced (fôrst, fōrst) *adj.* **1.** Imposed by force; involuntary: *forced labor.* **2.** Produced under strain; not spontaneous: *forced laughter.* See Usage Note at **forceful.**

force-feed (fôrs′fēd′, fōrs′-) *tr.v.* **-fed** (-fĕd′), **-feed•ing, -feeds. 1.** To compel to ingest food; feed forcibly, esp. by mechanical means. **2.** To force to assimilate.

force field *n.* See **field of force.**

force•ful (fôrs′fəl, fōrs′-) *adj.* Characterized by or full of force; effective. **—force′ful•ly** *adv.* **—force′ful•ness** *n.*

Usage Note: *Forceful, forcible,* and *forced* have distinct, though related meanings. *Forceful* is used to describe someone or something that possesses or is filled with strength or force: *a forceful speaker. Forceful measures* may or may not involve the use of actual physical force. *Forcible,* by contrast, is most often used of actions accomplished by the application of physical force: *There had been a forcible entry. Forced* is used to describe an act or a condition brought about by control or an outside influence: *a forced landing.*

force ma•jeure (fôrs′ mä-zhûr′, fōrs′) *n.* **1.** Superior or overpowering force. **2.** An unexpected or uncontrollable event. [Fr. : *force,* force + *majeure,* greater.]

force•meat (fôrs′mēt′, fōrs′-) *n.* Finely ground and highly spiced meat, fish, or poultry that is served alone or used in stuffing. [*Force* (alteration of FARCE) + MEAT.]

force of habit *n.* Behavior that has become automatic through long practice or frequent repetition.

force-out (fôrs′out′, fōrs′-) *n. Baseball.* The act or fact of putting out a base runner on a force play.

force play *n. Baseball.* A play in which a runner is put out when forced by the batter to move to the next base.

for•ceps (fôr′səps, -sĕps) *n., pl.* **forceps. 1.** A pincerlike instrument used for grasping, manipulating, or extracting, esp. such an instrument used by a surgeon. **2.** A pincerlike pair of movable posterior appendages in certain insects, such as earwigs. [Lat., fire tongs, pincers. See **gʷher-*.**]

Betty Ford
Photographed in 1982

force pump *n.* A pump with a solid piston and valves used to raise a liquid or expel it under pressure.

forc•i•ble (fôr′sə-bəl, fōr′-) *adj.* **1.** Effected against resistance by using force. **2.** Characterized by force; powerful. See Usage Note at **forceful. —forc′i•ble•ness** *n.* **—forc′i•bly** *adv.*

ford (fôrd, fōrd) *n.* A shallow place in a body of water where one can cross by walking or riding. *—tr.v.* **ford•ed, ford•ing, fords.** To cross (a body of water) at a ford. [ME < OE. See **per-²*.**] **—ford′a•ble** *adj.*

Ford (fôrd, fōrd), **Elizabeth ("Betty") Bloomer.** b. 1918. First Lady of the U.S. (1974–77) who supported the Equal Rights Amendment, the arts, and programs for disabled children.

Ford, Ford Madox. 1873–1939. British writer and editor noted for his novel *The Good Soldier* (1915).

Ford, Gerald Rudolph. b. 1913. The 38th President of the U.S. (1974–77), who was appointed Vice President on the resignation of Spiro Agnew (1973) and became President after Richard Nixon's resignation over the Watergate scandal.

Ford, Henry. 1863–1947. Amer. automobile manufacturer who developed a gasoline-powered automobile (1893) and mass-produced the Model T (1908–27).

Gerald Ford

Ford, John¹. 1586–1639. English playwright whose works include *'Tis Pity She's a Whore* (1633).

Ford, John². 1895–1973. Amer. filmmaker whose motion pictures include *The Grapes of Wrath* (1940).

for•do also **fore•do** (fôr-do͞o′, fōr-) *tr.v.* **-did** (-dĭd′), **-done** (-dŭn′), **-do•ing, -does** (-dŭz′). *Archaic.* **1.** To bring to ruin; destroy. **2.** To exhaust utterly. [ME *fordon* < OE *fordōn* : *for-,* for- + *dōn,* to do; see **dhē-*.**]

fore (fôr, fōr) *adj.* **1.** Located at or toward the front; forward. **2.** Earlier in order of occurrence; former. *—n.* **1.** Something that is located at or toward the front. **2.** The front part. *—adv.* **1.** At, toward, or near the front; forward. **2.** At an earlier time. *—prep.* also **'fore.** Before. *—interj. Sports.* Used by a golfer to warn those ahead that a ball is headed in their direction. *—idiom.* **to the fore.** In, into, or toward a position of prominence. [ME, beforehand, before, in front of < OE. See **per¹*.**]

fore– *pref.* **1.** Before; earlier: *foredoom.* **2.** In front of; front: *foredeck.* [ME *for-, fore-* < OE < *fore,* in front. See **per¹*.**]

fore and aft *adv.* **1.** *Naut.* **a.** From the bow of a ship to the stern; lengthwise. **b.** In, at, or toward both ends of a ship. **2.** In or at the front and back.

fore-and-aft (fôr′ən-ăft′, fōr′-) *adj.* Parallel with the length of a structure, such as a ship or house; running lengthwise.

fore-and-aft•er (fôr′ən-ăf′tər, fōr′-) *n. Naut.* A sailing ship, such as a schooner, with a fore-and-aft rig.

fore-and-aft rig *n. Naut.* A rig on a sailing ship that has quadrilateral and triangular sails set to the fore-and-aft line.

fore-and-aft sail *n. Naut.* A sail set along the fore-and-aft line of a vessel, having its luff attached to the mast.

fore•arm¹ (fôr-ärm′, fōr-) *tr.v.* **-armed, -arm•ing, -arms.** To arm or prepare in advance of a conflict.

fore•arm² (fôr′ärm′, fōr′-) *n.* **1.** The part of the arm between the wrist and the elbow. **2.** The corresponding part of the foreleg in certain quadrupeds, such as a horse.

fore•bear also **for•bear** (fôr′bâr′, fōr′-) *n.* A person from whom one is descended; an ancestor. See Syns at **ancestor.** [ME : *fore-,* fore- + *beer,* one who is (< *been,* to be; see BE).]

fore•bode (fôr-bōd′, fōr-) *v.* **-bod•ed, -bod•ing, -bodes.** *—tr.* **1.** To indicate the likelihood of; portend. **2.** To have a premonition of (a future misfortune). *—intr.* To prophesy or predict. **—fore•bod′er** *n.*

fore•bod•ing (fôr-bō′dĭng, fōr-) *n.* **1.** A sense of impending evil. **2.** An evil omen; a portent. *—adj.* Marked by or indicative of foreboding; ominous. **—fore•bod′ing•ly** *adv.* **—fore•bod′ing•ness** *n.*

fore•brain (fôr′brān′, fōr′-) *n.* **1.** The most anterior of the three primary regions of the embryonic brain. **2.** The segment of the adult brain that develops from the embryonic forebrain and includes the cerebrum, thalamus, and hypothalamus.

fore•cast (fôr′kăst′, fōr′-) *v.* **-cast** or **-cast•ed, -cast•ing, -casts.** *—tr.* **1.** To estimate or calculate in advance, esp. to predict (weather conditions) by analysis of meteorological data. **2.** To serve as an advance indication of; foreshadow. *—intr.* To calculate or estimate something in advance; predict the future. *—n.* A prediction, as of coming events. [ME *forecasten,* to plan beforehand : *fore-,* fore- + *casten,* to throw, calculate, prepare; see CAST.] **—fore•cast′a•ble** *adj.* **—fore′cast′er** *n.*

fore•cas•tle (fōk′səl, fôr′kăs′əl, fōr′-) also **fo'c's'le** (fōk′səl) *n. Naut.* **1.** The section of the upper deck of a ship located at the bow forward of the foremast. **2.** A superstructure at the bow of a merchant ship where the crew is housed. [ME *forecastel* : *fore-,* fore- + *castel,* fortification; see CASTLE.]

fore-check (fôr′chĕk′, fōr′-) *intr.v.* **-checked, -check•ing, -checks.** *Sports.* To check an ice-hockey opponent in the opponent's own defensive zone. **—fore′-check′er** *n.*

fore•close (fôr-klōz′, fōr-) *v.* **-closed, -clos•ing, -clos•es.** *—tr.* **1.a.** To deprive (a mortgagor) of the right to redeem mortgaged property, as when payments have not been made. **b.** To bar an equity or a right to redeem (a mortgage). **2.** To exclude or rule out; bar. **3.** To settle or resolve beforehand. *—intr.* To bar an equity or a right to redeem a mortgage. [ME *forclosen,* to exclude from an inheritance < OFr. *forclos,* shut out, p.part. of *forclore,* to exclude : *fors-,* outside (< Lat. *forīs*; see **dhwer-***) + *clore,* to close (< Lat. *claudere*).] **—fore•clos′a•ble** *adj.*

fore•clo•sure (fôr-klō′zhər, fōr-) *n.* The act of foreclosing, esp. a legal proceeding by which a mortgage is foreclosed.

fore•court (fôr′kôrt′, fōr′kōrt′) *n.* **1.** A courtyard in front of a building. **2.** *Sports.* The part of a court nearest the net or wall.

fore•deck (fôr′dĕk′, fōr′-) *n. Naut.* The forward part of the deck of a ship, usu. the main deck.

fore•do (fôr-do͞o′, fōr-) *v.* Var. of **fordo.**

fore•doom (fôr-do͞om′, fōr-) *tr.v.* **-doomed, -doom•ing, -dooms.** To doom or condemn beforehand.

fore•fa•ther (fôr′fä′*th*ər, fōr′-) *n.* An ancestor. See Syns at **ancestor.**

fore•feel (fôr-fēl′, fōr-) *tr.v.* **-felt** (-fĕlt′), **-feel•ing, -feels.** To feel beforehand; have a premonition of.

fore•fend (fôr-fĕnd′, fōr-) *v.* Var. of **forfend.**

fore•fin•ger (fôr′fĭng′gər, fōr′-) *n.* See **index finger.**

fore•foot (fôr′fo͝ot′, fōr′-) *n.* **1.** Either of the front feet of a quadruped. **2.** *Naut.* The part of a ship where the prow joins the keel.

fore•front (fôr′frŭnt′, fōr′-) *n.* **1.** The foremost part or area. **2.** The position of most importance, prominence, or responsibility; the vanguard: *in the forefront of the movement.*

fore•gath•er (fôr-găth′ər, fōr-) *v.* Var. of **forgather.**

fore•go¹ (fôr-gō′, fōr-) *tr.v.* **-went** (-wĕnt′), **-gone** (-gôn′, -gŏn′), **-go•ing, -goes** (-gōz′). To precede, as in time or place. [ME *foregon* < OE *foregān* : *fore-,* fore- + *gān,* go; see **ghē-*.**] **—fore•go′er** *n.*

fore•go² (fôr-gō′, fōr-) *v.* Var. of **forgo.**

fore•go•ing (fôr-gō′ĭng, fōr-, fôr′gō′ĭng, fōr′-) *adj.* Said, written, or encountered just before; previous.

fore•gone *adj.* (fôr′gôn′, -gŏn′, fōr′-). Having gone before; previous. [P.part. of FOREGO¹.]

foregone conclusion *n.* **1.** An end or a result regarded as inevitable. **2.** A conclusion formed before consideration.

fore•ground (fôr′ground′, fōr′-) *n.* **1.** The part of a scene or picture nearest and in front of the viewer. **2.** See **forefront** 2.

fore•gut (fôr′gŭt′, fōr′-) *n.* **1.** The part of the embryonic vertebrate alimentary canal from which the pharynx, lungs, esophagus, stomach, liver, pancreas, and duodenum develop. **2.** The first part of the alimentary canal of an arthropod or annelid, which includes the buccal cavity, esophagus, crop, and gizzard.

fore•hand (fôr′hănd′, fōr′-) *adj.* **1.** Made or done with the hand moving palm forward: *a forehand tennis stroke.* **2.** *Obsolete.* Taking place, done, or given beforehand; prior. —*n.* **1.** A forehand stroke, as in tennis. **2.** The part of a horse in front of the rider. —*adv.* With a forehand stroke or motion.

fore•hand•ed (fôr′hăn′dĭd, fōr′-) *adj.* **1.** Forehand, as in tennis. **2.a.** Looking or planning ahead; circumspect. **b.** Having ample financial resources; well-off. —**fore′hand′ed•ly** *adv.* —**fore′hand′ed•ness** *n.*

fore•head (fôr′ĭd, -hĕd′, fŏr′-) *n.* **1.** The part of the face between the eyebrows, the normal hairline, and the temples. **2.** The front part of something. [ME *forhed* < OE *forhēafod* : *for-*, fore- + *hēafod*, head; see HEAD.]

for•eign (fôr′ĭn, fŏr′-) *adj.* **1.** Located away from one's native country. **2.** Of, characteristic of, or from a place other than the one being considered. **3.** Conducted or involved with other nations or governments; not domestic. **4.** Situated in an abnormal or improper place in the body and typically introduced from outside. **5.** Not natural; alien. **6.** Not germane; irrelevant. **7.** Subject to another political unit's jurisdiction. [ME *forein* < OFr. *forain* < LLat. *forānus*, on the outside < Lat. *forās*, outside. See **dhwer-***.] —**for′eign•ness** *n.*

foreign affairs *pl.n.* Affairs concerning international relations and national interests in foreign countries.

foreign aid *n.* Aid offered by one nation to another.

foreign bill *n.* A draft for a sum of money to be paid in another country.

for•eign-born (fôr′ĭn-bôrn′, fŏr′-) *adj.* Foreign by birth; not native to the country in which one resides.

foreign correspondent *n.* A correspondent who sends news reports or commentary from a foreign country.

for•eign•er (fôr′ə-nər, fŏr′-) *n.* **1.** One who is from a foreign country or place. **2.** One who is from outside a particular group or community; an outsider.

foreign exchange *n.* **1.** Transaction of international monetary business, as between different governments. **2.** Negotiable bills drawn in one country to be paid in another.

for•eign•ism (fôr′ĭ-nĭz′əm, fŏr′-) *n.* A foreign idiom or custom.

foreign minister *n.* A cabinet minister in charge of a nation's foreign affairs.

foreign mission *n.* **1.** A permanent diplomatic legation established in a foreign country. **2.** A religious group esp. of Christians sent to a foreign country for missionary service.

foreign office *n.* The governmental department in charge of foreign affairs in certain countries.

foreign policy *n.* The diplomatic policy of a nation in its interactions with other nations.

For•eign Service (fôr′ĭn, fŏr′-) *n.* **1.** The diplomatic and consular staff of the United States. **2. foreign service.** The diplomatic and consular personnel of a nation's foreign office.

fore•judge also **for•judge** (fôr-jŭj′, fōr-) *tr.v.* **-judged, -judg•ing, -judg•es.** To judge beforehand without adequate examination or evidence; prejudge. —**fore•judg′ment** *n.*

fore•know (fôr-nō′, fōr-) *tr.v.* **-knew** (-nōō′, -nyōō′), **-known** (-nōn′), **-know•ing, -knows.** To have foreknowledge of, esp. by supernatural means or through revelation.

fore•knowl•edge (fôr-nŏl′ĭj, fōr-, fôr′nŏl′-, fōr′-) *n.* Awareness of something before its existence or occurrence.

fore•la•dy (fôr′lā′dē, fōr′-) *n.* See **forewoman.**

fore•land (fôr′lənd, fōr′-) *n.* A projecting land mass.

fore•leg (fôr′lĕg′, fōr′-) *n.* Either of the front legs of a quadruped.

fore•limb (fôr′lĭm′, fōr′-) *n.* An anterior appendage, such as a leg, wing, or flipper.

fore•lock[1] (fôr′lŏk′, fōr′-) *n.* A lock of hair that grows from or falls on the forehead, esp. the part of a horse's mane that falls forward between the ears.

fore•lock[2] (fôr′lŏk′, fōr′-) *n.* A cotter pin; a linchpin.

fore•man (fôr′mən, fōr′-) *n.* **1.** A man who leads a work crew. **2.** A man who chairs and speaks for a jury. —**fore′man•ship′** *n.*

fore•mast (fôr′məst, -măst′, fōr′-) *n.* *Naut.* The forward mast on a sailing vessel.

fore•milk (fôr′mĭlk′, fōr′-) *n.* See **colostrum.**

fore•most (fôr′mōst′, fōr′-) *adj.* **1.** First in time or place. **2.** Ahead of all others, esp. in position or rank; paramount. —*adv.* **1.** In the front or first position. **2.** So as to be most important. [Alteration of ME *formest*, superl. of *forme*, first < OE *forma*. See **per**[1]***.]

fore•moth•er (fôr′mŭth′ər, fōr′-) *n.* A woman ancestor.

fore•name (fôr′nām′, fōr′-) *n.* A name before one's surname; a first name.

fore•named (fôr′nāmd′, fōr′-) *adj.* Named previously.

fore•noon (fôr′nōōn′, fōr′-, fôr-nōōn′, fōr-) *n.* The period of time between sunrise and noon; morning.

fo•ren•sic (fə-rĕn′sĭk, -zĭk) *adj.* **1.** Relating to, used in, or appropriate for courts of law or for public discussion or argumentation. **2.** Of, relating to, or used in debate or argument; rhetorical. [< Lat. *forēnsis*, public, of a forum < *forum*, forum. See **dhwer-***.] —**fo•ren′si•cal•ly** *adv.*

forensic medicine *n.* The branch of medicine that interprets or establishes the facts in civil or criminal law cases.

fo•ren•sics (fə-rĕn′sĭks, -zĭks) *n.* *(used with a sing. v.)* The art or study of formal debate; argumentation.

fore•or•dain (fôr′ôr-dān′, fōr′-) *tr.v.* **-dained, -dain•ing, -dains.** To determine or appoint beforehand; predestine. —**fore′or•dain′ment, fore•or′di•na′tion** (-ôr′dn-ā′shən) *n.*

fore•part (fôr′pärt′, fōr′-) *n.* **1.** The first or early part of a period of time. **2.** The anterior part, as of an object.

fore•paw (fôr′pô′, fōr′-) *n.* The paw of an animal's foreleg.

fore•peak (fôr′pēk′, fōr′-) *n.* *Naut.* The section of the hold of a ship that is within the angle made by the bow.

fore•per•son (fôr′pûr′sən, fōr′-) *n.* **1.** The chair and spokesperson for a jury. **2.** The leader of a work crew.

fore•play (fôr′plā′, fōr′-) *n.* Sexual stimulation preceding intercourse.

fore•quar•ter (fôr′kwôr′tər, fōr′-) *n.* **1.** The front section of a side of meat. **2.** The foreleg, shoulder, and adjacent lateral parts of an animal, esp. a horse.

fore•reach (fôr-rēch′, fōr-) *v.* **-reached, -reach•ing, -reach•es.** —*tr.* To gain on or get ahead of (a sailing vessel). —*intr.* **1.** To forereach a sailing vessel. **2.** To continue moving forward after taking in sail, as when coming about.

fore•run (fôr-rŭn′, fōr-) *tr.v.* **-ran** (-răn′), **-run, -run•ning, -runs. 1.** To run before. **2.** To precede as an indication of what is to follow. **3.** To prevent from arriving or occurring.

fore•run•ner (fôr′rŭn′ər, fōr′-) *n.* **1.a.** One that precedes, as in time; a predecessor. **b.** An ancestor; a forebear. **2.a.** One that comes before and indicates the approach of another; a harbinger. **b.** A warning sign or symptom.

fore•said (fôr′sĕd′, fōr′-) *adj.* *Archaic.* Aforesaid.

fore•sail (fôr′səl, -sāl′, fōr′-) *n.* *Naut.* **1.** The principal sail hung from the foreyard of a square-rigged vessel. **2.** The principal sail hung from the foremast of a fore-and-aft-rigged vessel. **3.** A triangular sail hung from the forestay of a cutter or sloop; a jib.

fore•see (fôr-sē′, fōr-) *tr.v.* **-saw** (-sô′), **-seen** (-sēn′), **-see•ing, -sees.** To see or know beforehand: *foresaw the increase in unemployment.* —**fore•see′a•ble** *adj.* —**fore•se′er** *n.*

fore•shad•ow (fôr-shăd′ō, fōr-) *tr.v.* **-owed, -ow•ing, -ows.** To present an indication or a suggestion of beforehand; presage. —**fore•shad′ow•er** *n.*

fore•sheet (fôr′shēt′, fōr′-) *n.* *Naut.* **1.** A sheet used in trimming a foresail. **2. foresheets.** The space near the bow of an open boat.

fore•shock (fôr′shŏk′, fōr′-) *n.* A tremor that precedes an earthquake originating at approximately the same location.

fore•shore (fôr′shôr′, fōr′shōr′) *n.* **1.** The part of a shore that lies between high and low watermarks. **2.** The part of a shore between the water and occupied or cultivated land.

fore•short•en (fôr-shôr′tn, fōr-) *tr.v.* **-ened, -en•ing, -ens. 1.** To shorten the lines of (an object) in a drawing or other representation so as to produce an illusion of projection or extension in space. **2.** To reduce the length of; curtail.

fore•show (fôr-shō′, fōr-) *tr.v.* **-showed, -shown** (-shōn′) or **-showed, -show•ing, -shows.** To show in advance; prefigure.

fore•side (fôr′sīd′, fōr′-) *n.* The front or upper side or part.

fore•sight (fôr′sīt′, fōr′-) *n.* **1.** Perception of the significance and nature of events before they have occurred. **2.** Care in providing for the future; prudence. See Syns at **prudence. 3.** The act of looking forward. —**fore′sight′ed, fore′sight′ful** *adj.* —**fore′sight′ed•ly** *adv.* —**fore′sight′ed•ness** *n.*

fore•skin (fôr′skĭn′, fōr′-) *n.* The loose fold of skin that covers the glans of the penis.

fore•speak (fôr-spēk′, fōr-) *tr.v.* **-spoke** (-spōk′), **-spo•ken** (-spō′kən), **-speak•ing, -speaks. 1.** To predict. **2.** To arrange for in advance.

for•est (fôr′ĭst, fŏr′-) *n.* **1.** A dense growth of trees, plants, and underbrush covering a large area. **2.** Something that resembles a large dense growth of trees, as in density. **3.** A defined area of land formerly set aside in England as a royal hunting ground. —*tr.v.* **-est•ed, -est•ing, -ests.** To plant trees on. [ME < OFr. < Med.Lat. *forestis (silva)*, outside (forest) < Lat. *forīs*, outside. See **dhwer-***.] —**for′est•al, fo•res′tial** (fə-rĕs′chəl) *adj.* —**for′es•ta′tion** *n.*

fore•stage (fôr′stāj′, fōr′-) *n.* The part of a stage in front of the closed curtain.

fore•stall (fôr-stôl′, fōr-) *tr.v.* **-stalled, -stall•ing, -stalls. 1.** To delay, hinder, or prevent by taking precautionary measures. **2.** To deal with or think of beforehand; anticipate. **3.** To prevent or hinder normal sales in (a market) by buying up merchandise, discouraging persons from bringing their goods to market, or encouraging an increase in prices in goods already on sale. [ME *forestallen*, to waylay and rob < *forestal*, highway robbery, ambush < OE *foresteall* : *fore*, fore- + *steall*, position; see **stel-***.] —**fore•stall′er** *n.* —**fore•stall′ment** *n.*

forehand

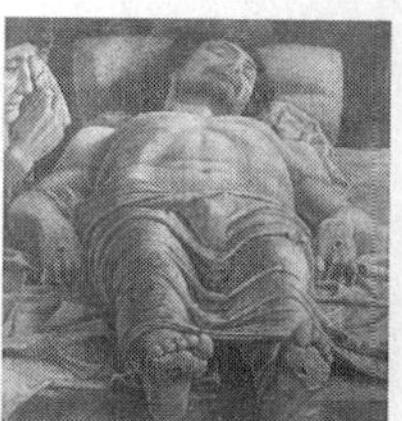
foreshorten
Detail of *The Dead Christ* by Andrea Mantegna

ă pat	oi boy
ā pay	ou out
âr care	ŏŏ took
ä father	ōō boot
ĕ pet	ŭ cut
ē be	ûr urge
ĭ pit	th thin
ī pie	*th* this
îr pier	hw which
ŏ pot	zh vision
ō toe	ə about, item
ô paw	

Stress marks:
′ (primary);
′ (secondary), as in dictionary (dĭk′shə-nĕr′ē)

fore•stay (fôr′stā′, fōr′-) *n. Naut.* A stay extending from the head of the foremast to the bowsprit of a ship.

fore•stay•sail (fôr′stā′səl, -sāl′, fōr′-) *n. Naut.* A triangular sail set on the forestay.

for•est•er (fôr′ĭ-stər, fŏr′-) *n.* **1.** One trained in forestry. **2.** One that inhabits a forest. **3.** Any of various chiefly black moths of the family Agaristidae.

For•est•er (fôr′ĭ-stər, fŏr′-), **C(ecil) S(cott).** 1899–1966. British writer known esp. for his novels featuring Horatio Hornblower.

For•est Hills (fôr′ĭst, fŏr′-). A residential section of New York City in central Queens on W Long I.; site of the U.S. Open tennis championship matches until 1978.

for•est•land (fôr′ĭst-lănd′, fŏr′-) *n.* A section of land covered with forest or set aside for the cultivation of forests.

Forest Park. 1. A city of NW GA, a suburb of Atlanta. Pop. 16,925. **2.** A city of SW OH, a suburb of Cincinnati. Pop. 18,609.

for•est•ry (fôr′ĭ-strē, fŏr′-) *n.* **1.a.** The science and art of cultivating, maintaining, and developing forests. **b.** The management of a forestland. **2.** A forestland.

fore•swear (fôr-swâr′, fōr-) *v.* Var. of **forswear.**

fore•taste (fôr′tāst′, fōr′-) *n.* **1.** An advance token or warning. **2.** A slight taste or sample in anticipation of something. —*tr.v.* (fôr-tāst′, fōr-, fôr′tāst′, fōr′-) **-tast•ed, -tast•ing, -tastes.** To have an anticipatory taste of.

fore•tell (fôr-tĕl′, fōr-) *tr.v.* **-told** (-tōld′), **-tell•ing, -tells.** To tell of or indicate beforehand; predict. —**fore•tell′er** *n.*

fore•thought (fôr′thôt′, fōr′-) *n.* **1.** Deliberation, consideration, or planning beforehand. **2.** Preparation or thought for the future. See Syns at **prudence.** —**fore′thought′ful** *adj.* —**fore′thought′ful•ly** *adv.* —**fore′thought′ful•ness** *n.*

fore•to•ken (fôr-tō′kən, fōr-) *tr.v.* **-kened, -ken•ing, -kens.** To indicate or give warning of beforehand; presage. —*n.* (fôr′tō′kən, fōr′-). An advance sign; a warning.

fore•top (fôr′tŏp′, fōr′-) *n.* **1.** (*also* -təp). *Naut.* A platform at the top of a ship's foremast. **2.** A forelock, esp. of a horse.

fore•top•gal•lant (fôr′tŏp-găl′ənt, fōr′-, fôr′tə-, fōr′-) *adj. Naut.* Of, relating to, or being the mast directly above the foretopmast.

fore•top•mast (fôr′tŏp′məst, fōr′-, fôr′təp-măst′, fōr′-) *n. Naut.* The mast that is above the foretop.

fore•top•sail (fôr′tŏp′səl, fōr′-, fôr′təp-, fōr′-) *n. Naut.* A sail hung from the foretopmast.

for•ev•er (fôr-ĕv′ər, fər-) *adv.* **1.** For everlasting time. **2.** At all times; incessantly. —*n.* A seemingly very long time.

for•ev•er•more (fôr-ĕv′ər-môr′, -mōr′, fər-) *adv.* Forever.

fore•warn (fôr-wôrn′, fōr-) *tr.v.* **-warned, -warn•ing, -warns.** To warn in advance.

fore•went (fôr-wĕnt′, fōr-) *v.* P.t. of **forego**[1].

fore•wing (fôr′wĭng′, fōr′-) *n.* Either of a pair of anterior wings of a four-winged insect.

fore•wom•an (fôr′wo͝om′ən, fōr′-) *n.* **1.** A woman who leads a work crew. **2.** A woman who chairs and speaks for a jury.

fore•word (fôr′wərd, fōr′-) *n.* A preface or an introductory note, as for a book, esp. by a person other than the author.

fore•worn (fôr-wôrn′, fōr-wōrn′) *adj.* Var. of **forworn.**

fore•yard (fôr′yärd′, fōr′-) *n. Naut.* The lowest yard on a foremast, from which the foresail is hung.

for•feit (fôr′fĭt) *n.* **1.** Something surrendered or subject to surrender as punishment, as for a crime, for example. **2.** *Games.* **a.** Something placed in escrow and then redeemed after payment of a fine. **b. forfeits.** A game in which forfeits are demanded. **3.** A forfeiture. —*adj.* Lost or subject to loss through forfeiture. —*tr.v.* **-feit•ed, -feit•ing, -feits. 1.** To surrender, be deprived of, or give up the right to, as on account of a crime, for example. **2.** To subject to seizure as a forfeit. [ME *forfet,* crime, penalty < OFr. *forfait,* p.part. of *forfaire,* to commit a crime, act outside the law : *fors,* beyond (< Lat. *forīs,* outside; see **dhwer-***) + *faire,* to do (< Lat. *facere;* see **dhē-***).] —**for′feit•a•ble** *adj.* —**for′feit•er** *n.*

for•fei•ture (fôr′fĭ-cho͝or′, -chər) *n.* **1.** The act of surrendering something as a forfeit. **2.** Something that is forfeited.

for•fend also **fore•fend** (fôr-fĕnd′, fōr-) *tr.v.* **-fend•ed, -fend•ing, -fends. 1.a.** To keep or ward off; avert. **b.** *Archaic.* To forbid. **2.** To defend or protect. [ME *forfenden* : *for-,* for- + *fenden,* to ward off; see FEND.]

for•gath•er also **fore•gath•er** (fôr-găth′ər, fōr-) *intr.v.* **-ered, -er•ing, -ers. 1.** To gather together; assemble. **2.** To meet another usu. by accident.

forge[1] (fôrj, fōrj) *n.* **1.** A furnace or hearth where metals are heated or wrought; a smithy. **2.** A workshop where pig iron is transformed into wrought iron. —*v.* **forged, forg•ing, forg•es.** —*tr.* **1.a.** To form (metal, for example) by heating in a forge and beating or hammering into shape. **b.** To form (metal) by a mechanical or hydraulic press. **2.** To give form or shape to, esp. by means of careful effort: *forge a relationship.* **3.** To reproduce for fraudulent purposes; counterfeit. —*intr.* **1.** To work at a forge or smithy. **2.** To make a forgery or counterfeit. [ME < OFr. < Lat. *fabrica* < *faber,* worker.] —**forge′a•bil′i•ty** *n.* —**forge′a•ble** *adj.* —**forg′er** *n.*

forge[2] (fôrj, fōrj) *intr.v.* **forged, forg•ing, forg•es. 1.** To advance gradually but steadily: *forged ahead.* **2.** To advance with an abrupt increase of speed. [Prob. < FORGE[1].]

for•ger•y (fôr′jə-rē, fōr′-) *n., pl.* **-ies. 1.** The act of forging, esp. the illegal production of something counterfeit. **2.** Something counterfeit, forged, or fraudulent.

for•get (fər-gĕt′, fôr-) *v.* **-got** (-gŏt′), **-got•ten** (-gŏt′n) or **-got, -get•ting, -gets.** —*tr.* **1.** To be unable to remember (something). **2.** To treat with thoughtless inattention; neglect. **3.** To leave behind unintentionally. **4.** To fail to mention. **5.a.** To banish from one's thoughts. **b.** *Informal.* To disregard on purpose. Usu. used in the imperative: *Oh, forget it.* —*intr.* **1.** To cease remembering. **2.** To fail or neglect to become aware at the proper or specified moment. —***idiom.* forget oneself.** To lose one's reserve, temper, or self-restraint. [ME *forgeten* < OE *forgietan.* See **ghend-***.] —**for•get′ter** *n.*

for•get•ful (fər-gĕt′fəl, fôr-) *adj.* **1.** Tending or likely to forget. **2.** Marked by neglectful or heedless failure to remember: *forgetful of one's responsibilities.* **3.** Causing one to be unable to remember. —**for•get′ful•ly** *adv.* —**for•get′ful•ness** *n.*

for•ge•tive (fôr′jĭ-tĭv, fōr′-) *adj. Archaic.* Capable of imagining or inventing. [Poss. < FORGE[1] + *-tive* (as in *inventive*).]

for•get-me-not (fər-gĕt′mē-nŏt′, fôr-) *n.* **1.** Any of various herbs of the genus *Myosotis,* having clusters of small blue flowers. **2.** Any of several similar or related plants.

for•get•ta•ble (fər-gĕt′ə-bəl, fôr-) *adj.* Fit or apt to be forgotten: *a very forgettable movie.*

for•give (fər-gĭv′, fôr-) *v.* **-gave** (-gāv′), **-giv•en** (-gĭv′ən), **-giv•ing, -gives.** —*tr.* **1.** To excuse for a fault or an offense; pardon. **2.** To renounce anger or resentment against. **3.** To absolve from payment of (a debt, for example). —*intr.* To accord forgiveness. [ME *forgiven* < OE *forgiefan.* See **ghabh-***.] —**for•giv′a•ble** *adj.* —**for•giv′a•bly** *adv.* —**for•giv′er** *n.*

Syns: *forgive, pardon, excuse, condone.* These verbs mean to refrain from imposing punishment on an offender or demanding satisfaction for an offense. The first three can be used as conventional ways of offering apology. More strictly, to *forgive* is to grant pardon without harboring resentment: *"Children begin by loving their parents; as they grow older they judge them; sometimes they forgive them"* (Oscar Wilde). *Pardon* more strongly implies release from the liability for or penalty entailed by an offense: *All political prisoners were pardoned.* To *excuse* is to pass over a mistake or fault without demanding punishment or redress: *"There are some acts of injustice which no national interest can excuse"* (J.A. Froude). To *condone* is to overlook an offense, usually a serious one, and often suggests tacit forgiveness: *Failure to protest may indicate willingness to condone.*

for•give•ness (fər-gĭv′nĭs, fôr-) *n.* The act of forgiving.

for•giv•ing (fər-gĭv′ĭng, fôr-) *adj.* **1.** Inclined or able to forgive. **2.** Providing a margin for error or shortcomings. —**for•giv′ing•ly** *adv.* —**for•giv′ing•ness** *n.*

for•go also **fore•go** (fôr-gō′, fōr-) *tr.v.* **-went** (-wĕnt′), **-gone** (-gôn′, -gŏn′), **-go•ing, -goes.** To abstain from; relinquish. [ME *forgon* < OE *forgān,* go away, forgo : *for-,* for- + *gān,* to go; see **ghē-***.] —**for•go′er** *n.*

fo•rint (fôr′ĭnt′) *n.* See table at **currency.** [Hung. < Ital. *fiorino,* florin. See FLORIN.]

for•judge (fôr-jŭj′, fōr-) *v.* Var. of **forejudge.**

fork (fôrk) *n.* **1.** A utensil with two or more prongs, used for eating or serving food. **2.** An implement with two or more prongs used for raising, carrying, piercing, or digging. **3.a.** A bifurcation or separation into two or more branches or parts. **b.** The point at which such a bifurcation or separation occurs. **c.** One of the branches of such a bifurcation or separation. **4.** *Games.* An attack by one chess piece on two pieces at the same time. —*v.* **forked, fork•ing, forks.** —*tr.* **1.** To raise, carry, pitch, or pierce with a fork. **2.** To give the shape of a fork to (one's fingers, for example). **3.** *Games.* To launch an attack on (two chess pieces). **4.** *Informal.* To pay. —*intr.* **1.** To divide into two or more branches. **2.a.** To use a fork, as in working. **b.** To turn at or travel along a fork. [ME *forke,* digging fork < OE *forca* and < ONFr. *forque,* both < Lat. *furca.*] —**fork′er** *n.* —**fork′ful′** *n.*

fork•ball (fôrk′bôl′) *n. Baseball.* A pitch with the ball placed between the index and middle fingers so that the ball takes a sharp dip near home plate. —**fork′ball′er** *n.*

forked (fôrkt, fôr′kĭd) *adj.* **1.** Containing or characterized by a fork: *a forked river.* **2.** Shaped like or similar to a fork.

fork•lift (fôrk′lĭft′) *n.* A small industrial vehicle with a power-operated pronged platform that can be inserted under a load to lift and move it. —**fork′lift′** *v.*

forklift

fork•y (fôr′kē) *adj.* **-i•er, -i•est.** Forked.

For•lì (fôr-lē′). A city of N Italy SE of Bologna; founded as a Roman trade center. Pop. 91,900.

for•lorn (fər-lôrn′, fôr-) *adj.* **1.a.** Appearing sad or lonely because deserted or abandoned. **b.** Forsaken or deprived: *forlorn of all hope.* **2.** Wretched or pitiful in appearance or condition. **3.** Nearly hopeless; desperate. [ME *forloren,* p.part. of *forlesen,* to abandon < OE *forlēosan.* See **leu-***.] —**for•lorn′ly** *adv.* —**for•lorn′ness** *n.*

forlorn hope *n.* **1.** An arduous or nearly hopeless undertaking.

2. An advance guard of troops sent on a hazardous mission. [By folk ety. < Du. *verloren hoop*, advance guard : *verloren*, p.part. of *verliezen*, to lose; see **leu-*** + *hoop*, troop.]

form (fôrm) *n.* **1.a.** The shape and structure of an object. **b.** The body or outward appearance of a person or an animal considered separately from the face or head; figure. **2.a.** The essence of something. **b.** The mode in which a thing exists, acts, or manifests itself; kind. **3.a.** Procedure as determined by regulation or custom. **b.** A fixed order of words or procedures, as for use in a ceremony; a formula. **4.** A document with blanks for the insertion of details or information. **5.a.** Manners or conduct as governed by etiquette, decorum, or custom. **b.** Behavior according to a fixed or accepted standard: *bad form to be late.* **c.** Performance considered with regard to acknowledged criteria: *unusual form as a bowler.* **6.a.** Proven ability to perform: *a musician in top form.* **b.** Fitness, as of an athlete, with regard to health or training. **c.** The past performance of a racehorse. **d.** A racing form. **7.a.** Method of arrangement or manner of coordinating elements in literary or musical composition or in organized discourse: *in outline form.* **b.** A particular type or example of such arrangement: *The essay is a literary form.* **c.** The design, structure, or pattern of a work of art: *symphonic form.* **8.a.** A mold for the setting of concrete. **b.** A model of the human figure or part of it used for displaying clothes. **c.** A proportioned model that may be adjusted for fitting clothes. **9.** A grade in a British secondary school or in some American private schools: *the sixth form.* **10.a.** A linguistic form. **b.** The external aspect of words with regard to their inflections, pronunciation, or spelling. **11.a.** *Chiefly British.* A long seat; a bench. **b.** The resting place of a hare. **12.** *Bot.* A subdivision of a variety usu. differing in one trivial characteristic. —*v.* **formed, form•ing, forms.** —*tr.* **1.a.** To give form to; shape. **b.** To develop in the mind; conceive. **2.a.** To shape or mold (dough, for example) into a particular form. **b.** To arrange oneself in. **c.** To organize or arrange. **d.** To fashion, train, or develop by instruction or precept. **3.** To come to have; develop or acquire. **4.** To constitute or compose a usu. basic element, part, or characteristic of. **5.a.** To produce (a tense, for example) by inflection. **b.** To make (a word) by derivation or composition. **6.** To put in order; arrange. —*intr.* **1.** To become formed or shaped. **2.** To come into being by taking form; arise. **3.** To assume a specified form, shape, or pattern. [ME *forme* < Lat. *fōrma.*] —**form′a•bil′i•ty** *n.* —**form′a•ble** *adj.*

–form *suff.* Having the form of: *plexiform.* [NLat. *-fōrmis* < Lat. *fōrma*, form.]

for•mal (fôr′məl) *adj.* **1.a.** Relating to or involving outward form or structure. **b.** Being or relating to essential form or constitution: *a formal principle.* **2.a.** Following or being in accord with accepted forms, conventions, or regulations: *a formal dinner.* **b.** Executed, carried out, or done in proper or regular form. **3.a.** Characterized by strict observation of forms; methodical: *formal in their transactions.* **b.** Stiffly ceremonious: *a formal greeting.* **4.** Having the outward appearance but lacking in substance. —*n.* Something, such as a gown, that is formal in nature. [ME < Lat. *fōrmālis* < *fōrma*, shape.] —**for′mal•ly** *adv.* —**for′mal•ness** *n.*

for•mal•de•hyde (fôr-măl′də-hīd′) *n.* A colorless gaseous compound, HCHO, the simplest aldehyde, used to make synthetic resins, as an embalming fluid, and in aqueous solution as a preservative and disinfectant. [FORM(IC ACID) + ALDEHYDE.]

for•ma•lin (fôr′mə-lĭn) *n.* An aqueous solution of formaldehyde that is 37 percent by weight. [Originally a trademark.]

for•mal•ism (fôr′mə-lĭz′əm) *n.* **1.** Rigorous or excessive adherence to recognized forms, as in art. **2.** An instance of formalism. —**for′mal•ist** *adj. & n.* —**for′mal•is′tic** *adj.* —**for′mal•is′ti•cal•ly** *adv.*

for•mal•i•ty (fôr-măl′ĭ-tē) *n., pl.* **-ties. 1.** The quality or condition of being formal. **2.** Rigorous or ceremonious adherence to established forms, rules, or customs. **3.** An established form, rule, or custom, esp. one followed merely for the sake of procedure or decorum.

for•mal•ize (fôr′mə-līz′) *tr.v.* **-ized, -iz•ing, -iz•es. 1.** To give a definite form or shape to. **2.a.** To make formal. **b.** To give formal standing or endorsement to; make official by the observance of proper procedure. —**for′mal•iz′a•ble** *adj.* —**for′mal•i•za′tion** (-mə-lĭ-zā′shən) *n.* —**for′mal•iz′er** *n.*

formal logic *n.* The study of the properties of propositions and deductive reasoning by abstraction and analysis of the form rather than the content of propositions under consideration.

for•mal•wear (fôr′məl-wâr′) *n.* Attire, such as evening gowns and tuxedos, for wear on formal occasions.

for•mant (fôr′mənt) *n.* Any of several frequency regions of relatively great intensity in a sound spectrum, which together determine the characteristic quality of a vowel sound. [Ger. < Lat. *fōrmāns, fōrmant-*, pr.part. of *fōrmāre*, to form < *fōrma*, form.]

for•mat (fôr′măt′) *n.* **1.** A plan for the organization and arrangement of a specified production. **2.** The material form or layout of a publication. **3.** *Comp. Sci.* **a.** The arrangement of data for storage or display. **b.** A method for achieving such an arrangement. —*tr.v.* **-mat•ted, -mat•ting, -mats. 1.** To plan or arrange in a specified form. **2.** *Comp. Sci.* **a.** To divide (a disk) into marked sectors so that it may store data. **b.** To determine the arrangement of (data) for storage or display. [Fr., ult. < Lat. *fōrmātus*, p.part. of *fōrmāre*, to form < *fōrma*, form.]

for•mate (fôr′māt′) *n.* A salt or an ester of formic acid that contains the $HCOO^-$ radical. [FORM(IC ACID) + –ATE[2].]

for•ma•tion (fôr-mā′shən) *n.* **1.** The act or process of forming something or of taking form. **2.** Something formed: *cloud formations.* **3.** The manner or style in which something is formed; structure. **4.** A specified arrangement or deployment, as of troops. **5.** *Geol.* The primary unit of lithostratigraphy, consisting of a body of rock useful for mapping or description. —**for•ma′tion•al** *adj.*

form•a•tive (fôr′mə-tĭv) *adj.* **1.** Forming or capable of forming. **2.a.** Susceptible to transformation by growth and development. **b.** *Biol.* Capable of producing new cells or tissue. **3.** Of or relating to formation, growth, or development: *the formative stages of a plot.* **4.** *Ling.* Relating to the formation or inflection of words. —*n. Gram.* A derivational or inflectional affix. —**form′a•tive•ly** *adv.*

form class *n. Ling.* A set of words that have one or more grammatical or syntactic characteristics in common.

form criticism *n.* A method of textual criticism, applied esp. to the Bible, for tracing the origin and history of certain passages through systematic study of the writings in terms of conventional literary forms.

form•er[1] (fôr′mər) *n.* **1.** One that forms; a maker or creator. **2.** *Chiefly British.* A member of a school form.

for•mer[2] (fôr′mər) *adj.* **1.a.** Occurring earlier in time. **b.** Of, relating to, or taking place in the past. **2.** Coming before in place or order; foregoing. **3.** Being the first of two mentioned. **4.** Having been in the past: *a former ambassador.* [ME, comp. of *forme*, first < OE *forma.* See **per[1]***.]

Usage Note: Grammarians have often insisted that the phrases *the former* and *the latter* should be used only to refer to the first of two things and the second of two things, respectively: *"But Flynn preceded Casey, as did also Jimmy Blake, and the former was a lulu and the latter was a fake."* It is not difficult to find violations of this rule in the works of reputable writers. But the fact that *former* and *latter* are plainly comparatives will make many readers uneasy when the words are used in enumerations of more than two things.

for•mer•ly (fôr′mər-lē) *adv.* At an earlier time; once.

form•fit•ting (fôrm′fĭt′ĭng) *adj.* Snugly fitting the contours of the body: *formfitting jeans.*

form genus *n. Bot.* A classification, as of fossil plants, based on morphological resemblance.

for•mic (fôr′mĭk) *adj.* **1.** Of or relating to ants. **2.** Of, derived from, or containing formic acid. [< Lat. *formīca*, ant.]

For•mi•ca (fôr-mī′kə). A trademark for a variety of laminated plastic sheets of synthetic resin used esp. as a surface on tables and counters.

formic acid *n.* A colorless caustic fuming liquid, HCOOH, used in dyeing and finishing textiles and paper and in fumigants and insecticides. [From its natural occurrence in ants.]

for•mi•car•y (fôr′mĭ-kĕr′ē) *n., pl.* **-ies.** A nest of ants; an anthill. [Med.Lat. *formīcārium* < Lat. *formīca*, ant.]

for•mi•civ•o•rous (fôr′mĭ-sĭv′ər-əs) *adj.* Feeding on ants. [Lat. *formīca*, ant + –VOROUS.]

for•mi•da•ble (fôr′mĭ-də-bəl) *adj.* **1.** Arousing fear, dread, or alarm. **2.** Inspiring awe, admiration, or wonder. **3.** Difficult to undertake, surmount, or defeat: *a formidable challenge.* [ME < OFr. < Lat. *formīdābilis* < *formīdāre*, to fear < *formīdō*, fear.] —**for′mi•da•bil′i•ty, for′mi•da•ble•ness** *n.* —**for′mi•da•bly** *adv.*

form•less (fôrm′lĭs) *adj.* **1.** Having no definite form; shapeless. **2.** Lacking order. **3.** Having no material existence. —**form′less•ly** *adv.* —**form′less•ness** *n.*

form letter *n.* A usu. impersonal letter in a standardized format that may be sent to different people.

For•mo•sa (fôr-mō′sə). See **Taiwan.**

Formosa Strait also **Tai•wan Strait** (tī′wän′). An arm of the Pacific Ocean between Taiwan and China linking the East China Sea with the South China Sea.

for•mu•la (fôr′myə-lə) *n., pl.* **-las** or **-lae** (-lē′). **1.a.** An established form of words or symbols for use in a ceremony or procedure. **b.** An utterance of conventional notions or beliefs; a hackneyed expression. **2.** A method of doing or treating something that relies on an established uncontroversial model or approach. **3.** *Chem.* **a.** A symbolic representation of the composition or of the composition and structure of a compound. **b.** The compound so represented. **4.a.** A prescription of ingredients in fixed proportion; a recipe. **b.** A liquid food for infants, containing most of the nutrients in human milk. **5.** *Math.* A statement, esp. an equation, of a rule, principle, or other factual relation. **6. Formula.** *Sports.* A set of specifications that determine a class of racing car. [Lat. *fōrmula*, dim. of *fōrma*, form.] —**for′mu•la′ic** (-lā′ĭk) *adj.* —**for′mu•la′i•cal•ly** *adv.*

for•mu•la•rize (fôr′myə-lə-rīz′) *tr.v.* **-rized, -riz•ing, -riz•es.**

ă pat	oi boy
ā pay	ou out
âr care	ŏŏ took
ä father	ōō boot
ĕ pet	ŭ cut
ē be	ûr urge
ĭ pit	th thin
ī pie	*th* this
îr pier	hw which
ŏ pot	zh vision
ō toe	ə about, item
ô paw	

Stress marks:
′ (primary);
′ (secondary), as in
dictionary (dĭk′shə-nĕr′ē)

To express as or reduce to a formula; formulate. **— for′mu•la•ri•za′tion** (-lər-ĭ-zā′shən) *n.* **— for′mu•la•riz′er** *n.*

for•mu•lar•y (fôr′myə-lĕr′ē) *n., pl.* **-ies. 1.** A book or other collection of stated and fixed forms, such as prayers. **2.** A statement expressed in formulas. **3.** A fixed form or pattern; a formula. **4.** A book containing a list of pharmaceutical substances, their formulas, uses, and methods of preparation.

for•mu•late (fôr′myə-lāt′) *tr.v.* **-lat•ed, -lat•ing, -lates. 1.a.** To state as or reduce to a formula. **b.** To express in systematic terms or concepts. **c.** To devise or invent: *formulate strategy.* **2.** To prepare according to a specified formula. **— for′mu•la′tion** *n.* **— for′mu•la′tor** *n.*

formula weight *n.* See **molecular weight.**

for•mu•lize (fôr′myə-līz′) *tr.v.* **-lized, -liz•ing, -liz•es.** To formulate. **— for′mu•li•za′tion** (-lĭ-zā′shən) *n.* **— for′mu•liz′er** *n.*

form word *n. Gram.* See **function word.**

for•myl (fôr′mĭl′) *n.* The negative univalent radical HCO, characteristic of aldehydes. [FORM(IC ACID) + -YL.]

For•nax (fôr′năks′) *n.* A constellation in the Southern Hemisphere near Eridanus. [Lat. *fornāx,* furnace, oven. See **gʷher-*.**]

for•nent (fər-nĕnt′) *prep. Upper Southern U.S.* Var. of **fernenst.**

for•ni•cate (fôr′nĭ-kāt′) *intr.v.* **-cat•ed, -cat•ing, -cates.** To engage in fornication. [LLat. *fornicārī, fornicāt-* < *fornix, fornic-,* vault, vaulted cellar, brothel. See **gʷher-*.**] **— for′ni•ca′tor** *n.*

for•ni•ca•tion (fôr′nĭ-kā′shən) *n.* Sexual intercourse between partners who are not married to each other.

Word History: The word *fornication* had a lowly beginning. The Latin word *fornix,* from which *fornicātiō,* the ancestor of *fornication,* is derived, meant "a vault, an arch." The term also referred to a vaulted cellar where prostitutes plied their trade. This sense of *fornix* in Late Latin yielded the verb *fornicārī,* "to commit fornication," from which is derived *fornicātiō,* "whoredom, fornication."

for•nix (fôr′nĭks) *n., pl.* **-ni•ces** (-nĭ-sēz′). An archlike anatomical structure or fold, such as the arched band of white matter located beneath the corpus callosum of the brain. [Lat., arch, vault. See **gʷher-*.**]

For•rest (fôr′ĭst, fŏr′-), **Nathan Bedford.** 1821–77. Amer. Confederate general who was the founder and first leader (1866–69) of the Ku Klux Klan.

for•sake (fôr-sāk′, fər-) *tr.v.* **-sook** (-so͝ok′), **-sak•en** (-sā′kən), **-sak•ing, -sakes. 1.** To give up (something held dear); renounce. **2.** To leave altogether; abandon. [ME *forsaken* < OE *forsacan.* See **sāg-*.**]

for•sooth (fôr-so͞oth′, fər-) *adv.* In truth; indeed. [ME *forsoth* < OE *forsōth* : *for,* for; see FOR + *sōth,* truth; see SOOTH.]

for•spent (fôr-spĕnt′, fər-) *adj. Archaic.* Worn out, as from exertion; exhausted.

For•ster (fôr′stər), **E(dward) M(organ).** 1879–1970. British writer whose novels include *A Room with a View* (1908).

for•swear also **fore•swear** (fôr-swâr′, fōr-) *—v.* **-swore** (fôr-swôr′, fōr-swōr′), **-sworn** (fôr-swôrn′, fōr-swōrn′), **-swear•ing, -swears.** *—tr.* **1.a.** To renounce or repudiate under oath. **b.** To renounce seriously. **2.** To disavow under oath; deny. **3.** To make (oneself) guilty of perjury. *—intr.* To swear falsely; commit perjury. [ME *forsweren* < OE *forswerian* : *for-,* wrongly; see FOR- + *swerian,* to swear; see SWEAR.]

fossil
Leaf

for•syth•i•a (fôr-sĭth′ē-ə, -sī′thē-ə, fər-) *n.* Any of several Asian shrubs of the genus *Forsythia,* having early-blooming yellow flowers. [NLat., genus name, after William *Forsyth* (1737–1804), Scottish horticulturist.]

fort (fôrt, fōrt) *n.* **1.** A fortified place or position stationed with troops. **2.** A permanent army post. [ME, strength, stronghold < OFr., strong, strength < Lat. *fortis.* See **bhergh-[2]*.**]

For•ta•le•za (fôr′tl-ā′zə, -tə-lĕ′-). A city of NE Brazil NW of Natal; founded 1609. Pop. 1,307,611.

for•ta•lice (fôr′tə-lĭs) *n. Archaic.* **1.** A defensive structure or position; a fortress. **2.** A small fort. [ME < Med.Lat. *fortalitia.* See FORTRESS.]

For•tas (fôr′təs), **Abraham ("Abe").** 1910–82. Amer. jurist; associate justice of the U.S. Supreme Court (1965–69).

Fort Col•lins (fôrt kŏl′ĭnz, fōrt). A city of N CO NNE of Boulder. Pop. 87,758.

Fort-de-France (fôr-də-fräɴs′). The cap. of Martinique, on the W coast on **Fort-de-France Bay,** an inlet of the Caribbean; settled by the French in 1762. Pop. 99,844.

Fort Dodge (dŏj). A city of central IA on the Des Moines R. NNW of Des Moines; settled in the 1840's. Pop. 25,894.

forte[1] (fôrt, fōrt, fôr′tā′) *n.* **1.** Something in which a person excels. **2.** The strong part of a sword blade, between the middle and the hilt. [Fr. *fort* < OFr., strong < Lat. *fortis.* See **bhergh-[2]*.**]

for•te[2] (fôr′tā′) *Mus. —adv. & adj.* In a loud forceful manner. *—n.* A note, passage, or chord played forte. [Ital., strong, forte < Lat. *fortis.* See **bhergh-[2]*.**]

for•te-pi•an•o (fôr′tā-pē-än′ō, -ä′nō) *adv. & adj. Mus.* In a loud, then suddenly soft manner. [Ital. : *forte,* loud; see FORTE[2] + *piano,* soft; see PIANO[2].]

Fort E•rie (îr′ē). A town of S Ontario, Canada, on the Niagara R. opposite Buffalo NY. Pop. 24,096.

forth (fôrth, fōrth) *adv.* **1.** Forward in time, place, or order; onward: *from this time forth.* **2.** Out into view: *put my ideas forth.* **3.** *Obsolete.* Away from a specified place; abroad. *—prep. Archaic.* Out of; forth from. [ME < OE. See **per[1]*.**]

Forth (fôrth, fōrth). A river of S-central Scotland flowing c. 187 km (116 mi) to the **Firth of Forth,** an inlet of the North Sea.

forth•com•ing (fôrth-kŭm′ĭng, fōrth-) *adj.* **1.** About to appear or take place; approaching. **2.a.** Available when required or as promised. **b.** Affable and outgoing: *a forthcoming person.* **c.** Candid and willing to cooperate. *—n.* (fôrth′kŭm′ĭng, fōrth′-). The act or an instance of coming forth.

forth•right (fôrth′rīt′, fōrth′-) *adj.* **1.** Direct and without evasion; straightforward. **2.** *Archaic.* Proceeding straight ahead. *—adv.* **1.a.** Directly ahead. **b.** Directly and frankly. **2.** *Archaic.* At once. **— forth′right′ly** *adv.* **— forth′right′ness** *n.*

forth•with (fôrth-wĭth′, -wĭth′, fōrth-) *adv.* At once.

for•ti•eth (fôr′tē-ĭth) *n.* **1.** The ordinal number matching the number 40 in a series. **2.** One of 40 equal parts. **— for′ti•eth** *adv. & adj.*

for•ti•fi•ca•tion (fôr′tə-fĭ-kā′shən) *n.* **1.a.** The science of fortifying. **b.** The act or process of fortifying. **2.** Something that serves to fortify, esp. military works erected to fortify a position or place.

for•ti•fied wine (fôr′tə-fīd′) *n.* Wine to which alcohol, usu. in the form of grape brandy, has been added.

for•ti•fy (fôr′tə-fī′) *v.* **-fied, -fy•ing, -fies.** *—tr.* To make strong, as: **a.** To strengthen and secure (a position) with fortifications. **b.** To reinforce by adding material. **c.** To impart physical strength or endurance to; invigorate. **d.** To give emotional, moral, or mental strength to; encourage. **e.** To strengthen or enrich (food, for example), as by adding vitamins. *—intr.* To build fortifications. [ME *fortifien* < OFr. *fortifier* < LLat. *fortificāre* < Lat. *fortis,* strong. See **bhergh-[2]*.**] **— for′ti•fi′a•ble** *adj.* **— for′ti•fi′er** *n.* **— for′ti•fy′ing•ly** *adv.*

for•tis (fôr′tĭs) *Ling. —adj.* Articulated with relatively strong pressure or tension of the respiratory muscles, as in English *p.* *—n.* A fortis consonant. [Lat., strong. See **bhergh-[2]*.**]

for•tis•si•mo (fôr-tĭs′ə-mō′) *Mus. —adv. & adj.* In a very loud manner. *—n., pl.* **-mos.** A note, chord, or passage played fortissimo. [Ital., superl. of *forte,* strong. See FORTE[2].]

for•ti•tude (fôr′tĭ-to͞od′, -tyo͞od′) *n.* Strength of mind that allows one to endure pain or adversity with courage. [ME < Lat. *fortitūdō* < *fortis,* strong. See **bhergh-[2]*.**] **— for′ti•tu′di•nous** (-to͞od′n-əs, -tyo͞od′-) *adj.*

Fort-La•my (fôr-lä-mē′). See **Ndjamena.**

Fort Lau•der•dale (lô′dər-dāl′). A city of SE FL on the Atlantic coast N of Miami Beach. Pop. 149,377.

Fort Lee (lē). A borough of NE NJ on the Hudson R. opposite Manhattan; settled c. 1700. Pop. 31,997.

Fort Mc•Mur•ray (mĭk-mûr′ē, -mŭr′ē). A city of NE Alberta, Canada, NNE of Edmonton. Pop. 31,000.

Fort My•ers (mī′ərz). A city of SW FL on an estuary of the Caloosahatchee R. NNE of Cape Coral. Pop. 45,206.

Fort Nel•son (nĕl′sən). A river, c. 418 km (260 mi), of NE British Columbia, Canada.

fort•night (fôrt′nīt′) *n.* A period of 14 days; two weeks. [Ult. < ME *fourtene night,* fourteen nights : OE *fēowertēne,* fourteen; see FOURTEEN + OE *niht,* night; see NIGHT.]

fort•night•ly (fôrt′nīt′lē) *adj.* Happening or appearing once in or every two weeks. *—adv.* Once in a fortnight. *—n., pl.* **-lies.** A publication issued once every two weeks.

Fort Pierce (pîrs). A city of E-central FL on the Indian R. lagoon NNW of Palm Beach. Pop. 36,830.

FOR•TRAN (fôr′trăn′) *n. Comp. Sci.* A high-level programming language for problems that can be expressed algebraically. [FOR(MULA) + TRAN(SLATION).]

for•tress (fôr′trĭs) *n.* A fortified place, esp. a large permanent military stronghold that often includes a town. [ME *forteress* < OFr. < Med.Lat. *fortalitia* < Lat. *fortis,* strong. See **bhergh-[2]*.**]

Fort Smith (smĭth). **1.** A region of SW Northwest Terrs., Canada, including Great Slave Lake and most of Great Bear Lake. **2.** A city of W AR on the OK border WNW of Little Rock; founded as a military post in 1817. Pop. 72,798.

Fort Thom•as (tŏm′əs). A city of N KY, a suburb of Covington. Pop. 16,032.

for•tu•i•tous (fôr-to͞o′ĭ-təs, -tyo͞o′-) *adj.* **1.** Happening by accident or chance. **2.** *Usage Problem.* **a.** Happening by a fortunate accident or chance. **b.** Lucky or fortunate. [< Lat. *fortuītus* < *forte,* by chance, ablative of *fors,* chance.] **— for•tu′i•tous•ly** *adv.* **— for•tu′i•tous•ness** *n.*

Usage Note: In its best-established sense *fortuitous* means "happening by accident or chance," with no implication as to the desirability of the outcome. In this century, however, the word is often used with particular reference to happy accidents, as in *The company's profits were the result of a fortuitous drop in the cost of RAM chips.* This use may have arisen because *fortuitous* resembles both *fortunate* and *felicitous*; it is well established in the writing of reputable authors. More controversial is the use of *fortuitous* to mean simply "lucky or fortunate."

for•tu•i•ty (fôr-to͞o′ĭ-tē, -tyo͞o′-) *n., pl.* **-ties. 1.** A chance occurrence or event. **2.** The quality or condition of being fortuitous.

For•tu•na (fôr-to͞o′nə, -tyo͞o′-) *n. Rom. Myth.* The goddess of fortune.

for•tu•nate (fôr′chə-nĭt) *adj.* **1.** Bringing something good and unforeseen; auspicious. **2.** Having unexpected good fortune; lucky. —*n.* One who has good fortune, esp. a wealthy person. [Lat. *fortūnātus* < *fortūna*, chance. See FORTUNE.] —**for′tu•nate•ly** *adv.* —**for′tu•nate•ness** *n.*

for•tune (fôr′chən) *n.* **1.a.** The chance happening of fortunate or adverse events; luck. **b. fortunes.** The turns of luck in the course of one's life. **c.** Success, esp. when at least partially resulting from luck. **2.a.** A person's condition or standing in life determined by material possessions or financial wealth. **b.** Extensive amounts of material possessions or money; wealth. **c.** A large sum of money. **3.** Often **Fortune.** A hypothetical, often personified force or power that favorably or unfavorably governs the events of one's life. **4.a.** Fate; destiny. **b.** A foretelling of one's destiny. —*v.* **-tuned, -tun•ing, -tunes.** —*tr.* **1.** *Archaic.* To endow with wealth. **2.** *Obsolete.* To ascribe or give good or bad fortune to. —*intr. Archaic.* To occur by chance; happen. [ME < OFr. < Lat. *fortūna* < *fors, fort-*, chance.]

fortune cookie *n.* A cookie folded and baked around a slip of paper bearing a prediction of fortune or a maxim.

fortune hunter *n.* A person who seeks wealth, esp. through marriage.

for•tune•tell•er (fôr′chən-tĕl′ər) *n.* One who professes to predict future events. —**for′tune•tell′ing** *adj. & n.*

Fort Wal•ton Beach (wôl′tən). A city of NW FL in the Panhandle E of Pensacola. Pop. 21,471.

Fort Wayne (wān). A city of NE IN NE of Indianapolis; built on the site of a 17th-cent. French fort. Pop. 173,072.

Fort Worth (wûrth). A city of NE TX W of Dallas; on the site of a military post estab. in the 1840's. Pop. 447,619.

for•ty (fôr′tē) *n., pl.* **-ties. 1.** The cardinal number equal to 4 × 10. **2. forties. a.** Often **Forties.** The decade from 40 to 49 in a century. **b.** A decade or the numbers from 40 to 49. [ME < OE *fēowertig.* See **kʷetwer-***.] —**for′ty** *adj. & pron.*

for•ty-five (fôr′tē-fīv′) *n.* **1.** A .45-caliber pistol. **2.** A phonograph record played at 45 revolutions per minute. —**for′ty-five′** *adj.*

for•ty-nin•er (fôr′tē-nī′nər) *n.* One who took part in the 1849 California gold rush.

forty winks *pl.n. (used with a sing. or pl. v.) Informal.* A short nap.

fo•rum (fôr′əm, fōr′-) *n., pl.* **fo•rums** also **fo•ra** (fôr′ə, fōr′ə). **1.a.** The public square or marketplace of an ancient Roman city that was the assembly place for judicial activity and public business. **b.** A public meeting place for open discussion. **c.** A medium of open discussion or voicing of ideas. **2.** A public meeting or presentation involving a discussion usu. among experts and often including audience participation. **3.** A court of law; a tribunal. [ME < Lat. See **dhwer-***.]

for•ward (fôr′wərd) *adj.* **1.a.** At, near, or belonging to the front or forepart; fore. **b.** Located ahead or in advance. **2.a.** Going, tending, or moving toward a position in front. **b.** *Sports.* Advancing toward an opponent's goal. **c.** Moving in a prescribed direction or order for normal use: *forward rolling of the cassette tape.* **3.a.** Ardently inclined; eager. **b.** Lacking restraint or modesty; presumptuous or bold. **4.a.** Being ahead of current economic, political, or technological trends; progressive. **b.** Deviating radically from convention or tradition; extreme. **5.** Exceptionally advanced; precocious. **6.** Of, relating to, or done in preparation for the future. —*adv.* **1.** Toward or tending to the front; frontward: *step forward.* **2.** Into consideration. **3.** In or toward the future. **4.a.** In the prescribed direction or sequence for normal use. **b.** In an advanced position or a configuration registering a future time: *set the clock forward.* **c.** At or to a different time; earlier or later. —*n. Sports.* **1.** A player in certain games, such as basketball, who is part of the forward line of the offense. **2.** The position played by such a person. —*tr.v.* **-ward•ed, -ward•ing, -wards. 1.** To send on to a subsequent destination or address. **2.** To help advance; promote. See Syns at **advance.** [ME < OE *foreweard* : *fore-*, fore- + *-weard*, -ward.] —**for′ward•ly** *adv.* —**for′ward•ness** *n.*

forward dive *n.* A dive in which the diver leaves the springboard or platform facing the open water and rotates the body forward.

for•ward•er (fôr′wər-dər) *n.* One that forwards, esp. an agent that helps received goods get to their destination.

for•ward-look•ing (fôr′wərd-lo͝ok′ĭng) *adj.* Concerned with or making provision for the future: *forward-looking plans.*

forward pass *n. Football.* A pass thrown from behind the line of scrimmage toward the opponent's end line.

for•wards (fôr′wərdz, fōr′-) *adv.* To or tending to the front; forward.

for•went (fôr-wĕnt′, fōr-) *v.* P.t. of **forgo.**

for•worn also **fore•worn** (fôr-wôrn′, fōr-wōrn′) *adj. Archaic.* Worn-out.

for•zan•do (fôrt-sän′dō) *adv., adj., & n. Mus.* Var. of **sforzando.**

FOS *abbr.* Free on steamer.

fos•sa (fŏs′ə) *n., pl.* **fos•sae** (fŏs′ē′). *Anat.* A small cavity or depression, as in a bone. [Lat., ditch < fem. p.part. of *fodere*, to dig.] —**fos′sate′** (fŏs′āt′) *adj.*

fosse also **foss** (fŏs) *n.* A ditch or moat. [ME < OFr. < Lat. *fossa.* See FOSSA.]

fos•sick (fŏs′ĭk) *v.* **-sicked, -sick•ing, -sicks.** —*intr.* **1.** To search for gold, esp. by reworking washings or waste piles. **2.** To rummage or search around, esp. for a possible profit. —*tr.* To search for by or as if by rummaging. [E. dial., to find out, dig up.] —**fos′sick•er** *n.*

fos•sil (fŏs′əl) *n.* **1.** A remnant or trace of an organism of a past geologic age, such as a skeleton, embedded and preserved in the earth's crust. **2.** One, such as a rigid theory, that is outdated or antiquated. **3.** *Ling.* **a.** A word or morpheme that is used only in certain restricted contexts, as *kempt* in *unkempt*, but is otherwise obsolete. **b.** An archaic syntactic rule or pattern used only in idioms, as *so be it.* —*adj.* **1.** Characteristic of or having the nature of a fossil. **2.** Being or similar to a fossil. **3.** Belonging to the past; antiquated. [< Lat. *fossilis*, dug up < *fossus*, p.part. of *fodere*, to dig.]

fossil fuel *n.* A hydrocarbon deposit, such as coal, derived from living matter of a previous geologic time and used for fuel.

fos•sil•if•er•ous (fŏs′ə-lĭf′ər-əs) *adj.* Containing fossils.

fos•sil•ize (fŏs′ə-līz′) *v.* **-ized, -iz•ing, -iz•es.** —*tr.* **1.** To convert into a fossil. **2.** To make outmoded or inflexible with time; antiquate. —*intr.* To become a fossil. —**fos′sil•i•za′tion** (-sə-lĭ-zā′shən) *n.*

fos•so•ri•al (fŏ-sôr′ē-əl, -sōr′-) *adj. Zool.* Adapted for or used in burrowing or digging. [< LLat. *fossōrius* < Lat. *fossus*, p.part. of *fodere*, to dig.]

fos•ter (fô′stər, fŏs′tər) *tr.v.* **-tered, -ter•ing, -ters. 1.** To bring up; nurture. See Syns at **nurture. 2.** To promote the growth and development of; cultivate. See Syns at **advance. 3.** To nurse; cherish. —*adj.* **1.** Providing parental care and nurture to children not related through legal or blood ties. **2.** Receiving parental care and nurture from those not related to one through legal or blood ties. [ME *fostren* < OE **fōstrian*, to nourish < *fōstor*, food, nourishing. See **pā-***.]

Fos•ter (fô′stər, fŏs′tər), **Stephen Collins.** 1826–64. Amer. songwriter whose works include "Oh! Susannah" (1848).

Stephen Foster
c. 1850 portrait attributed to Thomas Hicks (1823–1890)

Foster City. A city of W CA, a suburb of San Mateo. Pop. 28,176.

Fou•cault (fo͞o-kō′), **Jean Bernard Léon.** 1819–68. French physicist who measured the velocity of light (1850).

Foucault pendulum *n.* A simple pendulum suspended from a long wire whose plane of motion appears to turn clockwise in the Northern Hemisphere and counterclockwise in the Southern Hemisphere, demonstrating the axial rotation of the earth. [After Jean Bernard Léon FOUCAULT.]

Foucault pendulum

Fouc•quet (fo͞o-kā′). See **Fouquet.**

fou•droy•ant (fo͞o-droi′ənt, fo͞o′drwä-yäɴ′) *adj.* Dazzling or stunning in effect. [Fr. < pr.part. of *foudroyer*, to strike with lightning < *foudre*, lightning < OFr. *fouldre* < Lat. *fulgur* < *fulgēre*, to flash. See **bhel-¹***.]

fought (fôt) *v.* P.t. and p.part. of **fight.**

foul (foul) *adj.* **foul•er, foul•est. 1.** Offensive to the senses; revolting. **2.** Having an offensive odor; smelly. **3.** Rotten or putrid. **4.a.** Full of dirt or mud; dirty. **b.** Full of impurities; polluted. **5.** Morally detestable; wicked. **6.** Of a vulgar or obscene nature. **7.** Very disagreeable or displeasing; horrid. **8.** Bad or unfavorable: *foul weather.* **9.** Violating accepted standards or rules; dishonorable. **10.a.** *Sports.* Contrary to the rules of a game or sport. **b.** *Baseball.* Outside the foul lines. **11.** Entangled or twisted: *a foul anchor.* **12.** Clogged or obstructed; blocked. **13.** *Archaic.* Ugly; unattractive. —*n.* **1.a.** *Sports.* An infraction or a violation of the rules of play. **b.** *Baseball.* A foul ball. **2.** An entanglement or a collision. **3.** An instance of clogging or obstructing. —*adv.* In a foul manner. —*v.* **fouled, foul•ing, fouls.** —*tr.* **1.** To make dirty or foul; pollute. **2.** To bring into dishonor; besmirch. **3.** To clog or obstruct. **4.** To entangle or catch (a rope, for example). **5.** *Naut.* To encrust (a ship's hull) with foreign matter, such as barnacles. **6.a.** *Sports.* To commit a foul against. **b.** *Baseball.* To hit (a ball) outside the foul lines. —*intr.* **1.** To become foul. **2.a.** *Sports.* To commit a foul. **b.** *Baseball.* To foul a ball. **3.** To become entangled or twisted. **4.** To become clogged or obstructed. —***phrasal verbs.* foul out.** *Sports.* To be put out of a game for exceeding the number of permissible fouls. **foul up.** To blunder or cause to blunder because of mistakes or poor judgment. [ME < OE *fūl.* See **pū-***.] —**foul′ly** *adv.* —**foul′ness** *n.*

fou•lard (fo͞o-lärd′) *n.* **1.** A lightweight twill or plain-woven fabric of silk or silk and cotton, usu. having a small printed design. **2.** An article of clothing, esp. a necktie or scarf, made of this fabric. [Fr.]

foul ball *n. Baseball.* A batted ball that touches the ground outside of fair territory.

ă pat	oi boy
ā pay	ou out
âr care	o͝o took
ä father	o͞o boot
ĕ pet	ŭ cut
ē be	ûr urge
ĭ pit	th thin
ī pie	*th* this
îr pier	hw which
ŏ pot	zh vision
ō toe	ə about, item
ô paw	

Stress marks:
′ (primary);
′ (secondary), as in
dictionary (dĭk′shə-nĕr′ē)

foul•brood (foul′bro͝od′) *n.* A fatal disease of honeybee larvae.

foul line *n.* **1.** *Baseball.* Either of two straight lines extending from the rear of home plate to the outer edge of the playing field and indicating the area in which a fair ball can be hit. **2.** *Basketball.* A line 15 feet in front of each backboard from which players shoot foul shots. **3.** *Sports.* A boundary limiting the permissible movements of a player, as in a field event.

foul-mouthed (foul′mouthd′, -moutht′) *adj.* Using abusive or obscene language.

foul play *n.* Unfair or treacherous action, esp. when violent.

foul shot *n. Basketball.* An unobstructed shot from the foul line by a fouled player, worth one point if successful.

foul tip *n. Baseball.* A pitched ball that is deflected slightly off the bat toward the catcher.

foul-up (foul′ŭp′) *n.* **1.** A condition of confusion caused by mistakes or poor judgment. **2.** A mechanical failure.

fountain

found[1] (found) *tr.v.* **found•ed, found•ing, founds. 1.** To establish or set up, esp. with provision for continuing existence. **2.** To establish the foundation or basis of; base. [ME *founden* < OFr. *fonder* < Lat. *fundāre* < *fundus,* bottom.]

Syns: *found, create, establish, institute, organize.* The central meaning shared by these verbs is "to bring something into existence and set it in operation": *founded a colony; created a trust fund; establishing a business; instituted an annual benefit concert; organizing a field trip.*

found[2] (found) *tr.v.* **found•ed, found•ing, founds. 1.** To melt (metal) and pour into a mold. **2.** To make (objects) by pouring molten material into a mold. [ME *founden* < OFr. *fondre* < Lat. *fundere.* See **gheu-***.]

found[3] (found) *v.* P.t. and p.part. of **find.**

foun•da•tion (foun-dā′shən) *n.* **1.** The act of founding, esp. the establishment of an institution with provisions for future maintenance. **2.** The basis on which a thing stands, is founded, or is supported. **3.a.** Funds for the perpetual support of an institution; an endowment. **b.** An institution founded and supported by an endowment. **4.** A foundation garment. **5.** A cosmetic used as a base for facial makeup. **— foun•da′tion•al** *adj.*

foundation garment *n.* A woman's supporting undergarment, such as a corset or girdle.

foun•der[1] (foun′dər) *v.* **-dered, -der•ing, -ders.** *— intr.* **1.** To sink below the surface of the water. **2.** To cave in; sink. **3.** To fail utterly; collapse. **4.** To stumble, esp. to stumble and go lame. Used of horses. **5.** To become ill from overeating. Used of livestock. **6.** To be afflicted wtih laminitis. Used of horses. *— tr.* To cause to founder. *— n.* See **laminitis.** [ME *foundren,* to sink to the ground < OFr. *fondrer* < VLat. **funderāre* < **fundus,* **funder-,* bottom < Lat. *fundus, fund-.*]

Usage Note: The verbs *founder* and *flounder* are often confused. *Founder* comes from a Latin word meaning "bottom" (as in *foundation*) and originally referred to knocking enemies down; it is now used as well to mean "to fail utterly, collapse." *Flounder* means "to move clumsily, thrash about," and hence "to proceed in confusion."

found•er[2] (foun′dər) *n.* One who establishes something or formulates the basis for something.

Found•ing Father (foun′dĭng) *n.* **1.** A member of the convention that drafted the U.S. Constitution in 1787. **2. founding father.** A man who founds or establishes something.

found•ling (found′lĭng) *n.* An abandoned child of unknown parentage. [ME < *found,* p.part. of *finden,* to find. See FIND.]

found object *n.* A natural object or an artifact not intended as art, found and given aesthetic value. [Transl. of Fr. *objet trouvé* : *objet,* object + *trouvé,* p.part. of *trouver,* to find.]

four-poster

foun•dry (foun′drē) *n., pl.* **-dries. 1.** An establishment in which metal is melted and poured into molds. **2.a.** The skill or operation of founding. **b.** The castings made by founding.

fount[1] (fount) *n.* **1.** A fountain. **2.** One that initiates or dispenses. [ME < OE and OFr. *font,* both < Lat. *fōns, font-.*]

fount[2] (fount) *n. Chiefly British.* Var. of **font[2].**

foun•tain (foun′tən) *n.* **1.a.** An artificially created jet or stream of water. **b.** A structure, often decorative, from which a jet or stream of water issues. **2.** A spring, esp. the source of a stream. **3.** A reservoir or chamber containing a supply of liquid that can be siphoned off as needed. **4.** A soda fountain. **5.** A point of origin or dissemination; a source. *— intr. & tr.v.* **-tained, -tain•ing, -tains.** To flow or cause to flow like a fountain. [ME < OFr. *fontaine* < LLat. *fontāna* < Lat., fem. of *fontānus,* of a spring < *fōns, font-,* spring.]

foun•tain•head (foun′tən-hĕd′) *n.* **1.** A spring that is the source or head of a stream. **2.** A chief and copious source; an originator.

fountain pen *n.* A pen filled from an external source with an ink reservoir that automatically feeds the writing point.

Foun•tain Valley (foun′tən). A city of S CA SE of Los Angeles. Pop. 53,691.

Fou•quet also **Fouc•quet** (fo͞o-kā′), **Jean.** 1420?–80? French artist noted for his book illuminations.

Fouquet also **Foucquet, Nicolas.** 1615–80. French superintendent of finance (1653–61) who was convicted of embezzlement (1664).

four (fôr, fōr) *n.* **1.** The cardinal number equal to 3 + 1. **2.** The fourth in a set or sequence. **3.** Something having four parts, units, or members, such as a four-cylinder engine. ***— idiom.* all fours.** All four limbs of an animal or a person. [ME < OE *fēower.* See **k^wetwer-***.] **— four** *adj. & pron.*

four-by-four or **4 × 4** (fôr′bī-fôr′, fōr′bī-fōr′) *n.* A four-wheel drive motor vehicle.

four•chette (fo͝or-shĕt′) *n.* **1.** A narrow forked strip of material joining the front and back sections of the fingers of gloves. **2.** *Anat.* A small band or fold of mucous membrane forming the posterior margin of the vulva and connecting the posterior ends of the labia majora. **3.** *Zool.* See **furcula.** [Fr. < OFr. *forchete,* fork, dim. of *forche,* pitchfork < Lat. *furca.*]

four-col•or (fôr′kŭl′ər, fōr′-) *adj.* Of or being an overprinting or photographic process in which three primary colors and black are transferred by four different plates or filters to a surface, reproducing the colors of the subject matter.

Four Cor•ners (fôr kôr′nərz). A location in the SW U.S. where the boundaries of CO, NM, AZ, and UT meet.

four-di•men•sion•al (fôr′dĭ-mĕn′shə-nəl, fōr′-) *adj.* Of, having, or determined by four dimensions, esp. the three spatial dimensions and single temporal dimension of the relativity theory.

four-eyed fish (fôr′īd′, fōr′-) *n.* Either of two freshwater fishes *(Anableps anableps* or *A. microlepis)* of tropical America having bulging eyes divided into an upper part for vision above the water and a lower part for vision below the water.

four flush *n. Games.* A five-card poker hand containing four cards in the same suit.

four-flush (fôr′flŭsh′, fōr′-) *intr.v.* **-flushed, -flush•ing, -flush•es. 1.** *Games.* To bluff in poker with a four flush. **2.** *Slang.* To make empty claims; bluff. **— four′-flush′er** *n.*

four-foot•ed (fôr′fo͝ot′ĭd, fōr′-) *adj.* Having four feet.

four•gon (fo͝or-gôɴ′) *n., pl.* **-gons** (-gôɴ′, -gôɴz′). A wagon for carrying baggage. [Fr.]

four•hand•ed (fôr′hăn′dĭd, fōr′-) *adj.* **1.** *Games.* Involving or requiring four players. **2.** Designed for four hands.

Four-H Club (fôr′āch′, fōr′-) *n.* A youth organization sponsored by the Department of Agriculture and offering instruction in agriculture and home economics. [From its four goals: to improve head, heart, hands, and health.]

Four Hundred also **four hundred** *n.* The wealthiest and most exclusive social set of a community.

Fou•rier (fo͝or′ē-ā′, fo͞o-ryā′), **(François Marie) Charles.** 1772–1837. French social theorist who propounded the reorganization of society into phalanxes. **— Fou′ri•er•ism** *n.* **— Fou′ri•er•ist, Fou′ri•er•ite′** (-ə-rīt′) *n.*

Fourier, Baron **Jean Baptiste Joseph.** 1768–1830. French mathematician and physicist who formulated a method for analyzing periodic functions.

Fourier analysis *n. Math.* The approximation of a periodic function by a Fourier series.

Fourier series *n. Math.* An infinite series whose terms are constants multiplied by sine and cosine functions and that can, if uniformly convergent, approximate a wide variety of functions. [After Baron Jean Baptiste Joseph FOURIER.]

four-in-hand (fôr′ĭn-hănd′, fōr′-) *n.* **1.** A team of four horses controlled by one driver. **2.** A vehicle drawn by four horses. **3.** A necktie tied in a slipknot with long ends left hanging one in front of the other.

four-leaf clover (fôr′lēf′, fōr′-) *n.* A clover leaf having four leaflets instead of three, considered an omen of good luck.

four-let•ter word (fôr′lĕt′ər, fōr′-) *n.* Any of several short English words generally regarded as vulgar or obscene.

four-o'clock (fôr′ə-klŏk′, fōr′-) *n.* Any of several plants of the genus *Mirabilis,* esp. *M. jalapa,* native to tropical America and having tubular flowers that open late in the afternoon.

four•pen•ny nail (fôr′pĕn′ē, -pə-nē, fōr′-) *n.* A nail 1½ inches (3.8 centimeters) long.

four-post•er (fôr′pō′stər, fōr′-) *n.* A bed having tall corner posts originally intended to support curtains or a canopy.

four•ra•gère (fo͝or′ə-zhâr′) *n.* An ornamental braided cord usu. looped around the left shoulder of a uniform. [Fr. < *fourrage,* forage < OFr. *forrage.* See FORAGE.]

four•score (fôr′skôr′, fōr′skōr′) *adj.* Four times twenty.

four•some (fôr′səm, fōr′-) *n.* **1.** A group of four persons or things, esp. two couples. **2.** *Sports & Games.* **a.** A game, esp. a golf match, played by four persons, two on each side. **b.** The players in such a game. [ME *four-som* < OE *fēowra sum,* one of four : *fēowra,* genitive pl. of *fēower,* four; see FOUR + *sum,* one; see -SOME[2].]

four•square (fôr′skwâr′, fōr′-) *adj.* **1.** Having four equal sides and four right angles; square. **2.** Marked by firm unwavering conviction or expression; forthright. *— adv.* In a forthright manner; squarely. **— four′square′ly** *adv.*

four-star (fôr′stär′, fōr′-) *adj.* Of superlative quality.

four•teen (fôr-tēn′, fōr-) *n.* **1.** The cardinal number equal to 13 + 1. **2.** The 14th in a set or sequence. **3.** Something having 14 parts, units, or members. [ME *fourtene* < OE *fēowertēne.* See **k^wetwer-***.] **— four•teen′** *adj. & pron.*

four•teenth (fôr-tēnth′, fōr-) *n.* **1.** The ordinal number matching the number 14 in a series. **2.** One of 14 equal parts. **— four•teenth′** *adv. & adj.*

fourth (fôrth, fōrth) *n.* **1.** The ordinal number matching the number four in a series. **2.** One of four equal parts. **3.** *Mus.* **a.** A tone four degrees above or below a given tone in a diatonic scale. **b.** The interval between two such tones. **c.** The harmonic combination of these tones. **d.** The subdominant in a scale. **4.** The transmission gear or gear ratio used to produce forward speeds next higher to those of third in a motor vehicle. **5. Fourth.** The Fourth of July; Independence Day. [ME *fourthe* < OE *fēortha*. See **kʷetwer-***.] — **fourth** *adv. & adj.*

fourth-class (fôrth′klăs′, fōrth′-) *adj.* Of or being a class of mail consisting of merchandise and some printed matter weighing over eight ounces and not sealed against inspection. — *adv.* As or by fourth-class mail.

fourth dimension *n.* Time regarded as a coordinate dimension and required by relativity theory, along with three spatial dimensions, to specify completely the location of any event.

fourth estate *n.* Journalists considered as a group; the press.

Fourth of July *n.* See **Independence Day.**

Fourth World also **fourth world** *n.* The least-developed countries of the Third World.

4WD *abbr.* Four-wheel drive.

four-wheel (fôr′hwēl′, -wēl′, fōr′-) *adj.* **1.** Having or running on four wheels. **2.** Of or relating to four-wheel drive.

four-wheel drive *n.* An automotive drive system in which mechanical power is transmitted from the drive shaft to all four wheels.

four-wheel•er (fôr′hwē′lər, -wē′-, fōr′-) *n.* A small, one-person, four-wheel all-terrain motor vehicle with large tires.

fo•ve•a (fō′vē-ə) *n., pl.* **-ve•ae** (-vē-ē′). **1.** A small cuplike depression or pit in a bone or an organ. **2.** The fovea centralis. [Lat., small pit.] — **fo′ve•al** (-əl), **fo′ve•ate′** (-āt′) *adj.* — **fo′ve•i•form′** (-ə-fôrm′) *adj.*

fovea cen•tra•lis (sĕn-trā′lĭs) *n.* A small depression near the center of the retina, constituting the area of most acute vision.

fo•ve•o•la (fō-vē′ə-lə) *n., pl.* **-lae** (-lē′) or **-las.** A small fovea. [NLat., dim. of Lat. *fovea*, small pit.]

fowl (foul) *n., pl.* **fowl** or **fowls. 1.** Any of various birds of the order Galliformes, esp. the common domesticated chicken *(Gallus gallus).* **2.a.** A bird, such as the turkey or pheasant, that is used as food or hunted as game. **b.** The flesh of such birds used as food. **3.** A bird of any kind. — *intr.v.* **fowled, fowl•ing, fowls.** To hunt, trap, or shoot wildfowl. [ME *foul* < OE *fugol.* See **pleu-***.] — **fowl′er** *n.*

Fow•ler (fou′lər), **Henry Watson.** 1858–1933. British lexicographer who wrote *A Dictionary of Modern English Usage* (1926) and collaborated with his brother **Francis** (1870–1918) on *The King's English* (1906).

fowl•ing piece (fou′lĭng) *n.* A light shotgun for shooting birds and small animals.

fox (fŏks) *n., pl.* **fox•es** also **fox. 1.a.** Any of various carnivorous mammals of the genus *Vulpes* and related genera, related to the dogs and wolves and characteristically having upright ears, a pointed snout, and a long bushy tail. **b.** The fur of a fox. **2.** A crafty, sly, or clever person. **3.** *Slang.* An attractive young person. **4.** *Archaic.* A sword. — *v.* **foxed, fox•ing, fox•es.** — *tr.* **1.** To trick or fool by ingenuity or cunning; outwit. **2.** To baffle or confuse. **3.** To make (beer) sour by fermenting. **4.** To repair (a shoe) by attaching a new upper. **5.** *Obsolete.* To intoxicate. — *intr.* **1.** To act slyly or craftily. **2.** To turn sour in fermenting. Used of beer. [ME < OE.]

Fox (fŏks) *n., pl.* **Fox** or **Fox•es. 1.** A member of a Native American people formerly inhabiting various parts of southern Michigan, southern Wisconsin, northern Illinois, and eastern Iowa, with present-day populations in central Iowa and Oklahoma. **2.** The Algonquian language of the Fox.

Fox, Charles James. 1749–1806. British politician who supported American independence and the French Revolution.

Fox, George. 1624–91. English religious leader who founded the Society of Friends, or Quakers (1647–48).

Foxe (fŏks), **John.** 1516–87. English martyrologist who wrote *The Book of Martyrs* (1563).

foxed (fŏkst) *adj.* Discolored with yellowish-brown stains. [Perh. from the color of foxes.]

fox•fire (fŏks′fīr′) *n.* A phosphorescent glow, esp. that produced by certain fungi found on rotting wood.

fox•glove (fŏks′glŭv′) *n.* **1.** Any of several herbs of the genus *Digitalis*, esp. *D. purpurea* of Europe having a long cluster of large tubular pinkish-purple flowers and leaves that are the source of the drug digitalis. **2.** Any of several related plants.

fox grape *n.* A wild grape *(Vitis labrusca)* of the eastern United States that bears purplish-black berries and is the source of many cultivated grape varieties.

fox•hole (fŏks′hōl′) *n.* A shallow pit dug by a soldier in combat for immediate refuge against enemy fire.

fox•hound (fŏks′hound′) *n.* Any of various medium-sized short-haired hounds developed for fox hunting, esp. either of two breeds, the English foxhound and the American foxhound.

Fox River. 1. A river rising in SE WI and flowing c. 354 km (220 mi) SSW to the Illinois R. in NE IL. **2.** A river of central and E WI flowing c. 282 km (175 mi) to Green Bay.

fox•tail (fŏks′tāl′) *n.* Any of several grasses of the genus *Alopecurus,* having dense silky or bristly flowering spikes.

foxtail lily *n.* Eremurus.

fox terrier *n.* Any of various small wire-haired or smooth-coated terriers of a breed originating in England and having a white coat with dark markings.

fox•trot (fŏks′trŏt′) *intr.v.* **-trot•ted, -trot•ting, -trots.** To dance the fox trot.

fox trot *n.* **1.a.** A ballroom dance in 2/4 or 4/4 time with both slow and fast steps. **b.** The music for this dance. **2.** A slow broken gait of a horse, between a trot and a walk.

fox•y (fŏk′sē) *adj.* **-i•er, -i•est. 1.a.** Of or resembling a fox. **b.** Slyly clever; crafty. **2.** Having a reddish-brown color. **3.** Discolored, as by age or decay; foxed. **4.** *Slang.* Sensually attractive; sexy. **5.** Having a distinctive sharp flavor or aroma. — **fox′i•ly** *adv.* — **fox′i•ness** *n.*

foy (foi) *n. Scots.* A farewell feast, drink, or gift, as at a wedding. [Du. dial. *fooi* < MDu. *foye,* journey < OFr. *voie* < Lat. *via,* road. See **wegh-***.]

foxglove

foy•er (foi′ər, foi′ā′, fwä′yā′) *n.* **1.** A lobby or an anteroom, as of a hotel. **2.** An entrance hall; a vestibule. [Fr., social center < OFr. *foier,* fireplace, ult. < Lat. *focus,* fire.]

fp or **f.p.** *abbr.* Freezing point.

FPC *abbr.* **1.** Federal Power Commission. **2.** Fish protein concentrate. **3.** Friends Peace Committee.

fpl *abbr.* Fireplace.

fpm or **f.p.m.** *abbr.* Feet per minute.

FPO *abbr.* Fleet post office.

fps or **f.p.s.** *abbr.* **1.** Feet per second. **2.** Foot-pound-second. **3.** Frames per second.

Fr The symbol for the element **francium.**

fr. *abbr.* **1.** Frame. **2.** Franc. **3.** From.

Fr. *abbr.* **1.** Father (cleric). **2.** France; French. **3.** Frau. **4.** Friar. **5.** Friday.

f.r. *abbr. Lat.* Folio recto (right-hand page).

Fra (frä) *n. Rom. Cath. Ch.* Used as a title for an Italian monk or friar; brother. [Ital., short for *frate,* brother < Lat. *frāter.* See **bhrāter-***.]

fra•cas (frā′kəs, frăk′əs) *n.* A noisy disorderly fight or quarrel; a brawl. [Fr. < Ital. *fracasso* < *fracassare,* to make an uproar.]

frac•tal (frăk′təl) *n.* A geometric pattern repeated at ever smaller scales to produce irregular shapes and surfaces and used esp. in computer modeling of irregular patterns and structures in nature. [Fr. < Lat. *frāctus,* p.part. of *frangere,* to break. See FRACTION.]

fract•ed (frăk′tĭd) *adj. Obsolete.* Broken. [< Lat. *frāctus,* p.part. of *frangere,* to break. See FRACTION.]

frac•tion (frăk′shən) *n.* **1.** *Math.* An expression that indicates the quotient of two quantities. **2.** A disconnected piece; a fragment. **3.** A small part; a bit. **4.** A chemical component separated by fractionation. [ME *fraccioun,* a breaking < AN < LLat. *frāctiō, frāctiōn-* < Lat. *frāctus,* p.part. of *frangere,* to break. See **bhreg-***.]

frac•tion•al (frăk′shə-nəl) *adj.* **1.** Of, relating to, or constituting a fraction. **2.** Very small; insignificant. **3.** Being in fractions or pieces. — **frac′tion•al•ly** *adv.*

fractional currency *n.* Coin or paper currency in a denomination less than a standard monetary unit.

frac•tion•al•ize (frăk′shə-nə-līz′) *tr.v.* **-ized, -iz•ing, -iz•es.** To divide into separate parts or sections. — **frac′tion•al•i•za′tion** (-shə-nə-lĭ-zā′shən) *n.*

frac•tion•ate (frăk′shə-nāt′) *tr.v.* **-at•ed, -at•ing, -ates. 1.** To divide or separate into parts; break up. **2.** To separate (a chemical compound) into components, as by distillation or crystallization. — **frac′tion•a′tion** *n.* — **frac′tion•a′tor** *n.*

frac•tion•ize (frăk′shə-nīz′) *tr. & intr.v.* **-ized, -iz•ing, -iz•es.** To divide into parts or fractions. — **frac′tion•i•za′tion** (-shə-nĭ-zā′shən) *n.*

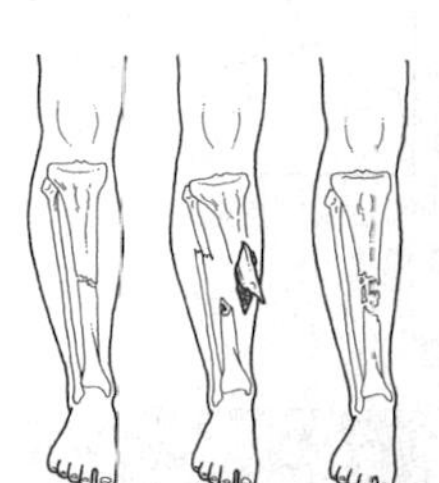
fracture
Left to right: Simple, compound, and comminuted fractures

frac•tious (frăk′shəs) *adj.* **1.** Inclined to make trouble; unruly. **2.** Having a peevish nature; cranky. [< FRACTION, discord (obsolete).] — **frac′tious•ly** *adv.* — **frac′tious•ness** *n.*

frac•ture (frăk′chər) *n.* **1.a.** The act or process of breaking. **b.** The condition of having been broken or ruptured. **2.** A break, rupture, or crack, esp. in bone or cartilage. **3.** *Mineral.* **a.** The characteristic manner in which a mineral breaks. **b.** The characteristic appearance of the surface of a broken mineral. **4.** *Geol.* A crack or fault in a rock. — *v.* **-tured, -tur•ing, -tures.** — *tr.* **1.** To cause to break. **2.** To disrupt or destroy as if by breaking. **3.** To abuse or misuse flagrantly, as by violating rules: *ignorant writers who fracture the language.* **4.** *Slang.* To cause to laugh heartily. — *intr.* To undergo a fracture. See Syns at **break.** [ME < OFr. < Lat. *frāctūra* < *frāctus,* p.part. of *frangere,* to break. See **bhreg-***.]

frae (frā) *prep. Scots.* From. [ME *fra* < ON *frā.* See FRO.]

frag•ile (frăj′əl, -īl′) *adj.* **1.** Easily broken, damaged, or destroyed; frail. **2.** Lacking physical or emotional strength. **3.** Lacking substance; tenuous or flimsy. [Fr. < OFr. < Lat. *fragilis* < *frangere, frag-,* to break. See **bhreg-***.] — **frag′ile•ly** *adv.* — **fra•gil′i•ty** (frə-jĭl′ĭ-tē), **frag′ile•ness** *n.*

Syns: *fragile, breakable, frangible, delicate, brittle.* These adjectives mean easily broken or damaged. *Fragile* applies to objects not made of strong or sturdy material and requiring

ă pat	oi boy
ā pay	ou out
âr care	ŏŏ took
ä father	ōō boot
ĕ pet	ŭ cut
ē be	ûr urge
ĭ pit	th thin
ī pie	*th* this
îr pier	hw which
ŏ pot	zh vision
ō toe	ə about, item
ô paw	

Stress marks:
′ (primary);
′ (secondary), as in
dictionary (dĭk′shə-nĕr′ē)

careful handling: *fragile porcelain. Breakable* and *frangible* mean capable of being broken but do not necessarily imply inherent weakness: *breakable toys; frangible artifacts. Delicate* refers to what is so soft, tender, or fine as to be susceptible to injury: *delicate fruit. Brittle* refers to inelasticity that makes something especially likely to fracture or snap when subjected to pressure: *brittle bones.*

frag•ment (frăg′mənt) *n.* **1.** A small part broken off or detached. **2.** An incomplete or isolated portion; a bit. — *v.* (-mĕnt′) **-ment•ed, -ment•ing, -ments.** — *tr.* To break or separate (something) into fragments. — *intr.* To become broken into fragments. [ME < Lat. *fragmentum* < *frangere, frag-*, to break. See **bhreg-***.]

Jean Fragonard

frag•men•tal (frăg-mĕn′tl) *adj.* **1.** Fragmentary. **2.** *Geol.* Consisting of broken rock, coal, or ore moved from its place of origin. — **frag•men′tal•ly** *adv.*

frag•men•tar•y (frăg′mən-tĕr′ē) *adj.* Consisting of small disconnected parts. — **frag′men•tar′i•ly** (-târ′ə-lē) *adv.* — **frag′men•tar′i•ness** *n.*

frag•men•ta•tion (frăg′mən-tā′shən, -mĕn-) *n.* **1.** The act or process of breaking into fragments. **2.** The scattering of the fragments of an exploding bomb or other projectile.

fragmentation bomb *n.* An aerial antipersonnel bomb that scatters shrapnel over a wide area upon explosion.

frag•men•tize (frăg′mən-tīz′) *tr. & intr.v.* **-tized, -tiz•ing, -tiz•es.** To fragment. — **frag′men•tiz′er** *n.*

Fra•go•nard (frăg′ə-när′, frä-gô-), **Jean Honoré.** 1732–1806. French artist best known for his rococo paintings of exotic landscapes and romantic scenes.

fra•grance (frā′grəns) *n.* **1.** The state or quality of having a pleasant odor. **2.** A sweet or pleasant odor; a scent.

fra•grant (frā′grənt) *adj.* Having a pleasant odor. [ME < Lat. *frāgrāns, frāgrant-*, p.part. of *frāgrāre*, to emit an odor.]

fraid•y cat (frā′dē) *n. Slang.* A timid or fearful person.

frail[1] (frāl) *adj.* **frail•er, frail•est. 1.** Physically weak; delicate. **2.** Not strong or substantial; slight: *frail evidence.* **3.** Easily broken or destroyed; fragile. **4.** Easily led astray; morally weak. [ME *frele* < OFr. < Lat. *fragilis* < *frangere, frag-*, to break. See **bhreg-***.] — **frail′ly** *adv.* — **frail′ness** *n.*

frail[2] (frāl) *n.* **1.** A rush basket for fruit, esp. dried fruit. **2.** The quantity of fruit that a frail can hold. [ME *fraiel* < OFr.]

frail•ty (frāl′tē) *n., pl.* **-ties. 1.** The condition or quality of being frail. **2.** A fault, esp. weakness of resolution, arising from the imperfections of human nature.

France

fraise (frāz) *n.* **1.** A defensive barrier of pointed inclined stakes or barbed wire. **2.** A ruff for the neck worn in the 16th century. [Fr. < OFr., mesentery (< its pleated shape) < *(feves) frasees*, shelled (beans) < Lat. *(faba) frēsa*, ground (bean), fem. p.part. of *frendere*, to crush. See FRENUM.]

frak•tur (fräk-to͝or′) *n.* A style of black letter formerly used in German manuscripts and printing. [Ger. < Lat. *fractūra*, a breaking (< the curlicues). See FRACTURE.]

fram•be•sia (frăm-bē′zhə, -zhē-ə) *n.* See **yaws.** [NLat. < Fr. *framboise*, raspberry < OFr., of Gmc. orig. See **bhā-**[1]*.]

frame (frām) *v.* **framed, fram•ing, frames.** — *tr.* **1.** To build by putting together the structural parts of; construct. **2.** To conceive or design. **3.** To arrange or adjust for a purpose: *a question framed to have one answer.* **4.a.** To put into words; formulate. **b.** To form (words) silently with the lips. **5.** To enclose in or as if in a frame. **6.** *Informal.* **a.** To make up evidence or contrive events so as to incriminate (a person) falsely. **b.** To prearrange (a contest) so as to ensure a desired fraudulent outcome; fix. — *intr.* **1.** *Archaic.* To go; proceed. **2.** *Obsolete.* To manage; contrive. — *n.* **1.** Something composed of parts fitted and joined together. **2.** A structure that gives shape or support. **3.a.** An open structure or rim for encasing, holding, or bordering. **b.** A closed, often rectangular border of drawn or printed lines. **4.** A pair of eyeglasses, excluding the lenses. Often used in the plural. **5.** The structure of a human or animal body; physique. **6.** A cold frame. **7.** A general structure or system. **8.** A general state or condition. **9.** *Sports & Games.* **a.** A round or period of play in some games, such as bowling and billiards. **b.** *Baseball.* An inning. **10.** A single picture on a roll of movie film. **11.** The total area of a complete picture in television broadcasting. **12.** *Informal.* A frame-up. **13.** A single step in a sequence of programmed instruction. **14.** *Obsolete.* Shape; form. [ME *framen* < OE *framian*, to further < *fram*, forward. See FROM.]

Francis I
Portrait of Francis I, King of France by Joos van Cleve (1490?–1540?)

frame of reference *n., pl.* **frames of reference. 1.** A set of coordinate axes in terms of which position or movement may be specified or with reference to which physical laws may be mathematically stated. **2.** A set of ideas in terms of which other ideas are interpreted or assigned meaning.

fram•er (frā′mər) *n.* **1.** One that frames. **2.** Often **Framer.** One of the people who wrote the U.S. Constitution.

frame•shift (frām′shĭft′) *n. Genet.* The insertion or deletion in a DNA chain of a number of nucleotides not divisible by three, resulting in the incorrect reading of the codon sequence during genetic transcription.

Francis Ferdinand

frame-up (frām′ŭp′) *n. Informal.* **1.** A scheme to incriminate an innocent person. **2.** A contest or deliberation the outcome of which is fraudulently prearranged.

frame•work (frām′wûrk′) *n.* **1.** A structure for supporting or enclosing something else, esp. the skeletal support of a physical construction. **2.** An external work platform; a scaffold. **3.** A fundamental structure, as for a written work.

fram•ing (frā′mĭng) *n.* A frame, framework, or system of frames.

Fra•ming•ham (frā′mĭng-hăm′). A town of E-central MA WSW of Boston; settled in 1650. Pop. 64,994.

franc (frăngk) *n.* See table at **currency.** [Fr. < OFr. < Med.Lat. *Francōrum rēx*, king of the Franks < LLat. *Francōrum*, genitive pl. of *Francus*, Frank. See FRANK.]

France (frăns). A country of W Europe on the Atlantic and the English Channel; settled by the Franks after the retreat of the Romans. Cap. Paris. Pop. 54,334,871.

France (frăns, fräNs), **Anatole.** Jacques Anatole François Thibault. 1844–1924. French critic and writer who won the 1921 Nobel Prize for literature.

Fran•ce•sca (frăn-chĕs′kə, frän-), **Piero della.** See **Piero della Francesca.**

Francesca da Ri•mi•ni (də rĭm′ĭ-nē, dä rē′mē-nē). d. c. 1285. Italian noblewoman who was murdered by her husband when he learned of her affair with his brother.

Franche-Com•té (fräNsh-kôN-tā′). A historical region and former province of E France; first occupied by a Celtic tribe in the 4th cent. B.C. and part of France after 1676.

fran•chise (frăn′chīz′) *n.* **1.** A privilege or right officially granted a person or a group by a government, esp.: **a.** The constitutional or statutory right to vote. **b.** The establishment of a corporation's existence. **c.** The granting of certain rights and powers to a corporation. **d.** Legal immunity from servitude, certain burdens, or other restrictions. **2.a.** Authorization granted to someone to sell or distribute a company's goods or services in a certain area. **b.** A business or group of businesses established or operated under such authorization. **3.** The territory or limits within which immunity, a privilege, or a right may be exercised. **4.** *Informal.* A professional sports team. — *tr.v.* **-chised, -chis•ing, -chis•es.** To grant a franchise to. [ME *fraunchise* < OFr. *franchise* < *franche*, fem. of *franc*, free, exempt. See FRANK[1].]

fran•chis•ee (frăn′chī-zē′) *n.* One that is granted a franchise, as to market a company's goods in a certain local area.

fran•chis•er or **fran•chi•sor** (frăn′chī′zər) *n.* One that grants a franchise.

Fran•cis I (frăn′sĭs). 1494–1547. King of France (1515–47) who waged four wars against Holy Roman Emperor Charles V from 1521 to 1544.

Francis II. 1768–1835. Last Holy Roman emperor (1792–1806) and emperor of Austria (1804–35) as Francis I, who was instrumental in the defeat of Napoleon (1813–15).

Fran•cis•can (frăn-sĭs′kən) *n. Rom. Cath. Ch.* A member of a religious mendicant order founded by Saint Francis of Assisi in 1209 and now divided into three independent branches. [NLat. *Franciscānus* < Med.Lat. *Franciscus* < Saint FRANCIS OF ASSISI.] — **Fran•cis′can** *adj.*

Francis Fer•di•nand (fûr′dn-ănd′). 1863–1914. Austrian archduke whose assassination precipitated World War I.

Francis Jo•seph I (jō′zəf, -səf, yō′zĕf) also **Franz Jo•sef I** (frănz jō′zəf, -səf, frănts, fränts yō′zĕf). 1830–1916. Emperor of Austria (1848–1916) and king of Hungary (1867–1916) whose ultimatum to Serbia led to World War I.

Francis of As•si•si (ə-sē′zē, -sē, ə-sĭs′ē), Saint. 1182?–1226. Italian Roman Catholic friar who founded the Franciscan order (1209) and was canonized in 1228.

Francis of Sales (sālz, säl), Saint. 1567–1622. French ecclesiastic who maintained that spiritual perfection is possible for people involved in secular pursuits.

fran•ci•um (frăn′sē-əm) *n. Symbol* **Fr** An extremely unstable radioactive element of the alkali metals, having approx. 19 isotopes, the most stable of which is Fr 223 with a half-life of 21 minutes. Atomic number 87; valence 1. See table at **element.** [After FRANCE.]

Franck (frängk, fräNk), **César Auguste.** 1822–90. French composer noted for his Symphony in D minor (1889).

Fran•co (frăng′kō, fräng′-), **Francisco.** "El Caudillo." 1892–1975. Spanish soldier and politician who directed the rebel armed forces that defeated the Republicans in the Spanish Civil War (1936–39) and ruled as dictator (1939–75).

Franco– *pref.* French: *Francophone.* [< LLat. *Francus*, a Frank. See FRANK.]

Fran•co-A•mer•i•can (frăng′kō-ə-mĕr′ĭ-kən) *n.* An American of French or French-Canadian descent. — *adj.* **1.** Of or relating to the Franco-Americans. **2.** Of or relating to France and America: *Franco-American relations.*

fran•co•lin (frăng′kə-lĭn) *n.* Any of various Eurasian or African birds of the genus *Francolinus*, related to and resembling the quails and partridges. [Fr. < Ital. *francolino.*]

Fran•co•ni•a (frăng-kō′nē-ə, -kōn′yə, frăn-). A region and former duchy of S Germany. — **Fran•co′ni•an** *adj. & n.*

Fran•co•phile (frăng′kə-fīl′) also **Fran•co•phil** (-fĭl′) *n.* One who admires France, its people, or its culture. — **Fran′co•phile′** *adj.* — **Fran′co•phil′i•a** (-fĭl′ē-ə, -fēl′yə) *n.*

Fran•co•phobe (frăng′kə-fōb′) *n.* One who dislikes or fears

France, its people, or its culture. — **Fran′co·phobe′, Fran′co·pho′bic** *adj.* — **Fran′co·pho′bi·a** *n.*
Fran·co·phone or **fran·co·phone** (frăng′kə-fōn′) —*n.* A French-speaking person, esp. in a region where two or more languages are spoken. —*adj.* French-speaking. — **Fran′co·phon′ic** (-fŏn′ĭk) *adj.*
fran·gi·ble (frăn′jə-bəl) *adj.* Capable of being broken; breakable. See Syns at **fragile.** [ME < OFr. < Med.Lat. *frangibilis* < Lat. *frangere,* to break. See **bhreg-*.**] — **fran′gi·bil′i·ty, fran′gi·ble·ness** *n.*
fran·gi·pan·i (frăn′jə-păn′ē, -pä′nē) *n., pl.* **-pan·is. 1.** Any of various tropical American deciduous shrubs or trees of the genus *Plumeria,* having fragrant, funnel-shaped, variously colored flowers. **2.** A perfume derived from or similar in scent to frangipani flowers. **3.** Also **fran·gi·pane** (frăn′jə-pān′). A creamy almond-flavored pastry filling. [Fr. *frangipane,* after Muzio *Frangipani,* 16th-cent. Italian marquis.]
Fran·glais (frän-glā′) *n.* French marked by many borrowings from English. [Blend of Fr. *français,* French (< OFr. *franceis* < *France,* France) and *anglais,* English (< OFr. *englois* < OE *Angel* < Lat. *Anglī,* the Angles; see ANGLE).]
frank¹ (frăngk) *adj.* **frank·er, frank·est. 1.** Open and sincere in expression; straightforward. **2.** Clearly manifest; evident. —*tr.v.* **franked, frank·ing, franks. 1.a.** To put an official mark on (a piece of mail) so that it can be sent free of charge. **b.** To send (mail) free of charge. **2.** To place a stamp or mark on (a piece of mail) to show the payment of postage. **3.** To enable (a person) to come and go freely. —*n.* **1.a.** A mark or signature placed on a piece of mail to indicate the right to send it free of charge. **b.** The right to send mail free. **2.** A franked piece of mail. [ME, free < OFr. *franc* < LLat. *Francus,* Frank. See FRANK.] — **frank′ness** *n.*

Syns: *frank, candid, outspoken, straightforward, open.* These adjectives mean revealing or disposed to reveal one's thoughts freely and honestly. *Frank* implies forthrightness, sometimes to the point of bluntness: *Please be frank and tell me what you think. Candid* often suggests refusal to evade difficult or unpleasant issues: *"Save, save, oh save me from the candid friend!"* (George Canning). *Outspoken* usually implies bold lack of reserve: *an outspoken activist. Straightforward* denotes directness of manner and expression: *"George was a straightforward soul . . 'See here!' he said. 'Are you engaged to anybody?' "* (Booth Tarkington). *Open* suggests freedom from all trace of reserve or secretiveness: *"I will be open and sincere with you"* (Joseph Addison).

frank² (frăngk) *n. Informal.* A frankfurter.
Frank (frăngk) *n.* A member of one of the Germanic tribes of the Rhine region in the early Christian era, esp. one of the Salian Franks who conquered Gaul about A.D. 500 and established an extensive empire. [ME < OE *Franca* and OFr. *Franc,* both < LLat. *Francus,* of Gmc. orig.]
Frank (frăngk, frängk), **Anne.** 1929–45. German Jewish diarist who fled from Nazi Germany to Amsterdam with her family (1933) and kept a diary during her years in hiding (1942–44). The diary was published in 1947.
Frank·en·stein (frăng′kən-stīn′) *n.* **1.** An agency or a creation that slips from the control of and ultimately destroys its creator. **2.** A monster having the appearance of a man. [From *Frankenstein,* the creator of the artificial monster in *Frankenstein* (1818) by Mary Wollstonecraft Shelley.]
Frank·en·thal·er (frăng′kən-thô′lər, -thŏl′ər), **Helen.** b. 1928. Amer. abstract expressionist painter whose works include *The Human Edge* (1967).
Frank·fort (frăngk′fərt). The cap. of KY, in the N-central part NW of Lexington; chosen as capital in 1792. Pop. 25,968.
Frank·furt (frănk′fərt, frängk′fo͝ort′). **1.** Also **Frankfurt an der O·der** (än dər ō′dər). A city of E Germany on the Oder R.; chartered 1253. Pop. 84,072. **2.** Also **Frankfurt am Main** (äm mīn′). A city of W-central Germany on the Main R.; founded in the 1st cent. B.C. Pop. 599,634.
frank·furt·er also **frank·fort·er** (frăngk′fər-tər) *n.* A sausage usu. of beef or beef and pork. [After FRANKFURT, W-central Germany.]
Frank·furt·er (frăngk′fər-tər), **Felix.** 1882–1965. Austrian-born Amer. jurist; associate justice of the U.S. Supreme Court (1939–62).
frank·in·cense (frăng′kĭn-sĕns′) *n.* An aromatic gum resin obtained from African and Asian trees of the genus *Boswellia* and used chiefly as incense and in perfumes. [ME *frank encens* < OFr. *franc encens* : *franc,* free, pure; see FRANK¹ + *encens,* incense; see INCENSE².]
Frank·ish (frăng′kĭsh) *adj.* Of or relating to the Franks or their language. —*n.* The West Germanic language of the Franks.
frank·lin (frăng′klĭn) *n.* A medieval English freeholder of non-noble birth holding extensive property. [ME *frankelein* < AN *fraunclein* < *franc.* See FRANK¹.]
Frank·lin (frăngk′lĭn). **1.** A former district of NE Northwest Terrs., Canada; created in 1895. **2.** A town of SE MA near the RI border SW of Boston; settled in 1660. Pop. 22,095. **3.** A city of SE WI, a suburb of Milwaukee. Pop. 21,855.
Franklin, Benjamin. 1706–90. Amer. public official, writer, scientist, and printer who published *Poor Richard's Almanac* (1732–57).
Franklin, Sir **John.** 1786–1847. British explorer who led a search for the Northwest Passage (1845–47).
Franklin, John Hope. b. 1915. Amer. historian noted for works such as *From Slavery to Freedom* (1947).
frank·lin·ite (frăng′klĭ-nīt′) *n.* A black, slightly magnetic mineral of zinc, iron, and manganese, $ZnFe_2O_4$, that is a valuable source of zinc. [After *Franklin,* a borough of N NJ.]
Franklin Square. A community of SE NY on SE Long I. Pop. 28,205.
Franklin stove *n.* A cast-iron heating stove shaped like a fireplace but employing metal baffles to increase its heating efficiency. [After Benjamin FRANKLIN.]
Franklin tree *n.* A deciduous tree or shrub *(Franklinia alatamaha)* originally native to Georgia and having large white fragrant flowers and woody capsules.
frank·ly (frăngk′lē) *adv.* **1.** In a frank manner; candidly. **2.** In truth; honestly: *Frankly, I don't care.*
frank·pledge (frăngk′plĕj′) *n.* **1.** An Anglo-Saxon legal system in which units or tithings composed of ten households were formed, in each of which members were held responsible for one another's conduct. **2.** A member of a unit in frankpledge. [ME *frankplegge* < AN *frauncpledge* : OFr. *franc,* free, frank; see FRANK¹ + OFr. *plege,* pledge; see PLEDGE.]
fran·se·ri·a (frăn-sîr′ē-ə) *n.* Any of various herbs or shrubs of the genus *Franseria,* native to western North America. [NLat. *Franseria,* genus name, after Antonio *Franseri,* 18th-cent. Spanish botanist.]
fran·tic (frăn′tĭk) *adj.* **1.** Highly excited with strong emotion or frustration; frenzied. **2.** Characterized by rapid and disordered or nervous activity. **3.** *Archaic.* Mad; insane. [ME *frantik* < OFr. *frenetique* < Lat. *phrenēticus.* See FRENETIC.] — **fran′ti·cal·ly, fran′tic·ly** *adv.* — **fran′tic·ness** *n.*
Franz Jo·sef I (frănz jō′zəf, -səf, fränts, fränts yō′zĕf). See **Francis Joseph I.**
Franz Josef Land (lănd, länt). An archipelago in the Arctic Ocean N of Novaya Zemlya.
frap (frăp) *tr.v.* **frapped, frap·ping, fraps.** *Naut.* **1.** To make secure by lashing. **2.** To take up the slack of; tighten. [ME *frapen,* to strike < OFr. *fraper.* See FRAPPÉ.]
frap·pé (fră-pā′, frăp) *n.* **1.** A frozen fruit-flavored mixture that is similar to sherbet and served as a dessert or appetizer. **2.** A beverage, usu. a liqueur, poured over shaved ice. **3.** Often **frappe** (frăp). *New England.* See **milk shake** 1. See Regional Note at **milk shake.** [Fr. < p.part. of *frapper,* to strike, chill < OFr. *fraper,* to strike, prob. of imit. orig.]
Fra·ser (frā′zər), **James Earle.** 1876–1953. Amer. sculptor whose works include the design for the buffalo nickel (1913).
Fraser River. A river of British Columbia, Canada, flowing c. 1,368 km (850 mi) from the Rocky Mts. near the Alberta boundary to the Strait of Georgia at Vancouver.
frat (frăt) *n. Informal.* A college fraternity.
fra·ter·nal (frə-tûr′nəl) *adj.* **1.a.** Of or relating to brothers. **b.** Showing comradeship; brotherly. **2.** Of or constituting a fraternity. **3.** *Biol.* Of, relating to, or being a twin developed from two separately fertilized ova; dizygotic. [ME, ult. < Lat. *frāternus* < *frāter,* brother. See **bhrāter-*.**] — **fra·ter′nal·ism** *n.* — **fra·ter′nal·ly** *adv.*
fra·ter·ni·ty (frə-tûr′nĭ-tē) *n., pl.* **-ties. 1.** A body of people associated for a common purpose or interest, such as a guild. **2.** A group joined by similar backgrounds, occupations, interests, or tastes. **3.** A chiefly social organization of men students at a college or university. **4.** The quality or condition of being brothers; brotherliness. [ME *fraternite* < OFr. < Lat. *frāternitās* < *frāternus,* fraternal. See FRATERNAL.]
frat·er·nize (frăt′ər-nīz′) *intr.v.* **-nized, -niz·ing, -niz·es. 1.** To associate with others in a brotherly or congenial way. **2.** To associate on friendly terms with an enemy or opposing group, often in violation of discipline or orders. [Ult. < Lat. *frāternus,* fraternal. See FRATERNAL.] — **frat′er·ni·za′tion** (-nĭ-zā′shən) *n.* — **frat′er·niz′er** *n.*
frat·ri·cide (frăt′rĭ-sīd′) *n.* **1.** The killing of one's brother or sister. **2.** One who has killed one's brother or sister. [ME < OFr. < Lat. *frātricīdium* and *frātricīda* : *frāter, frātr-,* brother; see **bhrāter-*** + *-cīdium* and *-cīda,* -cide.] — **frat′ri·cid′al** (-sīd′l) *adj.*
Frau (frou) *n., pl.* **Frau·en** (frou′ən). Used as a courtesy title in a German-speaking area before the surname or professional title of a woman. [Ger. < MHGer. *vrowe* < OHGer. *frouwa.* See **per¹*.**]
fraud (frôd) *n.* **1.** A deception deliberately practiced to secure unfair or unlawful gain. **2.** A piece of trickery; a trick. **3.a.** One that defrauds; a cheat. **b.** One who assumes a false pose; an impostor. [ME *fraude* < OFr. < Lat. *fraus, fraud-.*]
fraud·u·lent (frô′jə-lənt) *adj.* **1.** Engaging in fraud; deceitful. **2.** Characterized by, constituting, or gained by fraud. [ME < OFr. < Lat. *fraudulentus* < *fraus, fraud-,* deceit.] — **fraud′u·lence** *n.* — **fraud′u·lent·ly** *adv.*
fraught (frôt) *adj.* **1.** Filled with a specified element or elements; charged. **2.** Fully provided. **3.** Marked by distress; upsetting. —*n. Scots.* Freight; cargo. [ME, p.part. of *fraught-*

Benjamin Franklin
c. 1785 portrait by
Joseph Siffred Duplessis
(1725–1802)

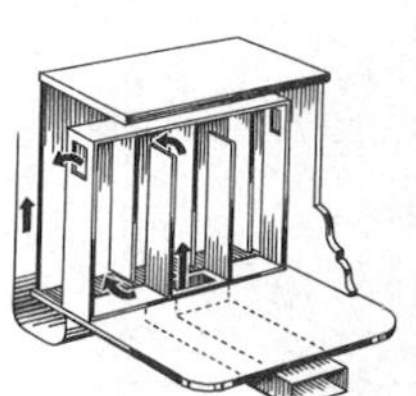

Franklin stove

ă pat	oi boy
ā pay	ou out
âr care	o͝o took
ä father	o͞o boot
ĕ pet	ŭ cut
ē be	ûr urge
ĭ pit	th thin
ī pie	*th* this
îr pier	hw which
ŏ pot	zh vision
ō toe	ə about, item
ô paw	

Stress marks:
′ (primary);
′ (secondary), as in
dictionary (dĭk′shə-nĕr′ē)

en, to load < *fraght*, cargo; see FREIGHT, and < MDu. *vrachten*, to load (< *vracht*, freight; see **ēik-***).]

Fräu•lein (froi′līn′, frou′-) *n., pl.* **Fräulein. 1.** Used as a courtesy title in a German-speaking area before the surname of a girl or sometimes an unmarried woman. **2. fräulein.** Used as a form of address for a girl or young woman in a German-speaking area. **3.** *Chiefly British.* A German governess. [Ger., dim. of *Frau*, woman. See FRAU.]

Fraun•ho•fer lines (froun′hō′fər) *pl.n.* A set of dark absorption lines appearing against the bright background of the continuous solar spectrum. [After Joseph von *Fraunhofer* (1787–1826), German physicist.]

frax•i•nel•la (frăk′sə-nĕl′ə) *n.* See **gas plant.** [NLat., dim. of Lat. *fraxinus*, ash tree. See **bherəg-***.]

fray[1] (frā) *n.* **1.** A scuffle; a brawl. **2.** A heated dispute or contest. — *tr.v.* **frayed, fray•ing, frays.** *Archaic.* **1.** To alarm; frighten. **2.** To drive away. [ME *frai*, alteration of *affrai*. See AFFRAY.]

fray[2] (frā) *v.* **frayed, fray•ing, frays.** — *tr.* **1.** To strain; chafe. **2.** To wear away (the edges of fabric, for example) by rubbing. — *intr.* To become worn away or tattered along the edges. — *n.* A frayed or threadbare spot, as on fabric. [ME *fraien*, to wear, bruise < OFr. *fraier*, to rub < Lat. *fricāre*.]

Fra•zer (frā′zər), Sir **James George.** 1854–1941. British anthropologist noted for *The Golden Bough* (1890).

fraz•zle (frăz′əl) *Informal.* — *v.* **-zled, -zling, -zles.** — *tr.* **1.** To wear away along the edges; fray. **2.** To exhaust physically or emotionally. — *intr.* **1.** To become worn away along the edges. **2.** To become exhausted physically or emotionally. — *n.* **1.** A frayed or tattered condition. **2.** A condition of exhaustion. [Perh. a blend of FRAY[2] and dial. *fazzle*, to unravel (< ME *facelyn*, to fray < *fasel*, frayed edge, prob. dim. of *fas*, rootlets < OE *fæs*).]

FRB *abbr.* Federal Reserve Board.

FRCP or **F.R.C.P.** *abbr.* Fellow of the Royal College of Physicians.

FRCS or **F.R.C.S.** *abbr.* Fellow of the Royal College of Surgeons.

freak[1] (frēk) *n.* **1.** A thing or an occurrence that is markedly unusual or irregular. **2.** An abnormally formed organism, esp. a person or animal regarded as a curiosity or monstrosity. **3.** A sudden capricious turn of mind; a whim. **4.** *Slang.* **a.** A drug user or addict. **b.** An eccentric or nonconformist person, esp. a member of a counterculture. **c.** An enthusiast. — *intr. & tr.v.* **freaked, freak•ing, freaks.** *Slang.* **1.** To experience or cause to experience frightening hallucinations or feelings of paranoia, esp. as a result of taking a drug. **2.** To behave or cause to behave irrationally and uncontrollably. **3.** To become or cause to become greatly excited or upset. In all three senses, often used with *out.* [?]

freak[2] (frēk) *n.* A fleck or streak of color. — *tr.v.* **freaked, freak•ing, freaks.** To speckle or streak with color. [< FREAK[1].]

freak•ing (frē′kĭng) *adj. Slang.* Used as an intensive. [Alteration of *frigging*, pr.part. of FRIG.]

freak•ish (frē′kĭsh) *adj.* **1.** Markedly unusual or abnormal; strange. **2.** Relating to or being a freak. **3.** Capricious or whimsical. — **freak′ish•ly** *adv.* — **freak′ish•ness** *n.*

freak-out or **freak•out** (frēk′out′) *n. Slang.* **1.** An experience of frightening feelings or hallucinations, esp. as a result of taking a drug. **2.** An experience or scene of unrestrained excitement or irrational behavior. **3.** One having such an experience or participating in such a scene.

freak•y (frē′kē) *adj.* **-i•er, -i•est. 1.** Strange or unusual; freakish. **2.** *Slang.* Frightening. — **freak′i•ly** *adv.*

freck•le (frĕk′əl) *n.* A small brownish spot on the skin, often turning darker or increasing in number upon exposure to the sun. — *tr. & intr.v.* **-led, -ling, -les.** To dot or become dotted with freckles or spots of color. [< ME *frakles*, freckles, alteration of *fraknes*, prob. of Scand. orig.] — **freck′ly** *adj.*

Fred•er•ick (frĕd′rĭk, -ər-ĭk). A city of N MD W of Baltimore. Pop. 40,148.

Frederick I. "Frederick Barbarossa." 1123?–90. Holy Roman emperor (1152–90) and king of Germany and Italy who conceded supremacy to Pope Alexander III (1177).

Frederick II[1]. 1194–1250. Holy Roman emperor (1212–50) and king of Sicily (1198–1250) as Frederick I who led the Sixth Crusade (1228–29), capturing Jerusalem.

Frederick II[2]. "Frederick the Great." 1712–86. King of Prussia (1740–86) who waged the War of the Austrian Succession (1740–48) and the Seven Years' War (1756–63).

Frederick IX. 1899–1972. King of Denmark (1947–72) who signed a constitutional amendment allowing the succession of a woman to the throne.

Fred•er•icks•burg (frĕd′rĭks-bûrg′, -ər-ĭks-). An independent city of NE VA N of Richmond; site of the Battle of Fredericksburg (Dec. 1862). Pop. 19,027.

Frederick Wil•liam (wĭl′yəm). "the Great Elector." 1620–88. Elector of Brandenburg (1640–88) who reorganized and rebuilt his domain after the Thirty Years' War.

Frederick William I. 1688–1740. King of Prussia (1713–40) who diversified the economy of his dominion.

Frederick William II. 1744–97. King of Prussia (1786–97) who fought a costly war with France (1792–95).

Frederick William III. 1770–1840. King of Prussia (1797–1840) whose long turbulent reign included participation in the Napoleonic Wars.

Fred•er•ic•ton (frĕd′rĭk-tən, -ər-ĭk-). The cap. of New Brunswick, Canada, in the S-central part NW of St. John; founded 1783. Pop. 43,723.

Fred•er•iks•berg (frĕd′rĭks-bûrg′, -ər-ĭks-, frĕ′*th*ə-rĕks-bärKH′). A city of E Denmark, a suburb of Copenhagen on Sjaelland I. Pop. 88,114.

free (frē) *adj.* **fre•er, fre•est. 1.** Not imprisoned or enslaved; being at liberty. **2.** Not controlled by obligation or the will of another. **3.a.** Having political independence. **b.** Governed by consent and possessing or granting civil liberties. **c.** Not subject to arbitrary interference by a government. **4.a.** Not affected or restricted by a given condition or circumstance. **b.** Not subject to a given condition; exempt. **5.** Not subject to external restraint. **6.** Not literal or exact: *a free translation.* **7.a.** Costing nothing; gratuitous. **b.** Publicly supported. **8.a.** Not occupied or used. **b.** Not taken up by scheduled activities. **9.** Unobstructed; clear. **10.** Unguarded in expression or manner; open; frank. **11.** Taking undue liberties; forward or overfamiliar. **12.** Liberal or lavish. **13.** Given, made, or done of one's own accord; voluntary or spontaneous. **14.** *Chem. & Phys.* **a.** Unconstrained; unconfined. **b.** Not fixed in position; capable of relatively unrestricted motion. **c.** Not chemically bound in a molecule. **d.** Involving no collisions or interactions. **e.** Empty: *a free space.* **f.** Unoccupied. **15.** Not bound, fastened, or attached. **16.** *Ling.* Being a vowel in an open syllable unchecked by a consonant. — *adv.* **1.** In a free manner; without restraint. **2.** Without charge. **3.** *Naut.* On a course other than close-hauled. — *tr.v.* **freed, free•ing, frees. 1.** To set at liberty; make free. **2.** To relieve of a burden, an obligation, or a restraint. **3.** To remove obstructions or entanglements from; clear. — ***idiom.* for free.** *Informal.* Without charge. [ME *fre* < OE *frēo*. V. < ME *freen* < OE *frēon*, to love, set free. See **prī-***.] — **free′ly** *adv.* — **free′ness** *n.*

free agent *n. Sports.* A professional player who is free to sign a contract with any team. — **free agency** *n.*

free alongside ship *adv. & adj.* Without charge to the purchaser for delivery to the point of loading aboard ship.

free-as•so•ci•ate (frē′ə-sō′shē-āt′, -sē-) *intr.v.* **-at•ed, -at•ing, -ates.** To engage in free association.

free association *n.* **1.** A spontaneous, logically unconstrained and undirected association of ideas, emotions, and feelings. **2.** A psychoanalytic technique in which a patient's articulation of free associations is encouraged in order to reveal unconscious thoughts and emotions.

free•base or **free-base** (frē′bās′) — *v.* **-based, -bas•ing, -bas•es.** — *tr.* **1.** To purify (cocaine) by dissolving it in a heated solvent and separating and drying the precipitate. **2.** To use (freebase) by burning it and inhaling the fumes. — *intr.* To prepare or use freebase. — *n.* Cocaine thus purified.

free•bie also **free•bee** (frē′bē) *n. Slang.* An article or service given free. [< FREE.]

free•board (frē′bôrd′, -bōrd′) *n.* **1.** *Naut.* The distance between the water line and the uppermost full deck of a ship. **2.** The distance between the ground and the undercarriage of an automobile. [Prob. ult. partial transl. of AN *franc bord*, land claimed outside the fence of a park or forest : *franc*, free + *bord*, border.]

freeboard deck *n. Naut.* The uppermost deck that is officially considered completely watertight.

free•boot (frē′bo͞ot′) *intr.v.* **-boot•ed, -boot•ing, -boots.** To act as a freebooter. [Back-formation < FREEBOOTER.]

free•boot•er (frē′bo͞o′tər) *n.* A person who pillages and plunders, esp. a pirate. [Du. *vrijbuiter* < *vrijbuit*, plunder : *vrij*, free; see **prī-*** + *buit*, booty (< MDu. *būte*, of MLGer. orig.).]

free•born (frē′bôrn′) *adj.* **1.** Born as a free person, not as a slave or serf. **2.** Relating to or befitting a person born free.

free city *n.* A city governed as an autonomous political unit under international auspices.

freed•man (frēd′mən) *n.* A man freed from slavery.

free•dom (frē′dəm) *n.* **1.** The condition of being free of restraints. **2.** Liberty of the person from slavery, detention, or oppression. **3.a.** Political independence. **b.** Possession of civil rights; immunity from the arbitrary exercise of authority. **4.** Exemption from an unpleasant or onerous condition. **5.** The capacity to exercise choice; free will. **6.** Ease or facility of movement. **7.** Frankness or boldness; lack of modesty or reserve. **8.a.** The right to unrestricted use; full access. **b.** The right of enjoying all the privileges of membership or citizenship. [ME *fredom* < OE *frēodōm* : *frēo*, free; see FREE + *-dōm*, -dom.]

Syns: *freedom, liberty, license.* These nouns refer to the power to act, speak, or think without externally imposed restraints. *Freedom* is the most general term: *"In giving freedom to the slave, we assure freedom to the free"* (Abraham Lincoln). *Liberty* often stresses the power of free choice: *"liberty, perfect liberty, to think, feel, do just as one pleases"* (William Hazlitt). *License* sometimes denotes deliberate deviation from normally applicable rules or practices to achieve a desired effect: *poetic license.* Frequently, though, it denotes undue freedom: *"the intolerable license with which the newspapers break . . . the rules of decorum"* (Edmund Burke).

freedom march *n.* An organized protest march in support of civil rights, esp. one aimed at ending racial segregation. — **freedom marcher** *n.*

freedom of the seas *n.* **1.** The doctrine that ships of any nation may travel through international waters unhampered. **2.** The right of neutral shipping in wartime to trade at will except where blockades are established.

freedom rider *n.* One of a group of civil rights activists in the early 1960's who rode buses in the southern United States to challenge racial segregation. — **freedom ride** *n.*

freed•wom•an (frēd′wo͝om′ən) *n.* A woman freed from slavery.

free energy *n.* **1.** A thermodynamic quantity that is the difference between the internal energy of a system and the product of its absolute temperature and entropy. **2.** A thermodynamic quantity that is the difference between the enthalpy and the product of the absolute temperature and entropy of a system.

free enterprise *n.* The freedom of private businesses to operate competitively for profit with minimal government regulation. — **free′-en′ter•prise′** (frē′ĕn′tər-prīz′) *adj.*

free fall or **free-fall** (frē′fôl′) *n.* **1.** The fall of a body within the atmosphere without a drag-producing device. **2.** The ideal falling motion of a body that is subject only to the earth's gravitational field. **3.** Rapid uncontrolled decline.

free-fire zone (frē′fīr′) *n.* A battle area or combat zone without restrictions on the use of arms or explosives.

free flight *n.* Flight, as of an aircraft or a spacecraft, after termination of powered flight.

free-float•ing (frē′flō′tĭng) *adj.* **1.** Not committed or decided. **2.** Experienced without an obvious basis or cause.

free-for-all (frē′fər-ôl′) *n.* A disorderly fight, argument, or competition in which everyone present takes part.

free•form (frē′fôrm′) *adj.* **1.** Having or characterized by a usu. flowing asymmetrical shape or outline. **2.** Characterized by an unconventional or variable form. — **free′form′** *adv.*

free form *n. Ling.* A morpheme, such as *cat* or *write,* that is capable of standing alone and retaining meaning.

free•hand (frē′hănd′) *adj.* Drawn by hand without the aid of tracing or drafting devices. — **free′hand′** *adv.*

free hand *n.* Freedom to do or decide as one sees fit.

free•hand•ed (frē′hăn′dĭd) *adj.* Openhanded; generous. See Syns at **liberal.** — **free′hand′ed•ly** *adv.* — **free′hand′ed•ness** *n.*

free•heart•ed (frē′här′tĭd) *adj.* **1.** Unreserved; open. **2.** Generous; liberal. — **free′heart′ed•ly** *adv.*

free•hold (frē′hōld′) *n.* **1.** *Law.* **a.** An estate held in fee or for life. **b.** The tenure by which such an estate is held. **2.** A tenure of an office or a dignity for life. [ME *frehold,* transl. of AN *fraunc tenement* : *fraunc,* free + *tenement,* possession.] — **free′hold′er** *n.*

free•lance also **free lance** (frē′lăns′) — *n.* **1.** A person, esp. a writer or an artist, who sells his or her services to employers without a long-term commitment. **2.** An uncommitted independent, as in politics. **3.** A medieval mercenary. — *v.* **-lanced, -lanc•ing, -lanc•es.** — *intr.* To work as a freelance. — *tr.* To produce and sell as a freelance. — *adj.* Of, relating to, or working as a freelance. — **free′lanc′er** *n.*

free-liv•ing (frē′lĭv′ĭng) *adj.* **1.** Given to self-indulgence. **2.** *Biol.* **a.** Living independently of another organism. **b.** Moving independently; not sessile.

free•load (frē′lōd′) *intr.v.* **-load•ed, -load•ing, -loads.** *Slang.* To take advantage of the charity, generosity, or hospitality of others. — **free′load′er** *n.*

free love *n.* The belief in or practice of sexual relations without marriage and without formal obligations.

free lunch *n. Slang.* Something acquired without due effort or without cost.

free•man (frē′mən) *n.* **1.** A person not in slavery or serfdom. **2.** One who possesses the rights or privileges of a citizen.

free•mar•tin (frē′mär′tn) *n.* A sterile or otherwise sexually imperfect female calf, usu. born as the twin of a bull calf. [?]

free•ma•son (frē′mā′sən) *n.* **1. Freemason.** A member of the Free and Accepted Masons, an international fraternal and charitable organization with secret rites and signs. **2.** A member of a medieval guild of skilled itinerant masons.

free•ma•son•ry (frē′mā′sən-rē) *n.* **1. Freemasonry.** The institutions, precepts, and rites of the Freemasons. **2.** Spontaneous fellowship and sympathy among a number of people.

free on board *adj. & adv.* Without charge to the purchaser for delivery on board or into a carrier at a specified point or location.

free port *n.* A port or an area of a port in which imported goods can be held or processed free of customs duties before reexport.

Free•port (frē′pôrt′, -pōrt′). **1.** A city of NW Bahamas on Grand Bahama I. Pop. 25,000. **2.** A city of NW IL W of Rockford. Pop. 25,840. **3.** A village of SE NY on the S shore of Long I. Pop. 39,894.

free radical *n.* **1.** An atom or group of atoms having at least one unpaired electron. **2.** An organic compound in which some of the valence electrons are unpaired.

free rein *n.* Unlimited freedom to act or make decisions.

free ride *n. Slang.* Something acquired without the ordinary effort or cost. — **free rider** *n.*

free•sia (frē′zhə, -zhē-ə, -zē-ə) *n.* Any of several plants of the genus *Freesia,* native to southern Africa and having one-sided flower clusters. [NLat., after Friedrich Heinrich Theodor *Freese* (1795–1876), German physician.]

freesia

free silver *n.* The free coinage of silver, esp. at a fixed ratio to gold.

free soil *n.* U.S. territory in which slavery was prohibited before the Civil War.

free-soil (frē′soil′) *adj.* **1.** Prohibiting slavery. **2.a.** Opposing the extension of slavery before the U.S. Civil War. **b. Free-Soil.** Of or being a U.S. political party founded in 1848 to oppose the extension of slavery into U.S. territories and the admission of slave states into the Union.

free speech *n.* The right to express any opinion in public without censorship or restraint by the government.

free spirit *n.* One who is not restrained, as by convention.

free-spo•ken (frē′spō′kən) *adj.* Candid in expression; outspoken. — **free′-spo′ken•ness** *n.*

free•stand•ing (frē′stăn′dĭng) *adj.* Standing or operating independently of anything else.

free•stone (frē′stōn′) *n.* **1.** A stone, such as limestone, soft enough to be cut easily without shattering or splitting. **2.** A fruit, esp. a peach, that has a stone not adhering to the pulp. [ME *freston,* transl. of OFr. *franche pere,* high-grade stone.]

free•style (frē′stīl′) *n. Sports.* **1.a.** A swimming event in which the contestants may choose any stroke. **b.** The crawl. **2.** A competition, as in figure skating, in which any maneuver or movement is allowed and competitors are judged on their artistic expression, acrobatic skill, and athletic expertise. **3.** A style of wrestling in which all noninjurious holds or tactics are permitted. — **free′style′** *adv. & adj.*

free-swim•ming (frē′swĭm′ĭng) *adj.* Able to swim freely; not sessile or attached. — **free′-swim′mer** *n.*

free-swing•ing (frē′swĭng′ĭng) *adj.* Bold and uninhibited.

free•think•er (frē′thĭng′kər) *n.* One who has rejected authority and dogma, esp. in religious thinking, in favor of rational inquiry and speculation. — **free′think′ing** *adj. & n.*

free thought *n.* Thought that rejects authority and dogma, esp. in religion; freethinking.

free throw *n. Basketball.* See **foul shot.**

free-throw line (frē′thrō′) *n. Basketball.* See **foul line** 2.

Free•town (frē′toun′). The cap. of Sierra Leone, in the W part on the Atlantic Ocean; settled in 1787. Pop. 300,000.

free trade *n.* Trade between nations without protective customs tariffs. — **free trader** *n.*

free verse *n.* Verse composed of variable, usu. unrhymed lines having no fixed metrical pattern. [Transl. of Fr. *vers libre* : *vers,* verse + *libre,* free.]

free•way (frē′wā′) *n.* **1.** See **expressway. 2.** A highway without tolls.

free•wheel (frē′hwēl′, -wēl′) *intr.v.* **-wheeled, -wheel•ing, -wheels. 1.** To continue turning or spinning after disengagement from the drive mechanism. **2.** To live or move freely and sometimes aimlessly or irresponsibly. **3.** To operate independently or free of restraints.

free wheel *n.* **1.** A power-transmission device that allows the drive shaft of a motor vehicle to continue turning when its speed is greater than that of the engine shaft. **2.** A clutch in the rear-wheel hub of a bicycle that permits the wheel to turn without pedal action.

free•wheel•ing (frē′hwē′lĭng, -wē′-) *adj.* **1.a.** Free of restraints or rules in organization, methods, or procedure. **b.** Heedless of consequences; carefree. **2.** Relating to or equipped with a free wheel.

free•will (frē′wĭl′) *adj.* Done of one's own accord; voluntary.

free will *n.* **1.** The ability or discretion to choose; free choice. **2.** The power, attributed esp. to human beings, of making free choices that are unconstrained by external circumstances or by an agency such as fate or divine will. [ME *fre wil,* transl. of LLat. *liberum arbitrium.*]

free world *n.* The countries of the world that have democratic and capitalistic or moderately socialistic systems rather than communist or totalitarian systems.

freeze (frēz) *v.* **froze** (frōz), **fro•zen** (frō′zən), **freez•ing, freez•es.** — *intr.* **1.a.** To pass from the liquid to the solid state by loss of heat. **b.** To acquire a surface or coat of ice from cold. **2.** To become clogged or jammed because of the formation of ice. **3.** To be at that degree of temperature at which ice forms. **4.** To be killed or harmed by cold or frost. **5.** To be or feel uncomfortably cold. **6.** To become fixed, stuck, or attached by or as if by frost. **7.a.** To become motionless or immobile, as from surprise or attentiveness. **b.** To become unable to act or react, as from fear. **8.** To become icily silent in manner. **9.** To become rigid and inflexible; solidify. — *tr.* **1.a.** To convert into ice. **b.** To cause ice to form upon. **c.** To cause to congeal or stiffen from extreme cold. **2.** To preserve (foods,

ă pat	oi boy
ā pay	ou out
âr care	o͝o took
ä father	o͞o boot
ĕ pet	ŭ cut
ē be	ûr urge
ĭ pit	th thin
ī pie	*th* this
îr pier	hw which
ŏ pot	zh vision
ō toe	ə about, item
ô paw	

Stress marks:
′ (primary);
′ (secondary), as in dictionary (dĭk′shə-nĕr′ē)

for example) by subjecting to freezing temperatures. **3.** To damage, kill, or make inoperative by cold or by the formation of ice. **4.** To make very cold; chill. **5.** To immobilize, as with fear or shock. **6.** To chill with an icy or formal manner. **7.** To stop the motion or progress of. **8.a.** To fix (prices or wages, for example) at a given or current level. **b.** To prohibit further manufacture or use of. **c.** To prevent or restrict the exchange, withdrawal, liquidation, or granting of by governmental action. **9.a.** To photograph (a subject) in midaction so as to produce a still image. **b.** To stop (a moving film) at a particular image. **10.** To anesthetize by chilling. **11.** *Sports.* To keep possession of (a ball or puck) so as to deny an opponent the opportunity to score. — *n.* **1.a.** The act of freezing. **b.** The state of being frozen. **2.** A spell of cold weather; a frost. **3.** A restriction that forbids a quantity from rising above a given or current level. — ***phrasal verb.*** **freeze out.** To shut out or exclude, as by cold treatment. — ***idiom.*** **freeze (someone's) blood.** To affect with terror or dread; horrify. [ME *fresen* < OE *frēosan*. See **preus-***.] — **freez′a•ble** *adj.*

French curve

freeze-dry (frēz′drī′) *tr.v.* **-dried, -dry•ing, -dries.** To preserve (food, for example) by rapid freezing and drying in a high vacuum.

freeze-etch•ing (frēz′ĕch′ĭng) *n.* A method of specimen preparation for electron microscopy in which a replica is made from a sample that has been rapidly frozen and then fractured along natural planes of weakness to reveal its internal structure. — **freeze′-etched′** (-ĕcht′) *adj.*

freeze-frame or **freeze frame** (frēz′frām′) *n.* **1.** A still picture in the course of a movie or television film, made by running a series of identical frames or by stopping a reel or videotape at one desired frame. **2.** A vivid, motionless scene or image.

freez•er (frē′zər) *n.* A thermally insulated compartment, cabinet, or room in which a subfreezing temperature is maintained for the rapid freezing and storing of perishable food.

freez•ing point (frē′zĭng) *n.* **1.** The temperature at which a liquid of specified composition solidifies under a specified pressure. **2.** The temperature at which the liquid and solid phases of a substance of specified composition are in equilibrium at atmospheric pressure.

free zone *n.* An area at a port or city where goods may be received and held without the payment of duty.

F region *n.* See **F layer** 1.

Frei•burg (frī′bûrg′, -bo͝ork′). Also **Freiburg im Breis•gau** (ĭm brīs′gou′). A city of SW Germany near the Rhine R. at the edge of the Black Forest; founded 1120. Pop. 181,304.

freight (frāt) *n.* **1.** Goods carried by a vessel or vehicle, esp. by a commercial carrier; cargo. **2.** A burden; a load. **3.a.** Commercial transportation of goods. **b.** The charge for transporting goods. **4.** A railway train carrying goods only. — *tr.v.* **freight•ed, freight•ing, freights. 1.** To convey commercially as cargo. **2.** To load with goods to be transported. **3.** To load; charge. [ME *fraught, freight* < MDu. or MLGer. *vracht, vrecht*; see **ēik-***.]

freight•age (frā′tĭj) *n.* **1.** See **freight** 3. **2.** Cargo.

freight car *n.* A railroad car designed for carrying freight.

freight•er (frā′tər) *n.* **1.** A vehicle, esp. a ship, used for carrying freight. **2.** A shipper of cargo.

freight train *n.* A railroad train made up of freight cars.

frem•i•tus (frĕm′ĭ-təs) *n.*, *pl.* **fremitus.** A palpable vibration, as felt by the hand on the chest during coughing or speaking. [Lat., a murmuring < p.part. of *fremere*, to murmur.]

French door
Doorway with two French doors

Fre•mont (frē′mŏnt′). **1.** A city of W CA on San Francisco Bay SE of Oakland. Pop. 173,339. **2.** A city of E-central NE on the Platte R. WNW of Omaha. Pop. 23,680. **3.** A city of N OH SE of Toledo. Pop. 17,648.

Fré•mont (frē′mŏnt′), **John Charles.** 1813–90. Amer. soldier and politician who explored much of the American West.

fre•na (frē′nə) *n. Anat.* Pl. of **frenum.**

french (frĕnch) *tr.v.* **frenched, french•ing, french•es. 1.** To cut (green beans, for example) into thin strips before cooking. **2.** To trim fat or bone from (a chop, for example). [< FRENCH.]

French (frĕnch) *adj.* **1.** Of, relating to, or characteristic of France or its people or culture. **2.** Of or relating to the French language. — *n.* **1.** The Romance language of France, parts of Switzerland and Belgium, and other countries formerly under French influence or control. **2.** The people of France. [ME < OE *frencisc*, Frankish < *Franca*, Frank. See FRANK.]

French, Daniel Chester. 1850–1931. Amer. sculptor whose works include the seated marble figure of Abraham Lincoln at the Lincoln Memorial in Washington DC.

French horn

French bulldog *n.* Any of a breed of small muscular dogs developed in France from toy English bulldogs and native breeds.

French Cam•e•roons (kăm′ə-ro͞onz′). A region and former French protectorate of W-central Africa.

French-Ca•na•di•an also **French Ca•na•di•an** (frĕnch′kə-nā′dē-ən) *n.* A Canadian of French descent. — **French′-Ca•na′di•an** *adj.*

French chalk *n.* Chalk made of a soft white variety of talc, used for marking fabrics and for removing grease spots.

French chop *n.* A rib chop with the meat and fat trimmed from the end of the rib.

French cuff *n.* A wide cuff for a shirt sleeve that is folded back and fastened with a cuff link.

French curve *n.* A flat drafting instrument with curved edges and scroll-shaped cutouts, used as a guide in drawing curves when constructing graphs or making engineering drawings.

French door *n.* A door, usu. one of a pair, of light construction with glass panes extending for most of its length.

French dressing *n.* **1.** A salad dressing of oil, vinegar, and seasonings. **2.** A commercially prepared creamy salad dressing that is usu. pinkish in color and often sweet.

French E•qua•to•ri•al Af•ri•ca (ē′kwə-tôr′ē-əl ăf′rĭ-kə, -tōr′-, ĕk′wə-). Formerly **French Con•go** (kŏng′gō). A former federation of W-central Africa (1910–58) comprising present-day Chad, Gabon, Congo, and Central African Republic.

French fry *n.* A thin strip of potato fried in deep fat. Often used in the plural.

French-fry (frĕnch′frī′) *tr.v.* **-fried, -fry•ing, -fries.** To fry (potato strips, for example) in deep fat.

French Gui•a•na (gē-ăn′ə, -ä′nə, gī-). A French overseas department of NE South America on the Atlantic Ocean; settled by the French after 1604. Cap. Cayenne. Pop. 72,012.

French heel *n.* A curved, moderately high heel used on women's shoes.

French horn *n. Mus.* A valved brass wind instrument that produces a mellow tone from a long, narrow tube that is coiled in a circle before ending in a flaring bell.

French•i•fy (frĕn′chə-fī′) *tr.v.* **-fied, -fy•ing, -fies.** To make French in character or quality. — **French′i•fi•ca′tion** (-fĭ-kā′shən) *n.*

French kiss *n. Slang.* A kiss in which the tongue enters the partner's mouth.

French knot *n.* A decorative embroidery stitch made by looping the thread two or more times around the needle, which is then inserted into the fabric.

French leave *n.* An informal, unannounced, or abrupt departure.

French•man (frĕnch′mən) *n.* A man who is a native or inhabitant of France.

French pastry *n.* Any of a wide variety of rich and elaborate pastries prepared in individual portions.

French Pol•y•ne•sia (pŏl′ə-nē′zhə, -shə). A French overseas island territory in the S-central Pacific; organized as a territory in 1903. Cap. Papeete. Pop. 166,753.

French provincial *n.* A style of architecture or furniture characteristic of the provinces in 17th- and 18th-century France.

French seam *n.* A seam stitched first on the right side and then turned in and stitched on the wrong side so that the raw edges are enclosed in the seam.

French telephone *n.* A telephone with the receiver and transmitter contained in a single unit.

French toast *n.* Sliced bread soaked in a batter of milk and egg and lightly fried.

French West Af•ri•ca (ăf′rĭ-kə). A former federation of W Africa (1895–1959) comprising present-day Benin, Guinea, Ivory Coast, Mali, Mauritania, Niger, Senegal, and Burkina Faso.

French West In•dies (ĭn′dēz). The French overseas departments of Guadeloupe and Martinique in the Lesser Antilles.

French window *n.* **1.** A pair or one of a pair of floor-length windows that open in the middle. **2.** A casement window.

French•wom•an (frĕnch′wo͝om′ən) *n.* A woman who is a native or inhabitant of France.

Fre•neau (frĭ-nō′), **Philip Morin.** 1752–1832. Amer. poet noted for his satirical attacks on the British.

fre•net•ic or **phre•net•ic** (frə-nĕt′ĭk) also **fre•net•i•cal** or **phre•net•i•cal** (-ĭ-kəl) *adj.* Wildly excited or active; frantic; frenzied. [ME *frenetik*, ult. < Gk. *phrenitikos* < *phrenitis*, brain disease < *phrēn*, mind. See **g^{w}hren-***.] — **fre•net′i•cal•ly** *adv.* — **fre•net′i•cism** (-ĭ-sĭz′əm) *n.*

fren•u•lum (frĕn′yə-ləm) *n.*, *pl.* **-la** (-lə). **1.** *Anat.* A small frenum. **2.** *Entomology.* A bristly structure on the hind wings of certain moths and butterflies that holds the forewings and hind wings together during flight. [NLat., dim. of Lat. *frēnum*, bridle. See FRENUM.]

fre•num (frē′nəm) *n.*, *pl.* **-nums** or **-na** (-nə). *Anat.* A membranous fold of skin or mucous membrane that supports or restricts the movement of a part or organ. [Lat. *frēnum*, bridle < *frendere*, to grind. See **ghrendh-***.]

fren•zied (frĕn′zēd) *adj.* Affected with or marked by frenzy; frantic: *a frenzied rush for the exits.* — **fren′zied•ly** *adv.*

fren•zy (frĕn′zē) *n.*, *pl.* **-zies. 1.** A state of violent mental agitation or wild excitement. **2.** Temporary madness or delirium. **3.** A mania; a craze. — *tr.v.* **-zied, -zy•ing, -zies.** To drive into a frenzy. [ME *frenesie* < OFr. < Med.Lat. *phrenēsia* < Lat. *phrenēsis*, back-formation < *phrenēticus*, delirious. See FRENETIC.]

Fre•on (frē′ŏn′). A trademark used for a variety of nonflammable gaseous or liquid fluorinated hydrocarbons used primarily in refrigeration and as aerosol propellants.

freq. *abbr.* **1.** Frequency. **2.** *Gram.* Frequentative. **3.** Frequently.

fre•quence (frē′kwəns) *n.* Frequency. [ME, multitude < OFr. < Lat. *frequentia.* See FREQUENCY.]

fre•quen•cy (frē′kwən-sē) *n., pl.* **-cies. 1.** The property or condition of occurring at frequent intervals. **2.** *Math. & Phys.* The number of times a specified phenomenon occurs within a specified interval, as: **a.** The number of repetitions of a complete sequence of values of a periodic function per unit variation of an independent variable. **b.** The number of complete cycles of a periodic process occurring per unit time. **3.** *Statistics.* **a.** The number of times a specified measurement occurs in a sample. **b.** The ratio of the number of times an event occurs in a series of trials of a chance experiment to the total number of trials. [Lat. *frequentia,* multitude < *frequēns, frequent-,* crowded, numerous, frequent.]

frequency distribution *n. Statistics.* A set of intervals, usu. adjacent and of equal width, into which the range of a statistical distribution is divided, each associated with a frequency indicating the number of measurements in that interval.

frequency modulation *n.* The encoding of a carrier wave by variation of its frequency in accordance with an input signal.

fre•quent (frē′kwənt) *adj.* Occurring or appearing quite often or at close intervals. —*tr.v.* (*also* frē-kwĕnt′) **-quent•ed, -quent•ing, -quents.** To pay frequent visits to; be in or at often. [ME, ample, profuse < OFr. < Lat. *frequēns, frequent-,* crowded, numerous, frequent.] —**fre′quen•ta′tion** *n.* —**fre•quent′er** (-kwĕn′tər) *n.* —**fre′quent•ness** *n.*

fre•quen•ta•tive (frē-kwĕn′tə-tĭv) *Gram.* —*adj.* Expressing repeated action. —*n.* A frequentative verb or verb form.

fre•quent•ly (frē′kwənt-lē) *adv.* At frequent intervals; often.

fres•co (frĕs′kō) *n., pl.* **-coes** or **-cos. 1.** The art of painting on fresh, moist plaster with pigments dissolved in water. **2.** A painting executed in this way. —*tr.v.* **-coed, -co•ing, -coes.** To paint in this way. [Ital., fresh (plaster), of Gmc. orig.] —**fres′co•er, fres′co•ist** *n.*

fresh (frĕsh) *adj.* **fresh•er, fresh•est. 1.** New to one's experience; not encountered before. **2.** Novel; different. See Syns at **new. 3.** Recently made, produced, or harvested; not stale or spoiled. **4.** Not preserved, as by canning or freezing. **5.** Not saline or salty. **6.** Not yet used or soiled; clean. **7.** Free from impurity or pollution; pure. **8.** Additional; new. **9.** Bright and clear; not dull or faded. **10.** Having the glowing, unspoiled appearance of youth. **11.** Untried; inexperienced. **12.** Having just arrived; straight. **13.** Revived or reinvigorated; refreshed. **14.** Fairly strong; brisk. **15.** *Informal.* Bold and saucy; impudent. **16.** Having recently calved and therefore with milk. Used of a cow. —*adv.* Recently; newly. —*n.* **1.** The early part. **2.** A freshet. [ME < OE *fersc,* pure, not salty, and < OFr. *freis* (fem. *fresche*) new, of Gmc. orig.] —**fresh′ly** *adv.* —**fresh′ness** *n.*

fresh•en (frĕsh′ən) *v.* **-ened, -en•ing, -ens.** —*intr.* **1.** To become fresh, as in vigor or appearance. **2.** To become brisk; increase. Used of the wind. **3.** To lose saltiness. **4.** To calve and begin to produce milk. Used of a cow. —*tr.* **1.** To make fresh. **2.** To add to or strengthen (a drink). —**fresh′en•er** *n.*

fresh•et (frĕsh′ĭt) *n.* **1.** A sudden overflow of a stream resulting from a heavy rain or a thaw. **2.** A stream of fresh water that empties into a body of salt water.

fresh•man (frĕsh′mən) *n.* **1.** A student in the first-year class of a high school, college, or university. **2.** A beginner; a novice. See Usage Note at **man.**

fresh•wa•ter (frĕsh′wô′tər, -wŏt′ər) *adj.* **1.** Of, relating to, living in, or consisting of water that is not salty: *freshwater fish.* **2.** Situated away from the sea; inland. **3.** *Naut.* Accustomed to sailing on inland waters only: *a freshwater sailor.*

Fres•nel (frā-nĕl′), **Augustin Jean.** 1788–1827. French physicist who investigated polarized light.

Fres•nel lens (frə-nĕl′) *n.* A thin optical lens consisting of concentric rings of segmental lenses, used in spotlights, beacons, and headlights. [After Augustin Jean FRESNEL.]

Fres•no (frĕz′nō). A city of central CA SSE of Sacramento in the San Joaquin Valley. Pop. 354,202.

fret¹ (frĕt) *v.* **fret•ted, fret•ting, frets.** —*tr.* **1.** To cause to be uneasy; vex. **2.a.** To gnaw or wear away; erode. **b.** To produce a hole or worn spot in; corrode. **3.** To form (a passage or channel) by erosion. **4.** To disturb the surface of (water or a stream); agitate. —*intr.* **1.** To be vexed or troubled; worry. See Syns at **brood. 2.** To be worn or eaten away; become corroded. **3.** To move agitatedly. **4.** To gnaw with the teeth in the manner of a rodent. —*n.* **1.** The act or an instance of fretting. **2.** A hole or worn spot made by abrasion or erosion. **3.** Irritation of mind; agitation. [ME *freten* < OE *fretan,* to devour. See **ed-***.]

fret² (frĕt) *Mus.* —*n.* One of the ridges set across the fingerboard of a stringed instrument, such as a guitar. —*tr.v.* **fret•ted, fret•ting, frets. 1.** To provide with frets. **2.** To press (the strings of an instrument) against the frets. [?]

fret³ (frĕt) *n.* **1.** An ornamental design consisting of repeated and symmetrical figures, often in relief, contained within a band or border. **2.** A headdress, worn by women of the Middle Ages, consisting of interlaced wire. —*tr.v.* **fret•ted, fret•ting, frets.** To provide with such a design or headdress. [ME, interlaced work < OFr. *frete.*]

fret•ful (frĕt′fəl) *adj.* **1.** Inclined to be vexed or troubled; peevish. **2.** Marked by worry and distress; troublesome. —**fret′ful•ly** *adv.* —**fret′ful•ness** *n.*

fret saw *n.* A long narrow-bladed saw with fine teeth, used in making curved cuts in thin wood or metal.

fret•work (frĕt′wûrk′) *n.* Ornamental work consisting of three-dimensional frets; geometric openwork.

Freud (froid), **Anna.** 1895–1982. Austrian-born British psychoanalyst who applied psychoanalysis to child therapy.

Freud, Sigmund. 1856–1939. Austrian founder of psychoanalysis. —**Freud′i•an** *adj. & n.* —**Freud′i•an•ism** *n.*

Freudian slip *n.* A verbal mistake that is thought to reveal an unconscious belief, thought, or emotion.

Freund's adjuvant (froindz) *n.* A substance consisting of killed microorganisms, such as mycobacteria, in an oil and water emulsion that is administered to induce and enhance the formation of antibodies. [After Jules T. *Freund* (1890–1960), Hungarian-born Amer. immunologist.]

Frey (frā) also **Freyr** (frâr) *n. Myth.* The Norse god who dispenses peace and prosperity; the brother of Freya.

Frey•a also **Frey•ja** (frā′ə) *n. Myth.* The Norse goddess of love and beauty; the sister of Frey.

F.R.G. or **FRG** *abbr.* Federal Republic of Germany.

Fri. *abbr.* Friday.

fri•a•ble (frī′ə-bəl) *adj.* Readily crumbled; brittle. [Lat. *friābilis* < *friāre,* to crumble.] —**fri′a•bil′i•ty, fri′a•ble•ness** *n.*

fri•ar (frī′ər) *n.* A member of a usu. mendicant Roman Catholic order. [ME *frere* < OFr. < Lat. *frāter,* brother. See **bhrāter-***.] —**fri′ar•ly** *adj.*

fri•ar's lantern (frī′ərz) *n.* See **ignis fatuus** 1.

fri•ar•y (frī′ə-rē) *n., pl.* **-ies.** A monastery of friars.

frib•ble (frĭb′əl) *v.* **-bled, -bling, -bles.** —*tr.* To waste (time, for example); fritter (something) away. —*intr.* To waste time; trifle. —*n.* **1.** A frivolity; a trifle. **2.** A frivolous person. [?] —**frib′bler** *n.*

fric•an•deau (frĭk′ən-dō′) *n.* A cut of veal that has been larded and braised. [Fr. < *fricasser,* to fricassee. See FRICASSEE.]

fric•as•see (frĭk′ə-sē′, frĭk′ə-sē′) *n.* Poultry or meat cut into pieces and stewed in gravy. —*tr.v.* **-seed, -see•ing, -sees.** To prepare (poultry or meat) as a fricassee. [Fr. *fricassée* < OFr. < fem. p.part. of *fricasser,* to fricassee : prob. *frire,* to fry (< Lat. *frīgere,* to roast, fry) + *casser,* to break, crack (< Lat. *quassāre,* to shake, shatter; see SQUASH²) or VLat. **coāctiāre,* to press together (< Lat. *coāctus,* p.part. of *cōgere,* to drive or bring together; see COGENT).]

fric•a•tive (frĭk′ə-tĭv) *Ling.* —*n.* A consonant, such as *f* or *s* in English, produced by the forcing of breath through a constricted passage. —*adj.* Of, relating to, or being a fricative. [NLat. *fricātīvus* < Lat. *fricātus,* p.part. of *fricāre,* to rub.]

Frick (frĭk), **Henry Clay.** 1849–1919. Amer. industrialist who bequeathed his art collection to New York City.

fric•tion (frĭk′shən) *n.* **1.** The rubbing of one object or surface against another. **2.** Conflict, as between persons having dissimilar ideas or interests; clash. **3.** *Phys.* A force that resists the relative motion or tendency to such motion of two bodies in contact. [Lat. *frictiō, frictiōn-* < *frictus,* p.part. of *fricāre,* to rub.] —**fric′tion•al** *adj.* —**fric′tion•al•ly** *adv.*

friction match *n.* A match that ignites when struck on an abrasive surface.

friction tape *n.* A moisture-resistant adhesive tape, usu. made of cloth, used chiefly to insulate electrical conductors.

Fri•day (frī′dē, -dā′) *n.* The sixth day of the week. [ME *Fridai* < OE *Frīgedæg.* See **prī-***.]

fridge (frĭj) *n. Informal.* A refrigerator.

Frid•ley (frĭd′lē). A city of E MN, a suburb of Minneapolis on the Mississippi R. Pop. 28,335.

fried (frīd) *v.* P.t. and p.part. of **fry¹.**

Fried (frēd, frēt), **Alfred Hermann.** 1864–1921. Austrian pacifist who shared the 1911 Nobel Peace Prize.

Frie•dan (frē-dăn′), **Betty Naomi.** b. 1921. Amer. feminist who wrote *The Feminine Mystique* (1963).

Fried•man (frēd′mən), **Milton.** b. 1912. Amer. economist who won a 1976 Nobel Prize.

friend (frĕnd) *n.* **1.** A person whom one knows, likes, and trusts. **2.** A person whom one knows; an acquaintance. **3.** A person with whom one is allied in a struggle or cause; a comrade. **4.** One who supports, sympathizes with, or patronizes a group, cause, or movement. **5. Friend.** A member of the Society of Friends; a Quaker. —*tr.v.* **friend•ed, friend•ing, friends.** *Archaic.* To befriend. [ME < OE *frēond.* See **prī-***.] —**friend′less** *adj.* —**friend′less•ness** *n.* —**friend′ship′** *n.*

friend•ly (frĕnd′lē) *adj.* **-li•er, -li•est. 1.** Of, relating to, or befitting a friend. **2.** Favorably disposed; not antagonistic. **3.** Warm; comforting. **4.a.** *Comp. Sci.* User-friendly. **b.** *Informal.* Easy to understand or use for a specified agent. —*adv.* In the manner of a friend; amicably. —*n., pl.* **-lies.** *Informal.* One fighting on or favorable to one's own side. —**friend′li•ly** *adv.* —**friend′li•ness** *n.*

Friend•ly Islands (frĕnd′lē). See **Tonga.**

fri•er (frī′ər) *n.* Var. of **fryer.**

fries (frīz) *v.* Third pers. sing. pr.t. of **fry¹.** —*n.* Pl. of **fry¹.**

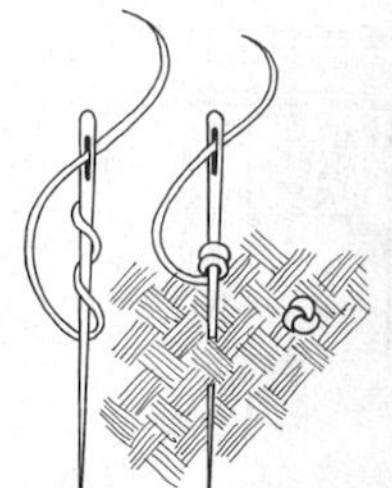

French knot

ᒥᒥᒥᒥ

fret³

Sigmund Freud

ă pat	oi boy
ā pay	ou out
âr care	ŏŏ took
ä father	ōō boot
ĕ pet	ŭ cut
ē be	ûr urge
ĭ pit	th thin
ī pie	*th* this
îr pier	hw which
ŏ pot	zh vision
ō toe	ə about, item
ô paw	

Stress marks:
′ (primary);
′ (secondary), as in
dictionary (dĭk′shə-nĕr′ē)

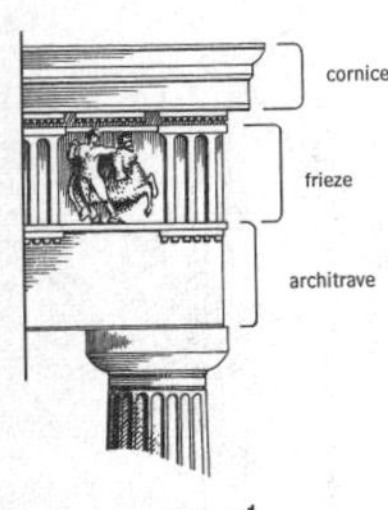

frieze[1]

frigate
Top: Modern U.S. Navy frigate
Bottom: Painting of the U.S.S. *Constitution,* also called "Old Ironsides"

fringe

Frie•sian (frē′zhən) *n.* Var. of **Frisian.**

Fries•land (frēz′lənd, -lănd′, frēs′-). A region of N Europe on the North Sea between the Scheldt and Weser rivers; conquered by the Franks in the 8th cent.

frieze[1] (frēz) *n. Archit.* **1.** A plain or decorated horizontal part of an entablature between the architrave and cornice. **2.** A decorative horizontal band, as along the upper part of a wall. [Fr. *frise* < Med.Lat. *frisium, frigium,* embroidery < Lat. *Phrygium (opus),* Phrygian (work) < PHRYGIA.]

frieze[2] (frēz) *n.* **1.** A coarse shaggy woolen cloth with an uncut nap. **2.** A dense low-pile surface, as in carpeting, resembling such cloth. [ME *frise* < OFr. < Med.Lat. *(pannī) frīsiī,* woolen garments < Lat. *Frīsiī,* the Frisians. See FRISIAN.]

frig (frĭg) *v.* **frigged, frig•ging, frigs.** — *tr.* To have sexual intercourse with. — *intr.* To have sexual intercourse. [ME, to quiver, poss. < OFr. *friquer,* to rub < Lat. *fricāre.*]

frig•ate (frĭg′ĭt) *n.* **1.** A U.S. warship larger than a destroyer and smaller than a cruiser, used primarily for escort duty. **2.** A high-speed medium-sized sailing war vessel of the 17th, 18th, and 19th centuries. [Fr. *frégate* < Ital. *fregata.*]

frigate bird *n.* Any of various tropical sea birds of the family Fregatidae that have long wings and dark plumage and characteristically snatch food from other birds in flight.

Frigg (frĭg) also **Frig•ga** (frĭg′ə) *n. Myth.* The Norse goddess of the heavens and wife of Odin. [ON. See **prī-***.]

fright (frīt) *n.* **1.** Sudden, intense fear; alarm. See Syns at **fear. 2.** *Informal.* Something extremely unsightly, alarming, or strange: *You look a fright.* — *tr.v.* **fright•ed, fright•ing, frights.** *Archaic.* To frighten. [ME < OE *fyrhto, fryhto.* V. < ME *frighten,* to frighten, be afraid < OE *fyrhtan.*]

fright•en (frīt′n) *v.* **-ened, -en•ing, -ens.** — *tr.* **1.** To fill with fear; alarm. **2.** To drive or force by arousing fear: *The suspect was frightened into confessing.* — *intr.* To become afraid. — **fright′en•er** *n.* — **fright′en•ing•ly** *adv.*

fright•ful (frīt′fəl) *adj.* **1.** Causing disgust or shock; horrifying. **2.** Causing fright; terrifying. **3.** *Informal.* **a.** Excessive; extreme: *a frightful liar.* **b.** Disagreeable; distressing: *frightful weather.* — **fright′ful•ly** *adv.* — **fright′ful•ness** *n.*

fright wig *n.* A wig with hair, esp. long or frizzy hair, standing up from the surface.

frig•id (frĭj′ĭd) *adj.* **1.** Extremely cold. See Syns at **cold. 2.** Lacking warmth of feeling. **3.** Stiff and formal in manner: *a frigid refusal to a request.* **4.** Persistently averse to sexual intercourse. [Lat. *frīgidus,* cold < *frīgus,* the cold.] — **fri•gid′i•ty** (frĭ-jĭd′ĭ-tē), **frig′id•ness** *n.* — **frig′id•ly** *adv.*

Frig•i•daire (frĭj′ĭ-dâr′). A trademark used for electric refrigerators and other household appliances.

Frig•id Zone (frĭj′ĭd). Either of two extreme latitude zones of the earth, the **North Frigid Zone,** between the North Pole and the Arctic Circle, or the **South Frigid Zone,** between the South Pole and the Antarctic Circle.

frig•o•rif•ic (frĭg′ə-rĭf′ĭk) also **frig•o•rif•i•cal** (-ĭ-kəl) *adj.* Causing coldness; chilling. [Lat. *frīgorificus* : *frīgus, frīgor-,* the cold + *-ficus,* -fic.]

fri•jol (frē-hōl′, frē′hōl′) also **fri•jo•le** (frē-hō′lē) *n., pl.* **fri•jo•les** (frē-hō′lēz, frē′hō′-). *Southwestern U.S.* A bean cultivated and used for food. [Sp., var. of *fréjol* < OSp. *frisol* < Catalan *fesol* < Lat. *phaseolus,* dim. of *phasēlus,* a type of legume < Gk. *phasēlos.*]

frill (frĭl) *n.* **1.** A ruffled, gathered, or pleated border or projection, such as a fabric edge used to trim clothing. **2.** A ruff of hair or feathers about the neck of an animal or a bird. **3.** A wrinkling of the edge of a photographic film. **4.** *Informal.* Something that is desirable but not a necessity; a luxury. — *v.* **frilled, frill•ing, frills.** — *tr.* **1.** To make into a ruffle or frill. **2.** To add a ruffle or frill to. — *intr.* To become wrinkled along the edge. [?] — **fril′li•ness** *n.* — **frill′y** *adj.*

frilled lizard (frĭld) *n.* An Australian lizard *(Chlamydosaurus kingi)* having a membrane that can be extended from the neck when the mouth is opened.

Friml (frĭm′əl), **Rudolf.** 1879–1972. Czech-born Amer. composer whose works include *The Vagabond King* (1925).

fringe (frĭnj) *n.* **1.** A decorative border or edging of hanging threads, cords, or strips, often attached to a separate band. **2.** Something that resembles such a border or edging. **3.** A marginal, peripheral, or secondary part. **4.** Those members of a group or political party holding extreme views. **5.** Any of the light or dark bands produced by the diffraction or interference of light. **6.** A fringe benefit. — *tr.v.* **fringed, fring•ing, fring•es. 1.** To decorate with or as if with a fringe. **2.** To serve as a fringe to. [ME *frenge* < OFr. < VLat. **frimbia,* alteration of LLat. *fimbria.* See FIMBRIA.] — **fring′y** *adj.*

fringe area *n.* A zone just outside of the range of a broadcasting station in which signals are weakened and distorted.

fringe benefit *n.* An employment benefit given in addition to one's wages or salary.

fringe tree *n.* A shrub or small tree *(Chionanthus virginicus)* of the southeast United States having drooping clusters of white flowers and dark blue fruit.

fring•ing reef (frĭn′jĭng) *n.* A coral reef formed close to a shoreline.

frip•per•y (frĭp′ə-rē) *n., pl.* **-ies. 1.** Pretentious showy finery. **2.** Pretentious elegance; ostentation. **3.** Something trivial or nonessential. [Fr. *friperie* < OFr. *freperie,* old clothes < *felpe, frepe* < Med.Lat. *faluppa,* worthless material.]

Fris. *abbr.* Frisian.

Fris•bee (frĭz′bē). A trademark used for a plastic disk-shaped toy that players throw and catch.

fri•sé (frē-zā′) *n.* See **frieze[2].** [Fr. < p.part. of *friser,* to curl. See FRIZZ[1].]

fri•sée (frĭ-zā′) *n.* See **endive** 1. [Fr. < fem. p.part. of *friser,* to curl. See FRIZZ[1].]

fri•sette also **fri•zette** (frĭ-zĕt′) *n.* A fringe of curled, often artificial hair, usu. worn on the forehead by a woman. [Fr. *frisette* < *friser,* to curl. See FRIZZ[1].]

fri•seur (frē-zûr′, -zœr′) *n.* A hairdresser; a coiffeur. [Fr. < *friser,* to curl. See FRIZZ[1].]

Fri•sian (frĭzh′ən, frē′zhən) also **Frie•sian** (frē′zhən) *n.* **1.** A native or inhabitant of the Frisian Islands or Friesland. **2.** The West Germanic language of the Frisians. [< Lat. *Frīsiī,* the Frisians, of Gmc. orig.] — **Fri′sian** *adj.*

Frisian Islands. A chain of islands in the North Sea off the coast of the Netherlands, Germany, and Denmark. The **West Frisian Islands** belong to the Netherlands; the **East Frisian Islands** and most of the **North Frisian Islands** are part of Germany; the other North Frisians are Danish.

frisk (frĭsk) *v.* **frisked, frisk•ing, frisks.** — *intr.* To move about briskly and playfully; frolic. — *tr.* To search (a person) for something concealed by passing the hands quickly over clothes or through pockets. — *n.* **1.** An energetic playful movement; a gambol. **2.** The act of frisking. [< ME *frisk,* lively < OFr. *frisque,* of Gmc. orig.] — **frisk′er** *n.*

frisk•y (frĭs′kē) *adj.* **-i•er, -i•est.** Energetic, lively, and playful: *a frisky kitten.* — **frisk′i•ly** *adv.* — **frisk′i•ness** *n.*

fris•son (frē-sōN′) *n., pl.* **-sons** (-sōNz′, -sōN′). A moment of intense excitement; a shudder. [Fr. < OFr. *friçons,* pl. of *friçon,* a trembling < VLat. **frīctiō, *frīctiōn-* < Lat. *frīgēre,* to be cold.]

frit (frĭt) *n.* **1.** The fused or partially fused materials used in making glass. **2.** A vitreous substance used in making porcelain, glazes, or enamels. — *tr.v.* **frit•ted, frit•ting, frits.** To make into frit. [Ital. *fritta* < fem. p.part. of *friggere,* to fry < Lat. *frīgere,* to roast, fry.]

frit fly *n.* Any of several flies of the family Chloropidae, esp. *Oscinella frit,* with larvae destructive to cereal plants. [?]

frith (frĭth) *n. Scots.* A firth. [Alteration of FIRTH.]

frit•il•lar•y (frĭt′l-ĕr′ē) *n., pl.* **-ies. 1.** Any of various bulbous plants of the genus *Fritillaria,* having nodding, often spotted or checkered flowers. **2.** Any of various butterflies of the family Nymphalidae, having brownish wings marked with black or silvery spots on the underside. [NLat. *Fritillāria,* genus name < Lat. *fritillus,* dice box.]

frit•ta•ta (frĭ-tä′tə, frē-tä′tə) *n.* An open-faced omelet, often cooked with meat, cheese, or vegetables. [Ital. < *fritto,* p.part. of *friggere,* to fry. See FRIT.]

frit•ter[1] (frĭt′ər) *tr.v.* **-tered, -ter•ing, -ters. 1.** To reduce or squander little by little. **2.** To break, tear, or cut into bits; shred. [Prob. < *fritter,* fragment, prob. alteration of *fitters* < *fitter,* to break into small pieces.]

frit•ter[2] (frĭt′ər) *n.* A small cake made of batter, often containing fruit, vegetables, or fish, sautéed or deep-fried. [ME *friture* < OFr. < LLat. *frīctūra* < Lat. *frīctus,* p.part. of *frīgere,* to roast, fry.]

fritz (frĭts) *n. Informal.* A condition in which something does not work properly: *Our TV is on the fritz.* [?]

Fri•u•li (frē-ŏŏ′lē, frē-ōō′lē). A historical region and former duchy of Italy in present-day NE Italy and W Slovenia.

Fri•u•li-Ve•ne•zia Giu•lia (frē′ə-lē′və-nĕt′sē-ə jōōl′yə, frē-ōō′lē-vĕ-nĕt′syä). A region of NE Italy bounded by Austria in the N and Slovenia in the E; formed in 1947.

friv•ol (frĭv′əl) *intr.v.* **-oled, -ol•ing, -ols** or **-olled, -ol•ling, -ols.** To behave frivolously. — **friv′ol•er** *n.*

fri•vol•i•ty (frĭ-vŏl′ĭ-tē) *n., pl.* **-ties. 1.** The quality or condition of being frivolous. **2.** A frivolous act or thing.

friv•o•lous (frĭv′ə-ləs) *adj.* **1.** Unworthy of serious attention; trivial. **2.** Inappropriately silly: *a frivolous purchase.* [ME, prob. < Lat. *frīvolus,* of little value, prob. < *friāre,* to crumble.] — **friv′o•lous•ly** *adv.* — **friv′o•lous•ness** *n.*

fri•zette (frĭ-zĕt′) *n.* Var. of **frisette.**

frizz[1] (frĭz) *tr. & intr.v.* **frizzed, frizz•ing, frizz•es.** To form or be formed into small tight curls or tufts. — *n.* **1.** The condition of being frizzed. **2.** A small tight curl or tuft. [Alteration (influenced by FRIZZLE[2]) of Fr. *friser* < OFr., poss. < *frire, fris-,* to fry < Lat. *frīgere,* to roast, fry.] — **frizz′er** *n.*

frizz[2] (frĭz) *v.* **frizzed, frizz•ing, frizz•es.** — *tr.* To fry or burn with a sizzling noise. — *intr.* To make a sizzling noise while frying or searing. [Poss. back-formation < FRIZZLE[1].]

friz•zle[1] (frĭz′əl) *v.* **-zled, -zling, -zles.** — *tr.* **1.** To fry (something) until crisp and curled: *frizzled the bacon.* **2.** To scorch or sear with heat. — *intr.* To fry or sear with a sizzling noise. [Poss. blend of FRY[1] and SIZZLE.]

friz•zle[2] (frĭz′əl) *tr. & intr.v.* **-zled, -zling, -zles.** To form or cause to be formed into small tight curls; frizz. — *n.* A small tight curl. [?]

friz•zly (frĭz′lē) *adj.* **-zli•er, -zli•est.** Tightly curled.
friz•zy (frĭz′ē) *adj.* **-zi•er, -zi•est.** Tightly curled; frizzly. — **friz′zi•ly** *adv.* — **friz′zi•ness** *n.*
fro (frō) *adv.* Away; back: *moving to and fro.* —*prep. Scots.* From. [ME, prob. < ON *frā*. See **per**[1]*.]
Fro•bish•er (frō′bĭ-shər, frŏb′ĭ-), Sir **Martin.** 1535?–94. English explorer who voyaged to the Canadian Arctic (1576, 1577, and 1578) in search of the Northwest Passage.
Frobisher Bay. An arm of the Atlantic Ocean extending into SE Baffin I. in Northwest Terrs., Canada.
frock (frŏk) *n.* **1.** A woman's dress. **2.** A long loose outer garment, as that worn by artists; a smock. **3.** A woolen garment formerly worn by sailors; a jersey. **4.** A robe worn by monks, friars, and other clerics; a habit. —*tr.v.* **frocked, frock•ing, frocks. 1.** To clothe in a frock. **2.** To invest with clerical office. [ME *frok*, a monk's habit < OFr. *froc* < Med.Lat. *froccus*, of Gmc. orig.]
frock coat *n.* A man's dress coat or suit coat with knee-length skirts.
froe also **frow** (frō) *n.* A cleaving tool having a heavy blade set at right angles to the handle. [< *frower*, poss. < FROWARD.]
Froe•bel also **Frö•bel** (frœ′bəl), **Friedrich Wilhelm August.** 1782–1852. German educator who established the first kindergarten (1837).
frog (frôg, frŏg) *n.* **1.** Any of numerous tailless amphibians of the order Anura, characteristically having a smooth moist skin, webbed feet, and long hind legs adapted for leaping. **2.** A wedge-shaped horny prominence in the sole of a horse's hoof. **3.** A loop fastened to a belt to hold a tool or weapon. **4.** An ornamental looped braid or cord with a button or knot for fastening the front of a garment. **5.** A device on intersecting railroad tracks that permits wheels to cross the junction. **6.** A spiked or perforated device used to support stems in a flower arrangement. **7.** *Informal.* Hoarseness or phlegm in the throat. **8.** *Offensive Slang.* Used as a disparaging term for a French person. [ME *frogge* < OE *frogga*.]
frog•eye (frôg′ī′, frŏg′ī′) *n.* A plant disease caused by fungi and characterized by rounded spots on the leaves.
frog•fish (frôg′fĭsh′, frŏg′-) *n., pl.* **frogfish** or **-fish•es.** Any of various bottom-dwelling fishes of the family Antennariidae, with a globose body and pectoral fins used for grasping.
frog•hop•per (frôg′hŏp′ər, frŏg′-) *n.* See **spittlebug.**
frog kick *n. Sports.* A swimming kick used in the breaststroke in which the knees are drawn up close to the hips and the feet are thrust outward and then drawn together.
frog•man (frôg′măn′, -mən, frŏg′-) *n.* A swimmer provided with breathing apparatus to execute underwater maneuvers.
frog spit *n.* **1.** A foamlike mat of small aquatic plants, such as green algae, on the surface of a pond. **2.** See **cuckoo spit.**
Frois•sart (froi′särt′, frwä-sär′), **Jean.** 1333?–1405? French historian noted for his chronicles of the Hundred Years' War.
frol•ic (frŏl′ĭk) *n.* **1.** Gaiety; merriment: *fun and frolic.* **2.** A gay, carefree time. **3.** A playful antic. —*intr.v.* **-icked, -ick•ing, -ics. 1.** To behave playfully and uninhibitedly; romp. **2.** To engage in merrymaking, joking, or teasing. —*adj. Archaic.* Merry. [< Du. *vrolijk*, merry < MDu. *vrolijc* : *vro*, happy + *-lijc*, -like; see **līk-***.] —**frol′ick•er** *n.*
frol•ic•some (frŏl′ĭk-səm) *adj.* Full of high-spirited fun.
from (frŭm, frŏm; frəm *when unstressed*) *prep.* **1.a.** Used to indicate a specified place or time as a starting point: *walked home from the station; from six o'clock on.* See Usage Note at **whence. b.** Used to indicate a specified point as the first of two limits: *from grades four to six.* **2.** Used to indicate a source, a cause, an agent, or an instrument: *a note from the teacher.* **3.** Used to indicate separation, removal, or exclusion: *keep someone from making a mistake.* **4.** Used to indicate differentiation: *know right from wrong.* **5.** Because of: *faint from hunger.* —*idiom.* **from away.** *Maine.* Not native to Maine. [ME < OE. See **per**[1]*.]
Fromm (frŏm, frŏm), **Erich.** 1900–80. German-born Amer. psychoanalyst whose works include *Escape from Freedom* (1941).
frond (frŏnd) *n.* **1.** The leaf of a fern. **2.** A large compound leaf of a palm. **3.** A leaflike thallus, as of a seaweed or lichen. [Lat. *frōns, frond-*, foliage.] —**frond′ed** *adj.*
fron•des•cent (frŏn-dĕs′ənt) *adj.* Bearing, resembling, or having a profusion of leaves or fronds. —**fron•des′cence** *n.*
fron•dose (frŏn′dōs′) *adj.* **1.** Bearing fronds. **2.** Resembling a frond. [Lat. *frondōsus*, abounding in foliage < *frōns, frond-*, foliage.] —**fron′dose′ly** *adv.*
frons (frŏnz) *n., pl.* **fron•tes** (frŏn′tēz). The anterior, uppermost part of the head of an insect. [Lat. *frōns, front-*.]
front (frŭnt) *n.* **1.** The forward part or surface, as of a building. **2.** The area, location, or position directly before or ahead. **3.** A position of leadership or superiority. **4.** The forehead or face, esp. of a bird or other animal. **5.a.** Demeanor or bearing, esp. in the presence of danger or difficulty. **b.** An outward, often feigned appearance or manner. **6.a.** Land bordering a lake, river, or street. **b.** A promenade along the water at a resort. **7.** A detachable part of a man's dress shirt covering the chest; a dickey. **8.a.** The most forward line of a combat force. **b.** The area of contact between opposing combat forces; a battlefront. **9.** *Meteorol.* The interface between air masses of different temperatures or densities. **10.** A field of activity. **11.a.** A group or movement uniting various individuals or organizations for the achievement of a common purpose; a coalition. **b.** A nominal leader lacking in real authority; a figurehead. **c.** An apparently respectable person, group, or business used as a cover for secret or illegal activities. **12.** *Archaic.* **a.** The first part; the beginning. **b.** The face; the countenance. —*adj.* **1.** Of, relating to, aimed at, or located in the front. **2.** *Ling.* Produced at or toward the front of the mouth. Used of vowels such as that in *green.* —*v.* **front•ed, front•ing, fronts.** —*tr.* **1.** To look out on; face. **2.** To meet in opposition; confront. **3.** To provide a front for. **4.** To serve as a front for. **5.** *Mus.* To lead (a group of musicians). **6.** *Informal.* To provide before payment. —*intr.* **1.** To have a front; face onto something else. **2.** To provide a cover for secret or illegal activities. [ME < OFr. < Lat. *frōns, front-*.]
front. *abbr.* Frontispiece.
front•age (frŭn′tĭj) *n.* **1.a.** The front part of a piece of property. **b.** The land between a building and the street. **c.** Land adjacent to something, such as a building, street, or body of water. **2.** The direction in which something faces.
fron•tal[1] (frŭn′tl) *adj.* **1.** Of, relating to, directed toward, or situated at the front: *a frontal attack.* **2.** *Anat.* Of or relating to the forehead or frontal bone. **3.** Of or relating to a meteorological front. —**fron′tal•ly** *adv.*
fron•tal[2] (frŭn′tl) *n.* **1.** A drapery covering the front of an altar. **2.** The façade of a building. [ME *frontel* < OFr. < Med.Lat. *frontāle* < Lat. *frōns, front-*, forehead, front.]
frontal bone *n. Anat.* A cranial bone consisting of a vertical portion corresponding to the forehead and a horizontal portion that forms the roofs of the orbital and nasal cavities.
frontal lobe *n. Anat.* The largest and most anterior part of each cerebral hemisphere.
frontal lobotomy *n.* A prefrontal lobotomy.
front bench *n.* The first bench on either side of the aisle in a parliament, reserved for ministers and leaders of the principal political parties.
front burner *n. Informal.* A position of relatively great importance.
front•court (frŭnt′kôrt′, -kōrt′) *n. Basketball.* **1.** The half of the court having the basket at which the offensive team shoots. **2.** The forwards and center on a team.
Fron•te•nac (frŏn′tə-năk′, frônt-näk′), Comte de. Louis de Buade. 1620?–98. French colonial administrator who governed New France (1672–82 and 1689–98).
front-end (frŭnt′ĕnd′) *adj.* **1.** Relating to the initial phase of a project. **2.** Relating to the forward parts of a vehicle.
front-end load *n.* The amount deducted from early payments to a mutual fund for expenses such as sales commissions.
fron•ten•is (frŭn-tĕn′ĭs, frŏn′tĕn′ĭs) *n. Sports.* A Latin-American tennis game played on a three-walled court. [Am.Sp., blend of Sp. *frontón*, jai alai court; see FRONTON, and Sp. *tenis*, tennis (< E. TENNIS).]
fron•tes (frŏn′tēz) *n.* Pl. of **frons.**
fron•tier (frŭn-tîr′, frŏn-, frŭn′tîr′, frŏn′-) *n.* **1.a.** An international border. **b.** The area along an international border. **2.** A region just beyond or at the edge of a settled area. **3.** An undeveloped area or field for discovery or research. [ME *frountier* < OFr. *frontier* < *front*, forehead, front. See FRONT.]
fron•tiers•man (frŭn-tîrz′mən, frŏn-) *n.* A man who lives on the frontier.
fron•tiers•wom•an (frŭn-tîrz′wo͝om′ən, frŏn-) *n.* A woman who lives on the frontier.
fron•tis•piece (frŭn′tĭ-spēs′) *n.* **1.** An illustration that faces or immediately precedes the title page of a book, book section, or magazine. **2.** *Archit.* **a.** A façade, esp. an ornamental façade. **b.** A small ornamental pediment, as on top of a door or window. **3.** *Archaic.* A title page. [Alteration (influenced by PIECE) of Fr. *frontispice* < LLat. *frontispicium*, façade of a building : Lat. *frontis*, genitive of *frōns*, forehead, front + Lat. *specere*, to look at; see **spek-***.]
front•let (frŭnt′lĭt) *n.* **1.** An ornament or a band worn on the forehead as a phylactery. **2.** The forehead of an animal. **3.** The forehead of a bird when of a different color or texture of plumage. **4.** An ornamental border for a frontal. [ME < OFr. *frontelet*, dim. of *frontel*. See FRONTAL[2].]
front•line also **front line** (frŭnt′līn′) —*n.* A front or boundary, esp. one between military, political, or ideological positions. —*adj.* or **front-line. 1.** Located or used at a military front. **2.** Of or relating to the most advanced or important position or activity in a field or undertaking.
front-load (frŭnt′-lōd′) *v.* **-load•ed, -load•ing, -loads.** —*tr.* To concentrate costs or benefits of (a financial obligation or deal) in an early period. —*intr.* To concentrate costs or benefits in an early period.
front man *n.* **1.** A man who serves as a nominal leader but lacks real authority. **2.** *Mus.* A leading singer with a group.
front matter *n.* The material, such as the preface, frontispiece, and title page, preceding the text in a book.
front money *n.* Money paid in advance, as for contracted goods or services.

frog
Bullfrog
Rana catesbeiana

ă pat	oi boy
ā pay	ou out
âr care	o͝o took
ä father	o͞o boot
ĕ pet	ŭ cut
ē be	ûr urge
ĭ pit	th thin
ī pie	*th* this
îr pier	hw which
ŏ pot	zh vision
ō toe	ə about, item
ô paw	

Stress marks:
′ (primary);
′ (secondary), as in
dictionary (dĭk′shə-nĕr′ē)

Fu•ji (fo͞o′jē), **Mount.** Also **Fu•ji•ya•ma** (fo͞o′jē-yä′mə, -mä) or **Fu•ji•no•ya•ma** (-nō-) or **Fu•ji•san** (-sän′). A dormant volcano, 3,778.6 m (12,389 ft), in central Honshu, Japan, WSW of Tokyo.

Fu•jian[1] (fo͞o′jyän′, fü′-) also **Fu•kien** (kyĕn′). A province of SE China on the East China Sea and the Formosa Strait. Cap. Fuzhou. Pop. 27,130,000.

Fu•jian[2] (fo͞o′jyän′, fü′-) also **Fu•kien** (-kyĕn′) *n.* A dialect of Chinese spoken in Fujian province, eastern Guangdong province, and Taiwan.

Fu•ji•sa•wa (fo͞o′jē-sä′wə, -wä). A city of E-central Honshu, Japan, a suburb of Tokyo. Pop. 328,387.

Fu•ku•o•ka (fo͞o′ko͞o-ō′kə, -kä). A city of NW Kyushu, Japan, on an inlet of the Sea of Japan. Pop. 1,160,402.

Fu•ku•ya•ma (fo͞o′kə-yä′mə, -ko͞o-yä′mä). A city of SW Honshu, Japan, on the Inland Sea E of Kure. Pop. 360,264.

-ful *suff.* **1.a.** Full of: *playful.* **b.** Characterized by; resembling: *masterful.* **c.** Tending, given, or able to: *useful.* **2.** A quantity that fills: *armful.* [ME < OE < *full,* full. See FULL[1].]

Usage Note: The plurals of nouns ending in *-ful* are usually formed by adding the letter *s* to the end of the suffix: *cupfuls; glassfuls; spoonfuls.*

Fu•la•ni (fo͞o′lä′nē, fo͞o-lä′-) also **Fu•la** (fo͞o′lə) *n., pl.* **Fulani** or **-nis** also **Fula** or **-las. 1.** A member of a pastoral, largely Muslim people inhabiting parts of West Africa from northern Nigeria to Mali and the Atlantic coast. **2.** The West Atlantic language of this people.

Ful•bright (fo͝ol′brīt′), **J(ames) William.** b. 1905. Amer. politician who proposed the Fulbright Act (1946), establishing an exchange program for educators and students.

ful•crum (fo͝ol′krəm, fŭl′-) *n., pl.* **-crums** or **-cra** (-krə). **1.** The point or support on which a lever pivots. **2.** *Zool.* An anatomical structure that acts as a hinge or a point of support. **3.** An agent through which vital powers are exercised. [Lat., bedpost < *fulcīre,* to support.]

Ful•da (fo͝ol′də). A city of central Germany SSE of Kassel on the **Fulda River,** c. 217 km (135 mi). Pop. 55,441.

ful•fill also **ful•fil** (fo͝ol-fĭl′) *tr.v.* **-filled, -fill•ing, -fills** also **-fils. 1.** To bring into actuality; effect: *fulfilled his promises.* **2.** To carry out (an order, for example). **3.** To measure up to; satisfy. See Syns at **satisfy. 4.** To bring to an end; complete. [ME *fulfillen* < OE *fullfyllan* : *full,* full; see FULL[1] + *fyllan,* to fill; see FILL.] **—ful•fill′er** *n.* **—ful•fill′ment** *n.*

ful•gent (fo͝ol′jənt, fŭl′-) *adj.* Shining brilliantly; radiant. [ME < Lat. *fulgēns, fulgent-,* pr.part. of *fulgēre,* to flash, shine. See **bhel-**[1*].] **—ful′gent•ly** *adv.*

ful•gu•rant (fo͝ol′gyər-ənt, -gər-, fŭl′-) *adj.* Flashing like lightning; dazzlingly bright. [Lat. *fulgurāns, fulgurant-,* pr.part. of *fulgurāre,* to lighten. See FULGURATE.]

ful•gu•rate (fo͝ol′gyə-rāt′, -gə-, fŭl′-) *v.* **-rat•ed, -rat•ing, -rates.** *—intr.* To emit flashes of lightning. *—tr.* **1.** To emit (light) in flashes. **2.** *Medic.* To destroy (abnormal tissue, for example) by electric current. [Lat. *fulgurāre, fulgurāt-* < *fulgur,* lightning. See **bhel-**[1*].] **—ful′gu•ra′tion** *n.*

ful•gu•rite (fo͝ol′gyə-rīt′, -gə-, fŭl′-) *n.* A slender, usu. tubular glassy rock produced by lightning striking and then fusing dry sand. [Lat. *fulgur,* lightning; see FULGURATE + -ITE[1].]

ful•gu•rous (fo͝ol′gyər-əs, -gər-, fŭl′-) *adj.* **1.** Emitting flashes of lightning. **2.** Emitting flashes similar to lightning. [Lat. *fulgur,* lightning; see FULGURATE + -OUS.]

fu•lig•i•nous (fyo͞o-lĭj′ə-nəs) *adj.* **1.** Sooty. **2.** Colored by or as if by soot. [LLat. *fūlīginōsus* < Lat. *fūlīgō, fūlīgin-,* soot.] **—fu•lig′i•nous•ly** *adv.*

full[1] (fo͝ol) *adj.* **full•er, full•est. 1.** Containing all that is normal or possible. **2.** Complete in every particular: *a full account.* **3.** *Baseball.* **a.** Amounting to three balls and two strikes. Used of a count. **b.** Having base runners at first, second, and third base. **4.a.** Of maximum or highest degree. **b.** Being at the peak of development or maturity. **5.** Having a great deal or many: *full of errors.* **6.** Totally qualified, accepted, or empowered. **7.a.** Rounded in shape; plump. **b.** Having or made with a generous amount of fabric. **8.a.** Having an appetite completely satisfied, esp. for food or drink. **b.** Providing an abundance, esp. of food. **9.** Having depth and body; rich: *a full aroma.* **10.** Completely absorbed or preoccupied: *full of himself.* **11.** Possessing both parents in common. *—adv.* **1.** To a complete extent; entirely. **2.** Exactly; directly. *—v.* **fulled, full•ing, fulls.** *—tr.* To make (a garment) full, as by pleating or gathering. *—intr.* To become full. Used of the moon. *—n.* **1.** The maximum or complete size or amount. **2.** The highest degree or state. [ME *ful* < OE *full.* See **pelə-**[1*].] **—full′ness, ful′ness** *n.*

full[2] (fo͝ol) *tr.v.* **fulled, full•ing, fulls.** To increase the weight and bulk of (cloth) by shrinking and beating or pressing. [ME *fullen* < OFr. *fouler* < VLat. **fullāre* < Lat. *fullō,* fuller. See **bhel-**[2*].]

full•back (fo͝ol′băk′) *n.* **1.** *Football.* **a.** An offensive backfield player whose position is behind the quarterback and halfbacks. **b.** The position of this player. **2.** *Sports.* **a.** A defensive backfield player in field hockey, soccer, or rugby. **b.** The position of this player.

full blood *n.* **1.** Relationship through the same set of parents. **2.** A person or an animal of unmixed race or breed.

full-blood•ed (fo͝ol′blŭd′ĭd) *adj.* **1.a.** Of unmixed ancestry; purebred. **b.** Related by way of having the same parents. **2.a.** Not pale or anemic; florid or ruddy. **b.** Vigorous and vital. **3.** Complete in all respects. **—full′-blood′ed•ness** *n.*

full-blown (fo͝ol′blōn′) *adj.* **1.** Having blossomed or opened completely. **2.** Fully developed or matured. **3.** Having or displaying all the characteristics necessary for completeness.

full-bod•ied (fo͝ol′bŏd′ēd) *adj.* **1.** Having a rich and intense flavor or aroma: *a full-bodied wine.* **2.** Rich and intense.

full circle *adv.* Back to one's starting point.

full-court press (fo͝ol′kôrt′, -kōrt′) *n.* **1.** *Basketball.* A defensive strategy in which one or two players harass the ball handler over the entire court. **2.** A strong, diversified effort.

full dress *n.* Attire appropriate for formal or ceremonial events.

full-dress (fo͝ol′drĕs′) *adj.* **1.** Of, appropriate for, or requiring full dress; formal. **2.** Complete or thorough.

full•er[1] (fo͝ol′ər) *n.* One that fulls cloth.

full•er[2] (fo͝ol′ər) *n.* **1.** A hammer used by a blacksmith for grooving or spreading iron. **2.** A groove made by such a hammer. [Poss. < FULL[1], to pleat.]

Ful•ler (fo͝ol′ər), **Melville Weston.** 1833–1910. Amer. jurist; chief justice of the U.S. Supreme Court (1888–1910).

Fuller, R(ichard) Buckminster. 1895–1983. Amer. architect and inventor noted for designing the geodesic dome.

Fuller, (Sarah) Margaret. 1810–50. Amer. writer and critic who wrote *Woman in the Nineteenth Century* (1845).

ful•ler•ene (fo͝ol′ə-rēn′) *n.* Any of various soccerball-shaped molecules that constitute the third form of carbon after graphite and diamond, including the extraordinarily stable fullerene C_{60}, the roundest molecule known. [After Richard Buckminster FULLER (from the resemblance of their configurations to his geodesic domes) + -ENE.]

full•er's earth (fo͝ol′ərz) *n.* A highly adsorbent claylike substance consisting of hydrated aluminum silicates, used formerly in fulling woolen cloth and now used in decolorizing oils and fats.

Ful•ler•ton (fo͝ol′ər-tən). A city of S CA SE of Los Angeles; founded 1887. Pop. 114,144.

full-fash•ioned (fo͝ol′făsh′ənd) *adj.* Knitted in a shape that conforms closely to body lines.

full-fledged (fo͝ol′flĕjd′) *adj.* **1.** Having reached full development; mature. **2.** Having full status or rank: *a full-fledged lawyer.* **3.** Having fully developed adult plumage.

full gainer *n.* *Sports.* A forward dive in which the diver executes a full back somersault before entering the water.

full house *n.* *Games.* A poker hand containing three of a kind and a pair, ranked above a flush and below four of a kind.

full-length (fo͝ol′lĕngkth′, -lĕngth′) *adj.* **1.** Showing or fitted to the entire length, esp. of the human body: *a full-length mirror.* **2.** Of a normal or standard length: *a full-length novel.*

full moon *n.* **1.** The moon visible as a fully illuminated disk. **2.** The period of the month when such a moon occurs.

full-mouthed (fo͝ol′mouthd′, -moutht′) *adj.* **1.** Having a complete set of teeth. Used of cattle and other livestock. **2.** Uttered loudly or noisily.

full nelson *n.* *Sports.* A wrestling hold in which both hands are thrust under the opponent's arms from behind and then pressed against the back of the opponent's neck.

full rhyme *n.* See **perfect rhyme** 1.

full-scale (fo͝ol′skāl′) *adj.* **1.** Of actual or full size; not reduced. **2.** Employing all resources; not limited or partial.

full-serv•ice (fo͝ol′sûr′vĭs) *adj.* Associated with or offering complete service: *full-service banks.*

full-size (fo͝ol′sīz′) *adj.* **1.** Of the standard or normal size: *a full-size car.* **2.a.** Measuring 54 by 75 inches. Used of a bed. **b.** Being of a size that will fit such a bed.

full stop *n.* **1.** A period indicating the end of a sentence. **2.** A complete halt, as one made by a motor vehicle.

full-time (fo͝ol′tīm′) *adj.* Employed for or involving a standard number of hours of working time. **—full′-time′** *adv.*

ful•ly (fo͝ol′ē) *adv.* **1.** Totally or completely. **2.** At least.

ful•mar (fo͝ol′mər, -mär′) *n.* **1.** A gull-like bird *(Fulmarus glacialis)* of Arctic regions having smoky gray plumage. **2.** Any of several similar or related birds. [Dial. : prob. < ON *fūll,* foul; see **pū-*** + *mār,* mew; akin to OE *mǣw.*]

ful•mi•nant (fo͝ol′mə-nənt, fŭl′-) *adj.* **1.** Exploding or detonating. **2.** *Pathol.* Occurring suddenly, rapidly, and with great severity or intensity. [Lat. *fulmināns, fulminant-,* pr.part. of *fulmināre,* to strike with lightning. See FULMINATE.]

ful•mi•nate (fo͝ol′mə-nāt′, fŭl′-) *v.* **-nat•ed, -nat•ing, -nates.** *—intr.* **1.** To issue a thunderous verbal attack or denunciation. **2.** To explode or detonate. *—tr.* **1.** To issue (a denunciation, for example) thunderously. **2.** To cause to explode. *—n.* An explosive salt of fulminic acid. [ME *fulminaten* < Lat. *fulmināre, fulmināt-,* to strike with lightning < *fulmen, fulmin-,* lightning that strikes. See **bhel-**[1*].] **—ful′mi•na′tion** *n.* **—ful′mi•na′tor** *n.* **—ful′mi•na•to′ry** (-nə-tôr′ē, -tōr′ē) *adj.*

ful•mine (fo͝ol′mĭn, fŭl′-) *tr. & intr.v.* **-mined, -min•ing, -mines.** *Archaic.* To fulminate. [< Lat. *fulmināre,* to strike with lightning. See FULMINATE.]

ful•min•ic acid (fo͝ol-mĭn′ĭk, fŭl-) *n.* An unstable acid, HONC, that forms highly explosive salts. [Lat. *fulmen, fulmin-*, lightning that strikes; see FULMINATE + -IC.]

ful•some (fo͝ol′səm) *adj.* **1.** Offensively flattering or insincere. **2.** Offensive to the taste or sensibilities. **3.** *Usage Problem.* Copious or abundant. [ME *fulsom*, abundant, well-fed, arousing disgust : *ful*, full; see FULL[1] + *-som*, adj. suff.; see -SOME[1].] —**ful′some•ly** *adv.* —**ful′some•ness** *n.*

Usage Note: The word *fulsome* is often used, particularly in the expression *fulsome praise*, to mean simply "abundant," without any implication of excess or insincerity. This usage is etymologically justified but may invite misunderstandings.

Ful•ton (fo͝ol′tən), **Robert.** 1765–1815. Amer. engineer who produced the first practical steamboat in 1807.

Fu Man•chu mustache (fo͞o′ măn-cho͞o′) *n.* A mustache with ends that hang downward toward or below the chin. [After *Fu Manchu*, character in novels by Sax Rohmer, pen name of Arthur Sarsfield Ward (1886–1959), British mystery writer.]

fu•ma•rate (fyo͞o′mə-rāt′) *n.* A salt or ester of fumaric acid. [FUMAR(IC ACID) + -ATE[2].]

fu•mar•ic acid (fyo͞o-măr′ĭk) *n.* An organic acid, $C_4H_4O_4$, found in living cells or synthesized and used in making dyes. [< NLat. *Fūmāria*, genus of herbaceous plants (< LLat. *fūmāria*, fumitory < Lat. *fūmus*, smoke) + -IC.]

fu•ma•role (fyo͞o′mə-rōl′) *n.* A hole in a volcanic area from which hot smoke and gases escape. [Ital. *fumarola* < LLat. *fūmāriolum*, smoke hole, dim. of Lat. *fūmārium*, smoke chamber < *fūmus*, smoke.] —**fu′ma•rol′ic** (-rŏl′ĭk) *adj.*

fu•ma•to•ry (fyo͞o′mə-tôr′ē, -tōr′ē) *adj.* Of or relating to smoke or fumigation. [< Lat. *fūmāre*, to smoke < *fūmus*, smoke.]

fum•ble (fŭm′bəl) *v.* **-bled, -bling, -bles.** —*intr.* **1.** To touch or handle nervously or idly. **2.** To grope awkwardly to find or to accomplish something. **3.** To proceed awkwardly and uncertainly; blunder. **4.a.** *Football.* To drop a ball that is in play. **b.** *Baseball.* To mishandle a ground ball. —*tr.* **1.** To touch or handle clumsily or idly. **2.** To make a mess of; bungle. See Syns at **botch. 3.** To feel or make (one's way) awkwardly. **4.a.** *Football.* To drop (a ball) while in play. **b.** *Baseball.* To mishandle (a ground ball). —*n.* **1.** The act or an instance of fumbling. **2.** *Sports.* A ball that has been fumbled. [ME *fomelen*, to grope.] —**fum′bler** *n.*

fume (fyo͞om) *n.* **1.** Vapor, gas, or smoke, esp. if irritating, harmful, or strong. **2.** A strong or acrid odor. **3.** A state of resentment or vexation. —*v.* **fumed, fum•ing, fumes.** —*tr.* **1.** To subject to or treat with fumes. **2.** To give off in or as if in fumes. —*intr.* **1.** To emit fumes. **2.** To rise in fumes. **3.** To feel or show resentment or vexation. [ME < OFr. *fum* < Lat. *fūmus.*]

fu•mi•gant (fyo͞o′mĭ-gənt) *n.* A chemical compound used in its gaseous state as a pesticide or disinfectant. [Lat. *fūmigāns, fūmigant-*, pr.part. of *fūmigāre*, to smoke. See FUMIGATE.]

fu•mi•gate (fyo͞o′mĭ-gāt′) *v.* **-gat•ed, -gat•ing, -gates.** —*tr.* To subject to smoke or fumes, usu. in order to exterminate pests or disinfect. —*intr.* To employ smoke or fumes in order to exterminate or disinfect. [Lat. *fūmigāre, fūmigāt-*, to smoke : *fūmus*, smoke + *agere*, to drive, make; see **ag-***.] —**fu′mi•ga′tion** *n.* —**fu′mi•ga′tor** *n.*

fu•mi•to•ry (fyo͞o′mĭ-tôr′ē, -tōr′ē) *n., pl.* **-ries.** An herb *(Fumaria officinalis)* native to Eurasia and having spurred purplish flowers. [ME *fumetere* < OFr. *fumeterre* < Med.Lat. *fūmus terrae* : Lat. *fūmus*, smoke + Lat. *terrae*, genitive of *terra*, dry land, earth; see **ters-***.]

fun (fŭn) *n.* **1.** A source of enjoyment, amusement, or pleasure. **2.** Enjoyment; amusement: *have fun at the beach.* **3.** Playful, often noisy activity. —*intr.v.* **funned, fun•ning, funs.** *Informal.* To behave playfully; joke. —*adj. Informal.* Enjoyable; amusing: *a fun day.* —*idiom.* **for** (or **in**) **fun.** As a joke; playfully. [Poss. < *fon*, to make a fool of < ME *fonnen*, to fool, poss. < *fonne*, fool.]

Usage Note: The use of *fun* as an attributive adjective, as in *a fun time, a fun place*, most likely originated in a playful reanalysis of the use of the word in sentences such as *It is fun to ski*, where *fun* behaves syntactically like an adjective such as *amusing* or *swell*. The day may come when this usage is entirely unremarkable. At present, however, writers who want to stay on the safe side are advised to avoid the attributive use of *fun* in contexts in which a light tone is not appropriate.

Fu•na•ba•shi (fo͞o′nə-bä′shē, -nä-). A city of E-central Honshu, Japan, a suburb of Tokyo on Tokyo Bay. Pop. 506,967.

fu•nam•bu•list (fyo͞o-năm′byə-lĭst) *n.* One who performs on a tightrope or a slack rope. [< Lat. *fūnambulus* : *fūnis*, rope + *ambulāre*, to walk; see **ambhi***.] —**fu•nam′bu•lism** *n.*

func•tion (fŭngk′shən) *n.* **1.** The action for which one is particularly fitted or employed. **2.a.** Assigned duty or activity. **b.** A specific occupation or role. **3.** An official ceremony or a formal social occasion. **4.** Something closely related to another thing and dependent on it for its existence, value, or significance. **5.** *Math.* A rule of correspondence between two sets such that there is a unique element in the second set assigned to each element in the first set. —*intr.v.* **-tioned, -tion•ing, -tions.** To have or perform a function; serve. [Lat. *fūnctiō, fūnctiōn-*, performance, execution < *fūnctus*, p.part. of *fungī*, to perform, execute.] —**func′tion•less** *adj.*

Syns: *function, duty, office, role.* The central meaning shared by these nouns is "the actions and activities assigned to, required of, or expected of a person": *the function of a teacher; a bank clerk's duty; assumed the office of financial adviser; the role of a parent.*

func•tion•al (fŭngk′shə-nəl) *adj.* **1.a.** Of or relating to a function. **b.** Of, relating to, or indicating a mathematical function or functions. **2.** Designed for or adapted to a particular function or use: *functional architecture.* **3.** Capable of performing; operative: *functional brakes.* **4.** *Pathol.* Involving functions rather than a physiological or structural cause. —**func′tion•al′i•ty** (-shə-năl′ĭ-tē) *n.* —**func′tion•al•ly** *adv.*

functional group *n.* A group of atoms, such as a carboxyl group, that characterizes the properties of a family of organic compounds.

functional illiterate *n.* A person whose skills in reading and writing are insufficient for ordinary practical needs.

func•tion•al•ism (fŭngk′shə-nə-lĭz′əm) *n.* **1.** The doctrine that the function of an object should determine its design and materials. **2.** A doctrine stressing purpose, practicality, and utility. —**func′tion•al•ist′** *adj. & n.*

functional shift *n. Ling.* A shift in the syntactic function of a word, as when a noun serves as a verb.

func•tion•ar•y (fŭngk′shə-nĕr′ē) *n., pl.* **-ies.** One who holds an office or a trust or performs a particular function.

function word *n. Gram.* A word, such as a preposition, that chiefly indicates a grammatical relationship.

func•tor (fŭngk′tər) *n.* **1.** One that performs an operation or a function. **2.** *Gram.* See **function word.** [NLat. < Lat. *fūnctiō*, performance, function. See FUNCTION.]

fund (fŭnd) *n.* **1.** A source of supply; a stock: *a fund of goodwill.* **2.a.** A sum of money or other resources set aside for a specific purpose: *a pension fund.* **b. funds.** Available money; ready cash: *short on funds.* **3. funds.** The stock of the British permanent national debt, considered as public securities. Used with *the.* **4.** An organization established to administer a sum of money. —*tr.v.* **fund•ed, fund•ing, funds. 1.** To provide money for paying off the interest or principal of (a debt). **2.** To convert into a long-term or floating debt with fixed interest payments. **3.** To place in a fund for accumulation. **4.** To furnish a fund for. [Lat. *fundus*, bottom, piece of land.]

fun•da•ment (fŭn′də-mənt) *n.* **1.a.** The buttocks. **b.** The anus. **2.** The natural features of a land surface unaltered by human beings. **3.** A foundation, as of a building. **4.** An underlying theoretical basis or principle. [ME *foundement* < OFr. *fondement* < Lat. *fundāmentum* < *fundāre*, to lay the foundation < *fundus*, bottom.]

fun•da•men•tal (fŭn′də-mĕn′tl) *adj.* **1.a.** Of or relating to the foundation or base; elementary. **b.** Forming or serving as an essential component of a system or structure; central. **c.** Of great significance or entailing major change. **2.** *Phys.* **a.** Of or relating to the component of lowest frequency of a periodic wave or quantity. **b.** Of or relating to the lowest possible frequency of a vibrating element or system. **3.** *Mus.* Having the root in the bass: *a fundamental chord.* —*n.* **1.** An essential part of a system or object. **2.** *Phys.* The lowest frequency of a periodically varying quantity or a vibrating system. —**fun′da•men′tal•ly** *adv.*

fun•da•men•tal•ism (fŭn′də-mĕn′tl-ĭz′əm) *n.* **1.a.** Often **Fundamentalism.** An organized, militant Evangelical movement originating in the United States in 1920 in opposition to Liberalism and secularism. **b.** Adherence to its theology. **2.** A movement or point of view characterized by rigid adherence to fundamental or basic principles. —**fun′da•men′tal•ist** *adj. & n.* —**fun′da•men′tal•ist′ic** *adj.*

fundamental particle *n. Phys.* See **elementary particle.**

fund•raise or **fund-raise** also **fund raise** (fŭnd′rāz′) *intr.v.* **-raised, -rais•ing, -rais•es.** To engage in fundraising.

fund•rais•er also **fund-rais•er** (fŭnd′rā′zər) *n.* **1.** One that raises funds. **2.** A social function held for raising funds.

fund•rais•ing or **fund-rais•ing** (fŭnd′rā′zĭng) *n.* The organized activity or an instance of soliciting money or pledges, as for political campaigns. —**fund′rais′ing** *adj.*

fun•dus (fŭn′dəs) *n., pl.* **-di** (-dī′). *Anat.* The portion of a hollow organ opposite or farthest from its opening. [Lat., bottom.] —**fun′dic** *adj.*

Fun•dy (fŭn′dē), **Bay of.** An inlet of the Atlantic Ocean in SE Canada between New Brunswick and Nova Scotia.

fu•ner•al (fyo͞o′nər-əl) *n.* **1.a.** The ceremonies held in connection with the burial or cremation of a dead person. **b.** *Archaic.* The eulogy delivered or the sermon preached at such a ceremony. **2.** The burial procession accompanying a body to the grave. **3.** An end or a cessation of existence. **4.** *Slang.* A source of concern or care. —*adj.* Of, relating to, or resembling a funeral. [ME *funerelles*, funeral rites < OFr. *funerailles* < Med.Lat. *fūnerālia*, neut. pl. of *fūnerālis*, funereal < LLat. < Lat. *fūnus, fūner-*, death rites.]

funeral director *n.* One whose business is to arrange for the burial or cremation of the dead and assist at the funeral rites and who is usu. an embalmer.

ă pat	oi boy
ā pay	ou out
âr care	o͝o took
ä father	o͞o boot
ĕ pet	ŭ cut
ē be	ûr urge
ĭ pit	th thin
ī pie	*th* this
îr pier	hw which
ŏ pot	zh vision
ō toe	ə about, item
ô paw	

Stress marks:
′ (primary);
′ (secondary), as in **dictionary** (dĭk′shə-nĕr′ē)

funeral home *n.* An establishment in which the dead are prepared for burial or cremation and in which wakes and funerals may be held.

fu•ner•ar•y (fyo͞o′nə-rĕr′ē) *adj.* Of or suitable for a funeral or burial. [Lat. *fūnerārius* < *fūnus, fūner-*, funeral.]

fu•ne•re•al (fyo͞o-nîr′ē-əl) *adj.* **1.** Of or relating to a funeral. **2.** Appropriate for or suggestive of a funeral. [< Lat. *fūnereus* < *fūnus, fūner-*, funeral.] —**fu•ne′re•al•ly** *adv.*

fun fair *n. Chiefly British.* An amusement park.

fun•gal (fŭng′gəl) also **fun•gous** (-gəs) *adj.* **1.** Of, resembling, or characteristic of a fungus. **2.** Caused by a fungus.

fun•gi•ble (fŭn′jə-bəl) *adj.* **1.** *Law.* Returnable or negotiable in kind or by substitution, as a quantity of grain for an equal amount of the same kind of grain. **2.** Interchangeable. —*n.* Something that is exchangeable or substitutable. Often used in the plural. [Med.Lat. *fungibilis* < Lat. *fungī (vice)*, to perform (in place of).] —**fun′gi•bil′i•ty** *n.*

fun•gi•cide (fŭn′jĭ-sīd′, fŭng′gĭ-) *n.* A chemical substance that destroys or inhibits the growth of fungi. —**fun′gi•cid′al** (-sīd′l) *adj.* —**fun′gi•cid′al•ly** *adv.*

fun•gi•form (fŭn′jə-fôrm′, fŭng′gə-) *adj.* Shaped like a mushroom. [FUNG(US) + -FORM.]

fun•gi•stat (fŭn′jĭ-stăt′, fŭng′gĭ-) *n.* A substance that inhibits the growth of fungi.

fun•giv•or•ous (fŭn-jĭv′ər-əs, fŭng-gĭv′-) *adj.* Feeding on fungi.

fun•go (fŭng′gō) *n., pl.* **-goes.** *Baseball.* A practice fly ball hit by a player who tosses the ball up and hits it on its way down with a long, thin, light bat. [?]

fun•goid (fŭng′goid′) *adj.* Of, relating to, resembling, or being a fungus. —*n.* A fungus.

fun•gus (fŭng′gəs) *n., pl.* **fun•gi** (fŭn′jī, fŭng′gī) or **fun•gus•es.** Any of numerous eukaryotic organisms of the kingdom Fungi, such as mushrooms, that lack chlorophyll and vascular tissue and range from a single cell to a body mass of branched filamentous hyphae that often produce specialized fruiting bodies. [Lat.; perh. akin to Gk. *spongos, sphongos*, sponge.]

fun house also **fun•house** (fŭn′hous′) *n.* A building or an attraction in an amusement park or a carnival that features devices intended to surprise, frighten, bewilder, or amuse.

fu•nic•u•lar (fyo͞o-nĭk′yə-lər, fə-) *adj.* **1.** Of, relating to, or like a rope or cord. **2.** Operated or moved by a cable. **3.** Of, relating to, or being a funiculus. —*n.* A cable railway on a steep incline, esp. one with counterbalanced ascending and descending cars.

fu•nic•u•lus (fyo͞o-nĭk′yə-ləs, fə-) also **fu•ni•cle** (fyo͞o′nĭ-kəl) *n., pl.* **-li** (-lī′) also **-cles.** **1.** *Anat.* A slender cordlike strand or band, esp.: **a.** A bundle of nerve fibers in a nerve trunk. **b.** One of three major divisions of white matter in the spinal cord, consisting of fasciculi. **c.** The umbilical cord. **2.** *Bot.* A stalk connecting an ovule or a seed with the placenta. [Lat. *fūniculus*, slender rope, dim. of *fūnis*, rope.]

funk[1] (fŭngk) *n.* **1.a.** A state of cowardly fright; a panic. **b.** A state of severe depression. **2.** A cowardly fearful person. —*v.* **funked, funk•ing, funks.** —*tr.* **1.** To shrink from in fright or dread. **2.** To be afraid of. —*intr.* To shrink in fright. [Prob. < obsolete Flem. *fonck*, disturbance, agitation.]

funk[2] (fŭngk) *n.* **1.** *Mus.* **a.** An earthy quality, as in jazz or soul. **b.** A type of popular music combining elements of jazz, blues, and soul and characterized by syncopated rhythm and a heavy repetitive bass line. **2.** *Slang.* An unsophisticated quality or atmosphere of a region or locality.

funk hole *n.* A dugout or similar place of shelter or refuge.

funk•y[1] (fŭng′kē) *adj.* **-i•er, -i•est.** Frightened; panicky.

funk•y[2] (fŭng′kē) *adj.* **-i•er, -i•est.** **1.a.** Having a moldy or musty smell: *funky cheese.* **b.** Having a strong, offensive, unwashed odor. **2.** *Slang.* **a.** Of or relating to music that has an earthy quality reminiscent of the blues. **b.** Earthy and uncomplicated; natural. **3.** *Slang.* **a.** Marked by self-expression, originality, and modishness; unconventional. **b.** Outlandishly vulgar or eccentric in a humorous or tongue-in-cheek manner; campy. [< *funk*, strong smell, tobacco smoke, perh. < Fr. dial. *funquer*, to give off smoke < OFr. *fungier* < Lat. *fūmigāre*. See FUMIGATE.] —**funk′i•ness** *n.*

funicular

fun•nel (fŭn′əl) *n.* **1.a.** A conical utensil with a small hole or narrow tube at the apex, used to channel the flow of a substance, as into a small opening. **b.** Something resembling this utensil in shape. **2.** A shaft, flue, or stack for ventilation or the passage of smoke, esp. the smokestack of a ship or locomotive. —*v.* **-neled, -nel•ing, -nels** or **-nelled, -nel•ling, -nels.** —*intr.* **1.** To take the shape of a funnel. **2.** To move through or as if through a funnel. —*tr.* **1.** To cause to take the shape of a funnel. **2.** To cause to move through or as if through a funnel. [ME *fonel* < Prov. *fonilh* < LLat. *fundibulum* < Lat. *īnfundibulum* < *īnfundere*, to pour in. See INFUSE.]

fun•nel•form (fŭn′əl-fôrm′) *adj. Bot.* Shaped like a funnel.

fun•ny (fŭn′ē) *adj.* **-ni•er, -ni•est.** **1.a.** Causing laughter or amusement. **b.** Intended or designed to amuse. **2.** Strangely or suspiciously odd; curious. **3.** Tricky or deceitful. —*n., pl.* **-nies.** *Informal.* **1.** A joke; a witticism. **2. funnies. a.** Comic strips. **b.** The section of a newspaper containing comic strips. [< FUN.] —**fun′ni•ly** *adv.* —**fun′ni•ness** *n.*

funny bone *n. Informal.* **1.** A point on the elbow where the ulnar nerve runs close to the surface and tingles sharply if knocked against the bone. **2.** A sense of humor.

funny book *n.* See **comic book.**

funny farm *n. Slang.* A mental health facility or hospital.

funny money *n. Informal.* **1.** Counterfeit currency. **2.** Money from an obscure or questionable source.

funny paper *n.* The section of a newspaper with comic strips.

fur (fûr) *n.* **1.** The thick coat of soft hair covering a mammal's skin. **2.** The hair-covered dressed pelt of such a mammal, used in the making of garments and as trimming or decoration. **3.** A garment made of or lined with the dressed pelt of a mammal. **4.** A coating similar to the pelt of a mammal. —*tr.v.* **furred, fur•ring, furs.** **1.** To cover, line, or trim with fur. **2.** To provide fur garments for. **3.** To cover or coat as if with fur. **4.** To line (a wall or floor) with furring. [ME *furre*, prob. < *furren*, to line with fur < OFr. *forrer* < *forre, fuerre*, sheath, lining, of Gmc. orig. See **pā-***.]

fur. *abbr.* Furlong.

fu•ran (fyo͝or′ăn′, fyo͞o-răn′) *n.* **1.** One of a group of volatile heterocyclic organic compounds containing a ring of four carbon atoms and one oxygen atom, used in the synthesis of furfural. **2.** The simplest such compound, C_4H_4O. [FUR(FURAL) + -AN[2].]

fu•ra•nose (fyo͝or′ə-nōs′) *n.* A sugar having a cyclic structure resembling that of furan.

fur•bear•er also **fur-bear•er** (fûr′bâr′ər) *n.* An animal with fur, esp. commercially valued fur. —**fur′bear′ing** *adj.*

fur•be•low (fûr′bə-lō′) *n.* **1.** A ruffle or flounce on a garment. **2.** A piece of showy ornamentation. —*tr.v.* **-lowed, -low•ing, -lows.** To decorate with a ruffle or flounce. [Prob. alteration of Prov. *farbello, farbella*, fringe, perh. alteration of Ital. *faldella*, pleat, dim. of *falda*, flap, loose end, of Gmc. orig. See **pel-**[2]*.]

fur•bish (fûr′bĭsh) *tr.v.* **-bished, -bish•ing, -bish•es.** **1.** To brighten by cleaning or rubbing; polish. **2.** To restore to attractive or serviceable condition. [ME *furbishen* < OFr. *fourbir, fourbiss-* < Frankish **furbjan*.] —**fur′bish•er** *n.*

fur•cate (fûr′kāt′) *intr.v.* **-cat•ed, -cat•ing, -cates.** To divide into branches; fork. —*adj.* Divided into branches; forked. [LLat. *furcātus*, forked < Lat. *furca*, fork.] —**fur′cate′ly** *adv.* —**fur•ca′tion** *n.*

fur•cu•la (fûr′kyə-lə) *n., pl.* **-lae** (-lē′). *Zool.* A forked part or bone, such as a wishbone. [Lat., dim. of *furca*, fork.] —**fur′cu•lar** *adv.*

fur•fur (fûr′fər) *n., pl.* **-fu•res** (-fyə-rēz′). An epidermal scale, as that associated with dandruff. [Lat., bran, scales.]

fur•fu•ra•ceous (fûr′fə-rā′shəs, -fyə-) *adj.* **1.** Made of or covered with scaly particles, such as dandruff. **2.** Relating to or resembling bran. [< LLat. *furfurāceus*, branlike, scaly : Lat. *furfur*, bran + Lat. *-āceus*, -aceous.]

fur•fu•ral (fûr′fə-răl′, -fyə-) *n.* A sweet-smelling mobile liquid, C_4H_3OCHO, used as a solvent, in making resins, and as a fungicide. [FURFUR + -AL[3].]

fur•fu•ran (fûr′fə-răn′, -fyə-) *n.* See **furan** 2. [FURFUR(AL) + -AN[2].]

fu•ri•o•so (fyo͝or′ē-ō′sō, -zō) *adv. & adj. Mus.* In a tempestuous and vigorous manner. [Ital. < Lat. *furiōsus*, furious. See FURIOUS.]

fu•ri•ous (fyo͝or′ē-əs) *adj.* **1.** Full of or characterized by extreme anger; raging. **2.** Suggestive of extreme anger in action or appearance; fierce. [ME < OFr. *furieus* < Lat. *furiōsus* < *furia*, fury. See FURY.] —**fu′ri•ous•ly** *adv.*

furl (fûrl) *v.* **furled, furl•ing, furls.** —*tr.* To roll up and secure (a flag or sail, for example) to something else. —*intr.* To be or become rolled up. —*n.* **1.** The act or an instance of rolling up. **2.** A single roll or a rolled section. [Perh. < Fr. *ferler* < OFr. *ferlier*, to fasten : *ferm*, firm; see FIRM[1] + *lier*, to bind (< Lat. *ligāre*; see **leig-***).]

fur•long (fûr′lông′, -lŏng′) *n.* A unit for measuring distance, equal to ⅛ mile (201 meters). See table at **measurement.** [ME < OE *furlang* : *furh*, furrow + *lang*, long; see LONG[1].]

fur•lough (fûr′lō) *n.* **1.a.** A leave of absence or vacation, esp. one granted to a member of the armed forces. **b.** A usu. temporary layoff from work. **c.** A leave of absence from prison granted to a prisoner. **2.** The papers or documents authorizing a leave. —*tr.v.* **-loughed, -lough•ing, -loughs.** **1.** To grant a leave to. **2.** To lay off (workers). [Alteration of *vorloffe, furlogh* < Du. *verlof* < MDu. See **leubh-***.]

fur•mi•ty (fûr′mĭ-tē) *n.* Var. of **frumenty.**

furn. *abbr.* Furnished.

fur•nace (fûr′nĭs) *n.* **1.** An enclosure in which energy in a nonthermal form is converted to heat, esp. such an enclosure in which heat is generated by the combustion of a suitable fuel. **2.** An intensely hot place. **3.** A severe test or trial. [ME < OFr. *fornais* < Lat. *fornāx, fornāc-*, oven. See **gʷher-***.]

fur•nish (fûr′nĭsh) *tr.v.* **-nished, -nish•ing, -nish•es.** **1.** To equip with what is needed, esp. to provide furniture for. **2.** To supply; give. [ME *furnisshen* < OFr. *fournir, fourniss-*, of Gmc. orig. See **per**[1]*.] —**fur′nish•er** *n.*

fur•nish•ing (fûr′nĭ-shĭng) *n.* **1.** A piece of equipment necessary or useful for comfort or convenience. **2. furnishings.** The furniture, appliances, and other movable articles in a home or other building. **3. furnishings.** Wearing apparel and accessories.

fur•ni•ture (fûr′nĭ-chər) *n.* **1.** The movable articles in a room or an establishment that make it fit for living or working. **2.** *Archaic.* The necessary equipment for a saddle horse. [OFr. *fourniture* < *fournir*, to furnish. See FURNISH.]

Fur•ni•vall (fûr′nə-vəl), **Frederick James.** 1825–1910. British philologist who proposed the *Oxford English Dictionary* (1857).

fu•ror (fyo͝or′ôr′, -ər) *n.* **1.** A general commotion; public disorder or uproar. **2.** Violent anger; frenzy. **3.** A fashion adopted enthusiastically by the public; a fad. **4.** A state of intense excitement or ecstasy. [ME *furour*, wrath, fury < OFr. *fureur* < Lat. *furor* < *furere*, to rage.]

fu•rore (fyo͝or′ôr′, -ōr′) *n. Chiefly British.* Var. of **furor** 1, 3. [Ital. < Lat. *furor*, frenzy. See FUROR.]

fu•ro•se•mide (fyo͞o-rō′sə-mīd′) *n.* A crystalline powder, $C_{12}H_{11}ClN_2O_5S$, used as a diuretic. [FUR(FURAL) + S(ULFO)- + -*emide* (alteration of AMIDE).]

furred (fûrd) *adj.* **1.** Bearing fur. **2.** Made, covered, or trimmed with fur. **3.** Wearing fur garments. **4.** Covered or coated as if with fur. **5.** Provided with furring, as a wall.

fur•ri•er (fûr′ē-ər) *n.* **1.** One that deals in furs. **2.** One whose occupation is the dressing, designing, cleaning, or repairing of furs. [Alteration (influenced by CLOTHIER) of ME *furrer* < AN *furrere* < OFr. *forrer*, to line with fur. See FUR.]

fur•ri•er•y (fûr′ē-ə-rē) *n., pl.* **-ies. 1.** Fur garments and trimmings considered as a group. **2.** The business of a furrier.

fur•ring (fûr′ĭng) *n.* **1.** Trimming or lining made of fur. **2.** A furlike coating, as on the tongue. **3.a.** The preparation of a wall, ceiling, or floor with strips of wood or metal to provide a level substratum for plaster, flooring, or another surface or to create an air space. **b.** Strips of material used in furring.

fur•row (fûr′ō, fŭr′ō) *n.* **1.** A long, narrow, shallow trench made in the ground by a plow. **2.** A rut, groove, or narrow depression. **3.** A deep wrinkle in the skin, as on the forehead. —*v.* **-rowed, -row•ing, -rows.** —*tr.* **1.** To make long, narrow, shallow trenches in; plow. **2.** To form grooves or deep wrinkles in. —*intr.* To become furrowed or wrinkled. [ME *forwe* < OE *furh.*]

fur•ry (fûr′ē, fŭr′ē) *adj.* **-ri•er, -ri•est. 1.** Consisting of or similar to fur. **2.a.** Covered with, wearing, or trimmed with fur. **b.** Covered with a furlike substance. **3.** Having a furlike quality, as in tone; fuzzy: *a furry voice.* **—fur′ri•ness** *n.*

fur seal *n.* Any of several eared seals of the genera *Callorhinus* or *Arctocephalus,* whose underfur is used in making garments.

fur seal
Antarctic fur seal
Arctocephalus gazella

Fürth (fo͝ort, fürt). A city of S-central Germany, a suburb of Nuremberg; founded in the late 8th cent. Pop. 97,623.

fur•ther (fûr′*th*ər) *adj.* A comp. of **far. 1.** More distant in degree, time, or space. **2.** Additional. —*adv.* A comp. of **far. 1.** To a greater extent; more. **2.** In addition; furthermore. **3.** At or to a more distant or advanced point. See Usage Note at **farther.** —*tr.v.* **-thered, -ther•ing, -thers.** To help the progress of; advance. See Syns at **advance.** [ME < OE *furthra* < *furthor*, farther. Adv. < ME < OE *furthor.* See **per**[1]*.] **—fur′ther•er** *n.*

fur•ther•ance (fûr′*th*ər-əns) *n.* The act of furthering, advancing, or helping forward.

fur•ther•more (fûr′*th*ər-môr′, -mōr′) *adv.* In addition.

fur•ther•most (fûr′*th*ər-mōst′) *adj.* Most distant or remote.

fur•thest (fûr′*th*ĭst) *adj.* A superl. of **far.** Most distant in degree, time, or space. —*adv.* A superl. of **far. 1.** To the greatest extent or degree. **2.** At or to the most distant point in space or time. [ME < *further*, more distant. See FURTHER.]

fur•tive (fûr′tĭv) *adj.* **1.** Characterized by stealth; surreptitious. **2.** Expressive of hidden motives or purposes; shifty. [Fr. *furtif* < OFr. < Lat. *furtīvus* < *furtum*, theft < *fūr*, thief. See **bher-**[1]*.] **—fur′tive•ly** *adv.* **—fur′tive•ness** *n.*

fu•run•cle (fyo͝or′ŭng′kəl) *n.* See **boil**[2]. [Lat. *fūrunculus*, knob on a vine that "steals" the sap, dim. of *fūr*, thief. See **bher-**[1]*.] **—fu•run′cu•lar** (fyo͞o-rŭng′kyə-lər), **fu•run′cu•lous** (-ləs) *adj.*

fu•run•cu•lo•sis (fyo͞o-rŭng′kyə-lō′sĭs) *n.* A skin condition characterized by the development of recurring boils. [Lat. *fūrunculus*, furuncle; see FURUNCLE + -OSIS.]

fu•ry (fyo͝or′ē) *n., pl.* **-ries. 1.** Violent anger; rage. See Syns at **anger. 2.** Violent, uncontrolled action; turbulence. **3. Furies.** *Gk. & Rom. Myth.* The three winged goddesses, Alecto, Megaera, and Tisiphone, who pursue and punish doers of unavenged crimes. **4.** A woman regarded as angry or spiteful. [ME *furie* < OFr. < Lat. *furia* < *furere*, to rage.]

furze (fûrz) *n.* See **gorse.** [ME *furse* < OE *fyrs.*]

fu•sain (fyo͞o-zān′, fyo͞o′zān) *n.* **1.a.** Fine charcoal in stick form, made from spindle tree wood. **b.** A sketch or drawing made with this charcoal. **2.** A dull dark gray, brittle, porous type of bituminous coal resembling charcoal. [Fr., spindle tree, charcoal made from its wood < VLat. *fūsāgō, *fūsāgin-, spindle < Lat. *fūsus.*]

Fu•san (fo͞o′sän′). See **Pusan.**

fu•sar•i•um (fyo͞o-zâr′ē-əm) *n., pl.* **-i•a** (-ē-ə). Any of various pathogenic fungi of the genus *Fusarium,* chiefly inhabiting temperate climates and infecting both plants and animals, including human beings. [NLat., genus name, poss. < Lat. *fūsus*, spindle (< its shape).]

fus•cous (fŭs′kəs) *adj.* Dark brownish-gray in color. [< Lat. *fuscus.*]

fuse[1] also **fuze** (fyo͞oz) —*n.* **1.** A cord of readily combustible material that is lighted at one end to detonate an explosive at the other end. **2.** Often **fuze.** A mechanical or electrical mechanism used to detonate an explosive charge or a device such as a bomb or grenade. —*tr.v.* **fused, fus•ing, fus•es** also **fuzed, fuz•ing, fuz•es.** To equip with a mechanical or electrical fuse. [< Ital. *fuso*, spindle < Lat. *fūsus.*]

fuse[2] (fyo͞oz) *v.* **fused, fus•ing, fus•es.** —*tr.* **1.** To liquefy or reduce to a plastic state by heating; melt. **2.** To mix (constituent elements) together by or as if by melting; blend. —*intr.* **1.** To become liquefied from heat. **2.** To become mixed or united by or as if by melting together. —*n.* A safety device that protects an electric circuit from excessive current, consisting of or containing a metal element that melts when current exceeds a specific amperage, thereby opening the circuit. [Lat. *fundere, fūs-*, to melt. See **gheu-***.]

fused quartz (fyo͞ozd) *n.* See **quartz glass.**

fused silica *n.* See **quartz glass.**

fu•see also **fu•zee** (fyo͞o-zē′) *n.* **1.** A lucifer or a vesuvian. **2.** A colored flare used as a warning signal for trucks and railroad trains. **3.** A conical pulley with a spiral groove, used in a cord- or chain-winding clock to maintain even travel as the force of the mainspring lessens in unwinding. **4.** A combustible fuse for detonating explosives. [< Fr. *fusée*, spindle, rocket, flare, fuse < OFr., spindleful of thread < *fus*, spindle < Lat. *fūsus.*]

fu•se•lage (fyo͞o′sə-läzh′, -zə-) *n.* The central body of an aircraft, to which the wings and tail assembly are attached and which accommodates the crew, passengers, and cargo. [Fr. < *fuselé*, spindle-shaped < OFr. *fusel*, spindle < VLat. *fūsellus, dim. of Lat. *fūsus.*]

Fu•sel•i (fyo͞o′zə-lē′), **Henry.** 1741–1825. Swiss-born British painter whose works include *The Nightmare* (1781).

fu•sel oil (fyo͞o′zəl) *n.* An acrid, oily, poisonous liquid mixture of amyl alcohols, occurring in incompletely distilled alcoholic liquids and used as a solvent and in explosives and pure amyl alcohols. [Ger. *Fusel*, bad liquor < LGer.]

Fu•shun (fo͞o′sho͞on′, fü′shün′). A city of NE China E of Shenyang. Pop. 1,240,000.

fu•si•ble (fyo͞o′zə-bəl) *adj.* Capable of being fused or melted by heating. **—fu′si•bil′i•ty, fu′si•ble•ness** *n.*

fusible metal *n.* A metal alloy having a low melting point, used as solder and for safety plugs and fuses.

fu•si•form (fyo͞o′zə-fôrm′) *adj.* Tapering at each end; spindle-shaped. [Lat. *fūsus*, spindle + -FORM.]

fu•sil (fyo͞o′zəl) *n.* A light flintlock musket. [Fr., steel in a flintlock, firearm < OFr. *fuisil*, steel for a tinderbox < VLat. *focīlis (petra), fire-(stone) < LLat. *focus*, fire < Lat., hearth.]

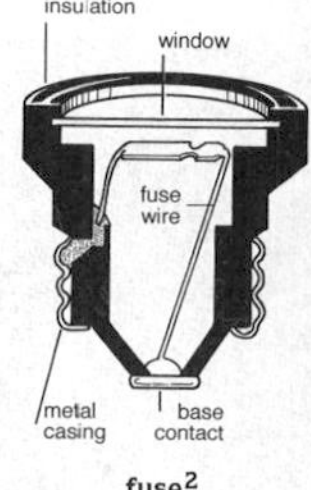

fuse[2]

fu•sile (fyo͞o′zəl, -zīl′) *adj. Archaic.* **1.** Formed by melting or casting. **2.** Capable of being fused; fusible. [ME < Lat. *fūsilis* < *fūsus*, p.part. of *fundere*, to melt. See **gheu-***.]

fu•sil•ier also **fu•sil•eer** (fyo͞o′zə-lîr′) *n.* **1.** A soldier in any of certain British army regiments formerly armed with fusils. **2.** A soldier armed with a fusil. [Fr., musketeer < *fusil*, musket. See FUSIL.]

fu•sil•lade (fyo͞o′sə-läd′, -lād′, -zə-, fyo͞o′sə-läd′, -lād′, -zə-) *n.* **1.** A discharge from a number of firearms, fired simultaneously or in rapid succession. **2.** A rapid outburst or barrage, as of insults. —*tr.v.* **-lad•ed, -lad•ing, -lades.** To attack with a fusillade. [Fr. < *fusiller*, to shoot < *fusil*, firearm. See FUSIL.]

Fu•sin (fo͞o′shĭn′, fü′-). See **Fuxin.**

fu•sion (fyo͞o′zhən) *n.* **1.** The act or procedure of liquefying or melting by the application of heat. **2.** The liquid or melted state induced by heat. **3.a.** The merging of different elements into a union: *fusion of metals in an alloy.* **b.** A union resulting from fusing: *a fusion of religion and politics.* **4.** *Phys.* A nuclear reaction in which light nuclei combine to form a heavier nucleus with the release of energy. **5.** *Mus.* Jazz-rock. [Lat. *fūsiō, fūsiōn-* < *fūsus*, p.part. of *fundere*, to melt. See **gheu-***.]

fusion bomb *n.* A nuclear bomb, esp. a hydrogen bomb, that derives its released energy principally from fusion reactions.

fu•sion•ism (fyo͞o′zhə-nĭz′əm) *n.* The theory or practice of forming coalitions, esp. political ones. **—fu′sion•ist** *n.*

fuss (fŭs) *n.* **1.** Needlessly nervous or useless activity; commotion. **2.a.** A state of excessive and unwarranted concern over an unimportant matter. **b.** An objection; a protest. **3.** A quarrel. **4.** A display of affectionate excitement and attention. —*v.* **fussed, fuss•ing, fuss•es.** —*intr.* **1.** To trouble or worry over trifles. **2.** To be excessively careful or solicitous. **3.** To get into or be in a state of nervous or useless activity; fidget. **4.** To object; complain. —*tr.* To disturb or vex with unimportant matters. [?] **—fuss′er** *n.*

fuss•budg•et also **fuss•bud•get** (fŭs′bŭj′ĭt) *n.* A person who fusses over trifles.

fuss•pot (fŭs′pŏt′) *n.* See **fussbudget.**

fuss•y (fŭs′ē) *adj.* **-i•er, -i•est. 1.** Easily upset; given to bouts

ă pat	oi boy
ā pay	ou out
âr care	o͝o took
ä father	o͞o boot
ĕ pet	ŭ cut
ē be	ûr urge
ĭ pit	th thin
ī pie	*th* this
îr pier	hw which
ŏ pot	zh vision
ō toe	ə about, item
ô paw	

Stress marks:
′ (primary);
′ (secondary), as in
dictionary (dĭk′shə-nĕr′ē)

of ill temper. **2.** Paying great or excessive attention to personal tastes and appearance; fastidious. **3.** Calling for or requiring great attention to sometimes trivial details. **4.** Full of superfluous details. —**fuss′i•ly** *adv.* —**fuss′i•ness** *n.*

fus•tian (fŭs′chən) *n.* **1.a.** A coarse sturdy cloth made of cotton and flax. **b.** Any of several thick twilled cotton fabrics, such as corduroy, having a short nap. **2.** Pretentious speech or writing; pompous language. —*adj.* **1.** Made of or as if of fustian. **2.** Pompous, bombastic, and ranting. [ME < OFr. *fustaigne* < Med.Lat. *fustāneum*, poss. < Lat. *fūstis*, wooden stick, club (loan transl. of Gk. *xulina (lina)*, wood-linen, cotton) or from *El Fostat* (El Fustat), a section of Cairo, Egypt.]

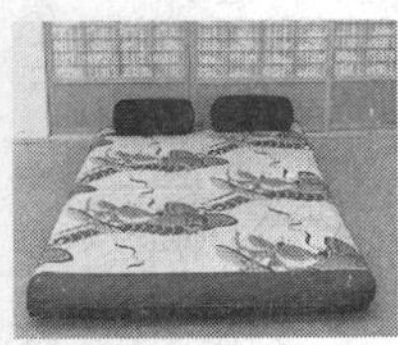
futon

fus•tic (fŭs′tĭk) *n.* **1.** A small dioecious tropical American tree *(Chlorophora tinctoria)* having wood that yields a yellow dyestuff. **2.** The wood of this plant. **3.** A dyestuff obtained from the wood of this plant. [ME *fustik* < OFr. *fustoc* < Ar. *fustuq* < Gk. *pistakē*, pistachio. See PISTACHIO.]

fus•ti•gate (fŭs′tĭ-gāt′) *tr.v.* **-gat•ed, -gat•ing, -gates. 1.** To beat with a club; cudgel. **2.** To criticize harshly. [LLat. *fūstigāre, fūstigāt-* : < Lat. *fūstis*, club + *agere*, to do; see **ag-***.] —**fus′ti•ga′tion** *n.*

fus•ty (fŭs′tē) *adj.* **-ti•er, -ti•est. 1.** Smelling of mildew or decay; musty. **2.** Old-fashioned; antique. [ME < OFr. *fust*, piece of wood, wine cask < Lat. *fūstis*, stick, club.] —**fus′ti•ly** *adv.* —**fus′ti•ness** *n.*

fu•su•ma (fo͞o-so͞o′mä) *n., pl.* **fusuma.** A sliding partition of thick paper mounted in grooves on the floor and ceiling of a Japanese house and variously positioned to form rooms. [J.]

fut. *abbr.* **1.** *Gram.* Future. **2.** *Bus.* Futures.

fu•thark (fo͞o′thärk′) *n.* **1.** The common Germanic runic alphabet. **2.** Also **fu•thorc** or **fu•thork** (-thôrk′). The Old English runic alphabet. [< the first six letters of the alphabet: *f, u, th, a, r, k* (or *c*).]

fu•tile (fyo͞ot′l, fyo͞o′tīl′) *adj.* **1.** Having no useful result. **2.** Trifling and frivolous; idle. [Lat. *fūtilis*. See **gheu-***.] —**fu′tile•ly** *adv.* —**fu′tile•ness** *n.*

Syns: *futile, barren, bootless, fruitless, unavailing, useless, vain.* The central meaning shared by these adjectives is "producing no result or effect": *a futile effort; a barren search; bootless entreaties; fruitless labors; an unavailing attempt; a useless discussion; vain regrets.* **Ant:** *useful.*

fu•til•i•tar•i•an (fyo͞o-tĭl′ĭ-târ′ē-ən) *adj.* Holding or based on the view that human endeavor is futile. —*n.* One who holds the view that human endeavor is futile. [FUTILIT(Y) + -ARIAN.] —**fu•til′i•tar′i•an•ism** *n.*

fu•til•i•ty (fyo͞o-tĭl′ĭ-tē) *n., pl.* **-ties. 1.** The quality of having no useful result; uselessness. **2.** Lack of importance or purpose; frivolousness. **3.** A futile act.

fu•ton (fo͞o′tŏn) *n., pl.* **futon** or **-tons.** An article of bedding consisting of a pad of tufted cotton batting or similar material, used on a floor or a raised frame as a mattress. [J., bedclothes, bedding.]

fut•tock (fŭt′ək) *n. Naut.* One of the curved timbers that forms a rib in the frame of a ship. [ME *fottek*, perh. alteration of *fothok* : *fot*, foot; see FOOT + *hok*, hook; see HOOK.]

futtock plate *n. Naut.* An iron plate attached horizontally to the top of the lower mast to secure the topmast rigging and the upper ends of the futtock shrouds.

futtock shroud *n. Naut.* One of the iron rods extending from a band on the lower mast to the futtock plate, used to brace the base of the topmast.

Fu•tu•na Islands (fə-to͞o′nə, fo͞o-) also **Hoorn Islands** (hôrn, hōrn). An island group of the French overseas territory of Wallis and Futuna in the SW Pacific NE of Fiji; annexed by France in 1887.

futurism
Unique Forms of Continuity in Space, 1913, by Umberto Boccioni. *Bronze (cast 1913), 43⅞" × 34⅞" × 15¾". The Museum of Modern Art, New York. Acquired through the Lillie P. Bliss Bequest.*

fu•ture (fyo͞o′chər) *n.* **1.** The indefinite time yet to come. **2.** Something that will happen in time to come. **3.** A prospective or expected condition, esp. one considered with regard to growth, advancement, or development: *a business with no future.* **4. futures.** *Bus.* Commodities or stocks bought or sold upon agreement of delivery in time to come. **5.** *Gram.* **a.** The form of a verb used in speaking of action that has not yet occurred or of states not yet in existence. **b.** A verb form in the future tense. —*adj.* That is to be or to come; of or existing in later time. [ME < OFr. *futur* < Lat. *futūrus*, about to be. See **bheuə-***.]

fu•ture•less (fyo͞o′chər-lĭs) *adj.* Having no prospect or hope of success in one's future. —**fu′ture•less•ness** *n.*

future perfect *n. Gram.* A verb tense that expresses action completed by a specified time in the future, formed in English by combining *will have* or *shall have* with a past participle.

future shock *n.* A condition of distress and disorientation due to inability to cope with rapid technological change. [After the book *Future Shock* by Alvin Toffler (b. 1928).]

future tense *n. Gram.* A verb tense expressing future time.

fu•tur•ism (fyo͞o′chə-rĭz′əm) *n.* **1.** A belief that the meaning of life and one's personal fulfillment lie in the future. **2.** An artistic movement originating in Italy around 1910 whose aim was to express the energetic, dynamic, and violent quality of contemporary life. —**fu′tur•ist** *n.*

fu•tur•is•tic (fyo͞o′chə-rĭs′tĭk) *adj.* **1.** Of or relating to the future. **2.a.** Of, characterized by, or expressing a vision of the future. **b.** Being ahead of the times; innovative or revolutionary. **3.** Of or relating to futurism. —**fu′tur•is′ti•cal•ly** *adv.*

fu•tur•ist•ics (fyo͞o′chə-rĭs′tĭks) *n.* *(used with a sing. v.)* Futurology.

fu•tu•ri•ty (fyo͞o-to͝or′ĭ-tē, -tyo͝or′-, -cho͝or′-) *n., pl.* **-ties. 1.** The future. **2.** The quality or condition of being in or of the future. **3.** A future event or possibility. **4.** *Sports.* A futurity race.

futurity race *n. Sports.* A race for horses in which the competitors are entered at or before their birth.

fu•tur•ol•o•gy (fyo͞o′chə-rŏl′ə-jē) *n.* The study or forecasting of potential developments, as in science and society, based on current conditions and trends. —**fu′tur•o•log′i•cal** (fyo͞o′-chər-ə-lŏj′ĭ-kəl) *adj.* —**fu′tu•rol′o•gist** *n.*

futz (fŭts) *intr.v.* **futzed, futz•ing, futz•es.** *Slang.* To waste time or effort on frivolities; fool. Often used with *around.* [Poss. blend of FUCK and PUTZ.]

Fu•xin also **Fu•sin** (fo͞o′shĭn′, fü′-). A city of NE China WNW of Shenyang. Pop. 551,300.

fuze (fyo͞oz) *n. & v.* Var. of **fuse[1]**.

fu•zee (fyo͞o-zē′) *n.* Var. of **fusee.**

Fu•zhou (fo͞o′jō′) also **Foo•chow** or **Fu•chou** (fo͞o′jō′, -chou′). A city of SE China on the Min R. delta; the cap. of Fujian province since the 10th cent. Pop. 754,500.

fuzz[1] (fŭz) *n.* A mass or coating of fine light fibers, hairs, or particles; down. —*v.* **fuzzed, fuzz•ing, fuzz•es.** —*tr.* **1.** To cover with fuzz. **2.** To make blurred or indistinct: *fuzzing up the details.* —*intr.* To become blurred or obscure. [Perh. back-formation < FUZZY.]

fuzz[2] (fŭz) *n. Slang.* The police. [?]

fuzz•y (fŭz′ē) *adj.* **-i•er, -i•est. 1.** Covered with fuzz. **2.** Of or resembling fuzz. **3.** Not clear; indistinct: *a fuzzy recollection.* **4.** Not coherent; confused: *a fuzzy plan.* [Perh. < LGer. *fussig*, spongy. See **pū̆-***.] —**fuzz′i•ly** *adv.* —**fuzz′i•ness** *n.*

fuzz•y•head•ed (fŭz′ē-hĕd′ĭd) *adj.* **1.a.** Marked by unclear confused thinking. **b.** Giddy; silly. **2.** Having a head covered with fuzz. —**fuzz′y•head′ed•ness** *n.*

f.v. *abbr. Lat.* Folio verso (on the back of the page).

FWB *abbr.* Four-wheel brake.

fwd *abbr. Sports.* Forward.

FWD *abbr.* **1.** Four-wheel drive. **2.** Front-wheel drive.

FX *abbr.* Foreign exchange.

FY *abbr.* Fiscal year.

-fy or **-ify** *suff.* Cause to become; make. *basify.* [ME *-fien* < OFr. *-fier* < Lat. *-ficāre, -ficārī* < *-ficus*, -fic.]

FYI *abbr.* For your information.

fyke (fīk) *n.* A long bag-shaped fishing net held open by hoops. [Du. *fuik* < MDu. *fūke*.]

fyl•fot (fĭl′fŏt′) *n.* A swastika. [Originally perh. a device for the foot of a painted window : FILL + FOOT.]

Fyn (fĭn, fün). An island of S-central Denmark W of Sjaelland.

FZS or **F.Z.S.** *abbr.* Fellow of the Zoological Society.

Gg

gable roof
Three of the gables on the House of the Seven Gables, Salem, Massachusetts

g[1] or **G** (jē) *n., pl.* **g's** or **G's. 1.** The seventh letter of the modern English alphabet. **2.** Any of the speech sounds represented by the letter *g*. **3.** *Mus.* **a.** The fifth tone in the scale of C major or the seventh tone in the relative minor scale. **b.** A key or scale in which G is the tonic. **4.** A unit of acceleration equal to the acceleration caused by gravity at the earth's surface, about 9.8 meters (32 feet) per second per second.

g[2] *abbr.* **1.** Acceleration of gravity. **2.** Gram.

G[1] (jē) *n.* A movie rating that allows admission to all ages. [Short for GENERAL.]

G[2] (jē) *n., pl.* **G's.** *Slang.* One thousand dollars. [G(RAND), one thousand dollars.]

G[3] The symbol for **conductance.**

G[4] *abbr.* **1.** *Phys.* Gauss. **2.** Also **G.** Good. **3.** Gravitational constant. **4.** Guanine.

g. *abbr.* **1.** *Gram.* Gender. **2.** *Gram.* Genitive. **3.** Also **G.**

Gourde. **4.** Also **G.** Guilder. **5.** Also **G.** Guinea. **6.** Also **G.** Gulf.

Ga[1] The symbol for the element **gallium.**

Ga[2] *abbr. Bible.* Galatians.

GA *abbr.* **1.** General agent. **2.** Also **G.A.** General Assembly. **3.** Also **Ga.** Georgia.

ga. *abbr.* Gauge.

G.A. *abbr.* General average.

gab (găb) *Slang.* —*intr.v.* **gabbed, gab•bing, gabs.** To talk idly or incessantly, as about trivial matters. —*n.* Idle talk; chatter. [ME *gabben,* to scoff, speak foolishly < ON *gabba,* to scoff.] —**gab′ber** *n.*

GABA *abbr.* Gamma-aminobutyric acid.

gab•ar•dine (găb′ər-dēn′, găb′ər-dēn′) *n.* **1.** A sturdy, tightly woven fabric of cotton, wool, or rayon twill. **2.** See **gaberdine** 1. **3.** *Chiefly British.* A laborer's long loose smock; a gaberdine. [Alteration of GABERDINE.]

gab•ble (găb′əl) *v.* **-bled, -bling, -bles.** —*intr.* **1.** To speak rapidly or incoherently; jabber. **2.** To make rapid low muttering or quacking sounds, as a goose or duck. —*tr.* To utter rapidly or incoherently. —*n.* **1.** Rapid, incoherent, or meaningless speech. **2.** The gabble of a goose or duck. [Prob. freq. of GAB.] —**gab′bler** *n.*

gab•bro (găb′rō) *n., pl.* **-bros.** A usu. coarse-grained igneous rock composed chiefly of calcic plagioclase and pyroxene. [Ital., perh. < Lat. *glaber,* bald, beardless.] —**gab•bro′ic** (gă-brō′ĭk) *adj.* —**gab′broid′** (găb′roid′) *adj.*

gab•by (găb′ē) *adj.* **-bi•er, -bi•est.** *Slang.* Tending to talk excessively; garrulous. —**gab′bi•ness** *n.*

ga•belle (gə-bĕl′) *n.* A tax, esp. the salt tax imposed in France before 1790. [ME *gabel* < OFr. < OItal. *gabella* < Ar. *qabāla,* tribute < *qabila,* to receive.]

gab•er•dine (găb′ər-dēn′, găb′ər-dēn′) *n.* **1.** A long coarse cloak or frock. **2.** *Chiefly British.* A loose smock worn by laborers. **3.** See **gabardine** 1. [Obsolete Fr. *gauvardine* < OFr. *galvardine,* perh. < MHGer. *wallevart,* pilgrimage : *wallen,* to roam (< OHGer. *wallōn;* see **wel-[2]***) + *vart,* journey (< OHGer. < *faran,* to go; see **per-[2]***).]

gab•fest (găb′fĕst′) *n. Slang.* **1.** An informal gathering or session for the exchange of news, opinions, and gossip. **2.** A long animated conversation or discussion.

ga•bi•on (gā′bē-ən) *n.* **1.** A cylindrical wicker basket filled with earth and stones, formerly used in building fortifications. **2.** A hollow metal cylinder used esp. in dams and foundations. [Fr. < Ital. *gabbione,* aug. of *gabbia,* cage < Lat. *cavea.*]

ga•ble (gā′bəl) *n.* **1.a.** The generally triangular section of wall at the end of a pitched roof, occupying the space between the two slopes of the roof. **b.** The whole end wall of a building or wing having a gable roof. **2.** A triangular, usu. ornamental architectural section, as one above an arched door or window. [ME *gable, gavel* < Norman Fr. *gable* (perh. of Celt. orig.) and < ON *gafl;* see **ghebh-el-***.] —**ga′bled** *adj.*

Ga•ble (gā′bəl), **(William) Clark.** 1901–60. Amer. actor whose films include *It Happened One Night* (1934).

gable roof *n.* A pitched roof having a gable at each end.

Ga•bo (gä′bō, -bə), **Naum.** 1890–1977. Russian-born Amer. sculptor known for his experiments with constructivism.

Ga•bon (gă-bōN′). A country of W-central Africa on the Atlantic Ocean; achieved independence from France in 1960. Cap. Libreville. Pop. 1,312,000.

Ga•bor (gä′bôr, gə-bôr′), **Dennis.** 1900–79. Hungarian-born British physicist who won a 1971 Nobel Prize.

Ga•bo•rone (gä′bə-rōn′, -rō′nē). The cap. of Botswana, in the SE part; founded c. 1890. Pop. 72,000.

Ga•bri•el (gā′brē-əl) *n. Bible.* An archangel acting as the messenger of God.

ga•by (gā′bē) *n., pl.* **-bies.** *Chiefly British.* A person of deficient intelligence. [?]

gad[1] (găd) *intr.v.* **gad•ded, gad•ding, gads.** To move about restlessly and with little purpose. See Syns at **wander.** [ME *gadden,* to hurry.] —**gad′der** *n.*

gad[2] (găd) *n.* **1.** A pointed tool, such as a spike, used for breaking rock or ore. **2.** A goad, as for prodding cattle. —*tr.v.* **gad•ded, gad•ding, gads.** To break up (ore, for example) with a gad. [ME < ON *gaddr.*]

Gad[1] (găd). In the Bible, a son of Jacob and the forebear of one of the tribes of Israel.

Gad[2] (găd) *interj.* Used to express surprise or dismay. [Alteration of GOD.]

gad•a•bout (găd′ə-bout′) *n.* One who roams or roves about, as in search of amusement or social activity.

gad•fly (găd′flī′) *n., pl.* **-flies. 1.** A persistent, irritating critic; a nuisance. **2.** One that acts as a provocative stimulus; a goad. **3.** Any of various flies, esp. of the family Tabanidae, that bite or annoy livestock and other animals.

gadg•et (găj′ĭt) *n.* A small specialized mechanical or electronic device; a contrivance. [?] —**gadg′et•y** *adj.*

gadg•e•teer (găj′ĭ-tîr′) *n.* A person who designs, builds, or delights in the use of gadgets.

gadg•et•ry (găj′ĭ-trē) *n.* **1.** Gadgets considered as a group. **2.** The design or construction of gadgets.

ga•doid (gā′doid′, găd′oid′) also **ga•did** (gā′dĭd) —*adj.* Of or belonging to the fish family Gadidae, which includes the cods and the hakes. —*n.* A fish of the family Gadidae. [NLat. *Gadus,* fish genus (< Gk. *gados,* a kind of fish) + -OID.]

gad•o•lin•ite (găd′l-ə-nīt′) *n.* A dark green or greenish-black silicate mineral, $Be_2FeY_2Si_2O_{10}$, containing several of the rare earths in combination with iron.

gad•o•lin•i•um (găd′l-ĭn′ē-əm) *n. Symbol* **Gd** A malleable, ductile metallic rare-earth element obtained from monazite and used in improving ferromagnetic characteristics of iron, cerium, and related alloys. Atomic number 64; atomic weight 157.25; melting point 1,312°C; boiling point approx. 3,000°C; specific gravity from 7.8 to 7.896; valence 3. See table at **element.** [After Johan *Gadolin* (1760–1852), Finnish chemist.]

ga•droon (gə-dro͞on′) *n.* **1.** *Archit.* A band of convex molding carved with ornamental beading or reeding. **2.** An ornamental band, used esp. in silverwork, embellished with fluting, reeding, or another continuous pattern. [Fr. *godron* < OFr. *goderon,* perh. ult. < Lat. *guttus,* flask < *gutta,* drop.] —**ga•drooned′** *adj.* —**ga•droon′ing** *n.*

Gads•den (gădz′dən). A city of NE AL NE of Birmingham. Pop. 42,523.

Gadsden, James. 1788–1858. Amer. diplomat, politician, and railroad promoter who negotiated the Gadsden Purchase.

Gadsden Purchase. An area in extreme S NM and AZ S of the Gila R.; purchased by the U.S. from Mexico in 1853.

gad•wall (găd′wôl′) *n.* A North American duck *(Anas strepera)* having gray or brown plumage. [?]

gad•zooks (găd′zo͞oks′) *interj.* Used as a mild or ironic oath.

Gae•a (jē′ə) also **Gai•a** (gā′ə) *n. Gk. Myth.* The goddess of the earth, who bore and married Uranus.

Gael (gāl) *n.* **1.** A Gaelic-speaking Celt of Scotland, Ireland, or the Isle of Man. **2.** A Scottish Highlander. [Sc.Gael. *Gaidheal* and Ir.Gael. *Gaedheal,* both < OIr. *Goídil.* See GOIDELIC.]

Gael•ic (gā′lĭk) *adj.* Of or relating to the Gaels or their culture or languages. —*n.* **1.** Goidelic. **2.** A Goidelic language.

gaff[1] (găf) *n.* **1.** A large iron hook attached to a pole or handle and used to land large fish. **2.** *Naut.* A spar attached to the mast and used to extend the upper edge of a fore-and-aft sail. **3.a.** A sharp metal spur or spike fastened to the leg of a gamecock. **b.** A climbing hook used by telephone and electric line workers. **4.** *Slang.* A trick or gimmick, esp. one used in a swindle or to rig a game. **5.** *Slang.* Harshness of treatment; abuse. —*tr.v.* **gaffed, gaf•fing, gaffs. 1.** To hook or land (a fish) using a gaff. **2.** To equip (a gamecock) with a gaff. **3.** *Slang.* **a.** To take in or defraud; swindle. **b.** To rig or fix in order to cheat. [ME *gaffe* < OFr. < OProv. *gaf* < *gafar,* to seize, of Gmc. orig. See **kap-***.]

gaff[2] (găf) *n. Chiefly British.* A public place of entertainment, esp. a cheap or disreputable music hall or theater. [?]

gaff[3] (găf) *n.* Var. of **gaffe.**

gaffe also **gaff** (găf) *n.* **1.** A clumsy social error. **2.** A blatant mistake or misjudgment. [Fr. < OFr., hook. See GAFF[1].]

gaf•fer (găf′ər) *n.* **1.** An electrician in charge of lighting on a movie or television set. **2.** *Chiefly British.* An old man or a rustic. **3.** *Chiefly British.* A boss or foreman. [Prob. alteration (influenced by GRANDFATHER) of GODFATHER.]

gaff rig *n. Naut.* A rig with a fore-and-aft sail that has its upper edge supported by a gaff.

gaff-top•sail (găf′tŏp′səl, -sāl′) *n. Naut.* A light triangular or quadrilateral sail set above a gaff.

gag (găg) *n.* **1.** Something forced into or put over the mouth to prevent speaking or crying out. **2.** An obstacle to or a censoring of free speech. **3.** A device placed in the mouth to keep it open, as in dentistry. **4.a.** A practical joke. **b.** A comic effect or remark. **5.** The act or an instance of gagging or choking. —*v.* **gagged, gag•ging, gags.** —*tr.* **1.** To prevent from speaking or crying out by using a gag. **2.** To stop or restrain from exercising free speech. **3.** To cause to choke, retch, or gag. **4.** To keep (the mouth) open by using a gag. **5.** To block off or obstruct (as a pipe). —*intr.* **1.a.** To experience a regurgitative spasm in the throat, as from revulsion to a food. **b.** To retch or choke. **2.** To make jokes or quips. [< ME *gaggen,* to suffocate, perh. of imit. orig.]

ga•ga (gä′gä′) *adj. Informal.* **1.** Silly; crazy. **2.** Completely absorbed, infatuated, or excited: *gaga over the album.* **3.** Senile; doddering. [Fr., old fool, gaga, of imit. orig.]

Ga•ga•rin (gə-gär′ĭn), **Yuri Alekseyevich.** 1934–68. Soviet cosmonaut who was the first person to travel in space (1961).

gage[1] (gāj) *n.* **1.** Something deposited or given as security against an obligation; a pledge. **2.** Something, such as a glove, offered or thrown down as a pledge or challenge to fight. **3.** A challenge. —*tr.v.* **gaged, gag•ing, gag•es.** *Archaic.* **1.** To pledge as security. **2.** To offer as a stake in a bet; wager. [ME < OFr., of Gmc. orig.]

gage[2] (gāj) *n.* Any of several varieties of plum. [After Sir William *Gage,* 18th-cent. British botanist.]

gage[3] (gāj) *n. & v.* Var. of **gauge.**

Gage (gāj), **Thomas.** 1721–87. British colonial administrator who served as governor of Massachusetts (1774–75).

gag•er (gā′jər) *n.* Var. of **gauger.**

gag•ger (găg′ər) *n.* One that gags.

Gabon

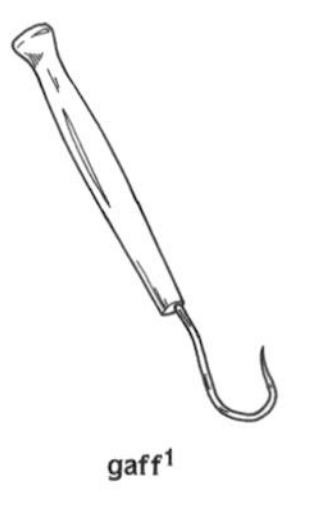

gaff[1]

Yuri Gagarin

ă pat	oi boy
ā pay	ou out
âr care	o͝o took
ä father	o͞o boot
ĕ pet	ŭ cut
ē be	ûr urge
ĭ pit	th thin
ī pie	*th* this
îr pier	hw which
ŏ pot	zh vision
ō toe	ə about,
ô paw	item

Stress marks:
′ (primary);
′ (secondary), as in
dictionary (dĭk′shə-nĕr′ē)

fem. of *gallus*, cock. See **gal-***.] —**gal′li•na′cean** *n.*

Gal•li•nas (gä-yē′näs), **Point.** A cape of N Colombia, the northernmost point of South America.

gall•ing (gô′lĭng) *adj.* Causing extreme irritation or chagrin; vexing: *a galling delay.* —**gall′ing•ly** *adv.*

gal•li•nip•per (găl′ə-nĭp′ər) *n.* A large mosquito or other insect capable of inflicting a painful bite. [?]

gal•li•nule (găl′ə-no͞ol′, -nyo͞ol′) *n.* Any of various wading and swimming birds of the family Rallidae, having dark iridescent plumage and a red bill tipped with yellow. [Lat. *gallinula*, pullet, dim. of *gallīna*, hen. See GALLINACEOUS.]

gal•li•pot (găl′ə-pŏt′) *n.* A small glazed earthenware jar formerly used by druggists for medicaments. [ME *galy pott* : prob. *galei*, galley; see GALLEY + *pott*, pot; see POT[1].]

gal•li•um (găl′ē-əm) *n. Symbol* **Ga** A rare metallic element that is liquid near room temperature, expands on solidifying, is found as a trace element in coal, bauxite, and other minerals, and is used in semiconductor technology. Atomic number 31; atomic weight 69.72; melting point 29.78°C; boiling point 2,403°C; specific gravity 5.907; valence 2, 3. See table at **element.** [< Lat. *gallus*, cock, translation of surname of Paul Émile *Lecoq* de Boisbaudran (1838–1912), French chemist, : Fr. *le*, the + *coq*, rooster.]

gallium arsenide *n.* A crystalline compound, GaAs, used in transistors, solar cells, and semiconducting lasers.

gal•li•vant also **gal•a•vant** (găl′ə-vănt′) *intr.v.* **-vant•ed, -vant•ing, -vants. 1.** To roam about in search of pleasure or amusement. See Syns at **wander. 2.** To play around amorously; flirt. [Perh. alteration of GALLANT.]

gal•li•wasp (găl′ə-wŏsp′, -wôsp′) *n.* Any of several long-bodied lizards of the genus *Diploglossus,* native to marshy regions of Central America and the West Indies. [?]

gall midge *n.* Any of various small mosquitolike flies of the family Cecidomyiidae, having larvae that mature in galls.

gall mite *n.* Any of various mites of the family Eriophyidae that produce galls on plants.

gall•nut (gôl′nŭt′) *n.* See **nutgall.**

gal•lo•glass or **gal•low•glass** (găl′ō-glăs′) *n.* An armed retainer or mercenary in the service of an Irish chieftain. [Ir. Gael. *galloglach* : *gall*, foreigner + *oglach*, soldier (< *ōg* < OIr. *ōac*; see **yeu-***).]

gal•lon (găl′ən) *n.* **1.a.** A unit of volume in the U.S. Customary System, used in liquid measure, equal to 4 quarts (3.785 liters). **b.** A unit of volume in the British Imperial System, used in liquid and dry measure, equal to 4 quarts (4.546 liters). See table at **measurement. 2.** A container with a capacity of one gallon. [ME, a liquid measure < ONFr. *galon.*]

gal•lon•age (găl′ə-nĭj) *n.* An amount measured in gallons.

gal•loon (gə-lo͞on′) *n.* A narrow band or braid used as trimming and commonly made of lace, metallic thread, or embroidery. [Fr. *galon* < OFr. *galonner*, to ribbon hair.]

gal•loot (gə-lo͞ot′) *n. Slang.* Var. of **galoot.**

gal•lop (găl′əp) *n.* **1.a.** A natural three-beat gait of a horse, faster than a canter, in which all four feet are off the ground at the same time during each stride. **b.** A fast running motion of other quadrupeds. **2.** A ride taken at a gallop. **3.** A rapid pace. —*v.* **-loped, -lop•ing, -lops.** —*tr.* **1.** To cause to gallop. **2.** To transport at or as if at a gallop. —*intr.* **1.** To ride a horse at a gallop. **2.** To move swiftly. [< ME *galopen*, to go at a gallop < OFr. *galoper*, of Gmc. orig. See **wel-**[1]*.]

Gambia

gal•lo•pade (găl′ə-păd′, -päd′) *n.* Var. of **galop.**

gal•lop•ing (găl′ə-pĭng) *adj.* **1.** Of or resembling a gallop, esp. in rhythm or rapidity. **2.** Developing at an accelerated rate and leading to death. Used of certain diseases.

Gal•lo•way (găl′ə-wā′). A region of SW Scotland. The **Mull of Galloway,** a promontory on a peninsula on its SW coast, is the southernmost point in Scotland.

gal•lows (găl′ōz) *n., pl.* **gallows** or **-lows•es. 1.a.** A device usu. consisting of two upright posts supporting a crossbeam from which a noose is suspended and used for execution by hanging; a gallows tree. **b.** A similar structure used for supporting or suspending. **2.** Execution by hanging. [ME *galwes*, pl. of *galwe*, gallows < OE *gealga, galga.*]

gallows bird *n. Informal.* One who is destined or deserves to be hanged.

gallows humor *n.* Humor about a grave or dire situation.

gallows tree *n.* A gallows.

gall•stone (gôl′stōn′) *n.* A small hard pathological concretion, composed chiefly of cholesterol, calcium salts, and bile pigments, formed in the gallbladder or in a bile duct.

Gal•lup (găl′əp). A city of NW NM near the AZ border WNW of Albuquerque. Pop. 19,154.

Gallup, George Horace. 1901–84. Amer. public-opinion analyst who accurately predicted the outcome of the 1936 presidential election.

gal•lus•es (găl′ə-sĭz) *pl.n.* Suspenders for trousers. [Var. of *gallowses*, pl. of GALLOWS.]

gall wasp *n.* Any of various wasps of the family Cynipidae whose larvae produce galls on oaks and other plants.

gambrel roof

Ga•lois theory (găl-wä′) *n.* The part of mathematical group theory concerned with the conditions under which a polynomial equation of power *n* with coefficients in a given mathematical field can be solved by repeating given operations and extracting the *n*th roots. [After Évariste *Galois* (1811–32), French mathematician.]

ga•loot also **gal•loot** (gə-lo͞ot′) *n. Slang.* A person, esp. a clumsy or uncouth one. [?]

gal•op (găl′əp) also **gal•o•pade** or **gal•lo•pade** (găl′ə-păd′, -päd′) *n.* **1.** A lively round dance in duple time, popular in the 19th century. **2.** The music for this dance. [Fr. < OFr., gallop < *galoper*, to gallop. See GALLOP.]

ga•lore (gə-lôr′, -lōr′) *adj.* In great numbers; in abundance. [Ir.Gael. *go leór*, enough : *go*, adv. particle + *leór*, enough (< OIr. *lour*, alteration of *roar*; see **wēro-***).]

ga•losh (gə-lŏsh′) *n.* **1.** A waterproof overshoe. **2.** *Obsolete.* A sturdy heavy-soled boot or shoe. [ME *galoche*, wooden soled shoe < OFr.]

Gals•wor•thy (gôlz′wûr′*thē*), **John.** 1867–1933. British writer who won the 1932 Nobel Prize for literature.

ga•lumph (gə-lŭmf′) *intr.v.* **-lumphed, -lumph•ing, -lumphs.** To move or run clumsily or heavily. [Perh. blend of GALLOP and TRIUMPH.]

galv. *abbr.* Galvanized.

Gal•va•ni (găl-vä′nē, gäl-), **Luigi.** 1737–98. Italian physiologist whose experiments stimulated research on electricity.

gal•van•ic (găl-văn′ĭk) *adj.* **1.** Of or relating to direct-current electricity, esp. when produced chemically. **2.a.** Having the effect of an electric shock. **b.** Produced as if by an electric shock. [GALVAN(ISM) + -IC.] —**gal•van′i•cal•ly** *adv.*

galvanic cell *n.* See **primary cell.**

gal•va•nism (găl′və-nĭz′əm) *n.* **1.** Direct-current electricity, esp. when produced chemically. **2.** Therapeutic application of direct-current electricity, esp. the electric stimulation of nerves and muscle. [After Luigi GALVANI.]

gal•va•nize (găl′və-nīz′) *tr.v.* **-nized, -niz•ing, -niz•es. 1.** To stimulate or shock with an electric current. **2.** To arouse to awareness or action; spur. **3.** To coat (iron or steel) with rust-resistant zinc. —**gal′va•ni•za′tion** (-nĭ-zā′shən) *n.* —**gal′va•niz′er** *n.*

galvano– *pref.* Galvanism; galvanic: *galvanometer.*

gal•va•no•mag•net•ic (găl′və-nō-măg-nĕt′ĭk, găl-văn′ō-) *adj.* Of or relating to the generation of an electric field by a magnetic field in semiconductors and metals.

gal•va•nom•e•ter (găl′və-nŏm′ĭ-tər) *n.* An instrument used to detect, measure, and determine the direction of small electric currents, usu. by means of mechanical effects produced by a coil in a magnetic field. —**gal′va•no•met′ric** (-nō-mĕt′rĭk), **gal′va•no•met′ri•cal** *adj.* —**gal′va•nom′e•try** *n.*

Gal•ves•ton (găl′vĭ-stən). A city of SE TX SSE of Houston on **Galveston Island** at the entrance to **Galveston Bay,** an arm of the Gulf of Mexico. Pop. 59,070.

Gal•way (gôl′wā′). A region of W-central Ireland bordering on **Galway Bay,** an inlet of the Atlantic. The city of **Galway** (pop. 37,835) was incorp. in the late 14th cent.

gal•yak (găl′yăk′) *n.* A flat glossy fur made from the pelt of a stillborn lamb or kid. [Russ. dial. *golyak*, sheepskin coat of smooth fur < Russ. *golyĭ*, smooth, bald, naked.]

gam[1] (găm) *n.* **1.** A social visit or friendly interchange, esp. between whalers or seafarers. **2.** A herd of whales or a social congregation of whalers, esp. at sea. —*v.* **gammed, gam•ming, gams.** —*intr.* To hold a visit, esp. while at sea. —*tr.* **1.** To visit with. **2.** To spend (time) talking or visiting. [Perh. short for GAMMON[2] or var. of GAME[1].]

gam[2] (găm) *n. Slang.* A person's leg. [Prob. < Polari (theatrical argot) < Ital. *gamba* < LLat., hoof. See GAMBOL.]

gam– *pref.* Var. of **gamo–.**

Ga•ma (găm′ə, gä′mə), **Vasco da.** 1460?–1524. Portuguese explorer and first European to sail to India (1497–98).

ga•may (gă-mā′, găm′ā) *n.* A variety of red grape used for making red wines, esp. Beaujolais. [Fr., after *Gamay*, a village of E-central France.]

gam•ba (găm′bə, găm′-) *n. Mus.* See **viola da gamba.**

gam•ba•do[1] (găm-bā′dō) *n., pl.* **-does** or **-dos. 1.** A low leap of a horse in which all four feet are off the ground. **2.** A leaping or gamboling movement. [Alteration of Fr. *gambade* < Ital. *gambata* < OItal. See GAMBOL.]

gam•ba•do[2] (găm-bā′dō) *n., pl.* **-does** or **-dos. 1.** Either of a pair of protective leather gaiters attached to a saddle. **2.** A rider's legging. [< Ital. *gamba*, leg < OItal. See GAMBOL.]

Gam•bi•a (găm′bē-ə). A country of W Africa on the Atlantic Ocean; gained independence from Great Britain in 1965. Cap. Banjul. Pop. 696,000. —**Gam′bi•an** *adj. & n.*

Gambia River. A river of W Africa flowing c. 1,126 km (700 mi) from N Guinea to the Atlantic Ocean at Banjul.

gam•bier also **gam•bir** (găm′bîr) *n.* A resinous astringent extract obtained from the leaves of a woody vine *(Uncaria gambir)* of Malaysia and Indonesia, used medicinally and in tanning and dyeing. [Malay *gambir.*]

Gam•bier Islands (găm′bîr′). A group of small islands of French Polynesia in the S-central Pacific Ocean.

gam•bit (găm′bĭt) *n.* **1.** *Games.* An opening in chess in which a minor piece, or pieces, is offered in exchange for a favorable position. **2.** A maneuver, stratagem, or ploy, esp. one used at an initial stage. **3.** A remark intended to open a conversation.

[Ult. < Sp. *gambito* < Ital. *gambetto*, act of tripping someone up in wrestling < *gamba*, leg < OItal. See GAMBOL.]

Usage Note: Critics familiar with the nature of chess gambits have sometimes maintained that the word should not be used in an extended sense except to refer to maneuvers that involve the tactical sacrifice of some advantage. But *gambit* is well established in the general sense of "maneuver" and in the related sense of "a remark intended to open a conversation."

gam•ble (găm′bəl) *v.* **-bled, -bling, -bles.** — *intr.* **1.a.** To bet on an uncertain outcome, as of a contest. **b.** *Games.* To play a game of chance for stakes. **2.** To take a risk in the hope of gaining an advantage or a benefit. **3.** To engage in reckless or hazardous behavior. — *tr.* **1.** *Games.* To put up as a stake in gambling; wager. **2.** To expose to hazard; risk. — *n.* **1.** *Games.* A bet, wager, or other gambling venture. **2.** An act or undertaking of uncertain outcome; a risk. [Perh. < obsolete *gamel*, to play games < ME *gamen, gamenen*, to play < OE *gamenian* < *gamen*, fun.] — **gam′bler** *n.*

gam•boge (găm-bōj′, -bo͞ozh′) *n.* **1.** A brownish or orange resin obtained from several trees of the genus *Garcinia* of south-central Asia and yielding a golden yellow pigment. **2.** *Color.* A strong yellow. [NLat. *cambugium, gambogium*, after CAMBODIA.] — **gam•boge′** *adj.*

gam•bol (găm′bəl) *intr.v.* **-boled, -bol•ing, -bols** or **-bolled, -bol•ling, -bols.** To leap about playfully; frolic. — *n.* A playful skipping or frolicking about. [Alteration of Fr. *gambade*, horse's jump < OFr., perh. < OItal. *gambata* < *gamba*, leg < LLat., hoof, perh. < Gk. *kampē*, bend.]

gam•brel (găm′brəl) *n.* **1.** The hock of a horse or other animal. **2.** A frame used by butchers for hanging carcasses by the legs. [Fr. dial. *gamberel* < ONFr. < *gambe*, leg < LLat. *gamba*, hoof. See GAMBOL.]

gambrel roof *n.* A ridged roof with two slopes on each side, the lower slope having the steeper pitch.

gam•bu•sia (găm-byo͞o′zhə) *n.* Any of various small livebearers of the genus *Gambusia* that feed on mosquito larvae and are often used in mosquito control. [NLat. *Gambusia*, genus name < Am.Sp. *gambusino*, idle fisherman.]

game[1] (gām) *n.* **1.** An activity providing entertainment or amusement; a pastime. **2.a.** A competitive activity or sport in which players contend with each other according to a set of rules. **b.** A single instance of such an activity. **c. games.** An organized athletic program or contest. **d.** A period of competition or challenge. **3.a.** The total number of points required to win a game. **b.** The score accumulated at any given time in a game. **4.** The equipment needed for playing certain games. **5.** A particular style or manner of playing a game. **6.** *Informal.* **a.** An active interest or pursuit, esp. one involving competitive engagement or adherence to rules. **b.** A business or occupation; a line. **c.** An illegal activity; a racket. **7.** *Informal.* **a.** Evasive, trifling, or manipulative behavior. **b.** A calculated strategy or approach; a scheme. **8.** *Math.* A model of a competitive situation that identifies interested parties and stipulates rules governing all aspects of the competition, used in game theory. **9.a.** Wild animals, birds, or fish hunted for food or sport. **b.** The flesh of these animals, eaten as food. **10.a.** An object of attack, ridicule, or pursuit. **b.** Mockery; sport. — *v.* **gamed, gam•ing, games.** — *tr. Archaic.* To waste or lose by gambling. — *intr.* To play for stakes; gamble. — *adj.* **gam•er, gam•est. 1.** Plucky and unyielding in spirit; resolute. **2.** Ready and willing. — ***idiom.* the only game in town.** *Informal.* The only alternative. [ME < OE *gamen.*] — **game′ly** *adv.* — **game′ness** *n.*

game[2] (gām) *adj.* **gam•er, gam•est.** Crippled; lame. [?]

game bird *n.* A bird that is widely hunted for sport.

game•cock (gām′kŏk′) *n.* A rooster trained for cockfighting.

game fish *n.* A fish prized for the sport involved in catching it.

game fowl *n.* Any of several breeds of domestic fowl raised esp. for cockfighting.

game•keep•er (gām′kē′pər) *n.* One who is employed to protect and maintain game birds and animals.

gam•e•lan (găm′ə-lăn′) *n. Mus.* An Indonesian orchestra composed mainly of tuned percussion instruments such as bamboo xylophones and gongs. [Javanese : *gamêl*, to make music + *-an*, suff. indicating means.]

game law *n.* A regulation intended for the management or conservation of game animals.

game of chance *n. Games.* A game in which the winner is determined by a chance event, as by drawing numbers.

game plan *n.* **1.** *Sports.* The strategy devised before or used during an event. **2.** A strategy for reaching an objective.

game point *n. Sports & Games.* **1.** A situation in a game, esp. tennis, in which one side or player needs only one point to win. **2.** The winning point.

game show *n. Games.* A television show in which contestants compete for prizes by playing games of knowledge or chance.

games•man•ship (gāmz′mən-shĭp′) *n.* **1.** The art or practice of using tactical maneuvers to further one's aims or better one's position. **2.** *Sports & Games.* The use in a sport or game of aggressive, often dubious tactics, to win.

game•some (gām′səm) *adj.* Frolicsome; playful. — **game′some•ly** *adv.* — **game′some•ness** *n.*

game•ster (gām′stər) *n. Games.* One who plays games, esp. a gambler.

gam•e•tan•gi•um (găm′ĭ-tăn′jē-əm) *n., pl.* **-gi•a** (-jē-ə). An organ or a cell in which gametes are produced. [GAMET(O)- + Gk. *angeion*, vessel, dim. of *angos*, vessel + -IUM.] — **gam′e•tan′gi•al** (-əl) *adj.*

gam•ete (găm′ēt′, gə-mēt′) *n.* A reproductive cell having the haploid number of chromosomes, esp. a mature sperm or egg capable of fusing with a gamete of the opposite sex to produce the fertilized egg. [NLat. *gameta* < Gk. *gametē*, wife and *gametēs*, husband < *gamein*, to marry < *gamos*, marriage. See **gemə-***.] — **ga•met′ic** (-mĕt′ĭk) *adj.*

game theory *n.* A mathematical method of decision-making in which a competitive situation is analyzed to determine the optimal course of action for an interested party.

gameto– or **gamet–** *pref.* Gamete: *gametogenesis.* [< NLat. *gameta*, gamete. See GAMETE.]

ga•me•to•cyte (gə-mē′tə-sīt′) *n.* A cell from which gametes develop by meiotic division, esp. a spermatocyte or an oocyte.

ga•me•to•gen•e•sis (gə-mē′tə-jĕn′ĭ-sĭs) *n.* The formation or production of gametes. — **ga•me′to•gen′ic, gam′e•tog′e•nous** (găm′ĭ-tŏj′ə-nəs) *adj.*

ga•me•to•phore (gə-mē′tə-fôr′, -fōr′) *n.* A structure, as in liverworts and mosses, on which gametangia are borne. — **ga•me′to•phor′ic** (-fôr′ĭk, -fŏr′-) *adj.*

ga•me•to•phyte (gə-mē′tə-fīt′) *n. Bot.* The gamete-producing phase in a plant characterized by alternation of generations. — **ga•me′to•phyt′ic** (-fĭt′ĭk) *adj.*

gam•ey (gā′mē) *adj.* Var. of **gamy.**

gam•ic (găm′ĭk) *adj.* Of or requiring fertilization to reproduce; sexual.

gam•in (găm′ĭn) *n.* An often homeless boy who roams about the streets; an urchin. [Fr.]

ga•mine (gă-mēn′, găm′ēn) *n.* **1.** An often homeless girl who roams about the streets; an urchin. **2.** A girl or woman of impish appeal. [Fr., fem. of *gamin*, gamin.]

gam•ing (gā′mĭng) *n. Games.* Gambling.

gam•ma (găm′ə) *n.* **1.** The third letter of the Greek alphabet. **2.** The third item in a series or system of classification. **3.** A unit of magnetic field strength equal to one hundred thousandth (10^{-5}) of an oersted. **4.** A unit of mass equal to one millionth (10^{-6}) of a gram. **5.** *Chem.* The third position from a designated carbon atom in an organic molecule at which an atom or a radical may be substituted. [ME < Gk., of Phoenician orig.; akin to Heb. *gīmel*, gimel.]

gam•ma-a•mi•no•bu•tyr•ic acid (găm′ə-ə-mē′nō-byo͞o-tîr′ĭk, -ăm′ə-nō-) *n.* An amino acid, $C_4H_9NO_2$, that occurs in the central nervous system and is associated with the transmission of nerve impulses.

gamma globulin *n.* A protein fraction of blood serum containing numerous antibodies, used in the prevention and treatment of measles, poliomyelitis, and hepatitis, for example.

gamma ray *n.* Electromagnetic radiation emitted by radioactive decay and having energies in a range from ten thousand (10^4) to ten million (10^7) electron volts.

gam•mer (găm′ər) *n. Chiefly British.* An elderly woman. [Prob. alteration (influenced by GRANDMOTHER) of GODMOTHER.]

gam•mon[1] (găm′ən) *Games.* — *n.* A victory in backgammon reached before the loser has succeeded in removing a single piece. — *tr.v.* **-moned, -mon•ing, -mons.** To defeat in backgammon by scoring a gammon. [Prob. < ME *gamen, gammen*, game < OE *gamen.*]

gam•mon[2] (găm′ən) *Chiefly British.* — *n.* Misleading or nonsensical talk; humbug. — *v.* **-moned, -mon•ing, -mons.** — *tr.* To mislead by deceptive talk. — *intr.* To talk misleadingly or deceptively. [?] — **gam′mon•er** *n.*

gam•mon[3] (găm′ən) *n.* **1.** A cured or smoked ham. **2.** The lower part of a side of bacon. [ME *gambon* < ONFr. < *gambe*, leg < LLat. *gamba*, hoof. See GAMBOL.]

gam•mon[4] (găm′ən) *tr.v.* **-moned, -mon•ing, -mons.** *Naut.* To fasten (a bowsprit) to the stem of a ship. [?]

gamo– or **gam–** *pref.* **1.** United; joined: *gamopetalous.* **2.** Sexual: *gamogenesis.* [Gk., marriage < *gamos.* See **gemə-***.]

gam•o•gen•e•sis (găm′ə-jĕn′ĭ-sĭs) *n.* Sexual reproduction. — **gam′o•ge•net′ic** (-jə-nĕt′ĭk) *adj.*

gam•o•pet•al•ous (găm′ə-pĕt′l-əs) *adj. Bot.* Having or being a corolla with partially or wholly fused petals.

gam•o•phyl•lous (găm′ə-fĭl′əs) *adj. Bot.* Having or being united leaves or leaflike parts.

gam•o•sep•al•ous (găm′ə-sĕp′ə-ləs) *adj. Bot.* Having or being united or partly united sepals.

–gamous *suff.* **1.a.** Having a specified number of marriages: *monogamous.* **b.** Practicing a specified kind of marriage: *exogamous.* **2.** Having a specified kind of reproduction or reproductive organs: *heterogamous.* [< Gk. *-gamos* < *gamos*, marriage. See **gemə-***.]

Ga•mow (gā′mou, găm′ôf, -ŏf), **George.** 1904–68. Russian-born Amer. nuclear physicist known for his work on radioactivity and genetic information.

gamp (gămp) *n. Chiefly British.* A large, baggy umbrella. [After Mrs. Sarah *Gamp*, in *Martin Chuzzlewit* by Dickens.]

gamopetalous
Wild potato vine
Ipomoea pandurata

ă pat	oi boy
ā pay	ou out
âr care	o͝o took
ä father	o͞o boot
ĕ pet	ŭ cut
ē be	ûr urge
ĭ pit	th thin
ī pie	*th* this
îr pier	hw which
ŏ pot	zh vision
ō toe	ə about, item
ô paw	

Stress marks:
′ (primary);
′ (secondary), as in
dictionary (dĭk′shə-nĕr′ē)

gam•ut (găm′ət) *n.* **1.** A complete range or extent. **2.** *Mus.* The entire series of recognized notes. [ME, the musical scale < Med.Lat. *gamma ut*, low G : *gamma*, lowest note of the medieval scale (< Gk., gamma; see GAMMA) + *ut*, first note of the lowest hexachord (after *ut*, first word in a Latin hymn to St. John the Baptist, the initial syllables of successive lines of which were sung to the notes of an ascending scale CDEFGA: *Ut* queant laxis *re*sonare fibris *Mi*ra gestorum *fa*muli tuorum, *Sol*ve polluti *la*bii reatum, Sancte Iohannes).]

gam•y also **gam•ey** (gā′mē) *adj.* **-i•er, -i•est. 1.a.** Having the flavor or odor of game, esp. game that is slightly spoiled. **b.** Ill-smelling; rank. **2.** Showing an unyielding spirit; plucky. **3.a.** Corrupt; tainted. **b.** Sordid; seamy. **— gam′i•ly** *adv.* **— gam′i•ness** *n.*

–gamy *suff.* **1.** Marriage: *exogamy.* **2.** Procreative or propagative union: *allogamy.* **3.** The possession of a specified manner of fertilization or specified reproductive organs: *apogamy.* [Gk. *-gamia* < *gamos*, marriage. See **gemə-*.**]

gan•der (găn′dər) *n.* **1.** A male goose. **2.** *Informal.* A look or glance. **3.** *Informal.* A simpleton; a ninny. [ME < OE *gandra.* See **ghans-*.**]

Gan•der (găn′dər). A town of NE Newfoundland, Canada; long used as a refueling stop for transatlantic flights. Pop. 10,404.

Gan•dhi (gän′dē, găn′-), **Indira Nehru.** 1917–84. Indian politician and prime minister (1966–77 and 1980–84).

Indira Gandhi
Photographed in 1982

Gandhi, Mohandas Karamchand. "Mahatma Gandhi." 1869–1948. Indian nationalist and spiritual leader who developed the practice of nonviolent disobedience that forced Great Britain to grant independence to India (1947).

gan•dy dancer (găn′dē) *n. Slang.* **1.** A railroad worker. **2.** An itinerant laborer. [?]

ga•nef or **ga•nof** also **gon•if** (gä′nəf) *n.* A thief, scoundrel, or rascal. [Yiddish; akin to Heb. *gannāb.*]

gang¹ (găng) *n.* **1.** A group of criminals or hoodlums who band together for mutual protection and profit. **2.** A group of adolescents who band together, esp. a group of delinquents. **3.** *Informal.* A group of people who associate regularly on a social basis. **4.** A group of laborers organized together on one job or under one supervisor. **5.** A matched or coordinated set, as of tools. **6.a.** A pack of wolves or wild dogs. **b.** A herd, esp. of buffalo or elk. **—** *v.* **ganged, gang•ing, gangs.** **—** *intr.* To band together as a group or gang. **—** *tr.* **1.** To arrange or assemble into a group, as for simultaneous operation or production. **2.** To attack as an organized group. **—** ***phrasal verb.*** **gang up. 1.** To join together in opposition or attack. **2.** To act together as a group. [ME, band of men < OE, journey and ON *gangr*, journey, group.]

Mahatma Gandhi

gang² (găng) *n.* Var. of **gangue.**

gang•bang or **gang-bang** (găng′băng′) *n. Vulgar Slang.* **1.** Rape or sexual intercourse involving one person and several others in succession. **2.** Sexual intercourse involving several partners who change indiscriminately. **— gang′bang′** *v.*

gang•bus•ter (găng′bŭs′tər) *n. Slang.* A law enforcement officer who breaks up organized criminal groups. **—** ***idiom.*** **like gangbusters.** *Slang.* With great impact, vigor, or zeal.

Gan•ges (găn′jēz′) also **Gan•ga** (gŭng′gə). A river of N India and Bangladesh rising in the Himalaya Mts. and flowing c. 2,510 km (1,560 mi) to the Bay of Bengal.

gang•land (găng′lănd′, -lənd) *n.* The underworld of organized criminal gangs. **— gang′land′** *adj.*

gan•gli•at•ed (găng′glē-ā′tĭd) also **gan•gli•ate** (-ĭt, -āt′) *adj.* Having ganglia.

gan•gling (găng′glĭng) *adj.* Awkwardly tall or long-limbed. [Perh. < dial. *gang*, to go < ME *gangen* < OE *gangan.*]

gan•gli•on (găng′glē-ən) *n., pl.* **-gli•a** (-glē-ə) or **-gli•ons. 1.** *Anat.* A group of nerve cells forming a nerve center, esp. one located outside the brain or spinal cord. **2.** A center of power, activity, or energy. **3.** *Pathol.* A benign cystic lesion resembling a tumor, occurring in a tendon sheath or joint capsule. [< Gk., cystlike tumor, nerve bundle.] **— gan′gli•on′ic** (-ŏn′ĭk) *adj.*

Federico García Lorca

gan•gli•o•side (găng′glē-ə-sīd′) *n.* Any of a group of galactose-containing cerebrosides found in the surface membranes of nerve cells. [GANGLI(ON) + -OS(E)² + -IDE.]

gan•gly (găng′glē) *adj.* **-gli•er, -gli•est.** Gangling.

gang•plank (găng′plăngk′) *n. Naut.* A board or ramp used as a removable footway between a ship and a pier. [< GANG¹, way (obsolete and dialectal).]

gang•plow (găng′plou′) *n.* A plow equipped with several blades that make parallel furrows.

gan•grel (găng′rəl) *n. Scots.* A vagabond; a drifter. [ME, prob. < *gangen*, to go. See GANGLING.]

gan•grene (găng′grēn′, găng-grēn′) *n.* Death and decay of body tissue, often occurring in a limb, caused by insufficient blood supply and usu. following injury or disease. **—** *tr. & intr.v.* **-grened, -gren•ing, -grenes.** To affect or become affected with gangrene. [Med.Lat. *cancrēna* < Lat. *gangrēna* < Gk. *gangraina.*] **— gan′gre•nous** (găng′grə-nəs) *adj.*

gang•ster (găng′stər) *n.* A member of an organized group of criminals. **— gang′ster•dom** *n.* **— gang′ster•ism** *n.*

James A. Garfield

gangue also **gang** (găng) *n.* Worthless rock or other material in which valuable minerals are found. [Fr. < Ger. *Gang*, lode < MHGer. *ganc* < OHGer. *gang*, a going.]

gang•way (găng′wā′) *n.* **1.** *Naut.* **a.** A passage along either side of a ship's upper deck. **b.** See **gangplank. c.** An opening in the bulwark of a ship through which passengers may board. **2.** A narrow passageway, as of boards laid on the ground. **3.** The main level of a mine. **4.** *Chiefly British.* **a.** The aisle that divides the front and rear seating sections of the House of Commons. **b.** An aisle between seating sections, as in a theater. **—** *interj.* Used to clear a passage through a crowded area. [< GANG¹, way, passage (obsolete, dial.).]

gan•is•ter also **gan•nis•ter** (găn′ĭ-stər) *n.* **1.** A fine-grained quartzite used to line refractory furnaces. **2.** A mixture of fire clay and ground quartz lining metallurgical furnaces. [?]

gan•ja (gän′jə) *n.* Marijuana, esp. of a highly resinous form prepared from the flowering tops and leaves of selected plants. [Hindustani *gāṁjhā*, hemp resin < Skt. *gāñjyā-*, of hemp < *gañjaḥ*, hemp, alteration of *gṛñjaḥ.*]

Gan Jiang (gän′ jyäng′) also **Kan River** (kăn). A river of SE China flowing c. 885 km (550 mi) generally N to the Yangtze R. (Chang Jiang) N of Nanchang.

gan•net (găn′ĭt) *n.* Any of several large sea birds of the genus *Morus*, esp. *M. bassanus* of northern Atlantic coastal regions, having white plumage with black wingtips. [ME *ganet* < OE *ganot.* See **ghans-*.**]

ga•nof (gä′nəf) *n.* Var. of **ganef.**

gan•oid (găn′oid′) *adj.* Of, relating to, or characteristic of certain bony fishes, such as the gar, having armorlike scales of bony plates covered with layers of dentine and enamel. [< NLat. *Ganoidei*, subclass name < Gk. *ganos*, brightness < *ganusthai*, to rejoice. See **gāu-*.**] **— gan′oid′** *n.*

Gan•su (gän′so͞o′) also **Kan•su** (kän′so͞o′, gän′-). A province of N-central China; long a corridor for the Silk Road to Turkistan, India, and Persia. Cap. Lanzhou. Pop. 20,410,000.

gant•let¹ (gônt′lĭt, gänt′-) *n.* A section of double railroad tracks formed by the temporary convergence of two parallel tracks so that each set remains independent, affording passage at a narrow place without need of switching. **—** *tr.v.* **-let•ed, -let•ing, -lets.** To converge (railroad tracks) to form a gantlet. [Var. of GAUNTLET².]

gant•let² (gônt′lĭt, gänt′-) *n.* Var. of **gauntlet¹.**

gant•let³ (gônt′lĭt, gänt′-) *n.* Var. of **gauntlet².**

gan•try (găn′trē) *n., pl.* **-tries. 1.** A mount for a traveling crane consisting of a large archlike or bridgelike frame designed to move along a set of tracks. **2.** A similar spanning frame supporting a group of railway signals over several tracks. **3.** *Aerospace.* A massive vertical frame structure used in assembling or servicing a rocket. **4.** A support for a barrel lying on its side. [ME *ganter, gauntre*, wooden stand for barrels < ONFr. *gantier*, wooden frame < Lat. *canthērius* < Gk. *kanthēlios*, pack ass < *kanthēlia*, panniers.]

Gan•y•mede (găn′ə-mēd′) *n.* **1.** *Gk. Myth.* A beautiful boy carried away by Zeus to be the gods' cupbearer. **2.** One of the satellites of Jupiter. [Lat. *Ganymēdēs* < Gk. *Ganumēdēs.*]

GAO *abbr.* General Accounting Office.

gaol (jāl) *n. & v. Chiefly British.* Var. of **jail.**

gap (găp) *n.* **1.a.** An opening in a solid structure or surface; a cleft or breach. **b.** A break in a line of defense. **2.** An opening through mountains; a pass. **3.** A space between objects or points; an aperture. **4.** An interruption of continuity. **5.a.** A conspicuous difference or imbalance; a disparity. **b.** A problematic situation resulting from such a disparity. **6.** A spark gap. **7.** *Comp. Sci.* An absence of information on a recording medium, often used to signal the end of a segment of information. **8.** *Electron.* The distance between the head of a recording device and the surface of the recording medium. **—** *v.* **gapped, gap•ping, gaps. —** *tr.* To make an opening in. **—** *intr.* To be or become open. [ME < ON, chasm.]

gape (gāp, găp) *intr.v.* **gaped, gap•ing, gapes. 1.** To open the mouth wide; yawn. **2.** To stare wonderingly or stupidly, often with the mouth open. **3.** To open wide. **—** *n.* **1.** The act or an instance of gaping. **2.** A large opening. **3.** *Zool.* The width of the space between the open jaws or mandibles of a vertebrate. **4. gapes.** *(used with a sing. v.) Veterinary Medic.* A disease of birds caused by gapeworms and resulting in obstructed breathing. **5. gapes.** A fit of yawning. [ME *gapen* < ON *gapa.*]

gape•worm (gāp′wûrm′, găp′-) *n.* A nematode worm *(Syngamus trachea)* that infects certain birds and causes gapes.

gap•ing (gā′pĭng) *adj.* Deep and wide open. **— gap′ing•ly** *adv.*

gar¹ (gär) *n.* **1.** Any of several ganoid fishes of the family Lepisosteidae of North and Central America, having long narrow jaws, an elongated body, and a long snout. **2.** A similar or related fish, such as the needlefish. [Short for GARFISH.]

gar² (gär) *tr.v.* **garred, gar•ring, gars.** *Scots.* To cause or compel. [ME *geren* < ON *gera*, to make.]

GAR or **G.A.R.** *abbr.* Grand Army of the Republic.

ga•rage (gə-räzh′, -räj′) *n.* **1.** A building or indoor space in which to park or keep a motor vehicle. **2.** A commercial establishment where cars are repaired, serviced, or parked. **—** *tr.v.* **-raged, -rag•ing, -rag•es.** To put or store in a garage.

[Fr. < *garer*, to shelter < OFr. *garer, guerrer*, of Gmc. orig. See **wer-⁴***.] — **ga•rage′a•ble** *adj.*

garage sale *n.* A sale of used household items or clothing held at the home of the seller.

Gar•a•mond (găr′ə-mŏnd′, gä-rä-môN′), **Claude.** 1480?–1561. French type designer known for establishing the roman-style letter as the standard in printing.

garb (gärb) *n.* **1.** A distinctive style or form of clothing; dress. **2.** An outward appearance; a guise. — *tr.v.* **garbed, garb•ing, garbs.** To cover with or as if with clothing; dress. [Obsolete Fr. *garbe*, grace < Ital. *garbo* < *garbare*, to please, of Gmc. orig.]

gar•bage (gär′bĭj) *n.* **1.a.** Food wastes, as from a kitchen. **b.** Refuse; trash. **2.a.** Worthless or nonsensical matter; rubbish. **b.** Inferior or offensive literary or artistic material. **3.** *Comp. Sci.* Incorrect, meaningless, or unwanted information in input, output, or memory. [ME, offal from fowls.]

gar•ban•zo (gär-bän′zō) *n., pl.* **-zos.** See **chickpea.** [Sp., alteration of OSp. *arvanço*, perh. < Gk. *erebinthos*.]

gar•ble (gär′bəl) *tr.v.* **-bled, -bling, -bles. 1.** To mix up or distort so as to make misleading or incomprehensible. **2.** To scramble (a signal or message), as by faulty transmission. **3.** *Archaic.* To sort out; cull. — *n.* The act or an instance of garbling. [ME *garbelen*, to clean spices < AN *garbeler*, to sift, and < Med.Lat. *garbellāre*, both < Ar. *garbala*, to select < *ġirbāl*, sieve < LLat. *crībellum*, dim. of Lat. *crībrum*. See **krei-***.] — **gar′bler** (-blər) *n.*

Gar•bo (gär′bō), **Greta.** 1905–90. Swedish-born Amer. actress whose films include *Camille* (1937).

gar•board (gär′bôrd′, -bōrd′) *n. Naut.* The first range or strake of planks laid next to a ship's keel. [Obsolete Du. *gaarboord* : poss. Du. *gaar*, cooked, done (< MDu. *gaer*) + Du. *boord*, board (< MDu. *boort*).]

gar•boil (gär′boil′) *n. Archaic.* Confusion; uproar. [Obsolete Fr. *garbouil*, ult. perh. < Lat. *bullīre*, to boil.]

Gar•cí•a Lor•ca (gär-sē′ə lôr′kə, gär-thē′ä), **Federico.** 1898–1936. Spanish writer whose works include *House of Bernarda Alba* (1936).

Gar•cí•a Már•quez (gär-sē′ə mär′kəs, -kĕs), **Gabriel.** b. 1928. Colombian-born writer who won the 1982 Nobel Prize for literature.

Gar•cí•a Ro•bles (gär-sē′ə rō′bləs, -blĕs), **Alfonso.** 1911–91. Mexican diplomat who shared the 1982 Nobel Peace Prize.

gar•çon (gär-sôN′) *n., pl.* **-çons** (-sôN′). A waiter. [Fr. < OFr. *garçun*, servant, accusative of *gars*, boy, soldier, prob. of Gmc. orig.]

Gar•da (gär′də), **Lake.** A lake of N Italy E of Milan.

gar•dant (gär′dnt) *adj. Her.* Var. of **guardant.**

gar•den (gär′dn) *n.* **1.** A plot of land for the cultivation of flowers, vegetables, herbs, or fruit. **2.** Grounds laid out with flowers, trees, and ornamental shrubs, used for recreation or display. Often used in the plural. **3.** A yard or lawn. **4.** A fertile, well-cultivated region. **5.a.** An open-air establishment serving refreshments. **b.** A large public auditorium or arena. — *v.* **-dened, -den•ing, -dens.** — *tr.* **1.** To cultivate (a plot) as a garden. **2.** To furnish with a garden. — *intr.* **1.** To plant or tend a garden. **2.** To work as a gardener. — *adj.* **1.** Of, suitable to, or used in a garden. **2.** Provided with open areas and greenery. **3.** Garden-variety. — ***idiom.* lead** (or **take**) **down the garden path.** To mislead or deceive (another). [ME *gardin* < ONFr. < *gart*, of Gmc. orig. See **gher-¹***.]

Gar•den (gär′dn), **Alexander.** 1730?–91. Scottish-born Amer. naturalist and physician who contributed to the classification of New World plants.

Gar•de•na (gär-dē′nə). A city of S CA, a suburb of Los Angeles. Pop. 49,847.

garden apartment *n.* A unit in a low-rise apartment complex that includes open, usu. landscaped ground.

garden city *n.* A residential community combining a pleasant environment with low-density housing and open public land.

Garden City. 1. A city of SW KS WNW of Dodge City. Pop. 24,097. **2.** A city of SE MI, a suburb of Detroit. Pop. 31,846. **3.** A village of SE NY on W Long I.; starting point for Charles A. Lindbergh's 1927 transatlantic flight. Pop. 21,686.

garden cress *n.* An annual herb *(Lepidium sativum)* of the mustard family, usu. grown as a salad plant.

gar•den•er (gärd′nər, gär′dn-ər) *n.* One who works in or tends a garden for pleasure or hire.

Garden Grove. A city of S CA, a residential suburb of Long Beach and Los Angeles. Pop. 143,050.

garden heliotrope *n.* A widely cultivated valerian *(Valeriana officinalis)* having small fragrant flowers and strong-smelling rhizomes formerly used in medicine.

gar•de•nia (gär-dēn′yə) *n.* **1.** Any of various shrubs and trees of the Old World tropics that belong to the genus *Gardenia*, esp. *G. jasminoides* native to China, having glossy evergreen leaves and large, fragrant, usu. white flowers. **2.** The flower of this plant. [NLat., genus name, after Alexander GARDEN.]

Garden of Eden *n.* See **Eden¹** 1.

gar•den-va•ri•e•ty (gär′dn-və-rī′ĭ-tē) *adj.* Common; unremarkable.

garde•robe (gärd′rōb′) *n. Archaic.* **1.a.** A chamber for storing clothes; a wardrobe. **b.** The contents of a wardrobe. **2.** A private chamber. [ME < OFr. : *garder*, to keep (of Gmc. orig.; see GUARD) + *robe*, robe (of Gmc. orig.; see ROBE).]

Gar•di•ner (gärd′nər, gär′dn-ər), **Samuel Rawson.** 1829–1902. British historian known for his *History of England* (10 volumes, 1863–82).

Gar•di•ners Island (gärd′nərz, gär′dn-ərz). An island of SE NY in **Gardiners Bay** between two peninsulas of E Long I.; settled in 1639.

Gard•ner (gärd′nər). A city of N-central MA W of Fitchburg. Pop. 20,125.

Gardner, Erle Stanley. 1889–1970. Amer. lawyer and detective novelist best known for his character Perry Mason.

Gar•eth (găr′ĭth) *n.* In Arthurian legend, a nephew of King Arthur and one of the Knights of the Round Table.

Gar•field (gär′fēld′). A city of NE NJ on the Passaic R. SE of Paterson; settled by the Dutch in 1679. Pop. 26,727.

Garfield, James Abram. 1831–81. The 20th President of the U.S. (1881); assassinated by Charles Guiteau (1841–82), a frustrated office-seeker.

Garfield Heights. A city of NE OH, a suburb of Cleveland. Pop. 31,739.

gar•fish (gär′fĭsh′) *n., pl.* **garfish** or **-fish•es.** See **gar¹** 2. [ME : *gare*, spear (< OE *gār*) + *fish*, fish; see FISH.]

gar•gan•tu•a (gär-găn′cho͞o-ə) *n.* A person of great size or stature and voracious physical or intellectual appetites. [After the hero of *Gargantua and Pantagruel* by François Rabelais.]

gar•gan•tu•an (gär-găn′cho͞o-ən) *adj.* Of immense size, volume, or capacity; gigantic.

gar•get (gär′gĭt) *n.* Mastitis of domestic animals, esp. cattle. [Perh. < ME, throat < OFr. *gargate*.]

gar•gle (gär′gəl) *v.* **-gled, -gling, -gles.** — *intr.* **1.** To force exhaled air through a liquid held in the back of the mouth, with the head tilted back, in order to cleanse or medicate the mouth or throat. **2.** To produce the sound of gargling when speaking or singing. — *tr.* **1.** To rinse or medicate by gargling. **2.** To circulate or apply by gargling. **3.** To utter with a gargling sound. — *n.* **1.** A medicated solution for gargling. **2.** A gargling sound. [Fr. *gargouiller* < OFr.]

gar•goyle (gär′goil′) *n.* **1.** A roof spout in the form of a grotesque or fantastic creature projecting from a gutter to carry rainwater clear of the wall. **2.** A grotesque ornamental figure or projection. **3.** A person of bizarre or grotesque appearance. [ME *gargoile* < OFr. *gargole, gargouille*, throat, waterspout.]

gargoyle
On the Cathedral of Notre Dame, Paris

gar•i•bal•di (găr′ə-bôl′dē) *n.* **1.** A loose high-necked blouse styled after the red shirts worn by Garibaldi and his soldiers. **2.** A bright orange or yellow-orange damselfish *(Hypsypops rubicundus)* native to coastal marine waters of southern California. [After Giuseppe GARIBALDI.]

Gar•i•bal•di (găr′ə-bôl′dē, gä′rē-bäl′dē), **Giuseppe.** 1807–82. Italian general whose conquests led to the formation of the kingdom of Italy (1861).

Giuseppe Garibaldi
Wearing the shirt he made popular

gar•ish (gâr′ĭsh, găr′-) *adj.* **1.a.** Marred by strident color or excessive ornamentation; gaudy. **b.** Loud and flashy. **2.** Glaring; dazzling. [?] — **gar′ish•ly** *adv.* — **gar′ish•ness** *n.*

gar•land (gär′lənd) *n.* **1.a.** A wreath or festoon, esp. one of plaited flowers or leaves, worn on the body or draped as a decoration. **b.** A representation of such a wreath or festoon, used as an architectural ornament or a heraldic device. **2.** A mark of honor or tribute; an accolade. **3.** An anthology, as of poems. — *tr.v.* **-land•ed, -land•ing, -lands. 1.** To ornament or deck with a garland. **2.** To form into a garland. [ME < OFr. *garlande*, perh. of Gmc. orig. See **wei-***.]

Gar•land (gär′lənd). A city of NE TX, a suburb of Dallas. Pop. 180,650.

Garland, (Hannibal) Hamlin. 1860–1940. Amer. writer whose works include *Son of the Middle Border* (1917).

Garland, Judy. 1922–69. Amer. actress and singer best known for her performance as Dorothy in *The Wizard of Oz* (1939).

garland chrysanthemum *n.* An annual Mediterranean herb *(Chrysanthemum coronarium)* of the composite family, with yellow flower heads and aromatic, bipinnately lobed leaves.

garland flower *n.* A European evergreen shrub *(Daphne cneorum)* having fragrant rose, pink, or white flowers grouped in dense terminal heads.

gar•lic (gär′lĭk) *n.* **1.** An onionlike plant *(Allium sativum)* of southern Europe having a bulb that separates into cloves with a strong distinctive odor and flavor. **2.** The bulb of this plant. — *tr.v.* **-licked, -lick•ing, -licks.** To season or flavor (a food) with garlic. [ME < OE *gārlēac* : *gār*, spear + *lēac*, leek.]

garlic chive *n.* See **Chinese chive.**

gar•lick•y (gär′lĭ-kē) *adj.* Containing, tasting of, or smelling of garlic.

gar•ment (gär′mənt) *n.* An article of clothing. — *tr.v.* **-ment•ed, -ment•ing, -ments.** To clothe; dress. [ME < OFr. *garnement* < *garnir*, to equip, of Gmc. orig. See **wer-⁴***.]

gar•ner (gär′nər) *tr.v.* **-nered, -ner•ing, -ners. 1.** To gather and store in or as if in a granary. **2.** To amass; acquire. — *n.* A granary. [ME < *garner, gerner*, granary < OFr. *gernier, grenier* < Lat. *grānārium*. See GRANARY.]

Gar•ner (gär′nər), **John Nance.** 1868–1967. Vice President of the U.S. (1933–41).

ă pat	oi boy
ā pay	ou out
âr care	o͝o took
ä father	o͞o boot
ĕ pet	ŭ cut
ē be	ûr urge
ĭ pit	th thin
ī pie	*th* this
îr pier	hw which
ŏ pot	zh vision
ō toe	ə about, item
ô paw	

Stress marks:
′ (primary);
′ (secondary), as in
dictionary (dĭk′shə-nĕr′ē)

gar•net[1] (gär′nĭt) *n.* **1.** Any of several common aluminum or calcium silicate minerals occurring in two internally isomorphic series, (Mg, Mn, Fe)$_3$Al$_2$Si$_3$O$_{12}$ and Ca$_3$(Cr, Al, Fe)$_2$Si$_3$O$_{12}$, generally crystallized, colored red, brown, black, green, yellow, or white, and used as gemstones and abrasives. **2.** *Color.* A dark to very dark red. [ME < OFr. *grenate* < *grenat*, pomegranate-red, prob. < Lat. *grānātum*, pomegranate < neut. of *grānātus*, seedy. See POMEGRANATE.]

gar•net[2] (gär′nĭt) *n. Naut.* A tackle for hoisting light cargo. [ME *garnett*, prob. < MDu. *garnaat*.]

gar•net•if•er•ous (gär′nĭ-tĭf′ər-əs) *adj.* Containing garnets.

gar•ni•er•ite (gär′nē-ə-rīt′) *n.* A pale green or apple-green mineral, (Ni, Mg)$_3$Si$_2$O$_5$(OH)$_4$, used as a gemstone and as a nickel ore. [After Jules *Garnier*, 19th-cent. French geologist.]

gar•nish (gär′nĭsh) *tr.v.* **-nished, -nish•ing, -nish•es. 1.a.** To enhance in appearance by adding decorative touches; embellish. **b.** To decorate (prepared food or drink) with colorful or savory items. **2.** *Law.* To garnishee. —*n.* **1.a.** Ornamentation; embellishment. **b.** An embellishment used to garnish a prepared food or drink. **2.** *Slang.* An unwarranted fee, such as one extorted from a new prisoner by a jailer. [ME *garnishen* < OFr. *garnir, garniss-*, of Gmc. orig. See **wer-**[4]*.]

gar•nish•ee (gär′nĭ-shē′) *Law.* —*n.* A third party who has been notified that money or property in his or her hands but belonging to a defendant has been attached. —*tr.v.* **-eed, -ee•ing, -ees. 1.** To attach by garnishment. **2.** To serve with a garnishment.

gar•nish•ment (gär′nĭsh-mənt) *n.* **1.** *Law.* **a.** A legal proceeding whereby money or property due a debtor but in the possession of another is applied to the payment of the debt to the plaintiff. **b.** A court order directing a third party who holds money or property of a defendant to withhold it and appear in court. **2.** Ornamentation; embellishment.

gar•ni•ture (gär′nĭ-chər) *n.* Something that garnishes; an embellishment. [Fr. < OFr. < *garnir*, to garnish. See GARNISH.]

Ga•ronne (gä-rôn′). A river of SW France flowing c. 563 km (350 mi) to the Dordogne R. N of Bordeaux.

gar•pike (gär′pīk′) *n.* See **gar**[1] 2.

gar•ret (găr′ĭt) *n.* A room on the top floor of a house, typically under a pitched roof; an attic. [ME < OFr. *garite*, watchtower < *garir*, to defend, of Gmc. orig. See **wer-**[4]*.]

Gar•rick (găr′ĭk), **David.** 1717–79. British actor and theater manager noted for his Shakespearean roles.

gar•ri•son (găr′ĭ-sən) *n.* **1.** A military post, esp. one that is permanently established. **2.** The troops stationed at a military post. —*tr.v.* **-soned, -son•ing, -sons. 1.** To assign (troops) to a military post. **2.** To supply (a post) with troops. **3.** To occupy as or convert into a military post. [ME *garison*, fortified place < OFr. < *garir*, to defend, of Gmc. orig. See **wer-**[4]*.]

Gar•ri•son (găr′ĭ-sən), **William Lloyd.** 1805–79. Amer. abolitionist leader who founded and published *The Liberator* (1831–65), an antislavery journal.

garrison cap *n.* A soft cloth military cap without a visor.

Garrison finish *n. Sports.* A finish in a contest or race in which the winner comes from behind at the last moment. [After Edward ("Snapper") *Garrison*, 19th-cent. Amer. jockey.]

gar•rote or **gar•rotte** (gə-rŏt′, -rōt′) —*n.* **1.a.** A method of execution in which a tightened iron collar is used to strangle or break the neck. **b.** The iron collar used for such an execution. **2.a.** Strangulation, esp. in order to rob. **b.** A cord or wire for strangling. —*tr.v.* **-rot•ed, -rot•ing, -rotes** or **-rot•ted, -rot•ting, -rottes. 1.** To execute by garrote. **2.** To strangle in order to rob. [Sp., cudgel, poss. < OFr. *garrot*, perh. < *garoquier*, to struggle.] —**gar•rot′er** *n.*

gar•ru•li•ty (gə-ro͞o′lĭ-tē) *n.* Excessive talkativeness.

gar•ru•lous (găr′ə-ləs, găr′yə-) *adj.* **1.** Given to excessive and often trivial or rambling talk; tiresomely talkative. **2.** Wordy and rambling. [< Lat. *garrulus* < *garrīre*, to chatter.] —**gar′ru•lous•ly** *adv.* —**gar′ru•lous•ness** *n.*

gar•ter (gär′tər) *n.* **1.a.** An elasticized band worn around the leg to hold up a stocking or sock. **b.** A suspender strap with a fastener attached to a girdle or belt to hold up a woman's stocking. **c.** An elasticized band worn around the arm to keep the sleeve pushed up. **2. Garter. a.** The badge of the Order of the Garter. **b.** The order itself. **c.** Membership in the order. —*tr.v.* **-tered, -ter•ing, -ters. 1.** To fasten and hold with a garter. **2.** To put a garter on. [ME, band to support socks < ONFr. *gartier* < *garet*, bend of the knee, prob. of Celt. orig.]

garter snake *n.* Any of various striped nonvenomous North and Central American snakes of the genus *Thamnophis.*

garth (gärth) *n.* **1.** A grassy quadrangle surrounded by cloisters. **2.** *Archaic.* A yard, garden, or paddock. [ME, enclosed yard < ON *gardhr*. See **gher-**[1]*.]

Gar•vey (gär′vē), **Marcus (Moziah) Aurelius.** 1887–1940. Jamaican Black nationalist who founded the Universal Negro Improvement Association (1914).

Gar•y (gâr′ē, găr′ē). A city of NW IN on Lake Michigan near the IL border; founded c. 1905. Pop. 116,646.

gas (găs) *n., pl.* **gas•es** or **gas•ses. 1.a.** The state of matter distinguished from the solid and liquid states by relatively low density and viscosity and the spontaneous tendency to become distributed uniformly throughout any container. **b.** A substance in the gaseous state. **2.** A gaseous fuel, such as natural gas. **3.** Gasoline. **4.** The speed control of a gasoline engine. **5.** A gaseous asphyxiant, irritant, or poison. **6.** A gaseous anesthetic, such as nitrous oxide. **7.a.** Flatulence. **b.** Flatus. **8.** *Slang.* Idle or boastful talk. **9.** *Slang.* Someone or something exceptionally exciting or entertaining. —*v.* **gassed, gas•sing, gas•es** or **gas•ses.** —*tr.* **1.** To treat chemically with gas. **2.** To overcome, disable, or kill with poisonous fumes. —*intr.* **1.** To give off gas. **2.** *Slang.* To talk excessively. —***phrasal verb.*** **gas up.** To supply a vehicle with gas or gasoline. [Du., an occult physical principle supposed in all bodies, alteration of Gk. *khaos*, chaos, empty space, coined by Jan Baptista van Helmont (1577–1644), Flem. chemist.]

gas•bag (găs′băg′) *n.* **1.** An expansible bag for holding gas. **2.** *Slang.* One given to empty or boastful talk.

gas burner *n.* A nozzle or jet on a fitting through which combustible gas is released to burn.

gas chamber *n.* A sealed enclosure in which condemned prisoners are executed by poison gas.

gas•con (găs′kən) *n.* A braggart. [< GASCON.]

Gas•con (găs′kən) *n.* A native or inhabitant of Gascony. —*adj.* Of or relating to Gascony, the Gascons, or their language or culture.

gas•con•ade (găs′kə-nād′) *n.* Boastfulness; bravado. [Fr. *gasconnade* < *Gascon*, Gascon < Lat. *Vascō, Vascon-*.] —**gas′con•ade′** *v.* —**gas′con•ad′er** *n.*

Gas•con•ade (găs′kə-nād′). A river rising in the Ozark Plateau of S-central MO and flowing c. 426 km (265 mi) to the Missouri R. E of Jefferson City.

gas constant *n. Symbol* **R** *Phys.* The constant of proportionality in the equation relating the product of the pressure and volume of a gas to its absolute temperature, equal to 8.314 joules per kelvin.

Gas•co•ny (găs′kə-nē). A historical region and former province of SW France; settled orig. by Basque peoples and part of the French royal domain after 1607.

gas•e•ous (găs′ē-əs, găsh′əs) *adj.* **1.** Of, relating to, or existing as a gas. **2.** Lacking substance or concreteness; indefinite. **3.** Full of or containing gas; gassy. —**gas′e•ous•ness** *n.*

gas fitter *n.* One who installs or repairs gas pipes, fixtures, or appliances.

gas gangrene *n.* Gangrene occurring in a wound infected with bacteria of the genus *Clostridium*, esp. *C. perfringens*, and characterized by the presence of gas in the affected tissue.

gas-guz•zler (găs′gŭz′lər) *n. Informal.* An automotive vehicle that gets relatively low gas mileage. —**gas′-guz′zling** *adj.*

gash (găsh) *tr.v.* **gashed, gash•ing, gash•es.** To make a long deep cut in; slash deeply. —*n.* **1.** A long deep cut. **2.** A deep flesh wound. [Alteration of ME *garsen*, to scarify < ONFr. *garser* < LLat. *charaxāre*, to scratch, engrave < Gk. *kharassein*.]

Gash•er•brum (gŭsh′ər-bro͞om′, -bro͝om′). A series of four peaks in the Karakoram Range of the Himalaya Mts. in N Kashmir. **Gasherbrum I** is the highest, at 8,073.4 m (26,470 ft), although **Gasherbrum IV**, 7,930 m (26,000 ft), has been called more difficult to climb than Everest. The other two peaks are 8,039.8 m (26,360 ft) and 7,957.5 m (26,090 ft).

gas•hold•er (găs′hōl′dər) *n.* A storage container for fuel gas, esp. a large, telescoping cylindrical tank.

gas•house (găs′hous′) *n.* See **gasworks.**

gas•i•form (găs′ə-fôrm′) *adj.* In the form of gas; gaseous.

gas•i•fy (găs′ə-fī′) *tr. & intr.v.* **-fied, -fy•ing, -fies.** To convert into or become gas. —**gas′i•fi′a•ble** *adj.* —**gas′i•fi•ca′tion** (-fĭ-kā′shən) *n.* —**gas′i•fi′er** *n.*

gas jet *n.* **1.** See **gas burner. 2.** The flame from a gas burner.

Gas•kell (găs′kəl), **Elizabeth Cleghorn Stevenson.** 1810–1865. British writer noted for her *Life of Charlotte Brontë* (1857) and her novels, including *Mary Barton* (1848).

gas•ket (găs′kĭt) *n.* **1.** Any of a wide variety of seals or packings used between matched machine parts or around pipe joints to prevent the escape of a gas or fluid. **2.** *Naut.* A cord or canvas strap used to secure a furled sail to a yard boom or gaff. [Perh. alteration of Fr. *garcette*, small cord, dim. of *garce*, girl < OFr., fem. of *gars*, boy, soldier. See GARÇON.]

gas•kin (găs′kĭn) *n.* **1.** The part of the hind leg of a horse or related animal between the stifle and the hock. **2. gaskins.** *Obsolete.* Galligaskins. [Prob. short for GALLIGASKINS.]

gas•light (găs′līt′) *n.* **1.** Light produced by burning illuminating gas. **2.** A gas burner or lamp.

gas log *n.* A gas burner shaped like a log for use in a fireplace.

gas main *n.* A major pipeline conveying gas to smaller pipes for distribution to consumers.

gas mask *n.* A respirator with a chemical air filter, worn over the face as protection against toxic gases and aerosols.

gas•o•hol (găs′ə-hôl′) *n.* A fuel consisting of a blend of ethyl alcohol and unleaded gasoline. [GAS(OLINE) + (ALC)OHOL.]

gas•o•line (găs′ə-lēn′, găs′ə-lēn′) *n.* A volatile mixture of flammable liquid hydrocarbons derived chiefly from crude petroleum and used as a fuel, a solvent, an illuminant, and a thinner. [GAS + -OL(E) + -INE[2].]

gas•om•e•ter (gă-sŏm′ĭ-tər) *n.* **1.** An apparatus for measuring gases. **2.** See **gasholder.**

gas mask

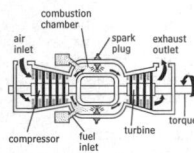

gas turbine
Simple, open-cycle gas turbine

gasp (găsp) *v.* **gasped, gasp•ing, gasps.** —*intr.* **1.** To draw in the breath sharply, as from shock. **2.** To breathe convulsively or laboriously. —*tr.* To utter in a breathless manner. —*n.* A short convulsive intake or catching of the breath. [ME *gaspen, gaispen,* to gape, yawn < ON *geispa,* to yawn.]

Gas•par (găs′pär, -pər). See **Caspar.**

Gas•pé (găs-pā′). A city of E Quebec, Canada, on **Gaspé Bay,** an inlet of the Gulf of St. Lawrence. Pop. 17,261.

Gaspé Peninsula. A peninsula of E Quebec, Canada, between Chaleur Bay and the mouth of the St. Lawrence R.

gasp•er (găs′pər) *n. Chiefly British.* A cigarette.

gas plant *n.* A Eurasian plant *(Dictamnus albus)* having aromatic foliage and emitting a flammable vapor.

gas•ser (găs′ər) *n.* **1.** A well or drilling that yields natural gas. **2.** *Slang.* Something highly entertaining or remarkable. **3.** *Slang.* A talkative or boastful person.

gas station *n.* See **service station** 1.

gas•sy (găs′ē) *adj.* **-si•er, -si•est. 1.** Containing or full of gas. **2.** Resembling gas. **3.** *Slang.* Bombastic; boastful. —**gas′si•ness** *n.*

Gas•to•ni•a (gă-stō′nē-ə). A city of S NC near the SC border W of Charlotte. Pop. 54,732.

gastr– *pref.* Var. of **gastro–.**

gas•trec•to•my (gă-strĕk′tə-mē) *n., pl.* **-mies.** Surgical excision of part or all of the stomach.

gas•tric (găs′trĭk) *adj.* Of, relating to, or associated with the stomach.

gastric juice *n.* The watery acidic digestive fluid secreted by various glands in the mucous membrane of the stomach, consisting chiefly of hydrochloric acid, pepsin, rennin, and mucin.

gastric ulcer *n.* An ulcer in the stomach mucous membrane.

gas•trin (găs′trĭn) *n.* A hormone secreted by glands in the mucous membrane of the stomach that stimulates the production of gastric juice.

gas•tri•tis (gă-strī′tĭs) *n.* Chronic or acute inflammation of the stomach, esp. of the mucous membrane of the stomach.

gastro– or **gastr–** *pref.* **1.a.** Belly: *gastropod.* **b.** Stomach: *gastritis.* **2.** Gastric: *gastrin.* [Gk. < *gastēr, gastr-,* belly.]

gas•troc•ne•mi•us (găs′trŏk-nē′mē-əs, găs′trə-) *n., pl.* **-mi•i** (-mē-ī′). The largest muscle of the calf of the leg, the action of which extends the foot and bends the knee. [NLat. < Gk. *gastroknēmia,* calf of the leg : *gastro-,* gastro- + *knēmē,* leg.]

gas•tro•en•ter•ic (găs′trō-ĕn-tĕr′ĭk) *adj.* Gastrointestinal.

gas•tro•en•ter•i•tis (găs′trō-ĕn′tə-rī′tĭs) *n.* Inflammation of the mucous membrane of the stomach and intestines.

gas•tro•en•ter•ol•o•gy (găs′trō-ĕn′tə-rŏl′ə-jē) *n.* The branch of medicine that studies disorders affecting the stomach, intestines, and associated organs. —**gas′tro•en′ter•o•log′ic** (-ə-lŏj′ĭk), **gas′tro•en′ter•o•log′i•cal** *adj.* —**gas′tro•en′ter•ol′o•gist** *n.*

gas•tro•in•tes•ti•nal (găs′trō-ĭn-tĕs′tə-nəl) *adj.* Of or relating to the stomach and intestines.

gas•tro•lith (găs′trə-lĭth′) *n.* **1.** A pathological stony mass formed in the stomach. **2.** A small stone found in the stomach of some reptiles, fish, and birds that helps grind food.

gas•trol•o•gy (gă-strŏl′ə-jē) *n.* The medical study of the stomach and its diseases. —**gas′tro•log′i•cal, gas′tro•log′ic** *adj.* —**gas•trol′o•gist** *n.*

gas•tro•nome (găs′trə-nōm′) also **gas•tron•o•mer** (gă-strŏn′ə-mər) or **gas•tron•o•mist** (gă-strŏn′ə-mĭst) *n.* A connoisseur of good food and drink; a gourmet.

gas•tro•nom•ic (găs′trə-nŏm′ĭk) also **gas•tro•nom•i•cal** (-ĭ-kəl) *adj.* Of or relating to gastronomy. —**gas′tro•nom′i•cal•ly** *adv.*

gas•tron•o•my (gă-strŏn′ə-mē) *n., pl.* **-mies. 1.** The art or science of good eating. **2.** A style of cooking.

gas•tro•pod (găs′trə-pŏd′) *n.* Any of various mollusks of the class Gastropoda, such as the snail, characteristically having a single, usu. coiled shell or no shell at all, a ventral muscular foot, and eyes and feelers. [< NLat. *Gastropoda,* class name : GASTRO– + *-poda,* -pod.] —**gas′tro•pod′, gas•trop′o•dan** (gă-strŏp′ə-dn), **gas•trop′o•dous** (-dəs) *adj.*

gas•tro•scope (găs′trə-skōp′) *n.* An endoscope that is inserted through the mouth to examine the interior of the stomach. —**gas′tro•scop′ic** (-skŏp′ĭk) *adj.* —**gas•tros′co•pist** (gă-strŏs′kə-pĭst) *n.* —**gas•tros′co•py** (-kə-pē) *n.*

gas•trot•o•my (gă-strŏt′ə-mē) *n., pl.* **-mies.** A surgical incision into the stomach.

gas•tro•trich (găs′trə-trĭk) *n.* Any of various minute aquatic animals of the phylum Gastrotricha, having a wormlike ciliated body. [< NLat. *Gastrotricha,* phylum name : GASTRO– + Gk. *-trikha,* neut. pl. of *-trikhos,* -trichous.]

gas•tro•vas•cu•lar (găs′trō-văs′kyə-lər) *adj.* Having both a digestive and a circulatory function.

gas•tru•la (găs′trə-lə) *n., pl.* **-las** or **-lae** (-lē′). An embryo at the stage following the blastula, consisting of a hollow two-layered sac of ectoderm and endoderm surrounding an archenteron. [NLat. : Gk. *gastēr, gastr-,* belly + Lat. *-ula,* fem. dim. suff.] —**gas′tru•lar** (-lər) *adj.* —**gas′tru•late′** *v.* —**gas′tru•la′tion** *n.*

gas turbine *n.* An internal-combustion engine consisting of an air compressor, a combustion chamber, and a turbine wheel turned by the expanding products of combustion.

gas•works (găs′wûrks′) *pl.n. (used with a sing. v.)* A factory where gas for heating and lighting is produced.

gat[1] (găt) *n.* A narrow passage extending inland from a shore; a channel. [Prob. Du. < MDu.]

gat[2] (găt) *n. Slang.* A pistol. [Short for GAT(LING GUN).]

gat[3] (găt) *v. Archaic.* A p.t. of **get.**

gate[1] (gāt) *n.* **1.** A structure that can be swung, drawn, or lowered to block an entrance or a passageway. **2.a.** An opening in a wall or fence for entrance or exit. **b.** The structure surrounding such an opening. **3.a.** A means of access. **b.** A passageway, as in an airport, through which passengers proceed for embarkation. **4.** A mountain pass. **5.** The total paid attendance or admission receipts at a public event. **6.** A device for controlling the passage of water or gas through a dam or conduit. **7.** The channel through which molten metal flows into a shaped cavity of a mold. **8.** *Sports.* A passage between two upright poles through which a skier must go in a slalom race. **9.** *Electron.* A circuit with multiple inputs and one output that is energized only when a designated set of input pulses is received. —*tr.v.* **gat•ed, gat•ing, gates. 1.** *Chiefly British.* To confine (a student) to the grounds of a college as punishment. **2.** *Electron.* To select part of (a wave) for transmission, reception, or processing by magnitude or time interval. —***idioms.*** **get the gate.** *Slang.* To be dismissed or rejected. **give (someone) the gate.** *Slang.* **1.** To discharge from a job. **2.** To reject or jilt. [ME < OE *geat.*]

gate[1]
Floodgate

gate[2] (gāt) *n.* **1.** *Chiefly British.* A particular way of acting. **2.** *Archaic.* A path or way. [ME < ON *gata.* See **ghē-*.**]

gâ•teau or **ga•teau** (gă-tō′, gä-) *n., pl.* **gâ•teaux** or **ga•teaux** (gă-tō′, gä-). A cake or pastry, esp. a light, filled one. [Fr. < OFr. *gastel,* cake < Frankish **wastil,* food.]

gate•crash•er (gāt′krăsh′ər) *n. Slang.* One who gains admittance, as to a party or concert, without being invited or without paying. —**gate′crash′** *v.*

gate•fold (gāt′fōld′) *n. Print.* A foldout, esp. one that opens to double the page size.

gate•house (gāt′hous′) *n.* **1.** A lodge at the entrance to the driveway of an estate. **2.** A fortified structure built over the gateway to a city or castle. **3.** A building that houses the controls of a dam or canal lock.

gatehouse

gate•keep•er (gāt′kē′pər) *n.* **1.** One in charge of passage through a gate. **2.** One who monitors or oversees others.

gate-leg table (gāt′lĕg′) *n.* A drop leaf table with paired legs that swing out to support the leaves.

gate•post (gāt′pōst′) *n.* An upright post on which a gate is hung or against which it closes.

ga•ter also **'ga•ter** (gā′tər) *n. Informal.* Var. of **gator.**

Gates (gāts), **Horatio.** 1728?–1806. Amer. Revolutionary general who won the Battle of Saratoga (1777).

Gates•head (gāts′hĕd′). A borough of NE England on the Tyne R. opposite Newcastle; dating probably to Saxon times. Pop. 214,100.

gate•way (gāt′wā′) *n.* **1.** An opening or a structure framing an opening, such as an arch, that may be closed by a gate. **2.** Something that serves as an entrance or a means of access.

Gath (găth). An ancient city of Palestine ENE of Gaza; one of the five Philistine city-kingdoms and the home of Goliath.

gath•er (găth′ər) *v.* **-ered, -er•ing, -ers.** —*tr.* **1.** To cause to come together; convene. **2.a.** To accumulate (something) gradually; amass. **b.** To harvest or pick. **3.** To gain by a process of gradual increase. **4.** To collect into one place; assemble. **5.** To pick up and enfold. **6.** *Print.* To arrange (signatures) in sequence for bookbinding. **7.a.** To draw into small folds or puckers, as by pulling a thread through cloth. **b.** To contract and wrinkle (the brow). **8.** To bring closer to or draw about something else. **9.** To conclude; infer. **10.** To summon up; muster: *gathered up his courage.* **11.** To attract or be a center of attraction for. —*intr.* **1.** To come together in a group; assemble. **2.** To accumulate. **3.** To grow or increase by degrees. **4.** To come to a head, as a boil; fester. **5.** To forage for wild foodstuffs. —*n.* **1.a.** The act or an instance of gathering. **b.** A quantity gathered. **2.** A small fold or pucker made by gathering cloth. [ME *getheren, gaderen* < OE *gadrian.* See **ghedh-*.**] —**gath′er•er** *n.*

Syns: *gather, collect, assemble, congregate, accumulate, amass.* These verbs mean to bring or come together in a group or agregate. *Gather* is the most widely applicable: *Students gathered. Collect* frequently refers to the careful selection of like or related things that become part of an organized whole: *collected stamps. Assemble* implies a definite and usually close relationship: *The legislature assembled in January. The curator is assembling interesting Stone Age artifacts. Congregate* refers chiefly to the coming together of a large number of persons or animals: *The physicians congregated to compare notes. Accumulate* applies to the increase of like or related things over an extended period: *Old newspapers are accumulating. Amass* refers to the collection or accumulation of things, especially valuable things, to form an imposing quantity: *Their families had amassed great fortunes.*

gath•er•ing (găth′ər-ĭng) *n.* **1.a.** The action of one that gath-

ă pat	oi boy
ā pay	ou out
âr care	ŏŏ took
ä father	ōō boot
ĕ pet	ŭ cut
ē be	ûr urge
ĭ pit	th thin
ī pie	*th* this
îr pier	hw which
ŏ pot	zh vision
ō toe	ə about, item
ô paw	

Stress marks:
′ (primary);
′ (secondary), as in
dictionary (dĭk′shə-nĕr′ē)

ers. **b.** That which is gathered or amassed; a collection or an accumulation. **2.** An assembly of persons; a meeting. **3.** The collecting of food that grows wild, such as berries. **4.** A gather in cloth. **5.** A suppurated swelling; a boil or an abscess.

Gat•i•neau (găt′n-ō′, gä-tē-nō′). A town of SW Quebec, Canada, NE of Hull near the mouth of the **Gatineau River,** which rises in the Laurentian Plateau and flows c. 386 km (240 mi) SW to the Ottawa R. Pop. 74,988.

Gatling gun *n.* A machine gun having a cluster of barrels that are fired in sequence as the cluster is rotated. [After Richard Jordan *Gatling* (1818–1903), Amer. firearms inventor.]

ga•tor or **ga•ter** also **'ga•tor** or **'ga•ter** (gā′tər) *n. Informal.* An alligator.

GATT *abbr.* General Agreement on Tariffs and Trade.

Ga•tún Lake (gə-to͞on′, gä-). An artificial lake of central Panama, a major link in the Panama Canal system.

gauntlet[1]

gauche (gōsh) *adj.* Lacking social polish; tactless. [Fr., awkward < OFr. < *gauchir*, to turn aside, walk clumsily, of Gmc. orig.] — **gauche′ly** *adv.* — **gauche′ness** *n.*

gau•che•rie (gō′shə-rē′) *n.* **1.** An awkward or tactless act, manner, or expression. **2.** A lack of tact; awkwardness. [Fr. < *gauche*, gauche. See GAUCHE.]

gau•cho (gou′chō) *n., pl.* **-chos. 1.** A cowboy of the South American pampas. **2. gauchos.** Calf-length pants with flared legs. [Am.Sp., prob. < Quechua *wáhcha*, vagabond.]

gaud (gôd) *n.* A gaudy or showy ornament or trinket. [ME *gaud, gaudi*, sing. of *gaudies*, large, ornamental beads on a rosary, trinkets < Med.Lat. *gaudia* < Lat., pl. of *gaudium*, joy (referring to the Joyful Mysteries of the Virgin Mary) < *gaudēre*, to rejoice. See **gāu-***.]

gaud•er•y (gô′də-rē) *n., pl.* **-ies.** Showy or gaudy decoration; ostentatious or pretentious show.

Gau•dí (gou′dē, gou-dē′), **Antonio.** 1852–1926. Spanish architect whose most celebrated work is the façade of the Expiatory Church of the Holy Family in Barcelona.

gaud•y[1] (gô′dē) *adj.* **-i•er, -i•est.** Showy in a tasteless or vulgar way. [Poss. < GAUDY[2] (influenced by GAUD).] — **gaud′i•ly** *adv.* — **gaud′i•ness** *n.*

gaud•y[2] (gô′dē) *n., pl.* **-ies.** *Chiefly British.* A feast, esp. an annual university dinner. [ME *gaudi, gaud*, prank, trick, poss. < OFr. *gaudie*, merriment (< *gaudir*, to enjoy, make merry < Lat. *gaudēre*, to rejoice) and < Lat. *gaudium*, enjoyment, merry-making (< *gaudēre*, to rejoice; see **gāu-***).]

gauf•fer (gŏf′ər, gô′fər) *v. & n.* Var. of **goffer.**

Gau•ga•me•la (gô′gə-mē′lə). An ancient village of Assyria NE of Nineveh where Alexander the Great defeated the Persians under Darius III in 331 B.C.

gaur
Bos gaurus

gauge also **gage** (gāj) — *n.* **1.a.** A standard or scale of measurement. **b.** A standard dimension, quantity, or capacity. **2.** An instrument for measuring or testing. **3.** A means of estimating or evaluating; a test. **4.a.** The distance between the two rails of a railroad. **b.** The distance between two wheels on an axle. **5.** The interior diameter of a shotgun barrel as determined by the number of lead balls of a size exactly fitting the barrel required to make one pound. **6.** The amount of plaster of Paris combined with common plaster to speed setting of the mixture. **7.** Thickness or diameter, as of sheet metal or wire. **8.** The fineness of knitted cloth as determined by the number of loops per 1½ inches. — *tr.v.* **gauged, gaug•ing, gaug•es** also **gaged, gag•ing, gag•es. 1.** To measure precisely. **2.** To determine the capacity, volume, or contents of. **3.** To evaluate or judge. **4.** To adapt to a specified measurement. **5.** To mix (plaster) in specific proportions. **6.** To chip or rub (bricks or stones) to size. [ME < ONFr., gauging rod, of Gmc. orig.] — **gauge′a•ble** *adj.*

gaug•er also **gag•er** (gā′jər) *n. Chiefly British.* A revenue officer who inspects bulk goods subject to duty.

Gau•guin (gō-găɴ′), **(Eugène Henri) Paul.** 1848–1903. French artist whose paintings include *Ia Orana Maria* (1891).

Gaul[1] (gôl) *n.* **1.** A Celt of ancient Gaul. **2.** A French person.

Gaul[2] (gôl). Formerly **Gal•li•a** (găl′ē-ä). An ancient region of W Europe S and W of the Rhine R., W of the Alps, and N of the Pyrenees, corresponding roughly to modern-day France and Belgium; conquered by Julius Caesar in the Gallic Wars (58–51 B.C.).

Gaul•ish (gô′lĭsh) *n.* The Celtic language of ancient Gaul.

Gaull•ism (gō′lĭz′əm, gô′-) *n.* **1.** The movement supporting Gen. Charles de Gaulle as leader of the French government in exile during World War II. **2.** The movement headed by Charles de Gaulle after World War II. — **Gaull′ist** *n.*

gaum (gôm) *tr.v.* **gaumed, gaum•ing, gaums.** *Upper Southern U.S.* To smudge or smear. [Perh. alteration of obsolete *gome*, grease, var. of *coom*, soot, mixture of dirt and axle grease, var. of CULM[2].]

gaunt (gônt) *adj.* **gaunt•er, gaunt•est. 1.** Thin and bony; angular. See Syns at **lean[2]. 2.** Emaciated and haggard; drawn. **3.** Bleak and desolate; barren. [ME, perh. < OFr. *gant*, poss. of Scand. orig.] — **gaunt′ly** *adv.* — **gaunt′ness** *n.*

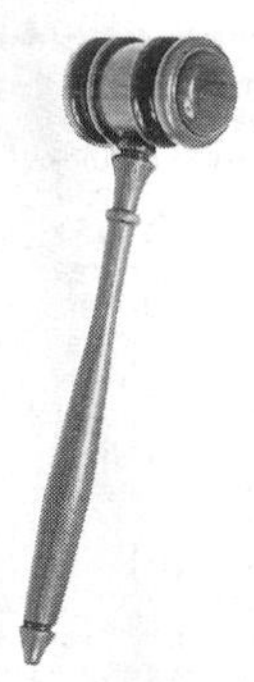

gavel[1]

gaunt•let[1] also **gant•let** (gônt′lĭt, gänt′-) *n.* **1.** A protective glove worn with medieval armor. **2.** A protective glove with a flared cuff, used in manual labor, in certain sports, and for driving. **3.** A challenge. **4.** A dress glove cuffed above the wrist. [ME < OFr. *gantelet*, dim. of *gant*, glove, of Gmc. orig.]

Word History: A perennial usage question is whether the spelling *gauntlet* is acceptable for both *gauntlet*[1] and *gauntlet*[2]. *Gauntlet*[1], as in *to throw down the gauntlet,* comes from the Old French word *gantelet,* a diminutive of *gant,* "glove." From the time of its appearance in Middle English, the word has been spelled with an *au* as well as an *a,* still a possible spelling. But the other *gauntlet,* as in *to run the gauntlet,* is an alteration of the earlier English form *gantlope,* which came from the Swedish word *gatlopp,* a compound of *gata,* "lane," and *lopp,* "course." The English word was influenced by the spelling of the word *gauntlet,* "glove," and in 1676 we find the first recorded instance of the spelling *gauntlet* for this word, although *gantelope* is found as late as 1836. Although one could say that the *a* spelling is preferable because it reflects the Swedish source, in regard to a word that has been so altered in form, this seems a rather fine point.

gaunt•let[2] also **gant•let** (gônt′lĭt, gänt′-) *n.* **1.a.** A form of punishment in which a person is forced to run between two lines of men armed to strike, as with sticks. **b.** The lines of men so arranged. **2.** An onslaught or attack from all sides. **3.** A severe trial; an ordeal. [Alteration (influenced by GAUNTLET[1]) of *gantlope* < Swed. *gatlopp* : *gata*, lane (< OSwed.; see **ghē-***) + *lopp*, course, running (< MLGer. *lōp*).]

gaur (gour) *n.* A large dark-coated wild ox *(Bos gaurus)* of southeast Asia. [Hindi < Skt. *gauraḥ*. See **gʷou-***.]

gauss (gous) *n., pl.* **gauss** or **gauss•es.** *Phys.* The centimeter-gram-second unit of magnetic induction, equal to one maxwell per square centimeter. [After Karl Friedrich GAUSS.]

Gauss (gous), **Karl Friedrich.** 1777–1855. German mathematician and astronomer known for his contributions to algebra, differential geometry, probability theory, and number theory.

Gauss•i•an distribution (gou′sē-ən) *n.* See **normal distribution.** [After Karl Friedrich GAUSS.]

Gau•ta•ma (gô′tə-mə, gou′-), **Siddhartha.** See **Buddha.**

Gau•tier (gō-tyā′), **Théophile.** 1811–72. French writer whose works include *Enamels and Cameos* (1852).

gauze (gôz) *n.* **1.a.** A thin transparent fabric with a loose open weave. **b.** A thin, loosely woven surgical dressing, usu. made of cotton. **c.** A thin plastic or metal woven mesh. **2.** A mist or haze. [Fr. *gaze*, poss. < Sp. *gasa* < Ar. *qazz*, raw silk, poss. < Pers. *kazh*.] — **gauz′i•ly** *adv.* — **gauz′i•ness** *n.*

gauz•y (gô′zē) *adj.* **-i•er, -i•est.** Resembling gauze in thinness or transparency. See Syns at **airy.** — **gauz′i•ly** *adv.* — **gauz′i•ness** *n.*

ga•vage (gə-väzh′) *n.* Introduction of nutritive material into the stomach by means of a tube. [Fr. < *gaver*, to force down the throat, ult. < OFr. *gave*, throat < OLat. **gaba*.]

gave (gāv) *v.* P.t. of **give.**

gav•el[1] (găv′əl) *n.* **1.** A small mallet used by a presiding officer or an auctioneer to signal for attention or order or mark the conclusion of a transaction. **2.** A maul used by masons in fitting stones. — *tr.v.* **-eled, -el•ing, -els** also **-elled, -el•ling, -els.** To bring about or compel by using a gavel. [?]

gav•el[2] (găv′əl) *n.* Tribute or rent in ancient and medieval England. [ME < OE *gafol*. See **ghabh-***.]

gav•el•kind (găv′əl-kīnd′) *n.* A former English system of land tenure that provided for the equal division of land among all qualified heirs. [ME *gavelkinde* : OE *gafol*, gavel; see GAVEL[2] + OE *gecynd*, kind; see KIND[2].]

ga•vi•al (gā′vē-əl) *n.* A large reptile *(Gavialis gangeticus)* of southern Asia, related to and resembling the crocodiles and having a long slender snout. [Fr. < Hindi *ghaṛiyāl*.]

ga•votte (gə-vŏt′) *n.* **1.** A French peasant dance resembling the minuet. **2.** Music for this dance in moderately quick 4/4 time. [Fr. < Prov. *gavoto* < *gavot*, native of the Alps, poss. < *gava*, crop of a bird < OLat. **gaba*, gullet, throat.]

GAW *abbr.* Guaranteed annual wage.

Ga•wain (gə-wān′, gä′wān′, gou′ən, gä′wən) *n.* A nephew of King Arthur and a Knight of the Round Table.

gawk (gôk) *n.* An awkward, loutish person; an oaf. — *intr.v.* **gawked, gawk•ing, gawks.** To stare or gape stupidly. [Perh. alteration of obsolete *gaw*, to gape < ME *gawen* < ON *gā*, to heed.] — **gawk′er** *n.*

gawk•y (gô′kē) *adj.* **-i•er, -i•est.** Awkward; ungainly. — **gawk′i•ly** *adv.*

gay (gā) *adj.* **gay•er, gay•est. 1.** Showing or characterized by cheerfulness and lighthearted excitement; merry. **2.** Bright or lively, esp. in color. **3.** Of, relating to, or sharing the lifestyle and concerns of the homosexual community. **4.** Homosexual. **5.** Given to social pleasures. **6.** Dissolute; licentious. — *n.* A gay person, esp. an openly gay person in contemporary society. [ME *gai* < OFr., poss. of Gmc. orig.] — **gay′ness** *n.*

Usage Note: The word *gay* is now standard in its use to refer to the American homosexual community and its members; in this use it is generally lowercased. *Gay* is distinguished from *homosexual* in emphasizing the cultural and social aspects of homosexuality. Many writers reserve *gay* for male homosexuals, but the word is used to refer to both sexes; when the intended meaning is not clear in the context, the phrase *gay and lesbian* should be used. *Gay* may be regarded as offensive when used as a noun to refer to particular individuals, as in *There were two gays on the panel*; here a phrase such as *gay people* should be used instead. But there is no objection to the use of the noun in the plural to refer to the general gay community.

Gay (gā), **John.** 1685–1732. English writer known esp. for his play *The Beggar's Opera* (1728).

Ga•ya (gə-yä′, gī′ə). A city of NE India S of Patna; a sacred area to Buddhist and Hindu pilgrims. Pop. 247,075.

ga•yal (gə-yäl′) *n.* A domesticated bovine mammal *(Bos frontalis)* of India and Burma, with thick pointed horns and a dark coat. [Bengali *gayāl*, prob. < Skt. *gauḥ*, ox. See **gʷou-***.]

gay•e•ty (gā′ĭ-tē) *n.* Var. of **gaiety.**

gay feather *n.* See **blazing star** 2.

Gay-Lus•sac (gā′lə-săk′, -lü-säk′), **Joseph Louis.** 1778–1850. French chemist and physicist who isolated boron (1809) and formulated a law of combining volumes of gases.

gay•ly (gā′lē) *adv.* Var. of **gaily.**

gaz. *abbr.* Gazette; gazetteer.

Ga•za (gä′zə, găz′ə, gā′zə). A city of SW Asia in the **Gaza Strip,** a narrow coastal area along the Mediterranean adjoining Israel and Egypt. Part of the British mandate for Palestine (1917–48), the territory passed to Egypt in 1949 and was occupied by Israel in 1967. Pop. 118,272.

gaze (gāz) *intr.v.* **gazed, gaz•ing, gaz•es.** To look steadily, intently, and with fixed attention. —*n.* A steady fixed look. [ME *gasen*, prob. of Scand. orig.] **—gaz′er** *n.*

ga•ze•bo (gə-zā′bō, -zē′-) *n., pl.* **-bos** or **-boes. 1.** A freestanding roofed, usu. open-sided structure providing a shady resting place. **2.** See **belvedere.** [?]

gaze•hound (gāz′hound′) *n.* A dog, such as the Afghan hound or the greyhound, that hunts its prey by sight.

ga•zelle (gə-zĕl′) *n.* Any of various small swift antelopes of the genus *Gazella* and related genera of Africa and Asia, with a slender neck and annulate horns. [Fr. < OFr. < Ar. *ġazāl.*]

ga•zette (gə-zĕt′) *n.* **1.** A newspaper. **2.** An official journal. **3.** *Chiefly British.* An announcement in an official journal. —*tr.v.* **-zet•ted, -zet•ting, -zettes.** *Chiefly British.* To announce or publish in an official journal or a newspaper. [Fr. < Ital. *gazzetta*, prob. < Ital. dial. *gazeta*, a small coin.]

gaz•et•teer (găz′ĭ-tîr′) *n.* **1.** A geographic dictionary or index. **2.** *Archaic.* A writer for a gazette; a journalist.

Ga•zi•an•tep (gä′zē-än-tĕp′). Formerly **Ain•tab** (īn-tăb′). A city of S Turkey N of Aleppo, Syria. Pop. 374,290.

gaz•pa•cho (gə-spä′chō, gəz-pä′-) *n., pl.* **-chos.** A chilled soup made with chopped tomatoes, cucumbers, onions, peppers, herbs, and sometimes bread. [Sp.]

G.B. *abbr.* Great Britain.

Gbe (bĕ, gbĕ) *n.* A closely related group of languages, including Ewe and Fon, that are spoken in coastal Ghana, Togo, Benin, and Nigeria. [Gbe, language, voice.]

GCA *abbr.* Ground-controlled approach.

G.C.B. *abbr.* Knight of the Grand Cross, Order of the Bath.

gcd or **g.c.d.** *abbr. Math.* Greatest common divisor.

gcf or **g.c.f.** *abbr. Math.* Greatest common factor.

G clef *n. Mus.* See **treble clef.**

GCT *abbr.* Greenwich civil time.

Gd The symbol for the element **gadolinium.**

gd. *abbr.* Good.

G.D. *abbr.* Grand duchy.

Gdańsk (gə-dänsk′, -dănsk′, -dĭnsk′) also **Dan•zig** (dăn′sĭg, dän′tsĭk). A city of N Poland on the **Gulf of Gdańsk,** an inlet of the Baltic Sea. The Treaty of Versailles (1919) declared Gdańsk a free city, although it came under Nazi control in 1935. It was liberated by the Russians in 1945 and subsequently restored to Poland. Pop. 467,200.

G.D.R. or **GDR** *abbr.* German Democratic Republic.

gds. *abbr.* Goods.

Gdy•ni•a (gə-dĭn′ē-ə, -dĭn′yə). A city of N Poland on the Gulf of Gdańsk NW of Gdańsk. Pop. 243,100.

Ge The symbol for the element **germanium.**

ge– *pref.* Var. of **geo–.**

ge•an•ti•cline (jē-ăn′tĭ-klīn′) *n.* A large upward fold of the earth's crust. **—ge•an′ti•cli′nal** *adj.*

gear (gîr) *n.* **1.a.** A toothed machine part, such as a wheel or cylinder, that meshes with another toothed part to transmit motion or to change speed or direction. **b.** A complete assembly that performs a specific function in a larger machine. **c.** A transmission configuration for a specific ratio of engine to axle torque in a motor vehicle. **2.** Equipment, such as tools, used for a particular activity; paraphernalia. **3.a.** Clothing and accessories. **b.** Personal belongings, including clothing. **4.** The harness for a horse. **5.** *Naut.* **a.** A ship's rigging. **b.** A sailor's personal effects. —*v.* **geared, gear•ing, gears.** —*tr.* **1.a.** To equip with gears. **b.** To connect by gears. **c.** To put into gear. **2.** To adjust or adapt so as to make suitable. **3.** To provide with gear; equip. —*intr.* **1.** To come into or be in gear. **2.** To become adjusted so as to fit or blend. ***—phrasal verb.* gear up.** To get ready for a coming action or event. [ME *gere*, equipment < ON *gervi.*]

gear•box (gîr′bŏks′) *n.* **1.** See **transmission** 3. **2.** A protective casing for a system of gears.

gear•ing (gîr′ĭng) *n.* **1.** A system of gears and associated elements by which motion is transferred within a machine. **2.** The act or technique of providing with gears.

gear ratio *n.* The ratio of the speed of rotation of the powered gear of a gear train to that of the final or driven gear.

gear•shift (gîr′shĭft′) *n.* A mechanism for changing from one gear to another in a transmission.

gear train *n.* A system of interconnected gears.

gear•wheel also **gear wheel** (gîr′hwēl′, -wēl′) *n.* A wheel with a toothed rim.

Geat (gēt, yăt) *n.* A member of an ancient Germanic people of southern Sweden conquered by the Swedes in the sixth century A.D. [OE *Gēat.*]

Ge•bel Mu•sa (jĕb′əl mo͞o′sə, -sä). See **Jebel Musa.**

Ge•ber (jē′bər, gā′-) also **Ja•bir** (jä′bər, jä′bîr). fl. 8th cent.? Arab scholar and alchemist who wrote *Summa Perfectionis.*

geck•o (gĕk′ō) *n., pl.* **-os** or **-oes.** Any of various usu. small tropical and subtropical lizards of the family Gekkonidae, having toes containing numerous suction cups that enable them to climb on vertical surfaces. [Malay (Javanese) *ge'kok.*]

gecko

GED *abbr.* **1.** General equivalency diploma. **2.** General educational development.

Ged•des (gĕd′ēz), **Norman Bel.** 1893–1958. Amer. designer who popularized the concept of streamlining.

gee[1] (jē) *n.* The letter *g.*

gee[2] (jē) *interj.* Used to command a horse or an ox to turn to the right. —*intr.v.* **geed, gee•ing, gees.** To turn to the right.

gee[3] also **jee** (jē) *interj.* Used as a mild expletive or exclamation, as of surprise or sympathy. [Alteration of JESUS.]

gee[4] (jē) *n. Slang.* A thousand dollars. [< GEE[1] < the first letter of GRAND.]

Gee•chee (gē′chē) *n.* **1.** *Southeastern U.S.* Gullah. **2.** The local dialect of English spoken in Charleston, South Carolina. [After the OGEECHEE R., in the environs of which a Black English dialect called Geechee was spoken.]

geek (gēk) *n. Slang.* **1.** An odd or ridiculous person. **2.** A carnival performer whose show consists of bizarre acts, such as biting the head off a live chicken. [Perh. alteration of dial. *geck*, fool < LGer. *gek* < MLGer.] **—geek′y** *adj.*

Gee•long (jə-lông′). A city of SE Australia SW of Melbourne. Met. area pop. 137,173.

geese (gēs) *n.* Pl. of **goose.**

gee whiz *interj.* Used to express mild surprise, amazement, or enthusiasm.

gee•zer (gē′zər) *n.* An eccentric old man. [Prob. alteration of dial. *guiser*, masquerader < ME *gysar* < *gysen*, to dress < *gyse, guise*, fashion. See GUISE.]

ge•fil•te fish (gə-fĭl′tə) *n.* Finely chopped fish mixed with crumbs, eggs, and seasonings, cooked in a broth in oval-shaped cakes or balls and usu. served chilled. [Yiddish : *gefilt*, p.part. of *filn*, to fill, stuff + *fish*, fish.]

ge•gen•schein (gā′gən-shīn′) *n.* A faint glowing spot in the sky, exactly opposite the position of the sun. [Ger. : *gegen*, against + *Schein*, light.]

Ge•hen•na (gĭ-hĕn′ə) *n.* **1.** A place or state of torment or suffering. **2.** The abode of condemned souls; hell. [LLat. < Gk. *Geenna* < Heb. *Gê' Hinnōm*, poss. short for *Gē ben Hinnōm*, valley of the son of Hinnom, a valley S of the Old City Jerusalem.]

Geh•rig (gĕr′ĭg), **Henry Louis ("Lou").** 1903–41. Amer. baseball player who was a member of the New York Yankees (1925–39).

Lou Gehrig
Photographed in the late 1930's

Gei•ger counter (gī′gər) *n.* An instrument that detects radiation, consisting of a tube filled with gas that is ionized by passing charged particles, producing a voltage pulse which triggers a counter. [After Hans Wilhelm *Geiger* (1882–1945), German physicist.]

Gei•sel (gī′zəl), **Theodor Seuss.** Dr. Seuss. 1904–91. Amer. writer and illustrator of children's books whose works include *The Cat in the Hat* (1957).

gei•sha (gā′shə, gē′-) *n., pl.* **geisha** or **-shas.** A woman in Japan trained from girlhood in conversation, dancing, and singing in order to lend an atmosphere of gaiety to professional or social gatherings of men. [J. : *gei*, art + *sha*, person.]

gel (jĕl) *n.* **1.** A colloid in which the disperse phase has combined with the dispersion medium to produce a semisolid material. **2.** A gelatin used in theatrical lighting. **3.** A jellylike substance used in styling hair. —*intr.v.* **gelled, gel•ling, gels.** To become a gel. [Short for GELATIN.] **—gel′a•ble** *adj.*

ge•län•de•sprung (gə-lĕn′də-shpro͝ong′) *n. Sports.* A jump in skiing made from a crouching position with the use of both poles. [Ger. : *Gelände*, open field (< MHGer. *gelende* < OHGer. *gilanti* < *lant*, land; see **lendh-***) + *Sprung*, jump (< MHGer. *sprunc* < OHGer. < *springan*, to jump).]

gel•ate (jĕl′āt′) *intr.v.* **-at•ed, -at•ing, -ates.** To gel.

gel•a•tin also **gel•a•tine** (jĕl′ə-tn) *n.* **1.a.** A colorless or slightly yellow transparent brittle protein obtained from the skin, bones, and connective tissue of animals and used in foods, drugs, and photographic film. **b.** Any of various similar substances. **2.** A jelly made with gelatin. **3.** A thin transparent membrane over a theatrical light to color it. [Fr. *gélatine* <

ă pat	oi boy
ā pay	ou out
âr care	o͝o took
ä father	o͞o boot
ĕ pet	ŭ cut
ē be	ûr urge
ĭ pit	th thin
ī pie	*th* this
îr pier	hw which
ŏ pot	zh vision
ō toe	ə about, item
ô paw	

Stress marks:
′ (primary);
′ (secondary), as in
dictionary (dĭk′shə-nĕr′ē)

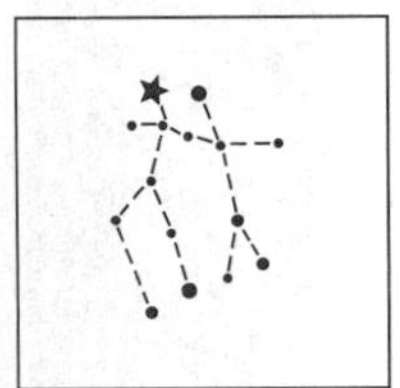
Gemini

Ital. *gelatina*, dim. of *gelata*, jelly < fem. p.part. of *gelare*, to freeze < Lat. *gelāre*. See **gel-***.]

ge•lat•i•nize (jə-lăt′n-īz′, jĕl′ə-tn-īz′) *v.* **-nized, -niz•ing, -niz•es.** —*tr.* **1.** To convert to gelatin or jelly. **2.** To coat with gelatin. —*intr.* To become gelatinous. —**ge•lat′i•ni•za′tion** (-lăt′n-ĭ-zā′shən) *n.*

ge•lat•i•nous (jə-lăt′n-əs) *adj.* **1.** Resembling gelatin; viscous. **2.** Of, relating to, or containing gelatin. —**ge•lat′i•nous•ly** *adv.* —**ge•lat′i•nous•ness** *n.*

ge•la•tion (jĕ-lā′shən) *n.* **1.** Solidification by cooling or freezing. **2.** The process of forming a gel. [Lat. *gelātiō, gelātiōn-* < *gelātus*, p.part. of *gelāre*, to freeze. See **gel-***.]

ge•la•to (jə-lä′tō, jĕ-) *n., pl.* **-ti** (-tē). An Italian ice cream or ice. [Ital. < p.part. of *gelare*, to freeze. See GELATIN.]

geld¹ (gĕld) *tr.v.* **geld•ed** or **gelt** (gĕlt), **geld•ing, gelds. 1.** To castrate (a horse, for example). **2.** To deprive of strength or vigor; weaken. [ME *gelden* < ON *gelda.*]

geld² (gĕld) *n.* A tax paid to the crown by English landholders under Anglo-Saxon and Norman kings. [ME *geld* and Med. Lat. *geldum*, both < OE *geld, gield*, payment.]

Gel•der•land (gĕl′dər-lănd′, KHĕl′dər-länt′). A region and former duchy of E-central Netherlands; passed to the Hapsburgs (1543) and then to the Netherlands (1579).

geld•ing (gĕl′dĭng) *n.* A castrated animal, esp. a horse. [ME < ON *geldingr* < *gelda*, to geld.]

gel•id (jĕl′ĭd) *adj.* Very cold; icy. See Syns at **cold.** [Lat. *gelidus* < *gelū*, frost. See **gel-***.] —**ge•lid′i•ty** (jə-lĭd′ĭ-tē), **gel′id•ness** *n.* —**gel′id•ly** *adv.*

gel•ig•nite (jĕl′ĭg-nīt′) *n.* An explosive mixture composed of nitroglycerine, guncotton, wood pulp, and potassium nitrate. [GEL(ATIN) + Lat. *ignis*, fire + -ITE¹.]

Gell-Mann (gĕl′män′), **Murray.** b. 1929. Amer. physicist who won a 1969 Nobel Prize.

Gel•sen•kir•chen (gĕl′zən-kîr′kən, -KHən). A city of W-central Germany NE of Essen. Pop. 287,956.

gelt¹ (gĕlt) *n. Slang.* Money. [Yiddish < MHGer. *geld* < OHGer. *gelt*, recompense.]

gelt² (gĕlt) *v.* A p.t. and p.part. of **geld¹**.

gem (jĕm) *n.* **1.** A pearl or mineral that has been cut and polished for use as an ornament. **2.a.** Something valued for its beauty or perfection. **b.** A beloved or highly prized person. **3.** A type of muffin. —*tr.v.* **gemmed, gem•ming, gems.** To adorn with or as if with precious or semiprecious stones. [ME *gemme* < OFr. < Lat. *gemma*. See **gembh-***.]

Ge•ma•ra (gə-mär′ə, -môr′ə) *n.* The second part of the Talmud, consisting primarily of commentary on the Mishnah. [Aram. *gĕmārā*, completion < *gĕmar*, to complete.] —**Ge•ma′ric** *adj.* —**Ge•ma′rist** *n.*

gem clip *n. Chiefly Southern U.S.* See **paper clip.** [?]

gem•i•nate (jĕm′ə-nāt′) *v.* **-nat•ed, -nat•ing, -nates.** —*tr.* **1.** To double. **2.** To arrange in pairs. —*intr.* To occur in pairs. —*adj.* (-nĭt, -nāt′). Forming a pair; doubled. —*n.* (-nĭt, -nāt′). *Ling.* A double or long consonant. [Lat. *gemināre, gemināt-* < *geminus*, twin.] —**gem′i•na′tion** *n.*

Gem•i•ni (jĕm′ə-nī′, -nē′) *pl.n. (used with a sing. v.)* **1.** A constellation in the Northern Hemisphere containing the stars Castor and Pollux. **2.a.** The third sign of the zodiac in astrology. **b.** One who is born under this sign. [ME < Lat. *Geminī*, pl. of *geminus*, twin.]

gem•ma (jĕm′ə) *n., pl.* **gem•mae** (jĕm′ē′). An asexual budlike propagule, as in liverworts, capable of developing into a new individual; a bud. [Lat., bud. See **gembh-***.]

gem•mate (jĕm′āt′) *adj.* Having or reproducing by gemmae. —*intr.v.* **-mat•ed, -mat•ing, -mates.** To produce gemmae or reproduce by means of gemmae. [< Lat. *gemmātus*, p.part. of *gemmāre*, to bud < *gemma*, bud. See **gembh-***.] —**gem•ma′tion** (jĕ-mā′shən) *n.*

gem•mip•a•rous (jĕ-mĭp′ər-əs) *adj. Bot.* Reproducing by buds or gemmae. [Lat. *gemma*, bud; see GEMMA + -PAROUS.] —**gem•mip′a•rous•ly** *adv.*

gem•mule (jĕm′yo͞ol) *n.* **1.** A small gemma or similar structure, esp. a reproductive structure in some sponges. **2.** A hypothetical particle of heredity in the theory of pangenesis. [Fr. < Lat. *gemmula*, dim. of *gemma*, bud. See **gembh-***.] —**gem′mu•lif′er•ous** (jĕm′yo͞o-lĭf′ər-əs) *adj.*

gem•my (jĕm′ē) *adj.* **1.** Full of or set with gems. **2.** Glittering like a gem.

gem•ol•o•gy or **gem•mol•o•gy** (jĕ-mŏl′ə-jē) *n.* The study of gems. —**gem′o•log′i•cal** (jĕm′ə-lŏj′ĭ-kəl) *adj.* —**gem•ol′o•gist** *n.*

ge•mot also **ge•mote** (gə-mōt′) *n.* A public meeting or local judicial assembly in Anglo-Saxon England. [OE *gemōt* : *ge-*, collective pref.; see **kom*** + *mōt*, assembly.]

gems•bok (gĕmz′bŏk′) *n.* A large antelope *(Oryx gazella)* of southern Africa having long straight horns, a tufted tail, and distinctive black and white markings on the head. [Afr. < Du. < Ger. *Gemsbock* : *Gemse*, chamois (ult. < LLat. *camox*) + *Bock*, buck (< MHGer. *boc* < OHGer.).]

gemsbok
Oryx gazella

gem•stone (jĕm′stōn′) *n.* A precious or semiprecious stone that may be used as a jewel when cut and polished.

ge•müt•lich (gə-mo͞ot′lĭk, -müt′lĭKH) *adj.* Warm and congenial; pleasant or friendly. [Ger. < MHGer. *gemüetlich* < *gemüete*, spirit, feelings < OHGer. *gimuoti* < *muot*, mind, spirit, joy. See **mē-¹***.]

ge•müt•lich•keit (gə-müt′lĭKH-kīt′, -mo͞ot′-) *n.* Warm friendliness; amicability. [Ger. See GEMÜTLICH.]

gen. *abbr.* **1.** Gender. **2.** General; generally. **3.** Generator. **4.** Generic. **5.** *Gram.* Genitive. **6.** Genus.

Gen. *abbr.* **1.** General. **2.** *Bible.* Genesis.

-gen or **-gene** *suff.* **1.** Producer: *androgen.* **2.** One that is produced: *phosgene.* [Fr. *-gène* < Gk. *-genēs*, born. See **genə-***.]

gen•darme (zhän′därm′) *n.* **1.** A member of the French national police organization constituting a branch of the armed forces. **2.** *Slang.* A police officer. [Fr. < OFr. *gent d'armes*, sing. of *gens d'armes*, men-at-arms : *gens*, men (< Lat. *gentes*, pl. of *gēns*, clan; see **genə-***) + *de*, of (< Lat. *dē*; see DE-) + *armes*, pl. of *arme*, weapon; see ARM².]

gen•dar•me•rie (zhän-där′mə-rē) *n.* **1.** A body of French gendarmes. **2.** *Slang.* A group of police officers. [Fr. < OFr., calvary < *gendarme*, mounted soldier. See GENDARME.]

gen•der (jĕn′dər) *n.* **1.** *Gram.* **a.** A grammatical category used in the analysis of nouns, pronouns, adjectives, and, in some languages, verbs that may be arbitrary or based on characteristics such as sex or animacy and that determines agreement with or selection of modifiers, referents, or grammatical forms. **b.** One category of such a set. **c.** The classification of a word or grammatical form in such a category. **d.** The distinguishing form or forms used. **2.** Sexual identity, esp. in relation to society or culture. —*tr.v.* **-dered, -der•ing, -ders.** To engender. [ME *gendre* < OFr., kind, gender < Lat. *genus, gener-*. See **genə-***.] —**gen′der•less** *adj.*

Usage Note: Traditionally, *gender* has been used primarily to refer to the grammatical categories of "masculine," "feminine," and "neuter"; but in recent years the word has become well established in its use to refer to sex-based categories, as in *the politics of gender.* This usage is supported by the practice of many anthropologists, who reserve *sex* for reference to biological categories, while using *gender* to refer to social or cultural categories. According to this rule, one would say *The effectiveness of the medication depends on the sex of the patient,* but *In peasant societies, gender roles are more clearly defined.* This distinction, however, is by no means widely observed.

gender gap or **gen•der-gap** (jĕn′dər-găp′) *n.* A disproportionate difference, as in attitudes, between the sexes.

gene (jēn) *n.* A hereditary unit that occupies a specific location on a chromosome and determines a particular characteristic in an organism. [< Gk. *genos*, race, offspring. See **genə-***.]

ge•ne•al•o•gy (jē′nē-ŏl′ə-jē, -ăl′-, jĕn′ē-) *n., pl.* **-gies. 1.** A record or table of the descent of a person, family, or group from an ancestor or ancestors; a family tree. **2.** Direct descent from an ancestor; lineage or pedigree. **3.** The study or investigation of ancestry and family histories. [ME *genealogie* < OFr. < LLat. *geneālogia* < Gk. : *genea*, family; see **genə-*** + *-logia*, -logy.] —**ge′ne•a•log′i•cal** (-ə-lŏj′ĭ-kəl) *adj.* —**ge′ne•a•log′i•cal•ly** *adv.* —**ge′ne•al′o•gist** *n.*

gene amplification *n.* A cellular process characterized by the production of multiple copies of a particular gene or genes to amplify the phenotype that the gene confers on the cell.

gene flow *n.* Transfer of genes from one population to another of the same species, as by migration.

gene frequency *n.* The frequency of occurrence of an allele in relation to that of other alleles of the same gene in a population.

gene pool *n.* The collective genetic information contained within a population of sexually reproducing organisms.

gen•er•a (jĕn′ər-ə) *n.* Pl. of **genus.**

gen•er•a•ble (jĕn′ər-ə-bəl) *adj.* Capable of being generated. [Lat. *generābilis* < *generāre*, to produce. See GENERATE.]

gen•er•al (jĕn′ər-əl) *adj.* **1.** Concerned with, applicable to, or affecting the whole or every member of a class or category. **2.** Affecting or characteristic of the majority of those involved; prevalent. **3.** Being usu. the case; true or applicable in most instances. **4.a.** Not limited in scope, area, or application. **b.** Not limited to or dealing with one class of things; diversified. **5.** Involving only the main features rather than precise details. **6.** Highest or superior in rank. —*n.* **1.a.** A commissioned rank in the U.S. Army, Air Force, or Marine Corps that is above lieutenant general. **b.** One who holds this rank or a similar rank in another military organization. **2.** A general officer. **3.** A statement, principle, or fact that embraces or is applicable to the whole. **4.** *Archaic.* The public. —***idiom.*** **in general.** Generally. [ME < Lat. *generālis* < *genus, gener-*, kind. See **genə-***.] —**gen′er•al•ness** *n.*

Syns: *general, common, generic, universal.* The central meaning shared by these adjectives is "belonging to, relating to, or affecting the whole": *the general welfare; a common enemy; generic similarities; universal hopes.* ***Ant:*** *particular.*

Gen•er•al American (jĕn′ər-əl) *n.* The speech of native English speakers of the upper Midwestern United States, considered by some to be representative of that of the majority.

general assembly *n.* **1.** A legislative body, esp. a U.S. state legislature. **2. General Assembly.** The principal deliberative body of the United Nations. **3.** The supreme governing body of some religious denominations.

General Court *n.* **1.** A legislative body having judicial powers in colonial New England. **2.** The state legislature of Massachusetts and New Hampshire.

general delivery *n.* **1.** A department of a post office that holds mail for addressees until called for. **2.** Mail directed here.

general election *n.* An election involving all or most constituencies of a state or nation in the choice of candidates.

gen•er•al•is•si•mo (jĕn′ər-ə-lĭs′ə-mō′) *n., pl.* **-mos.** The commander in chief of all the armed forces in certain countries. [Ital., superl. of *generale*, a general < Lat. *generālis*, general. See GENERAL.]

gen•er•al•ist (jĕn′ər-ə-lĭst) *n.* One who has broad general knowledge and skills in several areas.

gen•er•al•i•ty (jĕn′ə-răl′ĭ-tē) *n., pl.* **-ties. 1.** The state or quality of being general. **2.** An observation or a principle having general application; a generalization. **3.** An imprecise or vague statement or idea. **4.** The greater portion or number.

gen•er•al•i•za•tion (jĕn′ər-ə-lĭ-zā′shən) *n.* **1.** The act or an instance of generalizing. **2.** A principle, a statement, or an idea having general application.

gen•er•al•ize (jĕn′ər-ə-līz′) *v.* **-ized, -iz•ing, -iz•es.** *—tr.* **1.a.** To reduce to a general form, class, or law. **b.** To render indefinite or unspecific. **2.a.** To infer from many particulars. **b.** To draw inferences or a general conclusion from. **3.a.** To make generally or universally applicable. **b.** To popularize. *—intr.* **1.a.** To form a concept inductively. **b.** To form general notions or conclusions. **2.** To deal in generalities; speak or write vaguely. **3.** *Medic.* To spread through the body.

gen•er•al•ized (jĕn′ər-ə-līzd′) *adj.* **1.** *Biol.* Not specifically adapted to a particular environment or function; not specialized. **2.** Generally prevalent: *generalized discontent.*

gen•er•al•ly (jĕn′ər-ə-lē) *adv.* **1.** Popularly; widely: *generally known.* **2.a.** As a rule; usually. **b.** For the most part. **3.** Without reference to particular instances or details.

general officer *n.* An officer in the U.S. Army, Air Force, or Marine Corps ranking above colonel.

General of the Air Force *n.* The highest commissioned officer in the U.S. Air Force.

General of the Army *n.* The highest commissioned officer in the U.S. Army.

general paresis *n.* A brain disease occurring as a late consequence of syphilis, characterized by dementia, progressive muscular weakness, and paralysis.

general practitioner *n.* A physician whose practice covers a variety of medical problems in patients of all ages.

gen•er•al-pur•pose (jĕn′ər-əl-pûr′pəs) *adj.* Designed for or suitable to more than one use; broadly useful.

general relativity *n.* The geometric theory of gravitation proposed by Albert Einstein, extending the theory of special relativity to accelerated frames of reference and introducing the principle that gravitational and inertial forces are equivalent.

general semantics *n. (used with a sing. v.)* A discipline developed by Alfred Korzybski that proposes to improve human behavioral responses by using words and symbols more critically.

gen•er•al•ship (jĕn′ər-əl-shĭp′) *n.* **1.** The rank, office, or tenure of a general. **2.** Leadership or skill in the conduct of a war. **3.** Skillful management or leadership.

general staff *n.* A group of military officers charged with assisting the commander of a division or higher unit in planning, coordinating, and supervising operations.

general store *n.* A retail store, usu. in a rural area, selling a wide variety of merchandise but not divided into departments.

general strike *n.* A strike by all or most of the workers in an industry or throughout a country or an area.

gen•er•ate (jĕn′ə-rāt′) *tr.v.* **-at•ed, -at•ing, -ates. 1.a.** To bring into being; give rise to. **b.** To produce as a result of a chemical or physical process. **2.** To engender (offspring); procreate. **3.** *Math.* To form (a geometric figure) by describing a curve or surface. **4.** *Comp. Sci.* To produce (a specialized program) by instructing a computer to follow given parameters that select or complete parts of a general program. [Lat. *generāre, generāt-*, to produce < *genus, gener-*, birth. See **genə-***.]

gen•er•a•tion (jĕn′ə-rā′shən) *n.* **1.** All of the offspring that are at the same stage of descent from a common ancestor. **2.** *Biol.* A form or stage in the life cycle of an organism. **3.** The average interval of time between the birth of parents and the birth of their offspring. **4.a.** A group of individuals born and living about the same time. **b.** A group of generally contemporaneous individuals regarded as having common cultural or social characteristics and attitudes. **5.a.** A period of sequential technological development and innovation. **b.** A class of objects derived from a preceding class: *a new generation of computers.* **6.** The act or process of generating; origination, production, or procreation. **—gen•er•a′tion•al** *adj.*

generation gap *n.* A broad difference in values and attitudes between one generation and another.

Gen•er•a•tion X (jĕn′ə-rā′shən) *n.* A group of people born between 1961 and 1972 typified by a college education, dissatisfaction with career opportunities, and pessimism. [After *Generation X* by Douglas Coupland.]

gen•er•a•tive (jĕn′ər-ə-tĭv, -ə-rā′-) *adj.* **1.** Having the ability to originate, produce, or procreate. **2.** Of or relating to the production of offspring. **—gen′er•a•tive•ly** *adv.* **—gen′er•a•tive•ness** *n.*

generative grammar *n.* A linguistic theory that attempts to describe a native speaker's tacit grammatical knowledge by a system of rules that can generate any grammatical sentence of a given language.

gen•er•a•tor (jĕn′ə-rā′tər) *n.* **1.a.** One that generates, esp. a machine that converts mechanical energy into electrical energy. **b.** An apparatus that generates vapor or gas. **2.** A circuit that generates a specified waveform. **3.** *Math.* See **generatrix. 4.** *Comp. Sci.* A program that produces specific programs from the definition of an operation.

gen•er•a•trix (jĕn′ə-rā′trĭks) *n., pl.* **-er•a•tri•ces** (-ə-rā′trĭ-sēz′, -ər-ə-trī′sēz). *Math.* A geometric element that generates a geometric figure, esp. a straight line that generates a surface by moving in a specified fashion.

ge•ner•ic (jə-nĕr′ĭk) *adj.* **1.** Relating to or descriptive of an entire group or class; general. See Syns at **general. 2.** *Biol.* Of or relating to a genus. **3.** Not having a trademark or brand name. *—n.* **1.** A generic product. **2.** A wine that is a blend of grape varieties and is named for no specific grape. [< Lat. *genus, gener-*, kind. See **genə-***.] **—ge•ner′i•cal•ly** *adv.*

gen•er•os•i•ty (jĕn′ə-rŏs′ĭ-tē) *n., pl.* **-ties. 1.** Liberality in giving or willingness to give. **2.** Nobility of thought or behavior; magnanimity. **3.** Amplitude; abundance. **4.** A generous act. [ME *generosite* < OFr. < Lat. *generōsitās* < *generōsus*, magnanimous. See GENEROUS.]

gen•er•ous (jĕn′ər-əs) *adj.* **1.** Liberal in giving or sharing. See Syns at **liberal. 2.** Characterized by nobility and forbearance in thought or behavior; magnanimous. **3.** Marked by abundance; ample. **4.** Having a rich bouquet and flavor. **5.** *Obsolete.* Of noble lineage. [Fr. *genereux*, of noble birth, magnanimous < Lat. *generōsus* < *genus, gener-*, birth. See **genə-***.] **—gen′er•ous•ly** *adv.* **—gen′er•ous•ness** *n.*

Gen•e•see (jĕn′ĭ-sē′, jĕn′ĭ-sē′). A river rising in N PA and flowing c. 241 km (150 mi) to Lake Ontario.

gen•e•sis (jĕn′ĭ-sĭs) *n., pl.* **-ses** (-sēz′). **1.** The coming into being of something; the origin. See Syns at **beginning. 2. Genesis.** See table at **Bible.** [Lat. < Gk. See **genə-***.]

-genesis *suff.* Origin; production: *abiogenesis.* [Lat. < Gk., birth, orig. See **genə-***.]

gene-splic•ing (jēn′splī′sĭng) *n.* The process in which fragments of DNA from one or more different organisms are combined to form recombinant DNA and are made to function within the cells of a host organism.

gen•et[1] (jĕn′ĭt, jə-nĕt′) *n.* Any of several Old World carnivorous mammals of the genus *Genetta,* having a long ringed tail. [ME < OFr. *genete.*]

gen•et[2] (jĕn′ĭt) *n.* Var. of **jennet.**

Ge•net (zhə-nā′), **Jean.** 1910–86. French writer who is best known for his absurdist plays, including *The Balcony* (1956).

Ge•nêt (zhə-nā′). See Janet **Flanner.**

Genêt or **Genet Edmond Charles Edouard.** "Citizen Genêt." 1763–1834. French diplomat who attempted (1793) to draw the U.S. into France's war against Great Britain and Spain.

gene therapy *n.* The treatment of certain disorders, esp. those caused by genetic anomalies or deficiencies, by introducing specific engineered genes into a patient's cells.

ge•net•ic (jə-nĕt′ĭk) also **ge•net•i•cal** (-ĭ-kəl) *adj.* **1.a.** Of or relating to genetics or genes. **b.** Affecting or affected by genes: *a genetic disorder.* **2.** Of, relating to, or influenced by the origin or development of something. **3.** *Ling.* Of or relating to the relationship between or among languages that are descendants of a protolanguage. [< Gk. *genetikos*, genitive < *genesis*, origin See GENESIS.] **—ge•net′i•cal•ly** *adv.*

genetic code *n.* The nucleotide sequence in DNA that specifies the amino acid sequence in the synthesis of proteins and is the basis of heredity. **—genetic coding** *n.*

genetic drift *n.* Random fluctuations in the frequency of the appearance of a gene in a small isolated population.

genetic engineering *n.* Scientific alteration of the structure of genetic material in a living organism, used, for example, to create bacteria that synthesize insulin. **—genetic engineer** *n.*

ge•net•i•cist (jə-nĕt′ĭ-sĭst) *n.* One who specializes in genetics.

genetic load *n.* The difference in fitness between the theoretically most fit genotype within a population and the average genotype.

genetic map *n.* A graphic representation of the arrangement of genes or mutable sites on a chromosome.

genetic marker *n.* A known DNA sequence associated with a particular gene or trait that is used to indicate the presence of that gene or trait.

ge•net•ics (jə-nĕt′ĭks) *n.* **1.** *(used with a sing. v.)* The branch of biology that deals with heredity, esp. the mechanisms of hereditary transmission and the variation of inherited characteristics among similar or related organisms. **2.** *(used with a pl. v.)* The genetic makeup of an individual, a group, or a class.

ă **pat**	oi **boy**
ā **pay**	ou **out**
âr **care**	o͝o **took**
ä **father**	o͞o **boot**
ĕ **pet**	ŭ **cut**
ē **be**	ûr **urge**
ĭ **pit**	th **thin**
ī **pie**	*th* **this**
îr **pier**	hw **which**
ŏ **pot**	zh **vision**
ō **toe**	ə **about, item**
ô **paw**	

Stress marks:
′ (primary);
′ (secondary), as in **dictionary** (dĭk′shə-nĕr′ē)

Ge•ne•va (jə-nē′və). A city of SW Switzerland located on Lake Geneva and bisected by the Rhone R.; a focal point of the Reformation. Pop. 159,500.

Geneva, Lake. Also **Lake Le•man** (lē′mən, lə-măɴ′). A lake on the Swiss-French border between the Alps and the Jura Mts.

Geneva bands *pl.n.* Two strips of white cloth that hang from the front of the collar of some clerical and academic robes.

Geneva Convention *n.* One of a series of agreements first formulated at an international convention held in Geneva, Switzerland, in 1864, establishing rules for the treatment of prisoners of war, the sick, and the wounded.

Geneva cross *n.* A red Greek or St. George's cross on a white ground, used as a symbol by the Red Cross and as a sign of neutrality. [After GENEVA, Switzerland.]

Geneva gown *n.* A loose black academic or clerical gown with wide sleeves. [After GENEVA, Switzerland.]

Ge•ne•van (jə-nē′vən) also **Gen•e•vese** (jĕn′ə-vēz′, -vēs′) — *adj.* **1.** Of or relating to Geneva or its inhabitants. **2.** Of or relating to the teachings of John Calvin in Geneva; Calvinistic. — *n.* **1.** A native or inhabitant of Geneva. **2.** A Calvinist.

Genghis Khan
Portrait from a 16th-century Persian manuscript

Gen•ghis Khan (jĕng′gĭs kän′, gĕng′-) also **Jen•ghis Khan** or **Jen•ghiz Khan** (jĕn′gĭz kän′, -gĭs, jĕng′-). 1162?–1227. Mongol conqueror who united the Mongol tribes and annexed N China, central Asia, Iran, and S Russia.

gen•ial[1] (jēn′yəl) *adj.* **1.** Having a pleasant or friendly disposition or manner. **2.** Conducive to life, growth, or comfort; mild. **3.** *Obsolete.* Relating to or marked by genius. **4.** *Obsolete.* Of or relating to marriage; nuptial. [Lat. *geniālis*, festive < *genius*, spirit of festivity. See **genə-***.] — **ge′ni•al′i•ty** (jē′nē-ăl′ĭ-tē), **gen′ial•ness** *n.* — **gen′ial•ly** *adv.*

ge•ni•al[2] (jĭ-nī′əl) *n.* Of or relating to the chin. [< Gk. *geneion*, chin < *genus*, jaw. See **genu-**[2]***.]

gen•ic (jē′nĭk, jĕn′ĭk) *adj.* Of, relating to, produced by, or being genes or a gene. — **gen′i•cal•ly** *adv.*

-genic *suff.* **1.** Producing; generating: *dysgenic.* **2.** Produced or generated by: *cryptogenic.* **3.** Suitable for production or reproduction by a specified medium: *photogenic.* [-GEN + -IC.]

ge•nic•u•late (jə-nĭk′yə-lĭt) also **ge•nic•u•lat•ed** (-lā′tĭd) *adj.* **1.** Bent abruptly, as a knee. **2.** Having kneelike joints; able to bend at an abrupt angle. [Lat. *geniculātus*, with bended knee < *geniculum*, dim. of *genū*, knee. See **genu-**[1]***.] — **ge•nic′u•late•ly** *adv.* — **ge•nic′u•la′tion** *n.*

ge•nie (jē′nē) *n.* **1.** A supernatural creature who does one's bidding when summoned. **2.** A jinni. [Fr. *génie*, spirit < Lat. *genius*, guardian spirit. See GENIUS.]

ge•ni•i (jē′nē-ī′) *n. Rom. Myth.* Pl. of **genius** 4.

gen•ip (jĕn′əp) *n.* **1.** A tropical American tree *(Melicoccus bijugatus)* having small fruits with a green leathery rind and a juicy translucent pulp. **2.** The sweet edible fruit of this plant. **3.** See **genipap** 2. [Poss. alteration of GENIPAP.]

gen•i•pap (jĕn′ə-păp′) *n.* **1.** A tropical American evergreen tree *(Genipa americana)* having yellowish-white flowers and edible fruits used in preserves or drinks. **2.** The reddish-brown fruit of this plant. [Port. *genipapo* < Tupi *jenipapo* < *yandiipab*, genipap fruit.]

genit. *abbr. Gram.* Genitive.

gen•i•tal (jĕn′ĭ-tl) *adj.* **1.** Of or relating to biological reproduction. **2.** Of or relating to the genitalia. **3.** *Psychol.* Of or relating to the stage of psychosexual development in psychoanalytic theory beginning in puberty and during which the genitals become the focus of sexual gratification. — *n.* A reproductive organ, esp. one of the external sex organs. Often used in the plural. [ME < Lat. *genitālis* < *genitus*, p.part. of *gignere*, to beget. See **genə-***.] — **gen′i•tal•ly** *adv.*

genital herpes *n.* A highly contagious, sexually transmitted viral infection of the genital and anal regions caused by herpes simplex and characterized by small clusters of painful lesions.

gen•i•ta•li•a (jĕn′ĭ-tā′lē-ə, -tāl′yə) *pl.n.* The genitals. [Lat. *genitālia* < neut. pl. of *genitālis*, genital. See GENITAL.]

genital wart *n.* A pointed papilloma typically found on the skin or mucous membranes of the anus and external genitalia and caused by a virus transmitted through sexual contact.

gen•i•ti•val (jĕn′ĭ-tī′vəl) *adj. Gram.* Of, relating to, or in the genitive case. — **gen′i•ti′val•ly** *adv.*

gen•i•tive (jĕn′ĭ-tĭv) *Gram.* — *adj.* **1.** Of, relating to, or being a case that expresses possession, measurement, or source. **2.** Of or relating to an affix or a construction, such as a prepositional phrase, characteristic of the genitive case. — *n.* **1.** The genitive case. **2.** A form or construction in this case. [ME *genetif* < Lat. *genetīvus* < *genitus*, p.part. of *gignere*, to beget. See **genə-***.]

gen•i•tor (jĕn′ĭ-tər) *n.* **1.** One who produces or creates. **2.** *Anthro.* A natural father or mother. [ME *genitour* < OFr. *genitor* < Lat. < *genitus*, p.part. of *gignere*, to beget. See **genə-***.]

gen•i•to•u•ri•nar•y (jĕn′ĭ-tō-yo͝or′ə-nĕr′ē) *adj.* Of or relating to the genital and urinary organs or their functions.

gen•ius (jēn′yəs) *n., pl.* **-ius•es. 1.a.** Extraordinary intellectual and creative power. **b.** A person of extraordinary intellect and talent. **c.** A person who has an exceptionally high intelligence quotient, typically above 140. **2.a.** A strong natural talent, aptitude, or inclination. **b.** One who has such a talent or inclination. **3.** The prevailing spirit or distinctive character, as of a place, a person, or an era. **4.** *pl.* **ge•ni•i** (jē′nē-ī′). *Rom. Myth.* A tutelary deity or guardian spirit of a person or place. **5.** A person who has great influence over another. **6.** A jinni in Muslim mythology. [ME, guardian spirit < Lat. See **genə-***.]

ge•ni•us lo•ci (jē′nē-əs lō′sī′, -kē, -kī) *n.* **1.** The distinctive atmosphere or pervading spirit of a place. **2.** The guardian deity of a place. [Lat. *genius locī* : *genius*, spirit + *locī*, genitive sing. of *locus*, place.]

genl. *abbr.* General.

gen•o•a (jĕn′ō-ə) *n. Naut.* A large jib used on a sloop, overlapping the mainsail. [After GENOA.]

Gen•o•a (jĕn′ō-ə). A city of NW Italy on the **Gulf of Genoa**, an arm of the Ligurian Sea. Pop. 760,300. — **Gen′o•ese′** (-ēz′, -ēs′), **Gen′o•vese′** (-vēz′, -vēs′) *adj. & n.*

genoa jib *n. Naut.* See **genoa.**

gen•o•cide (jĕn′ə-sīd′) *n.* The systematic and planned extermination of an entire national, racial, political, or ethnic group. [Gk. *genos*, race; see **genə-*** + -CIDE.] — **gen′o•cid′al** (-sīd′l) *adj.* — **gen′o•cid′al•ly** *adv.*

ge•nome (jē′nōm′) also **ge•nom** (-nŏm) *n.* A complete haploid set of chromosomes with its associated genes. [GEN(E) + -OME.] — **ge•nom′ic** (-nŏm′ĭk) *adj.*

gen•o•type (jĕn′ə-tīp′, jē′nə-) *n.* **1.** The genetic constitution of an organism or a group of organisms. **2.** A group or class of organisms having the same genetic constitution. [Gk. *genos*, race; see **genə-*** + Lat. *typus*, type; see TYPE.] — **gen′o•typ′ic** (-tĭp′ĭk), **gen′o•typ′i•cal** *adj.* — **gen′o•typ′i•cal•ly** *adv.* — **gen′o•ty•pic′i•ty** (-tī-pĭs′ĭ-tē) *n.*

-genous *suff.* **1.** Producing; generating: *hematogenous.* **2.** Produced by or in a specified manner: *hypogenous.*

gen•re (zhän′rə) *n.* **1.** A type or class. **2.a.** An established class or category of artistic composition, as in music or literature. **b.** A realistic style of painting that depicts scenes from everyday life. [Fr. < OFr., kind < Lat. *genus*, *gener-*. See **genə-***.]

gen•ro (gĕn′rō′) *n., pl.* **-ros.** Any of a group of elder male politicians in Japan who formerly advised the emperor. [J. *genrō* : Chin. *yuán*, first + Chin. *lăo*, elder.]

gens (jĕnz) *n., pl.* **gen•tes** (jĕn′tēz′). **1.** A patrilineal clan of ancient Rome composed of several families of the same name claiming a common ancestor and belonging to a common religious cult. **2.** *Anthro.* An exogamous patrilineal clan. [Lat. *gēns*. See **genə-***.]

Gen•ser•ic (jĕn′sə-rĭk′, gĕn′-) also **Gai•ser•ic** (gī′zə-). d. A.D. 477. King of the Vandals (428–477) who invaded Africa (429), captured Carthage (439), and sacked Rome (455).

gent[1] (jĕnt) *adj. Archaic.* Graceful; elegant. [ME, noble, excellent < OFr., well-born < Lat. *genitus*, p.part. of *gignere*, to beget. See **genə-***.]

gent[2] (jĕnt) *n. Informal.* A gentleman. [Short for GENTLEMAN.]

Gent (gĕnt, KHĕnt). See **Ghent.**

gen•ta•mi•cin (jĕn′tə-mī′sĭn) *n.* A broad-spectrum antibiotic derived from an actinomycete of the genus *Micromonospora* and used in its sulfate form to treat various infections. [Alteration of *gentamycin* : GENT(I)A(N VIOLET) + -MYCIN.]

gen•teel (jĕn-tēl′) *adj.* **1.** Refined in manner; well-bred and polite. **2.** Free from vulgarity or rudeness. **3.** Elegantly stylish. **4.a.** Striving to convey a manner or an appearance of refinement and respectability. See Syns at **polite. b.** Marked by affected and somewhat prudish refinement. [Fr. *gentil* < OFr. See GENTLE.] — **gen•teel′ly** *adv.* — **gen•teel′ness** *n.*

gen•teel•ism (jĕn-tēl′ĭz′əm) *n.* A word or an expression thought by its user to be more refined than another.

gen•tian (jĕn′shən) *n.* **1.** Any of numerous plants of the genus *Gentiana,* characteristically having showy, variously colored flowers. **2.** The dried rhizome and roots of a yellow-flowered European gentian, *G. lutea,* sometimes used as a tonic. [ME *gencian* < OFr. *genciane* < Lat. *gentiāna*, perh. after *Gentius*, 2nd-cent. B.C. king of Illyria.]

gentian violet *n.* A dye used as a biological stain and as a bactericide, a fungicide, and an anthelmintic.

gen•tile (jĕn′tīl′) *n.* **1.** Often **Gentile.** One who is not of the Jewish faith or is of a non-Jewish nation. **2.** Often **Gentile.** A Christian. **3.** A pagan or heathen. **4.** Often **Gentile.** *Mormon Ch.* A non-Mormon. — *adj.* **1.** Of or relating to a Gentile. **2.** Of or relating to a gens, tribe, or people. **3.** *Gram.* Expressing national or local origins. [ME *gentil* < LLat. *gentīlis*, pagan < Lat., of the same clan. See GENTLE.]

Gen•ti•le•schi (jĕn′tē-lĕs′kē), **Artemisia.** 1593?–1652? Italian Renaissance painter whose works include self-portraits.

gen•ti•lesse (jĕn′tə-lĕs′) *n. Archaic.* Refinement and courtesy resulting from good breeding. [ME < OFr. < *gentil*, noble. See GENTLE.]

gen•til•i•ty (jĕn-tĭl′ĭ-tē) *n.* **1.** The quality of being well-mannered; refinement. **2.** The condition of being born to the gentry. **3.** Persons of high social standing considered as a group. **4.** An attempt to convey or maintain the appearance of refinement and elegance. [ME *gentilete*, nobility of birth < OFr. < Lat. *gentīlitās* < *gentīlis*, of the same clan. See GENTLE.]

gen•tle (jĕn′tl) *adj.* **-tler, -tlest. 1.** Considerate or kindly in disposition; amiable and tender. **2.** Not harsh or severe; mild and soft. **3.** Easily managed or handled; docile. **4.** Not steep or sudden; gradual. **5.a.** Of good family; wellborn. **b.** Suited to one of good breeding; refined and polite. **6.** *Archaic.* Noble; chivalrous. —*n. Archaic.* One of good birth or relatively high station. —*tr.v.* **-tled, -tling, -tles. 1.** To make less severe or intense. **2.** To soothe, as by stroking; pacify. **3.** To tame or break (a domestic animal, for instance). **4.** To raise to the status of a noble. [ME *gentil,* courteous, noble < OFr. < Lat. *gentīlis,* of the same clan < *gēns, gent-,* clan. See **genə-*.**] —**gen′tle•ness** *n.* —**gen′tly** *adv.*

gen•tle•folk (jĕn′tl-fōk′) also **gen•tle•folks** (-fōks′) *pl.n.* Persons of good family and relatively high station.

gen•tle•man (jĕn′tl-mən) *n.* **1.** A man of gentle or noble birth or superior social position. **2.** A well-mannered and considerate man with high standards of proper behavior. See Usage Note at **lady. 3.** A man of independent means who does not need to have a wage-paying job. **4.** A man. **5. gentlemen.** Used as a form of address for a group of men. **6.** A manservant; a valet. —**gen′tle•man•ly** *adj.*

gen•tle•man-at-arms (jĕn′tl-mən-ət-ärmz′) *n., pl.* **gen•tle•men-at-arms** (-mĭn-). One of a military corps of 40 gentlemen who attend the British sovereign on state occasions.

gentleman farmer *n., pl.* **gentlemen farmers.** A man of independent means who farms chiefly for pleasure.

gen•tle•man's agreement or **gen•tle•men's agreement** (jĕn′tl-mənz) *n., pl.* **gentleman's agreements** or **gentlemen's agreements.** An unwritten agreement guaranteed only by the pledged word or secret understanding of the participants.

gentleman's gentleman *n.* A manservant; a valet.

gen•tle•per•son (jĕn′tl-pûr′sən) *n.* A person of good breeding; a lady or a gentleman.

gen•tle•wom•an (jĕn′tl-wo͝om′ən) *n.* **1.** A woman of gentle or noble birth or superior social position. **2.** A well-mannered and considerate woman with high standards of proper behavior. **3.** A woman personal attendant to a lady of rank.

gen•tri•fi•ca•tion (jĕn′trə-fĭ-kā′shən) *n.* The restoration and upgrading of deteriorated urban property by the middle classes, often resulting in displacement of lower-income people.

gen•tri•fy (jĕn′trə-fī′) *tr.v.* **-fied, -fy•ing, -fies.** To subject to gentrification. [GENTR(Y) + -FY.] —**gen′tri•fi′er** *n.*

gen•try (jĕn′trē) *n., pl.* **-tries. 1.** People of gentle birth, good breeding, or high social position. **2.a.** An upper or ruling class. **b.** The class of English landowners ranking below the nobility. **3.** People of a particular class or group. [ME *gentri,* nobility of birth < OFr. *genterie,* var. of *genterise, gentilise* < *gentil,* noble. See GENTLE.]

gen•u•flect (jĕn′yə-flĕkt′) *intr.v.* **-flect•ed, -flect•ing, -flects. 1.** To bend the knee or touch one knee to the floor or ground, as in worship. **2.** To be servilely deferential; grovel. [LLat. *genūflectere* : Lat. *genū,* knee; see **genu-¹*** + Lat. *flectere,* to bend.] —**gen′u•flec′tion** (-flĕk′shən) *n.*

gen•u•ine (jĕn′yo͞o-ĭn) *adj.* **1.** Possessing the alleged or apparent attribute or character: *genuine leather.* **2.** Not spurious or counterfeit; authentic. See Syns at **authentic. 3.a.** Honestly felt or experienced. **b.** Actual; real. **4.** Free from hypocrisy or dishonesty; sincere. **5.** Being of pure or original stock: *a genuine Hawaiian.* [Lat. *genuīnus,* natural, poss. < alteration of *ingenuus,* native, freeborn. See INGENUOUS.] —**gen′u•ine•ly** *adv.* —**gen′u•ine•ness** *n.*

ge•nus (jē′nəs) *n., pl.* **gen•er•a** (jĕn′ər-ə). **1.** *Biol.* A taxonomic category ranking below a family and above a species and usu. consisting of a group of species exhibiting similar characteristics. See table at **taxonomy. 2.** *Logic.* A class of objects divided into subordinate species having certain common attributes. **3.** A class, group, or kind with common attributes. [Lat., kind. See **genə-*.**]

-geny *suff.* Production; generation; origin: *ontogeny.* [Gk. *-geneia* < *-genēs,* born. See **genə-*.**]

geo– or **ge–** *pref.* **1.** Earth: *geocentric.* **2.** Geography: *geopolitical.* [Gk. *geō-* < *gē,* earth.]

ge•o•bot•a•ny (jē′ō-bŏt′n-ē) *n.* See **phytogeography.** —**ge′o•bo•tan′ic** (-bə-tăn′ĭk), **ge′o•bo•tan′i•cal** *adj.* —**ge′o•bo•tan′i•cal•ly** *adv.* —**ge′o•bot′a•nist** (bŏt′n-ĭst) *n.*

ge•o•cen•tric (jē′ō-sĕn′trĭk) *adj.* **1.** Relating to, measured from, or with respect to the center of the earth. **2.** Having the earth as a center. —**ge′o•cen′tri•cal•ly** *adv.*

ge•o•chem•is•try (jē′ō-kĕm′ĭ-strē) *n.* The chemistry of the composition and alterations of the solid matter of the earth or a celestial body. —**ge′o•chem′i•cal** (-ĭ-kəl) *adj.* —**ge′o•chem′i•cal•ly** *adv.* —**ge′o•chem′ist** *n.*

ge•o•chro•nol•o•gy (jē′ō-krə-nŏl′ə-jē) *n.* The chronology of the earth as determined by geologic events. —**ge′o•chron′o•log′ic** (-krŏn′ə-lŏj′ĭk), **ge′o•chron′o•log′i•cal** *adj.* —**ge′o•chro•nol′o•gist** *n.*

ge•o•chro•nom•e•try (jē′ō-krə-nŏm′ĭ-trē) *n.* Measurement of geologic time, as through isotopic radioactive decay. —**ge′o•chron′o•met′ric** (-krŏn′ə-mĕt′rĭk) *adj.*

ge•o•co•ro•na (jē′ō-kə-rō′nə) *n.* The outermost region of the earth's atmosphere, consisting chiefly of ionized hydrogen.

ge•ode (jē′ōd′) *n.* A hollow, usu. spheroidal rock with crystals lining the inside wall. [Fr. *géode* < Lat. *geōdēs,* a precious stone < Gk., earthlike : *gē,* earth + *-ōdēs, -oeidēs,* -oid.]

ge•o•des•ic (jē′ə-dĕs′ĭk, -dē′sĭk) *adj.* **1.** *Math.* Of or relating to the geometry of geodesics. **2.** Of or relating to geodesy. —*n. Math.* The shortest line between two points on any mathematically defined surface. [< GEODESY.]

geodesic dome *n.* A domed or vaulted structure of lightweight straight elements that form interlocking polygons.

ge•od•e•sy (jē-ŏd′ĭ-sē) *n.* The geologic science of the size and shape of the earth. [NLat. *geōdaesia* < Gk. *geōdaisia* : *geō-,* geo- + *daiesthai,* to divide; see **dā-*.**] —**ge•od′e•sist** *n.*

ge•o•det•ic (jē′ə-dĕt′ĭk) also **ge•o•det•i•cal** (-ĭ-kəl) *adj.* Geodesic. —**ge′o•det′i•cal•ly** *adv.*

geodetic survey *n.* A survey of a large area of land in which corrections are made to account for the curvature of the earth.

geo•duck also **gwe•duc** (go͞o′ē-dŭk′) *n.* A large edible clam *(Panope generosa)* of the Pacific coast of northwest North America. [< Puget Salish *gʷídəq.*]

ge•o•ec•o•nom•ics also **ge•o-ec•o•nom•ics** (jē′ō-ĕk′ə-nŏm′ĭks, -ē′kə-) *n. (used with a sing. v.)* **1.** The study of the relationship between politics and economics, esp. internationally. **2.** A governmental policy employing geoeconomics. **3.** The international economic and political factors relating to or influencing a nation or region. —**ge′o•ec′o•nom′ic** *adj.*

Geof•frey of Mon•mouth (jĕf′rē; mŏn′məth). 1100?–54. English prelate and chronicler whose *Historia Regum Britanniae* (c. 1139) is a source of Arthurian legend.

geode

geog. *abbr.* **1.a.** Geographer. **b.** Geography. **2.** Geographic.

ge•o•graph•ic (jē′ə-grăf′ĭk) also **ge•o•graph•i•cal** (-ĭ-kəl) *adj.* **1.** Of or relating to geography. **2.** Concerning the topography of a specific region. —**ge′o•graph′i•cal•ly** *adv.*

geographic mile *n.* A nautical mile.

ge•og•ra•phy (jē-ŏg′rə-fē) *n., pl.* **-phies. 1.** The study of the earth and its features and of the distribution of life on the earth, including human life and the effects of human activity. **2.** The physical characteristics, esp. the surface features, of an area. **3.** A book on geography. **4.** An ordered arrangement of constituent elements. —**ge•og′ra•pher** *n.*

ge•oid (jē′oid′) *n.* The hypothetical surface of the earth that coincides everywhere with mean sea level. [Ger. < Gk. *geoeidēs,* earthlike : *gē,* earth + *-oeidēs,* -oid.] —**ge•oid′al** (-oid′l) *adj.*

geol. *abbr.* **1.** Geologic; geological. **2.a.** Geologist. **b.** Geology.

geologic time *n.* The time covering the physical formation and development of the earth, esp. prior to human history.

ge•ol•o•gize (jē-ŏl′ə-jīz′) *intr.v.* **-gized, -giz•ing, -giz•es.** To study geology or make geologic investigations.

ge•ol•o•gy (jē-ŏl′ə-jē) *n., pl.* **-gies. 1.** The scientific study of the origin, history, and structure of the earth. **2.** The structure of a specific region of the earth's crust. **3.** A book on geology. **4.** The scientific study of the origin, history, and structure of the solid matter of a celestial body. —**ge′o•log′ic** (jē′ə-lŏj′ĭk), **ge′o•log′i•cal** *adj.* —**ge′o•log′i•cal•ly** *adv.* —**ge•ol′o•gist** *n.*

geom. *abbr.* **1.** Geometric. **2.** Geometry.

geomagnetic equator *n.* The imaginary great circle on the earth's surface formed by the intersection of a plane passing through the earth's center perpendicular to the axis connecting the north and south magnetic poles.

geodesic dome

geomagnetic storm *n.* See **magnetic storm.**

ge•o•mag•ne•tism (jē′ō-măg′nĭ-tĭz′əm) *n.* **1.** The magnetism of the earth. **2.** The study of the earth's magnetism. —**ge′o•mag•net′ic** (-nĕt′ĭk) *adj.*

ge•o•man•cy (jē′ə-măn′sē) *n.* Divination by means of lines and figures or by geographic features. [Ult. < Gk. *geō-,* geo- + Gk. *manteia,* divination; see -MANCY.] —**ge′o•man′cer** *n.* —**ge′o•man′tic** (-tĭk) *adj.*

ge•o•met•ric (jē′ə-mĕt′rĭk) also **ge•o•met•ri•cal** (-rĭ-kəl) *adj.* **1.** *Math.* **a.** Of or relating to geometry and its methods and principles. **b.** Increasing or decreasing in a geometric progression. **2.** Using simple geometric forms such as circles and squares in design and decoration. —**ge′o•met′ri•cal•ly** *adv.*

geometric isomer *n.* Any of a set of isomers that differ because of a structural asymmetry about a double bond in the molecule.

ge•o•met•ri•cize (jē′ə-mĕt′rĭ-sīz′) *tr.v.* **-cized, -ciz•ing, -ciz•es.** To design or form in geometric patterns or figures.

geometric mean *n. Math.* The *n*th root, usu. the positive *n*th root, of a product of *n* factors.

geometric pace *n.* See **pace¹** 3a.

geometric progression *n. Math.* A sequence, such as the numbers 1, 3, 9, 27, 81, in which each term is multiplied by the same factor in order to obtain the following term.

ge•o•met•rics (jē′ə-mĕt′rĭks) *n. (used with a pl. v.)* **1.** *Math.* Geometric qualities or properties. **2.** A pattern or design characterized by the use of geometric figures.

geometric series *n. Math.* An infinite series of the form $a + ax + ax^2 + ax^3 + \ldots$

ge•om•e•trid (jē-ŏm′ĭ-trĭd) *n.* Any of various moths of the family Geometridae, having caterpillars commonly known as measuring worms that move by looping the body. [< NLat. *Geōmetridae,* family name < Lat. *geōmetrēs,* geometrician, land-measurer < Gk. < *geōmetrein,* to measure land. See GEOMETRY.] —**ge•om′e•trid** *adj.*

ă pat	oi boy
ā pay	ou out
âr care	o͝o took
ä father	o͞o boot
ĕ pet	ŭ cut
ē be	ûr urge
ĭ pit	th thin
ī pie	*th* this
îr pier	hw which
ŏ pot	zh vision
ō toe	ə about, item
ô paw	

Stress marks:
′ (primary);
′ (secondary), as in **dictionary** (dĭk′shə-nĕr′ē)

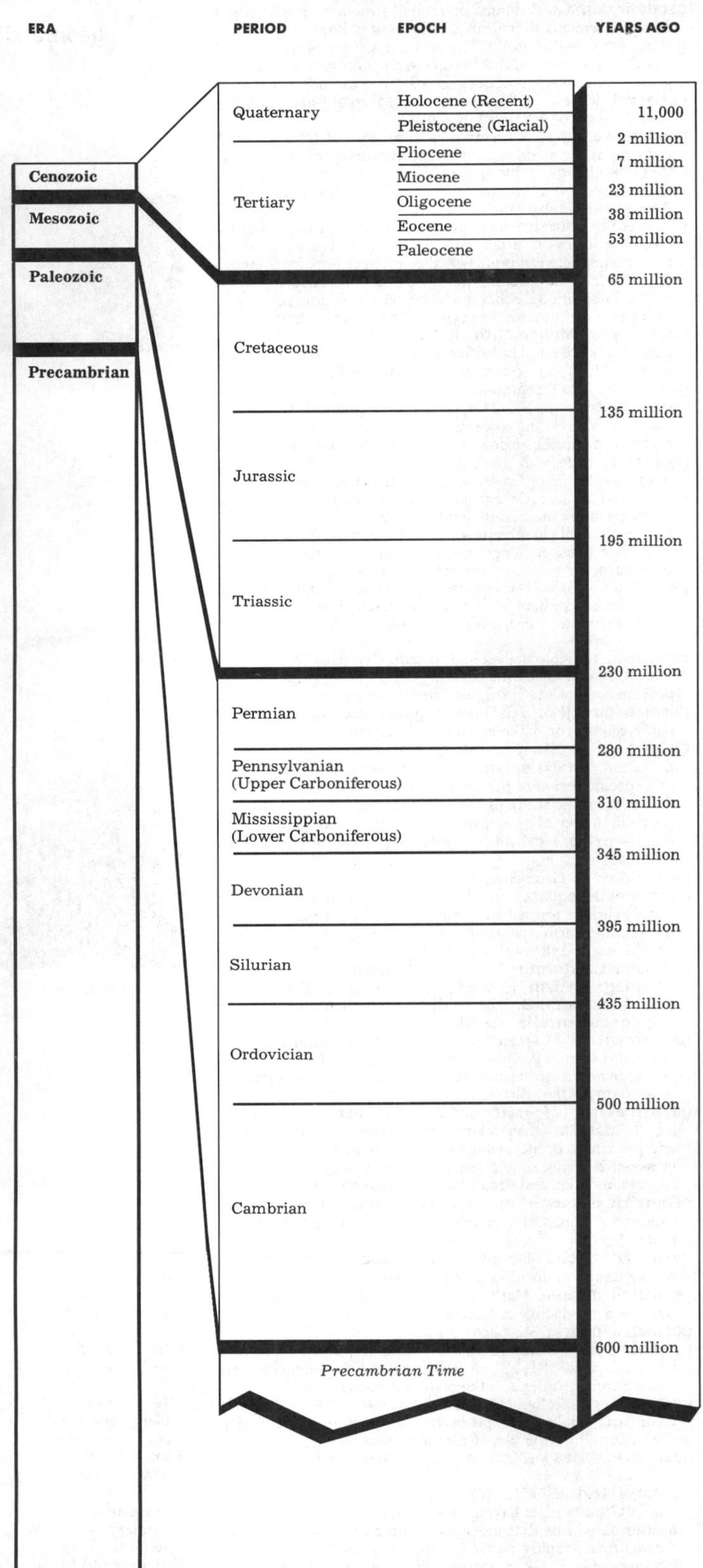

ge•om•e•trize (jē-ŏm′ĭ-trīz′) *v.* **-trized, -triz•ing, -triz•es.** —*intr.* **1.** To study geometry. **2.** To apply the methods of geometry. —*tr.* **1.** To present in geometric form. **2.** To bring into conformance with the laws and principles of geometry.

ge•om•e•try (jē-ŏm′ĭ-trē) *n., pl.* **-tries. 1.a.** The mathematics of the properties, measurement, and relationships of points, lines, angles, surfaces, and solids. **b.** A system of geometry. **c.** A geometry restricted to a class of problems or objects. **d.** A book on geometry. **2.a.** Configuration; arrangement. **b.** A surface shape. **3.** A physical arrangement suggesting geometric forms or lines. [ME *geometrie* < OFr. < Lat. *geōmetria* < Gk. < *geōmetrein*, to measure land : *gē*, earth + *metron*, measure; see **mē-²***.] —**ge•om′e•tri′cian** (jē-ŏm′ĭ-trĭsh′ən, jē′ə-mĭ-), **ge•om′e•ter** *n.*

ge•o•mor•phic (jē′ə-môr′fĭk) *adj.* Of or resembling the earth or its shape or surface configuration.

ge•o•mor•phol•o•gy (jē′ō-môr-fŏl′ə-jē) *n.* The study of the evolution and configuration of landforms. —**ge′o•mor′pho•log′ic** (-môr′fə-lŏj′ĭk), **ge′o•mor′pho•log′i•cal** (-ĭ-kəl) *adj.* —**ge′o•mor•phol′o•gist** *n.*

ge•oph•a•gy (jē-ŏf′ə-jē) *n.* The eating of earthy substances, such as clay. —**ge•oph′a•gism** *n.* —**ge•oph′a•gist** *n.*

ge•o•phone (jē′ə-fōn′) *n.* An electronic receiver designed to pick up seismic vibrations.

ge•o•phys•ics (jē′ō-fĭz′ĭks) *n.* *(used with a sing. v.)* The physics of the earth and its environment, including the physics of fields such as meteorology, oceanography, and seismology. —**ge′o•phys′i•cal** *adj.* —**ge′o•phys′i•cal•ly** *adv.* —**ge′o•phys′i•cist** (-ĭ-sĭst) *n.*

ge•o•phyte (jē′ə-fīt′) *n.* A perennial plant, such as a tulip, propagated by buds on underground bulbs, tubers, or corms.

ge•o•pol•i•tics (jē′ō-pŏl′ĭ-tĭks) *n.* *(used with a sing. v.)* **1.** The study of the relationship among politics and geography, demography, and economics, esp. with respect to the foreign policy of a nation. **2.a.** A governmental policy employing geopolitics. **b.** A Nazi doctrine holding that the geographic, economic, and political needs of Germany justified its invasion and seizure of other lands. **3.** A combination of geographic and political factors relating to or influencing a nation or region. —**ge′o•po•lit′i•cal** (-pə-lĭt′ĭ-kəl) *adj.*

ge•o•pon•ic (jē′ə-pŏn′ĭk) *adj.* Of or relating to agriculture or farming. [Gk. *geōponikos* < *geōponein*, to till : *gē*, earth + *ponein*, to toil; see **(s)pen-***.]

ge•o•pon•ics (jē′ə-pŏn′ĭks) *n.* *(used with a sing. v.)* The study or science of agriculture.

ge•o•pres•sured (jē′ō-prĕsh′ərd) also **ge•o•pres•sur•ized** (jē′ō-prĕsh′ə-rīzd′) *adj.* Under high pressure within the earth.

Geor•die¹ (jôr′dē) *n. Chiefly British.* **1.** A native or inhabitant of Newcastle upon Tyne, England, or its environs. **2.** Their dialect of English. [Sc., dim. of *George*.]

Geor•die² (jôr′dē) *n. Scots.* A former British gold coin worth one pound and five pence; a guinea. [Sc., dim. of *George*, after St. GEORGE.]

George (jôrj) *n.* **1.** A jeweled figure of Saint George killing the dragon, used as an insignia of the Knights of the Garter. **2.** An English coin during the reign of Henry VIII.

George, Saint. d. c. A.D. 303. Christian martyr and patron of England who according to legend slew a fearsome dragon.

George I¹. 1660–1727. Elector of Hanover (1698–1727) and king of Great Britain and Ireland (1714–27) who left the affairs of his country in the hands of Sir Robert Walpole.

George I². 1845–1913. King of Greece (1863–1913) who introduced a democratic constitution (1864).

George II¹. 1683–1760. King of Great Britain and Ireland and elector of Hanover (1727–60) who won the Battle of Dettingen (1743) in S-central present-day Germany.

George III. 1738–1820. King of Great Britain and Ireland (1760–1820) and of Hanover (1815–20) whose policies fed American colonial discontent, leading to revolution in 1776.

George IV. 1762–1830. King of Great Britain and Ireland and of Hanover (1820–30) who caused controversy when he attempted to divorce his estranged wife.

George V. 1865–1936. King of Great Britain and Northern Ireland and emperor of India (1910–36) who gave up his German titles during World War I.

George V Coast also **George V Land.** A region of Antarctica between Wilkes Land and Victoria Land; claimed by Australia.

George VI. 1895–1952. King of Great Britain and Northern Ireland (1936–52) and emperor of India (1936–47) noted for his dedication to his duty, esp. during World War II.

George, Henry. 1839–97. Amer. journalist and reformer whose works include *Progress and Poverty* (1879).

George, Lake. A glacial lake of NE NY in the foothills of the Adirondack Mts. S of Lake Champlain.

George River. A river of NE Quebec, Canada, rising on the Quebec-Labrador border and flowing c. 563 km (350 mi) to Ungava Bay.

Geor•ges Bank (jôr′jĭz). A submerged sandbank in the Atlantic Ocean E of Cape Cod.

George•town (jôrj′toun′). **1.** Also **George Town.** The cap. of the Cayman Is., on Grand Cayman in the West Indies W of

Jamaica. Pop. 7,617. **2.** The cap. of Guyana, in the N part on the Atlantic Ocean; founded by the British in 1781. Pop. 78,500. **3.** A section of W Washington DC; settled c. 1665 and annexed by Washington DC in 1878.

George Town. **1.** Also **Pi•nang** or **Pe•nang** (pə-näng′, pē′-näng′). A city of W Malaysia on Pinang I. in the Strait of Malacca. Pop. 250,578. **2.** See **Georgetown** 1.

geor•gette (jôr-jĕt′) *n.* A sheer strong silk or silklike clothing fabric with a dull, creped surface. [Originally a trademark.]

Geor•gia (jôr′jə). **1.** A region and republic of Asia Minor in the Caucasus S of Russia; acquired by Russia between 1801 and 1829 and a constituent republic of the U.S.S.R. from 1936 to 1991. Cap. Tbilisi. Pop. 5,201,000. **2.** A state of the SE U.S.; admitted as one of the original Thirteen Colonies in 1788. Cap. Atlanta. Pop. 6,508,419.

Georgia, Strait of. A channel between Vancouver I. and mainland British Columbia, Canada, and N WA linking Puget Sound with Queen Charlotte Sound.

Geor•gian (jôr′jən) *adj.* **1.** Of, relating to, or characteristic of the reigns of the four Georges who ruled Great Britain from 1714 to 1830. **2.** Of or relating to the U.S. state of Georgia or its inhabitants. **3.** Of or relating to the Georgian republic or its people, non-Indo-European language, or culture. **— Geor′gian** *adj.*

Georgian Bay. An extension of Lake Huron in SE Ontario, Canada.

geor•gic (jôr′jĭk) *adj.* also **geor•gi•cal** (-jĭ-kəl). Of or relating to agriculture or rural life. *— n.* A poem concerning farming or rural life. [Lat. *geōrgicus* < Gk. *geōrgikos* < *geōrgos*, farmer : *geō-*, geo- + *ergon*, work; see **werg-***.]

ge•o•sci•ence (jē′ō-sī′əns) *n.* Any of the sciences, such as geology or geochemistry, that deals with the earth.

ge•o•sta•tion•ar•y (jē′ō-stā′shə-nĕr′ē) *adj.* **1.** Of, relating to, or being a satellite that travels above Earth's equator from west to east at an altitude of approx. 35,900 kilometers (22,300 miles) and at a speed matching that of Earth's rotation, thus remaining stationary in relation to Earth. **2.** Of, relating to, or being the orbit of such a satellite.

ge•o•strat•e•gy (jē′ō-străt′ə-jē) *n., pl.* **-gies. 1.** The branch of geopolitics that deals with strategy. **2.** The geopolitical and strategic factors that characterize a certain geographic area. **3.** Governmental strategy based on geopolitics. **— ge′o•stra•te′gic** (-strə-tē′jĭk) *adj.* **— ge′o•strat′e•gist** *n.*

ge•o•stroph•ic (jē′ə-strŏf′ĭk) *adj.* Of or relating to force caused by the earth's rotation. [GEO- + Gk. *strophē*, a turning; see STROPHE + -IC.] **— ge′o•stroph′i•cal•ly** *adv.*

ge•o•syn•chro•nous (jē′ō-sĭng′krə-nəs, -sĭn′-) *adj.* Geostationary. **— ge′o•syn′chro•nous•ly** *adv.*

ge•o•syn•cline (jē′ō-sĭn′klīn′) *n.* An extensive, usu. linear depression in the earth's crust. **— ge′o•syn•cli′nal** (-sĭn-klī′nəl) *adj.*

ge•o•tax•is (jē′ō-tăk′sĭs) *n. Biol.* Movement of a motile organism using the earth's gravity for orientation. **— ge′o•tac′tic** (-tĭk) *adj.* **— ge′o•tac′ti•cal•ly** *adv.*

ge•o•tec•ton•ic (jē′ō-tĕk-tŏn′ĭk) *adj.* Of or relating to the shape, structure, and arrangement of the rock masses resulting from structural deformation of the earth's crust.

ge•o•ther•mal (jē′ō-thûr′məl) also **ge•o•ther•mic** (-mĭk) *adj.* Of or relating to the internal heat of the earth.

ge•ot•ro•pism (jē-ŏt′rə-pĭz′əm) *n. Biol.* The growth of a living organism in response to gravity, as the downward growth of plant roots. **— ge′o•tro′pic** (jē′ə-trō′pĭk, -trŏp′ĭk) *adj.*

ger. *abbr. Gram.* Gerund.

Ger. *abbr.* German; Germany.

Ge•ra (gĕr′ə). A city of E-central Germany SSW of Leipzig; chartered in the early 13th cent. Pop. 129,891.

ge•rah (gîr′ə) *n.* An ancient Hebrew coin and unit of weight. [Heb. *gērâ*, grain, bean.]

ge•ra•ni•al (jə-rā′nē-əl) *n.* A structural isomer of citral obtained from the oxidation of geraniol. [GERANI(OL) + -AL³.]

ge•ra•ni•ol (jə-rā′nē-ôl′, -ōl′, -ŏl′) *n.* A fragrant pale yellow liquid alcohol, $C_9H_{17}COH$, derived chiefly from the oils of geranium and citronella and used in cosmetics and flavorings.

ge•ra•ni•um (jə-rā′nē-əm) *n.* **1.** Any of various plants of the genus *Geranium,* having pink or purplish flowers. **2.** Any of various chiefly southern African plants of the genus *Pelargonium,* having showy clusters of red, pink, or white flowers. **3.** *Color.* A strong to vivid red. [NLat. *Geranium*, genus name < Lat. *geranium*, cranesbill < Gk. *geranion*, dim. of *geranos*, crane. See **gerə-²***.]

ger•bil (jûr′bəl) *n.* Any of various mouselike rodents of the subfamily Gerbillinae of Africa and Asia Minor, having long hind legs and a long tail and often kept as pets. [Fr. *gerbille* < NLat. *Gerbillus*, genus name, dim. of *gerbō*, jerboa. See JERBOA.]

ge•rent (jîr′ənt) *n.* One that rules or manages. [< Lat. *gerēns*, *gerent-*, pr.part. of *gerere*, to manage.]

ger•e•nuk (gĕr′ə-no͝ok′) *n.* An African gazelle *(Litocranius walleri)* having long legs, a long slender neck, and backward-curving horns in the male. [Somali *garanūg*, Waller's gazelle.]

ger•fal•con (jûr′făl′kən, -fôl′-, -fô′-) *n.* Var. of **gyrfalcon.**

ger•i•at•ric (jĕr′ē-ăt′rĭk) *adj.* **1.** Of or relating to geriatrics. **2.** Of or relating to the aged or the aging process. *— n.* An aged person. [Back-formation < GERIATRICS.]

ger•i•a•tri•cian (jĕr′ē-ə-trĭsh′ən) also **ger•i•at•rist** (-ăt′-rĭst) *n.* A physician who specializes in geriatrics.

ger•i•at•rics (jĕr′ē-ăt′rĭks) *n.* *(used with a sing. v.)* The branch of medicine that deals with the diagnosis and treatment of diseases and problems specific to the aged. [Gk. *gēras*, old age; see **gerə-¹*** + -IATRICS.]

Gé•ri•cault (zhā-rē-kō′), **(Jean Louis André) Théodore.** 1791–1824. French painter noted for his boldly colored, unorthodox works, such as *The Raft of the Medusa* (1819).

Saint George
Early 15th-century Italian tempera painting by an unknown artist of the Byzantine School

germ (jûrm) *n.* **1.** *Biol.* A small mass of protoplasm or cells from which a new organism or one of its parts may develop. **2.** A seed, bud, or spore. **3.** A microorganism, esp. a pathogen. **4.** A possible basis of further growth or development. [ME < OFr. *germe* < Lat. *germen*, bud. See **genə-***.]

ger•man¹ (jûr′mən) *n.* **1.** An intricate dance for many couples. **2.** A party for dancing at which this dance is featured. [Short for *German cotillion.*]

ger•man² (jûr′mən) *adj.* Having the same parents or the same grandparents on either the mother's or the father's side. Often used in combination: *a cousin-german.* [ME *germain* < OFr. < Lat. *germānus* < *germen*, offshoot. See **genə-***.]

Ger•man (jûr′mən) *adj.* **1.** Of, relating to, or characteristic of Germany or its people. **2.** Of or relating to the German language. *— n.* **1.a.** A native or inhabitant of Germany. **b.** A person of German ancestry. **2.** The West Germanic language of Germany, Austria, and part of Switzerland. [ME < Lat. *Germānus.*]

German cockroach *n.* A small light brown cockroach *(Blatella germanica)* that is a common household pest.

ger•man•der (jər-măn′dər) *n.* Any of various usu. aromatic plants of the genus *Teucrium,* with purplish or reddish flowers. [ME *germandre* < OFr. *germandree*, alteration of Med. Lat. *germandrea* < LGk. *khamandrua* < Gk. *khamaidrus* : *khamai*, on the ground; see **dhghem-*** + *drus*, oak; see **deru-***.]

ger•mane (jər-mān′) *adj.* Being both pertinent and fitting. [ME *germain*, having the same parents, closely connected. See GERMAN².] **— ger•mane′ly** *adv.* **— ger•mane′ness** *n.*

George III

German East Af•ri•ca (ăf′rĭ-kə). A former German protectorate of E Africa including much of what is now Tanzania, Rwanda, and Burundi.

Ger•ma•ni•a (jər-mā′nē-ə, -mān′yə). **1.** An ancient region of central Europe N of the Danube and E of the Rhine. **2.** A part of the Roman Empire W of the Rhine R. in present-day NE France and sections of Belgium and the Netherlands.

Ger•man•ic (jər-măn′ĭk) *adj.* **1.a.** Of, relating to, or characteristic of Germany or its people, language, or culture. **b.** Of or relating to the Teutons. **c.** Of or relating to speakers of a Germanic language. **2.** Of, relating to, or constituting Germanic. *— n.* A branch of the Indo-European language family that comprises North Germanic, West Germanic, and the extinct East Germanic.

Ger•man•i•cus Cae•sar (jər-măn′ĭ-kəs sē′zər). 15 B.C.–A.D. 19. Roman general noted for his military triumphs in the Rhineland (A.D. 11–16).

Ger•man•ism (jûr′mə-nĭz′əm) *n.* **1.** An attitude, a custom, or a feature that seems characteristically German. **2.** A German idiom or phrasing in another language. **3.** Esteem for Germany and emulation of German ways.

German shepherd

Ger•man•ist (jûr′mə-nĭst) *n.* A specialist in the study of German or Germanic culture, literature, or language.

ger•ma•ni•um (jər-mā′nē-əm) *n. Symbol* **Ge** A brittle crystalline gray-white metalloid element, widely used as a semiconductor, as an alloying agent and catalyst, and in certain optical glasses. Atomic number 32; atomic weight 72.59; melting point 937.4°C; boiling point 2,830°C; specific gravity 5.323 (at 25°C); valence 2, 4. See table at **element.** [After GERMANIA.]

Ger•man•ize (jûr′mə-nīz′) *v.* **-ized, -iz•ing, -iz•es.** *— tr.* **1.** To give a German quality to. **2.** *Archaic.* To translate into German. *— intr.* To have or adopt German customs or attitudes. **— Ger′man•i•za′tion** (-mə-nĭ-zā′shən) *n.* **— Ger′man•iz′er** *n.*

German measles *n.* *(used with a sing. or pl. v.)* See **rubella.**

Ger•man•o•phile (jər-măn′ə-fīl′) *n.* One who admires Germany, its people, and its culture. **— Ger•man′o•phile′** *adj.*

Ger•man•o•phobe (jər-măn′ə-fōb′) *n.* One who dislikes or fears Germany, its people, and its culture. **— Ger•man′o•phobe′** *adj.* **— Ger•man′o•pho′bi•a** *n.*

German shepherd *n.* Any of a breed of large dog developed in Germany, having a dense grayish to brownish or black coat and often trained to assist the police and guide the blind.

German shorthaired pointer *n.* Any of a breed of medium to large hunting dog, developed in Germany and having a short white and reddish coat.

German silver *n.* See **nickel silver.**

German Southwest Af•ri•ca (ăf′rĭ-kə). A former German colony of SW Africa; awarded to South Africa in 1919.

Ger•man•town (jûr′mən-toun′). A town of extreme SW TN, a suburb of Memphis. Pop. 32,893.

ă pat	oi boy
ā pay	ou out
âr care	o͝o took
ä father	o͞o boot
ĕ pet	ŭ cut
ē be	ûr urge
ĭ pit	th thin
ī pie	*th* this
îr pier	hw which
ŏ pot	zh vision
ō toe	ə about,
ô paw	item

Stress marks:
′ (primary);
′ (secondary), as in
dictionary (dĭk′shə-nĕr′ē)

German wirehaired pointer *n.* Any of a breed of medium to large hunting dog, developed in Germany and having a flat, wiry, white and reddish coat.

Ger•ma•ny (jûr′mə-nē). A country of N-central Europe bordered on the N by the Baltic and North seas; occupied since c. 500 B.C. by Germanic tribes and divided between **West Germany** and **East Germany** from 1949 to 1990. Cap. Berlin. Bonn is the seat of government. Pop. 77,750,743.

Germany

germ cell *n.* An ovum or a sperm cell or one of its developmental precursors.

germ•free (jûrm′frē′) *adj.* Free of microorganisms.

ger•mi•cide (jûr′mĭ-sīd′) *n.* An agent that kills germs, esp. pathogenic microorganisms; a disinfectant. **—ger′mi•cid′al** (-sīd′l) *adj.*

ger•mi•nal (jûr′mə-nəl) *adj.* **1.** Of, relating to, or having the nature of a germ cell. **2.** Of, relating to, or occurring in the earliest stage of development. [Fr. < Lat. *germen, germin-,* seed. See **genə-***.] **—ger′mi•nal•ly** *adv.*

germinal disk *n. Embryol.* A disklike region of cells from which the embryo develops in the fertilized ovum of many vertebrates.

germinal vesicle *n.* The enlarged nucleus of an oocyte before the end of meiosis.

ger•mi•nate (jûr′mə-nāt′) *v.* **-nat•ed, -nat•ing, -nates.** *—tr.* To cause to sprout or grow. *—intr.* **1.** To begin to sprout or grow. **2.** To come into existence. [Lat. *germināre, germināt-,* to sprout < *germen, germin-,* seed. See **genə-***.] **—ger′mi•na′tion** *n.* **—ger′mi•na′tive** *adj.* **—ger′mi•na′tor** *n.*

germ layer *n.* Any of three cellular layers in the gastrula, the ectoderm, endoderm, or mesoderm, from which the organs and tissues of the body develop.

germ plasm *n.* **1.** The cytoplasm of a germ cell, esp. that part containing the chromosomes. **2.** Germ cells as distinguished from other body cells. **3.** Hereditary material; genes.

germ theory *n.* The doctrine holding that infectious diseases are caused by the activity of microorganisms within the body.

germ warfare *n.* The use of injurious microorganisms, such as bacteria or viruses, as weapons in warfare.

germ•y (jûr′mē) *adj.* **-i•er, -i•est.** Full of germs. **—germ′i•ness** *n.*

Gé•rôme (zhā-rōm′, -rôm′), **Jean Léon.** 1824–1904. French painter of historical genre works, such as *Cockfight* (1847).

Geronimo
1907 photogravure by Edward Sheriff Curtis (1868–1952)

Ge•ron•i•mo (jə-rŏn′ə-mō′). 1829–1909. Apache leader who led a series of raids against settlements in the Southwest (1876–86).

ge•ron•tic (jə-rŏn′tĭk) *adj.* Of or relating to old age.

geronto– or **geront–** *pref.* Old age; aged one: *gerontology.* [Fr. *géronto-* < Gk. *geronta-* < *gerōn, geront-,* old man. See **gerə-¹***.]

ger•on•toc•ra•cy (jĕr′ən-tŏk′rə-sē) *n., pl.* **-cies. 1.** Governmental rule by elders. **2.** A governing group of elders.

ger•on•tol•o•gy (jĕr′ən-tŏl′ə-jē) *n.* The study of the biological, psychological, and sociological phenomena associated with old age and aging. **—ge•ron′to•log′i•cal** (jə-rŏn′tə-lŏj′ĭ-kəl), **ge•ron′to•log′ic** (-lŏj′ĭk) *adj.* **—ger′on•tol′o•gist** *n.*

Ger•ry (gĕr′ē), **Elbridge.** 1744–1814. Amer. politician who served as governor of MA (1810–11) and Vice President of the U.S. (1813–14).

ger•ry•man•der (jĕr′ē-măn′dər, gĕr′-) *tr.v.* **-dered, -der•ing, -ders.** To divide (a geographic area) into voting districts so as to give unfair advantage to one party in elections. *—n.* **1.** The act, process, or an instance of gerrymandering. **2.** A district or configuration of districts differing widely in size or population because of gerrymandering. [After Elbridge GERRY + (SALA)MANDER (< the shape of an election district created while Gerry was governor of MA).]

George and Ira Gershwin
Photographed in the 1930's

Gersh•win (gûrsh′wĭn), **George.** 1898–1937. Amer. composer whose works include *Rhapsody in Blue* (1924) and *Porgy and Bess* (1935), written with his brother **Ira** (1896–1983).

ger•und (jĕr′ənd) *n. Gram.* **1.** In Latin, a noun derived from a verb and having all case forms except the nominative. **2.** In other languages, a verbal noun analogous to the Latin gerund, such as the English form ending in *-ing.* [LLat. *gerundium* < Lat. *gerundum,* var. of *gerendum,* gerundive of *gerere,* to carry on.] **—ge•run′di•al** (jə-rŭn′dē-əl) *adj.*

ge•run•dive (jə-rŭn′dĭv) *n.* A verbal adjective in Latin that in the nominative case expresses fitness or obligation and in other cases functions as a future passive participle. [ME *gerundif* < LLat. *gerundīvus* < *gerundium,* gerund. See GERUND.]

Ge•ry•on (jîr′ē-ən, gĕr′-) *n. Gk. Myth.* A monster with three bodies that was slain by Hercules.

Ge•sell (gĭ-zĕl′), **Arnold Lucius.** 1880–1961. Amer. psychologist noted for researching child development.

Ges•ner (gĕs′nər), **Konrad von.** 1516–65. Swiss encyclopedist and naturalist whose *Historia Animalium* (1551–58) is considered the basis of modern zoology.

ges•ne•ri•ad (gĕs-nîr′ē-ăd′, jĕs-) *n.* Any of numerous tropical herbs or shrubs of the family Gesneriaceae, including African violets and gloxinia. [< NLat. *Gesneria,* type genus, after Konrad von GESNER.]

ges•so (jĕs′ō) *n., pl.* **-soes. 1.** A preparation of plaster of Paris and glue used as a base for low relief or as a surface for painting. **2.** A surface of gesso. [Ital. < Lat. *gypsum,* gypsum. See GYPSUM.] **—ges′soed** *adj.*

gest or **geste** (jĕst) *n.* **1.** An adventure or exploit. **2.a.** A verse romance or tale. **b.** A prose romance. [ME *geste.* See JEST.]

ge•stalt or **Ge•stalt** (gə-shtält′, -shtôlt′, -stält′, -stôlt′) *n., pl.* **-stalts** or **-stalt•en** (-shtält′n, -shtôlt′n, -stält′n, -stôlt′n). A physical, biological, psychological, or symbolic pattern of elements so unified that its properties cannot be derived from the sum of its parts. [Ger., shape < MHGer. < p.part. of *stellen,* to place < OHGer. See **stel-***.]

Ge•stalt•ist (gə-shtäl′tĭst, -shtôl′-, -stäl′-, -stôl′-) *n.* An adherent or a practitioner of Gestalt psychology.

Gestalt psychology *n.* The school or theory in psychology that considers psychological, physiological, and behavioral phenomena to be irreducible wholes rather than simple summations of discrete perceptual elements.

Ge•sta•po (gə-stä′pō, -shtä′-) *n.* **1.** The internal security police of Nazi Germany, known for its terrorist methods. **2. gestapo,** *pl.* **-pos.** A police organization that employs terroristic methods to control a populace. [Ger. *Ge(heime) Sta(ats)po(lizei),* secret state police : *geheim,* secret + *Staat,* state + *Polizei,* police.] **—Ge•sta′po** *adj.*

ges•tate (jĕs′tāt′) *v.* **-tat•ed, -tat•ing, -tates.** *—tr.* **1.** To carry within the uterus from conception to delivery. **2.** To conceive and develop in the mind. *—intr.* **1.** To gestate offspring. **2.** To develop gradually.

ges•ta•tion (jĕ-stā′shən) *n.* **1.** The period of development in the uterus from conception until birth; pregnancy. **2.** The conception and development of a plan or an idea in the mind. [LLat. *gestātiō, gestātiōn-* < Lat., a carrying < *gestātus,* p.part. of *gestāre,* freq. of *gerere,* to carry.] **—ges′ta•to′ry** (jĕs′tə-tôr′ē, -tōr′ē), **ges•ta′tion•al** *adj.*

ges•tic (jĕs′tĭk) *adj.* Relating to bodily movements or gestures, esp. in dancing. [< obsolete *gest,* bearing < Fr. *geste* < OFr. < Lat. *gestus.* See GESTURE.]

ges•tic•u•late (jĕ-stĭk′yə-lāt′) *v.* **-lat•ed, -lat•ing, -lates.** *—intr.* To make gestures esp. while speaking, as for emphasis. *—tr.* To say or express by gestures. [Lat. *gesticulārī, gesticulāt-* < *gesticulus,* gesticulation, dim. of *gestus,* gesture, bearing. See GESTURE.] **—ges•tic′u•la′tive, ges•tic′u•la•to′ry** (-lə-tôr′ē, -tōr′ē) *adj.* **—ges•tic′u•la′tor** *n.*

ges•tic•u•la•tion (jĕ-stĭk′yə-lā′shən) *n.* **1.** The act of gesticulating. **2.** A deliberate vigorous motion or gesture.

ges•ture (jĕs′chər) *n.* **1.** A motion of the limbs or body made to express thought or to emphasize speech. **2.** The act of gesturing. **3.** An act or a remark made as a formality or a sign of intention or attitude. *—v.* **-tured, -tur•ing, -tures.** *—intr.* To make gestures. *—tr.* To show, express, or direct by gestures. [ME < Med.Lat. *gestūra,* bearing < Lat. *gestus* < p.part. of *gerere,* to behave.] **—ges′tur•al** *adj.* **—ges′tur•al•ly** *adv.* **—ges′tur•er** *n.*

ge•sund•heit (gə-zo͝ont′hīt′) *interj.* Used to wish good health to a person who has just sneezed. [Ger., health < MHGer. *gesuntheit* < *gesunt,* healthy < OHGer. *gisunt.*]

get (gĕt) *v.* **got** (gŏt), **got•ten** (gŏt′n) or **got, get•ting, gets.** *—tr.* **1.a.** To come into possession or use of; receive. **b.** To meet with or incur. **2.a.** To go after and obtain. **b.** To go after and bring: *Get me a pillow.* **c.** To purchase; buy. **3.a.** To acquire as a result of action or effort **b.** To earn: *got high marks in math.* **c.** To accomplish or attain as a result of military action. **4.** To obtain by concession or request. **5.a.** To arrive at; reach. **b.** To reach and board; catch: *got the bus.* **6.** To succeed in communicating with, as by telephone. **7.** To become affected with (an illness, for example) by infection or exposure. **8.a.** To be subjected to; undergo: *got a concussion.* **b.** To receive as retribution or punishment. **c.** To sustain a stated injury to: *got my arm broken.* **9.a.** To gain or have understanding of. **b.** To learn (a poem, for example) by heart; memorize. **c.** To find or reach by calculating. **d.** To perceive by hearing. **10.** To procreate; beget. **11.a.** To cause to become or be in a specified condition: *got the shirt clean.* **b.** To make ready; prepare. **c.** To cause to come or go: *got the car home.* **d.** To cause to move or leave: *Get me out of here!* **12.** To cause to undertake or perform; prevail on: *got the baby to eat squash.* **13.a.** To take, esp. by force; seize. **b.** *Informal.* To overcome or destroy. **c.** To evoke an emotional response or reaction in. **d.** To annoy or irritate. **e.** To present a difficult problem to; puzzle. **f.** To take revenge on, esp. to kill in revenge for a wrong. **g.** *Informal.* To hit or strike. **14.** *Baseball.* To put out. **15.** To begin or start. Used with the present participle: *Let's get working.* **16.a.** To have current possession of. Used in the present perfect form with the meaning of the present: *We've got cash.* **b.** To have as an obligation. Used in the present perfect form with the meaning of the present: *I have got to leave early.* *—intr.* **1.a.** To become or grow to be: *got well.* **b.** To be successful in coming or going: *When will we get to New York?* **2.** To be able or permitted: *got to see Europe.* **3.a.** To be successful in becoming: *The dog got loose.* **b.** Used with the past participle of transitive verbs as a passive voice auxiliary: *got stung.* **c.** To become drawn in, entangled,

ă pat | oi boy
ā pay | ou out
âr care | o͝o took
ä father | o͞o boot
ĕ pet | ŭ cut
ē be | ûr urge
ĭ pit | th thin
ī pie | *th* this
îr pier | hw which
ŏ pot | zh vision
ō toe | ə about, item
ô paw |

Stress marks:
′ (primary);
ʹ (secondary), as in **dictionary** (dĭk′shə-nĕr′ē)

or involved: *got into debt.* **4.** *Informal.* To depart immediately. **5.** To work for gain or profit; make money. —*n.* **1.a.** The act of begetting. **b.** Progeny; offspring. **2.** *Sports.* A return in tennis on a shot that seems impossible to reach. —***phrasal verbs.* get about.** To be out of bed and beginning to walk again, as after an illness. **get across. 1.** To make understandable or clear. **2.** To be convincing or understandable. **get after.** To urge or scold. **get along. 1.** To be or continue to be on harmonious terms. **2.** To manage or fare with reasonable success. **3.a.** To make progress. **b.** To advance, esp. in years. **4.** To go away; leave. **get around. 1.** To circumvent or evade. **2.** *Informal.* To convince or win over by flattering or cajoling. **3.** To travel from place to place. **4.** To become known; circulate: *Word got around.* **get at. 1.** To touch or reach successfully. **2.** To try to make understandable; hint at or suggest. **3.** To discover or understand. **4.** *Informal.* To influence by improper or illegal means. **get away. 1.** To break free; escape. **2.** To leave or go away. **get back.** To return to a person, place, or condition. **get by. 1.** To pass or outstrip. **2.** To succeed at a level of minimal acceptability or with the minimal amount of effort. **3.** To succeed in managing; survive. **4.** To be unnoticed or ignored by. **get down. 1.** To descend. **2.** To give one's attention. Often used with *to: Let's get down to work.* **3.** To exhaust, discourage, or depress. **4.** To swallow. **5.** To describe in writing. **6.** *Informal.* To lose one's inhibitions; enjoy oneself wholeheartedly. **get in. 1.a.** To enter. **b.** To arrive. **2.** To become or cause to become involved. **3.** To become accepted, as in a club. **4.** To succeed in making or doing. **get into. 1.** To become involved in. **2.** *Informal.* To be interested in. **get off. 1.** To start, as on a trip; leave. **2.a.** To fire (a round of ammunition, for example). **b.** To write and send (a letter, for example). **3.** To escape, as from punishment. **4.** To obtain a release or lesser penalty for. **5.** *Slang.* To act or speak with effrontery. **6.** *Slang.* To have an orgasm. **7.** *Slang.* **a.** To feel great pleasure or gratification. **b.** To experience euphoria, as from taking a drug. **8.** To get permission to leave one's workplace. **get on. 1.** To be or continue on harmonious terms. **2.** To manage or fare with reasonable success. **3.a.** To make progress; continue. **b.** To advance in years. **4.** To acquire understanding or knowledge. **get out. 1.a.** To leave or escape. **b.** To cause to leave or escape. **2.** To become known. **3.** To publish (a newspaper, for example). **get over. 1.** To prevail against; overcome. **2.** To recover from. **3.** To get across. **get through. 1.** To arrive at the end of; finish or complete. **2.a.** To succeed in making contact; reach. **b.** To make oneself understood. **get to. 1.a.** To begin. Used with the present participle: *got to reminiscing.* **b.** To start to deal with. **2.** To influence or affect, esp. adversely. **get together. 1.** To bring together; gather. **2.** To come together. **3.** To arrive at an agreement. **get up. 1.a.** To arise from bed or rise to one's feet. **b.** To climb. **2.** To act as the creator or organizer of. **3.** To dress or adorn. **4.** To find within oneself: *trying to get up the nerve.* —***idioms.* get around to.** To find the time or occasion for. **get away with.** To escape the consequences of. **get back at.** To take revenge on. **get cracking.** To begin to work; get started. **get even.** To obtain revenge. **get even with.** To repay with an equivalent act, as for revenge. **get going.** To make a beginning; get started. **get it.** *Informal.* To be punished or scolded. **get it on.** *Slang.* **1.** To become filled with energy or excitement. **2.** To engage in sexual intercourse. **get nowhere.** To make no progress. **get on the stick.** To begin to work. **get (someone's) goat.** To make angry or vexed. **get somewhere.** *Informal.* To make progress. **get there.** *Informal.* To make progress or achieve success. **get wind of.** To learn of. [ME *geten* < ON *geta.* See **ghend-***.] —**get′a•ble, get′ta•ble** *adj.*

Usage Note: The use of *get* in the passive, as in *We got sunburned at the beach,* is generally avoided in formal writing. In less formal contexts, however, the construction does provide a useful distinction in attributing a more active role to its subject than would the corresponding passive with *be.* Thus if Jones has committed a flagrant breach of law in order to test a particular statute, the situation might best be described by the sentence *Jones got arrested by the police;* whereas if Jones did nothing to provoke the police action, the sentence *Jones was arrested by the police* would be preferred.

ge•ta (gĕt′ə, gĕ′tä) *n., pl.* **geta** or **ge•tas.** A wooden-soled shoe worn by the Japanese. [J.]

Ge•ta•fe (hĕ-tä′fĕ). A town of central Spain S of Madrid. Pop. 128,522.

get•a•way (gĕt′ə-wā′) *n.* **1.** The act or an instance of escaping: *made a quick getaway.* **2.** The start, as of a race. **3.** A place appropriate for a vacation.

geth•sem•a•ne (gĕth-sĕm′ə-nē) *n.* An instance or a place of great suffering.

Geth•sem•a•ne (gĕth-sĕm′ə-nē). In the Bible, a garden E of Jerusalem near the foot of the Mt. of Olives; scene of Jesus's agony and betrayal.

get•ter (gĕt′ər) *n.* A material added in small amounts during a chemical or metallurgical process to absorb impurities.

get-to•geth•er (gĕt′tə-gĕth′ər) *n. Informal.* **1.** A meeting. **2.** A casual social gathering.

get-tough (gĕt′tŭf′) *adj. Informal.* Marked by resoluteness, aggressiveness, or austerity: *a get-tough policy on crime.*

Get•tys•burg (gĕt′ĕz-bûrg′). A town of S PA ESE of Chambersburg; site of a major Union victory in the Civil War (Jul. 1–3, 1863) and of Abraham Lincoln's Gettysburg Address (Nov. 19, 1863). Pop. 7,025.

get•up (gĕt′ŭp′) *n.* **1.** *Informal.* An outfit or a costume. **2.** *Print.* Arrangement and production style, as of a magazine.

get-up-and-go (gĕt′ŭp′ən-gō′) *n. Informal.* Initiation of action motivated by energy and ambition.

get-well (gĕt′wĕl′) *adj.* Expressing wishes for one's recovery.

GeV *abbr. Phys.* Giga-electron volts.

gew•gaw (gyōō′gô′, gōō′-) *n.* A decorative trinket; a bauble. [ME *giuegaue.*]

Ge•würz•tra•mi•ner (gə-vōōrts′trə-mē′nər, -wûrts′-) *n.* **1.** A dry white wine produced in the Alsace region of France. **2.** A similar wine produced elsewhere. [Ger. : *Gewürz,* spice (< *würze* < MHGer. *wirze* < OHGer. *wurz,* plant; see **wrād-***) + *Traminer,* grape variety (< *Tramin,* wine-growing district of the S Tyrol).]

gey•ser (gī′zər) *n.* **1.** A natural hot spring that intermittently ejects a column of water and steam into the air. **2.** (gē′zər). *Chiefly British.* A gas-operated hot-water heater. [After Icelandic *Geysir,* name of a hot spring of SW Iceland < *geysa,* to gush < ON. See **gheu-***.]

gey•ser•ite (gī′zə-rīt′) *n.* A white or grayish opaline siliceous deposit formed around natural hot springs.

Ge•zer (gē′zər). An ancient city of Canaan on the coastal Plain of Sharon NW of Jerusalem.

Ge•zi•ra (jə-zîr′ə), **El.** A region of E-central Sudan between the Blue Nile and the White Nile.

Gha•gha•ra (gä′gə-rä′) or **Gha•ghra** (gä′grə, -grä) also **Gog•ra** (gŏg′rə, -rä). A river rising in SW Tibet and flowing c. 965 km (600 mi) to the Ganges R. in N India.

Gha•li (gä-lē′), **Boutros Boutros.** b. 1922. Egyptian politician and diplomat who became secretary-general of the United Nations in 1992.

Gha•na (gä′nə, găn′ə). **1.** A medieval African kingdom in what is now E Senegal, SW Mali, and S Mauritania; probably founded in the 6th cent. A.D. **2.** A country of W Africa on the Gulf of Guinea; gained independence from Great Britain in 1957. Cap. Accra. Pop. 12,205,574. —**Gha′na•ian, Gha′ni•an** *adj. & n.*

gha•ri•al (gŭr′ē-əl) *n.* See **gavial.**

ghast•ly (găst′lē) *adj.* **-li•er, -li•est. 1.** Inspiring shock, revulsion, or horror, as death does; terrifying. **2.** Suggestive of or resembling ghosts. **3.** Extremely unpleasant or bad. **4.** Very serious or great. [Alteration of ME *gastli* < *gasten,* to terrify. See AGHAST.] —**ghast′li•ness** *n.* —**ghast′ly** *adv.*

ghat also **ghaut** (gôt, gät) *n.* A broad flight of steps leading down to the bank of a river in India, used esp. by bathers. [Hindi *ghāt* < Skt. *ghaṭṭaḥ* < *ghaṭṭate,* he shakes, rubs.]

Ghats (gôts). Two mountain ranges of S India separated by the Deccan Plateau into the **Eastern Ghats** along the Bay of Bengal and the **Western Ghats** along the Arabian Sea.

ghee (gē) *n.* A clarified semifluid butter used esp. in Indian cooking. [Hindi *ghī* < Skt. *ghṛtam,* poss. < *gharati,* he sprinkles.]

Ghent (gĕnt) also **Gent** (gĕnt, KHĕnt). A city of W Belgium WNW of Brussels; founded in the 7th cent. Pop. 236,540.

gher•kin (gûr′kĭn) *n.* **1.** A West Indian vine *(Cucumis anguria)* whose immature fruits are used for pickling. **2.** The fruit of this plant. **3.** A small cucumber, esp. one used for pickling. [Du. *gurken,* pl. of *gurk,* cucumber, short for *agurk,* poss. < Pol. *ogorek,* perh. < LGk. *angourion.*]

ghet•to (gĕt′ō) *n., pl.* **-tos** or **-toes. 1.** A section of a city occupied by a minority group who live there esp. because of social, economic, or legal pressure. **2.** A walled quarter in a European city to which Jews were restricted. **3.** Something resembling the restriction or isolation of a ghetto. [Ital.]

ghetto blaster *n. Slang.* A portable stereo.

ghet•to•ize (gĕt′ō-īz′) *tr.v.* **-ized, -iz•ing, -iz•es. 1.** To set apart in or as if in a ghetto; isolate. **2.** To make into or similar to a ghetto. —**ghet′to•i•za′tion** (-ĭzā′shən) *n.*

Ghib•el•line (gĭb′ə-lēn′, -līn′, -lĭn) *n.* A member of the aristocratic political faction who fought during the Middle Ages for German imperial control of Italy, in opposition to the Guelphs and the papacy. [Ital. *Ghibellino* < MHGer. **wībeling,* name of a Hohenstaufen estate.]

Ghi•ber•ti (gē-bĕr′tē), **Lorenzo.** 1378?–1455. Florentine sculptor known for his bronze panels *Gates of Paradise* (1425–52) for the baptistery of Florence Cathedral.

ghil•lie (gĭl′ē) *n.* Var. of **gillie.**

Ghir•lan•da•io also **Ghir•lan•da•jo** (gîr-län-dä′yō), **Domenico.** 1449–94. Florentine painter whose narrative frescoes include *Scenes from the Life of St. Francis* (1483–85).

ghost (gōst) *n.* **1.** The spirit of a dead person, esp. one believed to appear to living persons or to haunt former habitats. **2.** The center of spiritual life; the soul. **3.** A demon or spirit. **4.** A returning or haunting memory or image. **5.a.** A slight or faint trace. **b.** The tiniest bit. **6.** A faint, false image, as: **a.** A secondary image on a television or radar screen caused by

geta
A pair of geta

geyser
Old Faithful,
Yellowstone National Park

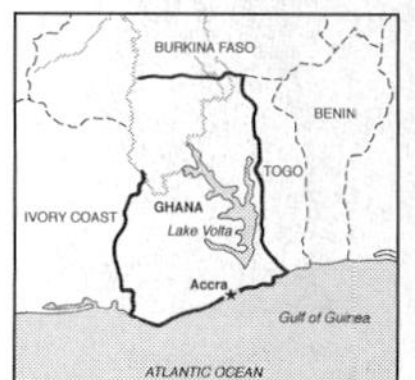

Ghana

reflected waves. **b.** A displaced image in a photograph caused by the optical system of the camera. **7.** *Informal.* A ghostwriter. **8.a.** A nonexistent publication listed in bibliographies. **b.** A fictitious employee or business. — *v.* **ghost•ed, ghost•ing, ghosts.** — *intr.* **1.** *Informal.* To engage in ghostwriting. **2.** To move noiselessly like a ghost. — *tr.* **1.** To haunt. **2.** *Informal.* To ghostwrite. [ME *gost* < OE *gāst*, breath, spirit.] — **ghost′y** *adj.*

ghost dance *n.* Either of two group dances related to a messianic religious movement among late-19th-century Native American peoples of the Southwest and Great Plains.

ghost•ing (gō′stĭng) *n.* The appearance of one or more false images on a television screen.

ghost•ly (gōst′lē) *adj.* **-li•er, -li•est. 1.** Of, relating to, or resembling a ghost or an apparition. **2.** Of or relating to the soul or spirit; spiritual. — **ghost′li•ness** *n.* — **ghost′ly** *adv.*

ghost story *n.* A story having supernatural or frightening elements, esp. a story featuring ghosts or spirits of the dead.

ghost town *n.* A once thriving town, esp. a boomtown of the American West, that has been completely abandoned.

ghost word *n.* A word introduced to a language by a misreading of a manuscript, a typographical error, or a misunderstanding.

ghost•write (gōst′rīt′) *v.* **-wrote** (-rōt′), **-writ•ten** (-rĭt′n), **-writ•ing, -writes.** — *intr.* To work as a ghostwriter. — *tr.* To write (a speech, for example) as a ghostwriter.

ghost•writ•er (gōst′rī′tər) *n.* One who writes for and gives credit of authorship to another.

ghoul (go͞ol) *n.* **1.** One who delights in the revolting, morbid, or loathsome. **2.** A grave robber. **3.** An evil spirit or demon in Muslim folklore believed to plunder graves and feed on corpses. [Ar. *ġūl*, demon < *ġāla*, to seize suddenly.] — **ghoul′ish** *adj.* — **ghoul′ish•ly** *adv.* — **ghoul′ish•ness** *n.*

GHQ *abbr.* General headquarters.

GHz *abbr.* Gigahertz.

gi *abbr.* Gill (liquid measure).

GI[1] (jē′ī′) *n.*, *pl.* **GIs** or **GI's.** An enlisted person in or a veteran of any of the U.S. armed forces, esp. the army. — *adj.* **1.** Relating to or characteristic of an enlisted person. **2.** Conforming to or in accordance with U.S. military regulations or procedures. **3.** Issued by a U.S. military supply department. [< abbreviation of *galvanized iron* (applied to trash cans, etc.) later reinterpreted as *government issue.*]

GI[2] *abbr.* **1.** Galvanized iron. **2.** Gastrointestinal. **3.** General issue. **4.** Also **G.I.** Government Issue.

Gia•co•met•ti (jä-kə-mĕt′ē, -kô-mĕt′tē), **Alberto.** 1901–66. Swiss sculptor, painter, and exponent of surrealism known for elongated sculptures, such as *Walking Man* (1960).

gi•ant (jī′ənt) *n.* **1.a.** A person or thing of great size. **b.** A person of extraordinary power or importance. **2.a.** *Gk. Myth.* One of a race of humanlike beings of enormous size, destroyed in battle with the Olympians. **b.** A being in folklore or myth similar to one of these beings. — *adj.* Marked by great size, magnitude, or power. [ME < OFr. *geant, jaiant* < VLat. **gagās, gagant-* < Lat. *gigās* < Gk. *gigas.*]

gi•ant•ess (jī′ən-tĭs) *n.* A female giant.

gi•ant•ism (jī′ən-tĭz′əm) *n.* **1.** The quality or condition of being a giant. **2.** See **gigantism** 2.

giant panda *n.* See **panda** 1.

Gi•ant's Causeway (jī′ənts). A basaltic formation on the N coast of Northern Ireland consisting of thousands of columns forming three natural platforms.

giant schnauzer *n.* Any of a breed of dog developed in Germany, similar to but larger than the standard schnauzer.

giant sequoia *n.* A very tall coniferous evergreen tree *(Sequoiadendron giganteum)* of California having a massive trunk and reddish wood.

giant slalom *n. Sports.* A downhill skiing race in which participants must pass between pairs of gates set along a course that is larger and often steeper than a slalom course.

giant star *n.* Any of a class of highly luminous, exceptionally massive stars.

giaour (jour) *n. Islam.* A nonbeliever; an infidel. [Alteration of obsolete *gower, gour* < Turk. *gâvur* < Pers. *gabr*, infidel, Zoroastrian < Ar. *kāfir*, infidel < *kafara*, not to believe.]

gi•ar•di•a•sis (jē′är-dī′ə-sĭs) *n.* Intestinal infection with the protozoan *Giardia lamblia.* [After Alfred Mathieus *Girard* (1846–1908), French zoologist.]

gib[1] (gĭb) *n.* A plain or notched, often wedge-shaped piece of wood or metal designed to hold parts of a machine or structure in place or provide a bearing surface, usu. adjusted by a screw or key. — *tr.v.* **gibbed, gib•bing, gibs.** To fasten with a gib. [?]

gib[2] (gĭb) *n.* A male cat, esp. a castrated one. [ME, prob. short for the personal name *Gilbert.*]

Gib. *abbr.* Gibraltar.

gib•ber (jĭb′ər) *intr.v.* **-bered, -ber•ing, -bers.** To prattle and chatter unintelligibly. — *n.* Unintelligible or foolish talk. [Prob. back-formation < GIBBERISH.]

gib•ber•el•lic acid (jĭb′ə-rĕl′ĭk) *n.* A hormone, $C_{19}H_{22}O_6$, obtained from the fungus *Gibberella fujikuroi* and used to promote plant growth. [< GIBBERELLIN.]

gibbon
Lar gibbon
Hylobates lar

Gibson girl
Created by
Charles Dana Gibson

gib•ber•el•lin (jĭb′ə-rĕl′ĭn) *n.* Any of several plant hormones, such as gibberellic acid, used to promote stem elongation. [< NLat. *Gibberella (fujikoroi)*, fungus (first source of gibberellin) < Lat. *gibberella*, fem. dim. of *gibber*, hump.]

gib•ber•ish (jĭb′ər-ĭsh) *n.* **1.** Unintelligible or nonsensical talk or writing. **2.a.** Highly technical or esoteric language. **b.** Unnecessarily pretentious or vague language. [Prob. *gibber-*, of imit. orig. + -ISH.]

gib•bet (jĭb′ĭt) *n.* **1.** A device used for hanging a person until dead; a gallows. **2.** An upright post with a crosspiece, forming a T-shaped structure from which executed criminals were formerly hung for public viewing. — *tr.v.* **-bet•ed, -bet•ing, -bets** or **-bet•ted, -bet•ting, -bets. 1.** To execute by hanging on a gibbet. **2.a.** To hang on a gibbet for public viewing. **b.** To expose to infamy or public ridicule. [ME *gibet* < OFr., dim. of *gibe*, staff, prob. < Frankish **gibb*, forked stick.]

gib•bon (gĭb′ən) *n.* Any of several small slender arboreal apes of the genus *Hylobates* of southeast Asia. [Fr.]

Gib•bon (gĭb′ən), **Edward.** 1737–94. British historian who wrote *The History of the Decline and Fall of the Roman Empire* (1776–88).

gib•bos•i•ty (gĭ-bŏs′ĭ-tē) *n.*, *pl.* **-ties. 1.** The condition of being gibbous. **2.** A rounded hump or protuberance.

gib•bous (gĭb′əs) *adj.* **1.a.** Characterized by convexity; protuberant. **b.** More than half but less than fully illuminated. Used of the moon or a planet. **2.** Having a hump; humpbacked. [ME, bulging < LLat. *gibbōsus*, hunch-backed < Lat. *gibbus*, hump.] — **gib′bous•ly** *adv.* — **gib′bous•ness** *n.*

Gibbs (gĭbz), **Josiah Willard.** 1839–1903. Amer. mathematician and physicist who formulated the theoretical foundation of physical chemistry and developed vector analysis.

Gibbs free energy *n.* See **free energy** 2.

gibe also **jibe** (jīb) — *v.* **gibed, gib•ing, gibes** also **jibed, jib•ing, jibes.** — *intr.* To make taunting, heckling, or jeering remarks. See Syns at **ridicule.** — *tr.* To deride with gibes. — *n.* A derisive remark. [Poss. < obsolete Fr. *giber*, to handle roughly, play < OFr.] — **gib′er** *n.* — **gib′ing•ly** *adv.*

Gib•e•on (gĭb′ē-ən). An ancient village of Palestine near Jerusalem. — **Gib′e•o•nite′** *n.*

gib•lets (jĭb′lĭts) *pl.n.* The edible heart, liver, or gizzard of a fowl. [< ME *gibelet* < OFr., game stew, perh. alteration of **giberet* < *gibier*, game.]

Gi•bral•tar[1] (jə-brôl′tər). A British colony at the NW end of the **Rock of Gibraltar,** a peninsula on the S-central coast of Spain in the **Strait of Gibraltar,** connecting the Mediterranean and the Atlantic between Spain and N Africa. Gibraltar was captured by Arabs in 711 and passed to the Spanish in 1462; Great Britain took control in 1704. Pop. 29,648.

Gi•bral•tar[2] (jĭ-brôl′tər) *n.* An invincible stronghold.

Gibraltar fever *n.* See **brucellosis** 1.

Gib•ran (jə-brän′), **(Gibran) Kahlil.** 1883–1931. Syrian-born Amer. mystic poet and painter best known for his prose poem *The Prophet* (1923).

Gib•son (gĭb′sən) *n.* A dry martini garnished with a small pickled onion. [< the name *Gibson.*]

Gibson, Althea. b. 1927. Amer. tennis player who was the first Black American to play at Wimbledon (1951), where she won singles and doubles titles in 1957 and 1958.

Gibson Desert. A desert of W-central Australia bounded by the Great Sandy Desert and Great Victoria Desert.

Gibson girl *n.* The American young woman of the 1890's in idealized sketches by the American illustrator Charles Dana Gibson (1867–1944). — *adj.* Of a clothing style marked by a high neck, puffed sleeves, and a tight waistline.

gid (gĭd) *n.* A disease of herbivores, esp. sheep, caused by larvae of the tapeworm *Multiceps multiceps* in the brain and marked by a staggering gait. [Back-formation < GIDDY.]

gid•dap (gĭ-dăp′, -dŭp′) also **gid•dy•ap** (gĭd′ē-ăp′, -ŭp′) or **gid•dy•up** (-ŭp′) *interj.* Used to command a horse to go ahead or go at a faster pace. [Alteration of *get up.*]

gid•dy (gĭd′ē) *adj.* **-di•er, -di•est. 1.a.** Having a reeling lightheaded sensation; dizzy. **b.** Causing or capable of causing dizziness: *a giddy height.* **2.** Frivolous and lighthearted; flighty. — *intr. & tr.v.* **-died, -dy•ing, -dies.** To become or make giddy. [ME *gidi*, crazy < OE *gidig.* See **gheu(ə)-*.**] — **gid′di•ly** *adv.* — **gid′di•ness** *n.*

Gide (zhēd), **André.** 1869–1951. French writer who won the 1947 Nobel Prize for literature.

Gid•e•on[1] (gĭd′ē-ən). A Hebrew judge who opposed the Baal cult and defeated the Midianites.

Gid•e•on[2] (gĭd′ē-ən) *n.* A member of an interdenominational and international society known for placing Bibles in hotel rooms. [< *Gideons International*, after GIDEON[1].]

gie (gē) *v. Scots.* Var. of **give.**

Giel•gud (gĭl′go͝od′, gēl′-), Sir **(Arthur) John.** b. 1904. British actor and director particularly noted for his Shakespearean productions.

gift (gĭft) *n.* **1.** Something bestowed voluntarily and without compensation. **2.** The act, right, or power of giving. **3.** A talent, an endowment, an aptitude, or a bent. — *tr.v.* **gift•ed, gift•ing, gifts. 1.** *Usage Problem.* To present with as a gift. **2.** To endow with. [ME < ON. See **ghabh-*.**]

Usage Note: The verbal use of *gift* in Modern English is irredeemably tainted (as is its derivative *giftable*) by its association with the language of advertising and publicity. In an earlier survey the usage was rejected by a large majority of the Usage Panel. Where clarity is required, substitutes such as *give as a gift, bestow,* or *donate* are recommended. • The increasing currency of the phrase *free gift* is indicative mainly of the degree to which the word *gift* itself has been expropriated by advertisers to refer to merchandise offerings to which an obligation is attached. It is perhaps this use of *gift,* rather than *free gift,* that is most objectionable.

gift•a•ble (gĭf′tə-bəl) *Usage Problem. adj.* Appropriate for a gift. See Usage Note at **gift.** — **gift′a•ble** *n.*

gift certificate *n.* A certificate usu. presented as a gift that entitles the recipient to merchandise of an indicated cash value.

gift•ed (gĭf′tĭd) *adj.* **1.** Endowed with great natural ability, intelligence or talent: *a gifted pianist.* **2.** Revealing special talent. — **gift′ed•ly** *adv.* — **gift′ed•ness** *n.*

gift of tongues *n.* An ecstatic utterance that is unintelligible to hearers, esp. considered as a charismatic gift in certain Christian congregations. [< Acts 2:4.]

gift•ware (gĭft′wâr′) *n.* Merchandise appropriate for gifts.

gift-wrap (gĭft′răp′) *tr.v.* **-wrapped, -wrap•ping, -wraps.** To wrap (a gift) in a decorative manner. — *n.* Gift-wrapping.

gift-wrap•ping (gĭft′răp′ĭng) *n.* Decorative wrapping paper.

Gi•fu (gē′fo͞o′). A city of central Honshu, Japan, NNW of Nagoya; rebuilt after an earthquake in 1891. Pop. 411,740.

gig¹ (gĭg) *n.* **1.** A light two-wheeled carriage drawn by one horse. **2.** *Naut.* **a.** A long light ship's boat, usu. reserved for the ship's captain. **b.** A fast light rowboat. **3.a.** An object that whirls. **b.** *Games.* A three-digit selection in a numbers game. — *intr.v.* **gigged, gig•ging, gigs.** To ride in a gig. [Perh. < obsolete *gig,* spinning top < ME *gyg-,* poss. of Scand. orig.]

gig² (gĭg) *n.* **1.** An arrangement of barbless hooks that is dragged through a school of fish to hook them in their bodies. **2.** A pronged spear for fishing or catching frogs. — *v.* **gigged, gig•ging, gigs.** — *tr.* To fish for or catch with a gig. — *intr.* To catch a fish or frog with a gig. [Short for FISHGIG.]

gig³ (gĭg) *Slang.* — *n.* A demerit given in the military. — *tr.v.* **gigged, gig•ging, gigs.** To give a military demerit to. [?]

gig⁴ (gĭg) *Slang.* — *n.* A job, esp. a booking for musicians. — *intr.v.* **gigged, gig•ging, gigs.** To work as a musician. [?]

giga– *pref.* One billion (10^9): *gigahertz.* [< Gk. *gigas,* giant.]

gig•a•bit (jĭg′ə-bĭt′, gĭg′-) *n. Comp. Sci.* A unit of information equal to one billion (10^9) bits.

gig•a•byte (jĭg′ə-bīt′, gĭg′-) *n. Comp. Sci.* A unit of information equal to one billion (10^9) bytes.

gig•a•hertz (jĭg′ə-hûrtz′, gĭg′-) *n.* A unit of frequency equal to one billion (10^9) hertz.

gi•gan•tesque (jī′găn-tĕsk′) *adj.* Of enormous size or magnitude; huge. [Fr. < Ital. *gigantesco* < *gigante,* giant < Lat. *gigās, gigant-.* See GIANT.]

gi•gan•tic (jī-găn′tĭk) *adj.* **1.** Relating to or suggestive of a giant. **2.a.** Exceedingly large of its kind: *a gigantic toadstool.* **b.** Very large or extensive: *a gigantic corporation.* [< Lat. *giga, gigant-,* giant; see GIANT, or < Gk. *gigantikos* (< *gigas, gigant-,* giant).] — **gi•gan′ti•cal•ly** *adv.*

gi•gan•tism (jī-găn′tĭz′əm) *n.* **1.** The quality or state of being gigantic; abnormally large size. **2.** Excessive growth of the body or any of its parts.

gig•a•watt (jĭg′ə-wŏt′, gĭg′-) *n.* One billion (10^9) watts.

gig•gle (gĭg′əl) *v.* **-gled, -gling, -gles.** — *intr.* To laugh with repeated short spasmodic sounds. — *tr.* To utter while giggling. — *n.* A short spasmodic laugh. [Of imit. orig.] — **gig′gler** *n.* — **gig′gling•ly** *adv.* — **gig′gly** *adj.*

GIGO (gī′gō, gē′-) *n. Comp. Sci.* An informal rule holding that the integrity of output is dependent on the integrity of input. [*g(arbage) i(n) g(arbage) o(ut).*]

gig•o•lo (jĭg′ə-lō′, zhĭg′-) *n., pl.* **-los. 1.** A man who has a continuing sexual relationship with and receives financial support from a woman. **2.** A man hired as a woman's escort or dancing partner. [Fr., perh. < *gigolette,* dancing girl, prostitute < *giguer,* to dance < *gigue,* fiddle < OFr. See GIGOT.]

gig•ot (jĭg′ət, zhē-gō′) *n.* **1.** A leg of mutton, lamb, or veal for cooking. **2.** A leg-of-mutton sleeve. [Fr. < OFr., dim. of *gigue,* fiddle < MHGer. *gīge* < OHGer. *gīga.*]

gigue (zhēg) *n.* See **jig** 1. [Fr., prob. < JIG.]

Gi•jón (hē-hōn′). A city of NW Spain on the Bay of Biscay W of Santander; of pre-Roman origin. Pop. 262,395.

Gi•ku•yu (gĭ-ko͞o′yo͞o) *n.* Var. of **Kikuyu.**

Gi•la monster (hē′lə) *n.* A black and orange venomous lizard *(Heloderma suspectum)* of the southwest United States and western Mexico. [After the GILA R.]

Gila River. A river rising in the mountains of W NM and flowing c. 1,014 km (630 mi) across S AZ to the Colorado R.

gil•bert (gĭl′bərt) *n.* The centimeter-gram-second electromagnetic unit of magnetomotive force, equal to $10/4\pi$ ampere-turn. [After William *Gilbert* (1544–1603), English physician.]

Gil•bert (gĭl′bərt), **Cass.** 1859–1934. Amer. architect whose design of the 60-story Woolworth Building in New York City (1913) greatly influenced the development of the skyscraper.

Gilbert, Sir **Humphrey.** 1539?–1583. English navigator who established in Newfoundland (1583) the first English colony in North America.

Gilbert, Sir **William Schwenck.** 1836–1911. British playwright and lyricist known for his comic operas, including *H.M.S. Pinafore* (1878), written with composer Sir Arthur Sullivan.

Gilbert Islands. A group of islands of W Kiribati in the central Pacific; made a British protectorate in 1892 and later became part of the **Gilbert and Ellice Islands Colony** (1915–76). Full independence was achieved in 1979.

gild¹ (gĭld) *tr.v.* **gild•ed** or **gilt** (gĭlt), **gild•ing, gilds. 1.** To cover with or as if with a thin layer of gold. **2.** To give an often deceptively attractive or improved appearance to. **3.** *Archaic.* To smear with blood. — ***idiom.* gild the lily. 1.** To adorn unnecessarily something already beautiful. **2.** To make superfluous additions to what is already complete. [ME *gilden* < OE *gyldan.* See **ghel-²*.**] — **gild′er** *n.*

gild² (gĭld) *n.* Var. of **guild.**

gild•ing (gĭl′dĭng) *n.* **1.** The art or process of applying gilt to a surface. **2.** Gold leaf or a paint containing or simulating gold. **3.** Something used to give a superficially attractive appearance.

Gil•e•ad (gĭl′ē-əd). A mountainous region of ancient Palestine E of the Jordan R. in what is now NW Jordan.

Gil•ga•mesh (gĭl′gə-mĕsh′) *n. Myth.* The semidivine king of Erech, a city of southern Babylonia, and hero of an epic that tells of a flood covering the earth.

gill¹ (gĭl) *n.* **1.** *Zool.* The respiratory organ of most aquatic animals that breathe water to obtain oxygen. **2.a.** The wattle of a bird. Often used in the plural. **b. gills.** *Informal.* The area around the chin and neck. **3.** *Bot.* One of the thin plates on the underside of the cap of a mushroom or similar fungus. — *v.* **gilled, gill•ing, gills.** — *tr.* **1.** To catch (fish) in a gill net. **2.** To gut or clean (fish). — *intr.* To become entangled in a gill net. Used of fish. — ***idiom.* to the gills.** *Informal.* As full as possible; completely. [ME *gile,* of Scand. orig.] — **gilled** *adj.*

gill² (jĭl) *n.* **1.** A unit of volume or capacity in the U.S. Customary System, used in liquid measure, equal to ¼ of a pint or four ounces (118 milliliters). See table at **measurement. 2.** A unit of volume or capacity, used in dry and liquid measure, equal to ¼ of a British Imperial pint (142 milliliters). [ME *gille* < OFr., wine measure < LLat. *gillō,* vessel for cooling liquids.]

gill³ (gĭl) *n. Chiefly British.* **1.** A ravine. **2.** A narrow stream. [ME *gille* < ON *gil.*]

gill⁴ also **jill** or **Gill** (jĭl) *n.* A girl or a sweetheart. Used esp. with *Jack.* [ME *gille* < *Gille,* a woman's name.]

gill arch (gĭl) *n.* **1.** One of several bony or cartilaginous arches on either side of the pharynx that support the gills in fish and amphibians. **2.** *Embryol.* One of several corresponding arches in the embryo of a higher vertebrate.

gill cleft (gĭl) *n.* See **gill slit** 1.

Gilles de la Tour•ette syndrome (zhēl də lä to͞o-rĕt′) *n.* See **Tourette's syndrome.**

Gil•les•pie (gə-lĕs′pē), **John Birks ("Dizzy").** 1917–93. Amer. jazz musician and composer.

gill fungus (gĭl) *n.* A fleshy fungus having a cap with gills on the underside.

gil•lie also **ghil•lie** (gĭl′ē) *n., pl.* **-lies. 1.** *Scots.* A professional fishing and hunting guide. **2.** A low-cut sports shoe with fringed laces. [Sc.Gael. *gille,* boy < OIr. *gilla* < *gildae.*]

gill•net (gĭl′nĕt′) *tr.v.* **-net•ted, -net•ting, -nets.** To catch (fish) by means of a gill net.

gill net (gĭl) *n.* A fishing net set vertically in the water so that fish swimming into it are entangled by the gills in its mesh.

gill-net•ter (gĭl′nĕt′ər) *n.* **1.** One who uses a gill net to catch fish. **2.** *Naut.* A boat used in fishing with gill nets.

gill slit (gĭl) *n.* **1.** One of several narrow external openings connecting with the pharynx, characteristic of sharks, through which water passes to the exterior, thereby bathing the gills. **2.** *Embryol.* One of several rudimentary invaginations in the surface of the embryo, corresponding to the functional gill slits of aquatic species.

gil•ly•flow•er (gĭl′ē-flou′ər) *n.* **1.** The carnation or a similar plant of the genus *Dianthus.* **2.** Any of several plants, such as the wallflower, that have fragrant flowers. [Alteration (influenced by FLOWER) of ME *gilofre* < OFr. *gilofre, girofle,* clove < LLat. *gariofilum* < Gk. *karuophullon* : *karuon,* nut; see **kar-*** + *phullon,* leaf; see **bhel-³*.**]

Gil•man (gĭl′mən), **Charlotte Anna Perkins.** 1860–1935. Amer. writer whose works include *Women and Economics* (1898), a call for the economic independence of women.

Gil•mer (gĭl′mər), **Elizabeth Meriwether.** Dorothy Dix. 1870–1951. Amer. journalist noted for her syndicated advice column for the lovelorn (1896–1949).

Gil•roy (gĭl′roi′). A city of W CA SE of San Jose in the Santa Clara Valley. Pop. 31,487.

Gil•son•ite (gĭl′sə-nīt′). A trademark for a natural black bitumen used in road construction and waterproof coatings.

gilt¹ (gĭlt) *v.* A p.t. and p.part. of **gild¹.** — *adj.* **1.** Covered with gold or gilt. **2.** Resembling gold, as in color or luster. — *n.* **1.** A thin layer of gold or something simulating gold applied

Gila monster
Heloderma suspectum

ă pat	oi boy
ā pay	ou out
âr care	o͝o took
ä father	o͞o boot
ĕ pet	ŭ cut
ē be	ûr urge
ĭ pit	th thin
ī pie	*th* this
îr pier	hw which
ŏ pot	zh vision
ō toe	ə about, item
ô paw	

Stress marks:
′ (primary);
′ (secondary), as in
dictionary (dĭk′shə-nĕr′ē)

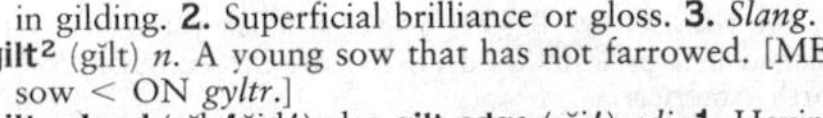

in gilding. **2.** Superficial brilliance or gloss. **3.** *Slang.* Money.

gilt[2] (gĭlt) *n.* A young sow that has not farrowed. [ME, young sow < ON *gyltr.*]

gilt-edged (gĭlt′ĕjd′) also **gilt-edge** (-ĕj′) *adj.* **1.** Having gilded edges. **2.** Of the highest quality or value. **3.** Very wealthy.

gim•bal (gĭm′bəl, jĭm′-) *n.* A device consisting of two rings mounted on axes at right angles to each other so that an object will remain suspended in a horizontal plane between them regardless of any motion of its support. Often used in the plural. —*tr.v.* **-baled, -bal•ing, -bals** or **-balled, -bal•ling, -bals.** To supply with or support on gimbals. [Alteration of obsolete *gemel,* double ring. See GIMMAL.]

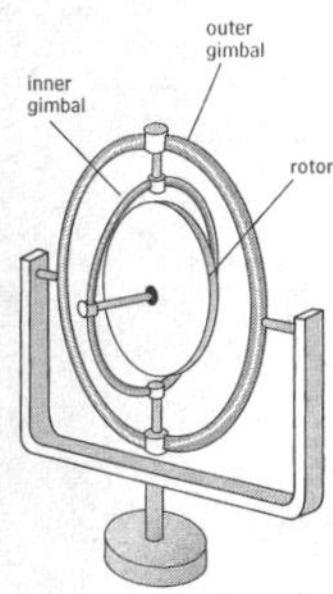

gimbal
Two-degree-of-freedom gyroscope

gim•crack (jĭm′krăk′) *n.* A cheap, showy, useless object. —*adj.* Cheap and tasteless; gaudy. [Poss. alteration of ME *gibecrake,* small ornament.] —**gim′crack′er•y** *n.*

gim•el (gĭm′əl) *n.* The third letter of the Hebrew alphabet. [Heb. *gīmel.*]

gim•let (gĭm′lĭt) *n.* **1.** A small hand tool having a spiraled shank, a screw tip, and a cross handle and used for boring holes. **2.** A cocktail made with vodka or gin, sweetened lime juice, and sometimes effervescent water. —*tr.v.* **-let•ed, -let•ing, -lets.** To penetrate with or as if with a gimlet. —*adj.* Having a penetrating or piercing quality. [ME < AN *guimbelet,* perh. < MDu. *wimmelkijn,* dim. of *wimmel,* auger.]

gim•let-eyed (gĭm′lĭt-īd′) *adj.* Having keen vision.

gim•mal (gĭm′əl, jĭm′-) *n.* **1.** A ring made of two or more interlocked rings. **2.** Any of various linkages allowing one part to rotate within another rotating part, used esp. in clockworks. [Alteration of obsolete *gemel* < ME, sing. of *gemeles,* twins < OFr. < Lat. *gemellus,* dim. of *geminus,* twin.]

gim•mick (gĭm′ĭk) *n.* **1.a.** A device used to cheat, deceive, or trick, esp. a mechanism to control a gambling apparatus. **b.** An innovative or unusual mechanical contrivance; a gadget. **2.a.** An innovative stratagem or scheme employed esp. to promote a project. **b.** A significant feature that is obscured, misrepresented, or not readily evident; a catch. **3.** A small object whose name escapes one. —*tr.v.* **-micked, -mick•ing, -micks. 1.** To add gimmicks to; clutter with gadgets or attention-getting details. Often used with *up.* **2.** To change or affect by means of a gimmick. [?] —**gim′mick•y** *adj.*

gim•mick•ry (gĭm′ĭk-rē) *n., pl.* **-ries. 1.** An array or abundance of gimmicks. **2.** The use of gimmicks.

gimp[1] (gĭmp) *n.* A narrow flat braid or rounded cord of fabric used for trimming. [Perh. < Fr. *guimpe.* See GUIMPE.]

gimp[2] (gĭmp) *Slang.* —*n.* **1.** A limp or a limping gait. **2.** A person who limps. —*intr.v.* **gimped, gimp•ing, gimps.** To walk with a limp. [?] —**gimp′y** *adj.*

gimp[3] (gĭmp) *n.* Spirit; pep. [?]

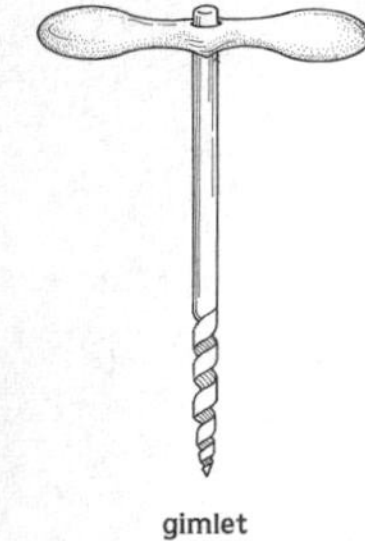
gimlet

gin[1] (jĭn) *n.* A strong colorless alcoholic beverage made by distilling grain spirits and adding juniper berries or aromatics as flavoring. [Alteration of *geneva* < Du. *jenever,* ult. < Lat. *iūniperus.*] —**gin′ny** *adj.*

gin[2] (jĭn) *n.* **1.** Any of several machines or devices, esp.: **a.** A machine for hoisting or moving heavy objects. **b.** A pile driver. **c.** A snare or trap for game. **d.** A pump operated by a windmill. **2.** A cotton gin. —*tr.v.* **ginned, gin•ning, gins. 1.** To remove the seeds from (cotton) with a cotton gin. **2.** To trap in a gin. [ME < OFr., short for *engin,* skill. See ENGINE.]

gin[3] (jĭn) *n. Games.* Gin rummy.

gin•ger (jĭn′jər) *n.* **1.** A plant *(Zingiber officinale)* of tropical southeast Asia having yellowish-green flowers and a pungent aromatic rhizome. **2.** The rhizome of this plant, often powdered and used as a spice. **3.a.** Any of several related plants. **b.** Wild ginger. **4.** *Color.* A strong brown. **5.** *Informal.* Spirit and liveliness; vigor. —*tr.v.* **-gered, -ger•ing, -gers. 1.** To spice with ginger. **2.** *Informal.* To make lively. [ME *gingivere* < OE *gingifer* and < OFr. *gingivre,* both < Med.Lat. *gingiber* < Lat. *zingiberi* < Gk. *zingiberis,* of Middle Indic orig. (akin to Pali *singiveram*) < Dravidian : akin to Tamil *iñci,* ginger (of SE Asian orig.) + Tamil *vēr,* root.] —**gin′ger•y** *adj.*

ginger ale *n.* An effervescent sweetened soft drink flavored with ginger.

ginger beer *n.* A nonalcoholic drink similar to ginger ale but flavored with fermented ginger.

gin•ger•bread (jĭn′jər-brĕd′) *n.* **1.a.** A molasses cake flavored with ginger. **b.** A molasses and ginger cookie cut in various shapes and sometimes elaborately decorated. **2.a.** Elaborate ornamentation. **b.** Superfluous or tasteless embellishment, esp. in architecture. [ME *gingebred,* a stiff pudding, preserved ginger, alteration of OFr. *gingembrat,* ult. < *gingiber,* ginger. See GINGER.] —**gin′ger•bread′, gin′ger•bread′y** *adj.*

gingerbread palm *n.* See **doom palm.**

gin•ger•ly (jĭn′jər-lē) *adv.* With great care or delicacy; cautiously. —*adj.* Cautious; careful. [Poss. alteration of obsolete Fr. *gensor,* delicate < OFr., comp. of *gent,* gentle. See GENT[1].] —**gin′ger•li•ness** *n.*

gin•ger•root (jĭn′jər-ro͞ot′, -ro͝ot′) *n.* See **ginger** 2.

gin•ger•snap (jĭn′jər-snăp′) *n.* A flat brittle cookie spiced with ginger and sweetened with molasses.

ging•ham (gĭng′əm) *n.* A yarn-dyed cotton fabric woven in stripes, checks, plaids, or solid colors. [Du. *ginggang* < Malay < *genggang,* at intervals.]

ginkgo
Ginkgo biloba

gin•gi•va (jĭn′jə-və, jĭn-jī′-) *n., pl.* **-vae** (-vē′). See **gum**[2]. [Lat. *gingīva.*]

gin•gi•val (jĭn′jə-vəl, jĭn-jī′-) *adj.* **1.** Of or relating to the gums. **2.** *Ling.* Alveolar.

gin•gi•vec•to•my (jĭn′jə-vĕk′tə-mē) *n., pl.* **-mies.** Surgical removal of gum tissue.

gin•gi•vi•tis (jĭn′jə-vī′tĭs) *n.* Inflammation of the gums.

gink (gĭnk) *n. Slang.* A man, esp. one regarded as foolish or contemptible. [?]

gink•go also **ging•ko** (gĭng′kō) *n., pl.* **-goes** also **-koes.** A deciduous dioecious tree *(Ginkgo biloba)* native to China and having fan-shaped leaves and fleshy yellow seeds. [J. *ginkyō.*]

gin mill *n. Slang.* A bar or saloon.

gin rummy *n. Games.* A variety of rummy for two or more persons in which a player may win by matching all his or her cards or may end the game by melding with unmatched cards that add up to ten points or fewer.

Gins•berg (gĭnz′bərg), **Allen.** b. 1926. Amer. poet of the beat generation whose works include *Howl* (1956).

gin•seng (jĭn′sĕng′) *n.* **1.** Any of several plants of the genus *Panax,* esp. *P. pseudoginseng* or *P. quinquefolius,* having small greenish flowers and forked roots believed to have medicinal properties. **2.** The roots of these plants. [Chin. (Mandarin) *rén shēn* : *rén,* man + *shēn,* ginseng.]

Gin•za (gĭn′zə). A shopping and entertainment district of Tokyo, Japan.

gin•zo (gĭn′zō) *n., pl.* **-zoes.** *Offensive Slang.* Used as a disparaging term for a person of Italian ancestry. [?]

Gior•gio•ne (jôr-jō′nē, -nĕ). 1478?–1510. Italian painter and early master of the Venetian school whose ascribed works include *The Tempest* (c. 1505).

Giot•to (jô′tō, jŏt′ō). 1267?–1337. Florentine painter, architect, and sculptor renowned for his frescoes.

gip (jĭp) *v. & n. Slang.* Var. of **gyp.**

Gip•sy (jĭp′sē) *n.* Var. of **Gypsy.**

gi•raffe (jə-răf′) *n., pl.* **-raffes** or **giraffe.** An African ruminant *(Giraffa camelopardalis)* having a very long neck and legs, short horns, and a tan coat with orange-brown to black blotches, often reaching a height of 5 meters (16½ feet). [Fr. *girafe* < Ital. *giraffa* < Ar. dial. *zirāfah,* prob. of African orig.] —**gi•raff′ish** *adj.*

gir•an•dole (jĭr′ən-dōl′) *n.* **1.** A composition or structure in radiating form or arrangement, such as a rotating display of fireworks. **2.** An ornamental branched candleholder, sometimes backed by a mirror. [Fr. < Ital. *girandola* < *girare,* to turn < LLat. *gȳrāre.* See GYRATE.]

Gi•rard (jə-rärd′), **Stephen.** 1750–1831. French-born Amer. philanthropist who helped finance the War of 1812.

gir•a•sol (jĭr′ə-sôl′, -sōl′, -sŏl′) *n.* **1.** Also **gir•o•sol.** See **fire opal. 2.** Also **gir•a•sole.** See **Jerusalem artichoke.** [Ital. *girasole,* sunflower, opal : *girare,* to turn (< LLat. *gȳrāre;* see GYRATE) + *sole,* sun (< Lat. *sōl;* see **sāwel-***).]

Gi•rau•doux (zhē-rō-do͞o′), **(Hippolyte) Jean.** 1882–1944. French writer primarily known for his dramas, such as *Electra* (1937), that are based on Greek mythology or biblical stories.

gird[1] (gûrd) *v.* **gird•ed** or **girt** (gûrt), **gird•ing, girds.** —*tr.* **1.a.** To encircle with a belt or band. **b.** To fasten or secure (clothing, for example) with a belt or band. **c.** To surround. **2.** To equip or endow. **3.** To prepare (oneself) for action. —*intr.* To prepare for action. —*idiom.* **gird (up) (one's) loins.** To summon up one's inner resources in preparation for action. [ME *girden* < OE *gyrdan.* See **gher-**[1]***.]

gird[2] (gûrd) *intr. & tr.v.* **gird•ed, gird•ing, girds.** To jeer or jeer at. —*n.* A sarcastic remark. [ME *girden,* to strike.]

gird•er (gûr′dər) *n.* A horizontal beam, as of steel or wood, used as a main support for a building or bridge.

gir•dle (gûr′dl) *n.* **1.a.** A belt or sash worn around the waist. **b.** Something that encircles like a belt. **c.** A woman's elasticized flexible undergarment worn over the waist and hips. **2.** A band made around the trunk of a tree by the removal of a strip of bark. **3.** The edge of a cut gem held by the setting. **4.** *Anat.* The pelvic or pectoral girdle. —*tr.v.* **-dled, -dling, -dles. 1.** To encircle with or as if with a belt. **2.** To circle around. **3.** To remove a band of bark and cambium from the circumference of (a tree), usu. in order to kill it. [ME *girdel* < OE *gyrdel.* See **gher-**[1]***.]

gird•ler (gûrd′lər) *n.* **1.** One that makes girdles. **2.** Any of several insects that chew bands around twigs or stems.

girl (gûrl) *n.* **1.** A female child. **2.** An immature or inexperienced woman, esp. a young woman. **3.** A daughter. **4.** *Informal.* A grown woman: *a night out with the girls.* **5.** A female who comes from or belongs to a particular place: *a city girl.* **6.** *Offensive.* A female servant, such as a maid. **7.** A female sweetheart. [ME *girle,* child, girl.] —**girl′hood′** *n.*

girl Friday *n. Informal.* An efficient and faithful woman aide or employee. [GIRL + (MAN) FRIDAY.]

girl•friend also **girl friend** (gûrl′frĕnd′) *n.* **1.** A favored female companion or sweetheart. **2.** A female friend.

Girl Guide (gûrl) *n.* A member of the Girl Guides, a British organization of young women and girls founded in 1910.

girl•ie also **girl•y** (gûr′lē) *adj. Informal.* Featuring minimally clothed or naked women typically in pornographic contexts.

girl•ish (gûr′lĭsh) *adj.* Characteristic of or befitting a girl: *girlish charm.* —**girl′ish•ly** *adv.* —**girl′ish•ness** *n.*

Girl Scout *n.* A member of the Girl Scouts, an organization of young women and girls, founded in the United States in 1912 on the plan of the Girl Guides.

girn (gûrn) *intr.v.* **girned, girn•ing, girns.** *Scots.* **1.** To complain in a whining voice. **2.** To contort one's face, grimace. [ME *girnen*, var. of *grinnen, grennan.* See GRIN.] —**girn** *n.*

Gi•ronde[1] (jə-rŏnd′, zhē-rôNd′). An estuary of SW France formed by the Garonne and Dordogne rivers and opening into the Bay of Biscay.

Gi•ronde[2] (jə-rŏnd′, zhĭ-) *n.* A moderate republican political party of Revolutionary France (1791–1793). [After *Gironde*, a department of SW France.] —**Gi•rond′ist** *n.*

gir•o•sol (jĭr′ə-sôl′, -sōl′, -sŏl′) *n.* Var. of **girasol** 1.

girt[1] (gûrt) *v.* **girt•ed, girt•ing, girts.** —*tr.* **1.** To gird. **2.** To secure with a girth. **3.** To measure the girth of. —*intr.* To measure in girth. [Var. of GIRD[1].]

girt[2] (gûrt) *v.* A p.t. and p.part. of **gird**[1].

girth (gûrth) *n.* **1.** The distance around something; the circumference. **2.** Size; bulk. **3.** A strap around an animal's body that secures a load or saddle on its back; a cinch. —*tr.v.* **girthed, girth•ing, girths. 1.** To measure the circumference of. **2.** To encircle. **3.** To secure with a girth. [ME *gerth*, girth strap < ON *gjördh*, girdle. See **gher-**[1]*.]

gi•sarme (gĭ-zärm′) *n.* A halberd with a two-sided blade, carried by medieval foot soldiers. [ME < OFr. *guisarme*, poss. < OHGer. *getīsarn* : *getan*, to weed + *īsarn*, iron; see **eis-***.]

Gis•card d'Es•taing (zhē-skär′ dĕs-tăng′, -tăN′), **Valéry.** b. 1926. French politician who served as president (1974–81).

Gish (gĭsh), **Lillian Diana.** 1893–1993. Amer. actress known for her roles in silent films, such as *The Birth of a Nation* (1915). Her sister **Dorothy** (1898–1968) was also a film actress.

gis•mo (gĭz′mō) *n.* Var. of **gizmo.**

Gis•sing (gĭs′ĭng), **George Robert.** 1857–1903. British writer whose works include *New Grub Street* (1891).

gist (jĭst) *n.* **1.** The central idea; the essence. **2.** *Law.* The grounds for action in a suit. [< AN *(cest action) gist*, (this action) lies, third pers. sing. of *gesir*, to lie < Lat. *iacēre.* See **yē-***.]

gite (zhēt) *n.* A simple, usu. inexpensive rural vacation retreat, esp. in France. [Fr. *gîte*, lodging, lair < OFr. *giste* < fem. p.part. of *gesir*, to lie. See GIST.]

git•tern (gĭt′ərn) *n. Mus.* A medieval guitar. [ME *giterne* < OFr. *guiterne* < Lat. *cithara.* See CITHARA.]

give (gĭv) *v.* **gave** (gāv), **giv•en** (gĭv′ən), **giv•ing, gives.** —*tr.* **1.** To make a present of. **2.** To place in the hands of; pass. **3.a.** To deliver in exchange or recompense; pay. **b.** To let go for a price; sell. **4.a.** To administer: *give him medicine.* **b.** To convey by a physical action: *gave me a punch in the nose.* **c.** To inflict as punishment. **d.** *Law.* To accord by verdict. **5.a.** To bestow, esp. officially; confer. **b.** To accord or tender to another: *Give him your confidence.* **c.** To put temporarily at the disposal of. **d.** To entrust to another, usu. for a specified reason. **e.** To convey or offer for conveyance: *Give him my best.* **f.** *Law.* To execute and deliver. Used esp. in the phrase *give bond.* **6.a.** To endure the loss of; sacrifice. **b.** To devote or apply completely. **c.** To furnish or contribute. **d.** To offer in good faith; pledge. **7.a.** To allot as a portion or share. **b.** To bestow (a name, for example). **c.** To attribute (blame, for example) to someone; assign. **d.** To award as due: *gave us first prize.* **8.** To emit or utter. **9.** To submit for consideration, acceptance, or use: *give an opinion.* **10.a.** To proffer to another: *gave the toddler my hand.* **b.** To consent to engage (oneself) in sexual intercourse with a man. **11.a.** To perform for an audience. **b.** To present to view: *gave the sign to begin.* **12.a.** To offer as entertainment: *give a party.* **b.** To propose as a toast. **13.a.** To be a source of; afford: *His remark gave offense.* **b.** To cause to catch or be subject to (a disease or bodily condition). **c.** To guide or direct, as by persuasion or behavior. Used with an infinitive phrase: *You gave me to imagine you approved of him.* **14.a.** To yield or produce: *Cows give milk.* **b.** To bring forth or bear. **c.** To produce as a result of calculation: *5 × 12 gives 60.* **15.a.** To manifest or show. **b.** To carry out (a physical movement). **16.** To permit one to have or take: *gave us an hour to finish.* **17.** To take an interest to the extent of. —*intr.* **1.** To make gifts or donations. **2.a.** To yield to physical force. **b.** To collapse from force or pressure. **c.** To yield to change. **3.** To afford access to or a view of; open. **4.** *Slang.* To be in progress; happen. —*n.* **1.** Capacity or inclination to yield under pressure. **2.** The quality or condition of resilience; springiness. —***phrasal verbs.*** **give away. 1.** To make a gift of. **2.** To present (a bride) to the bridegroom at a wedding ceremony. **3.a.** To reveal or make known, often accidentally. **b.** To betray. **give back.** To return. **give in. 1.** To hand in; submit. **2.** To cease opposition; yield. **give of.** To devote or contribute. **give off.** To send forth; emit. **give out. 1.** To allow to be known; declare publicly. **2.** To send forth; emit. **3.** To distribute: *gave out the food.* **4.** To stop functioning; fail. **5.** To become used up or exhausted; run out. **give over. 1.** To hand over; entrust. **2.a.** To devote to a particular purpose or use. **b.** To surrender (oneself) completely; abandon. **3.** To cause an activity to stop. **give up. 1.a.** To surrender. **b.** To devote (oneself) completely. **2.a.** To cease to do or perform. **b.** To desist from; stop. **3.** To part with; relinquish: *gave up all hope.* **4.a.** To lose hope for. **b.** To lose hope of seeing. **5.** To admit defeat. **6.** To abandon what one is doing or planning to do. —***idioms.*** **give a good account of (oneself).** To behave or perform creditably. **give birth to. 1.** To bear as offspring. **2.** To be the origin of. **give ground.** To yield to a more powerful force; retreat. **give it to.** *Informal.* To punish or reprimand severely. **give or take.** Plus or minus (a small specified amount). **give rise to.** To be the cause or origin of; bring about. **give (someone) the eye.** To look at admiringly or invitingly. **give the lie to. 1.** To show to be inaccurate or untrue. **2.** To accuse of lying. **give up the ghost.** To cease living or functioning; die. **give way. 1.a.** To retreat or withdraw. **b.** To yield the right of way. **c.** To relinquish ascendancy or position. **2.a.** To collapse from or as if from physical pressure. **b.** To yield to urging or demand; give in. **3.** To abandon oneself. [ME *given* < OE *giefan* and ON *gefa*; see **ghabh-***.]

give•a•way (gĭv′ə-wā′) *n. Informal.* **1.** The act or an instance of giving something away. **2.** Something given away at no charge. **3.** Something that accidentally exposes or betrays.

give•back (gĭv′băk′) *n.* **1.** A cutback in wages or benefits conceded by a union, as in exchange for other benefits. **2.** Something rebated or returned.

giv•en (gĭv′ən) *v.* P.part. of **give.** —*adj.* **1.a.** Specified; fixed. **b.** Granted as a supposition; acknowledged or assumed. **2.** Having a tendency; inclined. **3.** Bestowed as a gift; presented. **4.** *Law.* Issued on a specified date. Used of legal documents. —*n.* Something assumed or taken for granted.

given name *n.* A name given to a person at birth or at baptism.

giv•er (gĭv′ər) *n.* **1.** One that gives. **2.** A donor or contributor.

Gi•za (gē′zə). A city of N Egypt, a suburb of Cairo; near the site of the Great Pyramids and the Sphinx. Pop. 1,608,400.

giz•mo also **gis•mo** (gĭz′mō) *n., pl.* **-mos.** A mechanical device or part whose name is forgotten or unknown. [?]

giz•zard (gĭz′ərd) *n.* **1.** A modified, thickly lined muscular pouch behind the stomach in birds, often containing ingested grit, that aids in the mechanical breakdown of food. **2.** A similar digestive organ in certain invertebrates. [Alteration of ME *giser* < OFr. < VLat. **gicērium* < Lat. *gigēria*, cooked entrails of poultry, prob. < Pers. *jigar*, liver. See **yĕkʷr̥***.]

Gjel•le•rup (gĕl′ə-ro͝op′), **Karl.** 1857–1919. Danish writer who shared the 1917 Nobel Prize for literature.

Gk. *abbr.* Greek.

gl. *abbr.* Gloss (explanatory note).

gla•bel•la (glə-bĕl′ə) *n., pl.* **-bel•lae** (-bĕl′ē). The smooth area between the eyebrows. [NLat. < Lat. *glabellus*, hairless, dim. of *glaber.*] —**gla•bel′lar** *adj.*

gla•brous (glā′brəs) *adj.* Having no hairs, projections, or pubescence; smooth: *glabrous leaves.* [< Lat. *glaber, glabr-*, bald.] —**gla′brous•ness** *n.*

gla•cé (glă-sā′) *adj.* **1.** Having a smooth glazed or glossy surface, such as certain silks or leathers. **2.** Coated with a sugar glaze; candied. —*tr.v.* **-céed, -cé•ing, -cés. 1.** To glaze. **2.** To candy. [Fr. < p.part. of *glacer*, to glaze, freeze < OFr., to freeze < Lat. *glaciāre.* See GLACIATE.]

Glace Bay (glās). A town of NE Nova Scotia, Canada, on the Atlantic coast of Cape Breton I. Pop. 21,466.

gla•cial (glā′shəl) *adj.* **1.a.** Of, relating to, or derived from a glacier. **b.** Suggesting the extreme slowness of a glacier. **2.a.** Often **Glacial.** Characterized or dominated by glaciers. Used of a geologic epoch. **b.** Pleistocene. See table at **geologic time. 3.** Extremely cold; icy. See Syns at **cold. 4.** Having the appearance of ice. **5.a.** Lacking warmth and friendliness. **b.** Coldly detached. [French < OFr., icy < Lat. *glaciālis* < *glaciēs*, ice. See **gel-***.] —**gla′cial•ly** *adv.*

glacial acetic acid *n.* Acetic acid that is at least 99.8 percent pure.

gla•ci•ate (glā′shē-āt′, -sē-) *tr.v.* **-at•ed, -at•ing, -ates. 1.a.** To cover with ice or a glacier. **b.** To subject to or affect by glacial action. **2.** To freeze. [Lat. *glaciāre, glaciāt-*, to freeze < *glaciēs*, ice. See **gel-***.] —**gla′ci•a′tion** *n.*

gla•cier (glā′shər) *n.* A huge mass of ice slowly flowing over a land mass, formed from compacted snow in an area where snow accumulation exceeds melting and sublimation. [Fr. < OFr., cold place < *glace*, ice < VLat. **glacia* < Lat. *glaciēs.* See **gel-***.] —**gla′ciered** *adj.*

Gla•cier Bay (glā′shər). A narrow inlet of the Pacific Ocean in SE AK NW of Juneau; named for the surrounding mountain peaks with spectacular glaciers.

glacier meal *n.* See **rock flour.**

gla•ci•ol•o•gy (glā′shē-ŏl′ə-jē, -sē-) *n.* The scientific study of glaciers and their effects on the landscape. [GLACI(ER) + -LOGY.] —**gla′ci•o•log′ic** (-ə-lŏj′ĭk), **gla′ci•o•log′i•cal** *adj.* —**gla′ci•ol′o•gist** *n.*

gla•cis (glă-sē′, glăs′ē, glā′sĭs) *n., pl.* **glacis. 1.a.** A gentle slope; an incline. **b.** A slope extending down from a fortification. **2.** A neutral area separating conflicting forces. [Fr. < OFr. < *glacer*, to slide < *glace*, ice < VLat. **glacia* < Lat. *glaciēs.* See **gel-***.]

giraffe
Masai giraffe
Giraffa tippelskirchi

girandole
c. 1810 American

ă pat	oi boy
ā pay	ou out
âr care	o͝o took
ä father	o͞o boot
ĕ pet	ŭ cut
ē be	ûr urge
ĭ pit	th thin
ī pie	*th* this
îr pier	hw which
ŏ pot	zh vision
ō toe	ə about, item
ô paw	

Stress marks:
′ (primary);
′ (secondary), as in **dictionary** (dĭk′shə-nĕr′ē)

glints. — *intr.* To gleam or flash briefly. — *tr.* To cause to gleam or flash. [ME *glent,* of Scand. orig. See **ghel-**[2*].]
glint•y (glĭn′tē) *adj.* **-i•er, -i•est. 1.** Sparkling; glittery. **2.** Cheap and flashy.
gli•o•ma (glē-ō′mə, glī-) *n., pl.* **-mas** or **-ma•ta** (-mä′tə). A tumor originating in the neuroglia of the brain or spinal cord.
glis•sade (glĭ-säd′, -sād′) *n.* **1.** A gliding step in ballet. **2.** A controlled slide used in descending a steep icy or snowy incline. — *intr.v.* **-sad•ed, -sad•ing, -sades.** To perform a glissade. [Fr. < *glisser,* to slide < OFr., poss. alteration of *glier,* to glide, of Gmc. orig. See **ghel-**[2*].] — **glis•sad′er** *n.*
glis•san•do (glĭ-sän′dō) *n., pl.* **-di** (-dē) or **-dos.** *Mus.* A rapid slide through a series of consecutive tones in a scalelike passage. [Fr. *glissade;* see GLISSADE + *-ando,* as in ACCELERANDO.]

globe

glis•ten (glĭs′ən) *intr.v.* **-tened, -ten•ing, -tens.** To shine by reflection with a sparkling luster. — *n.* A sparkling lustrous shine. [ME *glisnen* < OE *glisnian.* See **ghel-**[2*].]
glis•ter (glĭs′tər) *intr.v.* **-tered, -ter•ing, -ters.** To glisten. — *n.* Glitter; brilliance. [ME *glisteren,* prob. < MDu. *glinsteren* or MLGer. *glisteren;* see **ghel-**[2*].]
glitch (glĭch) *n.* **1.** A minor malfunction, mishap, or technical problem; a snag: *a computer glitch.* **2.** A false or spurious electronic signal caused by a brief unwanted surge of electric power. **3.** *Astron.* A sudden change in the period of rotation of a neutron star. [Prob. < Yiddish *glitsh,* a slip, lapse < *glitshn,* to slip < MHGer. *glitschen,* alteration of *gliten,* to glide < OHGer. *glītan.* See **ghel-**[2*].] — **glitch′y** *adj.*
glit•ter (glĭt′ər) *n.* **1.** A sparkling or glistening light. **2.** Brilliant or showy, often superficial attractiveness. **3.** Small pieces of light-reflecting decorative material. — *intr.v.* **-tered, -ter•ing, -ters. 1.a.** To sparkle brilliantly; glisten. **b.** To sparkle coldly or malevolently: *eyes that glittered.* **2.** To be brilliantly, often deceptively attractive. [< ME *gliteren,* to sparkle < ON *glitra.* See **ghel-**[2*].] — **glit′ter•ing•ly** *adv.* — **glit′ter•y** *adj.*
glit•te•ra•ti (glĭt′ə-rä′tē) *pl.n. Informal.* Highly fashionable celebrities; the smart set. [GLITTER + (LITER)ATI.]
glitz (glĭts) *Informal.* — *n.* Ostentatious showiness; flashiness. — *tr.v.* **glitz•ed, glitz•ing, glitz•es.** To invest with an ostentatiously showy quality. [Back-formation < *glitzy,* flashy, showy, prob. < Ger. *glitzern,* to glitter < MHGer. *glitzen,* to shine < OHGer. *glīzan.* See **ghel-**[2*].] — **glitz′i•ness** *n.* — **glitz′y** *adj.*
Gli•wi•ce (glĭ-vēt′sə, glē-vē′tsě). A city of S-central Poland WNW of Katowice; chartered 1276. Pop. 212,500.
gloam (glōm) *n. Archaic.* Twilight; gloaming.
gloam•ing (glō′mĭng) *n.* Twilight; dusk. [ME *gloming* < OE *glōmung* < *glōm,* dusk. See **ghel-**[2*].]
gloat (glōt) *intr.v.* **gloat•ed, gloat•ing, gloats.** To feel or express great, often malicious pleasure or self-satisfaction. — *n.* **1.** The act of gloating. **2.** A feeling of gloating. [Perh. of Scand. orig. See **ghel-**[2*].] — **gloat′er** *n.*
glob (glŏb) *n.* **1.** A small drop; a globule. **2.** A soft thick lump or mass: *globs of red mud.* [ME *globbe,* large mass < Lat. *globus,* globular mass.]

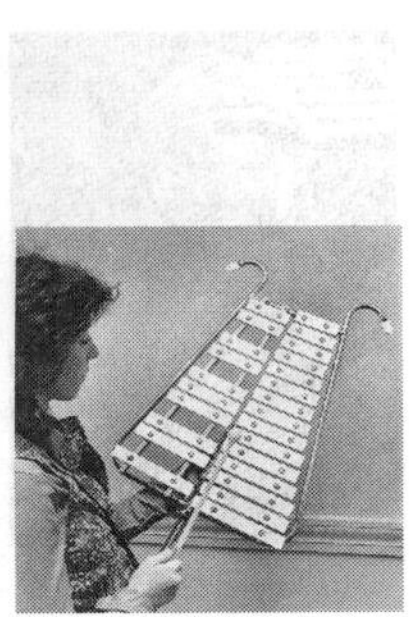
glockenspiel

glob•al (glō′bəl) *adj.* **1.** Having the shape of a globe; spherical. **2.** Of, relating to, or involving the entire earth; worldwide. **3.** Comprehensive; total. **4.** *Comp. Sci.* Of or relating to an entire program, document, or file. — **glob′al•ly** *adv.*
glob•al•ism (glō′bə-lĭz′əm) *n.* A policy in which the world is seen as the appropriate sphere for a state's influence. — **glob′al•ist** *n.*
glob•al•ize (glō′bə-līz′) *tr.v.* **-ized, -iz•ing, -iz•es.** To make global or worldwide in scope or application. — **glob′al•i•za′tion** *n.* — **glob′al•iz′er** *n.*
global village *n.* The entire world and its inhabitants.
globe (glōb) *n.* **1.** A body with the shape of a sphere, esp. a representation of the earth in the form of a hollow ball. **2.a.** The earth. **b.** A planet. **3.** A spherical or bowllike container, esp. a glass cover for a light bulb. **4.** A sphere emblematic of sovereignty; an orb. — *intr. & tr.v.* **globed, glob•ing, globes.** To assume the shape of or form into a sphere. [ME < OFr. < Lat. *globus.*]
globe•fish (glōb′fĭsh′) *n., pl.* **globefish** or **-fish•es.** Any of various fishes, esp. the ocean sunfish or puffer, having or capable of assuming a globular shape.
globe•flow•er (glōb′flou′ər) *n.* Any of several plants of the genus *Trollius,* having globose, usu. yellow flowers.
globe•trot (glōb′trŏt′) *intr.v.* **-trot•ted, -trot•ting, -trots.** To travel far and often, esp. for pleasure. — **globe′trot′ter** *n.*
glo•bin (glō′bĭn) *n.* A constituent protein of hemoglobin.
glo•boid (glō′boid′) *adj.* Having a globelike shape; spheroid. — *n.* A globe-shaped object.
glo•bose (glō′bōs′) also **glo•bous** (-bəs) *adj.* Spherical; globular. — **glo′bose′ly** *adv.* — **glo′bose′ness, glo•bos′i•ty** (-bŏs′ĭ-tē) *n.*
glob•u•lar (glŏb′yə-lər) *adj.* **1.** Having the shape of a globe or globule; spherical. **2.** Consisting of globules. **3.** Worldwide; global. — **glob′u•lar•ly** *adv.* — **glob′u•lar•ness** *n.*
glob•ule (glŏb′yo͞ol) *n.* A small spherical mass, esp. a small drop of liquid. [Fr. < Lat. *globulus,* dim. of *globus,* sphere.]
glob•u•lif•er•ous (glŏb′yə-lĭf′ər-əs) *adj.* Composed of or producing globules.
glob•u•lin (glŏb′yə-lĭn) *n.* Any of a class of proteins that are soluble in dilute salt solution and are found extensively in plant and animal tissue. [GLOBUL(E) + -IN.]
glo•chid•i•um (glō-kĭd′ē-əm) *n., pl.* **-i•a** (-ē-ə). **1.** *Zool.* The parasitic larva of certain freshwater mussels of the family Unionidae, having hooks for attaching to the external parts of a host fish. **2.** Also **glo•chid** (glō′kĭd). *Bot.* A minute barbed hair or bristle on certain plants, such as the prickly pear. [NLat. *glōchidium* < Gk. *glōkhis, glōkhid-,* barb of an arrow.] — **glo•chid′i•ate** (-ĭt, -āt′) *adj.*
glock•en•spiel (glŏk′ən-spēl′, -shpēl′) *n. Mus.* A percussion instrument with a series of metal bars tuned to the chromatic scale and played with two light hammers. [Ger. : *Glocken,* pl. of *Glocke,* bell (< MHGer. < OHGer. *glocka,* of imit. origin) + *Spiel,* play; see SPIEL.]
glogg (glŏg) also **glögg** (glœg) *n.* A hot punch made of red wine, brandy, and sherry with almonds, raisins, and orange peel. [Swed. *glögg,* alteration of *glödgat,* mulled < p.part. of *glödga,* to mull < *glöd,* ember. See **ghel-**[2*].]
glom (glŏm) *Slang.* — *v.* **glommed, glom•ming, gloms.** — *tr.* **1.** To steal. **2.** To seize; grab. **3.** To look or stare at. — *intr.* To seize upon or latch on to something. — *n.* A glimpse; a look. [Prob. < Sc. *glam,* to snatch at < Sc.Gael.]
glom•er•ate (glŏm′ər-ĭt) *adj.* Formed into a compact rounded mass; tightly clustered. [Lat. *glomerātus,* p.part. of *glomerāre,* to wind into a ball < *glomus, glomer-,* ball.]
glom•er•ule (glŏm′ə-ro͞ol′)) *n.* **1.** *Bot.* A compact cymose cluster of flowers. **2.** *Anat.* A glomerulus. [NLat. *glomerulus.* See GLOMERULUS.] — **glo•mer′u•late** (glō-mĕr′yə-lĭt) *adj.*
glo•mer•u•lus (glō-mĕr′yə-ləs) *n., pl.* **-li** (-lī′). *Anat.* **1.** A small cluster or mass of blood vessels or nerve fibers. **2.** A tuft of capillaries situated within a Bowman's capsule in the vertebrate kidney that filters waste products from the blood. [NLat., dim. of Lat. *glomus, glomer-,* ball.]
Glom•ma (glô′mə, -mä). See **Glåma.**
gloom (glo͞om) *n.* **1.a.** Partial or total darkness; dimness. **b.** A partially or totally dark place, area, or location. **2.a.** An atmosphere of melancholy or depression. **b.** A state of melancholy or depression. — *v.* **gloomed, gloom•ing, glooms.** — *intr.* **1.** To be or become dark, shaded, or obscure. **2.** To feel, appear, or act despondent, sad, or mournful. — *tr.* **1.** To make dark, shaded, or obscure. **2.** *Archaic.* To make despondent; sadden. [Prob. < ME *gloumen,* to become dark.]
gloom•y (glo͞o′mē) *adj.* **-i•er, -i•est. 1.** Partially or totally dark, esp. dismal and dreary: *a damp, gloomy day.* **2.** Showing or filled with gloom. **3.a.** Causing or producing gloom; depressing. **b.** Marked by hopelessness; very pessimistic. — **gloom′i•ly** *adv.* — **gloom′i•ness** *n.*
glop (glŏp) *n. Slang.* **1.** A soft soggy mixture, as of food. **2.** Something, such as a piece of writing, that is judged worthless. [Prob. imit. of the sound of food being mixed.] — **glop** *v.* — **glop′py** *adj.*
Glo•ri•a (glôr′ē-ə, glōr′-) *n.* **1.a.** A Latin doxology beginning with the words *Gloria Patri.* **b.** A Latin doxology beginning with the words *Gloria in excelsis Deo.* **c.** A musical setting for either of these doxologies. **2. gloria.** A halo or nimbus. [ME < LLat. *Glōria* < Lat. *glōria,* glory.]
glo•ri•fy (glôr′ə-fī′, glōr′-) *tr.v.* **-fied, -fy•ing, -fies. 1.** To give glory, honor, or high praise to; exalt. **2.** To cause to be or seem more glorious or excellent than is actually the case. **3.** To give glory to, esp. through worship. [ME *glorifien* < OFr. *glorefier* < Lat. *glōrificāre* : *glōria,* glory + *-ficāre,* -fy.] — **glo′ri•fi•ca′tion** (-fĭ-kā′shən) *n.* — **glo′ri•fi′er** *n.*
glo•ri•ole (glôr′ē-ōl′, glōr′-) *n.* See **glory** 8. [Fr. < Lat. *glōriola,* dim. of *glōria,* glory.]
glo•ri•ous (glôr′ē-əs, glōr′-) *adj.* **1.** Having or deserving glory; famous. **2.** Conferring or advancing glory: *a glorious achievement.* **3.** Characterized by great beauty and splendor; magnificent: *a glorious sunset.* **4.** Delightful; wonderful. — **glo′ri•ous•ly** *adv.* — **glo′ri•ous•ness** *n.*
glo•ry (glôr′ē, glōr′ē) *n., pl.* **-ries. 1.** Great honor, praise, or distinction accorded by common consent; renown. **2.** Something conferring honor or renown. **3.** A highly praiseworthy asset. **4.** Adoration, praise, and thanksgiving offered in worship. **5.** Majestic beauty and splendor; resplendence. **6.** The splendor and bliss of heaven; perfect happiness. **7.** A height of achievement, enjoyment, or prosperity. **8.** A halo, nimbus, or aureole. — *intr.v.* **-ried, -ry•ing, -ries.** To rejoice triumphantly; exult. [ME *glorie* < OFr. < Lat. *glōria.*]
gloss[1] (glôs, glŏs) *n.* **1.** A surface shininess or luster. **2.** A superficially or deceptively attractive appearance. — *v.* **glossed, gloss•ing, gloss•es.** — *tr.* **1.** To give a bright sheen or luster to. **2.** To make attractive or acceptable by deception or superficial treatment: *glossed over my errors.* — *intr.* To become shiny or lustrous. [Perh. of Scand. orig.; akin to Icel. *glossi,* a spark. See **ghel-**[2*].]
gloss[2] (glôs, glŏs) *n.* **1.a.** A brief explanatory note or translation usu. inserted in the margin or between lines of a text or manuscript. **b.** A collection of such notes; a glossary. **2.** An extensive commentary, often accompanying a text or publication. **3.** A purposefully misleading interpretation or explanation. — *tr.v.* **glossed, gloss•ing, gloss•es. 1.** To provide

(an expression or a text) with a gloss or glosses. **2.** To give a false interpretation to. [ME *glose* < OFr. < Med.Lat. *glōsa* < LLat. *glōssa,* foreign word requiring explanation < Gk., tongue, language.] **—gloss′er** *n.*

gloss. *abbr.* Glossary.

glos•sa (glô′sə, glŏs′ə) *n., pl.* **glos•sae** (glô′sē, glŏs′ē) or **glos•sas. 1.** *Anat.* The tongue. **2.** *Zool.* A tonguelike structure in the labium of an insect. [Gk. *glōssa,* tongue.]

glos•sal (glô′səl, glŏs′əl) *adj.* Of or relating to the tongue.

glos•sa•ry (glô′sə-rē, glŏs′ə-) *n., pl.* **-ries.** A list of often difficult or specialized words with their definitions, often placed at the back of a book. [ME *glosarie* < LLat. *glōssārium* < *glōssa,* foreign word. See GLOSS[2].] **—glos•sar′i•al** (glô-sâr′ē-əl, glŏ-) *adj.* **—glos′sa•rist** *n.*

glos•si•tis (glô-sī′tĭs, glŏ-) *n.* Inflammation of the tongue. **—glos•sit′ic** (-sĭt′ĭk) *adj.*

glos•sog•ra•phy (glô-sŏg′rə-fē, glŏ-) *n.* The compilation of glosses or glossaries. **—glos•sog′ra•pher** *n.*

glos•so•la•li•a (glô′sə-lā′lē-ə, glŏs′ə-) *n.* **1.** Fabricated and meaningless speech, esp. when associated with a trance state or certain schizophrenic syndromes. **2.** See **gift of tongues.** [NLat. : Gk. *glōssa,* tongue + Gk. *lalein,* to babble.]

gloss•y (glô′sē, glŏs′ē) *adj.* **-i•er, -i•est. 1.** Having a smooth shiny lustrous surface: *glossy satin.* **2.** Superficially and often speciously attractive; showy. —*n., pl.* **-ies. 1.** A photographic print on smooth shiny paper. **2.** *Chiefly British.* A popular magazine printed on smooth-coated stock. **—gloss′i•ly** *adv.* **—gloss′i•ness** *n.*

glot•tal (glŏt′l) *adj. Ling.* Relating to or articulated in the glottis.

glottal stop *n. Ling.* A speech sound produced by closure of the glottis, followed by an explosive release.

glot•tis (glŏt′ĭs) *n., pl.* **-tis•es** or **glot•ti•des** (glŏt′ĭ-dēz′). **1.** The opening between the vocal cords at the upper part of the larynx. **2.** The vocal apparatus of the larynx. [Gk. *glōttis* < *glōtta, glōssa,* tongue.]

Glouces•ter (glŏs′tər, glô′stər). **1.** A borough of SW-central England on the Severn R. WNW of London; once the Saxon capital of Mercia. Pop. 91,600. **2.** A city of NE MA on Cape Ann and the Atlantic Ocean NE of Boston. Pop. 28,716.

glove (glŭv) *n.* **1.a.** A fitted covering for the hand with a separate sheath for each finger and the thumb. **b.** A gauntlet. **2.a.** *Baseball.* An oversize padded leather covering for the hand, used in catching balls. **b.** *Sports.* A boxing glove. —*v.* **gloved, glov•ing, gloves.** —*tr.* **1.** To furnish with gloves. **2.** To cover with or as if with a glove. —*intr.* To don gloves, as before surgery. [ME < OE *glōf.*]

glove box *n.* See **glove compartment.**

glove compartment *n.* A small dashboard storage container.

Glov•ers•ville (glŭv′ərz-vĭl′). A city of E-central NY NW of Schenectady. Pop. 16,656.

glow (glō) *intr.v.* **glowed, glow•ing, glows. 1.** To shine brightly and steadily, esp. without a flame. **2.a.** To have a bright, warm, usu. reddish color. **b.** To flush; blush. **3.** To be exuberant or radiant: *glowing with pride.* —*n.* **1.** A light produced by a body heated to luminosity; incandescence. **2.** Brilliance or warmth of color, esp. redness. **3.** A sensation of physical warmth. **4.** A warm feeling, as of pleasure or well-being. [ME *glouen* < OE *glōwan.* See **ghel-**[2]*.]

glow•er (glou′ər) *intr.v.* **-ered, -er•ing, -ers.** To look or stare angrily or sullenly. —*n.* An angry or sullen look or stare. [ME *gloren,* prob. of Scand. orig. See **ghel-**[2]*.]

glow plug *n.* An electric heating element in a diesel engine that facilitates starting by preheating the air in a cylinder.

glow•worm (glō′wûrm′) *n.* Any of various luminous female beetles or beetle larvae of the families Phengodidae and Lampyridae, esp. the larva or wingless female of a firefly.

glox•in•i•a (glŏk-sĭn′ē-ə) *n.* Any of several tropical South American plants of the genus *Sinningia,* esp. *S. speciosa,* having showy, variously colored flowers. [NLat., after Benjamin Peter *Gloxin,* 18th-cent. German botanist.]

gloze (glōz) *v.* **glozed, gloz•ing, gloz•es.** —*tr.* To minimize or underplay; gloss: *glozed over the embarrassing part.* —*intr. Archaic.* To use flattery or cajolery. [ME *glosen,* to interpret, explain away < OFr. *gloser* < *glose,* gloss. See GLOSS[2].]

glu•ca•gon (glo͞o′kə-gŏn′) *n.* A pancreatic hormone that stimulates an increase in blood sugar levels. [Prob. GLUC(O)– + Gk. *agōn,* pr.part. of *agein,* to lead, drive; see **ag-***.]

Gluck (glo͝ok), **Christoph Willibald.** 1714–87. German operatic composer whose works include *Orfeo ed Euridice* (1762).

gluco– or **gluc–** *pref.* Glucose: *glucagon.* [< GLUCOSE.]

glu•co•cor•ti•coid (glo͞o′kō-kôr′tĭ-koid′) *n.* Any of a group of corticoids, such as cortisone, that are involved in carbohydrate, protein, and fat metabolism and have anti-inflammatory properties.

glu•co•ne•o•gen•e•sis (glo͞o′kə-nē′ə-jĕn′ĭ-sĭs) *n.* The formation of glucose, esp. by the liver, from noncarbohydrates, such as proteins and fats.

glu•cose (glo͞o′kōs′) *n.* **1.** A monosaccharide sugar, $C_6H_{12}O_6$, common in most plant and animal tissue, that is the major energy source of the body. **2.** A colorless to yellowish syrupy mixture of dextrose, maltose, dextrins, and water, used in confectionery, alcoholic fermentation, tanning, and treating tobacco. [Fr. < Gk. *gleukos,* sweet wine.]

glu•co•side (glo͞o′kə-sīd′) *n.* A glycoside containing glucose. **—glu′co•sid′ic** (-sĭd′ĭk) *adj.* **—glu′co•sid′i•cal•ly** *adv.*

glue (glo͞o) *n.* **1.a.** A strong liquid adhesive obtained by boiling collagenous animal parts such as bones, hides, and hooves into hard gelatin and then adding water. **b.** Any of various similar adhesives, such as paste. **2.** An adhesive force or factor. —*tr.v.* **glued, glu•ing, glues. 1.** To stick or fasten with or as if with glue. **2.** To fasten on something attentively: *Our eyes were glued to the stage.* [ME *glu* < OFr. < LLat. *glūs, glūt-* < Lat. *glūten.*] **—glu′ey** *adj.* **—glu′i•ness** *n.*

glum (glŭm) *adj.* **glum•mer, glum•mest. 1.** Moody and melancholy; dejected. **2.** Gloomy; dismal. —*n.* **1.** The quality or state of being glum or an instance of it. **2. glums.** *Chiefly British.* The blues. [Prob. akin to ME *gloumen,* to become dark. See GLOOM.] **—glum′ly** *adv.* **—glum′ness** *n.*

glu•ma•ceous (glo͞o-mā′shəs) *adj.* Having or resembling glumes.

glume (glo͞om) *n.* One of the two chaffy basal bracts of a grass spikelet. [Lat. *glūma,* husk. See **gleubh-***.]

glu•on (glo͞o′ŏn) *n.* A hypothetical massless, neutral elementary particle believed to mediate the strong interaction that binds quarks together. [GLU(E) + –ON[1].]

glut (glŭt) *v.* **glut•ted, glut•ting, gluts.** —*tr.* **1.** To fill beyond capacity, esp. with food; satiate. **2.** To supply (a market) with goods in excess of demand. —*intr.* To eat or indulge to excess. —*n.* An oversupply. [ME *glotten,* prob. < OFr. *glotoiier,* to eat greedily < Lat. *gluttīre.*]

glu•tam•ic acid (glo͞o-tăm′ĭk) *n.* A nonessential amino acid, $C_5H_9NO_4$, common in plant and animal tissue and having a salt used as a seasoning. [GLUT(EN) + AM(IDE) + –IC.]

glu•ta•mine (glo͞o′tə-mēn′) *n.* A nonessential amino acid, $C_5H_{10}N_2O_3$, common in plant and animal tissue and produced commercially for use in research. [GLUT(EN) + AMINE.]

glu•ten (glo͞ot′n) *n.* A mixture of plant proteins occurring in cereal grains, used as an adhesive and as a flour substitute. [Fr. < Lat. *glūten,* glue.] **—glu′ten•ous** *adj.*

glu•teth•i•mide (glo͞o-tĕth′ə-mīd′) *n.* A nonbarbiturate hypnotic drug, $C_{13}H_{15}NO_2$. [GLUTE(N) + THI(O)– + (A)MIDE.]

glu•te•us (glo͞o′tē-əs, glo͞o-tē′-) *n., pl.* **glu•te•i** (glo͞o′tē-ī′, glo͞o-tē′ī′). Any of the three large muscles of each buttock, esp. the gluteus maximus, that extend, abduct, and rotate the thigh. [NLat. < Gk. *gloutos,* buttock.] **—glu′te•al** *adj.*

gluteus max•i•mus (măk′sə-məs) *n., pl.* **glutei max•i•mi** (măk′sə-mī′). The largest and outermost gluteus. [NLat.]

glu•ti•nous (glo͞ot′n-əs) *adj.* Of the nature of or resembling glue; sticky. [ME < Lat. *glūtinōsus* < *glūten, glūtin-,* glue.] **—glu′ti•nous•ly** *adv.* **—glu′ti•nous•ness, glu′ti•nos′i•ty** (-ŏs′ĭ-tē) *n.*

glut•ton (glŭt′n) *n.* **1.** A person who eats or consumes immoderately. **2.** A person with an inordinate capacity to receive or withstand something. **3.** See **wolverine** 1. [ME *glotoun* < OFr. *gloton* < Lat. *gluttō, gluttōn-.*]

glut•ton•ous (glŭt′n-əs) *adj.* **1.** Given to or marked by gluttony. **2.** Indulging in something, such as an activity, to excess; voracious. **—glut′ton•ous•ly** *adv.*

glut•ton•y (glŭt′n-ē) *n., pl.* **-ies.** Excess in eating or drinking.

glyc•er•al•de•hyde (glĭs′ə-răl′də-hīd′) *n.* A sweet colorless crystalline solid, $C_3H_6O_3$, that is an intermediate compound in carbohydrate metabolism. [GLYCER(IN) + ALDEHYDE.]

gly•cer•ic acid (glĭ-sĕr′ĭk) *n.* A colorless syrupy acid, $C_3H_6O_4$, obtained from oxidation of glycerol. [< GLYCERIN.]

glyc•er•ide (glĭs′ə-rīd′) *n.* A natural or synthetic ester of glycerol and fatty acids. [GLYCER(IN) + –IDE.]

glyc•er•in also **glyc•er•ine** (glĭs′ər-ĭn) *n.* Glycerol. [Fr. *glycérine* < Gk. *glukeros,* sweet.]

glyc•er•ol (glĭs′ə-rôl′, -rōl′, -rŏl′) *n.* A syrupy sweet colorless or yellowish liquid, $C_3H_8O_3$, obtained from the saponification of fats and oils and used as a solvent and sweetener and in dynamite and cosmetics. [GLYCER(IN) + –OL[1].]

glyc•er•yl (glĭs′ər-əl) *n.* A trivalent radical, CH_2CHCH_2, of glycerol. [GLYCER(IN) + –YL.]

gly•cine (glī′sēn′, -sĭn) *n.* A sweet-tasting crystalline nonessential amino acid, $C_2H_5NO_2$, that is the principal amino acid occurring in sugar cane. [GLYC(O)– + –INE[2].]

glyco– or **glyc–** *pref.* **1.** Sugar: *glycoprotein.* **2.** Glycogen: *glycogenesis.* [< Gk. *glukus,* sweet.]

gly•co•gen (glī′kə-jən) *n.* A polysaccharide, $(C_6H_{10}O_5)_n$, that is the main form of carbohydrate storage in animals and occurs primarily in the liver and muscle tissue. **—gly′co•gen′ic** (-jĕn′ĭk) *adj.*

gly•co•gen•e•sis (glī′kə-jĕn′ĭ-sĭs) *n.* The formation or synthesis of glycogen. [GLYCO– + –GENESIS.] **—gly′co•ge•net′ic** (-jə-nĕt′ĭk) *adj.*

gly•col (glī′kôl′, -kōl′, -kŏl′) *n.* **1.** Ethylene glycol. **2.** Any of various alcohols containing two hydroxyl groups.

gly•col•ic acid (glī-kŏl′ĭk) *n.* A colorless crystalline compound, $C_2H_4O_3$, found in sugar beets and unripe grapes and used in leather processing.

gly•co•lip•id (glī′kə-lĭp′ĭd) *n.* A lipid that contains carbohydrate groups.

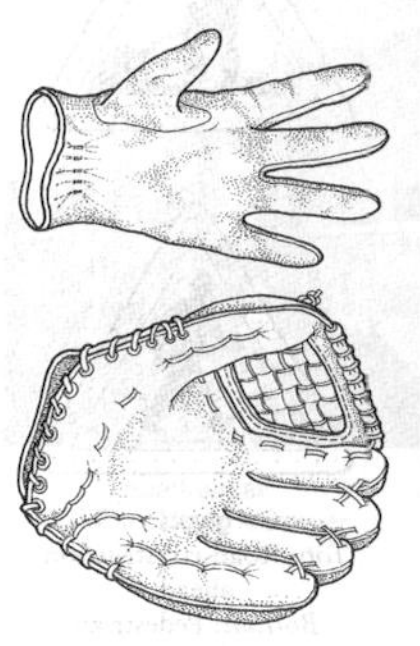

glove
Top: Winter glove
Bottom: Baseball outfielder's glove

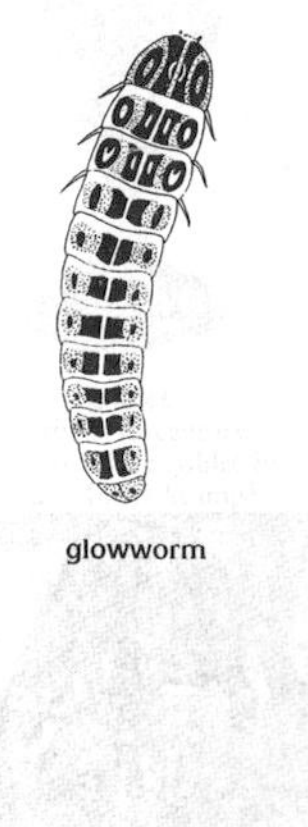

glowworm

ă pat · ā pay · âr care · ä father · ĕ pet · ē be · ĭ pit · ī pie · îr pier · ŏ pot · ō toe · ô paw · oi boy · ou out · o͝o took · o͞o boot · ŭ cut · ûr urge · th thin · *th* this · hw which · zh vision · ə about, item

Stress marks:
′ (primary);
′ (secondary), as in
dictionary (dĭk′shə-nĕr′ē)

goggles

golden eagle
Aquila chrysaetos

golf
Preparing to putt

1. Located in a dismal or remote area. 2. Desolate; forlorn.

God•frey of Bouil•lon (gŏd′frē; bo͞o-yôN′). 1061?–1100. French leader of the First Crusade (1096–99).

god•head (gŏd′hĕd′) *n.* **1.** Divinity; godhood. **2. Godhead. a.** The Christian God, esp. the Trinity. **b.** The essential and divine nature of God, regarded abstractly. [ME *godhode, godhede* < OE *godhād* : *god,* god; see GOD + *-hād,* -hood.]

god•hood (gŏd′ho͝od′) *n.* The quality or state of being a god.

god•less (gŏd′lĭs) *adj.* **1.** Recognizing or worshiping no god. **2.** Wicked, impious, or immoral. **—god′less•ly** *adv.* **—god′less•ness** *n.*

god•like (gŏd′līk′) *adj.* Resembling or of the nature of a god or God; divine. **—god′like′ness** *n.*

god•ling (gŏd′lĭng) *n.* A minor god.

god•ly (gŏd′lē) *adj.* **-li•er, -li•est. 1.** Having great reverence for God; pious. **2.** Divine. **—god′li•ness** *n.*

god•moth•er (gŏd′mŭ*th*′ər) *n.* **1.** A woman who sponsors a person, as at baptism. **2.** One that has a relationship to another person or to something that is the equivalent of being a baptismal sponsor. *—tr.v.* **-ered, -er•ing, -ers.** To serve as or as if a godmother to.

god•par•ent (gŏd′pâr′ənt, -păr′-) *n.* A godfather or a godmother.

God's acre (gŏdz) *n.* A churchyard or burial ground.

god•send (gŏd′sĕnd′) *n.* Something wanted or needed that comes or happens unexpectedly. [Alteration of ME *goddes sand,* God's message : *goddes,* genitive of *God,* God; see GOD + *sand,* message (< OE; see **sent-***).]

god•son (gŏd′sŭn′) *n.* A male godchild.

God•speed (gŏd′spēd′) *n.* Success or good fortune. [ME *God spede (you),* may God prosper (you) : *God,* god; see GOD + *spede,* third pers. sing. pr. subjunctive of *speden,* to prosper (< OE *spēdan* < *spēd,* success; see SPEED).]

Godt•håb (gôt′hôp′). The cap. of Greenland, on the SW coast of the island on **Godthåb Fjord;** founded 1721. Pop. 10,559.

Go•du•nov (go͝od′n-ôf′, gŏd′-, gə-do͞o-nôf′), **Boris Fyodorovich.** 1551?–1605. Czar of Russia (1598–1605) whose reign was marked by the colonization of Siberia.

God•win (gŏd′wĭn), **William.** 1756–1836. British writer and political theorist whose most important work is *Enquiry Concerning Political Justice* (1793).

Godwin Aus•ten (ô′stən), **Mount.** See **K2.**

god•wit (gŏd′wĭt′) *n.* Any of various large shore birds of the genus *Limosa,* with a slender, slightly upturned bill. [?]

Goeb•bels (gœ′bəls), **(Paul) Joseph.** 1897–1945. German Nazi propaganda minister (1933–45) who led propaganda attacks on the Jews and other groups.

Goe•ring (gĕr′ĭng, gûr′-, gœ′rĭng), **Hermann Wilhelm.** See Hermann Wilhelm **Göring.**

goes (gōz) *v.* Third pers. sing. pr.t. of **go**[1].

Goe•thals (gō′thəlz), **George Washington.** 1858–1928. Amer. army officer who directed the construction of the Panama Canal (1907–14).

Goe•the (gœ′tə), **Johann Wolfgang von.** 1749–1832. German writer renowned for his two-part dramatic poem *Faust* (published 1808 and 1832). **—Goe′the•an** (-tē-ən) *adj.*

goe•thite (gō′thīt′, gœ′tīt′) *n.* A brown mineral, $HFeO_2$, a common constituent of rust.

go•fer also **go-fer** (gō′fər) *n. Slang.* An employee who runs errands in addition to regular duties. [Alteration of *go for,* from that person's having to go for or after things.]

gof•fer also **gauf•fer** (gŏf′ər, gô′fər) *—tr.v.* **-fered, -fer•ing, -fers.** To press ridges or narrow pleats into (a frill, for example). *—n.* **1.** An iron used for goffering. **2.** Ridges or pleats produced in this manner. [Fr. *gaufrer,* to emboss < OFr. < *gaufre,* honeycomb, waffle, of Gmc. orig. See **webh-***.]

go-get•ter (gō′gĕt′ər, -gĕt′-) *n. Informal.* An enterprising person.

gog•gle (gŏg′əl) *v.* **-gled, -gling, -gles.** *—intr.* **1.** To stare with wide and bulging eyes. **2.** To roll or bulge. Used of the eyes. *—tr.* To roll or bulge (the eyes). *—n.* **1.** A stare or leer. **2. goggles.** A pair of tight-fitting eyeglasses, often tinted or having side shields, worn to protect the eyes. [ME *gogelen,* to squint.] **—gog′gly** *adj.*

gog•gle-eyed (gŏg′əl-īd′) *adj.* Having prominent or rolling eyes.

Gogh (gō, gôKH, KHôKH), **Vincent van.** See Vincent **van Gogh.**

go-go[1] also **go•go** (gō′gō′) *adj. Informal.* Of or relating to discotheques or to their music and dancing. [< À GOGO.]

go-go[2] also **go•go** (gō′gō′) *adj. Informal.* Marked by assertive action. [Intensive redup. of GO[1].]

Go•gol (gô′gəl, gō′gôl), **Nikolai Vasilievich.** 1809–52. Russian writer whose works include the novel *Dead Souls* (1842).

Gog•ra (gŏg′rə, -rä). See **Ghaghara.**

Goi•â•ni•a (goi-ăn′ē-ə, -ä′nē-ə). A city of S-central Brazil SW of Brasília. Pop. 702,858.

Goi•del•ic (goi-dĕl′ĭk) *n.* A branch of the Celtic languages that includes Irish Gaelic, Scottish Gaelic, and Manx. *—adj.* **1.** Of or relating to the Gaels. **2.** Of, relating to, or characteristic of Goidelic. [< OIr. *Goídil,* Gael, poss. < Old Welsh *-guoidel, Gwyddel.*]

go•ing (gō′ĭng) *n.* **1.** Departure. **2.** The condition underfoot as it affects walking or riding. **3.** *Informal.* Progress toward a goal; headway. *—adj.* **1.** Working; running. **2.** In full operation; flourishing. **3.** Current; prevailing. **4.** To be found; available. *—idiom.* **going on.** Approaching.

go•ing-o•ver (gō′ĭng-ō′vər) *n., pl.* **go•ings-o•ver** (gō′ĭngz-). *Informal.* **1.** An examination; an inspection. **2.a.** A severe beating. **b.** A severe reprimand.

go•ings-on (gō′ĭngz-ŏn′, -ôn′) *pl.n. Informal.* Actions or behavior, esp. when regarded with disapproval.

goi•ter (goi′tər) *n.* A noncancerous enlargement of the thyroid gland, visible as a swelling at the front of the neck, that is often associated with iodine deficiency. [Fr. *goitre* < Prov. *goitron* < VLat. **guttūriō, guttūriōn-,* throat < Lat. *guttur.*] **—goi′trous** (-trəs) *adj.*

Go•lan Heights (gō′län′). A region between NE Israel and SW Syria NE of the Sea of Galilee; captured by Israel in the 1967 Arab-Israeli War and formally annexed in 1981.

Gol•con•da[1] (gŏl-kŏn′də). A ruined city of S-central India W of Hyderabad; cap. of an ancient kingdom (c. 1364–1512) and later one of the five Muslim kingdoms of the Deccan. Golconda was once known for the diamonds found nearby and cut in the city.

Gol•con•da[2] (gŏl-kŏn′də) *n.* A source of great riches, such as a mine. [After GOLCONDA[1].]

gold (gōld) *n.* **1.a.** *Symbol* **Au** A soft yellow malleable metallic element, occurring in veins and alluvial deposits. A good thermal and electrical conductor, it is used as an international monetary standard, in jewelry, for decoration, and as a plated coating on a wide variety of electrical and mechanical components. Atomic number 79; atomic weight 196.967; melting point 1,063.0°C; boiling point 2,966.0°C; specific gravity 19.32; valence 1, 3. See table at **element. b.** Coinage made of this element. **c.** A gold standard. **2.** Money; riches. **3.** *Color.* A light olive-brown to dark yellow or a moderate strong to vivid yellow. **4.** Something regarded as having great value or goodness: *a heart of gold.* **5.a.** A medal, as in the Olympics, made of gold. **b.** A gold record. *—adj.* Having the color of gold. [ME < OE. See **ghel-**[2]*.]

gold•beat•ing (gōld′bē′tĭng) *n.* The act, process, or art of beating sheets of gold into gold leaf. **—gold′beat′er** *n.*

gold beetle *n.* See **gold bug** 1.

Gold•berg (gōld′bərg), **Arthur Joseph.** 1908–90. Amer. jurist and diplomat; associate justice of the U.S. Supreme Court (1962–65) and a delegate to the United Nations (1965–68).

Goldberg, Reuben ("Rube") Lucius. 1883–1970. Amer. cartoonist noted for his diagrams of complicated impractical contraptions designed to effect comparatively simple results.

gold•brick (gōld′brĭk′) *Slang.* *—n.* A person, esp. a soldier, who avoids assigned duties or work; a shirker. *—v.* **-bricked, -brick•ing, -bricks.** *—intr.* To shirk one's assigned duties or responsibilities. *—tr.* To cheat; swindle. **—gold′brick′er** *n.*

gold brick *n.* **1.** A bar of gilded cheap metal that appears to be genuine gold. **2.** A fraudulent worthless substitute.

gold bug *n.* **1.** Any of several North American beetles, esp. *Metriona bicolor,* with a golden luster. **2.** A supporter of the gold standard. **3.** A gold speculator or purchaser.

gold coast *n. Informal.* **1.** A rich neighborhood. **2.** The executive suite or suites in a company's headquarters.

Gold Coast (gōld). **1.** A section of coastal W Africa along the Gulf of Guinea on the S shore of Ghana; named for the large quantities of gold formerly sold there. **2.** A former British colony in the S part of the Gold Coast, now part of Ghana.

gold digger *n. Informal.* A woman who seeks money and expensive gifts from men.

gold•en (gōl′dən) *adj.* **1.** Of, relating to, made of, or containing gold. **2.a.** *Color.* Having the color of gold or a yellow color suggestive of gold. **b.** Lustrous; radiant. **c.** Suggestive of gold, as in richness or splendor. **3.** Of the greatest value or importance; precious. **4.** Marked by peace, prosperity, and often creativeness. **5.** Very favorable or advantageous; excellent. **6.** Having a promising future; seemingly assured of success. **7.** Of or relating to a 50th anniversary. **—gold′en•ly** *adv.* **—gold′en•ness** *n.*

golden age *n.* **1.** A period of great peace, prosperity, and happiness. **2.** *Gk. & Rom. Myth.* The first age of the world, a prosperous era during which people lived in ideal happiness.

golden aster *n.* Any of various North American plants of the genus *Chrysopsis,* having yellow rayed flower heads.

golden bantam *n.* A variety of corn having large bright yellow kernels on a relatively small ear.

golden calf *n.* **1.** A golden image of a sacrificial calf fashioned by Aaron and worshiped by the Israelites. **2.a.** Money as an object of worship; mammon. **b.** The subject of intense veneration.

golden club *n.* An aquatic plant *(Orontium aquaticum)* of the eastern United States having a clublike golden-yellow spadix.

golden eagle *n.* A large eagle *(Aquila chrysaetos)* of mountainous areas of the Northern Hemisphere having dark plumage with brownish-yellow feathers on the back of the head and neck.

gol•den•eye (gōl′dən-ī′) *n.* **1.** Either of two yellow-eyed diving ducks *(Bucephala clangula* or *B. islandica)* of northern regions. **2.** Any of various lacewings of the family Chrysopidae having yellow or copper-colored eyes.

Gold•en Fleece (gōl′dən) *n. Gk. Myth.* The fleece of the golden ram, stolen by Jason and the Argonauts from Colchis.

Golden Gate. A strait in W CA connecting the Pacific Ocean and San Francisco Bay; first sighted by Sir Francis Drake in 1579.

golden glow *n.* A tall plant *(Rudbeckia laciniata)* cultivated for its large yellow many-rayed double flower heads.

Golden Horde *n.* The Mongol army that swept over eastern Europe in the 13th century and established a suzerain in Russia. [From the golden tent of their commander.]

Golden Horn. An inlet of the Bosporus in NW Turkey forming the harbor of Istanbul.

golden mean *n.* The ethical midpoint between unethical extremes.

golden oldie *n.* A recording, movie, or other form of entertainment that was very popular in the past.

golden parachute *n. Slang.* An agreement guaranteeing a key executive lucrative severance benefits when a company changes hands followed by management shifts.

golden pheasant *n.* A brilliantly colored pheasant *(Chrysolophus pictus)* of China and Tibet.

gold•en•rod (gōl′dən-rŏd′) *n.* Any of numerous chiefly North American plants of the genus *Solidago,* having clusters of small yellow flower heads that bloom in late summer or fall.

golden rule *n.* The biblical teaching of treating others as one would be treated.

gold•en•seal (gōl′dən-sēl′) *n.* A woodland plant *(Hydrastis canadensis)* of eastern North America having small greenish-white flowers and a yellow root formerly used medicinally.

golden section *n.* A ratio, observed esp. in the fine arts, between the two dimensions of a plane figure or the two divisions of a line such that the smaller is to the larger as the larger is to the sum of the two, a ratio of roughly three to five.

Golden Valley. A city of SE MN, a suburb of Minneapolis. Pop. 20,971.

gold•field (gōld′fēld′) *n.* An area containing abundant deposits of gold or gold ore.

gold-filled (gōld′fĭld′) *adj.* Made of a hard base metal with an outer layer of gold.

gold•finch (gōld′fĭnch′) *n.* **1.** Any of several American finches of the genus *Carduelis,* esp. *C. tristis* of which the male has yellow plumage with a black forehead, wings, and tail. **2.** A Eurasian finch *(Carduelis carduelis)* having dark plumage marked with yellow and a red face.

gold•fish (gōld′fĭsh′) *n., pl.* **goldfish** or **-fish•es.** An Asian freshwater fish *(Carassius auratus),* having brassy or reddish coloring and bred as an aquarium fish.

gold foil *n.* Gold rolled or beaten into sheets somewhat thicker than gold leaf.

Gold•ing (gōl′dĭng), **William Gerald.** b. 1911. British writer noted for his dark novels, such as *The Lord of the Flies* (1954), who won the 1983 Nobel Prize for literature.

gold leaf *n.* Gold beaten into extremely thin sheets used esp. for gilding.

Gold•man (gōld′mən), **Emma.** 1869–1940. Russian-born Amer. anarchist who advocated opposition to military conscription and was deported to the Soviet Union in 1919.

gold mine *n. Informal.* A rich or plentiful source of something desired.

Gol•do•ni (gŏl-dō′nē), **Carlo.** 1707–93. Italian dramatist whose plays include *The Mistress of the Inn* (1753).

gold rush *n.* **1.** A rush of migrants to an area where gold has been discovered. **2.** Headlong pursuit of wealth and success.

Golds•bor•o (gōldz′bûr′ō). A city of E-central NC SE of Raleigh. Pop. 40,709.

gold•smith (gōld′smĭth′) *n.* **1.** An artisan who fashions objects of gold. **2.** A trader or dealer in gold articles.

Gold•smith (gōld′smĭth′), **Oliver.** 1730?–74. British writer renowned for his novel *The Vicar of Wakefield* (1766).

gold standard *n.* A monetary standard under which the basic unit of currency is equal in value to and exchangeable for a specified amount of gold.

gold•stone (gōld′stōn′) *n.* An aventurine with gold-colored inclusions.

gold•thread (gōld′thrĕd′) *n.* Any of several plants of the genus *Coptis,* having white flowers and slender yellow roots.

Gold•wa•ter (gōld′wô′tər, -wŏt′ər), **Barry Morris.** b. 1909. Amer. politician who ran unsuccessfully for President in 1964.

Gold•wyn (gōld′wĭn), **Samuel.** 1882–1974. Polish-born Amer. film producer who joined with Louis B. Mayer to form Metro-Goldwyn-Mayer (1925).

go•lem (gō′ləm) *n.* In Jewish folklore, an artificially created human being supernaturally endowed with life. [Heb. *gōlem,* lump, clod, fool < *gālam,* to wrap up.]

golf (gŏlf, gôlf) *n. Sports.* A game played on an outdoor course with a series of 9 or 18 holes spaced far apart, the object being to propel a small ball with the use of various clubs into each hole with as few strokes as possible. —*intr.v.* **golfed, golf•ing, golfs.** To play this game. [ME.] —**golf′er** *n.*

golf club *n. Sports.* **1.** One of a set of clubs having a slender shaft and a head of wood or iron, used in golf. **2.** An organization of golfers.

golf course *n. Sports.* A large tract of land laid out for golf.

Gol•gi apparatus (gôl′jē) *n.* A network of membranous vesicles present in most living cells that functions in the formation of cellular secretions. [After Camillo *Golgi* (1844?–1926), Italian histologist.]

gol•go•tha (gŏl′gə-thə) *n.* A place or occasion of great suffering. [After *Golgotha* (Calvary).]

Gol•go•tha (gŏl′gə-thə, gŏl-gŏth′ə). See **Calvary[1].**

gol•iard (gōl′yərd, -yär′) *n.* A wandering student in medieval Europe, noted for writing and singing ribald and satirical Latin songs. [ME < OFr., glutton, goliard < *gole,* throat < Lat. *gula.*] —**gol•iar′dic** (gōl-yär′dĭk) *adj.*

Go•li•ath[1] (gə-lī′əth). In the Bible, a giant Philistine warrior who was slain by David with a stone and sling.

Go•li•ath[2] (gə-lī′əth) *n.* A person or thing of colossal power or achievement.

gol•li•wog or **gol•li•wogg** (gŏl′ē-wŏg′) *n.* A doll fashioned in grotesque caricature of a Black male. [After *Golliwog,* a character in books by Florence Upton (d. 1922).]

gol•ly (gŏl′ē) *interj.* Used to express mild surprise or wonder. [Alteration of God.]

gom•been (gŏm-bēn′) *n. Irish.* Usury. [Ir.Gael. *gaimbín,* dim. of *gamba,* leg, lump (perh. influenced by *glamba,* heap).]

Go•mel (gō′məl, gô′-, gô′myĭl). A city of E Belorussia SE of Minsk; first mentioned in 1142. Pop. 465,000.

Go•mor•rah[1] (gə-môr′ə, -mŏr′ə). An ancient city of Palestine near Sodom, possibly covered by the waters of the Dead Sea. According to the Bible, the city was destroyed by fire because of its wickedness.

Go•mor•rah[2] (gə-môr′ə, -mŏr′ə) *n.* A wicked place.

Gom•pers (gŏm′pərz), **Samuel.** 1850–1924. British-born Amer. labor leader who served as president of the American Federation of Labor (1886–1924, except 1895).

gon– *pref.* Var. of **gono–.**

–gon *suff.* A figure having a specified kind or number of angles: *isogon.* [Gk. *-gōnon* < neut. of *gōnos,* angled < *gōnia,* angle. See **genu-[1]*.**]

go•nad (gō′năd′) *n.* An organ in animals that produces gametes, esp. a testis or an ovary. [NLat. *gonas, gonad-* < Gk. *gonos,* procreation, genitals. See **genə-*.**] —**go•nad′al** (gō-năd′l), **go•nad′ic** *adj.*

go•nad•o•trop•ic (gō-năd′ə-trŏp′ĭk, -trō′pĭk) also **go•nad•o•troph•ic** (-trŏf′ĭk, -trō′fĭk) *adj.* Acting on or stimulating the gonads: *a gonadotropic hormone.*

go•nad•o•tro•pin (gō-năd′ə-trō′pĭn, -trŏp′ĭn) also **go•nad•o•tro•phin** (-trō′fĭn, -trō′pĭn) *n.* A hormone that stimulates the growth and activity of the gonads.

Go•na•ïves (gō′nə-ēv′, gô-nä-). A city of W Haiti on an arm of the Caribbean Sea NNW of Port-au-Prince. Haitian independence was proclaimed here in 1804. Pop. 34,209.

Gon•court (gôN-ko͝or′), **Edmond Louis Antoine Huot de.** 1822–96. French writer who collaborated with his brother **Jules Alfred Huot de Goncourt** (1830–70) on works such as *Madame Gervaisais* (1869).

Gond (gŏnd) *n.* A member of a Dravidian people inhabiting central India.

Gon•dar (gŏn′dər, -där′) also **Gon•der** (-dər). A town of NW Ethiopia on Lake Tana; an early cap. of Ethiopia that flourished c. 1630 to c. 1860. Pop. 85,941.

Gon•di (gŏn′dē) *n.* The Dravidian language of the Gonds.

gon•do•la (gŏn′dl-ə, gŏn-dō′lə) *n.* **1.** *Naut.* **a.** A lightweight narrow barge with ends that curve up into a point and often a small cabin in the middle, propelled with a single oar from the stern. **b.** A flatbottom riverboat. **2.** A gondola car. **3.** A basket, an enclosure, or an instrument sling suspended from and carried aloft by a balloon. **4.** An enclosed structure suspended from a cable, used for conveying passengers, as to and from a ski slope. [Ital. < OItal. *gondula.*]

gondola car *n.* An open railroad freight car with low sides.

gon•do•lier (gŏn′dl-îr′) *n. Naut.* One who propels a gondola. [Fr. < Ital. *gondoliere* < *gondola,* gondola. See gondola.]

Gond•wa•na•land (gŏnd-wä′nə-lănd′) *n.* The supercontinent of the Southern Hemisphere, a hypothetical landmass that according to the theory of plate tectonics broke up into India, Australia, Antarctica, Africa, and South America. [After *Gondwana,* a region of central India < Gond.]

gone (gôn, gŏn) *v.* P.part. of **go[1].** —*adj.* **1.** Past; bygone. **2.** Advanced beyond hope or recall. **3.** Dying or dead. **4.** Ruined; lost. **5.** Carried away; absorbed. **6.** Used up; exhausted. **7.** *Slang.* Infatuated. **8.** *Slang.* Pregnant.

gon•er (gô′nər, gŏn′ər) *n. Slang.* One ruined or doomed.

gon•fa•lon (gŏn′fə-lŏn′, -lən) *n.* A banner suspended from a crosspiece, esp. as a standard in an ecclesiastical procession or as the ensign of a medieval Italian republic. [Ital. *gonfalone,* of Gmc. orig. See **gʷhen-*.**]

gon•fa•lon•ier (gŏn′fə-lə-nîr′) *n.* The bearer of a gonfalon. [Fr. < Ital. *gonfaloniere* < *gonfalone.* See gonfalon.]

gong (gông, gŏng) *n.* **1.** A rimmed metal disk that produces a loud sonorous tone when struck with a padded mallet. **2.** A usu. saucer-shaped bell that is struck with a mechanically op-

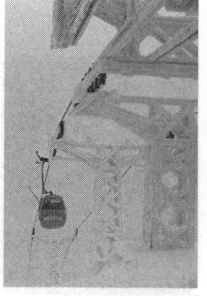

gondola
Ski lift gondola

gonfalon

ă pat	oi boy
ā pay	ou out
âr care	o͝o took
ä father	o͞o boot
ĕ pet	ŭ cut
ē be	ûr urge
ĭ pit	th thin
ī pie	*th* this
îr pier	hw which
ŏ pot	zh vision
ō toe	ə about, item
ô paw	

Stress marks:
′ (primary);
′ (secondary), as in
dictionary (dĭk′shə-nĕr′ē)

age. **2.** Any of several similar or related hawks. [ME *goshauk* < OE *gōshafoc* : *gōs*, goose; see GOOSE + *hafoc*, hawk; see HAWK[1].]

Go•shen (gō′shən). **1.** A region of ancient Egypt on the E delta of the Nile R.; inhabited by the Israelites from the time of Jacob until the Exodus. **2.** A city of N IN ESE of South Bend. Pop. 23,797.

Go•siute (gō′sho͞ot) *n., pl.* **Gosiute** or **-siutes. 1.** A member of a Native American people inhabiting an area southwest of Great Salt Lake. **2.** The Uto-Aztecan language of this people, a dialect of Shoshone.

gos•ling (gŏz′lĭng) *n.* **1.** A young goose. **2.** A naive or inexperienced young person. [ME, var. of *gesling* < ON *gæslingr*, dim. of *gās*, goose. See **ghans-***.]

gos•pel (gŏs′pəl) *n.* **1.** Often **Gospel.** The proclamation of redemption preached by Jesus and the Apostles, which is the central content of Christian revelation. **2.a. Gospel.** *Bible.* One of the first four books of the New Testament, presenting the life, teaching, death, and resurrection of Jesus. **b.** A similar narrative. **3.** Often **Gospel.** A lection from any of the four Gospels included as part of a religious service. **4.** A teaching or doctrine of a religious teacher. **5.** *Mus.* Gospel music. **6.** Something, such as an idea, accepted without question. [ME < OE *gōdspel* (ult. transl. of Gk. *euangelion*; see EVANGEL) : *gōd*, good; see GOOD + *spel*, news.]

gos•pel•er also **gos•pel•ler** (gŏs′pə-lər) *n.* **1.** One who teaches or professes faith in a gospel. **2.** One who reads or sings the Gospel as part of a church service.

gospel music *n. Mus.* A kind of American music that originated in Black Protestantism and is based on folk music, spirituals, and jazz.

gospel side also **Gospel side** *n.* The left side of an altar or a chancel as the congregation faces it.

gos•port (gŏs′pôrt′, -pōrt′) *n.* A flexible speaking tube used for one-way communication between individual compartments or cockpits of an airplane. [After GOSPORT.]

Gos•port (gŏs′pôrt′, -pōrt′). A municipal borough of S England W of Portsmouth; an embarkation point for the invasion of France in 1944. Pop. 77,400.

gos•sa•mer (gŏs′ə-mər) *n.* **1.** A soft sheer gauzy fabric. **2.** Something delicate, light, or flimsy. **3.** A fine film of cobwebs often seen floating in the air or caught on bushes or grass. —*adj.* Sheer, light, delicate, or tenuous. See Syns at **airy.** [ME *gossomer*, cobwebs : *gos*, goose; see GOOSE + *somer*, summer; see SUMMER[1].] —**gos′sa•mer•y** *adj.*

gos•sip (gŏs′əp) *n.* **1.** Rumor or talk of a personal, sensational, or intimate nature. **2.** A person who habitually spreads gossip. **3.** Trivial, chatty talk or writing. **4.** A close friend or companion. **5.** *Chiefly British.* A godparent. —*intr.v.* **-siped, -sip•ing, -sips.** To engage in or spread gossip. [ME *godsib, gossip*, godparent < OE *godsibb* : *god*, god; see GOD + *sibb*, kinsman; see **s(w)e-***.] —**gos′sip•er** *n.* —**gos′sip•ry** *n.* —**gos′sip•y** *adj.*

gos•sip•mon•ger (gŏs′əp-mŭng′gər, -mŏng′-) *n.* One who relates gossip.

gos•sy•pol (gŏs′ə-pôl′, -pōl′, -pŏl′) *n.* A toxic pigment, $C_{30}H_{30}O_8$, obtained from cottonseed oil and detoxified by heating, that inhibits sperm production. [NLat. *Gossypium*, genus name (< Lat. *gossypion*, cotton plant) + -OL[1].]

got (gŏt) *v.* P.t. and p.part. of **get.**

Gö•ta Canal (yœ′tə). A system of rivers, lakes, and canals of S Sweden extending from the Kattegat at the mouth of the **Göta River,** c. 93 km (58 mi), to the Baltic Sea.

Gö•te•borg (yœ′tə-bôr′ē). A city of SW Sweden on the Göta Canal; founded 1604. Pop. 424,085.

Goth (gŏth) *n.* A member of a Germanic people who invaded the Roman Empire in the early Christian era. [< ME *Gothes*, Goths < LLat. *Gothī* (of Gmc. orig.) and < OE *Gotan*.]

Goth. *abbr.* Gothic.

Go•tha (gō′thə, -tä). A city of central Germany W of Erfurt. The *Almanach de Gotha*, a record of Europe's aristocratic and royal houses, was first published here in 1763. Pop. 57,662.

Goth•am (gŏth′əm). New York City. The nickname was popularized by Washington Irving in *Salmagundi*, a series of satirical sketches (1807–08). —**Goth′am•ite′** (-ə-mīt′) *n.*

Goth•ic (gŏth′ĭk) *adj.* **1.a.** Of or relating to the Goths or their language. **b.** Germanic; Teutonic. **2.** Of or relating to the Middle Ages; medieval. **3.a.** Of or relating to an architectural style prevalent in western Europe from the 12th through the 15th century and marked by pointed arches, rib vaulting, and flying buttresses. **b.** Of or relating to an architectural style derived from medieval Gothic. **4.** Of or relating to painting or other art forms prevalent in northern Europe from the 12th through the 15th century. **5.** Often **gothic.** Of or relating to a style of fiction that emphasizes the grotesque, mysterious, and desolate. **6. gothic.** Barbarous; crude. —*n.* **1.** The extinct East Germanic language of the Goths. **2.** Gothic art or architecture. **3.** Often **gothic.** *Print.* **a.** See **black letter. b.** See **sans serif. 4.** A gothic novel. —**Goth′i•cal•ly** *adv.*

Gothic arch *n.* A pointed arch, esp. one with a jointed apex.

Goth•i•cism (gŏth′ĭ-sĭz′əm) *n.* **1.** The use or imitation of Gothic style. **2.** A barbarous or crude manner or style.

Goth•i•cize also **goth•i•cize** (gŏth′ĭ-sīz′) *tr.v.* **-cized, -ciz•ing, -ciz•es.** To make Gothic.

Got•land (gŏt′lənd, gôt′lŭnd). An island region of SE Sweden in the Baltic Sea, including **Gotland Island.**

got•ten (gŏt′n) *v.* A p.part. of **get.**

göt•ter•däm•mer•ung or **Göt•ter•däm•mer•ung** (gŏt′ər-dăm′ə-rŭng′, gœt′ər-dĕm′ə-ro͝ong′) *n.* A turbulent ending of a regime or an institution. [Ger., after *Götterdämmerung*, an opera by Richard Wagner : Ger. *Götter-*, genitive pl. of *Gott*, god (< MHGer. *got* < OHGer.; see **gheu(ə)-***) + Ger. *Dämmerung*, twilight (ult. < OHGer. *demar*, twilight).]

Göt•tin•gen (gœt′ĭng-ən). A city of central Germany NE of Kassel; chartered 1210. Pop. 132,454.

Gott•schalk (gŏch′ôk′, gŏt′shôk′), **Louis Moreau.** 1829–69. Amer. composer whose works include *The Dying Poet* (1864).

gouache (gwäsh, go͞o-äsh′) *n.* **1.a.** A method of painting with opaque watercolors mixed with a preparation of gum. **b.** An opaque pigment used when painting in this way. **2.** A painting executed in this manner. [Fr. < Ital. *guazzo* < Lat. *aquātiō*, watering < *aquātus*, p.part. of *aquārī*, to fetch water < *aqua*, water. See **akʷ-ā-***.]

Gou•da[1] (gou′də, go͞o′-, KHOU′dä). A city of W Netherlands NE of Rotterdam; chartered 1272. Pop. 60,026.

Gou•da[2] (go͞o′də, gou′-) *n.* A mild close-textured cheese made from whole or partially skimmed milk. [After GOUDA[1].]

Gou•dy (gou′dē), **Frederic William.** 1865–1947. American printer and designer of more than 90 typefaces.

gouge (gouj) *n.* **1.** A chisel with a rounded troughlike blade. **2.a.** A scooping or digging action, as with such a chisel. **b.** A groove or hole scooped with or as if with such a chisel. **3.** *Informal.* A large amount, as of money, exacted or extorted. —*tr.v.* **gouged, goug•ing, goug•es. 1.** To cut or scoop out with or as if with a gouge. **2.a.** To force out the eye of (a person) with one's thumb. **b.** To thrust one's thumb into the eye of. **3.** *Informal.* To extort from. **4.** *Slang.* To swindle. [ME < OFr. < LLat. *gubia*, var. of *gulbia*, of Celt. orig.] —**goug′er** *n.*

gou•lash (go͞o′läsh′, -lăsh′) *n.* A stew of beef or veal and vegetables, seasoned mainly with paprika. [Hung. *gulyás (hús)*, herdsman's (meat), goulash < *gulya*, herdsman.]

Gould (go͞old), **Jay.** 1836–92. Amer. financier who with James Fisk caused the financial panic of Sep. 24, 1869, with an attempt to corner the gold market.

Gou•nod (go͞o′nō, go͞o-nō′), **Charles François.** 1818–93. French composer whose operas include *Faust* (1859).

gou•ra•mi (go͞o-rä′mē, go͝or′ə-) *n., pl.* **-mis.** Any of various freshwater fishes of the family Anabantidae of southeast Asia, which can breathe air. [Malay *gurami*, carp, of Javanese orig.]

gourd (gôrd, gōrd, go͝ord) *n.* **1.** Any of several trailing or climbing plants related to the pumpkin, squash, and cucumber and bearing fruits with a hard rind. **2.a.** The fruit of a gourd, often of unusual shape. **b.** The dried and hollowed-out shell of such a fruit, often used as a drinking utensil. [ME *gourde* < AN, ult. < Lat. *cucurbita*.]

gourde (go͝ord) *n.* See table at **currency.** [Haitian < fem. of Fr. *gourd*, dull < LLat. *gurdus*, blunt < Lat., dullard.]

gour•mand (go͝or-mänd′, go͝or′mənd) *n.* **1.** A lover of good food. **2.** A gluttonous eater. See Usage Note at **gourmet.** [ME *gourmant*, glutton < OFr. *gormant*.]

gour•man•dise (go͝or′mən-dēz′) *n.* A taste and relish for good food. [ME *gromandise*, gluttony < OFr. *gormandise* < *gormant*, glutton.]

gour•met (go͝or-mā′, go͝or′mā′) *n.* A connoisseur of fine food and drink. [Fr. < OFr., alteration of *groumet*, servant, valet in charge of wines < ME *grom*, boy, valet.]

Usage Note: A *gourmet* is a person with discriminating taste in food and wine, as is a *gourmand*. *Gourmand* can also mean one who enjoys food in great quantities. An *epicure* is much the same as a *gourmet*, but the word may sometimes carry overtones of excessive refinement.

Gour•mont (go͝or-môN′), **Rémy de.** 1858–1915. French writer whose symbolic novels include *A Virgin Heart* (1907).

gout (gout) *n.* **1.** *Pathol.* A disturbance of uric-acid metabolism occurring predominantly in males, characterized by painful inflammation of the joints, esp. of the feet and hands, and arthritic attacks that can become chronic and result in deformity. **2.** A large blob or clot. [ME *goute* < OFr., drop, gout < Med.Lat. *gutta* < Lat., drop (< ascribing gout to drops of morbid humors).] —**gout′i•ness** *n.* —**gout′y** *adj.*

gov. *abbr.* **1.** Government. **2.** Or **Gov.** Governor.

gov•ern (gŭv′ərn) *v.* **-erned, -ern•ing, -erns.** —*tr.* **1.** To make and administer the public policy and affairs of; exercise sovereign authority in. **2.** To control the speed or magnitude of; regulate. **3.** To control the actions or behavior of. **4.** To keep under control; restrain. **5.** To exercise a deciding or determining influence on. **6.** *Gram.* To require (a specific morphological form) of accompanying words. —*intr.* **1.** To exercise political authority. **2.** To have or exercise a determining influence. [ME *governen* < OFr. *governer* < Lat. *gubernāre* < Gk. *kubernan*.] —**gov′ern•a•ble** *adj.*

Gothic
Cathedral of Notre Dame, Rheims, France

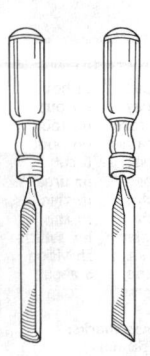

gouge
Left: Hollow gouge
Right: Parting gouge

Go•ver•na•dor Va•la•da•res (guv′ər-nə-dôr′ văl′ə-där′ĭs, gô′vĭr-nä-dôr′ vä′lä-där′ĭs). A city of E Brazil NE of Belo Horizonte. Pop. 173,624.

gov•er•nance (gŭv′ər-nəns) *n.* **1.** The act, process, or power of governing; government. **2.** The state of being governed.

gov•er•ness (gŭv′ər-nĭs) *n.* A woman employed to educate and train the children of a private household. [ME *governesse*, short for *governouresse* < OFr. *governeresse*, fem. of *governeor*, governor < Lat. *gubernātor*. See GUBERNATORIAL.]

gov•er•nes•sy (gŭv′ər-nĭs′ē, -nĭ-sē) *adj.* Fastidious, esp. about matters of learning; prim.

gov•ern•ment (gŭv′ərn-mənt) *n.* **1.** The act or process of governing, esp. the control and administration of public policy in a political unit. **2.** The office, function, or authority of one who governs or a governing body. **3.** Exercise of authority in a political unit; rule. **4.** The agency or apparatus through which one that governs exercises authority and performs its functions. **5.** A governing body or organization, as: **a.** The ruling political party or coalition in a parliamentary system. **b.** The cabinet in a parliamentary system. **c.** The persons who make up a governing body. **6.** A system or policy by which a political unit is governed. **7.** Management or administration of an organization, a business, or an institution. **8.** Political science. **—gov′ern•men′tal** (-mĕn′tl) *adj.* **—gov′ern•men′tal•ly** *adv.*

Usage Note: In American usage *government* always takes a singular verb. In British usage *government,* in the sense of a governing group of officials, is usually construed as a plural collective taking a plural verb: *The government are divided.* See Usage Note at **collective noun.**

gov•er•nor (gŭv′ər-nər) *n.* **1.** A person who governs, esp.: **a.** The chief executive of a state in the United States. **b.** An official appointed to govern a colony or territory. **c.** A member of a governing body. **2.** The manager or administrative head of an organization, a business, or an institution. **3.** A military commandant. **4.** *Chiefly British.* Used as a form of polite address for a man. **5.** A feedback device on a machine or an engine that provides automatic control, as of speed.

gov•er•nor-gen•er•al (gŭv′ər-nər-jĕn′ər-əl) *n., pl.* **gov•er•nors-gen•er•al** (gŭv′ər-nərz-) or **gov•er•nor-gen•er•als** (-jĕn′ər-əlz). A governor who has jurisdiction over subordinate governors. **—gov′er•nor-gen′er•al•ship′** *n.*

gov•er•nor•ship (gŭv′ər-nər-shĭp′) *n.* The office, term, or jurisdiction of a governor.

Gov•er•nors Island (gŭv′ər-nərz). An island of SE NY in Upper New York Bay S of Manhattan; a residence for British colonial governors in the 17th and 18th cent.

govt. *abbr.* Government.

gow•an (gou′ən) *n. Scots.* A yellow or white wildflower, esp. the Old World daisy. [Prob. alteration of ME *gollan*, a plant with yellow flowers; akin to ON *gullinn*, golden < *gull*, gold. See **ghel-**[2*].]

Gow•er (gou′ər, gôr′, gōr′), **John.** 1325?–1408. English poet whose allegorical works include *Vox Clamantis* (1382?–84).

gown (goun) *n.* **1.** A long, loose, flowing garment, such as a robe. **2.** A long, usu. formal dress for a woman. **3.** A robe or smock worn in hospitals as a guard against contamination. **4.** A distinctive outer robe worn on ceremonial occasions, as by scholars. **5.** The faculty and student body of a university: *town and gown.* —*intr. & tr.v.* **gowned, gown•ing, gowns.** To dress oneself in or invest (another) with a gown. [ME *goune* < OFr. < LLat. *gunna*, leather garment.]

gowns•man (gounz′mən) *n.* One who wears a distinctive gown as a mark of profession or office.

goy (goi) *n., pl.* **goy•im** (goi′ĭm) or **goys.** *Offensive.* Used as a disparaging term for a gentile. [Yiddish < Heb. *gôy*, nation, non-Jew.] **—goy′ish** *adj.*

Go•ya y Lu•ci•en•tes (goi′ə ē lo͞o-syĕn′tēs, gô′yä ē lo͞o-thyĕn′tĕs), **Francisco José de.** 1746–1828. Spanish painter and etcher whose works include *The Third of May 1808* (1814).

G.P. or **GP** *abbr.* General practitioner.

GPA *abbr.* Grade point average.

g.p.d. *abbr.* Gallons per day.

g.p.m. *abbr.* Gallons per minute.

GPO *abbr.* **1.** General post office. **2.** Government Printing Office.

g.p.s. *abbr.* Gallons per second.

GQ *abbr.* General quarters.

gr. *abbr.* **1.** Grade. **2.** Grain. **3.** Gram. **4.** Gravity. **5.** Great. **6.** Gross. **7.** Group.

Gr. *abbr.* Greece; Greek

Graaf•i•an follicle (grä′fē-ən, grăf′ē-) *n.* Any of the fluid-filled vesicles in the mammalian ovary containing a maturing ovum. [After Regnier de *Graaf* (1641–73), Dutch physician and anatomist.]

grab[1] (grăb) *v.* **grabbed, grab•bing, grabs.** —*tr.* **1.** To take or grasp suddenly. **2.** To capture or restrain; arrest. **3.** To obtain or appropriate unscrupulously or forcibly. **4.** To take hurriedly: *grabbed my hat and left.* **5.** *Slang.* To capture the attention of. —*intr.* To make a grasping or snatching motion. —*n.* **1.** Sudden seizure of something or someone; a snatch. **2.** One that is grabbed. **3.** A mechanical device for gripping an object. **—*idiom.* up for grabs.** *Slang.* Available for anyone to take or win. [Obsolete Du. or LGer. *grabben* < MDu. or MLGer.; see **ghrebh-**[1*].] **—grab′ber** *n.*

grab[2] (grăb) *n. Naut.* An Oriental coastal vessel with two or three masts. [Ar. *ġurāb*, raven, swift galley.]

grab bag *n.* **1.** A container filled with articles, such as gifts, to be drawn unseen. **2.** *Slang.* A miscellaneous collection.

grab•ble (grăb′əl) *intr.v.* **-bled, -bling, -bles.** **1.** To feel around with the hands; grope. **2.** To fall down; sprawl. [Prob. < Du. *grabbelen* < MDu., freq. of *grabben*, to grab. See GRAB[1].] **—grab′bler** *n.*

grab•by (grăb′ē) *adj.* **-bi•er, -bi•est.** *Informal.* Inclined to grab; greedy. **—grab′bi•ness** *n.*

gra•ben (grä′bən) *n.* A usu. elongated depression between geologic faults. [Ger. *Graben* < MHGer. *grabe*, trench < OHGer. *grabo* < *graban*, to dig. See **ghrebh-**[2*].]

Grac•chi (grăk′ī). See **Gracchus.**

Grac•chus (grăk′əs), **Tiberius Sempronius.** 163–133 B.C. Roman social reformer who with his brother **Gaius Sempronius Gracchus** (153–121 B.C.), known together as "the Gracchi," initiated reforms to aid farmers.

grace (grās) *n.* **1.** Seemingly effortless beauty or charm of movement, form, or proportion. **2.** A characteristic or quality pleasing for its charm or refinement. **3.** A sense of fitness or propriety. **4.a.** A disposition to be generous or helpful; goodwill. **b.** Mercy; clemency. **5.** A favor rendered by one who need not do so; indulgence. **6.** A temporary immunity or exemption; a reprieve. **7. Graces.** *Gk. & Rom. Myth.* Three sister goddesses who dispense charm and beauty. **8.** *Theol.* **a.** Divine love and protection bestowed freely on people. **b.** The state of being protected or sanctified by the favor of God. **c.** An excellence or a power granted by God. **9.** A short prayer said before or after a meal. **10. Grace.** Used with *His, Her,* or *Your* as a title and form of address for a duke, a duchess, or an archbishop. **11.** *Mus.* An embellishment such as an appoggiatura or a trill. —*tr.v.* **graced, grac•ing, grac•es.** **1.** To honor or favor. **2.** To give beauty, elegance, or charm to. **3.** *Mus.* To embellish with grace notes. **—*idioms.* in the bad graces of.** Out of favor with. **in the good graces of.** In favor with. **with bad grace.** In a grudging manner. **with good grace.** In a willing manner. [ME < OFr. < Lat. *grātia* < *grātus*, pleasing. See **gʷerə-**[2*].]

grace cup *n.* **1.** A cup used at the end of a meal, usu. after grace, for the final toast. **2.** The final toast of a meal.

grace•ful (grās′fəl) *adj.* Showing grace of movement, form, or proportion. **—grace′ful•ly** *adv.* **—grace′ful•ness** *n.*

grace•less (grās′lĭs) *adj.* **1.** Lacking grace; clumsy. **2.** Having or exhibiting no sense of propriety or decency. **3.** Inferior or clumsy in treatment or performance: *a graceless production of the play.* **—grace′less•ly** *adv.* **—grace′less•ness** *n.*

grace note *n. Mus.* A note, esp. an appoggiatura, added as an embellishment.

grace period *n.* **1.** A period in which a debt may be paid without accruing interest or penalty. **2.** A period in which an insurance policy is effective though the premium is past due.

grac•ile (grăs′əl, -īl′) *adj.* **1.** Gracefully slender. **2.** Graceful. [Lat. *gracilis*.] **—gra•cil′i•ty** (grə-sĭl′ĭ-tē) *n.*

gra•ci•o•so (grä′sē-ō′sō, -zō) *n., pl.* **-sos.** A clown or buffoon in Spanish comedies. [Sp. < Lat. *grātiōsus*. See GRACIOUS.]

gra•cious (grā′shəs) *adj.* **1.** Marked by kindness and warm courtesy. **2.** Marked by tact and propriety. **3.** Of a merciful or compassionate nature. **4.** Condescendingly courteous; indulgent. **5.** Marked by charm or beauty; graceful. **6.** Marked by elegance and good taste. **7.** *Archaic.* Enjoying favor or grace; acceptable or pleasing. —*interj.* Used to express surprise or mild emotion. [ME < OFr. *gracieus* < Lat. *grātiōsus* < *grātia*, good will. See GRACE.] **—gra′cious•ly** *adv.* **—gra′cious•ness** *n.*

grack•le (grăk′əl) *n.* **1.** Any of several American blackbirds of the family Icteridae, esp. of the genus *Quiscalus,* having iridescent blackish plumage. **2.** Any of several Asian mynas of the genus *Gracula.* [NLat. *Grācula*, genus name < Lat. *grāculus*, jackdaw. See **gerə-**[2*].]

grad (grăd) *n. Informal.* A graduate of a school or college.

grad. *abbr.* **1.** Gradient. **2.** Graduated.

gra•date (grā′dāt′) *v.* **-dat•ed, -dat•ing, -dates.** —*intr.* To pass imperceptibly from one degree, shade, or tone to another. —*tr.* **1.** To cause to gradate. **2.** To arrange in or according to grades. [Back-formation < GRADATION.]

gra•da•tion (grā-dā′shən) *n.* **1.a.** A series of gradual successive stages; a systematic progression. **b.** A degree or stage in such a progression. **2.** A passing by barely perceptible degrees from one tone or shade, as of color, to another. **3.** The act of gradating or arranging in grades. **4.** *Ling.* See **ablaut.** [Lat. *gradātiō*, *gradātiōn-* < *gradus*, step. See GRADE.] **—gra•da′tion•al** *adj.* **—gra•da′tion•al•ly** *adv.*

grade (grād) *n.* **1.** A stage or degree in a process. **2.** A position in a scale of size, quality, or intensity. **3.** An accepted level or standard. **4.** A set whose members fall in the same specified limits; a class. **5.a.** A class at a school or the pupils in it. **b. grades.** Elementary school. **6.** A mark indicating a stu-

Francisco Goya
1799 self-portrait
from a series of satirical paintings and prints entitled *Los Caprichos*

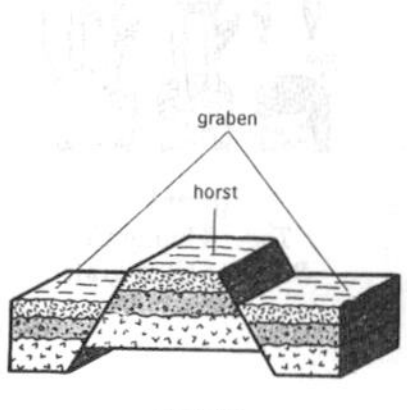

graben

ă pat	oi boy
ā pay	ou out
âr care	o͝o took
ä father	o͞o boot
ĕ pet	ŭ cut
ē be	ûr urge
ĭ pit	th thin
ī pie	*th* this
îr pier	hw which
ŏ pot	zh vision
ō toe	ə about,
ô paw	item

Stress marks:
′ (primary);
′ (secondary), as in
dictionary (dĭk′shə-nĕr′ē)

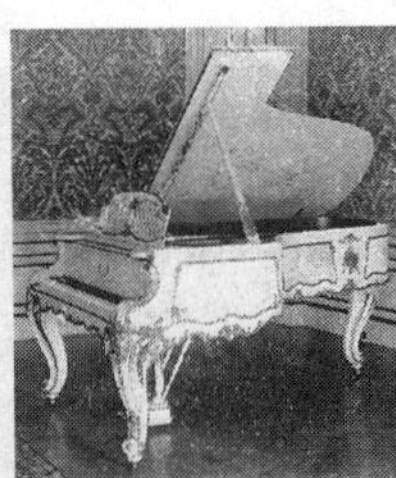
grand piano
Rococo style

Ulysses S. Grant

grape

Grande-Terre (grăn′târ′, gräɴd-). An island of E Guadeloupe in the Leeward Is. of the West Indies.
gran•deur (grăn′jər, -jo͝or′) *n.* **1.** The quality or condition of being grand; magnificence. **2.** Nobility or greatness of character. [ME < OFr. < *grand*, great < Lat. *grandis*.]
Grand Falls. See **Churchill Falls.**
grand•fa•ther (grănd′fä′*th*ər, grăn′-) *n.* **1.** The father of one's mother or father. **2.** A forefather; an ancestor. —*tr.v.* **-thered, -ther•ing, -thers.** To exempt (one already involved in an activity or a business) from new regulations.
grandfather clause *n.* **1.** A provision in a statute exempting those already involved in a regulated activity from the new regulations in the statute. **2.** A clause in the constitutions of several southern states before 1915, intended to disfranchise Black people by exempting from stringent voting requirements all lineal descendants of persons registered before 1867.
grandfather clock *n.* A pendulum clock enclosed in a tall narrow cabinet. [From the song *My Grandfather's Clock* by Henry C. Work.]
grand•fa•ther•ly (grănd′fä′*th*ər-lē, grăn′-) *adj.* **1.** Of or befitting a grandfather. **2.** Having the qualities of a grandfather.
Grand Forks. A city of E ND on the Red R. N of Fargo; estab. as a fur-trading post in 1801. Pop. 49,425.
Grand Gui•gnol (gräɴ gē-nyôl′) *n.* Drama emphasizing the horrifying or the macabre. [After Le *Grand Guignol*, a theater in Paris.]
gran•dil•o•quence (grăn-dĭl′ə-kwəns) *n.* Pompous or bombastic speech or expression. [< GRANDILOQUENT < Lat. *grandiloquus* : *grandis*, great + *loquī*, to speak; see **tolkʷ-*.**] —**gran•dil′o•quent** *adj.* —**gran•dil′o•quent•ly** *adv.*
gran•di•ose (grăn′dē-ōs′, grăn′dē-ōs′) *adj.* **1.** Marked by greatness of scope or intent. See Syns at **grand. 2.** Marked by feigned or affected grandeur; pompous. [Fr. < Ital. *grandioso* < *grande*, great < Lat. *grandis*.] —**gran′di•ose′ly** *adv.* —**gran′di•os′i•ty** (-ŏs′ĭ-tē), **gran′di•ose′ness** *n.*
gran•di•o•so (grän′dē-ō′sō, -zō, grăn′) *adv. & adj. Mus.* In a grand and noble style. [Ital. See GRANDIOSE.]
Grand Island. A city of SE-central NE W of Lincoln; orig. settled on the Platte R. in 1857. Pop. 39,386.
Grand Junc•tion (jŭngk′shən). A city of W CO at the junction of the Gunnison and Colorado rivers. Pop. 29,034.
grand jury *n. Law.* A jury of 12 to 23 persons convened in private session to evaluate accusations against persons charged with crime and determine whether a bill of indictment is warranted.
grand•kid (grănd′kĭd′, grăn′-) *n. Informal.* A grandchild.
Grand Lama *n.* Either of two high lamas of Tibetan Buddhism, the Dalai Lama or the Panchen Lama.
grand larceny *n. Law.* The theft of property of a value exceeding the amount constituting petit larceny.
grand•ma (grănd′mä′, grăn′-, grăm′mä′, grăm′ə) *n. Informal.* A grandmother.
grand mal (grăn′ mäl′, măl′, grănd′) *n.* A severe form of epilepsy characterized by seizures involving spasms and loss of consciousness. [Fr. : *grand*, great + *mal*, illness.]
Grand Ma•nan Island (mə-năn′). An island of S New Brunswick, Canada, in the Bay of Fundy separated from the coast of ME by **Grand Manan Channel.**
grand master or **grand•mas•ter** (grănd′măs′tər) *n.* **1.** *Games.* A chess player regarded as having the highest level of ability. **2.** A person of the highest competence or accomplishment in a field.
grand•moth•er (grănd′mŭ*th*′ər, grăn′-) *n.* **1.** The mother of one's father or mother. **2.** A female ancestor.
grand•moth•er•ly (grănd′mŭ*th*′ər-lē, grăn′-) *adj.* **1.** Characteristic of or befitting a grandmother. **2.** Having the qualities of a grandmother.
grand•neph•ew (grănd′nĕf′yo͞o, grăn′-) *n.* A son of one's nephew or niece.
grand•niece (grănd′nēs′, grăn′-) *n.* A daughter of one's nephew or niece.
grand opera *n. Mus.* A serious or melodramatic drama having the entire text set to music.
grand•pa (grănd′pä′, grăn′-, grăm′pä′, grăm′pə) *n. Informal.* A grandfather.
grand•par•ent (grănd′pâr′ənt, -păr′-, grăn′-) *n.* A parent of one's mother or father; a grandmother or grandfather. —**grand′par′ent•hood′** *n.*
grand piano *n. Mus.* A piano having the strings strung in a horizontal harp-shaped frame supported usu. on three legs.
Grand Prairie. A city of NE TX between Dallas and Fort Worth. Pop. 99,616.
Grand Pré (grăn′ prā′, gräɴ′). A village of W Nova Scotia, Canada, on an arm of the Bay of Fundy; settled by Acadians and the setting for Longfellow's poem *Evangeline* (1847).
Grand Prix (gräɴ′ prē′) *n., pl.* **Grand Prix** (prēz′, prē′). *Sports.* Any of several competitive international road races for sports cars of specific engine size over an exacting, usu. risky course. [Fr., short for *Grand Prix de Paris*, originally an international horserace established in 1863 at Longchamp in Paris.]
Grand Rapids (grănd). A city of W-central MI on the Grand R. WNW of Lansing. Pop. 189,126.
Grand River. 1. A river rising in SE IA and flowing c. 483 km (300 mi) across NW MO to the Missouri R. **2.** A river of S MI flowing c. 418 km (260 mi) to Lake Michigan.
grand•sire (grănd′sīr′, grăn′-) also **grand•sir** (-sər) *n. Archaic.* **1.** A grandfather. **2.** A male ancestor; a forefather. **3.** An old man.
grand slam *n.* **1.** *Games.* The winning of all the tricks during the play of one hand in bridge and other whist-derived card games. **2.** *Sports.* The winning of all the major or specified events, esp. on a professional circuit. **3.** *Baseball.* A home run hit when three runners are on base.
grand•son (grănd′sŭn′, grăn′-) *n.* A son of one's son or daughter.
grand•stand (grănd′stănd′, grăn′-) *n.* **1.** A roofed stand for spectators at a stadium or racetrack. **2.** The spectators or audience at an event. —*intr.v.* **-stand•ed, -stand•ing, -stands.** To perform ostentatiously so as to impress. —**grand′stand′er** *n.*
Grand Te•ton (tē′tŏn′, tēt′n). A mountain, 4,198.6 m (13,766 ft), of the Teton Range in NW WY.
grand tour *n.* **1.** A comprehensive tour or survey. **2.** An extended tour of continental Europe formerly considered a finishing course for young English gentlemen.
Grand Turk (tûrk). The chief island of the Turks and Caicos Is. in the Atlantic SE of the Bahamas. The town of **Grand Turk** (pop. 3,146) is the cap. of the island group.
grand•un•cle (grănd′ŭng′kəl) *n.* See **great-uncle.**
grand unified theory *n. Phys.* A theory of elementary particles that unites the weak, strong, and electromagnetic interactions into one field theory, viewing the known interactions as low-energy manifestations of a single unified interaction.
Grand•view (grănd′vyo͞o′). A city of W MO bordered on three sides by S Kansas City. Pop. 24,967.
grange (grānj) *n.* **1. Grange. a.** An association of farmers founded in the United States in 1867. **b.** One of the branch lodges of this association. **2.** *Chiefly British.* A farm, esp. the residence and outbuildings of a gentleman farmer. **3.** *Archaic.* A granary. [ME, granary < OFr. < VLat. **grānica* < Lat. *grānum*, seed. See **grə-no-*.**]
grani– *pref.* Grain; seed: *granivorous.* [Lat. *grāni-* < *grānum*, seed. See GRAM².]
gran•ite (grăn′ĭt) *n.* **1.** A common, coarse-grained, hard igneous rock consisting chiefly of quartz, orthoclase or microcline, and mica, used for building. **2.** Unyielding endurance; steadfastness. [Ital. *granito* < p.part. of *granire*, to make grainy < *grano*, grain < Lat. *grānum.* See **grə-no-*.**] —**gra•nit′ic** (grā-nĭt′ĭk, grə-), **gran′it•oid′** (grăn′ĭ-toid′) *adj.*
Gran•ite City (grăn′ĭt). A city of SW IL, a suburb of East St. Louis on the Mississippi R. Pop. 32,862.
gran•ite•ware (grăn′ĭt-wâr′) *n.* **1.** Iron utensils with a mottled enamel resembling granite. **2.** Earthenware with a speckled glaze resembling granite.
gra•niv•o•rous (grə-nĭv′ər-əs) *adj.* Feeding on grain and seeds.
gran•ny or **gran•nie** (grăn′ē) *n., pl.* **-nies. 1.** *Informal.* A grandmother. **2.** *Informal.* A fussy person. **3.** *Chiefly Southern U.S.* See **midwife** 1. [Short for GRANDMOTHER or GRANDAM.]
granny knot *n.* A knot resembling a square knot but with the second tie crossed incorrectly. [So called in contempt.]
grano– *pref.* Granite: *granolith.* [Ger. < *Granit*, granite < Ital. *granito.* See GRANITE.]
gra•no•la (grə-nō′lə) *n.* Rolled oats and various ingredients, such as nuts. [Originally a trademark.]
gran•o•lith (grăn′ə-lĭth′) *n.* A paving stone of crushed granite and cement. —**gran′o•lith′ic** *adj.*
gran•o•phyre (grăn′ə-fīr′) *n.* A fine-grained granite porphyry having a groundmass with irregular intergrowths of quartz and feldspar. [Ger. *Granophyr* : *grano-*, grano- + *Porphyr*, porphyry (< Med.Lat. *porphyrium*; see PORPHYRY).]
grant (grănt) *tr.v.* **grant•ed, grant•ing, grants. 1.** To consent to the fulfillment of. **2.** To accord as a favor, prerogative, or privilege. **3.a.** To bestow; confer: *grant aid.* **b.** To transfer (property) by a deed. **4.** To concede; acknowledge. —*n.* **1.** The act of granting. **2.a.** Something granted. **b.** A giving of funds for a specific purpose. **3.** *Law.* **a.** A transfer of property by deed. **b.** The property so transferred. **c.** The deed by which the property is so transferred. **4.** One of several tracts of land in New Hampshire, Maine, and Vermont originally granted to an individual or a group. [ME *granten* < OFr. *granter*, var. of *creanter* < VLat. **crēdentāre*, to assure < Lat. *crēdēns*, *crēdent-*, pr.part. of *crēdere*, to believe. See **kerd-*.**] —**grant′a•ble** *adj.* —**grant′er** *n.*
Grant (grănt), **Cary.** 1904–86. British-born Amer. actor whose films include *The Philadelphia Story* (1940).
Grant, Ulysses Simpson. 1822–85. The 18th President of the U.S. (1869–77) and a Civil War general. After his victorious Vicksburg campaign (1862–63) he was made commander in chief of the Union Army (1864) and accepted the surrender of Gen. Robert E. Lee at Appomattox (1865).
grant•ee (grăn-tē′) *n. Law.* One to whom a grant is made.
grant-in-aid (grănt′ĭn-ād′) *n., pl.* **grants-in-aid** (grănts′-). **1.** A giving of federal funds to a state or local government to sub-

sidize a public project. **2.** A giving of funds to an institution or a person in order to subsidize a project or program.

gran•tor (grăn′tər, -tôr′) *n. Law.* One that makes a grant.

gran•u•lar (grăn′yə-lər) *adj.* **1.** Composed or appearing to be composed of granules or grains. **2.** Having a grainy texture. **3.** *Biol.* Containing granules: *granular cells.* **—gran′u•lar′i•ty** (-lăr′ĭ-tē) *n.* **—gran′u•lar•ly** *adv.*

gran•u•late (grăn′yə-lāt′) *v.* **-lat•ed, -lat•ing, -lates.** *—tr.* **1.** To form into grains or granules. **2.** To make rough and grainy. *—intr.* To become granular or grainy. **—gran′u•la′tive** *adj.* **—gran′u•la′tor** *n.*

gran•u•la•tion (grăn′yə-lā′shən) *n.* **1.a.** The act or process of granulating. **b.** The condition or appearance of being granulated. **2.** *Physiol.* **a.** Small fleshy beadlike outgrowths of new capillaries on the surface of a wound that is healing. **b.** The formation of these protuberances. **3.** *Astron.* The transient brilliant granular markings on the photosphere of the sun.

gran•ule (grăn′yo͞ol) *n.* **1.** A small grain or pellet; a particle. **2.** *Geol.* A rock fragment larger than a sand grain and smaller than a pebble, between 2 and 4 millimeters in diameter. **3.** *Astron.* One of the transient brilliant markings on the photosphere of the sun. **4.** *Biol.* A cellular or cytoplasmic particle, esp. one that stains readily. [LLat. *grānulum,* dim. of Lat. *grānum,* grain. See **grə-no-***.]

gran•u•lite (grăn′yə-līt′) *n.* A fine-grained metamorphic rock often banded in appearance and composed chiefly of feldspar and quartz. **—gran′u•lit′ic** (-lĭt′ĭk) *adj.*

gran•u•lo•cyte (grăn′yə-lō-sīt′) *n.* Any of a group of white blood cells having cytoplasmic granules.

gran•u•lo•ma (grăn′yə-lō′mə) *n., pl.* **-mas** or **-ma•ta** (-mə-tə). A mass of inflamed granulation tissue, usu. associated with infections. **—gran′u•lo′ma•tous** (-mə-təs) *adj.*

gran•u•lose (grăn′yə-lōs′) *adj.* Having a surface covered with granules.

gra•num (grā′nəm) *n. Bot.* A stacked chlorophyll-containing structure within a chloroplast that is the site of the light reactions of photosynthesis. [Lat. *grānum,* seed. See GRAIN.]

Gran•ville-Bar•ker (grăn′vĭl-bär′kər), **Harley Granville.** 1877–1946. British actor, playwright, and theater manager known for his Shakespearean criticism.

grape (grāp) *n.* **1.** Any of numerous woody vines of the genus *Vitis,* bearing edible berries and cultivated in many species and varieties. **2.** The fleshy smooth-skinned purple, red, or green berry of a grape, eaten raw or dried as a raisin and used in winemaking. **3.** *Color.* A dark violet to dark grayish purple. **4.** Grapeshot. [ME < OFr., bunch of grapes, hook, of Gmc. orig.]

grape fern *n.* Any of various ferns of the genus *Botrychium,* having a fertile frond bearing grapelike clusters of spore cases.

grape•fruit (grāp′fro͞ot′) *n.* **1.** A tropical or semitropical evergreen *(Citrus paradisi)* cultivated for its edible fruit. **2.** Its large round fruit having juicy, somewhat acid pulp.

grape hyacinth *n.* Any of various Eurasian plants of the genus *Muscari,* having rounded, usu. blue flowers.

grape•shot (grāp′shŏt′) *n.* A cluster of small iron balls formerly used as a cannon charge.

grape sugar *n.* Dextrose obtained from grapes.

grape•vine (grāp′vīn′) *n.* **1.** A vine on which grapes grow. **2.a.** The informal transmission of information, gossip, or rumor. **b.** A source of confidential information.

grap•ey or **grap•y** (grā′pē) *adj.* **-i•er, -i•est.** Of or resembling grapes: *a wine with a grapey taste.* **—grap′i•ness** *n.*

graph[1] (grăf) *n.* **1.** A diagram that shows the relation, often functional, between two sets of numbers as a set of points having coordinates determined by the relation. **2.** A pictorial device, such as a pie chart, used to illustrate quantitative relationships. *—tr.v.* **graphed, graph•ing, graphs. 1.** To represent by a graph. **2.** To plot (a function) on a graph. [Short for *graphic formula.*]

graph[2] (grăf) *n.* **1.** The spelling of a word. **2.** Any of the possible forms of a grapheme. **3.** A written character that represents a phoneme, syllable, word, or other expression and cannot be further analyzed. [Gk. *graphē,* writing. See GRAPHIC.]

-graph *suff.* **1.** Something written or drawn: *monograph.* **2.** An instrument for writing, drawing, or recording: *seismograph.* [Fr. *-graphe* < LLat. *-graphus* < Gk. *-graphos* < *graphein,* to write. See **gerbh-***.]

graph•eme (grăf′ēm′) *n.* **1.** A letter of an alphabet. **2.** All of the letters and letter combinations that represent a phoneme, as *f, ph,* and *gh* for the phoneme /f/. [GRAPH[2] + -EME.] **—gra•phe′mic** (gră-fē′mĭk) *adj.* **—gra•phe′mi•cal•ly** *adv.*

-grapher *suff.* One who writes about a specified subject or in a specified manner: *stenographer.* [< LLat. *-graphus* < Gk. *-graphos* < *graphein,* to write. See **gerbh-***.]

graph•ic (grăf′ĭk) *adj.* also **graph•i•cal** (-ĭ-kəl). **1.a.** Of or relating to written representation. **b.** Of or relating to pictorial representation. **2.** Of, relating to, or represented by or as if by a graph. **3.a.** Described in vivid detail. **b.** Clearly outlined or set forth. **4.** Of or relating to the graphic arts. **5.** Of or relating to graphics. **6.** *Geol.* Having crystals resembling printed characters. *—n.* **1.** A work of graphic art. **2.** A pictorial device used for illustration, as a slide. **3.** A graphic display generated by a computer or an imaging device. [Lat. *graphicus* < Gk. *graphikos* < *graphē,* writing < *graphein,* to write. See **gerbh-***.] **—graph′i•cal•ly** *adv.* **—graph′ic•ness** *n.*

Syns: graphic, lifelike, realistic, vivid. The central meaning shared by these adjectives is "strikingly sharp and accurate": *a graphic account of the battle; a lifelike portrait; a realistic description; a vivid recollection.*

graphic arts *pl.n.* **1.** The visual arts and associated techniques involving the application of lines and strokes to a two-dimensional surface. **2.** The visual arts and associated techniques in which images are made by blocks, plates, or type.

graph•ics (grăf′ĭks) *n.* **1.a.** *(used with a sing. v.)* The making of drawings in accordance with the rules of mathematics. **b.** *(used with a pl. v.)* Calculations from such drawings. **2.** *Comp. Sci.* **a.** *(used with a sing. or pl. v.)* The pictorial representation and manipulation of data, as used in computer-aided design, typesetting, the graphic arts, and educational and recreational programs. **b.** *(used with a sing. v.)* The process by which a computer displays data pictorially.

graph•ite (grăf′īt′) *n.* A soft, gray to black, hexagonally crystallized allotrope of carbon with a metallic luster, used in lead pencils, lubricants, and coatings and fabricated into a variety of forms such as molds and electrodes. [Gk. *graphein,* to write; see **gerbh-*** + -ITE[1].] **—gra•phit′ic** (gră-fĭt′ĭk) *adj.*

graph•i•tize (grăf′ĭ-tīz′) *tr.v.* **-tized, -tiz•ing, -tiz•es. 1.** To convert into graphite, as by heating. **2.** To coat or impregnate with graphite. **—graph′i•ti•za′tion** (-tĭ-zā′shən) *n.*

gra•phol•o•gy (gră-fŏl′ə-jē) *n.* The study of handwriting, esp. for analyzing character. [Gk. *graphē,* writing; see GRAPHIC + -LOGY.] **—gra•phol′o•gist** *n.*

graph paper *n.* Paper ruled usu. into small squares of equal size for use in drawing charts, graphs, or diagrams.

-graphy *suff.* **1.** A writing or representation produced in a specified manner or by a specified process: *photography.* **2.a.** A writing about a specified subject: *oceanography.* **b.** A representation of a specified object: *phonography.* [Lat. *-graphia* < Gk. < *graphein,* to write. See **gerbh-***.]

grap•nel (grăp′nəl) *n.* **1.** *Naut.* A small anchor with three or more flukes, esp. for anchoring a small vessel. **2.** See **grapple** 1a. [ME *grapenel,* prob. ult. < OFr. *grapin,* hook, dim. of *grape.* See GRAPE.]

grap•pa (grä′pə) *n.* An Italian brandy distilled from the pomace of grapes used in winemaking. [Ital. < Ital. dial., grape stalk, brandy, of Gmc. orig.]

grap•ple (grăp′əl) *n.* **1.a.** An iron shaft with claws at one end, usu. thrown by a rope and used for grasping and holding, esp. of an enemy ship alongside. **b.** *Naut.* See **grapnel** 1. **2.** The act of grappling. **3.** *Sports.* **a.** A contest in which the participants attempt to clutch or grip each other. **b.** A grasp or grip in such a contest. *—v.* **-pled, -pling, -ples.** *—tr.* **1.** To seize and hold, as with a grapple. **2.** To seize firmly, as with the hands. *—intr.* **1.** To hold onto something with or as if with a grapple. **2.** To use a grapple or similar device. **3.** To struggle in or as if in wrestling. [ME *grapel* < OFr. *grapil,* dim. of *grape,* hook. See GRAPE.] **—grap′pler** *n.*

grap•pling (grăp′lĭng) *n.* **1.** See **grapple** 1a. **2.** *Naut.* See **grapnel** 1.

grappling hook *n.* See **grapple** 1a.

grappling iron *n.* See **grapple** 1a.

grap•to•lite (grăp′tə-līt′) *n.* Any of numerous extinct colonial marine animals chiefly of the orders Dendroidea and Graptoloidea of the late Cambrian to the early Mississippian periods, whose fossils help date Paleozoic rocks. [Gk. *graptos,* written (< *graphein,* to write; see GRAPHIC) + -LITE.]

grap•y (grā′pē) *adj.* **-i•er, -i•est.** Var. of **grapey.**

GRAS *abbr.* Generally recognized as safe.

Gras•mere (grăs′mîr′). A lake of NW England in the Lake District. Dove Cottage, in the former village of **Grasmere,** was the home of William Wordsworth from 1799 to 1808.

grasp (grăsp) *v.* **grasped, grasp•ing, grasps.** *—tr.* **1.** To take hold of or seize firmly with or as if with the hand. **2.** To clasp firmly with or as if with the hand. **3.** To take hold of intellectually; comprehend. See Syns at **apprehend.** *—intr.* **1.** To make a motion of seizing, snatching, or clutching. **2.** To show eager and prompt willingness or acceptance. *—n.* **1.** The act of grasping. **2.a.** A firm hold or grip. **b.** An embrace. **3.** The ability or power to seize or attain; reach. **4.** Understanding; comprehension. [ME *graspen.* See **ghrebh-[1]***.]

grasp•ing (grăs′pĭng) *adj.* Exceedingly eager for material gain; avaricious. **—grasp′ing•ly** *adv.* **—grasp′ing•ness** *n.*

grass (grăs) *n.* **1.a.** The grass family. **b.** The members of the grass family considered as a group. **2.** Any of various plants having slender leaves characteristic of the grass family. **3.** An expanse of ground covered with grass or similar plants. **4.** Grazing land; pasture. **5.** *Slang.* Marijuana. **6.** *Electron.* Small variations in amplitude of an oscilloscope display caused by electrical noise. *—v.* **grassed, grass•ing, grass•es.** *—tr.* **1.a.** To cover with grass. **b.** To grow grass on. **2.** To feed (livestock) with grass. *—intr.* **1.** To become covered with grass. **2.** To graze. [ME *gras* < OE *græs.* See **ghrē-***.]

Grass (gräs), **Günter Wilhelm.** Born 1927. German writer best known for his novel *The Tin Drum* (1959).

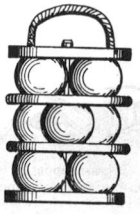

grapeshot

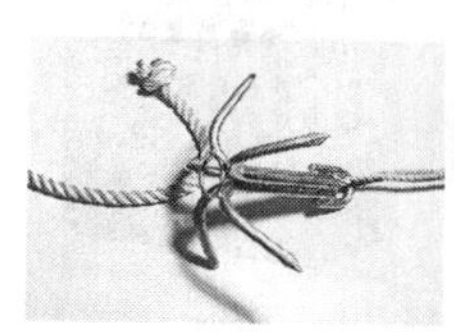

grapple

ă pat	oi boy
ā pay	ou out
âr care	o͝o took
ä father	o͞o boot
ĕ pet	ŭ cut
ē be	ûr urge
ĭ pit	th thin
ī pie	*th* this
îr pier	hw which
ŏ pot	zh vision
ō toe	ə about,
ô paw	item

Stress marks:
′ (primary);
′ (secondary), as in
dictionary (dĭk′shə-nĕr′ē)

great seal
Great Seal of the United States

Canada. The **Great Bear River**, c. 113 km (70 mi), flows W from the lake to the Mackenzie R.

great blue heron *n.* An American heron *(Ardea herodias)* with blue-gray plumage, a white head, and a dark crest.

Great Brit•ain (brĭt′n). **1.** An island off the W coast of Europe comprising England, Scotland, and Wales. **2.** See **United Kingdom.**

great circle *n.* **1.** A circle described by the intersection of the surface of a sphere with a plane passing through the center of the sphere. **2.** A segment of such a circle representing the shortest distance between two terrestrial points.

great•coat (grāt′kōt′) *n.* A heavy overcoat.

Great Dane *n.* Any of various large strong dogs of a breed developed in Germany, having a short smooth coat and a narrow head.

great divide *n.* **1.** A large or major watershed of a landmass. **2.** A major point of division, esp. death.

Great Di•vide (dĭ-vīd′). See **Continental Divide.**

Great Di•vid•ing Range (dĭ-vī′dĭng). A chain of mountains curving along the E coast of Australia.

great•en (grāt′n) *tr. & intr.v.* **-ened, -en•ing, -ens.** *Archaic.* To make or become great or greater.

great•er also **Great•er** (grā′tər) *adj.* Of, relating to, or being a city together with its populous suburbs.

Greater An•til•les (ăn-tĭl′ēz). An island group of the N West Indies including Cuba, Jamaica, Hispaniola, and Puerto Rico.

greater omentum *n.* A fold of the peritoneum, passing from the stomach to the transverse colon.

great•est common divisor (grā′tĭst) *n. Math.* The largest number that divides evenly into each of a given set of numbers.

Great Falls. A city of central MT on the Missouri R. NNE of Helena. Pop. 55,097.

great•heart•ed (grāt′här′tĭd) *adj.* **1.** Noble or courageous in spirit. **2.** Generous; magnanimous. **—great′heart′ed•ly** *adv.* **—great′heart′ed•ness** *n.*

great horned owl *n.* A large North American owl *(Bubo virginianus)* with prominent ear tufts and brownish plumage.

Great In•di•an Desert (ĭn′dē-ən). See **Thar Desert.**

Great Kar•roo (kə-ro͞o′). See **Karroo.**

Great Lakes. A group of five freshwater lakes of central North America between the U.S. and Canada, including Lakes Superior, Huron, Erie, Ontario, and Michigan; first sighted by French traders in the early 17th cent.

great laurel *n.* See **rosebay** 1.

Great Mi•am•i River (mī-ăm′ē, -ăm′ə). See **Miami River.**

Great Ouse River (o͞oz). See **Ouse River** 1.

Great Pee Dee (pē′ dē′). See **Pee Dee.**

Great Plains. A vast grassland region of central North America E of the Rocky Mts.

Great Power *n.* One of the nations having great political, social, and economic influence in international affairs.

Great Pyrenees *n.* Any of a breed of large heavy-boned dogs having a thick white coat and developed to guard sheep.

Great Rift Valley. A geologic depression of SW Asia and E Africa extending from the Jordan R. valley to Mozambique.

Great Russian *n.* A member of the Russian-speaking people inhabiting Russia.

Great Saint Ber•nard Pass (sānt′ bər-närd′). An Alpine pass, 2,473.6 m (8,110 ft), on the Italian-Swiss border.

Great Salt Lake (sôlt). A shallow body of salt water of NW UT between the Wasatch Range and the **Great Salt Lake Desert.**

Great Sand•y Desert (săn′dē). A vast arid area of NW Australia N of the Gibson Desert.

great seal *n.* The principal seal of a government or state, with which official documents are stamped.

great skua *n.* A predatory gull-like sea bird *(Catharacta skua)* of northern regions, having brownish plumage.

Great Slave Lake (slāv). A lake of S Northwest Terrs., Canada.

Great Smok•y Mountains (smō′kē). A range of the Appalachians on the NC–TN border rising to 2,026.1 m (6,643 ft).

Great Spirit *n.* The principal deity in the religion of many Native American peoples.

great-un•cle or **great uncle** (grāt′ŭng′kəl) *n.* A brother of one's grandparent.

Great Vic•to•ri•a Desert (vĭk-tôr′ē-ə, -tōr′-). An arid region of S-central Australia.

Great Vowel Shift *n.* A series of phonetic changes in Early Modern English that raised the Middle English low and mid long vowels, so that (ä) became (ā), for example, while the high long vowels became diphthongs.

Great Wall of China
Section at Gubeikou, northeast of Beijing

Great Wall of Chi•na (chī′nə). A line of fortifications extending c. 2,414 km (1,500 mi) across N China; built in the 3rd cent. B.C.

Great War *n.* World War I.

great white shark *n.* A shark *(Carcharodon carcharias)* of temperate and tropical waters that grows to about 7 meters (23 feet) and feeds regularly on marine mammals.

greave (grēv) *n.* Leg armor worn below the knee. Often used in the plural. [Sing. of ME *greves* < OFr., shins.]

greaves (grēvz) *pl.n. (used with a sing. or pl. v.)* The unmelted residue from rendered animal fat. [< LGer. *greven.*]

grebe (grēb) *n.* Any of various swimming and diving birds of the family Podicipedidae, having a pointed bill and lobed fleshy membranes along each toe. [Fr. *grèbe.*]

Gre•cian (grē′shən) *adj.* Greek. —*n.* A native or inhabitant of Greece. [< Lat. *Graecia,* Greece < *Graecus,* Gk. See GREEK.]

Gre•cism (grē′sĭz′əm) *n.* **1.** The style or spirit of Greek culture, art, or thought. **2.** Something done in imitation of Greek style or spirit. **3.** An idiom of the Greek language.

Gre•cize (grē′sīz′) *tr.v.* **-cized, -ciz•ing, -ciz•es.** To make Greek or Hellenic in form or style. [Fr. *gréciser* < LLat. *graecizāre* < Gk. *graikizein,* to speak Gk. < *Graikos,* Gk.]

Gre•co (grĕk′ō), **El.** Doménikos Theotokópoulos. 1541–1614. Greek-born Spanish painter of religious works characterized by elongated human figures and deep shadows.

El Greco
c. 1609 self-portrait

Greco– or **Graeco–** *pref.* Greece; Greek: *Greco-Roman.* [< Lat. *Graecus,* Gk. See GREEK.]

Grec•o-Ro•man (grĕk′ō-rō′mən, grē′kō-) *adj.* Of or relating to both Greece and Rome: *Greco-Roman mythology.*

gree (grē) *n. Scots.* Superiority; preeminence. [ME *gre* < OFr., step < Lat. *gradus.* See GRADE.]

Greece (grēs) Formerly **Hel•las** (hĕl′əs). A country of SE Europe on the S Balkan Peninsula and including numerous islands in the Mediterranean, Aegean, and Ionian seas. One of the most important centers of early civilization, it was ruled by the Ottoman Turks from the 15th cent. until its independence in 1829. Cap. Athens. Pop. 9,740,417.

greed (grēd) *n.* An excessive desire to acquire or possess more than one needs or deserves, esp. of material wealth.

greed•y (grē′dē) *adj.* **-i•er, -i•est. 1.** Having greed. **2.** Wanting to eat or drink more than one can reasonably consume; gluttonous. **3.** Extremely eager or desirous. [ME *gredi* < OE *grǣdig.* See **gher-**[2]*.] **—greed′i•ly** *adv.* **—greed′i•ness** *n.*

Greek (grēk) *n.* **1.a.** The Indo-European language of the Greeks. **b.** Greek language and literature from the middle of the eighth century B.C. to the end of the third century A.D., esp. the Attic Greek of the fifth and fourth centuries B.C. **2.a.** A native or inhabitant of Greece. **b.** A person of Greek ancestry. **3.** *Informal.* A member of a fraternity or sorority with a name composed of Greek letters. **4.** *Informal.* Something unintelligible. —*adj.* Of or relating to Greece or its people, language, or culture. [ME *Grek* < OE *Grēcas,* the Greeks < Lat. *Graecus,* Greek < Gk. *Graikos,* tribal name.]

Greek Catholic *n.* **1.** A member of the Eastern Orthodox Church. **2.** A member of a Uniat church.

Greek Church *n.* The Eastern Orthodox Church.

Greek cross *n.* A cross formed by two bars of equal length crossing in the middle at right angles to each other.

Greek fire *n.* An incendiary preparation first used by the Byzantine Greeks to set fire to enemy ships.

Greek Orthodox Church *n.* The state church of Greece, an autonomous part of the Eastern Orthodox Church.

Greek revival *n.* An architectural style imitating elements of ancient Greek temple design, popular in the United States and Europe in the first half of the 19th century.

Gree•ley (grē′lē). A city of N-central CO NNE of Denver; founded 1870. Pop. 60,536.

Greeley, Horace. 1811–72. Amer. journalist and politician who founded and edited the *New York Tribune* (1841–72).

green (grēn) *n.* **1.** *Color.* The hue of the portion of the visible spectrum between yellow and blue, evoked in the human observer by radiant energy with wavelengths of approx. 490 to 570 nanometers; any of a group of colors whose hue is that of the emerald or somewhat less yellow than that of growing grass; one of the additive or light primaries; one of the psychological primary hues. **2.** Something green in color. **3. greens.** Green growth or foliage, esp.: **a.** The branches and leaves of plants used for decoration. **b.** Leafy plants or plant parts eaten as vegetables. **4.** A grassy lawn or plot, esp.: **a.** A common. **b.** *Sports.* A putting green. **5. greens.** A green uniform. **6.** *Slang.* Money. **7. Green.** A supporter of a social and political movement that espouses global environmental protection, social responsibility, and nonviolence. —*adj.* **green•er, green•est. 1.** *Color.* Of the color green. **2.** Abounding in or covered with green growth or foliage. **3.** Made with green or leafy vegetables. **4.** Characterized by mild or temperate weather. **5.** Youthful; vigorous. **6.** Not mature or ripe; young. **7.** Brand-new; fresh. **8.** Not yet fully processed, esp.: **a.** Not aged: *green wood.* **b.** Not cured or tanned: *green pelts.* **9.** Lacking training or experience. **10.a.** Lacking sophistication or worldly experience; naive. **b.** Easily duped or deceived; gullible. **11.** Having a sickly or unhealthy pallor indicative of nausea or jealousy, for example. —*tr. & intr.v.* **greened, green•ing, greens.** To make or become green. **—*idiom.* green around** (or **about) the gills.** Pale or sickly in appearance. [ME *grene* < OE *grēne.* See **ghrē-***.] **—green′ly** *adv.* **—green′ness** *n.*

Green, Paul Eliot. 1894–1981. Amer. playwright noted for dramas such as *In Abraham's Bosom* (1926).

Green, William. 1873–1952. Amer. labor leader who was president of the American Federation of Labor (1924–52).

green alga *n.* Any of the numerous algae of the division Chlorophyta having chlorophyll unmasked by other pigments.

Gree•na•way (grē′nə-wā′), **Catherine ("Kate").** 1846–1901. British artist and writer noted for her children's books.
green•back (grēn′băk′) *n.* A note of U.S. currency.
Green Bay. A city of E WI on **Green Bay,** an arm of Lake Michigan; founded 1634. Pop. 96,466.
green bean *n.* See **string bean** 1.
green•belt (grēn′bĕlt′) *n.* A belt of recreational parks, farmland, or uncultivated land surrounding a community.
Green•belt (grēn′bĕlt′). A city of central MD, a suburb of Washington DC. Pop. 21,096.
Green Beret *n.* A member of the U.S. Army Special Forces.
green•bri•er (grēn′brī′ər) *n.* See **catbrier.**
green card *n.* A card issued by the U.S. government to aliens, allowing them to work legally in the United States.
green corn *n.* Young, tender ears of sweet corn.
green dragon *n.* A tuberous plant *(Arisaema dracontium)* of eastern North America having minute flowers at the base of a spadix projecting from a narrow green spathe.
Greene (grēn), **(Henry) Graham.** 1904–91. British writer whose novels include *The Power and the Glory* (1940).
Greene, Nathanael. 1742–86. Amer. Revolutionary general noted for his campaigns in the S colonies.
Greene, Robert. 1558?–92. English writer whose plays include *Friar Bacon and Friar Bungay* (c. 1589).
green•er•y (grē′nə-rē) *n., pl.* **-ies. 1.a.** Green foliage; verdure. **b.** Greenery used as decoration. **2.** A place where plants are grown.
green-eyed (grēn′īd′) *adj.* Jealous.
Green•field (grēn′fēld′). **1.** A town of NW MA N of Northampton. Pop. 18,666. **2.** A city of SE WI, a suburb of Milwaukee. Pop. 33,403.
Greenfield Park. A town of southern Quebec, Canada, a suburb of Montreal. Pop. 18,527.
green•finch (grēn′fĭnch′) *n.* A common Eurasian finch *(Carduelis chloris)* having green and yellow plumage.
green•fly (grēn′flī′) *n.* A green aphid commonly occurring as a destructive pest of various cultivated plants.
green•gage (grēn′gāj′) *n.* A variety of plum *(Prunus domestica)* having yellowish-green skin and sweet flesh. [GREEN + *gage,* after Sir William *Gage,* 18th-cent. English botanist.]
green•gro•cer (grēn′grō′sər) *n. Chiefly British.* A retail seller of fresh fruits and vegetables. **— green′gro′cer•y** *n.*
green•head (grēn′hĕd′) *n.* A male mallard duck.
green•heart (grēn′härt′) *n.* **1.a.** A tropical American tree *(Ocotea rodioei)* having greenish dark durable wood. **b.** Any of various similar trees. **2.** The wood of any of these trees.
green•horn (grēn′hôrn′) *n.* **1.** An inexperienced or immature person, esp. one easily deceived. **2.** A newcomer, esp. one unfamiliar with a place or group. [ME *greene horn,* horn of a newly slaughtered animal.]
green•house (grēn′hous′) *n.* A structure, primarily of glass, in which temperature and humidity can be controlled for the cultivation or protection of plants.
greenhouse effect *n.* **1.** The phenomenon whereby the earth's atmosphere traps solar radiation, caused by the presence of gases such as carbon dioxide that allow incoming sunlight to pass through but absorb heat radiated back from the earth's surface. **2.** A similar retention of solar radiation.
green•ie (grē′nē) *n. Slang.* A green amphetamine pill.
green•ing[1] (grē′nĭng) *n.* Restoration of vitality or freshness; rejuvenation.
green•ing[2] (grē′nĭng) *n.* Any of several varieties of green-skinned apples.
green•ish (grē′nĭsh) *adj.* Somewhat green.
Green•land (grēn′lənd, -lănd′). An island of Denmark in the N Atlantic off NE Canada; discovered by Eric the Red in the 10th cent. **— Green•land′ic** (-lăn′dĭk) *adj.*
Greenland Sea. A section of the S Arctic Ocean off the E coast of Greenland.
Greenland spar *n.* See **cryolite.**
green•let (grēn′lĭt) *n.* Any of various small greenish birds of the genus *Hylophilus* of Central and South America.
green light *n.* **1.** The green-colored light that signals traffic to proceed. **2.** *Informal.* Permission to proceed.
green•ling (grēn′lĭng) *n.* Any of various northern Pacific marine food fishes of the family Hexagrammidae.
green•mail (grēn′māl′) *n.* An antitakeover maneuver in which the target firm purchases the raider's stock at a price above that available to other stockholders. [GREEN, money + (BLACK-)MAIL.] **— green′mail′er** *n.*
green manure *n.* A growing crop, such as clover or grass, that is plowed under the soil to improve fertility.
green monkey *n.* A long-tailed African monkey *(Cercopithecus aethiops* subsp. *sabaeus)* with greenish yellowish-gray fur.
Green Mountains. A range of the Appalachian Mts. extending from S Quebec, Canada, through VT to W MA and rising to 1,339.9 m (4,393 ft).
green•ock•ite (grē′nə-kīt′) *n.* A yellow to brown or red mineral, CdS, the only ore of cadmium. [After Charles Murray Cathcart, 2nd Earl *Greenock* (1783–1859).]
Gree•nough (grē′nō′), **Horatio.** 1805–52. Amer. sculptor whose principal work is the neoclassical statue of George Washington at the Smithsonian Institution in Washington DC.
green pepper *n.* The unripened green fruit of pepper plants of the genus *Capsicum.*
green plover *n.* See **lapwing.**
green revolution *n.* A significant increase in agricultural productivity due to the use of high-yield varieties of grains, pesticides, and improved management techniques.
Green River. 1. A river rising in central KY and flowing c. 595 km (370 mi) to the Ohio R. near Evansville IN. **2.** A river, c. 1,175 km (730 mi), rising in W WY and flowing through NW CO and E UT to the Colorado R.
green•room (grēn′ro͞om′, -ro͝om′) *n.* A waiting room or lounge in a theater or concert hall for performers off-stage.
green•sand (grēn′sănd′) *n.* A sand or sediment having a dark greenish color caused by the presence of glauconite.
Greens•bor•o (grēnz′bûr′ə, -bûr′ō). A city of N-central NC E of Winston-Salem; settled in 1749. Pop. 183,521.
Greens•burg (grēnz′bûrg′). A city of SW PA ESE of Pittsburgh; settled in the late 1700's. Pop. 16,318.
green•shank (grēn′shăngk′) *n.* A European wading bird *(Tringa nebularia)* having greenish legs and a long bill.
green•sick•ness (grēn′sĭk′nĭs) *n.* See **chlorosis** 2.
greens•keep•er (grēnz′kē′pər) *n. Sports.* One who is responsible for the maintenance of a golf course.
green snake *n.* Any of several slender yellow-green nonvenomous North American snakes of the genus *Opheodrys.*
green soap *n.* A translucent yellowish-green soap made chiefly from vegetable oils and used to treat skin disorders.
green•stick fracture (grēn′stĭk′) *n.* A partial bone fracture in which the bone is bent but broken only on one side.
green•stone (grēn′stōn′) *n.* Any of various altered basic igneous rocks colored green by chlorite, hornblende, or epidote.
green•sward (grēn′swôrd′) *n.* Grassy green ground; turf.
green tea *n.* Tea made from unfermented dried leaves.
green thumb *n.* An extraordinary ability to make plants grow.
green turtle *n.* A large marine turtle *(Chelonia mydas)* having greenish flesh that is prized as food, esp. in turtle soup.
Green•ville (grēn′vĭl′). **1.** A city of W MS on the Mississippi R. N of Vicksburg. Pop. 45,226. **2.** A city of E NC SE of Rocky Mount; founded 1786. Pop. 44,972. **3.** A city of NW SC NW of Columbia; laid out in 1797. Pop. 58,282. **4.** A city of NE TX NE of Dallas. Pop. 23,071.
Green•wich. 1. (grĕn′ĭch, grĭn′ĭj). A borough of Greater London in SE England on the Thames R.; site of the original Royal Observatory, through which passes the prime meridian, or longitude 0°. **2.** (grĕn′ĭch, grĭn′-, grēn′wĭch′). A town of SW CT on Long Island Sound; settled in 1640. Pop. 58,441.
Green•wich time (grĕn′ĭch, grĭn′ĭj) *n.* See **universal time.**
Green•wich Village (grĕn′ĭch, -ĭj, grĭn′-). A section of lower Manhattan in New York City; noted as an artists' and writers' community since the early 1900's.
green-winged teal (grēn′wĭngd′) *n.* A small freshwater duck *(Anas crecca)* with an iridescent green speculum in the male.
green•wood (grēn′wo͝od′) *n.* A wood or forest with green foliage.
Green•wood (grēn′wo͝od′). **1.** A city of central IN, a suburb of Indianapolis. Pop. 26,265. **2.** A city of W-central MS E of Greenville. Pop. 18,906. **3.** A city of W SC WNW of Columbia; settled in 1824. Pop. 20,807.
greet (grēt) *tr.v.* **greet•ed, greet•ing, greets. 1.** To salute or welcome in a friendly and respectful way. **2.** To receive with a specified reaction. **3.** To be perceived by: *A din greeted our ears.* [ME *greten* < OE *grētan.*] **— greet′er** *n.* **— greet′ing** *n.*
greeting card *n.* A folded card with a greeting or another sentiment, usu. for a special occasion or holiday.
greg•a•rine (grĕg′ə-rīn′) *n.* Any of various sporozoan protozoans of the order Gregarinida that are parasitic within the digestive tracts of various invertebrates including arthropods and annelids. [< NLat. *Gregarina,* type genus < Lat. *gregārius,* of a flock. See GREGARIOUS.] **— greg′a•rine′** *adj.*
gre•gar•i•ous (grĭ-gâr′ē-əs) *adj.* **1.** Seeking and enjoying the company of others; sociable. **2.** Tending to move in or form a group with others of the same kind. **3.** *Bot.* Growing in groups that are close together but not densely clustered or matted. [< Lat. *gregārius,* of a flock < *grex, greg-,* flock. See **ger-*.**] **— gre•gar′i•ous•ly** *adv.* **— gre•gar′i•ous•ness** *n.*
Gre•go•ri•an calendar (grĭ-gôr′ē-ən, -gōr′-) *n.* The solar calendar used in most of the world, sponsored by Pope Gregory XIII in 1582 to correct the Julian calendar.
Gregorian chant *n. Rom. Cath. Ch.* A monodic, rhythmically unstructured liturgical chant sung without accompaniment. [After Saint GREGORY I.]
Greg•o•ry I (grĕg′ə-rē), Saint. "Gregory the Great." 540?–604. Pope (590–604) who sponsored the missionary expedition of St. Augustine to Britain (596).
Gregory VII. Hildebrand. 1020?–85. Pope (1073–85) who sought to establish papal supremacy.
Gregory XIII. 1502–85. Pope (1572–85) who sponsored the adoption of the Gregorian calendar (1582).
Gregory, Lady **Isabella Augusta Persse.** 1852–1932. Irish playwright who was a founder (1899) and director (1904–32) of the Abbey Theatre.

Greece

FORMS	NAME	SOUND
Α α	alpha	a
Β β	beta	b
Γ γ	gamma	g (n)
Δ δ	delta	d
Ε ε	epsilon	e
Ζ ζ	zēta	z
Η η	ēta	ē
Θ θ	thēta	th
Ι ι	iota	i
Κ κ	kappa	k
Λ λ	lambda	l
Μ μ	mu	m
Ν ν	nu	n
Ξ ξ	xi	x
Ο ο	omicron	o
Π π	pi	p
Ρ ρ	rhō	r (rh)
Σ σ	sigma	s
Τ τ	tau	t
Υ υ	upsilon	u
Φ φ	phi	ph
Χ χ	chi, khi	kh
Ψ ψ	psi	ps
Ω ω	ōmega	ō

Greek

ă pat	oi boy
ā pay	ou out
âr care	o͝o took
ä father	o͞o boot
ĕ pet	ŭ cut
ē be	ûr urge
ĭ pit	th thin
ī pie	*th* this
îr pier	hw which
ŏ pot	zh vision
ō toe	ə about, item
ô paw	

Stress marks:
′ (primary);
′ (secondary), as in **dictionary** (dĭk′shə-nĕr′ē)

Gregory of Nys•sa (nĭs′ə), Saint. A.D. 335?–394? Eastern theologian who led the conservative faction during the Trinitarian controversy.

Gregory of Tours (to͝or, to͞or), Saint. 538–594. Frankish prelate and historian who wrote a history of the 6th-cent. Franks.

greige (grā, grāzh) *adj.* Not bleached or dyed; unfinished. Used of textiles. [Fr. *grège* < Ital. *(seta) greggia,* raw (silk) < *greggio,* gray, of Gmc. orig.]

grei•sen (grī′zən) *n.* A granitic rock composed chiefly of quartz and mica. [Ger. < *greissen,* to split.]

grem•lin (grĕm′lĭn) *n.* **1.** An imaginary gnomelike creature to whom mechanical problems, esp. in aircraft, are attributed. **2.** A maker of mischief. [Perh. blend of Ir. *gruaimín,* bad-tempered little guy (< MIr. *gruaim,* gloom) and GOBLIN.]

Gre•na•da (grə-nā′də). A country in the Windward Is. of the West Indies comprising the island of **Grenada** and the S Grenadines; achieved independence from Great Britain in 1974. Cap. St. George's. Pop. 110,100.

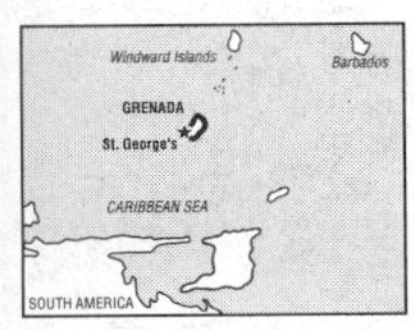

Grenada

gre•nade (grə-nād′) *n.* **1.** A missile containing priming and bursting charges, designed to be thrown by hand or deployed by a launcher. **2.** A glass container filled with a chemical that is dispersed by throwing and smashing the container. [Fr. < OFr. *(pome) grenate,* pomegranate. See POMEGRANATE.]

gren•a•dier (grĕn′ə-dîr′) *n.* **1.a.** A member of the British Grenadier Guards, the first regiment of the royal household infantry. **b.** A soldier in a special corps or regiment. **c.** A soldier equipped with grenades. **2.** Any of various deep-sea fishes of the family Macrouridae, having a long tapering tail and no tail fin. [Fr. < *grenade,* grenade. See GRENADE.]

gren•a•dine (grĕn′ə-dēn′, grĕn′ə-dēn′) *n.* **1.** A thick sweet syrup made from pomegranates and used as a flavoring, esp. in beverages. **2.** A thin, loosely woven fabric of silk, cotton, or synthetic fiber. [Fr. < *grenade,* pomegranate < OFr. *grenate.* See POMEGRANATE.]

Gren•a•dines (grĕn′ə-dēnz′). An archipelago in the Windward Is. of the E Caribbean. The S islands are part of Grenada; the others are part of St. Vincent and the Grenadines.

Gren•del (grĕn′dl) *n.* The male monster, descended from Cain, slain by Beowulf in the Old English epic *Beowulf.*

Gren•fell (grĕn′fĕl′, -fəl), Sir **Wilfred Thomason.** 1865–1940. British missionary who estab. medical facilities in Labrador.

Gre•no•ble (grə-nō′bəl, -nôbl′). A city of SE France on the Isère R. SSW of Chambéry. Pop. 156,637.

Gren•ville (grĕn′vĭl′, -vəl), **George.** 1712–70. British political leader who served as prime minister (1763–65).

Gresh•am (grĕsh′əm). A city of NW OR, a suburb of Portland. Pop. 68,235.

Gresham, Sir **Thomas.** 1519–79. English financier who is traditionally credited with Gresham's law.

Gresh•am's law (grĕsh′əmz) *n.* The theory holding that if two kinds of money in circulation have the same denominational value but different intrinsic values, the money with higher intrinsic value will be hoarded and driven out of circulation by the other money. [After Sir Thomas GRESHAM.]

greyhound

gres•so•ri•al (grĕ-sôr′ē-əl, -sōr′-) *adj.* Adapted for walking or having limbs adapted for walking. Used of flightless birds. [< NLat. *gressōrius* < Lat. *gressus,* step < p.part. of *gradī,* to walk. See **ghredh-***.]

Gret•na (grĕt′nə). A city of SE LA on the Mississippi R. opposite New Orleans. Pop. 17,208.

Gretna Green. A village of S Scotland on the English border; formerly noted as a site of runaway marriages.

Greuze (grœz), **Jean Baptiste.** 1725–1805. French painter of moralistic genre works.

grew (gro͞o) *v.* P.t. of **grow.**

grey (grā) *adj., n., & v.* Var. of **gray.**

Grey (grā), **Charles.** 2nd Earl Grey. 1764–1845. British politician who as prime minister (1830–34) implemented the abolition of slavery throughout the British Empire.

griffin
Sixth- to seventh-century Persian bowl

Grey, Lady **Jane.** 1537–54. Queen of England for nine days (1553) who was beheaded for treason.

Grey, Zane. 1875–1939. Amer. writer of Western adventure novels, including *Riders of the Purple Sage* (1912).

grey•hen (grā′hĕn′) *n.* The female of the black grouse.

grey•hound (grā′hound′) *n.* Any of a breed of tall slender dogs, having a smooth coat, a narrow head, and long legs and capable of running swiftly.

grey•lag (grā′lăg′) *n.* Var. of **graylag.**

grib•ble (grĭb′əl) *n.* Any of several small wood-boring marine isopod crustaceans of the genus *Limnoria,* esp. *L. lignorum.* [Poss. dim. of GRUB.]

D.W. Griffith

grid (grĭd) *n.* **1.a.** A framework of crisscrossed or parallel bars; a grating or mesh. **b.** A cooking surface of parallel metal bars; a gridiron. **2.** Something resembling a grid. **3.** A pattern of regularly spaced horizontal and vertical lines forming squares on a map, a chart, an aerial photograph, or an optical device, used for locating points. **4.** *Elect.* **a.** An interconnected system for the distribution of electricity or electromagnetic signals over a wide area, esp. a network of high-tension cables and power stations. **b.** A corrugated or perforated conducting plate in a storage battery. **c.** A network or coil of fine wires located between the plate and the filament in an electron tube. **5.** *Football.* The gridiron. **6.** *Sports.* The starting positions of cars on a racecourse. **7.** *Print.* A device in a photocomposition machine on which the characters used in composition are etched. [Short for GRIDIRON.] **—grid′ded** *adj.*

grid•der (grĭd′ər) *n. Football.* A player.

grid•dle (grĭd′l) *n.* A flat metal surface used for cooking by dry heat. [ME *gridel,* gridiron < ONFr. *gredil* < Lat. *crātīcula,* dim. of *crātis,* hurdle, lattice.] **—grid′dle** *v.*

grid•dle•cake (grĭd′l-kāk′) *n.* See **pancake.**

grid•i•ron (grĭd′ī′ərn) *n.* **1.** *Football.* **a.** The field of play. **b.** The game itself. **2.** A metal structure high above the stage of a theater, from which ropes or cables are strung to scenery and lights. **3.a.** A flat framework of parallel metal bars for broiling food. **b.** An object resembling a griddle. [ME *gridirne,* alteration of *gridere,* alteration of *gridel.* See GRIDDLE.]

grid•lock (grĭd′lŏk′) *n.* **1.** A traffic jam in which no vehicular movement is possible. **2.** A complete lack of movement or progress. **—grid′lock′** *v.* **—grid′locked′** *adj.*

grief (grēf) *n.* **1.** Deep mental anguish, as from bereavement. See Syns at **regret. 2.** A source of deep mental anguish. **3.** Annoyance or frustration. **4.** Trouble or difficulty. **5.** *Archaic.* A grievance. [ME < OFr. < *grever,* to harm. See GRIEVE.]

Grieg (grēg, grĭg), **Edvard Hagerup.** 1843–1907. Norwegian composer known for his works incorporating folk music.

Grier (grîr), **Robert Cooper.** 1794–1870. Amer. jurist; associate justice of the U.S. Supreme Court (1846–70).

griev•ance (grē′vəns) *n.* **1.a.** A circumstance seen as just cause for protest. **b.** A complaint or protestation based on a grievance. **2.** Indignation or resentment stemming from feeling wronged. **3.** *Obsolete.* **a.** The act of inflicting hardship or harm. **b.** The cause of hardship or harm. [ME *grevaunce* < OFr. *grevance* < *grever,* to harm. See GRIEVE.]

grieve (grēv) *v.* **grieved, griev•ing, grieves.** —*tr.* **1.** To cause to be sorrowful; distress. **2.** *Archaic.* To hurt or harm. —*intr.* To experience or express grief. [ME *greven* < OFr. *grever,* to harm < Lat. *gravāre,* to burden < *gravis,* heavy. See **gʷerə-¹***.] **—griev′er** *n.* **—griev′ing•ly** *adv.*

Syns: *grieve, lament, mourn, sorrow.* The central meaning shared by these verbs is "to feel, show, or express grief, sadness, or regret": *grieved over the loss; lamenting over declining standards; mourning for lost hopes; sorrowed over our poverty.* ***Ant:*** *rejoice.*

griev•ous (grē′vəs) *adj.* **1.** Causing grief, pain, or anguish. **2.** Serious or dire; grave: *a grievous crime.* **—griev′ous•ly** *adv.* **—griev′ous•ness** *n.*

grif•fin also **grif•fon** or **gryph•on** (grĭf′ən) *n.* A fabulous beast with the head and wings of an eagle and the body of a lion. [ME *griffoun* < OFr. *griffon* < *grif* < LLat. *grȳphus,* var. of Lat. *grȳps, grȳph-* < Gk. *grups.*]

Grif•fin (grĭf′ĭn). A city of W-central GA SSE of Atlanta. Pop. 21,347.

Grif•fith (grĭf′ĭth). A town of extreme NW IN S of Hammond. Pop. 17,916.

Griffith, D(avid Lewelyn) W(ark). 1875–1948. Amer. filmmaker whose works include *The Birth of a Nation* (1915).

grif•fon (grĭf′ən) *n.* **1.** Any of a breed of dog originating in Belgium and having a short bearded muzzle. **2.** Any of various wirehaired hunting dogs of a breed originating in the Netherlands in the late 19th century. **3.** Var. of **griffin.** [Fr. < OFr. See GRIFFIN.]

grift (grĭft) *Slang.* —*n.* **1.** Money made by grifting. **2.** A swindle or confidence game. —*v.* **grift•ed, grift•ing, grifts.** —*intr.* To engage in swindling or cheating. —*tr.* To obtain by grifting. [Perh. alteration of GRAFT².] **—grift′er** *n.*

grig (grĭg) *n.* A lively, bright person. [ME, dwarf.]

gri•gri also **gris-gris** (grē′grē) *n., pl.* **gri•gris** also **gris-gris** (grē′grē). An African charm, fetish, or amulet. [Fr., of West African orig.; akin to Bulanda *grigri,* amulet.]

grill (grĭl) *tr.v.* **grilled, grill•ing, grills. 1.** To broil on a gridiron. **2.** To torture or afflict as if by broiling. **3.** *Informal.* To question relentlessly; cross-examine. **4.** To mark or emboss with a gridiron. —*n.* **1.** A cooking surface of parallel metal bars; a gridiron. **2.** Food cooked by broiling or grilling. **3.** A grillroom. **4.** A series of marks grilled or embossed on a surface. **5.** Var. of **grille.** [Fr. *griller* < *gril,* gridiron < OFr. *greille* < Lat. *crātīcula,* dim. of *crātis,* lattice.] **—grill′er** *n.*

gril•lage (grĭl′ĭj) *n.* A network or frame of timber or steel serving as a foundation, usu. on wet or soft ground. [Fr. < OFr., trellis < *greille,* gridiron. See GRILL.]

grille also **grill** (grĭl) *n.* **1.** A grating used as a screen, divider, barrier, or decorative element, as in a window. **2.** An opening covered with a grating. [Fr. < OFr. *greille.* See GRILL.]

grill•er•y (grĭl′ə-rē) *n., pl.* **-ies.** A grill; a grillroom.

grill•room (grĭl′ro͞om′, -ro͝om′) *n.* A place where grilled foods are served to customers.

grill•work (grĭl′wûrk′) *n.* Material formed into a grille.

grilse (grĭls) *n., pl.* **grilse.** A young Atlantic salmon first returning to fresh or brackish waters. [< ME *grills* (pl.).]

grim (grĭm) *adj.* **grim•mer, grim•mest. 1.** Unrelenting; rigid. **2.** Uninviting or unnerving in aspect; forbidding. **3.** Ghastly; sinister. **4.** Dismal; gloomy. **5.** Ferocious; savage. [ME < OE, fierce, severe.] **—grim′ly** *adv.* **—grim′ness** *n.*

grim·ace (grĭm′ĭs, grĭ-mās′) *n.* A sharp contortion of the face expressive of pain, contempt, or disgust. [Fr. < OFr. *grimache*, alteration of *grimuche*, prob. < Frankish **grīma*, mask.] — **grim′ace** *v.* — **grim′ac·er** *n.*

gri·mal·kin (grĭ-môl′kĭn, -măl′-) *n.* **1.** A cat, esp. an old female cat. **2.** An ill-tempered old woman. [Var. of *graymalkin* : GRAY + obsolete *Malkin*, dim. of *Matilda*.]

grime (grīm) *n.* Black dirt or soot, esp. such dirt clinging to or ingrained in a surface. [ME *grim*; akin to MDu. *grīme*. See **ghrēi-***.] — **grime** *v.*

Grim·ké (grĭm′kē), **Sarah Moore.** 1792–1873. Amer. feminist and abolitionist who with her sister **Angelina Emily Grimké** (1805–79) campaigned publicly against slavery.

Grimm (grĭm), **Jakob Ludwig Karl.** 1785–1863. German philologist and folklorist who formulated Grimm's Law (1819) and with his brother **Wilhelm Karl** (1786–1859) compiled *Grimm's Fairy Tales* (1812–15).

Grimm's Law (grĭmz) *n.* A formula showing how Indo-European stops changed in Germanic, stating that Indo-European *p, t,* and *k* became Germanic *f, th,* and *h*; *b, d,* and *g* became *p, t,* and *k*; and *bh, dh,* and *gh* became *b, d,* and *g*. [After Jakob Ludwig Karl GRIMM.]

Grims·by (grĭmz′bē). Officially **Great Grimsby.** A borough of E England SE of Hull. Pop. 91,800.

grim·y (grī′mē) *adj.* **-i·er, -i·est.** Covered or smudged with grime. — **grim′i·ly** *adv.* — **grim′i·ness** *n.*

grin (grĭn) *v.* **grinned, grin·ning, grins.** — *intr.* To draw back the lips and bare the teeth, as in mirth. — *tr.* To express with a grin. — *n.* **1.** The act of grinning. **2.** The facial expression in grinning. [ME *grennen*, to grimace < OE *grennian*.] — **grin′ner** *n.* — **grin′ning·ly** *adv.*

grind (grīnd) *v.* **ground** (ground), **grind·ing, grinds.** — *tr.* **1.a.** To crush, pulverize, or reduce to powder by friction, esp. by rubbing between two hard surfaces. **b.** To shape, sharpen, or refine with friction: *grind a lens.* **2.** To rub (two surfaces) together harshly; gnash: *grind the teeth.* **3.** To bear down on harshly; crush. **4.** To oppress or weaken gradually. **5.a.** To operate by turning a crank. **b.** To produce or process by turning a crank. **6.** To produce mechanically or without inspiration: *grinds out work.* **7.** To instill or teach by persistent repetition. — *intr.* **1.** To grind something. **2.** To become crushed, pulverized, or powdered by friction. **3.** To move with noisy friction; grate. **4.** *Informal.* To devote oneself to study or work: *grinding away at math.* **5.** *Slang.* To rotate the pelvis erotically, as in the manner of a stripteaser. — *n.* **1.** The act of grinding. **2.** A crunching or grinding noise. **3.** A specific grade or degree of pulverization, as of coffee beans. **4.** *Informal.* A laborious task, routine, or study. **5.** *Informal.* A student who works or studies excessively. **6.** *Slang.* An erotic rotation of the pelvis. [ME *grinden* < OE *grindan*. See **ghrendh-***.] — **grind′ing·ly** *adv.*

grind·er (grīn′dər) *n.* **1.** One that grinds, esp.: **a.** One who sharpens cutting edges. **b.** A mechanical device that grinds. **2.** A molar. **3. grinders.** *Informal.* The teeth. **4.** *New England.* See **submarine** 2. See Regional Note at **submarine.**

grind·stone (grīnd′stōn′) *n.* **1.** A revolving stone disk used for grinding, polishing, or sharpening tools. **2.** A millstone. — *idiom.* **put (one's) nose to the grindstone.** *Informal.* To work in earnest.

grin·go (grĭng′gō) *n., pl.* **-gos.** *Offensive Slang.* Used as a disparaging term for a foreigner in Latin America, esp. an American or English person. [Sp., foreign, foreign language, gibberish, prob. alteration of *griego*, Gk. < Lat. *Graecus.* See GREEK.]

Word History: The word *gringo* may be an alteration of *griego*, the Spanish development of Latin *Graecus*, "Greek." *Griego* first meant "Greek, Grecian, Greek language." The saying "It's Greek to me" exists in both Spanish and English and helps explain why *griego* came to mean "unintelligible language" and perhaps, by further extension, "stranger, one who speaks a foreign language." The altered form *gringo* kept the senses "unintelligible language," "foreigner, especially an English person," and in Latin America, "North American or Britisher."

gri·ot (grē-ō′, grē′ō, grē′ŏt) *n.* A storyteller in western Africa who perpetuates the oral tradition of a village or family. [Fr., alteration of *guiriot*, perh. ult. < Port. *criado*, servant < Lat. *creātus*, one trained < p.part. of *creāre*, to bring up. See CREATE.]

grip¹ (grĭp) *n.* **1.a.** A tight hold; a firm grasp. **b.** The pressure or strength of such a grasp. **c.** A manner of grasping and holding. **2.a.** Intellectual hold; understanding. **b.** Ability to function properly or well; competence. **3.a.** A mechanical device that grasps and holds. **b.** A part, such as a handle, that is designed to be grasped and held. **4.** A suitcase or valise. **5.a.** A stagehand who helps in shifting scenery. **b.** A member of a film crew who adjusts sets and props and sometimes assists the camera operator. — *v.* **gripped, grip·ping, grips.** — *tr.* **1.** To secure and maintain a grip on; seize firmly. **2.** To hold the interest or attention of. — *intr.* To maintain a secure grasp. [ME < OE *gripe*, grasp and *gripa*, handful.] — **grip′per** *n.* — **grip′ping·ly** *adv.*

grip² (grĭp) *n.* Var. of **grippe.**

gripe (grīp) *v.* **griped, grip·ing, gripes.** — *intr.* **1.** *Informal.* To complain naggingly or petulantly; grumble. **2.** To have sharp pains in the bowels. — *tr.* **1.** *Informal.* To irritate; annoy. **2.** To cause sharp pain in the bowels of. **3.** To grasp; seize. **4.** To oppress or afflict. — *n.* **1.** *Informal.* A complaint. **2. gripes.** Sharp spasmodic pains in the bowels. **3.** A firm hold; a grasp. **4.** A grip; a handle. [ME *gripen*, to seize < OE *grīpan*.] — **grip′er** *n.*

grippe also **grip** (grĭp) *n.* See **influenza** 1. [Fr. < OFr., claw, quarrel < *gripper*, to seize, grasp < Frankish **grīpan*.] — **grip′py** *adj.*

grip·sack (grĭp′săk′) *n.* A small suitcase.

Gris (grēs), **Juan.** 1887–1927. Spanish painter whose works include *Homage to Picasso* (1912).

gri·saille (grĭ-zī′, -zāl′) *n.* **1.** A style of monochromatic painting in shades of gray, used esp. to depict relief sculpture. **2.** A painting or design in this style. **3.a.** Vitrifiable glass paint. **b.** A lacy pattern painted on light glass with grisaille and fired. [Fr. < *gris*, gray < OFr. < Frankish **grīs*.]

gris·e·o·ful·vin (grĭz′ē-ə-fŭl′vĭn) *n.* An antibiotic, $C_{17}H_{17}ClO_6$, used to treat ringworm and other fungal infections. [< NLat. *griseofulvum*, species of penicillium : Med.Lat. *grīseus*, griseous; see GRISEOUS + Lat. *fulvum*, neut. of *fulvus*, tawny; see **ghel-²***.]

gris·e·ous (grĭz′ē-əs, grĭs′-) *adj.* Mottled with gray, esp. bluish gray; grizzled. [Med.Lat. *grīseus*, of Gmc. orig.]

gris-gris (grē′grē) *n.* Var. of **grigri.**

gris·ly (grĭz′lē) *adj.* **-li·er, -li·est.** Repugnant; gruesome. [ME *grisli* < OE *grislīc.* See **ghrēi-***.] — **gris′li·ness** *n.*

gri·son (grī′sən, grĭz′ən) *n.* Either of two small carnivorous mammals *(Galictis vittata* or *G. cuja)* of Central and South America having grizzled fur, a slender body, and short legs. [Fr. < OFr., gray fur < *gris*, gray. See GRISAILLE.]

grist (grĭst) *n.* **1.** Grain or a quantity of grain for grinding. **2.** Ground grain. — *idiom.* **grist for (one's) (**or **the) mill.** Something that can be used to advantage. [ME < OE *grīst.* See **ghrendh-***.]

gris·tle (grĭs′əl) *n.* Cartilage, esp. in meat. [ME < OE.]

gris·tly (grĭs′lē) *adj.* **-tli·er, -tli·est. 1.** Composed of or containing gristle. **2.** Resembling gristle. — **gris′tli·ness** *n.*

grist·mill (grĭst′mĭl′) *n.* A mill for grinding grain.

grit (grĭt) *n.* **1.** Minute rough granules, as of sand. **2.** The texture or fineness of sand or stone used in grinding. **3.** A coarse hard sandstone used in grindstones and millstones. **4.** *Informal.* Indomitable spirit; pluck. — *v.* **grit·ted, grit·ting, grits.** — *tr.* **1.** To clamp (the teeth) together. **2.** To cover or treat with grit. — *intr.* To make a grinding noise. [ME *gret*, sand < OE *grēot*.]

grith (grĭth) *n.* Protection or sanctuary provided by Old English law to persons in certain circumstances, as when in a church. [ME < OE < ON *gridh*, domicile, asylum.]

grits (grĭts) *pl.n. (used with a sing. or pl. v.)* **1.** A ground, usu. white meal of dried and hulled corn kernels that is boiled and eaten. **2.** Coarsely ground grain, esp. corn. [Alteration of ME *grutta*, coarse meal < OE *grytta*, pl. of *grytt*.]

grit·ty (grĭt′ē) *adj.* **-ti·er, -ti·est. 1.** Containing, covered with, or resembling grit. **2.** Showing resolution and fortitude; plucky. — **grit′ti·ly** *adv.* — **grit′ti·ness** *n.*

griv·et (grĭv′ĭt) *n.* A long-tailed African monkey *(Cercopithecus aethiops)* with a greenish-gray coat and tufts of white hair on the face. [Fr.]

griz·zle (grĭz′əl) *tr. & intr.v.* **-zled, -zling, -zles.** To make or become gray. — *n.* **1.a.** The color of a grizzled animal. **b.** A grizzled animal. **2.** *Archaic.* Gray hair. — *adj.* **1.** Gray. **2.** Grizzled. [< ME *grisel*, gray < OFr., dim. of *gris*, gray. See GRISAILLE.]

griz·zled (grĭz′əld) *adj.* **1.** Streaked with or partly gray. **2.** Having brownish fur or hair tipped with gray.

griz·zly (grĭz′lē) *adj.* **-zli·er, -zli·est.** Grayish or flecked with gray. — *n., pl.* **-zlies.** A grizzly bear.

grizzly bear *n.* The brown bear of northwest North America, now considered a subspecies *(Ursus arctos* subsp. *horribilis)*.

gro. *abbr.* Gross.

groan (grōn) *v.* **groaned, groan·ing, groans.** — *intr.* **1.** To voice a deep inarticulate sound, as of pain. **2.** To make a sound expressive of stress or strain. — *tr.* To utter or express by groaning. — *n.* The sound made in groaning. [ME *gronen* < OE *grānian*.] — **groan′er** *n.* — **groan′ing·ly** *adv.*

groat (grōt) *n.* An English silver coin worth four pence, used from the 14th to the 17th century. [ME *grot* < MDu. *groot*, a thick large coin, transl. of Med.Lat. *(dēnārius) grossus*.]

groats (grōts) *pl.n. (used with a sing. or pl. v.)* Hulled, usu. crushed grain, esp. oats. [ME *grotes* < OE *grotan*.]

gro·cer (grō′sər) *n.* A seller of foodstuffs and various household supplies. [ME, wholesaler < AN *grosser* < Med.Lat. *grossārius, grocerius* < LLat. *grossus*, thick.]

gro·cer·y (grō′sə-rē) *n., pl.* **-ies. 1.** A store selling groceries. **2. groceries.** Commodities sold by a grocer.

Grod·no (grôd′nō, -nə, grŏd′-). A city of W Belorussia on the Neman R. near the Polish border. Pop. 247,000.

grog (grŏg) *n.* An alcoholic liquor, esp. rum diluted with water.

grindstone

ă **pat**	oi **boy**
ā **pay**	ou **out**
âr **care**	o͝o **took**
ä **father**	o͞o **boot**
ĕ **pet**	ŭ **cut**
ē **be**	ûr **urge**
ĭ **pit**	th **thin**
ī **pie**	*th* **this**
îr **pier**	hw **which**
ŏ **pot**	zh **vision**
ō **toe**	ə **a**bout,
ô **paw**	it**e**m

Stress marks:
′ (primary);
′ (secondary), as in
dictionary (dĭk′shə-nĕr′ē)

[After Old *Grog*, nickname of Edward Vernon (1684–1757), British admiral who ordered that grog be served his sailors < GROGRAM (< his wearing a grogram cloak).]

grog·gy (grŏg′ē) *adj.* **-gi·er, -gi·est.** Unsteady and dazed; shaky. [< GROG.] **—grog′gi·ly** *adv.* **—grog′gi·ness** *n.*

grog·ram (grŏg′rəm, grō′grəm) *n.* A coarse, often stiffened fabric made of silk, mohair, wool, or a blend of these fibers. [Alteration of Fr. *gros grain*, coarse texture. See GROSGRAIN.]

groin

groin (groin) *n.* **1.** *Anat.* The crease or hollow at the junction of the inner part of each thigh with the trunk, together with the adjacent region and often including the external genitals. **2.** *Archit.* The curved edge at the junction of two intersecting vaults. **3.** A small jetty extending from a shore to protect a beach against erosion or trap shifting sands. *—tr.v.* **groined, groin·ing, groins.** To provide or build with groins. [Alteration of ME *grinde*, perh. < OE *grynde*, abyss, hollow.]

grok (grŏk) *tr.v.* **grok·ked, grok·king, groks.** *Slang.* To understand profoundly through intuition or empathy. [Coined in *Stranger in a Strange Land* by Robert A. Heinlein (1907–88), Amer. writer.]

grom·met (grŏm′ĭt) also **grum·met** (grŭm′-) *n.* **1.a.** A reinforced eyelet, as in cloth, through which a fastener may be passed. **b.** A small metal or plastic ring used to reinforce a grommet. **2.** *Naut.* A loop of rope or metal used for securing the edge of a sail to its stay. [Prob. < obsolete Fr. *gromette*, chain joining the ends of a bit < OFr. < *gourmer*, to bridle.]

grom·well (grŏm′wəl, -wĕl′) *n.* See **puccoon** 1. [Alteration of ME *gromil* < OFr. : *gro-*; perh. akin to *graine*, grain + *mil*, millet (< Lat. *milium*; see MILLET).]

Gro·my·ko (grə-mē′kō, grō-), **Andrei Andreyevich.** 1909–89. Soviet politician who served as ambassador to the U.S. (1943–46) and the United Nations (1946–48).

Gro·ning·en (grō′nĭng-ən, KHrō′-). A city of NE Netherlands NNE of Apeldoorn. Pop. 167,866.

groom (gro͞om, gro͝om) *n.* **1.** A man or boy employed to take care of horses. **2.** A bridegroom. **3.** One of several officers in an English royal household. **4.** *Archaic.* **a.** A man. **b.** A male servant. *—v.* **groomed, groom·ing, grooms.** *—tr.* **1.** To care for the appearance of; to make neat and trim. **2.** To clean and brush (an animal). **3.** To prepare, as for a specific purpose. **4.** *Sports.* To prepare (a trail) for skiers, as by leveling moguls. *—intr.* To care for one's appearance. [ME *grom*. N., sense 2, short for BRIDEGROOM.] **—groom′er** *n.*

grooms·man (gro͞omz′mən, gro͝omz′-) *n.* A man who attends the bridegroom at a wedding.

grotesque

groove (gro͞ov) *n.* **1.** A long narrow furrow or channel. **2.** *Slang.* A settled routine. **3.** *Slang.* A situation or an activity that one enjoys or to which one is well suited. **4.** *Slang.* A very pleasurable experience. *—v.* **grooved, groov·ing, grooves.** *—tr.* To cut a groove or grooves in. *—intr. Slang.* **1.a.** To take great pleasure or satisfaction; enjoy oneself. **b.** To be pleasurably excited. **2.** To react or interact harmoniously. [ME *groof*, mining shaft, prob. < MDu. *groeve*, ditch. See **ghrebh-**[2]***.**]

groov·y (gro͞o′vē) *adj.* **-i·er, -i·est.** *Slang.* Very pleasing; wonderful. **—groov′i·ness** *n.*

grope (grōp) *v.* **groped, grop·ing, gropes.** *—intr.* **1.** To reach about uncertainly; feel one's way. **2.** To search blindly or uncertainly. *—tr.* **1.** To make (one's way) by reaching about uncertainly. **2.** *Slang.* To handle or fondle for sexual pleasure. *—n.* The act or an instance of groping. [ME *gropen* < OE *grāpian*.] **—grop′er** *n.* **—grop′ing·ly** *adv.*

Gro·pi·us (grō′pē-əs), **Walter Adolph.** 1883–1969. German-born Amer. architect and founder of the Bauhaus school.

gros·beak (grōs′bēk′) *n.* Any of various finches of the family Fringillidae of Europe and America, having a thick conical bill. [Partial transl. of Fr. *grosbec* : *gros*, thick, large (< OFr.; see GROSS) + *bec*, beak.]

gro·schen (grō′shən) *n.*, *pl.* **groschen.** See table at **currency.** [Ger. < MHGer. *grosse* < Med.Lat. *(dēnārius) grossus*, thick (denarius) < LLat. *grossus*, thick.]

gros·grain (grō′grān′) *n.* **1.** A closely woven silk or rayon fabric with narrow horizontal ribs. **2.** A ribbon made of this fabric. [Fr. *gros grain*, coarse texture : *gros*, coarse, thick (< OFr.; see GROSS) + *grain*, texture, grain (< OFr. *graine*, grain, seed; see GRAIN).]

gross (grōs) *adj.* **gross·er, gross·est. 1.a.** Exclusive of deductions; total. See Syns at **whole. b.** Unmitigated in any way; utter. **2.** Glaringly obvious; flagrant. **3.a.** Brutishly coarse, as in behavior; crude. **b.** Offensive; disgusting. **c.** Lacking sensitivity or discernment; unrefined. **d.** Carnal; sensual. **4.a.** Overweight; corpulent. **b.** Dense; profuse. **5.** Broad; general: *gross outlines.* *—n.* **1.** *pl.* **gross·es.** The gross amount or body, as of income. **2.** *pl.* **gross.** A group of 144 items; 12 dozen. *—tr.v.* **grossed, gross·ing, gross·es.** To earn as a gross income or profit. ***—phrasal verb.*** **gross out.** *Slang.* To fill with disgust; nauseate. [ME, large < OFr. *gros* < LLat. *grossus*, thick. N., sense 2, ME *grosse* < OFr. *grosse (douzain)*, large (dozen), fem. of *gros*.] **—gross′er** *n.* **—gross′ly** *adv.* **—gross′ness** *n.*

gross anatomy *n.* The study of the organs, parts, and structures of a body that are visible to the naked eye.

gross index *n. Comp. Sci.* The general index that is consulted first in locating a specific record.

gross national product *n.* The total market value of all the goods and services produced by a nation in a specified period.

gross-out (grōs′out′) *n. Slang.* Something that disgusts.

gros·su·la·rite (grŏs′yə-lə-rīt′) also **gros·su·lar** (-lər) *n.* A pale green, pink, brown, or black garnet, $Ca_3Al_2(SiO_4)_3$, occurring alone or as a constituent of the common garnet. [Ger. *Grossularit* < NLat. *Grossulāria*, former genus of gooseberry < Fr. *groseille*, gooseberry < OFr. *grosele*, of Gmc. orig.]

Gros Ventre (grō′ vänt′) *n.*, *pl.* **Gros Ventre** or **Gros Ventres** (vänt′). **1.** See **Atsina. 2.** See **Hidatsa.** [Fr. : *gros*, big + *ventre*, belly.]

grosz (grôsh) *n.*, *pl.* **gro·szy** (grô′shē). See table at **currency.** [Pol. < Czech *groš* < Med.Lat. *(dēnārius) grossus*, thick (denarius). See GROSCHEN.]

Grosz (grōs), **George.** 1893–1959. German-born Amer. artist known for his biting antimilitaristic caricatures of the 1920's.

grot (grŏt) *n.* A grotto. [Fr. *grotte* < Ital. *grotta*. See GROTTO.]

Grote (grōt), **George.** 1794–1871. British historian noted for his *History of Greece* (1846–56).

gro·tesque (grō-tĕsk′) *adj.* **1.** Marked by ludicrous or incongruous distortion, as of appearance. **2.** Outlandish or bizarre, as in character. See Syns at **fantastic. 3.** Of, relating to, or being the grotesque style in art or a work executed in this style. *—n.* **1.** One that is grotesque. **2.a.** A style of painting, sculpture, and ornamentation in which natural forms and monstrous figures are intertwined in bizarre or fanciful combinations. **b.** A grotesque work of art. [< Fr., grotesque style < Ital. *grottesca* < fem. of *grottesco*, of a grotto < *grotta*, grotto. See GROTTO.] **—gro·tesque′ly** *adv.* **—gro·tesque′ness** *n.*

gro·tes·que·ry also **gro·tes·que·rie** (grō-tĕs′kə-rē) *n.*, *pl.* **-ries. 1.** Grotesqueness. **2.** Something grotesque.

Gro·ti·us (grō′shē-əs, -shəs), **Hugo.** Orig. Huig de Groot. 1583–1645. Dutch jurist and politician known for *Of the Law of War and Peace* (1625).

Grot·on (grŏt′n). A town of SE CT on the Thames R. opposite New London. Pop. 45,144.

grot·to (grŏt′ō) *n.*, *pl.* **-toes** or **-tos. 1.** A small cave or cavern. **2.** An artificial structure or excavation made to resemble a cave or cavern. [Alteration of Ital. *grotta* < VLat. **grupta* < Lat. *crypta*, vault. See CRYPT.]

grot·ty (grŏt′ē) *adj.* **-ti·er, -ti·est.** *Chiefly British.* Wretched; miserable. [Alteration of GROTESQUE.] **—grot′ti·ness** *n.*

grouch (grouch) *n.* **1.** A habitually complaining or irritable person. **2.** A grumbling or sulky mood. **3.** A complaint; a grudge. *—intr.v.* **grouched, grouch·ing, grouch·es.** To grumble or sulk. [< ME *grucchen*, to grumble, complain. See GRUDGE.]

grouch·y (grou′chē) *adj.* **-i·er, -i·est.** Tending to grouch; peevish or grumpy. **—grouch′i·ly** *adv.* **—grouch′i·ness** *n.*

ground[1] (ground) *n.* **1.a.** The solid surface of the earth. **b.** The floor of a body of water, esp. the sea. **2.** Soil; earth. **3.** An area of land designated for a particular purpose. Often used in the plural. **4.** The land surrounding or forming part of a house or another building. Often used in the plural. **5.** An area or a position that is contested in or as if in battle. **6.** Something that serves as a foundation or means of attachment for something else. **7.** A surrounding area; a background. **8.** The foundation for an argument, a belief, or an action; a basis. Often used in the plural. **9.** The underlying condition prompting an action; a cause. Often used in the plural. **10.** An area of reference or discussion; a subject. **11. grounds.** The sediment at or from the bottom of a liquid. **12.** *Elect.* **a.** A large conducting body, such as the earth, used as an arbitrary zero of potential. **b.** A conducting object, such as a wire, connected to such a position of zero potential. *—v.* **ground·ed, ground·ing, grounds.** *—tr.* **1.** To place on or cause to touch the ground. **2.** To provide a basis for (a theory, for example); justify. **3.** To supply with basic information; instruct in fundamentals. **4.a.** To prevent (an aircraft or a pilot) from flying. **b.** *Informal.* To restrict (someone) esp. to a certain place as a punishment. **5.** *Elect.* To connect (an electric circuit) to a ground. **6.** *Naut.* To run (a vessel) aground. **7.a.** *Baseball.* To hit (a ball) onto the ground. **b.** *Football.* To throw (a ball) to the ground in order to stop play and avoid being tackled behind the line of scrimmage. *—intr.* **1.** To touch or reach the ground. **2.** *Baseball.* To hit a ground ball. **3.** *Naut.* To run aground. ***—phrasal verb.*** **ground out.** *Baseball.* To be put out by hitting a ground ball that is fielded and thrown to first base. ***—idioms.*** **drive (or run) into the ground.** To belabor (a subject). **from the ground up.** From the most basic level to the highest level; completely. **off the ground.** Under way, as if in flight. **on (one's) own ground.** In a situation where one has knowledge or competence. [ME < OE *grund*.]

ground[2] (ground) *v.* *P.t. and p.part. of* **grind.**

ground ball also **ground·ball** (ground′bôl′) *n. Baseball.* A batted ball that rolls or bounces along the ground.

ground bass (bās) *n. Mus.* A short musical passage continually repeated in the bass under the changing harmonies and melodies of the upper range.

ground beetle *n.* See **carabid.**
ground•break•er (ground′brāʹkər) *n.* One that is original or innovative.
ground•break•ing (ground′brāʹkĭng) *n.* The act or ceremony of breaking ground to begin a construction project. —*adj.* **1.** Of, relating to, or being a ceremony of breaking ground. **2.** Characterized by originality and innovation.
ground cedar *n.* See **ground pine.**
ground cherry *n.* Any of various chiefly New World plants of the genus *Physalis,* having small globose fleshy fruit enclosed in a papery bladderlike persistent calyx.
ground cloth *n.* **1.** A waterproof cover used to protect an area of ground, such as a baseball field. **2.** A waterproof sheet placed under camp bedding as a protection against moisture.
ground-con•trolled approach (ground′kən-trōldʹ) *n.* A control mode in which an aircraft is talked down for landing through the use of surveillance and precision approach radar.
ground cover also **ground•cov•er** (ground′kŭvʹər) *n.* **1.** Small plants other than saplings, such as mosses and undershrubs, growing on a forest floor; undergrowth. **2.a.** A low-growing dense growth of plants, such as pachysandra, planted to prevent soil erosion in areas where turf is difficult or impossible to grow, as in deep shade. **b.** A plant used for such a growth.
ground crew *n.* A team of mechanics and technicians that maintain and service aircraft on the ground.
ground-ef•fect machine (ground′ĭ-fĕktʹ) *n.* See **air-cushion vehicle.** [< *ground effect,* a peculiarity of certain aircraft when landing, in which a cushion of air directed off the wings prevents touchdown.]
ground•er (groun′dər) *n. Baseball.* A ground ball.
ground fish *n.* A fish, such as a cod, that lives at the bottom of a body of water.
ground floor *n.* **1.** The floor of a building at or nearest ground level. **2.** *Informal.* The beginning of a venture, esp. as a position of advantage.
ground glass *n.* **1.** Glass that has been ground or etched to create a roughened nontransparent surface. **2.** Glass that has been ground into fine particles, as for use as an abrasive.
ground hemlock *n.* A low-growing yew *(Taxus canadensis)* of northeast North America.
ground•hog also **ground hog** (ground′hôgʹ, -hŏgʹ) *n.* See **woodchuck.** See Regional Note at **woodchuck.**
Ground•hog Day (ground′hôgʹ, -hŏgʹ) *n.* February 2, on which popular legend predicts an early spring if the groundhog does not see its shadow upon emerging from its burrow or six more weeks of winter if it does.
ground ivy *n.* A creeping or trailing aromatic plant *(Glechoma hederacea)* having rounded scalloped leaves and small purplish flowers.
ground•keep•er (ground′kēʹpər) *n.* Var. of **groundskeeper.**
ground•less (ground′lĭs) *adj.* Having no ground or foundation; unsubstantiated. —**ground′less•ness** *n.*
ground level *n. Phys.* See **ground state.**
ground•ling (ground′lĭng) *n.* **1.a.** A plant or an animal living on or near the ground. **b.** See **ground fish. 2.** A person with uncultivated tastes. **3.** A spectator in the cheap standing-room section of an Elizabethan theater.
ground loop *n.* A sharp horizontal turn made by an aircraft on the ground when taxiing, landing, or taking off.
ground•mass (ground′măsʹ) *n.* The fine-grained crystalline base of porphyritic rock in which larger crystals are embedded.
ground meristem *n. Bot.* The tissue at the tip of a growing stem or root that differentiates into the pith and cortex.
ground•nut (ground′nŭtʹ) *n.* **1.a.** A climbing vine *(Apios americana)* of eastern North America having compound leaves and small edible tubers. **b.** Any of several plants having underground tubers or nutlike parts. **c.** The tuber or nutlike part of such a plant. **2.** *Chiefly British.* A peanut.
ground•out (ground′outʹ) *n. Baseball.* A play in which a batter grounds out.
ground pine *n.* A club moss, esp. *Lycopodium obscurum* or *L. complanatum* or a similar species.
ground plan *n.* **1.** A plan of a floor of a building drawn as if seen from overhead. **2.** A preliminary plan or strategy.
ground plum *n.* **1.** A perennial plant *(Astragalus crassicarpus)* of the central and western United States having compound leaves and plumlike edible fruit. **2.** The fruit of this plant.
ground rent *n. Chiefly British.* Rent paid for land to be used chiefly for building.
ground robin *n.* See **towhee** 1.
ground rule *n.* **1.** *Sports.* A rule governing the playing of a game on a particular field, course, or court. **2.** A basic rule of procedure or behavior. Often used in the plural.
ground•sel¹ (ground′səl, groun′-) *n.* Any of various plants of the genus *Senecio,* having rayed, usu. yellow flower heads. [ME *groundeswille* < OE *grundeswylige,* alteration of *gundeswilge* : *gund,* pus + *swelgan,* to swallow (used in reducing abscesses); see **swel-*.**]
ground•sel² (ground′səl, groun′-) *n.* Var. of **groundsill.**
ground sheet *n.* See **ground cloth.**
ground•side (ground′sīdʹ) *n.* The part of an airport used for operations unrelated to the departure and arrival of aircraft.
ground•sill (ground′sĭlʹ) also **ground•sel** (ground′səl, groun′-) *n.* The horizontal timber nearest the ground in the frame of a building.
grounds•keep•er (groundz′kēʹpər) also **ground•keep•er** (ground′-) *n.* One who maintains grounds, as of an estate.
ground speed also **ground•speed** (ground′spēdʹ) *n.* The speed of an airborne aircraft relative to the ground it traverses in a given period of time.
ground squirrel *n.* Any of several burrowing or terrestrial squirrels of the genus *Citellus* or *Spermophilus.*
ground state *n. Phys.* The state of least possible energy in a physical system, as of elementary particles.
ground•stroke (ground′strōkʹ) *n. Sports.* A swing of a tennis racquet at a ball that has bounced from the ground.
ground substance *n.* **1.** The intercellular material in which the cells and fibers of connective tissue are embedded. **2.** See **hyaloplasm.**
ground•swell (ground′swĕlʹ) *n.* **1.** A sudden gathering of force, as of public opinion. **2.** A broad deep undulation of the ocean, often caused by a distant storm or an earthquake.
ground water also **ground•wa•ter** (ground′wôʹtər, -wŏtʹər) *n.* Water beneath the earth's surface, often between saturated soil and rock, that supplies wells and springs.
ground wave *n.* A radio wave traveling along the earth's surface.
ground•work (ground′wûrkʹ) *n.* A foundation; a basis.
ground zero *n.* **1.** The target of a projectile, such as a missile or bomb. **2.** The site directly below, directly above, or at the point of detonation of a nuclear weapon.
group (gro͞op) *n.* **1.** An assemblage of persons or objects gathered or located together; an aggregation. **2.** Two or more figures that make up a unit or design, as in sculpture. **3.** A number of individuals or things considered together because of similarities. **4.** *Ling.* A category of related languages that is less inclusive than a family. **5.a.** A military unit consisting of two or more battalions and a headquarters. **b.** A unit of two or more squadrons in the U.S. Air Force, smaller than a wing. **6.** A class or collection of related objects or entities, as: **a.** Two or more atoms behaving or regarded as behaving as a single chemical unit. **b.** A column in the periodic table of the elements. **c.** A stratigraphic unit, esp. a unit of two or more formations deposited during a single geologic era. **7.** *Math.* A set with an associative binary operation under which the set is closed, which contains an identity element and an inverse for every element in the set. —*adj.* Of, relating to, constituting, or being a member of a group. —*v.* **grouped, group•ing, groups.** —*tr.* To place or arrange in a group. —*intr.* To belong to or form a group. [Fr. *groupe* < Ital. *gruppo,* prob. of Gmc. orig.]

Usage Note: *Group* as a collective noun can be followed by a singular or plural verb. It takes a singular verb when those making up the group are considered collectively: *The group is here. Group* takes a plural verb when those constituting it are considered individually: *The group were divided about that.* See Usage Note at **collective noun.**

grou•per (gro͞o′pər) *n., pl.* **grouper** or **-pers.** Any of various often large food and game fishes of the genera *Epinephelus, Mycteroperca,* and related genera. [Port. *garupa.*]
group•ie (gro͞o′pē) *n. Slang.* A fan, esp. a young woman, who follows a rock group around on tours.
group•ing (gro͞o′pĭng) *n.* **1.** The act or process of uniting into groups. **2.** People or things united into a group.
group insurance *n.* Insurance purchased by a group of persons, such as union members, often at a reduced individual rate.
group practice *n.* **1.** The practice of health care by an association of professionals who share premises and other resources. **2.** An association engaged in group practice.
group theory *n.* The branch of mathematics concerned with the discovery of groups and the description of their properties.
group therapy *n.* A form of psychotherapy in which several clients guided by a therapist confront their problems together. —**group therapist** *n.*
group•think (gro͞op′thĭngkʹ) *n.* **1.** The act or practice of reasoning or decision-making by a group. **2.** Blind conformity in such reasoning or decision-making.
grouse¹ (grous) *n., pl.* **grouse** or **grous•es.** Any of various plump chickenlike game birds of the family Tetraonidae, chiefly of the Northern Hemisphere and having mottled brown or grayish plumage. [?]
grouse² (grous) *Informal.* —*intr.v.* **groused, grous•ing, grous•es.** To complain; grumble. —*n.* A cause for complaint; a grievance. [Perh. < Fr. dial. *groucer* < OFr. *groucier.* See GRUDGE.] —**grous′er** *n.*
grout (grout) *n.* **1.a.** A thin mortar used to fill cracks and crevices in masonry. **b.** A thin plaster for finishing walls and ceilings. **2.** *Chiefly British.* Sediment; lees. Often used in the plural. —*tr.v.* **grout•ed, grout•ing, grouts.** To fill or finish with grout. [ME, grain used for making malt, mud < OE *grūt,* coarse meal.] —**grout′er** *n.*
grove (grōv) *n.* **1.** A small wood or stand of trees lacking dense undergrowth. **2.** A group of trees planted and cultivated for

ă pat	oi boy
ā pay	ou out
âr care	o͝o took
ä father	o͞o boot
ĕ pet	ŭ cut
ē be	ûr urge
ĭ pit	th thin
ī pie	*th* this
îr pier	hw which
ŏ pot	zh vision
ō toe	ə about, item
ô paw	

Stress marks:
′ (primary);
ʹ (secondary), as in
dictionary (dĭk′shə-nĕrʹē)

gueridon

Guernsey[2]
Guernsey cow

guide dog

Guinea

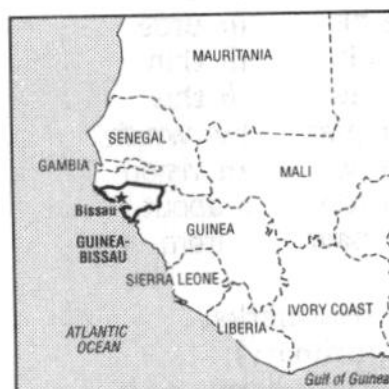

Guinea-Bissau

in the S-central part; founded 1776. Pop. 754,243. — **Gua′te•ma′lan** *adj. & n.*

gua•va (gwä′və) *n.* **1.** Any of various tropical American shrubs and trees of the genus *Psidium*, esp. *P. guajava*, having white flowers and edible fruit. **2.** The fruit of this plant. [Sp. *guayaba*, of Caribbean Indian orig.]

Gua•via•re (gwäv-yär′ē, -yä′rĕ). A river of central and E Colombia flowing c. 1,046 km (650 mi) to the Orinoco R.

Gua•ya•quil (gwī′ə-kēl′). A city of W Ecuador near the **Gulf of Guayaquil**, an inlet of the Pacific. Pop. 1,204,532.

Guay•na•bo (gwī-nä′bō). A city of NE Puerto Rico, a suburb of San Juan. Pop. 65,075.

gua•yu•le (gwī-ōō′lē) *n.* A shrub *(Parthenium argentatum)* of the southwest United States and Mexico. [Am.Sp. < Nahuatl *cuauhuli* : *cuahu(itl)*, tree + *uli*, latex gum.]

gu•ber•na•to•ri•al (gōō′bər-nə-tôr′ē-əl, -tōr′-, gyōō′-) *adj.* Of or relating to a governor. [< Lat. *gubernātor*, governor < *gubernāre*, to govern. See GOVERN.]

guck (gŭk, gŏŏk) also **gook** (gŏŏk, gōōk) *n. Slang.* A thick messy substance, such as sludge. [Poss. G(OO) + (M)UCK.]

gudg•eon[1] (gŭj′ən) *n.* **1.a.** A small Eurasian freshwater fish *(Gobio gobio)* related to the carp and used for bait. **b.** Any of various similar or related fishes. **2.** *Slang.* One who is easily duped. [ME *gojoun* < OFr. *goujon* < Lat. *gōbiō, gōbiōn-*, var. of *gōbius*. See GOBY.]

gudg•eon[2] (gŭj′ən) *n.* **1.** A metal pivot or journal at the end of a shaft or an axle, around which a wheel or other device turns. **2.** The socket of a hinge into which a pin fits. **3.** A metal pin that joins two pieces of stone. [ME *gudyon* < OFr. *gojon*, peg, dim. of *gouge*, gouge. See GOUGE.]

gudgeon pin *n.* See **wrist pin.**

Gud•run (gŏŏd′rōōn′) also **Guth•run** (gŏŏth′-) *n. Myth.* The daughter of the king of the Nibelungs and wife of Sigurd, later of Atli, in the *Volsunga Saga.*

guel•der rose (gĕl′dər) *n.* A Eurasian shrub *(Viburnum opulus)* having clusters of white flowers and small red fruit. [After *Guelderland* (Gelderland), the Netherlands.]

Guelph[1] (gwĕlf). A city of S Ontario, Canada, W of Toronto. Pop. 71,207.

Guelph[2] also **Guelf** (gwĕlf) *n.* A member of a faction in medieval Italy that supported the pope and the city-states against the German emperors and the Ghibellines. [Ital. *Guelfo* < MHGer. *Welf*, the founder of a German princely family.]

Guen•e•vere (gwĕn′ə-vîr) *n.* Var. of **Guinevere.**

gue•non (gə-nōn′) *n.* Any of various African monkeys, primarily of the genus *Cercopithecus*, having a long tail. [Fr.]

guer•don (gûr′dn) *n.* A reward; recompense. — *tr.v.* **-doned, -don•ing, -dons.** To reward. [ME < OFr. < Med.Lat. *widerdōnum*, alteration of OHGer. *widarlōn* : *widar*, back, against; see **wi-*** + *lōn*, reward; see **lau-*.**]

gue•ri•don (gĕr′ĭ-dŏn′, gā-rē-dôN′) *n.* A small round table. [Fr. *guéridon* < the proper name *Guéridon.*]

Guer•ni•ca (gwâr′nĭ-kə, gĕr-nē′kä) also **Guernica y Lu•no** (ē lōō′nō). A town of N-central Spain NE of Bilbao. Its Apr. 1937 bombing by German planes during the Spanish Civil War inspired Picasso's famous paintings. Pop. 12,100.

Guern•sey[1] (gûrn′zē). An island of S Great Britain, one of the Channel Is. in the English Channel off NW France.

Guern•sey[2] (gûrn′zē) *n., pl.* **-seys.** Any of a breed of brown and white dairy cattle originally developed on the island of Guernsey and noted for producing a rich golden milk.

guer•ril•la or **gue•ril•la** (gə-rĭl′ə) *n.* A member of an irregular, usu. indigenous military unit operating in small bands to undermine the enemy. [Sp., raiding party, dim. of *guerra*, war, of Gmc. orig. See **wers-*.**]

guerrilla theater *n.* See **street theater.**

guess (gĕs) *v.* **guessed, guess•ing, guess•es.** — *tr.* **1.a.** To predict (a result or event) without sufficient information. **b.** To assume or assert (a fact) without sufficient information. **2.** To form a correct estimate or conjecture of. **3.** To suppose; think. — *intr.* **1.** To make an estimate or conjecture. **2.** To estimate or conjecture correctly. — *n.* **1.** An act or instance of guessing. **2.** A conjecture arrived at by guessing. [ME *gessen*, prob. of Scand. orig. See **ghend-*.**] — **guess′er** *n.*

guess•ti•mate (gĕs′tə-mĭt) *n. Informal.* An estimate based on conjecture. [Blend of GUESS and ESTIMATE.] — **guess′ti•mate′** (-māt′) *v.*

guess•work (gĕs′wûrk′) *n.* **1.** The process of making guesses. **2.** An estimate or judgment made by guessing.

guest (gĕst) *n.* **1.** One who is a recipient of hospitality at the home or table of another. **2.** One to whom entertainment or hospitality has been extended by another, as at a party. **3.** One who patronizes a restaurant, hotel, or other establishment. **4.** A distinguished visitor to whom the hospitality of an institution, a city, or a government is extended. **5.** A visiting performer, speaker, or contestant, as on a radio program. **6.** *Zool.* A commensal organism, esp. an insect that lives in the nest or burrow of another species. — *v.* **guest•ed, guest•ing, guests.** — *tr.* To entertain as a guest. — *intr.* To appear as a guest. — *adj.* **1.** Provided for guests. **2.** Participating as a guest: *a guest conductor.* [ME *gest* < ON *gestr.* See **ghos-ti-*.**]

Guest (gĕst), **Edgar Albert.** 1881–1959. British-born Amer. journalist known for his widely syndicated homey rhymes.

guest•house (gĕst′hous′) *n.* A small house or cottage adjacent to a main house, used for lodging guests.

guest worker *n.* A foreigner who is permitted to work in a country on a temporary basis, as for farm labor.

Gue•va•ra (gə-vär′ə, gĕ-vä′rä), **Ernesto.** "Che." 1928–67. Argentine-born Cuban revolutionary leader who was Fidel Castro's chief lieutenant in the Cuban revolution (1956–59) and later served as minister of industry (1961–65).

guff (gŭf) *n. Slang.* **1.** Nonsense; baloney. **2.** Insolent talk; back talk. [Perh. imit.]

guf•faw (gə-fô′) *n.* A hearty boisterous burst of laughter. — *intr.v.* **-fawed, -faw•ing, -faws.** To laugh heartily and boisterously. [Prob. imit.]

Gui•an•a (gē-ăn′ə, -ä′nə, gī-). A region of NE South America including SE Venezuela, part of N Brazil, and French Guiana, Suriname, and Guyana.

Guiana High•lands (hī′ləndz). A mountainous tableland region of N South America extending from SE Venezuela into Guyana and N Brazil.

guid•ance (gīd′ns) *n.* **1.** The act or process of guiding. **2.** Counseling, such as that provided for students about vocational and educational matters. **3.** Any of various processes for guiding a vehicle by means of built-in equipment.

guide (gīd) *n.* **1.a.** One who shows the way by leading, directing, or advising. **b.** One who serves as a model for others, as in a course of conduct. **2.** A person employed to conduct others and give information. **3.a.** Something, such as a pamphlet, that offers basic information or instruction. **b.** A guidebook. **4.a.** Something that serves to direct or indicate. **b.** A device, such as a ruler or bar, that serves as an indicator or a regulator. **5.** A soldier stationed at the right or left of a column of marchers to control alignment, show direction, or mark the point of pivot. — *v.* **guid•ed, guid•ing, guides.** — *tr.* **1.** To serve as a guide for; conduct. **2.** To direct the course of; steer. **3.** To exert control or influence over. **4.** To supervise the training or education of. — *intr.* To serve as a guide. [ME < OFr. < OProv. *guida* < *guidar*, to guide, of Gmc. orig. See **weid-*.**] — **guid′a•ble** *adj.* — **guid′er** *n.*

guide•book (gīd′bŏŏk′) *n.* A handbook of directions and other information, esp. for travelers or tourists.

guid•ed missile (gī′dĭd) *n.* A self-propelled missile that can be guided while it is in flight.

guide dog *n.* A dog that has been specially trained to guide a visually impaired or sightless person.

guide•line (gīd′līn′) *n.* A statement or other indication of policy or procedure by which to determine a course of action.

guide•post (gīd′pōst′) *n.* **1.** A post with a sign giving directions for travelers, usu. placed at a crossroad. **2.** Something that serves as a guide or an example; a guideline.

guide•word (gīd′wûrd′) *n.* A word or term that appears at the top of each page or column in a reference book, such as a dictionary, to indicate the first or last entry.

Gui•do d'A•rez•zo (gwē′dō dä-rĕt′sō) or **Guido A•re•ti•no** (är′ĕ-tē′nō). 990?–1050. Benedictine monk who devised the four-line staff, thereby allowing precise musical notation.

gui•don (gī′dŏn′, gīd′n) *n.* **1.** A small flag or pennant carried as a standard by a military unit. **2.** A soldier bearing such a flag or pennant. [Fr. < OFr. < OItal. *guidone* < *guidare*, to guide < OProv. *guidar.* See GUIDE.]

Gui•enne or **Guy•enne** (gē-ĕn′). A historical region and former province of SW France; part of England from 1152 to 1453.

guild also **gild** (gĭld) *n.* **1.** An association of persons of the same trade or pursuits, formed to protect mutual interests and maintain standards. **2.** A similar association, as of artisans, in medieval times. [ME *gild* < ON *gildi*, payment, guild.]

guil•der (gĭl′dər) *n.* See table at **currency.** [ME *gilder*, alteration of MDu. *gulden*, golden. See **ghel-[2]*.**]

guild•hall (gĭld′hôl′) *n.* **1.** The meeting hall of a guild. **2.** A town hall.

guilds•man (gĭldz′mən) *n.* **1.** A member of a guild. **2.** An advocate of guild socialism.

guild socialism *n.* An English socialist doctrine of the early 20th century according to which industry would be owned by the state but managed by guilds of workers.

guile (gīl) *n.* **1.** Treacherous cunning; skillful deceit. **2.** *Obsolete.* A trick or stratagem. — *tr.v.* **guiled, guil•ing, guiles.** *Archaic.* To beguile; deceive. [ME < OFr., of Gmc. orig.]

guile•ful (gīl′fəl) *adj.* Full of guile; treacherously cunning. — **guile′ful•ly** *adv.* — **guile′ful•ness** *n.*

guile•less (gīl′lĭs) *adj.* Free of guile; artless. See Syns at **naive.**

Guil•ford (gĭl′fərd). A town of S CT E of New Haven; settled in 1639. Pop. 19,848.

Gui•lin (gwē′lĭn′) also **Kwei•lin** (kwā′-). A city of SE China NW of Guangzhou; orig. founded in the 6th cent. A.D. Pop. 325,000.

Guil•lain Bar•ré Syndrome (gē-yăN′ bə-rā′) *n.* A temporary inflammation of the nerves, causing pain, weakness, and paralysis in the extremities and often progressing to the chest and face. [After Georges *Guillain* (1876–1961) and Jean Alexandre *Barré* (1880–1967), French neurologists.]

guil•le•mot (gĭl′ə-mŏt′) *n.* Any of several auks of the genus *Cepphus,* having black plumage with white markings. [Fr., dim. of the personal name *Guillaume.*]

guil•loche (gĭ-lōsh′, gē-yōsh′) *n. Archit.* An ornamental border formed of two or more curved bands that interlace to repeat a circular design. [Fr. *guilloch.*]

guil•lo•tine (gĭl′ə-tēn′, gē′ə-) *n.* **1.** A device consisting of a heavy blade held aloft between upright guides and dropped to behead the victim below. **2.** An instrument, such as a paper cutter, similar in action to a guillotine. —*tr.v.* **-tined, -tin•ing, -tines. 1.** To behead with a guillotine. **2.** To cut with or as if with a guillotine. [Fr., after Joseph Ignace *Guillotin* (1738–1814), French physician.]

guilt (gĭlt) *n.* **1.** The fact of being responsible for the commission of an offense. See Syns at **blame. 2.** *Law.* Culpability for a crime or lesser breach of regulations that carries a legal penalty. **3.a.** Remorseful awareness of having done something wrong. **b.** Self-reproach for supposed inadequacy or wrongdoing. **4.** Guilty conduct; sin. [ME *gilt* < OE *gylt,* crime.]

guilt•less (gĭlt′lĭs) *adj.* Free of guilt; innocent.

guilt•y (gĭl′tē) *adj.* **-i•er, -i•est. 1.** Responsible for or chargeable with a reprehensible act; culpable. **2.** *Law.* Adjudged to have committed a crime. **3.** Suffering from or prompted by a sense of guilt: *a guilty conscience.* **4.** Hinting at or entailing guilt: *a guilty smirk.* —**guilt′i•ly** *adv.* —**guilt′i•ness** *n.*

guimpe (gămp, gĭmp) *n.* **1.** A blouse worn under a jumper. **2.** A yoke insert for a low-necked dress. **3.** A starched cloth covering the neck and shoulders as part of a nun's habit. **4.** See **gimp[1].** [Fr. < OFr. *guimple* < OHGer. *wimpal.* See **weip-*.**]

Guin. *abbr.* Guinea.

guin•ea (gĭn′ē) *n.* **1.a.** A gold coin issued in England from 1663 to 1813 and worth one pound and one shilling. **b.** The sum of one pound and one shilling. **2.** *Offensive Slang.* Used as a disparaging term for an Italian or a person of Italian descent. [After the GUINEA coast of Africa.]

Guin•ea (gĭn′ē). A country of W Africa on the Atlantic Ocean; a French colony from 1898 until 1958. Cap. Conakry. Pop. 4,830,000. —**Guin′e•an** *adj. & n.*

Guinea, Gulf of. A broad inlet of the Atlantic Ocean formed by the great bend in the W-central coast of Africa.

Guin•ea-Bis•sau (gĭn′ē-bĭ-sou′). A country of W Africa on the Atlantic Ocean; achieved independence from Portugal in 1974. Cap. Bissau. Pop. 777,214.

guinea fowl *n.* Any of several pheasantlike birds of the family Numididae native to Africa, esp. a domesticated species *(Numida meleagris)* having blackish plumage marked with small white spots. [After the GUINEA coast of Africa.]

guinea hen *n.* See **guinea fowl.**

guinea pig *n.* **1.** Any of various small short-eared domesticated rodents of the genus *Cavia,* having no visible tail and often kept as pets and used as experimental animals. **2.** *Informal.* A person who is used as a subject for experimentation or research. [Perh. alteration (influenced by GUINEA, used as a name for any faraway unknown country) of GUIANA.]

guinea worm *n.* A long nematode worm *(Dracunculus medinensis)* of tropical Asia and Africa that is a subcutaneous parasite of human beings and other mammals.

Guin•e•vere (gwĭn′ə-vîr′) also **Guen•e•vere** (gwĕn′-) *n.* The wife of King Arthur and lover of Lancelot.

Guin•ness (gĭn′ĭs), Sir **Alec.** b. 1914. British actor whose films include *The Bridge on the River Kwai* (1957).

gui•pure (gĭ-po͝or′, -pyo͝or′) *n.* **1.** A coarse large-patterned lace without a net ground. **2.** See **gimp[1].** [Fr. < OFr. < *guiper,* to cover with silk, of Gmc. orig. See **weip-*.**]

guise (gīz) *n.* **1.** Outward appearance or aspect; semblance. **2.** False appearance; pretense: *under the guise of friendship.* **3.** Mode of dress; garb. **4.** *Obsolete.* Custom; habit. [ME, manner, fashion < OFr., of Gmc. orig. See **weid-*.**]

Guise (gēz), 2nd Duke. François de Lorraine. 1519–63. French general and politician who suppressed the Huguenots.

Guise, 3rd Duke. Henri de Lorraine. 1550–88. French military leader who helped plan the massacre of Huguenots on St. Bartholomew's Day, 1572.

gui•tar (gĭ-tär′) *n. Mus.* An instrument having a large flat-backed sound box, a long fretted neck, and usu. six strings, played by strumming or plucking. [Fr. *guitare* < Sp. *guitarra* < alteration of Gk. *kithara,* cithara.] —**gui•tar′ist** *n.*

gui•tar•fish (gĭ-tär′fĭsh′) *n., pl.* **guitarfish** or **-fish•es.** Any of several marine fishes of the family Rhinobatidae, having a guitar-shaped body and related to the skates and rays.

Gui•yang (gwē′yäng′) also **Kwei•yang** (kwā′-). A city of SW China ENE of Kunming; cap. of Guizhou. Pop. 871,000.

Gui•zhou (gwē′jō′) also **Kwei•chow** (kwā′chō′). A province of SE China; passed under Chinese suzerainty in the 10th cent. Cap. Guiyang. Pop. 29,680,000.

Gu•ja•rat (go͞o′jə-rät′, go͝oj′ə-). A region of W India bordering on the Arabian Sea; annexed by the Moguls in 1572.

Gu•ja•ra•ti (go͞o′jə-rä′tē, go͝oj′ə-) *n., pl.* **Gujarati** or **-tis. 1.** The Indic language of Gujarat. **2.** A native or inhabitant of Gujarat.

Guj•ran•wa•la (go͝oj′rən-wä′lə, go͝oj′-). A city of NE Pakistan N of Lahore; a center of Sikh influence. Pop. 597,000.

gu•lag also **Gu•lag** (go͞o′läg) *n.* **1.** A network of forced labor camps in the former Soviet Union. **2.** A forced labor camp or prison, esp. for political dissidents. [Russ. *Gulag* < *G(lavnoe) u(pravlenie) (ispravitel'no-trudovykh) lag(ereĭ),* Chief Administration of (Correctional Labor) Camps.]

gu•lar (go͞o′lər, gyo͞o′-) *adj.* Of, relating to, or located on the throat. [Lat. *gula,* throat + -AR.]

gulch (gŭlch) *n.* A small ravine, esp. one cut by a torrent. [Perh. < dial. *gulch,* (of land) to sink in < ME *gulchen,* to spew.]

gul•den (go͞ol′dən, go͝ol′-) *n., pl.* **-dens** or **gulden.** A guilder. [ME < Du. *gulden (florijn),* golden (florin) < MDu. See **ghel-[2]*.**]

gules (gyo͞olz) *n. Her.* The color red, indicated on a blazon by vertical lines. [ME *goules* < OFr., red fur neckpiece, pl. of *gole,* throat < Lat. *gula.*]

gulf (gŭlf) *n.* **1.** A large area of a sea or ocean partially enclosed by land. **2.** A deep wide chasm; an abyss. **3.** A wide gap, as in understanding. **4.** Something, such as a whirlpool, that draws down or engulfs. —*tr.v.* **gulfed, gulf•ing, gulfs.** To engulf. [ME *goulf* < OFr. *golfe* < OItal. *golfo* < LLat. *colpus, colfus* < Gk. *kolpos,* bosom, gulf.]

Gulf In•tra•coas•tal Waterway (gŭlf ĭn′trə-kō′stəl). An inland waterway of bays, canals, and rivers from NW FL to Brownsville TX, approx. 1,770 km (1,100 mi) long.

Gulf of. For names of actual gulfs, see the specific element of the name; for example, **Mexico, Gulf of.**

Gulf•port (gŭlf′pôrt′, -pōrt′). A city of SE MS on an arm of the Gulf of Mexico W of Biloxi; settled in 1891. Pop. 40,775.

Gulf States. 1. The countries bordering the Persian Gulf in SW Asia, including Iran, Iraq, Kuwait, Saudi Arabia, Bahrain, Qatar, United Arab Emirates, and Oman. **2.** The states of the S U.S. with coastlines on the Gulf of Mexico, including FL, AL, MS, LA, and TX.

Gulf Stream. A warm ocean current of the N Atlantic off E North America flowing from the Gulf of Mexico through the Straits of Florida to the North Atlantic Drift.

gulf•weed also **gulf weed** (gŭlf′wēd′) *n.* Any of several brownish seaweeds of the genus *Sargassum* of tropical Atlantic waters, having round air sacs. [After the *Gulf* of Mexico.]

gull[1] (gŭl) *n.* Any of various chiefly coastal aquatic birds of the family Laridae, having long wings, webbed feet, and usu. gray and white plumage. [ME *gulle,* poss. of Brythonic orig.]

gull[2] (gŭl) *n.* A person who is easily tricked or cheated; a dupe. —*tr.v.* **gulled, gull•ing, gulls.** To deceive or cheat. [Prob. < *gull,* to swallow (obsolete) < ME *golen,* to pretend to swallow < *gole,* throat, perh. < OFr. *goule.* See GULLET.]

Gul•lah (gŭl′ə) *n.* **1.** One of a group of people of African ancestry inhabiting the Sea Islands and coastal areas of South Carolina, Georgia, and northern Florida. **2.** The creolized language of the Gullahs, based on English but including elements and features from several African languages. [Perh. alteration of ANGOLA or < *Gola,* a people of Sierra Leone and Liberia.]

gul•let (gŭl′ĭt) *n.* **1.** The esophagus. **2.** The throat. **3.** *Zool.* An invagination into the cytoplasm of some ciliates for food intake. [ME *golet* < OFr. *goulet* < *goule,* throat < Lat. *gula.*]

gul•li•ble (gŭl′ə-bəl) *adj.* Easily deceived or duped. [< GULL[2].] —**gul′li•bil′i•ty** *n.* —**gul′li•bly** *adv.*

Gul•li•ver (gŭl′ə-vər) *n.* An Englishman who travels to imaginary lands such as Lilliput and Brobdingnag in Jonathan Swift's satire *Gulliver's Travels* (1726).

gull•wing (gŭl′wĭng′) *adj.* Hinged at the top so as to swing upward. Used of a type of automobile door.

gul•ly[1] (gŭl′ē) *n., pl.* **-lies.** A deep ditch or channel cut in the earth by running water after a prolonged downpour. —*v.* **-lied, -ly•ing, -lies.** —*tr.* To wear a deep ditch or channel in. —*intr.* To form a deep ditch or channel. [Perh. alteration of ME *golet,* throat, channel. See GULLET.]

gul•ly[2] (gŭl′ē) *n., pl.* **-lies.** *Chiefly British.* A large knife. [Short for dial. *gully knife* : *gully* (prob. alteration of ME *golet,* throat; see GULLET) + KNIFE.]

gulp (gŭlp) *v.* **gulped, gulp•ing, gulps.** —*tr.* **1.** To swallow greedily or rapidly in large amounts. **2.** To choke back by or as if by swallowing. —*intr.* **1.** To choke or gasp, as in gulping liquid. **2.** To swallow air audibly, as in nervousness. —*n.* **1.** The act of gulping. **2.** A large amount gulped at one time. [< ME *gulpen* or < Flem. or Du. *gulpen.*] —**gulp′er** *n.*

gum[1] (gŭm) *n.* **1.a.** Any of various viscous substances exuded by certain plants and trees that dry into water-soluble noncrystalline brittle solids. **b.** A similar plant exudate, such as a resin. **c.** Any of various adhesives made from such exudates or other sticky substances. **2.** A substance resembling gum, as in stickiness. **3.a.** Any of various trees of the genera *Eucalyptus, Liquidambar,* or *Nyssa* that are sources of gum. **b.** The wood of such a tree; gumwood. **4.** Chewing gum. —*v.* **gummed, gum•ming, gums.** —*tr.* To cover, smear, seal, fill, or fix in place with or as if with gum. —*intr.* **1.** To exude or form gum. **2.** To become sticky or clogged. —***phrasal verb.* gum up.** To ruin or bungle. [ME *gomme* < OFr. < LLat. *gumma,* var. of Lat. *gummi, cummi* < Gk. *kommi,* perh. < Egypt. *kmj-t.*]

gum[2] (gŭm) *n.* The firm connective tissue covered by mucous

guinea fowl
Vulturine guinea fowl
Acryllium vulturinum

guitar

gullwing

ă pat	oi boy
ā pay	ou out
âr care	o͝o took
ä father	o͞o boot
ĕ pet	ŭ cut
ē be	ûr urge
ĭ pit	th thin
ī pie	*th* this
îr pier	hw which
ŏ pot	zh vision
ō toe	ə about, item
ô paw	

Stress marks:
′ (primary);
′ (secondary), as in
dictionary (dĭk′shə-nĕr′ē)

on the Atlantic Ocean; a British colony from 1814 until 1966. Cap. Georgetown. Pop. 918,000. — **Guy′a•nese′** (-nēz′, -nēs′) *adj. & n.*

Guy•enne (gē-ĕn′). See **Guienne.**

Guy Fawkes Day (gī′ fôks′) *n.* November 5, observed in Great Britain to commemorate the foiling of the attempt led by Guy Fawkes in 1605 to blow up the king and Parliament in retaliation for increasing repression of Roman Catholics.

guy•ot (gē′ō) *n.* A flat-topped submarine mountain. [After Arnold Henri *Guyot* (1807–84), Amer. geologist.]

guz•zle (gŭz′əl) *v.* **-zled, -zling, -zles.** — *tr.* **1.** To drink greedily or habitually. **2.** To consume to excess. — *intr.* To drink, esp. liquor, greedily or habitually. [?] — **guz′zler** *n.*

GW *abbr.* Gigawatt.

Gwa•li•or (gwä′lē-ôr′). A city of N-central India S of Agra. Pop. 539,015.

gwe•duc (go͞o′ē-dŭk′) *n.* Var. of **geoduck.**

Gwin•net (gwə-nĕt′), **Button.** 1735?–77. Amer. Revolutionary patriot primarily known for the value of his autographs.

Gwyn or **Gwynne** (gwĭn), **Eleanor ("Nell").** 1650?–87. English actress who was the lover of Charles II after c. 1668.

gybe (jīb) *v. & n. Naut.* Var. of **jibe**[1].

gym (jĭm) *n. Sports.* **1.** A gymnasium. **2.** A school course in physical education. **3.** A metal frame supporting equipment used in outdoor play.

gym. *abbr. Sports.* Gymnastics.

gym•kha•na (jĭm-kä′nə) *n. Sports.* **1.** Any of various meets at which contests are held to test the skill of the competitors, as in equestrianship or gymnastics. **2.** The place where such an event is held. [Prob. alteration of Hindi *gend-khānā*, racket court : *gend*, ball + *khānā*, house (< Pers.).]

gym•na•si•um (jĭm-nā′zē-əm) *n., pl.* **-si•ums** or **-si•a** (-zē-ə). **1.** *Sports.* A room or building equipped for indoor sports. **2.** (gĭm-nä′zē-o͝om′). An academic high school in some central European countries, esp. Germany, that prepares students for the university. [Lat., school < Gk. *gumnasion* < *gumnazein*, to exercise naked < *gumnos*, naked. See **nogʷ-*.**]

gym•nast (jĭm′năst′, -nəst) *n. Sports.* A person who is trained and skilled in gymnastics. [Fr. *gymnaste* < Gk. *gumnastēs*, athletic trainer < *gumnazein*, to exercise. See GYMNASIUM.]

gym•nas•tic (jĭm-năs′tĭk) *adj. Sports.* Of or relating to gymnastics. — **gym•nas′ti•cal•ly** *adv.*

gym•nas•tics (jĭm-năs′tĭks) *n.* **1.** *Sports.* **a.** *(used with a pl. v.)* Physical exercises designed to develop and display strength, balance, and agility, esp. those performed on or with specialized apparatus. **b.** *(used with a sing. v.)* The art or practice of such exercises. **2.** *(used with a pl. v.)* **a.** Complex intellectual or artistic exercises. **b.** *Informal.* Feats of physical agility.

gym•nos•o•phist (jĭm-nŏs′ə-fĭst) *n.* One of an ancient sect of Hindu ascetics who wore little or no clothing and were devoted to mystical contemplation. [ME *gumnosophist* < sing. of Lat. *gymnosophistae* < Gk. *gumnosophistai* : *gumnos*, naked; see **nogʷ-*** + *sophistēs*, expert; see SOPHIST.]

gypsy moth
Lymantria dispar

gym•no•sperm (jĭm′nə-spûrm′) *n.* A plant, such as a cycad or conifer, whose seeds are not enclosed within an ovary. [< NLat. *Gymnospermae*, class name < Gk. *gumnospermos* : *gumnos*, naked; see **nogʷ-*** + *sperma*, seed; see SPERM[1].] — **gym′no•sper′mous** *adj.* — **gym′no•sper′my** *n.*

gyn. *abbr.* **1.** Gynecological. **2.** Gynecologist. **3.** Gynecology.

gyn– *pref.* Var. of **gyno–.**

gy•nan•dro•morph (jī-năn′drə-môrf′, gī-, jĭ-) *n.* An organism having both male and female characteristics, esp. an insect exhibiting a mixture of male and female tissues or sex organs. — **gy•nan′dro•mor′phic, gy•nan′dro•mor′phous** *adj.* — **gy•nan′dro•mor′phism, gy•nan′dro•mor′phy** *n.*

gy•nan•drous (jī-năn′drəs, gī-, jĭ-) *adj.* Having the stamens and pistil united to form a column, as in orchids.

gyn•ar•chy (jĭn′är′kē, jī′när′-, gī′-) *n., pl.* **-chies.** Government by women. — **gyn•ar′chic** *adj.*

–gyne *suff.* Female reproductive organ: *trichogyne.* [< Gk. *gunē*, woman. See **gʷen-*.**]

gyneco– or **gynec–** *pref.* Woman: *gynecology.* [Gk. *gunaiko-* < *gunē, gunaik-*, woman. See GYNO–.]

gyn•e•coc•ra•cy (jĭn′ĭ-kŏk′rə-sē, gī′-nĭ-, jī′-) or **gy•noc•ra•cy** (jĭ-nŏk′rə-sē, gī-, jī-) *n., pl.* **-cies.** **1.** Government by women. **2.** A society ruled by women. [Gk. *gunaikokratia* : *gunē, gunaik-*, woman; see **gʷen-*** + *-kratia*, -cracy.]

gyn•e•coid (jĭn′ĭ-koid′, gī′nĭ-, jī′-) *adj.* Characteristic of a woman.

gynecol. *abbr.* **1.** Gynecological. **2.** Gynecologist. **3.** Gynecology.

gy•ne•col•o•gy (gī′nĭ-kŏl′ə-jē, jĭn′ĭ-, jī′nĭ-) *n.* The branch of medicine dealing with the administration of health care to women, esp. the diagnosis and treatment of disorders affecting the female reproductive organs. — **gy′ne•co•log′i•cal** (-kə-lŏj′ĭ-kəl), **gy′ne•co•log′ic** *adj.* — **gy′ne•col′o•gist** *n.*

gyn•e•co•mas•ti•a (jĭn′ĭ-kō-măs′tē-ə, gī′nĭ-, jī′-) *n.* Abnormal enlargement of the breasts in a male.

gyno– or **gyn–** *pref.* **1.** Woman: *gynarchy.* **2.** Female reproductive organ; pistil: *gynophore.* [< Gk. *gunē*, woman. See **gʷen-*.**]

gy•noe•ci•um (jĭ-nē′sē-əm, gī-, jī-) *n., pl.* **-ci•a** (-sē-ə). The female reproductive organs of a flower; the pistil or pistils considered as a group. [NLat., alteration of Lat. *gynaecēum*, women's apartments < Gk. *gunaikeion* < neut. of *gunaikeios*, of women < *gunē, gunaik-*, woman. See **gʷen-*.**]

gyn•o•gen•e•sis (jĭn′ə-jĕn′ĭ-sĭs, gī′nə-, jī′-) *n.* Parthenogenesis in which the egg is activated by sperm but without fusion of the egg and sperm nuclei.

gyn•o•phore (jĭn′ə-fôr′, -fōr′, gī′nə-, jī′-) *n.* The stalk of a pistil. — **gyn′o•phor′ic** (-fôr′ĭk, -fŏr′-) *adj.*

–gynous *suff.* **1.** Of, relating to, or having a specified number or kind of females: *heterogynous.* **2.a.** Of, relating to, or situated in a specified place with respect to female plant organs: *epigynous.* **b.** Having a specified number or kind of female plant organs: *protogynous.* [< NLat. *-gynus* < Gk. *gunē*, woman. See **gʷen-*.**]

–gyny *suff.* **1.** The state or condition of having a specified number of women or females: *monogyny.* **2.a.** The condition of being situated in a specified place with respect to female plant organs: *epigyny.* **b.** The condition of having a specified number or kind of female plant organs: *protogyny.* [< Gk. *gunē*, woman. See **gʷen-*.**]

Győr (dyûr, dyœr). A city of NW Hungary near the Slovakian border; once a Magyar stronghold. Pop. 128,252.

gyo•za (gyō′zə, gyô′zä′) *n.* A Japanese dish consisting of fried pockets of dough stuffed, as with minced pork. [J.]

gyp also **gip** (jĭp) *Slang.* — *tr.v.* **gypped, gyp•ping, gyps** also **gipped, gip•ping, gips.** To deprive (another) of something by fraud; cheat or swindle. — *n.* **1.** A fraud or swindle. **2.** One who defrauds. [Prob. short for GYPSY.] — **gyp′per** *n.*

gyp•sif•er•ous (jĭp-sĭf′ər-əs) *adj.* Containing gypsum.

gyp•soph•i•la (jĭp-sŏf′ə-lə) *n.* Any of various plants of the genus *Gypsophila*, having small white or pink flowers and including baby's breath. [NLat. *Gypsophila*, genus name : Gk. *gupsos*, chalk; see GYPSUM + Gk. *philos*, loving; see –PHILE.]

gyp•sum (jĭp′səm) *n.* A widespread colorless, white, or yellowish mineral, $CaSO_4{\cdot}2H_2O$, used in plaster of Paris, Portland cement, and wallboard. [ME *gipsum* < Lat. *gypsum* < Gk. *gupsos*, prob. of Semitic orig.]

gypsum board *n.* See **plasterboard.**

Gyp•sy also **Gip•sy** (jĭp′sē) *n., pl.* **-sies.** **1.** A member of a nomadic people that migrated to Europe from northern India around the 14th century, now also living in North America and Australia. **2.** See **Romany** 2. **3. gypsy.** One inclined to a nomadic, unconventional way of life. **4.** A person who moves from place to place as required for employment. [Alteration of ME *gypcian*, short for *Egipcien*, Egyptian (so called because they were thought to have come from Egypt).]

gypsy cab *n.* A taxicab that is licensed only to respond to calls but often cruises the streets for passengers.

gypsy moth *n.* A European moth *(Lymantria dispar)* having hairy caterpillars that feed on foliage.

gy•ral (jī′rəl) *adj.* **1.** Moving in a circle or spiral; gyratory. **2.** Of or relating to a gyrus. — **gy′ral•ly** *adv.*

gy•rate (jī′rāt′) *intr.v.* **-rat•ed, -rat•ing, -rates.** **1.** To revolve around a fixed point or axis. **2.** To revolve in or as if in a circle or spiral. — *adj. Biol.* In rings; coiled or convoluted. [LLat. *gȳrāre, gȳrāt-* < Lat. *gȳrus*, circle. See GYRE.] — **gy•ra′tion** *n.* — **gy′ra′tor** *n.*

gy•ra•to•ry (jī′rə-tôr′ē, -tōr′ē) *adj.* Having a circular or spiral motion.

gyre (jīr) *n.* **1.** A circular or spiral form; a vortex. **2.** A circular or spiral motion, esp. a circular ocean current. — *intr.v.* **gyred, gyr•ing, gyres.** To whirl. [Lat. *gȳrus* < Gk. *guros*.]

gy•rene (jī-rēn′) *n. Slang.* A member of the U.S. Marine Corps. [Perh. alteration of GI[1] + (MA)RINE.]

gyr•fal•con also **ger•fal•con** (jûr′făl′kən, -fôl′-, -fô′-) *n.* A large falcon *(Falco rusticolus)* of Arctic regions, having color phases that range from black to gray to white. [ME *girfaucoun* < OFr. *girfaut, gerfaucon* : OHGer. *gīr*, vulture + OFr. *faucon*, falcon; see FALCON.]

gy•ri (jī′rī′) *n.* Pl. of **gyrus.**

gy•ro[1] (jī′rō) *n., pl.* **-ros.** **1.** A gyroscope. **2.** A gyrocompass.

gy•ro[2] (jī′rō, jē′-) *n., pl.* **-ros.** A sandwich made usu. of sliced roasted lamb, onion, and tomato stuffed in pita bread. [< Mod.Gk. *guros*, a turning < Gk., circle (< the turning spit).]

gyro– *pref.* **1.** Spinning: *gyromagnetic.* **2.** Circle; spiral: *gyroplane.* **3.** Gyroscopic: *gyrostabilizer.* [Gk. *guro-*, circular < *guros*, circle.]

gy•ro•com•pass (jī′rō-kŭm′pəs, -kŏm′-) *n.* A compass with a motorized gyroscope whose angular momentum interacts with the force produced by the earth's rotation to maintain a north-south orientation of the gyroscopic spin axis.

gy•ro•mag•net•ic (jī′rō-măg-nĕt′ĭk) *adj.* Of or relating to the magnetic properties of a spinning charged particle.

gyromagnetic ratio *n.* The ratio of the magnetic moment of a system to its angular momentum.

gy•ro pilot (jī′rō) *n.* An automatic pilot incorporating a gyroscope that maintains a preset course and altitude.

gy•ro•plane (jī′rə-plān′) *n.* An aircraft, such as a helicopter, equipped with wings that rotate about an approximately vertical axis.

gy•ro•scope (jī′rə-skōp′) *n.* A device consisting of a spinning mass, typically a disk or wheel, mounted on a base so that its axis can turn freely in one or more directions and thereby maintain its orientation regardless of any movement of the base. —**gy′ro•scop′ic** (-skŏp′ĭk) *adj.* —**gy′ro•scop′i•cal•ly** *adv.*

gy•ro•sta•bi•liz•er (jī′rō-stā′bə-lī′zər) *n.* An instrument having a heavy gyroscope whose axis spins in a vertical plane to reduce the rolling of a ship or aircraft.

gy•ro•stat (jī′rə-stăt′) *n.* A gyroscope consisting of a rotating wheel in a rigid case. —**gy′ro•stat′ic** *adj.*

gy•rus (jī′rəs) *n., pl.* **-ri** (-rī′). Any of the prominent rounded elevated convolutions on the surfaces of the cerebral hemispheres. [Lat. *gȳrus*, circle. See GYRE.]

GySgt *abbr.* Gunnery sergeant.

gyve (jīv) *Archaic.* —*n.* A shackle or fetter, esp. for the leg. —*tr.v.* **gyved, gyv•ing, gyves.** To shackle or fetter. [< ME *gives*, gyves.]

H h

h^{1} or **H** (āch) *n., pl.* **h's** or **H's. 1.** The eighth letter of the modern English alphabet. **2.** Any of the speech sounds represented by the letter *h.* **3.** The eighth in a series. **4.** Something shaped like the letter H.

h^{2} The symbol for **Planck's constant.**

h^{3} *abbr.* **1.** Also **h.** Hit. **2.** Hour.

H^{1} **1.** The symbol for the element **hydrogen. 2.** The symbol for **enthalpy.**

H^{2} *abbr.* **1.** *Phys.* Hamiltonian. **2.** Henry. **3.** Humidity.

h. also **H.** *abbr.* **1.** Harbor. **2.** Hard; hardness. **3.** Height. **4.** High. **5.** *Mus.* Horn. **6.** Hundred. **7.** Husband.

ha^{1} also **hah** (hä) *interj.* Used to express surprise, wonder, triumph, puzzlement, or pique.

ha^{2} *abbr.* **1.** Hectare. **2.** *Lat.* Hoc anno (this year). **3.** Hour angle.

Haa•kon VII (hô′kən, -ko͞on′). 1872–1957. King of Norway (1905–57) who headed the exiled government in London during the Nazi occupation of his country (1940–45).

Haar•lem (här′ləm). A city of W Netherlands near the North Sea W of Amsterdam; chartered 1245. Pop. 152,511.

Haar•lem•mer•meer (här′lə-mər-mâr′). A city of W Netherlands WNW of Amsterdam. Pop. 83,428.

Ha•bak•kuk (hăb′ə-kŭk′, -ko͝ok′, hə-băk′ək) *n. Bible.* **1.** A Hebrew prophet of the late 7th cent. B.C. **2.** See table at **Bible.**

ha•ba•ne•ra (hä′bə-nâr′ə, ä′bə-) *n.* **1.** A slow Cuban dance. **2.** The music for this dance, in duple time. [Sp. *(danza) habanera*, (dance) of Havana < *La Habana*, Havana, Cuba.]

hab. corp. *abbr. Law.* Habeas corpus.

ha•be•as corpus (hā′bē-əs) *n. Law.* One of a variety of writs that may be issued to bring a party before a court or judge, serving to release the party from unlawful restraint. [ME < Med.Lat. *habeās corpus* : Lat. *habeās*, second pers. sing. pr. subjunctive of *habēre*, to have + Latin *corpus*, body.]

Ha•ber (hä′bər), **Fritz.** 1868–1934. German chemist who won a 1918 Nobel Prize.

hab•er•dash•er (hăb′ər-dăsh′ər) *n.* **1.** A dealer in men's furnishings. **2.** *Chiefly British.* A dealer in sewing notions and small wares. [ME, prob. < AN *hapertas*, petty wares.]

hab•er•dash•er•y (hăb′ər-dăsh′ə-rē) *n., pl.* **-ies. 1.** A haberdasher's shop. **2.** The goods sold by a haberdasher.

hab•er•geon (hăb′ər-jən) also **hau•ber•geon** (hô′-) *n.* **1.** A short sleeveless coat of mail. **2.** A hauberk. [Middle English < OFr. *hauberjon* < *hauberc*, hauberk. See HAUBERK.]

hab•ile (hăb′ĭl) *adj.* Generally able or adroit; handy. [ME *habil* < OFr. *habile* < Lat. *habilis* < *habēre*, to handle. See **ghabh-*.**]

ha•bil•i•ment (hə-bĭl′ə-mənt) *n.* **1.a.** The special dress associated with an occasion or office. Often used in the plural. **b.** Clothes. Often used in the plural. **2. habiliments.** Characteristic furnishings or equipment; trappings. [ME *habilement* < OFr. *habillement* < *habiller*, to clothe, alteration of *abiller*, to prepare, strip a tree of its branches : *a-*, toward (< Lat. *ad-*; see AD-) + *bille*, log; see BILLET^{2}.]

ha•bil•i•tate (hə-bĭl′ĭ-tāt′) *v.* **-tat•ed, -tat•ing, -tates.** —*tr.* **1.** To clothe. **2.** To fit out or equip (a mine) for operation. **3.** *Obsolete.* To impart an ability or capacity to. —*intr.* To qualify oneself for a post or office. [LLat. *habilitāre*, *habilitāt-*, to enable < Lat. *habilitās*, *habilitāt-*, ability < *habilis*, able. See HABILE.] —**ha•bil′i•ta′tion** *n.*

hab•it (hăb′ĭt) *n.* **1.a.** A recurrent, often unconscious pattern of behavior acquired through frequent repetition. **b.** An established disposition of the mind or character. **2.** Customary manner or practice. **3.** An addiction, esp. to a narcotic drug. **4.** Physical constitution. **5.** Characteristic appearance, form, or manner of growth, esp. of a plant or crystal. **6.a.** A distinctive dress or costume, esp. of a religious order. **b.** The outfit typically worn by a horseback rider. —*tr.v.* **-it•ed, -it•ing, -its.** To clothe; dress. [ME, clothing < OFr., clothing, behavior, custom < Lat. *habitus* < p.part. of *habēre*, to have. See **ghabh-*.**]

Syns: *habit, practice, custom, usage.* These nouns denote patterns of behavior established by continual repetition. *Habit* applies to a way of acting so ingrained in an individual that it is done without conscious thought: *a habit of interrupting. Practice* often denotes a chosen pattern of behavior: *"You will find it a very good practice always to verify your references, sir"* (Martin Joseph Routh). *Custom* is established by long practice and especially by accepted conventions: *"No written law has ever been more binding than unwritten custom supported by popular opinion"* (Carrie Chapman Catt). *Usage* refers to an accepted standard for a group that regulates individual behavior: *"laws . . . . corrected, altered, and amended by acts of parliament and common usage"* (William Blackstone).

hab•it•a•ble (hăb′ĭ-tə-bəl) *adj.* Suitable to inhabit. [ME < OFr. < Lat. *habitābilis* < *habitāre*, to dwell, freq. of *habēre*, to have. See **ghabh-*.**] —**hab′it•a•bil′i•ty, hab′it•a•ble•ness** *n.* —**hab′it•a•bly** *adv.*

hab•i•tant (hăb′ĭ-tənt) *n.* **1.** An inhabitant. **2.** Also **ha•bi•tan** (ă′bē-täɴ′). An inhabitant of French descent living in Canada, esp. Quebec, or in Louisiana. [ME < OFr. < pr.part. of *habiter*, to dwell < Lat. *habitāre*. See HABITABLE.]

hab•i•tat (hăb′ĭ-tăt′) *n.* **1.** The environment in which an organism normally lives or occurs. **2.** The place in which a person or thing is most likely to be found. [Lat., it dwells, third pers. sing. pr. of *habitāre*, to dwell. See HABITABLE.]

hab•i•ta•tion (hăb′ĭ-tā′shən) *n.* **1.** The act of inhabiting or the state of being inhabited. **2.a.** A natural environment or locality. **b.** A place of abode; a residence. [ME *habitacioun* < Lat. *habitātiō*, *habitātiōn-* < *habitātus*, p.part. of *habitāre*, to dwell. See HABITABLE.]

hab•it-form•ing (hăb′ĭt-fôr′mĭng) *adj.* **1.** Capable of leading to physiological or psychological dependence: *a habit-forming drug.* **2.** Tending to become habitual.

ha•bit•u•al (hə-bĭch′o͞o-əl) *adj.* **1.a.** Of the nature of a habit: *habitual lying.* **b.** Being such by force of habit: *a habitual liar.* **2.** Established by long use; usual. See Syns at **usual.** —**ha•bit′u•al•ly** *adv.* —**ha•bit′u•al•ness** *n.*

ha•bit•u•ate (hə-bĭch′o͞o-āt′) *v.* **-at•ed, -at•ing, -ates.** —*tr.* To accustom by frequent repetition or prolonged exposure. —*intr.* **1.** To cause physiological or psychological habituation, as to a drug. **2.** *Psychol.* To experience habituation. [< ME, accustomed < LLat. *habituātus*, p.part. of *habituārī*, to be in a condition < Lat. *habitus*, condition, habit. See HABIT.]

ha•bit•u•a•tion (hə-bĭch′o͞o-ā′shən) *n.* **1.** The process of habituating or the state of being habituated. **2.a.** Physiological tolerance to a drug resulting from repeated use. **b.** Psychological dependence on a drug. **3.** *Psychol.* The decline of a conditioned response following repeated exposure to the conditioned stimulus.

hab•i•tude (hăb′ĭ-to͞od′, -tyo͞od′) *n.* A habitual tendency or way of behaving. [ME < Lat. *habitūdō*, condition < *habitus*. See HABIT.]

ha•bit•u•é (hə-bĭch′o͞o-ā′, hə-bĭch′o͞o-ā′) *n.* A person who frequents a particular place, esp. one with a specific pleasurable activity. [Fr. < p.part. of *habituer*, to frequent < OFr. < LLat. *habituārī*, to be in a state. See HABITUATE.]

hab•i•tus (hăb′ĭ-təs) *n., pl.* **habitus.** The physical and constitutional characteristics of an individual, esp. as related to the tendency toward a certain disease. [Lat., state. See HABIT.]

ha•boob (hə-bo͞ob′) *n.* A violent sandstorm or dust storm, occurring chiefly in Arabia, North Africa, and India. [Ar. *habūb*, strong wind < *habba*, to blow.]

Habs•burg (hăps′bûrg′, häps′bo͝ork′). See **Hapsburg.**

ha•ček (hä′chĕk′) *n.* A diacritical mark (ˇ) that is used over certain letters, such as *č*, to indicate quality of pronunciation. [Czech *háček*, dim. of *hák*, hook < MHGer. *hāken* < OHGer. *hāko*. See **keg-*.**]

Ha•chi•o•ji (hä′chē-ō′jē). A city of E-central Honshu, Japan, W of Tokyo. Pop. 426,650.

ha•chure (hă-sho͝or′, hăsh′o͝or) *n.* One of the short lines used on maps to shade or to indicate topography. —*tr.v.* (hă-sho͝or′) **-chured, -chur•ing, -chures.** To make hatching on (a map). [Fr. < OFr. < *hacher*, to crosshatch. See HATCH^{3}.]

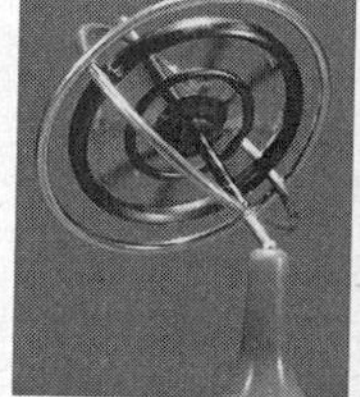

gyroscope

ă pat	oi boy
ā pay	ou out
âr care	o͝o took
ä father	o͞o boot
ĕ pet	ŭ cut
ē be	ûr urge
ĭ pit	th thin
ī pie	*th* this
îr pier	hw which
ŏ pot	zh vision
ō toe	ə about,
ô paw	item

Stress marks:
′ (primary);
′ (secondary), as in
dictionary (dĭk′shə-nĕr′ē)

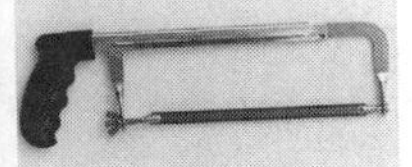

hacksaw

ha•ci•en•da (hä′sē-ĕn′də) *n.* **1.** A large estate or plantation in Spanish-speaking countries. **2.** The house of the owner of such an estate. [Sp. < Lat. *facienda*, things to be done, neut. pl. gerundive of *facere*, to do. See **dhē-***.]

hack[1] (hăk) *v.* **hacked, hack•ing, hacks.** —*tr.* **1.** To cut or chop with repeated and irregular blows. **2.** To break up the surface of (soil). **3.** *Slang.* To cut or mutilate as if by hacking. **4.** *Slang.* To cope with successfully; manage. —*intr.* **1.** To chop or cut something by hacking. **2.** *Comp. Sci.* To work or perform as a hacker. **3.** To cough roughly or harshly. —*n.* **1.** A rough irregular cut made by hacking. **2.** A tool, such as a hoe, used for hacking. **3.** A blow made by hacking. **4.** A rough dry cough. [ME *hakken* < OE *-haccian.* See **keg-***. V., intr., sense 2, back-formation < HACKER[1].] —**hack′a•ble** *adj.*

hack[2] (hăk) *n.* **1.** A horse used for riding or driving; a hackney. **2.** A worn-out horse for hire; a jade. **3.a.** One who undertakes distasteful tasks for money or reward; a hireling. **b.** A writer hired to produce hack writing. **4.** A carriage or hackney for hire. **5.** *Informal.* **a.** A taxicab. **b.** See **hackie.** —*v.* **hacked, hack•ing, hacks.** —*tr.* **1.** To let out (a horse) for hire. **2.** To make banal or hackneyed with indiscriminate use. —*intr.* **1.** To drive a taxicab for a living. **2.** To work as a hack writer. **3.** To ride on horseback at an ordinary pace. —*adj.* **1.** By, characteristic of, or being routine or commercial writing. **2.** Hackneyed; banal. [Short for HACKNEY.]

hack•a•more (hăk′ə-môr′, -mōr′) *n.* A simple bridle with an adjustable noseband and no bit, used esp. in breaking horses. [Alteration of Sp. *jáquima*, halter < OSp. *xaquima* < Ar. *šakīma*, bit of a bridle.]

hack•ber•ry (hăk′bĕr′ē) *n.* **1.** Any of various trees or shrubs of the genus *Celtis*, having inconspicuous flowers and small, usu. ovoid drupes. **2.** The fruit of such a plant. **3.** The soft, yellowish wood of these trees or shrubs. [Alteration of obsolete *hagberry* : *hag-* (of Scand. orig.) + BERRY.]

hack•but (hăk′bŭt′) *n.* See **harquebus.** [Fr. *haquebute* < OFr. *hacquebute*, alteration of MDu. *hakebus.* See HARQUEBUS.] —**hack′but•eer′** (-bə-tîr′), **hack′but′ter** *n.*

Hack•en•sack (hăk′ən-săk′). A city of NE NJ ESE of Paterson on the **Hackensack River,** c. 64 km (40 mi). Pop. 37,049.

hack•er[1] (hăk′ər) *n.* **1.** *Comp. Sci.* **a.** One who is proficient at using or programming a computer; a computer buff. **b.** One who illegally enters another's electronic system, as to gain secret information. **2.** *Sports.* One who enthusiastically pursues a game or sport. [Perh. < *hacker*, amateurish golfer or tennis player (poss. < HACK[1]) or < *hack*, practical joke (< dial. *hack*, to play a trick on).]

hack•er[2] (hăk′ər) *n.* See **hackie.**

hack•ie (hăk′ē) *n.* A taxicab driver.

hack•le[1] (hăk′əl) *n.* **1.** Any of the long slender feathers on the neck of a bird, esp. a male domestic fowl. **2. hackles.** The erectile hairs along the back of the neck of an animal, esp. of a dog. **3.a.** A tuft of cock feathers trimming an artificial fishing fly. **b.** An artificial fishing fly so trimmed. —*tr.v.* **-led, -ling, -les.** To trim (an artificial fishing fly) with a hackle. —***idiom.* get (one's) hackles up.** To be extremely insulted or irritated. [ME *hakell*, plumage, poss. < OE *hacele*, cloak.]

hack•le[2] (hăk′əl) *v.* **-led, -ling, -les.** —*tr.* To chop roughly; mangle by hacking. —*intr.* To hack. [Freq. of HACK[1].]

hack•ly (hăk′lē) *adj.* Nicked or notched; jagged. [< HACKLE[2].]

hack•ma•tack (hăk′mə-tăk′) *n.* See **balsam poplar.** [Perh. < Western Abenaki.]

hack•ney (hăk′nē) *n., pl.* **-neys. 1.** Often **Hackney.** A horse of a breed developed in England, having a gait characterized by pronounced flexion of the knee. **2.** A trotting horse suited for routine riding or driving; a hack. **3.** A coach or carriage for hire. —*tr.v.* **-neyed, -ney•ing, -neys. 1.** To cause to become banal and trite through overuse. **2.** To hire out; let. —*adj.* **1.** Banal; trite. **2.** Having been hired. [ME *hakenei*, prob. after *Hakenei*, Hackney, a borough of London.]

hack•neyed (hăk′nēd) *adj.* Overfamiliar through overuse.

hack•saw (hăk′sô′) *n.* A saw having a tough fine-toothed blade, used for cutting metal. [Alteration of ME *hagge-saue*, a kind of saw : *haggen*, to cut, chop; see HAGGLE + *sawe*, saw; see SAW[1].] —**hack′saw′** *v.*

Hadrian

had (hăd) *v.* P.t. and p.part. of **have.**

ha•dal (hād′l) *adj.* Of or relating to the deepest regions of the ocean, below about 6,000 meters (20,000 feet). [Fr. < *Hadès*, Hades < Gk. *Haidēs.* See **weid-***.]

had•dock (hăd′ək) *n., pl.* **haddock** or **-docks.** A food fish *(Melanogrammus aeglefinus)* of northern Atlantic waters, related to and resembling the cod. [ME *haddok.*]

hade (hād) *n. Geol.* The angle of inclination from the vertical of a vein, fault, or lode. [?]

Ha•des (hā′dēz) *n.* **1.** *Gk. Myth.* **a.** The god of the netherworld and dispenser of earthly riches. **b.** This netherworld kingdom, the abode of the shades of the dead. **2.** Also **hades.** Hell. [Gk. *Haidēs.* See **weid-***.]

hadj (hăj) *n. Islam.* Var. of **haj.**

hadj•i (hăj′ē) *n. Islam.* Var. of **haji.**

had•n't (hăd′nt). Had not.

Ha•dri•an (hā′drē-ən). A.D. 76–138. Emperor of Rome (117–138) who ordered construction of Hadrian's Wall (122).

Ha•dri•an's Wall (hā′drē-ənz). An ancient Roman wall that marked the N defensive boundary of Roman Britain.

had•ron (hăd′rŏn′) *n.* Any of a class of subatomic particles that are composed of quarks and take part in the strong interaction. See table at **subatomic particle.** [Gk. *hadros*, thick; see **sā-*** + -ON[1].] —**had•ron′ic** *adj.*

had•ro•saur (hăd′rə-sôr′) *n.* Any of various amphibious dinosaurs of the genus *Anatosaurus* and related genera that had webbed feet and a ducklike bill. [NLat. *Hadrosaurus*, genus name : Gk. *hadros*, thick; see HADRON + *sauros*, lizard.]

hadst (hădst) *v. Archaic.* A second pers. sing. p.t. of **have.**

hae (hā, hă) *tr.v.* **haed, haen** (hān, hăn), **hae•ing, haes.** *Scots.* To have.

Haeck•el (hĕk′əl), **Ernst Heinrich.** 1834–1919. German philosopher and naturalist.

Haeck•el's law (hĕk′əlz) *n.* See **biogenetic law.** [After Ernst Heinrich HAECKEL.]

haem– also **haema–** or **haemo–** *pref.* Var. of **hemo–.**

haemat– or **haemato–** *pref.* Var. of **hemato–.**

–haemia *suff.* Var. of **–emia.**

haen (hān, hăn) *v. Scots.* P.part. of **hae.**

haet (hāt) *n. Scots.* A minute amount; a jot. [Sc., short for *hae it*, take it.]

ha•fiz (hä′fĭz) *n. Islam.* **1.** One who has memorized the Koran. **2.** Used as a title of respect for such a person. [Pers. < Ar. *ḥāfiẓ* < *ḥafiẓa*, to memorize, guard.]

Ha•fiz (hä-fĭz′, -fēz′). fl. 14th cent. Persian poet whose sensuous verses are interpreted allegorically by Sufic Muslims.

haf•ni•um (hăf′nē-əm) *n. Symbol* **Hf** A metallic element found with zirconium and used in nuclear reactor control rods and in tungsten alloys in filaments. Atomic number 72; atomic weight 178.49; melting point 2,220°C; boiling point 5,400°C; specific gravity 13.3; valence 4. See table at **element.** [After *Hafnia*, Medieval Latin name for Copenhagen, Denmark.]

haft (hăft) *n.* A handle or hilt, esp. of a tool or weapon. —*tr.v.* **haft•ed, haft•ing, hafts.** To fit into or equip with a hilt or handle. [ME < OE *hæft.* See **kap-***.]

haf•ta•rah or **haf•to•rah** (häf′tä-rä′, häf-tôr′ə, -tōr′ə) *n.* Var. of **haphtarah.**

hag[1] (hăg) *n.* **1.** An old woman considered ugly or frightful. **2.a.** A witch; a sorceress. **b.** *Obsolete.* A female demon. **3.** A hagfish. [ME *hagge*, perh. short for OE *hægtesse*, witch.] —**hag′gish** *adj.* —**hag′gish•ly** *adv.* —**hag′gish•ness** *n.*

hag[2] (hăg) *n. Chiefly British.* **1.** A boggy area; a quagmire. **2.** A spot in boggy land that is softer or more solid than the surrounding area. **3.** A cutting in a peat bog. [ME, gap, chasm, of Scand. orig.; akin to ON *högg.* See **kau-***.]

Hag. *abbr. Bible.* Haggai.

Ha•gar (hā′gər, -gär). In the Bible, the Egyptian servant of Abraham's wife, Sarah, and the mother of Ishmael.

Ha•gen (hä′gən). A city of W-central Germany NE of Cologne; chartered 1746. Pop. 207,636.

Hag•ers•town (hā′gərz-toun′). A city of N MD NW of Frederick. Pop. 35,445.

hag•fish (hăg′fĭsh′) *n., pl.* **hagfish** or **-fish•es.** Any of various primitive eel-shaped marine fishes of the family Myxinidae, having a jawless sucking mouth equipped with rasping teeth with which they bore into and feed on other fishes.

Hag•ga•dah also **Hag•ga•da** (hä′gä-dä′, hə-gä′də, -gô′də) *n., pl.* **-doth** (-dôt′, -dōt′, -dōs, -dəz). *Judaism.* **1.** Traditional Jewish literature, esp. the nonlegal part of the Talmud. **2.** The book containing the story of the Exodus and the ritual of the Seder, read at the Passover Seder. [Heb. *haggādâ*, narration, telling < *higgîd*, to narrate, tell.]

hag•gad•ic also **Hag•gad•ic** (hə-găd′ĭk, -gä′dĭk, -gôdĭk) *adj. Judaism.* Of or relating to the Haggadah.

hag•ga•dist (hə-gä′dĭst, -gô′-) *n. Judaism.* **1.** A haggadic writer. **2.** A student of haggadic literature.

Hag•ga•i (hăg′ē-ī′, hăg′ī′) *n. Bible.* **1.** A Hebrew prophet of the 6th cent. B.C. **2.** See table at **Bible.** [Heb. *Ḥaggay.*]

hag•gard (hăg′ərd) *adj.* **1.a.** Appearing worn and exhausted; gaunt. **b.** Wild or distraught in appearance. **2.** Wild and intractable. Used of a hawk in falconry. —*n.* An adult hawk captured for training. [Fr. *hagard*, wild < OFr., wild hawk, raptor, perh. of Gmc. orig.] —**hag′gard•ly** *adv.* —**hag′gard•ness** *n.*

Hag•gard (hăg′ərd), Sir **(Henry) Rider.** 1856–1925. British writer whose novels include *King Solomon's Mines* (1885).

hag•gis (hăg′ĭs) *n.* A Scottish dish consisting of the minced heart, lungs, and liver of a sheep or calf mixed with suet, oatmeal, and seasonings and boiled in the stomach of the slaughtered animal. [ME *hagese*; perh. akin to *haggen*, to chop. See HAGGLE.]

hag•gle (hăg′əl) *v.* **-gled, -gling, -gles.** —*intr.* **1.** To bargain, as over the price of something; dicker. **2.** To argue in an attempt to come to terms. —*tr.* **1.** To cut (something) in a crude manner; hack. **2.** *Archaic.* To harass or worry by wrangling. —*n.* An instance of bargaining or arguing. [Freq. of dial. *hag*, to chop, hack < ME *haggen* < ON *höggva.* See **kau-***.] —**hag′gler** *n.*

hag•i•ar•chy (hăg′ē-är′kē, hā′jē-) *n., pl.* **-chies.** Government by holy men, such as priests or saints.

hagio– or **hagi–** *pref.* **1.** Saint: *hagiography.* **2.** Holy: *hagioscope.* [Gk. *hagios*, holy.]

hag·i·oc·ra·cy (hăg′ē-ŏk′rə-sē, hā′jē-) *n., pl.* **-cies.** See **hagiarchy.**

Hag·i·og·ra·pha (hăg′ē-ŏg′rə-fə, hā′jē-) *pl.n. (used with a sing. or pl. v.) Bible.* The Writings. [LLat. < LGk. < neut. pl. of *hagiographos*, written by inspiration, scriptural : Gk. *hagio-*, hagio- + Gk. *-graphos*, written (< *graphein*, to write; see -GRAPH).]

hag·i·og·ra·phy (hăg′ē-ŏg′rə-fē, hā′jē-) *n., pl.* **-phies. 1.** Biography of saints. **2.** A worshipful or idealizing biography. **— hag′i·og′raph·er** *n.* **— hag′i·o·graph′ic** (-ə-grăf′ĭk), **hag′i·o·graph′i·cal** *adj.*

hag·i·ol·o·gy (hăg′ē-ŏl′ə-jē, hā′jē-) *n., pl.* **-gies. 1.** Literature dealing with the lives of saints. **2.** A collection of sacred writings. **3.** An authoritative list of saints. **— hag′i·o·log′ic** (-ə-lŏj′ĭk), **hag′i·o·log′i·cal** *adj.* **— hag′i·ol′o·gist** *n.*

hag·i·o·scope (hăg′ē-ə-skōp′, hā′jē-) *n.* A small opening in an interior wall of a church, enabling those in the transept to view the main altar. **— hag′i·o·scop′ic** (-skŏp′ĭk) *adj.*

hag·rid·den (hăg′rĭd′n) *adj.* **1.** Harassed by or as if by a witch. **2.** Tormented or harassed, as by unreasoning fears.

Hague (hāg), **The.** Also **'s Gra·ven·ha·ge** (skrä′vən-hä′gə, sKHrä′vən-hä′KHə). The de facto cap. of the Netherlands, in the W part near the North Sea. Pop. 445,213.

hah (hä) *interj.* Var. of **ha[1].**

ha-ha[1] (hä′hä′) also **haw-haw** (hô′hô′) *— n.* **1.** A sound made in imitation of laughter. **2. ha-ha.** *Slang.* An instance of amusement. *— interj.* Used to express amusement or scorn.

ha-ha[2] (hä′hä′) also **haw-haw** (hô′hô′) *n.* A moat, walled ditch, or hedge sunk in the ground to serve as a fence without impairing the view or scenic appeal. [Fr.]

Hahn (hän), **Otto.** 1879–1968. German chemist who won a 1944 Nobel Prize.

Hah·ne·mann (hä′nə-mən, -män′), **(Christian Friedrich) Samuel.** 1755–1843. German founder of homeopathy.

hah·ni·um (hä′nē-əm) *n.* Element 105. [After Otto HAHN.]

Hai·da (hī′də) *n., pl.* **Haida** or **-das. 1.** A member of a Native American people inhabiting the Queen Charlotte Islands of British Columbia and Prince of Wales Island in Alaska. **2.** Any or all of the Haida language varieties. **— Hai′dan** *adj.*

Hai·fa (hī′fə). A city of NW Israel on the **Bay of Haifa**, an inlet of the Mediterranean; probably founded in the 3rd cent. A.D. Pop. 224,700.

Haig (hāg), **Douglas.** 1st Earl Haig. 1861–1928. British field marshal who led British forces in France in World War I.

Haight-Ash·bu·ry (hāt′ăsh′bĕr-ē, -bə-rē). A section of central San Francisco; a gathering place for hippies and followers of the drug culture in the 1960's.

Hai·kou (hī′kou′, -kō′). A city of S China on Hainan I. in the South China Sea; cap. of Hainan province. Pop. 266,302.

hai·ku (hī′ko͞o) *n., pl.* **haiku** also **-kus. 1.** A Japanese lyric verse form having three unrhymed lines of five, seven, and five syllables, traditionally invoking an aspect of nature or the seasons. **2.** A poem written in this form. [J. : *hai*, amusement (< Chin. *pá*, farce) + *ku*, sentence (< Chin. *jù*).]

hail[1] (hāl) *n.* **1.** Precipitation in the form of spherical or irregular pellets of ice larger than 5 millimeters (0.2 inches) in diameter. **2.** Something with the force and quantity of a shower of ice. *— v.* **hailed, hail·ing, hails.** *— intr.* **1.** To precipitate in pellets of ice. **2.** To fall like hailstones. *— tr.* To pour (something) down or forth. [ME < OE *hægel.*]

hail[2] (hāl) *v.* **hailed, hail·ing, hails.** *— tr.* **1.a.** To salute or greet. **b.** To greet or acclaim enthusiastically. **2.** To call out to in order to catch the attention of. *— intr. Naut.* To signal or call to a passing ship as a greeting or an identification. *— n.* **1.** The act of greeting or acclaiming. **2.** A shout made to catch someone's attention or to greet. **3.** Hailing distance. *— interj.* Used to express a greeting or tribute. ***— phrasal verb.* hail from.** To come or originate from. [ME *heilen* < (*wæs*) *hæil*, (be) healthy. See WASSAIL.]

hail·er (hā′lər) *n.* **1.** One that greets, acclaims, or catches someone's attention. **2.** A bullhorn.

Hai·le Se·las·sie (hī′lē sə-lăs′ē, -lä′sē). Ras Taffari Makonnen. 1892–1975. Emperor of Ethiopia (1930–74) who was deposed in a military coup.

hail-fel·low (hāl′fĕl′ō) also **hail-fel·low-well-met** (-wĕl′-mĕt′) *adj.* Heartily friendly and congenial. [< the obsolete greeting *hail, fellow!*] **— hail′-fel′low** *n.*

Hail Mar·y (hāl′ mâr′ē) *n., pl.* **Hail Mar·ys.** *Rom. Cath. Ch.* A prayer based on the greetings of Gabriel and Saint Elizabeth to the Virgin Mary.

hail·stone (hāl′stōn′) *n.* A pellet of hail.

hail·storm (hāl′stôrm′) *n.* A storm with hail.

haim·ish (hā′mĭsh) *adj. Slang.* Warm and comfortable; homey; folksy. [Yiddish *heymish* < MHGer. *heimisch* < OHGer. *heimisc* < *heim*, home. See **tkei-*.**]

Hai·nan (hī′nän′). An island and province of S China in the South China Sea separated from Leizhou Peninsula by a narrow strait. Cap. Haikou. Pop. 6,000,000.

Hai·naut (hā-nō′, ĕ-nō′). A historical region of SW Belgium and N France.

haint (hānt) *n. Chiefly Southern U.S.* Var. of **haunt** 2.

Hai·phong (hī′fŏng′). A city of NE Vietnam on the Red R. delta near the Gulf of Tonkin; heavily bombed by U.S. forces during the Vietnam War. Pop. 330,755.

hair (hâr) *n.* **1.a.** Any of the cylindrical, keratinized, often pigmented filaments characteristically growing from the epidermis of a mammal. **b.** A growth of such filaments, as that covering the scalp of a human being. **2.** A filamentous projection or bristle similar to a hair, such as an epidermal process of a plant. **3.** Fabric made from the hair of certain animals. **4.a.** A minute distance or narrow margin. **b.** A precise or exact degree. [ME *her* < OE *hǣr.*]

hair·ball (hâr′bôl′) *n.* A small mass of hair located in the stomach or intestine of an animal, such as a cat, that accumulates each time the animal licks its coat.

hair·breadth (hâr′brĕdth′) *adj.* Extremely close: *a hairbreadth escape.* *— n.* Var. of **hairsbreadth.**

hair·brush (hâr′brŭsh′) *n.* A brush for the hair.

hair cell *n.* A cell in the organ of Corti having fine hairlike processes.

hair·cloth (hâr′klôth′, -klŏth′) *n.* A wiry fabric woven esp. from horsehair or camel's hair.

hair·cut (hâr′kŭt′) *n.* **1.** The act or an instance of cutting the hair. **2.** A style in which hair is cut. **— hair′cut′ter** *n.* **— hair′cut′ting** *adj. & n.*

hair·do (hâr′do͞o′) *n., pl.* **-dos.** A hairstyle.

hair·dress·er (hâr′drĕs′ər) *n.* One who cuts or arranges hair.

hair·dress·ing (hâr′drĕs′ĭng) *n.* **1.** The occupation of a hairdresser. **2.** The act of dressing or arranging the hair. **3.** A cosmetic or medicinal preparation for dressing the hair.

haired (hârd) *adj.* Having a specified kind of hair. Often used in combination: *a longhaired cat; a shorthaired dog.*

hair follicle *n.* A tubular infolding of the epidermis containing the root of a hair.

hair·less (hâr′lĭs) *adj.* Having little or no hair.

hair·line (hâr′līn′) *n.* **1.** The outline of the growth of hair on the head, esp. across the front. **2.** A very slender line. **3.** *Print.* **a.** A very fine line on a typeface. **b.** A style of type using such lines. **4.a.** A textile design having thin threadlike stripes. **b.** A fabric, usu. a worsted, with such stripes.

hair·piece (hâr′pēs′) *n.* A covering or bunch of human or artificial hair used to conceal baldness or shape a coiffure.

hair·pin (hâr′pĭn′) *n.* **1.** A thin strip of metal or other material bent in the shape of a long U, used to secure a hairdo or headdress. **2.** Something shaped like a hairpin.

hair-rais·ing (hâr′rā′zĭng) *adj.* Causing excitement, terror, or thrills.

hairs·breadth or **hair's-breadth** (hârz′brĕdth′) also **hair·breadth** (hâr′-) *n.* A small space, distance, or margin.

hair seal *n.* Any of various seals of the family Phocidae, having a stiff hairlike coat and ears visible only as small indentations.

hair shirt *n.* A coarse haircloth garment worn next to the skin by religious ascetics as penance.

hair space *n. Print.* The narrowest of the metal spaces used for separating words or letters.

hair·split·ting (hâr′splĭt′ĭng) *n.* The making of unreasonably fine distinctions. **— hair′split′ter** *n.* **— hair′split′ting** *adj.*

hair spray also **hair·spray** (hâr′sprā′) *n.* A commercial product sprayed on the hair to keep it in place.

hair·spring (hâr′sprĭng′) *n.* A fine coiled spring that regulates the movement of the balance wheel in a watch or clock.

hair·streak (hâr′strēk′) *n.* Any of numerous butterflies of the subfamily Theclinae, having transverse streaks on the underside of the wings and hairlike projections on the hind wings.

hair stroke *n.* A very fine line in writing or printing.

hair·style (hâr′stīl′) *n.* The design of a coiffure. **— hair′styl′ing** *n.* **— hair′styl′ist** *n.*

hair trigger *n.* A gun trigger adjusted to respond to a very slight pressure.

hair-trig·ger (hâr′trĭg′ər) *adj.* Responding to the slightest provocation or stimulation: *a hair-trigger temper.*

hair·worm (hâr′wûrm′) *n.* **1.** Any of various slender, parasitic nematode worms of the genus *Trichostrongylus,* which infest cattle, sheep, and related animals. **2.** See **horsehair worm.**

hair·y (hâr′ē) *adj.* **-i·er, -i·est. 1.** Covered with hair or hairlike projections. **2.** Consisting of or resembling hair. **3.** *Slang.* Fraught with difficulties: *a hairy escape.* **— hair′i·ness** *n.*

Hai·ti (hā′tē). **1.** A country of the West Indies comprising the W part of the island of Hispaniola and two offshore islands; became independent in 1804 following a slave revolt led by Toussaint L'Ouverture. Cap. Port-au-Prince. Pop. 5,053,791. **2.** See **Hispaniola.**

Hai·tian (hā′shən, -tē-ən) *adj.* Of or relating to Haiti or its people or culture. *— n.* **1.** A native or inhabitant of Haiti. **2.** Haitian Creole.

Haitian Creole *n.* A language spoken by the majority of Haitians, based on French and various African languages.

haj or **hajj** also **hadj** (hăj) *n., pl.* **haj·es** or **hajj·es** also **hadj·es.** *Islam.* A pilgrimage to Mecca during Dhu'l Hijja, made as an objective of the religious life of a Muslim. [Ar. *ḥajj* < *ḥajja*, to go on a pilgrimage.]

haj·i or **haj·ji** also **hadj·i** (hăj′ē) *n., pl.* **haj·is** or **haj·jis** also

hadrosaur
Corythosaurus

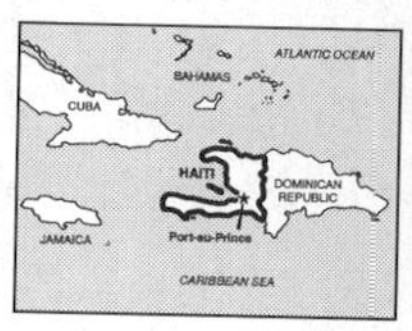

Haiti

ă **pat**	oi **boy**
ā **pay**	ou **out**
âr **care**	o͝o **took**
ä **father**	o͞o **boot**
ĕ **pet**	ŭ **cut**
ē **be**	ûr **urge**
ĭ **pit**	th **thin**
ī **pie**	*th* **this**
îr **pier**	hw **which**
ŏ **pot**	zh **vision**
ō **toe**	ə **a**bout,
ô **paw**	it**e**m

Stress marks:
′ (primary);
′ (secondary), as in
dictionary (dĭk′shə-nĕr′ē)

haku

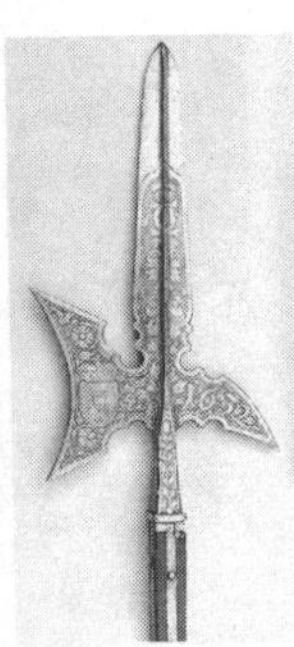
halberd
Austrian

Edmund Halley

hadj•is. *Islam.* **1.** One who has made a pilgrimage to Mecca. **2.** Often used as a form of address for one who has made such a pilgrimage. [Ar. *ḥājjī* < *ḥajj*, pilgrimage. See HAJ.]

hake (hāk) *n., pl.* **hake** or **hakes.** Any of various marine food fishes of the genera *Merluccius* and *Urophycis,* related to and resembling the cod. [ME, poss. < OE *haca*, hook (< the shape of its lower jaw). See **keg-*.**]

Ha•ken•kreuz (hä**′**kən-kroits′) *n.* A swastika. [Ger. : *Haken,* hook (< MHGer. *hāken*; see HAČEK) + *Kreuz,* cross (< MHGer. *kriuze*; see KREUZER).]

ha•kim¹ also **ha•keem** (hä**′**kēm) *n., pl.* **-kims** also **-keems.** A Muslim physician, usu. male. [Ar. *ḥakīm*, wise, wise man < *ḥakama*, to be judicious, exercise authority.]

ha•kim² (hä**′**kĭm) *n., pl.* **-kims.** A male Muslim ruler, provincial governor, or judge. [Ar. *ḥākim* < *ḥakama*, to exercise authority.]

Hak•luyt (hăk**′**lo͞ot′), **Richard.** 1552?–1616. English geographer noted for *Principal Navigations, Voyages, and Discoveries of the English Nation* (1589).

Ha•ko•da•te (hä′kô-dä**′**tĕ). A city of SW Hokkaido, Japan, on Tsugaru Strait. Pop. 319,190.

ha•ku (hä**′**ko͞o) *n. Hawaii.* A crown made of fresh flowers. [Hawaiian < *haku,* to put in order, make a wreath.]

hal– *pref.* Var. of **halo–.**

Ha•la•kah also **Ha•la•cha** (hä′lä-KHä**′**, hä-lä**′**KHə, -lô**′**-) *n. Judaism.* The legal part of Talmudic literature, an interpretation of the scriptural laws. [Mishnaic Heb. *hălākâ*, rule, tradition < *hālak*, to go.] **— Ha•lak′ic** (hə-lăk**′**ĭk, -lä**′**KHĭk) *adj.*

ha•lal (hə-läl**′**) *Islam.* —*n.* Meat that has been slaughtered in the manner prescribed by the shari'a. —*adj.* **1.** Of or being meat slaughtered in this way. **2.** In accordance with or permitted under the shari'a. [Ar. *ḥalāl*, that which is lawful.]

ha•la•la (hə-lä**′**lə) *n., pl.* **halala** or **-las.** See table at **currency.** [Ar. *halalah.*]

ha•la•tion (hā-lā**′**shən) *n.* **1.** A blurring or spreading of light around bright areas on a photographic image. **2.** A glow around a bright object on a television screen. [< HALO.]

ha•la•vah (hä′lə-vä**′**) *n.* Var. of **halvah.**

hal•berd (hăl**′**bərd, hôl**′**-) also **hal•bert** (-bərt) *n.* A weapon of the 15th and 16th centuries having an axlike blade and a steel spike mounted on the end of a long shaft. [Fr. *hallebarde* < OFr. *alabarde* < OItal. *alabarda* < MHGer. *helmbarde, halmbarte* : *helm*, handle + *barte*, ax (< OHGer. *barta*; see **bhardh-ā-***).] **— hal′ber•dier′** (-bər-dîr**′**) *n.*

hal•cy•on (hăl**′**sē-ən) *n.* **1.** A kingfisher, esp. one of the genus *Halcyon.* **2.** A fabled bird, identified with the kingfisher, believed to be able to calm the wind and the waves while it nested on the sea during the winter solstice. —*adj.* **1.** Calm and peaceful; tranquil. See Syns at **calm. 2.** Prosperous; golden: *halcyon years.* [ME *alcioun* < Lat. *alcyōn, halcyōn* < Gk. *halkuōn*, a mythical bird, kingfisher, alteration of *alkuōn*.]

Hal•dane (hôl**′**dā′, -dən). Family of Scottish intellectuals, including **Richard Burdon Haldane** (1856–1928), a philosopher and politician; his sister **Elizabeth Sanderson Haldane** (1862–1937), a writer and Scotland's first woman justice of the peace (1920); their brother **John Scott Haldane** (1860–1936), a physiologist; and his son **John Burdon Sanderson Haldane** (1892–1964), a geneticist.

hale¹ (hāl) *adj.* **hal•er, hal•est.** Free from infirmity or illness; sound. See Syns at **healthy.** [ME < OE *hāl*. See **kailo-*.**] **— hale′ness** *n.*

hale² (hāl) *tr.v.* **haled, hal•ing, hales. 1.** To compel to go. **2.** *Archaic.* To pull, draw, drag, or hoist. [ME *halen*, to pull, drag < OFr. *haler*, of Gmc. orig. See **kelə-²*.**]

Hale (hāl), **Edward Everett.** 1822–1909. Amer. Unitarian cleric and writer whose works include the story "The Man Without a Country" (1863). His sister **Lucretia Peabody Hale** (1820–1900) was a writer of children's books.

Hale, George Ellery. 1868–1938. Amer. astrophysicist who invented the spectroheliograph (1891).

Hale, Nathan. 1755–76. Amer. Revolutionary soldier who was hanged by the British as a spy.

Hale, Sarah Josepha Buell. 1788–1879. Amer. writer and editor of *Godey's Lady's Book* (1837–77).

Ha•le•a•ka•la Crater (hä′lē-ä′kə-lä**′**). A volcanic crater, 829.6 m (2,720 ft) deep, of E Maui, HI.

ha•ler (hä**′**lər, -lĕr**′**) *n., pl.* **-lers** or **-le•ru** (-lə-ro͞o′). See table at **currency.** [Czech *haléř* < MHGer. *haller*, an early Ger. silver coin, after Schwäbisch *Hall*, a town of SW Germany.]

Ha•lé•vy (ä-lā-vē**′**), **(Jacques François) Fromental (Élie).** 1799–1862. French composer whose operatic works include *La Juive* and *L'Eclair* (both 1835).

Ha•ley (hā**′**lē), **Alex.** 1921–92. Amer. writer best known for *Roots* (1976), a fictionalized chronicle tracing his family history back to its African origins.

half (hăf, häf) *n., pl.* **halves** (hăvz, hävz). **1.a.** One of two equal parts that together make a whole. **b.** One part approximately equal to the remaining part. **2.** *Informal.* A 50-cent piece. **3.** *Sports.* **a.** One of the two periods into which certain games are divided. **b.** A halfback. **4.** *Chiefly British.* A school term; a semester. **5.** Half an hour. —*adj.* **1.a.** Being one of two equal parts. **b.** Being approximately a half. **2.** Partial or incomplete. —*adv.* **1.** To the extent of exactly or nearly 50 percent. **2.** Not completely or sufficiently; partly. ***— idioms.* by half. 1.** By a considerable extent. **2.** By an excessive amount. **by halves.** In a reluctant manner; unenthusiastically. **in half.** Into halves. **not half.** Not at all. **not the half of.** Only a fraction or a small part of. [ME < OE *healf*. See **skel-¹*.**]

Usage Note: The phrases *a half, half of,* and *half a* or *half an* are all correct, though they may differ slightly in meaning. For example, *a half day* is used when *day* has the special sense "a working day," and the phrase then means "4 hours." *Half of a day* and *half a day* are not restricted in this way and can mean either 4 or 12 hours.

half-and-half (hăf**′**ənd-hăf**′**, häf**′**ənd-häf**′**) *adj.* Being half one thing and half another. —*adv.* In equal portions. —*n.* **1.** A mixture of two things in equal portions, esp. milk and cream. **2.** *Chiefly British.* A blend of malt liquors, esp. porter and ale.

half-assed (hăf**′**ăst′, häf**′**äst′) *adj. Vulgar Slang.* **1.** Not well planned or executed. **2.** Incompetent. **— half′-assed′** *adv.*

half•back (hăf**′**băk′, häf**′**-) *n.* **1.** *Football.* One of the two players positioned near the flanks behind the line of scrimmage. **2.** *Sports.* One of several players in various sports stationed behind the forward line.

half-baked (hăf**′**bākt′, häf**′**-) *adj.* **1.** Only partly baked. **2.** *Informal.* Insufficiently thought out; ill-conceived. **3.** *Informal.* Exhibiting a lack of common sense: *a half-baked visionary.*

half binding *n. Print.* A bookbinding in which the back and often the corners of the volume are bound in a material differing from the rest of the cover.

half blood also **half-blood** (hăf**′**blŭd′, häf**′**-) *n.* **1.a.** The relationship between people having one parent in common. **b.** A person in such a relationship. **2.** *Offensive.* A person of mixed ancestry. **3.** A half-blooded domestic animal.

half-blood•ed (hăf**′**blŭd**′**ĭd, häf**′**-) *adj.* **1.** Having only one parent in common. **2.** Having one pedigreed parent and one of unknown or mixed ancestry. Used of animals.

half boot *n.* A low boot extending just above the ankle.

half-breed (hăf**′**brēd′, häf**′**-) *n. Offensive.* A person of mixed ancestry. —*adj.* Half-blooded; hybrid. Used of animals.

half brother *n.* A brother related through one parent only.

half-caste (hăf**′**kăst′, häf**′**käst′) *Offensive.* —*n.* A person of mixed racial descent. —*adj.* Of mixed racial descent.

half-cell (hăf**′**sĕl′, häf**′**-) *n.* Either of the two connected parts of an electrochemical cell, consisting of one electrode in a conductive fluid.

half cock *n.* The position of the hammer of a firearm when it is locked halfway up so that the trigger cannot be pulled.

half•cocked (hăf**′**kŏkt**′**, häf**′**-) *adj.* **1.** *Informal.* Inadequately or poorly prepared: *a halfcocked plan.* **2.** Being at the position of half cock. Used of a firearm. **— half′cocked′** *adv.*

half-crown (hăf**′**kroun**′**, häf**′**-) *n.* A coin formerly used in Great Britain, worth two shillings and sixpence.

half-dol•lar (hăf**′**dŏl′ər, häf**′**-) *n.* A U.S. silver 50-cent coin.

half gainer *n. Sports.* A dive in which the diver springs from the board facing forward, rotates in a half backward somersault, and enters the water headfirst, facing the board.

half•heart•ed (hăf**′**här**′**tĭd, häf**′**-) *adj.* Exhibiting or feeling little interest or enthusiasm; uninspired. **— half′heart′ed•ly** *adv.* **— half′heart′ed•ness** *n.*

half hitch *n.* A knot or hitch made by looping a rope or strap around an object and then back around itself, bringing the end of the rope through the loop.

half-hour (hăf**′**our**′**, häf**′**-) *n.* **1.** A period of 30 minutes. **2.** The middle point of an hour. **— half′-hour′ly** *adv. & adj.*

half-length (hăf**′**lĕngkth′, -lĕngth′, häf**′**-) *n.* A portrait that shows only the upper half and hands of a person. —*adj.* **1.** Of or relating to a half-length. **2.** Of half the full length.

half-life (hăf**′**līf′, häf**′**-) *n.* **1.** *Phys.* The time required for half the nuclei in a sample of a specific isotopic species to undergo radioactive decay. **2.** *Biol.* **a.** The time required for half the quantity of a drug or other substance deposited in a living organism to be metabolized or eliminated normally. **b.** The time required for the radioactivity of material taken in by a living organism to be halved from its initial value.

half-light (hăf**′**līt′, häf**′**-) *n.* The soft subdued light seen at dusk or dawn or in dimly lit interiors.

half-line or **half line** (hăf**′**līn′, häf**′**-) *n. Math.* See **ray¹** 4.

half-mast (hăf**′**măst**′**, häf**′**mäst**′**) *n.* The position about halfway up a mast or pole at which a flag is flown as a symbol of mourning or a signal of distress. —*tr.v.* **-mast•ed, -mast•ing, -masts.** To place (a flag) halfway up a mast or pole.

half-moon (hăf**′**mo͞on**′**, häf**′**-) *n.* **1.** The moon when only half its disk is illuminated. **2.** Something shaped like a crescent.

half nelson *n. Sports.* A wrestling hold with one arm under the opponent's arm from behind to the back of the neck.

half note *n. Mus.* A note worth one half of a whole note.

half•pen•ny (hā**′**pə-nē, hăp**′**nē) *n., pl.* **half•pence** (hā**′**pəns) or **half•pen•nies. 1.a.** A British coin worth one half of a new penny. **b.** A British coin worth one half of an old penny, no longer in circulation. **2.** The sum of one half of a penny.

half-pint (hăf**′**pīnt′, häf**′**-) *n. Slang.* A small person or animal.

half relief *n.* Sculptural relief composed of modeled forms that project approximately halfway from the background.

half rhyme *n.* See **off rhyme.**
half sister *n.* A sister related through one parent only.
half-slip (hăf′slĭp′, häf′-) *n.* A woman's slip that hangs from the waist.
half sole *n.* A shoe sole that extends from the shank to the toe.
half-sole (hăf′sōl′, häf′-) *tr.v.* **-soled, -sol•ing, -soles.** To fit or repair with a half sole.
half-staff (hăf′stăf′, häf′stäf′) *n.* See **half-mast.**
half step *n.* **1.** *Mus.* See **semitone. 2.** A marching step of 15 inches (38 centimeters) at quick time and 18 inches (46 centimeters) at double time.
half-tim•bered (hăf′tĭm′bərd, häf′-) also **half-tim•ber** (-bər) *adj.* Having a wooden framework with plaster, brick, stone, or other masonry filling the spaces.
half•time (hăf′tīm′, häf′-) *n. Sports.* The intermission between halves in certain games, such as basketball or football.
half title *n. Print.* The title of a book at the top of the first page of the text or on a full page preceding the main title page.
half•tone (hăf′tōn′, häf′-) *n.* **1.** A tone or value halfway between a highlight and a dark shadow. **2.a.** A picture in which gradations of light are obtained by photographing the subject through a fine screen. **b.** A picture made by such a process.
half tone *n. Mus.* See **semitone.**
half-track (hăf′trăk′, häf′-) *n.* A lightly armored military motor vehicle, with caterpillar treads in place of wheels.
half-truth (hăf′tro͞oth′, häf′-) *n.* A statement, esp. one intended to deceive, that omits some facts.
half volley *n. Sports.* A stroke in certain games in which the ball is hit immediately after it bounces off the ground.
half•way (hăf′wā′, häf′-) *adj.* **1.** Midway between two points or conditions. **2.** Reaching or including only half or a portion; partial: *halfway measures.* **— half′way′** *adv.*
halfway house *n.* **1.** A rehabilitation center, esp. for people who have left an institution. **2.** A stopping place that marks the midpoint of a journey.
half-wit (hăf′wĭt′, häf′-) *n. Offensive.* A person regarded as foolish or stupid. **— half′-wit′ted** *adj.*
hal•i•but (hăl′ə-bət, hŏl′-) *n., pl.* **halibut** or **-buts.** Any of several large edible flatfishes of the genus *Hippoglossus* and related genera of northern Atlantic or Pacific waters. [ME : *hali, holi,* holy (< its being eaten on holy days); see HOLY + *butte,* flatfish (< MDu.; see **bhau-***).]
Hal•i•car•nas•sus (hăl′ĭ-kär-năs′əs). An ancient Greek city of SW Asia Minor on the Aegean Sea; site of the tomb of King Mausolus, one of the Seven Wonders of the World.
hal•ide (hăl′īd′, hā′līd′) *n.* A chemical compound of a halogen with a more electropositive element or group.
hal•i•dom (hăl′ĭ-dəm) *n. Obsolete.* **1.** Something considered holy. **2.** A sanctuary. [ME < OE *hāligdōm* : *hālig,* holy; see HOLY + *-dōm,* -dom.]
Hal•i•fax (hăl′ə-făks′). **1.** The cap. of Nova Scotia, Canada, in the S-central part on the Atlantic Ocean; founded 1749. Pop. 114,594. **2.** A borough of NE England NE of Manchester. Pop. 192,500.
hal•ite (hăl′īt′, hā′līt′) *n.* **1.** A colorless or white mineral, NaCl, occurring as cubic crystals and found in dried lakebeds in acrid climates, used as table salt. **2.** Rock salt.
hal•i•to•sis (hăl′ĭ-tō′sĭs) *n.* The condition of having stale or foul-smelling breath. [Lat. *hālitus,* breath + -OSIS.]
hall (hôl) *n.* **1.** A corridor or passageway in a building. **2.** A large entrance room or vestibule in a building; a lobby. **3.a.** A building for public gatherings or entertainments. **b.** The large room in which such events are held. **4.** A building used for the meetings, entertainments, or living quarters of a social or religious organization. **5.a.** A building belonging to a school, college, or university that provides classroom, dormitory, or dining facilities. **b.** A large room in such a building. **c.** *Chiefly British.* A meal served in such a building. **6.** The main house on a landed estate. **7.a.** The castle or house of a medieval monarch or noble. **b.** The principal room in such a hall. [ME *halle,* large residence < OE *heall.* See **kel-**¹*.]
Hall (hôl), **Charles Francis.** 1821–71. Amer. Arctic explorer who led three expeditions (1860–62, 1864–69, and 1871).
Hall, Charles Martin. 1863–1914. Amer. chemist who developed a method of producing aluminum from bauxite (1886).
Hall, Granville Stanley. 1844–1924. Amer. psychologist who founded child psychology.
hal•lah (KHä′lə, hä′-) *n.* Var. of **challah.**
Hal•lam (hăl′əm), **Henry.** 1777–1859. British historian whose works include *Europe During the Middle Ages* (1818). The death of his son **Arthur Henry Hallam** (1811–33) inspired Tennyson's poem *In Memoriam.*
Hal•lan•dale (hăl′ən-dāl′). A city of SE FL on the Atlantic S of Fort Lauderdale. Pop. 30,996.
Hal•le (hä′lə). A city of central Germany WNW of Leipzig; first mentioned in the 9th cent. Pop. 236,139.
hal•lel (hä-lāl′, hä′lāl) *n. Judaism.* A chant of praise consisting of Psalms 113 through 118, recited on certain holidays. [Heb. *hallēl,* song of praise < *hillēl,* to praise.]
hal•le•lu•jah (hăl′ə-lo͞o′yə) *interj.* Used to express praise or joy. **—** *n.* **1.** An exclamation of "hallelujah." **2.** *Mus.* A composition expressing praise and based on the word "hallelujah." [Heb. *hallĕlûyāh,* praise the Lord : *hallĕlu,* pl. imper. of *hillēl,* to praise + *Yāh,* God (short for *Yahweh*).]
Hal•ley (hăl′ē), **Edmund** or **Edmond.** 1656–1742. English astronomer who first applied Newton's laws of motion to predict correctly the period of a comet (1705).
Hal•ley's comet (hăl′ēz, hā′lēz) *n.* A comet with a period of approx. 76 years, first predicted by Edmund Halley. [After Edmund HALLEY.]

Halley's comet
In 1986

hal•liard (hăl′yərd) *n. Naut.* Var. of **halyard.**
hall•mark (hôl′märk′) *n.* **1.** A mark indicating quality or excellence. **2.** A mark used in England to stamp gold and silver articles that meet established standards of purity. **3.** A conspicuous feature or characteristic. **—** *tr.v.* **-marked, -mark•ing, -marks.** To stamp (gold and silver articles) with a hallmark. [After Goldsmith's *Hall* in London, England.]
hall of fame *n., pl.* **halls of fame. 1.** A group of persons judged outstanding, as in a sport or profession. **2.** A building housing memorial items honoring illustrious persons.
hal•loo (hə-lo͞o′) also **hal•loa** (-lō′) **—** *interj.* **1.** Used to catch someone's attention. **2.** Used to urge on hounds in a hunt. **—** *n., pl.* **-loos** also **-loas.** A shout or call of "halloo." **—** *v.* **-looed, -loo•ing, -loos** also **-loaed, -loa•ing, -loas. —** *intr.* To shout "halloo." **—** *tr.* **1.** To urge on or pursue by calling "halloo" or shouting. **2.** To call out to. **3.** To shout or yell (something). [Alteration of obsolete *holla,* stop! See HELLO.]
hal•low (hăl′ō) *tr.v.* **-lowed, -low•ing, -lows. 1.** To make or set apart as holy. **2.** To respect or honor greatly; revere. [ME *halwen* < OE *hālgian.* See **kailo-***.]
hal•lowed (hăl′ōd) *adj.* **1.** Sanctified; consecrated. **2.** Highly venerated; sacrosanct.
Hal•low•een also **Hal•low•e'en** (hăl′ə-wēn′, hŏl′-) *n.* October 31, celebrated by children going door to door in costume begging treats and playing pranks. [Short for *All Hallow Even* : ALLHALLOW(MAS) + EVEN².]
Hal•low•mas also **Hal•low•mass** (hăl′ō-məs, -măs′) *n. Archaic.* All Saints' Day. [Short for ALLHALLOWMAS.]
Hall•statt (hôl′stăt′, häl′shtät′) *adj.* Of or relating to a dominant Iron Age culture of central and western Europe, probably chiefly Celtic, that flourished from approx. 900 to 500 B.C. [After the type-site at *Hallstatt* in N Austria.]
hal•lu•ci•nate (hə-lo͞o′sə-nāt′) *v.* **-nat•ed, -nat•ing, -nates. —** *intr.* To undergo hallucination. **—** *tr.* To cause to have hallucinations. [Lat. *hallūcinārī, hallūcināt-,* to dream, be deceived, var. of *ālūcinārī.*] **— hal•lu′ci•na′tor** *n.*
hal•lu•ci•na•tion (hə-lo͞o′sə-nā′shən) *n.* **1.a.** False or distorted perception of objects or events with a compelling sense of their reality. **b.** The objects or events so perceived. **2.** A false or mistaken idea; a delusion. **— hal•lu′ci•na′tion•al, hal•lu′ci•na′tive** *adj.*
hal•lu•ci•na•to•ry (hə-lo͞o′sə-nə-tôr′ē, -tōr′ē) *adj.* **1.** Of or characterized by hallucination. **2.** Inducing hallucination.
hal•lu•cin•o•gen (hə-lo͞o′sə-nə-jən) *n.* A substance that induces hallucination. [HALLUCIN(ATION) + -GEN.] **— hal•lu′cin•o•gen′ic** (-jĕn′ĭk) *adj.*
hal•lu•ci•no•sis (hə-lo͞o′sə-nō′sĭs) *n.* An abnormal condition or mental state characterized by hallucination.
hal•lux (hăl′əks) *n., pl.* **hal•lu•ces** (hăl′yə-sēz′, hăl′ə-). **1.** The innermost or first digit on the hind foot of certain mammals. **2.** A homologous digit of a bird, a reptile, or an amphibian. [Lat. *hallux, hallus.*]
hall•way (hôl′wā′) *n.* **1.** A corridor in a building. **2.** An entrance hall.
halm (hôm) *n.* Var. of **haulm.**
Hal•ma•he•ra (hăl′mə-hĕr′ə, häl′mä-hĕ′rä). An island of E Indonesia in the Moluccas E of Sulawesi.
ha•lo (hā′lō) *n., pl.* **-los** or **-loes. 1.a.** A circular band of colored light around a light source, as around the sun, caused by the refraction and reflection of light by ice particles suspended in the intervening atmosphere. **b.** Something resembling this band. **2.** A luminous ring or disk of light surrounding sacred figures in religious paintings; a nimbus. **3.** The aura of majesty or glory surrounding a person, a thing, or an event that is regarded with reverence, awe, or sentiment. **—** *tr.v.* **-loed, -lo•ing, -loes.** To encircle with or as if with a halo. [Med.Lat. *halō* < accusative of Lat. *halōs* < Gk.]

halo
Detail of a chasuble

halo– or **hal–** *pref.* **1.** Salt: *halophyte.* **2.** Halogen: *halocarbon.* [Fr. < Gk. < *hals, hal-,* salt, sea. See **sal-***.]
hal•o•car•bon (hăl′ə-kär′bən) *n.* A compound, such as a fluorocarbon, of carbon and one or more halogens.
hal•o•cline (hăl′ə-klīn′) *n.* A vertical gradient in ocean salinity.
hal•o•gen (hăl′ə-jən) *n.* Any of the chemically related elements fluorine, chlorine, bromine, iodine, and astatine. **— ha•log′e•nous** (hă-lŏj′ə-nəs) *adj.*
hal•o•ge•nate (hăl′ə-jə-nāt′) *tr.v.* **-nat•ed, -nat•ing, -nates.** To treat or combine with a halogen. **— hal′o•ge•na′tion** *n.*
hal•o•per•i•dol (hăl′ō-pĕr′ĭ-dôl′, -dŏl′, -dōl′) *n.* A tranquilizer, $C_{21}H_{23}ClFNO_2$, used esp. in the treatment of psychotic disorders. [HALO- + (PI)PERID(INE) + -OL¹.]
hal•o•phile (hăl′ə-fīl′) *n.* An organism that requires a salty environment. **— hal′o•phil′ic** (-fĭl′ĭk), **ha•loph′i•lous** (hă-lŏf′ə-ləs) *adj.*

ă pat	oi boy
ā pay	ou out
âr care	o͝o took
ä father	o͞o boot
ĕ pet	ŭ cut
ē be	ûr urge
ĭ pit	th thin
ī pie	*th* this
îr pier	hw which
ŏ pot	zh vision
ō toe	ə about, item
ô paw	

Stress marks:
′ (primary);
′ (secondary), as in dictionary (dĭk′shə-nĕr′ē)

hand•fast (hănd′făst′) *n. Archaic.* A handclasp used to signify a pledge, such as a contract or marriage. [< ME *hondfast,* p.part. of *hondfesten,* to betroth < ON *handfesta,* to strike a bargain : *hönd,* hand + *festa,* to fasten; see **past-*.**]

hand•ful (hănd′fo͝ol′) *n., pl.* **-fuls. 1.** The amount that a hand can hold. **2.** A small, undefined number or quantity. **3.** *Informal.* One that is too difficult to control or handle easily.

hand glass *n.* **1.** A small magnifying glass held in the hand. **2.** A mirror with a handle.

hand•grip (hănd′grĭp′) *n.* **1.** A grip of or by the hand. **2.** Something, such as a handle, that is suited to a grip by the hand. **3. handgrips.** Hand-to-hand combat.

hand•gun (hănd′gŭn′) *n.* A firearm used with one hand.

hand•hold (hănd′hōld′) *n.* **1.** A grip of or by the hand. **2.** Something that one can hold onto for support.

hand•hold•ing (hănd′hōl′dĭng) *n.* Strong personal support and reassurance, esp. that given to alleviate anxiety.

hand•i•cap (hăn′dē-kăp′) *n.* **1.** *Sports & Games.* **a.** A race or contest in which advantages or compensations are given different contestants to equalize the chances of winning. **b.** Such an advantage or penalty. **2.** A physical or mental disability. See Syns at **disadvantage. 3.** A hindrance. — *tr.v.* **-capped, -cap•ping, -caps. 1.** *Sports & Games.* To assign handicaps or a handicap to (a contestant). **2.** To cause to be at a disadvantage; impede. [< obsolete *hand in cap,* a game in which forfeits were held in a cap.]

hand•i•capped (hăn′dē-kăpt′) *adj.* Physically or mentally disabled: *a pool equipped for handicapped swimmers.*

Usage Note: Although *handicapped* is widely used in both law and everyday speech to refer to people having physical or mental disabilities, those described by the word tend to prefer the expressions *disabled* or *people with disabilities.* The term *handicapped* may imply an inequality in functioning, while *disability* implies fuctioning equally but in different ways. The word *handicapped,* therefore, is best reserved to describe a disabled person who is unable to function owing to some property of the environment. Thus people with a physical disability requiring a wheelchair may or may not be *handicapped,* depending on whether wheelchair ramps are made available to them.

hand•i•cap•per (hăn′dē-kăp′ər) *n.* **1.** *Sports & Games.* One who assigns handicaps. **2.** *Games.* One who predicts the winners in a horserace, esp. one who publishes such predictions as a guide.

hand•i•craft (hăn′dē-krăft′) also **hand•craft** (hănd′krăft′) *n.* **1.** Skill and facility with the hands. **2.** A craft or an occupation requiring skilled use of the hands. **3.** Work produced by skilled hands. [ME *handecraft* < OE *handcræft* : *hand,* hand + *cræft,* craft.]

Han•dies Peak (hăn′dēz). A mountain, 4,284.6 m (14,048 ft), in the San Juan Mts. of SW CO.

hand•i•ly (hăn′dĭ-lē, -dl-ē) *adv.* **1.** In an easy manner. **2.** In a convenient manner.

hand in glove or **hand and glove** *adv.* On intimate terms or in close association.

hand in hand *adv.* In cooperation; jointly.

hand•i•work (hăn′dē-wûrk′) *n.* **1.** Work performed by hand. **2.** The product of a person's efforts and actions. [ME *handiwerk* < OE *handgeweorc* : *hand,* hand + *geweorc,* work (*ge-,* collective pref.; see **kom*** + *weorc,* work; see WORK).]

hand•ker•chief (hăng′kər-chĭf, -chēf′) *n., pl.* **-chiefs** also **-chieves** (-chĭvz, -chēvz′). **1.** A small square of cloth used esp. for wiping the nose or mouth. **2.** A large piece of cloth worn as a decorative article; a scarf.

han•dle (hăn′dl) *v.* **-dled, -dling, -dles.** — *tr.* **1.** To touch, lift, or hold with the hands. **2.** To operate with the hands; manipulate. **3.** To deal with or have responsibility for; conduct. See Syns at **treat. 4.** To cope with or dispose of. **5.a.** To direct, execute, or dispose of. **b.** To manage, administer to, or represent. **6.** To deal or trade in the purchase or sale of. — *intr.* To act or function in a given way while in operation. — *n.* **1.** A part that is designed to be held or operated with the hand. **2.** An opportunity or a means for achieving a purpose. **3.** *Slang.* A person's name. **4.** *Games.* The total amount of money bet on an event or over a set period of time. — ***idiom.* get (or have) a handle on.** *Informal.* To achieve an understanding of. [ME *handelen* < OE *handlian.*]

han•dle•bar (hăn′dl-bär′) *n.* A curved metal steering bar, as on a bicycle. Often used in the plural.

handlebar mustache *n.* A long, curved mustache resembling a handlebar.

han•dler (hănd′lər) *n.* **1.** One that handles or directs something or someone: *the candidate's campaign handlers.* **2.** *Sports.* **a.** One who trains or exhibits an animal, such as a dog. **b.** One who acts as the trainer or second of a boxer.

han•dling (hănd′lĭng) *n.* **1.** The act of one that handles something. **2.** The way in which a matter, esp. a delicate one, is taken care of. **3.** The way in which a presentation, esp. an artistic or theatrical work, is treated.

hand•made (hănd′mād′) *adj.* Made or prepared by hand rather than by machine.

hand•maid (hănd′mād′) also **hand•maid•en** (-mād′n) *n.* **1.** A woman attendant or servant. **2.** Often **handmaiden.** Something that serves a useful but subordinate purpose.

hand-me-down (hănd′mē-doun′) *adj.* **1.** Handed down to one person after use by another. **2.** Of inferior quality; shabby. — *n.* Something passed on from one person to another.

hand•off (hănd′ôf′, -ŏf′) *n. Football.* A play in which one player hands the ball to another.

hand organ *n. Mus.* A barrel organ operated by turning a crank by hand.

hand•out (hănd′out′) *n.* **1.** Food, clothing, or money given to the needy. **2.** A folder or leaflet circulated free of charge. **3.** A prepared news or publicity release.

hand over fist *adv.* At a tremendous rate: *made money hand over fist.* [From the way sailors haul in or climb up a rope.]

hand•pick (hănd′pĭk′) *tr.v.* **-picked, -pick•ing, -picks. 1.** To gather or pick by hand. **2.** To select personally. — **hand′-picked′** *adj.*

hand press *n.* A printing press operated by hand.

hand•print (hănd′prĭnt′) *n.* An outline or indentation left by a hand.

hand puppet *n.* A puppet operated by hand.

hand•rail (hănd′rāl′) *n.* A narrow railing to be grasped with the hand for support.

hand•saw (hănd′sô′) *n.* A small saw operated by one hand.

hand's-breadth or **hand's breadth** (hăndz′brĕdth′) *n.* Var. of **handbreadth.**

hands down (hăndz) *adv.* **1.** With no trouble; easily. **2.** Unquestionably. — **hands′-down′** (hăndz′doun′) *adj.*

hand•sel (hănd′səl) also **han•sel** (hăn′-) *Chiefly British.* — *n.* **1.** A gift to express good wishes at the beginning of a new year or enterprise. **2.** The first money or barter taken in, as by a new business, esp. when considered good luck. **3.a.** A first payment. **b.** A specimen or foretaste of what is to come. — *tr.v.* **-seled, -sel•ing, -sels** or **-selled, -sel•ling, -sels. 1.** To give a handsel to. **2.** To launch with a ceremonial gesture or gift. **3.** To do or use the first time. [ME *hanselle* < OE *handselen,* a handing over (*hand,* hand + *selen,* gift) and < ON *handsal,* legal transfer (*hand* + *sal,* a giving).]

hand•set (hănd′sĕt′) *n.* The part of a telephone containing the receiver and transmitter and often a dial or push buttons.

hand•shake (hănd′shāk′) *n.* The grasping of hands by two people, as in greeting or leave-taking.

hands-off (hăndz′ôf′, -ŏf′) *adj.* Marked by nonintervention.

hand•some (hăn′səm) *adj.* **-som•er, -som•est. 1.** Pleasing and dignified in form or appearance. **2.** Generous or copious: *a handsome reward.* See Syns at **liberal. 3.** Marked by or requiring skill or dexterity. **4.** Appropriate or fitting. **5.** Large: *a handsome price.* [ME *handsom,* handy : *hand,* hand (< OE) + *-som,* n. suff.; see -SOME[1].] — **hand′some•ly** *adv.* — **hand′some•ness** *n.*

hands-on (hăndz′ŏn′, -ôn′) *adj.* Involving active participation; applied, as opposed to theoretical.

hand•spike (hănd′spīk′) *n.* A bar used as a lever. [Alteration of Du. *handspaak* : *hand,* hand (< MDu. *hant*) + *spaak,* spoke (< MDu. *spāke,* stick).]

hand•spring (hănd′sprĭng′) *n. Sports.* A gymnastic feat in which the body is flipped forward or backward from an upright position, landing first on the hands and then on the feet.

hand•stand (hănd′stănd′) *n. Sports.* The act of balancing on the hands with one's feet in the air.

hand-to-hand (hănd′tə-hănd′) *adj.* Being at close quarters: *hand-to-hand combat.* — **hand to hand** *adv.*

hand-to-mouth (hănd′tə-mouth′) *adj.* Having or providing only the bare essentials: *a hand-to-mouth way of life.*

hand•work (hănd′wûrk′) *n.* Work done by hand rather than by machine.

hand•wo•ven (hănd′wō′vən) *adj.* **1.** Woven on a hand-operated loom. **2.** Woven by hand: *handwoven baskets.*

hand•writ•ing (hănd′rī′tĭng) *n.* **1.** Writing done with the hand. **2.** The writing characteristic of a particular person.

hand•y (hăn′dē) *adj.* **-i•er, -i•est. 1.** Skillful in using one's hands; manually adroit. See Syns at **dexterous. 2.** Readily accessible. **3.** Useful; convenient. **4.** Easy to use or handle: *a handy book.* [< HAND.] — **hand′i•ness** *n.*

Han•dy (hăn′dē), **William Christopher ("W.C.").** 1873–1958. Amer. composer whose works include "The Memphis Blues" (1911).

hand•y•man also **handy man** (hăn′dē-măn′) *n.* A man who does odd jobs or various small tasks.

Han•ford (hăn′fərd). A city of central CA SSE of Fresno. Pop. 30,897.

hang (hăng) *v.* **hung** (hŭng), **hang•ing, hangs.** — *tr.* **1.** To fasten from above with no support from below; suspend. **2.** To suspend or fasten so as to allow free movement at or about the point of suspension: *hang a door.* **3.** *p.t. and p.part.* **hanged** (hăngd). **a.** To execute by suspending by the neck. **b.** Used to express exasperation or disgust: *Hang it all!* **4.** To fix or attach at an appropriate angle: *hang a scythe to its handle.* **5.** To alter the hem of (a garment) so as to fall evenly at a specified height. **6.** To furnish, decorate, or appoint by suspending objects around or about: *hang a room with curtains.* **7.** To hold or incline downward; let droop. **8.a.** To

hand press
Used by Benjamin Franklin in England, 1725–1726

attach to a wall: *hang wallpaper.* **b.** To display, as in a gallery. **9.** *Informal.* To give (a nickname or label) to someone. **10.** To deadlock (a jury) by failing to render a unanimous verdict. **11.** *Baseball.* To throw (a pitch) in such a manner as to fail to break. — *intr.* **1.** To be attached from above with no support from below. **2.** To die as a result of hanging. **3.** To remain suspended or poised over a place or an object; hover. **4.** To attach oneself as a dependent or an impediment; cling. **5.** To incline downward; droop. **6.** To depend. **7.** To pay strict attention. **8.** To remain unresolved or uncertain. **9.** To fit the body in loose lines. **10.** To be on display, as in a gallery. **11.** *Baseball.* To fail to break or move in the intended way, as a curve ball. **12.** To be imminent; loom. **13.** To be or become burdensome. — *n.* **1.** The way in which something hangs. **2.** A downward inclination or slope. **3.** Particular meaning or significance. **4.** *Informal.* The proper method for doing or using something: *got the hang of it.* **5.** A suspension of motion; a slackening. ***— phrasal verbs.*** **hang around. 1.** To spend time idly; loiter. **2.** To keep company; consort. **hang back.** To be averse; hold back. **hang in.** *Informal.* To persevere. **hang off.** To hold back; be averse. **hang on. 1.** To cling tightly to something. **2.** To continue persistently; persevere. **3.** To keep a telephone connection open. **4.** To wait for a short period of time. **hang out.** *Slang.* **1.** To spend one's free time in a certain place. **2.** To pass time idly; loiter. **3.** To keep company; date. **hang together. 1.** To stand united; stick together. **2.** To make sense as a unity; cohere. **hang up. 1.** To suspend on a hook or hanger. **2.a.** To replace (a telephone receiver) on its base or cradle. **b.** To end a telephone conversation. **3.a.** To delay or impede; hinder. **b.** To become halted or snagged. **c.** *Informal.* To have or cause to have emotional difficulties or inhibitions. ***— idioms.*** **hang a left.** *Informal.* To make a left turn, as in an automobile. **hang a right.** *Informal.* To make a right turn, as in an automobile. **hang fire. 1.** To delay. **2.** To be slow in firing, as a gun. **hang in there.** *Informal.* To persevere despite difficulties. **hang it up.** *Informal.* To give up; quit. **hang loose.** *Slang.* To stay calm or relaxed. **hang on to.** To hold firmly; keep fast. **hang tough.** *Informal.* To remain firmly resolved. [ME *hongen* < OE *hangian,* to be suspended, and < OE *hōn,* to hang; see **konk-*.**]

Usage Note: *Hanged,* as a past tense and a past participle of *hang,* is used in the sense of "to put to death by hanging." In the following example *hung* would be unacceptable to a majority of the Usage Panel: *Frontier courts hanged many a prisoner after a summary trial.* In all other senses of the word, *hung* is the preferred form as past tense and past participle.

han•gar (hăng′ər, hăng′gər) *n.* A shelter esp. for housing or repairing aircraft. [Fr. < OFr. *hangard,* of Gmc. orig. See **tkei-*.**]

Hang•chow or **Hang•chou** (hăng′chou′, hăng′jō′). See **Hangzhou.**

hang•dog (hăng′dôg′, -dŏg′) *adj.* **1.** Shamefaced or guilty. **2.** Downcast; intimidated. — *n.* A sneaky or despicable person.

hang•er (hăng′ər) *n.* **1.** One who hangs something. **2.** A contrivance on which something hangs or by which something is hung, as: **a.** A device around which a garment is draped for hanging from a hook or rod. **b.** A loop or strap by which something is hung. **3.** A bracket on the spring shackle of a motor vehicle, designed to hold it to the chassis. **4.** A decorative strip of cloth hung on a garment or wall. **5.** A short sword that may be hung from a belt.

hang•er-on (hăng′ər-ŏn′, -ôn′) *n., pl.* **hang•ers-on** (hăng′-ərz-). A sycophant; a parasite.

hang-glide (hăng′glīd′) *intr.v.* **-glid•ed, -glid•ing, -glides.** To fly by means of a hang glider.

hang glider *n.* **1.** A kitelike device from which a harnessed rider hangs while gliding from a height. **2.** Its rider.

hang•ing (hăng′ĭng) *n.* **1.** Execution on a gallows. **2.** Something, such as a tapestry, that is hung. **3.** A descending slope or an inclination. — *adj.* **1.** Situated on a sharp declivity. **2.** Projecting downward; overhanging. **3.** Suited for holding something that hangs. **4.a.** Deserving death by hanging. **b.** Disposed to inflict severe sentences.

hanging indention *n.* Indention of every line in a paragraph except the first.

hang•man (hăng′mən) *n.* A man employed to execute condemned prisoners by hanging.

hang•nail (hăng′nāl′) *n.* A small piece of dead skin at the side or the base of a fingernail that is partly detached from the rest of the skin. [Alteration of AGNAIL.]

hang•out (hăng′out′) *n. Slang.* A frequently visited place.

hang•o•ver (hăng′ō′vər) *n.* **1.** Unpleasant physical effects following the heavy use of alcohol. **2.** A letdown, as after a period of excitement. **3.** A vestige; a holdover.

hang•tag (hăng′tăg′) *n.* A tag attached to a piece of merchandise giving information about its composition, care, and use.

hang-up (hăng′ŭp′) *n. Informal.* **1.** A psychological or emotional difficulty or inhibition. **2.** An obstacle to smooth progress or development.

Hang•zhou (häng′jō′) also **Hang•chow** or **Hang•chou** (hăng′chou′, häng′jō′). A city of E China at the head of Hangzhou Bay, an inlet of the East China Sea; founded 606 and the cap. of Zhehjiang province. Pop. 1,250,000.

hank (hăngk) *n.* **1.** A coil or loop. **2.** *Naut.* A ring or clip by which a jib or staysail is attached to its stay. **3.** A looped bundle, as of yarn. [ME < ON *hönk.*]

han•ker (hăng′kər) *intr.v.* **-kered, -ker•ing, -kers.** To have a strong, often restless desire. [Perh. < Du. dial. *hankeren.* See **konk-*.**] — **hank′er•er** *n.*

han•kie also **han•ky** (hăng′kē) *n., pl.* **-kies.** *Informal.* A handkerchief.

han•ky-pan•ky (hăng′kē-păng′kē) *n. Slang.* **1.** Devious or mischievous activity. **2.** Illicit sexual activity. [Alteration of *hokey-pokey,* alteration of HOCUS-POCUS.]

Han•na (hăn′ə), **Marcus ("Mark") Alonzo.** 1837–1904. Amer. financier and politician who managed the 1896 and 1900 presidential campaigns of William McKinley.

Han•ni•bal¹ (hăn′ə-bəl). 247–183? B.C. Carthaginian general who crossed the Alps in 218 with c. 35,000 men and routed Roman armies at Lake Trasimeno (217) and Cannae (216).

Han•ni•bal² (hăn′ə-bəl). A city of NE MO on the Mississippi R. NW of St. Louis; boyhood home of Mark Twain. Pop. 18,004.

Ha•noi (hă-noi′, hə-). The cap. of Vietnam, in the N part on the Red R.; cap. of French Indochina (after 1887) and of North Vietnam (1954–75). Pop. 819,913.

Han•o•ver¹ (hăn′ō′vər). British ruling family (1714–1901).

Han•o•ver² or **Han•no•ver** (hăn′ō′vər, hä-nō′-). **1.** A former kingdom and province of NW Germany; an electorate of the Holy Roman Empire from 1692 to 1805. **2.** A city of NW Germany SE of Bremen; chartered 1241. Pop. 514,010.

Han•o•ve•ri•an (hăn′ō-vîr′ē-ən) *adj.* **1.** Of, relating to, or characteristic of the royal family of Hanover. **2.** Of, belonging to, or characteristic of the kingdom or province of Hanover.

Hanover Park. A village of NE IL, a suburb of Chicago. Pop. 32,895.

Han River (hän). A river, c. 1,126 km (700 mi), of E-central China flowing to the Yangtze R. (Chang Jiang).

Han•sard (hăn′sərd) *n.* The official report of the proceedings and debates of a legislature in the Commonwealth of Nations, esp. of the British or Canadian parliament. [After Luke *Hansard* (1752–1828), British printer.]

Hans•ber•ry (hănz′bĕr-ē), **Lorraine.** 1930–65. Amer. playwright known esp. for *A Raisin in the Sun* (1959).

hanse (hăns) *n.* A medieval merchant guild or trade association. [ME < OFr. < MLGer. < OHGer. *hansa,* military troop.] — **han′se•at′ic** (hăn′sē-ăt′ĭk) *adj.*

Han•se•at•ic League (hăn′sē-ăt′ĭk). A former economic and defensive confederation of free towns in N Germany and neighboring areas; reached the height of its power in the 14th cent. and held its last official assembly in 1669.

han•sel (hăn′səl) *n. & v.* Var. of **handsel.**

Han•sen's disease (hăn′sənz) *n.* Leprosy. [After Gerhard H.A. *Hansen* (1841–1912), Norwegian physician.]

han•som (hăn′səm) *n.* A two-wheeled covered carriage with the driver's seat above and behind. [After Joseph Aloysius *Hansom* (1803–82), British architect.]

Han•tan (hän′dän′). See **Handan.**

Ha•nuk•kah or **Ha•nu•kah** also **Cha•nu•kah** (KHä′nə-kə, hä′-) *n. Judaism.* An eight-day festival beginning on the 25th of Kislev, commemorating the victory in 165 B.C. of the Maccabees over Antiochus Epiphanes (c. 215–164 B.C.) and the rededication of the Temple at Jerusalem. [Heb. *ḥănukkâ,* dedication < *ḥānak,* to dedicate.]

hao (hou) *n.* See table at **currency.** [Vietnamese *hào* < Chin. (Mandarin) *háo.*]

hao•le (hou′lē, -lā) *n. Hawaii.* A person, esp. a white person, who is not a native Hawaiian. See Regional Note at **ukulele.** [Hawaiian.]

hap (hăp) *n.* **1.** Fortune; chance. **2.** A happening; an occurrence. — *intr.v.* **happed, hap•ping, haps.** To happen. [ME < ON *happ.* See **kob-*.**]

ha•pax le•go•me•non (hā′păks′ lĭ-gŏm′ə-nŏn′) *n., pl.* **ha•pax le•go•me•na** (-nə). A word or form that occurs only once in the recorded corpus of a language. [Gk. : *hapax,* once + *legomenon,* neut. sing. passive part. of *legein,* to say.]

hap•haz•ard (hăp-hăz′ərd) *adj.* Dependent upon or characterized by mere chance. See Syns at **chance.** — *n.* Mere chance; fortuity. — *adv.* By chance; casually. — **hap•haz′ard•ly** *adv.* — **hap•haz′ard•ness** *n.*

haph•ta•rah also **haf•ta•rah** or **haf•to•rah** (häf′tä-rä′, häf-tôr′ə, -tōr′ə) *n., pl.* **-ta•roth** or **-to•roth** or **-to•rot** or **-to•ros** (-tä-rōt′, -rōs′, -tôr′ōt′, -ōs′, -tōr′-). *Judaism.* A selection from the Prophets, read in synagogue services on the Sabbath following each lesson from the Torah. [Mishnaic Heb. *hapṭārâ,* conclusion < *hipṭîr,* to conclude, dismiss < Heb. *'pāṭar,* to separate, discharge.]

hap•less (hăp′lĭs) *adj.* Luckless; unfortunate. — **hap′less•ly** *adv.* — **hap′less•ness** *n.*

hap•lite (hăp′līt′) *n.* Var. of **aplite.**

hap•loid (hăp′loid′) *Genet.* — *adj.* **1.** Having the same number of sets of chromosomes as a germ cell or half as many as a somatic cell. **2.** Having a single set of chromosomes. — *n.*

hang glider

hansom

ă pat	oi boy
ā pay	ou out
âr care	o͝o took
ä father	o͞o boot
ĕ pet	ŭ cut
ē be	ûr urge
ĭ pit	th thin
ī pie	*th* this
îr pier	hw which
ŏ pot	zh vision
ō toe	ə about,
ô paw	item

Stress marks:
′ (primary);
′ (secondary), as in dictionary (dĭk′shə-nĕr′ē)

An organism having haploid cells. [< Gk. *haplous*, single; see **sem-**[1]* + -OID.] — **hap′loi′dy** (-loi′dē) *n.*

hap•lol•o•gy (hăp-lŏl′ə-jē) *n.* The loss of one of two identical or similar adjacent syllables in a word, as in Latin *nūtrīx*, "nurse," from earlier **nūtrītrīx*. [Gk. *haplos, haplous*, single, simple; see HAPLOID + -LOGY.]

hap•lont (hăp′lŏnt) *n. Genet.* An organism with haploid somatic cells but a diploid zygote, as in many algae and fungi. [Gk. *haplous*, single, simple; see HAPLOID + -ONT.]

hap•lo•sis (hăp-lō′sĭs) *n. Genet.* Meiotic reduction of the diploid number of chromosomes by one half, resulting in haploidy. [Gk. *haplos, haplous*, single; see HAPLOID + -OSIS.]

hap•ly (hăp′lē) *adv.* By chance or accident.

hap•pen (hăp′ən) *intr.v.* **-pened, -pen•ing, -pens. 1.a.** To come to pass. **b.** To come into being. **2.** To take place or occur by chance. **3.** To come upon something by chance. **4.** To come or go casually; make an appearance: *He happened by.* [ME *happenen* < *hap*, chance. See HAP.]

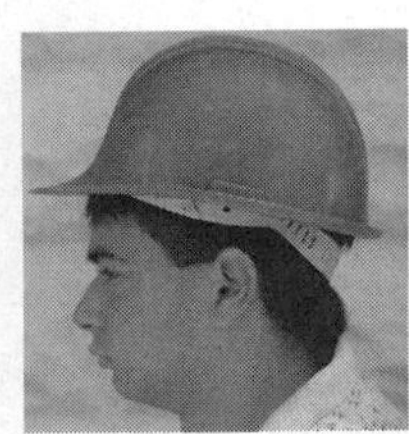

hardhat

hap•pen•chance (hăp′ən-chăns′) *n.* A happenstance.

hap•pen•ing (hăp′ə-nĭng) *n.* **1.** Something that takes place; an occurrence. See Syns at **occurrence. 2.** An improvised spectacle or performance, esp. one involving the audience.

hap•pen•stance (hăp′ən-stăns′) *n.* A chance circumstance. [HAPPEN + (CIRCUM)STANCE.]

hap•pi coat (hăp′ē) *n.* A Japanese jacket made of cotton or similar material and having an open front, often fastened with ties. [J. *happi* : Chin. (Mandarin) *bàn*, half + Chin. (Mandarin) *bèi*, to wear.]

hap•py (hăp′ē) *adj.* **-pi•er, -pi•est. 1.** Characterized by good luck; fortunate. **2.** Enjoying, showing, or marked by pleasure, satisfaction, or joy. See Syns at **glad**[1]. **3.** Well-adapted; felicitous. **4.** Cheerful; willing. **5.a.** Characterized by a spontaneous or obsessive inclination to use something. Often used in combination: *trigger-happy.* **b.** Inordinately enthusiastic about or involved with. Often used in combination: *clothes-happy.* [ME < *hap*, luck. See HAP.] — **hap′pi•ly** *adv.* — **hap′pi•ness** *n.*

hap•py-go-luck•y (hăp′ē-gō-lŭk′ē) *adj.* Taking things easily; carefree.

happy hour *n.* A period during which a bar or lounge serves drinks at reduced prices or free hors d'oeuvres.

Haps•burg also **Habs•burg** (hăps′bûrg′, häps′bo͝ork′). A royal German family that supplied rulers to various European states from the late Middle Ages to the early 20th cent.

hap•ten (hăp′tĕn′) also **hap•tene** (-tēn′) *n.* An antibody-specific substance that cannot induce antibody formation unless bound to a carrier protein or other molecule. [Ger. : Gk. *haptein*, to fasten + Ger. *-en*, n. suff. (< Gk. *-ēnē*, -ene).]

hap•tic (hăp′tĭk) *adj.* Of or relating to the sense of touch; tactile. [Gk. *haptikos* < *haptesthai*, to grasp, touch.]

hap•to•glo•bin (hăp′tə-glō′bĭn) *n.* A plasma protein that binds free hemoglobin in the bloodstream. [Gk. *haptein*, to bind, fasten + (HEMO)GLOBIN.]

ha•ra-ki•ri (hăr′ĭ-kîr′ē, hä′rē-) also **ha•ri-ka•ri** (hăr′ē-kăr′ē, hăr′ē-kăr′ē) *n., pl.* **-ris.** Ritual suicide by disembowelment formerly practiced by Japanese samurai. [J. : *hara*, abdomen, bowels + *kiri*, to cut.]

ha•rangue (hə-răng′) *n.* **1.** A long, pompous speech, esp. one delivered before a gathering. **2.** A speech or piece of writing characterized by strong feeling or expression; a tirade. — *v.* **-rangued, -rangu•ing, -rangues.** — *tr.* To deliver a harangue to. — *intr.* To deliver a harangue. [ME *arang*, a speech to an assembly < OFr. *harangue* < OItal. *aringa* < *aringare*, to speak in public, prob. < *aringo, arringa*, public square, meeting place, of Gmc. orig. See **koro-*.**] — **ha•rangu′er** *n.*

Ha•rap•pa (hə-răp′ə). A locality in the Indus R. valley of the Punjab in Pakistan; site of archaeological finds dating to the 3rd millennium B.C.

Florence Harding

Ha•ra•re (hə-rär′ā). Formerly (until 1982) **Salis•bur•y** (sôlz′bĕr′ē, -brē). The cap. of Zimbabwe, in the NE part; founded by the British in 1890. Pop. 656,011.

ha•rass (hăr′əs, hə-răs′) *tr.v.* **-rassed, -rass•ing, -rass•es. 1.** To irritate or torment persistently. **2.** To wear out; exhaust. **3.** To impede and exhaust (an enemy) by repeated attacks or raids. [Fr. *harasser*, poss. < OFr. *harer*, to set a dog on < *hare*, interj. used to set a dog on, of Gmc. orig.] — **ha•rass′er** *n.* — **ha•rass′ment** *n.*

Syns: *harass, harry, hound, badger, pester, plague, bait.* These verbs mean to trouble persistently or incessantly. *Harass* and *harry* imply systematic persecution by besieging with repeated annoyances, threats, or demands: *"of all the griefs that harass the distress'd"* (Samuel Johnson). *A customer harried the storekeeper. Hound* suggests unrelenting pursuit to gain a desired end: *Reporters hounded the celebrity.* To *badger* is to nag or tease persistently: *The child badgered his parents for toys.* To *pester* is to inflict a succession of petty annoyances: *"How she would have pursued and pestered me with questions"* (Charlotte Brontë). *Plague* refers to an affliction likened to an epidemic disease: *"As I have no estate, I am plagued with no tenants or stewards"* (Henry Fielding). To *bait* is to torment by or as if by taunting, insulting, or ridiculing: *Hecklers baited the speaker.*

Usage Note: In a recent survey 50 percent of the Usage Panel preferred a pronunciation of *harass* with stress on the first syllable, while 50 percent preferred stress on the second syllable.

Har•bin (här′bĭn′). A city of NE China N of Jilin; cap. of Heilongjiang province. Pop. 2,630,000.

har•bin•ger (här′bĭn-jər) *n.* One that indicates or foreshadows what is to come. — *tr.v.* **-gered, -ger•ing, -gers.** To signal the approach of; presage. [ME *herbengar*, one sent to arrange lodgings < OFr. *herbergeor* < *herbergier*, to lodge < *herberge*, lodging, of Gmc. orig. See **koro-*.**]

har•bor (här′bər) *n.* **1.** A sheltered part of a body of water deep enough to provide anchorage for ships. **2.** A place of shelter; a refuge. — *tr.v.* **-bored, -bor•ing, -bors. 1.** To give shelter to: *harbor refugees.* **2.** To provide a place, home, or habitat for. **3.** To entertain or nourish (a thought or feeling): *harbor a grudge.* [ME *herberwe*, prob. < OE *herebeorg*, lodging. See **koro-*.**] — **har′bor•er** *n.*

har•bor•age (här′bər-ĭj) *n.* **1.** Shelter and anchorage for ships. **2.** Shelter; refuge.

har•bor•mas•ter (här′bər-măs′tər) *n.* An officer who oversees and enforces the regulations of a harbor.

harbor seal *n.* A hair seal *(Phoca vitulina)* of coastal waters of the Northern Hemisphere having a spotted coat.

har•bour (här′bər) *n.* & *v. Chiefly British.* Var. of **harbor.**

hard (härd) *adj.* **hard•er, hard•est. 1.** Resistant to pressure; not readily penetrated. See Syns at **firm**[1]. **2.a.** Physically toughened; rugged. **b.** Mentally toughened; strong-minded. **3.a.** Requiring great effort or endurance. **b.** Performed with or marked by great diligence or energy. **c.** Difficult to resolve, accomplish, or finish. **d.** Difficult to understand or impart. **4.a.** Intense in force or degree. **b.** Inclement: *a hard winter.* **5.a.** Stern or strict in nature or comportment. **b.** Resistant to persuasion or appeal; obdurate. **c.** Making few concessions. **6.a.** Difficult to endure. **b.** Oppressive or unjust in nature or effect. **c.** Lacking compassion or sympathy; callous. **7.a.** Harsh or severe in effect or intention: *said some hard things.* **b.** Bitter; resentful. **8.a.** Causing damage or premature wear. **b.** Bad; adverse: *hard luck.* **9.** Proceeding or performing with force, vigor, or persistence; assiduous. **10.a.** Real and unassailable: *hard evidence.* **b.** Definite; firm. **c.** Close; penetrating: *a hard look at the situation.* **d.** Free from illusion or bias; practical. **e.** Using or based on data that are readily quantified or verified. **11.a.** Marked by sharp outline or definition; stark. **b.** Lacking in delicacy, shading, or nuance. **12.a.** Metallic, as opposed to paper. Used of currency. **b.** Backed by bullion rather than by credit. Used of currency. **c.** High and stable. Used of prices. **13.a.** Durable; lasting: *hard merchandise.* **b.** Written or printed rather than stored in electronic media. **14.** Erect; tumid. Used of a penis. **15.a.** Having high alcoholic content; intoxicating. **b.** Rendered alcoholic by fermentation; fermented. **16.** Containing dissolved salts. Used of water. **17.** *Ling* Velar, as *c* in *cake* or *g* in *log*, as opposed to palatal or soft. **18.** *Phys.* Of relatively high energy; penetrating: *hard x-rays.* **19.** High in gluten content. **20.** *Chem.* Resistant to biodegradation. **21.** Physically addictive. Used of certain illegal drugs, such as heroin. **22.** Resistant to blast, heat, or radiation. Used esp. of nuclear weapons. — *adv.* **1.** With strenuous effort; intently. **2.** With great force, vigor, or energy. **3.** In such a way as to cause great damage or hardship. **4.** With great distress, grief, or bitterness. **5.** Firmly; securely. **6.** Toward or into a solid condition: *concrete that sets hard within a day.* **7.** Near in space or time; close. **8.** *Naut.* Completely; fully: *hard alee.* — ***idioms.* hard and fast.** Defined, fixed, and invariable. **hard of hearing.** Having a partial loss of hearing. **hard put.** Undergoing great difficulty. **hard up.** *Informal.* In need; poor. [ME < OE *heard.* See **kar-*.**]

hard•back (härd′băk′) *Print.* — *adj.* Bound in cloth, cardboard, or leather rather than paper. Used of books. — *n.* A hardback book.

hard•ball (härd′bôl′) *n.* **1.** *Sports.* Baseball. **2.** *Informal.* The use of any means, however ruthless, to attain an objective.

hard-bit•ten (härd′bĭt′n) *adj.* Toughened by experience.

hard•board (härd′bôrd′, -bōrd′) *n.* A construction board made by compressing fibers of wood chips usu. with a binder.

hard-boiled (härd′boild′) *adj.* **1.** Cooked by boiling in the shell to a solid consistency. Used of eggs. **2.** Callous; unfeeling. **3.** Unsentimental and practical; tough.

hard•bound (härd′bound′) *adj.* & *n. Print.* Hardback.

hard coal *n.* See **anthracite.**

hard core *n.* **1.** The most dedicated, loyal faction of a group or an organization. **2.** An intractable core or nucleus of a society, esp. one resistant to improvement or change.

hard-core also **hard•core** (härd′kôr′, -kōr′) *adj.* **1.** Intensely loyal; die-hard: *a hard-core golfer.* **2.** Stubbornly resistant to improvement or change. **3.** Extremely graphic or explicit.

hard•cov•er (härd′kŭv′ər) *adj.* & *n. Print.* Hardback.

hard disk *n. Comp. Sci.* A rigid magnetic disk fixed within a drive unit and used for storing computer data.

Har•de•ca•nute or **Har•di•ca•nute** (här′dĭ-kə-no͞ot′, -nyo͞ot′). 1019?–42. King of England (1040–42) and of

Denmark (1035–42) who claimed the English throne after the death of Harold I.

hard•edge (härd′ĕj′) *n.* A form of abstract painting characterized by clearly defined geometric shapes.

hard-edged (härd′ĕjd′) *adj.* Inclined to hold a position; severe.

hard•en (här′dn) *v.* **-ened, -en•ing, -ens.** —*tr.* **1.** To make hard or harder. **2.** To enable to withstand physical or mental hardship. **3.** To make unfeeling, unsympathetic, or callous. **4.** To make sharp, as in outline. —*intr.* **1.** To become hard or harder. **2.** To rise and become stable. Used of prices. **3.** To become inured.

hard•en•er (här′dn-ər) *n.* One that hardens, esp. a substance added to varnish or paint to give it a harder finish.

hard•en•ing (här′dn-ĭng) *n.* **1.** The act or process of becoming hard or harder. **2.** Something that hardens, as a substance added to iron to yield steel. **3.** Gradual exposure of plants to cold weather.

hardening of the arteries *n.* Arteriosclerosis.

hard-fist•ed (härd′fĭs′tĭd) *adj.* Tightfisted; stingy.

hard•hack (härd′hăk′) *n.* A downy plant *(Spiraea tomentosa)* of eastern North America having small rose-purple flowers.

hard-hand•ed (härd′hăn′dĭd) *adj.* **1.** Having hands calloused or hardened by work. **2.** Oppressive; tyrannical.

hard•hat or **hard-hat** (härd′hăt′) *n.* **1.a.** A lightweight protective helmet, usu. of metal or reinforced plastic, worn by workers in industrial settings. **b.** *Informal.* A construction worker. **2.** *Slang.* An extremely patriotic or conservative person. —**hard′hat** *adj.*

hard•head (härd′hĕd′) *n.* **1.** A shrewd tough person. **2.** A stubborn unmovable person. **3.** *pl.* **hardhead** or **-heads.** Any of several fishes having a bony head, esp. the Atlantic croaker.

hard•head•ed (härd′hĕd′ĭd) *adj.* **1.** Stubborn; willful. **2.** Realistic; pragmatic. —**hard′head′ed•ness** *n.*

hard•heart•ed (härd′här′tĭd) *adj.* Lacking in feeling or compassion; pitiless and cold. —**hard′heart′ed•ly** *adv.* —**hard′heart′ed•ness** *n.*

hard-hit•ting (härd′hĭt′ĭng) *adj.* Effective; forceful.

Har•di•ca•nute (här′dĭ-kə-no͞ot′, -nyo͞ot′). See **Hardecanute.**

har•di•hood (här′dē-ho͝od′) *n.* **1.** Boldness and daring. **2.** Impudence or insolence.

Har•ding (här′dĭng), **Chester.** 1792–1866. Amer. portrait painter whose subjects included Daniel Webster.

Harding, Florence Mabel King. 1860–1924. First Lady of the U.S. (1921–23).

Harding, Warren Gamaliel. 1865–1923. The 29th President of the U.S. (1921–23).

hard labor *n.* Compulsory physical labor coincident with a prison term imposed as punishment for a crime.

hard line *n.* A firm uncompromising policy, position, or stance.

hard-line also **hard•line** (härd′līn′) *adj.* Firm and uncompromising, as in policy or position. —**hard′-lin′er** *n.*

hard•ly (härd′lē) *adv.* **1.** Barely; just. **2.** To almost no degree; almost not. **3.** Probably or almost surely not. **4.** With severity; harshly. **5.** With great difficulty; painfully. [ME *hardli* < OE *heardlīce,* harshly < *heard,* hard. See HARD.]

Usage Note: The use of *hardly* with a negative is avoided in Standard English. Some critics have been puzzled that adverbs such as *hardly, rarely,* and *scarcely* should be treated as negatives in the traditional strictures against double negation. The fact is that adverbs such as *hardly* are semantically negative in that they qualify a state or an event relative to the limiting case of nonoccurrence. Thus the meaning of *hardly* is, roughly, "almost not at all"; the meaning of *rarely* is "practically never"; and so forth. These adverbs are felt to have a negative component in their meaning, and grammarians have reacted to the use of *hardly* with negatives just as they have reacted to the use of pairs of negatives such as *not* and *none.* See Usage Notes at **double negative, rarely, scarcely.**

hard maple *n.* See **sugar maple.**

hard•ness (härd′nĭs) *n.* **1.** The quality or condition of being hard. **2.** *Mineral.* The relative resistance of a mineral to scratching, as measured by the Mohs scale. **3.** The relative resistance of a metal or other material to denting, scratching, or bending.

hard-nosed (härd′nōzd′) *adj.* Hardheaded.

hard-on (härd′ŏn′, -ôn′) *n. Vulgar Slang.* An erection of the penis.

hard palate *n.* The bony anterior portion of the palate.

hard•pan (härd′păn′) *n.* **1.** A layer of hard subsoil or clay. **2.** Hard unbroken ground. **3.** A foundation; bedrock.

hard-pressed (härd′prĕst′) *adj.* Experiencing great difficulty or distress: *financially hard-pressed.*

hard rock *n. Mus.* A style of rock 'n' roll marked by a harsh amplified sound, often using electronic modulations.

hard rubber *n.* Ebonite.

hard sauce *n.* A creamy sauce of butter and sugar with rum, brandy, or vanilla flavoring, served with some desserts.

hard•scrab•ble (härd′skrăb′əl) *adj.* Earning a bare subsistence; marginal. —*n.* Barren or marginal farmland.

hard sell *n. Informal.* **1.** Aggressive, high-pressure selling or promotion. **2.** A difficult sales prospect.

hard-set (härd′sĕt′) *adj.* Fixed; rigid.

hard-shell (härd′shĕl′) *n.* A hard-shell clam or crab. —*adj.* also **hard-shelled** (-shĕld′). **1.** Having a thick, heavy, or hardened shell. **2.** Uncompromising; confirmed.

hard-shell clam *n.* See **quahog.**

hard-shell crab *n.* A crab, esp. an edible marine crab, with a fully hardened shell.

hard•ship (härd′shĭp′) *n.* **1.** Extreme privation; suffering. **2.** A cause of privation or suffering. See Syns at **difficulty.**

hard•stand (härd′stănd′) *n.* A hard-surfaced area for parking aircraft or ground vehicles.

hard•tack (härd′tăk′) *n.* A hard biscuit or bread made with flour and water.

hard•top (härd′tŏp′) *n.* An automobile designed to look like a convertible but having a rigidly fixed hard top.

hard•ware (härd′wâr′) *n.* **1.** Metal goods and utensils such as locks, tools, and cutlery. **2.a.** *Comp. Sci.* A computer and the associated physical equipment directly involved in the performance of data-processing or communications functions. **b.** Machines and other physical equipment directly involved in performing an industrial, technological, or military function. **3.** *Informal.* Weapons, esp. military weapons.

hard-wired (härd′wīrd′) *adj.* **1.** *Comp. Sci.* Of, relating to, or implemented through logic circuitry permanently connected within a device. **2.** Directly connected by electrical wires or cables. —**hard′wire′** *v.*

hard•wood (härd′wo͝od′) *n.* **1.** The wood of a dicotyledonous tree. **2.** A dicotyledonous tree.

har•dy[1] (här′dē) *adj.* **-di•er, -di•est.** **1.** Being in robust and sturdy good health. See Syns at **healthy. 2.** Courageous; intrepid. **3.** Brazenly daring; audacious. **4.** Capable of surviving unfavorable conditions, such as cold weather. Used esp. of cultivated plants. [ME < OFr. *hardi,* p.part. of *hardir,* make hard, embolden, of Gmc. orig. See **kar-*.**] —**har′di•ly** *adv.* —**har′di•ness** *n.*

har•dy[2] (här′dē) *n., pl.* **-dies.** A square-shanked chisel that fits into a square hole in an anvil. [Prob. < HARD.]

Har•dy (här′dē), **Oliver.** 1892–1957. Amer. comedian famous for his slapstick routines with Stan Laurel.

Hardy, Thomas. 1840–1928. British writer whose works include *Tess of the d'Urbervilles* (1891).

hare (hâr) *n.* Any of various mammals of the family Leporidae, esp. of the genus *Lepus,* similar to rabbits but having longer ears and legs and giving birth to active, furred young. —*intr.v.* **hared, har•ing, hares.** To move hurriedly, as if hunting a swift quarry. [ME < OE *hara.* See **kas-*.**]

hare and hounds *n. Games.* A game in which one group leaves a trail of paper scraps for a pursuing group to follow.

hare•bell (hâr′bĕl′) *n.* A perennial plant *(Campanula rotundifolia)* having bell-shaped blue or white flowers.

hare•brained (hâr′brānd′) *adj.* Foolish; flighty.

Usage Note: The first part of the compound *harebrained* is often misspelled *hair* in the belief that the meaning of the word is "with a hair-sized brain" rather than "with no more sense than a hare."

Ha•re Krish•na (hä′rē krĭsh′nə) *n., pl.* **Hare Krish•nas.** **1.** A chant to the Hindu god Krishna. **2.** *Informal.* **a.** A member of the International Society for Krishna Consciousness (ISKCON), founded in the United States in 1966. **b.** The society itself. [< the chant *Hare Krishna* : Skt. *hare,* vocative of *Hariḥ,* a name of Vishnu (< *hari-,* yellow-green, tawny yellow; see **ghel-[2]*)** + Skt. *Kṛṣṇā,* Krishna.]

hare•lip (hâr′lĭp′) *n. Offensive.* A cleft lip.

har•em (hâr′əm, hăr′-) *n.* **1.** A house or a section of a house reserved for women members of a Muslim household. **2.** The women occupying such a place. **3.** A group of women sexual partners for one man. [Turk. < Pers. *ḥaram* < Ar. *ḥarīm,* sacred, forbidden place < *ḥarama,* to be prohibited.]

Har•greaves (här′grēvz′), **James.** d. 1778. British inventor of the spinning jenny (c. 1764; patented 1770).

har•i•cot[1] (hăr′ĭ-kō′) *n.* The edible pod or seed of any of several beans, esp. the kidney bean. [Fr., poss. alteration of Nahuatl *ayacotli.*]

har•i•cot[2] (hăr′ĭ-kō′) *n.* A highly seasoned mutton or lamb stew with vegetables. [Fr. < OFr. *hericot, hericoq,* poss. < *harigoter,* to cut into pieces, prob. of Gmc. orig.]

ha•ri-ka•ri (här′ē-kär′ē, hăr′ē-kăr′ē) *n.* Var. of **hara-kiri.**

Ha•ri Rud (här′ē ro͞od′). A river, c. 1,126 km (700 mi), of NW Afghanistan, NE Iran, and S Turkmenistan.

hark (härk) *intr.v.* **harked, hark•ing, harks.** To listen attentively. —***idiom.*** **hark back.** To return to a previous point, as in a narrative. [ME *harken, herken* < OE **heorcian.*]

har•ken (här′kən) *v.* Var. of **hearken.**

Har•lan (här′lən), **John Marshall.** 1833–1911. Amer. jurist; associate justice of the U.S. Supreme Court (1877–1911). His grandson **John Marshall Harlan** (1899–1971) also served as an associate justice of the Court (1955–71).

Har•lem (här′ləm). A section of New York City in N Manhattan bordering on the Harlem and East rivers; estab. as the settlement of Nieuw Haarlem in 1658. —**Har′lem•ite′** *n.*

Harlem River. A channel in New York City separating the N end of Manhattan I. from the Bronx and with Spuyten Duyvil Creek connecting the Hudson and East rivers.

Warren G. Harding

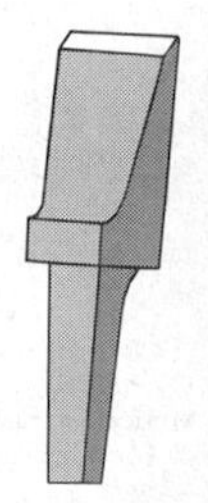

hardy[2]

hare
European hare
Lepus europaeus

ă pat	oi boy
ā pay	ou out
âr care	o͝o took
ä father	o͞o boot
ĕ pet	ŭ cut
ē be	ûr urge
ĭ pit	th thin
ī pie	*th* this
îr pier	hw which
ŏ pot	zh vision
ō toe	ə about,
ô paw	item

Stress marks:
′ (primary);
′ (secondary), as in
dictionary (dĭk′shə-nĕr′ē)

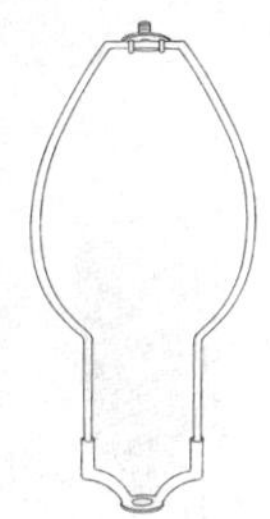

harp
Top: Musical instrument
Bottom: For a lampshade

Benjamin Harrison[2]

George Harrison

har•le•quin (här′lĭ-kwĭn, -kĭn) *n.* **1. Harlequin.** A buffoon of the commedia dell'arte, traditionally presented in a mask and parti-colored tights. **2.** A clown; a buffoon. *—adj.* Having a pattern of brightly colored diamond shapes. [Obsolete Fr. < OFr. *Herlequin, Hellequin*, a demon, perh. < ME **Herleking* < OE *Herla cyning*, King Herla, a mythical figure identified with Woden.]

har•le•quin•ade (här′lĭ-kwə-nād′) *n.* **1.** A comedy or pantomime featuring Harlequin. **2.** Clowning or buffoonery. [Obsolete Fr. < *harlequin*, harlequin. See HARLEQUIN.]

harlequin bug *n.* A brightly colored stinkbug *(Murgantia histrionica)* that is destructive to some cruciferous plants.

Har•lin•gen (här′lĭn-jən). A city of extreme S TX NW of Brownsville. Pop. 48,735.

har•lot (här′lət) *n.* A prostitute. [ME, vagabond, lecher, harlot < OFr. *arlot, herlot*, vagabond.] **—har′lot•ry** (-lə-trē) *n.*

Har•low (här′lō). An urban district of SE England NE of London; designated a new town in 1946. Pop. 79,400.

Harlow, Jean. 1911–37. Amer. actress whose films include *Hell's Angels* (1930) and *Red Dust* (1932).

harm (härm) *n.* **1.** Physical or psychological injury or damage. **2.** Wrong; evil. *—tr.v.* **harmed, harm•ing, harms.** To do harm to. See Syns at **spoil.** [ME < OE *hearm.*]

har•mat•tan (här′mə-tăn′, här-măt′n) *n.* A dry dusty wind that blows along the northwest coast of Africa. [Akan (Twi) *haramata*, poss. < Ar. *ḥarām*, evil thing.]

harm•ful (härm′fəl) *adj.* Causing or capable of causing harm; injurious. **—harm′ful•ly** *adv.* **—harm′ful•ness** *n.*

harm•less (härm′lĭs) *adj.* **1.** Incapable of causing harm. **2.** Free from loss or legal liability: *held harmless if the other parties defaulted.* **—harm′less•ness** *n.*

har•mon•ic (här-mŏn′ĭk) *adj.* **1.** *Mus.* **a.** Of or relating to harmony. **b.** Pleasing to the ear. **c.** Characterized by harmony. **2.** Of or relating to harmonics. **3.** Integrated in nature. *—n.* **1.** *Mus.* **a.** A tone in the harmonic series of overtones produced by a fundamental tone. **b.** A tone produced on a stringed instrument by lightly touching an open or stopped vibrating string so that both segments vibrate. **2.** A wave whose frequency is a whole-number multiple of that of another. **3. harmonics.** *(used with a sing. v.)* The theory or study of the physical properties and characteristics of musical sound. [Lat. *harmonicus* < Gk. *harmonikos* < *harmonia*, harmony. See HARMONY.] **—har•mon′i•cal•ly** *adv.*

har•mon•i•ca (här-mŏn′ĭ-kə) *n. Mus.* **1.** A small rectangular instrument consisting of a row of free reeds set back in air holes, played by exhaling or inhaling. **2.** A glass harmonica. **3.** An instrument consisting of tuned strips of metal or glass fixed to a frame and struck with a hammer. [Alteration of obsolete *armonica*, glass harmonica < Ital., fem. of *armonico*, harmonious < Lat. *harmonicus*, harmonic. See HARMONIC.]

harmonic analysis *n. Math.* The representation of functions by means of linear operations on characteristic sets of functions, esp. such representation by Fourier series.

harmonic mean *n. Math.* The reciprocal of the arithmetic mean of the reciprocals of a specified set of numbers.

harmonic motion *n.* A periodic vibration, as of a violin string, in which the motions are symmetrical about a region of equilibrium.

harmonic progression *n. Math.* A sequence of quantities whose reciprocals form an arithmetic progression.

harmonic series *n.* **1.** *Math.* A series whose terms are in harmonic progression, as $1 + \frac{1}{3} + \frac{1}{5} + \frac{1}{7} + \ldots$ **2.** *Mus.* A series of tones consisting of a fundamental tone and the overtones produced by it, and whose frequencies are consecutive integral multiples of the frequency of the fundamental.

har•mo•ni•ous (här-mō′nē-əs) *adj.* **1.** Exhibiting accord in feeling or action. **2.** Having component elements pleasingly or appropriately combined: *a harmonious blend of architectural styles.* **3.** Characterized by harmony of sound; melodious. **—har•mo′ni•ous•ly** *adv.* **—har•mo′ni•ous•ness** *n.*

har•mo•nist (här′mə-nĭst) *n. Mus.* One skilled in harmony. **—har′mo•nis′tic** *adj.* **—har′mo•nis′ti•cal•ly** *adv.*

har•mo•ni•um (här-mō′nē-əm) *n. Mus.* A keyboard instrument having free metal reeds actuated by a bellows. [Fr. < *harmonie*, harmony < OFr. See HARMONY.]

har•mo•nize (här′mə-nīz′) *v.* **-nized, -niz•ing, -niz•es.** *—tr.* **1.** To bring into agreement or harmony. **2.** *Mus.* To provide harmony for (a melody). *—intr.* **1.** To be in or come into agreement; be harmonious. **2.** *Mus.* To sing or play in harmony. **—har′mo•ni•za′tion** (-nĭ-zā′shən) *n.* **—har′mo•niz′er** *n.*

har•mo•ny (här′mə-nē) *n., pl.* **-nies. 1.** Agreement in feeling or opinion; accord. **2.** A pleasing combination of elements in a whole. See Syns at **proportion. 3.** *Mus.* **a.** The study of the structure, progression, and relation of chords. **b.** Simultaneous combination of notes in a chord. **c.** The structure of a work or passage as considered from the point of view of its chordal characteristics and relationships. **d.** A combination of sounds considered pleasing to the ear. **4.** A collation of parallel passages, esp. from the Gospels, with a commentary. [ME *armonie* < OFr. < Lat. *harmonia* < Gk., articulation, agreement, harmony < *harmos*, joint. See **ar-*.**]

Harms•worth (härmz′wûrth′), **Alfred Charles William.** Viscount Northcliffe. 1865–1922. British publisher who founded the *Daily Mail* (1896) and the *Daily Mirror* (1903).

har•ness (här′nĭs) *n.* **1.** The gear or tackle, other than a yoke, with which a draft animal pulls a vehicle or an implement. **2.** Something resembling such gear or tackle, as the straps used to hold a parachute to the body. **3.** A device that raises and lowers the warp threads on a loom. **4.** *Archaic.* Armor for a man or horse. *—tr.v.* **-nessed, -ness•ing, -ness•es. 1.a.** To put a harness on (a draft animal). **b.** To fasten by the use of a harness. **2.** To bring under control and direct the force of. ***—idiom.* in harness.** On duty or at work. [ME *harnes* < OFr. *harneis*, of Gmc. orig. See **nes-**[1]***.**]

harness race *n. Sports.* A horserace between pacers or trotters harnessed to sulkies. **—harness racing** *n.*

Har•old I (hăr′əld). "Harold Harefoot." d. 1040. King of England (1035–40) who was the illegitimate son of Canute and claimed the English throne after his father's death.

Harold II. 1022?–66. King of England (1066) who was killed fighting the invasion of William the Conqueror.

Ha•roun al-Ra•schid (hä-ro͞on′ äl-rä-shēd′). See **Harun al-Rashid.**

harp (härp) *n.* **1.** *Mus.* An instrument consisting of an upright, open triangular frame with usu. 46 strings of graded lengths played by plucking with the fingers. **2.** Something, such as a pair of vertical supports for a lampshade, that resembles this musical instrument. *—intr.v.* **harped, harp•ing, harps.** To play a harp. ***—phrasal verb.* harp on.** To talk or write about to an excessive, tedious degree. [ME < OE *hearpe* and < OFr. *harpe*, of Gmc. orig.] **—harp′er** *n.* **—harp′ist** *n.*

Har•pers Ferry (här′pərz). A locality of extreme NE WV; scene of John Brown's rebellion (1859), in which he briefly seized the U.S. arsenal.

har•poon (här-po͞on′) *n.* A spearlike weapon with a barbed head used in hunting whales and large fish. *—tr.v.* **-pooned, -poon•ing, -poons.** To strike, kill, or capture with or as if with a harpoon. [Prob. < Du. *harpoen* < MDu. < OFr. *harpon*, poss. < *harpe*, clamp, claw < Lat. *harpa*, sickle < Gk. *harpē*.] **—har•poon′er** *n.*

harp seal *n.* An earless seal *(Pagophilus groenlandicus)* of the North Atlantic and Arctic oceans. [< the shape of the markings on its shoulders and sides.]

harp•si•chord (härp′sĭ-kôrd′, -kōrd′) *n. Mus.* A keyboard instrument whose strings are plucked with quills or plectrums. [Alteration of obsolete Fr. *harpechorde* < Ital. *arpicordo* : *arpa*, harp (< LLat. *harpa*, of Gmc. orig.) + *corda*, string (< Lat. *chorda* < Gk. *khordē*; see **gherə-***).] **—harp′si•chord′ist** *n.*

Har•py (här′pē) *n., pl.* **-pies. 1.** *Gk. Myth.* One of several monsters with the head and trunk of a woman and the tail, wings, and talons of a bird. **2. harpy.** A predatory person. **3. harpy.** A woman held to be shrewish.

har•que•bus (här′kə-bəs, -kwə-) also **ar•que•bus** (är′-) *n.* A heavy portable matchlock gun invented during the 15th century. [Obsolete Fr. *harquebuse* < OFr., alteration of MDu. *hakebus* : *hake*, hook; see **keg-*** + *busse*, gun (< LLat. *buxis*, box; see BOX[1]).]

har•ri•dan (hăr′ĭ-dn) *n.* A woman regarded as scolding and vicious. [Poss. < Fr. *haridelle*, gaunt woman, old horse, nag.]

har•ri•er[1] (hăr′ē-ər) *n.* **1.** One that harries. **2.** Any of various slender narrow-winged hawks of the genus *Circus* that prey on small animals. [Sense 2, alteration (influenced by HARRY) of obsolete *harrower* < HARROW[2].]

har•ri•er[2] (hăr′ē-ər) *n.* **1.** Any of a breed of small hound used to hunt hares and rabbits. **2.** *Sports.* A cross-country runner. [ME *hairer, eirer*, poss. alteration of OFr. *errier*, wanderer < *errer*, to wander. See ERR.]

Har•ri•man (hăr′ə-mən), **Edward Henry.** 1848–1909. Amer. railway magnate who joined J.P. Morgan and James J. Hill to form the Northern Securities Company

Harriman, (William) Averell. 1891–1986. Amer. financier who served as ambassador to the U.S.S.R. (1943–46).

Har•ris (hăr′ĭs), **Benjamin.** fl. 1673–1713. English publisher and journalist in Massachusetts whose *Publick Occurrences* was the first newspaper printed in America (1690).

Harris, Frank. 1856–1931. Irish-born Amer. writer known for *My Life and Loves* (three volumes, 1923–27).

Harris, Joel Chandler. 1848–1908. Amer. writer and journalist who wrote *Uncle Remus: His Songs and His Sayings* (1880).

Harris, Roy Ellsworth. 1898–1979. Amer. composer known especially for his folk-inspired symphonies.

Har•ris•burg (hăr′ĭs-bûrg′). The cap. of PA, in the SE-central part WNW of Philadelphia; settled in the early 1700's. Pop. 52,376.

Har•ri•son (hăr′ĭ-sən). A village of SE NY, a residential suburb of New York City. Pop. 23,308.

Harrison, Benjamin[1]**.** 1726–91. Amer. Revolutionary leader who served in the Continental Congress (1774–78).

Harrison, Benjamin[2]**.** 1833–1901. The 23rd President of the U.S. (1889–93).

Harrison, George. b. 1943. British singer and songwriter who was a member of the Beatles.

Harrison, William Henry. 1773–1841. The 9th President of the U.S. (1841); died of pneumonia after one month in office.
Har•ri•son•burg (hăr′ĭ-sən-bûrg′). An independent city of N-central VA NW of Charlottesville. Pop. 30,707.
har•row[1] (hăr′ō) *n.* A farm implement consisting of a heavy frame with sharp teeth or upright disks, used to break up and even off plowed ground. — *tr.v.* **-rowed, -row•ing, -rows. 1.** To break up and level with a harrow. **2.** To inflict great distress or torment on. [ME *harwe.*] —**har′row•er** *n.*
har•row[2] (hăr′ō) *tr.v.* **-rowed, -row•ing, -rows.** *Archaic.* To plunder; sack. [ME *herwen*, var. of *harien.* See HARRY.]
Har•row (hăr′ō). A mainly residential district of NE Greater London; site of the public school Harrow (founded 1571).
har•row•ing (hăr′ō-ĭng) *adj.* Extremely distressing.
har•rumph (hə-rŭmf′) *intr.v.* **-rumphed, -rumph•ing, -rumphs. 1.** To make a show of clearing one's throat. **2.** To offer usu. brief critical comments. [Imit.] —**har•rumph′** *n.*
har•ry (hăr′ē) *tr.v.* **-ried, -ry•ing, -ries. 1.** To disturb or distress by or as if by repeated attacks; harass. See Syns at **harass. 2.** To raid, as in war; sack or pillage. [ME *harien* < OE *hergian.* See **koro-***.]
harsh (härsh) *adj.* **harsh•er, harsh•est. 1.** Unpleasantly coarse and rough to the touch. **2.** Disagreeable to the senses, esp. to the sense of hearing. **3.** Extremely severe or exacting; stern. [ME *harsk*, of Scand. orig.] —**harsh′ly** *adv.* —**harsh′ness** *n.*
harsh•en (här′shən) *tr. & intr.v.* **-ened, -en•ing, -ens.** To make or become harsh.
hars•let (här′slĭt) *n.* Var. of **haslet.**
hart (härt) *n., pl.* **harts** or **hart.** A male deer, esp. a male red deer over five years old. [ME < OE *heorot.* See **ker-**[1]*.]
Hart (härt), **Lorenz Milton.** 1895–1943. Amer. lyricist whose songs include "My Funny Valentine" and "Blue Moon."
Hart, Moss. 1904–61. Amer. playwright, librettist, and director whose collaborations with George S. Kaufman include *The Man Who Came to Dinner* (1939).
Harte (härt), **(Francis) Bret.** 1836–1902. Amer. writer whose works include "The Luck of Roaring Camp" (1868).
har•te•beest (här′tə-bēst′, härt′bēst′) *n., pl.* **-beests** or **hartebeest.** Any of various large reddish-brown African antelopes of the genus *Alcelaphus*, having ringed outward-curving horns. [Obsolete Afr. < MDu., var. of *hertebeest* : *hert*, deer; see **ker-**[1]* + *beest*, beast (< OFr. *beste*; see BEAST).]
Hart•ford (härt′fərd). The capital of CT, in the N-central part on the Connecticut R.; settled 1635–36 by Massachusetts colonists on the site of a Dutch trading post. Pop. 139,739.
Har•tle•pool (härt′lē-pōōl′, här′tl-). A borough of NE England on the North Sea SSE of Newcastle. Pop. 94,600.
hart's-tongue (härts′tŭng′) *n.* A European evergreen fern *(Phyllitis scolopendrium)* with narrow undivided fronds.
har•um-scar•um (hâr′əm-skâr′əm, hăr′əm-skăr′əm) *adj.* Lacking a sense of responsibility; reckless. — *adv.* With abandon; recklessly. [< *hare*, to frighten + SCARE.]
Ha•run al-Ra•shid or **Ha•roun al-Ra•schid** (hä-rōōn′ äl-rä-shēd′) also **Harun ar-Ra•shid** (är′-). 763?–809. Caliph of Baghdad (786–809) noted for the splendor of his court.
ha•rus•pex (hə-rŭs′pĕks′, hăr′ə-spĕks′) also **a•rus•pex** (ə-rŭs′pĕks′) *n., pl.* **ha•rus•pi•ces** (hə-rŭs′pĭ-sēz′) also **a•rus•pi•ces** (ə-rŭs′pĭ-sēz′). A priest in ancient Rome who practiced divination by the inspection of the entrails of animals. [Lat. See **gherə-***.]
Har•vard (här′vərd), **John.** 1607–38. Amer. cleric and philanthropist who left his library and half his estate to the college in Cambridge MA that now bears his name.
Harvard, Mount. A peak, 4,398.1 m (14,420 ft), in the Sawatch Range of the Rocky Mts. in central CO.
har•vest (här′vĭst) *n.* **1.** The act or process of gathering a crop. **2.a.** The crop that ripens or is gathered in a season. **b.** The amount or measure of the crop gathered in a season. **c.** The time or season of such gathering. **3.** The result or consequence of an activity. — *v.* **-vest•ed, -vest•ing, -vests.** — *tr.* **1.** To gather (a crop). **2.** To gather a crop from. **3.** To receive (the benefits or consequences of an action). — *intr.* To gather a crop. [ME < OE *hærfest.* See **kerp-***.]
har•vest•er (här′vĭ-stər) *n.* **1.** One who gathers a crop. **2.** A machine for harvesting crops; a reaper.
harvest fly *n.* Any of several cicadas of the genus *Tibicen.*
harvest home *n.* **1.** The completion of a harvest. **2.a.** The time of completing a harvest. **b.** A festival held at this time. **c.** A song sung at this time.
har•vest•man (här′vĭst-mən) *n.* **1.** A man who harvests. **2.** See **daddy longlegs** 1.
harvest mite *n.* See **chigger** 1.
harvest moon *n.* The full moon that occurs nearest the autumnal equinox.
Har•vey (här′vē). A city of NE IL, a suburb of Chicago. Pop. 29,771.
Harvey, William. 1578–1657. English physician and anatomist who discovered human blood circulation (1628).
Harz Mountains (härts). A mountain range of central Germany extending c. 97 km (60 mi) between the Weser and the Elbe and rising to 1,142.8 m (3,747 ft).
has (hăz) *v.* Third pers. sing. pr.t. of **have.**
has-been (hăz′bĭn′) *n., pl.* **has-beens.** *Informal.* One that is no longer famous, popular, successful, or useful.
Has•dru•bal (hăz′drōō′bəl, hăz-drōō′-). d. 207 B.C. Carthaginian general who was defeated by Roman forces (207) during the Second Punic War.
ha•sen•pfef•fer (hä′zən-fĕf′ər, -sən-) *n.* A highly seasoned stew of marinated rabbit meat. [Ger. : *Hase*, rabbit (< MHGer. < OHGer. *haso*; see **kas-***) + *Pfeffer*, pepper (< OHGer. *pfeffar* < Lat. *piper*; see PEPPER).]
hash[1] (hăsh) *n.* **1.** A dish of chopped meat, potatoes, and sometimes vegetables, usu. browned. **2.a.** A jumble; a hodgepodge. **b.** *Informal.* A mess. **3.** A reworking or restatement of familiar material. — *tr.v.* **hashed, hash•ing, hash•es. 1.** To chop into pieces; mince. **2.** *Informal.* To make a mess of; mangle. **3.** *Informal.* To discuss carefully; review: *hash over plans.* —***idiom.*** **settle (someone's) hash.** *Slang.* To silence or subdue. [Var. of ME *hache* < OFr., p.part. of *hacher, hachier*, to chop up < *hache*, ax, of Gmc. orig. See HATCHET.]
hash[2] (hăsh) *n. Slang.* Hashish.
hash browns (brounz) *pl.n.* Chopped cooked potatoes, fried until brown.
hash house *n. Slang.* A cheap restaurant.
hash•ish (hăsh′ēsh′, -ĭsh, hă-shēsh′, hä-) also **hash•eesh** (hăsh′ēsh′, hă-shēsh′, hä-) *n.* A purified resin prepared from the female cannabis plant and smoked or chewed as a narcotic or an intoxicant. [Ar. *ḥašīš*, hemp, dried grass.]
hash mark *n.* **1.** A service stripe on the sleeve of an enlisted person's uniform. **2.** *Football.* A mark in either of two series placed on the field perpendicular to the yard lines and used for spotting the ball. [Alteration of HATCH[3].]
hash slinger *n. Slang.* One who provides food in a cheap restaurant.
Ha•sid or **Has•sid** also **Chas•sid** (KHä′sĭd, KHô-, hä-) *n., pl.* **Ha•si•dim** or **Has•si•dim** also **Chas•si•dim** (KHä-sē′dĭm, KHô-, hä-). *Judaism.* A member of a movement of popular mysticism founded in eastern Europe in the 18th century. [< Heb. *ḥāsîd*, pious.] —**Ha•si′dic** *adj.* —**Ha•si′dism** *n.*
has•let (hăs′lĭt, hāz′-) also **hars•let** (här′slĭt) *n.* The edible viscera of an animal, esp. hog viscera. [ME *hastelet* < OFr., dim. of *haste*, roast meat, spit, perh. < Lat. *hasta*, spear, or of Gmc. orig.]
has•n't (hăz′ənt). Has not.
hasp (hăsp) *n.* A metal fastener with a hinged slotted part that fits over a staple and is secured by a pin, bolt, or padlock. — *tr.v.* **hasped, hasp•ing, hasps.** To close or lock with a hasp. [ME < OE *hæsp, hæpse.*]
Has•sam (hăs′əm), **(Frederick) Childe.** 1859–1935. Amer. painter whose works include *Rainy Day in Boston* (1885).
Has•sel (hä′səl), **Odd.** 1897–1981. Norwegian chemist who shared a 1969 Nobel Prize.
has•sle (hăs′əl) *Informal.* — *n.* **1.** An argument or a fight. **2.** Trouble; bother. — *v.* **-sled, -sling, -sles.** — *intr.* To argue or fight. — *tr.* To bother or harass. [?]
has•sock (hăs′ək) *n.* **1.** A thick cushion used as a footstool or for kneeling. **2.** A dense clump of grass. [ME *hassok*, clump of grass < OE *hassuc.*]
hast (hăst) *v. Archaic.* Second pers. sing. pr.t. of **have.**
has•tate (hăs′tāt′) *adj. Bot.* Having the shape of an arrowhead but with the basal lobes pointing outward at right angles. [< Lat. *hasta*, spear.] —**has′tate′ly** *adv.*
haste (hāst) *n.* **1.** Rapidity of action or motion. **2.** Overeagerness to act. **3.** Rash or headlong action; precipitateness. — *intr. & tr.v.* **hast•ed, hast•ing, hastes.** To hasten or cause to hasten. —***idiom.*** **make haste.** To move or act swiftly; hurry. [ME < OFr., of Gmc. orig.]
Syns: *haste, celerity, dispatch, expedition, hurry, speed.* The central meaning shared by these nouns is "rapidity or promptness of movement or activity": *left in haste; a legal system known for celerity; advanced with all possible dispatch; cleaned up with remarkable expedition; worked without hurry; driving with excessive speed.* ***Ant:*** *deliberation.*
has•ten (hā′sən) *v.* **-tened, -ten•ing, -tens.** — *intr.* To move or act swiftly. — *tr.* **1.** To cause to hurry. **2.** To speed up; accelerate: *fanned the paint to hasten drying.*
Has•tings (hā′stĭngz). **1.** A borough of SE England on the English Channel at the entrance to the Strait of Dover; near the site of William the Conqueror's victory over the Saxons (Oct. 14, 1066). Pop. 75,900. **2.** A city of S NE S of Grand I. Pop. 22,837.
Hastings, Warren. 1732–1818. British colonial administrator who served as governor-general of India (1773–85).
hast•y (hā′stē) *adj.* **-i•er, -i•est. 1.** Characterized by speed; rapid. See Syns at **fast**[1]. **2.** Done or made too quickly to be accurate or wise; rash. **3.** Easily angered; irritable. —**hast′i•ly** *adv.* —**hast′i•ness** *n.*
hasty pudding *n.* **1.** Cornmeal mush served with maple syrup, brown sugar, or other sweetening. **2.** *Chiefly British.* A mush made with flour or oatmeal.
hat (hăt) *n.* **1.** A covering for the head, esp. one with a shaped crown and brim. **2.a.** A head covering of distinctive color and shape worn as a symbol of office. **b.** The office symbolized by the wearing of such a head covering. **3.** A role or an office

William Henry Harrison

hartebeest
Hunter's hartebeest
Damaliscus hunteri

ă pat	oi boy
ā pay	ou out
âr care	ŏŏ took
ä father	ōō boot
ĕ pet	ŭ cut
ē be	ûr urge
ĭ pit	th thin
ī pie	*th* this
îr pier	hw which
ŏ pot	zh vision
ō toe	ə about,
ô paw	item

Stress marks:
′ (primary);
′ (secondary), as in
dictionary (dĭk′shə-nĕr′ē)

Hayne (hān), **Robert Young.** 1791–1839. Amer. politician who as U.S. senator from SC (1823–32) engaged Daniel Webster in a debate on federal power vs. states' rights (1830).

hay•rack (hā′răk′) *n.* **1.** A rack from which livestock feed. **2.a.** A rack fitted to a wagon for carrying hay. **b.** A wagon fitted with such a rack.

hay•rick (hā′rĭk′) *n.* See **haystack.**

hay•ride (hā′rīd′) *n.* A ride taken for amusement usu. by people in a wagon or other vehicle piled with hay or straw.

Hay River. A river of NW Canada rising in NE British Columbia and flowing c. 853 km (530 mi) across NW Alberta to Great Slave Lake in S Northwest Terrs.

Hays (hāz). A city of central KS W of Salina; founded near the site of Fort Hays (estab. 1865). Pop. 17,767.

hay•seed (hā′sēd′) *n.* **1.** Grass seed shaken out of hay. **2.** Pieces of chaff or straw that fall from hay. **3.** *Slang.* A bumpkin.

hay•stack (hā′stăk′) *n.* A large stack of hay for winter storage in the open.

Hay•ward (hā′wərd). A city of W CA SE of Oakland. Pop. 111,498.

hay•wire (hā′wīr′) *n.* Wire used in baling hay. —*adj. Informal.* **1.** Mentally confused or erratic; crazy. **2.** Not functioning properly; broken. [Adj. < the use of baling wire for makeshift repairs.]

Hay•wood (hā′wo͝od′), **William Dudley.** "Big Bill Haywood." 1869–1928. Amer. labor leader who helped found the Industrial Workers of the World (1905).

haz•ard (hăz′ərd) *n.* **1.** A chance; an accident. **2.** A chance of being injured or harmed; danger. **3.** A possible source of danger. **4.** *Games.* A dice game similar to craps. **5.** *Sports.* An obstacle found on a golf course. —*tr.v.* **-ard•ed, -ard•ing, -ards. 1.** To expose to danger or harm. See Syns at **endanger. 2.** To venture (something); dare. [ME *hasard,* dice game < OFr., poss. < OSp. *azar,* poss. < Ar. *az-zahr,* gaming die.]

haz•ard•ous (hăz′ər-dəs) *adj.* **1.** Marked by danger; perilous. **2.** Depending on chance; risky. —**haz′ard•ous•ly** *adv.* —**haz′ard•ous•ness** *n.*

hazardous waste *n.* A substance, such as nuclear waste, that is potentially damaging to the environment and harmful to the health of humans and other living organisms.

haze[1] (hāz) *n.* **1.a.** Atmospheric moisture, dust, smoke, and vapor that diminishes visibility. **b.** A partially opaque covering. **2.** A vague or confused state of mind. —*intr.v.* **hazed, haz•ing, haz•es.** To become misty or hazy; blur.

haze[2] (hāz) *tr.v.* **hazed, haz•ing, haz•es. 1.** To persecute or harass with meaningless, difficult, or humiliating tasks. **2.** To initiate, as into a college fraternity, by exacting humiliating performances from or playing rough practical jokes upon. [Perh. < obsolete *haze,* to frighten < obsolete Fr. *haser,* to annoy < OFr.] —**haz′er** *n.*

ha•zel (hā′zəl) *n.* **1.** Any of various shrubs or small trees of the genus *Corylus,* esp. the European species *C. avellana* or the American species *C. americana,* bearing edible nuts. **2.** A hazelnut. **3.** *Color.* A light brown or yellowish brown. [ME *hasel* < OE *hæsel.*] —**ha′zel** *adj.*

ha•zel•nut (hā′zəl-nŭt′) *n.* The edible nut of a hazel, having a hard smooth brown shell.

Ha•zel Park (hā′zəl). A city of SE MI, a suburb of Detroit. Pop. 20,051.

Haz•let (hăz′lĭt). A community of E-central NJ ESE of New Brunswick. Pop. 23,013.

Ha•zle•ton (hā′zəl-tən). A city of E-central PA S of Wilkes-Barre. Pop. 24,730.

Haz•litt (hăz′lĭt, hāz′-), **William.** 1778–1830. British essayist whose works include *The Spirit of the Age* (1825).

haz•y (hā′zē) *adj.* **-i•er, -i•est. 1.** Marked by the presence of haze; misty: *hazy sunshine.* **2.** Not clearly defined; unclear or vague. [?] —**haz′i•ly** *adv.* —**haz′i•ness** *n.*

haz•zan (KHä′zən) *n.* Var. of **chazan.**

hb or **hb.** *abbr. Sports.* Halfback.

Hb *abbr.* Hemoglobin.

H-bomb (āch′bŏm′) *n.* A hydrogen bomb.

h.c. *abbr. Lat.* Honoris causa (by reason of honor).

H.C. *abbr.* **1.** Holy Communion. **2.** House of Commons.

H.C.F. also **h.c.f.** or **hcf** *abbr. Math.* Highest common factor.

HCG *abbr.* Human chorionic gonadotropin.

hd. *abbr.* Head.

hdbk. *abbr.* Handbook.

hdkf. *abbr.* Handkerchief.

HDL *abbr.* High-density lipoprotein.

hdqrs. *abbr.* Headquarters.

HDTV *abbr.* High-definition television.

hdwe. *abbr.* Hardware.

he[1] (hē) *pron.* **1.a.** Used to refer to the man or boy previously mentioned or implied. **b.** Used to refer to a male animal. **2.** *Usage Problem.* Used to refer to a person whose gender is unspecified or unknown: *"He who desires but acts not, breeds pestilence"* (William Blake). —*n.* A male person or animal: *Is the cat a he?* [ME < OE *hē.* See **ko-*.**]

Usage Note: Traditionally, English speakers have used the pronouns *he, him,* and *his* generically in contexts in which the grammatical form of the antecedent requires a singular pronoun, as in *Every member of Congress is answerable to* his *constituents.* Beginning early in the 20th century, however, the traditional usage has come under increasing criticism for reflecting and perpetuating gender discrimination. There is something plainly disconcerting, for example, about sentences such as *Each of the stars of* It Happened One Night [i.e., Clark Gable and Claudette Colbert] *won an Academy Award for his performance.* In this case, the use of *his* forces the reader to envision a single male who stands as the representative member of this group. Thus *he* is not really a gender-neutral pronoun; rather, it refers to a male who is to be taken as the representative member of the group referred to by its antecedent. • Many writers sidestep the problem by avoiding the relevant constructions. In place of *Every student handed in* his *assignment,* they write *All the students handed in their assignments.* Even when using the relevant constructions, however, many writers never use masculine pronouns as generics. In a series of sample sentences such as *A patient who doesn't accurately report _____ sexual history to the doctor runs the risk of misdiagnosis,* an average of 46 percent of the Usage Panel chose a coordinate form (*her/his, his or her,* and so on), 3 percent chose the plural pronoun (although the actual frequency of the plural in writing is far higher than this number would suggest), 2 percent chose the feminine pronoun, another 2 percent chose an indefinite or a definite article, and 7 percent gave no response or felt that no pronoun was needed to complete the sentence. • As a substitute for coordinate forms such as *his/her* or *her and his,* third person plural forms, such as *their,* may be the only sensible choice in informal style. But in formal style this option is risky for an individual writer, who may be misconstrued as being careless or ignorant. What is more, this solution ignores a persistent intuition that expressions such as *everyone* and *each student* should in fact be treated as grammatically singular. Writers who are concerned about avoiding both grammatical and social problems are best advised to use coordinate forms such as *his or her.* • Many writers continue to use the masculine pronoun as generic in all cases. For the same series of sample sentences the average percentage of Usage Panel members who consistently completed the sentences with *his* was 37. This course is grammatically unexceptionable, but the writer who follows it must be prepared to incur the displeasure of readers who regard this pattern as a mark of insensitivity or gender discrimination. The entire question is unlikely to be resolved in the near future. See Usage Notes at **any, anyone, each, every, neither, one.**

he[2] (hā) *n.* The fifth letter of the Hebrew alphabet. [Heb. *hē.*]

He The symbol for the element **helium.**

HE *abbr.* High explosive.

H.E. *abbr.* **1.** His Eminence. **2.** Her, or His, Excellency.

head (hĕd) *n.* **1.a.** The uppermost or forwardmost part of the body of a vertebrate, containing the brain and the eyes, ears, nose, mouth, and jaws. **b.** The analogous part of an invertebrate organism. **c.** The length or height of such a part. **2.** The seat of the faculty of reason; intelligence, intellect, or mind. **3.** Mental ability or aptitude. **4.** Freedom of choice or action. **5.** *Slang.* **a.** A habitual drug user. **b.** An enthusiast. **6.** A portrait or representation of a person's head. **7.** The side of a coin having the principal design and the date. Often used in the plural with a singular verb. **8.** *Informal.* A headache. **9.a.** An individual; a person. **b.** *pl.* **head.** A single animal: *20 head of cattle.* **10.a.** A person who leads, rules, or is in charge. **b.** A headmaster or headmistress. **11.** The foremost or leading position. **12.** A headwaiter. **13.a.** The difference in depth of a liquid at two given points. **b.** The measure of pressure at the lower point expressed in terms of this difference. **c.** The pressure exerted by a liquid or gas. **d.** The liquid or gas exerting the pressure. **14.** The froth or foam that rises to the top in pouring an effervescent liquid, such as beer. **15.** The tip of an abscess, a boil, or a pimple, in which pus forms. **16.** A turning point; a crisis. **17.a.** A projection, weight, or fixture at the end of an elongated object: *the head of a pin.* **b.** *Anat.* The proximal end of a long bone. **c.** The working end of a tool or an implement. **d.** The part of an explosive device that carries the explosive; a warhead. **18.a.** An attachment to or part of a machine that holds or contains the operative device. **b.** The magnetic head of a tape recorder. **19.** A rounded compact mass, as of leaves or buds. **20.** *Bot.* A flower head. **21.** The uppermost part; the top. **22.** The end considered the most important: *the head of the table.* **23.** Either end of an object, such as a drum, whose two ends are interchangeable. **24.** *Naut.* **a.** The forward part of a vessel. **b.** The top part or upper edge of a sail. **25.** A toilet, esp. on a ship. **26.** A passage or gallery in a coal mine. **27.** *Print.* **a.** The top of a book or of a page. **b.** A headline or heading. **c.** A distinct topic or category. **28.** Headway; progress. **29.** *Ling.* The word in a construction that has the same grammatical function as the construction as a whole and that determines relationships of concord to other parts of the construction or sentence in which the construction occurs. —*adj.* **1.** Of, relating to, or intended for the head. Often used in combination: *headwrap.* **2.** Foremost in rank or importance. **3.** Placed at the top or the

headdress
Top: Chinese
Bottom: Native American

front. **4.** *Slang.* Of, relating to, or for drugs or drug users. —*v.* **head•ed, head•ing, heads.** —*tr.* **1.** To be in charge of; lead. **2.** To be in the first or foremost position of. **3.** To aim, point, or turn in a certain direction. **4.** To remove the head or top of. **5.** *Sports.* To hit (a soccer ball) in the air with one's head. **6.** To provide with a head: *head each column with a number.* —*intr.* **1.** To proceed or go in a certain direction. **2.** To form a head, as lettuce or cabbage. **3.** To originate, as a stream or river; rise. —***phrasal verb.*** **head off.** To block the progress or completion of; intercept. —***idioms.*** **head and shoulders above.** Far superior to. **head over heels. 1.** Rolling, as in a somersault. **2.** Completely; hopelessly. **keep (one's) head.** To remain calm; remain in control of oneself. **lose (one's) head.** To lose one's poise or self-control. **off (or out of) (one's) head.** Insane; crazy. **put heads together.** To consult and plan together. [ME < OE *hēafod.* See **kaput-*.**]

head•ache (hĕd′āk′) *n.* **1.** A pain in the head. **2.** *Informal.* Something that causes annoyance or trouble.

head•band (hĕd′bănd′) *n.* **1.** A band worn around the head. **2.** *Print.* An ornamental strip at the top of a page or beginning of a chapter or paragraph. **3.** *Print.* A cloth band attached to the top of the spine of a book.

head•board (hĕd′bôrd′, -bōrd′) *n.* A board or panel that forms the head, as of a bed.

head•cheese (hĕd′chēz′) *n.* A jellied loaf or sausage made from chopped and boiled parts of the feet, head, and sometimes the tongue and heart of an animal, usu. a hog.

head cold *n.* A common cold mainly affecting the mucous membranes of the nasal passages, characterized by congestion, headache, and sneezing.

head•dress (hĕd′drĕs′) *n.* **1.** A covering or an ornament for the head. **2.** A hairdo; a coiffure.

head•ed (hĕd′ĭd) *adj.* **1.** Growing or grown into a head. **2.** Having a head or heading. **3.** Having a specified kind or number of heads. Often used in combination: *three-headed Cerberus.* **4.** Having a mentality of a certain type. Often used in combination: *a cool-headed pilot.*

head•er (hĕd′ər) *n.* **1.** One that fits a head on an object. **2.** One that removes a head from an object, esp. a machine that reaps and gathers the heads of grain. **3.** A pipe that connects two or more smaller pipes. **4.** A beam that crosses and supports the ends of joists, studs, or rafters. **5.** A brick laid across rather than parallel with a wall. **6.** *Informal.* A headlong dive or fall. **7.** *Sports.* A pass or shot made in soccer by heading the ball. **8.** *Comp. Sci.* Printed matter or information at the top margin of a page and usu. repeated throughout a document. **9.** A raised tank or hopper that maintains a constant pressure or supply to a system, esp. the small tank that supplies water to a central heating system.

head•first (hĕd′fûrst′) also **head•fore•most** (-fôr′mōst′, -məst, -fōr′-) *adv.* **1.** With the head leading; headlong. **2.** Impetuously; brashly. —**head′first′** *adj.*

head•ful (hĕd′fo͝ol′) *n. Informal.* **1.** A relatively great amount of knowledge. **2.** Something that covers one's head.

head gate *n.* **1.** A control gate upstream of a lock or canal. **2.** A floodgate that controls the flow of water, as in a ditch.

head•gear (hĕd′gîr′) *n.* **1.** A covering for the head. **2.** The part of a harness that fits about a horse's head. **3.** The rigging for hauling or lifting located at the head of a mine shaft.

head•hunt•ing (hĕd′hŭn′tĭng) *n.* **1.** The custom of cutting off and preserving the heads of enemies as trophies. **2.** *Slang.* The process of attempting to remove influence and power from enemies, esp. political enemies. **3.** *Slang.* The business of recruiting personnel, esp. executive personnel, as for a corporation. —**head′hunt′** *v. & n.* —**head′hunt′er** *n.*

head•ing (hĕd′ĭng) *n.* **1.** The title, subtitle, or topic that stands at the top or beginning, as of a paragraph, letter, or chapter. **2.** The course or direction of a ship or an aircraft. **3.a.** A gallery or drift in a mine. **b.** The end of a gallery or drift.

head•lamp (hĕd′lămp′) *n.* See **headlight** 1.

head•land (hĕd′lənd, -lănd′) *n.* **1.** A point of land, usu. high, extending out into a body of water; a promontory. **2.** The unplowed land at the end of a plowed furrow.

head•less (hĕd′lĭs) *adj.* **1.a.** Formed without a head. **b.** Decapitated. **2.** Lacking a leader or director. **3.** Lacking intelligence and prudence; stupid or foolish. —**head′less•ness** *n.*

head•light (hĕd′līt′) *n.* **1.** A light with a reflector and lens mounted on the front of a vehicle. **2.** A lamp mounted on a miner's or spelunker's hard hat.

head•line (hĕd′līn′) *n.* **1.** The title or caption of a newspaper article, usu. set in large type. **2.** An important or sensational piece of news. Often used in the plural. **3.** A line at the head of a page or passage giving information such as the title, author, and page number. —*tr.v.* **-lined, -lin•ing, -lines. 1.** To supply (a page or passage) with a headline. **2.a.** To present or promote as a headliner. **b.** To serve as the headliner of.

head•lin•er (hĕd′lī′nər) *n.* A performer who receives prominent billing; a star.

head•lock (hĕd′lŏk′) *n. Sports.* A hold in which one wrestler encircles the other's head and locks it with the arm and body.

head•long (hĕd′lông′, -lŏng′) *adv.* **1.** With the head leading; headfirst. **2.** In an impetuous manner; rashly. **3.** At breakneck speed or with uncontrolled force. —*adj.* (hĕd′lông′, -lŏng′). **1.** Done with the head leading; headfirst. **2.** Impetuous; rash. **3.** Uncontrollably forceful or fast. **4.** *Archaic.* Steep; sheer. [< ME *(bi) hedlong* < *hed,* head. See HEAD.]

head•man (hĕd′mən, -măn′) *n.* **1.** The leader or chief man of a primitive small village or community. **2.** A headsman.

head•mas•ter also **head master** (hĕd′măs′tər) *n.* A man who is the principal of a school, usu. a private school.

head•mis•tress also **head mistress** (hĕd′mĭs′trĭs) *n.* A woman who is the principal of a school, usu. a private school.

head•most (hĕd′mōst′, -məst) *adj.* Leading; foremost.

head-on (hĕd′ŏn′, -ôn′) *adv.* **1.** With the head or front first. **2.** In open conflict; in direct opposition. —*adj.* **1.** Facing forward; frontal. **2.** With the front end foremost.

head•phone (hĕd′fōn′) *n.* A receiver, as for a telephone, radio, or stereo, held to the ear by a headband.

head•piece (hĕd′pēs′) *n.* **1.** A protective covering for the head. **2.** A set of headphones; a headset. **3.** See **headstall. 4.** An ornamental design, esp. at the top of a page. **5.** The seat of intelligence; brains.

head pin *n. Sports.* See **kingpin** 1.

head•quar•ter (hĕd′kwôr′tər) *v.* **-tered, -ter•ing, -ters.** —*tr.* To provide with headquarters. —*intr.* To establish headquarters.

Usage Note: The verb *headquarter* occurs in both transitive and intransitive senses: *The magazine has headquartered him* (or *He headquarters*) *in a building that houses many foreign journalists.* Although ample citational evidence exists for these usages, writers who wish to avoid criticism should consider the use of alternative expressions, for example: *The magazine has just assigned him to* (or *has stationed him in*) *Europe. He will make his headquarters in Paris.*

head•quar•ters (hĕd′kwôr′tərz) *pl.n. (used with a sing. or pl. v.)* **1.** The offices of a commander, as of a military unit, from which orders are issued. **2.** A center of operations or administration. See Syns at **center.**

Usage Note: The noun *headquarters* is used with either a singular or a plural verb. The plural is more common: *The headquarters are in Boston.* But the singular is sometimes preferred when reference is to authority rather than to physical location: *Battalion headquarters has approved the retreat.*

head•race (hĕd′rās′) *n.* A watercourse that feeds water into a mill, water wheel, or turbine.

head•rest (hĕd′rĕst′) *n.* **1.** A support for the head, as at the back of a chair. **2.** A cushion attached to the top of the back of an automotive vehicle's seat, esp. to prevent whiplash.

head•room (hĕd′ro͞om′, -ro͝om′) *n.* **1.** Space above one's head; clearance. **2.** *Electron.* Dynamic headroom.

head•sail (hĕd′səl, -sāl′) *n. Naut.* A sail, such as a jib, set forward of a foremast.

head•set (hĕd′sĕt′) *n.* **1.** A pair of headphones. **2.** A pair of headphones with a voice transmitter attached.

head•ship (hĕd′shĭp′) *n.* **1.** The position or office of a head or leader; primacy or command. **2.** *Chiefly British.* The position of a headmaster or headmistress.

head shrinker *n.* **1.** A headhunter who shrinks the heads of victims. **2.** *Slang.* A psychiatrist, esp. a psychoanalyst.

heads•man (hĕdz′mən) *n.* A public executioner who beheads condemned prisoners.

head•spring (hĕd′sprĭng′) *n.* A fountainhead; a source.

head•stall (hĕd′stôl′) *n.* The section of a bridle that fits over a horse's head.

head•stand (hĕd′stănd′) *n.* A position in which one supports oneself vertically on one's head with one's hands.

head start *n.* **1.** *Sports.* A start before other contestants in a race. **2.** An early start that confers an advantage.

head•stock (hĕd′stŏk′) *n.* A nonmoving part of a machine or tool that supports a revolving part, as the spindle of a lathe.

head•stone (hĕd′stōn′) *n.* **1.** A memorial stone set at the head of a grave. **2.** Also **head stone.** *Archit.* See **keystone** 1.

head•strong (hĕd′strông′, -strŏng′) *adj.* **1.** Stubbornly and often recklessly willful. See Syns at **obstinate, unruly. 2.** Resulting from willfulness and obstinacy.

heads up (hĕdz) *interj.* Used as a warning to watch out for a potential source of danger, as at a construction site.

heads-up (hĕdz′ŭp′) *adj.* Showing an alert competent style.

head-to-head (hĕd′tə-hĕd′) *adv. & adj.* **1.** In direct confrontation or conflict at close quarters. **2.** Arranged in lines running in opposite directions. **3.** Running close together in the same direction; neck and neck.

head•wait•er (hĕd′wā′tər) *n.* The supervisor of the waiters and waitresses in a restaurant, often responsible for taking reservations and seating guests.

head wall *n.* A steep slope or precipice rising at the head of a valley or glacial cirque.

head•wa•ter (hĕd′wô′tər, -wŏt′ər) *n.* The water from which a river rises; a source. Often used in the plural.

head•way (hĕd′wā′) *n.* **1.** Forward movement or the rate of forward movement, esp. of a ship. **2.** Progress toward a goal. **3.** The clear vertical space beneath a ceiling or archway; clearance. **4.** The distance in time or space that separates two vehicles traveling the same route.

headset

headstand

ă pat	oi boy
ā pay	ou out
âr care	o͝o took
ä father	o͞o boot
ĕ pet	ŭ cut
ē be	ûr urge
ĭ pit	th thin
ī pie	*th* this
îr pier	hw which
ŏ pot	zh vision
ō toe	ə about, item
ô paw	

Stress marks:
′ (primary);
′ (secondary), as in
dictionary (dĭk′shə-nĕr′ē)

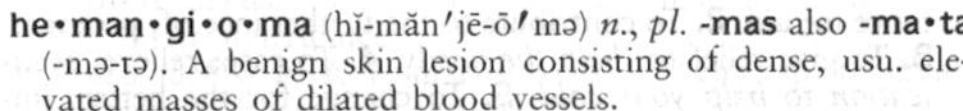

Ernest Hemingway

he•man•gi•o•ma (hĭ-măn′jē-ō′mə) *n.*, *pl.* **-mas** also **-ma•ta** (-mə-tə). A benign skin lesion consisting of dense, usu. elevated masses of dilated blood vessels.

he•ma•te•in (hē′mə-tē′ĭn, hē′mə-tēn′) *n.* A reddish-brown crystalline compound, $C_{16}H_{12}O_6$, used as an indicator and a biological stain.

he•mat•ic (hĭ-măt′ĭk) *adj.* Of, relating to, resembling, containing, or acting on blood. —*n. Medic.* A hematinic. [Gk. *haimatikos* < *haima*, blood.]

he•ma•tin (hē′mə-tĭn) *n.* A blue to blackish-brown compound, $C_{34}H_{32}N_4O_4{\cdot}FeOH$, formed in the decomposition of hemoglobin.

he•ma•tin•ic (hē′mə-tĭn′ĭk) *adj.* **1.** Acting to increase the amount of hemoglobin in the blood. **2.** Of, relating to, or derived from hematin. —*n.* A hematinic drug.

he•ma•tite (hē′mə-tīt′) *n.* A black or blackish-red to brick-red mineral, Fe_2O_3, the chief ore of iron. [ME *emathite*, *ematites* < Lat. *haematītēs* < Gk. *(lithos) haimatitēs*, bloodlike (stone) < *haima*, *haimat-*, blood.]

hemato– or **hemat–** also **haemat–** or **haemato–** *pref.* Blood: *hematology.* [Gk. *haimato-* < *haima*, *haimat-*, blood.]

he•ma•to•blast (hē′mə-tə-blăst′, hĭ-măt′ə-) *n.* An immature blood cell. —**he′ma•to•blas′tic** *adj.*

he•mat•o•crit (hĭ-măt′ə-krĭt′) *n.* **1.** The percentage by volume of packed red blood cells in a given sample of blood after centrifugation. **2.** A centrifuge used to determine the volume of blood cells and plasma in a given sample of blood. [HEMATO– + Gk. *kritēs*, judge (< *krinein*, to judge; see **krei-***).]

he•ma•tog•e•nous (hē′mə-tŏj′ə-nəs) *adj.* **1.** Producing blood. **2.** Originating in or spread by the blood.

he•ma•tol•o•gy (hē′mə-tŏl′ə-jē) *n.* The science encompassing the medical study of the blood and blood-producing organs. —**he′ma•to•log′ic** (-tə-lŏj′ĭk), **he′ma•to•log′i•cal** *adj.* —**he′ma•to•log′i•cal•ly** *adv.* —**he′ma•tol′o•gist** *n.*

he•ma•to•ma (hē′mə-tō′mə) *n.*, *pl.* **-mas** or **-ma•ta** (-mə-tə). A localized swelling filled with blood resulting from a break in a blood vessel.

he•ma•to•poi•e•sis (hē′mə-tō-poi-ē′sĭs, hĭ-măt′ə-) also **he•mo•poi•e•sis** (hē′mə-poi-ē′-sĭs) *n.* Formation of blood or blood cells in the body. —**he′ma•to•poi•et′ic** (-ĕt′ĭk) *adj.*

he•ma•tox•y•lin (hē′mə-tŏk′sə-lĭn) *n.* A yellow or red crystalline compound, $C_{16}H_{14}O_6{\cdot}3H_2O$, that is used in dyes, inks, and stains. [NLat. *Haematoxylon*, a genus of plants (Gk. *haimato-*, hemato- + XYL–) + –IN.]

he•ma•to•zo•on (hē′mə-tō-zō′ŏn′, hĭ-măt′ə-) *n.*, *pl.* **-zo•a** (-zō′ə). A parasitic protozoan or similar organism found in blood. —**he′ma•to•zo′al**, **he′ma•to•zo′ic** *adj.*

he•ma•tu•ri•a (hē′mə-to͝or′ē-ə, -tyo͝or′-) *n.* The presence of blood in the urine. —**he′ma•tu′ric** *adj.*

heme (hēm) *n.* The deep red nonprotein ferrous component of hemoglobin, $C_{34}H_{32}FeN_4O_4$. [Short for HEMATIN.]

he•mel•y•tron (hĕ-mĕl′ĭ-trŏn′) *n.*, *pl.* **-tra** (-trə). One of the forewings of a hemipterous insect, having a thick membranous apex. [HEM(I)– + ELYTRON.]

hem•er•a•lo•pi•a (hĕm′ər-ə-lō′pē-ə) *n.* A visual defect characterized by the inability to see as clearly in bright light as in dim. [NLat. < Gk. *hēmeralōps*, suffering from hemeralopia : *hēmera*, day + *alaos*, blind + *ōps*, eye; see NYCTALOPIA.] —**hem′er•a•lop′ic** (-lŏp′ĭk) *adj.*

hem•er•o•cal•lis (hĕm′ər-ə-kăl′ĭs) *n.* See **day lily.** [NLat. < Gk. *hēmerokalles*, a lily : *hēmera*, day + *kallos*, beauty.]

Hem•et (hĕm′ĭt). A city of S CA E of Santa Ana. Pop. 36,094.

hemi– *pref.* **1.** Half: *hemihedral.* **2.** Partial; partially: *hemiparasite.* [Gk. *hēmi-*. See **sēmi-***.]

–hemia *suff.* Var. of **–emia.**

hem•i•al•gi•a (hĕm′ē-ăl′jē-ə, -jə) *n.* Pain affecting one half of the body.

he•mic (hē′mĭk) *adj.* Of or relating to the blood.

hem•i•cel•lu•lose (hĕm′ĭ-sĕl′yə-lōs′, -lōz′) *n.* Any of several polysaccharides more complex than a sugar and less complex than cellulose, found in plant cell walls.

hem•i•chor•date (hĕm′ĭ-kôr′dāt′, -dĭt) *n.* Any of various wormlike marine animals of the phylum Hemichordata, having a primitive notochord. —**hem′i•chor′date′** *adj.*

hem•i•cy•cle (hĕm′ĭ-sī′kəl) *n.* **1.** A semicircle. **2.** A semicircular structure or arrangement. [Fr. *hémicycle* < Lat. *hēmicyclium* < Gk. *hēmikuklion* : *hēmi-*, hemi- + *kuklion*, neut. of *kuklios*, circular (< *kuklos*, circle; see CYCLE).]

hem•i•dem•i•sem•i•qua•ver (hĕm′ē-dĕm′ē-sĕm′ē-kwā′-vər) *n. Chiefly British.* A sixty-fourth note.

hem•i•he•dral (hĕm′ĭ-hē′drəl) *adj.* Exhibiting only half the faces required for complete symmetry. Used of a crystal.

hem•i•hy•drate (hĕm′ĭ-hī′drāt′) *n.* A hydrate in which the molecular ratio of water molecules to anhydrous compound is 1:2. —**hem′i•hy′drat′ed** *adj.*

hem•i•me•tab•o•lous (hĕm′ē-mə-tăb′ə-ləs) also **hem•i•met•a•bol•ic** (-mĕt′ə-bŏl′ĭk) *adj.* Undergoing a metamorphosis that lacks a pupal stage. Used of certain insects. —**hem′i•me•tab′o•lism** (-ə-lĭz′əm) *n.*

hem•i•mor•phic (hĕm′ĭ-môr′fĭk) *adj.* Asymmetrical at the axial ends. Used of a crystal.

hemlock
Eastern hemlock
Tsuga canadensis

hem•i•mor•phite (hĕm′ĭ-môr′fīt′) *n.* A usu. white or colorless mineral, $Zn_4Si_2O_7(OH)_2{\cdot}H_2O$, an important ore of zinc.

he•min (hē′mĭn) *n.* The crystalline chloride of heme, $C_{34}H_{32}N_4O_4FeCl$, produced when hemoglobin reacts with glacial acetic acid and sodium chloride in a test for the presence of blood.

Hem•ing•way (hĕm′ĭng-wā′), **Ernest Miller.** 1899–1961. Amer. writer whose works include *For Whom the Bell Tolls* (1940). He won the 1954 Nobel Prize for literature.

hem•i•par•a•site (hĕm′ĭ-păr′ə-sīt′) *n.* **1.** A plant, such as mistletoe, that obtains nourishment from its host but also photosynthesizes. **2.** An organism that can live independently or as a parasite. —**hem′i•par′a•sit′ic** (-sĭt′ĭk) *adj.*

hem•i•ple•gia (hĕm′ĭ-plē′jə, -jē-ə) *n.* Complete paralysis in only one side of the body. —**hem′i•ple′gic** *adj. & n.*

he•mip•ter•an (hĭ-mĭp′tər-ən) *adj.* Hemipterous. —*n.* also **he•mip•ter•on** (-tə-rŏn′). A hemipterous insect; a true bug.

he•mip•ter•ous (hĭ-mĭp′tər-əs) *adj.* Of or belonging to the insect order Hemiptera, including the suborders Heteroptera and Homoptera, marked by piercing or sucking mouthparts and two pairs of wings.

hem•i•sphere (hĕm′ĭ-sfîr′) *n.* **1.a.** A half of a sphere bounded by a great circle. **b.** A half of a symmetrical, approximately spherical object as divided by a plane of symmetry. **2.** Either half of the celestial sphere as divided by the ecliptic, the celestial equator, or the horizon. **3.** Either the northern or southern half of the earth as divided by the equator or the eastern or western half as divided by a meridian. **4.** *Anat.* Either of the lateral halves of the cerebrum; a cerebral hemisphere. —**hem′i•spher′ic** (-sfîr′ĭk, -sfĕr′-), **hem′i•spher′i•cal** *adj.* —**hem′i•spher′i•cal•ly** *adv.*

hem•i•stich (hĕm′ĭ-stĭk′) *n.* **1.** A half line of verse, esp. when separated rhythmically from the rest of the line by a caesura. **2.** An incomplete or imperfect line of verse. [Lat. *hemistichium* < Gk. *hēmistikhion* : *hēmi-*, hemi- + *stikhos*, line; see **steigh-***.]

hem•line (hĕm′līn′) *n.* **1.** The bottom edge of a skirt, dress, or coat. **2.** The height of a hem from the floor.

hem•lock (hĕm′lŏk′) *n.* **1.a.** Any of various coniferous evergreen trees of the genus *Tsuga* of North America and eastern Asia, having small cones and short flat leaves with two white bands underneath. **b.** The wood of such trees. **2.a.** Any of several poisonous plants of the genera *Conium* and *Cicuta*, such as the poison hemlock. **b.** A poison obtained from the poison hemlock. [ME *hemlok*, poisonous hemlock < OE *hymlice*, *hemlic.*]

hemo– or **hema–** or **hem–** also **haemo–** or **haema–** or **haem–** *pref.* Blood: *hemacyte.* [Gk. *haimo-* < *haima.*]

he•mo•chro•ma•to•sis (hē′mə-krō′mə-tō′sĭs) *n.* A hereditary disorder of iron metabolism in which iron accumulates in the body tissues.

he•mo•coel (hē′mə-sēl′) *n.* A cavity or series of spaces between the organs of most arthropods and mollusks through which the blood circulates.

he•mo•cy•a•nin (hē′mō-sī′ə-nĭn) *n.* A bluish copper-containing respiratory pigment similar to hemoglobin, present in the blood of certain mollusks and arthropods.

he•mo•cyte (hē′mə-sīt′) *n.* A cellular component of the blood, esp. of an invertebrate.

he•mo•di•al•y•sis (hē′mō-dī-ăl′ĭ-sĭs) *n.*, *pl.* **-ses** (-sēz′). A procedure for removing metabolic waste products or toxic substances from the bloodstream by dialysis.

he•mo•dy•nam•ics (hē′mə-dī-năm′ĭks) *n.* *(used with a sing. v.)* The study of the forces involved in the circulation of blood. —**he′•mo•dy•nam′•ic** *adj.*

he•mo•flag•el•late (hē′mō-flăj′ə-lāt′, -lĭt, -flə-jĕl′ĭt) *n.* A flagellate protozoan that is parasitic in the blood.

he•mo•glo•bin (hē′mə-glō′bĭn) *n.* The iron-containing respiratory pigment in red blood cells of vertebrates, consisting of about 6 percent heme and 94 percent globin. [Ult. short for *hematinoglobulin* : HEMATIN + GLOBULIN.]

he•mo•glo•bi•nu•ri•a (hē′mə-glō′bə-no͝or′ē-ə, -nyo͝or′-) *n.* The presence of hemoglobin in the urine. —**he′mo•glo′bi•nu′ric** *adj.*

he•mo•lymph (hē′mə-lĭmf′) *n.* The circulatory fluid of certain invertebrates, analogous to lymph in other invertebrates.

he•mo•ly•sin (hē′mə-lī′sĭn, hĭ-mŏl′ĭ-) *n.* An agent or a substance, such as an antibody, that causes hemolysis.

he•mol•y•sis (hĭ-mŏl′ĭ-sĭs, hē′mə-lī′sĭs) *n.* The destruction or dissolution of red blood cells, with subsequent release of hemoglobin. —**he′mo•lyt′ic** (hē′mə-lĭt′ĭk) *adj.* —**he′mo•lyze′** (hē′mə-līz′) *v.*

hemolytic anemia *n.* Anemia resulting from the lysis of red blood cells, as in certain inherited blood disorders.

he•mo•phil•i•a (hē′mə-fĭl′ē-ə, -fēl′yə) *n.* Any of several sex-linked blood-coagulation disorders in which the blood fails to clot normally because of a defective clotting factor.

he•mo•phil•i•ac (hē′mə-fĭl′ē-ăk′, -fē′lē-) *n.* A person, almost exclusively a male, who is affected with hemophilia.

he•mo•phil•ic (hē′mə-fĭl′ĭk) *adj.* **1.** Of, relating to, or affected by hemophilia. **2.** Growing well in blood or in a culture containing blood. Used of certain bacteria.

he•mo•pho•bi•a (hē′mə-fō′bē-ə) *n.* An abnormal fear of blood. — **he′mo•pho′bic** *adj.*

he•mo•poi•e•sis (hē′mə-poi-ē′sĭs) *n.* Var. of **hematopoiesis.**

he•mop•ty•sis (hĭ-mŏp′tĭ-sĭs) *n.* The coughing or spitting up of blood from the respiratory tract. [HEMO- + Gk. *ptusis*, a spitting (< *ptuein*, to spit).]

hem•or•rhage (hĕm′ər-ĭj) *n.* **1.** Excessive discharge of blood from the blood vessels; profuse bleeding. **2.** A copious loss of something valuable: *a hemorrhage of profit.* — *v.* **-rhaged, -rhag•ing, -rhag•es.** — *intr.* **1.** To bleed copiously. **2.** To undergo a rapid and sudden loss. — *tr.* To lose (something valuable) rapidly and in quantity. [Ult. < Gk. *haimorrhagia* : *haimo-*, hemo- + *-rrhagia*, -rrhagia.] — **hem′or•rhag′ic** (hĕm′ə-răj′ĭk) *adj.*

hemorrhagic measles *n. (used with a sing. v.)* See **black measles.**

hem•or•rhoid (hĕm′ə-roid′) *n.* **1.** An itching or painful mass of dilated veins in swollen anal tissue. **2. hemorrhoids.** The pathological condition in which hemorrhoids occur. [Ult. < Gk. *haimorrhoïdes*, pl. of *haimorrhoïs* < *haimorrhoos*, flowing with blood : *haimo-*, hemo- + *rhein*, to flow; see **sreu-***.]

hem•or•rhoi•dal (hĕm′ə-roid′l) *adj.* **1.** Of or relating to hemorrhoids. **2.** *Anat.* Supplying the region of the rectum and anus. Used of certain arteries.

hem•or•rhoid•ec•to•my (hĕm′ə-roi-dĕk′tə-mē) *n., pl.* **-mies.** Surgical removal of hemorrhoids.

he•mo•sid•er•in (hē′mō-sĭd′ər-ĭn) *n.* A protein that stores iron in the body, derived chiefly from the hemoglobin released during hemolysis.

he•mo•sta•sis (hē′mə-stā′sĭs, hē-mŏs′tə-) also **he•mo•sta•sia** (hē′mə-stā′zhə, -zhē-ə, -zē-ə) *n.* **1.** The stoppage of bleeding or hemorrhage. **2.** The stoppage of blood flow through a blood vessel or body part.

he•mo•stat (hē′mə-stăt′) *n.* **1.** An agent that stops bleeding. **2.** A clamplike instrument used to compress a blood vessel to reduce or arrest the flow of blood during surgery.

he•mo•stat•ic (hē′mə-stăt′ĭk) *adj.* Acting to arrest bleeding or hemorrhage. — *n.* A hemostatic device or agent. [HEMO- + Gk. *statikos*, causing to stop; see STATIC.]

hemp (hĕmp) *n.* **1.** Cannabis. **2.** The tough, coarse fiber of the cannabis plant, used to make cordage. **3.a.** Any of various plants similar to cannabis, esp. one yielding a similar fiber. **b.** The fiber of such a plant. [ME < OE *hænep*.]

hemp agrimony *n.* An Old World plant *(Eupatorium cannabinum)* having clusters of reddish-purple flower heads.

hemp•en (hĕm′pən) *adj.* Of, relating to, or resembling hemp.

hemp nettle *n.* Any of various Eurasian plants of the genus *Galeopsis,* having bristly stems and flowers with two lips.

Hemp•stead (hĕmp′stĕd′, -stĭd). A village of SE NY on W Long I. SE of Mineola; settled c. 1643. Pop. 49,453.

hem•stitch (hĕm′stĭch′) *n.* **1.** A decorative stitch usu. bordering a hem, made by drawing out several parallel threads and catching together the cross threads in uniform groups. **2.** Needlework using this stitch. — *tr.v.* **-stitched, -stitch•ing, -stitch•es.** To embroider with hemstitches.

hen (hĕn) *n.* **1.** A female bird, esp. the adult female of the domestic fowl. **2.** The female of certain aquatic animals, such as an octopus. **3.** *Offensive Slang.* A woman, esp. an older woman viewed as fussy. [ME < OE. See **kan-***.] — **hen′nish** *adj.* — **hen′nish•ly** *adv.* — **hen′nish•ness** *n.*

He•nan (hœ′nän′) also **Ho•nan** (hō′-). A province of E-central China. Cap. Zhengzhou. Pop. 77,130,000.

hen-and-chick•ens (hĕn′ən-chĭk′ənz) *n., pl.* **hens-and-chick•ens** (hĕnz′-). Any of several plants having many runners or offshoots, esp. the houseleek.

hen•bane (hĕn′bān′) *n.* A poisonous Eurasian plant *(Hyoscyamus niger)* having an unpleasant odor, sticky leaves, and funnel-shaped flowers and serving as a source of hyoscamine.

hen•bit (hĕn′bĭt′) *n.* A Eurasian plant *(Lamium amplexicaule)* having toothed opposite leaves and small white or purplish-red flowers with two lips. [HEN + BIT[1].]

hence (hĕns) *adv.* **1.a.** For this reason; therefore: *handmade and hence expensive.* **b.** From this source: *They grew up in the Sudan, hence their interest in Nubian art.* **2.** From this time; from now. **3.a.** From this place; away from here: *Get you hence!* **b.** From this life. [ME *hennes*, from here : *henne* (< OE *heonan*; see **ko-***) + *-es*, adverbial suff.; see *-s*[3].]

hence•forth (hĕns′fôrth′) *adv.* From this time forth.

hence•for•ward (hĕns-fôr′wərd) *adv.* Henceforth.

hench•man (hĕnch′mən) *n.* **1.** A loyal and trusted follower or subordinate. **2.** A person who supports a political figure chiefly from selfish interests. **3.** A member of a criminal gang. **4.** *Obsolete.* A page to a person of high rank. [ME *hengsman, henshman*, servant to a person of rank : *hengest*, horse (< OE) + *man*, man; see MAN.]

hen•coop (hĕn′ko͞op′) *n.* A coop or cage for poultry.

hen•dec•a•syl•lab•ic (hĕn-dĕk′ə-sĭ-lăb′ĭk) *adj.* Containing 11 syllables. — *n.* A verse of 11 syllables. [< Lat. *hendecasyllabus*, a line of 11 syllables < Gk. *hendekasullabos* : *hendeka*, eleven (*hen*, neut. of *heis*, one; see **sem-**[1]* + *deka*, ten; see DECADE) + *sullabē*, syllable; see SYLLABLE.] — **hen•dec′a•syl′la•ble** (-sĭl′ə-bəl) *n.*

Hen•der•son (hĕn′dər-sən). **1.** A city of NW KY on the Ohio R. S of Evansville IN; settled in the late 1700's. Pop. 25,945. **2.** A city of SE NV SE of Las Vegas; founded 1942. Pop. 64,942.

Henderson, Arthur. 1863–1935. British politician and president of the World Disarmament Conference (1932–35) who won the 1934 Nobel Peace Prize.

Hen•der•son•ville (hĕn′dər-sən-vĭl′). A city of N TN NE of Nashville. Pop. 32,188.

hen•di•a•dys (hĕn-dī′ə-dĭs) *n.* A figure of speech in which two words joined by a conjunction express a notion normally expressed by an adjective and a substantive, such as *grace and favor* instead of *gracious favor.* [LLat. < Gk. *hen dia duoin*, one by means of two : *hen*, neut. of *heis*, one; see **sem-**[1]* + *dia*, through + *duoin*, genitive of *duō*, two; see **dwo-***.]

Hen•dricks (hĕn′drĭks), **Thomas Andrews.** 1819–85. Vice President of the U.S. (1885); died in office.

Jimi Hendrix

Hen•drix (hĕn′drĭks), **Jimi.** 1942–70. Amer. musician whose innovative electric guitar playing greatly influenced the development of rock music.

hen•e•quen also **hen•e•quin** (hĕn′ĭ-kwĭn) *n.* **1.** A tropical American plant *(Agave fourcroydes)* having large sword-shaped leaves that yield a fiber used in making rope. **2.** This fiber. [Sp. *henequén*, perh. of Arawakan orig.]

Heng•e•lo (hĕng′ə-lō′). A city of E Netherlands near the German border NW of Enschede. Pop. 76,855.

Heng•yang (hŭng′yäng′, hœng′-). A city of SE China SSW of Wuhan. Pop. 350,000.

hen harrier *n.* See **northern harrier.**

Hen•ie (hĕn′ē), **Sonja.** 1912–69. Norwegian-born figure skater who won ten world championships (1927–36).

Hen•ley (hĕn′lē) or **Hen•ley-on-Thames** (-ŏn-tĕmz′, -ôn-). A municipal borough of S-central England W of London; site of an annual rowing regatta (estab. 1839). Pop. 10,976.

hen•na (hĕn′ə) *n.* **1.a.** A tree or shrub *(Lawsonia inermis)* of the Middle East having fragrant white or reddish flowers. **b.** A reddish-orange dyestuff prepared from the leaves of this plant. **2.** *Color.* A moderate or strong reddish brown to strong brown. — *tr.v.* **-naed, -na•ing, -nas.** To dye (hair, for example) with henna. [Ar. *ḥinnā'*.] — **hen′na** *adj.*

hen•ner•y (hĕn′ə-rē) *n., pl.* **-ies. 1.** A poultry farm. **2.** See **hencoop.**

hen•o•the•ism (hĕn′ə-thē-ĭz′əm) *n.* Belief in one god without denying the existence of others. [Gk. *heno-* (< *hen*, neut. of *heis*, one; see **sem-**[1]*) + THE(O)- + -ISM.] — **hen′o•the′ist** *n.* — **hen′o•the•is′tic** *adj.*

hen•peck (hĕn′pĕk′) *tr.v.* **-pecked, -peck•ing, -pecks.** *Informal.* To dominate or nag (one's husband).

Hen•ri (hĕn′rē), **Robert.** 1865–1929. Amer. painter and member of the Ashcan School.

hen•ry (hĕn′rē) *n., pl.* **-ries** or **-rys.** The unit of inductance in which an induced electromotive force of one volt is produced when the current is varied at the rate of one ampere per second. See table at **measurement.** [After Joseph HENRY.]

Hen•ry I (hĕn′rē). "Henry Beauclerc." 1068–1135. King of England (1100–35) who conquered Normandy (1106).

Henry II[1]. 1133–89. King of England (1154–89) who founded the Plantagenet royal line.

Henry II[2]. 1519–59. King of France (1547–59) who regained Calais from the English (1558).

Henry III[1]. 1207–72. King of England (1216–72) whose reign was marred by opposition led by Simon de Montfort.

Henry III[2]. 1551–89. King of France (1574–89) who helped plot the St. Bartholomew's Day Massacre (1572).

Henry IV[1]. 1050–1106. Holy Roman emperor and king of Germany (1056–1106) who vied with Pope Gregory VII.

Henry IV[2]. "Henry Bolingbroke." 1366?–1413. King of England (1399–1413) and founder of the Lancastrian line.

Henry IV[3]. "Henry of Navarre." 1553–1610. King of France (1589–1610) who founded the Bourbon royal line and gave rights to French Protestants in the Edict of Nantes (1598).

Henry VIII

Henry V[1]. 1081–1125. Holy Roman emperor and king of Germany (1106–1125).

Henry V[2]. 1387–1422. King of England (1413–22) who defeated the French at Agincourt (1415).

Henry VI. 1421–71. King of England (1422–61 and 1470–71) who was captured at the Battle of Barnet and murdered in the Tower of London.

Henry VII. "Henry Tudor." 1457–1509. King of England (1485–1509) and founder of the Tudor line.

Henry VIII. 1491–1547. King of England (1509–47) whose divorce from Catherine of Aragon compelled him to break from the Catholic Church by the Act of Supremacy (1534).

Henry, Cape. A promontory of SE VA at the entrance to Chesapeake Bay E of Norfolk.

Henry, Joseph. 1791–1878. Amer. physicist who conducted extensive studies of electromagnetic phenomena.

Henry, O. See William Sydney **Porter.**

Henry, Patrick. 1736–99. Amer. Revolutionary leader and orator who spurred the creation of the Virginia militia with his words "Give me liberty, or give me death" (1775).

Henry the Navigator. 1394–1460. Prince of Portugal who es-

ă pat	oi boy
ā pay	ou out
âr care	o͝o took
ä father	o͞o boot
ĕ pet	ŭ cut
ē be	ûr urge
ĭ pit	th thin
ī pie	*th* this
îr pier	hw which
ŏ pot	zh vision
ō toe	ə about, item
ô paw	

Stress marks:
′ (primary);
′ (secondary), as in
dictionary (dĭk′shə-nĕr′ē)

the works ascribed to him. **b.** Having to do with the occult sciences, esp. alchemy; magical. [NLat. *hermēticus*, alchemical < Med.Lat. *Hermēs Trismegistus*. See HERMES TRISMEGISTUS.] — **her•met′i•cal•ly** *adv.*

her•mit (hûr′mĭt) *n.* **1.** One who has withdrawn from society and lives alone; a recluse. **2.** A spiced cookie made with molasses, raisins, and nuts. [ME *heremite* < OFr. < Med.Lat. *heremīta* < LLat. *erēmīta* < Gk. *erēmitēs* < *erēmia*, desert < *erēmos*, solitary.] — **her•mit′ic, her•mit′i•cal** *adj.* — **her•mit′i•cal•ly** *adv.*

her•mit•age (hûr′mĭ-tĭj) *n.* **1.a.** The habitation of a hermit or group of hermits. **b.** A monastery or an abbey. **2.** A place where one can live in seclusion; a retreat. **3.** The condition or way of life of a hermit. [ME < OFr. *hermitage* < *heremite*, hermit. See HERMIT.]

hermit crab *n.* Any of various crabs of the order Decapoda that protect their unarmored abdomens by taking over the empty shells of snails or other univalve mollusks.

hermit thrush *n.* A North American bird *(Catharus guttatus)* with brown plumage, a spotted breast, and a reddish tail.

Her•mon (hûr′mən), **Mount.** A peak, 2,815.8 m (9,232 ft), of the Anti-Lebanon Range on the Syria-Lebanon border; traditionally considered the site of Jesus's transfiguration.

Her•mo•sa Beach (hər-mō′sə). A city of S CA on the Pacific Ocean SSW of Los Angeles. Pop. 18,219.

Her•mo•sil•lo (ĕr′mô-sē′ô). A city of NW Mexico near the Gulf of CA W of Chihuahua; estab. c. 1700. Pop. 297,175.

hern (hûrn) *n.* A heron. [Var. of HERON.]

Her•ne (hĕr′nə). A city of W-central Germany in the Ruhr district ENE of Essen. Pop. 173,226.

her•ni•a (hûr′nē-ə) *n., pl.* **-ni•as** or **-ni•ae** (-nē-ē′). The protrusion of an organ or other structure through the wall that normally contains it; a rupture. [ME < Lat. See **gherə-*.**] — **her′ni•al** *adj.*

her•ni•ate (hûr′nē-āt′) *intr.v.* **-at•ed, -at•ing, -ates.** To protrude through a ruptured body wall. — **her′ni•a′tion** *n.*

he•ro (hîr′ō) *n., pl.* **-roes. 1.** In mythology and legend, a man, often of divine ancestry, who is endowed with great courage and strength, celebrated for bold exploits, and favored by the gods. **2.** A person noted for feats of courage or nobility of purpose, esp. one who has risked or sacrificed his or her life. **3.** A person noted for special achievement in a particular field: *the heroes of medicine.* **4.** The principal male character in a novel, poem, or dramatic presentation. See Usage Note at **heroine. 5.** See **submarine** 2. See Regional Note at **submarine.** [Prob. alteration of Lat. *hērōs* < Gk. See **ser-[1]*.**]

He•ro[1] (hîr′ō) *n. Gk. Myth.* A priestess of Aphrodite beloved by Leander.

He•ro[2] (hē′rō, hîr′ō) or **He•ron** (hē′rŏn′). 1st cent. A.D. Alexandrian scientist who devised a formula for determining the area of a triangle.

Her•od (hĕr′əd). "the Great." 73?–4 B.C. King of Judea (40–4) who according to the Bible attempted to kill the infant Jesus by ordering the death of all children under the age of two in Bethlehem.

Herod An•ti•pas (ăn′tĭ-păs′, -pəs). d. c. A.D. 40. Ruler of Judea and tetrarch in Galilee (4 B.C.–A.D. 40).

He•ro•di•as (hĭ-rō′dē-əs). d. c. A.D. 39. The niece and second wife of Herod Antipas and the mother of Salome.

He•rod•o•tus (hĭ-rŏd′ə-təs). "the Father of History." 5th cent. B.C. Greek historian whose writings are the earliest known examples of narrative history.

he•ro•ic (hĭ-rō′ĭk) *adj.* also **he•ro•i•cal** (-ĭ-kəl). **1.** Of, relating to, or resembling the heroes of literature, legend, or myth. **2.** Having, showing, or characteristic of the qualities appropriate to a hero; courageous. **3.a.** Impressive in size or scope; grand. **b.** Of a size or scale that is larger than life. — *n.* **1.** A line of heroic verse. **2. heroics.** Melodramatic behavior or language. — **he•ro′i•cal•ly** *adv.* — **he•ro′i•cal•ness** *n.*

heroic couplet *n.* A verse unit consisting of two rhymed lines in iambic pentameter.

heroic drama *n.* Restoration tragedy or tragicomedy in heroic couplets and marked by exoticism, bombastic rhetoric, and exaggerated characters.

heroic meter *n.* See **heroic verse.**

heroic stanza *n.* A stanza consisting of four lines in iambic pentameter rhyming *abab* or *aabb.*

heroic verse *n.* One of several verse forms traditionally used in epic and dramatic poetry, esp.: **a.** The dactylic hexameter in Greek and Latin. **b.** The iambic pentameter in English. **c.** The alexandrine in French.

her•o•in (hĕr′ō-ĭn) *n.* An odorless, bitter crystalline compound, $C_{17}H_{17}NO(C_2H_3O_2)_2$, derived from morphine and a highly addictive narcotic. [Ger., originally a trademark.]

Word History: The word *heroin* is a good example of how the concerns of a later age can distort the etymology of a word. For most of this century etymologists assumed that the drug name *heroin* was derived from Greek *hērōs*, "hero," because the euphoria associated with the drug made one "feel like a hero." A derivative of the opiate morphine, heroin was first marketed in 1898 by the German chemical firm Friedrich Bayer & Company. The drug was sold to doctors and pharmacists as a treatment for coughs and other respiratory ailments. Because heroin was much more powerful than morphine or codeine, the two drugs most commonly prescribed for respiratory problems in the 19th century, doctors believed that by giving smaller doses they could avoid the side effects of morphine and codeine, most importantly, addiction. Thus, *heroin* was derived from the Greek word for "hero" not in order to appeal to drug addicts interested in its euphoria but to appeal to doctors who wished to relieve their patients' symptoms. Heroin was sold as the "hero" of such drugs, the most powerful opiate available. The trade-namer was also relying on echoes with the medical expression *heroisches Mittel,* which is very similar to the English phrase *heroic remedy,* a powerful, daring, or extreme treatment. Yet by 1900 doctors were already prescribing opiates less and less, and in the first decades of this century there was a large public outcry against opiate addiction. By the 1920's heroin was known as an evil menace associated with criminal drug use and trafficking, and its origin, as the "hero" of the opiates, was forgotten.

heron
Great egret
Casmerodius albus

her•o•ine (hĕr′ō-ĭn) *n.* **1.** A woman noted for courage and daring action. **2.** A woman noted for special achievement in a particular field. **3.** The principal female character in a novel, poem, or dramatic presentation. [Lat. *hērōinē, hērōīna* < Gk. *hērōinē*, fem. of *hērōs*, hero. See HERO.]

Usage Note: The word *hero* should no longer be regarded as restricted to men in the sense "a person noted for courageous action," though *heroine* is always restricted to women. The distinction between *heroine* and *hero* is still useful in referring to the principal character of a fictional work.

her•o•in•ism (hĕr′ō-ĭ-nĭz′əm) *n.* Addiction to heroin.

her•o•ism (hĕr′ō-ĭz′əm) *n.* **1.** Heroic conduct or behavior. **2.** Heroic characteristics or qualities; courage.

her•on (hĕr′ən) *n.* Any of various wading birds of the family Ardeidae, having a long neck, long legs, a long pointed bill, and usu. white, gray, or bluish-gray plumage. [ME < OFr., of Gmc. orig.]

He•ron (hē′rŏn′). See **Hero[2].**

her•on•ry (hĕr′ən-rē) *n., pl.* **-ries.** A place where herons nest and breed.

hero worship *n.* Intense or excessive admiration for a hero or a person regarded as a hero.

he•ro-wor•ship (hîr′ō-wûr′shĭp) *tr.v.* **-shiped, -ship•ing, -ships** or **-shipped, -ship•ping, -ships. 1.** To revere as an ideal. **2.** To adulate. — **he′ro-wor′ship•er** *n.*

her•pes (hûr′pēz) *n.* Any of several viral diseases causing the eruption of vesicles on the skin or mucous membranes, esp. herpes simplex or herpes zoster. [ME < Lat. *herpēs* < Gk. < *herpein*, to creep.] — **her•pet′ic** (hər-pĕt′ĭk) *adj.*

herpes la•bi•a•lis (lā′bē-ā′lĭs) *n.* See **cold sore.** [NLat. *herpēs labiālis* : Lat. *herpēs*, herpes + Med.Lat. *labiālis*, of the lip.]

herpes sim•plex (sĭm′plĕks′) *n.* **1.** A recurrent viral disease caused by the herpes simplex virus, type one, and marked by the eruption of vesicles on the mouth, lips, or face. **2.** A recurrent viral disease caused by the herpes simplex virus, type two, and marked by the eruption of vesicles on the genitals. [NLat. *herpēs simplex.*]

her•pes•vi•rus (hûr′pēz-vī′rəs) *n., pl.* **-rus•es.** Any of a group of DNA-containing animal viruses that form characteristic inclusion bodies within the nuclei of host cells and cause diseases such as chickenpox and herpes simplex.

herpes zos•ter (zŏs′tər, zō′stər) *n.* See **shingles.** [NLat. *herpēs zōstēr* : Lat. *herpēs*, herpes + Gk. *zōstēr*, girdle.]

her•pe•tol•o•gy (hûr′pĭ-tŏl′ə-jē) *n.* The branch of zoology that deals with reptiles and amphibians. [Gk. *herpeton*, reptile (< *herpein*, to creep) + -LOGY.] — **her′pe•to•log′ic** (-tə-lŏj′ĭk), **her′pe•to•log′i•cal** *adj.* — **her′pe•tol′o•gist** *n.*

Herr (hĕr) *n., pl.* **Her•ren** (hĕr′ən). Used as a male courtesy title in a German-speaking area, prefixed to a surname or professional title. [Ger. < MHGer. *hërre* < OHGer. *hērro*, lord, master, alteration of *hēriro*, older, more venerable, comp. of *hēr*, proud, holy, splendid, noble.]

Her•rick (hĕr′ĭk), **Robert.** 1591–1674. English Cavalier poet whose works include "Delight in Disorder" (1648).

her•ring (hĕr′ĭng) *n., pl.* **herring** or **-rings.** Any of various fishes of the family Clupeidae, esp. a commercially important food fish *(Clupea harengus)* of Atlantic and Pacific waters. [ME *hering* < OE *hǣring.*]

her•ring•bone (hĕr′ĭng-bōn′) *n.* **1.a.** A decorative pattern of rows of slanted parallel lines with the direction of the slant alternating row by row. **b.** A twilled fabric woven in this pattern. **2.** *Sports.* A method of climbing a ski slope with the tips of the skis pointed outward. — *v.* **-boned, -bon•ing, -bones.** — *tr.* To arrange or decorate with a herringbone pattern. — *intr.* **1.** To produce a herringbone pattern. **2.** *Sports.* To ascend a ski slope with the ski tips pointed outward.

herring gull *n.* A common seagull *(Larus argentatus)* of the Northern Hemisphere having gray and white plumage with black wing tips.

hers (hûrz) *pron. (used with a sing. or pl. v.)* Used to indicate the one or ones belonging to her: *Whose hat? Hers.* [ME *hires, hirs* : *hire*, her; see HER + *-es*, possessive suff.; see -'s.]

Her•schel (hûr′shəl). Family of British astronomers, including

Sir **William** (1738–1822), who discovered Uranus (1781); his sister **Caroline** (1750–1848) who published a star catalog; and his son Sir **John Frederick William** (1792–1871), who conducted research on light, photography, and astrophysics.

her•self (hûr-sĕlf′) *pron.* **1.** That one identical with her: **a.** Used reflexively as the direct or indirect object of a verb or the object of a preposition: *She bought herself a car.* **b.** Used for emphasis: *She herself was certain.* **c.** Used in an absolute construction: *In office herself, she helped him get a job.* **2.** Her normal or healthy condition or state: *She's feeling herself again.* [ME *hire self* < OE *hire selfre*, dative of *hēo self* : *hēo*, she; see SHE + *self*, self; see SELF.]

her•sto•ry (hûr′stə-rē) *n., pl.* **-sto•ries. 1.** The experiences and accomplishments of women, esp. as seen in a historical context. **2.** The experiences making up a woman's life.

hertz (hûrts) *n., pl.* **hertz.** A unit of frequency equal to one cycle per second. See table at **measurement.** [After Heinrich Rudolf HERTZ.]

Hertz (hûrts, hĕrts), **Heinrich Rudolf.** 1857–1894. German physicist who was the first to produce radio waves artificially.

Hertz•i•an wave (hûrt′sē-ən, hĕrt′-) *n.* An electromagnetic wave, usu. of radio frequency, produced by the oscillation of electricity in a conductor. [After Heinrich Rudolf HERTZ.]

Hert•zog (hûrt′sŏg′, -sôg′, hĕr′tsôKH), **James Barry Munnik.** 1866–1942. South African general and politician who as prime minister (1924–39) instituted apartheid policies.

Hertz•sprung-Rus•sell diagram (hĕrts′sprŭng-rŭs′əl, -sprŏŏng-) *n.* A graph of the absolute magnitude of stars plotted against their surface temperature or color, used in the study of stellar evolution. [After Ejnar *Hertzsprung* (1873–1967), Danish astronomer, and Henry Norris RUSSELL.]

Herz•berg (hûrts′bûrg′), **Gerhard.** b. 1904. German-born Canadian physicist who won a 1971 Nobel Prize for chemistry.

Her•ze•go•vi•na (hĕrt′sə-gō-vē′nə, hûrt′-). The S region of Bosnia-Herzegovina; conquered by Serbs in the 13th cent. and joined with Bosnia since the 15th cent. **—Her′ze•go•vi′ni•an** *adj. & n.*

Her•zl (hĕrt′səl), **Theodor.** 1860–1904. Hungarian-born Austrian who organized the Zionist World Congress (1897).

he's (hēz). **1.** He is: *He's going.* **2.** He has: *He's been there.*

Hesh•van also **Hesh•wan** (KHĕsh′vən, -vän) *n.* The second month of the year in the Jewish calendar. [Heb. *ḥešwān* < *marḥešwān*, October/November < Akkadian *araḫsamnu*.]

He•si•od (hē′sē-əd, hĕs′ē-). fl. 8th cent. B.C. Greek poet whose epics include *Works and Days* and *Theogony.*

hes•i•tan•cy (hĕz′ĭ-tən-sē) *n., pl.* **-cies. 1.** The state or quality of being hesitant. **2.** An instance of hesitating.

hes•i•tant (hĕz′ĭ-tənt) *adj.* Inclined or tending to hesitate.

hes•i•tate (hĕz′ĭ-tāt′) *intr.v.* **-tat•ed, -tat•ing, -tates. 1.a.** To be slow to act, speak, or decide. **b.** To pause in uncertainty; waver. **2.** To be reluctant. **3.** To speak haltingly; falter. [Lat. *haesitāre*, *haesitāt-*, to hesitate, freq. of *haerēre*, to hold fast.] **—hes′i•tat′er** *n.* **—hes′i•tat′ing•ly** *adv.*

hes•i•ta•tion (hĕz′ĭ-tā′shən) *n.* **1.** The act or an instance of hesitating. **2.** The state of being hesitant. **3.** A pause or faltering in speech.

Hes•pe•ri•an (hĕ-spîr′ē-ən) *adj.* Of or relating to the west. [< Lat. *Hesperius* < Gk. *hesperios* < *hesperos*, evening. See **wes-pero-***.]

Hes•per•i•des (hĕ-spĕr′ĭ-dēz′) *pl.n. Gk. Myth.* **1.** The nymphs who together with a dragon watch over a garden in which golden apples grow. **2.** *(used with a sing. v.)* A garden at the western end of the earth, in which golden apples grow. [Lat. < Gk., pl. of *hesperis*, fem. of *hesperios*, of the evening, western. See HESPERIAN.] **—Hes′per•id′i•an, Hes′per•id′e•an** (hĕs′pə-rĭd′ē-ən) *adj.*

hes•per•i•din (hĕ-spĕr′ĭ-dĭn) *n.* A crystalline compound, $C_{28}H_{34}O_{15}$, occurring in citrus fruit. [HESPERID(IUM) + -IN.]

hes•per•id•i•um (hĕs′pə-rĭd′ē-əm) *n., pl.* **-i•a** (-ē-ə). A berry having a leathery rind and juicy pulp divided into segments, as a citrus fruit. [NLat. < HESPERIDES, land of golden apples.]

Hes•per•us (hĕs′pər-əs) *n.* The planet Venus as the evening star. [ME < Lat. < Gk. *hesperos*. See HESPERIAN.]

Hess (hĕs), **Victor Franz.** 1883–1964. Austrian-born Amer. physicist who shared a 1936 Nobel Prize.

Hess, (Walter Richard) Rudolf. 1894–1987. German Nazi leader who at the Nuremburg trials (1946) was sentenced to life imprisonment for war crimes.

Hess, Walter Rudolf. 1881–1973. Swiss physiologist who shared a 1949 Nobel Prize.

Hesse (hĕs). A region and former grand duchy of W-central Germany; divided after 1567 into four regions ruled by various branches of the Hesse family.

Hes•se (hĕs′ə), **Hermann.** 1877–1962. German-born Swiss writer whose works include *Siddhartha* (1922). He won the 1946 Nobel Prize for literature.

Hes•sian (hĕsh′ən) *adj.* Of or relating to Hesse or its inhabitants. *—n.* **1.** A native or inhabitant of Hesse. **2.** A German mercenary in the British army in America during the Revolutionary War. **3.** A mercenary soldier.

Hessian boot *n.* A man's high tasseled boot introduced into England by Hessians in the 19th century.

Hessian fly *n.* A small fly *(Mayetiola destructor)* having larvae that infest and destroy wheat and other grain plants.

hes•so•nite (hĕs′ə-nīt′) *n.* Var. of **essonite.**

hest (hĕst) *n. Archaic.* Command; behest. [ME, alteration of *hes* < OE *hǣs*. See **kei-²***.]

Hes•ti•a (hĕs′tē-ə) *n. Gk. Myth.* The goddess of the hearth and the daughter of Cronus and Rhea.

he•tae•ra (hĭ-tîr′ə) also **he•tai•ra** (-tīr′ə) *n., pl.* **-tae•rae** (-tîr′ē) or **-tae•ras** also **-tai•rai** (-tīr′ī′) or **-tai•ras.** An ancient Greek courtesan, esp. one of a special class of cultivated female companions. [Gk. *hetaira*, fem. of *hetairos*, companion.] **—he•tae′ric** *adj.*

het•er•o (hĕt′ə-rō′) *n., pl.* **-os.** *Informal.* A heterosexual person. **—het′er•o** *adj.*

hetero– or **heter–** *pref.* **1.** Other; different: *heterochromatic.* **2.** Containing different kinds of atoms: *heterocyclic.* [Gk. < *heteros*, other. See **sem-¹***.]

het•er•o•at•om (hĕt′ə-rō-ăt′əm) *n.* An atom other than carbon in the structure of a heterocyclic compound.

heterocercal
Shark with heterocercal tail

het•er•o•cer•cal (hĕt′ə-rō-sûr′kəl) *adj.* Relating to, having, or being a tail fin in which the upper lobe is larger than the lower as in sharks. [HETERO– + Gk. *kerkos*, tail + –AL¹.]

het•er•o•chro•mat•ic (hĕt′ə-rō-krō-măt′ĭk) *adj.* **1.** Of or characterized by different colors. **2.** Consisting of different wavelengths or frequencies. **3.** Of or relating to heterochromatin. **—het′er•o•chro′ma•tism** (-krō′mə-tĭz′əm) *n.*

het•er•o•chro•ma•tin (hĕt′ə-rō-krō′mə-tĭn) *n.* Tightly coiled chromosomal material that stains deeply during interphase and is believed to be genetically inactive.

het•er•o•cy•clic (hĕt′ə-rō-sī′klĭk, -sĭk′lĭk) *adj.* Containing more than one kind of atom joined in a ring. **—het′er•o•cy′cle** (-sī′kəl) *n.* **—het′er•o•cy′clic** *n.*

het•er•o•cyst (hĕt′ər-ə-sĭst′) *n.* A large transparent cell that occurs along the filaments of certain cyanobacteria.

het•er•o•dox (hĕt′ər-ə-dŏks′) *adj.* **1.** Not in agreement with accepted beliefs, esp. church doctrine or dogma. **2.** Holding unorthodox opinions. [Gk. *heterodoxos* : *hetero-*, hetero- + *doxa*, opinion (< *dokein*, to think; see **dek-***).]

het•er•o•dox•y (hĕt′ər-ə-dŏk′sē) *n., pl.* **-ies. 1.** The condition or quality of being heterodox. **2.** A heterodox opinion.

het•er•o•dyne (hĕt′ər-ə-dīn′) *adj.* Having alternating currents of two different frequencies that are combined to produce two new frequencies, the sum and difference of the original frequencies. *—tr.v.* **-dyned, -dyn•ing, -dynes.** To combine (a radio frequency wave) with a locally generated wave of different frequency in order to produce a new frequency equal to the sum or difference of the two. [HETERO– + *-dyne*, power, frequency (< Gk. *dunamis*, power; see DYNE).]

het•er•oe•cious (hĕt′ə-rē′shəs) *adj.* Spending different stages of a life cycle on different, usu. unrelated hosts. Used of parasites such as tapeworms. [HETERO– + Gk. *oikia*, house; see **weik-¹*** + –OUS.] **—het′er•oe′cism** (-sĭz′əm) *n.*

het•er•o•gam•ete (hĕt′ə-rō-găm′ēt′, -gə-mēt′) *n.* Either of two conjugating gametes that differ in structure or behavior.

het•er•o•ga•met•ic (hĕt′ə-rō-gə-mĕt′ĭk) *adj.* **1.** Producing dissimilar gametes, such as human males, who produce spermatazoa bearing X-chromosomes or Y-chromosomes. **2.** Of or relating to heterogametes.

het•er•og•a•mous (hĕt′ə-rŏg′ə-məs) *adj.* **1.** *Biol.* **a.** Reproducing by the fusion of unlike gametes. **b.** Heterogonous. **2.** *Bot.* Bearing male and female flowers.

het•er•og•a•my (hĕt′ə-rŏg′ə-mē) *n.* **1.** Alternation of sexual and parthenogenic generations, as in some aphids. **2.** The state or condition in which conjugating gametes are dissimilar in structure and size as well as in function. **—het′er•o•gam′ic** (-rō-găm′ĭk) *adj.*

het•er•o•ge•ne•i•ty (hĕt′ə-rō′jə-nē′ĭ-tē) *n.* The quality or state of being heterogeneous.

het•er•o•ge•ne•ous (hĕt′ər-ə-jē′nē-əs, -jēn′yəs) *adj.* **1.** Also **het•er•og•e•nous** (hĕt′ə-rŏj′ə-nəs). Consisting of dissimilar elements or parts; not homogeneous. See Syns at **miscellaneous. 2.** Completely different; incongruous. [< Med.Lat. *heterogeneus* < Gk. *heterogenēs* : *hetero-*, hetero- + *genos*, kind, race; see **genə-***.] **—het′er•o•ge′ne•ous•ly** *adv.* **—het′er•o•ge′ne•ous•ness** *n.*

het•er•og•e•nous¹ (hĕt′ə-rŏj′ə-nəs) also **het•er•o•gen•ic** (-rō-jĕn′ĭk) *adj.* Not arising within the body; derived from another individual or species. **—het′er•og′e•ny** *n.*

het•er•og•e•nous² (hĕt′ə-rŏj′ə-nəs) *adj.* Var. of **heterogeneous** 1.

het•er•og•o•nous (hĕt′ə-rŏg′ə-nəs) *adj.* Characterized by the alternation of sexual and parthenogenic generations. [HETERO– + –GON(Y) + –OUS.] **—het′er•og′o•ny** *n.*

het•er•o•graft (hĕt′ə-rō-grăft′) *n.* A type of tissue graft in which the donor and recipient are of different species.

het•er•o•kar•y•on (hĕt′ər-ə-kăr′ē-ŏn′, -ən) *n.* A cell having two or more genetically different nuclei. [HETERO– + KARY(O)– + –ON¹.] **—het′er•o•kar′y•ot′ic** (-ŏt′ĭk) *adj.*

het•er•o•lec•i•thal (hĕt′ə-rō-lĕs′ə-thəl) *adj. Embryol.* Having the yolk unevenly distributed throughout the egg. [HETERO– + Gk. *lekithos*, egg yolk + –AL¹.]

het•er•ol•o•gous (hĕt′ə-rŏl′ə-gəs) *adj.* **1.** Derived from a

ă pat	oi boy
ā pay	ou out
âr care	ŏŏ took
ä father	ōō boot
ĕ pet	ŭ cut
ē be	ûr urge
ĭ pit	th thin
ī pie	*th* this
îr pier	hw which
ŏ pot	zh vision
ō toe	ə about, item
ô paw	

Stress marks:
′ (primary);
′ (secondary), as in
dictionary (dĭk′shə-nĕr′ē)

hex sign
On the side of a barn

Thor Heyerdahl

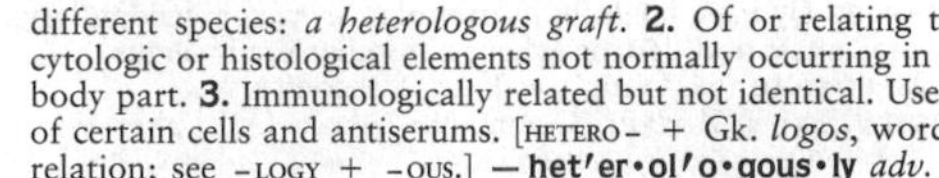

different species: *a heterologous graft.* **2.** Of or relating to cytologic or histological elements not normally occurring in a body part. **3.** Immunologically related but not identical. Used of certain cells and antiserums. [HETERO– + Gk. *logos*, word, relation; see –LOGY + –OUS.] — **het′er•ol′o•gous•ly** *adv.*

het•er•ol•o•gy (hĕt′ə-rŏl′ə-jē) *n.* Lack of correspondence between body parts, as in structure, due to different origins.

het•er•ol•y•sis (hĕt′ə-rŏl′ĭ-sĭs, -ə-rō-lī′sĭs) *n., pl.* **-ses** (-sēz′). **1.** *Biol.* Dissolution of cells or proteins in one species by the action of lysins or enzymes of another. **2.** *Chem.* An organic reaction in which the breaking of bonds leads to the formation of ion pairs. — **het′er•o•lyt′ic** (-ə-rō-lĭt′ĭk) *adj.*

het•er•om•er•ous (hĕt′ə-rŏm′ər-əs) *adj.* Having unequal or differing parts within the same structure or similar structures.

het•er•o•mor•phic (hĕt′ə-rō-môr′fĭk) *adj.* **1.** Having different forms at different periods of the life cycle. **2.** Nonstandard in size or structure. — **het′er•o•mor′phism** *n.*

het•er•on•o•mous (hĕt′ə-rŏn′ə-məs) *adj.* **1.** Subject to external or foreign laws or domination; not autonomous. **2.** *Biol.* Differing in development or manner of specialization. [HETERO– + Gk. *nomos*, law; see –NOMY + –OUS.] — **het′er•on′o•mous•ly** *adv.*

het•er•o•nym (hĕt′ər-ə-nĭm′) *n.* One of two or more words with identical spellings but different meanings and pronunciations, such as *row* (a series arranged in a line), pronounced (rō), and *row* (a fight), pronounced (rou).

het•er•on•y•mous (hĕt′ə-rŏn′ə-məs) *adj.* **1.** Being, relating to, or of the nature of a heteronym. **2.** Being different names or terms but having correspondence or relationship, as *mother* and *daughter.* [< LGk. *heterōnumos* < Gk., with a different denominator : Gk. *hetero-*, hetero- + Gk. *onoma*, name; see **nō-men-***.]

het•er•oph•o•ny (hĕt′ə-rŏf′ə-nē) *n. Mus.* The simultaneous playing or singing of one melody by different instruments or singers. — **het′er•o•phon′ic** (-ər-ə-fŏn′ĭk) *adj.*

het•er•o•phyl•lous (hĕt′ə-rō-fĭl′əs) *adj.* Having dissimilar leaves on one plant. — **het′er•o•phyl′ly** *n.*

het•er•o•phyte (hĕt′ər-ə-fīt′) *n.* A plant, as a parasite, that feeds on other organisms. — **het′er•o•phyt′ic** (-fĭt′ĭk) *adj.*

het•er•o•plas•ty (hĕt′ər-ə-plăs′tē) *n., pl.* **-ties.** The surgical grafting of tissue from one individual or species to another. — **het′er•o•plas′tic** *adj.*

het•er•o•ploid (hĕt′ər-ə-ploid′) *adj.* Having a chromosome number that is not a whole-number multiple of the haploid chromosome number for that species. — **het′er•o•ploid′** *n.* — **het′er•o•ploi′dy** *n.*

het•er•op•ter•ous (hĕt′ə-rŏp′tər-əs) *adj.* Of or belonging to the hemopterous insect suborder Heteroptera, which includes the true bugs, marked by differing forewings and hind wings.

het•er•o•sex•ism (hĕt′ə-rō-sĕk′sĭz′əm) *n.* Discrimination against people who are homosexual or bisexual by people who are heterosexual. — **het′er•o•sex′ist**

het•er•o•sex•u•al (hĕt′ə-rō-sĕk′sho͞o-əl) *adj.* **1.** Sexually oriented to persons of the opposite sex. **2.** Of or relating to different sexes. — *n.* A heterosexual person. — **het′er•o•sex′u•al•ly** *adv.*

het•er•o•sex•u•al•i•ty (hĕt′ə-rō-sĕk′sho͞o-ăl′ĭ-tē) *n.* **1.** Sexual orientation to persons of the opposite sex. **2.** Sexual activity with another of the opposite sex.

het•er•o•sis (hĕt′ə-rō′sĭs) *n.* See **hybrid vigor.** [LGk. *heterōsis*, alteration, alteration of Gk. *heteroiōsis* < *heteroioun*, to alter < *heteroios*, different in kind < *heteros*, other. See HETERO–.] — **het′er•ot′ic** (-rŏt′ĭk) *adj.*

het•er•o•spo•rous (hĕt′ər-ə-spôr′əs, -spōr′-, hĕt′ə-rŏs′pər-əs) *adj.* Producing two types of spores differing in size and sex. — **het′er•o•spo′ry** *n.*

het•er•o•tax•is (hĕt′ə-rō-tăk′sĭs) also **het•er•o•tax•y** (hĕt′ər-ə-tăk′sē) or **het•er•o•tax•i•a** (hĕt′ə-rō-tăk′sē-ə) *n., pl.* **-tax•es** (-tăk′sēz) also **-tax•ies** or **-tax•i•as.** Abnormal structural arrangement, as of body parts. — **het′er•o•tac′tic** (-tăk′tĭk), **het′er•o•tac′tous** (-tăk′təs) *adj.*

het•er•o•thal•lic (hĕt′ə-rō-thăl′ĭk) *adj.* Producing male and female gametangia in different structures or plants, as in some algae and fungi. — **het′er•o•thal′lism** *n.*

het•er•o•to•pi•a (hĕt′ər-ə-tō′pē-ə) also **het•er•ot•o•py** (hĕt′ə-rŏt′ə-pē) *n.* Moving of an organ or other body part to an abnormal location. — **het′er•o•top′ic** (-tŏp′ĭk) *adj.*

het•er•o•troph (hĕt′ər-ə-trŏf′, -trōf′) *n.* An organism that cannot synthesize its own food and is dependent on complex organic substances for nutrition. [HETERO– + Gk. *trophos*, feeder; see –TROPHY.] — **het′er•o•tro′phic** *adj.* — **het′er•o•tro′phi•cal•ly** *adv.* — **het′er•ot′ro•phy** (-ə-rŏt′rə-fē) *n.*

het•er•o•typ•ic (hĕt′ə-rō-tĭp′ĭk) also **het•er•o•typ•i•cal** (-ĭ-kəl) *adj.* **1.** *Biol.* Of, relating to, or being the reduction division of meiosis. **2.** Of a different type or form.

het•er•o•zy•go•sis (hĕt′ə-rō-zī-gō′sĭs) *n.* **1.** The formation of a zygote by the union of genetically different gametes. **2.** The condition of being a heterozygote.

het•er•o•zy•gote (hĕt′ə-rō-zī′gōt′) *n.* An organism that has different alleles at a particular gene locus on homologous chromosomes.

het•er•o•zy•gous (hĕt′ər-ə-zī′gəs) *adj.* **1.** Having different alleles at one or more corresponding chromosomal loci. **2.** Of or relating to a heterozygote.

heth (KHĕt, KHĕs) *n.* The eighth letter of the Hebrew alphabet. [Heb. *ḥêt.*]

het•man (hĕt′mən) *n., pl.* **-mans.** See **ataman.** [Ukrainian *het'man* < Pol. *hetman* < Ger. dial. *hetmann*, captain; akin to Ger. *Hauptmann* < MHGer. *houbetman* : OHGer. *houbit*, head; see **kaput-*** + OHGer. *man*, man; see FUGLEMAN.]

heu•land•ite (hyo͞o′lən-dīt′) *n.* A white, red, or yellow zeolite mineral, $CaO{\cdot}Al_2O_3{\cdot}6SiO_2{\cdot}5H_2O$. [After Henry *Heuland*, 19th-cent. British mineralogist.]

heu•ris•tic (hyo͞o-rĭs′tĭk) *adj.* **1.** Of or relating to a usu. speculative formulation guiding the investigation or solution of a problem. **2.** Of, relating to, or constituting an educational method in which students learn through their own investigations. **3.** *Comp. Sci.* Relating to or using a problem-solving technique in which the most appropriate solution is selected at successive stages of a program for use in the next step of the program. — *n.* **1.** A heuristic method or process. **2. heuristics.** *(used with a sing. v.)* The study and application of heuristic methods and processes. [< Gk. *heuriskein*, to find.] — **heu•ris′ti•cal•ly** *adv.*

hew (hyo͞o) *v.* **hewed, hewn** (hyo͞on) or **hewed, hew•ing, hews.** — *tr.* **1.** To make or shape with or as if with an ax: *hew a path.* **2.** To cut down with an ax; fell: *hew an oak.* **3.** To strike or cut; cleave. — *intr.* **1.** To cut something by repeated blows, as of an ax. **2.** To adhere or conform strictly; hold. [ME *hewen* < OE *hēawan.* See **kau-***.] — **hew′er** *n.*

HEW *abbr.* Department of Health, Education, and Welfare.

hex¹ (hĕks) *n.* **1.** An evil spell; a curse. **2.** One that brings bad luck. — *tr.v.* **hexed, hex•ing, hex•es. 1.** To put a hex on. **2.** To bring or wish bad luck to. [Penn.Du. < Ger. *hexen*, to hex < *Hexe*, witch < MHGer. *hecse* < OHGer. *hagzissa.*] — **hex′er** *n.*

hex² (hĕks) *adj.* Hexagonal. Used of hardware.

hex. *abbr.* Hexagon; hexagonal.

hexa– or **hex–** *pref.* **1.** Six: *hexagram.* **2.** Containing six atoms, molecules, or groups: *hexose.* [Gk. < *hex*, six. See **s(w)eks***.]

hex•a•chlo•ro•eth•ane (hĕk′sə-klôr′ō-ĕth′ān′, -klōr′-) also **hex•a•chlor•eth•ane** (-klôr-ĕth′ān′, -klōr-) *n.* A colorless crystalline compound, Cl_3CCCl_3, used as a camphor substitute and in explosives and veterinary medicine.

hex•a•chlo•ro•phene (hĕk′sə-klôr′ə-fēn′, -klōr′-) *n.* An almost odorless white powder, $(C_6HCl_3OH)_2CH_2$, used as a disinfectant and an antibacterial agent in soaps. [HEXA– + CHLORO– + PHEN(OL).]

hex•a•chord (hĕk′sə-kôrd′) *n. Mus.* A sequence of six tones with a semitone between the third and fourth tones, the others being whole tones, that was used in medieval music. [Med. Lat. *hexachordum* < Lat. *hexachordos*, having six strings or stops : Gk. *hexa-*, hexa- + Gk. *-khordos*, string, note (< *khordē*; see CORD).]

hex•ad (hĕk′săd′) *n.* A group or series of six. [LLat. *hexas, hexad-*, the number six < Gk. < *hex*, six. See **s(w)eks***.] — **hex•ad′ic** (hĕk-săd′ĭk) *adj.*

hex•a•dec•i•mal (hĕk′sə-dĕs′ə-məl) *adj.* **1.** Of, relating to, or based on the number 16: *the hexadecimal number system.* **2.** Of or relating to sixteenths. — *n.* A sixteenth.

hex•a•gon (hĕk′sə-gŏn′) *n.* A polygon having six sides.

hex•ag•o•nal (hĕk-săg′ə-nəl) *adj.* **1.** Having six sides. **2.** Containing or shaped like a hexagon. **3.** *Mineral.* Having three equal axes intersecting at angles of 60° in one plane and one axis of variable length that is perpendicular to the others. — **hex•ag′o•nal•ly** *adv.*

hex•a•gram (hĕk′sə-grăm′) *n.* **1.** A six-pointed star formed by extending each of the sides of a regular hexagon into equilateral triangles. **2.** A figure of six lines or sides.

hex•a•he•dron (hĕk′sə-hē′drən) *n., pl.* **-drons** or **-dra** (-drə). A polyhedron, such as a cube, that has six faces. — **hex′a•he′dral** (-drəl) *adj.*

hex•am•er•ous (hĕk-săm′ər-əs) *adj.* **1.** Having six similar parts or divisions. **2.** *Bot.* Having flower parts in sets of six. — **hex•am′er•ism** *n.*

hex•am•e•ter (hĕk-săm′ĭ-tər) *n.* **1.** A line of verse consisting of six metrical feet. **2.** In classical prosody, a line in which the first four feet are either dactylic or spondaic, the fifth is dactylic, and the sixth is spondaic. [Lat. < Gk. *hexametros*, having six metrical feet : *hexa-*, hexa- + *metron*, meter; see METER¹.] — **hex′a•met′ric** (hĕk-sə-mĕt′rĭk), **hex′a•met′ri•cal** (-rĭ-kəl) *adj.*

hex•a•meth•yl•ene•tet•ra•mine (hĕk′sə-mĕth′ə-lēn-tĕt′rə-mēn′) *n.* See **methenamine.**

hex•ane (hĕk′sān′) *n.* A flammable liquid, C_6H_{14}, derived from the fractional distillation of petroleum and used as a solvent and a working fluid in some thermometers.

hex•a•pod (hĕk′sə-pŏd′) *n.* A six-legged arthropod of the class Insecta (formerly Hexapoda); an insect. — *adj.* **1.** Of or belonging to the class Insecta. **2.** Having six legs or feet. [< NLat. *Hexapoda*, class name : Gk. *hexa-*, hexa- + NLat. *-poda*, -pod.] — **hex•ap′o•dous** (hĕk-săp′ə-dəs) *adj.*

Hex•a•teuch (hĕk′sə-to͞ok′, -tyo͞ok′) *n. Bible.* The first six books of the Old Testament. [HEXA- + (PENTA)TEUCH.]

hex•o•san (hĕk′sə-săn′) *n.* Any of several polysaccharides that have the general formula $(C_6H_{10}O_5)_n$ and form a hexose on hydrolysis.

hex•ose (hĕk′sōs′) *n.* Any of various simple sugars, such as glucose, that have six carbon atoms per molecule.

hex sign *n.* Any of various round signs with designs thought to be magical, painted on barns to ward off evil.

hex•yl (hĕk′səl) *n.* The hydrocarbon radical, C_6H_{13}, having valence 1.

hex•yl•re•sor•ci•nol (hĕk′səl-rĭ-zôr′sə-nôl′, -nōl′, -nŏl′) *n.* A yellowish-white crystalline phenol, $C_6H_{13}C_6H_3(OH)_2$, used as an antiseptic and anthelmintic.

hey (hā) *interj.* Used to attract attention or express surprise, appreciation, wonder, or pleasure.

hey•day (hā′dā′) *n.* The period of greatest popularity, success, or power; prime. [Perh. alteration of *heyda*, exclamation of pleasure, prob. alteration of ME *hey*, hey.]

Hey•er•dahl (hā′ər-däl′, hī′-), **Thor.** b. 1914. Norwegian ethnologist and explorer who led the Kon Tiki expedition (1947) on a raft across the Pacific from Peru to Tuamotu to demonstrate that Polynesians may be of South American origin.

Hey•rov•sky (hā-rôf′skē), **Jaroslav.** 1890–1967. Czech chemist who won a 1959 Nobel Prize.

Hey•ward (hā′wərd), **(Edwin) DuBose.** 1885–1940. Amer. writer best known for the novel *Porgy* (1925).

Hez•e•ki•ah (hĕz′ĭ-kī′ə) also **Ez•e•ki•as** (ĕz′ĭ-kī′əs). fl. 715?–686? B.C. King of Judah who according to the Bible sought to abolish idolatry and restore worship of Jehovah.

Hf The symbol for the element **hafnium.**

HF or **hf** *abbr.* High frequency.

hf. *abbr.* Half.

hfs *abbr.* Hyperfine structure.

hg *abbr.* Hemoglobin.

Hg The symbol for the element **mercury** 1. [NLat. *hydrargyrum*, mercury < Lat. *hydrargyrus* < Gk. *hudrarguros* : *hydr-, hudro-*, hydro- + *arguros*, silver; see LITHARGE.]

HG or **H.G.** *abbr.* High German.

hgb. *abbr.* Hemoglobin.

HGH *abbr.* Human growth hormone.

hgt. *abbr.* Height.

hgwy. *abbr.* Highway.

H.H. *abbr.* **1.** Her Highness; His Highness. **2.** His Holiness.

hhd *abbr.* Hogshead.

HH.D. *abbr. Lat.* Humanitatum Doctor (Doctor of Humanities).

HHFA *abbr.* Housing and Home Finance Agency.

HHS *abbr.* Department of Health and Human Services.

hi (hī) *interj. Informal.* Used to express greeting.

HI *abbr.* **1.** Hawaii. **2.** High intensity. **3.** Humidity index.

H.I. *abbr.* Hawaiian Islands.

Hi•a•le•ah (hī′ə-lē′ə). A city of SE FL NW of Miami; noted esp. for its racetrack. Pop. 188,004.

hiatal hernia *n.* A hernia in which part of the stomach protrudes through the esophageal opening of the diaphragm.

hi•a•tus (hī-ā′təs) *n., pl.* **-tus•es** or **hiatus. 1.** A gap or an interruption in space, time, or continuity; a break. **2.** *Ling.* A slight pause between two adjacent vowels in consecutive syllables, as in *naive.* **3.** *Anat.* A separation, an aperture, a fissure, or a short passage in an organ or a body part. [Lat. *hiātus* < p.part. of *hiāre*, to gape.] **— hi•a′tal** (-āt′l) *adj.*

hiatus hernia *n.* See **hiatal hernia.**

Hi•a•wa•tha (hī′ə-wŏth′ə, -wô′thə, hē′ə-). fl. 1570. Onondagan leader credited with the organization of the Iroquois confederacy.

hi•ba•chi (hĭ-bä′chē) *n., pl.* **-chis.** A portable charcoal-burning brazier with a grill, used chiefly for cooking. [J. : *hi*, fire + *bachi*, bowl.]

Hib•bing (hĭb′ĭng). A city of NE MN in the Mesabi Range NW of Duluth. Pop. 18,046.

hi•ber•nac•u•lum (hī′bər-năk′yə-ləm) *n., pl.* **-la** (-lə). *Biol.* **1.** A protective covering or structure in which an organism remains dormant for the winter. **2.** The shelter of a hibernating animal. [Lat. *hībernāculum*, winter residence < *hībernāre*, to winter < *hībernus*, of winter. See **ghei-***.]

hi•ber•nal (hī-bûr′nəl) *adj.* Of or relating to winter. [Lat. *hībernālis* < *hībernus*, wintry. See HIBERNACULUM.]

hi•ber•nate (hī′bər-nāt′) *intr.v.* **-nat•ed, -nat•ing, -nates. 1.** To pass the winter in a dormant or torpid state. **2.** To be in an inactive or dormant state or period. [Lat. *hībernāre, hībernāt-*, to winter < *hībernus*, relating to winter. See **ghei-***.] **— hi′ber•na′tion** *n.* **— hi′ber•na′tor** *n.*

Hi•ber•ni•a (hī-bûr′nē-ə). The island of Ireland. **— Hi•ber′ni•an** *adj. & n.*

Hi•ber•no-Eng•lish (hī-bûr′nō-ĭng′glĭsh) *n.* See **Irish English.**

hi•bis•cus (hī-bĭs′kəs) *n.* Any of various chiefly tropical shrubs or trees of the genus *Hibiscus*, having large showy flowers with numerous stamens united into a tube surrounding the style. [LLat., var. of Lat. *hibiscum*, marsh mallow, perh. of Celt. orig.]

hic•cup also **hic•cough** (hĭk′əp) *— n.* **1.a.** A spasm of the diaphragm resulting in a rapid involuntary inhalation stopped by the sudden closure of the glottis and accompanied by a sharp distinctive sound. **b. hiccups.** An attack of these spasms. Often used with *the.* **2.** The sound made by such a spasm or a sound resembling it. *— intr.v.* **-cupped, -cup•ping, -cups** also **-coughed, -cough•ing, -coughs. 1.** To make a hiccup or a sound like a hiccup. **2.** To have a hiccup attack. [Imit.]

hick (hĭk) *Informal. — n.* A person regarded as gullible or provincial. *— adj.* Provincial; unsophisticated: *a hick town.* [After *Hick*, a nickname for *Richard* < ME *Hikke.*]

hick•ey (hĭk′ē) *n., pl.* **-eys.** *Informal.* **1.** A device or contrivance; a gadget. **2.a.** A reddish mark on the skin caused by kissing, biting, or sucking, as in lovemaking. **b.** A pimple. **3.** A pipe-bending apparatus. **4.** A threaded electrical fitting to connect a fixture to an outlet box. [?]

Hick•ok (hĭk′ŏk′), **James Butler.** "Wild Bill Hickok." 1837–76. Amer. frontier scout and marshal noted for his legendary exploits against outlaws.

hick•o•ry (hĭk′ə-rē) *n., pl.* **-ries. 1.** Any of several chiefly North American deciduous trees of the genus *Carya*, having compound leaves and hard smooth stones or nuts, each containing an edible seed and surrounded by a four-valved husk. **2.a.** The hard, tough, heavy wood of such a tree. **b.** A walking stick or switch made from such wood. [Short for Virginia Algonquian *pocohiquara*, pressed hickory nut drink.]

Hick•o•ry (hĭk′ə-rē, hĭk′rē). A city of W-central NC NW of Charlotte at the foot of the Blue Ridge. Pop. 28,301.

Hicks (hĭks), **Edward.** 1780–1849. Amer. painter of primitive works, notably *The Peaceable Kingdom.*

Hicks•ville (hĭks′vĭl). A community of SE NY on W Long I. NE of Mineola; founded 1648. Pop. 40,174.

hi•dal•go (hĭ-dăl′gō, ē-*th*äl′gô) *n., pl.* **-gos.** A member of the minor nobility in Spain. [Sp., alteration of *hijo dalgo* < OSp. *fijo dalgo* : *fijo*, son (< Lat. *fīlius*; see **dhē(i)-***) + *de*, of (< Lat. *dē*; see DE-) + *algo*, something, possession (< Lat. *aliquō*, ablative of *aliquid* : *alius*, some; see **al-**[1]* + *quid*, something; see **k**[w]**o-***).]

Hi•dat•sa (hē-dät′sä) *n., l.* **Hidatsa** or **-sas. 1.a.** A member of a Native American people living along the Missouri River in western North Dakota. **2.** Their Siouan language.

hid•den•ite (hĭd′n-īt′) *n. Mineral.* A transparent emerald-green variety of spodumene, used as a gemstone. [After William E. *Hidden* (1832–1918), Amer. mineralogist.]

hide[1] (hīd) *v.* **hid** (hĭd), **hid•den** (hĭd′n) or **hid, hid•ing, hides.** *— tr.* **1.** To put or keep out of sight; secrete. **2.** To prevent the disclosure or recognition of; conceal. **3.** To cut off from sight; cover up. **4.** To avert (one's gaze), esp. in shame or grief. *— intr.* **1.** To keep oneself out of sight. **2.** To seek refuge. ***— phrasal verb.* hide out.** To be in hiding, as from a pursuer. [ME *hiden* < OE *hȳdan.* See **(s)keu-***.]

Syns: *hide, conceal, secrete, cache, screen, bury, cloak.* These verbs mean to keep from the sight or knowledge of others. *Hide* and *conceal* are the most general and are often used interchangeably: *I used a throw rug to hide* (or *conceal*) *the stain. She smiled to hide* (or *conceal*) *her feelings. Secrete* and *cache* involve concealment in a place unknown to others; *cache* often implies storage for later use: *The lioness secreted her cubs in the grass. The mountain climbers cached their food in a cave.* To *screen* is to shield or block from the view of others: *Tall shrubs screen the home. Bury* implies covering over: *buried the treasure.* To *cloak* is to conceal something by masking or disguising it: *"On previously cloaked issues, the Soviets have suddenly become forthcoming"* (John McLaughlin). See also Syns at **block.**

hide[2] (hīd) *n.* The skin of an animal, esp. the skin or pelt of a large animal. *— tr.v.* **hid•ed, hid•ing, hides.** To beat severely; flog. ***— idiom.* hide nor hair.** A trace; a vestige: *haven't seen hide nor hair of them.* [ME < OE *hȳd.* See **(s)keu-***.]

hide[3] (hīd) *n.* An old English measure of land, usu. the amount held adequate for one free family and its dependents. [ME < OE *hīd.* See **kei-**[1]*.]

hide-and-go-seek (hīd′n-gō-sēk′) *n. Games.* See **hide-and-seek.**

hide-and-seek (hīd′n-sēk′) *n. Games.* A children's game in which a player tries to catch others who are hiding.

hide•a•way (hīd′ə-wā′) *n.* **1.** A place of concealment; a hideout. **2.** A secluded or isolated place.

hide•bound (hīd′bound′) *adj.* **1.** Stubbornly prejudiced, narrow-minded, or inflexible. **2.** Having abnormally dry stiff skin that adheres closely to the underlying flesh. Used of domestic animals such as cattle. **3.** Having the bark so contracted and unyielding as to hinder growth. Used of trees.

hid•e•ous (hĭd′ē-əs) *adj.* **1.** Repulsive, esp. to the sight; revoltingly ugly. **2.** Offensive to moral sensibilities; despicable. [ME, var. of *hidous* < AN < OFr. *hide, hisde*, fear, poss. of Gmc. orig.] **— hid′e•ous•ly** *adv.* **— hid′e•ous•ness, hid′e•os′i•ty** (-ŏs′ĭ-tē) *n.*

hide•out (hīd′out′) *n.* A place of shelter or concealment.

hid•ey-hole (hī′dē-hōl′) *n. Informal.* A secluded hideaway.

hi•dro•sis (hĭ-drō′sĭs) *n., pl.* **-ses** (-sēz). **1.** The formation and excretion of sweat. **2.** Sweat, esp. in excessive or abnormal amounts. [Gk. *hidrōsis*, sweating < *hidrōs*, sweat. See **sweid-***.] **— hi•drot′ic** (-drŏt′ĭk) *adj.*

hibiscus
Rose of Sharon
Hibiscus syriacus

Wild Bill Hickok

ă pat	oi boy
ā pay	ou out
âr care	o͝o took
ä father	o͞o boot
ĕ pet	ŭ cut
ē be	ûr urge
ĭ pit	th thin
ī pie	*th* this
îr pier	hw which
ŏ pot	zh vision
ō toe	ə about, item
ô paw	

Stress marks:
′ (primary);
′ (secondary), as in
dictionary (dĭk′shə-nĕr′ē)

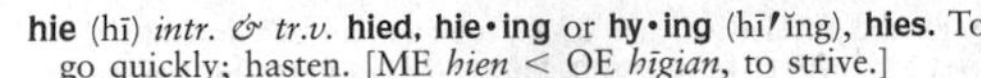

hie (hī) *intr. & tr.v.* **hied, hie•ing** or **hy•ing** (hī′ĭng), **hies.** To go quickly; hasten. [ME *hien* < OE *hīgian*, to strive.]

hi•e•mal (hī′ə-məl) *adj.* Of or relating to winter. [Lat. *hiemālis* < *hiems*, winter. See **ghei-***.]

hi•er•arch (hī′ə-rärk′, hī′rärk′) *n.* One who occupies a position of authority in a religious or other hierarchy. [< ME *jerarchis*, hierarchs < Med.Lat. *hierarcha*, dignitary, prelate < Gk. *hierarkhēs*, high priest : *hieros*, holy; see **eis-*** + *-arkhēs*, -arch.]

hi•er•ar•chi•cal (hī′ə-rär′kĭ-kəl, hī-rär′-) or **hi•er•ar•chic** (-kĭk) or **hi•er•ar•chal** (-rär′kəl) *adj.* Of or relating to a hierarchy. **—hi′er•ar′chi•cal•ly** *adv.*

hi•er•ar•chize (hī′ə-rär-kīz′, hī′rär-) *tr.v.* **-chized, -chiz•ing, -chiz•es.** To arrange in a hierarchy. **—hi′er•ar•chi•za′tion** (-kĭ-zā′shən) *n.*

hi•er•ar•chy (hī′ə-rär′kē, hī′rär′-) *n., pl.* **-chies. 1.** A body of persons having authority. **2.a.** Categorization of a group of people according to ability or status. **b.** The group so categorized. **3.** A series in which each element is graded or ranked. **4.a.** A body of clergy organized into successive ranks or grades. **b.** Religious rule by a group of ranked clergy. **5.** One of the divisions of angels. [ME *ierarchie* < OFr. < Med.Lat. *hierarchia* < Gk. *hierarkhia*, rule of a high priest < *hierarkhēs*, high priest. See HIERARCH.]

hi•er•at•ic (hī′ə-răt′ĭk, hī-răt′-) *adj.* **1.** Of or associated with sacred persons or offices; sacerdotal. **2.** Constituting or relating to a simplified cursive style of Egyptian hieroglyphics. **3.** Extremely formal or stylized, as in a work of art. [Lat. *hierāticus* < Gk. *hieratikos* < *hierateia*, priesthood < *hierasthai*, to be a priest < *hiereus*, priest < *hieros*, holy. See **eis-***.] **—hi′er•at′i•cal•ly** *adv.*

hieroglyphic
Detail from false door to the tomb of Hesire

hiero– or **hier–** *pref.* Sacred; holy: *hierology.* [Gk. < *hieros*, holy. See **eis-***.]

hi•er•oc•ra•cy (hī′ə-rŏk′rə-sē, hī-rŏk′-) *n., pl.* **-cies.** Government by the clergy; ecclesiastical rule. **—hi′er•o•crat′ic** (hī′ər-ə-krăt′ĭk, hī′rə-krăt′-), **hi′er•o•crat′i•cal** *adj.*

hi•er•o•dule (hī′ər-ə-do͞ol′, -dyo͞ol′) *n.* An ancient Greek temple slave serving a deity. [LLat. *hierodūlus* < Gk. *hierodoulos* : *hieron*, temple < neut. of *hieros*, hiero- + *doulos*, slave.] **—hi′er•o•du′lic** (-do͞o′lĭk, -dyo͞o′-) *adj.*

hi•er•o•glyph (hī′ər-ə-glĭf′, hī′rə-) *n.* **1.** A symbol used in hieroglyphic writing. **2.** Something that suggests a hieroglyph.

hi•er•o•glyph•ic (hī′ər-ə-glĭf′ĭk, hī′rə-) also **hi•er•o•glyph•i•cal** (-ĭ-kəl) *—adj.* **1.a.** Of, relating to, or being a system of writing, such as that of ancient Egypt, in which pictorial symbols are used to represent meaning or sounds or a combination of them. **b.** Written with such symbols. **2.** Difficult to read or decipher. *—n.* **1.a.** A hieroglyph. **b.** Often **hieroglyphics.** *(used with a sing. or pl. v.)* Hieroglyphic writing, esp. of the ancient Egyptians. **2.** Something, such as illegible writing, that resembles a hieroglyph. [Fr. *hiéroglyphique* < LLat. *hieroglyphicus* < Gk. *hierogluphikos* : *hieros*, holy; see **eis-*** + *gluphē*, carving (< *gluphein*, to carve; see **gleubh-***).] **—hi′er•o•glyph′i•cal•ly** *adv.*

Hi•er•o•glyph•ic Luvian (hī′ər-ə-glĭf′ĭk, hī′rə-) or **Hieroglyphic Luwian** *n.* A dialect of the Luvian branch of the extinct Anatolian branch of Indo-European, found in documents and inscriptions in an indigenous hieroglyphic script from the late second and early first millenniums B.C. in Anatolia and northern Syria.

hi•er•ol•o•gy (hī′ə-rŏl′ə-jē, hī-rŏl′-) *n., pl.* **-gies.** The sacred literature of a people.

hi•er•o•phant (hī′ər-ə-fănt′, hī′rə-, hī-ĕr′ə-fənt) *n.* **1.** An ancient Greek priest who interpreted sacred mysteries, esp. the Eleusinian mysteries. **2.** An interpreter of sacred mysteries or arcane knowledge. **3.** One who explains or makes a commentary. [LLat. *hierophanta* < Gk. *hierophantēs* : *hieros*, holy; see **eis-*** + *-phantēs*, one who shows (< *phainein*, *phan-*, to show; see **bhā-**[1]*).] **—hi′er•o•phan′tic** *adj.*

hi•fa•lu•tin (hī′fə-lo͞ot′n) *adj.* Var. of **highfalutin.**

hi-fi (hī′fī′) *n., pl.* **-fis.** *Informal.* **1.** High fidelity. **2.** An electronic system for reproducing high-fidelity sound from radio or recordings. [HI(GH), FI(DELITY).] **—hi′-fi′** *adj.*

Hi•ga•shi•o•sa•ka (hē-gä′shē-ō-sä′kä). A city of S Honshu, Japan, a suburb of Osaka. Pop. 522,798.

Hig•gin•son (hĭg′ən-sən), **Thomas Wentworth Storrow.** 1823–1911. Amer. writer and soldier who led the first Black Union Army regiment (1862–64).

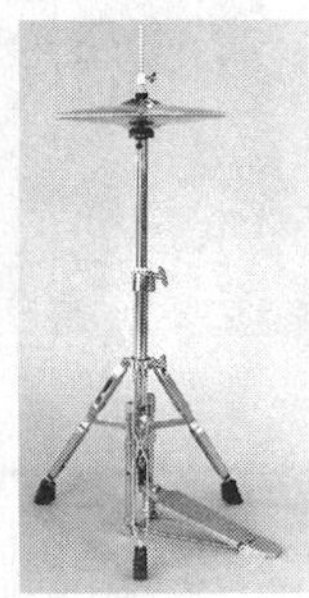

high-hat cymbal

hig•gle (hĭg′əl) *intr.v.* **-gled, -gling, -gles.** To haggle. [Prob. alteration of HAGGLE.] **—hig′gler** *n.*

hig•gle•dy-pig•gle•dy (hĭg′əl-dē-pĭg′əl-dē) *adv.* In utter disorder or confusion. *—adj.* Topsy-turvy; jumbled. [?]

high (hī) *adj.* **high•er, high•est. 1.a.** Having a relatively great elevation; extending far upward: *a high mountain.* **b.** Extending a specified distance upward. **2.a.** Being at or near the peak or culminating stage: *high summer.* **b.** Advanced in development or complexity. **c.** Far removed in time; remote: *high antiquity.* **3.a.** Slightly spoiled or tainted; gamy. Used of meat. **b.** Having a bad smell; malodorous. **4.a.** Having a pitch corresponding to a relatively large number of sound wave cycles per second: *the high tones of a flute.* **b.** Raised in pitch; not soft or hushed: *a high voice.* **5.** Situated relatively far from the equator. **6.a.** Of great importance. **b.** Eminent in rank or status. **c.** Serious; grave. **d.** Constituting a climax; crucial. **e.** Characterized by lofty or stirring events or themes: *high drama.* **7.** Lofty or exalted in quality or character: *high morals.* **8.a.** Greater than usual or expected, as in quantity, magnitude, cost, or degree. **b.** Favorable: *a high opinion of himself.* **9.** Of great force or violence: *high winds.* **10.a.** Filled with excitement or euphoria. **b.** *Slang.* Intoxicated by alcohol or a drug, such as marijuana. **11.** Luxurious; extravagant. **12.** *Ling.* Of or relating to vowels produced with part of the tongue close to the palate, as in the vowel of *tree.* **13.** Of, relating to, or being the gear configuration, as in an automotive transmission, that produces the greatest vehicular speed with respect to engine speed. *—adv.* **higher, highest. 1.** At, in, or to a lofty position, level, or degree. **2.** In an extravagant or luxurious way. *—n.* **1.** A lofty place or region. **2.** A lofty level or degree. **3.** The high gear of a transmission. **4.** A center of high atmospheric pressure; an anticyclone. **5.** *Slang.* An intoxicated or euphoric condition induced by or as if by a drug. **—*idioms.* high and dry. 1.** In a position of helplessness; stranded. **2.** *Naut.* Out of water. Used of a ship, for example. **high and low.** Here and there; everywhere. **on high. 1.** High in the sky. **2.** In heaven. **3.** In a position of authority. [ME < OE *hēah.*] **—high′ly** *adv.*

high-and-might•y (hī′ən-mī′tē) *adj.* Marked by arrogance; haughty and overbearing. **—high and mighty** *adv. & n.*

high•ball (hī′bôl′) *n.* **1.** A cocktail served in a tall glass and consisting of liquor mixed with water or a carbonated beverage. **2.a.** A railroad signal indicating full speed ahead. **b.** A high-speed train. *—intr.v.* **-balled, -ball•ing, -balls.** *Slang.* To move ahead at full speed.

high beam *n.* The beam of a vehicle's headlight that provides long-range illumination.

high•bind•er (hī′bīn′dər) *n.* **1.** A corrupt politician. **2.** A member of a Chinese-American secret society of paid assassins and blackmailers. [After the *Highbinders*, a group of ruffians in New York City c. 1806.]

high blood pressure *n.* Hypertension.

high•born (hī′bôrn′) *adj.* Of noble birth.

high•boy (hī′boi′) *n.* A tall chest of drawers usu. divided into two sections and supported on four legs.

high•bred (hī′brĕd′) *adj.* Of superior breed or stock.

high•brow (hī′brou′) *adj.* also **high•browed** (-broud′). Of, relating to, or being highly cultured or intellectual. *—n.* One who has or affects a high degree of culture or learning.

high•bush cranberry (hī′bo͝osh′) *n.* See **cranberry bush.**

high•chair (hī′châr′) *n.* A very young child's feeding chair that has long legs, a footrest, and a usu. detachable tray.

High-Church (hī′chûrch′) *adj.* Of or relating to a group in the Anglican Church that maintains traditional definitions of authority, the episcopacy, and the sacraments.

high-class (hī′klăs′) *adj.* Of superior quality; first-class.

high comedy *n.* Comedy of a sophisticated and witty nature, often satirizing genteel society.

high commissioner *n.* **1.** A chief commissioner or one of high rank. **2.** A chief representative of the government of one country who is assigned to an ambassadorial post in another.

high-count (hī′kount′) *adj.* Having a large number of warp and filling threads per square inch. Used of a woven fabric.

high court *n. Law.* See **Supreme Court** 2.

high-def•i•ni•tion television (hī′dĕf′ə-nĭsh′ən) *n.* A television system that has twice the standard number of scanning lines per frame and so produces greater detail.

high-den•si•ty (hī′dĕn′sĭ-tē) *adj.* Having a high concentration: *high-density urban areas.*

high-density lipoprotein *n.* A complex of lipids and proteins that transports cholesterol in the blood.

high-end (hī′ĕnd′) *adj. Informal.* Sophisticated and discerning: *the high-end consumer.*

high-en•er•gy (hī′ĕn′ər-jē) *adj.* **1.** Of or relating to elementary particles with energies exceeding hundreds of thousands of electron volts. **2.** Yielding a large amount of energy in a chemical reaction. **3.** Vigorous; dynamic.

high•er criticism (hī′ər) *n.* Critical study of biblical texts to ascertain their history and meaning. **—higher critic** *n.*

higher education *n.* Education beyond the secondary level.

higher law *n.* A moral or religious principle that takes precedence over the constitutions or statutes of society.

high•er-up (hī′ər-ŭp′) *n. Informal.* One who has a rank, position, or status superior to others.

high•est common factor (hī′ĭst) *n. Math.* See **greatest common divisor.**

high explosive *n.* An explosive that combusts nearly instantaneously, thereby producing a violent shattering effect.

high•fa•lu•tin or **hi•fa•lu•tin** (hī′fə-lo͞ot′n) also **high•fa•lu•ting** (-lo͞ot′n, -lo͞o′tĭng) *adj. Informal.* Pompous or pretentious. [?]

high fashion *n.* **1.** See **high style. 2.** See **haute couture.**

high fidelity *n.* The electronic reproduction of sound, esp. from broadcast or recorded sources, with minimal distortion. **—high′-fi•del′i•ty** (hī′fĭ-dĕl′ĭ-tē, -fī-) *adj.*

high-five (hī′fīv′) *n. Slang.* A gesture, as of greeting, in which one person slaps an upraised palm against that of another.

high•fli•er also **high•fli•er** (hī′flī′ər) *n.* **1.** One who is extravagant or extreme in manner or opinions. **2.** A stock that sells well above its original value.

high-flown (hī′flōn′) *adj.* **1.** Exceedingly lofty or exalted. **2.** Highly pretentious or inflated: *high-flown rhetoric.*

high•fly•ing (hī′flī′ĭng) *adj.* **1.** Rising to a great height. **2.** Unusually extravagant, affected, or ambitious.

high frequency *n.* A radio frequency in the range between 3 and 30 megahertz.

High German (hī) *n.* **1.** German as spoken and written in central and southern Germany. **2.** See **German** 2. [Transl. of Ger. *Hochdeutsch* : *hoch*, high (< the area's mountainous terrain) + *Deutsch*, German.]

high-grade (hī′grād′) *adj.* Of superior grade or quality.

high•hand•ed (hī′hăn′dĭd) *adj.* Arrogant; overbearing. — **high′hand′ed•ly** *adv.* — **high′hand′ed•ness** *n.*

high hat *n.* **1.** See **top hat. 2.** *Mus.* A set of high-hat cymbals.

high-hat (hī′hăt′) *Informal.* — *tr.v.* **-hat•ted, -hat•ting, -hats.** To treat in a condescending or supercilious manner. — *adj.* Snobbish; haughty.

high-hat cymbal *n. Mus.* One of a pair of cymbals positioned to be worked by a foot pedal.

High Holy Day *n. Judaism.* **1.** Rosh Hashanah or Yom Kippur. **2. High Holy Days.** The period from Rosh Hashanah to the end of Yom Kippur.

high horse *n. Informal.* A mood or an attitude of stubborn arrogance or contempt.

high•jack (hī′jăk′) *Informal. v. & n.* Var. of **hijack.**

high jinks or **hi•jinks** (hī′jĭnks′) *pl.n.* Playful, often noisy and rowdy activity, usu. involving mischievous pranks.

high jump *n. Sports.* **1.** A jump for height made over a horizontal bar in a track-and-field contest. **2.** A contest in which high jumps are made. — **high jumper** *n.*

high•land (hī′lənd) *n.* **1.** Elevated land. **2. highlands.** A mountainous or hilly section of a country. — **high′land** *adj.* — **high′land•er** *n.*

High•land (hī′lənd). A town of NW IN, a suburb in the Chicago-Gary area. Pop. 23,696.

Highland fling *n.* A lively folk dance originating in the Highlands of Scotland.

Highland Park. 1. A city of NE IL, a suburb of Chicago on Lake Michigan. Pop. 30,575. **2.** A city of SE MI surrounded by Detroit. Pop. 20,121.

High•lands (hī′ləndz). A region of central and N Scotland including the Grampian Mts. — **High′land** *adj.* — **High′land•er** *n.*

high-lev•el (hī′lĕv′əl) *adj. Comp. Sci.* Of, relating to, or being a language, such as BASIC, in which each instruction corresponds to several instructions in machine language.

high•life or **high life** (hī′līf′) *n. Informal.* An extravagant or luxurious style of living. — **high′-lif′er** *n.*

high•light (hī′līt′) *n.* **1.** A strongly illuminated area or spot in a drawing, painting, or photograph. **2.** An esp. significant or interesting detail or event. — *tr.v.* **-light•ed, -light•ing, -lights. 1.** To give a highlight to (the subject of a painting, for example). **2.a.** To make prominent; emphasize. **b.** To be a highlight of. **3.** To mark (text) with a highlighter.

high•light•er (hī′lī′tər) *n.* **1.** A usu. fluorescent marker used to mark important passages of text. **2.** A cosmetic for emphasizing areas of the face, such as the eyes or cheekbones.

high-low (hī′lō′) *n. Games.* **1.** A poker game in which both high and low hands can win. **2.** A signal chiefly in bridge for one's partner to lead a suit.

High Mass *n. Rom. Cath. Ch.* A form of Mass, now obsolete, in which the celebrant was assisted by a deacon and a subdeacon and accompanied by acolytes, a thurifer, and a choir.

high-mind•ed (hī′mīn′dĭd) *adj.* Characterized by elevated ideals or conduct; noble. — **high′-mind′ed•ly** *adv.* — **high′-mind′ed•ness** *n.*

high muckamuck *n. Slang.* An important, often overbearing person. [< Chinook Jargon *hayo makamak*, plenty to eat.]

high•ness (hī′nĭs) *n.* **1.** The quality or condition of being high. **2. Highness.** Used with *His, Her,* or *Your* as a title and form of address for a prince or princess: *Her Royal Highness.*

high noon *n.* **1.** Exactly noon. **2.** The highest or most advanced stage or period: *the high noon of her creativity.*

high-oc•tane (hī′ŏk′tān) *adj.* **1.** Having a high octane number and thus good antiknock properties and high efficiency: *high-octane gas.* **2.** *Slang.* High-powered; dynamic.

high-pitched (hī′pĭcht′) *adj.* **1.** High in pitch, as a voice or musical tone. **2.** Steeply sloped, as a roof. **3.** Marked by or indicating intense emotion: *a high-pitched debate.*

high place *n.* In early Semitic religions, a place of worship built usu. on top of a hill.

[illegible]**int.** A city of N-central NC SW of Greensboro; settled [illegible]0. Pop. 69,496.

[illegible]**d** (hī′pou′ərd) also **high-pow•er** (-pou′ər) *adj.* [illegible] power or energy; dynamic.

[illegible] (hī′prĕsh′ər) *adj.* **1.** Of or relating to pres[illegible] normal, esp. higher than atmospheric pres[illegible] **a.** Using aggressive, persistent persuasive tactics. **b.** Full of or imposing great stress or tension.

high priest *n.* **1.** *Judaism.* A chief priest from among the male priesthood descended from Aaron. **2.** The head or chief proponent, as of a movement. — **high priesthood** *n.*

high priestess *n.* The female head or chief proponent, as of a movement.

high relief *n.* Sculptural relief in which the modeled forms project from the background by at least half their depth.

high-res•o•lu•tion (hī′rĕz′ə-lo͞o′shən) *adj.* **1.** Relating to an image that has fine detail. **2.** *Comp. Sci.* Relating to an output device whose images contain a large number of pixels.

high-rise (hī′rīz′) *adj.* **1.** Being a high-rise. **2.** Of, relating to, or marked by multistoried buildings: *a high-rise district.* — *n.* or **high rise.** A multistoried building equipped with elevators.

high-risk (hī′rĭsk′) *adj.* **1.** Of, relating to, or marked by risk. **2.** Being particularly subject to potential danger or hazard.

high•road or **high road** (hī′rōd′) *n.* **1.a.** The easiest or surest path or course. **b.** The most positive, diplomatic, or optimistic course. **2.** *Chiefly British.* A main road; a highway.

high roller *n. Slang.* **1.** One that spends or invests freely, rashly, or extravagantly. **2.** One who gambles rashly or for high stakes. — **high′-roll′ing** (hī′rō′lĭng) *adj.*

high school *n.* A secondary school that usu. includes grades 9 through 12 or 10 through 12. — **high′-school′** (hī′sko͞ol′) *adj.* — **high school′er** *n.*

high seas *pl.n.* The open waters of an ocean or a sea beyond the limits of the territorial jurisdiction of a country.

high sign *n. Informal.* An often prearranged secret sign or signal intended esp. to warn or inform.

high-sound•ing (hī′soun′dĭng) *adj.* Pretentiously impressive; pompous: *high-sounding oratory.*

high-speed (hī′spēd′) *adj.* **1.** Operated or designed for operation at high speed. **2.** Taking place at high speed: *a high-speed chase.* **3.** Having a speed of 50–500 frames per second to record events that occur too rapidly for usual photography.

high-spir•it•ed (hī′spĭr′ĭ-tĭd) *adj.* **1.** Having a proud or unbroken spirit: *a high-spirited horse.* **2.** Vivacious; lively. — **high′-spir′it•ed•ly** *adv.* — **high′-spir′it•ed•ness** *n.*

high-stick•ing (hī′stĭk′ĭng) *n. Sports.* The act of carrying the blade of an ice hockey stick at a height ruled illegal.

high street *n. Chiefly British.* A main street.

high-strung (hī′strŭng′) *adj.* Very nervous and easily excited.

high style *n.* The latest in fashion or design, usu. intended for an exclusive clientele. — **high′-style′** (hī′stīl′) *adj.*

hight (hīt) *adj. Archaic.* Named or called. [ME, p.part. of *highten, hihten*, to call, be called < *hehte, hight*, p.t. of *hoten* < OE *hātan.* See **kei-²*.**]

high•tail (hī′tāl′) *intr.v.* **-tailed, -tail•ing, -tails.** *Slang.* To go as fast as possible, esp. in retreating: *hightailed out of town.* [< those animals that raise their tails when fleeing.]

high tea *n. Chiefly British.* A fairly substantial meal that includes tea and is served in the late afternoon or early evening.

high tech (tĕk) *Informal.* — *n.* **1.** High technology. **2.** A style of interior decoration marked by the use of industrial materials, equipment, or design. — *adj.* also **hi-tech** (hī′tĕk′). Of, relating to, or resembling high technology.

high technology *n.* Technology that involves highly advanced or specialized systems or devices. — **high′-tech•nol′o•gy** (hī′tĕk-nŏl′ə-jē) *adj.*

high-ten•sion (hī′tĕn′shən) *adj.* Having a high voltage.

high-test (hī′tĕst′) *adj.* **1.** Of or relating to highly volatile high-octane gasoline. **2.** Meeting exacting requirements.

high tide *n.* **1.a.** The tide at its fullest, when the water reaches its highest level. **b.** The time at which this tide occurs. **2.** A point of culmination; a climax.

high-toned (hī′tōnd′) *adj.* **1.** Intellectually, morally, or socially superior. **2.** *Informal.* Pretentiously elegant or fashionable.

high-tops (hī′tŏps′) *pl.n.* Sneakers or athletic shoes that lace up to the ankle.

high treason *n.* Treason against one's country or sovereign.

high water *n.* **1.** High tide. **2.** The state of a body of water that has reached its highest level.

high-wa•ter mark (hī′wô′tər, -wŏt′ər) *n.* **1.** A mark indicating the highest level reached by a body of water. **2.** The highest point, as of achievement; the apex.

high•way (hī′wā′) *n.* A main public road, esp. one connecting towns and cities.

high•way•man (hī′wā′mən) *n.* A man who holds up and robs travelers on a road.

highway patrol *n.* A state law enforcement organization whose police officers patrol the public highways.

highway robbery *n.* **1.** Robbery usu. of travelers on or near a public road. **2.** *Informal.* The exaction of an exorbitantly high price or fee. — **highway robber** *n.*

high wire *n.* A tightrope for aerialists that is stretched very high above the ground. — **high′-wire′** (hī′wīr′) *adj.*

H.I.H. *abbr.* **1.** Her Imperial Highness. **2.** His Imperial Highness.

hi•jack also **high•jack** (hī′jăk′) *Informal.* — *tr.v.* **-jacked, -jack•ing, -jacks. 1.a.** To stop and rob (a vehicle in transit). **b.** To steal (goods) from a vehicle in transit. **c.** To seize control of (a moving vehicle) by use of force, esp. to reach an alter-

high jump
Fosbury flop technique

high relief

ă pat	oi boy
ā pay	ou out
âr care	o͝o took
ä father	o͞o boot
ĕ pet	ŭ cut
ē be	ûr urge
ĭ pit	th thin
ī pie	*th* this
îr pier	hw which
ŏ pot	zh vision
ō toe	ə about, item
ô paw	

Stress marks:
′ (primary);
′ (secondary), as in
dictionary (dĭk′shə-nĕr′ē)

nate destination. **2.a.** To steal from as if by hijacking. **b.** To swindle or subject to extortion. — *n.* The act or an instance of hijacking. [Prob. back-formation < *highjacker*, perh. < *jacker*, holdup man < JACK, to jacklight.] — **hi′jack′er** *n.*

hi•jinks (hī′jĭngks′) *pl.n.* Var. of **high jinks.**

hike (hīk) *v.* **hiked, hik•ing, hikes.** — *intr.* **1.** To go on an extended walk for pleasure or exercise. **2.** To rise, esp. to rise upward out of place: *My coat had hiked up in the back.* — *tr.* **1.** To increase or raise in amount, esp. abruptly. **2.** To pull or raise with a sudden motion; hitch: *hiked up her knee socks.* **3.** *Football.* To snap (the ball). — *n.* **1.** A long walk or march. **2.** An often abrupt increase or rise. **3.** *Football.* See **snap** 13. — ***phrasal verb.* hike out.** *Naut.* To sit facing the sail and lean far backward and over the side of a small boat in order to reduce excessive heeling. — ***idiom.* take a hike.** *Slang.* To leave because one is unwanted. [?] — **hik′er** *n.*

hi•la (hī′lə) *n.* Pl. of **hilum.**

hi•lar•i•ous (hĭ-lâr′ē-əs, -lăr′-, hī-) *adj.* Characterized by or causing great merriment. [Lat. *hilarus, hilaris*, cheerful; see HILARITY + -IOUS.] — **hi•lar′i•ous•ly** *adv.*

hi•lar•i•ty (hĭ-lăr′ĭ-tē, -lâr′-, hī-) *n.* Great merriment. [ME *hilarite*, good spirits < OFr. < Lat. *hilaritās* < *hilaris*, cheerful < Gk. *hilaros.*]

Hil•de•brand (hĭl′də-brănd′). See **Gregory VII.**

Hil•des•heim (hĭl′dəs-hīm′, -dĕs-). A city of central Germany SSE of Hanover; passed to Prussia in 1866. Pop. 101,017.

hill (hĭl) *n.* **1.** A well-defined natural elevation smaller than a mountain. **2.** A small heap, pile, or mound. **3.a.** A mound of earth piled around and over a plant. **b.** A plant thus covered. **4.** An incline, esp. of a road; a slope. **5. Hill. a.** Capitol Hill. **b.** The U.S. Congress. — *tr.v.* **hilled, hill•ing, hills. 1.** To form into a hill, pile, or heap. **2.** To cover (a plant) with a mound of soil. — ***idiom.* over the hill.** *Informal.* Past one's prime. [ME *hil* < OE *hyll.* See **kel-**[2]***.**] — **hill′er** *n.*

Hill, Ambrose Powell. 1825–65. Amer. Confederate officer whose charge began the Battle of Gettysburg (1863).

Hill, J(ames) J(erome). 1838–1916. Amer. railroad magnate who promoted the Great Northern Railway.

Hil•la•ry (hĭl′ə-rē), Sir **Edmund Percival.** b. 1919. New Zealand explorer who in 1959 with Tenzing Norgay first attained the summit of Mt. Everest.

hill•bil•ly (hĭl′bĭl′ē) *n., pl.* **-lies.** *Informal.* A person from the backwoods or a remote mountain area. [HILL + *Billy*, a nickname for William.]

hillbilly music *n. Mus.* A type of country music originating in the Appalachian Mountains, based on traditional folk music.

Hill•crest Heights (hĭl′krĕst′). A community of W-central MD, a suburb of Washington DC. Pop. 17,136.

Hil•lel (hĭl′ĕl, -āl, hē-lĕl′). fl. 1st cent. B.C.–A.D. 1st cent. Palestinian rabbi who influenced the interpretation of Judaic law.

hill myna *n.* A starling *(Gracula religiosa)* native to Europe and North America that is able to mimic human speech.

hill•ock (hĭl′ək) *n.* **1.** A small hill. **2.** *Biol.* A small protuberance or elevation, as from an organ, a tissue, or a structure. [ME *hillok* < *hil*, hill. See HILL.] — **hill′ock•y** *adj.*

Hills•bor•o (hĭlz′bûr′ō, -bŭr′ō). A city of NW OR W of Portland; settled in the 1840's. Pop. 37,520.

hill•side (hĭl′sīd′) *n.* The side or slope of a hill, situated between the foot and the summit.

Hill•side (hĭl′sīd′). A community of NE NJ N of Elizabeth. Pop. 21,044.

hill•top (hĭl′tŏp′) *n.* The crest or top of a hill.

hill•y (hĭl′ē) *adj.* **-i•er, -i•est. 1.** Having many hills. **2.** Similar to a hill; steep. — **hill′i•ness** *n.*

Hi•lo (hē′lō). A city of HI on the E coast of Hawaii I. on **Hilo Bay,** an inlet of the Pacific; settled in the 1820's. Pop. 37,808.

hilt (hĭlt) *n.* The handle of a weapon or tool. — ***idiom.* to the hilt.** To the limit; completely. [ME < OE.]

Hil•ton (hĭl′tən), **James.** 1900–54. British novelist whose works include *Lost Horizon* (1933).

Hilton Head Island. An island off the S coast of SC in the Sea Is. of the Atlantic Ocean.

hi•lum (hī′ləm) *n., pl.* **-la** (-lə). **1.** *Bot.* **a.** The scar on a seed, such as a bean, indicating the point of attachment to the funiculus. **b.** The nucleus of a starch grain. **2.** *Anat.* The area through which ducts, nerves, or blood vessels enter and leave an organ or a gland. [Lat. *hīlum*, trifle.] — **hi′lar** (-lər) *adj.*

Hil•ver•sum (hĭl′vər-səm). A city of central Netherlands SE of Amsterdam. Pop. 88,417.

him (hĭm) *pron.* The objective case of **he. 1.** Used as the direct object of a verb: *They saw him.* **2.** Used as the indirect object of a verb: *They offered him a ride.* **3.** Used as the object of a preposition: *This call is for him.* **4.** *Informal.* Used as a predicate nominative: *It's him.* See Usage Note at **I**[1]. — *n.* A male: *The dog is a him.* [ME < OE. See **ko-*.**]

H.I.M. *abbr.* **1.** Her Imperial Majesty. **2.** His Imperial Majesty.

Him•a•la•ya Mountains (hĭm′ə-lā′ə, hĭ-mäl′yə). A mountain system of S-central Asia extending c. 2,414 km (1,500 mi) through Kashmir, N India, S Tibet, Nepal, Sikkim, and Bhutan. — **Him′a•la′yan** *adj. & n.*

hi•mat•i•on (hĭ-măt′ē-ŏn′) *n., pl.* **-i•a** (-ē-ə). A rectangular cloak worn in ancient Greece. [Gk., dim. of *hima, himat-*, garment, var. of *heima* < *hennunai*, to clothe. See **wes-**[2]***.**]

Hi•me•ji (hē′mĕ-jē′, hē-mĕ′jē). A city of SW Honshu, Japan, WNW of Kobe. Pop. 452,916.

Himm•ler (hĭm′lər), **Heinrich.** 1900–45. German Nazi leader who directed the Nazi elite forces, the SS (1929–45), and coordinated the operation of the concentration and extermination camps (1941–45).

him•self (hĭm-sĕlf′) *pron.* **1.** That one identical with him: **a.** Used reflexively as the direct or indirect object of a verb or the object of a preposition: *He praised himself.* **b.** Used for emphasis: *He himself came.* **c.** Used in an absolute construction: *In the black himself, he could help his cousin.* **2.** His normal or healthy condition or state: *He's feeling himself again.* See Usage Note at **myself.** [ME < OE *himselfum* : *him*, him; see HIM + *selfum*, dative of *self*, self; see SELF.]

Him•yar•ite (hĭm′yə-rīt′) *adj.* Of or relating to the Himyarites, their language, or their culture. — *n.* **1.** A member of an ancient tribe of southwest Arabia. **2.** The Semitic language of the ancient Himyarites. [After *Himyar*, a legendary king of Yemen.] — **Him′yar•it′ic** (-rĭt′ĭk) *adj.*

hin (hĭn) *n.* A unit of liquid measure used by the ancient Hebrews, equal to about five liters. [ME < LLat. < Gk. < Heb. *hīn*, of Egypt. orig.]

Hi•na•ya•na (hē′nə-yä′nə) *n. Buddhism.* A conservative branch of Buddhism following the Pali scriptures and the nontheistic ideal of self-purification to nirvana. [Skt. *hīnayānam*, lesser vehicle : *hīna-*, inferior; see **ghē-*** + *yānam*, vehicle, way; see **ei-*.**] — **Hi′na•ya′nist** *n.*

hind[1] (hīnd) also **hind•er** (hīn′dər) *adj.* Located at or forming the back or rear; posterior: *an animal's hind legs.* [ME *hinde*, short for *bihinde*, behind < OE *bihindan.* See **ko-*.**]

hind[2] (hīnd) *n.* **1.** A female red deer. **2.** Any of several fishes of the genus *Epinephelus* of Atlantic waters, related to the groupers. [ME < OE.]

hind[3] (hīnd) *n.* **1.** *Chiefly British.* A farm laborer, esp. a skilled worker. **2.** *Archaic.* A country bumpkin; a rustic. [Alteration of ME *hine*, household servants, poss. < OE *hīne*, genitive of *hīgan, hīwan*, members of a household. See **kei-**[1]***.**]

Hind. *abbr.* **1.** Hindi. **2.** Hindustani.

hind•brain (hīnd′brān′) *n.* See **rhombencephalon.**

Hin•de•mith (hĭn′də-mĭth, -mĭt), **Paul.** 1895–1963. German composer of chamber music, instrumental works, and operas.

Hin•den•burg (hĭn′dən-bûrg′, -bŏŏrk′), **Paul von.** 1847–1934. German politician who was president of the Weimar Republic (1925–34).

hin•der[1] (hĭn′dər) *v.* **-dered, -der•ing, -ders.** — *tr.* **1.** To be or get in the way of. **2.** To obstruct or delay the progress of. — *intr.* To interfere with action or progress. [ME *hindren* < OE *hindrian.* See **ko-*.**] — **hin′der•er** *n.*

hind•er[2] (hīn′dər) *adj.* Var. of **hind**[1].

hind•gut (hīnd′gŭt′) *n.* The caudal portion of the embryonic alimentary canal in vertebrates.

Hin•di (hĭn′dē) *n.* **1.** A group of Indic dialects of northern India. **2.** The literary and official language of northern India, based on these dialects. [Hindi *Hindī* < *Hind*, India < Pers. < OPers. *Hindu*, the Indus R. < Skt. *sindhuḥ*, river.] — **Hin′di** *adj.*

hind limb *n.* A posterior appendage, such as a leg or wing.

hind•most (hīnd′mōst′) also **hind•er•most** (hīn′dər-) *adj.* Farthest to the rear; last.

hind•quar•ter (hīnd′kwôr′tər) *n.* **1.** The posterior portion of a side of beef, lamb, veal, or mutton, including a hind leg and one or two ribs. **2. hindquarters.** The posterior part of a quadruped, adjacent to the hind legs.

hin•drance (hĭn′drəns) *n.* **1.a.** The act of hindering. **b.** The condition of being hindered. **2.** One that hinders. [ME *hindraunce*, harm < *hindren*, to hinder. See HINDER[1].]

hind•sight (hīnd′sīt′) *n.* **1.** Perception of the significance and nature of events after they have occurred. **2.** The rear sight of a firearm.

Hin•du (hĭn′do͞o) *adj.* **1.** Of or relating to Hinduism. **2.** Of or relating to the Hindus and their culture. — *n.* An adherent of Hinduism. [Pers. *Hindū* < *Hind*, India. See HINDI.]

Hindu calendar *n.* The lunisolar calendar of Hindu religious life, dating in its classic form from the fourth century A.D.

Hin•du•ism (hĭn′do͞o-ĭz′əm) *n.* A diverse body of religion, philosophy, and culture native to India, characterized esp. by a belief in reincarnation and a supreme being of many forms and natures.

Hindu Kush (ko͝osh, kŭsh). A mountain range of SW Asia extending more than 805 km (500 mi) from N Pakistan to NE Afghanistan and rising to 7,695.2 m (25,230 ft).

Hin•du•stan (hĭn′do͞o-stăn′, -stän′). A historical region of India considered at various times to include only the upper Ganges R. plateau or all of N India from the Himalaya Mts. t... Deccan Plateau and from the Punjab to Assam. Th... also been applied to the entire Indian subconti...

Hin•du•sta•ni (hĭn′do͞o-stä′nē, -stăn′ē) *n.* A ... dialects that includes Urdu and Hindi. — *a*... to Hindustan, its people, or the Hindustar...

Hines (hīnz), **Earl ("Fatha").** 1905–83. Am... first gained wide recognition in the 192...

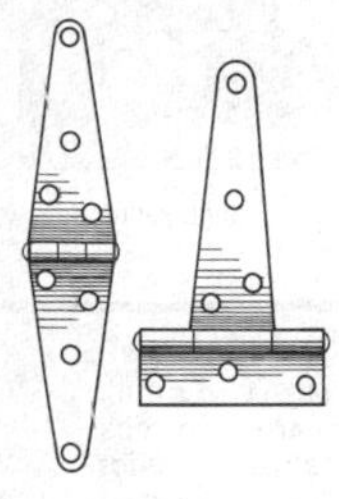

hinge
Left: Strap hinge
Right: T hinge

hinge (hĭnj) *n.* **1.a.** A jointed or flexible device that allows the turning or pivoting of a part, such as a door, on a stationary frame. **b.** A similar structure or part. **2.** A small folded paper rectangle gummed on one side, used esp. to fasten stamps in an album. **3.** A point or circumstance on which subsequent events depend. — *v.* **hinged, hing•ing, hing•es.** — *tr.* **1.** To attach by or equip with or as if with hinges or a hinge. **2.** To consider or make (something) dependent on something else; predicate. — *intr.* To be contingent on a single factor; depend. [ME. See **konk-*.**]

hinge joint *n.* A joint, such as the elbow, in which a convex part of one bone fits into a concave part of another.

Hing•ham (hĭng′əm). A town of E MA on Massachusetts Bay SE of Boston. Pop. 19,821.

hin•ny (hĭn′ē) *n., pl.* **-nies.** The hybrid offspring of a male horse and a female donkey. [Alteration of Lat. *hinnus* < Gk. *ginnos, innos.*]

Hin•shel•wood (hĭn′shəl-wŏŏd′, -chəl-), Sir **Cyril Norman.** 1897–1967. British chemist who shared a 1956 Nobel Prize.

hint (hĭnt) *n.* **1.** A slight indication or intimation: *a hint of scandal.* **2.a.** A brief or indirect suggestion; a tip. **b.** A statement conveying information in an indirect fashion; a clue. **3.** A barely perceptible amount: *a hint of color.* **4.** *Archaic.* An occasion; an opportunity. — *v.* **hint•ed, hint•ing, hints.** — *tr.* To indicate or make known in an indirect manner. — *intr.* To give a hint. See Syns at **suggest.** [Prob. < ME *hinten, henten,* to catch, grasp < OE *hentan.*] — **hint′er** *n.*

hin•ter•land (hĭn′tər-lănd′) *n.* **1.** The land next to and inland from a coast. **2.a.** A region remote from urban areas; backcountry. **b.** A region far from metropolitan culture. [Ger. : *hinter-*, behind (< MHGer. *hinter* < OHGer. *hintar;* see **ko-***) + *Land,* land (< MHGer. *lant* < OHGer.; see **lendh-***).]

hip¹ (hĭp) *n.* **1.a.** The laterally projecting prominence of the pelvis or pelvic region from the waist to the thigh. **b.** A homologous posterior part in quadrupeds. **c.** The hip joint. **2.** *Archit.* The external angle formed by the meeting of two adjacent sloping sides of a roof. [ME < OE *hype.*]

hip² (hĭp) also **hep** (hĕp) *adj.* **hip•per, hip•pest** also **hep•per, hep•pest.** *Slang.* **1.** Keenly aware of, knowledgeable about, or interested in the latest developments. **2.** Cognizant; wise. **3.** Very fashionable or stylish. [Perh. < Wolof *hipi, hepi,* to open one's eyes, be aware.] — **hip** *n. & v.* — **hip′ly** *adv.*

hip³ (hĭp) *n.* A rose hip. [ME *hipe* < OE *hēope.*]

hip⁴ (hĭp) *interj.* Usu. used to begin a cheer: *Hip, hip, hooray!*

hip•bone (hĭp′bōn′) *n.* Either of two large flat bones each forming one of the lateral halves of the pelvis and consisting of the fused ilium, ischium, and pubis.

hip boot *n.* A very high boot extending to the hips.

hip-hop (hĭp′hŏp′) *n.* The popular culture of big-city and esp. inner-city youth, characterized by graffiti art, break dancing, and rap music. — *adj.* Of, relating to, or characteristic of this culture. [Prob. HIP² + HOP¹.]

hip-hug•gers (hĭp′hŭg′ərz) *pl.n.* Tight-fitting pants whose waistline rests at hip level.

hip joint *n.* The ball-and-socket joint formed by the head of the femur and the cup-shaped cavity of the hipbone.

Hip•par•chus¹ (hĭ-pär′kəs). d. 514 B.C. Athenian tyrant (527–514) who ruled with his brother Hippias.

Hip•par•chus² (hĭ-pär′kəs). fl. 2nd cent. B.C. Greek astronomer who mapped the earliest known star chart.

hipped¹ (hĭpt) *adj.* Having hips, esp. of a given kind. Often used in combination: *slim-hipped; large-hipped.*

hipped² (hĭpt) *adj. Slang.* Interested or preoccupied to a great degree. [Prob. < *hip,* to make aware < HIP².]

hipped³ (hĭpt) *adj. Chiefly British.* Melancholy; depressed. [Shortening and alteration of HYPOCHONDRIAC.]

Hip•pi•as (hĭp′ē-əs). d. 490 B.C. Athenian tyrant (527–510) who governed with his brother Hipparchus until 514 and was exiled by the Spartans (510).

hip•pie also **hip•py** (hĭp′ē) *n., pl.* **-pies.** *Slang.* A person who rejects many of the conventional standards and customs of society, esp. one who advocates extreme liberalism. [< HIP².]

hip•po (hĭp′ō) *n., pl.* **-pos.** A hippopotamus.

Hip•po (hĭp′ō) also **Hippo Re•gi•us** (rē′jē-əs). An ancient city of NW Africa in present-day NE Algeria S of Annaba.

hip•po•cam•pus (hĭp′ə-kăm′pəs) *n., pl.* **-pi** (-pī′). *Anat.* A ridge in the floor of each lateral ventricle of the brain that consists mainly of gray matter and has a central role in memory processes. [LLat., a sea horse with a horse's forelegs and a dolphin's tail (< its shape in cross section) < Gk. *hippokampos* : *hippos,* horse; see **ekwo-*** + *kampos,* sea monster.] — **hip′po•cam′pal** (-pəl) *adj.*

hip•po•cras (hĭp′ə-krăs′) *n.* A cordial made from spiced wine, formerly used as a medicine. [ME *ipocras* < OFr. *ypocras,*
High Po... < alteration of *Hippocras,* Hippocrates.]
before 17... **tes** (hĭ-pŏk′rə-tēz′). "the Father of Medicine."
high-pow•ere... c. Greek physician who laid the foundations of
Having great ... ine. — **Hip′po•crat′ic** (hĭp′ə-krăt′ĭk) *adj.*
high-pres•sure ... *n.* An oath of ethical professional behavior
sures higher tha... ew physicians, falsely attributed to Hippoc-
sure. **2.** *Informa*...

Hip•po•crene (hĭp′ə-krēn′, hĭp′ə-krē′nē) *n. Gk. Myth.* A fountain on Mount Helicon, Greece, sacred to the Muses and a source of poetic inspiration. [Lat. *Hippocrēnē* < Gk. *Hippokrēnē* : *hippos,* horse (< the myth that Pegasus's hoof created it); see **ekwo-*** + *krēnē,* fountain.]

hip•po•drome (hĭp′ə-drōm′) *n.* **1.** *Sports.* An arena for equestrian shows. **2.** An open-air stadium with an oval course for horse and chariot races in ancient Greece and Rome. [Fr. < OFr. *ypodrome* < Lat. *hippodromos* < Gk. : *hippos,* horse; see **ekwo-*** + *dromos,* racecourse.]

hip•po•griff also **hip•po•gryph** (hĭp′ə-grĭf′) *n. Myth.* A monster having the wings, claws, and head of a griffin and the body and hindquarters of a horse. [Fr. *hippogriffe* < Ital. *ippogrifo* : *ippo-*, horse (< Gk. *hippos;* see **ekwo-***) + *grifo,* griffin (< Lat. *grȳphus;* see GRIFFIN).]

Hip•pol•y•ta (hĭ-pŏl′ĭ-tə) *n. Gk. Myth.* A queen of the Amazons who was defeated by Hercules.

Hip•pol•y•tus (hĭ-pŏl′ĭ-təs) *n. Gk. Myth.* A son of Hippolyta and Theseus who was killed by Poseidon.

Hip•pom•e•nes (hĭ-pŏm′ə-nēz) *n. Gk. Myth.* The suitor who tricked and thereby outran Atalanta.

hip•po•pot•a•mus (hĭp′ə-pŏt′ə-məs) *n., pl.* **-mus•es** or **-mi** (-mī′). **1.** A large, chiefly aquatic African herbivorous mammal *(Hippopotamus amphibius)* having thick skin, short legs with four toes, and a broad wide-mouthed muzzle. **2.** The pygmy hippopotamus. [Lat. < Gk. *hippopotamos* : *hippos,* horse; see **ekwo-*** + *potamos,* river; see **pet-*.**]

Hippo Re•gi•us (rē′jē-əs). See **Hippo.**

hip•py (hĭp′ē) *n. Slang.* Var. of **hippie.**

hip roof *n.* A roof having sloping edges and sides.

hip•ster (hĭp′stər) *n. Slang.* One who is interested in the latest trends and tastes, esp. a devotee of modern jazz.

hip•ster•ism (hĭp′stə-rĭz′əm) *n. Slang.* **1.** The quality or condition of being hip. **2.** The lifestyle characteristic of hipsters.

hi•ra•ga•na (hîr′ə-gä′nə) *n.* A cursive kana used for polite, informal, or casual writing. [J. : *hira,* ordinary, plain + *kana,* kana; see KANA.]

Hi•ra•ka•ta (hē′rä-kä′tä, hē-rä′kä-tä′). A city of S Honshu, Japan, a suburb of Osaka. Pop. 382,257.

hir•cine (hûr′sīn′, -sĭn) *adj.* Of or characteristic of a goat, esp. in strong odor. [ME *hircyne* < Lat. *hircīnus* < *hircus,* goat.]

hire (hīr) *v.* **hired, hir•ing, hires.** — *tr.* **1.a.** To engage the services of (a person) for a fee; employ. **b.** To engage the temporary use of for a fee; rent. **2.** To grant the services of or the temporary use of for a fee. — *intr.* To obtain work: *hired on today.* — *n.* **1.a.** The act of hiring. **b.** The condition or fact of being hired. **2.a.** Payment for services; wages. **b.** Payment for the use of something. **3.** *Informal.* One hired. [ME *hiren* < OE *hȳrian.*] — **hir′a•ble, hire′a•ble** *adj.* — **hir′er** *n.*

hired gun (hīrd) *n. Slang.* **1.** One hired to kill another person. **2.** One hired to fight for or protect another.

hired hand *n.* **1.** A paid employee, esp. on a farm or ranch. **2.** *Informal.* A paid employee.

hire•ling (hīr′lĭng) *n.* One who works solely for compensation, esp. one who performs tasks considered menial or offensive.

hire purchase *n. Chiefly British.* Purchase of a commodity on an installment plan.

hir•ing hall (hīr′ĭng) *n.* A union-operated placement center where jobs are allotted to applicants according to a set order.

Hi•ro•hi•to (hîr′ō-hē′tō). 1901–89. Emperor of Japan (1926–89) who advocated the Japanese government's unconditional surrender that ended World War II (1945).

Hirohito
Photographed in 1984

Hi•ro•shi•ge (hîr′ō-shē′gä, hē′rô-shē′gĕ), **Ando.** 1797–1858. Japanese artist whose color woodblock prints include *Fifty-three Stages of the Tokaido* (1832).

Hi•ro•shi•ma (hîr′ə-shē′mə, hĭ-rō′shə-mə). A city of SW Honshu, Japan, on the Inland Sea W of Osaka; destroyed by U.S. forces in World War II with the first atomic bomb used in warfare (Aug. 6, 1945). Pop. 1,044,129.

hir•sute (hûr′sōōt′, hîr′-, hər-sōōt′) *adj.* **1.** Covered with hair; hairy. **2.** *Bot.* Covered with stiff or coarse hairs. [Lat. *hirsūtus,* hairy, bristly.] — **hir′sute′ness** *n.*

hir•sut•ism (hûr′sōō-tĭz′əm, hîr′-, hər-sōō′-) *n.* Heavy growth of hair, often in abnormal distribution.

hir•u•din (hîr-ōōd′n, hîr′ə-dən, -yə-) *n.* A substance extracted from the salivary glands of leeches and used as an anticoagulant. [Originally a trademark < Lat. *hirūdō,* leech.]

his (hĭz) *adj.* The possessive form of **he.** Used as a modifier before a noun: *his boots.* — *pron. (used with a sing. or pl. v.)* Used to indicate the one or ones belonging to him: *If you can't find your hat, take his.* [ME < OE. See **ko-*.**]

His•pan•ic (hĭ-spăn′ĭk) *adj.* **1.** Of or relating to Spain or Spanish-speaking Latin America. **2.** Of or relating to a Spanish-speaking people or culture. — *n.* **1.** A Spanish-speaking person. **2.** A U.S. citizen or resident of Latin-American or Spanish descent. [Lat. *Hispānicus* < *Hispānia,* Spain.]

Usage Note: There are a number of words denoting persons who trace their origins to a Spanish-speaking country or culture. *Hispanic* encompasses all Spanish-speaking peoples in both hemispheres and emphasizes the common denominator of language between communities that sometimes have little

ă pat	oi boy
ā pay	ou out
âr care	ŏŏ took
ä father	ōō boot
ĕ pet	ŭ cut
ē be	ûr urge
ĭ pit	th thin
ī pie	*th* this
îr pier	hw which
ŏ pot	zh vision
ō toe	ə about, item
ô paw	

Stress marks:
′ (primary);
′ (secondary), as in
dictionary (dĭk′shə-nĕr′ē)

else in common. It is widely used in both official and unofficial contexts and is entirely acceptable. *Latino* is also in wide use, but it is somewhat less formal in most contexts and is generally restricted to persons of Latin-American descent. See Usage Note at **Chicano.**

Hispanic American *n.* **1.** A U.S. citizen or resident of Hispanic descent. **2.** A Spanish American. — **His•pan′ic-A•mer′i•can** (hĭ-spăn′ĭk-ə-mĕr′ĭ-kən) *adj.*

His•pan•i•cize (hĭ-spăn′ĭ-sīz′) *tr.v.* **-cized, -ciz•ing, -ciz•es. 1.** To make Spanish in form, style, or character. **2.** To bring under Hispanic influence or control. — **His•pan′i•ci•za′tion** (-sĭ-zā′shən) *n.*

His•pan•io•la (hĭs′pən-yō′lə). Formerly **Hai•ti** (hā′tē). An island of the West Indies E of Cuba, divided between Haiti and the Dominican Republic.

His•pa•nism (hĭs′pə-nĭz′əm) or **His•pan•i•cism** (hĭ-spăn′ĭ-sĭz′əm) *n.* A Spanish word, phrase, or linguistic feature occurring in another language.

His•pa•nist (hĭs′pə-nĭst) *n.* A specialist in Spanish language or literature or in the languages and literatures of Spain, Portugal, and Latin America.

His•pa•no (hĭ-spăn′ō, -spä′nō) *n., pl.* **-nos. 1.** A native or resident of Spanish descent in the southwest United States. **2.** A Hispanic. [Short for *Hispano-American* < Sp. *hispano,* Spanish < Lat. *Hispānus* < *Hispānī,* the Spaniards.]

Hispano– *pref.* Spanish; Hispanic: *Hispanophile.* [< Lat. *Hispānus.* See HISPANO.]

his•pid (hĭs′pĭd) *adj.* Covered with stiff or rough hairs; bristly: *hispid stems.* [Lat. *hispidus.*] — **his•pid′i•ty** (hĭ-spĭd′ĭ-tē) *n.*

hiss (hĭs) *n.* **1.** A sharp sibilant sound similar to a sustained *s.* **2.** An expression of disapproval, contempt, or dissatisfaction conveyed by a hiss. — *v.* **hissed, hiss•ing, hiss•es.** — *intr.* To make a hiss. — *tr.* **1.** To utter with a hiss. **2.** To express (a negative view or reaction) by uttering a hiss. [ME *hissen,* to hiss, of imit. orig.] — **hiss′er** *n.* — **hiss′ing•ly** *adv.*

Hiss (hĭs), **Alger.** b. 1904. Amer. public official who was accused of espionage at the height of the Communist scare and was convicted of perjury (1950) in a controversial case.

his•sy fit (hĭs′ē) *n. Chiefly Southern U.S.* See **tantrum.**

hist. *abbr.* **1.** Historian. **2.** Historical. **3.** History.

his•tam•i•nase (hĭ-stăm′ə-nās′, -nāz′, hĭs′tə-mə-) *n.* An enzyme found in the digestive system that inactivates histamine.

his•ta•mine (hĭs′tə-mēn′, -mĭn) *n.* A physiologically active amine, $C_5H_9N_3$, found in plant and animal tissue and released in humans as part of an allergic reaction. [HIST(IDINE) + AMINE.] — **his′ta•min′ic** (-mĭn′ĭk) *adj.*

his•ti•dine (hĭs′tĭ-dēn′, -dĭn) *n.* An essential amino acid, $C_6H_9N_3O_2$, important for the growth and repair of tissues. [HIST(O)– + –ID(E) + –INE[2].]

his•ti•o•cyte (hĭs′tē-ə-sīt′) *n.* A relatively inactive immobile macrophage found in normal connective tissue. [Gk. *histion,* web, dim. of *histos;* see **stā-*** + –CYTE.]

histo– or **hist–** *pref.* Body tissue: *histogenesis.* [< Gk. < *histos,* web. See **stā-*.**]

his•to•chem•is•try (hĭs′tō-kĕm′ĭ-strē) *n.* The study of the chemical composition of body cells and tissues. — **his′to•chem′i•cal** (-ĭ-kəl) *adj.* — **his′to•chem′i•cal•ly** *adv.*

his•to•com•pat•i•bil•i•ty (hĭs′tō-kəm-păt′ə-bĭl′ĭ-tē) *n., pl.* **-ties.** A state in which the absence of immunological interference permits the grafting of tissue or the transfusion of blood without rejection. — **his′to•com•pat′i•ble** *adj.*

his•to•gen•e•sis (hĭs′tō-jĕn′ĭ-sĭs) *n.* The formation and development of body tissues. — **his′to•ge•net′ic** (-jə-nĕt′ĭk), **his′to•gen′ic** (-jĕn′ĭk) *adj.* — **his′to•ge•net′i•cal•ly, his′to•gen′i•cal•ly** *adv.*

his•to•gram (hĭs′tə-grăm′) *n.* A bar graph of a frequency distribution in which the widths of the bars are proportional to the classes into which the variable has been divided and the heights of the bars are proportional to the class frequencies.

his•tol•o•gy (hĭ-stŏl′ə-jē) *n., pl.* **-gies. 1.** The anatomical study of the microscopic structure of animal and plant tissues. **2.** The microscopic structure of tissue. — **his′to•log′i•cal** (hĭs′tə-lŏj′ĭ-kəl), **his′to•log′ic** *adj.* — **his′to•log′i•cal•ly** *adv.* — **his•tol′o•gist** *n.*

his•tol•y•sis (hĭ-stŏl′ĭ-sĭs) *n.* The breakdown and disintegration of organic tissue. — **his′to•lyt′ic** (hĭs′tə-lĭt′ĭk) *adj.* — **his′to•lyt′i•cal•ly** *adv.*

his•tone (hĭs′tōn′) *n.* Any of several small basic proteins most commonly found in association with the DNA in chromatin.

his•to•pa•thol•o•gy (hĭs′tō-pə-thŏl′ə-jē, -pă-) *n.* The study of the microscopic anatomical changes in diseased tissue. — **his′to•path′o•log′ic** (-păth′ə-lŏj′ĭk), **his′to•path′o•log′i•cal** *adj.* — **his′to•pa•thol′o•gist** *n.*

his•to•phys•i•ol•o•gy (hĭs′tō-fĭz′ē-ŏl′ə-jē) *n.* The branch of physiology that deals with the structure and function of tissues. — **his′to•phys′i•o•log′ic** (-ē-ə-lŏj′ĭk), **his′to•phys′i•o•log′i•cal** (-ĭ-kəl) *adj.*

his•to•plas•mo•sis (hĭs′tō-plăz-mō′sĭs) *n., pl.* **-ses** (-sēz). A disease caused by the inhalation of spores of the fungus *Histoplasma capsulatum,* most often asymptomatic but occasionally producing acute pneumonia or an influenzalike illness.

his•to•ri•an (hĭ-stôr′ē-ən, -stōr′-, -stŏr′-) *n.* **1.** A writer, student, or scholar of history. **2.** One who writes or compiles a chronological record of events; a chronicler.

his•tor•ic (hĭ-stôr′ĭk, -stŏr′-) *adj.* **1.** Having importance in or influence on history. **2.** Historical.

Usage Note: *Historic* and *historical* are differentiated in usage, though their senses overlap. *Historic* refers to what is important in history: *the historic first voyage to outer space.* It is also used of what is famous or interesting because of its association with persons or events in history: *a historic house. Historical* refers to whatever existed in the past, whether regarded as important or not: *a historical character. Historical* refers also to anything concerned with history or the study of the past: *a historical novel.* The words are often used interchangeably: *historic times* or *historical times.*

his•tor•i•cal (hĭ-stôr′ĭ-kəl, -stŏr′-) *adj.* **1.a.** Of or relating to the character of history. **b.** Based on or concerned with events in history. **c.** Used in the past: *historical costumes.* **2.** Important or famous in history. See Usage Note at **historic. 3.** Diachronic. — **his•tor′i•cal•ly** *adv.* — **his•tor′i•cal•ness** *n.*

historical linguistics *n.* *(used with a sing. v.)* The study of linguistic change over time in language or in a particular language or language family.

historical materialism *n.* A major tenet in the Marxist theory of history that regards material economic forces as the base on which sociopolitical institutions and ideas are built.

historical present *n.* The present tense used in the narration of events set in the past.

historical school *n.* A school of theorists, as in law or economics, stressing the influence of historical conditions.

his•tor•i•cism (hĭ-stôr′ĭ-sĭz′əm, -stŏr′-) *n.* **1.** A theory that events are determined or influenced by conditions beyond human control. **2.** A theory that stresses the significant influence of history as a criterion of value. — **his•tor′i•cist** *adj. & n.*

his•to•ric•i•ty (hĭs′tə-rĭs′ĭ-tē) *n.* Historical authenticity.

his•tor•i•cize (hĭ-stôr′ĭ-sīz′, -stŏr′-) *v.* **-cized, -ciz•ing, -ciz•es.** — *tr.* To make or make appear historical. — *intr.* To use historical details or materials. — **his•tor′i•ci•za′tion** (-sĭ-zā′shən) *n.*

his•to•ried (hĭs′tə-rēd) *adj.* Having an interesting history.

his•to•ri•og•ra•pher (hĭ-stôr′ē-ŏg′rə-fər, -stōr′-) *n.* **1.** A specialist in historiography. **2.** A historian, esp. one designated by a group or public institution.

his•to•ri•og•ra•phy (hĭ-stôr′ē-ŏg′rə-fē, -stōr′-) *n.* **1.** The principles and methodology of historical research and presentation. **2.** The writing of history based on the analysis and selection of sources. **3.** A body of historical literature. [Fr. *historiographie* < OFr. < Gk. *historiographia* : *historia,* history; see HISTORY + *-graphia,* -graphy.] — **his•to′ri•o•graph′ic** (-ē-ə-grăf′ĭk), **his•to′ri•o•graph′i•cal** (-ĭ-kəl) *adj.*

his•to•ry (hĭs′tə-rē) *n., pl.* **-ries. 1.** A narrative of events; a story. **2.a.** A chronological record of events, as of the development of a people, often including an explanation of or commentary on those events. **b.** A formal written account of related natural phenomena. **c.** A record of a patient's medical background. **3.** The discipline that records and analyzes past events. **4.a.** The events forming the subject matter of a historical account. **b.** Something that belongs to the past. **c.** An interesting past. **5.** A drama based on historical events. [ME *histoire* < OFr. < Lat. *historia* < Gk. < *historein,* to inquire < *histōr,* learned man. See **weid-*.**]

his•tri•on•ic (hĭs′trē-ŏn′ĭk) also **his•tri•on•i•cal** (-ĭ-kəl) *adj.* **1.** Of or relating to actors or acting. **2.** Excessively dramatic or emotional; affected. [LLat. *histriōnicus* < Lat. *histriō, histriōn-,* actor, prob. of Etruscan orig.]

his•tri•on•ics (hĭs′trē-ŏn′ĭks) *n.* **1.** *(used with a pl. v.)* Theatrical arts or performances. **2.** *(used with a sing. or pl. v.)* Exaggerated emotional behavior calculated for effect.

hit (hĭt) *v.* **hit, hit•ting, hits.** — *tr.* **1.a.** To come into contact with forcefully; strike. **b.** To reach with or as if with a blow: *The bullet hit him.* **2.a.** To cause to come into contact. **b.** To deal a blow to. **c.** To strike with a missile. **3.** To press or push (a key or button, for example). **4.** *Sports.* **a.** To reach with a propelled object. **b.** To score in this way. **c.** To perform (a shot or maneuver) successfully. **d.** To propel with a stroke or blow. **5.** *Baseball.* **a.** To execute (a base hit) successfully. **b.** To bat against (a pitcher or kind of pitch) successfully. **6.** To affect, esp. adversely. **7.** *Informal.* To come upon or discover, esp. by chance. **8.a.** *Informal.* To attain or reach. **b.** To accord with; suit: *The idea hit my fancy.* **c.** To produce or represent accurately: *trying to hit the right note.* **9.** *Games.* To deal cards to. **10.** *Slang.* To give a drink of liquor or a dose of a narcotic to. — *intr.* **1.** To strike or deal a blow. **2.a.** To come into contact with something; collide. **b.** To attack. **c.** To happen or occur. **3.** To achieve or find something desired or sought: *hit on the answer.* **4.** *Baseball.* To bat. **5.** To ignite a mixture of air and fuel in the cylinders. Used of an internal-combustion engine. — *n.* **1.a.** A collision or an impact. **b.** A successfully executed shot, blow, thrust, or throw. **2.** A successful or popular venture: *a Broadway hit.* **3.** An apt or effective remark. **4.** *Baseball.* A base hit. **5.** *Slang.* **a.** A dose of a narcotic drug. **b.** A puff of a cigarette or a marijuana cigarette or pipe. **6.** *Slang.* A murder carried out usu. by a member of an un-

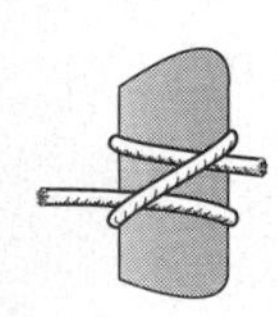

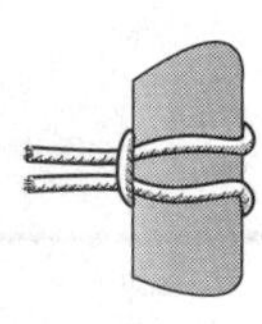

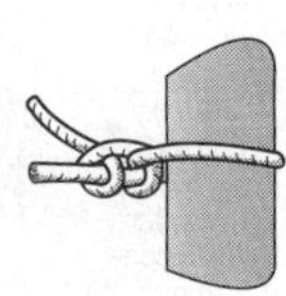

hitch
Top: Clove hitch
Center: Cow hitch
Bottom: Two half hitches

derworld syndicate. *—phrasal verbs.* **hit on.** *Slang.* To pay unsolicited and usu. unwanted sexual attention to. **hit up.** *Slang.* To approach and ask (someone) for something, esp. for money. *—idioms.* **hit it big.** *Slang.* To be successful. **hit it off.** *Informal.* To get along well together. **hit the books.** *Informal.* To study, esp. with concentrated effort. **hit the bottle.** *Slang.* To engage in drinking alcoholic beverages. **hit the ground running.** *Informal.* To begin a venture with great energy, involvement, and competence. **hit the hay (or sack).** *Slang.* To go to bed. **hit the jackpot.** To become highly and unexpectedly successful, esp. to win a great deal of money. **hit the nail on the head.** To be absolutely right. **hit the road.** *Slang.* To set out, as on a trip; leave. **hit the roof (or ceiling).** *Slang.* To express anger, esp. vehemently. **hit the spot.** To give total or desired satisfaction, as food or drink. [ME *hitten* < OE *hyttan* < ON *hitta.*] **—hit′ta•ble** *adj.*

hit-and-miss (hĭt′n-mĭs′) *adj.* Sometimes succeeding and sometimes not.

hit-and-run (hĭt′n-rŭn′) *adj.* **1.** Being or involving the driver of a motor vehicle who leaves the scene of an accident, esp. one in which a pedestrian or another vehicle has been struck. **2.** *Baseball.* Relating to or being a play in which a base runner starts to run on the pitch and the batter attempts to hit the ball to protect the runner. **3.** Involving or designed for swift action or effect.

hitch (hĭch) *v.* **hitched, hitch•ing, hitch•es.** *—tr.* **1.** To fasten or catch temporarily with or as if with a loop, hook, or noose. **2.** To connect or attach, as to a vehicle. **3.** To move or raise by pulling or jerking: *hitch up one's suspenders.* **4.** *Informal.* To hitchhike. *—intr.* **1.** To move haltingly; hobble. **2.** To become entangled, snarled, or fastened. **3.** *Slang.* To marry. **4.** *Informal.* To hitchhike. *—n.* **1.** Any of various knots used as a temporary fastening. **2.** A device used to connect one thing to another. **3.** A short jerking motion; a tug. **4.** A hobble or limp. **5.** An impediment or a delay: *a hitch in our plans.* **6.** A term of service, esp. of military service. **7.** *Informal.* A free ride obtained along a road. [Prob. < ME *hytchen, icchen,* to move, jerk.] **—hitch′er** *n.*

Hitch•cock (hĭch′kŏk′), Sir **Alfred Joseph.** 1899–1980. British director known for suspense films such as *The 39 Steps* (1935) and *Psycho* (1960).

hitch•hike (hĭch′hīk′) *v.* **-hiked, -hik•ing, -hikes.** *—intr.* To travel by hitchhiking rides. *—tr.* To solicit or get (a free ride) along a road. **—hitch′hike′** *n.* **—hitch′hik′er** *n.*

hitch•ing post (hĭch′ĭng) *n.* A post to which an animal, esp. a horse, is hitched.

hi-tech (hī′tĕk′) *adj.* Var. of **high tech.**

hith•er (hĭ*th*′ər) *adv.* To or toward this place: *Come hither.* *—adj.* Located on the near side. *—idiom.* **hither and thither (or yon).** In or to many places; here and there: *ran hither and yon.* [ME < OE *hider.* See **ko-*.**]

hith•er•most (hĭ*th*′ər-mōst′) *adj.* Nearest to this place or side.

hith•er•to (hĭ*th*′ər-to͞o′, hĭ*th*′ər-to͞o′) *adv.* Until this time.

hith•er•ward (hĭ*th*′ər-wərd) also **hith•er•wards** (-wərdz) *adv.* Hither.

Hit•ler (hĭt′lər), **Adolf.** "Der Führer." 1889–1945. Austrian-born founder of the German Nazi Party, chancellor of the Third Reich (1933–45), and absolute dictator (1934–45). **—Hit•ler′i•an** (hĭt-lîr′ē-ən) *adj.* **—Hit′ler•ism** (hĭt′lə-rĭz′-əm) *n.* **—Hit′ler•ite′** (-lə-rīt′) *adj. & n.*

hit list *n. Slang.* **1.** A list of potential murder victims. **2.** A list designating a target, as for attack, coercion, or elimination.

hit man *n. Slang.* **1.** A man hired by a crime syndicate as a professional killer. **2.** A hatchet man.

hit-or-miss (hĭt′ər-mĭs′) *adj.* Marked by a lack of care, accuracy, or organization; random. **—hit or miss** *adv.*

hit parade *n.* **1.** *Mus.* A ranked group or listing of the currently most popular songs. **2.** A collection or listing of the most popular or excellent items or people of a certain kind.

hit squad *n. Slang.* **1.** A squad or team of hired executioners. **2.** A group of political terrorists.

hit•ter (hĭt′ər) *n.* **1.** One who hits or strikes something. **2.** *Baseball.* A batter.

Hit•tite (hĭt′īt′) *n.* **1.** A member of an ancient people living in Anatolia and northern Syria about 2000–1200 B.C. **2.** The Indo-European language of the Hittites. *—adj.* Of or relating to the Hittites, their language, or their culture. [< Heb. *ḥittī* < Akkadian *ḫatti* < Hittite *Hatti.*]

HIV (āch′ī-vē′) *n.* A retrovirus that causes AIDS, formerly known as HTLV-III. [H(UMAN) I(MMUNODEFICIENCY) V(IRUS).]

hive (hīv) *n.* **1.a.** A structure for housing bees, esp. honeybees. **b.** A colony of bees living in such a structure. **2.** A place swarming with activity. *—v.* **hived, hiv•ing, hives.** *—tr.* **1.** To collect into a hive. **2.** To store (honey) in a hive. **3.** To store up; accumulate. *—intr.* **1.** To enter and occupy a beehive. **2.** To live closely with many others. *—phrasal verb.* **hive off.** To set apart from a group. [ME < OE *hӯf.*]

hives (hīvz) *pl.n. (used with a sing. or pl. v.)* A skin condition characterized by intensely itching welts and caused by an allergic reaction, an infection, or a nervous condition. [?]

hl *abbr.* Hectoliter.

H.L. *abbr.* House of Lords.

H.M. *abbr.* **1.** Her Majesty. **2.** His Majesty.

HMO (āch′ĕm-ō′) *n.* A corporation financed by insurance premiums whose physicians and staff provide curative and preventive medicine to enrolled volunteer members and their families. [H(EALTH) M(AINTENANCE) O(RGANIZATION).]

Hmong (hmông) *n., pl.* **Hmong** or **Hmongs. 1.** A member of a people inhabiting the mountainous regions of southern China and adjacent areas. **2.** The Miao-Yao language of the Hmong.

HMS or **H.M.S.** *abbr.* Her, or His, Majesty's Ship.

ho (hō) *interj.* Used to express surprise or joy, to attract attention to something sighted, or to urge onward: *Land ho!*

Ho¹ The symbol for the element **holmium.**

Ho² *abbr. Bible.* Hosea.

ho. *abbr.* House.

hoa•gie also **hoa•gy** (hō′gē) *n., pl.* **-gies.** *Chiefly Pennsylvania & New Jersey.* See **submarine** 2. See Regional Note at **submarine.** [Alteration of *hoggy.*]

hoar (hôr, hōr) *adj.* Hoary. *—n.* Hoarfrost. [ME *hor* < OE *hār.*]

hoard (hôrd, hōrd) *n.* A hidden fund or supply stored for future use; a cache. *—v.* **hoard•ed, hoard•ing, hoards.** *—intr.* To gather or accumulate a hoard. *—tr.* **1.** To accumulate a hoard of. **2.** To keep hidden or private. [ME *hord* < OE. See **(s)keu-*.**] **—hoard′er** *n.*

hoard•ing (hôr′dĭng, hōr′-) *n.* **1.** A temporary wooden fence around a building or structure under construction or repair. **2.** *Chiefly British.* A billboard. [Obsolete *hoard, hourd* < Fr. dial. *hourd,* fence, scaffold, hurdle < OFr., of Gmc. orig.]

hoar•frost (hôr′frôst′, -frŏst′, hōr′-) *n.* Frozen dew that forms a white coating on a surface.

hoarse (hôrs, hōrs) *adj.* **hoars•er, hoars•est. 1.** Rough or grating in sound: *a hoarse cry.* **2.** Having or characterized by a husky grating voice. [ME *hos, hors* < OE *hās.*] **—hoarse′ly** *adv.* **—hoarse′ness** *n.*

hoars•en (hôr′sən, hōr′-) *tr. & intr.v.* **-ened, -en•ing, -ens.** To make or become hoarse.

hoar•y (hôr′ē, hōr′ē) *adj.* **-i•er, -i•est. 1.** Gray or white with or as if with age. **2.** Covered with grayish hair or pubescence: *hoary leaves.* **3.** So old as to inspire veneration; ancient. **—hoar′i•ly** *adv.* **—hoar′i•ness** *n.*

hoary alyssum *n.* An annual European herb *(Berteroa incana)* of the mustard family, having silvery foliage.

hoat•zin (wät-sēn′) *n.* A crested brownish bird *(Opisthocomus hoazin)* of tropical South America. [Am.Sp. *hoazín* < Nahuatl *uatzin,* pheasant or small game bird.]

hoax (hōks) *n.* **1.** An act intended to deceive or trick. **2.** Something that has been established or accepted by fraudulent means. *—tr.v.* **hoaxed, hoax•ing, hoax•es.** To deceive or cheat with a hoax. [Perh. alteration of HOCUS.] **—hoax′er** *n.*

hob¹ (hŏb) *n.* **1.** A shelf or projection at the back or side of a fireplace, used for keeping food or utensils warm. **2.** A tool used for cutting the teeth of machine parts. [?]

hob² (hŏb) *n.* **1.** *Chiefly British.* A hobgoblin or an elf. **2.** Mischievous behavior. [< ME *Hob,* a nickname for Robert.]

Ho•bart. 1. (hō′bärt′). A city of SE Tasmania, Australia, on an inlet of the Tasman Sea; founded as a penal colony in 1804. Pop. 47,920. **2.** (hō′bərt). A city of NW IN SE of Gary. Pop. 21,822.

Ho•bart (hō′bärt′, -bərt), **Garret Augustus.** 1844–99. Vice President of the U.S. (1897–99).

Hob•be•ma (hŏb′ə-mə, hô′bə-mä), **Meindert.** 1638–1709. Dutch landscape painter whose works include *The Hermitage, St. Petersburg* (1663).

Hobbes (hŏbz), **Thomas.** 1588–1679. English political philosopher best known for *Leviathan* (1651). **—Hobbes′i•an** *adj.*

Hobb•ism (hŏb′ĭz′əm) *n.* A political theory propounded by Thomas Hobbes, advocating absolute monarchy to deal with inherently selfish, aggrandizing humanity.

hob•bit (hŏb′ĭt) *n.* An imaginary creature resembling a diminutive human being and being naturally peace-loving, domestic, and sociable. [< pseudo-OE *holbӯtla,* hole-builder (coined by J.R.R. Tolkien) : OE *hol,* hole; see HOLE + OE *bӯtla,* builder, hammerer (< *bӯtl, bīetel,* mallet; see BEETLE³).]

hob•ble (hŏb′əl) *v.* **-bled, -bling, -bles.** *—intr.* To walk or move along haltingly or with difficulty; limp. *—tr.* **1.** To put a device around the legs of (a horse, for example) to hamper but not prevent movement. **2.** To cause to limp. **3.** To hamper the action or progress of; impede. *—n.* **1.** A hobbling walk or gait. **2.** A device, such as a rope or strap, used to hobble an animal. **3.** *Archaic.* An awkward situation. [ME *hobblen,* of LGer. orig.] **—hob′bler** *n.*

hob•ble•bush (hŏb′əl-bo͝osh′) *n.* A deciduous shrub *(Viburnum alnifolium)* of eastern North America having flat clusters of white flowers.

hob•ble•de•hoy (hŏb′əl-dē-hoi′) *n., pl.* **-hoys.** A gawky adolescent boy. [?]

hobble skirt *n.* A long skirt, popular between 1910 and 1914, so narrow below the knees that it restricted normal stride.

Hobbs (hŏbz). A city of SE NM near the TX border. Pop. 29,115.

hob•by¹ (hŏb′ē) *n., pl.* **-bies.** An activity or interest pursued

Alfred Hitchcock
Photographed in 1960

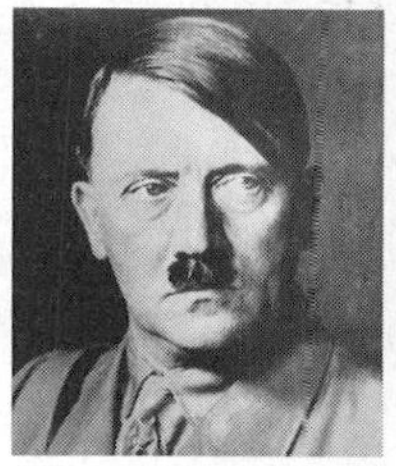

Adolf Hitler

ă pat	oi boy
ā pay	ou out
âr care	o͝o took
ä father	o͞o boot
ĕ pet	ŭ cut
ē be	ûr urge
ĭ pit	th thin
ī pie	*th* this
îr pier	hw which
ŏ pot	zh vision
ō toe	ə about, item
ô paw	

Stress marks:
′ (primary);
′ (secondary), as in
dictionary (dĭk′shə-nĕr′ē)

outside one's regular occupation, primarily for pleasure. [ME *hobi, hobyn*, small horse, hobby horse, perh. < *Hobin, Hobby*, nickname for *Robert*.] — **hob′by•ist** *n.*

hob•by² (hŏb′ē) *n., pl.* **-bies.** Any of several small falcons of the genus *Falco*, formerly used for catching small birds or game. [ME *hobi* < OFr. *hobe, hobel*.]

hob•by•horse (hŏb′ē-hôrs′) *n.* **1.a.** A child's riding toy that consists of a long stick with an imitation horse's head on one end. **b.** See **rocking horse. 2.a.** A figure of a horse worn at the waist by a mummer. **b.** A person wearing such a figure. **3.a.** A favorite hobby. **b.** A topic with which one is obsessed.

hob•gob•lin (hŏb′gŏb′lĭn) *n.* **1.** An ugly mischievous elf or goblin. **2.** An object or a source of fear, dread, or harassment.

hob•nail (hŏb′nāl′) *n.* A short nail with a thick head used to protect the soles of shoes or boots. [HOB¹, peg, projection (obsolete) + NAIL.] — **hob′nailed′** *adj.*

hob•nob (hŏb′nŏb′) *intr.v.* **-nobbed, -nob•bing, -nobs.** To associate familiarly. [< the phrase *(drink) hob or nob*, (toast) one another alternately < obsolete and dial. *hab nab*, have or have not : prob. ME *habbe*, have; see HAVE + ME *nabbe* (contraction of *ne habbe*, have not : OE *ne*, not; see NOT + *habbe*, have).]

ho•bo (hō′bō) *n., pl.* **-boes** or **-bos. 1.** A homeless person, esp. an impoverished vagrant. **2.** A migrant worker. — *intr.v.* **-boed, -bo•ing, -boes.** To live or wander like a vagrant. [?]

Ho•bo•ken (hō′bō′kən). A city of NE NJ on the Hudson R. opposite Manhattan. Pop. 33,397.

Hob•son's choice (hŏb′sənz) *n.* An apparently free choice that offers no real alternative. [After Thomas *Hobson* (1544?–1630), English keeper of a livery stable, from his requirement that customers take the horse nearest the stable door or none.]

Ho Chi Minh (hō′ chē′ mĭn′). 1890–1969. Vietnamese leader and first president of North Vietnam (1954–69).

Ho Chi Minh City. Formerly **Sai•gon** (sī-gŏn′). A city of S Vietnam near the South China Sea; cap. of South Vietnam (1954–75). Pop. 2,441,185.

hock¹ (hŏk) *n.* **1.a.** The tarsal joint of the hind leg of a digitigrade quadruped, such as a horse, corresponding to the human ankle but bending in the opposite direction. **b.** A joint in the leg of a domestic fowl similar to the hock of a quadruped. **2.** A small cut of meat, esp. ham, from the front or hind leg directly above the foot. — *tr.v.* **hocked, hock•ing, hocks.** To disable by cutting the tendons of the hock; hamstring. [ME < OE *hōh*, heel.]

hock² (hŏk) *n. Chiefly British.* Rhine wine. [Short for obsolete *Hockamore*, alteration of Ger. *Hochheimer* < *Hochheim*, a town of W-central Germany.]

hock³ (hŏk) *Slang.* — *tr.v.* **hocked, hock•ing, hocks.** To pawn. — *n.* **1.** The state of being pawned: *put the diamonds in hock.* **2.** The state of being in debt. [Prob. < Du. *hok*, prison.]

hock•ey (hŏk′ē) *n. Sports.* **1.** Ice hockey. **2.** Field hockey. [?]

hockey stick *n. Sports.* A long-handled stick with one curved end that is used in hockey.

hock•shop (hŏk′shŏp′) *n. Slang.* A pawnshop.

ho•cus (hō′kəs) *tr.v.* **-cused, -cus•ing, -cus•es** or **-cussed, -cus•sing, -cus•ses. 1.** To fool or deceive; hoax. **2.** To infuse (food or drink) with a drug. [Short for HOCUS-POCUS.]

ho•cus-po•cus (hō′kəs-pō′kəs) *n.* **1.** Nonsense words or phrases used as a formula by quack conjurers. **2.** A trick performed by a magician or juggler; sleight-of-hand. **3.** Foolishness or empty pretense used esp. to disguise deception or chicanery. — *tr.v.* **-cused, -cus•ing, -cus•es** or **-cussed, -cus•sing, -cus•ses.** To play tricks on; deceive. [Poss. < an alteration of Lat. *hoc est corpus (meum)*, this is (my) body (words used in the Eucharist).]

hod (hŏd) *n.* **1.** A trough carried over the shoulder for transporting loads. **2.** A coal scuttle. [Perh. alteration of dialectal *hot* < ME, pannier < OFr. *hotte*, of Gmc. orig.]

Ho•dei•da (hō-dā′də). A city of W Yemen on the Red Sea. Pop. 126,400.

hodge•podge (hŏj′pŏj′) *n.* A mixture of dissimilar ingredients; a jumble. [Alteration of ME *hochepot* < OFr., stew. See HOTCHPOTCH.]

Hodg•kin (hŏj′kĭn), Sir **Alan Lloyd.** b. 1914. British physiologist who shared a 1963 Nobel Prize.

Hodgkin, Dorothy Mary Crowfoot. b. 1910. Egyptian-born British chemist who won a 1964 Nobel Prize.

Hodg•kin's disease (hŏj′kĭnz) *n.* A sometimes fatal cancer marked by enlargement of the lymph nodes, spleen, and liver. [After Thomas *Hodgkin* (1798–1866), British physician.]

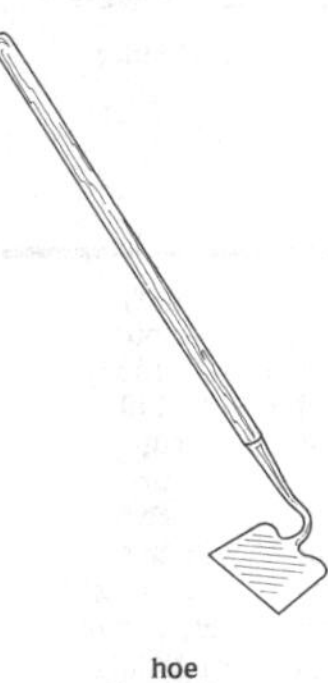
hoe
Garden hoe

hoe (hō) *n.* A tool with a flat blade attached approximately at a right angle to a long handle, used as for weeding or cultivating. — *v.* **hoed, hoe•ing, hoes.** — *tr.* To weed, cultivate, or dig up with a hoe. — *intr.* To work with a hoe. [ME *howe* < OFr. *houe*, of Gmc. orig. See **kau-*.**] — **ho′er** *n.*

hoe•cake (hō′kāk′) *n. Chiefly Southern U.S.* See **johnnycake.** See Regional Note at **johnnycake.** [Poss. because it was sometimes baked on the blade of a hoe.]

hoe•down (hō′doun′) *n.* **1.** A square dance. **2.** The music for a square dance. **3.** A square dance party.

Hoek van Hol•land (ho͝ok′ vän hō′länt). See **Hook of Holland.**

Ho•fei (hŭ′fā′). See **Hefei.**

Hoff•mann (hŏf′mən, hôf′män′), **August Heinrich.** 1798–1874. German writer and philologist whose patriotic verse includes "Deutschland, Deutschland über Alles" (1841).

Hoffmann, Roald. b. 1937. Polish-born Amer. chemist who shared a 1981 Nobel Prize.

Hof•mann (hŏf′mən, hôf′män′), **August Wilhelm von.** 1818–92. German chemist who discovered formaldehyde.

Hofmann, Hans. 1880–1966. German-born Amer. artist whose schools helped develop abstract expressionism.

Hof•manns•thal (hôf′mäns-täl′, hōf′-), **Hugo von.** 1874–1929. Austrian writer who wrote lyric poems and plays, including *Death and the Fool* (1893).

Hof•stadt•er (hŏf′stăt′ər), **Richard.** 1916–70. Amer. historian whose works include *The Age of Reform* (1955).

Hofstadter, Robert. b. 1915. Amer. physicist who shared a 1961 Nobel Prize.

hog (hôg, hŏg) *n.* **1.a.** Any of various mammals of the family Suidae, including the domesticated pig and wild species, such as the boar. **b.** A domesticated pig, esp. one weighing over 54 kilograms (120 pounds). **2.a.** A self-indulgent, gluttonous, or filthy person. **b.** One that uses too much of something. **3.a.** *Chiefly British.* A young sheep before it has been shorn. **b.** The wool from this sheep. **4.** *Slang.* A big, heavy motorcycle. — *v.* **hogged, hog•ging, hogs.** — *tr.* **1.** *Informal.* To take more than one's share of. **2.** To cause (the back) to arch like a hog's. **3.** To cut (a horse's mane) short and bristly. **4.** To shred (waste wood, for example) by machine. — *intr. Naut.* To arch upward in the middle. Used of a ship's keel. — ***idiom.*** **high on** (or **off**) **the hog.** *Slang.* In a lavish or extravagant manner. [ME < OE *hogg*, poss. of Celt. orig. See **sū-*.**]

ho•gan (hō′gän′, -gən) *n.* A usu. earth-covered Navajo dwelling traditionally built with the entrance facing east. [Navajo *hooghan*.]

Ho•gan (hō′gən), **William Benjamin ("Ben").** b. 1912. Amer. golfer who won the U.S. Open championship (1948, 1950, 1951, and 1953) and the P.G.A. championship (1948).

Ho•garth (hō′gärth′), **William.** 1697–1764. British artist whose satirical paintings attacked the contradiction of luxury and squalor in society. — **Ho•garth′i•an** *adj.*

hog•back (hôg′băk′, hŏg′-) *n.* A sharp ridge with steeply sloping sides, produced by erosion of the broken edges of highly tilted strata.

hog cholera *n.* A highly infectious, often fatal viral disease of swine, characterized by fever, loss of appetite, and diarrhea.

hog•fish (hôg′fĭsh′, hŏg′-) *n., pl.* **hogfish** or **-fish•es. 1.** A colorful fish *(Lachnolaimus maximus)* of warm Atlantic waters, having a long snout in the adult male. **2.** See **pigfish.**

hogg (hôg, hŏg) *n. Chiefly British.* Var. of **hog** 3.

Hogg (hôg, hŏg), **James.** 1770–1835. British writer known for his rustic verse, including *The Mountain Bard* (1807).

hog•gish (hô′gĭsh, hŏg′ĭsh) *adj.* **1.** Coarsely self-indulgent or gluttonous. **2.** Filthy. — **hog′gish•ness** *n.*

Hog•ma•nay (hŏg′mə-nā′, hŏg′mə-nā′) *n. Scots.* **1.** The eve of New Year's Day, on which children traditionally beg for presents. **2.** A present requested or given this day. [?]

hog•nose snake (hôg′nōz′, hŏg′-) *n.* Any of several thick-bodied nonvenomous North American snakes of the genus *Heterodon*, having an upturned snout.

hog peanut *n.* A North American vine *(Amphicarpaea bracteata)* having pinkish or white flowers and bearing three-seeded pods and basal or underground one-seeded pods.

hogs•head (hôgz′hĕd′, hŏgz′-) *n.* **1.** Any of various units of volume or capacity ranging from 63 to 140 gallons (238 to 530 liters), esp. a unit of capacity used in liquid measure in the United States, equal to 63 gallons (238 liters). **2.** A large barrel or cask with this capacity.

hog-tie also **hog•tie** (hôg′tī′, hŏg′-) *tr.v.* **-tied, -tie•ing** or **-ty•ing, -ties. 1.** To tie together the feet or legs of. **2.** *Informal.* To impede or disrupt in movement or action.

hog•wash (hôg′wŏsh′, -wôsh′, hŏg′-) *n.* **1.** Worthless, false, or ridiculous speech or writing. **2.** Garbage fed to hogs; swill.

hog•weed (hôg′wēd′, hŏg′-) *n.* Any of certain coarse weedy plants of the genera *Ambrosia, Erigeron,* or *Heracleum.*

hog-wild (hôg′wīld′, hŏg′-) *adj. Informal.* **1.** So wildly excited as to be irrational or devoid of good judgment. **2.** Wildly enthusiastic. — **hog′-wild′** *adv.*

Ho•hen•stau•fen (hō′ən-shtou′fən). Family of German rulers of the Holy Roman Empire (1138–1208 and 1215–54) and Sicily (1194–1268).

Ho•hen•zol•lern (hō′ən-zŏl′ərn, -tsôl′-). German royal family who ruled Brandenburg, Prussia, and the German Empire (1415–1918).

Hoh•hot (hō′hōt′) also **Hu•he•hot** (ho͞o′hā-). A city of N China WNW of Beijing; cap. of Nei Monggol (Inner Mongolia) autonomous region. Pop. 542,800.

Ho•ho•kam (hə-hō′kəm) *n.* A Native American culture flourishing from about the 3rd century B.C. to the mid-15th century A.D. in south-central Arizona, noted for an extensive system of irrigation canals. [< Papago *huhugam*, those who are gone.]

ho hum (hō′ hŭm′) *interj.* Used to express boredom, weariness, or contempt.

ho-hum (hō′hŭm′) *adj. Informal.* Boring and dull; routine.
hoicks (hoiks) *interj.* Var. of **yoicks.**
hoi pol•loi (hoi′ pə-loi′) *n.* The common people; the masses. [Gk., the many : *hoi*, nominative pl. of *ho*, the; see **so-*** + *polloi*, nominative pl. of *polus*, many; see **pelə-[1]*.**]
hoi•sin sauce (hoi′sĭn, hoi-sĭn′) *n.* A thick sweet pungent sauce used in Chinese cooking. [Chin. (Cantonese) *hoisin*, seafood : *hoi*, ocean + *sin*, delicacy, seafood.]
hoist (hoist) *v.* **hoist•ed, hoist•ing, hoists.** —*tr.* To raise or haul up with or as if with a mechanical apparatus. See Syns at **lift.** —*intr.* To become raised or lifted. —*n.* **1.** An apparatus for lifting heavy or cumbersome objects. **2.** The act of hoisting; a lift. **3.** *Naut.* **a.** The height or vertical dimension of a flag or of any square sail other than a course. **b.** A group of flags raised together as a signal. [Alteration of dial. *hoise*, perh. var. of ME *hisse*, heave!, poss. < MDu. *hissen*, to haul.] —**hoist′er** *n.*
hoi•ty-toi•ty (hoi′tē-toi′tē) *adj.* **1.** Pretentiously self-important; pompous. **2.** Given to frivolity or silliness. [< redup. of dial. *hoit*, to romp; perh. akin to HOYDEN.]
Ho•kan (hō′kən) *n.* A proposed grouping of a number of Native American language families of western North America.
hoke (hōk) *tr.v.* **hoked, hok•ing, hokes.** *Slang.* To give an impressive but artificial or false quality to. [< HOKUM.]
hok•ey (hō′kē) *adj.* **-i•er, -i•est.** *Slang.* **1.** Mawkishly sentimental; corny. **2.** Noticeably contrived; artificial. —**hok′i•ly** *adv.* —**hok′i•ness, hok′ey•ness** *n.*
Hok•kai•do (hŏ-kī′dō, hô′kī-dō′). An island of Japan N of Honshu; became part of Japan in the medieval period (c. 1600) and was called Yezo or Ezo until 1868.
hok•ku (hō′ko͞o) *n., pl.* **hokku.** A haiku. [J. : *hok*, opening, first + *ku*, stanza.]
ho•kum (hō′kəm) *n.* **1.** Something apparently impressive or legitimate but actually untrue or insincere; nonsense. **2.** A stock technique for eliciting a desired response from an audience. [Perh. HO(CUS-POCUS) + (BUN)KUM.]
Ho•ku•sai (hō′ko͞o-sī′, hō′ko͞o-sī′). 1760–1849. Japanese artist noted for his historical scenes and landscapes.
hol– *pref.* Var. of **holo–.**
ho•lan•dric (hō-lăn′drĭk, hŏ-) *adj.* Relating to a trait encoded by a gene on the Y-chromosome and therefore occurring only in males. [HOL(O)– + ANDR(O)– + –IC.]
Hol•arc•tic (hō-lärk′tĭk, -lär′tĭk, hŏ-) *adj.* Of, relating to, or being the zoogeographic region that is divided into Nearctic and Palearctic regions.
Hol•bein (hōl′bīn, hôl′-), **Hans[1].** "the Elder." 1465?–1524. German painter whose religious works include the altar piece of the Augsburg Cathedral (1493).
Hol•bein (hōl′bīn, hôl′-), **Hans[2].** "the Younger." 1497?–1543. German-born artist in Switzerland and England noted for his portraits and religious paintings.
hold[1] (hōld) *v.* **held** (hĕld), **hold•ing, holds.** —*tr.* **1.a.** To have and keep in one's grasp. **b.** To aim or direct; point. **c.** To keep from falling or moving; support. **d.** To sustain the pressure of. **2.a.** To keep from departing or getting away. **b.** To keep in custody. **c.** To retain the attention or interest of. **d.** To avoid letting out or expelling: *held her breath.* **3.a.** To be filled by; contain. **b.** To be capable of holding. See Syns at **contain. c.** To have as a chief characteristic or quality. **d.** To have in store: *what the future holds.* **4.a.** To have and maintain in one's possession. **b.** To have as a responsible position or a privilege. **c.** To have in recognition of achievement or superiority: *holds our respect.* **5.a.** To maintain control over: *The dam held the floodwaters.* **b.** To maintain occupation of by force or coercion. **c.** To withstand the efforts or advance of (an opposing team, for example). **d.** To maintain in a given condition, situation, or action: *held himself in readiness.* **6.a.** To impose control or restraint on; curb: *She held her temper.* **b.** To stop the movement or progress of. **c.** To reserve or keep back from use: *Please hold two tickets.* **d.** To defer the immediate handling of. **7.a.** To be the legal possessor of. **b.** To bind by a contract. **c.** To adjudge or decree. **d.** To make accountable; obligate: *held me to my promise.* **8.a.** To keep in the mind or convey as a judgment, conviction, or point of view. **b.** To assert or affirm, esp. formally. **c.** To regard in a certain way: *I hold you in high esteem.* **9.a.** To cause to take place; carry on: *hold a yard sale.* **b.** To assemble for and conduct the activity of; convene. **10.a.** To carry or support (the body or a body part) in a certain position. **b.** To cover (the ears or the nose, for example) esp. for protection. —*intr.* **1.a.** To maintain a grasp or grip on something. **b.** To stay securely fastened. **2.a.** To maintain a desired or accustomed position or condition. **b.** To withstand stress, pressure, or opposition. **3.** To continue in the same direction. **4.** To be valid, applicable, or true. **5.** To have legal right or title. Often used with *of* or *from.* **6.** To halt an intended action. Often used in the imperative. **7.** To stop the countdown during a missile or spacecraft launch. **8.** *Slang.* To have in one's possession illicit or illegally obtained material or goods, esp. narcotics. —*n.* **1.a.** The act or a means of grasping. **b.** A manner of grasping an opponent, as in wrestling or aikido. **2.** Something that may be grasped or gripped, as for support. **3.a.** A bond or force that attaches or restrains, or by which something is affected or dominated. **b.** Complete control. **c.** Full understanding. **4.** *Mus.* **a.** The sustaining of a note longer than its indicated time value. **b.** The symbol designating this pause; a fermata. **5.a.** A direction or an indication that something is to be reserved or deferred. **b.** A temporary halt, as in a countdown. **6.a.** A prison cell. **b.** The state of being in confinement; custody. **7.** *Archaic.* A fortified place; a stronghold. —***phrasal verbs.*** **hold back. 1.** To retain in one's possession or control. **2.** To impede the progress of. **3.** To restrain oneself. **hold down. 1.** To limit. **2.** To have (a job): *holds down two jobs.* **hold forth.** To talk at great length. **hold off. 1.** To keep at a distance; resist. **2.** To stop or delay doing something. **hold on. 1.** To maintain one's grip; cling. **2.** To continue to do something; persist. **3.** To wait for something wanted or requested, esp. to keep a telephone connection open. **hold out. 1.** To present or proffer as something attainable. **2.** To continue to be in supply or service; last. **3.** To continue to resist. **4.** To refuse to reach or satisfy an agreement. **hold over. 1.a.** To postpone or delay. **b.** To keep in a position or state from an earlier period of time. **2.** To continue a term of office past the usual length of time. **3.** To prolong the engagement of: *The film was held over for weeks.* **hold to.** To remain loyal or faithful to. **hold up. 1.** To obstruct or delay. **2.** To rob while armed, often at gunpoint. **3.** To offer or present as an example. **4.** To continue to function without losing force or effectiveness; cope. **hold with.** To agree with; support. —***idioms.*** **get hold of. 1.** To come into possession of; find. **2.** To communicate with, as by telephone. **3.** To gain control of. Often used reflexively: *Get hold of yourself!* **hold a candle to.** To compare favorably with. **hold (one's) own.** To do reasonably well despite difficulty or criticism. **hold out on (someone).** To withhold something from. **hold (someone's) feet to the fire.** To pressure (someone) to consent to or undertake something. **hold sway.** To have a controlling influence; dominate. **hold the bag.** *Informal.* **1.** To be left with empty hands. **2.** To be forced to assume total responsibility when it ought to have been shared. **hold the fort.** *Informal.* **1.** To assume responsibility, esp. in another's absence. **2.** To maintain a secure position. **hold the line.** To maintain the existing position or state of affairs. **hold the phone.** *Slang.* To stop doing what one is engaged in doing. Often used in the imperative. **hold water.** To stand up to critical examination. **no holds barred.** Without limits or restraints. **on hold. 1.** Into a state of temporary interruption without total disconnection during a telephone call. **2.** *Informal.* Into a state of delay or indeterminate suspension. [ME *holden* < OE *healdan.*]
hold[2] (hōld) *n.* The lower interior part of a ship or an airplane in which cargo is stored. [Alteration (influenced by HOLD[1]) of ME *hole*, husk, hull of a ship < OE *hulu.* See **kel-[1]*.**]
hold•all (hōld′ôl′) *n.* **1.** A container for holding items. **2.** A case or bag for carrying miscellaneous items.
hold•back (hōld′băk′) *n.* **1.a.** The act of holding back. **b.** Something held back. **2.** A device that retains or restrains. **3.** A strap or an iron between the shaft and the harness on a drawn wagon, allowing the horse to stop or back up.
hold-down (hōld′doun′) *n.* **1.a.** The act of holding down. **b.** A limit or restraint. **2.** Something, such as a clamp, used to hold an object in place.
hold•en (hōl′dən) *v. Archaic.* A p.part. of **hold[1].**
hold•er (hōl′dər) *n.* **1.** One that holds, as: **a.** One that possesses something; an owner: *the holder of farmland.* **b.** One, esp. a tenant, that occupies or controls something. **c.** *Law.* One that legally possesses and is entitled to the payment of a check, bill, or promissory note. **2.** A device for holding.
hold•fast (hōld′făst′) *n.* **1.** Any of various devices used to fasten something securely. **2.** *Biol.* An organ or a structure of attachment, esp. the basal rootlike formation by which certain seaweeds or other algae are attached to a substrate.
hold•ing (hōl′dĭng) *n.* **1.a.** Land rented or leased from another. **b.** Legally owned property, such as land, capital, or stocks. Often used in the plural. **2.** *Law.* A court ruling, esp. a ruling on a point of law raised in an official proceeding. **3.** *Sports.* Illegal obstruction of the movements of an opponent. —*adj.* **1.** Tending to impede or delay progress: *a holding action.* **2.** Designed for usually short-term storage or retention.
holding company *n.* A company controlling partial or complete interest in another company or other companies.
holding pattern *n.* **1.** A usu. circular pattern flown by aircraft awaiting clearance to land at an airport. **2.** *Informal.* A state of waiting or delay; a static situation.
hold•out (hōld′out′) *n.* One that withholds agreement or consent upon which progress is contingent.
hold•o•ver (hōld′ō′vər) *n.* One that is held over, esp. an officeholder who is retained after an expired term of office.
hold•up (hōld′ŭp′) *n.* **1.** An interruption or a delay. **2.** An armed robbery.
hole (hōl) *n.* **1.** A cavity in a solid. **2.a.** An opening or a perforation: *a hole in the clouds.* **b.** *Sports.* An opening in a defensive formation. **c.** A fault or flaw: *holes in the argument.* **3.** A deep place in a body of water. **4.** An animal's hollowed-out habitation, such as a burrow. **5.** An ugly, squalid, or de-

ă pat	oi boy
ā pay	ou out
âr care	o͝o took
ä father	o͞o boot
ĕ pet	ŭ cut
ē be	ûr urge
ĭ pit	th thin
ī pie	*th* this
îr pier	hw which
ŏ pot	zh vision
ō toe	ə about, item
ô paw	

Stress marks:
′ (primary);
′ (secondary), as in
dictionary (dĭk′shə-nĕr′ē)

pressing dwelling. **6.** A deep or isolated place of confinement; a dungeon. **7.** An awkward situation; a predicament. **8.** *Sports.* **a.** The small pit into which a golf ball must be hit. **b.** One of the divisions of a golf course, from tee to cup. **9.** *Phys.* A vacant position in a crystal left by the absence of an electron, esp. a position in a semiconductor that acts as a carrier of positive electric charge. — *v.* **holed, hol•ing, holes.** — *tr.* **1.** To put a hole in. **2.** To put or propel into a hole. — *intr.* To make a hole in something. — ***phrasal verbs.*** **hole out.** *Sports.* To hit a golf ball into the hole. **hole up. 1.** To hibernate in or as if in a hole. **2.** *Informal.* To take refuge in or as if in a hideout. — ***idioms.*** **hole in one.** *Sports.* The driving of a golf ball from the tee into the hole in only one stroke. **in the hole. 1.** Having a score below zero. **2.** In debt. **3.** At a disadvantage. [ME < OE *hol.* See **kel-**[1]*.]

hole-and-cor•ner (hōl′ən-kôr′nər) *adj.* Being in a secret place; conducted secretly.

hole card *n.* **1.** *Games.* A card in stud poker that the holder is not obliged to reveal before the showdown. **2.** *Informal.* Something held in reserve until it can be used advantageously.

hole-in-the-wall (hōl′ĭn-thə-wôl′) *n., pl.* **holes-in-the-wall** (hōlz′-). A small, very modest, often out-of-the-way place.

hol•ey (hō′lē) *adj.* **-i•er, -i•est.** Having holes or full of holes.

Hol•guín (ôl-gēn′). A city of E Cuba NNW of Santiago de Cuba. Pop. 186,236.

hol•i•day (hŏl′ĭ-dā′) *n.* **1.** A day on which general business activity halts to commemorate or celebrate a particular event. **2.** A religious feast day; a holy day. **3.** A day free from work that one may spend at leisure; a day off. **4.** *Chiefly British.* A vacation. — *intr.v.* **-dayed, -day•ing, -days.** *Chiefly British.* To pass a holiday or vacation. [ME *holidai,* holy day < OE *hālig dæg* : *hālig,* holy; see HOLY + *dæg,* day; see DAY.]

holly

Hol•i•day (hŏl′ĭ-dā′), **Eleanora ("Billie").** 1915–59. Amer. singer who was the leading female jazz vocalist of her time.

hol•i•day•mak•er (hŏl′ĭ-dā-mā′kər) *n. Chiefly British.* One who goes on vacation.

ho•li•er-than-thou (hō′lē-ər-*thən-thou*′) *adj.* Exhibiting an attitude of superior virtue; self-righteously pious.

ho•li•ness (hō′lē-nĭs) *n.* **1.** The state or quality of being holy; sanctity. **2. Holiness.** *Rom. Cath. Ch.* Used with *His* or *Your* as a title and form of address for a pope.

Hol•in•shed (hŏl′ən-shĕd′, -ĭnz-hĕd′) also **Hol•lings•head** (-ĭngz-hĕd′), **Raphael.** d. c. 1580. English historian whose *Chronicles of England, Scotland, and Ireland* (1577) was used extensively by Shakespeare and other Elizabethan dramatists.

ho•lism (hō′lĭz′əm) *n.* **1.** The theory that living matter or reality is made up of organic or unified wholes that are greater than the simple sum of their parts. **2.** A holistic investigation or system of treatment. — **ho′list** *n.*

ho•lis•tic (hō-lĭs′tĭk) *adj.* **1.** Of or relating to holism. **2.a.** Emphasizing the importance of the whole and the interdependence of its parts. **b.** Concerned with wholes rather than analysis or separation into parts. — **ho•lis′ti•cal•ly** *adv.*

Hol•la•day (hŏl′ə-dā′). A community of N-central UT, a suburb of Salt Lake City. Pop. 22,189.

hol•land (hŏl′ənd) *n.* A cotton or linen fabric, usu. sized or glazed, used esp. for window shades, bookbinding, and upholstery. [ME *holand,* after *Holand* (Holland), a former province of the Netherlands < MDu.]

Hol•land (hŏl′ənd). **1.** A city of SW MI SW of Grand Rapids; founded in 1847. Pop. 30,745. **2.** See **Netherlands.**

Holland, John Philip. 1840–1914. Irish-born Amer. inventor whose submarine was the first purchased by the U.S. government (1900).

hol•lan•daise sauce (hŏl′ən-dāz′) *n.* A rich creamy sauce made of butter, egg yolks, and lemon juice or vinegar. [< Fr. *(sauce) Hollandaise,* Holland-style < *Hollande,* Holland.]

hol•ler[1] (hŏl′ər) *v.* **-lered, -ler•ing, -lers.** — *intr.* **1.** To yell or shout. **2.** *Informal.* To complain. — *tr.* To shout out (words or phrases). See Syns at **shout.** — *n.* **1.** A yell or shout; a call. **2.** *Informal.* A complaint or gripe. [< obsolete *hollo,* hail!, stop! See HELLO.]

hol•ler[2] (hŏl′ər) *adj. & v. Upper Southern U.S.* Var. of **hollow.** — *n.* **1.** *Upper Southern U.S.* Var. of **hollow** 1, 2, 3. **2.** *Appalachian Mountains.* Var. of **hollow** 4.

Regional Note: One feature of Upper Southern English and specifically of Appalachian English is its pronunciation of the final unstressed syllable in words such as *hollow, window,* and *potato* as (-ər). *Holler, winder,* and *tater* are merely variant pronunciations reflected in spelling.

Oliver Wendell Holmes

Hol•ler•ith (hŏl′ə-rĭth′), **Herman.** 1860–1929. Amer. inventor who founded the company that became IBM (1924).

Hollerith card *n. Comp. Sci.* See **punch card.**

Hollerith code *n. Comp. Sci.* A code used for recording alphanumeric information on punch cards.

Hol•li•day (hŏl′ĭ-dā′), **Judith ("Judy") Tuvim.** 1922–65. Amer. comedian best remembered for her performance in the play (1946–50) and film (1950) *Born Yesterday.*

Hol•lings•head (hŏl′ĭngz-hĕd′), **Raphael.** See Raphael **Holinshed.**

hol•low (hŏl′ō) *adj.* **-er, -est. 1.** Having a cavity, gap, or space within: *a hollow wall.* **2.** Deeply indented or concave; sunken. **3.** Without substance or character: *a hollow person.* **4.** Devoid of truth or validity; specious. **5.** Having a reverberating, sepulchral sound: *hollow footsteps.* — *n.* **1.** A cavity, gap, or space. **2.** An indented or concave surface or area. **3.** A void; an emptiness. **4.** Also **hol•ler** (hŏl′ər). *Appalachian Mountains.* A small valley between mountains. — *v.* **-lowed, -low•ing, -lows.** — *tr.* **1.** To make hollow: *hollow out a pumpkin.* **2.** To scoop or form by making concave: *hollow out a nest in the sand.* — *intr.* To become hollow or empty. [ME *holwe, holowe* < *holgh,* hole, burrow < OE *holh.* See **kel-**[1]*.] — **hol′low•ly** *adv.* — **hol′low•ness** *n.*

hol•low•ware (hŏl′ō-wâr′) *n.* Pieces of tableware, such as bowls, pitchers, or serving dishes, that have depth or volume.

hol•ly (hŏl′ē) *n., pl.* **-lies. 1.a.** Any of numerous trees or shrubs of the genus *Ilex,* usu. having red berries and evergreen leaves with spiny margins. **b.** Branches of these plants, traditionally used for Christmas decoration. **2.** Any of various similar or related plants. [ME *holin, holi* < OE *holen.*]

hol•ly•hock (hŏl′ē-hŏk′) *n.* A tall plant *(Alcea rosea)* native to the Middle East and widely cultivated for its showy clusters of very large, variously colored flowers. [ME *holihocke,* marsh mallow : *holi,* holy; see HOLY + *hoc,* mallow (< OE).]

holly oak *n.* See **holm oak.**

Hol•ly•wood[1] (hŏl′ē-wo͝od′). **1.** A district of Los Angeles CA; long a film and entertainment center. **2.** A city of SE FL on the Atlantic N of Miami Beach. Pop. 121,697.

Hol•ly•wood[2] (hŏl′ē-wo͝od′) *n.* **1.** The U.S. film industry. **2.** Flashy vulgarity associated with the U.S. film industry. — *adj.* **1.** Of or relating to the U.S. film industry. **2.** Flashy and vulgar.

hol•ly•wood bed (hŏl′ē-wo͝od′) *n.* A mattress on a box spring supported by a metal frame or attached low legs, often with an upholstered headboard.

holm (hōm, hōlm) *n. Chiefly British.* An island in a river. [ME < ON *hōlmr.* See **kel-**[2]*.]

Holmes (hōmz, hōlmz), **Oliver Wendell.** 1809–94. Amer. physician and writer of humorous conversational pieces, including *The Autocrat of the Breakfast Table* (1858).

Holmes, Oliver Wendell, Jr. 1841–1935. Amer. jurist; associate justice of the U.S. Supreme Court (1902–32).

hol•mic (hōl′mĭk) *adj.* Relating to trivalent holmium.

hol•mi•um (hōl′mē-əm) *n. Symbol* **Ho** A soft malleable rare-earth element found in monazite and other rare-earth minerals. Atomic number 67; atomic weight 164.930; melting point 1,461°C; boiling point 2,600°C; specific gravity 8.803; valence 3. See table at **element.** [From *Holmia* (Stockholm).]

holm oak *n.* A Mediterranean evergreen tree *(Quercus ilex)* whose leaves are dark green on top and yellow or white underneath. [ME *holm,* alteration of *holin,* holly. See HOLLY.]

holo– or **hol–** *pref.* Whole; entire; entirely: *holoblastic.* [Gk. < *holos,* whole. See **sol-***.]

hol•o•blas•tic (hŏl′ə-blăs′tĭk, hō′lə-) *adj. Embryol.* Exhibiting cleavage in which the entire egg separates into individual blastomeres. — **hol′o•blas′ti•cal•ly** *adv.*

hol•o•caust (hŏl′ə-kôst′, hō′lə-) *n.* **1.** Great or total destruction, esp. by fire. **2.a.** Widespread destruction. **b.** A great disaster. **3.a. Holocaust.** The genocide of European Jews, Gypsies, and others by the Nazis during World War II. **b.** A massive slaughter. **4.** A sacrificial offering that is consumed entirely by flames. [ME, burnt offering < OFr. *holocauste* < Lat. *holocaustum* < Gk. *holokauston* < neut. of *holokaustos,* burnt whole : *holo-,* holo- + *kaustos,* burnt (< *kaiein,* to burn).] — **hol′o•caus′tal, hol′o•caus′tic** *adj.*

Usage Note: When referring to the massive destruction of human beings by other human beings, *holocaust* has a secure place in the language. Fully 99 percent of the Usage Panel accepts the use of *holocaust* in the phrase *nuclear holocaust.* When the word with its associations with genocide is used to refer to death brought about by natural causes, the percentage of the Panel's acceptance drops sharply. Only 31 percent of the Panel accepts the sentence *In East Africa five years of drought have brought about a holocaust in which millions have died.* This suggests that other figurative usages such as *the huge losses in the Savings and Loan holocaust* may be viewed as overblown or in poor taste.

Word History: Totality of destruction has been central to the meaning of *holocaust* since it first appeared in Middle English in the 14th century and referred to the biblical sacrifice in which a male animal was wholly burnt on the altar in worship of God. *Holocaust* comes from Greek *holokauston* ("that which is completely burnt"), which was a translation of Hebrew *ôlâ* (literally "that which goes up," that is, in smoke). In the 17th century the meaning of *holocaust* broadened to "something totally consumed by fire," and the word eventually was applied to fires of extreme destructiveness. In the 20th century *holocaust* has taken on a variety of figurative meanings, summarizing the effects of war, rioting, storms, epidemic diseases, and even economic failures. Most of these usages arose after World War II, but it is unclear whether they permitted or resulted from the use of *holocaust* in reference to the mass murder of European Jews and others by the Nazis. This application of the word occurred as early as 1942, but the phrase *the Holocaust* did not become established until the late 1950's. This sense of *holocaust* has since broadened to include the mass slaughter of other peoples, but when capitalized it refers specifically to the destruction of Jews and other Europeans by the Nazis and may also encompass the Nazi persecution of Jews that preceded the outbreak of the war.

Hol•o•cene (hŏl′ə-sēn′, hō′lə-) *adj.* Of or belonging to the more recent of the two epochs of the Quaternary Period, extending from the end of the Pleistocene Epoch to the present. See table at **geologic time.** —*n.* The Holocene Epoch or its deposits.

hol•o•crine (hŏl′ə-krĭn, -krīn′, -krēn′, hō′lə-) *adj.* Of or relating to a gland whose output consists of disintegrated secretory cells along with the secretory product itself. [HOLO– + Gk. *krinein*, to separate; see ENDOCRINE.]

hol•o•en•zyme (hŏl′ō-ĕn′zīm′, hō′lō-) *n.* An active complex enzyme consisting of an apoenzyme and a coenzyme.

ho•log•a•mous (hə-lŏg′ə-məs) *adj.* Of or relating to an organism whose germ cells morphologically resemble its somatic cells.

hol•o•gram (hŏl′ə-grăm′, hō′lə-) *n.* **1.** The pattern produced on a photosensitive medium that has been exposed by holography and then photographically developed. **2.** The photosensitive medium so treated.

hol•o•graph (hŏl′ə-grăf′, hō′lə-) *n.* **1.** A document written wholly in the handwriting of the person whose signature it bears. **2.** See **hologram.**

hol•o•graph•ic (hŏl′ə-grăf′ĭk, hō′lə-) also **hol•o•graph•i•cal** (-ĭ-kəl) *adj.* **1.** Of or relating to holography or holograms. **2.** Also **hol•o•graph** (hŏl′ə-grăf, hō′lə-). Of or being a document written wholly in the handwriting of the person whose signature it bears. **—ho′lo•graph′i•cal•ly** *adv.*

ho•log•raph•y (hō-lŏg′rə-fē) *n.* A method of producing a three-dimensional image of an object by recording on a photographic plate or film the pattern of interference formed by a split laser beam and then illuminating the pattern.

hol•o•gyn•ic (hŏl′ə-jĭn′ĭk, -gī′nĭk, hō′lə-) *adj.* Passing to successive generations only in females: *a hologynic trait.*

hol•o•he•dral (hŏl′ə-hē′drəl, hō′lə-) *adj.* Having the required planes for complete symmetry in a given crystal system.

hol•o•me•tab•o•lism (hŏl′ō-mə-tăb′ə-lĭz′əm, hō′lō-) *n.* Metamorphosis at every stage of an insect's development. **—hol′o•me•tab′o•lous** *adj.*

Ho•lon (hō-lōn′, KHô-lôn′). A city of W-central Israel near Tel Aviv–Jaffa; estab. 1941. Pop. 137,800.

hol•o•phras•tic (hŏl′ə-frăs′tĭk, hō′lə-) *adj.* Polysynthetic. [HOLO– + Gk. *phrastikos*, expressive (< *-phrastos*, speakable, thought of < *phrazein*, to show; see **gʷhren-***).]

hol•o•plank•ton (hŏl′ə-plăngk′tən, hō′lə-) *n.* Plankton that remains free-swimming through all stages of its life cycle.

hol•o•thu•ri•an (hŏl′ə-thŏŏr′ē-ən, -thyŏŏr′-, hō′lə-) *n.* Any of various echinoderms of the class Holothuroidea, which includes the sea cucumbers. [< Lat. *holothūria*, water polyp < Gk. *holothourion*.] **—hol′o•thu′ri•an** *adj.*

hol•o•type (hŏl′ə-tīp′, hō′lə-) *n.* The specimen used as the basis of the first published description of a taxonomic group and later designated as the type specimen.

hol•o•zo•ic (hŏl′ə-zō′ĭk, hō′lə-) *adj.* Obtaining nourishment by the ingestion of organic material, as animals do.

holp (hōlp) *v. Archaic.* A p.t. of **help.**

hol•pen (hōl′pən) *v. Archaic.* A p.part. of **help.**

Hol•stein[1] (hōl′stīn′, -stēn′). A region and former duchy of N Germany at the base of the Jutland Peninsula.

Hol•stein[2] (hōl′stīn′, -stēn′) *n.* Any of a breed of black and white dairy cattle developed in Friesland. [After HOLSTEIN[1].]

Hol•stein-Frie•sian (hōl′stīn-frēzhən, -stēn-) *n.* A Holstein.

hol•ster (hōl′stər) *n.* **1.** A leather case shaped to hold a pistol. **2.** A belt with loops or slots for carrying small tools or other equipment. —*tr.v.* **hol•stered, hol•ster•ing, hol•sters.** To put (a gun, for example) in a holster. [Prob. Du., alteration of *holfter, hulfter* < MHGer. *hulffter*, case, sheath, quiver, covering < *hulft* < OHGer. See **kel-¹***.] **—hol′stered** *adj.*

holt (hōlt) *n. Archaic.* A wood or grove; a copse. [ME < OE.]

ho•ly (hō′lē) *adj.* **-li•er, -li•est. 1.** Of, derived from, or associated with a divine power; sacred. **2.** Regarded with or worthy of worship or veneration; revered. **3.** Living according to a strict or highly moral religious or spiritual system; saintly. **4.** Specified or set apart for a religious purpose: *a holy place.* **5.** Solemnly undertaken; sacrosanct: *a holy pledge.* **6.** Regarded with or deserving special respect or reverence. **7.** *Informal.* Used as an intensive. [ME *holi* < OE *hālig*. See **kailo-***.] **—ho′li•ly** *adv.* **—ho′li•ness** *n.*

Ho•ly Ark (hō′lē) *n. Judaism.* The cabinet in a synagogue in which the scrolls of the Torah are kept.

Holy Communion *n.* The sacrament of the Eucharist received by a congregation.

Holy Cross (krôs′, krŏs′), **Mount of the.** A peak, 4,271.5 m (14,005 ft), in the Sawatch Range of the Rocky Mts. in W-central CO.

holy day also **ho•ly•day** (hō′lē-dā′) *n.* A day specified for religious observance.

holy day of obligation also **holyday of obligation** *n. Rom. Cath. Ch.* A feast on which the faithful are obliged to hear Mass and abstain from servile work.

Holy Father *n. Rom. Cath. Ch.* Used as a title and form of address for the pope.

Holy Ghost *n.* The Holy Spirit. [ME *holi gost*, holy spirit < OE *hālig gāst* : *hālig*, holy; see HOLY + *gāst*, spirit.]

Holy Grail *n.* See **grail** 1.

Holy In•no•cents' Day (ĭn′ə-sənts) *n. Eccles.* December 28, observed in commemoration of the slaughter of male infants in Bethlehem when Herod the Great tried to kill Jesus.

Holy Island or **Lin•dis•farne** (lĭn′dĭs-färn′). An island off the coast of NE England near the Scottish border; site of a monastery founded by St. Aidan (d. 651) in 635.

Holy Land. The biblical region of Palestine.

Holy Office *n. Rom. Cath. Ch.* A Roman congregation of the Curia that deals with protection of the faith and morals.

holy of ho•lies (hō′lēz) *n.* **1.** *Judaism.* The sanctuary inside the tabernacle in the Temple of Jerusalem, in which the Ark of the Covenant was kept. **2.** *Eastern Orthodox Ch.* The bema or sanctuary in a church. **3.** A place of awe. [Transl. of LLat. *sanctum sanctōrum* : *sanctum*, holy + *sanctōrum*, neut. genitive pl. of *sanctus*, holy.]

holy oil *n. Eccles.* **1.** See **chrism** 1. **2.** Olive oil blessed by a bishop and used to anoint the sick and in sacramentals.

Hol•yoke (hōl′yōk′). A city of SW MA on the Connecticut R. N of Springfield; settled in 1745. Pop. 43,704.

holy order also **Holy Order** *n. Eccles.* **1.** The sacrament or rite of ordination. Often used in the plural. **2.** The rank of an ordained Christian minister or priest. Often used in the plural. **3.** A principal order of clergy, esp. the rank of bishop, priest, and deacon, in the Roman Catholic, Eastern Orthodox, and Anglican churches.

Holy Roller *n. Offensive.* Used as a disparaging term for a member of a religious denomination in which spiritual fervor is expressed by shouts and violent body movements.

Holy Ro•man Empire (rō′mən). A loosely federated European political entity that began with the papal coronation of the German king Otto I as the first emperor in 962 and lasted until Francis II's renunciation of the title in 1806.

Holy Saturday *n.* The Saturday before Easter.

Holy Scripture *n.* See **Scripture** 2.

Holy See *n. Rom. Cath. Ch.* **1.** The see of the bishop of Rome. **2.** The authority, jurisdiction, and governmental functions associated with the papacy.

Holy Spirit *n.* The third person of the Christian Trinity.

ho•ly•stone (hō′lē-stōn′) *n.* A piece of soft sandstone used for scouring the wooden decks of a ship. —*tr.v.* **-stoned, -ston•ing, -stones.** To scrub or scour with a piece of holystone. [?]

Holy Synod *n.* The governing body of any of the Eastern Orthodox churches.

Holy Thursday *n.* **1.** See **Maundy Thursday. 2.** See **Ascension Day.**

holy war also **Holy War** *n.* A war deemed to have a religious or high moral purpose, as to extend or defend a religion.

holy water *n.* Water blessed by a priest and used esp. for religious purposes.

Holy Week *n.* The week before Easter.

holy writ *n.* **1.** Often **Holy Writ.** The Bible. **2.** *Informal.* A document held to be the most authoritative of its kind.

hom– *pref.* Var. of **homo–.**

hom•age (hŏm′ĭj, ŏm′-) *n.* **1.** Ceremonial acknowledgment by a vassal of allegiance to a feudal lord. **2.** Special honor or respect shown or expressed publicly. [ME < OFr., prob. < *omne, homme*, man < Lat. *homō, homin-*. See **dhghem-***.]

hom•bre[1] (ŏm′brā′, -brē) *n. Slang.* A man; a fellow. [Sp. < OSp. *omne* < Lat. *homō, homin-*. See **dhghem-***.]

hom•bre[2] (hŏm′bər, ŏm′-) *n. Games.* Var. of **ombre.**

Hom•burg also **hom•burg** (hŏm′bûrg′) *n.* A man's felt hat having a soft dented crown and a shallow, slightly rolled brim. [After (BAD) HOMBURG.]

home (hōm) *n.* **1.** A place where one lives; a residence. **2.** The physical structure within which one lives, such as a house. **3.** A dwelling place together with the social unit that occupies it; a household. **4.a.** An environment offering security and happiness. **b.** A valued place regarded as a refuge or place of origin. **5.** The place, such as a town, where one was born or has lived for a long period. **6.** The native habitat, as of a plant. **7.** The place where something is discovered, founded, developed, or promoted; a source. **8.** A headquarters; a home base. **9.a.** *Baseball.* Home plate. **b.** *Games.* Home base. **10.** An institution where people are cared for. —*adj.* **1.a.** Of or relating to a home, esp. to one's household or house: *home cooking.* **b.** Taking place in the home. **2.** Of, relating to, or being a place of origin or headquarters. **3.** *Sports.* Relating to or played at a team's place of origin. —*adv.* **1.** At, to, or toward the direction of home. **2.** On or into the point at which something is directed. **3.** To the center or heart of something; deeply. —*v.* **homed, hom•ing, homes.** —*intr.* **1.** To go or return to one's residence or base of operations. **2.** To be guided to a target automatically, as by means of radio waves. **3.** To move or lead toward a goal: *homing in on*

Holstein[2]

Homburg
Worn by Edward VII

ă pat	oi boy
ā pay	ou out
âr care	ŏŏ took
ä father	ōō boot
ĕ pet	ŭ cut
ē be	ûr urge
ĭ pit	th thin
ī pie	*th* this
îr pier	hw which
ŏ pot	zh vision
ō toe	ə about, item
ô paw	

Stress marks:
′ (primary);
′ (secondary), as in
dictionary (dĭk′shə-nĕr′ē)

the truth. — *tr.* To guide (a missile or an aircraft) to a target automatically. — ***idioms.*** **at home. 1.** Available to receive visitors. **2.** Comfortable and relaxed; at ease. **3.** Feeling an easy competence and familiarity. **home free.** Free of tension or stress, usu. after expending considerable effort. [ME < OE *hām*. See **tkei-***.]

home base *n.* **1.a.** *Games.* An objective toward which players of certain games, such as backgammon, progress. **b.** *Baseball.* Home plate. **2.** A base of operations; a headquarters.

home•bod•y (hōm′bŏd′ē) *n., pl.* **-ies.** One whose interests center on the home.

home•bound[1] (hōm′bound′) *adj.* Heading homeward.

home•bound[2] (hōm′bound′) *adj.* Restricted or confined to home.

home•boy (hōm′boi′) *n. Slang.* **1.** A male friend or acquaintance from one's hometown or neighborhood. **2.** A fellow male gang member.

home•bred (hōm′brĕd′) *adj.* Raised, bred, or reared at home.

home-brew (hōm′brōō′) *n.* An alcoholic beverage, esp. beer, that is made at home. — **home′-brewed′** *adj.*

home•com•ing (hōm′kŭm′ĭng) *n.* **1.** A coming to or returning home. **2.** An annual event at schools, colleges, and universities for visiting graduates.

home computer *n. Comp. Sci.* A microcomputer intended for use in the home.

home economics *n. (used with a sing. or pl. v.)* The science and art of home management. — **home economist** *n.*

home front *n.* The civilian population or the civilian activities of a country at war.

home fry *n.* A potato that has been peeled, boiled, sliced, and then fried. Often used in the plural.

home•girl (hōm′gûrl′) *n. Slang.* A female friend or acquaintance from one's hometown or neighborhood.

home•grown (hōm′grōn′) *adj.* **1.** Raised or grown at home. **2.** Originating in or characteristic of a locality.

home-help•er (hōm′hĕl′pər) *n.* One who aids someone requiring long-term care in a private residence.

home•land (hōm′lănd′) *n.* **1.** One's native land. **2.** A state, region, or territory identified with a particular people or ethnic group. **3.** Any of the ten regions designated by South Africa as semiautonomous territorial states for the Black population.

home•less (hōm′lĭs) *adj.* Having no home or haven. — *n.* People without homes considered as a group.

home•ly (hōm′lē) *adj.* **-li•er, -li•est. 1.** Not attractive or good-looking. **2.** Lacking elegance or refinement: *homely furniture.* **3.** Of a simple or unpretentious nature; plain: *homely truths.* **4.** Typical of the home or of home life. — **home′li•ness** *n.*

home•made (hōm′mād′) *adj.* **1.** Made or prepared in the home. **2.** Made by oneself. **3.** Crudely or simply made.

home•mak•er (hōm′mā′kər) *n.* One who manages a household. — **home′mak′ing** *n.*

homeo– or **homoio–** *pref.* Like; similar: *homeostasis.* [Gk. *homoio-* < *homoios* < *homos*, same. See **sem-**[1]***.]

ho•me•o•mor•phism (hō′mē-ə-môr′fĭz′əm) *n.* **1.** *Chem.* A close similarity in the crystal forms of unlike compounds. **2.** *Math.* A one-to-one correspondence between the points of two geometric figures that is continuous in both directions. — **ho′me•o•mor′phous** *adj.*

ho•me•op•a•thy (hō′mē-ŏp′ə-thē) *n., pl.* **-thies.** A system for treating disease based on the administration of minute doses of a drug that in massive amounts produces symptoms in healthy individuals similar to those of the disease itself. — **ho′me•o•path′** (-ə-păth′), **ho′me•op′a•thist** *n.* — **ho′me•o•path′ic** *adj.* — **ho′me•o•path′i•cal•ly** *adv.*

ho•me•o•sta•sis (hō′mē-ō-stā′sĭs) *n.* The ability or tendency of an organism or a cell to maintain internal equilibrium by adjusting its physiological processes. — **ho′me•o•stat′ic** (-stăt′ĭk) *adj.*

ho•me•o•therm (hō′mē-ə-thûrm′) also **ho•moi•o•therm** (hō-moi′ə-) *n.* A homeothermic organism; an endotherm.

ho•me•o•ther•mal (hō′mē-ə-thûr′məl) also **ho•moi•o•ther•mal** (hō-moi′ə-) *adj.* Homeothermic.

ho•me•o•ther•mic (hō′mē-ə-thûr′mĭk) also **ho•moi•o•ther•mic** (hō-moi′ə-) *adj.* Maintaining a relatively constant body temperature independent of the environment.

ho•me•o•ther•mous (hō′mē-ə-thûr′məs) also **ho•moi•o•ther•mous** (hō-moi′ə-) *adj.* Homeothermic.

home•own•er (hōm′ō′nər) *n.* One who owns a home. — **home′own′er•ship′** *n.*

home plate *n. Baseball.* The base at which a batter stands when hitting and which a base runner must finally touch in order to score.

home port also **home•port** (hōm′pôrt′, -pōrt′) *n.* **1.** The port in which a vessel is registered or permanently based. **2.** The port from which a merchant vessel primarily operates, regardless of its registry.

hom•er[1] (hō′mər) *n.* **1.** *Baseball.* A home run. **2.** A homing pigeon. — **hom′er** *v.*

ho•mer[2] (hō′mər) *n.* A unit of capacity used by the ancient Hebrews, equal to 10 ephahs (about 10 bushels) or 10 baths (about 100 gallons). [Heb. *ḥōmer*.]

Winslow Homer
Photographed in 1867

Ho•mer (hō′mər). fl. 850 B.C. Greek epic poet and the traditional author of the *Iliad* and the *Odyssey.*

Homer, Winslow. 1836–1910. Amer. painter known for his realistic seascapes, such as *Eight Bells* (1886).

home range *n.* The geographic area to which an organism normally confines its activity.

Ho•mer•ic (hō-mĕr′ĭk) *adj.* **1.** Of, relating to, or characteristic of Homer, his works, or his subject matter. **2.** Heroic in proportion, degree, or character; epic. — **Ho•mer′i•cal•ly** *adv.*

Homeric simile *n.* See **epic simile.**

home•room (hōm′rōōm′, -rŏŏm′) *n.* A school classroom to which a group of pupils is required to report each day.

home rule *n.* The principle or practice of self-government in the internal affairs of a dependent country or other political unit.

home run *n. Baseball.* A hit that allows the batter to make a complete circuit of the diamond and score a run.

home•sick (hōm′sĭk′) *adj.* Acutely longing for one's family or home. — **home′sick′ness** *n.*

home•spun (hōm′spŭn′) *adj.* **1.** Spun or woven in the home: *homespun linen.* **2.** Made of a homespun fabric. **3.** Simple and homely; unpretentious. — *n.* **1.** A plain, coarse, usu. woolen cloth made of homespun yarn. **2.** A similar fabric made on a power loom.

home stand *n. Sports.* A succession of games played esp. by a baseball team at the team's home field or court.

home•stead (hōm′stĕd′) *n.* **1.** A house, esp. a farmhouse, with adjoining buildings and land. **2.** *Law.* Property claimed as a householder's home and protected by law from forced sale to meet debts. **3.** Land claimed by a settler or squatter, esp. under the Homestead Act. **4.** The place where one's home is. — *v.* **-stead•ed, -stead•ing, -steads.** — *intr.* To settle and farm land, esp. under the Homestead Act. — *tr.* To claim and settle (land) as a homestead. — **home′stead′er** *n.*

Home•stead (hōm′stĕd′). A city of SE FL SW of Miami. Pop. 20,866.

Homestead Act *n.* An act passed by Congress in 1862 promising ownership of a 160-acre tract of public land to a citizen or head of a family who had resided on and cultivated the land for five years after the initial claim.

homestead law *n.* Any of several laws passed in most states exempting a householder's homestead from attachment or forced sale to meet general debts.

home•stretch (hōm′strĕch′) *n.* **1.** *Sports.* The portion of a racetrack from the last turn to the finish line. **2.** *Informal.* The final stages of an undertaking.

home study *n.* A course of study in which instruction is offered at home, usu. by mail.

home•town (hōm′toun′) *n.* The town or city of one's birth, rearing, or main residence.

home truth *n.* A central or basic truth, esp. one that is discomforting to acknowledge.

home video *n.* Videotapes for viewing in the home.

home•ward (hōm′wərd) *adv. & adj.* Toward or at home. — **home′wards** (-wərdz) *adv.*

Home•wood (hōm′wŏŏd′). **1.** A city of central AL, a suburb of Birmingham. Pop. 22,922. **2.** A village of NE IL, a suburb of Chicago. Pop. 19,278.

home•work (hōm′wûrk′) *n.* **1.** Work, such as schoolwork, that is done at home. **2.** Preparatory or preliminary work.

hom•ey also **hom•y** (hō′mē) *adj.* **-i•er, -i•est.** *Informal.* Having a feeling of home; comfortable; cozy. — **hom′ey•ness** *n.*

hom•i•cid•al (hŏm′ĭ-sīd′l, hō′mĭ-) *adj.* **1.** Of or relating to homicide. **2.** Capable of or conducive to homicide.

hom•i•cide (hŏm′ĭ-sīd′, hō′mĭ-) *n.* **1.** The killing of one person by another. **2.** A person who kills another person. [ME < OFr. < Lat. *homicīdium* and *homicīda* : *homō*, person; see **dhghem-*** + *-cīdium* and *-cīda*, -cide.]

hom•i•let•ic (hŏm′ə-lĕt′ĭk) also **hom•i•let•i•cal** (-ĭ-kəl) *adj.* **1.** Relating to or of the nature of a homily. **2.** Relating to homiletics. [LLat. *homīlēticus* < Gk. *homīlētikos*, of conversation < *homilētos*, conversation < *homilein*, to converse with < *homilos*, crowd. See HOMILY.]

hom•i•let•ics (hŏm′ə-lĕt′ĭks) *n. (used with a sing. v.)* The art of preaching.

hom•i•ly (hŏm′ə-lē) *n., pl.* **-lies. 1.** A sermon, esp. on a scriptural text. **2.** A tedious moralizing lecture or admonition. [ME *omelie* < OFr. < LLat. *homīlia* < Gk., discourse < *homilos*, crowd. See **sem-**[1]***.] — **hom′i•list** *n.*

hom•ing pigeon (hō′mĭng) *n.* A pigeon trained to return to its home roost.

hom•i•nid (hŏm′ə-nĭd) *n.* A primate of the family Hominidae, of which *Homo sapiens* is the only extant species. [< NLat. *Hominidae*, family name < Lat. *homō, homin-*, man. See **dhghem-***.] — **hom′i•nid** *adj.*

hom•i•ni•za•tion (hŏm′ə-nĭ-zā′shən) *n.* The evolutionary process leading to the human characteristics that distinguish hominids from other primates. [Lat. *homō, homin-*, man; see HOMO[1] + -IZATION.]

hom•i•noid (hŏm′ə-noid′) *adj.* **1.** Of or belonging to the superfamily Hominoidea, which includes apes and human beings. **2.** Resembling a human being. — *n.* A member of the Hominoidea. [< NLat. *Hominoidea*, superfamily name :

Homō, type genus (< Lat. *homō, homin-*, man; see HOMO[1]) + *-oidea*, resembling (< Gk. *-oeidēs*, -oid).]

hom•i•ny (hŏm′ə-nē) *n.* Hulled and dried kernels of corn boiled as food. [Short for Virginia Algonquian *uskatahomen*.]

hominy grits *pl.n.* Grits, esp. eaten as a breakfast food. See Regional Note at **pone.**

hom•mos (ho͝om′əs, hŭm′-) *n.* Var. of **hummus.**

ho•mo[1] (hō′mō) *n.* A member of the genus *Homo*, which includes the extinct and extant species of human beings. [Lat. *homō*, man. See **dhghem-***.]

ho•mo[2] (hō′mō) *n., pl.* **-mos.** *Offensive.* Used as a disparaging term for a gay or lesbian person.

homo– or **hom–** *pref.* Same; like: *homophone.* [Gk. < *homos*, same. See **sem-**[1]*.]

ho•mo•cen•tric (hō′mə-sĕn′trĭk, hŏm′ə-) *adj.* Having the same center.

ho•mo•cer•cal (hō′mə-sûr′kəl, hŏm′ə-) *adj.* Relating to, being, or characterized by a tail fin having two symmetrical lobes extending from the end of the vertebral column, as in most bony fishes. [HOMO– + Gk. *kerkos*, tail + –AL[1].]

ho•mo•chro•mat•ic (hō′mə-krō-măt′ĭk, hŏm′ə-) *adj.* Of or characterized by one color; monochromatic.

ho•moe•cious (hō-mē′shəs, hō-) *adj.* Of or being a parasite that spends its entire life cycle on the same host. [HOMO– + Gk. *oikia*, house; see HETEROECIOUS + –OUS.]

Ho•mo e•rec•tus (hō′mō ĭ-rĕk′təs) *n.* An extinct species of human beings, regarded as an ancestor of *Homo sapiens.* [Lat. *homō*, man + *ērēctus*, upright.]

ho•mo•e•rot•ic (hō′mō-ĭ-rŏt′ĭk) *adj.* **1.** Of or concerning homosexual love and desire. **2.** Arousing such desire.

ho•mo•e•rot•i•cism (hō′mō-ĭ-rŏt′ĭ-sĭz′əm) also **ho•mo•er•o•tism** (-ĕr′ə-tĭz′əm) *n.* A homoerotic quality or theme.

ho•mo•ga•met•ic (hō′mō-gə-mĕt′ik) *adj.* Producing gametes that contain only one type of sex chromosome.

ho•mog•a•mous (hō-mŏg′ə-məs) *adj. Bot.* **1.** Having one kind of flower on the same plant. **2.** Having stamens and pistils that mature simultaneously.

ho•mo•ge•ne•i•ty (hō′mə-jə-nē′ĭ-tē, -nā′-, hŏm′ə-) *n., pl.* **-ties.** The state or quality of being homogeneous.

ho•mo•ge•ne•ous (hō′mə-jē′nē-əs, -jēn′yəs) *adj.* **1.** Of the same or similar nature or kind. **2.** Uniform in structure or composition. **3.** *Math.* Consisting of terms of the same degree or elements of the same dimension. [< Med.Lat. *homogeneus* < Gk. *homogenēs* : *homo-*, homo- + *genos*, kind; see HETEROGENEOUS.] **—ho′mo•ge′ne•ous•ness** *n.*

ho•mog•e•nize (hə-mŏj′ə-nīz′, hō-) *tr.v.* **-nized, -niz•ing, -niz•es. 1.** To make homogeneous. **2.a.** To reduce to particles and disperse throughout a fluid. **b.** To make uniform in consistency, esp. to make (milk) so by emulsifying the fat content. [< HOMOGENEOUS.] **—ho•mog′e•ni•za′tion** (-nĭ-zā′shən) *n.*

ho•mog•e•nous[1] (hə-mŏj′ə-nəs, hō-) *adj. Biol.* Of or exhibiting homogeny.

ho•mog•e•nous[2] (hə-mŏj′ə-nəs, hō-) *adj.* Homogeneous. [Alteration of HOMOGENEOUS.]

ho•mog•e•ny (hə-mŏj′ə-nē, hō-) *n., pl.* **-nies.** Similarity of structure between organs or parts of common descent, regardless of function. [Gk. *homogenia*, community of origin < *homogenēs*, of the same race, kind. See HOMOGENEOUS.]

ho•mo•graft (hō′mə-grăft′, hŏm′ə-) *n.* See **allograft.**

hom•o•graph (hŏm′ə-grăf′, hō′mə-) *n.* One of two or more words that have the same spelling but differ in origin, meaning, and sometimes pronunciation. **—hom′o•graph′ic** *adj.*

Ho•mo hab•i•lis (hō′mō hăb′ə-ləs) *n.* An extinct species of human beings considered to be an ancestor of modern human beings and the earliest hominid to make tools. [Lat. *homō*, man + Lat. *habilis*, skillful.]

homoio– *pref.* Var. of **homeo–.**

ho•moi•o•therm (hō-moi′ə-thûrm′) *n.* Var. of **homeotherm.**

ho•moi•o•ther•mal (hō-moi′ə-thûr′məl) *adj.* Var. of **homeothermal.**

ho•moi•o•ther•mic (hō-moi′ə-thûr′mĭk) *adj.* Var. of **homeothermic.**

ho•moi•o•ther•mous (hō-moi′ə-thûr′məs) *adj.* Var. of **homeothermous.**

Ho•moi•ou•si•an (hō′moi-o͞o′sē-ən, -zē-) *n.* A member of a Christian sect in the fourth century A.D. that held that Jesus and God the Father were similar but not the same in substance. [< Gk. *homoiousios*, of similar substance : *homoio-*, homeo- + *ousia*, substance (< neut. pr.part. of *einai*, to be; see **es-***).]

ho•mo•lec•i•thal (hō′mə-lĕs′ə-thəl) *adj.* Having a yolk that is evenly distributed throughout: *a homolecithal egg.* [HOMO– + Gk. *lekithos*, egg yolk + –AL[1].]

ho•mol•o•gate (hə-mŏl′ə-gāt′, hō-) *tr.v.* **-gat•ed, -gat•ing, -gates.** *Scots.* To approve, esp. to confirm officially. [Med. Lat. *homologāre, homologāt-* < Gk. *homologein*, to agree < *homologos*, agreeing. See HOMOLOGOUS.]

ho•mo•log•i•cal (hō′mə-lŏj′ĭ-kəl, hŏm′ə-) also **ho•mo•log•ic** (-lŏj′ĭk) *adj.* Homologous. **—ho′mo•log′i•cal•ly** *adv.*

ho•mol•o•gize (hə-mŏl′ə-jīz′, hō-) *tr.v.* **-gized, -giz•ing, -giz•es. 1.** To make homologous. **2.** To show to be homologous. **—ho•mol′o•giz′er** *n.*

ho•mol•o•gous (hə-mŏl′ə-gəs, hō-) *adj.* **1.** Corresponding or similar in position, value, structure, or function. **2.** *Biol.* Similar in structure and evolutionary origin, though not necessarily in function, as the flippers of a seal and the hands of a human being. **3.** *Immunol.* Relating to the correspondence between an antigen and its antibody. **4.** *Genet.* Having the same morphology and linear sequence of gene loci as another chromosome. **5.** *Chem.* Belonging to or being a series of organic compounds each successive member of which differs from the preceding by a constant increment, esp. by a CH_2 group. [< Gk. *homologos*, agreeing : *homo-*, homo- + *logos*, word, proportion; see **leg-***.]

hom•o•lo•graph•ic (hŏm′ə-lə-grăf′ĭk) *adj.* Maintaining the ratio of parts. [Gk. *homalos*, even; see **sem-**[1]* + GRAPHIC.]

homolographic projection *n.* A map projection reproducing the ratios of areas as they exist on the earth's surface.

hom•o•logue also **hom•o•log** (hŏm′ə-lôg′, -lŏg′, hō′mə-) *n.* Something homologous. [Fr. < Gk. *homologon*, neut. of *homologos*, agreeing. See HOMOLOGOUS.]

homocercal
Swordfish with homocercal tail

ho•mol•o•gy (hə-mŏl′ə-jē, hō-) *n., pl.* **-gies. 1.** The quality or condition of being homologous. **2.** A homologous relationship or correspondence. **3.** *Chem.* **a.** The relation of the elements of a periodic family or group. **b.** The relation of the organic compounds in a homologous series. **4.** *Math.* A topologic classification of configurations into distinct types that imposes an algebraic structure on families of geometric figures. [Gk. *homologia*, agreement < *homologos*, agreeing. See HOMOLOGOUS.]

ho•mol•o•sine projection (hō-mŏl′ə-sīn′, -sĭn, hə-) *n.* A map of the earth's surface based on sinusoidal curves, with the ocean areas distorted so that the continents appear with minimal distortion. [HOMOLO(GRAPHIC) + SINE + PROJECTION.]

ho•mo•mor•phism (hō′mə-môr′fĭz′əm, hŏm′ə-) *n.* **1.** *Biol.* Similarity of external form or appearance but not of structure or origin. **2.** *Zool.* A resemblance in form between an animal's immature and adult stages. **3.** *Math.* A transformation from one set into another that preserves algebraic operations. **—ho′mo•mor′phic, ho′mo•mor′phous** *adj.*

hom•o•nym (hŏm′ə-nĭm′, hō′mə-) *n.* **1.** One of two or more words that have the same sound and often the same spelling but differ in meaning. **2.a.** A word that is used to designate several different things. **b.** A namesake. **3.** *Biol.* A taxonomic name identical to one previously applied to a different species or genus and therefore unacceptable in its new use. [Lat. *homōnymum* < Gk. *homōnumon* < neut. of *homōnumos*, homonymous. See HOMONYMOUS.] **—hom′o•nym′ic** *adj.*

ho•mon•y•mous (hō-mŏn′ə-məs, hə-) *adj.* **1.** Having the same name. **2.** Of the nature of a homonym; homonymic. [< Lat. *homōnymus* < Gk. *homōnumos* : *homo-*, homo- + *onuma*, name; see **nō̆-men-***.] **—ho•mon′y•mous•ly** *adv.*

ho•mon•y•my (hō-mŏn′ə-mē, hə-) *n., pl.* **-mies.** The quality or condition of being homonymous.

Ho•mo•ou•si•an (hō′mō-o͞o′sē-ən, -zē-) *n.* A Christian supporting the Council of Nicaea's Trinitarian definition of Jesus as consubstantial with God the Father. [LLat. *homoūsiānus* < *homoūsius*, of same substance < Gk. *homoousios* : *homo-*, homo- + *ousia*, substance; see HOMOIOUSIAN.]

ho•mo•phile (hō′mə-fīl′) *adj.* **1.** Gay or lesbian. **2.** Being actively concerned with gay or lesbian rights and welfare. **—ho′mo•phile′** *n.*

ho•mo•pho•bi•a (hō′mə-fō′bē-ə) *n.* **1.** Aversion to gay or lesbian people or their lifestyle or culture. **2.** Behavior or an act based on homophobia. [HOMO(SEXUAL) + –PHOBIA.] **—ho′mo•phobe′** *n.* **—ho′mo•pho′bic** (-fō′bĭk) *adj.*

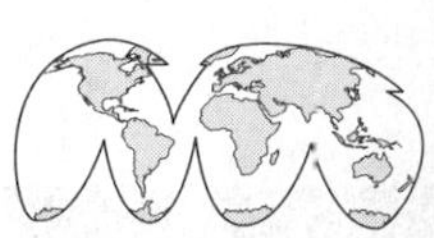

homolosine projection

hom•o•phone (hŏm′ə-fōn′, hō′mə-) *n.* One of two or more words, such as *night* and *knight*, that are pronounced the same but differ in meaning, origin, and sometimes spelling. **—ho•moph′o•nous** (hō-mŏf′ə-nəs) *adj.*

hom•o•phon•ic (hŏm′ə-fŏn′ĭk, hō′mə-) *adj.* **1.** Sounding alike. **2.** *Mus.* Having or characterized by a single melodic line with accompaniment. [< Gk. *homophōnos* : *homo-*, homo- + *phōnē*, sound; see PHONE[2].]

ho•moph•o•ny (hō-mŏf′ə-nē) *n., pl.* **-nies. 1.** The quality or condition of being homophonic. **2.** *Mus.* Homophonic music.

ho•mo•phy•ly (hō′mə-fī′lē, hŏm′ə-, hō-mŏf′ə-lē) *n., pl.* **-lies.** *Zool.* Resemblance arising from common ancestry. [HOMO– + PHYL(UM) + –Y[2].] **—ho′mo•phyl′ic** (-fĭl′ĭk) *adj.*

ho•mo•plas•tic (hō′mə-plăs′tĭk, hŏm′ə-) *adj.* **1.** Of, relating to, or exhibiting homoplasy. **2.** Of, relating to, or derived from a different individual of the same species.

ho•mo•pla•sy (hō′mə-plā′sē, -plăs′ē, hŏm′ə-) *n.* Correspondence between parts or organs due to evolutionary convergence.

ho•mop•ter•an (hō-mŏp′tər-ən) *n.* A homopterous insect. [< NLat. *Homoptera*, order name : Gk. *homo-*, homo- + Gk. *pteron*, wing; see –PTER.] **—ho•mop′ter•an** *adj.*

ho•mop•ter•ous (hō-mŏp′tər-əs) *adj.* Of or belonging to the order Homoptera, which includes the cicadas and scale insects and is characterized by sucking mouthparts. [< NLat. *Homoptera*, order name. See HOMOPTERAN.]

Ho•mo sa•pi•ens (hō′mō sā′pē-ənz, -ĕnz′) *n.* The modern species of human beings, the only extant species of the pri-

ă pat	oi boy
ā pay	ou out
âr care	o͝o took
ä father	o͞o boot
ĕ pet	ŭ cut
ē be	ûr urge
ĭ pit	th thin
ī pie	*th* this
îr pier	hw which
ŏ pot	zh vision
ō toe	ə about, item
ô paw	

Stress marks:
′ (primary);
′ (secondary), as in dictionary (dĭk′shə-nĕr′ē)

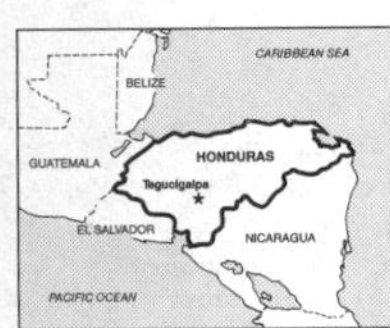

Honduras

mate family Hominidae. [NLat. *Homō sapiēns* : *Homō*, genus name + Lat. *sapiēns*, pr.part. of *sapere*, to be wise.]

ho•mo•sex•u•al (hō′mə-sĕk′sho͞o-əl, -mō-) *adj.* Of, relating to, or having a sexual orientation to persons of the same sex. —*n.* A homosexual person; a gay man or a lesbian.

ho•mo•sex•u•al•i•ty (hō′mə-sĕk′sho͞o-ăl′ĭ-tē, -mō-) *n.* **1.** Sexual orientation to persons of the same sex. **2.** Sexual activity with another of the same sex.

ho•mo•spo•rous (hō′mə-spôr′əs, -spōr′-, hŏm′ə-, hō-mŏs′pər-əs) *adj. Bot.* Producing spores of one kind only. —**ho′mo•spo′ry** *n.*

ho•mo•tax•is (hō′mō-tăk′sĭs, hŏm′ō-) *n.* Similarity of stratigraphic arrangement and fossils in noncontemporaneous or widely separated geologic deposits. —**ho′mo•tax′ic** (-tăk′sĭk), **ho′mo•tax′i•al** (-tăk′sē-əl) *adj.*

ho•mo•thal•lic (hō′mō-thăl′ĭk, hŏm′ō-) *adj. Bot.* Having male and female reproductive structures on the same thallus.

ho•mo•zy•go•sis (hō′mō-zī-gō′sĭs, -mə-, hŏm′ə-) *n.* The union of genetically identical gametes, resulting in the formation of a homozygote. —**ho′mo•zy•got′ic** (-gŏt′ĭk) *adj.*

ho•mo•zy•gote (hō′mō-zī′gōt′, -mə-, hŏm′ə-) *n. Genet.* A homozygous organism.

ho•mo•zy•gous (hō′mō-zī′gəs, -mə-, hŏm′ə-) *adj. Genet.* Having the same alleles at a particular gene locus on homologous chromosomes. —**ho′mo•zy•gos′i•ty** (-gŏs′ĭ-tē) *n.* —**ho′mo•zy′gous•ly** *adv.*

Homs (hômz, hôms). A city of W-central Syria N of Damascus; birthplace of the emperor Heliogabalus. Pop. 346,871.

ho•mun•cu•lus (hō-mŭng′kyə-ləs, hə-) *n., pl.* **-li** (-lī′). **1.** A diminutive human being. **2.** A miniature, fully formed individual believed by adherents of the early biological theory of preformation to be present in the sperm cell. [Lat., dim. of *homō*, man. See **dhghem-***.]

hom•y (hō′mē) *adj.* Var. of **homey.**

Hon. *abbr.* **1.** Honorable. **2. hon.** Honorary.

ho•nan also **Ho•nan** (hō′năn′) *n.* A pongee fabric of even color made originally from silk produced by the silkworms of Henan (formerly Honan), China.

Honan. See **Henan.**

hon•cho (hŏn′chō) *Slang. n., pl.* **-chos.** One who is in charge; a manager or leader. [J. *hanchō*, squad leader : *han*, squad + *chō*, chief.] —**hon′cho** *v.*

Hond. *abbr.* Honduras.

Hon•du•ras (hŏn-do͝or′əs, -dyo͝or′-). A country of N Central America; colonized by the Spanish in the early 1500's and proclaimed its independence in 1821. Cap. Tegucigalpa. Pop. 4,092,000. —**Hon•du′ran** *adj. & n.*

Honduras, Gulf of. An inlet of the W Caribbean Sea bordering on Belize, Honduras, and Guatemala.

hone[1] (hōn) *n.* **1.** A fine-grained whetstone for giving a keen edge to a cutting tool. **2.** A tool with a rotating abrasive tip for enlarging holes to precise dimensions. —*tr.v.* **honed, hon•ing, hones. 1.** To sharpen on a fine-grained whetstone. **2.** To perfect or make more intense or effective: *honed her skills.* [ME < OE *hān*, stone. See **kō-***.]

hone[2] (hōn) *intr.v.* **honed, hon•ing, hones.** *Informal.* **1.** To whine or moan. **2.** To hanker; yearn. [Obsolete Fr. *hoigner* < OFr., perh. < *hon*, cry of discontent.]

Hon•eg•ger (hŏn′ĭ-gər, hō′nĕg′ər, ô-nĕ-gĕr′), **Arthur.** 1892–1955. French-born Swiss composer whose works include *Pacific 231* (1923).

hon•est (ŏn′ĭst) *adj.* **1.** Marked by or displaying integrity; upright. **2.** Not deceptive or fraudulent; genuine. **3.** Equitable; fair. **4.a.** Truthful; not false. **b.** Sincere; frank. **5.a.** Of good repute; respectable. **b.** Without affectation; plain. **6.** Virtuous; chaste. [ME < OFr. *honeste* < Lat. *honestus*, honorable < *honōs*, honor.]

honest broker *n.* A neutral agent, as in mediation.

hon•est•ly (ŏn′ĭst-lē) *adv.* **1.** In an honest manner. **2.** Used as an intensive: *I honestly don't care.* —*interj.* Used to express mild disapproval or dismay: *Honestly! Look at this mess!*

hon•es•ty (ŏn′ĭ-stē) *n., pl.* **-ties. 1.** The quality or condition of being honest; integrity. **2.** Truthfulness; sincerity. **3.** *Archaic.* Chastity. **4.** *Bot.* A European plant *(Lunaria annua)* having round, flat, papery silver-white seedpods.

Syns: *honesty, honor, integrity, probity, rectitude.* These nouns denote the quality of being upright in principle and action. *Honesty* implies truthfulness, fairness, and refusal to engage in fraud, deceit, or dissembling: *Honesty is the best policy. Honor* implies a worthy adherence to a strict moral or ethical code: *"Never give in except to convictions of honor and good sense"* (Winston S. Churchill). *Integrity* is moral soundness, especially when one's steadfastness of purpose, responsibility, or trust is tested: *"Integrity without knowledge is weak and useless, and knowledge without integrity is dangerous and dreadful"* (Samuel Johnson). *Probity* is proven integrity: *a person of unquestioned probity. Rectitude* is moral righteousness: *"The name of Brutus would be a guaranty to the people of rectitude of intention"* (J.A. Froude).

hone•wort (hōn′wûrt′, -wôrt′) *n.* An eastern North American plant *(Cryptotaenia canadensis)* having umbels of small whitish flowers. [*hone-*, of unknown meaning + WORT[1].]

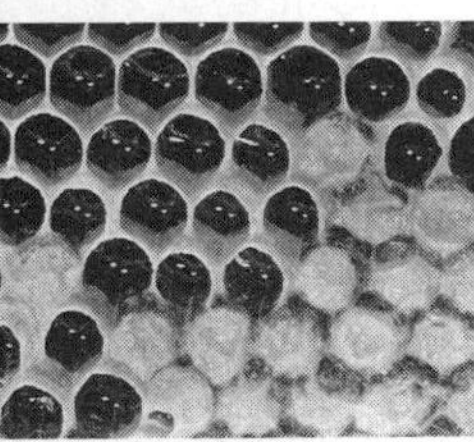

honeycomb
Close-up of hexagon-shaped cells

hon•ey (hŭn′ē) *n., pl.* **-eys. 1.a.** A sweet yellowish or brownish viscid fluid produced by various bees from the nectar of flowers and used as food. **b.** A similar substance made by certain other insects. **2.** A sweet substance, such as nectar. **3.** Sweetness; pleasantness. **4.** Sugary or ingratiating words; flattery. **5.** *Informal.* Sweetheart; dear. **6.** *Informal.* Something remarkably fine. —*tr.v.* **-eyed** or **-ied** (hŭn′ēd), **-ey•ing, -eys. 1.** To sweeten with or as if with honey. **2.** To cajole with sweet talk. [ME *honi* < OE *hunig.*]

honey badger *n.* See **ratel.**

honey bear *n.* See **kinkajou.**

hon•ey•bee (hŭn′ē-bē′) *n.* Any of several honey-producing social bees of the genus *Apis*, esp. *A. mellifera,* raised for honey and beeswax.

hon•ey•ber•ry (hŭn′ē-bĕr′ē) *n.* See **genip** 2.

hon•ey•comb (hŭn′ē-kōm′) *n.* **1.** A beeswax structure of hexagonal thin-walled cells made by honeybees to hold honey and larvae. **2.** Something resembling this structure in configuration or pattern. —*tr.v.* **-combed, -comb•ing, -combs. 1.** To fill with holes or compartments; riddle. **2.** To form in or cover with a pattern like that of a honeycomb.

hon•ey•creep•er (hŭn′ē-krē′pər) *n.* **1.** Any of various small tropical American birds of the family Coerebidae, having a curved bill adapted for sucking nectar from flowers. **2.** Any of several similar birds of the family Drepanididae of Hawaii.

hon•ey•dew (hŭn′ē-do͞o′, -dyo͞o′) *n.* **1.** A sweet sticky substance excreted by various insects, esp. aphids, on plant leaves. **2.** A sweet exudate similar to honeydew on plant leaves. **3.** A honeydew melon.

honeydew melon *n.* A kind of melon *(Cucumis melo)* having a smooth whitish rind and green flesh.

hon•ey•eat•er (hŭn′ē-ē′tər) *n.* Any of various birds of the family Meliphagidae of Australia, having a long extensible tongue adapted for sucking nectar from flowers.

hon•eyed (hŭn′ēd) *adj.* also **hon•ied. 1.** Containing, full of, or sweetened with honey. **2.** Ingratiating; sugary: *honeyed words.* **3.** Sweet; dulcet: *a honeyed voice.*

honey guide *n.* Any of various tropical Old World birds of the family Indicatoridae, some species of which lead to the nests of wild honeybees in their own quest for food.

honey locust *n.* Any of several trees of the genus *Gleditsia*, esp. *G. triacanthos,* having deciduous compound leaves, small flowers in racemes, and large indehiscent pods.

honey mesquite *n.* See **mesquite** a.

hon•ey•moon (hŭn′ē-mo͞on′) *n.* **1.** A holiday or trip taken by a newly married couple. **2.** An early harmonious period in a relationship. —*intr.v.* **-mooned, -moon•ing, -moons.** To spend a honeymoon. [Perh. < a comparison of the moon, which wanes as soon as it is full, to the affections of a newly married couple.] —**hon′ey•moon′er** *n.*

hon•ey•suck•le (hŭn′ē-sŭk′əl) *n.* **1.** Any of various shrubs or vines of the genus *Lonicera,* having opposite leaves, fragrant, usu. paired tubular flowers, and small berries. **2.** Any of various similar or related plants. [ME *honysoukel,* alteration of *honisouke* < OE *hunīsūce* : *hunig*, honey + *sūcan*, to suck; see SUCK.]

Hong Ha (hông′ hä′). See **Red River** 1.

Hong Kong (hŏng′kŏng′, -kŏng′, hông′kông′, -kông′). A British crown colony on the SE coast of China SE of Guangzhou, including **Hong Kong Island** and adjacent areas. The colony will revert to Chinese sovereignty in 1997. Cap. Victoria. Pop. 5,021,066.

Hong•shui He also **Hung•shui He** (ho͝ong′shwā′ hə′). A river rising in SW China and flowing c. 1,448 km (900 mi) to the Xiang Jiang.

Ho•ni•a•ra (hō′nē-är′ə). The cap. of the Solomon Is., on the NW coast of Guadalcanal. Pop. 16,125.

hon•ied (hŭn′ēd) *v.* A p.t. and p.part. of **honey.** —*adj.* Var. of **honeyed.**

honk (hôngk, hŏngk) *n.* **1.** The raucous resonant sound typical of a wild goose. **2.a.** A sound like a goose's honk. **b.** The sound of a motor vehicle horn. —*v.* **honked, honk•ing, honks.** —*intr.* To emit a honk. —*tr.* To cause (a horn) to produce a honk. [Imit.] —**honk′er** *n.*

hon•ky or **hon•kie** also **hon•key** (hông′kē, hŏng′-) *n., pl.* **-kies** also **-keys.** *Offensive Slang.* Used as a disparaging term for a white person. [Poss. blend of Wolof *honq*, red, pink, of light complexion, and HUNKY.]

hon•ky-tonk (hông′kē-tôngk′, hŏng′kē-tŏngk′) *n. Slang.* A cheap, noisy bar or dance hall. —*adj.* **1.** *Slang.* Of or relating to such a bar or dance hall; tawdry. **2.** *Mus.* Of, relating to, or being a type of ragtime played on a tinny-sounding piano. —*intr.v.* **-tonked, -tonk•ing, -tonks.** *Slang.* To visit cheap, noisy bars or dance halls. [Perh. < HONK.]

Hon•o•lu•lu (hŏn′ə-lo͞o′lo͞o). The cap. of HI, on the SE coast of Oahu; first settled in 1816. Pop. 365,272.

hon•or (ŏn′ər) *n.* **1.** High respect, as for special merit; esteem. **2.a.** Good name; reputation. **b.** A source or cause of credit. **3.a.** Glory or recognition; distinction. **b.** A mark, token, or gesture of respect or distinction. **c.** A military decoration. **d.** A title conferred for achievement. **4.** Nobility of mind; probity or integrity. See Syns at **honesty. 5.** High rank. **6.** The dignity accorded to position. **7.** Great privilege: *May I have the honor of this dance?* **8. Honor.** Used with *His, Her,* or *Your* as a title and form of address for certain officials: *Her Honor the Mayor.* **9.a.** A code of integrity, dignity, and pride, chiefly among men, maintained in some societies, as in feudal Europe, by force of arms. **b.** A woman's chastity or reputation for chastity. **10. honors.** Social courtesies offered to guests. **11. honors. a.** Special recognition for unusual academic achievement. **b.** A program of individual advanced study for exceptional students. **12.** *Sports.* The right of being first at the tee in golf. **13.** *Games.* **a.** Any of the four or five highest cards in each suit, esp. in bridge. **b. honors.** A bonus score, esp. in bridge, awarded for having certain honor cards in one's hand. — *tr.v.* **-ored, -or•ing, -ors. 1.a.** To hold in respect; esteem. **b.** To show respect for. **c.** To bow to (another dancer) in square dancing. **2.** To confer distinction on. **3.** To accept or pay as valid. — ***idiom.*** **honor bound.** Under an obligation enforced by the personal integrity of the one obliged. [ME < OFr. < Lat.] — **hon′or•er** *n.*

hon•or•a•ble (ŏn′ər-ə-bəl) *adj.* **1.** Deserving or earning honor and respect. **2.** Bringing distinction or recognition: *honorable service.* **3.** Possessing and characterized by honor. **4.** Consistent with honor or good name. **5.** Distinguished; illustrious. **6.** Attended by marks of recognition and honor. **7. Honorable. a.** Used as a title of respect for certain high government officials. **b.** Used as a courtesy title for the children of barons and viscounts and the younger sons of earls. **c.** Used in the House of Commons as a title of respect for members. — **hon′or•a•ble•ness** *n.* — **hon′or•a•bly** *adv.*

honorable discharge *n.* Discharge from the armed forces with a commendable record.

honorable mention *n.* A citation to one who has performed well in a competition but has not been awarded a prize.

hon•o•rar•i•um (ŏn′ə-râr′ē-əm) *n., pl.* **-i•ums** or **-i•a** (-ē-ə). A payment given to a professional person for services for which fees are not required. [Lat. *honōrārium* < neut. of *honōrārius*, honorary < *honor, honōr-*, honor.]

hon•or•ar•y (ŏn′ə-rĕr′ē) *adj.* **1.** Held or given as a mark of honor, esp. conferred as an honor without the usual adjuncts. **2.a.** Holding an office or title given as an honor, without payment. **b.** Voluntary. **3.** Relying on honor and not legally enforceable, as a duty.

hon•or•ee (ŏn′ə-rē′) *n.* The recipient of an honor.

hon•or•if•ic (ŏn′ə-rĭf′ĭk) *adj.* Conferring or showing respect or honor. — *n.* A title, phrase, or grammatical form conveying respect, used esp. for a social superior. [Lat. *honōrificus* : *honor, honōr-*, honor + *-ficus*, -fic.] — **hon′or•if′i•cal•ly** *adv.*

Ho•no•ri•us (hō-nôr′ē-əs, -nōr′-), **Flavius.** A.D. 384–423. Roman emperor of the West (395–423).

honor society *n.* An organization to which students are admitted in recognition of academic achievement.

honor system *n.* A system in which persons are trusted without supervision in situations that might allow for dishonesty.

hon•our (ŏn′ər) *n. & v. Chiefly British.* Var. of **honor.**

Hon•shu (hŏn′sho͞o). An island of central Japan between the Sea of Japan and the Pacific.

hooch[1] also **hootch** (ho͞och) *n. Slang.* **1.** Alcoholic liquor, esp. inferior or bootleg liquor. **2.** Marijuana. [Short for *hoochinoo* < *Hoochinoo*, a Tlingit village where illegal liquor was distilled < Tlingit *xutsnuuwú*.]

hooch[2] also **hootch** (ho͞och) *n. Slang.* A dwelling, esp. a thatched hut. [Alteration of J. *uchi*, inside, interior.]

hood[1] (ho͝od) *n.* **1.** A loose pliable covering for the head and neck, usu. attached to a robe or jacket. **2.** An ornamental draping of cloth hung from the shoulders of an academic or ecclesiastical robe. **3.** A sack placed over a falcon's head to keep the bird quiet. **4.a.** A metal cover or cowl for a hearth or stove. **b.** A carriage top. **c.** The hinged metal lid over the engine of a motor vehicle. **5.** *Zool.* An expanded part, crest, or marking on or near the head of an animal. — *tr.v.* **hood•ed, hood•ing, hoods.** To supply or cover with a hood. [ME *hod* < OE *hōd.*]

hood[2] (ho͝od) *n. Slang.* A hoodlum; a thug. [Short for HOODLUM.]

Hood (ho͝od), **John Bell.** 1831–79. Amer. Confederate soldier who commanded the Atlanta Campaign (1864).

Hood, Mount. A volcanic peak, 3,426.7 m (11,235 ft), in the Cascade Range of NW OR.

Hood, Thomas. 1799–1845. British poet and editor whose verses include "The Song of the Shirt" (1843).

–hood *suff.* **1.a.** Condition; state; quality: *manhood.* **b.** An instance of a specified state or quality: *falsehood.* **2.** A group sharing a specified state or quality: *sisterhood.* [ME *-hed, -hode* < OE **-hǣde, -hād.*]

'hood (ho͝od) *n. Slang.* A neighborhood.

hood•ed (ho͝od′ĭd) *adj.* **1.** Covered with or having a hood. **2.** Shaped like a hood or cowl. **3.** *Zool.* **a.** Having coloration or a crest suggesting a hood. **b.** Having elastic skin at the neck that when distended resembles a hood, as that of the cobra.

hooded seal *n.* A seal *(Cystophora cristata)* of northern seas, having a grayish spotted coat and an inflatable hoodlike or bladderlike pouch near the nose.

hood•lum (ho͝od′ləm, ho͞od′-) *n.* A gangster; a tough. [?]

hood•mold (ho͝od′mōld′) *n.* See **dripstone** 1.

hoo•doo (ho͞o′do͞o) *n., pl.* **-doos. 1.** See **voodoo** 3. **2.a.** Bad luck. **b.** One that brings bad luck. **3.** *Geol.* A column of eccentrically shaped rock, produced by differential weathering. — *tr.v.* **-dooed, -doo•ing, -doos.** To bring bad luck to. [Of West African orig., poss. < VOODOO.] — **hoo′doo•ism** *n.*

hood•wink (ho͝od′wĭngk′) *tr.v.* **-winked, -wink•ing, -winks. 1.** To take in by deceptive means; deceive. **2.** *Archaic.* To blindfold. **3.** *Obsolete.* To conceal. — **hood′wink′er** *n.*

hoo•ey (ho͞o′ē) *n. Slang.* Nonsense. [?]

hoof (ho͝of, ho͞of) *n., pl.* **hoofs** or **hooves** (ho͝ovz, ho͞ovz). **1.a.** The horny sheath covering the toes or lower part of the foot of a mammal of the orders Perissodactyla and Artiodactyla, such as an ox. **b.** The foot of such an animal, esp. a horse. **2.** *Slang.* The human foot. — *v.* **hoofed, hoof•ing, hoofs.** — *tr.* **1.** To trample with the hoofs. **2.** *Slang.* To walk. — *intr. Slang.* **1.** To dance, esp. professionally. **2.** To go on foot; walk. — ***idiom.*** **on the hoof.** Not yet butchered; alive. Used esp. of cattle. [ME *hof* < OE *hōf.*]

hoof-and-mouth disease (ho͝of′ən-mouth′, ho͞of′-) *n.* See **foot-and-mouth disease.**

hoof•bound (ho͝of′bound′, ho͞of′-) *adj.* Afflicted with drying and contraction of the hoof, resulting in lameness. Used of a horse.

hoofed (ho͝oft, ho͞oft) *adj.* Having hoofs; ungulate.

hoof•er (ho͝of′ər, ho͞o′fər) *n. Slang.* A professional dancer, esp. a tap dancer.

Hoogh•ly (ho͞o′glē). A channel, c. 257 km (160 mi), of the Ganges R. in E India between Calcutta and the Bay of Bengal.

hoo-hah (ho͞o′hä′) *n. Slang.* **1.** A fuss; a disturbance. **2.** A chortle or laugh. [Perh. < Yiddish *hu-ha*, to-do, uproar.]

hook (ho͝ok) *n.* **1.a.** A curved or sharply bent device, usu. of metal, used to catch, pull, suspend, or fasten something. **b.** A fishhook. **2.** Something shaped like a hook, esp.: **a.** A curved or barbed plant or animal part. **b.** A short angled or curved line on a letter. **c.** A sickle. **3.a.** A sharp bend or curve, as in a river. **b.** A point or spit of land with a sharply curved end. **4.** A means of catching or ensnaring; a trap. **5.** *Slang.* **a.** A means of attracting interest or attention; an enticement. **b.** *Mus.* A catchy motif or refrain. **6.** *Sports.* **a.** A short swinging blow in boxing delivered with a crooked arm. **b.** A golf stroke that sends the ball to the left of a right-handed player or the right of a left-handed player. — *v.* **hooked, hook•ing, hooks.** — *tr.* **1.a.** To catch, suspend, or connect with a hook. **b.** *Informal.* To snare. **c.** *Slang.* To steal; snatch. **2.** To fasten by or as if by a hook. **3.** To pierce or gore with or as if with a hook. **4.** *Slang.* **a.** To take strong hold of; captivate. **b.** To cause to become addicted. **5.** To make (a rug) by looping yarn through canvas with a hook. **6.** *Sports.* **a.** To hit with a hook in boxing. **b.** To hit (a golf ball) in a hook. — *intr.* **1.** To bend like a hook. **2.** To fasten by means of a hook or a hook and eye. **3.** *Slang.* To work as a prostitute. — ***phrasal verb.*** **hook up. 1.** To assemble or wire (a mechanism). **2.** To connect a mechanism and a source of power. **3.** *Slang.* To join; associate with. — ***idioms.*** **by hook or by crook.** By whatever means possible, fair or unfair. **get the hook.** *Slang.* To be unceremoniously dismissed or terminated. **hook, line, and sinker.** *Informal.* Without reservation; completely. **off the hook.** *Informal.* Freed, as from blame or a vexatious obligation. **on (one's) own hook.** By one's own efforts. [ME *hok* < OE *hōc.* See **keg-*.**]

hook•ah (ho͝ok′ə) *n.* An Eastern smoking pipe having a long tube passing through an urn of water that cools the smoke. [Urdu < Ar. *ḥuqqah*, the hookah's water urn.]

hook and eye *n.* **1.** A clothes fastener consisting of a small blunt metal hook that is inserted in a corresponding loop or eyelet. **2.** A latch consisting of a hook that is inserted in a screw eye.

hook-and-lad•der truck (ho͝ok′ən-lăd′ər) *n.* A fire engine equipped with extension ladders and hooked poles.

Hooke (ho͝ok), **Robert.** 1635–1703. English physicist who formulated the theory of planetary movement.

hooked (ho͝okt) *adj.* **1.** Bent or angled like a hook. **2.** Having a hook. **3.** Made by hooking yarn: *a hooked rug.* **4.** *Slang.* **a.** Captivated by or devoted to a custom or thing. **b.** Addicted to a narcotic. — **hook′ed•ness** (ho͝ok′ĭd-nĭs) *n.*

hook•er[1] (ho͝ok′ər) *n. Naut.* **1.** A single-masted fishing smack used off the coast of Ireland. **2.** An old worn-out or clumsy ship. [Du. *hoeker* < MDu. *hoeckboot* : *hoec*, fishhook; see **keg-*** + *boot*, boat.]

hook•er[2] (ho͝ok′ər) *n.* **1.** One that hooks. **2.** *Slang.* A prostitute.

Hook•er (ho͝ok′ər), **Joseph.** "Fighting Joe." 1814–79. Amer. Union army officer who was defeated by Robert E. Lee at Chancellorsville (1863).

Hooker, Richard. 1554?–1600. English theologian noted for his *Laws of Ecclesiastical Polity* (1594).

Hooker, Thomas. 1586?–1647. English-born Amer. colonizer and cleric who founded Hartford in Connecticut (1636).

hook•nose (ho͝ok′nōz′) *n.* An aquiline nose. — **hook′nosed′** *adj.*

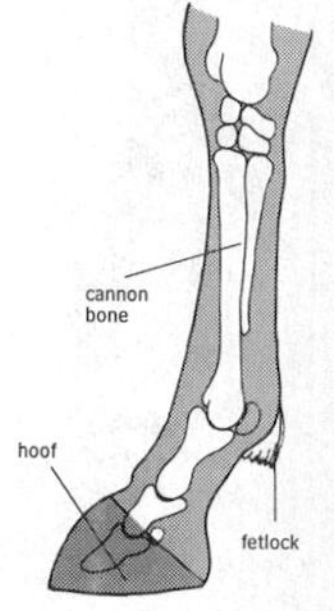

hoof
Of a horse

ă pat	oi boy
ā pay	ou out
âr care	o͝o took
ä father	o͞o boot
ĕ pet	ŭ cut
ē be	ûr urge
ĭ pit	th thin
ī pie	*th* this
îr pier	hw which
ŏ pot	zh vision
ō toe	ə about, item
ô paw	

Stress marks:
′ (primary);
′ (secondary), as in **dictionary** (dĭk′shə-nĕr′ē)

hoopoe
European hoopoe
Upupa epops

Hook of Hol•land (ho͝ok; hŏl′ənd) also **Hoek van Hol•land** (ho͝ok′ vän hô′länt). A cape and harbor of SW Netherlands on the North Sea W of Rotterdam.

hook shot *n. Basketball.* A shot made by arcing the far hand upward while being positioned or moving sideways to the basket.

hook•up (ho͝ok′ŭp′) *n.* **1.** A system of electric circuits and electrically powered equipment designed to operate together. **2.a.** A configuration of mechanical parts or devices providing a link between a supply source and a user. **b.** A plan or schematic drawing of such a system or configuration. **3.** *Informal.* A linkage or connection, often between unlikely associates or factors.

hook•worm (ho͝ok′wûrm′) *n.* Any of numerous small parasitic nematode worms of the family Ancylostomatidae, having hooked mouthparts with which they fasten themselves to the intestinal walls of their hosts, causing ancylostomiasis.

hookworm disease *n.* See **ancylostomiasis.**

hook•y (ho͝ok′ē) *n. Informal.* Absence without leave; truancy: *play hooky from school.* [Perh. < *hook it,* to make off.]

hoo•li•gan (ho͞o′lĭ-gən) *n. Informal.* A young ruffian; a hoodlum. [?] **—hoo′li•gan•ism** *n.*

hoop (ho͞op, ho͝op) *n.* **1.** A circular band of metal or wood put around a cask or barrel to bind the staves together. **2.** A large wooden, plastic, or metal ring, esp. one used as a toy. **3.** One of the lightweight circular supports for a hoop skirt. **4.** A circular ringlike earring. **5.** One of a pair of circular frames used to hold material taut for needlework. **6.** *Basketball.* **a.** The basket. **b.** The game of basketball. **7.** *Sports.* A croquet wicket. —*tr.v.* **hooped, hoop•ing, hoops. 1.** To hold together or support with or as if with a hoop. **2.** To encircle. **—*idiom.* jump (or go) through the hoop.** To undergo a rigorous trial or examination. [ME *hop.*]

hoop•er (ho͞o′pər, ho͝op′ər) *n.* A maker or repairer of barrels and tubs; a cooper.

hoop•la (ho͞op′lä′, ho͝op′-) *n. Slang.* **1.a.** Boisterous, jovial commotion or excitement. **b.** Extravagant publicity. **2.** Talk intended to mislead or confuse. [Perh. < Fr. *houp-là,* upsy-daisy! : *houp* (of imit. orig.) + *là,* there; see VOILÀ.]

hoo•poe (ho͞o′po͞o, -pō) *n.* Any of several Old World birds, esp. *Upupa epops,* having a fanlike crest and a slender downward-curving bill. [Alteration (influenced by Lat. *ūpupa*) of obsolete *hoop* < Fr. *huppe* < OFr. < VLat. **ūppa,* alteration of Lat. *upupa, ūpupa,* of imit. orig.]

hoop skirt *n.* A long full skirt belled out with a series of connected circular supports.

hoop snake *n.* Any of several snakes said to grasp the tail in the mouth and move with a rolling hooplike motion.

hoo•ray (ho͝o-rā′, hə-) *interj., n., & v.* Var. of **hurrah.**

Hoorn Islands (hôrn, hōrn). See **Futuna Islands.**

hoose•gow (ho͞os′gou′) *n. Slang.* A jail. [Sp. *juzgado,* tribunal, courtroom < p.part. of *juzgar,* to judge < Lat. *iūdicāre* < *iūdex, iūdic-,* judge. See JUDGE.]

Hoo•sier (ho͞o′zhər) *n.* Used as a nickname for a native or resident of Indiana. [?]

hoot[1] (ho͞ot) *v.* **hoot•ed, hoot•ing, hoots.** —*intr.* **1.** To utter the hoot of an owl. **2.** To make a loud raucous cry, esp. of derision or contempt. —*tr.* **1.** To shout down or drive off with jeers. **2.** To express or convey by hooting. —*n.* **1.a.** The characteristic cry of an owl. **b.** A sound suggesting the cry of an owl, esp. the sound of a horn. **2.** A cry of scorn or derision. **3.** *Informal.* One that is hilariously funny. **—*idiom.* not give (or care) a hoot.** To be completely indifferent to. [ME *houten,* perh. of imit. orig.] **—hoot′er** *n.*

hoot[2] (ho͞ot, o͞ot) also **hoots** (ho͞ots, o͞ots) *interj. Scots.* Used to express annoyance or objection.

hootch[1] (ho͞och) *n.* Var. of **hooch[1].**

hootch[2] (ho͞och) *n.* Var. of **hooch[2].**

hootch•y-kootch•y (ho͞o′chē-ko͞o′chē) *n., pl.* **-kootch•ies.** A deliberately sensual form of belly dance, typically part of a carnival. [?]

Herbert Hoover

hoot•en•an•ny (ho͞ot′n-ăn′ē) *n., pl.* **-nies. 1.** *Mus.* An informal performance by folk singers, typically with participation by the audience. **2.** *Informal.* An unidentified or unidentifiable gadget. [?]

hoot owl *n.* Any of various owls having a hooting cry.

Hoo•ver (ho͞o′vər). A city of N-central AL, a suburb of Birmingham. Pop. 39,788.

Hoover, Herbert Clark. 1874–1964. The 31st President of the U.S. (1929–33), whose fiscal policies failed to stem the effects of the crash of 1929.

Hoover, J(ohn) Edgar. 1895–1972. Amer. director of the FBI (1924–72) remembered for his vigorous anti-Communist campaign after World War II.

Hoover, Lou Henry. 1874–1944. First Lady of the U.S. (1929–33).

Hoo•ver•ville (ho͞o′vər-vĭl′) *n.* A crudely built camp put up usu. on the edge of a town to house the destitute during the depression of the 1930's. [After Herbert Clark HOOVER.]

Lou Hoover

hooves (ho͝ovz, ho͞ovz) *n.* Pl. of **hoof.**

hop[1] (hŏp) *v.* **hopped, hop•ping, hops.** —*intr.* **1.a.** To move with light bounding skips or leaps. **b.** *Informal.* To move

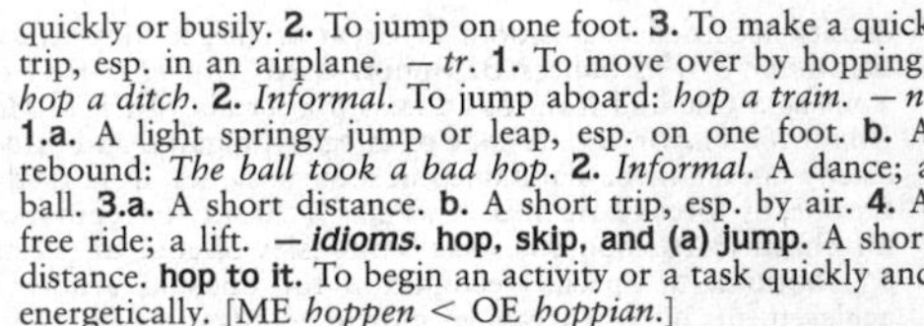

quickly or busily. **2.** To jump on one foot. **3.** To make a quick trip, esp. in an airplane. —*tr.* **1.** To move over by hopping: *hop a ditch.* **2.** *Informal.* To jump aboard: *hop a train.* —*n.* **1.a.** A light springy jump or leap, esp. on one foot. **b.** A rebound: *The ball took a bad hop.* **2.** *Informal.* A dance; a ball. **3.a.** A short distance. **b.** A short trip, esp. by air. **4.** A free ride; a lift. **—*idioms.* hop, skip, and (a) jump.** A short distance. **hop to it.** To begin an activity or a task quickly and energetically. [ME *hoppen* < OE *hoppian.*]

hop[2] (hŏp) *n.* **1.** A twining vine *(Humulus lupulus)* having lobed leaves and green female flowers arranged in conelike spikes. **2. hops.** The dried ripe flowers of this plant, containing a bitter aromatic oil and used in brewing beer to prevent bacterial action and add the characteristic bitter taste. **3.** *Slang.* Opium. —*tr.v.* **hopped, hop•ping, hops.** To flavor with hops. **—*phrasal verb.* hop up.** *Slang.* **1.** To increase the power or energy of: *hop up a car.* **2.** To stimulate with or as if with a narcotic. [ME *hoppe* < MDu.]

HOP *abbr.* High oxygen pressure.

hop clover *n.* A Eurasian clover *(Trifolium agrarium)* or one of its relatives, having yellow flower heads that resemble hops when withered.

hope (hōp) *v.* **hoped, hop•ing, hopes.** —*intr.* **1.** To wish for something with expectation of its fulfillment. **2.** *Archaic.* To have confidence; trust. —*tr.* **1.** To look forward to with confidence or expectation. **2.** To expect and desire. See Syns at **expect.** —*n.* **1.** A wish or desire accompanied by confident expectation of its fulfillment. **2.** Something hoped for or desired: *Success is our hope.* **3.** A source of or reason for hope. **4.** Often **Hope.** *Theol.* Trust in God's mercy, tempered by fear of divine justice. **5.** *Archaic.* Trust; confidence. **—*idiom.* hope against hope.** To hope with little reason or justification. [ME *hopen* < OE *hopian.*] **—hop′er** *n.*

Hope, Anthony. See Sir Anthony Hope **Hawkins.**

Hope, Bob. b. 1903. British-born Amer. entertainer known esp. for his films and variety shows.

hope chest *n.* A chest traditionally used by a young woman for clothing and household goods in anticipation of marriage.

hope•ful (hōp′fəl) *adj.* **1.** Having or manifesting hope. **2.** Inspiring hope; promising. —*n.* A person who aspires to success or who shows promise of succeeding, esp. as a political candidate: *presidential hopefuls.* **—hope′ful•ness** *n.*

hope•ful•ly (hōp′fə-lē) *adv.* **1.** In a hopeful manner. **2.** *Usage Problem.* It is to be hoped.

Usage Note: Writers who use *hopefully* as a sentence adverb, as in *Hopefully, the measures will be adopted,* should be aware that the usage is unacceptable to many critics, including a large majority of the Usage Panel. But it is not easy to explain why critics dislike this use of *hopefully.* It is justified by analogy to the unexceptionable uses of many other adverbs, as in *Mercifully, the play was brief.* The well-attested acceptance of the usage reflects an implicit popular recognition of its usefulness; there is no precise substitute. Someone who says *Hopefully, the treaty will be ratified* makes a hopeful prediction about the fate of the treaty, whereas someone who says *I hope* (or *We hope* or *It is hoped*) *the treaty will be ratified* expresses a bald statement about what is desired. Only the latter could be continued with a clause such as *but it isn't likely.* Some may choose to avoid the usage, whether motivated by discretion or civility.

Ho•pei or **Ho•peh** (hō′pā′, hŭ′bā′). See **Hebei.**

hope•less (hōp′lĭs) *adj.* **1.** Having no hope; despairing. **2.** Offering no hope; bleak. **3.** Incurable. **4.** Having no possibility of solution; impossible. **—hope′less•ly** *adv.*

hope•less•ness (hōp′lĭs-nĭs) *n.* The condition or quality of being hopeless.

Hope•well[1] (hōp′wĕl′, -wəl) *n.* An early Native American culture centered in the Ohio River valley from about the second century B.C. to the fourth century A.D., noted for extensive earthworks and large burial mounds. [After the owner of a farm in Ross County, OH.]

Hope•well[2] (hōp′wĕl′). An independent city of SE VA SSE of Richmond; founded 1913. Pop. 23,101.

hop•head (hŏp′hĕd′) *n. Slang.* A drug addict. [HOP[2] + HEAD.]

hop hornbeam *n.* Any of several deciduous trees of the genus *Ostrya,* esp. *O. virginiana* of eastern North America, having fruit clusters resembling hops.

Ho•pi (hō′pē) *n., pl.* **Hopi** or **-pis. 1.** A member of a Pueblo people occupying a number of mesa-top pueblos on reservation land in northeast Arizona. **2.** The Uto-Aztecan language of the Hopi. [Hopi *hópi,* peaceable, a Hopi.]

Hop•kins (hŏp′kĭnz), Sir **Frederick Gowland.** 1861–1947. British biochemist who shared a 1929 Nobel Prize.

Hopkins, Gerard Manley. 1844–89. British poet known for his posthumously published works, including "The Wreck of the Deutschland."

Hopkins, Johns. 1795–1873. Amer. financier whose bequest funded the creation of the Baltimore hospital and university that bear his name.

Hopkins, Mark. 1802–87. Amer. educator and theologian who was president of Williams College (1836–72).

Hop•kin•son (hŏp′kĭn-sən), **Francis.** 1737–91. Amer. Revolutionary leader known for his satires against the British.

Hop•kins•ville (hŏp′kĭnz-vĭl′). A city of SW KY WSW of Bowling Green. Pop. 29,809.

hop•lite (hŏp′līt′) *n.* A heavily armed foot soldier of ancient Greece. [Gk. *hoplitēs* < *hoplon*, armor.]

hop•per (hŏp′ər) *n.* **1.** One that hops. **2.a.** A funnel-shaped container in which materials, such as grain, are stored for later dispensation. **b.** *Informal.* A place in which something is held for later use or consideration. **c.** A freight car with a door in the floor through which materials are unloaded.

Hop•per (hŏp′ər), **Edward.** 1882–1967. Amer. painter famous for his realist style in works such as *Nighthawks* (1942).

hop•per•grass (hŏp′ər-grăs′) *n. Chiefly Southern U.S.* See **grasshopper** 1. See Regional Note at **everwhere.**

hop•sack•ing (hŏp′săk′ĭng) also **hop•sack** (-săk′) *n.* A loosely woven coarse fabric of cotton or wool used in clothing. [< its being used for bags by hop growers.]

hop•scotch (hŏp′skŏch′) *n. Games.* A children's game in which players toss an object into numbered spaces drawn on the ground and then hop or jump through the spaces to retrieve the object. —*intr.v.* **-scotched, -scotch•ing, -scotch•es.** To move in or as if in irregular jumps. [HOP[1] + SCOTCH[1], a score, line.]

hor. *abbr.* Horizontal.

ho•ra also **ho•rah** (hôr′ə, hōr′ə) *n.* A traditional round dance of Romania and Israel. [Mod.Heb. *hōrâ* < Romanian *horă* < Turk. *hora*, perh. < Mod.Gk. *khoro*, accusative of *khoros*, round dance < Gk. See **gher-¹***.]

Hor•ace (hôr′əs, hŏr′-). 65–8 B.C. Roman lyric poet noted for his *Odes* and *Satires.* —**Ho•ra′tian** (hə-rā′shən) *adj.*

ho•ra•ry (hôr′ə-rē, hōr′-) *adj.* **1.** Of an hour or hours. **2.** Occurring once an hour; hourly. [Med.Lat. *hōrārius* < Lat. *hōra*, hour. See HOUR.]

Horatian ode *n.* An ode with a fixed stanzaic pattern.

horde (hôrd, hōrd) *n.* **1.** A large group or crowd; a swarm. **2.a.** A nomadic Mongol tribe. **b.** A nomadic tribe or group. [Ult. (via Pol. *horda*) < NW Turkic *ordï*, residence, court < Old Turkic.]

hore•hound (hôr′hound′, hōr′-) *n.* **1.a.** An aromatic Eurasian plant *(Marrubium vulgare)* having square stems and opposite leaves covered with white pubescence and yielding a bitter extract used in flavoring and as a cough remedy. **b.** A candy or preparation flavored with horehound. **2.** Any of similar plants, such as the black horehound. [ME, alteration of *horhune* < OE *hārehūne* : *hār*, hoary + *hūne*, a plant.]

ho•ri•zon (hə-rī′zən) *n.* **1.** The apparent intersection of the earth and sky as seen by an observer. **2.** *Astron.* **a.** The sensible horizon. **b.** The celestial horizon. **c.** The limit of the theoretically possible universe. **3.** The range of one's knowledge, experience, or interest. **4.** *Geol.* **a.** A specific position in a stratigraphic column, such as the location of one or more fossils, that serves to identify the stratum. **b.** A specific layer of soil or subsoil in a vertical cross section of land. [ME *orizon* < OFr. < Lat. < Gk. *horizōn (kuklos)*, limiting (circle), horizon < pr.part. of *horizein*, to limit < *horos*, boundary.]

hor•i•zon•tal (hôr′ĭ-zŏn′tl, hŏr′-) *adj.* **1.** Of, relating to, or near the horizon. **2.a.** Parallel to or in the plane of the horizon. **b.** At right angles to a vertical line. **3.** Occupying or restricted to the same level in a hierarchy. —*n.* Something, such as a plane, that is horizontal. [Fr. < Lat. *horizōn*, *horizont-*, horizon. See HORIZON.] —**hor′i•zon′tal•ly** *adv.*

horizontal union *n.* See **craft union.**

hor•mone (hôr′mōn′) *n.* **1.** A substance, usu. a peptide or steroid, produced by one tissue and conveyed by the bloodstream to another to effect physiological activity, such as growth. **2.** Any of various similar substances in plants and insects that regulate development. [< Gk. *hormōn*, pr.part. of *horman*, to urge on < *hormē*, impulse. See **er-¹***.] —**hor•mon′al** (-mō′nəl), **hor•mon′ic** (-mŏn′ĭk) *adj.*

Hor•muz (hôr′mŭz′, hôr-mo͞oz′), **Strait of.** Also **Strait of Or•muz** (ôr′mŭz′, ôr-mo͞oz′). A strategic waterway linking the Persian Gulf with the Gulf of Oman.

horn (hôrn) *n.* **1.** One of the hard, usu. permanent structures projecting from the head of certain mammals, such as sheep, consisting of a bony core covered with a sheath of keratinous material. **2.** A hard protuberance, such as an antler, that is similar to or suggestive of a horn. **3.a.** The hard smooth keratinous material forming the outer covering of the horns of cattle or related animals. **b.** A natural or synthetic substance resembling this material. **4.** A container made from a horn. **5.** Something shaped like a horn, esp.: **a.** Either of the ends of a crescent moon. **b.** The point of an anvil. **c.** The pommel of a saddle. **d.** A device for projecting sound waves, as in a loudspeaker. **e.** An electromagnetic transmission antenna with a circular or rectangular cross section. **6.** *Mus.* **a.** A wind instrument made of an animal horn. **b.** A brass wind instrument, such as a tuba. **c.** A French horn. **d.** A wind instrument, such as a saxophone, used in a jazz band. **7.a.** A usu. electrical signaling device that produces a loud resonant sound: *a car horn.* **b.** Any of various noisemakers operated by blowing or by squeezing a hollow rubber ball. **8.** *Slang.* A telephone. —*intr.v.* **horned, horn•ing, horns.** To join without being invited; intrude. Used with *in.* —***idioms.*** **blow** (or **toot**) **(one's) own horn.** *Informal.* To brag or boast about oneself. **draw** (or **haul** or **pull**) **in (one's) horns.** *Informal.* **1.** To restrain oneself; draw back. **2.** To retreat from a previously taken position, view, or stance. **3.** To economize. **on the horns of a dilemma.** Faced with two equally undesirable alternatives. [ME < OE. See **ker-¹***.] —**horn** *adj.* —**horn′ist** *n.*

Horn (hôrn), **Cape.** A headland of extreme S Chile in the Tierra del Fuego archipelago; first rounded by the Dutch in 1616.

horn•beam (hôrn′bēm′) *n.* **1.** Any of various trees of the genus *Carpinus*, having smooth grayish bark and hard whitish wood. **2.** The wood of one of these trees.

horn•bill (hôrn′bĭl′) *n.* Any of various tropical Old World birds of the family Bucerotidae, having a very large bill often surmounted by an enlarged protuberance at the base.

horn•blende (hôrn′blĕnd′) *n.* An amphibolic mineral, $CaNa(Mg,Fe)_4(Al,Fe,Ti)_3Si_6O_{22}(OH,F)_2$, commonly green to black in color, formed late in the cooling of igneous rock. [Ger. : *Horn*, horn (< MHGer. *horn* < OHGer.; see **ker-¹***) + *Blende*, blende; see BLENDE.]

horn•book (hôrn′bo͝ok′) *n.* **1.** A one-page primer protected by a transparent sheet of horn, once used to teach children to read. **2.** A text teaching basic skills or introducing a subject.

Horne (hôrn), **Lena.** b. 1917. Amer. singer and actress.

Horne, Marilyn. b. 1934. Amer. operatic soprano who made her debut at the Metropolitan Opera in *Norma* (1970).

horned (hôrnd) *adj.* Having a horn, horns, or a hornlike growth.

horned lizard *n.* See **horned toad.**

horned owl *n.* Any of various owls with characteristic ear tufts that resemble horns.

horned toad *n.* Any of several lizards of the genus *Phrynosoma* of western North America and Central America, with hornlike projections on the head and a flat spiny body.

horned viper *n.* A venomous African snake *(Cerastes cornutus)* having a hornlike projection above each eye.

hor•net (hôr′nĭt) *n.* Any of various large stinging wasps of the family Vespidae, chiefly of the genera *Vespa* and *Vespula*, characteristically building large papery nests. [ME *hornet*, alteration of *hernet* < OE *hyrnet.* See **ker-¹***.]

hor•nets' nest (hôr′nĭts) *n.* A violent or highly contentious situation.

Hor•ney (hôr′nī), **Karen Danielsen.** 1885–1952. German-born Amer. psychoanalyst who emphasized environmental and cultural factors in the development of neurosis.

horn•fels (hôrn′fĕlz′) *n., pl.* **hornfels.** A fine-grained metamorphic rock composed of quartz, feldspar, mica, and other minerals, formed by the action of intrusive rock upon sedimentary rock, esp. shale. [Ger. : *Horn*, horn; see HORNBLENDE + *Fels*, rock, cliff (< MHGer. *vels* < OHGer. *felis*).]

horn fly *n.* A small black European fly *(Haematobia irritans)* that sucks blood from cattle, usu. at the base of the horn.

horn•ing (hôr′nĭng) *n. Upstate New York & Western New England.* See **shivaree.** See Regional Note at **shivaree.**

hor•ni•to (hôr-nē′tō) *n., pl.* **-tos.** A low mound of volcanic origin, sometimes emitting smoke or vapor. [Sp., dim. of *horno*, oven < Lat. *furnus.* See **gʷher-***.]

horn of plenty *n., pl.* **horns of plenty.** See **cornucopia** 1.

horn•pipe (hôrn′pīp′) *n.* **1.** *Mus.* An instrument with a single reed, finger holes, and a bell and mouthpiece made of horn. **2.a.** A spirited British folk dance originally accompanied by this instrument. **b.** The music accompanying such a dance.

horn•swog•gle (hôrn′swŏg′əl) *tr.v.* **-gled, -gling, -gles.** *Chiefly Northern, Midland & Western U.S.* To bamboozle; deceive. [?]

horn•tail (hôrn′tāl′) *n.* Any of various sawflies of the family Siricidae, the female of which has a long stout ovipositor.

horn•worm (hôrn′wûrm′) *n.* The larva of the hawk moth, having a hornlike posterior segment.

horn•wort (hôrn′wûrt′, -wôrt′) *n.* Any of several submerged plants of the genus *Ceratophyllum*, forming branched masses in quiet water and having finely dissected whorled leaves.

horn•y (hôr′nē) *adj.* **-i•er, -i•est.** **1.** Having horns or hornlike projections. **2.** Made of horn or a similar substance. **3.** Tough and calloused: *horny skin.* **4.** *Vulgar Slang.* **a.** Desirous of sexual activity. **b.** Sexually aroused. [Sense 4 < HORN, an erection.] —**horn′i•ness** *n.*

horol. *abbr.* Horology.

hor•o•loge (hôr′ə-lōj′, hŏr′-) *n.* A device, such as a clock, for telling time. [ME *orloge* < OFr. < Lat. *hōrologium* < Gk. *hōrologion* : *hōra*, hour, season; see **yēr-*** + *legein*, to speak; see **leg-***.]

hor•o•log•ic (hôr′ə-lŏj′ĭk, hŏr′-) also **hor•o•log•i•cal** (-ĭ-kəl) *adj.* Of or relating to horology or a horologe.

ho•rol•o•gist (hô-rŏl′ə-jĭst) also **ho•rol•o•ger** (-jər) *n.* One who practices or is skilled in horology.

Hor•o•lo•gi•um (hôr′ə-lō′jē-əm, hŏr′-) *n.* A constellation in the Southern Hemisphere near Hydrus, Eridanus, and Reticulum. [Lat. *hōrologium*, horologe. See HOROLOGE.]

ho•rol•o•gy (hô-rŏl′ə-jē) *n.* **1.** The science of measuring time. **2.** The art of making timepieces. [Gk. *hōra*, hour, season; see **yēr-*** + -LOGY.]

hopper
At a lumberyard

hornbill
Yellow-billed hornbill
Tockus flavirostris

Lena Horne

ă pat	oi boy
ā pay	ou out
âr care	o͝o took
ä father	o͞o boot
ĕ pet	ŭ cut
ē be	ûr urge
ĭ pit	th thin
ī pie	*th* this
îr pier	hw which
ŏ pot	zh vision
ō toe	ə about, item
ô paw	

Stress marks:
′ (primary);
′ (secondary), as in dictionary (dĭk′shə-nĕr′ē)

hor•o•scope (hôr′ə-skōp′, hŏr′-) *n.* **1.a.** The aspect of the planets and stars at a given moment, as of a person's birth, used by astrologers. **b.** A diagram of the signs of the zodiac based on such an aspect. **2.** An astrological forecast, as of a person's future, based on such a diagram. [Fr. < OFr. < Lat. *hōroscopus* < Gk. *hōroskopos* : *hōra*, hour, season; see **yēr-*** + *skopos*, observer; see **spek-***.]

Ho•ro•witz (hôr′ə-wĭts, hŏr′-), **Vladimir.** 1904–89. Russian-born Amer. pianist noted for his interpretations of Chopin and Liszt.

hor•ren•dous (hô-rĕn′dəs, hə-) *adj.* Hideous; dreadful. [< Lat. *horrendus* < gerundive of *horrēre*, to tremble.] **—hor•ren′dous•ly** *adv.*

Vladimir Horowitz

hor•rent (hôr′ənt, hŏr′-) *adj. Archaic.* Covered with bristles; bristling. [Lat. *horrēns*, *horrent-*, pr.part. of *horrēre*, to tremble, bristle.]

hor•ri•ble (hôr′ə-bəl, hŏr′-) *adj.* **1.** Arousing or tending to arouse horror; dreadful. **2.** Very unpleasant; disagreeable. [ME < OFr. < Lat. *horribilis* < *horrēre*, to tremble.] **—hor′ri•ble•ness** *n.* **—hor′ri•bly** *adv.*

hor•rid (hôr′ĭd, hŏr′-) *adj.* **1.** Causing horror; dreadful. **2.** Extremely disagreeable; offensive. **3.** *Archaic.* Bristling; rough. [Alteration (influenced by Lat. *horridus*, bristling < *horrēre*, to bristle) of ME *horred*, p.part. of *horren*, to bristle < Lat. *horrēre*, to tremble, bristle.] **—hor′rid•ly** *adv.* **—hor′rid•ness** *n.*

hor•rif•ic (hô-rĭf′ĭk, hŏ-) *adj.* Causing horror; terrifying. [Lat. *horrificus* : *horrēre*, to tremble + *-ficus*, -fic.] **—hor•rif′i•cal•ly** *adv.*

hor•ri•fy (hôr′ə-fī′, hŏr′-) *tr.v.* **-fied, -fy•ing, -fies. 1.** To cause to feel horror. See Syns at **dismay. 2.** To cause unpleasant surprise to; shock. [Lat. *horrificāre* < *horrificus*, horrific. See HORRIFIC.] **—hor′ri•fi•ca′tion** (-fĭ-kā′shən) *n.*

hor•rip•i•la•tion (hô-rĭp′ə-lā′shən, hŏ-) *n.* The bristling of the body hair, as from fear; goose bumps. [LLat. *horripilātiō*, *horripilātiōn-* < Lat. *horripilātus*, p.part. of *horripilāre*, to bristle with hairs : *horrēre*, to tremble + *pilāre*, to grow hair (< *pilus*, hair).] **—hor•rip′i•late′** *v.*

hor•ror (hôr′ər, hŏr′-) *n.* **1.** An intense painful feeling of repugnance and fear. See Syns at **fear. 2.** Intense dislike; abhorrence. **3.** A cause of horror. **4.** *Informal.* Something unpleasant, ugly, or disagreeable. **5. horrors.** *Informal.* Intense nervous depression or anxiety. Often used with *the.* [ME *horrour* < OFr. *horreur* < Lat. *horror* < *horrēre*, to tremble.]

hors de com•bat (ôr′ də kôN-bä′) *adv. & adj.* Out of action; disabled. [Fr. : *hors*, out + *de*, of + *combat*, combat.]

hors d'oeuvre (ôr dûrv′) *n., pl.* **hors d'oeuvres** (ôr dûrvz′) or **hors d'oeuvre.** An appetizer served before a meal. [Fr. : *hors*, outside + *de*, of + *oeuvre*, (the main) work.]

horse (hôrs) *n.* **1.a.** A large hoofed mammal *(Equus caballus)* having a short-haired coat, a long mane, and a long tail, domesticated for riding and for drawing or carrying loads. **b.** An adult male horse; a stallion. **c.** Any of various equine mammals, such as certain extinct forms that are related ancestrally to the modern horse. **2.** A frame or device, usu. with four legs, used for supporting or holding. **3.** *Sports.* A piece of gymnastic equipment with an upholstered body used esp. for vaulting. **4.** *Slang.* Heroin. **5.** Horsepower. Often used in the plural. **6.** Cavalry. **7.** *Geol.* **a.** A block of rock interrupting a vein and containing no minerals. **b.** A displaced rock caught along a fault. *—v.* **horsed, hors•ing, hors•es.** *—tr.* **1.** To provide with a horse. **2.** To haul or hoist energetically. *—intr.* To be in heat. Used of a mare. *—adj.* **1.** Of or relating to a horse. **2.** Mounted on horses. **3.** Drawn or operated by a horse. **4.** Larger or cruder than others of its kind. ***—phrasal verb.*** **horse around.** *Informal.* To indulge in horseplay or frivolous activity. ***—idioms.*** **a horse of another (**or **a different) color.** Another matter entirely; something else. **beat (**or **flog) a dead horse. 1.** To continue to pursue a hopeless cause. **2.** To dwell tiresomely on a decided matter. **be (**or **get) on (one's) high horse.** To be or become disdainful, superior, or conceited. **hold (one's) horses.** To restrain oneself. **the horse's mouth.** A source of information regarded as original or unimpeachable. [ME < OE *hors.*]

horse•back (hôrs′băk′) *n.* **1.** The back of a horse. **2.** A natural ridge; a hogback. *—adv. & adj.* On the back of a horse.

horse bean *n.* See **broad bean.**

horse chestnut *n.* **1.** Any of several trees of the genus *Aesculus,* esp. the European species *A. hippocastanum,* having opposite, palmately compound leaves, erect flower clusters, and spiny or smooth capsules containing large brown seeds. **2.** The seed of any of these plants.

horse chestnut
Aesculus hippocastanum

horse•feath•ers (hôrs′fĕth′ərs) *Slang.* *—n. (used with a sing. v.)* Nonsense; foolishness. *—interj.* Used to express disagreement or exasperation. [Alteration of HORSESHIT.]

horse•flesh (hôrs′flĕsh′) *n.* **1.** The flesh of a horse. **2.** Horses considered as a group, esp. for driving, riding, or racing.

horse•fly also **horse fly** (hôrs′flī′) *n.* Any of numerous large flies of the family Tabanidae, the females of which suck the blood of various mammals.

horse gentian *n.* Any of various plants of the genus *Triosteum,* having small purplish-brown flowers and leathery fruit.

horse•hair (hôrs′hâr′) *n.* **1.** The hair of a horse, esp. from the mane or tail. **2.** Cloth made of the hair of horses.

horsehair worm *n.* Any of various aquatic worms of the phylum Nematomorpha, the larvae of which are parasitic within insects.

horse•hide (hôrs′hīd′) *n.* **1.** The hide of a horse. **2.** Leather made from the hide of a horse.

horse latitudes *pl.n.* Either of two belts of latitudes located over the oceans at about 30° to 35° north and south, having high barometric pressure, calms, and light changeable winds. [Poss. < Sp. *golfo de las yeguas*, mares' sea.]

horse•laugh (hôrs′lăf′, -läf′) *n. Informal.* A loud coarse laugh; a guffaw.

horse•leech (hôrs′lēch′) *n.* Any of several large leeches of the genus *Haemopis.*

horse•less carriage (hôrs′lĭs) *n.* An automobile.

horse mackerel *n.* **1.** See **saurel** 1. **2.** Any of several tunas or related fishes.

horse•man (hôrs′mən) *n.* **1.a.** A man who rides a horse. **b.** A man skilled in equitation. **2.** A man who breeds horses.

horse•man•ship (hôrs′mən-shĭp′) *n.* The skill of riding horses; equitation.

horse•mint (hôrs′mĭnt′) *n.* **1.** A perennial aromatic eastern North American plant *(Monarda punctata)* having opposite leaves and yellowish flowers with purple spots. **2.** A Eurasian wild mint *(Mentha longifolia)* having long opposite leaves and dense spikelike clusters of flowers.

horse nettle *n.* A prickly-stemmed plant *(Solanum carolinense)* of eastern and central North America having purplish or white star-shaped flowers and yellowish berries.

horse opera *n.* A film or other theatrical work about the American West.

horse•play (hôrs′plā′) *n.* Rowdy or rough play.

horse•play•er (hôrs′plā′ər) *n. Games.* One who regularly bets on horseraces.

horse•pow•er (hôrs′pou′ər) *n.* **1.** A unit of power in the U.S. Customary System, equal to 745.7 watts or 33,000 foot-pounds per minute. **2.** The power of a horse in pulling.

horse•race or **horse race** (hôrs′rās′) *n.* **1.** *Sports.* A contest in which horses ridden by jockeys are raced. **2.** A closely fought contest or competition. **—horse′rac′ing** *n.*

horse•rad•ish (hôrs′răd′ĭsh) *n.* **1.** A Eurasian plant *(Armoracia rusticana)* in the mustard family, having a pungent root, large basal leaves, and white flowers. **2.a.** The roots of this plant. **b.** A sharp condiment made of the roots of this plant.

horse sense *n. Informal.* Common sense; gumption.

horse•shit (hôrs′shĭt′, hôrsh′-) *n.* **1.** *Vulgar.* Horse feces. **2.** *Vulgar Slang.* Meaningless or insincere talk or action.

horse•shoe (hôrs′sho͞o′, hôrsh′-) *n.* **1.** A flat U-shaped metal plate fitted and nailed to the bottom of a horse's hoof for protection. **2.** A U-shaped object similar to a horseshoe. **3. horseshoes.** *(used with a sing. v.) Games.* A game in which players toss horseshoes at a stake. *—tr.v.* **-shoed, -shoe•ing, -shoes.** To fit with horseshoes.

horseshoe crab *n.* Any of various marine arthropods of the class Merostomata, esp. *Limulus polyphemus* or *Xiphosura polyphemus* of eastern North America, having a large rounded body and a stiff pointed tail.

Horse•shoe Falls (hôrs′sho͞o′, hôrsh′-). See **Canadian Falls.**

horse•tail (hôrs′tāl′) *n.* Any of various nonflowering plants of the genus *Equisetum,* having a jointed hollow stem and narrow, sometimes much reduced leaves.

horse-trad•ing (hôrs′trā′dĭng) *n.* Negotiation characterized by hard bargaining and shrewd exchange. **—horse trade** *n.* **—horse′-trade′** *v.* **—horse trader** *n.*

horse•weed (hôrs′wēd′) *n.* A weedy North American plant *(Erigeron canadensis)* having narrow leaves and numerous small white or greenish flower heads grouped in panicles.

horse•whip (hôrs′hwĭp′, -wĭp′) *n.* A whip used to control a horse. *—tr.v.* **-whipped, -whip•ping, -whips.** To beat with or as if with a horsewhip.

horse•wom•an (hôrs′wo͝om′ən) *n.* **1.a.** A woman who rides a horse. **b.** A woman skilled in equitation. **2.** A woman who breeds horses.

horst (hôrst) *n.* A mass of the earth's crust that lies between two faults and is higher than the surrounding land. [Ger. < MHGer. *hurst*, thicket < OHGer.]

hors•y also **hors•ey** (hôr′sē) *adj.* **-i•er, -i•est. 1.** Of, relating to, or resembling horses or a horse. **2.** Devoted to horses and equitation: *the horsy set.* **3.** Large and clumsy: *a horsy bureau.* **—hors′i•ly** *adv.* **—hors′i•ness** *n.*

hort. *abbr.* **1.** Horticultural. **2.** Horticulture.

hor•ta•tive (hôr′tə-tĭv) *adj.* Hortatory. [LLat. *hortātīvus* < Lat. *hortātus*, p.part. of *hortārī*, to exhort. See **gher-²***.]

hor•ta•to•ry (hôr′tə-tôr′ē, -tōr′ē) *adj.* Marked by exhortation or strong urging: *a hortatory speech.* [LLat. *hortātōrius* < Lat. *hortātus*, exhorted. See HORTATIVE.]

hor•ti•cul•ture (hôr′tĭ-kŭl′chər) *n.* **1.** The science or art of cultivating fruits, vegetables, flowers, or ornamental plants. **2.** The cultivation of a garden. [Lat. *hortus*, garden; see **gher-¹*** + (AGRI)CULTURE.] **—hor′ti•cul′tur•al** *adj.* **—hor′ti•cul′tur•al•ly** *adv.* **—hor′ti•cul′tur•ist** *n.*

Hor•ton River (hôr′tn). A river, c. 443 km (275 mi), of N Northwest Terrs., Canada, flowing into Franklin Bay, an inlet of the Beaufort Sea.

Ho•rus (hôr′əs, hōr′-) *n. Myth.* The ancient Egyptian god of the sun, son of Osiris and Isis.

Hos. *abbr. Bible.* Hosea.

ho•san•na also **ho•san•nah** (hō-zăn′ə) *— interj.* Used to express praise or adoration to God. *— n.* **1.** A cry of "hosanna." **2.** A shout of fervent and worshipful praise. [ME *osanna* < OE < LLat. *ōsanna* < Gk. *hōsanna* < Heb. *hôša' nā'* < *hôša' nā'*, save (us), I pray.]

hose (hōz) *n., pl.* **hose** or **hos•es. 1.** *pl.* **hose.** Stockings; socks. Used only in the plural. **2.** *pl.* **hose. a.** Close-fitting breeches or leggings reaching up to the hips and fastened to a doublet, formerly worn by men. Used only in the plural. **b.** Breeches reaching down to the knees. Used only in the plural. **3.** *pl.* **hos•es.** A flexible tube for conveying liquids or gases under pressure. *— tr.v.* **hosed, hos•ing, hos•es. 1.** To water, drench, or wash with a hose: *hosed down the deck.* **2.** *Slang.* To attack and kill (someone), typically by use of a firearm. [ME, a stocking < OE *hosa*, leg covering. See **(s)keu-*.**]

Ho•se•a (hō-zē′ə, -zā′ə) *n. Bible.* **1.** A Hebrew prophet of the 8th cent. B.C. **2.** See table at **Bible.**

ho•sey (hō′zē) *intr.v.* **-seyed, -sey•ing, -seys.** *New England.* To choose sides for a children's game. [Perh. < Fr. *(je) choisis*, (I) choose, first pers. sing. pr. of *choisir*, to choose < OFr. See CHOICE.]

ho•sier•y (hō′zhə-rē) *n.* **1.** Socks and stockings; hose. **2.** *Chiefly British.* Stockings, socks, and underclothing. [< *hosier*, stocking maker < ME (< *hose*, stocking; see HOSE).]

hosp. *abbr.* Hospital.

hos•pice (hŏs′pĭs) *n.* **1.** A shelter or lodging, as for travelers, esp. one maintained by a monastic order. **2.** A program or facility that provides palliative care and attends to the needs of the terminally ill. [Fr. < OFr. < Lat. *hospitium*, hospitality < *hospes, hospit-*, host. See **ghos-ti-*.**]

hos•pi•ta•ble (hŏs′pĭ-tə-bəl, hŏ-spĭt′ə-bəl) *adj.* **1.** Disposed to treat guests with warmth and generosity. **2.** Indicative of cordiality toward guests: *a hospitable act.* **3.** Having an open mind; receptive. **4.** Favorable to growth and development; agreeable. [Obsolete Fr. < Med.Lat. **hospitābilis* < Lat. *hospitāre*, to put up as a guest < *hospes, hospit-*, guest, host. See **ghos-ti-*.**] **— hos′pi•ta•bly** *adv.*

hos•pi•tal (hŏs′pĭ-tl, -pĭt′l) *n.* **1.** An institution that provides care and treatment for the sick or the injured. **2.** *Chiefly British.* A charitable institution, such as an orphanage. **3.** A repair shop for specified items: *a doll hospital.* **4.** *Archaic.* A hospice for travelers or pilgrims. [ME, hospice < OFr. *ospital* < Med.Lat. *hospitāle* < Lat. *hospitālis*, of a guest < *hospes, hospit-*, guest. See **ghos-ti-*.**]

Hos•pi•tal•er also **Hos•pi•tal•ler** (hŏs′pĭt′l-ər) *n.* **1.** A member of a military religious order founded among crusaders in 12th-century Jerusalem to care for sick and needy pilgrims. **2.** A member of any of several religious orders who care for sick or needy persons. [ME *Hospiteler* < OFr. *hospitalier* < Med.Lat. *hospitālārius*, giver of hospitality < *hospitāle*, hospice. See HOSPITAL.]

Hos•pi•ta•let (hŏs′pĭt-l-ĕt′, ôs′pē-tä-lĕt′). A city of NE Spain, a suburb of Barcelona. Pop. 288,290.

hos•pi•tal•i•ty (hŏs′pĭ-tăl′ĭ-tē) *n., pl.* **-ties. 1.** Cordial and generous reception of or disposition toward guests. **2.** An instance of such treatment. [ME *hospitalite* < OFr. < Lat. *hospitālitās* < *hospitālis*, of a guest. See HOSPITAL.]

hos•pi•tal•i•za•tion (hŏs′pĭ-tl-ĭ-zā′shən) *n.* **1.a.** The act of placing a person in a hospital as a patient. **b.** The condition of being hospitalized. **2.** Insurance that fully or partially covers a patient's hospital expenses.

hos•pi•tal•ize (hŏs′pĭt-l-īz′) *tr.v.* **-ized, -iz•ing, -iz•es.** To place in a hospital for treatment, care, or observation.

host¹ (hōst) *n.* **1.** One who receives or entertains guests in a social or an official capacity. **2.** A person who manages an inn or a hotel. **3.** One that furnishes facilities and resources for a function or an event. **4.** The emcee or interviewer on a radio or television program. **5.** *Biol.* The animal or plant on which or in which another organism lives. **6.** *Medic.* The recipient of a transplanted tissue or organ. *— tr.v.* **host•ed, host•ing, hosts.** *Usage Problem.* To serve as host to or at. [ME, host, guest < OFr. < Lat. *hospes, hospit-*. See **ghos-ti-*.**]

Usage Note: The usage of *host* as a verb occurs particularly in contexts relating to institutional gatherings or television and radio shows, a usage better accepted by the Panel in the former than in the latter context. In our most recent survey 53 percent of the Panelists accepted the usage in the phrase *a reception hosted by the Secretary of State.* Only 31 percent of the Panel accepted the use of the verb in the sentence *Students have watched* Sex, Drugs and AIDS, *a graphic film hosted by actress Rae Dawn Chong.* • The verb *cohost* has become established in its use to refer to those who collaborate in assuming responsibility for an occasion. Fifty-eight percent of the Usage Panel accepted this use in the sentence *The Department of Architecture and the Department of History will be cohosting a reception for conference participants.*

host² (hōst) *n.* **1.** An army. **2.** A great number; a multitude. [ME < OFr. < LLat. *hostis* < Lat., enemy. See **ghos-ti-*.**]

host³ also **Host** (hōst) *n. Eccles.* The consecrated bread of the Eucharist. [ME < Lat. *hostia*, sacrifice.]

hos•ta (hō′stə, hŏs′tə) *n.* See **plantain lily.** [NLat. *Hosta*, genus name, after N.T. *Host* (1761–1834), botanist.]

hos•tage (hŏs′tĭj) *n.* **1.** A person held by one party in a conflict as security that specified terms will be met by the opposing party. **2.** One that serves as security against an implied threat. **3.** One that is manipulated by the demands of another. [ME < OFr., prob. < *host*, guest, host. See HOST¹.]

hos•tel (hŏs′təl) *n.* **1.** An inexpensive lodging place for travelers, esp. young travelers. **2.** An inn; a hotel. *— intr.v.* **-teled, -tel•ing, -tels.** To stay at hostels while traveling. [ME, lodging < OFr. < Med.Lat. *hospitāle*, hospice, inn. See HOSPITAL.]

hos•tel•er (hŏs′tə-lər) *n.* **1.** A traveler who stays at hostels. **2.** *Archaic.* An innkeeper.

hos•tel•ry (hŏs′təl-rē) *n., pl.* **-ries.** An inn; a hotel. [ME *hostelrie* < OFr. *hostelerie* < *hostel*, lodging, inn. See HOSTEL.]

host•ess (hō′stĭs) *n.* **1.** A woman who receives or entertains guests in a social or official capacity. **2.** A woman who manages an inn or a hotel. **3.** A woman who is the emcee or interviewer on a radio or television program. **4.** A woman who is employed to greet and assist patrons, as in a restaurant. **5.** A woman who is employed to dance with customers in a dance hall or nightclub. See Usage Note at **-ess.**

hos•tile (hŏs′təl, -tīl′) *adj.* **1.** Of, relating to, or characteristic of an enemy: *hostile acts.* **2.** Feeling or showing enmity or ill will; antagonistic. **3.** Unfavorable to health or well-being; inhospitable or adverse: *a hostile climate.* *— n.* **1.** An antagonistic person or thing. **2.** An enemy in warfare. [Lat. *hostīlis* < *hostis*, enemy. See **ghos-ti-*.**] **— hos′tile•ly** *adv.*

hos•til•i•ty (hŏ-stĭl′ĭ-tē) *n., pl.* **-ties. 1.** The state of being hostile; antagonism or enmity. **2.a.** A hostile act. **b. hostilities.** Acts of war; overt warfare.

hos•tler (hŏs′lər, ŏs′-) also **os•tler** (ŏs′-) *n.* **1.** One who is employed to tend horses, esp. at an inn. **2.** One who services a large vehicle or engine, such as a locomotive. [ME < AN *hostiler* < OFr. *hostel*, lodging. See HOSTEL.]

hot (hŏt) *adj.* **hot•ter, hot•test. 1.a.** Having or giving off heat capable of burning. **b.** Being at a high temperature. **2.** Being at or exhibiting a temperature higher than normal or desirable: *a hot forehead.* **3.** Causing a burning sensation, as in the mouth; spicy. **4.a.** Charged or energized with electricity. **b.** Radioactive, esp. to a dangerous degree. **5.a.** Marked by intensity of emotion; ardent or fiery. **b.** Having or displaying great enthusiasm; eager. **6.a.** *Informal.* Arousing intense interest, excitement, or controversy. **b.** *Informal.* Marked by excited activity or energy. **c.** Violent; raging. **7.** *Slang.* Sexually excited or exciting. **8.** *Slang.* **a.** Recently stolen. **b.** Wanted by the police. **9.** Close to a successful solution or conclusion: *hot on the trail.* **10.** *Informal.* **a.** Most recent; new or fresh. **b.** Currently very popular or successful. **c.** Requiring immediate action or attention: *a hot opportunity.* **11.** *Slang.* Very good or impressive. Often used in the negative: *I'm not so hot at math.* **12.** *Slang.* Funny or absurd. **13.** *Slang.* **a.** Performing with great skill and daring: *a hot drummer.* **b.** Fast and responsive: *a hot sports car.* **c.** Unusually lucky. **14.** *Mus.* Of, relating to, or being an emotionally charged style of performance marked by strong rhythms and improvisation. **15.** *Color.* Bold and bright. *— n.* **hots.** *Slang.* Strong sexual attraction or desire. *— adv.* **1.** In a hot manner; hotly. **2.** While hot. *— tr.v.* **hot•ted, hot•ting, hots.** *Informal.* To cause to increase in intensity or excitement. Often used with *up.* ***— idioms.*** **hot and bothered.** *Informal.* In a state of agitated excitement; flustered. **hot to trot.** *Slang.* **1.** Sexually avid; lascivious. **2.** Ready and willing; eager. **hot under the collar.** *Informal.* Angry. **make it hot for.** *Slang.* To make things uncomfortable or dangerous for. [ME < OE *hāt.* See **kai-*.**] **— hot′ness** *n.*

hot air *n. Slang.* Empty, exaggerated talk.

hot•bed (hŏt′bĕd′) *n.* **1.** An environment conducive to vigorous growth or development, esp. of something undesirable: *a hotbed of intrigue.* **2.** A glass-covered bed of heated soil, used for the germination of seeds or for protecting tender plants.

hot-blood•ed (hŏt′blŭd′ĭd) *adj.* Easily excited or aroused. **— hot′-blood′ed•ness** *n.*

hot•box (hŏt′bŏks′) *n.* An axle or journal box, as on a railway car, that has become overheated by excessive friction.

hot•cake also **hot cake** (hŏt′kāk′) *n.* See **pancake.** ***— idiom.*** **go (**or **sell) like hotcakes.** *Informal.* To be disposed of quickly; be in great demand.

hotch (hŏch) *intr.v.* **hotched, hotch•ing, hotch•es.** *Scots.* To fidget. [ME, perh. < OFr. *hocher*, to shake, poss. of Gmc. orig.]

hotch•potch (hŏch′pŏch′) *n.* A hodgepodge. [ME *hochepoche*, alteration of *hochepot* < OFr., mixture, stew : *hocher*, to shake together; see HOTCH + *pot*, pot.]

hot cross bun *n.* A sweet bun marked on top with a cross of frosting, traditionally eaten during Lent.

hot dog or **hot•dog** (hŏt′dôg′, -dŏg′) *— n.* **1.** A frankfurter, esp. one served hot in a roll. **2.** *Slang.* One who performs

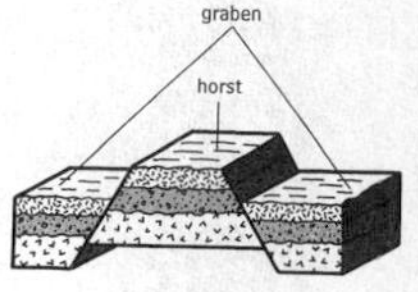

horst

hot dog

ă pat | oi boy
ā pay | ou out
âr care | o͝o took
ä father | o͞o boot
ĕ pet | ŭ cut
ē be | ûr urge
ĭ pit | th thin
ī pie | *th* this
îr pier | hw which
ŏ pot | zh vision
ō toe | ə about, item
ô paw

Stress marks:
′ (primary);
′ (secondary), as in
dictionary (dĭk′shə-nĕr′ē)

Harry Houdini
With shackled wrists and ankles

showy, often dangerous stunts, as in skiing or surfing. — *interj. Informal.* Used to express delight or enthusiasm.

hot-dog (hŏt′dôg′, -dŏg′) *intr.v.* **-dogged, -dog•ging, -dogs.** *Slang.* To perform daring stunts or acrobatic feats, as while surfing. — **hot′-dog′ger** *n.* — **hot′-dog′ging** *adj. & n.*

ho•tel (hō-tĕl′) *n.* An establishment that provides lodging and usu. meals and other services for travelers and other paying guests. [Fr. *hôtel* < OFr. *hostel*, hostel. See HOSTEL.]

ho•te•lier (ō′təl-yā′, hō′-) *n.* A manager or an owner of a hotel. [Fr. *hôtelier* < OFr. *hostilier* < *hostel*, inn. See HOSTEL.]

ho•tel•keep•er (hō-tĕl′kē′pər) *n.* See **hotelier.**

hot flash *n.* **1.** A sudden brief sensation of heat, caused by a transient dilation of the blood vessels of the skin. **2.** *Slang.* A brief important piece of news or other information.

hot•foot (hŏt′fo͝ot′) *intr.v.* **-foot•ed, -foot•ing, -foots.** *Informal.* To go in haste. Often used with *it.* — *adv.* In haste. — *n., pl.* **-foots.** The practical joke of lighting a match secretly inserted between the sole and upper of a victim's shoe.

hot•head (hŏt′hĕd′) *n.* A quick-tempered or impetuous person.

hot•head•ed (hŏt′hĕd′ĭd) *adj.* **1.** Easily angered; quick-tempered. **2.** Impetuous; rash. — **hot′head′ed•ness** *n.*

hot•house (hŏt′hous′) *n.* A heated greenhouse for plants that require an even, relatively warm temperature. — *adj.* **1.** Grown in a hothouse: *a hothouse orchid.* **2.** Delicate and sensitive, as if from growing up in a protective environment.

hot line or **hot•line** (hŏt′līn′) *n.* **1.** A direct and immediate telephone linkup, esp. between heads of government, as for use in a crisis. **2.** A telephone line that gives quick and direct access to a source of information or help.

hot•ly (hŏt′lē) *adv.* In an intense or fiery way: *answered hotly.*

hot metal *n. Print.* Type cast from molten metal.

hot money *n.* Money moved by its owner quickly from one form of investment to another.

hot pants *pl.n.* **1.** *Vulgar Slang.* Strong sexual desire. **2.** Very brief tight shorts worn by women.

hot pepper *n.* **1.** The pungent fruit of any of several varieties of *Capsicum frutescens.* **2.** See **pepper** 4.

hot plate *n.* **1.** An electrically heated plate for cooking or warming food. **2.** A tabletop cooking device with burners.

hot pot *n. Chiefly British.* A stew of lamb or beef and potatoes cooked in a tightly covered pot.

hot potato *n. Informal.* A problem that is so controversial or sensitive that those handling it risk unpleasant consequences.

hot rod also **hot-rod** (hŏt′rŏd′) *n. Slang.* An automobile that has been rebuilt or modified to increase its speed and acceleration. — **hot′-rod′** *v.* — **hot rodder, hot′-rod′der** *n.*

hot seat *n.* **1.** *Slang.* The electric chair. **2.** *Informal.* A position in which one is subjected to extreme stress or discomfort.

hot•shot (hŏt′shŏt′) *n.* **1.** *Slang.* A person of impressive skill and daring, esp. one who is highly successful and self-assured. **2.** A nonstop freight train. — **hot′shot′** *adj.*

hot spot also **hot•spot** (hŏt′spŏt′) *n.* **1.** An area in which there is dangerous unrest or hostile action. **2.** *Informal.* A lively and popular place, such as a nightclub. **3.** An area of intense heat, radiation, or activity.

hot spring *n.* A natural spring that issues warm water.

Hot Springs (hŏt). A city of W-central AR WSW of Little Rock; noted for its thermal springs. Pop. 32,462.

Hot•ten•tot (hŏt′n-tŏt′) *n., pl.* **Hottentot** or **-tots.** *Offensive.* **1.** A Khoikhoin. **2.** Any of the Khoikhoin group of languages. [Afr.]

hot•tish (hŏt′ĭsh) *adj.* Somewhat hot.

hot toddy *n.* A drink consisting of whiskey, brandy, or other liquor mixed with hot water, sugar, and spices.

hot tub *n.* A very large tub filled with hot water in which one or more bathers may soak.

hot war *n.* Armed open conflict between nations or factions.

hot water *n.* Trouble; difficulty: *is in political hot water.*

hot-wa•ter bottle (hŏt′wô′tər, -wŏt′ər) *n.* A stoppered container, usu. made of plastic or rubber, filled with hot water and applied to a part of the body for warmth.

hot-wire (hŏt′wīr′) *tr.v.* **-wired, -wir•ing, -wires.** *Informal.* To start the engine of (an automobile, for example) without a key, as by short-circuiting the ignition system.

hou•dah (hou′də) *n.* Var. of **howdah.**

Hou•dan (ho͞o′dăn′) *n.* A domesticated fowl characterized by black-and-white plumage and a V-shaped comb. [Fr., after *Houdan*, a village of N-central France.]

Hou•di•ni (ho͞o-dē′nē), **Harry.** 1874–1926. Amer. magician known for his spectacular escapes.

Hou•don (ho͞o′dŏn′, o͞o-dôɴ′), **Jean Antoine.** 1741–1828. French sculptor noted esp. for his statues of Washington and Voltaire.

Hough•ton (hōt′n), **Henry Oscar.** 1823–95. Amer. publisher who founded (1852) the printing office that became the Houghton Mifflin Company.

Hou•ma (hō′mə, ho͞o′-). A city of SE LA on the Intracoastal Waterway SW of New Orleans. Pop. 30,495.

hound (hound) *n.* **1.a.** A domestic dog of any of various breeds commonly used for hunting, characteristically having drooping ears, a short coat, and a deep resonant voice. **b.** A dog. **2.** A contemptible person; a scoundrel. **3.a.** One who eagerly pursues something. **b.** A devotee or an enthusiast. — *tr.v.* **hound•ed, hound•ing, hounds. 1.** To pursue relentlessly and tenaciously. See Syns at **harass. 2.** To urge insistently; nag. [ME < OE *hund.* See **kwon-***.] — **hound′er** *n.*

hound's-tongue
Burgundy hound's-tongue
Cynoglossum officinale

hound's-tongue (houndz′tŭng′) *n.* Any of several Eurasian plants of the genus *Cynoglossum*, having hairy leaves, small reddish-purple flowers, and prickly, clinging fruit.

hounds•tooth check or **hound's-tooth check** (houndz′-to͞oth′) *n.* A textile design of small broken checks.

houndstooth check
Detail of fabric

hour (our) *n.* **1.** One of the 24 equal parts of a day. **2.a.** One of the points on a timepiece marking off 12 or 24 successive intervals of 60 minutes, from midnight to noon and noon to midnight or from midnight to midnight. **b.** The time of day indicated by a 12-hour clock. **c. hours.** The time of day determined on a 24-hour basis. **3.** A unit of measure of longitude or right ascension, equal to 15° or 1⁄24 of a great circle. **4.a.** A customary or fixed time: *the dinner hour.* **b. hours.** A set period of time for a specified activity: *banking hours.* **5.a.** A particular time. **b.** A significant time. **c.** The present time. **6.a.** The work that can be accomplished in an hour. **b.** The distance that can be traveled in an hour. **7.a.** A single session of a school day or class. **b.** A credit hour. **8. hours.** *Eccles.* The canonical hours. [ME < OFr. *houre* < Lat. *hōra* < Gk., season, time. See **yēr-***.]

hour angle *n.* The angular distance, measured westward along the celestial equator, between the celestial meridian of the observer and the hour circle passing through a celestial body.

hour circle *n.* A great circle passing through the poles of the celestial sphere and intersecting the celestial equator at right angles.

hour•glass (our′glăs′) *n.* An instrument for measuring time, consisting of two glass chambers connected by a narrow neck and containing a quantity of a flowing substance that trickles from the upper chamber to the lower in a fixed amount of time. — *adj.* Shaped like an hourglass: *an hourglass design.*

hou•ri (ho͝or′ē, ho͞o′rē) *n., pl.* **-ris. 1.** A voluptuous, alluring woman. **2.** One of the beautiful virgins of the Koranic paradise. [Fr. < Pers. *ḥūrī* < Ar. *ḥūr*, pl. of *haurā'*, dark-eyed woman.]

hour•long or **hour-long** (our′lông′, -lŏng′) *adj.* Lasting an hour: *an hourlong television episode.*

hour•ly (our′lē) *adj.* **1.** Occurring every hour: *hourly chimes.* **2.** Frequent; continual. **3.** By the hour as a unit: *hourly pay.* — *adv.* **1.** At or during every hour. **2.** Frequently; continually. — *n., pl.* **-lies.** *Informal.* An employee paid by the hour.

Hou•sa•ton•ic (ho͞o′sə-tŏn′ĭk). A river rising in W MA and flowing c. 209 km (130 mi) to Long Island Sound.

house (hous) *n., pl.* **hous•es** (hou′zĭz, -sĭz). **1.a.** A structure serving as a dwelling for one or more persons, esp. for a family. **b.** A household or family. **2.** Something, such as a burrow or shell, that serves as a shelter or habitation for a wild animal. **3.** A dwelling for a group of people, such as students, who live together as a unit. **4.** A building that functions as the primary shelter or location of something. **5.a.** A facility, such as a theater or restaurant, that provides entertainment or food for the public. **b.** The audience or patrons of such an establishment. **6.a.** A commercial firm. **b.** A publishing company. **c.** A gambling casino. **d.** *Slang.* A house of prostitution. **7.** A residential college within a university. **8.a.** Often **House.** A legislative or deliberative assembly. **b.** The hall or chamber in which such an assembly meets. **c.** A quorum of such an assembly. **9.** Often **House.** A family line, esp. of a royal or noble family: *the House of Orange.* **10.a.** One of the 12 parts into which the heavens are divided in astrology. **b.** The sign of the zodiac indicating the seat or station of a planet in the heavens. — *v.* (houz) **housed, hous•ing, hous•es.** — *tr.* **1.** To provide living quarters for; lodge. **2.** To shelter, keep, or store in or as if in a house. **3.** To contain; harbor. **4.** To fit into a socket or mortise. **5.** *Naut.* To secure or stow safely. — *intr.* **1.** To reside; dwell. **2.** To take shelter. — ***idioms.*** **like a house on fire** (or **afire**). *Informal.* In an extremely speedy manner. **on the house.** At the expense of the establishment; free. **put** (or **set**) **(one's) house in order.** To organize one's affairs in a sensible, logical way. [ME < OE *hūs.*]

house arrest *n. Law.* Confinement to one's quarters, rather than prison, by administrative or judicial order.

house•boat (hous′bōt′) *n.* **1.** *Naut.* A barge designed and equipped for use as a dwelling or cruiser. **2.** See **banana split.** See Regional Note at **milk shake.**

house•boy (hous′boi′) *n.* A male servant in a house.

house•break (hous′brāk′) *tr.v.* **-broke** (-brōk′), **-bro•ken** (-brō′kən), **-break•ing, -breaks. 1.** To train to have excretory habits that are acceptable for indoor living: *housebreak a puppy.* **2.** To subdue; tame. — *n.* Burglary of a dwelling.

house•break•ing (hous′brā′kĭng) *n. Law.* The act of unlawfully breaking into and entering another's house. — **house′-break′er** *n.*

house•bro•ken (hous′brō′kən) *adj.* **1.** Trained to have excretory habits that are appropriate for indoor living: *The dog is housebroken.* **2.** Trained to be docile or compliant.

house call *n.* A professional visit made to a home, esp. by a physician.

house•carl (hous′kärl′) *n.* A member of the bodyguard or household troops of a Danish or Anglo-Saxon king or noble.

house•clean•ing (hous′klē′nĭng) *n.* **1.** The cleaning and tidying of a house and its contents. **2.** *Informal.* Removal of personnel, methods, or policies in an effort at reform.

house•coat (hous′kōt′) *n.* A woman's garment, usu. long and loose, used for informal wear at home.

house detective *n.* A detective employed by an establishment, such as a hotel, to prevent theft or misconduct.

house•dress (hous′drĕs′) *n.* A simple washable dress worn for housework.

house finch *n.* See **linnet** 2.

house•fly (hous′flī′) *n.* A widely distributed fly *(Musca domestica)* that frequents human dwellings, breeds in moist or decaying organic matter, and transmits many diseases.

house•ful (hous′fo͝ol) *n.* The amount or number that a house can hold or accommodate: *a houseful of furniture.*

house•guest (hous′gĕst′) *n.* A person who stays in a home as a guest.

house•hold (hous′hōld′) *n.* **1.a.** A domestic unit consisting of the members of a family who live together along with nonrelatives. **b.** The living spaces and possessions belonging to such a unit. **2.** A person or group of people occupying a single dwelling: *nonfamily households.* —*adj.* **1.** Of, relating to, or used in a household. **2.** Commonly known; familiar. [ME : *house*, house; see HOUSE + *hold*, possession, holding (< OE < *healdan*, to hold; see HOLD[1]).]

household arts *pl.n. (used with a sing. or pl. v.)* See **home economics.**

house•hold•er (hous′hōl′dər) *n.* **1.** One who occupies or owns a house. **2.** The head of a household.

household word *n.* Someone or something widely known.

house•hus•band (hous′hŭz′bənd) *n.* A married man who manages the household as his main occupation.

house•keep•er (hous′kē′pər) *n.* **1.** One who is employed to perform or direct the domestic tasks in a household. **2.** A housewife. **3.** An employee of an establishment, such as an inn or a hotel, who manages other employees engaged in domestic tasks.

house•keep•ing (hous′kē′pĭng) *n.* **1.** Performance or management of household tasks. **2.** Management and maintenance of the property and equipment of an institution or organization. **3.** Routine tasks and procedures carried out in the functioning of an operation or a system. —**house′keep′** *v.*

hou•sel (hou′zəl) *Archaic.* —*n.* The Eucharist. —*tr.v.* **-seled, -sel•ing, -sels.** To administer the Eucharist to. [ME < OE *hūsel.*]

house•leek (hous′lēk′) *n.* Any of various Old World plants of the genus *Sempervivum*, esp. *S. tectorum* having a basal rosette of leaves and a cluster of pinkish or purplish flowers.

house•lights (hous′līts′) *pl.n.* The lights that illuminate the audience section of a concert hall, a theater, or an auditorium.

house•maid (hous′mād′) *n.* A woman or girl employed to do housework.

house•maid's knee (hous′mādz′) *n.* Bursitis in the knee.

house•man (hous′măn′, -mən) *n.* A man employed for cleaning, maintenance, and other general work in a house or hotel.

house martin *n.* An Old World bird *(Delichon urbica)* having blue-black plumage, white underparts, and a forked tail.

house•mas•ter (hous′măs′tər) *n.* A male teacher in charge of a residence hall at a school.

house•mate (hous′māt′) *n.* One who shares a house with another.

house•moth•er (hous′mŭth′ər) *n.* A woman employed as supervisor or housekeeper of a residence hall for young people.

house mouse *n.* A gray or brownish-gray mouse *(Mus musculus)* that lives in or near buildings and often carries disease.

House of Burgesses *n.* The lower house of the legislature in colonial Virginia.

House of Commons *n.* The lower house of Parliament in the United Kingdom and Canada.

house of correction *n., pl.* **houses of correction.** An institution for persons convicted of minor criminal offenses.

House of Delegates *n.* The lower house of the state legislature in Maryland, Virginia, and West Virginia.

House of Lords *n.* The upper house of Parliament in the United Kingdom, made up of nobles and high-ranking clergy.

house of prostitution *n., pl.* **houses of prostitution.** An establishment in which the services of prostitutes are available on the premises.

House of Representatives *n.* The lower house of the U.S. Congress and of most state legislatures.

house organ *n.* A periodical published by a business organization for its employees or clients.

house party *n.* A party at which guests stay overnight or for several days in a residence, such as the home of the host.

house physician *n.* **1.** A physician, esp. an intern or a resident, who cares for hospitalized patients under the supervision of the surgical and medical staff of a hospital. **2.** A physician employed by a hotel or another establishment.

house•plant (hous′plănt′) *n.* Any of a wide variety of plants grown indoors, often for decorative purposes.

house-proud (hous′proud′) *adj.* Proud of one's house or its furnishings or upkeep.

house-rais•ing (hous′rā′zĭng) *n.* The construction of a house or its framework by a group of friends or neighbors.

house•room (hous′ro͞om′, -ro͝om′) *n.* Space or accommodation in or as if in a house.

house sitter *n.* One who lives in and cares for a house while the usual occupant is away. —**house′sit′** (hous′sĭt′) *v.*

house snake *n.* See **milk snake.**

house sparrow *n.* A small bird *(Passer domesticus)* native to the Old World but widely naturalized and having brown and gray plumage with a black throat in the adult male.

house•top (hous′tŏp′) *n.* The roof of a house. —***idiom.* shout (or proclaim) from the housetops.** To make known publicly.

house•train also **house-train** (hous′trān′) *tr.v.* **-trained, -train•ing, -trains.** *Chiefly British.* To housebreak.

house•wares (hous′wârz′) *pl.n.* Cooking utensils and other articles used in a household, esp. in the kitchen.

house•warm•ing (hous′wôr′mĭng) *n.* A celebration of the occupancy of a new home.

house•wife (hous′wīf′) *n., pl.* **-wives** (-wīvz′). **1.** A woman who manages the household as her main occupation. **2.** (hŭz′ĭf). A small container for sewing equipment.

house•wife•ly (hous′wīf′lē) *adj.* Of, relating to, or suited to a housewife; domestic. —**house′wife′li•ness** *n.*

house•wif•er•y (hous′wī′fə-rē, -wīf′rē) *n.* The function or duties of a housewife; housekeeping.

house•work (hous′wûrk′) *n.* The tasks, such as cleaning and cooking, performed in housekeeping. —**house′work′er** *n.*

hous•ing[1] (hou′zĭng) *n.* **1.a.** Buildings or other shelters in which people live. **b.** A place to live; a dwelling. **2.** Provision of lodging or shelter. **3.** Something that covers, protects, or supports, esp.: **a.** A frame, bracket, or box for holding or protecting a mechanical part: *a wheel housing.* **b.** An enclosing frame in which a shaft revolves. **4.** A hole, groove, or slot in a piece of wood into which another piece is inserted. **5.** A niche for a statue.

hous•ing[2] (hou′zĭng) *n.* **1.** An ornamental or protective covering for a saddle. **2.** Trappings for a horse. Often used in the plural. [< ME *house* < OFr. *houce* < Med.Lat. *hucia, hulcia, hultia*, protective covering, of Gmc. orig. See **kel-[1]*.**]

housing development *n.* A group of houses or apartment buildings on a site, usu. under a single management.

housing project *n.* A publicly funded and administered housing development, usu. for low-income families.

Hous•man (hous′mən), **Alfred Edward.** 1859–1936. British poet whose works include *A Shropshire Lad* (1896).

Hous•ton (hyo͞o′stən). A city of SE TX NW of Galveston connected with Galveston Bay and the Gulf of Mexico by the **Houston Ship Channel;** founded 1836. Pop. 1,630,553. —**Hous•to′ni•an** (hyo͞o-stō′nē-ən) *n.*

Houston, Samuel. 1793–1863. Amer. general who was president of the Republic of Texas (1836–38 and 1841–44).

hove (hōv) *v.* —*tr.* P.t. and p.part. of **heave** 4. —*intr.* P.t. and p.part. of **heave** 5.

hov•el (hŭv′əl, hŏv′-) *n.* **1.** A small miserable dwelling. **2.** An open low shed. [ME, hut.]

hov•er (hŭv′ər, hŏv′-) *intr.v.* **-ered, -er•ing, -ers. 1.** To remain floating, suspended, or fluttering in the air: *gulls hovering over the waves.* **2.** To remain or linger in or near a place. **3.** To remain in an uncertain state; waver. —*n.* The act or state of hovering. [ME *hoveren*, freq. of *hoven.*] —**hov′er•er** *n.* —**hov′er•ing•ly** *adv.*

hov•er•craft (hŭv′ər-krăft′, hŏv′-) *n.* See **air-cushion vehicle.**

how (hou) *adv.* **1.** In what manner or way; by what means: *How does this machine work?* **2.** In what state or condition: *How are you today?* **3.** To what extent, amount, or degree: *How bad was it?* **4.** For what reason or purpose; why: *How is it that he left early?* **5.** With what meaning: *How should I take that remark?* **6.** By what name: *How is she called?* **7.** By what measure; in what units: *How do you sell this corn?* **8.** What. Usu. used in requesting that something be said again: *How's that again?* **9.** Used as an intensive: *How we laughed!* —*conj.* **1.** The manner or way in which. **2.** That. **3.** In whatever way or manner; however: *Cook it how you please.* —*n.* A manner or method of doing something. —***idioms.* and how.** *Informal.* Most certainly; you bet. **how about.** What is your thought, feeling, or desire regarding. **how about that.** *Informal.* Used rhetorically to express surprise or wonder at or approval for something. **how come.** *Informal.* How is it that; why. **how so.** How is it so. [ME *howe* < OE *hū.* See **k^wo-*.**]

How•ard (hou′ərd), **Catherine.** 1520?–42. Queen of England as the fifth wife of Henry VIII (1540–42); executed for adultery.

Howard, Henry. 1st Earl of Surrey. 1517?–47. English poet and soldier noted for his sonnets.

Howard, Roy Wilson. 1883–1964. Amer. journalist who was president (1936–53) of the United Press Association.

hourglass

Sam Houston
c. 1845 daguerreotype

ă pat	oi boy
ā pay	ou out
âr care	o͝o took
ä father	o͞o boot
ĕ pet	ŭ cut
ē be	ûr urge
ĭ pit	th thin
ī pie	*th* this
îr pier	hw which
ŏ pot	zh vision
ō toe	ə about, item
ô paw	

Stress marks:
′ (primary);
′ (secondary), as in
dictionary (dĭk′shə-nĕr′ē)

Howard, Sidney Coe. 1891–1939. Amer. playwright best known for *They Knew What They Wanted* (1924).

how•be•it (hou-bē′ĭt) *adv.* Be that as it may; nevertheless. — *conj. Obsolete.* Although.

how•dah also **hou•dah** (hou′də) *n.* A seat, usu. fitted with a canopy and railing, placed on the back of an elephant or a camel. [Urdu *haudah* < Ar. *hawdaj* < *hadaja,* to shuffle along, totter.]

how•dy (hou′dē) *interj.* Used to express a greeting. [< *how do ye,* how do you do.]

Howe (hou), **Elias.** 1819–67. Amer. inventor and manufacturer who designed early sewing machines (1845 and 1846).

Howe, Julia Ward. 1819–1910. Amer. writer who was active in the women's suffrage movement and wrote "Battle Hymn of the Republic" (published 1862).

Howe, Richard. Earl Howe. 1726–99. British admiral who conducted naval operations in America (1776–78).

Howe, Sir **William.** 5th Viscount Howe. 1729–1814. British general in America who defeated George Washington in a number of battles but could not force a surrender.

huarache
Pair of huaraches

How•ells (hou′əlz), **William Dean.** 1837–1920. Amer. writer and editor (1871–81) of the *Atlantic Monthly* whose novels include *The Rise of Silas Lapham* (1885).

how•ev•er (hou-ev′ər) *adv.* **1.** In whatever manner or way: *However he did it, it was very clever.* **2.** To whatever degree or extent. **3.** In what way. Used as an intensive of *how: However did you get here so soon?* **4.** In spite of that; nevertheless; yet: *The book is expensive; however, it's worth it.* **5.** On the other hand; by contrast. — *conj.* **1.** In whatever manner or way: *Dress however you like.* **2.** *Archaic.* Notwithstanding that; although.

Usage Note: Although some grammarians have insisted that *however* should not be used to begin a sentence, this rule has been ignored by a number of reputable writers. See Usage Notes at **but, whatever.**

how•it•zer (hou′ĭt-sər) *n.* A relatively short cannon that delivers shells at a medium muzzle velocity, usu. by a high trajectory. [Du. *houwitser* < Ger. *Haubitze,* alteration of obsolete *haufnitz,* catapult < Old Czech *haufnice* : *hauf,* group, heap (of Gmc. orig.) + *-nice,* fem. n. suff.]

howl (houl) *v.* **howled, howl•ing, howls.** — *intr.* **1.** To utter a long, mournful, plaintive sound. **2.** To cry or wail loudly, as in pain. **3.** *Slang.* To laugh heartily. **4.** *Slang.* To go on a spree. — *tr.* To express or utter with a howl. See Syns at **shout.** — *n.* **1.** A long wailing cry. **2.** *Slang.* Something uproariously funny or absurd. — ***phrasal verb.*** **howl down.** To drown out or silence by loud derisive calls. [ME *houlen.*]

howl•er (hou′lər) *n.* **1.** One that howls. **2.** A howler monkey. **3.** *Slang.* A laughably stupid blunder.

howler monkey *n.* Any of several monkeys of the genus *Alouatta* of tropical America, having a long prehensile tail and an extremely loud howling call.

howl•ing (hou′lĭng) *adj.* **1.** Marked by the sound of howling. **2.** Desolate; dreary. **3.** *Slang.* Very great; tremendous.

How•rah (hou′rə, -rä). A city of E India on the Hooghly R. opposite Calcutta. Pop. 744,429.

how•so•ev•er (hou′sō-ev′ər) *adv.* **1.** To whatever degree or extent. **2.** By whatever means.

how-to (hou′to͞o′) *Informal.* — *adj.* Offering practical advice and detailed instruction in an activity. — *n., pl.* **how-tos.** Something, such as a book or learning situation, that provides practical advice and detailed instruction in an activity.

hoy[1] (hoi) *n. Naut.* **1.** A small sloop-rigged coasting ship. **2.** A heavy barge used for freight. [ME *hoie* < MDu. *hoey, hoede.*]

hoy[2] (hoi) *interj.* Used to attract attention.

hoy•a (hoi′ə) *n.* Any of several evergreen climbing vines or shrubs of the genus *Hoya,* having opposite simple leaves and axillary umbellate flower clusters. [NLat. *Hoya,* genus name, after Thomas *Hoy* (1750?–1822), British gardener.]

hoy•den (hoid′n) *n.* A high-spirited or boisterous girl. — *adj.* High-spirited; boisterous. [< earlier *hoyden,* a rude youth, prob. < Du. *heiden,* heathen, boor < MDu. See **kaito-*.**] — **hoy′den•ish** *adj.*

Henry Hudson

Hoyle (hoil) *n. Games.* A reference book of rules for card games and other indoor games. — ***idiom.*** **according to Hoyle.** In accord with the prescribed rules or regulations. [After Edmond *Hoyle* (1672?–1769), British writer on games.]

hp *abbr.* Horsepower.

HP *abbr.* High pressure.

HQ or **h.q.** or **H.Q.** *abbr.* Headquarters.

hr *abbr.* Hour.

Hr. *abbr.* Herr.

h.r. *abbr. Baseball.* Home run.

H.R. *abbr.* **1.** Home rule. **2.** House of Representatives.

Hra•dec Krá•lo•vé (rä′dĕts krä′lə-və, -lô-vĕ, hrä′-). A city of N-central Czech Republic E of Prague; founded in the 10th cent. Pop. 98,476.

H. Rept. *abbr.* House Report.

H. Res. *abbr.* House Resolution.

H.R.H. *abbr.* **1.** Her Royal Highness. **2.** His Royal Highness.

Hrolf (rŏlf, hrŏlf). See **Rollo.**

hrs *abbr.* Hours.

HS or **H.S.** *abbr.* High school.

H.S.H. *abbr.* **1.** Her Serene Highness. **2.** His Serene Highness.

Hsian (shyän). See **Xi'an.**

Hsiang Kiang (shyäng′ kyäng′). See **Xiang Jiang.**

Hsin•king (shĭn′gĭng′). See **Changchun.**

HST *abbr.* **1.** Or **H.S.T.** Hawaiian Standard Time **2.** Hypersonic transport.

ht *abbr.* Height.

HT *abbr.* **1.** *Sports.* Halftime. **2.** High-tension. **3.** High tide.

HTLV–I (āch′tē-ĕl′vē-wŭn′) *n.* A retrovirus that causes diseases similar to multiple sclerosis. [H(UMAN) T(-CELL) L(YMPHOTROPIC) V(IRUS) I.]

HTLV–III (āch′tē-ĕl′vē-thrē′) *n.* HIV. [H(UMAN) T(-CELL) L(YMPHOTROPIC) V(IRUS) III.]

Hts. *abbr.* Heights.

HUAC *abbr.* House Un-American Activities Committee.

Huai•nan (hwī′nän′). A city of E-central China WNW of Nanjing. Pop. 603,200.

Hua•la•pai or **Wa•la•pai** (wä′lə-pī′) *n.* **1.** A member of a Native American people inhabiting northwest Arizona south of the Grand Canyon. **2.** Their Yuman language.

Hual•la•ga (wä-yä′gä). A river rising in W-central Peru and flowing c. 1,126 km (700 mi) to the Marañón R.

Huang He (hwäng′ hə′) also **Hwang Ho** (hō′) or **Yel•low River** (yĕl′ō). A river of N China rising in the Kunlun Mts. and flowing c. 4,827 km (3,000 mi) to the Gulf of Bo Hai.

hua•ra•che (wə-rä′chē, hə-) *n.* A flat-heeled sandal with an upper of woven leather strips. [Am.Sp., prob. < J. *warachi,* straw sandal.]

Huás•car (wäs′kär′). d. 1532. Incan chieftain who fought with his brother Atahualpa over the division of the empire and was assassinated after the Spanish conquest.

Huas•ca•rán (wäs′kə-rän′, -kä-). An extinct volcano, 6,770.4 m (22,198 ft), in the Andes of W-central Peru.

hub (hŭb) *n.* **1.** The center part of a wheel, fan, or propeller. **2.** A center of activity or interest; a focal point. See Syns at **center.** [Prob. alteration of HOB[1].]

Hub•bard (hŭb′ərd), **Mount.** A peak, 4,559.8 m (14,950 ft), in the Coast Mts. of SE AK.

hub•bard squash (hŭb′ərd) *n. Northern & Western U.S.* A variety of winter squash. [< the surname *Hubbard.*]

Hub•ble (hŭb′əl), **Edwin Powell.** 1889–1953. Amer. astronomer who discovered (1929) that the velocities of nebulae increase with distance.

hub•ble-bub•ble (hŭb′əl-bŭb′əl) *n.* **1.** An uproar; a hubbub. **2.** See **hookah.** [Redup. and alteration of BUBBLE.]

Hub•ble's constant (hŭb′əlz) *n.* A ratio expressing the rate of apparent expansion of the universe, equal to the velocity at which a typical galaxy is receding from Earth divided by its distance from Earth. [After Edwin Powell HUBBLE.]

hub•bub (hŭb′ŭb′) *n.* **1.** Loud noise; din. See Syns at **noise.** **2.** Confusion; tumult. [Prob. of Ir.Gael. orig.]

hub•by (hŭb′ē) *n., pl.* **-bies.** *Informal.* A husband. [Alteration of HUSBAND.]

hub•cap (hŭb′kăp′) *n.* A round covering over the hub of the wheel of a motor vehicle.

Hu•bei (ho͞o′bā′, hü′-) also **Hu•pei** or **Hu•peh** (-pā′). A province of E-central China. Cap. Wuhan. Pop. 49,310,000.

Hu•bel (hyo͞o′bəl), **David.** b. 1926. Amer. neurobiologist who shared a 1981 Nobel Prize.

Hu•ber Heights (hyo͞o′bər). A community of SW OH, a suburb of Dayton. Pop. 38,696.

Hu•bli-Dhar•war (ho͝ob′lē-där-wär′). A city of SW India NW of Bangalore; estab. 1961. Pop. 527,108.

hu•bris (hyo͞o′brĭs) *n.* Overbearing pride or presumption; arrogance. [Gk., excessive pride, wanton violence. See **ud-*.**] — **hu•bris′tic** (-brĭs′tĭk) *adj.* — **hu•bris′tic•al•ly** *adv.*

huck•a•back (hŭk′ə-băk′) *n.* A coarse absorbent cotton or linen fabric used esp. for toweling. [?]

huck•le•ber•ry (hŭk′əl-bĕr′ē) *n.* **1.** Any of various New World shrubs of the genus *Gaylussacia,* related to the blueberries. **2.** The glossy, blackish, many-seeded edible berry of these plants. [Prob. alteration of *hurtleberry,* whortleberry.]

huck•ster (hŭk′stər) *n.* **1.** One who sells wares or provisions in the street; a peddler or hawker. **2.** One who uses aggressive, showy, and sometimes devious methods to promote or sell a product. **3.** *Informal.* One who writes advertising copy, esp. for radio or television. — *v.* **-stered, -ster•ing, -sters.** — *tr.* **1.** To sell; peddle. **2.** To promote or attempt to sell in an overaggressive or showy manner. **3.** To haggle over; deal in. — *intr.* To engage in haggling. [ME, prob. of LGer. orig.; akin to MDu. *hokester.*] — **huck′ster•ism** *n.*

HUD *abbr.* Department of Housing and Urban Development.

Hud•ders•field (hŭd′ərz-fēld′). A borough of N-central England NE of Manchester; first settled in Roman times. Pop. 125,800.

hud•dle (hŭd′l) *n.* **1.** A densely packed group or crowd, as of people or animals. **2.** *Football.* A brief gathering of a team's players behind the line of scrimmage. **3.** A small private conference or meeting. — *v.* **-dled, -dling, -dles.** — *intr.* **1.** To crowd together, as from cold or fear. **2.** To draw or curl one's limbs close to one's body; crouch. **3.** *Football.* To gather in a huddle. **4.** *Informal.* To gather together for conference or consultation. — *tr.* **1.** To cause to crowd together. **2.** To draw (oneself) together in a crouch. **3.** *Chiefly British.* To arrange, do, or make hastily or carelessly. [Poss. < LGer. *hudeln,* to crowd together. See **(s)keu-*.**] — **hud′dler** *n.*

Hu•di•bras•tic (hyo͞o′də-brăs′tĭk) *adj.* Of or relating to a style of mock-heroic verse composed in rhymed iambic pentameter couplets. [After *Hudibras,* a satiric epic by Samuel Butler.]

Hud•son (hŭd′sən). A town of E-central MA NE of Worcester. Pop. 17,233.

Hudson, Henry. d. 1611. English navigator and first European to explore the Hudson R. (1609).

Hudson, William Henry. 1841–1922. British naturalist and writer whose works include *Green Mansions* (1904).

Hudson Bay. An inland sea of E-central Canada connected to the Atlantic by **Hudson Strait,** lying between S Baffin I. and N Quebec; explored and named by Henry Hudson in 1610.

Hudson River. A river rising in the Adirondack Mts. of NE NY and flowing c. 507 km (315 mi) to Upper New York Bay at New York City.

Hudson seal *n.* Muskrat fur treated to resemble seal. [After HUDSON (BAY).]

hue (hyo͞o) *n.* **1.** The property of colors by which they can be perceived as ranging from red through yellow, green, and blue, as determined by the dominant wavelength of the light. **2.** A particular gradation of color; a shade or tint. **3.** Color. **4.** Appearance; aspect. [ME, color, form < OE *hīw, hēo.*]

Hue (hyo͞o-ā′, hwā). A city of central Vietnam near the South China Sea NW of Da Nang; probably dating from the 3rd cent. A.D. Pop. 165,865.

hue and cry *n.* **1.** A public clamor, as of protest or demand. **2.a.** The pursuit of a felon with loud shouts to alert others who were then legally obliged to give chase. **b.** The loud outcry formerly used in such a pursuit. [ME *hew and cri* < AN *hu e cri* : *hu,* outcry, clamor (< OFr. *huer,* to shout, of imit. orig.) + *cri,* cry (< OFr. *crier,* to cry; see CRY).]

hued (hyo͞od) *adj.* Having a given hue, aspect, or character. Often used in combination: *rosy-hued; dark-hued.*

Huel•va (wĕl′və, -vä). A city of SW Spain near the Gulf of Cádiz; founded by Carthaginians. Pop. 137,453.

huff (hŭf) *n.* A fit of anger or annoyance; a pique. — *v.* **huffed, huff•ing, huffs.** — *intr.* **1.** To puff; blow. **2.** To make empty threats; bluster. **3.** To react indignantly; take offense. — *tr.* **1.** To cause to puff up; inflate. **2.** To treat insolently; bully. **3.** To anger; annoy. [Imit. of puffing.]

huff•ish (hŭf′ĭsh) *adj.* **1.** Peevish; sulky. **2.** Arrogant; insolent. — **huff′ish•ly** *adv.* — **huff′ish•ness** *n.*

huff•y (hŭf′ē) *adj.* **-i•er, -i•est.** **1.** Easily offended; touchy. **2.** Irritated or annoyed; indignant. **3.** Arrogant; haughty. — **huff′i•ly** *adv.* — **huff′i•ness** *n.*

hug (hŭg) *v.* **hugged, hug•ging, hugs.** — *tr.* **1.** To clasp or hold closely, esp. in the arms, as in affection; embrace. **2.** To hold steadfastly to; cherish. **3.** To stay close to. — *intr.* To embrace or cling together closely. — *n.* **1.** A close affectionate embrace. **2.** A crushing embrace, as in wrestling. [Prob. of Scand. orig.] — **hug′ga•ble** *adj.* — **hug′ger** *n.*

huge (hyo͞oj) *adj.* **hug•er, hug•est.** **1.** Of exceedingly great size, extent, or quantity; tremendous. **2.** Of exceedingly great scope or nature. [ME < OFr. *ahuge.*] — **huge′ly** *adv.* — **huge′ness** *n.*

huge•ous (hyo͞o′jəs) *adj.* Huge.

hug•ger•mug•ger or **hug•ger-mug•ger** (hŭg′ər-mŭg′ər) — *n.* **1.** Disorderly confusion; muddle. **2.** Secrecy; concealment. — *adj.* **1.** Disorderly; jumbled. **2.** Secret; clandestine. — *v.* **-gered, -ger•ing, -gers.** — *tr.* To keep secret; conceal. — *intr.* To act in a secretive manner. [?] — **hug′ger•mug′ger** *adv.* — **hug′ger•mug′ger•y** *n.*

Hugh Ca•pet (hyo͞o′ kā′pĭt, kăp′ĭt, kă-pā′). See **Capet.**

Hughes (hyo͞oz), **Charles Evans.** 1862–1948. Amer. jurist; associate justice (1910–16) and chief justice (1930–41) of the Supreme Court.

Hughes, Howard Robard. 1905–76. Amer. industrialist, film producer, and aviator who broke the airplane speed record (1935) and flew around the world in record time (1938).

Hughes, (James) Langston. 1902–67. Amer. writer whose works include *The Ways of White Folks* (1934).

Hughes, Ted. b. 1930. British poet whose work is noted for its violence, passion, and natural imagery.

Hu•go (hyo͞o′gō, ü-gō′), **Victor Marie.** 1802–85. French writer whose novels include *Les Misérables* (1862).

Hu•gue•not (hyo͞o′gə-nŏt′) *n.* A French Protestant of the 16th and 17th centuries. [Fr. < OFr. *huguenot,* member of a Swiss political movement, ult. < MHGer. *eitgenōz,* confederate : *eit,* oath (< OHGer. *eid*) + *genōz,* companion (< OHGer. *ginōz*).] — **Hu′gue•not′ic** *adj.* — **Hu′gue•not′ism** *n.*

huh (hŭ) *interj.* Used to express interrogation, surprise, contempt, or indifference.

Hu•he•hot (ho͞o′hā-hōt′). See **Hohhot.**

Hui (hwē) also **Hwei** (hwā) *n., pl.* **Hui** or **Huis** also **Hwei** or **Hweis.** A member of a Muslim people of northwest China, descended chiefly from the Han.

Hui•zing•a (hī′zĭng-ə, hoi′zĭng-ä), **Johan.** 1872–1945. Dutch historian noted for *The Waning of the Middle Ages* (1919).

hu•la (ho͞o′lə) also **hu•la-hu•la** (ho͞o′lə-ho͞o′lə) *n.* A Polynesian dance characterized by undulating hips and miming movements of the arms and hands. [Hawaiian.]

Hu•la-Hoop (ho͞o′lə-ho͞op′). A trademark used for a light plastic hoop that is whirled around the body by the hips.

hulk (hŭlk) *n.* **1.** *Naut.* **a.** A heavy unwieldy ship. **b.** The hull of an old, unseaworthy, or wrecked ship. **c.** An old or unseaworthy ship used as a prison or warehouse. Often used in the plural. **2.** One, such as a person or an object, that is bulky, clumsy, or unwieldy. — *intr.v.* **hulked, hulk•ing, hulks.** **1.** To appear as a massive or towering form; loom. **2.** To move clumsily. [ME < OE *hulc* < Med.Lat. *hulcus,* prob. < Gk. *holkas,* merchant ship, ship that is towed < *helkein,* to pull.]

hulk•ing (hŭl′kĭng) also **hulk•y** (hŭl′kē) *adj.* Unwieldy or bulky; massive.

hull (hŭl) *n.* **1.a.** The dry outer covering of a fruit, seed, or nut; a husk. **b.** The enlarged calyx of a fruit, such as a strawberry, that is usu. green and easily detached. **2.a.** *Naut.* The frame or body of a ship, exclusive of masts, engines, or superstructure. **b.** The main body of various other large vehicles, such as a tank or an airship. **3.** The outer casing of a rocket, guided missile, or spaceship. — *tr.v.* **hulled, hull•ing, hulls.** To remove the hulls of (fruit or seeds). [ME *hulle,* husk < OE *hulu.* See **kel-¹*.**] — **hull′er** *n.*

Hull (hŭl). **1.** A city of SW Quebec, Canada, opposite Ottawa, Ontario. Pop. 56,225. **2.** Also **King•ston-up•on-Hull** (kĭng′stən-ə-pŏn-hŭl′, -pôn-). A borough of NE-central England on the N shore of the Humber estuary at the influx of the **Hull River;** chartered 1299. Pop. 272,500.

Hull, Cordell. 1871–1955. Amer. public official who as secretary of state (1933–44) laid the groundwork for the founding of the United Nations.

Hull, Isaac. 1773–1843. Amer. naval officer who commanded the *Constitution* during the War of 1812.

hul•la•ba•loo also **hul•la•bal•loo** (hŭl′ə-bə-lo͞o′) *n., pl.* **-loos.** Great noise or excitement; uproar. See Syns at **noise.** [Alteration of obsolete *hollo-ballo,* prob. < *holla,* hello. See HELLO.]

hul•lo (hə-lō′) *interj., n., & v.* Var. of **hello.**

hum (hŭm) *v.* **hummed, hum•ming, hums.** — *intr.* **1.a.** To emit a continuous low droning sound like that of the speech sound (m) when prolonged. **b.** To emit the hum of a bee on the wing; buzz. **c.** To give forth a low continuous drone blended of many sounds. **2.** To be in a state of busy activity. **3.** To hum a tune. — *tr.* To sing (a tune) without opening the lips or forming words. — *n.* **1.** The sound produced by humming. **2.** The act of humming. — *interj.* Used to indicate hesitation, surprise, or displeasure. [ME *hummen,* of imit. orig.] — **hum′ma•ble** *adj.* — **hum′mer** *n.*

hu•man (hyo͞o′mən) *adj.* **1.** Of, relating to, or characteristic of human beings. **2.** Having or showing those positive aspects of nature and character that distinguish human beings from the lower animals. **3.** Subject to or indicative of the weaknesses, imperfections, and fragility associated with human beings. **4.** Having the form of a human being. **5.** Made up of human beings. — *n.* A human being; a person. [ME *humain* < OFr. < Lat. *hūmānus.* See **dhghem-*.**] — **hu′man•hood′** *n.* — **hu′man•ness** *n.*

human being *n.* **1.** A member of the genus *Homo* and esp. of the species *H. sapiens.* **2.** A person: *a fine human being.*

human chorionic gonadotropin *n.* A placental hormone that maintains the corpus luteum during pregnancy.

hu•mane (hyo͞o-mān′) *adj.* **1.** Characterized by kindness, mercy, or compassion: *a humane judge.* **2.** Marked by an emphasis on humanistic values and concerns. [ME *humain,* human. See HUMAN.] — **hu•mane′ly** *adv.* — **hu•mane′ness** *n.*

Syns: *humane, compassionate, humanitarian, merciful.* The central meaning shared by these adjectives is "marked or motivated by concern with the alleviation of suffering": *a humane physician; compassionate toward disadvantaged people; released the prisoner for humanitarian reasons; is merciful to the repentant.* ***Ant:*** *inhumane.*

human ecology *n.* See **ecology** 2, 3.

human engineering *n.* See **ergonomics** 1.

human factors engineering *n.* See **ergonomics** 1.

human im•mu•no•de•fi•cien•cy virus (ĭm′yə-nō-dĭ-fĭsh′ən-sē) *n.* HIV.

hu•man•ism (hyo͞o′mə-nĭz′əm) *n.* **1.** A system of thought that centers on humans and their values, capacities, and worth. **2.** Concern with the interests, needs, and welfare of humans. **3.** The study of the humanities; learning in the liberal arts. **4. Humanism.** A movement of the Renaissance that emphasized secular concerns as a result of the rediscovery and study of the culture of ancient Greece and Rome.

hu•man•ist (hyo͞o′mə-nĭst) *n.* **1.** A believer in the principles of humanism. **2.** One who is concerned with or displays humanism. **3.a.** A classical scholar. **b.** A student of the liberal arts. **4. Humanist.** A Renaissance scholar devoted to Humanism. — **hu′man•is′tic** *adj.* — **hu′man•is′ti•cal•ly** *adv.*

hu•man•i•tar•i•an (hyo͞o-măn′ĭ-târ′ē-ən) *n.* One who is de-

Langston Hughes
Photographed in 1932 by Edward Weston

hula

ă pat	oi boy
ā pay	ou out
âr care	o͝o took
ä father	o͞o boot
ĕ pet	ŭ cut
ē be	ûr urge
ĭ pit	th thin
ī pie	*th* this
îr pier	hw which
ŏ pot	zh vision
ō toe	ə about, item
ô paw	

Stress marks:
′ (primary);
′ (secondary), as in
dictionary (dĭk′shə-nĕr′ē)

voted to the promotion of human welfare and the advancement of social reforms. — *adj.* Of or characteristic of a hu manitarian or humanitarianism. See Syns at **humane.**

hu•man•i•tar•i•an•ism (hyo͞o-măn′ĭ-târ′ē-ə-nĭz′əm) *n.* **1.** Concern for human welfare, esp. as manifested through philanthropy. **2.** The belief that the sole moral obligation of humankind is the improvement of human welfare. **3.** *Theol.* The doctrine holding that Jesus was human, not divine.

hu•man•i•ty (hyo͞o-măn′ĭ-tē) *n., pl.* **-ties. 1.** Human beings considered as a group; the human race. **2.** The condition or quality of being human; humanness. **3.** The quality of being humane; benevolence. **4.** A humane characteristic, attribute, or act. **5. humanities. a.** The languages and literatures of ancient Greece and Rome; the classics. **b.** Those branches of knowledge, such as literature and art, that are concerned with human thought and culture; the liberal arts. [ME *humanite* < OFr. < Lat. *hūmānitās* < *hūmānus*, human. See HUMAN.]

hu•man•ize (hyo͞o′mə-nīz′) *tr.v.* **-ized, -iz•ing, -iz•es. 1.** To portray or endow with human characteristics or attributes; make human. **2.** To imbue with humaneness or human kindness; civilize. **— hu′man•i•za′tion** (-mə-nĭ-zā′shən) *n.* **— hu′man•iz′er** *n.*

hu•man•kind (hyo͞o′mən-kīnd′) *n.* The human race.

hu•man•ly (hyo͞o′mən-lē) *adv.* **1.** In a human way. **2.** Within the scope of human means, capabilities, or powers. **3.** According to human experience or knowledge.

human nature *n.* The sum of qualities and traits shared by all human beings.

hu•man•oid (hyo͞o′mə-noid′) *adj.* Having human characteristics or form. — *n.* **1.** A being having human form. **2.** See **android.**

human rights *pl.n.* The basic rights and freedoms of all human beings, often held to include the right to life and liberty, freedom of thought and expression, and equality before the law.

human T–cell lymphotropic virus I (tē′sĕl′) *n.* HTLV-I.

human T–cell lymphotropic virus III *n.* HTLV-III.

Hum•ber (hŭm′bər). An estuary of the Trent and Ouse rivers in NE-central England.

hum•ble (hŭm′bəl) *adj.* **-bler, -blest. 1.** Marked by meekness or modesty in behavior, attitude, or spirit; not arrogant or prideful. **2.** Showing deferential or submissive respect: *a humble apology.* **3.** Low in rank, quality, or station; unpretentious or lowly. — *tr.v.* **-bled, -bling, -bles. 1.** To curtail or destroy the pride of; humiliate. **2.** To cause to be meek or modest in spirit. **3.** To give a lower condition or station to; abase. See Syns at **degrade.** [ME < OFr. < Lat. *humilis*, low, lowly < *humus*, ground. See **dhghem-*.**] **— hum′ble•ness** *n.* **— hum′bler** *n.* **— hum′bly** *adv.*

hum•ble•bee (hŭm′bəl-bē′) *n.* See **bumblebee.** [ME *humbulbe* : poss. MDu. *hummel* + ME *be, bee*, bee; see BEE[1].]

humble pie *n.* A pie formerly made from the edible organs of a deer or hog. — ***idiom.* eat humble pie.** To be forced to apologize abjectly or admit one's faults in humiliating circumstances. [Alteration (influenced by HUMBLE) of obsolete *umble pie* : ME *umbles*, edible animal organs (var. of *numbles* < Norman Fr. *nombles* < OFr., loin of veal, prob. < alteration of Lat. *lumbulus*, dim. of *lumbus*, loin) + PIE[1].]

Hum•boldt (hŭm′bōlt′, ho͝om′bôlt′), Baron **(Friedrich Heinrich) Alexander von.** 1769–1859. German naturalist and writer who advanced the science of ecology.

Hum•boldt Bay (hŭm′bōlt′). A sheltered inlet of the Pacific Ocean in NW CA.

Humboldt Current *n.* A cold ocean current flowing north along the western coast of South America. [After Baron Friedrich Heinrich Alexander von HUMBOLDT.]

Humboldt Peak. A mountain, 4,289.5 m (14,064 ft), in the Sangre de Cristo Mts. of S-central CO.

Humboldt River. A river rising in NE NV and meandering c. 467 km (290 mi) to the **Humboldt Sink**, a lake in W NV.

hum•bug (hŭm′bŭg′) *n.* **1.** Something intended to deceive; a hoax or fraud. **2.** A person who claims to be other than what he or she is; an impostor. **3.** Nonsense; rubbish. **4.** Pretense; deception. — *interj.* Used to express disbelief or disgust. — *v.* **-bugged, -bug•ging, -bugs.** — *tr.* To deceive or trick. — *intr.* To practice deception or trickery. [?] **— hum′bug′ger** *n.* **— hum′bug′ger•y** *n.*

hum•ding•er (hŭm′dĭng′ər) *n. Slang.* One that is extraordinary or remarkable. [?]

hum•drum (hŭm′drŭm′) *adj.* Lacking variety or excitement; dull. See Syns at **boring.** — *n.* Monotonous talk or routine. [Prob. < HUM.]

Hume (hyo͞om), **David.** 1711–76. British philosopher who argued that human knowledge comes from sense experience.

hu•mec•tant (hyo͞o-mĕk′tənt) *n.* A humectant substance. — *adj.* Promoting retention of moisture. [< Lat. *hūmectāns, hūmectānt-*, pr.part. of *hūmectāre*, to moisten < *hūmectus*, moist < *hūmēre*, to be moist.]

hu•mer•al (hyo͞o′mər-əl) *adj.* **1.** Of, relating to, or located in the region of the humerus or the shoulder. **2.** Relating to or being a body part analogous to the humerus.

humeral veil *n. Rom. Cath. Ch.* A vestment resembling a shawl worn over the shoulders during certain rituals.

hu•mer•us (hyo͞o′mər-əs) *n., pl.* **-mer•i** (-mə-rī′). The long bone of the arm or forelimb, extending from the shoulder to the elbow. [Lat., upper arm.]

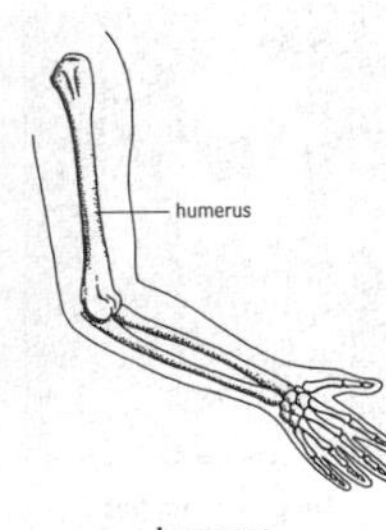

humerus

hu•mic (hyo͞o′mĭk) *adj.* Of or derived from humus.

hu•mid (hyo͞o′mĭd) *adj.* Containing or characterized by a high amount of water or water vapor: *humid air.* See Syns at **wet.** [Lat. *hūmidus* < *hūmēre*, to be moist.] **— hu′mid•ly** *adv.*

hu•mid•i•fi•er (hyo͞o-mĭd′ə-fī′ər) *n.* A device for increasing the humidity in a room, greenhouse, or other enclosure.

hu•mid•i•fy (hyo͞o-mĭd′ə-fī′) *tr.v.* **-fied, -fy•ing, -fies.** To make humid. **— hu•mid′i•fi•ca′tion** (-fĭ-kā′shən) *n.*

hu•mid•i•stat (hyo͞o-mĭd′ĭ-stăt′) *n.* An instrument designed to indicate or control the relative humidity of the air.

hu•mid•i•ty (hyo͞o-mĭd′ĭ-tē) *n.* **1.** Dampness, esp. of the air. **2.** Relative humidity. [ME *humidite* < OFr. < Med.Lat. *hūmiditās* < Lat. *hūmidus*, humid. See HUMID.]

hu•mi•dor (hyo͞o′mĭ-dôr′) *n.* A container designed for storing cigars or other tobacco products at a constant level of humidity. [HUMID + -OR[1].]

hu•mil•i•ate (hyo͞o-mĭl′ē-āt′) *tr.v.* **-at•ed, -at•ing, -ates.** To lower the pride, dignity, or self-respect of. See Syns at **degrade.** [LLat. *humiliāre, humiliāt-*, to humble < *humilis*, humble. See HUMBLE.]

hu•mil•i•a•tion (hyo͞o-mĭl′ē-ā′shən) *n.* **1.** The act of humiliating; degradation. **2.** The state of being humiliated or disgraced; shame. **3.** A humiliating condition or circumstance.

hu•mil•i•ty (hyo͞o-mĭl′ĭ-tē) *n.* The quality or condition of being humble. [ME *humilite* < OFr. < LLat. *humilitās* < *humilis*, humble. See HUMBLE.]

hum•ming•bird (hŭm′ĭng-bûrd′) *n.* Any of numerous New World birds of the family Trochilidae, usu. very small and having brilliant iridescent plumage, a slender bill, and wings that can beat rapidly, enabling the bird to hover.

hummingbird

hum•mock (hŭm′ək) *n.* **1.** A low mound or ridge of earth; a knoll. **2.** Also **ham•mock** (hăm′ək). A tract of forested land that rises above an adjacent marsh in the southern United States. **3.** A ridge or hill of ice in an ice field. [?] **— hum′mock•y** *adj.*

hum•mus also **hum•us** or **hom•mos** (ho͝om′əs, hŭm′-) *n.* A mixture of mashed chickpeas, tahini, oil, lemon juice, and garlic, eaten esp. as a dip. [Ar. *ḥummuṣ*, chickpea.]

hu•mon•gous (hyo͞o-mŏng′gəs, -mŭng′-) or **hu•mun•gous** (-mŭng′-) *adj. Slang.* Extremely large; enormous. [Perh. blend of HUGE and MONSTROUS or TREMENDOUS.]

hu•mor (hyo͞o′mər) *n.* **1.** The quality that makes something laughable or amusing; funniness. **2.** That which is intended to induce laughter or amusement. **3.** The ability to perceive, enjoy, or express what is amusing, comical, incongruous, or absurd. **4.** One of the four fluids of the body, blood, phlegm, choler, and black bile, whose relative proportions were thought in ancient physiology to determine disposition and general health. **5.** *Physiol.* **a.** A body fluid, such as blood, lymph, or bile. **b.** Aqueous humor. **c.** Vitreous humor. **6.** Disposition or temperament. **7.** An often temporary state of mind; a mood. **8.a.** A sudden, unanticipated whim. See Syns at **mood[1]. b.** Capricious or peculiar behavior. — *tr.v.* **-mored, -mor•ing, -mors. 1.** To comply with the wishes or ideas of; indulge. **2.** To adapt or accommodate oneself to. — ***idiom.* out of humor.** In a bad mood; irritable. [ME, fluid < OFr. *umor* < Lat. *ūmor.*]

hu•mor•al (hyo͞o′mər-əl) *adj.* **1.** *Physiol.* Relating to body fluids, esp. serum. **2.** Of or arising from any of the body humors.

humoral immunity *n.* The component of the immune response involving the transformation of B-lymphocytes into plasma cells that produce and secrete antibodies to a specific antigen.

hu•mor•esque (hyo͞o′mə-rĕsk′) *n. Mus.* A whimsical or light-spirited composition. [Ger. *Humoreske* < *Humor*, humor < E. HUMOR.]

hu•mor•ist (hyo͞o′mər-ĭst) *n.* **1.** A person with a good sense of humor. **2.** A performer or writer of humorous material.

hu•mor•less (hyo͞o′mər-lĭs) *adj.* **1.** Lacking a sense of humor. **2.** Said or done without humor. **— hu′mor•less•ly** *adv.* **— hu′mor•less•ness** *n.*

hu•mor•ous (hyo͞o′mər-əs) *adj.* **1.** Full of or characterized by humor; funny: *a humorous story.* **2.** Employing or showing humor; witty: *a humorous writer.* **3.** *Archaic.* Given to moods or whims; capricious. **4.** *Obsolete.* Damp; moist. **— hu′mor•ous•ly** *adv.* **— hu′mor•ous•ness** *n.*

hu•mour (hyo͞o′mər) *n. & v. Chiefly British.* Var. of **humor.**

Hungary

hump (hŭmp) *n.* **1.** A rounded mass or protuberance, such as the fleshy structure on the back of a camel or of some cattle. **2.** A deformity of the back in humans caused by an abnormal convex curvature of the upper spine. **3.a.** A low mound of earth; a hummock. **b.** A mountain range. **4.** *Chiefly British.* A fit of depression; an emotional slump. — *v.* **humped, hump•ing, humps.** — *tr.* **1.** To bend or round into a hump; arch. **2.** *Slang.* **a.** To exert (oneself). **b.** To carry, esp. on the back. **3.** *Vulgar Slang.* To engage in sexual intercourse with. — *intr.* **1.** *Slang.* To exert oneself. **2.** *Slang.* To hurry. **3.** *Vulgar Slang.* To engage in sexual intercourse. — ***idiom.* over the hump.** Past the worst or most difficult part or stage. [Prob. of LGer. orig.] **— humped** (hŭmpt) *adj.*

hump·back (hŭmp′băk′) *n.* **1.** See **hunchback** 1. **2.** A humped upper back. **3.** A humpback whale. — **hump′backed′** *adj.*

humpback salmon *n.* See **pink salmon.**

humpback whale *n.* A baleen whale *(Megaptera novaeangliae)* having a rounded back and long knobby flippers.

Hum·per·dinck (ho͝om′pər-dĭngk′, hŭm′-), **Engelbert.** 1854–1921. German composer who wrote the fairy tale opera *Hansel and Gretel* (1893).

humph (hŭmf, həmf) *interj.* Used to express doubt, displeasure, or contempt.

Hum·phrey (hŭm′frē, hŭmp′-), **Hubert Horatio.** 1911–78. Vice President of the U.S. (1965–69).

hump·y (hŭm′pē) *adj.* **-i·er, -i·est. 1.** Covered with or containing humps. **2.** Resembling a hump.

hu·mun·gous (hyo͞o-mŭng′gəs) *adj. Slang.* Var. of **humongous.**

hu·mus¹ (hyo͞o′məs) *n.* An organic substance of decayed vegetable or animal matter that provides plants nutrients and increases soil water retention. [Lat., soil. See **dhghem-***.]

hum·us² (ho͞om′əs, hŭm′-) *n.* Var. of **hummus.**

Hun (hŭn) *n.* **1.** A member of a nomadic pastoralist people who invaded Europe in the fourth and fifth centuries A.D. and were defeated in 455. **2.** Often **hun.** A barbarous or destructive person. **3.** *Offensive Slang.* Used as a disparaging term for a German. [< LLat. *Hunnī*, the Huns < Turki *Hunyü.*]

Hu·nan (ho͞o′nän′). A province of SE-central China; under Chinese rule since the 3rd cent. B.C. Cap. Changsha. Pop. 56,220,000.

hunch (hŭnch) *n.* **1.** An intuitive feeling or a premonition. **2.** A hump. **3.** A lump or chunk. — *v.* **hunched, hunch·ing, hunch·es.** — *tr.* **1.** To bend or draw up into a hump. **2.** To push or shove. — *intr.* **1.** To assume a crouched or cramped posture. **2.** To thrust oneself forward. [?]

hunch·back (hŭnch′băk′) *n.* **1.** An individual whose back is hunched due to abnormal convex curvature of the upper spine. **2.** An abnormally curved or hunched back. **3.** Kyphosis. — **hunch′backed′** *adj.*

hun·dred (hŭn′drĭd) *n., pl.* **hundred** or **-dreds. 1.** The cardinal number equal to 10 × 10 or 10^2. **2.** The number in the third position left of the decimal point in an Arabic numeral. **3.** A note of currency worth 100 dollars. **4. hundreds.** The numbers between 100 and 999. **5.** An administrative division of some counties in England and the United States. [ME < OE. See **dekm̥***.] — **hun′dred** *adj.*

hun·dredth (hŭn′drĭdth) *n.* **1.** The ordinal number matching the number 100 in a series. **2.** One of 100 equal parts. — **hun′dredth** *adj.*

hun·dred·weight (hŭn′drĭd-wāt′) *n., pl.* **hundredweight** or **-weights. 1.** A unit of weight in the U.S. Customary System equal to 100 pounds (45.36 kilograms). **2.** A unit of weight in the British Imperial System equal to 112 pounds (50.80 kilograms).

hung (hŭng) *v.* P.t. and p.part. of **hang.** See Usage Note at **hang.**

Hung. *abbr.* Hungarian; Hungary.

Hun·gar·i·an (hŭng-gâr′ē-ən) *adj.* Of or relating to Hungary or its people, language, or culture. — *n.* **1.** A native or inhabitant of Hungary. **2.** The Finno-Ugric language of the Magyars that is the official language of Hungary.

Hun·ga·ry (hŭng′gə-rē). A country of central Europe. An independent kingdom (until 1526) and later part of the Ottoman Empire and then the dual monarchy of Austria-Hungary (1867–1918), Hungary came under Communist rule in 1949. A new constitution, guaranteeing free multiparty elections, was adopted in 1989. Cap. Budapest. Pop. 10,657,000.

hun·ger (hŭng′gər) *n.* **1.a.** A strong desire or need for food. **b.** The discomfort, weakness, or pain caused by a prolonged lack of food. **2.** A strong desire or craving. — *v.* **-gered, -ger·ing, -gers.** — *intr.* **1.** To have a need or desire for food. **2.** To have a strong desire or craving. — *tr.* To cause to experience hunger; make hungry. [ME < OE *hungor.*]

hunger strike *n.* A voluntary fast undertaken as a means of protest, as by a prisoner. — **hunger striker** *n.*

hung jury *n. Law.* A jury that is unable to agree on a verdict.

Hung·nam (ho͝ong′näm′). A city of E-central North Korea on the Sea of Japan NNE of Seoul, South Korea. Pop. 260,000.

hung-over also **hung over** or **hung·o·ver** (hŭng′ō′vər) *adj.* Suffering from a hangover.

hun·gry (hŭng′grē) *adj.* **-gri·er, -gri·est. 1.** Experiencing a desire or need for food. **2.** Extremely desirous; avid. **3.** Characterized by or expressing hunger or craving. **4.** Lacking richness or fertility. [ME *hungri* < OE *hungrig* < *hungor*, hunger.] — **hun′gri·ly** *adv.* — **hun′gri·ness** *n.*

Hung·shui He (ho͝ong′shwā′ hœ). See **Hongshui He.**

hung up *adj. Informal.* **1.** Delayed; hindered: *motorists hung up in traffic.* **2.** Also **hung-up** (hŭng′ŭp′). Anxious; nervous. **3.** Over involved or preoccupied.

hunk (hŭngk) *n.* **1.** *Informal.* A large piece; a chunk. **2.** *Slang.* A man with a well-developed physique considered sexually attractive. [Perh. < Flem. *hunke*, a piece of food.]

hun·ker (hŭng′kər) *intr.v.* **-kered, -ker·ing, -kers. 1.** To squat close to the ground; crouch: *hunkered down to avoid the icy wind.* **2.** To hold stubbornly to a position. — *n.* **hunkers.** The haunches. [Perh. of Scand. orig.]

Hunk·pa·pa (hŭngk′pä′pä) *n., pl.* **Hunkpapa** or **-pas.** A member of a Native American people constituting a subdivision of the Teton Sioux.

hun·ky (hŭng′kē) *n., pl.* **-kies.** *Offensive Slang.* Used as a disparaging term for a person, esp. a laborer, from east-central Europe. [Prob. alteration of BOHUNK.]

hun·ky-do·ry (hŭng′kē-dôr′ē, -dōr′ē) *adj. Slang.* Perfectly satisfactory; fine. [Prob. alteration of *hunky*, safe, all right < obsolete *hunk*, goal < Du. *honk* < Frisian *hunk.*]

Hun·nish (hŭn′ĭsh) *adj.* **1.** Of, relating to, or characteristic of the Huns. **2.** Often **hunnish.** Barbarous; destructive. — **Hun′nish·ness** *n.*

hunt (hŭnt) *v.* **hunt·ed, hunt·ing, hunts.** — *tr.* **1.** To pursue or lie in wait for (game) for food or sport. **2.** To search through (an area) for prey. **3.** To make use of (hounds, for example) in pursuing game. **4.** To pursue intensively so as to capture or kill. **5.** To seek out; search for. **6.** To drive out forcibly, esp. by harassing; chase away. — *intr.* **1.** To pursue game. **2.** To make a search; seek. **3.** *Engineering.* **a.** To oscillate about a selected value. Used of a machine, an instrument, or a system. **b.** To swing back and forth; oscillate. Used of an indicator on a display or an instrument panel. — *n.* **1.** The act or sport of hunting. **2.a.** A hunting expedition or outing, usu. with horses and hounds. **b.** Those taking part in such an expedition or outing. **3.** A diligent search or pursuit. [ME *hunten* < OE *huntian.*]

Hunt (hŭnt), **(James Henry) Leigh.** 1784–1859. British writer and editor of the *Examiner* (1806–21).

Hunt, Richard Morris. 1827–95. Amer. architect who designed an extension of the U.S. Capitol (1855).

Hunt, Ward. 1810–86. American jurist; associate justice of the U.S. Supreme Court (1873–82).

Hunt, (William) Holman. 1827–1910. British painter who with Rossetti and Millais founded the Pre-Raphaelite Brotherhood.

hunt-and-peck (hŭnt′ən-pĕk′) *n.* A slow method of typing in which an untrained typist finds each key before striking it.

hunt·er (hŭn′tər) *n.* **1.** One who hunts game. **2.** A dog bred or trained for use in hunting. **3.** A horse, typically a strong fast jumper, that has been bred or trained for use in hunting. **4.** One who searches for or seeks something.

hunt·er-gath·er·er (hŭn′tər-gath′ər-ər) *n.* A member of a people subsisting on food obtained by hunting and foraging.

hunt·ing (hŭn′tĭng) *n.* **1.** The activity or sport of pursuing game. **2.** The act of conducting a search for something: *house hunting.* **3.** *Electron.* The periodic variation in speed of a synchronous motor with respect to the current.

Hun·ting·ton (hŭn′tĭng-tən). **1.** A city of NE IN SW of Fort Wayne. Pop. 16,389. **2.** A city of W WV on the Ohio R. W of Charleston; founded 1871. Pop. 54,844.

Huntington, Collis Potter. 1821–1900. Amer. transportation executive who built the W section of the first U.S. transcontinental railroad (completed 1869).

Huntington, Samuel. 1731–96. Amer. Revolutionary leader who was president of the Continental Congress (1779–81 and 1783) and a signer of the Declaration of Independence.

Huntington Beach. A city of S CA on the Pacific Ocean SE of Long Beach. Pop. 181,519.

Huntington Park. A city of S CA, a suburb of Los Angeles. Pop. 56,065.

Hun·ting·ton's chorea (hŭn′tĭng-tənz) *n.* A rare inherited disease of the central nervous system characterized by progressive dementia, abnormal posture, and involuntary movements. [After George *Huntington* (1851?–1916), Amer. physician.]

Huntington Station. A community of SE NY on the N shore of W Long I. Pop. 28,247.

hunt·ress (hŭn′trĭs) *n.* A woman who hunts.

hunts·man (hŭnts′mən) *n.* **1.** A man who hunts. **2.** A man who manages the hounds in the hunting field.

Hunts·ville (hŭnts′vĭl′). **1.** A city of N AL ENE of Decatur; settled in 1805. Pop. 159,789. **2.** A city of E-central TX N of Houston. Pop. 27,925.

Hu·nya·di or **Hu·nya·dy** (ho͝on′yä-dē, -yô-), **János.** 1387?–1456. Hungarian general and nationalist leader who fought to protect Hungary from Turkish conquest (1437–56).

Hu·pei or **Hu·peh** (ho͞o′pā′, hü′-). See **Hubei.**

hur·dle (hûr′dl) *n.* **1.** *Sports.* **a.** A light portable barrier over which competitors must leap in certain races. **b. hurdles.** A race in which a series of such barriers must be jumped without the competitors' breaking their stride. **2.** An obstacle or difficulty to be overcome. **3.** *Chiefly British.* A portable framework made of intertwined branches or wattle and used for temporary fencing. **4.** *Chiefly British.* A frame or sledge on which condemned persons were dragged to execution. — *v.* **-dled, -dling, -dles.** — *tr.* **1.** To leap over (a barrier) in or as if in a race. **2.** To overcome or deal with successfully; surmount. — *intr.* To leap over a barrier or other obstacle. [ME *hurdel*, portable fence panel < OE *hyrdel.*] — **hur′dler** *n.*

hur·dy-gur·dy (hûr′dē-gûr′dē, hûr′dē-gûr′dē) *n., pl.* **-dies.**

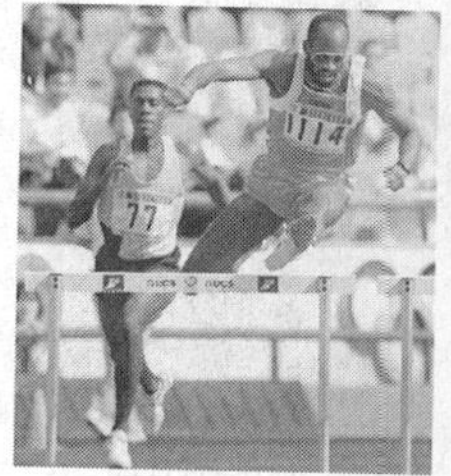

hurdle
Edwin Moses of the United States (#1114) and Allan Ince of Barbados (#77) at the Seoul Summer Olympics, 1988

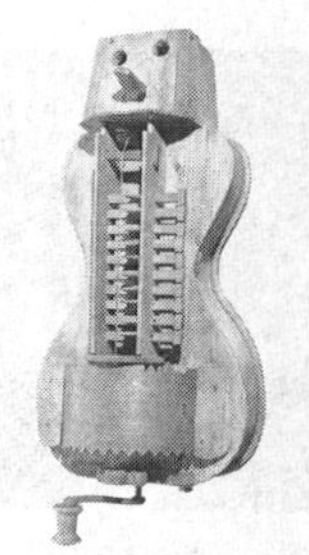
hurdy-gurdy
Early 19th-century American from northern Maine or eastern Canada

ă pat	oi boy
ā pay	ou out
âr care	o͝o took
ä father	o͞o boot
ĕ pet	ŭ cut
ē be	ûr urge
ĭ pit	th thin
ī pie	*th* this
îr pier	hw which
ŏ pot	zh vision
ō toe	ə about, item
ô paw	

Stress marks:
′ (primary);
′ (secondary), as in dictionary (dĭk′shə-nĕr′ē)

hurricane lamp

Mus. **1.** A medieval stringed instrument played by turning a rosined wheel with a crank and depressing keys connected to tangents on the strings. **2.** Any instrument, such as a barrel organ, played by turning a crank. [Prob. imit.]

hurl (hûrl) *v.* **hurled, hurl•ing, hurls.** —*tr.* **1.** To throw with great force; fling. See Syns at **throw. 2.** To send with great vigor; thrust. **3.** To throw down; overthrow. **4.** To utter vehemently. —*intr.* **1.** To move with great speed, force, or violence; hurtle. **2.** To throw something with force. **3.** *Baseball.* To pitch the ball. [ME *hurlen.*] —**hurl** *n.* —**hurl′er** *n.*

hurl•ing (hûr′lĭng) *n. Sports.* An Irish game resembling lacrosse played with a broad-bladed netless stick.

hur•ly-bur•ly (hûr′lē-bûr′lē) *n., pl.* **-lies.** Noisy confusion; tumult. [Alteration and redup. of *hurling,* gerund of HURL.]

Hu•ron (hyo͝or′ən, -ŏn′) *n., pl.* **Huron** or **-rons. 1.** A member of a Native American confederacy formerly inhabiting southeast Ontario around Lake Simcoe, with small present-day populations in Quebec and northeast Oklahoma, where they are known as Wyandot. **2.** The Iroquoian language of the Huron. [Fr., boor, Huron < OFr. *hure,* bristling hair.]

Huron, Lake. The second largest of the Great Lakes, between SE Ontario, Canada, and E MI.

hur•rah (ho͝o-rä′, -rô′, hə-) also **hoo•ray** or **hur•ray** (-rā′) —*interj.* Used as an exclamation of pleasure, approval, elation, or victory. —*n.* **1.** A shout of "hurrah." **2.** Excitement; fanfare. —*v.* **-rahed, -rah•ing, -rahs** also **-rayed, -ray•ing, -rays.** —*tr.* To applaud, cheer, or approve by shouting "hurrah." —*intr.* To shout "hurrah." [Alteration of HUZZAH.]

hur•ri•cane (hûr′ĭ-kān′, hŭr′-) *n.* **1.** A tropical cyclone originating in the equatorial regions of the Atlantic Ocean or Caribbean Sea, traveling north, northwest, or northeast from its point of origin, and usu. involving heavy rains. **2.** A wind with a speed greater than 74 miles (119 kilometers) per hour. **3.** Something resembling a hurricane in force or speed. [Sp. *huracán* < Carib *huracan, furacan.*]

hurricane deck *n. Naut.* The upper deck on a passenger steamship.

hurricane lamp *n.* A lamp with a candle, an oiled wick, or an electric bulb protected by a glass chimney.

hur•ried (hûr′ēd, hŭr′-) *adj.* **1.a.** Moving or acting rapidly. **b.** Required to move or act more rapidly; rushed. **2.** Done in great haste. —**hur′ried•ly** *adv.* —**hur′ried•ness** *n.*

hur•ry (hûr′ē, hŭr′-) *v.* **-ried, -ry•ing, -ries.** —*intr.* To move or act with speed or haste. —*tr.* **1.** To cause to move or act with speed or haste. **2.** To cause to move or act with undue haste; rush. **3.** To speed the progress or completion of; expedite. —*n., pl.* **-ries. 1.** The act or an instance of hurrying; hastened progress. **2.** Activity or motion that is often unduly hurried; haste. See Syns at **haste. 3.** The need or wish to hurry; a condition of urgency. [Poss. ME *horien,* perh. var. of *harien,* to harass. See HARRY.] —**hur′ri•er** *n.*

hur•ry-scur•ry also **hur•ry-skur•ry** (hûr′ē-skûr′ē, hŭr′ē-skŭr′ē) —*intr.v.* **-ried, -ry•ing, -ries.** To move or act with undue hurry and confusion. —*n., pl.* **-ries.** Confused haste; agitation. [Redup. of HURRY.]

Hurst (hûrst). A city of NE TX, a suburb of Fort Worth. Pop. 33,574.

Hussein
Photographed in 1987

Hur•ston (hûr′stən), **Zora Neale.** 1901?–60. Amer. writer whose works include *Their Eyes Were Watching God* (1937).

hurt (hûrt) *v.* **hurt, hurt•ing, hurts.** —*tr.* **1.** To cause physical damage or pain to; injure. **2.** To cause mental or emotional suffering to; distress. **3.** To damage or impair. See Syns at **spoil.** —*intr.* **1.** To have or produce a feeling of physical pain or discomfort. **2.a.** To cause distress or damage. **b.** To have an adverse effect. **3.** *Informal.* To experience distress, esp. of a financial kind; be in need. —*n.* **1.** Something that hurts; a pain, an injury, or a wound. **2.** Mental suffering; anguish. **3.** A wrong; harm. [ME *hurten,* poss. < OFr. *hurter,* to bang into, perh. of Gmc. orig.] —**hurt′er** *n.*

hurt•ful (hûrt′fəl) *adj.* Causing injury or suffering; damaging. —**hurt′ful•ly** *adv.* —**hurt′ful•ness** *n.*

hur•tle (hûr′tl) *v.* **-tled, -tling, -tles.** —*intr.* To move with or as if with great speed and a rushing noise: *A train hurtled past.* —*tr.* To fling with great force; hurl. [ME *hurtlen,* to collide, freq. of *hurten,* to knock against, damage. See HURT.]

hurt•less (hûrt′lĭs) *adj.* **1.** Causing no hurt; harmless. **2.** Having no hurt; unhurt.

Aldous Huxley

Hus (hŭs, ho͞os), **Jan.** See John **Huss.**

Hu•sain or **Hu•sayn** (ho͞o-sān′). See **Hussein.**

hus•band (hŭz′bənd) *n.* **1.** A man joined to a woman in marriage; a male spouse. **2.** *Chiefly British.* A manager or steward, as of a household. **3.** *Archaic.* A prudent thrifty manager. —*tr.v.* **-band•ed, -band•ing, -bands. 1.** To use sparingly or economically; conserve: *husband one's energy.* **2.** *Archaic.* To find a husband for. [ME *huseband* < OE *hūsbōnda* < ON *hūsbōndi* : *hūs,* house + *bōndi, būandi,* householder, pr.part. of *būa,* to dwell; see **bheuə-*.**]

hus•band•man (hŭz′bənd-mən) *n.* One whose occupation is husbandry; a farmer.

hus•band•ry (hŭz′bən-drē) *n.* **1.a.** The act or practice of cultivating crops and breeding and raising livestock; agriculture. **b.** The application of scientific principles to agriculture, esp. to animal breeding. **2.** Careful management or conservation of resources; economy. [ME *husbondri* < *huseband,* husband. See HUSBAND.]

hush (hŭsh) *v.* **hushed, hush•ing, hush•es.** —*tr.* **1.** To make silent or quiet. **2.** To calm; soothe. **3.** To keep from public knowledge; suppress mention of. Often used with *up.* —*intr.* To be or become silent or still. —*n.* A silence or stillness, esp. after noise. —*adj. Archaic.* Silent; quiet. [Prob. back-formation < ME *husht,* silent, of imit. orig.]

hush-hush (hŭsh′hŭsh′) *adj. Informal.* Secret; confidential.

hush money *n. Informal.* A bribe paid to keep a secret.

hush•pup•py or **hush puppy** (hŭsh′pŭp′ē) *n.* A small cake of cornmeal fried in deep fat. [?]

husk (hŭsk) *n.* **1.** The outer membranous or green envelope of some fruits or seeds, as that of a walnut or an ear of corn. **2.** A shell or outer covering, esp. when considered worthless. **3.** A framework serving as a support. —*tr.v.* **husked, husk•ing, husks.** To remove the husk from. [ME; prob. akin to *hose,* stocking, sheath. See HOSE.] —**husk′er** *n.*

husk•ing bee (hŭs′kĭng) *n.* See **cornhusking** 2.

husk tomato *n.* See **ground cherry.**

husk•y¹ (hŭs′kē) *adj.* **-i•er, -i•est. 1.** Hoarse or rough in quality: *a husky voice.* **2.a.** Resembling a husk. **b.** Containing husks. [< HUSK.] —**husk′i•ly** *adv.*

husk•y² (hŭs′kē) *adj.* **-i•er, -i•est. 1.** Strongly built; burly. **2.** Heavily built. —*n., pl.* **-ies.** A husky person. [Perh. < HUSK.]

hus•ky³ also **hus•kie** (hŭs′kē) *n., pl.* **-kies. 1.** Often **Husky** or **Huskie.** A dog of a breed developed in Siberia for pulling sleds and having a dense, variously colored coat. **2.** A similar dog of Arctic origin. [Prob. < alteration of ESKIMO.]

Huss or **Hus** (hŭs, ho͞os), **John** or **Jan.** 1372?–1415. Bohemian religious reformer who was excommunicated (1409) for attacking the corruption of the clergy. —**Huss′ite′** (hŭs′īt′, ho͞os′-) *adj. & n.* —**Huss′it′ism** *n.*

hus•sar (hə-zär′, -sär′) *n.* **1.** A horseman of the Hungarian light cavalry organized during the 15th century. **2.** A member of any similar European unit. [Hung. *huszár* < Serbian *husar,* highwayman < OItal. *corsaro.* See CORSAIR.]

Hus•sein or **Hu•sain** or **Hu•sayn** (ho͞o-sān′). b. 1935. King of Jordan (since 1952) who lost control of W Jordan in the Arab-Israeli War (1967).

Hussein, Saddam. b. 1937. Iraqi president (since 1979) who waged war against Iran over a territorial dispute (1980–88) and invaded and occupied Kuwait (1990–91).

Hus•serl (ho͞os′ərl, -ĕrl), **Edmund.** 1859–1938. Austrian-born German philosopher who helped develop phenomenology.

hus•sy (hŭz′ē, hŭs′ē) *n., pl.* **-sies. 1.** A woman considered brazen or immoral. **2.** A girl considered saucy or impudent. [Alteration of ME *houswif,* housewife.]

hust•ings (hŭs′tĭngz) *pl.n. (used with a sing. or pl. v.)* **1.a.** A place where political campaign speeches are made. **b.** The activities involved in political campaigning. **2.** *Chiefly British.* A court formerly held in some English cities and still held infrequently in London. **3.** *Chiefly British.* **a.** A platform on which candidates for Parliament formerly stood to address the electors. **b.** The proceedings of a parliamentary election. [< ME *husting,* court of common pleas < OE *hūsting,* court < ON *hūsthing* : *hūs,* house + *thing,* assembly.]

hus•tle (hŭs′əl) *v.* **-tled, -tling, -tles.** —*tr.* **1.** To jostle or shove roughly. **2.** To convey in a hurried or rough manner. **3.** To cause or urge to proceed quickly. **4.** To gain by energetic effort. **5.** *Slang.* **a.** To sell or get by questionable or aggressive means. **b.** To pressure into buying or doing something. —*intr.* **1.** To jostle and push. **2.** To work or move energetically and rapidly. **3.** To act aggressively, esp. in business dealings. **4.** *Slang.* To obtain something by deceitful or illicit means. **5.** *Slang.* To solicit customers. Used of a pimp or prostitute. —*n.* **1.** The act or an instance of jostling or shoving. **2.** Energetic activity; drive. **3.** *Slang.* An illicit or unethical way of doing business or obtaining money; a fraud or deceit. [Du. *husselen,* to shake < MDu. *husselen,* freq. of *hutsen.*] —**hus′tler** *n.*

Hus•ton (hyo͞o′stən), **John.** 1906–87. Amer. filmmaker whose works include *The African Queen* (1951).

hut (hŭt) *n.* **1.** A crude or makeshift dwelling or shelter; a shack. **2.** A temporary structure for sheltering troops. —*tr. & intr.v.* **hut•ted, hut•ting, huts.** To shelter or take shelter in a hut. [Fr. *hutte,* of Gmc. orig. See **(s)keu-*.**]

hutch (hŭch) *n.* **1.** A pen or coop for small animals, esp. rabbits. **2.** A cupboard with drawers for storage and usu. open shelves on top, often used for dishes. **3.** A chest or bin for storage. **4.** A hut. [ME *huche,* chest < OFr. < Med.Lat. *hūtica,* poss. of Gmc. orig.]

Hutch•ins (hŭch′ĭnz), **Robert Maynard.** 1899–1977. Amer. educator who was president (1929–45) and chancellor (1945–51) of the University of Chicago.

Hutch•in•son (hŭch′ĭn-sən). A city of S-central KS on the Arkansas R. NW of Wichita. Pop. 39,308.

Hutchinson, Anne. 1591–1643. English-born Amer. colonist who was banished from Boston (1637) for her religious beliefs.

Hutchinson, Thomas. 1711–80. Amer. colonial official who served as governor of Massachusetts (1771–74).

Hutch•in•son-Gil•ford syndrome (hŭch′ĭn-sən-gĭl′fərd) *n.* See **progeria.** [After Sir Jonathan *Hutchinson* (1828–1913) and Hastings *Gilford* (1861–1941), British physicians.]

hut•ment (hŭt′mənt) *n.* An encampment of huts.

Hut•ter•ite (hŭt′ə-rīt′, ho͝ot′-) *n.* A member of an Anabaptist sect originating in Moravia and now living communally in parts of Canada and the northwest United States. [After Jakob *Hutter* (d. 1536), Moravian Anabaptist leader.]

hutz•pah (ĸʜo͝ot′spə, ho͝ot′-) *n.* Var. of **chutzpah.**

Hux•ley (hŭks′lē), **Aldous Leonard.** 1894–1963. British writer whose best-known work is *Brave New World* (1932).

Huxley, Andrew Fielding. b. 1917. British physiologist who shared a 1963 Nobel Prize.

Huxley, Sir **Julian Sorell.** 1887–1975. British biologist and writer who was director general of UNESCO (1946–48).

Huxley, Thomas Henry. 1825–95. British biologist who championed Darwin's theory of evolution in works such as *Zoological Evidences as to Man's Place in Nature* (1863).

Hu Yao•bang (ho͞o′ you′bäng′, hü′) also **Hu Yao-pang** (-päng′). 1915–89. Chinese politician who served as general secretary of the Communist Party (1980–89).

Huy•gens (hī′gənz, hoi′gĕns), **Christiaan.** 1629–95. Dutch physicist who discovered Saturn's rings (1655) and pioneered the use of the pendulum in clocks (1657).

Huy•gens' principle (hī′gənz) *n.* The principle that any point on a wave front of light may be regarded as the source of secondary waves and that the surface that is tangent to the secondary waves can be used to determine the future position of the wave front. [After Christiaan Huygens.]

Huys•mans (wēs-mäɴs′), **Joris Karl.** 1848–1907. French writer whose realistic novels include *En Rade* (1887).

Huy•ton-with-Ro•by (hīt′n-wĭ*th*-rō′bē, -wĭth-). An urban district of NW England, a suburb of Liverpool. Pop. 174,100.

huz•zah also **huz•za** (hə-zä′) *—interj.* Used to express joy, encouragement, or triumph. *—n.* **1.** A shout of "huzzah." **2.** A cheer. [Perh. var. of ME *hisse,* heave!. See hoist.]

H.V. *abbr.* **1.** High velocity. **2.** High voltage.

HW *abbr.* **1.** High water. **2.** Hot water.

Hwang Ho (hwäng′ hō′). See **Huang He.**

Hwei (hwā) *n.* Var. of **Hui.**

hwy *abbr.* Highway.

hy•a•cinth (hī′ə-sĭnth) *n.* **1.a.** A bulbous Mediterranean plant *(Hyacinthus orientalis)* having narrow leaves and variously colored, usu. fragrant flowers, with a funnel-shaped perianth. **b.** Any of several similar or related plants, such as the grape hyacinth. **2.** *Gk. Myth.* A plant that sprang from the blood of the slain Hyacinthus. **3.** *Color.* A deep purplish blue to vivid violet. **4.a.** A reddish or cinnamon-colored variety of transparent zircon, used as a gemstone. **b.** A blue precious stone, perhaps the sapphire, known in antiquity. [Lat. *hyacinthus* < Gk. *huakinthos,* wild hyacinth.] **—hy′a•cin′thine** (-sĭn′thĭn, -thīn′) *adj.*

hyacinth bean *n.* A vine *(Dolichos lablab)* of the Old World tropics, having edible pods and seeds.

Hy•a•cin•thus (hī′ə-sĭn′thəs) *n. Gk. Myth.* A beautiful young man loved but accidentally killed by Apollo, from whose blood Apollo caused the hyacinth to grow.

Hy•a•des (hī′ə-dēz′) *pl.n.* **1.** *Gk. Myth.* The five daughters of Atlas and sisters of the Pleiades, placed by Zeus among the stars. **2.** A cluster of stars in the constellation Taurus. [Lat. < Gk. *Huades.*]

hy•ae•na (hī-ē′nə) *n.* Var. of **hyena.**

hy•a•lin (hī′ə-lĭn) also **hy•a•line** (-lĭn, -līn′) *n.* **1.** *Physiol.* The uniform matrix of hyaline cartilage. **2.** *Pathol.* A translucent product of some degenerative skin conditions. [Gk. *hualos,* glass + -in.]

hy•a•line (hī′ə-lĭn, -līn′) *adj.* Resembling glass, as in translucence or transparency; glassy. *—n.* Something translucent or transparent. [LLat. *hyalīnus* < Gk. *hualinos,* of glass < *hualos,* glass.]

hyaline membrane disease *n.* See **respiratory distress syndrome.**

hy•a•lite (hī′ə-līt′) *n.* A clear colorless opal. [Gk. *hualos,* glass + -ite[1].]

hy•a•loid (hī′ə-loid′) *adj.* Glassy or transparent in appearance; hyaline. [Gk. *hualoeidēs* : *hualos,* glass + *-oeidēs,* -oid.]

hy•a•lo•plasm (hī′ə-lō-plăz′əm) *n.* The clear fluid portion of cytoplasm as distinguished from the granular and netlike components. [Gk. *hualos,* glass + -plasm.]

hy•al•u•ron•ic acid (hī′ə-lo͞o-rŏn′ĭk) *n.* A gellike polysaccharide found in the tissue space, the synovial fluid of joints, and the vitreous humor of the eyes and acts as a binding, lubricating, and protective agent. [< Gk. *hualos,* glass.]

hy•a•lu•ron•i•dase (hī′ə-lo͞o-rŏn′ĭ-dās′, -dāz′) *n.* An enzyme that inactivates hyaluronic acid in the body, thereby increasing tissue permeability to fluids.

hy•brid (hī′brĭd) *n.* **1.** *Genet.* The offspring of genetically dissimilar parents or stock, esp. that of breeding plants or animals of different varieties, species, or races. **2.a.** Something of mixed origin or composition. **b.** Something, such as a computer or power plant, having two kinds of components that produce the same or similar results. **3.** A word whose elements are derived from different languages. [Lat. *hybrida.*] **—hy′brid•ism, hy•brid′i•ty** *n.* **—hy′brid•ist** *n.*

hy•brid•ize (hī′brĭ-dīz′) *intr. & tr.v.* **-ized, -iz•ing, -iz•es.** To produce or cause to produce hybrids; crossbreed. **—hy′brid•i•za′tion** (-brĭ-dĭ-zā′shən) *n.* **—hy′brid•iz′er** *n.*

hy•brid•o•ma (hī′brĭ-dō′mə) *n.* A cell produced in the laboratory from the fusion of an antibody-producing lymphocyte and a myeloma tumor cell and able to produce an antibody.

hybrid vigor *n.* Increased vigor or other superior qualities arising from the crossbreeding of genetically different plants or animals.

hy•da•thode (hī′də-thōd′) *n.* A water-excreting microscopic epidermal structure in many plants. [Gk. *hudōr, hudat-,* water; see **wed-**[1]***** + *hodos,* way, road.]

hy•da•tid (hī′də-tĭd) *n.* **1.** A cyst formed as a result of infestation by larvae of the tapeworm *Echinococcus granulosus.* **2.** The encysted larva of *E. granulosus.* [Gk. *hudatis, hudatid-,* watery vesicle < *hudōr, hudat-,* water. See **wed-**[1]*****.]

Hyde (hīd), **Douglas.** 1860–1949. Irish nationalist and writer who was president of Ireland (1938–45).

Hyde, Edward. 1st Earl of Clarendon. 1609–74. English politician who was adviser to Charles I during the Civil War.

Hyde Park[1]**.** A large public park in W-central London, England, famous for its soapbox orators.

Hyde Park[2]**.** A village of SE NY on the E bank of the Hudson R. N of Poughkeepsie; birth and burial place of President Franklin D. Roosevelt. Pop. 2,550.

Hy•der•a•bad (hī′dər-ə-băd′, -bäd′, hī′drə-). **1.** A city of S-central India ESE of Bombay; founded 1589. Pop. 2,187,262. **2.** A city of S Pakistan on the Indus R. NE of Karachi; founded 1768. Pop. 745,000.

hydr– *pref.* Var. of **hydro–.**

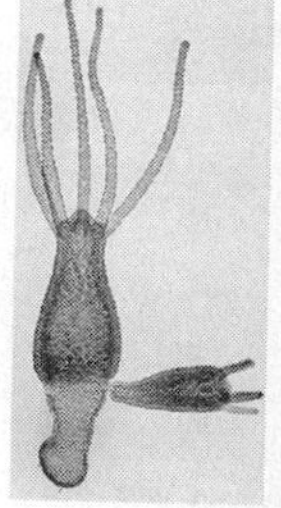

hydra

hy•dra (hī′drə) *n.* Any of several small freshwater polyps of the genus *Hydra* and related genera, having a naked cylindrical body and an oral opening surrounded by tentacles. [NLat. *Hydra,* genus name < Lat. *Hydra,* Hydra. See Hydra.]

Hy•dra (hī′drə) *n.* **1.** *Gk. Myth.* The many-headed serpent that was slain by Hercules. **2.** A constellation in the equatorial region of the southern sky near Cancer, Libra, and Centaurus. **3.** A persistent or multifaceted problem. [ME *Idra* < Lat. *Hydra* < Gk. *Hudra,* Hydra, a water serpent. See **wed-**[1]*****.]

hy•dran•gea (hī-drān′jə, -drăn′-) *n.* Any of various shrubs of the genus *Hydrangea,* having opposite leaves and large white, pink, or blue flowers. [NLat. *Hydrangēa,* genus name : Gk. *hudro-, hudr-,* hydro- + Gk. *angeion,* vessel; see angio–.]

hy•drant (hī′drənt) *n.* A fire hydrant.

hy•dranth (hī′drănth′) *n.* A feeding zooid in a hydroid colony, having an oral opening surrounded by tentacles. [hydr(a) + Gk. *anthos,* flower.]

hy•dras•tine (hī-drăs′tēn′, -tĭn) *n.* A poisonous white alkaloid, $C_{21}H_{21}NO_6$, obtained from the root of the goldenseal and formerly used locally to treat inflammation of mucous membranes. [NLat. *Hydrastis,* plant genus + -ine[2].]

hy•drate (hī′drāt′) *n.* A solid compound containing water molecules combined in a definite ratio as an integral part of the crystal. *—v.* **-drat•ed, -drat•ing, -drates.** *—tr.* **1.** To rehydrate. **2.** To supply water to (a person, for example) in order to restore or maintain fluid balance. *—intr.* To become a hydrate. **—hy•dra′tion** *n.* **—hy′dra′tor** *n.*

hydrant
Fire hydrant

hy•drat•ed (hī′drā′tĭd) *adj.* Chemically combined with water, esp. existing in the form of a hydrate.

hy•drau•lic (hī-drô′lĭk) *adj.* **1.** Of, involving, moved by, or operated by a fluid, esp. water, under pressure. **2.** Able to set and harden under water, as Portland cement. **3.** Of or relating to hydraulics. [Lat. *hydraulicus* < Gk. *hudraulikos* < *hudraulis,* water organ : *hudro-, hudr-,* hydro- + *aulos,* pipe, flute.] **—hy•drau′li•cal•ly** *adv.*

hydraulic press *n.* A machine in which a large force is exerted on the larger of two pistons in a pair of hydraulically coupled cylinders by a small force applied to the smaller piston.

hydraulic ram *n.* **1.** A water pump in which the downward flow of naturally running water is intermittently halted by a valve so that the flow is forced upward through an open pipe into a reservoir. **2.** The large piston of a hydraulic press.

hy•drau•lics (hī-drô′lĭks) *n. (used with a sing. v.)* The science and technology of the mechanics of fluids.

hy•dra•zine (hī′drə-zēn′, -zĭn) *n.* A fuming corrosive hygroscopic liquid, H_2NNH_2, used in jet and rocket fuels.

hy•dric (hī′drĭk) *adj.* Relating to, characterized by, or requiring considerable moisture.

hy•dride (hī′drīd′) *n.* A compound of hydrogen with another, more electropositive element or group.

hy•dri•od•ic acid (hī′drē-ŏd′ĭk) *n.* A clear colorless or pale yellow aqueous solution of hydrogen iodide, HI, that is a strong acid and reducing agent.

hy•dro (hī′drō) *adj.* Hydroelectric. *—n., pl.* **-dros. 1.** Hydroelectric power. **2.** A hydroelectric power plant.

hydro– or **hydr–** *pref.* **1.a.** Water: *hydroelectric.* **b.** Liquid: *hydrodynamics.* **2.** Hydrogen: *hydrochloride.* [Gk. *hudro-, hudr-* < *hudōr.* See **wed-**[1]*****.]

ă pat	oi boy
ā pay	ou out
âr care	o͝o took
ä father	o͞o boot
ĕ pet	ŭ cut
ē be	ûr urge
ĭ pit	th thin
ī pie	*th* this
îr pier	hw which
ŏ pot	zh vision
ō toe	ə about, item
ô paw	

Stress marks:
′ (primary);
′ (secondary), as in **dictionary** (dĭk′shə-nĕr′ē)

hy•dro•bi•ol•o•gy (hī′drō-bī-ŏl′ə-jē) *n.* The biological study of bodies of water. — **hy′dro•bi•ol′o•gist** *n.*

hy•dro•bro•mic acid (hī′drə-brō′mĭk) *n.* A highly acidic and corrosive aqueous solution of hydrogen bromide, HBr, used in the manufacture of bromides.

hy•dro•car•bon (hī′drə-kär′bən) *n.* Any of numerous organic compounds, such as benzene, that contain only carbon and hydrogen. — **hy′dro•car′bo•na′ceous** (-bə-nā′shəs), **hy′dro•car•bon′ic** (-bŏn′ĭk), **hy′dro•car′bon•ous** (-bə-nəs) *adj.*

hy•dro•cele (hī′drə-sēl′) *n.* A pathological accumulation of serum in a body cavity, esp. in the scrotum. [Lat. *hydrocēlē* < Gk. *hudrokēlē* : *hudro-*, hydro- + *kēlē*, tumor; see -CELE[1].]

hy•dro•ceph•a•lus (hī′drō-sĕf′ə-ləs) also **hy•dro•ceph•a•ly** (-lē) *n.* A usu. congenital condition in which an abnormal accumulation of fluid in the cerebral ventricles causes enlargement of the skull and compression of the brain, destroying much of the neural tissue. [NLat. < Gk. *hudrokephalon* : *hudro-*, hydro- + *kephalē*, head; see **ghebh-el-***.] — **hy′dro•ce•phal′ic** (-sə-făl′ĭk), **hy′dro•ceph′a•loid′** (-loid′), **hy′dro•ceph′a•lous** (-ləs) *adj.*

hy•dro•chlo•ric acid (hī′drə-klôr′ĭk, -klōr′-) *n.* A fuming, poisonous, highly acidic aqueous solution of hydrogen chloride, HCl, widely used in industry and found in the stomach in dilute form.

hy•dro•chlo•ride (hī′drə-klôr′īd′, -klōr′-) *n.* A compound resulting or regarded as resulting from the reaction of hydrochloric acid with an organic base.

hy•dro•col•loid (hī′drə-kŏl′oid′) *n.* A substance that forms a gel with water. — **hy′dro•col•loid′al** (-kə-loid′l) *adj.*

hy•dro•cor•ti•sone (hī′drə-kôr′tĭ-sōn′, -zōn′) *n.* **1.** A steroid hormone, $C_{21}H_{30}O_5$, produced by the adrenal cortex, that regulates carbohydrate metabolism and maintains blood pressure. **2.** A preparation of this hormone used to treat inflammatory conditions and adrenal failure.

hy•dro•crack•ing (hī′drə-krăk′ĭng) *n.* A process by which the hydrocarbon molecules of petroleum are broken into simpler molecules, as of gasoline, by the addition of hydrogen under high pressure and in the presence of a catalyst.

hy•dro•cy•an•ic acid (hī′drō-sī-ăn′ĭk) *n.* An aqueous solution of hydrogen cyanide.

hy•dro•dy•nam•ic (hī′drō-dī-năm′ĭk) also **hy•dro•dy•nam•i•cal** (-ĭ-kəl) *adj.* **1.** Of or relating to hydrodynamics. **2.** Of, relating to, or operated by the force of liquid in motion. — **hy′dro•dy•nam′i•cal•ly** *adv.*

hy•dro•dy•nam•ics (hī′drō-dī-năm′ĭks) *n.* **1.** *(used with a sing. v.)* The scientific study of the dynamics of fluids in motion. **2.** *(used with a pl. v.)* The dynamics of fluids in motion. — **hy′dro•dy•nam′i•cist** (-ĭ-sĭst) *n.*

hy•dro•e•lec•tric (hī′drō-ĭ-lĕk′trĭk) *adj.* **1.** Generating electricity by conversion of the energy of running water. **2.** Of or using electricity so generated. — **hy′dro•e•lec′tri•cal•ly** *adv.* — **hy′dro•e•lec•tric′i•ty** (-ĭ-lĕk-trĭs′ĭ-tē) *n.*

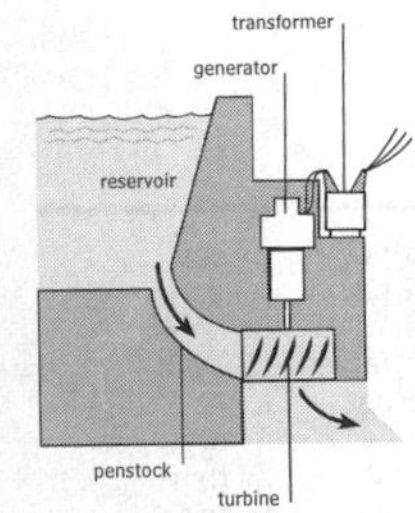

hydroelectric
Low head hydroelectric power plant

hy•dro•fluor•ic acid (hī′drō-flŏŏr′ĭk, -flôr′-, -flōr′-) *n.* A corrosive poisonous aqueous solution of hydrogen fluoride, HF, widely used as a fluorinating agent.

hy•dro•foil (hī′drə-foil′) *Naut. n.* **1.** A winglike structure attached to the hull of a boat that raises all or part of the hull out of the water when the boat is moving forward, thus reducing drag. **2.** A boat equipped with hydrofoils.

hy•dro•form•ing (hī′drə-fôr′mĭng) *n.* A process in which naphthas are converted to high-octane aromatics in the presence of hydrogen and a catalyst under pressure and heat.

hy•dro•gen (hī′drə-jən) *n. Symbol* **H** A colorless, highly flammable gaseous element, the most abundant in the universe, used in ammonia and methanol synthesis, in petroleum refining, in the hydrogenation of organic materials, and as a reducing atmosphere. Atomic number 1; atomic weight 1.00797; melting point −259.14°C; boiling point −252.8°C; density at 0°C 0.08987 gram per liter; valence 1. See table at **element.** [Fr. *hydrogène* : Gk. *hudro-*, hydro- + *-gène*, -gen.] — **hy•drog′e•nous** (-drŏj′ə-nəs) *adj.*

hy•dro•gen•ate (hī′drə-jə-nāt′, hī-drŏj′ə-) *tr.v.* **-at•ed, -at•ing, -ates.** To combine with or subject to the action of hydrogen, esp. to combine (an unsaturated oil) with hydrogen.

hydrogen bomb *n.* An explosive weapon of enormous destructive power caused by the fusion of the nuclei of various hydrogen isotopes in the formation of helium nuclei.

hydrogen bond *n.* A chemical bond in which a hydrogen atom of one molecule is attracted to an electronegative atom, esp. a nitrogen, oxygen, or flourine atom, usu. of another molecule.

hydrogen bromide *n.* An irritating colorless gas, HBr, used in the manufacture of barbiturates and synthetic hormones.

hydrogen chloride *n.* A colorless fuming corrosive suffocating gas, HCl, used in the manufacture of plastics.

hydrogen cyanide *n.* A colorless, volatile, extremely poisonous flammable liquid, HCN, miscible in water and used in the manufacture of dyes, fumigants, and plastics.

hydrogen fluoride *n.* A colorless fuming corrosive liquid or a highly soluble corrosive gas, HF, used in making hydrofluoric acid and as a reagent, catalyst, and fluorinating agent.

hydrogen iodide *n.* A corrosive colorless suffocating gas, HI, used to manufacture hydriodic acid.

hy•dro•gen•ol•y•sis (hī′drō-jə-nŏl′ĭ-sĭs) *n.* The breaking of a chemical bond by reaction with hydrogen.

hydrogen peroxide *n.* A colorless, heavy, strongly oxidizing liquid, H_2O_2, used principally in aqueous solution as a mild antiseptic, a bleaching agent, and a reagent.

hydrogen sulfide *n.* A colorless flammable poisonous gas, H_2S, having a characteristic rotten-egg odor.

hy•dro•ge•ol•o•gy (hī′drō-jē-ŏl′ə-jē) *n.* The branch of geology that deals with the occurrence, distribution, and effect of ground water. — **hy′dro•ge•ol′o•gist** *n.*

hy•drog•ra•phy (hī-drŏg′rə-fē) *n., pl.* **-phies. 1.** The scientific description and analysis of the physical conditions, boundaries, flow, and related characteristics of the earth's surface waters. **2.** The mapping of bodies of water. — **hy•drog′ra•pher** *n.* — **hy′dro•graph′ic** (hī′drə-grăf′ĭk) *adj.*

hy•droid (hī′droid′) *n.* **1.** Any of numerous characteristically colonial hydrozoan coelenterates having a polyp rather than a medusoid form as the dominant stage of the life cycle. **2.** The asexual polyp in the life cycle of a hydrozoan. — *adj.* Of, relating to, or characteristic of a hydroid. [HYDRA + -OID.]

hy•dro•ki•net•ic (hī′drō-kĭ-nĕt′ĭk, -kī-) also **hy•dro•ki•net•i•cal** (-ĭ-kəl) *adj.* **1.** Of or relating to hydrokinetics. **2.** Of or relating to the kinetic energy and motion of fluids.

hy•dro•ki•net•ics (hī′drō-kĭ-nĕt′ĭks, -kī-) *n. (used with a sing. v.)* The scientific study of fluids in motion.

hydrologic cycle *n.* See **water cycle.**

hy•drol•o•gy (hī-drŏl′ə-jē) *n.* The scientific study of the properties, distribution, and effects of water on the earth's surface, in the soil and underlying rocks, and in the atmosphere. — **hy′dro•log′ic** (-drə-lŏj′ĭk), **hy′dro•log′i•cal** *adj.* — **hy′dro•log′i•cal•ly** *adv.* — **hydrol′o•gist** *n.*

hy•drol•y•sate (hī-drŏl′ĭ-sāt′, hī′drə-lī′-) also **hy•drol•y•zate** (-zāt′) *n.* A product of hydrolysis.

hy•drol•y•sis (hī-drŏl′ĭ-sĭs) *n.* Decomposition of a chemical compound by reaction with water, such as the dissociation of a dissolved salt. — **hy′dro•lyte′** (-līt′) *n.* — **hy′dro•lyt′ic** (-drə-lĭt′ĭk) *adj.*

hy•dro•lyze (hī′drə-līz′) *tr. & intr.v.* **-lyzed, -lyz•ing, -lyz•es.** To subject to or undergo hydrolysis. — **hy′dro•lyz′a•ble** *adj.* — **hy′dro•ly•za′tion** (-lĭ-zā′shən) *n.*

hy•dro•mag•net•ics (hī′drō-măg-nĕt′ĭks) *n. (used with a sing. v.)* See **magnetohydrodynamics.** — **hy′dro•mag•net′ic** *adj.*

hy•dro•man•cy (hī′drə-măn′sē) *n.* Divination by the observation of water. [ME *ydromancy* < OFr. *ydromancie* < Lat. *hydromantīa* < Gk. *hudromanteia* : *hudro-*, hydro- + *manteia*, divination; see -MANCY.]

hy•dro•me•chan•ics (hī′drō-mĭ-kăn′ĭks) *n. (used with a sing. v.)* The scientific study of the mechanics of fluids or the laws of equilibrium and motion concerning fluids. — **hy′dro•me•chan′i•cal** *adj.*

hy•dro•me•du•sa (hī′drō-mĭ-dōō′sə, -dyōō′-) *n., pl.* **-sas** or **-sae** (-sē). A hydrozoan in the medusoid stage of its life cycle.

hy•dro•mel (hī′drə-mĕl′) *n.* A mixture of water and honey that becomes mead when fermented. [ME *ydromel* < OFr. < Lat. *hydromeli* < Gk. *hudromeli* : *hudro-*, hydro- + *meli*, honey; see **melit-***.]

hy•dro•met•al•lur•gy (hī′drō-mĕt′l-ûr′jē) *n.* The treatment of metal or the separation of metal from ores and ore concentrates by liquid processes.

hy•dro•me•te•or (hī′drō-mē′tē-ər, -ôr′) *n.* A precipitation product, such as rain, snow, fog, or clouds, formed from the condensation of water vapor in the atmosphere.

hy•dro•me•te•or•ol•o•gy (hī′drō-mē′tē-ə-rŏl′ə-jē) *n.* The study of hydrologic problems, such as flood control and irrigation. — **hy′dro•me′te•or•ol′o•gist** *n.*

hy•drom•e•ter (hī-drŏm′ĭ-tər) *n.* An instrument used to determine specific gravity, esp. a sealed graduated tube, weighted at one end, that sinks in a fluid to a depth used as a measure of the fluid's specific gravity. — **hy′dro•met′ric** (hī′drə-mĕt′rĭk), **hy′dro•met′ri•cal** *adj.* — **hy′dro•met′ri•cal•ly** *adv.* — **hy•drom′e•try** *n.*

hy•dro•ni•um (hī-drō′nē-əm) *n.* A hydrated hydrogen ion, H_3O^+. [HYDR(O)- + (AMM)ONIUM.]

hy•drop•a•thy (hī-drŏp′ə-thē) *n., pl.* **-thies.** Use of water as a therapeutic treatment for disease. — **hy′dro•path′ic** (hī′drə-păth′ĭk), **hy′dro•path′i•cal** *adj.* — **hy•drop′a•thist, hy′dro•path′** *n.*

hy•dro•phane (hī′drə-fān′) *n.* An opal that is almost opaque when dry but transparent when wet. — **hy•droph′a•nous** (hī-drŏf′ə-nəs) *adj.*

hy•dro•phil•ic (hī′drə-fĭl′ĭk) *adj.* Having an affinity for water; readily absorbing or dissolving in water. — **hy′dro•phile′** (-fīl′) *n.* — **hy′dro•phi•lic′i•ty** (-fə-lĭs′ĭ-tē) *n.*

hy•droph•i•lous (hī-drŏf′ə-ləs) *adj. Bot.* **1.** Growing or thriving in water. **2.** Pollinated by water, as the flowers of hornwort. — **hy•droph′i•ly** *n.*

hy•dro•pho•bi•a (hī′drə-fō′bē-ə) *n.* **1.** An abnormal fear of water. **2.** Rabies.

hy•dro•pho•bic (hī′drə-fō′bĭk, -fŏb′ĭk) *adj.* **1.** Repelling, tending not to combine with, or incapable of dissolving in water. **2.** Of or exhibiting hydrophobia. — **hy′dro·pho·bic′i·ty** (-bĭs′ĭ-tē) *n.*

hy·dro·phone (hī′drə-fōn′) *n.* An electrical instrument for detecting or monitoring sound under water.

hy·dro·phyte (hī′drə-fīt′) *n.* A plant adapted to grow in water. — **hy′dro·phyt′ic** (-fĭt′ĭk) *adj.*

hy·dro·plane (hī′drə-plān′) *n.* **1.** *Naut.* A motorboat designed to skim the surface at high speeds. **2.** *Naut.* See **hydrofoil** 2. **3.** A horizontal rudder on a submarine. — *intr.v.* **-planed, -plan·ing, -planes. 1.** To drive or ride in a hydroplane. **2.a.** To skim along on the surface of the water. **b.** To be or go out of control by skimming along the surface of a wet road. Used of a motor vehicle.

hy·dro·pon·ics (hī′drə-pŏn′ĭks) *n.* *(used with a sing. v.)* Cultivation of plants in nutrient solution rather than in soil. [HYDRO– + (GEO)PONICS.] — **hy′dro·pon′ic** *adj.* — **hy′dro·pon′i·cal·ly** *adv.* — **hy′dro·pon′i·cist** (-ĭ-sĭst), **hy′dro·pon′ist** (hī′drə-pŏn′ĭst, hī-drŏp′ə-nĭst) *n.*

hy·dro·pow·er (hī′drə-pou′ər) *n.* Hydroelectric power.

hy·dro·qui·none (hī′drō-kwĭ-nōn′, -kwĭn′ōn′) also **hy·dro·quin·ol** (-kwĭn′ôl′, -ōl′) *n.* A white crystalline compound, $C_6H_4(OH)_2$, used as a photographic developer, an antioxidant, a stabilizer, and a reagent.

hy·dro·scope (hī′drə-skōp′) *n.* An optical device used for viewing objects far below the surface of water. — **hy′dro·scop′ic** (-skŏp′ĭk) *adj.*

hy·dro·sol (hī′drə-sôl′, -sōl′, -sôl′) *n.* A colloid with water as the dispersing medium. — **hy′dro·sol′ic** (-sŏl′ĭk) *adj.*

hy·dro·space (hī′drə-spās′) *n.* The regions beneath the ocean's surface, esp. when considered as an area to be studied.

hy·dro·sphere (hī′drə-sfîr′) *n.* **1.** The waters of the earth's surface as distinguished from those of the lithosphere and the atmosphere. **2.** The water vapor in the earth's atmosphere. — **hy′dro·spher′ic** (-sfîr′ĭk, -sfĕr′-) *adj.*

hy·dro·stat·ic (hī′drə-stăt′ĭk) also **hy·dro·stat·i·cal** (-ĭ-kəl) *adj.* Of or relating to hydrostatics.

hy·dro·stat·ics (hī′drə-stăt′ĭks) *n.* *(used with a sing. v.)* The scientific study of fluids at rest and under pressure.

hy·dro·sul·fite (hī′drə-sŭl′fīt′) *n.* A salt of hyposulfurous acid.

hy·dro·sul·fu·rous acid (hī′drō-sŭl-fyŏŏr′əs, -sŭl′fər-əs) *n.* See **hyposulfurous acid.**

hy·dro·tax·is (hī′drə-tăk′sĭs) *n.* *Biol.* Movement of an organism in response to moisture. — **hy′dro·tac′tic** (-tăk′tĭk) *adj.*

hy·dro·ther·a·peu·tics (hī′drə-thĕr′ə-pyōō′tĭks) *n.* *(used with a sing. v.)* Hydrotherapy. — **hy′dro·ther′a·peu′tic** *adj.*

hy·dro·ther·a·py (hī′drə-thĕr′ə-pē) *n., pl.* **-pies.** External use of water in the medical treatment of certain diseases.

hy·dro·ther·mal (hī′drə-thûr′məl) *adj.* **1.** Of or relating to hot water. **2.** *Geol.* **a.** Of or relating to hot magmatic emanations rich in water. **b.** Of or relating to the rocks, ore deposits, and springs produced by such emanations.

hy·dro·tho·rax (hī′drə-thôr′ăks′, -thōr′-) *n.* Accumulation of serous fluid in one or both pleural cavities.

hy·drot·ro·pism (hī-drŏt′rə-pĭz′əm) *n.* Growth or movement in a sessile organism toward or away from water. — **hy′dro·tro′pic** (hī′drə-trō′pĭk, -trŏp′ĭk) *adj.*

hy·drous (hī′drəs) *adj.* Containing water, esp. water of crystallization or hydration.

hy·drox·ide (hī-drŏk′sīd′) *n.* A chemical compound containing the hydroxyl group.

hy·drox·y (hī-drŏk′sē) *adj.* Containing the hydroxyl group.

hy·drox·y·a·pa·tite (hī-drok′sē-ăp′ĭ-tīt′) *n.* The principal bone salt, $Ca_5(PO_4)_3OH$, which provides the compressional strength of vertebrate bone.

hy·drox·yl (hī-drŏk′sĭl) *n.* The univalent radical or group OH, a characteristic component of bases, certain acids, phenols, alcohols, carboxylic and sulfonic acids, and amphoteric compounds. [HYDR(O)– + OX(YGEN) + –YL.] — **hy′drox·yl′ic** (hī′-drŏk-sĭl′ĭk) *adj.*

hy·drox·yl·a·mine (hī-drŏk′sə-lə-mēn′, hī′drŏk-sĭl′ə-mēn′, -sə-lăm′ĭn) *n.* A colorless crystalline compound, NH_2OH, that is used as a reducing agent and in organic synthesis.

hy·drox·yl·ate (hī-drŏk′sə-lāt′) *tr.v.* **-at·ed, -at·ing, -ates.** To introduce hydroxyl into (a compound). — **hy·drox′y·la′tion** *n.*

hy·dro·zo·an (hī′drə-zō′ən) *n.* Any of numerous coelenterates of the class Hydrozoa, including the freshwater hydras, hydroids, and siphonophores. [< NLat. *Hydrozoa*, class : HYDRO– + *-zoa* (pl. of -ZOON).] — **hy′dro·zo′an** *adj.*

Hy·drus (hī′drəs) *n.* A constellation in the Southern Hemisphere near Tucana and Mensa. [Lat. < Gk. *hudros*, water snake. See **wed-¹*.**]

hy·e·na also **hy·ae·na** (hī-ē′nə) *n.* Any of several carnivorous mammals of the family Hyaenidae of Africa and Asia, which feed as scavengers and have powerful jaws and relatively short hind limbs. [ME *hiena* < OFr. *hiene* < Lat. *hyaena* < Gk. *huaina*, fem. of *hus*, swine. See **sū-*.**]

hy·e·tal (hī′ĭ-tl) *adj.* Of or relating to rain or rainy regions. [< Gk. *huetos*, rain. See **seuə-²*.**]

Hy·ge·ia (hī-jē′ə) *n.* *Gk. Myth.* The goddess of health.

hy·giene (hī′jēn′) *n.* **1.** The science that deals with the promotion and preservation of health. **2.** Conditions and practices that serve to promote or preserve health: *personal hygiene.* [Fr. *hygiène* and NLat. *hygieina*, both < Gk. *hugieinē (tekhnē)*, (art) of health < *hugiēs*, healthy. See **gʷei-*.**] — **hy·gien′ist** (hī-jē′nĭst, hī′jē′-, hī-jĕn′ĭst) *n.*

hy·gi·en·ic (hī′jē-ĕn′ĭk, hī-jĕn′-, -jē′nĭk) *adj.* **1.** Of or relating to hygiene. **2.** Tending to promote or preserve health. **3.** Sanitary. — **hy′gi·en′i·cal·ly** *adv.*

hy·gi·en·ics (hī′jē-ĕn′ĭks, hī-jĕn′-, -jē′nĭks) *n.* *(used with a sing. v.)* See **hygiene** 1.

hygro– *pref.* Moisture; humidity: *hygroscope.* [< Gk. *hugros*, wet, moist.]

hy·grom·e·ter (hī-grŏm′ĭ-tər) *n.* Any of several instruments that measure atmospheric humidity. — **hy′gro·met′ric** (hī′-grə-mĕt′rĭk) *adj.* — **hy·grom′e·try** *n.*

hy·gro·scope (hī′grə-skōp′) *n.* An instrument that indicates changes in atmospheric humidity.

hy·gro·scop·ic (hī′grə-skŏp′ĭk) *adj.* Readily absorbing moisture, as from the atmosphere. — **hy′gro·scop′i·cal·ly** *adv.* — **hy′gro·sco·pic′i·ty** (-skō-pĭs′ĭ-tē) *n.*

hy·gro·stat (hī′grə-stăt′) *n.* See **humidistat.**

hy·ing (hī′ĭng) *v.* A pr.part. of **hie.**

hy·lo·zo·ism (hī′lə-zō′ĭz′əm) *n.* The philosophical doctrine holding that all matter has life, which is a property or derivative of matter. [Gk. *hulē*, matter + Gk. *zoē*, life; see AZO– + –ISM.] — **hy′lo·zo′ic** *adj.* — **hy′lo·zo′ist** *n.*

hy·men (hī′mən) *n.* A tissue that partly or completely occludes the external vaginal orifice. [LLat. *hymēn* < Gk. *humēn*, thin skin, membrane. See **syū-*.**] — **hy′men·al** *adj.*

Hy·men (hī′mən) *n.* *Gk. Myth.* The god of marriage.

hy·me·ne·al (hī′mə-nē′əl) *adj.* Of or relating to a wedding or marriage. — *n.* **1.** A wedding song or poem. **2. hymeneals.** *Archaic.* A wedding; nuptials. [< Lat. *hymenaeus*, wedding song, wedding < Gk. *humēnaios* < *Humēn*, Hymen < *humēn*, membrane. See HYMEN.] — **hy′me·ne′al·ly** *adv.*

hy·me·ni·um (hī-mē′nē-əm) *n., pl.* **-ni·a** (-nē-ə) or **-ni·ums.** The spore-bearing layer of the fruiting body of certain fungi. [NLat. < Gk. *humenion*, dim. of *humēn*, membrane. See HYMEN.] — **hy·me′ni·al** (-əl) *adj.*

hy·me·nop·ter·an (hī′mə-nŏp′tər-ən) *adj.* Of or belonging to the Hymenoptera. — *n.* also **hy·me·nop·ter·on** (-tə-rŏn′). An insect of the order Hymenoptera, including the bees, wasps, and ants, often living in complex social groups and characteristically having two pairs of membranous wings. [< NLat. *Hymenoptera*, order name < Gk. *humenopteros*, membrane-winged : *humēn*, membrane; see HYMEN + *pteron*, wing; see –PTER.] — **hy′me·nop′ter·ous** (-tər-əs) *adj.*

Hy·met·tus (hī-mĕt′əs). A mountain ridge, rising to c. 1,028 m (3,370 ft), in E-central Greece near Athens.

hymn (hĭm) *n.* **1.** A song of praise or thanksgiving to God or a deity. **2.** A song of praise or joy; a paean. — *v.* **hymned, hymn·ing, hymns.** — *tr.* To praise, glorify, or worship in or as if in a hymn. — *intr.* To sing hymns. [ME *imne* < OFr. *ymne* < Lat. *hymnus*, song of praise < Gk. *humnos.*]

hym·nal (hĭm′nəl) *n.* A collection of church hymns. [ME *himnale* < Med.Lat. *hymnāle* < Lat. *hymnus*, hymn. See HYMN.]

hymnal stanza *n.* See **common measure** 3.

hym·na·ry (hĭm′nə-rē) *n.* See **hymnal.**

hymn·book (hĭm′bŏŏk′) *n.* See **hymnal.**

hym·no·dy (hĭm′nə-dē) *n., pl.* **-dies. 1.** The singing of hymns. **2.** The composing or writing of hymns. **3.** The hymns of a particular period or church. [Med.Lat. *hymnōdia* < Gk. *humnōidia* : *humnos*, hymn + *ōidē*, song; see **wed-²*.**] — **hym′no·dist** (-dĭst) *n.*

hym·nol·o·gy (hĭm-nŏl′ə-jē) *n.* **1.** Hymnody. **2.** The study of hymns. — **hym′no·log′ic** (hĭm′nə-lŏj′ĭk), **hym′no·log′i·cal** (-ĭ-kəl) *adj.* — **hym·nol′o·gist** *n.*

hy·oid (hī′oid′) *adj.* Of or relating to the hyoid. — *n.* A U-shaped bone at the base of the tongue, supporting the muscles of the tongue. [NLat. *hyoidēs*, the hyoid bone < Gk. *huoeidēs*, shaped like the letter upsilon : *hu*, name of the letter upsilon + *-oeidēs*, -oid.]

hy·o·scine (hī′ə-sēn′) *n.* See **scopolamine.** [Ger. *Hyoscin* < NLat. *Hyoscyamus*, henbane genus < Gk. *huoskuamos*, henbane : *huos*, genitive of *hus*, swine; see **sū-*** + *kuamos*, bean.]

hy·o·scy·a·mine (hī′ə-sī′ə-mēn′) *n.* A poisonous white crystalline alkaloid, $C_{17}H_{23}NO_3$, isometric with atropine and having similar uses but more potent effects. [NLat. *Hyoscyamus*, henbane genus; see HYOSCINE + –INE².]

hyp. *abbr.* **1.** *Math.* Hypotenuse. **2.** Hypothesis. **3.** Hypothetical.

hyp– *pref.* Var. of **hypo–.**

hyp·a·bys·sal (hĭp′ə-bĭs′əl, hī′pə-) *adj.* *Geol.* Solidifying chiefly as a minor intrusion, esp. as a dike or sill, before reaching the earth's surface. Used of rocks.

hy·pae·thral also **hy·pe·thral** (hĭ-pē′thrəl) *adj.* Wholly or partly open to the sky. [< Lat. *hypaethrus* < Gk. *hupaithros* : *hupo*, under; see HYPO– + *aithēr*, sky, air.]

hy·pan·thi·um (hī-păn′thē-əm) *n., pl.* **-thi·a** (-thē-ə). The

hyena
Spotted hyena
Crocuta crocuta

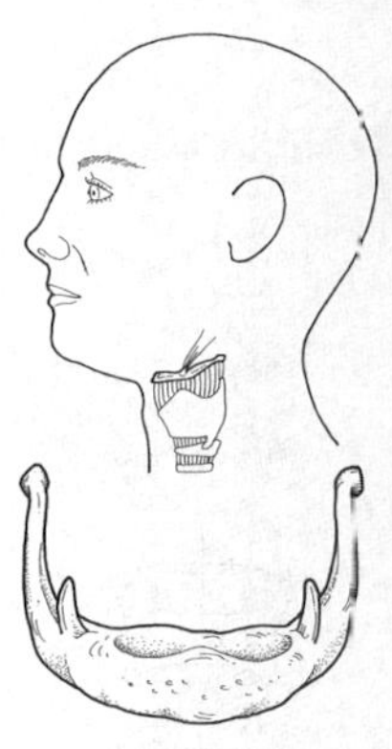
hyoid

ă pat	oi boy
ā pay	ou out
âr care	ŏŏ took
ä father	ōō boot
ĕ pet	ŭ cut
ē be	ûr urge
ĭ pit	th thin
ī pie	*th* this
îr pier	hw which
ŏ pot	zh vision
ō toe	ə about, item
ô paw	

Stress marks:
′ (primary);
′ (secondary), as in dictionary (dĭk′shə-nĕr′ē)

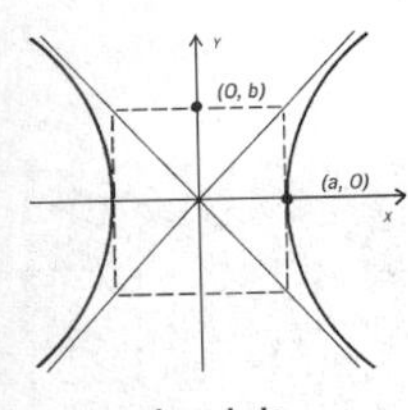

hyperbola

$$\frac{x^2}{a^2} - \frac{y^2}{b^2} = 1$$

structure of a flower on which the sepals, petals, and stamens are borne, as in the flowers of the rose or cherry. [NLat. : HYP(O)- + Gk. *anthos*, flower.] — **hy•pan′thi•al** *adj.*

hype^{1} (hīp) *Slang.* — *n.* **1.** Excessive publicity and the ensuing commotion. **2.** Exaggerated or extravagant claims made esp. in advertising or promotional material. **3.** An advertising or promotional ploy. **4.** Something deliberately misleading; a deception. — *tr.v.* **hyped, hyp•ing, hypes.** To publicize or promote, esp. by extravagant, inflated, or misleading claims. [Partly < *hype*, a swindle (perh. < HYPER-) and partly < HYPE(RBOLE).]

hype^{2} (hīp) *Slang.* — *n.* **1.** A hypodermic injection, syringe, or needle. **2.** A drug addict. — *tr.v.* **hyped, hyp•ing, hypes.** To stimulate with or as if with a hypodermic injection.

hyped-up (hīpt′ŭp′) *adj. Slang.* Stimulated with or as if with a hypodermic injection.

hy•per (hī′pər) *adj. Slang.* **1.** Having a very excitable or nervous temperament; high-strung. **2.** Emotionally stimulated or overexcited. [Short for HYPERACTIVE.]

hyper– *pref.* **1.** Over; above; beyond: *hypercharge.* **2.** Excessive; excessively: *hypercritical.* [Gk. *huper-* < *huper*, over, beyond. See **uper***.]

hy•per•ac•id (hī′pər-ăs′ĭd) *adj.* Excessively acidic. — **hy′per•a•cid′i•ty** (-ə-sĭd′ĭ-tē) *n.*

hy•per•ac•tive (hī′pər-ăk′tĭv) *adj.* **1.** Highly or excessively active. **2.a.** Having behavior characterized by constant overactivity. **b.** Afflicted with attention deficit disorder. — **hy′per•ac′tive•ly** *adv.* — **hy′per•ac•tiv′i•ty** (-ăk-tĭv′ĭ-tē) *n.*

hy•per•aes•the•sia (hī′pər-ĭs-thē′zhə) *n.* Var. of **hyperesthesia.**

hy•per•bar•ic (hī′pər-băr′ĭk) *adj.* Of, relating to, producing, operating, or occurring at pressures higher than normal atmospheric pressure. — **hy′per•bar′i•cal•ly** *adv.*

hy•per•ba•ton (hī-pûr′bə-tŏn′) *n.* A figure of speech, such as anastrophe, using deviation from normal or logical word order to produce an effect. [Gk. *huperbaton* < neut. of *huperbatos*, transposed < *huperbainein*, to step over : *huper-*, over, across; see HYPER- + *bainein*, to step; see **gwā-***.]

hy•per•bo•la (hī-pûr′bə-lə) *n., pl.* **-las** or **-lae** (-lē). *Math.* A plane curve having two branches, formed by the intersection of a plane with both halves of a right circular cone at an angle parallel to the axis of the cone. [NLat. < Gk. *huperbolē*, a throwing beyond, excess (from the relationship between the line joining the vertices of a conic and the line through its focus and parallel to its directrix). See HYPERBOLE.]

hy•per•bo•le (hī-pûr′bə-lē) *n.* A figure of speech in which exaggeration is used for emphasis or effect, as in *That book weighs a ton.* [Lat. *hyperbolē* < Gk. *huperbolē*, excess < *huperballein*, to exceed : *huper*, beyond; see HYPER- + *ballein*, to throw; see **gʷelə-***.] — **hy•per′bo•lize′** *v.*

hy•per•bol•ic (hī′pər-bŏl′ĭk) also **hy•per•bol•i•cal** (-ĭ-kəl) *adj.* **1.** Of, relating to, or employing hyperbole. **2.** *Math.* **a.** Of, relating to, or resembling a hyperbola. **b.** Of or relating to a geometry in which two or more lines can be drawn through any point in a plane and not intersect a given line in the plane. **c.** Of or relating to a hyperbolic function. — **hy′per•bol′i•cal•ly** *adv.*

hyperbolic function *n. Math.* Any of a set of six functions related to the hyperbola in a manner analogous to the relationship of the trigonometric functions to the circle, including the hyperbolic sine, the hyperbolic cosine, and the hyperbolic tangent.

hyperbolic paraboloid *n. Math.* A surface of which all sections parallel to one coordinate plane are hyperbolas and all sections parallel to another coordinate plane are parabolas.

hy•per•bo•lism (hī-pûr′bə-lĭz′əm) *n.* **1.** The use of hyperbole. **2.** An instance of hyperbole.

hy•per•bo•loid (hī-pûr′bə-loid′) *n. Math.* Either of two quadric surfaces generated by rotating a hyperbola about either of its main axes and having plane sections that are hyperbolas, ellipses, or circles.

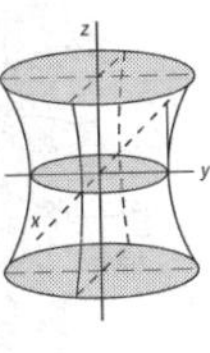

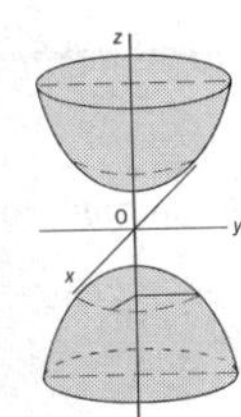

hyperboloid
Top: Hyperboloid of one sheet
Bottom: Hyperboloid of two sheets

Hy•per•bo•re•an (hī′pər-bôr′ē-ən, -bōr′-, -bə-rē′ən) *n. Gk. Myth.* An inhabitant of a perpetually warm and sunny land north of the source of the north wind. — *adj.* **1.** Of or relating to the Hyperboreans. **2. hyperborean. a.** Of or relating to the far north; Arctic. **b.** Very cold; frigid. [< Lat. *Hyperboreus* < *Hyperboreī*, the Hyperboreans < Gk. *Huperboreoi* : *huper-*, hyper- + *boreios*, northern, or *Boreas*, the north wind, the north.]

hy•per•cat•a•lec•tic (hī′pər-kăt′l-ĕk′tĭk) *adj.* Having an extra syllable or syllables at the end of a metrically complete line of verse or in a metrical foot. [Ult. < Gk. *huperkatalēktikos* : *huper-*, hyper- + *katalēktikos*, incomplete; see CATALECTIC.] — **hy′per•cat′a•lex′is** (-kăt′l-ĕk′sĭs) *n.*

hy•per•charge (hī′pər-chärj′) *n. Symbol* **Y** A quantum number equal to the sum of the strangeness and the baryon number of a particle.

hy•per•cor•rect (hī′pər-kə-rĕkt′) *adj.* Of, relating to, or marked by hypercorrection. — **hy′per•cor•rect′ly** *adv.* — **hy′per•cor•rect′ness** *n.*

hy•per•cor•rec•tion (hī′pər-kə-rĕk′shən) *n. Ling.* **1.** A construction or pronunciation produced by mistaken analogy with standard usage out of a desire to be correct, as in the substitution of *I* for *me* in *on behalf of my wife and I.* **2.** The production of such a construction or pronunciation.

hy•per•crit•ic (hī′pər-krĭt′ĭk) *n.* A person who is excessively critical.

hy•per•crit•i•cal (hī′pər-krĭt′ĭ-kəl) *adj.* Excessively critical; captious. — **hy′per•crit′i•cal•ly** *adv.* — **hy′per•crit′i•cism** (-ĭ-sĭz′əm) *n.*

hy•per•e•mi•a (hī′pə-rē′mē-ə) *n.* An increase in the quantity of blood flow to a body part; engorgement. — **hy′per•e′mic** (-mĭk) *adj.*

hy•per•es•the•sia also **hy•per•aes•the•sia** (hī′pər-ĭs-thē′zhə) *n.* An abnormal or pathological increase in sensitivity to sensory stimuli, as of the ear to sound. — **hy′per•es•thet′ic** (-thĕt′ĭk) *adj.*

hy•per•eu•tec•tic (hī′pər-yo͞o-tĕk′tĭk) *adj.* Having the minor component present in a larger amount than in the eutectic composition of the same components.

hy•per•ex•ten•sion (hī′pər-ĭk-stĕn′shən) *n.* Extension of a bodily joint beyond its normal range of motion. — **hy′per•ex•tend′** (-ĭk-stĕnd′) *v.*

hy•per•fine structure (hī′pər-fīn′) *n.* The splitting of a spectral line into two or more components as a result of the spin or magnetic moment of the atomic nucleus.

hy•per•gly•ce•mi•a (hī′pər-glī-sē′mē-ə) *n.* The presence of an abnormally high concentration of glucose in the blood. — **hy′per•gly•ce′mic** (-mĭk) *adj.*

hy•per•gol•ic (hī′pər-gŏl′ĭk) *adj.* **1.** Of or relating to a rocket propellant consisting of fuel and an oxidizer that ignite spontaneously on contact. **2.** Using such a fuel. [< Ger. *Hypergol*, a hypergolic fluid propellant : < *hyper-*, extreme (< Gk. *huper-*; see HYPER-) + Gk. *ergon*, work; see ERG.] — **hy′per•gol′** (hī′pər-gôl′, -gōl′, -gŏl′) *n.* — **hy′per•gol′i•cal•ly** *adv.*

hy•per•in•su•lin•ism (hī′pər-ĭn′sə-lə-nĭz′əm) *n.* An abnormally high level of insulin in the blood, resulting in hypoglycemia.

Hy•pe•ri•on (hī-pîr′ē-ən) *n.* **1.** *Gk. Myth.* A Titan, the son of Gaea and Uranus and the father of Helios. **2.** A satellite of Saturn. [Gk. *Huperiōn*.]

hy•per•ker•a•to•sis (hī′pər-kĕr′ə-tō′sĭs) *n.* Hypertrophy of the cornea or the horny layer of the skin. — **hy′per•ker′a•tot′ic** (-tŏt′ĭk) *adj.*

hy•per•ki•ne•sia (hī′pər-kĭ-nē′zhə) also **hy•per•ki•ne•sis** (-sĭs) *n.* Pathologically increased muscular movement. [HYPER- + Gk. *kinēsis*, movement (< *kinein*, to move; see **kei-^{2}***) + -IA^{1}.] — **hy′per•ki•net′ic** (-nĕt′ĭk) *adj.*

hy•per•mar•ket (hī′pər-mär′kĭt) *n.* A large commercial establishment combining a department store and a supermarket.

hy•per•met•ric (hī′pər-mĕt′rĭk) *adj.* Having one or more syllables in addition to those found in a standard metrical unit or line of verse. — **hy•per′me•ter** (hī-pûr′mĭ-tər) *n.*

hy•per•me•tro•pi•a (hī′pər-mĭ-trō′pē-ə) *n.* See **hyperopia.** [Gk. *hupermetros*, beyond measure (*huper-*, hyper- + *metron*, measure; see METER^{2}) + -OPIA.] — **hy′per•me•tro′pic** (-trō′pĭk, -trŏp′ĭk), **hy′per•me•tro′pi•cal** *adj.* — **hy′per•met′ro•py** (-mĕt′rə-pē) *n.*

hy•perm•ne•sia (hī′pərm-nē′zhə) *n.* Exceptionally exact or vivid memory, esp. as associated with certain mental illnesses. [HYPER- + (A)MNESIA.] — **hy′perm•ne′sic** (-zĭk, -sĭk) *adj.*

hy•per•on (hī′pə-rŏn′) *n.* A semistable or unstable baryon with mass greater than the neutron. See table at **subatomic particle.**

hy•per•o•pi•a (hī′pə-rō′pē-ə) *n.* An abnormal condition of the eye in which vision is better for distant objects than for near objects. — **hy′per•ope′** (hī′pə-rōp′) *n.* — **hy′per•o′pic** (-ō′pĭk, -ŏp′ĭk) *adj.*

hy•per•os•to•sis (hī′pər-ŏ-stō′sĭs) *n., pl.* **-ses** (-sēz). Excessive or abnormal thickening or growth of bone tissue. [HYPER- + OST(EO)- + -OSIS.] — **hy′per•os•tot′ic** (-ŏ-stŏt′ĭk) *adj.*

hy•per•pi•tu•i•ta•rism (hī′pər-pĭ-to͞o′ĭ-tə-rĭz′əm, -tyo͞o′-) *n.* **1.** Pathologically excessive production of anterior pituitary hormones, esp. growth hormones. **2.** The condition resulting from an excess of pituitary hormones. — **hy′per•pi•tu′i•tar′y** (-tĕr′ē) *adj.*

hy•per•pla•sia (hī′pər-plā′zhə) *n.* An abnormal increase in the number of cells in an organ or a tissue with consequent enlargement. — **hy′per•plas′tic** (-plăs′tĭk) *adj.*

hy•per•ploid (hī′pər-ploid′) *adj.* Having a chromosome number greater than but not an exact multiple of the normal euploid number. — **hy′per•ploid′** *n.* — **hy′per•ploi′dy** *n.*

hy•perp•ne•a (hī′pərp-nē′ə, hī′pər-nē′ə) *n.* Abnormally deep or rapid breathing. [HYPER- + Gk. *pnoia, pnoē*, breath, breathing (< *pnein*, to breathe; see **pneu-***).] — **hy′perp•ne′ic** (-ĭk) *adj.*

hy•per•py•rex•i•a (hī′pər-pī-rĕk′sē-ə) *n.* Abnormally high fever. — **hy′per•py•rex′i•al, hy′per•py•ret′ic** (-rĕt′ĭk) *adj.*

hy•per•sen•si•tive (hī′pər-sĕn′sĭ-tĭv) *adj.* Highly or excessively sensitive. — **hy′per•sen′si•tive•ness, hy′per•sen′si•tiv′i•ty** (-tĭv′ĭ-tē) *n.*

hy•per•sex•u•al (hī′pər-sĕk′sho͞o-əl) *adj.* Excessively interested or involved in sexual activity. — **hy′per•sex′u•al′i•ty** (-sĕk′sho͞o-ăl′ĭ-tē) *n.*

hy•per•son•ic (hī′pər-sŏn′ĭk) *adj.* Of, relating to, or capable of speed equal to or exceeding five times the speed of sound.

hy•per•space (hī′pər-spās′) *n.* Space that has four or more dimensions.

hy•per•sthene (hī′pərs-thēn′) *n.* A green, brown, or black splintery cleavable pyroxene mineral, $(Fe,Mg)_2Si_2O_6$. [Fr. *hypersthène* : *hyper-*, extreme (< Gk. *huper-*; see HYPER–) + Gk. *sthenos*, strength.] — **hy′per•sthen′ic** (-thĕn′ĭk) *adj.*

hy•per•ten•sion (hī′pər-tĕn′shən) *n.* **1.** Arterial disease in which chronic high blood pressure is the primary symptom. **2.** Abnormally high blood pressure. — **hy′per•ten′sive** *adj.*

hy•per•text (hī′pər-tĕkst′) *n. Comp. Sci.* A computer-based text retrieval system that enables the user to provide access to or gain information related to a particular text.

hy•per•ther•mi•a (hī′pər-thûr′mē-ə) *n.* Unusually high body temperature. — **hy′per•ther′mal** *adj.*

hy•per•thy•roid (hī′pər-thī′roid′) *adj.* Of, relating to, or afflicted with hyperthyroidism.

hy•per•thy•roid•ism (hī′pər-thī′roi-dĭz′əm) *n.* **1.** Pathologically excessive production of thyroid hormones. **2.** The condition resulting from excessive activity of the thyroid gland.

hy•per•to•ni•a (hī′pər-tō′nē-ə) *n. Pathol.* The state of being hypertonic.

hy•per•ton•ic (hī′pər-tŏn′ĭk) *adj.* **1.** *Pathol.* Having extreme muscular or arterial tension. **2.** *Chem.* Having the higher osmotic pressure of two solutions. — **hy′per•to•nic′i•ty** (-tə-nĭs′ĭ-tē, -tō-) *n.*

hy•per•tro•phy (hī-pûr′trə-fē) *n., pl.* **-phies.** A nontumorous enlargement of an organ or a tissue due to an increase in the size rather than the number of constituent cells: *muscle hypertrophy.* — *intr. & tr.v.* **-phied, -phy•ing, -phies.** To grow or cause to grow abnormally large. — **hy′per•tro′phic** (-trō′fĭk, -trŏf′ĭk) *adj.*

hy•per•ven•ti•late (hī′pər-vĕn′tl-āt′) *v.* **-lat•ed, -lat•ing, -lates.** — *intr.* **1.** To breathe abnormally fast or deeply so as to effect hyperventilation. **2.** To breathe in this manner as from excitement or anxiety. — *tr.* To subject to hyperventilation.

hy•per•ven•ti•la•tion (hī′pər-vĕn′tl-ā′shən) *n.* Abnormally fast or deep respiration, which results in the loss of carbon dioxide from the blood.

hy•per•vi•ta•min•o•sis (hī′pər-vī′tə-mə-nō′sĭs) *n., pl.* **-ses** (-sēz). Any of various abnormal conditions produced by excessive intake of a vitamin.

hy•pes•the•sia (hī′pĭs-thē′zhə) *n.* Var. of **hypoesthesia.**

hy•pe•thral (hī-pē′thrəl) *adj.* Var. of **hypaethral.**

hy•pha (hī′fə) *n., pl.* **-phae** (-fē). Any of the threadlike filaments forming the mycelium of a fungus. [NLat. < Gk. *huphē*, web. See **webh-*.**] — **hy′phal** *adj.*

hy•phen (hī′fən) *n.* A punctuation mark (-) used between the parts of a compound word or name or between the syllables of a word, esp. when divided at the end of a line of text. — *tr.v.* **-phened, -phen•ing, -phens.** To hyphenate. [LLat. < Gk. *huphen*, a sign indicating a compound or two words which are to be read as one < *huph' hen*, in one : *hupo*, under; see HYPO– + *hen*, neut. of *heis*, one; see **sem-¹*.**]

hy•phen•ate (hī′fə-nāt′) *tr.v.* **-at•ed, -at•ing, -ates.** To divide or connect (syllables, word elements, or names) with a hyphen. — **hy′phen•a′tion** *n.*

hyp•na•gog•ic also **hyp•no•gog•ic** (hĭp′nə-gŏj′ĭk, -gō′jĭk) *adj.* **1.** Inducing sleep; soporific. **2.** Of or relating to the state of drowsiness preceding sleep. [Fr. *hypnagogique* : Gk. *hupnos*, sleep; see HYPNO– + Gk. *agōgos*, leading (< *agein*, to lead; see **ag-***).]

hypno– or **hypn–** *pref.* **1.** Sleep: *hypnophobia.* **2.** Hypnosis: *hypnoanalysis.* [< Gk. *hupnos*, sleep. See **swep-*.**]

hyp•no•a•nal•y•sis (hĭp′nō-ə-năl′ĭ-sĭs) *n., pl.* **-ses** (-sēz′). The use of hypnosis in conjunction with psychoanalytic techniques.

hyp•no•gen•e•sis (hĭp′nō-jĕn′ĭ-sĭs) *n.* The process of inducing or entering sleep or a hypnotic state. — **hyp′no•ge•net′ic** (-jə-nĕt′ĭk) *adj.* — **hyp′no•ge•net′i•cal•ly** *adv.*

hyp•noid (hĭp′noid′) also **hyp•noi•dal** (hĭp-noid′l) *adj.* Of or resembling hypnosis or sleep.

hyp•no•pe•di•a (hĭp′nə-pē′dē-ə) *n.* See **sleep-learning.** [HYPNO– + Gk. *paideia*, education; see ENCYCLOPEDIA.]

hyp•no•pho•bi•a (hĭp′nə-fō′bē-ə) *n.* An abnormal fear of falling asleep. — **hyp′no•pho′bic** *adj.*

hyp•no•pom•pic (hĭp′nə-pŏm′pĭk) *adj.* Of or relating to the partially conscious state that precedes complete awakening from sleep. [< HYPNO– + Gk. *pompē*, a sending away; see POMP.]

Hyp•nos (hĭp′nŏs′) *n. Gk. Myth.* The god of sleep.

hyp•no•sis (hĭp-nō′sĭs) *n., pl.* **-ses** (-sēz). **1.** A sleeplike state usu. induced by another person in which forgotten or suppressed memories, hallucinations, and heightened suggestibility may be experienced. **2.** Hypnotism. **3.** A sleeplike condition.

hyp•no•ther•a•py (hĭp′nō-thĕr′ə-pē) *n., pl.* **-pies.** Therapy based on or using hypnosis, esp. for chronic pain.

hyp•not•ic (hĭp-nŏt′ĭk) *adj.* **1.a.** Of or relating to hypnosis. **b.** Of or relating to hypnotism. **2.** Inducing or tending to induce sleep; soporific. — *n.* **1.a.** A person who is hypnotized. **b.** A person who can be hypnotized. **2.** An agent that causes sleep; a soporific. [Fr. *hypnotique* < LLat. *hypnōticus*, inducing sleep < Gk. *hupnōtikos* < *hupnoun*, to put to sleep < *hupnos*, sleep. See **swep-*.**] — **hyp•not′i•cal•ly** *adv.*

hyp•no•tism (hĭp′nə-tĭz′əm) *n.* **1.** The theory or practice of inducing hypnosis. **2.** The act of inducing hypnosis. — **hyp′no•tist** *n.*

hyp•no•tize (hĭp′nə-tīz′) *tr.v.* **-tized, -tiz•ing, -tiz•es. 1.** To put into a state of hypnosis. **2.** To fascinate by or as if by hypnosis. — **hyp′no•tiz′a•ble** *adj.* — **hyp′no•ti•za′tion** (-tĭ-zā′shən) *n.* — **hyp′no•tiz′er** *n.*

hy•po¹ (hī′pō) *n.* See **sodium thiosulfate.** [Short for HYPOSULFITE: HYPO– + SULFITE.]

hy•po² (hī′pō) *Informal.* — *n., pl.* **-pos. 1.** A hypodermic syringe. **2.** A hypodermic injection. — *tr.v.* **-poed, -po•ing, -pos.** To stimulate by or as if by hypodermic injection.

hypo– or **hyp–** *pref.* **1.** Below; beneath; under: *hypodermic.* **2.** Less than normal; deficient: *hypoesthesia.* **3.** In the lowest state of oxidation: *hypoxanthine.* [Gk. *hupo-* < *hupo*, under, beneath. See **upo*.**]

hy•po•al•ler•gen•ic (hī′pō-ăl′ər-jĕn′ĭk) *adj.* Having a decreased tendency to provoke an allergic reaction.

hy•po•bar•ic (hī′pə-băr′ĭk) *adj.* Below normal pressure. — **hy′po•bar′ism** *n.*

hy•po•blast (hī′pə-blăst′) *n.* See **endoderm.** — **hy′po•blas′tic** *adj.*

hy•po•caust (hī′pə-kôst′) *n.* A space under the floor of an ancient Roman building where heat from a furnace was accumulated to heat a room or a bath. [Lat. *hypocaustum* < Gk. *hupokauston* < *hupokaiein*, to light a fire beneath : *hupo-*, hypo- + *kaiein*, to burn.]

hy•po•cen•ter (hī′pə-sĕn′tər) *n.* The surface position directly beneath the center of a nuclear explosion. — **hy′po•cen′tral** (-sĕn′trəl) *adj.*

hy•po•chlo•rite (hī′pə-klôr′īt′, -klōr′-) *n.* A salt or ester of hypochlorous acid.

hy•po•chlo•rous acid (hī′pə-klôr′əs, -klōr′-) *n.* A weak unstable acid, HOCl, occurring only in solution and used as a bleach, an oxidizer, a deodorant, and a disinfectant.

hy•po•chon•dri•a (hī′pə-kŏn′drē-ə) *n.* The persistent neurotic conviction that one is or is likely to become ill. [LLat., abdomen < Gk. *hupokhondria*, pl. of *hupokhondrion*, abdomen (held to be the seat of melancholy), neut. of *hupokhondrios*, under the cartilage of the breastbone : *hupo-*, hypo- + *khondros*, cartilage; see **ghrendh-*.**]

hy•po•chon•dri•ac (hī′pə-kŏn′drē-ăk′) *n.* A person afflicted with hypochondria. — *adj.* **1.** Relating to or afflicted with hypochondria. **2.** *Anat.* Relating to or located in the hypochondrium. — **hy′po•chon•dri′a•cal** (-kŏn-drī′ə-kəl) *adj.*

hy•po•chon•dri•a•sis (hī′pə-kən-drī′ə-sĭs) *n., pl.* **-ses** (-sēz′). See **hypochondria.** [HYPOCHONDR(IA) + –IASIS.]

hy•po•chon•dri•um (hī′pə-kŏn′drē-əm) *n., pl.* **-dri•a** (-drē-ə). The upper lateral region of the abdomen, marked by the lower ribs. [NLat. < Gk. *hupokhondrion*, abdomen. See HYPOCHONDRIA.]

hy•poc•o•rism (hī-pŏk′ə-rĭz′əm, hī′pə-kôr′ĭz′əm, -kōr′-) *n.* **1.** A name of endearment; a pet name. **2.** The use of such names. [LLat. *hypocorisma* < Gk. *hupokorisma* < *hupokorizesthai*, to call by endearing names : *hypo*, beneath, secretly; see HYPO– + *korizesthai*, to caress (< *koros*, boy and *korē*, girl; see **ker-²***).] — **hy′po•co•ris′tic** (hī′pə-kə-rĭs′tĭk), **hy′po•co•ris′ti•cal** (-tĭ-kəl) *adj.* — **hy′po•co•ris′ti•cal•ly** *adv.*

hy•po•cot•yl (hī′pə-kŏt′l) *n.* The part of the axis of a plant embryo or seedling plant that is below the cotyledons. [HYPO– + COTYL(EDON).]

hy•poc•ri•sy (hĭ-pŏk′rĭ-sē) *n., pl.* **-sies. 1.** The practice of professing beliefs, feelings, or virtues that one does not hold or possess; falseness. **2.** An act or instance of such falseness. [ME *ipocrisie* < OFr. < LLat. *hypocrisis*, play-acting, pretense < Gk. *hupokrisis* < *hupokrinesthai*, to play a part, pretend : *hupo-*, hypo- + *krinesthai*, to explain (< *krinein*, to decide, judge; see **krei-***).]

hyp•o•crite (hĭp′ə-krĭt′) *n.* A person given to hypocrisy. [ME *ipocrite* < OFr. < LLat. *hypocrita* < Gk. *hupocritēs*, actor < *hupokrinesthai*, to play a part, pretend. See HYPOCRISY.]

hy•po•crit•i•cal (hĭp′ə-krĭt′ĭ-kəl) *adj.* **1.** Characterized by hypocrisy. **2.** Being a hypocrite. — **hyp′o•crit′i•cal•ly** *adv.*

hy•po•cy•cloid (hī′pō-sī′kloid′) *n. Math.* The plane locus of a point fixed on a circle that rolls on the inside circumference of a fixed circle.

hy•po•der•mal (hī′pə-dûr′məl) *adj.* **1.** Of or relating to the hypodermis. **2.** Lying below the epidermis.

hy•po•der•mic (hī′pə-dûr′mĭk) *adj.* **1.** Of or relating to the layer just beneath the epidermis. **2.** Relating to the hypodermis. **3.** Injected in or beneath the skin. — *n.* **1.** A hypodermic injection. **2.** A hypodermic needle. **3.** A hypodermic syringe. — **hy′po•der′mi•cal•ly** *adv.*

hypodermic needle *n.* **1.** A hollow needle used with a hypodermic syringe. **2.** A hypodermic syringe including the needle.

hypodermic syringe *n.* A piston syringe that is fitted with a hypodermic needle for giving injections.

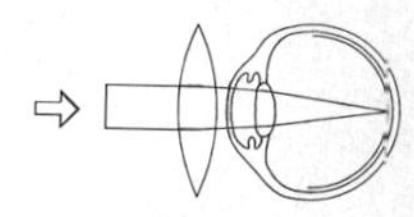

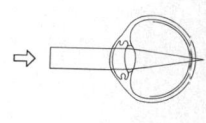

hyperopia
Top: Before correction
Bottom: After correction

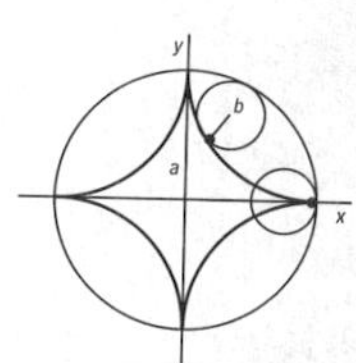

hypocycloid
a = radius of fixed circle
b = radius of rotating circle

ă pat	oi boy
ā pay	ou out
âr care	ŏŏ took
ä father	ōō boot
ĕ pet	ŭ cut
ē be	ûr urge
ĭ pit	th thin
ī pie	*th* this
îr pier	hw which
ŏ pot	zh vision
ō toe	ə about, item
ô paw	

Stress marks:
′ (primary);
′ (secondary), as in
dictionary (dĭk′shə-nĕr′ē)

hy•po•der•mis (hī′pə-dûr′mĭs) also **hy•po•derm** (hī′pə-dûrm′) *n.* **1.** An epidermal layer of cells that secretes an overlying chitinous cuticle, as in arthropods. **2.** *Bot.* A layer of cells lying immediately below the epidermis. **3.** *Anat.* A subcutaneous layer of tissue containing a number of fat cells.

hy•po•es•the•sia (hī′pō-ĭs-thē′zhə) also **hy•pes•the•sia** (hī′pĭs-) *n.* Partial loss of sensation; diminished sensibility.

hy•po•eu•tec•tic (hī′pō-yo͞o-tĕk′tĭk) *adj. Chem.* Having the minor component present in a smaller amount than in the eutectic composition of the same components.

hy•po•gas•tri•um (hī′pə-găs′trē-əm) *n., pl.* **-tri•a** (-trē-ə). The lowest of the three median regions of the abdomen. [NLat. < Gk. *hypogastrion* : *hupo*, hypo- + *gastrion*, dim. of *gastēr*, belly.] **— hy′po•gas′tric** *adj.*

hy•po•ge•al (hī′pə-jē′əl) also **hy•po•ge•an** (-ən) or **hy•po•ge•ous** (-əs) *adj.* **1.** Located under the earth's surface. **2.** *Bot.* Of or relating to seed germination in which the cotyledons remain below the surface of the ground. [< Lat. *hypogēus* < Gk. *hupogeios* : *hupo*, hypo- + *gē*, earth.]

hy•po•gene (hī′pə-jēn′) *adj.* Formed or situated below the earth's surface. Used of rocks.

hy•pog•e•nous (hī-pŏj′ə-nəs) *adj. Bot.* Growing on a lower surface of a structure, as fungi on leaves.

hy•po•ge•um (hī′pə-jē′əm) *n., pl.* **-ge•a** (-jē′ə). **1.** A subterranean chamber of an ancient building. **2.** An ancient subterranean burial chamber, such as a catacomb. [Lat. *hypogēum* < Gk. *hupogeion* < neut. of *hupogeios*, underground. See HYPOGEAL.]

hy•po•glos•sal (hī′pə-glŏs′əl) *adj.* **1.** Of or relating to the area under the tongue. **2.** Of or relating to the hypoglossal nerve. [HYPO– + Gk. *glōssa*, tongue.]

hypoglossal nerve *n.* Either of the 12th pair of cranial nerves that innervate the muscles of the tongue.

hy•po•gly•ce•mi•a (hī′pō-glī-sē′mē-ə) *n.* An abnormally low level of glucose in the blood.

hy•po•gly•ce•mic (hī′pō-glī-cē′mĭk) *adj.* **1.** Of or relating to hypoglycemia. **2.** Lowering the concentration of glucose in the blood: *a hypoglycemic drug.*

hy•pog•y•nous (hī-pŏj′ə-nəs) *adj. Bot.* Having the floral parts, such as sepals, petals, and stamens, borne on the receptacle beneath the ovary. **— hy•pog′y•ny** (-nē) *n.*

hy•po•lim•ni•on (hī′pə-lĭm′nē-ŏn′, -ən) *n.* The layer of water in a thermally stratified lake that lies below the thermocline, is noncirculating, and remains perpetually cold. [HYPO– + Gk. *limnion*, dim. of *limnē*, lake, pool.] **— hy′po•lim•net′ic** (-lĭm-nĕt′ĭk), **hy′po•lim′ni•al** *adj.*

hy•po•ma•ni•a (hī′pə-mā′nē-ə, -mān′yə) *n.* A mild state of mania, esp. as a phase of a manic-depressive cycle. **— hy′po•man′ic** (-măn′ĭk) *adj.*

hy•po•nas•ty (hī′pə-năs′tē) *n., pl.* **-ties.** An upward bending of leaves or other plant parts, resulting from growth of the lower side. **— hy′po•nas′tic** *adj.*

hy•po•phos•phite (hī′pō-fŏs′fīt′) *n.* A salt of hypophosphorous acid.

hy•po•phos•pho•rous acid (hī′pō-fŏs′fər-əs, -fŏs-fôr′əs, -fōr′-) *n.* A clear colorless or slightly yellow liquid, H_3PO_2, used as a reducing agent.

hy•poph•y•sis (hī-pŏf′ĭ-sĭs) *n., pl.* **-ses** (-sēz′). See **pituitary gland.** [NLat. < Gk. *hupophusis*, attachment underneath < *hupophuein*, to grow up beneath : *hupo-*, hypo- + *phuein*, to make grow; see **bheuə-*.**] **— hy•poph′y•se′al** (hī-pŏf′ĭ-sē′əl), **hy′po•phys′i•al** (hī′pə-fĭz′ē-əl) *adj.*

hy•po•pi•tu•i•ta•rism (hī′pō-pĭ-to͞o′ĭ-tə-rĭz′əm, -tyo͞o′-) *n.* **1.** Deficient or diminished production of pituitary hormones. **2.** The condition resulting from a deficiency in pituitary hormone, esp. growth hormone, marked by dwarfism in children and by decreased activity of the thyroid, adrenal, or gonadal glands. **— hy′po•pi•tu′i•tar′y** (-tĕr′ē) *adj.*

hy•po•pla•sia (hī′pō-plā′zhə, -zhē-ə) *n.* Incomplete or arrested development of an organ or a part. **— hy′po•plas′tic** (-plăs′tĭk) *adj.*

hy•po•ploid (hī′pō-ploid′) *adj. Genet.* Having a chromosome number lower by only a few chromosomes than the normal diploid number. **— hy′po•ploi′dy** *n.*

hy•pop•ne•a (hī-pŏp′nē-ə, hī′pō-nē′ə) *n.* Abnormally slow shallow breathing. [HYPO– + Gk. *pnoia*, *pnoē*, breath; breathing (< *pnein*, to breathe; see **pneu-*).]** **— hy′pop•ne′ic** *adj.*

hy•po•sen•si•tiv•i•ty (hī′pō-sĕn′sĭ-tĭv′ĭ-tē) *n., pl.* **-ties.** Less than the normal ability to respond to stimuli. **— hy′po•sen′si•tive** *adj.*

hy•po•sen•si•tize (hī′pō-sĕn′sĭ-tīz′) *tr.v.* **-tized, -tiz•ing, -tiz•es.** To make less sensitive, as to an allergen; desensitize. **— hy′po•sen′si•ti•za′tion** (-tĭ-zā′shən) *n.*

hy•pos•ta•sis (hī-pŏs′tə-sĭs) *n., pl.* **-ses** (-sēz′). **1.** *Philos.* The substance, essence, or underlying reality. **2.** *Theol.* **a.** Any of the persons of the Trinity. **b.** The essential person of Jesus in which his human and divine natures are united. **3.** Something hypostatized. **4.a.** A settling of solid particles in a fluid. **b.** Something that settles to the bottom of a fluid; sediment. **5.** *Medic.* The settling of blood in the lower part of an organ or the body as a result of decreased blood flow. **6.** *Genet.* A condition in which the action of one gene conceals or suppresses the action of another gene that is not its allele but that affects the same part or biochemical process in an organism. [LLat. < Gk. *hupostasis* : *hupo-*, hypo- + *stasis*, a standing; see **stā-*.**] **— hy′po•stat′ic** (hī′pə-stăt′ĭk), **hy′po•stat′i•cal** *adj.* **— hy′po•stat′i•cal•ly** *adv.*

hy•pos•ta•tize (hī-pŏs′tə-tīz′) *tr.v.* **-tized, -tiz•ing, -tiz•es.** To ascribe material existence to. [< Gk. *hupostatos*, placed under, substantial < *huphistasthai*, to stand under, exist : *hupo*, beneath; see HYPO– + *histasthai*, middle voice of *histanai*, to set, place; see EPISTASIS.] **— hy•pos′ta•ti•za′tion** (-tĭ-zā′shən) *n.*

hy•po•style (hī′pə-stīl′) *adj.* Having a roof or ceiling supported by rows of columns. **—** *n.* A hypostyle building. [< Gk. *hupostulos*, resting upon pillars : *hupo-*, hypo- + *stulos*, pillar; see **stā-*.**]

hy•po•sul•fu•rous acid (hī′pō-sŭl-fyo͝or′əs, -sŭl′fər-əs) *n.* An unstable acid, $H_2S_2O_4$, known only in aqueous solution and used as a bleaching and reducing agent.

hy•po•tax•is (hī′pə-tăk′sĭs) *n. Gram.* The dependent subordinate relationship of clauses and connectives. [Gk. *hupotaxis*, subjection < *hupotassein*, to arrange under : *hupo-*, hypo- + *tassein*, *tag-*, to arrange.] **— hy′po•tac′tic** *adj.*

hy•po•ten•sion (hī′pə-tĕn′shən) *n.* Abnormally low blood pressure.

hy•pot•e•nuse (hī-pŏt′n-o͞os′, -yo͞os′) also **hy•poth•e•nuse** (-pŏth′ə-no͞os′, -nyo͞os′) *n. Math.* The side of a right triangle opposite the right angle. [Lat. *hypotēnūsa* < Gk. *hupoteinousa*, fem. sing. pr.part. of *hupoteinein*, to stretch or extend under : *hupo-*, hypo- + *teinein*, to stretch; see **ten-*.**]

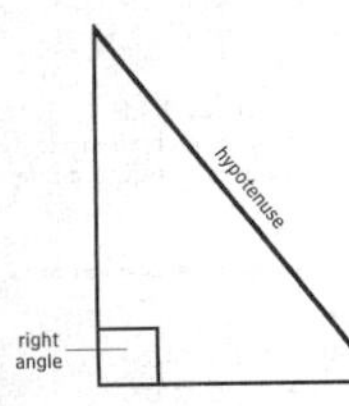

hypotenuse

hypoth. *abbr.* Hypothesis.

hy•po•thal•a•mus (hī′pō-thăl′ə-məs) *n.* The part of the brain below the thalamus, forming the major portion of the ventral region of the diencephalon and regulating bodily temperature and other autonomic activities. **— hy′po•tha•lam′ic** (-thə-lăm′ĭk) *adj.*

hy•poth•e•cate (hī-pŏth′ĭ-kāt′) *tr.v.* **-cat•ed, -cat•ing, -cates.** To pledge (property) as security or collateral for a debt without transfer of title or possession. [Med.Lat. *hypothēcāre*, *hypothēcāt-* < Lat. *hypothēca*, pledge, deposit < Gk. *hupothēkē* < *hupotithenai*, to give as a pledge, suppose. See HYPOTHESIS.] **— hy•poth′e•ca′tion** *n.* **— hy•poth′e•ca′tor** *n.*

hy•po•ther•mal (hī′pō-thûr′məl) *adj. Geol.* Of, relating to, or being mineral deposits formed at great depths and high temperatures.

hy•po•ther•mi•a (hī′pə-thûr′mē-ə) *n.* Abnormally low body temperature. [HYPO– + Gk. *thermē*, heat; see **gʷher-*** + -IA[1].] **— hy′po•ther′mic** (-mĭk) *adj.*

hy•poth•e•sis (hī-pŏth′ĭ-sĭs) *n., pl.* **-ses** (-sēz′). **1.** A tentative explanation that accounts for a set of facts and can be tested by further investigation; a theory. **2.** Something taken to be true for the purpose of argument or investigation; an assumption. **3.** The antecedent of a conditional statement. [Lat., subject for a speech < Gk. *hupothesis*, proposal, supposition < *hupotithenai*, to suppose : *hupo-*, hypo- + *tithenai*, to place; see **dhē-*.**]

hy•poth•e•size (hī-pŏth′ĭ-sīz′) *v.* **-sized, -siz•ing, -siz•es.** **—** *tr.* To assert as a hypothesis. **—** *intr.* To form a hypothesis.

hy•po•thet•i•cal (hī′pə-thĕt′ĭ-kəl) also **hy•po•thet•ic** (-thĕt′ĭk) *adj.* **1.** Of, relating to, or based on a hypothesis. **2.a.** Suppositional; uncertain. **b.** Conditional; contingent. [< Gk. *hupothetikos* < *hupothetos*, placed under, supposed < *hupotithenai*, to suppose. See HYPOTHESIS.] **— hy′po•thet′i•cal** *n.* **— hy′po•thet′i•cal•ly** *adv.*

hy•po•thy•roid (hī′pō-thī′roid′) *adj.* Affected by or manifesting hypothyroidism.

hy•po•thy•roid•ism (hī′pō-thī′roi-dĭz′əm) *n.* **1.** Insufficient production of thyroid hormones. **2.** A pathological condition resulting from severe thyroid insufficiency.

hy•po•ton•ic (hī′pō-tŏn′ĭk) *adj.* **1.** *Pathol.* Having less than normal tone or tension, as of muscles or arteries. **2.** *Chem.* Having the lower osmotic pressure of two fluids. **— hy′po•to•nic′i•ty** (-tə-nĭs′ĭ-tē) *n.*

hy•po•xan•thine (hī′pō-zăn′thēn′) *n.* A white powder, $C_5H_4N_4O$, that is an intermediate in the metabolism of animal purines.

hy•pox•e•mi•a (hī′pŏk-sē′mē-ə) *n.* Insufficient oxygenation of the blood.

hy•pox•i•a (hī-pŏk′sē-ə, hĭ-) *n.* Deficiency in the amount of oxygen reaching body tissues. **— hy•pox′ic** *adj.*

hypso– or **hyps–** *pref.* Height: *hypsometer.* [< Gk. *hupsos*, height, top. See **upo*.**]

hyp•sog•ra•phy (hĭp-sŏg′rə-fē) *n., pl.* **-phies. 1.a.** The scientific study of the earth's topologic configuration above sea level, esp. the measurement and mapping of land elevations. **b.** A representation or description of the earth's topologic features above sea level. **2.** Hypsometry. **— hyp′so•graph′ic** (hĭp′sə-grăf′ĭk), **hyp′so•graph′i•cal** *adj.*

hyp•som•e•ter (hĭp-sŏm′ĭ-tər) *n.* An instrument using atmospheric pressure to determine land elevations.

hyp•som•e•try (hĭp-sŏm′ĭ-trē) *n.* The measurement of elevation relative to sea level. **— hyp′so•met′ric** (hĭp′sə-mĕt′rĭk), **hyp′so•met′ri•cal** *adj.* **— hyp•som′e•trist** *n.*

hy•rax (hī′răks′) *n., pl.* **-rax•es** or **-ra•ces** (-rə-sēz′). Any of several herbivorous mammals of the family Procaviidae of Africa and adjacent Asia, resembling woodchucks or similar rodents but more closely related to the hoofed mammals. [Gk. *hurax,* shrew mouse.]

hy•son (hī′sən) *n.* A type of Chinese green tea with twisted leaves. [Chin. (Mandarin) *xī chūn* : *xī,* warm, sunny + *chūn,* springlike.]

hys•sop (hĭs′əp) *n.* **1.** A woody Eurasian plant *(Hyssopus officinalis)* having spikes of small blue flowers and aromatic leaves used in perfumery and as a condiment. **2.** Any of several similar or related plants. **3.** An unidentified plant mentioned in the Bible as the source of twigs used for sprinkling in certain Hebraic purificatory rites. [ME *ysope* < OE *ȳsōpe* < Lat. *hȳsōpum, hyssōpus* < Gk. *hussōpos,* prob. of Semitic orig.; akin to Heb. *'ēzôb.*]

hys•ter•ec•to•my (hĭs′tə-rĕk′tə-mē) *n., pl.* **-mies.** Surgical removal of part or all of the uterus.

hys•ter•e•sis (hĭs′tə-rē′sĭs) *n., pl.* **-ses** (-sēz). The lagging of an effect behind its cause, as when the change in magnetism of a body lags behind changes in the magnetic field. [Gk. *husterēsis,* a shortcoming < *husterein,* to come late < *husteros,* late. See **ud-***.] **—hys′ter•et′ic** (-rĕt′ĭk) *adj.*

hys•ter•i•a (hĭ-stĕr′ē-ə, -stîr′-) *n.* **1.** A neurosis characterized by the presentation of a physical ailment without an organic cause and various other mental and behavioral aberrations. **2.** Excessive or uncontrollable emotion, such as fear or panic. [NLat. : HYSTER(IC) + -IA[1].]

hys•ter•ic (hĭ-stĕr′ĭk) *n.* **1.** A person suffering from hysteria. **2. hysterics.** *(used with a sing. or pl. v.)* **a.** A fit of uncontrollable laughing or crying. **b.** An attack of hysteria. *—adj.* Hysterical. [< Lat. *hystericus,* hysterical < Gk. *husterikos* < *hustera,* womb (< the former idea that disturbances in the womb caused hysteria).]

hys•ter•i•cal (hĭ-stĕr′ĭ-kəl) *adj.* **1.** Of, characterized by, or arising from hysteria. **2.** Having or prone to having hysterics. **3.** *Informal.* Extremely funny. **—hys•ter′i•cal•ly** *adv.*

hystero– or **hyster–** *pref.* **1.** Uterus: *hysterectomy.* **2.** Hysteria: *hysteroid.* [< Gk. *hustera,* womb.]

hys•ter•o•gen•ic (hĭs′tə-rō-jĕn′ĭk) *adj.* Inducing hysteria.

hys•ter•oid (hĭs′tə-roid′) *adj.* Resembling hysteria.

hys•ter•on prot•er•on (hĭs′tə-rŏn′ prŏt′ə-rŏn′) *n.* **1.** A figure of speech in which the natural or rational order of its terms is reversed, as in *bred and born* instead of *born and bred.* **2.** The logical fallacy of assuming as true and using as a premise a proposition that is yet to be proved. [LLat. < Gk. *husteron proteron,* latter first : *husteron,* neut. sing. of *husteros,* latter, later; see **ud-*** + *proteron,* neut. sing. of *proteros,* former; see **per[1]***.]

hys•ter•ot•o•my (hĭs′tə-rŏt′ə-mē) *n., pl.* **-mies.** Surgical incision of the uterus, as in a cesarean section.

Hz *abbr.* Hertz.

hyrax

I i

i[1] or **I** (ī) *n., pl.* **i's** or **I's. 1.** The ninth letter of the modern English alphabet. **2.** Any of the speech sounds represented by the letter *i.* **3.** The ninth in a series. **4.** Something shaped like the letter I.

i[2] also **I** *Elect.* The symbol for **current 4.**

i[3] *abbr. Math.* Imaginary unit.

I[1] (ī) *pron.* Used to refer to oneself as speaker or writer. *—n., pl.* **I's.** The self; the ego. [ME < OE *ic.* See **eg***.]

Usage Note: The question of when to use nominative forms of the personal pronouns (for example, *I, she, they*) and when to use objective forms (for example, *me, her, them*) has always created controversy among grammarians and uncertainty among speakers and writers. When pronouns are joined with other nouns or pronouns by *and* or *or,* there is a widespread tendency to use the objective form even when the phrase is the subject of the sentence: *Robert and her are not speaking to each other.* This usage is natural in colloquial speech, but the nominative forms should be used in formal speech and writing: *John and she will be giving the talk.* • When pronouns joined by a conjunction occur as the object of a preposition such as *between, according to,* or *like,* many people use the nominative form where the traditional grammatical rule would require the objective; they say *between you and I* rather than *between you and me* and so forth. Such constructions are best avoided. The objective form sounds most natural when the pronoun is not grammatically related to an accompanying verb or preposition. Thus, in response to the question *"Who cut down the cherry tree?"* we more colloquially say *"Me,"* even though some grammarians have argued that *I* must be correct here by analogy to the form *"I did."* See Usage Notes at **be, but, we.**

I[2] 1. The symbol for the element **iodine** 1. **2.** Also **i** The symbol for the Roman numeral 1.

I[3] *abbr.* **1.** Institute. **2.** Intelligence. **3.** Interstate. **4.** Isospin.

i. *abbr.* **1.** Incisor. **2.** Interest. **3.** *Gram.* Intransitive. **4.** Or **I.** Island; isle.

–i–. Used as a connective to join word elements: *setiform.* [ME < OFr. < Lat., stem vowel of nouns and adjectives used in combination.]

IA or **Ia.** *abbr.* Iowa.

i.a. *abbr.* In absentia.

–ia[1] *suff.* **1.** Disease; pathological or abnormal condition: *anoxia.* **2.** Territory; country: *Australia.* [NLat. < Lat. and Gk., n. suff.]

–ia[2] *suff.* Things derived from, relating to, or belonging to: *personalia.* [Lat., neut. pl. of *-ius,* and Gk., neut. pl. of *-ios,* and adj. suffixes.]

–ial *suff.* Of, relating to, or characterized by: *baronial.* [ME < OFr. < Lat. *-iālis.*]

i•amb (ī′ămb′, ī′ăm′) also **i•am•bus** (ī-ăm′bəs) *n., pl.* **i•ambs** also **-bus•es** or **-bi** (-bī′). A metrical foot consisting of an unstressed syllable followed by a stressed syllable or a short syllable followed by a long syllable. [Fr. *iambe* < Lat. *iambus* < Gk. *iambos.*]

i•am•bic (ī-ăm′bĭk) *adj.* Consisting of iambs or characterized by their predominance: *iambic pentameter.* *—n.* **1.** An iamb. **2.** Often **iambics.** A verse, stanza, or poem written in iambs.

–ian *suff.* **1.** Of, relating to, or resembling: *Bostonian.* **2.** One relating to, belonging to, or resembling: *academician.* [ME *-ien, -ian* < OFr. *-ien* < Lat. *-iānus,* adj. and n. suff.]

–iana *suff.* Var. of **–ana.**

I•ap•e•tus (ī-ăp′ĭ-təs, ē-ăp′-) *n. Gk. Myth.* A Titan who was the father of Prometheus and Atlas and an ancestor of the human race. [Lat. *Īapetus* < Gk. *Iapetos.*]

IAS *abbr.* Indicated air speed.

Ia•şi (yäsh, yä′shē). A city of NE Romania NNE of Bucharest; cap. of the country until 1861. Pop. 305,598.

–iasis *suff.* A pathological condition characterized or produced by: *teniasis.* [NLat. < Gk., n. suff.]

–iatric *suff.* Of or relating to a specified kind of medical practice, treatment, or healing: *geriatric.* [< Gk. *iatrikos,* medical < *iatros,* physician < *iasthai,* to heal.]

–iatrics *suff.* Medical treatment: *pediatrics.* [< -IATRIC.]

i•at•ro•gen•ic (ī-ăt′rə-jĕn′ĭk) *adj.* Induced in a patient by a physician's activity, manner, or therapy. [Gk. *iatros,* physician; see -IATRIC + -GENIC.] **—i•at′ro•gen′i•cal•ly** *adv.*

–iatry *suff.* Medical treatment: *psychiatry.* [Gk. *-iatreia,* art of healing < *iatros,* physician. See -IATRIC.]

ib. *abbr.* Ibidem.

I•ba•dan (ē-bäd′n, ē-bä′dän). A city of SW Nigeria NNW of Lagos; founded in the 1830's. Pop. 1,009,400.

I•ba•gué (ē-bä-gĕ′). A city of W-central Colombia W of Bogotá. Pop. 265,598.

I-beam (ī′bēm′) *n.* A steel joist or girder with short flanges and a cross section formed like the letter I.

I•be•ri•a (ī-bîr′ē-ə). **1.** An ancient country of Transcaucasia roughly equivalent to the E part of present-day Georgia; became a Byzantine province in the 6th cent. A.D. **2.** See **Iberian Peninsula.**

I•be•ri•an (ī-bîr′ē-ən) *adj.* **1.** Of or relating to ancient Iberia in Transcaucasia or its peoples, languages, or cultures. **2.** Of or relating to the Iberian Peninsula or its peoples, languages, or cultures. *—n.* **1.** A native or inhabitant of ancient Iberia in Transcaucasia. **2.a.** A native or inhabitant of the Iberian Peninsula. **b.** A member of one of the ancient peoples that inhabited the Iberian Peninsula. **3.** Any of the languages of these peoples.

Iberian Peninsula also **I•be•ri•a** (ī-bîr′ē-ə). A peninsula of SW Europe separated from the rest of Europe by the Pyrenees and from Africa by the Strait of Gibraltar.

I•ber•ville (ē-bĕr-vēl′), **Pierre Le Moyne.** Sieur d'Iberville. 1661–1706. Canadian-born French explorer who established settlements in what is now S LA.

i•bex (ī′bĕks′) *n., pl.* **ibex** or **i•bex•es.** Any of several wild goats of the genus *Capra,* esp. *C. ibex,* native to mountainous regions of Eurasia and northern Africa and having long, ridged, backward-curving horns. [Lat.]

I•bib•i•o (ĭ-bĭb′ē-ō) *n., pl.* **Ibibio** or **-os. 1.** A member of a people of southeast Nigeria. **2.** The South Central Niger Congo language of the Ibibio, closely related to Efik.

ă pat	oi boy
ā pay	ou out
âr care	o͝o took
ä father	o͞o boot
ĕ pet	ŭ cut
ē be	ûr urge
ĭ pit	th thin
ī pie	*th* this
îr pier	hw which
ŏ pot	zh vision
ō toe	ə about, item
ô paw	

Stress marks:
′ (primary);
′ (secondary), as in
dictionary (dĭk′shə-nĕr′ē)

i•bi•dem (ĭb′ĭ-dĕm′, ĭ-bī′dəm) *adv.* In the same place. Used in footnotes and bibliographies to refer to the reference cited just before. [Lat. *ibīdem.* See **i-***.]

–ibility *suff.* Var. of **–ability.**

i•bis (ī′bĭs) *n., pl.* **ibis** or **i•bis•es. 1.** Any of various storklike wading birds of the family Threskiornithidae of temperate and tropical regions, having a slender downward-curving bill. **2.** The wood ibis. [ME *ibin* < Lat. *ībis* < Gk. < Egypt. *hbj.*]

I•bi•za also **I•vi•za** (ē-bē′sə, ē-vē′thä). A Spanish island of the Balearic Is. in the W Mediterranean SW of Majorca.

I•bi•zan hound (ĭ-bē′zən, -zän) *n.* A swift slender hunting dog bred primarily in the Balearic Islands and having a short, solid or spotted red and white or tawny coat. [After Ibiza.]

–ible *suff.* Var. of **–able.**

ibn-Sa•ud (ĭb′ən-sä-o͞od′), **Abdul Aziz.** 1880?–1953. Arab leader who was the first king of Saudi Arabia (1932–53).

ibis
White ibis
Eudocimus albus

I•bo (ē′bō) also **Ig•bo** (ĭg′bō) *n., pl.* **Ibo** or **I•bos** also **Igbo** or **-bos. 1.** A member of a people of southeast Nigeria. **2.** The South Central Niger Congo language of the Ibo.

Ib•sen (ĭb′sən, ĭp′-), **Henrik.** 1828–1906. Norwegian playwright whose works include *Peer Gynt* (1867) and *A Doll's House* (1879). **— Ib•sen′i•an** (-sē′nē-ən, -sĕn′ē-) *adj.*

i•bu•pro•fen (ī′byo͞o-prō′fən) *n.* A nonsteroidal anti-inflammatory medication, $C_{13}H_{18}O_2$, used esp. in the treatment of arthritis and commonly taken as an analgesic and antipyretic. [Alteration of chemical name *i(so)bu(tyl)phen(yl) pro(pionic acid).*]

IC *abbr.* Integrated circuit.

–ic *suff.* **1.** Of, relating to, or characterized by: *seismic.* **2.** Having a valence higher than that of a specified element in compounds or ions named with adjectives ending in *–ous: sulfuric acid.* **3.** One relating to or characterized by: *academic.* [ME < OFr. *-ique* < Lat. *-icus* < Gk. *-ikos.*]

I•ca (ē′kə, ē′kä). A city of SW Peru SSE of Lima; settled by the Spanish in 1563. Pop. 114,786.

I•car•i•a (ĭ-kâr′ē-ə, ī-kâr′-). See **Ikaria.**

Ic•a•rus (ĭk′ər-əs) *n. Gk. Myth.* The son of Daedalus who in escaping from Crete on wings made for him by his father flew so close to the sun that the wax fastening his wings melted and he fell into the Aegean Sea. [Lat. < Gk. *Ikaros.*]

ICBM *abbr.* Intercontinental ballistic missile.

ICC *abbr.* **1.** Indian Claims Commission. **2.** International Chamber of Commerce. **3.** Interstate Commerce Commission.

Henrik Ibsen

ice (īs) *n.* **1.** Water frozen solid. **2.** A surface, layer, or mass of frozen water. **3.** Something resembling frozen water. **4.** A dessert consisting of sweetened and flavored crushed ice. **5.** Cake frosting; icing. **6.** *Slang.* Diamonds. **7.** *Sports.* The playing field in ice hockey; the rink. **8.** Extreme unfriendliness or reserve. **9.** *Slang.* A payment over the listed price of a ticket for a public event. *— v.* **iced, ic•ing, ic•es.** *— tr.* **1.** To coat or slick with solidly frozen water. **2.** To cause to become ice; freeze. **3.** To chill by setting in or as if in ice. **4.** To cover or decorate (a cake, for example) with a sugar coating. **5.** *Slang.* To ensure of victory, as in a game; clinch. **6.** *Sports.* To shoot (the puck) far out of defensive territory in ice hockey. **7.** *Slang.* To kill; murder. *— intr.* To turn into or become coated with ice; freeze: *The pond iced over.* **— *idiom.* on ice.** *Slang.* **1.** In reserve or readiness. **2.** Held incommunicado. [ME *ise* < OE *īs.*]

ICE *abbr.* **1.** Internal-combustion engine. **2.** International Cultural Exchange.

Ice. *abbr.* Iceland; Icelandic.

ice age *n.* **1.** A cold period marked by episodes of extensive glaciation alternating with episodes of relative warmth. **2. Ice Age.** The most recent glacial period, which occurred during the Pleistocene Epoch.

ice ax *n.* An ax used by mountaineers for cutting steps in ice.

ice bag *n.* See **ice pack** 2.

ice barrier *n. Geol.* A section of the Antarctic ice shelf beyond the coastline, resting partly on the ocean floor.

ice•berg (īs′bûrg′) *n.* **1.** A massive floating body of ice broken away from a glacier. **2.** *Informal.* A cold aloof person. [Partial transl. of Du. *ijsberg* < MDu. *ijsbergh* : *ijs,* ice + *bergh,* mountain (< MDu.; see **bhergh-²***).]

iceberg lettuce *n.* A crisp round compact head of lettuce with light green, tightly folded leaves. [From its pale color.]

ice•blink (īs′blĭngk′) *n.* **1.** A yellowish glare in the sky over an ice field. **2.** A coastal ice cliff.

ice blue (īs′blo͞o′) *n. Color.* A very pale blue.

iceboat

ice•boat (īs′bōt′) *n. Naut.* **1.** A boatlike vehicle set on sharp runners, used for sailing on ice. **2.** See **icebreaker** 1.

ice•bound (īs′bound′) *adj.* Locked in or covered over by ice.

ice•box (īs′bŏks′) *n.* **1.** An insulated chest or box into which ice is placed to cool and preserve food. **2.** A refrigerator.

ice•break•er (īs′brā′kər) *n.* **1.** *Naut.* A sturdy ship built to break a passage through icebound waters. **2.** A protective pier or dock apron used as a buffer against floating ice. **3.a.** Something done or said to relax an unduly formal atmosphere or situation. **b.** A beginning; a start. **— ice′break′ing** *n.*

ice hockey

ice bucket *n.* **1.** A small insulated container with a lid, used to hold ice. **2.** A similar container without a lid, used to cool bottles placed inside it.

ice•cap or **ice cap** (īs′kăp′) *n.* An extensive dome-shaped or platelike perennial cover of ice and snow that spreads out from a center and covers a large area, esp. of land.

ice-cold (īs′kōld′) *adj.* Extremely cold.

ice cream *n.* A dessert food prepared from a frozen mixture of milk products, sugar, and flavorings.

ice-cream cone *n.* **1.** A conical wafer used to hold a scoop of ice cream. **2.** A cone with ice cream in it.

ice-cream parlor *n.* An establishment serving ice cream.

ice-cream social *n. Northern U.S.* A picnic featuring ice cream, often held for the purpose of raising money for charity. Also called regionally *ice-cream sociable.*

ice-cream soda *n.* A refreshment consisting of scoops of ice cream in a mixture of soda water and syrup.

iced (īst) *adj.* **1.** Covered over with ice. **2.** Chilled with ice. **3.** Decorated or coated with icing.

ice•fall (īs′fôl′) *n.* **1.** The part of a glacier resembling a frozen waterfall flowing down a steep slope. **2.** An ice avalanche.

ice field *n.* A large level expanse of floating ice that is more than eight kilometers (five miles) in its greatest dimension.

ice floe *n.* A flat expanse of ice smaller than an ice field.

ice fog *n.* A fog of ice particles.

ice foot *n.* A belt or ledge of ice along Arctic shorelines.

ice-free (īs′frē′) *adj.* **1.** Free of ice and passable: *an ice-free river.* **2.** Lacking obstructive ice: *an ice-free period.*

ice hockey *n. Sports.* A game played on ice in which two opposing teams of skaters, using curved sticks, try to drive a puck into the opponent's goal.

ice•house (īs′hous′) *n.* A place where ice is made, stored, or sold.

Icel. *abbr.* Iceland; Icelandic.

Ice•land (īs′lənd). An island country in the North Atlantic near the Arctic Circle; gained independence from Denmark in 1944. Cap. Reykjavík. Pop. 240,443. **— Ice′land•er** *n.*

Ice•land•ic (īs-lăn′dĭk) *adj.* Of or relating to Iceland or its people, language, or culture. *— n.* The North Germanic language of Iceland.

Iceland moss *n.* A brittle grayish-brown Arctic lichen *(Cetraria islandica)* sometimes used as a food or in medicine.

Iceland spar *n.* A doubly refracting transparent calcite used in optical instruments.

ice•mak•er (īs′mā′kər) *n.* A machine, often built into a refrigerator, that freezes water into ice cubes.

ice•man (īs′mən) *n.* **1.** A man who cuts, sells, or delivers ice. **2.** *Slang.* A hired killer.

ice milk *n.* A dessert food prepared from a frozen mixture of milk products and sugar.

ice-mi•nus (īs′mī′nəs) *adj.* Of or relating to a strain of genetically altered bacteria that are applied to crop plants to inhibit the formation of frost.

ice needle *n.* A long thin ice crystal floating high in the atmosphere under certain conditions of temperature and humidity.

I•ce•ni (ī-sē′nī′) *pl.n.* An ancient Celtic tribe of eastern Britain who under Queen Boudicca fought unsuccessfully against the Romans about A.D. 60. [Lat. *Icēnī.*] **— I•ce′nic** (-nĭk) *adj.*

ice pack *n.* **1.** A floating mass of compacted ice fragments. **2.** A folded sac filled with crushed ice and applied to parts of the body to reduce pain and inflammation.

ice pick *n.* A pointed awl for chipping or breaking ice.

ice plant *n.* A succulent annual *(Mesembryanthemum crystallinum)* native to southern Africa and having fleshy leaves and stems covered with glistening papillae.

ice point *n.* The temperature, equal to 1.0°C (33.8°F), at which pure water and ice are in equilibrium in a mixture at 1 atmosphere of pressure.

ice show *n.* An entertainment consisting of figure skating, ice dancing, acrobatic stunts, and buffoonery performed on ice.

ice skate *n. Sports.* A shoe or light boot with a metal runner or blade fitted to the sole, used for skating on ice. **— ice′-skate′** (īs′skāt′) *v.* **— ice skater** *n.*

ice storm *n.* A storm in which snow or rain freezes on contact, forming a coat of ice on the surfaces it touches.

ice water *n.* **1.** Very cold or chilled water, esp. for drinking, often with ice in it. **2.** Melted ice.

ICFTU *abbr.* International Confederation of Free Trade Unions.

I•chi•ka•wa (ē-chē′kä-wä′). A city of E-central Honshu, Japan, a suburb of Tokyo. Pop. 397,806.

I Ching (ē jĭng) *n.* An ancient Chinese book consisting of 64 interrelated hexagrams along with commentaries that may be consulted as an oracle. [Chin. (Mandarin) *Yì Jīng* : *Yì,* divination + *Jīng,* classic, book.]

I•chi•no•mi•ya (ē′chē-nō′mē-ä′, -yä′). A city of central Honshu, Japan, a suburb of Nagoya. Pop. 257,392.

ich•neu•mon (ĭk-no͞o′mən, -nyo͞o′-) *n.* **1.** A large mongoose *(Herpestes ichneumon)* of Africa and southern Europe having a gray coat and black tail tufts. **2.** The ichneumon fly. [Lat. *ichneumōn,* weasel, ichneumon fly < Gk. *ikhneumōn* < *ikhneuein,* to track < *ikhnos,* track.]

ichneumon fly *n.* Any of various wasplike insects of the family Ichneumonidae, whose larvae are parasitic on the larvae of other insects.

ich•nite (ĭk′nīt′) also **ich•no•lite** (-nō-līt′) *n.* A fossilized footprint. [Gk. *ikhnos*, track + -ITE[1].]

ich•nog•ra•phy (ĭk-nŏg′rə-fē) *n., pl.* **-phies. 1.** The art or process of drawing ground plans. **2.** A ground plan of a building. [Lat. *ichnographia* : Gk. *ikhnos*, track + Lat. *-graphia*, -graphy.]

i•chor (ī′kôr′, ī′kər) *n.* **1.** *Gk. Myth.* The rarefied fluid running in the veins of the gods. **2.** *Pathol.* A watery acrid discharge from a wound or ulcer. [ME *icor* < LLat. *ichōr* < Gk. *ikhōr*.] — **i′chor•ous** (ī′kər-əs) *adj.*

ichth. *abbr.* Ichthyology.

ich•thy•ic (ĭk′thē-ĭk) *adj.* Of or characteristic of fishes.

ichthyo– or **ichthy–** *pref.* Fish: *ichthyophagous.* [Lat. < Gk. *ikhthuo-* < *ikhthus*, fish.]

ich•thy•o•fau•na (ĭk′thē-ə-fô′nə) *n.* The fish of a particular region.

ich•thy•oid (ĭk′thē-oid′) *n.* A fish or fishlike vertebrate. — **ich′thy•oid′, ich′thy•oi′dal** (ĭk′thē-oid′l) *adj.*

ich•thy•ol•o•gy (ĭk′thē-ŏl′ə-jē) *n.* The branch of zoology that deals with the study of fishes. — **ich′thy•o•log′ic** (-ə-lŏj′ĭk), **ich′thy•o•log′i•cal** *adj.* — **ich′thy•ol′o•gist** *n.*

ich•thy•oph•a•gous (ĭk′thē-ŏf′ə-gəs) *adj.* Feeding on fish.

ich•thy•or•nis (ĭk′thē-ôr′nĭs) *n.* Any of various extinct birds of the genus *Ichthyornis* that existed during the Cretaceous Period. [ICHTHY(O)– + Gk. *ornis*, bird; see **or-***.]

ich•thy•o•saur (ĭk′thē-ə-sôr′) also **ich•thy•o•sau•rus** (ĭk′-thē-ə-sôr′əs) *n., pl.* **-saurs** also **-sau•ri** (-sôr′ī′). Any of various extinct marine reptiles of the order Ichthyosauria of the Triassic Period to the Cretaceous Period, having a porpoiselike head and an elongated toothed snout. [< NLat. *ichthyosaurus* : Gk. *ikhthuo-*, ichthyo- + Gk. *sauros*, lizard.]

ich•thy•o•sis (ĭk′thē-ō′sĭs) *n.* A congenital, often hereditary skin disease characterized by dry thickened scaly skin.

–ician *suff.* One who practices; a specialist: *technician.* [ME < OFr. *-icien* : *-ique*, n. suff.; see –IC + *-ien*, adj. and n. suff.; see –IAN.]

i•ci•cle (ī′sĭ-kəl) *n.* **1.** A tapering spike of ice formed by the freezing of dripping or falling water. **2.** *Informal.* An aloof or emotionally unresponsive person. [ME *isikel* : *is, ise*, ice; see ICE + *ikel*, icicle (< OE *gicel*; see **yeg-***).]

icicle plant *n.* See **fig marigold.** [< its glistening papillae.]

ic•ing (ī′sĭng) *n.* **1.** A sweet glaze made of sugar, butter, water, and egg whites or milk, used to cover or decorate baked goods. **2.** *Sports.* The act of intentionally shooting the puck far out of defensive territory in ice hockey.

ICJ *abbr. Law.* International Court of Justice.

ick•y (ĭk′ē) *adj.* **-i•er, -i•est.** *Informal.* **1.** Disagreeably sticky. **2.** Offensive; distasteful. [?] — **ick′i•ness** *n.*

i•con also **i•kon** (ī′kŏn′) *n.* **1.a.** An image; a representation. **b.** An enduring symbol. **2.** A representation or picture of a sacred or sanctified Christian personage, traditional to the Eastern Church. **3.** The object of great attention and devotion; an idol. **4.** *Comp. Sci.* A picture on a screen representing a specific command. [Ult. < Gk. *eikōn*.]

i•con•ic (ī-kŏn′ĭk) *adj.* **1.** Of, relating to, or characteristic of an icon. **2.** Conventional or formulaic. Used of memorial statues and busts.

icono– or **icon–** *pref.* Image; icon: *iconolatry.* [Gk. *eikono-* < *eikōn*, image.]

i•con•o•clasm (ī-kŏn′ə-klăz′əm) *n.* The beliefs, practices, or doctrine of an iconoclast. [< ICONOCLAST.]

i•con•o•clast (ī-kŏn′ə-klăst′) *n.* **1.** One who attacks and seeks to overthrow traditional or popular ideas or institutions. **2.** One who destroys sacred religious images. [Fr. *iconoclaste* < Med.Gk. *eikonoklastēs*, smasher of religious images : Gk. *eikono-*, icono- + Gk. *-klastēs*, breaker (< *klan, klas-*, to break).] — **i•con′o•clas′tic** *adj.*

i•co•nog•ra•phy (ī′kə-nŏg′rə-fē) *n., pl.* **-phies. 1.a.** Pictorial illustration of a subject. **b.** The collected representations illustrating a subject. **2.** A set of specified or traditional symbolic forms associated with the theme of a stylized work of art. **3.** A treatise or book dealing with iconography. [LLat. *īconographia*, description < Gk. *eikonographia* : *eikono-*, icono- + *-graphia*, -graphy.] — **i′co•nog′ra•pher** *n.* — **i•con′o•graph′ic** (ī-kŏn′ə-grăf′ĭk), **i•con′o•graph′i•cal** *adj.*

i•co•nol•a•try (ī′kə-nŏl′ə-trē) *n.* Worship of icons or images. — **i′co•nol′a•ter** *n.* — **i′con•o•lat′ric** (ī′kŏn-ə-lăt′rĭk) *adj.*

i•co•nol•o•gy (ī′kə-nŏl′ə-jē) *n.* The branch of art history that deals with the description, analysis, and interpretation of icons or iconic representations. — **i•con′o•log′i•cal** (ī-kŏn′-ə-lŏj′ĭ-kəl) *adj.* — **i′co•nol′o•gist** *n.*

i•con•o•scope (ī-kŏn′ə-skōp′) *n.* An early form of a television-camera tube, equipped for rapid scanning of a photoactive mosaic. [Originally a trademark.]

i•co•nos•ta•sis (ī′kə-nŏs′tə-sĭs) *n., pl.* **-ses** (-sēz′). The screen with icons that divides the sanctuary from the nave of an Eastern Orthodox church. [< LGk. *eikonostasion*, shrine : Gk. *eikono-*, icono- + Gk. *stasis*, a standing; see **stā-***.]

i•co•sa•he•dron (ī-kō′sə-hē′drən, ī-kŏs′ə-) *n., pl.* **-drons** or **-dra** (-drə). A polyhedron having 20 faces. [Gk. *eikosaedron* : *eikosi*, twenty; see **wīkm̥tī*** + *-edron*, -hedron.] — **i•co′sa•he′dral** (-drəl) *adj.*

ICRC *abbr.* International Committee of the Red Cross.

–ics *suff.* **1.** Science; art; study; knowledge; skill: *graphics.* **2.** Actions, activities, or practices of: *athletics.* **3.** Qualities or operations of: *mechanics.* [–IC + –S[1] (transl. of Gk. *-ika* < neut. pl. of *-ikos*, adj. suff).]

ic•ter•ic (ĭk-tĕr′ĭk) *adj.* **1.** Relating to or affected with jaundice. **2.** Used to treat jaundice. — *n.* A remedy for jaundice. [Lat. *ictericus* < Gk. *ikterikos* < *ikteros*, jaundice.]

ic•ter•us (ĭk′tər-əs) *n.* See **jaundice.** [NLat. < Gk. *ikteros*.]

Ic•ti•nus (ĭk-tī′nəs). fl. 5th cent. B.C. Greek architect and the chief designer of the Parthenon at Athens.

ic•tus (ĭk′təs) *n., pl.* **ictus** or **-tus•es.** *Medic.* **1.** A sudden attack, blow, stroke, or seizure. **2.** The accent that falls on a stressed syllable in a line of scanned verse. [Lat., stroke < p.part. of *īcere*, to strike.]

ICU *abbr.* Intensive care unit.

ic•y (ī′sē) *adj.* **ic•i•er, ic•i•est. 1.** Containing or covered with ice. **2.** Bitterly cold. See Syns at **cold. 3.a.** Resembling ice. **b.** Chilling in manner. — **ic′i•ly** *adv.* — **ic′i•ness** *n.*

id (ĭd) *n.* In Freudian theory, the unconscious part of the psyche that serves as the source of instinctual impulses and demands immediate satisfaction of primitive needs. [NLat. (transl. of Ger. *Es*, a special use of *es*, it, as a psychoanalytic term) < Lat., it. See **i-***.]

ID[1] (ī′dē′) *n., pl.* **ID's** or **IDs.** *Informal.* An ID card.

ID[2] *abbr.* **1. Id.** Idaho. **2.** Also **I.D.** Identification. **3.** Intelligence Department.

id. *abbr.* Idem.

–id *suff.* Body; particle: *chromatid.* [Lat. *-is, -id-*, fem. patronymic suff. < Gk.]

I'd (īd). **1.** I had. **2.** I would. **3.** I should.

I•da (ī′də), **Mount.** A peak, 2,457.7 m (8,058 ft), of central Crete; associated with the worship of Zeus in ancient times.

I•da•ho (ī′də-hō′). A state of the NW U.S.; admitted as the 43rd state in 1890. The region was held jointly by Great Britain and the U.S. from 1818 to 1846. Cap. Boise. Pop. 1,011,986. — **I′da•ho′an** *adj. & n.*

Idaho Falls. A city of SE ID NNE of Pocatello. Pop. 43,929.

ID card *n.* A card, often bearing a photograph, that gives identifying data, such as name and age, about a person.

–ide *suff.* **1.** Group of related chemical compounds: *monosaccharide.* **2.** Binary compound: *sodium chloride, hydrogen cyanide.* **3.** Chemical element with properties similar to another: *lanthanide.* [< (OX)IDE.]

i•de•a (ī-dē′ə) *n.* **1.** Something, such as a thought, that potentially or actually exists in the mind because of mental activity. **2.** An opinion, a conviction, or a principle. **3.** A plan, scheme, or method. **4.** The gist of a specific situation; significance. **5.** A notion; a fancy. **6.** *Mus.* A theme or motif. **7.** *Philos.* **a.** In the philosophy of Plato, an archetype of which a corresponding being in phenomenal reality is an imperfect replica. **b.** In the philosophy of Kant, a transcendent but nonempirical concept of reason. **c.** In the philosophy of Hegel, absolute truth; the complete and ultimate product of reason. **8.** *Obsolete.* A mental image of something remembered. [ME < Lat. < Gk. See **weid-***.]

Syns: idea, thought, notion, concept, conception. These nouns refer to what is formed or represented in the mind as the product of mental activity. *Idea* has the widest range: *"Human history is in essence a history of ideas"* (H.G. Wells). *Thought* is distinctively intellectual and thus stresses contemplation and reasoning: *"Language is the dress of thought"* (Samuel Johnson). *Notion* often refers to a vague, general, or even fanciful idea: *"She certainly has some notion of drawing"* (Rudyard Kipling). *Concept* and *conception* are applied to mental formulations on a broad scale: *no concept of time; ancient conceptions of divinity.*

i•de•al (ī-dē′əl, ī-dēl′) *n.* **1.** A conception of something in its absolute perfection. **2.** One seen as a standard or model of perfection or excellence. **3.** An ultimate object of endeavor; a goal. **4.** An honorable or worthy principle or aim. — *adj.* **1.a.** Of, relating to, or embodying an ideal. **b.** Conforming to an ultimate form or standard of perfection or excellence. **2.** Considered the best of its kind. **3.** Completely or highly satisfactory. **4.a.** Existing only in the mind; imaginary. **b.** Lacking practicality or the possibility of realization. **5.** Of, relating to, or consisting of ideas or mental images. **6.** *Philos.* **a.** Existing as an archetype or pattern, esp. as a Platonic idea. **b.** Of or relating to idealism. [< ME, of divine archetypes < LLat. *ideālis* < Lat. *idea*, idea. See IDEA.]

i•de•al•ism (ī-dē′ə-lĭz′əm) *n.* **1.** The act or practice of envisioning things in an ideal form. **2.** Pursuit of one's ideals. **3.** Idealized treatment of a subject in literature or art. **4.** *Philos.* The theory that the object of external perception consists of ideas.

i•de•al•ist (ī-dē′ə-lĭst) *n.* **1.** One whose conduct is influenced by ideals that often conflict with practical considerations. **2.** One who is unrealistic and impractical; a visionary. **3.** An artist or a writer whose work shows idealism. **4.** An adherent of any system of philosophical idealism.

i•de•al•is•tic (ī-dē′ə-lĭs′tĭk) *adj.* Of, relating to, or having the nature of an idealist or idealism. — **i′de•al•is′ti•cal•ly** *adv.*

Iceland

ichthyosaur

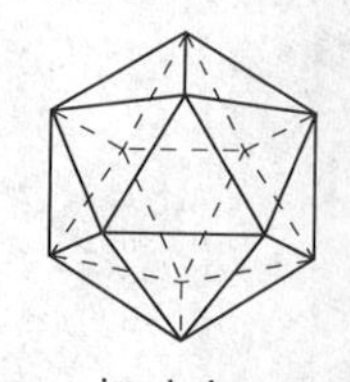
icosahedron

ă pat	oi boy
ā pay	ou out
âr care	o͝o took
ä father	o͞o boot
ĕ pet	ŭ cut
ē be	ûr urge
ĭ pit	th thin
ī pie	*th* this
îr pier	hw which
ŏ pot	zh vision
ō toe	ə about, item
ô paw	

Stress marks:
′ (primary);
′ (secondary), as in **dictionary** (dĭk′shə-nĕr′ē)

i•de•al•i•ty (ī′dē-ăl′ĭ-tē) *n., pl.* **-ties. 1.** The state or quality of being ideal. **2.** Existence in idea only.

i•de•al•ize (ī-dē′ə-līz′) *v.* **-ized, -iz•ing, -iz•es.** — *tr.* **1.** To regard as ideal. **2.** To make or envision as ideal. — *intr.* **1.** To render something as an ideal. **2.** To conceive an ideal. — **i•de′al•i•za′tion** (-ə-lĭ-zā′shən) *n.* — **i•de′al•iz′er** *n.*

i•de•al•ly (ī-dē′ə-lē) *adv.* **1.** In conformity with an ideal; perfectly. **2.** In theory or imagination; theoretically.

i•de•ate (ī′dē-āt′) *v.* **-at•ed, -at•ing, -ates.** — *tr.* To form an idea of; imagine or conceive. — *intr.* To conceive mental images; think. — **i′de•a′tion** *n.* — **i′de•a′tion•al** *adj.*

i•dée fixe (ē-dā fēks′) *n., pl.* **i•dées fixes** (ē-dā fēks′). A fixed idea; an obsession. [Fr. : *idée*, idea + *fixe*, fixed.]

i•dem (ī′dĕm′) *pron.* Something that has been mentioned previously; the same. [Lat. < *id*, it. See **i-***.]

i•den•tic (ī-dĕn′tĭk) *adj.* **1.** Being or constituting a diplomatic action or language in which governments agree to use the same forms in their relations with other governments. **2.** Identical. [Med.Lat. *identicus*, identical. See IDENTICAL.]

i•den•ti•cal (ī-dĕn′tĭ-kəl) *adj.* **1.** Being the same. **2.** Exactly equal and alike. **3.** Having such a close similarity or resemblance as to be essentially equal or interchangeable. **4.** *Biol.* Of or relating to a twin or twins developed from the same fertilized ovum and having the same genetic makeup and closely similar appearance; monozygotic. [< Med.Lat. *identicus* < LLat. *identitās*, identity. See IDENTITY.] — **i•den′ti•cal•ly** *adv.* — **i•den′ti•cal•ness** *n.*

Usage Note: Either *with* or *to* is now acceptable after *identical.*

identical rhyme *n.* **1.** Repetition of the same word in the rhyme position. **2.** See **rime riche.**

i•den•ti•fi•ca•tion (ī-dĕn′tə-fĭ-kā′shən) *n.* **1.a.** The act of identifying. **b.** The state of being identified. **2.** Proof or evidence of identity. **3.** *Psychol.* **a.** A person's association with the qualities, traits, or views of another person or group. **b.** An unconscious process by which a person transfers the response appropriate to one person or group to a different person or group.

identification card *n.* An ID card.

i•den•ti•fi•er (ī-dĕn′tə-fī′ər) *n. Comp. Sci.* A symbol that serves to identify, indicate, or name a body of data.

i•den•ti•fy (ī-dĕn′tə-fī′) *v.* **-fied, -fy•ing, -fies.** — *tr.* **1.** To establish the identity of. **2.** To ascertain the origin, nature, or characteristics of. **3.** *Biol.* To determine the taxonomic classification of (an organism). **4.** To consider as identical or united; equate. **5.** To associate or affiliate (oneself) closely with a person or group. — *intr.* To establish an identification with another or others. [Med.Lat. *identificāre*, to make to resemble : LLat. *identitās*, identity; see IDENTITY + Lat. *-ficāre*, -fy.] — **i•den′ti•fi′a•ble** *adj.* — **i•den′ti•fi′a•bly** *adv.* — **i•den′ti•fi′er** *n.*

i•den•ti•ty (ī-dĕn′tĭ-tē) *n., pl.* **-ties. 1.** The set of characteristics by which a thing is recognized or known. **2.** The set of behavioral or personal traits by which an individual is recognizable as a member of a group. **3.** The quality or condition of being the same as something else. **4.** The distinct personality of an individual regarded as a persisting entity; individuality. **5.** *Math.* **a.** An equation that is satisfied by any number that replaces the letter for which the equation is defined. **b.** Identity element. [Fr. *identité* < OFr. *identite* < LLat. *identitās* < Lat. *idem*, the same < *id*, it. See **i-***.]

identity crisis *n.* **1.** A psychosocial state or condition of disorientation and role confusion occurring esp. in adolescents as a result of conflicting pressures and expectations and often producing acute anxiety. **2.** An analogous state of confusion occurring in a social structure, such as a corporation.

identity element *n. Math.* The element of a set that when combined with another element in an operation leaves that element unchanged.

identity matrix *n. Math.* A square matrix with numeral 1's along the diagonal from upper left to lower right and 0's in all other positions.

identity sign *n. Math.* The symbol (≡), used to designate identity rather than equality.

ideo– *pref.* Idea: *ideography.* [Fr. *idéo-* < Gk. *idea*, form, idea. See **weid-***.]

id•e•o•gram (ĭd′ē-ə-grăm′, ī′dē-) *n.* **1.** A character or symbol representing an idea or a thing without expressing the pronunciation of the words for it, as in many traffic signs. **2.** See **logogram. 3.** A graphic symbol, such as &. — **id′e•o•gram•mat′ic** (grə-măt′ĭk) *adj.*

id•e•o•graph (ĭd′ē-ə-grăf′) *n.* See **ideogram** 1. — **id′e•o•graph′ic** *adj.* — **id′e•o•graph′i•cal•ly** *adv.*

id•e•og•ra•phy (ĭd′ē-ŏg′rə-fē, ī′dē-) *n.* **1.** The representation of ideas by graphic symbols. **2.** The use of ideograms to express ideas.

i•de•o•log•i•cal (ī′dē-ə-lŏj′ĭ-kəl, ĭd′ē-) also **i•de•o•log•ic** (-lŏj′ĭk) *adj.* **1.** Of or relating to ideology. **2.** Of or concerned with ideas.

i•de•o•logue (ī′dē-ə-lôg′, -lŏg′, ĭd′ē-) *n.* An advocate of a particular ideology. [Fr. *idéologue*, back-formation < *idéologie*, ideology. See IDEOLOGY.]

i•de•ol•o•gy (ī′dē-ŏl′ə-jē, ĭd′ē-) *n., pl.* **-gies. 1.** The body of ideas reflecting the social needs and aspirations of an individual, a group, a class, or a culture. **2.** A set of doctrines or beliefs that form the basis of a political, economic, or other system. — **i′de•ol′o•gist** *n.*

i•de•o•mo•tor (ī′dē-ə-mō′tər, ĭd′ē-) *adj. Psychol.* Of or relating to an unconscious or involuntary body movement made in response to a thought rather than to a sensory stimulus.

ides (īdz) *pl.n. (used with a sing. or pl. v.)* The 15th day of March, May, July, or October or the 13th day of the other months in the ancient Roman calendar. [ME < OFr. < Lat. *īdūs*.]

idio– *pref.* **1.** One's own; private; personal: *idiolect.* **2.** Distinct; separate: *idioblast.* [Gk. < *idios*, personal, private. See **s(w)e-***.]

id•i•o•blast (ĭd′ē-ə-blăst′) *n.* A plant cell that differs noticeably in form from neighboring cells. — **id′i•o•blas′tic** *adj.*

id•i•o•cy (ĭd′ē-ə-sē) *n., pl.* **-cies. 1.** Extreme folly or stupidity. **2.** A foolish or stupid utterance or deed. **3.** *Psychol.* Profound mental retardation. No longer in scientific use. [< IDIOT.]

id•i•o•lect (ĭd′ē-ə-lĕkt′) *n.* One individual's speech considered linguistically unique among speakers of the same language or dialect. [IDIO– + (DIA)LECT.] — **id′i•o•lec′tal, id′i•o•lec′tic** *adj.*

id•i•om (ĭd′ē-əm) *n.* **1.** A speech form or an expression of a given language that is peculiar to itself grammatically or cannot be understood from the individual meanings of its elements, as in *keep tabs on.* **2.** The specific grammatical, syntactic, and structural character of a given language. **3.** Regional speech or dialect. **4.a.** A specialized vocabulary used by a group; jargon. **b.** A style or manner of expression peculiar to a given people. **5.** A style of artistic expression characteristic of a particular individual, school, period, or medium. [LLat. *idiōma*, *idiōmat-* < Gk. < *idiousthai*, to make one's own < *idios*, own, personal, private. See **s(w)e-***.]

id•i•o•mat•ic (ĭd′ē-ə-măt′ĭk) *adj.* **1.** Peculiar to or characteristic of a given language. **2.** Resembling or having the nature of an idiom. **3.** Using many idioms. **4.** Peculiar to or characteristic of a given group. — **id′i•o•mat′i•cal•ly** *adv.*

id•i•o•path•ic (ĭd′ē-ə-păth′ĭk, ĭd′ē-ō-) *adj. Medic.* Of, relating to, or being a disease having no known cause.

id•i•op•a•thy (ĭd′ē-ŏp′ə-thē) *n. Medic.* A disease of unknown origin or cause. [NLat. *idiopathīa*, primary disease < Gk. *idiopatheia* : *idio-*, idio- + *-patheia*, -pathy.]

id•i•o•syn•cra•sy (ĭd′ē-ō-sĭng′krə-sē) *n., pl.* **-sies. 1.** A structural or behavioral characteristic peculiar to an individual or a group. **2.** A physiological or temperamental peculiarity. **3.** An unusual individual reaction to food or a drug. [Gk. *idiosunkrasia* : *idio-*, idio- + *sunkrasis*, mixture, temperament (*sun-*, syn- + *krasis*, a mixing; see **kerə-***).] — **id′i•o•syn•crat′ic** (-sĭn-krăt′ĭk) *adj.* — **id′i•o•syn•crat′i•cal•ly** *adv.*

id•i•ot (ĭd′ē-ət) *n.* **1.** A foolish or stupid person. **2.** A person of profound mental retardation having a mental age below three years. The term is no longer in scientific use and is now considered offensive. [ME, ignorant person < OFr. *idiote* < Lat. *idiōta* < Gk. *idiōtēs*, private person, layman < *idios*, own, private. See **s(w)e-***.]

idiot box *n. Slang.* A television.

id•i•ot•ic (ĭd′ē-ŏt′ĭk) *adj.* **1.** Showing foolishness or stupidity. **2.** Exhibiting idiocy. — **id′i•ot′i•cal•ly** *adv.*

idiot savant *n., pl.* **idiot savants.** A mentally retarded person who exhibits genius in a highly specialized area, such as mathematics or music. [Fr. : *idiot*, idiot + *savant*, learned.]

i•dle (īd′l) *adj.* **i•dler, i•dlest. 1.a.** Not employed or busy: *idle carpenters.* See Syns at **inactive. b.** Avoiding work or employment; lazy. **c.** Not in use or operation: *idle hands.* **2.** Lacking substance, value, or basis. — *v.* **i•dled, i•dling, i•dles.** — *intr.* **1.** To pass time without working or while avoiding work. **2.** To move lazily and without purpose. **3.** To run at a slow speed or out of gear. Used of a motor vehicle. — *tr.* **1.** To pass (time) without working or while avoiding work; waste. **2.** To make or cause to be unemployed or inactive. **3.** To cause (a motor, for example) to idle. [ME *idel* < OE *īdel.*] — **i′dle•ness** *n.* — **i′dler** (īd′lər) *n.* — **i′dly** *adv.*

idle character *n. Comp. Sci.* An alphanumeric or digital character that is transmitted over a communications line but does not appear in the output of the receiving terminal.

idle pulley also **idler pulley** *n.* A pulley on a shaft that rests on or presses against a drive belt to guide it or take up slack.

idle wheel *n.* **1.** A gear, wheel, or roller interposed between two similar parts to convey motion from one to the other without change in speed or direction of motion. **2.** See **idle pulley.**

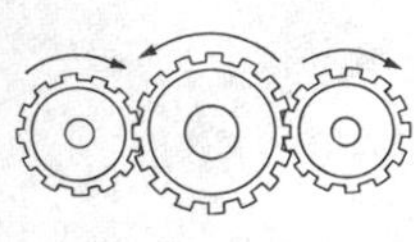

idle wheel

i•do•crase (ī′də-krās′, -krāz′, ĭd′ə-) *n.* See **vesuvianite.** [Fr. : Gk. *eidos*, form; see **weid-*** + *krasis*, mixture; see IDIOSYNCRASY.]

i•dol (īd′l) *n.* **1.a.** An image used as an object of worship. **b.** A false god. **2.** One that is adored, often blindly or excessively. **3.** Something visible but without substance. [ME < OFr. *idole* < LLat. *īdōlum* < Gk. *eidōlon*, phantom, idol < *eidos*, form. See **weid-***.]

Ignatius of Loyola

i•dol•a•ter or **i•dol•a•tor** (ī-dŏl′ə-tər) *n.* **1.** One who worships idols. **2.** One who blindly or excessively admires or adores another. [ME *idolatre* < OFr. < Lat. *īdōlolatrēs* < Gk. *eidōlolatrēs* : *eidōlon*, idol; see IDOL + *-latrēs*, worshiper.]

i•dol•a•trous (ī-dŏl′ə-trəs) *adj.* **1.** Of or constituting idolatry. **2.** Given to blind or excessive devotion to something. **— i•dol′a•trous•ly** *adv.* **— i•dol′a•trous•ness** *n.*

i•dol•a•try (ī-dŏl′ə-trē) *n., pl.* **-tries. 1.** Worship of idols. **2.** Blind or excessive devotion to something. [ME *idolatrie* < OFr. < Lat. *īdōlolatrīa* < Gk. *eidōlolatria* : *eidōlon*, idol; see IDOL + *latreia*, service.]

i•dol•ize (īd′l-īz′) *tr.v.* **-ized, -iz•ing, -iz•es. 1.** To regard with idolatrous devotion. See Syns at **revere**[1]. **2.** To worship as an idol. **— i′dol•i•za′tion** (-ĭ-zā′shən) *n.* **— i′dol•iz′er** *n.*

IDP *abbr.* **1.** *Comp. Sci.* Integrated data processing. **2.** International driving permit.

i•dyll also **i•dyl** (īd′l) *n.* **1.a.** A short poem or prose piece depicting a rural or pastoral scene, usu. in idealized terms. **b.** A narrative poem treating an epic or romantic theme. **2.** A scene or an event of a simple and tranquil nature. **3.a.** A carefree episode or experience: *a summer idyll in France.* **b.** A romantic interlude. [Lat. *īdyllium* < Gk. *eidullion*, dim. of *eidos*, form, figure. See **weid-***.] **— i•dyl′li•cal•ly** *adv.*

i•dyl•lic (ī-dĭl′ĭk) *adj.* **1.** Of or having the nature of an idyll. **2.** Simple and carefree: *an idyllic vacation.*

i•dyl•list (īd′l-ĭst) *n.* A writer of idylls.

IE or **I.E.** *abbr.* **1.** Industrial engineer. **2.** Industrial engineering. **3.** Indo-European.

i.e. *abbr. Lat.* Id est (that is).

-ie *suff.* Var. of **-y**[3].

Ie•per (yā′pər) also **Y•pres** (ē′prə). A city of W Belgium near the French border S of Ostend; site of three World War I battles (1914, 1915, and 1917). Pop. 21,200.

if (ĭf) *conj.* **1.a.** In the event that: *If I were to go, I would be late.* **b.** Granting that: *If that is true, what next?* **c.** On the condition that: *She will sing only if paid.* **2.** Although possibly; even though: *a handsome if useless trinket.* **3.** Whether: *Ask if he plans to come.* **4.** Used to introduce an exclamatory clause, indicating a wish: *If they had only come!* —*n.* A possibility, condition, or stipulation. [ME < OE *gif.* See **i-***.]

Usage Note: In informal writing both *if* and *whether* are standard in their use to introduce a clause indicating uncertainty after a verb such as *ask, doubt, know, learn,* or *see*: *We shall soon learn whether* (or *if*) *it is true.* In such contexts, however, the use of *if* can sometimes create ambiguities. Depending on the intended meaning, the sentence *Let her know if she is invited* might be better paraphrased as *Let her know whether she is invited* or *If she is invited, let her know.* • In conditional sentences the clause introduced by *if* may contain either a past subjunctive verb (*if I were going*) or an indicative verb (*if I was going*), depending on the intended meaning. According to the traditional rule, the subjunctive should be used to describe an occurrence that is presupposed to be contrary to fact, as in *if I were ten years younger.* The main verb of such a sentence must then contain the modal verb *would* or (less frequently) *should*: *If I were you, I should* (or *would*) *buy new shirts.* When the situation described by the *if* clause is not presupposed to be false, however, that clause must contain an indicative verb, and the choice of verb in the main clause will depend on the intended meaning: *If Kevin was out all day, then he couldn't call back.* • Again according to the traditional rule, the subjunctive is not correctly used following verbs such as *ask* or *wonder* in *if* clauses that express indirect questions, even if the content of the question is presumed to be contrary to fact: *We wondered if dinner was* (not *were*) *included in the room price.* See Usage Notes at **should, wish.**

IF or **i.f.** *abbr.* Intermediate frequency.

I•fe (ē′fā). A city of SW Nigeria E of Ibadan; center of a powerful Yoruba kingdom until the late 17th cent. Pop. 209,100.

if•fy (ĭf′ē) *adj.* **-fi•er, -fi•est.** *Informal.* Doubtful; uncertain.

If•ni (ēf′nē). A former Spanish possession (1860–1969) on the Atlantic coast of SW Morocco.

IFO *abbr.* Identified flying object.

I formation *n. Football.* An alignment of the offensive team in which all the backs line up in single file behind the center.

IFR *abbr.* Instrument flight rules.

-ify *suff.* Var. of **-fy.**

Ig *abbr.* Immunoglobulin.

IG or **I.G.** *abbr.* Inspector general.

igg (ĭg) *tr.v.* **igged, igg•ing, iggs.** *Northern U.S.* To ignore.

Regional Note: *Igg*, a shortened form of *ignore*, seems to have come into American speech from jive, the special jargon of Black jazz musicians in the 1930's. Its use has spread from the musicians' jargon into the Black communities of Northern U.S. cities. Such reduction of a word to its initial syllable is a common source of slang or informal words.

Ig•bo (ĭg′bō) *n.* Var. of **Ibo.**

ig•loo (ĭg′lo͞o) *n., pl.* **-loos. 1.** An Eskimo dwelling, esp. a dome-shaped dwelling built of blocks of packed snow. **2.** A dome-shaped structure or building. [Canadian Eskimo *iglu*, house.]

ign. *abbr.* Ignition.

Ig•na•tius (ĭg-nā′shəs), Saint. d. c. A.D. 110. Bishop of Antioch who was martyred during the reign of Trajan.

Ignatius of Loy•o•la (loi-ō′lə), Saint. 1491–1556. Spanish ecclesiastic who founded the Jesuits.

ig•ne•ous (ĭg′nē-əs) *adj.* **1.** Of, relating to, or characteristic of fire. **2.** *Geol.* **a.** Formed by solidification from a molten state. Used of rocks. **b.** Of or relating to rock so formed; pyrogenic. [< Lat. *igneus* < *ignis*, fire.]

ig•nim•brite (ĭg′nĭm-brīt′) *n.* A volcanic rock formed by the welding together of tuffs from an explosive volcanic eruption. [Lat. *ignis*, fire + *imber, imbr-*, rain + -ITE[1].]

ig•nis fat•u•us (ĭg′nĭs făch′o͞o-əs) *n., pl.* **ig•nes fat•u•i** (ĭg′nēz făch′o͞o-ī′). **1.** A phosphorescent light that hovers or flits over swampy ground at night, possibly from spontaneous combustion of gases emitted by rotting organic matter. **2.** Something that misleads or deludes; an illusion. [Med.Lat. : Lat. *ignis*, fire + Lat. *fatuus*, foolish.]

ig•nite (ĭg-nīt′) *v.* **-nit•ed, -nit•ing, -nites.** —*tr.* **1.a.** To cause to burn. **b.** To set fire to. **2.** To subject to great heat, esp. to make luminous by heat. **3.** To arouse the passions of; excite: *The insults ignited my anger.* —*intr.* **1.** To begin to burn. **2.** To begin to glow. [LLat. *ignīre, ignīt-* < Lat. *ignis*, fire.] **— ig•nit′a•ble, ig•nit′i•ble** *adj.* **— ig•nit′er, ig•ni′tor** *n.*

ig•ni•tion (ĭg-nĭsh′ən) *n.* **1.** The raising of a substance to its ignition point, as by electric current. **2.a.** An electrical system, typically powered by a battery or magneto, that provides the spark to ignite the fuel mixture in an internal-combustion engine. **b.** A switch that activates this system.

ignition point *n.* The minimum temperature at which a substance will continue to burn without additional external heat.

ig•ni•tron (ĭg-nī′trŏn′, ĭg′nĭ-) *n.* A single-anode mercury-vapor rectifier in which current passes as an arc between an anode and cathode, consisting of liquid mercury, used in power rectification. [IGNI(TE) + -TRON.]

ig•no•ble (ĭg-nō′bəl) *adj.* **1.** Not noble in quality, character, or purpose; base or mean. **2.** Not of the nobility; common. [ME, of low birth < OFr. < Lat. *ignōbilis* : *i-, in-*, not; see IN-[1] + *nōbilis, gnōbilis*, noble; see NOBLE.] **— ig′no•bil′i•ty** (-bĭl′ĭ-tē), **ig•no′ble•ness** *n.* **— ig•no′bly** *adv.*

ig•no•min•i•ous (ĭg′nə-mĭn′ē-əs) *adj.* **1.** Marked by shame or disgrace. **2.** Deserving disgrace or shame; despicable. **3.** Degrading; debasing: *an ignominious task.* **— ig′no•min′i•ous•ly** *adv.* **— ig′no•min′i•ous•ness** *n.*

ig•no•min•y (ĭg′nə-mĭn′ē, -mə-nē) *n., pl.* **-ies. 1.** Great personal dishonor or humiliation. **2.** Shameful or disgraceful action, conduct, or character. [Fr. *ignominie* < OFr. < Lat. *ignōminia* : *i-, in-*, not; see IN-[1] + *nōmen, nōmin-*, name, reputation; see **nō-men-***.]

ig•no•ra•mus (ĭg′nə-rā′məs) *n., pl.* **-mus•es.** An ignorant person. [Ult. < Lat. *ignōrāmus*, we do not know, first pers. pl. pr.t. of *ignōrāre*, to be ignorant. See IGNORE.]

ig•no•rance (ĭg′nər-əns) *n.* The condition of being uneducated, unaware, or uninformed.

ig•no•rant (ĭg′nər-ənt) *adj.* **1.** Lacking education or knowledge. **2.** Showing or arising from a lack of education or knowledge: *an ignorant mistake.* **3.** Unaware or uninformed. [ME *ignoraunt* < OFr. *ignorant* < Lat. *ignōrāns, ignōrant-*, pr.part. of *ignōrāre*, to be ignorant, not to know. See **gnō-***.] **— ig′no•rant•ly** *adv.*

ig•nore (ĭg-nôr′, -nōr′) *tr.v.* **-nored, -nor•ing, -nores.** To refuse to pay attention to; disregard. See Regional Note at **igg.** [Fr. *ignorer* < OFr. < Lat. *ignōrāre.* See **gnō-***.] **— ig•nor′a•ble** *adj.* **— ig•nor′er** *n.*

I•go•rot (ĭg′ə-rōt′, ē′gə-) *n., pl.* **Igorot** or **-rots. 1.** A member of any of several peoples of the mountains of northern Luzon in the Philippines. **2.** Any of the Austronesian languages of the Igorot.

I•gua•çú also **I•guas•sú** (ē′gwə-so͞o′). A river of S Brazil flowing c. 1,199 km (745 mi) to the Paraná R. at the Argentina-Paraguay-Brazil border. Just above the junction it forms **Iguaçú Falls,** a series of cataracts averaging 61 m (200 ft) high.

i•gua•na (ĭ-gwä′nə) *n.* Any of various large tropical American lizards of the family Iguanidae, often having spiny projections along the back. [Sp. < Arawak *iwana.*]

i•guan•o•don (ĭ-gwä′nə-dŏn′) *n.* Any of various large dinosaurs of the genus *Iguanodon*, of the Jurassic and Cretaceous periods. [NLat. *Iguanodon*, genus name : IGUANA + -ODON.]

ihp or **i.hp.** *abbr.* Indicated horsepower.

ih•ram (ē-räm′) *n. Islam.* **1.** The sacred dress of Muslim pilgrims, consisting of two lengths of white cotton. **2.** The sacred state of Muslim pilgrims wearing this dress at a time of great self-denial. [Ar. *'iḥrām*, prohibition, ihram < *'aḥrama*, to consecrate.]

IHS *abbr.* Jesus (Greek ΙΗΣΟΥΣ with S for sigma).

IJs•sel or **IJs•sel** (ī′səl). A river, c. 113 km (70 mi) of E Netherlands flowing from the Lower Rhine R. to the Ijsselmeer.

IJs•sel•meer or **IJs•sel•meer** (ī′səl-mâr′, -mār′). A shallow dike-enclosed lake of NW Netherlands; formed from the Zuider Zee by the construction of two dams (completed 1932).

I•ka•ri•a (ē′kä-rē′ä) also **I•car•i•a** (ĭ-kâr′ē-ə, ī-kâr′-). An island of SE Greece in the Aegean Sea W of Samos.

iguana
Common iguana
Iguana iguana

iguanodon
Ouranosaurus

ă pat	oi boy
ā pay	ou out
âr care	o͝o took
ä father	o͞o boot
ĕ pet	ŭ cut
ē be	ûr urge
ĭ pit	th thin
ī pie	*th* this
îr pier	hw which
ŏ pot	zh vision
ō toe	ə about, item
ô paw	

Stress marks:
′ (primary);
′ (secondary), as in
dictionary (dĭk′shə-nĕr′ē)

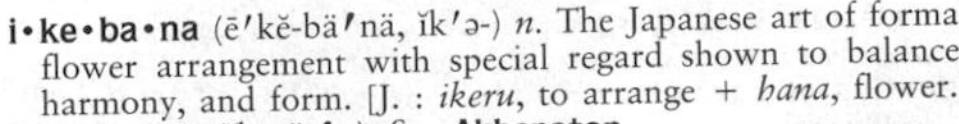

i•ke•ba•na (ē′kĕ-bä′nä, ĭk′ə-) *n.* The Japanese art of formal flower arrangement with special regard shown to balance, harmony, and form. [J. : *ikeru*, to arrange + *hana*, flower.]
Ikh•na•ton (ĭk-nät′n). See **Akhenaton.**
i•kon (ī′kŏn′) *n.* Var. of **icon.**
IL *abbr.* Illinois.
il–[1] *pref.* Var. of **in–**[1].
il–[2] *pref.* Var. of **in–**[2].
IL–1 *abbr.* Interleukin–1.
IL–2 *abbr.* Interleukin–2.
ILA *abbr.* International Longshoremen's Association.
i•lang-i•lang (ē′läng-ē′läng) *n.* Var. of **ylang-ylang.**
–ile[1] *suff.* Of, relating to, or capable of: *audile.* [ME < OFr. < Lat. *-ilis, -īlis.*]
–ile[2] *suff.* A division of a specified size in the range of a statistic: *percentile.* [Prob. < -ILE[1].]
il•e•ac[1] (ĭl′ē-ăk′) *adj.* Of, relating to, or having the nature of ileus.
il•e•ac[2] (ĭl′ē-ăk′) *adj.* Of, relating to, or involving the ileum.
Île-de-France (ēl′də-fräNs′). A historical region and former province of N-central France in the Paris basin; became the nucleus of the crown lands in 987 with the choice of Hugh Capet, Count of Paris, as the French king.
il•e•i•tis (ĭl′ē-ī′tĭs) *n.* Inflammation of the ileum.
il•e•os•to•my (ĭl′ē-ŏs′tə-mē) *n., pl.* **-mies.** Surgical construction of an artificial excretory opening through the abdominal wall into the ileum. [ILE(UM) + -STOMY.]

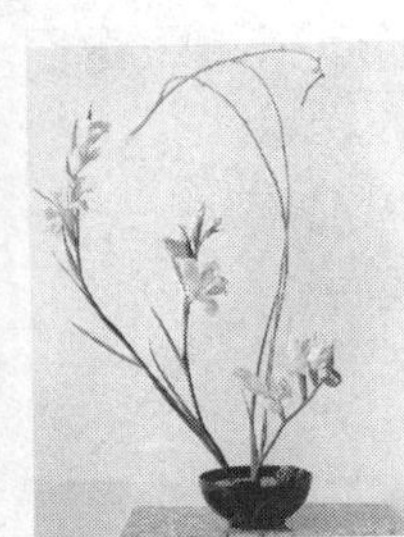
ikebana

il•e•um (ĭl′ē-əm) *n., pl.* **-e•a** (-ē-ə). The terminal portion of the small intestine extending from the jejunum to the cecum. [LLat. *īleum*, groin, flank, var. of Lat. *īlia.*] — **il′e•al** *adj.*
il•e•us (ĭl′ē-əs) *n.* Intestinal obstruction causing colic, vomiting, and constipation. [Lat. *īleus* < Gk. *eileos* < *eilein*, to squeeze, hold in check. See **wel-**[2]*.]
i•lex (ī′lĕks′) *n.* Any of various trees or shrubs of the genus *Ilex*; holly. [ME, holm oak < Lat. *īlex.*]
ILGWU or **I.L.G.W.U.** *abbr.* International Ladies' Garment Workers' Union.
I•li (ē′lē′). A river, c. 1,287 km (800 mi), of NW China and SE Kazakhstan flowing into Lake Balkhash.
il•i•ac (ĭl′ē-ăk′) *adj.* Of, relating to, or situated near the ilium.
Il•i•on (ĭl′ē-ən, -ŏn′). See **Troy** 1.
il•i•um (ĭl′ē-əm) *n., pl.* **-i•a** (-ē-ə). The uppermost and widest of the three bones constituting either of the lateral halves of the pelvis. [LLat. *ilium*, groin, flank, var. of Lat. *īlia.*] — **il′i•ac′** (-ăk′) *adj.*
Il•i•um (ĭl′ē-əm). See **Troy** 1.
ilk[1] (ĭlk) *n.* Type or kind: *people of that ilk.* — *pron. Scots.* The same. Used following a name to indicate that the one named resides in an area bearing the same name: *Duncan of that ilk.* [ME, same < OE *ilca.* See **i-***.]
ilk[2] (ĭlk) *adj.* Var. of **ilka.**
il•ka (ĭl′kə) also **ilk** (ĭlk) *adj. Scots.* Each; every. [ME *ilk a*, each one : *ilk* (var. of *ech*, each; see EACH) + *a*, one, a; see A[2].]
ill (ĭl) *adj.* **worse** (wûrs), **worst** (wûrst). **1.** Not healthy; sick. **2.** Not normal; unsound. **3.** Resulting in suffering; distressing. **4.a.** Having evil intentions; hostile or unfriendly. **b.** Ascribing an objectionable quality. **c.** Harmful; cruel. **5.** Not favorable; unpropitious. **6.** Not measuring up to recognized standards of excellence, as of conduct. — *adv.* **worse, worst. 1.** In a sickly or unsound manner; not well. **2.** Scarcely or with difficulty. — *n.* **1.** Evil; sin. **2.** Disaster, distress, or harm. **3.** Something that causes suffering; trouble. **4.** Something that reflects in an unfavorable way on one. [ME < ON *illr*, bad.]
ill. *abbr.* **1.** Illustrated. **2.** Illustration. **3.** Illustrator.
Ill. *abbr.* Illinois.
I'll (īl). **1.** I will. **2.** I shall.
ill-ad•vised (ĭl′əd-vīzd′) *adj.* Performed, carried out, or done without wise counsel or careful deliberation. — **ill′-ad•vis′ed•ly** (-vī′zĭd-lē) *adv.*
Il•lam•pu (ē-yäm′po͞o). A peak, 6,366.3 m (20,873 ft), in the Andes of W Bolivia NW of La Paz.
ill at ease *adj.* Nervously uncomfortable.
il•la•tion (ĭ-lā′shən) *n.* **1.** The act of inferring or drawing conclusions. **2.** A conclusion drawn; a deduction. [LLat. *illātiō*, *illātiōn-* < Lat. *illātus*, p.part. of *īnferre*, to carry in, infer : *in-*, in; see IN–[2] + *lātus*, brought; see **telə-***.]
il•la•tive (ĭl′ə-tĭv, ĭ-lā′-) *adj.* **1.** Of, relating to, or of the nature of an illation. **2.** Expressing or preceding an inference. Used of a word. **3.** *Ling.* Of, relating to, or being a grammatical case indicating motion toward or into, as in Finnish *Helsinkiin*, "to Helsinki." — *n.* **1.** A word or phrase, such as *hence*, that expresses an inference. **2.** See **illation** 2. — **il′la•tive•ly** *adv.*

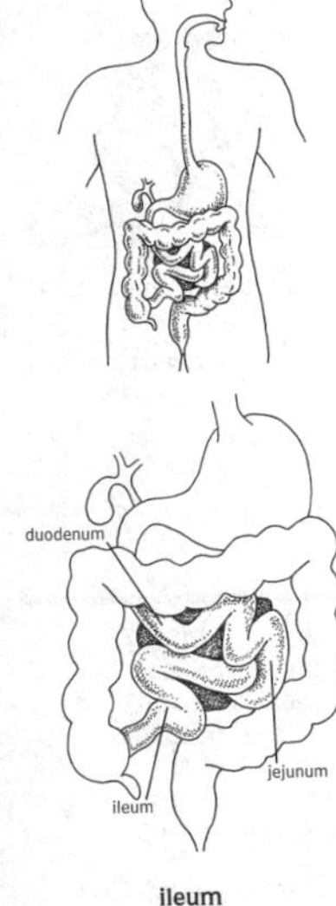

ileum

ill-be•ing (ĭl′bē′ĭng) *n.* Lack of prosperity, happiness, or health.
ill-bred (ĭl′brĕd′) *adj.* **1.** Badly brought up; impolite and crude. **2.** Not thoroughbred; underbred. Used of animals.
il•le•gal (ĭ-lē′gəl) *adj.* **1.** Prohibited by law. **2.** Prohibited by official rules. **3.** *Comp. Sci.* Unacceptable to or not performable by a computer. — *n.* An illegal immigrant. — **il•le′gal•ly** *adv.*
il•le•gal•i•ty (ĭl′ē-găl′ĭ-tē) *n., pl.* **-ties. 1.** The quality or state of being illegal. **2.** An illegal act.
il•leg•i•ble (ĭ-lĕj′ə-bəl) *adj.* Not legible or decipherable. — **il•leg′i•bil′i•ty, il•leg′i•ble•ness** *n.* — **il•leg′i•bly** *adv.*
il•le•git•i•ma•cy (ĭl′ĭ-jĭt′ə-mə-sē) *n.* **1.** The quality or condition of being illegitimate. **2.** Bastardy.
il•le•git•i•mate (ĭl′ĭ-jĭt′ə-mĭt) *adj.* **1.** Against the law; illegal. **2.** Born out of wedlock. **3.** *Gram.* Not in correct usage. **4.** Incorrectly deduced; illogical. **5.** *Biol.* Unacceptable as a scientific name because of contradiction to the international rules of nomenclature. — **il′le•git′i•mate•ly** *adv.*
ill-fat•ed (ĭl′fā′tĭd) *adj.* **1.** Destined for misfortune; doomed. **2.** Marked by or causing misfortune; unlucky.
ill-fa•vored (ĭl′fā′vərd) *adj.* **1.** Having an ugly or unattractive face. **2.** Objectionable; offensive.
ill feeling *n.* A feeling of animosity or rancor.
ill-found•ed (ĭl′foun′dĭd) *adj.* Having no factual basis.
ill-got•ten (ĭl′gŏt′n) *adj.* Obtained in an evil manner or by dishonest means: *ill-gotten gains.*
ill health *n.* Poor health; sickness.
ill humor *n.* An irritable state of mind; surliness.
ill-hu•mored (ĭl′hyo͞o′mərd) *adj.* Irritable; surly.
il•lib•er•al (ĭ-lĭb′ər-əl) *adj.* **1.** Narrow-minded; bigoted. **2.** *Archaic.* Ungenerous, mean, or stingy. **3.** *Archaic.* **a.** Lacking liberal culture. **b.** Ill-bred; vulgar. — **il•lib′er•al•ism** *n.* — **il•lib′er•al′i•ty** (-ə-răl′ĭ-tē), **il•lib′er•al•ness** *n.* — **il•lib′er•al•ly** *adv.*
il•lic•it (ĭ-lĭs′ĭt) *adj.* Not sanctioned by custom or law; unlawful. — **il•lic′it•ly** *adv.* — **il•lic′it•ness** *n.*
Il•li•ma•ni (ē′yē-mä′nē). A mountain, 6,461.1 m (21,184 ft), in the Andes of W Bolivia E of La Paz.
il•lim•it•a•ble (ĭ-lĭm′ĭ-tə-bəl) *adj.* Impossible to limit or circumscribe; limitless. See Syns at **infinite.** — **il•lim′it•a•bil′i•ty, il•lim′it•a•ble•ness** *n.* — **il•lim′it•a•bly** *adv.*
Il•li•noi•an (ĭl′ə-noi′ən) *adj.* Of or relating to the third glacial stage of the Pleistocene in North America. [After ILLINOIS[2].]
Il•li•nois[1] (ĭl′ə-noi′, -noiz′) *n., pl.* **Illinois. 1.** A member of a confederacy of Native American peoples formerly inhabiting southern Wisconsin, northern Illinois, and parts of eastern Iowa and Missouri, with present-day descendants mostly in Oklahoma. **2.** The Algonquian language of the Illinois. [Fr., of Algonquian orig.]
Il•li•nois[2] (ĭl′ə-noi′, -noiz′). A state of the N-central U.S.; admitted as the 21st state in 1818. Cap. Springfield. Pop. 11,466,682. — **Il′li•nois′an** (-noi′ən, -zən) *adj. & n.*
Illinois River. A river rising in NE IL and flowing c. 439 km (273 mi) to the Mississippi R. in W-central IL.
Illinois Waterway. A system of rivers and canals of N and W IL, linking Lake Michigan with the Mississippi R.
il•liq•uid (ĭ-lĭk′wĭd) *adj.* **1.** Not readily converted into cash. **2.** Lacking cash or liquid assets. — **il′li•quid′i•ty** *n.*
il•lit•er•a•cy (ĭ-lĭt′ər-ə-sē) *n., pl.* **-cies. 1.** The state of being unable to read and write. **2.** An error, as in speech, made by or thought typical of an illiterate.
il•lit•er•ate (ĭ-lĭt′ər-ĭt) *adj.* **1.a.** Unable to read and write. **b.** Having little or no formal education. **2.a.** Inferior to an expected standard of familiarity with language and literature. **b.** Violating prescribed standards of speech or writing. **3.** Ignorant of the fundamentals of a given art or branch of knowledge. — **il•lit′er•ate** *n.* — **il•lit′er•ate•ly** *adv.* — **il•lit′er•ate•ness** *n.*
ill-man•nered (ĭl′măn′ərd) *adj.* Lacking or indicating a lack of good manners; rude. — **ill′-man′nered•ly** *adv.*
ill nature *n.* A disagreeable or malevolent disposition.
ill-na•tured (ĭl′nā′chərd) *adj.* **1.** Having an ill nature. **2.** Spiteful; nasty. — **ill′-na′tured•ness** *n.*
ill•ness (ĭl′nĭs) *n.* **1.a.** Disease of body or mind; poor health; sickness. **b.** A disease. **2.** *Obsolete.* Evil; wickedness.
ill-nour•ished (ĭl′nûr′ĭsht, -nŭr′-) *adj.* Inadequately or poorly nourished; malnourished.
il•log•ic (ĭ-lŏj′ĭk) *n.* A lack of logic.
il•log•i•cal (ĭ-lŏj′ĭ-kəl) *adj.* **1.** Contradicting or disregarding the principles of logic. **2.** Without logic; senseless. — **il•log′i•cal′i•ty** (-kăl′ĭ-tē), **il•log′i•cal•ness** *n.* — **il•log′i•cal•ly** *adv.*
ill-o•mened (ĭl′ō′mənd) *adj.* Marked by bad omens; inauspicious.
ill-sort•ed (ĭl′sôr′tĭd) *adj.* Badly matched.
ill-starred (ĭl′stärd′) *adj.* Ill-fated; unlucky.
ill-tem•pered (ĭl′tĕm′pərd) *adj.* Having a bad temper; irritable. — **ill′-tem′pered•ly** *adv.*
ill-timed (ĭl′tīmd′) *adj.* Done or occurring at an inappropriate time; untimely.
ill-treat (ĭl′trēt′) *tr.v.* **-treat•ed, -treat•ing, -treats.** To treat unkindly or harshly; maltreat. See Syns at **abuse.** — **ill′-treat′ment** *n.*
il•lume (ĭ-lo͞om′) *tr.v.* **-lumed, -lum•ing, -lumes.** To illuminate. [Short for ILLUMINE.]
il•lu•mi•nance (ĭ-lo͞o′mə-nəns) *n. Phys.* See **illumination** 7.
il•lu•mi•nant (ĭ-lo͞o′mə-nənt) *n.* Something that gives off light. [Lat. *illūmināns*, *illūminant-*, pr.part. of *illūmināre*, to illuminate. See ILLUMINATE.]

il•lu•mi•nate (ĭ-lo͞o′mə-nāt′) *v.* **-nat•ed, -nat•ing, -nates.** —*tr.* **1.** To provide or brighten with light. **2.** To decorate or hang with lights. **3.** To make understandable; clarify. **4.** To enlighten intellectually or spiritually; enable to understand. **5.** To endow with fame or splendor; celebrate. **6.** To adorn (a page of a book, for example) with designs, miniatures, or lettering in brilliant colors or precious metals. **7.** To expose to or reveal by radiation. —*intr.* **1.** To become lighted; glow. **2.** To provide intellectual or spiritual enlightenment and understanding. **3.** To be exposed to or revealed by radiation. —*n.* (-nĭt). One who has or professes to have an unusual degree of enlightenment. [ME *illuminaten* < Lat. *illūmināre*, *illūmināt-* : *in-*, in; see IN–^{2} + *lūmināre*, to light up (< *lūmen*, *lūmin-*, light; see **leuk-***).] —**il•lu′mi•nat′ing•ly** *adv.*

il•lu•mi•na•ti (ĭ-lo͞o′mə-nä′tē) *pl.n.* **1.** People claiming to have enlightenment in a subject. **2. Illuminati.** Any of various groups claiming special religious enlightenment. [Lat., pl. of *illūminātus*, p.part. of *illūmināre*, to illuminate. See ILLUMINATE.]

il•lu•mi•na•tion (ĭ-lo͞o′mə-nā′shən) *n.* **1.a.** The act of illuminating. **b.** The state of being illuminated. **2.** A source of light. **3.** Decorative lighting. **4.** Spiritual or intellectual enlightenment. **5.** Clarification; elucidation. **6.a.** The art or act of decorating a text with designs, miniatures, or lettering. **b.** An example of this art. **7.** *Phys.* The luminous flux per unit area at any point on a surface exposed to incident light.

il•lu•mi•na•tive (ĭ-lo͞o′mə-nā′tĭv) *adj.* Of, causing, or capable of causing illumination.

il•lu•mi•na•tor (ĭ-lo͞o′mə-nā′tər) *n.* **1.** One that illuminates, esp. a device for producing, concentrating, or reflecting light. **2.** One who illuminates manuscripts or other objects.

il•lu•mine (ĭ-lo͞o′mĭn) *tr.v.* **-mined, -min•ing, -mines.** To give light to; illuminate. [ME *illuminen* < OFr. *illuminer* < Lat. *illūmināre.* See ILLUMINATE.] —**il•lu′min•a•ble** *adj.*

il•lu•mi•nism (ĭ-lo͞o′mə-nĭz′əm) *n.* **1.** Belief in or proclamation of a special personal enlightenment. **2. Illuminism.** The ideas and principles of various groups of Illuminati. [Fr. *illuminisme* < *illuminé*, an illuminist < p.part. of *illuminer*, to illuminate < OFr. See ILLUMINE.] —**il•lu′mi•nist** *n.*

illus. *abbr.* **1.** Illustrated. **2.** Illustration. **3.** Illustrator.

ill-us•age (ĭl′yo͞o′sĭj, -zĭj) *n.* Bad treatment; ill-use.

ill-use (ĭl′yo͞oz′) *tr.v.* **-used, -us•ing, -us•es.** To maltreat. —*n.* (ĭl′yo͞os′). Unjust or poor treatment; ill-usage.

il•lu•sion (ĭ-lo͞o′zhən) *n.* **1.a.** An erroneous perception of reality. **b.** An erroneous concept or belief. **2.** The condition of being deceived by an illusion. **3.** Something, such as a fantastic plan, that causes an erroneous belief or perception. **4.** Illusionism in art. **5.** A fine transparent cloth, used for dresses or trimmings. [ME < OFr. < LLat. *illūsiō*, *illūsiōn-* < Lat., a mocking, irony < *illūsus*, p.part. of *illūdere*, to mock : *in-*, against; see IN–^{2} + *lūdere*, to play; see **leid-***.] —**il•lu′sion•al, il•lu′sion•ar′y** (-zhə-nĕr′ē) *adj.*

il•lu•sion•ism (ĭ-lo͞o′zhə-nĭz′əm) *n.* **1.** *Philos.* The doctrine that the material world is an immaterial product of the senses. **2.** The use of illusionary techniques in art or decoration. —**il•lu′sion•is′tic** *adj.* —**il•lu′sion•is′ti•cal•ly** *adv.*

il•lu•sion•ist (ĭ-lo͞o′zhə-nĭst) *n.* **1.** *Philos.* An adherent of the doctrine of illusionism. **2.** An artist whose work is marked by illusionism. **3.** A magician or ventriloquist.

il•lu•sive (ĭ-lo͞o′sĭv) *adj.* Illusory. —**il•lu′sive•ly** *adv.* —**il•lu′sive•ness** *n.*

il•lu•so•ry (ĭ-lo͞o′sə-rē, -zə-rē) *adj.* Produced by, based on, or having the nature of an illusion; deceptive.

il•lus•trate (ĭl′ə-strāt′, ĭ-lŭs′trāt′) *v.* **-trat•ed, -trat•ing, -trates.** —*tr.* **1.a.** To clarify, as by examples. **b.** To clarify by serving as an example or comparison. **2.** To provide (a publication) with explanatory or decorative features. **3.** *Obsolete.* To illuminate. —*intr.* To present a clarification, an example, or an explanation. [Lat. *illūstrāre*, *illūstrāt-* : *in-*, in; see IN–^{2} + *lūstrāre*, to make bright; see **leuk-***.] —**il′lus•trat′a•ble** *adj.* —**il′lus•tra′tor** *n.*

il•lus•tra•tion (ĭl′ə-strā′shən) *n.* **1.a.** The act of clarifying or explaining. **b.** The state of being clarified or explained. **2.** Material used to clarify or explain. **3.** Visual matter used to clarify or decorate a text. **4.** *Obsolete.* Illumination. —**il′lus•tra′tion•al** *adj.*

il•lus•tra•tive (ĭ-lŭs′trə-tĭv, ĭl′ə-strā′tĭv) *adj.* Acting or serving as an illustration. —**il•lus′tra•tive•ly** *adv.*

il•lus•tri•ous (ĭ-lŭs′trē-əs) *adj.* **1.** Well known and very distinguished; eminent. See Syns at **noted. 2.** *Obsolete.* Shining brightly. [< Lat. *illūstris* < *illūstrāre*, to give glory to, shine upon. See ILLUSTRATE.] —**il•lus′tri•ous•ly** *adv.* —**il•lus′tri•ous•ness** *n.*

il•lu•vi•ate (ĭ-lo͞o′vē-āt′) *intr.v.* **-at•ed, -at•ing, -ates.** To undergo illuviation. [Back-formation < ILLUVIATION.]

il•lu•vi•a•tion (ĭ-lo͞o′vē-ā′shən) *n.* The deposition in an underlying soil layer of colloids, soluble salts, and mineral particles leached out of an overlying soil layer. [*illuvial*, resulting from illuviation (IN–^{2} + *-luvial*, relating to the action of flowing water, as in ALLUVIAL) + –ATION.]

ill will *n.* Unfriendly feeling; enmity.

ill-wish•er (ĭl′wĭsh′ər) *n.* One who wishes another no good.

il•ly (ĭl′lē) *adv.* Badly; ill.

Il•lyr•i•a (ĭ-lĭr′ē-ə) also **Il•lyr•i•cum** (-ĭ-kəm). An ancient region of the Balkan Peninsula on the Adriatic coast; became the Roman province of Illyricum after 33 B.C. and was later coextensive with the Illyrian Provinces (1809–15) and the kingdom of Illyria, a division of Austria (1816–49).

Il•lyr•i•an (ĭ-lîr′ē-ən) *adj.* Of or relating to ancient Illyria or its peoples, languages, or cultures. —*n.* **1.** A member of one of the ancient peoples that inhabited Illyria. **2.** Any of the Indo-European languages of these peoples.

il•men•ite (ĭl′mə-nīt′) *n.* A lustrous black to brownish titanium ore, essentially $FeTiO_3$. [After the *Ilmen* Mts., a range of the S Ural Mts.]

ILO *abbr.* International Labor Organization.

I•lo•ca•no also **I•lo•ka•no** (ē′lō-kä′nō) —*n., pl.* **Ilocano** or **-nos** also **Ilokano** or **-nos. 1.** A member of an agricultural people of northern Luzon in the Philippines. **2.** The Austronesian language of the Ilocano. —*adj.* Of or relating to the Ilocano or their language or culture. [Sp. *Ilócano* < *Iloko*, Austronesian people of the Philippines.]

I•lo•i•lo (ē′lō-ē′lō). A city of SE Panay, Philippines, on **Iloilo Strait,** an inlet of the Sulu Sea. Pop. 244,827.

I•lo•rin (ē′lə-rēn′, ĭ-lôr′ən). A city of SW Nigeria NNE of Lagos; cap. of a Yoruba kingdom c. 1800–25. Pop. 355,400.

ILS *abbr.* Instrument landing system.

im–^{1} *pref.* Var. of **in–^{1}.**

im–^{2} *pref.* Var. of **in–^{2}.**

I'm (īm). I am.

im•age (ĭm′ĭj) *n.* **1.** A reproduction of a person or an object, esp. a sculptured likeness. **2.** *Phys.* An optically or electronically formed representative reproduction of an object, esp. an optical reproduction formed by a lens or mirror. **3.** One that closely or exactly resembles another; a double. **4.a.** The public's opinion or concept of something. **b.** The character projected to the public, as by a person, esp. as interpreted by the mass media. **5.** A personification of something specified. **6.** A mental picture of something not real or present. **7.a.** A vivid description or representation. **b.** A figure of speech, esp. a metaphor or simile. **c.** A concrete representation, as in art, that expresses or evokes something else. **8.** *Math.* A set of values of a function corresponding to a given subset of a domain. **9.** *Comp. Sci.* A copy of data in a file transferred to another medium. **10.** *Obsolete.* An apparition. —*tr.v.* **-aged, -ag•ing, -ag•es. 1.** To make or produce a likeness of. **2.** To mirror or reflect. **3.** To symbolize or typify. **4.** To picture (something) mentally; imagine. **5.** To describe, esp. so as to evoke a mental picture of. **6.** *Comp. Sci.* To translate (photographs or other pictures) by computer into numbers that can be transmitted to and reconverted into pictures by another computer. **7.** To visualize (something), as by magnetic resonance imaging. [ME < OFr. < Lat. *imāgō.*]

im•age-mak•er (ĭm′ĭj-mā′kər) *n. Informal.* One who creates a favorable public view, as in the mass media. —**im′age-mak′ing** *n.*

image orthicon *n.* See **orthicon.**

im•age•ry (ĭm′ĭj-rē) *n., pl.* **-ries. 1.** A set of mental pictures or images. **2.a.** The use of vivid or figurative language to represent objects, actions, or ideas. **b.** The use of expressive or evocative images in art, literature, or music. **c.** A group or body of related images, as in a poem. **3.a.** Representative images, esp. statues or icons. **b.** The art of making them.

i•mag•i•na•ble (ĭ-măj′ə-nə-bəl) *adj.* Conceivable in the imagination. —**i•mag′i•na•bil′i•ty** *n.* —**i•mag′i•na•bly** *adv.*

i•ma•gi•nal (ĭ-mā′gə-nəl, ĭ-mä′-) *adj.* Of, relating to, or having the form of an insect imago.

i•mag•i•nar•y (ĭ-măj′ə-nĕr′ē) *adj.* **1.** Having existence only in the imagination; unreal. **2.** *Math.* **a.** Of, relating to, or being the coefficient of the imaginary unit in a complex number. **b.** Of, relating to, involving, or being an imaginary number. —*n., pl.* **-ies.** *Math.* An imaginary number. —**i•mag′i•nar′i•ly** *adv.* —**i•mag′i•nar′i•ness** *n.*

imaginary number *n. Math.* A complex number in which the real part is zero and the coefficient of the imaginary unit is not zero.

imaginary unit *n. Math.* The positive square root of −1.

i•mag•i•na•tion (ĭ-măj′ə-nā′shən) *n.* **1.a.** The formation of a mental image of something that is neither perceived as real nor present to the senses. **b.** The mental image so formed. **c.** The ability or tendency to form such images. **2.** The ability to confront and deal with reality creatively; resourcefulness. **3.** A traditional or widely held belief or opinion. **4.** *Archaic.* **a.** An unrealistic idea or notion; a fancy. **b.** A plan or scheme. —**i•mag′i•na′tion•al** *adj.*

i•mag•i•na•tive (ĭ-măj′ə-nə-tĭv, -nā′tĭv) *adj.* **1.** Having a lively or creative imagination. **2.** Created by, indicative of, or characterized by imagination or creativity. **3.** Tending to indulge in the fanciful or in make-believe. **4.** Having no truth. —**i•mag′i•na•tive•ly** *adv.* —**i•mag′i•na•tive•ness** *n.*

i•mag•ine (ĭ-măj′ĭn) *v.* **-ined, -in•ing, -ines.** —*tr.* **1.** To form a mental picture or image of. **2.** To think; conjecture. **3.** To have a notion of or about without adequate foundation; fancy. —*intr.* **1.** To employ the imagination. **2.** To guess; con-

illumination
From *The Hours of Jeanne d'Evreaux* illuminated by Jean Pucelle (1300?–1355)

ă pat	oi boy
ā pay	ou out
âr care	o͝o took
ä father	o͞o boot
ĕ pet	ŭ cut
ē be	ûr urge
ĭ pit	th thin
ī pie	*th* this
îr pier	hw which
ŏ pot	zh vision
ō toe	ə about, item
ô paw	

Stress marks:
′ (primary);
′ (secondary), as in **dictionary** (dĭk′shə-nĕr′ē)

jecture. [ME *imaginen* < OFr. *imaginer* < Lat. *imāginārī* < *imāgō, imāgin-*, image.] — **i•mag′in•er** *n.*

im•ag•ing (ĭm′ĭ-jĭng) *n.* **1.** *Medic.* Visualization of internal body parts using specialized instruments and techniques, such as ultrasonography, for diagnostic purposes. **2.** *Psychol.* The use of mental images to influence bodily processes.

im•a•gism also **Im•a•gism** (ĭm′ə-jĭz′əm) *n.* A literary movement launched by British and American poets early in the 20th century that advocated the use of free verse, common speech patterns, and concrete images. — **im′a•gist** *n.* — **im′a•gis′tic** *adj.* — **im′a•gis′ti•cal•ly** *adv.*

i•ma•go (ĭ-mā′gō, ĭ-mä′-) *n., pl.* **-goes** or **-gi•nes** (-gə-nēz′). **1.** An insect in its sexually mature adult stage after metamorphosis. **2.** *Psychol.* An often idealized image of a person, usu. a parent, formed in childhood and persisting unconsciously into adulthood. [Lat. *imāgō, imāgin-*, image.]

i•mam also **I•mam** (ĭ-mäm′) *n. Islam.* **1.a.** In law and theology, the caliph who succeeds Muhammad as the supreme leader of the Islamic community. **b.** The male prayer leader in a mosque. **c.** The Muslim worshiper who leads the recitation of prayer when two or more worshipers are present. **2.a.** A male leader regarded by Shiites as a descendant of Muhammad divinely appointed to guide human beings. **b.** A male earthly representative of the 12 such leaders recognized by Imamites. **3.** A male ruler claiming descent from Muhammad and exercising authority in an Islamic state. **4.a.** Any one of the founders of the four schools of law and theology. **b.** An authoritative scholar who founds a school of law or theology. **5.** Used as a title for an imam. [Ar. *'imām*, leader, imam < *'amma*, to lead.]

i•mam•ate (ĭ-mä′māt′) *n. Islam.* The office of a ruling imam.

I•mam•ite (ĭ-mä′mīt′) *n.* A member of the largest branch of Shiism, marked by its acceptance of 12 divinely appointed imams.

i•ma•ret (ĭ-mä′rĕt) *n.* An inn or hostel for pilgrims in Turkey. [Turk. < Ar. *'imārah* < *'amara*, to build.]

im•bal•ance (ĭm-băl′əns) *n.* A lack of balance, as in distribution or functioning. — **im•bal′anced** *adj.*

im•be•cile (ĭm′bə-sĭl, -səl) *n.* **1.** A stupid or silly person; a dolt. **2.** A person whose mental acumen is well below par. **3.** A person of moderate to severe mental retardation having a mental age of from three to seven years. The term is no longer in scientific use and is now considered offensive. — *adj.* also **im•be•cil•ic** (ĭm′bə-sĭl′ĭk). **1.** Stupid; silly. **2.** Well below par in mental acumen. [< obsolete Fr. *imbécille*, weak, feeble < OFr. < Lat. *imbēcillus* : *in-*, not; see IN-[1] + poss. *bacillum*, staff, dim. of *baculum*, rod; see **bak-***.]

im•be•cil•i•ty (ĭm′bə-sĭl′ĭ-tē) *n., pl.* **-ties. 1.a.** Great stupidity or foolishness. **b.** Something stupid or foolish, such as an act. **2.** *Psychol.* The state or condition of being an imbecile; moderate or severe mental retardation.

im•bed (ĭm-bĕd′) *v.* Var. of **embed.**

im•bibe (ĭm-bīb′) *v.* **-bibed, -bib•ing, -bibes.** — *tr.* **1.** To drink. **2.** To absorb or take in as if by drinking. **3.** To receive and absorb into the mind. **4.** *Obsolete.* To permeate; saturate. — *intr.* To drink alcoholic beverages. [ME *embiben*, to soak up, saturate < Lat. *imbibere*, to drink in, imbibe : *in-*, in; see IN-[2] + *bibere*, to drink; see **pō(i)-***.] — **im•bib′er** *n.*

im•bi•bi•tion (ĭm′bə-bĭsh′ən) *n.* **1.** The act of imbibing. **2.** *Chem.* Absorption of fluid by a solid or colloid that causes swelling.

im•bri•cate (ĭm′brĭ-kāt′) *adj.* Having the edges overlapping in a regular arrangement, as roof tiles. — *v.* **-cat•ed, -cat•ing, -cates.** — *tr.* To overlap in a regular pattern. — *intr.* To be arranged with regular overlapping edges. [Lat. *imbricātus*, p.part. of *imbricāre*, to cover with roof tiles < *imbrex, imbric-*, roof tile < *imber, imbr-*, rain.] — **im′bri•ca′tion** *n.*

imbricate
Roof tiles

im•bro•glio (ĭm-brōl′yō) *n., pl.* **-glios. 1.a.** A difficult or intricate situation; an entanglement. **b.** A confused or complicated disagreement. **2.** A confused heap; a tangle. [Ital. < OItal. < *imbrogliare*, to tangle, confuse : *in-*, in (< Lat.; see IN-[2]) + *brogliare*, to mix, stir (prob. < OFr. *brooiller, brouiller*; see BROIL[2]).]

im•brue (ĭm-bro͞o′) also **em•brue** (ĕm-) *tr.v.* **-brued, -bru•ing, -brues. 1.** To saturate. **2.** To stain. [ME *embrewen* < OFr. *embreuver* < VLat. **imbiberāre* : Lat. *in-*, in; see IN-[2] + LLat. *biber*, beverage (< Lat. *bibere*, to drink; see BEVERAGE).]

im•brute (ĭm-bro͞ot′) *tr. & intr.v.* **-brut•ed, -brut•ing, -brutes.** To make or become brutal.

im•bue (ĭm-byo͞o′) *tr.v.* **-bued, -bu•ing, -bues. 1.** To inspire, permeate, or invade. **2.** To stain or dye deeply. [ME *enbuen, imbeuen* < Lat. *imbuere*, to moisten, stain.]

IMF *abbr.* International Monetary Fund.

im•id•az•ole (ĭm′ĭ-dăz′ōl′) *n.* An organic crystalline base, $C_3H_4N_2$, that is an inhibitor of histamine. [IMID(E) + AZOLE.]

im•ide (ĭm′īd′) *n.* A compound derived from ammonia and containing the bivalent NH group combined with a bivalent acid group or two monovalent acid groups. [Alteration of AMIDE.]

im•i•do (ĭm′ĭ-dō′) *adj.* Of or relating to imides or an imide. [< *imido-* < IMIDE.]

im•ine (ĭm′ēn′, -ĭn, ĭ-mēn′) *n.* A compound derived from ammonia and containing the bivalent NH group combined with a bivalent nonacid group. [Alteration of AMINE.]

im•i•no (ĭm′ə-nō′) *adj.* Of or relating to imines or an imine. [< *imino-* < IMINE.]

i•mip•ra•mine (ĭ-mĭp′rə-mēn′) *n.* A tricyclic compound, $C_{19}H_{24}N_2$, used to treat depression and enuresis. [IMI(DE) + PR(OPYL) + AMINE.]

imit. *abbr.* Imitation; imitative.

im•i•ta•ble (ĭm′ĭ-tə-bəl) *adj.* **1.** That can be imitated. **2.** Worthy of imitation.

im•i•tate (ĭm′ĭ-tāt′) *tr.v.* **-tat•ed, -tat•ing, -tates. 1.** To use or follow as a model. **2.a.** To copy the actions, appearance, mannerisms, or speech of; mimic. **b.** To copy or use the style of. **3.** To copy exactly; reproduce. **4.** To appear like; resemble. [Lat. *imitārī, imitāt-*.] — **im′i•ta′tor** *n.*

Syns: *imitate, copy, mimic, ape, parody, simulate.* These verbs mean to follow something or someone taken as a model. To *imitate* is to act like or follow a pattern or style set by another: *"Art imitates Nature"* (Richard Franck). To *copy* is to duplicate an original as precisely as possible: *tried to copy her cultivated accent.* To *mimic* is to make a close imitation, often with an intent to ridicule: mimicked her dialect. To *ape* is to follow another's lead slavishly but often with an absurd result: *"Those* [superior] *states of mind do not come from aping an alien culture"* (John Russell). To *parody* is either to imitate with comic effect or to attempt a serious imitation and fail: *"All these peculiarities* [of Samuel Johnson's literary style] *have been imitated by his admirers and parodied by his assailants"* (Macaulay). To *simulate* is to feign or falsely assume the appearance or character of something: *"I . . . lay there simulating death"* (W.H. Hudson).

im•i•ta•tion (ĭm′ĭ-tā′shən) *n.* **1.** The act or an instance of imitating. **2.** Something derived or copied from an original. **3.** *Mus.* Repetition of a phrase or sequence often with variations in key, rhythm, and voice. — *adj.* Made to resemble another, usu. superior material. — **im′i•ta′tion•al** *adj.*

im•i•ta•tive (ĭm′ĭ-tā′tĭv) *adj.* **1.** Of or involving imitation. **2.** Not original; derivative. **3.** Tending to imitate. **4.** Onomatopoeic. — **im′i•ta′tive•ly** *adv.* — **im′i•ta′tive•ness** *n.*

im•mac•u•la•cy (ĭ-măk′yə-lə-sē) *n.* The quality or condition of being immaculate.

im•mac•u•late (ĭ-măk′yə-lĭt) *adj.* **1.** Impeccably clean; spotless. See Syns at **clean. 2.** Free from stain or blemish; pure. **3.** Free from fault or error. **4.** Having no markings. [ME *immaculat* < Lat. *immaculātus* : *in-*, not; see IN-[1] + *maculātus*, p.part. of *maculāre*, to blemish (< *macula*, spot).] — **im•mac′u•late•ly** *adv.* — **im•mac′u•late•ness** *n.*

Im•mac•u•late Conception (ĭ-măk′yə-lĭt) *n. Rom. Cath. Ch.* **1.** The doctrine that the Virgin Mary was conceived free from original sin. **2.** The feast of the Immaculate Conception, celebrated on December 8.

im•ma•nent (ĭm′ə-nənt) *adj.* **1.** Existing or remaining within; inherent. **2.** Restricted entirely to the mind; subjective. [LLat. *immanēns, immanent-*, pr.part. of *immanēre*, to remain in : Lat. *in-*, in; see IN-[2] + Lat. *manēre*, to remain; see **men-[3]***.] — **im′ma•nence, im′ma•nen•cy** *n.* — **im′ma•nent•ly** *adv.*

im•ma•nent•ism (ĭm′ə-nən-tĭz′əm) *n.* Any of various religious theories postulating that a deity, mind, or spirit is immanent in the world and in the individual. — **im′ma•nent•ist** *adj. & n.*

im•ma•te•ri•al (ĭm′ə-tîr′ē-əl) *adj.* **1.** Of no importance or relevance; inconsequential or irrelevant. **2.** Having no material body or form. — **im′ma•te′ri•al•ly** *adv.*

im•ma•te•ri•al•ism (ĭm′ə-tîr′ē-ə-lĭz′əm) *n.* A metaphysical doctrine asserting the nonexistence of corporeal reality. — **im′ma•te′ri•al•ist** *adj. & n.*

im•ma•te•ri•al•i•ty (ĭm′ə-tîr′ē-ăl′ĭ-tē) *n., pl.* **-ties. 1.** The state or quality of being immaterial. **2.** Something immaterial.

im•ma•te•ri•al•ize (ĭm′ə-tîr′ē-ə-līz′) *tr.v.* **-ized, -iz•ing, -iz•es.** To render immaterial.

im•ma•ture (ĭm′ə-tyo͝or′, -to͝or′, -cho͝or′) *adj.* **1.** Not fully grown or developed. **2.** Marked by or suggesting a lack of maturity. [Lat. *immātūrus* : *in-*, not; see IN-[1] + *mātūrus*, mature; see **mā-[1]***.] — **im′ma•ture′ly** *adv.* — **im′ma•tur′i•ty, im′ma•ture′ness** *n.*

im•meas•ur•a•ble (ĭ-mĕzh′ər-ə-bəl) *adj.* **1.** Impossible to measure. See Syns at **incalculable. 2.** Vast; limitless. — **im•meas′ur•a•bil′i•ty, im•meas′ur•a•ble•ness** *n.* — **im•meas′ur•a•bly** *adv.*

im•me•di•a•cy (ĭ-mē′dē-ə-sē) *n., pl.* **-cies. 1.** The state or quality of being immediate. **2.** Lack of an intervening or mediating agency; directness: *the immediacy of TV.* **3.** Something immediate, as in importance.

im•me•di•ate (ĭ-mē′dē-ĭt) *adj.* **1.** Occurring at once; instant. **2.a.** Of or near the present time. **b.** Of or relating to the present time and place; current. **3.** Close at hand; near. See Syns at **close. 4.** Next in line or relation. **5.** Directly apprehended or perceived. **6.** Acting or occurring without the interposition of another agency or object; direct. [ME *immediat* < OFr. < LLat. *immediātus* : Lat. *in-*, not; see IN-[1] + Lat. *mediātus*, p.part. of *mediāre*, to be in the middle; see MEDIATE.] — **im•me′di•ate•ness** *n.*

immediate constituent *n. Ling.* Any meaningful constituent, such as a word, that enters directly into the formation of a linguistic construction, such as a phrase.

im•me•di•ate•ly (ĭ-mē′dē-ĭt-lē) *adv.* **1.** Without delay. **2.** With no intermediary; directly. —*conj.* As soon as; directly.

im•med•i•ca•ble (ĭ-mĕd′ĭ-kə-bəl) *adj.* Incurable.

Im•mel•mann turn (ĭm′əl-mən, -män′) *n.* A maneuver in which an airplane first completes half a loop and then half a roll in order to gain altitude and change flight direction simultaneously. [After Max *Immelmann* (1890–1916), German aviator.]

im•me•mo•ri•al (ĭm′ə-môr′ē-əl, -mōr′-) *adj.* Exceeding the limits of memory, tradition, or recorded history. —**im′me•mo′ri•al•ly** *adv.*

im•mense (ĭ-mĕns′) *adj.* **1.** Extremely large; huge. **2.** Boundless or immeasurable in size or extent. **3.** *Informal.* Surpassingly good; excellent. [ME < OFr. < Lat. *immēnsus* : *in-*, not; see IN-[1] + *mēnsus*, p.part. of *mētīrī*, to measure; see **mē-**[2]*.] —**im•mense′ly** *adv.* —**im•mense′ness** *n.*

im•men•si•ty (ĭ-mĕn′sĭ-tē) *n., pl.* **-ties. 1.** The quality or state of being immense. **2.** Something immense.

im•men•sur•a•ble (ĭ-mĕn′shər-ə-bəl) *adj.* Immeasurable.

im•merge (ĭ-mûrj′) *intr.v.* **-merged, -merg•ing, -merg•es.** To submerge or disappear in or as if in a liquid. [Lat. *immergere.* See IMMERSE.] —**im•mer′gence** *n.*

im•merse (ĭ-mûrs′) *tr.v.* **-mersed, -mers•ing, -mers•es. 1.** To cover completely in a liquid; submerge. **2.** To baptize by submerging in water. **3.** To engage wholly or deeply; absorb: *immersed in study.* [< ME *immersed*, embedded deeply < Lat. *immersus*, p.part. of *immergere*, to immerse : *in-*, in; see IN-[2] + *mergere*, to dip.]

im•mers•i•ble (ĭ-mûr′sə-bəl) *adj.* Capable of being completely immersed in water without suffering damage.

im•mer•sion (ĭ-mûr′zhən, -shən) *n.* **1.a.** The act or an instance of immersing. **b.** The state of being immersed. **2.** Baptism performed by submerging a person in water. **3.** *Astron.* The obscuring of a celestial body by another or by the shadow of another.

im•mesh (ĭm-mĕsh′) *v.* Var. of **enmesh.**

im•mi•grant (ĭm′ĭ-grənt) *n.* **1.** A person who leaves one country to settle permanently in another. **2.** A plant or an animal that establishes itself where it previously did not exist.

im•mi•grate (ĭm′ĭ-grāt′) *v.* **-grat•ed, -grat•ing, -grates.** —*intr.* To enter and settle in a land to which one is not native. See Usage Note at **migrate.** —*tr.* To send or introduce as immigrants. [Lat. *immigrāre, immigrāt-*, to go into : *in-*, in; see IN-[2] + *migrāre*, to depart.] —**im′mi•gra′tion** *n.*

im•mi•nence (ĭm′ə-nəns) *n.* **1.** The quality or condition of being about to occur. **2.** Something about to occur.

im•mi•nen•cy (ĭm′ə-nən-sē) *n., pl.* **-cies.** Imminence.

im•mi•nent (ĭm′ə-nənt) *adj.* About to occur; impending. [Ult. < Lat. *imminēns, imminent-*, pr.part. of *imminēre*, to overhang : *in-*, in; see IN-[2] + *-minēre*, to jut, threaten; see **men-**[2]*.] —**im′mi•nent•ly** *adv.* —**im′mi•nent•ness** *n.*

im•mis•ci•ble (ĭ-mĭs′ə-bəl) *adj.* That cannot undergo mixing or blending. —**im•mis′ci•bil′i•ty** *n.* —**im•mis′ci•bly** *adv.*

im•mit•i•ga•ble (ĭ-mĭt′ĭ-gə-bəl) *adj.* That cannot be mitigated: *immitigable circumstances.* —**im•mit′i•ga•bil′i•ty, im•mit′i•ga•ble•ness** *n.* —**im•mit′i•ga•bly** *adv.*

im•mit•tance (ĭ-mĭt′ns) *n.* Electrical impedance or admittance. [IM(PEDANCE) + (AD)MITTANCE.]

im•mix (ĭ-mĭks′) *tr.v.* **-mixed, -mix•ing, -mix•es.** To commingle; blend. [Ult. < Lat. *immīxtus*, p.part. of *immīscēre*, to blend : *in-*, in; see IN-[2] + *mīscēre*, to mix; see **meik-***.] —**im•mix′ture** (-mĭks′chər) *n.*

im•mo•bile (ĭ-mō′bəl, -bēl′, -bīl′) *adj.* **1.** Immovable; fixed. **2.** Not moving; motionless. —**im′mo•bil′i•ty** (-bĭl′ĭ-tē) *n.*

im•mo•bi•lize (ĭ-mō′bə-līz′) *tr.v.* **-lized, -liz•ing, -liz•es. 1.** To render immobile. **2.** To fix the position of (a joint or fractured limb), as with a cast. **3.** To impede movement or use of: *A storm immobilized us.* **4.** *Econ.* **a.** To withdraw (specie) from circulation and reserve as security for other money. **b.** To convert (floating capital) into fixed capital. —**im•mo′bi•li•za′tion** (-lĭ-zā′shən) *n.* —**im•mo′bi•liz′er** *n.*

im•mod•er•a•cy (ĭ-mŏd′ər-ə-sē) *n., pl.* **-cies. 1.** The quality or state of being immoderate. **2.** Something immoderate.

im•mod•er•ate (ĭ-mŏd′ər-ĭt) *adj.* Exceeding normal or appropriate bounds; extreme: *immoderate spending.* See Syns at **excessive.** [ME < Lat. *immoderātus* : *in-*, not; see IN-[1] + *moderātus*, p.part. of *moderārī*, to moderate; see **med-***.] —**im•mod′er•ate•ly** *adv.* —**im•mod′er•ate•ness, im•mod′er•a′tion** *n.*

im•mod•est (ĭ-mŏd′ĭst) *adj.* **1.** Lacking modesty. **2.a.** Offending against sexual mores in conduct or appearance; indecent: *immodest dress.* **b.** Not properly restrained in expression or self-assertion; boastful: *immodest claims.* **3.** Arrogant. [Lat. *immodestus* : *in-*, not; see IN-[1] + *modestus*, moderate, modest; see **med-***.] —**im•mod′est•ly** *adv.* —**im•mod′es•ty** *n.*

im•mo•late (ĭm′ə-lāt′) *tr.v.* **-lat•ed, -lat•ing, -lates. 1.** To kill as a sacrifice. **2.** To kill (oneself) by fire. **3.** To destroy. [Lat. *immolāre, immolāt-*, to sacrifice, sprinkle with sacrificial meal : *in-*, on; see IN-[2] + *mola*, meal, millstone; see **melə-***.] —**im′mo•la′tion** *n.* —**im′mo•la′tor** *n.*

im•mor•al (ĭ-môr′əl, -mŏr′-) *adj.* Contrary to established moral principles. —**im•mor′al•ly** *adv.*

im•mor•al•ist (ĭ-môr′ə-lĭst, -mŏr′-) *n.* An advocate of immorality.

im•mor•al•i•ty (ĭm′ô-răl′ĭ-tē, ĭm′ə-) *n., pl.* **-ties. 1.** The quality or condition of being immoral. **2.** An immoral act or practice.

im•mor•tal (ĭ-môr′tl) *adj.* **1.** Not subject to death. **2.** Never to be forgotten; everlasting: *immortal words.* **3.** Of or relating to immortality. **4.** *Biol.* Capable of indefinite growth or division. Used of cells in culture. —*n.* **1.** One not subject to death. **2.** One whose fame is enduring. [ME < OFr. *immortel* < Lat. *immortālis.* See **mer-***.] —**im•mor′tal•ly** *adv.*

im•mor•tal•i•ty (ĭm′ôr-tăl′ĭ-tē) *n.* **1.** The quality or condition of being immortal. **2.** Endless life or existence. **3.** Enduring fame.

im•mor•tal•ize (ĭ-môr′tl-īz′) *tr.v.* **-ized, -iz•ing, -iz•es.** To make immortal.

im•mor•telle (ĭm′ôr-tĕl′) *n.* A plant with flowers of lasting color. [Fr. < fem. of *immortel*, immortal < OFr. See IMMORTAL.]

im•mo•tile (ĭ-mōt′l, ĭ-mō′tīl′) *adj.* Not moving or lacking the ability to move. —**im′mo•til′i•ty** (-tĭl′ĭ-tē) *n.*

im•mov•a•ble (ĭ-mo͞o′və-bəl) *adj.* **1.a.** Impossible to move. **b.** Incapable of movement. **2.** Unalterable: *immovable plans.* **3.** Unyielding in principle, purpose, or adherence; steadfast. **4.** Incapable of being moved emotionally. —*n.* One that cannot move or be moved. —**im•mov′a•bil′i•ty, im•mov′a•ble•ness** *n.* —**im•mov′a•bly** *adv.*

immun. *abbr.* **1.** Immunity. **2.** Immunization.

im•mune (ĭ-myo͞on′) *adj.* **1.** Not subject to an obligation imposed on others; exempt: *immune from taxation.* **2.** Not affected by a given influence; unresponsive: *immune to persuasion.* **3.** *Immunol.* Of, relating to, or having immunity to infection by a specific pathogen. —*n.* A person who is immune. [ME < Lat. *immūnis.* See **mei-**[1]*.]

immune reaction *n.* The reaction due to the recognition and binding of an antigen by its specific antibody or by a previously sensitized lymphocyte.

immune response *n.* An integrated bodily response to an antigen, esp. one mediated by lymphocytes and involving an immune reaction.

immune system *n.* The integrated body system of organs, tissues, cells, and cell products that identifies nonself and neutralizes potentially pathogenic organisms or substances.

im•mu•ni•ty (ĭ-myo͞o′nĭ-tē) *n., pl.* **-ties. 1.** The quality or condition of being immune. **2.** *Immunol.* Inherited, acquired, or induced resistance to infection by a specific pathogen. **3.** *Law.* **a.** Exemption from legal duties, penalties, or liabilities, granted to a group. **b.** Exemption from legal prosecution, often granted a witness in exchange for testimony.

im•mu•nize (ĭm′yə-nīz′) *tr.v.* **-nized, -niz•ing, -niz•es. 1.** To render immune. **2.** To produce immunity in, as by inoculation. **3.** *Law.* To grant immunity from prosecution: *immunize a witness.* —**im′mu•ni•za′tion** (-nĭ-zā′shən) *n.*

immuno– *pref.* Immune; immunity: *immunoelectrophoresis.* [< IMMUNE.]

im•mu•no•as•say (ĭm′yə-nō-ăs′ā, ĭ-myo͞o′-) *n.* A laboratory or clinical technique that makes use of the specific binding between an antigen and its homologous antibody in order to identify and quantify a substance in a sample.

im•mu•no•chem•is•try (ĭm′yə-nō-kĕm′ĭ-strē, ĭ-myo͞o′-) *n.* The chemistry of immunologic phenomena.

im•mu•no•com•pe•tent (ĭm′yə-nō-kŏm′pĭ-tənt, ĭ-myo͞o′-) *adj.* Having the normal bodily capacity to develop an immune response following exposure to an antigen. —**im′mu•no•com′pe•tence** *n.*

im•mu•no•de•fi•cien•cy (ĭm′yə-nō-dĭ-fĭsh′ən-sē, ĭ-myo͞o′-) *n., pl.* **-cies.** An inability to develop a normal immune response. —**im′mu•no•de•fi′cient** *adj.*

im•mu•no•e•lec•tro•pho•re•sis (ĭm′yə-nō-ĭ-lĕk′trə-fə-rē′sĭs, ĭ-myo͞o′-) *n.* The separation and identification of proteins based on differences in electrical charge and reactivity with antibodies.

im•mu•no•fluo•res•cence (ĭm′yə-nō-flo͝o-rĕs′əns, -flô-, -flō-) *n.* Any of various techniques that use antibodies chemically linked to a fluorescent dye to identify or quantify antigens in a tissue sample. —**im′mu•no•fluo•res′cent** *adj.*

im•mu•no•ge•net•ics (ĭm′yə-nō-jə-nĕt′ĭks) *n.* (*used with a sing. v.*) **1.** The study of the interrelation between immunity to disease and genetic makeup. **2.** The branch of immunology that deals with the molecular and genetic bases of the immune response. —**im′mu•no•ge•net′i•cist** (-ĭ-sĭst) *n.*

im•mu•no•gen•ic (ĭm′yə-nō-jĕn′ĭk, ĭmyo͞o′-) *adj.* Producing an immune response; antigenic.

im•mu•no•glob•u•lin (ĭm′yə-nō-glŏb′yə-lĭn, ĭ-myo͞o′-) *n.* Any of a group of large glycoproteins secreted by plasma cells in vertebrates that function as antibodies in the immune response by binding to specific antigens.

im•mu•nol•o•gy (ĭm′yə-nŏl′ə-jē) *n.* The branch of biomed-

ă pat	oi boy
ā pay	ou out
âr care	o͝o took
ä father	o͞o boot
ĕ pet	ŭ cut
ē be	ûr urge
ĭ pit	th thin
ī pie	*th* this
îr pier	hw which
ŏ pot	zh vision
ō toe	ə about, item
ô paw	

Stress marks:
′ (primary);
′ (secondary), as in **dictionary** (dĭk′shə-nĕr′ē)

icine concerned with the structure and function of the immune system, innate and acquired immunity, the bodily distinction of self from nonself, and laboratory techniques involving the interaction of antigens with specific antibodies. — **im′mu·no·log′ic** (-nə-lŏj′ĭk), **im′mu·no·log′i·cal** *adj.* — **im′mu·no·log′i·cal·ly** *adv.* — **im′mu·nol′o·gist** *n.*

im·mu·no·sup·pres·sion (ĭm′yə-nō-sə-prĕsh′ən, ĭ-myo͞o′-) *n.* Suppression of the immune response, as by drugs, in order to prevent the rejection of grafts or transplants or control autoimmune diseases. — **im′mu·no·sup·pres′sant** (-prĕs′-ənt) *n.* — **im′mu·no·sup·pres′sive** *adj.*

im·mu·no·ther·a·py (ĭm′yə-nō-thĕr′ə-pē, ĭ-myo͞o′-) *n., pl.* **-pies.** Treatment of disease by inducing, enhancing, or suppressing an immune response. — **im′mu·no·ther′a·peu′tic** (-pyo͞o′tĭk) *adj.* — **im′mu·no·ther′a·pist** *n.*

impala
Male impala
Aepyceros melampus

im·mure (ĭ-myo͝or′) *tr.v.* **-mured, -mur·ing, -mures. 1.** To confine within or as if within walls; imprison. **2.** To build into a wall. **3.** To entomb in a wall. [Med.Lat. *immūrāre* : Lat. *in-*, in; see IN-² + Lat. *mūrus*, wall.] — **im·mure′ment** *n.*

im·mu·ta·ble (ĭ-myo͞o′tə-bəl) *adj.* Not subject or susceptible to change. — **im·mu′ta·bil′i·ty, im·mu′ta·ble·ness** *n.* — **im·mu′ta·bly** *adv.*

imp (ĭmp) *n.* **1.** A mischievous child. **2.** A small demon. **3.** *Obsolete.* A graft. —*tr.v.* **imped, imp·ing, imps. 1.** To graft (new feathers) onto the wing of a trained falcon or hawk to repair damage or increase flying capacity. **2.** To furnish with wings. [ME *impe*, scion, sprig, offspring < OE *impa*, young shoot < *impian*, to graft, ult. < Med.Lat. *impotus*, graft < Gk. *emphutos*, grafted < *emphuein*, to implant : *en-*, in; see EN-² + *phuein*, to make grow; see **bheuə-***.]

imp. *abbr.* **1.** Imperative. **2.** Imperfect. **3.** Imperial. **4.a.** Import. **b.** Imported; importer. **5.** Important. **6.** Imprimatur.

im·pact (ĭm′păkt′) *n.* **1.** The striking of one body against another; collision. **2.** The force or impetus transmitted by a collision. **3.** The effect or impression of one thing on another. **4.** The power of making a strong, immediate impression. —*v.* (ĭm-păkt′) **-pact·ed, -pact·ing, -pacts.** —*tr.* **1.** To pack firmly together. **2.** To strike forcefully. **3.** *Usage Problem.* To have an effect or impact on. —*intr. Usage Problem.* To have an effect or impact. [< Lat. *impāctus*, p.part. of *impingere*, to push against. See IMPINGE.] — **im·pac′tion** *n.*

Usage Note: Eighty-four percent of the Usage Panel disapproves of the construction *to impact on*, as in the phrase *social pathologies, common to the inner city, that impact heavily on such a community*; and fully 95 percent disapproves of the use of *impact* as a transitive verb in the sentence *Companies have used disposable techniques that have a potential for impacting our health.* • It may be that the particular pretentiousness associated with the verbal use of *impact* is caused by its derivation from an already questionable metaphoric use of the noun *impact,* as in phrases such as *the political impact of the decision,* in which no more is usually meant than might have been expressed by *effects* or *consequences*. But *impact* has by now become so common in corporate and institutional contexts that younger speakers appear to regard it as wholly standard and straightforward usage. Within a few years, accordingly, the usage is likely to be no more objectionable than the use of *contact* as a verb. See Usage Note at **contact.**

impatiens
Spotted jewelweed
Impatiens capensis

Word History: The often criticized use of *impact,* as in "social pathologies that impact on a community," illustrates how one part of speech can have an impact on another. The noun *impact* comes from the past participle *impāctus* of the Latin verb *impingere,* which means "to bring into violent contact," "to drive persons or other creatures onto or against," and "to fix, fasten onto." Our noun, first recorded in 1781, derived its sense from the "contact" sense of *impingere*. First recorded in a scientific context having to do with the collision of bodies, it was much used in scientific contexts and later, in the 19th century, took on a figurative sense, "the effect of one thing upon another." The verb *impact,* on the other hand, also coming from Latin *impāctus,* is found much earlier than the noun, that is, it is first recorded in 1601, deriving its sense from the "driving" and "fixing" senses of *impingere* and meaning "to press closely into something, pack in." This old sense is still with us, but the later noun had an influence on the verb, giving us senses such as "to strike forcefully" and "to have an effect."

im·pact·ed (ĭm-păk′tĭd) *adj.* **1.** Wedged together at the broken ends. Used of a fractured bone. **2.** Placed in the alveolus and prohibiting eruption into a normal position. Used of a tooth. **3.** Wedged or packed in, so as to fill or block an organ or a passage.

im·pair (ĭm-pâr′) *tr.v.* **-paired, -pair·ing, -pairs.** To cause to diminish, as in strength or quality: *An injury impaired my hearing.* See Syns at **spoil.** [ME *empairen* < OFr. *empeirer* < VLat. **impēiōrāre* : Lat. *in-*, causative pref.; see IN-² + LLat. *pēiōrāre*, to worsen (< Lat. *pēior*, *pēiōr-*, worse; see **ped-***).] — **im·pair′ment** *n.*

im·pa·la (ĭm-păl′ə) *n.* A reddish African antelope *(Aepyceros melampus)* noted for its leaping ability and having ridged curved horns in the male. [Nguni (Zulu) *im-pala.*]

im·pale (ĭm-pāl′) also **em·pale** (ĕm-) *tr.v.* **-paled, -pal·ing, -pales. 1.a.** To pierce with a sharp stake or point. **b.** To torture or kill by impaling. **2.** To render helpless as if by impaling. [Med.Lat. *impālāre* : Lat. *in-*, in; see IN-² + Lat. *pālus*, stake; see **pag-***.] — **im·pale′ment** *n.* — **im·pal′er** *n.*

im·pal·pa·ble (ĭm-păl′pə-bəl) *adj.* **1.** Not perceptible to the touch; intangible. **2.** Difficult to perceive or grasp by the mind. — **im·pal′pa·bil′i·ty** *n.* — **im·pal′pa·bly** *adv.*

im·pan·el (ĭm-păn′əl) also **em·pan·el** (ĕm-) *tr.v.* **-eled, -el·ing, -els** or **-elled, -el·ling, -els.** *Law.* To enroll (a jury) upon a panel or list. [ME *empanellen* < AN *empaneller* : *en-*, in (< Lat. *in-*; see IN-²) + *panel*, piece of paper listing jurors, jury; see PANEL.] — **im·pan′el·ment** *n.*

im·par·i·ty (ĭm-păr′ĭ-tē) *n., pl.* **-ties.** Inequality; disparity. [LLat. *imparitās* < Lat. *impār*, not equal : *in-*, not; see IN-¹ + *pār*, equal; see **perə-²***.]

im·part (ĭm-pärt′) *tr.v.* **-part·ed, -part·ing, -parts. 1.** To grant a share of; bestow. **2.** To make known; disclose. [Ult. < Lat. *impertīre, impartīre* : *in-*, in; see IN-² + *partīre*, to share (< *pars, part-*, part; see **perə-²***).]

im·par·tial (ĭm-pär′shəl) *adj.* Not partial or biased; unprejudiced. See Syns at **fair¹.** — **im′par·ti·al′i·ty** (-shē-ăl′ĭ-tē), **im·par′tial·ness** *n.* — **im·par′tial·ly** *adv.*

im·part·i·ble (ĭm-pär′tə-bəl) *adj.* Not partible; indivisible. — **im·part′i·bil′i·ty** *n.* — **im·part′i·bly** *adv.*

im·pass·a·ble (ĭm-păs′ə-bəl) *adj.* Impossible to pass, cross, or overcome. — **im·pass′a·bil′i·ty, im·pass′a·ble·ness** *n.* — **im·pass′a·bly** *adv.*

im·passe (ĭm′păs′) *n.* **1.** A road or passage having no exit; a cul-de-sac. **2.** A situation in which no progress can be made; a deadlock or a stalemate. [Fr. : *in-*, not (< Lat. *in-*; see IN-¹) + *passe*, a passing (< OFr. < *passer*, to pass; see PASS).]

im·pas·si·ble (ĭm-păs′ə-bəl) *adj.* **1.** Not subject to suffering or pain. **2.** Unfeeling; impassive. — **im·pas′si·bil′i·ty, im·pas′si·ble·ness** *n.* — **im·pas′si·bly** *adv.*

im·pas·sion (ĭm-păsh′ən) *tr.v.* **-sioned, -sion·ing, -sions.** To arouse the passions of. [Ital. *impassionare* : *in-*, in (< Lat.; see IN-²) + *passione*, passion (< Lat. *passiō*, *passiōn-*, emotion; see PASSION).]

im·pas·sioned (ĭm-păsh′ənd) *adj.* Full of passion; fervent.

im·pas·sive (ĭm-păs′ĭv) *adj.* **1.** Devoid of or not subject to emotion. **2.** Revealing no emotion; expressionless. **3.** Incapable of physical sensation. **4.** Motionless; still. [IN-¹ + PASSIVE, suffering (obsolete).] — **im·pas′sive·ly** *adv.* — **im·pas′sive·ness, im′pas·siv′i·ty** *n.*

im·paste (ĭm-pāst′) *tr.v.* **-past·ed, -past·ing, -pastes. 1.** To enclose with or as if with a paste or crust. **2.** To paint by applying thick layers of pigment.

im·pas·to (ĭm-păs′tō, -pä′stō) *n., pl.* **-tos. 1.** The application of thick layers of pigment to a canvas or other surface in painting. **2.** The paint so applied. [Ital. < *impastare*, to make into a paste : *in-*, in (< Lat.; see IN-²) + *pasta*, paste (< LLat.; see PASTE¹).]

im·pa·tience (ĭm-pā′shəns) *n.* The quality or condition of being impatient.

im·pa·tiens (ĭm-pā′shənz, -shəns) *n.* Any of various plants of the genus *Impatiens,* which includes the jewelweed. [Lat. *impatiēns*, impatient (so called because the ripe pods burst open when touched). See IMPATIENT.]

im·pa·tient (ĭm-pā′shənt) *adj.* **1.** Unable to wait patiently or tolerate delay; restless. **2.** Unable to endure irritation or opposition; intolerant: *impatient of criticism.* **3.** Expressing or produced by impatience. **4.** Restively eager or desirous; anxious. [Ult. < Lat. *impatiēns*, *impatient-* : *in-*, not; see IN-¹ + *patiēns*, pr.part. of *patī*, to suffer, endure; see PATIENT.]

im·peach (ĭm-pēch′) *tr.v.* **-peached, -peach·ing, -peach·es. 1.a.** To accuse. **b.** To charge (a public official) with improper conduct in office before a proper tribunal. **2.** To challenge the validity of; try to discredit: *impeach one's credibility.* [ME *empechen*, to impede, accuse < AN *empecher* < LLat. *impedicāre*, to entangle : Lat. *in-*, in; see IN-² + Lat. *pedica*, fetter; see **ped-***.] — **im·peach′er** *n.* — **im·peach′ment** *n.*

im·peach·a·ble (ĭm-pē′chə-bəl) *adj.* **1.** Capable of being impeached: *impeachable mayors.* **2.** Making one liable to impeachment: *impeachable offenses.* — **im·peach′a·bil′i·ty** *n.*

im·pearl (ĭm-pûrl′) *tr.v.* **-pearled, -pearl·ing, -pearls. 1.** To form (something) into pearls. **2.** To adorn with or as if with pearls.

im·pec·ca·ble (ĭm-pĕk′ə-bəl) *adj.* **1.** Flawless; perfect. See Syns at **perfect. 2.** Incapable of sin or wrongdoing. [Lat. *impeccābilis* : *in-*, not; see IN-¹ + *peccāre*, to sin; see **ped-***.] — **im·pec′ca·bil′i·ty** *n.* — **im·pec′ca·bly** *adv.*

im·pe·cu·ni·ous (ĭm′pĭ-kyo͞o′nē-əs) *adj.* Lacking money; penniless. See Syns at **poor.** [IM-¹ + *pecunious*, rich (< ME < OFr. *pecunios* < Lat. *pecūniōsus* < *pecūnia*, money, wealth; see **peku-***).] — **im′pe·cu′ni·ous·ly** *adv.* — **im′pe·cu′ni·ous·ness, im′pe·cu′ni·os′i·ty** (-ŏs′ĭ-tē) *n.*

im·pe·dance (ĭm-pēd′ns) *n. Symbol* **Z** A measure of the total opposition to current flow in an alternating current circuit, usu. represented in complex notation as $Z = R + iX$, where R is the ohmic resistance, X is the reactance, and i is the imaginary unit.

impedance match•ing (măchʹĭng) *n.* The optimization of power transfer in a system by equalizing the impedance of a load and the internal impedance of the power source.

im•pede (ĭm-pēdʹ) *tr.v.* **-ped•ed, -ped•ing, -pedes.** To retard or obstruct the progress of. [Lat. *impedīre.* See **ped-*.**] **— im•pedʹer** *n.*

im•ped•i•ment (ĭm-pĕdʹə-mənt) *n.* **1.** Something that impedes; a hindrance or an obstruction. **2.** An organic defect preventing clear articulation: *a speech impediment.* **3.** *Law.* Something that obstructs the making of a legal contract. [ME < OFr. < Lat. *impedīmentum* < *impedīre,* to impede. See IMPEDE.] **— im•pedʹi•menʹtal** (-mĕnʹtl), **im•pedʹi•menʹta•ry** (-mĕnʹtə-rē) *adj.*

im•ped•i•men•ta (ĭm-pĕdʹə-mĕnʹtə) *pl.n.* Objects, such as provisions, that impede or encumber. [Lat. *impedīmenta,* pl. of *impedīmentum,* impediment. See IMPEDIMENT.]

im•pel (ĭm-pĕlʹ) *tr.v.* **-pelled, -pel•ling, -pels. 1.** To urge to action through moral pressure; drive. **2.** To drive forward; propel. [ME *impellen* < Lat. *impellere* : *in-,* against; see IN-^{2} + *pellere,* to drive; see **pel-^{5}*.**]

im•pel•ler (ĭm-pĕlʹər) *n.* **1.** One that impels, as a rotating device moving fluid under pressure. **2.** A rotor or rotor blade.

im•pend (ĭm-pĕndʹ) *intr.v.* **-pend•ed, -pend•ing, -pends. 1.** To be about to take place. **2.** To threaten to happen; menace. **3.** *Archaic.* To jut out; hang suspended. [Lat. *impendēre* : *in-,* over; see IN-^{2} + *pendēre,* to hang; see **(s)pen-*.**]

im•pen•e•tra•bil•i•ty (ĭm-pĕnʹĭ-trə-bĭlʹĭ-tē) *n.* **1.** The quality or condition of being impenetrable. **2.** The inability of two bodies to occupy the same space at the same time.

im•pen•e•tra•ble (ĭm-pĕnʹĭ-trə-bəl) *adj.* **1.** Impossible to penetrate or enter. **2.** Impossible to understand; incomprehensible. **3.** Impervious to sentiment or argument. **— im•penʹe•tra•ble•ness** *n.* **— im•penʹe•tra•bly** *adv.*

im•pen•i•tent (ĭm-pĕnʹĭ-tənt) *adj.* Not penitent; unrepentant. **— im•penʹi•tence** *n.* **— im•penʹi•tent** *n.* **— im•penʹi•tent•ly** *adv.*

im•per•a•tive (ĭm-pĕrʹə-tĭv) *adj.* **1.** Expressing a command or plea; peremptory. **2.** Having the power or authority to command or control. **3.** *Gram.* Of, relating to, or being the mood that expresses a command or request. **4.** Impossible to deter or evade; pressing. See Syns at **urgent.** *— n.* **1.a.** A command; an order. **b.** An obligation; a duty. **2.** A rule, a principle, or an instinct that compels a certain behavior: *imperatives of survival.* **3.** *Gram.* **a.** The imperative mood. **b.** A verb in the imperative. [ME *imperatif,* relating to the imper. mood < OFr. < LLat. *imperātīvus* < Lat. *imperātus,* p.part. of *imperāre,* to command. See EMPEROR.] **— im•perʹa•tive•ly** *adv.* **— im•perʹa•tive•ness** *n.*

im•pe•ra•tor (ĭmʹpə-räʹtôrʹ, -tər) *n.* **1.a.** An army commander in the Roman Republic. **b.** Used as a form of address and salutation by soldiers to a victorious Roman general. **2.** The supreme power of the Roman emperor. **3.** The head of state and supreme commander in the Roman Empire, in whose name all victories were won. [Lat. *imperātōr.* See EMPEROR.] **— im•perʹa•to•riʹal** (ĭm-pĕrʹə-tôrʹē-əl, -tōrʹ-) *adj.*

im•per•cep•ti•ble (ĭmʹpər-sĕpʹtə-bəl) *adj.* **1.** Impossible or difficult to perceive by the mind or senses: *an imperceptible drop in temperature.* **2.** So subtle, slight, or gradual as to be barely perceptible. **— imʹper•cepʹti•bilʹi•ty, imʹper•cepʹti•ble•ness** *n.* **— imʹper•cepʹti•bly** *adv.*

im•per•cep•tive (ĭmʹpər-sĕpʹtĭv) *adj.* Lacking perception; not perceptive. **— imʹper•cepʹtive•ness, imʹper•cep•tivʹi•ty** *n.*

im•per•fect (ĭm-pûrʹfĭkt) *adj.* **1.** Not perfect. **2.** *Gram.* Of or being the tense of a verb that shows, usu. in the past, an action or a condition as incomplete, continuous, or coincident with another action. **3.** *Bot.* Having either stamens or a pistil only. Used of a flower. **4.** *Law.* Not legally enforceable: *an imperfect contract.* *— n.* **1.** A flawed but usable piece of merchandise, usu. sold at a discount. **2.** *Gram.* **a.** The imperfect tense. **b.** A verb in the imperfect. **— im•perʹfect•ly** *adv.* **— im•perʹfect•ness** *n.*

imperfect fungus *n.* Any of various fungi of the order Fungi Imperfecti, which reproduce only by asexual means.

im•per•fec•tion (ĭmʹpər-fĕkʹshən) *n.* **1.** The quality or state of being imperfect. **2.** Something imperfect; a defect or flaw.

im•per•fec•tive (ĭmʹpər-fĕkʹtĭv) *adj. Gram.* Of or being the verbal aspect not marked for completion, inception, causality, or modality. *— n.* **1.** The imperfective aspect. **2.** A verb in the imperfective.

im•per•fo•rate (ĭm-pûrʹfər-ĭt) *adj.* **1.** Having no opening; not perforated. **2.** Not separated by rows of perforations: *imperforate stamps.* **3.** *Medic.* Lacking a normal opening: *an imperforate anus.* *— n.* An imperforate stamp.

im•pe•ri•al (ĭm-pîrʹē-əl) *adj.* **1.** Of or suggestive of an empire or a sovereign, esp. an emperor or empress. **2.** Ruling over extensive territories or over colonies or dependencies. **3.a.** Having supreme authority; sovereign. **b.** Regal; majestic. **4.** Outstanding in size or quality. **5.** Of or belonging to the British Imperial System of weights and measures. *— n.* **1.** An emperor or empress. **2.** The top of a carriage. **3.** Something outstanding in size or quality. **4.** A variable size of paper, usu. 23 by 33 inches. **5.** A pointed beard grown from the lower lip and chin. [ME < OFr. < Lat. *imperiālis* < *imperium,* command. See EMPIRE.] **— im•peʹri•al•ly** *adv.*

Im•pe•ri•al Beach (ĭm-pîrʹē-əl). A city of S CA on the Pacific Ocean at the Mexican border. Pop. 26,512.

im•pe•ri•al•ism (ĭm-pîrʹē-ə-lĭzʹəm) *n.* **1.** The policy of extending a nation's authority by territorial acquisition or by establishing economic and political hegemony over other nations. **2.** The system, policies, or practices of such a government. **— im•peʹri•al•ist** *adj. & n.* **— im•peʹri•al•isʹtic** *adj.* **— im•peʹri•al•isʹti•cal•ly** *adv.*

imperial moth *n.* A large New World moth *(Eacles imperialis)* having yellow wings with purplish or brownish markings.

Imperial Valley. A fertile irrigated region of SE CA and NE Baja California, Mexico.

im•per•il (ĭm-pĕrʹəl) *tr.v.* **-iled, -il•ing, -ils** or **-illed, -il•ling, -ils.** To put into peril; endanger. See Syns at **endanger. — im•perʹil•ment** *n.*

im•pe•ri•ous (ĭm-pîrʹē-əs) *adj.* **1.** Arrogantly domineering or overbearing. **2.** Urgent; pressing. **3.** *Obsolete.* Regal; imperial. [< Lat. *imperiōsus* < *imperium,* imperium. See EMPIRE.] **— im•peʹri•ous•ly** *adv.* **— im•peʹri•ous•ness** *n.*

im•per•ish•a•ble (ĭm-pĕrʹĭ-shə-bəl) *adj.* Not perishable: *imperishable food.* **— im•perʹish•a•bilʹi•ty, im•perʹish•a•ble•ness** *n.* **— im•perʹish•a•bly** *adv.*

im•pe•ri•um (ĭm-pîrʹē-əm) *n., pl.* **-pe•ri•a** (-pîrʹē-ə). **1.** Absolute rule; supreme power. **2.** A sphere of power or dominion; an empire. [Lat. See EMPIRE.]

im•per•ma•nent (ĭm-pûrʹmə-nənt) *adj.* Not lasting; not permanent. **— im•perʹma•nence, im•perʹma•nen•cy** *n.*

im•per•me•a•ble (ĭm-pûrʹmē-ə-bəl) *adj.* Impossible to permeate: *an impermeable fortress.* **— im•perʹme•a•bilʹi•ty, im•perʹme•a•ble•ness** *n.* **— im•perʹme•a•bly** *adv.*

im•per•mis•si•ble (ĭmʹpər-mĭsʹə-bəl) *adj.* Not permitted; not permissible: *impermissible behavior.* **— imʹper•misʹsi•bilʹi•ty** *n.* **— imʹper•misʹsi•bly** *adv.*

imperial
Shown on Napoleon III

im•per•son•al (ĭm-pûrʹsə-nəl) *adj.* **1.** Lacking personality; not being a person: *an impersonal force.* **2.a.** Showing no emotion or personality. **b.** Having no personal reference or connection. **c.** Not responsive to or expressive of human personalities: *an impersonal corporation.* **3.** *Gram.* **a.** Of, relating to, or being the action of a verb that expresses the action of an unspecified or expletive subject, as in *It snowed.* **b.** Indefinite. Used of pronouns. **— im•perʹson•alʹi•ty** (-sə-nălʹĭ-tē) *n.* **— im•perʹson•al•ly** *adv.*

im•per•son•al•ize (ĭm-pûrʹsə-nə-līzʹ) *tr.v.* **-ized, -iz•ing, -iz•es.** To make impersonal.

im•per•son•ate (ĭm-pûrʹsə-nātʹ) *tr.v.* **-at•ed, -at•ing, -ates. 1.** To assume the character or appearance of, esp. fraudulently: *impersonate a police officer.* **2.** To imitate the appearance, voice, or manner of; mimic. **3.** *Archaic.* To embody; personify. **— im•perʹson•aʹtion** *n.* **— im•perʹson•aʹtor** *n.*

im•per•ti•nence (ĭm-pûrʹtn-əns) *n.* **1.** The quality or condition of being impertinent, esp.: **a.** Insolence. **b.** Irrelevance. **2.** An impertinent act or statement.

im•per•ti•nen•cy (ĭm-pûrʹtn-ən-sē) *n., pl.* **-cies.** Impertinence.

im•per•ti•nent (ĭm-pûrʹtn-ənt) *adj.* **1.** Exceeding the limits of propriety or good manners; improperly forward or bold. **2.** Not pertinent; irrelevant. **— im•perʹti•nent•ly** *adv.*

im•per•turb•a•ble (ĭmʹpər-tûrʹbə-bəl) *adj.* Unshakably calm and collected. **— imʹper•turbʹa•bilʹi•ty, imʹper•turbʹa•ble•ness** *n.* **— imʹper•turbʹa•bly** *adv.*

im•per•vi•ous (ĭm-pûrʹvē-əs) *adj.* **1.** Impossible to penetrate. **2.** Impossible to affect. **— im•perʹvi•ous•ly** *adv.* **— im•perʹvi•ous•ness** *n.*

im•pe•ti•go (ĭmʹpĭ-tīʹgō) *n., pl.* **-gos.** A contagious bacterial skin infection, usu. of children, that is characterized by the eruption of superficial pustules and the formation of thick yellow crusts, commonly on the face. [ME < Lat. *impetīgō* < *impetere,* to attack. See IMPETUS.]

im•pet•u•os•i•ty (ĭm-pĕchʹo͞o-ŏsʹĭ-tē) *n., pl.* **-ties. 1.** The quality or condition of being impetuous. **2.** An impetuous act.

im•pet•u•ous (ĭm-pĕchʹo͞o-əs) *adj.* **1.** Marked by sudden and forceful energy or emotion; impulsive and passionate. **2.** Having or marked by violent force: *impetuous waves.* [ME, violent < OFr. *impetueux* < LLat. *impetuōsus* < Lat. *impetus,* impetus. See IMPETUS.] **— im•petʹu•ous•ly** *adv.* **— im•petʹu•ous•ness** *n.*

im•pe•tus (ĭmʹpĭ-təs) *n., pl.* **-tus•es. 1.** An impelling force; an impulse. **2.** The force or energy associated with a moving body. **3.a.** Something that incites; a stimulus. **b.** Increased activity in response to a stimulus: *The deadline gave impetus to the work.* [Lat. < *impetere,* to attack : *in-,* against; see IN-^{2} + *petere,* to go towards, seek; see **pet-*.**]

im•pi•e•ty (ĭm-pīʹĭ-tē) *n., pl.* **-ties. 1.** The quality or state of being impious. **2.** An impious act. **3.** Undutifulness.

im•pinge (ĭm-pĭnjʹ) *v.* **-pinged, -ping•ing, -ping•es.** *— intr.* **1.** To collide or strike. **2.** To encroach; trespass: *impinged on my privacy.* *— tr.* To encroach upon. [Lat. *impingere* : *in-,* against; see IN-^{2} + *pangere,* to fasten; see **pag-*.**] **— im•pingeʹment** *n.* **— im•pingʹer** *n.*

ă **pat**	oi **boy**
ā **pay**	ou **out**
âr **care**	o͝o **took**
ä **father**	o͞o **boot**
ĕ **pet**	ŭ **cut**
ē **be**	ûr **urge**
ĭ **pit**	th **thin**
ī **pie**	*th* **this**
îr **pier**	hw **which**
ŏ **pot**	zh **vision**
ō **toe**	ə **about, item**
ô **paw**	

Stress marks:
ʹ (primary);
ʹ (secondary), as in
dictionary (dĭkʹshə-nĕrʹē)

im•pi•ous (ĭm′pē-əs, ĭm-pī′-) *adj.* **1.** Lacking reverence; not pious. **2.** Lacking due respect or dutifulness: *impious toward one's parents.* — **im′pi•ous•ly** *adv.* — **im′pi•ous•ness** *n.*

imp•ish (ĭm′pĭsh) *adj.* Of or befitting an imp; mischievous. — **imp′ish•ly** *adv.* — **imp′ish•ness** *n.*

im•plac•a•ble (ĭm-plăk′ə-bəl, -plā′kə-) *adj.* Impossible to placate or appease: *implacable foes.* — **im•plac′a•bil′i•ty, im•plac′a•ble•ness** *n.* — **im•plac′a•bly** *adv.*

im•plant (ĭm-plănt′) *v.* **-plant•ed, -plant•ing, -plants.** — *tr.* **1.** To set in firmly, as into the ground: *implant fence posts.* **2.** To establish securely, as in the mind; instill. **3.** *Medic.* **a.** To insert or embed (an object or a device) surgically. **b.** To graft or insert (a tissue) within the body. — *intr. Embryol.* To become attached to and embedded in the uterine lining. Used of a fertilized egg. — *n.* (ĭm′plănt′). Something implanted, esp. surgically: *a dental implant.* [ME *implanten* < Med.Lat. *implantāre* : Lat. *in-*, in; see IN-^{2} + Lat. *plantāre*, to plant (< *planta*, a shoot; see PLANT).] — **im•plant′a•ble** *adj.*

im•plan•ta•tion (ĭm′plăn-tā′shən) *n.* **1.a.** The act or an instance of implanting. **b.** The condition of being implanted. **2.** *Embryol.* The process by which a fertilized egg implants in the uterine lining.

im•plau•si•ble (ĭm-plô′zə-bəl) *adj.* Difficult to believe; not plausible. — **im•plau′si•bil′i•ty, im•plau′si•ble•ness** *n.* — **im•plau′si•bly** *adv.*

im•plead (ĭm-plēd′) *tr.v.* **-plead•ed, -plead•ing, -pleads.** *Law.* To sue in court in response to an earlier pleading. [ME *empleden* < AN *empleder*, var. of OFr. *emplaider* : *en-*, intensive pref. (< Lat. *in-*; see IN-^{2}) + *plaidier*, to plead; see PLEAD.]

im•ple•ment (ĭm′plə-mənt) *n.* **1.** A tool or an instrument used in doing work. See Syns at **tool. 2.** An article used to outfit or equip. **3.** A means of achieving an end; an instrument or agent. — *tr.v.* (-mĕnt′) **-ment•ed, -ment•ing, -ments. 1.** To put into practical effect; carry out: *implement the plan.* **2.** To supply with implements. [ME, supplementary payment < OFr. *emplement*, act of filling < LLat. *implēmentum* < Lat. *implēre*, to fill up : *in-*, intensive pref.; see IN-^{2} + *plēre*, to fill; see **pelə-^{1}***.] — **im′ple•men•ta′tion** (-mən-tā′shən, -mĕn-) *n.* — **im′ple•ment′er** *n.*

Usage Note: The obvious usefulness of the verb *implement,* meaning "to put into practice, carry out," appears to have outweighed the reservations of critics. Eighty-nine percent of the Usage Panel accepts the usage in the sentence *The mayor's office announced that a special task force will be responsible for implementing the new policy.*

im•pli•cate (ĭm′plĭ-kāt′) *tr.v.* **-cat•ed, -cat•ing, -cates. 1.** To involve or connect intimately or incriminatingly. **2.** To have as a consequence or an inference; imply. **3.** *Archaic.* To interweave or entangle; entwine. [ME, to convey a truth in a fable < Lat. *implicāre, implicāt-*, to entangle, unite : *in-*, in; see IN-^{2} + *plicāre*, to fold; see **plek-***.]

im•pli•ca•tion (ĭm′plĭ-kā′shən) *n.* **1.** The act of implicating or the condition of being implicated. **2.** The act of implying or the condition of being implied. **3.** Something that is implied, esp.: **a.** An indirect indication; a suggestion. **b.** An implied meaning; implicit significance. **c.** An inference. — **im′pli•ca′tive** *adj.* — **im′pli•ca′tive•ly** *adv.*

im•plic•it (ĭm-plĭs′ĭt) *adj.* **1.** Implied or understood though not directly expressed. **2.** Contained in the nature of something though not readily apparent. **3.** Having no doubts or reservations; unquestioning. [Lat. *implicitus*, var. of *implicātus*, p.part. of *implicāre*, to entangle. See IMPLICATE.] — **im•plic′it•ly** *adv.* — **im•plic′it•ness** *n.*

implicit differentiation *n. Math.* The process of finding the derivative of a dependent variable of an implicit function by differentiating each term of the function separately and solving the resulting expression for the desired derivative.

implicit function *n. Math.* A function in which the dependent variable is not directly expressed but must be solved for. In the equation $2x + 3y = 0$, for example, x is an implicit function of y.

im•plode (ĭm-plōd′) *v.* **-plod•ed, -plod•ing, -plodes.** — *intr.* To collapse inward violently. — *tr.* **1.** To cause to implode. **2.** To demolish (a building) by causing to implode. [IN-^{2} + (EX)PLODE.]

im•plore (ĭm-plôr′, -plōr′) *v.* **-plored, -plor•ing, -plores.** — *tr.* **1.** To appeal to in supplication; beseech: *implored the judge for mercy.* **2.** To beg for urgently: *implored her mercy.* — *intr.* To make an earnest appeal. [Lat. *implōrāre* : *in-*, toward; see IN-^{2} + *plōrāre*, to weep.] — **im′plo•ra′tion** *n.* — **im•plor′er** *n.* — **im•plor′ing•ly** *adv.*

im•plo•sion (ĭm-plō′zhən) *n.* **1.** A violent collapse inward. **2.** Violent compression. **3.** The controlled imploding of a building whose structural members are weakened and broken by explosives. **4.** *Ling.* The pronunciation of an implosive. [IN-^{2} + (EX)PLOSION.]

im•plo•sive (ĭm-plō′sĭv) *n. Ling.* A stop consonant pronounced with the breath drawn in. — **im•plo′sive** *adj.*

im•ply (ĭm-plī′) *tr.v.* **-plied, -ply•ing, -plies. 1.** To involve by logical necessity; entail. **2.** To express or indicate indirectly: *His tone implied disapproval.* See Syns at **suggest.** See Usage Note at **infer. 3.** *Obsolete.* To entangle. [ME *implien* < OFr. *emplier*, to enfold < Lat. *implicāre*. See IMPLICATE.]

implosion
Four stages of demolition by implosion; Abraham Lincoln Hotel, Springfield, Illinois, December 17, 1978

im•po•lite (ĭm′pə-līt′) *adj.* Not polite; discourteous. [Lat. *impolītus*, unpolished, inelegant : *in-*, not; see IN-^{1} + *polītus*, polished, p.part. of *polīre*, to polish; see POLISH.] — **im′po•lite′ly** *adv.* — **im′po•lite′ness** *n.*

im•pol•i•tic (ĭm-pŏl′ĭ-tĭk) *adj.* Not wise or expedient; not politic: *an impolitic speech.* — **im•pol′i•tic•ly** *adv.*

im•pon•der•a•ble (ĭm-pŏn′dər-ə-bəl) *adj.* That cannot undergo precise evaluation: *imponderable problems.* — **im•pon′der•a•ble** *n.* — **im•pon′der•a•bil′i•ty, im•pon′der•a•ble•ness** *n.* — **im•pon′der•a•bly** *adv.*

im•port (ĭm-pôrt′, -pōrt′, ĭm′pôrt′, -pōrt′) *v.* **-port•ed, -port•ing, -ports.** — *tr.* **1.** To bring or carry in from an outside source, esp. from abroad for trade or sale. **2.** *Comp. Sci.* To transfer (a file, for example) from one database to another. **3.** To carry or hold the meaning of; signify: *high inflation importing hard times.* **4.** To imply. **5.** *Archaic.* To have importance for. — *intr.* To be significant. See Syns at **count^1.** — *n.* (ĭm′pôrt′, -pōrt′). **1.** Something imported. **2.** The act or occupation of importing goods or materials. **3.** Meaning; signification. See Syns at **meaning. 4.** Importance; significance. See Syns at **importance.** [ME *importen*, to convey a meaning < Med.Lat. *importāre* and < OFr. *importer*, to cause, both < Lat. *importāre*, to carry in, cause : *in-*, in; see IN-^{2} + *portāre*, to carry; see **per-^{2}***.] — **im•port′a•bil′i•ty** *n.* — **im•port′a•ble** *adj.* — **im•port′er** *n.*

im•por•tance (ĭm-pôr′tns) *n.* **1.** The quality or condition of being important; significance. **2.** Personal status; standing. **3.** *Obsolete.* An important matter. **4.** *Obsolete.* Meaning; import. **5.** *Obsolete.* Importunity.

Syns: *importance, consequence, moment, significance, import, weight.* These nouns refer to the state or quality of being significant, influential, or worthy of note or esteem. *Importance* is the most general term: *the importance of a proper diet. Consequence* is especially applicable to persons or things of notable rank or position (*scholars of consequence*) and to what is important because of its possible outcome, result, or effect (*tax laws of consequence to investors*). *Moment* implies importance or consequence that is readily apparent: *decisions of great moment. Significance* and *import* refer to the quality of something, often not obvious, that gives it special meaning or value: *an event of real significance; works of great social import. Weight* often suggests a personal evaluation or judgment of importance: *"The popular faction at Rome . . . was led by men of weight"* (J.A. Froude).

im•por•tant (ĭm-pôr′tnt) *adj.* **1.** Strongly affecting the course of events or the nature of things; significant. **2.** Having or suggesting a consciousness of high position or authority; authoritative. **3.** *Obsolete.* Importunate. [ME < OFr. < Med. Lat. *importāns, important-*, pr.part. of *importāre*, to mean < Lat., to import. See IMPORT.] — **im•por′tant•ly** *adv.*

Usage Note: Some critics have objected to the use of the phrase *more importantly* in place of *more important* as a means of introducing an assertion. But there is no obvious reason for preferring one or the other.

im•por•ta•tion (ĭm′pôr-tā′shən, -pōr-) *n.* **1.a.** The act or business of importing. **b.** The condition or process of being imported. **2.** Something imported; an import.

im•por•tu•nate (ĭm-pôr′chə-nĭt) *adj.* Troublesomely urgent or persistent in requesting: *an importunate beggar.* — **im•por′tu•nate•ly** *adv.* — **im•por′tu•nate•ness** *n.*

im•por•tune (ĭm′pôr-to͞on′, -tyo͞on′, ĭm-pôr′chən) *v.* **-tuned, -tun•ing, -tunes.** — *tr.* **1.** To beset with insistent or repeated requests; entreat pressingly. **2.** *Archaic.* To ask for urgently or repeatedly. **3.** To annoy; vex. — *intr.* To plead or urge irksomely, often persistently. — *adj.* Importunate. [Fr. *importuner* < OFr. *importun*, inopportune < Lat. *importūnus* : *in-*, not; see IN-^{1} + *portus*, port, refuge; see **per-^{2}***.] — **im′por•tune′ly** *adv.* — **im′por•tun′er** *n.*

im•por•tu•ni•ty (ĭm′pôr-to͞o′nĭ-tē, -tyo͞o′-) *n., pl.* **-ties. 1.** An importunate request. **2.** The quality of being importunate.

im•pose (ĭm-pōz′) *v.* **-posed, -pos•ing, -pos•es.** — *tr.* **1.** To establish or apply as compulsory; levy. **2.** To apply or make prevail by or as if by authority. See Syns at **dictate. 3.** To obtrude or force (oneself, for example) on another or others. **4.** *Print.* To arrange (type or plates) on an imposing stone. **5.** To offer or circulate fraudulently; pass off. — *intr.* To take unfair advantage. [ME *imposen* < OFr. *imposer*, alteration (influenced by *poser*, to put, place; see POSE^1) of Lat. *impōnere*, to place upon : *in-*, on; see IN-^{2} + *pōnere*, to place; see **apo-***.] — **im•pos′er** *n.*

im•pos•ing (ĭm-pō′zĭng) *adj.* Impressive, as in power. See Syns at **grand.** — **im•pos′ing•ly** *adv.*

imposing stone *n. Print.* A stone or metal slab on which material to be printed is arranged.

im•po•si•tion (ĭm′pə-zĭsh′ən) *n.* **1.** The act of imposing or the condition of being imposed. **2.** Something imposed, such as a tax or a fraud. **3.** A burdensome or unfair demand, as upon someone's time. **4.** *Print.* The arrangement of printed matter to form a sequence of pages.

im•pos•si•bil•i•ty (ĭm-pŏs′ə-bĭl′ĭ-tē) *n., pl.* **-ties. 1.** The state or quality of being impossible. **2.** Something impossible.

im•pos•si•ble (ĭm-pŏs′ə-bəl) *adj.* **1.** Incapable of existing or occurring. **2.** Not capable of being accomplished. **3.** Unacceptable; intolerable. **4.** Extremely difficult to deal with or tolerate. **— im•pos′si•bly** *adv.*

im•post[1] (ĭm′pōst′) *n.* **1.** Something, such as a tax, that is imposed. **2.** *Sports.* The weight a horse must carry in a handicap race. [Obsolete Fr. < OFr. < Med.Lat. *impostum* < Lat., neut. of *impostus*, var. of *impositus*, p.part. of *impōnere*, to place upon. See IMPOSE.]

im•post[2] (ĭm′pōst′) *n. Archit.* The uppermost part of a column or pillar supporting an arch. [Fr. *imposte* < Ital. *imposta* < Lat., fem. p.part. of *impōnere*, to place upon. See IMPOSE.]

im•pos•tor (ĭm-pŏs′tər) *n.* One who engages in deception under an assumed name or identity. [Fr. *imposteur* < Lat. *impostor*, var. of *impositor*, one who assigns a name < *impositus*, p.part. of *impōnere*, to place upon. See IMPOSE.]

im•pos•ture (ĭm-pŏs′chər) *n.* The act or instance of engaging in deception under an assumed name or identity. [Fr. < OFr. < LLat. *impostūra* < Lat. *impostus*, var. of *impositus*, p.part. of *impōnere*, to place upon. See IMPOSE.]

im•po•tence (ĭm′pə-təns) also **im•po•ten•cy** (-tən-sē) *n.* The quality or condition of being impotent.

im•po•tent (ĭm′pə-tənt) *adj.* **1.** Lacking physical strength or vigor; weak. **2.** Lacking in power, as to act effectively; helpless. **3.a.** Incapable of sexual intercourse, often because unable to achieve or sustain an erection. **b.** Sterile. Used of males. **4.** *Obsolete.* Lacking self-restraint. **— im′po•tent•ly** *adv.*

im•pound (ĭm-pound′) *tr.v.* **im•pound•ed, im•pound•ing, im•pounds. 1.** To confine in or as if in a pound: *impound stray dogs.* **2.** To seize and retain in legal custody. **3.** To set aside in a fund rather than spend as prescribed. **4.** To accumulate and store in a reservoir. **— im•pound′age, im•pound′ment** *n.* **— im•pound′er** *n.*

im•pov•er•ish (ĭm-pŏv′ər-ĭsh) *tr.v.* **-ished, -ish•ing, -ish•es. 1.** To reduce to poverty; make poor. **2.** To deprive of natural richness or strength: *impoverish the soil by overuse.* See Syns at **deplete.** [ME *empoverishen* < OFr. *empovrir, empovriss-* : *en-*, causative pref.; see EN-[2] + *povre*, poor (< Lat. *pauper*; see PAUPER).] **— im•pov′er•ish•ment** *n.*

im•pov•er•ished (ĭm-pŏv′ər-ĭsht) *adj.* **1.** Reduced to poverty; poverty-stricken. See Syns at **poor. 2.** Deprived of natural richness or strength; depleted.

im•prac•ti•ca•ble (ĭm-prăk′tĭ-kə-bəl) *adj.* **1.** Impossible to do or carry out. **2.** Unfit for passage: *roads impracticable in winter.* **3.** *Archaic.* Unmanageable; intractable. **— im•prac′ti•ca•bil′i•ty, im•prac′ti•ca•ble•ness** *n.* **— im•prac′ti•ca•bly** *adv.*

Usage Note: *Impracticable* applies to a course of action that is impossible to carry out; *impractical*, though it can be used in this way, also can be weaker in sense, suggesting that the course of action would yield an insufficient return or would have little practical value. A plan for a new baseball stadium might be *impracticable* if the site was too marshy to permit safe construction; but if the objection was that the site was too remote for patrons to attend games easily, the plan would be *impractical.* See Usage Note at **practicable.**

im•prac•ti•cal (ĭm-prăk′tĭ-kəl) *adj.* **1.** Unwise to implement or maintain in practice. **2.** Incapable of dealing efficiently with practical matters, esp. finances. **3.** Not a part of experience, fact, or practice; theoretical. **4.** Impracticable. See Usage Note at **impracticable. — im•prac′ti•cal′i•ty** (-kăl′ĭ-tē), **im•prac′ti•cal•ness** *n.*

im•pre•cate (ĭm′prĭ-kāt′) *tr.v.* **-cat•ed, -cat•ing, -cates.** To invoke evil upon; curse. [Lat. *imprecārī, imprecāt-* : *in-*, towards; see IN-[2] + *precārī*, to pray, ask; see **prek-*.**] **— im′pre•ca′tor** *n.* **— im′pre•ca•to′ry** (-kə-tôr′ē, -tōr′ē) *adj.*

im•pre•ca•tion (ĭm′prĭ-kā′shən) *n.* A curse.

im•pre•cise (ĭm′prĭ-sīs′) *adj.* Not precise. **— im′pre•cise′ly** *adv.* **— im′pre•ci′sion** (-sĭzh′ən) *n.*

im•preg•na•ble[1] (ĭm-prĕg′nə-bəl) *adj.* **1.** Impossible to capture or enter by force: *an impregnable fortress.* **2.** Difficult or impossible to attack, challenge, or refute with success: *an impregnable argument.* [ME < OFr. *imprenable* : *in-*, not (< Lat. *in-*; see IN-[1]) + *pregnable*, pregnable; see PREGNABLE.]

im•preg•na•ble[2] (ĭm-prĕg′nə-bəl) *adj.* Capable of being impregnated. [IMPREGN(ATE) + -ABLE.]

im•preg•nate (ĭm-prĕg′nāt) *tr.v.* **-nat•ed, -nat•ing, -nates. 1.** To make pregnant; inseminate. **2.** To fertilize (an ovum, for example). **3.** To fill throughout; saturate. **4.** To permeate or imbue. *— adj.* (*also* -nĭt). Saturated or filled. [Prob. < LLat. *impraegnātus*, pregnant : Lat. *in-*, in; see IN-[2] + Lat. *praegnātus*, var. of *praegnās*, pregnant. See PREGNANT[1].] **— im′preg•na′tion** *n.* **— im•preg′na′tor** *n.*

im•pre•sa (ĭm-prā′zə) *n.* An emblem or a device with a motto. [Ital., undertaking, impresa. See IMPRESARIO.]

im•pre•sa•ri•o (ĭm′prĭ-sär′ē-ō′, -sâr′-) *n., pl.* **-os. 1.** One who sponsors or produces entertainment, esp. the director of an opera company. **2.** A manager; a producer. [Ital. < *impresa*, undertaking < fem. p.part. of *imprendere*, to undertake < VLat. **imprendere*. See EMPRISE.]

im•press[1] (ĭm-prĕs′) *tr.v.* **-pressed, -press•ing, -press•es. 1.** To affect strongly, often favorably. **2.** To produce or attempt to produce a vivid impression or image of. **3.** To mark or stamp with or as if with pressure. **4.** To apply with pressure; press. *— n.* (ĭm′prĕs′). **1.** The act of impressing. **2.** A mark or pattern produced by or as if by impressing. **3.** A stamp or seal meant to be impressed. [ME *impressen*, to imprint < OFr. *empresser* < Lat. *impressus*, p.part. of *imprimere* : *in-*, in; see IN-[2] + *premere*, to press; see **per-[4]*.**]

im•press[2] (ĭm-prĕs′) *tr.v.* **-pressed, -press•ing, -press•es. 1.** To compel (a person) to serve in a military force. **2.** To seize (property) by force or authority; confiscate. *— n.* (ĭm′-prĕs). Impressment. [IN-[2] + PRESS[2] (influenced by IMPREST, advance on a soldier's pay (obsolete)).]

im•press•i•ble (ĭm-prĕs′ə-bəl) *adj.* Susceptible to impressions; malleable: *impressible young minds.* **— im•press′i•bil′i•ty** *n.* **— im•press′i•bly** *adv.*

im•pres•sion (ĭm-prĕsh′ən) *n.* **1.** An effect, a feeling, or an image retained as a consequence of experience. **2.** A vague notion, remembrance, or belief. **3.** A mark produced on a surface by pressure. **4.** The act or process of impressing. **5.** *Print.* **a.** All the copies of a publication printed at one time from the same set of type. **b.** A single copy of such a printing. **6.** A humorous imitation of the voice and mannerisms of a celebrity. **7.** An initial or single coat of color or paint. **8.** *Dentistry.* An imprint of the teeth and surrounding tissues, used as a mold to make dentures, inlays, or plastic models.

im•pres•sion•a•ble (ĭm-prĕsh′ə-nə-bəl) *adj.* **1.** Readily or easily influenced; suggestible. **2.** Capable of receiving an impression; plastic: *impressionable plaster.* **— im•pres′sion•a•bil′i•ty, im•pres′sion•a•ble•ness** *n.*

im•pres•sion•ism (ĭm-prĕsh′ə-nĭz′əm) *n.* **1.** Often **Impressionism.** A theory or style of painting originating in France during the 1870's, marked by concentration on the immediate visual impression produced by a scene and by the use of unmixed primary colors and small strokes to simulate reflected light. **2.** A literary style marked by the use of details and mental associations to evoke subjective and sensory impressions rather than objective reality. **3.** *Mus.* A style of the late 19th and early 20th centuries, using lush vague harmony and rhythm to evoke mood, place, and natural phenomena. **4.** The practice of expressing or developing one's subjective response to art or experience.

impressionism
Mother and Children, 1874, by Pierre Auguste Renoir

im•pres•sion•ist (ĭm-prĕsh′ə-nĭst) *n.* **1.** An artist, a composer, or a writer who practices or upholds impressionism. **2.** An entertainer who does impressions. *— adj.* Impressionistic, esp. in painting.

im•pres•sion•is•tic (ĭm-prĕsh′ə-nĭs′tĭk) *adj.* **1.** Of, relating to, or practicing impressionism. **2.** Of, relating to, or predicated on impression as opposed to reason or fact. **3.** Impressionable. **— im•pres′sion•is′ti•cal•ly** *adv.*

im•pres•sive (ĭm-prĕs′ĭv) *adj.* Making a strong or vivid impression; striking or remarkable: *an impressive ceremony.* **— im•pres′sive•ly** *adv.* **— im•pres′sive•ness** *n.*

im•press•ment (ĭm-prĕs′mənt) *n.* The act or policy of seizing people or property for public service or use.

im•pres•sure (ĭm-prĕsh′ər) *n. Archaic.* A mark produced by pressure; an impression.

im•prest (ĭm-prĕst′) *n.* An advance or a loan of funds, esp. for services rendered to a government. [< obsolete Ital. *impresto*, loan < p.part. of *imprestare*, to lend : *in-*, toward (< Lat.; see IN-[2]) + *prestare*, to lend (< Lat. *praestāre*, to give < *praestō*, at hand).]

im•pri•ma•tur (ĭm′prə-mä′to͝or, -mā′tər) *n.* **1.** Official approval or license to print or publish, esp. under conditions of censorship. **2.a.** Official approval; sanction. **b.** A mark of official approval. [NLat. *imprimātur*, let it be printed, third pers. sing. pr. subjunctive passive of Lat. *imprimere*, to imprint. See IMPRESS[1].]

im•pri•mis (ĭm-prī′mĭs) *adv.* In the first place. [ME *in primis* < Lat. *in prīmīs* : *in*, among; see IN-[2] + *prīmīs*, ablative pl. of *prīmus*, first; see **per[1]*.**]

im•print (ĭm-prĭnt′) *tr.v.* **-print•ed, -print•ing, -prints. 1.** To produce (a mark or pattern) on a surface by pressure. **2.** To produce a mark on (a surface) by pressure. **3.** To impart a strong or vivid impression of. **4.** To fix firmly, as in the mind. *— n.* (ĭm′prĭnt′). **1.** A mark or pattern produced by imprinting. **2.** A distinguishing influence or effect. **3.** A publisher's name, often with the address, printed at the bottom of a title page of a publication. [ME *emprenten* < OFr. *empreinter* < *empreinte*, impression < fem. p.part. of *empreindre*, to print < Lat. *imprimere*, to impress. See IMPRESS[1].]

im•print•ing (ĭm′prĭn′tĭng) *n.* A process occurring early in the life of a social animal in which a specific behavior is learned through association with a parent or other role model.

im•pris•on (ĭm-prĭz′ən) *tr.v.* **-oned, -on•ing, -ons.** To put in or as if in prison; confine. [ME *emprisonen* < OFr. *emprisoner* : *en-*, in (< Lat. *in-*; see IN-[2]) + *prison*, prison; see PRISON.] **— im•pris′on•a•ble** *adj.* **— im•pris′on•ment** *n.*

im•prob•a•bil•i•ty (ĭm-prŏb′ə-bĭl′ĭ-tē) *n., pl.* **-ties. 1.** The quality or condition of being improbable. **2.** Something improbable.

ă pat	oi boy
ā pay	ou out
âr care	o͝o took
ä father	o͞o boot
ĕ pet	ŭ cut
ē be	ûr urge
ĭ pit	th thin
ī pie	*th* this
îr pier	hw which
ŏ pot	zh vision
ō toe	ə about, item
ô paw	

Stress marks:
′ (primary);
′ (secondary), as in **dictionary** (dĭk′shə-nĕr′ē)

im•prob•a•ble (ĭm-prŏb′ə-bəl) *adj.* Unlikely to take place or be true. **—im•prob′a•ble•ness** *n.* **—im•prob′a•bly** *adv.*

im•pro•bi•ty (ĭm-prō′bĭ-tē) *n.* Lack of probity; dishonesty. [ME *improbite,* shameless persistence < OFr., dishonesty < Lat. *improbitās* < *improbus,* dishonest : *in-,* not; see IN-[1] + *probus,* honest, good; see **per**[1]*.]

im•promp•tu (ĭm-prŏmp′to͞o, -tyo͞o) *adj.* **1.** Prompted by the occasion rather than being planned in advance. **2.** Spoken, performed, done, or composed with little or no preparation; extemporaneous: *impromptu remarks.* —*adv.* With little or no preparation; extemporaneously. —*n.* **1.** Something impromptu, such as a speech. **2.** *Mus.* A short lyrical composition, esp. for the piano. [Fr. < Lat. *in prōmptū,* at hand : *in,* in; see IN-[2] + *prōmptū,* ablative of *prōmptus,* readiness < p.part. of *prōmere,* to bring forth; see PROMPT.]

im•prop•er (ĭm-prŏp′ər) *adj.* **1.** Not suited to circumstances or needs; unsuitable. **2.** Not in keeping with conventional mores; indecorous. **3.** Not consistent with established truth, fact, or rule; incorrect. **4.** Irregular or abnormal. **—im•prop′er•ly** *adv.* **—im•prop′er•ness** *n.*

improper fraction *n. Math.* A fraction in which the numerator is larger than or equal to the denominator.

improper integral *n. Math.* An integral having at least one nonfinite limit or an integrand that becomes infinite between the limits of integration.

im•pro•pri•e•ty (ĭm′prə-prī′ĭ-tē) *n., pl.* **-ties. 1.** The quality or condition of being improper. **2.** An improper act. **3.** An improper or unacceptable usage in speech or writing.

im•prove (ĭm-pro͞ov′) *v.* **-proved, -prov•ing, -proves.** —*tr.* **1.** To raise to a more desirable or more excellent quality or condition; make better. **2.** To increase the productivity or value of (land or property). **3.** To put to good use; use profitably. —*intr.* **1.** To become better. **2.** To make beneficial additions or changes. [ME *improwen,* to enclose land for cultivation < AN *emprouwer,* to turn to profit : OFr. *en-,* causative pref. (< Lat. *in;* see IN-[2]) + OFr. *prou,* profit (< LLat. *prōde,* advantageous; see PROUD).]

Syns: *improve, better, help, ameliorate.* These verbs mean to advance to a more desirable, valuable, or excellent state. *Improve* and *better,* the most general terms, are often interchangeable: *improve* (or *better*) *the mind through study. Help* usually implies limited relief or change: *Gargling helps a sore throat.* To *ameliorate* is to improve circumstances that demand change: *Volunteers were able to ameliorate conditions in the refugee camp.*

im•prove•ment (ĭm-pro͞ov′mənt) *n.* **1.a.** The act or process of improving. **b.** The state of being improved. **2.** A change or an addition that improves.

im•prov•i•dent (ĭm-prŏv′ĭ-dənt) *adj.* **1.** Not providing for the future; thriftless. **2.** Rash; incautious. **—im•prov′i•dence** *n.* **—im•prov′i•dent•ly** *adv.*

im•prov•i•sa•tion (ĭm-prŏv′ĭ-zā′shən, ĭm′prə-vĭ-) *n.* **1.** The act of improvising. **2.** Something improvised, esp. a dramatic skit.

im•prov•i•sa•tor (ĭm-prŏv′ĭ-zā′tər) *n.* One who improvises.

im•prov•i•sa•to•ry (ĭm-prŏv′ĭ-zə-tôr′ē, -tōr′ē, ĭm′prə-vĭ′-) also **im•prov•i•sa•to•ri•al** (ĭm-prŏv′ĭ-zə-tôr′ē-əl, -tōr′-) *adj.* **1.** Made up without preparation; improvised. **2.** Of or relating to improvisation: *improvisatory skill.*

im•pro•vise (ĭm′prə-vīz′) *v.* **-vised, -vis•ing, -vis•es.** —*tr.* **1.** To invent, compose, or recite without preparation. **2.** To make or provide from available materials. —*intr.* To invent, compose, recite, or execute something offhand. [Fr. *improviser* < Ital. *improvvisare* < *improvviso,* unforeseen < Lat. *imprōvīsus* : *in-,* not; see IN-[1] + *prōvīsus,* p.part. of *prōvidēre,* to foresee; see PROVIDE.] **—im′pro•vis′er** *n.*

im•pru•dence (ĭm-pro͞od′ns) *n.* **1.** The quality or condition of being imprudent. **2.** An imprudent act.

im•pru•dent (ĭm-pro͞od′nt) *adj.* Unwise or indiscreet; not prudent.

im•pu•dence (ĭm′pyə-dəns) also **im•pu•den•cy** (-dən-sē) *n.* **1.** The quality of being offensively bold. **2.** Offensively bold behavior.

im•pu•dent (ĭm′pyə-dənt) *adj.* **1.** Marked by offensive boldness; insolent. **2.** *Obsolete.* Immodest. [ME < Lat. *impudēns, impudent-* : *in-,* not; see IN-[1] + *pudēns,* pr.part. of *pudēre,* to be ashamed.] **—im′pu•dent•ly** *adv.*

im•pu•dic•i•ty (ĭm′pyo͞o-dĭs′ĭ-tē) *n.* Immodesty; shamelessness. [LLat. *impudīcitās* < Lat. *impudīcus,* immodest : *in-,* not; see IN-[1] + *pudīcus,* modest (< *pudēre,* to be ashamed).]

im•pugn (ĭm-pyo͞on′) *tr.v.* **-pugned, -pugn•ing, -pugns.** To attack as false or questionable; challenge in argument: *impugn an opponent's record.* [ME *impugnen* < OFr. *impugner* < Lat. *impugnāre* : *in-,* against; see IN-[2] + *pugnāre,* to fight; see **peuk-***.] **—im•pugn′a•ble** *adj.* **—im•pugn′er** *n.*

im•pu•is•sance (ĭm-pyo͞o′ĭ-səns, ĭm-pwĭs′əns) *n.* Lack of power or effectiveness; weakness. [ME *impuissaunce* < OFr. *impuissance* : *in-,* not; see IN-[1] + *puissance,* power; see PUISSANCE.] **—im•pu′is•sant** *adj.*

im•pulse (ĭm′pŭls′) *n.* **1.a.** An impelling force; an impetus. **b.** The motion produced by such a force. **2.** A sudden wish or urge that prompts an unpremeditated act or feeling; abrupt inclination. **3.** A motivating force or tendency. **4.** *Electron.* A surge of electrical power in one direction. **5.** *Phys.* The product obtained by multiplying the average value of a force by the time during which it acts, equal to the change in momentum produced by the force in this time interval. **6.** *Physiol.* The electrochemical transmission of a signal along a nerve fiber that produces an excitatory or inhibitory response at a target tissue, such as a muscle. —*adj.* Marked by impulsiveness or acting on impulse. [Lat. *impulsus* < p.part. of *impellere,* to impel. See IMPEL.]

im•pul•sion (ĭm-pŭl′shən) *n.* **1.** The act of impelling or the condition of being impelled. **2.** An impelling force; a thrust. **3.** Motion produced by an impelling force; momentum. **4.** A wish or an urge from within; an impulse.

im•pul•sive (ĭm-pŭl′sĭv) *adj.* **1.** Inclined to act on impulse rather than thought. **2.** Motivated by or resulting from impulse: *impulsive generosity.* **3.** Having force or power to impel or incite; forceful. **4.** *Phys.* Acting within brief time intervals. Used esp. of a force. **—im•pul′sive•ly** *adv.* **—im•pul′sive•ness, im′pul•siv′i•ty** *n.*

im•pu•ni•ty (ĭm-pyo͞o′nĭ-tē) *n., pl.* **-ties.** Exemption from punishment, penalty, or harm. [Lat. *impūnitās* < *impūne,* without punishment : *in-,* not; see IN-[1] + *poena,* penalty (< Gk. *poinē;* see **k[w]ei-**[1]*).]

im•pure (ĭm-pyo͝or′) *adj.* **-pur•er, -pur•est. 1.** Not pure or clean; contaminated. **2.** Not purified by religious rite; unclean. **3.** Immoral or obscene. **4.** Mixed with another, usu. inferior substance; adulterated. **5.** *Color.* Being a composite of more than one color or mixed with black or white. **6.** Deriving from more than one source, style, or convention; eclectic. **7.** Not consistent in grammar, vocabulary, idiom, or usage. **—im•pure′ly** *adv.* **—im•pure′ness** *n.*

im•pu•ri•ty (ĭm-pyo͝or′ĭ-tē) *n., pl.* **-ties. 1.** The quality or condition of being impure, esp.: **a.** Contamination or pollution. **b.** Lack of consistency or homogeneity; adulteration. **c.** A state of immorality; sin. **2.** Something that renders something else impure; an inferior component or additive.

im•put•a•ble (ĭm-pyo͞o′tə-bəl) *adj.* Possible to impute or ascribe; attributable. **—im•put′a•bly** *adv.*

im•pu•ta•tion (ĭm′pyo͞o-tā′shən) *n.* **1.** The act of imputing or attributing. **2.** Something imputed or attributed. **—im•pu′ta•tive** (ĭm-pyo͞o′tə-tĭv) *adj.* **—im•pu′ta•tive•ly** *adv.*

im•pute (ĭm-pyo͞ot′) *tr.v.* **-put•ed, -put•ing, -putes. 1.** To charge with the fault or responsibility for. **2.** To attribute; credit. [ME *imputen* < OFr. *emputer* < Lat. *imputāre* : *in-,* in; see IN-[2] + *putāre,* to settle an account; see **peu-***.]

in[1] (ĭn) *prep.* **1.a.** Within the limits, bounds, or area of: *in the garden.* **b.** From the outside to a point within; into: *threw the pin in the cup.* **2.** To or at a situation or condition of: *in debt.* **3.a.** Having the activity, occupation, or function of: *work in politics.* **b.** During the act or process of: *tripped in running.* **4.a.** With the arrangement or order of: *fabric that fell in luxuriant folds.* **b.** After the style or form of: *a poem in couplets.* **5.** With the characteristic, attribute, or property of: *a man in an overcoat.* **6.a.** By means of: *paid in cash.* **b.** Made with or through the medium of: *written in German.* **7.** With the aim or purpose of: *in pursuit.* **8.** With reference to: *six inches in depth.* **9.** Used to indicate the second and larger term of a ratio or proportion: *one in ten.* —*adv.* **1.** To or toward the inside: *knocked and came in.* **2.** To or toward a destination or goal: *closed in.* **3.** *Baseball.* So as to score; to home base: *runs driven in.* **4.** Within a place, as of business or residence: *The boss stayed in.* **5.** So as to include or incorporate: *Fold in the egg whites.* **6.** So as to occupy a position of success or favor: *was voted in.* **7.** In a particular relationship: *got in bad with their supervisor.* —*adj.* **1.** Located inside; inner. **2.** Incoming; inward: *the in bus.* **3.** Holding office; having power: *the in party.* **4.** *Informal.* **a.** Currently fashionable: *the in thing to wear.* **b.** Concerned with or attuned to the latest fashions: *the in crowd.* —*n.* **1.** One with position, influence, or power. **2.** *Informal.* Influence; power. —***idioms.* in for.** Guaranteed to get or have. **in that.** For the reason that. [ME < OE. See **en***.]

in[2] or **in.** *abbr.* Inch.

In The symbol for the element **indium.**

IN *abbr.* Indiana.

in-[1] or **il-** or **im-** or **ir-** *pref.* Not: *inarticulate.* Before *l, in-* is usu. assimilated to *il-,* before *r* to *ir-,* and before *b, m,* and *p* to *im-.* [ME < OFr. < Lat. See **ne***.]

in-[2] or **il-** or **im-** or **ir-** *pref.* **1.** In; into; within: *illuviation.* Before *l, in-* is usu. assimilated to *il-,* before *r* to *ir-,* and before *b, m,* and *p* to *im-.* **2.** Var. of **en-**[1]. [ME < OE (< *in,* in; see IN[1]) and < OFr. (< Lat. < *in,* in, within; see **en***).]

-in *suff.* **1.** Neutral chemical compound, esp.: **a.** Neutral carbohydrate: *inulin.* **b.** Protein or protein derivative: *albumin.* **c.** Lipid or lipid derivative: *lecithin.* **d.** Enzyme: *pancreatin.* **e.** Glycoside: *chitin.* **2.** A pharmaceutical: *rifampin.* **3.** An antibiotic: *penicillin.* **4.** Antigen: *tuberculin.* **5.** Var. of **-ine**[2] 1. [Var. of -INE[2].]

in•a•bil•i•ty (ĭn′ə-bĭl′ĭ-tē) *n.* Lack of ability or means.

in ab•sen•tia (ĭn ăb-sĕn′shə, -shē-ə) *adv.* While or although not present; in absence. [Lat. *in absentiā.*]

in•ac•ces•si•ble (ĭn′ăk-sĕs′ə-bəl) *adj.* Not accessible; unapproachable: *inaccessible executives.* — **in′ac•ces′si•bil′i•ty** *n.* — **in′ac•ces′si•bly** *adv.*
in•ac•cu•ra•cy (ĭn-ăk′yər-ə-sē) *n., pl.* **-cies. 1.** The quality or condition of being inaccurate. **2.** An instance of being inaccurate; an error.
in•ac•cu•rate (ĭn-ăk′yər-ĭt) *adj.* Mistaken or incorrect; not accurate. — **in•ac′cu•rate•ly** *adv.* — **in•ac′cu•rate•ness** *n.*
in•ac•tion (ĭn-ăk′shən) *n.* Lack or absence of action.
in•ac•ti•vate (ĭn-ăk′tə-vāt′) *tr.v.* **-vat•ed, -vat•ing, -vates.** To render inactive. — **in•ac′ti•va′tion** *n.*
in•ac•tive (ĭn-ăk′tĭv) *adj.* **1.** Not active or tending to be active. **2.a.** Not functioning or operating; out of use: *inactive machinery.* **b.** Not being in continuous use or operation: *an inactive account.* **3.** Retired from duty or service. **4.** *Chem.* Not readily participating in chemical reactions. **5.** *Biol.* Having no significant effect on or interaction with living organisms. **6.** *Medic.* Quiescent. Used esp. of a disease. **7.** *Phys.* Showing no optical activity in polarized light. — **in•ac′tive•ly** *adv.* — **in′ac•tiv′i•ty, in•ac′tive•ness** *n.*
Syns: *inactive, idle, inert, passive, dormant.* These adjectives mean not involved in or disposed to movement or functioning. *Inactive* simply indicates absence of activity: *retired but not inactive. Idle* refers to persons who are not doing anything or are not busy (*can't bear being idle*); it also refers to what is not in use or operation (*idle hands*). *Inert* describes things powerless to move themselves or to produce a desired effect; applied to persons, it implies lethargy or sluggishness, especially of mind or spirit: *"The Honorable Mrs. Jamieson . . . was fat and inert, and very much at the mercy of her old servants"* (Elizabeth C. Gaskell). *Passive* implies being reactive instead of proactive: *"in an hour like this, when the mind has a passive sensibility, but no active strength"* (Nathaniel Hawthorne). *Dormant* refers principally to a state of suspended activity but often implies the possibility of renewal: *Her dormant feelings of affection.*
in•ad•e•qua•cy (ĭn-ăd′ĭ-kwə-sē) *n., pl.* **-cies. 1.** The quality or condition of being inadequate. **2.** An instance of being inadequate; a failing or lack.
in•ad•e•quate (ĭn-ăd′ĭ-kwĭt) *adj.* Not adequate to fulfill a need or requirement; insufficient. — **in•ad′e•quate•ly** *adv.*
in•ad•mis•si•ble (ĭn′əd-mĭs′ə-bəl) *adj.* Not admissible. — **in′ad•mis′si•bil′i•ty** *n.* — **in′ad•mis′si•bly** *adv.*
in•ad•ver•tence (ĭn′əd-vûr′tns) *n.* **1.** The quality of being inadvertent. **2.** An instance of being inadvertent; an oversight or a slip. [ME < OFr. < Med.Lat. *inadvertentia* : Lat. *in-*, not; see IN-[1] + Lat. *advertēns, advertent-*, pr.part. of *advertere*, to turn toward; see ADVERSE.]
in•ad•ver•ten•cy (ĭn′əd-vûr′tn-sē) *n., pl.* **-cies.** Inadvertence.
in•ad•ver•tent (ĭn′əd-vûr′tnt) *adj.* **1.** Not duly attentive. **2.** Marked by unintentional lack of care. — **in′ad•ver′tent•ly** *adv.*
in•ad•vis•a•ble (ĭn′əd-vī′zə-bəl) *adj.* Not recommended; unwise. — **in′ad•vis′a•bil′i•ty** *n.*
in ae•ter•num (ē-tûr′nəm) *adv.* To eternity; forever. [Lat. : *in*, in + *aeternum*, forever < neut. of *aeternus*, eternal.]
in•al•ien•a•ble (ĭn-āl′yə-nə-bəl, -ā′lē-ə-) *adj.* That cannot be transferred to another or others: *inalienable rights.* — **in•al′ien•a•bil′i•ty** *n.* — **in•al′ien•a•bly** *adv.*
in•al•ter•a•ble (ĭn-ôl′tər-ə-bəl) *adj.* Impossible to alter. — **in•al′ter•a•bil′i•ty** *n.* — **in•al′ter•a•bly** *adv.*
in•am•o•ra•ta (ĭn-ăm′ə-rä′tə) *n., pl.* **-tas.** A woman with whom one is in love or has an intimate relationship. [Ital., fem. of *inamorato*, inamorato. See INAMORATO.]
in•am•o•ra•to (ĭn-ăm′ə-rä′tō) *n., pl.* **-tos.** A man with whom one is in love or has an intimate relationship. [Ital. < p.part. of *inammorare*, to enamor : *in-*, into (< Lat.; see IN-[2]) + *amore*, love (< Lat. *amor* < *amāre*, to love).]
in-and-in (ĭn′ənd-ĭn′) *adv.* Repeatedly within the same or closely related stocks: *breeding in-and-in.* — **in′-and-in′** *adj.*
in•ane (ĭn-ān′) *adj.* **-an•er, -an•est.** Lacking sense or substance; empty. [Lat. *inānis*.] — **in•ane′ly** *adv.*
in•an•i•mate (ĭn-ăn′ə-mĭt) *adj.* **1.** Not having the qualities associated with active, living organisms; not animate. **2.** Not animated or energetic; dull. **3.** *Gram.* Belonging to the class of nouns that stand for nonliving things. — **in•an′i•mate•ly** *adv.* — **in•an′i•mate•ness** *n.*
in•a•ni•tion (ĭn′ə-nĭsh′ən) *n.* **1.** Exhaustion, as from lack of nourishment. **2.** The condition or quality of being empty. [ME *inanisioun*, emptiness < OFr. *inanicion*, exhaustion from hunger < LLat. *inānītiō, inānītiōn-*, emptiness < Lat. *inānītus*, p.part. of *inānīre*, to make empty < *inānis*, empty.]
in•an•i•ty (ĭ-năn′ĭ-tē) *n., pl.* **-ties. 1.** The condition or quality of being inane. **2.** Something empty of meaning or sense.
in•ap•peas•a•ble (ĭn′ə-pē′zə-bəl) *adj.* Difficult or impossible to appease: *inappeasable resentment.*
in•ap•pe•tence (ĭn-ăp′ĭ-təns) also **in•ap•pe•ten•cy** (-tən-sē) *n.* Lack of appetite. — **in•ap′pe•tent** *adj.*
in•ap•pli•ca•ble (ĭn-ăp′lĭ-kə-bəl, ĭn′ə-plĭk′ə-) *adj.* Not applicable: *inapplicable rules.* — **in•ap′pli•ca•bil′i•ty** *n.* — **in•ap′pli•ca•bly** *adv.*
in•ap•po•site (ĭn-ăp′ə-zĭt) *adj.* Not pertinent; unsuitable. — **in•ap′po•site•ly** *adv.* — **in•ap′po•site•ness** *n.*
in•ap•pre•cia•ble (ĭn′ə-prē′shə-bəl) *adj.* Too small to be noticed or make a significant difference; negligible. — **in′ap•pre′cia•bly** *adv.*
in•ap•pre•cia•tive (ĭn′ə-prē′shə-tĭv, -shē-ā′tĭv, shē-ə-) *adj.* Feeling or showing no appreciation; unappreciative. — **in′ap•pre′cia•tive•ly** *adv.* — **in′ap•pre′cia•tive•ness** *n.*
in•ap•proach•a•ble (ĭn′ə-prō′chə-bəl) *adj.* Not approachable: *a cold, inapproachable person.* — **in′ap•proach′a•bil′i•ty** *n.* — **in′ap•proach′a•bly** *adv.*
in•ap•pro•pri•ate (ĭn′ə-prō′prē-ĭt) *adj.* Unsuitable or improper; not appropriate. — **in′ap•pro′pri•ate•ly** *adv.* — **in′ap•pro′pri•ate•ness** *n.*
in•apt (ĭn-ăpt′) *adj.* **1.** Inappropriate: *inapt remarks.* **2.** Inept: *inapt work.* — **in•apt′ly** *adv.* — **in•apt′ness** *n.*
in•ap•ti•tude (ĭn-ăp′tĭ-to͞od′, -tyo͞od′) *n.* **1.** Lack of talent or ability. **2.** The quality or state of being inappropriate.
I•na•ri (ĭn′ə-rē, ē′när′ē), **Lake.** A lake of N Finland with an outlet to the Arctic Ocean.
in•ar•tic•u•late (ĭn′är-tĭk′yə-lĭt) *adj.* **1.** Uttered without the use of normal words or syllables; incomprehensible as speech or language. **2.** Unable to speak; speechless: *inarticulate with shock.* See Syns at **dumb. 3.** Unable to speak with clarity or eloquence. **4.** Going unexpressed: *inarticulate sorrow.* **5.** *Biol.* Not having joints or segments. — **in′ar•tic′u•late•ly** *adv.* — **in′ar•tic′u•late•ness, in′ar•tic′u•la•cy** (-lə-sē) *n.*
in•ar•tis•tic (ĭn′är-tĭs′tĭk) *adj.* **1.** Not conforming to the principles or criteria of art. **2.** Lacking taste or interest in art. — **in′ar•tis′tic•al•ly** *adv.*
in•as•much as (ĭn′əz-mŭch′) *conj.* **1.** Because of the fact that; since. **2.** To the extent that; insofar as.
in•at•ten•tion (ĭn′ə-tĕn′shən) *n.* Lack of attention, notice, or regard.
in•at•ten•tive (ĭn′ə-tĕn′tĭv) *adj.* Exhibiting a lack of attention; not attentive. — **in′at•ten′tive•ly** *adv.* — **in′at•ten′tive•ness** *n.*
in•au•di•ble (ĭn-ô′də-bəl) *adj.* Impossible to hear. — **in•au′di•bil′i•ty** *n.* — **in•au′di•bly** *adv.*
in•au•gu•ral (ĭn-ô′gyər-əl) *adj.* **1.** Of, relating to, or characteristic of an inauguration. **2.** Initial; first: *the inaugural issue of a magazine.* — *n.* **1.** An inauguration. **2.** A speech given by a person being formally inducted into office.
in•au•gu•rate (ĭn-ô′gyə-rāt′) *tr.v.* **-rat•ed, -rat•ing, -rates. 1.** To induct into office by a formal ceremony. **2.** To cause to begin, esp. officially or formally. **3.** To open or begin use of with a ceremony; dedicate. [Lat. *inaugurāre, inaugurāt-* : *in-*, intensive pref.; see IN-[2] + *augurāre*, to augur (< *augur*, soothsayer; see **aug-***).] — **in•au′gu•ra′tor** *n.*
in•au•gu•ra•tion (ĭn-ô′gyə-rā′shən) *n.* **1.** Formal induction into office. **2.** A formal beginning or introduction.
in•aus•pi•cious (ĭn′ô-spĭsh′əs) *adj.* Not favorable; not auspicious. — **in′aus•pi′cious•ness** *n.*
in•au•then•tic (ĭn′ô-thĕn′tĭk) *adj.* Not genuine or authentic. — **in′au•then•tic′i•ty** (-tĭs′ĭ-tē) *n.*
in between *prep. & adv.* Between.
in-be•tween (ĭn′bĭ-twēn′) *adj.* Intermediate: *an in-between age.* — *n.* An intermediate.
in•board (ĭn′bôrd′, -bōrd′) *adj.* **1.** *Naut.* Within the hull or toward the center of a vessel. **2.** Relatively close to the fuselage of an aircraft: *the inboard engines.* — *n. Naut.* A motor on the inside of the hull of a boat. — **in′board′** *adv.*
in•born (ĭn′bôrn′) *adj.* **1.** Possessed by an organism at birth. **2.** Inherited or hereditary.
in•bound[1] (ĭn′bound′) *adj.* Bound or headed inward.
in•bound[2] (ĭn′bound′) *v.* **-bound•ed, -bound•ing, -bounds.** — *tr.* To put (the ball) into play by passing it from out of bounds to a teammate on the court. — *intr.* To execute an inbounds pass.
in•bounds (ĭn′boundz′) *adj.* **1.** *Basketball.* Involving putting the ball into play by passing it from out of bounds to a teammate on the court. **2.** *Sports.* Within the designated boundaries.
in•breathe (ĭn′brēth′) *tr.v.* **-breathed, -breath•ing, -breathes.** To breathe (something) in; inhale.
in•bred (ĭn′brĕd′) *adj.* **1.** Produced by inbreeding. **2.** Fixed in the character or disposition as if inherited; deep-seated.
in•breed (ĭn′brēd′) *tr.v.* **-bred** (-brĕd′), **-breed•ing, -breeds. 1.** To breed by the continued mating of closely related individuals, esp. to preserve desirable traits in a stock. **2.** To breed or develop within; engender. — **in•breed′er** *n.*
in•breed•ing (ĭn′brē′dĭng) *n.* **1.** The breeding of related individuals within an isolated or a closed group of organisms or people. **2.** The inbreeding of closely related individuals.
in•built (ĭn′bĭlt′) *adj.* Built-in; inherent.
inc. *abbr.* **1.** Income. **2.** Incomplete. **3.** Also **Inc.** Incorporated. **4.** Increase.
In•ca (ĭng′kə) *n., pl.* **Inca** or **-cas. 1.a.** A member of the group of Quechuan peoples of highland Peru who established an empire from northern Ecuador to central Chile before the Spanish conquest. **b.** A ruler or high-ranking member of the Inca empire. **2.** A member of any of the peoples ruled by the Incas. [Sp. < Quechua *inka*, ruler, man of royal lineage.]

ă pat	oi boy
ā pay	ou out
âr care	o͝o took
ä father	o͞o boot
ĕ pet	ŭ cut
ē be	ûr urge
ĭ pit	th thin
ī pie	*th* this
îr pier	hw which
ŏ pot	zh vision
ō toe	ə about, item
ô paw	

Stress marks:
′ (primary);
′ (secondary), as in **dictionary** (dĭk′shə-nĕr′ē)

in•cal•cu•la•ble (ĭn-kăl′kyə-lə-bəl) *adj.* **1.a.** Impossible to calculate: *a mass of incalculable figures.* **b.** Too great to be calculated or reckoned: *incalculable wealth.* **2.** Impossible to foresee; unpredictable. **—in•cal′cu•la•bil′i•ty, in•cal′cu•la•ble•ness** *n.* **—in•cal′cu•la•bly** *adv.*

Syns: *incalculable, countless, immeasurable, incomputable, inestimable, infinite, innumerable, measureless.* The central meaning shared by these adjectives is "being greater than can be calculated or reckoned": *incalculable riches; countless hours; an immeasurable distance; an incomputable amount; jewels of inestimable value; infinite reasons; innumerable difficulties; measureless power.* ***Ant:*** *calculable.*

in•ca•les•cent (ĭn′kə-lĕs′ənt) *adj.* Growing hotter or more ardent. [Lat. *incalēscēns, incalēscent-,* pr.part. of *incalēscere,* to grow warm : *in-,* intensive pref.; see IN-[2] + *calēscere,* to grow warm, inchoative of *calēre,* to be warm; see **kelə-[1]*.**] **—in′ca•les′cence** *n.*

in cam•er•a (kăm′ər-ə) *adv.* **1.** In secret; privately. **2.** *Law.* In private with a judge rather than in open court. [NLat. *in camerā* : Lat. *in,* in + Med.Lat. *camerā,* chamber.]

In•can (ĭng′kən) *adj.* Of or relating to the Inca, their civilization, or their language. *—n.* **1.** An Inca. **2.** Quechua.

in•can•desce (ĭn′kən-dĕs′) *tr. & intr.v.* **-desced, -desc•ing, -desc•es.** To make or become incandescent. [Lat. *incandēscere,* to glow : *in-,* intensive pref.; see IN-[2] + *candēscere,* to glow, inchoative of *candēre,* to shine; see **kand-*.**]

in•can•des•cence (ĭn′kən-dĕs′əns) *n.* **1.** The emission of visible light by a hot object. **2.** The light emitted by such an object. **3.** A high degree of emotion, intensity, or brilliance.

in•can•des•cent (ĭn′kən-dĕs′ənt) *adj.* **1.** Emitting visible light as a result of being heated. **2.** Shining brilliantly; very bright. See Syns at **bright. 3.** Characterized by ardent emotion, intensity, or brilliance. **—in′can•des′cent•ly** *adv.*

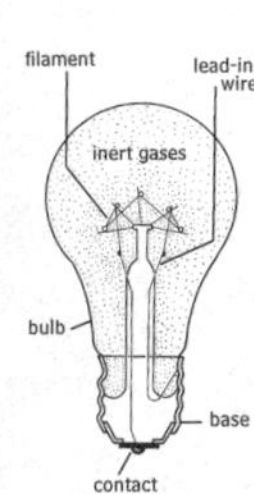

incandescent lamp

incandescent lamp *n.* An electric lamp in which a filament is heated to incandescence by an electric current.

in•can•ta•tion (ĭn′kăn-tā′shən) *n.* **1.** Ritual recitation of charms or spells to produce a magic effect. **2.a.** A formula used in ritual recitation; a charm or spell. **b.** A conventionalized utterance repeated without thought or aptness; a formula. [ME *incantacioun* < OFr. *incantation* < LLat. *incantātiō, incantātiōn-,* spell < Lat. *incantātus,* p.part. of *incantāre,* to enchant. See ENCHANT.] **—in′can•ta′tion•al** *adj.* **—in•can′ta•to′ry** (-tə-tôr′ē, -tōr′ē) *adj.*

in•ca•pa•ble (ĭn-kā′pə-bəl) *adj.* **1.a.** Lacking the necessary ability, capacity, or power: *incapable of love.* **b.** Unable to perform adequately; incompetent. **2.** Not admitting or permitting; not susceptible. **3.** *Law.* Lacking legal qualifications or requirements; ineligible. **—in•ca′pa•bil′i•ty, in•ca′pa•ble•ness** *n.* **—in•ca′pa•bly** *adv.*

in•ca•pac•i•tant (ĭn′kə-păs′ĭ-tənt) *n.* A device or substance, such as tear gas, used to incapacitate individuals temporarily.

in•ca•pac•i•tate (ĭn′kə-păs′ĭ-tāt′) *tr.v.* **-tat•ed, -tat•ing, -tates. 1.** To deprive of strength or ability; disable. **2.** To make legally ineligible; disqualify. **—in′ca•pac′i•ta′tion** *n.*

in•ca•pac•i•ty (ĭn′kə-păs′ĭ-tē) *n., pl.* **-ties. 1.** Inadequate strength or ability; lack of capacity. **2.** A defect or handicap; a disability. **3.** *Law.* Something that renders one incapable.

in•cap•su•late (ĭn-kăp′sə-lāt′) *v.* Var. of **encapsulate.**

in•car•cer•ate (ĭn-kär′sə-rāt′) *tr.v.* **-at•ed, -at•ing, -ates. 1.** To put into jail. **2.** To shut in; confine. [Med.Lat. *incarcerāre, incarcerāt-* : Lat. *in-,* in; see IN-[2] + Lat. *carcer,* prison.] **—in•car′cer•a′tion** *n.* **—in•car′cer•a′tor** *n.*

in•car•na•dine (ĭn-kär′nə-dīn′, -dēn′, -dĭn) *adj.* **1.** Flesh-colored. **2.** Blood-red. *—tr.v.* **-dined, -din•ing, -dines.** To make incarnadine, esp. to redden. [Fr. *incarnadin* < Ital. *incarnatino,* dim. of *incarnato* : *in,* in (< Lat.; see IN-[2]) + *carne,* flesh (< Lat. *carō, carn-;* see INCARNATE).]

in•car•nate (ĭn-kär′nĭt) *adj.* **1.a.** Invested with bodily nature and form: *an incarnate spirit.* **b.** Embodied in human form; personified: *a villain who is evil incarnate.* **2.** Incarnadine. *—tr.v.* (-nāt′) **-nat•ed, -nat•ing, -nates. 1.a.** To give bodily, esp. human, form to. **b.** To personify. **2.** To realize in action or fact; actualize. [ME < LLat. *incarnātus,* p.part. of *incarnāre,* to make flesh : Lat. *in-,* causative pref.; see IN-[2] + Lat. *carō, carn-,* flesh; see **sker-[1]*.**] **—in•car′na′tor** *n.*

in•car•na•tion (ĭn′kär-nā′shən) *n.* **1.a.** The act of incarnating. **b.** The condition of being incarnated. **2. Incarnation.** *Theol.* The Christian doctrine that the Son of God was conceived in the womb of Mary and that Jesus is true God and true man. **3.** A bodily manifestation of a supernatural being. **4.** One believed to personify a given abstract quality or idea. **5.** A period of time passed in a given bodily form or condition: *hopes for a better life in another incarnation.*

in•case (ĭn-kās′) *v.* Var. of **encase.**

in•cau•tious (ĭn-kô′shəs) *adj.* Not cautious; rash. **—in•cau′tious•ly** *adv.* **—in•cau′tious•ness** *n.*

in•cen•di•ar•y (ĭn-sĕn′dē-ĕr′ē) *adj.* **1.a.** Causing or capable of causing fire. **b.** Of or containing chemicals that produce intensely hot fire when exploded: *an incendiary bomb.* **c.** Of or involving arson. **2.** Tending to inflame; inflammatory. *—n., pl.* **-ies. 1.** An arsonist. **2.** An incendiary device. **3.** One who creates or stirs up factionism or sedition; an agitator. [ME < Lat. *incendiārius* < *incendium,* fire < *incendere,* to set on fire. See INCENSE[1].] **—in•cen′di•a•rism** (-ə-rĭz′əm) *n.*

in•cense[1] (ĭn-sĕns′) *tr.v.* **-censed, -cens•ing, -cens•es.** To cause to be extremely angry; infuriate. [ME *encensen* < OFr. *incenser* < LLat. *incēnsāre,* to sacrifice, burn < Lat. *incēnsus,* p.part. of *incendere,* to set on fire. See **kand-*.**]

in•cense[2] (ĭn′sĕns′) *n.* **1.a.** An aromatic substance, such as wood or a gum, that is burned to produce a pleasant odor. **b.** The smoke or odor produced by the burning of such a substance. **2.** A pleasant smell. **3.** Flattering or fawning attention; homage. *—tr.v.* **-censed, -cens•ing, -cens•es. 1.** To perfume with incense. **2.** To burn incense to, as a ritual offering. [ME *encens* < OFr. < Lat. *incēnsum* < neut. p.part. of *incendere,* to set on fire. See **kand-*.**]

incense cedar *n.* Any of several coniferous evergreen trees of the genera *Calocedrus* and *Libocedrus,* having flattened branches with scalelike leaves.

in•cen•tive (ĭn-sĕn′tĭv) *n.* Something, such as a reward or punishment, that induces action or motivates effort. *—adj.* Serving to induce or motivate. [ME < LLat. *incentīvum* < neut. of *incentīvus,* inciting < Lat., setting the tune < *incentus,* p.part. of *incinere,* to sound : *in-,* intensive pref.; see IN-[2] + *canere,* to sing; see **kan-*.**]

in•cept (ĭn-sĕpt′) *tr.v.* **-cept•ed, -cept•ing, -cepts.** To take in; ingest. [Lat. *incipere, incept-,* to begin, take up. See INCEPTION.] **—in•cep′tor** *n.*

in•cep•tion (ĭn-sĕp′shən) *n.* The beginning of something, such as an undertaking; a commencement. See Syns at **origin.** [ME *incepcion* < Lat. *inceptiō, inceptiōn-* < *inceptus,* p.part. of *incipere,* to begin, take up : *in-,* in; see IN-[2] + *capere,* to take; see **kap-*.**]

in•cep•tive (ĭn-sĕp′tĭv) *adj.* **1.** Incipient; beginning. **2.** *Gram.* Inchoative. *—n. Gram.* An inchoative verb.

in•cer•ti•tude (ĭn-sûr′tĭ-to͞od′, -tyo͞od′) *n.* **1.** Uncertainty. **2.** Absence of confidence; doubt. **3.** Insecurity or instability.

in•ces•sant (ĭn-sĕs′ənt) *adj.* Continuing without interruption. See Syns at **continual.** [ME *incessaunte* < LLat. *incessāns, incessant-* : Lat. *in-,* not; see IN-[1] + Lat. *cessāns,* pr.part. of *cessāre,* to stop; see CEASE.] **—in•ces′san•cy** *n.* **—in•ces′sant•ly** *adv.*

in•cest (ĭn′sĕst′) *n.* **1.** Sexual relations between persons so closely related that their marriage is illegal or forbidden by custom. **2.** The statutory crime of sexual relations with such a relative. [ME < Lat. *incestum,* neut. of *incestus,* impure, unchaste : *in-,* not; see IN-[1] + *castus,* pure, chaste; see **kes-*.**]

in•ces•tu•ous (ĭn-sĕs′cho͞o-əs) *adj.* **1.** Of, involving, or suggestive of incest. **2.** Having committed incest. **3.** Improperly intimate or interconnected. **—in•ces′tu•ous•ly** *adv.* **—in•ces′tu•ous•ness** *n.*

inch[1] (ĭnch) *n.* **1.** A unit of length in the U.S. Customary and British Imperial systems, equal to 1/12 of a foot (2.54 centimeters). See table at **measurement. 2.** A fall, as of rain or snow, sufficient to cover a surface to the depth of one inch. **3.** A unit of atmospheric pressure that is equal to the pressure exerted by a one-inch column of mercury at the earth's surface at a temperature of 0°C. **4.** A very small degree or amount. *—intr. & tr.v.* **inched, inch•ing, inch•es.** To move or cause to move slowly or by small degrees. ***—idioms.* every inch.** In every respect; entirely. **inch by inch.** Very gradually or slowly. **within an inch of.** Almost to the point of. [ME < OE *ynce* < Lat. *uncia,* one twelfth of a unit. See **oi-no-*.**]

inch[2] (ĭnch) *n. Scots.* A small island. [ME < Sc.Gael. *innis* < OIr. *inis.*]

inch•er (ĭn′chər) *n.* Something measuring a specified number of inches. Often used in combination: *an 18-incher.*

inch•meal (ĭnch′mēl′) *adv.* Little by little; gradually. [INCH[1] + (PIECE)MEAL.]

in•cho•ate (ĭn-kō′ĭt) *adj.* **1.** In an initial or early stage; incipient. **2.** Imperfectly formed or developed: *a vague, inchoate idea.* [Lat. *inchoātus,* p.part. of *inchoāre,* to begin, alteration of *incohāre* : *in-,* in; see IN-[2] + *cohum,* strap from yoke to harness.] **—in•cho′ate•ly** *adv.* **—in•cho′ate•ness** *n.*

in•cho•a•tive (ĭn-kō′ə-tĭv) *adj.* **1.** Beginning; initial. **2.** *Gram.* Of or being a verb or verbal form that designates the beginning of an action, a state, or an event. **—in•cho′a•tive** *n.* **—in•cho′a•tive•ly** *adv.*

In•chon (ĭn′chŏn′). A city of NW South Korea on an inlet of the Yellow Sea SW of Seoul. Pop. 1,387,000.

inch•worm (ĭnch′wûrm′) *n.* See **measuring worm.**

in•ci•dence (ĭn′sĭ-dəns) *n.* **1.** The act or an instance of happening; occurrence. **2.** Extent or frequency of occurrence: *a high incidence of malaria.* **3.** *Phys.* **a.** The arrival of radiation or a projectile at a surface. **b.** Angle of incidence.

in•ci•dent (ĭn′sĭ-dənt) *n.* **1.** A definite and separate occurrence; an event. See Syns at **occurrence. 2.** A usu. minor event or condition subordinate to another. **3.** Something contingent on or related to something else. **4.** An occurrence or event that interrupts normal procedure or precipitates a crisis: *an international incident.* *—adj.* **1.** Tending to arise or occur as a result or an accompaniment. **2.** Related to or dependent on another thing. **3.** *Phys.* Falling upon or striking a surface: *incident radiation.* [ME < OFr., apt to happen, an incident <

Lat. *incidēns, incident-*, pr.part. of *incidere*, to happen : *in-*, on; see IN-[2] + *cadere*, to fall; see **kad-***.]

in·ci·den·tal (ĭn′sĭ-dĕn′tl) *adj.* **1.** Occurring or likely to occur as an unpredictable or minor accompaniment. **2.** Of a minor, casual, or subordinate nature: *incidental expenses.* —*n.* A minor accompanying item or expense.

in·ci·den·tal·ly (ĭn′sĭ-dĕn′tl-ē) *adv.* **1.** As a minor or subordinate matter: *a lawyer and incidentally a musician.* **2.** (*also* -dĕnt′lē). Apart from the main subject; parenthetically.

incidental music *n. Mus.* Music accompanying the action or dialogue of a drama or filling intervals between scenes or acts.

in·cin·er·ate (ĭn-sĭn′ə-rāt′) *v.* **-at·ed, -at·ing, -ates.** —*tr.* To cause to burn to ashes. —*intr.* To burn completely. [Med. Lat. *incinerāre, incinerāt-* : Lat. *in-*, causative pref.; see IN-[2] + Lat. *cinis, ciner-*, ashes.] —**in·cin′er·a′tion** *n.*

in·cin·er·a·tor (ĭn-sĭn′ə-rā′tər) *n.* One that incinerates, esp. an apparatus, such as a furnace, for burning waste.

in·cip·i·ent (ĭn-sĭp′ē-ənt) *adj.* Beginning to exist or appear: *detecting incipient tumors.* [Lat. *incipiēns, incipient-*, pr.part. of *incipere*, to begin. See INCEPTION.] —**in·cip′i·en·cy, in·cip′i·ence** *n.* —**in·cip′i·ent·ly** *adv.*

in·ci·pit (ĭn′sĭ-pĭt′, ĭng′kĭ-) *n.* The beginning or opening words of the text of a medieval manuscript or early printed book. [Lat., third pers. sing. pr.t. of *incipere*, to begin. See INCEPTION.]

in·cise (ĭn-sīz′) *tr.v.* **-cised, -cis·ing, -cis·es. 1.** To cut into, as with a sharp instrument: *incised the tablet with chisels.* **2.a.** To engrave (designs, for example) into a surface; carve. **b.** To engrave designs, writing, or other marks into. [Fr. *inciser* < OFr. *enciser* < VLat. **incīsāre*, freq. of Lat. *incīdere, incīs-* : *in-*, in; see IN-[2] + *caedere*, to cut; see **kaə-id-***.]

in·cised (ĭn-sīzd′) *adj.* **1.** Cut into a surface; engraved. **2.** Made with or as if with a sharp instrument. **3.** Deeply and sharply cut: *the incised margin of a leaf.*

in·ci·sion (ĭn-sĭzh′ən) *n.* **1.** The act of incising. **2.** *Medic.* **a.** A cut into a body tissue or organ, esp. during surgery. **b.** The scar resulting from such a cut. **3.** A notch, as in the edge of a leaf. **4.** The condition or quality of being incisive.

in·ci·sive (ĭn-sī′sĭv) *adj.* Penetrating, clear, and sharp, as in expression. —**in·ci′sive·ly** *adv.* —**in·ci′sive·ness** *n.*

in·ci·sor (ĭn-sī′zər) *n.* A tooth for cutting or gnawing, located at the front of the mouth along the apex of the dental arch.

in·cite (ĭn-sīt′) *tr.v.* **-cit·ed, -cit·ing, -cites.** To provoke and urge on: *inciting workers to strike.* [ME *encyten* < OFr. *enciter* < Lat. *incitāre*, to urge forward : *in-*, intensive pref.; see IN-[2] + *citāre*, to stimulate, freq. of *ciēre*, to put in motion; see **kei-**[2]*****.] —**in·cite′ment** *n.* —**in·cit′er** *n.* —**in′ci·ta′tion** *n.*

in·ci·vil·i·ty (ĭn′sĭ-vĭl′ĭ-tē) *n., pl.* **-ties. 1.** The quality or condition of being uncivil. **2.** An uncivil or discourteous act.

incl. *abbr.* **1.** Including. **2.** Inclusive.

in·clasp (ĭn-klăsp′) *v.* Var. of **enclasp.**

in·clem·ent (ĭn-klĕm′ənt) *adj.* **1.** Stormy: *inclement weather.* **2.** Showing no clemency; unmerciful. —**in·clem′en·cy** *n.*

in·clin·a·ble (ĭn-klī′nə-bəl) *adj.* **1.** Having a specified tendency or disposition; inclined. **2.** Favorably disposed; amenable.

in·cli·na·tion (ĭn′klə-nā′shən) *n.* **1.** The act of inclining or the state of being inclined; a bend or tilt. **2.a.** A deviation or the degree of deviation from the horizontal or vertical; a slant. **b.** An inclined surface; a slope. **3.** A tendency toward a certain condition. **4.** A characteristic disposition to do, prefer, or favor one thing rather than another; a propensity.

in·cline (ĭn-klīn′) *v.* **-clined, -clin·ing, -clines.** —*intr.* **1.** To deviate from the horizontal or vertical; slant. **2.** To be disposed to a certain preference, opinion, or course of action. **3.** To lower or bend the head or body, as in a nod or bow. —*tr.* **1.** To cause to lean, slant, or slope. **2.** To influence to have a certain tendency; dispose. **3.** To bend or lower in a nod or bow. —*n.* (ĭn′klīn′). An inclined surface; a slope or gradient. [ME *enclinen* < OFr. *encliner* < Lat. *inclīnāre* : *in-*, into, toward; see IN-[2] + *-clīnāre*, to lean; see **klei-***.] —**in·clin′er** *n.*

Syns: *incline, bias, dispose, predispose.* The central meaning shared by these verbs is "to influence or be influenced toward a particular attitude or course of action": *inclined to believe him; is biased in her favor; were disposed to admire him; predisposed to studying.* See also Syns at **slant.**

in·clined (ĭn-klīnd′) *adj.* **1.** Sloping, slanting, or leaning. **2.** Having a preference, disposition, or tendency.

inclined plane *n.* A plane set at an angle to the horizontal, esp. to raise or lower a load by rolling or sliding.

in·cli·nom·e·ter (ĭn′klə-nŏm′ĭ-tər) *n.* **1.** An instrument used to determine the angle of the earth's magnetic field in respect to the horizontal plane. **2.** An instrument for showing the inclination of an aircraft or a ship relative to the horizontal. **3.** See **clinometer.**

in·close (ĭn-klōz′) *v.* Var. of **enclose.**

in·clude (ĭn-klo͞od′) *tr.v.* **-clud·ed, -clud·ing, -cludes. 1.** To take in as a part, an element, or a member. **2.** To contain as a secondary or subordinate element. **3.** To consider with or place into a group, class, or total. [ME *includen* < Lat. *inclūdere*, to enclose : *in-*, in; see IN-[2] + *claudere*, to close.] —**in·clud′a·ble, in·clud′i·ble** *adj.*

Usage Note: Some writers have insisted that *include* be used only when it is followed by a partial list of the contents of the referent of the subject. One may write *New England includes Connecticut and Rhode Island,* but one must use *comprise* or *consist of* when a full enumeration is provided: *New England comprises Connecticut, Rhode Island, Massachusetts, Vermont, New Hampshire, and Maine. Include,* however, does not rule out the possibility of a complete listing. Thus the sentence *The bibliography should include all the journal articles you have used* does not entail that the bibliography must contain something other than journal articles, though it does leave that possibility open. When one wants to make clear that the listing is exhaustive, however, the use of *comprise* or *consist of* will avoid ambiguity. See Usage Note at **comprise.**

in·clud·ed (ĭn-klo͞o′dĭd) *adj.* **1.** *Bot.* Not protruding beyond a surrounding part, as stamens that do not project from a corolla. **2.** *Math.* Formed by and between two intersecting straight lines: *an included angle.*

in·clu·sion (ĭn-klo͞o′zhən) *n.* **1.** The act of including or the state of being included. **2.** Something included. **3.** *Geol.* A solid, liquid, or gaseous foreign body enclosed in a mineral or rock. **4.** *Biol.* A nonliving mass, such as fat, in the cytoplasm of a cell. **5.** *Comp. Sci.* A logical operation that assumes the second statement of a pair is true if the first one is true. [Lat. *inclūsiō, inclūsiōn-* < *inclūsus*, p.part. of *inclūdere*, to enclose. See INCLUDE.] —**in·clu′sion·ar′y** (-zhə-nĕr′ē) *adj.*

inclusion body *n.* An abnormal structure in a cell nucleus or cytoplasm having characteristic staining properties and associated esp. with certain viral infections, such as rabies.

in·clu·sive (ĭn-klo͞o′sĭv) *adj.* **1.** Taking a great deal or everything within its scope; comprehensive. **2.** Including the specified extremes or limits and the area between them. —**in·clu′sive·ly** *adv.* —**in·clu′sive·ness** *n.*

inclusive of *prep.* Taking into consideration; including.

in·co·er·ci·ble (ĭn′kō-ûr′sə-bəl) *adj.* Difficult or impossible to coerce or control forcibly: *incoercible rebel leaders.*

incog. *abbr.* Incognita; incognito.

in·cog·i·tant (ĭn-kŏj′ĭ-tənt) *adj.* Thoughtless; inconsiderate. [Lat. *incōgitāns, incōgitant-* : *in-*, not; see IN-[1] + *cōgitāns*, pr.part. of *cōgitāre*, to think; see COGITATE.]

in·cog·ni·ta (ĭn′kŏg-nē′tə, ĭn-kŏg′nĭ-tə) *adv. & adj.* With one's identity disguised or concealed. Used of a woman. [Ital., fem. of *incognito*. See INCOGNITO.] —**in′cog·ni′ta** *n.*

in·cog·ni·to (ĭn′kŏg-nē′tō, ĭn-kŏg′nĭ-tō′) *adv. & adj.* With one's identity disguised or concealed. —*n., pl.* **-tos. 1.** One whose identity is disguised or concealed. **2.** The condition of having a disguised or concealed identity. [Ital. < Lat. *incognitus*, unknown : *in-*, not; see IN-[1] + *cognitus*, p.part. of *cognōscere*, to learn, recognize; see COGNITION.]

in·cog·ni·zant (ĭn-kŏg′nĭ-zənt) *adj.* Lacking knowledge or awareness; unaware.

in·co·her·ence (ĭn′kō-hîr′əns) *n.* **1.** The condition or quality of being incoherent. **2.** Something incoherent. —**in′co·her′en·cy** *n.*

in·co·her·ent (ĭn′kō-hîr′ənt) *adj.* **1.** Lacking cohesion, connection, or harmony; not coherent. **2.** Unable to think or express one's thoughts in a clear or orderly manner. —**in′co·her′ent·ly** *adv.* —**in′co·her′ent·ness** *n.*

in·com·bus·ti·ble (ĭn′kəm-bŭs′tə-bəl) *adj.* Incapable of burning. —*n.* An incombustible object or material. —**in′com·bus′ti·bil′i·ty** *n.* —**in′com·bus′ti·bly** *adv.*

in·come (ĭn′kŭm′) *n.* **1.** The amount of money or its equivalent received during a period of time for labor or services, from the sale of goods or property, or as profit from financial investments. **2.** The act of coming in; entrance. [ME, arrival, entrance < *incomen*, to come in < OE *incuman* : *in*, in; see IN[1] + *cuman*, to come; see COME.]

income tax *n.* A tax levied on net personal or business income.

in·com·ing (ĭn′kŭm′ĭng) *adj.* **1.** Coming in or about to come in; entering: *incoming trains.* **2.** About to assume an office or a position: *the incoming governor.* —*n.* **1.** The act of coming in; arrival. **2.** Income; revenue. Often used in the plural.

in·com·men·su·ra·ble (ĭn′kə-mĕn′sər-ə-bəl, -shər-) *adj.* **1.a.** Impossible to measure or compare. **b.** Lacking a common quality on which to make a comparison. **2.** *Math.* Having no common measure or number of which all the given lengths or measures are integral multiples. —*n.* One that is incommensurable. —**in′com·men′su·ra·bil′i·ty** *n.* —**in′com·men′su·ra·bly** *adv.*

in·com·men·su·rate (ĭn′kə-mĕn′sər-ĭt, -shər-) *adj.* **1.a.** Not commensurate; disproportionate: *a reward incommensurate with their efforts.* **b.** Inadequate. **2.** Incommensurable. —**in′com·men′su·rate·ly** *adv.* —**in′com·men′su·rate·ness** *n.*

in·com·mode (ĭn′kə-mōd′) *tr.v.* **-mod·ed, -mod·ing, -modes.** To cause to be inconvenienced; disturb. [Fr. *incommoder* < OFr. < Lat. *incommodāre* < *incommodus*, inconvenient : *in-*, not; see IN-[1] + *commodus*, convenient; see COMMODIOUS.]

in·com·mo·di·ous (ĭn′kə-mō′dē-əs) *adj.* Inconvenient or uncomfortable, as by not affording sufficient space. —**in′com·mo′di·ous·ly** *adv.* —**in′com·mo′di·ous·ness** *n.*

ă pat	oi boy
ā pay	ou out
âr care	o͝o took
ä father	o͞o boot
ĕ pet	ŭ cut
ē be	ûr urge
ĭ pit	th thin
ī pie	*th* this
îr pier	hw which
ŏ pot	zh vision
ō toe	ə about, item
ô paw	

Stress marks:
′ (primary);
′ (secondary), as in dictionary (dĭk′shə-nĕr′ē)

in•com•mod•i•ty (ĭn′kə-mŏd′ĭ-tē) *n., pl.* **-ties. 1.** Inconvenience. **2.** Something inconvenient.

in•com•mu•ni•ca•ble (ĭn′kə-myo͞o′nĭ-kə-bəl) *adj.* **1.** Impossible to be transmitted; not communicable. **2.** Incommunicative. **—in′com•mu′ni•ca•bil′i•ty** *n.* **—in′com•mu′ni•ca•bly** *adv.*

in•com•mu•ni•ca•do (ĭn′kə-myo͞o′nĭ-kä′dō) *adv. & adj.* Without the means or right of communicating with others. [Sp. *incomunicado,* p.part. of *incomunicar,* to deny communication : *in-,* not (< Lat.; see IN-[1]) + *comunicar,* to communicate (< Lat. *commūnicāre;* see COMMUNICATE).]

in•com•mu•ni•ca•tive (ĭn′kə-myo͞o′nĭ-kə-tĭv, -kā′tĭv) *adj.* Not disposed to be forthcoming or communicative; uncommunicative. **—in′com•mu′ni•ca•tive•ly** *adv.* **—in′com•mu′ni•ca•tive•ness** *n.*

in•com•mut•a•ble (ĭn′kə-myo͞o′tə-bəl) *adj.* **1.** Not able to be exchanged one for another. **2.** That cannot be changed; unalterable. **—in′com•mut′a•bil′i•ty, in′com•mut′a•ble•ness** *n.* **—in′com•mut′a•bly** *adv.*

in•com•pa•ra•ble (ĭn-kŏm′pər-ə-bəl) *adj.* **1.** Being such that comparison is impossible. **2.** So outstanding as to be beyond comparison; unsurpassed. **—in•com′pa•ra•bil′i•ty, in•com′pa•ra•ble•ness** *n.* **—in•com′pa•ra•bly** *adv.*

in•com•pat•i•bil•i•ty (ĭn′kəm-păt′ə-bĭl′ĭ-tē) *n., pl.* **-ties. 1.** The state or quality of being incompatible. **2. incompatibilities.** Mutually exclusive or antagonistic qualities or things.

in•com•pat•i•ble (ĭn′kəm-păt′ə-bəl) *adj.* **1.** Incapable of associating or blending or of being associated or blended because of disharmony, incongruity, or antagonism. **2.** Impossible to be held simultaneously by one person: *the incompatible offices of prosecutor and judge.* **3.** *Logic.* That cannot be simultaneously true; mutually exclusive. **4.** *Medic.* **a.** Producing an undesirable effect when combined with a particular substance. **b.** Not immunologically compatible. **—***n.* One that is incompatible. **—in′com•pat′i•ble•ness** *n.* **—in′com•pat′i•bly** *adv.*

in•com•pe•tent (ĭn-kŏm′pĭ-tənt) *adj.* **1.** Not qualified in legal terms: *incompetent to stand trial.* **2.** Inadequate for or unsuited to a particular purpose or application. **3.** Devoid of qualities requisite for effective conduct or action. **—***n.* An incompetent person. **—in•com′pe•tence, in•com′pe•ten•cy** *n.* **—in•com′pe•tent•ly** *adv.*

in•com•plete (ĭn′kəm-plēt′) *adj.* **1.** Not complete. **2.** *Football.* Not caught or not caught in bounds. **—in′com•plete′ly** *adv.* **—in′com•plete′ness, in′com•ple′tion** *n.*

in•com•pli•ant (ĭn′kəm-plī′ənt) *adj.* Not willing to comply; unyielding. **—in′com•pli′ance, in′com•pli′an•cy** *n.*

in•com•pre•hen•si•ble (ĭn′kŏm-prĭ-hĕn′sə-bəl, ĭn-kŏm′-) *adj.* **1.a.** Difficult or impossible to understand; unintelligible. **b.** Impossible to know or fathom. **2.** *Archaic.* Having no limits; boundless. **—in′com•pre•hen′si•bil′i•ty, in′com•pre•hen′si•ble•ness** *n.* **—in′com•pre•hen′si•bly** *adv.*

in•com•pre•hen•sion (ĭn′kŏm-prĭ-hĕn′shən, ĭn-kŏm′-) *n.* Lack of comprehension or understanding.

in•com•pre•hen•sive (ĭn′kŏm-prĭ-hĕn′sĭv, ĭn-kŏm′-) *adj.* Limited in scope; not all-inclusive. **—in′com•pre•hen′sive•ly** *adv.* **—in′com•pre•hen′sive•ness** *n.*

in•com•press•i•ble (ĭn′kəm-prĕs′ə-bəl) *adj.* Impossible to compress; resisting compression.

in•com•put•a•ble (ĭn′kəm-pyo͞o′tə-bəl) *adj.* Impossible to compute or be computed; incalculable. See Syns at **incalculable. —in′com•put′a•bil′i•ty** *n.*

in•con•ceiv•a•ble (ĭn′kən-sē′və-bəl) *adj.* **1.** Impossible to comprehend or grasp fully: *inconceivable folly.* **2.** So unlikely or surprising as to have been thought impossible; unbelievable: *an inconceivable victory.* **—in′con•ceiv′a•bil′i•ty, in′con•ceiv′a•ble•ness** *n.* **—in′con•ceiv′a•bly** *adv.*

in•con•cin•ni•ty (ĭn′kən-sĭn′ĭ-tē) *n.* Lack of congruity or harmony; unsuitability.

in•con•clu•sive (ĭn′kən-klo͞o′sĭv) *adj.* Not conclusive. **—in′con•clu′sive•ly** *adv.* **—in′con•clu′sive•ness** *n.*

in•con•den•sa•ble also **in•con•den•si•ble** (ĭn′kən-dĕn′sə-bəl) *adj.* Difficult or impossible to condense: *an incondensable judicial opinion.* **—in′con•den′sa•bil′i•ty** *n.*

in•con•dite (ĭn-kŏn′dĭt, -dīt′) *adj.* Badly constructed; crude. [Lat. *inconditus* : *in-,* not; see IN-[1] + *conditus,* p.part. of *condere,* to put together; see **dhē-***.] **—in•con′dite•ly** *adv.*

in•con•form•i•ty (ĭn′kən-fôr′mĭ-tē) *n.* Lack of conformity; disagreement.

in•con•gru•ent (ĭn-kŏng′gro͞o-ənt, ĭn′kŏn-gro͞o′ənt) *adj.* **1.** Not congruent. **2.** Incongruous. **—in•con′gru•ence** *n.* **—in•con′gru•ent•ly** *adv.*

in•con•gru•i•ty (ĭn′kŏn-gro͞o′ĭ-tē) *n., pl.* **-ties. 1.** Lack of congruence. **2.** The state or quality of being incongruous. **3.** Something incongruous.

in•con•gru•ous (ĭn-kŏng′gro͞o-əs) *adj.* **1.** Lacking in harmony; incompatible. **2.** Not in agreement, as with principles; inconsistent. **3.** Not in keeping with what is correct, proper, or logical; inappropriate. **—in•con′gru•ous•ly** *adv.* **—in•con′gru•ous•ness** *n.*

in•con•se•quent (ĭn-kŏn′sĭ-kwənt) *adj.* **1.** Having no importance or significance. **2.** Inconsistent or illogical. **3.** Proceeding without a natural or logical sequence; haphazard. **—in•con′se•quence** *n.* **—in•con′se•quent•ly** *adv.*

in•con•se•quen•tial (ĭn-kŏn′sĭ-kwĕn′shəl, ĭn′kŏn-) *adj.* **1.** Lacking importance. **2.** Not following from premises or evidence; illogical. **—***n.* A triviality. **—in•con′se•quen′ti•al′i•ty** (-kwĕn′shē-ăl′ĭ-tē), **in•con′se•quen′tial•ness** (-shəl-nĭs) *n.* **—in•con′se•quen′tial•ly** *adv.*

in•con•sid•er•a•ble (ĭn′kən-sĭd′ər-ə-bəl) *adj.* Too small or unimportant to merit attention or consideration; trivial. **—in′con•sid′er•a•ble•ness** *n.* **—in′con•sid′er•a•bly** *adv.*

in•con•sid•er•ate (ĭn′kən-sĭd′ər-ĭt) *adj.* **1.** Thoughtless of others; heedless. **2.** Not well considered or carefully thought out; ill-advised. **—in′con•sid′er•ate•ly** *adv.* **—in′con•sid′er•ate•ness, in′con•sid′er•a′tion** (-ā′shən) *n.*

in•con•sis•tence (ĭn′kən-sĭs′təns) *n.* Inconsistency.

in•con•sis•ten•cy (ĭn′kən-sĭs′tən-sē) *n., pl.* **-cies. 1.** The state or quality of being inconsistent. **2.** Something inconsistent.

in•con•sis•tent (ĭn′kən-sĭs′tənt) *adj.* **1.** Displaying or marked by a lack of consistency, esp.: **a.** Not regular or predictable; erratic: *inconsistent behavior.* **b.** Lacking in correct logical relation; contradictory: *inconsistent statements.* **c.** Not in agreement or harmony; incompatible. **2.** *Math.* Not solvable by the same set of values for the unknowns. Used of two or more equations or inequalities. **—in′con•sis′tent•ly** *adv.*

in•con•sol•a•ble (ĭn′kən-sō′lə-bəl) *adj.* Impossible or difficult to console; despondent. **—in′con•sol′a•bil′i•ty, in′con•sol′a•ble•ness** *n.* **—in′con•sol′a•bly** *adv.*

in•con•so•nant (ĭn-kŏn′sə-nənt) *adj.* Lacking harmony, agreement, or compatibility; discordant. **—in•con′so•nance** *n.* **—in•con′so•nant•ly** *adv.*

in•con•spic•u•ous (ĭn′kən-spĭk′yo͞o-əs) *adj.* Not readily noticeable. **—in′con•spic′u•ous•ly** *adv.* **—in′con•spic′u•ous•ness** *n.*

in•con•stan•cy (ĭn-kŏn′stən-sē) *n., pl.* **-cies. 1.** The state or quality of being eccentrically variable or fickle. **2.** An instance of being eccentrically variable or fickle.

in•con•stant (ĭn-kŏn′stənt) *adj.* **1.** Changing or varying, esp. often and without discernible pattern or reason. **2.** Fickle; faithless. **—in•con′stant•ly** *adv.*

in•con•sum•a•ble (ĭn′kən-so͞o′mə-bəl) *adj.* That cannot be consumed. **—in′con•sum′a•bly** *adv.*

in•con•test•a•ble (ĭn′kən-tĕs′tə-bəl) *adj.* Impossible to contest; unquestionable. **—in′con•test′a•bil′i•ty, in′con•test′a•ble•ness** *n.* **—in′con•test′a•bly** *adv.*

in•con•ti•nence (ĭn-kŏn′tə-nəns) *n.* The quality or state of being incontinent.

in•con•ti•nent (ĭn-kŏn′tə-nənt) *adj.* **1.** Not restrained; uncontrolled: *incontinent rage.* **2.** Lacking normal voluntary control of excretory functions. **3.** Lacking sexual restraint; unchaste. **—in•con′ti•nent•ly** *adv.*

in•con•trol•la•ble (ĭn′kən-trō′lə-bəl) *adj.* Being such that control is impossible: *incontrollable rage.*

in•con•tro•vert•i•ble (ĭn-kŏn′trə-vûr′tə-bəl, ĭn′kŏn-) *adj.* Impossible to dispute; unquestionable. **—in•con′tro•vert′i•bil′i•ty, in•con′tro•vert′i•ble•ness** *n.* **—in•con′tro•vert′i•bly** *adv.*

in•con•ven•ience (ĭn′kən-vēn′yəns) *n.* **1.** The state or quality of being inconvenient. **2.** Something inconvenient. **—***tr.v.* **-ienced, -ienc•ing, -ienc•es.** To cause inconvenience to; trouble: *The snow inconvenienced the travelers.*

in•con•ven•ient (ĭn′kən-vēn′yənt) *adj.* Not convenient, esp.: **a.** Not accessible; hard to reach. **b.** Not suited to one's comfort, purpose, or needs. **c.** Inopportune. **—in′con•ven′ient•ly** *adv.*

in•con•vert•i•ble (ĭn′kən-vûr′tə-bəl) *adj.* Not redeemable for money in coin. **—in′con•vert′i•bil′i•ty, in′con•vert′i•ble•ness** *n.* **—in′con•vert′i•bly** *adv.*

in•con•vinc•i•ble (ĭn′kən-vĭn′sə-bəl) *adj.* Not convincible.

in•co•or•di•nate (ĭn′kō-ôr′dn-ĭt, -āt′) *adj.* Lacking coordination; uncoordinated. **—in′co•or′di•nate•ly** *adv.*

in•co•or•di•na•tion (ĭn′kō-ôr′dn-ā′shən) *n.* Lack of coordination, esp. a lack of normal voluntary and harmonious control of muscular movement.

in•cor•po•rate (ĭn-kôr′pə-rāt′) *v.* **-rat•ed, -rat•ing, -rates. —***tr.* **1.** To unite (one thing) with something else already in existence. **2.** To admit as a member to a corporation or similar organization. **3.** To cause to merge or combine together into a united whole. **4.** To cause to form into a legal corporation. **5.** To give substance or material form to; embody. **—***intr.* **1.** To become united or combined into an organized body. **2.** To become or form a legal corporation. **—***adj.* (-pər-ĭt). **1.** Combined into one united body; merged. **2.** Formed into a legal corporation. [ME *incorporaten* < LLat. *incorporāre, incorporāt-,* to form into a body : Lat. *in-,* in; see IN-[2] + Lat. *corpus, corpor-,* body; see CORPUS.] **—in•cor′po•ra•ble** (-pər-ə-bəl) *adj.* **—in•cor′po•ra′tion** *n.* **—in•cor′po•ra′tive** *adj.* **—in•cor′po•ra′tor** *n.*

in•cor•po•rat•ed (ĭn-kôr′pə-rā′tĭd) *adj.* **1.** United into one body; combined. **2.** Formed into or organized and maintained as a legal corporation.

in•cor•po•rat•ing (ĭn-kôr′pə-rā′tĭng) *adj. Ling.* Polysynthetic, as Eskimo or Mohawk.

in•cor•po•re•al (ĭn′kôr-pôr′ē-əl, -pōr′-) *adj.* **1.** Lacking material form or substance. **2.** *Law.* Intangible, as a right or patent. —**in′cor•po′re•al′i•ty** (ăl′ĭ-tē) *n.* —**in′cor•po′re•al•ly** *adv.*

in•cor•po•re•i•ty (ĭn-kôr′pə-rē′ĭ-tē) *n.* The state or quality of being incorporeal; immateriality.

in•cor•rect (ĭn′kə-rĕkt′) *adj.* **1.** Not correct; erroneous or wrong. **2.** Defective; faulty. **3.** Improper; inappropriate. —**in′cor•rect′ly** *adv.* —**in′cor•rect′ness** *n.*

in•cor•ri•gi•ble (ĭn-kôr′ĭ-jə-bəl, -kŏr′-) *adj.* **1.** Incapable of being corrected or reformed. **2.** Firmly rooted; ineradicable: *incorrigible habits.* **3.** Difficult or impossible to control: *an incorrigible child.* —*n.* One that cannot be corrected or reformed. [ME < Lat. *incorrigibilis* : *in-*, not; see IN-[1] + *corrigere*, to correct; see CORRECT.] —**in•cor′ri•gi•bil′i•ty, in•cor′ri•gi•ble•ness** *n.* —**in•cor′ri•gi•bly** *adv.*

in•cor•rupt (ĭn′kə-rŭpt′) *adj.* **1.** Free of corruption or immorality. **2.** Not decayed; unspoiled. **3.** Free of errors or faults. —**in′cor•rupt′ly** *adv.* —**in′cor•rupt′ness** *n.*

in•cor•rupt•i•ble (ĭn′kə-rŭp′tə-bəl) *adj.* **1.** Incapable of being morally corrupted. **2.** Not subject to corruption or decay. —**in′cor•rupt′i•bil′i•ty** *n.* —**in′cor•rupt′i•bly** *adv.*

incr. *abbr.* **1.** Increase. **2.** Incremental.

in•crease (ĭn-krēs′) *v.* **-creased, -creas•ing, -creas•es.** —*intr.* **1.** To become greater or larger. **2.** To multiply; reproduce. —*tr.* To make greater or larger. —*n.* (ĭn′krēs′). **1.** The act or process of increasing. **2.** The amount or rate by which something is increased. **3.** *Obsolete.* Reproduction and spread; propagation. —***idiom.* on the increase.** Increasing, esp. in frequency of occurrence. [ME *encresen* < OFr. *encreistre, encreiss-* < Lat. *incrēscere* : *in-*, intensive pref.; see IN-[2] + *crēscere*, to grow; see **ker-**[2*].] —**in•creas′a•ble** *adj.* —**in•creas′er** *n.* —**in•creas′ing•ly** *adv.*

Syns: *increase, expand, enlarge, extend, augment, multiply.* These verbs mean to make or become greater or larger. *Increase* sometimes suggests steady growth: *"Absence diminishes mediocre passions and increases great ones"* (La Rochefoucauld). To *expand* is to increase in size, area, volume, bulk, or range: *"Work expands so as to fill the time available for its completion"* (C. Northcote Parkinson). *Enlarge* refers to expansion in size, extent, capacity, or scope: *The landowner enlarged her property by repeated purchases.* To *extend* is to lengthen in space or time or to broaden in range: *The baseball season may be extended. Augment* usually applies to what is already developed or well under way: *augmented her collection of books.* To *multiply* is to increase in number, especially by propagation or procreation: *"As for my cats, they multiplied"* (Daniel Defoe).

in•cre•ate (ĭn′krē-āt′, ĭn-krē′ĭt) *adj.* Existing without having been created. [ME *increat* < LLat. *increātus* : Lat. *in-*, not; see IN-[1] + Lat. *creātus*, p.part. of *creāre*, to create; see CREATE.]

in•cred•i•ble (ĭn-krĕd′ə-bəl) *adj.* **1.** So implausible as to elicit disbelief. **2.** Astonishing. —**in•cred′i•bil′i•ty, in•cred′i•ble•ness** *n.* —**in•cred′i•bly** *adv.*

in•cre•du•li•ty (ĭn′krĭ-do͞o′lĭ-tē, -dyo͞o′-) *n.* The state or quality of being incredulous; disbelief.

in•cred•u•lous (ĭn-krĕj′ə-ləs) *adj.* **1.** Skeptical; disbelieving. **2.** Expressive of disbelief: *an incredulous stare.* —**in•cred′u•lous•ly** *adv.* —**in•cred′u•lous•ness** *n.*

in•cre•ment (ĭn′krə-mənt, ĭng′-) *n.* **1.** The process of increasing in number, size, quantity, or extent. **2.** Something added or gained. **3.** A slight, often barely perceptible augmentation. **4.** One of a series of regular additions or contributions: *accumulating a fund by increments.* **5.** *Math.* A small positive or negative change in the value of a variable. [ME < Lat. *incrēmentum* < *incrēscere*, to increase. See INCREASE.] —**in′cre•men′tal** (-mĕn′tl) *adj.* —**in′cre•men′tal•ly** *adv.*

in•cre•men•tal•ism (ĭn′krə-mĕn′tl-ĭz′əm) *n.* Social or political gradualism. —**in′cre•men′tal•ist** *n.*

in•cres•cent (ĭn-krĕs′ənt) *adj.* Showing an ever larger lighted surface; waxing: *the increscent moon.* [Lat. *incrēscēns, incrēscent-*, pr.part. of *incrēscere*, to increase. See INCREASE.]

in•cre•tion (ĭn-krē′shən) *n.* **1.** The process of internal secretion characteristic of endocrine glands. **2.** The product of this process; a hormone. [IN-[2] + (SE)CRETION[1].]

in•crim•i•nate (ĭn-krĭm′ə-nāt′) *tr.v.* **-nat•ed, -nat•ing, -nates. 1.** To accuse of a crime or other wrongful act. **2.** To cause to appear guilty of a crime or fault; implicate. [LLat. *incrīmināre, incrīmināt-* : Lat. *in-*, causative pref.; see IN-[2] + Lat. *crīmen, crīmin-*, crime; see CRIME.] —**in•crim′i•na′tion** *n.* —**in•crim′i•na•to′ry** (-nə-tôr′ē, -tōr′ē) *adj.*

in•crust (ĭn-krŭst′) *v.* Var. of **encrust.**

in•crust•a•tion (ĭn′krŭ-stā′shən) also **en•crust•a•tion** (ĕn′-) *n.* **1.a.** The act of encrusting. **b.** The state of being encrusted. **2.** A material encrusted on a surface. **3.** *Biol.* A coating of hardened exudate or other material on a body or body part; a scab or scale.

in•cu•bate (ĭn′kyə-bāt′, ĭng′-) *v.* **-bat•ed, -bat•ing, -bates.** —*tr.* **1.** To sit on (eggs) to provide heat, promote embryonic development, and hatch the young; brood. **2.** To maintain (living tissue or a chemical system, for example) at suitable conditions for growth and development or for a particular reaction. **3.** To form or consider slowly and protectively, as if hatching: *incubated the idea for a while.* —*intr.* **1.** To brood eggs. **2.** To develop and hatch. **3.** To undergo incubation. [Lat. *incubāre, incubāt-*, to lie down on : *in-*, on; see IN-[2] + *cubāre*, to lie down.] —**in′cu•ba′tive** *adj.*

in•cu•ba•tion (ĭn′kyə-bā′shən, ĭng′-) *n.* **1.a.** The act of incubating. **b.** The state of being incubated. **2.** *Medic.* The development of an infection from the entrance of the pathogen into the body until the appearance of signs or symptoms. **3.** *Medic.* The maintenance of an infant in an incubator. —**in′cu•ba′tion•al** *adj.*

in•cu•ba•tor (ĭn′kyə-bā′tər, ĭng′-) *n.* **1.** An apparatus in which the environment can be controlled, often used for growing suitable bacterial cultures, hatching eggs artificially, or providing suitable conditions for a chemical or biological reaction. **2.** *Medic.* An apparatus for controlling the temperature, humidity, and oxygen level surrounding an infant.

in•cu•bus (ĭn′kyə-bəs, ĭng′-) *n., pl.* **-bus•es** or **-bi** (-bī′). **1.** An evil spirit believed to descend upon and have sexual intercourse with women as they sleep. **2.** A nightmare. **3.** An oppressive or nightmarish burden. [ME < LLat. < Lat. *incubō* < *incubāre*, to lie down on. See INCUBATE.]

in•cu•des (ĭng-kyo͞o′dēz) *n.* Pl. of **incus.**

in•cul•cate (ĭn-kŭl′kāt′, ĭn′kŭl-) *tr.v.* **-cat•ed, -cat•ing, -cates. 1.** To impress (something) upon the mind of another by frequent instruction or repetition; instill: *inculcating sound principles.* **2.** To teach (others) by frequent instruction or repetition; indoctrinate. [Lat. *inculcāre, inculcāt-*, to force upon : *in-*, on; see IN-[2] + *calcāre*, to trample (< *calx, calc-*, heel).] —**in′cul•ca′tion** *n.* —**in•cul′ca′tor** *n.*

in•cul•pa•ble (ĭn-kŭl′pə-bəl) *adj.* Free of guilt; blameless.

in•cul•pate (ĭn-kŭl′pāt′, ĭn′kŭl-) *tr.v.* **-pat•ed, -pat•ing, -pates.** To incriminate. [Lat. *inculpāre, inculpāt-* : *in-*, on; see IN-[2] + *culpāre*, to blame (< *culpa*, fault).] —**in′cul•pa′tion** *n.* —**in•cul′pa•to′ry** (-pə-tôr′ē, -tōr′ē) *adj.*

in•cult (ĭn-kŭlt′) *adj.* Not cultured; coarse. [Lat. *incultus* : *in-*, not; see IN-[1] + *cultus*, p.part. of *colere*, to till; see **k**ʷ**el-**[1*].]

in•cum•ben•cy (ĭn-kŭm′bən-sē) *n., pl.* **-cies. 1.** The quality or condition of being incumbent. **2.** Something incumbent; an obligation. **3.a.** The holding of an office or ecclesiastical benefice. **b.** The term of an office or a benefice.

in•cum•bent (ĭn-kŭm′bənt) *adj.* **1.** Imposed as an obligation or a duty; obligatory. **2.** Lying, leaning, or resting on something else. **3.** Currently holding a specified office. —*n.* A person who holds an office or ecclesiastical benefice. [ME, holder of an office < Med.Lat. *incumbēns, incumbent-* < Lat., pr.part. of *incumbere*, to lean upon : *in-*, on; see IN-[2] + *-cumbere*, to recline.] —**in•cum′bent•ly** *adv.*

in•cu•na•ble (ĭn-kyo͞o′nə-bəl) *n.* An incunabulum. [Fr. < NLat. *incūnābulum.* See INCUNABULUM.]

in•cu•nab•u•lum (ĭn′kyə-năb′yə-ləm, ĭng′-) *n., pl.* **-la** (-lə). **1.** A book printed before 1501. **2.** An artifact of an early period. [NLat. *incūnābulum* < sing. of Lat. *incūnābula*, swaddling clothes : *in-*, in; see IN-[2] + *cūnābula*, infancy (< *cūnae*, cradle; see **kei-**[1*]).] —**in′cu•nab′u•lar** (-lər) *adj.*

in•cur (ĭn-kûr′) *tr.v.* **-curred, -cur•ring, -curs. 1.** To acquire or come into (something usu. undesirable); sustain. **2.** To become subject to as a result of one's actions; bring upon oneself. [ME *incurren* < OFr. *encorir* < Lat. *incurrere*, to run upon : *in-*, on; see IN-[2] + *currere*, to run; see **kers-***.]

in•cur•a•ble (ĭn-kyo͝or′ə-bəl) *adj.* **1.** Impossible to cure: *an incurable disease.* **2.** Impossible to alter, as in disposition or habits: *an incurable optimist.* —**in•cur′a•bil′i•ty, in•cur′a•ble•ness** *n.* —**in•cur′a•ble** *n.* —**in•cur′a•bly** *adv.*

in•cu•ri•ous (ĭn-kyo͝or′ē-əs) *adj.* Lacking curiosity; uninterested. —**in•cu′ri•os′i•ty** (-ŏs′ĭ-tē), **in•cu′ri•ous•ness** *n.* —**in•cu′ri•ous•ly** *adv.*

in•cur•rent (ĭn-kûr′ənt, -kŭr′-) *adj.* Affording passage to an inflowing current. [Lat. *incurrēns, incurrent-*, pr.part. of *incurrere*, to run upon. See INCUR.]

in•cur•sion (ĭn-kûr′zhən, -shən) *n.* **1.** A raid or invasion into foreign territory. **2.** The act of entering another's territory or domain. **3.** The act of entering or running into. [ME < OFr. < Lat. *incursiō, incursiōn-* < *incursus*, p.part. of *incurrere*, to run upon. See INCUR.]

in•cur•vate (ĭn-kûr′vāt′, ĭn′kûr-) *tr.v.* **-vat•ed, -vat•ing, -vates.** To cause to bend into an inward curve. —*adj.* Curved inward. —**in′cur•va′tion** *n.* —**in•cur′va•ture′** *n.*

in•curve (ĭn-kûrv′, ĭn′kûrv′) *tr. & intr.v.* **-curved, -curv•ing, -curves.** To cause to bend or to bend into an inward curve. —*n.* (ĭn′kûrv′). An inward curve. [ME *incurven*, to twist, distort < Lat. *incurvāre*, to curve in, be crooked : *in-*, in; see IN-[2] + *curvus*, curve; see CURVE.]

in•cus (ĭng′kəs) *n., pl.* **in•cu•des** (ĭng-kyo͞o′dēz). **1.** *Anat.* An anvil-shaped bone between the malleus and the stapes in the mammalian middle ear. **2.** A thunderhead. [Lat. *incūs, incūd-*, anvil < *incūsus*, p.part. of *incūdere*, to forge with a hammer : *in-*, intensive pref.; see IN-[2] + *cūdere*, to beat, forge; see **kau-***.]

in•cuse (ĭn-kyo͞oz′, -kyo͞os′) *adj.* Formed by hammering, stamping, or pressing: *an incuse design on a coin.* [Lat. *incūdere, incūs-*, to forge with a hammer. See INCUS.]

incuse
1793 copper penny

ă pat	oi boy
ā pay	ou out
âr care	o͝o took
ä father	o͞o boot
ĕ pet	ŭ cut
ē be	ûr urge
ĭ pit	th thin
ī pie	*th* this
îr pier	hw which
ŏ pot	zh vision
ō toe	ə about,
ô paw	item

Stress marks:
′ (primary);
′ (secondary), as in
dictionary (dĭk′shə-nĕr′ē)

ind. *abbr.* **1.** Independence; independent. **2.** Index. **3.** Indigo. **4.** Industrial; industry.

Ind. *abbr.* **1.** Indian. **2.** Indiana. **3.** Indies.

in•da•mine (ĭn′də-mēn′) *n.* Any of a group of organic bases forming unstable bluish or greenish salts and used in making dyes. [IND(IGO) + AMINE.]

in•debt•ed (ĭn-dĕt′ĭd) *adj.* Morally, socially, or legally obligated to another; beholden. [ME *endetted* < OFr. *endette,* p.part. of *endetter,* to oblige : *en-,* causative pref.; see EN-[1] + *dette,* debt; see DEBT.]

in•debt•ed•ness (ĭn-dĕt′ĭd-nĭs) *n.* **1.** The state of being indebted. **2.** Something owed to another.

in•de•cen•cy (ĭn-dē′sən-sē) *n., pl.* **-cies. 1.** The state or quality of being unseemly or immodest. **2.** Something indecent.

in•de•cent (ĭn-dē′sənt) *adj.* **1.** Offensive to good taste; unseemly. **2.** Offensive to public morals; immodest. **—in•de′cent•ly** *adv.*

in•de•ci•pher•a•ble (ĭn′dĭ-sī′fər-ə-bəl) *adj.* Impossible to decipher. **—in′de•ci′pher•a•bil′i•ty, in′de•ci′pher•a•ble•ness** *n.* **—in′de•ci′pher•a•bly** *adv.*

in•de•ci•sion (ĭn′dĭ-sĭzh′ən) *n.* Reluctance or an inability to make up one's mind; irresolution.

in•de•ci•sive (ĭn′dĭ-sī′sĭv) *adj.* **1.** Prone to or characterized by indecision; irresolute. **2.** Inconclusive: *an indecisive battle.* **3.** Not clearly defined; indefinite: *indecisive boundaries.* **—in′de•ci′sive•ly** *adv.* **—in′de•ci′sive•ness** *n.*

in•de•clin•a•ble (ĭn′dĭ-klī′nə-bəl) *adj.* **1.** Without grammatical inflection. **2.** Of, relating to, or being a word that lacks grammatical inflection though belonging to a form class whose members are usu. inflected.

in•de•com•pos•a•ble (ĭn-dē′kəm-pō′zə-bəl) *adj.* That cannot be separated into components: *indecomposable matter.*

in•dec•o•rous (ĭn-dĕk′ər-əs) *adj.* Lacking propriety or good taste. **—in•dec′o•rous•ly** *adv.* **—in•dec′o•rous•ness** *n.*

in•de•cor•um (ĭn′dĭ-kôr′əm, -kōr′-) *n.* **1.** Lack of propriety or good taste; impropriety. **2.** An instance of such behavior.

in•deed (ĭn-dēd′) *adv.* **1.** Without a doubt; certainly: *very cold indeed.* **2.** In fact; in reality. *—interj.* Used to express surprise, skepticism, or irony. [ME *in dede,* in fact : *in,* in; see IN[1] + *dede,* deed, fact; see DEED.]

indef. *abbr.* Indefinite.

in•de•fat•i•ga•ble (ĭn′dĭ-făt′ĭ-gə-bəl) *adj.* Incapable or seemingly incapable of being fatigued; tireless. [Obsolete Fr. *indéfatigable* < Lat. *indēfatīgābilis* : < *in-,* not; see IN-[1] + *dēfatīgāre,* to tire out (*dē-,* intensive pref.; see DE- + *fatīgāre,* to weary).] **—in′de•fat′i•ga•bil′i•ty, in′de•fat′i•ga•ble•ness** *n.* **—in′de•fat′i•ga•bly** *adv.*

in•de•fea•si•ble (ĭn′dĭ-fē′zə-bəl) *adj.* That cannot be annulled or made void: *an indefeasible claim.* **—in′de•fea′si•bil′i•ty** *n.* **—in′de•fea′si•bly** *adv.*

in•de•fec•ti•ble (ĭn′dĭ-fĕk′tə-bəl) *adj.* **1.** Having the ability to resist decay or failure; lasting. **2.** Having no flaw or defect; perfect. **—in′de•fec′ti•bil′i•ty** *n.* **—in′de•fec′ti•bly** *adv.*

in•de•fen•si•ble (ĭn′dĭ-fĕn′sə-bəl) *adj.* **1.** Inexcusable; unpardonable. **2.** Invalid; untenable. **3.** Vulnerable to physical attack. **—in′de•fen′si•bil′i•ty, in′de•fen′si•ble•ness** *n.* **—in′de•fen′si•bly** *adv.*

India

in•de•fin•a•ble (ĭn′dĭ-fī′nə-bəl) *adj.* Impossible to define, describe, or analyze: *an indefinable quality.* *—n.* One that is indefinable. **—in′de•fin′a•bil′i•ty, in′de•fin′a•ble•ness** *n.* **—in′de•fin′a•bly** *adv.*

in•def•i•nite (ĭn-dĕf′ə-nĭt) *adj.* Not definite, esp.: **a.** Unclear; vague. **b.** Lacking precise limits. **c.** Uncertain; undecided. **—in•def′i•nite•ly** *adv.* **—in•def′i•nite•ness** *n.*

indefinite article *n. Gram.* An article, such as English *a* or *an,* that does not fix the identity of the noun modified.

indefinite integral *n. Math.* A function whose derivative is a given function.

indefinite pronoun *n. Gram.* A pronoun, such as English *any* or *some,* that does not specify the identity of its object.

in•de•his•cent (ĭn′dĭ-hĭs′ənt) *adj. Bot.* Not splitting open at maturity: *indehiscent fruit.* **—in′de•his′cence** *n.*

in•del•i•ble (ĭn-dĕl′ə-bəl) *adj.* **1.** Impossible to remove, erase, or wash away; permanent: *indelible ink.* **2.** Making a mark not easily erased or washed away: *an indelible pen.* [Lat. *indēlēbilis* : *in-,* not; see IN-[1] + *dēlēbilis,* capable of being effaced (< *dēlēre,* to wipe out).] **—in•del′i•bil′i•ty, in•del′i•ble•ness** *n.* **—in•del′i•bly** *adv.*

in•del•i•ca•cy (ĭn-dĕl′ĭ-kə-sē) *n., pl.* **-cies. 1.** The quality or condition of being indelicate. **2.** Something indelicate.

in•del•i•cate (ĭn-dĕl′ĭ-kĭt) *adj.* **1.** Offensive to established standards of propriety; improper. **2.** Marked by a lack of good taste; coarse. **3.** Lacking in consideration for the feelings of others; tactless. **—in•del′i•cate•ly** *adv.* **—in•del′i•cate•ness** *n.*

in•dem•ni•fi•ca•tion (ĭn-dĕm′nə-fĭ-kā′shən) *n.* **1.a.** The act of indemnifying. **b.** The condition of being indemnified. **2.** Something that indemnifies; a compensation for loss.

in•dem•ni•fy (ĭn-dĕm′nə-fī′) *tr.v.* **-fied, -fy•ing, -fies. 1.** To protect against damage, loss, or injury; insure. **2.** To make compensation to for damage, loss, or injury suffered. [Lat. *indemnis,* uninjured (*in-,* not; see IN-[1] + *damnum,* harm, damage entailing liability) + -FY.] **—in•dem′ni•fi′er** *n.*

in•dem•ni•ty (ĭn-dĕm′nĭ-tē) *n., pl.* **-ties. 1.** Security against damage, loss, or injury. **2.** A legal exemption from liability for damages. **3.** Compensation for damage, loss, or injury suffered. [ME *indempnite* < AN < LLat. *indemnitās* < Lat. *indemnis,* uninjured. See INDEMNIFY.]

in•de•mon•stra•ble (ĭn′dĭ-mŏn′strə-bəl) *adj.* Impossible to prove or demonstrate. **—in′de•mon′stra•ble•ness, in′de•mon′stra•bil′i•ty** *n.* **—in′de•mon′stra•bly** *adv.*

in•dene (ĭn′dēn′) *n.* An organic liquid, C_9H_8, obtained from coal tar and used in preparing synthetic resins. [IND(OLE) + -ENE.]

in•dent[1] (ĭn-dĕnt′) *v.* **-dent•ed, -dent•ing, -dents.** *—tr.* **1.** *Print.* To set (the first line of a paragraph, for example) in from the margin. **2.a.** To cut or tear (a document with two or more copies) along an irregular line so that the parts can later be matched for establishing authenticity. **b.** To draw up (a document) in duplicate or triplicate. **3.a.** To notch or serrate the edge of; make jagged. **b.** To make notches, grooves, or holes in (wood, for example) for the purpose of mortising. **c.** To fit or join together by or as if by mortising. **4.** *Chiefly British.* To order (goods) with an indent. *—intr.* **1.** To make or form an indentation. **2.** *Chiefly British.* To draw up or order an indent. *—n.* (ĭn-dĕnt′, ĭn′dĕnt′). **1.** The act of indenting or the condition of being indented. **2.** *Print.* A blank space before the beginning of an indented line. **3.** An indenture. **4.** *Chiefly British.* An official requisition or purchase order for goods. [ME *endenten,* to notch < AN and OFr. *endenter,* both < Med.Lat. *indentāre* : Lat. *in-,* in; see IN-[2] + Lat. *dēns, dent-,* tooth; see **dent-***.]

in•dent[2] (ĭn-dĕnt′) *tr.v.* **-dent•ed, -dent•ing, -dents. 1.** To make a dent in. **2.** To impress (a design, for example); stamp. *—n.* (ĭn-dĕnt′, ĭn′dĕnt′). An indentation.

in•den•ta•tion (ĭn′dĕn-tā′shən) *n.* **1.a.** The act of indenting. **b.** The condition of being indented. **2.** *Print.* The blank space between a margin and the beginning of an indented line. **3.** A notch or jagged cut in an edge. **4.** A recess, as in a border or coastline.

in•den•tion (ĭn-dĕn′shən) *n.* **1.a.** The act of indenting. **b.** The condition of being indented. **2.** *Print.* The blank space between a margin and the beginning of an indented line. **3.** *Archaic.* An indentation or a dent.

in•den•ture (ĭn-dĕn′chər) *n.* **1.** A contract binding one party into the service of another for a specified term. Often used in the plural. **2.a.** A document in duplicate having indented edges. **b.** A deed or legal contract executed between two or more parties. **c.** An official or authenticated inventory, list, or voucher. **3.** Indentation. *—tr.v.* **-tured, -tur•ing, -tures. 1.** To bind into the service of another by indenture. **2.** *Archaic.* To form a small depression in (a surface). [ME *endenture,* a written agreement < AN < *endenter,* to indent (from the matching notches on multiple copies of the documents). See INDENT[1].]

in•de•pend•ence (ĭn′dĭ-pĕn′dəns) *n.* **1.** The state or quality of being independent. **2.** *Archaic.* Sufficient income for comfortable self-support; a competence.

In•de•pend•ence (ĭn′dĭ-pĕn′dəns). A city of W MO, a suburb of Kansas City. Pop. 112,301.

Independence Day *n.* July 4, celebrated in the United States to commemorate the adoption in 1776 of the Declaration of Independence.

in•de•pend•en•cy (ĭn′dĭ-pĕn′dən-sē) *n., pl.* **-cies. 1.** Independence. **2.** An independent territory or state. **3. Independency.** The Independent movement in 17th-century England.

in•de•pend•ent (ĭn′dĭ-pĕn′dənt) *adj.* **1.** Not governed by a foreign power; self-governing. **2.** Free from the influence, guidance, or control of another or others; self-reliant. **3.** Not determined or influenced by someone or something else; not contingent. **4.** Often **Independent.** Affiliated with or loyal to no one political party or organization. **5.** Not dependent on or affiliated with a larger or controlling group or system. **6.a.** Not relying on others for support, care, or funds; self-supporting. **b.** Providing or being sufficient income to enable one to live without working. **7.** *Math.* **a.** Not dependent on other variables. **b.** Of or relating to a system of equations no one of which can be derived from another equation in the system. **8. Independent.** Of or relating to the 17th-century English Independents. *—n.* **1.** Often **Independent.** One that is independent, esp. a voter, an officeholder, or a political candidate not committed to a political party. **2. Independent.** A member of a movement in England in the 17th century advocating the political and religious independence of individual congregations. **3. Independent.** *Chiefly British.* A Congregationalist.

independent clause *n. Gram.* See **main clause.**

independent variable *n.* **1.** *Math.* A variable whose value determines the value of other variables. **2.** *Statistics.* A manipulated variable in an experiment or a study whose presence or degree determines the change in the dependent variable.

in-depth (ĭn′dĕpth′) *adj.* Detailed; thorough.

in•de•scrib•a•ble (ĭn′dĭ-skrī′bə-bəl) *adj.* **1.** Impossible to describe: *indescribable views.* **2.** Exceeding description.

— **in′de•scrib′a•bil′i•ty, in′de•scrib′a•ble•ness** *n.* — **in′-de•scrib′a•bly** *adv.*

in•de•struc•ti•ble (ĭn′dĭ-strŭk′tə-bəl) *adj.* Impossible to destroy. — **in′de•struc′ti•bil′i•ty, in′de•struc′ti•ble•ness** *n.* — **in′de•struc′ti•bly** *adv.*

in•de•ter•min•a•ble (ĭn′dĭ-tûr′mə-nə-bəl) *adj.* **1.** Impossible to fix or measure. **2.** Impossible to settle or decide: *indeterminable questions.* — **in′de•ter′min•a•bly** *adv.*

in•de•ter•mi•na•cy (ĭn′dĭ-tûr′mə-nə-sē) *n.* The state or quality of being indeterminate.

in•de•ter•mi•nate (ĭn′dĭ-tûr′mə-nĭt) *adj.* **1.a.** Not precisely determined, determinable, or established. **b.** Not precisely fixed, as to extent, size, nature, or number. **c.** Lacking clarity or precision, as in meaning; vague. **d.** Not fixed or known in advance. **e.** Not leading up to a definite result or ending. **2.** *Bot.* Continuing to grow at the apex and not terminating in a flower. — **in′de•ter′mi•nate•ly** *adv.* — **in′de•ter′mi•nate•ness, in′de•ter′mi•na′tion** (-nā′shən) *n.*

indeterminate vowel *n. Ling.* See **schwa** 1.

in•de•ter•min•ism (ĭn′dĭ-tûr′mə-nĭz′əm) *n.* **1.** Unpredictability. **2.** *Philos.* The doctrine that the will is free and that human action is not necessarily or not at all predetermined by physiological and psychological antecedents. — **in′de•ter′-min•ist** *n.* — **in′de•ter′min•is′tic** *adj.*

in•dex (ĭn′dĕks′) *n., pl.* **-dex•es** or **-di•ces** (-dĭ-sēz′). **1.** Something that serves to guide, point out, or facilitate reference, esp.: **a.** An alphabetized list of names, places, and subjects in a printed work, giving the page or pages on which each item is mentioned. **b.** A thumb index. **c.** A table, file, or catalog. **2.** Something that reveals or indicates; a sign. **3.** *Print.* A character (☞) used in printing to call attention to a particular paragraph or section. **4.** An indicator or a pointer, as on a scientific instrument. **5.a.** *Math.* A number or symbol, often written as a subscript or superscript, that indicates an operation to be performed on, an ordering relation involving, or a use of its associated expression. **b.** A number derived from a formula, used to characterize a set of data. **6. Index.** *Rom. Cath. Ch.* A list formerly published by Church authority, restricting or forbidding the reading of certain books. — *tr.v.* **-dexed, -dex•ing, -dex•es. 1.** To furnish with an index: *index a book.* **2.** To enter in an index. **3.** To indicate or signal. **4.** To adjust through indexation. [ME, forefinger < Lat. See **deik-*.**] — **in′dex′er** *n.*

in•dex•a•tion (ĭn′dĕk-sā′shən) *n.* The automatic adjustment of an economic variable, such as wages, taxes, or pension benefits, to a cost-of-living index, so that the variable rises or falls in accordance with the rate of inflation.

index finger *n.* The finger next to the thumb.

index fossil *n.* The fossil remains of an organism that lived in a particular geologic age, used to identify or date the rock or rock layer in which it is found.

index of refraction *n.* The ratio of the speed of light in a vacuum to the speed of light in a given medium.

In•di•a (ĭn′dē-ə). **1.** A peninsula and subcontinent of S Asia S of the Himalaya Mts. **2.** A country of S Asia; site of one of the oldest civilizations in the world, centered in the Indus R. valley c. 2500 to 1500 B.C. India gained independence from Great Britain in 1947. Cap. New Delhi. Pop. 685,184,692.

India ink *n.* **1.** A black pigment made from lampblack mixed with a binding agent and molded into cakes or sticks. **2.** A liquid ink made from this pigment.

In•di•a•man (ĭn′dē-ə-mən) *n. Naut.* A large merchant ship formerly used on trade routes to India.

In•di•an (ĭn′dē-ən) *adj.* **1.** Of or relating to India or the East Indies or to their peoples, languages, or cultures. **2.** Of or relating to any of the Native American peoples. — *n.* **1.** A native or inhabitant of India or the East Indies. **2.** See **Native American.** See Usage Note at **Native American. 3.** Any of the languages of the Native Americans. **4.** See **Indus**[2].

In•di•an•a (ĭn′dē-ăn′ə). A state of the N-central U.S.; admitted as the 19th state in 1816. The area was controlled by France until 1763 and by Great Britain until 1783. Cap. Indianapolis. Pop. 5,564,228. — **In′di•an′an, In′di•an′i•an** *adj. & n.*

In•di•an•ap•o•lis (ĭn′dē-ə-năp′ə-lĭs). The cap. of IN, in the central part; settled in 1820. Pop. 741,952.

Indian bean *n.* See **catalpa.**

Indian bread *n.* Any of various edible plants, such as the breadroot, used by certain Native American peoples for food.

Indian club *n. Sports.* A bottle-shaped wooden club swung in the hand for gymnastic exercise.

Indian corn *n.* See **corn**[1] 1.

Indian currant *n.* See **coralberry.**

Indian file *n.* See **single file.** — **Indian file** *adv.*

Indian giver *n. Offensive.* One who gives something to another and then takes or demands the gift back.

Indian hemp *n.* Cannabis.

Indian licorice *n.* See **rosary pea.**

Indian mallow *n.* See **flowering maple.**

Indian meal *n.* See **cornmeal.**

Indian mustard *n.* An annual plant *(Brassica juncea)* in the mustard family, having yellow flowers and oil-rich seeds.

Indian Ocean. A body of water extending from S Asia to Antarctica and from E Africa to SE Australia.

Indian paintbrush *n.* Any of various partly parasitic plants of the genus *Castilleja,* having spikes of flowers surrounded by showy, brightly colored bracts.

Indian pipe *n.* A waxy white or sometimes pinkish saprophytic woodland plant *(Monotropa uniflora)* having scalelike leaves and a solitary nodding flower.

Indian pony *n.* A small hardy horse of western North America, often used for crossbreeding.

Indian pudding *n. New England.* A pudding consisting of milk, cornmeal, egg, and molasses baked for several hours in a heavy casserole. [< INDIAN (MEAL).]

Indian red *n.* An iron oxide used as a paint and pigment.

Indian River. A lagoon extending c. 265 km (165 mi) along the coast of E-central FL.

Indian summer *n.* **1.** A period of mild weather occurring in late autumn. **2.** A pleasant, tranquil, or flourishing period occurring near the end of something.

Indian Territory. A region of the S-central U.S. mainly in present-day OK; set aside by the government as a homeland for forcibly displaced Native Americans in 1834.

Indian tobacco *n.* A poisonous North American plant *(Lobelia inflata)* having light blue to white flowers and rounded seedpods enclosed by an inflated persistent calyx.

Indian turnip *n. Midland U.S.* See **jack-in-the-pulpit.**

Indian wrestling *n. Sports.* **1.** A form of wrestling in which two opponents, lying supine in reversed position, lock their near arms, raise and lock their near legs, and attempt to force the other's leg down. **2.** A form of wrestling in which two opponents stand facing each other with usually right hands interlocked and the outsides of their near feet set together and attempt to unbalance each other.

India paper *n.* **1.** A thin uncoated delicate paper made of vegetable fiber, used esp. for taking impressions of engravings. **2.** See **Bible paper.**

India rubber *n.* See **rubber**[1] 1.

In•dic (ĭn′dĭk) *adj.* **1.** Of or relating to India or its peoples or cultures. **2.** Of, relating to, or constituting Indic. — *n.* A branch of the Indo-European language family that comprises the languages of the Indian subcontinent and Sri Lanka.

indic. *abbr.* **1.** *Gram.* Indicative. **2.** Indicator.

in•di•can (ĭn′dĭ-kăn′) *n.* **1.** A potassium salt, $C_8H_6NO_4SK$, in sweat and urine, formed by the conversion of tryptophan to indole by intestinal bacteria. **2.** A glucoside, $C_{14}H_{17}NO_6$, occurring in the indigo plant and a source of indigo dye. [Lat. *indicum,* indigo; see INDIGO + -AN[2].]

in•di•cant (ĭn′dĭ-kənt) *n.* Something, such as a typographical device, that serves to indicate.

in•di•cate (ĭn′dĭ-kāt′) *tr.v.* **-cat•ed, -cat•ing, -cates. 1.** To show the way to or the direction of; point out. **2.** To serve as a sign, symptom, or token of; signify. **3.** To suggest or demonstrate the necessity, expedience, or advisability of. **4.** To state or express briefly. [Lat. *indicāre, indicāt-,* to show < *index,* forefinger, indicator. See **deik-*.**] — **in′di•ca•to′ry** (-kə-tôr′ē, -tōr′ē) *adj.*

in•di•ca•tion (ĭn′dĭ-kā′shən) *n.* **1.** The act of indicating. **2.** Something that serves to indicate; a sign. **3.** Something indicated as necessary or expedient. **4.** The degree indicated by a measuring instrument.

in•dic•a•tive (ĭn-dĭk′ə-tĭv) *adj.* **1.** Serving to indicate. **2.** *Gram.* Of, relating to, or being the mood of the verb used in ordinary objective statements. — *n. Gram.* **1.** The indicative mood. **2.** A verb in this mood. — **in•dic′a•tive•ly** *adv.*

in•di•ca•tor (ĭn′dĭ-kā′tər) *n.* **1.** One that indicates, esp.: **a.** A pointer or an index. **b.** An instrument used to monitor the operation or condition of an engine, an electrical network, or another physical system; a meter or gauge. **c.** The needle, dial, or other registering device on such an instrument. **2.** *Chem.* Any of various substances, such as litmus, that indicate the presence or concentration of another substance or the degree of a reaction by means of a characteristic change, esp. in color. **3.** Any of various statistical values that together provide an indication of the condition or direction of the economy.

in•di•ces (ĭn′dĭ-sēz′) *n.* Pl. of **index.**

in•di•cia (ĭn-dĭsh′ə, -dĭsh′ē-ə) *pl.n.* **1.** Identifying marks; indications. **2.** Markings on bulk mailings used as a substitute for stamps or cancellations. [Lat., pl. of *indicium,* sign < *index, indic-,* indicator. See INDEX.]

in•dict (ĭn-dīt′) *tr.v.* **-dict•ed, -dict•ing, -dicts. 1.** To accuse of wrongdoing; charge. **2.** *Law.* To make a formal accusation or indictment against (a party) by the findings of a jury, esp. a grand jury. [Alteration of ME *enditen.* See INDITE.] — **in′dict•ee′** (ĭn′dī-tē′) *n.* — **in•dict′er, in•dict′or** *n.*

in•dict•a•ble (ĭn-dī′tə-bəl) *adj.* **1.** Capable of being indicted: *indictable for the crime.* **2.** Making one liable to indictment.

in•dic•tion (ĭn-dĭk′shən) *n.* A 15-year cycle used as a chronological unit in ancient Rome and incorporated in some medieval systems. [ME *indiccioun* < LLat. *indictiō, indictiōn-,* proclamation, period of 15 years < Lat. *indictus,* p.part. of *indīcere,* to proclaim : *in-,* toward; see IN-[2] + *dīcere,* to say; see INDITE.]

Indian club

Indian tobacco
Lobelia inflata

ă pat | oi boy
ā pay | ou out
âr care | o͝o took
ä father | o͞o boot
ĕ pet | ŭ cut
ē be | ûr urge
ĭ pit | th thin
ī pie | *th* this
îr pier | hw which
ŏ pot | zh vision
ō toe | ə about, item
ô paw |

Stress marks:
′ (primary);
′ (secondary), as in dictionary (dĭk′shə-nĕr′ē)

in•dict•ment (ĭn-dīt′mənt) *n.* **1.a.** The act of indicting. **b.** The condition of being indicted. **2.** *Law.* A written statement charging a party with committing an offense, drawn up by a prosecuting attorney and found and presented by a grand jury.

In•dies (ĭn′dēz). **1.** See **East Indies. 2.** See **West Indies.**

in•dif•fer•ence (ĭn-dĭf′ər-əns, -dĭf′rəns) *n.* The state or quality of being indifferent.

in•dif•fer•en•cy (ĭn-dĭf′ər-ən-sē, -dĭf′rən-) *n. Archaic.* Indifference.

in•dif•fer•ent (ĭn-dĭf′ər-ənt, -dĭf′rənt) *adj.* **1.** Characterized by a lack of partiality; unbiased. **2.** Not mattering one way or the other. **3.** Having no marked feeling for or against. **4.** Having no particular interest in or concern for; apathetic. **5.** Being neither too much nor too little; moderate. **6.** Being neither good nor bad; mediocre. See Syns at **average. 7.** Being neither right nor wrong. **8.** Not active or involved; neutral: *an indifferent chemical in a reaction.* **9.** *Biol.* Undifferentiated, as cells or tissue. **— in•dif′fer•ent•ly** *adv.*

in•dif•fer•ent•ism (ĭn-dĭf′ər-ən-tĭz′əm, -dĭf′rən-) *n.* The belief that all religions are equally valid.

in•di•gen (ĭn′dĭ-jən, -jĕn′) also **in•di•gene** (-jən, -jēn′) *n.* One that is native or indigenous to an area. [Fr. *indigène,* native, a native < Lat. *indigena.* See **genə-*.**]

in•di•gence (ĭn′dĭ-jəns) *n.* Poverty; neediness.

in•dig•e•nous (ĭn-dĭj′ə-nəs) *adj.* **1.** Originating and growing or living in an area or environment. **2.** Intrinsic; innate. [< Lat. *indigena,* a native. See INDIGEN.] **— in•dig′e•nous•ly** *adv.* **— in•dig′e•nous•ness** *n.*

in•di•gent (ĭn′dĭ-jənt) *adj.* **1.** Experiencing want or need; impoverished. See Syns at **poor. 2.** *Archaic.* Lacking or deficient. *— n.* A needy or destitute person. [ME < OFr. < Lat. *indigēns, indigent-,* pr.part. of *indigēre,* to need : *indu-,* in; see **en*** + *egēre,* to lack.] **— in′di•gent•ly** *adv.*

in•di•gest•ed (ĭn′dĭ-jĕs′tĭd, -dī-) *adj.* **1.** Not digested; undigested: *indigested food.* **2.** *Archaic.* **a.** Not carefully thought over or considered. **b.** Formless or shapeless.

in•di•gest•i•ble (ĭn′dĭ-jĕs′tə-bəl, -dī-) *adj.* Difficult or impossible to digest: *an indigestible meal.* **— in′di•gest′i•bil′i•ty** *n.* **— in′di•gest′i•bly** *adv.*

in•di•ges•tion (ĭn′dĭ-jĕs′chən, -dī-) *n.* **1.** Inability to digest or difficulty in digesting something, esp. food. **2.** Discomfort or illness resulting from this inability or difficulty.

In•di•gir•ka (ĭn′dĭ-gîr′kə). A river of NE Russia flowing c. 1,789 km (1,112 mi) to the East Siberian Sea.

in•dign (ĭn-dīn′) *adj.* **1.** *Archaic.* Unworthy. **2.** *Obsolete.* Shameful; disgraceful. [ME *indigne* < OFr. < Lat. *indignus* : *in-,* not; see IN-[1] + *dignus,* worthy; see **dek-*.**]

in•dig•nant (ĭn-dĭg′nənt) *adj.* Characterized by or filled with indignation. [Lat. *indignāns, indignant-,* pr.part. of *indignārī,* to be indignant < *indignus,* unworthy. See INDIGN.] **— in•dig′nant•ly** *adv.*

in•dig•na•tion (ĭn′dĭg-nā′shən) *n.* Anger aroused by something unjust, mean, or unworthy. See Syns at **anger.** [ME *indignacioun* < OFr. *indignation* < Lat. *indignātiō, indignātiōn-* < *indignātus,* p.part. of *indignārī,* to regard as unworthy < *indignus,* unworthy. See INDIGN.]

in•dig•ni•ty (ĭn-dĭg′nĭ-tē) *n., pl.* **-ties. 1.** Humiliating, degrading, or abusive treatment. **2.** A source of offense, as to a person's pride or sense of dignity; an affront. **3.** *Obsolete.* Lack of dignity or honor. [Fr. *indignité* < OFr. < Lat. *indignitās* < *indignus,* unworthy. See INDIGN.]

in•di•go (ĭn′dĭ-gō′) *n., pl.* **-gos** or **-goes. 1.a.** Any of various shrubs or herbs of the genus *Indigofera* in the pea family, having odd-pinnate leaves and usu. red or purple flowers in axillary racemes. **b.** A blue dye obtained from these plants or produced synthetically. **2.** Any of several related plants, esp. those of the genera *Amorpha* or *Baptisia.* **3.** *Color.* The hue of that portion of the visible spectrum lying between blue and violet, evoked in the human observer by radiant energy with wavelengths of approximately 420 to 450 nanometers; a dark blue to grayish purple blue. [Sp. *índigo* and Du. *indigo* (< Port. *endego*), both < Lat. *indicum* < Gk. *Indikon (pharmakon),* Indian (dye) < neut. of *Indikos,* of India < *India,* India < *Indos,* the Indus R. < OPers. *Hindu.* See HINDI.] **— in′di•go′** *adj.*

indigo bunting *n.* A finch *(Passerina cyanea)* of North and Central America, the male of which has deep blue plumage.

indigo snake *n.* A nonvenomous bluish-black snake *(Drymarchon corais)* of southern North America.

in•dig•o•tin (ĭn-dĭg′ə-tĭn, ĭn′dĭ-gō′-) *n.* A dark blue crystalline compound, $C_{16}H_{10}N_2O_2$, the principal coloring matter of indigo. [INDIGO + -IN.]

In•di•o (ĭn′dē-ō′). A city of SE CA E of Santa Ana. Pop. 36,793.

in•di•rect (ĭn′dĭ-rĕkt′, -dī-) *adj.* **1.** Diverging from a direct course; roundabout. **2.a.** Not proceeding straight to the point or object. **b.** Not forthright and candid; devious. **3.** Not directly planned for; secondary: *indirect benefits.* **4.** Reporting the words of another with the changes necessary to bring the original statement into grammatical conformity with the sentence in which it is included: *indirect discourse.* **5.** *Logic.* Involving, relating to, or being the proof of a statement by the demonstration of the impossibility or absurdity of the statement's negation. **— in′di•rect′ly** *adv.* **— in′di•rect′ness** *n.*

in•di•rec•tion (ĭn′dĭ-rĕk′shən, -dī-) *n.* **1.** The quality or state of being indirect. **2.a.** Lack of straightforwardness; deviousness. **b.** A devious act or statement. **3.** Lack of direction; aimlessness.

indirect lighting *n.* Illumination by reflected or diffused light.

indirect object *n. Gram.* An object indirectly affected by the action of a verb, as *me* in *Sing me a song.*

indirect tax *n.* A tax levied on goods or services that is ultimately paid by consumers in the form of higher prices.

in•dis•cern•i•ble (ĭn′dĭ-sûr′nə-bəl, -zûr′-) *adj.* Difficult or impossible to discern or perceive; imperceptible. **— in′dis•cern′i•bly** *adv.*

in•dis•ci•pline (ĭn-dĭs′ə-plĭn) *n.* Lack of discipline or restraint. **— in•dis′ci•plined** *adj.*

in•dis•creet (ĭn′dĭ-skrēt′) *adj.* Lacking discretion; injudicious. **— in′dis•creet′ly** *adv.* **— in′dis•creet′ness** *n.*

in•dis•crete (ĭn′dĭ-skrēt′) *adj.* Not divided or divisible into separate parts: *layers that were fused into an indiscrete mass.*

in•dis•cre•tion (ĭn′dĭ-skrĕsh′ən) *n.* **1.** Lack of discretion; injudiciousness. **2.** An indiscreet act or remark.

in•dis•crim•i•nate (ĭn′dĭ-skrĭm′ə-nĭt) *adj.* **1.** Not making or based on careful distinctions; unselective. **2.** Random; haphazard. **3.** Confused; chaotic. **4.** Unrestrained or wanton; profligate: *indiscriminate spending.* **— in′dis•crim′i•nate•ly** *adv.* **— in′dis•crim′i•nate•ness** *n.* **— in′dis•crim′i•na′tive** *adj.*

in•dis•crim•i•nat•ing (ĭn′dĭ-skrĭm′ə-nā′tĭng) *adj.* Not discriminating: *an indiscriminating audience.*

in•dis•crim•i•na•tion (ĭn′dĭ-skrĭm′ə-nā′shən) *n.* Lack of discrimination or judgment.

in•dis•pen•sa•ble (ĭn′dĭ-spĕn′sə-bəl) *adj.* **1.** Not to be dispensed with; essential. **2.** Obligatory; unavoidable. *— n.* One that is indispensable. **— in′dis•pen′sa•bil′i•ty, in′dis•pen′sa•ble•ness** *n.* **— in′dis•pen′sa•bly** *adv.*

***Syns:** indispensable, essential, necessary, needful, requisite.* The central meaning shared by these adjectives is "pressingly needed": *foods indispensable to good nutrition; funds essential to the project; necessary tools and materials; provided them with all things needful; lacking the requisite qualifications.* ***Ant:** dispensable.*

in•dis•pose (ĭn′dĭ-spōz′) *tr.v.* **-posed, -pos•ing, -pos•es. 1.** To make averse; disincline. **2.** To cause to be or feel ill; sicken. **3.** To render unfit; disqualify.

in•dis•posed (ĭn′dĭ-spōzd′) *adj.* **1.** Mildly ill. **2.** Averse; disinclined: *was clearly indisposed to grant their request.*

in•dis•po•si•tion (ĭn-dĭs′pə-zĭsh′ən) *n.* **1.** Disinclination; unwillingness. **2.** A minor ailment.

in•dis•put•a•ble (ĭn′dĭ-spyōō′tə-bəl) *adj.* Beyond dispute or doubt; undeniable: *indisputable evidence.* **— in′dis•put′a•ble•ness** *n.* **— in′dis•put′a•bly** *adv.*

in•dis•sol•u•ble (ĭn′dĭ-sŏl′yə-bəl) *adj.* **1.** Permanent; binding: *an indissoluble contract.* **2.** Impossible to dissolve, disintegrate, or decompose. **— in′dis•sol′u•bil′i•ty, in′dis•sol′u•ble•ness** *n.* **— in′dis•sol′u•bly** *adv.*

in•dis•tinct (ĭn′dĭ-stĭngkt′) *adj.* **1.** Not clearly or sharply delineated. **2.** Faint; dim. **3.a.** Hazy; vague: *an indistinct memory.* **b.** Difficult to understand or make out. **— in′dis•tinct′ly** *adv.* **— in′dis•tinct′ness** *n.*

in•dis•tinc•tive (ĭn′dĭ-stĭngk′tĭv) *adj.* Lacking distinguishing qualities; not distinctive. **— in′dis•tinc′tive•ly** *adv.* **— in′dis•tinc′tive•ness** *n.*

in•dis•tin•guish•a•ble (ĭn′dĭ-stĭng′gwĭ-shə-bəl) *adj.* **1.** Not distinguishable, esp.: **a.** Impossible to differentiate or tell apart. **b.** Impossible to discern; imperceptible. **2.** Difficult to understand or make out; vague: *indistinguishable speech.* **— in′dis•tin′guish•a•ble•ness, in′dis•tin′guish•a•bil′i•ty** *n.* **— in′dis•tin′guish•a•bly** *adv.*

in•dite (ĭn-dīt′) *tr.v.* **-dit•ed, -dit•ing, -dites. 1.** To write; compose. **2.** To set down in writing. **3.** *Obsolete.* To dictate. [ME *enditen* < OFr. *enditer* < VLat. **indictāre* : Lat. *in-,* toward; see IN-[2] + Lat. *dictāre,* to compose, to say habitually, freq. of *dīcere,* to say; see **deik-*.**] **— in•dit′er** *n.*

in•di•um (ĭn′dē-əm) *n. Symbol* **In** A soft malleable metallic element found primarily in ores of zinc used as a plating and in some semiconductor compounds. Atomic number 49; atomic weight 114.82; melting point 156.61°C; boiling point 2,000°C; specific gravity 7.31; valence 1, 2, 3. See table at **element.** [IND(IGO) + -IUM (< the indigo blue lines in its spectrum).]

in•di•vid•u•al (ĭn′də-vĭj′ōō-əl) *adj.* **1.a.** Of or relating to an individual, esp. a single human being. **b.** By or for one person. **2.** Existing as a distinct entity; separate. **3.a.** Distinctive; individualistic. **b.** Special; particular. **c.** Serving to identify or set apart. *— n.* **1.a.** A single human being considered apart from a society or community. **b.** A human being regarded as unique. **c.** A person distinguished from others by a special quality. **d.** A person. **2.** A single animal or plant as distinguished from a species, community, or group. **3.** A member of a collection or set; a specimen. [ME, single, indivisible < OFr.

< Med.Lat. *indīviduālis* < Lat. *indīviduus* : *in-*, not; see IN-[1] + *dīviduus*, divisible (< *dīvidere*, to divide).] — **in′di•vid′u•al•ly** *adv.*

Usage Note: The noun *individual* is used to refer to an individual person as opposed to a larger social group or as distinguished from others by some special quality: *"This is not only a crisis of individuals, but also of a society"* (Raymond Williams). Critics have objected, however, to use of the word to mean "a person" where no larger contrast is implied, as in *Two individuals were arrested*. In such contexts the words *person* and *people* will usually do the same semantic job with less affectation.

in•di•vid•u•al•ism (ĭn′də-vĭj′o͞o-ə-lĭz′əm) *n.* **1.a.** Belief in the primary importance of the individual and in the virtues of self-reliance and personal independence. **b.** Acts or an act based on this belief. **2.** A doctrine of freedom from government regulation of personal economic or social goals. **3.** The doctrine that the interests of the individual should take precedence over the interests of the group. **4.a.** The quality of being an individual; individuality. **b.** An individual characteristic; a quirk.

in•di•vid•u•al•ist (ĭn′də-vĭj′o͞o-ə-lĭst) *n.* **1.** One that asserts individuality by independence of thought and action. **2.** An advocate of individualism. — **in′di•vid′u•al•is′tic** *adj.* — **in′di•vid′u•al•is′ti•cal•ly** *adv.*

in•di•vid•u•al•i•ty (ĭn′də-vĭj′o͞o-ăl′ĭ-tē) *n., pl.* **-ties. 1.a.** The aggregate of qualities and characteristics that distinguish one person or thing from others; character. **b.** An individual or distinguishing feature. **2.** The quality or state of being individual; singularity. **3.** A single, distinct entity. **4.** *Archaic.* Indivisibility.

in•di•vid•u•al•ize (ĭn′də-vĭj′o͞o-ə-līz′) *tr.v.* **-ized, -iz•ing, -iz•es. 1.** To give individuality to. **2.** To consider or treat individually; particularize. **3.** To modify to suit a particular individual. — **in′di•vid′u•al•i•za′tion** (-ə-lĭ-zā′shən) *n.*

in•di•vid•u•ate (ĭn′də-vĭj′o͞o-āt′) *tr.v.* **-at•ed, -at•ing, -ates. 1.** To give individuality to; individualize. **2.** To form into a separate distinct entity.

in•di•vid•u•a•tion (ĭn′də-vĭj′o͞o-ā′shən) *n.* **1.** The act or process of individuating, esp. the process by which social individuals become differentiated. **2.** The condition of being individuated; individuality. **3.** *Philos.* **a.** The development of the individual from the general or universal. **b.** The distinction or determination of the individual within the general or universal. **4.** *Embryol.* Formation of distinct organs or structures in adjacent tissues.

in•di•vis•i•ble (ĭn′də-vĭz′ə-bəl) *adj.* **1.** Incapable of undergoing division: *an indivisible union of states.* **2.** *Math.* Incapable of being divided without a remainder. — **in′di•vis′i•ble•ness, in′di•vis′i•bil′i•ty** *n.* — **in′di•vis′i•bly** *adv.*

indn. *abbr.* Indication.

Indo– *pref.* **1.** India; East Indies: *Indochina.* **2.** Indo-European: *Indo-Hittite.* [Gk. < *Indos*, the Indus R. See INDIGO.]

In•do-Ar•y•an (ĭn′dō-âr′ē-ən, -ăr′-) *adj.* **1.** Of, relating to, or being any of the peoples of the Indian subcontinent who speak an Indo-European language. **2.** Indo-Iranian. — *n.* **1.** A member of any of the Indo-Aryan peoples. **2.** The Indo-Iranian languages.

In•do•chi•na (ĭn′dō-chī′nə). **1.** A peninsula of SE Asia comprising Vietnam, Laos, Cambodia, Thailand, Burma, and the mainland territory of Malaysia. **2.** The former French colonial empire (c. 1862–1954) in SE Asia. — **In′do•chi′nese′** (-nēz′, -nēs′) *adj. & n.*

in•doc•ile (ĭn-dŏs′əl) *adj.* Resistant to authority or discipline; recalcitrant. — **in′do•cil′i•ty** (ĭn′dŏ-sĭl′ĭ-tē, -dō-) *n.*

in•doc•tri•nate (ĭn-dŏk′trə-nāt′) *tr.v.* **-nat•ed, -nat•ing, -nates. 1.a.** To instruct in a body of doctrine or principles. **b.** To initiate by means of doctrinal instruction: *indoctrinate new members.* **2.** To imbue with a partisan or ideological point of view. — **in•doc′tri•na′tion** *n.*

In•do-Eu•ro•pe•an (ĭn′dō-yo͝or′ə-pē′ən) *n.* **1.a.** A family of languages consisting of most of the languages of Europe as well as those of Iran, the Indian subcontinent, and other parts of Asia. **b.** Proto-Indo-European. **2.** A member of any of the peoples speaking an Indo-European language. — **In′do-Eu′ro•pe′an** *adj.* — **In′do-Eu′ro•pe′an•ist** *n.*

In•do-Ger•man•ic (ĭn′dō-jər-măn′ĭk) *n.* See **Indo-European** 1. — **In′do-Ger•man′ic** *adj.*

In•do-Hit•tite (ĭn′dō-hĭt′īt′) *n.* **1.** A language family that includes Indo-European and Anatolian. **2.** The hypothetical parent language of Indo-European and Anatolian.

In•do-I•ra•ni•an (ĭn′dō-ĭ-rā′nē-ən) *n.* **1.** A subfamily of the Indo-European language family that comprises the Indic and Iranian branches. **2.** A member of any of the peoples speaking an Indo-Iranian language. — **In′do-I•ra′ni•an** *adj.*

in•dole (ĭn′dōl′) *n.* **1.** A crystalline compound, C_8H_7N, obtained from coal tar or various plants and produced by the bacterial decomposition of tryptophan in the intestine. **2.** A derivative of this compound. [IND(IGO) + -OLE.]

in•dole•a•ce•tic acid (ĭn′dō-lə-sē′tĭk) *n.* A plant hormone, $C_{10}H_9NO_2$, that stimulates growth.

in•dole•bu•tyr•ic acid (ĭn′dōl-byo͞o-tîr′ĭk) *n.* A synthetic compound, $C_{12}H_{13}NO_2$, used to regulate plant growth.

in•do•lence (ĭn′də-ləns) *n.* Habitual laziness; sloth.

in•do•lent (ĭn′də-lənt) *adj.* **1.a.** Disinclined to exert oneself; habitually lazy. **b.** Conducive to inactivity or laziness; lethargic. **2.a.** Causing little or no pain. **b.** Slow to heal, grow, or develop; inactive. [LLat. *indolēns, indolent-*, painless : Lat. *in-*, not; see IN-[1] + Lat. *dolēns*, pr.part. of *dolēre*, to feel pain.] — **in′do•lent•ly** *adv.*

in•do•meth•a•cin (ĭn′dō-mĕth′ə-sĭn) *n.* A nonsteroidal anti-inflammatory drug, $C_{19}H_{16}ClNO_4$, used esp. in the treatment of arthritis. [INDO(LE) + METH- + AC(ETIC ACID) + -IN.]

in•dom•i•ta•ble (ĭn-dŏm′ĭ-tə-bəl) *adj.* Incapable of being overcome or subdued; unconquerable. [LLat. *indomitābilis* : Lat. *in-*, not; see IN-[1] + Lat. *domitāre*, to tame, freq. of *domāre*, to subdue; see **demə-***.] — **in•dom′i•ta•bil′i•ty, in•dom′i•ta•ble•ness** *n.* — **in•dom′i•ta•bly** *adv.*

In•do•ne•sia (ĭn′də-nē′zhə, -shə, -dō-). Formerly **Dutch East In•dies** (dŭch; ĭn′dēz). A country of SE Asia in the Malay Archipelago; achieved full independence from the Netherlands in 1949. Cap. Jakarta. Pop. 147,490,298.

Indonesia

In•do•ne•sian (ĭn′də-nē′zhən, -shən) *n.* **1.** A native or inhabitant of Indonesia. **2.** A native or inhabitant of the Malay Archipelago. **3.** A subfamily of Austronesian that includes Malay, Tagalog, and the languages of Indonesia. **4.** A dialect of Malay that is the official language of Indonesia. — *adj.* Of or relating to Indonesia, the Indonesians, or their languages or cultures.

in•door (ĭn′dôr′, -dōr′) *adj.* **1.** Of, situated in, or intended for use in the interior of a building. **2.** Carried on within doors.

in•doors (ĭn-dôrz′, -dōrz′) *adv.* In or into a house or building.

in•do•phen•ol (ĭn′dō-fē′nôl, -nōl, -nŏl) *n.* Any of various synthetic blue or green dyes. [IND(IGO) + PHENOL.]

In•dore (ĭn-dôr′, -dōr′). A city of W-central India NNE of Bombay; founded 1715. Pop. 829,327.

in•dorse (ĭn-dôrs′) *v.* Var. of **endorse.**

In•dra (ĭn′drə) *n. Hinduism.* A principal Vedic deity associated with rain and thunder.

in•draft (ĭn′drăft′) *n.* **1.** An inward flow or current, as of air. **2.** A pulling or drawing inward.

in•drawn (ĭn′drôn′) *adj.* **1.** Drawn in: *an indrawn gasp.* **2.** Emotionally unresponsive or reserved, withdrawn.

in•dri (ĭn′drē) *n.* A large arboreal lemur *(Indri indri)* of Madagascar having large eyes and a rudimentary tail. [Prob. ult. of Malagasy orig.]

in•du•bi•ta•ble (ĭn-do͞o′bĭ-tə-bəl, -dyo͞o′-) *adj.* Too apparent to be doubted; unquestionable. — **in•du′bi•ta•bly** *adv.*

in•duce (ĭn-do͞os′, -dyo͞os′) *tr.v.* **-duced, -duc•ing, -duc•es. 1.** To lead or move, as to a course of action, by influence or persuasion. **2.** To bring about or stimulate; cause: *a drug used to induce labor.* **3.** To infer by inductive reasoning. **4.** *Phys.* **a.** To produce (an electric current or a magnetic charge) by induction. **b.** To produce (radioactivity, for example) artificially by bombardment, as with neutrons. **5.** *Biochem.* To initiate or increase the production of (an enzyme or other protein) at the level of genetic transcription. [ME *inducen* < OFr. *inducer* < Lat. *indūcere* : *in-*, in; see IN-[2] + *dūcere*, to lead; see **deuk-***.] — **in•duc′i•ble** *adj.*

Indra
Riding his white elephant, Airavata

in•duce•ment (ĭn-do͞os′mənt, -dyo͞os′-) *n.* **1.** Something that helps bring about an action or a desired result; an incentive. **2.** The act or process of inducing: *inducement of sleep.*

in•duc•er (ĭn-do͞o′sər, -dyo͞o′-) *n.* **1.** One that induces, esp. a substance that is capable of activating specific genes within a cell. **2.** A part or structure in an embryo that influences the differentiation of another part.

in•duct (ĭn-dŭkt′) *tr.v.* **-duct•ed, -duct•ing, -ducts. 1.** To place ceremoniously or formally in an office or a position; install. **2.a.** To admit as a member; receive. **b.** To admit to military service. **c.** To introduce, as to new experience or knowledge; initiate. **3.** *Phys.* To induce. [ME *inducten* < Lat. *indūcere, induct-*. See INDUCE.]

in•duc•tance (ĭn-dŭk′təns) *n.* **1.** The property of an electric circuit by which an electromotive force is induced in it or in a nearby circuit by a change of current in either circuit. **2.** A circuit element in which electromotive force is generated by electromagnetic induction.

in•duct•ee (ĭn′dŭk-tē′) *n.* One who is inducted, esp. a person newly admitted to military service.

in•duc•tion (ĭn-dŭk′shən) *n.* **1.a.** The act or an instance of inducting. **b.** A ceremony or formal act by which a person is inducted, as into office. **2.** *Elect.* **a.** The generation of electromotive force in a closed circuit by a varying magnetic flux through the circuit. **b.** The charging of an isolated conducting object by momentarily grounding it while a charged body is nearby. **3.** *Logic.* **a.** The process of deriving general principles from particular facts or instances. **b.** A conclusion reached by this process. **4.** *Math.* A method of proving a theorem involving a positive integral variable by which the theorem is verified for the smallest admissible value of the integer and it is then proven that if the theorem is true for any value of the integer, it is true for the next greater value. **5.** The act of inducing. **6.** Presentation of material in support of an argument or a proposition. **7.** A preface or prologue. **8.** *Biochem.*

ă pat	oi boy
ā pay	ou out
âr care	o͝o took
ä father	o͞o boot
ĕ pet	ŭ cut
ē be	ûr urge
ĭ pit	th thin
ī pie	*th* this
îr pier	hw which
ŏ pot	zh vision
ō toe	ə about, item
ô paw	

Stress marks:
′ (primary);
′ (secondary), as in
dictionary (dĭk′shə-nĕr′ē)

The process of initiating or increasing the production of an enzyme or other protein at the level of genetic transcription. **9.** *Embryol.* The change in form or shape caused by the action of one tissue of an embryo on adjacent tissues.

induction coil *n.* A transformer in which an interrupted low-voltage direct current in the primary is converted into an intermittent high-voltage current in the secondary.

in•duc•tive (ĭn-dŭk**′**tĭv) *adj.* **1.** Of, relating to, or using logical induction: *inductive reasoning.* **2.** *Elect.* Of or arising from inductance. **3.** Causing or influencing; inducing. **4.** Introductory. **— in•duc′tive•ly** *adv.* **— in•duc′tive•ness** *n.*

inductive statistics *n.* *(used with a sing. v.)* The branch of statistics that deals with generalizations, predictions, estimations, and decisions from data initially presented.

in•duc•tor (ĭn-dŭk**′**tər) *n.* One that inducts, esp. a device that functions by or introduces inductance into a circuit.

in•due (ĭn-do͞o**′**, -dyo͞o**′**) *v.* Var. of **endue.**

in•dulge (ĭn-dŭlj**′**) *v.* **-dulged, -dulg•ing, -dulg•es.** *— tr.* **1.** To yield to the desires and whims of; humor. **2.a.** To yield to; gratify. **b.** To allow (oneself) unrestrained gratification. **3.** To grant an ecclesiastical indulgence or dispensation to. *— intr.* **1.** To indulge oneself. **2.** To engage or take part, esp. freely or avidly. [Lat. *indulgēre.*] **— in•dulg′er** *n.*

in•dul•gence (ĭn-dŭl**′**jəns) *n.* **1.a.** The act or an instance of indulging; gratification. **b.** The state of being indulgent. **2.a.** The act of indulging in something. **b.** Something indulged in. **3.** Liberal or lenient treatment; tolerance. **4.** Self-indulgence. **5.a.** Something granted as a favor or privilege. **b.** Permission to extend the time of payment or performance. **c.** Patient attention. **6.** *Rom. Cath. Ch.* The remission of temporal punishment still due for a sin that has been sacramentally absolved. *— tr.v.* **-genced, -genc•ing, -genc•es.** *Rom. Cath. Ch.* To attach an indulgence to.

in•dul•gent (ĭn-dŭl**′**jənt) *adj.* Showing, characterized by, or given to indulgence; lenient. **— in•dul′gent•ly** *adv.*

in•dult (ĭn-dŭlt**′**) *n.* *Rom. Cath. Ch.* A faculty granted by the pope to deviate from the common law of the Church. [ME < Med.Lat. *indultum* < LLat., concession, gift < Lat. *indultum,* neut. p.part. of *indulgēre,* to be kind.]

in•du•pli•cate (ĭn-do͞o**′**plĭ-kĭt, -dyo͞o**′**-) *adj.* *Bot.* Having the edges folded or turned inward.

in•du•rate (ĭn**′**də-rāt′, -dyə-) *v.* **-rat•ed, -rat•ing, -rates.** *— tr.* **1.** To make hard; harden. **2.** To inure, as to hardship. **3.** To make callous or obdurate. *— intr.* **1.** To grow hard; harden. **2.** To become firmly fixed or established. *— adj.* (ĭn**′**do͝o-rĭt, -dyə-). Hardened; obstinate; unfeeling. [Lat. *indūrāre, indūrāt-* : *in-,* intensive pref.; see IN-[2] + *dūrus,* hard; see **deru-*.**] **— in′du•ra′tive** *adj.*

in•du•ra•tion (ĭn′də-rā**′**shən, -dyə-) *n.* **1.** The quality or condition of being hardened. **2.** The act or process of becoming hardened. **3.** *Pathol.* The hardening of a normally soft tissue or organ, as because of inflammation.

In•dus[1] (ĭn**′**dəs). A river of S-central Asia rising in SW Tibet and flowing c. 3,057 km (1,900 mi) through N India and Pakistan to the Arabian Sea. Its valley was the site of an advanced civilization lasting c. 2500–1500 B.C.

In•dus[2] (ĭn**′**dəs) *n.* A constellation in the Southern Hemisphere near Tucana and Pavo. [Lat. *Indus,* an Indian < Gk. *Indos,* the Indus R., an Indian. See INDIGO.]

indus. *abbr.* Industrial; industry.

in•du•si•um (ĭn-do͞o**′**zē-əm, -zhē-, -dyo͞o**′**-) *n., pl.* **-si•a** (-zē-ə, -zhē-ə). An enclosing membrane, as that covering the sorus of a fern. [Lat., tunic, perh. alteration of Gk. *endusis,* dress < *enduein,* put on : *en-,* in; see EN-[2] + *duein,* to sink.]

in•dus•tri•al (ĭn-dŭs**′**trē-əl) *adj.* **1.** Of, relating to, or resulting from industry. **2.** Having highly developed industries: *an industrial nation.* **3.** Employed, required, or used in industry. *— n.* **1.** A firm engaged in industry. **2.** A stock or bond issued by an industrial enterprise. **3.** A person employed in industry. **— in•dus′tri•al•ly** *adv.*

industrial arts *n.* *(used with a sing. v.)* A subject of study aimed at developing the manual and technical skills required to work with tools and machinery.

industrial disease *n.* Occupational disease.

industrial engineering *n.* The branch of engineering that is concerned with the efficient production of industrial goods. **— industrial engineer** *n.*

in•dus•tri•al•ism (ĭn-dŭs**′**trē-ə-lĭz′əm) *n.* An economic and social system based on large-scale industries.

in•dus•tri•al•ist (ĭ-dŭs**′**trē-ə-lĭst) *n.* One who owns, directs, or has a substantial financial interest in an industry.

in•dus•tri•al•ize (ĭn-dŭs**′**trē-ə-līz′) *v.* **-ized, -iz•ing, -iz•es.** *— tr.* **1.** To develop industry in. **2.** To organize (the production of something) as an industry. *— intr.* To become industrial. **— in•dus′tri•al•i•za′tion** (-ə-lĭ-zā**′**shən) *n.*

industrial park *n.* An area usu. located on the outskirts of a city and zoned for a group of industries and businesses.

industrial psychology *n.* The branch of applied psychology that is concerned with efficient management of an industrial labor force. **— industrial psychologist** *n.*

industrial relations *pl.n.* Relations between the management of an industrial enterprise and its employees.

industrial revolution also **Industrial Revolution** *n.* The complex of radical socioeconomic changes brought about by the extensive mechanization of production.

industrial union *n.* A labor union to which all the workers of a particular industry can belong regardless of occupation.

in•dus•tri•ous (ĭn-dŭs**′**trē-əs) *adj.* **1.** Assiduous in work or study; diligent. **2.** *Obsolete.* Skillful; clever. **— in•dus′tri•ous•ly** *adv.* **— in•dus′tri•ous•ness** *n.*

in•dus•try (ĭn**′**də-strē) *n., pl.* **-tries. 1.** Commercial production and sale of goods. **2.** A specific branch of manufacture and trade. See Syns at **business. 3.** The sector of an economy made up of manufacturing enterprises. **4.** Industrial management. **5.** Energetic devotion to a task or an endeavor; diligence. **6.** Ongoing work or study associated with a specified subject or figure. [ME *industrie,* skill < OFr. < Lat. *industria,* diligence < fem. of *industrius,* diligent. See **ster-[2]*.**]

in•dwell (ĭn-dwĕl**′**) *v.* **-dwelt** (-dwĕlt**′**), **-dwell•ing, -dwells.** *— intr.* **1.** To exist as an animating or divine inner spirit, force, or principle. **2.** To be located or implanted inside something. *— tr.* To inhabit or reside within. **— in′dwell′er** *n.*

In•dy (ăn**′**dē, ăɴ-dē**′**), **(Paul Marie Théodore) Vincent d'.** 1851–1931. French composer who was a founder (1894) and director of the Schola Cantorum in Paris.

–ine[1] *suff.* **1.** Of or relating to: *Benedictine.* **2.** Made of; resembling: *opaline.* [ME *-in, -ine* < OFr. < Lat. *-īnus, -īna,* adj. suff., and < Lat. *-inus* (< Gk. *-inos*).]

–ine[2] *suff.* **1.** Also **-in.** A chemical substance, esp.: **a.** Halogen: *bromine.* **b.** Basic compound: *amine.* **c.** Alkaloid: *quinine.* **2.** Amino acid: *glycine.* **3.** A mixture of compounds: *gasoline.* **4.** Commercial material: *glassine.* [Ult. < Lat. *-īnus* and *-inus,* adj. suffixes; see -INE[1].]

in•e•bri•ant (ĭn-ē**′**brē-ənt) *adj.* Serving to intoxicate. *— n.* An intoxicant.

in•e•bri•ate (ĭn-ē**′**brē-āt′) *tr.v.* **-at•ed, -at•ing, -ates. 1.** To make drunk; intoxicate. **2.** To exhilarate or stupefy as if with alcohol. *— adj.* (-ĭt). Intoxicated. *— n.* (-ĭt). An intoxicated person. [Lat. *inēbriāre, inēbriāt-* : *in-,* intensive pref.; see IN-[2] + *ēbriāre,* to intoxicate (< *ēbrius,* drunk; see **ēgʷh-***).] **— in•e′bri•a′tion** *n.*

in•e•bri•at•ed (ĭn-ē**′**brē-ā′tĭd) *adj.* Exhilarated or stupefied by or as if by alcohol; intoxicated.

in•e•bri•e•ty (ĭn′ĭ-brī**′**ĭ-tē) *n.* Intoxication; drunkenness.

in•ed•i•ble (ĭn-ĕd**′**ə-bəl) *adj.* Unfit to be eaten; not edible. **— in•ed′i•bil′i•ty** *n.* **— in•ed′i•bly** *adv.*

in•ed•it•ed (ĭn-ĕd**′**ĭ-tĭd) *adj.* **1.** Not edited. **2.** Not published.

in•ed•u•ca•ble (ĭn-ĕj**′**ə-kə-bəl) *adj.* Incapable of being educated. **— in•ed′u•ca•bil′i•ty** *n.*

in•ef•fa•ble (ĭn-ĕf**′**ə-bəl) *adj.* **1.** Incapable of being expressed; indescribable or unutterable. **2.** Not to be uttered; taboo. [ME < OFr. < Lat. *ineffābilis* : *in-,* not; see IN-[1] + *effābilis,* utterable (< *effārī,* to utter : *ex-,* ex- + *fārī,* to speak; see **bhā-[2]***).] **— in•ef′fa•bil′i•ty, in•ef′fa•ble•ness** *n.* **— in•ef′fa•bly** *adv.*

in•ef•face•a•ble (ĭn′ĭ-fā**′**sə-bəl) *adj.* Impossible to efface; indelible. **— in′ef•face′a•bil′i•ty** *n.* **— in′ef•face′a•bly** *adv.*

in•ef•fec•tive (ĭn′ĭ-fĕk**′**tĭv) *adj.* **1.** Not producing an intended effect; ineffectual. **2.** Inadequate; incompetent. **— in′ef•fec′tive•ly** *adv.* **— in′ef•fec′tive•ness** *n.*

in•ef•fec•tu•al (ĭn′ĭ-fĕk**′**cho͞o-əl) *adj.* **1.a.** Insufficient to produce a desired effect: *an ineffectual effort.* **b.** Useless; worthless. **2.** Lacking forcefulness or effectiveness; weak: *an ineffectual ruler.* **— in′ef•fec′tu•al′i•ty** (-ăl**′**ĭ-tē), **in′ef•fec′tu•al•ness** *n.* **— in′ef•fec′tu•al•ly** *adv.*

in•ef•fi•ca•cious (ĭn-ĕf′ĭ-kā**′**shəs) *adj.* Not capable of producing a desired effect or result; ineffective. **— in•ef′fi•ca′cious•ly** *adv.* **— in•ef′fi•ca′cious•ness** *n.*

in•ef•fi•ca•cy (ĭn-ĕf**′**ĭ-kə-sē) *n.* The state or quality of being incapable of producing a desired effect or result.

in•ef•fi•cien•cy (ĭn′ĭ-fĭsh**′**ən-sē) *n., pl.* **-cies. 1.** The quality, condition, or fact of being inefficient. **2.** An inefficient act, design, or procedure.

in•ef•fi•cient (ĭn′ĭ-fĭsh**′**ənt) *adj.* **1.** Not efficient, as: **a.** Lacking the ability or skill to perform effectively; incompetent. **b.** Not producing the intended result; ineffective. **2.** Wasteful of time, energy, or materials. **— in′ef•fi′cient•ly** *adv.*

in•e•gal•i•tar•i•an (ĭn′ĭ-găl′ĭ-târ**′**ē-ən) *adj.* Marked by or accepting of social, economic, or political inequality.

in•e•las•tic (ĭn′ĭ-lăs**′**tĭk) *adj.* Lacking elasticity; unyielding or unadaptable. See Syns at **stiff. — in′e•las•tic′i•ty** (-ĭ-lă-stĭs**′**ĭ-tē) *n.*

inelastic collision *n.* A collision between two particles in which part of their kinetic energy is transformed to another form of energy, the total amount of energy remaining the same.

in•el•e•gance (ĭn-ĕl**′**ĭ-gəns) *n.* Lack of refinement or polish.

in•el•e•gant (ĭn-ĕl**′**ĭ-gənt) *adj.* Lacking refinement or polish; not elegant. **— in•el′e•gant•ly** *adv.*

in•el•i•gi•ble (ĭn-ĕl**′**ĭ-jə-bəl) *adj.* **1.** Disqualified by law, rule, or provision. **2.** Unworthy of being chosen; unfit. **— in•el′i•gi•ble** *n.* **— in•el′i•gi•bly** *adv.*

in•el•o•quent (ĭn-ĕl**′**ə-kwənt) *adj.* Lacking eloquence. **— in•el′o•quence** *n.* **— in•el′o•quent•ly** *adv.*

in•e•luc•ta•ble (ĭn′ĭ-lŭk**′**tə-bəl) *adj.* Not to be avoided or escaped; inevitable. [Lat. *inēluctābilis* : *in-*, not; see IN-[1] + *ēluctābilis*, penetrable (< *ēluctārī*, to struggle out of : *ex-*, ex- + *luctārī*, to struggle).] — **in′e·luc′ta·bil′i·ty** *n.* — **in′e·luc′ta·bly** *adv.*

in·ept (ĭn-ĕpt′) *adj.* **1.** Not apt or fitting; inappropriate. **2.a.** Displaying a lack of judgment, sense, or reason; foolish. **b.** Bungling or clumsy; incompetent. [Lat. *ineptus* : *in-*, not; see IN-[1] + *aptus*, suitable; see APT.] — **in·ept′ly** *adv.* — **in·ept′ness, in·ep′ti·tude′** (-ĕp′tĭ-to͞od′, -tyo͞od′) *n.*

in·e·qual·i·ty (ĭn′ĭ-kwŏl′ĭ-tē) *n.*, *pl.* **-ties. 1.a.** The condition of being unequal. **b.** An instance of being unequal. **2.a.** Lack of equality, as of opportunity. **b.** Social or economic disparity: *the growing inequality between rich and poor.* **3.** Lack of smoothness or regularity; unevenness. **4.** Variability; changeability. **5.** *Math.* An algebraic expression showing that a quantity is greater than or less than another quantity.

in·eq·ui·ta·ble (ĭn-ĕk′wĭ-tə-bəl) *adj.* Not equitable; unfair. — **in·eq′ui·ta·bly** *adv.*

in·eq·ui·ty (ĭn-ĕk′wĭ-tē) *n.*, *pl.* **-ties. 1.** Injustice; unfairness. **2.** An instance of injustice or unfairness.

in·e·rad·i·ca·ble (ĭn′ĭ-răd′ĭ-kə-bəl) *adj.* Impossible to eradicate or be eradicated. — **in′e·rad′i·ca·bly** *adv.*

in·er·ran·cy (ĭn-ĕr′ən-sē) *n.* Freedom from error or untruths.

in·er·rant (ĭn-ĕr′ənt) *adj.* **1.** Incapable of erring; infallible. **2.** Containing no errors.

in·er·ran·tism (ĭn-ĕr′ən-tiz′əm) *n.* Belief in the inerrancy or literal truth of a particular writing or document. — **in·er′ran·tist′** *adj. & n.*

in·ert (ĭn-ûrt′) *adj.* **1.** Unable to move or act. **2.** Sluggish in action or motion; lethargic. See Syns at **inactive. 3.** *Chem.* Not readily reactive with other elements. [Lat. *iners*, *inert-* : *in-*, not; see IN-[1] + *ars*, skill; see **ar-***.] — **in·ert′ly** *adv.* — **in·ert′ness** *n.*

inert gas *n.* See **noble gas.**

in·er·tia (ĭ-nûr′shə) *n.* **1.** *Phys.* The tendency of a body at rest to remain at rest or of a body in motion to stay in motion in a straight line unless acted on by an outside force. **2.** Resistance or disinclination to motion, action, or change: *bureaucratic inertia.* [Lat., idleness < *iners*, *inert-*, inert. See INERT.] — **in·er′tial** *adj.* — **in·er′tial·ly** *adv.*

inertial guidance *n.* Guidance of an aircraft or a spacecraft in which gyroscopic and accelerometer data are used by a computer to maintain a predetermined course.

in·es·cap·a·ble (ĭn′ĭ-skā′pə-bəl) *adj.* Impossible to escape or avoid; inevitable. — **in′es·cap′a·bly** *adv.*

in·es·sen·tial (ĭn′ĭ-sĕn′shəl) *adj.* **1.** Not essential; unessential. **2.** Without essence. — *n.* Something that is not essential. — **in′es·sen′ti·al′i·ty** (-shē-ăl′ĭ-tē) *n.*

in·es·ti·ma·ble (ĭn-ĕs′tə-mə-bəl) *adj.* **1.** Impossible to estimate or compute. See Syns at **incalculable. 2.** Of immeasurable value; invaluable. — **in·es′ti·ma·bly** *adv.*

in·ev·i·ta·ble (ĭn-ĕv′ĭ-tə-bəl) *adj.* **1.** Impossible to avoid or prevent. **2.** Invariably occurring or appearing; predictable. — **in·ev′i·ta·bil′i·ty** *n.* — **in·ev′i·ta·bly** *adv.*

in·ex·act (ĭn′ĭg-zăkt′) *adj.* **1.** Not strictly accurate; not exact: *an inexact quotation.* **2.** Not rigorous or meticulous: *an inexact method.* — **in′ex·act′ly** *adv.* — **in′ex·act′ness** *n.*

in·ex·act·i·tude (ĭn′ĭg-zăk′tĭ-to͞od′, -tyo͞od′) *n.* Lack of exactitude; inexactness.

in·ex·cus·a·ble (ĭn′ĭk-skyo͞o′zə-bəl) *adj.* Impossible to excuse or justify; unpardonable: *inexcusable behavior.* — **in′ex·cus′a·ble·ness** *n.* — **in′ex·cus′a·bly** *adv.*

in·ex·haust·i·ble (ĭn′ĭg-zô′stə-bəl) *adj.* **1.** That cannot be depleted or used up. **2.** Never wearying; tireless: *an inexhaustible campaigner.* — **in′ex·haust′i·bil′i·ty, in′ex·haust′i·ble·ness** *n.* — **in′ex·haust′i·bly** *adv.*

in·ex·is·tent (ĭn′ĭg-zĭs′tənt) *adj.* Having no existence; nonexistent. — **in′ex·is′tence** *n.*

in·ex·o·ra·ble (ĭn-ĕk′sər-ə-bəl) *adj.* Incapable of being persuaded by entreaty; relentless. [Lat. *inexōrābilis* : *in-*, not; see IN-[1] + *exōrābilis*, pliant (< *exōrāre*, to prevail upon : *ex-*, intensive pref.; see EX- + *ōrāre*, to argue).] — **in·ex′o·ra·bil′i·ty, in·ex′o·ra·ble·ness** *n.* — **in·ex′o·ra·bly** *adv.*

in·ex·pe·di·ent (ĭn′ĭk-spē′dē-ənt) *adj.* Not expedient; inadvisable: *an inexpedient tactic.* — **in′ex·pe′di·ence, in′ex·pe′di·en·cy** *n.* — **in′ex·pe′di·ent·ly** *adv.*

in·ex·pen·sive (ĭn′ĭk-spĕn′sĭv) *adj.* Not high in price; cheap. — **in′ex·pen′sive·ly** *adv.* — **in′ex·pen′sive·ness** *n.*

in·ex·pe·ri·ence (ĭn′ĭk-spîr′ē-əns) *n.* **1.** Lack of experience. **2.** Lack of the knowledge gained from experience. — **in′ex·pe′ri·enced** *adj.*

in·ex·pert (ĭn-ĕk′spûrt′) *adj.* Not expert; unskilled. — **in·ex′pert′ly** *adv.* — **in·ex′pert′ness** *n.*

in·ex·pi·a·ble (ĭn-ĕk′spē-ə-bəl) *adj.* **1.** Impossible to expiate or atone for: *inexpiable crimes.* **2.** *Obsolete.* Implacable. — **in·ex′pi·a·bly** *adv.*

in·ex·plain·a·ble (ĭn′ĭk-splā′nə-bəl) *adj.* Difficult or impossible to explain; inexplicable. — **in′ex·plain′a·bly** *adv.*

in·ex·pli·ca·ble (ĭn-ĕk′splĭ-kə-bəl, ĭn′ĭk-splĭk′ə-bəl) *adj.* Difficult or impossible to account for. — **in·ex′pli·ca·bil′i·ty, in·ex′pli·ca·ble·ness** *n.* — **in·ex′pli·ca·bly** *adv.*

in·ex·plic·it (ĭn′ĭk-splĭs′ĭt) *adj.* Not explicit; indefinite.

in·ex·press·i·ble (ĭn′ĭk-sprĕs′ə-bəl) *adj.* Impossible to express; indescribable: *finally overcame her inexpressible grief.* — **in′ex·press′i·bil′i·ty, in′ex·press′i·ble·ness** *n.* — **in′ex·press′i·bly** *adv.*

in·ex·pres·sive (ĭn′ĭk-sprĕs′ĭv) *adj.* **1.** Lacking expression; blank. **2.** Devoid of emotion or style; flat or dull. — **in′ex·pres′sive·ly** *adv.* — **in′ex·pres′sive·ness** *n.*

in·ex·pug·na·ble (ĭn′ĭk-spŭg′nə-bəl, -spyo͞o′nə-) *adj.* **1.** Impossible to overcome or overthrow by force. **2.** Impossible to put aside or drive away: *inexpugnable dislike.* [ME < OFr. < Lat. *inexpugnābilis* : *in-*, not; see IN-[1] + *expugnābilis*, capable of being overcome (< *expugnāre* : *ex-*, completely; see EX- + *pugnāre*, to fight; see IMPUGN).] — **in′ex·pug·na·bil′i·ty** *n.* — **in′ex·pug′na·bly** *adv.*

in·ex·ten·si·ble (ĭn′ĭk-stĕn′sə-bəl) *adj.* Not extensible.

in ex·ten·so (ĭn ĕk-stĕn′sō) *adv.* At full length. [Lat. : *in*, at + *extēnsō*, ablative of *extēnsus*, stretch.]

in·ex·tin·guish·a·ble (ĭn′ĭk-stĭng′gwĭ-shə-bəl) *adj.* Difficult or impossible to extinguish. — **in′ex·tin′guish·a·bly** *adv.*

in·ex·tir·pa·ble (ĭn′ĭk-stûr′pə-bəl) *adj.* Difficult or impossible to eradicate or destroy.

in ex·tre·mis (ĭn ĕk-strē′mĭs) *adv.* **1.** At the point of death. **2.** In grave or extreme circumstances. [Lat. : *in*, in + *extrēmīs*, ablative pl. of *extrēmus*, extreme.]

in·ex·tri·ca·ble (ĭn-ĕk′strĭ-kə-bəl, ĭn′ĭk-strĭk′ə-bəl) *adj.* **1.a.** So intricate or entangled as to make escape impossible: *an inextricable maze.* **b.** Difficult or impossible to disentangle or untie. **c.** Too involved or complicated to solve. **2.** Unavoidable; inescapable. — **in·ex′tri·ca·bil′i·ty, in·ex′tri·ca·ble·ness** *n.* — **in·ex′tri·ca·bly** *adv.*

inf. *abbr.* **1.** Also **Inf.** Infantry. **2.** Inferior. **3.** Infinitive. **4.** Infinity. **5.** Information.

in·fal·li·ble (ĭn-făl′ə-bəl) *adj.* **1.** Incapable of erring. **2.** Incapable of failing; certain. **3.** *Rom. Cath. Ch.* Incapable of error in expounding doctrine on faith or morals. — **in·fal′li·bil′i·ty, in·fal′li·ble·ness** *n.* — **in·fal′li·bly** *adv.*

in·fa·mous (ĭn′fə-məs) *adj.* **1.** Having an exceedingly bad reputation; notorious. **2.** Causing or deserving infamy; heinous: *an infamous deed.* **3.** *Law.* **a.** Punishable by severe measures, such as death or long imprisonment. **b.** Convicted of a crime that carries such a punishment. [ME *infamis* < Lat. *īnfāmis* : *in-*, not; see IN-[1] + *fāma*, renown, fame; see **bhā-**[2]*.] — **in′fa·mous·ly** *adv.* — **in′fa·mous·ness** *n.*

in·fa·my (ĭn′fə-mē) *n.*, *pl.* **-mies. 1.** Evil fame or reputation. **2.** The condition of being infamous. **3.** An evil or criminal act that is publicly known. [ME *infamie*, dishonor < OFr. < Lat. *īnfāmia* < *īnfāmis*, infamous. See INFAMOUS.]

in·fan·cy (ĭn′fən-sē) *n.*, *pl.* **-cies. 1.** The earliest period of childhood, esp. before the ability to walk has been acquired. **2.** The state of being an infant. **3.** An early stage of existence. **4.** *Law.* The state or period of being a minor.

in·fant (ĭn′fənt) *n.* **1.** A child in infancy. **2.** *Law.* A person under the legal age of majority; a minor. — *adj.* **1.** Of or being in infancy. **2.** Intended for infants or young children. **3.** Newly begun or formed. [ME < OFr. *enfant* < Lat. *īnfāns*, *īnfant-* < *īnfāns*, not able to speak, young : *in-*, not; see IN-[1] + *fāns*, pr.part. of *fārī*, to speak; see **bhā-**[2]*.]

in·fan·ta (ĭn-făn′tə, -făn′-) *n.* A daughter of a Spanish or Portuguese king. [Sp. and Port., fem. of *infante*, infante; see INFANTE.]

in·fan·te (ĭn-făn′tē, -făn′tā) *n.* A son of a Spanish or Portuguese king other than the heir to the throne. [Sp. and Port., both < Lat. *īnfāns*, *īnfant-*, infant. See INFANT.]

in·fan·ti·cide (ĭn-făn′tĭ-sīd′) *n.* **1.** The act of killing an infant. **2.** The practice of killing newborn infants. **3.** One who kills an infant. [LLat. *īnfanticīdium*, the killing of a child and *īnfanticīda*, killer of a child : Lat. *īnfāns*, *īnfant-*, infant; see INFANT + Lat. *-cīdium* and *-cīda*, -cide.] — **in·fan′ti·cid′al** (-sīd′l) *adj.*

in·fan·tile (ĭn′fən-tīl′, -tĭl) *adj.* **1.** Of or relating to infants or infancy. **2.** Displaying or suggesting a lack of maturity; extremely childish: *infantile behavior.* [ME *infantil* < Lat. *īnfantīlis* < *īnfāns*, *īnfant-*, infant. See INFANT.]

infantile autism *n.* *Psychol.* A severe disorder of childhood characterized by withdrawal, preoccupation with fantasy, language impairment, and ritualistic behavior.

infantile paralysis *n.* See **poliomyelitis.**

in·fan·til·ism (ĭn′fən-tl-ĭz′əm, ĭn-făn′tl-) *n.* **1.** A state of arrested development in an adult, characterized by retention of infantile mentality and accompanied by stunted growth and sexual immaturity and often by dwarfism. **2.a.** Extreme immaturity, as in behavior or character. **b.** An infantile act or remark.

in·fan·til·ize (ĭn′fən-tl-īz′, ĭn-făn′-) *tr.v.* **-ized, -iz·ing, -iz·es. 1.** To reduce to an infantile state or condition. **2.** To treat or condescend to as if still a young child. — **in·fan′til·i·za′tion** (-ĭ-zā′shən) *n.*

in·fan·tine (ĭn′fən-tīn′, -tĭn) *adj.* Infantile; childish.

in·fan·try (ĭn′fən-trē) *n.*, *pl.* **-tries.** The combat arm made up of units trained to fight on foot. [Fr. *infanterie* < OFr. < OItal. *infanteria* < *infante*, youth, foot soldier < Lat. *īnfāns*, *īnfant-*, infant. See INFANT.]

infanta
The Infanta Margarita, c. 1653, by Velázquez

ă pat	oi boy
ā pay	ou out
âr care	o͝o took
ä father	o͞o boot
ĕ pet	ŭ cut
ē be	ûr urge
ĭ pit	th thin
ī pie	*th* this
îr pier	hw which
ŏ pot	zh vision
ō toe	ə about, item
ô paw	

Stress marks:
′ (primary);
′ (secondary), as in **dictionary** (dĭk′shə-nĕr′ē)

in•fan•try•man (ĭn′fən-trē-mən) *n.* A soldier in the infantry.

infant school *n. Chiefly British.* A kindergarten.

in•farct (ĭn′färkt′, ĭn-färkt′) *n. Pathol.* An area of tissue that undergoes necrosis as a result of obstruction of local blood supply. [< Lat. *īnfarctus*, p.part. of *īnfarcīre*, to cram : *in-*, in; see IN-² + *farcīre*, to stuff.] — **in•farct′ed** *adj.*

in•farc•tion (ĭn-färk′shən) *n.* **1.** The formation or development of an infarct. **2.** An infarct.

in•fat•u•ate (ĭn-făch′o͞o-āt′) *tr.v.* **-at•ed, -at•ing, -ates. 1.** To inspire with unreasoning love or attachment. **2.** To cause to behave foolishly. —*adj.* (-ĭt, -āt′). Infatuated. [Lat. *īnfatuāre, īnfatuāt-* : *in-*, causative pref.; see IN-² + *fatuus*, foolish.]

in•fat•u•at•ed (ĭn-făch′o͞o-ā′tĭd) *adj.* Possessed by an unreasoning passion or attraction. — **in•fat′u•at′ed•ly** *adv.*

in•fat•u•a•tion (ĭ-făch′o͞o-ā′shən) *n.* **1.** A foolish, unreasoning, or extravagant passion or attraction. See Syns at **love. 2.** An object of extravagant, short-lived passion.

in•fau•na (ĭn′fô′nə) *n.* Aquatic animals that live in the substrate of a body of water. [IN-² + FAUNA.]

in•fea•si•ble (ĭn-fē′zə-bəl) *adj.* Not feasible; impracticable.

in•fect (ĭn-fĕkt′) *tr.v.* **-fect•ed, -fect•ing, -fects. 1.** To contaminate with a pathogen. **2.** To communicate a pathogen or disease to. **3.** To invade and produce infection in. **4.** To contaminate or corrupt. **5.** To affect in a contagious way. [ME *infecten*, to afflict with disease < Lat. *īnficere, īnfect-*, to stain, infect : *in-*, in; see **in-*** + *facere*, to do; see **dhē-*.**]

in•fec•tion (ĭn-fĕk′shən) *n.* **1.a.** Invasion by and multiplication of pathogenic microorganisms in a body tissue. **b.** An instance of being infected. **c.** An agent or a contaminated substance responsible for one's becoming infected. **d.** The pathological state resulting from having been infected. **2.** An infectious disease. **3.a.** Moral contamination or corruption. **b.** Ready communication of an emotion or attitude by contact or example.

in•fec•tious (ĭn-fĕk′shəs) *adj.* **1.** Capable of causing infection. **2.** Caused by or capable of being transmitted by infection. **3.** Easily or readily communicated: *an infectious laugh.* — **in•fec′tious•ly** *adv.* — **in•fec′tious•ness** *n.*

infectious enterohepatitis *n.* See **blackhead** 2.

infectious hepatitis *n.* See **hepatitis A.**

infectious mononucleosis *n.* An acute infectious disease caused by Epstein-Barr virus and characterized by fever, swollen lymph nodes, sore throat, and lymphocyte abnormalities.

in•fec•tive (ĭn-fĕk′tĭv) *adj.* Capable of producing infection; infectious. — **in•fec′tive•ness, in′fec•tiv′i•ty** *n.*

in•fe•lic•i•tous (ĭn′fĭ-lĭs′ĭ-təs) *adj.* **1.** Inappropriate; ill-chosen: *an infelicitous remark.* **2.** Not happy; unfortunate.

in•fe•lic•i•ty (ĭn′fĭ-lĭs′ĭ-tē) *n., pl.* **-ties. 1.** The quality or condition of being infelicitous. **2.** Something inappropriate or unpleasing. [ME *infelicite* < Lat. *īnfēlīcitās* < *īnfēlīx, īnfēlīc-*, unhappy : *in-*, not; see IN-¹ + *fēlīx*, happy; see **dhē(i)-*.**]

in•fer (ĭn-fûr′) *v.* **-ferred, -fer•ring, -fers.** —*tr.* **1.** To conclude from evidence or premises. **2.** To reason from circumstance; surmise. **3.** To lead to as a consequence or conclusion: *"Socrates argued that a statue inferred the existence of a sculptor"* (Academy). **4.** *Usage Problem.* To hint; imply. —*intr.* To draw inferences. [Lat. *īnferre*, to bring in, adduce : *in-*, in; see IN-² + *ferre*, to bear; see **bher-¹*.**] — **in•fer′a•ble** *adj.* — **in•fer′a•bly** *adv.* — **in•fer′rer** *n.*

Usage Note: The traditional distinction between *imply* and *infer* is a useful one. When we say that a speaker or sentence implies something, we mean that it is conveyed or suggested without being stated outright: *When the mayor said that she would not rule out a business tax increase, she implied* (not *inferred*) *that some taxes might be raised.* Inference, on the other hand, is the activity performed by a reader or interpreter in deriving conclusions that are not explicit in what is said: *When the mayor said that she would not rule out a tax increase, we inferred that she had been consulting with some new financial advisers, since her old advisers were in favor of tax reductions.*

in•fer•ence (ĭn′fər-əns) *n.* **1.a.** The act or process of deriving logical conclusions from premises known or assumed to be true. **b.** The act of reasoning from factual knowledge or evidence. **2.a.** Something inferred. **b.** *Usage Problem.* A hint or suggestion. See Usage Note at **infer.**

in•fer•en•tial (ĭn′fə-rĕn′shəl) *adj.* **1.** Of, relating to, or involving inference. **2.** Derived or capable of being derived by inference. — **in′fer•en′tial•ly** *adv.*

in•fe•ri•or (ĭn-fîr′ē-ər) *adj.* **1.** Low or lower in order, degree, or rank. **2.a.** Low or lower in quality, value, or estimation: *felt inferior to his older sibling.* **b.** Second-rate; poor. **3.** Situated under or beneath. **4.** *Bot.* Located below the perianth and other floral parts. Used of an ovary. **5.** *Anat.* Located beneath or directed downward. **6.** *Print.* Set below the normal line of type; subscript. **7.** *Astron.* **a.** Orbiting between the earth and the sun. **b.** Lying below the horizon. —*n.* **1.** A person lower in rank, status, or accomplishment than another. **2.** *Print.* An inferior character, such as the number 2 in CO_2. [ME < Lat. *īnferior*, comp. of *īnferus*, low. See **n̥dher-*.**] — **in•fe′ri•or′i•ty** (-ôr′ĭ-tē, -ŏr′-) *n.*

inferiority complex *n.* A persistent sense of inadequacy or a tendency to self-diminishment.

in•fer•nal (ĭn-fûr′nəl) *adj.* **1.a.** Of or relating to a lower world of the dead. **b.** Of or relating to hell. **2.** Fiendish; diabolical: *infernal instruments of war.* **3.** Abominable; awful. [ME < OFr. < LLat. *īnfernālis* < *īnfernus*, hell < Lat., lower, underground. See **n̥dher-*.**] — **in•fer′nal•ly** *adv.*

infernal machine *n. Law.* An explosive device maliciously designed to harm or destroy.

in•fer•no (ĭn-fûr′nō) *n., pl.* **-nos. 1.** A place or condition suggestive of hell. **2.** A place of fiery heat or destruction. [Ital., hell < LLat. *īnfernus*. See INFERNAL.]

in•fer•tile (ĭn-fûr′tl) *adj.* **1.** Not fertile; unproductive or barren. **2.** *Biol.* Incapable of producing offspring; sterile.

in•fer•til•i•ty (ĭn′fər-tĭl′ĭ-tē) *n.* **1.** Absent or diminished fertility. **2.** The persistent inability to conceive a child.

in•fest (ĭn-fĕst′) *tr.v.* **-fest•ed, -fest•ing, -fests. 1.** To inhabit or overrun in numbers large enough to be harmful, threatening, or obnoxious. **2.** To live as a parasite in or on: *livestock infested with tapeworms.* [ME *infesten*, to distress < OFr. *infester* < Lat. *īnfestāre* < *īnfestus*, hostile. See **gʷhedh-*.**] — **in′fes•ta′tion** *n.* — **in•fest′er** *n.*

in•fi•del (ĭn′fĭ-dəl, -dĕl′) *n.* **1.** An unbeliever with respect to a particular religion, esp. Christianity or Islam. **2.** One who has no religious beliefs. **3.** One who doubts or rejects a particular doctrine, system, or principle. [ME *infidele* < OFr. < Lat. *īnfidēlis*, disloyal : *in-*, not; see IN-¹ + *fidēlis*, faithful (< *fidēs*, faith; see **bheidh-***).]

in•fi•del•i•ty (ĭn′fĭ-dĕl′ĭ-tē) *n., pl.* **-ties. 1.a.** Unfaithfulness to a sexual partner, esp. a spouse. **b.** An act of sexual unfaithfulness. **2.** Lack of loyalty. **3.** Lack of religious belief.

in•field (ĭn′fēld′) *n.* **1.** *Baseball.* **a.** The area of the field bounded by home plate and first, second, and third bases. **b.** The defensive positions of first base, second base, third base, and shortstop considered as a unit. **2.** *Sports.* The area inside a racetrack or running track. **3.** A field located near a farmhouse.

in•field•er (ĭn′fēl′dər) *n. Baseball.* An infield player.

in•fight•ing (ĭn′fī′tĭng) *n.* **1.** Contentious rivalry or disagreement among members or groups within an organization. **2.** *Sports.* Fighting or boxing at close range. — **in′fight′er** *n.*

in•fil•trate (ĭn-fĭl′trāt′, ĭn′fĭl-) *v.* **-trat•ed, -trat•ing, -trates.** —*tr.* **1.a.** To pass (troops, for example) surreptitiously into enemy-held territory. **b.** To penetrate with hostile intent. **2.** To enter or take up positions in gradually or surreptitiously, as for espionage. **3.** To cause (a liquid, for example) to permeate by passing through interstices or pores. **4.** To permeate (a porous substance) with a liquid or gas. —*intr.* To gain entrance gradually or surreptitiously. —*n.* One that infiltrates, esp. an abnormal substance that accumulates gradually in cells or body tissues. — **in•fil′tra•tive** (-trə-tĭv) *adj.* — **in•fil′tra•tor** *n.*

in•fil•tra•tion (ĭn′fĭl-trā′shən) *n.* **1.** The act or process of infiltrating. **2.** The state of being infiltrated. **3.** Something that infiltrates.

infin. *abbr.* Infinitive.

in•fi•nite (ĭn′fə-nĭt) *adj.* **1.** Having no boundaries or limits. **2.** Immeasurably great or large; boundless: *infinite importance.* **3.** *Math.* **a.** Existing beyond or being greater than any arbitrarily large value. **b.** Unlimited in spatial extent. **c.** Of or relating to a set capable of being put into one-to-one correspondence with a proper subset of itself. —*n.* Something infinite. — **in′fi•nite•ly** *adv.* — **in′fi•nite•ness** *n.*

Syns: *infinite, boundless, eternal, illimitable, sempiternal.* The central meaning shared by these adjectives is "having no beginning or end": *infinite wisdom; boundless ambition; eternal beauty; illimitable space; sempiternal truth.* See also Syns at **incalculable.** ***Ant:*** *finite.*

Usage Note: *Infinite* is sometimes grouped with absolute terms such as *unique, absolute,* and *omnipotent,* since in its strict mathematical sense it allows no degree modification or comparison; one quantity cannot be more infinite than another. Unlike other absolute terms, however, *infinite* also does not permit modification by adverbs such as *nearly* and *almost.* In nontechnical usage *infinite* is often used metaphorically to refer to an unimaginably large degree or amount, and here the comparison of the word is unexceptionable. See Usage Note at **unique.**

in•fin•i•tes•i•mal (ĭn′fĭn-ĭ-tĕs′ə-məl) *adj.* **1.** Immeasurably or incalculably minute. **2.** *Math.* Capable of having values approaching zero as a limit. —*n.* **1.** An infinitesimal amount or quantity. **2.** *Math.* An infinitesimal function or variable. [< NLat. *īnfīnītēsimus*, infinite in rank < Lat. *īnfīnītus*, infinite. See INFINITE.] — **in′fin•i•tes′i•mal•ly** *adv.*

infinitesimal calculus *n. Math.* Differential and integral calculus.

in•fin•i•ti•val (ĭn′fĭn-ĭ-tī′vəl) *adj.* Relating to the infinitive.

in•fin•i•tive (ĭn-fĭn′ĭ-tĭv) *n.* A verb form that functions as a substantive while retaining certain verbal characteristics and that in English may be preceded by *to,* as in *We want to go too,* or may also occur without *to,* as in *We may finish today.* See Usage Note at **split infinitive.** [< ME *infinitif*, of an infinitive < OFr. < LLat. *īnfīnītīvus*, unlimited, indefinite, infinitive < Lat. *īnfīnītus*, infinite. See INFINITE.]

in•fin•i•tude (ĭn-fĭn′ĭ-to͞od′, -tyo͞od′) *n.* **1.** The state or quality of being infinite. **2.** An immeasurably large quantity, number, or extent.

in•fin•i•ty (ĭn-fĭn′ĭ-tē) *n., pl.* **-ties. 1.** The quality or condition of being infinite. **2.** Unbounded space, time, or quantity. **3.** An indefinitely large number or amount. **4.** *Math.* The limit that a function f is said to approach at $x = a$ when for x close to a, $f(x)$ is larger than any preassigned number. **5.a.** A range in relation to an optical system in which light rays reflected from objects may be regarded as parallel. **b.** A distance setting, as on a camera, beyond which the entire field is in focus.

in•firm (ĭn-fûrm′) *adj.* **1.** Weak in body, esp. from old age or disease; feeble. **2.** Lacking firmness of will, character, or purpose; irresolute. **3.** Not strong or stable; shaky. [ME *infirme* < OFr. < Lat. *īnfirmus* : *in-*, not; see IN-^{1} + *firmus*, strong, firm; see **dher-***.] **—in•firm′ly** *adv.*

in•fir•ma•ry (ĭn-fûr′mə-rē) *n., pl.* **-ries.** A place for the care of the infirm, sick, or injured, esp. a small hospital or dispensary in an institution. [ME *infirmarie* < Med.Lat. *īnfirmāria* < Lat. *īnfirmus*, infirm. See INFIRM.]

in•fir•mi•ty (ĭn-fûr′mĭ-tē) *n., pl.* **-ties. 1.** A bodily ailment or weakness, esp. one brought on by old age. **2.** Frailty; feebleness. **3.** A condition or disease producing weakness. **4.** A failing or defect in a person's character.

in•fix (ĭn-fĭks′) *tr.v.* **-fixed, -fix•ing, -fix•es. 1.** To fix in the mind; instill. **2.** *Ling.* To insert (a morphological element) into the body of a word. —*n.* (ĭn′fĭks′). An inflectional or derivational element appearing in the body of a word. [Ult. < Lat. *īnfixus*, p.part. of *īnfīgere*, to fasten in : *in-*, in; see IN-^{2} + *fīgere*, to fasten; see **dhīgʷ-***.]

infl. *abbr.* **1.** Influence **2.** Influenced.

in•flame (ĭn-flām′) *v.* **-flamed, -flam•ing, -flames.** —*tr.* **1.** To arouse to passionate feeling or action. **2.** To make more violent; intensify. **3.a.** To cause (the skin) to redden or grow hot. **b.** To turn red or make glow. **4.** To produce inflammation in (a tissue or an organ). **5.** To set on fire; kindle. —*intr.* **1.** To become excited or aroused. **2.** To be affected by inflammation. **3.** To catch fire. [Ult. < Lat. *īnflammāre* : *in-*, intensive pref.; see IN-^{2} + *flammāre*, to set on fire (< *flamma*, flame; see **bhel-**^{1}*).] **—in•flam′er** *n.*

in•flam•ma•ble (ĭn-flăm′ə-bəl) *adj.* **1.** Easily ignited and capable of burning rapidly; flammable. See Usage Note at **flammable. 2.** Quickly or easily aroused to strong emotion; excitable. [Ult. < Lat. *īnflammāre*, to inflame. See INFLAME.] **—in•flam′ma•bil′i•ty** *n.* **—in•flam′ma•ble** *n.* **—in•flam′ma•bly** *adv.*

in•flam•ma•tion (ĭn′flə-mā′shən) *n.* **1.** The act of inflaming or the state of being inflamed. **2.** A localized protective reaction of tissue to irritation, injury, or infection, characterized by pain, redness, swelling, and sometimes loss of function.

in•flam•ma•to•ry (ĭn-flăm′ə-tôr′ē, -tōr′ē) *adj.* **1.** Arousing passion or strong emotion, such as anger. **2.** Characterized or caused by inflammation. **—in•flam′ma•to′ri•ly** *adv.*

in•flat•a•ble (ĭn-flā′tə-bəl) *adj.* Designed to be filled with air or gas before use: *an inflatable mattress.* —*n.* An object that can be filled with air or gas, esp.: **a.** A small rubber boat or raft. **b.** A large helium or hot-air balloon.

in•flate (ĭn-flāt′) *v.* **-flat•ed, -flat•ing, -flates.** —*tr.* **1.** To fill (something) with air or gas so as to make it swell. **2.a.** To enlarge or amplify unduly or improperly; aggrandize. **b.** To raise or expand abnormally or improperly. See Syns at **exaggerate. 3.** To cause (a currency or an economy) to undergo inflation. —*intr.* To become inflated. [ME *inflaten* < Lat. *īnflāre*, *īnflāt-* : *in-*, in; see IN-^{2} + *flāre*, to blow; see **bhlē-***.] **—in•fla′tor, in•flat′er** *n.*

in•flat•ed (ĭn-flā′tĭd) *adj.* **1.** Filled or expanded by gas or air. **2.** Unduly enlarged or aggrandized; swollen: *an inflated estimate.* **3.** Full of empty or pretentious language; bombastic. **4.** Raised or expanded to abnormal levels: *an inflated economy.* **5.** Hollow and enlarged: *an inflated calyx.*

in•fla•tion (ĭn-flā′shən) *n.* **1.** The act of inflating or the state of being inflated. **2.** A persistent increase in the level of consumer prices or a persistent decline in the purchasing power of money, caused by an increase in available currency and credit beyond the proportion of available goods and services.

in•fla•tion•ar•y (ĭn-flā′shə-nĕr′ē) *adj.* Of, associated with, or tending to cause inflation: *inflationary prices.*

in•fla•tion•ist (ĭn-flā′shə-nĭst) *n.* An advocate of deliberate inflation achieved by increasing available currency and credit. **—in•fla′tion•ism** *n.* **—in•fla′tion•ist** *adj.*

in•flect (ĭn-flĕkt′) *v.* **-flect•ed, -flect•ing, -flects.** —*tr.* **1.** To alter (the voice) in tone or pitch; modulate. **2.** *Gram.* To alter (a word) by inflection. **3.** To turn from a course or a specified alignment; bend. —*intr. Gram.* **1.** To be modified by inflection. **2.** To give all of the inflected forms of a word; to provide a paradigm. [ME *inflecten*, to bend down < Lat. *īnflectere* : *in-*, in; see IN-^{2} + *flectere*, to bend.] **—in•flec′tive** *adj.* **—in•flec′tor** *n.*

in•flec•tion (ĭn-flĕk′shən) *n.* **1.** The act of inflecting or the state of being inflected. **2.** Alteration in pitch or tone of the voice. **3.** *Gram.* **a.** An alternation of the form of a word by adding affixes or by changing the form of a base in order to indicate grammatical features such as number, person, mood, or tense. **b.** The paradigm of a word. **c.** A pattern of forming paradigms. **4.** A turning or bending away from a course or position of alignment. **—in•flec′tion•al** *adj.* **—in•flec′tion•al•ly** *adv.*

in•flexed (ĭn-flĕkst′) *adj.* Bent or curved inward or downward, as petals. [< Lat. *īnflexus*, p.part. of *īnflectere*, to bend. See INFLECT.]

in•flex•i•ble (ĭn-flĕk′sə-bəl) *adj.* **1.** Not easily bent; stiff or rigid. See Syns at **stiff. 2.** Incapable of being changed; unalterable. **3.** Unyielding in purpose, principle, or temper; immovable. **—in•flex′i•bil′i•ty, in•flex′i•ble•ness** *n.* **—in•flex′i•bly** *adv.*

in•flex•ion (ĭn-flĕk′shən) *n. Chiefly British.* Var. of **inflection.**

in•flict (ĭn-flĭkt′) *tr.v.* **-flict•ed, -flict•ing, -flicts. 1.** To deal or mete out (something punishing or burdensome); impose. **2.** To afflict. [Lat. *īnflīgere*, *īnflīct-* : *in-*, on; see IN-^{2} + *flīgere*, to strike.] **—in•flict′er, in•flic′tor** *n.*

in•flic•tion (ĭn-flĭk′shən) *n.* **1.** The act or process of imposing or meting out something unpleasant. **2.** Something, such as punishment, that is imposed. **—in•flic′tive** *adj.*

in-flight (ĭn′flīt′) *adj.* **1.** Occurring, carried out, or present while in flight. **2.** Provided or offered during a flight.

in•flo•res•cence (ĭn′flə-rĕs′əns) *n.* **1.a.** A characteristic arrangement of flowers on a stem. **b.** A flower cluster. **2.** A flowering. [NLat. *īnflōrēscentia* < LLat. *īnflōrēscēns*, *īnflōrēscent-*, pr.part. of *īnflōrēscere*, to begin to flower : Lat. *in-*, intensive pref.; see IN-^{2} + Lat. *flōrēscere*, to begin to blossom; see FLORESCENCE.] **—in′flo•res′cent** *adj.*

in•flow (ĭn′flō′) *n.* **1.** The act or process of flowing in or into. **2.** Something that flows in or into: *a freshwater inflow.*

in•flu•ence (ĭn′flo͞o-əns) *n.* **1.** A power affecting a person, thing, or course of events, esp. without direct or apparent effort. **2.a.** Power to sway or affect based on prestige, wealth, ability, or position. **b.** One exercising such power: *You are a bad influence on me.* **c.** An effect or change produced by such power. **3.** In astrology, a factor determining one's tendencies and characteristics, believed to be caused by the positions of the stars and planets at the time of one's birth. —*tr.v.* **-enced, -enc•ing, -enc•es. 1.** To produce an effect on by imperceptible or intangible means; sway. **2.** To affect the nature, development, or condition of; modify. —***idiom.* under the influence.** Intoxicated, esp. with alcohol. [ME < OFr. < Med.Lat. *īnfluentia*, influx < Lat. *īnfluēns*, *īnfluent-*, pr.part. of *īnfluere*, to flow in : *in-*, in; see IN-^{2} + *fluere*, to flow; see **bhleu-***.] **—in′flu•ence•a•ble** *adj.* **—in′flu•enc•er** *n.*

in•flu•ent (ĭn′flo͞o-ənt, ĭn-flo͞o′-) *adj.* Flowing in or into. —*n.* **1.** An inflow, esp. a tributary. **2.** *Ecol.* A nondominant organism in a community that modifies it in an important way. [ME < Lat. *īnfluēns*, *īnfluent-*, pr.part. of *īnfluere*, to flow in. See INFLUENCE.]

in•flu•en•tial (ĭn′flo͞o-ĕn′shəl) *adj.* Having or exercising influence. —*n.* One that is of considerable importance or influence. **—in′flu•en′tial•ly** *adv.*

in•flu•en•za (ĭn′flo͞o-ĕn′zə) *n.* **1.** An acute contagious viral infection characterized by inflammation of the respiratory tract and by fever, chills, muscular pain, and prostration. **2.** Any of various viral infections of domestic animals characterized generally by fever and respiratory involvement. [Ital. < Med.Lat. *īnfluentia*, influence (so called apparently from the belief that epidemics were due to the influence of the stars). See INFLUENCE.] **—in′flu•en′zal** *adj.*

in•flux (ĭn′flŭks′) *n.* **1.** A flowing in: *an influx of capital.* **2.** A mass arrival or incoming: *an influx of visitors.* [LLat. *īnflūxus* < Lat., p.part. of *īnfluere*, to flow in. See INFLUENCE.]

in•fo (ĭn′fō) *n. Informal.* Information.

in•fold (ĭn-fōld′) *v.* **-fold•ed, -fold•ing, -folds.** —*intr.* To fold inward. —*tr.* To enfold. **—in•fold′er** *n.* **—in•fold′ment** *n.*

in•form (ĭn-fôrm′) *v.* **-formed, -form•ing, -forms.** —*tr.* **1.a.** To impart information to; make aware of something. **b.** To acquaint (oneself) with knowledge of a subject. **2.** To give form or character to; imbue with a quality or an essence. **3.** To be a pervasive presence in; animate. **4.** *Obsolete.* To form (the mind or character) by teaching or training. —*intr.* **1.** To give or provide information. **2.** To disclose confidential or incriminating information to an authority. [ME *enfourmen*, *informen* < OFr. *enfourmer* < Lat. *īnfōrmāre* : *in-*, in; see IN-^{2} + *fōrmāre*, to fashion (< *fōrma*, form).]

in•for•mal (ĭn-fôr′məl) *adj.* **1.** Not formal or ceremonious; casual. **2.** Not being in accord with prescribed regulations or forms; unofficial. **3.** Suited for everyday wear or use. **4.** Being more appropriate for use in the spoken language than in the written language. **—in•for′mal•ly** *adv.*

in•for•mal•i•ty (ĭn′fôr-măl′ĭ-tē) *n., pl.* **-ties. 1.** The state or quality of being informal. **2.** An informal act.

in•form•ant (ĭn-fôr′mənt) *n.* **1.a.** One that gives information. **b.** One who informs against others; an informer. **2.** One who furnishes linguistic or cultural information to a researcher.

in•for•mat•ics (ĭn′fər-măt′ĭks) *n.* (*used with a sing. v.*) *Chief-*

inflatable
In Macy's Thanksgiving Parade, New York City

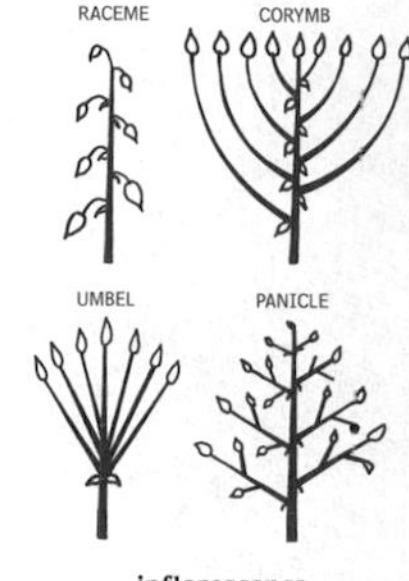

inflorescence

ă pat	oi boy
ā pay	ou out
âr care	o͝o took
ä father	o͞o boot
ĕ pet	ŭ cut
ē be	ûr urge
ĭ pit	th thin
ī pie	*th* this
îr pier	hw which
ŏ pot	zh vision
ō toe	ə about, item
ô paw	

Stress marks:
′ (primary);
′ (secondary), as in
dictionary (dĭk′shə-nĕr′ē)

Jean Auguste Dominique Ingres
After a self-portrait originally painted in 1804 and reworked in 1850

ly British. Information science. [INFORMAT(ION) + -ICS.]

in•for•ma•tion (ĭn′fər-mā′shən) *n.* **1.** Knowledge derived from study, experience, or instruction. **2.** Knowledge of a specific event or situation; intelligence. **3.** A collection of facts or data: *statistical information.* **4.** The act of informing or the condition of being informed; communication of knowledge: *for the information of our passengers.* **5.** *Comp. Sci.* A nonaccidental signal or character used as an input to a computer or communications system. **6.** A numerical measure of the uncertainty of an experimental outcome. **7.** *Law.* A formal accusation of a crime made by a public officer rather than by grand jury indictment. **—in′for•ma′tion•al** *adj.*

information retrieval *n. Comp. Sci.* The process of searching for and recovering specific data from large quantities of information stored in a computer.

information science *n.* The science that is concerned with the gathering, manipulation, classification, storage, and retrieval of recorded knowledge.

information theory *n.* The theory of the probability of transmission of messages with specified accuracy when the bits of information constituting the messages are subject, with certain probabilities, to transmission errors and noise.

in•form•a•tive (ĭn-fôr′mə-tĭv) *adj.* Serving to inform; providing or disclosing information; instructive. **—in•form′a•tive•ly** *adv.* **—in•form′a•tive•ness** *n.*

in•form•a•to•ry (ĭn-fôr′mə-tôr′ē, -tōr′ē) *adj.* Informative.

in•formed (ĭn-fôrmd′) *adj.* **1.** Possessing, displaying, or based on reliable information. **2.** Knowledgeable; educated.

informed consent *n.* Consent by a patient to a surgical or medical procedure or participation in a clinical study after understanding the medical facts and the risks involved.

in•form•er (ĭn-fôr′mər) *n.* An informant, esp. one who informs against others, often for compensation.

infra– *pref.* Inferior to, below, or beneath: *infrasonic.* [< Lat. *īnfrā,* below. See **ndher-***.]

in•fra•class (ĭn′frə-klăs′) *n.* A taxonomic category of related organisms ranking below a subclass and above an order.

in•fract (ĭn-frăkt′) *tr.v.* **-fract•ed, -fract•ing, -fracts.** To infringe; violate. [Lat. *īnfringere, īnfrāct-,* to destroy. See INFRINGE.] **—in•frac′tor** *n.*

in•frac•tion (ĭn-frăk′shən) *n.* The act or an instance of infringing; a violation. See Syns at **breach.**

in•fra dig (ĭn′frə dĭg′) *adj.* Beneath one's dignity. [Short for Lat. *īnfrā dignitātem* : *īnfrā,* below + *dignitātem,* dignity.]

in•fra•hu•man (ĭ′frə-hyo͞o′mən) *adj.* Of a lower order than human beings; subhuman. **—in′fra•hu′man** *n.*

in•fran•gi•ble (ĭn-frăn′jə-bəl) *adj.* **1.** Difficult or impossible to break or separate into parts. **2.** Inviolable: *infrangible human rights.* [LLat. *īnfrangibilis* : Lat. *in-,* not; see IN-¹ + Lat. *frangere,* to break; see **bhreg-***.] **—in•fran′gi•bil′i•ty** *n.* **—in•fran′gi•bly** *adv.*

in•fra•red (ĭn′frə-rĕd′) *adj.* **1.** Of or relating to the range of invisible radiation wavelengths from about 750 nanometers, just longer than red in the visible spectrum, to 1 millimeter, on the border of the microwave region. **2.** Generating, using, or sensitive to infrared radiation. —*n.* Infrared light or the infrared part of the spectrum.

in•fra•son•ic (ĭn′frə-sŏn′ĭk) *adj.* Generating or using waves or vibrations with frequencies below that of audible sound.

in•fra•sound (ĭn′frə-sound′) *n.* Vibrations of the air with frequencies below that of human hearing.

in•fra•struc•ture (ĭn′frə-strŭk′chər) *n.* **1.** An underlying base or foundation, esp. for an organization or a system. **2.** The basic facilities, services, and installations needed for the functioning of a community or society, such as transportation and communications systems.

in•fre•quent (ĭn-frē′kwənt) *adj.* **1.** Not occurring regularly; occasional or rare: *an infrequent guest.* **2.** Situated or placed at rather wide intervals, as in time or space. **—in•fre′quence, in•fre′quen•cy** *n.* **—in•fre′quent•ly** *adv.*

in•fringe (ĭn-frĭnj′) *v.* **-fringed, -fring•ing, -fring•es.** —*tr.* **1.** To transgress or exceed the limits of; violate: *infringe a contract.* **2.** *Obsolete.* To defeat; invalidate. —*intr.* To encroach on someone or something. [Lat. *īnfringere,* to destroy : *in-,* intensive pref.; see IN-² + *frangere,* to break; see **bhreg-***.] **—in•fring′er** *n.*

in•fringe•ment (ĭn-frĭnj′mənt) *n.* **1.** A violation, as of a law, a regulation, or an agreement; a breach. **2.** An encroachment, as of a right or privilege. See Syns at **breach.**

in•fruc•tes•cence (ĭn′frŭk-tĕs′əns) *n.* The fruiting stage of an inflorescence. [Fr. : Lat. *in-,* in; see IN-² + Lat. *frūctus,* fruit; see FRUIT.]

in•fun•dib•u•li•form (ĭn′fən-dĭb′yə-lə-fôrm′) *adj.* Shaped like a funnel.

in•fun•dib•u•lum (ĭn′fən-dĭb′yə-ləm) *n., pl.* **-la** (-lə). *Anat.* Any of various funnel-shaped body passages, openings, or parts, esp.: **a.** The stalk of the pituitary gland. **b.** The calyx of a kidney. **c.** The ovarian opening of a fallopian tube. [Lat., funnel < *īnfundere,* to pour in. See INFUSE.] **—in′fun•dib′u•lar** (-lər), **in′fun•dib′u•late′** (-lāt′, -lĭt) *adj.*

in•fu•ri•ate (ĭn-fyo͝or′ē-āt′) *tr.v.* **-at•ed, -at•ing, -ates.** To make furious; enrage. —*adj.* (ĭn-fyo͝or′ē-ĭt). *Archaic.* Furious. [Med.Lat. *īnfuriāre, īnfuriāt-* : Lat. *in-,* intensive pref.; see IN-² + Lat. *furiāre,* to enrage (< *furia,* fury; see FURY).] **—in•fu′ri•at′ing•ly** *adv.* **—in•fu′ri•a′tion** *n.*

in•fuse (ĭn-fyo͞oz′) *tr.v.* **-fused, -fus•ing, -fus•es. 1.** To put into or introduce as if by pouring. **2.** To fill or cause to be filled with something. **3.** *Chem.* To steep or soak without boiling in order to extract soluble elements or active principles. **4.** To introduce (a solution) into the body through a vein for therapeutic purposes. [ME *infusen* < OFr. *infuser* < Lat. *īnfundere, īnfūs-* : *in-,* in; see IN-² + *fundere,* to pour; see **gheu-***.] **—in•fus′er** *n.* **—in•fus′i•bil′i•ty, in•fus′i•ble•ness** *n.* **—in•fus′i•ble** *adj.*

in•fu•sion (ĭn-fyo͞o′zhən) *n.* **1.** The act or process of infusing. **2.** Something infused or introduced. **3.** The liquid product obtained by infusing: *an infusion of medicinal herbs.* **4.a.** Introduction of a solution into the body through a vein for therapeutic purposes. **b.** The solution so introduced.

–ing¹ *suff.* **1.** Used to form the present participle of verbs: *seeing.* **2.** Used to form adjectives resembling present participles but not derived from verbs: *swashbuckling.* [ME, alteration (influenced by *-inge,* n. or gerund suff.; see -ING²) of *-ende, -inde* < OE *-ende,* pr.part. suff.]

–ing² *suff.* **1.a.** Action, process, or art: *dancing.* **b.** An instance of an action, a process, or an act: *a gathering.* **2.** An action or a process connected with a specified thing: *berrying.* **3.a.** Something necessary to perform an action or a process: *mooring.* **b.** The result of an action or a process: *a drawing.* **c.** Something connected with a specified thing or concept: *siding; offing.* [ME < OE *-ung, -ing.*]

–ing³ *suff.* One having a specified quality or nature: *wilding.* [ME < OE, belonging to, descended from.]

in•gath•er (ĭn′găth′ər) *v.* **-ered, -er•ing, -ers.** —*tr.* To gather in; collect. —*intr.* To come together in a central place.

Inge (ĭnj), **William.** 1913–73. Amer. playwright whose dramas include *Picnic* (1953).

Inge (ĭng), **William Ralph.** "the Gloomy Dean." 1860–1954. British prelate noted for his pessimistic sermons.

in•gen•ious (ĭn-jēn′yəs) *adj.* **1.** Marked by inventive skill and imagination. **2.** Having or arising from an inventive or cunning mind; clever: *an ingenious scheme.* See Syns at **clever. 3.** *Obsolete.* Having genius; brilliant. [ME < OFr. *ingenios* < Lat. *ingeniōsus* < *ingenium,* inborn talent. See **genə-***.] **—in•gen′ious•ly** *adv.* **—in•gen′ious•ness** *n.*

in•gé•nue (ăN′zhə-no͞o′) *n.* **1.** An artless, innocent girl or young woman. **2.a.** The role of an artless, innocent girl or young woman in a dramatic production. **b.** An actress playing such a role. [Fr., fem. of *ingénu,* guileless < Lat. *ingenuus,* ingenuous. See INGENUOUS.]

in•ge•nu•i•ty (ĭn′jə-no͞o′ĭ-tē, -nyo͞o′-) *n., pl.* **-ties. 1.** Inventive skill or imagination; cleverness. **2.** Imaginative and clever design or construction. **3.** An ingenious or imaginative contrivance. **4.** *Obsolete.* Ingenuousness. [Lat. *ingenuitās,* frankness (influenced by INGENIOUS) < *ingenuus,* ingenuous. See INGENUOUS.]

in•gen•u•ous (ĭn-jĕn′yo͞o-əs) *adj.* **1.** Lacking in sophistication or worldliness; artless. **2.** Openly straightforward or frank; candid. See Syns at **naive. 3.** *Obsolete.* Ingenious. [< Lat. *ingenuus,* honest, freeborn. See **genə-***.] **—in•gen′u•ous•ly** *adv.* **—in•gen′u•ous•ness** *n.*

In•ger•soll (ĭng′gər-sôl′, -sŏl′, -səl), **Robert Green.** 1833–99. Amer. politician and lecturer known for his support of scientific and humanistic rationalism.

in•gest (ĭn-jĕst′) *tr.v.* **-gest•ed, -gest•ing, -gests.** To take into the body by the mouth for digestion or absorption. [Lat. *ingerere, ingest-* : *in-,* in; see IN-² + *gerere,* to carry.] **—in•ges′tion** *n.* **—in•ges′tive** *adj.*

in•ges•ta (ĭn-jĕs′tə) *pl.n.* Ingested matter, esp. food taken into the body through the mouth. [NLat. < neut. pl. of Lat. *ingestus,* p.part. of *ingerere,* to carry in. See INGEST.]

in•gle (ĭng′gəl) *n.* **1.** An open fire in a fireplace. **2.** A fireplace. [Perh. Sc.Gael. *aingeal,* fire, light.]

in•gle•nook (ĭng′gəl-no͝ok′) *n.* **1.** A nook or corner beside an open fireplace. **2.** A bench, esp. either of two facing benches, placed in a nook or corner beside a fireplace. [INGLE + NOOK.]

In•gle•wood (ĭng′gəl-wo͝od′). A city of S CA, a suburb of Los Angeles. Pop. 109,602.

in•glo•ri•ous (ĭn-glôr′ē-əs, -glōr′-) *adj.* **1.** Ignominious; disgraceful. **2.** Not famous or renowned; obscure. **—in•glo′ri•ous•ly** *adv.* **—in•glo′ri•ous•ness** *n.*

in•go•ing (ĭn′gō′ĭng) *adj.* **1.** Going in; entering. **2.** Initial; opening.

In•gol•stadt (ĭng′gəl-shtät′, -gôl-). A city of SE Germany on the Danube R. N of Munich; chartered c. 1250. Pop. 90,763.

in•got (ĭng′gət) *n.* **1.** A mass of metal cast in a standard shape for convenient storage or shipment. **2.** A casting mold for metal. [ME, mold for casting metal : prob. *in-,* in; see IN-² + OE *goten,* p.part. of *geotan,* to pour, or perh. < OFr. *lingot,* metal ingot (as if *l'ingot* : *le,* definite article + **ingot,* ingot).]

ingot iron *n.* A bar of iron that contains small quantities of other elements.

in•grain (ĭn-grān′) *tr.v.* **-grained, -grain•ing, -grains. 1.** To fix deeply or indelibly, as in the mind. **2.** *Archaic.* To dye or stain

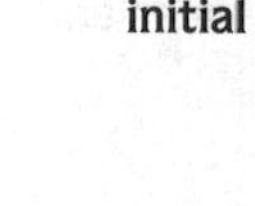

into the fiber of. —*adj.* (ĭn′grān′). **1.** Deep-seated; ingrained. **2.** Made of predyed fibers; thoroughly dyed. **3.** Made of fiber or yarn dyed before weaving, as a rug. —*n.* (ĭn′grān′). **1.** Yarn or fiber dyed before manufacture. **2.** An ingrain rug or carpet. [Var. of ENGRAIN.]

in•grained (ĭn-grānd′) *adj.* **1.** Firmly established; deep-seated. **2.** Worked deeply into the texture or fiber.

in•grate (ĭn′grāt′) *n.* An ungrateful person. [< ME *ingrat*, ungrateful < OFr. < Lat. *ingrātus* : *in-*, not; see IN–[1] + *grātus*, pleasing, thankful; see **gʷerə-[2]***.]

in•gra•ti•ate (ĭn-grā′shē-āt′) *tr.v.* **-at•ed, -at•ing, -ates.** To bring (oneself, for example) into another's favor, esp. deliberately. [Perh. < Ital. *ingraziare* < *in grazia*, into favor < Lat. *in grātiam* : *in*, in; see IN–[2] + *grātiam*, accusative of *grātia*, favor (< *grātus*, pleasing; see **gʷerə-[2]***).] —**in•gra′ti•a′tion** *n.* —**in•gra′ti•a•to′ry** (-shē-ə-tôr′ē, -tōr′ē) *adj.*

in•gra•ti•at•ing (ĭn-grā′shē-ā′tĭng) *adj.* **1.** Pleasing; agreeable. **2.** Calculated to please or win favor. —**in•gra′ti•at′ing•ly** *adv.*

in•grat•i•tude (ĭn-grăt′ĭ-to͞od′, -tyo͞od′) *n.* Lack of gratitude.

in•gre•di•ent (ĭn-grē′dē-ənt) *n.* An element in a mixture or compound; a constituent. See Syns at **element.** [ME < Lat. *ingrediēns*, *ingredient-*, pr.part. of *ingredī*, to enter. See INGRESS.]

In•gres (ăN′grə), **Jean Auguste Dominique.** 1780–1867. French painter best known for his historical works.

in•gress (ĭn′grĕs′) *n.* **1.** Also **in•gres•sion** (ĭn-grĕsh′ən). A going in or entering. **2.** Right or permission to enter. **3.** A means or place of entering. [ME *ingresse* < Lat. *ingressus* < p.part. of *ingredī*, to enter : *in-*, in; see IN–[2] + *gradī*, to step; see **ghredh-***.]

in•gres•sive (ĭn-grĕs′ĭv) *adj.* **1.** Of, relating to, or involving ingress. **2.** *Gram.* Inchoative. **3.** *Ling.* Of or being a speech sound produced with an inhalation of breath. —**in•gres′sive** *n.* —**in•gres′sive•ness** *n.*

in-group (ĭn′gro͞op′) *n.* A group of people united by common beliefs, attitudes, or interests and usu. excluding outsiders.

in•grow•ing (ĭn′grō′ĭng) *adj.* Growing inward or into, esp. into the flesh.

in•grown (ĭn′grōn′) *adj.* **1.** Grown abnormally into the flesh. **2.** Inbred; innate. **3.** Insular; self-contained.

in•growth (ĭn′grōth′) *n.* **1.** The act of growing inward or into. **2.** Something that grows inward or into.

in•gui•nal (ĭng′gwə-nəl) *adj.* Of, relating to, or located in the groin. [Lat. *inguinālis* < *inguen*, *inguin-*, groin.]

in•gur•gi•tate (ĭn-gûr′jĭ-tāt′) *tr.v.* **-tat•ed, -tat•ing, -tates.** To swallow greedily or in excessive amounts; gulp. [Lat. *ingurgitāre*, *ingurgitāt-* : *in-*, in; see IN–[2] + *gurges*, *gurgit-*, throat, whirlpool.] —**in•gur′gi•ta′tion** *n.*

INH A trademark used for the drug isoniazid.

in•hab•it (ĭn-hăb′ĭt) *v.* **-it•ed, -it•ing, -its.** —*tr.* **1.** To live or reside in. **2.** To be present in; fill. —*intr. Archaic.* To dwell. [ME *enhabiten* < OFr. *enhabiter* < Lat. *inhabitāre* : *in-*, in; see IN–[2] + *habitāre*, to dwell, freq. of *habēre*, to have; see **ghabh-***.] —**in•hab′it•a•bil′i•ty** *n.* —**in•hab′it•a•ble** *adj.* —**in•hab′i•ta′tion** *n.* —**in•hab′it•er** *n.*

in•hab•i•tan•cy (ĭn-hăb′ĭ-tən-sē) *n.*, *pl.* **-cies.** Occupancy.

in•hab•i•tant (ĭn-hăb′ĭ-tənt) *n.* One that inhabits a place, esp. as a permanent resident: *the inhabitants of a village.*

in•hab•it•ed (ĭn-hăb′ĭ-tĭd) *adj.* Having inhabitants; lived in.

in•ha•lant (ĭn-hā′lənt) *adj.* Used in or for inhaling. —*n.* **1.** Something inhaled. **2.** A medication or other compound in vapor or aerosol form, taken by inhalation.

in•ha•la•tion (ĭn′hə-lā′shən) *n.* **1.** The act or an instance of inhaling. **2.** An inhalant.

in•ha•la•tor (ĭn′hə-lā′tər) *n.* **1.** See **respirator** 1. **2.** See **inhaler** 2.

in•hale (ĭn-hāl′) *v.* **-haled, -hal•ing, -hales.** —*tr.* **1.** To draw (air or smoke, for example) into the lungs by breathing; inspire. **2.** *Informal.* To take in rapidly or eagerly; devour. —*intr.* **1.** To breathe in; inspire. **2.** To draw smoke into the lungs; puff. [Lat. *inhālāre*, to breathe upon : *in-*, in; see IN–[2] + *hālāre*, to breathe.]

in•hal•er (ĭn-hā′lər) *n.* **1.** One that inhales. **2.** A device that produces a vapor to ease breathing or is used to medicate by inhalation.

in•har•mon•ic (ĭn′här-mŏn′ĭk) *adj.* Not harmonic; discordant.

in•har•mo•ni•ous (ĭn′här-mō′nē-əs) *adj.* **1.** Not in harmony; discordant. **2.** Not in accord or agreement. —**in′har•mo′ni•ous•ly** *adv.* —**in′har•mo′ni•ous•ness** *n.*

in•har•mo•ny (ĭn-här′mə-nē) *n.*, *pl.* **-nies.** **1.** Lack of harmony; discord. **2.** An instance of such discord.

in•here (ĭn-hîr′) *intr.v.* **-hered, -her•ing, -heres.** To be inherent or innate. [Lat. *inhaerēre* : *in-*, in; see IN–[2] + *haerēre*, to stick.] —**in•her′ence** (-hîr′əns, -hĕr′-), **in•her′en•cy** *n.*

in•her•ent (ĭn-hîr′ənt, -hĕr′-) *adj.* Existing as an essential constituent or characteristic; intrinsic. [Lat. *inhaerēns*, *inhaerent-*, pr.part. of *inhaerēre*, to inhere. See INHERE.] —**in•her′ent•ly** *adv.*

in•her•it (ĭn-hĕr′ĭt) *v.* **-it•ed, -it•ing, -its.** —*tr.* **1.a.** To receive (property or a title, for example) from an ancestor by legal succession or will. **b.** To receive by bequest or as a legacy. **2.** To receive or take over from a predecessor. **3.** *Biol.* To receive (a characteristic) from one's parents by genetic transmission. **4.** To gain (something) as one's right or portion. —*intr.* To hold or take possession of an inheritance. [ME *enheriten* < OFr. *enheriter*, to make heir to < LLat. *inhērēditāre* : Lat. *in-*, in; see IN–[2] + LLat. *hērēditāre* (< Lat. *hērēs*, *hērēd-*, heir; see **ghē-***).] —**in•her′i•tor** *n.*

in•her•it•a•ble (ĭn-hĕr′ĭ-tə-bəl) *adj.* **1.** That can be inherited. **2.** Having the right to inherit or the capability of inheriting. —**in•her′it•a•bil′i•ty** *n.*

in•her•i•tance (ĭn-hĕr′ĭ-təns) *n.* **1.a.** The act of inheriting. **b.** Something inherited or to be inherited. **2.** Something regarded as a heritage. **3.** *Biol.* **a.** The process of genetic transmission of characteristics from parents to offspring. **b.** A characteristic so inherited. **c.** The sum of characteristics genetically transmitted from parents to offspring.

inheritance tax *n.* A tax imposed on the privilege of receiving property by inheritance or legal succession and assessed on the value of the property received.

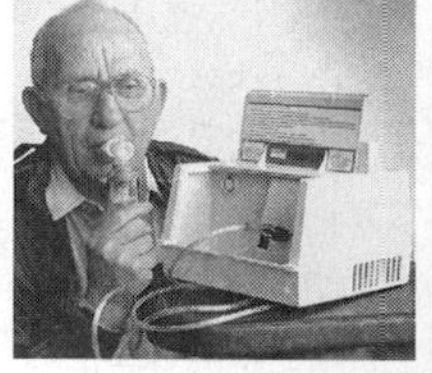

inhaler

in•hib•in (ĭn-hĭb′ĭn) *n.* A peptide that acts to inhibit follicle-stimulating hormonal secretion from the pituitary gland.

in•hib•it (ĭn-hĭb′ĭt) *tr.v.* **-it•ed, -it•ing, -its.** **1.** To hold back; restrain. **2.** To prohibit; forbid. **3.** *Psychol.* To suppress or restrain (an impulse, for example) consciously or unconsciously. **4.a.** *Chem.* To prevent or decrease the rate of (a reaction). **b.** *Biol.* To decrease, limit, or block the action or function of (an enzyme, for example). [ME *inhibiten*, to forbid < Lat. *inhibēre*, *inhibit-*, to restrain, forbid : *in-*, in; see IN–[2] + *habēre*, to hold; see **ghabh-***.] —**in•hib′it•a•ble** *adj.* —**in•hib′i•tive, in•hib′i•to′ry** (-tôr′ē, -tōr′ē) *adj.*

in•hi•bi•tion (ĭn′hə-bĭsh′ən, ĭn′ə-) *n.* **1.** The act of inhibiting or the state of being inhibited. **2.** Something that restrains, blocks, or suppresses. **3.** *Psychol.* Conscious or unconscious restraint of a behavioral process, a desire, or an impulse. **4.a.** *Chem.* The condition in which or the process by which a reaction is inhibited. **b.** *Biol.* The condition in which or the process by which an enzyme, for example, is inhibited.

in•hib•i•tor also **in•hib•it•er** (ĭn-hĭb′ĭ-tər) *n.* One that inhibits, as a substance that retards or stops a chemical reaction.

in•hold•ing (ĭn′hōl′dĭng) *n.* A privately owned parcel of land within the boundaries of a federal preserve. —**in′hold′er** *n.*

in•ho•mo•ge•ne•i•ty (ĭn-hō′mə-jə-nē′ĭ-tē, -nā′-, hŏm′ə-) *n.*, *pl.* **-ties.** **1.** Lack of homogeneity. **2.** Something that is not homogeneous or uniform.

in•hos•pi•ta•ble (ĭn-hŏs′pĭ-tə-bəl, ĭn′hŏ-spĭt′ə-bəl) *adj.* **1.** Displaying no hospitality; unfriendly. **2.** Unfavorable to life or growth; hostile: *the barren, inhospitable desert.* —**in•hos′pi•ta•ble•ness** *n.* —**in•hos′pi•ta•bly** *adv.*

in•hos•pi•tal•i•ty (ĭn′hŏs-pĭ-tăl′ĭ-tē) *n.* Lack of hospitality or friendliness.

in-house (ĭn′hous′) *adj.* Conducted within, coming from, or being within an organization or group. —**in′-house′** *adv.*

in•hu•man (ĭn-hyo͞o′mən) *adj.* **1.a.** Lacking kindness, pity, or compassion; cruel. See Syns at **cruel. b.** Deficient in emotional warmth; cold. **2.** Not suited for human needs: *an inhuman environment.* **3.** Not of ordinary human form; monstrous. —**in•hu′man•ly** *adv.* —**in•hu′man•ness** *n.*

in•hu•mane (ĭn′hyo͞o-mān′) *adj.* Lacking pity or compassion. —**in′hu•mane′ly** *adv.*

in•hu•man•i•ty (ĭn′hyo͞o-măn′ĭ-tē) *n.*, *pl.* **-ties.** **1.** Lack of pity or compassion. **2.** An inhuman or cruel act.

in•hume (ĭn-hyo͞om′) *tr.v.* **-humed, -hum•ing, -humes.** To place in a grave; bury. [Fr. *inhumer* < OFr. < Lat. *inhumāre* : *in-*, in; see IN–[2] + *humus*, earth; see **dhghem-***.] —**in′hu•ma′tion** *n.* —**in•hum′er** *n.*

in•im•i•cal (ĭ-nĭm′ĭ-kəl) *adj.* **1.** Injurious or harmful in effect; adverse. **2.** Unfriendly; hostile. [LLat. *inimīcālis* < Lat. *inimīcus*, enemy. See ENEMY.] —**in•im′i•cal•ly** *adv.*

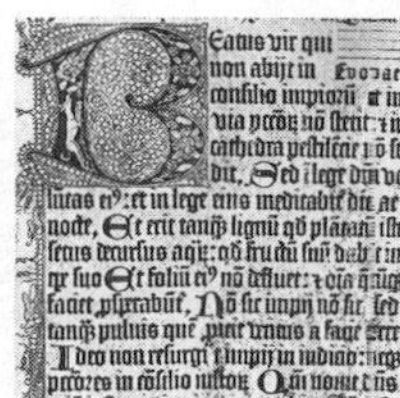

initial

in•im•i•ta•ble (ĭ-nĭm′ĭ-tə-bəl) *adj.* Defying imitation; matchless. [ME < Lat. *inimitābilis* : *in-*, not; see IN–[1] + *imitābilis*, imitable (< *imitārī*, to imitate).] —**in•im′i•ta•bil′i•ty, in•im′i•ta•ble•ness** *n.* —**in•im′i•ta•bly** *adv.*

in•i•on (ĭn′ē-ən) *n.* The most prominent projecting point of the occipital bone at the base of the skull. [Gk., occipital bone < *is*, *in-*, sinew, fiber. See **wei-***.]

in•iq•ui•tous (ĭ-nĭk′wĭ-təs) *adj.* Characterized by iniquity; wicked. —**in•iq′ui•tous•ly** *adv.* —**in•iq′ui•tous•ness** *n.*

in•iq•ui•ty (ĭ-nĭk′wĭ-tē) *n.*, *pl.* **-ties.** **1.** Gross immorality or injustice; wickedness. **2.** A grossly immoral act; a sin. [ME *iniquite* < OFr. < Lat. *inīquitās* < *inīquus*, unjust, harmful : *in-*, not; see IN–[1] + *aequus*, equal.]

in•i•tial (ĭ-nĭsh′əl) *adj.* **1.** Of, relating to, or occurring at the beginning; first. **2.** Being the first letter or letters of a word. —*n.* **1.a.** The first letter of a proper name. **b. initials.** The first letter of each word of a person's complete name considered as a unit. **2.** The first letter of a word. **3.** A large, often highly decorated letter set at the beginning of a chapter, verse, or paragraph. —*tr.v.* **-tialed, -tial•ing, -tials** also **-tialled, -tial•ling, -tials.** To mark or sign with initials, esp. for purposes of authorization or approval. [Lat. *initiālis* < *initium*, beginning. See **ei-***.] —**in•i′tial•ly** *adv.*

ă pat	oi boy
ā pay	ou out
âr care	o͝o took
ä father	o͞o boot
ĕ pet	ŭ cut
ē be	ûr urge
ĭ pit	th thin
ī pie	*th* this
îr pier	hw which
ŏ pot	zh vision
ō toe	ə about, item
ô paw	

Stress marks:
′ (primary);
′ (secondary), as in
dictionary (dĭk′shə-nĕr′ē)

inky cap
Coprinus atramentarius

inlay

in•i•tial•ize (ĭ-nĭsh′ə-līz′) *tr.v.* **-ized, -iz•ing, -iz•es.** *Comp. Sci.* To set to a starting position or value. **—in•i′tial•i•za′tion** (-shə-lĭ-zā′shən) *n.* **—in•i′tial•iz′er** *n.*

initial rhyme *n.* See **beginning rhyme.**

initial teaching alphabet *n.* An alphabet with 44 symbols representing sounds, used to teach reading of English.

in•i•ti•ate (ĭ-nĭsh′ē-āt′) *tr.v.* **-at•ed, -at•ing, -ates. 1.** To set going by taking the first step; begin: *initiated trade with developing nations.* **2.** To introduce to a new field, interest, skill, or activity. **3.** To admit into membership, as with ritual. *—adj.* (-ĭt). **1.** Initiated or admitted, as to membership. **2.a.** Instructed in esoteric knowledge. **b.** Introduced to something new. *—n.* (-ĭt). **1.** One who is being or has been initiated. **2.** One who has been introduced to or has attained knowledge in a particular field. [Lat. *initiāre, initiāt-* < *initium*, beginning. See **ei-*.**] **—in•i′ti•a′tor** *n.*

in•i•ti•a•tion (ĭ-nĭsh′ē-ā′shən) *n.* **1.a.** The act or an instance of initiating. **b.** The process of being initiated. **c.** The condition of being initiated. **2.** A ceremony, test, or period of instruction marking admission, as to an organization. **3.** The condition of being knowledgeable.

in•i•tia•tive (ĭ-nĭsh′ə-tĭv) *n.* **1.** The power or ability to begin or follow through energetically with a plan or task; enterprise and determination. **2.** A beginning or introductory step; an opening move. **3.a.** The power or right to introduce a new legislative measure. **b.** The right and procedure by which citizens can propose a law by petition and ensure its submission to the electorate. *—adj.* **1.** Of or relating to initiation. **2.** Used to initiate; initiatory. ***—idiom.* on (one's) own initiative.** Without prompting or direction from others; on one's own. **—in•i′tia•tive•ly** *adv.*

in•i•ti•a•to•ry (ĭ-nĭsh′ē-ə-tôr′ē, -tōr′ē) *adj.* **1.** Introductory; initial. **2.** Tending or used to initiate.

in•ject (ĭn-jĕkt′) *tr.v.* **-ject•ed, -ject•ing, -jects. 1.** To force or drive (a fluid) into something. **2.a.** *Medic.* To introduce (a drug, for example) into a body part. **b.** To treat by means of injection. **3.** To introduce into conversation or consideration. **4.** To place into an orbit, a trajectory, or a stream. [Lat. *inicere, iniect-*, to throw in : *in-*, in; see IN-[2] + *iacere*, to throw; see **yē-*.**] **—in•jec′tor** *n.*

in•ject•a•ble (ĭn-jĕk′tə-bəl) *adj.* That can be injected. Used of a drug. **—in•ject′a•ble** *n.*

in•jec•tion (ĭn-jĕk′shən) *n.* **1.** The act of injecting. **2.** Something injected, esp. a dose of medicine injected into the body.

in-joke (ĭn′jōk′) *n. Informal.* A joke originated or appreciated by the members of a particular group.

in•ju•di•cious (ĭn′jo͞o-dĭsh′əs) *adj.* Lacking or showing a lack of judgment or discretion; unwise. **—in′ju•di′cious•ly** *adv.* **—in′ju•di′cious•ness** *n.*

in•junc•tion (ĭn-jŭngk′shən) *n.* **1.** The act or an instance of enjoining; a command, a directive, or an order. **2.** *Law.* A court order prohibiting a party from a specific course of action. [ME *injunccion* < LLat. *iniūnctiō, iniūnctiōn-* < Lat. *iniūnctus*, p.part. of *iniungere*, to enjoin : *in-*, in; see IN-[2] + *iungere*, to join; see **yeug-*.**] **—in•junc′tive** *adj.*

in•jure (ĭn′jər) *tr.v.* **-jured, -jur•ing, -jures. 1.** To cause physical harm to; hurt. **2.** To cause damage to; impair. **3.** To cause distress to; wound. **4.** To commit an injustice or offense against; wrong. See Syns at **spoil.** [ME *injuren*, to wrong < OFr. *injurier* < Lat. *iniūriārī* < *iniūria*, a wrong. See INJURY.] **—in′jur•er** *n.*

in•ju•ri•ous (ĭn-jo͝or′ē-əs) *adj.* **1.** Causing or tending to cause injury; harmful. **2.** Slanderous; libelous. **—in•ju′ri•ous•ly** *adv.* **—in•ju′ri•ous•ness** *n.*

in•ju•ry (ĭn′jə-rē) *n., pl.* **-ries. 1.** Damage or harm. **2.** A particular form of hurt, damage, or loss. **3.** *Law.* Violation of the rights of another party for which legal redress is available. **4.** *Obsolete.* An insult. [ME *injurie* < AN < Lat. *iniūria*, a wrong, injustice < fem. of *iniūrius*, unjust : *in-*, not; see IN-[1] + *iūs, iūr-*, law; see **yewes-*.**]

in•jus•tice (ĭn-jŭs′tĭs) *n.* **1.** Violation of another's rights or of what is right; lack of justice. **2.** A specific unjust act; a wrong. [ME < OFr. < Lat. *iniūstitia* < *iniūstus*, unjust : *in-*, not; see IN-[1] + *iūstus*, just; see JUST[1].]

ink (ĭngk) *n.* **1.** A pigmented liquid or paste used esp. for writing or printing. **2.** A dark liquid ejected for protection by most cephalopods. *—tr.v.* **inked, ink•ing, inks. 1.** To mark, coat, or stain with ink. **2.** *Informal.* To append one's signature to (a contract, for example). [ME *inke* < OFr. *enque* < LLat. *encaustum*, purple ink < Gk. *enkauston*, painted in encaustic < *enkaiein*, to paint in encaustic, burn in. See ENCAUSTIC.] **—ink′er** *n.* **—ink′i•ness** *n.* **—ink′y** *adj.*

ink•ber•ry (ĭngk′bĕr′ē) *n.* **1.** A North American shrub *(Ilex glabra)* having black berrylike fruit. **2.** Its fruit.

ink•blot (ĭngk′blŏt′) *n.* **1.** A blotted pattern of spilled ink. **2.** A pattern resembling an inkblot used in inkblot tests.

inkblot test *n. Psychol.* A projective test in which a subject's interpretation of inkblots is analyzed.

ink•horn (ĭngk′hôrn′) *n.* A small container made of horn or a similar material, formerly used to hold ink for writing. *—adj.* Affectedly or ostentatiously learned; pedantic.

in•kle (ĭng′kəl) *n.* **1.** A colored linen tape woven on a simple narrow loom and used for trimmings. **2.** The yarn or thread used in making this tape. [?]

in•kling (ĭng′klĭng) *n.* **1.** A slight hint or indication. **2.** A slight understanding or vague idea or notion. [Prob. alteration of ME *(a) ningkiling*, (a) hint, suggestion, poss. alteration of *nikking* < *nikken*, to mark a text for correction < *nik*, notch, tally, perh. < var. of OFr. *niche*, niche. See NICHE.]

ink•stand (ĭngk′stănd′) *n.* **1.** A tray or rack for pens and bottles of ink. **2.** See **inkwell.**

Ink•ster (ĭngk′stər). A city of SE MI, a suburb of Detroit. Pop. 30,772.

ink•well (ĭngk′wĕl′) *n.* A small reservoir for ink.

inky cap *n.* Any of various mushrooms of the genus *Coprinus*, having gills that dissolve into a dark liquid after the spores mature.

in•lace (ĭn-lās′) *v.* Var. of **enlace.**

in•laid (ĭn′lād′) *adj.* **1.** Set into a surface in a decorative pattern. **2.** Decorated with a pattern set into a surface.

in•land (ĭn′lənd) *adj.* **1.** Of, relating to, or located in the interior part of a country or region. **2.** *Chiefly British.* Operating or applying within the borders of a country or region; domestic. *—adv.* In, toward, or into the interior of a country or region. *—n.* (-lănd′, -lənd). The interior of a country or region. **—in′land′er** *n.*

In•land Empire (ĭn′lənd, -lănd′). A region of the NW U.S. between the Cascade Range and the Rocky Mts. comprising E WA, E OR, N ID, and W MT.

Inland Passage. See **Inside Passage.**

Inland Sea. An arm of the Pacific Ocean in S Japan between Honshu, Shikoku, and Kyushu.

in-law (ĭn′lô′) *n.* A relative by marriage. [Back-formation < such compounds as *mother-in-law*.]

in•lay (ĭn′lā′, ĭn-lā′) *tr.v.* **-laid** (-lād′), **-lay•ing, -lays. 1.a.** To set (pieces of wood, for example) into a surface to form a design. **b.** To decorate by setting in such designs. **2.** To insert (a photograph, for example) within a mat in a book. *—n.* **1.a.** Contrasting material set into a surface in pieces to form a design. **b.** A design, pattern, or decoration made by inlaying. **2.** *Dentistry.* A solid filling fitted to a cavity in a tooth and cemented into place. **—in•lay′er** *n.*

in•let (ĭn′lĕt′, -lĭt) *n.* **1.a.** A recess, such as a bay or cove, along a coast. **b.** A stream or bay leading inland, as from the ocean; an estuary. **c.** A narrow passage of water, as between two islands. **d.** A drainage passage, as to a culvert. **2.** An opening providing a means of entrance or intake.

in•li•er (ĭn′lī′ər) *n.* An area or a formation of older rocks completely surrounded by younger layers. [IN[1] + (OUT)LIER.]

in lo•co pa•ren•tis (ĭn lō′kō pə-rĕn′tĭs) *adv.* In the position or place of a parent. [Lat. *in locō parentis*.]

in•ly (ĭn′lē) *adv.* **1.** In an inward manner; inwardly. **2.** With thorough knowledge or understanding.

in•ly•ing (ĭn′lī′ĭng) *adj.* Located farther in: *inlying streams.*

in•mate (ĭn′māt′) *n.* A resident of a dwelling that houses a number of occupants, esp. a person confined to an institution.

in me•di•as res (ĭn mē′dē-əs rās′) *adv.* In or into the middle of a sequence of events, as in a literary narrative. [Lat. *in mediās rēs*.]

in me•mo•ri•am (ĭn′ mə-môr′ē-əm, -mōr′-) *prep.* In memory of; as a memorial to. Used esp. in epitaphs. [< Lat. *in memoriam*, to the memory (of).]

in-mi•grate (ĭn′mī′grāt) *intr.v.* **-grat•ed, -grat•ing, -grates.** To move into a different region of the same country or territory. **—in′-mi′grant** (ĭn′mī′grənt) *n.*

in•most (ĭn′mōst′) *adj.* Farthest within; innermost.

inn (ĭn) *n.* **1.** A public lodging house serving food and drink to travelers; a hotel. **2.** A tavern or restaurant. **3.** *Chiefly British.* Formerly, a residence hall for students, esp. law students, in London. [ME < OE. See **en*.**]

Inn (ĭn). A river of E Switzerland, W Austria, and SE Germany flowing c. 515 km (320 mi) to the Danube R.

in•nards (ĭn′ərdz) *pl.n. Informal.* **1.** Internal bodily organs; viscera. **2.** The inner parts, as of a machine. [Alteration of *inwards*, pl. of INWARD.]

in•nate (ĭ-nāt′, ĭn′āt′) *adj.* **1.** Possessed at birth; inborn. **2.** Possessed as an essential characteristic; inherent. **3.** Of or produced by the mind rather than learned through experience: *innate knowledge.* [ME *innat* < Lat. *innātus*, p.part. of *innāscī*, to be born in : *in-*, in; see IN-[2] + *nāscī*, to be born; see **genə-*.**] **—in•nate′ly** *adv.* **—in•nate′ness** *n.*

in•ner (ĭn′ər) *adj.* **1.** Located or occurring farther inside: *an inner room.* **2.** Less apparent; deeper: *inner meaning.* **3.** Of or relating to the mind or spirit. **4.** More exclusive, influential, or important. [ME < OE *innera*. See **en*.**] **—in′ner** *n.* **—in′ner•ly** *adv. & adj.* **—in′ner•ness** *n.*

inner city *n.* The usu. older, central part of a city, esp. when characterized by crowded impoverished neighborhoods. **—in′ner-cit′y** (ĭn′ər-sĭ′tē) *adj.*

in•ner-di•rect•ed (ĭn′ər-dĭ-rĕk′tĭd, -dī-) *adj.* Guided in thought and behavior by one's own set of values.

inner ear *n.* The portion of the ear located within the temporal bone that is involved in both hearing and balance and includes the semicircular canals, vestibule, and cochlea.

In•ner Heb•ri•des (ĭn′ər hĕb′rĭ-dēzʹ). See **Hebrides.**

Inner Light *n.* In Quaker doctrine, a divine presence believed to be an enlightening and guiding force in the human soul.

Inner Mon•go•li•a (mŏng-gō′lē-ə, -gōl′yə, mŏn-). See **Nei Monggol.**

in•ner•most (ĭn′ər-mōstʹ) *adj.* **1.** Situated or occurring farthest within. **2.** Most intimate: *innermost feelings.* — *n.* The part situated farthest in.

inner planet *n.* Any of the four planets, Mercury, Venus, Earth, and Mars, whose orbits are closest to the sun.

inner product *n. Math.* See **scalar product.**

in•ner•sole (ĭn′ər-sōlʹ) *n.* See **insole.**

in•ner•spring (ĭn′ər-sprĭngʹ) *adj.* Having numerous coil springs enclosed by a padded cover: *an innerspring mattress.*

inner tube *n.* A flexible airtight hollow ring, usu. made of rubber, inside a pneumatic tire for holding compressed air.

in•ner•vate (ĭ-nûr′vātʹ, ĭn′ər-) *tr.v.* **-vat•ed, -vat•ing, -vates. 1.** To supply (an organ or a body part) with nerves. **2.** To stimulate (a nerve, muscle, or body part) to action. **— in′ner•va′tion** *n.* **— in′ner•va′tion•al** (-vā′shə-nəl) *adj.*

in•nerve (ĭ-nûrv′) *tr.v.* **-nerved, -nerv•ing, -nerves.** To give nervous energy to; stimulate.

In•ness (ĭn′ĭs), **George.** 1825–94. Amer. painter whose works include *Rainbow after a Storm* (1869).

in•ning (ĭn′ĭng) *n.* **1.a.** *Baseball.* One of nine periods of a game, in which each team has a turn at bat as limited by three outs. **b. innings.** *(used with a sing. v.) Sports.* The period in cricket during which one team is at bat. **2.** An opportunity to act or speak out; a chance for accomplishment. Often used in the plural with a singular or plural verb. **3.** The reclamation of flooded or marshy land. [ME *innynge*, a getting in < OE *innung*, gerund of *innian*, to put in < *in*, in. See IN[1].]

inn•keep•er (ĭn′kē′pər) *n.* One that owns or manages an inn or hotel.

in•no•cence (ĭn′ə-səns) *n.* **1.** The state, quality, or virtue of being innocent, as: **a.** Freedom from sin, moral wrong, or guilt through lack of knowledge of evil. **b.** Guiltlessness of a specific legal crime or offense. **c.** Freedom from guile, cunning, or deceit; simplicity or artlessness. **d.** Lack of worldliness or sophistication; naiveté. **e.** Lack of knowledge or understanding. **f.** Freedom from harmfulness; inoffensiveness. **2.** One that is innocent. **3.** *Bot.* See **blue-eyed Mary.**

in•no•cen•cy (ĭn′ə-sən-sē) *n., pl.* **-cies. 1.** Innocence. **2.** An innocent quality or action.

in•no•cent (ĭn′ə-sənt) *adj.* **1.** Uncorrupted by evil, malice, or wrongdoing; sinless. **2.a.** Not guilty of a specific crime or offense; legally blameless. **b.** Within, allowed by, or sanctioned by the law; lawful. **3.a.** Not dangerous or harmful; innocuous. **b.** Candid; straightforward. **4.a.** Not experienced or worldly; naive. **b.** Betraying or suggesting no deception or guile; artless. **5.a.** Not exposed to or familiar with something specified; ignorant. **b.** Unaware. **6.** Lacking, deprived, or devoid of something. — *n.* **1.** A person, esp. a child, who is free of evil or sin. **2.** A simple, guileless, inexperienced, or unsophisticated person. **3.** A very young child. [ME < OFr. < Lat. *innocēns, innocent-* : *in-*, not; see IN-[1] + *nocēns*, pr.part. of *nocēre*, to harm; see **nek-[1]*.**] **— in′no•cent•ly** *adv.*

In•no•cent III (ĭn′ə-sənt). 1161–1216. Pope (1198–1216) whose reign was marked by the Fourth Crusade.

in•noc•u•ous (ĭ-nŏk′yo͞o-əs) *adj.* **1.** Having no adverse effect; harmless. **2.** Not likely to offend or provoke to strong emotion; insipid. [< Lat. *innocuus* : *in-*, not; see IN-[1] + *nocuus*, harmful (< *nocēre*, to harm; see **nek-[1]***).] **— in•noc′u•ous•ly** *adv.* **— in•noc′u•ous•ness** *n.*

in•nom•i•nate (ĭ-nŏm′ə-nĭt) *adj.* **1.** Having no name. **2.** Anonymous. [LLat. *innōminātus* : Lat. *in-*, not; see IN-[1] + Lat. *nōminātus*, p.part. of *nōmināre*, to name; see NOMINATE.]

innominate bone *n.* See **hipbone.**

in•no•vate (ĭn′ə-vātʹ) *v.* **-vat•ed, -vat•ing, -vates.** — *tr.* To begin or introduce (something new) for or as if for the first time. — *intr.* To begin or introduce something new. [Fr. *innover* < OFr. < Lat. *innovāre, innovāt-*, to renew : *in-*, intensive pref.; see IN-[2] + *novāre*, to make new (< *novus*, new; see **newo-***).] **— in′no•va′tor** *n.* **— in′no•va•to′ry** (-və-tôr′ē, -tōr′ē) *adj.*

in•no•va•tion (ĭn′ə-vā′shən) *n.* **1.** The act of introducing something new. **2.** Something newly introduced. **— in′no•va′tion•al** *adj.*

in•no•va•tive (ĭn′ə-vā′tĭv) *adj.* Marked by or given to innovations. **— in′no•va′tive•ness** *n.*

Inns•bruck (ĭnz′bro͝okʹ, ĭns′-). A city of SW Austria WSW of Salzburg; settled c. 1180. Pop. 117,287.

Inns of Court (ĭnz) *pl.n. Law.* **1.** The four legal societies in England having the exclusive right to confer the title of barrister on law students. **2.** The buildings housing the Inns of Court.

in•nu•en•do (ĭn′yo͞o-ĕn′dō) *n., pl.* **-does.** An indirect or subtle, usu. derogatory implication in expression; an insinuation. [< Lat. *innuendō*, by hinting, ablative of *innuendum*, gerund of *innuere*, to nod to : *in-*, to, toward; see IN-[2] + *-nuere*, to nod.]

In•nu•it (ĭn′yo͞o-ĭt) *n.* Var. of **Inuit.**

in•nu•mer•a•ble (ĭ-no͞o′mər-ə-bəl, ĭ-nyo͞o′-) *adj.* Too numerous to be counted; numberless. See Syns at **incalculable. — in•nu′mer•a•ble•ness** *n.* **— in•nu′mer•a•bly** *adv.*

in•nu•mer•ate (ĭ-no͞o′mər-ĭt, ĭ-nyo͞o′-) *adj.* Unfamiliar with mathematical concepts and methods. — *n.* One who is innumerate. **— in•nu′mer•a•cy** *n.*

in•nu•mer•ous (ĭ-no͞o′mər-əs) *adj.* Innumerable. [< Lat. *innumerus* : *in-*, not; see IN-[1] + *numerus*, number; see NUMBER.]

in•nu•tri•tion (ĭn′no͞o-trĭsh′ən, -nyo͞o-) *n.* Poor nourishment; lack of good nutrition. **— in′nu•tri′tious** *adj.*

in•ob•ser•vance (ĭn′əb-zûr′vəns) *n.* **1.** Lack of heed or attention; disregard. **2.** Nonobservance, as of a law or custom. **— in′ob•ser′vant** *adj.*

in•ob•tru•sive (ĭn′əb-tro͞o′sĭv) *adj.* Not noticeable; unobtrusive.

in•oc•u•la•ble (ĭ-nŏk′yə-lə-bəl) *adj.* **1.** Susceptible to a disease spread by inoculation. **2.** That can be used in an inoculation. **3.** Transmissible by inoculation. **— in•oc′u•la•bil′i•ty** *n.*

in•oc•u•lant (ĭ-nŏk′yə-lənt) *n.* See **inoculum.**

in•oc•u•late (ĭ-nŏk′yə-lātʹ) *tr.v.* **-lat•ed, -lat•ing, -lates. 1.** To introduce a serum, a vaccine, or an antigenic substance into (the body), esp. to produce or boost immunity to a specific disease. **2.** To communicate a disease to (a living organism) by transferring its causative agent into the organism. **3.** To implant microorganisms or infectious material into (a culture medium). **4.** To safeguard as if by inoculation; protect. **5.** To introduce an idea or attitude into the mind of. [ME *inoculaten*, to graft a scion < Lat. *inoculāre, inoculāt-* : *in-*, in; see IN-[2] + *oculus*, eye, bud; see **okʷ-*.**] **— in•oc′u•la′tive** *adj.* **— in•oc′u•la′tor** *n.*

in•oc•u•la•tion (ĭ-nŏk′yə-lā′shən) *n.* The act or an instance of inoculating, esp. inoculating the body.

in•oc•u•lum (ĭ-nŏk′yə-ləm) *n., pl.* **-la** (-lə) or **-lums.** The material used in an inoculation. [NLat. < Lat. *inoculāre*, to graft a scion. See INOCULATE.]

in•o•dor•ous (ĭn-ō′dər-əs) *adj.* Having no odor.

in•of•fen•sive (ĭn′ə-fĕn′sĭv) *adj.* **1.** Giving no offense; unobjectionable. **2.** Causing no harm; harmless. **— in′of•fen′sive•ly** *adv.* **— in′of•fen′sive•ness** *n.*

I•nö•nü (ĭn′ə-no͞oʹ, ĭ-nœ-nü′), **Ismet.** 1884–1973. Turkish politician who served as president (1938–50).

in•op•er•a•ble (ĭn-ŏp′ər-ə-bəl, -ŏp′rə-) *adj.* **1.** Not functioning. **2.** Unsuitable for surgery. **— in•op′er•a•bly** *adv.*

in•op•er•a•tive (ĭn-ŏp′ər-ə-tĭv, -ŏp′rə-) *adj.* **1.** Not working or functioning. **2.** No longer in force, countermanded: *earlier instructions now inoperative.* **— in•op′er•a•tive•ness** *n.*

in•o•per•cu•late (ĭn′ō-pûr′kyə-lĭt) *adj. Biol.* Lacking an operculum. **— in′o•per′cu•late** *n.*

in•op•por•tune (ĭn-ŏp′ər-to͞onʹ, -tyo͞on′) *adj.* Inappropriate or ill-timed; not opportune. **— in•op′por•tune′ly** *adv.* **— in•op′por•tune′ness** *n.*

in•or•di•nate (ĭn-ôr′dn-ĭt) *adj.* **1.** Exceeding reasonable limits; immoderate. See Syns at **excessive. 2.** Not regulated; disorderly. [ME *inordinat* < Lat. *inōrdinātus*, disordered : *in-*, not; see IN-[1] + *ōrdinātus*, p.part. of *ōrdināre*, to set in order (< *ōrdō, ōrdin-*, order; see **ar-***).] **— in•or′di•na•cy, in•or′di•nate•ness** *n.* **— in•or′di•nate•ly** *adv.*

in•or•gan•ic (ĭn′ôr-găn′ĭk) *adj.* **1.a.** Involving no organic life or the products of organic life. **b.** Not composed of organic matter. **2.** *Chem.* Of or relating to compounds not containing hydrocarbon groups. **3.** Not arising in normal growth. **4.** Lacking system or structure. **— in′or•gan′i•cal•ly** *adv.*

in•os•cu•late (ĭn-ŏs′kyə-lātʹ) *v.* **-lat•ed, -lat•ing, -lates.** — *tr.* **1.** To unite (blood vessels, nerve fibers, or ducts) by small openings. **2.** To make continuous; blend. — *intr.* **1.** To open into one another. **2.** To unite so as to be continuous; blend. [IN-[2] + Lat. *ōsculāre, ōsculāt-*, to provide with an opening (< *ōsculum*, dim. of *ōs*, mouth; see **ōs-***).] **— in•os′cu•la′tion** *n.*

in•o•si•tol (ĭ-nō′sĭ-tôlʹ, -tōlʹ, ī-nō′-) *n.* Any of nine isomeric alcohols, $C_6H_{12}O_6 \cdot 2H_2O$, esp. one found in plant and animal tissue and classified as a member of the vitamin B complex. [Gk. *inos*, genitive of *is*, sinew; see **wei-*** + -IT(E)[2] + -OL[1].]

in•o•tro•pic (ē′nə-trō′pĭk, -trŏp′ĭk, ī′nə-) *adj.* Affecting the contraction of muscle, esp. heart muscle: *an inotropic drug.* [Gk. *is, in-*, tendon, sinew; see **wei-*** + -TROPIC.]

in•pa•tient (ĭn′pā′shənt) *n.* One admitted to a hospital or clinic for treatment that requires at least one overnight stay.

in per•so•nam (ĭn′ pər-sō′nəm) *adv. & adj. Law.* Against a person rather than against property. Used of an action or a judgment. [LLat. *in persōnam.*]

in pet•to (ĭn pĕt′ō) *adv. & adj. Rom. Cath. Ch.* In secret or private. Used of appointments of cardinals by the pope undisclosed in consistory. [Ital. : *in*, in + *petto*, breast.]

in•phase (ĭn′fāzʹ) *adj.* Having the same electrical phase.

in pos•se (ĭn pŏs′ē) *adv. & adj.* In potential but not in actuality. [Med.Lat. : Lat. *in*, in + Lat. *posse*, to be able.]

in pro•pri•a per•so•na (ĭn prō′prē-ə pər-sō′nə) *adv. Law.* In one's own person, esp. without representation by an attorney. [Med.Lat. *in propriā persōnā.*]

in•put (ĭn′po͝otʹ) *n.* **1.** Something put into a system or ex-

Innocent III
13th-century mosaic

Ismet Inönü

ă pat	oi boy
ā pay	ou out
âr care	o͝o took
ä father	o͞o boot
ĕ pet	ŭ cut
ē be	ûr urge
ĭ pit	th thin
ī pie	*th* this
îr pier	hw which
ŏ pot	zh vision
ō toe	ə about, item
ô paw	

Stress marks:
′ (primary);
ʹ (secondary), as in
dictionary (dĭk′shə-nĕrʹē)

pended in its operation to achieve output or a result, esp.: **a.** Energy, work, or power used to drive a machine. **b.** Current, electromotive force, or power supplied to an electric circuit, network, or device. **c.** *Comp. Sci.* Information put into a communications system for transmission or into a computer system for processing. **d.** *Comp. Sci.* A position, terminal, or station at which input enters a system. **e.** Any of the items, including materials, equipment, and funds, required for production. **2.a.** The act of putting in; infusion: *a steady input of fuel.* **b.** An amount put in. **3.** *Usage Problem.* **a.** Contribution of information or a comment or viewpoint. **b.** Information in general. — *tr.v.* **-put•ted** or **-put, -put•ting, -puts.** *Comp. Sci.* To enter (data or a program) into a computer.

Usage Note: The noun *input* has been used as a technical term for about a century in fields such as physics and electrical engineering, but its recent popularity grows out of its use in computer science. In general discourse *input* is now widely used to refer to the transmission of information and opinion. Although the usage is well established, care should be taken not to use the word merely as a way of pretending to a scientific precision unwarranted by the facts of the case.

in•quest (ĭn′kwĕst′) *n.* **1.** *Law.* **a.** A judicial inquiry into a matter usu. held before a jury, esp. into the cause of a death. **b.** A jury making such an inquiry. **c.** The finding based on such an inquiry. **2.** An investigation or inquiry. [ME *enqueste* < OFr. < VLat. **inquæsīta*, thing inquired into, alteration of Lat. *inquīsīta*, fem. p.part. of *inquīrere*, to inquire into. See INQUIRE.]

in•qui•e•tude (ĭn-kwī′ĭ-to͞od′, -tyo͞od′) *n.* A state of restlessness or uneasiness; disquietude. [ME, disturbance < LLat. *inquiētūdō*, restlessness < Lat. *inquiētus*, restless : *in-*, not; see IN-^{1} + *quiētus*, quiet; see QUIET.]

in•qui•line (ĭn′kwə-līn′, -lĭn, ĭng′-) *n.* An animal that characteristically lives commensally in the nest or burrow of an animal of another species. — *adj.* Being or living as an inquiline. [Lat. *inquilīnus*, lodger, tenant : *in-*, in; see IN-^{2} + *colere*, to inhabit; see **kʷel-**^{1}***.**] — **in′qui•lin•ism** (-lə-nĭz′əm), **in′qui•lin′i•ty** (-lĭn′ĭ-tē) *n.* — **in′qui•lin′ous** (-lī′nəs) *adj.*

in•quire (ĭn-kwīr′) also **en•quire** (ĕn-) — *v.* **-quired, -quir•ing, -quires.** — *intr.* **1.** To seek information by asking a question. **2.** To make an inquiry or investigation. — *tr.* **1.** To ask about. **2.** To ask. See Syns at **ask.** — ***phrasal verb.* inquire after.** To ask about the health or condition of. [ME *enquiren* < OFr. *enquerre* < VLat. **inquaerere*, alteration of Lat. *inquīrere* : *in-*, into; see IN-^{2} + *quaerere*, to seek.] — **in•quir′er** *n.* — **in•quir′ing•ly** *adv.*

in•quir•y (ĭn-kwīr′ē, ĭn′kwīr′ē, ĭn′kwə-rē, ĭng′-) also **en•quir•y** (ĕn-kwīr′ē, ĕn′kwə-rē) *n., pl.* **-ies. 1.** The act of inquiring. **2.** A question; a query. **3.** A close examination of a matter in a search for information or truth.

in•qui•si•tion (ĭn′kwĭ-zĭsh′ən, ĭng′-) *n.* **1.** The act of inquiring into a matter; an investigation. **2.** *Law.* **a.** An inquest. **b.** The verdict of a judicial inquiry. **3.a. Inquisition.** A tribunal formerly held in the Roman Catholic Church to suppress heresy. **b.** An investigation that violates the privacy or rights of individuals. **c.** A rigorous harsh interrogation. [ME *inquisicioun* < OFr. *inquisicion* < Lat. *inquīsītiō*, *inquīsītiōn-* < *inquīsītus*, p.part. of *inquīrere*, to inquire. See INQUIRE.] — **in′qui•si′tion•al** *adj.*

in•quis•i•tive (ĭn-kwĭz′ĭ-tĭv) *adj.* **1.** Unduly curious and inquiring. See Syns at **curious. 2.** Inclined to investigate; eager for knowledge. — **in•quis′i•tive•ly** *adv.* — **in•quis′i•tive•ness** *n.*

in•quis•i•tor (ĭn-kwĭz′ĭ-tər) *n.* One who inquires or makes an inquisition, esp. an excessively rigorous or harsh questioner.

in•quis•i•to•ri•al (ĭn-kwĭz′ĭ-tôr′ē-əl, -tōr′-) *adj.* **1.** Of, relating to, or having the function of an inquisitor. **2.** *Law.* **a.** Relating to a trial in which one party acts as both prosecutor and judge. **b.** Relating to a criminal proceeding conducted in secrecy. — **in•quis′i•to′ri•al•ly** *adv.*

in re (ĭn rā′, rē′) *prep. Law.* In the matter or case of; in regard to. [Lat. *in rē* : *in*, in + *rē*, ablative of *rēs*, thing, matter.]

in rem (ĭn rĕm′) *adv. & adj. Law.* Against a thing, such as property, status, or a right, rather than against a person. Used of an action or a judgment. [LLat. : Lat. *in*, against + Lat. *rem*, accusative of *rēs*, thing, matter.]

in-res•i•dence (ĭn-rĕz′ĭ-dəns) *adj.* Associated in an official specified position with an organization such as a university or college. Often used in combination: *artist-in-residence.*

I.N.R.I. *abbr. Lat.* Iesus Nazarenus Rex Iudaeorum (Jesus of Nazareth, King of the Jews).

inro
19th-century black lacquer inro

in•ro (ĭn′rō) *n., pl.* **inro.** A small, usu. ornamented box that hangs from the waist of a kimono and holds small objects such as cosmetics, perfumes, or medicines. [J.]

in•road (ĭn′rōd′) *n.* **1.** An invasion; a raid. **2.** An advance, esp. at another's expense; an encroachment. Often used in the plural. [IN^{1} + ROAD, riding, raid (obsolete).]

in•rush (ĭn′rŭsh′) *n.* A sudden rushing in; an influx.

INS *abbr.* **1.** Immigration and Naturalization Service. **2.** International News Service.

ins. *abbr.* **1.** Inches. **2.** Inspector. **3.** Insulation. **4.** Insurance.

in•sal•i•vate (ĭn-săl′ə-vāt′) *tr.v.* **-vat•ed, -vat•ing, -vates.** To mix (food) with saliva in chewing. — **in•sal′i•va′tion** *n.*

in•sa•lu•bri•ous (ĭn′sə-lo͞o′brē-əs) *adj.* Not promoting health; unwholesome. — **in′sa•lu′bri•ous•ly** *adv.* — **in′sa•lu′bri•ty** *n.*

ins and outs (ĭnz; outs) *pl.n.* **1.** The intricate details of a situation, decision, or process. **2.** The windings of a way.

in•sane (ĭn-sān′) *adj.* **1.a.** Of, exhibiting, or afflicted with insanity. **b.** Characteristic of or associated with persons afflicted with insanity. **c.** Intended for use by such persons. **2.** Immoderate; wild: *insane jealousy.* **3.** Very foolish; absurd: *insane risks.* [Lat. *īnsānus* : *in-*, not; see IN-^{1} + *sānus*, sane, healthy.] — **in•sane′ly** *adv.* — **in•sane′ness** *n.*

in•san•i•tar•y (ĭn-săn′ĭ-tĕr′ē) *adj.* So unclean as to be a likely cause of disease.

in•san•i•ty (ĭn-săn′ĭ-tē) *n., pl.* **-ties. 1.** Persistent mental disorder or derangement. **2.** *Law.* **a.** Unsoundness of mind sufficient to render a person unfit to maintain a contractual or other legal relationship or to warrant commitment to a mental health facility. **b.** In most criminal jurisdictions, a degree of mental malfunctioning sufficient to relieve the accused of legal responsibility for the act committed. **3.a.** Extreme foolishness; folly. **b.** Something extremely foolish.

Syns: *insanity, lunacy, madness, mania, dementia.* These nouns denote conditions of serious mental disability. *Insanity* is a grave, often prolonged condition that prevents a person from being held legally responsible for his or her actions: *was judged not guilty for reasons of insanity. Lunacy* often denotes derangement relieved intermittently by periods of clear-mindedness: *yelled wildly in a moment of utter lunacy. Madness* often stresses the violent aspect of mental illness: *a story about obsession and madness. Mania* refers principally to the excited phase of manic-depressive psychosis: *prescribed drugs to control the patient's periods of mania. Dementia* implies mental deterioration brought on by organic brain disorder: *underwent progressive stages of dementia.*

in•sa•tia•ble (ĭn-sā′shə-bəl, -shē-ə-) *adj.* Impossible to satiate or satisfy. — **in•sa′tia•bil′i•ty, in•sa′tia•ble•ness** *n.* — **in•sa′tia•bly** *adv.*

in•sa•ti•ate (ĭn-sā′shē-ĭt) *adj.* Insatiable. — **in•sa′ti•ate•ly** *adv.* — **in•sa′ti•ate•ness** *n.*

in•scribe (ĭn-skrīb′) *tr.v.* **-scribed, -scrib•ing, -scribes. 1.a.** To write, print, carve, or engrave (words or letters) on or in a surface. **b.** To mark or engrave (a surface) with words or letters. **2.** To enter (a name) on a list or in a register. **3.a.** To sign one's name or write a brief message in or on (a gift book, for example). **b.** To dedicate to someone. **4.** *Math.* To draw (one figure) within another figure so that every vertex of the enclosed figure touches the outer figure. [Lat. *īnscrībere* : *in-*, in, on; see IN-^{2} + *scrībere*, to write; see **skrībh-*.**] — **in•scrib′er** *n.*

in•scrip•tion (ĭn-skrĭp′shən) *n.* **1.** The act or an instance of inscribing. **2.** Something, such as the wording on a coin or seal, that is inscribed. **3.** An enrollment or a registration of names. **4.a.** A short signed message in a book or on a photograph given as a gift. **b.** The usu. informal dedication of a book or an artistic work. [ME *inscripcioun*, statement giving the author or title of a book < Lat. *īnscrīptiō*, *īnscrīptiōn-* < *īnscrīptus*, p.part. of *īnscrībere*, to inscribe. See INSCRIBE.] — **in•scrip′tion•al, in•scrip′tive** *adj.* — **in•scrip′tive•ly** *adv.*

in•scru•ta•ble (ĭn-skro͞o′tə-bəl) *adj.* Difficult to fathom or understand; impenetrable. See Syns at **mysterious.** — **in•scru′ta•bil′i•ty, in•scru′ta•ble•ness** *n.* — **in•scru′ta•bly** *adv.*

in•seam (ĭn′sēm′) *n.* **1.** The inside seam of a pant leg. **2.** The length or measurement of such a seam.

in•sect (ĭn′sĕkt′) *n.* **1.a.** Any of numerous usu. small arthropod animals of the class Insecta, having an adult stage characterized by three pairs of legs and a body segmented into head, thorax, and abdomen and usu. having two pairs of wings. **b.** Any of various similar arthropod animals, such as spiders, centipedes, or ticks. **2.** An insignificant or contemptible person. [Lat. *īnsectum* < neut. p.part. of *īnsecāre*, to cut up (transl. of Gk. *entomon*, segmented, cut up, insect; see ENTOMO-) : *in-*, in; see IN-^{2} + *secāre*, to cut; see **sek-*.**] — **in′sect′** *adj.* — **in′sec•ti′val** (ĭn′sĕk-tī′vəl) *adj.*

in•sec•tar•y (ĭn′sĕk′tə-rē, ĭn-sĕk′-) or **in•sec•tar•i•um** (ĭn′sĕk-târ′ē-əm) *n., pl.* **-tar•ies** also **-tar•i•a** (-târ′ē-ə). A place for keeping, breeding, or observing living insects.

in•sec•ti•cide (ĭn-sĕk′tĭ-sīd′) *n.* A chemical substance used to kill insects. — **in•sec′ti•cid′al** (-sīd′l) *adj.* — **in•sec′ti•cid′al•ly** *adv.*

in•sec•ti•vore (ĭn-sĕk′tə-vôr′, -vōr′) *n.* **1.** Any of various small, principally nocturnal mammals of the order Insectivora, characteristically feeding chiefly on insects. **2.** An organism that feeds mainly on insects. [NLat. *Īnsectivora*, order name : Lat. *īnsectum*, insect; see INSECT + Lat. *-vora*, neut. pl. of *-vorus*, -vorous.]

in•sec•tiv•o•rous (ĭn′sĕk-tĭv′ər-əs) *adj.* **1.** Feeding on insects. **2.** *Bot.* Capable of trapping and absorbing insects.

in•se•cure (ĭn′sĭ-kyo͝or′) *adj.* **1.** Not sure or certain; doubtful: *an insecure future.* **2.** Inadequately guarded or protected; unsafe. **3.** Not firm or fixed; unsteady. **4.a.** Lacking emotional stability; not well-adjusted. **b.** Lacking self-confidence; plagued by anxiety. **— in′se•cure′ly** *adv.* **— in′se•cure′ness** *n.* **— in′se•cu′ri•ty** (-kyo͝or′ĭ-tē) *n.*

in•sem•i•nate (ĭn-sĕm′ə-nāt′) *tr.v.* **-nat•ed, -nat•ing, -nates. 1.** To introduce or inject semen into the reproductive tract of (a female). **2.** To sow seed in. [Lat. *īnsēmināre, īnsēmināt-*, to implant, impregnate : *in-*, in; see IN-^{2} + *sēmināre*, to plant (< *sēmen, sēmin-*, seed; see SEMEN).] **— in•sem′i•na′tion** *n.* **— in•sem′i•na′tor** *n.*

in•sen•sate (ĭn-sĕn′sāt′, -sĭt) *adj.* **1.a.** Lacking sensation or awareness; inanimate. **b.** Unconscious. **2.** Lacking sensibility; unfeeling. **3.a.** Lacking sense or the power to reason. **b.** Foolish; witless. **— in•sen′sate′ly** *adv.* **— in•sen′sate′ness** *n.*

in•sen•si•ble (ĭn-sĕn′sə-bəl) *adj.* **1.a.** Imperceptible; inappreciable. **b.** Very small or gradual. **2.a.** Having lost consciousness, esp. temporarily; unconscious. **b.** Not invested with sensation; inanimate. **c.** Devoid of physical sensation or the power to react, as to pain or cold; numb. **3.a.** Unaware; unmindful. **b.** Not emotionally responsive; indifferent. **4.** Lacking meaning; unintelligible. **— in•sen′si•bil′i•ty, in•sen′si•ble•ness** *n.* **— in•sen′si•bly** *adv.*

in•sen•si•tive (ĭn-sĕn′sĭ-tĭv) *adj.* **1.** Not physically sensitive; numb. **2.a.** Lacking in sensitivity to the feelings or circumstances of others; unfeeling. **b.** Lacking in responsiveness: *insensitive to the customers.* **— in•sen′si•tive•ly** *adv.* **— in•sen′si•tiv′i•ty, in•sen′si•tive•ness** *n.*

in•sen•tient (ĭn-sĕn′shənt) *adj.* Devoid of sensation or consciousness; inanimate. **— in•sen′tience** *n.*

in•sep•a•ra•ble (ĭn-sĕp′ər-ə-bəl, -sĕp′rə-) *adj.* **1.** Impossible to separate or part. **2.** Very closely associated; constant. **— in•sep′a•ra•bil′i•ty, in•sep′a•ra•ble•ness** *n.* **— in•sep′a•ra•ble** *n.* **— in•sep′a•ra•bly** *adv.*

in•sert (ĭn-sûrt′) *tr.v.* **-sert•ed, -sert•ing, -serts. 1.** To put or set into, between, or among. **2.** To put or introduce into the body of something; interpolate. **3.** To place into an orbit, a trajectory, or a stream. *— n.* (ĭn′sûrt′). Something inserted or intended for insertion. [Lat. *īnserere, īnsert-* : *in-*, in; see IN-^{2} + *serere*, to join; see **ser-**^{2}*.] **— in•sert′er** *n.*

in•ser•tion (ĭn-sûr′shən) *n.* **1.** The act or process of inserting. **2.** Something inserted. **3.** *Anat.* The point or mode of attachment of a skeletal muscle to the bone or other body part that it moves. **4.** *Genet.* The addition, as by mutation, of one or more nucleotides to a chromosome. **— in•ser′tion•al** *adj.*

in-serv•ice (ĭn′sûr′vĭs) *adj.* **1.** Of, relating to, or being a full-time employee. **2.** Taking place or continuing while one is a full-time employee.

in•ses•so•ri•al (ĭn′sĕ-sôr′ē-əl, -sōr′-) *adj.* Perching or adapted for perching. [< NLat. *Īnsessores*, the perching birds < Lat. *īnsessus*, p.part. of *īnsidēre*, to sit upon. See INSIDIOUS.]

in•set (ĭn′sĕt′, ĭn-sĕt′) *tr.v.* **-set, -set•ting, -sets. 1.** To set in; insert. **2.** To furnish with an inset. *— n.* (ĭn′sĕt′). **1.** Something set in, as: **a.** A small map or illustration set within a larger one. **b.** A leaf or group of pages inserted into a publication. **c.** A piece of material set into a garment as decoration or trim. **2.a.** An inflow, as of water. **b.** A channel.

in•shore (ĭn′shôr′, -shōr′) *adv. & adj.* **1.** Close to a shore. **2.** Toward or coming toward a shore.

in•shrine (ĭn-shrīn′) *v.* Var. of **enshrine.**

in•side (ĭn-sīd′, ĭn′sīd′) *n.* **1.a.** An inner or interior part. **b.** Inward character, perceptions, or feelings. **2.** An inner side or surface. **3.** The part away from the edge; the middle part. **4. insides.** *Informal.* **a.** The inner organs; entrails. **b.** The inner parts or workings. **5.** *Slang.* Confidential or secret information. *— adj.* **1.** Inner; interior. **2.** Relating to, known to, or coming from an exclusive group. **3.** *Baseball.* Passing on the side of home plate nearer the batter. Used of a pitch. *— adv.* **1.** Into or in the interior; within. **2.** On the inner side. **3.** *Slang.* In prison. *— prep.* **1.** Within: *We'll be there inside an hour.* **2.a.** On the inner side or part of. **b.** Into the interior of. ***— idioms.*** **inside of.** *Usage Problem.* Within. **inside out. 1.** With the inner surface turned out; reversed. **2.** *Informal.* As completely as possible; thoroughly. **on the inside.** In a position of confidence or influence.

Usage Note: The construction *inside of* has been criticized as redundant or colloquial. But *inside of* is well established in formal writing, particularly in reference to periods of time: *They usually pay inside of* (or *inside*) *a month.*

inside job *n. Slang.* A crime perpetrated by or with the help of a person working for or trusted by the victim.

In•side Passage (ĭn′sīd′) also **In•land Passage** (ĭn′lənd). A natural protected waterway extending c. 1,529 km (950 mi) from Puget Sound to Skagway AK.

in•sid•er (ĭn-sī′dər) *n.* **1.** An accepted member of a group. **2.** One who has special knowledge or access to information.

inside track *n.* **1.** *Informal.* An advantageous position. **2.** *Sports.* The inside path in a curved racetrack.

in•sid•i•ous (ĭn-sĭd′ē-əs) *adj.* **1.** Working or spreading harmfully in a subtle or stealthy manner. **2.** Intended to entrap; treacherous. **3.** Beguiling but harmful; alluring. [< Lat. *īnsidiōsus* < *īnsidiae*, ambush < *īnsidēre*, to sit upon, lie in wait for : *in-*, in, on; see IN-^{2} + *sedēre*, to sit; see **sed-***.] **— in•sid′i•ous•ly** *adv.* **— in•sid′i•ous•ness** *n.*

in•sight (ĭn′sīt′) *n.* **1.** The capacity to discern the true nature of a situation; penetration. **2.** The act or outcome of grasping the inward nature of things or of perceiving in an intuitive manner.

in•sight•ful (ĭn′sīt′fəl, ĭn-sīt′-) *adj.* Showing or having insight; perceptive. **— in′sight′ful•ly** *adv.* **— in•sight′ful•ness** *n.*

in•sig•ni•a (ĭn-sĭg′nē-ə) also **in•sig•ne** (-nē) *n., pl.* **insignia** or **-ni•as. 1.** A badge of office, rank, membership, or nationality; an emblem. **2.** A distinguishing sign. [Lat. *īnsignia*, pl. of *īnsigne*, badge of office, mark < neut. of *īnsignis*, distinguished, marked : *in-*, in; see IN-^{2} + *signum*, sign; see **sek**^{w}**-1***.]

Usage Note: *Insignia* in Latin is the plural form of *insigne,* but it has long been used in English as both a singular and a plural form: *The insignia was visible on the wingtip. There are five insignia on various parts of the plane.* From the singular use of *insignia* comes the plural *insignias,* which is also common in reputable writing.

in•sig•nif•i•cance (ĭn′sĭg-nĭf′ĭ-kəns) *n.* The quality or state of being insignificant.

in•sig•nif•i•can•cy (ĭn′sĭg-nĭf′ĭ-kən-sē) *n., pl.* **-cies. 1.** Insignificance. **2.** One that is insignificant.

in•sig•nif•i•cant (ĭn′sĭg-nĭf′ĭ-kənt) *adj.* **1.** Not significant, esp.: **a.** Lacking in importance; trivial. **b.** Lacking power, position, or value; worthy of little regard. **c.** Small in size or amount. **2.** Having little or no meaning.

in•sin•cere (ĭn′sĭn-sîr′) *adj.* Not sincere; hypocritical. **— in′sin•cere′ly** *adv.* **— in′sin•cer′i•ty** (-sĕr′ĭ-tē) *n.*

in•sin•u•ate (ĭn-sĭn′yo͞o-āt′) *v.* **-at•ed, -at•ing, -ates.** *tr.v.* **1.** To introduce or otherwise convey (a thought, for example) gradually and insidiously. See Syns at **suggest. 2.** To introduce or insert (oneself) by subtle and artful means. *— intr.v.* To make insinuations. [Lat. *īnsinuāre, īnsinuāt-* : *in-*, in; see IN-^{2} + *sinuāre*, to curve (< *sinus*, curve).] **— in•sin′u•a′tive** *adj.* **— in•sin′u•a′tor** *n.* **— in•sin′u•a•tor′y** (-yo͞o-ə-tôr′ē, -tōr′ē) *adj.*

in•sin•u•at•ing (ĭn-sĭn′yo͞o-ā′tĭng) *adj.* **1.** Provoking gradual doubt or suspicion; suggestive. **2.** Artfully contrived to gain favor or confidence; ingratiating. **— in•sin′u•at′ing•ly** *adv.*

in•sin•u•a•tion (ĭn-sĭn′yo͞o-ā′shən) *n.* **1.** The act, process, or practice of insinuating. **2.** Something insinuated, esp. an artfully indirect, often derogatory suggestion.

in•sip•id (ĭn-sĭp′ĭd) *adj.* **1.** Lacking flavor or zest; not tasty. **2.** Lacking excitement, stimulation, or interest; dull. [Fr. *insipide* < LLat. *īnsipidus* : Lat. *in-*, not; see IN-^{1} + Lat. *sapidus*, savory (< *sapere*, to taste; see **sep-***).] **— in′si•pid′i•ty** (ĭn′sĭ-pĭd′ĭ-tē), **in•sip′id•ness** *n.* **— in•sip′id•ly** *adv.*

in•sip•i•ence (ĭn-sĭp′ē-əns) *n. Archaic.* Lack of wisdom. [ME < OFr. < Lat. *īnsipientia* < *īnsipiēns, insipient-*, not wise : *in-*, not; see IN-^{1} + *sapiēns*, wise; see SAPIENT.]

in•sist (ĭn-sĭst′) *v.* **-sist•ed, -sist•ing, -sists.** *— intr.* To be firm in a demand or course; refuse to yield. *— tr.* To assert or demand (something) vehemently and persistently: *We insist that you come along.* [Lat. *īnsistere*, to persist : *in-*, on; see IN-^{2} + *sistere*, to stand; see **stā-***.] **— in•sis′tence, in•sis′ten•cy** *n.* **— in•sist′er** *n.* **— in•sist′ing•ly** *adv.*

in•sis•tent (ĭn-sĭs′tənt) *adj.* **1.** Firm in asserting a demand or an opinion; unyielding. **2.** Demanding notice: *insistent hunger.* **3.** Repetitive and persistent. **— in•sis′tent•ly** *adv.*

in si•tu (ĭn sī′to͞o, sē′-) *adv. & adj.* In the original position. [Lat. *in situ* : *in*, in + *situ*, ablative of *situs*, place.]

in•snare (ĭn-snâr′) *v.* Var. of **ensnare.**

in•so•bri•e•ty (ĭn′sə-brī′ĭ-tē) *n.* Lack of sobriety; intemperance, esp. in drinking.

in•so•cia•ble (ĭn-sō′shə-bəl) *adj.* Not sociable. **— in•so′cia•bil′i•ty** *n.* **— in•so′cia•bly** *adv.*

in•so•far (ĭn′sō-fär′) *adv.* To such an extent.

insofar as *conj.* To the extent that.

insol. *abbr.* Insoluble.

in•so•late (ĭn′sō-lāt′, ĭn-sō′-) *tr.v.* **-lat•ed, -lat•ing, -lates.** To expose to sunlight. [Lat. *īnsōlāre, īnsōlāt-* : *in-*, in; see IN-^{2} + *sōl*, sun; see **sāwel-***.]

in•so•la•tion (ĭn′sō-lā′shən) *n.* **1.a.** The act or an instance of exposing to sunlight. **b.** Therapeutic exposure to sunlight. **2.** See **sunstroke. 3.a.** The solar radiation striking Earth or another planet. **b.** The rate of delivery of solar radiation per unit of horizontal surface.

in•sole (ĭn′sōl′) *n.* **1.** The inner sole of a shoe or boot. **2.** An extra strip of material put inside a shoe for comfort or protection.

in•so•lence (ĭn′sə-ləns) *n.* **1.** The quality or condition of being insolent. **2.** An instance of such behavior or speech.

in•so•lent (ĭn′sə-lənt) *adj.* **1.** Presumptuous and insulting in manner or speech; arrogant. **2.** Audaciously rude or disrespectful; impertinent. [ME < Lat. *īnsolēns, īnsolent-*, immoderate, arrogant : *in-*, not; see IN-^{1} + *solēns*, pr.part. of *solēre*, to be accustomed.] **— in′so•lent** *n.* **— in′so•lent•ly** *adv.*

in•sol•u•ble (ĭn-sŏl′yə-bəl) *adj.* **1.** That cannot be dissolved. **2.** Difficult or impossible to solve or explain; insolvable. **— in•sol′u•bil′i•ty, in•sol′u•ble•ness** *n.* **— in•sol′u•ble** *n.* **— in•sol′u•bly** *adv.*

ă pat	oi boy
ā pay	ou out
âr care	o͝o took
ä father	o͞o boot
ĕ pet	ŭ cut
ē be	ûr urge
ĭ pit	th thin
ī pie	*th* this
îr pier	hw which
ŏ pot	zh vision
ō toe	ə about, item
ô paw	

Stress marks:
′ (primary);
′ (secondary), as in
dictionary (dĭk′shə-nĕr′ē)

in•solv•a•ble (ĭn-sŏl′və-bəl) *adj.* Impossible to solve; having no solution. —**in•solv′a•bil′i•ty** *n.* —**in•solv′a•bly** *adv.*

in•sol•ven•cy (ĭn-sŏl′vən-sē) *n., pl.* **-cies. 1.** The condition of being insolvent. **2.** An instance of being insolvent.

in•sol•vent (ĭn-sŏl′vənt) *adj.* **1.a.** Unable to meet debts or discharge liabilities; bankrupt. **b.** Insufficient to meet all debts, as an estate or a fund. **2.** Of or relating to bankrupt persons or entities. —*n.* A bankrupt.

in•som•ni•a (ĭn-sŏm′nē-ə) *n.* Chronic inability to fall asleep or remain asleep for a length of time. [Lat. < *īnsomnis*, sleepless : *in-*, not; see IN-[1] + *somnus*, sleep; see **swep-***.]

in•som•ni•ac (ĭn-sŏm′nē-ăk′) *n.* One who suffers from insomnia. —*adj.* Having or causing insomnia.

in•so•much as (ĭn′sō-mŭch′) *conj.* **1.** To such extent or degree as. **2.** Inasmuch as; since.

insomuch that *conj.* With the result that; so.

in•sou•ci•ant (ĭn-so͞o′sē-ənt, ăN′so͞o-syäN′) *adj.* Marked by blithe unconcern; nonchalant. [Fr. : *in-*, not (< OFr.; see IN-[1]) + *souciant*, pr.part. of *soucier*, to trouble (< OFr. < VLat. **sollicītāre*, alteration of Lat. *sollicitāre*, to vex; see SOLICIT).] —**in•sou′ci•ance** *n.* —**in•sou′ci•ant•ly** *adv.*

in•soul (ĭn-sōl′) *v.* Var. of **ensoul.**

insp. *abbr.* **1.** Inspected. **2.** Inspector.

in•spect (ĭn-spĕkt′) *tr.v.* **-spect•ed, -spect•ing, -spects. 1.** To examine carefully and critically, esp. for flaws. **2.** To review or examine officially. [< Lat. *īnspicere, īnspect-* : *in-*, intensive pref.; see IN-[2] + *specere*, to look at; see **spek-***.] —**in•spec′tive** *adj.*

in•spec•tion (ĭn-spĕk′shən) *n.* **1.** The act of inspecting. **2.** Official examination or review. —**in•spec′tion•al** *adj.*

in•spec•tor (ĭn-spĕk′tər) *n.* **1.** One who is appointed or employed to inspect something. **2.** A police officer ranking next below superintendent. —**in•spec′to•ral, in′spec•to′ri•al** (-tôr′-ē-əl, -tōr′-) *adj.* —**in•spec′tor•ship′** *n.*

in•spec•tor•ate (ĭn-spĕk′tər-ĭt) *n.* **1.** The office or duties of an inspector. **2.** A staff of inspectors. **3.** An inspector's district.

inspector general *n., pl.* **inspectors general.** An officer with general investigative powers within a civil, military, or other organization.

in•sphere (ĭn-sfîr′) *v.* Var. of **ensphere.**

in•spi•ra•tion (ĭn′spə-rā′shən) *n.* **1.a.** Stimulation of the mind or emotions to a high level of feeling or activity. **b.** The condition of being so stimulated. **2.** An agency, such as a person or work of art, that moves the intellect or emotions or prompts action or invention. **3.** Something, such as a sudden creative act, that is inspired. **4.** The quality of inspiring or exalting. **5.** *Theol.* Divine guidance or influence exerted directly on the mind and soul of a human being. **6.** The act of drawing in, esp. the inhalation of air into the lungs.

in•spi•ra•tion•al (ĭn′spə-rā′shə-nəl) *adj.* **1.** Of or relating to inspiration. **2.** Providing or intended to convey inspiration. **3.** Resulting from inspiration. —**in′spi•ra′tion•al•ly** *adv.*

in•spi•ra•tor (ĭn′spə-rā′tər) *n.* A device, such as a respirator or an inhaler, by which a gas, vapor, or air is drawn in. [Lat. *īnspīrāre*, to breathe into; see INSPIRE + -ATOR.]

in•spir•a•to•ry (ĭn-spīr′ə-tôr′ē, -tōr′ē) *adj.* Of, relating to, or used for the drawing in of air.

in•spire (ĭn-spīr′) *v.* **-spired, -spir•ing, -spires.** —*tr.* **1.** To affect, guide, or arouse by divine influence. **2.** To fill with enlivening or exalting emotion. **3.a.** To stimulate to action; motivate. **b.** To affect or touch. **4.** To draw forth; elicit or arouse. **5.** To be the cause or source of; bring about. **6.** To draw in (air) by inhaling. **7.** *Archaic.* **a.** To breathe on. **b.** To breathe life into. —*intr.* **1.** To stimulate energies, ideals, or reverence. **2.** To inhale. [ME *enspiren* < OFr. *enspirer* < Lat. *īnspīrāre* : *in-*, into; see IN-[2] + *spīrāre*, to breathe.] —**in•spir′er** *n.*

in•spired (ĭn-spīrd′) *adj.* Of such surpassing brilliance or excellence as to suggest divine inspiration: *an inspired musician.* —**in•spir′ed•ly** (-spī′rĭd-lē, -spīrd′lē) *adv.*

in•spir•ing (ĭn-spīr′ĭng) *adj.* Tending to arouse or exalt: *an inspiring eulogy.* —**in•spir′ing•ly** *adv.*

in•spir•it (ĭn-spĭr′ĭt) *tr.v.* **-it•ed, -it•ing, -its.** To instill courage or life into; animate. —**in•spir′it•ing•ly** *adv.*

in•spis•sate (ĭn-spĭs′āt′, ĭn′spĭ-sāt′) *intr. & tr.v.* **-sat•ed, -sat•ing, -sates.** To undergo thickening or cause to thicken, as by boiling or evaporation; condense. [< LLat. *īnspissāre, īnspissāt-*, to thicken : Lat. *in-*, causative pref.; see IN-[2] + Lat. *spissus*, thick.] —**in′spis•sa′tion** *n.* —**in•spis′sa′tor** *n.*

inst. *abbr.* **1.** Instant. **2.** Or **Inst.** Institute; institution. **3.** Institutional.

in•sta•bil•i•ty (ĭn′stə-bĭl′ĭ-tē) *n., pl.* **-ties. 1.** Lack of physical stability; unsteadiness. **2.** The quality or condition of being erratic or undependable: *political instability.*

in•stall also **in•stal** (ĭn-stôl′) *tr.v.* **-stalled, -stall•ing, -stalls** also **-stals. 1.** To set in position and connect or adjust for use. **2.** To induct into an office, a rank, or a position: *install the new governor.* **3.** To settle in an indicated place or condition; establish. [ME *installen*, to place in office < OFr. *installer* < Med.Lat. *installāre* : *in-*, in (< Lat.; see IN-[2]) + *stallum*, stall, place; see **stel-***.] —**in•stall′er** *n.*

in•stal•la•tion (ĭn′stə-lā′shən) *n.* **1.a.** The act of installing. **b.** The state of being installed. **2.** A system of machinery or other apparatus set up for use. **3.** A permanent military base.

in•stall•ment[1] also **in•stal•ment** (ĭn-stôl′mənt) *n.* **1.** One of a number of successive payments in settlement of a debt. **2.a.** A portion of something, such as a publication, issued at intervals. **b.** A chapter or part of a literary work presented serially. [Alteration of obsolete *estallment* < AN < OFr. *estaler*, to place, fix < *estal*, place, of Gmc. orig. See **stel-***.]

in•stall•ment[2] also **in•stal•ment** (ĭn-stôl′mənt) *n.* See **installation** 1.

installment plan *n.* A credit system by which payment for merchandise is made in installments over a fixed period.

in•stance (ĭn′stəns) *n.* **1.a.** An example that is cited to prove or invalidate a contention or illustrate a point. **b.** A case or an occurrence. **2.** *Law.* A legal proceeding or process; a suit. **3.** A step in a process or series of events. **4.a.** A suggestion or request. **b.** *Archaic.* Urgent solicitation. **5.** *Obsolete.* An impelling motive. —*tr.v.* **-stanced, -stanc•ing, -stanc•es. 1.** To offer as an example; cite. **2.** To demonstrate or show by an example; exemplify. —***idiom.* for instance.** As an example; for example. [ME *instaunce* < OFr. *instance*, request, instant, and < Med.Lat. *īnstantia*, example, both < Lat., presence < *īnstāns, īnstant-*, present. See INSTANT.]

in•stan•cy (ĭn′stən-sē) *n., pl.* **-cies. 1.** The quality or condition of being insistent; urgency. **2.** Immediacy of occurrence.

in•stant (ĭn′stənt) *n.* **1.** An almost imperceptible space of time. **2.** A particular time. **3.** The current month. **4.** A food or beverage designed for quick preparation. —*adj.* **1.** Occurring at once; immediate. **2.** Imperative; urgent. **3.** Now under consideration; present. **4.a.** Commercially prepared or processed for quick and easy final preparation. **b.** Readily soluble in water. **c.** Appearing, done, or taking place with or as if with maximum quickness and ease. —*adv.* At once; instantly. [ME < OFr. < Lat. *īnstāns, īnstant-*, present, pr.part. of *īnstāre*, to approach : *in-*, on; see IN-[2] + *stāre*, to stand; see **stā-***.]

in•stan•ta•ne•ous (ĭn′stən-tā′nē-əs) *adj.* **1.** Occurring or completed without perceptible delay. **2.** Done or made as quickly or directly as possible. **3.** Present or occurring at a specific instant. [< Med.Lat. *īnstantāneus* < Lat. *īnstāns, īnstant-*, present. See INSTANT.] —**in•stan′ta•ne′i•ty** (ĭn-stăn′tə-nē′ĭ-tē, ĭn′stən) *n.* —**in′stan•ta′ne•ous•ly** *adv.* —**in′stan•ta′ne•ous•ness** *n.*

in•stan•ter (ĭn-stăn′tər) *adv.* Instantly. [Med.Lat. < Lat., urgently < *īnstāns, īnstant-*, present. See INSTANT.]

in•stant•ly (ĭn′stənt-lē) *adv.* **1.** At once. **2.** With insistence; urgently. —*conj. Chiefly British.* As soon as.

instant replay *n.* **1.a.** The recording and immediate playback of part of a live television broadcast, as of a sports play. **b.** The part so recorded and replayed. **2.** *Informal.* Something repeated directly or soon after its original occurrence.

in•star[1] (ĭn-stär′) *tr.v.* **-starred, -star•ring, -stars.** To stud with or as if with stars.

in•star[2] (ĭn′stär′) *n.* A stage of an insect or other arthropod between molts. [NLat. < Lat., image, form.]

in•state (ĭn-stāt′) *tr.v.* **-stat•ed, -stat•ing, -states.** To establish in office; install.

in•stau•ra•tion (ĭn′stô-rā′shən) *n.* **1.** Renovation; restoration. **2.** The institution or establishment of something. [Lat. *īnstaurātiō, īnstaurātiōn-* < *īnstaurātus*, p.part. of *īnstaurāre*, to renew. See **stā-***.]

in•stead (ĭn-stĕd′) *adv.* **1.** In the place of something previously mentioned; as a substitute or an equivalent. **2.** In preference; as an alternative. [< ME *in sted of*, in place of : *in*, in; see IN[1] + *stede*, place; see STEAD + *of*, of; see OF.]

instead of *prep.* In place of; rather than.

in•step (ĭn′stĕp′) *n.* **1.** The arched middle part of the human foot between the toes and the ankle. **2.** The part of a shoe or stocking covering the instep. [ME.]

in•sti•gate (ĭn′stĭ-gāt′) *tr.v.* **-gat•ed, -gat•ing, -gates. 1.** To urge on; goad. **2.** To stir up; foment. [Lat. *īnstīgāre, īnstīgāt-*. See **steig-***.] —**in′sti•ga′tion** *n.* —**in′sti•ga′tive** *adj.* —**in′sti•ga′tor** *n.*

in•still also **in•stil** (ĭn-stĭl′) *tr.v.* **-stilled, -still•ing, -stills** also **-stils. 1.** To introduce by gradual, persistent efforts; implant. **2.** To pour in (medicine, for example) drop by drop. [ME *instillen* < Lat. *īnstillāre* : *in-*, into; see IN-[2] + *stillāre*, to drip, drop (< *stilla*, drop).] —**in′stil•la′tion** (ĭn′stə-lā′shən) *n.* —**in•still′er** *n.* —**in•still′ment** *n.*

in•stinct (ĭn′stĭngkt′) *n.* **1.** An inborn pattern of behavior that is characteristic of a species and is often a response to specific environmental stimuli: *the spawning instinct.* **2.** A powerful motivation or impulse. **3.** An innate capability or aptitude. —*adj.* (ĭn-stĭngkt′). **1.** Deeply filled or imbued: *words instinct with love.* **2.** *Obsolete.* Impelled from within. [ME < Lat. *īnstīnctus*, impulse < p.part. of *īnstinguere*, to incite : *in-*, intensive pref.; see IN-[2] + *stinguere*, to prick; see **steig-***.]

in•stinc•tive (ĭn-stĭngk′tĭv) *adj.* **1.** Of, relating to, or prompted by instinct. **2.** Arising from impulse; spontaneous and unthinking. —**in•stinc′tive•ly** *adv.*

in•stinc•tu•al (ĭn-stĭngk′cho͞o-əl) *adj.* Of, relating to, or derived from instinct. —**in•stinc′tu•al•ly** *adv.*

in•sti•tute (ĭn′stĭ-to͞ot′, -tyo͞ot′) *tr.v.* **-tut•ed, -tut•ing, -tutes. 1.a.** To establish, organize, and set in operation. **b.** To initiate; begin. See Syns at **found**[1]. **2.** To establish or invest in an office or a position. — *n.* **1.a.** Something instituted, esp. an authoritative rule or precedent. **b. institutes.** A digest of the principles or rudiments of a particular subject, esp. a legal abstract. **2.** An organization founded to promote a cause: *a cancer research institute.* **3.a.** An educational institution, esp. for technical subjects. **b.** The building or buildings housing such an institution. **4.** An intensive workshop or seminar on a specific subject. [ME *instituten* < Lat. *īnstituere, īnstitūt-*, to establish : *in-*, in; see IN-[2] + *statuere*, to set up; see **stā-***.] — **in′sti•tut′er, in′sti•tu′tor** *n.*

in•sti•tu•tion (ĭn′stĭ-to͞o′shən, -tyo͞o′-) *n.* **1.** The act of instituting. **2.a.** A custom, practice, relationship, or behavioral pattern of importance in a community or society. **b.** *Informal.* One long associated with a specified place, position, or function. **3.a.** An established organization or foundation, as one dedicated to education or culture. **b.** The building or buildings housing an institution. **c.** A place for the care of persons who are destitute, disabled, or mentally ill.

in•sti•tu•tion•al (ĭn′stĭ-to͞o′shə-nəl, -tyo͞o′-) *adj.* **1.** Of or relating to an institution or institutions. **2.** Organized as or forming an institution: *institutional religion.* **3.** Characteristic or suggestive of an institution, esp. in being uniform, dull, or unimaginative. **4.** Of or relating to the principles or institutes of a subject such as law. — **in′sti•tu′tion•al•ly** *adv.*

in•sti•tu•tion•al•ism (ĭn′stĭ-to͞o′shə-nə-lĭz′əm, -tyo͞o′-) *n.* **1.** Adherence to or belief in established forms, esp. belief in organized religion. **2.** Use of public institutions for the care of those who are physically or mentally disabled, criminally delinquent, or incapable of independent living. — **in′sti•tu′tion•al•ist** *n.*

in•sti•tu•tion•al•ize (ĭn′stĭ-to͞o′shə-nə-līz′, -tyo͞o′-) *tr.v.* **-ized, -iz•ing, -iz•es. 1.a.** To make into, treat as, or give the character of an institution to. **b.** To make part of a structured and usu. well-established system. **2.** To place (a person) in the care of an institution. — **in′sti•tu′tion•al•i•za′tion** (-shə-nə-lĭ-zā′shən) *n.*

instr. *abbr.* **1.** Instruction. **2.** Instructor. **3.** Instrument.

in•stroke (ĭn′strōk′) *n.* An inward stroke, esp. a piston stroke moving away from the crankshaft.

in•struct (ĭn-strŭkt′) *v.* **-struct•ed, -struct•ing, -structs.** — *tr.* **1.** To provide with knowledge, esp. in a methodical way. See Syns at **teach. 2.** To give orders to; direct. — *intr.* To serve as an instructor. [ME *instructen* < Lat. *īnstruere, īnstrūct-*, to prepare, instruct : *in-*, on; see IN-[2] + *struere*, to build; see **ster-**[2]*.]

in•struc•tion (ĭn-strŭk′shən) *n.* **1.** The act, practice, or profession of instructing. **2.a.** Imparted knowledge. **b.** An imparted or acquired item of knowledge; a lesson. **3.** *Comp. Sci.* A machine code telling a computer to perform a particular operation. **4.a.** An authoritative direction to be obeyed; an order. Often used in the plural. **b. instructions.** Detailed directions on procedure. — **in•struc′tion•al** *adj.*

in•struc•tive (ĭn-strŭk′tĭv) *adj.* Conveying knowledge or information. — **in•struc′tive•ly** *adv.* — **in•struc′tive•ness** *n.*

in•struc•tor (ĭn-strŭk′tər) *n.* **1.** One who instructs; a teacher. **2.** A college or university teacher who ranks below an assistant professor. — **in•struc′tor•ship′** *n.*

in•stru•ment (ĭn′strə-mənt) *n.* **1.** A means by which something is done; an agency. **2.** One used by another to accomplish a purpose; a dupe. **3.** An implement used to facilitate work. See Syns at **tool. 4.** A device for recording, measuring, or controlling, esp. such a device functioning as part of a control system. **5.** *Mus.* A device for playing or producing music. **6.** A legal document. — *tr.v.* (-mĕnt′) **-ment•ed, -ment•ing, -ments. 1.** To provide or equip with instruments. **2.** *Mus.* To compose or arrange for performance. **3.** To address a legal document to. [ME < OFr. < Lat. *īnstrūmentum*, tool, implement < *īnstruere*, to prepare. See INSTRUCT.]

in•stru•men•tal (ĭn′strə-mĕn′tl) *adj.* **1.** Serving as a means or an agency; implemental: *instrumental in solving the crime.* **2.** Of, relating to, or accomplished with an instrument or a tool. **3.** *Mus.* Performed on or written for an instrument. **4.** *Gram.* Of or being a case used typically to express means, agency, or accompaniment. **5.** Of or relating to instrumentalism. — *n.* **1.a.** *Gram.* The instrumental case. **b.** A word in the instrumental case. **2.** *Mus.* A composition for one or more instruments. — **in′stru•men′tal•ly** *adv.*

in•stru•men•tal•ism (ĭn′strə-mĕn′tl-ĭz′əm) *n.* A pragmatic theory that ideas are instruments that guide action, their validity being determined by the success of the action.

in•stru•men•tal•ist (ĭn′-strə-mĕn′tl-ĭst) *n.* **1.** *Mus.* One who plays an instrument. **2.** An advocate or a student of instrumentalism. — **in′stru•men′tal•ist** *adj.*

in•stru•men•tal•i•ty (ĭn′strə-mĕn-tăl′ĭ-tē) *n., pl.* **-ties. 1.** The state or quality of being instrumental. **2.** A means; an agency. **3.** A subsidiary branch, as of a government, by means of which functions or policies are carried out.

in•stru•men•ta•tion (ĭn′strə-mĕn-tā′shən) *n.* **1.** The application or use of instruments. **2.** *Mus.* **a.** The study and practice of arranging music for instruments. **b.** The arrangement or orchestration resulting from such practice. **c.** A list of instruments used in an orchestration. **3.a.** The study, development, and manufacture of instruments, as for scientific use. **b.** Instruments for a specific purpose. **4.** Instrumentality.

instrument board *n.* See **instrument panel.**

instrument flying *n.* Aircraft navigation by reference to instruments only.

instrument landing *n.* An aircraft landing made by means of instruments and ground-based radio equipment only.

instrument panel *n.* A mounted array of instruments used to operate a machine, as in an aircraft.

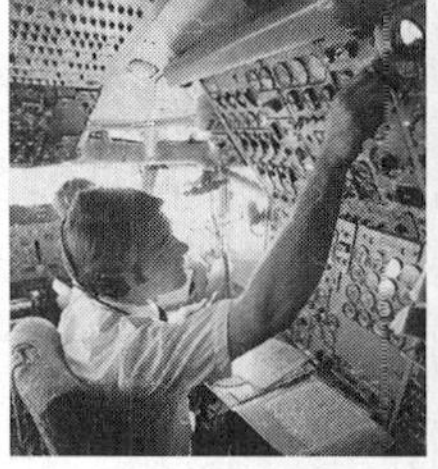

instrument panel
In an airplane cockpit

in•sub•or•di•nate (ĭn′sə-bôr′dn-ĭt) *adj.* Not submissive to authority: *insubordinate behavior.* — **in′sub•or′di•nate** *n.* — **in′sub•or′di•nate•ly** *adv.* — **in′sub•or′di•na′tion** *n.*

in•sub•stan•tial (ĭn′səb-stăn′shəl) *adj.* **1.** Lacking substance or reality. **2.a.** Not firm or solid; flimsy. **b.** Delicate; fine. — **in′sub•stan′ti•al′i•ty** (-shē-ăl′ĭ-tē) *n.*

in•suf•fer•a•ble (ĭn-sŭf′ər-ə-bəl, -sŭf′rə-) *adj.* Difficult or impossible to endure; intolerable. — **in•suf′fer•a•ble•ness** *n.* — **in•suf′fer•a•bly** *adv.*

in•suf•fi•cien•cy (ĭn′sə-fĭsh′ən-sē) *n., pl.* **-cies. 1.** The quality or state of being insufficient, esp.: **a.** Moral or mental incompetence. **b.** Inadequate supply: *an insufficiency of funds.* **c.** Inability of a body part or an organ to function normally: *cardiac insufficiency.* **2.** A failing; an inadequacy.

in•suf•fi•cient (ĭn′sə-fĭsh′ənt) *adj.* Not sufficient; inadequate. — **in′suf•fi′cient•ly** *adv.*

in•suf•flate (ĭn′sə-flāt′, ĭn-sŭf′lāt′) *tr.v.* **-flat•ed, -flat•ing, -flates. 1.** To blow or breathe into or on. **2.** *Medic.* To treat medically by blowing a powder, gas, or vapor into a bodily cavity. [Lat. *īnsufflāre, īnsufflāt-* : *in-*, into; see IN-[2] + *sufflāre*, to inflate; see SOUFFLÉ.] — **in′suf•fla′tor** *n.*

in•suf•fla•tion (ĭn′sə-flā′shən) *n.* **1.** The act or an instance of insufflating. **2.** *Eccles.* A ritual act of breathing on baptismal water or on the one being baptized.

in•su•lant (ĭn′sə-lənt, ĭns′yə-) *n.* A material used for insulation; an insulator.

in•su•lar (ĭn′sə-lər, ĭns′yə-) *adj.* **1.a.** Of, relating to, or constituting an island. **b.** Living or located on an island. **2.a.** Suggestive of the isolated life of an island. **b.** Circumscribed and detached in outlook and experience; narrow or provincial. **3.** *Anat.* Of or relating to isolated tissue or an island of tissue. [Fr. *insulaire* < LLat. *īnsulāris* < Lat. *īnsula*, island.] — **in′su•lar•ism, in′su•lar′i•ty** (-lăr′ĭ-tē) *n.* — **in′su•lar•ly** *adv.*

in•su•late (ĭn′sə-lāt′, ĭns′yə-) *tr.v.* **-lat•ed, -lat•ing, -lates. 1.** To cause to be in a detached or isolated position. **2.** To prevent the passage of heat, electricity, or sound into or out of, esp. by surrounding with a nonconducting material. [Lat. *īnsula*, island + -ATE[1].]

in•su•la•tion (ĭn′sə-lā′shən, ĭns′yə-) *n.* **1.** The act of insulating or the state of being insulated. **2.** A material or substance used in insulating: *soundproof cork insulation.*

in•su•la•tive (ĭn′sə-lā′tĭv, ĭns′yə-) *adj.* Serving to insulate or keep safe: *the insulative value of an animal's fur.*

in•su•la•tor (ĭn′sə-lā′tər, ĭns′yə-) *n.* **1.** A material that insulates, esp. a nonconductor of sound, heat, or electricity. **2.** A device that insulates.

in•su•lin (ĭn′sə-lĭn) *n.* **1.** A hormone secreted by the islets of Langerhans and regulating the metabolism of carbohydrates and fats, esp. the conversion of glucose to glycogen. **2.** Any of various pharmaceutical preparations containing this hormone, used to treat diabetes mellitus (type I). [NLat. *īnsula*, island (of Langerhans) (< Lat., island) + -IN.]

insulin shock *n.* Acute hypoglycemia usu. resulting from an overdose of insulin and characterized by sweating, trembling, dizziness, and if left untreated, convulsions and coma.

in•sult (ĭn-sŭlt′) *v.* **-sult•ed, -sult•ing, -sults.** — *tr.* **1.a.** To treat with gross insensitivity, insolence, or rudeness. **b.** To affront or demean. **2.** *Obsolete.* To make an attack on. — *intr. Archaic.* **1.** To behave arrogantly. **2.** To give offense; offend. — *n.* (ĭn′sŭlt′). **1.** An offensive action or remark. **2.** *Medic.* A bodily injury, irritation, or trauma. [Ult. < Lat. *īnsultāre*, to leap at, insult, freq. of *īnsilīre*, to leap upon : *in-*, on; see IN-[2] + *salīre*, to leap; see **sel-***.] — **in•sult′er** *n.* — **in•sult′ing•ly** *adv.*

in•su•per•a•ble (ĭn-so͞o′pər-ə-bəl) *adj.* Impossible to overcome; insurmountable. — **in•su′per•a•bil′i•ty, in•su′per•a•ble•ness** *n.* — **in•su′per•a•bly** *adv.*

in•sup•port•a•ble (ĭn′sə-pôr′tə-bəl, -pōr′-) *adj.* **1.** Not endurable; intolerable: *insupportable anguish.* **2.** Lacking grounds or defense; unjustifiable: *an insupportable claim.* — **in′sup•port′a•ble•ness** *n.* — **in′sup•port′a•bly** *adv.*

in•sup•press•i•ble (ĭn′sə-prĕs′ə-bəl) *adj.* Impossible to suppress or control; irrepressible. — **in′sup•press′i•bly** *adv.*

in•sur•ance (ĭn-sho͝or′əns) *n.* **1.a.** The act, business, or system of insuring. **b.** The state of being insured. **c.** A means of being insured. **2.a.** Coverage by a contract binding a party to indemnify another against specified loss in return for premiums paid. **b.** The sum or rate for which such a contract insures something. **c.** The periodic premium paid for this coverage. **3.** A protective measure.

ă pat	oi boy
ā pay	ou out
âr care	o͝o took
ä father	o͞o boot
ĕ pet	ŭ cut
ē be	ûr urge
ĭ pit	th thin
ī pie	*th* this
îr pier	hw which
ŏ pot	zh vision
ō toe	ə about, item
ô paw	

Stress marks:
′ (primary);
′ (secondary), as in
dictionary (dĭk′shə-nĕr′ē)

in•sure (ĭn-sho͝or′) *v.* **-sured, -sur•ing, -sures.** —*tr.* **1.** To cover with insurance. **2.** To make sure, certain, or secure. See Usage Note at **assure.** —*intr.* To buy or sell insurance. [ME *ensuren,* to assure < OFr. *enseurer,* poss. var. of *assurer.* See ASSURE.] —**in•sur′a•bil′i•ty** *n.* —**in•sur′a•ble** *adj.*

in•sured (ĭn-sho͝ord′) *n., pl.* **insured** or **-sureds. 1.** The party who stands to benefit from an insurance policy. **2.** The party insured.

in•sur•er (ĭn-sho͝or′ər) *n.* One that insures, esp. an insurance underwriter.

in•sur•gence (ĭn-sûr′jəns) *n.* The action or an instance of rebellion; an insurrection.

in•sur•gen•cy (ĭn-sûr′jən-sē) *n., pl.* **-cies. 1.** The quality or circumstance of being rebellious. **2.** An instance of rebellion.

in•sur•gent (ĭn-sûr′jənt) *adj.* Rising in revolt against civil authority or a government in power; rebellious. —*n.* **1.** One that is insurgent. **2.** A member of a political party who rebels against its leadership. [Lat. *īnsurgēns, īnsurgent-,* pr.part. of *īnsurgere,* to rise up : *in-,* intensive pref.; see IN-[2] + *surgere,* to rise; see SURGE.] —**in•sur′gent•ly** *adv.*

in•sur•mount•a•ble (ĭn′sər-moun′tə-bəl) *adj.* Impossible to surmount; insuperable. —**in′sur•mount′a•bil′i•ty, in′sur•mount′a•ble•ness** *n.* —**in′sur•mount′a•bly** *adv.*

in•sur•rec•tion (ĭn′sə-rĕk′shən) *n.* The act or an instance of open revolt against civil authority or a constituted government. See Syns at **rebellion.** [ME < OFr. < LLat. *īnsurrēctiō, īnsurrēctiōn-* < Lat. *īnsurrēctus,* p.part. of *īnsurgere,* to rise up. See INSURGENT.] —**in′sur•rec′tion•al** *adj.* —**in′sur•rec′tion•ar′y** (-shə-nĕr′ē) *adj.* & *n.* —**in′sur•rec′tion•ism** *n.* —**in′sur•rec′tion•ist** *n.*

in•sus•cep•ti•ble (ĭn′sə-sĕp′tə-bəl) *adj.* Not susceptible. —**in•sus•cep′ti•bil′i•ty** *n.* —**in′sus•cep′ti•bly** *adv.*

int. *abbr.* **1.** Intelligence. **2.** Intercept. **3.** Interest. **4.** Interim. **5.** Interior. **6.** *Gram.* Interjection. **7.** Intermediate. **8.** Internal. **9.** International. **10.** Intersection. **11.** Interval. **12.** Interview. **13.** *Gram.* Intransitive.

in•tact (ĭn-tăkt′) *adj.* **1.** Remaining sound, entire, or uninjured; not impaired in any way. **2.** Having all physical parts, esp.: **a.** Having the hymen unbroken. **b.** Not castrated. [ME < Lat. *intāctus* : *in-,* not; see IN-[1] + *tāctus,* p.part. of *tangere,* to touch; see **tag-*.**] —**in•tact′ly** *adv.* —**in•tact′ness** *n.*

in•ta•glio (ĭn-tăl′yō, -täl′-) *n., pl.* **-glios. 1.a.** A figure or design carved into or beneath the surface of hard metal or stone. **b.** The art or process of carving a design in this manner. **2.** A gemstone carved in intaglio. **3.** Printing done with a plate bearing an image in intaglio. **4.** A die incised so as to produce a design in relief. [Ital. < *intagliare,* to engrave : *in-,* in (< Lat.; see IN-[2]) + *tagliare,* to cut (< VLat. **talliāre*; see TAILOR).]

in•take (ĭn′tāk′) *n.* **1.** An opening by which a fluid is admitted into a container or conduit. **2.a.** The act of taking in. **b.** The quantity taken in. **c.** Something, esp. energy, taken in.

in•tan•gi•ble (ĭn-tăn′jə-bəl) *adj.* **1.** Incapable of being perceived by the senses. **2.** Incapable of being realized or defined. —*n.* Something intangible, esp. an asset that cannot be perceived by the senses. Often used in the plural. —**in•tan′gi•bil′i•ty, in•tan′gi•ble•ness** *n.* —**in•tan′gi•bly** *adv.*

in•tar•si•a (ĭn-tär′sē-ə) *n.* **1.** A decorative inlaid pattern in a surface, esp. a mosaic in wood. **2.** The art or practice of making such a pattern. [Ger. < Ital. *intarsio* < *intarsiare,* to inlay : *in-,* in (< Lat.; see EN-[1]) + *tarsia,* inlaid mosaic work (< Ar. *tarṣī*‘).]

intarsia

in•te•ger (ĭn′tĭ-jər) *n. Math.* **1.** A member of the set of positive whole numbers (1, 2, 3 . . .), negative whole numbers (−1, −2, −3 . . .), and zero (0). **2.** A complete unit or entity. [< Lat., whole, complete. See **tag-*.**]

in•te•gra•ble (ĭn′tĭ-grə-bəl) *adj. Math.* Capable of undergoing integration or of being integrated.

in•te•gral (ĭn′tĭ-grəl, ĭn-tĕg′rəl) *adj.* **1.** Essential or necessary for completeness; constituent: *A kitchen is integral to a house.* **2.** Possessing everything essential; entire. **3.** (ĭn′tĭ-grəl). *Math.* **a.** Expressed or expressible as or in terms of integers. **b.** Expressed as or involving integrals. —*n.* **1.** A complete unit; a whole. **2.** (ĭn′tĭ-grəl). *Math.* **a.** A definite integral. **b.** An indefinite integral. [ME < OFr. < Med.Lat. *integrālis,* making up a whole < Lat. *integer,* complete. See INTEGER.] —**in′te•gral′i•ty** (-grăl′ĭ-tē) *n.* —**in′te•gral•ly** *adv.*

integral calculus *n. Math.* The study of integration and its use in finding volumes, areas, and solutions of differential equations.

integral domain *n. Math.* A commutative ring with unity where the product of nonzero elements cannot be zero.

in•te•grand (ĭn′tĭ-grănd′) *n. Math.* A function or an equation to be integrated. [< Lat. *integrandus,* gerundive of *integrāre,* to integrate. See INTEGRATE.]

in•te•grant (ĭn′tĭ-grənt) *adj.* Constituting part of a whole; integral.

in•te•grate (ĭn′tĭ-grāt′) *v.* **-grat•ed, -grat•ing, -grates.** —*tr.* **1.** To make a whole by bringing all parts together; unify. **2.a.** To join with something else; unite. **b.** To make part of a larger unit. **3.** To open to people of all races or ethnic groups without restriction; desegregate. **4.** *Math.* **a.** To calculate the integral of. **b.** To perform integration on. **5.** *Psychol.* To bring about the integration of (personality traits). —*intr.* To become integrated or undergo integration. [< ME, intact < Lat. *integrātus,* p.part. of *integrāre,* to make whole < *integer,* complete. See **tag-*.**] —**in′te•gra′tive** *adj.*

in•te•grat•ed circuit (ĭn′tĭ-grā′tĭd) *n.* A slice or chip of material on which is etched or imprinted a complex of electronic components and their interconnections.

in•te•gra•tion (ĭn′tĭ-grā′shən) *n.* **1.a.** The act or process of integrating. **b.** The state of becoming integrated. **2.** The bringing of people of different racial or ethnic groups into unrestricted and equal association, as in society or an organization; desegregation. **3.** *Psychol.* The organization of the psychological or social traits and tendencies of a personality into a harmonious whole. **4.** *Math.* The process of finding the equation or function of which a given quantity or function is the derivative.

in•te•gra•tion•ist (ĭn′tĭ-grā′shə-nĭst) *n.* One who advocates or works for social integration. —**in′te•gra′tion•ist** *adj.*

in•te•gra•tor (ĭn′tĭ-grā′tər) *n.* **1.** One that integrates. **2.** An instrument for mechanically calculating definite integrals.

in•teg•ri•ty (ĭn-tĕg′rĭ-tē) *n.* **1.** Steadfast adherence to a strict ethical code. See Syns at **honesty. 2.** The state of being unimpaired; soundness. **3.** The quality or condition of being whole or undivided; completeness. [ME *integrite* < OFr. < Lat. *integritās,* soundness < *integer,* whole, complete. See **tag-*.**]

in•teg•u•ment (ĭn-tĕg′yo͞o-mənt) *n.* **1.** A natural outer covering, such as the membrane enclosing an organ. **2.** *Bot.* The envelope of an ovule. [Lat. *integumentum* < *integere,* to cover : *in-,* on; see IN-[2] + *tegere,* to cover; see **(s)teg-*.**] —**in•teg′u•men′ta•ry** (-mĕn′tə-rē, -mĕn′trē) *adj.*

in•tel•lect (ĭn′tl-ĕkt′) *n.* **1.a.** The ability to learn and reason; the capacity for knowledge and understanding. **b.** The ability to think abstractly or profoundly. **2.** A person of great intellectual ability. [ME < OFr. *intellecte* < Lat. *intellēctus,* perception < p.part. of *intellegere,* to perceive. See INTELLIGENT.]

in•tel•lec•tion (ĭn′tl-ĕk′shən) *n.* **1.** The act or process of using the intellect; thinking or reasoning. **2.** A thought or an idea. [ME *intelleccioun,* understanding < Lat. *intellēctiō, intellēctiōn-,* synecdoche < *intellēctus,* intellect. See INTELLECT.]

in•tel•lec•tive (ĭn′tl-ĕk′tĭv) *adj.* Of, relating to, or generated by the intellect. —**in′tel•lec′tive•ly** *adv.*

in•tel•lec•tu•al (ĭn′tl-ĕk′cho͞o-əl) *adj.* **1.a.** Of or relating to the intellect. **b.** Rational rather than emotional. **2.** Appealing to or engaging the intellect. **3.a.** Having or showing intellect, esp. to a high degree. See Syns at **intelligent. b.** Given to exercise of the intellect; inclined toward abstract thinking. —*n.* An intellectual person. [ME < OFr. *intellectuel* < LLat. *intellēctuālis* < Lat. *intellēctus,* intellect. See INTELLECT.] —**in′tel•lec′tu•al′i•ty** (-ăl′ĭ-tē), **in′tel•lec′tu•al•ness** *n.* —**in′tel•lec′tu•al•ly** *adv.*

in•tel•lec•tu•al•ism (ĭn′tl-ĕk′cho͞o-ə-lĭz′əm) *n.* **1.** Exercise or application of the intellect. **2.** Devotion to exercise or development of the intellect. —**in′tel•lec′tu•al•ist** *n.* —**in′tel•lec′tu•al•is′tic** *adj.*

in•tel•lec•tu•al•i•za•tion (ĭn′tl-ĕk′cho͞o-ə-lĭ-zā′shən) *n.* *Psychol.* **1.** The act or process of intellectualizing. **2.** Excessive reasoning as an unconscious means of protecting oneself from the anxiety of confronting painful fears or problems.

in•tel•lec•tu•al•ize (ĭn′tl-ĕk′cho͞o-ə-līz′) *tr.v.* **-ized, -iz•ing, -iz•es. 1.** To furnish a rational structure or meaning for. **2.** To avoid psychological insight into (an emotional problem) by intellectual analysis. —**in′tel•lec′tu•al•iz′er** *n.*

in•tel•li•gence (ĭn-tĕl′ə-jəns) *n.* **1.a.** The capacity to acquire and apply knowledge. **b.** The faculty of thought and reason. **c.** Superior powers of mind. **2.** *Theol.* An intelligent incorporeal being, esp. an angel. **3.** Information; news. **4.a.** Secret information, esp. about an enemy. **b.** An agency, a staff, or an office gathering intelligence. **c.** Espionage agents, organizations, and activities considered as a group.

intelligence quotient *n.* The ratio of tested mental age to chronological age, usu. expressed as a quotient multiplied by 100.

in•tel•li•genc•er (ĭn-tĕl′ə-jən-sər, -jĕn′-) *n.* **1.** One who conveys information. **2.** A secret agent, an informer, or a spy.

in•tel•li•gent (ĭn-tĕl′ə-jənt) *adj.* **1.** Having intelligence. **2.** Having a high degree of intelligence; mentally acute. **3.** Showing sound judgment and rationality. **4.** Appealing to the intellect; intellectual. **5.** *Comp. Sci.* Having certain data storage and processing capabilities. [Lat. *intelligēns, intelligent-,* pr.part. of *intellegere, intelligere,* to perceive : *inter-,* inter- + *legere,* to choose; see **leg-*.**] —**in•tel′li•gen′tial** (-jĕn′shəl) *adj.* —**in•tel′li•gent•ly** *adv.*

Syns: *intelligent, bright, brilliant, knowing, quick-witted, smart, intellectual.* These adjectives mean having or showing mental keenness. *Intelligent* usually implies the ability to cope with new problems and to use the power of reasoning and inference effectively: *an intelligent officer. Bright* implies quickness or ease in learning: *a bright child. Brilliant* suggests unusually impressive mental acuteness: *"The dullard's envy of brilliant men is always assuaged by the suspicion that they* *will come to a bad end"* (Max Beerbohm). *Knowing* implies the possession of knowledge, information, or understanding: *Knowing collectors bought all the paintings. Quick-witted* suggests mental alertness and prompt response: *quick-witted emergency medical staff. Smart* refers to quick intelligence and often a ready capability for taking care of one's own interests: *Smart lawyers can effectively manipulate juries. Intellectual* especially implies the capacity to grasp difficult or abstract concepts: *intellectual students.*

in•tel•li•gent•si•a (ĭn-tĕl′ə-jĕnt′sē-ə, -gĕnt′-) *n.* The intellectual elite of a society. [Russ. *intelligentsiya* < Lat. *intelligentia*, intelligence < *intelligēns, intelligent-*, intelligent. See INTELLIGENT.]

in•tel•li•gi•ble (ĭn-tĕl′ĭ-jə-bəl) *adj.* **1.** Capable of being understood. **2.** Capable of being apprehended by the intellect alone. [ME < OFr. < Lat. *intellegibilis, intelligibilis* < *intellegere*, to perceive. See INTELLIGENT.] **— in•tel′li•gi•bil′i•ty, in•tel′li•gi•ble•ness** *n.* **— in•tel′li•gi•bly** *adv.*

in•tem•per•ance (ĭn-tĕm′pər-əns, -prəns) *n.* **1.** Lack of temperance, as in the indulgence of an appetite or a passion. **2.** Excessive use of alcoholic beverages.

in•tem•per•ate (ĭn-tĕm′pər-ĭt, -prĭt) *adj.* Not temperate or moderate; excessive, esp. in the use of alcoholic beverages. **— in•tem′per•ate•ly** *adv.* **— in•tem′per•ate•ness** *n.*

in•tend (ĭn-tĕnd′) *v.* **-tend•ed, -tend•ing, -tends.** *— tr.* **1.** To have in mind; plan: *We intend to go.* **2.a.** To design for a specific purpose. **b.** To have in mind for a particular use. **3.** To signify or mean. *— intr.* To have a design or purpose in mind. [ME *entenden* < OFr. *entendre* < Lat. *intendere* : *in-*, toward; see IN-[2] + *tendere*, to stretch; see **ten-***.]

in•ten•dance (ĭn-tĕn′dəns) *n.* **1.** The function of an intendant; management. **2.** An administrative office or district.

in•ten•dan•cy (ĭn-tĕn′dən-sē) *n., pl.* **-cies. 1.** The position or function of an intendant. **2.** Intendants considered as a group. **3.** The district supervised by an intendant.

in•ten•dant (ĭn-tĕn′dənt) *n.* **1.** An administrative official serving a French, Spanish, or Portuguese monarch. **2.** A district administrator in some countries of Latin America. [Fr. < OFr., administrator < Lat. *intendēns, intendent-*, pr.part. of *intendere*, to intend. See INTEND.]

in•tend•ed (ĭn-tĕn′dĭd) *adj.* **1.** Deliberate; intentional. **2.** Prospective; future. *— n. Informal.* One who is engaged to be married. **— in•tend′ed•ly** *adv.*

in•tend•ing (ĭn-tĕn′dĭng) *adj.* Purposing to become or be; prospective.

in•tend•ment (ĭn-tĕnd′mənt) *n.* The true meaning or intention of something, esp. of a law.

in•ten•er•ate (ĭn-tĕn′ə-rāt′) *tr.v.* **-at•ed, -at•ing, -ates.** To make tender; soften. [IN-[2] + Lat. *tener*, tender; see TENDER[1] + -ATE[1].] **— in•ten′er•a′tion** *n.*

in•tense (ĭn-tĕns′) *adj.* **-tens•er, -tens•est. 1.** Possessing or displaying a distinctive feature to an extreme degree. **2.** Extreme in degree, strength, or size. **3.** Involving or showing strain or extreme effort. **4.a.** Deeply felt; profound. **b.** Tending to feel deeply. [ME < OFr. < Lat. *intēnsus*, stretched, intent < p.part. of *intendere*, to stretch, intend. See INTEND.] **— in•tense′ly** *adv.* **— in•tense′ness** *n.*

Usage Note: The meanings of *intense* and *intensive* are often subtly distinct. When used to describe human feeling or activity, *intense* often suggests a strength or concentration that arises from inner dispositions. *Intensive* is frequently applied when the strength or concentration of an activity is imposed from without. *Mark's intense study of German* suggests that Mark himself was responsible for the concentrated activity, whereas *Mark's intensive study of German* suggests that the program in which Mark was studying was designed to cover a great deal of material in a brief period.

in•ten•si•fi•er (ĭn-tĕn′sə-fī′ər) *n. Gram.* See **intensive.**

in•ten•si•fy (ĭn-tĕn′sə-fī′) *v.* **-fied, -fy•ing, -fies.** *— tr.* **1.** To make intense or more intense. **2.** To increase the contrast of (a photographic image). *— intr.* To become intense or more intense. **— in•ten′si•fi•ca′tion** (-fĭ-kā′shən) *n.*

in•ten•sion (ĭn-tĕn′shən) *n.* **1.** The state or quality of being intense; intensity. **2.** The act of becoming intense or more intense; intensification. **3.** *Logic.* The sum of the attributes contained in a term. [Lat. *intēnsiō, intēnsiōn-* < *intēnsus*, stretched. See INTENSE.] **— in•ten′sion•al** *adj.*

in•ten•si•ty (ĭn-tĕn′sĭ-tē) *n., pl.* **-ties. 1.** Exceptionally great concentration, power, or force. **2.** *Phys.* The amount or degree of strength of electricity, light, heat, or sound per unit area or volume. **3.** *Color.* **a.** The strength of a color, esp. the degree to which it lacks its complementary color. **b.** See **saturation** 5.

in•ten•sive (ĭn-tĕn′sĭv) *adj.* **1.** Of, relating to, or marked by intensity. See Usage Note at **intense. 2.** *Gram.* Tending to emphasize or intensify. **3.** Possessing or requiring to a high degree. Often used in combination: *research-intensive.* **4.** Relating to or being a method esp. of land cultivation intended to increase the productivity of a fixed area by means of an increase in capital and labor. **5.** *Phys.* Having the same value for any subdivision of a thermodynamic system: *intensive pressure. — n. Gram.* A linguistic element, such as the adverb *extremely*, that provides force or emphasis. **— in•ten′sive•ly** *adv.* **— in•ten′sive•ness** *n.*

intensive care *n.* Continuous and closely monitored health care that is provided to critically ill patients.

intensive care unit *n.* A specialized section of a hospital containing the equipment and staff to provide intensive care.

in•tent (ĭn-tĕnt′) *n.* **1.** Something that is intended; an aim or a purpose. See Syns at **intention. 2.** *Law.* The state of one's mind at the time one carries out an action. **3.** Meaning; purport. *— adj.* **1.** Firmly fixed; concentrated. **2.** Having the attention applied; engrossed. **3.** Having the mind and will on a specific purpose. ***— idiom.*** **for** (or **to**) **all intents and purposes.** In every practical sense; practically. [ME *entent* < OFr. < Med.Lat. *intentus* < Lat., an extending < *intentus*, attentive to < p.part. of *intendere*, to direct attention. See INTEND.] **— in•tent′ly** *adv.* **— in•tent′ness** *n.*

in•ten•tion (ĭn-tĕn′shən) *n.* **1.** A course of action that one intends to follow. **2.a.** An aim that guides action; an objective. **b. intentions.** Purpose with respect to marriage. **3.** *Philos.* A concept arising from directing the attention toward an object. **4.** *Medic.* The process by which or the manner in which a wound heals. **5.** *Archaic.* Import; meaning. [Ult. < Lat. *intentiō, intentiōn-* < *intentus*, intent < p.part. of *intendere*, to direct attention. See INTEND.]

Syns: *intention, intent, purpose, goal, end, aim, object, objective.* These nouns refer to what one plans to do or achieve. *Intention* simply signifies a course of action that one proposes to follow: *It is not my intention to argue with you. Intent* more strongly implies deliberateness: *our intent to plant a garden next year. Purpose* strengthens the idea of resolution or determination: *"His purpose was to discover how long these guests intended to stay"* (Joseph Conrad). *Goal* may suggest an idealistic or even a remote purpose: *set high goals for herself. End* suggests a long-range goal: *will use any means to achieve that end. Aim* stresses the direction one's efforts take in pursuit of an end: *The aim of most students is to study hard.* An *object* is an end that one tries to carry out: *The object of the game is to score points. Objective* often implies that the end or goal can be reached: *The report outlines the committee's objectives.*

in•ten•tion•al (ĭn-tĕn′shə-nəl) *adj.* **1.** Done deliberately; intended: *an intentional slight.* See Syns at **voluntary. 2.** Having to do with intention. **— in•ten′tion•al′i•ty** (-năl′ĭ-tē) *n.* **— in•ten′tion•al•ly** *adv.*

in•ter (ĭn-tûr′) *tr.v.* **-terred, -ter•ring, -ters.** To place in a grave or tomb; bury. [Ult. < Med.Lat. *interrāre* : Lat. *in-*, in; see IN-[2] + Lat. *terra*, earth; see **ters-***.]

inter. *abbr.* Intermediate.

inter– *pref.* **1.** Between; among: *international.* **2.** In the midst of; within: *intertropical.* **3.** Mutual; mutually: *interrelate.* **4.** Reciprocal; reciprocally: *intermingle.* [ME *entre-, inter-* < OFr. *entre-* < Lat. *inter-* < *inter*. See **en***.]

in•ter•a•bang (ĭn-tĕr′ə-băng′) *n.* Var. of **interrobang.**

in•ter•act (ĭn′tər-ăkt′) *intr.v.* **-act•ed, -act•ing, -acts.** To act on each other: *Students learn by interacting.*

in•ter•ac•tion (ĭn′tər-ăk′shən) *n.* **1.a.** The act or process of interacting. **b.** The state of undergoing interaction. **2.** *Phys.* Any of four fundamental ways in which bodies can influence each other, classified as strong, weak, electromagnetic, and gravitational.

in•ter•ac•tive (ĭn′tər-ăk′tĭv) *adj.* **1.** Acting or capable of acting on each other. **2.** *Comp. Sci.* Of or relating to a two-way electronic or communications system in which response is direct and continual. **3.** Of, relating to, or being a form of television entertainment in which the viewer participates directly. **— in′ter•ac′tive•ly** *adv.*

in•ter a•li•a (ĭn′tər ā′lē-ə, ä′lē-ə) *adv.* Among other things. [Lat.]

inter a•li•os (ā′lē-ōs′, ä′lē-ōs′) *adv.* Among other persons. [Lat. *inter aliōs*.]

in•ter•a•tom•ic (ĭn′tər-ə-tŏm′ĭk) *adj.* Occurring, operating, or situated between atoms.

in•ter•breed (ĭn′tər-brēd′) *v.* **-bred** (-brĕd′), **-breed•ing, -breeds.** *— intr.* **1.** To breed with another kind or species; hybridize. **2.** To breed within a narrow range or with closely related types or individuals; inbreed. *— tr.* To cause to interbreed.

in•ter•ca•lar•y (ĭn-tûr′kə-lĕr′ē, ĭn′tər-kăl′ə-rē) *adj.* **1.a.** Inserted in the calendar to make the calendar year correspond to the solar year. Used of a day or month. **b.** Having such a day or month inserted. Used of a year. **2.** Inserted between other elements or parts; interpolated. [Lat. *intercalārius, intercalāris* < *intercalāre*, to intercalate. See INTERCALATE.]

in•ter•ca•late (ĭn-tûr′kə-lāt′) *tr.v.* **-lat•ed, -lat•ing, -lates. 1.** To insert (a day or month) in a calendar. **2.** To insert, interpose, or interpolate. [Lat. *intercalāre, intercalāt-* : *inter-*, inter- + *calāre*, to proclaim; see **kelə-**[2]*.] **— in•ter′ca•la′tion** *n.* **— in•ter′ca•la′tive** *adj.*

in•ter•cede (ĭn′tər-sēd′) *intr.v.* **-ced•ed, -ced•ing, -cedes. 1.** To plead on another's behalf. **2.** To act as mediator in a dispute. [Lat. *intercēdere*, to intervene : *inter-*, inter- + *cēdere*, to go; see **ked-***.] **— in′ter•ced′er** *n.*

ă pat	oi boy
ā pay	ou out
âr care	o͝o took
ä father	o͞o boot
ĕ pet	ŭ cut
ē be	ûr urge
ĭ pit	th thin
ī pie	*th* this
îr pier	hw which
ŏ pot	zh vision
ō toe	ə about, item
ô paw	

Stress marks:
′ (primary);
′ (secondary), as in
dictionary (dĭk′shə-nĕr′ē)

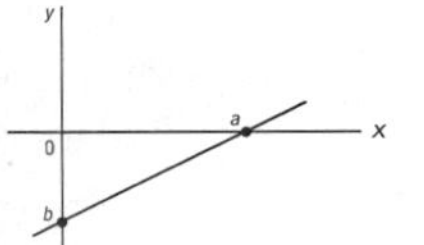

intercept
Intercept form of the equation of a line:
$\frac{x}{a} + \frac{y}{b} = 1$

in•ter•cel•lu•lar (ĭn′tər-sĕl′yə-lər) *adj. Biol.* Located among or between cells: *intercellular fluid.*

in•ter•cept (ĭn′tər-sĕpt′) *tr.v.* **-cept•ed, -cept•ing, -cepts. 1.a.** To stop, deflect, or interrupt the progress or intended course of. **b.** *Sports.* To take possession of by catching (an opponent's ball), esp. in football. **2.** *Math.* To include or bound (a part of a space or curve) between two points or lines. **3.** *Archaic.* To prevent. **4.** *Obsolete.* To cut off from access or communication. —*n.* (ĭn′tər-sĕpt′). **1.** *Math.* The distance from the origin to the point at which a line, curve, or surface intersects a coordinate axis. **2.a.** The interception of a missile by another missile or an aircraft by another aircraft. **b.** Interception of a radio transmission. **3.** An interceptor. [ME *intercepten* < Lat. *intercipere, intercept-* : *inter-*, inter- + *capere*, to seize; see **kap-***.] —**in′ter•cep′tive** *adj.*

in•ter•cep•tion (ĭn′tər-sĕp′shən) *n.* **1.** The act of intercepting or the state of being intercepted. **2.** Something that is intercepted. **3.** *Sports.* An intercepted pass.

in•ter•cep•tor also **in•ter•cept•er** (ĭn′tər-sĕp′tər) *n.* One that intercepts, esp. a plane or missile designed to intercept enemy aircraft.

in•ter•ces•sion (ĭn′tər-sĕsh′ən) *n.* **1.** Entreaty in favor of another, esp. a prayer or petition to God in behalf of another. **2.** Mediation in a dispute. [ME < OFr. < Lat. *intercessiō, intercessiōn-*, intervention < *intercessus*, p.part. of *intercēdere*, to intervene. See INTERCEDE.] —**in′ter•ces′sion•al** *adj.* —**in′ter•ces′sor** (-sĕs′ər) *n.* —**in′ter•ces′so•ry** *adj.*

in•ter•change (ĭn′tər-chānj′) *v.* **-changed, -chang•ing, -chang•es.** —*tr.* **1.** To switch each of (two things) into the place of the other. **2.** To give and receive mutually; exchange. **3.** To cause to succeed each other in a series or pattern; alternate. —*intr.* **1.** To change places with each other. **2.** To succeed each other; alternate. —*n.* (ĭn′tər-chānj′). **1.** The act or process of interchanging. **2.** A highway intersection designed to permit traffic to move freely from one road to another without crossing another line of traffic. —**in′ter•chang′er** *n.*

in•ter•change•a•ble (ĭn′tər-chān′jə-bəl) *adj.* That can be interchanged. —**in′ter•change′a•bil′i•ty, in′ter•change′a•ble•ness** *n.* —**in′ter•change′a•bly** *adv.*

in•ter•clav•i•cle (ĭn′tər-klăv′ĭ-kəl) *n.* A bone located in front of the sternum and between the clavicles in certain vertebrates, such as reptiles and amphibians. —**in′ter•cla•vic′u•lar** (-klə-vĭk′yə-lər) *adj.*

in•ter•coast•al (ĭn′tər-kōs′təl) *adj.* Relating to, involving, or connecting two or more coastlines: *intercoastal trade.*

in•ter•col•le•giate (ĭn′tər-kə-lē′jĭt, -jē-ĭt) *adj.* Involving or representing two or more colleges.

in•ter•co•lum•ni•a•tion (ĭn′tər-kə-lŭm′nē-ā′shən) *n.* **1.** The open spaces between the columns in a colonnade. **2.** The system by which intercolumniation is determined.

in•ter•com (ĭn′tər-kŏm′) *n.* An electronic intercommunication system, as between two rooms.

in•ter•com•mu•ni•cate (ĭn′tər-kə-myo͞o′nĭ-kāt′) *intr.v.* **-cat•ed, -cat•ing, -cates. 1.** To communicate with each other. **2.** To be connected or adjoined, as rooms. —**in′ter•com•mu′ni•ca′tion** *n.* —**in′ter•com•mu′ni•ca′tive** (-kā′tĭv, -kə-tĭv) *adj.*

in•ter•com•mun•ion (ĭn′tər-kə-myo͞on′yən) *n.* **1.** Communion, relationship, or association between persons or groups. **2.** The practice by which Christians of different denominations can receive Communion at one another's services or at a common service.

in•ter•con•nect (ĭn′tər-kə-nĕkt′) *v.* **-nect•ed, -nect•ing, -nects.** —*intr.* To be connected with each other. —*tr.* To connect reciprocally: *interconnected theories.* —**in′ter•con•nect′ed•ness** *n.* —**in′ter•con•nect′i•ble, in′ter•con•nect′a•ble** *adj.* —**in′ter•con•nec′tion** *n.*

in•ter•con•ti•nen•tal (ĭn′tər-kŏn′tə-nĕn′tl) *adj.* **1.** Extending or taking place between or among continents. **2.** Having the capability of traveling from one continent to another.

in•ter•con•ver•sion (ĭn′tər-kən-vûr′zhən, -shən) *n.* Mutual conversion. —**in′ter•con•vert′** *v.* —**in′ter•con•vert′i•bil′i•ty** *n.* —**in′ter•con•vert′i•ble** *adj.*

in•ter•cool•er (ĭn′tər-ko͞o′lər) *n.* A device for cooling a fluid between successive heating stages. —**in′ter•cool′** *v.*

in•ter•cos•tal (ĭn′tər-kŏs′təl) *adj.* Located or occurring between the ribs. —*n.* An intercostal space, muscle, or part. [NLat. *intercostālis* : INTER- + Lat. *costa*, rib; see **kost-***.]

in•ter•course (ĭn′tər-kôrs′, -kōrs′) *n.* **1.** Dealings or communications between persons or groups. **2.** Sexual intercourse. [ME *entercours*, commercial dealings < OFr. *entrecours* < Lat. *intercursus*, a running between, interposition < p.part. of *intercurrere*, to mingle with : *inter-*, inter- + *currere*, to run; see **kers-***.]

in•ter•crop (ĭn′tər-krŏp′) *v.* **-cropped, -crop•ping, -crops.** —*intr.* To grow more than one crop in the same field, esp. in alternating rows. —*tr.* To plant (a crop) in the same field with another. —**in′ter•crop′** *n.*

in•ter•cul•tur•al (ĭn′tər-kŭl′chər-əl) *adj.* Of, relating to, involving, or representing different cultures.

in•ter•cur•rent (ĭn′tər-kûr′ənt, -kŭr′-) *adj. Pathol.* Occurring at the same time as and usu. altering the course of another disease. [Lat. *intercurrēns, intercurrent-*, pr.part. of *intercurrere*, to mingle with. See INTERCOURSE.]

in•ter•cut (ĭn′tər-kŭt′) *tr.v.* **-cut, -cut•ting, -cuts.** To insert (scenes or camera shots) in a film sequence to achieve dramatic contrast or follow two or more actions taking place simultaneously. —**in′ter•cut′** *adj.*

in•ter•de•nom•i•na•tion•al (ĭn′tər-də-nŏm′ə-nā′shə-nəl) *adj.* Of or involving different religious denominations.

in•ter•den•tal (ĭn′tər-dĕn′tl) *adj.* **1.** Located or made for use between the teeth. **2.** *Ling.* Pronounced with the tip of the tongue between the teeth, as (*th*) in *that.* —*n. Ling.* An interdental consonant.

in•ter•de•part•men•tal (ĭn′tər-dē′pärt-mĕn′tl) *adj.* Involving or representing different departments, as of a business.

in•ter•de•pend•ent (ĭn′tər-dĭ-pĕn′dənt) *adj.* Mutually dependent. —**in′ter•de•pend′ence, in′ter•de•pend′en•cy** *n.*

in•ter•dict (ĭn′tər-dĭkt′) *tr.v.* **-dict•ed, -dict•ing, -dicts. 1.** To prohibit or place under an ecclesiastical or legal sanction. **2.** To forbid or debar, esp. authoritatively. See Syns at **forbid. 3.a.** To cut or destroy (a line of communication) by firepower so as to halt an enemy's advance. **b.** To confront and halt the activities, advance, or entry of. —*n.* (ĭn′tər-dĭkt′). **1.** *Law.* A prohibition by court order. **2.** *Rom. Cath. Ch.* An ecclesiastical censure that excludes a person or district from participation in most sacraments and from Christian burial. [Ult. < Lat. *interdīcere, interdict-*, to forbid : *inter-*, inter- + *dīcere*, to say; see **deik-***.] —**in′ter•dic′tion** *n.* —**in′ter•dic′tive, in′ter•dic′to•ry** (-dĭk′tə-rē) *adj.* —**in′ter•dic′tive•ly** *adv.* —**in′ter•dic′tor** *n.*

in•ter•dis•ci•pli•nar•y (ĭn′tər-dĭs′ə-plə-nĕr′ē) *adj.* Of, relating to, or involving two or more academic disciplines that are usu. considered distinct.

in•ter•est (ĭn′trĭst, -tər-ĭst, -trĕst′) *n.* **1.a.** A state of curiosity or concern about or attention to something. **b.** Something, such as a subject, that evokes this mental state. **2.** Regard for one's own benefit or advantage; self-interest. Often used in the plural. **3.a.** A right, claim, or legal share. **b.** Something in which such a right, claim, or share is held. **c.** A person or group of persons holding such a right, claim, or share. **4.** Involvement with or participation in something. **5.a.** A charge for a loan, usu. a percentage of the amount loaned. **b.** An excess or a bonus beyond what is expected or due. **6.a.** An interest group. **b.** The particular cause supported by an interest group. —*tr.v.* **-est•ed, -est•ing, -ests. 1.** To arouse the curiosity or hold the attention of. **2.** To cause to become involved or concerned with. **3.** *Obsolete.* To concern or affect. —***idiom.*** **in the interest (***or* **interests) of.** To the advantage of; for the sake of. [ME < OFr. < Lat., it is of importance, 3rd pers. sing. pr.t. of *interesse*, to be between, take part in : *inter-*, inter- + *esse*, to be; see **es-***.]

in•ter•est•ed (ĭn′trĭ-stĭd, -tər-ĭ-stĭd, -tə-rĕs′tĭd) *adj.* **1.** Having or showing curiosity, fascination, or concern. **2.** Possessing a right, claim, or stake. See Usage Note at **disinterested.** —**in′ter•est•ed•ly** *adv.* —**in′ter•est•ed•ness** *n.*

interest group *n.* A group of persons working on behalf of or strongly supporting a particular cause. —**in′ter•est-group′** (ĭn′trĭst-group′, -tər-ĭst, -trĕst-) *adj.*

in•ter•est•ing (ĭn′trĭ-stĭng, -tər-ĭ-stĭng, -tə-rĕs′tĭng) *adj.* Arousing or holding the attention; absorbing. —**in′ter•est•ing•ly** *adv.*

in•ter•face (ĭn′tər-fās′) *n.* **1.** A surface forming a common boundary between adjacent regions, bodies, substances, or phases. **2.** A point at which independent systems or diverse groups interact. **3.** *Comp. Sci.* The point of interaction or communication between a computer and any other entity, such as a printer. —*v.* (ĭn′tər-fās′) **-faced, -fac•ing, -fac•es.** —*tr.* **1.** To join by means of an interface. **2.** To serve as an interface for. —*intr.* **1.** To serve as an interface or become interfaced. **2.** To interact or coordinate smoothly.

in•ter•fac•ing (ĭn′tər-fā′sĭng) *n.* Material inserted between the layers of a garment to thicken or stiffen it.

in•ter•faith (ĭn′tər-fāth′) *adj.* Of, relating to, or involving persons of different religious faiths: *an interfaith marriage.*

in•ter•fas•cic•u•lar cambium (ĭn′tər-fə-sĭk′yə-lər) *n. Bot.* The cambium arising between the vascular bundles.

in•ter•fere (ĭn′tər-fîr′) *intr.v.* **-fered, -fer•ing, -feres. 1.** To come between so as to be a hindrance or an obstacle. **2.** *Sports.* To perform an act of interference. **3.** To intervene or intrude in the affairs of others; meddle. **4.** To strike one hoof against the opposite hoof or leg while moving. Used of a horse. **5.** *Phys. & Electron.* To cause interference. [ME *enterferen* < OFr. *s'entreferer*, to strike one another : *entre-*, between (< Lat. *inter-*; see INTER-) + *ferir*, to strike (< Lat. *ferīre*).] —**in′ter•fer′er** *n.* —**in′ter•fer′ing•ly** *adv.*

Syns: *interfere, meddle, tamper.* These verbs mean to intervene unasked in the affairs of others and often in an impudent or indiscreet manner. *Interfere* implies action that seriously hampers, hinders, or frustrates: *Restrictive clothing that interferes with movement. Meddle* stresses unwanted, unwarranted, or unnecessary intrusion: *"wholly unacquainted with the world in which they are so fond of meddling"* (Edmund Burke). To *tamper* is to interfere by making unsought, unwelcome, and often destructive changes or by trying to influence another in an improper way: *"persons accused of . . . tampering with ballot boxes"* (James Bryce).

in•ter•fer•ence (ĭn′tər-fîr′əns) *n.* **1.a.** The act or an instance of hindering, obstructing, or impeding. **b.** Something that hinders, obstructs, or impedes. **2.a.** *Sports.* Illegal obstruction or hindrance of the ball or an opposing player, esp. of a receiver in football. **b.** *Football.* The legal blocking of defensive tacklers to protect and make way for the ball carrier. **3.** *Phys.* The variation of wave amplitude that occurs when waves of the same or nearly the same frequency come together. **4.** *Electron.* **a.** The inhibition or prevention of clear reception of broadcast signals. **b.** The distorted portion of a received signal. **—in′ter•fer•en′tial** (-fə-rĕn′shəl) *adj.*

in•ter•fe•rom•e•ter (ĭn′tər-fə-rŏm′ĭ-tər) *n.* Any of several optical, acoustic, or radio frequency instruments that use interference phenomena between waves to determine wavelengths, wave velocities, and small distances and thicknesses. **—in′ter•fer′o•met′ric** (-fîr′ə-mĕt′rĭk) *adj.* **—in′ter•fer′o•met′ri•cal•ly** *adv.* **—in′ter•fe•rom′e•try** *n.*

in•ter•fer•on (ĭn′tər-fîr′ŏn′) *n.* Any of a group of glycoproteins produced by cells in response to infection by a virus that act to prevent viral replication and have the ability to induce resistance to viral antigens. [INTERFER(E) + -ON[3].]

in•ter•fer•tile (ĭn′tər-fûr′tl) *adj.* Capable of interbreeding. **—in′ter•fer•til′i•ty** (-fûr-tĭl′ĭ-tē) *n.*

in•ter•fluve (ĭn′tər-flo͞ov′) *n.* The region of higher land between two rivers that are in the same drainage system. [Back-formation < INTERFLUVIAL.] **—in′ter•flu′vi•al** *adj.*

in•ter•ga•lac•tic (ĭn′tər-gə-lăk′tĭk) *adj.* Being or occurring between galaxies. **—in′ter•ga•lac′ti•cal•ly** *adv.*

in•ter•gen•er•a•tion•al (ĭn′tər-jĕn′ə-rā′shə-nəl) *adj.* Being or occurring between generations.

in•ter•gla•cial (ĭn′tər-glā′shəl) *adj.* Occurring between glacial epochs. —*n.* A comparatively short period of warmth during an overall period of glaciation.

in•ter•gov•ern•men•tal (ĭn′tər-gŭv′ərn-mĕn′tl) *adj.* Being or occurring between two or more governments or divisions of a government. **—in′ter•gov′ern•men′tal•ly** *adv.*

in•ter•grade (ĭn′tər-grād′) *intr.v.* **-grad•ed, -grad•ing, -grades.** To merge into each other in a series of stages, forms, or types. —*n.* (ĭn′tər-grād′). A transitional stage, form, or type. **—in′ter•gra•da′tion** (-grā-dā′shən) *n.*

in•ter•im (ĭn′tər-ĭm) *n.* An interval of time between one event, process, or period and another. —*adj.* Belonging to, serving during, or taking place during an interim; temporary: *an interim agreement.* [< Lat., in the meantime. See **en***.]

in•ter•i•on•ic (ĭn′tər-ī-ŏn′ĭk) *adj. Phys. & Chem.* Located or occurring between ions.

in•te•ri•or (ĭn-tîr′ē-ər) *adj.* **1.** Of, relating to, or located on the inside; inner. **2.** Of or relating to one's mental or spiritual being. **3.** Situated away from a coast or border; inland. —*n.* **1.** The internal portion or area. **2.** One's mental or spiritual life. **3.** The inland part of a political or geographic entity. **4.** The internal affairs of a country or nation. **5.** A representation of the inside of a building or room, as in a photograph. [Ult. Lat., comp. adj. of *inter,* between. See **en***.] **—in•te′ri•or′i•ty** (-ôr′ĭ-tē, -ŏr′-) *n.* **—in•te′ri•or•ly** *adv.*

interior angle *n. Math.* **1.** Any of the four angles formed between two straight lines intersected by a third straight line. **2.** The angle formed inside a polygon by two adjacent sides.

interior decoration *n.* The planning and execution of the layout, decoration, and furnishing of an architectural interior. **—interior decorator** *n.*

in•te•ri•or•ize (ĭn-tîr′ē-ə-rīz′) *tr.v.* **-ized, -iz•ing, -iz•es.** To cause (feelings, for example) to become an interior or internal part of one's mental or spiritual being; internalize.

interior monologue *n.* A passage of writing presenting a character's inner thoughts and emotions directly.

In•te•ri•or Salish (ĭn-tîr′ē-ər) *n.* A group of Salish-speaking Native American peoples in parts of British Columbia, northern Washington, northern Idaho, and western Montana.

interj. *abbr.* Interjection.

in•ter•ject (ĭn′tər-jĕkt′) *tr.v.* **-ject•ed, -ject•ing, -jects.** To insert between other elements; interpose. [Lat. *interiicere, interiect-* : *inter-,* inter- + *iacere,* to throw; see **yē-***.] **—in•ter•jec′tor** *n.* **—in′ter•jec′to•ry** (-jĕk′tə-rē) *adj.*

in•ter•jec•tion (ĭn′tər-jĕk′shən) *n.* **1.** A sudden short utterance; an ejaculation. **2.** A part of speech usu. expressing emotion and capable of standing alone, such as *Ugh!* or *Wow!* **—in′ter•jec′tion•al** *adj.* **—in′ter•jec′tion•al•ly** *adv.*

in•ter•lace (ĭn′tər-lās′) *v.* **-laced, -lac•ing, -lac•es.** —*tr.* **1.** To connect by or as if by lacing together; interweave. **2.** To intersperse; intermix: *interlaced lies with truth.* —*intr.* To intertwine. **—in′ter•lace′ment** *n.*

In•ter•la•ken (ĭn′tər-lä′kən, ĭn′tər-lä′-). A town of central Switzerland SE of Bern in the Bernese Alps. Pop. 4,852.

in•ter•lam•i•nate (ĭn′tər-lăm′ə-nāt′) *tr.v.* **-nat•ed, -nat•ing, -nates.** **1.** To insert between layers. **2.** To arrange in alternating layers. **—in′ter•lam′i•na′tion** *n.*

in•ter•lard (ĭn′tər-lärd′) *tr.v.* **-lard•ed, -lard•ing, -lards.** To insert something foreign into. [ME *interlarden,* to mix fat into < OFr. *entrelarder* : *entre-,* between (< Lat. *inter-*; see INTER-) + *larder,* to lard (< *lard,* lard; see LARD).]

in•ter•leaf (ĭn′tər-lēf′) *n., pl.* **-leaves** (-lēvz′). *Print.* A blank leaf inserted between the regular pages of a book.

in•ter•leave (ĭn′tər-lēv′) *tr.v.* **-leaved, -leav•ing, -leaves.** *Print.* To provide with interleaves or an interleaf.

in•ter•leu•kin-1 (ĭn′tər-lo͞o′kĭn-wŭn′) *n.* Any of a group of protein substances, released by macrophages and other cells, that induce the production of interleukin-2 by helper T cells and stimulate the inflammatory response. [INTER- + Gk. *leukos,* white; see LEUKO- + -IN.]

in•ter•leu•kin-2 (ĭn′tər-lo͞o′kĭn-to͞o′) *n.* A lymphokine that is released by helper T cells in response to an antigen and interleukin-1 and stimulates the proliferation of helper T cells.

in•ter•line[1] (ĭn′tər-līn′) *tr.v.* **-lined, -lin•ing, -lines.** To insert between printed or written lines. **—in′ter•lin′e•a′tion** (-lĭn′ē-ā′shən) *n.*

in•ter•line[2] (ĭn′tər-līn′) *tr.v.* **-lined, -lin•ing, -lines.** To fit (a garment) with an interlining.

in•ter•lin•e•ar (ĭn′tər-lĭn′ē-ər) *adj. Print.* **1.** Inserted between the lines of a text. **2.** Written or printed with different languages or versions in alternating lines.

in•ter•lin•ing (ĭn′tər-lī′nĭng) *n.* An extra lining between the outer fabric and regular lining of a garment.

in•ter•link (ĭn′tər-lĭngk′) *tr.v.* **-linked, -link•ing, -links.** To link together or join (one) with another: *interlinked policies.*

in•ter•lock (ĭn′tər-lŏk′) *v.* **-locked, -lock•ing, -locks.** —*tr.* **1.** To unite or join closely as by hooking or dovetailing. **2.** To connect together (parts of a mechanism, for example) so that individual parts affect each other in motion or operation. —*intr.* To become interlocked. —*n. Comp. Sci.* (ĭn′tər-lŏk′). A device or an instruction that coordinates processes and prevents one operation from interfering with another.

in•ter•lo•cu•tion (ĭn′tər-lō-kyo͞o′shən) *n.* Speech between two or more persons; conversation. [Lat. *interlocūtiō, interlocūtiōn-* < *interlocūtus,* p.part. of *interloquī,* to interrupt : *inter-,* inter- + *loquī,* to speak; see **tolk**ʷ-*.]

in•ter•loc•u•tor (ĭn′tər-lŏk′yə-tər) *n.* One who takes part in a conversation, often formally or officially.

in•ter•loc•u•to•ry (ĭn′tər-lŏk′yə-tôr′ē, -tōr′ē) *adj. Law.* Pronounced or decided during the course of an action or a suit and temporary or provisional in nature.

in•ter•lop•er (ĭn′tər-lō′pər) *n.* **1.** One that interferes with the affairs of others, often for selfish reasons; a meddler. **2.** *Archaic.* **a.** One that trespasses on a trade monopoly. **b.** A ship or other vessel used in such trade. [INTER- + prob. MDu. *loper,* runner (< *loopen,* to run).] **—in′ter•lope′** *v.*

in•ter•lude (ĭn′tər-lo͞od′) *n.* **1.** An intervening episode, feature, or period of time. **2.a.** A short farcical entertainment performed between the acts of a medieval mystery or morality play. **b.** A 16th-century genre of comedy derived from this. **c.** An entertainment between the acts of a play. **3.** *Mus.* A short piece inserted between the parts of a longer composition. [Ult. < Med.Lat. *interlūdium* : Lat. *inter-,* inter- + Lat. *lūdus,* play; see **leid-***.]

in•ter•lu•nar (ĭn′tər-lo͞o′nər) *adj.* Of or relating to the four-day period between the old and new moon.

in•ter•mar•ry (ĭn′tər-măr′ē) *intr.v.* **-ried, -ry•ing, -ries.** **1.** To marry a member of another group. **2.** To be bound together by the marriages of members. **3.** To marry within one's family, tribe, or clan. **—in′ter•mar′riage** (-măr′ĭj) *n.*

in•ter•med•dle (ĭn′tər-mĕd′l) *intr.v.* **-dled, -dling, -dles.** To interfere in the affairs of others; meddle. [ME *entermedlen* < OFr. *entremedler* : *entre-,* between (< Lat. *inter-*; see INTER-) + *medler,* to mix; see MEDDLE.] **—in′ter•med′dler** *n.*

in•ter•me•di•ar•y (ĭn′tər-mē′dē-ĕr′ē) *adj.* **1.** Existing or occurring between; intermediate. **2.** Acting as a mediator or an agent between persons or things. —*n., pl.* **-ies.** **1.** One that acts as a mediator. **2.** One that acts as an agent between persons or things; a means. **3.** An intermediate state or stage. [Prob. Fr. *intermédiaire* < Lat. *intermedius,* intermediate. See INTERMEDIATE.]

in•ter•me•di•ate (ĭn′tər-mē′dē-ĭt) *adj.* Lying or occurring between two extremes or in a middle position or state: *an intermediate school.* —*n.* **1.** One that is in a middle position or state. **2.** An intermediary. **3.** *Chem.* A substance formed as a necessary stage in the manufacture of a desired end product. **4.** An automobile that is smaller than a full-sized model but larger than a compact. —*intr.v.* (-āt′) **-at•ed, -at•ing, -ates.** **1.** To act as an intermediary; mediate. **2.** To intervene. [ME < Med.Lat. *intermediātus* < Lat. *intermedius* : *inter-,* inter- + *medius,* middle; see **medhyo-***.] **—in′ter•me′di•a•cy** *n.* **—in′ter•me′di•ate•ly** *adv.* **—in′ter•me′di•ate•ness** *n.* **—in′ter•me′di•a′tion** *n.* **—in′ter•me′di•a′tor** *n.*

in•ter•me•din (ĭn′tər-mēd′n) *n.* See **melanocyte-stimulating hormone.** [NLat. *(pars) intermed(ia),* middle part of the hypophysis < Lat., fem. of *intermedius*; see INTERMEDIATE + -IN.]

in•ter•ment (ĭn-tûr′mənt) *n.* The act or ritual of interring.

in•ter•mez•zo (ĭn′tər-mĕt′sō, -mĕd′zō) *n., pl.* **-zos** or **-zi** (-sē, -zē). **1.** A brief entertainment between two acts of a play; an entr'acte. **2.** *Mus.* **a.** A short movement separating the major

ă pat	oi boy
ā pay	ou out
âr care	o͝o took
ä father	o͞o boot
ĕ pet	ŭ cut
ē be	ûr urge
ĭ pit	th thin
ī pie	*th* this
îr pier	hw which
ŏ pot	zh vision
ō toe	ə about, item
ô paw	

Stress marks:
′ (primary);
′ (secondary), as in **dictionary** (dĭk′shə-nĕr′ē)

in•ter•view (ĭn′tər-vyo͞o′) *n.* **1.** A formal meeting in person, esp. one arranged for the assessment of the qualifications of an applicant. **2.a.** A conversation, such as one conducted by a reporter, in which facts or statements are elicited from another. **b.** An account or a reproduction of such a conversation. — *v.* **-viewed, -view•ing, -views.** — *tr.* To obtain an interview from. — *intr.* To have an interview: *interviewed for the job.* [Fr. *entrevue* < OFr. < fem. p.part. of *entrevoir,* to see : *entre-,* between (< Lat. *inter-*; see INTER-) + *voir,* to see (< Lat. *vidēre;* see **weid-***).] — **in′ter•view′a•ble** *adj.* — **in′ter•view•ee′** *n.* — **in′ter•view′er** *n.*

in•ter vi•vos (ĭn′tər vē′vōs′, vī′-) *adj. Law.* Between living persons: *an inter vivos trust.* [Lat. *inter vivōs.*]

in•ter•vo•cal•ic (ĭn′tər-vō-kăl′ĭk) *adj.* Occurring between vowels.

in•ter•weave (ĭn′tər-wēv′) *v.* **-wove** (-wōv′), **-wo•ven** (-wō′vən), **-weav•ing, -weaves.** — *tr.* **1.** To weave together. **2.** To blend together; intermix. — *intr.* To intertwine.

in•tes•tate (ĭn-tĕs′tāt′, -tĭt) *Law.* — *adj.* **1.** Having made no legal will. **2.** Not disposed of by a legal will. — *n.* One who dies without a legal will. — **in•tes′ta•cy** (-tə-sē) *n.*

in•tes•ti•nal (ĭn-tĕs′tə-nəl) *adj.* Of, relating to, or constituting the intestine: *intestinal bacteria.* — **in•tes′ti•nal•ly** *adv.*

intestinal fortitude *n.* Courage; endurance.

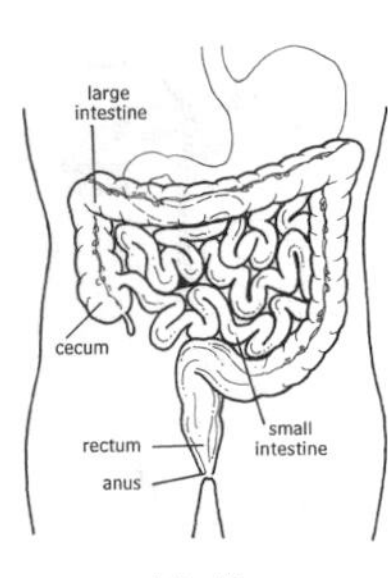

intestine

in•tes•tine (ĭn-tĕs′tĭn) *n.* The portion of the alimentary canal extending from the stomach to the anus and in human beings and other mammals consisting of two segments, the small intestine and the large intestine. Often used in the plural. — *adj.* Internal; civil: *intestine affairs.* [ME < OFr. *intestin* < Lat. *intestīna,* intestines < neut. pl. of *intestīnus,* internal < *intus,* within. See **en***.]

in•thrall (ĭn-thrôl′) *v.* Var. of **enthrall.**

in•throne (ĭn-thrōn′) *v.* Var. of **enthrone.**

in•ti (ĭn′tē) *n.* See table at **currency.** [Am.Sp. < Quechua, sun.]

in•ti•ma (ĭn′tə-mə) *n., pl.* **-mae** (-mē′) or **-mas.** *Anat.* The innermost membrane of an organ or a part, esp. the inner lining of a lymphatic vessel, an artery, or a vein. [Lat. < fem. of *intimus,* innermost. See **en***.] — **in′ti•mal** *adj.*

in•ti•ma•cy (ĭn′tə-mə-sē) *n., pl.* **-cies. 1.** The condition of being intimate. **2.** An instance of being intimate.

in•ti•mate[1] (ĭn′tə-mĭt) *adj.* **1.** Marked by close acquaintance, association, or familiarity. **2.** Relating to or indicative of one's deepest nature. **3.** Essential; innermost. **4.** Marked by informality and privacy. **5.** Very personal; private. **6.** Of or involved in a sexual relationship. — *n.* A close friend or confidant. [Lat. *intimātus,* p.part. of *intimāre,* to make familiar with. See INTIMATE[2].] — **in′ti•mate•ly** *adv.* — **in′ti•mate•ness** *n.*

in•ti•mate[2] (ĭn′tə-māt′) *tr.v.* **-mat•ed, -mat•ing, -mates. 1.** To make known subtly and indirectly; hint. See Syns at **suggest. 2.** To announce; proclaim. [Lat. *intimāre, intimāt-,* to make known < *intimus,* innermost. See **en***.] — **in′ti•mat′er** *n.* — **in′ti•ma′tion** *n.*

in•time (ăN-tēm′) *adj.* Intimate; private: *an intime dining corner.* [Fr. < OFr. < Lat. *intimus,* innermost. See INTIMATE[2].]

in•tim•i•date (ĭn-tĭm′ĭ-dāt′) *tr.v.* **-dat•ed, -dat•ing, -dates. 1.** To make timid; fill with fear. **2.** To coerce or inhibit by or as if by threats. [Med.Lat. *intimidāre, intimidāt-* : Lat. *in-,* in, into; see IN-[2] + Med.Lat. *timidāre,* to be timorous, to frighten (< Lat. *timidus,* timid; see TIMID).] — **in•tim′i•dat′ing•ly** *adv.* — **in•tim′i•da′tion** *n.* — **in•tim′i•da′tor** *n.*

in•tinc•tion (ĭn-tĭngk′shən) *n. Eccles.* The administration of the Eucharist by dipping the host into the wine and thus offering both simultaneously to the communicant. [LLat. *intīnctiō, intīnctiōn-,* a dipping in < Lat. *intīnctus,* p.part. of *intingere,* to dip in : *in-,* in; see IN-[2] + *tingere,* to moisten.]

in•tine (ĭn′tēn′) *n.* The innermost wall of a spore or pollen grain. [Ger. < Lat. *intus,* within. See **en***.]

in•tit•ule (ĭn-tĭch′o͞ol) *tr.v.* **-uled, -ul•ing, -ules.** *Chiefly British.* To give a designation or title to (a legislative act, for example). [Ult. < LLat. *intitulāre* : Lat. *in-,* in; see IN-[2] + LLat. *titulāre,* to entitle (< Lat. *titulus,* title).]

intl. *abbr.* International.

in•to (ĭn′to͞o) *prep.* **1.** To the inside or interior of. **2.a.** To the activity or occupation of: *went into banking.* **b.** To the condition, state, or form of: *changed into a butterfly.* **c.** So as to be in or be included in: *entering into an agreement.* **d.** *Informal.* Interested in or involved with: *into jogging.* **3.** To a point within the limits of a period of time or extent of space. **4.** In the direction of; toward. **5.** Against: *crashed into a tree.* **6.** As a divisor of: *3 goes into 9 three times.*

in•tol•er•a•ble (ĭn-tŏl′ər-ə-bəl) *adj.* Impossible to tolerate or endure; unbearable: *intolerable agony.* — **in•tol′er•a•bil′i•ty, in•tol′er•a•ble•ness** *n.* — **in•tol′er•a•bly** *adv.*

in•tol•er•ance (ĭn-tŏl′ər-əns) *n.* **1.** The quality or condition of being intolerant; lack of tolerance. **2.** *Medic.* Extreme sensitivity or allergy to a substance: *lactose intolerance.*

in•tol•er•ant (ĭn-tŏl′ər-ənt) *adj.* Not tolerant, esp.: **a.** Unwilling to tolerate differences in opinions or beliefs, esp. religious beliefs. **b.** Unable or unwilling to endure or support: *intolerant of interruptions.* — **in•tol′er•ant•ly** *adv.*

in•to•nate (ĭn′tə-nāt′) *tr.v.* **-nat•ed, -nat•ing, -nates. 1.** To intone. **2.** To utter with a particular tone of voice. [Med.Lat. *intonāre, intonāt-.* See INTONE.]

in•to•na•tion (ĭn′tə-nā′shən, -tō-) *n.* **1.a.** The act of intoning or chanting. **b.** An intoned utterance. **2.** A manner of producing tones, esp. with regard to accurate pitch. **3.** *Ling.* The use of pitch to convey syntactic information: *a questioning intonation.* **4.** A use of pitch characteristic of a speaker or dialect. **5.** *Mus.* The opening phrase of a plainsong composition sung as a solo. — **in′to•na′tion•al** *adj.*

in•tone (ĭn-tōn′) *v.* **-toned, -ton•ing, -tones.** — *tr.* **1.** To recite in a singing tone. **2.** To utter in a monotone. — *intr.* **1.** To speak with a singing tone or with a particular intonation. **2.** *Mus.* To sing a plainsong intonation. [Ult. < Med.Lat. *intonāre* : Lat. *in-,* in; see IN-[2] + Lat. *tonus,* tone; see TONE.] — **in•tone′ment** *n.* — **in•ton′er** *n.*

in to•to (ĭn tō′tō) *adv.* Totally; altogether: *He accepted her ideas in toto.* [Lat. : *in,* in + *tōtō,* ablative of *tōtus,* all.]

in•tox•i•cant (ĭn-tŏk′sĭ-kənt) *n.* An agent that intoxicates, esp. an alcoholic beverage. — **in•tox′i•cant** *adj.*

in•tox•i•cate (ĭn-tŏk′sĭ-kāt′) *v.* **-cat•ed, -cat•ing, -cates.** — *tr.* **1.** To stupefy or excite, as by a drug or alcohol. **2.** To stimulate or excite: *The sea breeze intoxicated him.* **3.** To poison. — *intr.* To cause stupefaction, stimulation, or excitement by or as if by a chemical substance. [ME, to poison < Med.Lat. *intoxicāre, intoxicāt-* : Lat. *in-,* in; see IN-[2] + LLat. *toxicāre,* to smear with poison (< Lat. *toxicum,* poison; see TOXIC).] — **in•tox′i•cat′ing•ly** *adv.* — **in•tox′i•ca′tion** *n.* — **in•tox′i•ca′tive** *adj.* — **in•tox′i•ca′tor** *n.*

intr. *abbr. Gram.* Intransitive.

intra– *pref.* Within: *intraocular.* [LLat. *intrā-* < Lat. *intrā.* See **en***.]

in•tra-ar•te•ri•al (ĭn′trə-är-tîr′ē-əl) *adj.* Within an artery.

in•tra-a•tom•ic (ĭn′trə-ə-tŏm′ĭk) *adj.* Within an atom.

in•tra•car•di•ac (ĭn′trə-kär′dē-ăk′) *adj.* Within the heart.

in•tra•cel•lu•lar (ĭn′trə-sĕl′yə-lər) *adj.* Occurring or situated within a cell or cells. — **in′tra•cel′lu•lar•ly** *adv.*

In•tra•coas•tal Waterway (ĭn′trə-kōs′təl). A system of artificial and natural channels and canals along the Atlantic and Gulf coasts of the E and SE U.S.

in•tra•cer•e•bral (ĭn′trə-sə-rē′brəl, -sĕr′ə-) *adj.* Occurring or situated within the cerebrum. — **in′tra•cer•e′bral•ly** *adv.*

in•tra•cra•ni•al (ĭn′trə-krā′nē-əl) *adj.* Occurring or situated within the cranium. — **in′tra•cra′ni•al•ly** *adv.*

in•trac•ta•ble (ĭn-trăk′tə-bəl) *adj.* **1.** Difficult to manage or govern; stubborn. See Syns at **unruly. 2.** Difficult to mold or manipulate: *intractable materials.* **3.** Difficult to alleviate, remedy, or cure: *intractable pain.* — **in•trac′ta•bil′i•ty, in•trac′ta•ble•ness** *n.* — **in•trac′ta•bly** *adv.*

in•tra•cu•ta•ne•ous (ĭn′trə-kyo͞o-tā′nē-əs) *adj.* Within the skin; intradermal. — **in′tra•cu•ta′ne•ous•ly** *adv.*

in•tra•day (ĭn′trə-dā′) *adj.* Occurring within a single day.

in•tra•der•mal (ĭn′trə-dûr′məl) *adj.* Within or between the layers of the skin. — **in′tra•der′mal•ly** *adv.*

intradermal test *n.* A test for hypersensitivity or allergy in which some of the suspected allergen is injected into the skin.

in•tra•dos (ĭn′trə-dŏs′, -dō′, ĭn-trā′dŏs, -dōs′) *n., pl.* **-dos** (-dōz′) or **-dos•es** (-dŏs′ĭz). *Archit.* The inner curve of an arch. [Fr. : *intra-,* within (< LLat. *intrā-;* see INTRA-) + *dos,* back (< OFr. < Lat. *dorsum*).]

in•tra•ga•lac•tic (ĭn′trə-gə-lăk′tĭk) *adj.* Occurring or situated within the space of a galaxy.

in•tra•mo•lec•u•lar (ĭn′trə-mə-lĕk′yə-lər) *adj.* Within a molecule. — **in′tra•mo•lec′u•lar•ly** *adv.*

in•tra•mu•ral (ĭn′trə-myo͝or′əl) *adj.* **1.** Existing or carried on within the bounds of an institution, esp. a school: *intramural athletics.* **2.** *Anat.* Occurring or situated within the wall of a cavity or an organ. — **in′tra•mu′ral•ly** *adv.*

in•tra•mus•cu•lar (ĭn′trə-mŭs′kyə-lər) *adj.* Within a muscle: *an intramuscular injection.* — **in′tra•mus′cu•lar•ly** *adv.*

in•tra•na•sal (ĭn′trə-nā′zəl) *adj.* Within the nose.

in•tran•si•gent also **in•tran•si•geant** (ĭn-trăn′sə-jənt, -zə-) *adj.* Refusing to moderate a position, esp. an extreme one; uncompromising. [Fr. *intransigeant* < Sp. *intransigente* : *in-,* not (< Lat.; see IN-[1]) + *transigente,* pr.part. of *transigir,* to compromise (< Lat. *trānsigere,* to come to an agreement : *trāns-,* trans- + *agere,* to drive; see **ag-***).] — **in•tran′si•gence, in•tran′si•gen•cy** *n.* — **in•tran′si•gent** *n.* — **in•tran′si•gent•ly** *adv.*

in•tran•si•tive (ĭn-trăn′sĭ-tĭv, -zĭ-) *Gram.* — *adj.* Being a verb or verb construction that does not require or cannot take a direct object. — *n.* An intransitive verb. — **in•tran′si•tive•ly** *adv.* — **in•tran′si•tive•ness** *n.*

in•tra•nu•cle•ar (ĭn′trə-no͞o′klē-ər, -nyo͞o′-) *adj.* Situated or occurring within the nucleus of an atom or a cell.

in•tra•oc•u•lar (ĭn′trə-ŏk′yə-lər) *adj.* Situated or occurring within the eyeball: *intraocular pressure.*

in•tra•per•son•al (ĭn′trə-pûr′sə-nəl) *adj.* Existing or occurring within the individual self or mind. — **in′tra•per′son•al•ly** *adv.*

in•tra•pre•neur (ĭn′trə-prə-nûr′) *n.* A person in a large corporation empowered to create new products without being constrained by standard procedures. [*intra(corporate)* + (EN-

TRE)PRENEUR.] — **in′tra•pre•neur′i•al** *adj.* — **in′tra•pre•neur′i•al•ism** *n.* — **in′tra•pre•neur′i•al•ly** *adv.*

in•tra•psy•chic (ĭn′trə-sī′kĭk) *adj.* Existing or taking place within the mind or psyche. — **in′tra•psy′chi•cal•ly** *adv.*

in•tra•spe•cif•ic (ĭn′trə-spĭ-sĭf′ĭk) also **in•tra•spe•cies** (-spē′shēz, -sēz) *adj.* Arising or occurring within a species.

in•tra•state (ĭn′trə-stāt′) *adj.* Relating to or existing within the boundaries of a state.

in•tra•u•ter•ine (ĭn′trə-yo͞o′tər-ĭn, -tə-rīn′) *adj.* Occurring or situated within the uterus.

intrauterine device *n.* A birth control device, such as a plastic loop, that is inserted into the uterus to prevent implantation.

in•tra•va•sa•tion (ĭn-trăv′ə-sā′shən) *n. Pathol.* Entry of foreign matter into a blood vessel. [INTRA– + (EXTRA)VASATION.]

in•tra•vas•cu•lar (ĭn′trə-văs′kyə-lər) *adj.* Within blood vessels or a blood vessel. — **in′tra•vas′cu•lar•ly** *adv.*

in•tra•ve•nous (ĭn′trə-vē′nəs) *adj.* Within or administered into a vein. — *n.* A drug, nutrient solution, or other substance administered into a vein. — **in′tra•ve′nous•ly** *adv.*

in•tra•vi•tal (ĭn′trə-vīt′l) *adj.* Occurring in or performed on a living organism: *intravital staining.* — **in′tra•vi′tal•ly** *adv.*

in•treat (ĭn-trēt′) *v.* Var. of **entreat.**

in•trench (ĭn-trĕnch′) *v.* Var. of **entrench.**

in•trep•id (ĭn-trĕp′ĭd) *adj.* Resolutely courageous; fearless. See Syns at **brave.** [Lat. *intrepidus* : *in-*, not; see IN–[1] + *trepidus*, alarmed.] — **in′tre•pid′i•ty** (-trə-pĭd′ĭ-tē), **in•trep′id•ness** *n.* — **in•trep′id•ly** *adv.*

in•tri•ca•cy (ĭn′trĭ-kə-sē) *n., pl.* **-cies. 1.** The condition or quality of being intricate; complexity. **2.** Something intricate.

in•tri•cate (ĭn′trĭ-kĭt) *adj.* **1.** Having many complexly arranged elements; elaborate. **2.** Solvable or comprehensible only with painstaking effort. See Syns at **complex.** [Middle English < Lat. *intrīcātus*, p.part. of *intrīcāre*, to entangle, perplex : *in-*, in; see IN–[2] + *trīcae*, perplexities, wiles.] — **in′tri•cate•ly** *adv.* — **in′tri•cate•ness** *n.*

in•trigue (ĭn′trēg′, ĭn-trēg′) *n.* **1.a.** A secret or underhand scheme; a plot. **b.** The practice of or involvement in such schemes. **2.** A clandestine love affair. — *v.* (ĭn-trēg′) **-trigued, -trigu•ing, -trigues.** — *intr.* To engage in secret or underhand schemes; plot. — *tr.* **1.** To effect through such schemes. **2.** To arouse the interest or curiosity of. [Prob. < Fr. *intriguer*, to plot < Ital. *intrigare*, to plot < Lat. *intrīcāre*, to entangle. See INTRICATE.] — **in•trigu′er** *n.* — **in′trigu′ing•ly** *adv.*

Usage Note: The introduction of the verb *intrigue* to mean "to arouse the interest or curiosity of" was initially resisted by writers on usage as an unneeded French substitute for available English words such as *interest, fascinate,* or *puzzle,* but it now appears to be well established. Seventy-eight percent of the Usage Panel accepts it in the sentence *The special-quota idea intrigues some legislators, who have asked a Washington think tank to evaluate it,* whereas only 52 percent accepted it in a 1968 survey.

in•trin•sic (ĭn-trĭn′zĭk, -sĭk) *adj.* **1.** Of or relating to the essential nature of a thing; inherent. **2.** *Anat.* Situated within or belonging solely to the organ or body part on which it acts. Used of certain nerves and muscles. [ME *intrinsique*, inner < OFr. *intrinseque* < LLat. *intrīnsecus*, inward < Lat., inwardly. See **en*.**] — **in•trin′si•cal•ly** *adv.*

intrinsic factor *n.* A substance that is secreted by the gastric mucous membrane and is essential for the absorption of vitamin B_{12} in the intestines.

in•tro (ĭn′trō′) *n., pl.* **-tros.** *Informal.* An introduction.

intro. *abbr.* Introductory.

intro– *pref.* **1.** In; into: *introjection.* **2.** Inward: *introvert.* [Lat. < *intrō*, to the inside. See **en*.**]

in•tro•duce (ĭn′trə-do͞os′, -dyo͞os′) *tr.v.* **-duced, -duc•ing, -duc•es. 1.a.** To present (someone) by name to another in order to establish an acquaintance. **b.** To present (a performer, for example) to the public for the first time. **2.** To bring forward (a plan, for example) for consideration. **3.** To provide with a beginning knowledge or first experience of something. **4.a.** To bring in and establish in a new place or environment. **b.** To bring into currency, use, or practice; originate. **5.** To put inside or into; insert or inject. **6.** To open or begin; preface. [ME *introducen*, to bring into < Lat. *intrōdūcere* : *intrō-*, within; see **en*** + *dūcere*, to lead; see **deuk-*.**] — **in′tro•duc′er** *n.* — **in′tro•duc′i•ble** *adj.*

in•tro•duc•tion (ĭn′trə-dŭk′shən) *n.* **1.** The act or process of introducing or the state of being introduced. **2.** A means, such as a personal letter, of presenting one person to another. **3.** Something recently introduced; an innovation. **4.** Something presented in beginning or introducing something, esp.: **a.** A preface, as to a book. **b.** *Mus.* A short preliminary movement in a larger work. **c.** A basic introductory text or course of study. [Ult. < Lat. *intrōductiō, intrōductiōn-* < *intrōductus*, p.part. of *intrōdūcere*, to bring in. See INTRODUCE.]

in•tro•duc•to•ry (ĭn′trə-dŭk′tə-rē) *adj.* **1.** Of, relating to, or constituting an introduction. **2.** Serving to introduce. — **in′tro•duc′to•ri•ly** *adv.*

in•tro•gres•sion (ĭn′trə-grĕsh′ən) *n.* Infiltration of the genes of one species into the gene pool of another through repeated backcrossing of an interspecific hybrid with one of its parents. [< Lat. *intrōgressus*, p.part. of *intrōgredī*, to step in : *intrō-*, intro- + *gradī*, to step; see INGRESS.] — **in′tro•gres′sive** (-grĕs′ĭv) *adj.*

in•tro•it also **In•tro•it** (ĭn′trō′ĭt, -troit′, ĭn-trō′ĭt) *n.* **1.** A hymn or psalm sung at the opening of a Christian service, esp. in the Anglican Church. **2.** *Rom. Cath. Ch.* The beginning of the Mass, usu. consisting of a psalm verse, an antiphon, and the Gloria Patri. [Ult. < Med.Lat. *introitus*, sung passage at entrance of celebrant < Lat. *introitus*, entrance < p.part. of *introīre*, to enter : *intrō-*, in; see **en*** + *īre*, to go; see **ei-*.**]

in•tro•ject (ĭn′trə-jekt′) *tr.v. Psychiat.* To incorporate (characteristics of a person or an object) into one's own psyche unconsciously. [Back-formation < INTROJECTION < Ger. *Introjektion* : Lat. *intrō-*, intro- + Lat. *-iectiō, -iectiōn-*, throwing (< *iactus*, p.part. of *iacere*, to throw; see INJECT).] — **in′tro•jec′tion** *n.*

in•tro•mis•sion (ĭn′trə-mĭsh′ən) *n.* The act or process of intromitting; introduction or admission. [Med.Lat. *intrōmissiō, intrōmissiōn-*, usurpation < Lat. *intrōmissus*, p.part. of *intrōmittere*, to intromit. See INTROMIT.] — **in′tro•mis′sive** (-mĭs′ĭv) *adj.*

in•tro•mit (ĭn′trə-mĭt′) *tr.v.* **-mit•ted, -mit•ting, -mits.** To cause or permit to enter; introduce or admit. [ME *intromitten*, to deal illegally with others < Lat. *intrōmittere*, to send in, let into : *intrō-*, in; see **en*** + *mittere*, to send.] — **in′tro•mit′tent** *adj.* — **in′tro•mit′ter** *n.*

in•tron (ĭn′trŏn) *n.* A segment of a gene situated between axons that does not function in coding for protein synthesis. [*intragenic*, within a gene (INTRA– + GENIC) + –ON[1].]

in•trorse (ĭn′trôrs′) *adj. Bot.* Facing inward; turned toward the axis. Used esp. of anthers. [Lat. *intrōrsus*, contraction of *intrōversus*, inwards : *intrō-*, to the inside; see **en*** + *versus*, p.part. of *vertere*, to turn; see **wer-[2]*.**]

in•tro•spect (ĭn′trə-spĕkt′, ĭn′trə-spĕkt′) *intr.v.* **-spect•ed, -spect•ing, -spects.** To engage in introspection. [Lat. *intrōspicere, intrōspect-*, to look into : *intrō-*, within; see **en*** + *specere*, to look at; see **spek-*.**] — **in′tro•spec′tive** *adj.* — **in′tro•spec′tive•ly** *adv.* — **in′tro•spec′tive•ness** *n.*

in•tro•spec•tion (ĭn′trə-spĕk′shən) *n.* Contemplation of one's own thoughts, feelings, and sensations; self-examination. — **in′tro•spec′tion•al** *adj.*

in•tro•ver•sion (ĭn′trə-vûr′zhən, -shən) *n.* **1.** The act or process of introverting or the condition of being introverted. **2.** *Psychol.* Introverting or the tendency to introvert one's interests. — **in′tro•ver′sive** (-vûr′sĭv) *adj.*

in•tro•vert (ĭn′trə-vûrt′, ĭn′trə-vûrt′) *tr.v.* **-vert•ed, -vert•ing, -verts. 1.** To turn or direct inward. **2.** *Psychol.* To concentrate (one's interests) upon oneself. **3.** *Medic.* To turn (a tubular organ or part) inward upon itself. — *n.* (ĭn′trə-vûrt′). **1.** *Psychol.* An introverted person. **2.** *Medic.* An anatomical structure that is capable of being introverted. [INTRO– + Lat. *vertere*, to turn; see **wer-[2]*.**]

in•trude (ĭn-tro͞od′) *v.* **-trud•ed, -trud•ing, -trudes.** — *tr.* **1.** To put or force in inappropriately, esp. without invitation, fitness, or permission. **2.** *Geol.* To thrust (molten rock) into preexisting rock. — *intr.* To come in rudely or inappropriately; enter as an improper or unwanted element. [ME *intruden* < Lat. *intrūdere, intrūs-*, to thrust in : *in-*, in; see IN–[2] + *trūdere*, to thrust; see **treud-*.**] — **in•trud′er** *n.*

in•tru•sion (ĭn-tro͞o′zhən) *n.* **1.** The act of intruding or the state of being intruded on. **2.** An inappropriate or unwelcome addition. **3.** *Geol.* **a.** The intruding of molten rock. **b.** The rock mass produced by an intrusive process.

in•tru•sive (ĭn-tro͞o′sĭv, -zĭv) *adj.* **1.** Intruding or tending to intrude. **2.** Of or relating to igneous rock that is forced while molten into cracks or between other layers of rock. **3.** Epenthetic. — **in•tru′sive•ly** *adv.* — **in•tru′sive•ness** *n.*

in•trust (ĭn-trŭst′) *v.* Var. of **entrust.**

in•tu•bate (ĭn′to͞o-bāt′, -tyo͞o-) *tr.v.* **-bat•ed, -bat•ing, -bates.** *Medic.* To insert a tube into (a hollow organ or body passage). — **in′tu•ba′tion** *n.* — **in′tu•ba′tion•al** *adj.*

in•tu•it (ĭn-to͞o′ĭt, -tyo͞o′-) *tr.v.* **-it•ed, -it•ing, -its.** *Usage Problem.* To know intuitively. [Back-formation < INTUITION.]

Usage Note: The verb *intuit* is well established in reputable writing, but some critics have objected to it. Only 34 percent of the Usage Panel accepts it in the sentence *Claude often intuits my feelings about things long before I am really aware of them myself.* The source of the objections most likely lies in the fact that the verb is often used in reference to more trivial sorts of insight than would be permitted by a full appreciation of the traditional meaning of *intuition.* In this connection a somewhat greater percentage of the Panel, 46 percent, does accept *intuit* in the sentence *Mathematicians sometimes intuit the truth of a theorem long before they are able to prove it.*

in•tu•i•tion (ĭn′to͞o-ĭsh′ən, -tyo͞o-) *n.* **1.a.** The act or faculty of knowing or sensing without the use of rational processes; immediate cognition. **b.** Knowledge gained by the use of this faculty; a perceptive insight. **2.** A sense of something not evident or deducible; an impression. [ME *intuicioun*, insight < LLat. *intuitiō, intuitiōn-*, a looking at < Lat. *intuitus*, a look < p.part. of *intuērī*, contemplate : *in-*, on; see IN–[2] + *tuērī*,

ă pat	oi boy
ā pay	ou out
âr care	o͝o took
ä father	o͞o boot
ĕ pet	ŭ cut
ē be	ûr urge
ĭ pit	th thin
ī pie	*th* this
îr pier	hw which
ŏ pot	zh vision
ō toe	ə about, item
ô paw	

Stress marks:
′ (primary);
′ (secondary), as in
dictionary (dĭk′shə-nĕr′ē)

to look at.] — **in′tu·i′tion·al** *adj.* — **in′tu·i′tion·al·ly** *adv.*

in·tu·i·tion·ism (ĭn′to͞o-ĭsh′ə-nĭz′əm, -tyo͞o-) *n. Philos.* **1.** The theory that truth or certain truths are known by intuition rather than reason. **2.** The theory that external objects of perception are immediately known to be real by intuition. **3.** The theory that ethical principles are known to be valid and universal through intuition. — **in′tu·i′tion·ist** *n.*

in·tu·i·tive (ĭn-to͞o′ĭ-tĭv, -tyo͞o′-) *adj.* **1.** Of, relating to, or arising from intuition. **2.** Known or perceived through intuition. **3.** Possessing or demonstrating intuition. — **in·tu′i·tive·ly** *adv.* — **in·tu′i·tive·ness** *n.*

in·tu·mesce (ĭn′to͞o-mĕs′, -tyo͞o-) *intr.v.* **-mesced, -mesc·ing, -mesc·es. 1.** To swell or expand; enlarge. **2.** To bubble up, esp. due to heating. [Lat. *intumēscere* : *in-*, intensive pref.; see IN-[2] + *tumēscere*, to begin to swell, inchoative of *tumēre*, to swell; see **teuə-***.]

in·tu·mes·cence (ĭn′to͞o-mĕs′əns, -tyo͞o-) *n.* **1.** The act or process of swelling or the condition of being swollen. **2.** A swollen organ or body part. — **in′tu·mes′cent** *adj.*

in·tus·sus·cept (ĭn′tə-sə-sĕpt′) *tr.v.* **-cept·ed, -cept·ing, -cepts.** To take within, as in telescoping one part of the intestine into another; invaginate.

in·tus·sus·cep·tion (ĭn′tə-sə-sĕp′shən) *n.* **1.** *Medic.* Invagination, esp. an infolding of one part of the intestine into another. **2.** *Biol.* Assimilation of new substances into the existing components of living tissue. [Med.Lat. *intussusceptiō, intussusceptiōn-*, a taking in, admission < *intussusceptus*, p.part. of *intussuscipere*, to take in : Lat. *intus*, within; see **en*** + Lat. *suscipere*, to take up (*sub*, sub- + *capere*, to take; see **kap-***).]

in·twine (ĭn-twīn′) *v.* Var. of **entwine.**

in·twist (ĭn-twĭst′) *v.* Var. of **entwist.**

In·u·it also **In·nu·it** (ĭn′yo͞o-ĭt) *n., pl.* **Inuit** or **-its** also **Innuit** or **-its. 1.** A member of any of the Eskimo peoples of North America and esp. of Arctic Canada and Greenland. **2.** Any or all of the Eskimo languages of the Inuit. [Eastern Eskimo, people.]

in·u·lase (ĭn′yə-lās′) *n.* An enzyme that catalyzes the conversion of inulin to fructose. [INUL(IN) + -ASE.]

in·u·lin (ĭn′yə-lĭn) *n.* A polysaccharide with the general formula $(C_6H_{10}O_5)_n$ that is found in the roots of various composite plants and yields fructose when hydrolyzed. [NLat. *Inula*, plant genus (< Lat. *inula*, elecampane < Gk. *helenion*; see **wel-[2]***) + -IN.]

in·unc·tion (ĭn-ŭngk′shən) *n.* **1.** The process of applying and rubbing in an ointment. **2.** The act of anointing, as in a ceremony. [ME, anointing < Lat. *inūnctiō, inūnctiōn-* < *inūnctus*, p.part. of *inunguere*, to anoint : *in-*, on; see IN-[2] + *unguere*, to smear.]

in·un·date (ĭn′ŭn-dāt′, ĭn′ən-) *tr.v.* **-dat·ed, -dat·ing, -dates. 1.** To cover with water, esp. floodwaters. **2.** To overwhelm as if with a flood; swamp: *inundated with work.* [Lat. *inundāre, inundāt-* : *in-*, in; see IN-[2] + *undāre*, to surge (< *unda*, wave; see **wed-[1]***).] — **in′un·da′tion** *n.* — **in′un·da′tor** *n.* — **in·un′da·to′ry** (-də-tôr′ē, -tōr′ē) *adj.*

in·ure also **en·ure** (ĭn-yo͝or′) *tr.v.* **-ured, -ur·ing, -ures.** To habituate to something undesirable, esp. by prolonged subjection; accustom. [ME, back-formation < *enured*, customary < *in ure* : *in*, in; see IN[1] + *ure*, use (< OFr. *euvre, uevre*, work < Lat. *opera*, activity associated with work; see **op-***).] — **in·ure′ment** *n.*

in·urn (ĭn-ûrn′) *tr.v.* **-urned, -urn·ing, -urns. 1.** To put in an urn. **2.** To bury or entomb; inter.

in u·ter·o (ĭn yo͞o′tə-rō) *adv. & adj.* In the uterus. [NLat.]

in·u·tile (ĭn-yo͞ot′l, -yo͞o′tīl′) *adj.* Lacking in utility or serviceability; not useful. [ME < OFr. < Lat. *inūtilis* : *in-*, not; see IN-[1] + *ūtilis*, useful; see UTILE.] — **in·u′tile·ly** *adv.* — **in′u·til′i·ty** (ĭn′yo͞o-tĭl′ĭ-tē) *n.*

I·nu·vik (ĭ-no͞o′vĭk). A region of NW Northwest Terrs., Canada.

inv. *abbr.* **1.** Invented; inventor. **2.** Invention. **3.** Invoice.

in vac·u·o (ĭn văk′yo͞o-ō′) *adv.* **1.** In a vacuum. **2.** In isolation; without reference to related evidence. [NLat. *in vacuō*.]

in·vade (ĭn-vād′) *v.* **-vad·ed, -vad·ing, -vades.** — *tr.* **1.** To enter by force in order to conquer or pillage. **2.** To encroach or intrude on; violate. **3.** To overrun as if by invading; infest. **4.** To enter and permeate, esp. harmfully. — *intr.* To make an invasion. [ME < OFr. *invader* < Lat. *invādere* : *in-*, in; see IN-[2] + *vādere*, to go.] — **in·vad′er** *n.*

in·vag·i·nate (ĭn-văj′ə-nāt′) *v.* **-nat·ed, -nat·ing, -nates.** *tr. & intr.v.* **1.** To enclose or become enclosed in or as if in a sheath. **2.** To turn or become turned inward. **3.** To infold or become infolded so as to form a hollow space within a previously solid structure, as in the formation of a gastrula from a blastula. [Med.Lat. *invāgināre, invāgināt-* : Lat. *in-*, in; see IN-[2] + Lat. *vāgina*, sheath.]

in·vag·i·na·tion (ĭn-văj′ə-nā′shən) *n.* **1.** The act or process of invaginating or the condition of being invaginated. **2.** An invaginated organ or part. **3.** *Embryol.* The infolding of a portion of the outer layer of a blastula in the formation of a gastrula.

in·va·lid[1] (ĭn′və-lĭd) *n.* One who is incapacitated by a chronic illness or disability. — *adj.* **1.** Incapacitated by illness or injury. **2.** Of, relating to, or intended for invalids. — *tr.v.* **-lid·ed, -lid·ing, -lids. 1.** To incapacitate physically. **2.** *Chiefly British.* To release or exempt from duty because of ill health. [< INVALID[2] (influenced by Fr. *invalide*, sickly, infirm).]

in·val·id[2] (ĭn-văl′ĭd) *adj.* **1.** Not legally or factually valid; null: *an invalid license.* **2.** Falsely based or reasoned; faulty: *an invalid argument.* [Lat. *invalidus*, weak : *in-*, not; see IN-[1] + *validus*, strong (< *valēre*, to be strong; see **wal-***).] — **in′va·lid′i·ty** (-və-lĭd′ĭ-tē) *n.* — **in·val′id·ly** *adv.*

in·val·i·date (ĭn-văl′ĭ-dāt′) *tr.v.* **-dat·ed, -dat·ing, -dates.** To make invalid; nullify. — **in·val′i·da′tion** *n.* — **in·val′i·da′tor** *n.*

in·va·lid·ism (ĭn′və-lĭ-dĭz′əm) *n.* The condition of being incapacitated by an illness or disability.

in·val·u·a·ble (ĭn-văl′yo͞o-ə-bəl) *adj.* Of inestimable value; priceless: *invaluable help.* — **in·val′u·a·ble·ness** *n.* — **in·val′u·a·bly** *adv.*

in·var·i·a·ble (ĭn-vâr′ē-ə-bəl) *adj.* Not changing or subject to change; constant. — **in·var′i·a·bil′i·ty, in·var′i·a·ble·ness** *n.* — **in·var′i·a·bly** *adv.*

in·var·i·ant (ĭn-vâr′ē-ənt) *adj.* **1.** Not varying; constant. **2.** *Math.* Unaffected by a designated operation, as a transformation of coordinates. — *n.* An invariant quantity, function, configuration, or system. — **in·var′i·ance** *n.*

in·va·sion (ĭn-vā′zhən) *n.* **1.** The act of invading, esp. the entrance of an armed force into a territory to conquer. **2.** A large-scale onset of something injurious or harmful, such as a disease. **3.** An intrusion or encroachment. [ME *invasioun* < OFr. *invasion* < LLat. *invāsiō, invāsiōn-* < *invāsus*, p.part. of *invādere*, to invade. See INVADE.]

in·va·sive (ĭn-vā′sĭv) *adj.* **1.** Of, engaging in, or given to armed aggression. **2.** Marked by the tendency to spread, esp. into healthy tissue: *an invasive carcinoma.* **3.** Of or relating to a medical procedure in which a part of the body is entered, as by incision. **4.** Tending to intrude or encroach, as upon privacy. — **in·va′sive·ly** *adv.* — **in·va′sive·ness** *n.*

in·vec·tive (ĭn-vĕk′tĭv) *n.* **1.** Denunciatory or abusive language; vituperation. **2.** Denunciatory or abusive expression or discourse. [< ME *invectif*, denunciatory < OFr. < LLat. *invectīvus*, reproachful, abusive < Lat. *invectus*, p.part. of *invehī*, to inveigh against. See INVEIGH.] — **in·vec′tive** *adj.* — **in·vec′tive·ly** *adv.* — **in·vec′tive·ness** *n.*

in·veigh (ĭn-vā′) *intr.v.* **-veighed, -veigh·ing, -veighs.** To give vent to angry disapproval; protest vehemently. [Lat. *invehī*, to attack with words, inveigh against, passive of *invehere*, to carry in : *in-*, in; see IN-[2] + *vehere*, to carry; see **wegh-***.] — **in·veigh′er** *n.*

in·vei·gle (ĭn-vā′gəl, -vē′-) *tr.v.* **-gled, -gling, -gles. 1.** To win over by coaxing, flattery, or artful talk. **2.** To obtain by cajolery: *inveigle a free museum pass.* [ME *envegle*, alteration of OFr. *aveugler*, to blind < *aveugle*, blind < VLat. **aboculus* : Lat. *ab–*, away from; see AB-[1] + Lat. *oculus*, eye; see **okʷ-***.] — **in·vei′gle·ment** *n.* — **in·vei′gler** *n.*

in·vent (ĭn-vĕnt′) *tr.v.* **-vent·ed, -vent·ing, -vents. 1.** To produce or contrive (something previously unknown) by ingenuity or imagination. **2.** To make up; fabricate. [Lat. *invenīre, invent-*, to find : *in-*, on, upon; see IN-[2] + *venīre*, to come; see **gʷā-***.] — **in·vent′i·ble** *adj.* — **in·ven′tor** *n.*

in·ven·tion (ĭn-vĕn′shən) *n.* **1.** The act or process of inventing. **2.** A new device, method, or process developed from study and experimentation. **3.** A mental fabrication, esp. a falsehood. **4.** Skill in inventing; inventiveness. **5.** *Mus.* A short composition developing a single theme contrapuntally. **6.** A discovery; a finding. [Ult. < Lat. *inventiō, inventiōn-*, inventiveness < *inventus*, p.part. of *invenīre*, to find. See INVENT.] — **in·ven′tion·al** *adj.*

in·ven·tive (ĭn-vĕn′tĭv) *adj.* **1.** Of, relating to, or characterized by invention. **2.** Adept or skillful at inventing; creative. — **in·ven′tive·ly** *adv.* — **in·ven′tive·ness** *n.*

in·ven·to·ry (ĭn′vən-tôr′ē, -tōr′ē) *n., pl.* **-ries. 1.a.** A detailed itemized record of things in one's possession, esp. a periodic survey of all goods and materials in stock. **b.** The process of making such a record. **c.** The items listed in such a record. **d.** The quantity of goods and materials on hand; stock. **2.** An evaluation or a survey, as of resources. — *tr.v.* **-ried, -ry·ing, -ries. 1.** To make an inventory of. **2.** To include in an inventory. [ME *inventorie* < Med.Lat. *inventōrium*, alteration of LLat. *inventārium* < Lat. *inventus*, p.part. of *invenīre*, to find. See INVENT.] — **in′ven·to′ri·al** *adj.* — **in′ven·to′ri·al·ly** *adv.*

in·ve·rac·i·ty (ĭn′və-răs′ĭ-tē) *n., pl.* **-ties. 1.** Lack of veracity; untruthfulness. **2.** An untruth; a falsehood.

In·ver Grove Heights (ĭn′vər). A city of SE MN, a suburb of St. Paul. Pop. 22,477.

in·ver·ness also **In·ver·ness** (ĭn′vər-nĕs′) *n.* **1.** A long loose overcoat with a detachable cape having a round collar. **2.** The cape of such an overcoat. [After INVERNESS.]

In·ver·ness (ĭn′vər-nĕs′). A burgh of N Scotland on the Moray Firth; chartered c. 1200. Pop. 39,700.

in·verse (ĭn-vûrs′, ĭn′vûrs′) *adj.* **1.** Reversed in order, nature, or effect. **2.** *Math.* Of or relating to an inverse or an inverse

inverness
Edward VII wearing an inverness coat

function. **3.** *Archaic.* Turned upside down; inverted. —*n.* (ĭn′vûrs′, ĭn-vûrs′). **1.** Something that is opposite, as in sequence; the reverse. **2.** *Math.* One of a pair of elements in a set whose result under the operation of the set is the identity element, esp.: **a.** The reciprocal of a given quantity. **b.** The negative of a given quantity. [ME < Lat. *inversus*, p.part. of *invertere*, to invert. See INVERT.] —**in•verse′ly** *adv.*

inverse function *n. Math.* A function that replaces another function's independent variable with a value of its dependent value.

in•ver•sion (ĭn-vûr′zhən, -shən) *n.* **1.a.** The act of inverting. **b.** The state of being inverted. **2.** An interchange of position of adjacent objects in a sequence, esp.: **a.** A change in normal word order, such as the placement of a verb before its subject. **b.** *Mus.* A rearrangement of pitches in which higher and lower voices exchange positions or in which the direction of each interval in a melody is reversed. **3.** *Psychol.* **a.** The taking on of the gender role of the opposite sex. **b.** Homosexuality. Now rare in scientific use. **4.** *Chem.* Conversion of a compound in which the direction of optical rotation is reversed, as from the dextrorotatory to the levorotatory form. **5.** *Meteorol.* An atmospheric condition in which the air temperature rises with increasing altitude, holding surface air down and preventing dispersion of pollutants. **6.** *Genet.* A chromosomal defect in which a segment of the chromosome breaks off and reattaches in the reverse direction. [Lat. *inversiō, inversiōn-* < *inversus*, p.part. of *invertere*, to invert. See INVERT.]

in•vert (ĭn-vûrt′) *v.* **-vert•ed, -vert•ing, -verts.** —*tr.* **1.** To turn inside out or upside down. **2.** To reverse the position, order, or condition of. **3.** To subject to inversion. —*intr.* To be subjected to inversion. —*n.* (ĭn′vûrt′). **1.** Something inverted. **2.** *Psychol.* **a.** One who takes on the gender role of the opposite sex. **b.** A homosexual person. Now rare in scientific use. [Lat. *invertere* : *in-*, in; see IN-[2] + *vertere*, to turn; see **wer-**[2]*.] —**in•vert′i•ble** *adj.*

in•ver•tase (ĭn-vûr′tās′, ĭn′vər-tās′, -tāz′) *n.* An enzyme that catalyzes the hydrolysis of sucrose into glucose and fructose.

in•ver•te•brate (ĭn-vûr′tə-brĭt, -brāt′) *adj.* **1.** Lacking a backbone or spinal column; not vertebrate. **2.** Of or relating to invertebrates. —*n.* An invertebrate animal.

in•vert•ed comma (ĭn-vûr′tĭd) *n. Chiefly British.* A quotation mark.

inverted mordent *n. Mus.* See **pralltriller.**

in•vert•er (ĭn-vûr′tər) *n.* **1.** One that inverts or produces inversion. **2.** A device used to convert direct current into alternating current.

invert sugar *n.* A mixture of equal parts of glucose and fructose resulting from the hydrolysis of sucrose.

in•vest (ĭn-vĕst′) *v.* **-vest•ed, -vest•ing, -vests.** —*tr.* **1.** To commit (money or capital) in order to gain a financial return. **2.a.** To spend or devote for future advantage or benefit. **b.** To devote morally or psychologically, as to a purpose; commit. **3.** To endow with authority or power. **4.** To install in office with ceremony. **5.** To endow with an enveloping or pervasive quality. **6.** To clothe; adorn. **7.** To cover completely; envelop. **8.** To surround with troops or ships; besiege. —*intr.* To make investments or an investment. [Ult. < Lat. *investīre*, to clothe, surround : *in-*, in; see IN-[2] + *vestīre*, to clothe (< *vestis*, clothes; see **wes-**[2]*).] —**in•vest′a•ble** *adj.* —**in•ves′tor** *n.*

in•ves•ti•gate (ĭn-vĕs′tĭ-gāt′) *v.* **-gat•ed, -gat•ing, -gates.** —*tr.* To observe or inquire into in detail; examine systematically. —*intr.* To make a detailed inquiry or systematic examination. [Lat. *investīgāre, investīgāt-* : *in-*, in; see IN-[2] + *vestīgāre*, to track (< *vestīgium*, footprint).] —**in•ves′ti•ga•ble** (-gə-bəl) *adj.* —**in•ves′ti•ga•to′ry** (-gə-tôr′ē, -tōr′ē)

in•ves•ti•ga•tion (ĭn-vĕs′tĭ-gā′shən) *n.* **1.** The act or process of investigating. **2.** A detailed inquiry or systematic examination. —**in•ves′ti•ga′tion•al** *adj.*

in•ves•ti•ga•tive (ĭn-vĕs′tĭ-gā′tĭv) *adj.* **1.** Of or relating to investigation. **2.** Marked by or engaged in investigation; uncovering and reporting hidden information.

in•ves•ti•ga•tor (ĭn-vĕs′tĭ-gā′tər) *n.* One, esp. a detective, who investigates. —**in•ves′ti•ga•to′ri•al** (-gə-tôr′ē-əl, -tōr′-) *adj.*

in•ves•ti•ture (ĭn-vĕs′tə-cho͝or′, -chər) *n.* **1.** The act or ceremony of conferring the authority and symbols of a high office. **2.** An adornment or a cover. [ME < Med.Lat. *investītūra* < Lat. *investīre*, to clothe. See INVEST.]

in•vest•ment (ĭn-vĕst′mənt) *n.* **1.** The act of investing. **2.** An amount invested. **3.** A property or possession acquired for future financial benefit. **4.** A commitment, as of time. **5.** A military siege. **6.** *Archaic.* **a.** A garment; a vestment. **b.** An outer covering.

in•vet•er•ate (ĭn-vĕt′ər-ĭt) *adj.* **1.** Firmly and long established; deep-rooted. **2.** Persisting in an ingrained habit; habitual. [ME < Lat. *inveterātus*, p.part. of *inveterārī*, to grow old, endure : *in-*, causative pref.; see IN-[2] + *vetus, veter-*, old; see **wet-**[2]*.] —**in•vet′er•a•cy** (-ər-ə-sē), **in•vet′er•ate•ness** *n.* —**in•vet′er•ate•ly** *adv.*

in•vi•a•ble (ĭn-vī′ə-bəl) *adj.* Unable to survive or develop normally: *an inviable newborn calf.* —**in•vi•a•bil′i•ty** *n.*

in•vid•i•ous (ĭn-vĭd′ē-əs) *adj.* **1.** Tending to rouse ill will, animosity, or resentment: *invidious accusations.* **2.** Containing or implying a slight; discriminatory: *invidious policies.* **3.** Envious. [< Lat. *invidiōsus*, envious, hostile < *invidia*, envy. See ENVY.] —**in•vid′i•ous•ly** *adv.* —**in•vid′i•ous•ness** *n.*

in•vig•or•ate (ĭn-vĭg′ə-rāt′) *tr.v.* **-at•ed, -at•ing, -ates.** To impart vigor, strength, or vitality to; animate. [Poss. obsolete *invigor* (< Fr. *envigorer* < OFr. *envigourer* : *en-*, in; see IN-[2] + *vigour*, vigor; see VIGOR) + -ATE[1].] —**in•vig′or•at′ing•ly** *adv.* —**in•vig′or•a′tion** *n.* —**in•vig′or•a′tor** *n.*

in•vin•ci•ble (ĭn-vĭn′sə-bəl) *adj.* Incapable of being overcome or defeated; unconquerable. —**in•vin′ci•bil′i•ty, in•vin′ci•ble•ness** *n.* —**in•vin′ci•bly** *adv.*

in•vi•o•la•ble (ĭn-vī′ə-lə-bəl) *adj.* **1.** Secure from violation or profanation. **2.** Impregnable to assault or trespass; invincible. —**in•vi′o•la•bil′i•ty, in•vi′o•la•ble•ness** *n.* —**in•vi′o•la•bly** *adv.*

in•vi•o•late (ĭn-vī′ə-lĭt) *adj.* Not violated or profaned; intact. [ME < Lat. *inviolātus* : *in-*, not; see IN-[1] + *violātus*, p.part. of *violāre*, to violate; see VIOLATE.] —**in•vi′o•la•cy** (-lə-sē), **in•vi′o•late•ness** *n.* —**in•vi′o•late•ly** *adv.*

in•vis•cid (ĭn-vĭs′ĭd) *adj.* **1.** Having no viscosity. **2.** *Phys. & Chem.* Of or relating to a fluid with no viscosity.

in•vis•i•ble (ĭn-vĭz′ə-bəl) *adj.* **1.** Impossible to see; not visible. **2.** Not accessible to view; hidden. **3.** Not easily noticed or detected; inconspicuous. **4.** Not published in financial statements: *an invisible asset.* —**in•vis′i•ble** *n.* —**in•vis′i•bil′i•ty, in•vis′i•ble•ness** *n.* —**in•vis′i•bly** *adv.*

invisible ink *n.* Ink that is colorless and invisible until treated by a chemical, heat, or special light.

in•vi•ta•tion (ĭn′vĭ-tā′shən) *n.* **1.** The act of inviting. **2.** A request for someone's presence or participation. **3.** An allurement or enticement. **4.** *Chiefly Southern U.S.* See **altar call.**

in•vi•ta•tion•al (ĭn′vĭ-tā′shə-nəl) *adj.* Restricted to invited participants. —*n.* An invitational event, esp. a sports tournament.

in•vi•ta•to•ry (ĭn-vī′tə-tôr′ē, -tōr′ē) *adj.* Constituting or containing an invitation.

in•vite (ĭn-vīt′) *tr.v.* **-vit•ed, -vit•ing, -vites. 1.** To ask for the presence or participation of. **2.** To request formally. **3.** To welcome; encourage. **4.** To tend to bring on; provoke. **5.** To entice; tempt. —*n.* (ĭn′vīt′). *Informal.* An invitation. [Fr. *inviter* < OFr. < Lat. *invītāre*.]

in•vi•tee (ĭn′vī-tē′) *n.* One that is invited.

in•vit•ing (ĭn-vī′tĭng) *adj.* Attractive; tempting: *an inviting dessert.* —**in•vit′ing•ly** *adv.*

in vi•tro (ĭn vē′trō) *adv. & adj.* In an artificial environment outside the living organism: *in vitro fertilization.* [NLat. *in vitrō* : Lat. *in*, in + Lat. *vitrō*, ablative of *vitrum*, glass.]

in vi•vo (vē′vō) *adv. & adj.* Within a living organism. [NLat.]

in•vo•cate (ĭn′və-kāt′) *tr.v.* **-cat•ed, -cat•ing, -cates.** *Archaic.* To invoke. [Lat. *invocāre, invocāt-*, to invoke. See INVOKE.]

in•vo•ca•tion (ĭn′və-kā′shən) *n.* **1.** The act or an instance of invoking, esp. an appeal to a higher power for assistance. **2.** A prayer or other formula used in invoking. **3.a.** The act of conjuring up a spirit by incantation. **b.** An incantation used in conjuring. [ME *invocacion* < OFr. < Lat. *invocātiō, invocātiōn-* < *invocātus*, p.part. of *invocāre*, to invoke. See INVOKE.] —**in′vo•ca′tion•al** *adj.*

in•voc•a•to•ry (ĭn-vŏk′ə-tôr′ē, -tōr′ē) *adj.* Of or having the nature of an invocation.

in•voice (ĭn′vois′) *n.* **1.** A detailed list of goods shipped or services rendered, with an account of all costs; an itemized bill. **2.** The goods or services itemized in an invoice. —*tr.v.* **-voiced, -voic•ing, -voic•es. 1.** To make an invoice of (goods or services). **2.** To send an invoice to; bill. [Alteration of obsolete *invoyes*, pl. of *invoy*, invoice < Fr. *envoi*, a sending, shipment < *envoyer*, to send. See ENVOY[1].]

in•voke (ĭn-vōk′) *tr.v.* **-voked, -vok•ing, -vokes. 1.** To call on (a higher power) for assistance, support, or inspiration. **2.** To appeal to or cite in support or justification. **3.** To call for earnestly; solicit. **4.** To summon with incantations; conjure. **5.** To resort to; use or apply. [ME *envoken* < OFr. *invoquer* < Lat. *invocāre* : *in-*, in; see IN-[2] + *vocāre*, to call; see **wekʷ-***.] —**in•vok′er** *n.*

in•vol•u•cel (ĭn-vŏl′yə-sĕl′) *n. Bot.* A secondary involucre, as at the base of an umbel within a compound umbel. [NLat. *involūcellum*, dim. of *involūcrum*, involucre. See INVOLUCRUM.]

in•vo•lu•cre (ĭn′və-lo͞o′kər) *n.* A series of bracts beneath or around a flower or flower cluster. [Fr. < Lat. *involūcrum*, wrapper, envelope. See INVOLUCRUM.] —**in′vo•lu′cral** (-krəl), **in′vo•lu′crate** (-krĭt, -krāt′) *adj.*

in•vo•lu•crum (ĭn′və-lo͞o′krəm) *n., pl.* **-cra** (-krə). An enveloping sheath or envelope. [NLat. *involūcrum* < Lat., wrapper, envelope < *involvere*, to enwrap. See INVOLVE.]

in•vol•un•tar•y (ĭn-vŏl′ən-tĕr′ē) *adj.* **1.** Acting or done without or against one's will. **2.** Not subject to control of the volition. —**in•vol′un•tar′i•ly** (-târ′ə-lē) *adv.* —**in•vol′un•tar′i•ness** *n.*

in•vo•lute (ĭn′və-lo͞ot′) *adj.* **1.** Intricate; complex. **2.** *Bot.* **a.** Having the margins rolled inward. **b.** Having whorls that obscure the axis or other volutions, as the shell of a cowrie.

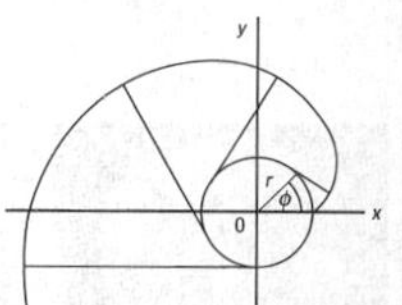

involute
Involute of a circle:
$x = r\cos\phi + r\phi\sin\phi$
$y = r\sin\phi - r\phi\cos\phi$

ă pat	oi boy
ā pay	ou out
âr care	o͝o took
ä father	o͞o boot
ĕ pet	ŭ cut
ē be	ûr urge
ĭ pit	th thin
ī pie	*th* this
îr pier	hw which
ŏ pot	zh vision
ō toe	ə about, item
ô paw	

Stress marks:
′ (primary);
′ (secondary), as in
dictionary (dĭk′shə-nĕr′ē)

— *intr.v.* **-lut•ed, -lut•ing, -lutes. 1.** To curl inward. **2.** To return to a normal or former condition. — *n.* The curve traced by a point on a taut inextensible string as it unwinds from another curve. [Lat. *involūtus*, p.part. of *involvere*, to enwrap. See INVOLVE.] — **in′vo•lute′ly** *adv.*

in•vo•lu•tion (ĭn′və-lo͞o′shən) *n.* **1.a.** The act of involving. **b.** The state of being involved. **2.** Intricacy; complexity. **3.** Something that is intricate or complex. **4.** *Math.* The multiplying of a quantity by itself a specified number of times; the raising to a power. **5.** *Embryol.* The ingrowth and curling inward of a group of cells, as in the formation of a gastrula from a blastula. **6.** *Medic.* **a.** A decrease in size of an organ, as of the uterus after childbirth. **b.** A progressive decline or degeneration of normal physiological function, caused by the aging process. [Lat. *involūtiō*, *involūtiōn-* < *involūtus*, p.part. of *involvere*, to enwrap. See INVOLVE.] — **in′vo•lu′tion•al** *adj.*

io moth
Automeris io

in•volve (ĭn-vŏlv′) *tr.v.* **-volved, -volv•ing, -volves. 1.** To contain as a part; include. **2.** To have as a necessary feature or consequence; entail. **3.** To engage as a participant; embroil. **4.a.** To connect closely and often incriminatingly; implicate. **b.** To influence or affect. **5.** To occupy or engage the interest of. **6.** To make complex or intricate; complicate. **7.** To wrap; envelop. **8.** *Archaic.* To wind or coil about. [ME *involven* < Lat. *involvere*, to enwrap : *in-*, in; see IN-[2] + *volvere*, to roll, turn; see **wel-**[2]*.] — **in•volve′ment** *n.* — **in•volv′er** *n.*

in•volved (ĭn-vŏlvd′) *adj.* **1.** Complicated; intricate. See Syns at **complex. 2.** Curled inward; coiled or involute. **3.** Confused; tangled. **4.** Connected by participation or association. **5.a.** Emotionally committed. **b.** Having a sexual relationship. — **in•volv′ed•ly** (-vŏl′vĭd-lē) *adv.*

Eugène Ionesco
Receiving an honorary degree at Brown University in 1984

in•vul•ner•a•ble (ĭn-vŭl′nər-ə-bəl) *adj.* **1.** Immune to attack; impregnable. **2.** Impossible to damage, injure, or wound. — **in•vul′ner•a•bil′i•ty, in•vul′ner•a•ble•ness** *n.* — **in•vul′ner•a•bly** *adv.*

in•ward (ĭn′wərd) *adj.* **1.** Located inside; inner. **2.** Directed or moving toward the interior. **3.** Of, relating to, or being in the mind. **4.** Intimate; familiar. — *adv.* **1.** Toward the inside, center, or interior. **2.** Toward the mind or the self: *looked inward.* — *n.* **1.** An inner or a central part. **2.** An inner essence or spirit. **3. inwards.** Entrails; innards. [ME < OE *inweard.* See **wer-**[2]*.] — **in′wards** *adv.*

inward dive *n.* A dive in which the diver, standing on the end of the board with the back to the water, leaps up and rotates forward.

in•ward•ly (ĭn′wərd-lē) *adv.* **1.** On or in the inside; within. **2.** Privately; to oneself.

in•ward•ness (ĭn′wərd-nĭs) *n.* **1.** Intimacy; familiarity. **2.** Preoccupation with one's own thoughts or feelings; introspection.

in•weave (ĭn-wēv′) *tr.v.* **-wove** (-wōv′), **-wo•ven** (-wō′vən), **-weav•ing, -weaves.** To weave into a fabric or design.

in•wind (ĭn-wīnd′) *v.* Var. of **enwind.**

in•wrap (ĭn-răp′) *v.* Var. of **enwrap.**

in•wreathe (ĭn-rēth′) *v.* Var. of **enwreathe.**

Ionic order

in•wrought (ĭn-rôt′, ĭn′rôt′) *adj.* **1.** Worked or woven in: *an inwrought design.* **2.** Having an inwrought decorative pattern.

I•o (ī′ō, ē′ō) *n.* **1.** *Gk. Myth.* A young woman whom Zeus loved and Hera transformed into a heifer. **2.** A satellite of Jupiter. [Lat. *Īō* < Gk.]

I/O *abbr.* Input/output.

IOC *abbr.* International Olympic Committee.

i•o•date (ī′ə-dāt′) *tr.v.* **-dat•ed, -dat•ing, -dates.** To combine, impregnate, or treat with iodine. — *n.* (-dāt′, -dĭt). A salt of iodic acid. — **i′o•da′tion** *n.*

i•od•ic acid (ī-ŏd′ĭk) *n.* A crystalline powder, HIO_3, used as an astringent and a disinfectant. [Fr. *iodique* < *iode*, iodine. See IODINE.]

Iran

i•o•dide (ī′ə-dīd′) *n.* A compound of iodine with a more electropositive element or group.

i•o•dine (ī′ə-dīn′, -dĭn, -dēn′) *n.* *Symbol* **I 1.** A poisonous halogen element having compounds used as germicides, antiseptics, and food supplements, with radioactive isotopes, esp. I 131, used in thyroid disease diagnosis and therapy. Atomic number 53; atomic weight 126.9044; melting point 113.5°C; boiling point 184.35°C; specific gravity (solid, at 20°C) 4.93; valence 1, 3, 5, 7. See table at **element. 2.** A liquid containing iodine dissolved in ethyl alcohol, used as an antiseptic for wounds. [Fr. *iode*, iodine (< Gk. *ioeidēs*, violet-colored : *ion*, violet + *-oeidēs*, -oid) + -INE[2].]

i•o•dize (ī′ə-dīz′) *tr.v.* **-dized, -diz•ing, -diz•es.** To treat or combine with iodine or an iodide: *iodize salt.* — **i′o•di•za′tion** (-dĭ-zā′shən) *n.*

Iraq

iodo– or **iod–** *pref.* Iodine: *iodoform.* [< Fr. *iode*, iodine. See IODINE.]

i•o•do•form (ī-ō′də-fôrm′, ī-ŏd′ə-) *n.* A crystalline iodine compound, CHI_3, used as an antiseptic. [IODO– + FORM(YL).]

i•o•do•phor (ī-ō′də-fôr′) *n.* A substance consisting of iodine and a solubilizing agent that releases free iodine when in solution. [IODO– + –PHOR(E).]

i•o•dop•sin (ī′ə-dŏp′sĭn) *n.* A violet light-sensitive pigment found in the retinal cones of the eye.

i•o moth (ī′ō, ē′ō) *n.* A large yellowish North American moth (*Automeris io*) having a prominent eyelike spot on each hind wing. [After Io, who was tormented by gadflies sent by Hera as a punishment (from the stinging spines of its larvae).]

i•on (ī′ən, ī′ŏn′) *n.* An atom or a group of atoms that has acquired a net electric charge by gaining or losing one or more electrons. [Gk. *ion*, something that goes, neut. pr.part. of *ienai*, to go. See **ei-***.]

Ion. *abbr.* Ionic.

–ion *suff.* **1.a.** Action or process: *completion.* **b.** Result of an action or process: *indention.* **2.** State or condition: *dehydration.* [ME < OFr. < Lat. *-iō*, *-iōn-*, n. suff.]

I•o•na (ī-ō′nə). An island of W Scotland in the S Inner Hebrides.

ion engine *n.* A rocket engine that develops thrust by expelling ions rather than gaseous combustion products.

Io•nes•co (ē′ə-nĕs′kō, yə-), **Eugène.** b. 1912. Romanian-born French dramatist whose plays include *Rhinoceros* (1959).

ion exchange *n.* A reversible chemical reaction between an insoluble solid and a solution during which ions may be interchanged, used in water softening, for example.

I•o•ni•a (ī-ō′nē-ə). An ancient region of W Asia Minor along the Aegean Sea; colonized by Greeks before 1000 B.C.

I•o•ni•an (ī-ō′nē-ən) *n.* **1.** A native or inhabitant of Ionia. **2.** One of a Hellenic people of Mycenaean origin that inhabited Attica, the Peloponnesus along the Saronic Gulf, Euboea, the Cyclades, and Ionia. — **I•o′ni•an** *adj.*

Ionian Islands. A chain of islands of W Greece in the Ionian Sea; ceded to Greece by Great Britain in 1864.

Ionian Sea. An arm of the Mediterranean Sea between W Greece and S Italy.

i•on•ic (ī-ŏn′ĭk) *adj.* Of, containing, or involving ions.

I•on•ic (ī-ŏn′ĭk) *adj.* **1.** Of or relating to Ionia or the Ionians. **2.** *Archit.* Of or belonging to the Ionic order. — *n.* The ancient Greek dialect of Ionia.

ionic bond *n.* A chemical bond between two ions with opposite charges, characteristic of salts.

Ionic order *n.* *Archit.* An order of classical Greek architecture characterized by two opposed volutes in the capital.

ionic propulsion *n.* Propulsion by the reactive thrust of a high-speed beam of similarly charged ions from an ion engine.

i•on•i•za•tion (ī′ə-nĭ-zā′shən) *n.* **1.** The formation of or separation into ions by heat, electrical discharge, radiation, or chemical reaction. **2.** The state of being ionized.

ionization chamber *n.* A gas-filled enclosure containing two electrodes that measures the amount of radiation passing through the enclosure by the degree of ionization caused.

ionization potential *n.* The energy required to remove completely an electron from its atom.

i•on•ize (ī′ə-nīz′) *tr. & intr.v.* **-ized, -iz•ing, -iz•es.** To convert or be converted into ions. — **i′on•iz′er** *n.*

i•on•iz•ing radiation (ī′ə-nī′zĭng) *n.* High-energy radiation capable of ionizing the substances through which it passes.

ion microscope *n.* A field-ion microscope.

i•o•none (ī′ə-nōn′) *n.* A liquid, $C_{13}H_{20}O$, having a strong odor of violets and used in perfumes. [Formerly a trademark.]

i•on•o•phore (ī-ŏn′ə-fôr, -fōr′) *n.* Any of a group of organic compounds facilitating ion transport across the cell membrane.

i•on•o•sphere (ī-ŏn′ə-sfîr′) *n.* A region of the earth's atmosphere extending from a height of 50 kilometers (30 miles) to 400 kilometers (250 miles) above the surface, where ionization caused by solar radiation affects the transmission of radio waves. — **i•on′o•spher′ic** (-sfîr′ĭk, -sfĕr′-) *adj.*

ion propulsion *n.* See **ionic propulsion.**

ion rocket *n.* **1.** A rocket using ionic propulsion. **2.** See **ion engine.**

ion trap *n.* A device, such as a magnet, used to prevent ions in an electron beam from striking other apparatus.

i•o•ta (ī-ō′tə) *n.* **1.** The ninth letter of the Greek alphabet. **2.** A very small amount; a bit. [Lat. *iōta* < Gk., of Phoenician orig.; akin to Heb. *yôd*, yod.]

i•o•ta•cism (ī-ō′tə-sĭz′əm) *n.* The conversion of other vowel sounds in Greek, such as eta, to the sound of iota. [LLat. *iōtacismus* < Gk. *iōtakismos* < *iōta*, iota. See IOTA.]

IOU (ī′ō-yo͞o′) *n., pl.* **IOU's** or **IOUs.** A promise to pay a debt, esp. a signed paper stating the amount owed and often bearing the letters IOU. [From the pronunciation of *I owe you.*]

–ious *suff.* Having; having the qualities of; full of: *bilious.* [ME, partly < Lat. *-ius* and partly < OFr. *-ieus*, *-ieux*, -ieux < Lat. *-iōsus.*]

I•o•wa[1] (ī′ə-wə) *n., pl.* **Iowa** or **-was. 1.** A member of a Native American people formerly inhabiting parts of Iowa and southwest Minnesota, with present-day descendants in Nebraska, Kansas, and Oklahoma. **2.** The Siouan language of the Iowa. [< Fr. *ayoés*, ult. < Dakota *ayúxba.*]

I•o•wa[2] (ī′ə-wə). A state of the N-central U.S.; admitted as the 29th state in 1846. Cap. Des Moines. Pop. 2,787,424. — **I′o•wan** *adj. & n.*

Iowa City. A city of E IA on the Iowa R. SSE of Cedar Rapids. Pop. 59,738.

Iowa River. A river rising in N IA and flowing c. 529 km (329 mi) SE to the Mississippi R.

IPA *abbr.* **1.** Also **I.P.A.** International Phonetic Alphabet. **2.** International Phonetic Association. **3.** Isopropyl alcohol.

ip•e•cac (ĭp′ĭ-kăk′) also **ip•e•cac•u•an•ha** (ĭp′ĭ-kăk′yo͞o-ăn′ə) *n.* **1.a.** A low-growing tropical American shrub *(Cephaelis ipecacuanha)* having roots and rhizomes that yield emetine. **b.** The dried roots and rhizomes of this shrub. **2.** A medicinal preparation made from this shrub and used as an emetic. [Short for Port. *ipecacuanha* < Tupi *ipekaaguéne* : *ipeh*, low + *kaâ*, leaves + *guéne*, vomit.]

Iph•i•ge•ni•a (ĭf′ə-jə-nī′ə, -nē′ə) *n. Gk. Myth.* The daughter of Clytemnestra and Agamemnon who was offered as a sacrifice by Agamemnon but rescued by Artemis.

ipm *abbr.* Inches per minute.

I•poh (ē′pō). A city of W Malaysia NNW of Kuala Lumpur. Pop. 300,325.

i•pro•ni•a•zid (ī′prə-nī′ə-zĭd) *n.* A compound, $C_9H_{13}N_3O$, used as an antidepressant and formerly used to treat tuberculosis. [I(SO)PRO(PYL ALCOHOL) + NI(COTINE) + AZ- + -ID.]

ips or **i.p.s.** *abbr.* Inches per second.

ip•se dix•it (ĭp′sē dĭk′sĭt) *n.* An unsupported assertion, usu. by a person of standing; a dictum. [Lat. *ipse dīxit*, he himself said (it).]

ip•si•lat•er•al (ĭp′sə-lăt′ər-əl) *adj.* Located on or affecting the same side of the body. [Alteration of Lat. *ipse*, self + LATERAL.] **— ip′si•lat′er•al•ly** *adv.*

ip•sis•si•ma ver•ba (ĭp-sĭs′ə-mə vûr′bə) *pl.n.* The very words. [NLat.]

ip•so fac•to (ĭp′sō făk′tō) *adv.* By the fact itself; by that very fact. [NLat. *ipsō factō*.]

ipso ju•re (jo͝or′ē) *adv. Law.* By the law itself. [NLat. *ipsō iūre*.]

Ips•wich (ĭp′swĭch′). A borough of E England near the North Sea NE of London. Pop. 118,900.

IQ or **I.Q.** *abbr.* Intelligence quotient.

i.q. *abbr. Lat.* Idem quod (the same as).

I•qui•que (ĭ-kē′kĕ). A city of NW Chile on the Pacific Ocean; founded in the 16th cent. Pop. 110,153.

I•qui•tos (ĭ-kē′tōs, ē-kē′tôs). A city of NE Peru on the Amazon R. NE of Lima. Pop. 178,738.

Ir The symbol for the element **iridium.**

IR *abbr.* **1.** Information retrieval. **2.** Infrared.

Ir. *abbr.* Irish.

ir–[1] *pref.* Var. of **in–**[1].

ir–[2] *pref.* Var. of **in–**[2].

IRA *abbr.* **1.** Individual Retirement Account. **2.** Individual Retirement Arrangement. **3.** Also **I.R.A.** Irish Republican Army.

I•rá•kli•on (ĭ-rä′klē-ôn′) also **Can•di•a** (kăn′dē-ə). A city of S Greece on the N coast of Crete; founded by Saracens in the 9th cent. Pop. 102,398.

I•ran (ĭ-răn′, ĭ-rän′, ī-răn′). Formerly **Per•sia** (pûr′zhə, -shə). A country of SW Asia; first inhabited c. 4000 B.C. and officially called Iran since 1935. Cap. Tehran. Pop. 40,777,000.

I•ra•ni•an (ĭ-rā′nē-ən, ĭ-rä′-, ī-rā′-) *adj.* Of or relating to Iran or its people, language, or culture. **—** *n.* **1.** A native or inhabitant of Iran. **2.** A branch of the Indo-European language family that includes Persian, Kurdish, Pashto, and other languages of Iran, Afghanistan, and western Pakistan.

I•ra•pua•to (îr′ə-pwä′tō, ē′rä-). A city of central Mexico E of Guadalajara. Pop. 170,138.

I•raq (ĭ-răk′, ĭ-räk′). A country of SW Asia; site of a number of flourishing ancient Mesopotamian civilizations and independent since 1921. Cap. Baghdad. Pop. 15,584,987.

I•ra•qi (ĭ-răk′ē, ĭ-rä′kē) *adj.* Of or relating to Iraq or its people, language, or culture. **—** *n., pl.* **-qis. 1.** A native or inhabitant of Iraq. **2.** The modern dialect of Arabic spoken in Iraq.

i•ras•ci•ble (ĭ-răs′ə-bəl, ī-răs′-) *adj.* **1.** Prone to outbursts of temper; easily angered. **2.** Characterized by or resulting from anger. [ME < OFr. < LLat. *īrāscibilis* < Lat. *īrāscī*, to be angry < *īra*, anger. See **eis-***.] **— i•ras′ci•bil′i•ty, i•ras′ci•ble•ness** *n.* **— i•ras′ci•bly** *adv.*

i•rate (ī-rāt′, ī′rāt′) *adj.* **1.** Extremely angry; enraged. **2.** Characterized or occasioned by anger: *an irate phone call.* [Lat. *īrātus*, p.part. of *īrāscī*, to be angry < *īra*, anger. See **eis-***.] **— i•rate′ly** *adv.* **— i•rate′ness** *n.*

Ir•bil (îr′bĭl) also **Er•bil** (îr′bĭl, ĕr′-). A city of N Iraq N of Baghdad; built on the site of ancient Arbela. Pop. 333,903.

IRBM *abbr.* Intermediate-range ballistic missile.

ire (īr) *n.* Anger; wrath. See Syns at **anger.** [ME < OFr. < Lat. *īra*. See **eis-***.]

Ire. *abbr.* Ireland.

Ire•dell (īr′dĕl′), **James.** 1751–99. Amer. jurist; associate justice of the U.S. Supreme Court (1790–99).

ire•ful (īr′fəl) *adj.* Full of ire; wrathful. **— ire′ful•ly** *adv.*

Ire•land[1] (īr′lənd). An island in the N Atlantic Ocean W of Great Britain; joined Great Britain in 1801 but after 1921 was split into the independent Irish Free State (now Ireland) and Northern Ireland, which is allied with Great Britain.

Ire•land[2] (īr′lənd). Formerly **I•rish Free State** (ī′rĭsh) also **Eir•e** (âr′ə, ī′rə, âr′ē, ī′rē) A country occupying most of the island of Ireland. Estab. as the Irish Free State in 1922, Ireland became Eire in 1937 and the Republic of Ireland in 1949. Cap. Dublin. Pop. 3,443,405.

Ireland, Northern. See **Northern Ireland.**

i•ren•ic (ī-rĕn′ĭk, ī-rē′nĭk) also **i•ren•i•cal** (-ĭ-kəl, -nĭ-kəl) *adj.* Promoting peace; conciliatory. [Gk. *eirēnikos* < *eirēnē*, peace.] **— i•ren′i•cal•ly** *adv.*

irid. *abbr.* Iridescent.

ir•i•da•ceous (ĭr′ĭ-dā′shəs) *adj.* Of or belonging to the iris family. [< NLat. *Īridācea*, iris family < *Īris, Īrid-*, type genus < Lat. *īris*, iris. See IRIS.]

ir•i•dec•to•my (ĭr′ĭ-dĕk′tə-mē, ī′rĭ-) *n., pl.* **-mies.** Surgical removal of part of the iris of the eye.

ir•i•des•cent (ĭr′ĭ-dĕs′ənt) *adj.* **1.** Producing a display of lustrous rainbowlike colors: *iridescent plumage.* **2.** Brilliant, lustrous, or colorful in effect or appearance. **— ir′i•des′cence** *n.*

i•rid•ic (ĭ-rĭd′ĭk, ī-rĭd′-) *adj.* Of or relating to the iris of the eye.

i•rid•i•um (ĭ-rĭd′ē-əm) *n. Symbol* **Ir** A hard, brittle, corrosion-resistant metallic element occurring in platinum ores and used principally to harden platinum and in high-temperature materials, electrical contacts, and wear-resistant bearings. Atomic number 77; atomic weight 192.2; melting point 2,410°C; boiling point 4,130°C; specific gravity 22.42 (at 17°C); valence 3, 4. See table at **element.** [Lat. *īris, īrid-*, rainbow; see IRIDO- + -IUM.]

irido– or **irid–** *pref.* **1.** Rainbow: *iridescent.* **2.** Iris of the eye: *iridectomy.* **3.** Iridium: *iridosmine.* [Lat. *īris, īrid-*, rainbow < Gk. See **wei-***.]

ir•i•dol•o•gy (ĭr′ĭ-dŏl′ə-jē, ī′rĭ-) *n.* The study of the iris of the eye, esp. as associated with disease. **— ir′i•dol′o•gist** *n.*

ir•i•dos•mine (ĭr′ĭ-dŏz′mĕn) *n.* See **osmiridium.** [IRID(O)- + OSM(IUM) + -INE[2].]

i•ris (ī′rĭs) *n., pl.* **i•ris•es** or **i•ri•des** (ī′rĭ-dēz′, ĭr′ĭ-). **1.** The pigmented round contractile membrane of the eye that regulates the amount of light entering the eye. **2.** Any of numerous plants of the genus *Iris*, having narrow sword-shaped leaves and variously colored flowers. **3.** A rainbow or rainbowlike display of colors. [ME, rainbow < Lat. *īris, īrid-* < Gk., rainbow, iris of the eye. See **wei-***.]

I•ris (ī′rĭs) *n. Gk. Myth.* The goddess of the rainbow and messenger of the gods. [Lat. *Īris* < Gk. See **wei-***.]

iris diaphragm *n.* A device with a variable diameter, used on cameras to regulate the amount of light admitted to a lens.

I•rish (ī′rĭsh) *adj.* Of Ireland, its people, language, or culture. **—** *n.* **1.** The people of Ireland. **2.a.** See **Irish Gaelic. b.** See **Irish English. 3.** *Informal.* Fieriness of temper or passion; high spirit. [ME < OE *Īras*, the Irish. See **peiə-***.]

Irish coffee *n.* A beverage of sweetened hot coffee and Irish whiskey, topped with whipped cream.

Irish elk *n.* A large extinct European deer of the genus *Megaceros* of the Pliocene Epoch and the Pleistocene Epoch.

Irish English *n.* English as spoken by the Irish.

Irish Free State. See **Ireland**[2]**.**

Irish Gaelic *n.* The Goidelic language of Ireland.

I•rish•ism (ī′rĭsh-ĭz′əm) *n.* An Irish idiom or custom.

I•rish•man (ī′rĭsh-mən) *n.* A man of Irish birth or ancestry.

Irish moss *n.* An edible North Atlantic seaweed *(Chondrus crispus)* that yields a mucilaginous substance used medicinally and in preparing jellies.

I•rish•ry (ī′rĭsh-rē) *n., pl.* **-ries. 1.** The Irish people, esp. those of Celtic descent. **2.a.** Irish character. **b.** An Irish trait, custom, or locution; an Irishism.

Irish Sea. An arm of the N Atlantic Ocean between Ireland and Great Britain.

Irish setter *n.* Any of a breed of setters having a silky reddish-brown coat.

Irish stew *n.* A stew of meat and vegetables.

Irish terrier *n.* Any of a breed of terriers having a wiry reddish-brown coat.

Irish whiskey *n.* Whiskey made by the distillation of barley.

Irish wolfhound *n.* Any of an ancient breed of large powerful dogs having a rough, shaggy coat.

I•rish•wom•an (ī′rĭsh-wo͝om′ən) *n.* A woman of Irish birth or ancestry.

i•ri•tis (ī-rī′tĭs) *n.* Inflammation of the iris of the eye. [IR(IS) + -ITIS.] **— i•rit′ic** (ī-rĭt′ĭk) *adj.*

irk (ûrk) *tr.v.* **irked, irk•ing, irks.** To be irritating, wearisome, or vexing to. [ME *irken*, to weary, poss. < ON *yrkja*, to work, make verses, harangue. See **werg-***.]

irk•some (ûrk′səm) *adj.* Causing annoyance, weariness, or vexation; tedious: *irksome restrictions.* See Syns at **boring. — irk′some•ly** *adv.* **— irk′some•ness** *n.*

Ir•kutsk (îr-ko͞otsk′). A city of S-central Russia near the S end of Lake Baikal. Pop. 597,000.

IRO *abbr.* International Refugee Organization.

i•ron (ī′ərn) *n.* **1.** *Symbol* **Fe** A lustrous, malleable, ductile, magnetic or magnetizable metallic element occurring abundantly in ores such as hematite and magnetite and used alloyed in a wide range of important structural materials. Atomic number 26; atomic weight 55.847; melting point 1,535°C; boiling point 2,750°C; specific gravity 7.874 (at 20°C); valence 2, 3, 4, 6. See table at **element. 2.** An implement made of iron alloy or similar metal, esp. a heated bar used to brand, curl hair, or cauterize. **3.** Great hardness or

Ireland[2]

Irish moss
Chondrus crispus

Irish setter

Irish wolfhound

ă pat	oi boy
ā pay	ou out
âr care	o͝o took
ä father	o͞o boot
ĕ pet	ŭ cut
ē be	ûr urge
ĭ pit	th thin
ī pie	*th* this
îr pier	hw which
ŏ pot	zh vision
ō toe	ə about, item
ô paw	

Stress marks:
′ (primary);
′ (secondary), as in
dictionary (dĭk′shə-nĕr′ē)

strength; firmness. **4.** *Sports.* A golf club with a metal head, numbered from one to nine in order of increasing loft. **5.** A metal appliance with a handle and a weighted flat bottom, used when heated to press wrinkles from fabric. **6.** A harpoon. **7. irons.** Fetters; shackles. **8.** A pill or other medication containing iron and taken as a dietary supplement. *—adj.* **1.** Made of or containing iron. **2.** Very hard and strong. **3.** Hardy; robust. **4.** Inflexible; unyielding. *—v.* **i•roned, i•ron•ing, i•rons.** *—tr.* **1.a.** To press and smooth with a heated iron. **b.** To remove (creases) by pressing. **2.** To put into irons; fetter. **3.** To fit or clad with iron. *—intr.* To iron clothes. ***—phrasal verb.* iron out.** To settle through discussion or compromise; work out. ***—idiom.* iron in the fire.** An undertaking in progress. [ME *iren* < OE *īren.* See **eis-*.**]

I•ron Age (ī′ərn) *n.* The period in human cultural development after the Bronze Age, in Europe beginning around the eighth century B.C., marked by the introduction of iron metallurgy.

iron blue *n.* Any of various light-resistant and heat-resistant, semitransparent blue pigments of powerful tinctorial strength, used chiefly in industrial finishes, ink, and artists' colors.

i•ron•bound (ī′ərn-bound′) *adj.* **1.** Bound with iron. **2.** Rigid and unyielding. **3.** Bound with rocks and cliffs.

i•ron•clad (ī′ərn-klăd′) *adj.* **1.** Sheathed with iron plates for protection. **2.** Rigid; fixed: *an ironclad rule.* *—n. Naut.* A 19th-century warship having sides armored with metal plates.

iron curtain *n.* **1.** Often **Iron Curtain.** The military, political, and ideological barrier existing between the Soviet bloc and western Europe from 1945 to 1990. **2.** A barrier that prevents free exchange of ideas and information.

ironwork
Window grille

I•ron•de•quoit (ĭ-rŏn′dĭ-kwoit′, -kwŏt′). A town of W NY W of Rochester; settled in 1791. Pop. 52,322.

Iron Gate. A narrow gorge of the Danube R. on the border of Serbia and Romania; created by a gap between the Carpathian and Balkan mountains.

iron gray *n. Color.* A dark gray with a slightly greenish tinge.

iron hand *n.* Rigorous or despotic control. **—i′ron•hand′ed** (ī′ərn-hăn′dĭd) *adj.* **—i′ron•hand′ed•ness** *n.*

iron horse *n. Informal.* A railroad locomotive.

i•ron•ic (ī-rŏn′ĭk) also **i•ron•i•cal** (ī-rŏn′ĭ-kəl) *adj.* **1.** Characterized by or constituting irony. **2.** Given to the use of irony. **3.** Poignantly contrary to what was expected or intended. **—i•ron′i•cal•ly** *adv.* **—i•ron′i•cal•ness** *n.*

Usage Note: The words *ironic, irony,* and *ironically* are sometimes used of events and circumstances that might better be described as simply "coincidental" or "improbable," in that they suggest no particular lessons about human vanity or folly. Thus 78 percent of the Usage Panel rejects the use of *ironically* in the sentence *In 1969 Susie moved from Ithaca to California where she met her husband-to-be, who, ironically, also came from upstate New York.* By contrast, 73 percent accepted the sentence *Ironically, even as the government was fulminating against American policy, American jeans and videocassettes were the hottest items in the stalls of the market,* where the incongruity can be seen as an example of human inconsistency.

i•ron•ing (ī′ər-nĭng) *n.* **1.** The act or process of pressing clothes with an iron. **2.** Clothing ironed or to be ironed.

ironing board *n.* A long narrow padded board, often with collapsible supporting legs, on which to iron.

i•ro•nist (ī′rə-nĭst) *n.* A notable user of irony, esp. a writer.

iron lung *n.* An airtight metal tank that encloses all of the body except the head and forces the lungs to inhale and exhale through regulated changes in air pressure.

iron maiden *n.* A medieval instrument of torture consisting of an iron frame in the form of a person in which the victim was enclosed and impaled on interior spikes.

i•ron•mon•ger (ī′ərn-mŭng′gər, -mŏng′-) *n. Chiefly British.* A hardware merchant.

i•ron•mon•ger•y (ī′ərn-mŭng′gə-rē, -mŏng′-) *n., pl.* **-ies.** *Chiefly British.* **1.** Ironware. **2.** The shop or business of an ironmonger.

iron oxide *n.* Any of various oxides of iron, such as ferric oxide or ferrous oxide.

iron pyrites *n.* See **pyrite.**

i•ron•smith (ī′ərn-smĭth′) *n.* One that makes iron articles; a blacksmith.

i•ron•stone (ī′ərn-stōn′) *n.* **1.** A hard white pottery. **2.** A rock containing enough iron to permit commercial extraction; an iron ore.

i•ron•ware (ī′ərn-wâr′) *n.* Iron utensils and ironwork.

i•ron•weed (ī′ərn-wēd′) *n.* Any of various plants of the genus *Vernonia,* having alternate leaves and purplish flower clusters.

i•ron•wood (ī′ərn-wo͝od′) *n.* **1.** Any of numerous trees, such as the hornbeam and the hop hornbeam, that have very hard wood. **2.** The wood of any of these trees.

i•ron•work (ī′ərn-wûrk′) *n.* Work in iron, such as gratings.

i•ron•work•er (ī′ərn-wûr′kər) *n.* **1.** A construction worker who builds steel structures. **2.** One who is employed in an ironworks. **3.** One who makes iron articles.

i•ron•works (ī′ərn-wûrks′) *pl.n. (used with a sing. or pl. v.)* A building or an establishment where iron is smelted or where heavy iron products are made.

Washington Irving
1832 engraving by Hatch (1805? – 1867) and Smillie (1807 – 1885)

i•ro•ny (ī′rə-nē, ī′ər-) *n., pl.* **-nies. 1.a.** The use of words to express something different from and often opposite to their literal meaning. **b.** An expression or utterance marked by irony. **c.** A literary style employing irony for humorous or rhetorical effect. **2.a.** Incongruity between what might be expected and what actually occurs. **b.** An occurrence, a result, or a circumstance notable for such incongruity. See Usage Note at **ironic. 3.** Dramatic irony. **4.** Socratic irony. [Fr. *ironie* < OFr. < Lat. *īrōnīa* < Gk. *eirōneia,* feigned ignorance < *eirōn,* dissembler, prob. < *eirein,* to say. See **wer-[5]*.**]

Ir•o•quoi•an (îr′ə-kwoi′ən) *n.* **1.** A family of North American Indian languages of the eastern part of Canada and the United States that includes Cayuga, Mohawk, Oneida, Onondaga, Seneca, Tuscarora, Cherokee, Erie, Huron, and Wyandot. **2.** A member of an Iroquoian-speaking people. *—adj.* Of or constituting the Iroquoian language family.

Ir•o•quois (îr′ə-kwoi′) *n., pl.* **Iroquois** (-kwoi′, -kwoiz′). **1.a.** A Native American confederacy inhabiting New York State and composed of the Mohawk, Oneida, Onondaga, Cayuga, Seneca, and, after 1722, Tuscarora peoples. **b.** A member of this confederacy or of any of its peoples. **2.** Any or all of the languages of the Iroquois. [?] **—Ir′o•quois′** *adj.*

ir•ra•di•ant (ĭ-rā′dē-ənt) *adj.* Sending forth radiant light. **—ir•ra′di•ance, ir•ra′di•an•cy** *n.*

ir•ra•di•ate (ĭ-rā′dē-āt′) *v.* **-at•ed, -at•ing, -ates.** *—tr.* **1.a.** To expose to radiation. **b.** To treat with radiation. **2.** To shed light on; illuminate. **3.** To manifest so as to suggest the emission of light; radiate. *—intr. Archaic.* **1.** To send forth rays; radiate. **2.** To become radiant. [Lat. *irrradiāre, irradiāt-,* to illuminate : *in-,* on; see IN-[2] + *radiāre,* to shine; see RADIATE.] **—ir•ra′di•a′tive** *adj.* **—ir•ra′di•a′tor** *n.*

ir•ra•di•a•tion (ĭ-rā′dē-ā′shən) *n.* **1.** The act of exposing to radiation or the condition of being so exposed. **2.** Therapy or treatment by exposure to radiation.

ir•rad•i•ca•ble (ĭ-răd′ĭ-kə-bəl) *adj.* Impossible to uproot or destroy; ineradicable. [Med.Lat. *irrādīcābilis* : Lat. *in-,* not; see IN-[1] + Lat. *rādīx, rādīc-,* root; see ERADICATE.] **—ir•rad′i•ca•bly** *adv.*

ir•ra•tion•al (ĭ-răsh′ə-nəl) *adj.* **1.a.** Not endowed with reason. **b.** Affected by loss of usual or normal mental clarity; incoherent, as from shock. **c.** Marked by a lack of accord with reason or sound judgment: *an irrational dislike.* **2.a.** Being a syllable in Greek and Latin prosody whose length does not fit the meter. **b.** Being a metric foot containing such a syllable. **3.** *Math.* Of or relating to an irrational number. **—ir•ra′tion•al•ly** *adv.* **—ir•ra′tion•al•ness** *n.*

ir•ra•tion•al•ism (ĭ-răsh′ə-nə-lĭz′əm) *n.* **1.** Irrational thought, expression, or behavior; irrationality. **2.** Belief in instinct or other nonrational forces rather than reason.

ir•ra•tion•al•i•ty (ĭ-răsh′ə-năl′ĭ-tē) *n., pl.* **-ties. 1.** The state or quality of being irrational. **2.** Something irrational.

irrational number *n. Math.* A real number that cannot be expressed as an integer or as a ratio of two integers.

Ir•ra•wad•dy (îr′ə-wŏd′ē, -wô′dē). A river of Burma flowing c. 1,609 km (1,000 mi) to the Bay of Bengal.

ir•re•claim•a•ble (ĭr′ĭ-klā′mə-bəl) *adj.* Impossible to reclaim: *irreclaimable wasteland.* **—ir′re•claim′a•bil′i•ty, ir′re•claim′a•ble•ness** *n.* **—ir′re•claim′a•bly** *adv.*

ir•rec•on•cil•a•ble (ĭ-rĕk′ən-sī′lə-bəl, ĭ-rĕk′ən-sī′-) *adj.* Impossible to reconcile. *—n.* **1.** A person, esp. a group member who will not compromise, adjust, or submit. **2.** One of two or more irreconcilable ideas or beliefs. **—ir•rec′on•cil′a•bil′i•ty** *n.* **—ir•rec′on•cil′a•bly** *adv.*

ir•re•cov•er•a•ble (ĭr′ĭ-kŭv′ər-ə-bəl) *adj.* Impossible to recover; irreparable: *irrecoverable losses.* **—ir′re•cov′er•a•ble•ness** *n.* **—ir′re•cov′er•a•bly** *adv.*

ir•re•cu•sa•ble (ĭr′ĭ-kyo͞o′zə-bəl) *adj.* Not subject to challenge or objection: *an irrecusable premise.* [Fr. *irrécusable* < LLat. *irrecūsābilis* : Lat. *in-,* not; see IN-[1] + LLat. *recūsābilis,* deserving of rejection (< Lat. *recūsāre,* to refuse; see RECUSE).] **—ir′re•cu′sa•bly** *adv.*

ir•re•deem•a•ble (ĭr′ĭ-dē′mə-bəl) *adj.* **1.** That cannot be bought back or paid off: *irredeemable sales.* **2.** Not convertible into coin. **3.** Impossible to remedy. **4.** Impossible to redeem or reform: *irredeemable evil.* **—ir′re•deem′a•bly** *adv.*

ir•re•den•tist (ĭr′ĭ-dĕn′tĭst) *n.* One who advocates the recovery of land culturally or historically related to one's nation but now under foreign control. [Ital. *irredentista* < *irredento* : *in-,* not (< Lat. *in-*; see IN-[1]) + *redento,* redeemed (< Lat. *redemptus,* p.part. of *redimere,* to redeem; see REDEEM).] **—ir′re•den′tism** *n.* **—ir′re•den′tist** *adj.*

ir•re•duc•i•ble (ĭr′ĭ-do͞o′sə-bəl, -dyo͞o′-) *adj.* Impossible to reduce to a desired, simpler, or smaller form or amount. **—ir′re•duc′i•bil′i•ty, ir′re•duc′i•ble•ness** *n.* **—ir′re•duc′i•bly** *adv.*

ir•ref•ra•ga•ble (ĭ-rĕf′rə-gə-bəl) *adj.* Impossible to refute or controvert; indisputable. [LLat. *irrefrāgābilis* : Lat. *in-,* not; see IN-[1] + Lat. *refrāgārī,* to oppose, resist; see **bhreg-*.**] **—ir•ref′ra•ga•bil′i•ty** *n.* **—ir•ref′ra•ga•bly** *adv.*

ir•re•fran•gi•ble (ĭr′ĭ-frăn′jə-bəl) *adj.* **1.** Impossible to break; indestructible: *irrefrangible cooking ware.* **2.** *Phys.* That cannot be refracted. **—ir′re•fran′gi•bly** *adv.*

ir•ref•u•ta•ble (ĭ-rĕf′yə-tə-bəl, ĭr′ĭ-fyōō′-) *adj.* Impossible to refute or disprove; incontrovertible: *irrefutable arguments.* — **ir•ref′u•ta•bil′i•ty** *n.* — **ir•ref′u•ta•bly** *adv.*

irreg. *abbr.* Irregular.

ir•re•gard•less (ĭr′ĭ-gärd′lĭs) *adv. Non-Standard.* Regardless. [Perh. < IR(RESPECTIVE) + REGARDLESS.]

Usage Note: The label *Non-Standard* does only approximate justice to the status of *irregardless.* More precisely, it is a form that many people mistakenly believe to be a correct usage in formal style but that in fact has no legitimate antecedents in either standard or nonstandard varieties. The word was likely coined from a blend of *irrespective* and *regardless.*

ir•reg•u•lar (ĭ-rĕg′yə-lər) *adj.* **1.** Contrary to rule, accepted order, or general practice. **2.** Not conforming to legality, moral law, or social convention. **3.** Not straight, uniform, or symmetrical. **4.** Of uneven rate, occurrence, or duration. **5.** Deviating from a type; atypical. **6.** *Bot.* Having differing floral parts, as of a zygomorphic flower. **7.** Falling below the manufacturer's standard or usual specifications; imperfect. **8.** *Gram.* Departing from the usual pattern of inflection, derivation, or word formation, as the plural noun *children.* **9.** Not belonging to a permanent organized military force. — *n.* **1.** One that is irregular. **2.** A soldier who is not part of a regular military force. — **ir•reg′u•lar•ly** *adv.*

ir•reg•u•lar•i•ty (ĭ-rĕg′yə-lăr′ĭ-tē) *n., pl.* **-ties. 1.** The quality or state of being irregular. **2.** Something irregular: *found the firm's books riddled with irregularities.* **3.** Constipation.

ir•rel•a•tive (ĭ-rĕl′ə-tĭv) *adj.* **1.** Having no correlative relationship; unconnected. **2.** Irrelevant. — **ir•rel′a•tive•ly** *adv.*

ir•rel•e•vance (ĭ-rĕl′ə-vəns) *n.* **1.** The quality or state of being irrelevant. **2.** Something irrelevant.

ir•rel•e•van•cy (ĭ-rĕl′ə-vən-sē) *n., pl.* **-cies.** Irrelevance.

ir•rel•e•vant (ĭ-rĕl′ə-vənt) *adj.* Unrelated to the matter at hand. — **ir•rel′e•vant•ly** *adv.*

ir•re•lig•ion (ĭr′ĭ-lĭj′ən) *n.* Hostility or indifference to religion.

ir•re•lig•ious (ĭr′ĭ-lĭj′əs) *adj.* Hostile or indifferent to religion. — **ir′re•lig′ious•ly** *adv.* — **ir′re•lig′ious•ness** *n.*

ir•re•me•a•ble (ĭ-rē′mē-ə-bəl) *adj. Archaic.* Affording no possibility of return. [Lat. *irremeābilis* : *in-*, not; see IN-[1] + *remeāre*, to return (*re-*, re- + *meāre*, to go; see **mei-**[1]*).]

ir•re•me•di•a•ble (ĭr′ĭ-mē′dē-ə-bəl) *adj.* Impossible to remedy, correct, or repair. — **ir′re•me′di•a•bly** *adv.*

ir•re•mis•si•ble (ĭr′ĭ-mĭs′ə-bəl) *adj.* Not remissible; unpardonable. — **ir′re•mis′si•bil′i•ty** *n.* — **ir′re•mis′si•bly** *adv.*

ir•re•mov•a•ble (ĭr′ĭ-mōō′və-bəl) *adj.* Impossible to remove. — **ir′re•mov′a•bil′i•ty** *n.* — **ir′re•mov′a•bly** *adv.*

ir•rep•a•ra•ble (ĭ-rĕp′ər-ə-bəl) *adj.* Impossible to repair, rectify, or amend. — **ir•rep′a•ra•bil′i•ty, ir•rep′a•ra•ble•ness** *n.* — **ir•rep′a•ra•bly** *adv.*

ir•re•peal•a•ble (ĭr′ĭ-pē′lə-bəl) *adj.* Impossible to repeal.

ir•re•place•a•ble (ĭr′ĭ-plā′sə-bəl) *adj.* Impossible to replace: *irreplaceable antiques.* — **ir′re•place′a•bil′i•ty, ir′re•place′a•ble•ness** *n.* — **ir′re•place′a•bly** *adv.*

ir•re•press•i•ble (ĭr′ĭ-prĕs′ə-bəl) *adj.* Difficult or impossible to control or restrain. — **ir′re•press′i•bil′i•ty, ir′re•press′i•ble•ness** *n.* — **ir′re•press′i•bly** *adv.*

ir•re•proach•a•ble (ĭr′ĭ-prō′chə-bəl) *adj.* Perfect or blameless in every respect; faultless. — **ir′re•proach′a•bil′i•ty, ir′re•proach′a•ble•ness** *n.* — **ir′re•proach′a•bly** *adv.*

ir•re•sis•ti•ble (ĭr′ĭ-zĭs′tə-bəl) *adj.* **1.** Impossible to resist. **2.** Having an overpowering appeal. — **ir′re•sis′ti•bil′i•ty, ir′re•sis′ti•ble•ness** *n.* — **ir′re•sis′ti•bly** *adv.*

ir•re•sol•u•ble (ĭr′ĭ-zŏl′yə-bəl) *adj.* Impossible to resolve: *irresoluble conflicts.*

ir•res•o•lute (ĭ-rĕz′ə-lōōt′) *adj.* **1.** Unsure of how to act; undecided. **2.** Lacking in resolution; indecisive. — **ir•res′o•lute′ly** *adv.* — **ir•res′o•lute′ness, ir•res′o•lu′tion** *n.*

ir•re•solv•a•ble (ĭr′ĭ-zŏl′və-bəl) *adj.* **1.** Irresoluble. **2.** Impossible to separate into component parts; irreducible.

ir•re•spec•tive (ĭr′ĭ-spĕk′tĭv) *adj. Archaic.* Characterized by disregard; heedless. — **ir′re•spec′tive•ly** *adv.*

irrespective of *prep.* Without consideration of; regardless of.

ir•res•pi•ra•ble (ĭ-rĕs′pər-ə-bəl, ĭr′ĭ-spīr′-) *adj.* Not fit for breathing; not respirable.

ir•re•spon•si•ble (ĭr′ĭ-spŏn′sə-bəl) *adj.* **1.** Marked by a lack of responsibility: *irresponsible claims.* **2.** Not responsible; unreliable or untrustworthy. **3.** *Law.* Mentally or financially unfit for responsibility. **4.** Not accountable to a higher authority. — *n.* **1.** One with no sense of responsibility. **2.** *Law.* One who is mentally or financially unfit for responsibility. **3.** One who is unlikely to be called to account by a higher authority. — **ir′re•spon′si•bil′i•ty, ir′re•spon′si•ble•ness** *n.* — **ir′re•spon′si•bly** *adv.*

ir•re•spon•sive (ĭr′ĭ-spŏn′sĭv) *adj.* **1.** Not responsive, as to treatment or stimuli. **2.** Not responding or answering readily. — **ir′re•spon′sive•ly** *adv.* — **ir′re•spon′sive•ness** *n.*

ir•re•triev•a•ble (ĭr′ĭ-trē′və-bəl) *adj.* Difficult or impossible to retrieve or recover. — **ir′re•triev′a•ble•ness, ir′re•triev′a•bil′i•ty** *n.* — **ir′re•triev′a•bly** *adv.*

ir•rev•er•ence (ĭ-rĕv′ər-əns) *n.* **1.** Lack of reverence or due respect. **2.** A disrespectful act or remark.

ir•rev•er•ent (ĭ-rĕv′ər-ənt) *adj.* **1.** Lacking reverence; disrespectful. **2.** Critical of what is generally accepted or respected; satirical. — **ir•rev′er•ent•ly** *adv.*

ir•re•vers•i•ble (ĭr′ĭ-vûr′sə-bəl) *adj.* Impossible to reverse: *an irreversible action.* — **ir′re•vers′i•bil′i•ty, ir′re•vers′i•ble•ness** *n.* — **ir′re•vers′i•bly** *adv.*

ir•rev•o•ca•ble (ĭ-rĕv′ə-kə-bəl) *adj.* Impossible to retract or revoke: *an irrevocable decision.* — **ir•rev′o•ca•bil′i•ty, ir•rev′o•ca•ble•ness** *n.* — **ir•rev′o•ca•bly** *adv.*

ir•ri•ga•ble (ĭr′ĭ-gə-bəl) *adj.* That can be irrigated.

ir•ri•gate (ĭr′ĭ-gāt′) *v.* **-gat•ed, -gat•ing, -gates.** — *tr.* **1.** To supply (dry land) with water by means of ditches, pipes, or streams. **2.** To wash out (a body cavity or wound) with water or a medicated fluid. **3.** To make fertile or vital as if by watering. — *intr.* To irrigate land. [Lat. *irrigāre, irrigāt-* : *in-*, in; see IN-[2] + *rigāre*, to water.] — **ir′ri•ga′tion** *n.* — **ir′ri•ga′tion•al** *adj.* — **ir′ri•ga′tor** *n.*

ir•ri•ta•bil•i•ty (ĭr′ĭ-tə-bĭl′ĭ-tē) *n., pl.* **-ties. 1.** The quality or state of being irritable; testiness or petulance. **2.** *Pathol.* Abnormal or excessive sensitivity of a body organ or part to a stimulus. **3.** *Physiol.* The capacity to respond to stimuli.

ir•ri•ta•ble (ĭr′ĭ-tə-bəl) *adj.* **1.** Easily irritated or annoyed. **2.** *Pathol.* Abnormally sensitive to a stimulus. **3.** *Physiol.* Capable of responding to stimuli. [Ult. < Lat. *irrītābilis* < *irrītāre*, to irritate.] — **ir′ri•ta•ble•ness** *n.* — **ir′ri•ta•bly** *adv.*

ir•ri•tant (ĭr′ĭ-tənt) *adj.* Causing irritation, esp. physical irritation. — *n.* A source of irritation.

ir•ri•tate (ĭr′ĭ-tāt′) *v.* **-tat•ed, -tat•ing, -tates.** — *tr.* **1.** To make impatient or angry; annoy. **2.** To chafe or inflame. — *intr.* To be a cause of impatience or anger. [Lat. *irrītāre, irrītāt-.*] — **ir′ri•tat′ing•ly** *adv.* — **ir′ri•ta′tor** *n.*

ir•ri•ta•tion (ĭr′ĭ-tā′shən) *n.* **1.a.** The act of irritating. **b.** The condition of being irritated; vexation. **2.** A source of irritation. **3.** *Pathol.* A condition of inflammation, soreness, or irritability of a body organ or part.

ir•ri•ta•tive (ĭr′ĭ-tā′tĭv) *adj.* Involving irritation.

ir•ro•ta•tion•al (ĭr′ō-tā′shə-nəl) *adj.* Involving no rotation.

ir•rupt (ĭ-rŭpt′) *intr.v.* **-rupt•ed, -rupt•ing, -rupts. 1.** To break or burst in. **2.** *Ecol.* To increase rapidly and irregularly in number. [Lat. *irrumpere, irrupt-* : *in-*, in; see IN-[2] + *rumpere*, to break; see **reup-***.] — **ir•rup′tion** *n.*

ir•rup•tive (ĭ-rŭp′tĭv) *adj.* **1.** Irrupting or tending to irrupt. **2.** *Geol.* Intrusive.

IRS *abbr.* Internal Revenue Service.

Ir•tysh or **Ir•tish** (ĭr-tĭsh′). A river of NW China, E Kazakhstan, and central Russia flowing c. 4,264 km (2,650 mi) to the Ob R.

Ir•vine (ûr′vīn′). A city of S CA SE of Santa Ana. Pop. 110,330.

Ir•ving (ûr′vĭng). A town of NE TX, a suburb of Dallas. Pop. 155,037.

Irving, John. b. 1942. Amer. writer whose novels include *The World According to Garp* (1978).

Irving, Washington. 1783–1859. Amer. writer best remembered for his stories "Rip Van Winkle" and "The Legend of Sleepy Hollow" in *The Sketch Book* (1819–20).

Ir•ving•ton (ûr′vĭng-tən). A town of NE NJ, a suburb of Newark; settled in 1692. Pop. 59,774.

is (ĭz) *v.* Third pers. sing. pr. indic. of **be.** [ME < OE. See **es-***.]

is. or **Is.** *abbr.* Island.

Is. *abbr. Bible.* Isaiah.

is– *pref.* Var. of **iso–.**

Isa. *abbr. Bible.* Isaiah.

I•saac (ī′zək). In the Bible, the son of Abraham and Sarah who was offered as a sacrifice to God.

Is•a•bel•la I (ĭz′ə-bĕl′ə). "Isabella the Catholic." 1451–1504. Queen of Castile (1474–1504) whose marriage in 1469 to Ferdinand V of Castile and León (later Ferdinand II of Aragon) marked the beginning of a unified Spanish state.

Isabella I

I•sa•iah (ī-zā′ə, ī-zī′ə) *n. Bible.* **1.** A Hebrew prophet of the 8th cent. B.C. **2.** See table at **Bible.**

i•sal•lo•bar (ī-săl′ə-bär′) *n.* A line on a weather map connecting places having equal changes in atmospheric pressure within a given period of time. [IS(O)- + ALLO- + Gk. *baros*, weight; see **gʷerə-**[1]*.]

–isation *suff.* Var. of **–ization.**

ISBN *abbr.* International Standard Book Number.

is•che•mi•a (ĭ-skē′mē-ə) *n.* A decrease in the blood supply to a body organ, tissue, or part caused by constriction or obstruction of the blood vessels. [NLat. *ischaemia* < Gk. *iskhaimos*, a stopping of the blood : *iskhein*, to keep back; see **segh-*** + *haima*, blood.] — **i•sche′mic** *adj.*

Is•chi•a (ĭs′kē-ə, ē′skyä). An island of S Italy in the Tyrrhenian Sea at the entrance to the Bay of Naples.

is•chi•um (ĭs′kē-əm) *n., pl.* **-chi•a** (-kē-ə). The lowest of the three major bones that constitute each half of the pelvis. [Lat., hip joint < Gk. *iskhion.*] — **is′chi•al** (-əl) *adj.*

–ise *suff.* Var. of **–ize.**

I•se Bay (ē′sā, ē′sĕ′). An arm of the Pacific Ocean on the S-central coast of Honshu, Japan.

Ise•lin (ĭz′lĭn). A community of E-central NJ NW of Perth Amboy. Pop. 16,141.

ă pat	oi boy
ā pay	ou out
âr care	ŏŏ took
ä father	ōō boot
ĕ pet	ŭ cut
ē be	ûr urge
ĭ pit	th thin
ī pie	*th* this
îr pier	hw which
ŏ pot	zh vision
ō toe	ə about, item
ô paw	

Stress marks:
′ (primary);
′ (secondary), as in
dictionary (dĭk′shə-nĕr′ē)

is•en•tro•pic (ī′sən-trō′pĭk, -trŏp′ĭk) *adj.* Without change in entropy; at constant entropy. [IS(O)– + ENTROP(Y) + –IC.]

I•sère (ē-zâr′). A river of SE France rising in the Graian Alps and flowing c. 290 km (180 mi) to the Rhone R.

I•ser•lohn (ē′zər-lōn′, ē′zər-lōn′). A city of W-central Germany NE of Cologne; founded in the 13th cent. Pop. 89,951.

I•seult (ĭ-so͞olt′) also **I•sol•de** (ĭ-sōl′də, ĭ-zōl′-) *n.* In Arthurian legend, an Irish princess who married the king of Cornwall and had a love affair with his knight Tristan.

Is•fa•han (ĭs′fə-hän′) or **Es•fa•han** (ĕs′-). A city of central Iran S of Tehran; cap. of Persia from 1598 to 1722. Pop. 927,000.

–ish *suff.* **1.** Of, relating to, or being: *Swedish.* **2.a.** Characteristic of: *girlish.* **b.** Having the usu. undesirable qualities of: *childish.* **3.** Approximately; somewhat: *greenish.* **4.** Tending toward; preoccupied with: *selfish.* [ME < OE *-isc.*]

Ish•er•wood (ĭsh′ər-wo͝od′), **Christopher William Bradshaw.** 1904–86. British-born Amer. writer best known for his works about Berlin in the early 1930's.

I•shim (ĭ-shĭm′). A river, c. 1,818 km (1,130 mi), rising in the steppe region of Kazakhstan and flowing to the Irtysh R. in S-central Russia.

Isis[1]

Ish•ma•el[1] (ĭsh′mē-əl, -mā-). In the Bible, the son of Abraham and Hagar who was cast out after the birth of Isaac.

Ish•ma•el[2] (ĭsh′mē-əl, -mā-) *n.* An outcast.

Ish•ma•el•ite (ĭsh′mē-ə-līt′, -mā-) *n.* **1.** A descendant of Ishmael. **2.** An outcast. — **Ish′ma•el•it′ism** *n.*

Ish•tar (ĭsh′tär′) *n. Myth.* The ancient Assyrian and Babylonian goddess of love, fertility, and war.

Is•i•dore of Se•ville (ĭz′ĭ-dôr′, -dōr′; sə-vĭl′), Saint. 560?–636. Spanish ecclesiastic who wrote the encyclopedia *Etymologiae.*

i•sin•glass (ī′zən-glăs′, ī′zĭng-) *n.* **1.** A transparent, almost pure gelatin prepared from the air bladder of the sturgeon and certain other fishes and used as an adhesive and a clarifying agent. **2.** Mica in thin transparent sheets. [By folk ety. (influenced by GLASS) < obsolete Du. *huizenblas* < MDu. *huusblase* : *huus*, sturgeon + *blase*, bladder; see **bhlē-***.]

I•sis[1] (ī′sĭs) *n. Myth.* An ancient Egyptian goddess of fertility, the sister and wife of Osiris.

I•sis[2] (ī′sĭs). The upper Thames R. in S-central England in the vicinity of Oxford. The name is used locally and in literature.

Is•ken•de•run (ĭs-kĕn′də-ro͞on′, -kĕn′dĕ-ro͞on′). Formerly **Al•ex•an•dret•ta** (ăl′ĭg-zăn-drĕt′ə). A city of S Turkey on an inlet of the E Mediterranean Sea; founded by Alexander the Great c. 333 B.C. Pop. 124,824.

isl. *abbr.* Island.

Is•lam (ĭs-läm′, ĭz-, ĭs′läm′, ĭz′-) *n.* **1.** The monotheistic religion based on the doctrine of submission to God and of Muhammad as the chief and last prophet of God. **2.a.** The people or nations that practice Islam; the Muslim world. **b.** The civilization based on Islam. [Ar. *'islām*, submission < *'aslama*, to surrender, resign oneself < Syriac *'ašlem.*] — **Is•lam′ic** *adj.*

Is•lam•a•bad (ĭs-lä′mə-bäd′, ĭz-lăm′ə-băd′). The cap. of Pakistan, in the NE part NE of Rawalpindi; replaced Karachi as the cap. in 1967. Pop. 201,000.

Is•lam•ism (ĭs′lə-mĭz′əm, ĭz′-) *n. Offensive.* The religious faith, principles, or cause of Islam. — **Is•lam′ist** (-lä′mĭst) *n.*

Is•lam•ize (ĭs′lə-mīz′, ĭz′-) *tr.v.* **-ized, -iz•ing, -iz•es. 1.** To convert to Islam. **2.** To cause to conform to Islamic law or precepts. — **Is′lam•i•za′tion** (-lə-mĭ-zā′shən) *n.*

is•land (ī′lənd) *n.* **1.** A land mass, esp. one smaller than a continent, entirely surrounded by water. **2.** Something resembling an island, esp. in being isolated or surrounded: *islands of people on the empty prairie.* **3.** The superstructure, as of an aircraft carrier. **4.** *Anat.* A cluster of cells differing in structure or function from those in the surrounding tissue. — *tr.v.* **-land•ed, -land•ing, -lands.** To make into or as if into an island; insulate. [Alteration (influenced by ISLE) of ME *ilond* < OE *īegland* : *īg*, *īeg*; see **ak^w-ā-*** + *land*, land; see **lendh-***.]

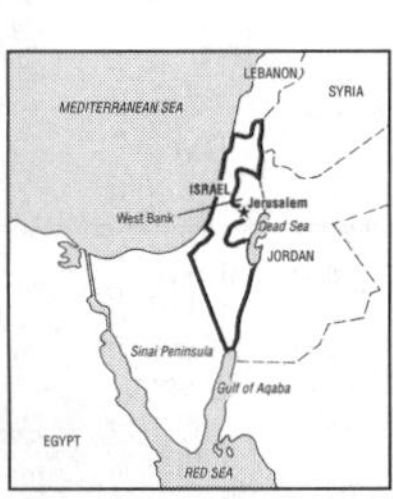

Israel[2]

is•land•er (ī′lən-dər) *n.* An inhabitant of an island.

is•lands of Lang•er•hans (ī′ləndz; läng′ər-häns′) *pl.n.* See **islets of Langerhans.**

Is•la Vis•ta (ī′lə vĭs′tə). A community of S CA on the Pacific Ocean W of Santa Barbara. Pop. 20,395.

Is•lay (ī′lā, ī′lə). An island of the S Inner Hebrides of W Scotland.

isle (īl) *n.* An island, esp. a small one. [ME *ile* < OFr. *isle* < Lat. *īnsula.*]

Isle of (īl). For names of actual isles, see the specific element of the name; for example, **Wight, Isle of.**

Isle Roy•ale (roi′əl). An island of N MI in Lake Superior near the coast of Ontario; named by French fur traders in 1671.

is•let (ī′lĭt) *n.* A very small island.

is•lets of Lang•er•hans (ī′lĭts; läng′ər-häns′) *pl.n.* Irregular clusters of endocrine cells scattered throughout the tissue of the pancreas that secrete insulin and glucagon. [After Paul *Langerhans* (1847–88), German pathologist.]

ism (ĭz′əm) *n. Informal.* A distinctive doctrine, system, or theory. [< –ISM.]

–ism *suff.* **1.** Action, process; practice: *terrorism.* **2.** Characteristic behavior or quality: *heroism.* **3.a.** State; condition; quality: *pauperism.* **b.** State or condition due to an excess of something specified: *strychninism.* **4.** Distinctive or characteristic trait: *Latinism.* **5.a.** Doctrine; theory; system of principles: *pacifism.* **b.** An attitude of prejudice against a given group: *racism.* [ME *-isme* < OFr. < Lat. *-ismus* < Gk. *-ismos*, n. suff.]

Is•ma•i•li (ĭs′mä-ē′lē) also **Is•ma•i•li•an** (-ē′lē-ən) *n.* A member of a branch of Shiism that follows a living imam and is noted for esoteric philosophy. [Ar. *Isma'īlīy*, after *Isma'īl* (d. 760), son of the sixth imam, Jafar (700?–765).]

Is•ma•i•li•a (ĭz′mā-ə-lē′ə, ĭs′-). A city of NE Egypt on the Suez Canal; founded in 1863. Pop. 191,700.

is•n't (ĭz′ənt). Is not.

iso– or **is–** *pref.* **1.** Equal; uniform: *isobar.* **2.** Isomeric: *isopropyl.* [Gk. < *isos*, equal.]

i•so•ag•glu•ti•na•tion (ī′sō-ə-glo͞ot′n-ā′shən) *n.* The agglutination of the red blood cells of an individual by antibodies in the serum of another individual of the same species.

i•so•ag•glu•ti•nin (ī′sō-ə-glo͞ot′n-ĭn) *n.* An isoantibody normally present in the serum of an individual that causes isoagglutination.

i•so•an•ti•bod•y (ī′sō-ăn′tē-bŏd′ē) *n., pl.* **-ies.** An antibody produced by or derived from the same species as the antigen with which it reacts.

i•so•an•ti•gen (ī′sō-ăn′tĭ-jən) *n.* A protein or other antigenic substance present in only some members of a species and therefore able to stimulate antibody production in those members that lack it. — **i′so•an′ti•gen′ic** (-jĕn′ĭk) *adj.*

i•so•bar (ī′sə-bär′) *n.* **1.** A line on a weather map connecting points of equal atmospheric pressure. **2.** Any of two or more kinds of atoms having the same atomic mass but different atomic numbers. [ISO– + Gk. *baros*, weight; see **g^werə-[1]***.] — **i′so•bar′ic** (-bär′ĭk, -băr′-) *adj.*

i•so•chro•mat•ic (ī′sə-krō-măt′ĭk) *adj.* **1.** Having the same color or wavelength. Used of light. **2.** Orthochromatic.

i•soch•ro•nal (ī-sŏk′rə-nəl) or **i•soch•ro•nous** (-nəs) *adj.* **1.** Equal in duration. **2.** Marked by or occurring at equal intervals of time. [< NLat. *isochronus* < Gk. *isokhronos* : *iso-*, iso- + *khronos*, time.] — **i•soch′ro•nal•ly** *adv.* — **i•soch′ro•nism** *n.* — **i•soch′ro•nize′** *tr.v.*

i•soch•ro•ous (ī-sŏk′rō-əs) *adj.* Having the same color throughout. [Gk. *isokhroos* : *iso-*, iso- + *khrōs*, flesh, color.]

i•so•cli•nal (ī′sə-klī′nəl) or **i•so•clin•ic** (-klĭn′ĭk) — *adj.* Having the same magnetic inclination or dip. — *n.* See **isoclinic line.** — **i′so•cli′nal•ly** *adv.*

i•so•cline (ī′sə-klīn′) *n. Geol.* An anticline or a syncline in which the rock beds of the two sides are nearly parallel.

isoclinic line *n.* A line on a map connecting points of equal magnetic dip.

I•soc•ra•tes (ī-sŏk′rə-tēz′). 436–338 B.C. Athenian rhetorician whose letters are a valuable source of Greek thought.

i•so•di•a•met•ric (ī′sō-dī′ə-mĕt′rĭk) *adj.* Having equal diameters or axes.

i•so•dy•nam•ic (ī′sō-dī-năm′ĭk) *adj.* **1.** Having equal force or strength. **2.** Connecting points of equal magnetic intensity.

i•so•e•lec•tric (ī′sō-ĭ-lĕk′trĭk) *adj.* Having equal electric potential.

i•so•e•lec•tron•ic (ī′sō-ĭ-lĕk-trŏn′ĭk, -ē′lĕk-) *adj.* Having equal numbers of electrons or the same electronic configuration.

i•so•en•zyme (ī′sō-ĕn′zīm′) *n.* Any of the chemically distinct forms of an enzyme that perform the same biochemical function. — **i′so•en•zy′mic** *adj.*

i•so•ga•mete (ī′sō-găm′ēt′, -gə-mēt′) *n.* A gamete that has the same size and structure as the one with which it unites.

i•sog•a•my (ī-sŏg′ə-mē) *n., pl.* **-mies.** Reproduction by the fusion or conjugation of isogametes. — **i•sog′a•mous** *adj.*

i•sog•e•nous (ī-sŏj′ə-nəs) *adj.* Having the same or similar origin, as parts derived from the same embryonic tissue.

i•so•gloss (ī′sə-glôs′, -glŏs′) *n.* A geographic boundary line delimiting the area in which a given linguistic feature occurs. [ISO– + Gk. *glōssa*, language, tongue.] — **i′so•gloss′al** *adj.*

i•so•gon (ī′sə-gŏn′) *n.* A polygon whose angles are equal. — **i′so•gon′ic, i•sog′o•nal** (ī-sŏg′ə-nəl) *adj.*

isogonic line *n.* A line on a map connecting points of equal magnetic declination.

i•so•gram (ī′sə-grăm′) *n.* See **isoline.**

i•so•hel (ī′sō-hĕl′) *n.* A line drawn on a map connecting points that receive equal amounts of sunlight. [ISO– + Gk. *hēlios*, sun; see **sāwel-***.]

i•so•hy•et (ī′sō-hī′ĭt) *n.* A line drawn on a map connecting points that receive equal amounts of rainfall. [ISO– + Gk. *huetos*, rain; see **seuə-[2]***.]

i•so•la•ble (ī′sə-lə-bəl) also **i•so•lat•a•ble** (-lā′tə-bəl) *adj.* Possible to isolate: *isolable viruses.*

i•so•late (ī′sə-lāt′) *tr.v.* **-lat•ed, -lat•ing, -lates. 1.** To set apart or cut off from others. **2.** To place in quarantine. **3.** *Chem.* To separate (a substance) out of a combined mixture. **4.** To render free of external influence; insulate. **5.** *Microbiol.* To separate (a pure strain) from a mixed bacterial or fungal culture. — *adj.* (-lĭt, -lāt′). Solitary; alone.

—*n. Microbiol.* An isolated strain. —**i′so•la′tor** *n.*

i•so•lat•ed (ī′sə-lā′tĭd) *adj.* Separated from others; solitary. [< Fr. *isolé* < Ital. *isolato* < Lat. *īnsulātus*, made into an island < *īnsula*, island.]

i•so•la•tion (ī′sə-lā′shən) *n.* **1.** The act of isolating. **2.** The quality or condition of being isolated.

i•so•la•tion•ism (ī′sə-lā′shə-nĭz′əm) *n.* A national policy of abstaining from political or economic relations with other countries. —**i′so•la′tion•ist** *n.*

I•sol•de (ĭ-sōl′də, ĭ-zōl′-) *n.* Var. of **Iseult.**

i•so•leu•cine (ī′sə-lo͞o′sēn′) *n.* An essential amino acid, $C_6H_{13}NO_2$, that is isomeric with leucine.

i•so•line (ī′sə-līn′) *n.* A line on a map, chart, or graph connecting points of equal value.

i•so•mag•net•ic (ī′sō-măg-nĕt′ĭk) *adj.* Of, relating to, or being lines connecting points of equal magnetic force.

i•so•mer (ī′sə-mər) *n.* **1.** *Chem.* Any of two or more substances that are composed of the same elements in the same proportions but differ in properties because of differences in the arrangement of atoms. **2.** *Phys.* Any of two or more nuclei with the same mass number and atomic number but different energy states and radioactive properties. —**i′so•mer′ic** (-mĕr′ĭk) *adj.*

i•som•er•ase (ī-sŏm′ə-rās′) *n.* One of a group of enzymes that catalyzes the conversion of one isomer into another.

i•som•er•ism (ī-sŏm′ə-rĭz′əm) *n.* **1.** The existence of isomers. **2.** The complex of phenomena characteristic of or attributable to isomers. **3.** The state or condition of being an isomer.

i•som•er•ize (ī-sŏm′ə-rīz′) *v.* **-ized, -iz•ing, -iz•es.** —*tr.* To cause to change into an isomeric form. —*intr.* To become changed into an isomeric form. —**i•som′er•i•za′tion** (-ər-ĭ-zā′shən) *n.*

i•som•er•ous (ī-sŏm′ər-əs) *adj.* **1.** Having an equal number of parts, as organs or markings. **2.** Having or being floral whorls with equal numbers of parts.

i•so•met•ric (ī′sə-mĕt′rĭk) also **i•so•met•ri•cal** (-rĭ-kəl) —*adj.* **1.** Of or exhibiting equality in dimensions or measurements. **2.** Of or being a crystal system of three equal axes lying at right angles to each other. **3.** *Physiol.* Of or involving muscular contraction against resistance in which the length of the muscle remains the same. —*n.* A line connecting isometric points. [< Gk. *isometros*, of equal measure : *iso-*, iso- + *metron*, measure; see **mē-²*.**]

i•so•met•rics (ī′sə-mĕt′rĭks) *n. (used with a sing. or pl. v.)* Exercise or a system of exercises in which isometric muscular contraction is used to strengthen and tone muscles.

i•so•me•tro•pi•a (ī′sō-mĭ-trō′pē-ə) *n.* Equality of refraction in both eyes. [Gk. *isometros*, isometric + -OPIA.]

i•som•e•try (ī-sŏm′ĭ-trē) *n.* **1.** Equality of measure. **2.** Equality of elevation above sea level.

i•so•morph (ī′sə-môrf′) *n.* An object, an organism, or a substance exhibiting isomorphism.

i•so•mor•phic (ī′sə-môr′fĭk) *adj.* **1.** *Biol.* Having a similar structure or appearance but being of different ancestry. **2.** Related by an isomorphism.

i•so•mor•phism (ī′sə-môr′fĭz′əm) *n.* **1.** *Biol.* Similarity in form, as in organisms of different ancestry. **2.** *Math.* A one-to-one correspondence between two sets such that an operation on elements of one set corresponds to the analogous operation on their images in the other set. **3.** A close similarity in the crystalline structure of two or more substances of similar chemical composition. —**i′so•mor′phous** *adj.*

i•so•ni•a•zid (ī′sə-nī′ə-zĭd) *n.* A crystalline antibacterial compound, $C_6H_7N_3O$, used in the treatment of tuberculosis. [*isoni(cotinic acid)*, isomer of nicotinic acid (ISO- + NICOTINIC ACID) + *(hydr)azid(e)* (HYDR(O)- + AZ(O)- + -IDE).]

i•so•oc•tane (ī′sō-ŏk′tān′) *n.* A flammable liquid, $(CH_3)_2CHCH_2C(CH_3)_3$, used to determine octane numbers.

i•so•pi•es•tic (ī′sō-pī-ĕs′tĭk, -pē-) *adj.* Marked by or indicating equal pressure; isobaric. —*n.* See **isobar** 1. [ISO- + Gk. *piestos*, able to be compressed (< *piezein*, to press tight; see **sed-***) + -IC.]

i•so•pod (ī′sə-pŏd′) *n.* Any of numerous crustaceans of the order Isopoda, characterized by a flattened body bearing seven pairs of legs. [< NLat. *Isopoda*, order name : ISO- + NLat. *-poda*, -pod.] —**i′so•pod′** *adj.*

i•so•prene (ī′sə-prēn′) *n.* A colorless volatile liquid, C_5H_8, used chiefly to make synthetic rubber. [ISO- + PR(OPYL)ENE.]

i•so•pro•pyl alcohol (ī′sə-prō′pəl) *n.* A clear colorless flammable mobile liquid, $(CH_3)_2CHOH$, used in antifreeze compounds, in lotions and cosmetics, and as a solvent.

i•sos•ce•les (ī-sŏs′ə-lēz′) *adj. Math.* Having two equal sides. [LLat. *īsoscelēs* < Gk. *isoskelēs* : *iso-*, iso- + *skelos*, leg.]

i•so•seis•mic (ī′sə-sīz′mĭk) also **i•so•seis•mal** (-məl) *adj.* Of or exhibiting equal intensity of earthquake shock.

i•sos•mot•ic (ī′sŏz-mŏt′ĭk, -sŏs-) *adj.* Of or exhibiting equal osmotic pressure.

i•so•spin (ī′sə-spĭn′) *n.* A quantum number related to the number of charge states of a baryon or meson. [ISO(TOPIC) + SPIN.]

i•sos•ta•sy (ī-sŏs′tə-sē) *n.* Equilibrium in the earth's crust such that the forces tending to elevate landmasses balance the forces tending to depress landmasses. [ISO- + Gk. *stasis*, a standstill; see **stā-*** + -Y².]

i•so•therm (ī′sə-thûrm′) *n.* A line drawn on a weather map or chart linking all points of equal or constant temperature.

i•so•ther•mal (ī′sə-thûr′məl) *adj.* **1.** Of, relating to, or indicating equal or constant temperatures. **2.** Of or being changes of pressure and volume at constant temperature. **3.** Of or relating to an isotherm. —*n.* An isotherm.

i•so•tone (ī′sə-tōn′) *n.* One of two or more atoms whose nuclei have the same number of neutrons but different numbers of protons. [Alteration of ISOTOPE (with *n* for *neutron* replacing *p* for *proton*).]

i•so•ton•ic (ī′sə-tŏn′ĭk) *adj.* **1.** Of equal tension. **2.** Isosmotic. **3.** Having the same concentration of solutes as the blood. **4.** *Physiol.* Of or involving muscular contraction in which the muscle stays under relatively constant tension while changing length. [ISO- + Gk. *tonos*, tension; see TONE + -IC.] —**i′so•ton′i•cal•ly** *adv.* —**i′so•to•nic′i•ty** (-tə-nĭs′ĭ-tē) *n.*

i•so•tope (ī′sə-tōp′) *n.* One of two or more atoms having the same atomic number but different mass numbers. [ISO- + Gk. *topos*, place (the isotopes of a chemical element occupying the same position in the periodic table of elements).] —**i′so•top′ic** (-tŏp′ĭk) *adj.* —**i′so•top′i•cal•ly** *adv.*

isotopic spin *n.* An isospin.

i•so•tro•pic (ī′sə-trō′pĭk, -trŏp′ĭk) *adj.* Identical in all directions; invariant with respect to direction. —**i•sot′ro•py** (ī-sŏt′rə-pē), **i•sot′ro•pism** (-pĭz′əm) *n.*

i•so•zyme (ī′sə-zīm′) *n.* An isoenzyme. [ISO- + (EN)ZYME.]

Isr. *abbr.* Israel; Israeli.

Is•ra•el¹ (ĭz′rē-əl) *n.* **1.** *Bible.* **a.** Jacob. **b.** The descendants of Jacob. **2.** *Judaism.* The Hebrew people, regarded as the chosen people of God by the covenant of Jacob. [ME < OE < Lat. < Gk. *Israēl* < Heb. *yiśrā'ēl.*]

Is•ra•el² (ĭz′rē-əl). **1.** An ancient kingdom of SW Asia founded by Saul c. 1025 B.C. After 933 it split into the Northern Kingdom, or kingdom of Israel, and the kingdom of Judah to the S. **2.** A country of SW Asia on the E Mediterranean Sea; created in 1948 on recommendation of the United Nations. Cap. Jerusalem. Pop. 4,141,400.

Is•rae•li (ĭz-rā′lē) *n., pl.* **-lis.** A native or inhabitant of modern-day Israel. —**Is•rae′li** *adj.*

Is•ra•el•ite (ĭz′rē-ə-līt′) *n.* **1.** A native or inhabitant of ancient Israel. **2.** A descendant of Jacob; a Jew. **3.** A Jew not descended from the tribe of Levi. **4.** A member of a people regarded as the chosen people of God. —*adj.* also **Is•ra•el•it•ic** (ĭz′rē-ə-lĭt′ĭk). Of or relating to ancient Israel, the ancient Israelites, or their culture.

Is•sa•char (ĭs′ə-kär′). In the Bible, a son of Jacob and Leah and the forebear of one of the tribes of Israel.

is•sei (ēs′sā′) *n., pl.* **issei** or **-seis.** A Japanese immigrant, esp. one to the United States. [J. : *is*, first + *sei*, generation.]

ISSN *abbr.* International Standard Serial Number.

is•su•a•ble (ĭsh′o͞o-ə-bəl) *adj.* **1.** Authorized for issue or to be issued: *issuable currency.* **2.** Open to debate or litigation. **3.** That can be accrued: *issuable profits.*

is•su•ance (ĭsh′o͞o-əns) *n.* **1.** The act of issuing. **2.** An issue.

is•su•ant (ĭsh′o͞o-ənt) *adj.* **1.** *Her.* Being an animal with only the upper part depicted. **2.** *Archaic.* Emerging.

issuant

is•sue (ĭsh′o͞o) *n.* **1.a.** The act or an instance of flowing, passing, or giving out. **b.** The act of circulating, distributing, or publishing by an office or official group. **2.** Something produced, published, or offered, as: **a.** An item or set of items, as stamps or coins, made available at one time by an office or bureau. **b.** A single copy of a periodical. **c.** A distinct set of copies of an edition of a book distinguished from others by print variations. **d.** A final result or conclusion, as a solution to a problem. **e.** Proceeds from estates or fines. **f.** Something proceeding from a specified source. **3.** Offspring; progeny. **4.a.** A point or matter of discussion, debate, or dispute. **b.** A matter of public concern. **c.** The essential point; crux. **d.** A culminating point leading to a decision. **5.** A place of egress; an outlet. **6.** *Pathol.* **a.** A discharge, as of blood or pus. **b.** A lesion, a wound, or an ulcer producing such a discharge. **7.** *Archaic.* Termination; close. —*v.* **-sued, -su•ing, -sues.** —*intr.* **1.** To go or come out. **2.** To accrue as proceeds or profit. **3.** To be born or be descended. **4.** To be circulated or published. **5.** To spring or proceed from a source. See Syns at **stem¹.** **6.** To terminate or result. —*tr.* **1.** To cause to flow out; emit. **2.** To circulate or distribute in an official capacity. **3.** To publish. —***idioms.*** **at issue. 1.** In question; in dispute. **2.** At variance; in disagreement. **join issue. 1.** To enter into controversy. **2.** *Law.* To submit an issue for decision. **take issue.** To take an opposing point of view; disagree. [ME < OFr. *eissue*, *issue* < VLat. **exūta*, alteration of Lat. *exita*, fem. p.part. of *exīre*, to go out : *ex-*, ex- + *īre*, to go; see **ei-*.**] —**is′su•er** *n.*

Is•sus (ĭs′əs). An ancient town of SE Asia Minor; site of Alexander the Great's defeat of Darius III of Persia (333 B.C.).

Is•syk-Kul (ĭs′ĭk-ko͝ol′, ē-sĭ′ko͝ol′). A lake of NE Kirghiz in the Tien Shan near the NW Chinese border.

–ist *suff.* **1.a.** One that performs a specified action: *lobbyist.* **b.** One that produces, makes, operates, plays, or is connected

ă pat	oi boy
ā pay	ou out
âr care	o͝o took
ä father	o͞o boot
ĕ pet	ŭ cut
ē be	ûr urge
ĭ pit	th thin
ī pie	*th* this
îr pier	hw which
ŏ pot	zh vision
ō toe	ə about, item
ô paw	

Stress marks:
′ (primary);
′ (secondary), as in **dictionary** (dĭk′shə-nĕr′ē)

with a specified thing: *novelist.* **2.** A specialist in a specified art, science, or skill: *biologist.* **3.** An adherent or advocate of a specified doctrine, theory, or school of thought: *anarchist.* **4.** One that is characterized by a specified trait or quality: *romanticist.* [ME *-iste* < OFr. < Lat. *-istēs, -ista* < Gk. *-istēs,* agent n. suff.]

Is•tan•bul (ĭs′tăn-bo͞ol′, -tän-, ĭ-stän′bo͞ol). Formerly **Con•stan•ti•no•ple** (kŏn′stăn-tə-nō′pəl). A city of NW Turkey on both sides of the Bosporus at its entrance into the Sea of Marmara. Founded c. 660 B.C. as Byzantium, it was renamed Constantinople in A.D. 330 by Constantine the Great. Istanbul was chosen as the official name in 1930. Pop. 2,772,708.

isth. *abbr.* Isthmus.

isth•mi•an (ĭs′mē-ən) *adj.* **1.** Of, relating to, or forming an isthmus. **2.** Of or relating to the Isthmus of Corinth, esp. to the ancient Pan-Hellenic games held there.

isth•mus (ĭs′məs) *n., pl.* **-mus•es** or **-mi** (-mī′). **1.** A strip of land connecting two larger masses of land. **2.** *Anat.* **a.** A strip of tissue joining two larger organs or parts of an organ. **b.** A narrow passage connecting two larger cavities. [Lat. < Gk. *isthmos.*]

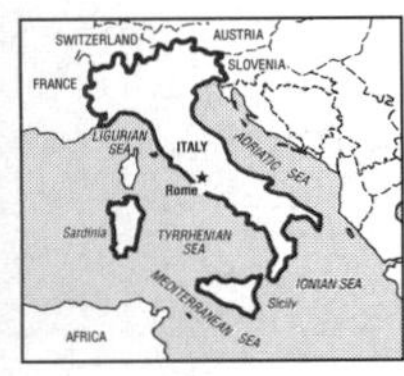

Italy

is•tle also **ix•tle** (ĭs′lē, ĭst′-) *n.* See **pita[2]** 1. [Am.Sp. *ixtle* < Nahuatl *ixtli,* fibrous stem.]

Is•tri•a (ĭs′trē-ə). A peninsula in the NE Adriatic Sea; conquered by Rome in the 2nd cent. A.D. **— Is′tri•an** *adj. & n.*

it (ĭt) *pron.* **1.** Used to refer to that one previously mentioned. Used of a nonhuman entity; an animate being whose sex is unspecified, unknown, or irrelevant; a group of objects or individuals; or an abstraction. **2.** Used as the subject of an impersonal verb: *It is snowing.* **3.a.** Used as an anticipatory subject or object: *Is it certain that they will win?* **b.** Used as an anticipatory subject to emphasize a term that is not itself a subject: *It was on Friday that all the snow fell.* **4.** Used to refer to a general condition or state of affairs: *She couldn't stand it.* **5.** *Informal.* Used to refer to something that is the best, the most desirable, or without equal: *He thinks he's it.* *— n. Games.* A player, as in tag, who attempts to find or catch the other players. [ME < OE *hit.* See **ko-***.]

It. *abbr.* Italian; Italy.

ITA or **I.T.A.** *abbr.* Initial teaching alphabet.

it•a•col•u•mite (ĭt′ə-kŏl′yə-mīt′) *n.* A variety of sandstone that is flexible when cut into thin slabs. [After *Itacolumi* (Itacolomi), a mountain of E-central Brazil.]

ital. *abbr.* **1.** Italic. **2.** Italics.

Ital. *abbr.* Italian.

I•tal•ian (ĭ-tăl′yən) *adj.* Of or relating to Italy or its people, language, or culture. *— n.* **1.a.** A native or inhabitant of Italy. **b.** A person of Italian descent. **2.** The Romance language of the Italians and an official language of Switzerland. **3.** *Midland U.S.* See **submarine** 2. See Regional Note at **submarine.** [ME < Lat. *Italiānus* < *Italia,* Italy.]

I•tal•ian•ate (ĭ-tăl′yə-nāt′, -nĭt) *adj.* Italian in character.

Italian East Af•ri•ca (ăf′rĭ-kə). A former federation (1936–41) of Italian-held territories in E Africa, including Ethiopia and part of present-day Somalia.

I•tal•ian•ism (ĭ-tăl′yə-nĭz′əm) *n.* **1.** An Italian idiom or custom. **2.** A quality characteristic of Italy or its people.

I•tal•ian•ize (ĭ-tăl′yə-nīz′) *v.* **-ized, -iz•ing, -iz•es.** *— tr.* To give an Italian aspect to. *— intr.* To adopt Italian speech or ways. **— I•tal′ian•i•za′tion** (-yə-nĭ-zā′shən) *n.*

Italian sandwich *n. Chiefly Maine.* See **submarine** 2.

Italian So•ma•li•land (sō-mä′lē-lănd′, sə-). A former Italian colony of E Africa; part of Italian East Africa after 1936.

Italian sonnet *n.* See **Petrarchan sonnet.**

ivory
Nigerian belt mask of ivory, metal, and stone

I•tal•ic (ĭ-tăl′ĭk, ī-tăl′-) *adj.* **1.** Of or relating to ancient Italy or its peoples or cultures. **2.** Of or relating to Italic. **3. italic.** Of or being a style of printing type patterned on a Renaissance script with the letters slanting to the right. *— n.* **1.** A branch of the Indo-European language family that includes Latin and other ancient languages. **2.** Italic print or typeface. Often used in the plural. [Lat. *Italicus* < Gk. *Italikos* < *Italia,* Italy < Lat.]

I•tal•i•cism (ĭ-tăl′ĭ-sĭz′əm) *n.* An Italianism, esp. a word or an idiom borrowed from or suggestive of Italian.

i•tal•i•cize (ĭ-tăl′ĭ-sīz′, ī-tăl′-) *tr.v.* **-cized, -ciz•ing, -ciz•es.** **1.** To print in italic type. **2.** To underscore (written matter) with a single line to indicate italics. **3.** To emphasize. **— i•tal′i•ci•za′tion** (-sĭ-zā′shən) *n.*

It•a•ly (ĭt′l-ē). **1.** A peninsula of S Europe projecting into the Mediterranean between the Tyrrhenian and Adriatic seas. **2.** A country of S Europe comprising the peninsula of Italy, Sardinia, Sicily, and several smaller islands; settled by Ligurian peoples and later by Etruscans (before 800 B.C.), who were supplanted by the Latin Romans by 270 B.C. Cap. Rome. Pop. 56,243,935.

I•tas•ca (ī-tăs′kə). A lake of NW MN; identified in 1832 as the source of the Mississippi R.

itch (ĭch) *n.* **1.** An irritating skin sensation causing a desire to scratch. **2.** Any of various skin disorders, such as scabies, marked by intense irritation and itching. **3.** A restless desire or craving for something: *an itch to travel.* *— v.* **itched, itch•ing, itch•es.** *— intr.* **1.a.** To feel, have, or produce an itch. **b.** To have a desire to scratch. **2.** To have a persistent, restless craving. *— tr.* **1.** To cause to itch. **2.** To scratch (an itch). [ME *yicche* < OE *gicce* < *giccan,* to itch.]

itch mite *n.* A parasitic mite *(Sarcoptes scabiei)* that burrows into the skin and causes scabies.

itch•y (ĭch′ē) *adj.* **-i•er, -i•est. 1.** Having or causing an itching sensation. **2.** Restless or nervous. **— itch′i•ness** *n.*

it'd (ĭt′əd). **1.** It would. **2.** It had.

-ite[1] *suff.* **1.** Native or resident of: *New Jerseyite.* **2.a.** Descendant of: *Levite.* **b.** Adherent or follower of: *Luddite.* **3.** A part of an organ, body, or bodily part: *somite.* **4.a.** Rock; mineral: *graphite.* **b.** Fossil: *trilobite.* **5.a.** Product: *metabolite.* **b.** A commercial product: *ebonite.* [ME < OFr. < Lat. *-ītēs, -īta* < Gk. *-ītēs.*]

-ite[2] *suff.* A salt or ester of an acid named with an adjective ending in *-ous: sulfite.* [Alteration of -ATE[2].]

i•tem (ī′təm) *n.* **1.** A single article or unit in a collection, an enumeration, or a series. **2.** A clause of a document, such as a bill. **3.** An entry in an account. **4.a.** A bit of information; a detail. **b.** A short piece in a newspaper or magazine. *— adv.* Also; likewise. Used to introduce each article in an enumeration or a list. *— tr.v.* **i•temed, i•tem•ing, i•tems.** *Archaic.* To compute. [< ME, also, moreover < Lat. See **i-***.]

Syns: *item, detail, particular.* The central meaning shared by these nouns is "an individual, often specialized element of a whole": *a list with numerous items; discussed all the details of their trip; gave the particulars of the accident.*

i•tem•ize (ī′tə-mīz′) *v.* **-ized, -iz•ing, -iz•es.** *— tr.* To set down item by item; list. *— intr.* To list deductions from taxable income on a tax return. **— i′tem•i•za′tion** (ī′tə-mĭ-zā′shən) *n.* **— i′tem•iz′er** *n.*

item veto *n.* Authority, as of a state governor, to reject provisions of a bill individually.

it•er•ance (ĭt′ər-əns) *n.* Iteration.

it•er•ant (ĭt′ər-ənt) *adj.* Marked by iteration; repeating.

it•er•ate (ĭt′ə-rāt′) *tr.v.* **-at•ed, -at•ing, -ates.** To say or perform again; repeat. See Syns at **repeat.** [Lat. *iterāre, iterāt-* < *iterum,* again. See **i-***.]

it•er•a•tion (ĭt′ə-rā′shən) *n.* **1.** The act or an instance of iterating; repetition. **2.** *Math.* A computational procedure in which the desired result is approached through repeated cycles of successively better approximations. **3.** *Comp. Sci.* The process of repeating a set of instructions a specified number of times or until a specific result is achieved.

it•er•a•tive (ĭt′ə-rā′tĭv, -ər-ə-tĭv) *adj.* **1.** Characterized by or involving repetition, recurrence, reiteration, or repetitiousness. **2.** *Gram.* Frequentative.

Ith•a•ca (ĭth′ə-kə). A city of SW-central NY SSW of Syracuse; seat of Cornell University (chartered 1865). Pop. 29,541.

I•thá•ki (ē-thä′kē) also **Ith•a•ca** (ĭth′ə-kə). An island of W Greece in the Ionian Is.; traditional home of Odysseus.

ith•y•phal•lic (ĭth′ə-făl′ĭk) *adj.* **1.** Of or relating to the phallus carried in the ancient festival of Bacchus. **2.** Having the penis erect. Used of graphic and sculptural representations. **3.** Lascivious; salacious. [LLat. *ithyphallicus* < Gk. *ithuphallikos* < *ithuphallos,* erect phallus : *ithus,* straight + *phallos,* phallus; see **bhel-[2]***.]

i•tin•er•an•cy (ī-tĭn′ər-ən-sē, ĭ-tĭn′-) also **i•tin•er•a•cy** (-ə-sē) *n., pl.* **-cies.** A state or system of itinerating, esp. in the role or office of public speaker, minister, or judge.

i•tin•er•ant (ī-tĭn′ər-ənt, ĭ-tĭn′-) *adj.* Traveling from place to place, esp. to perform work or a duty. *— n.* One who is itinerant. [LLat. *itinerāns, itinerant-,* pr.part. of *itinerārī,* to travel < Lat. *iter, itiner-,* journey. See **ei-***.]

i•tin•er•ar•y (ī-tĭn′ə-rĕr′ē, ĭ-tĭn′-) *n., pl.* **-ies. 1.** A route or proposed route of a journey. **2.** An account or a record of a journey. **3.** A guidebook for travelers. *— adj.* **1.** Of or relating to a journey or route. **2.** Traveling from place to place; itinerant. [Ult. < Lat. *itinerārius,* of traveling < Lat. *iter, itiner-,* journey. See **ei-***.]

i•tin•er•ate (ī-tĭn′ə-rāt′, ĭ-tĭn′-) *intr.v.* **-at•ed, -at•ing, -ates.** To travel around. [LLat. *itinerārī, itinerāt-* < Lat. *iter, itiner-,* journey. See ITINERARY.] **— i•tin′er•a′tion** *n.*

-itis *suff.* **1.** Inflammation or disease of: *laryngitis.* **2.** Excessive preoccupation with, indulgence in, reliance on, or possession of the qualities of: *televisionitis.* [Gk., n. suff.]

it'll (ĭt′l). **1.** It will. **2.** It shall.

ITO *abbr.* International Trade Organization.

its (ĭts) *adj.* The possessive form of **it.** Used as a modifier before a noun: *The airline canceled its early flight to New York.* [Alteration of *it's* : IT + -'s.]

Usage Note: *Its,* the possessive form of the pronoun *it,* is never written with an apostrophe. The contraction *it's* (for *it is* or *it has*) is always written with an apostrophe.

it's (ĭts). **1.** It is. **2.** It has. See Usage Note at **its.**

it•self (ĭt-sĕlf′) *pron.* **1.** That one identical with it: **a.** Used reflexively as the direct or indirect object of a verb or the object of a preposition: *The cat scratched itself.* **b.** Used for emphasis: *The trouble is in the machine itself.* **c.** Used in an absolute construction: *Itself no great poem, it still reveals talent.* **2.** Its normal or healthy condition or state: *The car is acting itself again.*

I•tsu•ku•shi•ma (ĭt′sōō-kōō′shĭ-mə). An island of SW Japan in the Inland Sea SW of Hiroshima.

it•ty-bit•ty (ĭt′ē-bĭt′ē) also **it•sy-bit•sy** (ĭt′sē-bĭt′sē) *adj. Informal.* Very small. [Prob. alteration of *little bit.*]

It•u•rae•a (ĭch′ə-rē′ə). An ancient country of NE Palestine; first inhabited by Arabians and later controlled by Judea and Rome. **— It′u•rae′an** *adj. & n.*

I•tur•bi•de (ē′tŏŏr-bē′dā, ē-tŏŏr′vē-*thĕ*), **Agustín de.** 1783–1824. Mexican revolutionary who estab. Mexican independence from Spain (1821) and served as emperor (1822–23).

–ity *suff.* State; quality: *abnormality.* [ME *-itie* < OFr. *-ite* < Lat. *-itās*, var. of *-tās*, -ty.]

IU *abbr.* International unit.

IUD *abbr.* Intrauterine device.

–ium *suff.* Chemical element or group: *californium.* [Alteration of *-um*, neut. suff.]

IV *abbr.* **1.** Intravenous. **2.** Intravenously.

I•van III Va•sil•ie•vich (ī′vən, ē-vän′; və-sĭl′yə-vĭch′). "Ivan the Great." 1440–1505. Grand duke of Muscovy (1462–1505) who laid the foundations for Russian unity.

Ivan IV Vasilievich. "Ivan the Terrible." 1530–84. The first czar of Russia (1547–84), who conducted unsuccessful wars against Sweden and Livonia.

I•va•no-Fran•kovsk (ĭ-vä′nō-fräng-kôfsk′, ē-vä′nə-frŭn-). A city of SW Ukraine SW of Kiev; chartered 1662. Pop. 210,000.

I•va•no•vo (ĭ-vä′nə-və). A city of W-central Russia NE of Moscow. Pop. 474,000.

–ive *suff.* Performing or tending toward a specified action: *demonstrative.* [ME < OFr. < Lat. *-īvus*, adj. suff.]

I've (īv). I have.

Ives (īvz), **Charles Edward.** 1874–1954. Amer. composer whose works include the Third Symphony (1904–11).

Ives, James Merritt. 1824–95. Amer. lithographer best known for his works with Nathaniel Currier.

i•vied (ī′vēd) *adj.* Overgrown or cloaked with ivy.

I•vi•za (ē-bē′sə, ē-vē′thä). See **Ibiza.**

i•vo•ry (ī′və-rē, īv′rē) *n., pl.* **-ries. 1.a.** A hard smooth yellowish-white substance obtained from the tusks of the elephant. **b.** A similar substance forming the tusks or teeth of certain other mammals. **2.** A tusk, esp. an elephant's tusk. **3.** An article made of ivory. **4.** A substance resembling ivory. **5.** *Color.* A pale or grayish yellow to yellowish white. **6.a.** *Mus.* Piano keys. Often used in the plural. **b.** *Games.* Dice. Often used in the plural. **c.** *Slang.* The teeth. Often used in the plural. [ME *ivorie* < OFr. *ivoire, ivurie* < Lat. *eboreus*, of ivory < *ebur, ebor-*, ivory < Coptic *ebou*, elephant < Egypt. *'bw.*] **— i′vo•ry** *adj.*

i•vo•ry-billed woodpecker (ī′və-rē-bĭld′, īv′rē-) *n.* A large, nearly extinct woodpecker *(Campephilus principalis)* of the southern United States and Cuba having black plumage, white wing patches, and an ivory-colored bill.

ivory black *n.* A black pigment prepared from charred ivory.

I•vo•ry Coast (ī′və-rē, īv′rē). A country of W Africa on the Gulf of Guinea; gained independence from France in 1960. Cap. Abidjan. Yamoussoukro was designated the new cap. in 1983. Pop. 7,920,000. **— I•vo′ri•an** (ī-vôr′ē-ən, ī-vōr′-), **I•voir′i•an** (ē-vwär′ē-ən) *adj. & n.*

ivory nut *n.* The seed of the ivory palm, having bony endosperm that is used as a substitute for true ivory.

ivory palm *n.* A stemless unarmed dioecious palm *(Phytelephas macrocarpa)* native to Brazil and Peru.

ivory tower *n.* A place or an attitude of retreat, esp. preoccupation with lofty, remote, or intellectual considerations rather than practical everyday life.

i•vy (ī′vē) *n., pl.* **i•vies.** Any of several woody climbing or trailing evergreen plants of the genus *Hedera* native to the Old World, esp. *H. helix,* having palmately lobed leaves and root-bearing young stems. [ME *ivi* < OE *īfig.*]

I•vy League (ī′vē) *n.* An association of eight universities and colleges in the northeast United States, comprising Brown, Columbia, Cornell, Dartmouth, Harvard, Princeton, the University of Pennsylvania, and Yale. **— Ivy Leaguer** *n.*

IW *abbr.* **1.** Index word. **2.** Isotopic weight.

i.w. *abbr.* Inside width.

I•wa•ki (ĭ-wä′kē). A city of E Honshu, Japan, on the Pacific Ocean NNE of Tokyo. Pop. 350,566.

i•wis also **y•wis** (ĭ-wĭs′) *adv. Archaic.* Certainly; assuredly. [ME < OE *gewis*, certain. See **weid-***.]

I•wo (ē′wō). A city of SW Nigeria ENE of Ibadan; cap. of a Yoruba kingdom from the 17th to the 19th cent. Pop. 255,100.

I•wo Ji•ma (ē′wə jē′mə, ē′wō). The largest of the Volcano Is. of Japan in the NW Pacific Ocean E of Taiwan.

IWW *abbr.* Industrial Workers of the World.

Ix•elles (ēk-sĕl′). A city of central Belgium, a suburb of Brussels. Pop. 76,146.

Ix•i•on (ĭk-sī′ən, ĭk′sē-ŏn′) *n. Gk. Myth.* A king of Thessaly whom Zeus punished for his temerity in seeking Hera's love by having him bound to a revolving wheel in Hades.

ix•tle (ĭs′lē, ĭst′-) *n.* Var. of **istle.**

Iy•yar also **I•yar** (ē-yär′, ē′yär′) *n.* The eighth month of the year in the Jewish calendar. [Heb. *'iyār.*]

–ization or **–isation** *suff.* Action, process, or result of doing or making: *colonization.* [–IZ(E) + –ATION.]

–ize or **–ise** *suff.* **1.a.** To cause to be or to become: *dramatize.* **b.** To cause to conform to or resemble: *Hellenize.* **c.** To treat as: *idolize.* **2.a.** To treat or affect with: *anesthetize.* **b.** To subject to: *tyrannize.* **3.** To treat according to or practice the method of: *pasteurize.* **4.** To become; become like: *materialize.* **5.** To perform, engage in, or produce: *botanize.* [ME *-isen* < OFr. *-iser* < LLat. *-izāre* < Gk. *-izein*, v. suff.]

Usage Note: The suffix *–ize* is a productive means of turning nouns or adjectives into verbs, as in well-established forms such as *formalize* or *criticize.* But the semantic versatility of the suffix can cause ambiguity. Thus *computerize* may mean "to furnish with computers" or "to enter on a computer." The meanings of verbs such as these may be obscure to people who will naturally tend to regard them as jargon. This is one reason that so many words formed with *–ize*, for example, *Americanize,* met with critical resistance when they were first introduced. Although some recent words of this type are unobjectionable, for example, *computerize, institutionalize,* and *radicalize,* many others are associated with bureaucratic and corporate jargon, for example, *accessorize, prioritize, privatize,* and in particular *finalize,* which despite its wide usage was judged unacceptable by 71 percent of the Usage Panel. Coinages of this sort should be used with caution until they have passed the tests of manifest utility and acceptance by reputable writers. See Usage Notes at **finalize, prioritize.**

I•zhevsk (ē-zhĕfsk′, ē-zhĭfsk′). Formerly **U•sti•nov** (ōō-stĭn′ôf). A city of W-central Russia NE of Kazan. Pop. 611,000.

Iz•mir (ĭz-mîr′). Formerly **Smyr•na** (smûr′nə). A city of W Turkey on the **Gulf of Izmir,** an inlet of the Aegean Sea; settled during the Bronze Age. Pop. 757,854.

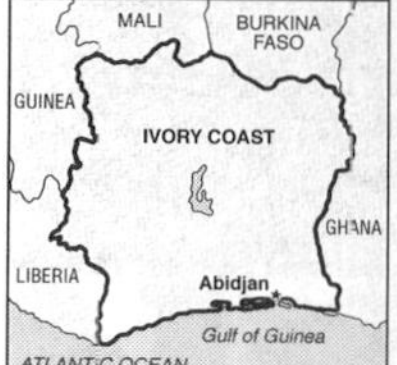

Ivory Coast

ivy

J j

j[1] or **J** (jā) *n., pl.* **j's** or **J's. 1.** The tenth letter of the modern English alphabet. **2.** Any of the speech sounds represented by the letter *j.* **3.** The tenth in a series. **4.** Something shaped like the letter J.

j[2] or **J** *Elect.* The symbol for **current density** 1.

j[3] or **J** *abbr.* Joule.

J *abbr. Games.* Jack.

J. *abbr.* **1.** Japanese. **2.** Or **j.** Journal. **3.** Or **j.** *Law.* Judge. **4.** Or **j.** *Law.* Justice.

JA *abbr.* **1.** Joint account. **2.** Also **J.A.** *Law.* Judge advocate.

jab (jăb) *v.* **jabbed, jab•bing, jabs.** *— tr.* **1.** To poke or thrust abruptly, esp. with something sharp. **2.** To stab or pierce. **3.** To thrust into or against with a rough, abrupt movement. **4.** To punch with short blows. *— intr.* **1.** To make an abrupt poking or thrusting motion. **2.** To deliver a quick punch. *— n.* **1.** A quick stab or blow. **2.** *Sports.* A short straight punch in boxing. [Var. of JOB[2].]

Jab•al•pur (jŭb′əl-pŏŏr′) also **Jub•bul•pore** (-pôr′, -pōr′). A city of central India SSE of Delhi. Pop. 614,162.

jab•ber (jăb′ər) *v.* **-bered, -ber•ing, -bers.** *— intr.* To talk rapidly, unintelligibly, or idly. *— tr.* To utter rapidly or unintelligibly. *— n.* Rapid or babbling talk. [ME *javeren*, of imit. orig.] **— jab′ber•er** *n.*

jab•ber•wock•y (jăb′ər-wŏk′ē) *n.* Nonsensical speech or writing. [< *"Jabberwocky,"* a poem by Lewis Carroll.]

Ja•bir (jā′bər, jä′bîr). See **Geber.**

jab•i•ru (jăb′ə-rōō′) *n.* A large tropical American stork *(Jabiru mycteria)* having white plumage with a pink band at the neck and a naked head. [Port. and Am.Sp. *jabirú.*]

jab•o•ran•di (jăb′ə-răn-dē′, -răn′dē) *n., pl.* **-dis. 1.** Either of two tropical American shrubs *(Pilocarpus jaborandi* or *P. microphyllus)* whose dried leaves yield the medicinal alkaloid pilocarpine. **2.** The dried leaves of these plants. [Port. and Am.Sp.]

ă pat	oi boy
ā pay	ou out
âr care	ŏŏ took
ä father	ōō boot
ĕ pet	ŭ cut
ē be	ûr urge
ĭ pit	th thin
ī pie	*th* this
îr pier	hw which
ŏ pot	zh vision
ō toe	ə about, item
ô paw	

Stress marks:
′ (primary);
′ (secondary), as in
dictionary (dĭk′shə-nĕr′ē)

je•june (jə-jo͞on′) *adj.* **1.** Not interesting; dull. **2.** Lacking maturity; childish. **3.** Lacking in nutrition. [< Lat. *iēiūnus*, meager, dry, fasting.] **—je•june′ly** *adv.* **—je•june′ness** *n.*

je•ju•num (jə-jo͞o′nəm) *n., pl.* **-na** (-nə). The section of the small intestine between the duodenum and the ileum. [ME < Med.Lat. *iēiūnum (intestīnum)*, fasting (intestine) (in dissection always being found empty), neut. of Lat. *iēiūnus*.]

Je•kyll and Hyde (jĕk′əl, jē′kəl; hīd′) *n. Informal.* One who has a dual personality that alternates between phases of good and evil behavior. [After *The Strange Case of Dr. Jekyll and Mr. Hyde* by Robert Louis Stevenson.]

Je•le•nia Gó•ra (yā-lĕn′yə go͝or′ə, yĕ-lĕ′nyä go͞o′rä). A city of SW Poland WSW of Poznań; chartered 1312. Pop. 90,400.

jell (jĕl) *v.* **jelled, jell•ing, jells.** *—intr.* **1.** To become firm or gelatinous; congeal. **2.** To take shape or fall into place; crystallize. *—tr.* **1.** To cause to become firm or gelatinous. **2.** To cause to take shape; make clear and definite; crystallize. [Prob. back-formation < JELLY.]

jel•la•ba (jə-lä′bə) *n.* Var. of **djellaba.**

Jel•li•coe (jĕl′ĭ-kō′), **John Rushworth.** 1st Earl Jellicoe. 1859–1935. British naval officer who commanded the fleet that fought the Germans at Jutland (1916).

jel•lied (jĕl′ēd) *adj.* **1.** Chilled or otherwise congealed into jelly. **2.** Coated with jelly. **3.** Prepared or cooked in or with jelly.

jel•li•fy (jĕl′ə-fī′) *intr. & tr.v.* **-fied, -fy•ing, -fies.** To become or make into jelly.

Jell-O (jĕl′ō). A trademark used for a gelatin dessert.

jel•ly (jĕl′ē) *n., pl.* **-lies. a.** A soft, semisolid food substance with a resilient consistency, esp. one made of fruit juice containing pectin boiled with sugar. **b.** Something, such as a petroleum ointment, having this consistency. *—v.* **-lied, -ly•ing, -lies.** *—tr.* To cause to have the consistency of jelly. *—intr.* To acquire the consistency of jelly. [ME *gelee* < OFr. < VLat. **gelāta* < Lat., fem. p.part. of *gelāre*, to freeze. See **gel-*.**]

jel•ly•bean (jĕl′ē-bēn′) *n.* A small ovoid candy with a hardened sugar coating over a chewy center.

jel•ly•fish (jĕl′ē-fĭsh′) *n., pl.* **jellyfish** or **-fish•es. 1.a.** Any of numerous marine coelenterates of the class Scyphozoa, existing as a gelatinous, tentacled, often bell-shaped medusa for most of its life cycle. **b.** Any of various similar or related coelenterates. **2.** *Informal.* One who lacks force of character; a weakling.

jel•ly•roll (jĕl′ē-rōl′) *n.* A thin sheet of sponge cake layered with jelly and then rolled up.

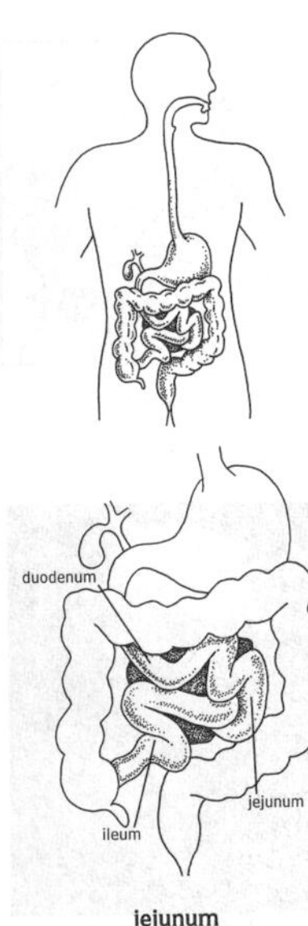

jejunum

jem•my (jĕm′ē) *n. & v. Chiefly British.* Var. of **jimmy².**

Je•na (yā′nə). A city of central Germany SW of Leipzig; site of Napoleon I's defeat of the Prussians (1806). Pop. 106,555.

je ne sais quoi (zhə′ nə sā kwä′, sĕ) *n.* A quality or an attribute that is difficult to describe or express. [Fr. : *je*, I + *ne*, not + *sais*, know + *quoi*, what.]

Jen•ghis Khan or **Jen•ghiz Khan** (jĕn′gĭz kän′, -gĭs, jĕng′-). See **Genghis Khan.**

Jen•i•son (jĕn′ĭ-sən). A community of W-central MI, a suburb of Grand Rapids. Pop. 17,882.

Jen•ner (jĕn′ər), **Edward.** 1749–1823. British physician who discovered that smallpox could be prevented by inoculation with the substance from cowpox lesions.

jen•net also **gen•et** (jĕn′ĭt) *n.* A small Spanish saddle horse. [ME *genet* < OFr. < Catalan *ginet* < Ar. *zinēti* < colloquial Ar. *Zenetī*, a Berber tribe famed for horsemanship.]

jen•ny (jĕn′ē) *n., pl.* **-nies. 1.** The female of certain animals, esp. the donkey and the wren. **2.** A spinning jenny. [< the name *Jenny*.]

Jen•sen (yĕn′sən, jĕn′-), **Johannes Vilhelm.** 1873–1950. Danish writer who won the 1944 Nobel Prize for literature.

jeop•ard•ize (jĕp′ər-dīz′) *tr.v.* **-ized, -iz•ing, -izes.** To expose to loss or injury; imperil. See Syns at **endanger.**

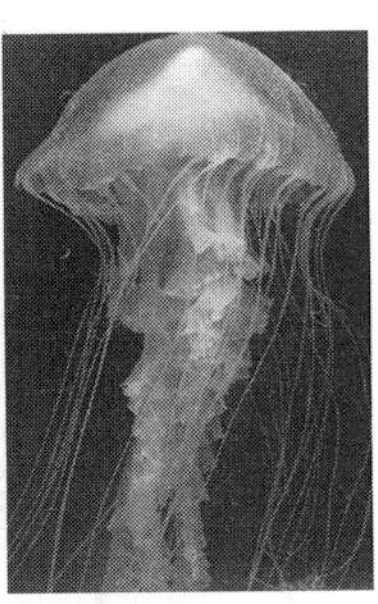
jellyfish
Sea nettle
Chrysaora quinquecirrha

jeop•ard•y (jĕp′ər-dē) *n., pl.* **-ies. 1.** Risk of loss or injury; peril or danger. **2.** *Law.* A defendant's risk or danger of conviction when put on trial. [ME *juperti* < OFr. *jeu parti*, even game, uncertainty : *jeu*, game (< Lat. *iocus*, joke, game; see **yek-***) + *parti*, p.part. of *partir*, to divide (< Lat. *partire* < *pars*, *part-*, part; see PART).]

Je•qui•tin•hon•ha (zhə-kēt′n-yōn′yə, zhĭ-kwē′tĭ-nyô′nyä). A river of E Brazil flowing c. 805 km (500 mi) to the Atlantic.

Jer. *abbr. Bible.* Jeremiah.

jer•bo•a (jər-bō′ə) *n.* Any of various small nocturnal rodents of the family Dipodidae of Asia and northern Africa, having long hind legs. [Med.Lat. *jerbōa* < Ar. *jarbū'*, loin flesh.]

jer•e•mi•ad (jĕr′ə-mī′əd) *n.* A literary work or speech expressing a bitter lament or a righteous prophecy of doom. [Fr. *jérémiade*, after *Jérémie*, Jeremiah, author of Lamentations.]

Jer•e•mi•ah (jĕr′ə-mī′ə) *n. Bible.* **1.** A Hebrew prophet of the 7th and 6th cent. B.C. **2.** See table at **Bible.** [Heb. *Yirmĕyāhû*.]

Je•rez (hĕ-rĕs′, -rĕth′) also **Jerez de la Fron•te•ra** (də lä frŭn-tĕr′ə, *thĕ* lä frôn-tĕ′rä). A city of SW Spain NE of Cádiz; held by the Moors from 711 to 1264. Pop. 138,700.

Jer•i•cho (jĕr′ĭ-kō′). An ancient city of Palestine near the NW shore of the Dead Sea.

Jersey
Jersey cow

jerk¹ (jûrk) *v.* **jerked, jerk•ing, jerks.** *—tr.* **1.** To give a sudden quick thrust, push, pull, or twist to. **2.** To throw or toss with a quick abrupt motion. **3.** To utter abruptly or sharply: *jerked out a sob.* **4.** To make and serve (ice-cream sodas, for example) at a soda fountain. *—intr.* **1.** To move in sudden abrupt motions; jolt. **2.** To make spasmodic motions. *—n.* **1.** A sudden abrupt motion, such as a yank. **2.** A jolting or lurching motion. **3.** *Physiol.* A sudden reflexive or spasmodic muscular movement. **4. jerks.** Involuntary convulsive twitching often resulting from excitement. Often used with *the.* **5.** *Slang.* A dull, stupid, or fatuous person. **6.** *Sports.* A lift in which the weight is heaved overhead from shoulder height with a quick motion. ***—phrasal verb.* jerk off.** *Vulgar Slang.* To masturbate. [?] **—jerk′er** *n.* **—jerk′ing•ly** *adv.*

jerk² (jûrk) *tr.v.* **jerked, jerk•ing, jerks.** To cut (meat) into long strips and dry in the sun or cure by exposing to smoke. *—adj.* Being or relating to a method of barbecuing meat that has been seasoned and wrapped in leaves of the allspice tree: *jerk chicken.* [Back-formation < JERKY².]

jer•kin (jûr′kĭn) *n.* **1.** A hip-length collarless and sleeveless jacket, worn over a doublet by men esp. in the 16th century. **2.** A short close-fitting, often sleeveless coat or jacket. [?]

jerk•wa•ter (jûrk′wô′tər, -wŏt′ər) *adj. Informal.* **1.** Remote, small, and insignificant: *a jerkwater town.* **2.** Contemptibly trivial: *jerkwater notions.* [< *jerkwater*, a branch-line train, so called because its small boiler had to be refilled often, requiring train crews to "jerk" or draw water from streams.]

jerk•y¹ (jûr′kē) *adj.* **-i•er, -i•est. 1.** Marked by jerks or jerking. **2.** *Slang.* Foolish. **—jerk′i•ly** *adv.* **—jerk′i•ness** *n.*

jerk•y² (jûr′kē) *n.* Jerked meat. [Alteration of CHARQUI.]

jer•o•bo•am (jĕr′ə-bō′əm) *n.* A wine bottle holding ⅘ of a gallon (3.03 liters). [After *Jeroboam I* (d. c. 901 B.C.), king of N Israel.]

Je•rome (jə-rōm′), Saint. 340?–420? Latin scholar who produced the *Vulgate*, a Latin translation of the Bible.

Jer•ry (jĕr′ē) *n., pl.* **-ries.** *Chiefly British.* A German, esp. a German soldier. [Alteration of GERMAN.]

jer•ry•build (jĕr′ē-bĭld′) *tr.v.* **-built** (-bĭlt′), **-build•ing, -builds.** To build shoddily and cheaply. [< dial. *jerry*, defective, perh. < the name *Jerry*.] **—jer′ry•build′er** *n.*

jer•sey (jûr′zē) *n., pl.* **-seys. 1.a.** A soft plain-knitted fabric. **b.** A garment made of this fabric. **2.** A close-fitting knitted pullover. **3.** Often **Jersey.** Any of a breed of fawn-colored dairy cattle developed on the island of Jersey. [After JERSEY.]

Jersey. The largest of the Channel Is. in the English Channel; annexed by the Normans in 933 and autonomous since 1204.

Jersey City. A city of NE NJ on the Hudson R. opposite Lower Manhattan; settled by the Dutch before 1650. Pop. 228,537.

Je•ru•sa•lem (jə-ro͞o′sə-ləm, -zə-). The cap. of Israel, in the E-central part in the West Bank; occupied as early as the 4th millennium B.C. Jerusalem is considered a holy city by Jews, Muslims, and Christians. Pop. 446,500.

Jerusalem artichoke *n.* **1.** A North American sunflower *(Helianthus tuberosus)* having yellow rayed flower heads and edible tubers. **2.** The edible tuber of this plant. [By folk ety. < obsolete Ital. *girasole*, sunflower. See GIRASOL.]

Jerusalem cherry *n.* An Old World ornamental shrub *(Solanum pseudocapsicum)* having inedible scarlet or yellow fruit.

Jerusalem oak *n.* A sticky Old World weed *(Chenopodium botrys)* having lobed leaves and a turpentinelike odor.

Jerusalem thorn *n.* A spiny tropical American tree *(Parkinsonia aculeata)* having bipinnately compound leaves.

Jes•per•sen (yĕs′pər-sən), **(Jens) Otto (Harry).** 1860–1943. Danish philologist noted for his contributions to phonetics and the teaching of languages.

jess (jĕs) *n.* A short strap fastened around the leg of a hawk or other bird, to which a leash may be fastened. *—tr.v.* **jessed, jess•ing, jess•es.** To put jesses or a jess on (a hawk, for example). [ME *ges* < OFr., pl. of *jet*, something thrown, ult. < Lat. *iactus*, p.part. of *iacere*, to throw. See **yē-*.**]

jes•sa•mine (jĕs′ə-mĭn) *n.* Var. of **jasmine.**

Jes•se (jĕs′ē). The father of King David and progenitor of the line of Jesus.

jest (jĕst) *n.* **1.** A playful or amusing act; a prank. **2.** A frolicsome or frivolous mood: *spoken in jest.* **3.** An object of ridicule; a laughingstock. **4.** A witty remark. *—v.* **jest•ed, jest•ing, jests.** *—intr.* **1.** To act or speak playfully. **2.** To make witty remarks. **3.** To utter scoffs; gibe. *—tr.* To make fun of; ridicule. [ME *geste*, tale < OFr. < Lat. *gesta*, deeds < neut. pl. p.part. of *gerere*, to perform.] **—jest′ing•ly** *adv.*

jest•er (jĕs′tər) *n.* **1.** One given to jesting. **2.** A fool or buffoon at medieval courts.

Jes•u•it (jĕzh′o͞o-ĭt, jĕz′o͞o-, -yo͞o-) *n.* **1.** *Rom. Cath. Ch.* A member of the Society of Jesus, an order founded by Ignatius of Loyola in 1534. **2.** Often **jesuit.** One given to subtle casuistry. [Fr. *Jésuite* < *Jésus*, Jesus.] **—Jes′u•it′i•cal** *adj.* **—Jes′u•it′i•cal•ly** *adv.*

Jes•u•it's bark (jĕzh′o͞o-ĭts, jĕz′o͞o-, -yo͞o-) *n.* See **cinchona** 2. [First known to Europeans through Jesuit missions in Peru.]

Je•sus (jē′zəs). A teacher and prophet who lived in the 1st cent. of this era and whose life and teachings form the basis of Christianity.

jet¹ (jĕt) *n.* **1.** A dense black coal that takes a high polish and is used for jewelry. **2.** *Color.* A deep black. *—adj.* **1.** Made of or resembling jet. **2.** Black as coal: *jet hair.* [ME < AN *geet* < Lat. *gagātēs* < Gk. *gagatēs,* after *Gagas,* a town of Lycia.]

jet[2] (jĕt) *n.* **1.a.** A high-velocity fluid stream forced out of a small-diameter opening or nozzle. **b.** An outlet used for emitting such a stream. **c.** Something emitted in or as if in a high-velocity fluid stream. **2.a.** A jet-propelled vehicle, esp. an aircraft. **b.** A jet engine. — *v.* **jet•ted, jet•ting, jets.** — *intr.* **1.** To travel by jet aircraft. **2.** To move very quickly. — *tr.* To propel outward or squirt, as under pressure. [Fr. < OFr. < *jeter,* to spout forth, throw < VLat. **iectāre,* alteration of Lat. *iactāre,* freq. of *iacere,* to throw. See **yē-*.**] —**jet′ful′** *n.*

jet boat *n. Naut.* A boat propelled by a powerful jet of water.

je•té (zhə-tā′) *n.* A leap in ballet in which the weight is transferred from one foot to the other. [Fr. < p.part. of *jeter,* to throw < OFr. See JET[2].]

jet engine *n.* An engine that develops thrust by ejecting a jet, esp. of gaseous combustion products.

jet•fight•er or **jet fighter** (jĕt′fī′tər) *n.* A jet-propelled fighter aircraft.

jet•foil (jĕt′foil′) *n. Naut.* A passenger-carrying hydrofoil that is propelled by a jet engine. [JET[2] + (HYDRO)FOIL.]

jet lag also **jet•lag** (jĕt′lăg′) *n.* A temporary disruption of body rhythms typically caused by high-speed travel across several time zones in a jet aircraft. —**jet′-lagged′** *adj.*

jet•lin•er (jĕt′lī′nər) *n.* A large passenger-carrying jet airplane.

jet•port (jĕt′pôrt′, -pōrt′) *n.* An airport for jet aircraft.

jet-pro•pelled (jĕt′prə-pĕld′) *adj.* Driven by jet propulsion.

jet propulsion *n.* Propulsion derived from the rearward expulsion of matter in a jet stream, esp. by jet engines.

jet•sam (jĕt′səm) *n.* **1.** Cargo or equipment thrown overboard to lighten a ship in distress. **2.** Discarded cargo or equipment found washed ashore. See Usage Note at **flotsam. 3.** Discarded odds and ends. [< earlier *jetson,* alteration of ME *jetteson,* a throwing overboard. See JETTISON.]

jet set *n.* An international social set made up of wealthy people who travel from one fashionable place to another. —**jet′-set′** (jĕt′sĕt′), **jet′-set′ting** (-sĕt′ĭng) *adj.* —**jet setter** *n.*

Jet Ski (jĕt). A trademark used for a jet-propelled recreational watercraft for one or two persons.

jet stream *n.* **1.** A high-speed meandering wind current, generally from a westerly direction at speeds often exceeding 400 kilometers (250 miles) per hour at altitudes of 15 to 25 kilometers (10 to 15 miles). **2.** A high-speed stream; a jet.

jet•ti•son (jĕt′ĭ-sən, -zən) *tr.v.* **-soned, -son•ing, -sons. 1.** To cast overboard or off. **2.** *Informal.* To discard (something) as unwanted or burdensome. — *n.* **1.** The act of discarding or casting overboard. **2.** Jetsam. [< ME *jetteson,* throwing jetsam < AN *getteson* < VLat. **iectātiō, iectātiōn-* < **iectātus,* p.part. of **iectāre,* to throw. See JET[2].]

jet•ty[1] (jĕt′ē) *n., pl.* **-ties. 1.** A structure, such as a pier, that projects into a body of water to influence the current or protect a harbor, for example. **2.** A wharf. [ME *getti, jettie* < OFr. *jetee* < fem. p.part. of *jeter,* to project, throw. See JET[2].]

jet•ty[2] (jĕt′ē) *adj.* **1.** Resembling jet, as in texture. **2.** Of the color jet; black. —**jet′ti•ness** *n.*

jeu•nesse do•rée (zhœ-nĕs′ dô-rā′) *n.* Fashionable and wealthy young people. [Fr. : *jeunesse,* youth + *dorée,* gilded.]

Jev•ons (jĕv′ənz), **William Stanley.** 1835–1882. British economist who codeveloped the marginal utility theory (published 1886), which explains the value of goods and services in terms of the subjective valuation of consumers.

Jew (jo͞o) *n.* **1.** A member by birth or conversion of the people tracing their descent from the ancient Hebrews and characterized by the religion and cultural heritage of Judaism. **2.** A native or inhabitant of the ancient kingdom of Judah. [ME *Jeu* < OFr. *giu* < Lat. *Iūdaeus* < Gk. *Ioudaios* < Aram. *yĕhûdāy* < Heb. *yĕhûdî,* after *yĕhûdâ,* Judah, son of Jacob and Leah.]

Usage Note: It is widely recognized that the attributive use of the noun *Jew,* in phrases such as *Jew lawyer* or *Jew ethics,* is both offensive and vulgar. In such contexts *Jewish* is the only acceptable possibility. But some people have become so wary of this construction that they avoid any use of the noun, a practice that carries risks of its own. In a sentence such as *There are now several Jews on the council,* which is unexceptionable, the substitution of a circumlocution like *Jewish people* or *persons of Jewish background* may unwittingly suggest an unwarranted and hence suspect delicacy.

jew•el (jo͞o′əl) *n.* **1.a.** A precious stone; a gem. **b.** A small natural or artificial gem used as a bearing in a watch. **2.** A costly ornament of precious metal or gems. **3.** One that is treasured or esteemed. — *tr.v.* **-eled, -el•ing, -els** or **-elled, -el•ling, -els. 1.** To adorn with jewels. **2.** To fit with jewels. [ME *juel* < AN, perh. < VLat. **iocāle* < neut. of **iocālis,* of play < Lat. *iocus,* joke. See **yek-*.**]

jew•el•er also **jew•el•ler** (jo͞o′ə-lər) *n.* One that makes, repairs, or deals in jewelry.

jew•el•fish (jo͞o′əl-fĭsh′) *n., pl.* **jewelfish** or **-fish•es.** A small, brilliantly colored freshwater fish *(Hemichromis bimaculatus)* of tropical Africa, popular in home aquariums.

jew•el•ry (jo͞o′əl-rē) *n.* Ornaments, such as bracelets or rings, made of precious metals set with gems or imitation gems.

jew•el•weed (jo͞o′əl-wēd′) *n.* Any of several plants of the genus *Impatiens* having yellowish spurred flowers and seedpods that dehisce into five valves when mature.

Jew•ess (jo͞o′ĭs) *n. Offensive.* A Jewish woman or girl.

Usage Note: The word *Jewess* has come to be widely regarded as offensive, since it seems to imply that the conjunction of Jewishness and female sex is sufficient to establish a distinct racial or social category. Where reference to gender is relevant, the phrase *Jewish woman* can be used.

Jew•ett (jo͞o′ĭt), **Sarah Orne.** 1849–1909. Amer. writer whose works include *The Country of the Pointed Firs* (1896).

jew•fish (jo͞o′fĭsh′) *n., pl.* **jewfish** or **-fish•es.** Any of several large marine fishes of the family Serranidae, esp. the grouper *Epinephelus itajara* of tropical waters.

Jew•ish (jo͞o′ĭsh) *adj.* Of or relating to the Jews or their culture or religion. See Usage Note at **Jew.** —**Jew′ish•ly** *adv.* —**Jew′ish•ness** *n.*

Jewish calendar *n.* The lunisolar calendar used to mark the events of the Jewish year, dating the creation of the world to 3761 B.C.

Jew•ry (jo͞o′rē) *n.* **1.** The Jewish people. **2.** A section of a medieval city inhabited by Jews.

jew's-harp also **jews'-harp** (jo͞oz′härp′) *n. Mus.* A small instrument consisting of a lyre-shaped metal frame held between the teeth and a projecting steel tongue that is plucked to produce a soft twanging sound.

jez•e•bel (jĕz′ə-bĕl′, -bəl) *n.* An evil and scheming woman.

Jez•e•bel (jĕz′ə-bĕl′). fl. 9th cent. B.C. Phoenician princess and queen of Israel, who according to the Bible encouraged idolatry.

jg *abbr.* Junior grade.

Jg. *abbr. Bible.* Judges.

Jhan•si (jän′sē). A city of N-central India SSE of Delhi. Pop. 246,172.

Jhe•lum (jā′ləm). A river, c. 772 km (480 mi), of N India and NE Pakistan; one of the five rivers of the Punjab.

JHVH or **JHWH** (yo͝od′hä′väv′hä′, yä′wā, yä′wĕ) *n.* Var. of **YHWH.**

Jia•ling also **Chia-ling** (jyä′lĭng′) or **Kia•ling** (kyä′-, jyä′-). A river, c. 965 km (600 mi), of central China flowing to the Chang Jiang (Yangtze River) at Chongqing.

Jia•mu•si (jyä′mo͞o′sē′, -mü′-) also **Chia•mus•su** (-mo͞o′-so͞o′) or **Kia•mu•sze** (kyä′mo͞o′so͞o′). A city of NE China ENE of Harbin. Pop. 350,000.

Jiang•su (jyäng′so͞o′, -sü′) also **Kiang•su** (kyäng′-). A province of E China bordering on the Yellow Sea. Cap. Nanjing. Pop. 62,130,000.

Jiang•xi (jyäng′shē′) also **Kiang•si** (kyäng′-). A province of SE China. Cap. Nanchang. Pop. 34,600,000.

jiao (jyou) also **chiao** (chyou) *n., pl.* **jiao** also **chiao.** See table at **currency.** [Chin. *jiăo,* one tenth of a dollar.]

jib[1] (jĭb) *n.* **1.** *Naut.* A triangular sail stretching from the foretopmast head to the jib boom and in small craft from the foremost mast to the bowsprit or stem. **2.a.** The arm of a mechanical crane. **b.** The boom of a derrick. [?]

jib[2] (jĭb) *intr.v.* **jibbed, jib•bing, jibs.** To stop short and turn restively from side to side; balk. [?] —**jib′ber** *n.*

jib boom *n. Naut.* A spar forming a continuation of the bowsprit.

jibe[1] also **gybe** (jīb) *Naut.* — *v.* **jibed, jib•ing, jibes** also **gybed, gyb•ing, gybes.** — *intr.* To shift a fore-and-aft sail from one side of a vessel to the other while sailing before the wind so as to sail on the opposite tack. — *tr.* To cause (a sail) to jibe. — *n.* The act of jibing. [Alteration (perh. influenced by JIB[1]) of *gybe* < obsolete Du. *gijben.*]

jibe[2] (jīb) *intr.v.* **jibed, jib•ing, jibes.** *Informal.* To be in accord; agree: *Your figures jibe with mine.* [?]

jibe[3] (jīb) *v. & n.* Var. of **gibe.**

ji•ca•ma (hē′kə-mə, hĭk′ə-) *n.* A crisp sweet turnip-shaped root vegetable used raw in salads or cooked in stews. [Am.Sp. *jícama* < Nahuatl *xicamatl.*]

Ji•ca•ril•la (hē′kə-rē′yə, -rēl′yə) *n., pl.* **Jicarilla** or **-las.** A member of an Apache tribe formerly inhabiting southeast Colorado and northern New Mexico and ranging eastward to the Great Plains, with a present-day population in northern New Mexico. [Am.Sp. *(Apaches de la) Jicarilla,* (Apaches of the) Jicarilla, prob. dim. of *jícara,* chocolate-cup (from the shape of a local hill), perh. < Nahuatl *xicalli,* gourd.]

Jid•da (jĭd′ə). A city of W-central Saudi Arabia on the Red Sea. Pop. 1,300,000.

jiff (jĭf) *n. Informal.* A jiffy.

jif•fy (jĭf′ē) *n., pl.* **jif•fies.** *Informal.* A short space of time; a moment. [?]

jig (jĭg) *n.* **1.a.** Any of various lively dances in triple time. **b.** The music for such a dance. **2.** A joke or trick. **3.** A typically metal fishing lure with one or more hooks, usu. deployed with a jiggling motion. **4.** An apparatus for cleaning or separating crushed ore by agitation in water. **5.** A device for guiding a tool or for holding machine work in place. — *v.* **jigged, jig•ging, jigs.** — *intr.* **1.** To dance or play a jig. **2.** To move or bob up and down jerkily and rapidly. **3.** To operate a jig.

Jerusalem artichoke
Helianthus tuberosus

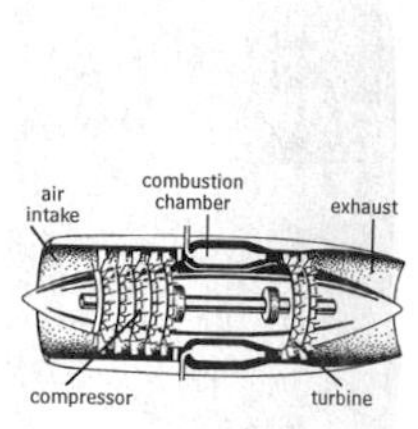

jet engine
Cutaway view of a turbojet engine

ă pat · ā pay · âr care · ä father · ĕ pet · ē be · ĭ pit · ī pie · îr pier · ŏ pot · ō toe · ô paw · oi boy · ou out · o͝o took · o͞o boot · ŭ cut · ûr urge · th thin · *th* this · hw which · zh vision · ə about, item

Stress marks:
′ (primary);
′ (secondary), as in
dictionary (dĭk′shə-nĕr′ē)

time required for a trip. **2.** A process or course likened to traveling; a passage. —*v.* **-neyed, -ney•ing, -neys.** —*intr.* To make a journey; travel. —*tr.* To travel over or through. [ME *journei,* day, day's travel, journey < OFr. *jornee* < VLat. **diurnāta* < LLat. *diurnum,* day < neut. of Lat. *diurnus,* of a day < *diēs,* day. See DIARY.] —**jour′ney•er** *n.*

journey cake *n. New England.* See **johnnycake.** See Regional Note at **johnnycake.** [Perh. by folk ety. < *jonakin.* See JOHNNYCAKE.]

jour•ney•man (jûr′nē-mən) *n.* **1.** One who has fully served an apprenticeship in a trade or craft and is a qualified worker in another's employ. **2.** An experienced and competent but undistinguished worker. [ME *journeiman* : *journei,* a day's work; see JOURNEY + *man,* man; see MAN.]

jour•ney•work (jûr′nē-wûrk′) *n.* The work of a journeyman.

joust (joust, jŭst, jo͞ost) also **just** (jŭst) —*n.* **1.a.** A combat between two mounted knights or men-at-arms using lances; a tilting match. **b. jousts.** A series of tilting matches; a tournament. **2.** A personal competition or combat suggestive of combat with lances. —*intr.v.* **joust•ed, joust•ing, jousts** also **just•ed, just•ing, justs. 1.** To engage in a joust. **2.** To engage in a personal combat or competition. [ME < OFr. *juste* < *juster,* to joust < VLat. **iuxtāre,* to be next to < Lat. *iuxtā,* close by. See **yeug-*.**] —**joust′er** *n.*

James Joyce

Jove (jōv) *n. Rom. Myth.* See **Jupiter** 1. —***idiom.* by Jove.** Used as a mild oath to express surprise or emphasis. [ME < OLat. *Iovis* or < Lat. *Iov-,* stem of *Iuppiter.* See **deiw-*.**]

jo•vi•al (jō′vē-əl) *adj.* Marked by hearty conviviality and good cheer. [Fr., prob. < Ital. *giovale* < OItal., of Jupiter (the source of happiness) < LLat. *Iovālis* < Lat. *Iovis,* Jupiter. See **deiw-*.**] —**jo′vi•al′i•ty** (-ăl′ĭ-tē) *n.* —**jo′vi•al•ly** *adv.*

Jo•vi•an[1] (jō′vē-ən). A.D. 331?–364. Emperor of Rome (363–364) who made peace with the Persians by giving up all Roman territories beyond the Tigris R.

Jo•vi•an[2] (jō′vē-ən) *adj.* **1.** *Rom. Myth.* Of, relating to, or resembling Jupiter. **2.** Of or resembling the planet Jupiter.

Jovian planet *n.* One of the four large, outer planets, Jupiter, Saturn, Uranus, and Neptune.

Jow•ett (jou′ĭt), **Benjamin.** 1817–93. British classical scholar known for his translations of Plato and Aristotle.

jowl[1] (joul) *n.* **1.** The jaw, esp. the lower jaw. **2.** The cheek. [ME *chavel, chaule, jaule* (influenced by *joue,* jaw or *jol,* head) < OE *ceafl.*]

jowl[2] (joul) *n.* **1.** The flesh under the lower jaw, esp. when plump or flaccid. **2.** A fleshy part similar to a jowl, such as the wattle of a fowl. [Alteration of ME *cholle* (influenced by ME *joue,* jaw or *jol,* head).]

jowl•y (jou′lē) *adj.* **-i•er, -i•est.** Having heavy or sagging jowls. —**jowl′i•ness** *n.*

joy (joi) *n.* **1.a.** Intense and ecstatic or exultant happiness. **b.** The expression or manifestation of such feeling. **2.** A source or an object of pleasure or satisfaction. —*v.* **joyed, joy•ing, joys.** —*intr.* To take great pleasure; rejoice. —*tr. Archaic.* **1.** To fill with ecstatic happiness, pleasure, or satisfaction. **2.** To enjoy. [ME *joie* < OFr. < Lat. *gaudia,* pl. of *gaudium,* joy < *gaudēre,* to rejoice. See **gāu-*.**]

Joyce (jois), **James.** 1882–1941. Irish writer whose works include *Ulysses* (1922) and *Finnegans Wake* (1939). —**Joyc′e•an** (joi′sē-ən) *adj.*

joy•ful (joi′fəl) *adj.* Feeling, causing, or indicating joy. See Syns at **glad[1].** —**joy′ful•ly** *adv.* —**joy′ful•ness** *n.*

joy•less (joi′lĭs) *adj.* Cheerless; dismal. —**joy′less•ly** *adv.* —**joy′less•ness** *n.*

joy•ous (joi′əs) *adj.* Feeling or causing joy; joyful. See Syns at **glad[1].** —**joy′ous•ly** *adv.* —**joy′ous•ness** *n.*

joy•pop (joi′pŏp′) *intr.v.* **-popped, -pop•ping, -pops.** *Slang.* To use narcotic drugs, esp. heroin, occasionally without becoming addicted. —**joy′pop′per** *n.*

joy ride *n. Slang.* **1.** A ride taken for fun and often for the thrills provided by reckless driving. **2.** A hazardous, reckless, often costly venture. —**joy rider** *n.*

joy•stick (joi′stĭk′) *n. Slang.* **1.** The control stick of an aircraft. **2.** A manual control or cursor device, as one attached to a computer.

J.P. or **JP** *abbr. Law.* Justice of the peace.

J particle *n.* An unusually massive neutral meson with an anomalously long lifetime. See table at **subatomic particle.**

Jr *abbr. Bible.* Jeremiah.

jr. or **Jr.** *abbr.* Junior.

JRC *abbr.* Junior Red Cross.

J.S.D. *abbr. Lat.* Juris Scientiae Doctor (Doctor of Juristic Science).

jt. *abbr.* Joint.

Juan Carlos
Receiving an honorary degree from Cambridge University in 1988

Juan Car•los (wän kär′ləs, -lôs, hwän). b. 1938. Spanish king (since 1975) who acceded after the death of Franco.

Juan de Fu•ca (də fo͞o′kə, fyo͞o′-), **Strait of.** A strait between NW WA and Vancouver I., British Columbia, Canada, linking Puget Sound and the Strait of Georgia with the Pacific Ocean.

Juan Fer•nán•dez Islands (fər-năn′dəs, fĕr-nän′dĕs). An island group of Chile, in the SE Pacific Ocean. Alexander Selkirk, a Scottish sailor and the inspiration for Defoe's *Robinson Crusoe,* lived on one of the islands from 1704 to 1709.

Juá•rez (wär′ĕz, hwä′rĕs). See **Ciudad Juárez.**

Juárez, Benito Pablo. 1806–72. Mexican politician who served as president (1858–72).

ju•ba (jo͞o′bə) *n.* An 18th- and 19th-century group dance, probably of West African origin, characterized by complex body movements and practiced on southern U.S. plantations. [?]

Ju•ba (jo͞o′bə, -bä). A river of S Ethiopia and S Somalia flowing c. 1,609 km (1,000 mi) to the Indian Ocean.

Ju•bal (jo͞o′bəl). In the Bible, a descendant of Cain who is said to have invented musical instruments.

Jub•bul•pore (jŭb′əl-pôr′, -pōr′). See **Jabalpur.**

ju•bi•lant (jo͞o′bə-lənt) *adj.* **1.** Exultingly joyful. **2.** Expressing joy. [Lat. *iūbilāns, iūbilant-,* pr.part. of *iūbilāre,* to raise a shout of joy.] —**ju′bi•lance** *n.* —**ju′bi•lant•ly** *adv.*

ju•bi•late (jo͞o′bə-lāt′) *intr.v.* **-lat•ed, -lat•ing, -lates.** To rejoice; exult. [Lat. *iūbilāre, iūbilāt-,* to raise a shout of joy.]

Ju•bi•la•te (yo͞o′bə-lä′tā, -tē, jo͞o′-) *n.* **1.a.** The 100th Psalm in the King James Bible and in most modern Catholic versions or the 99th in the Vulgate. **b.** A musical setting of the Jubilate. **2.** The third Sunday after Easter. **3.** A song or an outburst of joy and triumph. [ME < Lat. *iūbilātē,* second pers. pl. imper. of *iūbilāre,* to raise a shout of joy.]

ju•bi•la•tion (jo͞o′bə-lā′shən) *n.* **1.a.** The act of rejoicing. **b.** The condition or feeling of being jubilant. **2.** A celebration or other expression of joy.

ju•bi•lee (jo͞o′bə-lē′, jo͞o′bə-lē′) *n.* **1.a.** A specially celebrated anniversary, esp. a 50th anniversary. **b.** The celebration of such an anniversary. **2.** A season or an occasion of joyful celebration. **3.** Jubilation; rejoicing. **4.** Often **Jubilee.** *Bible.* A year of rest in the historic land of Israel when land is to be left untilled and slaves are to be freed and alienated property restored. **5.** Often **Jubilee.** *Rom. Cath. Ch.* A year during which plenary indulgence may be obtained by the performance of certain pious acts. [ME *jubile* < OFr. < LLat. *iūbilaeus,* the Jewish year of jubilee, alteration (influenced by *iubilāre,* to raise a shout of joy) of Gk. *iōbēlaios* < *iōbēlos* < Heb. *yôbēl.*]

Ju•dae•a (jo͞o-dē′ə, -dā′ə). See **Judea.**

Ju•dah[1] (jo͞o′də). In the Bible, a son of Jacob and Leah and the forebear of one of the tribes of Israel.

Ju•dah[2] (jo͞o′də). An ancient kingdom (931–586 B.C.) of SW Asia between the Mediterranean and the Dead Sea.

Ju•da•ic (jo͞o-dā′ĭk) also **Ju•da•i•cal** (-ĭ-kəl) *adj.* Of or characteristic of Jews or Judaism. —**Ju•da′i•cal•ly** *adv.*

Ju•da•ism (jo͞o′dē-ĭz′əm) *n.* **1.** The monotheistic religion of the Jews, tracing its origins to Abraham and having its spiritual and ethical principles embodied chiefly in the Bible and the Talmud. **2.** Conformity to the traditional ceremonies and rites of the Jewish religion. **3.** The cultural, religious, and social practices and beliefs of the Jews. **4.** The Jews considered as a people or community. [ME *Iudaisme* < OFr. *Judaisme* < LLat. *Iūdāismus* < Gk. *Ioudaismos* < *Ioudaios,* Jew. See JEW.]

Ju•da•ize (jo͞o′dē-īz′) *v.* **-ized, -iz•ing, -iz•es.** —*tr.* To bring into conformity with Judaism. —*intr.* To adopt Jewish customs and beliefs. —**Ju′da•i•za′tion** (-ĭ-zā′shən) *n.* —**Ju′da•i′zer** *n.*

Ju•das (jo͞o′dəs) *n.* **1.** One who betrays another under the guise of friendship. **2. judas.** A one-way peephole in a door. [ME < LLat. *Iūdas,* Judas Iscariot < Gk. *Ioudas* < Heb. *yĕhûdâ,* Judah.]

Judas Is•car•i•ot (ĭ-skăr′ē-ət). d. c. A.D. 30. One of the 12 Apostles and the betrayer of Jesus.

Judas tree *n.* See **redbud.** [< the belief that Judas Iscariot hanged himself on such a tree.]

jud•der (jŭd′ər) *intr.v.* **-dered, -der•ing, -ders.** To shake rapidly or spasmodically; vibrate conspicuously. —*n.* A rapid or spasmodic shaking. [Perh. J(ERK)[1] + (SH)UDDER.]

Jude (jo͞od) *n.* See table at **Bible.**

Jude, Saint. fl. 1st cent. A.D. One of the 12 Apostles, traditionally invoked in prayer when a situation seems hopeless.

Ju•de•a also **Ju•dae•a** (jo͞o-dē′ə, -dā′ə). An ancient region and kingdom of SW Asia comprising present-day S Israel and SW Jordan. —**Ju•de′an** *adj. & n.*

Ju•de•o-Span•ish (jo͞o-dā′ō-spăn′ĭsh) *n.* See **Ladino** 1. [< Lat. *Iūdaeus,* Jewish < Gk. *Ioudaios,* Jew. See JUDAISM.]

Judg. *abbr. Bible.* Judges.

judge (jŭj) *v.* **judged, judg•ing, judg•es.** —*tr.* **1.** To form an opinion or estimation of after careful consideration. **2.a.** *Law.* To hear and decide on in a court of law; try. **b.** *Obsolete.* To pass sentence on; condemn. **c.** To act as one appointed to decide the winners of. **3.** To determine or declare after consideration or deliberation. **4.** *Informal.* To have as an opinion or assumption; suppose. **5.** *Bible.* To govern; rule. Used of an ancient Israelite leader. —*intr.* **1.** To form an opinion or evaluation. **2.** To act or decide as a judge. —*n.* **1.** One who judges, esp.: **a.** One who makes estimates as to worth, quality, or fitness. **b.** *Law.* A public official who hears and decides cases brought before a court of law. **c.** *Law.* A bankruptcy referee. **d.** One appointed to decide the winners of a contest or competition. **2.** *Bible.* **a.** A leader of the Israelites during a period of about 400 years between the death of Joshua and the accession of Saul. **b. Judges.** *(used with a sing. v.)* See table at **Bible.** [ME *jugen* < AN *juger* < Lat. *iūdicāre* < *iūdex, iūdic-*, judge. See **deik-***.]

judge advocate *n., pl.* **judge advocates.** *Law.* **1.** A commissioned officer in the U.S. Army, Air Force, or Navy assigned to the Judge Advocate General's Corps. **2.** A staff officer serving as legal adviser to a commander. **3.** An officer acting as prosecutor at a court-martial.

judge advocate general *n., pl.* **judge advocates general** or **judge advocate generals.** The chief legal officer of a branch of the U.S. armed forces.

judge•ship (jŭj′shĭp′) *n. Law.* The office or jurisdiction of a judge.

judg•mat•ic (jŭj-măt′ĭk) also **judg•mat•i•cal** (-ĭ-kəl) *adj.* Judicious. [Perh. JUDG(MENT) + (DOG)MATIC.]

judg•ment also **judge•ment** (jŭj′mənt) *n.* **1.** The act or process of judging; the formation of an opinion after consideration or deliberation. **2.a.** The mental ability to perceive and distinguish relationships; discernment. **b.** The capacity to form an opinion by distinguishing and evaluating. **c.** The capacity to assess situations or circumstances and draw sound conclusions; good sense. **3.** An opinion or estimate formed after consideration or deliberation, esp. a formal or authoritative decision. **4.** *Law.* **a.** A determination of a court of law; a judicial decision. **b.** A court act creating or affirming an obligation, such as a debt. **c.** A writ in witness of such an act. **5.** An assertion of something believed. **6.** A misfortune believed to be sent by God as punishment for sin. **7. Judgment.** In traditional Christian eschatology, God's determination of which human beings shall be sent to heaven and which condemned to hell. [ME *jugement* < OFr. < *jugier*, to judge < Lat. *iūdicāre*. See JUDGE.]

judg•men•tal (jŭj-mĕn′tl) *adj.* **1.** Of, relating to, or dependent on judgment. **2.** Inclined to make judgments, esp. moral or personal ones. **—judg•men′tal•ly** *adv.*

Judgment Day *n.* **1.** In traditional Christian eschatology, the day at the end of the world when God judges all human beings, sending the saved to heaven and the damned to hell. **2. judgment day.** A day of reckoning or final judgment.

ju•di•ca•to•ry (jo͞o′dĭ-kə-tôr′ē, -tōr′ē) *Law.* — *n., pl.* **-ries.** A law court or system of law courts; a judiciary. — *adj.* Of or relating to the administration of justice. [LLat. *iūdicātōrium* < neut. of *iūdicātōrius*, judicial < Lat. *iūdicāre*, to judge. See JUDGE.]

ju•di•ca•ture (jo͞o′dĭ-kə-cho͝or′) *n. Law.* **1.** Administration of justice. **2.** The position, function, or authority of a judge. **3.** The jurisdiction of a law court or judge. **4.** A court or system of courts of law. [Med.Lat. *iūdicātūra* < fem. fut.part. of Lat. *iūdicāre*, to judge. See JUDGE.]

ju•di•cial (jo͞o-dĭsh′əl) *adj.* **1.** *Law.* **a.** Of, relating to, or proper to courts of law or to the administration of justice. **b.** Decreed by or proceeding from a court of justice. **c.** Belonging or appropriate to the office of a judge. **2.** Characterized by or expressing judgment. **3.** *Theol.* Proceeding from a divine judgment. [ME < AN < Lat. *iūdiciālis* < *iūdicium*, judgment < *iūdex, iūdic-*, judge. See **deik-***.] **—ju•di′cial•ly** *adv.*

ju•di•ci•ar•y (jo͞o-dĭsh′ē-ĕr′ē, -dĭsh′ə-rē) *n., pl.* **-ies.** *Law.* **1.** The judicial branch of government. **2.a.** A system of courts of law for the administration of justice. **b.** The judges of these courts. [Prob. < Lat. *iūdiciārius*, of the courts < *iūdicium*, judgment < *iūdex, iūdic-*, judge. See JUDGE.]

ju•di•cious (jo͞o-dĭsh′əs) *adj.* Having or exhibiting sound judgment; prudent. [< Fr. *judicieux* < Lat. *iūdicium*, judgment < *iūdex, iūdic-*, judge. See JUDGE.] **—ju•di′cious•ly** *adv.* **—ju•di′cious•ness** *n.*

Ju•dith (jo͞o′dĭth) *n. Bible.* **1.** A Jewish heroine who rescued her people by slaying an Assyrian general. **2.** See table at **Bible.**

ju•do (jo͞o′dō) *n.* A sport and method of physical training similar to wrestling, developed in Japan in the late 19th century and using principles of balance and leverage adapted from jujitsu. [J. *jūdō* : *jū*, soft + *dō*, way.] **—ju′do•ist** *n.*

Jud•son (jŭd′sən), **Edward Zane Carroll.** Ned Buntline. 1823–86. Amer. writer best remembered for his dime novels.

jug (jŭg) *n.* **1.a.** A large vessel of earthenware, glass, or metal with a small mouth, a handle, and usu. a stopper or cap. **b.** The amount a jug holds. **2.** A small pitcher. **3.** *Slang.* A jail. — *tr.v.* **jugged, jug•ging, jugs. 1.** To stew (meat) in an earthenware jug or jar. **2.** *Slang.* To jail. [ME *jugge*.]

ju•gate (jo͞o′gāt′, -gĭt) *adj.* Joined in or forming pairs or a pair. [Lat. *iugātus*, p.part. of *iugāre*, to join < Lat. *iugum*, yoke. See **yeug-***.]

jug band *n. Mus.* A group that uses unconventional or improvised instruments, such as jugs, kazoos, and washboards.

jug•ger•naut (jŭg′ər-nôt′) *n.* **1.** Something, such as a belief or an institution, that elicits blind devotion or sacrifice. **2.** An overwhelming, terrible, destructive force. **3. Juggernaut.** Used as a title for the Hindu deity Krishna. [Hindi *jagannāth*, title of Krishna < Skt. *jaganāthaḥ*, lord of the world : *jagat*, moving, the world (< *jigāti*, he goes; see **gʷā-***) + *nāthaḥ*, lord.]

jug•gle (jŭg′əl) *v.* **-gled, -gling, -gles.** — *tr.* **1.** To keep (two or more objects) in the air at one time by alternately tossing and catching them. **2.** To have difficulty holding; balance insecurely. **3.** To keep (more than two activities, for example) in motion or progress at one time. **4.** To manipulate in order to deceive. — *intr.* **1.** To juggle objects or perform other tricks of manual dexterity. **2.** To make rapid motions or manipulations. **3.** To use trickery; practice deception. — *n.* **1.** The act of juggling. **2.** Trickery for a dishonest end. [ME *jogelen*, to entertain with tricks < OFr. *jogler* < Lat. *ioculārī*, to jest < *ioculus*, dim. of *iocus*, joke. See **yek-***.] **—jug′gler** *n.*

jug•gler•y (jŭg′lə-rē) *n., pl.* **-ies. 1.** The skill or performance of a juggler. **2.** Trickery; deception.

jug•u•lar (jŭg′yə-lər) *adj. Anat.* Of, relating to, or located in the region of the neck or throat. — *n.* **1.** *Anat.* A jugular vein. **2.** The most vital part. [LLat. *iugulāris*, jugular < Lat. *iugulum*, collarbone, dim. of *iugum*, yoke. See **yeug-***.]

jugular vein *n. Anat.* Any of several large veins of the neck that drain blood from the head.

ju•gum (jo͞o′gəm) *n., pl.* **-ga** (-gə) or **-gums.** A yokelike structure in certain insects that joins the forewings to the hind wings. [Lat. *iugum*, yoke. See **yeug-***.]

jug wine *n.* Inexpensive table wine sold in large bottles.

juice (jo͞os) *n.* **1.a.** A fluid naturally contained in plant or animal tissue. **b.** A bodily secretion: *digestive juices.* **c.** The liquid contained in something that is chiefly solid. **2.** A substance or quality that imparts identity and vitality; essence. **3.** *Slang.* Vigorous life; vitality. **4.** *Slang.* Political power or influence; clout. **5.** *Slang.* **a.** Electric current. **b.** Fuel for an engine. **6.** *Slang.* Funds; money. **7.** *Slang.* Alcoholic drink; liquor. **8.** *Slang.* Racy or scandalous gossip. — *v.* **juiced, juic•ing, juic•es.** — *tr.* To extract the juice from. — *intr. Slang.* To drink alcoholic beverages excessively. **—*phrasal verb.* juice up.** *Slang.* To give energy, spirit, or interest to. [ME *jus* < OFr. < Lat. *iūs*.]

juiced (jo͞ost) *adj. Slang.* Intoxicated; drunk.

juice•head (jo͞os′hĕd′) *n. Slang.* A heavy drinker; an alcoholic.

juic•er (jo͞o′sər) *n.* **1.** An appliance used to extract juice from fruits and vegetables. **2.** *Slang.* One who drinks liquor or alcoholic beverages habitually or excessively.

juic•y (jo͞o′sē) *adj.* **-i•er, -i•est. 1.** Full of juice; succulent. **2.a.** Richly interesting. **b.** Racy; titillating: *a juicy bit of gossip.* **3.** Yielding profit; rewarding or gratifying. **—juic′i•ly** *adv.* **—juic′i•ness** *n.*

Juiz de Fo•ra (zhwēzh′ də fôr′ə). A city of SE Brazil N of Rio de Janeiro. Pop. 299,432.

ju•jit•su also **ju•jut•su** or **jiu•jit•su** or **jiu•jut•su** (jo͞o-jĭt′so͞o) *n.* An art of weaponless self-defense developed in China and Japan that uses throws, holds, and blows and derives added power from the attacker's own weight and strength. [J. *jūjitsu* : *jū*, soft + *jitsu*, arts.]

ju•ju (jo͞o′jo͞o) *n.* **1.** An object used as a fetish, a charm, or an amulet in West Africa. **2.** The supernatural power ascribed to such an object. [Hausa *jūjū*, fetish, evil spirit.] **—ju′ju•ism** *n.*

ju•jube (jo͞o′jo͞ob′) *n.* **1.a.** Any of several Old World trees of the genus *Ziziphus*, esp. *Z. jujuba* having palmately veined leaves, spiny stipules, and dark red fruit. **b.** The fleshy edible drupe of this tree. **2.** (*also* jo͞o′jo͞o-bē′). A fruit-flavored, usu. chewy candy or lozenge. [ME, jujube fruit < OFr. < Med. Lat. *jujuba* < Lat. *zizyphum* < Gk. *zizuphon*.]

juke¹ (jo͞ok) *Southeastern U.S.* — *n.* A roadside drinking establishment that offers inexpensive drinks, food, and music for dancing. — *intr.v.* **juked, juk•ing, jukes.** To dance, esp. in a roadside drinking establishment or to the music of a jukebox. [Prob. < Gullah *juke, joog*, disorderly, wicked, of West African orig.; akin to Wolof *dzug*, to live wickedly, Mandingo (Bambara) *dzugu*, wicked.]

Regional Note: Gullah, the English-based Creole language spoken by Black people off the coast of Georgia and South Carolina, retains a number of words from the West African languages brought over by slaves. One such word is *juke*, "bad, wicked, disorderly," the probable source of the English word *juke*. Used chiefly in the Southeastern states, *juke* (also appearing in the compound *juke joint*) means a roadside drinking establishment. "To juke" is to dance, particularly at a juke joint or to the music of a jukebox, whose name, no longer regional and having lost the connotation of sleaziness, contains the same word.

juke² (jo͞ok) *Football.* — *v.* — *tr.* To deceive or outmaneuver (a defender) by a feint; fake. — *intr.* To juke a defender. — *n.* A feint or fake. [ME *jowken*, to bend supply.]

juke•box (jo͞ok′bŏks′) *n.* A coin-operated phonograph equipped with push buttons for the selection of records. See Regional Note at **juke¹.**

juke joint *n. Informal.* A bar, tavern, or roadhouse featuring music played on a jukebox. See Regional Note at **juke¹.**

Jul. or **Jul** *abbr.* July.

ju•lep (jo͞o′lĭp) *n.* **1.** A mint julep. **2.** A sweet syrupy drink, esp. a medicinal one. [ME, a sugar syrup < OFr. < Med.Lat. < Ar. *julāb* < Pers. *gulāb*, rosewater : *gul*, rose (< MPers. *vardā*) + *āb*, water (< MPers. *āp* < OPers.).]

Jul•ian (jo͞ol′yən). A.D. 331?–363. Emperor of Rome (361–363) who attempted to restore the dominance of paganism.

judo

ă pat	oi boy
ā pay	ou out
âr care	o͝o took
ä father	o͞o boot
ĕ pet	ŭ cut
ē be	ûr urge
ĭ pit	th thin
ī pie	*th* this
îr pier	hw which
ŏ pot	zh vision
ō toe	ə about, item
ô paw	

Stress marks:
′ (primary);
′ (secondary), as in
dictionary (dĭk′shə-nĕr′ē)

jumping jack
c. 1827 American jumping jack of Puss in Boots

Carl Jung

juniper
Eastern red cedar
Juniperus virginiana

Ju•li•an•a (jo͞o′lē-ăn′ə). b. 1909. Queen of the Netherlands (1948–80) who abdicated in favor of her daughter Beatrix.

Julian Alps. A range of the E Alps in Slovenia and NE Italy rising to 2,864 m (9,390 ft).

Julian calendar *n.* The solar calendar introduced by Julius Caesar in Rome in 46 B.C., having a year of 12 months and 365 days and a leap year of 366 days every fourth year.

ju•li•enne (jo͞o′lē-ĕn′, zhü-lyĕn′) *n.* Consommé or broth garnished with long thin strips of vegetables. *—adj.* also **ju•li•enned.** Cut into long thin strips. [Fr., prob. < the name *Julienne.*]

Ju•lius II (jo͞ol′yəs). 1443–1513. Pope (1503–13) who commissioned Michelangelo to decorate the Sistine Chapel in the Vatican.

Ju•ly (jo͞o-lī′) *n.* The seventh month of the year in the Gregorian calendar. [ME *Julie* < ONFr. < Lat. *Iūlius* (see **deiw-***), after Julius CAESAR.]

Ju•ma•da (jo͞o-mä′dä) also **Jo•ma•da** (jə-) *n.* Either the fifth or the sixth month of the year in the Muslim calendar. [Ar. *jumādā* < *jamada*, to freeze.]

jum•ble (jŭm′bəl) *v.* **-bled, -bling, -bles.** *—tr.* **1.** To mix in a confused way; throw together carelessly. **2.** To muddle; confuse. *—intr.* To be mixed in a confused way. *—n.* **1.** A confused or disordered mass. **2.** A disordered state; a muddle. [?]

jum•bo (jŭm′bō) *n., pl.* **-bos.** An unusually large person, animal, or thing. [After *Jumbo*, a large elephant exhibited by P.T. Barnum, prob. < slang, clumsy person.] **—jum′bo** *adj.*

Jum•na (jŭm′nə). A river of N India rising in the Himalaya Mts. and flowing c. 1,384 km (860 mi) to the Ganges R.

jump (jŭmp) *v.* **jumped, jump•ing, jumps.** *—intr.* **1.a.** To spring off the ground or other base by a muscular effort of the legs and feet. **b.** To move suddenly and in one motion. **c.** To move involuntarily, as in surprise. **d.** To parachute from an aircraft. **2.a.** *Informal.* To move quickly; hustle. **b.** To take prompt advantage; respond quickly: *jump at a bargain.* **3.a.** To enter eagerly into an activity; plunge. **b.** To begin or start. Often used with *off*: *The project jumped off with great enthusiasm.* **4.** To form an opinion or a judgment hastily: *jump to conclusions.* **5.** To make a sudden verbal attack; lash out. **6.a.** To undergo a sudden and pronounced increase. **b.** To rise suddenly in position or rank. **7.** To move discontinuously or change after a short period. **8.** To be displaced, as by a sudden jerk. **9.** *Comp. Sci.* To move from one set of instructions in a program to another out of sequence. **10.** *Games.* **a.** To move over an opponent's playing piece in a board game. **b.** To make a jump bid in bridge. **11.** *Slang.* To be lively; bustle. *—tr.* **1.** To leap over or across. **2.** To leap onto. **3.** *Slang.* To spring upon in sudden attack; assault or ambush. **4.** To move or start prematurely before. **5.** To cause to leap. **6.** To cause to increase suddenly. **7.** To pass over; skip. **8.** To raise in rank or position; promote. **9.** *Games.* To move a piece over (an opponent's piece) in a board game, often thereby capturing the opponent's piece. **10.** To jump-start (a motor vehicle). **11.** To leave (a course), esp. through mishap: *The train jumped the rails.* **12.** *Slang.* **a.** To leave hastily; skip. **b.** To leave (an organization, for example) suddenly or in violation of an agreement. **13.** To seize or occupy illegally. **14.** To forfeit (bail) by failing to appear in court. *—n.* **1.a.** The act of jumping; a leap. **b.** The distance covered by a jump. **c.** An obstacle or a span to be jumped. **2.** A descent from an aircraft by parachute. **3.** *Sports.* Any of several track-and-field events in which contestants jump. **4.** *Informal.* An initial competitive advantage; a head start. **5.a.** A sudden pronounced rise, as in price or salary. **b.** An impressive promotion. **6.** A step or level. **7.** A sudden or major transition, as from one career or subject to another. **8.a.** A short trip. **b.** One in a series of moves and stopovers, as with a circus or road show. **9.** *Games.* A move in a board game over an opponent's piece. **10.** *Comp. Sci.* A movement from one set of instructions to another. **11.** An involuntary nervous movement; a start. **12.** A jump-start of a motor vehicle. **—*idiom.* jump the gun.** To start doing something too soon. [ME *jumpen*, to jump (sense uncertain).]

jump ball *n. Basketball.* A method of starting play or determining possession in which the ball is tossed up between two opposing players who try to tap the ball to a teammate.

jump bid *n. Games.* A bridge bid that skips at least one level of bidding.

jump cut *n.* A cut to slightly later action in a filmed scene, creating an effect of discontinuity or acceleration.

jump•er[1] (jŭm′pər) *n.* **1.** One that jumps. **2.** A type of coasting sled. **3.** *Elect.* A short length of wire used temporarily to complete a circuit or to bypass a break in a circuit. **4.** *Basketball.* See **jump shot. 5.** A saddle horse that has been trained to jump over obstacles.

jump•er[2] (jŭm′pər) *n.* **1.** A sleeveless dress worn over a blouse or sweater. **2.** A loose protective garment worn over other clothes. **3.** A child's garment of straight-legged pants attached to a biblike bodice. Often used in the plural. **4.** *Chiefly British.* A pullover sweater. [Prob. < *jump*, short coat.]

jump•er cable (jŭm′pər) *n.* See **booster cable.**

jump•ing bean (jŭm′pĭng) *n.* A seed, as of certain Mexican plants of the genera *Sebastiana* and *Sapium*, containing the larva of the moth *Laspeyresia saltitans*, whose movements cause the seed to jerk or roll.

jumping jack *n.* **1.** A toy figure with jointed limbs that can be made to dance by pulling an attached string. **2.** *Sports.* A physical exercise performed by jumping to a position with the legs spread wide and the hands touching overhead and then putting the feet together and the arms at the sides.

jumping mouse *n.* Any of various small Eurasian and North American rodents of the family Zapodidae, having a very long tail and long hind legs.

jump•ing-off place (jŭm′pĭng-ôf′, -ŏf′) *n.* **1.** A beginning point for a journey or venture. **2.** A very remote spot.

jump jet *n.* A jet aircraft capable of vertical takeoffs and landings.

jump-off (jŭmp′ôf′, -ŏf′) *n.* The commencement of a race or of a planned military attack.

jump rope *n.* A rope that is twirled and jumped over in children's games or in conditioning exercises.

jump seat *n.* **1.** A small folding seat, as in an automobile between the front and rear seats. **2.** A small rear seat in a sports car.

jump shot *n. Basketball.* A shot made by a player at the highest point of a jump.

jump-start (jŭmp′stärt′) *tr.v.* **-start•ed, -start•ing, -starts. 1.** To start (the engine of a motor vehicle) by using a booster cable connected to the battery of another vehicle or by engaging the drive train while the vehicle is rolling downhill or being pushed. **2.** *Informal.* To start or set in motion (something stalled or sluggish). **—jump′-start′** *n.*

jump suit *n.* **1.** A parachutist's uniform. **2.** Also **jump•suit** (jŭmp′so͞ot′). A one-piece garment consisting of a blouse or shirt with attached slacks or shorts.

jump•y (jŭm′pē) *adj.* **-i•er, -i•est. 1.** Characterized by fitful jerky movements. **2.** On edge; nervous. **—jump′i•ness** *n.*

jun. or **Jun.** *abbr.* Junior.

Jun. or **Jun** *abbr.* June.

junc. *abbr.* Junction.

jun•co (jŭng′kō) *n., pl.* **-cos** or **-coes.** Any of various small North American birds of the genus *Junco*, having predominantly gray plumage, a gray or black head, and white outer tail feathers. [Sp., reed < Lat. *iuncus.*]

junc•tion (jŭngk′shən) *n.* **1.** The act or process of joining or the condition of being joined. **2.** A place where two things join or meet, esp. a place where two roads or railway routes come together and one terminates. **3.** A transition layer or boundary between two different materials or regions, esp.: **a.** A connection between conductors or sections of a transmission line. **b.** The interface between two different semiconductor regions in a semiconductor device. **c.** A contact between different metals or other conductors. [Lat. *iūnctiō, iūnctiōn-* < *iūnctus*, p.part. of *iungere*, to join. See **yeug-***.] **—junc′tion•al** *adj.*

junction box *n.* An enclosure within which electric circuits are connected.

Junc•tion City (jŭngk′shən). A city of NE-central KS W of Topeka. Pop. 20,604.

junc•ture (jŭngk′chər) *n.* **1.** The act of joining or the condition of being joined. **2.** A place where two things are joined; a junction or joint. **3.** A point in time, esp. a critical point. **4.** The transition or mode of transition from one sound to another in speech. [ME < Lat. *iūnctūra* < *iūnctus*, p.part. of *iungere*, to join. See **yeug-***.]

Jun•dia•í (zho͞on′dyə-ē′). A city of SE Brazil NNW of São Paulo; estab. in the 17th cent. Pop. 221,888.

June (jo͞on) *n.* The sixth month of the year in the Gregorian calendar. [ME < OE *Junius* and < OFr. *juin*, both < Lat. *(mēnsis) Iūnius*, (month) of June < *Iūnō*, Juno.]

Ju•neau (jo͞o′nō′). The cap. of AK, in the Panhandle NE of Sitka; settled by gold miners in 1880. Pop. 26,751.

June beetle *n.* Any of various large North American scarabaeid beetles of the subfamily Melolonthinae, appearing in late spring and having larvae that are destructive to vegetation.

June•ber•ry (jo͞on′bĕr′ē) *n.* See **shadbush.**

June bug *n.* See **June beetle.**

Jung (yo͝ong), **Carl Gustav.** 1875–1961. Swiss psychiatrist and founder of analytical psychology whose works include *The Psychology of the Unconscious* (1912). **—Jung′i•an** *adj.*

Jung•frau (yo͝ong′frou′). A mountain, 4,160.8 m (13,642 ft), in the Bernese Alps of S-central Switzerland.

jun•gle (jŭng′gəl) *n.* **1.** Land densely overgrown with tropical vegetation. **2.** A dense thicket or growth. **3.** A dense confused mass; a jumble. **4.** A bewildering complex or maze. **5.** A place or milieu characterized by ruthless competition or struggle for survival. **6.** *Slang.* A place where hoboes camp. [Ult. < Skt. *jaṅgalam*, desert, wasteland, uncultivated area < *jaṅgala-*, desert, waste.] **—jun′gly** (-glē) *adj.*

jungle fever *n.* **1.** Malaria, esp. a severe form of the East Indies and other tropical regions. **2.** Any of various tropical diseases.

jungle fowl *n.* Any of several game birds of the genus *Gallus* of southeast Asia, esp. *G. gallus* considered to be the ancestor of the common domestic fowl.

jungle gym *n.* A structure of poles and bars for children to climb and play on. [Originally a trademark.]

jun·ior (jo͞on′yər) *adj.* **1.** Used to distinguish a son from his father when they have the same given name. **2.** Intended for or including youthful persons. **3.** Lower in rank or shorter in length of tenure. **4.** Of, for, or constituting students in the third year of a U.S. high school or college. **5.** Lesser in scale than the usual. —*n.* **1.** A person who is younger than another: *a sister four years my junior.* **2.** A person lesser in rank or time of participation or service; subordinate. **3.** A student in the third year of a U.S. high school or college. **4.** A class of clothing sizes for girls and slender women. [ME < Lat. *iunior,* comp. of *iuvenis,* young. See **yeu-***.]

junior college *n.* An educational institution offering a two-year course that is generally the equivalent of the first two years of a four-year undergraduate course.

junior high school *n.* A school in the U.S. system generally including the seventh, eighth, and sometimes ninth grades.

junior miss *n.* **1.** A teenage girl. **2.** See **junior** 4.

junior varsity *n. Sports.* A high-school or college team that competes in interschool sports on the level below varsity.

ju·ni·per (jo͞o′nə-pər) *n.* Any of various evergreen trees or shrubs of the genus *Juniperus,* having needlelike or scalelike leaves and aromatic berrylike seed-bearing cones. [ME < Lat. *iūniperus.*]

junk¹ (jŭngk) *n.* **1.** Discarded material, such as glass, rags, paper, or metal, that may be reused in some form. **2.** *Informal.* **a.** Articles that are worn-out or fit to be discarded. **b.** Cheap or shoddy material. **c.** Something meaningless, fatuous, or unbelievable. **3.** *Slang.* Heroin. **4.** Hard salt beef for consumption on board a ship. —*tr.v.* **junked, junk·ing, junks.** To throw away or discard as useless; scrap. —*adj.* **1.** Cheap, shoddy, or worthless. **2.** Having a superficial appeal or utility, but lacking substance. [ME *jonk,* an old cable or rope.]

Word History: The Middle English word *jonk,* ancestor of *junk,* originally had a very specific nautical meaning. First recorded in 1353, the word meant "an old cable or rope." On a sailing ship it made little sense to throw away useful material since new supplies might be distant. Old cable was used, for example, to make fenders, that is, material hung over the side of the ship to protect it from scraping other ships or wharves. *Junk* came to refer to this old cable as well. The big leap in meaning taken by the word seems to have occurred when *junk* was applied to discarded but useful material in general. This extension may also have taken place in a nautical context, for the earliest, more generalized use of *junk* is found in the compound *junk shop,* referring to a store where old materials from ships were sold. *Junk* has gone on to mean useless waste as well.

junk² (jŭngk) *n. Naut.* A Chinese flatbottom ship with a high stern and full-battened sails. [Port. *junco* or Du. *jonk,* both < Javanese *djong.*]

junk art *n.* Three-dimensional art made from junked materials, such as metal, glass, or wood.

junk bond *n.* A corporate bond high in yield and in risk.

junker (jŭng′kər) *n. Slang.* A car or truck that is old and in poor repair.

Jun·ker (yo͝ong′kər) *n.* A member of the Prussian landed aristocracy, a class formerly associated with political reaction and militarism. [Ger. < MHGer. *junchērre,* page, squire < OHGer. *junchērro* : *junc,* young; see **yeu-*** + *hērro,* lord; see HERR.] —**Jun′ker·dom** *n.*

jun·ket (jŭng′kĭt) *n.* **1.** A sweet food made from flavored milk and rennet. **2.** A party, banquet, or outing. **3.** A trip or tour, esp.: **a.** One taken by an official at public expense. **b.** One taken by a person as the guest of a business or an agency seeking favor or patronage. —*v.* **-ket·ed, -ket·ing, -kets.** —*intr.* **1.** To hold a party or banquet. **2.** To go on a junket. —*tr.* To fete at a party or banquet. [ME *jonket,* rush basket, a food served on rushes, feast, perh. < ONFr. *jonquette,* rush basket (prob. < *jonc,* rush) or < Med.Lat. *iuncāta,* rush basket, both < Lat. *iuncus,* rush.] —**jun′ket·er** *n.*

jun·ke·teer (jŭng′kĭ-tēr′) *n.* One who goes on a junket or junkets. —*intr.v.* **-teered, -teer·ing, -teers.** To junket.

junk food *n.* Any of various prepackaged snack foods high in calories but low in nutritional value.

junk·ie also **junk·y** (jŭng′kē) *n., pl.* **-ies.** *Slang.* **1.** A narcotics addict, esp. one using heroin. **2.** One who has an insatiable interest or devotion: *a sports junkie.*

junk mail *n.* Third-class mail, such as advertisements, mailed indiscriminately in large quantities.

junk·y¹ (jŭng′kē) *adj.* **-i·er, -i·est. 1.** Of or related to junk; worthy of being discarded. **2.** Meaningless, fatuous, or unbelievable: *a junky novel.*

junk·y² (jŭng′kē) *n.* Var. of **junkie.**

junk·yard (jŭngk′yärd′) *n.* A yard or lot that is used to store junk, such as scrap metal or resalable car parts.

Ju·no (jo͞o′nō) *n. Rom. Myth.* The principal goddess of the Pantheon, the wife and sister of Jupiter and the patron primarily of marriage and the well-being of women.

Ju·no·esque (jo͞o′nō-ĕsk′) *adj.* Having the stately bearing and imposing beauty of the goddess Juno.

jun·ta (ho͝on′tə, jŭn′-) *n.* **1.** A group of military officers ruling a country after seizing power. **2.** A council or small legislative body in a government, esp. in Central or South America. **3.** A junto. [Sp. and Port., conference, prob. < Lat. *iūncta,* fem. p.part. of *iungere,* to join. See **yeug-***.]

jun·to (jŭn′tō) *n., pl.* **-tos.** A small, usu. secret group united for a common interest. [Alteration of JUNTA.]

Ju·pi·ter (jo͞o′pĭ-tər) *n.* **1.** *Rom. Myth.* The supreme god, patron of the Roman state and brother and husband of Juno. **2.** *Astron.* The fifth planet from the sun, the largest and most massive in the solar system, having a sidereal period of revolution about the sun of 11.86 years at a mean distance of 777 million kilometers (483 million miles) and a mean diameter of approx. 138,000 kilometers (86,000 miles). [Lat. *Iūpiter.* See **deiw-***.]

ju·ral (jo͝or′əl) *adj.* **1.** Of or relating to law. **2.** Of or relating to rights and obligations. [< Lat. *iūs, iūr-,* law. See **yewes-***.] —**ju′ral·ly** *adv.*

Ju·ra Mountains (jo͝or′ə, zhü-rä′). A range along the French-Swiss border rising to 1,723.9 m (5,652 ft).

Ju·ras·sic (jo͝o-răs′ĭk) *adj.* Of, belonging to, or being the second period of the Mesozoic Era, marked by the existence of dinosaurs and the earliest mammals and birds. See table at **geologic time.** —*n.* The Jurassic Period or its deposits. [Fr. *jurassique,* after the JURA (MOUNTAINS).]

ju·rat (jo͝or′ăt′) *n. Law.* A certification on an affidavit declaring when, where, and before whom it was sworn. [ME, informant under oath < AN, member of a city ruling body < Med.Lat. *iūrātus,* juror < p.part. of Lat. *iūrāre,* to swear. See JURY¹.]

ju·rid·i·cal (jo͝o-rĭd′ĭ-kəl) also **ju·rid·ic** (-ĭk) *adj. Law.* Of or relating to the law and its administration. [< Lat. *iūridicus* : *iūs, iūr-,* law; see **yewes-*** + *dīcere, dic-,* to say; see **deik-***.] —**ju·rid′i·cal·ly** *adv.*

ju·ris·con·sult (jo͝or′ĭs-kŏn′sŭlt′) *n. Law.* A person learned in law; a jurist. [Lat. *iūrisconsultus* : *iūris,* genitive of *iūs,* law; see **yewes-*** + *cōnsultus,* skilled, p.part. of *cōnsulere,* to take counsel.]

ju·ris·dic·tion (jo͝or′ĭs-dĭk′shən) *n.* **1.** *Law.* The right and power to interpret and apply the law. **2.a.** Authority or control. **b.** The extent of authority or control. **3.** The territorial range of authority or control. [ME *jurisdiccioun* < OFr. *juridicion* < Lat. *iūrisdictiō, iūrisdictiōn-* : *iūris,* genitive of *iūs,* law; see **yewes-*** + *dictiō, dictiōn-,* declaration (< *dictus,* p.part. of *dīcere,* to say; see **deik-***).] —**ju′ris·dic′tion·al** *adj.* —**ju′ris·dic′tion·al·ly** *adv.*

ju·ris·pru·dence (jo͝or′ĭs-pro͞od′ns) *n. Law.* **1.** The philosophy or science of law. **2.** A division or department of law. [LLat. *iūrisprūdentia* : Lat. *iūris,* genitive of *iūs,* law; see **yewes-*** + Lat. *prūdentia,* knowledge (< *prūdēns, prūdent-,* knowing; see PRUDENT).] —**ju′ris·pru·den′tial** (-pro͞o-dĕn′shəl) *adj.* —**ju′ris·pru·den′tial·ly** *adv.*

ju·ris·pru·dent (jo͝or′ĭs-pro͞od′nt) *Law.* —*adj.* Versed in jurisprudence. —*n.* See **jurist.**

ju·rist (jo͝or′ĭst) *n. Law.* One who has thorough knowledge and experience of law, esp. an eminent judge, lawyer, or legal scholar. [ME < OFr. *juriste* < Med.Lat. *iurista* < Lat. *iūs, iūr-,* law. See **yewes-***.]

ju·ris·tic (jo͝o-rĭs′tĭk) also **ju·ris·ti·cal** (-tĭ-kəl) *adj. Law.* **1.** Of or relating to a jurist or to jurisprudence. **2.** Of or relating to law or legality. —**ju·ris′ti·cal·ly** *adv.*

ju·ror (jo͝or′ər, -ôr′) *n.* **1.** *Law.* **a.** One who serves as a member of a jury. **b.** One who awaits or is called for service on a jury. **2.** One who serves on a deliberative body analogous to a jury. [ME *jurour* < AN < Lat. *iūrātor,* swearer < *iūrāre,* to swear. See JURY¹.]

Ju·ru·á (zho͞o′ro͞o-ä′). A river of E Peru and NW Brazil flowing c. 1,931 km (1,200 mi) to the Amazon R.

ju·ry¹ (jo͝or′ē) *n., pl.* **-ries. 1.** *Law.* A body of persons sworn to judge and give a verdict on a given matter, esp. a body of persons summoned by law and sworn to hand down a verdict upon a case presented in court. **2.** A committee, usu. of experts, that judges contestants or applicants. —*tr.v.* **-ried, -ry·ing, -ries.** To judge or evaluate by a jury. [ME *jure* < AN *juree* < fem. p.part. of *jurer,* to swear < Lat. *iūrāre* < *iūs, iūr-,* law. See **yewes-***.]

ju·ry² (jo͝or′ē) *adj. Naut.* Intended or designed for temporary use; makeshift: *a jury sail.* [Ult. < OFr. *ajuri,* help < Lat. *adiūtāre,* to help. See AID.]

ju·ry-rig (jo͝or′ē-rĭg′) *tr.v.* **-rigged, -rig·ging, -rigs.** To rig or assemble for temporary emergency use; improvise.

jus gen·ti·um (yo͞os gĕn′tē-əm, jŭs jĕn′shē-əm) *n. Law.* The law of nations; international law. [Lat. *iūs gentium* : *iūs,* law + *gentium,* genitive pl. of *gēns,* nation.]

jus·sive (jŭs′ĭv) *n. Gram.* A word, mood, or form used to express a command. [< Lat. *iussus,* p.part. of *iubēre,* to command.] —**jus′sive** *adj.*

just¹ (jŭst) *adj.* **1.** Honorable and fair in one's dealings and actions. See Syns at **fair¹. 2.** Consistent with what is morally right; righteous. **3.** Properly due or merited. **4.** *Law.* Valid within the law; lawful. **5.** Suitable or proper in nature; fitting. **6.** Based on fact or sound reason; well-founded. —*adv.* (jəst,

junk²
In Victoria harbor,
Hong Kong

Jupiter
Photographed by Voyager I
in 1979 at a distance of
28.4 million kilometers
(17.6 million miles)

ă pat	oi boy
ā pay	ou out
âr care	o͝o took
ä father	o͞o boot
ĕ pet	ŭ cut
ē be	ûr urge
ĭ pit	th thin
ī pie	*th* this
îr pier	hw which
ŏ pot	zh vision
ō toe	ə about, item
ô paw	

Stress marks:
′ (primary);
′ (secondary), as in
dictionary (dĭk′shə-nĕr′ē)

Helen Keller
Photographed in the 1950's

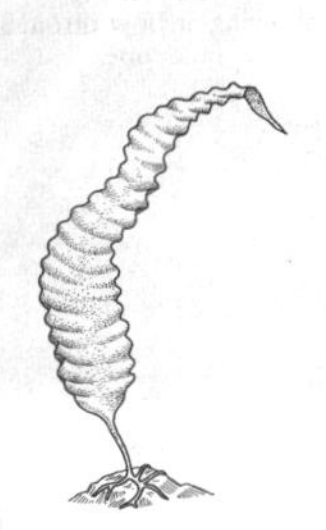
kelp
Common southern kelp
Laminaria agardhii

Jacqueline Kennedy
Photographed January 20, 1961, after the inauguration

John F. Kennedy

starred in silent film classics such as *The General* (1926).

Keats (kēts), **John.** 1795–1821. British poet whose melodic works include "The Eve of St. Agnes" and "Ode on a Grecian Urn" (both 1819). — **Keats′i•an** *adj.*

ke•bab or **ke•bob** also **ka•bob** (kə-bŏb′) *n.* Shish kebab.

Ke•ble (kē′bəl), **John.** 1792–1866. British cleric and poet known for his sermon "National Apostasy" (1833).

Kech•ua (kĕch′wə, -wä′) *n.* Var. of **Quechua.**

Kecs•ke•mét (kĕch′kĕ-māt′). A city of central Hungary SE of Budapest; known since the 4th cent. A.D. Pop. 81,300.

kedge (kĕj) *Naut.* — *n.* A light anchor used to warp a vessel. — *v.* **kedged, kedg•ing, kedg•es.** — *tr.* To warp (a vessel) by using a light anchor. — *intr.* To move by using a light anchor. [< *kedge*, to warp a vessel, perh. < ME *caggen*, to tie, perh. of Scand. orig.]

kedg•er•ee (kĕj′ə-rē′, kĕj′ə-rē′) *n.* A dish of flaked fish, boiled rice, and eggs. [Hindi *khichṛī* < Skt. *khiccā.*]

keek (kēk) *Scots.* — *intr.v.* **keeked, keek•ing, keeks.** To peek; peep. — *n.* A look, esp. a quick one; a peek. [ME *kiken, keken*, perh. < MDu. *kiken.*]

keel[1] (kēl) *n.* **1.** *Naut.* **a.** The principal structural member of a ship, running lengthwise along the center line from bow to stern, to which the frames are attached. **b.** A ship. **2.** A structure that resembles a ship's keel in function or shape. **3.** The principal structural member of an aircraft, resembling a ship's keel. **4.** A pair of united petals in certain flowers. — *intr. & tr.v.* **keeled, keel•ing, keels.** *Naut.* To capsize or cause to capsize. — ***phrasal verb.*** **keel over.** To collapse or fall into or as if into a faint. [ME *kele* < ON *kjölr.*]

keel[2] (kēl) *n.* **1.** *Naut.* **a.** A freight barge, esp. for carrying coal on the Tyne River in England. **b.** The load capacity of this barge. **2.** A British unit of weight formerly used for coal, equal to about 21.2 long tons. [ME *kele* < MDu. *kiel.*]

keel[3] (kēl) *tr.v.* **keeled, keel•ing, keels.** *Chiefly British.* To make cool. [ME *kelen* < OE *cēlan*, to cool. See **gel-*.**]

keel•boat (kēl′bōt′) *n. Naut.* A riverboat with a keel but without sails, used for carrying freight.

keel•haul (kēl′hôl′) *tr.v.* **-hauled, -haul•ing, -hauls. 1.** *Naut.* To discipline by dragging under the keel of a ship. **2.** To rebuke harshly. [Alteration of Du. *kielhalen* : *kiel*, keel of a ship (< MDu.) + *halen*, to haul (< MDu.); see **kelə-²*.**]

Kee•ling Islands (kē′lĭng). See **Cocos Islands.**

keel•son (kēl′sən, kĕl′-) also **kel•son** (kĕl′-) *n. Naut.* A timber or girder fastened above and parallel to the keel of a ship or boat for additional strength. [Alteration (influenced by KEEL[1]) of ME *kelswin*, prob. < ON **kjölsvīn* : *kjölr*, keel + *svīn*, swine, timber; see **sū-*.**]

Kee•lung (kē′lo͞ong′) also **Chi•lung** (jē′-, chē′-). A city of N Taiwan on the East China Sea. Pop. 349,686.

keen[1] (kēn) *adj.* **keen•er, keen•est. 1.** Having a fine sharp cutting edge or point. **2.** Having or marked by quick intelligence and acuity. See Syns at **sharp. 3.** Acutely sensitive. **4.** Sharp; vivid; strong. **5.** Intense; piercing: *a keen wind.* **6.** Pungent; acrid. **7.a.** Ardent; enthusiastic. **b.** Eagerly desirous. **8.** *Slang.* Great; splendid; fine. [ME *kene* < OE *cēne*, brave.] — **keen′ly** *adv.* — **keen′ness** *n.*

keen[2] (kēn) *n.* A loud wailing lament for the dead. — *intr.v.* **keened, keen•ing, keens.** To wail in lamentation, esp. for the dead. See Syns at **cry.** [< Ir.Gael. *caoineadh* < *caoinim*, I lament < OIr. *coínim.*] — **keen′er** *n.*

Keene (kēn). A city of SW NH W of Manchester; first settled in 1736. Pop. 22,430.

keep (kēp) *v.* **kept** (kĕpt), **keep•ing, keeps.** — *tr.* **1.** To retain possession of. **2.** To have as a supply. **3.** To support (a family, for example). **4.** To put customarily; store. **5.a.** To supply with room and board for a charge. **b.** To raise: *keep chickens.* **6.** To maintain for use or service. **7.** To manage, tend, or have charge of. **8.** To preserve (food). **9.** To cause to continue in a state or course of action. **10.a.** To maintain records in: *keep a diary.* **b.** To enter (data) in a book. **11.a.** To detain: *kept after school.* **b.** To restrain. **c.** To prevent or deter. **d.** To refrain from divulging. **e.** To save; reserve. **12.** To maintain: *keep late hours.* **13.** To adhere to; fulfill. **14.** To celebrate; observe. — *intr.* **1.** To remain in a state or condition; stay. **2.** To continue to do: *keep guessing.* **3.** To remain fresh or unspoiled. — *n.* **1.** Care; charge. **2.** The means by which one is supported. **3.a.** The stronghold of a castle. **b.** A jail. — ***phrasal verbs.*** **keep at.** To persevere in an action. **keep down.** To prevent from growing, accomplishing, or succeeding. **keep off.** To stay away from. **keep to.** To adhere to. **keep up. 1.** To maintain in good condition. **2.** To persevere in; carry on. **3.** To continue at the same level or pace. **4.** To match one's fellows in success or lifestyle. — ***idioms.*** **for keeps. 1.** For an indefinitely long period. **2.** Seriously and permanently. **keep an eye out.** To be watchful. **keep company.** To court: *kept company but never married.* **keep (one's) chin up.** To be courageous or optimistic in difficulties. **keep (one's) eyes open** (or **peeled**). To be on the lookout. **keep (one's) nose clean.** *Informal.* To stay out of trouble. **keep pace.** To stay even with others, as in a contest. **keep (someone) company.** To accompany or remain with. **keep time. 1.** To indicate the correct time. **2.** *Mus.* To maintain the tempo or rhythm. **keep to (oneself). 1.** To shun the company of others. **2.** To refrain from divulging. [ME *kepen* < OE *cēpan*, to observe, seize.]

Syns: *keep, retain, withhold, reserve.* These verbs mean to have and maintain in one's possession or control. *Keep* is the most general: *We received a tempting offer for the house but decided to keep it. Retain* means to continue to hold, especially in the face of possible loss: *Though unhappy, she retained her sense of humor. Withhold* implies reluctance or refusal to give, grant, or allow: *The tenants withheld their rent until the landlord repaired the boiler.* To *reserve* is to hold back for the future or for a special purpose: *The farmer reserved two acres for an orchard.*

keep•er (kē′pər) *n.* **1.** One that keeps, esp.: **a.** An attendant, a guard, or a warden. **b.** One in charge or care of something: *a lion keeper.* **2.** *Football.* A play made by the quarterback who keeps the ball after it is snapped and runs with it. **3.** *Informal.* One worth keeping, esp. a fish large enough to be legally caught.

keep•ing (kē′pĭng) *n.* **1.** The act of holding or supporting. **2.** Custody; care. See Syns at **care. 3.** Harmony; conformity.

keep•sake (kēp′sāk′) *n.* Something kept as a memento.

kees•hond (kās′hônt′, -hŏnd′) *n., pl.* **-hon•den** (-hôn′dən) or **-honds.** Any of a breed of dog originating in the Netherlands and having a thick grayish-black coat. [Du. : prob. the name *Kees* (nickname for *Cornelis*, Cornelius) + *hond*, dog (< MDu.; see **kwon-*.**)]

Kee•wa•tin (kē-wāt′n). A region of SE Northwest Terrs., Canada, including the E mainland and islands in Hudson Bay.

kef (kĕf, kēf, käf) *n.* Var. of **kif.**

Ke•fal•li•ní•a (kĕ′fä-lē-nē′ä). See **Cephalonia.**

ke•fir (kĕ-fîr′) *n.* A creamy drink made of fermented cow's milk. [Russ., prob. ult. < Old Turkic *köpür*, (milk) froth, foam < *köpürmäk*, to froth, foam.]

Kef•la•vík (kyĕb′lə-vēk′, kĕf′-). A town of SW Iceland on the Atlantic WSW of Reykjavík; site of an international airport built by the U.S. military during World War II. Pop. 6,907.

keg (kĕg) *n.* **1.a.** A small cask or barrel with a capacity of about 30 gallons (114 liters). **b.** Such a container and its contents. **2.** A unit of weight used for nails, equal to 100 pounds (45.5 kilograms). — *tr.v.* **kegged, keg•ging, kegs.** To put or store in a small cask or barrel. [ME *kag* < ON *kaggi.*]

keg•ler (kĕg′lər) *n. Sports.* A person who bowls; a bowler. [Ger. < *kegeln*, to bowl < *Kegel*, bowling pin < MHGer. *kegel* < OHGer. *kegil*, peg.]

keis•ter (kē′stər) *n. Slang.* **1.** The buttocks. **2.** The anus. [?]

Kei•tel (kīt′l), **Wilhelm.** 1882–1946. German general and chief of the supreme command of Nazi armed forces who signed an unconditional surrender (May 1945).

Kel•ler (kĕl′ər), **Helen Adams.** 1880–1968. Amer. memoirist who lectured widely on behalf of sightless people.

Kel•logg (kĕl′ôg′, -ŏg′), **Frank Billings.** 1856–1937. Amer. public official who cosponsored the Kellogg-Briand Pact (1928) and won the 1929 Nobel Peace Prize.

Kel•ly (kĕl′ē), **Emmett.** 1898–1979. Amer. circus clown who was famous as "Weary Willie," a sad-faced hobo with the Ringling Brothers and Barnum & Bailey Circus (1942–56).

Kelly, Grace Patricia. Princess Grace. 1929–82. Amer. actress who appeared in motion pictures such as *Country Girl* (1954) and married Prince Rainier III of Monaco (1956).

kel•ly green (kĕl′ē) *n. Color.* A strong yellowish green. [< the name *Kelly.*] — **kel′ly-green′** (kĕl′ē-grēn′) *adj.*

ke•loid also **che•loid** (kē′loid′) *n.* A red, raised formation of fibrous scar tissue caused by excessive tissue repair. [Fr. *kéloïde* : Gk. *khēlē*, claw + Fr. *-oïde*, resembling (< Gk. *-oeidēs*; see -OID).] — **ke•loid′al** (-loid′l) *adj.*

Ke•low•na (kə-lō′nə). A city of S British Columbia, Canada, on Okanagan Lake ENE of Vancouver. Pop. 59,196.

kelp (kĕlp) *n.* **1.** Any of various brown, often very large seaweeds of the order Laminariales. **2.** The ash of these seaweeds, used as a source of potash and iodine. [ME *culp.*]

kel•pie[1] also **kel•py** (kĕl′pē) *n., pl.* **-pies.** A malevolent water spirit of Scottish legend, usu. having the shape of a horse and rejoicing in or causing drownings. [Prob. of Celt. orig.; akin to Sc.Gael. *colpach*, heifer.]

kel•pie[2] (kĕl′pē) *n.* Any of an Austrian breed of sheepdog. [< *Kelpie*, the name of an early specimen of the breed.]

kel•son (kĕl′sən) *n. Naut.* Var. of **keelson.**

Kelt (kĕlt) *n.* Var. of **Celt.**

Kelt•ic (kĕl′tĭk) *n. & adj.* Var. of **Celtic.**

kel•vin (kĕl′vĭn) *n.* A unit of absolute temperature equal to 1/273.16 of the absolute temperature of the triple point of water and equal in magnitude to one Celsius degree. See table at **measurement.** [After First Baron KELVIN.]

Kel•vin (kĕl′vĭn), First Baron. William Thomson. 1824–1907. British physicist who developed the Kelvin scale (1848).

Kelvin scale *n.* An absolute scale of temperature in which each degree equals one kelvin, water freezing at 273.15 K and boiling at 373.15 K.

Ke•mal At•a•türk (kə-mäl′ ăt′ə-tûrk′, kĕ-mäl′ ä-tä-türk′). 1881–1938. Turkish nationalist politician who served as president of the Turkish Republic (1923–38).

Ke•me•ro•vo (kĕm′ə-rō′və, kyĕ′mər-ə-və). A city of S-central Russia ENE of Novosibirsk. Pop. 507,000.

Ke•mi•jo•ki (kĕm′ē-yô′kē). A river of N Finland flowing c. 555 km (345 mi) to the Gulf of Bothnia.

Kem•pis (kĕm′pĭs), **Thomas à.** See **Thomas à Kempis.**

kempt (kĕmpt) *adj.* Tidy; trim. [Back-formation < UNKEMPT.]

ken (kĕn) *n.* **1.** Perception; understanding. **2.a.** Range of vision. **b.** View; sight. —*v.* **kenned** or **kent** (kĕnt), **ken•ning, kens.** —*tr.* **1.** To know (a person or thing). **2.** To recognize. —*intr.* To have knowledge or an understanding. [< ME *kennen* < OE *cennan*, to declare. See **gnō-***.]

Ken. *abbr.* Kentucky.

Ke•nai Peninsula (kē′nī′). A peninsula of S-central AK between Cook Inlet and the Gulf of Alaska.

Ken•dal green (kĕn′dl) *n.* **1.** A coarse green woolen fabric similar to tweed. **2.** The color of this fabric. [After *Kendal*, a municipal borough of NW England.]

Ken•dall (kĕn′dl). A community of SE FL, a suburb of Miami. Pop. 51,000.

ken•do (kĕn′dō) *n.* The Japanese martial art of fencing with bamboo sticks. [J.]

Ken•drew (kĕn′drōō′), Sir **John Cowdery.** b. 1917. British biologist who shared the 1962 Nobel Prize for chemistry.

Ken•il•worth (kĕn′əl-wûrth′). An urban district of central England SE of Birmingham; site of the ruins of Kenilworth Castle, built c. 1120 and celebrated in Sir Walter Scott's novel *Kenilworth* (1821). Pop. 19,315.

Kenilworth ivy *n.* A European creeping herb *(Cymbalaria muralis)* with palmately lobed leaves and solitary, pale purple flowers. [After *Kenilworth* Castle, Kenilworth.]

Ken•more (kĕn′môr′, -mōr′). A village of W NY on the Niagara R. N of Buffalo. Pop. 17,180.

Ken•nan (kĕn′ən), **George Frost.** b. 1904. Amer. diplomat and historian who served as U.S. ambassador to the U.S.S.R. (1952) and Yugoslavia (1961–63).

Ken•ne•bec (kĕn′ə-bĕk′). A river of W-central and S Maine flowing c. 257 km (160 mi) to the Atlantic Ocean.

Ken•ne•dy (kĕn′ĭ-dē), **Anthony M.** b. 1936. Amer. jurist; associate justice of the U.S. Supreme Court (since 1988).

Kennedy, Cape. See Cape **Canaveral.**

Kennedy, Jacqueline Lee Bouvier. Now Jacqueline Kennedy Onassis. b. 1929. First Lady of the U.S. (1961–63) who supervised the redecoration of the White House.

Kennedy, John Fitzgerald. 1917–63. The 35th President of the U.S. (1961–63), who approved the failed invasion of the Bay of Pigs (1961) and forced Khrushchev to remove Soviet missiles from Cuba (1962). He was assassinated in Dallas, Texas, on Nov. 22, 1963.

Kennedy, Joseph Patrick. 1888–1969. Amer. financier who served as ambassador to Great Britain (1937–40).

Kennedy, Robert Francis. 1925–68. Amer. politician who served as U.S. attorney general (1961–64) and was assassinated in Los Angeles while campaigning for the presidency.

ken•nel[1] (kĕn′əl) *n.* **1.** A shelter for a dog. **2.** A pack of dogs, esp. hounds. **3.** An establishment where dogs are bred, trained, or boarded. **4.** The lair of a wild animal, such as a fox. —*v.* **-neled, -nel•ing, -nels** or **-nelled, -nel•ling, -nels.** —*tr.* To place or keep in or as if in a kennel. —*intr.* To take cover or lie in or as if in a kennel. [ME *kenel* < AN **kenil* < VLat. **canīle* < Lat. *canis*, dog. See **kwon-***.]

ken•nel[2] (kĕn′əl) *n.* A gutter along a street. [ME *cannel* < ONFr. *canel*, channel < Lat. *canālis*. See CANAL.]

Ken•nel•ly (kĕn′ə-lē), **Arthur Edwin.** 1861–1939. Amer. electrical engineer who concurrently with Oliver Heaviside predicted the existence of the ionosphere.

Ken•nel•ly-Heav•i•side layer (kĕn′ə-lē-hĕv′ē-sīd′) *n.* See **E layer.** [After Arthur Edwin KENNELLY and Oliver HEAVISIDE.]

Ken•ner (kĕn′ər). A city of SE LA, a suburb of New Orleans on the Mississippi R. Pop. 66,382.

Ken•ne•wick (kĕn′ə-wĭk′). A city of S WA on the Columbia R. WNW of Walla Walla. Pop. 42,155.

ken•ning (kĕn′ĭng) *n.* A figurative, usu. compound expression used in place of a name or noun, esp. in Old English and Old Norse poetry. [ON < *kenna*, to know, to name with a kenning. See **gnō-***.]

Ken•ny (kĕn′ē), **Elizabeth.** 1880?–1952. Australian nurse who developed a treatment for paralysis brought on by poliomyelitis.

ke•no (kē′nō) *n. Games.* A game of chance, similar to lotto, that uses balls rather than counters. [Fr. *quine*, set of five winning numbers (< Lat. *quīnī*, five each; see **penkʷe***) + *-o* (as in LOTTO).]

Ke•no•sha (kə-nō′shə). A city of extreme SE WI on Lake Michigan S of Milwaukee; founded 1835. Pop. 80,352.

ke•no•sis (kĭ-nō′sĭs) *n. Theol.* The relinquishment of the form of God by Jesus in becoming man and suffering death. [LGk. *kenōsis* < Gk., an emptying < *kenoun*, to empty < *kenos*, empty.] —**ke•not′ic** (-nŏt′ĭk) *adj.*

kent (kĕnt) *v. Scots.* A p.t. and p.part. of **ken.**

Kent (kĕnt). **1.** A region and former kingdom of SE England; settled by Jutes in the 5th cent. A.D. and one of the seven kingdoms of the Anglo-Saxon Heptarchy. **2.** A city of NE OH ENE of Akron; seat of Kent State University (founded 1910). Pop. 28,835. **3.** A city of W-central WA S of Seattle. Pop. 37,960.

Kent, Corita. "Sister Corita." 1918–86. Amer. artist noted for her serigraphs.

Kent, James. 1763–1847. Amer. jurist who as chief judge of the NY Supreme Court (1804–23) revived the use of equity.

Kent, Rockwell. 1882–1971. Amer. artist best known for his stark woodcuts in special editions of classic literary works.

Kent•ish (kĕn′tĭsh) *adj.* Of or relating to Kent, England, or its inhabitants. —*n.* The dialect of English spoken in Kent.

kent•ledge (kĕnt′lĭj) *n. Naut.* Pig iron used as permanent ballast. [?]

Ken•tuck•y (kən-tŭk′ē). A state of the E-central U.S.; admitted as the 15th state in 1792. Daniel Boone's Transylvania Co. settled the area in 1775. Cap. Frankfort. Pop. 3,698,969. —**Ken•tuck′i•an** *adj. & n.*

Kentucky bluegrass *n.* A perennial Eurasian and North African grass *(Poa pratensis)* that is commonly cultivated for pasture and lawns.

Kentucky coffee tree *n.* A deciduous North American tree *(Gymnocladus dioica)* having flat pulpy pods with large seeds formerly used as a coffee substitute.

Kentucky River. A river, of N-central KY flowing c. 417 km (259 mi) to the Ohio R.

Kent•wood (kĕnt′wŏŏd′). A city of W MI, a suburb of Grand Rapids. Pop. 37,826.

Ken•ya (kĕn′yə, kēn′-). A country of E-central Africa bordering on the Indian Ocean; gained independence from Great Britain in 1963. Cap. Nairobi. Pop. 15,327,061. —**Ken′yan** *adj. & n.*

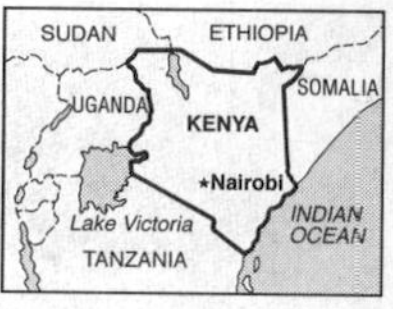

Kenya

Kenya, Mount. An extinct volcano, 5,202.7 m (17,058 ft), in central Kenya.

Ken•yat•ta (kĕn-yä′tə), **Jomo.** 1893?–1978. Kenyan nationalist and first president of independent Kenya (1964–78).

Ken•yon (kĕn′yən), **Dorothy.** 1888–1972. Amer. jurist noted for her work on labor disputes and women's rights.

Kenyon, Dame **Kathleen Mary.** 1906–78. British archaeologist who led the expedition credited with determining the accurate date and location of the walls of Jericho.

Ke•ogh plan (kē′ō) *n.* A retirement plan for the self-employed and their employees. [After Eugene James *Keogh* (b. 1907), former U.S. representative from NY.]

Ke•o•kuk (kē′ə-kŭk′). 1790?–1848? Amer. Sauk leader who negotiated peace between his people and the Sioux (1837).

keph•a•lin (kĕf′ə-lĭn) *n.* Var. of **cephalin.**

ke•pi (kā′pē, kĕp′ē) *n., pl.* **-pis.** A French military cap with a flat, circular top and a visor. [Fr. *képi* < Ger. dial. *Käppi*, ult. prob. < LLat. *cappa*, head covering.]

kepi

Kep•ler (kĕp′lər), **Johannes.** 1571–1630. German astronomer and mathematician who clarified the theory that the planets revolve around the sun.

kept (kĕpt) *v.* P.t. and p.part. of **keep.**

kerat– *pref.* Var. of **kerato–.**

ker•a•tec•to•my (kĕr′ə-tĕk′tə-mē) *n., pl.* **-mies.** Surgical removal of a part of the cornea.

ker•a•tin (kĕr′ə-tĭn) *n.* A tough insoluble protein and the chief constituent of hair, nails, horns, and hoofs. [Gk. *keras*, *kerat-*, horn; see **ker-¹*** + -IN.] —**ke•rat′i•nous** (kə-răt′n-əs) *adj.*

ker•a•tin•ize (kĕr′ə-tə-nīz′) *v.* **-ized, -iz•ing, -iz•es.** —*intr.* To produce or become like keratin. —*tr.* To convert (something) into keratin. —**ker′a•tin•i•za′tion** (-tə-nĭ-zā′shən) *n.*

ker•a•ti•tis (kĕr′ə-tī′tĭs) *n., pl.* **-tit•i•des** (-tĭt′ĭ-dēz′). Inflammation of the cornea.

kerato– or **kerat–** also **cerato–** or **cerat–** *pref.* **1.** Horn; horny: *keratosis.* **2.** Cornea: *keratectomy.* [Gk. *kerato-*, horn < *keras*, *kerat-*. See **ker-¹***.]

ker•a•to•sis (kĕr′ə-tō′sĭs) *n., pl.* **-ses** (-sēz). Excessive growth of horny tissue of the skin. —**ker′a•tot′ic** (-tŏt′ĭk) *adj.*

ker•a•tot•o•my (kĕr′ə-tŏt′ə-mē) *n., pl.* **-mies.** Surgical incision of the cornea.

kerb (kûrb) *n. Chiefly British.* Var. of **curb** 1.

Ker•be•la (kûr′bə-lə). See **Karbala.**

Kerch (kĕrch, kyĕrch). A city of S Ukraine on **Kerch Strait,** a shallow waterway connecting the Black Sea with the Sea of Azov and bordered on the W by the **Kerch Peninsula;** founded by Greek colonists in the 6th cent. B.C. Pop. 168,000.

ker•chief (kûr′chĭf, -chēf′) *n., pl.* **-chiefs** also **-chieves** (-chĭvz, -chēvz). **1.** A woman's square scarf, often worn as a head covering. **2.** A handkerchief. [ME *curchef* < AN *courchief* and < OFr. *couvrechef* : *covrir*, to cover (< Lat. *cooperīre*; see COVER) + *chef*, head (< Lat. *caput*; see **kaput-***).]

Ke•ren•sky (kə-rĕn′skē, kĕr′ən-, kyĕr′yĭn-), **Aleksandr Fedorovich.** 1881–1970. Russian revolutionary who became head of government (Jul. 1917) after the abdication of Nicholas II but was overthrown by the Bolsheviks (Oct. 1917).

Ker•e•san (kĕr′ĭ-sən) *n.* Any of a group of languages spoken by certain Pueblo peoples. —**Ker′e•san** *adj.*

kerf (kûrf) *n.* **1.** A groove or notch made by a cutting tool, such as a saw or an ax. **2.** The width of a groove made by a cutting tool. [ME < OE *cyrf*, a cutting. See **gerbh-***.]

Ker•gue•len Islands (kûr′gə-lən, -lĕn′). A French-

ă pat	oi boy
ā pay	ou out
âr care	ŏŏ took
ä father	ōō boot
ĕ pet	ŭ cut
ē be	ûr urge
ĭ pit	th thin
ī pie	*th* this
îr pier	hw which
ŏ pot	zh vision
ō toe	ə about, item
ô paw	

Stress marks:
′ (primary);
′ (secondary), as in
dictionary (dĭk′shə-nĕr′ē)

administered island group in the S Indian Ocean SE of South Africa.

Kér•ki•ra (kĕr′kē-rä′). See **Corfu.**

Ker•man (kər-män′, kĕr-). A city of E-central Iran SE of Tehran; long noted for its carpets. Pop. 239,000.

ker•mes (kûr′mēz) *n.* A red dyestuff once prepared from the dried bodies of various female scale insects of the genus *Kermes.* [Fr. *kermès,* short for *alkermès* < Ar. *al-qirmiz,* prob. < Skt. *kṛmi-ja-,* (red dye) produced by worms. See **kʷṛmi-*.**]

ker•mis also **ker•mess** or **kir•mess** (kûr′mĭs) *n.* **1.** An outdoor fair in the Low Countries. **2.** A fund-raising fair or carnival. [Du. < MDu. *kercmisse,* church dedication Mass : *kerc,* church (ult. < LGk. *kuriakon, kurikon,* of the lord; see CHURCH) + *misse,* Mass (< LLat. *missa;* see MASS).]

kettledrum

kern¹ also **kerne** (kûrn) *n.* **1.** A medieval Scottish or Irish foot soldier. **2.** A loutish person. [ME *kerne* < MIr. *ceithern,* band of soldiers < OIr.]

kern² (kûrn) *Print.* — *n.* The portion of a typeface that projects beyond the body or shank of a character. — *tr.v.* **kerned, kern•ing, kerns.** To provide (type) with a kern. [Fr. *carne,* corner < ONFr. < Lat. *cardō, cardin-,* hinge.]

Kern (kûrn), **Jerome David.** 1885–1945. Amer. composer of numerous songs and musicals, including *Show Boat* (1927).

ker•nel (kûr′nəl) *n.* **1.** A grain or seed, as of a cereal grass, enclosed in a husk. **2.** The inner, usu. edible seed of a nut or fruit stone. **3.** The most material and central part; the core. [ME < OE *cyrnel.* See **gr̥ə-no-*.**] — **ker′neled** *adj.*

kern•ite (kûr′nīt′) *n.* A colorless to white lustrous crystalline mineral, $Na_2B_4O_7{\cdot}4H_2O$, that is a major source of boron ore. [After *Kern,* a county of S CA.]

ker•o•gen (kĕr′ə-jən) *n.* A fossilized material in shale and other sedimentary rock that yields oil upon heating. [Gk. *kēros,* wax + -GEN.]

ker•o•sene also **ker•o•sine** (kĕr′ə-sēn′, kăr′-, kĕr′ə-sēn′, kăr′-) *n.* A thin oil distilled from petroleum or shale oil, used as a fuel and a denaturant for alcohol. [< Gk. *kēros,* wax.]

Ker•ou•ac (kĕr′o͞o-ăk′), **Jack.** 1922–69. Amer. writer of the beat generation who wrote *On the Road* (1957).

Ker•ry (kĕr′ē) *n., pl.* **-ries.** One of an Irish breed of small black dairy cattle. [After *Kerry,* a county of SW Ireland.]

Kerry blue terrier *n.* Any of an Irish breed of terriers having a bluish-gray coat. [After *Kerry,* a county of SW Ireland.]

ker•sey (kûr′zē) *n., pl.* **-seys. 1.** A twilled woolen fabric, sometimes with a cotton warp, used for coats. **2.** A garment made of this fabric. Often used in the plural. **3.** A woolen, often ribbed fabric formerly used for hose and trousers. [ME *kersei,* after *Kersey,* a village of SE England.]

ker•sey•mere (kûr′zē-mîr′) *n.* A fine woolen cloth with a fancy twill weave. [KERSEY + (CASSI)MERE.]

Ker•u•len (kĕr′o͞o-lĕn). A river rising in NE Mongolia and flowing c. 1,263 km (785 mi) to a lake in NE China.

ke•ryg•ma (kə-rĭg′mə) *n. Theol.* The proclamation of religious truths, esp. as taught in the Gospels. [Gk. *kērugma,* preaching, proclamation < *kērux, kērug-,* herald.]

kes•trel (kĕs′trəl) *n.* Any of various small falcons belonging to the genus *Falco,* esp. the American kestrel and the European kestrel. [Prob. < obsolete Fr. *cresserelle* < OFr. *cresserele,* prob. < *cresselle,* clacker, kestrel.]

ket– *pref.* Var. of **keto–.**

ketch (kĕch) *n. Naut.* A two-masted fore-and-aft-rigged sailing vessel with a mizzenmast stepped aft of a taller mainmast but forward of the rudder. [ME *cache* < *cacchen,* to catch. See CATCH.]

Ketch•i•kan (kĕch′ĭ-kăn′). A city of SE AK on an island in the Alexander Archipelago; a supply point for miners during the gold rush of the 1890's. Pop. 7,198.

ketch•up (kĕch′əp, kăch′-) also **catch•up** (kăch′əp, kĕch′-) or **cat•sup** (kăt′səp, kăch′əp, kĕch′-) *n.* A condiment consisting of a thick, smooth-textured, spicy sauce usu. made from tomatoes. [Prob. Malay *kēchap,* fish sauce, poss. < Chin. (Cantonese) *kē-tsiap.*]

Word History: The source of our word *ketchup* may be the Malay word *kēchap,* possibly taken into Malay from the Cantonese dialect of Chinese. *Kēchap,* like our word, referred to a kind of sauce but a sauce without tomatoes; rather, it contained fish brine, herbs, and spices. Sailors probably took the sauce to Europe, where it was made with local ingredients such as the juice of mushrooms or walnuts. When the juice of tomatoes was first used, ketchup as we know it was born. However, it is important to realize that in the 18th and 19th centuries *ketchup* was a generic term for sauces whose only common ingredient was vinegar. The word is first recorded in English in 1690 in the form *catchup,* in 1711 in the form *ketchup,* and in 1730 in the form *catsup.* These three spelling variants of a foreign borrowing remain current.

keystone

ke•tene (kē′tēn′) *n.* A pungent, toxic, colorless gas, C_2H_2O, used chiefly as an acetylation agent.

keto– or **ket–** *pref.* Ketone; ketone group: *ketosis.* [< KETONE.]

ke•to•gen•e•sis (kē′tō-jĕn′ĭ-sĭs) *n.* The formation of ketone bodies, as occurs in diabetes. — **ke′to•gen′ic** *adj.*

ke•tone (kē′tōn′) *n.* Any of a class of organic compounds having a carbonyl group linked to a carbon atom in each of two hydrocarbon radicals and the general formula R(CO)R′, where R may be the same as R′. [Ger. *Keton,* short for *Aketon,* acetone < Lat. *acētum,* vinegar. See ACETUM.] — **ke•ton′ic** (-tŏn′ĭk) *adj.*

ketone body *n.* A ketone-containing intermediate product of fatty acid metabolism produced excessively in individuals affected by starvation or uncontrolled diabetes mellitus.

ke•tose (kē′tōs′) *n.* Any of various carbohydrates containing a ketone group.

ke•to•sis (kē-tō′sĭs) *n., pl.* **-ses** (-sēz). A pathological increase in ketone bodies. — **ke•tot′ic** (-tŏt′ĭk) *adj.*

ke•to•ste•roid (kē′tō-stîr′oid′, -stĕr′-) *n.* A steroid containing a ketone group.

Ket•ter•ing (kĕt′ər-ĭng). A city of SW OH, a suburb of Dayton. Pop. 60,569.

Kettering, Charles Franklin. 1876–1958. Amer. electrical engineer and manufacturer who developed the first electric cash register (1905).

ket•tle (kĕt′l) *n.* **1.** A metal pot, usu. with a lid, for boiling or stewing. **2.** A teakettle. **3.** *Mus.* A kettledrum. **4.** *Geol.* A depression left in a mass of glacial drift, formed by the melting of an isolated block of glacial ice. **5.** A pothole. [ME *ketel* < ON *ketill* and OE *cetel,* both < Lat. *catillus,* dim. of *catīnus,* large bowl.]

ket•tle•drum (kĕt′l-drŭm′) *n. Mus.* A large copper or brass hemispherical drum with a parchment head that can be tuned by adjusting the tension.

kettle of fish *n., pl.* **kettles of fish. 1.** An awkward or embarrassing situation. **2.** A matter to be reckoned with.

Keu•ka Lake (kyo͞o′kə, kā-yo͞o′-). A lake of W-central New York, one of the Finger Lakes W of Seneca Lake.

keV *abbr.* Kiloelectron unit.

kev•el (kĕv′əl) *n. Naut.* A sturdy belaying pin for the heavier cables of a ship. [ME *kevil* < OFr. *keville,* wooden peg < Lat. *clāvicula,* dim. of *clāvis,* key.]

Kew (kyo͞o). A district of W Greater London in SE England; site of the Royal Botanic Gardens (estab. 1759).

kew•pie (kyo͞o′pē) *n.* A small fat-cheeked wide-eyed doll with a curl of hair on top of the head. [Originally a trademark.]

key¹ (kē) *n., pl.* **keys. 1.a.** A notched and grooved, usu. metal device that is turned to open or close a lock. **b.** A similar device for opening or winding: *the key of a clock.* **2.** A means of access, control, or possession. **3.a.** A vital, crucial element. **b.** A set of answers to a test. **c.** A table, gloss, or cipher for decoding or interpreting. **4.** A device, such as a wedge, inserted to lock together mechanical or structural parts. **5.** *Archit.* The keystone in an arch. **6.a.** A button or lever that is pressed to operate a machine. **b.** *Mus.* A button or lever that is pressed to produce or modulate the sound of an instrument, such as a clarinet. **7.** *Mus.* **a.** A tonal system consisting of seven tones in fixed relationship to a tonic; tonality. **b.** The principal tonality of a work: *an etude in the key of E.* **8.** The pitch of a voice or other sound. **9.** A characteristic tone or level of intensity, as of a speech. Often used in combination: *high-key; low-key.* **10.** *Bot.* The key fruit. **11.** An outline of the characteristics of a group of organisms, used in taxonomic identification. **12.** *Basketball.* An area at each end of the court between the base line and the foul line and including the jump-ball circle at the foul line. — *adj.* Of crucial importance; significant: *key decisions.* — *tr.v.* **keyed, key•ing, keys. 1.** To lock with or as if with a key. **2.** *Archit.* To furnish (an arch) with a keystone. **3.** *Mus.* To regulate the pitch of. **4.** To bring into harmony; adjust or adapt. **5.** To supply an explanatory key for. **6.a.** To operate (a device), as for typesetting with a keyboard. **b.** To enter (data) into a computer with a keyboard. **7.** To identify (a biological specimen). — ***phrasal verb.* key up.** To make intense, excited, or nervous. — ***idioms.* in key.** In consonance with other factors. **out of key.** Not in consonance with other factors. [ME *kai, kei* < OE *cǣg.*]

key² (kē) *n., pl.* **keys.** A low offshore island or reef, esp. in the Gulf of Mexico; a cay. [Alteration of Sp. *cayo.* See CAY.]

key³ (kē) *n., pl.* **keys.** *Slang.* A kilogram of marijuana, cocaine, or heroin. [Shortening and alteration of KILOGRAM.]

Key (kē), **Francis Scott.** 1779–1843. Amer. lawyer and poet who wrote "Defense of Fort M'Henry" (1814), which was later set to music, renamed "The Star-Spangled Banner," and adopted in 1931 by Congress as the national anthem.

key•board (kē′bôrd′, -bōrd′) *n.* **1.** A set of keys, as on a computer terminal, typewriter, or piano. **2.** *Mus.* Any one of various instruments played by a set of keys, often connected to a synthesizer or an amplifier. — *tr.v.* **-board•ed, -board•ing, -boards. 1.** *Print.* To set (copy) with a keyed typesetting machine. **2.** *Mus.* To play (a composition) on an instrument having a set of keys. — **key′board′er, key′board′ist** *n.*

key•card (kē′kärd′) *n.* A usu. plastic card with a magnetically coded strip that is scanned to operate a mechanism.

key club *n.* A private club featuring liquor and entertainment.

key fruit *n. Bot.* See **samara.** [From the shape of its bunches.]

key•hole (kē′hōl′) *n.* **1.** The hole in a lock into which a key fits. **2.** *Basketball.* The key.

Key Lar•go (lär′gō). An island in the Florida Keys off S FL.

key money *n.* Payment made to a landlord to assure a rental.

Keynes (kānz), **John Maynard.** 1st Baron of Tilton. 1883–1946. British economist who advocated government fiscal programs to increase employment and stimulate business activity. — **Keynes′i•an** *adj. & n.* — **Keynes′i•an•ism** *n.*

key•note (kē′nōt′) *n.* **1.** *Mus.* The tonic of a musical key. **2.** A prime underlying element or theme. — *tr.v.* **-not•ed, -not•ing, -notes. 1.** To give or set the keynote of. **2.** *Informal.* To give a keynote address at. — **key′not′er** *n.*

keynote address *n.* An opening address, as at a political convention, that outlines the issues to be considered.

keynote speech *n.* See **keynote address.**

key•pad (kē′păd′) *n. Comp. Sci.* An input device, sometimes part of a standard typewriter keyboard, consisting of a grid of numeric and function keys arranged for efficient data entry.

key•punch (kē′pŭnch′) *n.* A keyboard machine used to punch holes in cards or tapes for data-processing systems. — **key′-punch′** *v.* — **key′punch′er** *n.*

key signature *n. Mus.* The group of sharps or flats placed to the right of the clef on a staff to identify the key.

key•stone (kē′stōn′) *n.* **1.** *Archit.* The central wedge-shaped stone of an arch that locks its parts together. **2.** The central supporting element of a whole.

key•stroke (kē′strōk′) *n.* A stroke of a key, as on a word processor. — **key′stroke′** *v.*

key•way (kē′wā′) *n.* **1.** A slot for a key in the hub or shaft of a wheel. **2.** The keyhole of a cylinder lock.

Key West. A city of S FL on the island of **Key West,** the westernmost of the Florida Keys in the Gulf of Mexico. Pop. 24,832.

key•word also **key word** (kē′wûrd′) *n.* **1.** A word that serves as a key to a code or cipher. **2.** A significant or descriptive word. **3.** A word used as a reference point for finding other words or information.

kg *abbr.* Kilogram.

kG *abbr.* Kilogauss.

K.G. *abbr.* Knight of the Order of the Garter.

KGB or **K.G.B.** (kā′jē-bē′) *n.* The intelligence and internal security agency of the former Soviet Union. [Russ. < *K(omitét) G(osudárstvennoĭ) B(ezopásnosti)* : *komitet*, committee + *gosudarstvennoĭ*, genitive of *gosudarstvennyĭ*, of the state + *bezopasnosti*, genitive of *bezopasnost′*, security.]

kgf *abbr.* Kilogram force.

Kha•ba•rovsk (kə-bär′əfsk, KHə-). A city of SE Russia on the Amur R. near the Chinese border; built on the site of a fort estab. in 1652. Pop. 576,000.

Kha•cha•tu•ri•an (kä′chä-to͝or′ē-ən, kăch′ə-, KHə-chə-to͝or-yän′), **Aram Ilich.** 1903–78. Russian composer of Armenian parentage whose works include the ballet *Gayane* (1942).

Kha•da•fy (kə-dä′fē), **Muammar al-.** See Muammar al- **Qaddafi.**

khak•i (kăk′ē, kä′kē) *n.* **1.** *Color.* A light olive brown to moderate or light yellowish brown. **2.a.** A sturdy cloth of this color. **b. khakis.** A uniform made of this cloth. [Urdu *khākī*, dusty < Pers. < *khāk*, dust < MPers.] — **khak′i** *adj.*

Kha•lid (kä-lēd′, KHä-). 1913–82. King of Saudi Arabia (1975–82).

kha•lif (kā′lĭf, kăl′ĭf) *n.* Var. of **caliph.**

Khal•ki•dhi•kí (käl-kē′*thē*-kē′, KHäl-). See **Chalcidice.**

Khal•kís (käl-kēs′, KHäl-). See **Chalcis.**

kham•sin (kăm-sēn′) *n.* A usu. southerly hot wind from the Sahara that blows across Egypt from late March to early May. [Ar. *(rīḥ al-)hamsīn*, (wind of the) 50 (days), khamsin < *ḫamsūn*, fifty.]

khan[1] (kän, kăn) *n.* **1.** A ruler, an official, or an important person in India and some central Asian countries. **2.** A medieval ruler of a Mongol, Tartar, or Turkish tribe. [ME *caan* < OFr. *can* < Turk. *khān* (< Old Turkic *qaghan*) and < Mongolian *qā'ān*, ruler.]

khan[2] (kän, kăn) *n.* A caravansary in certain Asian countries. [Ar. *ḫān*, inn < Pers. *khān*, house < MPers.]

khan•ate (kä′nāt′, kăn′āt′) *n.* **1.** The realm of a khan. **2.** The position of a khan.

kha•pra beetle (kä′prə, kăp′rə) *n.* A beetle *(Trogoderma granurium)* accidentally brought into the United States that is a destructive grain pest. [Hindi *khaprā* < *khapnā*, to destroy.]

Khar•kov (kär′kôf′, KHär′kəf). A city of NE Ukraine E of Kiev; founded 1656. Pop. 1,554,000.

Khar•toum also **Khar•tum** (kär-to͞om′). The cap. of Sudan, in the E-central part at the confluence of the Blue Nile and the White Nile; founded c. 1821. Pop. 476,218.

khat (kät) *n.* **1.** An evergreen shrub *(Catha edulis)* of tropical East Africa with leaves that are chewed as a stimulant. **2.** A tealike beverage prepared from its leaves. [Ar. *qatt.*]

Kha•tan•ga (kə-tăng′gə, -tăng′-, KHä-tän′-). A river of N-central Russia flowing c. 1,150 km (715 mi) to **Khatanga Gulf,** an arm of the Laptev Sea.

Khay•yám (kī-yäm′, -ăm′), **Omar.** See **Omar Khayyám.**

khe•dive (kə-dēv′) *n.* One of several Turkish viceroys ruling Egypt from 1867 to 1914. [Fr. *khédive* < Turk. *hidiv* < Pers. *khidēw*, lord < MPers. *khwadāy* < OIran. *khvadāta-*. See **s(w)e-*.**]

Kher•son (kĕr-sôn′, KHyĭr-). A city of S-central Ukraine on the Dnieper R. near the Black Sea ENE of Odessa. Pop. 346,000.

khi (kī) *n.* Var. of **chi.**

Khí•os (kē′ôs, KHē′-). See **Chios.**

Khir•bet Qum•ran (kîr′bĕt ko͝om-rän′). See **Qumran.**

Khmer (kmâr) *n., pl.* **Khmer** or **Khmers. 1.** A member of a people of Cambodia whose civilization reached its height from the 9th to the 15th century. **2.** The Mon-Khmer language that is the official language of Cambodia.

Khmer Republic. See **Cambodia.**

Khoi•khoin (koi′koi′ĭn) or **Khoi•khoi** (koi′koi) *n., pl.* **Khoikhoin** or **-khoins** or **Khoikhoi** or **-khois. 1.** A member of a pastoral people of Namibia and South Africa. **2.** Any of the Khoisan languages of the Khoikhoin, including Nama. [Nama *khoi-khoi-n*, the Nama people : *khoi-khoi*, to speak Nama (< *khoi-*, human being) + *-n*, pl. common gender suff.]

Khoi•san (koi′sän′) *n.* A family of languages of southern Africa, including those of the Khoikhoin and the San. [Nama *khoi-khoi-n*, the Nama people; see KHOIKHOIN + *san*, the San people; see SAN.]

Kho•mei•ni (kō-mā′nē, KHō-, KHô′mā-nē′), Ayatollah **Ruholla.** 1900–89. Iranian Shiite leader and head of state (1979–89) who enforced strict observance of the Islamic code.

Kho•per (kə-pyôr′, KHŏ-). A river, c. 1,006 km (625 mi), of SE Russia flowing S to the Don R.

Kho•ra•na (kō-rä′nə), **Har Gobind.** b. 1922. Indian-born Amer. biochemist who shared a 1968 Nobel Prize.

khoum (ko͞om, ko͝om) *n.* See table at **currency.** [Native word in Mauritania.]

Nikita Khrushchev
Photographed in 1960 at the United Nations

Khru•shchev (kro͝osh′chĕf, -chôf, KHro͞o-shchyôf′), **Nikita Sergeyevich.** 1894–1971. Soviet politician who served as first secretary of the Communist Party (after 1953) and premier of the U.S.S.R. (1958–64).

Khu•fu (ko͞o′fo͞o′). See **Cheops.**

Khul•na (ko͝ol′nə). A city of SW Bangladesh near the Ganges R. delta. Pop. 623,184.

Khwa•riz•mi (kwär′ĭz-mē, KHwär′-), **al-.** Muhammad ibn-Musa al-Khwarizmi. 780?–850? Muslim mathematician whose works introduced Arabic numerals and algebraic concepts to Western mathematics.

Khy•ber Pass (kī′bər). A narrow pass, c. 53 km (33 mi) long and rising to c. 1,068 m (3,500 ft), through mountains on the border between W Afghanistan and N Pakistan.

kHz *abbr.* Kilohertz.

KIA (kā′ī-ā′) *n., pl.* **KIA's** also **KIAs.** A member of the armed services who is reported killed during a combat mission. [*k(illed) i(n) a(ction).*]

Kia•ling (kyä′lĭng′, jyä′-). See **Jialing.**

Kia•mu•sze (kyä′mo͞o′so͞o′). See **Jiamusi.**

ki•ang (kē-äng′) *n.* A large wild ass *(Equus hemionus* subsp. *kiang)* of the mountains of Asia. [Tibetan *rkyan.*]

Kiang•si (kyäng′shē′). See **Jiangxi.**

Kiang•su (kyäng′so͞o′, -sü′). See **Jiangsu.**

kiaugh (kyäKH) *n. Scots.* Trouble; anxiety. [Prob. < Sc.Gael. *cabhag.*]

kib•ble[1] (kĭb′əl) *n.* An iron bucket used in wells or mines for hoisting water, ore, or refuse to the surface. [Prob. < Ger. *Kübel*, pail < MHGer. *kübel* < OHGer. *-chublī* (in *miluhchublī*, milk pail) < VLat. **cupia* < Lat. *cūpa*, vat.]

kib•ble[2] (kĭb′əl) *tr.v.* **-bled, -bling, -bles.** To crush or grind (grain, for example) coarsely. — *n.* Meal ground by this process and used in pellets esp. for pet food. [?]

kib•butz (kĭ-bo͝ots′, -bo͞ots′) *n., pl.* **kib•but•zim** (kĭb′o͝ot-sēm′, -o͞ot-). A collective farm or settlement in modern Israel. [Heb. *qibbûṣ*, gathering < *qibbēṣ*, to gather.]

kib•butz•nik (kĭ-bo͝ots′nĭk, -bo͞ots′-) *n.* A member of a kibbutz.

kibe (kīb) *n.* A chapped or inflamed area on the skin, esp. on the heel, resulting from exposure to cold; an ulcerated chillblain. [ME *kybe.*]

Ki•bei (kē-bā′) *n., pl.* **Kibei** or **-beis.** A person born in the United States of Japanese immigrant parents and educated chiefly in Japan. [J., to go home, return to America, kibei.]

kib•itz (kĭb′ĭts) *intr.v.* **-itzed, -itz•ing, -itz•es.** *Informal.* **1.** To look on and offer unwanted, usu. meddlesome advice to others. **2.** To chat; converse. [Yiddish *kibitsen* < Ger. *kiebitzen* < *Kiebitz*, pewit, kibitzer < MHGer. *gībitz*, pewit, of imit. orig.] — **kib′itz•er** *n.*

kib•lah (kĭb′lə) *n. Islam.* The direction of the Kaaba, which Muslims face when praying. [Ar. *qiblah.*]

ki•bosh (kī′bŏsh′, kĭ-bŏsh′) *n. Informal.* A checking or restraining element: *put the kibosh on the plan.* [?]

kick (kĭk) *v.* **kicked, kick•ing, kicks.** — *intr.* **1.** To strike out with the foot or feet. **2.a.** *Sports.* To score or gain ground by kicking a ball. **b.** *Football.* To punt. **3.** To recoil: *The rifle kicked hard.* **4.** *Informal.* **a.** To express negative feelings vigorously; complain. **b.** To oppose by argument; protest. See Syns at **object.** — *tr.* **1.** To strike with the foot. **2.** To propel by striking with the foot. **3.** To spring back against suddenly. **4.** *Sports.* To score (a goal or point) by kicking a ball. — *n.* **1.a.** A vigorous blow with the foot. **b.** *Sports.* The thrusting motion of the legs in swimming. **2.** A jolting recoil. **3.** *Slang.*

ă pat	oi boy
ā pay	ou out
âr care	o͝o took
ä father	o͞o boot
ĕ pet	ŭ cut
ē be	ûr urge
ĭ pit	th thin
ī pie	*th* this
îr pier	hw which
ŏ pot	zh vision
ō toe	ə about, item
ô paw	

Stress marks: **′** (primary); ′ (secondary), as in **dictionary** (dĭk′shə-nĕr′ē)

A complaint; a protest. **4.** *Slang.* Power; force. **5.** *Slang.* **a.** A feeling of pleasurable stimulation. **b. kicks.** Fun. **6.** *Slang.* Temporary, often obsessive interest. **7.** *Slang.* A sudden striking surprise; a twist. **8.** *Sports.* **a.** The act or an instance of kicking a ball. **b.** A kicked ball. **c.** The distance spanned by a kicked ball. **—*phrasal verbs.* kick around.** *Informal.* **1.** To treat badly; abuse. **2.** To move from place to place. **3.** To give consideration or thought to (an idea). **kick back. 1.** To recoil unexpectedly and violently. **2.** *Slang.* To return (stolen items). **3.** *Slang.* To pay a kickback. **kick in. 1.** *Informal.* To contribute (one's share). **2.** *Slang.* To die. **kick off. 1.** *Sports.* To begin or resume play with a kickoff. **2.** *Informal.* To begin; start. **3.** *Slang.* To die. **kick out.** *Slang.* To throw out; dismiss. **kick over.** To begin to fire: *The engine kicked over.* **kick up.** *Informal.* **1.** To increase in amount or force; intensify. **2.** To stir up (trouble). **3.** To show signs of disorder. **—*idioms.* kick the bucket.** *Slang.* To die. **kick the habit.** *Slang.* To free oneself of an addiction, as to cigarettes. **kick up (one's) heels.** *Informal.* To cast off one's inhibitions and have a good time. **kick upstairs.** *Slang.* To promote to a higher yet less desirable position. [ME *kiken*, perh. of Scand. orig.]

kickboxing

Kick•a•poo (kĭk′ə-po͞o′) *n., pl.* **Kickapoo** or **-poos. 1.** A member of a Native American people formerly inhabiting southern Wisconsin and northern Illinois, with small present-day populations in Kansas, Oklahoma, and northern Mexico. **2.** The Algonquian language of the Kickapoo.

kick•back (kĭk′băk′) *n.* **1.** A sharp reaction; a repercussion. **2.** *Slang.* A return of a percentage of a sum of money already received, usu. as a result of coercion or a secret agreement.

kick•box•ing (kĭk′bŏk′sĭng) *n.* The martial art and sport of attack and defense, practiced in a boxing ring and combining many elements of karate and boxing. **—kick′box•er** *n.*

kick•er (kĭk′ər) *n.* **1.** One that kicks. **2.** *Informal.* **a.** A sudden surprising turn of events or ending; a twist. **b.** A tricky or concealed condition; a pitfall. **3.** A condition that imposes an automatic increase, as in a pension plan.

kick•off (kĭk′ôf′, -ŏf′) *n.* **1.** *Sports.* A place kick in football or soccer with which play is begun. **2.** *Informal.* A beginning.

kick plate *n.* A protective sheet of metal at the bottom of a door.

kick•shaw (kĭk′shô′) *n.* **1.** Fancy food; a delicacy. **2.** A trinket; a gewgaw. [By folk ety. < Fr. *quelque chose*, something : *quelque*, some + *chose*, thing.]

kick•stand (kĭk′stănd′) *n.* A swiveling metal bar for holding a two-wheeled vehicle upright when not being ridden.

kick•y (kĭk′ē) *adj.* **-i•er, -i•est.** *Slang.* So unusual or unconventional in character or nature as to provide a thrill.

kid (kĭd) *n.* **1.a.** A young goat. **b.** The young of a similar animal, such as an antelope. **2.a.** The flesh of a young goat. **b.** Leather made from the skin of a young goat; kidskin. **c.** An article made from this leather. **3.** *Informal.* **a.** A child. **b.** A young person. **4.** *Slang.* Pal. Used as a term of familiar address, esp. for a young person: *Hi, kid! What's up?* *—adj.* **1.** Made of kid. **2.** *Informal.* Younger than oneself: *my kid brother.* *—v.* **kid•ded, kid•ding, kids.** *—tr. Informal.* **1.** To mock playfully; tease. **2.** To deceive in fun; fool. *—intr.* **1.** *Informal.* To engage in teasing or good-humored fooling. **2.** To bear young. Used of a goat or an antelope. [ME *kide* < ON *kidh*.] **—kid′der** *n.* **—kid′ding•ly** *adv.*

Kid (kĭd), **Thomas.** See Thomas **Kyd.**

Kidd (kĭd), **William.** "Captain Kidd." 1645?–1701. British sea captain who turned to piracy after being hired to protect British ships in the Indian Ocean (1696).

killdeer
Charadrius vociferus

Kid•der•min•ster¹ (kĭd′ər-mĭn′stər). A municipal borough of W-central England WSW of Birmingham. Pop. 91,600.

Kid•der•min•ster² (kĭd′ər-mĭn′stər) *n.* An ingrain carpet originally made in Kidderminster.

kid•die or **kid•dy** (kĭd′ē) *n., pl.* **-dies.** *Slang.* A small child.

kid•do (kĭd′ō) *n., pl.* **-dos.** *Slang.* **1.a.** A child. **b.** A young person. **2.** Pal. Used as a term of familiar address.

Kid•dush (kĭd′əsh, kē-do͞osh′) *n.* *Judaism.* The traditional prayer recited over wine on the eve of the Sabbath or a festival. [Heb. *qiddûš* < *qāddēš*, to sanctify.]

kid glove *n.* A glove made of fine soft leather, esp. kidskin. **—*idiom.* with kid gloves.** Tactfully and cautiously.

kid•nap (kĭd′năp′) *tr.v.* **-napped, -nap•ping, -naps** or **-naped, -nap•ing, -naps.** To seize and detain unlawfully and usu. for ransom. [Prob. KID + *nap*, to snatch (perh. var. of NAB or of Scand. orig.).] **—kid′nap′** *n.* **—kid′nap′per, kid′nap′er** *n.*

kid•ney (kĭd′nē) *n., pl.* **-neys. 1.** *Anat.* Either one of a pair of organs in the dorsal region of the vertebrate abdominal cavity, functioning to maintain water and electrolyte balance, regulate acid-base concentration, and filter the blood of metabolic wastes. **2.** The kidney of certain animals, eaten as food. **3.** An excretory organ of certain invertebrates. **4.** Kind; sort. [ME *kidenere, kidenei.*]

kidney bean *n.* **1.** An annual plant *(Phaseolus vulgaris)* cultivated for its edible pods and seeds. **2.** Its pod or seed.

kidney stone *n.* A small hard mass in the kidney that forms from deposits chiefly of phosphates and urates.

kid•skin (kĭd′skĭn′) *n.* Soft leather made from the skin of a young goat.

kid stuff *n.* *Slang.* **1.** Something suitable only for children. **2.** Something very easy or uncomplicated.

Kiel (kēl). A city of N Germany on **Kiel Bay,** an arm of the Baltic Sea; chartered 1242. Pop. 245,751.

kiel•ba•sa (kĭl-bä′sə, kēl-) *n.* A spicy smoked Polish sausage. [Pol. *kiełbasa* < East and West Slav. **kŭlbasa* < East Turkic *kül bassï*, grilled cutlet < Turkic *kül bastï* : *kül*, coals, ashes + *bastï*, pressed (meat) (< *basmaq*, to press).]

Kiel Canal also **Nord-Ost•see Ka•nal** (nört-ôst′zā kä-näl′). An artificial waterway, 98.1 km (61 mi), of N Germany connecting the North Sea with the Baltic Sea; built (1887–95).

Kiel•ce (kyĕl′tsĕ). A city of SE-central Poland S of Warsaw; founded 1173. Pop. 200,500.

Kier•ke•gaard (kîr′kĭ-gärd′, -gôr′), **Søren Aaby.** 1813–55. Danish religious philosopher and precursor of modern existentialism whose works include *Either/Or* (1843).

kie•sel•guhr (kē′zəl-go͝or′) *n.* See **diatomite.** [Ger. *Kieselgur* : *Kiesel*, pebble (< MHGer. *kisel* < OHGer. *chisil*) + *Gur, Guhr*, ferment, earthy deposit from water (< *gären*, to ferment, blend of MHGer. *jësan* < OHGer., and MHGer. **jern*, to cause to ferment < OHGer. *jerian*; see **yes-***).]

kie•ser•ite (kē′zə-rīt′) *n.* A whitish to yellowish hydrous magnesium sulfate mineral, $MgSO_4 \cdot H_2O$, found in salt residues. [After Dietrich Georg *Kieser* (1779–1862), German physician.]

Ki•ev (kē′ĕf, -ĕv, kyĕ′yĭf). The cap. of Ukraine, in the N-central part on the Dnieper R.; center of the first Russian state. Pop. 2,448,000.

kif (kĭf, kēf) also **kef** (kĕf, kēf, kāf) *n.* **1.** Smoking material, such as Indian hemp, used esp. in the Maghreb. **2.** The euphoria caused by smoking kif. [Ar. *kayf, kef*, pleasure, well-being.]

Ki•ga•li (kĭ-gä′lē, kē-). The cap. of Rwanda, in the central part E of Lake Kivu. Pop. 156,700.

kike (kīk) *n.* *Offensive Slang.* Used as a disparaging term for a Jew. [?]

Ki•klá•dhes (kē-klä′thĕs). See **Cyclades.**

Ki•kon•go (kē-kŏng′gō) *n.* See **Kongo** 2.

Ki•ku•yu (kĭ-ko͞o′yo͞o) also **Gi•ku•yu** (gĭ-ko͞o′yo͞o) *n., pl.* **Kikuyu** or **-yus** also **Gikuyu** or **-yus. 1.** A member of a people of central and southern Kenya. **2.** Their Bantu language.

Ki•lau•e•a (kē′lou-ā′ə). An active volcanic crater on the SE slope of Mauna Loa in S-central Hawaii I.

kil•der•kin (kĭl′dər-kĭn) *n.* **1.** A cask. **2.** An obsolete English measure of capacity equal to about 18 gallons (68 liters). [ME, alteration of MFlem. *kinderkin* (var. of MDu. *kindekijn*) : *quintel, quintlein*, quintal (< Med.Lat. *quintāle*; see QUINTAL) + *-kijn*, dim. suff.]

ki•lim (kē-lēm′, kĭl′ĭm) *n.* A tapestry-woven Turkish rug or other textile with geometric designs in rich brilliant colors. [Turk. < Pers. *gilīm*.]

Kil•i•man•ja•ro (kĭl′ə-mən-jär′ō), **Mount.** A mountain of NE Tanzania near the Kenya border rising in two snow-capped peaks to 5,898.7 m (19,340 ft).

kill¹ (kĭl) *v.* **killed, kill•ing, kills.** *—tr.* **1.a.** To put to death. **b.** To deprive of life: *The Black Death killed millions.* **2.** To put an end to; extinguish. **3.a.** To destroy a vitally essential quality in. **b.** To cause to cease operating; turn off. **c.** To tire out completely; exhaust. **4.** To pass (time) in aimless activity. **5.** To consume entirely; finish off. **6.** To cause extreme pain or discomfort to. **7.** To mark for deletion; rule out. **8.** To thwart passage of; veto. **9.** *Informal.* To overwhelm with hilarity, pleasure, or admiration. **10.** *Sports.* **a.** To hit (a ball) with great force. **b.** To hit (a ball) with such force as to make a return impossible, esp. in a racquet game. *—intr.* **1.** To cause death or extinction; be fatal. **2.** To commit murder. *—n.* **1.** The act of killing. **2.a.** An animal killed, esp. in hunting. **b.** A person killed or to be killed. **c.** An enemy aircraft, vessel, or missile that has been attacked and destroyed. **3.** *Sports.* A kill shot. **—*phrasal verb.* kill off.** To destroy in such large numbers as to render extinct. **—*idiom.* in at** (or **on**) **the kill.** Present at the moment of triumph. [ME *killen*, perh. < OE **cyllan*. See **gʷelə-***.]

kill² (kĭl) *n.* *New York State.* See **creek** 1. See Regional Notes at **olicook, run.** [Du. *kil* < MDu. *kille.*]

Kil•lar•ney (kĭ-lär′nē), **Lakes of.** Three small lakes of SW Ireland near the market town of **Killarney** (pop. 7,693).

kill•deer (kĭl′dîr′) *n., pl.* **killdeer** or **-deers.** A New World plover *(Charadrius vociferus)* having a distinctive noisy cry and two black bands across its breast. [Prob. imit. of its call.]

Kil•leen (kĭ-lēn′). A city of central TX SW of Waco; founded 1882. Pop. 63,535.

kill•er (kĭl′ər) *n.* **1.** One that kills. **2.** *Slang.* Something extremely difficult to deal with or withstand.

killer bee *n.* See **Africanized bee.**

killer cell *n.* A large differentiated T cell that attacks and lyses target cells bearing specific antigens.

killer T cell *n.* See **killer cell.**

killer whale *n.* A black and white predatory whale *(Orcinus orca)* that mostly feeds on fish and squid.

kil•lick also **kil•lock** (kĭl′ĭk) *n.* *Naut.* A small anchor, esp. one made of a stone in a wooden frame. [?]

kil•lie (kĭl′ē) *n.* A killifish.

ă pat	oi boy
ā pay	ou out
âr care	o͝o took
ä father	o͞o boot
ĕ pet	ŭ cut
ē be	ûr urge
ĭ pit	th thin
ī pie	*th* this
îr pier	hw which
ŏ pot	zh vision
ō toe	ə about, item
ô paw	

Stress marks:
′ (primary);
′ (secondary), as in
dictionary (dĭk′shə-nĕr′ē)

kil•li•fish (kĭl′ĭ-fĭsh′) *n., pl.* **killifish** or **-fish•es.** Any of numerous small fishes of the family Cyprinodontidae, including the guppy and mosquito fish, inhabiting chiefly fresh and brackish waters in warm regions. [Perh. KILL[2] + FISH.]

kill•ing (kĭl′ĭng) *n.* **1.** Murder; homicide. **2.** A kill; a quarry. **3.** A sudden large profit: *made a killing on the market.* — *adj.* **1.** Intended or apt to kill; fatal. **2.** Thoroughly exhausting: *a killing pace.* **3.** *Informal.* Hilarious. — **kill′ing•ly** *adv.*

kill•joy (kĭl′joi′) *n.* One who spoils the fun of others.

kill shot *n. Sports.* A shot in various games, esp. racquet games, so hit or placed that it cannot be returned.

Kil•mer (kĭl′mər), **(Alfred) Joyce.** 1886–1918. Amer. poet whose best known work is "Trees" (1913).

kiln (kĭln, kĭl) *n.* Any of various ovens for hardening, burning, or drying substances such as grain, meal, or clay, esp. a brick-lined oven used to bake or fire ceramics. — *tr.v.* **kilned, kiln•ing, kilns.** To process in one of these ovens. [ME *kilne* < OE *cyln* < Lat. *culīna*, kitchen, stove. See **pekʷ-***.]

ki•lo (kē′lō) *n., pl.* **-los. 1.** A kilogram. **2.** A kilometer.

kilo– *pref.* One thousand (10^3): *kilowatt.* [Fr. < Gk. *khilioi*, thousand. See **gheslo-***.]

kil•o•bit (kĭl′ə-bĭt′) *n. Comp. Sci.* **1.** A unit of information equal to 1,024 (2^{10}) bits. **2.** One thousand bits.

kil•o•byte (kĭl′ə-bīt′) *n. Comp. Sci.* **1.** A unit of measurement of the memory capacity of a computer, equal to 1,024 (2^{10}) bytes. **2.** One thousand bytes.

kil•o•cal•o•rie (kĭl′ə-kăl′ə-rē) *n.* See **calorie** 3a.

kil•o•cu•rie (kĭl′ə-kyo͝or-ē′, -kyo͝o′rē) *n.* One thousand curies.

kil•o•cy•cle (kĭl′ə-sī′kəl) *n.* Kilohertz.

kil•o•gauss (kĭl′ə-gous′) *n.* A unit of magnetic induction equal to 1,000 (10^3) gauss.

kil•o•gram (kĭl′ə-grăm′) *n.* **1.** The base unit of mass in the International System, equal to 1,000 grams (2.2046 pounds). See table at **measurement. 2.** Kilogram force.

kilogram calorie *n.* See **calorie** 3a.

kilogram force *n.* A force equal to a kilogram weight or a one-kilogram mass times the acceleration of gravity.

kil•o•gram-me•ter (kĭl′ə-grăm-mē′tər) *n.* A unit of work in a gravitational system, equal to the work performed by a one-kilogram force acting through a distance of one meter.

kil•o•hertz (kĭl′ə-hûrts′) *n.* A unit of frequency equal to 1,000 hertz.

kil•o•me•ter (kĭ-lŏm′ĭ-tər, kĭl′ə-mē′tər) *n.* A metric unit of length equal to 1,000 meters (0.62 mile). See table at **measurement.** — **kil′o•met′ric** (kĭl′ə-mĕt′rĭk) *adj.*

kil•o•ton (kĭl′ə-tŭn′) *n.* **1.** A unit of weight or capacity equal to 1,000 tons. **2.** An explosive force equivalent to that of 1,000 metric tons of TNT.

kil•o•watt (kĭl′ə-wŏt′) *n.* A unit of power equal to 1,000 watts.

kil•o•watt-hour (kĭl′ə-wŏt-our′) *n.* A unit of electric power equal to the work done by one kilowatt acting for one hour.

kilt (kĭlt) *n.* **1.** A knee-length skirt with deep pleats, usu. of a tartan wool, worn as part of the dress for men in the Scottish Highlands. **2.** A similar skirt worn by women, girls, and boys. — *tr.v.* **kilt•ed, kilt•ing, kilts.** To tuck up (something) around the body. [< *kilt*, to tuck up < ME *kilten*, of Scand. orig.]

kil•ter (kĭl′tər) *n.* Good condition; proper form. [?]

Kim•ber•ley (kĭm′bər-lē). A city of central South Africa WNW of Bloemfontein; founded 1871. Pop. 70,920.

kim•ber•lite (kĭm′bər-līt′) *n.* A rock formation in South Africa containing peridotite, in which diamonds are formed. [After KIMBERLEY.] — **kim′ber•lit′ic** (-lĭt′ĭk) *adj.*

Kim•bun•du (kĭm-bo͝on′do͞o) *n.* See **Mbundu** 4.

ki•mo•no (kə-mō′nə, -nō) *n., pl.* **-nos. 1.** A long wide-sleeved Japanese robelike dress worn with an obi and often elaborately decorated. **2.** A loose robe worn chiefly by women. [J. : *ki*, to wear + *mono*, object.]

kin (kĭn) *n.* **1.** *(used with a pl. v.)* One's relatives; family; kinfolk. **2.** A kinsman or kinswoman. — *adj.* Related; akin. [ME < OE *cyn.* See **genə-***.]

-kin or **-kins** *suff.* Little one: *devilkin.* [ME, prob. < MDu. *-kijn, -kin.*]

ki•na (kē′nə) *n., pl.* **kina** or **-nas.** See table at **currency.** [Indigenous word in Papua New Guinea.]

ki•nase (kī′nās′, -nāz′, kĭn′ās′, āz′) *n.* Any of various enzymes that catalyze the transfer of a phosphate group from a donor, such as ADP, to an acceptor. [KIN(ETIC) + -ASE.]

kind[1] (kīnd) *adj.* **kind•er, kind•est. 1.** Of a friendly, generous, or warm-hearted nature. **2.** Sympathetic or understanding; charitable. **3.** Humane; considerate. **4.** Forbearing; tolerant. **5.** Generous; liberal. **6.** Agreeable; beneficial. [ME, natural, kind < OE *gecynde*, natural. See **genə-***.]

kind[2] (kīnd) *n.* **1.** A group of individuals linked by traits held in common. **2.** A particular variety; a sort. **3.** Fundamental underlying character as a determinant of the class to which a thing belongs; nature or essence. **4.** A doubtful or borderline member of a given category: *built a kind of shelter.* **5.** *Archaic.* Manner. — ***idioms.*** **all kinds of.** *Informal.* Plenty of; ample. **in kind. 1.** With produce or commodities rather than with money. **2.** In the same manner or with an equivalent. **kind of.** *Informal.* Rather; somewhat. [ME < OE *gecynd*, race, offspring, kind. See **genə-***.]

Usage Note: The use of the plural demonstratives *these* and *those* with *kind* and *sort*, as in *these kind* (or *sort*) *of films*, has been a traditional bugbear of American grammarians. We find reputable precedent, however, for *this kind of films are, these kind of films are, this kind of films is, these kind of films is,* and so on. When the plural *kinds* is used, the demonstrative and the verb must also be plural: *These kinds of films are popular.* By the same token, when both *kind* and the noun following it are singular, the verb must be singular: *This kind of film is popular.* To this may be added a word of caution to American writers: despite the existence of ample literary precedent for *these kind of films,* the construction has been so thoroughly stigmatized by native grammarians that its use would have to be reckoned indiscreet, if not strictly incorrect.

kiln
An intermittent kiln

kin•der•gar•ten (kĭn′dər-gär′tn, -dn) *n.* A program or class for four-year-old to six-year-old children that serves as an introduction to school. [Ger. : *Kinder*, genitive pl. of *Kind*, child (< MHGer. *kint* < OHGer. *kind*; see **genə-***) + *Garten*, garden (< MHGer. *garte* < OHGer. *garto*; see **gher-[1]***).]

kin•der•gart•ner also **kin•der•gar•ten•er** (kĭn′dər-gärt′nər, -gärd′-) *n.* **1.** A child who attends kindergarten. **2.** A teacher in a kindergarten. [Ger. *Kindergärtner* < *Kindergarten*, kindergarten. See KINDERGARTEN.]

kind•heart•ed (kīnd′här′tĭd) *adj.* Having or proceeding from a kind heart. — **kind′heart′ed•ly** *adv.* — **kind′heart′ed•ness** *n.*

kin•dle[1] (kĭn′dl) *v.* **-dled, -dling, -dles.** — *tr.* **1.a.** To build or fuel (a fire). **b.** To set fire to; ignite. **2.** To cause to glow; light up: *The sunset kindled the skies.* **3.** To arouse (an emotion, for example). — *intr.* **1.** To catch fire; burst into flame. **2.** To become bright; glow. **3.** To become inflamed. **4.** To be stirred up; rise. [ME *kindelen* (influenced by *kindelen*, to give birth to, cause; see KINDLE[2]), prob. < ON *kynda.*] — **kin′dler** *n.*

kin•dle[2] (kĭn′dl) *n.* A brood or litter, esp. of kittens. — *intr.v.* **-dled, -dling, -dles.** To give birth to young. Used esp. of rabbits. [ME *kindelen* < *kindel*, offspring < OE *gecynd.* See KIND[2].]

kind•less (kīnd′lĭs) *adj.* **1.** Exhibiting or feeling no kindness or compassion; heartless. **2.** *Obsolete.* Inhuman.

kind•li•ness (kīnd′lē-nĭs) *n.* **1.** The quality or state of being kindly. **2.** A kindly deed.

kin•dling (kĭnd′lĭng) *n.* Easily ignited material, such as dry sticks of wood, used to start a fire. Also called regionally *lightwood.* See Regional Note at **lightwood.**

kindling point *n.* See **ignition point.**

kind•ly (kīnd′lē) *adj.* **-li•er, -li•est. 1.** Of a sympathetic, helpful, or benevolent nature. **2.** Agreeable; pleasant: *a kindly breeze.* **3.a.** *Archaic.* Within the law; lawful. **b.** *Obsolete.* Natural to its kind. — *adv.* **1.** Out of kindness. **2.** In a kind manner. **3.** Pleasantly; agreeably. **4.** In an accommodating manner: *Would you kindly sign?* **5.** *Obsolete.* In a way or course that is natural; fittingly.

kind•ness (kīnd′nĭs) *n.* **1.** The quality or state of being kind. **2.** An instance of kind behavior.

kin•dred (kĭn′drĭd) *n.* **1.** A group of related persons, as a clan or tribe. **2.** *(used with a pl. v.)* One's relatives; kinfolk. — *adj.* **1.** Of the same ancestry or family. **2.** Having a similar or related origin, nature, or character. [ME *kinrede, kindrede* < OE *cynrēde* : *cyn*, kin; see **genə-*** + *-rēde*, condition (var. of *rǣden*; see **ar-***).] — **kin′dred•ness** *n.*

kine (kīn) *n. Archaic.* Pl. of **cow[1].** [ME *kyn* < OE *cȳna*, genitive pl. of *cū*, cow. See COW[1].]

kin•e•mat•ics (kĭn′ə-măt′ĭks) *n.* *(used with a sing. v.)* The branch of mechanics that studies the motion of a body or a system without consideration given to mass or force. [< Gk. *kinēma*, *kinēmat-*, motion < *kinein*, to move. See **kei-[2]***.] — **kin′e•mat′ic, kin′e•mat′i•cal** *adj.*

kin•e•scope (kĭn′ĭ-skōp′, kī′nĭ-) *n.* **1.** See **picture tube. 2.** A film of a transmitted television program. — *tr.v.* **-scoped, -scop•ing, -scopes.** To make a kinescope of. [Originally a trademark.]

ki•ne•sics (kə-nē′sĭks, -zĭks, kī-) *n.* *(used with a sing. v.)* The study of nonlinguistic bodily movements, such as gestures and facial expressions, as a systematic mode of communication. [< Gk. *kinēsis*, movement < *kinein*, to move. See **kei-[2]***.] — **ki•ne′sic** (-sĭk, -zĭk) *adj.*

ki•ne•si•ol•o•gy (kə-nē′sē-ŏl′ə-jē, -zē-) *n.* The study of muscles, esp. the mechanics of human motion. [Gk. *kinēsis*, movement (< *kinein*, to move; see **kei-[2]***) + -LOGY.] — **ki•ne′si•ol′o•gist** *n.*

-kinesis *suff.* Motion: *photokinesis.* [< Gk. *kinēsis*, movement < *kinein*, to move. See **kei-[2]***.]

kin•es•the•sia (kĭn′ĭs-thē′zhə, kī′nĭs-) *n.* The sense that detects bodily position, weight, or movement of the muscles, tendons, and joints. [Gk. *kinein*, to move; see **kei-[2]*** + ESTHESIA.] — **kin′es•thet′ic** (-thĕt′ĭk) *adj.*

ki•net•ic (kĭ-nĕt′ĭk, kī-) *adj.* Of, relating to, or produced by motion. [Gk. *kinētikos* < *kinētos*, moving < *kinein*, to move. See **kei-[2]***.] — **ki•net′i•cal•ly** *adv.*

kilt

kimono

king
Chess piece

Martin Luther King, Jr.
Photographed in 1964

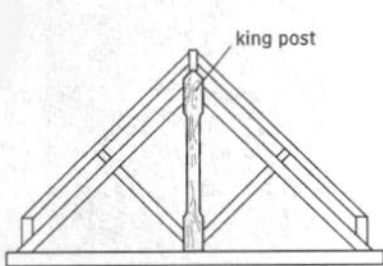

king post

kinkajou
Potos flavus

kiosk

kinetic art *n.* An art form, such as a sculpture, made up of parts to be set in motion by an internal mechanism or an external stimulus, such as light or air. — **kinetic artist** *n.* — **ki•net′i•cism** (-ĭ-sĭz′əm) *n.* — **ki•net′i•cist** *n.*

kinetic energy *n.* The energy possessed by a body because of its motion, equal to one half the mass of the body times the square of its speed.

ki•net•ics (kĭ-nĕt′ĭks, kī-) *n. (used with a sing. v.)* **1.** See **dynamics** 1a. **2.** The branch of chemistry that is concerned with the rates of chemical reactions.

kinetic theory *n.* A statistical theory of the thermodynamic behavior of matter, esp. gases, that explains properties, such as temperature and pressure, in terms of the kinetic energies of the rapidly moving atoms and molecules composing a system.

ki•ne•tin (kī′nə-tĭn) *n.* A plant hormone that promotes cell division.

kineto– *pref.* Movement: *kinetoplast.* [Gk. *kinēto-* < *kinētos,* moving. See KINETIC.]

ki•net•o•chore (kĭ-nĕt′ə-kôr′, -kōr′, -nē′tə-, kī-) *n. Biol.* Either of two submicroscopic attachment points for chromosomal microtubules, present on each centromere during cell division. [KINETO– + Gk. *khōros,* place; see –CHORE.]

ki•net•o•plast (kĭ-nĕt′ə-plăst′, -nē′tə-, kī-) *n. Microbiol.* An independently replicating structure lying near the base of the flagellum in certain protozoans.

ki•net•o•some (kĭ-nĕt′ə-sōm′, -nē′tə-, kī-) *n.* See **basal body.**

kin•folk (kĭn′fōk′) also **kins•folk** (kĭnz′-) or **kin•folks** (kĭn′fōks′) *pl.n.* Relatives; kindred.

king (kĭng) *n.* **1.** A male sovereign. **2.** One that is supreme or preeminent in a particular group, category, or sphere. **3. King. a.** The perfect, omniscient, omnipotent being; God. **b.** Jesus. **4.** *Games.* **a.** A playing card bearing the figure of a king, ranking above a queen. **b.** The principal chess piece, which can move one square in any direction and must be protected against checkmate. **c.** A piece in checkers that has been moved to the last row on the opponent's side of the board and been crowned. **5. Kings.** *(used with a sing. v.)* See table at **Bible.** — *adj.* Principal or chief, as in size or importance. — *tr.v.* **kinged, king•ing, kings.** *Games.* To make (a piece in checkers) into a king; crown. [ME < OE *cyning.* See **genə-*.**]

King, Billie Jean Moffitt. b. 1943. Amer. tennis player who won 20 titles at Wimbledon and 4 U.S. Open championships (1967, 1971, 1972, and 1974).

King, Coretta Scott. b. 1927. Amer. civil rights leader noted for her work for the Southern Christian Leadership Conference and the Martin Luther King, Jr., Memorial Foundation.

King, Martin Luther, Jr. 1929–68. Amer. cleric who led the civil rights movement in the 1950's and 1960's. He won the 1964 Nobel Peace Prize, four years before he was assassinated in Memphis TN.

King, William Lyon Mackenzie. 1874–1950. Canadian prime minister (1921–26, 1926–30, and 1935–48).

King, William Rufus de Vane. 1786–1853. Vice President of the U.S. (1853).

king•bird (kĭng′bûrd′) *n.* Any of various American flycatchers of the genus *Tyrannus,* esp. *T. tyrannus.*

king•bolt (kĭng′bōlt′) *n.* A vertical bolt that joins the body of a vehicle to its front axle and usu. acts as a pivot.

King Charles spaniel *n.* Any of a variety of English toy spaniel with a curly black-and-tan coat and long ears. [After *King* CHARLES II.]

king cobra *n.* A large venomous snake *(Ophiophagus hannah)* of southeast Asia and the Philippines.

king crab *n.* **1.** A large edible crab *(Paralithodes camtschatica)* inhabiting the coastal waters of Alaska, Japan, and Siberia. **2.** See **horseshoe crab.**

king•craft (kĭng′krăft′) *n.* The exercise of power by a king.

king•cup (kĭng′kŭp′) *n. Chiefly British.* **1.** Any of several plants with yellow flowers. **2.** The marsh marigold.

king•dom (kĭng′dəm) *n.* **1.** A political or territorial unit ruled by a sovereign. **2.a.** The eternal spiritual sovereignty of God or Christ. **b.** The realm of this sovereignty. **3.** A realm or sphere in which one thing is dominant. **4.** One of the three main divisions (animal, vegetable, and mineral) into which natural organisms and objects are classified. **5.** The highest taxonomic classification into which organisms are grouped, based on fundamental similarities and common ancestry. See table at **taxonomy.** [ME < OE *cyningdōm* : *cyning,* king; see KING + *-dōm,* -dom.]

kingdom come *n. Informal.* **1.** The next world. **2.** The end of time. [< *thy kingdom come* in the Lord's Prayer.]

king•fish (kĭng′fĭsh′) *n., pl.* **kingfish** or **-fish•es. 1.a.** Any of several food and game fishes of the drum family, esp. of the genus *Menticirrhus,* indigenous to warm Atlantic waters. **b.** Any of several similar or related fishes, indigenous to the Pacific Ocean. **2.** *Informal.* A person in a position of uncontested authority or influence.

king•fish•er (kĭng′fĭsh′ər) *n.* Any of various birds of the family Alcedinidae, characteristically having a crested head, a long stout beak, a short tail, and brilliant coloration.

King James Bible *n. Bible.* An English translation of the Bible from Hebrew and Greek published in 1611 under the auspices of James I.

king•let (kĭng′lĭt) *n.* **1.** Any of several small grayish North American birds of the genus *Regulus,* having a yellowish or reddish patch on the crown of the head. **2.** A king ruling a kingdom considered small or unimportant.

king•ly (kĭng′lē) *adj.* **-li•er, -li•est. 1.** Having the status or rank of king. **2.** Of, like, or befitting a king; majestic and regal. — *adv.* In a royal way; royally. — **king′li•ness** *n.*

king mackerel *n.* A food and game fish *(Scomberomorus cavalla)* of warm Atlantic waters.

king•mak•er (kĭng′mā′kər) *n.* One who has the political power to influence the selection of a candidate for high public office. — **king′mak′ing** *adj. & n.*

king-of-arms (kĭng′əv-ärmz′) *n., pl.* **kings-of-arms** (kĭngz′-). A high-ranking heraldic officer in Great Britain.

king•pin (kĭng′pĭn′) *n.* **1.** *Sports.* The foremost or central pin in an arrangement of bowling pins. **2.** One that is the most important in an enterprise or a system. **3.** See **kingbolt.**

king post *n. Archit.* A supporting post extending vertically from a crossbeam to the apex of a triangular truss.

king salmon *n.* See **Chinook salmon.**

King's Bench (kĭngz) *n. Law.* A division of the British superior court system that hears criminal and civil cases. Used when the sovereign is a man.

King's Counsel *n. Law.* A barrister appointed as counsel to the British crown. Used when the sovereign is a man.

King's English *n.* English speech or usage that is considered standard or accepted; Received Standard English.

king•ship (kĭng′shĭp′) *n.* **1.** The position, power, or province of a king. **2.** The domain ruled by a king; a kingdom. **3.** The period or tenure of a king; a reign. **4.** Used with *his* as a title for a king. **5.** A monarchy.

king-size (kĭng′sīz′) or **king-sized** (-sīzd′) *adj.* **1.** Larger than the usual or standard size: *a king-size desk.* **2.a.** Measuring about 76 inches by 80 inches (1.9 meters by 2.0 meters). Used of a bed. **b.** Being of a size that will fit such a bed.

king snake *n.* Any of various nonvenomous constricting New World snakes of the genus *Lampropeltis,* having a black or brown body with white, yellow, or reddish markings.

kings-of-arms (kĭngz′əv-ärmz′) *n.* Pl. of **king-of-arms.**

Kings•port (kĭngz′pôrt′, -pōrt′). A city of NE TN near the VA border ENE of Knoxville. Pop. 36,365.

Kings River (kĭngz). A river, c. 201 km (125 mi), of central CA rising in **Kings Canyon** in the Sierra Nevada.

King•ston (kĭng′stən). **1.** A city of SE Ontario, Canada, on Lake Ontario near the head of the St. Lawrence R.; founded by Loyalists in 1783 and the former cap. of Canada (1841–44). Pop. 52,616. **2.** The cap. of Jamaica, in the SE part on the Caribbean Sea; founded c. 1692. Pop. 586,930. **3.** A city of SE NY on the Hudson R. N of Poughkeepsie; permanently estab. in 1652. Pop. 23,095.

King•ston-up•on-Hull (kĭng′stən-ə-pŏn-hŭl′, -pôn-). See **Hull** 2.

Kings•town (kĭngz′toun′). The cap. of St. Vincent and the Grenadines, on the SW coast of St. Vincent I. Pop. 18,378.

Kings•ville (kĭngz′vĭl′, -vəl). A city of S TX SW of Corpus Christi. Pop. 25,276.

Kings•wood (kĭngz′wo͝od′). An urban district of SW England, a suburb of Bristol. Pop. 84,200.

King•teh•chen (kĭng′tə′chœn′). See **Jingdezhen.**

king•wood (kĭng′wo͝od′) *n.* **1.** A South American tree *(Dalbergia cearensis)* with hard fine-textured purplish-brown wood used in cabinetmaking. **2.** The wood of this tree.

ki•nin (kī′nĭn) *n.* Any of various structurally related polypeptides, such as bradykinin, that act locally to induce vasodilation and contraction of smooth muscle. [Short for *bradykinin* : BRADY– + Gk. *kinein,* to move; see **kei-**[2]* + –IN.]

kink (kĭngk) *n.* **1.** A tight curl, twist, or bend in a length of thin material, as one caused by the tensing of a looped section of wire. **2.** A painful muscle spasm, as in the neck; a crick. **3.** A difficulty or flaw that is likely to impede operation, as in a plan. **4.** A mental peculiarity; a quirk. **5.** An unusual or eccentric idea. — *intr. & tr.v.* **kinked, kink•ing, kinks.** To form or cause to form a kink or kinks. [Du., twist in a rope.]

kink•a•jou (kĭng′kə-jo͞o′) *n.* An arboreal mammal *(Potos flavus)* of Central and South America having brownish fur and a long prehensile tail. [Fr. *quincajou,* wolverine, prob. blend of Ojibwa *gwiingwa'aage* and Montagnais (Cree) *kuàkuàtsheu.*]

kink•y (kĭng′kē) *adj.* **-i•er, -i•est. 1.** Tightly twisted or curled: *kinky hair.* **2.** *Slang.* Showing or appealing to bizarre or deviant tastes, esp. of a sexual or erotic nature. — **kink′i•ly** *adv.* — **kink′i•ness** *n.*

kin•ni•kin•nick also **kin•ni•kin•nic** (kĭn′ĭ-kĭ-nĭk′) *n.* **1.** A preparation made from dried leaves, bark, and sometimes tobacco and smoked esp. by certain Native American peoples. **2.** See **bearberry.** [Unami Delaware *kələkkəníikkan,* literally, item for mixing in, kinnikinnick.]

ki•no (kē′nō) *n., pl.* **-nos.** A reddish resin obtained from several Old World trees of the genera *Eucalyptus, Pterocarpus,* and *Butea* and from tropical American trees of the genera *Coccoloba* and *Dipteryx*. [NLat., of West African orig.; akin to Mandingo *keno*.]

–kins *suff.* Var. of **–kin.**

Kin•sey (kĭn′zē), **Alfred Charles.** 1894–1956. Amer. biologist whose works include *Sexual Behavior in the Human Male* (1948) and *Sexual Behavior in the Human Female* (1953).

kins•folk (kĭnz′fōk′) *pl.n.* Var. of **kinfolk.**

Kin•sha•sa (kĭn-shä′sə). Formerly (before 1966) **Le•o•pold•ville** (lē′ə-pōld-vĭl′, lā′-). The cap. of Zaire, in the W part on the Congo R.; founded 1881. Pop. 2,653,558.

kin•ship (kĭn′shĭp′) *n.* **1.** Connection by blood, marriage, or adoption. **2.** Relationship by nature or character; affinity.

kins•man (kĭnz′mən) *n.* **1.** A male relative. **2.** A man sharing the same racial, cultural, or national background as another.

Kin•ston (kĭn′stən). A city of E-central NC SE of Raleigh. Pop. 25,295.

kins•wom•an (kĭnz′wo͝om′ən) *n.* **1.** A female relative. **2.** A woman sharing the same racial, cultural, or national background as another.

Kin•yar•wan•da (kĭn′yär-wän′də) *n.* A Bantu language of Rwanda, closely related to Kirundi and an official language of Rwanda.

Ki•o•ga or **Ky•o•ga** (kē-ō′gə), **Lake.** An irregularly shaped lake of central Uganda; noted for its papyrus swamps.

ki•osk (kē′ŏsk′, kē-ŏsk′) *n.* **1.** A small open gazebo or pavilion. **2.** A small structure, often open on one or more sides, used as a newsstand or booth. **3.** A cylindrical structure on which advertisements are posted. [Fr. *kiosque* < Turk. *köşk* < MPers. *gōshak*, corner < Avestan **gaoshaka-*, dim. of *gaosha-*, ear.]

Word History: The lowly kiosk where one buys a newspaper or on which one posts advertisements is like a child in a fairy tale who though raised by humble parents is really the descendant of kings. The word *kiosk* was originally taken into English from Turkish, in which its source *köşk* meant "pavilion." The open structures referred to by the Turkish word were used as pavilions and summerhouses in Turkey and Persia. The first recorded use of *kiosk* in English (1625) has reference to these Middle Eastern structures. In France and Belgium, where the Turkish word had also been borrowed, their word *kiosque* was applied to something lower on the scale, structures resembling these pavilions but used as places to sell newspapers or as bandstands. England borrowed this lowly structure from France and reborrowed the word, first recorded in 1865 with reference to a place to buy newspapers.

Ki•o•wa (kī′ə-wô′, -wä′, -wā′) *n., pl.* **Kiowa** or **-was. 1.a.** A member of a Native American people formerly inhabiting the southern Great Plains, with a present-day population in southwest Oklahoma. **2.** The Tanoan language of the Kiowa.

Kiowa Apache *n., pl.* **Kiowa Apache** or **Kiowa Apaches. 1.a.** A member of a Native American people of the southern Great Plains who formed part of the Kiowa tribe although speaking an unrelated Athabaskan language. **2.** The Athabaskan language of the Kiowa Apache.

kip¹ (kĭp) *n., pl.* **kip.** See table at **currency.** [Thai.]

kip² (kĭp) *n.* **1.** The untanned hide of a small or young animal, such as a calf. **2.** A set or bundle of such hides. [ME, bundle of animal hides, perh. < MDu. or MLGer.]

kip³ (kĭp) *Chiefly British.* —*n.* **1.** A rooming house. **2.** A place to sleep; a bed. **3.** Sleep. —*intr.v.* **kipped, kip•ping, kips.** To sleep. [Perh. < Dan. *kippe*, cheap inn.]

kip⁴ (kĭp) *n.* A unit of weight equal to 1,000 pounds (455 kilograms). [KI(LO)- + P(OUND)¹.]

Kip•ling (kĭp′lĭng), **(Joseph) Rudyard.** 1865–1936. British writer who wrote *The Jungle Book* (1894) and *Kim* (1901) and won the 1907 Nobel Prize for literature.

kip•per (kĭp′ər) *n.* **1.** A male salmon or sea trout during or shortly after the spawning season. **2.** A herring or salmon that has been split, salted, and smoked. —*tr.v.* **-pered, -per•ing, -pers.** To prepare (fish) by splitting, salting, and smoking. [ME *kipre* < OE *cypera*, spawning male salmon, prob. < *cyperen*, of copper < *coper*, copper (because of the fish's color during the spawning season). See COPPER¹.]

kir also **Kir** (kîr) *n.* A drink consisting of dry white wine or champagne flavored with cassis. [After Canon Félix *Kir* (1876–1968), mayor of Dijon, France.]

Kirch•hoff (kîr′kôf′, kïrKH′hôf), **Gustav Robert.** 1824–87. German physicist noted for his research in spectrum analysis, optics, and electricity.

Kirch•ner (kîrk′nər, kîrKH′-), **Ernst Ludwig.** 1880–1938. German artist whose works include *The Street* (1913).

Kir•ghiz¹ or **Kir•giz** (kîr-gēz′) *n., pl.* **Kirghiz** or **-ghiz•es** or **Kirgiz** or **-giz•es. 1.** A member of a traditionally nomadic people living principally in Kirghiz. **2.** The Turkic language of the Kirghiz.

Kir•ghiz² or **Kir•giz** (kîr-gēz′, -gyēs′) also **Kir•ghiz•stan** or **Kir•giz•stan** or **Kyr•gyz•stan** (-gē-stän′, -gyē-). A region and republic of W-central Asia bordering on NW China; probably inhabited before the 13th cent. by a Turkic-speaking Mongolian people and a constituent republic of the U.S.S.R. from 1936 to 1991. Cap. Bishkek. Pop. 3,967,000.

Ki•ri•ba•ti (kēr′ə-bä′tē, kîr′ə-băs′). An island country of the W-central Pacific including the former Gilbert Is. and the Phoenix and Line islands; became independent from Great Britain in 1979. Administrative center, Bairiki. Pop. 56,213.

Ki•rin (kē′rĭn′). See **Jilin.**

kirk (kûrk) *n.* **1.** *Scots.* A church. **2. Kirk.** *Chiefly British.* The Presbyterian Church of Scotland. Used with *the.* [ME < ON *kirkja* < OE *cirice*, church. See CHURCH.]

Kirk•land (kûrk′lənd). A city of W-central WA on Lake Washington NE of Seattle. Pop. 40,052.

Kirk•pat•rick (kûrk-păt′rĭk), **Mount.** A mountain, 4,531.1 m (14,856 ft), of Antarctica near the edge of the Ross Ice Shelf.

Kirks•ville (kûrks′vĭl′). A city of N MO NW of Hannibal. Pop. 17,152.

Kir•kuk (kîr-ko͞ok′). A city of NE Iraq SE of Mosul; built on the site of a settlement dating to 3000 B.C. Pop. 207,900.

Kirk•wood (kûrk′wo͝od′). A city of E MO, a suburb of St. Louis. Pop. 27,291.

Kir•li•an photography (kîr′lē-ən) *n.* The process of photographing an object by exposing film in a dark room to ultraviolet light that results from electronic and ionic interactions caused by an applied electric field. [After S.D. and V.K. *Kirlian*, 20th-cent. Russian electricians.]

Kir•man (kĭr-män′, kər-) *n.* A Persian rug with a pastel background, a center medallion, and an ornately patterned border. [After KERMAN.]

kir•mess (kûr′mĭs) *n.* Var. of **kermis.**

Ki•rov (kē′rôf′, kyē′-rəf). A city of W-central Russia ENE of Moscow; founded c. 1174. Pop. 411,000.

Ki•ro•va•bad (kĭ-rō′və-băd′, kyĭ′rə-və-bät′). A city of W Azerbaijan SE of Tbilisi. Pop. 261,000.

Ki•ro•vo•grad (kĭ-rō′və-grăd′, kyĭ′rə-va-grät′). A city of central Ukraine SSE of Kiev. Pop. 263,000.

kirsch (kîrsh) *n.* A colorless brandy made from the fermented juice of cherries. [Fr., short for Ger. *kirschwasser.* See KIRSCHWASSER.]

kirsch•was•ser (kîrsh′vä′sər) *n.* Kirsch. [Ger. : *Kirsch*, cherry (< MHGer. *kirse* < OHGer. *kirsa* < VLat. **ceresia*; see CHERRY) + *Wasser*, water (< MHGer. *wasser* < OHGer. *wassar*; see **wed-¹***).]

kir•tle (kûr′tl) *n. Archaic.* **1.** A man's knee-length tunic or coat. **2.** A woman's dress or skirt. [ME *kirtel* < OE *cyrtel*, prob. ult. < Lat. *curtus*, short. See **sker-¹*.**]

Ki•run•di (kē-ro͞on′dē) *n.* A Bantu language, closely related to Kinyarwanda, that is an official language of Burundi.

Ki•san•ga•ni (kē′sän-gä′nē, kĭ-zăng′gä-nē). Formerly **Stan•ley•ville** (stăn′lē-vĭl′). A city of N Zaire on the Congo R. NE of Kinshasa; founded 1883. Pop. 282,650.

Kish (kĭsh). An ancient city of Mesopotamia in the Euphrates R. valley of present-day central Iraq.

Ki•shi•nev (kĭsh′ə-nĕf′, -nôf′, kyĭ′shĭ-nyôf′). The cap. of Moldavia, near the Romanian border NW of Odessa; founded as a monastery center in the early 15th cent. Pop. 624,000.

kish•ke also **kish•ka** (kĭsh′kə) *n.* See **derma².** [Yiddish < Russ. *kishka*, intestine. See **(s)keu-*.**]

Ki•si (kē′sē′, -shē′). See **Jixi.**

Kis•lev (kĭs′ləv, kēs-lĕv′) *n.* The third month of the year in the Jewish calendar. [Heb. *kislēw* < Akkadian *kislimu*.]

kis•met (kĭz′mĕt′, -mĭt) *n.* Fate; fortune. [Turk. < Pers. *qismat* < Ar. *qismah*, lot < *qasama*, to divide, allot.]

kiss (kĭs) *v.* **kissed, kiss•ing, kiss•es.** —*tr.* **1.** To touch or caress with the lips as an expression of affection, greeting, respect, or amorousness. **2.** To touch lightly or gently: *leaves kissed by dew.* **3.** To strike lightly; brush against. —*intr.* **1.** To engage in mutual touching or caressing with the lips. **2.** To come into light contact. —*n.* **1.** A caress or touch with the lips. **2.** A slight or gentle touch. **3.** A small piece of candy, esp. of chocolate. **4.** A drop cookie made of egg whites and sugar. —***phrasal verb.*** **kiss off.** *Slang.* **1.** To dismiss or reject. **2.** To give up or regard as lost: *He can kiss off that promotion.* **3.** To leave or disappear from notice. —***idioms.*** **kiss ass.** *Vulgar Slang.* To act submissively or obsequiously to gain favor. **kiss good-bye.** *Informal.* To regard as lost, ruined, or hopeless. [ME *kissen* < OE *cyssan.*] —**kiss′a•ble** *adj.*

kiss-and-tell (kis′ən-tĕl′) *Informal. adj.* Revealing confidential or embarrassing information based on firsthand knowledge.

kiss•er (kĭs′ər) *n.* **1.** One that kisses. **2.** *Slang.* The mouth. **3.** *Slang.* The face.

kiss•ing bug (kĭs′ĭng) *n.* See **conenose.**

kissing cousin *n.* **1.** A distant relative known well enough to be kissed when greeted. **2.** One of two or more things that are closely akin.

kissing disease *n. Informal.* Infectious mononucleosis.

Kis•sin•ger (kĭs′ĭn-jər), **Henry Alfred.** b. 1923. German-born Amer. diplomat who was U.S. secretary of state (1973–77) and shared the 1973 Nobel Peace Prize.

kiss of death *n.* Something ultimately ruinous, destructive, or fatal. [< Judas's kiss of betrayal (Mark 14:44–46).]

kiss-off (kĭs′ôf′, -ŏf′) *n. Slang.* A dismissal, as from a job.

kiss of life *n.* Mouth-to-mouth resuscitation.

kiss of peace *n.* A ceremonial gesture, such as a kiss, used in some churches during the Eucharist.

Kirghiz²

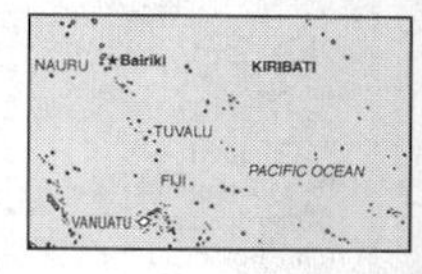

Kiribati

Henry Kissinger

ă pat	oi boy
ā pay	ou out
âr care	o͝o took
ä father	o͞o boot
ĕ pet	ŭ cut
ē be	ûr urge
ĭ pit	th thin
ī pie	*th* this
îr pier	hw which
ŏ pot	zh vision
ō toe	ə about,
ô paw	item

Stress marks:
′ (primary);
′ (secondary), as in
dictionary (dĭk′shə-nĕr′ē)

kist (kĭst) *n.* Var. of **cist**[2].

Kist•na (kĭst′nə) or **Krish•na** (krĭsh′-). A river of S India rising in the Western Ghats and flowing c. 1,287 km (800 mi) to the Bay of Bengal.

Ki•swa•hi•li (kē′swä-hē′lē) *n.* See **Swahili** 2.

kit[1] (kĭt) *n.* **1.a.** A set of articles or implements used for a specific purpose: *a shaving kit.* **b.** A container for such a set. **2.** A set of parts or materials to be assembled: *a model airplane kit.* **3.** A packaged set of related materials: *a sales kit.* **4.a.** A collection of personal effects used for travel. **b.** A container, such as a bag, for storing or holding such a collection. **—*idiom.* the (whole) kit and caboodle.** *Informal.* The entire collection or lot. [ME *kitte,* wooden tub, prob. < MDu.]

kit[2] (kĭt) *n.* **1.** A kitten. **2.** A young, often undersized furbearing animal. [Short for KITTEN.]

kit[3] (kĭt) *n. Mus.* A tiny narrow violin used by dancing masters in the 17th and 18th centuries. [?]

Ki•ta•kyu•shu (kē-tä′kyo͞o-sho͞o). A city of N Kyushu, Japan, NNE of Nagasaki. Pop. 1,056,400.

kit bag *n.* A traveling bag, such as a knapsack.

Kit Car•son Mountain (kĭt kär′sən). A peak, 4,320.3 m (14,165 ft), in the Sangre de Cristo Mts. of S-central CO.

kitch•en (kĭch′ən) *n.* **1.** A room or an area equipped for preparing and cooking food. **2.** A style of cooking; cuisine. **3.** A staff that prepares, cooks, and serves food. [ME *kichene* < OE *cycene,* prob. < VLat. **cocina* < LLat. *coquīna* < fem. of Lat. *coquīnus,* of cooking < *coquus,* cook < *coquere,* to cook. See **pek**^w^**-*.**]

kitchen cabinet *n.* A group of unofficial advisers to the head of a government. [< the story that Andrew Jackson met with his unofficial cabinet in the White House kitchen.]

Kitch•e•ner (kĭch′-nər, kĭch′ə-nər). A city of S Ontario, Canada, WSW of Toronto; settled in 1806. Pop. 139,734.

Kitchener, Horatio Herbert. 1st Earl Kitchener of Khartoum and of Broome. 1850–1916. British soldier who led Egyptian troops in the retaking of the Sudan (1898) and brought the Boer War (1899–1902) to a conclusion.

kitch•en•ette (kĭch′ə-nĕt′) *n.* A small kitchen.

kitchen garden *n.* A garden in which vegetables, fruits, and herbs are grown for household consumption.

kitchen midden *n.* **1.** A mound of kitchen refuse. **2.** *Archaeol.* A mound containing shells, animal bones, and other refuse that indicates the site of a human settlement.

kitchen police *n.* **1.** Enlisted military personnel assigned to work in a kitchen. **2.** Military duty assisting cooks.

kitch•en•ware (kĭch′ən-wâr′) *n.* Utensils, such as pots and pans, for use in a kitchen.

kite (kīt) *n.* **1.** A light framework covered with cloth, plastic, or paper, designed to be flown in the wind at the end of a long string. **2.** *Naut.* Any of the light sails of a ship used in a light wind. **3.** Any of various predatory birds of the hawk family Accipitridae, having a long, often forked tail and long pointed wings. **4.a.** A piece of negotiable paper representing a fictitious financial transaction and used temporarily to sustain credit or raise money. **b.** A bank check drawn on insufficient funds to take advantage of the time interval required for collection. **c.** A bank check altered to show a larger amount. *—v.* **kit•ed, kit•ing, kites.** *—intr.* **1.** To fly like a kite; soar or glide. **2.** To get money or credit with a kite. *—tr.* **1.** To use (a bad check) to sustain credit or raise money. **2.** To increase the amount of (a check) fraudulently. [ME, bird of prey < OE *cȳta.*]

kith and kin (kĭth′ ən kĭn′) *pl.n.* **1.** One's acquaintances and relatives. **2.** One's relatives. [ME *kith* < OE *cȳth,* kinsfolk, neighbors. See **gnō-*.**]

Kí•thi•ra (kē′thē-rä′). See **Cythera.**

Ki•tik•me•ot (kĭ-tĭk′mē-ŏt′). A region of central Northwest Terrs., Canada.

kitsch (kĭch) *n.* Art or artwork characterized by sentimental, often pretentious bad taste. *—adj.* Relating to or characterized by kitsch. [Ger., prob. of dial. orig.] **—kitsch′i•fy′** *v.* **—kitsch′y** *adj.*

kit•ten (kĭt′n) *n.* A young cat. *—intr.v.* **-tened, -ten•ing, -tens.** To bear kittens. [ME *kitoun,* prob. < ONFr. **caton,* dim. of *cat,* cat < LLat. *cattus.*]

kit•ten•ish (kĭt′n-ĭsh) *adj.* Playfully coy and frisky. **—kit′ten•ish•ly** *adv.* **—kit′ten•ish•ness** *n.*

kit•ti•wake (kĭt′ē-wāk′) *n.* Either of two cliff-nesting gulls *(Rissa tridactyla* or *R. brevirostris)* of northern regions, having a rudimentary hind toe. [Perh. imit. of its cry.]

kit•tle (kĭt′l) *Scots. —adj.* Touchy; unpredictable. *—tr.v.* **-tled, -tling, -tles. 1.** To tickle; arouse. **2.** To puzzle; perplex. [< ME *kitillen,* to tickle, prob. < OE **citelian* or ON *kitla.*]

Kit•tredge (kĭt′rĭj), **George Lyman.** 1860–1941. Amer. scholar noted for his works on Chaucer and Shakespeare.

kit•ty[1] (kĭt′ē) *n., pl.* **-ties. 1.** *Games.* A fund made up of a portion of each pot in a poker game. **2.** A pool of money, esp. one to which people have contributed for a designated purpose. **3.** See **widow** 3. [Prob. < KIT[1].]

kit•ty[2] (kĭt′ē) *n., pl.* **-ties.** A cat, esp. a kitten.

kit•ty-cor•nered (kĭt′ē-kôr′nərd) or **kit•ty-cor•ner** (-kôr′nər) *adj. & adv.* Var. of **cater-cornered.**

kiwi
Top: Common kiwi
Apteryx australis
Bottom: Botanical variety
Actinidia chinensis

Paul Klee

knight
Chess piece

Kit•ty Hawk (kĭt′ē hôk′). A village of NE NC on a sandy peninsula between Albemarle Sound and the Atlantic Ocean. Nearby Kill Devil Hill was the site of the Wright brothers' first two successful flights (Dec. 17, 1903).

ki•va (kē′və) *n.* An underground or partly underground chamber in a Pueblo village, used by men esp. for ceremonies or councils. [Hopi *kíva.*]

Ki•vu (kē′vo͞o), **Lake.** A lake on the Zaire-Rwanda border N of Lake Tanganyika at an altitude of 1,461 m (4,790 ft).

ki•wi (kē′wē) *n., pl.* **-wis. 1.** Any of several flightless birds of the genus *Apteryx,* native to New Zealand and having vestigial wings and a long slender bill. **2.a.** A woody Chinese vine *(Actinidia chinensis)* having brown edible fruit with a sweet green pulp. **b.** Its fruit. [Maori, perh. of imit. orig.]

Ki•zil Ir•mak also **Ki•zil-Ir•mak** (kĭ-zĭl′ îr-mäk′). A river of N-central Turkey flowing c. 1,150 km (715 mi) to the Black Sea.

KJV *abbr. Bible.* King James Version.

KKK or **K.K.K.** *abbr.* Ku Klux Klan.

kl *abbr.* Kiloliter.

Kla•gen•furt (klä′gən-fo͝ort′). A city of S Austria SW of Graz; chartered 1279. Pop. 87,321.

Klai•pe•da (klī′pĭ-də, -pĕ-dä). Formerly **Me•mel** (mā′məl). A city of W Lithuania on the Baltic Sea; founded as a fortress in 1252. Pop. 195,000.

Klam•ath (klăm′əth) *n., pl.* **Klamath** or **-aths. 1.** A member of a Native American people inhabiting an area of the Cascade Range in south-central Oregon and northern California. **2.** The Penutian language of the Klamath.

Klamath Falls. A city of S OR near the CA border ESE of Medford. Pop. 17,737.

Klamath River. A river flowing c. 423 km (263 mi) from SW OR through NW CA to the Pacific Ocean.

Klan (klăn) *n.* The Ku Klux Klan. **—Klans′man** (klănz′mən) *n.*

klav•ern (klăv′ərn) *n.* A local organizational unit of the Ku Klux Klan. [KL(AN) + (C)AVERN.]

Klax•on (klăk′sən). A trademark used for a loud electric horn.

Klee (klā), **Paul.** 1879–1940. Swiss artist noted for his expert use of line and color and his theories of abstract art.

Kleen•ex (klē′nĕks′). A trademark used for a soft facial tissue.

Klein bottle (klīn) *n.* A one-sided topologic surface having no inside or outside, formed by inserting the small end of a tapered tube through the side of the tube and making it contiguous with the larger end. [After Felix *Klein* (1849–1925), German mathematician.]

Kleist (klīst), **Heinrich von.** 1777–1811. German writer whose works include the comedy *The Broken Pitcher* (1811).

Klem•per•er (klĕm′pər-ər), **Otto.** 1885–1973. German conductor noted for his interpretations of Beethoven and Mahler.

klep•to•ma•ni•a (klĕp′tə-mā′nē-ə, -mān′yə) *n. Psychiat.* An obsessive impulse to steal regardless of economic need. [Gk. *kleptein,* to steal + -MANIA.] **—klep′to•ma′ni•ac′** (-nē-ăk′) *n.* **—klep′to•ma•ni′a•cal** (-mə-nī′ĭ-kəl) *adj.*

Kle•ve (klā′və) also **Cleves** (klēvz). A city of W-central Germany WSW of Münster. Pop. 44,223.

klez•mer (klĕz′mər) *n., pl.* **klez•mo•rim** (klĕz′mə-rēm′). *Mus.* **1.** A musician performing Jewish folk music of eastern Europe in a small band. **2.** The Jewish folk music played by small bands. [Yiddish < Heb. *kĕlê zemer,* musical instruments.]

klieg light (klēg) *n.* A powerful carbon-arc lamp producing an intense light and used esp. in making movies. [After John H. *Kliegl* (1869–1959) and his brother Anton T. *Kliegl* (1872–1927), German-born Amer. lighting experts.]

Klimt (klĭmt), **Gustav.** 1862–1918. Austrian painter whose art nouveau works include *The Kiss* (1908).

Kline (klīn), **Franz Joseph.** 1910–62. Amer. painter known for his abstract expressionist works.

klip•spring•er (klĭp′sprĭng′ər) *n.* A small agile African antelope *(Oreotragus oreotragus)* having large ears. [Afr. : Du. *klip,* cliff (< MDu. *klippe*) + Du. *springer,* jumper (< *springen,* to leap < MDu.).]

Klon•dike (klŏn′dīk′). A region of Yukon Terr., Canada, just E of AK and traversed by the **Klondike River,** c. 145 km (90 mi). Gold was discovered here in Aug. 1896, leading to the gold rush of 1897–98.

kloof (klo͞of) *n. South African.* A deep ravine. [Afr. < Du. < MDu. *clove,* cleft. See **gleubh-*.**]

kludge or **kluge** (klo͞oj) *n. Slang.* A system, esp. a computer system, constituted of poorly matched elements or of elements originally intended for other applications. [?] **—kludge** *v.* **—kludg′y** *adj.*

klutz (klŭts) *n. Slang.* **1.** A clumsy person. **2.** A person regarded as stupid. [Yiddish *klots* < MHGer. *kloz,* block, lump.] **—klutz′i•ness** *n.* **—klutz′y** *adj.*

kly•stron (klī′strŏn′) *n.* An electron tube used to amplify or generate ultrahigh frequency by means of velocity modulation. [Gk. *kluzein, klus-,* to wash + -TRON.]

km *abbr.* Kilometer.

K-me•son (kā′mĕz′ŏn, -mē′zŏn, -mĕs′ŏn, -mē′sŏn) *n.* See **kaon.**

kn. *abbr. Naut.* Knot.

knack (năk) *n.* **1.** A clever, expedient way of doing something. **2.** A specific talent for something, esp. one difficult to explain or teach. **3.** *Archaic.* **a.** A cleverly designed device. **b.** A knickknack. [ME *knakke* < MDu. *cnacken*, to strike, crack, prob. of imit. orig.]

knack•er (năk′ər) *n. Chiefly British.* **1.** A person who buys worn-out or old livestock and slaughters them to sell the meat or hides. **2.** A person who buys discarded structures and dismantles them to sell the materials. [Prob. of Scand. orig.] **— knack′er•y** (-ə-rē) *n.*

knack•wurst or **knock•wurst** (nŏk′wûrst′, -wŏŏrst′) *n.* A short, thick, highly seasoned sausage. [Ger. : *knacken*, to crack (< MHGer., of imit. orig.) + *Wurst*, sausage; see WURST.]

knap (năp) *tr.v.* **knapped, knap•ping, knaps. 1.** To break or chip (stone) with sharp blows, as in shaping flint into tools. **2.** *Chiefly British.* **a.** To strike sharply; rap. **b.** To snap at or bite. [ME *knappen*, prob. of imit. orig.] **— knap′per** *n.*

knap•sack (năp′săk′) *n.* A bag with shoulder straps, designed for carrying articles on the back. [Prob. LGer. *Knappsack* : *knappen*, to bite (prob. of imit. orig.) + *Sack*, bag (< MLGer. *sak* < OHGer. *sac* < LLat. *saccus*; see SACK[1]).]

knap•weed (năp′wēd′) *n.* Any of various thistles of the genus *Centaurea*, having variously colored flowers grouped in a head with a spiny involucre. [ME *knopwed* : *knop*, knob (< OE *cnop*) + *wed*, weed; see WEED[1].]

knar also **knaur** (när) *n.* A knot or burl on a tree or in wood. [ME *knarre*, prob. < OE **cnear* or < MDu. and MLGer. *knorre*.]

knave (nāv) *n.* **1.** An unprincipled, crafty man. **2.a.** A male servant. **b.** A man of humble birth. **3.** *Games.* See **jack** 3. [ME < OE *cnafa*, boy, male servant.] **— knav′ish** *adj.* **— knav′ish•ly** *adv.* **— knav′ish•ness** *n.*

knav•er•y (nā′və-rē) *n., pl.* **-ies. 1.** Dishonest or crafty dealing. **2.** An instance of trickery or mischief.

knawel (nôl) also **knawe** (nô) *n.* A low-growing weedy Eurasian annual *(Scleranthus annuus)* having narrow leaves and inconspicuous green flowers. [Ger. *Knäuel* < MHGer. *kliuwel, kniuwel*, dim. of *kliuwe*, ball of yarn < OHGer. *kliuwa*.]

knead (nēd) *tr.v.* **knead•ed, knead•ing, kneads. 1.** To mix and work into a uniform mass, as with the hands. **2.** To make or shape by or as if by folding, pressing, and stretching with the hands. **3.** To squeeze, press, or roll with the hands, as in massaging. [ME *kneden* < OE *cnedan*.] **— knead′er** *n.*

knee (nē) *n.* **1.a.** *Anat.* The joint between the thigh and the lower leg, formed by the articulation of the femur and the tibia and covered anteriorly by the patella. **b.** The region of the leg that encloses and supports this joint. **2.** An analogous joint or part of a leg of a quadruped vertebrate. **3.** Something resembling the human knee, such as a bent piece of pipe. **4.** The part of a garment that covers the knee. **5.** An abrupt woody projection arising from the roots of some swamp-growing trees: *cypress knees.* — *tr.v.* **kneed, knee•ing, knees.** To strike with the knee. [ME < OE *cnēo*. See **genu-**[1]*.]

knee action *n.* An automotive front-wheel suspension that permits independent vertical motion of each wheel.

knee breeches *pl.n.* Trousers extending to or below the knee.

knee•cap (nē′kăp′) *n.* **1.** See **patella** 1a. **2.** See **kneepad.** — *tr.v.* **-capped, -cap•ping, -caps.** To cripple by shooting in the legs, esp. in the knees.

knee-deep (nē′dēp′) *adj.* **1.** Reaching as high as the knees: *knee-deep water.* **2.** Submerged to the knees: *knee-deep in mud.* **3.** Deeply occupied or involved: *knee-deep in work.*

knee-high (nē′hī′) *adj.* Reaching up to the knees. — *n.* (nē′-hī′). A sock or stocking that extends just below the knee.

knee jerk *n.* A sudden involuntary extension of the leg, produced by a sharp tap to the tendon below the patella; patellar reflex.

knee-jerk (nē′jûrk′) *adj. Slang.* **1.** Easily predictable; automatic. **2.** Reacting spontaneously in the expected manner.

kneel (nēl) *intr.v.* **knelt** (nĕlt) or **kneeled, kneel•ing, kneels.** To go down or rest on one or both knees. [ME *knelen* < OE *cnēowlian*. See **genu-**[1]*.]

kneel•er (nē′lər) *n.* **1.** One who kneels, as to pray. **2.** Something, such as a stool, cushion, or board, on which to kneel.

knee•pad (nē′păd′) *n.* A protective covering for the knee.

knee sock *n.* A sock that reaches just below the knee.

knell (nĕl) *v.* **knelled, knell•ing, knells.** — *intr.* **1.** To ring slowly and solemnly, esp. for a funeral; toll. **2.** To give forth a mournful or ominous sound. — *tr.* To signal, summon, or proclaim by tolling. — *n.* **1.** The sound of a bell knelling; a toll. **2.** A signal of disaster or destruction. [ME *knellen* < OE *cnyllan*.]

Knes•set (knĕs′ĕt′) *n.* The unicameral parliament of Israel. [Mod.Heb. *Kneset* < Heb. (Mishnaic) *kĕneset*, assembly < *kānas*, to assemble.]

knew (nōō, nyōō) *v.* P.t. of **know.**

Knick•er•bock•er (nĭk′ər-bŏk′ər) *n.* **1.a.** A descendant of the Dutch settlers of New York. **b.** A native or inhabitant of New York. **2. knickerbockers.** Full breeches gathered and banded just below the knee; knickers. [After Diedrich *Knickerbocker*, fictional name used by Washington Irving.]

knick•ers (nĭk′ərz) *pl.n.* **1.a.** Long bloomers formerly worn as underwear by women and girls. **b.** *Chiefly British.* Panties. **2.** Full breeches gathered and banded just below the knee.

knick•knack also **nick•nack** (nĭk′năk′) *n.* A small ornamental article; a trinket. [Redup. of KNACK.]

knife (nīf) *n., pl.* **knives** (nīvz). **1.** A cutting instrument consisting of a sharp blade attached to a handle. **2.** A cutting edge; a blade. — *v.* **knifed, knif•ing, knifes.** — *tr.* **1.** To use a knife on, esp. to stab; wound with a knife. **2.** *Informal.* To betray or attempt to defeat by underhand means. — *intr.* To cut or slash a way through something with or as if with a knife. **— *idiom.* under the knife.** *Informal.* Undergoing surgery. [ME *knif* < OE *cnīf* < ON *knīfr*.] **— knif′er** *n.*

knife-edge (nīf′ĕj′) *n.* **1.** A sharp cutting edge. **2.** A sharp narrow edge or border. **3.** A wedge of metal used as a low-friction fulcrum for a balancing beam or lever.

knight (nīt) *n.* **1.a.** A medieval tenant serving a feudal landholder as a mounted man-at-arms. **b.** A medieval gentleman-soldier raised by a sovereign to privileged military status after training as a page and squire. **c.** A man holding a nonhereditary title conferred by a sovereign. **2.** A man belonging to an order or a brotherhood. **3.a.** A defender, champion, or zealous upholder of a cause or principle. **b.** The devoted champion of a lady. **4.** *Games.* A chess piece, usu. in the shape of a horse's head, that can be moved two squares horizontally and one vertically or two squares vertically and one horizontally. — *tr.v.* **knight•ed, knight•ing, knights.** To raise (a person) to knighthood. [ME < OE *cniht*.] **— knight′ly** *adj. & adv.* **— knight′li•ness** *n.*

knight bachelor *n., pl.* **knights bachelors** or **knight bachelors.** An English knight of the lowest rank; a bachelor.

knight-errant (nīt′ĕr′ənt) *n., pl.* **knights-errant** (nīts′-). **1.** A knight who wanders in search of adventures to prove his chivalry. **2.** One given to adventurous or quixotic conduct. **— knight′-er′rant•ry** (-ĕr′ən-trē) *n.*

knight•head (nīt′hĕd′) *n. Naut.* Either of two timbers rising from the keel of a sailing ship and supporting the inner end of the bowsprit. [< the fact that it was sometimes decorated with a carving of a man's head.]

knight•hood (nīt′hŏŏd′) *n.* **1.** The rank, dignity, or vocation of a knight. **2.** Behavior or qualities befitting a knight; chivalry. **3.** Knights considered as a group.

Knight of Columbus (nīt) *n., pl.* **Knights of Columbus.** A member of a society of Roman Catholic men founded in 1882.

Knight of Pythias *n., pl.* **Knights of Pythias.** A member of a secret philanthropic fraternal order founded in 1864.

Knights of the Round Table (nīts) *pl.n.* In Arthurian legend, the knights of King Arthur's court.

Knight Templar *n., pl.* **Knights Templars** or **Knights Templar. 1.** A member of an order of knights founded about 1118 to protect pilgrims in the Holy Land during the Second Crusade. **2.** A man belonging to a Masonic order in the United States.

knish (kə-nĭsh′) *n.* A piece of dough stuffed with potato, meat, or cheese and baked or fried. [Yiddish < Ukrainian *knysh*, prob. of Turkic orig.]

knit (nĭt) *v.* **knit** or **knit•ted, knit•ting, knits.** — *tr.* **1.** To make (a fabric or garment) by intertwining yarn or thread in a series of connected loops with knitting needles or on a machine. **2.** To form (yarn or thread) into fabric by intertwining. **3.** To join closely; unite securely. **4.** To draw (the brows) together in wrinkles; furrow. — *intr.* **1.** To make a fabric or garment by knitting. **2.** To become securely joined or mended together closely, as a fractured bone. **3.** To come together in wrinkles or furrows, as the brows. — *n.* **1.** A fabric or garment made by knitting. **2.** The way in which a fabric has been knit: *a loose knit.* [ME *knitten*, to tie in a knot < OE *cnyttan*.] **— knit′ter** *n.*

knit•ting (nĭt′ĭng) *n.* **1.** The act or process of producing something knitted. **2.** Material that has been knitted or is in the process of being knitted; knitted work.

knitting needle *n.* A long thin pointed rod used in pairs to knit yarn into cloth.

knit•wear (nĭt′wâr′) *n.* Knitted garments.

knives (nīvz) *n.* Pl. of **knife.**

knob (nŏb) *n.* **1.** A rounded protuberance. **2.a.** A rounded handle, as on a drawer or door. **b.** A rounded control switch or dial. **3.** A prominent rounded hill or mountain. [ME *knobbe*.] **— knobbed** (nŏbd) *adj.* **— knob′by** *adj.*

knob•ker•rie (nŏb′kĕr′ē) *n.* A short club with one knobbed end, used as a weapon by certain South African peoples. [Afr. *knopkierie* : *knop*, knob (< MDu. *cnoppe*) + *kieri*, club (< Khoikhoin *kirri*, stick).]

knock (nŏk) *v.* **knocked, knock•ing, knocks.** — *tr.* **1.** To strike with a hard blow. **2.** To affect in a specified way by striking hard. **3.** To cause to collide. **4.** To produce by hitting or striking. **5.** To instill with or as if with blows. **6.** *Slang.* To find fault with; criticize. — *intr.* **1.** To strike a sharp audible blow or series of blows, as on a door. **2.** To collide with something. **3.** To make a pounding or clanking noise. — *n.* **1.** An instance of striking or colliding; a blow. **2.** The sound of a sharp tap on a hard surface; a rap. **3.** A pounding or clanking noise made by an engine, often as a result of faulty fuel combustion.

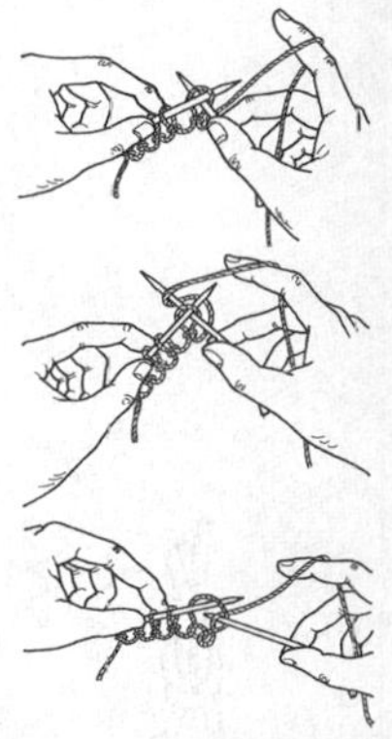

knit
Right-handed English knitting stitch

ă pat	oi boy
ā pay	ou out
âr care	ŏŏ took
ä father	ōō boot
ĕ pet	ŭ cut
ē be	ûr urge
ĭ pit	th thin
ī pie	*th* this
îr pier	hw which
ŏ pot	zh vision
ō toe	ə about, item
ô paw	

Stress marks:
′ (primary);
′ (secondary), as in **dictionary** (dĭk′shə-nĕr′ē)

4. *Slang.* A cutting, often petty criticism. ***—phrasal verbs.*** **knock around** (or **about**). **1.** To be rough or brutal with; maltreat. **2.** To wander from place to place. **3.** *Informal.* To discuss or consider. **knock back.** *Informal.* To gulp (an alcoholic drink). **knock down. 1.** To bring to the ground with a blow; topple. **2.** To disassemble into parts, as for storage or shipping. **3.** To declare sold at an auction, as by striking a blow with a gavel. **4.** *Informal.* To reduce, as in price. **5.** *Slang.* To receive as wages; earn. **knock off. 1.** *Informal.* **a.** To take a break or rest from; stop. **b.** To cease work. **2.** *Informal.* To complete, accomplish, or dispose of hastily or easily; finish. **3.** *Informal.* To get rid of; eliminate. **4.** *Slang.* To kill or overcome. **5.** *Slang.* To hold up or rob. **6.** *Informal.* To copy or imitate, esp. without permission. **knock out. 1.** To render unconscious. **2.** *Sports.* To defeat (a boxing opponent) by a knockout. **3.** To render useless or inoperative. **4.** *Informal.* To exert or exhaust (oneself or another) to the utmost. **knock together.** To make or assemble quickly or carelessly. **knock up. 1.** *Slang.* To make pregnant. **2.** *Chiefly British.* To wake up or summon, as by knocking at the door. **3.** *Chiefly British.* To wear out; exhaust. ***—idioms.*** **knock cold.** To render unconscious; knock out. **knock dead. 1.** To kill with a blow. **2.** *Slang.* To affect strongly and positively. **knock for a loop.** *Slang.* To surprise tremendously; astonish. **knock it off.** *Slang.* Quit it. Used in the imperative. **knock out of the box.** *Baseball.* To force the removal of (an opposing pitcher) by heavy hitting. **knock the** (or **someone's**) **socks off.** *Slang.* To overwhelm or amaze. [ME *knokken* < OE *cnocian.*]

knock•a•bout (nŏk′ə-bout′) *adj.* **1.** Boisterous; rowdy. **2.** Appropriate for rough wear or use. *—n. Naut.* A small sloop with a mainsail, jib, and keel but no bowsprit.

knock•down (nŏk′doun′) *n.* **1.a.** The act of knocking down. **b.** The condition of being knocked down. **2.** An overwhelming blow or shock. **3.** Something designed to be easily assembled or disassembled. *—adj.* **1.** Strong enough to knock down or overwhelm; powerful. **2.** Designed to be easily assembled or disassembled. **3.** Reduced: *knockdown prices.*

knock•down-drag•out (nŏk′doun′drăg′out′) *adj.* Marked by roughness, violence, and acrimony.

knock•er (nŏk′ər) *n.* **1.** A hinged fixture, such as a metal ring, used for knocking on a door. **2.** *Vulgar Slang.* A woman's breast.

knock-knee (nŏk′nē′) *n.* A deformity of the legs in which the knees are abnormally close together and the ankles are spread widely apart. **—knock′-kneed′** *adj.*

knock•off (nŏk′ôf′, -ŏf′) *n. Informal.* An unauthorized copy or imitation, as of designer clothing.

knock•out (nŏk′out′) *n.* **1.a.** The act of knocking out. **b.** The state of being knocked out. **c.** A blow that knocks out an opponent. **2.** *Sports.* **a.** A victory in boxing in which one's opponent is unable to rise from the canvas within a specified time after being knocked down. **b.** The act of winning a boxing match in this way. **3.** *Slang.* A strikingly attractive or impressive person or thing. *—adj.* Capable of knocking out.

knockout drop *n. Slang.* A solution put into a drink surreptitiously in order to render the drinker unconscious. Often used in the plural.

knock•wurst (nŏk′wûrst′, -wo͝orst′) *n.* Var. of **knackwurst.**

knoll[1] (nōl) *n.* A small rounded hill or mound; a hillock. [ME *knol* < OE *cnoll.*]

knoll[2] (nōl) *Archaic. —v.* **knolled, knoll•ing, knolls.** *—intr.* To ring mournfully; knell. *—tr.* To ring or sound (a bell, for example) mournfully; knell. *—n.* A knell. [ME *knollen,* prob. alteration of *knellen,* to knell. See KNELL.]

knop (nŏp) *n.* A small decorative knob or boss. [ME *knoppe* < OE *cnop.*]

Knos•sos also **Cnos•sos** or **Cnos•sus** (nŏs′əs). An ancient city of N Crete near present-day Iráklion; center of a Bronze Age culture that probably flourished c. 2000–1400 B.C.

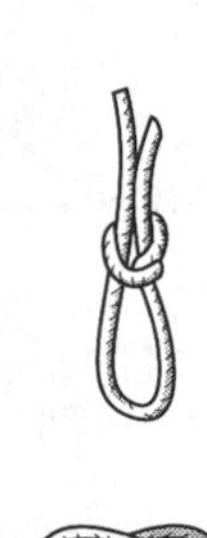

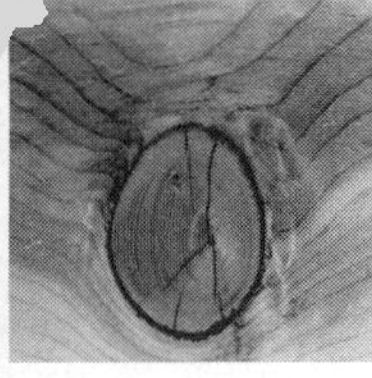

knot[1]
Top: Slipknot (*above*), square knot (*center*), and barrel knot (*below*)
Bottom: Cross section of cut lumber

knot[1] (nŏt) *n.* **1.a.** A compact intersection of interlaced material, such as cord, ribbon, or rope. **b.** A fastening made by tying together lengths of material, such as rope, in a prescribed way. **2.** A decorative bow of ribbon, fabric, or braid. **3.** A unifying bond, esp. a marriage bond. **4.** A tight cluster of persons or things. **5.** A feeling of tightness: *a knot in my stomach.* **6.** A complex problem. **7.a.** A hard place or lump, esp. on a tree, at a point from which a stem or branch grows. **b.** The round cross section of such a lump on a piece of cut lumber. **8.** A protuberant growth or swelling in a tissue. **9.a.** A division on a log line used to measure the speed of a ship. **b.** A unit of speed, one nautical mile per hour, approx. 1.85 kilometers (1.15 statute miles) per hour. **c.** A distance of one nautical mile. *—v.* **knot•ted, knot•ting, knots.** *—tr.* **1.** To tie in or fasten with a knot or knots. **2.** To snarl or entangle. **3.** To cause to form a knot or knots. *—intr.* **1.** To form a knot or knots. **2.** To become snarled or entangled. [ME < OE *cnotta.*]

Usage Note: In nautical usage *knot* is a unit of speed, not of distance, and has a built-in meaning of "per hour." Therefore, a ship would strictly be said to travel at ten knots (not ten knots per hour).

John Knox

knot[2] (nŏt) *n.* Either of two migratory sandpipers *(Calidris canutus* or *C. tenuirostris)* that breed in Arctic regions. [ME, of Scand. orig.]

knot•grass (nŏt′grăs′) *n.* **1.** A low-growing weedy grass *(Paspalum distichum)* with spikelets arranged in two rows along the rachis. **2.** Any of several weedy plants of the genus *Polygonum* that have stems with nodes.

knot•hole (nŏt′hōl′) *n.* A hole in a piece of lumber where a knot has dropped out or been removed.

knot•ty (nŏt′ē) *adj.* **-ti•er, -ti•est. 1.** Tied or snarled in knots. **2.** Covered with knots or knobs; gnarled. **3.** Difficult, as to understand or solve. See Syns at **complex. —knot′ti•ness** *n.*

knot•weed (nŏt′wēd′) *n.* Any of several plants of the genus *Polygonum,* with jointed stems and inconspicuous flowers.

knout (nout) *n.* A leather scourge used for flogging. *—v.* **knout•ed, knout•ing, knouts.** *—tr.* To flog with a knout. [Fr. < Russ. *knut* < ORuss. *knutŭ* < ON *knūtr,* knot in cord.]

know (nō) *v.* **knew** (no͞o, nyo͞o), **known** (nōn), **know•ing, knows.** *—tr.* **1.** To perceive directly; grasp in the mind with clarity or certainty. **2.** To regard as true beyond doubt. **3.** To have a practical understanding of, as through experience; be skilled in. **4.** To have fixed in the mind. **5.** To have experience of. **6.a.** To perceive as familiar; recognize. **b.** To be acquainted with. **7.** To be able to distinguish; recognize as distinct. **8.** To discern the character or nature of. **9.** *Archaic.* To have sexual intercourse with. *—intr.* **1.** To possess knowledge, understanding, or information. **2.** To be cognizant or aware. ***—idioms.*** **in the know.** *Informal.* Possessing special or secret information. **you know.** *Informal.* Used parenthetically in conversation, as to fill pauses or educe the listener's agreement or sympathy. [ME *knowen* < OE *cnāwan.* See **gnō-*.**] **—know′a•ble** *adj.* **—know′er** *n.*

know-how (nō′hou′) *n.* The knowledge and skill required to do something correctly.

know•ing (nō′ĭng) *adj.* **1.** Possessing knowledge, information, or understanding. See Syns at **intelligent. 2.** Showing clever awareness and resourcefulness; shrewd. **3.** Suggestive of secret or private knowledge: *a knowing glance.* **4.** Deliberate; conscious. **—know′ing•ly** *adv.* **—know′ing•ness** *n.*

know-it-all (nō′ĭt-ôl′) *n. Informal.* One who claims to know everything and rejects advice. **—know′-it-all′** *adj.*

knowl•edge (nŏl′ĭj) *n.* **1.** The state or fact of knowing. **2.** Familiarity, awareness, or understanding gained through experience or study. **3.** The sum or range of what has been perceived, discovered, or learned. **4.** Learning; erudition: *teachers of great knowledge.* **5.** Specific information about something. **6.** Carnal knowledge. [ME *knowlech* : *knowen,* to know; see KNOW + *-leche,* n. suff.]

knowl•edge•a•ble (nŏl′ĭ-jə-bəl) *adj.* Possessing or showing knowledge or intelligence; perceptive and well-informed. **—knowl′edge•a•bil′i•ty, knowl′edge•a•ble•ness** *n.* **—knowl′edge•ably** *adv.*

known (nōn) *adj.* Proved or generally recognized: *a known authority. —n.* Something that is known.

know-noth•ing (nō′nŭth′ĭng) *n.* **1.** A totally ignorant person; an ignoramus. **2.** An anti-intellectual. **3.** An agnostic. **4. Know-Nothing.** A member of a political party in the United States during the 1850's that was antagonistic toward recent immigrants and Roman Catholics.

Knox (nŏks), **Henry.** 1750–1806. Amer. Revolutionary soldier whose transport of 55 captured British cannon from Fort Ticonderoga helped force the British to evacuate Boston (1776).

Knox, John. 1514?–72. Scottish religious reformer and founder of Scottish Presbyterianism.

Knox•ville (nŏks′vĭl′, -vəl). A city of E TN on the Tennessee R. NE of Chattanooga; settled c. 1785. Pop. 165,121.

Knt *abbr.* Knight.

knuck•le (nŭk′əl) *n.* **1.** *Anat.* **a.** The prominence of the dorsal aspect of a joint of a finger, esp. of one of the joints connecting the fingers to the hand. **b.** A rounded protuberance formed by the bones in a joint. **2.** A cut of meat centering on the carpal or tarsal joint, as of a pig. **3.** The part of a hinge through which the pin passes. **4. knuckles.** Brass knuckles. *—tr.v.* **-led, -ling, -les. 1.** To press, rub, or hit with the knuckles. **2.** *Games.* To shoot (a marble) with the thumb over the bent forefinger. ***—phrasal verbs.*** **knuckle down.** To apply oneself earnestly to a task. **knuckle under.** To yield to pressure; give in. [ME *knokel.*]

knuckle ball or **knuck•le•ball** (nŭk′əl-bôl′) *n. Baseball.* A slow, randomly fluttering pitch thrown by gripping the ball with the tips or nails of two or three fingers.

knuck•le•bone (nŭk′əl-bōn′) *n.* A knobbed bone, as of a knuckle or joint.

knuck•le-dust•er (nŭk′əl-dŭs′tər) *n. Slang.* Brass knuckles.

knuck•le•head (nŭk′əl-hĕd′) *n. Informal.* A stupid person; a blockhead.

knuckle joint *n.* A hinged joint in which a pin fastens the ends of two rods, one of which has an eye that fits between the two perforated projections of the other.

knur (nûr) *n.* A bump or knot, as on a tree trunk; a gnarl. [ME *knarre, knor.* See KNAR.]

knurl (nûrl) *n.* **1.** A knob, knot, or other small protuberance.

2. One of a series of small ridges or grooves on the surface or edge of a metal object to aid in gripping. — *tr.v.* **knurled, knurl•ing, knurls.** To provide with knurls; mill. [Prob. dim. of KNUR.] — **knurled** (nûrld) *adj.* — **knurl′y** *adj.*

Knut (kə-no͞ot′, -nyo͞ot′). See **Canute.**

KO (kā′ō′) *Slang.* — *tr.v.* **KO'd, KO'ing, KO's.** To knock out, as in boxing. — *n.* (kā-ō′, kā′ō′), *pl.* **KO's.** A knockout, as in boxing.

ko•a•la (kō-ä′lə) *n.* An arboreal Australian marsupial *(Phascolarctos cinereus)* that has grayish fur, large ears, and sharp claws. [Dharuk (Aboriginal language of SE Australia) *gulawaŋ.*]

ko•an (kō′än′) *n.* A riddle in the form of a paradox used in Zen Buddhism as an aid to meditation and a means of gaining intuitive knowledge. [J. : *ko,* public + *an,* matter.]

kob (kŏb, kōb) *n.* An orange-brown antelope *(Kobus kob)* of southeast Africa. [Of African orig.]

Ko•be (kō′bē′, -bā′). A city of S Honshu, Japan, on Osaka Bay SSW of Kyoto. Pop. 1,410,843.

Ko•blenz also **Co•blenz** (kō′blĕnts′). A city of W-central Germany at the confluence of the Rhine and Moselle rivers SE of Bonn; founded as a Roman frontier station. Pop. 111,235.

ko•bo (kô′bô′) *n., pl.* **kobo.** See table at **currency.** [Poss. Yoruba *kọbọ* < E. COPPER[1], penny.]

ko•bold (kō′bôld′) *n.* **1.** An often mischievous household elf in German folklore. **2.** A gnome that haunts underground places in German folklore. [Ger. < MHGer. *kobolt.* See COBALT.]

Koch (kôk, kôKH), **Robert.** 1843–1910. German bacteriologist who won a 1905 Nobel Prize.

Ko•chi (kō′chē). A city of S Shikoku, Japan, on an inlet of the Pacific Ocean. Pop. 312,253.

Ko•dak (kō′dăk′). A trademark used for a hand-held camera and camera film.

Ko•dál•y (kō′dī′, kô′dä-yə), **Zoltán.** 1882–1967. Hungarian composer whose works include the opera *Háry János* (1926).

Ko•di•ak bear (kō′dē-ăk′) *n.* A brown bear inhabiting islands and coastal areas of Alaska and sometimes considered a separate species *(Ursus middendorffi).* [After KODIAK (ISLAND).]

Kodiak Island. An island of S AK in the Gulf of Alaska E of the Alaska Peninsula; site of the first permanent Russian settlement in the area (1784).

Koest•ler (kĕst′lər, kĕs′-), **Arthur.** 1905–83. Hungarian-born writer whose works include *Darkness at Noon* (1941).

K of C *abbr.* Knight of Columbus.

K of P *abbr.* Knight of Pythias.

kohl (kōl) *n.* A cosmetic preparation, such as powdered antimony sulfide, used esp. in Middle Eastern countries to darken the rims of the eyelids. [Ar. *kuḥl,* powder of antimony, kohl.]

kohl•ra•bi (kōl-rä′bē, -răb′ē) *n., pl.* **-bies.** A plant *(Brassica oleracea* var. *gongylodes)* in the mustard family, having a thick basal stem part that is eaten as a vegetable. [Ger., partial transl. (with Ger. *Kohl,* cabbage, ult. < Lat. *caulis)* of Ital. *cavoli rape,* pl. of *cavolo rapa* : *cavolo,* cabbage (< Lat. *caulis)* + *rapa,* turnip (< Lat. *rāpa).*]

Koi•ne (koi-nā′, koi′nā′) *n.* **1.** A dialect of Greek that became the common language of the Hellenistic world, from which later stages of Greek are descended. **2. koine.** A lingua franca. **3.** A regional dialect or language that becomes the standard language over a wider area, losing its most extreme local features. [< Gk. *(hē) koinē (dialektos),* common (language), fem. of *koinos,* common. See **kom***.]

Ko•kand (kō-kănd′). A city of E Uzbekistan SE of Tashkent; center of a powerful khanate in the 18th cent. Pop. 166,000.

Ko•ko•mo (kō′kə-mō′). A city of central IN N of Indianapolis; founded in the 1840's. Pop. 44,962.

Ko•ko Nor (kō′kō′ nôr′, nōr′). See **Qinghai Hu.**

Ko•kosch•ka (kə-kôsh′kə), **Oskar.** 1886–1980. Austrian expressionist painter noted for his portraits and landscapes.

kok-sa•ghyz (kōk′sə-gēz′) *n.* A central Asian dandelion *(Taraxacum koksaghyz)* having roots that yield a form of rubber. [Russ. < Turk. *kok-sagĭz* : *kok,* root + *sagĭz,* rubber.]

ko•la (kō′lə) *n.* Var. of **cola[4].**

Ko•la Peninsula (kō′lə). A peninsula of NW Russia between the White Sea and the Barents Sea.

Kol•ha•pur (kō′lə-po͝or′). A city of SW India SSE of Bombay; once the center of an important Deccan state. Pop. 340,625.

ko•lin•sky (kə-lĭn′skē) *n., pl.* **-skies. 1.** A northern Eurasian mink *(Mustela siberica)* having a dark brown coat with tawny markings. **2.** The tawny fur of this animal. [Russ. *kolinskiĭ,* of Kola < KOLA (PENINSULA).]

kol•khoz (kŏl-kôz′, kŭl-KHôs′) *n.* A collective farm in the former Soviet Union. [Russ. < *kol(lektivnoe) khoz(iaĭstvo)* : *kollektivnoe,* neut. of *kollektivnyĭ,* collective + *khozyaĭstvo,* economy, household farm.]

Kol•lon•tai (kŏl′ən-tī′), **Aleksandra Mikhailovna.** 1872–1952. Russian revolutionary and writer who advocated sweeping reforms in traditional customs and institutions.

Koll•witz (kōl′wĭts′, kôl′vĭts′), **Käthe** or **Kaethe.** 1867–1945. German artist noted for her sculptures and prints.

Köln (kœln). See **Cologne.**

Kol Nid•re (kōl nĭd′rā, -rə, kôl nē-drā′) *n. Judaism.* The opening prayer recited on the eve of Yom Kippur. [Aram. *kol nidhrê, all vows : kol, all + nidhrê, vows.]*

Ko•ly•ma (kə-lē′mə, kə-lē-mä′). A river of NE Russia rising in the Kolyma Mts. and flowing c. 2,148 km (1,335 mi) to the East Siberian Sea.

Kolyma Mountains. A range of NE Russia extending c. 1,126 km (700 mi) roughly parallel to the coast of Siberia.

Ko•man•dor•ski Islands also **Ko•man•dor•ski•ye Islands** (-skē-yĕ). An island group of NE Russia in the Bering Sea E of the Kamchatka Peninsula.

Ko•ma•ti (kə-mä′tē). A river of SE Africa flowing c. 805 km (500 mi) to an inlet of the Indian Ocean.

Ko•mo•do dragon (kə-mō′dō) *n.* An Indonesian monitor lizard *(Varanus komodoensis)* that is the largest living lizard. [After *Komodo,* an island of S-central Indonesia.]

Kom•so•molsk (kŏm′sə-môlsk′). A city of SE Russia N of Vladivostok; settled in 1932. Pop. 300,000.

Kon•go (kŏng′gō) *n., pl.* Kongo or **-gos. 1.** A member of a people living in west-central Africa along the lower Congo River. **2.** A Bantu language of the Kongo, a lingua franca in southern Congo, western Zaire, and northern Angola.

Kö•nigs•berg (kā′nĭg-bûrg′, kœ′nĭKHs-bĕrk′). See **Kaliningrad.**

Ko•no•ye (kə-nō′ā, kô′nô-yĕ′), Prince **Fumimaro.** 1891–1946. Japanese political leader who as premier (1937–39 and 1940–41) formed an alliance with Germany and Italy (1941).

Kon•stanz (kôn′stänts′) also **Con•stance** (kŏn′stəns). A city of SW Germany on the Lake of Constance S of Stuttgart; thought to have been founded c. A.D. 300. Pop. 68,605.

Kon•ya also **Kon•ia** (kôn-yä′). A city of SW-central Turkey S of Ankara; a powerful Seljuk sultanate from the 11th to the 13th cent. Pop. 329,139.

koo•doo (ko͞o′do͞o) *n.* Var. of **kudu.**

kook (ko͞ok) *n. Slang.* A person regarded as strange, eccentric, or crazy. [Poss. < CUCKOO.]

kook•a•bur•ra (ko͝ok′ə-bûr′ə, -bŭr′ə) *n.* A large kingfisher *(Dacelo gigas)* native to Australia and having a call that resembles raucous laughter. [Wiradhuri (Aboriginal language of SE Australia) *gugubarra.*]

kook•y also **kook•ie** (ko͞o′kē) *adj.* **-i•er, -i•est.** *Slang.* Characteristic of a kook; strange or crazy. — **kook′i•ness** *n.*

Koop•mans (ko͞op′mənz), **Tjalling Charles.** b. 1910. Dutch-born Amer. economist who shared a 1975 Nobel Prize.

Koo•te•nay River also **Koo•te•nai River** (ko͞ot′n-ā′). A river, c. 655 km (407 mi), flowing from SE British Columbia, Canada, through NW MT to N ID and again into British Columbia, where it widens to form **Kootenay Lake** before joining the Columbia R.

ko•peck or **ko•pek** also **co•peck** (kō′pĕk) *n.* See table at **currency.** [Russ. *kopeĭka* < Middle Russ. *kopeika* < *kopie,* spear.]

kor (kôr, kōr) *n.* See **homer[2].** [Heb. *kôr.*]

Kor. *abbr.* Korea; Korean.

Ko•ran or **Qur•'an** (kə-răn′, -rän′, kô-, kō-) *n.* The sacred text of Islam, considered by Muslims to contain the revelations of God to Muhammad. [Ar. *qur'ān,* reading, recitation, Koran < *qara'a,* to read, recite.] — **Ko•ran′ic** *adj.*

Kor•do•fan•i•an (kôr′də-făn′ē-ən) *n.* A small group of related languages spoken in Sudan and forming part of the Niger-Kordofanian language family.

Ko•re•a (kə-rē′ə, kô-, kō-). A peninsula and former country of E Asia between the Yellow Sea and the Sea of Japan; site of an ancient civilization dating to the 12th cent. B.C. The peninsula was divided into North Korea and South Korea after the Korean War (1950–53).

Korea Bay. An inlet of the Yellow Sea between NE China and W North Korea.

Ko•re•an (kə-rē′ən, kô-, kō-) *n.* **1.** A native or inhabitant of Korea. **2.** The language of the Koreans, possibly in the Altaic family. — *adj.* Of or relating to Korea or its people, language, or culture.

Korea Strait. A channel between SE South Korea and SW Japan connecting the East China Sea with the Sea of Japan.

Ko•rin•thos (kô′rĭn-thôs′). See **Corinth.**

Ko•ri•ya•ma (kôr′ē-ä′mə, -yä′mä). A city of N-central Honshu, Japan, N of Tokyo. Pop. 301,672.

Korn•berg (kôrn′bûrg′), **Arthur.** b. 1918. Amer. biochemist who shared a 1959 Nobel Prize.

Kor•sa•koff's syndrome (kôr′sə-kôfs′, -kŏfs′) *n. Psychiat.* A syndrome of severe mental impairment characterized by confusion and amnesia in which memory of recent events is esp. impaired. [After Sergei S. *Korsakoff* (1854–1900), Russian neurologist.]

Kort•rijk (kôrt′rĭk′) also **Cour•trai** (ko͝or-trā′, ko͝or-). A city of W Belgium W of Brussels. Pop. 75,587.

ko•ru•na (kôr′ə-nä′) *n.* See table at **currency.**

Kor•zyb•ski (kôr-zĭp′skē, kô-zhĭp′-), **Alfred Habdank Skarbek.** 1879–1950. Polish-born Amer. semanticist who wrote *Science and Sanity* (1933).

Kos also **Cos** (kŏs, kôs). An island of SE Greece in the N Dodecanese Is. at the entrance to the **Gulf of Kos,** an inlet of the Aegean Sea on the SW coast of Turkey.

koala
Adult female and young koala
Phascolarctos cinereus

kookaburra
Dacelo gigas

ă pat	oi boy
ā pay	ou out
âr care	o͝o took
ä father	o͞o boot
ĕ pet	ŭ cut
ē be	ûr urge
ĭ pit	th thin
ī pie	*th* this
îr pier	hw which
ŏ pot	zh vision
ō toe	ə about, item
ô paw	

Stress marks:
′ (primary);
′ (secondary), as in dictionary (dĭk′shə-nĕr′ē)

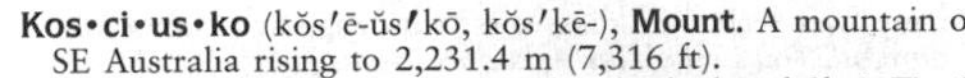

Kos•ci•us•ko (kŏs′ē-ŭs′kō, kŏs′kē-), **Mount.** A mountain of SE Australia rising to 2,231.4 m (7,316 ft).

Kos•ci•us•ko (kŏs′ē-ŭs′kō, kŏs′kē-, kôsh-cho͝osh′kō), **Thaddeus.** 1746–1817. Polish general and patriot who fought with the colonists in the American Revolution.

ko•sher (kō′shər) also **ka•sher** (kä′-) — *adj.* **1.** *Judaism.* **a.** Conforming to dietary laws; ritually pure: *kosher meat.* **b.** Selling or serving food prepared in accordance with dietary laws. **2.** *Slang.* **a.** Legitimate; permissible. **b.** Genuine; authentic. — *tr.v.* **-shered, -sher•ing, -shers.** To make proper or ritually pure. [Yiddish *kósher* < Heb. *kāšēr*, proper.]

Ko•ši•ce (kô′shĭ-tsĕ). A city of E Slovakia NE of Budapest, Hungary; chartered 1241. Pop. 218,238.

Ko•so•vo (kô′sə-vō′). A region of SW Serbia; under Turkish rule until 1913 and an autonomous region of the former republic of Yugoslavia after 1946.

Kublai Khan

Kos•suth (kŏs′o͞oth′, kô′sho͞ot′), **Lajos.** 1802–94. Hungarian revolutionary leader who sought Hungary's independence from Austria and briefly led a provisional government (1849).

Kos•tro•ma (kŏs′trə-mä′). A city of NW Russia on the Volga R. NE of Moscow; founded 1152. Pop. 269,000.

Ko•sy•gin (kə-sē′gən, -gyĭn), **Aleksei Nikolayevich.** 1904–80. Soviet premier (1964–80).

Ko•ta (kō′tə). A city of NW India SSW of Delhi. Pop. 358,241.

ko•to (kō′tō) *n., pl.* **-tos.** *Mus.* A Japanese instrument having 7 to 13 silk strings stretched over an oblong box. [J.]

Kott•bus (kŏt′bəs, kôt′bo͝os′). See **Cottbus.**

Kot•ze•bue Sound (kŏt′sə-byo͞o′). An inlet of the Chukchi Sea in NW AK N of Seward Peninsula.

kou•miss (ko͞o-mĭs′, ko͞o′mĭs) *n.* Var. of **kumiss.**

Kous•se•vitz•ky (ko͞o′sə-vĭt′skē), **Sergei Aleksandrovich.** 1874–1951. Russian-born Amer. conductor of the Boston Symphony Orchestra (1924–49).

Kow•loon (kou′lo͞on′). A city of Hong Kong on the SE coast of China on **Kowloon Peninsula** opposite Hong Kong I.; ceded to the British in 1860. Pop. 799,123.

kow•tow (kou-tou′, kou′tou′) *intr.v.* **-towed, -tow•ing, -tows. 1.** To kneel and touch the forehead to the ground in expression of deep respect, worship, or submission, as formerly done in China. **2.** To show servile deference; fawn. — *n.* **1.** The act of kneeling and touching the forehead to the ground. **2.** An obsequious act. [< Chin. (Mandarin) *kòu tóu*, a kowtow : *kòu*, to knock + *tóu*, head.]

Koy•u•kuk (kī′ə-kŭk′). A river of N AK flowing c. 805 km (500 mi) from the Brooks Range to the Yukon R.

Ko•zhi•kode (kō′zhĭ-kōd′). See **Calicut.**

KP (kā′pē′) *n.* Kitchen police. [K(ITCHEN) P(OLICE).]

Kr The symbol for the element **krypton.**

kr. *abbr.* **1.** Krona. **2.** Krone.

Kra (krä), **Isthmus of.** A narrow strip of land linking the Malay Peninsula with the Asian mainland.

kraal (krôl, kräl) *n. South African.* **1.** A rural village, typically consisting of huts surrounded by a stockade. **2.** An enclosure for livestock. [Afr. < Port. *curral*, pen, perh. < VLat. **currāle*, enclosure for carts. See CORRAL.]

Krafft-E•bing (krăft′ĕb′ĭng, kräft′ā′bĭng), Baron **Richard von.** 1840–1902. German physician and neurologist particularly known for his studies of sexual deviance.

kraft (krăft) *n.* A tough, usu. brown paper made from wood pulp and used chiefly for bags and wrapping paper. [Short for Swed. *kraftpapper* : *kraft* (< OSwed. *krapt*) + *papper*, paper.]

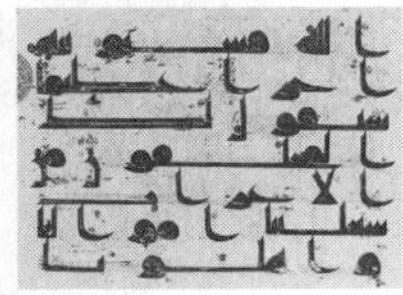

Kufic

krait (krīt) *n.* Any of several brightly banded, highly venomous snakes of the genus *Bungarus* of southeast Asia and adjacent islands. [Hindi *karait.*]

Kra•ka•tau (krăk′ə-tou′, krä′kə-) or **Kra•ka•to•a** (-tō′ə). A volcanic island of Indonesia between Sumatra and Java; blown apart by a violent explosion in Aug. 1883.

kra•ken (krä′kən) *n.* A huge sea monster in Norwegian legend. [Norw. dial. : *krake*, kraken + Norw. *-n*, suffixed definite article.]

Kra•ków (krăk′ou, krä′kou, -ko͝of). See **Cracow.**

Kra•ma•torsk (krä′mə-tôrsk′, krə-). A city of E Ukraine in the Donets Basin SSE of Kharkov. Pop. 192,000.

Kras•ner (krăz′nər), **Lee.** 1908–84. Amer. artist who was a founder of the New York School of abstract expressionism.

Kras•no•dar (krăs′nə-där′, krə-snə-där′). A city of SW Russia S of Rostov; founded 1794. Pop. 609,000.

Kras•no•yarsk (krăs′nə-yärsk′, krə-snə-). A city of S-central Russia on the upper Yenisei R. E of Novosibirsk; founded as a Cossack fortress in 1628. Pop. 872,000.

kra•ter or **cra•ter** (krā′tər) *n.* A wide two-handled bowl used in ancient Greece and Rome. [Gk. *kratēr.* See CRATER.]

K ration *n.* An emergency field ration for U.S. armed forces in World War II, consisting of a single packaged meal. [After Ancel Benjamin *Keys* (b. 1904), Amer. physiologist.]

kraut (krout) *n.* **1.** Sauerkraut. **2.** Often **Kraut.** *Offensive Slang.* Used as a disparaging term for a German. [Ger. See SAUERKRAUT.]

Krebs (krĕbz, krĕps), Sir **Hans Adolf.** 1900–81. German-born British biochemist who shared a 1953 Nobel Prize.

Krebs cycle (krĕbz) *n. Biochem.* A series of enzymatic reactions in aerobic organisms involving oxidation of acetyl units and producing high-energy phosphate compounds, which are the main source of cellular energy. [After Sir Hans Adolf KREBS.]

Kre•feld (krā′fĕld′, -fĕlt′). A city of W-central Germany on the Rhine R. NNW of Cologne; chartered 1373. Pop. 217,276.

Krei•sler (krī′slər), **Fritz.** 1875–1962. Austrian-born Amer. composer of the operetta *Apple Blossoms* (1919).

Kre•men•chug (krĕm′ən-cho͞ok′, -cho͞og′, kryĭ′mĭn-cho͞ok′). A city of E-central Ukraine on the Dnieper R. SE of Kiev; founded as a fortress in 1571. Pop. 224,000.

Krem•lin (krĕm′lĭn) *n.* **1.** The citadel of Moscow, housing government offices. **2.** The government of the former Soviet Union. **3. kremlin.** The citadel of a Russian city. [Obsolete Ger. *Kremelin* < ORuss. **kremlĭnŭ*, separate < *kremlĭ*, a separate place.]

Krem•lin•ol•o•gy (krĕm′lə-nŏl′ə-jē) *n.* The study of the policies of the Soviet government. — **Krem′lin•o•log′i•cal** (-lə-nə-lŏj′ĭ-kəl) *adj.* — **Krem′lin•ol′o•gist** *n.*

krep•lach (krĕp′ləкн, -läкн) *pl.n.* Small pockets of noodle dough filled with ground meat or cheese, usu. boiled and served in soups. [Yiddish *kreplech*, pl. of *krepel* < Ger. dial. *Kräppel*, fried pastry, var. of Ger. *Krapfen* < MHGer. *krapfe* < OHGer. *krapfo*, hook (< their hooklike shape).]

kreu•zer or **kreut•zer** (kroit′sər) *n.* Any of several coins of low value formerly used in Austria and Germany. [Ger. < MHGer. *kriuzer* < *kriuze*, cross (originally stamped with a cross) < OHGer. *krūzi* < Lat. *crux, cruc-*.]

krewe (kro͞o) *n. New Orleans.* Any of several groups whose members organize and participate in the annual Mardi Gras carnival. See Regional Note at **beignet.** [Alteration of CREW[1].]

Kriem•hild (krēm′hĭld′, -hĭlt′) also **Kriem•hil•de** (krēm-hĭl′də) *n.* The wife of Siegfried and sister of Gunther in the *Nibelungenlied.*

krill (krĭl) *n., pl.* **krill.** The collection of small marine crustaceans of the order Euphausiacea that are the principal food of baleen whales. [Norw. *kril*, young fry of fish.]

krim•mer (krĭm′ər) *n.* Gray curly fur made from the pelts of lambs of the Crimean region. [Ger. < *Krim*, Crimea.]

kris also **creese** (krēs) *n.* A Malayan dagger with a wavy double-edged blade. [Malay *kĕris.*]

Krish•na[1] (krĭsh′nə) *n. Hinduism.* The eighth and principal avatar of Vishnu, often depicted as a handsome young man playing a flute. — **Krish′na•ism** *n.*

Krish•na[2] (krĭsh′nə). See **Kistna.**

Kriss Krin•gle (krĭs′ krĭng′gəl) *n.* Santa Claus. [Alteration of Ger. dial. *Christkindl*, Christmas present : Ger. *Christ*, Christ (ult. < Lat. *Chrīstus*; see CHRIST) + Ger. dial. *Kindl* (dim. of Ger. *Kind*, child, ult. < OHGer. *kind*; see **genə-***).]

Kri•voi Rog or **Kri•voy Rog** (krĭ-voi′ rŏg′, rôk′). A city of S-central Ukraine NE of Odessa. Pop. 684,000.

Krogh (krôg, krôкн), **(Schack) August Steenberg.** 1874–1949. Danish physiologist who won a 1920 Nobel Prize.

kro•na[1] (krō′nə) *n., pl.* **-nur** (-nər). See table at **currency.** [Icel. *króna* < ON *krūna* < MLGer. *krūne, krōne*, ult. < Lat. *corōna*, wreath, crown. See CROWN.]

kro•na[2] (krō′nə) *n., pl.* **-nor** (-nôr′, -nər). See table at **currency.** [Swed. < OSwed. *krōna* < MLGer. *krūne, krōne.* See KRONA[1].]

kro•ne[1] (krō′nə) *n., pl.* **-ner** (-nər). See table at **currency.** [Norw. < ON *krūna.* See KRONA[1].]

kro•ne[2] (krō′nə) *n., pl.* **-ner** (-nər). See table at **currency.** [Dan. *krone* < ON *krūna.* See KRONA[1].]

Kro•pot•kin (krə-pŏt′kĭn, krō-), Prince **Pyotr Alekseyevich.** 1842–1921. Russian anarchist philosopher who advocated cooperation as the means of bettering the human condition.

Kru•ger (kro͞o′gər, krü′-), **Stephanus Johannes Paulus.** "Oom Paul." 1825–1904. South African politician who was a founder (1852) and president (1883–1900) of Transvaal.

Kru•ger•rand (kro͞o′gə-rănd′, -ränd′) *n.* A one-ounce gold coin of South Africa. [Afr. : after Stephanus Johannes Paulus KRUGER + *rand*, rand; see RAND.]

krumm•horn or **crum•horn** (krŭm′hôrn′) *n. Mus.* A wind instrument of the Renaissance with a curving tube and a double reed. [Ger. : *krumm*, crooked (< MHGer. *krump, krum* < OHGer. *krump*) + *Horn*, horn; see ALPENHORN.]

krumm•kake (kro͝om′kä′kə, krŭm′kāk′) *n. Upper Midwest.* A large thin cookie made from batter poured into an embossed mold with hinged plates. [Norw. *krumkake* : *krum*, curved, crooked (< MLGer. *krum* < OHGer. *krump*) + *kake*, cake (< ON *kaka*).]

Krung Thep (gro͞ong tĕp′). See **Bangkok.**

Krupp (kro͞op, krŭp). German family of steel and munitions manufacturers, including **Friedrich** (1787–1826), who founded the Krupp Works in Essen (1811). His great-granddaughter **Bertha** (1886–1957) and her husband **Gustav Krupp von Bohlen und Halbach** (1870–1950) were instrumental in the secret rearming of Germany after World War I.

Krup•ska•ya (kro͞op′skə-yə), **Nadezhda Konstantinovna.** 1869–1939. Russian revolutionary and wife of Vladimir Lenin who wrote *Memories of Lenin* (1930).

kryp•ton (krĭp′tŏn′) *n. Symbol* **Kr** A largely inert gaseous element used in gas fluorescent lamps. Atomic number 36; atomic weight 83.80; melting point −156.6°C; boiling point −152.30°C; density 3.73 grams per liter (0°C). See table at **element.** [Gk. *krupton*, neut. of *kruptos*, hidden < *kruptein*, to hide.]

KS *abbr.* Kansas.

Ksha•tri•ya (kə-shăt′rē-ə, -chăt′-) *n.* A member of the second of the four Hindu classes, responsible for justice and social harmony. [Skt. *kṣatriyaḥ* < *kṣatram*, rule, power.]

kt *abbr.* Kiloton.

Kt *abbr. Games.* Knight.

kt. also **kt** *abbr.* **1.** Karat. **2.** Knight. **3.** *Naut.* Knot.

Kua•la Lum•pur (kwä′lə lo͝om-po͝or′). The cap. of Malaysia, on the SW Malay Peninsula NW of Singapore; founded by tin miners in 1857. Pop. 937,817.

Ku•ban (ko͞o-băn′, -bän′). A river of SW Russia flowing c. 917 km (570 mi) to the Sea of Azov.

Ku•blai Khan (ko͞o′blī kän′) also **Ku•bla Khan** (-blə). 1215–94. Mongol emperor (1260–94) and founder of the Mongol dynasty in China.

ku•chen (ko͞o′kən, -KHən) *n.* A coffeecake leavened with yeast, often containing fruit and nuts. [Ger. < MHGer. *kuoche*, cake < OHGer. *kuocho*.]

ku•dos (ko͞o′dōz′, -dōs′, -dŏs′, kyo͞o′-) *n.* Acclaim or praise for exceptional achievement. [Gk., magical glory.]

Usage Note: *Kudos* is one of those words like *congeries* that look like plurals but are etymologically singular: correctness requires *Kudos* is *due her for her brilliant work.* Some writers have tried to defend the use of *kudos* with a plural verb, or even the introduction of a new singular form of *kudo*, on the grounds that these innovations follow the pattern whereby the English words *pea* and *cherry* were re-formed from nouns ending in *–s* that were thought to be plural. But at present *kudos* is still regarded as a pretentious variant for *praise* and can scarcely claim to be part of the linguistic folkways of the community.

ku•du also **koo•doo** (ko͞o′do͞o) *n., pl.* **kudu** or **-dus** also **koodoo** or **-doos.** Either of two large African antelopes *(Tragelaphus strepsiceros* or *T. imberbis)* having a brownish coat with narrow white vertical stripes and long, spirally curved horns in the male. [Afr. *koedoe* < Nguni (Xhosa) *i-quda, i-qudu*, poss. of Khoikhoin (Nama) orig.]

kud•zu (ko͝od′zo͞o) *n.* An eastern Asian vine *(Pueraria lobata)* having compound leaves and reddish-purple flowers. [J. *kuzu*.]

Ku•fic also **Cu•fic** (ko͞o′fĭk, kyo͞o′-) *adj.* Relating to or being an angular form of the Arabic alphabet used in making fine copies of the Koran. [After Al *Kufa*, a town of S-central Iraq.]

Kuhn (ko͞on), **Richard.** 1900–67. Austrian chemist who won a 1938 Nobel Prize.

Kui•by•shev or **Kuy•by•shev** (kwē′bə-shĕf′, -shĕv′, ko͞o′ē-bə-shĭf). A city of W Russia on the Volga R. ESE of Moscow; founded 1586. Pop. 1,257,000.

Ku Klux Klan (ko͞o′ klŭks klăn′, kyo͞o′) *n.* **1.** A secret society organized in the South after the Civil War to reassert white supremacy by terrorism. **2.** A secret fraternal organization of similar intent founded in Georgia in 1915. [Perh. alteration of Gk. *kuklos*, circle; see CYCLE + alteration of *clan*.] **— Ku Klux′er** (ko͞o klŭk′sər, kyo͞o) *n.*

ku•lak (ko͞o-lăk′, ko͞o′lăk′, -läk′) *n.* A relatively prosperous landed peasant in czarist Russia, characterized by the Communists during the October Revolution as an exploiter. [Russ., fist, kulak, prob. of Turkic orig.]

Kul•tur (ko͝ol-to͝or′) *n.* **1.** Culture; civilization. **2.** German culture and civilization as idealized during the Hohenzollern and Nazi regimes. [Ger. < Lat. *cultūra*, cultivation, care. See CULTURE.]

Kul•tur•kampf (ko͝ol-to͝or′kämpf′) *n.* The struggle (1871–1883) between the Roman Catholic Church and the German government under Bismarck for control over school and ecclesiastical appointments and civil marriage. [Ger. : *Kultur*, Kultur; see KULTUR + *Kampf*, struggle (< MHGer. *kampf* < OHGer. *kamph*, prob. ult. < Lat. *campus*, field).]

Ku•ma•mo•to (ko͞o′mə-mō′tō). A city of W Kyushu, Japan, E of Nagasaki. Pop. 555,722.

Ku•ma•si (ko͞o-mä′sē). A city of S-central Ghana NW of Accra; founded c. 1700. Pop. 348,880.

ku•miss also **kou•miss** (ko͞o-mĭs′, ko͞o′mĭs) *n.* The fermented milk of a mare or camel, used as a beverage. [Russ. *kumys* < ORuss. *komyzŭ* < Old Turkic *qïmïz* < *qammaq*, to shake.]

küm•mel (kĭm′əl, kü′məl) *n.* A colorless liqueur flavored chiefly with caraway seeds. [Ger. < MHGer. *kümel*, cumin seed, ult. < Lat. *cumīnum*. See CUMIN.]

küm•mel•weck (ko͞o′məl-vĕk′) *n. Buffalo.* A hard roll containing caraway seeds and coated with salt. [Ger. *kümmel*, cumin; see KÜMMEL + Ger. dial. *Weck*, roll; see WECK.]

kum•quat also **cum•quat** (kŭm′kwŏt′) *n.* **1.** Any of several trees or shrubs of the genus *Fortunella*, having small, edible orangelike fruit. **2.** The fruit of these plants. [Chin. (Cantonese) *kam kwat* : *kêm*, gold + *kwêt*, orange.]

Kun (ko͞on), **Béla.** 1886–1939? Hungarian politician who founded the Hungarian Communist Party (1918) and organized the revolution in Budapest (1919).

Ku•ne•ne (ko͞o-nā′nə). See **Cunene.**

kung fu (kŭng′ fo͞o′, ko͝ong′, go͝ong′) *Sports. n.* The Chinese martial arts, esp. those similar to karate. [Chin. (Cantonese).]

Kun•lun (ko͞on′lo͞on′). A mountain system of W China extending E from the Karakoram Range along the N edge of the Xizang (Tibet) plateau and rising to 7,729 m (25,341 ft).

Kun•ming (ko͞on′mĭng′). A city of S China SW of Chongqing; cap. of Yunnan province. Pop. 1,080,000.

kunz•ite (ko͝ont′sīt′) *n.* A lilac-colored spodumene used as a gemstone. [After George Frederick *Kunz* (1856–1932), Amer. gemologist.]

Kuo•pio (kwô′py-ô′). A city of S-central Finland NNE of Helsinki; chartered 1782. Pop. 77,371.

Kuo•yu (kwô′yo͞o′) *n.* Var. of **Guoyu.**

Ku•ra (ko͞o-rä′). A river of NE Turkey and S Azerbaijan flowing c. 1,514 km (941 mi) to the Caspian Sea S of Baku.

Ku•ra•shi•ki (ko͞o-rä′shē-kē). A city of W Honshu, Japan, a suburb of Okayama on the Inland Sea. Pop. 413,644.

kur•cha•tov•i•um (kûr′chə-tō′vē-əm) *n.* Element 104. [After Igor Vasilyevich *Kurchatov* (1903–60), Soviet physicist.]

Kurd (kûrd, ko͝ord) *n.* A member of a pastoral and agricultural people inhabiting the transnational region of Kurdistan.

Kurd•ish (kûr′dĭsh, ko͝or′-) *adj.* Of or relating to the Kurds or their language or culture. **—** *n.* Their Iranian language.

Kurd•i•stan (kûr′dĭ-stăn′, ko͝or′dĭ-stän′). An extensive plateau region of SW Asia divided among SE Turkey, NE Iraq, and NW Iran, with smaller sections in Syria and Armenia.

kumquat

Ku•re (ko͞o′rĕ′). A city of SW Honshu, Japan, on an arm of the Inland Sea SE of Hiroshima. Pop. 226,489.

kur•gan (ko͝or-gän′, -găn′) *n.* **1.** A type of tumulus or barrow characteristic of a culture located on the steppes of southern Russia about 5000 B.C. **2. Kurgan. a.** The culture that produced these tumuli or barrows. **b.** A member of the people or peoples sharing this culture. [Russ., fortified place, grave mound < Old Turkic *kurghan*, fortified place.]

Kur•gan (ko͝or-gän′). A city of W Russia ESE of Sverdlovsk; founded in the 17th cent. Pop. 343,000.

Ku•ril Islands also **Ku•rile Islands** (ko͝or′ĭl, ko͞o-rēl′). An island chain of E Russia extending c. 1,207 km (750 mi) in the Pacific Ocean between Kamchatka Peninsula and N Hokkaido, Japan. **— Ku•ril′i•an** *adj. & n.*

Kur•land (ko͝or′lənd). See **Courland.**

Ku•ro•sa•wa (ko͝or′ə-sä′wə, ko͞o′rô-sä′wä), **Akira.** b. 1910. Japanese filmmaker whose works include *Rashomon* (1950) and *Ran* (1985).

Ku•ro•shi•o Current (ko͞o-rō′shē-ō′) *n.* See **Japan Current.**

kur•ra•jong (kûr′ə-jông′, -jŏng′, kŭr′-) *n.* An Australian evergreen tree *(Brachychiton populneus)* having palmately lobed leaves, yellowish or reddish flowers, and long-stalked follicles. [Dharuk (Aboriginal language of SE Australia) *garajuŋ*.]

Kursk (ko͝orsk). A city of W Russia SSW of Moscow; destroyed by the Mongols in 1240 and rebuilt in 1586. Pop. 420,000.

kur•to•sis (kər-tō′sĭs) *n., pl.* **-ses** (-sēz′). The general form or a quantity indicative of the general form of a statistical frequency curve near the mean of the distribution. [Gk. *kurtōsis*, curvature < *kurtos*, bent. See **sker-**[2]*.]

ku•rus (kə-ro͞osh′, ko͞o-) *n., pl.* **kurus.** See table at **currency.** [Turk. *kuruş*, ult. < Lat. *(dēnārius) grossus*, thick (denarius). See GROSZ.]

Kush (kŭsh, ko͞osh). See **Cush**[2].

Kus•ko•kwim (kŭs′kə-kwĭm′). A river of SW AK flowing c. 965 km (600 mi) to **Kuskokwim Bay**, an inlet of the Bering Sea.

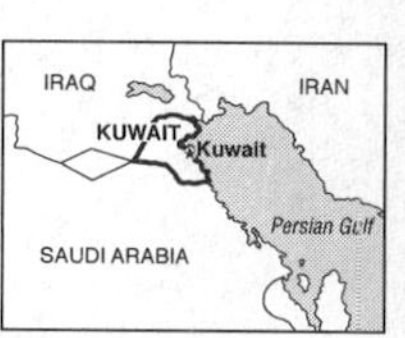

Kuwait

Ku•ta•i•si (ko͞o-tī′sē, ko͞o′tə-yē′syĭ). A city of W Georgia WNW of Tbilisi; cap. of ancient Colchis. Pop. 214,000.

Kutch (kŭch). See **Rann of Kutch.**

Kutch, Gulf of. An inlet of the Arabian Sea in W India adjoining the Rann of Kutch.

Ku•te•nai (ko͞ot′n-ā′, -n-ē′) *n., pl.* **Kutenai** or **-nais. 1.a.** A member of a Native American people inhabiting parts of southeast British Columbia, northeast Washington, and northern Idaho. **2.** The language of the Kutenai.

Ku•tu•zov (ko͞o-to͞o′zŏf, -zəf), **Mikhail Ilarionovich.** Prince of Smolensk. 1745–1813. Russian field marshal who commanded (1805–12) the Russian opposition to Napoleon.

Ku•wait (ko͞o-wāt′). **1.** A country of the NE Arabian Peninsula at the head of the Persian Gulf; a British protectorate from 1897 to 1961 and briefly annexed by Iraq (1990–91). Cap. Kuwait. Pop. 1,355,827. **2.** The cap. of Kuwait, in the E-central part on the Persian Gulf. Pop. 60,365. **— Ku•wait′i** (-wā′tē) *adj. & n.*

Kuy•by•shev (kwē′bə-shĕf′, -shĕv′, ko͞o′ē-bə-shĭf). See **Kuibyshev.**

Kuz•nets (ko͞oz′nĕts′, ko͞oz′nĭts), **Simon.** 1901–85. Russian-born Amer. economist who won a 1971 Nobel Prize.

Kuz•netsk Basin (ko͞oz-nĕtsk′, -nyĕtsk′). A coal-producing region of S-central Russia.

kV or **kv** *abbr.* Kilovolt.

kvass (kväs) *n.* A Russian fermented beverage similar to beer, made from rye or barley. [Russ. *kvas* < ORuss. *kvasŭ*.]

ă pat	oi boy
ā pay	ou out
âr care	o͝o took
ä father	o͞o boot
ĕ pet	ŭ cut
ē be	ûr urge
ĭ pit	th thin
ī pie	*th* this
îr pier	hw which
ŏ pot	zh vision
ō toe	ə about,
ô paw	item

Stress marks:
′ (primary);
′ (secondary), as in
dictionary (dĭk′shə-nĕr′ē)

kvetch (kvěch) *Slang.* — *intr.v.* **kvetched, kvetch•ing, kvetch•es.** To complain persistently and whiningly. — *n.* **1.** A chronic whining complainer. **2.** A nagging complaint. [Yiddish *kvetshn* < MHGer. *quetzen, quetschen,* to squeeze.]
kW *abbr.* Kilowatt.
Kwa (kwä) *n.* Any of several West African languages belonging to the South Central Niger-Congo language family, including Efik, Ewe, Ibibio, Ibo, and Yoruba.
kwa•cha (kwä′chə) *n.* See table at **currency.** [Bemba and Chewa, dawn : *kw-*, infinitive pref. + *-acha,* to dawn.]
Kwa•ja•lein (kwä′jə-lən, -lān′). An atoll in the Marshall Is. of the W Pacific Ocean; used as a Japanese air and naval base during World War II.
Kwa•ki•u•tl (kwä′kē-o͞ot′l) *n., pl.* **Kwakiutl** or **-tls. 1.** A member of a Native American people inhabiting parts of coastal British Columbia and northern Vancouver Island. **2.** The Wakashan language of the Kwakiutl.
Kwan•do (kwän′dō). A river rising in central Angola and flowing c. 965 km (600 mi) to the Zambezi R.
Kwang•chow (kwäng′chō′). See **Guangzhou.**
Kwang•ju (kwäng′jo͞o′, gwäng′-). A city of SW South Korea SSE of Seoul. Pop. 843,000.
Kwang•si Chuang (kwäng′sē′ chwäng′). See **Guangxi Zhuangzu.**
Kwang•tung (kwäng′to͝ong′, gwäng′do͝ong′). See **Guangdong.**
kwan•za (kwän′zə) *n., pl.* **kwanza** or **-zas.** See table at **currency.** [Bantu, poss. from *Kwanza* (Cuanza), a river of Angola, or < Swahili *kwanza,* first, or < *kuanza,* to begin.]
Kwan•za¹ (kwän′zə). See **Cuanza.**
Kwan•za² (kwän′zə) *n.* An African-American cultural festival, celebrated from December 26 to January 1. [Poss. < Swahili *kwanzaa,* first fruit of the harvest.]
kwa•shi•or•kor (kwä′shē-ôr′kôr′) *n.* Severe protein malnutrition, esp. in children, characterized by anemia, edema, potbelly, depigmentation of the skin, and loss of hair or change in hair color. [Gã (Niger-Congo language of Ghana) *kwashiɔkɔ.*]
Kwei•chow (kwā′chō′). See **Guizhou.**
Kwei•lin (kwā′lĭn′). See **Guilin.**
Kwei•yang (kwā′yäng′). See **Guiyang.**
kWh *abbr.* Kilowatt-hour.

kylix

kW-hr *abbr.* Kilowatt-hour.
KY or **Ky.** *abbr.* Kentucky.
ky•ack (kī′ăk′) *n.* A packsack that hangs on either side of a packsaddle. [Prob. < KAYAK.]
ky•a•nite (kī′ə-nīt′) also **cy•a•nite** (sī′ə-) *n.* A bluish-green to colorless mineral, Al_2SiO_5, used as a refractory. [Gk. *kuanos,* dark blue enamel + -ITE¹.]
kyat (chät) *n.* See table at **currency.** [Burmese.]
Kyd or **Kid** (kĭd), **Thomas.** 1558–94. English dramatist who wrote *The Spanish Tragedy* (c. 1584).
ky•lix (kī′lĭks, kĭl′ĭks) *n., pl.* **ky•li•kes** (kī′lĭ-kēz′, kĭl′ĭ-). A shallow stemmed two-handled drinking cup used in ancient Greece. [Gk. *kulix.*]
ky•mo•gram (kī′mə-grăm′) *n.* A graph or record made by a kymograph. [Gk. *kuma,* something swollen; see CYMA + -GRAM.]
ky•mo•graph (kī′mə-grăf′) *n. Physiol.* An instrument for recording variations in pressure or tension by means of a pen or stylus that marks a rotating drum. [Gk. *kuma,* something swollen; see CYMA + -GRAPH.] — **ky′mo•graph′ic** *adj.*
Ky•o•ga (kē-ō′gə), **Lake.** See Lake **Kioga.**
Kyo•to (kē-ō′tō, kyō′-). A city of W-central Honshu, Japan, NNE of Osaka; founded in the 8th cent. and former cap. of Japan (794–1869). Pop. 1,479,125.
ky•pho•sis (kī-fō′sĭs) *n.* Abnormal rearward curvature of the spine, resulting in protuberance of the upper back; hunchback. [Gk. *kuphōsis* < *kuphos,* bent.] — **ky•phot′ic** (-fŏt′ĭk) *adj.*
Kyr•gyz•stan (kîr-gē-stän′, -gyē-). See **Kirghiz.**
Kyr•i•e (kîr′ē-ā′) *n.* **1.** A brief petition and response used in various Christian liturgies, beginning with or composed of the words "Lord, have mercy." **2.** A musical setting for this prayer. [LLat. < Gk. *Kurie eleēson,* Lord, have mercy : *Kurie,* vocative of *kurios,* lord, master; see **keuə-*** + *eleēson,* aorist imper. of *elein,* to show mercy (< *eleos,* mercy).]
Kyrie e•le•i•son (ĭ-lā′ĭ-sŏn′, -sən) *n.* The Kyrie. [LLat. See KYRIE.]
Kyu•shu (kē-o͞o′sho͞o, kyo͞o′-). An island of SW Japan on the East China Sea and the Pacific Ocean.
Ky•zyl-Kum (kĭ-zĭl′ko͞om′). A desert of N-central Uzbekistan and S-central Kazakhstan SE of the Aral Sea between the Amu Darya and the Syr Darya.

L l

l¹ or **L** (ĕl) *n., pl.* **l's** or **L's. 1.** The 12th letter of the modern English alphabet. **2.** Any of the speech sounds represented by the letter *l.* **3.** The 12th in a series. **4.** Something shaped like the letter L.
l² *abbr.* Liter.
L¹ also **l** The symbol for the Roman numeral 50.
L² *abbr.* **1.** Lambert. **2.** Also **L.** Large.
l. *abbr.* **1.** Also **L.** Lake. **2.** Land. **3.** Late. **4.** Left. **5.** Length. **6.** Line. **7.** Lira.
L. *abbr.* Latin.
la¹ (lä) *n. Mus.* The sixth tone of the diatonic scale in solfeggio. [ME < Med.Lat. See GAMUT.]
la² (lä) *interj.* Used to express emphasis or indicate surprise.
La The symbol for the element **lanthanum.**
LA or **La.** *abbr.* Louisiana.
L.A. *abbr.* **1.** Legislative Assembly. **2.** Local agent. **3.** Also **LA** Los Angeles.
laa•ger (lä′gər) *n.* A defensive encampment encircled by armored vehicles or wagons. — *intr.v.* **-gered, -ger•ing, -gers.** To camp in a defensive encirclement. [Alteration of Obsolete Afr. *lager,* prob. < Ger. *Lager,* camp, lair < MHGer. *lēger,* bed, lair < OHGer. *legar.* See **legh-***.]
lab (lăb) *n.* A laboratory.
Lab. *abbr.* Labrador.
La Baie (lä bā′). A city of S-central Quebec, Canada, on the Saguenay R. SE of Chicoutimi. Pop. 20,935.
lab•a•rum (lăb′ər-əm) *n., pl.* **-a•ra** (-ər-ə). **1.** An ecclesiastical banner, esp. one carried in processions. **2.** The banner adopted by Constantine I after his conversion to Christianity. [Lat.]
lab•da•num (lăb′də-nəm) also **lad•a•num** (lăd′n-əm) *n.* A resin of certain Old World plants of the genus *Cistus,* yielding a fragrant essential oil used in flavorings and perfumes. [ME < Med.Lat. *lapdanum, labdanum,* alteration of Lat. *lādanum* < Gk. *lēdanon* < *lēdon,* rockrose, of Semitic orig.]
la•bel (lā′bəl) *n.* **1.** An item that serves to identify, esp. a small piece of paper or cloth attached to an article to designate its origin, owner, contents, use, or destination. **2.** A descriptive term; an epithet. **3.** A distinctive name or trademark identifying a product or manufacturer, esp. a recording company. **4.** *Comp. Sci.* A symbol or set of symbols identifying the contents of a file, memory, tape, or record. **5.** *Archit.* A molding over a door or window; a dripstone. **6.** *Her.* A figure in a field consisting of a narrow horizontal bar with several pendants. **7.** *Chem.* See **tracer** 4. — *tr.v.* **-beled, -bel•ing, -bels** or **-belled, -bel•ling, -bels. 1.** To attach a label to. **2.** To identify or designate with a label; describe or classify. See Syns at **mark¹. 3.** *Chem.* To add a tracer to (a compound). [ME, ornamental strip of cloth < OFr., prob. of Gmc. orig.] — **la′bel•er, la′bel•ler** *n.*
la•bel•lum (lə-bĕl′əm) *n., pl.* **-bel•la** (-bĕl′ə). **1.** The often enlarged petal of an orchid flower. **2.** A liplike part, as certain insect proboscis tips, used for lapping up liquids. [Lat., dim. of *labrum,* lip. See **leb-***.] — **la•bel′late** (-ĭt) *adj.*
la•bi•a (lā′bē-ə) *n.* Pl. of **labium.**
la•bi•al (lā′bē-əl) *adj.* **1.** Of or relating to the lips or labia. **2.** *Ling.* Articulated mainly by closing or partly closing the lips, as the sounds (b), (m), or (w). — *n.* **1.** *Ling.* A labial consonant. **2.** *Mus.* See **flue¹** 2a. [Med.Lat. *labiālis* < Lat. *labium,* lip. See **leb-***.] — **la′bi•al•ly** *adv.*
la•bi•al•ize (lā′bē-ə-līz′) *tr.v.* **-ized, -iz•ing, -iz•es.** *Ling.* To round (a vowel); make labial. — **la′bi•al•i•za′tion** (-ə-lĭ-zā′shən) *n.*
labia ma•jo•ra (mə-jôr′ə, -jōr′ə) *pl.n.* The two outer rounded folds of adipose tissue on either side of the vaginal opening that form the external lateral boundaries of the vulva. [NLat. *labia mājōra* : Lat. *labia,* lips + Lat. *māiōra,* larger.]
labia mi•no•ra (mə-nôr′ə, -nōr′ə) *pl.n.* The two thin inner folds of skin within the vestibule of the vagina enclosed within the cleft of the labia majora; nymphae. [NLat. *labia minōra* : Lat. *labia,* lips + Lat. *minōra,* smaller.]
la•bi•ate (lā′bē-ĭt, -āt′) *adj.* **1.** Having lips or liplike parts. **2.** *Bot.* **a.** Having or being flowers with the corolla divided into two liplike parts, as in the snapdragon. **b.** Of or belonging to the mint family Labiatae. — *n.* A plant belonging to the Labiatae. [Lat. *labium,* lip; see LABIUM + -ATE¹.]
la•bile (lā′bīl′, -bəl) *adj.* **1.** Open to change; adaptable. **2.** *Chem.* Constantly undergoing or likely to undergo change; unstable. [ME *labil,* wandering < OFr. *labile* < LLat. *lābilis,*

apt to slip < *lābī,* to slip.] — **la•bil′i•ty** (-bĭl′ĭ-tē) *n.*
labio– *pref.* Labial: *labiovelar.* [< Lat. *labium,* lip. See LABIUM.]
la•bi•o•den•tal (lā′bē-ō-dĕn′tl) *Ling.* — *adj.* Articulated with the lower lip and upper teeth, as the sounds (f) and (v). — *n.* A labiodental sound.
la•bi•o•na•sal (lā′bē-ō-nā′zəl) *Ling.* — *adj.* Simultaneously labial and nasal. — *n.* A labionasal sound.
la•bi•o•ve•lar (lā′bē-ō-vē′lər) *Ling.* — *adj.* Simultaneously labial and velar, as (kw) in *quick.* — *n.* A labiovelar sound.
la•bi•um (lā′bē-əm) *n., pl.* **-bi•a** (-bē-ə). **1.** *Anat.* Any of four folds of tissue of the female external genitalia. **2.** *Zool.* The floor of the mouth ... liplike structure, such as that forming the ... of certain invertebrates, esp. insects. **b.** The inner ... the opening of a gastropod shell. **3.** *Bot.* One of the divisions of a labiate corolla. [Lat., lip. See **leb-***.]
la•bor (lā′bər) *n.* **1.a.** Physical or mental exertion, esp. when difficult or exhausting; work. **b.** Something ... work or ... **2.** A specific task. **3.** A particular ... method of working: *manual labor.* **4.** ... for wages. ... on movement ... **5.a.** Workers considered as a group. **b.** The ... representing ... ment, esp. its officials. **6. Labor.** A political ... the physical ... the interests of workers, esp. in Great Britain ... efforts of childbirth; parturition. ... **-bor•ing,** **-bors.** — *intr.* **1.** To work; toil. **2.** ... painstakingly. **3.a.** To proceed with great effort; plod ... pitch and roll. **4.** To suffer from distress ... **5.** To undergo the efforts of childbirth. ... with in exhaustive or excessive detail; belabor ... *point in the argument.* **2.** To distress; burden ... or relating to labor. **2. Labor.** Of or relating ... representing the interests of the working ... *labour* < Lat. *labor.*] — **la′bor•er** *n.*
lab•o•ra•to•ry (lăb′rə-tôr′ē) *n.* ... **1.a.** A room or building equipped ... mentation or research. **b.** An academic ... work or study in such a place. **2.** A place ... chemicals are manufactured. **3.** A place ... or testing. [Med. Lat. *labōrātōrium* ... < *labor,* labor.]
Labor Day *n.* The ... holiday in some ... number, observed as a ... working people.
la•bored (lā′bərd) *adj.* **1.** Marked by or ... done with effort: *labored breathing* ... ase; strained.
la•bor-in•ten•sive ... *adj.* Requiring or having ... comparison to capital.
la•bo•ri•ous ... **1.** Marked by or requiring ... working; industrious. — **la•bo′ri•ous•ness** *n.*
... er or supporter of a labor ... A member of a political ...
la•bor•ing ... Designed to conserve human ... decrease the amount of ...
... organization of wage earners formed for the ... interests with respect to wages ... conditions ...
... *Chiefly British.* Var. of **labor.**
... (lăb′rə-dôr′) ... inland territory of Newfoundland, on the ... portion of the Labrador Peninsula ... by Norse ... as early as the 10th cent. — **Lab′ra•dor′e•an, Lab′ra•dor′i•an** *adj.* & *n.*
Labrador Current *n.* A cold current flowing southward along the coast of Labrador ... turning east.
lab•ra•dor•ite (lăb′rə-dô-rīt′) *n.* A variety of plagioclase feldspar found ... in rocks and characterized by brilliant colors. [After LABRADOR (PENINSULA).]
Labrador Peninsula. A ... E Canada between Hudson Bay and the Atlantic ...
Labrador retriever *n.* A breed of dog originating in Newfoundland, having ... yellow, black, or brown coat and a tapering tail. [After LABRADOR.]
la•bret (lā′brĭt) *n.* ... inserted into a perforation in the lip. [Lat. *labrum* ... **leb-*** + -ET.]
la•brum (lā′brəm) ... **1.** A lip or liplike structure. **2.** The outer ... opening of a gastropod shell. [Lat., lip. See ...]
La Bru•yère (lä brü-yĕr′, brü-), **Jean de.** 1645–96. French moralist whose works provide a critical account of ...
La•bu•an (lä′bo͞o-än′). An island of Malaysia off the NE coast ... became part of Malaysia in 1963.
la•bur•num ... Any of several trees or shrubs of the genus ... *L. anagyroides,* having drooping clusters ... [NLat. *Laburnum,* genus name < Lat. ... leaved bean trefoil, perh. of Etruscan orig.]
lab•y•rinth ... *n.* **1.a.** An intricate structure of interconnecting passages through which it is difficult to find one's way. **b. Labyrinth.** *Gk. Myth.* The maze in ... was confined. **2.** Something highly intricate in character, composition, or construction: ... **3.** *Anat.* **a.** A group of complex interconnecting anatomical cavities. **b.** See **inner ear.** [ME *laberinthe* < Lat. *labyrinthus* < Gk. *laburinthos.*]

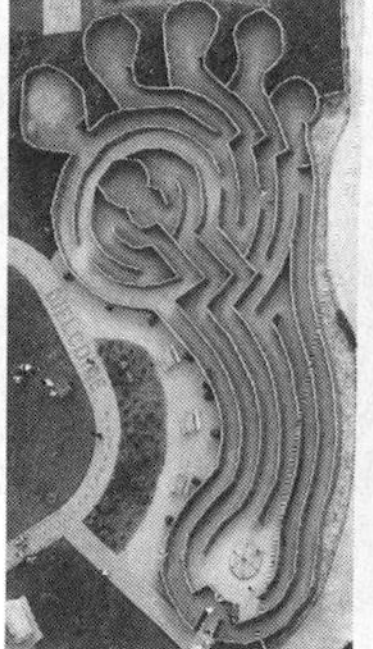

labyrinth

lab•y•rin•thine (lăb′ə-rĭn′thĭn, -thēn′) **lab•y•rin•thi•an** (-thē-ən) *adj.* Of, relating to, resembling, or being a labyrinth.
lac (lăk) *n.* A resinous secretion of various insects of the subfamily Lacciferinae, deposited on trees and used in making shellac. [Du. *lac* or Fr. *laque* (< OFr. *lacce* < Med.Lat. *lacca* < Ar. *lakk* < Pers. *lak*), both < Hindi *lākh* < Prakrit *lakkha* < Skt. *lākṣā,* red dye, resin, alteration of *rākṣā.*]
Lac•ca•dive Islands (lăk′ə-dīv′, lä′kə-dēv′). A group of islands and coral reefs in the Arabian Sea off the SW coast of India; now part of the region of Lakshadweep.
lac•co•lith (lăk′ə-lĭth′) *n.* A mass of igneous rock intruded between layers of sedimentary rock, resulting in uplift. [Gk. *lakkos,* cistern + -LITH.]
lace (lās) *n.* **1.** A cord or ribbon used to draw and tie together two opposite edges, as of a shoe. **2.** A delicate fabric made of yarn or thread in an open weblike pattern. **3.** Gold or silver braid ornamenting an officer's uniform. — *v.* **laced, lac•ing, lac•es.** — *tr.* **1.** To thread a cord through the eyelets or around the hooks of. **2.a.** To draw together and tie the laces of. **b.** To restrain or constrict by tightening laces, esp. of a corset. **3.** To pull or pass through; intertwine: *lace garlands through a trellis.* **4.** To trim or decorate with or as if with lace. **5.a.** To add a touch of liquor to. **b.** To add a touch of flavor or a dash of zest to. **6.** To streak with color. **7.** To give a beating to; thrash. — *intr.* To be fastened or tied with laces or a lace. — ***phrasal verb.*** **lace into.** *Informal.* To attack; assail: *laced into me.* [ME < OFr. *las,* noose, string < VLat. **laceum* < Lat. *laqueus,* noose; prob. akin to *lacere,* to entice, ensnare.] — **lace′less** *adj.* — **lac′er** *n.*
Lac•e•dae•mon (lăs′ĭ-dē′mən). See **Sparta.** — **Lac′e•dae•mo′ni•an** (-də-mō′nē-ən) *adj.* & *n.*
lac•er•ate (lăs′ə-rāt′) *tr.v.* **-at•ed, -at•ing, -ates. 1.** To rip, cut, or tear. **2.** To cause deep emotional pain to; distress. — *adj.* (-rĭt, -rāt′). **1.** Torn; mangled. **2.** Wounded. **3.** Having jagged, deeply cut edges: *lacerate leaves.* [ME *laceraten* < Lat. *lacerāre, lacerāt-* < *lacer,* torn.]
lac•er•a•tion (lăs′ə-rā′shən) *n.* A jagged wound or cut.
La•cer•ta (lə-sûr′tə) *n.* A constellation in the Northern Hemisphere near Cygnus and Andromeda. [Lat. *lacerta,* lizard.]
lace•wing (lās′wĭng′) *n.* Any of various insects of the superfamily Hemerobioidea, having four gauzy wings, threadlike antennae, and larvae that feed on insect pests such as aphids.
La•chaise (lə-shāz′, lä-shĕz′), **Gaston.** 1882–1935. French-born Amer. sculptor known for his large nude figures.
Lach•e•sis (lăk′ĭ-sĭs, lăch′-) *n. Gk. Myth.* One of the three Fates, the measurer of the thread of destiny.
La•chine (lə-shēn′, lä-). A city of S Quebec, Canada, on Montreal I.; first settled in 1668. Pop. 37,521.
La•chish (lā′kĭsh). An ancient city of S Palestine SW of Jerusalem; probably inhabited as early as 3200 B.C.
Lach•lan (lăk′lən). A river of SE Australia flowing c. 1,483 km (922 mi) to the Murrumbidgee R.
lach•ry•mal also **lac•ri•mal** (lăk′rə-məl) *adj.* **1.** Of or relating to tears. **2.** Of, relating to, or constituting the glands that produce tears. [ME *lacrimale* < OFr. *lacrymal* < Med.Lat. *lachrymālis* < Lat. *lacrima,* tear. See **dakru-***.]
lach•ry•ma•tion (lăk′rə-mā′shən) *n.* Var. of **lacrimation.**
lach•ry•ma•tor also **lac•ri•ma•tor** (lăk′rə-mā′tər) *n.* Tear gas. [Lat. *lacrimāre, lacrimātus,* to cry (< *lacrima,* tear; see LACHRYMAL) + -ATOR.]
lach•ry•mose (lăk′rə-mōs′) *adj.* **1.** Weeping or inclined to weep; tearful. **2.** Causing or tending to cause tears. [Lat. *lacrimōsus* < *lacrima,* tear. See LACHRYMAL.] — **lach′ry•mose′ly** *adv.* — **lach′ry•mos′i•ty** (-mŏs′ĭ-tē) *n.*
lac•ing (lā′sĭng) *n.* **1.** Something that laces; a lace. **2.** A touch of liquor added to a beverage or food. **3.** *Informal.* A beating or thrashing.
la•cin•i•ate (lə-sĭn′ē-ĭt, -āt′) *adj.* **1.** Having a fringe; fringed. **2.** Shaped or formed like a fringe, as a ligament. **3.** Slashed into narrow pointed lobes: *a laciniate leaf.* [Lat. *lacinia,* fringe, hem + -ATE[1].] — **la•cin′i•a′tion** *n.*
lack (lăk) *n.* **1.** A deficiency or an absence. **2.** Something needed or wanted. — *v.* **lacked, lack•ing, lacks.** — *tr.* **1.** To be entirely without or have very little of. **2.** To be in need of. — *intr.* **1.** To be wanting or deficient. **2.** To be in need of something. [ME, perh. < MDu. *lac,* deficiency, fault.]

Syns: *lack, want, need.* These verbs mean to be without something, especially something that is necessary or desirable. *Lack* emphasizes the absence or the inadequacy of something: *She lacks the money to buy new shoes. Want* and *need* stress the urgent necessity for filling a void or remedying an inadequacy: *"Her pens were uniformly bad and wanted fixing"* (Bret Harte). *The garden needs care.*

Usage Note: As an intransitive verb in the sense "to be wanting or deficient" *lack* is used chiefly in the present participle with *in: You will not be lacking in support from me.* In the sense "to be in need of something" it is often used with *for: "In the terrible, beautiful age of my prime/I lacked for sweet linen but never for time"* (E.B. White).

lack•a•dai•si•cal (lăk′ə-dā′zĭ-kəl) *adj.* Lacking spirit, liveli-

ă pat	oi boy
ā pay	ou out
âr care	o͝o took
ä father	o͞o boot
ĕ pet	ŭ cut
ē be	ûr urge
ĭ pit	th thin
ī pie	*th* this
îr pier	hw which
ŏ pot	zh vision
ō toe	ə about,
ô paw	item

Stress marks:
′ (primary);
′ (secondary), as in
dictionary (dĭk′shə-nĕr′ē)

ness, or interest; languid. [< *lackadaisy*, alteration of LACKADAY.] — **lack′a·dai′si·cal·ness** *n.*

lack·a·day (lăk′ə-dā′) *interj. Archaic.* Used to express regret or disapproval. [Alteration of *alack the day.*]

Lack·a·wan·na (lăk′ə-wŏn′ə). A city of W NY on Lake Erie S of Buffalo. Pop. 20,585.

lack·ey (lăk′ē) *n., pl.* **-eys. 1.** A liveried male servant; a footman. **2.** A servile follower; a toady. — *v.* **-eyed, -ey·ing, -eys.** — *tr.* To wait on as a footman; attend. — *intr.* To act in a servile manner; fawn. [Fr. *laquais* < OFr.]

lack·lus·ter (lăk′lŭs′tər) *adj.* Lacking brightness, luster, or vitality; dull.

La·co·ni·a (lə-kō′nē-ə). An ancient region of S Greece in the SE Peloponnesus; dominated by Sparta until the rise of the second Achaean League in the 3rd and 2nd cent. B.C.

lacrosse

la·con·ic (lə-kŏn′ĭk) *adj.* Using or marked by the use of few words; terse or concise. [Lat. *Lacōnicus*, Spartan < Gk. *Lakōnikos* < *Lakōn*, a Spartan (< the reputation of the Spartans for brevity of speech).] — **la·con′i·cal·ly** *adv.*

lac·o·nism (lăk′ə-nĭz′əm) *n.* Laconic style or expression.

La Co·ru·ña (lä′ kə-ro͞on′yə, kô-ro͞o′nyä). A city of NW Spain on the Atlantic Ocean W of Oviedo; point of departure for the Spanish Armada (1588). Pop. 240,463.

lac·quer (lăk′ər) *n.* **1.** Any of various clear or colored synthetic coatings made by dissolving cellulose derivatives together with plasticizers in volatile solvents and used to impart a high gloss to surfaces. **2.** A glossy resinous material, such as the exudation of the lacquer tree, used as a surface coating. **3.** A finish that is baked onto the inside of food and beverage cans. — *tr.v.* **-quered, -quer·ing, -quers. 1.** To coat with lacquer. **2.** To give a sleek glossy finish to. [Obsolete Fr. *lacre*, sealing wax < Port. < *lacca*, resin of the lac insect < Ar. *lakk*. See LAC.] — **lac′quer·er** *n.*

lacquer tree *n.* A poisonous eastern Asian tree *(Rhus verniciflua)* having pinnately compound leaves and a toxic exudation from which a black lacquer is obtained.

lac·ri·mal (lăk′rə-məl) *adj.* Var. of **lachrymal.**

lac·ri·ma·tion also **lach·ry·ma·tion** (lăk′rə-mā′shən) *n.* Secretion of tears, esp. in excess.

lac·ri·ma·tor (lăk′rə-mā′tər) *n.* Var. of **lachrymator.**

la·crosse (lə-krôs′, -krŏs′) *n. Sports.* A game of Native American origin played on a field by two teams of ten players each, in which participants use a long-handled stick with a webbed pouch to maneuver a ball into the opposing team's goal. [Canadian Fr. *la crosse* < Fr. *(jeu de) la crosse*, (game of) the hooked stick < OFr. *croce, crosse*, crosier, of Gmc. orig.]

La Crosse (lə krôs′, krŏs′). A city of W WI on the Mississippi R. NW of Madison. Pop. 51,003.

lact– *pref.* Var. of **lacto–.**

lac·tal·bu·min (lăk′tăl-byo͞o′mĭn) *n.* The albumin contained in milk and obtained from whey.

lac·tase (lăk′tās′) *n.* An enzyme occurring in certain yeasts and in the intestinal juices of mammals that is capable of splitting lactose into glucose and galactose.

lac·tate¹ (lăk′tāt′) *intr.v.* **-tat·ed, -tat·ing, -tates.** To secrete or produce milk. [Lat. *lactāre, lactāt-* < *lac, lact-*, milk. See LACTO–.]

lac·tate² (lăk′tāt′) *n.* A salt or an ester of lactic acid.

lac·ta·tion (lăk-tā′shən) *n.* **1.** Secretion or formation of milk by the mammary glands. **2.** The period during which the mammary glands secrete milk. — **lac·ta′tion·al** *adj.*

ladder-back
18th-century English ladder-back chair

lac·te·al (lăk′tē-əl) *adj.* **1.** Of, relating to, or resembling milk. **2.** *Anat.* Of or relating to any of numerous minute intestinal lymph-carrying vessels that convey chyle from the intestine. — *n. Anat.* A lacteal vessel. [< Lat. *lacteus* < *lac, lact-*, milk. See **melg-*.**] — **lac′te·al·ly** *adv.*

lac·tes·cent (lăk-tĕs′ənt) *adj.* **1.** Becoming milky. **2.** Milky. **3.** *Biol.* Secreting or yielding a milky juice, as certain plants and insects. [Lat. *lactēscēns, lactēscent-*, pr.part. of *lactēscere*, inchoative of *lactēre*, to be milky < *lac, lact-*, milk. See **melg-*.**] — **lac·tes′cence** *n.*

lac·tic (lăk′tĭk) *adj.* Of, relating to, or derived from milk.

lactic acid *n.* A syrupy water-soluble liquid, $C_3H_6O_3$, produced as a result of anaerobic glucose metabolism, present in sour milk and wines, and used in food preparation, industry, and pharmaceuticals.

lac·tif·er·ous (lăk-tĭf′ər-əs) *adj.* **1.** Producing, secreting, or conveying milk. **2.** *Bot.* Yielding latex.

lacto– or **lact–** *pref.* **1.** Milk: *lactoprotein.* **2.** Lactose: *lactase.* **3.** Lactic acid: *lactate.* [< Lat. *lac, lact-*, milk. See **melg-*.**]

lac·to·ba·cil·lus (lăk′tō-bə-sĭl′əs) *n., pl.* **-cil·li** (-sĭl′ī′). Any of various rod-shaped nonmotile aerobic bacteria of the genus *Lactobacillus* that ferment lactic acid from sugars.

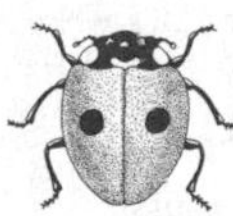

ladybug
Two-spotted ladybug
Adalia bipunctata

lac·to·fla·vin (lăk′tə-flā′vĭn, lăk′tə-flā′-) *n.* See **riboflavin.**

lac·to·gen·ic (lăk′tə-jĕn′ĭk) *adj.* Inducing lactation.

lac·tom·e·ter (lăk-tŏm′ĭ-tər) *n.* A device used to measure the specific gravity, and therefore the richness, of milk.

lac·tone (lăk′tōn′) *n.* An anhydride formed by the removal of a water molecule from the hydroxyl and carboxyl radicals of hydroxy acids. — **lac·ton′ic** (-tŏn′ĭk) *adj.*

lac·to·pro·tein (lăk′tō-prō′tēn′, -tē-ən) *n.* A protein normally present in milk.

lac·tose (lăk′tōs′) *n.* **1.** A disaccharide, $C_{12}H_{22}O_{11}$, found in milk, that may be hydrolyzed to yield glucose and galactose. **2.** A white crystalline substance obtained from whey and used as a diluent and excipient.

la·cu·na (lə-kyo͞o′nə) *n., pl.* **-nae** (-nē) or **-nas. 1.** An empty space or a missing part; a gap. **2.** *Anat.* A cavity, space, or depression, esp. in a bone, containing cartilage or bone cells. [Lat. *lacūna*. See LAGOON.] — **la·cu′nal** *adj.*

la·cu·nar (lə-kyo͞o′nər) *n.* **1.** A ceiling with recessed panels. **2.** *pl.* **la·cu·nar·i·a** (lăk′yə-nâr′ē-ə). A recessed panel in such a ceiling. [Lat. *lacūnar* < *lacūna*, hole. See LAGOON.]

la·cus·tri·ne (lə-kŭs′trĭn) *adj.* **1.** Of or relating to lakes. **2.** Growing in or along the edges of lakes. [Fr. or Ital. < Lat. *lacus*, lake) + -INE¹.]

lac·y (lā′sē) *adj.* **-i·er, -i·est.** Of, relating to, or resembling lace. — **lac′i·ness** *n.*

lad (lăd) *n.* **1.** A boy or young man; a youth. **2.** *Informal.* A man of any age; a fellow. [ME *ladde*, perh. of Scand. orig.]

lad·a·num (lăd′n-əm) *n.* Var. of **labdanum.**

lad·der (lăd′ər) *n.* **1.** A structure consisting of two long sides crossed by parallel rungs, used to climb up and down. **2.** Something resembling this device, esp. a run in a stocking. **2.a.** A means of ascent or descent. **b.** A series of ranked stages or levels. ... as a stocking does. ...

lad·der-back (lăd′ər-băk′) *adj.* Having a chair back consisting of two upright posts ... horizontal slats. **2.** A chair with such a back. ...

lad·die (lăd′ē) *n.* A lad.

lade (lād) *v.* **lad·ed, lad·en** ... **lad·ing, lades.** — *tr.* **1.a.** To load with. **b.** To place (something) as a load for or ... **2.** To burden or oppress; weigh down. **3.** To take up or remove (water) with a ladle or dipper. — *intr.* ... **2.** To ladle a liquid. [ME *laden* < OE ...]

lad·en (lād′n) *adj.* **1.** Weighed down with a load; heavy. **2.** Oppressed; burdened. ...

la-di-da also **la-de-da** (lä′dē-dä′) *adj.* ... affectedly genteel; pretentious. [Perh. ...]

la·dies' man (lā′dēz) *n.* ...

ladies' room *n.* A restroom ... women.

ladies' tresses also **lady's tresses** *pl.n.* ... *v.)* Any of various orchids of the genus ... spike or raceme of small ... flowers usu. ...

La·din (lə-dēn′) *n.* **1.** See Romansch. ... native speaker of Ladin. ... Rhaeto-Romanic ... Lat. See LATIN.]

lad·ing (lā′dĭng) *n.* **1.** The ... loading. ...

La·di·no (lə-dē′nō) *n., pl.* **-nos. 1.** A Romance language closely related to Medieval Spanish ... that has elements from Hebrew and is spoken ... in the Balkans. **2.** Also **ladino.** ... Sephardic Jews ... Spanish-speaking or acculturated Indian ... Central America ... mestizo. [Sp. ... < *Latinus*, Latin See LATIN.]

la·dle (lād′l) *n.* A long-handled ... deep ... serving liquids. — *tr.v.* **-dled, -dling, -dles.** To lift out with a long-handled spoon ... draw out, lade.] — **la′dler** *n.* [ME ... OE *hlædel* < ...]

Lad·o·ga (lä′də-gə), **Lake.** A ... NW Russia NE ... Petersburg.

la·dy (lā′dē) *n., pl.* **-dies. 1.** A ... woman with high standards of ... regarded as proper and ... behavior. **2.a.** A well-behaved girl ... **3.** A woman who is the head ... esp. when spoken of or to in ... **4.** A woman, whom a man is romantically ... **5.a.** A woman ... *Informal.* A wife. **6. Lady.** *Chiefly British.* A general ... title of nobility and other rank, specifically: **a.** ... title for the wife or widow of a knight or baronet ... form of address for a marchioness, countess, viscountess, or baroness. **c.** Used as a form of address ... a baron. **d.** Used as a courtesy title ... or widow of a marquis, or an earl. **e.** Used as ... of a younger son of a duke or marquis ... for the wife ... Often used with *Our.* **8.** *Slang.* ... Virgin Mary ... mistress of a household < OE *hlǣfdige.* See ...

Usage Note: *Lady*, a social ... parallel to *gentleman* to emphasize ... used as a ... society or in situations requiring ... civil ... *much of a lady to tell your secrets* ... *lady* as an attributive with an occupational ... *is too doctor,* is widely regarded as condescending ... of implication that the usual person ... role ...

lady beetle also **la·dy·bee·tle** (lā′dē-bēt′l) *n.* ...

la·dy·bird (lā′dē-bûrd′) *n.* See **ladybug.**

la·dy·bug (lā′dē-bŭg′) *n.* Any of numerous ... beetles of the family Coccinellidae, ... often reddish ... spots and feeding primarily on insect pests, such ...

Lady Chapel also **lady chapel** *n.* A chapel within a ... behind the sanctuary and dedicated to the Virgin ...

Lady Day *n. Chiefly British.* Annunciation, March ...

la·dy·fin·ger (lā′dē-fĭng′gər) also **la·dys·fin·ger** ...

n. A small oval sponge cake shaped like a human finger.
la•dy•fish (lā′dē-fĭsh′) *n., pl.* **ladyfish** or **-fish•es.** Any of several marine fishes, esp. the tarpon *Elops saurus.*
lady in waiting *n., pl.* **ladies in waiting.** A lady of a court appointed to attend a queen, princess, or royal duchess.
la•dy-kill•er (lā′dē-kĭl′ər) *n. Slang.* A man reputed to be exceptionally attractive to and often ruthless with women.
la•dy•like (lā′dē-līk′) *adj.* **1.** Characteristic of a lady; well-bred. **2.** Appropriate for or becoming to a lady. **—la′dy•like′ness** *n.*
la•dy•love (lā′dē-lŭv′) *n.* A woman or girl who is someone's sweetheart.
la•dy•ship also **La•dy•ship** (lā′dē-shĭp′) *n.* Used with *Your, Her,* or *Their* as a title and form of address for a woman or women holding the rank of lady.
la•dy's man also **la•dies' man** (lā′dēz) *n.* A man who enjoys and attracts the company of women.
lady's slipper *n., pl.* **lady's slippers.** Any of various orchids of the genus *Cypripedium,* having variously colored flowers with an inflated pouchlike lip.
lady's smock *n., pl.* **lady's smocks.** See **cuckooflower** 1.
lady's thumb *n., pl.* **lady's thumbs.** A European perennial weed *(Polygonum persicaria)* having very small pinkish flowers.
lady's tresses *pl.n. (used with a sing. or pl. v.)* Var. of **ladies' tresses.**
lady tulip *n.* A central Asian tulip *(Tulipa clusiana)* having red outer perianth segments with white margins.
La•er•tes (lā-ûr′tēz, -âr′-) *n. Gk. Myth.* The father of Odysseus.
la•e•trile (lā′ĭ-trĭl′, -trəl) *n.* A drug derived from amygdalin and purported to have antineoplastic properties.
La Farge (lə färzh′, färj′), **John.** 1835–1910. Amer. artist and art critic known for his murals and stained-glass designs.
La Farge, Oliver Hazard Perry. 1901–63. Amer. writer whose novels include *Laughing Boy* (1929).
La•fa•yette (lăf′ē-ĕt′, lä′fē-, -fā-). **1.** A city of W CA, a suburb in the San Francisco Bay area. Pop. 23,501. **2.** A city of W-central IN on the Wabash R. NW of Indianapolis. Pop. 43,764. **3.** A city of S-central LA WSW of Baton Rouge; settled by Acadians. Pop. 94,440.
Lafayette, Marquis **Marie Joseph Paul Yves Roch Gilbert du Motier de.** 1757–1834. French soldier and politician who served in the American Revolution and in the 1789 and 1830 French revolutions.
Laf•fer curve or **Laf•fer Curve** (lăf′ər) *n.* A curved graph illustrating the theory that if tax rates pass a certain level, economic growth is discouraged and government revenues reduced. [After Arthur *Laffer* (b. 1940), Amer. economist.]
Laf•fite or **La•fitte** (lə-fēt′, lä-), **Jean.** 1780?–1826? French pirate leader who aided U.S. troops in the War of 1812.
La Fol•lette (lə fŏl′ət), **Robert Marion.** 1855–1925. Amer. politician who served as a U.S. senator from WI (1906–25).
La•fon•taine (lə-fŏn-tān′, lä-fôN-tĕn′), **Henri Marie.** 1854–1943. Belgian politician who won the 1913 Nobel Peace Prize.
La Fon•taine (lə fŏn-tān′, lä fôN-tĕn′), **Jean de.** 1621–95. French writer known esp. for his collected *Fables* (1668–94).
lag¹ (lăg) *v.* **lagged, lag•ging, lags.** *—intr.* **1.** To fail to keep up a pace; straggle. **2.** To proceed or develop with comparative slowness. **3.** To fail, weaken, or slacken gradually; flag. **4.** *Games.* To determine the order of play in billiards by successively hitting the cue ball against the end rail, the ball rebounding closest to the head rail indicating the player to shoot first. *—tr.* **1.** To cause to hang back or fall behind. **2.** To shoot, throw, or pitch (a coin, for example) at a mark. *—n.* **1.** The act, process, or condition of lagging. **2.** One that lags. **3.** A condition of slowness or retardation. **4.a.** The extent or duration of lagging. **b.** An interval between events or phenomena considered together. [< earlier *lag,* last person < ME *lag-,* last, perh. of Scand. orig.] **—lag′ger** *n.*
lag² (lăg) *n.* **1.** A barrel stave. **2.** A strip, as of wood, that forms a part of the covering for a cylindrical object. *—tr.v.* **lagged, lag•ging, lags.** To furnish or cover with lags. [Prob. of Scand. orig.; akin to Swed. *lagg.* See **leu-*.**]
lag³ (lăg) *Chiefly British.* *—tr.v.* **lagged, lag•ging, lags. 1.** To arrest. **2.** To send to prison. *—n.* **1.a.** A convict. **b.** An ex-convict. **2.** A period of imprisonment; a sentence. [?]
lag•an (lăg′ən) also **li•gan** (lī′gən) or **lag•end** (lăg′ənd) *n. Naut.* Cargo or equipment thrown into the sea but attached to a float or buoy so that it can be recovered. [Fr. < OFr., poss. < ON *lögn, lagn-.* See **legh-*.**]
La•gash (lā′găsh). An ancient city of Sumer in S Mesopotamia; flourished c. 2400 B.C.
Lag b'O•mer (läg′ bō′mər, läg′ bə-ō′mĕr) *n.* A Jewish feast celebrated on the 33rd day of the Omer (the 18th day of Iyyar). [Heb. : *lag,* 33rd + *bā,* in, of + *'ōmer,* the Omer (second day of Passover to first day of Shavuoth).]
la•ger (lä′gər) *n.* A type of beer, originally brewed in Germany, that contains a relatively small amount of hops and is aged from six weeks to six months to allow sedimentation. [Ger., short for *Lagerbier* : *Lager,* storehouse, cellar (< MHGer. *leger* < OHGer. *legar,* bed, lair; see **legh-***) + *Bier,* beer.]
La•ger•kvist (lä′gər-kfĭst′), **Pär Fabian.** 1891–1974. Swedish writer who won the 1951 Nobel Prize for literature.
La•ger•löf (lä′gər-ləv, -lœf), **Selma Ottiliana Lovisa.** 1858–1940. Swedish writer who was the first woman to win the Nobel Prize for literature (1909).
lag•gard (lăg′ərd) *n.* One that lags; a straggler. *—adj.* Hanging back or falling behind; dilatory. **—lag′gard•ly** *adv.* **—lag′gard•ness** *n.*
lag•ging (lăg′ĭng) *n.* **1.** Insulation used to prevent heat diffusion, as from a steam pipe. **2.** A wooden frame built esp. to support an arch until the keystone is positioned. [< LAG².]
la•gniappe (lăn-yăp′, lăn′yăp′) *n. Chiefly Southern Louisiana.* **1.** A small gift presented by a storeowner to a customer with the customer's purchase. **2.** An extra or unexpected gift or benefit. Also called regionally *boot.* See Regional Note at **beignet.** [Louisiana Fr. < Am.Sp. *(la) ñapa,* (the) gift < Quechua *yapa* < *yapay,* to give more.]

Regional Note: *Lagniappe* derives from New World Spanish *la ñapa,* "the gift," and ultimately from Quechua *yapay,* "to give more." The word came into the rich Creole dialect mixture of New Orleans and there acquired a French spelling. Still used chiefly in southern Louisiana for a little bonus that a friendly shopkeeper might add to a purchase, it may also mean "an extra or unexpected gift or benefit."

lag•o•morph (lăg′ə-môrf′) *n.* Any of various plant-eating mammals having fully furred feet and two pairs of upper incisors and belonging to the order Lagomorpha, which includes the rabbits and hares. [< NLat. *Lagomorpha,* order name : Gk. *lagōs,* hare; see **slēg-*** + Gk. *morphē,* shape.] **—lag′o•mor′phic** (-fĭk), **lag′o•mor′phous** (-fəs) *adj.*
la•goon (lə-gōōn′) *n.* **1.** A shallow body of water, esp. one separated from a sea by sandbars or coral reefs. **2.** A shallow body of liquid waste material, as one in a dump. [Fr. *lagune* and Ital. *laguna,* both < Lat. *lacūna,* pool, hollow, gap < *lacus,* lake.]
La•gos (lā′gŏs′, lä′gōs). The cap. of Nigeria, in the SW part on the Gulf of Guinea. Pop. 1,404,000.
La•grange (lə-gränj′, lä-gräNzh′), Comte **Joseph Louis.** 1736–1813. French mathematician and astronomer who developed the calculus of variations (1755).
La Grange (lə grānj′). A city of W GA N of Columbus; incorp. 1828. Pop. 25,597.
lag screw *n.* A heavy wood screw having a square bolt head. [< LAG² (< its original use in securing barrel staves).]
La Guar•di•a (lə gwär′dē-ə), **Fiorello Henry.** "the Little Flower." 1882–1947. Amer. politician who served as mayor of New York City (1934–45).
La•gu•na Beach (lə-gōō′nə). A city of S CA SE of Long Beach. Pop. 23,170.
Laguna Hills. A city of S CA SE of Santa Ana. Pop. 46,731.
La Ha•bra (lə hä′brə). A city of S CA, a suburb of Los Angeles. Pop. 51,266.
la•har (lä′här′) *n.* **1.** A landslide or mudflow of volcanic fragments on the flanks of a volcano. **2.** The deposit produced by such a landslide. [Javanese, lava.]
La•hore (lə-hôr′, -hōr′). A city of NE Pakistan SE of Rawalpindi; a Mogul cap. in the 16th cent. Pop. 2,685,000.
Lah•ti (lä′tē, läKH′-). A city of S Finland NNE of Helsinki. Pop. 94,347.
la•ic (lā′ĭk) also **la•i•cal** (-ĭ-kəl) *—adj.* Of or relating to the laity; secular. *—n.* A layperson. [LLat. *lāicus.* See LAY².] **—la′i•cal•ly** *adv.*
la•i•cize (lā′ĭ-sīz′) *tr.v.* **-cized, -ciz•ing, -ciz•es. 1.** To free from ecclesiastical control; give over to laypeople. **2.** To change to lay status; secularize. **—la′i•ci•za′tion** (-sĭ-zā′shən) *n.*
laid (lād) *v.* P.t. and p.part. of **lay¹.**
laid-back (lād′băk′) *adj. Informal.* Having a relaxed or casual atmosphere or character; easygoing.
laid paper *n.* A paper made on wire molds that give it a characteristic watermark of close thin lines.
lain (lān) *v.* P.part. of **lie¹.**
Laing (lăng), **R(onald) D(avid).** 1927–89. British writer and psychiatrist whose works include *The Facts of Life* (1976).
lair (lâr) *n.* **1.** The den or dwelling of a wild animal. **2.** A den or hideaway. **3.** *Obsolete.* A resting place; a couch. [ME < OE *leger.* See **legh-*.**]
laird (lârd) *n. Scots.* The owner of a landed estate. [Sc. < ME *lard, lavered,* var. of *lord,* owner, master. See LORD.]
lais•sez faire also **lais•ser faire** (lĕs′ā fâr′) *n.* **1.** An economic doctrine that opposes governmental regulation of or interference in commerce. **2.** Noninterference in the affairs of others. [Fr. : *laissez,* let + *faire,* to do.] **—lais′sez-faire′** *adj.*
lais•sez-pas•ser (lĕs′ā-pä-sā′) *n.* A pass, esp. one used in lieu of a passport. [Fr. : *laissez,* let + *passer,* to pass.]
la•i•ty (lā′ĭ-tē) *n.* **1.** Laypeople considered as a group. **2.** Those who are not members of a given profession or other specialized field. [ME *laite* < *lay,* of the laity. See LAY².]
La•ius (lā′əs) *n. Gk. Myth.* A king of Thebes who was mistakenly killed by his son Oedipus.
lake¹ (lāk) *n.* **1.** A large inland body of fresh water or salt water. **2.** A scenic pond, as in a park. **3.** A large pool of

Marquis de Lafayette
Etching by Charles François Gabriel Levachez and son (fl. 1760–1820) tinted by Jean Duplessi-Bertaux (1747–1819)

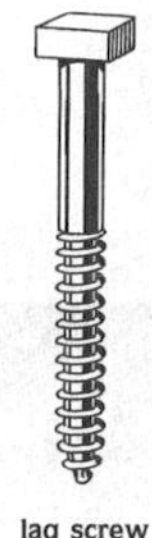
lag screw

ă pat	oi boy
ā pay	ou out
âr care	ŏŏ took
ä father	ōō boot
ĕ pet	ŭ cut
ē be	ûr urge
ĭ pit	th thin
ī pie	*th* this
îr pier	hw which
ŏ pot	zh vision
ō toe	ə about, item
ô paw	

Stress marks:
′ (primary);
′ (secondary), as in dictionary (dĭk′shə-nĕr′ē)

liquid. [ME < OFr. *lac* and < OE *lacu*, both < Lat. *lacus*.]

lake² (lāk) *n.* **1.** A pigment of organic coloring matter with an inorganic, usu. metallic base or carrier, used in dyes, inks, and paints. **2.** *Color.* A deep red. [< Fr. *laque*. See LAC.]

Lake or **Lake of** (lāk) or **Loch** (lŏk, lôKH). For the names of actual lakes, see the specific element of the name; for example, **Erie, Lake; Lucerne, Lake of; Lomond, Loch.**

lake•bed (lāk′bĕd′) *n.* The floor of a lake.

Lake Charles (chärlz). A city of SW LA E of Beaumont TX. Pop. 70,580.

Lake District. A scenic area of NW England including the Cumbrian Mts. and some 15 lakes.

lamb

lake dwelling *n.* A dwelling, esp. a prehistoric dwelling, built on piles in a shallow lake.

lake effect *n.* The effect of any lake, especially the Great Lakes, in modifying the weather in nearby areas.

lake•front (lāk′frŭnt′) *n.* The land along the edge of a lake.

lake herring *n.* A food fish, esp. the trout *Coregonus artedii* of the Great Lakes region, related to the cisco and whitefishes.

Lake•hurst (lāk′hûrst). A borough of E-central NJ S of Freehold. The dirigible *Hindenburg* was destroyed by fire at the naval air station here (May 6, 1937). Pop. 3,078.

Lake Jack•son (jăk′sən). A city of SE TX SW of Galveston. Pop. 22,776.

Lake•land (lāk′lənd). A city of central Florida ENE of Tampa. Pop. 70,576.

Lakeland terrier *n.* Any of a breed of small straight-legged slender dogs, originally bred in England for hunting foxes. [After *Lakeland*, a region of NW England.]

Lake Os•we•go (ŏs-wē′gō). A city of NW OR, a suburb of Portland. Pop. 30,576.

Lake Plac•id (plăs′ĭd). A village of NE NY in the Adirondack Mts. SW of Plattsburg; site of the Winter Olympics in 1932 and 1980. Pop. 2,485.

lak•er (lā′kər) *n.* **1.** A fish, such as the lake trout, that lives in a lake. **2.** *Naut.* A ship used on lakes.

lake•shore (lāk′shôr′, -shōr′) *n.* Land by a lake.

lake•side (lāk′sīd′) *n.* See **lakeshore.**

Lake Suc•cess (sək-sĕs′). An unincorp. village of SE NY on NW Long I. NW of Mineola; temporary headquarters of the United Nations (1946–51). Pop. 2,484.

lake trout *n.* A freshwater food and game fish *(Salvelinus namaycush)* of the Great Lakes.

Lake•wood (lāk′wo͝od′). **1.** A city of S CA, a suburb of Long Beach. Pop. 73,557. **2.** A city of N-central CO, a suburb of Denver. Pop. 126,481. **3.** A city of NE OH, a suburb of Cleveland on Lake Erie. Pop. 59,718. **4.** A community of W-central WA, a suburb of Tacoma. Pop. 58,412.

Lake Worth (wûrth). A city of SE FL S of West Palm Beach. Pop. 28,564.

La•ko•ta (lə-kō′tə) *n.*, *pl.* **Lakota** or **-tas.** See **Teton.**

Lak•shad•weep (lək-shäd′wēp′, lŭk′shə-dwēp′). A region of SW India comprising the Laccadive, Minicoy, and Amindivi islands.

lal•a•pa•loo•za (lŏl′ə-pə-lo͞o′zə) *n.* *Slang.* Var. of **lollapalooza.**

Lal•lan (lăl′ən) also **Lal•lans** (-ənz) *n.* *Scots.* **1.** The Lowlands of Scotland. **2.** Scots as spoken in southern and eastern Scotland. [Sc., alteration of LOWLAND.] **— Lal′lan** *adj.*

lal•la•pa•loo•za (lŏl′ə-pə-lo͞o′zə) *n.* *Slang.* Var. of **lollapalooza.**

lal•la•tion (lă-lā′shən) *n.* *Ling.* The substitution of the phoneme /l/ for /r/ or the mispronunciation of (l). [Lat. *lallāre*, *lallāt-*, to sing a lullaby + -ATION.]

lal•ly•gag (lăl′ē-găg′) *v.* Var. of **lollygag.**

La Lou•vière (lä lo͞o-vyĕr′). A city of SW Belgium S of Brussels. Pop. 76,534.

lam¹ (lăm) *v.* **lammed, lam•ming, lams.** — *tr.* To give a thorough beating to; thrash. — *intr.* To strike; wallop. [Prob. of Scand. orig.; akin to ON *lemja*, to cripple by beating, flog.]

lam² (lăm) *Slang.* — *intr.v.* **lammed, lam•ming, lams.** To escape, as from prison. — *n.* Flight, esp. from the law. [?]

lam. *abbr.* Laminated.

Lam. *abbr.* *Bible.* Lamentations.

la•ma (lä′mə) *n.* A Buddhist monk of Tibet or Mongolia. [Tibetan *bla-ma* < *bla*, superior.]

La•ma•ism (lä′mə-ĭz′əm) *n.* Tibetan Buddhism. **— La′ma•ist** *n.* **— La′ma•is′tic** *adj.*

La Man•cha (lä män′chə). A plateau region of S-central Spain; setting for Cervantes's *Don Quixote.*

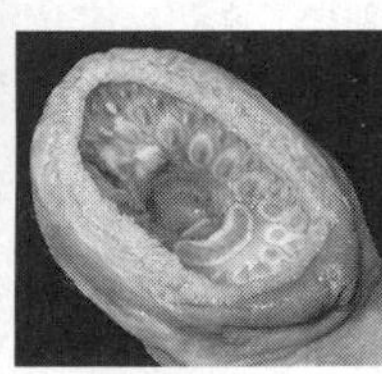

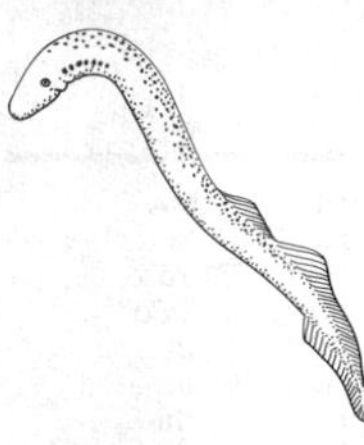

lamprey
Top: Close-up of mouth
Bottom: Full-length view

La•mar (lə-mär′), **Joseph Rucker.** 1857–1916. Amer. jurist; associate justice of the U.S. Supreme Court (1911–16).

Lamar, Lucius Quintus Cincinnatus. 1825–93. Amer. jurist; associate justice of the U.S. Supreme Court (1888–93).

La•marck (lə-märk′, lä-), Chevalier de **Jean Baptiste Pierre Antoine de Monet.** 1744–1829. French naturalist whose ideas about evolution influenced Darwin's theory. **— La•marck′i•an** *adj. & n.*

La•marck•ism (lə-mär′kĭz′əm) also **La•marck•i•an•ism** (-kē-ə-nĭz′əm) *n.* A theory of biological evolution holding that acquired traits can be inherited. [After LAMARCK.]

La•mar•tine (lä-mär-tēn′), **Alphonse Marie Louis de Prat de.** 1790–1869. French romantic poet who served briefly as minister of foreign affairs (1848).

la•ma•ser•y (lä′mə-sĕr′ē) *n.*, *pl.* **-ies.** A monastery of lamas. [Fr. *lamaserie* : *lama*, lama (< Tibetan *bla-ma*; see LAMA) + *-serie*, dwelling (prob. < Pers. *sarāī*, inn, palace).]

La•maze (lə-mäz′) *adj.* Relating to or being a method of childbirth in which a woman is prepared psychologically and physically to give birth without the use of drugs. [After Fernand *Lamaze* (1890–1957), French physician.]

lamb (lăm) *n.* **1.a.** A young sheep, esp. one that is not yet weaned. **b.** The flesh of a young sheep used as meat. **c.** Lambskin. **2.** A sweet, mild-mannered person; a dear. **3.** One who can be duped or cheated esp. in financial matters. **4. Lamb.** Jesus. — *intr.v.* **lambed, lamb•ing, lambs.** To give birth to a young sheep. [ME < OE.]

Lamb, Charles. "Elia." 1775–1834. British critic and essayist who with his sister **Mary Ann** (1764–1847) wrote the children's book *Tales from Shakespeare* (1807).

Lamb, William. 2nd Viscount Melbourne. 1779–1848. British politician who served as prime minister (1834 and 1835–41).

Lamb, Willis Eugene, Jr. b. 1913. Amer. physicist who shared a 1955 Nobel Prize.

lam•baste (lăm-bāst′) *tr.v.* **-bast•ed, -bast•ing, -bastes.** *Informal.* **1.** To give a thrashing to; beat. **2.** To scold sharply; berate. [Perh. LAM¹ + BASTE³.]

lamb•da (lăm′də) *n.* **1.** The 11th letter of the Greek alphabet. **2.** A lambda hyperon. [Gk., of Phoenician orig.; akin to Heb. *lāmed*, lamed.]

lambda hyperon *n.* An unstable, electrically neutral baryon. See table at **subatomic particle.**

lamb•doid (lăm′doid′) *adj.* **1.** Having the shape of the Greek letter lambda. **2.** *Anat.* Relating to the deeply serrated suture in the skull between the parietal bones and the occipital bone.

lam•bent (lăm′bənt) *adj.* **1.** Flickering lightly over or on a surface: *lambent moonlight.* **2.** Effortlessly light or brilliant: *lambent wit.* **3.** Having a gentle glow; luminous. See Syns at **bright.** [Lat. *lambēns*, *lambent-*, pr.part. of *lambere*, to lick.] **— lam′ben•cy** *n.* **— lam′bent•ly** *adv.*

lam•bert (lăm′bərt) *n.* A unit of brightness equivalent to the brightness of a perfectly diffusing surface that emits or reflects one lumen per square centimeter. [After Johann Heinrich *Lambert* (1728–77), German physicist and astronomer.]

lamb•kill (lăm′kĭl′) *n.* See **sheep laurel.**

Lamb of God *n.* Jesus.

lam•bre•quin (lăm′bər-kĭn, -brə-kĭn) *n.* **1.** A short ornamental drapery for the top of a window or door or the edge of a shelf. **2.** A cloth worn over a helmet in medieval times. [Fr., prob. < Du. *lamperkijn*, dim. of MDu. *lamper*, veil.]

lamb•skin (lăm′skĭn′) *n.* **1.** The hide of a lamb, esp. when dressed without removing the fleece, as for a garment. **2.** Leather made from the dressed hide of a lamb. **3.** Parchment made from such hide.

lamb's lettuce (lămz′) *n.* See **corn salad.**

lamb's quarters *pl.n.* *(used with a sing. or pl. v.)* See **pigweed** 1.

lame¹ (lām) *adj.* **lam•er, lam•est. 1.** Disabled so that movement, esp. walking, is difficult or impossible. **2.** Marked by pain or rigidness: *a lame back.* **3.** Weak and ineffectual; unsatisfactory: *a lame apology.* — *tr.v.* **lamed, lam•ing, lames.** To cause to become lame; cripple. [ME < OE *lama*.] **— lame′ly** *adv.* **— lame′ness** *n.*

lame² (lām) *n.* A thin metal plate, esp. one of the overlapping steel plates in medieval armor. [Fr. < OFr. < Lat. *lāmina*, thin plate.]

la•mé (lă-mā′) *n.* A brocaded fabric woven with metallic threads, often of gold or silver. [Fr., spangled, laminated, lamé < OFr. *lame*, thin metal plate. See LAME².]

lame•brain (lām′brān′) *n.* *Informal.* A person regarded as stupid. **— lame′brained′** (-brānd′) *adj.*

la•medh (lä′mĭd, -mĕd′) *n.* The 12th letter of the Hebrew alphabet. [Heb. *lāmed*.]

lame duck *n.* **1.** An elected officeholder continuing in office during the period before the inauguration of a successor. **2.** An ineffective person; a weakling. **— lame′-duck′** (lām′dŭk′) *adj.*

la•mel•la (lə-mĕl′ə) *n.*, *pl.* **-mel•lae** (-mĕl′ē′) or **-mel•las.** A thin scale, plate, or layer of bone or tissue. [Lat. *lāmella*, dim. of *lāmina*, thin plate.] **— la•mel′lar** *adj.*

la•mel•late (lə-mĕl′āt′, lăm′ə-lāt′) *adj.* **1.** Having, composed of, or arranged in lamellae. **2.** Resembling a lamella. **— lam′el•la′ted** *adj.* **— lam′el•la′tion** *n.*

lamelli– or **lamell–** *pref.* Lamella: *lamelliform.* [< LAMELLA.]

la•mel•li•branch (lə-mĕl′ə-brăngk′) *n.* Any of the bivalve mollusks of the class Lamellibranchia, including the clams, scallops, and oysters. [< NLat. *Lāmellibranchia*, class name : LAMELLI– + Lat. *branchia*, gill; see BRANCHIA.] **— la•mel′li•branch′** *adj.*

la•mel•li•corn (lə-mĕl′ĭ-kôrn′) *adj.* Of or belonging to the superfamily Lamellicornia, which includes the scarabs and other beetles that have club-shaped lamellate antennae. [< NLat. *Lāmellicornia*, superfamily name : LAMELLI– + Lat. *cornū*, horn; see **ker-¹***.] **— la•mel′li•corn** *n.*

la•mel•li•form (lə-mĕl′ə-fôrm′) *adj.* Having the form of a thin plate or lamella.

la•ment (lə-mĕnt′) *v.* **-ment•ed, -ment•ing, -ments.** —*tr.* **1.** To express grief for or about; mourn: *lament a death.* **2.** To regret deeply; deplore. —*intr.* **1.** To grieve audibly; wail. **2.** To express sorrow or regret. See Syns at **grieve.** —*n.* **1.** A feeling or an expression of grief. **2.** A song or poem expressing deep grief or mourning. [ME *lementen* < OFr. *lamenter* < Lat. *lāmentārī* < *lāmentum*, lament.] —**la•ment′er** *n.*

la•men•ta•ble (lə-mĕn′tə-bəl, lăm′ən-) *adj.* Inspiring or deserving of lament or regret; deplorable or pitiable. —**lam′en•ta•bly** *adv.*

lam•en•ta•tion (lăm′ən-tā′shən) *n.* **1.** The act of lamenting. **2.** A lament. **3. Lamentations.** *(used with a sing. v.)* See table at **Bible.**

la•ment•ed (lə-mĕn′tĭd) *adj.* Mourned for: *our late lamented president.* —**la•ment′ed•ly** *adv.*

La Me•sa (lə mā′sə). A city of S CA, a suburb of San Diego. Pop. 52,931.

la•mi•a (lā′mē-ə) *n., pl.* **-mi•as** or **-mi•ae** (-mē-ē′). **1.** *Gk. Myth.* A monster represented as part serpent and part woman and reputed to prey on humans, esp. children. **2.** A female vampire. [ME < Lat. < Gk.]

La•mi•a (lə-mē′ə, lä-mē′ä). A city of E-central Greece NW of Athens; founded c. 5th cent. B.C. Pop. 41,667. —**La•mi′an** *adj. & n.*

lam•i•na (lăm′ə-nə) *n., pl.* **-nae** (-nē′) or **-nas. 1.** A thin plate, sheet, or layer. **2.** *Bot.* The expanded area of a leaf or petal; a blade. **3.** A thin layer of bone, membrane, or other tissue. **4.** *Zool.* A thin scalelike or platelike structure. **5.** *Geol.* A narrow bed of rock. [Lat. *lāmina.*] —**lam′i•nar, lam′i•nal** *adj.*

laminar flow *n.* Nonturbulent flow of a viscous fluid in layers near a boundary, as that of lubricating oil in bearings.

lam•i•nate (lăm′ə-nāt′) *v.* **-nat•ed, -nat•ing, -nates.** —*tr.* **1.** To beat or compress into a thin plate or sheet. **2.** To divide into thin layers. **3.** To make by uniting several layers. **4.** To cover with thin sheets. —*intr.* To split into thin layers or sheets. —*adj.* (-nĭt, -nāt′). Consisting of, arranged in, or covered with laminae. —*n.* (-nāt′, -nĭt). A laminated product, such as plywood. —**lam′i•na′tor** *n.*

lam•i•nat•ed (lăm′ə-nā′tĭd) *adj.* **1.** Composed of layers bonded together. **2.** Arranged in laminae; laminate.

lam•i•na•tion (lăm′ə-nā′shən) *n.* **1.a.** The act or process of laminating. **b.** The state of being laminated. **2.** Something laminated. **3.** A lamina.

lam•i•nec•to•my (lăm′ə-nĕk′tə-mē) *n., pl.* **-mies.** Surgical removal of the posterior arch of a vertebra.

lam•i•ni•tis (lăm′ə-nī′tĭs) *n.* Inflammation of the sensitive vascular tissue laminae of the hoof, esp. in horses.

La Mi•ra•da (lä′ mə-rä′də). A city of S CA SE of Los Angeles. Pop. 40,452.

Lam•mas (lăm′əs) *n.* A feast formerly celebrated on August 1 in England, during which bread from the season's first wheat was consecrated at Mass. [ME *Lammasse* < OE *hlāfmæsse* : *hlāf*, loaf + *mæsse*, Mass; see **Mass.**]

lam•mer•gei•er also **lam•mer•gey•er** (lăm′ər-gī′ər) *n.* A large predatory bird *(Gypaetus barbatus)* of the vulture family, ranging from southern Europe to China and having a wide wingspan and black plumage. [Ger. *Lämmergeier* : *Lämmer*, genitive pl. of *Lamm*, lamb (< MHGer. *lamp* < OHGer. *lamb*) + *Geier*, vulture (< MHGer. *gīr* < OHGer.).]

lamp (lămp) *n.* **1.a.** A device that generates light, heat, or therapeutic radiation. **b.** A vessel containing oil or alcohol burned through a wick for illumination. **2.** A celestial body that gives off or reflects light. **3.** Something that illumines the mind or soul. [ME *lampe* < OFr. < Lat. *lampas* < Gk. < *lampein*, to shine.]

lamp•black (lămp′blăk′) *n.* Fine soot collected from incompletely burned carbonaceous materials, used as a pigment and in matches, explosives, lubricants, and fertilizers.

lam•per eel (lăm′pər) *n.* See **lamprey.** [Alteration of LAMPREY.]

lam•pi•on (lăm′pē-ən) *n.* An oil-burning lamp, often of colored glass, for outdoor use. [Fr. < Ital. *lampione*, aug. of *lampa*, lamp < OFr. *lampe.* See LAMP.]

lamp•light (lămp′līt′) *n.* The light shed by a lamp.

lamp•light•er (lămp′lī′tər) *n.* One that lights lamps.

lamp oil *n.* See **kerosene.**

lam•poon (lăm-po͞on′) *n.* **1.** A written attack ridiculing a person, a group, or an institution. **2.** A light good-humored satire. —*tr.v.* **-pooned, -poon•ing, -poons.** To ridicule or satirize in or as if in a lampoon. [Fr. *lampon*, perh. < *lampons*, let us drink (< drinking songs), first pers. pl. imper. of *lamper*, to gulp down, of Gmc. orig.] —**lam•poon′er, lam•poon′ist** *n.* —**lam•poon′er•y** *n.*

lamp•post (lămp′pōst′) *n.* A post supporting a street lamp.

lam•prey (lăm′prē) *n., pl.* **-preys.** Any of various primitive elongated freshwater or anadromous fishes of the family Petromyzontidae, with a sucking mouth and rasping teeth. [ME *lamprei* < OFr. *lampreie* < Med.Lat. *lampreda.*]

lamp•shade (lămp′shād′) *n.* Any of various protective or ornamental coverings used to screen a light bulb.

lamp•shell (lămp′shĕl′) *n.* See **brachiopod.**

lamp•work•ing (lămp′wûr′kĭng) *n.* The process of sculpting glass by twirling thin rods of glass over a gas-oxygen burner.

LAN (lăn) *n. Comp. Sci.* A system that links together electronic office equipment, such as computers, and forms a network within an office or a building. [*l(ocal) a(rea) n(etwork).*]

la•nai (lə-nī′, lä-) *n., pl.* **-nais.** A veranda or roofed patio. [Hawaiian.]

La•nai (lə-nī′). An island of central HI W of Maui; developed as a pineapple-growing area after 1922.

la•nate (lā′nāt′) *adj.* Having or consisting of woolly hairs. [Lat. *lānātus* < *lāna*, wool.]

Lan•ca•shire (lăng′kə-shîr′, -shər). A historical region of NW England on the Irish Sea; part of the kingdom of Northumbria in Anglo-Saxon times.

Lan•cas•ter[1] (lăng′kə-stər, -lăn′-). English royal house that from 1399 to 1461 produced three kings of England — Henry IV, Henry V, and Henry VI. During the Wars of the Roses its symbol was a red rose. —**Lan•cas′tri•an** (lăng-kăs′trē-ən) *adj. & n.*

Lan•cas•ter[2] (lăng′kə-stər, -kăs′tər, lăn′-). **1.** A municipal borough of NW England N of Liverpool; chartered 1193. Pop. 47,900. **2.** A city of S-central OH SE of Columbus. Pop. 34,507. **3.** A city of SE PA W of Philadelphia; settled by German Mennonites c. 1709. Pop. 55,551.

lance (lăns) *n.* **1.a.** A thrusting weapon with a long wooden shaft and a sharp metal head. **b.** A similar implement for spearing fish. **2.** A cavalry lancer. **3.** *Medic.* See **lancet** 1. —*tr.v.* **lanced, lanc•ing, lanc•es. 1.** To pierce with a lance. **2.** *Medic.* To make a surgical incision in; cut into. [ME < OFr. < Lat. *lancea*, prob. of Celt. orig.]

lance corporal *n.* A noncommissioned officer in the U.S. Marine Corps, ranking above private first class and below corporal. [< *lancepesade* < obsolete Fr. *lancepessade* < Ital. *lancia spezzata*, superior soldier < *lancia*, lance < Lat. *lancea.* See LANCE.]

lance•let (lăns′lĭt) *n.* Any of various small flattened marine organisms of the subphylum Cephalochordata.

Lan•ce•lot (lăn′sə-lət, -lŏt′, län′-) *n.* In Arthurian legend, a Knight of the Round Table whose love affair with Queen Guinevere resulted in a war with King Arthur.

lan•ce•o•late (lăn′sē-ə-lāt′) *adj.* Tapering from a rounded base toward an apex; lance-shaped: *lanceolate leaves.* [LLat. *lanceolātus* < Lat. *lanceola*, dim. of Lat. *lancea*, lance.]

lanc•er (lăn′sər) *n.* **1.** A cavalryman armed with a lance. **2.** A member of a regiment originally armed with lances. **3. lancers.** *(used with a sing. v.)* **a.** A form of quadrille. **b.** The music for this dance. [Fr. *lancier* < OFr., maker of lances < *lance*, lance. See LANCE.]

lan•cet (lăn′sĭt) *n.* **1.** *Medic.* A surgical knife with a short, wide, pointed double-edged blade. **2.** *Archit.* A lancet arch. **3.** A lancet window. [ME < OFr., dim. of *lance*, lance. See LANCE.]

lancet arch *n. Archit.* An arch that is narrow and pointed like the head of a spear.

lancet fish *n.* Either of two large elongated marine fishes *(Alepisauri ferox* or *A. brevirostris)* having long sharp teeth, a large dorsal fin, and no scales.

lancet window *n. Archit.* A tall narrow window set in a lancet arch.

lance•wood (lăns′wo͝od′) *n.* **1.** Any of several tropical American trees, esp. *Calycophyllum candidissimum*, having hard, durable, uniformly grained wood. **2.** The wood of this tree.

Lan•chow (län′jō′). See **Lanzhou.**

lan•ci•nat•ing (lăn′sə-nā′tĭng) *adj.* Characterized by a sensation of cutting, piercing, or stabbing. [< *lancinate*, to stab < Lat. *lancināre*, *lancināt-*, to lacerate.]

land (lănd) *n.* **1.** The solid ground of the earth. **2.a.** Ground or soil: *tilled the land.* **b.** A topographically or functionally distinct tract: *desert land.* **3.a.** A nation; a country. **b.** The people of a nation, district, or region. **c. lands.** Territorial possessions or property. **4.** Public or private landed property; real estate. **5.** An area or a realm: *the land of make-believe.* **6.** *Law.* **a.** A tract that may be owned, together with everything growing or constructed on it. **b.** A landed estate. **7.** The raised portion of a grooved surface, as on a phonograph record. —*v.* **land•ed, land•ing, lands.** —*tr.* **1.a.** To bring to and unload on land. **b.** To set (a vehicle) down on land or another surface. **2.** *Informal.* To cause to arrive in a place or condition. **3.a.** To catch and pull in (a fish). **b.** *Informal.* To win; secure. **4.** *Informal.* To deliver: *landed a blow.* —*intr.* **1.a.** To come to shore. **b.** To disembark. **2.** To descend toward and settle onto the ground or another surface. **3.** *Informal.* To arrive in a place or condition. **4.** To come to rest in a certain way or place: *land on one's feet.* [ME < OE. See **lendh-*.**]

Land (lănd), **Edwin Herbert.** 1909–91. Amer. inventor who developed a light-polarizing plastic film (1932).

lan•dau (lăn′dô′, -dou′) *n.* **1.** A four-wheeled carriage with facing passenger seats and a roof in two sections that can be lowered or detached. **2.** A style of automobile with a similar roof. [After *Landau*, a city of SW Germany.]

lancet window

landau
With lowered roof

ă pat	oi boy
ā pay	ou out
âr care	o͝o took
ä father	o͞o boot
ĕ pet	ŭ cut
ē be	ûr urge
ĭ pit	th thin
ī pie	*th* this
îr pier	hw which
ŏ pot	zh vision
ō toe	ə about, item
ô paw	

Stress marks:
′ (primary);
′ (secondary), as in
dictionary (dĭk′shə-nĕr′ē)

Lan•dau (län-dou′), **Lev Davidovich.** 1908–68. Soviet physicist who won a 1962 Nobel Prize.

land bank *n.* A bank that issues long-term loans on real estate in return for mortgages.

land bridge *n.* An isthmus.

land•ed (lăn′dĭd) *adj.* **1.** Owning land: *the landed gentry.* **2.** Consisting of land or real estate: *landed property.*

land•er (lăn′dər) *n.* A space vehicle designed to land on a celestial body, such as the moon or a planet.

land•fall (lănd′fôl′) *n.* **1.** The act or an instance of sighting or reaching land after a voyage or flight. **2.** The land sighted or reached after a voyage or flight.

land•fill (lănd′fĭl′) *n.* **1.** A method of solid waste disposal in which refuse is buried between layers of dirt so as to fill in or reclaim low-lying ground. **2.** A site of such disposal. — *v.* **-filled, -fill•ing, -fills.** — *tr.* **1.** To dispose of (waste material) in a landfill. **2.** To fill in or reclaim (land) by this method. — *intr.* To dispose of refuse or reclaim land by filling in low-lying ground.

Lillie Langtry

land•form (lănd′fôrm′) *n.* One of the features making up the earth's surface, such as a plain, mountain, or valley.

land grant *n.* A government grant of public land for a railroad, highway, or state college.

land•grave (lănd′grāv′) *n.* **1.** A man in medieval Germany who had jurisdiction over a particular territory. **2.** Used as the title for such a nobleman. [< MLGer. : *lant*, land; see **lendh-*** + *grave*, count.]

land•gra•vi•ate (lănd-grā′vē-ĭt, -āt′) *n.* The rank and office of a landgrave or landgravine.

land•gra•vine (lănd′grə-vēn′) *n.* **1.** A woman holding the title to a landgraviate. **2.** The wife or widow of a landgrave. **3.** Used as the title for such a noblewoman. [< MLGer. *landgravin*, fem. of *landgrave*, landgrave. See LANDGRAVE.]

land•hold•er (lănd′hōl′dər) *n.* One that owns land. — **land′hold′ing** *n.*

land•ing (lăn′dĭng) *n.* **1.a.** The act or process of coming to land or rest, esp. after a voyage or flight. **b.** A termination, esp. of a voyage or flight. **2.** A site for loading and unloading passengers and cargo. **3.a.** An intermediate platform on a flight of stairs. **b.** The area at the top or bottom of a staircase.

landing craft *n.* A naval craft designed to convey troops and equipment from ship to shore.

landing field *n.* A tract of land used by aircraft for landing and taking off.

landing gear *n.* The components of an aircraft or a spacecraft that support the weight of the craft and its load and give it mobility on ground or water.

landing strip *n.* An aircraft runway without airport facilities.

land•la•dy (lănd′lā′dē) *n.* **1.** A woman who owns and rents land, buildings, or dwelling units. **2.** A woman who runs a rooming house or an inn; an innkeeper.

land•less (lănd′lĭs) *adj.* Owning or having no land.

land•locked (lănd′lŏkt′) *adj.* **1.** Entirely or almost entirely surrounded by land: *a landlocked country.* **2.** Confined to inland waters, as certain salmon.

land•lord (lănd′lôrd′) *n.* **1.** A person who owns and rents land, buildings, or dwelling units. **2.** A man who runs a rooming house or an inn; an innkeeper.

land•lub•ber (lănd′lŭb′ər) *n.* A person unfamiliar with the sea or seamanship. — **land′lub′ber•ly** *adj.*

land•mark (lănd′märk′) *n.* **1.** A prominent identifying feature of a landscape. **2.** A fixed marker, such as a concrete block, that indicates a boundary line. **3.** An event marking an important stage of development or a turning point in history. **4.** A building or site that has historical significance, esp. one marked for preservation by a municipal or national government. — *adj.* Having great import or significance.

land•mass (lănd′măs′) *n.* A large unbroken area of land.

land mine *n.* **1.** An explosive mine laid usu. just below the surface of the ground. **2.** *Informal.* A concealed yet incipient crisis.

land office *n.* A government office that handles and keeps records of the sale or transfer of public land.

land-of•fice business (lănd′ô′fĭs, -ŏf′ĭs) *n.* A thriving, extensive, or rapidly moving volume of trade.

Lan•don (lăn′dən), **Alfred ("Alf") Mossman.** 1887–1987. Amer. politician who served as governor of KS (1933–37) and ran unsuccessfully for President in 1936.

Lan•dor (lăn′dôr, -dər), **Walter Savage.** 1775–1864. British writer best known for his *Imaginary Conversations of Literary Men and Statesmen* (1824–29).

land•own•er (lănd′ō′nər) *n.* One that owns land. — **land′own′er•ship′** *n.* — **land′own′ing** *adj.* & *n.*

Lan•dow•ska (lăn-dôf′skə, län-dôf′skä), **Wanda.** 1879?–1959. Polish-born harpsichordist.

land-poor (lănd′po͝or′) *adj.* Owning much unprofitable land but lacking the capital to improve or maintain it.

land reform *n.* Measures taken to bring about an equitable apportionment of agricultural land.

land•scape (lănd′skāp′) *n.* **1.** An expanse of scenery that can be seen in a single view. **2.** A picture depicting an expanse of scenery. **3.** The branch of art dealing with the representation of natural scenery. **4.** The aspect of the land characteristic of a particular region. **5.** An extensive mental view; an interior prospect. — *v.* **-scaped, -scap•ing, -scapes.** — *tr.* To adorn or improve (a section of ground) by contouring and by planting flowers, shrubs, or trees. — *intr.* To arrange grounds artistically as a profession. [Du. *landschap* < MDu. *landscap*, region : *land*, land; see **lendh-*** + *-scap*, state, condition (collective suff.).] — **land′scap′er** *n.*

landscape architect *n.* One whose profession is the decorative and functional alteration and planting of grounds, esp. at or around a building site. — **landscape architecture** *n.*

landscape gardener *n.* One whose occupation is the decoration of land by planting trees and shrubs and designing gardens. — **landscape gardening** *n.*

land•scap•ist (lănd′skā′pĭst) *n.* A painter of landscapes.

Land•seer (lănd′sîr′), Sir **Edwin Henry.** 1802–73. British painter best known for his sentimental paintings of animals.

Land's End or **Lands End** (lăndz′ ĕnd′). A peninsula of SW England in Cornwall.

land•side (lănd′sīd′) *n.* The flat side of a plow opposite the furrow.

lands•leit (länts′līt′) *n.* Pl. of **landsman[2]**. [Yiddish *landslayt* < MHGer. *lantsliute*, natives, compatriots : OHGer. *lant*, land; see LANDSMAN[2] + OHGer. *liuti*, pl. of *liut*, person, people; see **leudh-***.]

land•slide (lănd′slīd′) *n.* **1.a.** The downward sliding of a relatively dry mass of earth and rock. **b.** The mass that slides. **2.a.** An overwhelming majority of votes for a political party or candidate. **b.** An election that sweeps a party or candidate into office. **3.** A great victory.

land•slip (lănd′slĭp′) *n.* See **landslide** 1.

Lands•mål (länts′môl′) *n.* See **New Norwegian.** [Norw. : *land*, country (< ON; see **lendh-***) + *mål*, speech (< ON *māl*).]

lands•man[1] (lăndz′mən) *n.* One who lives and works on land.

lands•man[2] (länts′mən) *n., pl.* **lands•leit** (-līt′). A Jew from one's place of origin, esp. in Eastern Europe. [Yiddish < MHGer. *lantsman*, countryman : OHGer. *lant*, land; see **lendh-*** + OHGer. *man*, man; see **man-[1]***.]

Land•stei•ner (lănd′stī′nər, länt′-shtī′-), **Karl.** 1868–1943. Austrian-born pathologist who won a 1930 Nobel Prize.

Land•tag (länt′täk′) *n.* **1.** A legislative assembly of a German state. **2.** A diet or an assembly in some German states in the 19th century. [Ger. : *Land*, country (< MHGer. *lant* < OHGer.; see LANDSMAN[2]) + *Tag*, day, diet, assembly (< MHGer. < OHGer.; see **agh-***).]

land•ward (lănd′wərd) *adv.* & *adj.* To or toward land: *sailing landward; the landward side.* — **land′wards** *adv.*

lane (lān) *n.* **1.a.** A narrow country road. **b.** A narrow way or passage between walls, hedges, or fences. **2.** A narrow passage, course, or track, esp.: **a.** A prescribed course for ships or aircraft. **b.** A strip delineated on a street or highway for a single line of vehicles. **c.** *Sports.* One of a set of parallel courses marking the bounds for contestants in a race, esp. in swimming or track. **d.** *Sports.* A wood-surfaced passageway or alley along which a bowling ball is rolled. [ME < OE.]

lang (lăng) *adj. Scots.* Long.

Lang (lăng), **Andrew.** 1844–1912. British writer and anthropologist best known for *The Blue Fairy Book* (1889).

Lang, Fritz. 1890–1976. Austrian-born Amer. filmmaker whose films include *M* (1931) and *Fury* (1936).

lang. *abbr.* Language.

lang•bein•ite (lăng′bī-nīt′, läng′-) *n.* An evaporite mineral, $K_2Mg_2(SO_4)_3$, used as a source of potassium sulfate for fertilizer. [After A. *Langbein*, 19th-cent. German chemist.]

Lang•e (läng′ə), **Christian Louis.** 1869–1938. Norwegian historian who shared the 1921 Nobel Peace Prize.

Lange (lăng), **Dorothea.** 1895–1965. Amer. photographer noted for her portraits of rural workers during the Depression.

Lang•er (lăng′ər), **Susanne Knauth.** 1895–1985. Amer. educator and philosopher whose works include *Philosophy in a New Key* (1942).

Lang•land (lăng′lənd), **William.** 1332?–1400. English poet credited with the authorship of *Piers Plowman.*

lang•lauf (läng′louf′) *n. Sports.* A cross-country ski run. [Ger. : *lang*, long (< OHGer.; see **del-[1]***) + *Lauf*, race (< MHGer. *louf* < OHGer. *hlouf*).] — **lang′lauf′er** *n.*

lang•ley (lăng′lē) *n., pl.* **-leys.** A unit equal to one gram calorie per square centimeter of irradiated surface, used to measure solar radiation. [After Samuel Pierpoint LANGLEY.]

Lang•ley (lăng′lē), **Mount.** A peak, 4,227.9 m (14,026 ft), in the Sierra Nevada of S CA.

Langley, Samuel Pierpoint. 1834–1906. Amer. astronomer who built the first successful heavier-than-air flying machines.

Lang•muir (lăng′myo͝or′), **Irving.** 1881–1957. Amer. chemist who won a 1932 Nobel Prize.

Lan•go•bard (lăng′gə-bärd′) *n.* See **Lombard[1]** 1. [Lat. *Langobardus.* See LOMBARD[1].] — **Lan′go•bar′dic** *adj.*

lan•gouste (läN-go͞ost′) *n.* See **spiny lobster.** [Fr. < OFr. < OProv. *langosta* < VLat. *lacusta < Lat. *locusta*, lobster, locust.]

lan•gous•tine (lăng′gə-stēn′) *n.* A large edible prawn. [Fr., dim. of *langouste*, langouste. See LANGOUSTE.]

lan•grage (lăng′grĭj) *n.* A type of shot consisting of scrap iron loaded into a case and formerly used in naval warfare to damage sails and rigging. [?]

lang•syne also **lang syne** (lăng-zīn′) *Scots.* — *adv.* Long ago; long since. — *n.* Time long past; times past. [Sc. *lang syne* < ME *lang sine* : *long, lang,* long; see LONG[1] + *sine,* since (contraction of *sithen, sithens;* see SINCE).]

Lang•try (lăng′trē), **Lillie.** "the Jersey Lily." 1853–1929. British actress famous for her love affair with Edward VII.

lan•guage (lăng′gwĭj) *n.* **1.a.** The use by human beings of voice sounds, and often written symbols representing these sounds, in combinations and patterns to express and communicate thoughts and feelings. **b.** A system of words formed from such combinations and patterns, used by the people of a particular country or by a group of people with a shared history or set of traditions. **2.a.** A nonverbal method of communicating ideas, as by a system of signs, symbols, gestures, or rules: *the language of algebra.* **b.** *Comp. Sci.* A system of symbols and rules used for communication with or between computers. **3.** Body language; kinesics. **4.** The special vocabulary and usages of a scientific, professional, or other group. **5.** A characteristic style of speech or writing. **6.** A particular manner of utterance: *gentle language.* **7.** The manner or means of communication between living creatures other than human beings. **8.** Verbal communication as a subject of study. **9.** The wording of a legal document or statute as distinct from the spirit. [ME < OFr. *langage* < *langue,* tongue, language < Lat. *lingua.* See **dn̥ghū-*.**]

language laboratory *n.* A room for learning foreign languages, having equipment such as tape recorders connected to monitoring devices.

langue (läng, läɴg) *n. Ling.* Language viewed as a system including the vocabulary, grammar, and pronunciation of a particular community. [Fr. < OFr. See LANGUAGE.]

Lan•gue•doc (läng-dôk′, läɴg-). A historical region and former province of S-central France on the Gulf of Lions; included in the French royal domain in 1271.

langue d'oc (dôk′) *n.* The Romance language spoken in and around Provence and Roussillon, surviving in Provençal. [Fr. < OFr. : *langue,* language + *de,* of + OProv. *oc,* yes.]

langue d'o•ïl (doil′, doi′, dô-ēl′) *n.* The Romance language of Gaul north of the Loire River, on which modern French is based. [Fr. < OFr. : *langue,* language + *de,* of + *oil,* yes.]

lan•guet (lăng′gwĭt, lăng-gwĕt′) *n.* A tongue-shaped thing, part, or process. [ME < OFr. *languete,* dim. of *langue,* tongue < Lat. *lingua.* See **dn̥ghū-*.**]

lan•guid (lăng′gwĭd) *adj.* **1.** Lacking energy or vitality; weak: *a languid wave.* **2.** Showing little or no spirit or animation; listless. **3.** Lacking vigor or force; slow: *languid breezes.* [Fr. *languide* < Lat. *languidus* < *languēre,* to be languid. See LANGUISH.] — **lan′guid•ly** *adv.* — **lan′guid•ness** *n.*

lan•guish (lăng′gwĭsh) *intr.v.* **-guished, -guish•ing, -guish•es. 1.** To be or become weak or feeble; lose strength or vigor. **2.** To exist or continue in miserable or disheartening conditions. **3.** To remain unattended or be neglected. **4.** To become downcast; pine. **5.** To affect a wistful or languid air, esp. to gain sympathy. [ME *languishen* < OFr. *languir, languiss-* < Lat. *languēre,* to be languid. See **slēg-*.**] — **lan′guish•er** *n.* — **lan′guish•ing•ly** *adv.* — **lan′guish•ment** *n.*

lan•guor (lăng′gər, lăng′ər) *n.* **1.** Lack of physical or mental energy; listlessness. **2.** A dreamy, lazy mood or quality. **3.** Oppressive quiet or stillness. [ME < OFr. < Lat. < *languēre,* to be languid. See LANGUISH.] — **lan′guor•ous** *adj.* — **lan′guor•ous•ly** *adv.* — **lan′guor•ous•ness** *n.*

lan•gur (läng-go͝or′) *n.* Any of various slender long-tailed Asian monkeys of the genus *Presbytis* and related genera that eat leaves, fruits, and seeds and have a chin tuft and bushy eyebrows. [Hindi *lan̄gūr,* perh. < Skt. *lāṅgūlam,* tail.]

lan•iard (lăn′yərd) *n.* Var. of **lanyard.**

La•nier (lə-nîr′), **Sidney.** 1842–81. Amer. writer and musician noted for his melodic poems and his novel *Tiger Lilies* (1867).

la•nif•er•ous (lə-nĭf′ər-əs) *adj.* Having wool or woollike hair. [Lat. *lānifer* (*lāna,* wool + *-fer,* -fer) + -OUS.]

lank (lăngk) *adj.* **lank•er, lank•est. 1.** Long and lean. See Syns at **lean[2]. 2.** Long, straight, and limp: *lank hair.* [ME < OE *hlanc.*] — **lank′ly** *adv.* — **lank′ness** *n.*

lank•y (lăng′kē) *adj.* **-i•er, -i•est.** Tall, thin, and ungainly. See Syns at **lean[2].** — **lank′i•ly** *adv.* — **lank′i•ness** *n.*

lan•ner (lăn′ər) *n.* **1.** A falcon (*Falco biarmicus*) of Africa, the Mediterranean, and southern Asia. **2.** A female of this species, used in falconry. [ME *laner* < OFr. *lanier,* woolweaver, coward < Lat. *lānārius,* woolworker < *lāna,* wool.]

lan•ner•et (lăn′ə-rĕt′) *n.* A male lanner, smaller than the female, used in falconry. [ME *laneret* < OFr., dim. of *lanier,* lanner. See LANNER.]

lan•o•lin (lăn′ə-lĭn) *n.* A fatty substance obtained from wool and used in soaps, cosmetics, and ointments. [Ger. : < Lat. *lāna,* wool + Lat. *oleum,* oil.]

la•nose (lā′nōs′) *adj.* Woolly. [Lat. *lānōsus* < *lāna,* wool.]

Lans•dale (lănz′dāl′). A borough of SE PA N of Philadelphia. Pop. 16,362.

Lan•sing (lăn′sĭng). **1.** A village of NE IL, a suburb of Chicago. Pop. 28,086. **2.** The cap. of MI, in the S-central part NW of Detroit. Pop. 127,321.

lan•ta•na (lăn-tä′nə, -tăn′ə) *n.* Any of various aromatic, chiefly tropical shrubs of the genus *Lantana,* having dense spikes or heads and small colorful flowers. [NLat. *Lantana,* genus name < Ital. dial. *lantana,* wayfaring tree, viburnum.]

lan•tern (lăn′tərn) *n.* **1.a.** An often portable case with transparent or translucent sides for holding and protecting a light. **b.** A decorative casing for a light, often of paper. **c.** A light and its protective or decorative case. **2.a.** The room at the top of a lighthouse where the light is located. **b.** *Obsolete.* A lighthouse. **3.** A structure built on top of a roof with open or windowed walls to admit light and air. [ME < OFr. *lanterne* < Lat. *lanterna* < Gk. *lamptēr* < *lampein,* to shine.]

lantern fish *n.* Any of numerous small deep-sea fishes of the family Myctophidae, having phosphorescent light organs along each body wall.

lantern fly *n.* Any of various chiefly tropical insects of the family Fulgoridae, having an enlarged elongated head, once thought to be luminescent.

lantern jaw *n.* **1.** A lower jaw that protrudes beyond the upper jaw. **2.** A long thin jaw that gives the face a gaunt appearance. — **lan′tern-jawed′** (lăn′tərn-jôd′) *adj.*

lantern wheel *n.* A small pinion consisting of circular disks connected by cylindrical bars that serve as teeth.

lantern wheel

lan•tha•nide (lăn′thə-nīd′) *n.* See **rare-earth element.** [LANTHAN(UM) + -IDE.]

lanthanide series *n.* The set of chemically related elements with properties similar to those of lanthanum, with atomic numbers from 57 to 71; the rare-earth elements.

lan•tha•num (lăn′thə-nəm) *n. Symbol* **La** A soft malleable metallic rare-earth element, obtained chiefly from monazite and bastnaesite and used in glass manufacture. Atomic number 57; atomic weight 138.91; melting point 920°C; boiling point 3,469°C; specific gravity 5.98 to 6.186; valence 3. See table at **element.** [NLat. < Gk. *lanthanein,* to escape notice (< the finding of the element hidden in oxide of cerium).]

lant•horn (lănt′hôrn′, lăn′tərn) *n. Chiefly British.* A lantern. [Alteration of LANTERN.]

la•nu•gi•nous (lə-no͞o′jə-nəs, -nyo͞o′-) also **la•nu•gi•nose** (-nōs′) *adj.* Covered with soft short hair; downy. [< Lat. *lānūginōsus* < *lānūgō, lānūgin-,* lanugo. See LANUGO.] — **la•nu′gi•nous•ness** *n.*

la•nu•go (lə-no͞o′gō, -nyo͞o′-) *n., pl.* **-gos.** A covering of fine soft hair, as on a leaf or a newborn child. [ME, pith < Lat. *lānūgō,* down < *lana,* wool.]

lan•yard also **lan•iard** (lăn′yərd) *n.* **1.** *Naut.* A short rope or gasket used for fastening something or securing rigging. **2.** A cord worn around the neck for carrying something, such as a knife. **3.** A cord with a hook at one end used to fire a cannon. [Perh. alteration of ME *lainere,* strap < OFr. *laniere* < *lasne,* perh. alteration of **nasle,* lace, of Gmc. orig.]

Lan•zhou also **Lan•chow** (län′jō′). A city of central China on the Huang He (Yellow River) N of Chengdu; cap. of Gansu province. Pop. 1,060,000.

Lao (lou) *n., pl.* **Lao** or **Laos** (louz). **1.** A member of a Buddhist people inhabiting the area bordering the Mekong River in Laos and Thailand. **2.** The Tai language of the Lao. — *adj.* Of or relating to the Lao or their language or culture.

La•oc•o•on (lā-ŏk′ō-ŏn′) *n. Gk. Myth.* A Trojan priest of Apollo who was killed along with his two sons by two sea serpents for having warned his people of the Trojan horse.

La•od•i•ce•a (lā-ŏd′ĭ-sē′ə, lā′ə-dĭ-). An ancient city of W Asia Minor in present-day W Turkey; built by the Seleucids in the 3rd cent. B.C.

La•od•i•ce•an (lā-ŏd′ĭ-sē′ən) *adj.* **1.** Of or relating to Laodicea. **2.** Indifferent or lukewarm esp. in matters of religion. — *n.* A native or inhabitant of Laodicea. [Adj., sense 2, in reference to Revelation 3:14–16.]

La•om•e•don (lā-ŏm′ĭ-dŏn′) *n. Gk. Myth.* The founder and first king of Troy and father of Priam.

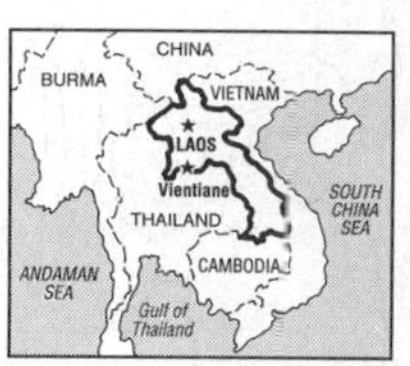

Laos

La•os (lous, lā′ŏs′). A country of SE Asia; became part of French Indochina in 1893 and gained its independence in 1953. Cap. Vientiane. Pop. 3,811,000.

La•o•tian (lā-ō′shən, lou′shən) *adj.* **1.** Of or relating to Laos or its people, language, or culture. **2.** Of or relating to the Lao people. — *n.* **1.** A native or inhabitant of Laos. **2.** A Lao.

Lao-tzu (lou′dzŭ′) also **Lao-tse** or **Lao•zi** (-dzə′). fl. 6th cent. B.C. Chinese philosopher regarded as the founder of Taoism.

lap[1] (lăp) *n.* **1.a.** The front area from the waist to the knees of a seated person. **b.** The portion of a garment that covers the lap. **2.** A hanging or flaplike part, esp. of a garment. **3.** An area of responsibility, interest, or control. — ***idiom.* the lap of luxury.** Conditions of great affluence or material comfort. [ME *lappe,* lappet, lap < OE *læppa,* lappet.] — **lap′ful′** *n.*

lap[2] (lăp) *v.* **lapped, lap•ping, laps.** — *tr.* **1.a.** To place or lay (something) so as to overlap another. **b.** To lie partly over or on: *each shingle lapping the next.* **2.** To fold (something) over onto itself. **3.** To wrap or wind around (something); encircle. **4.** To envelop in something; swathe: *lapped in furs.* **5.** To join (pieces, as of wood) by means of a scarf or lap joint. **6.** To get ahead of (an opponent) in a race by one or more complete

ă pat	oi boy
ā pay	ou out
âr care	o͝o took
ä father	o͞o boot
ĕ pet	ŭ cut
ē be	ûr urge
ĭ pit	th thin
ī pie	*th* this
îr pier	hw which
ŏ pot	zh vision
ō toe	ə about,
ô paw	item

Stress marks:
′ (primary);
′ (secondary), as in
dictionary (dĭk′shə-nĕr′ē)

circuits of the course. **7.** To convert (cotton or other fibers) into a sheet or layer. **8.a.** To polish (a surface) until smooth. **b.** To hone (two mating parts) against each other until closely fitted. — *intr.* **1.** To lie partly on or over something; overlap. **2.** To form a lap or fold. **3.** To wind around or enfold something. — *n.* **1.a.** A part that overlaps. **b.** The amount by which one part overlaps another. **2.a.** One complete round or circuit, esp. of a racetrack. **b.** One complete length of a straight course, as of a swimming pool. **3.** A segment or stage, as of a trip. **4.a.** A length, as of rope, required to make one complete turn around something. **b.** The act of lapping or encircling. **5.** A continuous band or layer of fiber. **6.** A wheel, disk, or slab of leather or metal, used for polishing and smoothing. [ME *lappen* < *lappe*, lap, lappet. See LAP^{1}.]

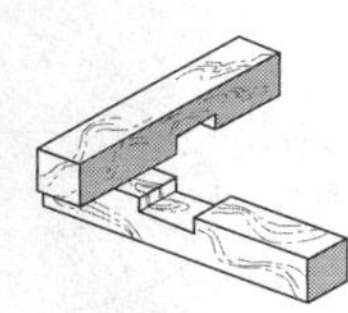

lap joint

lap^{3} (lăp) *v.* **lapped, lap•ping, laps.** — *tr.* **1.** To take in (a liquid or food) by lifting it with the tongue. **2.** To wash or slap against with soft liquid sounds. — *intr.* **1.** To lap a liquid or food. **2.** To lap against something. — *n.* **1.a.** The act or an instance of lapping. **b.** The amount taken in by lapping. **2.** The sound of lapping. **3.** A watery food or drink. — ***phrasal verb.*** **lap up.** To receive eagerly or greedily: *lapping up praise.* [ME *lapen* < OE *lapian.*]

lap•a•ro•scope (lăp′ər-ə-skōp′) *n.* A slender tubular endoscope inserted through an incision in the abdominal wall to examine the abdominal or pelvic cavities. [Gk. *lapara*, flank (< *laparos*, soft) + -SCOPE.]

lap•a•ros•co•py (lăp′ə-rŏs′kə-pē) *n., pl.* **-pies.** An operation in which a laparoscope is used, as in an examination of the liver. [Gk. *lapara*, flank; see LAPAROSCOPE + -SCOPY.] — **lap′a•ro•scop′ic** (-ər-ə-skŏp′ĭk) *adj.* — **lap′a•ros′co•pist** *n.*

lap•a•rot•o•my (lăp′ə-rŏt′ə-mē) *n., pl.* **-mies.** Surgical incision into the abdominal wall, esp. into the flank. [Gk. *lapara*, flank; see LAPAROSCOPE + -TOMY.]

La Paz (lə päz′, lä päs′). The administrative cap. of Bolivia, in the W part near Lake Titicaca. Pop. 992,592.

lap belt *n.* A seat belt that fastens across the lap.

lap•board (lăp′bôrd′, -bōrd′) *n.* A flat board held on the lap as a substitute for a table or desk.

lap dissolve *n.* See **dissolve.**

lap dog *n.* **1.** A small pet dog. **2.** *Informal.* One that is eager to do another's bidding, esp. so as to maintain a position of privilege or favor.

la•pel (lə-pĕl′) *n.* The part of a garment, such as a coat, that is an extension of the collar and folds back against the breast. [< LAP^{1}.] — **la•peled′, la•pelled′** *adj.*

lap•i•dar•i•an (lăp′ĭ-dâr′ē-ən) *adj.* Of or relating to the working of stone or gems; lapidary. [< Lat. *lapidārius*, stonecutter. See LAPIDARY.]

lap•i•dar•y (lăp′ĭ-dĕr′ē) *n., pl.* **-ies. 1.** One who cuts, polishes, or engraves gems. **2.** A dealer in precious or semiprecious stones. — *adj.* **1.** Of or relating to precious stones or the art of working with them. **2.a.** Engraved in stone. **b.** Marked by conciseness, precision, or refinement of expression: *lapidary prose.* **c.** Sharply or finely delineated. [ME *lapidarie* < OFr. *lapidaire* < Lat. *lapidārius* < *lapis, lapid-*, stone.]

la•pil•lus (lə-pĭl′əs) *n., pl.* **-pil•li** (-pĭl′ī′). A small solidified fragment of lava. [Lat., dim. of *lapis*, stone.]

lap•in (lăp′ĭn, lä-păN′) *n.* Rabbit fur, esp. when dyed to imitate a more expensive fur. [Fr. < OFr. *lapriel.*]

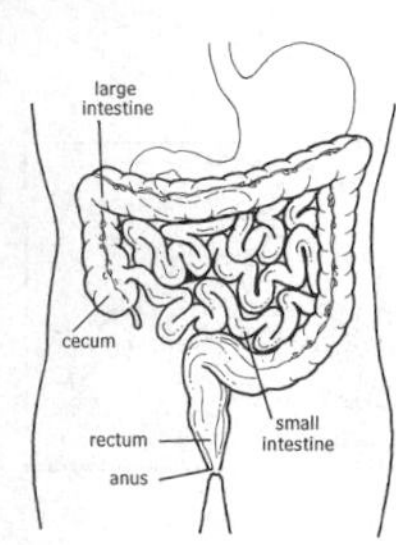

large intestine

lap•is laz•u•li (lăp′ĭs lăz′ə-lē, -yə-, lăzh′ə-) *n.* An opaque to translucent blue, violet-blue, or greenish-blue semiprecious gemstone composed mainly of lazurite and calcite. [ME < OFr. < Med.Lat. *lapis lazulī* : Lat. *lapis*, stone + Med.Lat. *lazulī*, genitive of *lazulum*, lapis lazuli (< Ar. *lāzaward* < Pers. *lajward*).]

Lap•ith (lăp′ĭth) *n. Gk. Myth.* One of a Thessalian tribe who at the wedding of their king defeated the drunken centaurs.

lap joint *n.* A joint, as between two boards or metal parts, in which the ends or edges are overlapped and fastened together.

La•place or **La Place** (lə-plās′). A village of SE LA on the Mississippi R. WNW of New Orleans. Pop. 24,194.

La•place (lə-pläs′, lä-), Marquis **Pierre Simon de.** 1749–1827. French mathematician and astronomer noted for his theory of a nebular origin of the solar system.

Lap•land (lăp′lănd′, -lənd). A region of extreme N Europe including N Norway, Sweden, and Finland and the Kola Peninsula of NW Russia. — **Lap′land•er** *n.*

La Pla•ta (lä plä′tä). A city of E-central Argentina SE of Buenos Aires; founded 1882. Pop. 454,884.

La Pla•ta Peak (lə plä′tə). A mountain, 4,380.1 m (14,361 ft), in the Sawatch Range of the Rocky Mts. in central CO.

La Porte (lə pôrt′, pōrt′). **1.** A city of NW IN WSW of South Bend; settled in 1832. Pop. 21,507. **2.** A city of SE TX on Galveston Bay E of Houston. Pop. 27,910.

largemouth bass
Micropterus salmoides

Lapp (lăp) *n.* **1.** A member of a people of nomadic herding tradition inhabiting Lapland. **2.** Any of the Finnic languages of the Lapps. [Swed. < OSwed. *lapper*, piece, perh. of Finn. orig.] — **Lap′pish** (lăp′ĭsh) *adj.*

lap•pet (lăp′ĭt) *n.* **1.** A decorative flap or loose fold on a garment or headdress. **2.** A flaplike structure, such as the earlobe.

lap robe *n.* A blanket or fur piece for the lap, legs, and feet.

lapse (lăps) *v.* **lapsed, laps•ing, laps•es.** — *intr.* **1.a.** To fall from a previous level or standard, as of accomplishment or conduct. **b.** To deviate from a prescribed or accepted way. **c.** To pass gradually or smoothly; slip. **2.a.** To come to an end, esp. gradually or temporarily. **b.** To be no longer valid or active; expire. **3.** *Law.* To pass to another through neglect or omission. Used of a right or privilege, a benefice, or an estate. **4.** To go by; elapse. — *tr.* To allow to lapse. — *n.* **1.** The act or an instance of lapsing, as: **a.** A usu. minor or temporary failure; a slip. **b.** A deterioration or decline. **c.** A moral fall. **2.** A break in continuity; a pause. **3.** A period of time; an interval. **4.** *Law.* The termination of a right or privilege through disuse, neglect, or death. [ME *lapsen*, to deviate from the normal < *laps*, lapse of time, sin (< OFr., lapse of time < Lat. *lāpsus* < p.part. of *lābī*, to lapse) and < Lat. *lāpsāre*, freq. of *lābī* < *lābī, lāps-*, to lapse.] — **laps′er** *n.*

lapsed (lăpst) *adj.* No longer active or practicing.

lapse rate *n.* The rate of decrease of atmospheric temperature with increase in altitude.

lap•strake (lăp′strāk′) also **lap•streak** (-strēk′) *adj. Naut.* Clinker-built.

Lap•tev Sea (lăp′tĕf′, -tĕv′, läp′tyĭf). A section of the Arctic Ocean N of E Russia between the Taimyr Peninsula and the New Siberian Is.

lap•top (lăp′tŏp′) *n. Comp. Sci.* A microcomputer small enough to use on one's lap.

La Pu•en•te (lä′ po͝o-ĕn′tē, pwĕn′tā). A city of S CA, a suburb of Los Angeles. Pop. 36,955.

La•pu•tan (lə-pyo͞ot′n) *adj.* Absurdly impractical or visionary. [After the flying island of *Laputa* in *Gulliver's Travels.*]

lap•wing (lăp′wĭng′) *n.* Any of several Old World birds of the genus *Vanellus*, esp. *V. vanellus*, related to the plovers and having a narrow crest. [ME, by folk ety. (perh. influenced by *lapen*, to lap; see LAP^{3}, and *wing*, wing; see WING) < OE *hlēapewince* : *hlēapan*, to leap + *-wince*, to waver.]

L'A•qui•la (lăk′wə-lə, lä′kwē-lä) also **A•qui•la** (ăk′wə-lə, ä′kwē-lä). A city of central Italy NE of Rome. Pop. 63,465.

Lar (lär) *n., pl.* **Lar•es** (lâr′ēz, lär′-). A tutelary deity or spirit of an ancient Roman household. [Lat. *Lār*, prob. of Etruscan orig.]

Lar•a•mie (lăr′ə-mē). A city of SE WY WNW of Cheyenne; settled in 1868. Pop. 26,687.

lar•board (lär′bərd) *Naut.* — *n.* See **port^{2}.** — *adj.* On the port side. [Alteration (influenced by *starboard*) of ME *laddebord* : prob. *laden*, to load; see LADE + *borde*, side of a ship; see STARBOARD.]

lar•ce•nist (lär′sə-nĭst) also **lar•ce•ner** (-nər) *n.* One who commits larceny.

lar•ce•nous (lär′sə-nəs) *adj.* **1.** Of or involving larceny. **2.** Guilty of or given to larceny. — **lar′ce•nous•ly** *adv.*

lar•ce•ny (lär′sə-nē) *n., pl.* **-nies.** *Law.* The unlawful taking and removing of another's personal property with the intent of permanently depriving the owner; theft. [ME < AN *larcin*, theft < Lat. *latrōcinium*, robbery < *latrō*, robber, mercenary, utimately < Gk. *latron*, pay, hire.]

larch (lärch) *n.* **1.** Any of several deciduous coniferous trees of the genus *Larix*, having needlelike leaves clustered on short shoots and heavy durable wood. **2.** The wood of these trees. [Ger. *Lärche* < MHGer. *larche* < Lat. *larix, laric-*.]

Larch River (lärch). A river of N Quebec, Canada, flowing c. 434 km (270 mi) NE to join the Caniapiscau R.

lard (lärd) *n.* The white solid or semisolid rendered fat of a hog. — *v.* **lard•ed, lard•ing, lards.** — *tr.* **1.** To cover or coat with lard or a similar fat. **2.** To insert strips of fat or bacon in (meat) before cooking. **3.** To enrich or lace heavily with extra material; embellish: *larded the report with quotations.* [ME < OFr. *larde* < Lat. *lārdum.*] — **lard′y** *adj.*

lar•der (lär′dər) *n.* **1.** A place, such as a pantry or cellar, where food is stored. **2.** A supply of food. [ME < AN < Med.Lat. *lārdārium* < Lat. *lārdum*, bacon.]

Lard•ner (lärd′nər), **Ringgold ("Ring") Wilmer.** 1885–1933. Amer. humorist noted for his satirical short stories.

La•re•do (lə-rā′dō). A city of S TX on the Rio Grande SSW of San Antonio; settled in 1755. Pop. 122,899.

lar•ee (lâr′ē) *n.* See table at **currency.** [Ult. < Pers. *lārī.*]

Lar•es (lâr′ēz) *n.* Pl. of **Lar.**

lar•es and penates (lâr′ēz, lär′-) *pl.n.* Treasured household possessions. [Transl. of Lat. *Larēs et Penātēs* : *Larēs*, pl. of *Lār*, Lar + *et*, and + *Penātēs*, Penates.]

large (lärj) *adj.* **larg•er, larg•est. 1.** Of greater than average size, extent, quantity, or amount; big. **2.** Of greater than average scope, breadth, or capacity; comprehensive. **3.** Important; significant. **4.a.** Understanding and tolerant; liberal. **b.** Of great magnitude or intensity; grand. **5.a.** Pretentious; boastful. Used of speech or manners. **b.** *Obsolete.* Gross; coarse. Used of speech or language. **6.** *Naut.* Favorable. Used of a wind. — ***idiom.*** **at large. 1.** Not in confinement or captivity; at liberty. **2.** As a whole; in general. **3.** Representing a nation, state, or district as a whole. Often used in combination: *councilor-at-large.* **4.** Not assigned to a particular country. Often used in combination: *ambassador-at-large.* **5.** At length; copiously. [ME < OFr. < Lat. *largus*, generous.] — **large′ness** *n.*

Syns: *large, big, great.* The central meaning shared by these adjectives is "being notably above the average in size or magnitude": *a large sum of money; a big barn; a great old oak.* ***Ant:*** *small.*

large calorie *n.* See **calorie** 3a.

large-heart•ed (lärj′här′tĭd) *adj.* Having a generous disposition; sympathetic. — **large′-heart′ed•ness** *n.*

large intestine *n.* The portion of the intestine that extends from the ileum to the anus, arching around the small intestine and including the cecum, colon, rectum, and anal canal.

large•ly (lärj′lē) *adv.* **1.** For the most part; mainly. **2.** On a large scale; amply.

large-mind•ed (lärj′mīn′dĭd) *adj.* Marked by breadth or tolerance of views; broad-minded. — **large′-mind′ed•ly** *adv.* — **large′-mind′ed•ness** *n.*

large•mouth bass (lärj′mouth′) *n.* A North American freshwater food and game fish *(Micropterus salmoides)* with a large upper jaw extending past the eye.

larg•er than life (lär′jər) *adj.* So impressive or imposing as to exceed most others of a class.

large-scale (lärj′skāl′) *adj.* **1.** Large in scope or extent. **2.** Drawn or made large to show detail.

lar•gess also **lar•gesse** (lär-zhĕs′, -jĕs′, lär′jĕs′) *n.* **1.a.** Liberality in bestowing gifts. **b.** Money or gifts bestowed. **2.** Generosity of spirit or attitude. [ME *largesse* < OFr. < *large,* generous < Lat. *largus.*]

large-toothed aspen (lärj′tōōtht′, -tōōthd′) *n.* An eastern North American deciduous tree *(Populus grandidentata)* having ovate leaves with coarsely toothed margins.

lar•ghet•to (lär-gĕt′ō) *Mus.* — *adv. & adj.* In a dignified style and slow tempo, usu. considered to be slightly faster than largo but slower than adagio. — *n., pl.* **-tos.** A larghetto passage or movement. [Ital., dim. of *largo,* largo. See LARGO.]

larg•ish (lär′jĭsh) *adj.* Fairly large.

lar•go (lär′gō) *Mus.* — *adv. & adj.* In a very slow tempo, usu. considered to be slower than adagio, and with great dignity. — *n., pl.* **-gos.** A largo passage or movement. [Ital. < Lat. *largus,* generous.]

Lar•go (lär′gō). A city of W FL on the Gulf of Mexico NW of St. Petersburg. Pop. 65,674.

lar•i•at (lăr′ē-ət) *n.* **1.** See **lasso. 2.** A rope for picketing grazing horses or mules. [Sp. *la reata* : *la,* the (< Lat. *illa;* see ALERT) + *reatar,* to tie again (*re-,* again < Lat.; see RE- + *atar,* to tie < Lat. *aptāre,* to join < *aptus,* p.part. of *apere,* to tie).]

Lá•ri•sa (lä′rē-sä) or **La•ris•sa** (lə-rĭs′ə). A city of E Greece near the Aegean; chief city of ancient Thessaly. Pop. 102,048.

lark[1] (lärk) *n.* **1.** Any of various chiefly Old World birds of the family Alaudidae, esp. the skylark, having a sustained melodious song. **2.** Any of several similar birds, such as the meadowlark. [ME *laveroc, larke* < OE *lāwerce.*]

lark[2] (lärk) *n.* **1.** A carefree or spirited adventure. **2.** A harmless prank. — *intr.v.* **larked, lark•ing, larks.** To engage in spirited fun or merry pranks. [Perh. short for SKYLARK, to frolic, and poss. alteration of dial. *lake,* play (< ME *leik, laik* < ON *leikr*).] — **lark′er** *n.* — **lark′ish, lark′y** *adj.*

lark•spur (lärk′spûr′) *n.* See **delphinium.**

La Roche•fou•cauld (lä rōsh-fōō-kō′, -rôsh-), Duc **François de.** 1613–80. French writer noted for his *Maxims* (1665).

La Ro•chelle (lä′ rə-shĕl′, rô-). A city of W France on the Bay of Biscay SW of Tours. Pop. 75,840.

La•rousse (lä-rōōs′), **Pierre Athanase.** 1817–75. French lexicographer, grammarian, and encyclopedist who compiled the *Grand Dictionnaire Universel du XIXe Siècle* (1866–76).

lar•ri•gan also **Lar•ri•gan** (lăr′ĭ-gən) *n.* A moccasin with knee-high leggings made of oiled leather. [?]

lar•rup (lăr′əp) *tr.v.* **-ruped, -rup•ing, -rups.** To beat, flog, or thrash. — *n.* A blow. [Perh. < Du. *larpen,* to slap, thrash < *larp,* rod, whip.]

lar•um (lăr′əm) *n.* An alarm. [ME *larum-,* as in *larumbelle,* short for *alarum.* See ALARUM.]

lar•va (lär′və) *n., pl.* **-vae** (-vē) or **-vas. 1.** The newly hatched, wingless, often wormlike form of many insects before metamorphosis. **2.** The earliest stage of any of various animals that undergo metamorphosis, differing markedly in form and appearance from the adult. **3.** *Rom. Myth.* A malevolent spirit of the dead; a lemur. [Lat. *lārva,* specter, mask (because it acts as a specter of or a mask for the adult form).] — **lar′val** *adj.*

Word History: The Latin word *lārva,* meaning "evil spirit, demon, devil," was used for a terrifying mask, and in Medieval Latin *larva* could mean "mask or visor." *Larva* was therefore an appropriate term for that stage of an insect's life during which its final form is still hidden or masked, and New Latin *lārva* was thus applied by Carolus Linnaeus, the Swedish botanist who originated our system of classifying plants and animals. The word *larva* is first recorded in English in its scientific sense in 1768, although it had been used in its "spirit" sense in 1651 and in a way that foreshadowed the usage by Linnaeus in 1691.

lar•vi•cide (lär′vĭ-sīd′) *n.* An insecticide designed to kill larval pests. — **lar′vi•cid′al** (-sīd′l) *adj.*

la•ryn•ge•al (lə-rĭn′jē-əl, -jəl, lăr′ən-jē′əl) also **la•ryn•gal** (lə-rĭng′gəl) — *adj.* **1.** Of, affecting, or near the larynx. **2.** Produced in or with the larynx; glottal. — *n.* **1.** A laryngeal sound. **2.** Any of a set of *h*-like sounds reconstructed for early Proto-Indo-European and partially preserved in Anatolian. [< NLat. *laryngeus* < Gk. *larunx, larung-,* larynx.]

lar•yn•gec•to•my (lăr′ən-jĕk′tə-mē) *n., pl.* **-mies.** Surgical removal of part or all of the larynx.

lar•yn•gi•tis (lăr′ən-jī′tĭs) *n.* Inflammation of the larynx. — **lar′yn•git′ic** (-jĭt′ĭk) *adj.*

laryngo– or **laryng–** *pref.* Larynx: *laryngoscope.* [NLat. < Gk. *larungo-* < *larunx, larung-,* larynx.]

lar•yn•gol•o•gy (lăr′ən-gŏl′ə-jē) *n.* The branch of medicine that studies and treats the larynx, pharynx, and fauces.

la•ryn•go•phar•ynx (lə-rĭng′gō-făr′ĭngks) *n.* The portion of the pharynx just above the larynx.

la•ryn•go•scope (lə-rĭng′gə-skōp′, -rĭn′jə-) *n.* A tubular endoscope inserted into the larynx through the mouth and used for observing the interior of the larynx. — **la•ryn′go•scop′ic** (-skŏp′ĭk), **la•ryn′go•scop′i•cal** *adj.* — **la•ryn′go•scop′i•cal•ly** *adv.* — **lar′yn•gos′co•py** (lăr′ən-gŏs′kə-pē) *n.*

lar•ynx (lăr′ĭngks) *n., pl.* **la•ryn•ges** (lə-rĭn′jēz) or **lar•ynx•es.** The part of the respiratory tract between the pharynx and the trachea, having walls of cartilage and muscle and containing the vocal cords. [NLat. < Gk. *larunx.*]

la•sa•gna also **la•sa•gne** (lə-zän′yə) *n.* **1.** Flat wide strips of pasta. **2.** A dish made by baking such pasta with tomato sauce and fillings such as cheese, meat, or vegetables. [Ital., poss. < VLat. **lasania* < Lat. *lasanum,* cooking pot < Gk. *lasanon.*]

La Salle (lə săl′, lä). A city of S Quebec, Canada, on Montreal I., a suburb of Montreal. Pop. 76,299.

La Salle, Sieur de. Robert Cavelier. 1643–87. French explorer in North America who claimed Louisiana for France (1682).

La Salle

las•car (lăs′kər) *n.* An East Indian sailor, army servant, or artillery trooper. [Urdu *lashkar,* army < Pers. < Ar. *al-'askar,* the army : *al,* the + *'askar,* army.]

Las Ca•sas (läs kä′səs, -säs), **Bartolomé de.** "Apostle of the Indies." 1474–1566. Spanish missionary who sought to abolish the oppression of native peoples in the Americas.

Las•caux (lă-skō′). A cave of SW France in the Dordogne R. valley containing important Paleolithic paintings.

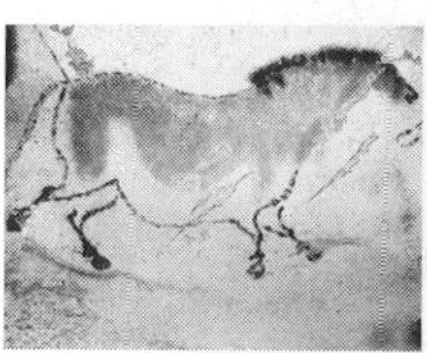

Lascaux
Bister and black horse with arrows in the Painted Gallery

las•civ•i•ous (lə-sĭv′ē-əs) *adj.* **1.** Given to or expressing lust; lecherous. **2.** Exciting sexual desires; salacious. [ME < LLat. *lascīviōsus* < Lat. *lascīvia,* lewdness, playfulness < *lascīvus,* lustful, playful. See **las-***.] — **las•civ′i•ous•ly** *adv.* — **las•civ′i•ous•ness** *n.*

Las Cru•ces (läs krōō′sĭs). A city of S NM on the Rio Grande NNW of El Paso TX. Pop. 62,126.

lase (lāz) *intr.v.* **lased, las•ing, las•es.** To function as a laser; emit coherent radiation by the action of a laser.

la•ser (lā′zər) *n.* Any of several devices that convert incident electromagnetic radiation of mixed frequencies to one or more discrete frequencies of highly amplified and coherent ultraviolet, visible, or infrared radiation. [*l(ight) a(mplification by) s(timulated) e(mission of) r(adiation).*]

laser disk *n.* See **optical disk.**

laser printer *n.* A printer that uses a laser to make an image on a rotating drum and electrostatically transfers the image to paper.

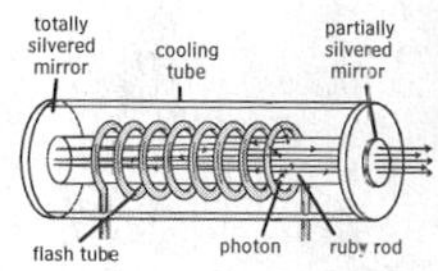

laser
Ruby laser

lash[1] (lăsh) *n.* **1.a.** A stroke or blow with or as if with a whip. **b.** A whip. **c.** The flexible portion of a whip, such as a plait. **2.** Punishment administered with a whip. **3.a.** A lacerating presence or power. **b.** A caustic verbal attack. **4.** An eyelash. — *v.* **lashed, lash•ing, lash•es.** — *tr.* **1.** To strike with or as if with a whip. **2.** To strike against with force or violence. **3.** To beat or swing rapidly. **4.** To make a scathing verbal attack against. **5.** To drive or goad; sting. — *intr.* **1.** To move swiftly or violently; thrash. **2.a.** To aim a sudden blow; strike: *The mule lashed out with its hind legs.* **b.** To beat; flail. **3.** To make a scathing verbal attack. [ME, prob. < *lashen,* to deal a blow, perh. of imit. orig.]

lash[2] (lăsh) *tr.v.* **lashed, lash•ing, lash•es.** To secure or bind, as with a rope, cord, or chain. [ME *lashen, lasen,* to lace < OFr. *lachier, lacier* < VLat. **laceāre* < Lat. *laqueāre,* to ensnare < *laqueus,* snare. See LACE.]

lash•er[1] (lăsh′ər) *n.* One that lashes, as with a whip.

lash•er[2] (lăsh′ər) *n.* One who lashes so as to secure or bind.

lash•ing (lăsh′ĭng) *n.* Something used for securing or binding.

lash•ings (lăsh′ĭngz) *pl.n. Chiefly British.* Lavish quantities. [< LASH[1], to lavish (obsolete).]

Las•ki (lăs′kē), **Harold Joseph.** 1893–1950. British political scientist who led the British Labor Party (1945–46).

Las Pal•mas (läs päl′mäs). The chief city of the Canary Is. of Spain, on the NE coast of Grand Canary I. Pop. 377,353.

La Spe•zia (lä spĕt′sē-ə, spĕ′tsyä). A city of NW Italy ESE of Genoa on the **Gulf of La Spezia,** an arm of the Ligurian Sea. Pop. 115,215.

lass (lăs) *n.* **1.** A girl or young woman. **2.** A sweetheart. [ME *las,* prob. of Scand. orig.]

Las•sa fever (lä′sə, lăs′ə) *n.* An acute, often fatal viral disease endemic to West Africa and marked by high fever, headache, ulcers of the mucous membranes, and disturbances of the gastrointestinal tract. [After *Lassa,* a village of NE Nigeria.]

ă pat	oi boy
ā pay	ou out
âr care	ŏŏ took
ä father	ōō boot
ĕ pet	ŭ cut
ē be	ûr urge
ĭ pit	th thin
ī pie	*th* this
îr pier	hw which
ŏ pot	zh vision
ō toe	ə about, item
ô paw	

Stress marks:
′ (primary);
′ (secondary), as in
dictionary (dĭk′shə-nĕr′ē)

Las•salle (lə-săl′, lä-säl′), **Ferdinand.** 1825–64. German politician who was a founder (1863) of the predecessor of the Social Democratic Party.

Las•sen Peak (lăs′ən). An active volcano, 3,188.2 m (10,453 ft), in the Cascade Range of northern CA.

las•sie (lăs′ē) *n.* A lass.

las•si•tude (lăs′ĭ-to͞od′, -tyo͞od′) *n.* A state or feeling of weariness, diminished energy, or listlessness. [ME < OFr. < Lat. *lassitūdō* < *lassus*, weary. See **lē-***.]

las•so (lăs′ō, lă-so͞o′) *n., pl.* **-sos** or **-soes.** A long rope with a running noose at one end, used esp. to catch horses and cattle. — *tr.v.* **-soed, -so•ing, -sos** or **-soes.** To catch with or as if with a lasso. [Sp. *lazo* < VLat. **laceum*, noose. See LACE.] — **las′so•er** *n.*

last[1] (lăst) *adj.* **1.** Being, coming, or placed after all others; final. **2.** Being the only one left. **3.** Just past; most recent. **4.** Most up-to-date; newest: *the last news.* **5.** Highest in extent or degree; utmost. **6.** Most valid, authoritative, or conclusive. **7.a.** Least likely or expected. **b.** The least desirable or suitable. **8.** Being the latest possible. **9.** Lowest in rank or importance. **10.** Used as an intensive: *every last dollar.* **11.** Of or relating to a terminal period or stage, as of life. — *adv.* **1.** After all others in chronology or sequence. **2.** Most recently: *last seen in 1986.* **3.** At the end; finally. — *n.* **1.** One that is at the end or last. **2.** The end. **3.** The final mention or appearance. — ***idioms.* at last.** After a considerable length of time; finally. **at long last.** After a lengthy or troublesome wait or delay. [ME < OE *latost*, superl. of *læt*, late. See **lē-***.] — **last′ly** *adv.*

Syns: *last, final, terminal, eventual, ultimate.* These adjectives mean coming after all others in chronology or sequence. *Last* applies to what comes at the end of a series: *the last day of the month. Final* stresses the definitiveness and decisiveness of the conclusion: *"I believe that unarmed truth and unconditional love will have the final word in reality"* (Martin Luther King, Jr.). *Terminal* applies to what marks or forms a limit or boundary, as in space, time, or development: *The railroad chose as its terminal city a town with a large harbor.* Something *eventual* will inevitably come about as a result of a particular circumstance or contingency: *Incautious investing led to the eventual closing of the bank. Ultimate* applies to what concludes a series, process, or progression, to what constitutes a final result or objective, and to what is most distant or remote, as in time: *our ultimate goal.*

last[2] (lăst) *v.* **last•ed, last•ing, lasts.** — *intr.* **1.a.** To continue in time; go on. **b.** To continue; survive: *The regime couldn't last.* **2.a.** To remain in good or usable condition. **b.** To continue in force or practice. **3.** To remain in adequate supply. — *tr.* **1.** To keep adequately supplied. **2.** To persist or endure for the entire length of; survive. [ME *lasten* < OE *lǣstan.* See **leis-**[1]***.**]

last[3] (lăst) *n.* A block or form shaped like a human foot and used in making or repairing shoes. — *tr.v.* **last•ed, last•ing, lasts.** To mold or shape on a last. [ME *leste, laste* < OE *lǣste* < *lǣst, lāst*, sole of the foot. See **leis-**[1]***.**]

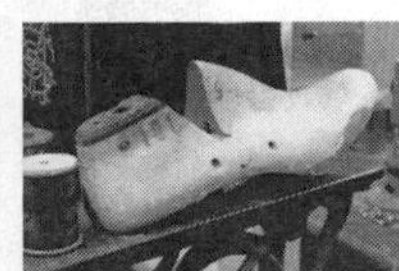

last[3]

last[4] (lăst) *n. Chiefly British.* A unit of volume or weight varying for different commodities and in different districts, equal to about 80 bushels, 640 gallons, or 2 tons. [ME, load, a kind of measure < OE *hlæst*, load.]

last-ditch (lăst′dĭch′) *adj.* Done or made as a final recourse, esp. to prevent a crisis or disaster: *a last-ditch effort.*

last hurrah *n.* A final appearance or effort, esp. at the end of a career. [After *The Last Hurrah*, a novel by Edwin O'Connor (1918–68), Amer. writer.]

last-in, first-out (lăst′ĭn′ fûrst′out′) *n. Accounting.* A method of inventory accounting in which the most recently acquired items are assumed to have been the first sold.

lateen

last•ing (lăs′tĭng) *adj.* Continuing or remaining for a long time; enduring: *a lasting peace.* — *n.* A sturdy twilled fabric. — **last′ing•ly** *adv.* — **last′ing•ness** *n.*

Last Judgment (lăst) *n.* The final judgment by God of all humankind, esp. in Christian, Jewish, and Islamic scriptures.

last minute *n.* The period just before a significant moment such as a deadline. — **last′-min′ute** (lăst′mĭn′ĭt) *adj.*

last rites *pl.n.* **1.** Rites performed in connection with a death or burial. **2.** A rite or sacrament administered to a dying person.

last straw *n.* The last of a series of troubles that leads one to a final loss of patience, trust, or hope. [From the proverb "It's the last straw that breaks the camel's back."]

Last Supper *n.* Jesus's supper with his disciples on the night before his crucifixion, at which he instituted the Eucharist.

last word *n.* **1.** The final statement in a verbal argument. **2.a.** A conclusive or authoritative statement or treatment. **b.** Power or authority of ultimate decision. **3.** *Informal.* The newest or most fashionable example of its kind; the latest thing.

Las Ve•gas (läs vā′gəs). A city of SE NV near the CA and AZ borders; known for its casinos. Pop. 258,295.

lat. *abbr.* Latitude.

Lat. *abbr.* **1.** Latin. **2.** Latvia; Latvian.

Latin cross

latch (lăch) *n.* **1.** A fastening, as for a door or gate, typically consisting of a bar that fits into a notch or slot and is lifted from either side by a lever or string. **2.** A spring lock, as for a door, that is opened from the outside by a key. — *v.* **latched, latch•ing, latch•es.** — *tr.* To close or lock with or as if with a latch. — *intr.* **1.** To have or be closed with a latch. **2.** To shut tightly so that the latch is engaged. — ***idiom.* latch on to** (or **onto**). To get hold of; obtain. [ME *latche* < *lacchen*, to seize < OE *læccan.*]

latch•et (lăch′ĭt) *n.* A leather thong or strap used to fasten a shoe or sandal on the foot. [ME *lachet* < OFr. *lacet, lachet* < *lace*, lace. See LACE.]

latch•key (lăch′kē′) *n.* A key for opening a latch or lock.

latchkey child *n.* A child who regularly spends time unsupervised at home while the parents are at work.

latch•string (lăch′strĭng′) *n.* A cord attached to a latch and often passed through a hole in the door to allow lifting of the latch from the outside.

late (lāt) *adj.* **lat•er, lat•est. 1.** Coming, occurring, or remaining after the correct, usual, or expected time; delayed. **2.a.** Beginning after or continuing past the usual or expected hour. **b.** Occurring at an advanced hour, esp. well into the evening or night: *a late movie.* **3.** Of or toward the end or more advanced part, as of a period or stage. **4.a.** Having begun or occurred just previous to the present time; recent. **b.** Contemporary; up-to-date: *the latest fashion.* **5.a.** Having recently occupied a position or place: *The late president spoke.* **b.** Dead, esp. if recently deceased. — *adv.* **later, latest. 1.** After the expected, usual, or proper time. **2.a.** At or until an advanced hour. **b.** At or into an advanced period or stage: *won late in her career.* **3.** Recently. — ***idiom.* of late.** Recently; lately. [ME < OE *læt.* See **lē-***.] — **late′ness** *n.*

Usage Note: It is technically correct to use a phrase such as *our late treasurer* to refer to a person who is still alive but who no longer holds the relevant post, but the use of *former* in this context will avoid any embarrassing misunderstanding.

late blight *n.* A disease of potato plants caused by the fungus *Phytophthora infestans* and marked by decaying foliage and tubers.

late•com•er (lāt′kŭm′ər) *n.* **1.** One that arrives late. **2.** A recent arrival, participant, or convert.

lat•ed (lā′tĭd) *adj.* Belated. [< LATE.]

la•teen (lə-tēn′, lă-) *Naut.* — *adj.* Being, relating to, or rigged with a triangular sail hung on a long yard that is attached at an angle to the top of a short mast. — *n.* **1.** A lateen-rigged boat. **2.** A lateen sail. [Fr. *(voile) latine*, lateen (sail), fem. of *latin*, Latin (from use in the Mediterranean) < OFr. See LATIN.]

Late Greek (lāt) *n.* The Greek language as used from the fourth to the ninth century A.D.

Late Hebrew *n.* The Hebrew language as used from the 12th to the 18th century.

Late Latin *n.* The Latin language as used from the third to the seventh century A.D.

late•ly (lāt′lē) *adv.* Not long ago; recently.

lat•en (lāt′n) *tr. & intr.v.* **-ened, -en•ing, -ens.** To make or grow late.

la•ten•cy (lāt′n-sē) *n., pl.* **-cies. 1.** The state or quality of being latent. **2.** The psychoanalytic stage of development, from about five years to puberty, when a child represses sexual urges and prefers to be with members of the same sex.

La Tène (lä tĕn′) *adj.* Of or relating to an Iron Age European civilization dating from the fifth to the first century B.C. [After *La Tène*, a district in Switzerland.]

la•tent (lāt′nt) *adj.* **1.** Present or potential but not evident or active. **2.** *Pathol.* In a dormant or hidden stage. **3.** *Biol.* Undeveloped but capable of normal growth under the proper conditions. **4.** *Psychol.* Present in the unconscious mind but not consciously expressed. — *n.* A fingerprint that is not apparent to the eye but can be made sufficiently visible, as by dusting, for use in identification. [ME < OFr. < Lat. *latēns, latent-*, pr.part. of *latēre*, to lie hidden.] — **la′tent•ly** *adv.*

latent heat *n.* The quantity of heat absorbed or released by a substance undergoing a change of state, such as ice changing to water, at constant temperature and pressure.

latent period *n.* **1.** The interval between exposure to an infectious organism or a carcinogen and the clinical appearance of disease. **2.** The interval between stimulus and response.

lat•er•al (lăt′ər-əl) *adj.* **1.** Of, relating to, or situated at or on the side. **2.** Of or constituting a change within an organization or a hierarchy to a position at a similar level, as in salary, to the one being left. **3.** *Ling.* Of, relating to, or being a sound produced by breath passing along one or both sides of the tongue. — *n.* **1.** A lateral part, projection, passage, or appendage. **2.** *Football.* A lateral pass. **3.** *Ling.* A lateral sound, such as (l). — *v.* **-aled, -al•ing, -als** also **-alled, -al•ling, -als.** — *intr.* To execute a lateral pass. — *tr.* To pass (the ball) sideways or backward. [ME < OFr. < Lat. *laterālis* < *latus, later-*, side.] — **lat′er•al•ly** *adv.*

lateral bud *n.* A bud located on the side of the stem, usu. in a leaf axil.

lat•er•al•i•za•tion (lăt′ər-ə-lĭ-zā′shən) *n.* Localization of function attributed to either the right or left side of the brain.

lateral line *n.* A series of sensory pores along the head and sides of fish and some amphibians by which water currents, vibrations, and pressure changes are detected.

lateral pass *n. Football.* A usu. underhand pass thrown side ways or somewhat backward with respect to downfield.

lat•er•ite (lăt′ə-rīt′) *n.* A red residual soil in humid tropical and subtropical regions that is leached of soluble minerals, aluminum hydroxides, and silica but still contains concentrations of iron oxides and iron hydroxides. [Lat. *later*, brick + -ITE[1].] — **lat′er•it′ic** (-rĭt′ĭk) *adj.*

lat•est (lā′tĭst) *adj.* Superl. of **late.** — *n.* Something that is the most recent or current of its kind. — ***idiom.*** **at the latest.** No later than: *by Tuesday at the latest.*

la•tex (lā′tĕks′) *n., pl.* **la•ti•ces** (lā′tĭ-sēz′, lăt′ĭ-) or **la•tex•es. 1.** The colorless or milky sap of certain plants, such as the milkweed, that coagulates on exposure to air. **2.** An emulsion of rubber or plastic globules in water, used esp. in paints and synthetic rubber. **3.** Latex paint. [Lat., fluid.] — **la′tex′** *adj.*

latex paint *n.* A paint having a latex binder.

lath (lăth) *n., pl.* **laths** (lă*th*z, lăths). **1.a.** A thin strip of wood or metal, usu. nailed in rows to framing supports as a substructure for plaster, shingles, slates, or tiles. **b.** A building material, such as a sheet of metal mesh, used for similar purposes. **2.a.** A quantity of laths; lathing. **b.** Work made with or from lath. — *tr.v.* **lathed, lath•ing, laths.** To build, cover, or line with laths. [ME *latthe*, prob. alteration (influenced by Welsh *llath*, rod) of OE *lætt*.]

lathe (lā*th*) *n.* A machine for shaping a piece of material, such as wood, by rotating it rapidly along its axis while pressing against a fixed cutting or abrading tool. — *tr.v.* **lathed, lath•ing, lathes.** To cut or shape on a lathe. [ME, a device used by coopers, perh. a turning lathe, prob. of Scand. orig.]

lath•er (lă*th*′ər) *n.* **1.** A foam formed by soap or detergent agitated in water, as in washing. **2.** Froth formed by profuse sweating, as on a horse. **3.** *Informal.* A condition of anxious or heated discomposure; agitation. — *v.* **-ered, -er•ing, -ers.** — *tr.* **1.** To spread with or as if with lather. **2.** *Informal.* To give a beating to; whip. — *intr.* **1.** To produce lather; foam. **2.** To become coated with lather. [Prob. < ME *latheren*, to wash or soak clothes < OE *lēthran*, to cover with lather. See **leu(ə)-*.**] — **lath′er•er** *n.* — **lath′er•y** *adj.*

lath•ing (lăth′ĭng, lă*th*′-) *n.* **1.** The act or process of building with laths. **2.** Work made of laths. **3.** A quantity of laths.

lath•y•rism (lăth′ə-rĭz′əm) *n.* A disease of human beings and animals from eating legumes of the genus *Lathyrus*, marked by spastic paralysis, hyperesthesia, and paresthesia. [< NLat. *Lathyrus*, genus name < Gk. *lathuros*, a type of pea.]

la•tic•i•fer (lā-tĭs′ə-fər) *n.* A plant duct containing latex. [Lat. *latex*, *latic-*, fluid; see LATEX + -FER.]

lat•i•cif•er•ous (lăt′ĭ-sĭf′ər-əs) *adj.* Producing or containing latex.

lat•i•fun•di•um (lăt′ə-fŭn′dē-əm) *n., pl.* **-di•a** (-dē-ə). A great landed estate, esp. of the ancient Romans. [Lat. *lātifundium* : *lātus*, broad + *fundus*, estate, base.]

Lat•i•mer (lăt′ə-mər), **Hugh.** 1485?–1555. English prelate who refused to recant his Protestantism after the accession of Mary I and was executed for heresy.

Lat•in (lăt′n) *n.* **1.a.** The Italic language of the ancient Latins and Romans. **b.** The Latin language and literature from the end of the third century B.C. to the end of the second century A.D. **2.** A member of a Latin people, esp. a native or inhabitant of Latin America. **3.** A native or resident of ancient Latium. — *adj.* **1.** Of, relating to, or composed in Latin: *Latin verse.* **2.a.** Of or relating to ancient Rome, its people, or its culture. **b.** Of or relating to Latium, its people, or its culture. **3.a.** Of or relating to the languages that developed from Latin, such as Spanish, or to the peoples that speak them. **b.** Of or relating to the peoples, countries, or cultures of Latin America. **4.** Of or relating to the Roman Catholic Church. [ME < OFr. and < OE *Latīn*, both < Lat. *Latīnus* < *Latium*, Latium.]

La•ti•na[1] (lə-tē′nə, lă-) *n.* **1.** A Latin-American woman or girl. **2.** A woman or girl of Spanish-speaking heritage, esp. in the United States. [Sp., Latin < Lat. *Latīna*, fem. of *Latīnus*. See LATIN.]

La•ti•na[2] (lə-tē′nə, lä-tē′nä). A city of W-central Italy SE of Rome. Pop. 81,000.

Latin alphabet *n.* The Roman alphabet adopted from the Greek by way of Etruscan, consisting of 23 letters upon which the modern western European alphabets are founded.

Latin A•mer•i•ca (ə-mĕr′ĭ-kə). The countries of the Western Hemisphere S of the U.S., esp. those speaking Spanish, Portuguese, or French.

Latin American *n.* **1.** A native or inhabitant of Latin America. **2.** A person of Latin-American descent. — **Lat′in-A•mer′i•can** (lăt′n-ə-mĕr′ĭ-kən) *adj.*

Lat•in•ate (lăt′n-āt′) *adj.* Of, derived from, or suggestive of Latin: *a Latinate word.*

Latin Church *n.* The Roman Catholic Church.

Latin cross *n.* A cross with a shorter horizontal bar intersecting a longer vertical bar above the midpoint.

Lat•in•ism (lăt′n-ĭz′əm) *n.* An idiom, a structure, or a word derived from or suggestive of Latin.

Lat•in•ist (lăt′n-ĭst) *n.* A specialist in Latin.

La•tin•i•ty (lə-tĭn′ĭ-tē) *n.* The manner in which Latin is used in speaking or writing.

Lat•in•ize (lăt′n-īz′) *v.* **-ized, -iz•ing, -iz•es.** — *tr.* **1.a.** To translate into Latin. **b.** To transliterate into the letters of the Latin alphabet; Romanize. **2.** To cause to adopt or acquire Latin characteristics or customs. **3.** To cause to follow or resemble the Roman Catholic Church in dogma or practices. — *intr.* To use Latinisms. — **Lat′in•i•za′tion** (-ĭ-zā′shən) *n.* — **Lat′in•iz′er** *n.*

La•ti•no (lə-tē′nō, lă-) *n., pl.* **-nos. 1.** A Latin American, esp. a man or a boy. **2.** A person, esp. a man or a boy, of Spanish-speaking heritage, esp. in the United States. See Usage Note at **Hispanic.** [Sp., Latin < Lat. *Latīnus*. See LATIN.]

Latin Quar•ter (kwôr′tər). A section of Paris on the S bank of the Seine R.

lat•ish (lā′tĭsh) *adv. & adj.* Fairly late.

la•tis•si•mus dor•si (lə-tĭs′ə-məs dôr′sī) *n., pl.* **la•tis•si•mi dorsi** (lə-tĭs′ə-mī′ dôr′sī). Either of two broad flat triangular muscles running from the vertebral column to the humerus. [NLat. *lātissimus dorsī* : Lat. *lātissimus*, superl. of *lātus*, wide + Lat. *dorsī*, genitive of *dorsum*, back.]

lattice
Pattern on a trellis

lat•i•tude (lăt′ĭ-to͞od′, -tyo͞od′) *n.* **1.a.** The angular distance north or south of the earth's equator, measured in degrees along a meridian, as on a map or globe. **b.** A region of the earth considered in relation to its distance from the equator. **2.** *Astron.* The angular distance of a celestial body north or south of the ecliptic. **3.** Freedom from normal restraints, limitations, or regulations. **4.** A range of values or conditions, esp. the range of exposures over which a photographic film yields usable images. **5.** Extent; breadth. [ME < OFr., width < Lat. *lātitūdō*, width, geographic latitude < *lātus*, wide.] — **lat′i•tu′din•al** (-to͞od′n-əl, -tyo͞od′-) *adj.* — **lat′i•tu′di•nal•ly** *adv.*

lat•i•tu•di•nar•i•an (lăt′ĭ-to͞od′n-âr′ē-ən, -tyo͞od′-) *adj.* Holding or expressing broad or tolerant views, esp. on religion. [Lat. *lātitūdō*, *lātitūdin-*, latitude; see LATITUDE + -ARIAN.] — **lat′i•tu′di•nar′i•an** *n.* — **lat′i•tu′di•nar′i•an•ism** *n.*

La•ti•um (lā′shē-əm, -shəm). An ancient country of W-central Italy bordering on the Tyrrhenian Sea; dominated by Rome after the 3rd cent. B.C.

lat•ke (lät′kə) *n.* A pancake, esp. of grated potato. [Yiddish < Ukrainian *oladka* < ORuss., dim. of *olad'ya* < Gk. *eladia*, pl. of *eladion*, little oily thing, dim. of *elaion*, olive oil.]

lat•o•sol (lăt′ə-sôl′, -sŏl′) *n.* Soil that is rich in iron, alumina, or silica and formed in hot and humid tropical woodlands. [LAT(ERITE) + *-sol*, soil (< Lat. *solum*).]

La Tour (lə to͝or′, lä to͝or′), **Georges de.** 1593–1652. French painter of religious subjects and genre scenes.

la•trine (lə-trēn′) *n.* A communal toilet of a type often used in a camp or barracks. [< Fr. *latrines*, privies < OFr. < Lat. *lātrīna*, bath, privy < *lavātrīna*. See **leu(ə)-*.**]

La•trobe (lə-trōb′), **Benjamin Henry.** 1764–1820. British-born Amer. architect whose works include the chambers of the U.S. Congress and Supreme Court.

-latry *suff.* Worship: *bibliolatry.* [< Gk. *latreia*, service, worship.]

lat•te (lät′tē) *n.* A strong espresso coffee topped with steamed frothed milk. [Ital. *(caffè e) latte*, (coffee with) milk < Lat. *lac*. See **melg-*.**]

lat•ten (lăt′n) *n.* **1.** Brass or an alloy resembling brass, hammered thin and formerly used in the manufacture of church vessels. **2.** A thin sheet of metal, esp. of tin. [ME *laton* < OFr. < Ar. *lātūn*, prob. < Old Turkic *altun*, gold.]

Latvia

lat•ter (lăt′ər) *adj.* **1.** Being the second of two persons or things mentioned. See Usage Note at **former[2]. 2.** Near or nearer to the end: *the latter part of the book.* **3.** Further advanced in time or sequence; later: *popular in latter times.* [ME, later < OE *lætra*. See **lē-*.**] — **lat′ter•ly** *adv.*

lat•ter-day (lăt′ər-dā′) *adj.* Belonging to present or recent times; modern.

Lat•ter-day Saint (lăt′ər-dā′) *n.* See **Mormon** 2.

lat•tice (lăt′ĭs) *n.* **1.a.** An open framework made of strips of metal, wood, or similar material overlapped or overlaid in a regular, usu. crisscross pattern. **b.** A structure, such as a screen, made of or containing a lattice framework. **2.** Something, such as a heraldic bearing, that resembles an open, patterned framework. **3.** *Phys.* **a.** A regular periodic configuration of points, particles, or objects throughout an area or a space, esp. the arrangement of ions or molecules in a crystalline solid. **b.** The spatial arrangement of fissionable and nonfissionable materials in a nuclear reactor. — *tr.v.* **-ticed, -tic•ing, -tic•es.** To construct or furnish with a lattice or latticework. [ME *latis* < OFr. *lattis* < *latte*, lath, of Germanic origin.] — **lat′ticed** *adj.*

lat•tice•work (lăt′ĭs-wûrk′) *n.* **1.** A lattice or latticelike structure. **2.** An open crisscross pattern or weave.

Lat•vi•a (lăt′vē-ə). A country of N Europe on the Baltic Sea. Conquered by the Livonian Brothers of the Sword in the 13th cent., Latvia passed under Russian control in the 18th cent. It officially became a constituent republic of the U.S.S.R. in 1940. Latvia declared independence in Mar. 1990 and joined the United Nations in Sep. 1991. Cap. Riga. Pop. 2,604,000.

ă pat	oi boy
ā pay	ou out
âr care	o͝o took
ä father	o͞o boot
ĕ pet	ŭ cut
ē be	ûr urge
ĭ pit	th thin
ī pie	*th* this
îr pier	hw which
ŏ pot	zh vision
ō toe	ə about, item
ô paw	

Stress marks:
′ (primary);
′ (secondary), as in
dictionary (dĭk′shə-nĕr′ē)

launch pad
Apollo 15 prior to launching on July 26, 1971

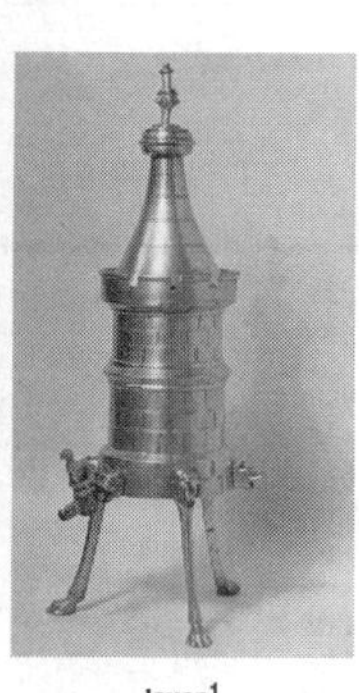

laver[1]
14th- to 15th-century bronze turret-shaped laver

Lat•vi•an (lăt′vē-ən) *adj.* Of or relating to Latvia or its people, language, or culture. —*n.* **1.** A native or inhabitant of Latvia. **2.** The Baltic language of the Latvians.

laud (lôd) *tr.v.* **laud•ed, laud•ing, lauds.** To give praise to; glorify. See Syns at **praise.** —*n.* **1.** Praise; glorification. **2.** A hymn or song of praise. **3.** The service of prayers following the matins. Often used in the plural with a singular or plural verb. [ME *lauden* < OFr. *lauder* < Lat. *laudāre* < *laus, laud-*, praise.] —**laud′er** *n.*

Laud (lôd), **William.** 1573–1645. English prelate who as archbishop of Canterbury (1633–45) was a strident supporter of Charles I and absolutism in church and state.

laud•a•ble (lô′də-bəl) *adj.* Commendable; praiseworthy. —**laud′a•bil′i•ty, laud′a•ble•ness** *n.* —**laud′a•bly** *adv.*

lau•da•num (lôd′n-əm) *n.* A tincture of opium, formerly used as a drug. [NLat., perh. alteration of Med.Lat. *labdanum*, labdanum. See LABDANUM.]

laud•a•tion (lô-dā′shən) *n.* The act of lauding; praise.

laud•a•tive (lô′də-tĭv) *adj.* Laudatory.

laud•a•to•ry (lô′də-tôr′ē, -tōr′ē) *adj.* Expressing or conferring praise: *a laudatory review of the new book.*

Lau•der•dale Lakes (lô′dər-dāl′). A city of SE FL, a suburb of Fort Lauderdale. Pop. 27,341.

Lau•der•hill (lô′dər-hĭl′). A city of SE FL, a suburb of Fort Lauderdale. Pop. 49,708.

laugh (lăf, läf) *v.* **laughed, laugh•ing, laughs.** —*intr.* **1.** To express certain emotions, esp. mirth or derision, by a series of spontaneous, usu. unarticulated sounds. **2.** To show or feel amusement or good humor. **3.a.** To feel or express derision or contempt; mock. **b.** To feel a triumphant or exultant sense of well-being. **4.** To produce sounds resembling laughter: *laughing parrots.* —*tr.* **1.** To affect or influence by laughter: *laughed the proposal down.* **2.** To say with a laugh. —*n.* **1.a.** The act of laughing. **b.** The sound of laughing; laughter. **2.** *Informal.* Something amusing, absurd, or contemptible; a joke. **3.** *Informal.* Fun; amusement. Often used in the plural: *just for laughs.* —***phrasal verbs.* laugh at.** To treat lightly; scoff at. **laugh off** (or **away**). To dismiss as ridiculously or laughably trivial. —***idiom.* laugh up** (or **in**) **(one's) sleeve.** To rejoice or exult in secret, as at another's error or defeat. [ME *laughen* < OE *hlæhhan*, prob. ult. of imit. orig.] —**laugh′er** *n.* —**laugh′ing•ly** *adv.*

laugh•a•ble (lăf′ə-bəl, lä′fə-) *adj.* Causing or deserving laughter or derision. —**laugh′a•ble•ness** *n.* —**laugh′a•bly** *adv.*

laugh•ing gas (lăf′ĭng, lä′fĭng) *n.* Nitrous oxide, esp. as used as an anesthetic.

laughing jackass *n.* See **kookaburra.**

laugh•ing•stock (lăf′ĭng-stŏk′, lä′fĭng-) *n.* An object of jokes or ridicule; a butt.

laugh•ter (lăf′tər, läf′-) *n.* **1.** The act of laughing. **2.** The sound produced by laughing. **3.** *Archaic.* A cause or subject for laughter. [ME < OE *hleahtor*, prob. ult. of imit. orig.]

laugh track *n.* Recorded laughter added to a soundtrack.

launce (lăns, läns, lôns) *n.* See **sand lance.** [Perh. alteration of LANCE.]

launch[1] (lônch, länch) *v.* **launched, launch•ing, launch•es.** —*tr.* **1.a.** To throw or propel with force; hurl. **b.** To set or thrust (a self-propelled craft or projectile) in motion. **2.** *Naut.* To put (a boat) into the water in readiness for use. **3.** To set going; initiate. **4.** To introduce to the public or to a market. **5.** To give (someone) a start, as in a career or vocation. —*intr.* **1.** To begin a new venture or phase; embark: *launched out on her own.* **2.** To enter enthusiastically into something; plunge: *launched into a speech.* —*n.* The act of launching. [ME *launchen* < ONFr. *lancher* < Lat. *lanceāre*, to wield a lance < *lancea*, lance. See LANCE.]

launch[2] (lônch, länch) *n.* *Naut.* **1.** A large ship's boat. **2.** A large open motorboat. [Prob. alteration of Malay *lancha.*]

launch•er (lôn′chər, län′-) *n.* One that launches, as: **a.** A rifle attachment for firing grenades. **b.** A device, such as an attached tube or a portable unit, for firing rockets.

launch•ing pad (lôn′chĭng, län′-) *n.* A launch pad.

launch pad *n.* **1.** The base or platform from which a rocket or space vehicle is launched. **2.** A foundation or starting point.

launch vehicle *n.* A rocket used to launch a spacecraft or satellite into an orbit or a trajectory.

launch window *n.* A brief period during which a spacecraft or a projectile must be launched to achieve its mission.

laun•der (lôn′dər, län′-) *v.* **-dered, -der•ing, -ders.** —*tr.* **1.a.** To wash (clothes, for example). **b.** To wash, fold, and iron. **2.** To disguise the source or nature of (illegal funds, for example) by channeling through an intermediate agent. **3.** To make more acceptable or presentable, sanitize. —*intr.* **1.** To undergo washing in a specified way: *This material launders well.* **2.** To wash or prepare laundry. —*n.* A trough or flume used in washing ore. [< ME *launder, lavender*, launderer < OFr. *lavandier* < VLat. **lavandārius* < Lat. *lavandāria*, things to be washed < *lavanda*, neut. pl. gerundive of *lavāre*, to wash. See **leu(ə)-*.**] —**laun′der•er** *n.*

laun•der•ette (lôn′də-rĕt′, län′-) *n.* A self-service laundry.

laun•dress (lôn′drĭs, län′-) *n.* A woman employed to launder clothes or linens.

Laun•dro•mat (lôn′drə-măt′, län′-). A service mark used for a commercial establishment equipped with washing machines and dryers, usu. coin-operated and self-service.

laun•dry (lôn′drē, län′-) *n., pl.* **-dries. 1.** Soiled or laundered clothes and linens; wash. **2.a.** A commercial establishment for laundering clothes or linens. **b.** A room or an area, as in a house, for doing the wash. [ME *lavendrye, laundry* < OFr. *lavanderie* < *lavandier.* See LAUNDER.]

laundry list *n.* *Informal.* An item-by-item enumeration.

Laur•a•sia (lô-rā′zhə, -shə) *n.* The hypothetical supercontinent of the Northern Hemisphere, which according to the theory of plate tectonics broke up into North America, Europe, and Asia. [NLat. *Laur(entia)*, geologic precursor of North America (after the SAINT LAWRENCE RIVER) + (EUR)ASIA.]

lau•re•ate (lôr′ē-ĭt, lŏr′-) *adj.* **1.** Worthy of the greatest honor or distinction. **2.** Crowned or decked with laurel as a mark of honor. **3.** *Archaic.* Made of laurel sprigs, as a wreath or crown. —*n.* **1.** One honored or awarded a prize for great achievements esp. in the arts or sciences: *a Nobel laureate.* **2.** A poet laureate. [ME < Lat. *laureātus*, adorned with laurel < *laurea*, crown of laurel < fem. of *laureus*, of laurel < *laurus*, laurel.] —**lau′re•ate•ship′** *n.*

lau•rel (lôr′əl, lŏr′-) *n.* **1.** A Mediterranean evergreen tree *(Laurus nobilis)* having aromatic simple leaves and blackish berries. **2.** A shrub or tree having a similar aroma or leaf shape. **3.a.** A wreath of laurel conferred as a mark of honor in ancient times upon poets, heroes, and athletes. Often used in the plural. **b.** Honor and glory won for great achievement. Often used in the plural. —*tr.v.* **-reled, -rel•ing, -rels** also **-relled, -rel•ling, -rels. 1.** To crown with laurel. **2.** To honor, esp. with an award or a prize. [ME < OFr. *laureole* < Lat. *laureola*, dim. of *laurea.* See LAUREATE.]

Lau•rel (lôr′əl, lŏr′-). A city of SE MS SW of Meridian. Pop. 18,827.

Laurel, Arthur Stanley Jefferson ("Stan"). 1890–1965. British-born Amer. comedian who with Oliver Hardy formed the first great comedy team of talking films.

Lau•ren•cin (lô-räN-săN′), **Marie.** 1885–1956. French artist noted for her soft pastel technique in portraiture.

Lau•rens (lôr′ənz, lŏr′-), **Henry.** 1724–92. Amer. Revolutionary leader who was president (1777–78) of the Continental Congress.

Lau•ren•tian (lô-rĕn′shən) *adj.* **1.** Of, relating to, or being in the vicinity of the St. Lawrence River. **2.** *Geol.* Of or relating to the Precambrian gneissic granite of the Lake Superior area. [< Lat. *Laurentius*, Lawrence.]

Laurentian Mountains. A range of S Quebec, Canada, N of the St. Lawrence R. rising to 960.8 m (3,150 ft).

Laurentian Plateau or **Laurentian Highlands** also **Ca•na•di•an Shield** (kə-nā′dē-ən). A plateau region of E Canada extending from the Great Lakes and the St. Lawrence R. to the Arctic Ocean.

lau•ric acid (lôr′ĭk, lŏr′-) *n.* A fatty acid, $CH_3(CH_2)_{10}COOH$, obtained chiefly from coconut and laurel oils and used in making soaps and lauryl alcohol. [Lat. *laurus*, laurel + -IC.]

Lau•ri•er (lôr′ē-ā′, lŏr′-), Sir **Wilfrid.** 1841–1919. Canadian politician who served as prime minister (1896–1911).

lau•ryl alcohol (lôr′əl, lŏr′-) *n.* A colorless solid alcohol, $CH_3(CH_2)_{11}OH$, used in synthetic detergents and pharmaceuticals. [LAUR(EL) + -YL.]

Lau•sanne (lō-zăn′, -zän′). A city of W Switzerland on the N shore of Lake Geneva. Pop. 126,200.

lav. *abbr.* Lavatory.

la•va (lä′və, lăv′ə) *n.* **1.** Molten rock that reaches the earth's surface through a volcano or fissure. **2.** The rock formed by the cooling and solidifying of molten rock. [Ital., perh. < Lat. *lābēs*, fall < Lat. *lābī*, to fall.]

la•va•bo (lə-vā′bō, -vä′-) *n., pl.* **-boes. 1.** Often **Lavabo.** In some Christian churches, the washing of the hands by the celebrant during the Eucharist. **2.** A washbowl attached to a wall and filled from a water tank fastened above. [Lat. *lavābō*, first pers. fut. indic. of *lavāre*, to wash. See LAVE.]

lav•age (lăv′ĭj, lä-väzh′) *n.* A washing, esp. of a hollow organ, such as the stomach, with repeated injections of water. [Fr. < OFr. < *laver*, to wash < Lat. *lavāre.* See **leu(ə)-*.**]

La•val (lə-văl′, lä-väl′). A city of S Quebec, Canada, on an island opposite Montreal. Pop. 268,335.

Laval, Pierre. 1883–1945. French politician who served as prime minister (1931–32 and 1935–36) and head of the Vichy government (1942) after the surrender of France.

la•va-la•va (lä′və-lä′və) *n.* A Polynesian, esp. Samoan, garment consisting of a rectangular piece of printed cotton tied loosely around the waist. [Samoan.]

lav•a•liere (lăv′ə-lîr′) also **la•val•lière** (lä′vä-lyâr′) *n.* A pendant worn on a chain around the neck. [Fr. *lavallière*, type of necktie, after Duchesse de LA VALLIÈRE.]

La Val•lière (lä vəl-yĕr′, vä-lyâr′), Duchesse de. Françoise Louise de la Baume Le Blanc. 1644–1710. French noblewoman and lover of Louis XIV.

la•va•tion (lă-vā′shən, lā-) *n.* The process of washing; a cleansing. [Lat. *lavātiō, lavātiōn-* < *lavātus*, p.part. of *lavāre*, to wash. See LAVE.]

lav•a•to•ry (lăv′ə-tôr′ē, -tōr′ē) *n., pl.* **-ries. 1.** A room with washing and often toilet facilities; a bathroom. **2.** A washbowl or basin, esp. one permanently installed with running water. **3.** A flush toilet. [ME, piscina < LLat. *lavātōrium* < *lavātor*, launderer < Lat. *lavāre*, to wash. See **leu(ə)-*.**]

lave (lāv) *v.* **laved, lav•ing, laves.** —*tr.* **1.** To wash; bathe. **2.** To lap or wash against. **3.** To refresh or soothe as if by washing: *"The quiet and the cool laved her"* (Edna Ferber). —*intr. Archaic.* To wash oneself. [ME *laven* < OE *gelafian* and < OFr. *laver*, both < Lat. *lavāre*. See **leu(ə)-*.**]

lav•en•der (lăv′ən-dər) *n.* **1.a.** Any of various aromatic Old World plants of the genus *Lavandula*, esp. *L. angustifolia* having small purplish flower clusters that yield an oil used in perfumery. **b.** The fragrant dried leaves, stems, and flowers of this plant. **2.** *Color.* A pale to light purple to very light or pale violet. [ME *lavendre* < AN < Med.Lat. *livendula, lavendula*, perh. < Lat. *līvidus*, bluish. See LIVID.] —**lav′en•der** *adj.*

la•ver¹ (lā′vər) *n.* **1.** A large basin used in the Temple in Jerusalem by a priest for ablutions before a sacrificial offering. **2.** *Archaic.* A vessel, stone basin, or trough used for washing. [ME, water pitcher < OFr. *laveoir*, prob. < LLat. *lavātōrium*. See LAVATORY.]

la•ver² (lā′vər) *n.* Any of several dried edible seaweeds of the genera *Porphyra* (the red algae) and *Ulva* (the green algae). [ME, a water plant < OE *læfer* < Lat.]

La Vé•ren•drye (lä vā-räN-drē′), Sieur de. Pierre Gaultier de Varennes. 1685–1749. French-Canadian explorer who established a chain of trading posts in New France.

La Verne (lə vûrn′). A city of S CA E of Los Angeles. Pop. 30,897.

lav•ish (lăv′ĭsh) *adj.* **1.** Marked by or produced with extravagance and profusion. **2.** Immoderate in giving or bestowing; unstinting. —*tr.v.* **-ished, -ish•ing, -ish•es.** To give or bestow in abundance; shower. [ME *laves*, prob. < OFr. *lavasse*, downpour < *laver*, to wash < Lat. *lavāre*. See LAVE.] —**lav′ish•er** *n.* —**lav′ish•ly** *adv.* —**lav′ish•ness** *n.*

La•voi•sier (lə-vwä′zē-ā′, lä-vwä-zyā′), **Antoine Laurent.** 1743–94. French chemist and founder of modern chemistry.

law (lô) *n.* **1.** A rule of conduct or procedure established by custom, agreement, or authority. **2.a.** The body of rules and principles governing the affairs of a community and enforced by a political authority; a legal system. **b.** The condition of social order and justice created by adherence to such a system: *a breakdown of law and order.* **3.** A set of rules or principles dealing with a specific area of a legal system: *tax law.* **4.** A piece of enacted legislation. **5.a.** The system of judicial administration giving effect to the laws of a community. **b.** Legal action or proceedings; litigation. **c.** An impromptu or extralegal system of justice substituted for established judicial procedure. **6.a.** An agency or agent responsible for enforcing the law: *The law caught up with them.* **b.** *Informal.* A police officer. **7.a.** The science and study of law; jurisprudence. **b.** Knowledge of law. **c.** The profession of an attorney. **8.** Something, such as an order or a dictum, having absolute or unquestioned authority. **9. Law. a.** The body of principles or precepts held to express the divine will, esp. as set forth in the Bible. **b.** The first five books of the Bible; Torah. **10.** A code of principles based on morality, conscience, or nature. **11.a.** A rule or custom generally established in a particular domain: *the laws of decency.* **b.** A way of life: *the law of the jungle.* **12.a.** A formulation describing a relationship observed to be invariable between or among phenomena for all cases in which the specified conditions are met: *the law of gravity.* **b.** A generalization based on consistent experience or results: *the law of supply and demand.* **13.** *Math.* A general principle or rule that is assumed or has been proven to hold between expressions. **14.** A principle of organization, procedure, or technique: *the laws of grammar.* —*intr.v.* **lawed, law•ing, laws.** To go to law; litigate. —***idioms.* a law unto (oneself).** A totally independent operator. **take the law into (one's) own hands.** To mete out justice as one sees fit without recourse to law enforcement agencies or the courts. [ME < OE *lagu* < ON **lagu*, sing. of *lög*, pl. of *lag*, that which is laid down. See **legh-*.**]

Law, (Andrew) Bonar. 1858–1923. Canadian-born British politician who served as prime minister (1922–23).

Law, John. 1671–1729. Scottish financier active in France who devised an ultimately disastrous speculation scheme for the development of Louisiana.

law-a•bid•ing (lô′ə-bī′dĭng) *adj.* Adhering to the law.

law•break•er (lô′brā′kər) *n.* One that breaks the law.

law clerk *n.* A person, typically an attorney, who assists a judge or another attorney, thereby gaining legal experience.

law•ful (lô′fəl) *adj.* **1.** Being within the law; allowed by law: *lawful dissent.* **2.** Established, sanctioned, or recognized by the law: *the lawful heir.* **3.** Obeying the law; law-abiding. —**law′ful•ly** *adv.* —**law′ful•ness** *n.*

law•giv•er (lô′gĭv′ər) *n.* **1.** One who gives a code of laws to a people. **2.** See **lawmaker.**

law•less (lô′lĭs) *adj.* **1.** Unrestrained by law; unruly. **2.** Contrary to the law; unlawful. **3.** Not governed by law. —**law′less•ly** *adv.* —**law′less•ness** *n.*

law•mak•er (lô′mā′kər) *n.* One who makes or enacts laws; a legislator. —**law′mak′ing** *n.*

law•man (lô′măn′, -mən) *n.* A law officer, such as a sheriff.

law merchant *n., pl.* **laws merchant.** A body of principles and regulations applied to commercial transactions and deriving from the established customs of merchants and traders rather than the jurisprudence of a particular nation or state.

lawn¹ (lôn) *n.* A plot of grass, usu. tended or mowed, as one in a park. [Alteration of ME *launde*, glade < OFr., heath, pasture, wooded area. See **lendh-*.**]

lawn² (lôn) *n.* A light cotton or linen fabric of very fine weave. [ME *laun*, after *Laon*, a city of N France.]

lawn bowling *n. Sports & Games.* A game played on a level lawn in which balls are rolled as close as possible to a smaller target ball.

Lawn•dale (lôn′dāl′). A city of S CA SW of Los Angeles near the Pacific Ocean. Pop. 27,331.

lawn mower also **lawn•mow•er** (lôn′mō′ər) *n.* A machine with a rotating blade for cutting grass.

lawn tennis *n. Sports.* See **tennis** 1.

law of averages *n.* The principle holding that probability will influence all occurrences in the long term.

law of diminishing returns *n.* The tendency for continuing work toward a particular project or goal to decline in effectiveness after a certain level of result has been achieved.

law of independent assortment *n.* See **Mendel's law** 2.

law of large numbers *n. Statistics.* The theorem that a large number of items chosen at random from a population will, on the average, have the characteristics of the population.

Law of Moses *n.* See **Mosaic Law.**

law of nations *n.* See **international law.**

law of parsimony *n.* See **Ockham's razor.**

law of segregation *n.* See **Mendel's law** 1.

Law•rence (lôr′əns, lŏr′-). **1.** A city of central IN, a suburb of Indianapolis. Pop. 26,763. **2.** A city of NE KS on the Kansas R. ESE of Topeka; scene of a proslavery raid (1856) that sparked retaliatory killings by the abolitionist John Brown. Pop. 65,608. **3.** A city of NE MA on the Merrimack R. NNE of Lowell; laid out in 1845. Pop. 70,207.

Lawrence, D(avid) H(erbert). 1885–1930. British writer whose novels include *Lady Chatterley's Lover* (1928).

Lawrence, Ernest Orlando. 1901–58. Amer. physicist who won a 1939 Nobel Prize.

Lawrence, Gertrude. 1898–1952. British actress remembered for her performances in *Private Lives* (1930) and *The King and I* (1951).

Lawrence, T(homas) E(dward). "Lawrence of Arabia." 1888–1935. Welsh-born British soldier, adventurer, and writer who led an Arab revolt against the Turks (1916–18) and wrote *The Seven Pillars of Wisdom* (1926).

law•ren•ci•um (lô-rĕn′sē-əm, lō-) *n. Symbol* **Lr** A radioactive synthetic element produced from californium and having isotopes with mass numbers 255 through 260 and half-lives of a few seconds to three minutes; atomic number 103. See table at **element.** [After Ernest Orlando LAWRENCE.]

law•suit (lô′so͞ot′) *n.* An action or a suit brought before a court, as to recover a right or redress a grievance.

Law•ton (lôt′n). A city of SW OK SW of Oklahoma City. Pop. 80,561.

law•yer (lô′yər) *n.* One whose profession is to give legal advice and assistance to clients and represent them in legal matters. [ME *lauier* < *law*, law. See LAW.] —**law′yer•ly** *adv.*

law•yer•ing (lô′yər-ĭng) *n.* The profession or work of practicing law.

lax (lăks) *adj.* **lax•er, lax•est. 1.** Lacking in rigor, strictness, or firmness. **2.** Not taut, firm, or compact; slack. See Syns at **loose. 3.** Loose and not easily retained or controlled. Used of bowel movements. **4.** *Ling.* Pronounced with the muscles of the tongue and jaw relatively relaxed, as the vowel *e* in *let.* [ME < Lat. *laxus*, loose, lax. See **slēg-*.**] —**lax•a′tion** *n.* —**lax′ly** *adv.* —**lax′ness** *n.*

lax•a•tive (lăk′sə-tĭv) *n.* A food or drug that stimulates evacuation of the bowels. —*adj.* Of or being a laxative. [ME < OFr. *laxatif* < Med.Lat. *laxātīvus*, preventing constipation < LLat., assuaging < Lat. *laxātus*, p.part. of *laxāre*, to relax < *laxus*, loose. See LAX.]

lax•i•ty (lăk′sĭ-tē) *n.* The state or quality of being lax.

Lax•ness (läks′nĕs′), **Halldór Kiljan.** b. 1902. Icelandic novelist who won the 1955 Nobel Prize for literature.

lay¹ (lā) *v.* **laid** (lād), **lay•ing, lays.** —*tr.* **1.** To cause to lie down. **2.a.** To place in or bring to a particular state or position. **b.** To bury. **3.** To put or set down: *lay railroad track.* **4.** To produce and deposit: *lay eggs.* **5.** To cause to subside; calm or allay. **6.** To put up to or against: *lay an ear to the door.* **7.** To put forward as a reproach or an accusation. **8.** To put or set in order or readiness for use: *lay the table.* **9.** To devise; contrive: *lay plans.* **10.** To spread over a surface. **11.** To place or give (importance). **12.** To impose as a burden or punishment. **13.** To present for examination: *lay a case before a committee.* **14.** To put forward as a demand or an assertion. **15.** *Games.* To place (a bet); wager. **16.** To aim (a gun or cannon). **17.a.** To place together (strands) to be twist-

Antoine Lavoisier
Detail from *Antoine Laurent Lavoisier and his Wife* by Jacques Louis David

T.E. Lawrence

ă pat	oi boy
ā pay	ou out
âr care	o͝o took
ä father	o͞o boot
ĕ pet	ŭ cut
ē be	ûr urge
ĭ pit	th thin
ī pie	*th* this
îr pier	hw which
ŏ pot	zh vision
ō toe	ə about, item
ô paw	

Stress marks:
′ (primary);
′ (secondary), as in **dictionary** (dĭk′shə-nĕr′ē)

lazy tongs

ed into rope. **b.** To make in this manner: *lay up cable.* **18.** *Vulgar Slang.* To have sexual intercourse with. —*intr.* **1.** To produce and deposit eggs. **2.** To bet; wager. **3.** *Non-Standard.* To lie. **4.** To engage energetically in an action. **5.** *Naut.* To put oneself into the position indicated. —*n.* **1.a.** The direction the strands of a rope or cable are twisted in. **b.** The amount of such twist. **2.** The state of one that lays eggs. **3.** *Vulgar Slang.* **a.** Sexual intercourse. **b.** A partner in sexual intercourse. —***phrasal verbs.*** **lay about.** To strike blows on all sides. **lay aside. 1.** To give up; abandon. **2.** To save for the future. **lay away. 1.** To reserve for the future; save. **2.** To put aside and hold for future delivery. **lay by.** To save for future use. **lay down. 1.** To give up and surrender. **2.** To specify: *laid down the rules.* **3.** To store for the future. **4.** *Non-Standard.* To lie down. **lay for.** *Informal.* To be waiting to attack. **lay in.** To store for future use. **lay into.** *Slang.* **1.** To scold sharply. **2.** To attack physically; beat up. **lay off. 1.** To terminate the employment of (a worker), esp. temporarily. **2.** To mark off. **3.** *Slang.* To stop doing something; quit. **4.** *Games.* To place all or a part of (an accepted bet) with another bookie in order to reduce the risk. **lay on. 1.** To apply (something) by or as if by spreading onto a flat surface. **2.** To prepare, usu. in an elaborate fashion; arrange. **3.** *Slang.* To present or reveal to; confront with. **lay out. 1.** To make a detailed plan for. **2.** To clothe and prepare (a corpse) for burial. **3.** To rebuke harshly. **4.** To knock to the ground or unconscious. **5.** To expend; spend. **6.** To display: *lay out merchandise.* **lay over.** To make a stopover in the course of a journey. **lay to.** *Naut.* To bring (a ship) to a stop in open water. **lay up. 1.** To stock for future use. **2.** *Informal.* To confine with an illness or injury. **3.** *Naut.* To put (a ship) in dock, as for repairs. —***idioms.*** **lay it on thick.** *Informal.* **1.** To exaggerate; overstate. **2.** To flatter effusively. **lay of the land.** The nature, arrangement, or disposition of something. **lay waste.** To ravage. [ME *leien* < OE *lecgan.* See **legh-*.**]

Usage Note: *Lay* ("to put, place, or prepare") and *lie* ("to recline or be situated") are frequently confused. *Lay* is basically a transitive verb and takes an object: *He laid* (not *lay*) *the newspaper on the table. She was laying carpet. The table was laid for four. Lie* is an intransitive verb and does not take an object: *She often lies down after lunch. When I lay down, I fell asleep. The rubbish had lain there a week. I was lying in bed when he called.* There are a few exceptions to these rules. The phrasal verb *lay for* and the nautical use of *lay,* as in *lay at anchor,* though intransitive, are well established.

lay[2] (lā) *adj.* **1.** Of, relating to, or involving the laity: *a lay preacher.* **2.** Not of or belonging to a particular profession; nonprofessional: *a lay opinion on the law.* [ME < OFr. *lai* < LLat. *lāicus* < Gk. *laikos,* of the people < *laos,* the people.]

lay[3] (lā) *n.* **1.** A narrative poem, such as one sung by medieval minstrels; a ballad. **2.** A song; a tune. [ME < OFr. *lai.*]

lay[4] (lā) *v.* P.t. of **lie[1].**

lay•a•bout (lā′ə-bout′) *n.* A lazy or idle person; a loafer.

Lay•a•mon (lā′ə-mən, lī′-). fl. 13th cent. English poet who wrote *The Brut* (c. 1205), the first English account of King Arthur.

lay•a•way (lā′ə-wā′) *n.* **1.** A payment plan in which a buyer reserves merchandise by placing a deposit until the balance is paid in full. **2.** An article reserved under such a plan.

lay•er (lā′ər) *n.* **1.a.** One that lays: *a tile layer.* **b.** A hen kept for laying eggs. **2.a.** A single thickness of a material covering a surface or forming an overlying part or segment: *a layer of dust.* **b.** A usu. horizontal deposit or expanse; a stratum. **c.** A depth or level: *several layers of meaning.* **3.** *Bot.* A stem, branch, or twig that is covered with soil for rooting while still part of the living plant. —*v.* **-ered, -er•ing, -ers.** —*tr.* **1.** To divide or form into layers. **2.** To cut (hair) into different, usu. overlapping lengths. **3.** *Bot.* To propagate (a plant) by means of a layer. —*intr.* **1.** To form or come apart as layers. **2.** *Bot.* To take root as a result of layering.

lay•ette (lā-ĕt′) *n.* Clothing and other equipment for a newborn child. [Fr. < OFr., chest of drawers, dim. of *laie,* box < MDu. *laeye.*]

lay figure *n.* **1.** See **mannequin** 2. **2.** A subservient or insignificant person. [< obsolete *layman* < Du. *leeman,* var. of *ledenman* : obsolete Du. *led,* limb (< MDu. *lit*) + *man,* man (< MDu.; see MANIKIN).]

lay•man (lā′mən) *n.* **1.** A man who is not a cleric. **2.** A man who is a nonprofessional. See Usage Note at **man.**

lay•off (lā′ôf′, -ŏf′) *n.* **1.** Suspension or dismissal of employees, esp. for lack of work. **2.** A period of temporary inactivity or rest.

lay•out (lā′out′) *n.* **1.** The act or an instance of laying out. **2.** An arrangement or a plan, esp. the schematic arrangement of parts or areas: *the layout of a factory.* **3.** *Print.* **a.** The art or process of arranging printed or graphic matter on a page. **b.** The overall design of a page, spread, or book, including elements such as page and type size. **c.** A page or set of pages marked to indicate this design. **4.** *Informal.* An establishment or property, esp. a large residence or estate. **5.** A midair position in sports such as gymnastics in which the body is kept straight and the arms are extended at the sides.

lay•o•ver (lā′ō′vər) *n.* A short stop or break in a journey, usu. imposed by scheduling requirements.

lay•peo•ple or **lay people** (lā′pē′pəl) *n.* Laymen and laywomen considered as a group.

lay•per•son (lā′pûr′sən) *n.* A layman or a laywoman.

lay reader *n.* A member of the laity in the Anglican or Roman Catholic church authorized by a bishop to read some parts of the service.

Lay•san Island (lī′săn′). An island of HI in the Leeward Is. NW of the main islands.

Lay•ton (lāt′n). A city of N-central UT N of Salt Lake City. Pop. 41,784.

lay-up (lā′ŭp′) *n.* **1.** *Basketball.* A usu. one-handed banked shot made close to the basket after driving in. **2.** The act or an instance of laying up.

lay•wom•an (lā′wo͝om′ən) *n.* **1.** A woman who is not a cleric. **2.** A woman who is a nonprofessional.

la•zar (lā′zər, lăz′ər) *n. Archaic.* A diseased person; a leper. [ME < OFr. *lazre* < LLat. *Lazarus,* Lazarus, the beggar full of sores in a New Testament parable (Luke 16:20).]

laz•a•ret•to (lăz′ə-rĕt′ō) also **laz•a•ret** or **laz•a•rette** (lăz′ə-rĕt′) *n., pl.* **-tos** also **-rets** or **-rettes. 1.** A hospital treating contagious diseases. **2.** A building or ship used as a quarantine station. **3.** Often **lazaret.** *Naut.* A storage space between the decks of a ship. [Ital. *lazzaretto* : *lazzaro,* lazar (< LLat. *Lazarus*; see LAZAR) + Ital. dial. *Nazareto,* popular name for a hospital maintained in Venice by the Church of Santa Maria di Nazaret.]

Laz•a•rus (lăz′ər-əs). In the Bible, the brother of Mary and Martha.

Lazarus, Emma. 1849–87. Amer. writer whose poem "The New Colossus" is inscribed on the Statue of Liberty.

laze (lāz) *v.* **lazed, laz•ing, laz•es.** —*intr.* To be lazy; loaf. —*tr.* To spend (time) in loafing. [Back-formation < LAZY.]

laz•u•lite (lăz′yo͞o-līt′, lăz′ə-, lăzh′ə-) *n.* A relatively rare blue mineral, $(Mg, Fe)Al_2(PO_4)_2(OH)_2$, with a vitreous luster. [Med.Lat. *lazulum,* lapis lazuli; see LAPIS LAZULI + -ITE[1].]

laz•u•rite (lăz′yo͞o-rīt′, lăz′ə-, lăzh′ə-) *n.* A relatively rare blue, violet-blue, or greenish-blue translucent mineral, $Na_{4-5}Al_3Si_3O_{12}S$, the chief component of lapis lazuli. [Med. Lat. *lāzur,* lapis lazuli (< Ar. *lāzaward*; see LAPIS LAZULI) + -ITE[1].]

la•zy (lā′zē) *adj.* **-zi•er, -zi•est. 1.** Resistant to work or exertion; disposed to idleness. **2.** Slow-moving; sluggish: *a lazy river.* **3.** Conducive to idleness or indolence. **4.** Depicted as reclining or lying on its side. Used of a brand on livestock. [Prob. of LGer. orig.] —**la′zi•ly** *adv.* —**la′zi•ness** *n.*

la•zy•bones (lā′zē-bōnz′) *pl.n. (used with a sing. v.) Informal.* A lazy person.

lazy eye *n.* See **amblyopia.**

lazy Su•san (so͞o′zən) *n.* A revolving tray for food.

lazy tongs *pl.n. (used with a sing. or pl. v.)* Tongs having a jointed extensible framework operated by scissorslike handles, used for grasping an object at a distance.

lb. *abbr.* **1.** Libra (ancient Roman weight). **2.** Pound (modern weight).

LBO *abbr.* Leveraged buyout.

lc also **l.c.** *abbr.* Lowercase.

LC *abbr.* **1.** Landing craft. **2.** Also **L.C.** Library of Congress.

L/C *abbr.* Letter of credit.

l.c.d. *abbr. Math.* Least common denominator.

LCD *abbr.* Liquid-crystal display.

l.c.m. *abbr. Math.* Least common multiple.

LCT *abbr.* **1.** Land conservation trust. **2.** Local civil time.

ld. *abbr.* **1.** *Print.* Lead. **2.** Load.

Ld. *abbr.* **1.a.** Limited. **b.** Limited company. **2.** Lord.

LDC *abbr.* Less-developed country.

ldg. *abbr.* **1.** Landing. **2.** Loading.

LDL *abbr.* Low-density lipoprotein.

L-do•pa (ĕl-dō′pə) *n.* The levorotatory form of dopa, used to treat Parkinson's disease. [L(EVOROTATORY) + DOPA.]

lea (lē, lā) also **ley** (lā, lē) *n.* A grassland; a meadow. [ME *leie* < OE *lēah.* See **leuk-*.**]

lea. *abbr.* League (measurement).

leach (lēch) *v.* **leached, leach•ing, leach•es.** —*tr.* **1.** To remove soluble or other constituents from by the action of a percolating liquid. **2.** To empty; drain. —*intr.* To be dissolved or passed out by a percolating liquid. —*n.* **1.** The act or process of leaching. **2.** A porous, perforated, or sievelike vessel that holds material to be leached. **3.** The substance through which a liquid is leached. [< ME *leche,* leachate < OE **lece,* muddy stream; akin to *leccan,* to moisten.] —**leach′a•bil′i•ty** *n.* —**leach′a•ble** *adj.* —**leach′er** *n.*

leach•ate (lē′chāt) *n.* A solution formed by leaching, esp. one containing contaminants leached from soil.

Lea•cock (lē′kŏk′), **Stephen Butler.** 1869–1944. Canadian economist whose works include *Literary Lapses* (1910).

lead[1] (lēd) *v.* **led** (lĕd), **lead•ing, leads.** —*tr.* **1.** To show the way to by going in advance. **2.** To guide or direct in a course. **3.a.** To serve as a route for; take: *The path led them home.* **b.** To be a channel or conduit for (water or electricity, for example). **4.** To guide the behavior or opinion of; induce. **5.a.** To direct the performance or activities of. **b.** To inspire the conduct of: *led the nation.* **6.** To play a principal or guiding role in: *lead a discussion.* **7.a.** To go or be at the head of: *My name led the list.* **b.** To be ahead of. **c.** To be foremost in or among. **8.** To pass or go through; live. **9.** To begin or open with, as in games: *led an ace.* **10.** To guide (a partner) in dancing. **11.** To aim in front of (a moving target). —*intr.* **1.** To be first; be ahead. **2.** To go first as a guide. **3.** To act as commander, director, or guide. **4.** To afford a passage, course, or route. **5.** To tend toward a certain goal or result. **6.** To make the initial play, as in a game or contest. **7.** To begin a presentation or an account in a given way. **8.a.** To guide a dance partner. **b.** To start a dance step on a specified foot. **9.** *Baseball.* To advance a few paces toward the next base while the pitcher is in the delivery. Used of a base runner. **10.** *Sports.* To begin an attack in boxing with a specified hand or punch. —*n.* **1.a.** The first or foremost position. **b.** One occupying such a position; a leader. **c.** The initiative. **2.** The margin by which one holds a position of advantage or superiority. **3.a.** Information pointing toward a possible solution; a clue. **b.** An indication of potential opportunity; a tip. **4.** Command; leadership. **5.** An example; a precedent. **6.a.** The principal role in a dramatic production. **b.** The person playing such a role. **7.a.** The introductory portion of a news story. **b.** An important, usu. prominently displayed news story. **8.** *Games.* **a.** The first play. **b.** The prerogative or turn to make the first play. **c.** A card played first in a round. **9.** *Baseball.* A position taken by a base runner away from one base in the direction of the next. **10.** A leash. **11.** *Geol.* **a.** A deposit of gold ore in an old riverbed. **b.** See **lode** 1. **12.** *Electron.* A conductor by which one circuit element is electrically connected to another. **13.** *Naut.* The direction in which a line runs. **14.** The distance aimed in front of a moving target. —***phrasal verbs.* lead off. 1.** To begin; start. **2.** *Baseball.* To be the first batter in an inning. **lead on. 1.** To keep in a state of expectation or hope; entice. **2.** To mislead; deceive. —***idiom.* lead up to. 1.** To result in by a series of steps. **2.** To proceed toward (a main topic) with preliminary remarks. [ME *leden* < OE *lǣdan.* See **leit-*.**]

lead² (lĕd) *n.* **1.** *Symbol* **Pb** A soft ductile dense metallic element, extracted chiefly from galena and used in pipes, solder and type metal, bullets, radiation shielding, paints, and antiknock compounds. Atomic number 82; atomic weight 207.19; melting point 327.5°C; boiling point 1,744°C; specific gravity 11.35; valence 2, 4. See table at **element. 2.** A lead weight suspended by a line, used to make soundings. **3.** Bullets from or for firearms; shot. **4. leads.** Strips of lead used to hold the panes of a window. **5.** *Print.* **a.** A thin strip of metal used to separate lines of type. **b.** A similar space between lines of photocomposed or computer-generated type. **6. leads.** *Chiefly British.* A flat roof covered with sheets of lead. **7.a.** Any of various, often graphitic compositions used as the writing substance in pencils. **b.** A thin stick of such material. —*v.* **lead•ed, lead•ing, leads.** —*tr.* **1.** To cover, line, weight, or fill with lead. **2.** *Print.* To provide space between (lines of type) with leads. **3.** To secure (window glass) with leads. **4.** To treat with lead or a lead compound: *leaded paint.* —***idiom.* get the lead out.** *Informal.* To start moving or move more rapidly. [ME *led* < OE *lēad,* prob. of Celt. orig.] —**lead** *adj.*

lead acetate (lĕd) *n.* A poisonous crystalline compound, $Pb(C_2H_3O_2)_2 \cdot 3H_2O$, used in waterproofing and varnishes.

lead carbonate (lĕd) *n.* A poisonous white amorphous powder, $PbCO_3$, used as a paint pigment.

lead chromate (lĕd) *n.* A poisonous yellow crystalline compound, $PbCrO_4$, used as a paint pigment.

lead colic (lĕd) *n.* See **painter's colic.**

lead dioxide (lĕd) *n.* A poisonous brown crystalline compound, PbO_2, used as an oxidizing agent, as in batteries.

lead•en (lĕd′n) *adj.* **1.** Made of or containing lead. **2.a.** Heavy and inert. **b.** Listless; sluggish. **3.** Lacking liveliness or sparkle; dull. **4.** Downcast; depressed. **5.** Dull dark gray in color: *a leaden sky.* —**lead′en•ly** *adv.* —**lead′en•ness** *n.*

lead•er (lē′dər) *n.* **1.** One that leads or guides. **2.** One who is in charge or in command of others. **3.a.** One who heads a political party or organization. **b.** One who has influence or power, esp. politically. **4.** *Mus.* **a.** A conductor, esp. of an orchestra, a band, or a choral group. **b.** The principal performer in an orchestral section or a group. **5.** The foremost animal, such as a dog, in a harnessed team. **6.** A loss leader. **7.** *Chiefly British.* The main editorial in a newspaper. **8. leaders.** *Print.* Dots or dashes in a row leading the eye across a page, as in an index entry. **9.** A pipe for conducting liquid. **10.** A short length of gut, wire, or similar material by which a hook is attached to a fishing line. **11.** A blank strip at the end of a film or tape used in threading or winding. **12.** *Bot.* The growing apex or main shoot of a shrub or tree. **13.** An economic indicator.

lead•er•ship (lē′dər-shĭp′) *n.* **1.** The position or office of a leader. **2.** Capacity or ability to lead. **3.** A group of leaders. **4.** Guidance; direction: *the leadership of the new president.*

lead glass (lĕd) *n.* See **flint glass.**

lead-in (lēd′ĭn′) *n.* **1.** Opening or introductory matter. **2.** A program, as for radio, scheduled to precede another. **3.** The wire between an outdoor antenna and an electronic transmitter or receiver.

lead•ing¹ (lē′dĭng) *adj.* **1.** Having a position in the lead; foremost. **2.** Chief; principal. **3.** Of or performing a lead in a theatrical production. **4.** Formulated so as to elicit a desired response: *a leading question.* —**lead′ing•ly** *adv.*

lead•ing² (lĕd′ĭng) *n.* **1.** A border or rim of lead, as around a windowpane. **2.** *Print.* The spacing between lines, usu. measured in points.

lead•ing economic indicator (lē′dĭng) *n.* An economic or a financial variable that tends to move ahead of and in the same direction as general economic activity.

lead•ing edge (lē′dĭng) *n.* **1.** *Naut.* The edge of a sail that faces the wind. **2.** The front edge of an airplane propeller blade or wing. **3.** The foremost position in a trend or movement; the vanguard. —**lead′ing-edge′** (lē′dĭng-ĕj′) *adj.*

lead•ing tone (lē′dĭng) *n. Mus.* The seventh tone or degree of a scale, a half tone below the tonic; a subtonic.

lead line (lĕd) *n. Naut.* See **sounding line.**

lead monoxide (lĕd) *n.* See **litharge.**

lead•off (lēd′ôf′, -ŏf′) *n.* **1.** An opening play or move. **2.** One that leads off. —**lead′off′** *adj.*

lead pencil (lĕd) *n.* A pencil that uses graphite as its marking substance.

lead•plant (lĕd′plănt′) *n.* A deciduous shrub *(Amorpha canescens)* of central North America having pinnately compound leaves covered with whitish hairs.

lead poisoning (lĕd) *n.* Acute or chronic poisoning by lead or any of its salts, causing anemia and damage to the gastrointestinal tract and nervous system.

leads•man (lĕdz′mən) *n. Naut.* The person using the lead line in taking soundings.

lead tetraethyl (lĕd) *n.* Tetraethyl lead.

lead-time (lēd′tīm′) *n.* The time between the start of a project or policy and the results: *a long lead-time in oil production.*

lead•wort (lĕd′wûrt′, -wôrt′) *n.* **1.** Any of various chiefly tropical plants of the genus *Plumbago,* having clusters of variously colored flowers. **2.** Any of several similar plants.

leaf (lēf) *n., pl.* **leaves** (lēvz). **1.** A usu. green, flattened lateral structure attached to a stem and functioning as a principal organ of photosynthesis and transpiration in most plants. **2.** A leaflike organ or structure. **3.a.** Leaves considered as a group; foliage. **b.** The state or time of having or showing leaves: *trees in full leaf.* **4.** The leaves of a plant used or processed for a specific purpose: *tobacco leaf.* **5.** Any of the sheets of paper bound in a book, each side of which constitutes a page. **6.a.** A very thin sheet of material, esp. metal. **b.** Such leaves considered as a group. **7.** A hinged or removable section for a table top. **8.** A hinged or otherwise movable section of a folding door, shutter, or gate. **9.** One of several metal strips forming a leaf spring. —*v.* **leafed, leaf•ing, leafs.** —*intr.* **1.** To produce leaves; put forth foliage. **2.** To turn pages, as in searching or browsing. —*tr.* To turn through the pages of. [ME < OE *lēaf.*]

leaf•age (lē′fĭj) *n.* Foliage.

leaf butterfly *n.* Any of several butterflies of the genus *Kallima,* having wings that resemble leaves.

leaf fat *n.* Layered fat that encloses the kidneys of a hog, used in making lard.

leaf•hop•per (lēf′hŏp′ər) *n.* Any of numerous insects of the family Cicadellidae that suck juices from plants, often damaging crops.

leaf insect *n.* Any of various chiefly Asian insects of the family Phyllidae that resemble leaves in color and form.

leaf lard *n.* High-grade lard made from leaf fat.

leaf•let (lē′flĭt) *n.* **1.** One of the segments of a compound leaf. **2.** A small leaf or leaflike part. **3.** A printed, usu. folded handbill or flier intended for free distribution. —*v.* **-let•ed, -let•ing, -lets** also **-let•ted, -let•ting, -lets.** —*intr.* To hand out leaflets. —*tr.* To hand out leaflets to or in.

leaf miner *n.* Any of numerous small flies and moths that in the larval stage dig into and feed on leaf tissue.

leaf mold *n.* Humus or compost consisting of decomposed leaves and other organic material.

leaf spot *n.* Any of various plant diseases resulting in well-defined necrotic areas on the leaves.

leaf spring *n.* A composite spring, used esp. in automotive suspensions, consisting of several layers of flexible metallic strips joined to act as a single unit.

leaf•stalk or **leaf stalk** (lēf′stôk′) *n.* See **petiole** 1.

leaf•y (lē′fē) *adj.* **-i•er, -i•est. 1.** Covered with or having leaves. **2.** Consisting of leaves. **3.** Similar to or resembling a leaf. —**leaf′i•ness** *n.*

league¹ (lēg) *n.* **1.** An association of states, organizations, or individuals for common action; an alliance. **2.** *Sports.* An association of teams or clubs that compete chiefly among themselves. **3.** A class or level of competition. —*v.* **leagued, leagu•ing, leagues.** —*intr.* To come together in or as if in a league. —*tr.* To bring together in or as if in a league. [Al-

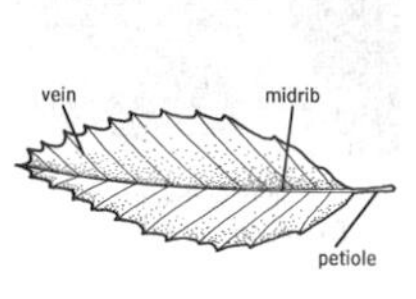

leaf
Simple leaf

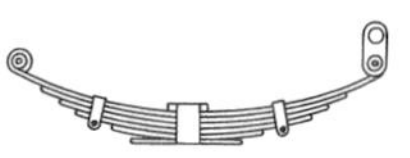
leaf spring

ă pat	oi boy
ā pay	ou out
âr care	ŏŏ took
ä father	ōō boot
ĕ pet	ŭ cut
ē be	ûr urge
ĭ pit	th thin
ī pie	*th* this
îr pier	hw which
ŏ pot	zh vision
ō toe	ə about,
ô paw	item

Stress marks:
′ (primary);
′ (secondary), as in
dictionary (dĭk′shə-nĕr′ē)

word *corp,* "body." *Corp* is borrowed from Latin *corpus.* Here is a piece of evidence attesting to the deep influence of Church Latin on the Irish language.

lep•ro•sar•i•um (lĕp′rə-sâr′ē-əm) *n., pl.* **-i•ums** or **-i•a** (-ē-ə). A hospital for the treatment of leprosy. [Med.Lat. *leprōsārium* < LLat. *leprōsus,* leprous. See LEPROUS.]

lep•rose (lĕp′rōs′) *adj.* Scurfy or scaly; leprous. [LLat. *leprōsus.* See LEPROUS.]

lep•ro•sy (lĕp′rə-sē) *n.* A chronic, mildly contagious granulomatous disease, caused by the bacillus *Mycobacterium leprae* and characterized by ulceration of the skin, loss of sensation, paralysis, gangrene, and deformation. [ME *lepruse* < *leprus,* leprous. See LEPROUS.] **—lep•rot′ic** (lĕ-prŏt′ĭk) *adj.*

lep•rous (lĕp′rəs) *adj.* **1.** Having leprosy. **2.** Of, relating to, or resembling leprosy. **3.** *Biol.* Having or consisting of loose scurfy scales. [ME *leprus* < OFr. *lepros* < LLat. *leprōsus* < *lepra,* leprosy. See LEPER.] **—lep′rous•ly** *adv.* **—lep′rous•ness** *n.*

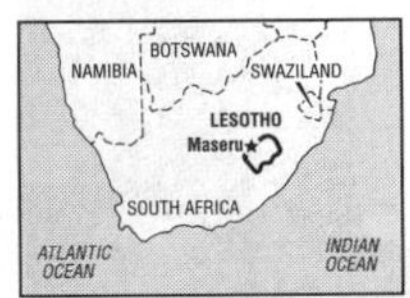

Lesotho

–lepsy *suff.* Fit; seizure: *narcolepsy.* [NLat. *-lēpsia* < Gk. < *lēpsis,* seizure < *lambanein, lēp-,* to take, seize.]

Lep•tis Mag•na (lĕp′tĭs măg′nə). An ancient city of N Africa in present-day Libya E of Tripoli; founded by Phoenicians.

lepto– or **lept–** *pref.* Slender; thin; fine: *leptocephalus.* [Gk. < *leptos,* fine, thin < *lepein,* to peel.]

lep•to•ceph•a•lus (lĕp′tə-sĕf′ə-ləs) *n., pl.* **-li** (-lī′). One of the small flat larvae of eels and certain other fishes, characterized by a long narrow head. [NLat. : LEPTO– + *cephalus,* head (< Gk. *-kephalos,* -headed); see –CEPHALOUS.]

lep•ton¹ (lĕp′tŏn′) *n., pl.* **-ta** (-tə). See table at **currency.** [Mod. Gk. < Gk., small coin < neut. of *leptos,* fine, small. See LEPTO–.]

lep•ton² (lĕp′tŏn′) *n.* Any of a family of elementary particles that participate in the weak interaction, including the electron, the muon, and their associated neutrinos. See table at **subatomic particle.** [LEPTO– + –ON¹.] **—lep•ton′ic** *adj.*

lep•to•spi•ro•sis (lĕp′tō-spī-rō′sĭs) *n.* An infectious disease of domestic animals, esp. cattle, swine, and dogs, caused by spirochetes of the genus *Leptospira* and characterized by jaundice and fever. [NLat. *Leptospīra,* genus name (LEPTO– + Lat. *spīra,* coil; see SPIRAL) + –OSIS.]

Le•pus (lē′pəs) *n.* A constellation in the Southern Hemisphere near Orion and Columba. [Lat. < *lepus,* hare.]

Lé•ri•da (lā′rĭ-də, lĕ′rē-*thä*). A city of NE Spain W of Barcelona. Pop. 87,800.

Ler•mon•tov (lĕr′mən-tôf′, lyĕr′mən-təf), **Mikhail Yurievich.** 1814–41. Russian writer best remembered for the novel *A Hero of Our Time* (1840).

Ler•ner (lûr′nər), **Alan Jay.** 1918–86. Amer. lyricist who wrote a number of musicals with the composer Frederick Loewe, including *My Fair Lady* (1956).

Le•sage (lə-säzh′), **Alain René.** 1668–1747. French writer best known for his novel *Gil Blas* (1715–35).

les•bi•an (lĕz′bē-ən) *n.* A gay or homosexual woman. *—adj.* Of, relating to, or being a lesbian. [From the putative homosexuality of Sappho, lyric poet of Lesbos.]

Les•bi•an (lĕz′bē-ən) *n.* **1.** A native or inhabitant of Lesbos. **2.** The ancient Greek dialect of Lesbos. *—adj.* Of or relating to Lesbos. [< Lat. *Lesbius* < Gk. *Lesbios* < LESBOS.]

les•bi•an•ism (lĕz′bē-ə-nĭz′əm) *n.* Sexual orientation of women to other women.

Les•bos (lĕz′bŏs, -bōs) also **Lés•vos** (-vôs). An island of E Greece in the Aegean Sea near the NW coast of Turkey; noted for its lyric poets, including Sappho.

lese maj•es•ty also **lèse ma•jes•té** (lēz′ măj′ĭ-stē) *n., pl.* **lese maj•es•ties** or **lèse ma•jes•tés. 1.** An offense or a crime committed against the ruler or supreme power of a state. **2.** An affront to another's dignity. [Partial transl. of Fr. *lèse-majesté* < Lat. *(crimen) laesae māiestātis,* (the crime) of injured majesty.]

le•sion (lē′zhən) *n.* **1.** A wound or an injury. **2.** A localized pathological change in a body organ or tissue. **3.** An infected or diseased patch of skin. [ME *lesioun* < OFr. *lesion* < Lat. *laesiō, laesiōn-* < *laesus,* p.part. of *laedere,* to injure.]

Le•so•tho (lə-sō′tō, -sōō′tōō). Formerly **Ba•su•to•land** (bə-sōō′tō-lănd′). A country of S Africa forming an enclave within E-central South Africa; gained independence from Great Britain in 1966. Cap. Maseru. Pop. 1,213,960.

lesser celandine
Ranunculus ficaria

les•pe•de•za (lĕs′pĭ-dē′zə) *n.* See **bush clover.** [NLat. *Lespedeza,* genus name, after V.M. de *Céspedez* (misread as *Léspedez*; fl. 1785), Spanish governor of Florida.]

less (lĕs) *adj.* A comp. of **little. 1.** Not as great in amount or quantity. **2.** Lower in importance, esteem, or rank. **3.** Consisting of a smaller number. See Usage Note at **few.** *—prep.* With the deduction of; minus: *Five less two is three.* *—adv.* Comp. of **little.** To a smaller extent, degree, or frequency. *—n.* **1.** A smaller amount. **2.** Something not as important as something else. ***—idioms.*** **less than.** Not at all. **much (or still) less.** Certainly not. [ME *lesse* < OE *lǣssa* (adj.) and *lǣs* (adv.); see **leis-²*.**]

–less *suff.* **1.** Without; lacking: *blameless.* **2.** Unable to act or be acted on in a specified way: *dauntless.* [ME *-lesse* < OE *-lēas* < *lēas,* without. See **leu-*.**]

les•see (lĕ-sē′) *n.* One that holds a lease. [ME < AN < p.part. of *lesser,* to let out, lease. See LEASE.]

less•en (lĕs′ən) *v.* **-ened, -en•ing, -ens.** *—tr.* **1.** To make less; reduce. **2.** *Archaic.* To make little of; belittle. *—intr.* To become less; decrease. See Syns at **decrease.** [ME *lessen, lessenen* < *lesse,* less. See LESS.]

Les•seps (lĕs′əps, lĕ-sĕps′), Vicomte **Ferdinand Marie de.** 1805–94. French diplomat and engineer who supervised the construction of the Suez Canal (1859–69).

less•er (lĕs′ər) *adj.* A comp. of **little. 1.** Smaller in amount, value, or importance, esp. in a comparison between two things. **2.** Of a smaller size than other similar forms. [ME < *lesse,* less. See LESS.]

Less•er An•til•les (lĕs′ər ăn-tĭl′ēz). An island group of the E West Indies extending from Curaçao to the Virgin Is.

lesser celandine *n.* A Eurasian plant *(Ranunculus ficaria)* having heart-shaped leaves and solitary yellow flowers.

lesser omentum *n. Anat.* A fold of the peritoneum joining parts of the stomach and duodenum to the liver.

lesser panda *n.* See **panda** 2.

Les•sing (lĕs′ĭng), **Doris.** b. 1919. British writer noted for works such as *The Golden Notebook* (1962).

Lessing, Gotthold Ephraim. 1729–81. German playwright and critic whose works include *Nathan the Wise* (1779).

les•son (lĕs′ən) *n.* **1.** Something to be learned. **2.a.** A period of instruction; a class. **b.** An assignment or exercise in which something is to be learned. **c.** The act or an instance of instructing; teaching. **3.a.** An experience, example, or observation that imparts new knowledge or wisdom. **b.** The knowledge or wisdom so acquired. **4.** A rebuke or reprimand. **5.** Often **Lesson.** A reading from the Bible or other sacred text as part of a religious service. *—tr.v.* **-soned, -son•ing, -sons. 1.** To teach a lesson to; instruct. **2.** To rebuke or reprimand. [ME *lessoun* < OFr. *leson* < Lat. *lēctiō, lēctiōn-,* a reading < *lēctus,* p.part. of *legere,* to read. See **leg-*.**]

les•sor (lĕs′ôr′, lĕ-sôr′) *n.* One that lets property under a lease. [ME *lessour* < AN < *lesser,* to let out, lease. See LEASE.]

lest (lĕst) *conj.* For fear that: *anxious lest he become ill.* [ME < OE *thȳ lǣs the,* so that not < *lǣs,* less. See LESS.]

Lés•vos (lĕz′vôs). See **Lesbos.**

let¹ (lĕt) *v.* **let, let•ting, lets.** *—tr.* **1.** To give permission or opportunity to; allow. See Usage Note at **leave¹. 2.** To cause to; make. **3.a.** Used as an auxiliary in the imperative to express a command, request, or proposal: *Let x equal y.* **b.** Used as an auxiliary in the imperative to express a warning or threat: *Just let her try!* **4.** To permit to enter, proceed, or depart. **5.** To release from or as if from confinement. **6.** To rent or lease. **7.** To award, esp. after bids have been submitted. *—intr.* **1.** To become rented or leased. **2.** To be or become assigned, as to a contractor. ***—phrasal verbs.*** **let down. 1.** To cause to come down gradually; lower. **2.a.** To withdraw support from; forsake. **b.** To fail to meet the expectations of; disappoint. **let on. 1.** To allow to be known; admit. **2.** To pretend. **let out. 1.** To come to a close; end. **2.** To make known; reveal. **3.** To increase the size of (a garment, for example). **let up. 1.** To slow down; diminish. **2.** To come to a stop; cease. ***—idioms.*** **let alone.** Not to mention; much less. **let go.** To cease to employ; dismiss. **let off on.** *Informal.* To cause to diminish, as in pressure; ease up on. **let (one's) hair down.** To drop one's reserve or inhibitions. **let up on.** To be or become more lenient with. [ME *leten* < OE *lǣtan.* See **lē-*.**]

let² (lĕt) *n.* **1.** Something that hinders; an obstacle. **2.** *Sports.* An invalid stroke in net games that must be repeated. *—tr.v.* **let•ted** or **let, let•ting, lets.** *Archaic.* To hinder or obstruct. [ME *lette* < *letten,* to hinder < OE *lettan.* See **lē-*.**]

–let *suff.* **1.** Small one: *ringlet.* **2.** Something worn on: *armlet.* [ME < OFr. *-elet,* dim. suff. : *-el* (< Lat. *-ellus*) + *-et,* -et.]

letch also **lech** (lĕch) *n.* **1.** A strong, esp. sexual desire or craving. **2.** A lecher. [Perh. back-formation < obsolete *letcher,* var. of LECHER.]

let•down (lĕt′doun′) *n.* **1.** A decrease, decline, or relaxation, as of effort or energy. **2.** A disappointment. **3.** The descent made by an aircraft in order to land.

le•thal (lē′thəl) *adj.* **1.** Capable of causing death. **2.** Of, relating to, or causing death. **3.** Extremely harmful; devastating. [LLat. *lēthālis,* alteration of Lat. *lētālis* < *lētum,* death.] **—le•thal′i•ty** (lē-thăl′ĭ-tē) *n.* **—le′thal•ly** *adv.*

lethal gene *n.* A gene whose expression results in the death of the organism.

le•thar•gic (lə-thär′jĭk) *adj.* Of, causing, or characterized by lethargy. **—le•thar′gi•cal•ly** *adv.*

leth•ar•gy (lĕth′ər-jē) *n., pl.* **-gies. 1.** A state of sluggishness, inactivity, and apathy. **2.** A state of unconsciousness resembling deep sleep. [ME *letargie* < OFr. < LLat. *lēthārgia* < Gk. *lēthargia* < *lēthargos,* forgetful : *lēthē,* forgetfulness + *argos,* idle (*a-,* without; see A–¹ + *ergon,* work; see **werg-***).]

Leth•bridge (lĕth′brĭj′). A city of S Alberta, Canada, SSE of Calgary. Pop. 54,072.

le•the (lē′thē) *n.* **1. Lethe.** *Gk. Myth.* The river of forgetfulness, one of the five rivers in Hades. **2.** A condition of forgetfulness; oblivion. [Gk. *Lēthē.*] **—le′the•an** *adj.*

Le•to (lē′tō) *n. Gk. Myth.* A lover of Zeus and the mother of Apollo and Artemis.

let's (lĕts). Let us.

Lett (lĕt) *n.* A member of a Baltic people constituting the main population of Latvia. [Ger. *Lette* < Latvian *Latvi.*]

let•ter (lĕt′ər) *n.* **1.** A written symbol or character representing a speech sound and being a component of an alphabet. **2.** A written or printed communication directed to a person or an organization. **3.** A certified document granting rights to its bearer. Often used in the plural. **4.** Literal meaning: *the letter of the law.* **5. letters.** *(used with a sing. v.)* **a.** Literary culture; belles-lettres. **b.** Learning or knowledge, esp. of literature. **c.** Literature or writing as a profession. **6.** *Print.* **a.** A piece of type that prints a single character. **b.** A specific style of type. **c.** The characters in one style of type. **7.** An emblem in the shape of the initial of a school awarded for outstanding performance, esp. in varsity athletics. — *v.* **-tered, -ter•ing, -ters.** — *tr.* **1.** To write letters on. **2.** To write in letters. — *intr.* **1.** To write or form letters. **2.** To earn a school letter, as for outstanding athletic achievement. — *idiom.* **to the letter.** To the last detail; exactly: *followed instructions to the letter.* [ME < OFr. *lettre* < Lat. *littera*, perh. < Etruscan < Gk. *diphthera*, hide, leather, writing surface.] — **let′ter•er** *n.*

let•ter•box (lĕt′ər-bŏks′) *n.* See **mailbox** 2.

letter carrier *n.* A person who delivers mail.

let•tered (lĕt′ərd) *adj.* **1.a.** Educated to read and write; literate. **b.** Highly educated; learned. **2.** Of or relating to literacy or learning. **3.** Inscribed or marked with or as if with letters.

let•ter•form (lĕt′ər-fôrm′) *n.* The shape of an alphabet letter with regard to its development or design.

let•ter•head (lĕt′ər-hĕd′) *n.* **1.** The heading at the top of a sheet of letter paper, usu. consisting of a name and an address. **2.** Stationery imprinted with such a heading.

let•ter•ing (lĕt′ər-ĭng) *n.* **1.** The act, process, or art of forming letters. **2.** Letters inscribed, as on a sign.

let•ter•man (lĕt′ər-măn′, -mən) *n.* A student who has earned a letter in a particular activity, esp. a varsity sport.

letter of credence *n.* An official document conveying the credentials of a diplomatic envoy to a foreign government.

letter of credit *n., pl.* **letters of credit.** A letter issued by a bank authorizing the bearer to draw a stated amount of money from the issuing bank, its branches, or other associated banks or agencies.

letter of intent *n., pl.* **letters of intent.** A written statement expressing the intention of the undersigned to enter into a formal agreement, esp. a business arrangement or transaction.

letter of marque *n.* See **letters of marque.**

let•ter-per•fect (lĕt′ər-pûr′fĭkt) *adj.* Correct to the last detail, esp. being in or following the exact words.

let•ter•press (lĕt′ər-prĕs′) *n.* **1.a.** The process of printing from a raised inked surface. **b.** Something printed in this fashion. **2.** *Chiefly British.* The text, as of a book, distinct from illustrations or other ornamentation.

let•ter-qual•i•ty (lĕt′ər-kwŏl′ĭ-tē) *adj.* Of or producing printed characters similar in clarity to those produced by a conventional typewriter.

let•ters of administration (lĕt′ərz) *pl.n.* A legal document entrusting an individual with the administration of the estate of a deceased person.

letters of credence *pl.n.* See **letter of credence.**

letters of marque *pl.n.* **1.** A document issued by a nation allowing a private citizen to seize citizens or goods of another nation. **2.** A document issued by a nation allowing a private citizen to equip a ship with arms in order to attack enemy ships. [ME *letters of mark* < OFr. *marque*, mark, seizure, reprisal. See MARQUETRY.]

letters patent *pl.n.* A document issued by a government to a patentee granting an exclusive right to the enjoyment or possession of an invention.

letters testamentary *pl.n.* A document issued by a probate court or officer informing an executor of a will of his or her appointment and empowering the executor to discharge the appointed responsibilities.

Let•tish (lĕt′ĭsh) *adj.* Of or relating to the Letts or their language or culture. — *n.* See **Latvian** 2.

let•tuce (lĕt′əs) *n.* **1.a.** Any of various plants of the genus *Lactuca*, esp. *L. sativa*, having edible leaves. **b.** The leaves of *L. sativa*, used esp. in salads. **2.** *Slang.* Paper money. [ME *lettuse* < OFr. *laitues*, pl. of *laitue* < Lat. *lactūca* < *lac, lact-*, milk (< its milky juice). See **melg-***.]

let•up (lĕt′ŭp′) *n.* **1.** A reduction in pace, force, or intensity; a slowdown. **2.** A temporary stop; a pause.

le•u (lĕ′o͞o) *n., pl.* **lei** (lā). See table at **currency.** [Romanian < Lat. *leō*, lion. See LION.]

leu•cine (lo͞o′sēn′) *n.* An essential amino acid, $C_4H_9CH(NH_2)COOH$, derived from the hydrolysis of protein during digestion. [LEUC(O)- + -INE[2].]

leu•cite (lo͞o′sīt′) *n.* A white or gray mineral of potassium aluminum silicate, $KAlSi_2O_6$. — **leu•cit′ic** (-sĭt′ĭk) *adj.*

leu•co•plast (lo͞o′kə-plăst′) also **leu•co•plas•tid** (lo͞o′kə-plăs′tĭd) *n.* A colorless plastid in the cytoplasm of plant cells around which starch collects.

Leuc•tra (lo͞ok′trə). A village of ancient Greece SW of Thebes; site of a major Theban defeat of the Spartans (371 B.C.).

leu•ke•mi•a (lo͞o-kē′mē-ə) *n.* Any of various acute or chronic neoplastic diseases of the bone marrow in which unrestrained proliferation of white blood cells occurs, usu. accompanied by anemia and enlargement of the lymph nodes, liver, or spleen. — **leu•ke′mic** *adj. & n.*

leuko– or **leuk–** also **leuco–** or **leuc–** *pref.* **1.** White; colorless: *leukoderma.* **2.** Leukocyte: *leukopenia.* [Gk. < *leukos*, clear, white. See **leuk-***.]

leu•ko•cyte also **leu•co•cyte** (lo͞o′kə-sīt′) *n.* See **white blood cell.** — **leu′ko•cyt′ic** (-sĭt′ĭk) *adj.* — **leu′ko•cy′toid′** *adj.*

leu•ko•cy•to•sis also **leu•co•cy•to•sis** (lo͞o′kə-sī-tō′sĭs) *n., pl.* **-ses** (-sēz). An abnormally large increase in the number of white blood cells in the blood, often occurring during an acute infection or inflammation. — **leu′ko•cy•tot′ic** (-tŏt′ĭk) *adj.*

leu•ko•der•ma also **leu•co•der•ma** (lo͞o′kə-dûr′mə) *n.* Partial or total loss of skin pigmentation, often occurring in patches. — **leu′ko•der′mal, leu′ko•der′mic** *adj.*

leu•ko•pe•ni•a also **leu•co•pe•ni•a** (lo͞o′kə-pē′nē-ə) *n.* An abnormally low number of leukocytes in the circulating blood. — **leu′ko•pe′nic** *adj.*

leu•ko•pla•ki•a (lo͞o′kə-plā′kē-ə) *n.* An abnormal condition characterized by white spots or patches on mucous membranes, esp. of the mouth and vulva. [NLat. : LEUKO- + Gk. *plax, plak-*, flat area; see **plāk-**[1]* + -IA[1].]

leu•kor•rhe•a also **leu•cor•rhe•a** (lo͞o′kə-rē′ə) *n.* A thick whitish discharge from the vagina or cervical canal.

Leu•ven (lĕv′ən). See **Louvain.**

Leu•wen•hoek (lā′vən-ho͝ok′, lā′ü-wən-ho͝ok′), **Anton van.** See Anton van **Leeuwenhoek.**

lev (lĕf) *n., pl.* **lev•a** (lĕv′ə). See table at **currency.** [Bulgarian, lion, lev < Old Church Slavonic *lĭvŭ*, lion, prob. < OHGer. *lewo* < Lat. *leō.* See LION.]

lev– *pref.* Var. of **levo–.**

Lev. *abbr. Bible.* Leviticus.

Lev•al•loi•si•an (lĕv′ə-loi′zē-ən) *adj.* Of or relating to a western European stage in lower Paleolithic culture, characterized by a distinctive method of striking off flake tools from pieces of flint. [After, LEVALLOIS(-PERRET).]

Le•val•lois-Per•ret (lə-väl-wä′pĕ-rā′). A city of N-central France, a suburb of Paris on the Seine R. Pop. 53,500.

le•vant (lə-vănt′) *intr.v.* **-vant•ed, -vant•ing, -vants.** *Chiefly British.* To leave hurriedly or in secret to avoid unpaid debts. [Poss. < Sp. *levantar (el campo)*, to lift or break (camp) < VLat. **levantāre* < Lat. *levāns, levant-*, pr.part. of *levāre*, to raise. See LEVER.]

Le•vant[1] (lə-vănt′). The countries bordering on the E Mediterranean from Turkey to Egypt. — **Le′van•tine′** (lĕv′ən-tīn′, -tēn′, lə-văn′-) *adj. & n.*

Le•vant[2] (lə-vănt′) *n.* A heavy coarse-grained morocco leather often used in bookbinding. [After LEVANT[1].]

le•vant•er (lə-văn′tər) *n.* **1.** A strong easterly wind of the Mediterranean area. **2. Levanter.** A native or inhabitant of the Levant.

Levant morocco *n.* See **Levant**[2].

le•va•tor (lə-vā′tər) *n., pl.* **lev•a•to•res** (lĕv′ə-tôr′ēz, -tōr′-). **1.** *Anat.* A muscle that raises a bodily part. **2.** A surgical instrument for lifting the depressed fragments of a fractured skull. [NLat. < Med.Lat. *levātor*, one that raises < Lat. *levāre*, to raise. See LEVER.]

lev•ee[1] (lĕv′ē) *n.* **1.** An embankment raised to prevent a river from overflowing. **2.** A small ridge or raised area bordering an irrigated field. **3.** A landing place on a river; a pier. — *tr.v.* **lev•eed, lev•ee•ing, lev•ees.** To provide with a levee. [Fr. *levée* < OFr. *levee* < fem. p.part. of *lever*, to raise. See LEVER.]

levee[1]

lev•ee[2] (lĕv′ē, lə-vē′, -vā′) *n.* **1.** A reception held, as by royalty, upon arising from bed. **2.** A formal reception, as at a royal court. [< Fr. *lever*, a rising < OFr. < *lever*, to raise, rise. See LEVER.]

lev•el (lĕv′əl) *n.* **1.a.** Relative position or rank on a scale. **b.** A relative degree, as of achievement, intensity, or concentration. **2.** A natural or proper position, place, or stage. **3.** Position along a vertical axis; height or depth. **4.a.** A horizontal line or plane at right angles to the plumb. **b.** The position or height of such a line or plane. **5.** A flat horizontal surface. **6.** A land area of uniform elevation. **7.a.** An instrument for ascertaining whether a surface is horizontal, vertical, or at a 45° angle, consisting essentially of an encased liquid-filled tube containing an air bubble that moves to a center window when the instrument is set on an even plane. **b.** A level combined with a telescope and used in surveying. **c.** A computation of the difference in elevation between two points by using a level. — *adj.* **1.** Having a flat smooth surface. **2.** Being on a horizontal plane. **3.a.** Being at the same height or position as another; even. **b.** Being at the same degree of rank, standing, or advantage as another; equal. **4.** Exhibiting no abrupt variations; steady. **5.** Rational and balanced; sensible. **6.** Filled evenly to the top. — *v.* **-eled, -el•ing, -els** or **-elled, -el•ling, -els.** — *tr.* **1.** To make horizontal, flat, or even. **2.** To tear down; raze. **3.** To knock down with or as if with a blow. **4.** To place on the same level; equalize. **5.** To aim along a

ă pat	oi boy
ā pay	ou out
âr care	o͝o took
ä father	o͞o boot
ĕ pet	ŭ cut
ē be	ûr urge
ĭ pit	th thin
ī pie	*th* this
îr pier	hw which
ŏ pot	zh vision
ō toe	ə about, item
ô paw	

Stress marks:
′ (primary);
′ (secondary), as in
dictionary (dĭk′shə-nĕr′ē)

horizontal plane. **6.** To direct emphatically or forcefully toward someone: *leveled charges of dishonesty.* **7.** To measure the different elevations of (a tract of land) with a level. — *intr.* **1.** To bring persons or things to an equal level; equalize. **2.** To aim a weapon horizontally. **3.** *Informal.* To be frank and open. — *adv.* Along a flat or even line or plane. — ***phrasal verb.*** **level off. 1.** To move toward stability or consistency. **2.** To maneuver an aircraft into a flight attitude parallel to the surface of the earth after gaining or losing altitude. — ***idioms.*** **(one's) level best.** The best one can do in an earnest attempt. **on the level.** *Informal.* Without deception; honest. [ME, a level (instrument) < OFr. *livel* < VLat. **libellum* < Lat. *lībella*, dim. of *lībra*, balance.] — **lev′el·ly** *adv.* — **lev′el·ness** *n.*

level crossing *n. Chiefly British.* A grade crossing.

lev·el·er also **lev·el·ler** (lĕv′ə-lər) *n.* **1.** One that levels. **2.a.** One who advocates the abolition of social inequities. **b. Leveller.** A member of an English radical political movement arising in the 1640's and advocating universal male suffrage, parliamentary democracy, and religious tolerance.

lev·el·head·ed (lĕv′əl-hĕd′ĭd) *adj.* Characteristically self-composed and sensible. — **lev′el·head′ed·ness** *n.*

lev·el·ing rod (lĕv′ə-lĭng) *n.* A graduated pole or stick with a movable marker, used with a surveyor's level to measure differences in elevation.

level of significance *n., pl.* **levels of significance.** *Statistics.* The probability of a false rejection of the null hypothesis in a statistical test.

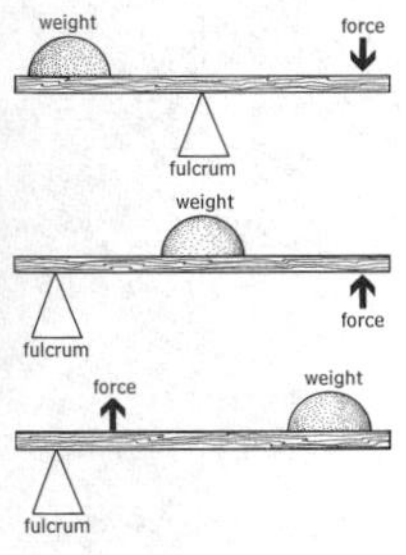

lever
Top: First-class lever, with fulcrum between weight and force
Center: Second-class lever, with weight between fulcrum and force
Bottom: Third-class lever, with force between fulcrum and weight

lev·er (lĕv′ər, lē′vər) *n.* **1.** A simple machine consisting of a rigid bar pivoted on a fixed point and used to transmit force, as in moving a weight at one end by pushing down on the other. **2.** A projecting handle used to adjust or operate a mechanism. **3.** A means of accomplishing; a tool: *friendship as a lever to obtain a job.* — *tr.v.* **-ered, -er·ing, -ers.** To move or lift with or as if with a lever. [ME < OFr. *levier* < *lever*, to raise < Lat. *levāre* < *levis*, light. See **legʷh-*.**]

lev·er·age (lĕv′ər-ĭj, lē′vər-) *n.* **1.a.** The action of a lever. **b.** The mechanical advantage of a lever. **2.** Positional advantage; power to act effectively. **3.** The use of credit or borrowed funds to improve one's speculative capacity and increase the rate of return from an investment, as in buying securities on margin. — *tr.v.* **-aged, -ag·ing, -ag·es. 1.a.** To provide (a company) with leverage. **b.** To supplement (money, for example) with leverage. **2.** To affect as if by leverage.

lev·er·aged buyout (lĕv′ər-ĭjd, lē′vər-ĭjd) *n.* The use of a target company's asset value to finance the debt incurred in acquiring the company.

lev·er·et (lĕv′ər-ĭt) *n.* A young hare, esp. one less than a year old. [ME < AN, dim. of *levere*, hare < Lat. *lepus, lepor-*.]

Le·ver·ku·sen (lā′vər-ko͞o′zən). A city of W-central Germany on the Rhine R. N of Cologne. Pop. 155,411.

Lé·vesque (lə-vĕk′), **René.** 1922–87. Canadian politician who cofounded (1967) the Parti Québecois.

Le·vi (lē′vī′). In the Bible, a son of Jacob and Leah and the forebear of one of the tribes of Israel.

lev·i·a·ble (lĕv′ē-ə-bəl) *adj.* **1.** That can be levied: *leviable taxes.* **2.** Liable to be taxed: *leviable imports.*

le·vi·a·than (lə-vī′ə-thən) *n.* **1.** Something unusually large of its kind, esp. a ship. **2.** A very large animal, esp. a whale. **3.** A monstrous sea creature mentioned in the Bible. [ME, huge biblical sea creature < LLat. < Heb. *liwyātān*.]

lev·i·gate (lĕv′ĭ-gāt′) *tr.v.* **-gat·ed, -gat·ing, -gates. 1.a.** To make into a smooth fine powder or paste, as by grinding when moist. **b.** To separate fine particles from coarse by grinding in water. **2.** To suspend in a liquid. **3.** To make smooth; polish. — *adj.* (-gāt′, -gĭt). Smooth. [Lat. *lēvigāre, lēvigāt-* : *lēvis*, smooth; see **lei-*** + *agere*, to make, do; see **ag-*.**] — **lev′i·ga′tion** *n.*

lev·in (lĕv′ĭn) *n. Archaic.* Lightning. [ME *levene, levin.* See **leuk-*.**]

lev·i·rate (lĕv′ər-ĭt, -ə-rāt′, lē′vər-ĭt, -və-rāt′) *n.* The practice of marrying the widow of one's brother to maintain his line, as required of Levite men by ancient Hebrew law. [< Lat. *lēvir*, husband's brother. See **daiwer-*.**]

Le·vi's (lē′vīz′). A trademark used for close-fitting trousers of heavy denim.

Lé·vis (lē′vĭs, lā-vē′). A city of S Quebec, Canada, on the St. Lawrence R.; settled in the mid-17th cent. Pop. 17,895.

Lé·vi-Strauss (lā′vē-strous′), **Claude.** b. 1908. French anthropologist who wrote *Structural Anthropology* (1958).

Levit. *abbr. Bible.* Leviticus.

lev·i·tate (lĕv′ĭ-tāt′) *intr. & tr.v.* **-tat·ed, -tat·ing, -tates.** To rise or cause to rise into the air and float in apparent defiance of gravity. [< Lat. *levis*, light. See LEVITY.] — **lev′i·ta′tion** *n.* — **lev′i·ta′tion·al** *adj.* — **lev′i·ta′tor** *n.*

Le·vite (lē′vīt′) *n. Bible.* A member of the tribe of Levi but not descended from Aaron, chosen to assist the Temple priests. [ME < LLat. *Lēvītēs, Lēvīta* < Gk. *Leuitēs* < *Leui*, Levi < Heb. *Lēwî*.]

Le·vit·i·cal (lə-vĭt′ĭ-kəl) also **Le·vit·ic** (-vĭt′ĭk) *adj. Bible.* **1.** Of or relating to the Levites. **2.** Of or relating to Leviticus.

Le·vit·i·cus (lə-vĭt′ĭ-kəs) *n.* See table at **Bible.** [ME < LLat. *Lēviticus* < Gk. *Leuitikos*, Levitical < *Leuitēs*, Levite. See LEVITE.]

Meriwether Lewis

Lev·it·town (lĕv′ĭt-toun′). **1.** An unincorp. community of SE NY on W Long I. ESE of Mineola; founded 1947. Pop. 53,286. **2.** A community of SE PA near the Delaware R. NE of Philadelphia. Pop. 55,362.

lev·i·ty (lĕv′ĭ-tē) *n., pl.* **-ties. 1.** Lightness of manner or speech, esp. when inappropriate; frivolity. **2.** Inconstancy; changeableness. **3.** The state or quality of being light; buoyancy. [Lat. *levitās* < *levis*, light. See **legʷh-*.**]

le·vo (lē′vō) *adj.* Levorotatory.

levo– or **lev–** *pref.* **1.** To the left: *levorotatory.* **2.** Levorotatory: *levulose.* [Fr. *lévo-* < Lat. *laevus*, left.]

le·vo·do·pa (lē′və-dō′pə) *n.* See **L-dopa.**

le·vo·ro·ta·tion (lē′və-rō-tā′shən) *n.* A counterclockwise rotation, esp. of the plane of polarized light.

le·vo·ro·ta·to·ry (lē′və-rō′tə-tôr′ē, -tōr′ē) also **le·vo·ro·ta·ry** (-tə-rē) *adj.* **1.** Turning or rotating the plane of polarization of light to the left, or counterclockwise. **2.** Of or relating to a chemical solution that rotates the plane of polarized light to the left, or counterclockwise.

lev·u·lose (lĕv′yə-lōs′, -lōz′) *n.* See **fructose.** [LEVO– + –UL(E) + –OSE[2].]

lev·y (lĕv′ē) *v.* **-ied, -y·ing, -ies.** — *tr.* **1.** To impose or collect (a tax, for example). **2.** To draft into military service. **3.** To declare and wage (a war). — *intr.* To confiscate property, esp. in accordance with a legal judgment. — *n., pl.* **-ies. 1.** The act or process of levying. **2.** Money, property, or troops levied. [ME *levien* < *leve*, levy, tax < OFr. *levee* < fem. p.part. of *lever*, to raise. See LEVER.] — **lev′i·er** *n.*

lewd (lo͞od) *adj.* **lewd·er, lewd·est. 1.a.** Preoccupied with sex and sexual desire; lustful. **b.** Obscene; indecent. **2.** *Obsolete.* Wicked. [ME *leued*, unlearned, lay, lascivious < OE *lǣwede*, ignorant, lay.] — **lewd′ly** *adv.* — **lewd′ness** *n.*

Lew·es River (lo͞o′ĭs). The upper course, c. 544 km (338 mi), of the Yukon R. above its junction with the Pelly R. in S Yukon Terr., Canada.

lew·is (lo͞o′ĭs) *n.* A dovetailed iron tenon designed to fit into a dovetail mortise in a large stone so that it can be lifted by a hoisting apparatus. [Perh. < the name *Lewis*.]

Lew·is (lo͞o′ĭs), **Cecil Day.** See Cecil **Day Lewis.**

Lewis, C(live) S(taples). 1898–1963. British writer and critic whose works include *The Screwtape Letters* (1942).

Lewis, (Harry) Sinclair. 1885–1951. Amer. novelist who was the first American to win a Nobel Prize for literature (1930).

Lewis, John Llewellyn. 1880–1969. Amer. labor leader who was president of the United Mine Workers of America (1920–60) and the Congress of Industrial Organizations (1935–40).

Lewis, Meriwether. 1774–1809. Amer. soldier and explorer who led the Lewis and Clark expedition (1803–06) from St. Louis to the mouth of the Columbia R.

Lewis, (Percy) Wyndham. 1884–1957. British writer and artist whose novels include *The Apes of God* (1930).

lew·is·ite (lo͞o′ĭ-sīt′) *n.* An oily colorless to violet or brown liquid, $C_2H_2AsCl_3$, used to make a highly toxic gas weapon. [After Winford Lee *Lewis* (1878–1943), Amer. chemist.]

lew·is·son (lo͞o′ĭ-sən) *n.* See **lewis.** [< LEWIS.]

Lew·is·ton (lo͞o′ĭ-stən). **1.** A city of NW ID on the border SSE of Spokane WA. Pop. 28,082. **2.** A city of SW ME on the Androscoggin R. N of Portland; settled in 1770. Pop. 39,757.

Lew·is·ville (lo͞o′ĭs-vĭl′, lo͞o′ē-). A city of NE TX, a suburb in the Dallas–Fort Worth area. Pop. 46,521.

Lewis with Har·ris (hăr′ĭs). An island of NW Scotland, the largest and northernmost of the Outer Hebrides.

lex (lĕks) *n., pl.* **le·ges** (lē′jēz′). Law. [Lat. *lēx.* See **leg-*.**]

lex. *abbr.* Lexicon.

lex·eme (lĕk′sēm′) *n.* The fundamental unit of the lexicon of a language; for example, *find, found,* and *finding* are members of the English lexeme *find.* [LEX(ICON) + –EME.]

lex·i·cal (lĕk′sĭ-kəl) *adj.* **1.** Of or relating to the vocabulary, words, or morphemes of a language. **2.** Of or relating to lexicography or a lexicon. [LEXIC(ON) + –AL[1].] — **lex′·i·cal′i·ty** (-kăl′ĭ-tē) *n.* — **lex′i·cal·ly** *adv.*

lex·i·cog·ra·phy (lĕk′sĭ-kŏg′rə-fē) *n.* The process or work of writing or compiling a dictionary. [LEXICO(N) + –GRAPHY.] — **lex′i·cog′ra·pher** *n.* — **lex′i·co·graph′ic** (-kə-grăf′ĭk), **lex′i·co·graph′i·cal** (-ĭ-kəl) *adj.*

lex·i·col·o·gy (lĕk′sĭ-kŏl′ə-jē) *n.* The branch of linguistics that deals with the lexical component of language. — **lex′i·co·log′i·cal** (-kə-lŏj′ĭ-kəl) *adj.* — **lex′i·col′o·gist** *n.*

lex·i·con (lĕk′sĭ-kŏn′) *n., pl.* **-cons** or **-ca** (-kə). **1.** A dictionary. **2.** A stock of terms used in a particular profession, subject, or style; a vocabulary. **3.** *Ling.* The morphemes of a language considered as a group. [Med.Lat. < Gk. *lexikon (biblion)*, word(book) < neut. of *lexikos*, of words < *lexis*, word < *legein*, to speak. See **leg-*.**]

Lex·ing·ton (lĕk′sĭng-tən). **1.** A city of NE-central Kentucky ESE of Louisville. Pop. 204,165. **2.** A town of NE MA, a suburb of Boston; site of the battle (Apr. 19, 1775) that marked the start of the American Revolution. Pop. 28,974.

lex·is (lĕk′sĭs) *n.* The total set of words in a language as distinct from morphology. [Gk., speech, word. See LEXICON.]

ley (lā, lē) *n.* Var. of **lea.**

Ley•den (līd′n). See **Leiden.**

Leyden jar *n.* An early form of capacitor consisting of a glass jar lined inside and out with tinfoil and a conducting rod. [After *Leyden* (Leiden).]

Ley•land (lā′lənd). An urban district of NW England NNE of Liverpool. Pop. 97,700.

Ley•te (lā′tē, -tĕ). An island of the E-central Philippines in the Visayan group N of Mindanao.

Leyte Gulf. An inlet of the W Pacific in the Philippines S of Samar and E of Leyte. An invasion force led by Gen. Douglas MacArthur defeated the Japanese here on Oct. 25–26, 1944.

lf *abbr. Print.* Lightface.

LF 1. *Baseball.* Left field; left fielder. **2.** Or **lf.** Low frequency.

lg. *abbr.* **1.** Large. **2.** Long.

lge. *abbr.* Large.

LH *abbr.* Luteinizing hormone.

Lha•sa (lä′sə, lăs′ə). A city of SW China, the cap. of Xizang (Tibet); long known as "the Forbidden City." Pop. 105,897.

Lhasa ap•so (ăp′sō) *n., pl.* **-sos.** Any of a breed of small dog originating in Tibet and having a long straight coat. [Lhasa + Tibetan *apso,* Lhasa apso.]

Lho•tse (lō′tsĕ′). A peak, 8,506.5 m (27,890 ft), of the central Himalaya Mts. on the Nepal-Xizang (Tibet) border.

li[1] (lē) *n., pl.* **li.** A traditional Chinese measure of distance, today standardized at 500 meters (547 yards). [Chin. (Mandarin) *lǐ.*]

li[2] *abbr.* Link.

Li The symbol for the element **lithium.**

L.I. *abbr.* Long Island.

li•a•bil•i•ty (lī′ə-bĭl′ĭ-tē) *n., pl.* **-ties. 1.** The state of being liable. **2.a.** Something for which one is liable; an obligation, a responsibility, or a debt. **b. liabilities.** The financial obligations entered in the balance sheet of a business enterprise. **3.** Something that holds one back; a handicap. **4.** Likelihood.

li•a•ble (lī′ə-bəl) *adj.* **1.** Legally obligated; responsible. See Syns at **responsible. 2.** At risk of or subject to experiencing or suffering something unpleasant. Used with *to.* **3.** Likely. Often used with reference to an unfavorable outcome. [ME, prob. < OFr. *lier,* to bind < Lat. *ligāre.* See **leig-*.**]

Usage Note: *Liable, apt,* and *likely* are often used interchangeably in constructions with following infinitives, as in *John is liable to lose, John is apt to lose,* and *John is likely to lose.* The three words are distinct in meaning. A widely repeated rule holds that *liable* should only be used if the subject would be adversely affected by the outcome expressed by the infinitive. The rule therefore permits *John is liable to fall out of his chair if he doesn't sit up straight* but not *The chair is liable to be slippery. Apt* usually suggests a natural tendency enhancing the probability of an outcome about which the speaker is apprehensive: *The fuel pump is apt to give out at any minute. Likely* ascribes no particular property to the subject that enhances the probability of the outcome: while *John is apt to lose the election* may suggest that the loss will result from something John does or fails to do, *John is likely to lose the election* does not. Nor does it suggest anything about the desirability of the outcome from the point of view of either the speaker or the subject. See Usage Note at **likely.**

li•aise (lē-āz′) *intr.v.* **-aised, -ais•ing, -ais•es. 1.** To effect or establish a liaison. **2.** To act or serve as a liaison officer.

li•ai•son (lē′ā-zŏn′, lē-ā′-) *n.* **1.a.** An instance or a means of communication between different groups or units of an organization, esp. in the armed forces. **b.** One that maintains communication: *the President's liaison with Congress.* **2.a.** A close relationship, connection, or link. **b.** An adulterous relationship; an affair. **3.** *Ling.* Pronunciation of the usu. silent final consonant of a word when followed by a word beginning with a vowel, esp. in French. [Fr. < OFr. < Lat. *ligātiō, ligātiōn-* < *ligātus,* p.part. of *ligāre,* to bind. See LIGATE.]

li•an•a (lē-ä′nə, -ăn′ə) also **li•ane** (-än′, -ăn′) *n.* Any of various climbing, woody, usu. tropical vines. [Alteration of Fr. *liane,* prob. < *lier,* to bind. See LIABLE.]

Liang (lyäng′). Two Chinese dynasties, the **Earlier Liang** (502–557) and the **Later Liang** (907–923).

Liao (lyou′). A Chinese dynasty that ruled from 916 to 1125.

Liao•dong (lyou′dŭng′) also **Liao•tung** (-to͝ong′), **Gulf of.** The N part of the Gulf of Bo Hai in NE China bordering on the **Liaodong Peninsula,** projecting SW into the Yellow Sea.

Liao He (hə′). A river of NE China flowing c. 1,448 km (900 mi) to the Gulf of Liaodong.

Liao•ning (lyou′nĭng′). A province of NE China on the Gulf of Bo Hai and Korea Bay; under Japanese control from 1932 to 1945. Cap. Shenyang. Pop. 36,860,000.

Liao•yang (lyou′yäng′). A city of NE China SSW of Shenyang; one of the oldest cities in Manchuria. Pop. 275,000.

li•ar (lī′ər) *n.* One that tells lies.

Li•ard (lē′ərd, lē-ärd′). A river rising in SE Yukon Terr., Canada, and flowing c. 1,215 km (755 mi) to the Mackenzie R. in SW Northwest Terrs.

lib (lĭb) *n. Informal.* A movement that seeks to achieve equal rights for a group; liberation.

lib. *abbr.* **1.** Or **Lib.** Liberal; Liberalism. **2.** Library.

li•ba•tion (lī-bā′shən) *n.* **1.a.** The pouring of a liquid offering as a religious ritual. **b.** The liquid so poured. **2.** *Informal.* **a.** A beverage, esp. an intoxicating beverage. **b.** The act of drinking an intoxicating beverage. [ME *libacioun* < Lat. *lībātiō, lībātiōn-* < *lībātus,* p.part. of *lībāre,* to pour out as an offering.] **—li•ba′tion•ar′y** (-shə-nĕr′ē) *adj.*

Lib•by (lĭb′ē), **Willard Frank.** 1908–80. Amer. chemist who won a 1960 Nobel Prize.

li•bel (lī′bəl) *Law.* —*n.* **1.a.** A false publication in writing, printing, or typewriting or in signs or pictures that maliciously damages a person's reputation. **b.** The act or an instance of presenting such a statement to the public. **2.** The written claims presented by a plaintiff in an action at admiralty law or to an ecclesiastical court. —*tr.v.* **-beled, -bel•ing, -bels** or **-belled, -bel•ling, -bels.** To communicate a false statement about in writing or by means of signs or pictures. [ME, litigant's written complaint < OFr. < Lat. *libellus,* dim. of *liber,* book.] **—li′bel•er, li′bel•ist** *n.*

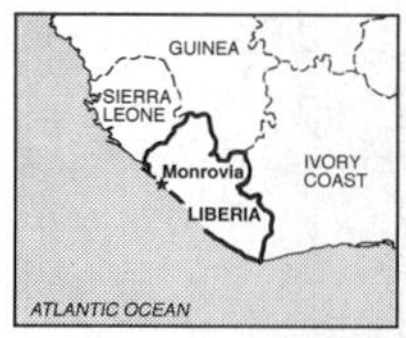

Liberia

li•bel•ant also **li•bel•lant** (lī′bə-lənt) *n. Law.* The plaintiff in a case of ecclesiastical or admiralty libel.

li•bel•ee also **li•bel•lee** (lī′bə-lē′) *n. Law.* The defendant in a case of ecclesiastical or admiralty libel.

li•bel•ous also **li•bel•lous** (lī′bə-ləs) *adj. Law.* Involving or constituting a libel; defamatory. **—li′bel•ous•ly** *adv.*

lib•er•al (lĭb′ər-əl, lĭb′rəl) *adj.* **1.a.** Not limited to or by traditional, orthodox, or authoritarian attitudes or dogmas; free from bigotry. **b.** Favoring proposals for reform, open to new ideas for progress, and tolerant of the ideas and behavior of others; broad-minded. **c.** Of, relating to, or characteristic of liberalism. **d. Liberal.** Of, being, or characteristic of a political party founded on or associated with principles of social and political liberalism, esp. in Great Britain and Canada. **2.a.** Tending to give freely; generous. **b.** Generous in amount; ample. **3.** Not strict or literal; loose or approximate: *a liberal translation.* **4.** Of, relating to, or based on the traditional arts and sciences of a college or university curriculum. **5.a.** *Archaic.* Permissible or appropriate for a person of free birth; befitting a lady or gentleman. **b.** *Obsolete.* Morally unrestrained; licentious. —*n.* **1.** A person with liberal ideas or opinions. **2. Liberal.** A member of a Liberal political party. [ME, generous < OFr. < Lat. *līberālis* < *līber,* free. See **leudh-*.**] **—lib′er•al•ly** *adv.* **—lib′er•al•ness** *n.*

Syns: *liberal, bounteous, bountiful, freehanded, generous, handsome, munificent, openhanded.* The central meaning shared by these adjectives is "willing or marked by a willingness to give unstintingly": *a liberal donor; a bounteous feast; bountiful compliments; a freehanded host; a generous donation; a handsome offer; a munificent gift; an openhanded grandfather.* See also Syns at **broad-minded.** ***Ant:*** *stingy.*

liberal arts *pl.n.* **1.** Academic disciplines, such as languages, literature, history, philosophy, mathematics, and science, that provide information of general cultural concern. **2.** The disciplines comprising the trivium and quadrivium. [ME, transl. of Med.Lat. *artēs līberālēs,* the trivium and quadrivium : Lat. *artēs,* pl. of Lat. *ars, art-,* subject of study + *līberālēs,* pl. of *līberālis,* proper to free persons.]

lib•er•al•ism (lĭb′ər-ə-lĭz′əm, lĭb′rə-) *n.* **1.** The state or quality of being liberal. **2.a.** A political theory favoring civil and political liberties, government by law with the consent of the governed, and protection from arbitrary authority. **b.** Often **Liberalism.** The tenets or policies of a Liberal party. **3.** An economic theory in favor of laissez-faire, the free market, and the gold standard. **4.a.** A 19th-century Protestant movement that favored free intellectual inquiry, stressed the ethical and humanitarian content of Christianity, and de-emphasized dogmatic theology. **b.** A 19th-century Roman Catholic movement that favored political democracy and ecclesiastical reform. **—lib′er•al•ist** *n.* **—lib′er•al•is′tic** (-lĭs′tĭk) *adj.*

lib•er•al•i•ty (lĭb′ə-răl′ĭ-tē) *n., pl.* **-ties. 1.** The quality or state of being liberal or generous. **2.** An instance of being liberal.

lib•er•al•ize (lĭb′ər-ə-līz′, lĭb′rə-) *v.* **-ized, -iz•ing, -iz•es.** —*tr.* To make liberal or more liberal. —*intr.* To become liberal or more liberal. **—lib′er•al•i•za′tion** (-lĭ-zā′shən) *n.* **—lib′er•al•iz′er** *n.*

lib•er•ate (lĭb′ə-rāt′) *tr.v.* **-at•ed, -at•ing, -ates. 1.** To set free, as from oppression, confinement, or foreign control. **2.** *Chem.* To release (a gas, for example) from combination. **3.** *Slang.* To obtain by illegal means, as by looting. [Lat. *līberāre, līberāt-* < *līber,* free. See **leudh-*.**] **—lib′er•a′tor** *n.*

lib•er•a•tion (lĭb′ə-rā′shən) *n.* **1.** The act of liberating or the state of being liberated. **2.** The act or process of trying to achieve equal rights and status. **—lib′er•a′tion•ist** *n.*

liberation theology *n.* A school of theology that finds in the Gospel a call to free people from political, social, and economic oppression. **—liberation theologian** *n.*

Li•be•rec (lĭb′ə-rĕts′). A city of N-central Czech Republic NNE of Prague; founded c. 1350. Pop. 100,048.

Li•be•ri•a (lī-bîr′ē-ə). A country of W Africa on the Atlantic Ocean; founded 1821 and gained independence in 1847. Cap. Monrovia. Pop. 1,911,000. **—Li•be′ri•an** *adj. & n.*

lib•er•tar•i•an (lĭb′ər-târ′ē-ən) *n.* **1.** One who believes in

ă **pat**	oi **boy**
ā **pay**	ou **out**
âr **care**	o͝o **took**
ä **father**	o͞o **boot**
ĕ **pet**	ŭ **cut**
ē **be**	ûr **urge**
ĭ **pit**	th **thin**
ī **pie**	*th* **this**
îr **pier**	hw **which**
ŏ **pot**	zh **vision**
ō **toe**	ə **about,**
ô **paw**	**item**

Stress marks:
′ (primary);
′ (secondary), as in
dictionary (dĭk′shə-nĕr′ē)

freedom of action and thought. **2.** One who believes in free will. [< LIBERTY.] — **lib′er•tar′i•an•ism** *n.*

lib•er•tin•age (lĭb′ər-tē′nĭj) *n.* Libertinism.

lib•er•tine (lĭb′ər-tēn′) *n.* **1.** One who acts without moral restraint; a dissolute person. **2.** One who defies established religious precepts; a freethinker. — *adj.* Morally unrestrained; dissolute. [ME, freedman < Lat. *lībertīnus* < *lībertus* < *līber*, free. See **leudh-***.]

lib•er•tin•ism (lĭb′ər-tē-nĭz′əm) *n.* **1.** The state or quality of being libertine. **2.** The behavior characteristic of a libertine.

lib•er•ty (lĭb′ər-tē) *n.*, *pl.* **-ties. 1.a.** The condition of being free from restriction or control. **b.** The right and power to act, believe, or express oneself in a manner of one's own choosing. **c.** The condition of being physically and legally free from confinement, servitude, or forced labor. See Syns at **freedom. 2.** Freedom from unjust or undue governmental control. **3.** A right and power to engage in certain actions without control or interference. **4.a.** A breach or overstepping of propriety or social convention. Often used in the plural. **b.** A statement, an attitude, or an action not warranted by conditions or actualities. Often used in the plural. **c.** An unwarranted risk; a chance. Often used in the plural. **5.** A period, usu. short, during which a sailor is authorized to go ashore. — ***idiom.* at liberty. 1.** Not in confinement or under constraint; free. **2.** Not employed, occupied, or in use. [ME *liberte* < OFr. < Lat. *lībertās* < *līber*, free. See **leudh-***.]

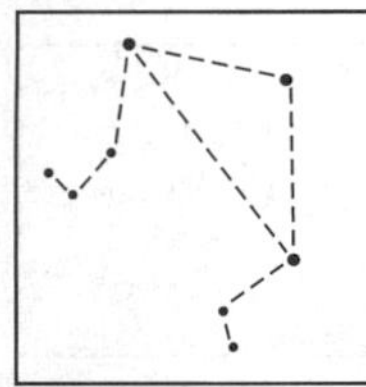
Libra

Lib•er•ty (lĭb′ər-tē). A city of W MO, a suburb of Kansas City. Pop. 20,459.

liberty cap *n.* A conical cap fitting snugly around the head, given to a slave in ancient Rome upon manumission and used as a symbol of liberty by the French revolutionaries.

Liberty Island. Formerly **Bed•loe's Island** (bĕd′lōz). An island of SE NY in Upper New York Bay SW of Manhattan; site of the Statue of Liberty.

Lib•er•ty•ville (lĭb′ər-tē-vĭl′). A village of NE IL SW of Waukegan. Pop. 19,174.

li•bid•i•nous (lĭ-bĭd′n-əs) *adj.* Having or exhibiting lustful desires; lascivious. [ME, ult. < *libīdō, libīdin-*, lust. See LIBIDO.] — **li•bid′i•nous•ly** *adv.* — **li•bid′i•nous•ness** *n.*

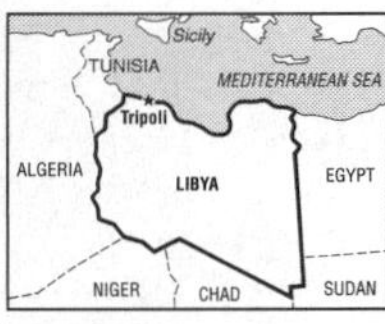

Libya

li•bi•do (lĭ-bē′dō, -bī′-) *n.*, *pl.* **-dos. 1.** The energy associated with instinctual biological drives. **2.a.** Sexual desire. **b.** Manifestation of the sexual drive. [Lat. *libīdō*, desire. See **leubh-***.] — **li•bid′i•nal** (-bĭd′n-əl) *adj.* — **li•bid′i•nal•ly** *adv.*

Li Bo (lē′ bō′). See **Li Po.**

li•bra (lē′brə) *n.*, *pl.* **-brae** (-brē′). A unit of weight in ancient Rome equivalent to about 12 ounces. [ME < Lat. *lībra.*]

Li•bra (lē′brə, lī′-) *n.* **1.** A constellation in the Southern Hemisphere near Scorpius and Virgo. **2.a.** The seventh sign of the zodiac in astrology. **b.** One born under this sign. [ME < Lat. *lībra*, balance, the constellation Libra.]

li•brar•i•an (lī-brâr′ē-ən) *n.* A specialist in library work. — **li•brar′i•an•ship′** *n.*

li•brar•y (lī′brĕr′ē) *n.*, *pl.* **-ies. 1.a.** A place in which literary and artistic materials, such as books, newspapers, and tapes, are kept for reading, reference, or lending. **b.** A collection of such materials, esp. when systematically arranged. **c.** A room in a private home for such a collection. **d.** An institution or a foundation maintaining such a collection. **2.** A commercial establishment that lends books for a fee. **3.** A series or set of books issued by a publisher. **4.** A collection of recorded data or tapes arranged for ease of use. **5.** *Comp. Sci.* A collection of standard programs, routines, or subroutines, often related to a specific application, that are available for general use. [ME *librarie* < AN < Lat. *librārium*, bookcase < neut. of *librārius*, of books < *liber, libr-*, book.]

lichen
Growing on a tree limb

library science *n.* The principles, practice, or study of library administration.

li•bra•tion (lī-brā′shən) *n.* A very slow oscillation, real or apparent, of a satellite as viewed from the larger celestial body around which it revolves. [Lat. *lībrātio, lībrātiōn-*, oscillation < *lībrātus*, p.part. of *lībrāre*, to balance < *lībra*, balance.] — **li•bra′tion•al** *adj.* — **li′bra•to′ry** (-brə-tôr′ē, -tōr′ē) *adj.*

li•bret•tist (lĭ-brĕt′ĭst) *n.* *Mus.* The author of a libretto.

li•bret•to (lĭ-brĕt′ō) *n.*, *pl.* **-bret•tos** or **-bret•ti** (-brĕt′ē). *Mus.* **1.** The text of a dramatic musical work, such as an opera. **2.** A book containing such a text. [Ital., dim. of *libro*, book < Lat. *liber, libr-*.]

Li•bre•ville (lē′brə-vĭl′, -vēl′). The cap. of Gabon, in the NW part on the Gulf of Guinea; named after freed slaves who settled there in 1848. Pop. 235,700.

Lib•ri•um (lĭb′rē-əm). A trademark used for preparations of chlordiazepoxide hydrochloride.

Lib•y•a (lĭb′ē-ə). A country of N Africa on the Mediterranean Sea; achieved independence in 1951. Cap. Tripoli. Pop. 3,096,000.

Liechtenstein

Lib•y•an (lĭb′ē-ən) *adj.* Of or relating to Libya or its people, language, or culture. — *n.* **1.** A native or inhabitant of Libya. **2.** A Berber language of ancient northern Africa.

Libyan Desert. A section of the Sahara Desert of NE Africa in Egypt, Libya, and Sudan.

lice (līs) *n.* Pl. of **louse** 1.

li•cence (lī′səns) *n.* & *v.* *Chiefly British.* Var. of **license.**

li•cense (lī′səns) *n.* **1.a.** Official or legal permission to do or own a specified thing. **b.** Proof of permission granted, usu. in the form of a document, card, plate, or tag: *a driver's license.* **2.** Deviation from normal rules, practices, or methods to achieve a certain end or effect. **3.** Latitude of action, esp. in behavior or speech. See Syns at **freedom. 4.a.** Lack of due restraint; excessive freedom. **b.** Heedlessness for the precepts of proper behavior; licentiousness. — *tr.v.* **-censed, -cens•ing, -cens•es. 1.** To give or yield permission to or for. **2.** To grant a license to or for; authorize. [ME *licence* < OFr. < Med.Lat. *licentia*, authorization < Lat., freedom < *licēns, licent-*, pr.part. of *licēre*, to be permitted.] — **li′cens•a•ble** *adj.* — **li′cens•er, li′cen•sor′** (-sən-sôr′) *n.*

li•censed practical nurse (lī′sənst) *n.* A nurse who has completed a practical nursing program and is licensed by a state to provide routine patient care under the direction of a registered nurse or a physician.

licensed vocational nurse *n.* A licensed practical nurse who is permitted by license to practice in California or Texas.

li•cens•ee (lī′sən-sē′) *n.* One granted a license.

li•cen•sure (lī′sən-shər, -shŏŏr′) *n.* The act or an instance of granting a license, usu. to practice a profession.

li•cen•ti•ate (lī-sĕn′shē-ĭt) *n.* **1.** One granted a license by an authorized body to practice a specified profession. **2.a.** A degree from certain European universities ranking just below that of a doctor. **b.** One holding such a degree. [ME < Med. Lat. *licentiātus* < p.part. of *licentiāre*, to allow < *licentia*, authorization. See LICENSE.]

li•cen•tious (lī-sĕn′shəs) *adj.* **1.** Lacking moral discipline or ignoring legal restraint, esp. in sexual conduct. **2.** Having no regard for accepted rules or standards. [< Lat. *licentiōsus* < *licentia*, freedom, license. See LICENSE.] — **li•cen′tious•ly** *adv.* — **li•cen′tious•ness** *n.*

li•chee (lē′chē) *n.* Var. of **litchi.**

li•chen (lī′kən) *n.* **1.** A fungus, usu. of the class Ascomycetes, that grows symbiotically with algae, resulting in a composite organism that characteristically forms a crustlike or branching growth on rocks or tree trunks. **2.** *Pathol.* Any of various skin diseases characterized by patchy eruptions of small firm papules. — *tr.v.* **-chened, -chen•ing, -chens.** To cover with lichens. [Lat. *līchēn*, a kind of plant < Gk. *leikhēn* < *leikhein*, to lick. See **leigh-***.] — **li′chen•ous** *adj.*

li•chen•ol•o•gy (lī′kə-nŏl′ə-jē) *n.* The branch of biology that deals with the study of lichens. — **li′chen•ol′o•gist** *n.*

lich gate (lĭch) *n.* Var. of **lych-gate.**

Lich•ten•stein (lĭk′tən-stīn′, -stēn′), **Roy.** b. 1923. Amer. pop artist best known for his depictions of comic book panels.

lic•it (lĭs′ĭt) *adj.* Permitted by law; legal. [ME < OFr. *licite* < Lat. *licitus*, p.part. of *licēre*, to be permitted.] — **lic′it•ly** *adv.*

lick (lĭk) *v.* **licked, lick•ing, licks.** — *tr.* **1.** To pass the tongue over or along. **2.** To lap up. **3.** To lap or flicker at like a tongue. **4.** *Slang.* To punish with a beating; thrash. **5.** *Slang.* To get the better of; defeat. — *intr.* To pass or lap quickly and rapidly. — *n.* **1.** The act or process of licking. **2.** A small quantity; a bit: *a lick of sense.* **3.** A deposit of exposed natural salt that is licked by passing animals. **4.** A sudden hard stroke; a blow. **5.** *Informal.* Speed; pace. **6.** *Mus.* A phrase improvised by a soloist, esp. on the guitar or banjo. — ***idioms.* lick and a promise.** A superficial effort made without care or enthusiasm. **lick into shape.** *Informal.* To bring into satisfactory condition or appearance. **lick (one's) chops.** To anticipate delightedly. **lick (one's) wounds.** To recuperate after a defeat. [ME *licken* < OE *liccian.* See **leigh-***.] — **lick′er** *n.*

lick•er•ish (lĭk′ər-ĭsh) *adj.* **1.** Lascivious; lecherous. **2.** Greedy; desirous. **3.a.** *Archaic.* Relishing good food. **b.** *Obsolete.* Arousing hunger; appetizing. [ME *likerous*, perh. < OFr. *lecheor, lekier.* See LECHER.] — **lick′er•ish•ness** *n.*

lick•e•ty-split (lĭk′ĭ-tē-splĭt′) *adv.* *Informal.* With great speed. [*lickety*, very fast, alteration of LICK, fast (dialectal) + SPLIT.]

lick•ing (lĭk′ĭng) *n.* *Slang.* **1.** A beating, thrashing, or spanking. **2.** A severe loss or defeat.

Lick•ing River (lĭk′ĭng). A river of NE KY flowing c. 515 km (320 mi) to the Ohio R.

lick•spit•tle (lĭk′spĭt′l) *n.* A fawning underling; a toady.

lic•o•rice (lĭk′ər-ĭs, -ĭsh) *n.* **1.a.** A Mediterranean perennial plant *(Glycyrrhiza glabra)* having blue flowers, pinnately compound leaves, and a sweet root. **b.** The root of this plant, used as a flavoring. **c.** A confection made from or flavored with the licorice root. **2.** Any of various similar plants. [ME < OFr. < LLat. *liquirītia*, alteration (influenced by Lat. *liquēre*, to flow) of Lat. *glycyrrhīza*, root of licorice < Gk. *glukurrhiza* : *glukus*, sweet + *rhiza*, root; see **wrād-***.]

lic•tor (lĭk′tər) *n.* A Roman functionary who carried fasces when attending a magistrate in public appearances. [< ME *littoures*, lictors < Lat. *lictōrēs*, pl. of *lictor.* See **leig-***.]

lid (lĭd) *n.* **1.** A removable or hinged cover for a hollow receptacle or box. **2.** An eyelid. **3.** *Biol.* A flaplike covering. **4.** A curb, restraint, or limit. **5.** *Informal.* An act of concealment; a cover. **6.** *Slang.* A hat. **7.** *Slang.* An ounce of marijuana. — *tr.v.* **lid•ded, lid•ding, lids.** To cover with or as if with a lid. [ME < OE *hlid.* See **klei-***.]

Li•di•ce (lĭd′ĭ-sē, -chā′, lyĭ′dĭ-tsĕ). A village of NW Czech Republic WNW of Prague. In reprisal for the murder of a Nazi official, German forces killed or deported its entire population to concentration camps (Jun. 9–10, 1942).
lid•less (lĭd′lĭs) *adj.* Having no lid or lids.
Li•do (lē′dō). An island reef of NE Italy separating the lagoon of Venice from the Adriatic Sea.
li•do•caine (lī′də-kān′) *n.* A synthetic amide, $C_{14}H_{22}N_2O$, used chiefly in the form of its hydrochloride as a local anesthetic and antiarrhythmic agent. [(ACETANI)LID(E) + -CAINE.]
lie[1] (lī) *intr.v.* **lay** (lā), **lain** (lān), **ly•ing** (lī′ĭng), **lies. 1.** To be or place oneself at rest in a flat, horizontal, or recumbent position; recline. **2.** To be placed on or supported by a surface that is usu. horizontal. See Usage Note at **lay**[1]. **3.** To be or remain in a specified condition. **4.** To exist; be inherent. **5.** To occupy a position or place. **6.** To extend: *Our land lies along the river.* **7.** *Law.* To be admissible or maintainable. **8.** *Archaic.* To stay for a night or short while. —*n.* **1.** The manner or position in which something is situated. **2.** A haunt or hiding place of an animal. **3.** *Sports.* The position of a golf ball that has come to a stop. —***phrasal verbs.*** **lie down.** To do little or nothing. **lie in.** To be in confinement for childbirth. **lie to.** *Naut.* To remain stationary while facing the wind. **lie with. 1.** To be decided by, dependent on, or up to. **2.** *Archaic.* To have sexual intercourse with. —***idiom.*** **lie (or lay) low. 1.** To keep oneself or one's plans hidden. **2.** To bide one's time but remain ready for action. [ME *lien* < OE *licgan.* See **legh-***.]
lie[2] (lī) *n.* **1.** A false statement deliberately presented as being true; a falsehood. **2.** Something meant to deceive or give a wrong impression. —*v.* **lied, ly•ing** (lī′ĭng), **lies.** —*intr.* **1.** To present false information with the intention of deceiving. **2.** To convey a false image or impression. —*tr.* To cause to be in a specific condition or affect in a specific way by telling falsehoods. [ME < OE *lyge.* See **leugh-***.]
Lie (lē), **Trygve Halvden.** 1896–1968. Norwegian politician and first secretary-general of the United Nations (1946–53).
Lie•big (lē′bĭg, -bĭKH), Baron **Justus von.** 1803–73. German chemist who pioneered laboratory-based education (1826).
Lieb•knecht (lēp′knĕkt′, -knĕKHt′), **Karl.** 1871–1919. German journalist and politician who founded (1918) the Spartacus Party, the precursor of the German Communist Party.
Liech•ten•stein (lĭk′tən-stīn′, lĭKH′tən-shtīn′). A small Alpine principality in central Europe between Austria and Switzerland; became independent in 1866. Cap. Vaduz. Pop. 27,076.
lied (lēt) *n., pl.* **lie•der** (lē′dər). *Mus.* A German art song for solo voice and piano. [Ger. *Lied,* ult. < OHGer. *liod.*]
Lie•der•kranz (lē′dər-kränts′, -krănts′). A trademark for a soft cheese resembling a mild Limburger.
lie detector *n.* A polygraph used to detect possible deception during an interrogation.
lief (lēf) *adv.* **lief•er, lief•est.** Readily; willingly. —*adj.* **liefer, liefest.** *Archaic.* **1.** Beloved; dear. **2.** Ready or willing. [ME *leve, lef,* dear, willingly < OE *lēof,* dear. See **leubh-***.]
liege (lēj) *n.* **1.** A lord or sovereign to whom allegiance and service are due according to feudal law. **2.** A vassal or subject owing allegiance and services to a lord or sovereign under feudal law. **3.** A loyal subject to a monarch. —*adj.* **1.a.** Entitled to the loyalty and services of vassals or subjects: *a liege lord.* **b.** Bound to give such allegiance and services to a lord or monarch. **2.** Loyal; faithful. [ME < OFr., entitled to feudal allegiance < LLat. *laeticus,* being a semifree colonist in Gaul < *laetus,* a semifree colonist, of Gmc. orig. See **lē-***.]
Li•ège (lē-āzh′, lyĕzh). A city of E Belgium near the Dutch and German borders; first mentioned in 558. Pop. 207,496.
liege•man (lēj′mən) *n.* **1.** A feudal vassal or subject. **2.** A loyal supporter, follower, or subject.
lien (lēn, lē′ən) *n. Law.* The right to take and hold or sell the property of a debtor as security or payment for a debt or duty. [Fr., tie, bond < OFr., constraint < Lat. *ligāmen,* bond < *ligāre,* to bind. See **leig-***.]
Lie•pa•ja (lē-ĕp′ə-yə, lyĕ′pä-yä). A city of SW Latvia on the Baltic Sea SW of Riga. Pop. 112,000.
li•erne (lē-ûrn′) *n. Archit.* A reinforcing rib used in Gothic vaulting to connect the intersections and bosses of the primary ribs. [Fr. < *lier,* to bind < OFr. See LIABLE.]
lieu (lo͞o) *n. Archaic.* Place; stead. —***idiom.*** **in lieu of.** In place of; instead of. [Fr. < OFr. < Lat. *locus.*]
lieu•ten•ant (lo͞o-tĕn′ənt) *n.* **1.a.** A commissioned officer in the U.S. Navy or Coast Guard ranking above lieutenant junior grade and below lieutenant commander. **b.** A first lieutenant. **c.** A second lieutenant. **2.** (lĕf-tĕn′ənt). A commissioned officer in the British and Canadian navies ranking just below a lieutenant commander. **3.** An officer in a police or fire department ranking below a captain. **4.** One who acts in place of or represents a superior; an assistant or a deputy. [ME, deputy < OFr. : *lieu,* lieu; see LIEU + *tenant,* pr.part. of *tenir,* to hold (< Lat. *tenēre;* see **ten-***).] —**lieu•ten′an•cy** *n.*
lieutenant colonel *n.* A commissioned officer in the U.S. Army, Air Force, or Marine Corps ranking above major and below colonel.
lieutenant commander *n.* A commissioned officer in the U.S. Navy or Coast Guard ranking above lieutenant and below commander.
lieutenant general *n.* A commissioned officer in the U.S. Army, Air Force, or Marine Corps ranking above major general and below general.
lieutenant governor *n.* **1.** An elected official ranking just below the governor of a state in the United States. **2.** The nonelective chief of government of a Canadian province.
lieutenant junior grade *n., pl.* **lieutenants junior grade.** A commissioned officer in the U.S. Navy or Coast Guard ranking above ensign and below lieutenant.
life (līf) *n., pl.* **lives** (līvz). **1.** *Biol.* **a.** The property or quality that distinguishes living organisms from dead organisms and inanimate matter, manifested in functions such as metabolism, growth, reproduction, and response to stimuli or adaptation to the environment originating from within the organism. **b.** The characteristic state or condition of a living organism. **2.** Living organisms considered as a group: *plant life.* **3.** A living being, esp. a person. **4.** The physical, mental, and spiritual experiences that constitute existence. **5.a.** The interval of time between birth and death. **b.** The interval of time between one's birth and the present. **c.** A particular segment of one's life. **d.** The period from an occurrence until death: *barred for life.* **e.** *Slang.* A sentence of imprisonment lasting till death. **6.** The time for which something exists or functions. **7.** A spiritual state regarded as a transcending of corporeal death. **8.** An account of a person's life; a biography. **9.** Human existence, relationships, or activity in general: *real life.* **10.a.** A manner of living: *led a hard life.* **b.** A specific characteristic manner of existence. Used of inanimate objects. **c.** The activities and interests of a particular area or realm. **11.a.** A source of vitality; an animating force. **b.** Liveliness or vitality; animation. **12.a.** Something that actually exists regarded as a subject for an artist: *painted from life.* **b.** Actual environment or reality; nature. —***idioms.*** **as big as life. 1.** Life-size. **2.** Actually present. **bring to life. 1.** To cause to regain consciousness. **2.** To put spirit into; to animate. **3.** To make lifelike. **come to life.** To become animated; grow excited. **for dear life.** Desperately or urgently. **for life.** Till the end of one's life. **for the life of (one).** Though trying hard. **not on your life.** *Informal.* Absolutely not; not for any reason whatsoever. **take (one's) life.** To commit suicide. **take (someone's) life.** To commit murder. **the good life.** A wealthy, luxurious way of living. **the life of Riley.** *Informal.* An easy life. **to save (one's) life.** No matter how hard one tries. **true to life.** Conforming to reality. [ME < OE *līf.* See **leip-***.]
life-and-death (līf′ən-dĕth′) or **life-or-death** (līf′ər-) *adj.* **1.** Involving or ending in life or death. **2.** Vitally important.
life belt *n.* A life preserver worn like a belt.
life•blood (līf′blŭd′) *n.* **1.** Blood regarded as essential for life. **2.** An indispensable or vital part.
life•boat (līf′bōt′) *n. Naut.* **1.** A boat carried on a ship for use if the ship has to be abandoned. **2.** A boat used for rescue.
life buoy *n.* A buoyant device, such as a cork or polystyrene ring, for keeping a person afloat in water.
life cycle *n.* **1.** The course of developmental changes through which an organism passes from its inception as a fertilized zygote to the mature state in which another zygote may be produced. **2.** A progression through a series of differing stages of development.
life expectancy *n.* The number of years that an individual is expected to live as determined by statistics.
life force *n.* See **élan vital.**
life form *n.* The characteristic morphology of a mature organism.
life•guard (līf′gärd′) *n.* An expert swimmer trained and employed to watch over other swimmers. —**life′guard′** *v.*
life history *n.* **1.** The history of changes undergone by an organism from inception or conception to death. **2.** The developmental history of an individual or a group in society.
life insurance *n.* Insurance that guarantees a sum of money to a beneficiary upon the death of the insured or to the insured if he or she lives beyond a certain age.
life jacket *n.* A life preserver in the form of a vest.
life•less (līf′lĭs) *adj.* **1.** Having no life; inanimate. **2.** Having lost life; dead. **3.** Not inhabited by living beings; not capable of sustaining life. **4.** Lacking vitality or animation; dull. —**life′less•ly** *adv.* —**life′less•ness** *n.*
life•like (līf′līk′) *adj.* Accurately representing real life: *a lifelike statue.* See Syns at **graphic.** —**life′like′ness** *n.*
life•line (līf′līn′) *n.* **1.** An anchored line thrown as a support to someone falling or drowning. **2.** *Naut.* **a.** A line shot to a ship in distress. **b.** A rope or wire along the deck of a ship, used as a handhold. **c.** A line used to raise and lower deep-sea divers. **3.a.** A means or route by which necessary supplies are transported. **b.** One regarded as a source of salvation in a crisis. **4.** A diagonal line crossing the palm of the hand and believed to indicate the major events and length of one's life.
life•long (līf′lông′, -lŏng′) *adj.* Continuing for a lifetime.
life-or-death (līf′ər-dĕth′) *adj.* Var. of **life-and-death.**
life preserver *n.* **1.** A buoyant device designed to keep a person

lierne

life jacket

ă pat	oi boy
ā pay	ou out
âr care	o͝o took
ä father	o͞o boot
ĕ pet	ŭ cut
ē be	ûr urge
ĭ pit	th thin
ī pie	*th* this
îr pier	hw which
ŏ pot	zh vision
ō toe	ə about, item
ô paw	

Stress marks:
′ (primary);
′ (secondary), as in dictionary (dĭk′shə-nĕr′ē)

afloat in the water. **2.** *Chiefly British.* A weapon, such as a blackjack.

lif•er (lī′fər) *n. Slang.* **1.a.** A prisoner serving a life sentence. **b.** One who makes a career in one of the armed forces. **2.** A right-to-lifer.

life raft *n. Naut.* A raft usu. made of inflatable material or wood and used in an emergency at sea.

life•sav•er (līf′sā′vər) *n.* **1.** One that saves a life. **2.** See **lifeguard. 3.** One that provides help in a crisis or emergency. **4.** A life preserver shaped like a ring. **— life′sav′ing** *n.*

life science *n.* Any of several branches of science, such as biology, medicine, or ecology, studying living organisms and their organization, life processes, and relationships to each other and their environment.

life-size (līf′sīz′) also **life-sized** (-sīzd′) *adj.* Being of the same size as an original: *a life-size statue.*

life span *n.* **1.** A lifetime. **2.** The average or maximum length of time an organism, a material, or an object can be expected to survive or last.

life•style also **life-style** or **life style** (līf′stīl′) *n.* A way of life or style of living that reflects the attitudes and values of a person or group.

Usage Note: *Lifestyle* has been criticized, perhaps because it appears to elevate habits of consumption, dress, and recreation to a primary basis of social classification. Such categories, however, do figure importantly in the schemes that Americans commonly invoke in explaining social values and social behavior. Fifty-three percent of the Usage Panel accepts the word in the sentence *Bohemian attitudes toward conventional society have been outstripped and outdated by the lifestyles of millions of young people,* and fully 70 percent accepts the word in the sentence *Salaries in the Bay Area may be higher, but it may cost employees as much as 30 percent more to maintain their lifestyles.*

ligature
Opening notes of "The Star-Spangled Banner"

life-sup•port system (līf′sə-pôrt′, -pōrt′) *n.* **1.** Equipment that creates a viable environment under conditions otherwise incompatible with life. **2.** Medical equipment that augments or substitutes for an essential bodily function, such as respiration, keeping a patient alive who might otherwise die.

life•time (līf′tīm′) *n.* **1.** The period of time during which an individual is alive. **2.** The period of time during which property, an object, a process, or a phenomenon exists or functions.

life•work (līf′wûrk′) *n.* The chief or entire work of a person's lifetime.

life zone *n. Ecol.* A geographic region or area defined by its characteristic life forms.

LIFO (lī′fō) *n. Accounting.* See **last-in, first-out.**

lift (lĭft) *v.* **lift•ed, lift•ing, lifts.** *— tr.* **1.a.** To direct or carry from a lower to a higher position; raise. **b.** To transport by air. **2.a.** To revoke by taking back; rescind: *lifted the embargo.* **b.** To bring an end to (a blockade or siege) by removing forces. **3.** To cease (artillery fire) in an area. **4.a.** To raise in condition, rank, or esteem. **b.** To uplift; elate. **5.** To remove (plants) from the ground for transplanting. **6.** To project or sound in loud, clear tones. **7.** *Informal.* To steal; pilfer. **8.** *Informal.* To copy from something already published; plagiarize. **9.** To pay off or clear (a debt or mortgage, for example). **10.** To perform cosmetic surgery on (the face), esp. to remove wrinkles or sagging skin. **11.a.** *Sports.* To hit (a golf ball) very high into the air. **b.** To pick up (a golf ball) to place it in a better lie. *— intr.* **1.a.** To rise; ascend. **b.** To yield to upward pressure: *These windows lift easily.* **2.a.** To disappear or disperse by or as if by rising: *The smog lifted.* **b.** To stop temporarily. **3.** To become elevated; soar: *Their spirits lifted.* *— n.* **1.** The act or process of rising or raising to a higher position. **2.** Power or force available for raising: *the lift of a pump.* **3.** An amount or a weight raised or capable of being raised at one time; a load. **4.a.** The extent or height to which something is raised or rises; the amount of elevation. **b.** The distance or space through which something is raised or rises. **5.** A rise or an elevation in the level of the ground. **6.** An elevation of one's spirits. **7.** A raised, high, or erect position, as of a part of the body: *the lift of his chin.* **8.** A machine or device designed to pick up, raise, or carry something. **9.** One of the layers making up the heel of a shoe. **10.** *Chiefly British.* A passenger or cargo elevator. **11.** A ride in a vehicle given to help someone reach a destination. **12.** Assistance or help. **13.** A set of pumps used in a mine. **14.** The component of the total aerodynamic force acting on an airfoil or on an entire aircraft perpendicular to the relative wind and normally exerted in an upward direction. ***— phrasal verb.* lift off.** To begin flight. [ME *liften* < ON *lypta.*] **— lift′a•ble** *adj.* **— lift′er** *n.*

lighthouse
West Quoddy lighthouse, Lubec, Maine

Syns: *lift, raise, rear, elevate, hoist, heave, boost.* These verbs mean to move something from a lower to a higher level or position. *Lift* sometimes stresses the expenditure of effort: *a trunk too heavy to lift. Raise* often implies movement to an approximately vertical position: *raising a monument. Rear* is frequently interchangeable with *raise: "Her family reared a sumptuous mausoleum over her remains"* (Macaulay). *Elevate* is sometimes synonymous with the preceding terms (*elevated his ankle*), but it more often suggests exalting, ennobling, or raising morally or intellectually: *"A generous and elevated mind is distinguished by nothing more certainly than an eminent degree of curiosity"* (Samuel Johnson). *Hoist* is applied principally to the lifting of heavy objects, often by mechanical means: *hoist a sunken ship.* To *heave* is to lift or raise with great effort or force: *heaved the pack up. Boost* suggests upward movement effected by or as if by pushing from below: *boosted the child into the saddle.*

lift•off (lĭft′ôf′, -ŏf′) *n.* The initial movement by which or the instant in which a rocket or other such craft commences flight.

lig•a•ment (lĭg′ə-mənt) *n.* **1.** *Anat.* A sheet or band of tough fibrous tissue connecting bones or cartilages at a joint or supporting an organ. **2.** A unifying or connecting tie or bond. [ME < Med.Lat. *ligāmentum* < Lat., bandage < *ligāre,* to bind. See LIEN.] **— lig′a•ment′al** (-mĕn′tl), **lig′a•men′ta•ry** (-mĕn′tə-rē, -mĕn′trē), **lig′a•men′tous** *adj.*

li•gan (lī′gən) *n.* Var. of **lagan.**

li•gand (lī′gənd, lĭg′ənd) *n.* An ion, a molecule, or a molecular group that binds to another chemical entity to form a larger complex. [< Lat. *ligandus,* gerundive of *ligāre,* to bind. See LIGATE.]

li•gase (lī′gās′, -gāz′) *n.* Any of a class of enzymes that catalyze the linkage of two molecules, generally utilizing ATP as the energy donor. [Lat. *ligāre,* to bind; see **leig-*** + -ASE.]

li•gate (lī′gāt′) *tr.v.* **-gat•ed, -gat•ing, -gates.** To tie or bind with a ligature. [Lat. *ligāre, ligāt-.* See **leig-*.**]

li•ga•tion (lī-gā′shən) *n.* **1.a.** The act of binding or of applying a ligature. **b.** The state of being bound. **2.** Something that binds; a ligature.

lig•a•ture (lĭg′ə-cho͝or′, -chər) *n.* **1.** The act of tying or binding. **2.** A cord, wire, or bandage used for tying or binding. **3.** A thread, wire, or cord used in surgery to close vessels or tie off ducts. **4.** Something that unites; a bond. **5.** A character, letter, or type, such as æ, combining two or more letters. **6.** *Mus.* **a.** A group of notes to be played or sung as one phrase. **b.** A curved line indicating such a phrase; a slur. *— tr.v.* **-tured, -tur•ing, -tures.** To ligate. [Ult. < LLat. *ligātūra* < Lat. *ligātus,* p.part. of *ligāre,* to bind. See **leig-*.**]

li•ger (lī′gər) *n.* The offspring of a male lion and a female tiger, usu. larger than either. [LI(ON) + (TI)GER.]

light¹ (līt) *n.* **1.** *Phys.* **a.** Electromagnetic radiation that has a wavelength in the range from about 4,000 (violet) to about 7,700 (red) angstroms and may be perceived by the normal unaided human eye. **b.** Electromagnetic radiation of any wavelength. **2.** The sensation of perceiving light; brightness. **3.a.** A source of light, such as a lamp. **b.** The illumination derived from a source of light. **c.** The particular quantity or quality of such illumination: *better light near the lamp.* **d.** The pathway or route of such illumination to a person. **4.** A mechanical device that uses illumination as a signal or warning, esp. a traffic signal. **5.a.** Daylight. **b.** Dawn; daybreak. **6.** Something, such as a window, that admits illumination. **7.** A source of fire, such as a match. **8.** Spiritual awareness; illumination. **9.a.** Something that provides information or clarification. **b.** A state of awareness or understanding. **10.** Public attention; general knowledge: *brought the scandal to light.* **11.** A way of looking at or considering a matter; an aspect. **12.** *Archaic.* Eyesight. **13. lights.** One's individual opinions, choices, or standards. **14.** A person who inspires or is adored by another. **15.** A prominent or distinguished person; a luminary. **16.** An expression of the eyes. **17. Light.** In Quaker doctrine, the guiding spirit or divine presence in each person. **18.** The representation of light in art. *— v.* **light•ed** or **lit** (lĭt), **light•ing, lights.** *— tr.* **1.** To set on fire; ignite or kindle. **2.** To cause to give out light; make luminous: *lit a lamp.* **3.** To provide, cover, or fill with light; illuminate. **4.** To signal, direct, or guide with or as if with illumination. **5.** To enliven or animate: *A smile lit her face.* *— intr.* **1.** To start to burn; be ignited or kindled. **2.** To emit light; be lighted: *The indicator lights up.* *— adj.* **light•er, light•est. 1.a.** *Color.* Having a greater rather than lesser degree of lightness. **b.** Of or being an additive primary color. **2.** Characterized by or filled with light; bright. **3.** Not dark in color; fair: *light hair.* **4.** Served with milk or cream. Used of coffee. ***— phrasal verb.* light up. 1.** To become or cause to become animated or cheerful. **2.** To start smoking a cigarette, cigar, or pipe. ***— idiom.* in (the) light of.** In consideration of; in relationship to. [ME < OE *lēoht, līht.* See **leuk-*.**]

Usage Note: *Lighted* and *lit* are equally acceptable as past tense and past participle of *light.* Both forms are well established as adjectives also: *a lit* (or *lighted*) *cigarette.*

light² (līt) *adj.* **light•er, light•est. 1.a.** Of relatively little weight; not heavy. **b.** Of relatively little weight for its size or bulk. **c.** Of less than the correct, standard, or legal weight: *a light pound.* **2.** Exerting little force or impact; gentle. **3.a.** Of little quantity; scanty: *light snow.* **b.** Consuming or using relatively moderate amounts; abstemious. **c.** Not harsh or severe. **4.** Demanding little exertion or effort; not burdensome. See Syns at **easy. 5.** Having little importance; insignificant. **6.** Intended primarily as entertainment; not serious or profound. **7.** Free from worries or troubles; blithe. **8.** Characterized by frivolity; silly or trivial. **9.** Liable to change; fickle. **10.** Mildly dizzy or faint. **11.** Lacking in ethical discrimination. **12.** Moving easily and quickly; nimble. **13.** Designed for ease and quickness of movement: *light aircraft.* **14.** Designed to carry relatively little weight: *a light truck.* **15.** Carrying little equipment or armament. **16.** Requiring relatively little equipment to produce consumer goods: *light industry.* **17.** Easily awakened or disturbed. **18.a.** Easily digested: *a light supper.* **b.** Having a spongy or flaky texture; well-leavened. **19.** Having a loose porous consistency: *light soil.* **20.** Containing a small amount of a potentially harmful ingredient, such as alcohol or fat. **21.** *Ling.* **a.** Of, relating to, or being a syllable ending in a short vowel or a short vowel plus a consonant. **b.** Of, relating to, or being a vowel or syllable pronounced with little or no stress. *—adv.* **lighter, lightest. 1.** In a light manner; lightly. **2.** With little weight and few burdens. *—intr.v.* **light•ed** or **lit** (lĭt), **light•ing, lights. 1.** To get down, as from a vehicle or horse; dismount. **2.** To descend to the ground after flight; land. **3.** To come upon one unexpectedly. **4.** To come upon by chance or accident. Used with *on* or *upon*: *lit on the solution.* ***—phrasal verbs.*** **light into.** *Informal.* To attack verbally or physically; assail. **light out.** *Informal.* To leave hastily; run off. ***—idiom.*** **go light on.** To treat casually or gingerly. [ME < OE *lēoht, līht.* See **legʷh-***.]

light adaptation *n.* The process, chiefly involving constriction of the pupil, by which the eye adapts to an increase in illumination. **—light′-a•dapt′ed** (līt′ə-dăp′tĭd) *adj.*

light bread *n. Chiefly Southern U.S.* See **white bread.**

light bulb *n.* An electric light in which a filament is heated to incandescence by an electric current.

light-e•mit•ting diode (līt′ĭ-mĭt′ĭng) *n.* LED.

light•en¹ (līt′n) *v.* **-ened, -en•ing, -ens.** *—tr.* **1.a.** To make light or lighter; illuminate or brighten. **b.** To make (a color) lighter. **2.** *Archaic.* To enlighten. *—intr.* **1.** To become lighter; brighten. **2.** To be luminous; shine. **3.** To give off flashes of lightning.

light•en² (līt′n) *v.* **-ened, -en•ing, -ens.** *—tr.* **1.** To make less heavy. **2.** To lessen the oppressiveness, trouble, or severity of. See Syns at **relieve. 3.** To relieve of cares or worries; gladden. *—intr.* **1.** To become less in weight. **2.** To become less oppressive, troublesome, or severe. **3.** To become cheerful.

light•er¹ (lī′tər) *n.* **1.** One that ignites or kindles. **2.** A mechanical device for lighting a cigarette, cigar, or pipe.

light•er² (lī′tər) *Naut. —n.* A large flatbottom barge, esp. one used to load and unload cargo ships. *—tr.v.* **-ered, -er•ing, -ers.** To convey (cargo) in a lighter. [ME, perh. < *lighten,* to make less heavy < OE *līhtan.* See **legʷh-***.]

light•er•age (lī′tər-ĭj) *n. Naut.* **1.** Transportation of goods on a lighter. **2.** The fee charged for lightering.

light•er-than-air (lī′tər-*th*ən-âr′) *adj.* Having a weight less than that of the air displaced. Used of certain aircraft.

light•face (līt′fās′) *n. Print.* A typeface or font of characters having relatively thin light lines. **—light′faced′** *adj.*

light-fin•gered (līt′fĭng′gərd) *adj.* **1.** Having quick and nimble fingers. **2.** Skilled at or given to petty thievery.

light-foot•ed (līt′fo͝ot′ĭd) also **light•foot** (-fo͝ot′) *adj.* Treading with light and nimble ease. **—light′-foot′ed•ly** *adv.*

light-hand•ed (līt′hăn′dĭd) *adj.* Having a light, delicate touch. **—light′-hand′ed•ly** *adv.*

light•head•ed (līt′hĕd′ĭd) *adj.* **1.** Faint, giddy, or delirious: *lightheaded with wine.* **2.** Given to frivolity; silly. **—light′head′ed•ly** *adv.* **—light′head′ed•ness** *n.*

light•heart•ed (līt′här′tĭd) *adj.* Not being burdened by trouble, worry, or care; happy and carefree. See Syns at **glad¹. —light′heart′ed•ly** *adv.* **—light′heart′ed•ness** *n.*

light heavyweight *n. Sports.* **1.** A professional boxer weighing more than 160 and not more than 175 pounds (approx. 72.5–79.5 kilograms), heavier than a middleweight and lighter than a heavyweight. **2.** A contestant in various other sports in a similar weight class.

light•house (līt′hous′) *n. Naut.* A tall structure topped by a powerful light used to aid marine navigation.

light•ing (lī′tĭng) *n.* **1.** The state of being lighted; illumination. **2.a.** The method or equipment used to provide artificial illumination. **b.** The illumination so provided. **3.** The act or process of igniting.

light•ly (līt′lē) *adv.* **1.** With little weight or force; gently. **2.** To a slight extent or amount: *apply paint lightly.* **3.a.** With little difficulty; easily. **b.** With agility and grace; nimbly. **4.a.** In a carefree manner; cheerfully: *took the news lightly.* **b.** Without sufficient care or consideration; indifferently.

light machine gun *n.* An air-cooled machine gun not greater than .30 caliber.

light meter *n.* See **exposure meter.**

light-mind•ed (līt′mīn′dĭd) *adj.* Frivolous, silly, or inanely giddy. **—light′-mind′ed•ly** *adv.* **—light′-mind′ed•ness** *n.*

light•ness¹ (līt′nĭs) *n.* **1.** The quality or condition of being illuminated. **2.** *Color.* The dimension of the color of an object by which the object appears to reflect or transmit more or less of the incident light, varying from black to white for surface colors and from black to colorless for transparent volume colors.

light•ness² (līt′nĭs) *n.* **1.** The state or quality of having little weight or force. **2.** Ease or quickness of movement; agility. **3.** Ease or cheerfulness in manner or style. **4.** Freedom from worry or trouble. **5.** Lack of appropriate seriousness; levity. **6.** Delicacy or subtlety in craft, performance, or effect.

light•ning (līt′nĭng) *n.* **1.a.** An abrupt discontinuous natural electric discharge in the atmosphere. **b.** The visible flash of light accompanying such a discharge. **2.** *Informal.* A sudden, usu. improbable stroke of fortune. *—intr.v.* **-ninged** (-nĭngd), **-ning, -nings.** To discharge a flash of lightning. *—adj.* Moving or occurring with remarkable speed or suddenness. [ME, gerund of *lightnen,* to illuminate, and *lighten* (*lightnen* < *lighten*) < OE *līhtan.* See **leuk-***.]

lightning

lightning arrester *n.* A protective device for electrical equipment that reduces excessive voltage resulting from lightning to a safe level by grounding the discharge.

lightning bug *n.* See **firefly.**

lightning rod *n.* **1.** A grounded metal rod placed high on a structure to prevent damage by conducting lightning to the ground. **2.** One that attracts and absorbs typically negative feelings and reactions, being a diversion from other issues.

light opera *n. Mus.* See **operetta.**

light pen *n. Comp. Sci.* A small photosensitive device connected to a computer and moved by hand over an output display to manipulate information in the computer.

light•proof (līt′pro͞of′) *adj.* Impenetrable by light.

lights (līts) *pl.n.* The lungs, esp. the lungs of an animal slaughtered for food. [ME *lightes* < *light,* light in weight (< the lightness of the lungs compared to other organs). See LIGHT².]

light•ship (līt′shĭp′) *n. Naut.* A ship with powerful lights or warning signals that is anchored in dangerous waters to alert other vessels.

light show *n.* A display of colored lights in shifting patterns, often accompanied by slides and film loops.

light•some¹ (līt′səm) *adj.* **1.** Providing light; luminous. **2.** Covered with or full of light; bright. **—light′some•ly** *adv.* **—light′some•ness** *n.*

light•some² (līt′səm) *adj.* **1.** Light, nimble, or graceful in movement. **2.** Free from worry or care; cheerful. **3.** Frivolous; silly. **—light′some•ly** *adv.* **—light′some•ness** *n.*

lights out *n.* **1.** A signal or command to extinguish lights for the night. **2.** Bedtime.

light-struck (līt′strŭk′) *adj.* Fogged by accidental exposure. Used of photosensitive materials.

light water *n. Phys. & Chem.* Ordinary water, H_2O.

light•weight (līt′wāt′) *n.* **1.** One that weighs relatively little or less than average. **2.** *Sports.* **a.** A professional boxer weighing more than 126 and not more than 135 pounds (approx. 57–61 kilograms), heavier than a featherweight and lighter than a welterweight. **b.** A contestant in various other sports in a similar weight class. **3.** A person of little ability, intelligence, influence, or importance. *—adj.* **1.** Weighing relatively little; not heavy. **2.** *Sports.* Of, relating to, or characteristic of a lightweight. **3.** Having no significance or influence.

light•wood (līt′wo͝od′) *n. Chiefly Southern U.S.* See **kindling.**

Regional Note: There are a number of regional equivalents for what Standard English calls *kindling. Lightwood,* derived from the verb *to light (a fire),* probably originated in Virginia, according to Craig M. Carver in *American Regional Dialects,* and is now used throughout the South Midland. *Fat pine, fatwood,* and *rich pine* all refer to the resinous pine native to the Gulf States.

light-year also **light year** (līt′yîr′) *n.* **1.** The distance that light travels in a vacuum in one year, approx. 9.46 trillion (9.46×10^{12}) kilometers or 5.88 trillion (5.88×10^{12}) miles. **2.** *Informal.* A long way. Often used in the plural.

lig•ne•ous (lĭg′nē-əs) *adj.* Consisting of or having the texture or appearance of wood; woody. [< Lat. *ligneus* < *lignum,* wood. See **leg-***.]

ligni– or **ligno–** or **lign–** *pref.* Wood: *lignocellulose.* [< Lat. *lignum,* wood. See **leg-***.]

lig•ni•fy (lĭg′nə-fī′) *v.* **-fied, -fy•ing, -fies.** *—intr.* To turn into wood or become woody through the formation and deposit of lignin in cell walls. *—tr.* To make woody or woodlike by the deposit of lignin. **—lig′ni•fi•ca′tion** (-fĭ-kā′shən) *n.*

lig•nin (lĭg′nĭn) *n.* A complex polymer, the chief noncarbohydrate constituent of wood, that binds to cellulose fibers and hardens and strengthens the cell walls of plants.

lig•nite (lĭg′nīt′) *n.* A soft brownish coal in which the alteration of vegetable matter is further along than in peat but not as far as in bituminous coal. **—lig•nit′ic** (-nĭt′ĭk) *adj.*

lig•no•cel•lu•lose (lĭg′nō-sĕl′yə-lōs′) *n.* A combination of lignin and cellulose that strengthens woody plant cells.

lig•num vi•tae (lĭg′nəm vī′tē) *n., pl.* **lignum vitaes. 1.** Either of two tropical American trees *(Guaiacum officinale* or *G. sanctum)* having evergreen leaves and very heavy durable wood. **2.** The wood of either of these trees. [NLat. *lignum vītae* : Lat. *lignum,* wood + Lat. *vītae,* genitive of *vīta,* life.]

lig•ro•in (lĭg′rō-ĭn) *n.* A volatile flammable fraction of petroleum, obtained by distillation and used as a solvent. [?]

ă pat	oi boy
ā pay	ou out
âr care	o͝o took
ä father	o͞o boot
ĕ pet	ŭ cut
ē be	ûr urge
ĭ pit	th thin
ī pie	*th* this
îr pier	hw which
ŏ pot	zh vision
ō toe	ə about, item
ô paw	

Stress marks:
′ (primary);
′ (secondary), as in
dictionary (dĭk′shə-nĕr′ē)

lig•u•la (lĭgʹyə-lə) *n., pl.* **-lae** (-lēʹ) or **-las.** A strap-shaped or tonguelike structure, esp. a mouth part in certain insects. [Lat., dim. of *lingua,* tongue. See **dn̥ghū-*.**]

lig•u•late (lĭgʹyə-lĭt, -lātʹ) *adj.* **1.** Strap-shaped. **2.** Having a ligule.

lig•ule (lĭgʹyo͞ol) *n.* A straplike structure, such as a membranous or hairy appendage between the sheaf and blade of a grass leaf. [Lat. *ligula,* dim. of *lingua,* tongue. See **dn̥ghū-*.**]

lig•ure (lĭgʹyo͝orʹ) *n.* A precious stone of ancient Israel. [ME *liguri* < LLat. *ligūrius* < Gk. *ligurion,* dim. of *liguros,* clear < *ligus.*]

Li•gu•ri•a (lĭ-gyo͝orʹē-ə). A region of NW Italy on the **Ligurian Sea,** an arm of the Mediterranean between NW Italy and Corsica; subdued by the Romans in the 2nd cent. B.C. and later (16th–19th cent. A.D.) controlled by Genoa. A small section of the coastline formed the **Ligurian Republic** (1797–1815). **—Li•guʹri•an** *adj. & n.*

Liliuokalani
c. 1891 photograph by Menzies Dickson (1840?–1891)

lik•a•ble also **like•a•ble** (līʹkə-bəl) *adj.* Pleasing; attractive. **—likʹa•ble•ness** *n.*

like[1] (līk) *v.* **liked, lik•ing, likes.** *—tr.* **1.** To find pleasant or attractive; enjoy. **2.** To want to have: *would like some coffee.* **3.** To feel about; regard. **4.** *Archaic.* To be pleasing to. *—intr.* **1.** To have an inclination or a preference: *If you like, we can go.* **2.** *Scots.* To be pleased. *—n.* Something that is liked; a preference. [ME *liken* < OE *līcian,* to please. See **līk-*.**]

like[2] (līk) *prep.* **1.** Possessing the characteristics of; resembling closely; similar to. **2.a.** In the typical manner of: *It's not like you to take offense.* **b.** In the same way as: *lived like royalty.* **3.** Inclined or disposed to: *felt like running away.* **4.** As if the probability exists for: *looks like a bad year for farmers.* **5.** Such as; for example: *saved things like old newspapers.* *—adj.* **1.** Possessing the same or almost the same characteristics; similar: *on this and like occasions.* **2.** Alike: *as like as two siblings.* **3.** Having equivalent value or quality. Usu. used in negative sentences: *There's nothing like a good night's sleep.* *—adv.* **1.** In the manner of being; as if. Used as an intensifier of action: *ran like crazy.* **2.** *Informal.* Probably; likely: *Like as not she'll change her mind.* **3.** *Non-Standard.* Used to provide emphasis or a pause: *Like let's get going.* *—n.* **1.** One similar to or like another. Used with *the*: *coughs and the like.* **2.** *Informal.* An equivalent or similar person or thing. Often used in the plural: *never seen the likes of this before.* *—conj. Usage Problem.* **1.** In the same way that; as: *to dance like she does.* **2.** As if: *It looks like we'll finish.* [ME < *like,* similar (< OE *gelīc* and ON *līkr*) and < *like,* similarly (< OE *gelīce* < *gelīc,* similar; see **līk-***).]

Usage Note: If one uses *like* as a conjunction in formal style, one incurs the risk of being accused of illiteracy or worse. Prudence requires *The dogs howled as* (not *like*) *we expected. Like* is more acceptably used as a conjunction in informal style with verbs such as *feel, look, seem, sound,* and *taste,* as in *It looks like we can't go.* But here too *as if* is to be preferred in formal writing. There can be no objection to the use of *like* as a conjunction when the following verb is not expressed, as in *He took to politics like a duck to water.* See Usage Notes at **as[1], together.**

like[3] (līk) also **liked** (līkt) *aux.v. Chiefly Southern U.S.* To be just on the point of; be or come near to. [ME *liken,* to compare < *like,* similar. See LIKE[2].]

-like *suff.* Resembling or characteristic of: *ladylike.* [ME < *like,* similar. See LIKE[2].]

like•li•hood (līkʹlē-ho͝odʹ) *n.* **1.** The state of being probable; probability. **2.** Something probable.

like•ly (līkʹlē) *adj.* **-li•er, -li•est. 1.** Possessing or displaying the qualities or characteristics that make something probable: *likely to become angry.* **2.** Within the realm of credibility; plausible: *not a likely excuse.* **3.** Apparently appropriate or suitable: *several likely candidates.* **4.** Apt to achieve success or yield a desired outcome; promising. **5.** Attractive; pleasant: *a likely spot for the picnic.* *—adv. Usage Problem.* Probably. [ME *likly* < OE *gelīclīc* (< *gelīc,* similar) and < ON *līkligr* (< *līkr,* similar; see **līk-***).]

Usage Note: Used as an adverb *likely* is most commonly preceded by a qualifier such as *very* or *quite*: *He will quite likely require some help with his classes.* But the unmodified use of *likely* is common enough in educated writing, and though it might be better avoided in highly formal style, it should not be regarded as incorrect: *They'll likely buy a new car this year.* See Usage Note at **liable.**

lily pad

like-mind•ed (līkʹmīnʹdĭd) *adj.* Of the same turn of mind.

lik•en (līʹkən) *tr.v.* **-ened, -en•ing, -ens.** To see, mention, or show as similar. [ME *liknen* < *like,* similar. See LIKE[2].]

like•ness (līkʹnĭs) *n.* **1.** The state, quality, or fact of being like; resemblance. **2.** An imitative appearance; a semblance. **3.** A pictorial, graphic, or sculptured representation of something.

Syns: *likeness, similarity, similitude, resemblance, analogy, affinity.* These nouns denote agreement or conformity. *Likeness* implies close agreement: *your likeness to my sister. Similarity* and *similitude* suggest agreement only in some respects or to some degree: *They were drawn to each other by similarity of interests. "A striking similitude between the brother and sister now first arrested my attention"* (Edgar Allan Poe). *Resemblance* refers to similarity in external or superficial details: *"The child . . . bore a remarkable resemblance to her grandfather"* (Lytton Strachey). *Analogy* is similarity, as of properties or functions, between things that are otherwise not comparable: *The computer presents an interesting analogy to the human brain. Affinity* is likeness deriving from kinship or from the possession of shared or compatible properties or sympathies: *the affinity between Brahms and Dvořák.*

like•wise (līkʹwīzʹ) *adv.* **1.** In the same way; similarly. **2.** As well; also.

lik•ing (līʹkĭng) *n.* **1.** A feeling of attraction or love; fondness. **2.** Preference or taste.

li•ku•ta (lē-ko͞oʹtä) *n., pl.* **ma•ku•ta** (mä-ko͞oʹtä). See table at **currency.** [Alteration of Port. *macuta,* an old West African unit of currency consisting originally of a piece of cloth : Bantu *li-,* sing. n. pref. + Kimbundu and Kongo *kuta,* cloth.]

li•lac (līʹlək, -lŏk, -lăk) *n.* **1.** Any of various shrubs of the genus *Syringa,* esp. *S. vulgaris,* having clusters of fragrant purplish or white flowers. **2.** *Color.* A pale to light or moderate purple. [Obsolete Fr. < Ar. *līlak* < MPers. *nīlak* < *nīl,* indigo < Skt. *nīlī* < *nīla-,* dark blue.] **—liʹlac** *adj.*

li•lan•ge•ni (lĭ-längʹgĕ-nē) *n., pl.* **em•a•lan•ge•ni** (ĕmʹə-läng-gĕnʹē). See table at **currency.** [Nguni : *li-,* sing. n. pref. + *langeni,* money.]

Lil•ith (lĭlʹĭth) *n.* **1.** A female spirit in ancient Semitic legend, alleged to haunt deserted places and attack children. **2.** The first wife of Adam in Jewish folklore, believed to have been created before Eve.

Li•li•u•o•ka•la•ni (lə-lēʹə-ō-kə-läʹnē, lē-lēʹo͞o-ō-kä-läʹnē). 1838–1917. Queen of the Hawaiian Is. (1891–93) who was the last Hawaiian ruler to govern the islands.

Lille (lēl). A city of N France NNE of Paris near the Belgian border; founded c. 1030. Pop. 168,424.

Lil•li•pu•tian also **lil•li•pu•tian** (lĭlʹə-pyo͞oʹshən) *—n.* A very small person or being. *—adj.* **1.** Very small; diminutive. **2.** Trivial; petty. [After the *Lilliputians,* a people in *Gulliver's Travels* by Jonathan Swift.]

Li•long•we (lĭ-lôngʹwā). The cap. of Malawi, in the S-central part; founded in the 1940's. Pop. 103,000.

lilt (lĭlt) *n.* **1.** A cheerful or lively manner of speaking, in which the pitch of the voice varies pleasantly. **2.** A light happy tune or song. **3.** A light or resilient manner of moving or walking. *—v.* **lilt•ed, lilt•ing, lilts.** *—tr.* To say, sing, or play (something) in a cheerful rhythmic manner. *—intr.* **1.** To speak, sing, or play with liveliness or rhythm. **2.** To move with lightness and buoyancy. [< ME *lulten, lilten,* to sound an alarm.]

lil•y (lĭlʹē) *n., pl.* **-ies. 1.** Any of various plants of the genus *Lilium,* having variously colored, often trumpet-shaped flowers. **2.** Any of various similar or related plants, such as the day lily or the water lily. **3.** The flower of any of these plants. [ME *lilie* < OE < Lat. *līlium.*]

lily family *n.* A large family of plants, the Liliaceae, marked by showy flowers with six perianth segments, six stamens, and a superior ovary and usu. producing bulbs or rhizomes.

lil•y-liv•ered (lĭlʹē-lĭvʹərd) *adj.* Cowardly; timid.

lily of the Nile *n., pl.* **lilies of the Nile.** See **African lily.**

lily of the valley *n., pl.* **lilies of the valley.** A widely cultivated ornamental European plant *(Convallaria majalis)* having one-sided racemes of fragrant bell-shaped white flowers.

lily pad *n.* One of the floating leaves of a water lily.

lil•y-trot•ter (lĭlʹē-trŏtʹər) *n.* See **jaçana.**

lil•y-white (lĭlʹē-hwītʹ, -wītʹ) *adj.* **1.** White as a lily. **2.** Beyond reproach; blameless. **3.** *Informal.* Excluding or seeking to exclude Black people.

lim. *abbr.* Limit.

Li•ma. 1. (lēʹmə). The cap. of Peru, in the W-central part near the Pacific Ocean; founded by Pizarro in 1535. Pop. 371,122. **2.** (līʹmə). A city of NW OH SSW of Toledo. Pop. 45,549.

li•ma bean (līʹmə) *n.* **1.** Any of several varieties of a tropical American plant *(Phaseolus limensis)* having flat pods containing large light green edible seeds. **2.** The seed of this plant. Also called regionally *butter bean.* [After LIMA, Peru.]

lim•a•cine (lĭmʹə-sēnʹ, līʹmə-) *adj.* Of, relating to, or resembling a slug. [< Lat. *līmāx, līmāc-,* slug, snail; akin to *līmus,* slime. See **lei-*.**]

limb[1] (lĭm) *n.* **1.** One of the larger branches of a tree. **2.** One of the jointed appendages of an animal used for locomotion or grasping. **3.** An extension or a projecting part, as of a building or mountain range. **4.** One regarded as an extension, a member, or a representative of a larger body or group. **5.** *Informal.* An impish child. *—tr.v.* **limbed, limb•ing, limbs.** To dismember. **—*idiom.* (out) on a limb.** *Informal.* In a difficult, awkward, or vulnerable position. [Alteration (prob. influenced by LIMB[2]) of ME *lim* < OE.]

limb[2] (lĭm) *n.* **1.** *Astron.* The circumferential edge of the apparent disk of a celestial body. **2.** *Math.* The edge of a graduated arc or circle used in an instrument to measure angles. **3.** *Bot.* The expanded tip of a plant organ, such as a petal or corolla lobe. [ME, graduated edge of an astronomical instrument < OFr. *limbe* < Lat. *limbus,* border.]

lim•bate (lĭmʹbātʹ) *adj. Bot.* Having an edge or a margin of a different color. [LLat. *limbātus*, bordered < Lat. *limbus*, border.]

lim•ber¹ (lĭm′bər) *adj.* **1.** Bending or flexing readily; pliable. **2.** Capable of moving, bending, or contorting easily; supple. —*v.* **-bered, -ber•ing, -bers.** —*tr.* To make limber: *limbered up his legs.* —*intr.* To make oneself limber. [?] —**lim′ber•ly** *adv.* —**lim′ber•ness** *n.*

lim•ber² (lĭm′bər) *n.* A two-wheeled horse-drawn vehicle used to tow a field gun or a caisson. [Alteration of ME *limour*, shaft of a cart, perh. < *limon* < OFr.]

lim•bers (lĭm′bərz) *pl.n. Naut.* Gutters or channels on each side of a ship's keelson that drain bilge water into the pump well. [Prob. alteration of Fr. *lumière*, one of the limbers < OFr. *lumiere*, opening, light < LLat. *lūminăria*, pl. of *lūminăre*, window < Lat., lamp. See LUMINARY.]

lim•bic (lĭm′bĭk) *adj.* **1.** Of, relating to, or characterized by a limbus. **2.** Of or relating to the limbic system. [Fr. *limbique* < *limbe*, edge < OFr., graduated edge. See LIMB².]

limbic system *n.* A group of interconnected deep brain structures, common to all mammals and involved in olfaction, emotion, motivation, behavior, and various autonomic functions.

lim•bo¹ (lĭm′bō) *n., pl.* **-bos. 1.** Often **Limbo.** *Theol.* The abode of just or innocent souls excluded from the beatific vision but not condemned to further punishment. **2.** A region or condition of oblivion or neglect: *Her promotion was in limbo for months.* **3.** A state or place of confinement. **4.** An intermediate place or state. [ME < Med.Lat. *(in) limbō*, (in) Limbo, ablative of *limbus*, Limbo < Lat., border.]

lim•bo² (lĭm′bō) *n., pl.* **-bos.** A West Indian dance in which the dancers keep bending over backward and passing under a pole that is lowered each time. [Prob. ult. of African orig.]

Lim•burg (lĭm′bûrg′, -bœrKH′). A former duchy of NW Europe; founded in the 11th cent. and divided into the Dutch and Belgian provinces of Limburg in 1839.

Lim•burg•er (lĭm′bûr′gər) *n.* A soft white cheese with a very strong odor and flavor. [Flem., one from Limburg, after *Limburg*, a province of NE Belgium.]

lim•bus (lĭm′bəs) *n., pl.* **-bi** (-bī′). *Biol.* A distinctive border or edge. [Lat., border.]

lime¹ (līm) *n.* **1.** A spiny Asian evergreen shrub or tree *(Citrus aurantifolia)* having leathery leaves, fragrant white flowers, and edible fruit. **2.** The fruit of this plant, having a green rind and acid juice used as flavoring. [Prob. French < Sp. *lima* < Ar. *līmah*, *līm*, prob. < *līmūn*, lemon. See LEMON.]

lime² (līm) *n.* See **linden.** [Alteration of ME *line* < OE *lind.*]

lime³ (līm) *n.* **1.a.** See **calcium oxide. b.** Any of various mineral and industrial forms of calcium oxide differing chiefly in water content and percentage of constituents such as silica, alumina, and iron. **2.** Birdlime. —*tr.v.* **limed, lim•ing, limes. 1.** To treat with lime. **2.** To smear with birdlime. **3.** To catch or snare with or as if with birdlime. [ME *lim* < OE *līm*, birdlime. See **lei-*.**] —**lim′y** *adj.*

lime•ade (lī-mād′) *n.* A sweetened beverage of lime juice and plain or carbonated water.

lime•kiln (līm′kĭl′, -kĭln′) *n.* A furnace used to reduce naturally occurring forms of calcium carbonate to lime.

lime•light (līm′līt′) *n.* **1.** A focus of public attention. **2.a.** An early stage light in which lime was heated to incandescence. **b.** The brilliant white light so produced.

li•men (lī′mən) *n., pl.* **li•mens** or **lim•i•na** (lĭm′ə-nə). The threshold of a physiological or psychological response. [Lat. *līmen*, threshold.] —**lim′i•nal** (lĭm′ə-nəl) *adj.*

lim•er•ick (lĭm′ər-ĭk) *n.* A light humorous, nonsensical, or bawdy verse of five anapestic lines usu. with the rhyme scheme *aabba.* [After LIMERICK.]

Lim•er•ick (lĭm′ər-ĭk, lĭm′rĭk). A borough of SW Ireland on the Shannon R. estuary; an important Norse settlement in the 9th and 10th cent. Pop. 60,736.

lime•stone (līm′stōn′) *n.* A common sedimentary rock consisting mostly of calcium carbonate, $CaCO_3$, used as a building stone and in the manufacture of lime, carbon dioxide, and cement.

lime•wa•ter (līm′wô′tər, -wŏt′ər) *n.* A clear colorless alkaline aqueous solution of calcium hydroxide, used in calamine lotion and other skin preparations.

lim•ey (lī′mē) *n., pl.* **-eys.** *Slang.* **1.** A British sailor. **2.** An English person. [Short for *lime juicer* (< the use of lime juice on British warships in order to prevent scurvy).]

li•mic•o•line (lī-mĭk′ə-līn′, -lĭn) *adj.* Of or relating to shore birds, esp. the plovers, sandpipers, and phalaropes. [< NLat. *Līmicolae*, group name < pl. of LLat. *līmicola*, living in mud : Lat. *līmus*, slime; see **lei-*** + Lat. *-cola*, inhabitant; see -COLOUS.]

li•mic•o•lous (lī-mĭk′ə-ləs) *adj.* Living in mud. [< LLat. *līmicola.* See LIMICOLINE.]

lim•it (lĭm′ĭt) *n.* **1.** The point, edge, or line beyond which something cannot or may not proceed. **2. limits.** The boundary surrounding a specific area; bounds. **3.** A confining or restricting object, agent, or influence. **4.** The greatest or least amount, number, or extent allowed or possible. **5.** *Games.* The largest amount that may be bet at one time in games of chance. **6.** *Math.* A number or point *k* that is closely approximated by a function *f(x)* when a suitable condition is placed on the independent variable *x*. **7.** *Informal.* One that approaches or exceeds certain limits. —*tr.v.* **-it•ed, -it•ing, -its. 1.** To confine or restrict within a boundary or bounds. **2.** To fix definitely; to specify. [ME *limite* < OFr., border < Lat. *līmes*, *līmit-*, border, limit.] —**lim′it•a•ble** *adj.*

lim•i•tar•y (lĭm′ĭ-tĕr′ē) *adj. Archaic.* **1.a.** Of or relating to a limit or boundary. **b.** Limiting; restrictive. **2.** Limited.

lim•i•ta•tion (lĭm′ĭ-tā′shən) *n.* **1.** The act of limiting or the state of being limited. **2.** A restriction. **3.** A shortcoming or defect. **4.** *Law.* A specified period during which, by statute, an action may be brought.

lim•it•ed (lĭm′ĭ-tĭd) *adj.* **1.** Confined or restricted within certain limits. **2.a.** Not attaining the highest goals or level of achievement. **b.** Having only mediocre talent or range of ability. **3.** Having governmental or ruling powers restricted by enforceable limitations, as a constitution. **4.** Of, relating to, or being a limited company. **5.** Of, relating to, or being transportation facilities, such as trains or buses, that make few stops and carry relatively few passengers. —*n.* A limited train or bus. —**lim′i•ted•ly** *adv.* —**lim′i•ted•ness** *n.*

limited company *n.* A firm, usu. British, organized in such a way as to give its owners limited liability.

limited edition *n.* An edition, as of a book or print, restricted to a specified number of copies.

limited liability *n.* The liability of a firm's owners for no more capital than they have invested in the business.

lim•it•er (lĭm′ĭt-ər) *n.* **1.** One that limits: *a limiter of choices.* **2.** *Electron.* A circuit that prevents the amplitude of a waveform from exceeding a specified value.

lim•it•ing (lĭm′ĭ-tĭng) *adj.* **1.** Acting as a limit. **2.** *Gram.* Restricting the range of application of the noun modified.

limit point *n. Math.* See **limit** 6.

limn (lĭm) *tr.v.* **limned, limn•ing** (lĭm′nĭng), **limns. 1.** To describe. **2.** To depict by painting or drawing. [ME *limnen*, to illuminate (a manuscript), prob. alteration of *luminen* < OFr. *luminer* < Lat. *lūmināre*, to illuminate, adorn < *lūmen*, *lūmin-*, light. See **leuk-*.**] —**limn′er** (lĭm′nər) *n.*

lim•net•ic (lĭm-nĕt′ĭk) *adj.* Of or occurring in the deeper open waters of lakes or ponds. [< Gk. *limnētēs*, marsh-dwelling < *limnē*, lake.]

limpet
Top: Overhead view
Bottom: Profile

lim•nol•o•gy (lĭm-nŏl′ə-jē) *n.* The scientific study of the life and phenomena of fresh water, esp. lakes and ponds. [Gk. *limnē*, lake + -LOGY.] —**lim′no•log′i•cal** (-nə-lŏj′ĭ-kəl) *adj.*

Lím•nos (lēm′nôs). See **Lemnos.**

lim•o (lĭm′ō) *n., pl.* **lim•os.** *Informal.* A limousine.

Li•moges (lē-mōzh′). A city of W-central France NE of Bordeaux; noted for its ceramic industry. Pop. 140,400.

lim•o•nene (lĭm′ə-nēn′) *n.* A liquid, $C_{10}H_{16}$, with a characteristic lemonlike fragrance, used as a solvent, wetting agent, and dispersing agent and in the manufacture of resins. [Fr. *limonène* < *limon*, lemon (obsolete) < OFr. See LEMON.]

li•mo•nite (lī′mə-nīt′) *n.* Any of a group of widely occurring iron oxide minerals, $Fe_2O_3{\cdot}nH_2O$, used as a minor ore of iron. [Ger. *Limonit* < Gk. *leimōn*, meadow.]

Li•mou•sin (lē-mo͞o-zăN′). A historical region and former province of central France W of the Auvergne Mts.; included in the dowry given by Eleanor of Aquitaine to Henry II of England in 1152 but reconquered by France (1370–74).

lim•ou•sine (lĭm′ə-zēn′, lĭm′ə-zēn′) *n.* Any of various large passenger vehicles, esp. a luxurious automobile usu. driven by a chauffeur. [Fr., perh. after LIMOUSIN.]

limp (lĭmp) *intr.v.* **limped, limp•ing, limps. 1.** To walk lamely, esp. with irregularity, as if favoring one leg. **2.** To move or proceed haltingly or unsteadily: *The project limped along.* —*n.* An irregular, jerky, or awkward gait. —*adj.* **limp•er, limp•est. 1.** Lacking or having lost rigidity, as of structure or substance. **2.** Lacking strength or firmness; weak or spiritless. [Prob. < obsolete *lymphault*, lame < OE *lempheallt* : *lemp-*, hanging loosely + *-healt*, lame, limping.] —**limp′ly** *adv.* —**limp′ness** *n.*

lim•pet (lĭm′pĭt) *n.* **1.** Any of numerous marine gastropod mollusks, as of the families Acmaeidae and Patellidae, having a conical shell and adhering to rocks of tidal areas. **2.** One that clings persistently. **3.** A type of explosive designed to cling to the hull of a ship and detonate on contact or signal. [Poss. ME *lempet*, European limpet (sense uncertain).]

lim•pid (lĭm′pĭd) *adj.* **1.** Characterized by transparent clearness; pellucid. **2.** Easily intelligible; clear. **3.** Calm and untroubled; serene. [Lat. *limpidus.*] —**lim•pid′i•ty, lim′pid•ness** *n.* —**lim′pid•ly** *adv.*

limp•kin (lĭmp′kĭn) *n.* A large brownish wading bird *(Aramus guarauna)* of warm swampy regions of the New World, having long legs and a drooping bill. [< its gait.]

Lim•po•po (lĭm-pō′pō) also **Croc•o•dile River** (krŏk′ə-dīl′). A river of SE Africa rising in NE South Africa and flowing c. 1,770 km (1,100 mi) to the Indian Ocean in S Mozambique.

lim•u•lus (lĭm′yə-ləs) *n., pl.* **-li** (-lī, -lē). See **horseshoe crab.** [Lat. *līmulus*, sidelong (< its motion), dim. of *līmus.*]

Lin (lĭn), **Maya.** b. 1959. Amer. sculptor and architect whose works include the Vietnam Veterans Memorial (1982).

ă pat	oi boy
ā pay	ou out
âr care	o͝o took
ä father	o͞o boot
ĕ pet	ŭ cut
ē be	ûr urge
ĭ pit	th thin
ī pie	*th* this
îr pier	hw which
ŏ pot	zh vision
ō toe	ə about, item
ô paw	

Stress marks:
′ (primary);
′ (secondary), as in **dictionary** (dĭk′shə-nĕr′ē)

Abraham Lincoln
1863 photograph by
Alexander Gardner
(1821–1882)

Mary Todd Lincoln
c. 1863–1865 photograph
attributed to
Mathew Brady

Charles Lindbergh
Photographed in 1927

lin. *abbr.* **1.** Lineal. **2.** Linear.

lin•ac (lĭn′ăk′) *n.* See **linear accelerator.** [LIN(EAR) AC(CELERATOR).]

lin•age also **line•age** (lī′nĭj) *n.* **1.** The number of lines of printed or written material. **2.** Payment for written work at a specified amount per line.

lin•al•o•ol (lĭ-năl′ō-ôl′, -ōl′, -ŏl′) *n.* A colorless fragrant liquid, $C_{10}H_{18}O$ distilled from essential oils, esp. rosewood and bergamot, and used in making perfume. [Sp. *lináloe*, aloe (< LLat. *lignum aloēs*, wood of the aloe : Lat. *lignum*, wood; see LIGNI- + Lat. *aloēs*, genitive of *aloē*, aloe; see ALOE) + -OL[1].]

Lin Biao (lĭn′ byou′) or **Lin Piao** (pyou′, byou′). 1907–71. Chinese political leader who fought to achieve a Communist takeover in China (1949).

linch•pin or **lynch•pin** (lĭnch′pĭn′) *n.* **1.** A locking pin inserted in the end of a shaft to prevent a wheel from slipping off. **2.** A central cohesive element. [ME *linspin* : *lins*, linchpin (< OE *lynis*) + *pin*, pin (< OE *pinn*; see PIN).]

Lin•coln[1] (lĭng′kən). **1.** A borough of E England NE of Nottingham; first chartered 1157. Pop. 75,900. **2.** The cap. of NE, in the SE part SW of Omaha; founded 1864. Pop. 191,972.

Lin•coln[2] (lĭng′kən) *n.* Any of a breed of sheep with long wool, developed in Lincolnshire, a county of eastern England.

Lincoln, Abraham. 1809–65. The 16th President of the U.S. (1861–65), who led the Union during the Civil War and emancipated slaves in the South (1863); assassinated by John Wilkes Booth. **—Lin′coln•esque′** *adj.*

Lincoln, Mary Todd. 1818–82. First Lady of the U.S. (1861–65); criticized for allegedly having Confederate sympathies.

Lincoln, Mount. A peak, 4,357.2 m (14,286 ft), in the Park Range of the Rocky Mts. in central CO.

Lincoln Park. A city of SE MI, a suburb of Detroit. Pop. 41,832.

lin•co•my•cin (lĭng′kə-mī′sĭn) *n.* An antibiotic derived from the bacterium *Streptomyces lincolnensis*, used in the treatment of certain infections. [*lincolnensis*, specific epithet + -MYCIN.]

Lind (lĭnd), **Jenny.** "the Swedish Nightingale." 1820–87. Swedish soprano who toured the U.S. (1850–52).

lin•dane (lĭn′dān) *n.* A white crystalline powder, $C_6H_6Cl_6$, used chiefly as an agricultural pesticide but also used topically in the treatment of scabies and pediculosis. [After Teunis van der *Linden*, 20th-cent. Dutch chemist.]

Lind•bergh (lĭnd′bûrg′, lĭn′-), **Anne Spencer Morrow.** b. 1906. Amer. aviator and writer whose works include *Gift from the Sea* (1955).

Lindbergh, Charles Augustus. "Lucky Lindy." 1902–74. Amer. aviator who made the first solo transatlantic flight (May 20–21, 1927).

lin•den (lĭn′dən) *n.* Any of various deciduous shade trees of the genus *Tilia,* having heart-shaped leaves. [ME, made of linden wood < OE < *lind*, linden.]

Lin•den (lĭn′dən). A city of NE NJ near Elizabeth. Pop. 36,701.

Lin•den•hurst (lĭn′dən-hûrst′). A village of SE NY on S Long I. near Babylon. Pop. 26,879.

Lin•den•wold (lĭn′dən-wōld′). A borough of SW NJ SE of Camden; settled in 1742. Pop. 18,734.

Lin•dis•farne (lĭn′dĭs-färn′). See **Holy Island.**

Lind•say (lĭn′zē), **(Nicholas) Vachel.** 1879–1931. Amer. poet who wrote *General William Booth Enters Heaven* (1913).

lin•dy or **Lin•dy** (lĭn′dē) *n.*, *pl.* **-dies.** A lively swing dance for couples. [After *Lindy*, nickname of Charles A. LINDBERGH.]

line[1] (līn) *n.* **1.** The path traced by a moving point. **2.a.** A thin continuous mark, as that made by a pen, pencil, or brush applied to a surface. **b.** A similar mark cut or scratched into a surface. **c.** A crease in the skin, esp. on the face; a wrinkle. **3.a.** A real or imaginary mark positioned in relation to fixed points of reference. **b.** A degree or circle of longitude or latitude drawn on a map or globe. **c.** The equator. **4.a.** A border or boundary. **b.** A demarcation. **c.** A contour or an outline. **5.a.** A mark used to define a shape or represent a contour. **b.** Any of the marks that make up the formal design of a picture. **6.a.** A cable, rope, string, cord, or wire. **b.** *Naut.* A rope put to use aboard a ship. **c.** A fishing line. **d.** A clothesline. **e.** A cord or tape used for measuring, leveling, or straightening. **7.** A pipe or system of pipes for conveying a fluid: *gas lines.* **8.** An electric-power transmission cable. **9.a.** A wire or system of wires connecting telephone or telegraph systems. **b.** An open or functioning telephone connection. **10.a.** A passenger or cargo system of public or private transportation usu. over a definite route. **b.** A company owning or managing such a system. **11.a.** A railway track or system of tracks. **b.** A particular section of a railway network. **12.** A course of progress or movement; a route. **13.a.** A general method, manner, or course of procedure. **b.** A manner or course of procedure determined by a specified factor: *along socialist lines.* **c.** An official or prescribed policy. **14.** A general concept or model. Often used in the plural. **15.** A condition of agreement; alignment. **16.a.** One's trade, occupation, or field of interest. **b.** Range of competence: *not in my line.* **17.** Merchandise or services of a similar or related nature: *a line of tools.* **18.** A group of persons or things arranged in a row or series. **19.a.** Ancestry or lineage. **b.** A series of persons, esp. from one family, who succeed each other. **c.** A strain, as of livestock or plants, developed and maintained by selective breeding. **20.a.** A sequence of related things that leads to a certain ending: *a line of argument.* **b.** An ordered system of operations that allows a sequential manufacture or assembly of goods. **c.** The personnel of an organization or a business who actually make a product or perform a service. **21.a.** A horizontal row of printed or written words or symbols. **b.** One of the horizontal scans forming a television image. **22.** A brief letter; a note. **23.a.** A unit of verse ending in a visual or typographic break and generally characterized by its length and meter. **b.** The dialogue of a theatrical presentation. Often used in the plural. **24.** *Informal.* Glib or insincere talk. **25. lines.** *Chiefly British.* **a.** A marriage certificate. **b.** A number of lines of prose or verse to be written out by a pupil as punishment. **26.** *Games.* A horizontal demarcation on a scorecard in bridge dividing the bonus points from the points for making the contract. **27.a.** A source of information. **b.** The information itself. **28.a.** *Mus.* One of the five parallel marks constituting a staff. **b.** A sustained melodic or harmonic part in a piece. **29.a.** A formation in which elements, such as troops, are arranged abreast of one another. **b.** The battle area closest to the enemy; the front. **c.** The combat troops or warships at the front. **d.** The regular forces of an army or a navy. **e.** The class of officers in direct command of warships or of army combat units. **f.** A bulwark or trench. **g.** An extended system of fortifications or defenses. **30.** *Sports.* **a.** A foul line. **b.** A real or imaginary mark demarcating a specified section of a playing area or field. **c.** A real or imaginary mark or point at which a race begins or ends. **d.** The center and two wings making up a hockey team's offensive unit. **31.a.** A line of scrimmage. **b.** The linemen considered as a group. **32.** *Informal.* The odds a bookmaker gives, esp. for sports events. **33.** The proportion of an insurance risk assumed by a particular underwriter or company. **34.** *Slang.* A small amount of cocaine arranged in a thin strip for sniffing. **35.** *Archaic.* One's lot or position in life. *—v.* **lined, lin•ing, lines.** *—tr.* **1.** To mark, incise, or cover with a line or lines. **2.** To represent with lines. **3.** To place in a series or row. **4.** To form a bordering line along. **5.** *Baseball.* To hit (a ball) sharply, usu. in a straight line. *—intr. Baseball.* To hit a line drive: *lined out to shortstop.* ***—phrasal verb.*** **line up. 1.** To arrange in or form a line. **2.** To organize and make ready. ***—idioms.*** **all along the line. 1.** In every place. **2.** At every stage or moment. **down the line. 1.** All the way; throughout. **2.** At a point or an end in the future. **in line for.** Next in order for. **on the line. 1.** Ready or available for immediate payment. **2.** So as to be risked; in jeopardy. **out of line. 1.** Uncalled-for; improper. **2.** Unruly and out of control. [ME < OE *līne* and < OFr. *ligne*, both < Lat. *līnea*, fem. sing. of *līneus*, of linen < *līnum*, thread, linen. See **līno-***.]

line[2] (līn) *tr.v.* **lined, lin•ing, lines. 1.** To fit a covering to the inside surface of. **2.** To cover the inner surface of. **3.** To fill plentifully, as with money or food. [ME *linen* < *line*, flax, linen cloth < OE *līn* < Lat. *līnum*. See **līno-***.]

lin•e•age[1] (lĭn′ē-ĭj) *n.* **1.a.** Direct descent from a particular ancestor; ancestry. **b.** Derivation. **2.** The descendants of a common ancestor considered to be the founder of the line. [ME *linage, lineage* < OFr. *lignage* < *ligne*, line. See LINE[1].]

line•age[2] (lī′nĭj) *n.* Var. of **linage.**

lin•e•al (lĭn′ē-əl) *adj.* **1.** Belonging to or being in the direct line of descent from an ancestor. **2.** Derived from or relating to a particular line of descent; hereditary. **3.** Linear. [ME < OFr. < LLat. *līneālis*, consisting of lines < Lat. *līnea*, line. See LINE[1].] **—lin′e•al•ly** *adv.*

lin•e•a•ment (lĭn′ē-ə-mənt) *n.* **1.** A distinctive shape, contour, or line, esp. of the face. **2.** A definitive or characteristic feature. Often used in the plural. [ME *liniament* < Lat. *līneāmentum* < *līnea*, line. See LINE[1].]

lin•e•ar (lĭn′ē-ər) *adj.* **1.** Of, relating to, or resembling a line; straight. **2.a.** In, of, describing, described by, or related to a straight line. **b.** Having only one dimension. **3.** Characterized by, composed of, or emphasizing drawn lines rather than painterly effects. **4.** *Bot.* Narrow and elongated with nearly parallel margins: *a linear leaf.* [Lat. *līneāris* < *līnea*, line. See LINE[1].] **—lin′e•ar•ly** *adv.*

Lin•e•ar A (lĭn′ē-ər) *n.* An undeciphered writing system used in Crete from the 18th to the 15th century B.C.

linear accelerator *n.* An electron, a proton, or a heavy-ion accelerator in which the paths of the particles accelerated are essentially straight lines rather than circles or spirals.

linear algebra *n.* *Math.* **1.** The branch of mathematics that deals with systems of linear equations, matrices, vector spaces, determinants, and linear transformations. **2.** A ring that is also a vector space with scalars from an associated field, the multiplication of which is of the form $(a\mathbf{A})(b\mathbf{B}) = (ab)(\mathbf{AB})$, where a and b are scalars and $\mathbf{A}$ and $\mathbf{B}$ are vectors.

Linear B *n.* A syllabic script used in Mycenaean Greek documents chiefly from Crete and Pylos, mostly from the 14th to the 12th century B.C.

linear combination *n. Math.* An expression of first order, composed of the sums and differences of elements with nonzero coefficients.
linear dependence *n. Math.* The property of a set that is not linearly independent.
linear equation *n. Math.* An algebraic equation, such as $y = 2x + 7$, in which the highest degree term in the variable or variables is of the first degree.
linear independence *n. Math.* The property of a set, with coefficients taken from another set, that has no linear combinations equal to zero unless all of the coefficients equal zero.
lin•e•ar•ize (lĭn′ē-ə-rīz') *tr.v.* **-ized, -iz•ing, -iz•es.** To put or project linearly. **— lin′e•ar•i•za′tion** (-ər-ĭ-zā′shən) *n.*
linear measure *n.* **1.** The measurement of length. **2.** A unit or system of units for measuring length.
linear momentum *n.* See **momentum** 1.
linear perspective *n.* A form of perspective in drawing and painting in which parallel lines are represented as converging so as to give the illusion of depth and distance.
lin•e•a•tion (lĭn'ē-ā′shən) *n.* **1.** The act of marking or outlining with lines. **2.** An outline. **3.** An arrangement of lines. [ME *lineacioun* < Lat. *līneātiō, līneātiōn-* < *līneātus,* p.part. of *līneāre,* to make straight < *līnea,* thread, line. See LINE[1].]
line•back•er (līn′băk'ər) *n. Football.* Any of the defensive players forming a second line of defense behind the ends and tackles. **— line′back′ing** *n.*
line breeding *n.* Selective inbreeding to perpetuate certain desired qualities or characteristics in a strain of livestock.
line cut *n.* A letterpress printing plate made from a line drawing by a photoengraving process.
line drawing *n.* A drawing made with lines only, esp. one used as copy for a line cut.
line drive *n. Baseball.* A batted ball hit sharply so that its path roughly describes a straight line.
line engraving *n.* **1.a.** A metal plate, used in intaglio printing, on which design lines have been engraved by hand. **b.** The process of making such an engraving. **c.** A print made from such an engraving. **2.** See **line cut.**
Line Islands (līn). A group of islands in the central Pacific Ocean S of Hawaii; now part of Kiribati.
line item *n.* A single item, esp. of a legislative appropriations bill. **— line′-i′tem** (līn′ī′təm) *adj.*
line•man (līn′mən) *n.* **1.** A person employed to install or repair telephone, telegraph, or electric power lines. **2.** *Football.* A player positioned on the forward line.
lin•en (lĭn′ən) *n.* **1.a.** Thread made from fibers of the flax plant. **b.** Cloth woven from this thread. **2.** Articles made from linen or a similar cloth; bed sheets and tablecloths. Often used in the plural. **3.** Paper made from flax fibers or having a linenlike luster. — *adj.* **1.** Made of flax or linen. **2.** Resembling linen. [ME < OE *līnen,* made of flax < Germanic **līnin-* < **līnam,* flax, prob. < Lat. *līnum.* See **līno-*.**]
line of credit *n., pl.* **lines of credit.** See **credit line** 2.
line officer *n.* A commissioned officer in the armed forces who is assigned to the line for duty.
line of force *n., pl.* **lines of force.** An imaginary line whose direction at any point is that of the field of force at that point.
line of scrimmage *n., pl.* **lines of scrimmage.** *Football.* An imaginary line across the field on which the ball rests and at which the teams line up for a new play.
line of sight *n., pl.* **lines of sight. 1.** An imaginary line from the eye to a perceived object. **2.** An unobstructed path between sending and receiving antennas.
lin•e•o•late (lĭn′ē-ə-lāt') *adj.* Marked with fine lines. [NLat. *līneolātus* < Lat. *līneola,* dim. of *līnea,* thread, line. See LINE[1].]
line printer *n.* A high-speed printing device, primarily used in data processing, that prints an entire line of type as a unit.
lin•er[1] (lī′nər) *n.* **1.** One that draws or makes lines. **2.** A large commercial ship or airplane, esp. one carrying passengers on a regular route. **3.** *Baseball.* A line drive.
lin•er[2] (lī′nər) *n.* **1.** One that makes or puts in linings. **2.a.** A lining. **b.** Material used as a lining.
lin•er•board (lī′nər-bôrd', -bōrd') *n.* A type of paperboard used in making corrugated cartons.
line score *n. Sports.* A summary of the scoring by period in a game displayed in a horizontal table, esp. an inning-by-inning record of the runs scored in a baseball game.
lines•man (līnz′mən) *n.* **1.a.** *Football.* An official who marks the downs and the position of the ball and watches for violations from the sidelines. **b.** *Sports.* A man in various court games who calls shots out of bounds. **2.** See **lineman** 1.
line spectrum *n.* A spectrum appearing as distinct lines characteristic of the chemical elements in a luminous gas.
line squall *n.* A squall or a series of squalls occurring along a narrow band of thunderstorms.
lines•wom•an (līnz′wo͝om'ən) *n. Sports.* A woman in various court games who calls shots out of bounds.
line•up also **line-up** (līn′ŭp') *n.* **1.** A line of people that is formed for inspection or identification. **2.** *Sports.* **a.** The members of a team chosen to start a game. **b.** A list of such players. **3.** A group of people, organizations, or things enlisted or arrayed for a purpose.
ling[1] (lĭng) *n., pl.* **ling** or **lings.** Any of various marine food fishes related to or resembling the cod, esp. *Molva molva.* [ME, poss. of LGer. orig. See **del-[1]*.**]
ling[2] (lĭng) *n.* See **heather** 1. [ME < ON *lyng.*]
ling. *abbr.* Linguistics.
–ling[1] *suff.* **1.** One connected with: *worldling.* **2.** One having a specified quality: *underling.* **3.** One that is young, small, or inferior: *duckling.* [ME < OE.]
–ling[2] *suff.* In a specified direction, manner, way, or condition: *darkling.* [ME < OE.]
Lin•ga•la (lĭng-gä′lə) *n.* A creole based on Bantu, widely spoken as a lingua franca in Zaire.
lin•gam (lĭng′gəm) also **lin•ga** (lĭn′-gə) *n. Hinduism.* A stylized phallus worshiped as a symbol of the god Shiva. [Skt. *liṅgam,* mark, penis.]
ling•ber•ry (lĭng′bĕr'ē) *n.* See **cowberry.** [Var. of LINGONBERRY.]
ling•cod (lĭng′kŏd') *n., pl.* **lingcod** or **-cods.** A large northern Pacific food fish *(Ophiodon elongatus).*
lin•ger (lĭng′gər) *v.* **-gered, -ger•ing, -gers.** — *intr.* **1.** To be slow in leaving, esp. out of reluctance; tarry. See Syns at **stay[1]. 2.** To remain feebly alive for some time before dying. **3.** To persist: *an aftertaste that lingers.* **4.** To proceed slowly; saunter. **5.** To be tardy in acting; procrastinate. — *tr.* To pass (a period of time) in a slow, leisurely, or aimless manner. [ME *lengeren,* freq. of *lengen,* to prolong < OE *lengan.* See **del-[1]*.**] **— lin′ger•er** *n.* **— lin′ger•ing•ly** *adv.*
lin•ge•rie (län'zhə-rā′, län′zhə-rē, lăɴ-zhə-rē′) *n.* **1.** Women's underclothes. **2.** *Archaic.* Linen articles, esp. garments. [Fr. < OFr. < *linge,* linen < Lat. *līneus,* made of linen < *līnum,* flax. See **līno-*.**]
lin•go (lĭng′gō) *n., pl.* **-goes. 1.** Language that is unintelligible or unfamiliar. **2.** The specialized vocabulary of a particular field or discipline. [Prob. < Port. *lingoa* < Lat. *lingua,* language. See **dn̥ghū-*.**]
lin•gon•ber•ry (lĭng′ən-bĕr'ē) *n.* See **cowberry.** [Swed. *lingon,* a kind of berry + BERRY.]
lin•gua (lĭng′gwə) *n., pl.* **-guae** (-gwē'). A tongue or tonguelike organ. [Lat., tongue, language. See **dn̥ghū-*.**]
lingua fran•ca (frăng′kə) *n., pl.* **lingua fran•cas** (-kəz) also **linguae fran•cae** (-kē). **1.** A medium of communication between peoples of different languages. **2.** A mixture of Italian with Provençal, French, Spanish, Arabic, Greek, and Turkish, formerly spoken on the eastern Mediterranean coast. [Ital. : *lingua,* language + *franca,* Frankish (that is, European).]
lin•gual (lĭng′gwəl) *adj.* **1.** Of, relating to, or situated near the tongue or a tonguelike organ. **2.** *Ling.* Pronounced with the tongue and other organs of speech. **3.** Of languages; linguistic. — *n. Ling.* A sound, such as (t), (l), and (n), that is pronounced with the tongue and other organs of speech.
lin•gui•ça (lĭng-gwē′sə, -sä, lĭn-) *n.* A highly seasoned Portuguese pork sausage flavored with garlic, onions, and pepper. [Port.]
lin•gui•ne also **lin•gui•ni** (lĭng-gwē′nē) *n.* Pasta in long flat thin strands. [Ital., pl. of *linguina,* dim. of *lingua,* tongue < Lat. See LINGUA.]
lin•guist (lĭng′gwĭst) *n.* **1.** A person who speaks several languages fluently. **2.** A specialist in linguistics. [Lat. *lingua,* language; see **dn̥ghū-*** + -IST.]
lin•guis•tic (lĭng-gwĭs′tĭk) *adj.* Of or relating to language or linguistics. **— lin•guis′ti•cal•ly** *adv.*
linguistic atlas *n.* A set of maps recording the geographic distribution of variations in speech.
linguistic form *n.* A meaningful unit of speech, such as an affix, a word, a phrase, or a sentence.
linguistic geography *n.* The branch of linguistics that studies regional variations of speech. **— linguistic geographer** *n.*
lin•guis•tics (lĭng-gwĭs′tĭks) *n. (used with a sing. v.)* The study of the nature and structure of human speech.
lin•gu•late (lĭng′gyə-lāt') *adj.* Shaped like a tongue. [Lat. *lingulātus* < *lingula,* dim. of *lingua,* tongue. See LINGUA.]
lin•i•ment (lĭn′ə-mənt) *n.* A medicinal fluid rubbed into the skin to soothe pain or relieve stiffness. [ME < LLat. *linīmentum* < Lat. *linere, linīre,* to rub over, anoint. See **lei-*.**]
lin•ing (lī′nĭng) *n.* **1.** A covering or coating for an inside surface. **2.** Material used for such covering or coating.
link[1] (lĭngk) *n.* **1.** One of the rings or loops forming a chain. **2.a.** A unit in a connected series of units. **b.** A unit in a transportation or communications system. **c.** A connecting element; a tie or bond. **3.a.** An association; a relationship. **b.** A causal, parallel, or reciprocal relationship; a correlation. **4.** A cuff link. **5.** A unit of length used in surveying, equal to 0.01 chain, 7.92 inches, or about 20.12 centimeters. **6.** A rod or lever transmitting motion in a machine. **7.** *Comp. Sci.* A pointer attached to an item in a data set or program to facilitate connection to other items. — *tr. & intr.v.* **linked, link•ing, links.** To connect or become connected with or as if with a link. See Syns at **join.** [ME *linke,* of Scand. orig.] **— link′er** *n.*
link[2] (lĭngk) *n.* A torch formerly used for lighting one's way in the streets. [Poss. < Med.Lat. *linchinus, lichnus,* candle < Lat. *lychnus* < Gk. *lukhnos,* lamp. See **leuk-*.**]
link•age (lĭng′kĭj) *n.* **1.a.** The act or process of linking. **b.** The

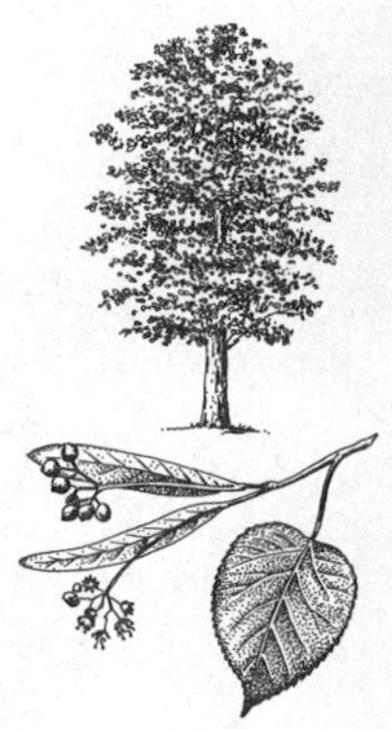

linden
American linden
Tilia americana

ă **pat**	oi **boy**
ā **pay**	ou **out**
âr **care**	o͝o **took**
ä **father**	o͞o **boot**
ĕ **pet**	ŭ **cut**
ē **be**	ûr **urge**
ĭ **pit**	th **thin**
ī **pie**	*th* **this**
îr **pier**	hw **which**
ŏ **pot**	zh **vision**
ō **toe**	ə **about, item**
ô **paw**	

Stress marks:
′ (primary);
' (secondary), as in
dictionary (dĭk′shə-nĕr'ē)

condition of being linked. **2.** A connection or relation; an association. **3.** A negotiating policy of making agreement on one issue dependent on progress toward another objective. **4.** A system of interconnected machine elements used to transmit power or motion. **5.** *Elect.* A measure of the induced voltage in a circuit, equal to the magnetic flux times the number of turns in the coil that surrounds it. **6.** *Genet.* An association between two or more genes such that the traits they control tend to be inherited together.

linkage group *n.* A pair or set of genes on a chromosome that tend to be transmitted together.

linked (lĭngkt) *adj.* **1.** Connected, esp. by or as if by links. **2.** *Genet.* Exhibiting linkage.

link•ing verb (lĭng′kĭng) *n.* See **copula** 1.

Lin•kö•ping (lĭn′chœ′pĭng). A city of SE Sweden SW of Stockholm; a noted intellectual center during the Middle Ages. Pop. 115,600.

links (lĭngks) *pl.n.* **1.** *Sports.* A golf course. **2.** *Scots.* Relatively flat or undulating sandy turf-covered ground usu. along a seashore. [< ME *link*, ridge of land, hill < OE *hlinc*, ridge.]

link•up (lĭngk′ŭp′) *n.* **1.** The act of linking or connecting. **2.** Something that serves to link or join; a connection. **3.** A set of linked elements that forms a functioning system.

linn (lĭn) *n. Scots.* **1.** A waterfall. **2.** A steep ravine. [Sc.Gael. *linne*, pool, waterfall.]

Lin•nae•us (lĭ-nē′əs, -nā′-), **Carolus.** 1707–78. Swedish botanist and founder of the modern classification system for plants and animals. — **Lin•nae′an, Lin•ne′an** *adj.*

lin•net (lĭn′ĭt) *n.* **1.** A small Old World finch *(Carduelis cannabina)* having brownish plumage. **2.** A similar bird *(Carpodacus mexicanus)* of Mexico and the western United States. [Obsolete Fr. *linette* < OFr. < *lin*, flax (< its feeding on flax seed) < Lat. *līnum*. See **līno-***.]

Linn•he (lĭn′ē), **Loch.** An inlet of the Atlantic on the W coast of Scotland, part of the Caledonian Canal waterway.

lin•o•le•ic acid (lĭn′ə-lē′ĭk) *n.* An unsaturated fatty acid, $C_{17}H_{31}COOH$, that is essential to the human diet and occurs widely in drying oils. [Gk. *linon*, flax; see **līno-*** + OLEIC ACID.]

lin•o•len•ic acid (lĭn′ə-lĕn′ĭk) *n.* An unsaturated fatty acid, $C_{17}H_{29}COOH$, that is essential to the human diet and occurs in natural drying oils. [Blend of LINOLEIC ACID and -ENE.]

li•no•le•um (lĭ-nō′lē-əm) *n.* A durable washable material made by pressing heated linseed oil, rosin, powdered cork, and pigments onto a burlap or canvas backing and used as a covering esp. for floors. [Originally a trademark.]

Li•no•type (lī′nə-tīp′). A trademark used for a machine that sets type on a metal slug, operated by a keyboard.

Lin Piao (lĭn′ pyou′, byou′). See **Lin Biao.**

lin•sang (lĭn′săng′) *n.* Any of several Asian or African catlike carnivorous mammals of the genera *Poiana* or *Prionodon,* having a spotted coat and a long banded tail. [Malay.]

lin•seed (lĭn′sēd′) *n.* The seed of flax, esp. when used as the source of linseed oil; flaxseed. [ME *linsed* < OE *līnsǣd* : *līn*, flax (< Lat. *līnum*; see **līno-***) + *sǣd*, seed; see SEED.]

linseed oil *n.* A drying oil extracted from flaxseed and used in paints, varnishes, printing inks, and synthetic resins.

lin•sey-wool•sey (lĭn′zē-wo͝ol′zē) *n., pl.* **-seys.** A coarse woven fabric of wool and cotton or of wool and linen. [ME *linsiwolsie* : alteration of *linen*, linen; see LINEN + *wolle*, wool; see WOOL.]

lin•stock (lĭn′stŏk′) *n.* A long forked stick for holding a match. [Obsolete *lyntstock*, alteration of Du. *lontstok* : *lont*, match + *stok*, stick (< MDu. *stoc*).]

lint (lĭnt) *n.* **1.** Clinging bits of fiber and fluff; fuzz. **2.** Downy material obtained by scraping linen cloth and used for dressing wounds. **3.** The mass of soft fibers surrounding the seeds of unginned cotton. [ME, var. of *linet* (< OFr. *linette*, grain of flax, dim. of *lin*, flax) or < Med.Lat. *linteum*, lint (< Lat., linen cloth), both < Lat. *līnum*, flax. See **līno-***.] — **lint′y** *adj.*

lin•tel (lĭn′tl) *n.* The horizontal beam over a window or door that supports the structure above it. [ME < OFr., prob. alteration of *lintier* < VLat. **līmitāris*, of a threshold < Lat., on a border < *līmes*, *līmit-*, boundary.]

lint•er (lĭn′tər) *n.* **1.** The short fibers that cling to cottonseeds after the first ginning. Often used in the plural. **2.** A machine that removes linters.

lint•white (lĭnt′hwīt′, -wīt′) *n.* A linnet. [By folk ety. < ME *linkwhitte*, alteration of OE *līnetwige* : *līn*, flax; see LINSEED + *-twige*, plucker, eater.]

Lin Yu•tang (lĭn′ yo͞o′tăng′). 1895–1976. Chinese-born Amer. philologist who wrote *Moment in Peking* (1939).

Linz (lĭnts). A city of N Austria on the Danube R. W of Vienna; orig. a Roman settlement. Pop. 199,910.

li•on (lī′ən) *n.* **1.** A large carnivorous feline mammal *(Panthera leo)* of Africa and northwest India having a short tawny coat and a long heavy mane in the male. **2.** Any of several large wildcats related to or resembling the lion. **3.a.** A very brave person. **b.** A person regarded as fierce or ferocious. **c.** An eminent person; a celebrity. — ***idiom.* lion's share.** The greatest or best part. [ME < OFr. < Lat. *leō*, *leōn-* < Gk. *leōn*, of Semitic orig.; akin to Heb. *lābî'*.]

Li•on (lī′ən) *n.* See **Leo.**

lion
Female and male lions
Panthera leo

li•on•ess (lī′ə-nĭs) *n.* A female lion.

li•on•fish (lī′ən-fĭsh′) *n., pl.* **lionfish** or **-fish•es.** Any of various brightly colored tropical Pacific scorpion fishes of the genus *Pterois,* having venomous spines in the dorsal fin.

li•on•heart•ed (lī′ən-här′tĭd) *adj.* Very courageous.

li•on•ize (lī′ə-nīz′) *tr.v.* **-ized, -iz•ing, -iz•es.** To look on or treat (a person) as a celebrity. — **li′on•iz′er** *n.*

Li•ons (lī′ənz), **Gulf of.** A wide inlet of the Mediterranean on the S coast of France.

lip (lĭp) *n.* **1.** *Anat.* Either of two fleshy folds that surround the opening of the mouth. **2.** A structure or part that encircles or bounds an orifice, as: **a.** *Anat.* A labium. **b.** The margin of flesh around a wound. **c.** Either of the margins of the aperture of a gastropod shell. **d.** A rim, as of a vessel or bell. **3.** *Bot.* One of the two divisions of a bilabiate corolla or calyx, as in the snapdragon. **4.** The tip of a pouring spout. **5.** *Slang.* Insolent talk. — *tr.v.* **lipped, lip•ping, lips. 1.a.** To touch the lips to. **b.** To kiss. **2.** To utter. **3.** To lap or splash against. **4.** *Sports.* To hit a golf ball so that it touches the edge of (the hole) without dropping in. [ME < OE *lippa*. See **leb-***.]

lip– *pref.* Var. of **lipo–.**

Li•pan (lĭ-pän′) *n.* **1.** *pl.* **Lipan** or **-pans.** A member of an Apache tribe formerly inhabiting western Texas, with a present-day population in southern New Mexico. **2.** The Apachean language of this tribe.

Lip•a•ri Islands (lĭp′ə-rē, lē′pä-). A group of volcanic islands of Italy off the NE coast of Sicily in the Tyrrhenian Sea.

lip•ase (lĭp′ās′, lī′pās′) *n.* Any of a group of enzymes that catalyze the hydrolysis of fats into glycerol and fatty acids.

Lip•chitz (lĭp′shĭts), **Jacques.** 1891–1973. Russian-born French sculptor whose works include *Rape of Europa* (1941).

lip•ec•to•my (lĭ-pĕk′tə-mē, lī-) *n., pl.* **-mies.** Surgical excision of subcutaneous fatty tissue.

Li•petsk (lē′pĕtsk′, lyĕ′pyĭtsk). A city of W-central Russia SSE of Moscow; orig. founded in the 13th cent. Pop. 447,000.

lip-gloss (lĭp′glôs′, -glŏs′) *n.* A cosmetic that gives shine or gloss to the lips.

lip•id (lĭp′ĭd, lī′pĭd) also **lip•ide** (lĭp′īd′, lī′pīd′) *n.* Any of a group of organic compounds, including the fats, oils, waxes, sterols, and glycerides, that are insoluble in water but soluble in organic solvents. [Fr. *lipide* : Gk. *lipos*, fat; see LIPO- + Fr. *-ide*, -ide.] — **lip•id′ic** *adj.*

Lip•mann (lĭp′mən), **Fritz Albert.** 1899–1986. German-born Amer. biochemist who shared a 1953 Nobel Prize.

Li Po (lē′ pō′, bō′) or **Li Bo** (bō′). d. c. 762. Chinese poet who composed romantic verse.

lipo– or **lip–** *pref.* Fat; fatty; fatty tissue: *lipolysis.* [< Gk. *lipos*, fat. See **leip-***.]

lip•oid (lĭp′oid′, lī′poid′) *n.* **1.** A lipid. **2.** Any of various substances, such as lecithin, that resemble fat. — *adj.* also **li•poi•dal** (lĭ-poid′l, lī-). Resembling fat; fatty.

li•pol•y•sis (lĭ-pŏl′ĭ-sĭs, lī-) *n., pl.* **-ses** (-sēz′). The hydrolysis of lipids. — **lip′o•lyt′ic** (lĭp′ə-lĭt′ĭk, lī′pə-) *adj.*

li•po•ma (lĭ-pō′mə, lī-) *n., pl.* **-ma•ta** (-mə-tə) or **-mas.** A benign fatty tumor. — **li•pom′a•tous** (-pŏm′ə-təs) *adj.*

lip•o•phil•ic (lĭp′ə-fĭl′ĭk, lī′pə-) *adj.* Having an affinity for, tending to combine with, or capable of dissolving in lipids.

lip•o•pol•y•sac•cha•ride (lĭp′ō-pŏl′ē-săk′ə-rīd′, lī′pō-) *n.* A polysaccharide combined with a lipid.

lip•o•pro•tein (lĭp′ō-prō′tēn′, -tē-ĭn, lī′pō-) *n.* Any of a group of conjugated proteins, such as cholesterol, in which at least one of the components is a lipid.

lip•o•some (lĭp′ə-sōm′, lī′pə-) *n.* An artificial microscopic vesicle consisting of an aqueous core enclosed in one or more phospholipid layers, used to convey vaccines, drugs, enzymes, or other substances to target cells or organs.

lip•o•suc•tion (lĭp′ō-sŭk′shən, lī′pō-) *n.* A usu. cosmetic surgical procedure in which excess fatty tissue is removed from a specific area of the body by means of suction.

lip•o•trop•ic (lĭp′ō-trŏp′ĭk, -trō′pĭk, lī′pō-) *adj.* **1.** Preventing accumulation of fat in the liver. **2.** Having an affinity for lipids. — **li•pot′ro•py** (lĭ-pŏt′rə-pē, lī-), **li•pot′ro•pism** *n.*

lip•o•tro•pin (lĭp′ə-trō′pĭn, lī′pə-) *n.* A hormone produced by the anterior pituitary gland that promotes the utilization of fat and is a precursor to the endorphins. [LIPOTROP(IC) + -IN.]

Lip•pi (lĭp′ē), **Filippino.** 1457?–1504? Italian painter who completed Masaccio's frescoes in the Brancacci Chapel in Florence.

Lippi, Fra **Filippo.** 1406?–69? Italian Renaissance painter whose works include *Madonna Enthroned* (1437).

Lipp•mann (lēp-män′), **Gabriel.** 1845–1921. French physicist who won a 1908 Nobel Prize.

Lipp•mann (lĭp′mən), **Walter.** 1889–1974. Amer. journalist who cofounded (1914) the weekly *New Republic.*

lip-read (lĭp′rēd′) *v.* **-read** (-rĕd′), **-read•ing, -reads.** — *tr.* To interpret (utterances) by lip reading. — *intr.* To interpret utterances by lip reading.

lip reading *n.* A technique for understanding unheard speech by interpreting the lip and facial movements of the speaker. — **lip reader** *n.*

Lip•scomb (lĭp′skəm), **William Nunn, Jr.** b. 1919. Amer. chemist who won a 1976 Nobel Prize.

lip service *n.* Verbal expression of agreement or allegiance, unsupported by real conviction or action; hypocritical respect.

lip•stick (lĭp′stĭk′) *n.* A small stick of waxy lip coloring enclosed in a cylindrical case.

lipstick tree *n.* See **annatto** 1.

lip-synch also **lip-sync** (lĭp′sĭngk′) — *v.* **-synched, -synch•ing, -synchs** also **-synced, -sync•ing, -syncs.** — *intr.* To move the lips in synchronization with recorded speech or song. — *tr.* To synchronize lip movement with (recorded speech or song).

Lip•tau•er (lĭp′tou′ər) *n.* **1.** A soft cheese originating in Hungary. **2.** A cheese spread made with Liptauer or a cream cheese substitute. [Ger., after *Liptau* (Liptó), Hungary.]

liq. *abbr.* **1.** Liquid. **2.** Liquor.

li•quate (lī′kwāt′) *tr.v.* **-quat•ed, -quat•ing, -quates.** To separate (the metals in an alloy) by melting the more fusible constituents while leaving the less fusible ones solid. [Lat. *liquāre, liquāt-*, to melt.] — **li•qua′tion** *n.*

liq•ue•fac•tion (lĭk′wə-făk′shən) *n.* **1.** The process of liquefying. **2.** The state of being liquefied. [ME *liquefaccion* < OFr. *liquefacion* < LLat. *liquefactiō, liquefactiōn-* < Lat. *liquefactus*, p.part. of *liquefacere*, to make liquid. See LIQUEFY.]

liq•ue•fy also **liq•ui•fy** (lĭk′wə-fī′) — *v.* **-fied, -fy•ing, -fies.** — *tr.* To cause to become liquid, esp.: **a.** To melt (a solid) by heating. **b.** To condense (a gas) by cooling. — *intr.* To become liquid. [ME *liquefien* < OFr. *liquefier* < Lat. *liquefacere* : *liquēre*, to be liquid + *facere*, to make; see FACT.] — **liq′ue•fi′er** *n.*

li•ques•cent (lĭ-kwĕs′ənt) *adj.* Becoming or tending to become liquid; melting. [Lat. *liquēscēns, liquēscent-*, pr.part. of *liquēscere*, to become liquid, inchoative of *liquēre*, to be liquid.] — **li•ques′cence, li•ques′cen•cy** *n.*

li•queur (lĭ-kûr′, -kyŏŏr′) *n.* Any of various strongly flavored alcoholic beverages typically served in small quantities after dinner. [Fr. < OFr. *licour*, a liquid. See LIQUOR.]

liq•uid (lĭk′wĭd) *n.* **1.a.** A state of matter characterized by a readiness to flow, little or no tendency to disperse, and relatively high incompressibility. **b.** Matter or a specific body of matter in this state. **2.** *Ling.* A consonant articulated without friction and capable of being prolonged like a vowel, such as English *l* and *r.* — *adj.* **1.** Of or being a liquid. **2.** Having been liquefied, esp.: **a.** Melted by heating. **b.** Condensed by cooling. **3.** Flowing readily; fluid. **4.** Having a flowing quality without harshness or abrupt breaks. **5.** *Ling.* Articulated without friction and capable of being prolonged like a vowel. **6.** Clear and shining. **7.** Readily convertible into cash. [< ME, of a liquid < OFr. *liquide* < Lat. *liquidus* < *liquēre*, to be liquid.] — **liq′uid•ly** *adv.* — **liq′uid•ness** *n.*

liq•uid•am•bar (lĭk′wĭd-ăm′bər) *n.* Any of several deciduous trees of the genus *Liquidambar,* such as the sweet gum. [NLat., genus name : Lat. *liquidus*, liquid; see LIQUID + Med.Lat. *ambar*, amber; see AMBER.]

liq•ui•date (lĭk′wĭ-dāt′) *v.* **-dat•ed, -dat•ing, -dates.** — *tr.* **1.a.** To pay off (a debt, for example); settle. **b.** To settle the affairs of (a business firm, for example) by determining the liabilities and applying the assets to their discharge. **2.** To convert (assets) into cash. **3.** To put an end to; abolish. **4.** To put to death; kill. — *intr.* **1.** To settle a debt, a claim, or an obligation. **2.** To liquidate a business or an estate. [LLat. *liquidāre, liquidāt-*, to melt < Lat. *liquidus*, liquid. See LIQUID.] — **liq′ui•da′tion** *n.* — **liq′ui•da′tor** *n.*

liquid crystal *n.* Any of various liquids in which the molecules are regularly arrayed in either one dimension or two dimensions, the order giving rise to characteristic optical properties.

liq•uid-crys•tal display (lĭk′wĭd-krĭs′təl) *n.* An alphanumeric display made up of a normally transparent liquid, sandwiched between layers of glass or plastic, that forms opaque patterns when an electric field is applied.

li•quid•i•ty (lĭ-kwĭd′ĭ-tē) *n.* **1.** The state of being liquid. **2.** The quality of being readily convertible into cash. **3.** Available cash or the capacity to obtain it on demand.

liquid measure *n.* **1.** The measurement of liquid capacity. **2.** A unit or system of units of liquid capacity.

liq•ui•fy (lĭk′wə-fī′) *v.* Var. of **liquefy.**

liq•uor (lĭk′ər) *n.* **1.** An alcoholic beverage made by distillation rather than by fermentation. **2.** A liquid, such as broth, produced in cooking. **3.** An aqueous solution of a nonvolatile substance. **4.** A solution, an emulsion, or a suspension for industrial use. — *tr.v.* **-uored, -uor•ing, -uors. 1.** To steep (malt, for example). **2.** *Slang.* To make drunk with alcoholic liquor. Often used with *up*: *was all liquored up.* [ME *licour*, a liquid < OFr. < Lat. *liquor* < *liquēre*, to be liquid.]

li•quo•rice (lĭk′ər-ĭs, -ĭsh) *n. Chiefly British.* Var. of **licorice.**

li•ra (lîr′ə, lē′rä) *n., pl.* **li•re** (lîr′ā, lē′rĕ) or **li•ras.** See table at **currency.** [Ital. < OItal. < OProv. *liura* < Lat. *lībra*, a unit of weight, pound.]

lir•i•pipe (lîr′ə-pīp′) *n.* A long scarf or cord attached to and hanging from a hood. [Med.Lat. *liripipium.*]

Lis•bon (lĭz′bən). The cap. of Portugal, in the W part on the Tagus R. estuary. An ancient Iberian settlement, it was devastated by a major earthquake in 1755. Pop. 807,167.

li•sen•te (lē-sĕn′tā) *n.* Pl. of **sente.**

lisle (līl) *n.* **1.** A fine, smooth, tightly twisted thread spun from long-stapled cotton. **2.** Fabric knitted of this thread, used esp. for hosiery and underwear. [After *Lisle* (Lille), France.]

lisp (lĭsp) *n.* **1.** A speech defect or mannerism characterized by mispronunciation of the sounds (s) and (z) as (th) and (*th*). **2.** A sound of or like a lisp. — *v.* **lisped, lisp•ing, lisps.** — *intr.* **1.** To speak with a lisp. **2.** To speak imperfectly, as a child does. — *tr.* To pronounce with a lisp. [< ME *lispen*, to lisp < OE *-wlispian* < *wlisp*, lisping.] — **lisp′er** *n.*

LISP (lĭsp) *n. Comp. Sci.* A programming language widely used in artificial intelligence research. [*lis(t) p(rocessing).*]

lis•some also **lis•som** (lĭs′əm) *adj.* **1.** Easily bent; supple. **2.** Having the ability to move with ease; limber. [Alteration of LITHESOME.] — **lis′some•ly** *adv.* — **lis′some•ness** *n.*

list[1] (lĭst) *n.* **1.** A series of names, words, or other items written, printed, or imagined one after the other: *guest list.* **2.** A considerable number; a long series. — *v.* **list•ed, list•ing, lists.** — *tr.* **1.** To make a list of; itemize. **2.** To enter in a list; register. **3.** To put (oneself) in a specific category. **4.** *Archaic.* To recruit. — *intr.* **1.** To have a stated list price. **2.** *Archaic.* To enlist in the armed forces. [Fr. *liste* < OFr. < OItal. *lista*, of Gmc. orig.] — **list′er** *n.*

Franz Liszt

list[2] (lĭst) *n.* **1.a.** A narrow strip, esp. of wood. **b.** *Archit.* See **listel. c.** A border or selvage of cloth. **2.** A stripe or band of color. **3.a.** An arena for jousting tournaments or other contests. Often used in the plural. **b.** A place of combat. Often used in the plural. **c.** An area of controversy. Often used in the plural. **4.** A ridge thrown up between two furrows by a lister in plowing. **5.** *Obsolete.* A boundary; a border. — *tr.v.* **list•ed, list•ing, lists. 1.** To cover, line, or edge with list. **2.** To cut a thin strip from the edge of. **3.** To furrow or plant (land) with a lister. [ME < OE *līste.*]

list[3] (lĭst) *n.* An inclination to one side, as of a ship; a tilt. — *intr. & tr.v.* **list•ed, list•ing, lists.** To lean or cause to lean to the side: *The ship listed badly to starboard.* [?]

list[4] (lĭst) *intr. & tr.v.* **list•ed, list•ing, lists.** *Archaic.* To listen or listen to. [ME *listen* < OE *hlystan.* See **kleu-*.**]

list[5] (lĭst) *Archaic.* — *v.* **list•ed, list•ing, lists.** — *tr.* To be pleasing to; suit. — *intr.* To be disposed; choose. — *n.* A desire or an inclination. [ME *listen*, to desire, please < OE *lystan.* See **las-*.**]

lis•tel (lĭs′təl) *n. Archit.* A narrow border, molding, or fillet. [Fr. < Ital. *listello*, dim. of *lista*, border, of Gmc. orig.]

lis•ten (lĭs′ən) *intr.v.* **-tened, -ten•ing, -tens. 1.** To make an effort to hear something: *listen to the radio.* **2.** To pay attention; heed. — ***phrasal verb.* listen in. 1.** To listen to a conversation between others; eavesdrop. **2.** To tune in and listen to a broadcast. [ME *listenen*, alteration (influenced by *listen*; see LIST[4]) of OE *hlysnan.* See **kleu-*.**] — **lis′ten•er** *n.*

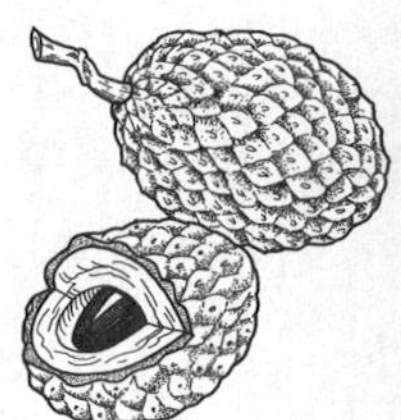

litchi
Litchi chinensis

lis•ten•a•ble (lĭs′ə-nə-bəl) *adj.* Being such that listening is pleasurable: *a listenable soundtrack.* — **lis′ten•a•bil′i•ty** *n.*

lis•ten•er•ship (lĭs′ə-nər-shĭp′, lĭs′nər-) *n.* The people who listen to a radio program or station.

list•er (lĭs′tər) *n.* A plow equipped with a double moldboard that turns up the soil on each side of the furrow. [< LIST[2].]

Lis•ter (lĭs′tər), **Joseph.** 1827–1912. British surgeon who demonstrated (1865) that carbolic acid was an effective antiseptic agent.

lis•te•ri•a (lĭ-stîr′ē-ə) *n.* Any of various rod-shaped gram-positive bacteria of the genus *Listeria.* [NLat. *Listeria*, genus name, after Joseph LISTER.]

lis•te•ri•o•sis (lĭ-stîr′ē-ō′sĭs) *n.* A bacterial disease caused by *Listeria monocytogenes*, affecting animals and occasionally human beings and marked by meningitis and encephalitis.

list•ing (lĭs′tĭng) *n.* **1.** An entry in a list or directory. **2.** A list or directory. **3.** *Comp. Sci.* A printout of a program or file.

list•less (lĭst′lĭs) *adj.* Lacking energy or disinclined to exert effort; lethargic: *listless resignation.* [ME *listles* : prob. < *liste*, desire (< *listen*, to desire; see LIST[5]) + *-les, -lesse*, -less.] — **list′less•ly** *adv.* — **list′less•ness** *n.*

list price *n.* A basic published or advertised price, often subject to discount.

Liszt (lĭst), **Franz.** 1811–86. Hungarian composer whose works include the *Dante Symphony* (1856).

lit[1] (lĭt) *v.* A p.t. and p.part. of **light**[1]. See Usage Note at **light**[1].

lit[2] (lĭt) *v.* A p.t. and p.part. of **light**[2].

lit. *abbr.* **1.** Liter. **2.a.** Literal. **b.** Literally. **3.** Literary. **4.** Literature.

lit•a•ny (lĭt′n-ē) *n., pl.* **-nies. 1.** A liturgical prayer consisting of a series of petitions recited by a leader alternating with fixed responses by the congregation. **2.** A repetitive or incantatory recital. [ME *letanie* < OFr. < Med.Lat. *letanīa* < LLat. *litanīa* < LGk. *litaneia* < Gk., entreaty < *litaneuein*, to entreat < *litanos*, entreating < *litē*, supplication.]

Lit.B. *abbr. Lat.* Litterarum Baccalaureus (Bachelor of Letters; Bachelor of Literature).

li•tchi also **li•chee** or **ly•chee** (lē′chē) *n.* **1.** A Chinese tree *(Litchi chinensis)* that bears bright red fruits, each of which has a large single seed with a white, fleshy, edible aril. **2.** The nutlike fruit of this tree. [Chin. (Mandarin) *lì zhī.*]

Lit.D. *abbr. Lat.* Litterarum Doctor (Doctor of Letters; Doctor of Literature).

lite (līt) *adj. Slang.* Having less substance or weight or fewer

ă pat	oi boy
ā pay	ou out
âr care	ŏŏ took
ä father	ōō boot
ĕ pet	ŭ cut
ē be	ûr urge
ĭ pit	th thin
ī pie	*th* this
îr pier	hw which
ŏ pot	zh vision
ō toe	ə about,
ô paw	item

Stress marks:
′ (primary);
′ (secondary), as in
dictionary (dĭk′shə-nĕr′ē)

calories than something else. [Alteration of LIGHT[2].]

–lite *suff.* Stone; mineral; fossil: *coprolite.* [Fr., alteration of *-lithe* < Gk. *lithos,* stone.]

li•ter (lē′tər) *n.* A metric unit of volume equal to approx. 1.056 liquid quarts, 0.908 dry quart, or 0.264 gallon. See table at **measurement.** [Fr. *litre* < obsolete *litron,* measure of capacity < Med.Lat. *lītra* < Gk. *litra,* unit of weight.]

lit•er•a•cy (lĭt′ər-ə-sē) *n.* The condition or quality of being literate, esp. the ability to read and write.

lit•er•al (lĭt′ər-əl) *adj.* **1.** Conforming or limited to the simplest, nonfigurative, or most obvious meaning of a word or words. **2.** Word for word; verbatim: *a literal translation.* **3.** Avoiding exaggeration, metaphor, or embellishment; factual; prosaic: *a literal mind.* **4.** Consisting of, using, or expressed by letters. —*n. Comp. Sci.* A word or symbol that represents a particular constant rather than a variable. [ME < OFr. < LLat. *litterālis,* of letters < Lat. *littera,* letter.] —**lit′er•al•ness** *n.*

lit•er•al•ism (lĭt′ər-ə-lĭz′əm) *n.* **1.** Adherence to the explicit sense of a given text or doctrine. **2.** Literal portrayal; realism. —**lit′er•al•ist** *n.* —**lit′er•al•is′tic** *adj.*

lit•er•al•ize (lĭt′ər-ə-līz′) *tr.v.* **-ized, -iz•ing, -iz•es.** To make literal.

lit•er•al•ly (lĭt′ər-ə-lē) *adv.* **1.** In a literal manner; word for word. **2.** In a literal or strict sense: *Don't take my remarks literally.* **3.** *Usage Problem.* **a.** Really; actually. **b.** Used as an intensive before a figurative expression.

Usage Note: For more than a hundred years critics have remarked on the incoherency of using *literally* in a way that suggests the exact opposite of its primary sense of "in a manner that accords with the literal sense of the words." The practice stems from a natural tendency to use the word as a general intensive meaning "without exaggeration," as in *It's literally roasting in here.* This looser use of the word *literally* does not usually create problems, but it can lead to an inadvertently comic effect when the word is used together with an idiomatic expression that has its source in a frozen figure of speech, such as in *I literally died laughing.*

Lithuania

lit•er•ar•y (lĭt′ə-rĕr′ē) *adj.* **1.** Of, relating to, or dealing with literature: *literary criticism.* **2.** Of or relating to writers or the profession of literature: *literary circles.* **3.** Versed in or fond of literature or learning. **4.a.** Appropriate to literature rather than everyday speech or writing. **b.** Bookish; pedantic. [Lat. *litterārius,* of reading and writing < *littera,* letter. See LETTER.] —**lit′er•ar′i•ly** (-râr′ə-lē) *adv.* —**lit′er•ar′i•ness** *n.*

lit•er•ate (lĭt′ər-ĭt) *adj.* **1.a.** Able to read and write. **b.** Knowledgeable or educated in several fields or a particular field. **2.** Familiar with literature; literary. **3.** Well-written; polished: *a literate essay.* —*n.* **1.** One who can read and write. **2.** A well-informed educated person. [ME *litterate* < Lat. *litterātus* < *littera,* letter. See LETTER.] —**lit′er•ate•ly** *adv.* —**lit′er•ate•ness** *n.*

lit•er•a•ti (lĭt′ə-rä′tē) *pl.n.* The literary intelligentsia. [Lat. *litterātī, līterātī,* pl. of *litterātus,* literate. See LITERATE.]

lit•er•a•tim (lĭt′ə-rā′tĭm, -rä′-) *adv.* Letter for letter: *a word transcribed literatim.* [Med.Lat. *līterātim, litterātim* < Lat. *littera,* letter. See LETTER.]

lit•er•a•ture (lĭt′ər-ə-cho͝or′, -chər) *n.* **1.** The body of written works of a language, period, or culture. **2.** Imaginative or creative writing, esp. of recognized artistic value. **3.** The art or occupation of a literary writer. **4.** The body of written work produced by scholars or researchers in a given field. **5.** Printed material. **6.** *Mus.* All the compositions of a certain kind or for a specific instrument or ensemble: *the symphonic literature.* [ME, book learning < OFr. *litterature* < Lat. *litterātūra* < *litterātus,* lettered. See LITERATE.]

lith. *abbr.* **1.** Lithograph; lithography. **2.** Lithographic.

Lith. *abbr.* Lithuania; Lithuanian.

lith– *pref.* Var. of **litho–.**

–lith *suff.* **1.** Rock; stone: *xenolith.* **2.** Stone implement or structure: *megalith.* **3.** Mineral concretion; calculus: *cystolith.* [< Gk. *lithos,* stone.]

lith•arge (lĭth′ärj′, lĭ-thärj′) *n.* A lead oxide, PbO, used in storage batteries and glass. [ME *litarge* < OFr., alteration of *litargire* < Lat. *lithargyrus* < Gk. *litharguros* : *lithos,* stone + *arguros,* silver; see **arg-*.**]

lithe (līth) *adj.* **lith•er, lith•est. 1.** Readily bent; supple. **2.** Marked by effortless grace. [ME < OE *līthe,* flexible, mild.] —**lithe′ly** *adv.* —**lithe′ness** *n.*

lithe•some (līth′səm) *adj.* Lithe; lissome.

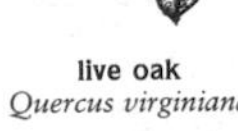
live oak
Quercus virginiana

lith•i•a (lĭth′ē-ə) *n.* See **lithium oxide.** [NLat. < *lithion* < Gk. *lithos,* stone.]

li•thi•a•sis (lĭ-thī′ə-sĭs) *n., pl.* **-ses** (-sēz′). Pathological formation of mineral concretions in the body.

lithia water *n.* Mineral water containing lithium salts.

lith•ic[1] (lĭth′ĭk) *adj.* Consisting of or relating to stone or rock.

lith•ic[2] (lĭth′ĭk) *adj.* Of or relating to lithium.

–lithic *suff.* Relating to or characteristic of a specified stage in the use of stone by human beings: *Eolithic.* [< LITHIC[1].]

lith•i•um (lĭth′ē-əm) *n. Symbol* **Li** A soft, highly reactive metallic element, used as a heat transfer medium and in various alloys, ceramics, and batteries. Atomic number 3; atomic weight 6.939; melting point 179°C; boiling point 1,317°C; specific gravity 0.534; valence 1. See table at **element.** [< LITHIA.]

lithium carbonate *n.* A granular powder, $LiCO_3$, used in glass and ceramics and in the treatment of manic-depressive illness.

lithium oxide *n.* A strongly alkaline white powder, Li_2O, used in ceramics and glass.

litho. *abbr.* **1.** Lithograph; lithography. **2.** Lithographic.

litho– or **lith–** *pref.* **1.** Stone: *lithosphere.* **2.** Lithium: *lithic.* **3.** Mineral concretion; calculus: *lithotomy.* [Gk. < *lithos,* stone.]

lithog. *abbr.* **1.** Lithograph; lithography. **2.** Lithographic.

lith•o•graph (lĭth′ə-grăf′) *n.* A print produced by lithography. —*tr.v.* **-graphed, -graph•ing, -graphs.** To produce by lithography. —**li•thog′raph•er** (lĭ-thŏg′rə-fər) *n.* —**lith′o•graph′ic, lith′o•graph′i•cal** *adj.* —**lith′o•graph′i•cal•ly** *adv.*

li•thog•ra•phy (lĭ-thŏg′rə-fē) *n.* A printing process in which the image to be printed is rendered on a flat surface, as on sheet zinc or aluminum, and treated to retain ink while the nonimage areas are treated to repel ink.

li•thol•o•gy (lĭ-thŏl′ə-jē) *n.* **1.** The gross physical character of a rock or rock formation. **2.** The description of rock, esp. sedimentary rock. —**lith′o•log′ic** (lĭth′ə-lŏj′ĭk), **lith′o•log′i•cal** *adj.* —**li•thol′o•gist** *n.*

lith•o•phyte (lĭth′ə-fīt′) *n.* **1.** *Bot.* A plant that grows on rock. **2.** *Zool.* An organism, such as coral, that has a stony structure. —**lith′o•phyt′ic** (-fĭt′ĭk) *adj.*

lith•o•pone (lĭth′ə-pōn′) *n.* A white pigment consisting of a mixture of zinc sulfide, zinc oxide, and barium sulfate. [LITHO– + Gk. *ponos,* toil, product; see **(s)pen-*.**]

lith•o•sphere (lĭth′ə-sfîr′) *n.* **1.** The solid part of the earth. **2.** The rocky crust of the earth. —**lith′o•spher′ic** *adj.*

lith•o•stra•tig•ra•phy (lĭth′ō-strə-tĭg′rə-fē) *n.* **1.** Stratigraphy based on the physical and petrographic properties of rocks. **2.** Interpretation of the physical characters of sedimentary rocks. —**lith′o•strat′i•graph′ic** (-străt′ĭ-grăf′ĭk) *adj.*

li•thot•o•my (lĭ-thŏt′ə-mē) *n., pl.* **-mies.** Surgical removal of a stone or stones from the urinary tract.

lith•o•trip•sy (lĭth′ə-trĭp′sē) *n., pl.* **-sies.** Pulverization of kidney stones by means of a lithotripter. [LITHO– + Gk. *tripsis,* a rubbing, pounding (< *tribein, trip-,* to rub, pound; see TRYPSIN) + -Y[2].]

lith•o•trip•ter (lĭth′ə-trĭp′tər) *n.* A device that uses shock waves to pulverize kidney stones, which can then be expelled in the urine. [Alteration of obsolete *lithotriptor,* ult. < Gk. *(pharmaka tōn en nephrōis) lithōn thruptika,* (drugs) crushing stones (in the kidneys) : *lithōn,* accusative pl. of *lithos,* stone + *thruptikos,* crushing (< *thruptein,* to crush; see **dhreu-*.**)]

li•thot•ri•ty (lĭ-thŏt′rĭ-tē) *n., pl.* **-ties.** A surgical procedure to pulverize stones in the urinary bladder or urethra. [< *lithotritor,* lithotripter, alteration of obsolete *lithotriptor.* See LITHOTRIPTER.]

Lith•u•a•ni•a (lĭth′o͞o-ā′nē-ə). A country of northern Europe on the Baltic Sea; perhaps settled as early as 1500 B.C. and a constituent republic of the U.S.S.R. from 1940 to 1990. Cap. Vilnius. Pop. 3,570,000.

Lith•u•a•ni•an (lĭth′o͞o-ā′nē-ən) *adj.* Of or relating to Lithuania or its people, language, or culture. —*n.* **1.a.** A native or inhabitant of Lithuania. **b.** A person of Lithuanian ancestry. **2.** The Baltic language of the Lithuanians.

lit•i•gant (lĭt′ĭ-gənt) *Law.* —*n.* A party engaged in a lawsuit. —*adj.* Engaged in a lawsuit.

lit•i•gate (lĭt′ĭ-gāt′) *v.* **-gat•ed, -gat•ing, -gates.** —*tr.* To subject to legal proceedings. —*intr.* To engage in legal proceedings. [Lat. *lītigāre, lītigāt-* : *līs, līt-,* lawsuit + *agere,* to drive; see **ag-*.**] —**lit′i•ga•ble** (-gə-bəl) *adj.* —**lit′i•ga′tion** *n.* —**lit′i•ga′tor** *n.*

li•ti•gious (lĭ-tĭj′əs) *adj. Law.* **1.** Of, relating to, or characterized by litigation. **2.** Tending to engage in lawsuits. [ME < OFr. < Lat. *lītigiōsus* < *lītigium,* dispute < *lītigāre,* to quarrel. See LITIGATE.] —**li•ti′gious•ly** *adv.* —**li•ti′gious•ness** *n.*

lit•mus (lĭt′məs) *n.* A water-soluble blue powder derived from certain lichens that changes to red with increasing acidity and to blue with increasing basicity. [ME *litmose,* of Scand. orig.; akin to ON *litmosi,* dyer's herbs : *litr,* color, dye + *mosi,* bog, moss.]

litmus paper *n.* An unsized white paper impregnated with litmus and used as a pH or acid-base indicator.

litmus test *n.* **1.** A test for chemical acidity or basicity using litmus paper. **2.** A test that uses a single indicator to prompt a decision.

li•to•tes (lī′tə-tēz′, lĭt′ə-, lī-tō′tēz) *n., pl.* **litotes.** A figure of speech consisting of an understatement in which an affirmative is expressed by negating its opposite, as in *This is no small problem.* [Gk. *litotēs* < *litos,* plain. See **lei-*.**]

li•tre (lē′tər) *n. Chiefly British.* Var. of **liter.**

Litt.B. *abbr. Lat.* Litterarum Baccalaureus (Bachelor of Letters; Bachelor of Literature).

Litt.D. *abbr. Lat.* Litterarum Doctor (Doctor of Letters; Doctor of Literature).

lit•ter (lĭt′ər) *n.* **1.a.** A disorderly accumulation of objects; a pile. **b.** Carelessly discarded refuse, such as wastepaper. **2.** The offspring produced at one birth by a multiparous mammal. **3.a.** Material, such as straw, used as bedding for animals. **b.** An absorbent material for covering the floor of an animal's cage or excretory box. **4.** An enclosed or curtained couch mounted on shafts and used to carry a single passenger. **5.** A flat supporting framework for carrying a disabled or dead person; a stretcher. **6.** The uppermost layer of the forest floor consisting chiefly of fallen leaves and other decaying organic matter. — *v.* **-tered, -ter•ing, -ters.** — *tr.* **1.** To give birth to (a litter). **2.** To make untidy by discarding rubbish carelessly. **3.** To scatter about. **4.** To supply (animals) with litter for bedding or floor covering. — *intr.* **1.** To give birth to a litter. **2.** To scatter litter. [ME, a litter < AN *litere* < Med. Lat. *lectāria* (influenced by OFr. *lit*, bed) < Lat. *lectus*, bed. See **legh-***.] — **lit′ter•er** *n.*

lit•té•ra•teur also **lit•ter•a•teur** (lĭt′ər-ə-tûr′, lĭt′rə-) *n.* One who is devoted to the study or writing of literature. [Fr. < Lat. *litterātor*, critic, lettered person < *littera*, letter. See LETTER.]

lit•ter•bag (lĭt′ər-băg′) *n.* A bag used for disposal of trash.

lit•ter•bug (lĭt′ər-bŭg′) *n. Informal.* A person who litters.

lit•ter•mate (lĭt′ər-māt′) *n.* One member of a given litter.

lit•tle (lĭt′l) *adj.* **lit•tler, lit•tlest** or **less** (lĕs), **least** (lēst). **1.** Small in size. See Syns at **small. 2.** Short in extent or duration; brief. **3.** Small in quantity or degree. **4.** Unimportant; trivial. **5.** Narrow; petty. **6.** Without much power or influence; of minor status. **7.** Being at an early stage of growth; young. — *adv.* **less, least. 1.** Not much; scarcely. **2.** Not in the least; not at all. — *n.* **1.** A small quantity or amount. **2.** Something much less than all: *I know little of their history.* **3.** A short distance or time. — ***idioms.*** **a little.** Somewhat; a bit. **little by little.** By small degrees or increments; gradually. [ME < OE *lȳtel.*] — **lit′tle•ness** *n.*

Lit•tle Al•föld (lĭt′l ôl′fəld). See **Alföld.**

Little A•mer•i•ca (ə-mĕr′ĭ-kə). A U.S. base for explorations in Antarctica on the Ross Ice Shelf.

little auk *n.* See **dovekie.**

Little Bear *n.* See **Ursa Minor.**

Little Big•horn River (bĭg′hôrn′). A river, c. 145 km (90 mi), rising in the Bighorn Mts. of N WY and flowing N to the Bighorn R. in S MT. Sioux and Cheyenne warriors defeated the forces of Gen. George A. Custer in the Little Bighorn valley on Jun. 25, 1876.

Little Cay•man (kā-măn′, kā′mən). See **Cayman Islands.**

Little Col•o•ra•do River (kŏl′ə-răd′ō, -rä′dō). A river of NE AZ flowing c. 507 km (315 mi) to the Colorado R.

Little Di•o•mede Island (dī′ə-mēd′). See **Diomede Islands.**

Little Dipper *n.* The seven bright stars that form the constellation Ursa Minor.

little finger *n.* The smallest finger of the human hand.

Little Kar•roo (kə-ro͞o′). See **Karroo.**

little magazine *n.* A literary magazine that publishes the work of relatively unknown writers.

Little Mis•sou•ri River (mĭ-zo͝or′ē, -zo͝or′ə). A river of the N U.S. rising in NE WY and flowing c. 901 km (560 mi) to the Missouri R. in W ND.

lit•tle•neck (lĭt′l-nĕk′) *n.* The quahog clam when small and suitable for eating raw. [After *Little Neck* Bay, Long I., NY.]

little owl *n.* A small European owl *(Athene noctua)* having streaked brownish plumage.

Little Rock. The cap. of AR, in the central part on the Arkansas R. Pop. 175,795.

Little Saint Ber•nard Pass (sānt′ bər-närd′). A mountain pass through the Savoy Alps between Italy and France.

little slam *n. Games.* The winning of all but one of the tricks during the play of one hand of bridge.

little theater *n.* A small theater usu. for a community, collegiate, or experimental drama group.

little toe *n.* The smallest toe of the human foot.

Lit•tle•ton (lĭt′l-tən). A city of N-central CO, a suburb of Denver. Pop. 33,685.

lit•to•ral (lĭt′ər-əl) *adj.* Of or on a shore, esp. a seashore: *the littoral zone.* — *n.* A coastal region; a shore. [Lat. *lītorālis* < *lītus, lītor-*, shore. N. < Ital. *littorale* < Lat. *lītorālis.*]

li•tur•gi•cal (lĭ-tûr′jĭ-kəl) also **li•tur•gic** (-tûr′jĭk) *adj.* **1.** Of, relating to, or in accordance with liturgy: *a book of liturgical forms.* **2.** Using or used in liturgy. — **li•tur′gi•cal•ly** *adv.*

li•tur•gics (lĭ-tûr′jĭks) *n. (used with a sing. v.)* The study of liturgies.

li•tur•gi•ol•o•gy (lĭ-tûr′jē-ŏl′ə-jē) *n.* See **liturgics.** — **li•tur′gi•ol′o•gist** *n.*

lit•ur•gist (lĭt′ər-jĭst) *n.* **1.** One who uses or advocates the use of liturgical forms. **2.** A scholar in liturgics. **3.** A writer or editor of a liturgy or liturgies.

lit•ur•gy (lĭt′ər-jē) *n., pl.* **-gies. 1.** Any form of public worship. **2.** A formulary for public worship. **3.** The act of public worship so prescribed. [LLat. *lītūrgia* < Gk. *leitourgia*, public service < *leitourgos*, public servant : *lēos, leit-*, people (var. of *laos*) + *ergon*, work; see **werg-***.]

Liu•zhou (lyo͞o′jō′) also **Liu•chow** (-chō′). A city of S China NNE of Nanning. Pop. 375,000.

liv•a•ble also **live•a•ble** (lĭv′ə-bəl) *adj.* **1.** Suitable to live in; habitable. **2.** Possible to bear; endurable. — **liv′a•ble•ness** *n.*

live[1] (lĭv) *v.* **lived, liv•ing, lives.** — *intr.* **1.** To be alive; exist. **2.** To continue to be alive. **3.** To support oneself; subsist. **4.** To reside; dwell. **5.** To conduct one's life in a particular manner: *lived frugally.* **6.** To pursue a positive, satisfying existence; enjoy life. **7.** To remain in human memory. — *tr.* **1.** To spend or pass (one's life). **2.** To go through; experience. **3.** To practice in one's life. — ***phrasal verbs.*** **live down.** To overcome or reduce the shame of (a misdeed, for example) over a period of time. **live in.** To reside in one's place of employment. **live out.** To live outside one's place of domestic employment. **live with.** To put up with; resign oneself to. — ***idioms.*** **live it up.** *Slang.* To engage in festive pleasures or extravagances. **live up to. 1.** To live or act in accordance with. **2.** To prove equal to. **3.** To carry out; fulfill. [ME *liven* < OE *libban, lifian.* See **leip-***.]

live[2] (līv) *adj.* **1.** Having life; alive. **2.** Of current interest or relevance. **3.** Glowing; burning: *live coals.* **4.** Not yet exploded but capable of being fired. **5.** *Elect.* Carrying an electric current. **6.** Not mined or quarried; in the natural state: *live ore.* **7.a.** Broadcast while actually being performed; not taped, filmed, or recorded. **b.** Involving performers or spectators who are physically present. **8.** *Print.* Not yet set into type: *live copy.* **9.** *Sports.* In play: *a live ball.* — *adv.* At, during, or from the time of actual occurrence or performance. [Short for ALIVE.] — **live′ness** *n.*

live•bear•er (līv′bâr′ər) *n.* A fish, esp. of the family Poeciliidae, that bears live young. — **live′-bear′ing** *adj.*

live-for•ev•er (lĭv′fər-ĕv′ər) *n.* **1.** See **orpine. 2.** See **houseleek.**

live-in (lĭv′ĭn′) *adj.* **1.** Residing in one's place of employment. **2.** Residing together with another, esp. in sexual intimacy.

live•li•hood (līv′lē-ho͝od′) *n.* Means of support; subsistence. [ME *livelyhed*, alteration of *livelode* < OE *līflād* : *līf*, life; see LIFE + *lād*, course; see **leit-***.]

live load (līv) *n.* A moving, variable weight added to the dead load or intrinsic weight of a structure or vehicle.

live•long (lĭv′lông′, -lŏng′) *adj.* Complete; whole: *the livelong day.* [ME : *leve, lefe*, dear, used as an intensive (< OE *lēof*, dear; see **leubh-***) + *long*, long; see LONG[1].]

live•ly (līv′lē) *adj.* **-li•er, -li•est. 1.** Full of life and energy; vigorous. **2.** Full of spirit; gay and animated. **3.** Marked by animated intelligence. **4.** Invigorating; refreshing. **5.** Effervescent; sparkling. **6.** Keen; brisk. **7.** Rebounding readily upon impact; resilient. — *adv.* With energy or vigor; briskly. [ME *lifli* < OE *līflīc* < *līf*, life. See **leip-***.] — **live′li•ly** *adv.* — **live′li•ness** *n.*

li•ven (lī′vən) *tr. & intr.v.* **-vened, -ven•ing, -vens.** To make or become more lively: *liven up a party.*

live oak (līv) *n.* Any of several American evergreen oaks, such as *Quercus virginiana* of Mexico and the southeast United States or *Q. agrifolia* of California.

liv•er[1] (lĭv′ər) *n.* **1.** *Anat.* A large reddish-brown glandular vertebrate organ located in the upper right portion of the abdominal cavity that secretes bile, makes certain blood proteins, and metabolizes carbohydrates, fats, and proteins. **2.** An organ in invertebrates that is similar to the vertebrate liver. **3.** The bile-secreting organ of an animal, used as food. **4.** *Color.* A dark reddish brown. — *adj.* **1.** Made of or flavored with liver: *liver pâté.* **2.** Of a dark reddish brown. [ME < OE *lifer.* See **leip-***.]

liv•er[2] (lĭv′ər) *n.* One who lives in a specified manner.

liver fluke *n.* **1.** Any of several parasitic trematode worms, esp. *Clonorchis sinensis*, that infest the liver of various animals, including human beings. **2.** Infestation with such worms.

liv•er•ied (lĭv′ə-rēd, lĭv′rēd) *adj.* Wearing livery.

liv•er•ish (lĭv′ər-ĭsh) *adj.* **1.** Resembling liver, esp. in color. **2.** Having a liver disorder; bilious. **3.** Having a disagreeable disposition; irritable. — **liv′er•ish•ness** *n.*

liv•er•leaf (lĭv′ər-lēf′) *n.* See **hepatica.**

Liv•er•more (lĭv′ər-môr′, -mōr′). A city of W CA ESE of Oakland. Pop. 56,741.

Livermore, Mary Ashton Rice. 1820–1905. American suffragist who founded (1869) *The Agitator.*

Liv•er•pool (lĭv′ər-po͞ol′). A borough of NW England on the Mersey R. near its mouth on the Irish Sea; chartered 1207. Pop. 518,900.

liver spot *n.* A benign localized brownish patch on the skin, often occurring in old age and in people with sun-damaged skin.

liv•er•wort (lĭv′ər-wûrt′, -wôrt′) *n.* Any of numerous small green nonvascular plants of the class Hepaticae.

liv•er•wurst (lĭv′ər-wûrst′, -wo͝orst′) *n.* A sausage made of or containing ground liver. [Partial transl. of Ger. *Leberwurst* : *Leber*, liver + *Wurst*, sausage; see WURST.]

liv•er•y (lĭv′ə-rē, lĭv′rē) *n., pl.* **-ies. 1.** A distinctive uniform worn by the male servants of a household. **2.** The distinctive dress worn by the members of a particular group; uniform. **3.** The costume or insignia worn by the retainers of a feudal lord. **4.a.** The boarding and care of horses for a fee. **b.** The hiring out of horses and carriages. **c.** A livery stable. **5.** A

liver

liver[1]

ă pat	oi boy
ā pay	ou out
âr care	o͝o took
ä father	o͞o boot
ĕ pet	ŭ cut
ē be	ûr urge
ĭ pit	th thin
ī pie	*th* this
îr pier	hw which
ŏ pot	zh vision
ō toe	ə about,
ô paw	item

Stress marks:
′ (primary);
′ (secondary), as in
dictionary (dĭk′shə-nĕr′ē)

business that offers vehicles for hire. **6.** *Law.* Official delivery of property, esp. land, to a new owner. [ME *liveri* < OFr. *livree*, delivery < fem. p.part. of *livrer*, to deliver < Lat. *līberāre*, to free < *līber*, free. See **leudh-***.]

liv•er•y•man (lĭv′ə-rē-mən, lĭv′rē-) *n.* A man who is employed in or keeps a livery stable.

livery stable *n.* A stable that boards horses and keeps horses and carriages for hire.

lives (līvz) *n.* Pl. of **life.**

live steam (līv) *n.* Steam coming from a boiler at full pressure.

live•stock (līv′stŏk′) *n.* Domestic animals, such as cattle or horses, raised for home use or for profit, esp. on a farm.

live wire (līv) *n.* **1.** A wire carrying electric current. **2.** *Informal.* A vivacious, alert, or energetic person.

llama
Lama glama

liv•id (lĭv′ĭd) *adj.* **1.** Discolored, as from a bruise; black-and-blue. **2.** Ashen or pallid. **3.** Extremely angry; furious. [ME *livide* < OFr. < Lat. *līvidus* < *līvēre*, to be bluish. See **slī-***.] **— li•vid′i•ty, liv′id•ness** *n.* **— liv′id•ly** *adv.*

liv•ing (lĭv′ĭng) *adj.* **1.** Possessing life. **2.** In active function or use: *a living language.* **3.** Of persons who are alive: *within living memory.* **4.** Full of life, interest, or vitality. **5.** True to life; realistic. **6.** *Informal.* Used as an intensive. **—** *n.* **1.** The condition or action of maintaining life. **2.** A manner or style of life. **3.** A means of maintaining life; livelihood. **4.** *Chiefly British.* A church benefice, including the revenue attached to it.

living death *n.* A situation or period of time characterized by unremitting pain and suffering.

living fossil *n.* An organism, such as a coelacanth, that is the sole survivor of an otherwise extinct taxonomic group.

living room *n.* A room in a private residence intended for general social and leisure activities.

Liv•ing•ston (lĭv′ĭng-stən). A community of NE NJ NW of Newark. Pop. 26,609.

Livingston, Henry Brockholst. 1757–1823. Amer. jurist; associate justice of the U.S. Supreme Court (1806–23).

Livingston, Robert R. 1746–1813. Amer. Revolutionary leader who served in the Continental Congress (1775–81) and helped draft the Declaration of Independence.

Liv•ing•stone (lĭv′ĭng-stən), **David.** 1813–73. Scottish missionary and explorer who attempted to find the source of the Nile with Henry M. Stanley.

living unit *n.* A dwelling for use by one family.

living wage *n.* A wage sufficient to provide minimally satisfactory living conditions.

living will *n.* A will in which the signer requests not to be kept alive by life-support systems in the event of a terminal illness.

Li•vo•ni•a (lĭ-vō′nē-ə, -vōn′yə). **1.** A region of S Estonia and N Latvia. The Livonian Brothers of the Sword conquered the area in the 13th cent. **2.** A city of SE MI, a suburb of Detroit. Pop. 100,850.

Li•vo•ni•an (lĭ-vō′nē-ən) *adj.* Of or relating to the region of Livonia or its people or culture. **—** *n.* A native or inhabitant of the region of Livonia.

Li•vor•no (lē-vôr′nō). See **Leghorn.**

li•vre (lē′vər, lē′vrə) *n.* A money of account formerly used in France and originally worth a pound of silver. [Fr. < OFr. < Lat. *lībra*, a unit of weight, pound.]

Liv•y (lĭv′ē). 59 B.C.–A.D. 17. Roman historian whose history of Rome consisted of 142 volumes, of which 35 survive.

lix•iv•i•ate (lĭk-sĭv′ē-āt′) *tr.v.* **-at•ed, -at•ing, -ates.** To wash or percolate the soluble matter from. [LLat. *lixīvium*, lye (< Lat. *lixīvius*, of lye < *lix*, lye) + -ATE[1].] **— lix•iv′i•a′tion** *n.*

liz•ard (lĭz′ərd) *n.* **1.** Any of numerous reptiles of the suborder Sauria or Lacertilia, having a scaly elongated body, movable eyelids, four legs, and a tapering tail. **2.** Leather made from lizard skin. [ME < OFr. *lesarde* < Lat. *lacertus, lacerta.*]

liz•ard•fish (lĭz′ərd-fĭsh′) *n., pl.* **lizardfish** or **-fish•es.** Any of various bottom-dwelling large-mouthed fishes of the family Synodontidae of warm seas, having a lizardlike head.

loblolly pine
Pinus taeda

Liz•ard Point or **Liz•ard Head** (lĭz′ərd). A cape of SW England at the S tip of **The Lizard,** a peninsula extending S into the English Channel.

Lju•blja•na (lo͞o′blē-ä′nə, lyo͞o′blyä-nä). The cap. of Slovenia, in the central part on the Sava R. WNW of Zagreb, Croatia; founded by Augustus in 34 B.C. Pop. 205,600.

Lk *abbr. Bible.* Luke.

ll or **ll.** *abbr.* Lines.

'll Shall; will: *We'll arrive later.*

lla•ma (lä′mə) *n.* **1.** A domesticated South American ruminant mammal *(Lama glama)* related to the camel, raised for its wool and used as a beast of burden. **2.** Any of various other mammals of the genus *Lama.* [Sp. < Quechua.]

lla•no (lä′nō, lăn′ō) *n., pl.* **-nos.** A large, grassy, almost treeless plain, esp. one in Latin America. [Sp., plain < Lat. *plānum* < neut. of *plānus*, level. See **pelə-**[2]*.]

lobster pot

Lla•no Es•ta•ca•do (lăn′ō ĕs′tə-kä′dō, lä′nō). An extensive semiarid plateau region of the S Great Plains in SE NM, W TX, and NW OK.

LL.B. *abbr. Lat.* Legum Baccalaureus (Bachelor of Laws).

LL.D. *abbr. Lat.* Legum Doctor (Doctor of Laws).

Llew•el•lyn (lo͞o-ĕl′ĭn), **Richard.** 1906–83. Welsh-born British writer best known for *How Green Was My Valley* (1940).

LL.M. *abbr. Lat.* Legum Magister (Master of Laws).

Lloyd (loid), **Henry Demarest.** 1847–1903. Amer. financial writer who was one of the first muckraking journalists.

Lloyd George (jôrj′), **David.** 1st Earl of Dwyfor. 1863–1945. British politician who served as prime minister (1916–22).

Llu•llai•lla•co (yo͞o′yī-yä′kō). A volcano, 6,727.4 m (22,057 ft), in the Andes of N Chile near the Argentine border.

lm *abbr. Phys.* Lumen.

Lm *abbr. Bible.* Lamentations.

LM *abbr.* **1.** Legion of Merit. **2.** Lunar module.

LMT *abbr.* Local mean time.

ln The symbol for **natural logarithm.**

LNG *abbr.* Liquefied natural gas.

lo (lō) *interj.* Used to attract attention or show surprise. [ME < OE *lā.*]

loach (lōch) *n.* Any of various Eurasian and African freshwater fishes of the family Cobitidae, having barbels around the mouth. [ME *loche* < OFr., perh. < VLat. **laukka*, fish, slug, poss. of Celt. orig.]

load (lōd) *n.* **1.a.** A weight or mass that is supported. **b.** The overall force to which a structure is subjected in supporting a weight or mass or in resisting externally applied forces. **2.a.** Something that is carried, as by a vehicle or a person. **b.** The quantity that is or can be carried at one time. **3.a.** The share of work allocated to or required of a person, a machine, a group, or an organization. **b.** The demand for services or performance made on a machine or system. **4.** The amount of material that can be inserted into a device or machine at one time. **5.** A single charge of ammunition for a firearm. **6.a.** A mental weight or burden. **b.** A responsibility regarded as oppressive. **7.** The external mechanical resistance against which a machine acts. **8.** *Elect.* **a.** The power output of a generator or power plant. **b.** A device or the resistance of a device to which power is delivered. **9.** A front-end load. **10.** *Informal.* A great number or amount. Often used in the plural: *loads of fun.* **11.** *Slang.* A satisfying view; an eyeful. **12.** Genetic load. **—** *v.* **load•ed, load•ing, loads.** **—** *tr.* **1.a.** To put (something) into or onto a structure, device, or conveyance. **b.** To put something into or onto (a structure, device, or conveyance). **2.** To provide or fill nearly to overflowing; heap. **3.** To weigh down; burden. **4.** To insert (a necessary material) into a device: *loaded bullets into the gun.* **5.** To insert a necessary material into: *loaded the camera.* **6.** *Games.* To make (dice) heavier on one side by adding weight. **7.** To charge with additional meanings, implications, or emotional import: *loaded the question.* **8.** To dilute, adulterate, or doctor. **9.** To raise the power demand in (an electrical circuit), as by adding resistance. **10.** To increase (a mutual fund share price, for example) by adding expenses or sale costs. **11.** *Baseball.* To have or put runners on (all three bases). **12.** *Comp. Sci.* **a.** To transfer (data) from a storage device into a computer's memory. **b.** To mount (an auxiliary storage device). **—** *intr.* **1.** To receive a load. **2.** To charge a firearm with ammunition. **3.** To put or place a load into or onto a structure, device, or conveyance. [ME *lode*, alteration (influenced by *laden*, to load; see LADE) of *lade*, course, way < OE *lād.* See **leit-***.]

load•ed (lō′dĭd) *adj.* **1.** Carrying a load. **2.** Heavy with meaning or emotional import. **3.** *Slang.* Intoxicated; drunk. **4.** *Slang.* Having a great deal of money.

load•er (lō′dər) *n. Comp. Sci.* A program that transfers data from off-line memory into internal storage.

load•ing (lō′dĭng) *n.* **1.** A weight placed on something else; a burden. **2.** A substance added to something else; a filler. **3.** An addition to an insurance premium. **4.** *Elect.* The addition of inductance to a circuit to improve its transmission characteristics.

load line *n. Naut.* See **Plimsoll mark.**

load•mas•ter (lōd′măs′tər) *n.* An aircraft crew member in charge of loading and unloading cargo or heavy weapons.

load•star (lōd′stär′) *n.* Var. of **lodestar.**

load•stone (lōd′stōn′) *n.* Var. of **lodestone.**

loaf[1] (lōf) *n., pl.* **loaves** (lōvz). **1.** A shaped mass of bread baked in one piece. **2.** A shaped, usu. rounded or oblong mass of food: *veal loaf.* [ME *lof* < OE *hlāf.*]

loaf[2] (lōf) *intr.v.* **loafed, loaf•ing, loafs.** To pass time at leisure; idle. [Prob. back-formation < LOAFER.]

loaf•er (lō′fər) *n.* One who is habitually idle. [Short for obsolete *land-loafer*, vagabond, idler, poss. partial transl. of obsolete Ger. *Landläufer* < MHGer. *landlöufer* : *land*, land + *löufer*, runner (< *loufen*, to run < OHGer. *hlouffan*).]

Loaf•er (lō′fər). A trademark used for a low leather step-in shoe with an upper resembling a moccasin but with a broad flat heel.

loam (lōm) *n.* **1.** Soil composed of a mixture of sand, clay, silt, and organic matter. **2.** A mixture of moist clay and sand, together with straw, used esp. in making bricks and foundry molds. **—** *tr.v.* **loamed, loam•ing, loams.** To fill, cover, or coat with loam. [ME *lam, lom*, clay < OE *lām.* See **lei-***.] **— loam′y** *adj.*

loan (lōn) *n.* **1.a.** Something lent for temporary use. **b.** A sum of money lent at interest. **2.** An act of lending; a grant for temporary use. **3.** A temporary transfer to a duty or place away from a regular job: *an auditor on loan from the main office.* —*tr.v.* **loaned, loan•ing, loans.** *Usage Problem.* To lend. [ME *lan, lon* < ON *lān.* See **leikʷ-*.**] —**loan′er** *n.*

Usage Note: The verb *loan* is well established in American usage and cannot be considered incorrect. But *loan* is used only to describe physical transactions, as of money or goods. For figurative transactions *lend* is the only possible form: *Distance lends enchantment. Lend* is also required in fixed expressions such as *lend-lease* and *moneylender.*

Lo•an•da (lō-ăn′də). See **Luanda.**

loan shark *n. Informal.* One who lends money at exorbitant interest rates, esp. one connected with organized crime.

loan translation *n.* A form of borrowing from one language to another whereby the semantic components of a given term are literally translated into their equivalents in the borrowing language, as *superman* from German *Übermensch.*

loan word or **loan•word** (lōn′wûrd′) *n.* A word adopted from another language and completely or partially naturalized, as *very* and *hors d'oeuvre,* both from French.

loath also **loth** (lōth, lō*th*) *adj.* Unwilling or reluctant; disinclined. [ME *loth* < OE *lāth,* hateful, loathsome.]

loathe (lō*th*) *tr.v.* **loathed, loath•ing, loathes.** To dislike (someone or something) greatly; abhor. [ME *lothen* < OE *lāthian.*] —**loath′er** *n.*

loath•ing (lō′*th*ĭng) *n.* Great dislike; abhorrence.

loath•ly (lō*th*′lē, lōth′-) *adj.* Loathsome. [ME *lothly* < OE *lāthlīc* : *lāth,* hateful + *-līc,* like; see -LY[1].]

loath•some (lō*th*′səm, lōth′-) *adj.* Arousing loathing; abhorrent. [ME *lothsome* : *loth,* hateful; see LOATH + *-som,* adj. suff.; see -SOME[1].] —**loath′some•ly** *adv.* —**loath′some•ness** *n.*

loaves (lōvz) *n.* Pl. of **loaf[1].**

lob (lŏb) *v.* **lobbed, lob•bing, lobs.** —*tr.* To hit, throw, or propel in a high arc. —*intr.* **1.** To lob a ball. **2.** To move heavily or clumsily. —*n.* **1.** A ball that is lobbed. **2.** *Chiefly British.* A clumsy dull person; a lout. [< ME, pollack, lout, prob. of LGer. orig.] —**lob′ber** *n.*

Lo•ba•chev•ski (lō′bə-chĕf′skē, lə-bə-chyĕf′-), **Nikolai Ivanovich.** 1792–1856. Russian mathematician who developed (1826) hyperbolic geometry.

lo•bar (lō′bər, -bär′) *adj.* Of or relating to a lobe or lobes.

lo•bate (lō′bāt′) also **lo•bat•ed** (-bā′tĭd) *adj.* **1.** Having lobes; lobed. **2.** Shaped like a lobe. **3.** Having separate toes, each bordered by a weblike lobe. Used of the feet of certain birds. —**lo′bate′ly** *adv.*

lo•ba•tion (lō-bā′shən) *n.* **1.** The state of being lobed. **2.** A structure or part resembling a lobe. **3.** A lobe.

lob•by (lŏb′ē) *n., pl.* **-bies. 1.** A hall, foyer, or waiting room at or near the entrance to a building, such as a hotel. **2.** A public room next to the assembly chamber of a legislative body. **3.** A group of persons engaged in trying to influence legislators or other public officials in favor of a specific cause: *the banking lobby.* —*v.* **-bied, -by•ing, -bies.** —*intr.* To try to influence the thinking of legislators or other public officials for or against a specific cause. —*tr.* **1.** To try to influence public officials on behalf of or against (proposed legislation, for example). **2.** To try to influence (an official) to take a desired action. [Med.Lat. *lobia,* monastic cloister, of Gmc. orig.] —**lob′by•er, lob′by•ist** *n.* —**lob′by•ism** *n.*

lobe (lōb) *n.* **1.** A rounded projection, esp. a rounded, projecting anatomical part. **2.** A subdivision of a bodily organ or part bounded by fissures, connective tissue, or other structures. [ME < OFr. < LLat. *lobus,* hull, pod < Gk. *lobos,* lobe, pod.]

lo•bec•to•my (lō-bĕk′tə-mē) *n., pl.* **-mies.** Surgical excision of a lobe, as of the lung.

lobed (lōbd) *adj.* Having a lobe or lobes: *lobed leaves.*

lobe•fin (lōb′fĭn′) *n.* Any of various mostly extinct bony fishes of the subclass Crossopterygii, including the coelacanth.

lo•be•li•a (lō-bē′lē-ə, -bēl′yə) *n.* Any of numerous plants of the genus *Lobelia,* having terminal racemes of variously colored flowers. [NLat. *Lobelia,* genus name, after Matthias de *Lobel* (1538–1616), Flemish botanist and physician.]

lob•lol•ly (lŏb′lŏl′ē) *n., pl.* **-lies. 1.** *Chiefly Southern U.S.* A mudhole; a mire. **2.** The loblolly pine. [Perh. dial. *lob,* to bubble + *lolly,* broth.]

loblolly pine *n.* A pine *(Pinus taeda)* of the southeast United States having needles in fascicles of three, oblong cones, and strong wood used as lumber and for paper pulp.

lo•bo (lō′bō) *n., pl.* **-bos.** *Western U.S.* The gray wolf. [Sp., wolf < Lat. *lupus.* See **wl̥kʷo-*.**]

lo•bot•o•mize (lə-bŏt′ə-mīz′, lō-) *tr.v.* **-mized, -miz•ing, -miz•es. 1.** To perform a lobotomy on (a patient). **2.** To deprive (a person) of energy or vitality.

lo•bot•o•my (lə-bŏt′ə-mē, lō-) *n., pl.* **-mies.** Surgical incision into the frontal lobe of the brain, a technique used to treat certain mental disorders. [LOBE + -TOMY.]

lob•scouse (lŏb′skous′) *n.* A sailor's stew made of meat, vegetables, and hardtack. [Perh. dial. *lob,* to bubble + *scouse,* of unknown orig.]

lob•ster (lŏb′stər) *n.* **1.** Any of several edible marine crustaceans of the family Homaridae, esp. of the genus *Homarus,* having long antennae and five pairs of legs, the first pair of which is modified into large pincers. **2.** Any of several crustaceans that are related to the lobsters. **3.** The flesh of a lobster used as food. —*intr.v.* **-stered, -ster•ing, -sters.** To search for and catch lobsters. [ME *lopster, lobstere* < OE *loppestre,* alteration (perh. influenced by *loppe, lobbe,* spider) of Lat. *locusta.*] —**lob′ster•er** *n.*

lob•ster•man (lŏb′stər-mən) *n.* **1.** A man whose occupation is catching lobsters. **2.** *Naut.* A boat used in locating and catching lobsters.

lobster pot *n.* A slatted cage with an opening covered by a funnel-shaped net, used for trapping lobsters.

lobster ther•mi•dor (thûr′mĭ-dôr′) *n.* A dish of cooked lobster meat mixed with a cream sauce, put into a lobster shell, sprinkled with cheese, and browned. [After Fr. *Thermidor,* the 11th calendar month during the French Revolution : Gk. *thermē,* heat; see THERM + Gk. *dōron,* gift; see **dō-*.**]

lob•u•late (lŏb′yə-lāt′) also **lob•u•lat•ed** (-lā′tĭd) *adj.* Having or consisting of lobules. —**lob′u•la′tion** *n.*

lob•ule (lŏb′yo͞ol) *n.* **1.** A small lobe. **2.** A section or subdivision of a lobe. —**lob′u•lar** (-yə-lər), **lob′u•lose′** (-yə-lōs′) *adj.* —**lob′u•lar•ly** *adv.*

lob•worm (lŏb′wûrm′) *n.* See **lugworm.** [Alteration (influenced by LOB, lump, something hanging) of LUGWORM.]

lo•cal (lō′kəl) *adj.* **1.a.** Of, relating to, or characteristic of a particular place. **b.** Of or relating to a city, town, or district rather than a larger area. **2.** Not broad or general; not widespread. **3.** *Medic.* Of or affecting a specific part of the body: *a local anesthetic.* **4.** Making all possible or scheduled stops on a route; not express: *a local train.* —*n.* **1.** A public conveyance that makes intermediate stops before reaching the final destination. **2.** A local chapter or branch of an organization, esp. of a labor union. **3.** *Informal.* A person from a particular locality. [ME < OFr. < LLat. *locālis* < Lat. *locus,* place.] —**lo′cal•ly** *adv.* —**lo′cal•ness** *n.*

local area network *n.* LAN.

local color *n.* **1.** The interest or flavor of a locality imparted by the customs and sights peculiar to it. **2.** The use of regional detail in a literary or an artistic work.

lo•cale (lō-kăl′) *n.* **1.** A place, esp. with reference to a particular event. **2.** The scene or setting, as of a novel. [< Fr. *local,* local, locale < OFr. See LOCAL.]

lo•cal•ism (lō′kə-lĭz′əm) *n.* **1.a.** A local linguistic feature. **b.** A local custom or peculiarity. **2.** Devotion to local interests and customs. —**lo′cal•ist** *n.*

lo•cal•i•ty (lō-kăl′ĭ-tē) *n., pl.* **-ties. 1.** A particular neighborhood, place, or district. **2.** The fact or quality of having position in space.

lo•cal•ize (lō′kə-līz′) *v.* **-ized, -iz•ing, -iz•es.** —*tr.* **1.** To make local. **2.** To confine or restrict to a particular locality. **3.** To attribute to a particular locality. —*intr.* To become local, esp. to become fixed in one area or part. —**lo′cal•i•za′tion** (-kə-lĭ-zā′shən) *n.*

local option *n.* The power granted to a local political subdivision to decide whether to apply a law within its jurisdiction.

Lo•car•no (lō-kär′nō). A town of S Switzerland at the N end of Lake Maggiore; first mentioned in historical records in 749. The Locarno Pact between Germany and various European powers was signed here on Dec. 1, 1925. Pop. 14,300.

lo•cate (lō′kāt′, lō-kāt′) *v.* **-cat•ed, -cat•ing, -cates.** —*tr.* **1.** To determine or specify the position or limits of. **2.** To find by searching, examining, or experimenting. **3.** To place at a certain location; station or situate. —*intr.* To become established; settle. [Lat. *locāre, locāt-,* to place < *locus,* place.] —**lo′cat′a•ble** *adj.* —**lo′cat′er** *n.*

lo•ca•tion (lō-kā′shən) *n.* **1.** The act or process of locating. **2.** A place where something is or could be located; a site. **3.** A site away from a studio at which part or all of a movie is shot. **4.** A tract of land that has been surveyed and marked off. —**lo•ca′tion•al** *adj.*

loc•a•tive (lŏk′ə-tĭv) *adj.* Of, relating to, or being a grammatical case in certain inflected languages that indicates place in or on which or time at which, as in Latin *domī,* "at home." —*n.* **1.** The locative case. **2.** A word in the locative case. [NLat. *locātīvus* < Lat. *locātus,* p.part. of *locāre,* to place. See LOCATE.]

lo•ca•tor (lō′kā′tər) *n.* One that locates, as a person who fixes the boundaries of mining claims.

loc. cit. *abbr. Lat.* Loco citato (in the place cited).

loch (lŏ*ĸʜ*, lŏk) *n. Scots.* **1.** A lake. **2.** An arm of the sea similar to a fjord. [ME *louch* < Sc.Gael. *loch* < OIr.]

Loch (lŏk, lŏ*ĸʜ*). See **Lake.**

lo•chi•a (lō′kē-ə, lŏk′ē-ə) *pl.n. Medic.* The normal uterine discharge of blood, tissue, and mucus from the vagina after childbirth. [Gk. *lokhia* < neut. pl. of *lokhios,* of childbirth < *lokhos,* childbirth. See **legh-*.**] —**lo′chi•al** *adj.*

lo•ci (lō′sī′, -kē, -kī′) *n.* Pl. of **locus.**

lock[1] (lŏk) *n.* **1.** A device operated by a key, combination, or keycard and used for holding, closing, or securing. **2.** A section of a waterway closed off with gates, in which vessels in transit are raised or lowered by raising or lowering the water

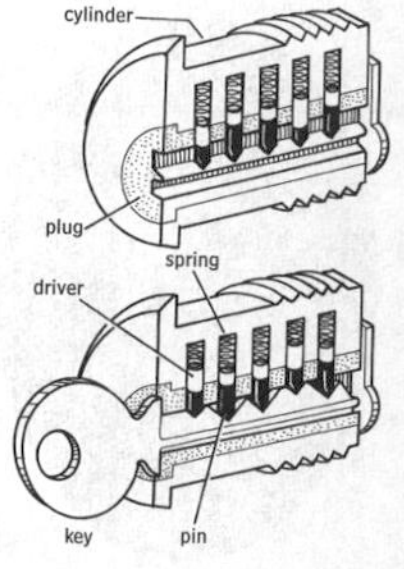

lock[1]
Top: Pin-tumbler cylinder lock
Bottom: River lock near Heidelberg, Germany

ă pat	oi boy
ā pay	ou out
âr care	o͝o took
ä father	o͞o boot
ĕ pet	ŭ cut
ē be	ûr urge
ĭ pit	th thin
ī pie	*th* this
îr pier	hw which
ŏ pot	zh vision
ō toe	ə about,
ô paw	item

Stress marks:
′ (primary);
′ (secondary), as in **dictionary** (dĭk′shə-nĕr′ē)

level. **3.** A mechanism in a firearm for exploding the charge. **4.** An interlocking or entanglement of elements or parts. **5.a.** *Sports.* A hold in wrestling or self-defense that is secured on a part of an opponent's body. **b.** A secure hold or grip. — *v.* **locked, lock•ing, locks.** — *tr.* **1.a.** To fasten the lock of. **b.** To shut or make secure with or as if with locks. **2.** To confine or exclude by or as if by means of a lock: *locked the dog in.* **3.** To fix in place so that movement or escape is impossible; hold fast. **4.a.** To sight and follow (a moving target) automatically. **b.** To aim (a weapon or other device) at a moving target so as to follow it automatically. **5.** To engage and interlock securely so as to be immobile. **6.** To clasp or link firmly; intertwine. **7.** To bind in close struggle or battle. **8.a.** To equip (a waterway) with locks. **b.** To pass (a vessel) through a lock. **9.** *Print.* **a.** To secure (letterpress type) in a chase or press bed by tightening the quoins. **b.** To fasten (a curved plate) to the cylinder of a rotary press. **10.** To invest (funds) in such a way that they cannot easily be converted into cash. **11.** *Comp. Sci.* To deny access to the contents of (a file or disk, for example). — *intr.* **1.** To become fastened by or as if by means of a lock. **2.** To become entangled; interlock. **3.** To become rigid or immobile. **4.** To pass through a lock or locks in a waterway. — ***phrasal verb.*** **lock out.** To withhold work from (employees) during a labor dispute. — ***idioms.*** **lock horns.** To become embroiled in conflict. **lock, stock, and barrel.** To the greatest or most complete extent; wholly. [ME < OE *loc,* bolt, bar.] — **lock′a•ble** *adj.*

John Locke

lock[2] (lŏk) *n.* **1.a.** A length or curl of hair; a tress. **b.** The hair of the head. Often used in the plural. **2.** A small wisp or tuft, as of wool or cotton. [ME < OE *locc.*]

lock•age (lŏk′ĭj) *n.* **1.** The passage of a ship through a lock. **2.** A toll paid for the use of a lock. **3.** A system of locks.

Locke (lŏk), **David Ross.** Petroleum V. Nasby. 1833–88. Amer. satirist who edited the *Toledo Blade* (1865–71).

Locke, John. 1632–1704. English philosopher whose *Essay Concerning Human Understanding* (1690) set out the principles of empiricism.

lock•er (lŏk′ər) *n.* **1.** One that locks: *a locker of doors.* **2.** A small, usu. metal compartment that can be locked for the safekeeping of clothing and valuables. **3.** A flat trunk for storage. **4.** A heavily insulated refrigerated cabinet, compartment, or room for storing frozen foods.

locomotive
Diesel locomotive

locker room *n.* A room furnished with lockers, as in a gymnasium, where clothes are changed and equipment is stored.

lock•er-room (lŏk′ər-ro͞om′, -ro͝om′) *adj.* Relating to, found in, or appropriate for a locker room: *locker-room language.*

lock•et (lŏk′ĭt) *n.* A small ornamental case for a picture or keepsake, usu. worn as a pendant. [ME *loket,* crossbar < OFr. *loquet,* latch, dim. of *loc,* lock, of Gmc. orig.]

lock•jaw (lŏk′jô′) *n.* **1.** See **tetanus** 1. **2.** An early sign of tetanus, in which the jaw is locked closed because of a tonic spasm of the muscles of mastication.

lock•keep•er (lŏk′kē′pər) *n.* One who is in charge of a lock on a waterway.

lock•mas•ter (lŏk′măs′tər) *n.* See **lockkeeper.**

lock•nut Also **lock nut** (lŏk′nŭt′) *n.* **1.** A usu. thin nut screwed down on another nut to prevent it from loosening. **2.** A self-locking nut.

lock•out (lŏk′out′) *n.* The withholding of work and closing down of a workplace by an employer during a labor dispute.

Lock•port (lŏk′pôrt′, -pōrt′). A city of W NY NNE of Buffalo. Pop. 24,426.

lock•set (lŏk′sĕt′) *n.* A set of hardware for shutting or locking a door.

lock•smith (lŏk′smĭth′) *n.* One that makes or repairs locks.

lock step or **lock•step** (lŏk′stĕp′) *n.* **1.** A way of marching in which the marchers follow each other as closely as possible. **2.** A standardized procedure followed closely and often mindlessly.

lock stitch *n.* A stitch made on a sewing machine by the interlocking of the upper thread and the bobbin thread.

lock•up (lŏk′ŭp′) *n.* **1.** *Informal.* A jail, esp. one in which offenders are held while awaiting a court hearing. **2.a.** The act or an instance of locking. **b.** The state of being locked.

Lock•wood (lŏk′wo͝od′), **Belva Ann Bennett.** 1830–1917. Amer. lawyer who was the first woman admitted to practice before the U.S. Supreme Court (1879).

Lock•yer (lŏk′yər), Sir **Joseph Norman.** 1836–1920. British astronomer who edited (1869–1919) *Nature* magazine.

lo•co[1] (lō′kō) *adj. Slang.* Mad; insane. — *n., pl.* **-cos. 1.** See **locoweed. 2.** See **loco disease.** — *tr.v.* **-coed, -co•ing, -cos. 1.** To poison with locoweed. **2.** *Slang.* To make insane; craze. [Sp., crazy, poss. < Ar. *lawqā,* foolish < *'alwaq,* stupid.]

lo•co[2] (lō′kō) *adv. & adj. Mus.* At the pitch written. [< Ital. *loco* < Lat. *locō,* ablative of *locus,* place.]

loco disease *n.* A disease of livestock caused by locoweed poisoning and marked by trembling and partial paralysis.

lo•co•ism (lō′kō-ĭz′əm) *n.* See **loco disease.**

locust
Top: Desert locust
Schistocerca gregaria
Bottom: Black locust
Robinia pseudoacacia

lo•co•mo•tion (lō′kə-mō′shən) *n.* **1.** The act of moving from place to place. **2.** The ability to move from place to place. [Lat. *locō,* from a place, ablative of *locus,* place + MOTION.]

lo•co•mo•tive (lō′kə-mō′tĭv) *n.* **1.** A self-propelled vehicle, usu. electric or diesel-powered, for pulling or pushing freight or passenger cars on railroad tracks. **2.** A driving or pulling force; an impetus. — *adj.* **1.a.** Of, relating to, or involved in locomotion. **b.** Serving to put into motion or propel forward. **2.** Able to move independently from place to place. **3.** Of or relating to a self-propelled locomotive. **4.** Of or relating to travel. [Lat. *locō,* from a place, ablative of *locus,* place + Med.Lat. *mōtīvus,* causing motion; see MOTIVE.]

lo•co•mo•tor (lō′kə-mō′tər) *adj.* Of or relating to locomotion; locomotive. [Lat. *locō,* from a place, ablative of *locus,* place + MOTOR.]

locomotor ataxia *n.* See **tabes dorsalis.**

lo•co•weed (lō′kō-wēd′) *n.* Any of several plants of the genera *Oxytropis* and *Astragalus* in the pea family, found in western North America and poisonous to livestock.

loc•u•lar (lŏk′yə-lər) also **loc•u•late** (-lāt′, -lĭt) or **loc•u•lat•ed** (-lā′tĭd) *adj.* Having, made of, or divided into small cavities or compartments. [LOCUL(US) + -AR.] — **loc′u•la′tion** *n.*

loc•ule (lŏk′yo͞ol) or **loc•u•lus** (-yə-ləs) *n., pl.* **-ules** or **-li** (-lī′). A small cavity or compartment within an animal or plant part, as in a plant ovary. [Lat. *loculus,* little place, dim. of *locus,* place.]

loc•u•li•cid•al (lŏk′yə-lə-sīd′l) *adj. Bot.* Longitudinally dehiscent along the capsule wall between the partitions of the locule, as in the fruits of irises and lilies. [LOCUL(US) + Lat. *-cīda,* one who cuts; see -CIDE + -AL[1].]

lo•cum te•nens (lō′kəm′ tē′nĕnz′, tĕn′ənz) *n., pl.* **locum te•nen•tes** (tə-nĕn′tēz). A person, esp. a physician or cleric, who substitutes temporarily for another. [Med.Lat. *locum tenēns* : Lat. *locum,* place + Lat. *tenēns,* holding.]

lo•cus (lō′kəs) *n., pl.* **-ci** (-sī′, -kē, -kī′). **1.** A locality; a place. **2.** A center or focus of great activity or intense concentration: *the locus of power.* **3.** *Math.* The set or configuration of all points whose coordinates satisfy a single equation or one or more algebraic conditions. **4.** The position of a given gene on a chromosome. [Lat.]

locus clas•si•cus (klăs′ĭ-kəs) *n., pl.* **loci clas•si•ci** (klăs′ĭ-sī′, -kī′). A passage from a classic or standard work that is cited as an illustration or instance. [NLat. : Lat. *locus,* place + Lat. *classicus,* belonging to the highest class.]

lo•cust (lō′kəst) *n.* **1.** Any of numerous grasshoppers of the family Acrididae, often migrating in immense swarms that devour vegetation and crops. **2.** The seventeen-year locust. **3.a.** Any of several North American deciduous trees of the genus *Robinia,* esp. *R. pseudoacacia,* having compound leaves and durable hard wood. **b.** Any of several similar or related trees, such as the carob. **c.** The wood of one of these trees. [ME < OFr. *locuste* < Lat. *locusta.*]

lo•cu•tion (lō-kyo͞o′shən) *n.* **1.** A particular word, phrase, or expression, esp. one used by a particular person or group. **2.** Style of speaking; phraseology. [ME *locucion* < OFr. *locution* < Lat. *locūtiō, locūtiōn-* < *locūtus,* p.part. of *loquī,* to speak. See **tolkʷ-*.**]

lode (lōd) *n.* **1.a.** The metalliferous ore that fills a fissure in a rock formation. **b.** A vein of mineral ore deposited between clearly demarcated layers of rock. **2.** A rich source or supply. [ME, way, load < OE *lād,* way. See **leit-*.**]

lode•star also **load•star** (lōd′stär′) *n.* **1.** A star, esp. Polaris, that is used as a point of reference. **2.** A guiding principle, interest, or ambition. [ME *lodesterre* : *lode,* way; see LODE + *sterre,* star; see STAR.]

lode•stone also **load•stone** (lōd′stōn′) *n.* **1.** A piece of magnetite that has magnetic properties and attracts iron or steel. **2.** One that attracts strongly. [ME *lode,* way; see LODE + STONE (< its use by sailors to show the way).]

lodge (lŏj) *n.* **1.a.** A cottage or cabin used as a temporary abode or shelter: *a ski lodge.* **b.** A small house on the grounds of an estate or a park, used by a caretaker or gatekeeper. **c.** An inn. **2.a.** Any of various Native American dwellings, such as a hogan or wigwam. **b.** The group living in such a dwelling. **3.a.** A local chapter of certain fraternal organizations. **b.** The meeting hall of such a chapter. **c.** The members of such a chapter. **4.** The den of certain animals, such as the dome-shaped structure built by beavers. — *v.* **lodged, lodg•ing, lodg•es.** — *tr.* **1.a.** To provide with temporary quarters, esp. for sleeping. **b.** To rent a room to. **c.** To place or establish in quarters. **2.** To serve as a depository for; contain. **3.** To place, leave, or deposit, as for safety. **4.** To fix, force, or implant. **5.** To register (a charge or complaint, for example) before an authority, such as a court; file. **6.** To vest (authority, for example). **7.** To beat (crops) down flat: *rye lodged by the cyclone.* — *intr.* **1.a.** To live in a place temporarily. **b.** To rent accommodations, esp. for sleeping. **2.** To be or become embedded. [ME < OFr. *loge,* of Gmc. orig.]

Lodge (lŏj), **Henry Cabot.** 1850–1924. Amer. politician who as Senate majority leader (1918–24) successfully opposed U.S. membership in the League of Nations.

Lodge, Henry Cabot, Jr. 1902–85. Amer. politician who served as ambassador to South Vietnam (1963–67).

lodge•pole pine (lŏj′pōl′) *n.* A pine *(Pinus contorta* var. *latifolia)* of western North America having light wood used in construction.

lodg•er (lŏj′ər) *n.* One that lodges, esp. one who rents and lives in a furnished room.

lodg•ing (lŏj′ĭng) *n.* **1.** A place to live. **2.** Sleeping accommodations. Often used in the plural. **3. lodgings.** Furnished rooms in another's house rented for accommodation.

lodg•ment also **lodge•ment** (lŏj′mənt) *n.* **1.a.** The act of lodging. **b.** The state of being lodged. **2.** A place for lodging. **3.** An accumulation or a deposit. **4.** A foothold or beachhead gained by troops in enemy or neutral territory.

Lo•di (lō′dī′). **1.** A city of central CA N of Stockton. Pop. 51,874. **2.** A borough of NE NJ NE of Passaic. Pop. 22,355.

lod•i•cule (lŏd′ĭ-kyo͞ol′) *n.* One of two or three small scales at the base of the ovary in a grass flower. [Lat. *lōdīcula,* small blanket, dim. of *lōdix, lōdīc-,* blanket.]

Łódź (lŏdz, wo͞och). A city of central Poland WSW of Warsaw; chartered 1423. Pop. 849,400.

Loeb (lōb), **Jacques.** 1859–1924. German-born Amer. physiologist noted for his work on parthenogenesis.

lo•ess (lō′əs, lĕs, lŭs) *n.* A buff to gray windblown deposit of fine-grained calcareous silt or clay. [Ger. *Löss* < Ger. dial. *Lösch* < *lösch,* loose. See **leu-***.] **—lo•es′si•al** (lō-ĕs′ē-əl, lĕs′ē-əl, lŭs′-) *adj.*

Loewe (lō), **Frederick.** 1901–87. Austrian-born Amer. composer who collaborated with Alan Jay Lerner on a number of musicals, including *My Fair Lady* (1956).

Loe•wy (lō′ē), **Raymond Fernand.** 1893–1986. French-born Amer. industrial designer noted for his streamlined designs.

loft (lôft, lŏft) *n.* **1.a.** A large, usu. unpartitioned floor over a factory, warehouse, or other commercial or industrial space. **b.** Such a floor converted into an apartment or artist's studio. **2.** An open space under a roof; an attic or a garret. **3.** A gallery or balcony. **4.** A hayloft. **5.** *Sports.* **a.** The backward slant of the face of a golf club head, designed to drive the ball in a high arc. **b.** A golf stroke that drives the ball in a high arc. **c.** The upward course of a ball driven in a high arc. **6.a.** The thickness of a fabric or yarn. **b.** The thickness of an item, such as a down coat, that is filled with compressible insulating material. *—v.* **loft•ed, loft•ing, lofts.** *—tr.* **1.** To put, store, or keep in a loft. **2.** To propel in a high arc. **3.** *Naut.* To lay out a full-size drawing of (the parts of a ship's hull, for example). *—intr.* **1.** To propel something, esp. a ball, in a high arc. **2.** To rise high into the air. [ME, sky, upstairs room < OE, air < ON *lopt,* upstairs room, sky, air.]

loft•y (lôf′tē, lŏf′-) *adj.* **-i•er, -i•est. 1.** Of imposing height. **2.** Elevated in character; exalted. **3.** Affecting grandness; pompous. **4.** Arrogant; haughty. [ME, noble < *loft,* upstairs room, sky. See LOFT.] **—loft′i•ly** *adv.* **—loft′i•ness** *n.*

log[1] (lôg, lŏg) *n.* **1.a.** A usu. large section of a trunk or limb of a fallen or felled tree. **b.** A long thick section of trimmed unhewn timber. **2.** *Naut.* **a.** A device trailed from a ship to determine its speed through the water. **b.** A record of a ship's speed, its progress, and any shipboard events of navigational importance. **c.** The book in which this record is kept. **3.** A record of a vehicle's performance, as the flight record of an aircraft. **4.** A record, as of the performance of a machine. *—v.* **logged, log•ging, logs.** *—tr.* **1.a.** To cut down, trim, and haul the timber of (a piece of land). **b.** To cut (timber) into unhewn sections. **2.** To enter in a record, as of a ship. **3.** To travel (a specified distance, time, or speed). **4.** To spend or accumulate (time). *—intr.* To cut down, trim, and haul timber. ***—phrasal verbs.*** **log in (or on).** *Comp Sci.* To enter into a computer the information required to begin a session. **log out (or off).** *Comp Sci.* To enter into a computer the command to end a session. [ME *logge.*]

log[2] (lôg, lŏg) *n. Math.* A logarithm.

log. *abbr.* Logic.

log– *pref.* Var. of **logo–.**

–log *suff.* Var. of **–logue.**

Lo•gan (lō′gən). A city of N-central UT N of Ogden; settled in the 1850's. Pop. 32,762.

Logan, Mount. A peak, 5,954.8 m (19,524 ft), of the St. Elias Mts. in SW Yukon Terr., Canada, near the AK border.

lo•gan•ber•ry (lō′gən-bĕr′ē) *n.* A trailing plant *(Rubus ursinus* var. *loganobaccus)* native to Oregon and south to Baja California and cultivated for its edible red fruit. [After James Harvey *Logan* (1841–1928), Amer. jurist.]

Lo•gans•port (lō′gənz-pôrt′, -pōrt′). A city of N-central IN NNW of Kokomo. Pop. 17,731.

log•a•rithm (lô′gə-rĭth′əm, lŏg′ə-) *n. Math.* The power to which a base, usu. 10, must be raised to produce a given number. If $n^x = a$, the logarithm of *a,* with *n* as the base, is *x*; symbolically, $\log_n a = x$. For example, $10^3 = 1{,}000$; therefore, $\log_{10} 1{,}000 = 3$. [NLat. *logarithmus* : Gk. *logos,* reason, proportion; see **leg-*** + Gk. *arithmos,* number; see **ar-***.] **—log′a•rith′mic** (-rĭ*th*′mĭk), **log′a•rith′mi•cal** (-mĭ-kəl) *adj.* **—log′a•rith′mi•cal•ly** *adv.*

log•book (lôg′bo͝ok′, lŏg′-) *n.* **1.** The official record book of a ship or an aircraft. **2.** A record book with periodic entries.

loge (lōzh) *n.* **1.** A small compartment, esp. a box in a theater. **2.** The front rows of the mezzanine in a theater. [Fr. < OFr., covered walk, lodge. See LODGE.]

log•ger (lô′gər, lŏg′ər) *n.* **1.a.** One who logs trees. **b.** One engaged in the logging business. **2.** A machine, such as a crane or tractor, that is used for hauling or loading logs.

log•ger•head (lô′gər-hĕd′, lŏg′ər-) *n.* **1.** A loggerhead turtle. **2.** An iron tool consisting of a long handle with a bulbous end heated to melt tar or warm liquids. **3.** *Naut.* A post on a whaleboat used to secure the harpoon rope. **4.** *Informal.* **a.** A blockhead; a dolt. **b.** A disproportionately large head. ***—idiom.*** **at loggerheads.** Engaged in a dispute. [Prob. dial. *logger,* wooden block (prob. < LOG[1]) + HEAD.]

loggerhead shrike *n.* A common North American bird *(Lanius ludovicianus)* having gray, black, and white plumage, a black facial mask, and a hooked beak. [< its large head.]

loggerhead turtle *n.* A large marine turtle *(Caretta caretta)* inhabiting warm ocean waters and having a large head.

log•gi•a (lô′jē-ə, lŏj′ē-ə) *n.* **1.** An open-sided roofed gallery or arcade along the front or side of a building, often at an upper level. **2.** An open balcony in a theater. [Ital. < OItal. < OFr. *loge.* See LOGE.]

log•ging (lô′gĭng, lŏg′ĭng) *n.* The work or business of felling and trimming trees and transporting the logs to a mill.

log•ic (lŏj′ĭk) *n.* **1.** The study of the principles of reasoning, esp. of the structure of propositions as distinguished from their content and of method and validity in deductive reasoning. **2.a.** A system of reasoning: *Aristotle's logic.* **b.** A mode of reasoning. **c.** The formal guiding principles of a discipline, school, or science. **3.** Valid reasoning. **4.** The relationship between elements and between an element and the whole in a set of objects, individuals, principles, or events: *There's a certain logic to gridlock.* **5.** *Comp. Sci.* **a.** The nonarithmetic operations performed by a computer, such as sorting, that involve yes-no decisions. **b.** Computer circuitry. **c.** Graphic representation of computer circuitry. [ME < OFr. *logique* < Lat. *logica* < Gk. *logikē (tekhnē),* (art) of reasoning, logic, fem. of *logikos,* of reasoning < *logos,* reason. See **leg-***.]

log•i•cal (lŏj′ĭ-kəl) *adj.* **1.** Of, relating to, in accordance with, or of the nature of logic. **2.** Based on earlier or otherwise known statements, events, or conditions; reasonable: *Rain was a logical expectation in April.* **3.** Reasoning or capable of reasoning in a clear and consistent manner. **—log′i•cal′i•ty** (-kăl′ĭ-tē), **log′i•cal•ness** *n.* **—log′i•cal•ly** *adv.*

logical positivism *n.* A philosophy asserting that in assessing truth observation has primacy and that metaphysical and subjective arguments not based on it are meaningless.

logic circuit *n. Comp. Sci.* A computer switching circuit that performs problem-solving functions.

lo•gi•cian (lō-jĭsh′ən) *n.* **1.** A practitioner of a system of logic. **2.** A student or scholar of logic.

logic operator *n. Comp. Sci.* A program instruction, such as OR, in which the quantity being operated on and the result of the operation each can have one of two values.

lo•gi•on (lō′gē-ŏn′) *n., pl.* **-gi•a** (-gē-ə). A supposed saying of Jesus not recorded in the Gospels. [Gk., oracle < *legein,* to speak. See **leg-***.]

lo•gis•tic (lō-jĭs′tĭk) also **lo•gis•ti•cal** (-tĭ-kəl) *adj.* **1.** Of or relating to symbolic logic. **2.** Of or relating to logistics. [Med. Lat. *logisticus,* of calculation < Gk. *logistikos,* skilled in calculating < *logistēs,* calculator < *logizesthai,* to calculate < *logos,* reckoning, reason. See **leg-***.] **—lo•gis′ti•cal•ly** *adv.* **—lo′gis•ti′cian** (-jĭ-stĭsh′ən) *n.*

lo•gis•tics (lō-jĭs′tĭks, lə-) *n. (used with a sing. or pl. v.)* **1.** The branch of military operations that deals with the procurement, distribution, maintenance, and replacement of materiel and personnel. **2.** The management of the details of an operation. [Fr. *logistiques* < *logistique,* logic < Med.Lat. *logisticus,* of calculation. See LOGISTIC.]

log•jam (lôg′jăm′, lŏg′-) *n.* **1.** An immovable mass of floating logs crowded together. **2.** A deadlock, as in talks; an impasse.

lo•go (lō′gō′) *n., pl.* **-gos.** A name, symbol, or trademark designed for easy recognition, esp. one borne on a single printing plate or piece of type. [Short for LOGOGRAM and LOGOTYPE.]

LO•GO (lō′gō) *n. Comp. Sci.* A programming language developed for teaching young children. [Alteration of Gk. *logos,* word. See LOGOS.]

logo– or **log–** *pref.* Word; speech: *logogram.* [Gk. < *logos,* word, speech. See **leg-***.]

log•o•gram (lô′gə-grăm′, lŏg′ə-) *n.* A written symbol representing a word without expressing its pronunciation; for example, for 4 read "four." **—log′o•gram•mat′ic** (-grə-măt′ĭk) *adj.* **—log′o•gram•mat′i•cal•ly** *adv.*

log•o•graph (lô′gə-grăf′, lŏg′ə-) *n.* See **logogram.** **—log′o•graph′ic** *adj.* **—log′o•graph′i•cal•ly** *adv.*

lo•gog•ra•phy (lō-gŏg′rə-fē) *n.* The use of logotypes in design and printing.

log•o•griph (lô′gə-grĭf′, lŏg′ə-) *n. Games.* A word puzzle, such as an anagram or one in which clues are given in a set of verses. [LOGO– + Gk. *griphos,* fishing basket, riddle.]

lo•gom•a•chy (lə-gŏm′ə-kē) *n., pl.* **-chies. 1.** A dispute about words. **2.** A dispute carried on in words only; a battle of words. [Gk. *logomakhia* < *logomakhein,* to fight about words : *logo-,* logo- + *makhē,* battle.]

log•or•rhe•a (lô′gə-rē′ə, lŏg′ə-) *n.* Excessive use of words.

Lo•gos (lō′gōs′, lŏg′ŏs′) *n.* **1.** *Philos.* **a.** In pre-Socratic phi-

loganberry
Rubus ursinus
var. *loganobaccus*

ă pat	oi boy
ā pay	ou out
âr care	o͝o took
ä father	o͞o boot
ĕ pet	ŭ cut
ē be	ûr urge
ĭ pit	th thin
ī pie	*th* this
îr pier	hw which
ŏ pot	zh vision
ō toe	ə about, item
ô paw	

Stress marks:
′ (primary);
′ (secondary), as in
dictionary (dĭk′shə-nĕr′ē)

Lombardy poplar
Populus nigra var. *italica*

Henry Wadsworth Longfellow
1870 photograph by George K. Warren (1824–1884)

losophy, the principle governing the cosmos, the source of this principle, or reasoning about the cosmos. **b.** Among the Sophists, the topics of rational argument or the arguments themselves. **c.** In Stoicism, the active, material, rational principle of the cosmos, identified with God and constituting the power of reason in the human soul. **2.** *Judaism.* **a.** In biblical Judaism, the creative word of God, which is God's medium of communication with the human race. **b.** In Hellenistic Judaism, a hypostasis associated with divine wisdom. **3.** *Theol.* In Saint John's Gospel, the creative word of God, which is itself God and incarnate in Jesus. [Gk. See **leg-***.]

lo•go•type (lô′gə-tīp′, lŏg′ə-) *n.* **1.** *Print.* A single piece of type bearing two or more elements. **2.** A logo.

log•roll (lôg′rōl′, lŏg′-) *v.* **-rolled, -roll•ing, -rolls.** *—tr.* To work toward the passage of (legislation) by logrolling. *—intr.* To engage in political logrolling.

log•roll•ing (lôg′rō′lĭng, lŏg′-) *n.* **1.** The exchanging of political favors, esp. the trading of influence or votes among legislators to achieve passage of projects that are of interest to one another. **2.** The exchanging of favors or praise, as among artists. **3.** See **birling.** [From the early American practice of neighbors gathering to help clear land by rolling off and burning felled timber.] **—log′roll′er** *n.*

Lo•gro•ño (lə-grōn′yə, lô-grô′nyô). A city of N Spain on the Ebro R. NNE of Madrid. Pop. 113,576.

–logue or **–log** *suff.* Speech; discourse: *travelogue.* [Fr. < Gk. *-logos* < *legein*, to speak. See **leg-***.]

log•wood (lôg′wo͝od′, lŏg′-) *n.* **1.** A spiny tropical American tree *(Haematoxylon campechianum)* in the pea family, having dark heartwood. **2.** The heartwood of this tree. **3.** The purplish-red dye obtained from the heartwood of this tree.

lo•gy (lō′gē) *adj.* **-gi•er, -gi•est.** Characterized by lethargy; sluggish. [Perh. < Du. *log*, heavy, or var. of E. *loggy*, heavy, sluggish (< LOG[1]).]

–logy *suff.* **1.** Discourse; expression: *phraseology.* **2.** Science; theory; study: *dermatology.* [ME *-logie* < OFr. < Lat. *-logia* < Gk. (< *logos*, word, speech; see **leg-***) and < *-logos*, one who deals with (< *legein*, to speak; see **leg-***).]

loin (loin) *n.* **1.** The part of the body of a human being or quadruped on either side of the backbone and between the ribs and hips. **2.** One of several cuts of meat, such as tenderloin, taken from this part of an animal's body, typically including the vertebrae. **3. loins. a.** The region of the hips, groin, and lower abdomen. **b.** The reproductive organs. [ME *loine* < OFr. *loigne* < VLat. **lumbea (carō)*, loin (meat), fem. of **lumbeus*, of the loin < Lat. *lumbus*, loin.]

loin•cloth (loin′klôth′, -klŏth′) *n.* A strip of cloth worn around the loins.

Loir (lwär). A river, c. 311 km (193 mi), of NW France flowing generally W to the Sarthe R.

Loire (lwär). The longest river of France, rising in the Cévennes and flowing c. 1,014 km (630 mi) to the Bay of Biscay.

loi•ter (loi′tər) *intr.v.* **-tered, -ter•ing, -ters. 1.** To stand idly about; linger aimlessly. **2.** To proceed slowly or with many stops. **3.** To delay or dawdle: *loiter over a job.* [ME *loitren*, prob. < MDu. *loteren*, to totter, be loose.] **—loi′ter•er** *n.*

Lo•ki (lō′kē) *n. Myth.* A Norse god who created discord, esp. among other gods.

Lo•li•ta (lō-lē′tə) *n.* An adolescent girl regarded as seductive. [After *Lolita*, heroine of *Lolita* by Vladimir Nabokov.]

loll (lŏl) *v.* **lolled, loll•ing, lolls.** *—intr.* **1.** To move, stand, or recline in an indolent or relaxed manner. **2.** To hang or droop laxly. *—tr.* To permit to hang or droop laxly. *—n. Archaic.* An act or attitude of lolling. [ME *lollen*, prob. < MDu., to doze.] **—loll′er** *n.* **—loll′ing•ly** *adv.*

Lol•land (lŏl′ənd, lô′län). An island of SE Denmark in the Baltic Sea S of Sjaelland.

lol•la•pa•loo•za also **lal•la•pa•loo•za** (lŏl′ə-pə-lo͞o′zə) *n. Slang.* Something outstanding of its kind. [?]

Lol•lard (lŏl′ərd) *n.* A member of a sect of religious reformers in England who were followers of John Wycliffe in the 14th and 15th centuries. [ME < MDu. *Lollaerd*, mumbler, mutterer, heretic < *lollen*, doze, to mumble.]

lol•li•pop also **lol•ly•pop** (lŏl′ē-pŏp′) *n.* A confection consisting of hard candy on the end of a small stick. [Perh. dial. *lolly*, tongue (< LOLL, to dangle the tongue) + POP[1].]

lol•lop (lŏl′əp) *intr.v.* **-loped, -lop•ing, -lops. 1.** To move with a bobbing motion. **2.** *Chiefly British.* To lounge about; loll. [Alteration of LOLL.] **—lol′lop•y** *adj.*

lol•ly (lŏl′ē) *n., pl.* **-lies.** *Chiefly British.* **1.a.** A piece of candy, esp. hard candy. **b.** A lollipop. **2.** Money. [Short for LOLLIPOP.]

lol•ly•gag (lŏl′ē-găg′) also **lal•ly•gag** (lăl′ē-) *intr.v.* **-gagged, -gag•ging, -gags.** To waste time by puttering aimlessly; dawdle. [?]

Lo•ma•mi (lō-mä′mē). A river of Zaire flowing c. 1,448 km (900 mi) to the Congo R.

Lo•mas de Za•mo•ra (lō′mäs də zə-môr′ə, -mōr′ə, *thĕ* sä-mô′rä). A city of E Argentina, a suburb of Buenos Aires. Pop. 508,620.

Lo•max (lō′măks′), **John Avery.** 1867–1948. Amer. folklorist who with his son **Alan Lomax** (b. 1915) toured the country recording blues and folk musicians for the Library of Congress.

Lom•bard[1] (lŏm′bərd, -bärd′, lŭm′-) *n.* **1.** A member of a Germanic people that invaded northern Italy in the sixth century A.D. **2.** A native or inhabitant of Lombardy. **3.** A banker or moneylender. [ME *Lumbarde* < OFr. *lombard* < OItal. *lombardo* < Med.Lat. *lombardus* < Lat. *Langobardus, Longobardus.* See **del-[1]***.]

Lom•bard[2] (lŏm′bärd′). A village of NE IL, a suburb of Chicago. Pop. 39,408.

Lom•bard (lŏm′bärd′, lŭm′-), **Peter.** 1100?–60? Italian theologian noted for his *Sententiarum Libri IV* (1148–51).

Lom•bar•dy (lŏm′bər-dē, lŭm′-). A region of N Italy bordering on Switzerland; center of the kingdom of the Lombards in the 6th cent. A.D.

Lombardy poplar *n.* A deciduous tree *(Populus nigra* var. *italica)* having upward-pointing branches that form a slender columnar outline. [After LOMBARDY.]

Lom•bok (lŏm-bŏk′). An island of S-central Indonesia in the Lesser Sundas E of Bali, from which it is separated by the **Lombok Strait.**

Lom•bro•so (lôm-brō′sō), **Cesare.** 1836–1909. Italian criminologist who suggested that individuals with innate criminal dispositions can be identified by physical characteristics.

Lo•mé (lō-mā′). The cap. of Togo, in the S part on the Gulf of Guinea. Pop. 369,926.

lo•ment (lō′mĕnt′) *n.* An indehiscent legume, as of the tick trefoil, usu. constricted between the seeds and separating at maturity into one-seeded segments. [Lat. *lōmentum*, skin conditioner made of bean meal < *lavere*, to wash. See **leu(ə)-***.]

Lo•mi•ta (lō-mē′tə). A city of southern CA, a suburb of Los Angeles. Pop. 19,382.

Lo•mond (lō′mənd), **Loch.** A lake in S-central Scotland; noted for its associations with the 18th-cent. outlaw Rob Roy.

Lom•poc (lŏm′pŏk′). A city of S CA WNW of Santa Barbara. Pop. 37,649.

Lon•don (lŭn′dən). **1.** A city of SE Ontario, Canada, SW of Toronto; settled in 1826. Pop. 283,668. **2.** The cap. of the United Kingdom, on the Thames R. in SE England; built on the site of a Roman outpost named Londinium. Pop. 6,851,400.

London, John ("Jack") Griffith. 1876–1916. Amer. writer whose adventure novels include *The Call of the Wild* (1903).

London broil *n.* Broiled flank steak cut into thin slices. [After LONDON, England.]

Lon•don•der•ry (lŭn′dən-dĕr′ē, lŭn′dən-dĕr′ē) also **Der•ry** (dĕr′ē). A borough of NW Northern Ireland NW of Belfast; built of the site of an abbey founded in 546. Pop. 68,000.

lone (lōn) *adj.* **1.a.** Without accompaniment; solitary. **b.** Without companionship; isolated or lonely. **2.** Being the only one; sole. **3.** Situated by itself. [ME, short for *alone.* See ALONE.]

lone•ly (lōn′lē) *adj.* **-li•er, -li•est. 1.a.** Without companions; lone. **b.** Characterized by aloneness; solitary. **2.** Unfrequented by people; desolate. **3.a.** Dejected by the awareness of being alone. See Syns at **alone. b.** Producing such dejection: *a lonely night of the week.* **—lone′li•ly** *adv.* **—lone′li•ness** *n.*

lone•ly-hearts or **lone•ly•hearts** (lōn′lē-härts′) *adj.* Of or relating to people who are looking for dates or partners.

lon•er (lō′nər) *n.* One who avoids company.

lone•some (lōn′səm) *adj.* **1.a.** Dejected because of a lack of companionship. See Syns at **alone. b.** Producing such dejection: *a lonesome hour.* **2.** Deserted; unfrequented: *a lonesome valley.* **3.** Solitary; lone. *—n. Informal.* Self: *He ate by his lonesome.* **—lone′some•ly** *adv.* **—lone′some•ness** *n.*

lone wolf *n.* One who prefers no company or help.

long[1] (lông, lŏng) *adj.* **long•er, long•est. 1.a.** Extending a relatively great distance. **b.** Having relatively great height; tall. **c.** Having the greater length of two or the greatest length of several. **2.** Of relatively great duration. **3.** Of a specified linear extent or duration: *a mile long.* **4.** Made up of many members or items: *a long list.* **5.** Extending beyond an average or a standard: *a long game.* **6.** Tediously protracted; lengthy. **7.** Concerned with distant issues; far-reaching: *a long view.* **8.** Involving substantial chance; risky: *long odds.* **9.** Having an abundance or excess. **10.** Holding a commodity or security in expectation of a rise in price. **11.** *Ling.* **a.** Having a great duration. Used of a vowel or consonant. **b.** Of, relating to, or being a vowel sound in English, as in *feet*, that is descended from a long vowel. **12.a.** Stressed or accented. Used of a syllable in accentual prosody. **b.** Being of relatively great duration. Used of a syllable in quantitative prosody. *—adv.* **1.** During or for an extended period of time. **2.** At or to a considerable distance; far. **3.** For or throughout a specified period: *all night long.* **4.** At a point of time distant from that referred to. **5.** Into or in a long position, as of a commodity market. *—n.* **1.** A long time: *It took long.* **2.** A long syllable, vowel, or consonant. **3.** One who acquires holdings in a security or commodity in expectation of a rise in price. **4.a.** A garment size for a tall person. **b. longs.** Trousers extending to the feet or ankles. **—*idioms.* any longer.** For more time. **as (or so) long as. 1.** During the time that. **2.** Inasmuch as; since. **3.** Under the condition that; provided that. **before long.**

Soon. **long ago. 1.** At a time or during a period well before the present. **2.** A time well before the present. **long in the tooth.** Growing old. **no longer.** Not now as formerly. **not long for.** Unlikely to remain for much more time in. **the long and the short of it.** The substance or gist. [ME < OE *lang.* See **del-¹*.**]

long² (lông, lŏng) *intr.v.* **longed, long•ing, longs.** To have an earnest, heartfelt desire, esp. for something beyond reach. [ME *longen* < OE *langian.* See **del-¹*.**]

Long (lông, lŏng), **Crawford Williamson.** 1815–78. Amer. surgeon among the first (1842) to use ether as an anesthetic.

Long, Huey Pierce. "the Kingfish." 1893–1935. Amer. politician who served as governor of LA (1928–32) and U.S. senator (1930–35).

long. *abbr.* Longitude.

lon•gan (lŏng′gən, lông′-) *n.* **1.** An Indian evergreen tree *(Euphoria longan)* having yellowish-brown drupes with edible flesh. **2.** Its fruit. [NLat. *longanum,* specific epithet < Chin. (Mandarin) *lóng yǎn* : *lóng,* dragon + *yǎn,* eye.]

lon•ga•nim•i•ty (lŏng′gə-nĭm′ĭ-tē, lông′-) *n.* Calmness in the face of suffering and adversity; forbearance. [ME *longanimite* < OFr. < LLat. *longanimitās* < *longanimis,* patient : Lat. *longus,* long; see LONGITUDE + Lat. *animus,* mind, reason; see **anə-*.**]

Long Beach. 1. A city of S CA on an arm of the Pacific Ocean SE of Los Angeles. Pop. 429,433. **2.** A city of SE NY on an island off S Long Island. Pop. 33,510.

long•boat (lông′bōt′, lŏng′-) *n. Naut.* The longest boat carried by a sailing ship, esp. by a merchant ship.

long•bow (lông′bō′, lŏng′-) *n.* A long hand-drawn bow, such as that used in medieval England, which sometimes exceeded 6 feet (1.8 meters) in length.

Long Branch. A city of E-central NJ on the Atlantic Ocean N of Asbury Park. Pop. 28,658.

long distance *n.* **1.** An operator or a system that places long-distance telephone calls. **2.** A long-distance telephone call.

long-dis•tance (lông′dĭs′təns, lŏng′-) *adj.* **1.** Covering a long distance. **2.** Of, relating to, or being telephone communication to a distant station. **—long′-dis′tance** *adv.*

long division *n. Math.* A process of division in arithmetic, usu. used with a large divisor, in which each step of the division is written out.

long dozen *n.* A baker's dozen; thirteen.

long-drawn-out (lông′drôn′out′, lŏng′-) *adj.* Greatly extended or protracted; prolonged: *a long-drawn-out speech.*

lon•ge•ron (lŏn′jər-ən) *n.* A major structural member of an aircraft fuselage, running from front to rear. [Fr. < OFr., beam < *long,* long < Lat. *longus.* See **del-¹*.**]

lon•gev•i•ty (lŏn-jĕv′ĭ-tē, lôn-) *n., pl.* **-ties. 1.a.** Long life; great duration of life. **b.** Length or duration of life. **2.** Long duration or continuance, as in an occupation. [LLat. *longaevitās* < Lat. *longaevus,* ancient : *longus,* long; see **del-¹*** + *aevum,* age; see **aiw-*.**] **—lon•ge′vous** (-jē′vəs) *adj.*

long face *n.* A discontented or sullen facial expression.

Long•fel•low (lông′fĕl′ō, lŏng′-), **Henry Wadsworth.** 1807–82. Amer. writer whose works include *The Song of Hiawatha* (1855).

long green *n. Slang.* Paper money.

long•hair (lông′hâr′, lŏng′-) *n. Informal.* **1.** One dedicated to the arts and esp. to classical music. **2.** One whose taste in the arts is considered overrefined. **3.** A person with long hair, esp. a hippie. **—long′hair′, long′haired′** *adj.*

long•hand (lông′hănd′, lŏng′-) *n.* Cursive writing.

long haul *n. Informal.* **1.** A long distance. **2.** A long period of time. **—long′-haul′** (lông′hôl′, lŏng′-) *adj.*

long•head (lông′hĕd′, lŏng′-) *n. Anthro.* **1.** A head having a cephalic index less than 76. **2.** A person having such a head.

long•head•ed also **long-head•ed** (lông′hĕd′ĭd, lŏng′-) *adj.* **1.** *Anthro.* Dolichocephalic. **2.** Foresighted; wise.

long•horn (lông′hôrn′, lŏng′-) *n.* **1.** Any of a breed of cattle with long horns. **2.** A kind of Cheddar cheese made in long cylinders.

long-horned beetle (lông′hôrnd′, lŏng′-) *n.* Any of numerous beetles of the family Cerambycidae, having long antennae.

long-horned grasshopper *n.* Any of various large insects of the family Tettigoniidae, having long slender antennae.

long•house or **long house** (lông′hous′) *n.* A long communal dwelling, esp. of the Iroquois, typically built of poles and bark, with family compartments in a central corridor.

lon•gi•corn (lŏn′jĭ-kôrn′) *n.* See **long-horned beetle.** —*adj.* **1.** Having long antennae. **2.** Of or belonging to the family Cerambycidae, which includes the long-horned beetles. [< NLat. *Longicornia,* former group name : Lat. *longus,* long; see LONGITUDE + Lat. *cornū,* horn; see **ker-¹*.**]

long•ing (lông′ĭng, lŏng′-) *n.* A strong persistent yearning or desire, esp. one that cannot be fulfilled. **—long′ing•ly** *adv.*

Lon•gi•nus (lŏn-jī′nəs), **Dionysius Cassius.** A.D. 210?–273. Greek philosopher. The volume of literary criticism *On The Sublime* is attributed to him.

Long Island. A long narrow island of SE NY bordered on the S by the Atlantic Ocean and separated from CT on the N by **Long Island Sound,** an arm of the Atlantic. The W part of Long I. includes two boroughs of New York City.

lon•gi•tude (lŏn′jĭ-to͞od′, -tyo͞od′, lôn′-) *n.* **1.** Angular distance on the earth's surface, measured east or west from the prime meridian at Greenwich, England, to the meridian passing through a position, expressed in degrees (or hours), minutes, and seconds. **2.** Celestial longitude. [ME, length, a measured length < OFr. < Lat. *longitūdō, longitūdin-* < *longus,* long. See **del-¹*.**]

lon•gi•tu•di•nal (lŏn′jĭ-to͞od′n-əl, -tyo͞od′-, lôn′-) *adj.* **1.a.** Of or relating to longitude or length. **b.** Concerned with the development of persons or groups over time. **2.** Placed or running lengthwise. **—lon′gi•tu′di•nal•ly** *adv.*

long johns *pl.n. Informal.* Long warm underwear. [< the name *John.*]

long jump *n. Sports.* A jump in track and field that is made for distance rather than height.

long•leaf pine (lông′lēf′, lŏng′-) *n.* An evergreen tree *(Pinus palustris)* of the southeast United States with long needles and resinous wood.

long-lived (lông′līvd′, -lĭvd′, lŏng′-) *adj.* **1.** Having a long life. **2.** Lasting a long time; persistent: *a long-lived rumor.* **3.** Functioning a long time; durable. **—long′-lived′ness** *n.*

long measure *n.* **1.** See **linear measure. 2.** See **long meter.**

long meter *n.* A quatrain in iambic tetrameter, rhyming in the second and fourth lines and often in the first and third.

Long•mont (lông′mŏnt′, lŏng′-). A city of N-central CO NNE of Boulder. Pop. 42,942.

long•neck (lông′nĕk′, lŏng′-) *n. Texas.* A glass beer bottle with an elongated neck.

long-play•ing (lông′plā′ĭng, lŏng′-) *adj.* Relating to or being a phonograph record that turns at 33⅓ revolutions per minute.

long-range (lông′rānj′, lŏng′-) *adj.* **1.** Of, suitable for, or reaching long distances: *long-range missiles.* **2.** Requiring or involving an extended span of time: *long-range planning.*

long run *n.* A long period of time: *It worked in the long run.*

long•shore (lông′shôr′, -shōr′, lŏng′-) *adj.* Occurring, living, or working along a seacoast. [Short for ALONGSHORE.]

long•shore•man (lông′shôr′mən, -shōr′-, lŏng′-) *n.* A dock worker who loads and unloads ships.

long shot *n.* **1.** *Sports & Games.* An entry, as in a horserace, with only a slight chance of winning. **2.a.** A bet made at great odds. **b.** A venture that offers a great reward but has very little chance of success. **3.** A photograph or a film or television shot taken at long range. **—*idiom.* by a long shot.** *Informal.* By any means. Usu. used in negative sentences.

long-sight•ed (lông′sī′tĭd, lŏng′-) *adj.* Farsighted. **—long′-sight′ed•ly** *adv.* **—long′-sight′ed•ness** *n.*

long•some (lông′səm, lŏng′-) *adj.* Tiresomely long.

Longs Peak (lôngz, lŏngz). A mountain, 4,347.8 m (14,255 ft), in the Front Range of the Rocky Mts. in N-central CO.

long•spur (lông′spûr′, lŏng′-) *n.* Any of several birds, esp. of the genus *Calcarius* of northern regions, having brownish plumage and long-clawed hind toes.

long-stand•ing (lông′stăn′dĭng, lŏng′-) *adj.* Of long duration or existence: *a long-standing friendship.*

Long•street (lông′strēt′, lŏng′-), **James.** 1821–1904. Amer. Confederate general whose delay in carrying out orders contributed to the Confederate defeat at Gettysburg (1863).

long-suf•fer•ing (lông′sŭf′ər-ĭng, lŏng′-) *adj.* Patiently enduring wrongs or difficulties. —*n.* Patient endurance. See Syns at **patience. —long′-suf′fer•ing•ly** *adv.*

long suit *n.* **1.** *Games.* The suit in which a given hand has the most cards. **2.** One's strongest asset in quality or talent.

long-tailed duck (lông′tāld′, lŏng′-) *n.* See **oldsquaw.**

long-term (lông′tûrm′, lŏng′-) *adj.* Involving, maturing after, or being in effect for a long time: *a long-term investment.*

long-time or **long•time** (lông′tīm′, lŏng′-) *adj.* Having existed or persisted for a long time.

long ton *n.* See **ton** 2.

Lon•gueil (lông-gāl′). A city of S Quebec, Canada, on the St. Lawrence R. opposite Montreal. Pop. 124,320.

lon•gueur (lông-gûr′, lŏng-) *n.* A tedious passage in a work of performing art or literature. [Fr. < OFr. *longor,* a protracted discussion < *long,* long < Lat. *longus.* See LONGITUDE.]

Long•view (lông′vyo͞o′, lŏng′-). **1.** A city of NE TX W of Shreveport LA. Pop. 70,311. **2.** A city of SW WA on the Columbia R. N of Vancouver. Pop. 31,499.

long-wind•ed (lông′wĭn′dĭd, lŏng′-) *adj.* **1.** Wearisomely verbose. **2.** Able to maintain breathing power during exertion. **—long′-wind′ed•ly** *adv.* **—long′-wind′ed•ness** *n.*

long•wise (lông′wīz′, lŏng′-) *adv. & adj.* Lengthwise.

loo¹ (lo͞o) *n., pl.* **loos.** *Games.* A card game in which each player contributes stakes to a pool. [Short for obsolete *lanterloo* < Fr. *lanturlu,* a meaningless refrain, loo.]

loo² (lo͞o) *n., pl.* **loos.** *Chiefly British.* A toilet. [?]

loo•fa or **loo•fah** (lo͞o′fə) also **luf•fa** (lo͞o′fə, lŭf′ə) *n.* **1.** Any of several Old World tropical vines of the genus *Luffa,* having cylindrical fruit with a fibrous spongelike interior. **2.** The interior, used as a washing sponge or filter. [Ar. *lūf, lūfah.*]

look (lo͝ok) *v.* **looked, look•ing, looks.** —*intr.* **1.a.** To employ one's sight, esp. in a given direction or on a given object.

longhorn

long jump

ă pat	oi boy
ā pay	ou out
âr care	o͝o took
ä father	o͞o boot
ĕ pet	ŭ cut
ē be	ûr urge
ĭ pit	th thin
ī pie	*th* this
îr pier	hw which
ŏ pot	zh vision
ō toe	ə about, item
ô paw	

Stress marks:
′ (primary);
′ (secondary), as in
dictionary (dĭk′shə-nĕr′ē)

b. To search. **2.a.** To turn one's glance or gaze. **b.** To turn one's attention; attend. **c.** To turn one's expectations: *looked to us for help.* **3.** To seem or appear to be. **4.** To face in a specified direction. — *tr.* **1.** To turn one's eyes on. **2.** To convey by one's expression. **3.a.** To have an appearance of conformity with: *He looks his age.* **b.** To appear to be. — *n.* **1.a.** The act or instance of looking. **b.** A gaze or glance expressive of something: *a mournful look.* **2.a.** Appearance or aspect: *a look of great age.* **b. looks.** Physical appearance, esp. when pleasing. **c.** A distinctive, unified manner of dress or fashion. — ***phrasal verbs.*** **look after.** To take care of. **look for. 1.** To search for; seek. **2.** To expect. **look on** (or **upon**). To regard in a certain way. **look out.** To be watchful or careful; take care. **look to. 1.** To expect to. **2.** To seem about to; promise to. **look up. 1.** To search for and find, as in a reference book. **2.** To visit. **3.** To become better; improve. — ***idioms.*** **look a gift horse in the mouth.** *Informal.* To be critical or suspicious of something one has received without expense. **look alive** (or **sharp**). *Informal.* To act or respond quickly. **look down on** (or **upon**). To regard with contempt or condescension. **look down (one's) nose at** (or **on**). To regard with contempt or condescension. **look forward to.** To think of (a future event) with pleasurable anticipation. **look up to.** To admire. [ME *loken* < OE *lōcian.*]

loom²

look-a•like (lo͝ok′ə-līk′) *n.* One that closely resembles another; a double.

look•er (lo͝ok′ər) *n.* **1.** One that looks, esp. a spectator or an onlooker. **2.** *Slang.* A very attractive person.

look•er-on (lo͝ok′ər-ŏn′, -ôn′) *n., pl.* **look•ers-on** (lo͝ok′ərz-). A spectator; an onlooker.

look-in (lo͝ok′ĭn′) *n.* **1.** A short visit. **2.** A quick glance.

look•ing glass (lo͝ok′ĭng) *n.* See **mirror** 1.

look•out (lo͝ok′out′) *n.* **1.** The act of observing or keeping watch. **2.** A high place or structure commanding a wide view, used for observation. **3.** One who keeps watch. **4.** Outlook; view. **5.** An object of concern or worry.

look-see (lo͝ok′sē′) *n. Informal.* A quick survey or glance.

look-up (lo͝ok′ŭp′) *n. Comp. Sci.* A procedure in which a table of values stored in a computer is searched until a specified value is found.

loon¹

loom¹ (lo͞om) *intr.v.* **loomed, loom•ing, looms. 1.** To come into view as a massive, distorted, or indistinct image. **2.** To appear to the mind in a magnified and threatening form. **3.** To seem imminent; impend: *Revolution loomed.* — *n.* A distorted, threatening appearance of something, as through fog or darkness. [Perh. of Scand. orig.]

loom² (lo͞om) *n.* An apparatus for making thread or yarn into cloth by weaving strands together at right angles. [ME *lome* < OE *gelōma*, tool : *ge-*, collective pref.; see YCLEPT + *-lōma*, tool, as in *andlōman*, tools.]

loon¹ (lo͞on) *n.* Any of several fish-eating diving birds of the genus *Gavia* of northern regions, having a short tail, webbed feet, and a laughlike cry. [Of Scand. orig.]

loon² (lo͞on) *n. Informal.* One who is crazy or deranged. [ME *louen*, rogue.]

loon•y or **loon•ey** also **lun•y** (lo͞o′nē) *Informal.* — *adj.* **-i•er, -i•est. 1.** Extremely foolish or silly. **2.** Crazy; insane. — *n., pl.* **-ies** also **-eys.** A foolish or crazy person. [Shortening and alteration (prob. influenced by LOON¹) of LUNATIC.] — **loon′i•ly** *adv.* — **loon′i•ness** *n.*

loony bin *n. Offensive Slang.* A mental health facility.

loosestrife

loop¹ (lo͞op) *n.* **1.a.** A length of line, thread, or other thin material that is curved or doubled over making an opening. **b.** The opening formed by such a doubled line. **2.** Something having a shape, order, or path of motion that is circular or curved over on itself. **3.** *Elect.* A closed circuit. **4.** *Comp. Sci.* A sequence of instructions that repeats either a specified number of times or until a particular condition prevails. **5.** A type of loop-shaped intrauterine device. **6.** A flight maneuver in which an aircraft flies a circular path in a vertical plane with the lateral axis of the aircraft remaining horizontal. **7.** *Sports.* See **league¹** 2. — *v.* **looped, loop•ing, loops.** — *tr.* **1.** To form into a loop. **2.** To fasten, join, or encircle with loops or a loop. **3.** To fly (an aircraft) in a loop. **4.** To move in a loop or an arc. **5.** *Elect.* To join (conductors) so as to complete a circuit. **6.** To add or substitute (words) in a film by altering the sound track. — *intr.* **1.** To form a loop. **2.** To move in a loop. **3.** To make a loop in an aircraft. [ME *loupe*, prob. < MIr. *lúb* (perh. influenced by ME *lep*, basket).]

loop² (lo͞op) *n. Archaic.* A loophole through which small arms may be fired. [ME *loupe.*]

looped (lo͞opt) *adj.* **1.** Formed into or having a loop or loops. **2.** *Slang.* Intoxicated; drunk.

loop•er (lo͞o′pər) *n.* **1.** One that makes loops. **2.** See **measuring worm.**

loop•hole (lo͞op′hōl′) *n.* **1.** A way of escaping a difficulty, esp. an omission or ambiguity in the wording of a contract or law that allows one to evade compliance. **2.** A small hole or slit in a wall, esp. one through which small arms may be fired.

loquat
Eriobotrya japonica

loop of Hen•le (hĕn′lē) *n.* The segment of the nephron of a vertebrate kidney between the proximal and distal convoluted tubules that helps transport ions and water and concentrate urine. [After Friedrich Gustav Jacob *Henle* (1809–85), German pathologist.]

loop•y (lo͞o′pē) *adj.* **-i•er, -i•est. 1.** Consisting of or covered with loops. **2.** Offbeat; crazy.

Loos (lo͞os), **Anita.** 1893?–1981. Amer. writer best known for *Gentlemen Prefer Blondes* (1925).

loose (lo͞os) *adj.* **loos•er, loos•est. 1.** Not fastened, restrained, or contained. **2.** Not taut, fixed, or rigid. **3.** Free from confinement or imprisonment; unfettered. **4.** Not tight-fitting or tightly fitted. **5.** Not bound, bundled, or gathered together. **6.** Not compact or dense in arrangement or structure: *loose gravel.* **7.** Lacking a sense of restraint or responsibility; idle: *loose talk.* **8.** Lacking conventional moral restraint in sexual behavior. **9.** Not literal or exact: *a loose translation.* **10.** Characterized by a free movement of fluids in the body. — *adv.* In a loose manner. — *v.* **loosed, loos•ing, loos•es.** — *tr.* **1.** To let loose; release. **2.** To make loose; undo. **3.** To cast loose; detach. **4.** To let fly; discharge. **5.** To release pressure or obligation from; absolve. **6.** To make less strict; relax. — *intr.* **1.** To become loose. **2.** To discharge a missile; fire. — ***idiom.*** **on the loose. 1.** At large; free. **2.** Acting in an uninhibited fashion. [ME *louse, los* < ON *lauss.* See **leu-*.**] — **loose′ly** *adv.* — **loose′ness** *n.*

Syns: *loose, lax, slack.* The central meaning shared by these adjectives is "not tautly bound, held, or fastened": *loose reins; a lax rope; slack sails.* ***Ant:*** *tight.*

loose cannon *n. Slang.* One that is uncontrolled and therefore poses danger. [< the threat posed by loose cannon rolling about a warship under sail.]

loose end *n.* A minor unresolved problem or difficulty. Often used in the plural.

loose-joint•ed (lo͞os′join′tĭd) *adj.* **1.** Having freely articulated, highly mobile joints. **2.** Limber or agile in movement.

loose-leaf (lo͞os′lēf′) *adj.* Relating to, having, or being leaves that are easy to remove, rearrange, or replace.

loos•en (lo͞o′sən) *v.* **-ened, -en•ing, -ens.** — *tr.* **1.** To untie or make looser. **2.** To free from restraint, pressure, or strictness. **3.** To free (the bowels) from constipation. — *intr.* To become loose or looser. [ME *lousnen, losnen* < *losen* < *los*, loose. See LOOSE.]

loose•strife (lo͞os′strīf′) *n.* **1.** Any of various plants of the genus *Lysimachia*, having usu. yellow flowers. **2.** Any of various plants of the genus *Lythrum*, having purple or white flowers. [Mistransl. of Lat. *lȳsimachīa* (as if < Gk. *lusis*, loosening, and Gk. *makhē*, battle) < Gk. *lusimakheios*, perh. after *Lusimakhos*, Lysimachos, early Greek physician.]

loot (lo͞ot) *n.* **1.** Valuables pillaged in time of war; spoils. **2.** Stolen goods. **3.** *Informal.* Goods illicitly obtained, as by bribery. **4.** *Informal.* Things of value, such as gifts, received on one occasion. **5.** *Slang.* Money. — *v.* **loot•ed, loot•ing, loots.** — *tr.* **1.** To pillage; spoil. **2.** To take as spoils; steal. — *intr.* To engage in pillaging. [Hindi *lūṭ* < Skt. *loptram, lotram*, plunder. See **reup-*.**] — **loot′er** *n.*

lop¹ (lŏp) *tr.v.* **lopped, lop•ping, lops. 1.** To cut off (a part); trim: *lopped her long curls.* **2.** To cut off from a tree or shrub. **3.** To eliminate or excise as superfluous. [Perh. < ME *loppe*, small branches and twigs.] — **lop′per** *n.*

lop² (lŏp) *intr. & tr.v.* **lopped, lop•ping, lops.** To hang or let hang loosely; droop. [?]

lope (lōp) *intr.v.* **loped, lop•ing, lopes.** To run or ride with a steady easy gait. — *n.* A steady easy gait. [ME *lopen*, to leap < ON *hlaupa.*] — **lop′er** *n.*

lop-eared (lŏp′îrd′) *adj.* Having bent or drooping ears.

Lop Nur (lŏp′ no͝or′) also **Lop Nor** (nôr′). A marshy depression of NW China, once a large salt lake.

lop•py (lŏp′ē) *adj.* **-pi•er, -pi•est.** Hanging limp; pendulous.

lop•sid•ed (lŏp′sī′dĭd) *adj.* **1.** Heavier, larger, or higher on one side than on the other. **2.** Sagging or leaning to one side. — **lop′sid′ed•ly** *adv.* — **lop′sid′ed•ness** *n.*

loq. *abbr. Lat.* Loquitur (speaks).

lo•qua•cious (lō-kwā′shəs) *adj.* Very talkative; garrulous. [< Lat. *loquāx, loquāc-* < *loquī*, to speak. See **tolkʷ-*.**] — **lo•qua′cious•ly** *adv.* — **lo•qua′cious•ness, lo•quac′i•ty** (lō-kwăs′ĭ-tē) *n.*

lo•quat (lō′kwŏt′, -kwăt′) *n.* **1.** A small evergreen tree *(Eriobotrya japonica)* native to China and Japan and having fragrant white flowers and yellow fruit. **2.** The edible fruit of this plant. [Chin. (Cantonese) *lo kwat* : *lo*, kind of tree + *kwêt*, an orange.]

Lo•rain (lə-rān′, lô-). A city of N OH on Lake Erie W of Cleveland; settled in 1807. Pop. 71,245.

lo•ran (lôr′ăn′, lōr′-) *n.* A long-range navigational system in which position is determined by an analysis involving the time intervals between pulsed radio signals from two or more pairs of ground stations of known position. [*lo(ng-)ra(nge) n(avigation).*]

Lor•ca (lôr′kə, -kä), **Federico García.** See Federico **García Lorca.**

lord (lôrd) *n.* **1.** A man of high rank in a feudal society or in one that retains feudal forms and institutions, esp.: **a.** A king. **b.** A territorial magnate. **c.** The proprietor of a manor. **2. Lords.** See **House of Lords. 3. Lord.** *Chiefly British.* The general masculine title of nobility and other rank: **a.** Used as a form of address for a marquis, an earl, or a viscount. **b.** Used as the usual style for a baron. **c.** Used as a courtesy title for a younger son of a duke or marquis. **d.** Used as a title for certain high officials and dignitaries. **e.** Used as a title for a bishop. **4.a. Lord.** God. **b. Lord.** Jesus. **c.** A man of renowned power or authority. **d.** A man with mastery in a given field or activity. **e.** *Archaic.* The male head of a household. **f.** *Archaic.* A husband. — *intr.v.* **lord•ed, lord•ing, lords.** To act like a lord; domineer. Often used with the indefinite *it*: *lorded it over their subordinates.* [ME < OE *hlāford* : *hlāf*, bread + *weard*, guardian; see **wer-**[3]*.]

Lord Chancellor *n., pl.* **Lords Chancellor.** The presiding officer of the House of Lords.

lord•ing (lôr′dĭng) *n.* **1.** *Archaic.* Used as a form of address for a lord. **2.** *Obsolete.* A lordling.

lord•ling (lôrd′lĭng) *n.* A lord regarded as immature or insignificant.

lord•ly (lôrd′lē) *adj.* **-li•er, -li•est. 1.** Of, relating to, or characteristic of a lord. **2.** Very dignified and noble: *lordly manners.* **3.** Pretentiously arrogant and overbearing. — *adv.* **1.** In a lordly manner. **2.** In a pretentiously arrogant and overbearing manner. — **lord′li•ness** *n.*

Lord of Misrule *n., pl.* **Lords of Misrule.** One who presided at English Christmas revelry during the 15th and 16th centuries.

lor•do•sis (lôr-dō′sĭs) *n., pl.* **-ses** (-sēz). An abnormal forward curvature of the spine in the lumbar region. [Gk. *lordōsis* < *lordos*, bent backward.] — **lor•dot′ic** (-dŏt′ĭk) *adj.*

Lord's Day or **Lord's day** (lôrdz) *n.* The Christian Sabbath, observed on Sunday.

lord•ship (lôrd′shĭp′) *n.* **1.** Often **Lordship.** Used with *Your, His,* or *Their* as a title and form of address for a man or men holding the rank of lord. **2.** The position or authority of a lord. **3.** The territory belonging to a feudal lord.

Lord's Prayer (prâr) *n.* The prayer taught by Jesus to his disciples.

Lord's Supper *n.* **1.** See **Last Supper. 2.** The sacrament of the Eucharist.

lore[1] (lôr, lōr) *n.* **1.** Accumulated facts, traditions, or beliefs about a particular subject. **2.** Knowledge acquired through education or experience. **3.** *Archaic.* Material taught or learned. [ME < OE *lār.* See **leis-**[1]*.]

lore[2] (lôr, lōr) *n.* The space between the eye and the base of the bill of a bird or between the eye and nostril of a snake. [Lat. *lōrum*, thong.]

Lo•re•lei (lôr′ə-lī′, lō′rə-) *n.* A siren of Germanic legend whose singing lures sailors to shipwreck.

Lo•rentz (lôr′ənts, lōr′-, lō′rĕnts), **Hendrik.** 1853–1928. Dutch physicist who shared a 1902 Nobel Prize.

Lorentz contraction *n.* See **Lorentz-Fitzgerald contraction.**

Lo•rentz-Fitz•ger•ald contraction (lôr′ənts-fĭts-jĕr′əld, lōr′-) *n.* The contraction in length of a moving body as it approaches the speed of light, as measured by an observer at rest with respect to the body. [After Hendrik LORENTZ and George Francis FITZGERALD.]

Lo•renz (lō′rĕnts′), **Konrad Zacharias.** 1903–89. Austrian psychologist who shared a 1973 Nobel Prize.

lor•gnette (lôrn-yĕt′) *n.* A pair of eyeglasses or opera glasses with a short handle. [Fr. < *lorgner*, to peer at < OFr. < *lorgne*, squinting, of Gmc. orig.]

lo•ri•ca (lô-rī′kə, lō-) *n., pl.* **-cae** (-sē). **1.** *Zool.* A protective external shell or case, as of a rotifer or certain other microscopic animals. **2.** A cuirass or corselet worn by Roman soldiers. [Lat. *lōrīca*, leather cuirass, perh. < *lōrum*, thong.] — **lor′i•cate′** (lôr′ĭ-kāt′, lōr′-), **lor′i•ca′ted** (-kā′tĭd) *adj.*

Lo•rient (lô-ryäN′). A city of NW France on the Bay of Biscay SE of Brest; estab. as a port in the 17th cent. Pop. 62,554.

lor•i•keet (lôr′ĭ-kēt′, lōr′-) *n.* Any of several small, often brilliantly colored Australasian parrots that feed primarily on fruits or nectar and pollen. [LOR(Y) + (PARA)KEET.]

lo•ris (lôr′ĭs, lōr′-) *n.* Any of several small slow-moving nocturnal prosimian primates of the genera *Loris* and *Nycticebus* of tropical Asia, having woolly fur and a vestigial tail. [Fr., poss. < obsolete Du. *loeris*, simpleton < *loer* < OFr. *lourt* < Lat. *lūridus*, pale. See LURID.]

lorn (lôrn) *adj.* Bereft; forlorn. [ME < OE *-loren*, p.part. of *-lēosan*, to lose, as in *forlēosan.* See **leu-***.]

Lorne also **Lorn** (lôrn), **Firth of.** An inlet of the Atlantic on the W coast of Scotland between Mull I. and the mainland.

Lor•rain (lō-rān′, lô-răN′), **Claude.** 1600–82. French painter known esp. for his landscapes.

Lor•raine (lô-rān′, lō-, lō-rĕn′). A historical region and former province of NE France; ceded with Alsace to Germany after the Franco-Prussian War (1871) and returned to France by the Treaty of Versailles (1919).

Lor•re (lôr′ē), **Peter.** 1904–64. Hungarian-born Amer. actor whose films include *The Maltese Falcon* (1941).

lor•ry (lôr′ē, lŏr′ē) *n., pl.* **-ries.** *Chiefly British.* A motor truck. [Perh. akin to dial. *lurry*, to lug, haul.]

lo•ry (lôr′ē, lōr′ē) *n., pl.* **-ries.** Any of various brightly colored Australasian parrots having a tongue with a brushlike tip that is used to feed on nectar and pollen. [Malay *luri.*]

LOS *abbr.* **1.** Length of stay. **2.** *Football.* Line of scrimmage. **3.** Line of sight.

Los Al•a•mos (lôs ăl′ə-mōs′, lŏs). An unincorp. community of N-central NM NW of Santa Fe; chosen in 1942 as a research site to produce the first atomic bombs. Pop. 11,455.

Los Al•tos (ăl′təs, -tōs). A city of W CA S of Palo Alto. Pop. 26,303.

Los An•ge•les (ăn′jə-ləs, -lēz′, ăng′gə-ləs). A city of S CA on the Pacific Ocean in a widespread metropolitan area; founded by the Spanish in 1781. Pop. 3,485,398.

lose (lo͞oz) *v.* **lost** (lôst, lŏst), **los•ing, los•es.** — *tr.* **1.** To be unsuccessful in retaining possession of; mislay. **2.a.** To come to be deprived of the ownership, care, or control of (something one has had), as by negligence, accident, or theft. **b.** To be deprived of (something one has had). **c.** To be bereaved of. **d.** To be unable to keep alive. **3.** To be unable to maintain, sustain, or keep. **4.** To fail to win; fail in. **5.** To fail to use or take advantage of. **6.** To fail to hear, see, or understand. **7.a.** To let (oneself) become unable to find the way. **b.** To remove (oneself), as from everyday reality into a fantasy world. **8.** To rid oneself of: *lost five pounds.* **9.** To consume aimlessly; waste. **10.** To stray or wander from. **11.a.** To elude or outdistance. **b.** To be outdistanced by. **12.** To become slow by (a specified amount of time). Used of a timepiece. **13.** To cause or result in the loss of. **14.** To cause to be destroyed. Usu. used in the passive: *Both planes were lost in the crash.* **15.** To cause to be damned. — *intr.* **1.** To suffer loss. **2.** To be defeated. **3.** To operate or run slow. Used of a timepiece. — ***phrasal verb.*** **lose out.** To fail to achieve or receive an expected gain. — ***idioms.*** **lose out on.** To miss (an opportunity, for example). **lose time. 1.** To operate too slowly. Used of a timepiece. **2.** To delay advancement. [ME *losen* < OE *losian*, to perish < *los*, loss. See **leu-***.]

lo•sel (lō′zəl, lo͞o′-, lŏz′əl) *n.* One that is worthless. [ME < *lōsen*, p.part. of *lēsen*, to lose < OE *-lēosan.* See LORN.]

los•er (lo͞o′zər) *n.* **1.a.** One that fails to win: *the losers of the game.* **b.** One who takes loss in a given way: *a graceful loser.* **2.a.** One that fails consistently, esp. a person with bad luck or poor skills. **b.** One that is bad in quality.

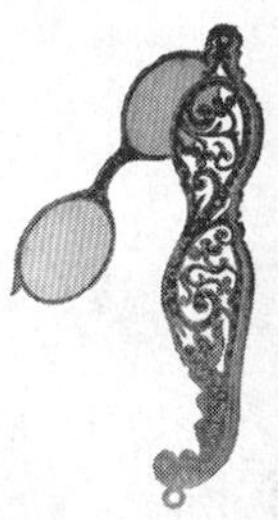

lorgnette

Los Ga•tos (lôs găt′əs, lŏs). A city of W CA, a suburb of San Jose. Pop. 27,357.

los•ing (lo͞o′zĭng) *adj.* **1.** Failing to win, as in a sport or game. **2.** Of or relating to one that fails to win: *a losing season.* — *n.* **1.** The act of one that loses; loss. **2.** Something lost, such as money at gambling. Often used in the plural.

loss (lôs, lŏs) *n.* **1.** The act or an instance of losing. **2.a.** One that is lost. **b.** The condition of being deprived or bereaved of something or someone. **c.** The amount of something lost. **3.** The harm or suffering caused by losing or being lost. **4. losses.** People lost in wartime; casualties. **5.** Destruction. **6.** *Elect.* The power decrease caused by resistance in a circuit, circuit element, or device. **7.** The amount of a claim on an insurer by an insured. — ***idiom.*** **at a loss. 1.** Below cost. **2.** Perplexed; puzzled. [ME *los* < OE. See LOSE.]

loss leader *n.* A commodity offered esp. by a retail store at cost or below cost to attract customers.

loss ratio *n.* The ratio between the premiums paid to an insurance company and the claims settled by the company.

lost (lôst, lŏst) *adj.* **1.** Unable to find one's way: *a lost child.* **2.a.** No longer in one's possession, care, or control: *a lost pen.* **b.** No longer known or practiced: *a lost art.* **3.** Unable to function, act, or make progress. **4.** Spiritually or physically destroyed. **5.** Completely involved or absorbed; rapt.

lost and found or **lost-and-found** (lôst′ən-found′, lŏst′-) *n.* A repository in a public place, as in a school, where found items are kept for reclaiming by their owners.

Lost River Range (lôst, lŏst). A chain of mountains in E-central ID rising to 3,861.9 m (12,662 ft).

lot (lŏt) *n.* **1.** An object used in making a determination or choice at random. **2.a.** The use of objects in making a determination or choice at random. **b.** The determination or choice so made. **3.** Something that befalls one because of or as if because of determination by lot. **4.** One's fortune in life; fate. **5.** A number of associated people or things. **6.** Kind; type. **7.** Miscellaneous articles sold as one unit. **8.** *Informal.* A large extent, amount, or number: *a lot of trouble; made lots of new friends.* Often used adverbially with *a* or in the plural: *felt a lot better; ran lots faster.* **9.a.** A piece of land having specific boundaries, esp. one constituting a part of a city, town, or block. **b.** A piece of land used for a given purpose. **c.** A film studio. — *tr.v.* **lot•ted, lot•ting, lots. 1.** To apportion by lots; allot. **2.** To divide (land) into lots. [ME < OE *hlot.*]

Lot[1] (lŏt). In the Bible, Abraham's nephew, whose wife was turned into a pillar of salt when she looked back as they fled Sodom.

Lot[2] (lŏt, lôt). A river of S France rising in the Cévennes and flowing c. 483 km (300 mi) to the Garonne R.

loth (lōth, lōth) *adj.* Var. of **loath.**

Lo•thair I (lō-thâr′, -târ′). 795?–855. Holy Roman emperor (840–855) who received the Middle Kingdom in 843.

Lothair II. 1070?–1137. King of Germany (1125–37) and Holy Roman emperor (1133–37) who invaded Italy in 1136.

ă pat	oi boy
ā pay	ou out
âr care	o͝o took
ä father	o͞o boot
ĕ pet	ŭ cut
ē be	ûr urge
ĭ pit	th thin
ī pie	*th* this
îr pier	hw which
ŏ pot	zh vision
ō toe	ə about, item
ô paw	

Stress marks:
′ (primary);
′ (secondary), as in
dictionary (dĭk′shə-nĕr′ē)

Lo•thar•i•o also **lo•thar•i•o** (lō-thâr′ē-ō) *n., pl.* **-os.** A man who seduces women. [After *Lothario,* a character in *The Fair Penitent,* a play by Nicholas Rowe (1674–1718).]

lo•ti (lō′tē) *n., pl.* **ma•lo•ti** (mä-). See table at **currency.** [Sotho, from *Maloti,* a range of mountains in Lesotho.]

Lo•ti (lō-tē′, lô-), **Pierre.** 1850–1923. French writer whose novels include *Aziyadé* (1879).

lo•tic (lō′tĭk) *adj.* Of, relating to, or living in moving water. [< Lat. *lōtus,* p.part. of *lavere,* to wash. See LOTION.]

lo•tion (lō′shən) *n.* **1.** A medicated liquid for external application. **2.** Any of various externally applied cosmetic liquids. [ME *locion* < OFr. *lotion* < Lat. *lōtiō, lōtiōn-,* a washing < *lōtus,* p.part. of *lavere,* to wash. See **leu(ə)-*.**]

lot•ter•y (lŏt′ə-rē) *n., pl.* **-ies. 1.** *Games.* A contest in which tokens are distributed or sold, the winning token or tokens being secretly predetermined or ultimately selected in a random drawing. **2.** A selection made by lot from a number of applicants or competitors. **3.** An activity or event regarded as having an outcome depending on fate: *Success seemed a lottery.* [Fr. *loterie,* prob. < Du. *loterije* < MDu. < *lot,* lot.]

lotus

lot•to (lŏt′ō) *n., pl.* **-tos.** *Games.* **1.** A game of chance similar to bingo. **2.** A lottery in which participants choose and play numbers in a random drawing. [Ital. and Fr. *loto,* both < Fr. *lot,* lot < OFr. < Frankish **lot.*]

lo•tus also **lo•tos** (lō′təs) *n.* **1.a.** An aquatic plant *(Nelumbo nucifera)* native to southern Asia and Australia and having large leaves, pinkish flowers, a perforated seedpod, and fleshy rhizomes. **b.** The edible seed, leaf, or rhizome of this plant. **c.** Any of several similar or related plants. **2.** A representation of any of various lotuses or similar or related plants in Egyptian or classical sculpture, architecture, or art. **3.** Any of several leguminous plants of the genus *Lotus.* **4.** *Gk. Myth.* **a.** A small Mediterranean tree or shrub whose fruit was eaten by the lotus-eaters. **b.** The fruit of this plant. [Lat. *lōtus,* name of several plants < Gk. *lōtos,* perh. of Semitic orig.]

lo•tus-eat•er (lō′təs-ē′tər) *n.* **1.** *Gk. Myth.* One of a people described in the *Odyssey* who fed on the lotus and hence lived in a drugged, indolent state. **2.** A lazy person devoted to pleasure and luxury.

lotus land *n. Informal.* A place or condition of irresponsibility and luxury.

lotus position *n.* A cross-legged sitting position used in yoga.

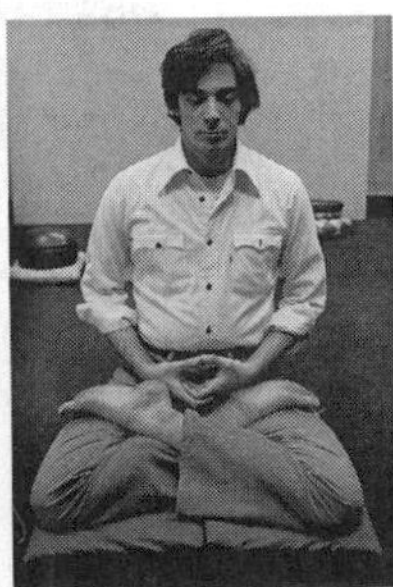

lotus position

louche (lo͞osh) *adj.* Of questionable taste or morality: *a louche painting.* [Fr. < OFr. *losche,* squint-eyed, fem. of *lois* < Lat. *luscus,* blind in one eye.]

loud (loud) *adj.* **loud•er, loud•est. 1.** Characterized by high volume and intensity. Used of sound. **2.** Producing sound of high volume and intensity. **3.** Clamorous and insistent: *loud denials.* **4.a.** Having offensively bright colors: *a loud necktie.* **b.** Having an offensively strong odor. **c.** Offensive in manner. — *adv.* **louder, loudest.** In a loud manner. [ME < OE *hlūd.* See **kleu-*.**] — **loud′ly** *adv.* — **loud′ness** *n.*

loud•en (loud′n) *tr. & intr.v.* **-ened, -en•ing, -ens.** To make or become louder.

loud•mouth (loud′mouth′) *n. Informal.* One given to loud, irritating, or indiscreet talk. — **loud′mouthed′** (-mouthd′, -moutht′) *adj.*

loud pedal *n. Mus.* See **sustaining pedal.**

loud•speak•er (loud′spē′kər) *n.* A device that converts electric signals to audible sound.

Lou Gehrig's disease (lo͞o′ gĕr′ĭgz) *n.* See **amyotrophic lateral sclerosis.** [After Henry Louis ("Lou") GEHRIG.]

lough (lŏKH, lŏk) *n. Irish.* **1.** A lake. **2.** A bay or an inlet of the sea. [ME < OE *luh,* ult. < OIr. *loch.*]

Louis XIV
1701 portrait by Hyacinthe Rigaud (1659–1743)

Lou•is VII (lo͞o′ē, lo͞o-ē′). 1120?–80. King of France (1137–80) who led the unsuccessful Second Crusade (1147–49).

Louis IX. "Saint Louis." 1214–70. King of France (1226–70) who led the Seventh Crusade (1248–54).

Louis XIII. 1601–43. King of France (1610–43) who relied heavily on his political adviser Cardinal Richelieu.

Louis XIV. "the Sun King." 1638–1715. King of France (1643–1715) whose reign was characterized by the expansion of French influence in Europe.

Louis XV. 1710–74. King of France (1715–74) who led France into the War of the Austrian Succession (1740–48) and the Seven Years' War (1756–63).

Louis XVI. 1754–93. King of France (1774–92) who summoned the Estates-General (1789) but did not grant the reforms demanded. Louis and his queen, Marie Antoinette, were guillotined in 1793.

Louis XVIII. 1755–1824. King of France (1814–24) whose reign was interrupted by Napoleon's return to power (1815).

Lou•is (lo͞o′ĭs), **Joe.** 1914–81. Amer. prizefighter who held the heavyweight title for nearly 12 years (1937–49).

Lou•is•burg or **Lou•is•bourg** (lo͞o′ĭs-bûrg′). A town of Nova Scotia, Canada, on E Cape Breton I. near the site of the fortress of Louisbourg, built c. 1712–40 by the French.

Lou•ise (lo͞o-ēz′), **Lake.** A lake of SW Alberta, Canada, in the Rocky Mts. near Banff.

Lou•i•si•an•a (lo͞o-ē′zē-ăn′ə, lo͞o′zē-). A state of the S U.S. on the Gulf of Mexico; admitted as the 18th state in 1812. Cap. Baton Rouge. Pop. 4,238,216.

Louisiana French *n.* French as spoken by the descendants of the original French settlers of Louisiana.

Louisiana Purchase. A territory of the W U.S. extending from the Mississippi R. to the Rocky Mts. between the Gulf of Mexico and the Canadian border; purchased from France on Apr. 30, 1803, for $15 million.

Lou•is Na•po•le•on (lo͞o′ē nə-pō′lē-ən). See **Napoleon III.**

Lou•is Phi•lippe (lo͞o′ē fĭ-lēp′, lo͞o-ē′ fē-lēp′). "the Citizen King." 1773–1850. King of France (1830–48) who ruled after the overthrow of the Bourbons in the July Revolution (1830) and abdicated during the Revolution of 1848.

Louis Qua•torze (kă-tôrz′) *adj.* Of, relating to, or characteristic of the baroque style in architecture, furniture, and decoration of the reign of Louis XIV. [Fr.]

Louis Quinze (kăNZ′) *adj.* Of, relating to, or characteristic of the rococo style in architecture, furniture, and decoration of the reign of Louis XV. [Fr.]

Louis Seize (sĕz′) *adj.* Of, relating to, or characteristic of the neoclassic style in architecture, furniture, and decoration of the reign of Louis XVI. [Fr.]

Louis Treize (trĕz′) *adj.* Of, relating to, or characteristic of the heavy late-Renaissance style in architecture, furniture, and decoration of the reign of Louis XIII. [Fr.]

Lou•is•ville (lo͞o′ē-vĭl′, -ə-vəl). A city of N-central KY on the Ohio R. W of Lexington. Pop. 269,063.

lounge (lounj) *v.* **lounged, loung•ing, loung•es.** — *intr.* **1.** To move or act in a lazy, relaxed way; loll. **2.** To pass time idly. — *tr.* To pass (time) in a lazy, relaxed, or idle way. — *n.* **1.** A public waiting room often having smoking or lavatory facilities. **2.** An establishment or a room in an establishment, as in a restaurant, where cocktails are served. **3.a.** A living room. **b.** A lobby. **4.** A long couch, esp. one having no back and a headrest at one end. [Poss. < Fr. *s'allonger,* to stretch out < OFr. *alongier,* to lengthen < Med.Lat. *allongāre* : Lat. *ad-,* ad- + Lat. *longus,* long; see LONG[1].] — **loung′er** *n.*

lounge car *n.* See **club car.**

lounge lizard *n. Slang.* **1.** A generally idle man who haunts establishments or gatherings frequented by the rich or fashionable; a social parasite. **2.** A habitué of cocktail lounges.

lounge•wear (lounj′wâr′) *n.* Clothing suitable for relaxing.

loupe (lo͞op) *n.* A small magnifying glass usu. set in an eyepiece and used chiefly by watchmakers and jewelers. [Fr. < OFr., flawed gem, prob. of Gmc. orig.]

loup-ga•rou (lo͞o′gə-ro͞o′, -gä-) *n., pl.* **loups-ga•rous** (lo͞o′gə-ro͞oz′, -gä-ro͞o′). A werewolf. [Fr. < OFr. *leu garoul* : *leu,* wolf (< Lat. *lupus;* see **wḷkʷo-***) + *garoul,* werewolf (of Gmc. orig.; see **wī-ro-***).]

loup•ing ill (lou′pĭng, lō′-) *n.* See **tremble** 3a. [< Sc. *loup,* to leap < ME *lopen.* See LOPE.]

Loup River (lo͞op). A river of E-central NE flowing a total length of c. 451 km (280 mi) to the Platte R.

lour (lour) *v. & n.* Var. of **lower[1].**

Lourdes (lo͝ord, lo͝ordz). A town of SW France at the foot of the Pyrenees; noted for its shrine marking the site where the Virgin Mary is said to have appeared to St. Bernadette in 1858. Pop. 17,425.

Lou•ren•ço Mar•ques (lə-rĕn′sō mär′kĕs, lô-rĕN′so͞o mär′-kĕsh). See **Maputo.**

lou•ry (lour′ē) *adj.* Var. of **lowery.**

louse (lous) *n.* **1.** *pl.* **lice** (līs). Any of numerous small wingless insects of the orders Mallophaga or Anoplura, many of which are external parasites on various animals, including human beings. **2.** *pl.* **lous•es.** *Slang.* A mean or despicable person. — *tr.v.* **loused, lous•ing, lous•es.** *Slang.* To bungle: *loused up the project.* [ME < OE *lūs.* See **lūs-*.**]

louse•wort (lous′wûrt′, -wôrt′) *n.* Any of numerous plants of the genus *Pedicularis,* having clusters of irregular, variously colored flowers.

lous•y (lou′zē) *adj.* **-i•er, -i•est. 1.** Infested with lice. **2.** Extremely contemptible; nasty. **3.** Very painful or unpleasant. **4.** Inferior or worthless. **5.** *Slang.* Abundantly supplied: *lousy with money.* — **lous′i•ly** *adv.* — **lous′i•ness** *n.*

lout[1] (lout) *n.* A person regarded as awkward and stupid; an oaf. [Poss. < LOUT[2].]

lout[2] (lout) *intr.v.* **lout•ed, lout•ing, louts. 1.** To bow or curtsy. **2.** To bend or stoop. [ME *louten* < OE *lūtan.*]

lout•ish (lou′tĭsh) *adj.* Having the characteristics of a lout; awkward and stupid. — **lout′ish•ly** *adv.* — **lout′ish•ness** *n.*

Lou•vain (lo͞o-văN′) also **Leu•ven** (lĕv′ən). A city of central Belgium E of Brussels. Pop. 85,068.

lou•ver also **lou•vre** (lo͞o′vər) *n.* **1.a.** A framed opening, as in a door, fitted with horizontal slats for admitting air and light and shedding rain. **b.** One of the slats used in such an opening. **c.** One of the narrow openings formed by such slats. **2.** A slatted ventilating opening, as on the hood of a motor vehicle. **3.** A lantern-shaped cupola on the roof of a medieval building for admitting air and providing for the escape of smoke. [ME *lover,* skylight, chimney < OFr. < MDu. *love,* gallery < MHGer. *lauble.*] — **lou′vered** *adj.*

Lou•ÿs (lo͞o-ē′, lwē), **Pierre.** 1870–1925. French writer whose novels include *Aphrodite* (1896).

lov•a•ble also **love•a•ble** (lŭv′ə-bəl) *adj.* Having characteristics that attract love or affection. —**lov′a•bil′i•ty, lov′a•ble•ness** *n.* —**lov′a•bly** *adv.*

lov•age (lŭv′ĭj) *n.* A Mediterranean perennial plant *(Levisticum officinale)* having small aromatic seedlike fruit used as seasoning. [ME < AN *luvesche* < OE *lufestice* < Med.Lat. *levistica* < LLat. *levisticum*, alteration of Lat. *ligusticum* < neut. of *ligusticus*, Ligurian.]

love (lŭv) *n.* **1.** A deep, tender feeling of affection and solicitude toward a person, such as that arising from kinship or a sense of oneness. **2.** A feeling of intense desire and attraction toward a person with whom one is disposed to make a pair; the emotion of sex and romance. **3.a.** Sexual passion. **b.** Sexual intercourse. **c.** A love affair. **4.** An intense emotional attachment, as for a pet or treasured object. **5.** A person who is the object of deep or intense affection or attraction; beloved. Often used as a term of endearment. **6.** An expression of one's affection: *Send him my love.* **7.a.** A strong predilection or enthusiasm. **b.** The object of such an enthusiasm. **8. Love.** *Myth.* Eros or Cupid. **9.** Often **Love.** *Theol.* Charity. **10.** *Sports.* A zero score in tennis. —*v.* **loved, lov•ing, loves.** —*tr.* **1.** To feel deep, tender affection and solicitude toward (a person). **2.** To feel intense desire and attraction toward (a person). **3.** To be emotionally attached to. **4.a.** To embrace or caress. **b.** To have sexual intercourse with. **5.** To like or desire enthusiastically. **6.** *Theol.* To have charity for. **7.** To thrive on; need. —*intr.* To experience deep affection or intense desire for another. —***idioms.*** **for love.** Out of compassion; with no thought for a reward. **for love or money.** Under any circumstances. Usu. used in negative sentences. **for the love of.** For the sake of; in consideration for. **no love lost.** No affection; animosity. [ME < OE *lufu*. See **leubh-*.**]

Syns: *love, affection, devotion, fondness, infatuation.* These nouns denote feelings of warm personal attachment or strong attraction to another person. *Love* is the most intense: *married for love. Affection* is a less ardent and more unvarying feeling of tender regard: *parental affection. Devotion* is earnest, affectionate dedication and implies selflessness: *A leader who inspires devotion. Fondness* is strong liking or affection: *evinces a fondness for small animals. Infatuation* is foolish or extravagant attraction, often of short duration: *Their infatuation blinded them to their differences.*

love affair *n.* **1.** An intimate sexual relationship or episode between lovers. **2.** A strong enthusiasm.

love apple *n.* A tomato. [Prob. transl. of Fr. *pomme d'amour*, (from the former belief in the tomato's aphrodisiacal powers) : *pomme*, apple + *de*, of + *amour*, love.]

love beads *pl.n.* Small beads on a necklace, esp. ones worn by hippies.

love•bird (lŭv′bûrd′) *n.* **1.** Any of various small Old World parrots, esp. of the genus *Agapornis*, often kept as cage birds and noted for the apparent affection between mates. **2. lovebirds.** *Informal.* An affectionate or demonstrative couple.

love child *n.* A child born of parents not legally married.

Love•craft (lŭv′krăft′), **H(oward) P(hillips).** 1890–1937. Amer. writer of *The Outsider and Others* (1939).

love feast *n.* **1.a.** A meal shared among early Christians as a symbol of love. **b.** A similar meal among modern Christians. **2.** A gathering meant to promote goodwill.

love handle *n. Slang.* A deposit of fat at the waistline.

love-in (lŭv′ĭn′) *n. Slang.* A gathering to engender and promote love.

love-in-a-mist (lŭv′ĭn-ə-mĭst′) *n.* A Mediterranean plant *(Nigella damascena)* having blue or whitish flowers surrounded by threadlike bracts.

love knot *n.* A knot symbolizing the constancy of two lovers.

Love•lace (lŭv′lās′), **Richard.** 1618–57? English Cavalier poet who is noted esp. for the lyrics "To Althea, from Prison" and "To Lucasta, Going to the Wars."

Love•land (lŭv′lənd). A city of N CO S of Fort Collins. Pop. 37,352.

love•less (lŭv′lĭs) *adj.* **1.** Characterized by an absence of love: *a loveless marriage.* **2.** Exhibiting or feeling no love; unloving: *a loveless glance.* **3.** Receiving no love; unloved.

love-lies-bleed•ing (lŭv′līz-blē′dĭng) *n.* A tropical Indian plant *(Amaranthus caudatus)* having clusters of small red flowers.

Lov•ell (lŭv′əl), Sir **(Alfred Charles) Bernard.** b. 1913. British radio astronomer who founded and directed (1951–81) the Jodrell Bank Experimental Station.

love life *n.* The amatory or sexual aspect of one's life.

love•lock (lŭv′lŏk′) *n.* A lock of hair hanging separately from the rest of the hair, as one tied with ribbon and worn by courtiers during the 17th and 18th centuries.

love•lorn (lŭv′lôrn′) *adj.* Bereft of love or one's lover.

love•ly (lŭv′lē) *adj.* **-li•er, -li•est. 1.** Full of love; loving. **2.** Inspiring love or affection. **3.** Having beauty that appeals to the emotions as well as to the eye. **4.** Enjoyable; delightful. —*n., pl.* **-lies. 1.** A beautiful person, esp. a woman. **2.** A lovely object. —**love′li•ness** *n.* —**love′ly** *adv.*

love•mak•ing (lŭv′mā′kĭng) *n.* **1.** Sexual activity, esp. sexual intercourse. **2.** Courtship; wooing.

lov•er (lŭv′ər) *n.* **1.** One who loves another, esp. one who feels sexual love. **2. lovers.** A couple in love with each other. **3.a.** A paramour. **b.** A sexual partner. **4.** One who is fond of or devoted to something. —**lov′er•ly** *adv. & adj.*

lov•ers' knot (lŭv′ərz) *n.* See **love knot.**

love seat or **love•seat** (lŭv′sēt′) *n.* A small sofa or double chair that seats two people.

love•sick (lŭv′sĭk′) *adj.* **1.** So affected by love as to be unable to act normally. **2.** Exhibiting a lover's yearning.

lov•ey-dov•ey (lŭv′ē-dŭv′ē) *adj. Informal.* Expressing affection in an extravagantly sentimental way; mushy.

lov•ing (lŭv′ĭng) *adj.* **1.** Feeling love; affectionate. **2.** Indicative of or exhibiting love.

loving cup *n.* **1.** A large ornamental wine vessel, usu. made of silver and having two or more handles. **2.** A large ornamental vessel awarded in modern sporting contests, for example.

low[1] (lō) *adj.* **low•er, low•est. 1.a.** Having little relative height; not high or tall. **b.** Rising only slightly above surrounding surfaces. **c.** Situated below normal height. **d.** Situated below the surrounding surfaces. **e.** Dead and buried. **f.** Cut to show the neck and chest; décolleté. **2.** Near or at the horizon. **3.** *Ling.* Produced with part or all of the tongue depressed, as *a*, pronounced (ä), in *father.* Used of vowels. **4.** Of less than usual or average depth; shallow. **5.** Humble in status or character. **6.** *Biol.* Of relatively simple structure in the scale of living organisms. **7.** Unrefined; coarse: *low humor.* **8.** Violating standards of decency; base. **9.a.** Lacking strength or vigor; weak. **b.** Emotionally or mentally depressed. **10.a.** Below average in degree, intensity, or amount. **b.** Below an average or a standard. **c.** Ranked near the beginning of an ascending series or scale. **d.** Relating to or being latitudes nearest to the equator. **e.** Relatively small. Used of a cost, price, or other value. **11.** Having a pitch corresponding to a relatively small number of sound-wave cycles per second. **12.** Not loud; soft. **13.** Being near total depletion. **14.** Not adequately provided or equipped; short. **15.** Depreciatory; disparaging. **16.** Brought down or reduced in health or wealth. **17.** Of, relating to, or being the gear configuration or setting, as in a car transmission, that produces the least vehicular speed with respect to engine speed. —*adv.* **1.a.** In or to a low position, level, or space. **b.** In or to a low condition or rank; humbly. **2.** In or to a reduced, humbled, or degraded condition. **3.** Softly; quietly. **4.** With a deep pitch. **5.** At a small price. —*n.* **1.** A low level, position, or degree. **2.** *Meteorol.* A region of atmospheric pressure that is below normal. **3.** The low gear configuration of a transmission. [ME *loue* < ON *lāgr*. See **legh-*.**] —**low′ness** *n.*

low[2] (lō) *n.* The characteristic sound uttered by cattle; a moo. —*intr.v.* **lowed, low•ing, lows.** To utter the sound made by cattle; moo. [< ME *lowen*, to moo < OE *hlōwan*. See **kelə-[2]*.**]

Low (lō), Sir **David Alexander Cecil.** 1891–1963. British political cartoonist who created the pompous Colonel Blimp.

Low, Juliette Magill Kinzie Gordon. 1860–1927. Amer. founder of the Girl Scouts (1912).

low-ball or **low•ball** (lō′bôl′) —*v.* **-balled, -bal•ling, -balls.** —*tr.* To underestimate or understate (a cost) deliberately. —*intr.* To engage in low-balling a cost. [From the card game of the same name.] —**low′-ball** *adj.*

low beam *n.* The beam of a vehicle's headlight that provides short-range illumination.

low blow *n.* An unscrupulous attack; an insult.

low•born (lō′bôrn′) *adj.* Of humble birth.

low•boy (lō′boi′) *n.* A low tablelike chest of drawers.

low•bred (lō′brĕd′) *adj.* Coarse; vulgar.

low•brow (lō′brou′) *n.* One with lowbrow tastes. —*adj.* also **low•browed** (-broud′). Uncultivated; vulgar. [LOW[1] + (HIGH)-BROW.]

Low Church *n.* The evangelical branch of the Anglican Church. —**Low′-Church′** (lō′chûrch′) *adj.*

low comedy *n.* Comedy characterized by slapstick, burlesque, and horseplay.

Low Countries. A region of NW Europe comprising Belgium, the Netherlands, and Luxembourg.

low-den•si•ty (lō′dĕn′sĭ-tē) *adj.* Having a low concentration.

low-density lipoprotein *n.* A complex of lipids and proteins that functions as a transporter of cholesterol in the blood.

low•down (lō′doun′) *n. Slang.* The whole truth.

low-down (lō′doun′) *adj.* **1.** Despicable; base. **2.** Emotionally depressed.

Low•ell (lō′əl). A city of NE MA on the Merrimack R. NW of Boston; settled in 1653. Pop. 103,439.

Lowell, Amy. 1874–1925. Amer. poet whose works include *Sword Blades and Poppy Seed* (1914).

Lowell, James Russell. 1819–91. Amer. poet and diplomat who edited the *Atlantic Monthly* (1857–61).

Lowell, Percival. 1855–1916. Amer. astronomer who founded the Lowell Observatory in AZ (1894).

Lowell, Robert Traill Spence, Jr. 1917–77. Amer. poet whose works include *The Dolphin* (1973).

low-end (lō′ĕnd′) *adj.* **1.** Cheapest in a line of merchandise. **2.** *Informal.* **a.** Appealing to unsophisticated and undiscerning customers. **b.** Unsophisticated and undiscerning.

Juliette Low

lowboy

ă pat	oi boy
ā pay	ou out
âr care	o͝o took
ä father	o͞o boot
ĕ pet	ŭ cut
ē be	ûr urge
ĭ pit	th thin
ī pie	*th* this
îr pier	hw which
ŏ pot	zh vision
ō toe	ə about, item
ô paw	

Stress marks:
′ (primary);
′ (secondary), as in **dictionary** (dĭk′shə-nĕr′ē)

2. To raise or lower (the boom of a crane or derrick). [ME *lof,* spar holding out the windward tack of a square sail < OFr., prob. of Gmc. orig.]

luf•fa (lo͞o′fə, lŭf′ə) *n.* Var. of **loofa.**

Luf•kin (lŭf′kĭn). A city of E TX NNE of Houston. Pop. 30,206.

Luft•waf•fe (lo͝oft′väf′ə) *n.* The German air force before and during World War II. [Ger. : *Luft,* air (< MHGer. < OHGer.) + *Waffe,* weapon (< MHGer. *wāfen* < OHGer. *waffan*).]

lug[1] (lŭg) *n.* **1.** A handle or projection used as a hold or support. **2.** A lug nut. **3.** *Naut.* A lugsail. **4.** A projection that helps to provide traction, as on a tire or the sole of a boot. **5.** A copper or brass fitting to which electrical wires can be soldered or otherwise connected. **6.** *Slang.* A clumsy fool; a blockhead. [ME *lugge,* earflap, prob. of Scand. orig.]

lug[2] (lŭg) *v.* **lugged, lug•ging, lugs.** *—tr.* **1.** To drag or haul (an object) laboriously. **2.** To pull or drag with short jerks. *—intr.* **1.** To pull something with difficulty; tug. **2.** To move along by jerks or as if under a heavy burden. **3.** To run poorly or hesitate because of strain. Used of an engine. *—n.* **1.** *Archaic.* **a.** The act of lugging. **b.** Something lugged. **2.** A box for shipping fruit or vegetables. [ME *luggen,* of Scand. orig.]

luge (lo͞ozh) *n. Sports.* **1.** A racing sled for one or two riders lying supine. **2.** A competition involving these sleds. [Fr. dial. < Med.Lat. *sludia,* perh. of Celt. orig.] **— luge** *v.* **— lug′er** *n.*

lug•gage (lŭg′ĭj) *n.* **1.** Containers for a traveler's belongings. **2.** The cases and belongings of a traveler. [Prob. LUG[2] + (BAG)GAGE.]

lug•ger (lŭg′ər) *n. Naut.* A small boat used for fishing, sailing, or coasting and having two or three masts, each with a lugsail, and two or three jibs set on the bowsprit. [< LUGSAIL.]

lug nut *n.* A heavy nut that fits over a bolt, used esp. to attach an automotive vehicle's wheel to its axle.

Lu•go•si (lo͞o-gō′sē, lə-), **Bela.** 1884–1956. Hungarian-born Amer. actor known for horror films such as *Dracula* (1931).

lug•sail (lŭg′səl) *n. Naut.* A quadrilateral sail that lacks a boom, has the foot larger than the head, and is bent to a yard hanging obliquely on the mast. [Poss. < LUG[1].]

lu•gu•bri•ous (lo͝o-go͞o′brē-əs, -gyo͞o′-) *adj.* Mournful, dismal, or gloomy, esp. to an exaggerated or ludicrous degree. [< Lat. *lūgubris* < *lūgēre,* to mourn.] **— lu•gu′bri•ous•ly** *adv.* **— lu•gu′bri•ous•ness** *n.*

lug•worm (lŭg′wûrm′) *n.* Any of various segmented, burrowing marine worms of the genus *Arenicola,* esp. *A. marina* often used as fishing bait. [?]

Lui•chow Peninsula (lwē′jō′). See **Leizhou Peninsula.**

Lui•se•ño (lwē-sān′yō) *n., pl.* **Luiseño** or **-ños. 1.** A member of a Native American people inhabiting the coastal area of California south of Los Angeles. **2.** The Uto-Aztecan language of the Luiseño. [Am.Sp., from San *Luis* Rey de Francia, a mission in S CA.]

Luke (lo͝ok) *n.* See table at **Bible.**

Luke, Saint. 1st cent. A.D. Companion of St. Paul and author of the third Gospel of the New Testament.

luke•warm (lo͝ok′wôrm′) *adj.* **1.** Mildly warm; tepid. **2.** Lacking conviction or enthusiasm; indifferent. [ME *leukwarm* : *leuk, luke* (poss. var. of *leu* < OE *-hlēow;* see **kelə-**[1]*) + *warm,* warm; see WARM.] **— luke′warm′ly** *adv.* **— luke′warm′ness** *n.*

Luks (lŭks), **George.** 1867–1933. Amer. painter known for his studies of urban life, including *The Spielers* (1905).

Lu•le•å (lo͞o′lĕ-ô′, lü′-). A city of NE Sweden on the Gulf of Bothnia; chartered 1621. Pop. 66,811.

Lu•le•älv (lo͞o′lĕ-ôlv′, lü′lə-ĕlv′). A river of N Sweden flowing c. 443 km (275 mi) to the Gulf of Bothnia.

lull (lŭl) *v.* **lulled, lull•ing, lulls.** *—tr.* **1.** To cause to sleep or rest; soothe or calm. **2.** To deceive into trustfulness. *—intr.* To become calm. *—n.* **1.** A relatively calm interval, as in a storm. **2.** An interval of lessened activity. [ME *lullen,* poss. of LGer. orig.]

lull•a•by (lŭl′ə-bī′) *n., pl.* **-bies.** *Mus.* A soothing song with which to lull a child to sleep. *—tr.v.* **-bied, -bying, -bies.** To quiet with or as if with a lullaby. [Obsolete *lulla,* word used in lullabies (< ME *lullai* < *lullen,* to lull; see LULL) + *by, bye* (as in GOOD-BYE).]

Lul•ly (lo͞o-lē′, lü-), **Jean Baptiste.** 1632–87. Italian-born French composer who founded the national French opera.

lu•lu (lo͞o′lo͞o) *n. Slang.* A remarkable person, object, or idea. [Alteration of obsolete *looly.*]

lum•ba•go (lŭm-bā′gō) *n.* A painful condition of the lower back, as one resulting from muscle strain or a slipped disk. [LLat. *lumbāgō* < Lat. *lumbus,* loin.]

lum•bar (lŭm′bər, -bär′) *adj.* Of, near, or situated in the part of the back and sides between the lowest ribs and the pelvis. *—n.* A lumbar artery, nerve, vertebra, or part. [NLat. *lumbāris* < Lat. *lumbus,* loin.]

lum•ber[1] (lŭm′bər) *n.* **1.** Timber sawed into boards, planks, or other structural members of standard or specified length. **2.** Something useless or cumbersome. **3.** *Chiefly British.* Miscellaneous stored articles. *—v.* **-bered, -ber•ing, -bers.** *—tr.* **1.a.** To cut down (trees) and prepare as marketable timber. **b.** To cut down the timber of. **2.** *Chiefly British.* To clutter with or as if with unused articles. *—intr.* To cut and prepare timber for marketing. [Perh. < LUMBER[2].] **— lum′ber** *adj.* **— lum′ber•er** *n.*

lum•ber[2] (lŭm′bər) *intr.v.* **-bered, -ber•ing, -bers. 1.** To walk or move with heavy clumsiness. See Syns at **blunder. 2.** To move with a rumbling noise. [ME *lomeren,* poss. of Scand. orig.] **— lum′ber•ing•ly** *adv.*

lum•ber•jack (lŭm′bər-jăk′) *n.* **1.** One who fells trees and transports the timber to a mill; a logger. **2.** A short warm outer jacket.

Lum•ber•ton (lŭm′bər-tən). A city of S NC S of Fayetteville. Pop. 18,601.

lum•ber•yard (lŭm′bər-yärd′) *n.* An establishment that sells lumber and other building materials from a yard.

lu•men (lo͞o′mən) *n., pl.* **-mens** or **-mi•na** (-mə-nə). **1.** *Anat.* The inner open space or cavity of a tubular organ, as of a blood vessel. **2.** *Phys.* The unit of luminous flux in the International System, equal to the amount of light given out through a solid angle by a source of one candela intensity radiating equally in all directions. See table at **measurement. 3.** *Bot.* The cavity bounded by a plant cell wall. [Lat. *lūmen,* an opening, light. See **leuk-***.] **— lu′men•al, lu′min•al** *adj.*

lu•mi•nance (lo͞o′mə-nəns) *n.* **1.** The condition or quality of being luminous. **2.** *Phys.* The intensity of light per unit area of its source.

lu•mi•nar•i•a (lo͞o′mə-nâr′ē-ə) *n.* **1.** *Southwestern U.S.* A votive candle in a small decorative paper bag weighted with sand and lined up with others as a holiday decoration. Also called regionally *farolito.* **2.** *New Mexico.* A bonfire in front of each house in a pueblo on Christmas Eve. [Sp. < Lat. *lūmināria,* pl. of *lūmināre,* lamp. See LUMINARY.]

lu•mi•nar•y (lo͞o′mə-nĕr′ē) *n., pl.* **-ies. 1.** An object, such as a celestial body, that gives light. **2.** A person who is an inspiration to others. **3.** A person who has achieved eminence in a field. [ME < OFr. *luminarie* < Lat. *lūmināre,* to shine < *lūmen, lūmin-,* light. See **leuk-***.] **— lu′mi•nar′y** *adj.*

lu•mi•nesce (lo͞o′mə-nĕs′) *intr.v.* **-nesced, -nesc•ing, -nesc•es.** To be or become luminescent.

lu•mi•nes•cence (lo͞o′mə-nĕs′əns) *n.* **1.** The emission of light that does not derive energy from the temperature of the emitting body, as in fluorescence, and is caused, for example, by radiation-induced excitation of atoms. **2.** The light so emitted.

lu•mi•nes•cent (lo͞o′mə-nĕs′ənt) *adj.* Capable of, suitable for, or exhibiting luminescence. [Lat. *lūmen, lūmin-,* light; see LUMEN + -ESCENT.]

lu•mi•nif•er•ous (lo͞o′mə-nĭf′ər-əs) *adj.* Generating, yielding, or transmitting light.

lu•mi•nos•i•ty (lo͞o′mə-nŏs′ĭ-tē) *n., pl.* **-ties. 1.** The condition or quality of being luminous. **2.** Something luminous. **3.** The ratio of luminous flux at a specific wavelength to the radiant flux at the same wavelength.

lu•mi•nous (lo͞o′mə-nəs) *adj.* **1.** Emitting light, esp. emitting self-generated light. **2.** Full of light; illuminated. See Syns at **bright. 3.a.** Easily comprehended; clear: *luminous prose.* **b.** Enlightened and intelligent; inspiring: *luminous ideas.* [ME < OFr. *lumineux* < Lat. *lūminōsus* < *lūmen, lūmin-,* light. See **leuk-***.] **— lu′mi•nous•ly** *adv.* **— lu′mi•nous•ness** *n.*

luminous energy *n.* The total radiant energy of light emitted by a source.

luminous flux *n.* The rate of flow of light per unit of time, esp. the flux of visible light expressed in lumens.

luminous intensity *n.* The luminous flux per solid angle as measured in a given direction relative to the emitting source.

lum•mox (lŭm′əks) *n. Informal.* A person regarded as clumsy or stupid. [?]

lump[1] (lŭmp) *n.* **1.** An irregularly shaped mass or piece. **2.** A small cube of sugar. **3.** *Pathol.* A swelling or small palpable mass. **4.** A collection or totality; an aggregate. **5.** A person regarded as ungainly or dull witted. **6. lumps.** *Informal.* **a.** Severe punishment or treatment, as an unsparing criticism. **b.** One's just deserts; comeuppance. *—adj.* **1.** Formed into lumps: *lump sugar.* **2.** Not broken or divided into parts: *a lump payment.* *—v.* **lumped, lump•ing, lumps.** *—tr.* **1.** To put together in a single group without discrimination. **2.** To move with heavy clumsiness. **3.** To make into lumps. *—intr.* **1.** To become lumpy. **2.** To move heavily. **—idiom. lump in (one's) throat.** A feeling of constriction in the throat caused by emotion. [ME *lumpe,* of LGer. orig.]

lump[2] (lŭmp) *tr.v.* **lumped, lump•ing, lumps.** *Informal.* To tolerate (what must be endured): *like it or lump it.* [Perh. < dial. *lump,* to look sullen.]

lump•ec•to•my (lŭm-pĕk′tə-mē) *n., pl.* **-mies.** Surgical excision of a tumor from the breast with the removal of a minimal amount of surrounding tissue.

lum•pen (lŭm′pən, lo͝om′-) *adj.* **1.** Of or relating to dispossessed, often displaced people who have been cut off from the socioeconomic class with which they would ordinarily be identified. **2.** Of or relating to the lumpenproletariat. **3.** Boorish or unenlightened. [< Ger. *Lumpenproletariat,* the lowest section of the proletariat. See LUMPENPROLETARIAT.]

lum•pen•pro•le•tar•i•at (lŭm′pən-prō′lĭ-târ′ē-ət, lo͝om′-) *n.* **1.** The lowest, most degraded stratum of the proletariat;

luna moth
Actias luna

originally in Marxist theory, those members of the proletariat who lacked class consciousness. **2.** The underclass of a human population. [Ger. : *Lumpen*, pl. of *Lump*, ragamuffin (< MHGer. *lumpe*, rag) + *Proletariat*, proletariat (< Fr. *prolétariat*; see PROLETARIAT).]

lump•fish (lŭmp′fĭsh′) *n., pl.* **lumpfish** or **-fish•es.** Any of various fishes of the family Cyclopteridae, esp. *Cyclopterus lumpus,* having prominent tubercles and pelvic fins united to form a suction disk. [Obsolete *lump* (perh. < Du. *lomp*, blenny, loach < MDu. *lompe*, cod) + FISH.]

lump•ish (lŭm′pĭsh) *adj.* **1.** Stupid or dull. **2.** Clumsy or cumbersome. — **lump′ish•ly** *adv.* — **lump′ish•ness** *n.*

lump sum *n.* A single sum of money that serves as complete payment. — **lump′-sum′** (lŭmp′sŭm′) *adj.*

lump•y (lŭm′pē) *adj.* **-i•er, -i•est. 1.** Covered or filled with lumps. **2.** Thickset or cumbersome. **3.** Exhibiting short jumbled waves. — **lump′i•ly** *adv.* — **lump′i•ness** *n.*

lumpy jaw *n.* See **actinomycosis.**

Lu•mum•ba (lo͞o-mo͝om′bə), **Patrice Emergy.** 1925–61. First prime minister (1960–61) of the Congo (now Zaire).

Lu•na (lo͞o′nə) *n. Rom. Myth.* The goddess of the moon. [Lat. *Lūna* < *lūna*, moon. See **leuk-*.**]

lu•na•cy (lo͞o′nə-sē) *n., pl.* **-cies. 1.** Insanity, esp. insanity relieved intermittently by periods of clear-mindedness. See Syns at **insanity. 2.a.** Great or wild foolishness. **b.** A wildly foolish act. **3.** *Archaic.* Intermittent mental derangement associated with the changing phases of the moon. [< LUNATIC.]

lu•na moth (lo͞o′nə) *n.* A large pale-green North American moth *(Actias luna)* having elongated taillike hind wings. [NLat. *lūna*, species name < Lat., moon. See LUNAR.]

lu•nar (lo͞o′nər) *adj.* **1.** Of, involving, caused by, or affecting the moon. **2.** Measured by the revolution of the moon. **3.** Of or relating to silver. [ME, crescent-shaped < OFr. *lunaire* < Lat. *lūnāris*, of the moon < *lūna*, moon. See **leuk-*.**]

lunar caustic *n.* Silver nitrate in the form of sticks used in cauterization.

lunar month *n.* The average time between successive new or full moons, equal to 29 days, 12 hours, 44 minutes.

lunar year *n.* An interval of 12 lunar months.

lu•nate (lo͞o′nāt′) also **lu•nat•ed** (-nā′tĭd) *adj.* Shaped like a crescent. [Lat. *lūnātus*, p.part. of *lūnāre*, to bend like a crescent < *lūna*, moon. See **leuk-*.**]

lu•na•tic (lo͞o′nə-tĭk) *adj.* **1.** Suffering from lunacy; insane. **2.** Of or for the insane. **3.** Wildly or giddily foolish. **4.** Characterized by lunacy or eccentricity. [ME *lunatik* < OFr. *lunatique* < Lat. *lūnāticus* < *lūna*, moon. See **leuk-*.**] — **lu′na•tic** *n.*

lunatic fringe *n.* The fanatical, extremist, or irrational members of a society or group.

lu•na•tion (lo͞o-nā′shən) *n.* The time that elapses between successive new moons, averaging 29 days, 12 hours, 44 minutes; a lunar month. [ME *lunacioun* < Med.Lat. *lūnātiō, lūnātiōn-* < Lat. *lūna*. See LUNAR.]

lunch (lŭnch) *n.* **1.** A meal eaten at midday. **2.** The food provided for a midday meal. — *intr.v.* **lunched, lunch•ing, lunch•es.** To eat a midday meal. — ***idiom.* out to lunch.** *Slang.* Not in touch with the real world; crazy. [Short for LUNCHEON.] — **lunch′er** *n.*

lunch•eon (lŭn′chən) *n.* **1.** A lunch, esp. a formal one. **2.** An afternoon party at which a light meal is served. [Prob. alteration of obsolete *nuncheon*, light snack < ME *nonschench* : *none*, noon; see NOON + *schench*, drink (< OE *scenc* < *scencan*, to pour out).]

lunch•eon•ette (lŭn′chə-nĕt′) *n.* A small restaurant that serves simple, easily prepared meals.

luncheon meat *n.* Prepackaged processed meat, often molded into a loaf and served sliced for use in sandwiches or salads.

lunch•room (lŭnch′ro͞om′, -ro͝om′) *n.* **1.** A luncheonette. **2.** A room in a facility where lunches are purchased or eaten.

Lund (lŭnd). A city of S Sweden N of Malmö. Pop. 81,199.

Lun•dy (lŭn′dē), **Benjamin.** 1789–1839. Amer. abolitionist who founded the *Genius of Universal Emancipation* (1821), one of the earliest antislavery newspapers.

lune (lo͞on) *n.* A crescent-shaped portion of a plane or sphere bounded by two arcs of circles. [Lat. *lūna*, moon. See **leuk-*.**]

Lü•nen (lo͞o′nən, lü′-). A city of W-central Germany ENE of Essen. Pop. 84,084.

lu•nette (lo͞o-nĕt′) *n.* **1.** *Archit.* **a.** A small circular or crescent-shaped opening in a vaulted roof. **b.** A crescent-shaped or semicircular space, as over a door, that may contain another window, a sculpture, or a mural. **2.** A fortification with two projecting faces and two parallel flanks. **3.** A broad, typically crescent-shaped mound of sandy or loamy matter formed by the wind. [Fr. < OFr. *lunete*, moon-shaped object, dim. of *lune*, moon < Lat. *lūna*. See LUNE.]

lung (lŭng) *n.* **1.** Either of two spongy saclike respiratory organs in the thorax of most vertebrates, removing carbon dioxide from the blood and providing it with oxygen. **2.** A similar organ in some invertebrates, including spiders. — ***idiom.* at the top of (one's) lungs.** As loudly as possible. [ME *lunge* < OE *lungen*, lungs. See **legʷh-*.**]

lunge (lŭnj) *n.* **1.** A sudden thrust or pass, as with a sword. **2.** A sudden forward movement or plunge. — *v.* **lunged, lung•ing, lung•es.** — *intr.* **1.** To make a sudden thrust or pass. **2.** To move with a sudden thrust. — *tr.* To cause (someone) to lunge. [< alteration of obsolete *allonge*, to thrust < Fr. *allonger* < OFr. *alongier*, to lengthen : *a*, to (< Lat. *ad*; see AD-) + *long*, long (< Lat. *longus*; see **del-¹*.**)]

lung•fish (lŭng′fĭsh′) *n., pl.* **lungfish** or **-fish•es.** Any of several elongated tropical freshwater fishes that have lunglike organs as well as gills and are able to breathe air.

lung•worm (lŭng′wûrm′) *n.* Any of various nematode worms, esp. of the family Metastrongylidae, that are parasitic in the lungs of mammals.

lung•wort (lŭng′wûrt′, -wôrt′) *n.* **1.** Any of various plants of the genus *Mertensia,* such as the Virginia cowslip, having drooping clusters of tubular, usu. blue flowers. **2.** Any of several European plants of the genus *Pulmonaria,* having long-stalked leaves and coiled clusters of blue or purple flowers and formerly used in treating respiratory disorders.

lu•ni•so•lar (lo͞o′nĭ-sō′lər) *adj.* Of or caused by both the sun and the moon. [Lat. *lūna*, moon; see LUNAR + SOLAR.]

lu•ni•ti•dal (lo͞o′nĭ-tīd′l) *adj.* Of or relating to tidal phenomena caused by the moon. [Lat. *lūna*, moon; see LUNAR + TIDAL.]

lunk•er (lŭng′kər) *n. Informal.* Something, esp. a game fish, that is large for its kind. [?]

lunk•head (lŭngk′hĕd′) *n. Slang.* A person regarded as stupid. [Prob. alteration of LUMP¹ + HEAD.] — **lunk′head′ed** *adj.*

Lunt (lŭnt), **Alfred.** 1893–1977. Amer. actor who performed with his wife Lynn Fontanne in productions such as *Pygmalion* (1926).

lu•nu•la (lo͞on′yə-lə) *n., pl.* **-lae** (-lē′). A small crescent-shaped structure or marking, esp. the white area at the base of a fingernail that resembles a half-moon. [NLat. *lūnula* < Lat., crescent-shaped ornament, dim. of *lūna*, moon. See **leuk-*.**]

lu•nu•lar (lo͞on′yə-lər) *adj.* Shaped like a crescent.

lu•nu•late (lo͞on′yə-lāt′, -lĭt) also **lu•nu•lat•ed** (-lā′tĭd) *adj.* **1.** Small and lunular. **2.** Having crescent-shaped markings.

lu•nule (lo͞on′yo͞ol) *n.* A lunula.

lun•y (lo͞o′nē) *adj. Informal.* Var. of **loony.**

Luo•yang (lwō′yäng′) also **Lo•yang** (lō′-). A city of E-central China ENE of Xi'an; cap. of several ancient dynasties, including the Han and Tang. Pop. 624,000.

Lu•per•ca•li•a (lo͞o′pər-kā′lē-ə, -kāl′yə) *n.* A fertility festival in ancient Rome, celebrated on February 15 in honor of the pastoral god Lupercus. [Lat. *Lupercālia* < *Lupercus*, Roman god of flocks.] — **Lu′per•ca′li•an** *adj.*

lu•pine¹ also **lu•pin** (lo͞o′pən) *n.* Any of numerous plants of the genus *Lupinus* in the pea family, having compound leaves and flowers grouped in spikes or racemes. [ME < OFr. *lupin* < Lat. *lupīnum* < neut. of *lupīnus*, wolflike. See LUPINE².]

lu•pine² (lo͞o′pīn′) *adj.* **1.** Resembling a wolf. **2.** Rapacious; ravenous. [Fr. < Lat. *lupīnus* < *lupus*, wolf. See **wl̥kʷo-*.**]

lu•pus (lo͞o′pəs) *n.* Any of several diseases, esp. systemic lupus erythematosus, that principally affect the skin and joints. [Med. Lat. < Lat., wolf. See **wl̥kʷo-*.**]

Lu•pus (lo͞o′pəs) *n.* A constellation of stars in the Southern Hemisphere near Centaurus and Scorpius. [Lat. < *lupus*, wolf. See LUPUS.]

lupus er•y•the•ma•to•sus (ĕr′ə-thē′mə-tō′səs, -thĕm′ə-) *n.* **1.** A chronic disease of unknown origin characterized by the appearance of red scaly lesions or patches on the face and upper portion of the trunk. **2.** Systemic lupus erythematosus. [NLat. *lupus erythēmatōsus* : LUPUS + *erythēmatōsus*, erythematous.]

lupus vul•gar•is (vŭl-gâr′ĭs) *n.* A cutaneous form of tuberculosis characterized by reddish-brown ulcerating nodules, usu. appearing on the face, that produce deep scars. [NLat. *lupus vulgāris*, common lupus : LUPUS + Lat. *vulgāris*, common.]

lurch¹ (lûrch) *intr.v.* **lurched, lurch•ing, lurch•es. 1.** To stagger. See Syns at **blunder. 2.** To roll or pitch suddenly or erratically. — *n.* **1.** A staggering or tottering movement or gait. **2.** An abrupt rolling or pitching. [?] — **lurch′ing•ly** *adv.*

lurch² (lûrch) *n. Games.* The losing position of a cribbage player who scores 30 points or less to the winner's 61. — ***idiom.* in the lurch.** In a difficult or embarrassing position. [Perh. back-formation < ME *lurching*, a total victory at *lorche* < *lorche*, a kind of game; perh. akin to *lurken*, to lurk. See LURK.]

lurch•er (lûr′chər) *n.* **1.** *Chiefly British.* A crossbred dog used by poachers. **2.** *Archaic.* A sneak thief. [ME < *lorchen*, to lurk, perh. < *lurken*. See LURK.]

lure (lo͝or) *n.* **1.a.** Something that tempts or attracts with the promise of pleasure or reward. **b.** An attraction or appeal. **2.** A decoy used in catching animals, esp. an artificial bait used in catching fish. **3.** A bunch of feathers attached to a long cord, used in falconry to recall the hawk. — *tr.v.* **lured, lur•ing, lures. 1.** To attract by wiles or temptation; entice. **2.** To recall (a falcon) with a lure. [ME < AN, of Gmc. orig.] — **lur′er** *n.* — **lur′ing•ly** *adv.*

lu•rid (lo͝or′ĭd) *adj.* **1.** Causing shock or horror; gruesome. **2.** Marked by sensationalism: *a lurid account of the crime.* **3.** Glowing or shining with the glare of fire through a haze: *lurid flames.* **4.** Sallow or pallid in color. [Lat. *lūridus*, pale <

A B C D

lune
Lune of a sphere bounded by arcs ABD and ACD

ă pat	oi boy
ā pay	ou out
âr care	o͝o took
ä father	o͞o boot
ĕ pet	ŭ cut
ē be	ûr urge
ĭ pit	th thin
ī pie	*th* this
îr pier	hw which
ŏ pot	zh vision
ō toe	ə about, item
ô paw	

Stress marks:
′ (primary);
′ (secondary), as in **dictionary** (dĭk′shə-nĕr′ē)

lūror, paleness.] —**lu′rid•ly** *adv.* —**lu′rid•ness** *n.*

lurk (lûrk) *intr.v.* **lurked, lurk•ing, lurks. 1.** To lie in wait, as in ambush. **2.** To move furtively; sneak. **3.** To exist unobserved or unsuspected: *danger lurking around every bend.* [ME *lurken,* poss. of Scand. orig.] —**lurk′ing•ly** *adv.*

Lur•ton (lûr′tn), **Horace Harmon.** 1844–1914. Amer. jurist; associate justice of the U.S. Supreme Court (1910–14).

Lu•sa•ka (lo͞o-sä′kə). The cap. of Zambia, in the S-central part; founded 1905. Pop. 535,830.

Lu•sa•ti•a (lo͞o-sā′shē-ə, -shə). A region of central Europe in E Germany and SW Poland; settled by descendants of the Wends, a Slavic people. —**Lu•sa′tian** *adj. & n.*

luster
Late 19th-century English

lus•cious (lŭsh′əs) *adj.* **1.** Sweet and pleasant to taste or smell. **2.** Having strong sensual or sexual appeal; seductive. **3.** Richly appealing to the senses or the mind. **4.** *Archaic.* Excessively sweet; cloying. [ME *lucius,* alteration of *licious,* perh. short for *delicious,* delicious. See DELICIOUS.] —**lus′cious•ly** *adv.* —**lus′cious•ness** *n.*

lush[1] (lŭsh) *adj.* **lush•er, lush•est. 1.a.** Having or characterized by luxuriant vegetation. **b.** Abundant; plentiful. **c.** Extremely productive; thriving. **2.a.** Luxurious; opulent. **b.** Extremely pleasing to the senses: *a lush scent.* **c.** Voluptuous or sensual. **3.** Overelaborate or extravagant: *lush rhetoric.* [ME, relaxed, soft, prob. alteration of *lache,* loose, weak < OFr., soft, succulent < *laschier,* to loosen < LLat. *laxicāre,* to become shaky, freq. of Lat. *laxāre,* to open, relax < *laxus,* loose. See LAX.] —**lush′ly** *adv.* —**lush′ness** *n.*

lush[2] (lŭsh) *Slang.* —*n.* A drunkard. —*intr.v.* **lushed, lush•ing, lush•es.** To drink liquor to excess. [?]

Lü•shun (lo͞o′sho͝on′, lü′-). A city of NE China at the tip of the Liaodong Peninsula, part of Lüda. Pop. 40,752.

Lu•si•ta•ni•a (lo͞o′sĭ-tā′nē-ə). An ancient region and Roman province of the Iberian Peninsula, corresponding roughly to modern-day Portugal. —**Lu′si•ta′ni•an** *adj. & n.*

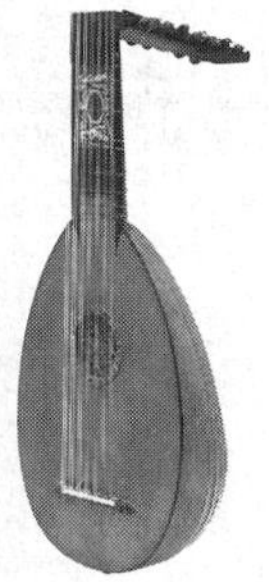

lute[1]
17th-century Italian

lust (lŭst) *n.* **1.** Intense or unrestrained sexual craving. **2.a.** An overwhelming desire or craving. **b.** Intense eagerness or enthusiasm. **3.** *Obsolete.* Pleasure; relish. —*intr.v.* **lust•ed, lust•ing, lusts.** To have an intense or obsessive desire, esp. one that is sexual. [ME < OE, desire. See **las-***.]

lus•ter (lŭs′tər) *n.* **1.** Soft reflected light; sheen. **2.** Brilliance or radiance of light; brightness. **3.** Glory, distinction, or splendor, as of beauty. **4.** A glass pendant, esp. on a chandelier. **5.** A decorative object that gives off light. **6.** Any of various substances, such as wax, used to give an object a gloss or polish. **7.** The surface glossiness of ceramic ware after glazing, esp. the metallic sheen of lusterware. **8.** A fabric, such as alpaca, having a glossy surface. **9.** The appearance of a mineral surface judged by its brilliance and ability to reflect light. —*v.* **-tered, -ter•ing, -ters.** —*tr.* **1.** To give a gloss, glaze, or sheen to. **2.** To give or add glory, distinction, or splendor to. —*intr.* To be or become lustrous. [Fr. *lustre* < OFr. < OItal. *lustro* < *lustrare,* to make bright < Lat. *lūstrāre* < *lūstrum,* purification. See **leuk-***.]

lus•ter•ware (lŭs′tər-wâr′) *n.* Pottery or porcelain having a metallic sheen produced by metallic oxides in the glaze.

lust•ful (lŭst′fəl) *adj.* Excited or driven by lust.

lus•tral (lŭs′trəl) *adj.* Of, relating to, or used in a rite of purification. [Lat. *lūstrālis* < *lūstrum,* purification. See LUSTER.]

lus•trate (lŭs′trāt′) *tr.v.* **lus•trat•ed, lus•trat•ing, lus•trates.** To purify by means of ceremony. [Lat. *lūstrāre, lūstrāt-,* to purify, make bright. See LUSTER.] —**lus•tra′tion** *n.*

lus•tre (lŭs′tər) *n. & v. Chiefly British.* Var. of **luster.**

lus•trous (lŭs′trəs) *adj.* **1.** Having a sheen or glow. **2.** Gleaming with or as if with brilliant light; radiant. See Syns at **bright.** —**lus′trous•ly** *adv.* —**lus′trous•ness** *n.*

lus•trum (lŭs′trəm) *n., pl.* **-trums** or **-tra** (-trə). **1.** A ceremonial purification of the entire ancient Roman population after the census every five years. **2.** A period of five years. [Lat. *lūstrum.* See LUSTER.]

Martin Luther
Portrait by Lucas Cranach

lust•y (lŭs′tē) *adj.* **-i•er, -i•est. 1.** Full of vigor or vitality; robust. **2.** Powerful; strong: *a lusty cry.* **3.** Lustful. **4.** Merry; joyous. —**lust′i•ly** *adv.* —**lust′i•ness** *n.*

lu•sus na•tu•rae (lo͞o′səs nə-to͝or′ē, -tyo͝or′ē) *n.* A freak or sport of nature. [NLat. *lūsus nātūrae.*]

Lü•ta (lo͞o′dä′, lü′-). See **Lüda.**

lute[1] (lo͞ot) *n. Mus.* A stringed instrument having a body shaped like a pear sliced lengthwise and a neck with a fretted fingerboard that is usu. bent just below the tuning pegs. [ME < OFr. *lut* < OProv. *laut* < Ar. *al-ʿud* : *al,* the + *ʿūd,* lute.]

lute[2] (lo͞ot) *n.* A substance, such as dried clay or cement, used to pack and seal pipe joints and other connections or coat a porous surface. —*tr.v.* **lut•ed, lut•ing, lutes.** To coat, pack, or seal with lute. [ME < OFr. *lut* < Lat. *lutum,* potter's clay.]

Luxembourg

lu•te•al (lo͞o′tē-əl) *adj.* Of, relating to, or involving the corpus luteum.

lu•te•fisk (lo͞o′tə-fĭsk′) also **lut•fisk** (lo͞ot′fĭsk′) *n.* A traditional Scandinavian dish prepared by soaking air-dried cod in a lye solution for several weeks before skinning, boning, and boiling it. [Norw. : *lut,* lye + *fisk,* fish (< ON *fiskr*).]

lu•te•in (lo͞o′tē-ĭn, -tēn′) *n.* **1.** A yellow carotenoid pigment, $C_{40}H_{56}O_2$, found widely in nature, as in corpus luteum, body fats, egg yolk, and green plants; xanthophyll. **2.** A dried preparation of corpus luteum. [Lat. *lūteum,* yellow, egg yolk < neut. of *lūteus,* yellow (< *lūtum,* yellowweed) + -IN.]

lu•te•in•ize (lo͞o′tē-ə-nīz′) *v.* **-ized, -iz•ing, -iz•es.** —*tr.* To cause the production of a corpus luteum in. —*intr.* To develop into or become part of the corpus luteum. —**lu′te•in•i•za′tion** (-ə-nĭ-zā′shən) *n.*

lu•te•in•iz•ing hormone (lo͞o′tē-ə-nī′zĭng) *n.* A hormone produced by the anterior lobe of the pituitary gland that stimulates ovulation and the development of the corpus luteum in the female and the production of testosterone in the male.

lu•te•nist also **lu•ta•nist** (lo͞ot′n-ĭst) *n. Mus.* A lute player. [Med.Lat. *lūtānista* < *lūtāna,* lute, poss. < OFr. *lut.* See LUTE[1].]

lu•te•ous (lo͞o′tē-əs) *adj. Color.* Of a light or moderate greenish yellow. [< Lat. *lūteus,* yellow. See LUTEIN.]

lu•te•ti•um also **lu•te•ci•um** (lo͞o-tē′shē-əm) *n. Symbol* **Lu** A rare-earth element that is difficult to separate from other rare-earth elements, used in nuclear research. Atomic number 71; atomic weight 174.97; melting point 1,663°C; boiling point 3,395°C; specific gravity 9.840 (at 25°C); valence 3. See table at **element.** [Lat. *Lutetia,* ancient name of Paris, France + -IUM.]

Lu•ther (lo͞o′thər), **Martin.** 1483–1546. German theologian and leader of the Reformation.

Lu•ther•an (lo͞o′thər-ən) *adj.* **1.** Of or relating to Luther or his religious teachings and esp. to the doctrine of justification by faith alone. **2.** Of or relating to the branch of the Protestant Church adhering to the views of Luther. —*n.* A member of the Lutheran Church. —**Lu′ther•an•ism, Lu′ther•ism** *n.*

lu•thi•er (lo͞o′tē-ər) *n. Mus.* One that makes or repairs stringed instruments, such as violins. [Fr. < *luth,* lute < OFr. *lut.* See LUTE[1].]

Lu•thu•li (lo͞o-to͞o′lē, -tyo͞o′-), **Albert John.** 1898–1967. Zulu leader who won the 1960 Nobel Peace Prize.

lut•ing (lo͞o′tĭng) *n.* See **lute**[2].

lut•ist (lo͞o′tĭst) *n. Mus.* **1.** A maker of lutes. **2.** See **lutenist.**

Lu•ton (lo͞ot′n). A borough of SE England NNW of London. Pop. 164,200.

Lutsk (lo͞otsk). A city of W-central Ukraine NE of Lvov; first mentioned in 1085. Pop. 172,000.

Lutz also **lutz** (lŭts) *n. Sports.* A jump in figure skating in which the skater takes off from the back outer edge of one skate and makes one full rotation before landing on the back outer edge of the other skate. [Perh. after Gustave *Lussi,* 20th-cent. Swiss figure skater.]

Lu•wi•an (lo͞o′wē-ən, -vē-ən) or **Lu•vi•an** (lo͞o′vē-ən) *n.* **1.** A language of the extinct Anatolian branch of Indo-European. **2.** A speaker of Luwian.

lux (lŭks) *n., pl.* **lux•es** or **lu•ces** (lo͞o′sēz). The International System unit of illumination, equal to one lumen per square meter. See table at **measurement.** [Lat. *lūx,* light. See **leuk-***.]

Lux. *abbr.* Luxembourg.

lux•ate (lŭk′sāt′) *tr.v.* **-at•ed, -at•ing, -ates.** To put out of joint; dislocate. [Lat. *luxāre, luxāt-* < *luxus,* dislocated.] —**lux•a′tion** *n.*

luxe (lo͝oks, lŭks) *n.* **1.** The condition of being elegantly sumptuous. **2.** Something luxurious; a luxury. [Fr., luxury < Lat. *luxus.*] —**luxe** *adj.*

Lux•em•bourg also **Lux•em•burg** (lŭk′səm-bûrg′). **1.** A country of NW Europe; created as a duchy in 1354 and declared a neutral territory in 1867. Cap. Luxembourg. Pop. 364,606. **2.** Also **Luxembourg City.** The cap. of Luxembourg, in the S part. Pop. 78,924.

Lux•em•burg (lŭk′səm-bûrg′, lo͝ok′səm-bo͝ork′), **Rosa.** 1870–1919. German socialist leader who cofounded (1918) the Spartacus Party.

Lux•or (lŭk′sôr′, lo͝ok′-). A city of central Egypt on the E bank of the Nile R.; built partially on the site of ancient Thebes. Pop. 137,300.

lux•u•ri•ant (lŭg-zho͝or′ē-ənt, lŭk-sho͝or′-) *adj.* **1.a.** Marked by rich or profuse growth. **b.** Producing or yielding in abundance. **2.** Excessively florid or elaborate. **3.** Marked by or displaying luxury; luxurious. [Lat. *luxuriāns, luxuriant-,* pr.part. of *luxuriāre,* to be luxuriant. See LUXURIATE.] —**lux•u′ri•ance** *n.* —**lux•u′ri•ant•ly** *adv.*

lux•u•ri•ate (lŭg-zho͝or′ē-āt′, lŭk-sho͝or′-) *intr.v.* **-at•ed, -at•ing, -ates. 1.** To take luxurious pleasure; indulge oneself. **2.** To proliferate. **3.** To grow profusely; thrive. [Lat. *luxuriāre, luxuriāt-,* to be luxuriant < *luxuria,* luxury. See LUXURY.]

lux•u•ri•ous (lŭg-zho͝or′ē-əs, lŭk-sho͝or′-) *adj.* **1.** Fond of or given to luxury. **2.** Marked by or contributing to luxury. **3.** Of a sumptuous, costly, or rich variety. —**lux•u′ri•ous•ness** *n.* —**lux•u′ri•ous•ly** *adv.*

lux•u•ry (lŭg′zhə-rē, lŭk′shə-) *n., pl.* **-ries. 1.** Something inessential but conducive to pleasure and comfort. **2.** Something expensive or hard to obtain. **3.** Sumptuous living or surroundings. [ME *luxurie,* lust < OFr. < Lat. *luxuria,* excess, luxury < *luxus.*]

Lu•zon (lo͞o-zŏn′). An island of the NW Philippines; the largest and most populous island in the archipelago.

Lv *abbr. Bible.* Leviticus.

lv. *abbr.* **1.** Leave. **2.** Livre.

LVN or **L.V.N.** *abbr.* Licensed vocational nurse.

Lvov (lvôf). A city of W-central Ukraine near the Polish border; founded 1256. Pop. 742,000.

LW *abbr.* Low water.

lwei (lwā) *n., pl.* **lwei.** See table at **currency.** [Of Bantu orig.]

LWV *abbr.* League of Women Voters.

lx *abbr.* Lux.

–ly[1] *suff.* **1.** Like; resembling; having the characteristics of: *sisterly.* **2.** Recurring at a specified interval of time: *hourly.* [ME *-li* < OE *-līc* (influenced by ON *-ligr*). See **līk-*.**]

–ly[2] *suff.* **1.** In a specified manner; in the manner of: *gradually.* **2.** At a specified interval of time: *weekly.* **3.** With respect to: *partly.* [ME *-li* < OE *-līce* (influenced by ON *-liga*) < *-līc*, adj. suff. See **līk-*.**]

Ly•all•pur (lī′əl-po͝or′). See **Faisalabad.**

ly•ase (lī′ās′) *n.* Any of a group of enzymes that catalyze the formation of double bonds without hydrolysis. [Gk. *luein*, to loosen; see **leu-*** + –ASE.]

ly•can•thrope (lī′kən-thrōp′, lī-kăn′-) *n.* A werewolf. [Gk. *lukanthrōpos* : *lukos*, wolf; see **wḷkʷo-*** + *anthrōpos*, man.]

ly•can•thro•py (lī-kăn′thrə-pē) *n.* In folklore, the magical ability to assume the form and characteristics of a wolf.

ly•cée (lē-sā′) *n.* A French public secondary school. [Fr. < OFr., lyceum < Lat. *Lycēum*. See LYCEUM.]

ly•ce•um (lī-sē′əm) *n.* **1.** A hall in which public lectures, concerts, and similar programs are presented. **2.** An organization sponsoring public programs and entertainment. **3.** A lycée. [Lat. *Lycēum* < Gk. *Lukeion*, the school outside Athens where Aristotle taught (335–323 B.C.).]

ly•chee (lē′chē) *n.* Var. of **litchi.**

lych-gate (lĭch′gāt′) or **lych gate** also **lich gate** (lĭch) *n.* A roofed gateway to a churchyard used originally as a resting place for a bier before burial. [ME *lycheyate* : *lyche*, corpse, body (< OE *līc*; see **līk-***) + *gate, yate*, gate; see GATE[1].]

lych•nis (lĭk′nĭs) *n.* Any of various plants of the genus *Lychnis*, which includes the campions. [NLat. *Lychnis*, genus name < Lat. *lychnis*, a red flower < Gk. *lukhnis*; akin to *lukhnos*, lamp. See **leuk-*.**]

Ly•ci•a (lĭsh′ē-ə, lĭsh′ə). An ancient country and Roman province of SW Asia Minor on the Aegean Sea; annexed by Rome in the 1st cent. A.D.

Ly•ci•an (lĭsh′ē-ən, lĭsh′ən) *adj.* Of or relating to Lycia or its people, language, or culture. —*n.* **1.** A language of the extinct Anatolian branch of Indo-European. **2.** A speaker of Lycian.

ly•co•po•di•um (lī′kə-pō′dē-əm) *n.* **1.** A plant of the genus *Lycopodium*, which includes the club mosses. **2.** The yellowish powdery spores of certain club mosses, esp. *Lycopodium clavatum*, used in fireworks and explosives and as a covering for pills. [NLat. *Lycopodium*, genus name : Gk. *lukos*, wolf; see **wḷkʷo-*** + Gk. *podion*, dim. of *pous*, foot; see **ped-*.**]

Ly•cra (lī′krə). A trademark used for a brand of spandex.

Ly•cur•gus (lī-kûr′gəs). fl. 9th cent. B.C. Spartan lawmaker who is considered the founder of the Spartan constitution.

lyd•dite (lĭd′īt′) *n.* An explosive consisting chiefly of picric acid. [After *Lydd*, a municipal borough of SE England.]

Lyd•gate (lĭd′gāt′, -gət), **John.** 1370?–1451? English poet who is best known for his long narrative works.

Lyd•i•a (lĭd′ē-ə). An ancient country of W-central Asia Minor on the Aegean Sea in present-day NW Turkey.

Lyd•i•an (lĭd′ē-ən) *adj.* Of or relating to Lydia or its people, language, or culture. —*n.* **1.** A language of the extinct Anatolian branch of Indo-European. **2.** A speaker of Lydian.

lye (lī) *n.* **1.** The liquid obtained by leaching wood ashes. **2.** See **potassium hydroxide. 3.** See **sodium hydroxide.** [ME *lie* < OE *lēag*. See **leu(ə)-*.**]

Ly•ell (lī′əl), Sir **Charles.** 1797–1875. British geologist whose *Principles of Geology* (1830–33) opposed the catastrophic theory of geologic change.

ly•gus bug (lī′gəs) *n.* Any of various North American bugs of the genus *Lygus*, including certain species that are destructive to plants. [NLat. *Lygus*, genus name < Gk. *lugaios*, murky.]

ly•ing[1] (lī′ĭng) *v.* Pr.part. of **lie[1].**

ly•ing[2] (lī′ĭng) *v.* Pr.part. of **lie[2].** —*adj.* Disposed to or characterized by untruth: *a lying witness.*

ly•ing-in (lī′ĭng-ĭn′) *n., pl.* **ly•ings-in** (lī′ĭngz-) or **ly•ing-ins.** The confinement of a woman in childbirth. —*adj.* Of or intended for use during childbirth: *a lying-in hospital.*

Lyl•y (lĭl′ē), **John.** 1554?–1606. English playwright who wrote a number of comedies that influenced English drama.

Lyme disease (līm) *n.* An inflammatory disease caused by a spirochete *(Borrelia burgdorferi)* that is transmitted by ticks, usu. characterized by a rash followed by flulike symptoms including fever, joint pain, and headache. [After *Lyme*, a town of SE CT.]

lymph (lĭmf) *n.* **1.** A clear watery fluid that contains white blood cells and circulates throughout the lymphatic system, removing bacteria and certain proteins from body tissues, transporting fat from the small intestine, and supplying mature lymphocytes to the blood. **2.** *Archaic.* A spring or stream of pure clear water. [Lat. *lympha*, water < Gk. *numphē*, water spirit.]

lym•phad•e•ni•tis (lĭm-făd′n-ī′tĭs, lĭm′fə-də-nī′-) *n.* Inflammation of one or more lymph nodes.

lym•phad•e•nop•a•thy (lĭm-făd′n-ŏp′ə-thē, lĭm′fə-dn-) *n., pl.* **-thies.** A chronic, abnormal enlargement of the lymph nodes. [LYMPH + ADENO– + –PATHY.]

lym•phan•gi•og•ra•phy (lĭm-făn′jē-ŏg′rə-fē) *n., pl.* **-phies.** Examination of the lymph nodes and lymphatic vessels following the injection of a radiopaque substance. —**lym•phan′gi•o•gram′** (-ə-grăm′) *n.*

lym•phat•ic (lĭm-făt′ĭk) *adj.* **1.** Of or relating to lymph, a lymph vessel, or a lymph node. **2.** Lacking energy or vitality; sluggish. —*n.* A vessel that conveys lymph. [NLat. *lymphaticus* < Lat. *lympha*, lymph. See LYMPH.] —**lym•phat′i•cal•ly** *adv.*

lymphatic system *n.* The interconnected system of spaces and vessels between body tissues and organs by which lymph circulates throughout the body.

lymph node *n.* Any of the small oval or round bodies, located along the lymphatic vessels, that supply lymphocytes to the bloodstream and remove bacteria and foreign particles from the lymph.

lympho– or **lymph–** *pref.* Lymphatic system; lymph: *lymphocyte.* [< LYMPH.]

lym•pho•blast (lĭm′fə-blăst′) *n.* A cell that gives rise to a mature lymphocyte. —**lym′pho•blas′tic** *adj.*

lym•pho•cyte (lĭm′fə-sīt′) *n.* Any of the nearly colorless cells formed in lymphoid tissue, as in the lymph nodes, that function in the development of immunity and include two specific types, B cells and T cells. —**lym′pho•cyt′ic** (-sĭt′ĭk) *adj.*

lym•pho•cy•to•sis (lĭm′fō-sī-tō′sĭs) *n.* A condition marked by an abnormal increase in the number of lymphocytes in the bloodstream. —**lym′pho•cy•tot′ic** (-tŏt′ĭk) *adj.*

lym•pho•gran•u•lo•ma ve•ne•re•um (lĭm′fə-grăn′yə-lō′mə və-nîr′ē-əm) *n.* A sexually transmitted disease caused by a bacterium *(Chlamydia trachomatis)* and characterized initially by a genital lesion followed by enlargement of the lymph nodes in the groin area. [NLat. : LYMPHO– + GRANULOMA + Lat. *venereum*, neut. of *venereus*, venereal.]

lym•phog•ra•phy (lĭm-fŏg′rə-fē) *n.* See **lymphangiography.**

lym•phoid (lĭm′foid′) *adj.* Of or relating to lymph or the lymphatic tissue where lymphocytes are formed.

lym•pho•kine (lĭm′fə-kīn′) *n.* Any of various substances released by T cells that function in the immune response through a variety of actions, including stimulating the production of nonsensitized lymphocytes and activating macrophages. [LYMPHO– + Gk. *kinein*, to move; see KININ.]

lym•pho•ma (lĭm-fō′mə) *n., pl.* **-ma•ta** (-mə-tə) or **-mas.** Any of various usu. malignant tumors that arise in the lymph nodes or in other lymphoid tissue. —**lym•pho′ma•toid′, lym•phom′a•tous** (-fŏm′ə-təs) *adj.*

lym•pho•poi•e•sis (lĭm′fō-poi-ē′sĭs) *n., pl.* **-ses** (-sēz′). The formation of lymphocytes. —**lym′pho•poi•et′ic** (-ĕt′ĭk) *adj.*

Lyn•brook (lĭn′bro͝ok′). A village of SE NY on SW Long I. E of Queens. Pop. 19,208.

lynch (lĭnch) *tr.v.* **lynched, lynch•ing, lynch•es.** To execute without due process of law, esp. to hang, as by a mob. [Short for LYNCH LAW.] —**lynch′er** *n.* —**lynch′ing** *n.*

Lynch•burg (lĭnch′bûrg′). An independent city of SW-central VA ENE of Roanoke. Pop. 66,049.

lynch law *n.* The punishment of persons suspected of crime without due process of law. [After William *Lynch* (d. 1820).]

lynch•pin (lĭnch′pĭn′) *n.* Var. of **linchpin.**

Lynd (lĭnd), **Robert Staughton.** 1892–1970. Amer. sociologist who wrote *Middletown: A Study in Contemporary American Culture* (1929) with his wife, **Helen Merrell Lynd** (1896–1982).

Lynn (lĭn). A city of NE MA, a suburb of Boston; formerly an important shoe-making center. Pop. 81,245.

Lynn Canal. An inlet of the Pacific Ocean in SE AK connecting Skagway with Juneau; a major route to the goldfields during the Alaskan gold rush (1896–98).

Lynn•wood (lĭn′wo͝od′). A city of W-central WA, a suburb of Seattle. Pop. 28,695.

Lyn•wood (lĭn′wo͝od′). A city of S CA, a suburb of Los Angeles. Pop. 61,945.

lynx (lĭngks) *n., pl.* **lynx** or **lynx•es.** Any of several wildcats of the genus *Lynx*, esp. *L. canadensis* of northern North America or *L. lynx* of Eurasia, having a black-tipped short tail and tufted ears. [ME < Lat. < Gk. *lunx*. See **leuk-*.**]

lynx

lynx-eyed (lĭngks′īd′) *adj.* Keen of vision.

lyo– *pref.* Dispersion; dissolution: *lyophilic.* [< Gk. *luein*, to loosen, dissolve. See **leu-*.**]

Ly•on (lī′ən), **Mary Mason.** 1797–1849. Amer. educator who founded (1837) Mount Holyoke College.

Ly•on•nais (lē-ô-nĕ′). A historical region and former province of E-central France; became part of the French royal domain in the 14th cent.

ly•on•naise (lī′ə-nāz′, lē′ə-nĕz′) *adj.* Cooked with onions: *lyonnaise potatoes.* [< Fr. *(à la) Lyonnaise*, (in the manner) of Lyons < LYONS.]

Ly•ons or **Ly•on** (lē-ōɴ′, lyôn). A city of E-central France at the confluence of the Rhone and Saône rivers S of Mâcon;

ă pat	oi boy
ā pay	ou out
âr care	o͝o took
ä father	o͞o boot
ĕ pet	ŭ cut
ē be	ûr urge
ĭ pit	th thin
ī pie	*th* this
îr pier	hw which
ŏ pot	zh vision
ō toe	ə about, item
ô paw	

Stress marks:
′ (primary);
′ (secondary), as in
dictionary (dĭk′shə-nĕr′ē)

founded 43 B.C. as a Roman colony. Pop. 413,095.

ly•o•phil•ic (lī′ə-fĭl′ĭk) *adj.* Characterized by strong attraction between the colloid medium and the dispersion medium of a colloidal system.

ly•oph•i•lize (lī-ŏf′ə-līz′) *tr.v.* **-lized, -liz•ing, -liz•es.** To freeze-dry (blood plasma or other biological substances).

ly•o•pho•bic (lī′ə-fō′bĭk) *adj.* Characterized by a lack of attraction between the colloid medium and the dispersion medium of a colloidal system.

Ly•ra (lī′rə) *n.* A constellation in the Northern Hemisphere near Cygnus and Hercules. [Lat. < *lyra*, lyre. See LYRE.]

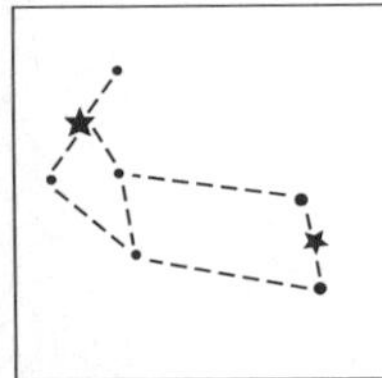

Lyra

ly•rate (lī′rāt′, -rĭt) *adj.* Having a form or curvature suggestive of a lyre.

lyre (līr) *n. Mus.* A stringed instrument of the harp family used to accompany a singer or reader of poetry, esp. in ancient Greece. [ME *lire* < OFr. < Lat. *lyra* < Gk. *lura*.]

lyre•bird (līr′bûrd′) *n.* Either of two Australian birds of the genus *Menura*, the male of which has long tail feathers that are spread in a lyre-shaped display during courtship.

lyr•ic (lĭr′ĭk) *adj.* **1.a.** Of or relating to a category of poetry that expresses subjective thoughts and feelings, often in a songlike style or form. **b.** Relating to or constituting a poem in this category, such as a sonnet or an ode. **c.** Of or relating to a writer of poems in this category. **2.** Lyrical. **3.** *Mus.* **a.** Having a singing voice of light volume and modest range. **b.** Of, relating to, or being musical drama, esp. opera. **c.** Of or relating to the lyre or harp. **d.** Appropriate for accompaniment by the lyre. —*n.* **1.** A lyric poem. **2.** *Mus.* The words of a song. Often used in the plural. [Fr. *lyrique*, of a lyre < OFr. < Lat. *lyricus* < Gk. *lurikos* < *lura*, lyre.]

lyr•i•cal (lĭr′ĭ-kəl) *adj.* **1.a.** Expressing deep personal emotion or observations. **b.** Highly enthusiastic; rhapsodic: *a lyrical description.* **2.** Lyric. —**lyr′i•cal•ly** *adv.* —**lyr′i•cal•ness** *n.*

lyr•i•cism (lĭr′ĭ-sĭz′əm) *n.* **1.a.** The character or quality of subjectivity and sensuality of expression, esp. in the arts. **b.** *Mus.* The quality or state of being melodious; melodiousness. **2.** An intense outpouring of exuberant emotion.

lyr•i•cist (lĭr′ĭ-sĭst) *n. Mus.* A writer of song lyrics.

lyr•i•cize (lĭr′ĭ-sīz′) *v.* **-ciz•ed, -ciz•ing, -ciz•es.** —*intr.* **1.** *Mus.* To write or sing lyrics. **2.** To write lyrically or in a lyric style. —*tr.* To treat (something) lyrically; put into lyric style.

lyre
c. 470 B.C. Etruscan painted terra-cotta plaque

lyr•ism (lĭr′ĭz′əm) *n.* Lyricism. [Fr. *lyrisme* < Gk. *lurismos*, played on the lyre < *lura*, lyre.]

lyr•ist (lĭr′ĭst) *n.* **1.** *Mus.* See **lyricist. 2.** (līr′ĭst). *Mus.* One who plays a lyre. **3.** A lyric poet. [Lat. *lyristēs*, lyre player < Gk. *luristēs* < *lura*, lyre.]

Lys (lēs). A river rising in N France and flowing c. 217 km (135 mi) NE to the Scheldt R.

lys– *pref.* Var. of **lyso–.**

Ly•san•der (lī-săn′dər). d. 395 B.C. Spartan military leader who defeated Athens (404) in the Peloponnesian War.

lyse (līs, līz) *intr. & tr.v.* **lysed, lys•ing, lys•es.** To undergo or cause to undergo lysis. [Back-formation < LYSIS.]

Ly•sen•ko (lĭ-sĕng′kō, -syĕn′kə), **Trofim Denisovich.** 1898–1976. Soviet biologist and director of the Institute of Genetics of the Soviet Academy of Sciences (1940–64).

Ly•sen•ko•ism (lĭ-sĕng′kō-ĭz′əm) *n.* A biological doctrine developed by Trofim Lysenko that maintains the possibility of inheriting environmentally acquired characteristics.

ly•ser•gic acid (lĭ-sûr′jĭk, lī-) *n.* A crystalline alkaloid, $C_{16}H_{16}N_2O_2$, derived from ergot and used in medical research as a psychotomimetic agent. [LYS(O)– + ERG(OT) + –IC.]

lysergic acid di•eth•yl•am•ide (dī′ĕth-əl-ăm′īd′) *n.* See **LSD**[1].

Ly•sim•a•chus (lī-sĭm′ə-kəs). 361?–281 B.C. Macedonian general who ruled the region from 287 to 286.

ly•sin (lī′sĭn) *n.* An antibody that causes lysis.

ly•sine (lī′sēn′, -sĭn) *n.* An essential amino acid, $C_6H_{14}N_2O_2$, derived from the hydrolysis of proteins and required by the body for optimum growth.

Ly•sip•pus (lī-sĭp′əs). fl. 4th cent. B.C. Greek sculptor who created figures that were more lifelike than traditional forms.

ly•sis (lī′sĭs) *n., pl.* **-ses** (-sēz). **1.** *Biochem.* The dissolution or destruction of cells, such as blood cells or bacteria, as by the action of a specific lysin. **2.** *Medic.* The gradual subsiding of the symptoms of an acute disease. [NLat. < Lat., a loosening < Gk. *lusis* < *luein*, to loosen. See **leu-***.]

–lysis *suff.* Decomposition; dissolving; disintegration: *electrolysis.* [NLat. < Gk. *lusis*, a loosening. See LYSIS.]

Ly•sith•e•a (lī-sĭth′ē-ə) *n.* A satellite of Jupiter. [Prob. < Gk. *Lusithoē*, daughter of Oceanus and mother of Herakles.]

lyso– or **lysi–** or **lys–** *pref.* Lysis: *lysin.* [< Gk. *lusis*, a loosening < *luein*, to loosen. See **leu-***.]

ly•so•gen (lī′sə-jən) *n.* A bacterium or bacterial strain that carries a prophage.

ly•so•gen•ic (lī′sə-jĕn′ĭk) *adj.* Carrying a prophage within the cell. Used of a bacterium.

ly•sog•e•nize (lī-sŏj′ĭ-nīz′) *tr.v.* **-nized, -niz•ing, -niz•es.** To make lysogenic. —**ly•sog′e•ni•za′tion** (-nĭ-zā′shən) *n.*

ly•sog•e•ny (lī-sŏj′ə-nē) *n.* The fusion of the nucleic acid of a bacteriophage with that of a host bacterium so that the potential exists for the newly integrated genetic material to be transmitted to daughter cells at each subsequent cell division.

Ly•sol (lī′sôl′, -sōl′, -sŏl′). A trademark used for a liquid antiseptic and disinfectant.

ly•so•some (lī′sə-sōm′) *n.* A membrane-bound organelle in the cytoplasm of most cells containing various hydrolytic enzymes that function in intracellular digestion.

ly•so•zyme (lī′sə-zīm′) *n.* An enzyme occurring naturally in egg white, human tears, saliva, and other body fluids, capable of destroying the cell walls of certain bacteria and thereby acting as a mild antiseptic.

–lyte *suff.* A substance that can be decomposed by a specified process: *electrolyte.* [< Gk. *lutos*, soluble < *luein*, to loosen. See **leu-***.]

lyt•ic (lĭt′ĭk) *adj.* **1.** Of, relating to, or causing lysis: *a lytic enzyme.* **2.** Of or relating to a lysin. [Gk. *lutikos*, able to loosen. See –LYTIC.]

–lytic *suff.* Of, relating to, or causing a specified kind of decomposition: *cellulolytic.* [< Gk. *lutikos*, able to loosen < *luein*, to loosen. See **leu-***.]

Lyt•ton (lĭt′n), First Baron. See Edward George Earle Lytton **Bulwer-Lytton.**

Lytton, First Earl of. Edward Robert Bulwer-Lytton. 1831–91. British politician who served as viceroy of India (1875–80) and ambassador to Paris (1887–91).

–lyze *suff.* To cause or undergo lysis: *pyrolyze.* [< –LYSIS.]

LZ *abbr.* Landing zone.

Mm

Douglas MacArthur
Photographed in 1945

m[1] or **M** (ĕm) *n., pl.* **m's** or **M's. 1.** The 13th letter of the modern English alphabet. **2.** Any of the speech sounds represented by the letter *m.* **3.** The 13th in a series.

m[2] *abbr.* **1.** Also **M.** *Print.* Em. **2.** *Phys.* Mass. **3.** Meter (measurement). **4.** Also **M.** *Phys.* Modulus.

M[1] also **m** The symbol for the Roman numeral 1,000.

M[2] *abbr.* **1.** *Bible.* Maccabees. **2.** Mach number. **3.** Metal. **4.** *Logic.* Middle term. **5.** *Chem.* Molar; molarity. **6.** *Phys.* Moment. **7.** *Phys.* Mutual inductance.

m. *abbr.* **1.** Or **M.** Male. **2.** Manual. **3.** Married. **4.** Or **M.** *Gram.* Masculine. **5.** Or **M.** Medium. **6.** Or **M.** *Lat.* Merides (noon). **7.** Or **M.** Meridian. **8.** Mile. **9.** Month. **10.** Morning.

M. *abbr.* **1.** Majesty. **2.** Mark (currency). **3.** Master. **4.** Medieval. **5.** Member. **6.** Mill (currency). **7.** Minim. **8.** Monday. **9.** Monsieur.

'm Am: *I'm feeling fine.*

ma (mä, mô) *n. Informal.* Mother. [Short for MAMA.]

mA *abbr.* Milliampere.

MA *abbr.* **1.** Maritime Administration. **2.** Massachusetts. **3.** Also **M.A.** Mental age.

M.A. or **MA** *abbr. Lat.* Magister Artium (Master of Arts).

ma'am (măm) *n.* Used as a form of polite address for a woman.

maar (mär) *n.* A circular volcanic crater of explosive origin that is often filled with water. [Ger. < VLat. **mara*, standing water, lake < Lat. *mare*, sea. See MARE[2].]

Maas (mäs). A section of the Meuse R. flowing through the S Netherlands to a joint delta with the Rhine R.

Maa•sai (mä-sī′, mä′sī) *n., pl.* **Maasai** or **-sais.** Var. of **Masai** 2.

Maas•tricht (mäs′trĭkt′, -trĭKHt′). A city of extreme SE Netherlands near the Belgian border; founded on the site of a Roman settlement. Pop. 113,277.

Ma•ble•ton (mā′bəl-tən). A community of NW GA, a suburb of Atlanta. Pop. 25,725.

mac (măk) *n. Chiefly British.* A mackintosh.

Mac (măk) *n. Slang.* Used as a form of address for a man whose name is unknown. [< *Mac-*, Scottish and Ir. surname pref.]

Mac. *abbr. Bible.* Maccabees.

ma•ca•bre (mə-kä′brə, mə-käb′, -kä′bər) *adj.* **1.** Suggesting the horror of death and decay; gruesome: *macabre tales of war.* **2.** Constituting or including a representation of death. [Ult. < OFr. *(Danse) Macabre*, (dance) of death, perh. alteration of *Macabe*, Maccabee < Lat. *Maccabaeus* < Gk. *Makkabios*.] — **ma·ca′bre·ly** *adv.*

ma·ca·co (mə-kä′kō) *n.*, *pl.* **-cos.** Any of various lemurs, esp. the species *Lemur macaco.* [Port., of Bantu orig.; akin to Kongo *ma-kako*, monkeys : *ma-*, pl. n. pref. + *kako*, monkey.]

mac·ad·am (mə-kăd′əm) *n.* Pavement of layers of compacted broken stone, now usu. bound with tar or asphalt. [After John L. *McAdam* (1756–1836), Scottish engineer.]

mac·a·da·mi·a nut (măk′ə-dā′mē-ə) *n.* The round hard-shelled nut or the edible seed of the Australian tree *Macadamia ternifolia.* [NLat. *Macadamia*, genus name, after John *Macadam* (1827–65), Scottish-born Australian chemist.]

mac·ad·am·ize (mə-kăd′ə-mīz′) *tr.v.* **-ized, -iz·ing, -iz·es.** To construct or pave (a road) with macadam. — **mac·ad′am·i·za′tion** (-ə-mĭ-zā′shən) *n.* — **mac·ad′am·iz′er** *n.*

Ma·cao also **Ma·cau** (mə-kou′). A Portuguese overseas province comprising **Macao Peninsula** and two offshore islands in the South China Sea W of Hong Kong; slated to come under Chinese control in 1999. The city of **Macao**, coextensive with the peninsula, is the cap. Pop. 350,000.

ma·caque (mə-kăk′, -käk′) *n.* Any of several short-tailed monkeys of the genus *Macaca* of southeast Asia, Japan, and northern Africa. [Fr. < Port. *macaco.* See MACACO.]

mac·a·ro·ni (măk′ə-rō′nē) *n.* **1.** *pl.* **macaroni.** A paste or pasta of wheat flour pressed into hollow tubes or other shapes, dried, and prepared for eating by boiling. **2.** *pl.* **macaronis** or **-nies. a.** A well-traveled young Englishman of the 18th and 19th centuries with foreign affectations. **b.** A fop. [Ital. dial. *maccaroni*, pl. of *maccarone*, dumpling, macaroni.]

mac·a·ron·ic (măk′ə-rŏn′ĭk) *adj.* **1.** Of or containing a mixture of vernacular words with Latin words or with vernacular words given Latinate endings. **2.** Of or involving a mixture of two or more languages. [NLat. *macaronicus* < Ital. dial. *maccarone*, dumpling, macaroni.] — **mac′a·ron′ic** *n.*

mac·a·roon (măk′ə-ro͞on′) *n.* A chewy cookie made with sugar, egg whites, and almond paste or coconut. [Fr. *macaron* < Ital. dial. *maccarone*, dumpling, macaroni.]

Mac·Ar·thur (mĭk-är′thər), **Charles.** 1895–1956. Amer. playwright who cowrote *The Front Page* (1928) with Ben Hecht.

MacArthur, Douglas. 1880–1964. Amer. general who served as U.S. chief of staff (1930–35), commanded Allied forces in the South Pacific during World War II, and led United Nations forces in Korea (1950–51).

Ma·cau·lay (mə-kô′lē), Dame **Rose.** 1881–1958. British writer whose witty urbane novels include *Potterism* (1920).

Macaulay, Thomas Babington. 1st Baron Macaulay. 1800–59. British historian noted for his *History of England* (1849–61).

ma·caw (mə-kô′) *n.* Any of various parrots of the genera *Ara* and *Anodorhynchus* of Central and South America, characterized by long tails, curved bills, and usu. brilliant plumage. [Port. *macaú* < *macaúba*, kind of palm tree < Tupi *macahuba*, palm tree : *maca*, palm + *ybá*, tree.]

Mac·beth (mək-bĕth′). d. 1057. King of Scotland (1040–57) who ascended the throne after killing King Duncan in battle.

Mac·Bride (mĭk-brīd′), **Sean.** 1904–88. Irish politician who shared the 1974 Nobel Peace Prize.

Macc. *abbr. Bible.* Maccabees.

Mac·ca·bees (măk′ə-bēz′) *pl.n. Bible.* **1.** A family of Jewish patriots of the 2nd and 1st cent. B.C., active in the liberation of Judea from Syrian rule. **2.** See table at **Bible.** — **Mac′ca·be′an** *adj.*

Mac·ca·be·us also **Mac·ca·bae·us** (măk′ə-bē′əs), **Judas** or **Judah.** d. 160 B.C. Jewish patriot of the Maccabees family who rededicated the Temple at Jerusalem (164 B.C.).

Mac·don·ald (mĭk-dŏn′əld), Sir **John Alexander.** 1815–91. Canadian politician and first prime minister of the Dominion of Canada (1867–73 and 1878–91).

Mac·Don·ald (mĭk-dŏn′əld), **(James) Ramsay.** 1866–1937. British prime minister (1924 and 1929–35).

Mac·Dow·ell (mĭk-dou′əl), **Edward Alexander.** 1861–1908. Amer. composer whose works include *Sea Pieces* (1898).

mace[1] (mās) *n.* **1.** A ceremonial staff borne or displayed as the symbol of authority of a legislative body. **2.** A macebearer. **3.** A heavy medieval war club with a spiked or flanged metal head, used to crush armor. [ME < OFr. *masse* < VLat. **mattea* < Lat. *mateola*, mallet.]

mace[2] (mās) *n.* An aromatic spice made from the dried waxy covering that partly encloses the kernel of the nutmeg. [ME < OFr. < Med.Lat. *macis*, alteration of Lat. *macir*, fragrant ailanthus resin < Gk. *makir*.]

Mace (mās). An alternate trademark used for Chemical Mace.

mace·bear·er (mās′bâr′ər) *n.* One who bears an official mace.

Maced. *abbr.* Macedonian.

mac·é·doine (măs′ə-dwän′) *n.* **1.** A mixture of finely cut vegetables or fruits. **2.** A mixture; a medley. [Fr. < *Macédoine*, Macedonia (perh. from its ethnic variety).]

Mac·e·do·ni·a (măs′ĭ-dō′nē-ə, -dōn′yə). **1.** Also **Mac·e·don** (-dən, -dŏn′). An ancient kingdom of N Greece; a powerful empire under Philip II and his son Alexander the Great (4th cent. B.C.). **2.** A historical region of SE Europe on the Balkan Peninsula, including modern Macedonia, N Greece, and SW Bulgaria. **3.** A region of the S-central Balkan Peninsula S of Serbia; a constituent republic of Yugoslavia from 1946 to 1991. Cap. Skopje. Pop. 1,623,598.

Mac·e·do·ni·an (măs′ĭ-dō′nē-ən) *n.* **1.** A native or inhabitant of ancient or modern Macedonia. **2.** The language of ancient Macedonia, of uncertain affiliation within Indo-European. **3.** The Slavic language of modern Macedonia, closely related to Bulgarian. — **Mac′e·do′ni·an** *adj.*

Ma·cei·ó (măs′ā-ō′, mä′sā-). A city of NE Brazil on the Atlantic Ocean SSW of Recife. Pop. 375,771.

mac·er (mā′sər) *n.* A macebearer.

mac·er·ate (măs′ə-rāt′) *v.* **-at·ed, -at·ing, -ates.** — *tr.* **1.** To make soft by soaking or steeping in a liquid. **2.** To separate into constituents by soaking. **3.** To cause to become lean, usu. by starvation; emaciate. — *intr.* To become soft or separated into constituents by soaking. — *n.* (-ĭt). A substance produced by macerating. [Lat. *mācerāre*, *mācerāt-*. See **mag-***.] — **mac′er·a′tion** *n.* — **mac′er·a′tor, mac′er·at′er** *n.*

Mach also **mach** (mäk) *n.* Mach number.

Mach (mäk, mäKH), **Ernst.** 1838–1916. Austrian physicist and philosopher who maintained that knowledge is the organization of sensory experience.

mach. *abbr.* Machine; machinery; machinist.

mache also **mâche** (mäsh) *n.* See **corn salad.** [Fr. *mâche* < dial. *pomache* < VLat. **pōmasca* < Lat. *pōmum*, fruit.]

ma·chet·e (mə-shĕt′ē, -chĕt′ē) *n.* A large knife with a broad blade, used as a weapon and for cutting vegetation. [Sp., dim. of *macho*, sledge hammer, alteration of *mazo*, club, prob. < *maza*, mallet < VLat. **mattea*, mace. See MACE[1].]

Mach·i·a·vel·li (măk′ē-ə-vĕl′ē, mä′kyä-), **Niccolò.** 1469–1527. Italian philosopher known for his treatise on political expediency, *The Prince* (1513).

Niccolò Machiavelli
Detail of a portrait by Santi di Tito (1536–1603)

Mach·i·a·vel·li·an (măk′ē-ə-vĕl′ē-ən) *adj.* **1.** Of or relating to Machiavelli or Machiavellianism. **2.** Suggestive of or characterized by expediency, deceit, and cunning. — **Mach′i·a·vel′li·an, Mach′i·a·vel′list** *n.*

Mach·i·a·vel·li·an·ism (măk′ē-ə-vĕl′ē-ə-nĭz′əm) also **Mach·i·a·vel·lism** (-vĕl′ĭz′əm) *n.* The political doctrine of Machiavelli, which denies the relevance of morality in politics and justifies craft and deceit.

ma·chic·o·late (mə-chĭk′ə-lāt′) *tr.v.* **-lat·ed, -lat·ing, -lates.** To provide or furnish with machicolations. [Med.Lat. *machicolāre*, *machicolāt-* < OFr. *machicoller* < *machicoleis*, machicolation < OProv. *machacol* : *macar*, to crush (< VLat. **maccāre*) + *col*, neck (< Lat. *collum*; see **k^{w}el-**[1]*).]

machicolation

ma·chic·o·la·tion (mə-chĭk′ə-lā′shən) *n.* **1.a.** A projecting gallery at the top of a castle wall, supported by corbeled arches and having openings through which stones and boiling liquids could be dropped on attackers. **b.** Such an opening. **2.** A row of corbeled arches used ornamentally.

Ma·chi·da (mə-chē′də, mä-chē′dä). A city of E-central Honshu, Japan, a suburb of Tokyo. Pop. 321,182.

mach·i·nate (măk′ə-nāt′, măsh′-) *v.* **-nat·ed, -nat·ing, -nates.** — *tr.* To devise (a plot). — *intr.* To engage in plotting. [Lat. *māchinārī*, *māchināt-*, to design, contrive < *māchina*, device. See MACHINE.] — **mach′i·na′tor** *n.*

mach·i·na·tion (măk′ə-nā′shən, măsh′-) *n.* **1.** The act of plotting. **2.** A crafty scheme or cunning design for the accomplishment of a sinister end.

ma·chine (mə-shēn′) *n.* **1.a.** A device consisting of fixed and moving parts that modifies mechanical energy and transmits it in a more useful form. **b.** A simple device, such as a lever, that alters the magnitude or direction, or both, of an applied force; a simple machine. **2.** A system or device for doing work, as a jackhammer, together with its power source and auxiliary equipment. **3.** A system or device, such as a computer, that performs or helps perform a human task. **4.** An intricate natural system or organism, such as the human body. **5.** A person who acts in a rigid, mechanical, or unconscious manner. **6.** An organized group of people whose members are or appear to be under the control of one or more leaders. **7.a.** A device used to produce a stage effect, esp. a mechanical means of lowering an actor onto the stage. **b.** A literary device used to produce an effect, esp. to resolve a plot. — *adj.* Of, relating to, or felt to resemble a machine. — *v.* **-chined, -chin·ing, -chines.** — *tr.* To cut, shape, or finish by machine. — *intr.* To be cut, shaped, or finished by machine. [Fr. < OFr. < Lat. *māchina* < Gk. *mēkhanē*, *makhana*. See **magh-***.] — **ma·chin′a·ble** *adj.*

machine bolt *n.* A bolt with a square or hexagonal head.

machine code *n. Comp. Sci.* See **machine language.**

machine gun *n.* A gun that fires rapidly and repeatedly.

ma·chine-gun (mə-shēn′gŭn′) *tr.v.* **-gunned, -gun·ning, -guns.** To fire at or kill with a machine gun. — *adj.* Fast and staccato: *machine-gun speech.* — **machine gunner** *n.*

machine language *n. Comp. Sci.* A set of instructions coded so that the computer can use it without further translation.

machine pistol *n.* A lightweight automatic or semiautomatic submachine gun designed to be fired one-handed like a pistol.

ma·chine-read·a·ble (mə-shēn′rē′də-bəl) *adj. Comp. Sci.* Easy to feed directly into a computer, as magnetically stored data.

ă pat	oi boy
ā pay	ou out
âr care	o͝o took
ä father	o͞o boot
ĕ pet	ŭ cut
ē be	ûr urge
ĭ pit	th thin
ī pie	*th* this
îr pier	hw which
ŏ pot	zh vision
ō toe	ə about,
ô paw	item

Stress marks:
′ (primary);
′ (secondary), as in
dictionary (dĭk′shə-nĕr′ē)

ma•chin•er•y (mə-shē′nə-rē, -shēn′rē) *n., pl.* **-ies. 1.** Machines or machine parts considered as a group. **2.** The working parts of a particular machine. **3.** A system of related elements that operate in a definable manner. **4.a.** A device or means of achieving or effecting a result. **b.** A literary device for bringing about an effect.

machine screw *n.* A screw with a thread along the entire length of the shaft.

machine shop *n.* A workshop where power-driven tools are used to make, finish, or repair machines or machine parts.

machine tool *n.* A power-driven tool, such as a lathe, used for machining. **— ma•chine′-tooled′** (mə-shēn′to͞old′) *adj.*

machine translation *n.* Automatic translation, as by computer, from one language to another.

ma•chine-wash (mə-shēn′wŏsh′, -wôsh′) *tr. & intr.v.* **-washed, -wash•ing, -wash•es.** To wash or undergo washing in a washing machine.

mackerel
Atlantic mackerel
Scomber scombrus

ma•chin•ist (mə-shē′nĭst) *n.* **1.** One who is skilled in operating machine tools. **2.** One who makes, operates, or repairs machines. **3.** A warrant officer who assists the engineering officer in the engine room of a naval vessel. **4.** *Archaic.* A person in charge of stage machinery.

ma•chis•mo (mä-chēz′mō) *n.* A strong sense of masculinity usu. entailing aggressiveness, domination of women, virility, and physical courage. [Sp. < *macho,* male. See MACHO.]

Mach•me•ter (mäk′mē′tər) *n.* An aircraft instrument that indicates speed in Mach numbers.

Mach number also **mach number** (mäk) *n.* The ratio of the speed of an object to the speed of sound in the surrounding medium. [After Ernst MACH.]

ma•cho (mä′chō) *adj.* Characterized or motivated by machismo. *— n., pl.* **-chos. 1.** Machismo. **2.** A person characterized by or exhibiting machismo. [Sp., male < Lat. *masculus.* See MASCULINE.] **— ma′cho•ism** *n.*

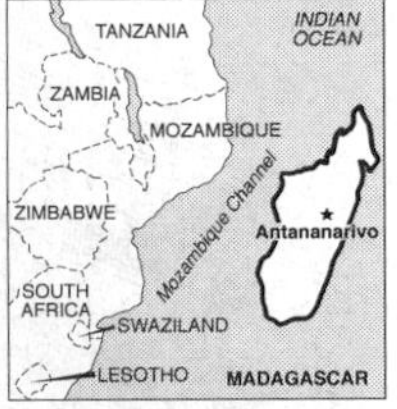

Madagascar

Ma•chu Pic•chu (mä′cho͞o pēk′cho͞o, pē′-). An ancient Inca fortress city in the Andes NW of Cuzco, Peru.

mach•zor (mäкн′zôr′, -zər, mäкн-zōr′) *n.* Var. of **mahzor.**

mac•in•tosh (măk′ĭn-tŏsh′) *n.* Var. of **mackintosh.**

Ma•cke (mä′kə), **August.** 1887–1914. German painter whose works include *Lady in a Green Jacket* (1913).

Mac•ken•zie (mə-kĕn′zē), **Alexander.** 1822–92. British-born Canadian politician who served as prime minister (1873–78).

Mackenzie, Sir **Alexander.** 1764–1820. British-born Canadian explorer who navigated the Mackenzie R. (1789).

Mackenzie, William Lyon. 1795–1861. British-born Canadian politician who led an armed insurrection in Toronto (1837) to protest colonial rule.

Mackenzie District. A former district of W and central Northwest Terrs., Canada.

Mackenzie Mountains. A range of the N Rocky Mts. in E Yukon Terr. and W Northwest Terrs., Canada, rising to 2,973.8 m (9,750 ft).

Mackenzie River. A river of NW Canada rising in Great Slave Lake in S Northwest Terrs. and flowing c. 1,802 km (1,120 mi) to **Mackenzie Bay,** an arm of the Beaufort Sea.

mack•er•el (măk′ər-əl, măk′rəl) *n., pl.* **mackerel** or **-els. 1.** Any of several marine fishes of the family Scombridae, esp. the Atlantic mackerel *(Scomber scombrus),* an important food fish. **2.** Any of the smaller fishes of the suborder Scombroidea, such as the Spanish mackerel. **3.** Any of various similar fishes. [ME *makerel* < OFr. *maquerel.*]

mackerel shark *n.* Any of various sharks of the family Lamnidae, including the great white shark, having a nearly symmetrical tail and a reputation for aggressiveness.

mackerel sky *n. Northeastern U.S.* A sky with many small cirrocumulus or altocumulus clouds, suggestive of the markings on a mackerel. Also called regionally *buttermilk sky.*

Dolley Madison
Detail of an 1804 portrait by Gilbert Stuart

Mack•i•nac Island (măk′ə-nô′). An island of N MI in the **Straits of Mackinac,** a passage connecting Lakes Huron and Michigan between the Upper and Lower peninsulas.

mack•i•naw (măk′ə-nô′) *n.* **1.** A short double-breasted coat of heavy, usu. plaid material. **2.** The cloth from which such a coat is made, usu. of wool, often with a heavy nap. **3.** *Naut.* A flatbottom boat with a pointed bow and square stern, once used on the upper Great Lakes. [After Old *Mackinac,* a fort on the site of *Mackinaw City* in N MI.]

Mack•i•naw blanket (măk′ə-nô′) *n.* A thick blanket in solid colors or stripes.

Mackinaw trout *n.* See **lake trout.**

mack•in•tosh also **mac•in•tosh** (măk′ĭn-tŏsh′) *n. Chiefly British.* **1.** A raincoat. **2.** A lightweight waterproof fabric that was originally of rubberized cotton. [After Charles *Macintosh* (1766–1843), Scottish inventor.]

mack•le (măk′əl) also **mac•ule** (măk′yo͞ol′) *— n.* A blurred or double impression in printing. *— v.* **-led, -ling, -les** also **-uled, -ul•ing, -ules.** *— tr.* To blur or double (a printed impression). *— intr.* To become blurred. [ME *macule,* spot < OFr. < Lat. *macula.*]

mac•le (măk′əl) *n.* **1.** Chiastolite. **2.** A twinned crystal. **3.** A dark spot or discoloration in a mineral. [Fr. < OFr., lozenge < Lat. *macula,* mesh.]

Mac•Leish (mĭk-lēsh′), **Archibald.** 1892–1982. Amer. poet who served as Librarian of Congress (1939–44).

Mac•Len•nan (mə-klĕn′ən), **Hugh.** b 1907. Canadian writer whose novels include *Two Solitudes* (1945).

Mac•leod (mə-kloud′), **John James Rickard.** 1876–1935. British physiologist who shared a 1923 Nobel Prize.

Mac•mil•lan (mĭk-mĭl′ən), **(Maurice) Harold.** 1894–1986. British politician who served as prime minister (1957–63).

Mac•Mil•lan (mĭk-mĭl′ən), **Donald Baxter.** 1874–1970. Amer. explorer noted for his use of aircraft in several Arctic explorations between 1913 and 1937.

Mac•Neice (mĭk-nēs′), **(Frederick) Louis.** 1907–63. Irish-born British poet whose works include *Blind Fireworks* (1929).

Ma•comb (mə-kōm′). A city of western IL WSW of Peoria. Pop. 19,952.

Ma•con (mā′kən). A city of central GA SE of Atlanta; settled in the early 1820's. Pop. 106,612.

Mâ•con (mä-kôɴ′). A city of E-central France on the Saône R. N of Lyons; noted for its Burgundy wines. Pop. 38,404.

Mac•pher•son (mək-fûr′sən), **James.** 1736–96. Scottish poet who claimed to have translated the works of Ossian, a 3rd-cent. A.D. Gaelic poet and warrior.

Mac•quar•ie (mə-kwär′ē, -kwôr′ē). A river of SE Australia flowing c. 949 km (590 mi) to the Darling R.

mac•ra•mé (măk′rə-mā′) *n.* Coarse lace work made by weaving and knotting cords into a pattern. [Fr. < Ital. *macramè* < Turk. *makrama,* towel < Ar. *miqramah,* embroidered veil.]

mac•ro (măk′rō′) *n., pl.* **-ros.** *Comp. Sci.* A single instruction in programming language that results in a series of instructions in machine language. [Short for MACROINSTRUCTION.]

macro– or **macr–** *pref.* **1.** Large: *macronucleus.* **2.** Long: *macrobiotics.* **3.** Inclusive: *macroinstruction.* [Gk. *makro-* < *makros,* large. See **māk-*.**]

mac•ro•bi•ot•ics (măk′rō-bī-ŏt′ĭks) *n. (used with a sing. v.)* The theory or practice of promoting well-being and longevity, principally by means of a diet consisting chiefly of whole grains and beans. **— mac′ro•bi•ot′ic** *adj.*

mac•ro•ceph•a•ly (măk′rō-sĕf′ə-lē) also **mac•ro•ce•pha•li•a** (-sə-fā′lē-ə, -fāl′yə) *n.* Abnormal largeness of the head. **— mac′ro•ce•phal′ic** (-sə-făl′ĭk), **mac′ro•ceph′a•lous** *adj.*

mac•ro•cli•mate (măk′rō-klī′mĭt) *n.* The climate of a large geographic area. **— mac′ro•cli•mat′ic** (-măt′ĭk) *adj.*

mac•ro•cosm (măk′rə-kŏz′əm) *n.* **1.** The entire world; the universe. **2.** A system reflecting on a large scale one of its component systems or parts. [Med.Lat. *macrocosmus* : Gk. *makro-,* macro- + Gk. *kosmos,* world.] **— mac′ro•cos′mic** *adj.* **— mac′ro•cos′mic•al•ly** *adv.*

mac•ro•cyte (măk′rō-sīt′) *n.* An abnormally large red blood cell, esp. one associated with pernicious anemia.

mac•ro•ec•o•nom•ics (măk′rō-ĕk′ə-nŏm′ĭks, -ē′kə-) *n. (used with a sing. v.)* The study of the overall aspects and workings of a national economy. **— mac′ro•ec′o•nom′ic** *adj.* **— mac′ro•e•con′o•mist** (-ĭ-kŏn′ə-mĭst) *n.*

mac•ro•ev•o•lu•tion (măk′rō-ĕv′ə-lo͞o′shən, -ē′və-) *n.* Large-scale evolution occurring over geologic time that results in the formation of new taxonomic groups.

mac•ro•gam•ete (măk′rō-găm′ēt, -gə-mēt′) *n.* The larger, usu. female of two conjugating gametes in a heterogamous organism.

ma•crog•ra•phy (mə-krŏg′rə-fē) *n.* **1.** Examination of objects with the unaided eye. **2.** Abnormally large handwriting, sometimes indicating a nervous disorder.

mac•ro•in•struc•tion (măk′rō-ĭn-strŭk′shən) *n. Comp. Sci.* A macro.

mac•ro•mere (măk′rə-mîr′) *n. Embryol.* A large blastomere.

mac•ro•mol•e•cule (măk′rō-mŏl′ĭ-kyo͞ol′) *n.* A large molecule, such as a protein, consisting of many smaller units linked together. **— mac′ro•mo•lec′u•lar** (-mə-lĕk′yə-lər) *adj.*

ma•cron (mā′krŏn′, -krən, măk′rŏn′) *n.* **1.** A symbol (¯) placed over a vowel indicating a long sound, as the *a* in *make.* **2.** A horizontal mark used to indicate a stressed or long syllable in verse. [Gk. *makron* < neut. of *makros,* long. See **māk-*.**]

mac•ro•nu•cle•us (măk′rō-no͞o′klē-əs, -nyo͞o′-) *n., pl.* **-cle•i** (-klē-ī′). The larger of two nuclei present in ciliate protozoans, which controls nonreproductive functions of the cell, such as metabolism. **— mac′ro•nu′cle•ar** *adj.*

mac•ro•nu•tri•ent (măk′rō-no͞o′trē-ənt, -nyo͞o′-) *n.* An element, such as carbon, required in large proportion for the normal growth and development of a plant.

mac•ro•phage (măk′rə-fāj′) *n.* Any of the large phagocytic cells of the reticuloendothelial system. **— mac′ro•phag′ic** (-făj′ĭk) *adj.*

mac•ro•phyte (măk′rə-fīt′) *n.* A macroscopic plant.

ma•crop•ter•ous (mə-krŏp′tər-əs) *adj.* Having very large fins or wings.

mac•ro•scop•ic (măk′rə-skŏp′ĭk) also **mac•ro•scop•i•cal** (-ĭ-kəl) *adj.* **1.** Large enough to be perceived or examined by the unaided eye. **2.** Relating to observations made by the unaided eye. **— mac′ro•scop′i•cal•ly** *adv.*

macroscopic anatomy *n.* See **gross anatomy.**

mac•ro•spo•ran•gi•um (măk′rō-spə-răn′jē-əm) *n., pl.* **-gi•a** (-jē-ə). See **megasporangium.**

mac•ro•spore (măk′rə-spôr′, -spōr′) *n.* See **megaspore.**

mac•u•la (măk′yə-lə) *n., pl.* **-lae** (-lē′) or **-las. 1.** Also **mac•ule** (-yo͞ol′). A spot, stain, or blemish, esp. an area of discoloration on the skin caused by excess or lack of pigment. **2.** *Anat.* A small area distinguishable from the surrounding tissue. **3.** A sunspot. [ME < Lat.] **—mac′u•lar** *adj.*

macula lu•te•a (lo͞o′tē-ə) *n., pl.* **maculae lu•te•ae** (lo͞o′tē-ē′). A minute yellowish area containing the fovea centralis located near the center of the retina where visual perception is most acute. [NLat. *macula lūtea* : Lat. *macula*, spot + Lat. *lūtea*, yellow.]

mac•u•late (măk′yə-lāt′) *tr.v.* **-lat•ed, -lat•ing, -lates.** To spot, blemish, or pollute. —*adj.* (-lĭt). **1.** Spotted or blotched. **2.** Stained; impure. [ME *maculaten* < Lat. *maculāre, maculāt-* < *macula*, spot.]

mac•u•la•tion (măk′yə-lā′shən) *n.* **1.** The act of spotting or staining or the condition of being spotted or stained. **2.** The spotted markings of a plant or an animal.

mac•ule[1] (măk′yo͞ol′) *n. & v.* Var. of **mackle.**

mac•ule[2] (măk′yo͞ol′) *n.* Var. of **macula** 1.

mad (măd) *adj.* **mad•der, mad•dest. 1.** Angry; resentful. **2.** Suffering from a disorder of the mind; insane. **3.** Temporarily or apparently deranged, as by violent emotions. **4.** Lacking restraint or reason; foolish. **5.** Feeling or showing strong liking or enthusiasm. **6.** Marked by extreme excitement, confusion, or agitation; frantic. **7.** Boisterously gay; hilarious. **8.** Affected by rabies; rabid. —*tr. & intr.v.* **mad•ded, mad•ding, mads.** To make or become mad; madden. —***idiom.*** **like mad.** *Informal.* **1.** Wildly; impetuously. **2.** To an intense degree or great extent. [ME < OE *gemǣdde*, p.part. of **gemǣdan*, to madden < *gemād*, insane. See **mei-**[1]*.] **—mad′dish** *adj.*

Mad. *abbr.* Madagascar.

Mad•a•gas•car (măd′ə-găs′kər). Formerly **Mal•a•gas•y Republic** (măl′ə-găs′ē) A country in the Indian Ocean off SE Africa comprising the island of **Madagascar** and several small islands; gained independence from France in 1960. Cap. Antananarivo. Pop. 9,230,000. **—Mad′a•gas′can** *adj. & n.*

Madagascar periwinkle *n.* A perennial plant *(Catharanthus roseus)* native to Madagascar and India that has flowers with a salverform corolla and is poisonous to domestic animals.

Mad•am (măd′əm) *n.* **1.** *pl.* **Mes•dames** (mā-dăm′, -däm′). Used formerly as a courtesy title before a woman's given name but now used only before a surname or title indicating rank or office: *Madam Ambassador.* **2.** Used as a salutation in a letter: *Dear Madam or Sir.* **3. madam.** Used as a form of polite address for a woman. **4. madam.** The mistress of a household. **5. madam.** A woman who manages a brothel. [ME *madame* < OFr. *ma dame.* See MADAME.]

Ma•dame (mə-dăm′, măd′əm) *n., pl.* **Mes•dames** (mā-dăm′, -däm′). **1.** Used as a courtesy title before the surname or full name of a married woman in a French-speaking area. **2. madame.** Used as a form of polite address for a woman in a French-speaking area. [Fr. < OFr. *ma dame* : *ma*, my (< Lat. *mea*, fem. of *meus*; see **me-**[1]*) + *dame*, lady (< Lat. *domina*, fem. of *dominus*, lord, master of a household; see **dem-***).]

mad•cap (măd′kăp′) *adj.* Behaving or acting impulsively or rashly; wild. [MAD + CAP[1], head.] **—mad′cap′** *n.*

MADD *abbr.* Mothers Against Drunk Driving.

mad•den (măd′n) *v.* **-dened, -den•ing, -dens.** —*tr.* **1.** To make angry; irritate. **2.** To drive insane. —*intr.* To become infuriated.

mad•den•ing (măd′n-ĭng) *adj.* **1.** Tending to anger or irritate. **2.** Tending to drive insane. **—mad′den•ing•ly** *adv.*

mad•der (măd′ər) *n.* **1.a.** A southwest Asian perennial plant *(Rubia tinctorum)* having small yellow flowers, whorled leaves, and a red root. **b.** The root of this plant, formerly a source of the dye alizarin. **c.** A red dye obtained from the roots of this plant. **2.** *Color.* A medium to strong red or reddish orange. [ME < OE *mædere.*]

mad•ding (măd′ĭng) *adj. Archaic.* In a state of frenzy.

made (mād) *v.* P.t. and p.part. of **make.** —*adj.* **1.** Produced or manufactured by constructing, shaping, or forming. Often used in combination: *handmade lace.* **2.** Produced or created artificially: *bought some made goods.* **3.** Having been invented; contrived. **4.** Assured of success: *a made woman.* —***idiom.*** **made for.** Perfectly suited for: *made for each other.*

Ma•dei•ra[1] (mə-dîr′ə, -dĕr′ə). A river of NW Brazil rising on the Bolivian border and flowing c. 3,315 km (2,060 mi) to the Amazon R. near Manaus.

Ma•dei•ra[2] (mə-dîr′ə) *n.* A fortified dessert wine, esp. from the island of Madeira.

Madeira Islands. An archipelago of Portugal in the NE Atlantic W of Morocco. **—Ma•dei′ran** *adj. & n.*

mad•e•leine (măd′ə-lĕn′) *n.* A small rich cake, baked in a shell-shaped mold. [After *Madeleine* Paulmier, 19th-cent. French pastry cook.]

Mad•e•moi•selle (măd′ə-mə-zĕl′, măd-mwä-zĕl′) *n., pl.* **Mad•e•moi•selles** (-zĕlz) or **Mes•de•moi•selles** (mād′-mwä-zĕl′). **1.** Used as a courtesy title before the surname or full name of a girl or an unmarried woman in a French-speaking area. **2. mademoiselle.** Used as a form of polite address for a girl or young woman in a French-speaking area. **3. mademoiselle,** *pl.* **mademoiselles.** A French governess. **4. mademoiselle,** *pl.* **mademoiselle** or **-selles.** See **silver perch.** [Fr. < OFr. *ma demoiselle* : *ma*, my; see MADAME + *demoiselle*, young lady (< *damisele* < VLat. **dominicella*, dim. of Lat. *domina*, lady, fem. of *dominus*, master of a household; see **dem-***).]

Ma•de•ra (mə-dĕr′ə). A city of central CA in the San Joaquin Valley NW of Fresno. Pop. 29,281.

Ma•de•ro (mə-dĕr′ō, mä-*th*ĕ′rô), **Francisco Indalecio.** 1873–1913. Mexican revolutionary who forced the resignation of Porfirio Díaz and assumed the presidency (1911).

made-to-or•der (măd′to͞o-ôr′dər) *adj.* **1.** Made to fit instructions or requirements; custom-made. **2.** Very suitable.

made-up (mād′ŭp′) *adj.* **1.** Having been fabricated; invented. **2.** Changed or adorned by the application of cosmetics or makeup. **3.a.** Complete; finished. **b.** Put together; arranged.

mad•house (măd′hous′) *n.* **1.** A mental health facility. **2.** *Informal.* A place of great disorder and confusion.

Mad•i•son (măd′ĭ-sən). The cap. of WI, in the S-central part W of Milwaukee; settled in 1836. Pop. 191,262.

Madison, Dolley Payne Todd. 1768–1849. First Lady of the U.S. (1809–17). She earlier served as White House hostess for the widowed Thomas Jefferson.

Madison, James. 1751–1836. The fourth President of the U.S. (1809–17). A member of the Constitutional Convention (1787) and a contributor to *The Federalist Papers* (1787–88). **—Mad′i•so′ni•an** (-sō′nē-ən) *adj.*

James Madison

Madison Avenue *n.* The American advertising industry. [After *Madison Avenue* in New York City.] **—Madison Avenue** *adj.*

Madison Heights. A city of SE MI, a suburb of Detroit. Pop. 32,196.

Mad•i•son•ville (măd′ĭ-sən-vĭl′). A city of W KY N of Hopkinsville. Pop. 16,200.

mad•ly (măd′lē) *adv.* **1.** In a crazy way; insanely. **2.** In a wild manner; frantically. **3.** In a foolish manner; rashly.

mad•man (măd′măn′, -mən) *n.* A man who is or seems to be mentally ill.

mad money *n. Slang.* A small sum of money kept for unlikely contingencies.

mad•ness (măd′nĭs) *n.* **1.** The quality or condition of being insane. See Syns at **insanity. 2.** Great folly. **3.** Fury; rage. **4.** Enthusiasm; excitement.

Ma•don•na (mə-dŏn′ə) *n.* **1.** The Virgin Mary. **2.** *Obsolete.* Used as a form of polite address for a married woman in an Italian-speaking area. [Ital. : *mia, ma*, my (< Lat. *mea*; see MADAME) + *donna*, lady (< Lat. *domina*, fem. of *dominus*, master of a household; see **dem-***).]

Madonna lily *n.* An eastern Mediterranean plant *(Lilium candidum)* having white bell-shaped flowers.

madroña
Arbutus menziesii

mad•ras (măd′rəs, mə-drăs′, -dräs′) *n.* **1.** A cotton cloth of fine texture, usu. with a plaid, striped, or checked pattern. **2.** A silk, generally striped cloth. **3.** A light cotton or rayon cloth used for drapery. **4.** A large handkerchief of brightly colored silk or cotton, often worn as a turban. [After MADRAS.]

Ma•dras (mə-drăs′, -dräs′). A city of SE India on the Coromandel Coast of the Bay of Bengal; founded by the British East India Company in 1639. Pop. 3,276,622.

ma•dra•sah (mä′drä-sä) *n.* An institute for higher education in Islamic studies.

Ma•dre de Di•os (mä′drā dā dē-ōs′, mä′*th*rĕ *th*ĕ dyôs′). A river of SE Peru and NW Bolivia flowing c. 1,126 km (700 mi) from the Andes to the Beni R.

mad•re•pore (măd′rə-pôr′, -pōr′) *n.* Any of various stony corals of the order Madreporaria, which includes the reef builders of tropical seas. [Ital. *madrepora* : *madre*, mother (< Lat. *māter, mātr-*; see **māter-***) + *-pora* (alteration of *poro*, tufa, pore < LLat. *porus*, passageway; see PORE[2], or < Lat. *pōrus*, calcareous stone, stalactite < Gk. *pōros*).] **—mad′re•po′ri•an, mad′re•por′ic** *adj.*

mad•re•por•ite (măd′rə-pôr′īt, -pōr′-) *n.* A perforated platelike structure in most echinoderms that forms the intake for their water-vascular systems. [So called because the perforations resemble those of a madrepore.]

Ma•drid (mə-drĭd′). The cap. of Spain, on the central plateau NNE of Toledo; became cap. in 1561. Pop. 3,200,234.

mad•ri•gal (măd′rĭ-gəl) *n.* **1.a.** *Mus.* An unaccompanied vocal composition for two or three voices, following a poetic form and developed in Italy in the late 13th and early 14th centuries. **b.** A short poem, often about love, suitable for being set to music. **2.** *Mus.* **a.** A polyphonic song using a secular text and intended for four to six voices, developed in Italy in the 16th century. **b.** A part song. [Ital. *madrigale*, prob. < dial. *madregal*, simple < LLat. *mātrīcālis*, invented, original < Lat., of the womb < *mātrix, mātrīc-*, womb < *māter, mātr-*, mother. See MATER.] **—mad′ri•gal•ist** *n.*

ma•dri•lène also **ma•dri•lene** (măd′rĭ-lĕn′) *n.* A consommé flavored with tomato, often served jellied and chilled. [Fr. *(consommé) madrilène*, Madrid (consommé) < Sp. *madrileño*, of Madrid < MADRID.]

ma•dro•ña (mə-drō′nyə) also **ma•dro•ño** (-drō′nyō) or **ma•dro•ne** (-drō′nə) *n., pl.* **-ñas** also **-ños** or **-nes.** An evergreen

ă pat	oi boy
ā pay	ou out
âr care	o͝o took
ä father	o͞o boot
ĕ pet	ŭ cut
ē be	ûr urge
ĭ pit	th thin
ī pie	*th* this
îr pier	hw which
ŏ pot	zh vision
ō toe	ə about,
ô paw	item

Stress marks:
′ (primary);
′ (secondary), as in
dictionary (dĭk′shə-nĕr′ē)

tree *(Arbutus menziesii)* native to Pacific North America and having leathery glossy leaves and orange or red edible berries. [Am.Sp. < Sp. *madroño,* strawberry tree.]

mad tom *n.* Any of several small freshwater North American catfishes of the genus *Noturus,* having poisonous spines.

Ma•du•rai (mä′də-rī′, măd′yo͞o-rī′). A city of S India SSW of Madras; a Hindu pilgrimage site. Pop. 820,891.

mad•wom•an (măd′wo͝om′ən) *n.* A woman who is or seems to be mentally ill.

mad•wort (măd′wûrt′, -wôrt′) *n.* **1.** A low-growing Eurasian plant *(Asperugo procumbens)* having rough stems and small blue flowers. **2.** See **alyssum** 2.

M.A.E. *abbr.* **1.** Master of Aeronautical Engineering. **2.** Master of Art Education. **3.** Master of Arts in Education.

Mae•an•der (mē-ăn′dər). The Menderes R. of W Turkey.

Mae•ce•nas (mē-sē′nəs, mī-), **Gaius.** 70?–8 B.C. Roman politician and patron of Horace and Virgil.

M.A.Ed. *abbr.* Master of Arts in Education.

mael•strom (māl′strəm) *n.* **1.** A violent or turbulent situation. **2.** A whirlpool of extraordinary size or violence. [Obsolete Du. : Du. *malen,* to grind, whirl (< MDu.; see **melə-***) + Du. *stroom,* stream (< MDu.; see **sreu-***).]

mae•nad (mē′năd′) *n.* **1.** *Gk. Myth.* A woman in the orgiastic cult of Dionysus. **2.** A frenzied woman. [Lat. *Maenas, Maenad-* < Gk. *mainas,* raving, madwoman, Maenad < *mainesthai,* to be mad. See **men-¹***.]

ma•es•to•so (mä-ĕs-tō′sō, -zō) *adv. & adj. Mus.* In a majestic and stately manner. [Ital. < *maestà,* majesty, greatness < Lat. *māiestās.* See **meg-***.]

maes•tro (mīs′trō) *n., pl.* **-tros** or **-tri** (-trē). A master in an art, esp. a composer, conductor, or music teacher. [Ital. < Lat. *magister, magistr-,* master. See **meg-***.]

Mae•ter•linck (mā′tər-lĭngk′, mĕt′ər-, mä-tĕr-lăɴ′), Count **Maurice.** 1862–1949. Belgian writer who won the 1911 Nobel Prize for literature.

Mae West (mā′ wĕst′) *n.* An inflatable vestlike life preserver. [After Mae WEST.]

Maf•e•king (mä′fĭ-kĭng′). Now **Maf•i•keng** (-kĕng′). A town of N-central South Africa W of Pretoria; site of a 217-day siege of a British garrison during the Boer War (1899–1900). Pop. 6,500.

maf•fick (măf′ĭk) *intr.v.* **-ficked, -fick•ing, -ficks.** *Chiefly British.* To rejoice or celebrate with boisterous public demonstrations. [After MAFEKING.]

Ma•fi•a (mä′fē-ə) *n.* **1.** A secret terrorist organization in Sicily, operating since the early 19th century in opposition to legal authority. **2.** An international criminal organization active, esp. in Italy and the United States, since the late 19th century. **3.** Often **mafia.** *Informal.* A tightly knit group of trusted associates, as of a political leader. [Ital., perh. < dial. *mafia,* bluster, boldness.]

maf•ic (măf′ĭk) *adj.* Containing or relating to a group of dark-colored minerals, composed chiefly of magnesium and iron, in igneous rocks. [MA(GNESIUM) + Lat. *ferrum,* iron + –IC.]

Ma•fi•o•so (mä′fē-ō′sō) *n., pl.* **-si** (-sē) or **-sos.** A member of the Mafia. [Ital. < *mafia,* mafia. See MAFIA.]

mag (măg) *n. Slang.* A magazine: *surfing mags.*

mag. *abbr.* **1.** Magnet. **2.** Magnetism. **3.** Magneto. **4.** Magnitude.

Ma•ga•dha (mä′gə-də). An ancient kingdom of NE India; esp. powerful from the 4th cent. B.C. to the 5th cent. A.D.

mag•a•zine (măg′ə-zēn′, măg′ə-zēn′) *n.* **1.** A periodical containing articles, stories, pictures, or other features. **2.a.** A place where goods, esp. ammunition and explosives, are stored. **b.** The contents of a storehouse, esp. a stock of ammunition. **3.a.** A compartment in some types of firearms, often detachable, from which cartridges are fed into the firing chamber. **b.** A compartment in a camera from which rolls or cartridges of film are fed through the exposure mechanism. **c.** Any of various compartments attached to machines, used for storing or supplying necessary material. —*adj.* Of or relating to periodicals. [Fr. *magasin,* storehouse < OFr. *magazin* (poss. via OItal. *magazzino*) < Ar. *maḫāzin,* pl. of *maḫzan* < *ḫazana,* to store.]

Mag•da•le•na (măg′də-lā′nə, mäg′*th*ä-lĕ′nä). A river rising in the Andes of SW Colombia and flowing c. 1,601 km (1,000 mi) to the Caribbean Sea.

Mag•da•le•ni•an (măg′də-lē′nē-ən) *adj. Archaeol.* Of or relating to the last upper Paleolithic culture of Europe, succeeding the Aurignacian. [Fr. *magdalénien,* after La *Madeleine,* a prehistoric site of SW France.]

Mag•de•burg (măg′də-bûrg′, mäg′də-bo͝ork′). A city of central Germany on the Elbe R. WSW of Berlin. Pop. 289,075.

Ma•gel•lan (mə-jĕl′ən), **Ferdinand.** 1480?–1521. Portuguese navigator who first sailed through the strait that now bears his name in 1520.

Magellan, Strait of. A channel between South America and Tierra del Fuego connecting the S Atlantic and Pacific oceans.

Mag•el•lan•ic Clouds (măj′ə-lăn′ĭk) *pl.n.* Two small, irregularly shaped galaxies that are the galaxies closest to the Milky Way. [After Ferdinand MAGELLAN.]

Ma•gen Da•vid also **Mo•gen Da•vid** (mŏ′gən dô′vĭd, dä′vĭd, mä-gĕn′ dä-vēd′) *n.* A six-pointed star, a symbol of Judaism, formed by placing two triangles together, one inverted over the other or interlaced. [Heb. *māgēn dāwid.*]

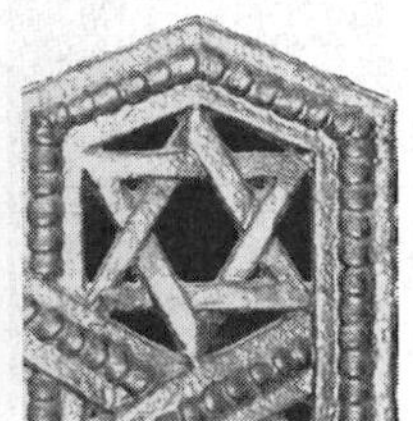

Magen David

ma•gen•ta (mə-jĕn′tə) *n.* **1.** See **fuchsin. 2.** *Color.* A moderate to vivid purplish red. [After *Magenta* in NW Italy.]

Mag•gio•re (mə-jôr′ē, -jōr′ē, mäd-jô′rĕ), **Lake.** An alpine lake of N Italy and S Switzerland.

mag•got (măg′ət) *n.* **1.** The legless soft-bodied wormlike larva of any of various flies of the order Diptera, often found in decaying matter. **2.** *Slang.* A despicable person. **3.** An extravagant notion; a whim. [ME *magot,* perh. alteration of *mathek, maddokk,* perh. < OE *matha.*] —**mag′got•y** *adj.*

Ma•ghreb or **Ma•ghrib** (mŭg′rəb). A region of NW Africa in Morocco, Algeria, and Tunisia.

ma•gi (mā′jī′) *n.* Pl. of **magus.**

mag•ic (măj′ĭk) *n.* **1.** The art that purports to control or forecast natural events, effects, or forces by invoking the supernatural. **2.a.** The practice of using charms, spells, or rituals to attempt to produce supernatural effects or control events in nature. **b.** The charms, spells, and rituals so used. **3.** The exercise of sleight of hand or conjuring for entertainment. **4.** A mysterious quality of enchantment. —*adj.* **1.** Of, relating to, or invoking the supernatural. **2.** Possessing distinctive qualities that produce unaccountable or baffling effects. —*tr.v.* **-icked, -ick•ing, -ics.** To produce or make by or as if by magic. [ME *magik* < OFr. *magique* < LLat. *magica* < Lat. *magicē* < Gk. *magikē* < fem. of *magikos,* of the Magi, magical < *magos,* magician, magus. See MAGUS.]

mag•i•cal (măj′ĭ-kəl) *adj.* **1.** Of, relating to, or produced by magic. **2.** Enchanting; bewitching. —**mag′i•cal•ly** *adv.*

magical realism *n.* A chiefly literary style or genre originating in Latin America that combines fantastic or dreamlike elements with reality.

ma•gi•cian (mə-jĭsh′ən) *n.* **1.** A sorcerer; a wizard. **2.** One who performs magic for entertainment or diversion. **3.** One whose skill or art seems to be magical.

magic lantern *n.* An optical device formerly used to project an enlarged image of a picture.

magic number *n. Phys. & Chem.* Any of the numbers, 2, 8, 20, 28, 50, 82, or 126, that represent the number of neutrons or protons in exceptionally stable and abundant atomic nuclei.

magic square *n.* A square that contains numbers arranged in equal rows and columns in such a way that the sum of each row or column, taken in any direction, is the same.

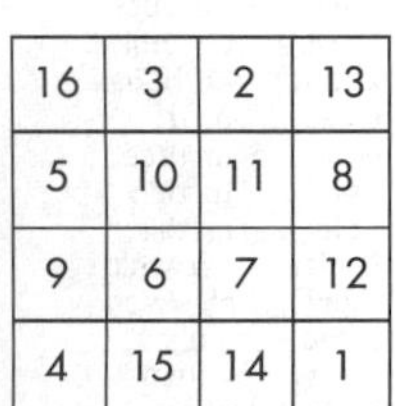

16	3	2	13
5	10	11	8
9	6	7	12
4	15	14	1

magic square
After a magic square in Albrecht Dürer's engraving *Melancolia I*

Ma•gi•not (măzh′ə-nō′, măj′-, mä-zhē-nō′), **André.** 1877–1932. French politician who proposed the Maginot Line of fortifications along France's border with Germany. The line was bypassed and captured by the Germans in 1940.

mag•is•te•ri•al (măj′ĭ-stîr′ē-əl) *adj.* **1.a.** Of, relating to, or characteristic of a master or teacher; authoritative. **b.** Sedately dignified in appearance or manner. **2.** Dogmatic; overbearing. **3.** Of or relating to a magistrate or a magistrate's official functions. [LLat. *magisteriālis* < *magisterius* < Lat. *magister,* master, teacher. See **meg-***.] —**mag′is•te′ri•al•ly** *adv.*

mag•is•te•ri•um (măj′ĭ-stîr′ē-əm) *n. Rom. Cath. Ch.* The authority to teach religious doctrine. [Lat., office of a teacher < *magister,* master. See MAGISTERIAL.]

mag•is•tra•cy (măj′ĭs-trə-sē) *n., pl.* **-cies. 1.** The position, function, or term of office of a magistrate. **2.** A body of magistrates. **3.** The district under jurisdiction of a magistrate.

mag•is•tral (măj′ĭ-strəl) *adj.* **1.** Of or relating to a magistrate; magisterial. **2.** Prepared as specified by a physician's prescription. **3.** Principal; main. [LLat. *magistrālis,* of a master < Lat. *magister, magistr-,* master. See **meg-***.]

mag•is•trate (măj′ĭ-strāt′, -strĭt) *n.* A civil officer with power to administer and enforce law, as: **a.** A local member of the judiciary having limited jurisdiction, esp. in criminal cases. **b.** A minor official, such as a justice of the peace, having administrative and limited judicial authority. [ME *magistrat* < OFr. < Lat. *magistrātus* < *magister, magistr-,* master. See **meg-***.]

mag•is•tra•ture (măj′ĭ-strā′chər, -strə-cho͝or′) *n.* Magistracy.

Ma•gle•mo•si•an (mä′glə-mō′zē-ən) *adj. Archaeol.* Of or relating to a Mesolithic forest culture of northern Europe. [After *Maglemose,* a Mesolithic site of W Sjaelland, Denmark.]

mag•lev or **Mag•lev** (măg′lĕv) *n.* Magnetic levitation.

mag•ma (măg′mə) *n., pl.* **-ma•ta** (-mä′tə) or **-mas. 1.** A mixture of finely divided solids with enough liquid to produce a pasty mass. **2.** *Geol.* The molten rock material under the earth's crust, from which igneous rock is formed by cooling. **3.** *Pharm.* A suspension of particles in a liquid, such as milk of magnesia. **4.** The residue of fruits after the juice has been expressed; pomace. [ME, sediment, dregs < Lat. < Gk., unguent < *massein, mag-,* to knead. See **mag-***.] —**mag•mat′ic** (-măt′ĭk) *adj.*

Mag•na Car•ta or **Mag•na Char•ta** (măg′nə kär′tə) *n.* **1.** The charter of English political and civil liberties granted by King John at Runnymede in June 1215. **2.** A document or piece of legislation guaranteeing basic rights. [ME < Med.Lat. : Lat. *magna,* great + Med.Lat. *charta,* charter.]

mag•na cum lau•de (mäg′nə ko͝om lou′də) *adv. & adj.* With high honors. Used to express high academic distinction. [Lat. *magnā cum laude* : *magnā*, fem. ablative sing. of *magnus*, great + *cum*, with + *laude*, ablative sing. of *laus*, praise.]

Magna Grae•cia (grē′shə). The ancient Greek seaport colonies of S Italy and Sicily from the 8th to the 4th cent. B.C.

mag•na•nim•i•ty (măg′nə-nĭm′ĭ-tē) *n.*, *pl.* **-ties. 1.** The quality of being magnanimous. **2.** A magnanimous act.

mag•nan•i•mous (măg-năn′ə-məs) *adj.* **1.** Courageously noble in mind and heart. **2.** Generous in forgiving; eschewing resentment or revenge; unselfish. [< Lat. *magnanimus* : *magnus*, great; see **meg-*** + *animus*, soul, mind; see **anə-***.] **—mag•nan′i•mous•ly** *adv.* **—mag•nan′i•mous•ness** *n.*

mag•nate (măg′nāt′, -nĭt) *n.* A powerful or influential person, esp. in business or industry: *an oil magnate.* [< ME *magnates*, magnates < LLat. *magnātēs*, pl. of *magnās*, magnate < Lat. *magnus*, great. See **meg-***.]

mag•ne•sia (măg-nē′zhə, -shə) *n.* Magnesium oxide. [ME, mineral ingredient of the philosophers' stone < Med.Lat. *magnēsia* < Gk., a kind of ore < *Magnēsia*, Magnesia, an ancient city of Asia Minor.] **—mag•ne′sian** *adj.*

mag•ne•site (măg′nə-sīt′) *n.* A white, yellowish, or brown mineral, magnesium carbonate, $MgCO_3$, used in the manufacture of magnesium oxide and carbon dioxide.

mag•ne•si•um (măg-nē′zē-əm, -zhəm) *n. Symbol* **Mg** A light metallic element that burns with a brilliant white flame and is used in structural alloys, pyrotechnics, flash photography, and incendiary bombs. Atomic number 12; atomic weight 24.312; melting point 649°C; boiling point 1,090°C; specific gravity 1.74 (at 20°C); valence 2. See table at **element.** [< MAGNESIA.]

magnesium carbonate *n.* A light odorless powdery compound, $MgCO_3$, used as a drying agent in a variety of manufactured products.

magnesium hydroxide *n.* A white powder, $Mg(OH)_2$, used as an antacid and a laxative.

magnesium oxide *n.* A white powdery compound, MgO, having a high melting point (2,800°C), used in high-temperature refractories, electrical insulation, and cosmetics.

magnesium sulfate *n.* A crystalline compound, $MgSO_4$, used in fireproofing, ceramics, matches, explosives, and fertilizers.

mag•net (măg′nĭt) *n.* **1.** An object that is surrounded by a magnetic field and has the property, either natural or induced, of attracting iron or steel. **2.** An electromagnet. **3.** A person, a place, an object, or a situation that exerts attraction. [ME < OFr. *magnete* < Lat. *magnēs*, *magnēt-* < Gk. *Magnēs (lithos)*, Magnesian (stone), magnet < *Magnēsia*, Magnesia, an ancient city of Asia Minor.]

mag•net•ic (măg-nĕt′ĭk) *adj.* **1.a.** Of or relating to magnetism or magnets. **b.** Having the properties of a magnet. **c.** Operating by means of magnetism. **d.** Capable of being magnetized or attracted by a magnet. **2.** Relating to the magnetic poles of the earth: *a magnetic compass.* **3.** Unusually attractive. **—mag•net′i•cal•ly** *adv.*

magnetic bottle *n.* A magnetic field used to confine plasma, as during controlled nuclear fusion.

magnetic bubble memory *n. Comp. Sci.* A memory in which data are stored in the form of bubbles, or circular areas, on a thin film of magnetic silicate.

magnetic card *n. Comp. Sci.* A card that has a magnetizable strip or surface on which data can be recorded.

magnetic compass *n.* An instrument that uses a magnetized steel bar to indicate direction relative to the earth's magnetic poles.

magnetic core *n.* See **core** 6b.

magnetic declination *n.* The angle between magnetic north and true north at a particular location.

magnetic dip *n.* The angle that a magnetic needle makes with the horizontal plane at any specific location.

magnetic disk *n. Comp. Sci.* **1.** A memory device covered with a magnetic coating on which information is stored by magnetization of microscopically small needles. **2.** A floppy disk. **3.** A hard disk.

magnetic equator *n.* A line connecting all points on the earth's surface at which a magnetic needle balances horizontally without dipping.

magnetic field *n.* A condition found in the region around a magnet or an electric current, characterized by the existence of a detectable magnetic force at every point in the region and by the existence of magnetic poles.

magnetic field strength *n.* **1.** Magnetic intensity. **2.** See **magnetic induction** 1.

magnetic flux *n.* A measure of the quantity of magnetism, being the total number of magnetic lines of force passing through a specified area in a magnetic field.

magnetic flux density *n. Symbol* **B** See **magnetic induction** 1.

magnetic force *n.* **1.** The force exerted between magnetic poles, producing magnetization. **2.** A force that exists between two electrically charged moving particles.

magnetic head *n.* An electromagnet, as in a tape recorder, that converts electrical impulses into variations in the magnetism of a surface for storage and retrieval.

magnetic inclination *n.* See **magnetic dip.**

magnetic induction *n.* **1.** The amount of magnetic flux in a unit area taken perpendicular to the direction of the magnetic flux. **2.** The process by which a substance, such as iron, becomes magnetized by a magnetic field.

magnetic intensity *n.* A quantity used in describing magnetic phenomena in terms of their magnetic fields and magnetization.

magnetic levitation *n.* A high-speed rail technology by which a train can travel free of friction while suspended on a magnetic cushion about half an inch above an elevated magnetic track.

magnetic lines of force *pl.n.* Curved lines used to represent a magnetic field, drawn such that the number of lines is related to the strength of the magnetic field at a given point and the tangent of any curve at a particular point is along the direction of magnetic force at that point.

magnetic meridian *n.* A line passing through both magnetic poles of the earth.

magnetic mine *n.* A marine mine detonated by a mechanism that responds to a mass of magnetic material.

magnetic moment *n.* The product of the pole strength of a magnet and the distance between the poles.

magnetic monopole *n.* A hypothetical particle that has only one pole of magnetic charge instead of the usual two.

magnetic needle *n.* A slender bar of magnetized steel usu. suspended on a low-friction mounting and used in various instruments, esp. in a magnetic compass, to indicate the direction of the earth's magnetic poles.

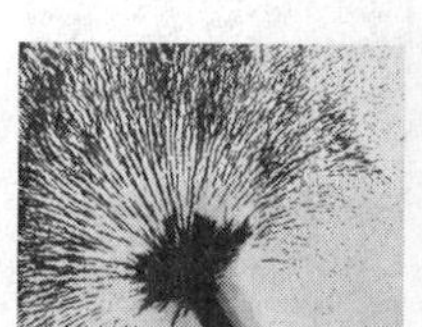
magnetic field
Magnet attracting iron filings

magnetic north *n.* The direction of the earth's magnetic pole, to which the north-seeking pole of a magnetic needle points when free from local magnetic influence.

magnetic pole *n.* **1.** Either of two limited regions in a magnet at which the magnet's field is most intense, each of which is designated by the approximate geographic direction to which it is attracted. **2.** Either of two variable points on the earth, close to but not coinciding with the geographic poles, where the earth's magnetic field is most intense and toward which a compass needle points.

magnetic pyrites *n.* See **pyrrhotite.**

magnetic recording *n.* **1.** The recording of a signal, such as sound, in a magnetic pattern on a magnetizable surface for storage and retrieval. **2.** A surface storing such a recording.

magnetic resonance *n.* The absorption of specific frequencies of radio and microwave radiation by atoms placed in a magnetic field, revealing molecular structure.

magnetic resonance imaging *n.* The use of a nuclear magnetic resonance spectrometer to produce electronic images of specific molecular structures in solids, esp. human tissues.

magnetic storm *n.* A disturbance or fluctuation in the earth's magnetic field, associated with solar flares.

magnetic tape *n.* A plastic tape coated with iron oxide for use in magnetic recording.

magnetic variation *n.* **1.** Differences in the earth's magnetic field in time and location. **2.** See **magnetic declination.**

mag•net•ism (măg′nĭ-tĭz′əm) *n.* **1.** The class of phenomena exhibited by a magnetic field. **2.** The study of magnets and their effects. **3.** The force exerted by a magnetic field. **4.** Unusual power to attract or influence. **5.** Animal magnetism.

mag•net•ite (măg′nĭ-tīt′) *n.* The mineral form of black iron oxide, Fe_3O_4, that often occurs with magnesium, zinc, and manganese and is an important ore of iron.

mag•net•i•za•tion (măg′nĭ-tĭ-zā′shən) *n.* **1.a.** The process of making a substance temporarily or permanently magnetic, as by insertion in a magnetic field. **b.** The extent to which an object is magnetized. **2.** The property of being magnetic.

mag•net•ize (măg′nĭ-tīz′) *tr.v.* **-ized, -iz•ing, -iz•es. 1.** To make magnetic. **2.** To attract, charm, or influence. **—mag′net•iz′a•ble** *adj.* **—mag′net•iz′er** *n.*

mag•ne•to (măg-nē′tō) *n.*, *pl.* **-tos.** A device that produces alternating current for distribution to the spark plugs, used in the ignition systems of some internal-combustion engines. [Short for *magnetoelectric machine.*]

magneto– or **magnet–** *pref.* **1.** Magnetism; magnetic: *magnetoelectric.* **2.** Magnetic field: *magnetometer.* [< MAGNET.]

mag•ne•to•e•lec•tric (măg-nē′tō-ĭ-lĕk′trĭk) *adj.* Of or relating to electricity produced by magnetic means. **—mag•ne′to•e•lec•tric′i•ty** (-ĭ-lĕk-trĭs′ĭ-tē, -ē′lĕk-) *n.*

mag•ne•to•hy•dro•dy•nam•ics (măg-nē′tō-hī′drō-dī-năm′ĭks) *n.* (*used with a sing. v.*) The study of the interaction of magnetic fields and electrically conducting liquids or gases, such as molten metal. **—mag•ne′to•hy′dro•dy•nam′ic** *adj.*

mag•ne•tom•e•ter (măg′nĭ-tŏm′ĭ-tər) *n.* An instrument for measuring the intensity and direction of a magnetic field. **—mag′ne•to•met′ric** (-tə-mĕt′rĭk) *adj.* **—mag′ne•tom′e•try** *n.*

mag•ne•to•mo•tive force (măg-nē′tō-mō′tĭv) *n.* The work required to carry a hypothetical isolated magnetic pole of unit strength completely around a magnetic circuit.

mag•ne•ton (măg′nĭ-tŏn′) *n.* A unit of the magnetic moment of a molecular, atomic, or subatomic particle, esp.: **a.** The Bohr magneton, calculated using the mass and charge of the electron. **b.** The nuclear magneton, calculated using the mass of the nucleon.

ă pat	oi boy
ā pay	ou out
âr care	ŏŏ took
ä father	ōō boot
ĕ pet	ŭ cut
ē be	ûr urge
ĭ pit	th thin
ī pie	*th* this
îr pier	hw which
ŏ pot	zh vision
ō toe	ə about,
ô paw	item

Stress marks:
′ (primary);
′ (secondary), as in
dictionary (dĭk′shə-nĕr′ē)

mag•ne•to•pause (măg-nē′tə-pôz′) *n.* The outer boundary of the magnetosphere.

mag•ne•to•sphere (măg-nē′tō-sfîr′) *n.* An asymmetrical region surrounding the earth, extending from about one hundred to several thousand kilometers above the surface, in which the earth's magnetic field controls charged particles.

mag•ne•to•stric•tion (măg-nē′tō-strĭk′shən) *n.* Deformation of a ferromagnetic material subjected to a magnetic field. [MAGNETO– + (CON)STRICTION.]

mag•ne•tron (măg′nĭ-trŏn′) *n.* A microwave tube in which electrons generated from a heated cathode are affected by magnetic and electric fields in such a way as to produce microwave radiation used in radar, for example.

magnet school *n.* A public school that attracts students from all parts of a city, provides a superior education, and serves as a means of desegregation.

mag•nif•ic (măg-nĭf′ĭk) also **mag•nif•i•cal** (-ĭ-kəl) *adj.* **1.** Magnificent. **2.** Imposingly large. **3.** Exalted. **4.** Pompous; grandiloquent. [ME *magnifique* < OFr. < Lat. *magnificus* : *magnus*, great; see **meg-*** + *-ficus*, -fic.] — **mag•nif′i•cal•ly** *adv.*

magpie
Black-billed magpie
Pica pica

Mag•nif•i•cat (măg-nĭf′ĭ-kăt′) *n.* **1.a.** The canticle beginning *Magnificat anima mea Dominum* ("My soul doth magnify the Lord," Luke 1:46). **b.** A musical setting of this canticle. **2. magnificat.** A song of praise. [ME < Med.Lat. < Lat. *magnificat*, it magnifies, third pers. sing. pr.t. of *magnificāre*, to magnify, extol. See MAGNIFY.]

mag•ni•fi•ca•tion (măg′nə-fĭ-kā′shən) *n.* **1.** The act of magnifying or the state of being magnified. **2.a.** The process of enlarging the size of something, as an optical image. **b.** Something that has been magnified; an enlargement. **3.** The ratio of the size of an image to the size of an object.

mag•nif•i•cence (măg-nĭf′ĭ-səns) *n.* **1.** Greatness or lavishness of surroundings; splendor. **2.** Grand or imposing beauty.

mag•nif•i•cent (măg-nĭf′ĭ-sənt) *adj.* **1.** Splendid in appearance; grand: *a magnificent palace.* **2.** Grand or noble in thought or deed; exalted. **3.** Outstanding of its kind; superlative: *a magnificent view.* See Syns at **grand.** [ME < OFr. < *magnificence*, splendor < Lat. *magnificentia* < *magnificus*, magnificent. See MAGNIFIC.] — **mag•nif′i•cent•ly** *adv.*

mag•nif•i•co (măg-nĭf′ĭ-kō′) *n., pl.* **-coes. 1.** A person of distinguished rank, importance, or appearance. **2.** A nobleman of the Venetian Republic. [Ital., magnificent, magnifico < Lat. *magnificus*. See MAGNIFIC.]

mag•ni•fi•er (măg′nə-fī′ər) *n.* **1.** One that magnifies, esp. a magnifying glass. **2.** A system of optical components that magnifies.

mag•ni•fy (măg′nə-fī′) *v.* **-fied, -fy•ing, -fies.** —*tr.* **1.** To make greater in size; enlarge. **2.** To cause to appear greater or seem more important than is in fact the case; exaggerate. See Syns at **exaggerate. 3.** To increase the apparent size of, esp. by means of a lens. **4.** To glorify or praise. —*intr.* To increase or have the power to increase the size or volume of an image or a sound. [ME *magnifien*, to extol < OFr. *magnifier* < Lat. *magnificāre* < *magnificus*, magnificent. See MAGNIFIC.]

mag•ni•fy•ing glass (măg′nə-fī′ĭng) *n.* A lens or combination of lenses that enlarges the image of an object.

mag•nil•o•quent (măg-nĭl′ə-kwənt) *adj.* Lofty and extravagant in speech; grandiloquent. [Back-formation < MAGNILOQUENCE < Lat. *magniloquentia* : *magnus*, great; see **meg-*** + *loquēns*, *loquent-*, pr.part. of *loquī*, to speak; see **tolkʷ-*.**] — **mag•nil′o•quence** *n.* — **mag•nil′o•quent•ly** *adv.*

Mag•ni•to•gorsk (măg-nē′tə-gôrsk′, məg-nyĭ-tə-gôrsk′). A city of SW Russia SSW of Chelyabinsk. Pop. 422,000.

mag•ni•tude (măg′nĭ-to͞od′, -tyo͞od′) *n.* **1.a.** Greatness of rank or position. **b.** Greatness in size or extent. **c.** Greatness in significance or influence. **2.** *Astron.* The degree of brightness of a celestial body according to a logarithmic scale, on which the brightest star has magnitude −1.4 and the faintest visible star has magnitude 6. **3.** *Math.* **a.** A number assigned to a quantity so that it may be compared with other quantities. **b.** A property that can be quantitatively described, such as the length of a vector. **4.** *Geol.* A measure of the amount of energy released by an earthquake, as indicated on the Richter Scale. [ME < OFr., size < Lat. *magnitūdō*, greatness, size < *magnus*, great. See **meg-*.**]

mag•no•lia (măg-nōl′yə) *n.* Any of numerous evergreen or deciduous trees and shrubs of the genus *Magnolia* of the Western Hemisphere and Asia, having aromatic twigs and showy flowers. [NLat. *Magnolia*, genus name, after Pierre *Magnol* (1638–1715), French botanist.]

magnolia warbler *n.* A black-and-yellow songbird *(Dendroica magnolia)* of northern North America.

mag•num (măg′nəm) *n.* **1.** A bottle, holding about two fifths of a gallon (1.5 liters), for wine or liquor. **2.** The amount of liquid that this bottle can hold. **3.** A firearm designed to shoot magnum cartridges. —*adj.* Of or relating to a cartridge that has more explosive charge than others of the same size. [< Lat., neut. of *magnus*, great. See **meg-*.**]

magnum opus *n.* **1.** A great work, esp. a literary or artistic masterpiece. **2.** The greatest single work of an artist, a writer, or a composer. [Lat. : *magnum*, great + *opus*, work.]

mag•nus hitch (măg′nəs) *n.* A clove hitch with one extra turn. [?]

ma•got (mă-gō′, măg′ət) *n.* **1.** See **Barbary ape. 2.** A fanciful, often grotesque figurine in the Japanese or Chinese style rendered in a crouching position. [Fr. < OFr. *magos*, a kind of monkey < *Magog, Magos*, Magog, name of biblical land (Ezekiel 38–39) and tribe (Revelation 20:8–9).]

mag•pie (măg′pī′) *n.* **1.** Any of various birds of the family Corvidae found worldwide, having a long tail and black, blue, or green plumage with white markings and noted for their chattering call. **2.** Any of various birds resembling the magpie. **3.** A person who chatters. [*Mag*, a name used in proverbs about chatterers (a nickname for *Margaret*) + PIE².]

M.Agr. *abbr.* Master of Agriculture.

Ma•gritte (mä-grēt′), **René.** 1898–1967. Belgian painter whose surreal works include *Steps of Summer* (1938).

ma•guey (mə-gā′, măg′wā) *n., pl.* **-gueys. 1.** Any of various American plants of the genus *Agave*, esp. the century plant. **2.** Any of various plants of the related genus *Furcraea*. **3.** The fiber obtained from any of these plants. [Sp., of Cariban orig.]

ma•gus (mā′gəs) *n.* **ma•gi** (mā′jī′). **1.** A member of the Zoroastrian priestly caste of the Medes and Persians. **2. Magus.** In the Bible, one of the wise men from the East who traveled to Bethlehem to pay homage to the infant Jesus. **3.** A sorcerer; a magician. [< ME *magi*, magi < Lat. *magī*, pl. of *magus*, sorcerer, magus < Gk. *magos* < OPers. *maguš*. See **magh-*.**] — **ma′gi•an** (mā′jē-ən) *adj.*

Mag•yar (măg′yär′, mäg′-, mŭd′-) *n.* **1.** A member of the principal ethnic group of Hungary. **2.** See **Hungarian** 2. [Hung.] — **Mag′yar** *adj.*

Ma•hal•la el Ku•bra (mə-hăl′ə ĕl ko͞o′brə). A city of N Egypt in the Nile R. delta N of Cairo. Pop. 362,700.

Ma•han (mə-hăn′), **Alfred Thayer.** 1840–1914. Amer. naval officer noted for *The Influence of Sea Power upon History, 1660–1783* (1890).

Ma•ha•na•di (mə-hä′nə-dē). A river of central India flowing c. 885 km (550 mi) to the Bay of Bengal.

ma•ha•ra•jah or **ma•ha•ra•ja** (mä′hə-rä′jə, -zhə) *n.* **1.** A king or prince in India ranking above a rajah, esp. the sovereign of one of the former native states. **2.** Used as a title for such a king or prince. [Hindi *mahārājā* < Skt. : *mahā-*, great; see **meg-*** + *rājā*, king; see **reg-*.**]

ma•ha•ra•ni or **ma•ha•ra•nee** (mä′hə-rä′nē) *n., pl.* **-nis** or **-nees. 1.** The wife of a maharajah. **2.** A princess in India ranking above a rani, esp. the sovereign ruler of one of the former native states. **3.** Used as a title for such a woman. [Hindi *mahārānī* < Skt. *mahārājñī* : *mahā-*, great; see **meg-*** + *rājñī*, queen; see **reg-*.**]

Ma•ha•rash•tra (mä′hə-räsh′trə). A historical region of W-central India; controlled by the Muslim rulers of India from the early 14th to the mid-17th cent.

ma•ha•ri•shi (mä′hə-rē′shē, mə-här′ə-shē) *n., pl.* **-shis.** *Hinduism.* **1.** A teacher of mysticism and spiritual knowledge. **2.** Used as a title for such a person. [Skt. *mahārṣiḥ* : *mahā-*, great; see **meg-*** + *ṛṣiḥ*, seer, sage, saint.]

ma•hat•ma (mə-hät′mə, -hăt′-) *n.* **1.** In India and Tibet, one of a class of persons venerated for great knowledge and love of humanity. **2. Mahatma.** *Hinduism.* Used as a title of respect for a person renowned for spirituality and high-mindedness. [Skt. *mahātmā* : *mahā-*, great; see **meg-*** + *ātmā*, life, spirit.]

Ma•ha•ya•na (mä′hə-yä′nə) *n.* One of the major schools of Buddhism, which teaches social concern and universal salvation. [Skt. *mahāyānam* : *mahā-*, great; see **meg-*** + *yānam*, vehicle; see **ei-*.**] — **Ma′ha•ya′nist** *n.*

Mah•di (mä′dē) *n., pl.* **-dis.** *Islam.* **1.** The messiah who, it is believed, will appear at the world's end and establish a reign of peace and righteousness. **2.** A leader who assumes the role of a messiah. [Ar. *mahdī*, rightly guided (one), Mahdi < *hadā*, to lead.] — **Mah′dism** *n.* — **Mah′dist** *n.*

Mah•fouz (mä-fo͞oz′), **Naguib.** b. 1911. Egyptian writer who won the 1988 Nobel Prize for literature.

Ma•hi•can (mə-hē′kən) also **Mo•hi•can** (mō-, mə-) *n., pl.* **Mahican** or **-cans** also **Mohican** or **-cans. 1.** A member of a Native American confederacy of subtribes formerly inhabiting the upper Hudson River valley from Albany south to the Catskill Mountains and north to Lake Champlain. **2.** The Algonquian language of the Mahican.

ma•hi-ma•hi also **ma•hi•ma•hi** (mä′hē-mä′hē) *n., pl.* **-his.** A tropical marine food fish *(Coryphaena hippurus)* having a blue body and a long dorsal fin. [Hawaiian.]

mah•jong also **mah•jongg** (mä′zhŏng′, -zhông′) *n. Games.* A game of Chinese origin usu. played by four persons with tiles resembling dominoes and bearing various designs. [Chin. (Mandarin) *má jiàng* : *má*, spotted + *jiàng*, main piece in Chinese chess.]

Mah•ler (mä′lər), **Gustav.** 1860–1911. Austrian composer and conductor of the State Opera House (1897–1907).

mahl•stick (môl′stĭk′) *n.* Var. of **maulstick.**

ma•hog•a•ny (mə-hŏg′ə-nē) *n., pl.* **-nies. 1.a.** Any of various tropical American evergreen trees of the genus *Swietenia*, valued for their hard reddish-brown wood. **b.** The wood of any of these trees, used in making furniture. **2.a.** Any of several trees having wood resembling true mahogany. **b.** The wood of any of these trees. **3.** *Color.* A moderate reddish brown. [Obsolete Sp. *mahogani*, perh. of Mayan orig.]

Ma•hón (mə-hōn′, mä-ôn′). A city of Spain on E Minorca; came under Spanish control in 1802. Pop. 22,926.

Mah•ra•ti (mə-rä′tē, -răt′ē) *n.* Var. of **Marathi.**

Mah•rat•ta (mə-rä′tə, -răt′ə) *n.* Var. of **Maratha.**

Mah•rat•ti (mə-rä′tē, -răt′ē) *n.* Var. of **Marathi.**

ma•huang (mä-hwäng′) *n.* Any of various Asian shrubs of the genus *Ephedra,* esp. *E. sinica,* the shrub from which the drug ephedrine is obtained. [Chin. (Mandarin) *má huáng* : *má,* hemp + *huáng,* yellow.]

mah•zor also **mach•zor** (mäKH′zôr′, -zər, mäKH-zōr′) *n., pl.* **-zor•im** (-zôr′ĭm, -zô-rēm′) or **-zors.** *Judaism.* The prayer book for the High Holidays. [Heb. *maḥăzôr,* cycle, mahzor.]

maid (mād) *n.* **1.a.** An unmarried girl or woman. **b.** A virgin. **2.** A woman servant. [ME *maide* < OE *mægden.* See **maghu-*.**]

maid•en (mād′n) *n.* **1.a.** An unmarried girl or woman. **b.** A virgin. **2.** A machine resembling the guillotine, used in Scotland in the 16th and 17th centuries to behead criminals. **3.** *Sports.* A racehorse that has never won a race. —*adj.* **1.** Of, relating to, or befitting a maiden. **2.** Being an unmarried girl or woman. **3.** Inexperienced; untried. **4.** Being a racehorse that has never won a race. **5.** First or earliest: *a maiden voyage.* [ME < OE *mægden.* See **maghu-*.**]

maid•en•hair fern (mād′n-hâr′) *n.* Any of various ferns of the genus *Adiantum,* having purplish to black stalks, usu. feathery fronds, and delicate fan-shaped leaflets with marginal sori. [From the fineness of its stems.]

maidenhair tree *n.* See **ginkgo.**

maid•en•head (mād′n-hĕd′) *n.* **1.** The condition or quality of being a maiden; virginity. **2.** The hymen. [ME *maidenhed* : *maiden,* maid; see MAIDEN + *-hed,* -hood.]

maid•en•hood (mād′n-ho͝od′) *n.* The condition or time of being a maiden.

maid•en•ly (mād′n-lē) *adj.* Of, relating to, or suitable for a maiden. —**maid′en•li•ness** *n.*

maiden name *n.* A woman's family name before marriage.

maid•hood (mād′ho͝od′) *n.* Maidenhood.

maid in waiting *n., pl.* **maids in waiting.** An unmarried woman attending a queen or princess.

Maid Mar•i•an (mād mâr′ē-ən, măr′-) *n.* Robin Hood's sweetheart.

maid of honor *n., pl.* **maids of honor. 1.** The chief unmarried woman attendant of a bride. **2.** An unmarried noblewoman attendant upon a queen or princess.

maid•ser•vant (mād′sûr′vənt) *n.* A woman servant.

Maid•stone (mād′stən, -stōn′). A municipal borough of SE England ESE of London; first chartered 1549. Pop. 72,500.

Mai•du (mī′do͞o) *n., pl.* **Maidu** or **-dus. 1.** A member of a Native American people inhabiting northeast California south of Lassen Peak. **2.** The Penutian language of the Maidu.

ma•ieu•tic (mā-yo͞o′tĭk, mī-) also **ma•ieu•ti•cal** (-tĭ-kəl) *adj.* Of or relating to the aspect of the Socratic method that induces a person to bring forth latent concepts through a logical sequence of questions. [Gk. *maieutikos* < *maieuesthai,* to act as midwife < *maia,* midwife, nurse. See **mā-²*.**]

mail¹ (māl) *n.* **1.a.** Materials, such as letters, handled in a postal system. **b.** Postal material for a specific person or organization. **c.** Material processed for distribution from a post office at a specified time. **2.** A system by which letters and other postal materials are transported. Often used in the plural. **3.** A vehicle by which mail is transported. —*v.* **mailed, mail•ing, mails.** —*tr.* To send by mail. —*intr.* To send postal material by mail. [ME *male,* bag < OFr., of Gmc. orig.] —**mail′a•ble** *adj.* —**mail′a•bil′i•ty** *n.*

mail² (māl) *n.* **1.** Flexible armor composed of small overlapping metal rings, loops of chain, or scales. **2.** The protective covering of certain animals, as the shell of a turtle. —*tr.v.* **mailed, mail•ing, mails.** To cover or armor with mail. [ME < OFr. *maile* < Lat. *macula,* blemish, mesh.]

mail³ (māl) *n. Scots.* Rent, payment, or tribute. [ME *mol, maile* < ON *māl,* lawsuit.]

mail•bag (māl′băg′) *n.* **1.** A large canvas sack used for transporting mail. **2.** A bag suspended from the shoulder, used by letter carriers for carrying mail.

mail•box (māl′bŏks′) *n.* **1.** A public container for deposit of outgoing mail. **2.** A private box for incoming mail.

mail carrier *n.* See **letter carrier.**

mail drop *n.* **1.** A receptacle or slot for the delivery of mail. **2.** An address or a place at which a nonresident person receives mail, often of a secret nature.

mailed (māld) *adj.* **1.** Covered with or made of plates of mail: *a mailed sleeve.* **2.** Having a hard covering of scales, spines, or horny plate, as an armadillo or a lobster.

mailed fist *n.* The threat of military force.

mail•er (mā′lər) *n.* **1.** One that uses the mails: *commercial mailers.* **2.** One who addresses or otherwise prepares mail. **3.** A container used to hold material to be mailed: *a book mailer.* **4.** An advertising leaflet included with a letter.

Mail•er (mā′lər), **Norman.** b. 1923. Amer. writer who established New Journalism in the 1960's.

Mail•gram (māl′grăm′). A trademark used for a telegram to a post office and delivered by the postal service.

mail•ing (mā′lĭng) *n.* **1.** Something sent by mail. **2.** A batch of mail dispatched at one time by a sender.

Mail•lol (mä-yôl′), **Aristide.** 1861–1944. French sculptor noted for his classically influenced statues of female nudes.

mail•lot (mä-yō′) *n.* **1.** A coarsely knitted stretchable jersey fabric. **2.** A pair of tights or a leotard of such fabric. **3.** A woman's one-piece swimsuit usu. cut high on the leg. [Fr. < OFr., swaddling clothes < *maille,* mesh < Lat. *macula.*]

mail•man (māl′măn′, -mən) *n.* A man who delivers mail.

mail order *n.* An order for goods to be shipped by mail.

mail-or•der house (māl′ôr′dər) *n.* A business that sells and provides merchandise or services through the mail.

mail•room (māl′ro͞om′, -ro͝om′) *n.* A room in which ingoing and outgoing mail is handled for an organization.

maim (mām) *tr.v.* **maimed, maim•ing, maims. 1.** To disable or disfigure, usu. by depriving of the use of a body part. **2.** To make imperfect or defective; impair. [ME *maimen* < OFr. *mahaignier,* prob. of Gmc. orig.] —**maim′er** *n.*

Mai•mon•i•des (mī-mŏn′ĭ-dēz′), **Moses.** Orig. Moses Ben Maimon. 1135–1204. Spanish-born Jewish philosopher and physician who codified the Talmud.

main (mān) *adj.* **1.** Most important; principal. **2.** Exerted to the utmost; sheer. **3.** *Naut.* Connected to or associated with the mainmast. **4.** *Gram.* Of, relating to, or being the principal clause or verb of a complex sentence. **5.** *Obsolete.* Of a continuous area or stretch. —*n.* **1.** The chief or largest part. **2.** The principal pipe or conduit in a system for conveying gas or other utility. **3.** Physical strength. **4.** A mainland. **5.** The open ocean. **6.** *Naut.* **a.** A mainsail. **b.** A mainmast. [ME < OE *mægen,* strength. See **magh-*.**]

Main (mān, mīn). A river rising in E Germany and flowing c. 499 km (310 mi) to the Rhine R. at Mainz.

main clause *n. Gram.* A clause in a complex sentence that contains at least a subject and a verb and can stand alone syntactically as a complete sentence.

main deck *n. Naut.* The principal deck of a large vessel.

main drag *n. Slang.* The principal street of a city or town.

Maine (mān). **1.** (*also* mĕn). A historical region and former province of NW France S of Normandy; passed to England in 1154 but reverted to the French crown in 1481. **2.** A state of the NE U.S.; admitted as the 23rd state in 1820. Cap. Augusta. Pop. 1,233,223.

main•frame (mān′frām′) *n. Comp. Sci.* **1.** A large powerful computer, often serving several terminals. **2.** The central processing unit of a computer.

main•land (mān′lănd′, -lənd) *n.* The principal landmass of a continent. —**main′land′er** *n.*

main•line (mān′līn′) *v.* **-lined, -lin•ing, -lines.** —*tr.* To inject (a drug) directly into a major vein. —*intr.* To inject a drug intravenously. —*adj.* Being in a principal or well-established position: *the mainline churches.* —**main′lin′er** *n.*

main line *n.* **1.** A principal section of a railroad line. **2.** *Slang.* A principal vein into which a drug can be injected.

main•ly (mān′lē) *adv.* For the most part; chiefly.

main•mast (mān′məst, -măst′) *n. Naut.* **1.** The principal mast of a vessel. **2.** The taller mast, whether forward or aft, of a two-masted sailing vessel. **3.** The second mast aft of a sailing ship with three or more masts.

main royalmast *n. Naut.* The section of the mainmast of a square-rigged vessel above the main topgallantmast.

main•sail (mān′səl, -sāl′) *n. Naut.* **1.** The principal sail of a vessel. **2.** A quadrilateral or triangular sail set from the after part of the mainmast on a fore-and-aft rigged vessel. **3.** A square sail set from the main yard on a square-rigged vessel.

main sequence *n.* The largest grouping of stars plotted on the Hertzsprung-Russell diagram.

main•sheet (mān′shēt′) *n. Naut.* The sheet that controls the angle at which a mainsail is trimmed and set.

main•spring (mān′sprĭng′) *n.* **1.** The principal spring in a mechanical device, esp. a watch or clock, that drives the mechanism by uncoiling. **2.** The chief motivating force.

main•stay (mān′stā′) *n.* **1.** A chief support. **2.** *Naut.* A stay leading forward from the mainmast of a sailing vessel.

main•stream (mān′strēm′) *n.* The prevailing current of thought, influence, or activity. —*adj.* Representing the prevalent attitudes and values of a society or group: *mainstream morality.* —*tr.v.* **-streamed, -stream•ing, -streams. 1.** To integrate (a physically or intellectually disadvantaged student) into regular school classes. **2.** To incorporate into a prevailing group. —**main′stream′er** *n.*

main street *n.* **1.** The principal street of a small town. **2. Main Street. a.** The inhabitants of small towns considered as a group. **b.** A place that represents narrowmindedness and smug complacency. [Sense 2, after *Main Street,* a novel by Sinclair Lewis.]

main•tain (mān-tān′) *tr.v.* **-tained, -tain•ing, -tains. 1.** To keep up or carry on; continue. **2.** To keep in an existing state; preserve or retain. **3.** To keep in a condition of good repair or

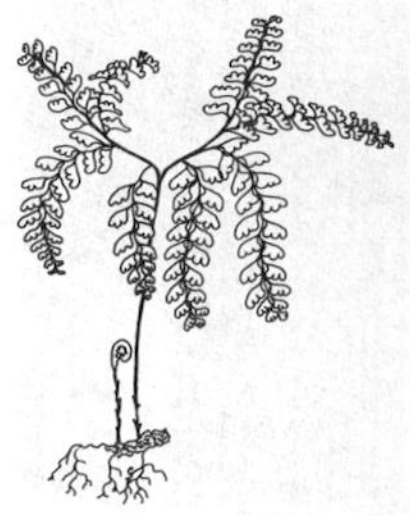

maidenhair fern
Northern maidenhair fern
Adiantum pedatum

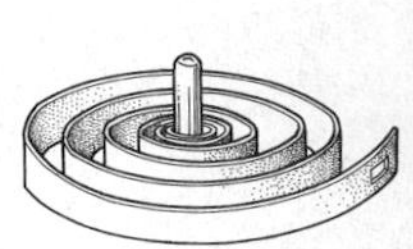

mainspring
Of a watch

ă pat	oi boy
ā pay	ou out
âr care	o͝o took
ä father	o͞o boot
ĕ pet	ŭ cut
ē be	ûr urge
ĭ pit	th thin
ī pie	*th* this
îr pier	hw which
ŏ pot	zh vision
ō toe	ə about, item
ô paw	

Stress marks:
′ (primary);
′ (secondary), as in **dictionary** (dĭk′shə-nĕr′ē)

efficiency. **4.a.** To provide for; support. **b.** To keep in existence; sustain. **5.** To defend or hold against criticism or attack. **6.** To declare to be true; affirm. [ME *maintainen* < OFr. *maintenir* < Med.Lat. *manutenēre* < Lat. *manū tenēre*, to hold in the hand : *manū*, ablative of *manus*, hand; see **man-**[2]* + *tenēre*, to hold; see **ten-***.] **— main•tain′a•bil′i•ty** *n.* **— main•tain′a•ble** *adj.* **— main•tain′er** *n.*

main•te•nance (mān′tə-nəns) *n.* **1.** The act of maintaining or the state of being maintained. **2.** The work of keeping something in proper condition; upkeep. **3.a.** Provision of support or livelihood. **b.** Means of support or livelihood. **4.** *Law.* The unlawful meddling in a suit by providing either party with the means to carry it on. [ME *maintenaunce* < OFr. *maintenance* < *maintenir*, to maintain. See MAINTAIN.]

maintop

Main•te•non (măN′tə-nôN′, mănt-nôN′), **Marquise de.** Françoise d'Aubigné. "Madame de Maintenon." 1635–1719. French consort of Louis XIV who secretly married the king (c. 1685) after the death of his first wife.

main•top (mān′tŏp′) *n. Naut.* A platform at the head of the mainmast on a square-rigged vessel.

main topgallant *n. Naut.* A sail or yard set from the topgallant section of a mainmast.

main top•gal•lant•mast (tə-găl′ənt-məst, tŏp-) *n. Naut.* The section of the mainmast next above the main topmast on a square-rigged sailing vessel.

main topmast *n. Naut.* The section of the mainmast on a square-rigged sailing vessel between the lower mast and the main topgallantmast.

main topsail *n. Naut.* The sail that is set above the mainsail.

main yard *n. Naut.* The lowest yard on a mainmast.

Mainz (mīnts). A city of W-central Germany at the confluence of the Rhine and Main rivers WSW of Frankfurt; built on the site of a Roman camp. Pop. 187,447.

mai tai (mī′ tī′) *n., pl.* **mai tais.** A cocktail made with rum, curaçao, and fruit juices. [Tahitian *maitai*, good.]

mai•tre d' (mā′trə dē′, mā′tər) *n., pl.* **mai•tre d's** (dēz′). *Informal.* A maitre d'hôtel.

mai•tre d'hô•tel (mā′trə dō-tĕl′) *n., pl.* **mai•tres d'hô•tel** (mā′trə dō-tĕl′). **1.** A headwaiter. **2.** A major-domo. **3.** A sauce of melted butter, chopped parsley, lemon juice, salt, and pepper. [Fr. *maître d'hôtel* : *maître*, master + *de*, of + *hôtel*, house.]

majolica
Early 16th-century
Italian plate

maize (māz) *n.* **1.** See **corn**[1] 1. **2.** *Color.* A light yellow to moderate orange yellow. [Sp. *maíz* < Cariban *mahiz*.]

Maj. *abbr.* Major.

ma•jes•tic (mə-jĕs′tĭk) also **ma•jes•ti•cal** (-tĭ-kəl) *adj.* Having or showing lofty dignity or nobility; stately. See Syns at **grand.** **— ma•jes′ti•cal•ly** *adv.*

maj•es•ty (măj′ĭ-stē) *n., pl.* **-ties. 1.a.** The greatness and dignity of a sovereign. **b.** The sovereignty and power of God. **2.** Supreme authority or power. **3.a.** A royal personage. **b. Majesty.** Used with *His, Her,* or *Your* as a title and form of address for a sovereign. **4.a.** Royal dignity of bearing or aspect; grandeur. **b.** Stately splendor; magnificence, as of style or character. [ME *mageste, maieste* < OFr. *majeste* < Lat. *māiestās*. See **meg-***.]

Maj. Gen. *abbr.* Major general.

ma•jol•i•ca (mə-jŏl′ĭ-kə, -yŏl′-) *n.* **1.** Tin-glazed earthenware, often richly colored and decorated, esp. an earthenware of this type made in Italy. **2.** Pottery made in imitation of this earthenware. [Ital. *maiolica* < Med.Lat. *Māiōlica*, Majorca (where it was made), alteration of LLat. *Māiōrica*.]

ma•jor (mā′jər) *adj.* **1.** Greater than others in importance or rank. **2.** Great in scope or effect. **3.** Great in number, size, or extent. **4.** Requiring great attention or concern; very serious. **5.** Of or relating to the field of academic study in which a student specializes. **6.** *Mus.* **a.** Having half steps between the third and fourth and the seventh and eighth degrees of a scale or mode. **b.** Equivalent to the distance between the tonic note and the second or third or sixth or seventh degrees of a major scale or mode. **c.** Based on a major scale: *major key.* —*n.* **1.a.** An officer in the U.S. Army, Air Force, or Marine Corps ranking above captain and below lieutenant colonel. **b.** A similar officer in another military or paramilitary organization. **2.** One that is superior in rank, importance, or ability. **3.a.** A field of study chosen as an academic specialty. **b.** A student specializing in such studies. **4.** *Logic.* **a.** A major premise. **b.** A major term. **5.** *Mus.* A major scale, key, interval, or mode. **6. majors.** *Sports.* The major leagues. —*intr.v.* **-jored, -jor•ing, -jors.** To pursue academic studies in a major. [ME *majour* < Lat. *māior*. See **meg-***.]

major scale

Ma•jor (mā′jər), **John.** b. 1943. British politician and prime minister (since 1990).

major axis *n. Math.* The longer of the two lines about which an ellipse is symmetrical.

Ma•jor•ca (mə-jôr′kə, -yôr′-) also **Mal•lor•ca** (mä-yôr′kä, -lyôr′-). An island of Spain in the W Mediterranean off the E-central coast of the mainland; center of an independent kingdom (1276–1343). **— Ma•jor′can** *adj. & n.*

ma•jor-do•mo (mā′jər-dō′mō) *n., pl.* **-mos. 1.** The head steward or butler in the household of a sovereign or great noble. **2.** A steward or butler. **3.** One who makes arrangements or directs affairs for another. [Ital. *maggiordomo* or Sp. *mayordomo*, both < Med.Lat. *māior domūs* : Lat. *māior*, chief; see **meg-*** + Lat. *domūs*, genitive of *domus*, house; see **dem-***.]

ma•jor•ette (mā′jə-rĕt′) *n.* A drum majorette. See Usage Note at **-ette.**

major general *n.* A commissioned officer in the U.S. Army, Air Force, or Marine Corps ranking above brigadier general and below lieutenant general.

ma•jor•i•tar•i•an•ism (mə-jôr′ĭ-târ′ē-ə-nĭz′əm, -jŏr′-) *n.* Rule by simple numerical majority in an organized group. **— ma•jor′i•tar′i•an** *adj. & n.*

ma•jor•i•ty (mə-jôr′ĭ-tē, -jŏr′-) *n., pl.* **-ties. 1.** The greater number or part; a number more than half of the total. **2.** The amount by which the greater number of votes cast, as in an election, exceeds the total number of remaining votes. **3.** The political party, group, or faction having the larger representation or electoral strength. **4.** The status of having reached full legal age. **5.** The military rank, commission, or office of a major. **6.** *Obsolete.* The fact or state of being greater; superiority. [Fr. *majorité* < Med.Lat. *māiōritās* < Lat. *māior*, greater. See **meg-***.]

Usage Note: When *majority* refers to a particular number of votes, it takes a singular verb: *Her majority was five votes.* When it refers to a group in the majority, it may take either a singular or plural verb, depending on whether the group is considered as a whole or individually. So we say *The majority elects the candidate it wants,* since the election is accomplished by the group as a whole, but *The majority of the voters live in the city,* since living in the city is something that each voter does individually.

majority leader *n.* The leader of the majority party in a legislature, as in the U.S. Senate or House of Representatives.

majority rule *n.* A doctrine by which a numerical majority of an organized group holds the power to make decisions binding on all in the group.

major league *n. Sports.* **1.** Either of the two principal groups of professional baseball teams in the United States. **2.** A league of principal importance in other professional sports. **— ma′jor-league′** (mā′jər-lēg′) *adj* **— ma′jor-lea′guer** (mā′jər-lē′gər) *n.*

major medical *n.* Insurance that covers all or most of the medical bills of major illnesses above a set amount.

major order *n. Eccles.* See **holy order** 3.

major premise *n. Logic.* The premise containing the major term in a syllogism.

Major Prophets *pl.n. Bible.* The Hebrew prophets Isaiah, Jeremiah, and Ezekiel.

major scale *n. Mus.* A diatonic scale having half steps between the third and fourth and the seventh and eighth tones.

major suit *n. Games.* A suit of superior scoring value, either spades or hearts in bridge.

major term *n. Logic.* The term of a syllogism that forms the predicate of the conclusion.

ma•jus•cule (mə-jŭs′kyo͞ol, măj′ə-skyo͞ol′) *n.* A large letter, either capital or uncial, used in writing or printing. [Fr. < Lat. *māiusculus*, somewhat larger, dim. of *māior*, greater. See **meg-***.] **— ma•jus′cule, ma•jus′cu•lar** (-kyə-lər) *adj.*

Mak•a•lu (mŭk′ə-lo͞o′). A mountain, 8,476 m (27,790 ft), in the Himalaya Mts. of NE Nepal.

mak•ar (mä′kər, mā′-) *n. Chiefly Scots.* A poet. [ME, var. of *maker*, maker, poet.]

Ma•kar•i•os III (mə-kăr′ē-əs, -ōs′, mä-kä′rē-ôs). 1913–77. Cypriot prelate and first president of Cyprus (1959–77).

Ma•kas•sar or **Ma•ka•sar** (mə-kăs′ər). See **Ujung Pandang.**

Makassar Strait. A strait between Borneo and Celebes connecting the Java Sea with the Celebes Sea.

make (māk) *v.* **made** (mād), **mak•ing, makes.** —*tr.* **1.** To cause to exist or happen; bring about; create. **2.** To bring into existence by shaping, modifying, or putting together material; construct. **3.** To form by assembling individuals or constituents. **4.** To change from one form or function to another: *make clay into bricks.* **5.a.** To cause to be or become. **b.** To cause to assume a specified function or role: *made Chicago his home.* **6.a.** To cause to act in a specified manner. **b.** To compel: *made him leave.* **7.a.** To form in the mind. **b.** To compose: *make verses.* **8.a.** To prepare; fix. **b.** To get ready or set in order for use: *made the bed.* **c.** To gather and light the materials for (a fire). **9.a.** To engage in. **b.** To carry out; perform: *make an incision.* **10.** To achieve, produce, or attain. **11.a.** To institute or establish; enact: *make laws.* **b.** To draw up and execute in a suitable form: *make a will.* **12.a.** To arrive at; reach. **b.** To reach in time. **13.a.** To attain the rank or position of. **b.** To acquire a place in or on: *made the team.* **14.a.** To gain or earn: *make money.* **b.** To behave so as to acquire: *make friends.* **c.** To score or achieve. **15.a.** To assure the success of. **b.** To favor the development of: *Practice makes a winning team.* **16.** To be suited for: *Oak makes strong furniture.* **17.** To develop into: *She will make a fine doctor.* **18.a.** To draw a conclusion as to the significance or nature of. **b.** To calculate as being; estimate. **c.** To consider as being: *wasn't the problem some people made it.* **19.a.** To constitute:

Twenty members make a quorum. **b.** To add up to: *Two and two make four.* **c.** To amount to: *makes no difference.* **20.** To constitute the essence or nature of. **21.** To cause to be very enjoyable or rewarding: *You made my day.* **22.** To appear to begin (an action): *She made to leave.* **23.** *Slang.* To persuade to have sexual intercourse. —*intr.* **1.** To act or behave in a specified manner: *make merry.* **2.** To begin or appear to begin an action: *made as if to shake my hand.* **3.** To cause something to be as specified: *make ready.* **4.** To proceed in a certain direction. **5.** *Slang.* To pretend to be; imitate. Used with *like.* **6.** To undergo fabrication or manufacture: *Wool makes up into a warm shawl.* **7.** To rise or accumulate: *The tide is making.* —*n.* **1.** The act or process of making; manufacturing. **2.** The style or manner in which a thing is made. **3.** The amount produced, esp. the output of a factory. **4.** A specific line of manufactured goods, identified by the manufacturer's name or trademark. **5.** The physical or moral nature of a person; character or disposition. **6.** *Slang.* Identification of a person or thing, often from police records. —***phrasal verbs.*** **make for. 1.** To have a particular effect or result: *details that make for comfort.* **2.** To help promote; further. **make off.** To depart in haste; run away. **make out. 1.** To discern or see, esp. with difficulty. **2.** To understand. **3.** To write out; draw up. **4.** To fill in (a form, for example). **5.** *Informal.* To imply or suggest. **6.** *Informal.* To try to establish or prove. **7.** To get along in a given way; fare. **8.** *Slang.* **a.** To neck; pet. **b.** To have sexual intercourse. **make over. 1.** To redo; renovate. **2.** To change or transfer the ownership of, usu. by means of a legal document. **make up. 1.** To put together; construct or compose: *make up a prescription.* **2.** To constitute; form. **3.a.** To alter one's appearance for a role on the stage, as with a costume and cosmetics. **b.** To apply cosmetics. **4.** To devise as a fiction or falsehood; invent. **5.a.** To make good (a deficit or lack). **b.** To compensate for. **6.** To resolve a quarrel. **7.** To make ingratiating or fawning overtures. Used with *to*: *made up to his boss.* **8.** To take (an examination or a course) again or at a later time because of previous absence or failure. **9.** To set in order: *make up a room.* **10.** *Print.* To select and arrange material for: *made up the front page.* **make with.** *Slang.* **1.** To bring into use. **2.** To put forth; produce: *always making with the jokes.* —***idioms.*** **make a clean breast of.** To confess fully. **make a face.** To distort the features of the face; grimace. **make a go of.** To achieve success in. **make away with. 1.** To carry off; steal. **2.** To use up or consume. **3.** To kill or destroy. **make believe.** To pretend. **make bold.** To venture. **make book.** *Games.* To accept bets on a race, game, or contest. **make do.** To manage to get along with the means available. **make ends meet.** To manage so that one's means are sufficient for one's needs. **make eyes.** To ogle. **make fun of.** To mock; ridicule. **make good. 1.** To carry out successfully. **2.** To fulfill. **3.** To make compensation for; make up for. **4.** To succeed. **make hay.** To turn to one's advantage. **make it. 1.** *Informal.* To be successful. **2.** *Slang.* To have sexual intercourse. **make light of.** To treat as unimportant. **make love. 1.** To engage in amorous caressing. **2.** To engage in sexual intercourse. **make much of.** To treat as of great importance. **make no bones about.** To be forthright and candid about; acknowledge freely. **make off with.** To snatch or steal. **make sail.** *Naut.* **1.** To begin a voyage. **2.** To set sails. **make the grade.** To measure up to a given standard. **make the most of.** To use to the greatest advantage. **make the scene.** *Slang.* **1.** To put in an appearance. **2.** To participate in a specified activity. **make time. 1.** To move or travel fast, as in an attempt to compensate for lost time. **2.** *Slang.* To make progress toward attracting. **make tracks.** *Slang.* To move or leave in a hurry. **make up (one's) mind.** To decide between alternatives; come to a definite decision or opinion. **make waves.** *Slang.* To cause a disturbance or controversy. **make way. 1.** To give room for passage; move aside. **2.** To make progress. **on the make.** *Slang.* **1.** Aggressively striving for financial or social improvement. **2.** Eagerly seeking a sexual partner. [ME *maken* < OE *macian.* See **mag-***.] —**mak′a•ble** *adj.*

make-be•lieve (māk′bĭ-lēv′) *n.* Playful or fanciful pretense. —**make′-be•lieve′** *adj.*

make•fast (māk′făst′) *n.* *Naut.* An object, such as a buoy, post, or pile, to which a boat is moored.

make-or-break (māk′ər-brāk′) *adj.* Resulting in great success or utter failure: *a make-or-break investment plan.*

mak•er (mā′kər) *n.* **1.** One that makes or manufactures. Often used in combination: *a policymaker.* **2.** *Law.* A party that signs a promissory note. **3. Maker.** God. **4.** *Archaic.* A poet.

make-read•y (māk′rĕd′ē) *n.* *Print.* The preparation of a form by adjusting and leveling the plates to get a clear impression.

make•shift (māk′shĭft′) *n.* A temporary or expedient substitute. —**make′shift′** *adj.*

make•up or **make-up** (māk′ŭp′) *n.* **1.** The way in which something is composed or arranged; composition or construction. **2.** *Print.* The arrangement or composition, as of type, on a page or in a book. **3.** The qualities or temperament that constitute a personality; disposition. **4.** Cosmetics applied esp. to the face. **5.** Materials, such as cosmetics, that an actor uses in portraying a role. **6.** A special examination for a student who has missed or failed a previous examination.

make•weight (māk′wāt′) *n.* **1.** Something added on a scale in order to meet a required weight. **2.** Something added only to fill a lack. **3.** A counterweight; a counterbalance.

make-work (māk′wûrk′) *n.* Work of little value assigned or taken on only to keep someone from being idle.

Ma•ke•yev•ka (mə-kē′əf-kə, -kyĕ′-). A city of E Ukraine NE of Donetsk. Pop. 451,000.

Ma•khach•ka•la (mə-käch′kə-lä′, -KHəch-). A city of SW Russia on the W coast of the Caspian Sea; founded 1844. Pop. 301,000.

ma•ki•mo•no (mä′kĭ-mō′nō) *n.*, *pl.* **-nos.** A horizontal Japanese decorative scroll featuring pictures or calligraphy. [J., scroll : *maki*, rolled + *mono*, thing.]

mak•ing (mā′kĭng) *n.* **1.a.** The act of one that makes. **b.** The process of coming into being. **2.** The means of gaining success or realizing potential. **3.a.** Something made. **b.** The quantity made at one time. **4.a.** The abilities or qualities needed for development. Often used in the plural. **b.** The material or ingredients needed for making or doing something. Often used in the plural. **5. makings.** *Informal.* The paper and tobacco for rolling a cigarette.

ma•ko (mä′kō) *n.*, *pl.* **-kos.** Either of two large mackerel sharks of the genus *Isurus.* [Maori.]

ma•ku•ta (mä-ko͞o′tä) *n.* Pl. of **likuta.**

Mal. *abbr.* **1.** *Bible.* Malachi. **2.** Malay.

mal– *pref.* **1.** Bad; badly: *maladminister.* **2.** Abnormal; abnormally: *malformation.* [ME < OFr. < Lat. < *male*, badly and *malus*, bad; see **mel-[3*]**.]

Mal•a•bar Coast (măl′ə-bär′). A region of SW India between the Arabian Sea and the Western Ghats.

Mal•a•bo (măl′ə-bō′, mä-lä′bō). Formerly **San•ta Is•a•bel** (săn′tə ĭz′ə-bĕl′, sän′tä ē-sä-bĕl′). The cap. of Equatorial Guinea, on Bioko in the Gulf of Guinea. Pop. 30,710.

mal•ab•sorp•tion (măl′əb-sôrp′shən, -zôrp′-) *n.* Defective or inadequate absorption of nutrients from the intestinal tract.

Ma•lac•ca (mə-lăk′ə, -lä′kə) *n.* The stem of the rattan palm, used for making canes and umbrella handles. [After *Malacca* (now Melaka), a town of W Malaysia.]

Malacca, Strait of. A channel between Sumatra and the Malay Peninsula connecting the Andaman and South China seas.

Mal•a•chi (măl′ə-kī′) *n.* *Bible.* **1.** A Hebrew prophet of the 6th cent. B.C. **2.** See table at **Bible.**

mal•a•chite (măl′ə-kīt′) *n.* A light to dark green carbonate mineral, $Cu_2CO_3(OH)_2$, used as a source of copper and for ornamental stoneware. [ME *melochite* < Lat. *molochītes* < Gk. *molokhitis* < *malakhē*, *molokhē*, mallow.]

mal•a•col•o•gy (măl′ə-kŏl′ə-jē) *n.* The branch of zoology that deals with mollusks. [Fr. *malacologie*, contraction of *malacozoologie* < NLat. *Malacozoa*, a classification that includes mollusks : Gk. *malakos*, soft; see **mel-[1*]** + NLat. *-zoa*, pl. of -ZOON.] —**mal′a•col′o•gist** *n.*

mal•ad•ap•ta•tion (măl′ăd-ăp-tā′shən) *n.* Faulty or inadequate adaptation.

mal•a•dap•ted (măl′ə-dăp′tĭd) *adj.* Poorly suited to a particular function or situation.

mal•a•dap•tive (măl′ə-dăp′tĭv) *adj.* **1.** Marked by faulty or inadequate adaptation. **2.** Not promoting adaptation.

mal•ad•just•ed (măl′ə-jus′tĭd) *adj.* **1.** Poorly adjusted: *a maladjusted carburetor.* **2.** *Psychol.* Inadequately adjusted to the demands or stresses of daily living.

mal•ad•just•ment (măl′ə-jŭst′mənt) *n.* **1.** Faulty or inadequate adjustment. **2.** *Psychol.* Inability to adjust to the stresses of daily living or of interpersonal relationships.

mal•ad•min•is•ter (măl′əd-mĭn′ĭ-stər) *tr.v.* **-tered, -ter•ing, -ters.** To administer or manage inefficiently or dishonestly. —**mal′ad•min′is•tra′tion** *n.*

mal•a•droit (măl′ə-droit′) *adj.* Marked by a lack of adroitness; inept. —*n.* An inept person. [Fr. : *mal-*, mal- + *adroit*, adroit; see ADROIT.] —**mal′a•droit′ly** *adv.* —**mal′a•droit′ness** *n.*

mal•a•dy (măl′ə-dē) *n.*, *pl.* **-dies. 1.** A disease, a disorder, or an ailment. **2.** An unwholesome condition: *the malady of discontent.* [ME *maladie* < OFr. < *malade*, sick < Lat. *male habitus*, in poor condition : *male*, badly; see **mel-[3*]** + *habitus*, p.part. of *habēre*, to hold; see **ghabh-***.]

Mal•a•ga (măl′ə-gə) *n.* A sweet fortified wine originally from Málaga, Spain.

Má•la•ga (măl′ə-gə, mä′lä-gä′). A city of S Spain NE of Gibraltar; founded in the 12th cent. B.C. Pop. 537,619.

Mal•a•gas•y (măl′ə-găs′ē) *n.*, *pl.* **Malagasy** or **-gas•ies. 1.** A native or inhabitant of Madagascar. **2.** The Austronesian language of the Malagasy. —*adj.* Of or relating to Madagascar, the Malagasy, or their language or culture.

Malagasy Republic. See **Madagascar.**

ma•la•gue•ña (mä′lə-gā′nyə) *n.* **1.** A dance native to Málaga, Spain, that is a variety of the fandango. **2.** Any of several Spanish folk tunes, esp. one native to Málaga that is similar to the fandango. [Sp., fem. of *malagueño*, of Málaga < MÁLAGA.]

mal•aise (mă-lāz′, -lĕz′) *n.* **1.** A vague feeling of bodily dis-

ă pat	oi boy
ā pay	ou out
âr care	o͝o took
ä father	o͞o boot
ĕ pet	ŭ cut
ē be	ûr urge
ĭ pit	th thin
ī pie	*th* this
îr pier	hw which
ŏ pot	zh vision
ō toe	ə about, item
ô paw	

Stress marks:
′ (primary);
′ (secondary), as in dictionary (dĭk′shə-nĕr′ē)

— *intr.v.* **-boed, -bo•ing, -bos.** To perform this dance. [Am. Sp. < *mamboo*, wooden cane, percussion instrument.]

Mam•e•luke (măm′ə-lo͝ok′) *n.* A member of a military caste, originally composed of Turkish slaves, that held the Egyptian throne from about 1250 until 1517 and remained powerful until 1811. [Fr. *mameluk* < Ar. *mamlūk*, slave, Mameluke < *malaka*, to possess.]

ma•mey (mä-mā′, -mē′) *n., pl.* **-meys. 1.** A West Indian tree *(Mammea americana)* having glossy leaves and large edible drupes with toxic seeds. **2.** Its fruit. [Sp. < Arawak or Taino.]

mam•ma¹ (mä′mə) *n.* Var. of **mama.**

mam•ma² (măm′ə) *n., pl.* **mam•mae** (măm′ē). An organ of female mammals that contains milk-producing glands; a mammary gland. [Lat. See **mā-²*.**] —**mam′mate′** (măm′āt′) *adj.*

mammoth
Woolly mammoth
Mammuthus primigenius

mam•mal (măm′əl) *n.* Any of various warm-blooded vertebrate animals of the class Mammalia, including human beings, characterized by a covering of hair on the skin and, in the female, mammary glands for nourishing the young. [< LLat. *mammālis*, of the breast < Lat. *mamma*, breast. See **mā-²*.**] —**mam•ma′li•an** (mă-mā′lē-ən) *adj. & n.*

mam•mal•o•gy (mă-măl′ə-jē, -mŏl′-) *n.* The branch of zoology that deals with mammals. —**mam′ma•log′i•cal** (măm′ə-lŏj′ĭ-kəl) *adj.* —**mam•mal′o•gist** *n.*

mam•ma•plas•ty or **mam•mo•plas•ty** (măm′ə-plăs′tē) *n., pl.* **-ties.** Reconstructive or cosmetic plastic surgery to alter the size or shape of the breast.

mam•ma•ry (măm′ə-rē) *adj.* Of or relating to a breast or mamma.

mammary gland *n.* Any of the milk-producing, typically paired glands in female mammals, consisting of lobes containing alveoli with ducts to convey the milk to an external nipple or teat.

Manchester terrier

mam•mee apple (mä-mā′, -mē′) *n.* See **mamey.**

mam•mif•er•ous (mă-mĭf′ər-əs) *adj.* Having mammary glands.

mam•mil•la (mă-mĭl′ə) *n., pl.* **-mil•lae** (-mĭl′ē). **1.** A nipple. **2.** A nipple-shaped protuberance. [Lat., dim. of *mamma*, breast. See **mā-²*.**] —**mam′mil•lar′y** (măm′ə-lĕr′ē) *adj.*

mam•mil•late (măm′ə-lāt′) also **mam•mil•lat•ed** (-lā′tĭd) *adj.* **1.** Having nipples or mammillae. **2.** Shaped like a nipple or mammilla. —**mam′mil•la′tion** *n.*

mam•mo•gram (măm′ə-grăm′) *n.* An x-ray image of the breast produced by mammography.

mam•mog•ra•phy (mă-mŏg′rə-fē) *n., pl.* **-phies.** X-ray examination of the breasts for early detection of tumors.

Mam•mon (măm′ən) *n.* **1.** *Bible.* Riches, avarice, and worldly gain personified as a false god in the Bible. **2.** Often **mammon.** Material wealth regarded as evil. [ME < LLat. *mammon* < Gk. *mamōnas* < Aram. *māmōnā*, riches.]

mam•moth (măm′əth) *n.* **1.** Any of various large hairy extinct elephants of the genus *Mammuthus*, esp. the woolly mammoth *(M. primigenius)* once widespread in the Northern Hemisphere. **2.** Something of great size. —*adj.* Of enormous size; huge. [Obsolete Russ. *mamut, mamot.*]

mam•my (măm′ē) *n., pl.* **-mies. 1.** Mother. **2.** *Offensive.* A Black nursemaid, esp. one formerly in the southern United States. [< dial. *mam*, var. of MAMA.]

manchineel
Hippomane mancinella

Ma•mo•ré (mä-mə-rā′). A river, c. 965 km (600 mi), of N Bolivia that joins the Beni R. to form the Madeira R.

man (măn) *n., pl.* **men** (mĕn). **1.** An adult male human being. **2.** A human being regardless of sex or age; a person. **3.** A human being or an adult male human being belonging to a specific occupation, nationality, or other category. Often used in combination: *a milkman; a freeman.* **4.** The human race; humankind. **5.** *Zool.* A member of the genus *Homo*, family Hominidae, order Primates, class Mammalia, characterized by erect posture and an opposable thumb, esp. a member of the species *Homo sapiens*, distinguished by a highly developed brain, the capacity for abstract reasoning, and the ability to communicate by means of organized speech and a variety of symbolic systems. **6.** A male human being and endowed with qualities considered characteristic of manhood. **7.** *Theol.* In Christianity and Judaism, a being composed of a body and a soul or spirit. **8.** *Informal.* **a.** A husband. **b.** A male lover or sweetheart. **9. men. a.** Workers. **b.** Enlisted personnel of the armed forces. **10.** A male representative, as of a company. **11.** A male servant or subordinate. **12.** *Informal.* Used as a familiar form of address for a man. **13.** One who swore allegiance to a lord in the Middle Ages; a vassal. **14.** *Games.* Any of the pieces used in a board game, such as chess. **15.** *Naut.* A ship. Often used in combination: *a man-of-war.* **16.** Often **Man.** *Slang.* A person or group felt to be in a position of power or authority. —*tr.v.* **manned, man•ning, mans. 1.** To supply with men. **2.** To take stations at. **3.** To fortify or brace. —*interj.* Used as an expletive to indicate intense feeling: *Man! What fun!* —***idioms.*** **as one man. 1.** In complete agreement; unanimously. **2.** With no exception. **one's own man.** Independent in judgment and action. **to a man.** Without exception. [ME < OE *mann.* See **man-¹*.**]

mandala
Earliest dated Hindu mandala known to exist, by Tejarama
(fl. early 15th century)

Usage Note: Traditionally, *man* and words derived from it have been used generically to designate any or all of the human race irrespective of sex. *Man* sometimes appears to have the sense of "person" or "people" when it is used as a count noun, as in *A man is known by the company he keeps.* Here the generic interpretation arises indirectly: if a man is known by the company he keeps, then so, by implication, is a woman. In almost all cases, however, the words *person* and *people* can be substituted for *man* and *men*, often with a gain in clarity. • By contrast, *man* functions more as a generic when it is used without an article in the singular to refer to the human race, as in sentences like *The capacity for language is unique to man.* In most contexts words such as *humanity* or *humankind* will convey the generic sense of this use of *man.* • On the whole, the Usage Panel accepts the generic use of *man*, the women members significantly less than the men. The sentence *If early man suffered from a lack of information, modern man is tyrannized by an excess of it* was acceptable to 81 percent of the Panel (including 58 percent of the women and 92 percent of the men). The Panel also accepted compound words derived from generic *man.* The sentence *The Great Wall is the only man-made structure visible from space* was acceptable to 86 percent (including 76 percent of the women and 91 percent of the men). • A related set of problems is raised by the use of *man* in forming the names of occupational and social roles such as *businessman, chairman, spokesman, layman,* and *freshman*, as well as in analogous formations such as *unsportsmanlike* and *showmanship.* Some condemn this use categorically; however, these words remained acceptable to a majority of the Usage Panel when they were used to refer to a role or class in the abstract but were rejected when they were used to refer to a woman. Thus the general use of *chairman* was acceptable to 67 percent of the Panel (including 52 percent of the women and 76 percent of the men) in the sentence *The chairman will be appointed by the Faculty Senate.* But only 48 percent (including 43 percent of the women and 50 percent of the men) accepted the use of the word in *Emily Owen, chairman of the Mayor's Task Force, issued a statement assuring residents that their views would be solicited*, where it is applied to a woman. • Several strategies have been suggested for replacing the categorical use of compounds formed with *man.* Parallel terms like *businesswoman, spokeswoman,* and *chairwoman* are increasingly used to refer to women. Also in use are common-gender terms coined with *person*, such as *businessperson, spokesperson,* and *chairperson.* For occupational titles ending in *man*, new standards of official usage have been established by the U.S. Department of Labor and other government agencies. In official contexts terms such as *firefighter* and *police officer* are now generally used in place of *fireman* and *policeman.* See Usage Notes at **-ess, people.**

Man, Isle of. An island of Great Britain in the Irish Sea off the NW coast of England; purchased by Parliament in 1765 and still an autonomous possession of the British crown.

man. *abbr.* Manual.

Man. *abbr.* Manitoba.

ma•na (mä′nə) *n.* **1.** A supernatural force believed to dwell in a person or sacred object. **2.** Power; authority. [Maori.]

man about town *n., pl.* **men about town.** A sophisticated, socially active man who frequents fashionable places.

man•a•cle (măn′ə-kəl) *n.* **1.** A device for confining the hands, usu. consisting of two metal rings that are fastened about the wrists and joined by a metal chain. **2.** Something that confines or restrains. —*tr.v.* **-cled, -cling, -cles.** To confine or restrain with or as if with manacles; fetter. [ME < OFr. *manicle* < Lat. *manicula*, dim. of *manus*, hand. See **man-²*.**]

man•age (măn′ĭj) *v.* **-aged, -ag•ing, -ag•es.** —*tr.* **1.** To direct or control the use of; handle. **2.a.** To exert control over. **b.** To make submissive to one's authority, discipline, or persuasion. **3.** To direct the affairs or interests of. **4.** To succeed in accomplishing or achieving, esp. with difficulty; contrive or arrange. —*intr.* **1.** To direct or conduct business affairs. **2.** To continue to get along; carry on. [Ital. *maneggiare* < VLat. **manidiāre* < Lat. *manus*, hand. See **man-²*.**]

man•age•a•ble (măn′ĭ-jə-bəl) *adj.* That can be managed or controlled: *manageable problems.* —**man′age•a•bil′i•ty, man′age•a•ble•ness** *n.* —**man′age•a•bly** *adv.*

man•age•ment (măn′ĭj-mənt) *n.* **1.** The act, manner, or practice of managing; handling, supervision, or control. **2.** The person or persons who control or direct a business or other enterprise. **3.** Skill in managing; executive ability.

man•ag•er (măn′ĭ-jər) *n.* **1.** One who handles, controls, or directs, esp.: **a.** One who directs a business or other enterprise. **b.** One who controls resources and expenditures. **2.** One who is in charge of an entertainer's business affairs. **3.** *Sports.* **a.** One who is in charge of the training and performance of an athlete or a team. **b.** A student who is in charge of the equipment and records of a school or college team. —**man′ag•er•ship′** *n.*

man•a•ge•ri•al (măn′ĭ-jîr′ē-əl) *adj.* Of or relating to a manager or management. —**man′a•ge′ri•al•ly** *adv.*

man•ag•ing editor (măn′-ĭ-jĭng) *n.* An editor who supervises and coordinates the editorial activities of a publishing house or publication, such as a newspaper.

Ma•na•gua (mə-näg′wə, mä-nä′gwä). The cap. of Nicaragua, in the W part on the S shore of **Lake Managua**; designated cap. in the 1850's. Pop. 644,588. **—Ma•na′guan** *adj. & n.*

man•a•kin (măn′ə-kĭn) *n.* Any of various small colorful birds of the family Pipridae, found in forests of Central and South America. [Alteration of MANIKIN.]

Ma•na•ma (mə-năm′ə, mă-) or **Al Ma•na•mah** (ăl mə-năm′-ə, mă-). The cap. of Bahrain, on the Persian Gulf; became cap. in 1971. Pop. 108,684.

ma•ña•na (mä-nyä′nə) *adv.* **1.** Tomorrow. **2.** At an unspecified future time. *—n.* An indefinite time in the future. [Sp. < VLat. **(crās) mānēāna*, early (tomorrow) < Lat. *māne*, morning. See **mā-**[1]*.]

Ma•nas•sas (mə-năs′əs). An independent city of NE VA W of Alexandria; the Civil War Battles of Bull Run (called the Battles of Manassas by the Confederates) were fought nearby in Jul. 1861 and Aug. 1862. Pop. 27,957.

Ma•nas•seh (mə-năs′ə). In the Bible, the eldest son of Joseph and the forebear of one of the tribes of Israel.

man-at-arms (măn′ət-ärmz′) *n., pl.* **men-at-arms** (mĕn′-). A soldier, esp. a medieval cavalryman supplied with heavy arms.

man•a•tee (măn′ə-tē′) *n.* Any of various herbivorous aquatic mammals of the genus *Trichechus*, found in warm coastal waters and having paddlelike front flippers. [Sp. *manatí* < Cariban, breast.]

Ma•naus (mə-nous′, mä-). A city of NW Brazil on the Rio Negro; founded in the 1660's. Pop. 611,763.

Man•ches•ter (măn′chĕs′tər, -chĭ-stər). **1.** A borough of NW England ENE of Liverpool; chartered 1301. The **Manchester Ship Canal** (completed in 1894) affords access for oceangoing vessels. Pop. 464,200. **2.** A town of N-central CT E of Hartford; settled in 1672. Pop. 51,618. **3.** A city of SE NH on the Merrimack R. N of Nashua; incorp. in 1751. Pop. 99,567.

Manchester terrier *n.* Any of various shorthaired black-and-tan dogs of a breed that originated in Manchester, England.

man-child (măn′chīd′) *n., pl.* **men-chil•dren** (mĕn′chĭl′drən). A male child; a boy; a son.

man•chi•neel (măn′chĭ-nēl′) *n.* A tropical American tree *(Hippomane mancinella)* having poisonous fruit and a milky vesicant sap. [Fr. *mancenille* < Sp. *manzanilla*, dim. of *manzana*, apple < OSp. < Lat. *(māla) Matiāna*, (apples) of Matius, poss. after Caius *Matius* Calvena (fl. 1st cent. B.C.), Roman cookbook author.]

Man•chu (măn′cho͞o, măn-cho͞o′) *n., pl.* **Manchu** or **-chus. 1.** A member of a people native to Manchuria who ruled China during the Qing dynasty. **2.** The Tungusic language of the Manchu. *—adj.* Of or relating to the Manchu or their language or culture. [Manchu *manju*.]

Man•chu•kuo (măn′cho͞o′kwō′) also **Man•chu•guo** (-gwō′). A former state of E Asia in Manchuria and E Nei Monggol (Inner Mongolia); estab. as a puppet state (1932) by the Japanese and returned to Chinese sovereignty in 1945.

Man•chu•ri•a (măn-cho͝or′ē-ə). A region of NE China comprising the modern-day provinces of Heilongjiang, Jilin, and Liaoning; homeland of the Manchu people who conquered China in the 17th cent. **—Man•chu′ri•an** *adj. & n.*

Man•chu-Tun•gus (măn′cho͞o-to͝ong-go͞oz′, -tŭn-, măn-cho͞o′-) *n.* See **Tungusic. —Man′chu-Tun•gus′ic** *adj.*

-mancy *suff.* Divination: *bibliomancy.* [ME < OFr. *-mancie* < LLat. *-mantīa* < Gk. *manteia, -manteia* < *manteuesthai*, to prophesy < *mantis*, prophet. See **men-**[1]*.]

Man•dae•an (măn-dē′ən) *n.* Var. of **Mandean.**

man•da•la (mŭn′də-lə) *n.* Any of various geometric designs symbolic of the universe and its powers, used in Hinduism and Buddhism to transform the adept through meditation. [Skt. *maṇḍalam*, circle, perh. < Tamil *muṭalai*, ball.] **—man•dal′ic** (mŭn-dăl′ĭk) *adj.*

Man•da•lay (măn′dl-ā′, măn′dl-ā′). A city of central Burma on the Irrawaddy R. N of Rangoon; cap. of the kingdom of Burma (1860–85). Pop. 532,895.

man•da•mus (măn-dā′məs) *Law. —n.* A writ issued by a superior court ordering a public official or body or a lower court to perform a specified duty. *—tr.v.* **-mused, -mus•ing, -mus•es.** To serve or compel with such a writ. [Lat. *mandāmus*, first pers. pl. of *mandāre*, to order. See **man-**[2]*.]

Man•dan[1] (măn′dăn′) *n., pl.* **Mandan** or **-dans. 1.** A member of a Native American people formerly living in south-central North Dakota, with present-day descendants in west-central North Dakota. **2.** The Siouan language of the Mandan. [Fr. *Mandane*, prob. < Dakota *mawátaɴɴa*.]

man•da•rin (măn′də-rĭn) *n.* **1.** A high public official in the Chinese Empire. **2.** A high government official or bureaucrat. **3.** A member of an elite group, esp. a person having influence or high status in intellectual or cultural circles. **4. Mandarin.** The official standard spoken language of China, based on the principal dialect spoken in and around Beijing. **5.** A mandarin orange; a tangerine. *—adj.* **1.** Of, relating to, or resembling a mandarin. **2.** Marked by elaborate and refined language or literary style. [< Sp. *mandarín*, ult. < Skt. *mantrī, mantrin-*, counselor < *mantraḥ*, counsel. See **men-**[1]*.]

mandarin collar *n.* A narrow upright collar usu. divided in front.

mandarin duck *n.* An Asian duck *(Aix galericulata)* having brightly colored plumage and a crested head.

mandarin orange *n.* See **tangerine** 2.

man•da•tar•y (măn′də-tĕr′ē) *n., pl.* **-ies.** A person or nation receiving a mandate.

man•date (măn′dāt′) *n.* **1.** An authoritative command or instruction. **2.** A command or an authorization given by a political electorate to its representative. **3.a.** A commission from the League of Nations authorizing a member nation to administer a territory. **b.** A region under such administration. **4.** *Law.* **a.** An order issued by a superior court or an official to a lower court. **b.** A contract by which one party agrees to perform services for another without payment. *—tr.v.* **-dat•ed, -dat•ing, -dates. 1.** To assign (a colony or territory) to a specified nation under a mandate. **2.** To make mandatory, as by law; decree or require. [Lat. *mandātum* < neut. p.part. of *mandāre*, to order. See **man-**[2]*.] **—man′da′tor** *n.*

man•da•to•ry (măn′də-tôr′ē, -tōr′ē) *adj.* **1.** Required or commanded by authority; obligatory. **2.** Of, having the nature of, or containing a mandate. **3.** Holding a League of Nations mandate over a territory. *—n., pl.* **-ries.** A mandatary.

man-day (măn′dā′) *n.* An industrial unit of production equal to the work one person can produce in a day.

Man•de (män′dā′) *n., pl.* **Mande** or **-des. 1.** A branch of the Niger-Congo language family, spoken in the upper Niger River valley. **2.** A member of a Mande-speaking people. [Mandingo *mandi, mande*, dim. of *ma*, mother.]

Man•de•an also **Man•dae•an** (măn-dē′ən) *n.* **1.** A member of a Gnostic sect in Iraq. **2.** A form of Aramaic used by the Mandeans. [Mandean *mandaya*, having knowledge < *manda*, knowledge.] **—Man•de′an** *adj.*

Man•de•kan (măn-dē′kən, män-dā′-) *n.* See **Mandingo** 2.

Man•de•la (măn-dĕl′ə), **Nelson Rolihlahla.** b. 1918. South African Black political leader imprisoned for nearly 30 years for his anti-apartheid activities; released in Feb. 1990.

Man•de•ville (măn′də-vĭl′), Sir **John.** Pen name of the unknown compiler of *The Voyage and Travels of Sir John Mandeville, Knight* (c. 1371).

man•di•ble (măn′də-bəl) *n.* **1.** The lower jaw of a vertebrate animal. **2.** Either the upper or lower part of the beak in birds. **3.** Any of various mouth organs of invertebrates used for seizing and biting food, esp. either of a pair of such organs in arthropods. [ME < OFr. < LLat. *mandibula* < Lat. *mandere*, to chew.] **—man•dib′u•lar** (-dĭb′yə-lər) *adj.*

man•dib•u•late (măn-dĭb′yə-lĭt, -lāt′) *adj.* Having a mandible or mandibles. *—n.* An insect having mandibles.

Man•din•go (măn-dĭng′gō) *n., pl.* **-gos** or **-goes. 1.** A member of any of various peoples inhabiting a large area of the upper Niger River valley. **2.** A group of related Mande languages including Bambara, Malinke, and Maninka, widely spoken in western Africa. [Mandingo < *mandi*, Mande. See MANDE.]

man•do•lin (măn′də-lĭn′, măn′dl-ĭn) *n. Mus.* A stringed instrument with a usu. pear-shaped body and a fretted neck. [Fr. *mandoline* < Ital. *mandolino*, dim. of *mandola*, lute < Fr. *mandore* < LLat. *pandūra*, three-string lute < Gk. *pandoura*.] **—man′do•lin′ist** *n.*

man•drag•o•ra (măn-drăg′ər-ə) *n.* See **mandrake** 1. [ME < OE < Lat. *mandragorās*. See MANDRAKE.]

man•drake (măn′drāk′) *n.* **1.a.** A southern European plant *(Mandragora officinarum)* once believed to have magical powers because its root resembles the human body. **b.** The root of this plant, containing the poisonous alkaloid hyoscyamine. **2.** See **May apple.** [ME, alteration of *mandragora* < OE < Lat. *mandragorās* < Gk.]

man•drel or **man•dril** (măn′drəl) *n.* **1.** A spindle or an axle used to secure or support material being machined or milled. **2.** A metal rod or bar around which material, such as metal or glass, may be shaped. **3.** A shaft on which a working tool is mounted, as in a dental drill. [Poss. alteration of Fr. *mandrin*, lathe < Prov. *mandre*, axle, crank < OProv., beam of a balance < Lat. *mamphur*, bow drill, perh. from Oscan.]

man•drill (măn′drəl) *n.* A large fierce baboon *(Papio sphinx)* of western Africa, having brilliant blue, purple, and scarlet facial markings in the adult male. [MAN + DRILL[4].]

mane (mān) *n.* **1.** The long hair along the top and sides of the neck of certain mammals, such as the horse. **2.** A long thick growth of hair on a person's head. [ME < OE *manu*.]

man-eat•er (măn′ē′tər) *n.* **1.** An animal that eats or is reputed to eat human flesh. **2.** A cannibal. **—man′-eat′ing** *adj.*

ma•nège also **ma•nege** (mă-nĕzh′) *n.* **1.** The art of training and riding horses. **2.** The movements and paces of a trained horse. **3.** A school for teaching equestrianship and training horses. [Fr. < Ital. *maneggio* < *maneggiare*, to manage. See MANAGE.]

ma•nes or **Ma•nes** (mā′nēz′, mä′nās′) *pl.n.* **1.** The spirits of the dead, regarded as minor supernatural powers in ancient Roman religion. **2.** *(used with a sing. v.)* The revered spirit of one who has died. [ME < Lat. *mānēs*, perh. < *mānis*, good. See **mā-**[1]*.]

Ma•nes (mā′nēz) also **Ma•ni** (mä′nē). A.D. 216?–276? Persian prophet and founder of Manichaeism.

Ma•net (mə-nā′, mă-), **Edouard.** 1832–83. French painter

mandarin duck
Male mandarin duck
Aix galericulata

Nelson Mandela
Photographed in Soweto, South Africa, in 1990

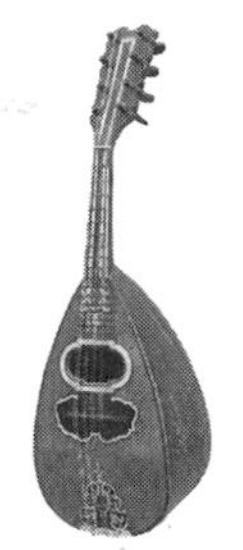

mandolin
Late 18th-century Italian

ă pat	oi boy
ā pay	ou out
âr care	o͝o took
ä father	o͞o boot
ĕ pet	ŭ cut
ē be	ûr urge
ĭ pit	th thin
ī pie	*th* this
îr pier	hw which
ŏ pot	zh vision
ō toe	ə about, item
ô paw	

Stress marks:
′ (primary);
′ (secondary), as in
dictionary (dĭk′shə-nĕr′ē)

— **man′o•met′ri•cal•ly** *adv.* — **ma•nom′e•try** *n.*

man on horseback *n.*, *pl.* **men on horseback. 1.** A man, usu. a military leader, whose popularity and power may make him a dictator, as in a crisis. **2.** A dictator.

man•or (măn′ər) *n.* **1.a.** A landed estate. **b.** The main house on an estate. **2.** A tract of land in certain North American colonies with hereditary rights granted to the proprietor by royal charter. **3.a.** The district over which a lord had domain in medieval western Europe. **b.** The lord's residence in such a district. [ME < OFr. *maneir, manoir*, to dwell, manor < Lat. *manēre*, to remain. See **men-**[3]*.] — **ma•no′ri•al** (mə-nôr′ē-əl, -nōr′-) *adj.*

manor house *n.* **1.** The main house on an estate. **2.** The house of the lord of a manor.

ma•no•ri•al•ism (mə-nôr′ē-ə-lĭz′əm, -nōr′-) *n.* The medieval manorial system or its precepts and practices.

man-o'-war bird (măn′ə-wôr′) *n.* See **frigate bird.**

man•pow•er (măn′pou′ər) *n.* **1.** The power of human physical strength. **2.** Power in terms of the workers available to a particular group or required for a particular task.

man•qué (mäɴ-kā′) *adj.* Unfulfilled or frustrated in the realization of one's ambitions or capabilities. [Fr. < p.part. of *manquer*, to fail < OFr. < OItal. *mancare* < *manco*, lacking < Lat. *mancus*, maimed, infirm. See **man-**[2]*.]

man•rope (măn′rōp′) *n. Naut.* A rope rigged as a handrail on a gangplank or ladder.

man•sard (măn′särd′) *n.* **1.** A roof having two slopes on all four sides, with the lower slope almost vertical and the upper almost horizontal. **2.** The upper story formed by the lower slope of a mansard roof. [Fr. *mansarde*, after François *Mansart* (1598–1666), French architect.] — **man′sard′ed** *adj.*

mansard

manse (măns) *n.* **1.** A Protestant cleric's house and land, esp. of a Presbyterian minister's residence. **2.** A large stately residence. **3.** *Archaic.* The dwellings belonging to a householder. [ME *manss*, a manor house < Med.Lat. *mansa*, a dwelling < Lat., fem. p.part. of *manēre*, to dwell, remain. See **men-**[3]*.]

man•ser•vant (măn′sûr′vənt) *n.*, *pl.* **men•ser•vants** (mĕn′sûr′vənts). A male servant, esp. a valet.

Mans•field (mănz′fēld′). **1.** A municipal borough of central England N of Nottingham. Pop. 99,900. **2.** A town of NE CT ENE of Hartford. Pop. 21,103. **3.** A city of N-central OH WSW of Akron. Pop. 50,627.

Mansfield, Katherine. 1888–1923. New Zealand-born British writer known for her short stories.

mantel

man•sion (măn′shən) *n.* **1.** A large stately house. **2.** A manor house. **3.** *Archaic.* **a.** A dwelling; an abode. **b. mansions.** A separate dwelling in a large house or structure. **4.a.** See **house** 10. **b.** Any one of the 28 divisions of the moon's monthly path. [ME, a dwelling < OFr. < Lat. *mānsiō, mānsiōn-* < *mānsus*, p.part. of *manēre*, to dwell, remain. See **men-**[3]*.]

man-sized (măn′sīzd′) also **man-size** (-sīz′) *adj.* **1.** *Informal.* Very large: *a man-sized piece of pie.* **2.** Calling for the strength traditionally attributed to a man: *a man-sized job.*

man•slaugh•ter (măn′slô′tər) *n. Law.* The unlawful killing of one human being by another without intent to do injury.

man•slay•er (măn′slā′ər) *n.* One that kills a human being.

man•sue•tude (măn′swĭ-to͞od′, -tyo͞od′) *n.* Gentleness of manner; mildness. [ME < OFr. < Lat. *mānsuētūdō* < *mānsuētus*, p.part. of *mānsuēscere*, to tame : *manus*, hand; see **man-**[2]* + *suēscere*, to accustom; see **s(w)e-***.]

Man•sur (măn-so͝or′), **al-.** 712?–775. Arab caliph (754–775) who founded Baghdad in 764.

man•ta (măn′tə) *n.* **1.** A rough-textured cotton fabric or blanket made and used in Spanish America and the southwest United States. **2.** Any of several rays of the family Mobulidae, having a large flattened body and winglike pectoral fins. [Sp., blanket, manta (< its blanketlike shape), alteration of *manto*, cloak, perh. < Lat. *mantellum, mantēlum*.]

man-tai•lored (măn′tā′lərd) *adj.* Tailored in the traditionally unadorned style of men's clothing.

manta ray *n.* See **manta** 2.

man•teau (măn-tō′) *n.*, *pl.* **-teaus** (-tōz′) or **-teaux** (-tō′). A loose cloak or mantle. [Fr. < OFr. *mantel*. See MANTLE.]

Man•te•ca (măn-tē′kə). A city of central CA S of Stockton. Pop. 40,773.

Man•te•gna (män-tān′yə, -tĕ′nyä), **Andrea.** 1431–1506. Italian artist noted for his works in the Renaissance style.

man•tel also **man•tle** (măn′tl) *n.* **1.** An ornamental facing around a fireplace. **2.** The protruding shelf over a fireplace. Also called regionally *fireboard* [ME *mantel*, as in *mantiltre*, beam over fireplace opening. See MANTLE.]

man•tel•et (măn′tl-ĭt, mănt′lĭt) *n.* **1.** A short cape. **2.** Also **mant•let** (mănt′lĭt). A mobile screen or shield formerly used to protect besieging soldiers. [ME < OFr., dim. of *mantel*, mantle. See MANTLE.]

man•tel•let•ta (măn′tə-lĕt′ə) *n.* A knee-length sleeveless vestment worn by Roman Catholic prelates. [Ital., prob. < Med.Lat. *mantellētum*, dim. of Lat. *mantellum*, mantle.]

man•tel•piece (măn′tl-pēs′) *n.* See **mantel** 2.

man•tel•shelf (măn′tl-shĕlf′) *n.* See **mantel** 2.

man•tel•tree (măn′tl-trē′) *n.* A beam, a stone, or an arch that supports the masonry above a fireplace.

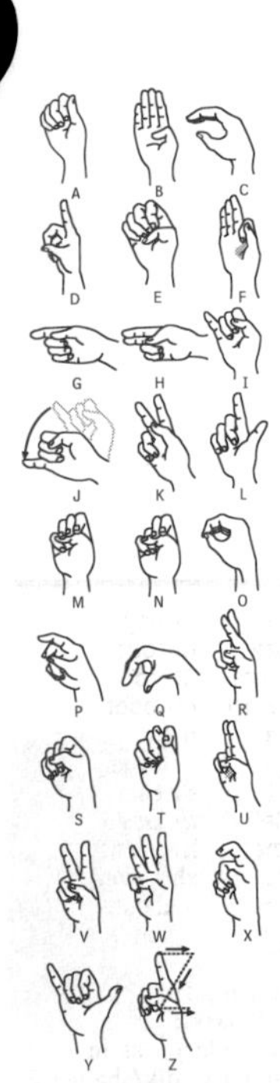

manual alphabet

man•tic (măn′tĭk) *adj.* Of, relating to, or having the power of divination; prophetic. [Gk. *mantikos* < *mantis*, seer. See **men-**[1]*.] — **man′tic•al•ly** *adv.*

man•ti•core (măn′tĭ-kôr′, -kōr′) *n.* A legendary monster having the head of a man, the body of a lion, and the tail of a dragon or scorpion. [ME *manticores* < Lat. *manticōra* < Gk. *mantikhōras*, var. of *martiokhōras* < OIran. **martiya-khvāra-*, man-eater : **martiya-*, man; akin to OPers. *martiya-*, man; see **mer-*** + **-khvāra-*, eater; akin to Avestan *khvar-*, to eat; see **swel-***.]

man•tid (măn′tĭd) *n.* See **mantis.** [< NLat. *Mantidae*, family name < *Mantis*, type genus < Gk. *mantis*, seer. See MANTIS.]

man•til•la (măn-tē′yə, -tĭl′ə) *n.* **1.** A lightweight lace or silk scarf worn over the head and shoulders, often over a high comb, by women in Spain and Latin America. **2.** A short cloak or cape. [Sp., dim. of *manta*, cape. See MANTA.]

Man•ti•ne•a (măn′tə-nē′ə). An ancient city of S Greece in the E Peloponnesus; site of a Theban defeat of Sparta (362 B.C.).

man•tis (măn′tĭs) *n.*, *pl.* **-tis•es** or **-tes** (-tēz). Any of various predatory insects of the family Mantidae, usu. pale green and having two pairs of walking legs and grasping forelimbs. [Gk., seer. See **men-**[1]*.]

mantis crab *n.* See **squilla.**

man•tis•sa (măn-tĭs′ə) *n. Math.* The decimal part of a logarithm; for example, in the logarithm 2.95424, the mantissa is 0.95424. [Lat., makeweight, perhaps of Etruscan orig.]

mantis shrimp *n.* See **squilla.**

man•tle (măn′tl) *n.* **1.** A loose sleeveless coat worn over outer garments; a cloak. **2.** Something that covers, envelops, or conceals. **3.** Var. of **mantel. 4.** The outer covering of a wall. **5.** A zone of hot gases around a flame. **6.** A sheath of threads in gas lamps that gives off brilliant illumination when heated by the flame. **7.** *Anat.* The cerebral cortex. **8.** *Geol.* The layer of the earth between the crust and the core. **9.** The outer wall and casing of a blast furnace above the hearth. **10.** The wings, shoulder feathers, and back of a bird when differently colored from the rest of the body. **11.** *Zool.* **a.** A fold or pair of folds of the body wall that lines the shell and secretes the substance that forms the shell in mollusks and brachiopods. **b.** The soft outer wall lining the shell of a tunicate or barnacle. — *v.* **-tled, -tling, -tles.** — *tr.* To cover with or as if with a mantle; conceal. — *intr.* **1.** To spread or become extended over a surface. **2.** To become covered with a coating, as froth on a liquid. **3.** To be overspread by blushes or colors. [ME < OE *mentel* and < OFr. *mantel*, both < Lat. *mantellum*.]

Man•tle (măn′tl), **Mickey Charles.** b. 1931. Amer. baseball player (1951–68) who hit 536 home runs.

mantle rock *n.* See **regolith.**

mant•let (mănt′lĭt) *n.* Var. of **mantelet** 2.

man-to-man (măn′tə-măn′) *adj.* **1.** Marked by forthrightness and honesty; heart-to-heart. **2.** *Sports.* Of, relating to, or being a system of defense in which a defensive player guards a specific offensive player.

Man•toux test (măn-to͞o′, män-) *n.* A tuberculin test in which a small amount of tuberculin is injected under the skin. [After Charles *Mantoux* (1877–1947), French physician.]

man•tra (măn′trə, mŭn′-) *n. Hinduism.* A sacred verbal formula repeated in prayer, meditation, or incantation. [Skt. *mantraḥ*. See **men-**[1]*.] — **man′tric** *adj.*

man•tu•a (măn′cho͞o-ə, -to͞o-ə) *n.* A loose gown open in front to reveal an underskirt, worn by European women in the 17th and 18th centuries. [Alteration of MANTEAU.]

Man•tu•a (măn′cho͞o-ə, -to͞o-ə). A city of N Italy SSW of Verona; orig. an Etruscan settlement. Pop. 60,932. — **Man′tu•an** *adj. & n.*

man•u•al (măn′yo͞o-əl) *adj.* **1.a.** Of or relating to the hands. **b.** Done by, used by, or operated with the hands. **c.** Employing human rather than mechanical energy. **2.** Of, relating to, or resembling a small reference book. — *n.* **1.** A small reference book, esp. one giving instructions. **2.** *Mus.* A keyboard of an organ played with the hands. **3.** A machine operated by hand. **4.** Prescribed movements in the handling of a weapon, esp. a rifle. [ME < OFr. *manuel* < Lat. *manuālis* < *manus*, hand. See MANUS.] — **man′u•al•ly** *adv.*

manual alphabet *n.* An alphabet used esp. by hearing-impaired people in which finger positions represent the letters.

manual training *n.* A course of training to develop manual dexterity in practical arts, such as woodworking.

ma•nu•bri•um (mə-no͞o′brē-əm, -nyo͞o′-) *n.*, *pl.* **-bri•a** (-brē-ə). **1.** A body part or process shaped like a handle. **2.a.** The broad upper division of the sternum with which the clavicle and first two ribs articulate. **b.** The long tapering process of the malleus attached to the central portion of the eardrum. [Lat., handle < *manus*, hand. See **man-**[2]*.]

manuf. *abbr.* Manufacture.

manufac. *abbr.* Manufacture.

man•u•fac•to•ry (măn′yə-făk′tə-rē) *n.*, *pl.* **-ries.** A factory or manufacturing plant. [Prob. MANUFACT(URE) + -ORY.]

man•u•fac•ture (măn′yə-făk′chər) *v.* **-tured, -tur•ing, -tures.** — *tr.* **1.a.** To make or process (a raw material) into a finished product, esp. by a large-scale industrial operation. **b.** To make or process (a product), esp. with industrial machines. **2.** To create, produce, or turn out in a mechanical manner. **3.** To concoct or invent; fabricate. *—intr.* To make or process goods, esp. in large quantities and by means of industrial machines. *—n.* **1.a.** The act, craft, or process of manufacturing products, esp. on a large scale. **b.** An industry in which mechanical power and machinery are employed. **2.** A product that is manufactured. **3.** The making or producing of something. [< Fr., manufacture < OFr. < Med.Lat. **manūfactūra* : Lat. *manū,* ablative of *manus,* hand; see **man-²*** + Lat. *factūra,* working of a metal < *factus,* p.part. of *facere,* to make. See **dhē-*.**] **—man′u·fac′tur·a·ble** *adj.* **—man′u·fac′tur·al** *adj.* **—man′u·fac′tur·ing** *n.*

man·u·fac·tured gas (măn′yə-făk′chərd) *n.* A gaseous fuel made from soft coal or various petroleum products.

man·u·fac·tur·er (măn′yə-făk′chər-ər) *n.* A person, an enterprise, or an entity that manufactures something.

man·u·mit (măn′yə-mĭt′) *tr.v.* **-mit·ted, -mit·ting, -mits.** To free from slavery or bondage; emancipate. [ME *manumitten* < OFr. *manumitter* < Lat. *manūmittere* : *manū,* ablative of *manus,* hand; see **man-²*** + *mittere,* to send from.] **—man′u·mis′sion** (-mĭsh′ən) *n.* **—man′u·mit′ter** *n.*

ma·nure (mə-no͝or′, -nyo͝or′) *n.* Material, esp. dung, often with discarded animal bedding, used to fertilize soil. *—tr.v.* **-nured, -nur·ing, -nures.** To fertilize (soil) by applying manure. [< ME *manuren,* to cultivate land < AN *mainouverer* < VLat. **manūoperāre,* to work with the hands : Lat. *manū,* ablative of *manus,* hand; see **man-²*** + Lat. *operārī,* to work; see **op-*.**] **—ma·nur′er** *n.* **—ma·nu′ri·al** *adj.*

ma·nus (mā′nəs, mä′-) *n., pl.* **manus.** The distal part of the forelimb of a vertebrate, including the wrist and hand or the carpus and forefoot. [Lat., hand. See **man-²*.**]

man·u·script (măn′yə-skrĭpt′) *n.* **1.** A book, document, or other composition written by hand. **2.** A typewritten or handwritten version of a book or other work, esp. the author's own copy, submitted for publication in print. **3.** Handwriting. [< Med.Lat. *manūscrīptum* < neut. of *manūscrīptus,* handwritten : Lat. *manū,* ablative of *manus,* hand; see **man-²*** + Lat. *scrīptus,* p.part. of *scrībere,* to write; see **skrībh-*.**]

Ma·nu·tius (mə-no͞o′shəs, -shē-əs, -nyo͞o′-), **Aldus.** 1450–1515. Italian scholar and printer who established (c. 1498) the Aldine Press to publish Greek and Latin classics.

man·ward (măn′wərd) *adv. & adj.* Of, at, or toward humankind. **—man′wards** *adv.*

man·wise (măn′wīz′) *adv.* In a manner characteristic of human beings.

Manx (măngks) *adj.* Of or relating to the Isle of Man or its people, language, or culture. *—n., pl.* **Manx. 1.** The people of the Isle of Man. **2.** The extinct Goidelic language of the Manx. **3.** A Manx cat. [Alteration of ON **Mansk* < *Mon, Man-,* Isle of Man.]

Manx cat (măngks) or **manx cat** *n.* Any of a breed of domestic cat having short hair and lacking an external tail.

Manx·man (măngks′mən) *n.* A man who is a native or inhabitant of the Isle of Man.

Manx·wom·an (măngks′wo͝om′ən) *n.* A woman who is a native or inhabitant of the Isle of Man.

man·y (mĕn′ē) *adj.* **more** (môr, mōr), **most** (mōst). **1.** Being one of a large indefinite number; numerous: *many a child.* **2.** Amounting to or consisting of a large indefinite number: *many friends.* *—n. (used with a pl. v.)* **1.** A large indefinite number: *A good many of us.* **2.** The majority of the people; the masses. *—pron. (used with a pl. v.)* A large number of persons or things: *Many came.* **—*idiom.* as many.** The same number of. [ME < OE *manig.* See **menegh-*.**]

man-year (măn′yîr′) *n.* A unit measuring the work of one person in a year, based on a standard number of man-days.

man·y·fold (mĕn′ē-fōld′) *adv.* By many times.

man·y·plies (mĕn′ĭ-plīz′) *n.* See **omasum.**

man·y-sid·ed (mĕn′ē-sī′dĭd) *adj.* **1.** Having many sides. **2.** Having many aspects, talents, or interests. **—man′y-sid′ed·ness** *n.*

Man·za·nil·la (măn′zə-nē′yə, -nĭl′ə) *n.* A pale dry sherry from Spain. [Sp., dim. of *manzana,* apple. See MANCHINEEL.]

man·za·ni·ta (măn′zə-nē′tə) *n.* Any of several evergreen shrubs or small trees of the genus *Arctostaphylos* of the Pacific coast of North America, esp. *A. manzanita,* bearing white or pink flowers and producing red berrylike drupes. [Sp., dim. of *manzana,* apple. See MANCHINEEL.]

Man·zo·ni (män-zō′nē, -dzō′-), **Alessandro.** 1785–1873. Italian writer best known for *The Betrothed* (1825–27).

MAO *abbr.* Monoamine oxidase.

Mao·ism (mou′ĭz′əm) *n.* Marxism-Leninism developed in China esp. by Mao Zedong. **—Mao′ist** *adj. & n.*

Mao·ri (mou′rē) *n., pl.* **Maori** or **-ris. 1.** A member of a people of New Zealand, of Polynesian-Melanesian descent. **2.** The Austronesian language of the Maori. *—adj.* Of or relating to the Maori or their language or culture.

mao-tai (mou′tī′) *n.* A clear, very strong Chinese liquor distilled from sorghum. [After *Mao-Tai,* a town of Guizhou province, China.]

Mao Ze·dong (mou′ dzə′do͝ng′) also **Mao Tse-tung** (tsə′to͝ong′). 1893–1976. Chinese political leader who was a founder of the Chinese Communist Party (1921) and proclaimed the People's Republic of China in 1949.

map (măp) *n.* **1.a.** A representation, usu. on a plane surface, of a region of the earth or heavens. **b.** Something that suggests such a representation, as in clarity. **2.** *Math.* The correspondence of one or more elements in one set to one or more elements in the same set or another set. **3.** *Slang.* The human face. **4.** *Genet.* A genetic map. *—tr.v.* **mapped, map·ping, maps. 1.a.** To make a map of. **b.** To depict as if on a map. **2.** To explore or make a survey of (a region) for the purpose of making a map. **3.** To plan or delineate, esp. in detail; arrange: *mapping out her future.* **4.** *Genet.* To locate (a gene or DNA sequence) in a specific region of a chromosome in relation to known genes or DNA sequences. **5.** *Math.* To establish a mapping of (an element or a set). **—*idioms.* put on the map.** To make well-known or famous. **wipe off the map.** To destroy completely; annihilate. [< ME *mapemounde* < OFr. *mapemond* < Med.Lat. *mappa (mundī),* map (of the world) < Lat., napkin, cloth (on which maps were drawn), perh. of Carthaginian orig.] **—map′pa·ble** *adj.* **—map′per** *n.*

ma·ple (mā′pəl) *n.* **1.** Any of numerous deciduous trees or shrubs of the genus *Acer* of the North Temperate Zone, having opposite, usu. palmate leaves and long-winged fruits. **2.** The wood of any of these trees, esp. of the sugar maple. **3.** The flavor of the concentrated sap of the sugar maple. [ME < OE *mapul-,* as in *mapultrēo.*]

Ma·ple Grove (mā′pəl). A city of SE MN, a suburb of Minneapolis. Pop. 38,763.

Maple Heights. A city of NE OH, a suburb of Cleveland. Pop. 27,089.

Maple Shade. A community of S-central NJ E of Camden. Pop. 19,211.

maple sugar *n.* A sugar made by boiling down maple syrup.

maple syrup *n.* **1.** A sweet syrup made from the sap of the sugar maple. **2.** Syrup made from various sugars and flavored with maple syrup or artificial maple flavoring.

Ma·ple·wood (mā′pəl-wo͝od′). **1.** A city of SE MN, a suburb of St. Paul. Pop. 30,954. **2.** A community of NE NJ E of Newark. Pop. 21,765.

map·mak·er (măp′mā′kər) *n.* A person who makes maps; a cartographer. **—map′mak·ing** (-māk′ĭng) *n.*

map·ping (măp′ĭng) *n.* **1.** The act or process of making a map. **2.** *Math.* A rule of correspondence between sets that associates each element of a set with an element in the same or another set.

Ma·pu·to (mə-po͞o′tō). Formerly **Lou·ren·ço Mar·ques** (lə-rĕn′sō mär′kĕs, lô-rĕɴ′so͞o mär′kĕsh). The cap. of Mozambique, in the S part on the Indian Ocean; founded in the late 18th cent. Pop. 755,300.

ma·quette (mă-kĕt′) *n.* A usu. small model of an intended work, such as a sculpture. [Fr. < Ital. *macchietta,* sketch, dim. of *macchia,* spot < Lat. *macula.*]

ma·qui (mä′kē) *n., pl.* **-quis. 1.** A Chilean evergreen shrub *(Aristotelia chilensis)* bearing edible purple berries. **2.** A Chilean wine made from maqui fruit. [Sp., of Araucanian orig.]

ma·qui·la (mə-kē′lə, mä-kē′lä) *n.* A maquiladora.

ma·qui·la·do·ra (mä-kē′lä-dô′rä) *n.* An assembly plant in Mexico, esp. one along the U.S. border, that finishes products for another company. [Am.Sp., place to pay miller's fee, maquiladora < Sp. *maquila,* miller's portion for milling one's grain < OSp. < Ar. *makīla,* measure < *kāla,* to measure.]

ma·quil·lage (mä′kē-äzh′) *n.* Cosmetic or theatrical makeup. [Fr. < *maquiller,* to apply makeup < OFr. *macquiller,* to work < ONFr. *maquier* < MDu. *maken,* to make. See **mag-*.**]

ma·quis (mă-kē′) *n., pl.* **maquis. 1.** A dense growth of small trees and shrubs in the Mediterranean area. **2. Maquis. a.** A member of the French Resistance that fought against the German occupation forces during World War II. **b.** The French Resistance. [Fr. < Ital. *macchie,* pl. of *macchia,* thicket, spot < Lat. *macula,* spot.]

Ma·qui·sard (măk′ē-zärd′, -zär′) *n.* See **maquis** 2a. [Fr. < *maquis,* the French underground. See MAQUIS.]

mar (mär) *tr.v.* **marred, mar·ring, mars. 1.** To inflict damage, esp. disfiguring damage, on. **2.** To impair the soundness, perfection, or integrity of; spoil. See Syns at **spoil.** *—n.* A disfiguring mark; a blemish. [ME *merren* < OE *mierran, merran,* to impede.]

mar. *abbr.* **1.** Maritime. **2.** Married.

Mar. or **Mar** *abbr.* March.

ma·ra (mə-rä′) *n.* Any of various long-eared and long-legged cavies of the genus *Dolichotis,* inhabiting central and southern Argentina. [Am.Sp. *mará,* perh. of Araucanian orig.]

mar·a·bou also **mar·a·bout** (măr′ə-bo͞o′) *n.* **1.** Any of several large African storks of the genus *Leptoptilos* that have a soft white down on the underside. **2.a.** The down of one of these storks or an imitation of it. **b.** A hat or garment trimmed with marabou. **3.a.** A raw silk that can be dyed without being separated from its coating of sericin. **b.** A fabric or an article of apparel made from such silk. [Fr. *marabout,* Muslim hermit, marabout. See MARABOUT¹.]

Mao Zedong

marabou
Leptoptilos crumeniferus

ă **pat**	oi **boy**
ā **pay**	ou **out**
âr **care**	o͝o **took**
ä **father**	o͞o **boot**
ĕ **pet**	ŭ **cut**
ē **be**	ûr **urge**
ĭ **pit**	th **thin**
ī **pie**	*th* **this**
îr **pier**	hw **which**
ŏ **pot**	zh **vision**
ō **toe**	ə **a**bout,
ô **paw**	it**e**m

Stress marks:
′ (primary);
′ (secondary), as in
dictionary (dĭk′shə-nĕr′ē)

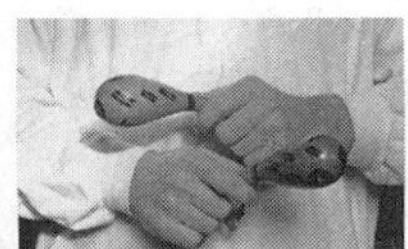

maraca
A pair of maracas

Jean Paul Marat
1793 portrait by Joseph Boze (1744–1826)

Marcel Marceau
As *Bip* in 1957

Margrethe II

mar•a•bout[1] (măr′ə-bo͞o′, -bo͞ot′) *n.* **1.** A Muslim hermit or saint, esp. in northern Africa. **2.** The tomb of such a hermit or saint. [Fr. < Port. *marabuto* < Ar. *murābiṭ*.]

mar•a•bout[2] (măr′ə-bo͞o′) *n.* Var. of **marabou.**

ma•ra•ca (mə-rä′kə) *n. Mus.* A percussion instrument consisting of a hollow gourd rattle containing pebbles or beans and often played in pairs. [Port. *maracá*, prob. from Tupi.]

Ma•ra•cai•bo (măr′ə-kī′bō, mä′rä-kī′vô). A city of NW Venezuela S of the Gulf of Venezuela at the outlet of **Lake Maracaibo;** founded 1571. Pop. 929,000.

Ma•ra•cay (mär′ə-kī′). A city of N Venezuela WSW of Caracas. Pop. 355,000.

Ma•ra•ñón (mär′ən-yōn′, mä′rä-nyôn′). A river flowing c. 1,609 km (1,000 mi) from W-central to NE Peru, where it joins the Ucayali R. to form the Amazon.

ma•ras•ca (mə-răs′kə) *n.* A European cultivar of the sour cherry tree *(Prunus cerasus)* bearing bitter red fruit from which maraschino is made. [Ital. See MARASCHINO.]

mar•a•schi•no (măr′ə-skē′nō, -shē′-) *n., pl.* **-nos.** A cordial made from the fermented juice and crushed pits of the marasca cherry. [Ital. < *marasca*, marasca < *amarasca* < *amaro*, bitter < Lat. *amārus*.]

maraschino cherry *n.* A cherry preserved in a syrup flavored with real or imitation maraschino.

ma•ras•mus (mə-răz′məs) *n. Pathol.* A progressive wasting of the body, occurring chiefly in young children and associated with insufficient intake or malabsorption of food. [NLat. < Gk. *marasmos* < *marainein*, to waste away. See **mer-*.**] —**ma•ras′mic** *adj.*

Ma•rat (mə-rä′, mä-), **Jean Paul.** 1743–93. Swiss-born French revolutionary who founded (1789) *L'Ami du Peuple*.

Ma•ra•tha also **Mah•rat•ta** (mə-rä′tə, -răt′ə) *n., pl.* **Maratha** or **-thas** also **Mahratta** or **-tas.** A member of a Hindu people inhabiting Maharashtra in west-central India. [Marathi *Marāṭhā* < Skt. *Mahārāṣṭraḥ*, Maharashtra.]

Ma•ra•thi also **Mah•ra•ti** or **Mah•rat•ti** (mə-rä′tē, -răt′ē) *n.* The principal Indic language of Maharashtra. [Marathi *Marāṭhī* < Skt. *Mahārāṣṭrī* < *Mahārāṣṭraḥ*, Maharashtra.]

mar•a•thon (măr′ə-thŏn′) *n.* **1.** *Sports.* **a.** A cross-country footrace of 26 miles, 385 yards (41.3 kilometers). **b.** A long-distance race other than a footrace. **2.a.** A contest of endurance. **b.** An event or activity that requires prolonged effort or endurance. [After MARATHON (a messenger having run from there to Athens to announce victory).]

Mar•a•thon (măr′ə-thŏn′). A plain of ancient Greece NE of Athens; site of a major victory over the Persians (490 B.C.).

mar•a•thon•er (măr′ə-thŏn′ər) *n.* One that participates in a marathon, esp. a marathon runner. —**mar′a•thon′ing** *n.*

ma•raud (mə-rôd′) *v.* **-raud•ed, -raud•ing, -rauds.** —*intr.* To rove and raid in search of booty. —*tr.* To raid or pillage for plunder. [Fr. *marauder* < *maraud*, tomcat, vagabond.]

mar•ble (mär′bəl) *n.* **1.a.** A metamorphic rock formed from limestone or dolomite, often irregularly colored by impurities and used esp. in architecture and sculpture. **b.** A piece of this rock. **c.** A sculpture made from this rock. **2.** Something resembling marble, as in hardness. **3.** *Games.* **a.** A small hard ball, usu. of glass, used in children's games. **b. marbles.** *(used with a sing. v.)* Any of various games played with marbles. **4. marbles.** *(used with a sing. v.) Slang.* Common sense; sanity. **5.** Marbling. —*tr.v.* **-bled, -bling, -bles.** To mottle and streak (paper, for example) with colors and veins in imitation of marble. —*adj.* **1.** Composed of marble. **2.** Resembling marble. [ME < OFr. *marbre* < Lat. *marmor* < Gk. *marmaros*.] —**mar′bly** *adj.*

marble cake *n.* A cake with a streaked or mottled appearance achieved by mixing light and dark batter.

mar•bled (mär′bəld) *adj.* **1.** Made of or covered with marble. **2.** Having a mix of fat and lean, as a cut of meat.

Mar•ble•head (mär′bəl-hĕd′, mär′bəl-hĕd′). A town of NE MA NE of Boston; founded in the 17th cent. Pop. 19,971.

mar•ble•ize (mär′bə-līz′) *tr.v.* **-ized, -iz•ing, -iz•es.** To marble.

mar•ble•wood (mär′bəl-wo͝od′) *n.* An Asian tree *(Diospyros kurzii)* having mottled gray wood used in cabinetwork.

mar•bling (mär′blĭng) *n.* **1.** A mottling or streaking that resembles marble. **2.** The process or operation of giving something the surface appearance of marble. **3.** The decorative marble patterns printed on page edges and endpapers of books. **4.** Flecks or thin strips of fat, esp. in a cut of meat.

Mar•burg (mär′bûrg′, -bo͝ork′). A city of W-central Germany N of Frankfurt; site of Europe's first Protestant university (founded 1527). Pop. 76,260.

marc (märk) *n.* **1.** The pulpy residue left after the juice has been pressed from fruits. **2.** Brandy distilled from grape or apple residue. [Fr. < OFr. *march* < *marchier*, to trample, of Gmc. orig. See **merg-*.**]

mar•ca•site (mär′kə-sīt′, -zīt′) *n.* **1.** A mineral with the same composition as pyrite, FeS_2, but differing in crystal structure. **2.** An ornament of pyrite, polished steel, or white metal. [ME < Med.Lat. *marcasīta* < Ar. *marqašītā* < Aram. *marqĕšītâ*, perh. < Assyrian *marḫašītu*, of Markhashi < *Markhashi*, region of perh. NE Persia.]

mar•ca•to (mär-kä′tō) *Mus.* —*adv. & adj.* With strong accentuation. —*n., pl.* **-tos.** A marcato passage or movement. [Ital., p.part. of *marcare*, to mark, accent < OItal. See DEMARCATION.]

Mar•ceau (mär-sō′), **Marcel.** b. 1923. French mime whose most famous character is Bip, a sad-faced clown.

mar•cel (mär-sĕl′) *n.* A hairstyle with deep regular waves made by a curling iron. —*v.* **-celled, -cell•ing, -cels.** —*tr.* To style (the hair) in a marcel. —*intr.* To make a marcel. [After *Marcel* Grateau (1852–1936), French hairdresser.]

Mar•cel•lus (mär-sĕl′əs), **Marcus Claudius.** 268?–208 B.C. Roman general in the Second Punic War.

mar•ces•cent (mär-sĕs′ənt) *adj. Bot.* Withering but not falling off, as a blossom. [Lat. *marcēscēns, marcēscent-*, p.part. of *marcēscere*, inchoative of *marcēre*, to wither.]

march[1] (märch) *v.* **marched, march•ing, march•es.** —*intr.* **1.** To walk steadily and rhythmically forward in step with others. **2.a.** To proceed directly and purposefully. **b.** To progress steadily onward; advance. **3.** To be arranged in an orderly fashion that suggests steady rhythmical progression. **4.** To participate in an organized walk, as for a public cause. —*tr.* **1.** To cause to move or otherwise progress in a steady rhythmical manner. **2.** To traverse by progressing steadily and rhythmically. —*n.* **1.** The act of marching, esp.: **a.** The steady forward movement of troops. **b.** A long tiring journey on foot. **2.** Steady forward movement or progression. **3.** A regulated pace: *quick march.* **4.** The distance covered within a certain period of time by marching. **5.** *Mus.* A composition in regularly accented, usu. duple meter that can accompany marching. **6.** An organized walk or procession by a group of people for a specific cause or issue. —***idioms.* on the march.** Advancing steadily; progressing. **steal a march on.** To get ahead of, esp. by quiet enterprise. [ME *marchen* < OFr. *marchier*, of Gmc. orig. See **merg-*.**]

march[2] (märch) *n.* **1.** The border or boundary of a country or an area of land; a frontier. **2.** A tract of land bordering on two countries and claimed by both. —*intr.v.* **marched, march•ing, march•es.** To have a common boundary. [ME < OFr. *marche*, of Gmc. orig. See **merg-*.**]

March (märch) *n.* The third month of the year in the Gregorian calendar. [ME < AN < Lat. *Mārtius (mēnsis)*, (month) of Mars < *Mārs, Mārt-*, Mars.]

March. *abbr.* Marchioness.

Marche[1] (märsh). A historical region and former province of central France; part of the crown lands after 1531.

Mar•che[2] (mär′kā) or **Mar•ches** (-chĭz). A region of E-central Italy extending from the E slopes of the Apennines to the Adriatic Sea; colonized by Rome in the 3rd cent. B.C.

Mär•chen (mĕr′KHən) *n., pl.* **Märchen.** A folktale or fairy story. [Ger. < MHGer. *merechyn*, short verse narrative, dim. of *mære*, narrative < OHGer. *māri*, famous, narrative. See **mē-**[3]***.**]

march•er[1] (mär′chər) *n.* One that marches, esp. for a cause.

march•er[2] (mär′chər) *n.* One who lives in a border district.

mar•che•sa (mär-kā′zə, -kĕ′zä) *n., pl.* **-se** (-zā, -zĕ). **1.** The wife or widow of a marchese. **2.** An Italian noblewoman ranking above a countess and below a princess. **3.** Used as the title for such a noblewoman. [Ital., fem. of *marchese*, marchese. See MARCHESE.]

mar•che•se (mär-kā′zā, -kĕ′zĕ) *n., pl.* **-si** (-zē). **1.** An Italian nobleman ranking above a count and below a prince. **2.** Used as the title for such a nobleman. [Ital. < Med.Lat. *(comēs) marcēnsis*, (count) of the border < *marca*, border region, of Gmc. orig. See **merg-*.**]

march•ing orders (mär′chĭng) *pl.n.* Orders to move on or depart.

mar•chio•ness (mär′shə-nĭs, mär′shə-nĕs′) *n.* **1.** The wife or widow of a marquis. **2.** A noblewoman ranking above a countess and below a duchess. **3.** Used as a title for such a noblewoman. [Med.Lat. *marchiōnissa*, fem. of *marchiō, marchiōn-*, marquis < *marca*, boundary, of Gmc. orig. See **merg-*.**]

march•land (märch′lănd′) *n.* A borderland.

march•pane (märch′pān′) *n. Archaic.* Marzipan. [Perh. obsolete Fr. *marcepain* < Ital. *marzapane*, marzipan. See MARZIPAN.]

Mar•cion•ism (mär′shə-nĭz′əm) *n.* A Christian heresy of the second and third centuries A.D. that rejected the Old Testament and denied the incarnation of God in Jesus as a human being. [After *Marcion* (d. c. A.D. 160), Pontic merchant and heretic in Rome.] —**Mar′cion•ite′** (-shə-nīt′) *n.*

Mar•co•ni (mär-kō′nē), **Guglielmo.** 1874–1937. Italian engineer and inventor who shared a 1909 Nobel Prize.

Marconi rig *n. Naut.* See **Bermuda rig.** [After Guglielmo MARCONI (< its resemblance to early aerials used by him).]

Mar•cos (mär′kōs), **Ferdinand Edralin.** 1917–89. Philippine president and dictator (1965–86).

Mar•cus Au•re•li•us An•to•ni•nus (mär′kəs ô-rē′lē-əs ăn′tə-nī′nəs). A.D. 121–180. Philosopher and emperor of Rome (161–180) noted for his *Meditations*.

Mar•cu•se (mär-ko͞o′zə), **Herbert.** 1898–1979. German-born Amer. philosopher who wrote *Eros and Civilization* (1955).

Mar del Pla•ta (mär′ dĕl plä′tə, *th*ĕl plä′tä). A city of E-central Argentina on the Atlantic SSE of Buenos Aires. Pop. 414,696.

Mar•di gras or **Mar•di Gras** (mär′dē grä′) *n.* **1.a.** The day before Ash Wednesday, celebrated in many places with carnivals, masquerades, and parades. **b.** A carnival period coming to a climax on this day. **2.** An occasion of great festivity and merrymaking. [Fr. : *Mardi*, Tuesday + *gras*, fat (< the feasting on Mardi gras before Lenten fasting).]

Mar•duk (mär′do͝ok) *n. Myth.* The chief Babylonian god.

mare[1] (mâr) *n.* A female horse or the female of other equine species. [ME, alteration of OE *mere* (influenced by forms of *mearh*, horse). See **marko-***.]

ma•re[2] (mä′rā) *n., pl.* **-ri•a** (-rē-ə). *Astron.* Any of the large dark areas on the moon or on Mars or other planets. [Lat., sea. See **mori-***.]

ma•re clau•sum (mä′rā klou′səm, klô′-) *n.* A navigable body of water under the jurisdiction of one nation and closed to all others. [NLat. : Lat. *mare*, sea + Lat. *clausum*, closed.]

ma•re li•be•rum (mä′rā lē′bə-ro͝om′) *n.* A navigable body of water open to navigation by vessels of all nations. [NLat. *mare līberum* : Lat. *mare*, sea + Lat. *līberum*, free.]

Ma•ren•go (mə-rĕng′gō) *adj.* Browned in oil and sautéed with tomatoes, mushrooms, garlic, onion, and white wine. [After *Marengo*, a village of NW Italy.]

ma•re nos•trum (mä′rā nō′strəm) *n.* A navigable body of water under the jurisdiction of one nation or shared by two or more nations. [Lat., the Mediterranean : *mare*, sea + *nostrum*, our.]

mare's nest (mârz) *n., pl.* **mare's nests** or **mares' nests. 1.** A hoax or fraud. **2.** An extraordinarily complicated situation.

mare's-tail (mârz′tāl′) *n., pl.* **mare's-tails** or **mares'-tails** (mârz′tālz′). **1.** A cosmopolitan aquatic herb *(Hippuris vulgaris)* having minute flowers and linear whorled leaves. **2.** A long narrow cirrus cloud with a flowing appearance.

Mar•fan syndrome (mär′făn) *n.* A hereditary disorder principally affecting connective tissue, manifested by excessive bone elongation and joint flexibility. [After Antonin Bernard Jean *Marfan* (1858–1942), French pediatrician.]

marg. *abbr.* Margin.

Mar•gar•et of An•jou (mär′gə-rət, -grət; ăn-jo͞o′, äN-zho͞o′). 1430–82. Queen of Henry VI of England who led the Lancastrians in the Wars of the Roses.

Margaret of Na•varre (nə-vär′, nä-). 1492–1549. Queen of Navarre (1527–49) who wrote the *Heptameron*.

Margaret of Val•ois (văl-wä′). 1553–1615. Queen consort whose marriage (1572) to Henry of Navarre, later Henry IV of France, was dissolved in 1599.

mar•gar•ic (mär-găr′ĭk) *adj.* Resembling pearl; pearly. [< Gk. *margaron*, pearl.]

margaric acid *n.* A synthetic crystalline fatty acid, $CH_3(CH_2)_{15}CO_2H$.

mar•ga•rine also **mar•ga•rin** (mär′jər-ĭn) *n.* A fatty solid butter substitute of hydrogenated vegetable oils, emulsifiers, and other ingredients. [Fr. < Gk. *margaron*, pearl.]

mar•ga•ri•ta (mär′gə-rē′tə) *n.* A cocktail made with tequila, an orange-flavored liqueur, and lemon or lime juice. [Sp. < the name *Margarita*, Margaret.]

mar•ga•rite (mär′gə-rīt′) *n.* **1.** A rock formation that resembles beads, found in glassy igneous rocks. **2.** *Archaic.* A pearl. [Ult. < Gk. *margaritēs*, pearl.]

Mar•gate (mär′gāt′). **1.** (*also* -gət). A borough of SE England E of London. Pop. 121,900. **2.** A city of SE FL NW of Fort Lauderdale. Pop. 42,985.

mar•gay (mär′gā′, mär-gā′) *n., pl.* **-gays.** A spotted Central and South American wildcat *(Felis wiedi)* resembling a small long-tailed ocelot. [Fr. < Port. *maracajá* < Tupi.]

mar•gin (mär′jĭn) *n.* **1.** An edge and the area immediately adjacent to it; a border. See Syns at **border. 2.** The blank space bordering the written or printed area on a page. **3.** A limit in a condition or process, beyond or below which something is no longer possible or acceptable. **4.** An amount allowed beyond what is needed. **5.** A measure, quantity, or degree of difference. **6.** *Econ.* **a.** The minimum return that an enterprise may earn and still pay for itself. **b.** The difference between the cost and the selling price of securities or commodities. **c.** The difference between the market value of collateral and the face value of a loan. **7.** An amount in money, or represented by securities, deposited by a customer with a broker as a provision against loss on transactions made on account. **8.** *Bot.* The border of a leaf. —*tr.v.* **-gined, -gin•ing, -gins. 1.** To provide with a margin. **2.** To be a margin to; border. **3.** To inscribe or enter in the margin of a page. **4.** *Econ.* **a.** To add margin to: *margin up a brokerage account.* **b.** To deposit margin for. **c.** To buy or hold (securities) by depositing or adding to a margin. [ME < OFr. < Lat. *margō, margin-*. See **merg-***.] —**mar′gined** *adj.*

mar•gin•al (mär′jə-nəl) *adj.* **1.** Of, relating to, located at, or constituting a margin, a border, or an edge. **2.** Being adjacent geographically. **3.** Written or printed in the margin of a book. **4.** Barely within a lower standard or limit of quality. **5.** *Econ.* **a.** Having to do with enterprises that produce goods or are capable of producing goods at a rate that barely covers production costs. **b.** Relating to commodities thus manufactured and sold. **6.** *Psychol.* Relating to or located at the fringe of consciousness. —*n.* One that is considered to be at a lower or outer limit, as of social acceptability. —**mar′gin•al′i•ty** (-jə-năl′ĭ-tē) *n.* —**mar′gin•al•ly** *adv.*

mar•gi•na•li•a (mär′jə-nā′lē-ə) *pl.n.* Notes in the margin or margins of a book. [NLat., neut. pl. of Med.Lat. *marginālis*, marginal < Lat. *margō, margin-*, margin. See MARGIN.]

mar•gin•al•ize (mär′jə-nə-līz′) *tr.v.* **-ized, -iz•ing, -iz•es.** To relegate or confine to a lower or outer limit or edge, as in society. —**mar′gin•al•i•za′tion** (-jə-nə-lĭ-zā′shən) *n.*

mar•gin•ate (mär′jə-nāt′) *tr.v.* **-at•ed, -at•ing, -ates. 1.** To provide with or be a margin to; border. **2.** To add margin to (a stock portfolio). —*adj.* (-nĭt, -nāt) also **mar•gin•at•ed** (-nā′tĭd). *Biol.* Having a border or an edge of distinctive color or pattern. —**mar′gin•a′tion** *n.*

mar•grave (mär′grāv′) *n.* **1.** The lord or military governor of a medieval German border province. **2.** Used as a hereditary title for certain princes in the Holy Roman Empire. [Prob. MDu. *marcgrāve* : *marc*, march, border; see **merg-*** + *grāve*, count.] —**mar•gra′vi•al** (-grā′vē-əl) *adj.*

mar•gra•vi•ate (mär-grā′vē-ĭt, -āt′) also **mar•gra•vate** (mär′grə-vāt′) *n.* The territory governed by a margrave.

mar•gra•vine (mär′grə-vēn′) *n.* **1.** The wife or widow of a margrave. **2.** Used as a title for such a woman. [Prob. MDu. *marcgravinne*, fem. of *marcgrāve*, margrave. See MARGRAVE.]

Mar•gre•the II (mär-grā′tə). b. 1940. Queen of Denmark who inherited the throne (1972) after the Danish constitution was amended to permit the accession of a woman.

mar•gue•rite (mär′gə-rēt′, -gyə-) *n.* **1.** Either of two plants, *Chrysanthemum frutescens* of the Canary Islands or *C. leucanthemum* of Eurasia, having white or pale yellow daisylike flowers. **2.** Any of several similar or related plants. [Fr. < OFr. *margarite*, daisy, pearl < Lat. *margarīta*, pearl < Gk. *margaritēs*.]

ma•ri•a (mä′rē-ə) *n. Astron.* Pl. of **mare**[2].

ma•ri•a•chi (mä′rē-ä′chē) *n., pl.* **-chis.** *Mus.* **1.** A street band in Mexico. **2.a.** The music performed by such a band. **b.** A musician belonging to such a band. [Am.Sp., perh. < Fr. *mariage*, marriage (so called because the music may have originated at weddings in Jalisco, Mexico). See MARRIAGE.]

mariachi

Mar•i•an[1] (mâr′ē-ən, măr′-) *adj.* **1.** Of or relating to the Virgin Mary, her cult, or her theology. **2.** Of or relating to Mary I of England or Mary Queen of Scots.

Mar•i•an[2] (mâr′ē-ən, măr′-) *adj.* Of Gaius Marius.

Mar•i•an•a Islands (măr′ē-ăn′ə, mâr′-, mä′rē-ä′nä). An island group and U.S. commonwealth in the W Pacific E of the Philippines. Guam, the largest island of the group, is independent of the commonwealth, known as the **Northern Mariana Islands.** Pop. 43,345.

Ma•ri•a The•re•sa (mə-rē′ə tə-rā′sə, -zə). 1717–80. Queen of Hungary and Bohemia (1740–80).

Ma•ri•bor (mär′ĭ-bôr′). A city of NE Slovenia on the Drava R. near the Austrian border. Pop. 105,100.

Mar•i•co•pa (măr′ĭ-kō′pə) *n., pl.* **Maricopa** or **-pas. 1.** A member of a Native American people sharing reservation lands with the Pima in south-central Arizona. **2.** The Yuman language of the Maricopa.

mar•i•cul•ture (măr′ĭ-kŭl′chər) *n.* Cultivation of marine organisms in their natural habitats, usu. for commercial purposes. [Lat. *mare, mari-*, sea; see **mori-*** + CULTURE.] —**mar′i•cul′tur•al** *adj.*

Ma•rie An•toi•nette (mə-rē′ ăn′twə-nĕt′). 1755–93. Queen of France (1774–93) as the wife of Louis XVI who was executed by the Revolutionary Tribunal.

Marie Antoinette
c. 1770 portrait attributed to Peter Adolf Hall (1739–1793)

Marie Byrd Land (bûrd′). A region of W Antarctica E of the Amundsen Sea; claimed for the U.S. in 1929.

Marie de Mé•di•cis (də mā′dē-sēs′). 1573–1642. Queen of France as the wife (1600–10) of Henry IV and regent (1610–17) for her son Louis XIII.

Marie Lou•ise (lo͞o-ēz′). 1791–1847. Austrian archduchess and empress of the French as the second wife of Napoleon.

Mar•i•et•ta (măr′ē-ĕt′ə, mâr′-). A city of NW GA NW of Atlanta. Pop. 44,129.

mar•i•gold (măr′ĭ-gōld′, mâr′-) *n.* **1.** Any of various American plants of the genus *Tagetes*, widely cultivated for their showy yellow or orange flowers. **2.** Any of several plants related to the marigold or having similar flowers. [ME : *Mari*, Mary, ult. < Gk. *Maria*; see MARIONETTE + *golde*, marigold (< OE *golde* ; prob. akin to GOLD).]

mar•i•jua•na or **mar•i•hua•na** (măr′ə-wä′nə) *n.* **1.** The cannabis plant. **2.** A preparation made from the dried flower clusters and leaves of the cannabis plant, usu. smoked or eaten to induce euphoria. [Sp. *mariguana*.]

ma•rim•ba (mə-rĭm′bə) *n. Mus.* A large wooden percussion instrument with resonators, resembling a xylophone. [Port., of Bantu orig.; akin to Kimbundu *ma-rimba* : *ma-*, pl. n. pref. + *rimba*, xylophone, hand piano.]

Mar•in (măr′ĭn), **John.** 1870–1953. Amer. painter noted for his expressionist watercolors.

ma•ri•na (mə-rē′nə) *n.* A boat basin that has docks, moorings,

ă pat	oi boy
ā pay	ou out
âr care	o͝o took
ä father	o͞o boot
ĕ pet	ŭ cut
ē be	ûr urge
ĭ pit	th thin
ī pie	*th* this
îr pier	hw which
ŏ pot	zh vision
ō toe	ə about, item
ô paw	

Stress marks:
′ (primary);
′ (secondary), as in
dictionary (dĭk′shə-nĕr′ē)

and other facilities for small boats. [Ital. and Sp., seashore < fem. of *marino*, of the sea < Lat. *marīnus*. See MARINE.]

Ma•ri•na (mə-rē′nə). A city of W CA on Monterey Bay W of Salinas. Pop. 26,436.

mar•i•nade (măr′ə-nād′) *n.* A liquid mixture, usu. of vinegar or wine and oil with various spices and herbs, in which meat, fowl, fish, or vegetables are soaked before cooking. —*tr.v.* (măr′ə-nād′) **-nad•ed, -nad•ing, -nades.** To soak (food) in such a mixture; marinate. [Fr., prob. < Ital. *marinare*, to marinate < Lat. *(aqua) marīna*, sea(water), brine, pickle < fem. of *marīnus*, of the sea. See MARINE.]

marionette
c. 1950 American

ma•ri•na•ra (măr′ə-năr′ə, mär′ə-när′ə) *adj.* Being or served with a sauce of tomatoes, onions, garlic, and spices. —*n.* Marinara sauce. [Ital. *(alla) marinara*, in sailor style, fem. of *marinaro*, sailor < *marino*, marine. See MARINA.]

mar•i•nate (măr′ə-nāt′) *v.* **-nat•ed, -nat•ing, -nates.** —*tr.* To soak (food) in a marinade. —*intr.* To become marinated. [Prob. < Ital. *marinato*, p.part. of *marinare*, to marinate < *marino*, marine. See MARINA.] —**mar′i•na′tion** *n.*

ma•rine (mə-rēn′) *adj.* **1.a.** Of or relating to the sea. **b.** Native to, inhabiting, or formed by the sea: *marine animals.* **2.** Of or relating to shipping or maritime affairs. **3.** Of or relating to sea navigation; nautical. See Syns at **nautical. 4.** Of or relating to the Marine Corps. —*n.* **1.a.** A soldier serving on a ship or at a naval installation. **b. Marine.** A member of the Marine Corps. **2.** The mercantile or naval ships or shipping fleet of a country. **3.** The governmental department in charge of naval affairs in some nations. **4.** A painting or photograph of the sea. [ME *marin, marine* < OFr. < Lat. *marīnus* < *mare*, sea. See **mori-***.]

Marine Corps *n.* A branch of the U.S. armed forces composed chiefly of amphibious troops under the authority of the Secretary of the Navy.

markhor
Male and
female markhor
Capra falconeri

mar•i•ner (măr′ə-nər) *n. Naut.* One who operates or helps operate a ship. [ME < OFr. *marinier* < *marin*, marine. See MARINE.]

Ma•ri•net•ti (măr′ə-nět′ē, mä′rē-nět′tē), **Emilio Filippo Tommaso.** 1876–1944. Italian writer who founded futurism with the publication of his 1909 manifesto.

Mar•i•ol•a•try (mâr′ē-ŏl′ə-trē) *n.* Excessive veneration or worship of the Virgin Mary. —**Mar′i•ol′a•ter** *n.* —**Mar′i•ol′a•trous** *adj.*

Mar•i•ol•o•gy also **Mar•y•ol•o•gy** (mâr′ē-ŏl′ə-jē) *n.* The theological study of the Virgin Mary and her role in the Incarnation. —**Mar′i•o•log′i•cal** *adj.*

Mar•i•on (măr′ē-ən, mâr′-). **1.** A city of NE-central IN NW of Muncie. Pop. 32,618. **2.** A city of E-central IA, a suburb of Cedar Rapids. Pop. 20,403. **3.** A city of central OH N of Columbus. Pop. 34,075.

Marion, Francis. "the Swamp Fox." 1732?–95. Amer. Revolutionary noted for his guerrilla tactics against the British.

mar•i•o•nette (măr′ē-ə-nět′) *n.* A jointed puppet manipulated from above by strings or wires attached to its limbs. [Fr. *marionnette* < OFr., musical instrument, dim. of *mariole*, the Virgin Mary < dim. of *Marie*, Mary (influenced by the name *Marion*) < LLat. *Maria* < Gk. < Heb. *Miryām*.]

mar•i•po•sa lily (măr′ə-pō′zə, -sə) *n.* Any of several bulbous plants of the genus *Calochortus* of western North America, having variously colored tuliplike flowers. [Prob. < Am.Sp. *mariposa* < Sp., butterfly : *mari-*, freq. pref. + *posar*, to perch (< LLat. *pausāre*, to pause < Lat. *pausa*, pause).]

Mar•ist (mâr′ĭst, măr′-) *n.* **1.** A member of the Society of Mary, a congregation of Roman Catholic missionary priests founded in 1824. **2.** A member of the Little Brothers of Mary, a Roman Catholic teaching congregation founded in 1817. [Fr. *Mariste* < *Marie*, the Virgin Mary < LLat. *Maria.* See MARIONETTE.]

Ma•ri•tain (măr′ĭ-tăN′, mä-rē-), **Jacques.** 1882–1973. French philosopher who wrote *Art and Scholasticism* (1920).

mar•i•tal (măr′ĭ-tl) *adj.* **1.** Of or relating to marriage: *marital problems.* **2.** Of or relating to a husband. [Lat. *marītālis* < *marītus*, married.] —**mar′i•tal•ly** *adv.*

mar•i•time (măr′ĭ-tīm′) *adj.* **1.** Of, relating to, or adjacent to the sea. **2.** Of or relating to marine shipping or navigation. See Syns at **nautical. 3.** Of or resembling a mariner. [Lat. *maritimus* < *mare, mari-*, sea. See **mori-***.]

marmot

Mar•i•time Alps (măr′ĭ-tīm′). A range of the SW Alps on the French-Italian border rising to 3,299.2 m (10,817 ft).

Maritime Provinces. Nova Scotia, New Brunswick, and Prince Edward Island. —**Mar′i•tim′er** *n.*

Ma•ri•tsa (mə-rēt′sə). A river of W Bulgaria and W Turkey flowing c. 483 km (300 mi) to the Aegean Sea.

Mar•i•us (mâr′ē-əs, măr′-), **Gaius.** 155?–86 B.C. Roman general and politician who lost a civil war (88) to Sulla.

Ma•ri•vaux (măr′ə-vō′, mä-rē-), **Pierre Carlet de Chamblain de.** 1688–1763. French writer noted for his sophisticated romantic comedies.

mar•jo•ram (mär′jər-əm) *n.* Any of several aromatic Eurasian or Mediterranean plants of the genus *Origanum*, esp. *O. majorana* or *O. vulgare*, having opposite leaves used as seasoning. [ME *majorane* < OFr. < Med.Lat. *maiorana*.]

mark¹ (märk) *n.* **1.** A visible trace or impression, such as a line or spot. **2.** A sign made in lieu of a signature. **3.** A written or printed symbol used for punctuation; a punctuation mark. **4.a.** A number, letter, or symbol used to indicate various grades of academic achievement. **b.** An appraisal; a rating. Often used in the plural: *earned high marks.* **5.a.** An inscription, name, stamp, label, or seal placed on an article to signify ownership, quality, manufacture, or origin. **b.** A notch in an animal's ear or hide indicating ownership. **6.** *Naut.* **a.** A knot or piece of material placed at various measured lengths on a sounding line to indicate the depth of the water. **b.** A Plimsoll mark. **7.a.** A distinctive trait or property: *Trust is the mark of friendship.* **b.** A lasting effect. **c. Mark.** A particular mode, brand, size, or quality of a product. **8.** A recognized standard of quality. **9.a.** Importance; prominence. **b.** Notice; attention. **10.** A target. **11.** Something that one wishes to achieve; a goal. **12.** An object or a point that serves as a guide. **13.** *Slang.* A person who is the intended victim of a swindler; a dupe. **14.a.** *Sports.* The place from which racers begin and sometimes end their contest. **b.** A point reached or gained. **c.** A record. **15.** *Sports.* **a.** A strike or spare in bowling. **b.** A stationary ball in lawn bowling; a jack. **16.** A boundary between countries. **17.** A tract of land in medieval England and Germany held in common by a community. **18.** *Comp. Sci.* A character or feature in a file or record used to locate a specific point or condition. —*v.* **marked, mark•ing, marks.** —*tr.* **1.a.** To make a visible trace or impression on, as with a spot, line, or dent. **b.** To form, make, or depict by making a mark. **c.** To supply with natural markings. **2.a.** To single out or indicate by or as if by a mark. **b.** To distinguish or characterize. **c.** To make conspicuous: *a concert marking the composer's birthday.* **3.** To set off or separate by or as if by a line or boundary: *marked off our property.* **4.** To attach or affix identification, such as a price tag, to. **5.** To evaluate (academic work) according to a scale of letters and numbers. **6.a.** To give attention to; notice. **b.** To take note of in writing; write down. **c.** *Sports & Games.* To record (the score) in various games. —*intr.* **1.** To make a visible impression. **2.** To receive a visible impression. **3.** *Sports & Games.* To keep score. **4.** To determine academic grades. **5.** *Archaic.* To pay attention; notice. —***phrasal verbs.*** **mark down.** To mark for sale at a lower price. **mark up. 1.** To deface by covering with marks. **2.** To mark for sale at a higher price. —***idioms.*** **beside the mark.** Beside the point; irrelevant. **mark time. 1.** To move the feet alternately in the rhythm of a marching step without advancing. **2.** To suspend progress for the time being; wait in readiness. **3.** To function in an apathetic or ineffective manner. [ME < OE *mearc.* See **merg-***.]

Syns: *mark, brand, label, tag, ticket.* The central meaning shared by these verbs is "to place a mark of identification on": *marked the items to be sold; branding cattle; labeled the boxes; tagging suitcases; ticketed the merchandise.*

mark² (märk) *n.* **1.** An English and Scottish monetary unit that was equal to 13 shillings and 4 pence. **2.** Any of several European units of weight that were equal to about 8 ounces (227 grams), used esp. for weighing gold and silver. [ME < OE *marc.* See **merg-***.]

Mark *n.* **1.** See table at **Bible. 2.** In Arthurian legend, a king of Cornwall who was the husband of Iseult and the uncle of her lover Tristan.

Mark, Saint. Disciple of St. Peter and author of the second Gospel in the New Testament.

Mark An•to•ny (ăn′tə-nē) or **Mark An•tho•ny** (ăn′thə-nē). Also **Marcus An•to•ni•us** (ăn-tō′nē-əs). 83?–30 B.C. Roman politician and soldier whose love affair with Cleopatra split the triumvirate he had formed with Octavian and Lepidus and led to war. Antony and Cleopatra were defeated in 31 B.C.

mark•down (märk′doun′) *n.* **1.** A reduction in price. **2.** The amount by which a price is reduced.

marked (märkt) *adj.* **1.** Having one or more distinguishing marks. **2.** Clearly defined and evident; noticeable: *a marked limp.* **3.** Singled out, esp. for a dire fate. —**mark′ed•ly** (mär′kĭd-lē) *adv.* —**mark′ed•ness** *n.*

mark•er (mär′kər) *n.* **1.** One that marks or serves as a mark, as: **a.** A bookmark. **b.** A tombstone. **c.** A milestone. **2.** An implement, esp. a felt-tipped pen, used for marking or writing. **3.** One who marks objects, esp. for industrial purposes. **4.** One who grades student papers. **5.** *Sports.* A device, such as a line, set on a playing field and showing the playing or scoring position. **6.** *Games.* **a.** One that keeps score in various games. **b.** A score in a game. **7.** *Slang.* A written, signed promissory note. **8.** A genetic marker. **9.** *Medic.* A physiological substance, such as human chorionic gonadotropin, that when present in abnormal amounts in the serum may indicate disease, as that caused by a malignancy. **10.** *Ling.* An element that indicates grammatical class or function; a derivational or inflectional morpheme.

mar•ket (mär′kĭt) *n.* **1.** A public gathering held for buying and selling merchandise. **2.** A place where goods are offered for sale. **3.** A store or shop that sells a particular type of merchandise: *a meat market.* **4.a.** The business of buying and selling a specified commodity: *the soybean market.* **b.** A market price. **c.** A geographic region considered as a place for sales. **d.** A subdivision of a population considered as buyers. **5.** The opportunity to buy or sell; extent of demand for merchandise. **6.a.** An exchange for buying and selling stocks or commodities. **b.** The entire enterprise of buying and selling commodities and securities. —*v.* **-ket•ed, -ket•ing, -kets.** —*tr.* **1.** To offer for sale. **2.** To sell. —*intr.* **1.** To deal in a market. **2.** To buy household supplies: *marketed for dinner.* —***idioms.*** **in the market.** Interested in buying. **on the market. 1.** Available for buying. **2.** Up for sale. [ME < ONFr. < VLat. **marcātus* < Lat. *mercātus* < p.part. of *mercārī*, to buy < *merx, merc-*, merchandise.]

mar•ket•a•ble (mär**′**kĭ-tə-bəl) *adj.* **1.** Fit for sale, as in a market: *marketable produce.* **2.** In demand by buyers or employers; salable: *marketable skills.* —**mar′ket•a•bil′i•ty** *n.*

market basket *n.* **1.** A grocery cart. **2.** A selection of foods needed for a statistical household of 3.2 persons or for a family of 4, considered in terms of its fluctuating cost.

mar•ket•er (mär**′**kĭ-tər) also **mar•ket•eer** (-kĭ-tîr**′**) *n.* One that sells goods or services in or to a market, esp. one that markets a specified commodity: *a major wine marketer.*

mar•ket•ing (mär**′**kĭ-tĭng) *n.* **1.** The act or process of buying and selling in a market. **2.** The commercial functions involved in transferring goods from producer to consumer. **3.** The act or business of promoting sales of a product, as by advertising and packaging.

market order *n.* An order to buy or sell stocks or commodities at the prevailing market price.

mar•ket•place also **market place** (mär**′**kĭt-plās′) *n.* **1.** An open area or square in a town where a public market or sale is set up. **2.** The world of business and commerce. **3.** A situation or place in which values, opinions, and ideas are put forward.

market price *n.* The prevailing price at which merchandise, securities, or commodities are sold.

market research *n.* The gathering and evaluation of data regarding consumers' preferences for products and services.

market value *n.* The amount that a seller may expect to obtain for merchandise, services, or securities in the open market.

Mark•ham (mär**′**kəm). A town of S Ontario, Canada, NNE of Toronto. Pop. 77,037.

Markham, Beryl. 1903–86. British aviator who was the first to fly solo across the Atlantic from E to W (1936).

Markham, (Charles) Edwin. 1852–1940. Amer. poet best known for "The Man with the Hoe" (1899).

Markham, Mount. A peak, 4,353 m (14,272 ft), of Victoria Land, Antarctica; discovered in 1902.

mar•khor (mär**′**kôr) *n., pl.* **markhor** or **-khors.** A large wild Himalayan goat *(Capra falconeri)* having spirally curved horns and a long mane in the male. [Pers. *mārkhōr* : *mār*, snake (< Avestan *mairya-*, treacherous) + *-khōr*, eater (< OIran. **-khāra-*; see MANTICORE).]

mark•ing (mär**′**kĭng) *n.* **1.a.** A making or giving of a mark. **b.** A mark or marks made. **2.** The characteristic pattern of coloration of a plant or an animal.

mark•ka (mär**′**kä′) *n., pl.* **-kaa** (-kä′). See table at **currency.** [Finn. < Swed. *mark*, a mark of money. See **merg-*.**]

Mar•ko•va (mär-kō**′**və, mär**′**kə-və), Dame **Alicia.** b. 1910. British ballerina known esp. for her performance in *Giselle.*

marks•man (märks**′**mən) *n.* A man skilled in shooting at a target. —**marks′man•ship′** *n.*

marks•wom•an (märks**′**wo͝om′ən) *n.* A woman skilled in shooting at a target.

mark•up (märk**′**ŭp′) *n.* **1.** A raise in the price of an item for sale. **2.** An amount added to a cost price in calculating a selling price, esp. one taking into account overhead and profit. **3.** A session of a U.S. congressional committee at which a legislative bill is put into final form. **4.** Typesetting instructions written on a manuscript.

marl (märl) *n.* A mixture of clays, calcium and magnesium carbonates, and shell remnants, used to fertilize lime-deficient soils. —*tr.v.* **marled, marl•ing, marls.** To fertilize with marl. [ME *marle* < OFr. < Med.Lat. *margila, marla*, dim. of Lat. *marga*, marl, of Celt. orig.] —**marl′y** *adj.*

Marl (märl). A city of W-central Germany in the Ruhr Valley N of Essen; first mentioned in the 9th cent. Pop. 87,231.

Marl•bor•ough or **Marl•bo•ro** (märl**′**bûr′ō, -bər-ə, -bŭr′ō). A city of E-central MA ENE of Worcester; settled in 1657. Pop. 31,813.

Marl•bor•ough (märl**′**bər-ə, -brə, môl**′**-), 1st Duke of. See John **Churchill.**

mar•lin¹ (mär**′**lĭn) *n.* Any of several large marine game fishes of the genera *Makaira* and *Tetrapturus,* having an elongated spearlike upper jaw. [Short for MARLINESPIKE.]

mar•lin² (mär**′**lĭn) *n. Naut.* Var. of **marline.**

mar•line also **mar•lin** (mär**′**lĭn) *n. Naut.* A light rope made of two loosely twisted strands. [ME.]

mar•line•spike also **mar•lin•spike** (mär**′**lĭn-spīk′) or **mar•ling•spike** (-lĭng-spīk′) *n. Naut.* A pointed metal spike, used to separate strands of rope in splicing.

mar•lite (mär**′**līt′) *n.* Marlstone. —**mar•lit′ic** (-lĭt′ĭk) *adj.*

Mar•lowe (mär**′**lō), **Christopher.** 1564–93. English playwright and poet whose works include *Tamburlaine* (c. 1587).

marl•stone (märl**′**stōn′) *n.* A rock containing clay materials and calcium and magnesium carbonates, with approximately the same composition as marl.

mar•ma•lade (mär**′**mə-lād′) *n.* A clear jellylike preserve made from the pulp and rind of fruits, esp. citrus fruits. [Fr. *marmelade* < Port. *marmelada* < *marmelo*, quince, alteration of Lat. *melimēlum*, a kind of sweet apple < Gk. *melimēlon* : *meli*, honey; see **melit-*** + *mēlon*, apple.]

marmalade box *n.* See **genipap** 2.

marmalade plum *n.* See **sapote.**

Mar•ma•ra (mär**′**mər-ə), **Sea of.** A sea of NW Turkey between Europe and Asia connected to the Black Sea through the Bosporus and to the Aegean through the Dardanelles.

mar•mite (mär**′**mīt, mär-mēt**′**) *n.* **1.a.** A large covered earthenware or metal cooking pot. **b.** A small covered earthenware casserole that holds an individual serving. **2.** A petite marmite. [Fr. < OFr., hypocritical, marmite : *marm-*; akin to *marmouser*, to murmur + *mite*, cat (of imit. orig.).]

Mar•mo•la•da (mär′mə-lä**′**də, -mô-lä**′**dä). A peak, 3,344.3 m (10,965 ft), in the Dolomite Alps of NE Italy.

mar•mo•re•al (mär-môr**′**ē-əl, -mōr**′**-) also **mar•mo•re•an** (-ē-ən) *adj.* Resembling marble, as in hardness. [< Lat. *marmoreus* < *marmor*, marble.] —**mar•mo′re•al•ly** *adv.*

mar•mo•set (mär**′**mə-sĕt′, -zĕt′) *n.* Any of various small, clawed monkeys of the genera *Callithrix* and *Cebuella* of the American tropics, having tufted ears and long tails. [ME *marmusette*, a small monkey < OFr. *marmouset*, grotesque figurine, alteration of *marmotte*, marmot. See MARMOT.]

mar•mot (mär**′**mət) *n.* Any of various burrowing rodents of the genus *Marmota,* having short legs and ears and short bushy tails. [Fr. *marmotte* < OFr., prob. < *marmotter*, to mumble, prob. of imit. orig.]

Marne (märn). A river of NE France flowing c. 523 km (325 mi) to the Seine R. near Paris; scene of heavy fighting in World War I and World War II.

Mar•o•nite (măr**′**ə-nīt′) *n.* A member of a Christian Uniat church, chiefly of Lebanon, the liturgy of which is in Syriac. [Med.Lat. *marōnīta*, after *Maro*, 4th-cent. A.D. Syrian religious leader.] —**Mar′o•nite′** *adj.*

ma•roon¹ (mə-ro͞on**′**) *tr.v.* **-rooned, -roon•ing, -roons. 1.** To put ashore on a deserted island or coast and intentionally abandon. **2.** To abandon or isolate with little hope of ready rescue or escape: *marooned by the blizzard.* —*n.* **1.** Often **Maroon. a.** A fugitive Black slave in the West Indies in the 17th and 18th centuries. **b.** A descendant of such a slave. **2.** A person who is marooned, as on an island. [< Fr. *marron*, fugitive slave < Am.Sp. *cimarrón*, wild, runaway, perh. < *cima*, summit < Lat. *cȳma*, sprout. See CYMA.]

Word History: The history of the word *maroon* takes us back to the days of slavery, when the noun *maroon* was a term in English for a Black person who lived in the mountains and forests of Dutch Guiana (Suriname) and the West Indies, a term that is still used in parts of the Caribbean. These were plantation slaves who had run away to live free in uncultivated parts. The English word is a borrowing of the French word *marron,* "runaway Black slave," which in turn was an alteration of American Spanish *cimarrón,* meaning "runaway slave." *Cimarrón* is perhaps from *cima,* "summit." English *maroon* came to be used as a verb meaning "to be lost in the wilds," from which our sense "to put ashore on a deserted island or coast" evolved.

ma•roon² (mə-ro͞on**′**) *n. Color.* A dark reddish brown to dark purplish red. [Fr. *marron*, chestnut < Ital. *marrone.*]

Ma•roon Peak (mə-ro͞on**′**). A mountain, 4,317.6 m (14,156 ft), in the Elk Mts. of W-central CO.

mar•plot (mär**′**plŏt′) *n.* A stupid officious meddler whose interference compromises an undertaking. [After *Marplot*, in a play by Susannah Centlivre (1669–1723).]

Mar•quand (mär-kwŏnd**′**), **John Phillips.** 1893–1960. Amer. writer whose works include *The Late George Apley* (1937).

marque (märk) *n.* A model or brand of a manufactured product, esp. an automobile. [Fr. < OFr. See MARQUETRY.]

mar•quee (mär-kē**′**) *n.* **1.** A large tent with open sides, used chiefly for outdoor entertainment. **2.** A rooflike structure, often bearing a signboard, projecting over an entrance, as to a theater. [Fr. *marquise*, marquise, marquee. See MARQUISE.]

Mar•que•san (mär-kā**′**zən, -sən) *n.* **1.** A native or inhabitant of the Marquesas Islands. **2.** The Austronesian language of the Marquesans. —**Mar•que′san** *adj.*

Mar•que•sas Islands (mär-kā**′**zəz, -səz, -səs). A volcanic archipelago in the S Pacific, part of French Polynesia since 1842.

mar•que•try also **mar•que•terie** (mär**′**kĭ-trē) *n., pl.* **-tries** also **-teries.** Material, such as ivory, inlaid piece by piece into a wood surface in an intricate design and veneered to another surface, esp. of furniture, for decoration. [Fr. *marqueterie* < OFr. < *marqueter*, to checker < *marque*, mark, ult. < ON *merki*, mark. See **merg-*.**]

Mar•quette (mär-kĕt**′**). A city of NW MI on the Upper Peninsula and Lake Superior. Pop. 21,977.

Marquette, Père Jacques. 1637–75. French missionary who accompanied Louis Jolliet on his 1673 exploration of the Wisconsin, Mississippi, and Illinois rivers.

marquee

marquetry

ă pat	oi boy
ā pay	ou out
âr care	o͝o took
ä father	o͞o boot
ĕ pet	ŭ cut
ē be	ûr urge
ĭ pit	th thin
ī pie	*th* this
îr pier	hw which
ŏ pot	zh vision
ō toe	ə about, item
ô paw	

Stress marks:
′ (primary);
′ (secondary), as in
dictionary (dĭk**′**shə-nĕr′ē)

mar•quis (mär′kwĭs, mär-kē′) or **mar•quess** (mär′kwĭs) *n.*, *pl.* **-quis•es** (-kwĭ-sĭz) or **mar•quis** (mär-kēz′) or **-quess•es** (-kwĭ-sĭz). **1.** A nobleman ranking below a duke and above an earl or a count. **2.** Used as a title for such a nobleman. [ME *marques* < OFr. *marchis, marquis* < *marche*, border country, of Gmc. orig. See **merg-*.**]

Mar•quis (mär′kwĭs), **Donald Robert Perry.** 1878–1937. Amer. writer who created *archy* the cockroach and *mehitabel* the cat.

mar•quis•ate (mär′kwĭ-zĭt, -sĭt) *n.* The rank or territory of a marquis.

mar•quise (mär-kēz′) *n.* **1.** See **marchioness** 2. **2.** See **marquee** 2. **3.a.** A finger ring set with a pointed oval stone or cluster of pointed oval stones. **b.** A pointed oval shape of a gem. [Fr., fem. of *marquis*, marquis. See MARQUIS.]

mar•qui•sette (mär′kĭ-zĕt′, -kwĭ-) *n.* A sheer fabric of cotton, rayon, silk, or nylon, used for clothing and curtains.

Mar•quis of Queens•ber•ry rules (mär′kwĭs, mär-kē′; kwēnz′bĕr′ē, -bə-rē) *pl.n. Sports.* A set of rules in modern boxing calling for the use of gloves, the division of matches into rounds, and the ten-second count for a knockout, among other provisions. [After 8th Marquis of QUEENSBERRY.]

martlet

Mar•ra•kesh or **Mar•ra•kech** (măr′ə-kĕsh′, mə-rä′kĕsh). A city of W-central Morocco in the foothills of the Atlas Mts.; founded 1062. Pop. 439,728.

mar•ram (măr′əm) *n.* See **beach grass.** [Of Scand. orig. See **mori-*.**]

Mar•ra•no (mə-rä′nō) *n.*, *pl.* **-nos.** *Offensive.* Used as a disparaging term for a Converso. [Sp., pig, Marrano (< the Jewish prohibition against eating pork), prob. < Ar. *maḥram*, something forbidden.]

Mar•re•ro (mə-răr′ō, -rĕr′ō). A community of SE LA, a suburb of New Orleans on the Mississippi R. Pop. 36,671.

mar•riage (măr′ĭj) *n.* **1.a.** The legal union of a man and woman as husband and wife. **b.** Wedlock. **2.** A wedding. **3.** A close union. **4.** *Games.* The combination of the king and queen of the same suit, as in pinochle. [ME *mariage* < OFr. < *marier*, to marry. See MARRY[1].]

mar•riage•a•ble (măr′ĭ-jə-bəl) *adj.* Suitable for marriage. —**mar′riage•a•bil′i•ty, mar′riage•a•ble•ness** *n.*

marriage of convenience *n.*, *pl.* **marriages of convenience.** A marriage or joint undertaking arranged for political, economic, or social benefit rather than from personal attachment.

mar•ried (măr′ēd) *adj.* **1.a.** Having a spouse. **b.** United in matrimony. **2.a.** Of or relating to the state of marriage. **b.** Acquired through marriage. **3.** Closely connected; united. —*n.*, *pl.* **marrieds** or **married.** A married person.

mar•ron (măr′ən, mă-rôN′) *n.* See **Spanish chestnut.** [Fr. See MAROON[2].]

mar•rons gla•cés (mă-rôN′ glă-sā′) *pl.n.* Chestnuts glazed with sugar or preserved in vanilla-flavored syrup. [Fr. : *marrons*, marrons + *glacés*, glazed.]

mar•row (măr′ō) *n.* **1.** Bone marrow. **2.a.** Spinal marrow. **b.** The spinal cord. **3.a.** The inmost, choicest, or essential part; the pith. **b.** Strength or vigor; vitality. [ME *marow* < OE *mearg*.]

mar•row•bone (măr′ō-bōn′) *n.* **1.** A bone for flavoring soup. **2. marrowbones.** *Informal.* The knees.

mar•row•fat (măr′ō-făt′) *n.* One of several varieties of pea that produces large seeds.

marrow squash *n.* An edible squash having very large elongated greenish fruit.

mar•ry[1] (măr′ē) *v.* **-ried, -ry•ing, -ries.** —*tr.* **1.a.** To join as spouses by exchanging vows. **b.** To take as a spouse. **c.** To give in marriage. **2.** To perform a marriage ceremony for. **3.** To obtain by marriage. **4.** *Naut.* To join (two ropes) end to end by interweaving their strands. **5.** To unite in a close, usu. permanent way. —*intr.* **1.** To take a spouse; wed. **2.** To combine or blend agreeably. [ME *marien* < OFr. *marier* < Lat. *marītāre* < *marītus*, married.]

Marx Brothers
Top to bottom: Groucho, Zeppo, Harpo, Chico, and Gummo (Milton, 1894–1977)

mar•ry[2] (măr′ē) *interj. Archaic.* Used as an exclamation of surprise or emphasis. [ME *Marie*, the Virgin Mary, ult. < Gk. *Maria*. See MARIONETTE.]

Mars (märz) *n.* **1.** *Rom. Myth.* The god of war. **2.** The fourth planet from the sun, having a sidereal period of revolution about the sun of 687 days at a mean distance of 227.8 million kilometers (141.6 million miles) and a mean diameter of approx. 6,726 kilometers (4,180 miles). [ME < Lat. *Mārs*.]

Mar•sa•la[1] (mär-sä′lə). A city of W Sicily on the Mediterranean; founded c. 397 B.C. Pop. 46,300.

Mar•sa•la[2] (mär-sä′lə) *n.* A sweet or dry fortified wine of Sicilian origin. —*adj.* Cooked or flavored with Marsala: *veal Marsala*. [Ital., after MARSALA[1].]

mar•seille (mär-sāl′) also **mar•seilles** (-sālz′) *n.* A heavy cotton fabric with a raised pattern of stripes or figures. [After MARSEILLES.]

Mar•seilles also **Mar•seille** (mär-sā′). A city of SE France on an arm of the Mediterranean WNW of Toulon; founded c. 600 B.C. Pop. 874,436.

marsh (märsh) *n.* An area of soft, wet, low-lying land, marked by grassy vegetation and often being a transition between water and land. [ME < OE *mersc*. See **mori-*.**]

Marsh (Märsh), **Ngaio.** 1899–1982. New Zealand writer whose detective novels include *A Man Lay Dead* (1934).

Marsh, Reginald. 1898–1954. Amer. painter whose works, such as *The Bowery* (1930), depict life in New York City.

mar•shal (mär′shəl) *n.* **1.a.** A military officer of the highest rank in some countries. **b.** A field marshal. **2.a.** A U.S. federal officer of a judicial district who carries out court orders and discharges duties similar to those of a sheriff. **b.** A city law enforcement officer in the United States who carries out court orders. **c.** The head, esp. of a fire department in the United States. **d.** A fire marshal. **3.** A person in charge of a parade or ceremony. **4.** A high official in a royal court, esp. one aiding the sovereign in military affairs. —*v.* **-shaled, -shal•ing, -shals** also **-shalled, marshal•ling, -shals.** —*tr.* **1.** To arrange or place (troops, for example) in line for a parade, maneuver, or review. **2.** To arrange, place, or set in methodical order. See Syns at **arrange. 3.** To enlist and organize. **4.** To guide ceremoniously; conduct or usher. —*intr.* **1.** To take up positions in or as if in a military formation. **2.** To take form or order. [ME < OFr. *mareschal*, of Gmc. orig.] —**mar′shal•cy, mar′shal•ship′** *n.*

Mar•shall (mär′shəl). A city of NE TX W of Shreveport, LA. Pop. 23,682.

Marshall, George Catlett. 1880–1959. Amer. soldier and diplomat who organized the European Recovery Program, or Marshall Plan, and received the 1953 Nobel Peace Prize.

Marshall, John. 1755–1835. Amer. jurist; chief justice of the U.S. Supreme Court (1801–35) who helped establish the practice of judicial review.

Marshall, Thomas Riley. 1854–1925. Vice President of the U.S. (1913–21).

Marshall, Thurgood. 1908–93. Amer. jurist; associate justice of the U.S. Supreme Court (1967–91).

Marshall Islands. A self-governing island group in the central Pacific; became a republic in 1986. Pop. 43,417.

Mar•shall•town (mär′shəl-toun′). A city of central IA NE of Des Moines. Pop. 25,178.

marsh elder *n.* Any of several herbs or shrubs of the genus *Iva* of North America, found in salt marshes and having greenish flower heads.

Marsh•field (märsh′fēld′). **1.** A town of SE MA on Massachusetts Bay SE of Boston. Pop. 21,531. **2.** A city of central WI SW of Wausau. Pop. 19,291.

marsh gas *n.* Methane.

marsh hawk *n.* See **northern harrier.**

marsh hen *n.* Any of various marsh birds of the family Rallidae, which includes the gallinules, coots, and rails.

marsh•land (märsh′lănd′) *n.* A marshy tract of land.

marsh•mal•low (märsh′mĕl′ō, -măl′ō) *n.* **1.a.** A light spongy confection made of corn syrup, gelatin, sugar, and starch. **b.** A confection of sweetened paste, once made from the marshmallow root. **2.** Often **marsh mallow.** *Bot.* A perennial plant *(Althaea officinalis)* native to Europe and having pink flowers and a mucilaginous root. **3.** *Slang.* A timid, cowardly, or ineffective person. —**marsh′mal′low•y** *adj.*

marsh marigold *n.* Any of several plants of the genus *Caltha*, esp. *C. palustris* growing in swampy places and having bright yellow flowers.

marsh•y (mär′shē) *adj.* **-i•er, -i•est. 1.** Of, resembling, or characterized by a marsh or marshes; boggy. **2.** Growing in marshes. —**marsh′i•ness** *n.*

Mar•ston (mär′stən), **John.** 1575?–1634. English playwright whose works include *The Malcontent* (1604).

Marston Moor. An area in N England W of York; site of the first Parliamentarian victory of the English Civil War (1644).

mar•su•pi•al (mär-so͞o′pē-əl) *n.* Any of various nonplacental mammals of the order Marsupialia, including kangaroos and wombats, found principally in Australia and the Americas. —*adj.* **1.** Of or belonging to the order Marsupialia. **2.** Of or relating to a marsupium. [< MARSUPIUM.]

mar•su•pi•um (mär-so͞o′pē-əm) *n.*, *pl.* **-pi•a** (-pē-ə). **1.** A pouch or fold on the abdomen of most female marsupials, containing the mammary glands and in which the young develop after leaving the uterus. **2.** A temporary egg pouch in various fishes and crustaceans. [LLat. *marsūpium*, pouch < Lat. *marsuppium* < Gk. *marsupion*, dim. of *marsuppos*, purse, perh. of Iran. orig.; akin to Avestan *marsū-*, belly, paunch.]

mart (märt) *n.* **1.** A trading center; a market. **2.** *Archaic.* A fair. [ME, prob. < MFlem. < VLat. **marcātus*. See MARKET.]

Mart. *abbr.* Martinique.

Mar•ta•ban (mär′tə-băn′, -bän′), **Gulf of.** An arm of the Andaman Sea off S Burma.

mar•ta•gon (mär′tə-gən) *n.* A Eurasian lily *(Lilium martagon)* usu. having spotted pinkish-purple flowers. [ME < OFr. < OSp. < Ottoman Turk. *mārtağān*, a kind of turban.]

Mar•tel (mär-tĕl′), **Charles.** See **Charles Martel.**

mar•ten (mär′tn) *n.*, *pl.* **marten** or **-tens. 1.** Any of several principally arboreal carnivorous mammals of the genus *Martes,* mainly inhabiting northern forests and having a slender body, bushy tail, and soft fur. **2.** The fur of the marten. [ME *martrin, marten* < OFr. *martrine* < fem. of *martrin*, of the marten (< *martre*, marten) and < Med.Lat. *martrīna*, both of Gmc. orig.]

mar·ten·site (mär′tn-zīt′) *n.* A solid solution of iron and up to 1 percent of carbon, the chief constituent of hardened carbon tool steels. [After Adolf *Martens* (1850–1914), German metallurgist.] **—mar′ten·sit′ic** (-zĭt′ĭk) *adj.*

Mar·tha (mär′thə). In the Bible, the sister of Lazarus and Mary and a friend of Jesus.

Mar·tha's Vine·yard (mär′thəz vĭn′yərd). An island of SE MA off the SW coast of Cape Cod; settled in 1642.

Mar·tí (mär-tē′), **José Julian.** 1853–95. Cuban revolutionary killed while fighting for Cuban independence from Spain.

mar·tial (mär′shəl) *adj.* **1.** Of, relating to, or suggestive of war. **2.** Relating to or connected with the armed forces or the profession of arms. **3.** Characteristic of or befitting a warrior. [ME < Lat. *Mārtiālis* < *Mārs, Mārt-*, Mars.] **—mar′tial·ism** *n.* **—mar′tial·ist** *n.* **—mar′tial·ly** *adv.*

Mar·tial (mär′shəl). fl. 1st cent. B.C. Roman poet known for his epigrams.

martial art *n.* Any of several Asian arts of combat or self-defense, such as aikido, karate, judo, or tae kwon do, usu. practiced as sport. Often used in the plural.

martial law *n.* **1.** Rule by military authorities, imposed on a civilian population esp. in time of war or when civil authority has broken down. **2.** The law imposed on an occupied territory by occupying military forces.

Mar·tian (mär′shən) *adj.* Of or relating to the planet Mars or its hypothetical inhabitants. —*n.* A hypothetical inhabitant of the planet Mars. [ME *marcien* < Lat. *Mārtius* < *Mārs, Mārt-*, Mars.]

mar·tin (mär′tn) *n.* Any of various swallows, such as the house martin or the purple martin. [ME *martoune*, prob. < the name *Martin*, Martin.]

Mar·tin I (mär′tn), Saint. d. 655. Pope (649–655) who was banished by Emperor Constans II (630–668).

Martin V. 1366–1431. Pope (1417–31) who restored the authority of the Church in the Papal States.

Martin, Archer John Porter. b. 1910. British chemist who shared a 1952 Nobel Prize.

Martin, Homer Dodge. 1836–1897. Amer. painter whose landscapes include *Lake Sanford* (1870).

Martin, Mary. 1913–90. Amer. actress who appeared in numerous Broadway hits, including *Peter Pan* (1954).

Mar·tin Du Gard (mär-tăN′ dü gär′), **Roger.** 1881–1958. French writer who won the 1937 Nobel Prize for literature.

Mar·ti·neau (mär′tn-ō), **Harriet.** 1802–76. British writer known for *Illustrations of Political Economy* (1832–34).

mar·ti·net (mär′tn-ĕt′) *n.* **1.** A rigid military disciplinarian. **2.** One who demands absolute adherence to forms and rules. [After Jean *Martinet* (d. 1672), French army officer.]

Mar·ti·nez (mär-tē′nəs). **1.** A city of W CA NE of Oakland. Pop. 31,808. **2.** A community of E GA, a suburb of Augusta. Pop. 33,731.

mar·tin·gale (mär′tn-gāl′) also **mar·tin·gal** (-găl′) *n.* **1.** The strap of a horse's harness that connects the girth to the noseband and prevents the horse from throwing back its head. **2.** *Naut.* Any of several parts of standing rigging strengthening the bowsprit and jib boom against the force of the head stays. **3.** *Games.* A method of gambling in which one doubles the stakes after each loss. **4.** A loose half belt or strap placed on the back of a garment, such as a coat. [Fr., perh. alteration of Sp. *almártaga, almártiga*, rein, harness, of Ar. orig.]

mar·ti·ni (mär-tē′nē) *n., pl.* **-nis.** A cocktail made of gin or vodka and dry vermouth. [?]

Mar·ti·nique (mär′tĭ-nēk′, -tn-ēk′). An island and overseas department of France in the Windward Is. of the West Indies; colonized by French settlers after 1635. Cap. Fort-de-France. Pop. 328,566.

Martin Luther King Day *n.* The third Monday in January, observed in honor of the birthday of Martin Luther King, Jr.

Mar·tin·mas (mär′tn-məs) *n.* A Christian feast commemorating the death and burial of Saint Martin of Tours, traditionally observed on November 11. [ME *martinmesse* : *Martin*, St. Martin of Tours + *messe, masse*, Mass; see MASS.]

Mar·tin of Tours (mär′tn, mär-tăN′; to͝or, to͞or), Saint. A.D. 316?–397? French prelate and patron saint of France.

Mar·tin·son (mär′tn-sôn′, -tēn-), **Harry Edmund.** 1904–78. Swedish writer who shared a 1974 Nobel Prize.

Mar·tins·ville (mär′tnz-vĭl′). An independent city of S VA in the foothills of the Blue Ridge near the NC border; founded 1793. Pop. 16,162.

mart·let (märt′lĭt) *n.* **1.** See **house martin. 2.** *Her.* An image of a bird without feet, used as a crest or bearing to indicate a fourth son. [Fr. *martelet* < *Martin*, St. Martin of Tours.]

mar·tyr (mär′tər) *n.* **1.** One who chooses to suffer death rather than renounce religious principles. **2.** One who makes great sacrifices or suffers much for a belief, cause, or principle. **3.a.** One who suffers greatly. **b.** One who makes a great show of suffering to arouse sympathy. —*tr.v.* **-tyred, -tyr·ing, -tyrs. 1.** To make a martyr of, esp. to put to death for religious beliefs. **2.** To inflict great pain on; torment. [ME, ult. < LGk. *martur* < Gk. *martus, martur-*, witness.]

mar·tyr·dom (mär′tər-dəm) *n.* **1.a.** The state of being a martyr. **b.** The suffering of death by a martyr. **2.** Extreme suffering of any kind.

mar·tyr·ize (mär′tə-rīz′) *tr.v.* **-ized, -iz·ing, -iz·es.** To martyr. **—mar′tyr·i·za′tion** (-tər-ĭ-zā′shən) *n.*

mar·tyr·ol·o·gy (mär′tə-rŏl′ə-jē) *n., pl.* **-gies. 1.** An official list or catalog of religious martyrs, esp. of Christian martyrs. **2.a.** An account of the life and manner of death of a martyr. **b.** The branch of ecclesiastical history or hagiography that deals with martyrs. **—mar′tyr·ol′o·gist** *n.*

mar·vel (mär′vəl) *n.* **1.** One that evokes surprise, admiration, or wonder. See Syns at **wonder. 2.** Strong surprise; astonishment. —*v.* **-veled, -vel·ing, -vels** also **-velled, -vel·ling, -vels.** —*intr.* To become filled with wonder or astonishment. —*tr.* To feel amazement or bewilderment at or about. [ME *marvail* < OFr. *merveille* < VLat. **mīribilia*, alteration of Lat. *mīrābilia*, wonderful things < neut. pl. of *mīrābilis*, wonderful < *mīrārī*, to wonder < *mīrus*, wonderful. See **smei-*.**]

Mar·vell (mär′vəl), **Andrew.** 1621–78. English metaphysical poet whose works include "To His Coy Mistress" (1650).

mar·vel·ous also **mar·vel·lous** (mär′və-ləs) *adj.* **1.** Causing wonder or astonishment. **2.** Miraculous; supernatural. **3.** Of the highest or best kind or quality; first-rate: *a marvelous library.* **—mar′vel·ous·ly** *adv.* **—mar′vel·ous·ness** *n.*

Marx (märks). Family of Amer. comedians, including the brothers **Julius** (1890–1977), "Groucho"; **Leonard** (1891–1961), "Chico"; **Arthur** (1893–1964), "Harpo"; and **Herbert** (1901–79), "Zeppo."

Marx, Karl. 1818–83. German philosopher, economist, and revolutionary who with Friedrich Engels wrote *The Communist Manifesto* (1848) and *Das Kapital* (1867–94).

Marx·i·an (märk′sē-ən) *n.* One that studies, advocates, or uses Marxism. **—Marx′i·an** *adj.* **—Marx′i·an·ism** *n.*

Marx·ism (märk′sĭz′əm) *n.* The political and economic ideas of Karl Marx and Friedrich Engels, specifically an ideology in which the concept of class struggle plays a primary role in analyzing society, which is seen as inevitably progressing from bourgeois oppression under capitalism to a socialist society and thence to Communism. **—Marx′ist** *n. & adj.*

Marx·ism-Len·in·ism (märk′sĭz′əm-lĕn′ĭ-nĭz′əm) *n.* The ideology derived from the expansion of Marxism to include both Lenin's concept of imperialism as the final form of capitalism and a focus on underdeveloped countries.

Mar·y¹ (mâr′ē). In the Bible, the mother of Jesus and the principal saint of many Christian churches.

Mar·y². In the Bible, a sister of Lazarus and Martha and a friend of Jesus.

Mar·y³ also **Mary of Teck** (tĕk). 1867–1953. Queen of George V of Great Britain.

Mary I or **Mary Tu·dor** (to͞o′dər, tyo͞o′-). 1516–58. Queen of England and Ireland (1553–58) who reestablished Roman Catholicism (1555).

Mary II. 1662–94. Queen of England, Scotland, and Ireland (1689–94) who ruled jointly with her husband, William III.

Mary Jane (jān′) *n. Slang.* Marijuana. [Poss. transl. of Sp. *María Juana*, Mary Jane, by folk ety. < *mariguana*, marijuana. See MARIJUANA.]

Mar·y·land (mĕr′ə-lənd). A state of the E-central U.S.; admitted as one of the original Thirteen Colonies in 1788. Cap. Annapolis. Pop. 4,798,622. **—Mar′y·land·er** *n.*

Mary Mag·da·lene (măg′də-lən, -lēn′). In the Bible, a woman whom Jesus cured of evil spirits. She is also identified with the repentent prostitute who washed the feet of Jesus.

Mar·y·ol·o·gy (mâr′ē-ŏl′ə-jē) *n.* Var. of **Mariology.**

Mary Queen of Scots (skŏts). also **Mary Stu·art** (sto͞o′ərt, styo͞o′-). 1542–87. Queen of Scotland (1542–67) who was forced to abdicate in favor of her son, the future James I of England.

Mar·y·ville (mâr′ē-vĭl′, mĕr′ĭ-vəl, -vĭl′). A city of E TN S of Knoxville. Pop. 19,208.

mar·zi·pan (mär′zə-păn′, märt′sə-pän′) *n.* A confection made of ground almonds or almond paste, egg whites, and sugar. [Ger. < Ital. *marzapane*, standard container, marzipan < obsolete Ital., coin or comfit box < Ar. *mawṭabān*, throned king, Byzantine coin with throned Christ.]

Ma·sac·cio (mə-sä′chē-ō, mä-sät′chô). 1401–28. Italian painter noted for his revolutionary use of linear perspective.

Ma·sa·da (mə-sä′də, -tsä-dä′). An ancient mountaintop fortress in SE Israel on the SW shore of the Dead Sea. In A.D. 73, after a two-year siege, members of the Zealot Jewish sect committed mass suicide rather than surrender to the Romans.

Ma·sai (mä-sī′, mä′sī) *n., pl.* **Masai** or **-sais. 1.** A member of a chiefly pastoral people of Kenya and parts of Tanzania. **2.** Also **Maa·sai.** The Nilotic language of this people.

Ma·san (mä′sän′). A city of SE South Korea W of Pusan. Pop. 424,000.

Mas·a·ryk (măs′ə-rĭk, mä′sä-), **Tomáš Garrigue.** 1850–1937. Czechoslovakian politician who served as the first president of independent Czechoslovakia (1918–35). His son **Jan Garrigue Masaryk** (1886–1948) was also a politician.

Mas·ba·te (mäs-bä′tē, -tĕ). An island of the central Philippines S of Luzon.

Mary Queen of Scots
Shown with her son, the future James I, in the Duff-Ogilvy portrait by an unknown artist

ă pat	oi boy
ā pay	ou out
âr care	o͝o took
ä father	o͞o boot
ĕ pet	ŭ cut
ē be	ûr urge
ĭ pit	th thin
ī pie	*th* this
îr pier	hw which
ŏ pot	zh vision
ō toe	ə about, item
ô paw	

Stress marks:
′ (primary);
′ (secondary), as in
dictionary (dĭk′shə-nĕr′ē)

esp. one who plans and directs a complex or difficult project. — *tr.v.* **-mind•ed, -mind•ing, -minds.** To direct, plan, or supervise (a project or an activity).

master of ceremonies *n., pl.* **masters of ceremonies. 1.** One who acts as host at a formal event, making the welcoming speech and introducing other speakers. **2.** One who conducts a program of entertainment by introducing other performers.

mas•ter•piece (măs′tər-pēs′) *n.* **1.** An outstanding work of art or craft. **2.** The greatest work, as of an artist. **3.** Something superlative of its kind. [Prob. transl. of Du. *meesterstuk* or Ger. *Meisterstück* : Du. *meester* and Ger. *Meister*, master + Du. *stuk* and Ger. *Stück*, piece of work.]

master race *n.* A people who consider themselves to be superior to other races and therefore suited to rule over them.

Mas•ters (măs′tərz), **Edgar Lee.** 1869–1950. Amer. poet known for his *Spoon River Anthology* (1915).

mas•ter's degree (măs′tərz) *n.* An academic degree conferred by a college or university upon those who complete at least one year of prescribed study beyond the bachelor's degree.

master sergeant *n.* **1.** A noncommissioned officer in the U.S. Army ranking above sergeant first class and below sergeant major. **2.** A noncommissioned officer in the U.S. Air Force ranking above technical sergeant and below senior master sergeant. **3.** A noncommissioned officer in the U.S. Marine Corps ranking above gunnery sergeant and below sergeant major.

mas•ter•ship (măs′tər-shĭp′) *n.* **1.** The office, function, or authority of a master. **2.** The skill or dexterity of a master.

mas•ter•sing•er (măs′tər-sĭng′ər) *n.* See **Meistersinger.**

Mas•ter•son (măs′tər-sən), **William Barclay ("Bat").** 1853–1921. Amer. frontier marshal famed for his exploits as an army scout, gambler, and law enforcer.

mas•ter•stroke (măs′tər-strōk′) *n.* An achievement or action revealing consummate skill.

mas•ter•work (măs′tər-wûrk′) *n.* See **masterpiece** 2.

mas•ter•y (măs′tə-rē) *n., pl.* **-ies. 1.** Possession of consummate skill. **2.** The status of master or ruler; control: *mastery of the seas.* **3.** Full command of a subject of study.

mast•head (măst′hĕd′) *n.* **1.** *Naut.* The top of a mast. **2.** The listing in a newspaper or periodical of information about its staff, operation, and circulation. **3.** The title of a newspaper or periodical on the first page, front cover, or title page.

mas•tic (măs′tĭk) *n.* **1.** The mastic tree. **2.** The aromatic resin of the mastic tree, used esp. in varnishes, lacquers, adhesives, and condiments and as an astringent. **3.** A pastelike cement used in highway construction, esp. one made with powdered lime or brick and tar. [ME, mastic resin < OFr. *mastich* < Lat. *mastichum, mastichē* < Gk. *mastikhē*, chewing gum, mastic < *mastikhan*, to grind the teeth.]

mas•ti•cate (măs′tĭ-kāt′) *v.* **-cat•ed, -cat•ing, -cates.** — *tr.* **1.** To chew (food). **2.** To grind and knead (rubber, for example) into a pulp. — *intr.* To chew food. [LLat. *masticāre, masticāt-*, to masticate < Gk. *mastikhan*, to grind the teeth.] **— mas′ti•ca′tion** *n.* **— mas′ti•ca′tor** *n.*

mas•ti•ca•to•ry (măs′tĭ-kə-tôr′ē, -tōr′ē) *adj.* **1.** Of, relating to, or used in mastication. **2.** Adapted for chewing. — *n., pl.* **-ries.** A medicinal substance chewed to increase salivation.

mastic tree *n.* A small evergreen shrub *(Pistacia lentiscus)* of the Mediterranean region, cultivated for its resin.

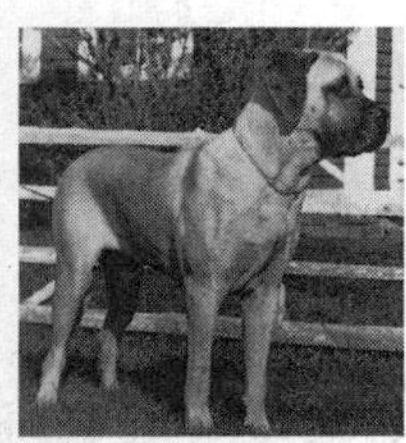

mastiff

mas•tiff (măs′tĭf) *n.* Any of an ancient breed of large strong dogs, probably originating in Asia and having a short, often fawn-colored coat. [ME *mastif*, alteration of OFr. *mastin* < VLat. **(canis) mānsuētīnus*, tame (dog) < Lat. *mānsuētus*, p.part. of *mānsuēscere*, to tame : *manus*, hand; see **man-**^{2}***** + *suēscere*, to accustom; see **s(w)e-*.**]

mastiff bat *n.* Any of various snub-nosed bats of the family Molossidae, found in warm regions of most parts of the world and having narrow wings and brown, gray, or black fur.

mas•ti•goph•o•ran (măs′tĭ-gŏf′ər-ən) *n.* Any of various protozoans of the class Mastigophora, having one or more flagella. [< NLat. *Mastigophora*, class name : Gk. *mastix, mastig-*, whip + NLat. *-phora* (< Gk., neut. pl. of *-phoros*, -phore).] **— mas′ti•goph′o•ran** *adj.*

mas•ti•tis (mă-stī′tĭs) *n.* Inflammation of the breast or udder.

masto– or **mast–** *pref.* Breast; mammary gland; nipple: *mastectomy.* [< Gk. *mastos*, breast.]

mas•to•don (măs′tə-dŏn′) *n.* Any of several very large extinct proboscidian mammals of the genus *Mammut* (sometimes *Mastodon*), resembling the elephant but having molar teeth of a different structure. [NLat. *Mastodōn*, genus name : Gk. *mastos*, nipple + Gk. *odōn, odont-*, tooth; see **dent-*.**]

mas•to•dont (măs′tə-dŏnt′) *adj.* Of, relating to, or characteristic of a mastodon. [< NLat. *Mastodōn*, genus name. See MASTODON.]

mas•toid (măs′toid′) *n.* The mastoid process. — *adj.* **1.** Of or relating to the mastoid process. **2.** Shaped like a breast or nipple. [NLat. *mastoidēs*, nipple-like, mastoid (< its shape) < Gk. *mastoeidēs* : *mastos*, breast + *-oeidēs*, -oid.]

mastoid bone *n.* See **mastoid process.**

mastoid cell *n.* Any of numerous air-filled spaces of various sizes in the mastoid process.

mas•toid•ec•to•my (măs′toi-dĕk′tə-mē) *n., pl.* **-mies.** Surgical removal of mastoid cells or part or all of the mastoid process.

mas•toid•i•tis (măs′toid-ī′tĭs) *n.* Inflammation of the mastoid process and mastoid cells.

mastoid process *n.* A conical protuberance of the temporal bone that is situated behind the ear in many vertebrates and serves as a site of muscle attachment.

mas•tur•bate (măs′tər-bāt′) *v.* **-bat•ed, -bat•ing, -bates.** — *intr.* To perform an act of masturbation. — *tr.* To perform an act of masturbation on. [Lat. *masturbārī, masturbāt-*.]

mas•tur•ba•tion (măs′tər-bā′shən) *n.* Excitation of one's own or another's genital organs, usu. to orgasm, by manual contact or means other than sexual intercourse. **— mas′tur•ba′tion•al, mas′tur•ba•to′ry** (-bə-tôr′ē, -tōr′ē) *adj.* **— mas′tur•ba′tor** *n.*

Ma•su•ri•a (mə-zo͝or′ē-ə). A historical region of NE Poland; assigned to Poland in 1945. **— Ma•su′ri•an** *adj.*

mat^{1} (măt) *n.* **1.** A flat piece of coarse fabric or other material, used for wiping one's shoes or feet or in various other forms as a floor covering. **2.** A small flat piece of decorated material placed under a lamp, dish of food, or other object. **3.** *Sports.* A floor pad to protect athletes. **4.** A densely woven or thickly tangled mass: *a mat of hair.* **5.** The solid part of a lace design. **6.** A heavy woven net of rope or wire cable placed over a blasting site to keep debris from scattering. — *v.* **mat•ted, mat•ting, mats.** — *tr.* **1.** To cover, protect, or decorate with mats or a mat. **2.** To pack or interweave into a thick mass. — *intr.* To be packed or interwoven into a thick mass; become entangled. [ME < OE *matte* < LLat. *matta*, poss. < Phoenician (Punic) *maṭṭâ*; akin to Heb. *miṭṭa*, bed, couch.]

mat^{2} (măt) *n.* **1.** A decorative border around a picture to serve as a frame or provide contrast between the picture and the frame. **2.** Also **matte. a.** A dull, often rough finish, as of paint, glass, metal, or paper. **b.** A special tool for producing such a surface or finish. **3.** *Print.* See **matrix** 10a. — *tr.v.* **mat•ted, mat•ting, mats. 1.** To put a mat around (a picture). **2.** To produce a dull finish on. — *adj.* also **matte.** Having a dull finish. [< Fr., dull < OFr., defeated, withered, perh. < Lat. *mattus*, stupefied, senseless, poss. < **maditus*, p.part. of *madēre*, to be wet.]

mat. *abbr.* Matinee.

M.A.T. *abbr.* Master of Arts in Teaching.

Mat•a•be•le (mä′tä-bĕl′ā) *n., pl.* **Matabele** or **-les.** See **Ndebele.**

Mat•a•be•le•land (mä′tə-bĕl′ā-lănd′). A region of W Zimbabwe inhabited by the Ndebele people after 1827.

mat•a•dor (măt′ə-dôr′) *n.* **1.** A bullfighter who performs the final passes and kills the bull. **2.** *Games.* One of the highest trumps in certain card games. [Sp. < *matar*, to kill, poss. < VLat. **mattāre*, to beat senseless, perh. < Lat. *mattus*, stupefied. See MAT^{2}.]

Ma•ta Ha•ri (mä′tə här′ē, măt′ə hăr′ē). 1876–1917. Dutch dancer who supposedly spied for Germany in World War I.

Ma•ta•mo•ros (măt′ə-môr′əs, -mōr′-, mä′tä-mô′rôs). A city of NE Mexico near the mouth of the Rio Grande opposite Brownsville TX. Pop. 188,745.

Ma•tan•zas (mə-tăn′zəs, mä-tän′säs). A city of NW-central Cuba E of Havana; founded 1693. Pop. 100,367.

Mat•a•pan (măt′ə-păn′), **Cape.** See Cape **Taínaron.**

Ma•ta•ró (mä′tə-rō′, -tä-). A city of NE Spain on the Mediterranean Sea NE of Barcelona. Pop. 99,126.

match^{1} (măch) *n.* **1.a.** One that is exactly like another; a counterpart. **b.** One that is like another in one or more specified qualities. **2.** One that is able to compete equally with another. **3.a.** One that closely resembles or harmonizes with another. **b.** A pair, each one of which resembles or harmonizes with the other. **4.** *Sports.* **a.** A game or contest in which two or more persons, animals, or teams oppose and compete with each other. **b.** A tennis contest won by the player or side that wins a specified number of sets. **5.** A marriage or an arrangement of marriage. **6.** A person viewed as a prospective marriage partner. — *v.* **matched, match•ing, match•es.** — *tr.* **1.a.** To be exactly like; correspond exactly to. **b.** To be like with respect to specified qualities. **2.** To resemble or harmonize with. **3.** To adapt or suit so that a balanced or harmonious result is achieved; cause to correspond. **4.** To find or produce a counterpart to. **5.** To fit together or cause to fit together. **6.** To join or give in marriage. **7.** To place in opposition or competition; pit. **8.** To provide with an adversary or a competitor. **9.** To do as well as or better than in competition; equal. **10.** To set in comparison; compare. **11.** To provide funds so as to equal or complement. **12.** To flip or toss (coins) and compare the sides that land face up. **13.** To couple (electric circuits) by means of a transformer. — *intr.* To be a close counterpart; correspond. [ME *macche* < OE *gemæcca*, companion, mate. See **mag-*.**] **— match′er** *n.*

match^{2} (măch) *n.* **1.** A narrow piece, usu. of wood or cardboard, coated on one end with a compound that ignites when scratched against a rough or chemically treated surface. **2.** An easily ignited cord or wick, formerly used to detonate powder charges or to fire cannons and muzzleloading firearms. [ME *matche*, lamp wick < OFr. *mesche* < VLat. **micca* < Lat.

myxa, a lamp's nozzle < Gk. *muxa*, mucus, lamp wick.]

match•a•ble (măch**′**ə-bəl) *adj.* That can be matched.

match•board (măch**′**bôrd′, -bōrd′) *n.* A board cut with a tongue on one side and a matching groove on the other to fit with other boards of similar cut.

match•book (măch**′**bo͝ok′) *n.* A small folder containing safety matches and having a striking surface along the bottom.

match•box (măch**′**bŏks′) *n.* A box for matches.

match•less (măch**′**lĭs) *adj.* Having no match or equal; unsurpassed. **— match′less•ly** *adv.* **— match′less•ness** *n.*

match•lock (măch**′**lŏk′) *n.* **1.** A gunlock in which powder is ignited by a match. **2.** A musket having such a gunlock.

match•mak•er (măch**′**mā′kər) *n.* **1.** One who arranges or tries to arrange marriages. **2.** *Sports.* One who arranges athletic competitions. **— match′mak′ing** *n.*

match play *n. Sports.* A method of scoring golf games by counting only the number of holes won by each side.

match point *n. Sports.* The final point needed to win a match.

match•stick (măch**′**stĭk′) *n.* **1.** A short slender piece of wood from which a match is made. **2.** Something similar to a matchstick, as in slenderness. *— adj.* Short and slender.

match•up (măch**′**ŭp′) *n.* The pairing of two people or things, as for athletic competition or for comparison.

match•wood (măch**′**wo͝od′) *n.* **1.** Wood in small pieces or splinters suitable esp. for making matches. **2.** Splinters.

mate[1] (māt) *n.* **1.** One of a matched pair: *the mate to this glove.* **2.** A spouse. **3.a.** Either of a pair of animals or birds that associate in order to propagate. **b.** Either of a pair of animals brought together for breeding. **4.a.** A person with whom one is in close association; an associate. **b.** A good friend or companion. **5.** A deck officer on a merchant ship ranking below the master. **6.** A U.S. Navy petty officer who is an assistant to a warrant officer. *— v.* **mat•ed, mat•ing, mates.** *— tr.* **1.** To join closely; pair. **2.** To unite in marriage. **3.** To pair (animals) for breeding. *— intr.* **1.** To become joined in marriage. **2.a.** To be paired for reproducing; breed. **b.** To copulate. [ME < MLGer. *māte, gemate*, messmate.]

mate[2] (māt) *Games. — n.* A checkmate. *— tr. & intr.v.* **mat•ed, mat•ing, mates.** To checkmate or achieve a checkmate. [ME < OFr. *mat*, checkmated < Ar. *māt*, dead. See CHECKMATE.]

ma•té or **ma•te** (mä**′**tā, mä-tā**′**) *n.* **1.** A South American evergreen tree *(Ilex paraguariensis),* the dried leaves of which are used to prepare a tealike beverage. **2.** This tealike beverage, popular in South America. [Fr. < Am.Sp. *mate* < Quechua, hollow gourd used to brew yerba maté.]

mat•e•lote (măt**′**l-ōt′, mä-tə-lōt**′**) also **mat•e•lotte** (-l-ŏt′, -lŏt**′**) *n.* A fish stew cooked in a wine sauce. [Fr. < *matelot*, sailor < OFr. *matenot*, bunkmate, sailor, poss. < MDu. *mattenoot* (perh. < *matte*, bed < LLat. *matta*; see MAT[1] + *noot*, fellow) or < ON *mötunautr*, messmate (*mata*, food, mess + *nautr*, companion).]

ma•ter (mā**′**tər) *n. Chiefly British.* Mother. [Lat. *māter*. See **māter-***.]

ma•ter•fa•mil•i•as (mā′tər-fə-mĭl**′**ē-əs) *n.* A woman who is the head of a household or the mother of a family. [Lat. *māterfamiliās* : *māter*, mother; see MATER + *familiās*, archaic genitive of *familia*, household; see FAMILY.]

ma•te•ri•al (mə-tîr**′**ē-əl) *n.* **1.** The substance or substances out of which a thing is or can be made. **2.** Something, such as an idea, that is to be refined and made or incorporated into a finished effort. **3. materials.** Tools or apparatus for the performance of a given task. **4.** Yard goods or cloth. **5.** A person qualified or suited for a position or activity. *— adj.* **1.** Of, relating to, or composed of matter. **2.** Of, relating to, or affecting physical well-being; bodily. **3.** Of or concerned with the physical as distinct from the intellectual or spiritual. **4.** Being both relevant and consequential; crucial. **5.** *Philos.* Of or relating to the matter of reasoning, rather than the form. [ME, consisting of matter, material < OFr. < LLat. *māteriālis* < Lat. *māteria*, matter. See **māter-***.] **— ma•te′ri•al•ness** *n.*

ma•te•ri•al•ism (mə-tîr**′**ē-ə-lĭz′əm) *n.* **1.** *Philos.* The theory that physical matter is the only reality and that everything can be explained in terms of matter and physical phenomena. **2.** The theory or doctrine that physical well-being and worldly possessions constitute the greatest good and highest value in life. **3.** A great or excessive regard for worldly concerns. **— ma•te′ri•al•ist** *n.* **— ma•te′ri•al•is′tic** *adj.*

ma•te•ri•al•i•ty (mə-tîr′ē-ăl**′**ĭ-tē) *n., pl.* **-ties. 1.** The state or quality of being material. **2.** Physical substance; matter.

ma•te•ri•al•ize (mə-tîr**′**ē-ə-līz′) *v.* **-ized, -iz•ing, -iz•es.** *— tr.* **1.** To cause to become real or actual. **2.** To cause to become materialistic. *— intr.* **1.** To assume material or effective form. **2.** To take physical form or shape. **3.** To appear, esp. suddenly. **— ma•te′ri•al•i•za′tion** (-ə-lĭ-zā**′**shən) *n.* **— ma•te′ri•al•iz′er** *n.*

ma•te•ri•al•ly (mə-tîr**′**ē-ə-lē) *adv.* **1.** With regard to the physical world. **2.** With regard to matter as distinguished from form. **3.** To a significant extent or degree; substantially.

ma•te•ri•als science (mə-tîr**′**ē-əlz) *n.* The study of the characteristics and uses of the various materials, such as ceramics and plastics, employed in science and technology.

ma•te•ri•a med•i•ca (mə-tîr**′**ē-ə mĕd**′**ĭ-kə) *n. Medic.* **1.** The scientific study of medicinal drugs and their sources, preparation, and use. **2.** Substances used in the preparation of medicinal drugs. [NLat. *māteria medica* (transl. of Gk. *hulē iatrikē*) : Lat. *māteria*, material + Lat. *medica*, medical.]

ma•te•ri•el or **ma•té•ri•el** (mə-tîr′ē-ĕl**′**) *n.* The equipment, apparatus, and supplies of a military force or other organization. [Fr. *matériel*, consisting of matter, materiel < OFr. *material*. See MATERIAL.]

ma•ter•nal (mə-tûr**′**nəl) *adj.* **1.** Relating to or characteristic of a mother or motherhood; motherly: *maternal instinct.* **2.** Inherited from one's mother. **3.** Related through one's mother. [ME < OFr. *maternel* < Med.Lat. *māternālis* < Lat. *māternus* < *māter*, mother. See **māter-***.] **— ma•ter′nal•ism** *n.* **— ma•ter′nal•ly** *adv.*

ma•ter•ni•ty (mə-tûr**′**nĭ-tē) *n., pl.* **-ties. 1.** The state of being a mother; motherhood. **2.** The feelings or characteristics associated with being a mother; motherliness. **3.** A maternity ward. *— adj.* Relating to or effective during pregnancy, childbirth, or the first months of motherhood: *maternity leave.* [Fr. *maternité* < Med.Lat. *māternitās* < Lat. *māternus*, maternal < *māter*, mother. See **māter-***.]

maternity ward *n.* The part of a hospital that provides care for women before and during childbirth and for their infants.

mat•ey (mā**′**tē) *adj. Chiefly British.* Sociable; friendly.

math (măth) *n.* Mathematics.

math. *abbr.* **1.** Mathematical. **2.** Mathematician.

math•e•mat•i•cal (măth′ə-măt**′**ĭ-kəl) also **math•e•mat•ic** (-ĭk) *adj.* **1.** Of or relating to mathematics. **2.a.** Precise; exact. **b.** Absolute; certain. **3.** Possible according to mathematics but highly improbable. [ME < Med.Lat. *mathēmaticālis* < Lat. *mathēmaticus* < Gk. *mathēmatikos* < *mathēma, mathēmat-*, science, learning < *manthanein*, to learn. See **mendh-***.] **— math′e•mat′i•cal•ly** *adv.*

mathematical induction *n. Math.* Induction.

mathematical logic *n.* See **symbolic logic.**

math•e•ma•ti•cian (măth′ə-mə-tĭsh**′**ən) *n.* A person skilled or learned in mathematics.

math•e•mat•ics (măth′ə-măt**′**ĭks) *n. (used with a sing. v.)* The study of the measurement, properties, and relationships of quantities, using numbers and symbols. [< ME *mathematik* < OFr. *mathematique* < Lat. *mathēmatica* < Gk. *mathēmatikē (tekhnē)*, mathematical (science), fem. of *mathēmatikos*, mathematical. See MATHEMATICAL.]

math•e•ma•tize (măth**′**ə-mə-tīz′) *tr.v.* **-tized, -tiz•ing, -tiz•es.** To reduce to or as if to mathematical formulas. **— math′e•ma•ti•za′tion** (-tĭ-zā**′**shən) *n.*

Math•er (măth**′**ər), **Increase.** 1639–1723. Amer. clergyman and writer who with his son **Cotton** (1663–1728) exerted great influence on the colony of Massachusetts.

Ma•thu•ra (mŭt**′**ər-ə) also **Mut•tra** (mŭt**′**rə). A city of N-central India NW of Agra; a Hindu pilgrimage site revered as the reputed birthplace of Krishna. Pop. 147,493.

ma•til•i•ja poppy (mə-tĭl**′**ē-hä′) *n.* A perennial herb *(Romneya coulteri)* of California and Baja California having very large white flowers. [After *Matilija* Canyon in SW CA.]

mat•in (măt**′**n) also **mat•in•al** (-əl) *adj.* Of or relating to matins or to the early part of the day. [ME < OFr., sing. of *matines*, matins. See MATINS.]

mat•i•nee or **mat•i•née** (măt′n-ā**′**) *n.* An entertainment, such as a dramatic or musical performance, given in the daytime, usu. in the afternoon. [Fr. *matinée* < *matin*, morning < OFr. *matines*, matins. See MATINS.]

mat•ins (măt**′**nz) *n. (used with a sing. or pl. v.)* **1.** *Eccles.* The office that formerly constituted the first of the seven canonical hours. **2.** Often **Matins.** See **Morning Prayer.** [ME *matines* < OFr. < Med.Lat. *(vigiliae) mātūtīnae*, morning (vigils), fem. pl. of Lat. *mātūtīnus*, of the morning < *Mātūta*, goddess of dawn. See **mā-**[1]***.**]

Ma•tisse (mə-tēs**′**, mä-), **Henri.** 1869–1954. French artist whose works include *The Dance* (1930–32).

mat•jes herring (mät**′**yĭs) *n.* Unspawned herring that are filleted and pickled. [Partial transl. of Du. *maatjesharing* : *maatjes* (alteration of *maeghdekins*, genitive of *maeghdekin*, maiden, dim. of *maagd*, maid; see **maghu-***) + *haring*, herring.]

matri– or **matro–** or **matr–** *pref.* Mother; maternal: *matrilineal.* [Lat. *mātri-* < *māter, mātr-*, mother. See MATER.]

ma•tri•arch (mā**′**trē-ärk′) *n.* **1.** A woman who rules a family, clan, or tribe. **2.** A woman who dominates a group or an activity. **3.** A highly respected mother. **— ma′tri•ar′chal** (-är**′**kəl), **ma′tri•ar′chic** *adj.* **— ma′tri•ar′chal•ism** *n.*

ma•tri•ar•chate (mā**′**trē-är′kĭt, -kāt′) *n.* **1.** See **matriarchy. 2.** A hypothetical stage in the evolution of a society in which authority is held by women.

ma•tri•ar•chy (mā**′**trē-är′kē) *n., pl.* **-chies. 1.** A social system in which the mother is head of the family and descent is traced through the mother's side. **2.** A family, community, or society based on this system or governed by women.

mat•ri•cide (măt**′**rĭ-sīd′) *n.* **1.** The act of killing one's mother. **2.** One who kills one's mother. **— mat′ri•cid′al** (-sīd**′**l) *adj.*

matilija poppy
Romneya coulteri

Henri Matisse

ă pat	oi boy
ā pay	ou out
âr care	o͝o took
ä father	o͞o boot
ĕ pet	ŭ cut
ē be	ûr urge
ĭ pit	th thin
ī pie	*th* this
îr pier	hw which
ŏ pot	zh vision
ō toe	ə about, item
ô paw	

Stress marks:
′ (primary);
′ (secondary), as in
dictionary (dĭk**′**shə-nĕr′ē)

ma•tric•u•late (mə-trĭk′yə-lāt′) *tr. & intr.v.* **-lat•ed, -lat•ing, -lates.** To admit or be admitted into a group, esp. a college or university. —*n.* (-lĭt, -lāt′). One who is admitted as a student to a college or university. [< Med.Lat. *mātrīculāre, mātrīculāt-* < LLat. *mātrīcula,* list, dim. of *mātrīx, mātrīc-.* See MATRIX.] —**ma•tric′u•lant** (mə-triək′yə-lənt) *n.* —**ma•tric′u•la′tion** *n.*

mat•ri•lin•e•age (măt′rə-lĭn′ē-ĭj) *n.* Line of descent as traced through the maternal side of a family.

mat•ri•lin•e•al (măt′rə-lĭn′ē-əl) *adj.* Relating to, based on, or tracing ancestral descent through the maternal line. —**mat′ri•lin′e•al•ly** *adv.*

mat•ri•lo•cal (măt′rə-lō′kəl) *adj. Anthro.* Of or relating to the residence of a wife's kin group or clan.

mat•ri•mo•ny (măt′rə-mō′nē) *n., pl.* **-nies.** The act or state of being married; marriage. [ME < OFr. *matrimoine* < Lat. *mātrimōnium* < *māter, mātr-,* mother. See **māter-***.] —**mat′ri•mo′ni•al** *adj.* —**mat′ri•mo′ni•al•ly** *adv.*

matrimony vine *n.* Any of various often thorny shrubs of the genus *Lycium,* some species of which are cultivated for their purplish flowers and brightly colored berries.

ma•trix (mā′trĭks) *n., pl.* **ma•tri•ces** (mā′trĭ-sēz′, măt′rĭ-) or **ma•trix•es. 1.** A situation or surrounding substance within which something else originates, develops, or is contained. **2.** The womb. **3.** *Anat.* **a.** The formative cells or tissue of a fingernail, toenail, or tooth. **b.** See **ground substance** 1. **4.** *Geol.* **a.** The solid matter in which a fossil or crystal is embedded. **b.** Groundmass. **5.** A mold or die. **6.** The principal metal in an alloy, as the iron in steel. **7.** A binding substance, as cement in concrete. **8.a.** *Math.* A rectangular array of numeric or algebraic quantities subject to mathematical operations. **b.** Something resembling such an array, as in the regular formation of elements into columns and rows. **9.** *Comp. Sci.* The network of intersections between input and output leads in a computer, functioning as an encoder or a decoder. **10.** *Print.* **a.** A mold used in stereotyping and designed to receive positive impressions of type or illustrations from which metal plates can be cast. **b.** A metal plate used for casting typefaces. [ME *matrice* < OFr. < LLat. *mātrīx, mātrīc-* < Lat., breeding-animal < *māter, mātr-,* mother. See **māter-***.]

matro– *pref.* Var. of **matri–.**

ma•tron (mā′trən) *n.* **1.** A married woman or a widow, esp. a mother of dignity, mature age, and established social position. **2.** A woman who acts as a supervisor or monitor in a public institution. [ME *matrone* < OFr. < Lat. *mātrōna* < *māter, mātr-,* mother. See **māter-***.] —**ma′tron•al** *adj.* —**ma′tron•li•ness** *n.* —**ma′tron•ly** *adv. & adj.*

matron of honor *n., pl.* **matrons of honor.** A married woman serving as chief attendant of the bride at a wedding.

mat•ro•nym•ic (măt′rə-nĭm′ĭk) *adj. & n.* Var. of **metronymic.**

Mat•su (măt′sōō′). An island administered by Taiwan in the East China Sea off the SE coast of mainland China.

Ma•tsu•do (mä-tsōō′dō). A city of E-central Honshu, Japan, a suburb of Tokyo. Pop. 427,479.

Ma•tsu•ya•ma (mä′tsōō-yä′mä). A city of W Shikoku, Japan, on the Inland Sea. Pop. 426,646.

Matt. *abbr. Bible.* Matthew.

Mat•tag•a•mi (mə-tăg′ə-mē). A river of E Ontario, Canada, rising in **Mattagami Lake** and flowing c. 443 km (275 mi) N to the Moose R.

matte¹ (măt) *n.* Var. of **mat²** 2. —*adj.* Var. of **mat².**

matte² (măt) *n.* A mixture of a metal and its sulfides, made by smelting the sulfide ores of copper, lead, or nickel. [Fr.]

mat•ted (măt′ĭd) *adj.* **1.** Covered with or made from mats. **2.** Tangled in a dense mass: *matted undergrowth.*

mat•ter (măt′ər) *n.* **1.a.** Something that occupies space and can be perceived by one or more senses; a physical body, a physical substance, or the universe as a whole. **b.** *Phys.* Something that has mass and exists as a solid, liquid, or gas. **2.** A specific type of substance: *inorganic matter.* **3.** Discharge or waste, such as pus or feces, from a living organism. **4.** *Philos.* In Aristotelian and Scholastic use, that which is in itself undifferentiated and formless and which, as the subject of change and development, receives form and becomes substance and experience. **5.** The substance of thought or expression as opposed to the manner in which it is stated or conveyed. **6.** A subject of concern, feeling, or action. See Syns at **subject. 7.** Trouble or difficulty. **8.** An approximated quantity, amount, or extent: *a matter of years.* **9.** Something printed or otherwise set down in writing: *reading matter.* **10.** Something sent by mail. **11.** *Print.* **a.** Composed type. **b.** Material to be set in type. —*intr.v.* **-tered, -ter•ing, -ters.** To be of importance. See Syns at **count¹.** —*idioms.* **as a matter of fact.** In fact; actually. **for that matter.** So far as that is concerned; as for that. **no matter.** Regardless of. [ME < OFr. *matere* < Lat. *māteria.* See **māter-***.]

Mat•ter•horn (măt′ər-hôrn′, mä′tər-). A mountain, 4,481.1 m (14,692 ft), in the Pennine Alps on the Italian-Swiss border.

Matterhorn

matter of course *n.* A natural or logical outcome.

mat•ter-of-fact (măt′ər-əv-făkt′) *adj.* **1.** Relating or adhering to facts; literal. **2.** Straightforward or unemotional. —**mat′ter-of-fact′ly** *adv.* —**mat′ter-of-fact′ness** *n.*

Mat•thew (măth′yōō) *n.* See table at **Bible.**

Matthew, Saint. 1st cent. A.D. One of the 12 Apostles and the author of the first Gospel of the New Testament.

Mat•thews (măth′yōōz), **Stanley.** 1824–89. Amer. jurist; associate justice of the U.S. Supreme Court (1881–89).

mat•ting¹ (măt′ĭng) *n.* **1.a.** Material formed into or considered a mat. **b.** A coarsely woven fabric used to cover floors, for example. **2.** The activity of making mats.

mat•ting² (măt′ĭng) *n.* **1.** A dull surface or finish. **2.** The process of dulling a surface, as of metal.

mat•tins (măt′nz) *n. (used with a sing. or pl. v.) Chiefly Brit-ish.* Var. of **matins.**

mat•tock (măt′ək) *n.* A digging tool with a flat blade set at right angles to the handle. [ME < OE *mattuc,* perh. < VLat. **matteūca,* club; akin to **mattea.* See MACE¹.]

Mat•toon (mə-tōōn′). A city of E-central IL SE of Decatur. Pop. 18,441.

mat•tress (măt′rĭs) *n.* **1.a.** A usu. rectangular pad of heavy cloth filled with soft material or an arrangement of coiled springs, used as or on a bed. **b.** An airtight inflatable pad used as or on a bed or as a cushion. **2.** A closely woven mat of brush and poles used to protect an embankment, a dike, or a dam from erosion. [ME *mattresse* < OFr. *materas* < OItal. *materasso* and < Med.Lat. *matracium,* both < Ar. *maṭraḥ,* place to throw something, mat, cushion < *ṭaraḥa,* to throw.]

Word History: During the earlier part of the Middle Ages, Arabic culture was more advanced than that of Europe. One of the amenities of life enjoyed by the Arabs was sleeping on cushions thrown on the floor. Derived from the Arabic word *ṭaraḥa,* "to throw," the word *maṭraḥ* meant "place where something is thrown" and "mat, cushion." This kind of sleeping surface was adopted by the Europeans during the Crusades, and the Arabic word was taken into Old Italian (*materasso*), Old French (*materas*), and Medieval Latin (*matracium*). English borrowed the word from Old French and Medieval Latin, *materas* being first recorded around 1300.

mat•u•rate (măch′ə-rāt′) *v.* **-ra•ted, -rat•ing, -rates.** —*intr.* **1.** To mature, ripen, or develop. **2.** To suppurate. —*tr.* To cause to suppurate. [Lat. *mātūrāre, mātūrāt-* < *mātūrus,* mature. See MATURE.] —**mat′u•ra′tive** *adj.*

mat•u•ra•tion (măch′ə-rā′shən) *n.* **1.** The process of becoming mature. **2.** Production or discharge of pus. **3.** *Biol.* **a.** The processes by which gametes are formed. **b.** The final differentiation processes in biological systems, such as those of a mature cell. —**mat′u•ra′tion•al** *adj.*

Somerset Maugham
Photographed in 1952

maturation division *n.* Either of the two successive cell divisions of meiosis, with only one duplication of the chromosomes, that results in the formation of haploid gametes.

ma•ture (mə-tyŏŏr′, -tŏŏr′, -chŏŏr′) *adj.* **-tur•er, -tur•est. 1.a.** Having reached full natural growth or development: *a mature cell.* **b.** Having reached a desired or final condition; ripe. **2.** Of, relating to, or characteristic of full development, either mental or physical. **3.a.** Suitable or intended for adults. **b.** Composed of adults. **4.** Worked out fully by the mind; considered. **5.** Having reached the limit of its time; due. **6.** No longer subject to great expansion or development. Used of an industry, a market, or a product. **7.** *Geol.* Having reached maximum development of form. Used of streams and landforms. —*v.* **-tured, -tur•ing, -tures.** —*tr.* **1.** To bring to full development; ripen. **2.** To work out fully in the mind. —*intr.* **1.** To evolve toward or reach full development. **2.** To become due. Used of notes and bonds. [ME < OFr. < Lat. *mātūrus.* See **mā-¹***.] —**ma•ture′ly** *adv.* —**ma•ture′ness** *n.*

Syns: *mature, age, develop, ripen.* The central meaning shared by these verbs is "to bring or come to full development or maximum excellence": *maturing wines in vats; aged the cheese; developed the flavor; fruits ripened on the vine.*

ma•ture-on•set diabetes (mə-tyŏŏr′ŏn′sĕt′, -ôn′, -tŏŏr′-, -chŏŏr′-) *n.* Diabetes mellitus.

ma•tur•i•ty (mə-tyŏŏr′ĭ-tē, -tŏŏr′-, -chŏŏr′-) *n., pl.* **-ties. 1.a.** The state or quality of being fully grown or developed. **b.** The state or quality of being mature. **2.a.** The time at which a note or bond is due. **b.** The state of a note or bond being due. **3.** *Geol.* A stage in the evolution of streams or landscapes at which maximum development has been reached or erosion is going on with maximum vigor. [ME *maturite* < OFr. < Lat. *mātūritās* < *mātūrus,* mature. See MATURE.]

Mauritania

ma•tu•ti•nal (mə-tōōt′n-əl, -tyōōt′-, măch′ōō-tī′nəl) *adj.* Of, relating to, or occurring in the morning; early. [LLat. *mātūtīnālis* < Lat. *mātūtīnus.* See MATINS.]

mat•zo or **mat•zah** (mät′sə, mät-sä′, -sô′) *n., pl.* **-zos** or **-zahs** (mät′səz, -səs, -sōs′) or **-zot** or **-zoth** (mät-sōt′). Flat unleavened bread, eaten esp. during Passover. [Yiddish *matse* < Heb. *maṣṣâ.*]

matzo ball *n.* A small dumpling made from matzo meal.

maud•lin (môd′lĭn) *adj.* Effusively or tearfully sentimental. [Alteration of (MARY) MAGDALENE, frequently depicted as a tearful penitent.] —**maud′lin•ly** *adv.* —**maud′lin•ness** *n.*

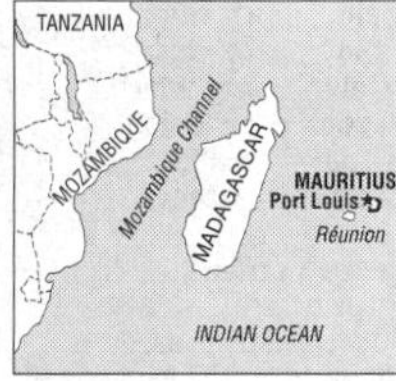

Mauritius

Maugham (môm), **W(illiam) Somerset.** 1874–1965. British writer whose works include *Of Human Bondage* (1915).

mau•gre (mô′gər) *prep. Archaic.* Notwithstanding. [ME < OFr. : *mal-*, *mau-*, bad; see MAL– + *gre*, pleasure (< Lat. *grātum* < neut. of *grātus*, pleasing; see **gʷerə-²***).]

Mau•i (mou′ē). An island of HI NW of Hawaii I.

maul also **mall** (môl) —*n.* **1.** A heavy long-handled hammer used esp. to drive stakes, piles, or wedges. **2.** A heavy hammer with a wedge-shaped head used for splitting logs. —*tr.v.* **mauled, maul•ing, mauls** also **malled, mall•ing, malls. 1.** To injure by or as if by beating. **2.** To handle roughly. **3.** To split (wood) with a maul and wedge. [ME *malle* < OFr. *mail* < Lat. *malleus*. See **melə-***.] —**maul′er** *n.*

Maul•din (môl′dĭn), **William Henry ("Bill").** b. 1921. Amer. editorial cartoonist noted for his realistic, bitterly comic drawings of front-line soldiers.

maul•stick also **mahl•stick** (môl′stĭk′) *n.* A long wooden stick used by painters as a support for the hand that holds the brush. [Partial transl. of obsolete Du. *maalstok* : *maalen*, to paint (< MDu. *malen*) + *stok*, stick.]

Mau•na Ke•a (mou′nə kā′ə, mô′nə kē′ə). An active volcano, c. 4,208 m (13,796 ft), of N-central Hawaii I.

Mauna Lo•a (lō′ə). An active volcano, 4,172.4 m (13,680 ft), of S-central Hawaii I.

maund (mônd) *n.* A unit of weight varying in different countries of Asia from 11.2 to 37.4 kilograms (24.8 to 82.6 pounds) avoirdupois, the latter being the official maund in India. [Hindi *man* < Skt. *mānam*, measure.]

maun•der (môn′dər, män′-) *intr.v.* **-dered, -der•ing, -ders. 1.** To talk incoherently or aimlessly. **2.** To move or act aimlessly or vaguely; wander. [?]

Maun•dy Thursday (môn′dē, män′-) *n.* The Thursday before Easter, commemorating the Last Supper. [< ME *maunde*, foot-washing ceremony on this day < OFr. *mande* < Lat. *(novum) mandātum*, (new) commandment (< Jesus's words in John 13:34). See MANDATE.]

Mau•pas•sant (mō′pə-sänt′, mō-pă-säN′), **(Henri René Albert) Guy de.** 1850–93. French writer known esp. for his realistic short stories, such as "The Necklace."

Mau•re•ta•ni•a (môr′ĭ-tā′nē-ə, -tān′yə, mär′-). An ancient district of the Roman Empire in present-day Morocco and Algeria; ruled by Rome from c. 100 B.C. to the 5th cent. A.D. —**Mau′re•ta′ni•an** *adj. & n.*

Mau•riac (môr′ē-äk′, môr-yäk′), **François.** 1885–1970. French writer who won the 1952 Nobel Prize for literature.

Mau•rice of Nas•sau (môr′ĭs, mŏr′-; năs′ô). Prince of Orange. 1567–1625. Dutch general who drove Spanish forces from Dutch territory (1590–1609).

Mau•ri•ta•ni•a (môr′ĭ-tā′nē-ə, -tān′yə, mär′-). A country of NW Africa bordering on the Atlantic; achieved independence from France in 1960. Cap. Nouakchott. Pop. 1,727,000. —**Mau′ri•ta′ni•an** *adj. & n.*

Mau•ri•tius (mô-rĭsh′əs, -ē-əs). An island country in the SW Indian Ocean comprising the island of **Mauritius** and small dependencies in the Mascarene Is.; achieved independence from Great Britain in 1968. Cap. Port Louis. Pop. 1,023,934. —**Mau•ri′tian** *adj. & n.*

Mau•rois (môr-wä′), **André. Émile Herzog.** 1885–1967. French writer noted for his essays, biographies, and novels.

Mau•ry (môr′ē), **Matthew Fontaine.** 1806–73. Amer. naval officer who charted the currents and winds of the Atlantic, Pacific, and Indian oceans.

mau•so•le•um (mô′sə-lē′əm, -zə-) *n., pl.* **-le•ums** or **-le•a** (-lē′ə). **1.** A large stately tomb or a building housing such a tomb or several tombs. **2.** A gloomy, usu. large room or building. [ME < Lat. *Mausōlēum* < Gk. *Mausōleion* < *Mausōlos*, Mausolus, ancient Persian satrap.] —**mau′so•le′an** *adj.*

mauve (mōv) *n. Color.* A grayish violet to reddish purple. [Fr. < OFr. *mallow* < Lat. *malva*.] —**mauve** *adj.*

ma•ven also **ma•vin** (mā′vən) *n.* A person who has special knowledge or experience; an expert. [Yiddish *meyvn* < Heb. *mēbīn*.]

mav•er•ick (măv′ər-ĭk, măv′rĭk) *n.* **1.** An unbranded range animal, esp. a calf separated from its mother. **2.** One that rejects the dictates of or resists adherence to a group; a dissenter. —*adj.* Independent in thought and action or exhibiting such independence. [Poss. after Samuel Augustus *Maverick* (1803–70), Amer. cattleman, or perh. after Samuel *Maverick* (1602?–76?), English-born colonist.]

ma•vis (mā′vĭs) *n.* See **song thrush.** [ME < OFr. *mauvis*, prob. < *mauve*, seagull, mew.]

ma•vour•neen also **ma•vour•nin** (mə-vo͝or′nēn′) *n. Irish.* My darling. [Ir.Gael. *mo mhuirnín* : *mo*, my (< OIr.; see **me-¹***) + *muirnín*, darling, dim. of *muirn*, delight (< OIr., tumult, revels).]

maw (mô) *n.* **1.** The mouth, stomach, jaws, or gullet of a voracious animal, esp. a carnivore. **2.** The opening into something felt to be insatiable. [ME *mawe* < OE *maga*.]

mawk•ish (mô′kĭsh) *adj.* **1.** Excessively and objectionably sentimental. **2.** Sickening or insipid in taste. [< ME *mawke*, maggot, var. of *magot*. See MAGGOT.] —**mawk′ish•ly** *adv.* —**mawk′ish•ness** *n.*

max (măks) *Slang. n.* The maximum. —**max** *adj., adv., & v.*

max. *abbr.* Maximum.

max•i (măk′sē) *n., pl.* **max•is.** A long skirt, coat, or dress that usu. extends to or just past the ankles. [< MAXIMUM.]

max•il•la (măk-sĭl′ə) *n., pl.* **max•il•lae** (măk-sĭl′ē) or **max•il•las. 1.** *Anat.* Either of a pair of bones of the human skull fusing in the midline and forming the upper jaw. **2.** A homologous bone of the skull in other vertebrates. **3.** Either of two laterally moving appendages situated behind the mandibles in insects and most other arthropods. [Lat., jawbone.]

max•il•lar•y (măk′sə-lĕr′ē) *adj.* Of or relating to a jaw or jawbone, esp. the upper one. —*n., pl.* **-ies.** A maxillary bone.

max•il•li•ped (măk-sĭl′ə-pĕd′) *n.* One of the three pairs of crustacean head appendages located just posterior to the maxillae and used in feeding. [MAXILL(A) + -PED.]

max•il•lo•fa•cial (măk-sĭl′ō-fā′shəl) *adj. Anat.* Relating to or involving the maxilla and the face.

max•im (măk′sĭm) *n.* A succinct formulation of a fundamental principle, general truth, or rule of conduct. [ME *maxime* < OFr. < Med.Lat. *maxima* < *maxima (prōpositiō)*, greatest (premise), fem. of Lat. *maximus*, greatest. See **meg-***.]

Max•im (măk′sĭm), Sir **Hiram Stevens.** 1840–1916. Amer.-born British inventor of an automatic recoil-operated machine gun (1884). His brother **Hudson** (1853–1927) invented smokeless gun powder, and his son **Hiram Percy** (1896–1936) developed a silencer for firearms.

max•i•mal (măk′sə-məl) *adj.* **1.** Of, relating to, or consisting of a maximum. **2.** Being the greatest or highest possible. —*n. Math.* An element in an ordered set that is followed by no other. —**max′i•mal•ly** *adv.*

max•i•mal•ist (măk′sə-mə-lĭst) *n.* One who advocates direct or radical action to secure a social or political goal in its entirety. [Russ. *maksimalist*, name of a splinter group of the Russian Socialist Revolutionary Party, ult. < Lat. *maximum*, maximum. See MAXIMUM.] —**max′i•mal•ist** *adj.*

Max•i•mil•ian (măk′sə-mĭl′yən). 1832–67. Austrian archduke and emperor of Mexico (1864–67) who was appointed emperor by the French and executed by Mexican republicans.

Maximilian I. 1459–1519. King of Germany (1486–1519) and Holy Roman emperor (1493–1519) who added greatly to the territory and power of the Hapsburgs.

Maximilian II. 1527–76. Holy Roman emperor (1564–76) who was tolerant of Lutheranism.

max•i•mize (măk′sə-mīz′) *tr.v.* **-mized, -miz•ing, -miz•es. 1.** To increase or make as great as possible. **2.** To assign the highest possible importance to. **3.** *Math.* To find the largest value of (a function). —**max′i•mi•za′tion** (-mĭ-zā′shən) *n.* —**max′i•miz′er** *n.*

max•i•mum (măk′sə-məm) *n., pl.* **-mums** or **-ma** (-mə). **1.a.** The greatest possible quantity or degree. **b.** The greatest quantity or degree reached or recorded; the upper limit of variation. **c.** The time or period during which the highest point or degree is attained. **2.** An upper limit permitted by law or other authority. **3.** *Astron.* **a.** The moment when a variable star is most brilliant. **b.** The magnitude of the star at such a moment. **4.** *Math.* **a.** The greatest value assumed by a function over a given interval. **b.** The largest number in a set. —*adj.* **1.** Having or being the maximum reached or attainable. **2.** Of, relating to, or making up a maximum. [Lat. < neut. of *maximus*, greatest. See **meg-***.]

max•well (măks′wĕl′, -wəl) *n.* The unit of magnetic flux in the centimeter-gram-second system, equal to 10_{-8} weber. [After James Clerk MAXWELL.]

Max•well (măks′wĕl′, -wəl), **James Clerk.** 1831–79. British physicist who made fundamental contributions to electromagnetic theory and the kinetic theory of gases.

may¹ (mā) *aux.v.* P.t. **might** (mīt). **1.** To be allowed or permitted to: *May I go?* **2.** Used to indicate a certain measure of likelihood or possibility: *It may rain.* **3.** Used to express a desire or fervent wish: *Long may he live!* **4.** Used to express contingency, purpose, or result in clauses introduced by *that* or *so that*: *so that you may understand.* **5.** To be obliged; must. Used in deeds and other legal documents. See Usage Note at **can¹**. [ME, to be able < OE *mæg*, first and third pers. sing. of *magan*, to be strong, be able. See **magh-***.]

may² (mā) *n. Chiefly British.* The blossoms of the hawthorn. [Fr. *mai*, hawthorn < *Mai*, May (when it blooms). See MAY.]

May (mā) *n.* **1.** The fifth month of the year in the Gregorian calendar. **2.** The springtime of life; youth. **3.** The celebration of May Day. [ME < OFr. *Mai* < Lat. *Maius (mēnsis)*, (the month) of Maia < *Maia*, an Italic goddess. See **meg-***.]

May, Cape. A peninsula of S NJ between the Atlantic and Delaware Bay. The S tip forms **Cape May Point.**

ma•ya (mä′yə) *n. Hinduism.* **1.** The power of a god or demon to transform a concept into an element of the sensible world. **2.** The transitory manifold appearance of the sensible world, which obscures the undifferentiated spiritual reality from which it originates. [Skt. *māyā*.]

Ma•ya (mä′yə) *n., pl.* **Maya** or **-yas. 1.a.** A member of a Mesoamerican Indian people inhabiting southeast Mexico, Guatemala, and Belize, whose civilization reached its height around A.D. 300–900. **b.** A modern-day descendant of this people. **2.** Any of the Mayan languages, esp. Quiché and Yucatec. [Sp.] —**Ma′ya** *adj.*

mausoleum
The Taj Mahal, Agra, India

Maximilian

ă pat	oi boy
ā pay	ou out
âr care	o͝o took
ä father	o͞o boot
ĕ pet	ŭ cut
ē be	ûr urge
ĭ pit	th thin
ī pie	*th* this
îr pier	hw which
ŏ pot	zh vision
ō toe	ə about,
ô paw	item

Stress marks:
′ (primary);
′ (secondary), as in
dictionary (dĭk′shə-nĕr′ē)

Mayan
Temple pyramid of Quetzalcoatl, Chichén Itzá, Mexico

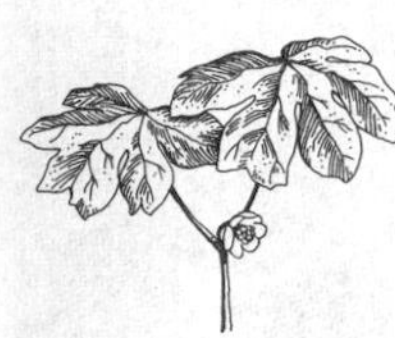
May apple
Podophyllum peltatum

Willie Mays

Paul McCartney
Photographed in 1989

Ma•ya•güez (mī′ə-gwĕz′, mä′yä-gwĕs′). A city of W Puerto Rico WSW of San Juan. Pop. 82,968.

Ma•ya•kov•ski (mä′yə-kôf′skē, mə-), **Vladimir Vladimirovich.** 1893–1930. Soviet poet who was a leader of futurism.

Ma•yan (mä′yən) *adj.* Of or relating to the Maya, their culture, their languages, or the language group to which Maya belongs. —*n.* **1.** A Maya. **2.** A linguistic stock of Central America that includes Quiché and Yucatec.

May apple *n.* **1.** A rhizomatous plant *(Podophyllum peltatum)* of eastern North America having a single nodding white flower and oval yellow fruit. **2.** The fruit of this plant.

may•be (mā′bē) *adv.* Perhaps; possibly. —*n. Informal.* **1.** An uncertainty. **2.** An uncertain reply.

May beetle *n.* See **June beetle.**

may•day (mā′dā′) *n.* An international radiotelephone signal word used by aircraft and ships in distress. [< Fr. *m'aidez,* help me!]

May Day *n.* **1.** May 1, observed in some countries in celebration of spring. **2.** May 1, observed as a holiday in some countries in honor of labor and labor organizations.

May•er (mā′ər), **Louis Burt.** 1885–1957. Russian-born Amer. motion-picture producer whose films include *Ben Hur* (1926).

may•est (mā′ĭst) or **mayst** (māst) *aux.v. Archaic.* Second pers. sing. pr.t. of **may[1].**

May•fair (mā′fâr′). A fashionable district in the West End of London, England.

May•field Heights (mā′fēld′). A city of NE OH, a suburb of Cleveland. Pop. 19,847.

may•flow•er (mā′flou′ər) *n.* **1.** Any of various plants that bloom in May. **2.** See **trailing arbutus.**

may•fly (mā′flī′) *n.* Any of various fragile winged insects of the order Ephemeroptera that develop from aquatic nymphs and live in the adult stage no longer than a few days.

may•hap (mā′hăp′, mā-hăp′) *adv.* Perhaps; perchance. [< the phrase *it may hap.*]

may•hem (mā′hĕm′, mā′əm) *n.* **1.** *Law.* The offense of willfully maiming or crippling a person. **2.** Infliction of violent injury on a person or thing; wanton destruction. **3.** A condition or state of violent disorder or riotous confusion; havoc. [ME *maim, mayhem* < AN *maihem* < OFr. *mahaigne,* injury < *mahaignier,* to maim < VLat. **mahanāre,* prob. of Gmc. orig.]

may•ing or **May•ing** (mā′ĭng) *n.* The celebration of May Day, esp. by the gathering of spring flowers.

may•n't (mā′ənt, mānt). May not.

may•o (mā′ō) *n. Informal.* Mayonnaise.

Ma•yo (mā′ō), **William James.** 1861–1939. Amer. surgeon who with his brother **Charles Horace Mayo** (1865–1939) founded the Mayo Clinic in Rochester MN.

Ma•yon (mä-yōn′), **Mount.** An active volcano, 2,461.4 m (8,070 ft), of SE Luzon, Philippines.

may•on•naise (mā′ə-nāz′, mā′ə-nāz′) *n.* A dressing made of beaten raw egg yolk, oil, lemon juice or vinegar, and seasonings. [Fr. *mahonnaise, mayonnaise,* poss. < Mahón, captured by the French in 1756 (mayonnaise being made in honor of the victory).]

may•or (mā′ər, mâr) *n.* The head of government of a city, town, borough, or municipal corporation. [ME *maire* < OFr. < Med.Lat. *māior* < Lat., greater, superior. See **meg-*.**] —**may′or•al** *adj.* —**may′or•ship′** *n.*

may•or•al•ty (mā′ər-əl-tē, mâr′əl-) *n., pl.* **-ties. 1.** The office of a mayor. **2.** The term of office of a mayor. [ME *mairalte* < AN < OFr. *maire,* mayor. See mayor.]

may•or•ess (mā′ər-ĭs, mâr′ĭs) *n.* **1.** A woman serving as the head of government of a city, town, borough, or municipal corporation. **2.** The wife of a mayor.

Ma•yotte (mä-yôt′). A French island territory of the E Comoros in the Mozambique Channel of the Indian Ocean.

May•pole also **may•pole** (mā′pōl′) *n.* A pole decorated with streamers that those celebrating May Day hold while dancing.

may•pop (mā′pŏp′) *n.* **1.** A vine *(Passiflora incarnata)* of the southeast United States having purple and white flowers, three-lobed leaves, and edible yellow fruit. **2.** The fruit of this plant. [Alteration of *maycock* < earlier *maracock,* perh. of Virginia Algonquian orig.]

Mays (māz), **Willie Howard, Jr.** b. 1931. Amer. baseball player (1951–72) who hit 660 home runs.

mayst (māst) *aux.v.* Var. of **mayest.**

may tree *n. Chiefly British.* The hawthorn.

may•weed (mā′wēd′) *n.* A weed *(Anthemis cotula)* with rank-smelling leaves and white-rayed flower heads. [ME *mayyen wed,* alteration of *maithe* < OE *mægtha.*]

May wine *n.* **1.** A still white wine with woodruff flavoring. **2.** A punch of champagne, claret, and Moselle or Rhine wine, flavored with woodruff. [Transl. of Ger. *Maiwein.*]

May•wood (mā′wo͝od′). **1.** A city of S CA, a suburb of Los Angeles. Pop. 27,850. **2.** A village of NE IL, a suburb of Chicago. Pop. 27,139.

Maz•a•rin (măz′ə-răɴ′), **Jules.** 1602–61. Italian-born French cardinal who served as chief minister to Louis XIV.

Ma•za•tlán (mä′sät-län′). A city of W Mexico on the Pacific NW of Guadalajara. Pop. 199,830.

Maz•da•ism also **Maz•de•ism** (măz′də-ĭz′əm) *n.* Zoroastrianism. [< Avestan *mazdā,* the good principle < *mazdā-,* wise. See Ahura Mazda.]

maze (māz) *n.* **1.a.** An intricate, usu. confusing network of interconnecting pathways; a labyrinth. **b.** A situation in which it is easy to get lost. **2.** A graphic puzzle, the solution of which is an uninterrupted path through an intricate pattern of line segments from a starting point to a goal. **3.** Something made up of many confused or conflicting elements; a tangle. —*tr.v.* **mazed, maz•ing, maz•es.** *Chiefly Southern U.S.* **1.** To bewilder or astonish. **2.** To stupefy; daze. See Regional Note at **possum.** [ME *mase,* confusion, maze < *masen,* to confuse, daze < OE *āmasian,* to confound.]

ma•zel tov also **ma•zal tov** (mä′zəl tôf′, tôv′, tōv′) *interj.* Used to express congratulations or best wishes. [LHeb. *mazzālṭôb* : *mazzāl,* luck + *ṭôb,* good.]

ma•zer (mā′zər) *n.* A large drinking bowl or goblet made of metal or hard wood. [ME < OFr. *masere,* kind of wood, maple burl, of Gmc. orig.]

ma•zu•ma (mə-zo͞o′mə) *n. Slang.* Money; cash. [Yiddish *mazume, mezumen,* cash < *binzumen,* in cash < Medieval Heb. *bimězummān,* in fixed currency < Mishnaic Heb. *mězummān,* fixed.]

ma•zur•ka also **ma•zour•ka** (mə-zûr′kə, -zo͝or′-) *n.* **1.** A lively Polish dance resembling the polka. **2.** A piece of music for such a dance, written in 3/4 or 3/8 time. [Russ., poss. < Pol. *(tańczyć) mazurka,* (to dance) the mazurka, accusative of *mazurek,* Mazovian dance < dim. of *Mazur,* person from Mazovia, historical region of E Poland.]

maz•y (mā′zē) *adj.* **-i•er, -i•est.** Mazelike, as in design; labyrinthine. —**maz′i•ly** *adv.* —**maz′i•ness** *n.*

maz•zard (măz′ərd) *n.* A wild sweet cherry *(Prunus avium)* often used as grafting stock. [Perh. alteration of ME *mazer,* goblet, hard wood. See mazer.]

Maz•zi•ni (mät-sē′nē), **Giuseppe.** 1805–72. Italian patriot who spurred the movement for an independent unified Italy.

mb *abbr.* Millibar.

MB *abbr.* **1.** Bachelor of medicine. **2.** Manitoba. **3.** Megabyte.

M.B.A. or **MBA** *abbr.* Master of Business Administration.

Mba•bane (əm-bä-bän′, -bä′nē). The cap. of Swaziland, in the NW part. Pop. 33,000.

mbi•ra (ĕm-bîr′ə, əm-) *n. Mus.* An African instrument consisting of a hollow gourd or wooden resonator and a number of usu. metal strips that vibrate when plucked. [Of Bantu orig.; akin to Shona *mbira.*]

Mbu•ji Ma•yi (əm-bo͞o′jē mä′yē). A city of S-central Zaire E of Kinshasa. Pop. 423,363.

Mbun•du (əm-bo͞on′do͞o) *n., pl.* **Mbundu** or **-dus. 1.** A member of a Bantu people inhabiting southern and central Angola. **2.** Their Bantu language. **3.** A member of a Bantu people inhabiting northern Angola. **4.** Their Bantu language.

mc *abbr.* Millicurie.

Mc *abbr.* Megacycle.

MC[1] (ĕm′sē′) *n.* A master of ceremonies.

MC[2] *abbr.* **1.** Marine Corps. **2.** Medical Corps. **3. M.C.** Member of Congress.

Mc•Al•es•ter (mĭ-kăl′ĭ-stər). A city of SE OK SE of Oklahoma City. Pop. 16,373.

Mc•Al•len (mĭ-kăl′ən). A city of S TX on the Rio Grande WNW of Brownsville. Pop. 84,021.

MCAT *abbr.* Medical College Admissions Test.

Mc•Car•thy (mə-kär′thē), **Joseph Raymond.** 1908–57. Amer. politician who as a U.S. senator from WI (1947–57) publicly accused many citizens of subversion.

McCarthy, Mary Therese. 1912–89. Amer. writer noted esp. for her novel *The Group* (1963).

Mc•Car•thy•ism (mə-kär′thē-ĭz′əm) *n.* **1.** The practice of publicizing accusations of political disloyalty or subversion with insufficient regard to evidence. **2.** The use of unfair investigatory or accusatory methods in order to suppress opposition. [After Joseph McCarthy.] —**Mc•Car′thy•ist** *n.*

Mc•Cart•ney (mə-kärt′nē), **(James) Paul.** b. 1942. British musician and composer who was a member of the Beatles.

Mc•Cau•ley (mə-kô′lē), **Mary Ludwig Hays.** "Molly Pitcher." 1754–1832. Amer. Revolutionary heroine of the Battle of Monmouth (Jun. 28, 1778).

Mc•Clel•lan (mə-klĕl′ən), **George Brinton.** 1826–85. Amer. commander of the Union Army (1861–62) whose overcautious tactics prompted Lincoln to relieve him of duty.

Mc•Clin•tock (mə-klĭn′tək, -tŏk′), **Barbara.** 1902–92. Amer. genetic botanist who won a 1983 Nobel Prize.

Mc•Cor•mack (mə-kôr′mək, -mĭk), **John.** 1884–1945. Irish-born Amer. operatic tenor.

Mc•Cor•mick (mə-kôr′mĭk), **Anne Elizabeth O'Hare.** 1882–1954. British-born Amer. journalist who was the first woman to receive a Pulitzer Prize for journalism (1937).

McCormick, Cyrus Hall. 1809–84. Amer. inventor and manufacturer who developed a mechanical harvester (1831).

Mc•Coy (mə-koi′) *n. Informal.* The authentic thing or quality; something that is not an imitation or substitute. [?]

Mc•Crae (mə-krā′), **John.** 1872–1918. Canadian poet noted for "In Flanders Fields" (1915).

Mc•Cul•lers (mə-kŭl′ərz), **Carson Smith.** 1917–67. Amer. writer noted for *The Heart is a Lonely Hunter* (1940).
mcf *abbr.* Thousand cubic feet.
Mc•Gov•ern (mə-gŭv′ərn), **George Stanley.** b. 1922. Amer. politician who ran unsuccessfully for President in 1972.
Mc•Guf•fey (mə-gŭf′ē), **William Holmes.** 1800–73. Amer. educator known for the *McGuffey Eclectic Readers* (1836–57).
mCi *abbr.* Millicurie.
Mc•In•tosh (măk′ĭn-tŏsh′) *n.* A variety of red eating apple. [After John *McIntosh* (fl. 1796), Canadian farmer.]
Mc•Kay (mə-kā′), **Claude.** 1890–1948. Jamaican-born Amer. writer whose novels include *Home to Harlem* (1928).
Mc•Kees•port (mĭ-kēz′pôrt′, -pōrt′). A city of SW PA ESE of Pittsburgh. Pop. 26,016.
Mc•Ken•na (mə-kĕn′ə), **Joseph.** 1843–1926. Amer. jurist; associate justice of the U.S. Supreme Court (1898–1925).
Mc•Kim (mə-kĭm′), **Charles Follen.** 1847–1909. Amer. architect whose designs include the Boston Public Library (1887).
Mc•Kin•ley (mə-kĭn′lē), **John.** 1780–1852. Amer. jurist; associate justice of the U.S. Supreme Court (1837–52).
McKinley, Mount. Also **De•na•li** (də-nä′lē). A peak, 6,197.6 m (20,320 ft), in the Alaska Range of S-central AK.
McKinley, William. 1843–1901. The 25th President of the U.S. (1897–1901), whose presidency was marked by the Spanish-American War (1898).
Mc•Kin•ney (mə-kĭn′ē). A city of NE TX NNE of Dallas. Pop. 21,283.
M.C.L. *abbr.* **1.** Master of Civil Law. **2.** Master of Comparative Law.
Mc•Lean (mə-klān′, -klēn′). A community of N VA, a suburb in the Washington DC area. Pop. 38,168.
Mc•Lean (mə-klēn′), **John.** 1785–1861. Amer. jurist; associate justice of the U.S. Supreme Court (1830–61).
Mc•Lu•han (mə-klo͞o′ən), **(Herbert) Marshall.** 1911–80. Canadian critic who wrote *The Medium is the Message* (1967).
Mc•Mil•lan (mĭk-mĭl′ən), **Edwin Mattison.** 1907–91. Amer. physicist and chemist who shared a 1951 Nobel Prize.
Mc•Mur•do Sound (mĭk-mûr′dō). An inlet of the Ross Sea in Antarctica off the coast of Victoria Land; site of a U.S. research and exploration base.
Mc•Pher•son (mĭk-fûr′sən), **Aimee Semple.** 1890–1944. Canadian-born Amer. evangelist who founded the International Church of the Foursquare Gospel (1927).
Mc•Rey•nolds (mĭk-rĕn′əldz), **James Clark.** 1862–1946. Amer. jurist; associate justice of the U.S. Supreme Court (1914–41).
Md The symbol for the element **mendelevium.**
MD *abbr.* **1.** Also **Md.** Maryland. **2.** Medical department. **3.** Also **M.D.** *Lat.* Medicinae Doctor (Doctor of Medicine). **4.** Muscular dystrophy.
M-day (ĕm′dā′) *n.* The day on which national mobilization for war is ordered; mobilization day.
Mde•wa•kan•ton (əm-dē-wô′kən-tŏn′, mĕd′ē-wô′-) *n., pl.* **Mdewakanton** or **-tons.** A member of a Sioux people of the Santee division.
M.Div. *abbr.* Master of Divinity.
Mdm. *abbr.* Madam.
M.D.S. *abbr.* Master of Dental Surgery.
mdse. *abbr.* Merchandise.
MDT *abbr.* Mountain Daylight Time.
me (mē) *pron.* The objective case of **I. 1.** Used as the direct object of a verb: *He assisted me.* **2.** Used as the indirect object of a verb: *They offered me a ride.* **3.** Used as the object of a preposition: *This letter is addressed to me.* **4.** *Informal.* Used as a predicate nominative: *It's me.* See Usage Notes at **be, but, I¹.** [ME < OE *mē.* See **me-¹*.**]
ME *abbr.* **1.** Also **Me.** Maine. **2.a.** Mechanical engineering. **b.** Mechanical engineer. **3.** Medical examiner. **4.** or **M.E.** Middle English.
me•a cul•pa (mā′ə kŭl′pə, mē′ə) *n.* An acknowledgment of a personal error or fault. [Lat. *meā culpā*, through my fault : *meā*, my + *culpā*, fault.]
mead¹ (mēd) *n.* An alcoholic beverage made from fermented honey and water. [ME < OE *meodu.* See **medhu-*.**]
mead² (mēd) *n. Archaic.* A meadow. [ME *mede* < OE *mǣd.* See **mē-⁴*.**]
Mead (mēd), **George Herbert.** 1863–1931. Amer. philosopher who was a leader in the development of social psychology.
Mead, Lake. A reservoir of SE NV and NW AZ formed by Hoover Dam on the Colorado R.
Mead, Margaret. 1901–78. Amer. anthropologist whose landmark studies include *Coming of Age in Samoa* (1928).
Meade (mēd), **George Gordon.** 1815–72. Amer. Union general who commanded the costly victory at Gettysburg (1863).
Meade, James Edward. b. 1907. British economist who shared a 1977 Nobel Prize.
mead•ow (mĕd′ō) *n.* A tract of grassland, in its natural state, as pasture, or for growing hay. [ME *medoue* < OE *mǣdwe*, var. of *mǣd.* See **mē-⁴*.**] **— mead′ow•y** *adj.*
meadow beauty *n.* Any of several North American plants of the genus *Rhexia,* growing in wet ground and having opposite leaves and showy purple flowers.
meadow fern *n.* See **sweet gale.**
meadow fescue *n.* A grass *(Festuca eliator)* grown for hay.
mead•ow•land (mĕd′ō-lănd′) *n.* A tract of land having the characteristics of or used for a meadow.
mead•ow•lark (mĕd′ō-lärk′) *n.* Any of various songbirds of the genus *Sturnella* of North America, esp. *S. magna,* the eastern meadowlark, and *S. neglecta,* the western meadowlark, having brownish plumage and a yellow breast.
meadow mouse *n.* See **field mouse.**
meadow mushroom *n.* A widely cultivated edible mushroom *(Agaricus campestris)* that thrives in moist soil.
meadow nematode *n.* Any of various nematodes of the genus *Pratylenchus* that are parasitic on the roots of plants.
meadow rue *n.* Any of various plants of the genus *Thalictrum,* having compound leaves and clusters of small white, yellowish, or purplish apetalous flowers.
meadow saffron *n.* See **autumn crocus.**
mead•ow•sweet (mĕd′ō-swēt′) *n.* **1.** Either of two North American shrubs *(Spiraea alba* or *S. latifolia)* having umbel-shaped clusters of white flowers. **2.** Any of various perennial herbs of the genus *Filipendula* in the rose family.
mea•ger also **mea•gre** (mē′gər) *adj.* **1.** Deficient in quantity, fullness, or extent; scanty. **2.** Deficient in richness, fertility, or vigor; feeble: *the meager soil of an eroded plain.* **3.** Having little flesh; lean. [ME *megre,* thin < OFr. < Lat. *macer.* See **māk-*.**] **— mea′ger•ly** *adv.* **— mea′ger•ness** *n.*
meal¹ (mēl) *n.* **1.** The edible whole or coarsely ground grains of a cereal grass. **2.** A granular substance produced by grinding. [ME *mele* < OE *melu.* See **melə-*.**]
meal² (mēl) *n.* **1.** The food served and eaten in one sitting. **2.** A customary time or occasion of eating food. [ME *mele* < OE *mǣl.* See **mē-²*.**]
meal•ie (mē′lē) *n. South African.* **1.** An ear of corn. **2. mealies.** Corn; maize. [Afr. *mielie* < Port. *milho,* millet < Lat. *milium.* See **melə-*.**]
meal ticket *n.* **1.** A card or ticket entitling the holder to a meal or meals. **2.** *Informal.* A person or thing depended on financially.
meal•time (mēl′tīm′) *n.* The usual time for eating a meal.
meal•worm (mēl′wûrm′) *n.* The larvae of various beetles of the genus *Tenebrio* that infest grain products such as flour.
meal•y (mē′lē) *adj.* **-i•er, -i•est. 1.** Resembling meal in texture or consistency; granular. **2.a.** Made of or containing meal. **b.** Sprinkled or covered with meal or a similar substance. **3.** Flecked with spots; mottled. **4.** Lacking healthy coloring; pale. **5.** Mealy-mouthed. **— meal′i•ness** *n.*
meal•y•bug (mē′lē-bŭg′) *n.* Any of various homopterous insects, esp. of the family Pseudococcidae, some of which are destructive to plants. [< its powdery covering.]
meal•y-mouthed (mē′lē-mouthd′, -moutht′) *adj.* Unwilling to state facts or opinions simply and directly.
mean¹ (mēn) *v.* **meant** (mĕnt), **mean•ing, means.** *— tr.* **1.a.** To be used to convey; denote. **b.** To act as a symbol of; signify or represent. **2.** To intend to convey or indicate. **3.** To have as a purpose or an intention; intend. **4.** To design, intend, or destine for a certain purpose or end. **5.** To have as a consequence; bring about. **6.** To have the importance or value of: *Their opinions meant nothing.* *— intr.* To have intentions of a specified kind; be disposed: *She means well.* ***— idiom.*** **mean business.** *Informal.* To be in earnest. [ME *menen* < OE *mǣnan,* to tell of. See **mei-no-*.**]
mean² (mēn) *adj.* **mean•er, mean•est. 1.a.** Selfish in a petty way; unkind. **b.** Cruel, spiteful, or malicious. **2.** Ignoble; base: *a mean motive.* **3.** Miserly; stingy. **4.a.** Low in quality or grade; inferior. **b.** Low in value or amount; paltry. **5.** Common or poor in appearance; shabby. **6.** Low in social status; of humble origins. **7.** Humiliated or ashamed. **8.** In poor physical condition; sick or debilitated. **9.** Extremely unpleasant or disagreeable: *a mean storm.* **10.** *Informal.* Ill-tempered. **11.** *Slang.* **a.** Hard to cope with; difficult or troublesome. **b.** Excellent; skillful: *a mean game of bridge.* [ME < OE *gemǣne,* common. See **mei-¹*.**]
mean³ (mēn) *n.* **1.** Something having a position, quality, or condition midway between extremes; a medium. **2.** *Math.* **a.** A number that typifies a set of numbers, such as a geometric mean or an arithmetic mean. **b.** The average value of a set of numbers. **3.** *Logic.* The middle term in a syllogism. **4. means.** *(used with a sing. or pl. v.)* A method, a course of action, or an instrument by which an act can be accomplished or an end achieved. **5. means.** *(used with a pl. v.)* **a.** Money, property, or other wealth. **b.** Great wealth: *a woman of means.* *— adj.* **1.** Occupying a middle or intermediate position between two extremes. **2.** Intermediate in size, extent, quality, time, or degree; medium. ***— idioms.*** **by all means.** Without fail; certainly. **by any means.** In any way possible; in any case. **by means of.** With the use of; owing to. **by no means.** In no sense; certainly not. [ME *mene,* middle < OFr. *meien* < Lat. *mediānus* < *medius.* See **medhyo-*.**]
Usage Note: In the sense of "financial resources" *means* takes a plural verb: *His means are more than adequate.* In the sense of "a way to an end" *means* is singular when referring to a particular strategy or method: *The best means of trav-*

William McKinley

Margaret Mead

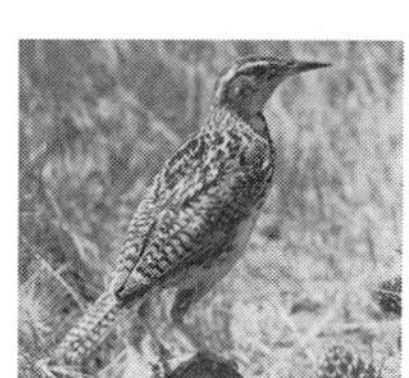
meadowlark
Western meadowlark
Sturnella neglecta

ă pat · ā pay · âr care · ä father · ĕ pet · ē be · ĭ pit · ī pie · îr pier · ŏ pot · ō toe · ô paw · oi boy · ou out · o͝o took · o͞o boot · ŭ cut · ûr urge · th thin · *th* this · hw which · zh vision · ə about, item

Stress marks:
′ (primary);
′ (secondary), as in
dictionary (dĭk′shə-nĕr′ē)

CONVERSION BETWEEN METRIC AND U.S. CUSTOMARY UNITS

FROM U.S. CUSTOMARY TO METRIC

WHEN YOU KNOW	MULTIPLY BY	TO FIND
inches	25.4	millimeters
	2.54	centimeters
feet	30.48	centimeters
yards	0.91	meters
miles	1.61	kilometers
teaspoons	4.93	milliliters
tablespoons	14.79	milliliters
fluid ounces	29.57	milliliters
cups	0.24	liters
pints	0.47	liters
quarts	0.95	liters
gallons	3.79	liters
cubic feet	0.028	cubic meters
cubic yards	0.76	cubic meters
ounces	28.35	grams
pounds	0.45	kilograms
short tons (2,000 lbs)	0.91	metric tons
square inches	6.45	square centimeters
square feet	0.09	square meters
square yards	0.84	square meters
square miles	2.60	square kilometers
acres	0.40	hectares

FROM METRIC TO U.S. CUSTOMARY

WHEN YOU KNOW	MULTIPLY BY	TO FIND
millimeters	0.04	inches
centimeters	0.39	inches
meters	3.28	feet
	1.09	yards
kilometers	0.62	miles
milliliters	0.20	teaspoons
	0.06	tablespoons
	0.03	fluid ounces
liters	1.06	quarts
	0.26	gallons
	4.23	cups
	2.12	pints
cubic meters	35.32	cubic feet
	1.35	cubic yards
grams	0.035	ounces
kilograms	2.21	pounds
metric ton (1,000 kg)	1.10	short ton
square centimeters	0.16	square inches
square meters	1.20	square yards
square kilometers	0.39	square miles
hectares	2.47	acres

TEMPERATURE CONVERSION BETWEEN CELSIUS AND FAHRENHEIT

°C = (°F − 32) 1.8

CONDITION	FAHRENHEIT	CELSIUS
Boiling point of water	212°	100°
A very hot day	104°	40°
Normal body temperature	98.6°	37°
A warm day	86°	30°
A mild day	68°	20°

°F = (°C × 1.8) + 32

CONDITION	FAHRENHEIT	CELSIUS
A cool day	50°	10°
Freezing point of water	32°	0°
Lowest temperature Gabriel Fahrenheit could obtain by mixing salt and ice	0°	−17.8°

U.S. CUSTOMARY SYSTEM

UNIT	RELATION TO OTHER U.S. CUSTOMARY UNITS	METRIC EQUIVALENT
LENGTH		
inch	1/12 foot	2.54 centimeters
foot	12 inches or 1/3 yard	0.3048 meter
yard	36 inches or 3 feet	0.9144 meter
rod	16½ feet or 5½ yards	5.0292 meters
furlong	220 yards or 1/8 mile	0.2012 kilometer
mile (statute)	5,280 feet or 1,760 yards	1.6093 kilometers
mile (nautical)	6,076 feet or 2,025 yards	1.852 kilometers
VOLUME OR CAPACITY (LIQUID MEASURE)		
ounce	1/16 pint	29.574 milliliters
gill	4 ounces	0.1183 liter
pint	16 ounces	0.4732 liter
quart	2 pints or ¼ gallon	0.9463 liter
gallon	128 ounces or 8 pints	3.7853 liters
barrel		
(wine)	31½ gallons	119.24 liters
(beer)	36 gallons	136.27 liters
(oil)	42 gallons	158.98 liters
VOLUME OR CAPACITY (DRY MEASURE)		
pint	½ quart	0.5506 liter
quart	2 pints	1.1012 liters
peck	8 quarts or ¼ bushel	8.8098 liters
bucket	2 pecks	17.620 liters
bushel	2 buckets or 4 pecks	35.239 liters
WEIGHT		
grain	1/7000 pound	64.799 milligrams
dram	1/16 ounce	1.7718 grams
ounce	16 drams	28.350 grams
pound	16 ounces	453.6 grams
ton (short)	2,000 pounds	907.18 kilograms
ton (long)	2,240 pounds	1,016.0 kilograms
GEOGRAPHIC AREA		
acre	4,840 square yards	4,047 square meters

COOKING MEASURES

UNIT	RELATION TO OTHER COOKING MEASURES	CONVERSION TO METRIC UNITS
drop	1/76 teaspoon	0.0649 milliliter
teaspoon	76 drops or 1/3 tablespoon	4.9288 milliliters
tablespoon	3 teaspoons	14.786 milliliters
cup	16 tablespoons or ½ pint	0.2366 liter
pint	2 cups	0.4732 liters
quart	4 cups or 2 pints	0.9463 liter

BRITISH IMPERIAL SYSTEM

UNIT	RELATION TO OTHER BRITISH IMPERIAL UNITS	CONVERSION TO U.S. CUSTOMARY UNITS	CONVERSION TO METRIC UNITS
VOLUME OR CAPACITY (LIQUID MEASURE)			
pint	½ quart	1.201 pints	0.5683 liter
quart	2 pints ¼ gallon	1.201 quarts	1.137 liters
gallon	8 pints 4 quarts	1.201 gallons	4.546 liters
VOLUME OR CAPACITY (DRY MEASURE)			
peck	¼ bushel	1.0314 pecks	9.087 liters
bushel	4 pecks	1.0320 bushels	36.369 liters

APOTHECARY WEIGHTS

UNIT	RELATION TO OTHER APOTHECARY UNITS	CONVERSION TO U.S. CUSTOMARY UNITS	CONVERSION TO METRIC UNITS
grain	1/60 dram 1/5760 pound	equal to the U.S. Customary grain	64.799 milligrams
dram	60 grains 1/8 ounce	2.1943 drams	3.8879 grams
ounce	8 drams	1.0971 ounces	31.1035 grams
pound	12 ounces 96 drams	0.8232 pound	373.242 grams

UNITS OF THE INTERNATIONAL SYSTEM

The **International System** (abbreviated **SI,** for Systeme International, the French name for the system) was adopted in 1960 by the 11th General Conference on Weights and Measures. An expanded and modified version of the metric system, the International System addresses the needs of modern science for additional and more accurate units of measurement. The key features of the International System are decimalization, a system of prefixes, and a standard defined in terms of an invariable physical measure.

BASE UNITS

The International System has base units from which all others in the system are derived. The standards for the base units, except for the kilogram, are defined by unchanging and reproducible physical occurrences. For example, the meter is defined as the distance traveled by light in a vacuum in 1/299,792,458 of a second. The standard for the kilogram is a platinum-iridium cylinder kept at the International Bureau of Weights and Standards in Sèvres, France.

UNIT	QUANTITY	SYMBOL
meter	length	m
kilogram	mass	kg
second	time	s
ampere	electric current	A
kelvin	temperature	K
mole	amount of matter	mol
candela	luminous intensity	cd

SUPPLEMENTARY UNITS

The International System uses two supplementary units that are based on abstract geometrical concepts rather than physical standards.

UNIT	QUANTITY	SYMBOL
radian	plane angles	rad
steradian	solid angles	sr

PREFIXES

A multiple of a unit in the International System is formed by adding a prefix to the name of that unit. The prefixes change the magnitude of the unit by orders of ten from 10^{18} to 10^{-18}.

PREFIX	SYMBOL	MULTIPLYING FACTOR
exa-	E	10^{18} = 1,000,000,000,000,000,000
peta-	P	10^{15} = 1,000,000,000,000,000
tera-	T	10^{12} = 1,000,000,000,000
giga-	G	10^{9} = 1,000,000,000
mega-	M	10^{6} = 1,000,000
kilo-	K	10^{3} = 1,000
hecto-	h	10^{2} = 100
deca-	da	10 = 10
deci-	d	10^{-1} = 0.1
centi-	c	10^{-2} = 0.01
milli-	m	10^{-3} = 0.001
micro-	μ	10^{-6} = 0.000,001
nano-	n	10^{-9} = 0.000,000,001
pico-	p	10^{-12} = 0.000,000,000,001
femto-	f	10^{-15} = 0.000,000,000,000,001
atto-	a	10^{-18} = 0.000,000,000,000,000,001

ADDITIONAL UNITS

Listed below are a few of the non-SI units that are commonly used with the International System.

UNIT	QUANTITY	SYMBOL
angstrom (= 10^{-10}m)	length	Å
electron-volt (= 0.160 aJ)	energy	eV
hectare (= 10,000 m^2)	land area	ha
liter (= 1.0 dm^3)	volume or capacity	l
standard atmosphere (= 101.3 kPa)	pressure	atm

DERIVED UNITS

Most of the units in the International System are derived units, that is units defined in terms of base units and supplementary units. Derived units can be divided into two groups—those that have a special name and symbol, and those that do not.

WITHOUT NAMES AND SYMBOLS

MEASURE OF	DERIVATION
acceleration	m/s^2
angular acceleration	rad/s^2
angular velocity	rad/s
density	kg/m^3
electric field strength	V/m
luminance	cd/m^2
magnetic field strength	A/m
velocity	m/s

WITH NAMES AND SYMBOLS

UNIT	MEASURE OF	SYMBOL	DERIVATION
coulomb	electric charge	C	A · s
farad	electric capacitance	F	A · s/V
henry	inductance	H	V · s/A
hertz	frequency	Hz	cycles/s
joule	quantity of energy	J	N · m
lumen	flux of light	lm	cd · sr
lux	illumination	lx	lm/m^2
newton	force	N	kg · m/s^2
ohm	electric resistance	Ω	V/A
pascal	pressure	Pa	N/m^2
tesla	magnetic flux density	T	Wb/m^2
volt	voltage	V	W/A
watt	power	W	J/s
weber	magnetic flux	Wb	V · s

boulevard strip, mall, medial strip, meridian, neutral ground. See Regional Note at **neutral ground.**

me•di•ant (mē′dē-ənt) *n. Mus.* The third tone in a diatonic musical scale, determining the major or minor quality of the tonic chord. [Ital. *mediante* < LLat. *mediāns, mediant-*, pr.part. of *mediāre*, to be in the middle < Lat. *medius*, middle. See MEDIUM.]

me•di•as•ti•num (mē′dē-ə-stī′nəm) *n., pl.* **-na** (-nə). *Anat.* The region in mammals between the pleural sacs, containing the heart and all of the thoracic viscera except the lungs. [NLat. < neut. of Med.Lat. *mediastīnus*, medial, alteration of *medius*, middle. See **medhyo-***.] — **me′di•as•ti′nal** *adj.*

me•di•ate (mē′dē-āt′) *v.* **-at•ed, -at•ing, -ates.** —*tr.* **1.** To settle (differences) by working with conflicting parties. **2.** To bring about (a settlement, for example) by working with conflicting parties. **3.** To effect or convey as an intermediate agent. —*intr.* **1.** To intervene between disputants to bring about an agreement or a compromise. **2.** To mediate differences. **3.** To have a relation to two differing persons or things. —*adj.* (-ĭt). **1.** Acting through, involving, or dependent on an intervening agency. **2.** Being in a middle position. [LLat. *mediāre, mediāt-*, to be in the middle < Lat. *medius*, middle. See **medhyo-***.] — **me′di•ate•ly** (-ĭt-lē) *adv.*

me•di•a•tion (mē′dē-ā′shən) *n.* **1.** The act of mediating; intervention. **2.** The state of being mediated. **3.** *Law.* An attempt to bring about a peaceful settlement between disputants through the intervention of a neutral party. — **me′di•a′tive, me′di•a•to′ry** (mē′dē-ə-tôr′ē, -tōr′ē) *adj.*

me•di•a•tize (mē′dē-ə-tīz′) *tr.v.* **-tized, -tiz•ing, -tiz•es.** To annex (a lesser state) to a greater state as a means of permitting the ruler of the lesser state to retain title and partial authority. [Prob. Fr. *médiatiser* < *médiat*, dependent < OFr., back-formation < *immediat*, independent < LLat. *immediātus*. See IMMEDIATE.] — **me′di•a•ti•za′tion** (-tĭ-zā′shən) *n.*

me•di•a•tor (mē′dē-ā′tər) *n.* **1.** One that mediates, esp. differences between disputants. **2.** *Physiol.* A substance or structure that mediates a specific response in a body tissue.

med•ic¹ or **med•ick** (mĕd′ĭk) *n.* Any of several Old World herbs of the genus *Medicago* in the pea family, having clusters of small, usu. yellow flowers and compound leaves with three leaflets. [ME *medike* < Lat. *Mēdica* < Gk. *Mēdikē* < fem. of *Mēdikos*, of Media < *Mēdos*, a Mede. See MEDE.]

med•ic² (mĕd′ĭk) *n.* **1.** A member of a military medical corps. **2.** A physician or surgeon. **3.** A medical student or intern. [Lat. *medicus*, physician. See MEDICAL.]

med•i•ca•ble (mĕd′ĭ-kə-bəl) *adj.* Potentially responsive to treatment with medicine; curable.

Med•i•caid also **med•i•caid** (mĕd′ĭ-kād′) *n.* A U.S. health care program reimbursing hospitals and physicians for care of those needing financial assistance. [MEDIC(AL) + AID.]

ă pat	oi boy
ā pay	ou out
âr care	o͝o took
ä father	o͞o boot
ĕ pet	ŭ cut
ē be	ûr urge
ĭ pit	th thin
ī pie	*th* this
îr pier	hw which
ŏ pot	zh vision
ō toe	ə about, item
ô paw	

Stress marks:
′ (primary);
′ (secondary), as in dictionary (dĭk′shə-nĕr′ē)

Meis•sen[2] (mī′sən) *n.* A delicate porcelain ware originally made in Meissen, Germany.

Meis•so•nier (mā′sən-yā′, -sôn-), **Jean Louis Ernest.** 1815–91. French painter noted for his genre and military scenes.

Meis•ter•sing•er (mīs′tər-sĭng′ər) *n., pl.* **Meistersinger** or **-ers.** A member of one of the guilds in German cities in the 14th, 15th, and 16th centuries that composed and performed music and poetry. [Ger. < MHGer. : *meister*, master (< OHGer. *meistar* < Lat. *magister*; see MASTER) + *singer*, singer (< *singen*, to sing < OHGer. *singan*; see **seng**[wh]**-***).]

Meit•ner (mīt′nər), **Lise.** 1878–1968. Austrian-born Swedish physicist and pioneer in the study of nuclear fission.

Mek•nes (mĕk-nĕs′). A city of N Morocco WSW of Fez; cap. of Moroccan sultans after c. 1672. Pop. 319,783.

Me•kong (mā′kông′, -kŏng′). A river of SE Asia flowing c. 4,183 km (2,600 mi) from SE China to the South China Sea through the vast **Mekong Delta** in S Vietnam.

mel•a•mine (mĕl′ə-mēn′) *n.* **1.** A white crystalline compound, $C_3H_6N_6$, used in making melamine resins and for tanning leather. **2.** A plastic made from such resin. [*Melam*, distillate of ammonium thiocyanate + AMINE.]

melamine resin *n.* A thermosetting resin used for molded products, adhesives, and surface coatings.

melan– *pref.* Var. of **melano–.**

mel•an•cho•li•a (mĕl′ən-kō′lē-ə) *n. Psychiat.* A mental disorder characterized by severe depression, apathy, and withdrawal. [LLat., melancholy. See MELANCHOLY.] —**mel′an•cho′li•ac** (-lē-ăk′) *adj. & n.*

mel•an•chol•ic (mĕl′ən-kŏl′ĭk) *adj.* **1.** Affected with or subject to melancholy. **2.** Of or relating to melancholia. —**mel′an•chol′ic** *n.* —**mel′an•chol′i•cal•ly** *adv.*

mel•an•chol•y (mĕl′ən-kŏl′ē) *n.* **1.** Sadness or depression of the spirits; gloom. **2.** Pensive reflection or contemplation. **3.** *Archaic.* **a.** Black bile. **b.** An emotional state characterized by sullenness and outbreaks of violent anger, believed to arise from black bile. —*adj.* **1.** Afflicted with or marked by depression of the spirits; sad. See Syns at **sad. 2.** Tending to promote sadness or gloom. **3.** Pensive; thoughtful. [ME *melancolie* < OFr. < LLat. *melancholia* < Gk. *melankholia* : *melas, melan-*, black + *kholē*, bile; see **ghel-**[2]*.] —**mel′an•chol′i•ly** *adv.* —**mel′an•chol′i•ness** *n.*

Me•lanch•thon (mə-lăngk′thən, mā-länкн′tôn), **Philipp.** 1497–1560. German theologian and Reformation leader.

Mel•a•ne•sia (mĕl′ə-nē′zhə, -shə). A division of Oceania in the SW Pacific NE of Australia and S of the equator.

Mel•a•ne•sian (mĕl′ə-nē′zhən, -shən) *adj.* Of or relating to Melanesia or its peoples, languages, or cultures. —*n.* **1.** A member of any of the indigenous peoples of Melanesia. **2.** A subfamily of the Austronesian languages that includes the languages of Melanesia.

Herman Melville

mé•lange also **me•lange** (mā-länzh′) *n.* A mixture. [Fr. < OFr. *meslance* < *mesler*, to mix. See MEDDLE.]

me•lan•ic (mə-lăn′ĭk) *adj.* **1.** Of, relating to, or exhibiting melanism. **2.** Of, relating to, or affected with melanosis.

mel•a•nin (mĕl′ə-nĭn) *n.* Any of a group of naturally occurring dark pigments, esp. one in skin, hair, fur, and feathers.

mel•a•nism (mĕl′ə-nĭz′əm) *n.* **1.** See **melanosis. 2.** Dark coloration of the skin, hair, fur, or feathers because of a high concentration of melanin. —**mel′a•nis′tic** *adj.*

melano– or **melan–** *pref.* Black; dark: *melanin.* [Gk. < *melas, melan-*, black.]

mel•a•no•blast (mĕl′ə-nō-blăst′, mə-lăn′ə-) *n.* A precursor cell of a melanocyte or melanophore.

mel•a•no•cyte (mĕl′ə-nō-sīt′) *n.* An epidermal cell capable of synthesizing melanin.

mel•a•no•cyte-stim•u•lat•ing hormone (mĕl′ə-nō-sīt′-stĭm′yə-lā′tĭng, mə-lăn′ə-) *n.* A hormone secreted by the pituitary gland that regulates skin color in human beings and other vertebrates by stimulating melanin dispersal.

mel•a•noid (mĕl′ə-noid′) *adj.* **1.** Of or related to melanin; black-pigmented. **2.** Of or affected with melanosis.

mel•a•no•ma (mĕl′ə-nō′mə) *n., pl.* **-mas** or **-ma•ta** (-mə-tə). *Pathol.* A dark-pigmented, usu. malignant tumor arising from a melanocyte and occurring most commonly in the skin.

mel•a•no•phore (mĕl′ə-nə-fôr′, -fōr′, mə-lăn′ə-) *n.* A pigment cell that contains melanin, esp. as found in the skin of amphibians and reptiles.

mel•a•no•sis (mĕl′ə-nō′sĭs) *n., pl.* **-ses** (-sēz). Abnormally dark pigmentation of the skin or other tissues, due to a disorder of pigment metabolism. —**mel′a•not′ic** (-nŏt′ĭk) *adj.*

mel•a•nous (mĕl′ə-nəs) *adj.* Having a swarthy or black complexion and black hair. —**mel′a•nos′i•ty** (-nŏs′ĭ-tē) *n.*

mel•a•phyre (mĕl′ə-fīr′) *n.* A dark igneous porphyry embedded with feldspar crystals. [Fr. *mélaphyre* : Gk. *melas*, black + Fr. *porphyre*, porphyry (< Med.Lat. *porphyrium*; see PORPHYRY).]

mel•a•to•nin (mĕl′ə-tō′nĭn) *n.* A hormone produced by the pineal gland that stimulates color change in the epidermis of amphibians and reptiles. [Gk. *melas*, black + TONE + –IN.]

Mel•ba (mĕl′bə), Dame **Nellie.** 1861–1931. Australian soprano associated primarily with London's Covent Garden (1889–1926).

Melba toast *n.* Very thinly sliced crisp toast. [After Dame Nellie MELBA.]

Mel•bourne (mĕl′bərn). **1.** A city of SE Australia SW of Canberra; settled in 1835. Met. area pop. 2,722,817. **2.** A city of E-central FL on Indian R. S of Cocoa Beach. Pop. 59,646.

Melbourne, 2nd Viscount. William Lamb. 1779–1848. British politician who served as prime minister (1834 and 1835–41).

Mel•chi•or (mĕl′kē-ôr′). In the Bible, one of the three wise men from the East who came bearing gifts for the infant Jesus.

Melchior, Lauritz Lebrecht Hommel. 1890–1973. Danish-born Amer. operatic tenor noted for his Wagnerian roles.

Mel•chite (mĕl′kīt) *n.* Var. of **Melkite.**

Mel•chiz•e•dek[1] (mĕl-kĭz′ĭ-dĕk′). In the Bible, the high priest and king of Salem who blessed Abraham.

Mel•chiz•e•dek[2] (mĕl-kĭz′ĭ-dĕk′) *n. Mormon Ch.* The higher order of priesthood. [After MELCHIZEDEK[1].]

meld[1] (mĕld) *Games.* —*v.* **meld•ed, meld•ing, melds.** —*tr.* To declare or display (a card or combination of cards in a hand) for inclusion in one's score in various card games, such as pinochle. —*intr.* To present a meld. —*n.* A combination of cards of value in scoring. [Prob. Ger. *melden*, to announce < MHGer. < OHGer. *meldōn*.]

meld[2] (mĕld) *v.* **meld•ed, meld•ing, melds.** —*tr.* To cause to merge. —*intr.* To become merged. —*n.* A blend or merger. [Perh. blend of MELT and WELD[2].]

me•lee (mā′lā′, mā-lā′) also **mê•lée** (mĕ-lā′) *n.* **1.a.** Confused hand-to-hand fighting in a pitched battle. **b.** A violent free-for-all. **2.** A confused tumultuous mingling, as of a crowd: *the rush-hour melee.* [Fr. *mêlée* < OFr. *meslee*, p.part. of *mesler*, to mix. See MEDDLE.]

me•le•na (mə-lē′nə) *n.* A condition marked by black tarry stool or vomit composed largely of blood that has been acted on by gastric juices, due to hemorrhage along the digestive tract. [NLat. *melēna* < Gk. *melaina*, fem. of *melas*, black.]

mel•ic (mĕl′ĭk) *adj.* Of or relating to verse intended to be sung, esp. Greek lyric verse of the seventh to the fifth century B.C. [Gk. *melikos* < *melos*, song.]

Me•lil•la (mā-lēl′yä). A Spanish city on the Mediterranean coast of NE Morocco; site of the army revolt that triggered the Spanish Civil War in 1936. Pop. 56,247.

mel•i•lot (mĕl′ə-lŏt′) *n.* Any of several Old World plants of the genus *Melilotus* in the pea family, having compound leaves with three leaflets and narrow racemes of small white or yellow flowers. [ME *melilote* < OFr. < Lat. *melilōtos* < Gk. : *meli*, honey; see **melit-*** + *lōtos*, lotus.]

mel•io•rate (mēl′yə-rāt′, mē′lē-ə-) *v.* **-rat•ed, -rat•ing, -rates.** —*tr.* To make better; improve. —*intr.* To grow better. [Lat. *meliōrāre, meliōrāt-* < *melior*, better. See **mel-**[2]*.] —**mel′io•ra•ble** (-rə-bəl) *adj.* —**mel′io•ra′tive** *adj. & n.* —**mel′io•ra′tor** *n.*

mel•io•ra•tion (mēl′yə-rā′shən, mē′lē-ə-) *n.* **1.a.** The act or process of improving something or the state of being improved. **b.** An improvement. **2.** The linguistic process by which a word becomes loftier in meaning or more positive in connotation.

mel•io•rism (mēl′yə-rĭz′əm, mē′lē-ə-) *n.* The belief that society has an innate tendency toward improvement that may be furthered through conscious effort. [Lat. *melior*, better; see **mel-**[2]* + –ISM.] —**mel′io•rist** *n.* —**mel′io•ris′tic** *adj.*

me•lis•ma (mə-lĭz′mə) *n., pl.* **-ma•ta** (-mə-tə) or **-mas.** *Mus.* A decorative passage of several notes sung to one syllable of text, as in Gregorian chant. [Gk., melody < *melizein*, to sing < *melos*, song.] —**mel′is•mat′ic** (mĕl′ĭz-măt′ĭk) *adj.*

Mel•kite or **Mel•chite** (mĕl′kīt) *n.* **1.** A member of the Christian churches in Egypt and Syria that accepted the Council of Chalcedon. **2.** A member of an eastern Christian church of the patriarchates of Alexandria, Antioch, or Jerusalem, esp. a Uniat Christian. [NLat. *Melchītae*, Melkites < Med.Gk. *Melkhitai* < Syriac *malkāyê*, royalists, pl. of *malkā*, king.]

mel•lif•er•ous (mə-lĭf′ər-əs) also **mel•lif•ic** (-lĭf′ĭk) *adj.* Forming or bearing honey. [< Lat. *mellifer* : *mel, mell-*, honey; see **melit-*** + *-fer*, -fer.]

mel•lif•lu•ent (mə-lĭf′lo͞o-ənt) *adj.* Mellifluous.

mel•lif•lu•ous (mə-lĭf′lo͞o-əs) *adj.* **1.** Flowing with sweetness or honey. **2.** Smooth and sweet: *a mellifluous voice.* [ME < LLat. *mellifluus* : Lat. *mel, mell-*, honey; see **melit-*** + Lat. *-fluus*, flowing; see **bhleu-***.] —**mel•lif′lu•ous•ly** *adv.* —**mel•lif′lu•ous•ness** *n.*

Mel•lon (mĕl′ən), **Andrew William.** 1855–1937. Amer. financier and patron of the arts.

mel•lo•phone (mĕl′ō-fōn′) *n. Mus.* A brass wind instrument, similar to the French horn. [MELLO(W) + –PHONE.]

mel•low (mĕl′ō) *adj.* **-er, -est. 1.a.** Soft, sweet, juicy, and full-flavored because of ripeness. **b.** Suggesting softness or sweetness. **2.** Rich and soft in quality. **3.** Having the gentleness, wisdom, or tolerance often characteristic of maturity. **4.** Relaxed and unhurried; easygoing. **5.** *Slang.* **a.** Slightly and pleasantly intoxicated. **b.** Pleasantly high from a drug, esp. from smoking marijuana. **6.** Moist, rich, soft, and loamy. Used of soil. —*tr. & intr.v.* **-lowed, -low•ing, -lows.** To make or become mellow. —***phrasal verb.* mellow out.** *Slang.* To become genial and pleasant; relax. [ME *melwe*, perh. <

melowe, var. of *mele*, ground grain, meal. See MEAL[1].] — **mel′low•ly** *adv.* — **mel′low•ness** *n.*

me•lo•de•on (mə-lō′dē-ən) *n. Mus.* A small reed organ. [Prob. alteration of *melodium* < MELODY.]

me•lod•ic (mə-lŏd′ĭk) *adj.* Of, relating to, or containing melody. — **me•lod′i•cal•ly** *adv.*

me•lo•di•ous (mə-lō′dē-əs) *adj.* **1.** Of, relating to, or containing a pleasing tune or melody. **2.** Agreeable to hear. — **me•lo′di•ous•ly** *adv.* — **me•lo′di•ous•ness** *n.*

mel•o•dize (mĕl′ə-dīz′) *v.* **-dized, -diz•ing, -diz•es.** — *tr.* **1.** To write a melody for (a lyric). **2.** To make melodious. — *intr.* To write a melody. — **mel′o•diz′er, mel′o•dist** *n.*

mel•o•dra•ma (mĕl′ə-drä′mə, -drăm′ə) *n.* **1.a.** A drama marked by exaggerated emotions, stereotypical characters, and interpersonal conflicts. **b.** The dramatic genre marked by this treatment. **2.** Behavior or occurrences having such characteristics. [Alteration of *melodrame* < Fr. *mélodrame*, spoken drama with some music, melodrama : Gk. *melos*, song + Fr. *drame*, drama (< LLat. *drāma*; see DRAMA).]

mel•o•dra•mat•ic (mĕl′ə-drə-măt′ĭk) *adj.* **1.** Having the excitement and emotional appeal of melodrama. **2.** Exaggeratedly emotional or sentimental; histrionic. **3.** Marked by false pathos and sentiment. — **mel′o•dra•mat′i•cal•ly** *adv.*

mel•o•dra•mat•ics (mĕl′ə-drə-măt′ĭks) *n.* **1.** *(used with a sing. v.)* Melodramatic theatrical performance. **2.** *(used with a pl. v.)* Exaggeratedly emotional behavior; histrionics.

mel•o•dy (mĕl′ə-dē) *n., pl.* **-dies. 1.** A pleasing succession or arrangement of sounds. **2.** Musical quality: *the melody of verse.* **3.** *Mus.* **a.** A rhythmic sequence of single related tones that make up a particular phrase or idea. **b.** Structure with respect to the arrangement of such tones. **c.** The leading part or the air in a harmonic composition. **4.** A poem suitable for setting to music or singing. [ME *melodie* < OFr. < LLat. *melōdia* < Gk. *melōidia*, singing choral song : *melos*, tune + *aoidē*, song; see **wed-**[2]*.]

mel•oid (mĕl′oid′, mĕl′ō-ĭd) *n.* See **blister beetle.** [< NLat. *Meloidae*, family name < *Meloe*, type genus.] — **mel′oid′** *adj.*

mel•on (mĕl′ən) *n.* **1.** Any of several varieties of two related vines *(Cucumis melo* or *Citrullus lanatus)* widely cultivated for their edible fruit. **2.** Their fruit, having a hard rind and juicy flesh. [Ult. < LLat. *mēlō*, *mēlōn-*, short for Lat. *mēlopepō* < Gk. *mēlopepōn* : *mēlon*, apple + *pepōn*, gourd.]

mel•on•gene (mĕl′ən-jēn′) *n.* See **eggplant** 1. [Fr. *mélongène* < OFr. *melonge* < Med.Lat. *melongēna* < OItal. *melongiane* < Med.Gk. *melintzana, melanzana*, alteration (influenced by Gk. *melas*, dark) of Ar. *bādinjān* < Pers. *bādingān*.]

Me•los (mē′lŏs). See **Milos.**

Mel•pom•e•ne (mĕl-pŏm′ə-nē′) *n. Gk. Myth.* The Muse of tragedy.

Mel•rose (mĕl′rōz′). A city of NE MA, a suburb of Boston. Pop. 28,150.

Melrose Park. A village of NE IL, a suburb of Chicago. Pop. 20,589.

melt (mĕlt) *v.* **melt•ed, melt•ing, melts.** — *intr.* **1.** To be changed from a solid to a liquid by heat or pressure or both. **2.** To dissolve. **3.** To disappear or vanish gradually as if by dissolving. **4.** To pass or merge imperceptibly into something else. **5.** To become softened in feeling. **6.** *Obsolete.* To be overcome or crushed, as by grief, dismay, or fear. — *tr.* **1.** To change (a solid) to a liquid by heat or pressure or both. **2.** To dissolve. **3.** To cause to disappear gradually; disperse. **4.** To cause (units) to blend. **5.** To soften (someone's feelings); make gentle or tender. — *n.* **1.** A melted solid; a fused mass. **2.** The state of being melted. **3.a.** The act or operation of melting. **b.** The quantity melted at a single operation or in one period. **4.** A usu. open sandwich topped with melted cheese. [ME *melten* < OE *meltan*. See **mel-**[1]*.] — **melt′a•bil′i•ty** *n.* — **melt′a•ble** *adj.* — **melt′er** *n.* — **melt′ing•ly** *adv.*

melt•age (mĕl′tĭj) *n.* **1.** The substance or quantity of a substance produced by melting. **2.** The act or process of melting.

melt•down (mĕlt′doun′) *n.* **1.** Severe overheating of a nuclear reactor core, resulting in its melting and the escape of radiation. **2.** *Informal.* A situation likened to a meltdown.

melt•ing point (mĕl′tĭng) *n. Chem.* **1.** The temperature at which a solid becomes a liquid at standard atmospheric pressure. **2.** The temperature at which a solid and its liquid are in equilibrium, at any fixed pressure.

melting pot *n.* **1.** A container in which a substance is melted. **2.** A place where immigrants of different cultures or races form an integrated society.

mel•ton (mĕl′tən) *n.* A heavy woolen cloth used chiefly for making overcoats and hunting jackets. [After *Melton* Mowbray, an urban district of central England.]

Mel•ville (mĕl′vĭl), **Herman.** 1819–91. Amer. writer whose works include the novel *Moby Dick* (1851). — **Mel•vil′le•an** (-vĭl′ē-ən) *adj.*

Melville, Lake. A saltwater lake of Newfoundland, Canada, in SE Labrador.

Melville Island. 1. An island of N Australia in the Timor Sea. **2.** An island of N Northwest Terrs., Canada, in the Queen Elizabeth Is. N of Victoria I.

Melville Peninsula. A peninsula of E Northwest Terrs., Canada, separated from Baffin I. by a narrow strait.

mem (mĕm) *n.* The 13th letter of the Hebrew alphabet. [Heb., perh. < *mayim*, water.]

mem. *abbr.* **1.** Member. **2.** Memoir. **3.** Memorandum. **4.** Memorial.

mem•ber (mĕm′bər) *n.* **1.** A distinct part of a whole, esp.: **a.** *Ling.* A syntactic unit of a sentence; a clause. **b.** *Logic.* A proposition of a syllogism. **c.** *Math.* An element in a set. **2.** A part or an organ of a human or animal body, as: **a.** A limb, such as an arm or a leg. **b.** The penis. **3.** A part of a plant. **4.** One that belongs to a group or an organization: *a member of the FDIC.* **5.** *Math.* The expression on either side of an equality sign. **6.** A structural unit, such as a beam or wall. [ME *membre* < OFr. < Lat. *membrum.*]

mem•ber•ship (mĕm′bər-shĭp′) *n.* **1.** The state of being a member. **2.** The total number of members in a group.

mem•brane (mĕm′brān′) *n.* **1.** *Biol.* **a.** A thin pliable layer of tissue covering, lining, or connecting surfaces or parts of an animal or a plant. **b.** Cell membrane. **2.** A piece of parchment. **3.** *Chem.* A thin sheet of natural or synthetic material that is permeable to substances in solution. [Lat. *membrāna*, skin < *membrum*, body member.] — **mem′bra•nal** (-brə-nəl) *adj.*

membrane bone *n.* A bone that forms directly in membranous connective tissue rather than in cartilage.

mem•bra•nous (mĕm′brə-nəs) *adj.* **1.** Relating to, made of, or similar to a membrane. **2.** *Pathol.* Characterized by the formation of a membrane or a layer similar to a membrane.

membranous labyrinth *n.* The fluid-filled membranous sacs of the inner ear that are associated with hearing and balance.

Me•mel (mā′məl). See **Klaipeda.**

me•men•to (mə-mĕn′tō) *n., pl.* **-tos** or **-toes.** A reminder of the past; a keepsake. [ME, commemoration of the living or the dead in the Canon of the Mass < Lat. *mementō*, imper. of *meminisse*, to remember. See **men-**[1]*.]

memento mo•ri (môr′ē) *n., pl.* **memento mori. 1.** A reminder of death or mortality, esp. a death's-head. **2.** A reminder of human failures or errors. [Med.Lat. **mementō morī*, be mindful of dying : Lat. *mementō*, imper. of *meminisse*, to remember + Lat. *morī*, to die.]

Mem•ling (mĕm′lĭng) also **Mem•linc** (-lĭngk), **Hans.** 1430?–94. Flemish painter of portraits and religious works.

Mem•non (mĕm′nŏn′) *n. Gk. Myth.* An Ethiopian king killed by Achilles and made immortal by Zeus.

mem•o (mĕm′ō) *n., pl.* **-os.** *Informal.* A memorandum.

mem•oir (mĕm′wär′, -wôr′) *n.* **1.** An account of an author's personal experiences. **2.** An autobiography. Often used in the plural. **3.** A biography or biographical sketch. **4.** A report, esp. on a scientific or scholarly topic. **5. memoirs.** The report of the proceedings of a learned society. [Fr. *mémoire* < OFr. *memoire*, memory < Lat., memoria. See MEMORY.] — **mem′oir•ist** *n.*

mem•o•ra•bil•i•a (mĕm′ər-ə-bĭl′ē-ə, -bĭl′yə) *pl.n.* **1.** Objects valued for their connection with historical events, culture, or entertainment. **2.** Events or experiences worthy of remembrance. [Lat. *memorābilia*, neut. pl. of *memorābilis*, memorable. See MEMORABLE.]

mem•o•ra•ble (mĕm′ər-ə-bəl) *adj.* Worth being remembered or noted; remarkable. [ME < OFr. < Lat. *memorābilis* < *memorāre*, to bring to remembrance < *memor*, mindful. See **(s)mer-**[1]*.] — **mem′o•ra•bil′i•ty, mem′o•ra•ble•ness** *n.* — **mem′o•ra•bly** *adv.*

mem•o•ran•dum (mĕm′ə-răn′dəm) *n., pl.* **-dums** or **-da** (-də). **1.** A short note written as a reminder. **2.** A written record or communication, as in business. **3.** *Law.* A short written statement of the terms of an agreement, transaction, or contract. **4.** A business statement made by a consignor about a shipment of goods that may be returned. **5.** A brief, unsigned diplomatic communication. [ME, to be remembered (a manuscript notation) < Lat., neut. sing. gerundive of *memorāre*, to bring to remembrance. See MEMORABLE.]

me•mo•ri•al (mə-môr′ē-əl, -mōr′-) *n.* **1.** Something, as a holiday, intended to celebrate or honor the memory of a person or an event. **2.** A written statement of facts or a petition presented to a legislature or an executive. — *adj.* **1.** Serving as a remembrance of a person or an event; commemorative. **2.** Of, relating to, or being in memory. [ME < OFr. < LLat. *memoriāle* < neut. of Lat. *memoriālis*, of memory < *memoria*, memory. See MEMORY.] — **me•mo′ri•al•ly** *adv.*

Me•mo•ri•al Day (mə-môr′ē-əl, -mōr′-) *n.* May 30, observed in the United States to commemorate members of the armed forces killed in war, officially observed on the last Monday in May.

me•mo•ri•al•ist (mə-môr′ē-ə-lĭst, -mōr′-) *n.* **1.** A person who writes memoirs. **2.** A person who writes or signs a memorial.

me•mo•ri•al•ize (mə-môr′ē-ə-līz′, mə-mōr′-) *tr.v.* **-ized, -iz•ing, -iz•es. 1.** To provide a memorial for; commemorate. **2.** To present a memorial to; petition. — **me•mo′ri•al•i•za′tion** (-ə-lĭ-zā′shən) *n.* — **me•mo′ri•al•iz′er** *n.*

memorial park *n.* A cemetery.

mem•o•rize (mĕm′ə-rīz′) *tr.v.* **-rized, -riz•ing, -riz•es. 1.** To

memorial
Vietnam Veterans Memorial
by Maya Yang Lin

ă **pat**	oi **boy**
ā **pay**	ou **out**
âr **care**	ŏŏ **took**
ä **father**	ōō **boot**
ĕ **pet**	ŭ **cut**
ē **be**	ûr **urge**
ĭ **pit**	th **thin**
ī **pie**	*th* **this**
îr **pier**	hw **which**
ŏ **pot**	zh **vision**
ō **toe**	ə **about,**
ô **paw**	**item**

Stress marks:
′ (primary);
′ (secondary), as in
dictionary (dĭk′shə-nĕr′ē)

commit to memory; learn by heart. **2.** *Comp. Sci.* To store in memory. **—mem′o•riz′a•ble** *adj.* **—mem′o•ri•za′tion** (-rĭ-zā′shən) *n.* **—mem′o•riz′er** *n.*

mem•o•ry (mĕm′ə-rē) *n., pl.* **-ries. 1.** The mental faculty of retaining and recalling past experience. **2.** The act or an instance of remembering; recollection. **3.** All that a person can remember. **4.** Something remembered. **5.** The fact of being remembered; remembrance: *dedicated to their memory.* **6.** The period of time covered by the remembrance or recollection of a person or group of persons. **7.** *Biol.* Persistent modification of behavior resulting from an animal's experience. **8.** *Comp. Sci.* **a.** A unit of a computer that preserves data for retrieval. **b.** Capacity for storing information. **9.** *Statistics.* The set of past events affecting a given event in a stochastic process. **10.** The capacity of a material, such as plastic or metal, to return to a previous shape after deformation. [ME *memorie* < AN < Lat. *memoria* < *memor*, mindful. See **(s)mer-**[1]*.]

Syns: *memory, remembrance, recollection, reminiscence.* These nouns denote the act or an instance of remembering or something remembered. *Memory* is the faculty of retaining and reviving impressions or recalling past experiences: *a bad memory for dates.* The word also applies to something recalled to the mind. *Remembrance* most often denotes the process or act of recalling: *Remembrance can be painful. Recollection* often suggests a deliberate, concentrated effort: *After a few minutes' recollection she produced the answer. Reminiscence* applies to experiences or events within one's personal knowledge: *"Her mind seemed wholly taken up with reminiscences of past gaiety"* (Charlotte Brontë). When the word refers to what is remembered, it may involve sharing with another or others: *The couple spent the evening in reminiscence.*

memory engram *n.* An engram.

memory trace *n.* An engram.

Mem•phis (mĕm′fĭs). **1.** An ancient city of Egypt S of Cairo; reputedly founded by Menes, the first king of united Egypt. **2.** A city of SW TN on the Mississippi R. near the MS border; estab. and named (1819) by Andrew Jackson on the site of a fort built in 1797. Pop. 610,337.

mem•sa•hib (mĕm′sä′ĭb) *n.* Used formerly as a form of respectful address for a European woman in colonial India. [MA'AM + SAHIB.]

men (mĕn) *n.* Pl. of **man.**

men– *pref.* Var. of **meno–.**

men•ace (mĕn′ĭs) *n.* **1.a.** A possible danger; a threat: *the menace of war.* **b.** The act of threatening. **2.** A troublesome or annoying person. *—v.* **-aced, -ac•ing, -ac•es.** *—tr.* **1.** To utter threats against. **2.** To constitute a threat to; endanger. *—intr.* To make threats. [ME < OFr. < VLat. **minācia*, sing. of Lat. *mināciæ*, threats, menaces < *mināx, mināc-*, threatening < *minārī*, to threaten < *minae*, threats. See **men-**[2]*.] **—men′ac•er** *n.* **—men′ac•ing•ly** *adv.*

men•a•di•one (mĕn′ə-dī′ōn′) *n.* A yellow crystalline powder, $C_{11}H_8O_2$, used in medicine as a vitamin K supplement. [ME(THYL) + NA(PHTHALENE) + DI-[1] + -ONE.]

mé•nage (mā-näzh′) *n.* **1.** People living together as a unit; a household. **2.** The management of a household. [Fr. < OFr. < *maneir*, to stay < Lat. *manēre*, to remain. See REMAIN.]

ménage à trois (ä trwä′) *n.* A relationship wherein three people, such as a married couple and a lover, live together. [Fr. : *ménage*, household + *à*, for + *trois*, three.]

me•nag•er•ie (mə-năj′ə-rē, -năzh′-) *n.* **1.a.** A collection of live wild animals on exhibition. **b.** An enclosure in which wild animals are kept. **2.** A diverse or miscellaneous group. [Fr. *ménagerie* < OFr. *menage*, ménage. See MÉNAGE.]

Me•nan•der (mə-năn′dər). 342–292 B.C. Greek dramatist whose works were influential in the development of comedy.

me•nar•che (mə-när′kē) *n.* The first menstrual period, usu. occurring during puberty. [MEN(O)- + Gk. *arkhē*, beginning (< *arkhein*, to begin).] **—me•nar′che•al** *adj.*

men-at-arms (mĕn′ət-ärmz′) *n.* Pl. of **man-at-arms.**

men-chil•dren (mĕn′chĭl′drən) *n.* Pl. of **man-child.**

Men•chu (mĕn′cho͞o), **Rigoberta.** b. 1959. Guatemalan leader who won the 1992 Nobel Peace Prize for her efforts toward improved economic, political, and social conditions for indigenous peoples.

Men•ci•us (mĕn′shē-əs). Orig. **Meng•zi** (mœng′zē′). 4th cent. B.C. Chinese Confucian philosopher who taught that human beings are innately good.

Menck•en (mĕng′kən), **H(enry) L(ouis).** 1880–1956. Amer. editor and critic who founded and edited (1924–33) the *American Mercury.* **—Menck•e′ni•an** (mĕng-kē′nē-ən) *adj.*

mend (mĕnd) *v.* **mend•ed, mend•ing, mends.** *—tr.* **1.** To make repairs or restoration to; fix. **2.** To reform or correct. *—intr.* **1.a.** To improve in health or condition. **b.** To heal. **2.** To make repairs or corrections. *—n.* **1.** The act of mending. **2.** A mended place. ***—idioms.*** **mend fences.** To improve poor relations, esp. in politics. **on the mend.** Improving, esp. in health. [ME *menden*, short for *amenden*, to amend. See AMEND.] **—mend′a•ble** *adj.* **—mend′er** *n.*

men•da•cious (mĕn-dā′shəs) *adj.* **1.** Lying; untruthful. **2.** False; untrue. [< Lat. *mendācium*, lie < *mendāx, mendāc-*, mendacious.] **—men•da′cious•ly** *adv.*

men•dac•i•ty (mĕn-dăs′ĭ-tē) *n., pl.* **-ties. 1.** The condition of being mendacious; untruthfulness. **2.** A lie; a falsehood.

Men•del (mĕn′dl), **Gregor Johann.** 1822–84. Austrian botanist and founder of the science of genetics. **—Men•de′li•an** (mĕn-dē′lē-ən, -dĕl′yən) *adj.*

Men•de•le•ev (mĕn′də-lā′əf, myĭn-dĭ-lē′yĕf), **Dmitri Ivanovich.** 1834–1907. Russian chemist who first devised and published the periodic table of the elements (1869).

men•de•le•vi•um (mĕn′də-lē′vē-əm) *n. Symbol* **Md** A synthetic radioactive element; its most stable isotope is Md 256 with a half-life of approx. 1.5 hours. Atomic number 101. See table at **element.** [After Dmitri Ivanovich MENDELEEV.]

Men•del•ism (mĕn′dl-ĭz′əm) also **Men•de•li•an•ism** (mĕn-dē′lē-ə-nĭz′əm) *n.* The theoretical principles of heredity formulated by Gregor Mendel; Mendel's laws.

Men•del's law (mĕn′dlz) *n.* **1.** The principle stating that the members of a pair of homologous chromosomes segregate during meiosis and are distributed to different gametes. **2.** The principle stating that each member of a pair of homologous chromosomes segregates during meiosis independently of the members of other pairs, so that alleles on different chromosomes are distributed randomly to the gametes.

Men•dels•sohn (mĕn′dl-sən, -zōn′), **Felix.** 1809–47. German conductor, pianist, and composer.

Mendelssohn, Moses. 1729–86. German philosopher noted for his writings on the inborn ability of human beings to recognize beauty, truth, and goodness.

Men•de•res (mĕn′də-rĕs′). A river of W Turkey flowing c. 402 km (250 mi) to the Aegean Sea.

Men•dès-France (mĕn′dĭs-frăns′, mäɴ-dĕs-fräɴs′), **Pierre.** 1907–82. French prime minister (1954–55).

men•di•cant (mĕn′dĭ-kənt) *adj.* Depending on alms for a living; practicing begging. *—n.* **1.** A beggar. **2.** A member of an order of friars forbidden to own property in common who work or beg for their living. [ME < OFr. < Lat. *mendicāns, mendicant-*, pr.part. of *mendicāre*, to beg < *mendīcus*, needy, beggar < *mendum*, physical defect.] **—men′di•can•cy, men•dic′i•ty** (-dĭs′ĭ-tē) *n.*

mend•ing (mĕn′dĭng) *n.* Articles, as clothes, needing repair.

Men•do•ci•no (mĕn′də-sē′nō), **Cape.** A promontory of NW CA SSW of Eureka.

Men•do•za (mĕn-dō′zə, -dô′sä). A city of W Argentina ENE of Santiago, Chile; founded c. 1560. Pop. 118,427.

men•eer (mə-nîr′) *n.* Var. of **mynheer.**

Men•e•la•us (mĕn′ə-lā′əs) *n. Gk. Myth.* The king of Sparta who was husband of Helen and brother of Agamemnon.

Men•e•lik II (mĕn′ə-lĭk). 1844–1913. Ethiopian emperor (1889–1913) who established independence from Italy.

Me•nén•dez de A•vi•lés (mə-nĕn′dəs dā ä′və-lās′, mĕ-nĕn′dĕth *th*ĕ ä′vē-lĕs′), **Pedro.** 1519–74. Spanish colonizer who founded the city of St. Augustine in Florida (1565).

Me•nes (mē′nēz). fl. 3000 B.C. King of Egypt who founded the first dynasty uniting Upper and Lower Egypt.

men•folk (mĕn′fōk′) or **men•folks** (-fōks′) *pl.n.* **1.** Men considered as a group. **2.** The males of a community or family.

Meng•zi (mœng′zē′). See **Mencius.**

men•ha•den (mĕn-hād′n) *n., pl.* **menhaden** or **-dens.** Any of several species of fish of the genus *Brevoortia*, esp. *B. tyrannus* of American Atlantic and Gulf waters. [Prob. blend of Narragansett *munnawhatteaûg* and E. dial. *poghaden* (prob. of Algonquian orig.).]

men•hir (mĕn′hîr′) *n.* Any of a type of prehistoric monument, chiefly of the British Isles and northern France, consisting of a tall upright megalith. [Fr. < Breton : *men*, stone (< Middle Breton) + *hir*, long (< Middle Breton).]

me•ni•al (mē′nē-əl, mēn′yəl) *adj.* **1.** Of or relating to work regarded as servile. **2.** Of, relating to, or appropriate for a servant. *—n.* **1.** A servant, esp. a domestic servant. **2.** A person of a servile or low nature. [ME *meinial*, belonging to a household < AN *meignial* < *meignee*, household < VLat. **mānsiōnāta* < Lat. *mānsiō, mānsiōn-*, house. See MANSION.] **—me′ni•al•ly** *adv.*

Mé•nière's disease (mān-yârz′) *n.* A disease of the inner ear characterized by dizziness, ringing in the ears, and progressive loss of hearing. [After Prosper *Ménière* (1799–1862), French physician.]

mening– *pref.* Var. of **meningo–.**

me•nin•ge•al (mə-nĭn′jē-əl) *adj.* Of, relating to, or affecting the meninges.

meningi– *pref.* Var. of **meningo–.**

me•nin•gi•o•ma (mə-nĭn′jē-ō′mə) *n., pl.* **-mas** or **-ma•ta** (-mə-tə). A slow-growing tumor of the meninges, occurring usu. in adults. [Short for *meningothelioma* : MENINGO- + (EN-DO)THELIOMA.]

men•in•gi•tis (mĕn′ĭn-jī′tĭs) *n.* Inflammation of the meninges usu. caused by a bacterium or virus and characterized by fever, vomiting, intense headache, and stiff neck. **—men′in•git′ic** (-jĭt′ĭk) *adj.*

meningo– or **meningi–** or **mening–** *pref.* Meninges: *meningococcus.* [< Gk. *mēninx, mēning-*, meninx.]

me•nin•go•coc•cus (mə-nĭng′gə-kŏk′əs, -nĭn′jə-) *n., pl.* **-coc•ci** (-kŏk′sī, -kī). A bacterium *(Neisseria meningitidis)* that causes cerebrospinal meningitis. **— me•nin′go•coc′cal** (-kŏk′əl), **me•nin′go•coc′cic** (-kŏk′sĭk) *adj.*

me•nin•go•en•ceph•a•li•tis (mə-nĭng′gō-ĕn-sĕf′ə-lī′tĭs) *n.* Inflammation of the brain and meninges. **— me•nin′go•en•ceph′a•lit′ic** (-lĭt′ĭk) *adj.*

me•ninx (mē′nĭngks) *n., pl.* **me•nin•ges** (mə-nĭn′jēz). A membrane, esp. one of the three membranes enclosing the brain and spinal cord in vertebrates. [Gk. *mēninx.*]

me•nis•cus (mə-nĭs′kəs) *n., pl.* **-nis•ci** (-nĭs′ī, -kī, -kē) or **-nis•cus•es. 1.** A crescent-shaped body. **2.** A concavo-convex lens. **3.** The concave or convex upper surface of a nonturbulent liquid in a container. **4.** *Anat.* A cartilage disk that acts as a cushion between the ends of bones that meet in a joint. [NLat. < Gk. *mēniskos,* dim. of *mēnē,* moon, month. See **mē-**[2*].] **— me•nis′cal** (-kəl), **me•nis′cate′** (-kăt′), **me•nis′coid′** (-koid′), **men′is•coi′dal** (mĕn′ĭs-koid′l) *adj.*

Men•lo Park (mĕn′lō). **1.** A city of W CA SE of San Francisco. Pop. 28,040. **2.** An unincorp. community of central NJ N of New Brunswick. Thomas Edison perfected the incandescent light bulb here (1879).

Men•ning•er (mĕn′ĭn-jər). Family of American psychiatrists, including **Charles Frederick** (1862–1953) and his sons **Karl Augustus** (1893–1990) and **William Claire** (1899–1966).

Men•non•ite (mĕn′ə-nīt′) *n.* A member of an Anabaptist church characterized particularly by simplicity of life, pacifism, and nonresistance. [Ger. *Mennonit,* after *Menno* Simons (1492–1559), Frisian religious leader.]

meno– or **men–** *pref.* **1.** Menstruation: *menarche.* **2.** Menses: *menorrhagia.* [Gk. < *mēn,* month. See **mē-**[2*].]

men-of-war (mĕn′ə-wôr′) *n.* Pl. of **man-of-war.**

Me•nom•i•nee (mə-nŏm′ə-nē) *n., pl.* **Menominee** or **-nees. 1.** A member of a Native American people formerly inhabiting an area along the Menominee River, with a present-day population in northeast Wisconsin. **2.** The Algonquian language of the Menominee.

Menominee River. A river rising in the Upper Peninsula of NW MI and flowing c. 190 km (118 mi) to Green Bay.

Me•nom•o•nee Falls (mə-nŏm′ə-nē). A village of SE WI, a suburb of Milwaukee. Pop. 26,840.

me•no mos•so (mā′nō môs′sō, mĕ′nō) *adv. & adj. Mus.* At a lower speed. [Ital. : *meno,* less + *mosso,* agitated.]

men•o•pause (mĕn′ə-pôz′) *n.* The period marked by the natural and permanent cessation of menstruation, occurring usu. between the ages of 45 and 55. [NLat. *mēnopausis* : MENO– + Gk. *pausis,* pause; see PAUSE.] **— men′o•paus′al** *adj.*

me•no•rah (mə-nôr′ə, -nōr′ə) *n. Judaism.* **1.** A nine-branched candelabrum used in celebration of Hanukkah. **2.** Often **Menorah.** A seven-branched candelabrum of the Jewish Temple symbolizing the seven days of the Creation. [Heb. *mənôrâ.*]

Me•nor•ca (mə-nôr′kə, mĕ-nôr′kä). See **Minorca**[1].

men•or•rha•gi•a (mĕn′ə-rā′jē-ə) *n.* Abnormally heavy or extended menstrual flow. **— men′or•rha′gic** (-jĭk) *adj.*

Me•not•ti (mə-nŏt′ē), **Gian Carlo.** b. 1911. Italian-born Amer. composer whose operas include *The Consul* (1950).

Men•sa (mĕn′sə) *n.* A southern constellation between Hydrus and Volans. [Lat. *mēnsa,* table.]

men•sal (mĕn′səl) *adj.* Belonging to or used at the table. [ME < LLat. *mēnsālis* < Lat. *mēnsa,* table.]

mensch or **mensh** (mĕnsh) *n., pl.* **mensch•en** (mĕn′shən) or **mensch•es.** *Informal.* A person having admirable characteristics, such as firmness of purpose. [Yiddish < MHGer., human being < OHGer. *mennisco.* See **man-**[1*].]

men•ses (mĕn′sēz) *pl.n. (used with a sing. or pl. v.)* The monthly flow of blood and cellular debris from the uterus that begins at puberty in women and the females of other primates. [Lat. *mēnsēs,* pl. of *mēnsis,* month. See **mē-**[2*].]

Men•she•vik (mĕn′shə-vĭk) *n., pl.* **-viks** or **-vi•ki** (-vē′kē). A member of the liberal faction of the Social Democratic Party that struggled against the Bolsheviks before and during the Russian Revolution. [Russ. *men'shevik* < *men'she,* less (< their relegation by Lenin to minority status). See **mei-**[2*].] **— Men′she•vism** *n.* **— Men′she•vist** *n.*

men's room (mĕnz) *n.* A restroom for men.

men•stru•al (mĕn′strōō-əl) also **men•stru•ous** (-əs) *adj.* **1.** Of or relating to menstruation. **2.a.** Taking place on a monthly basis. **b.** Lasting for one month. [ME < OFr. *menstruel* < Lat. *mēnstruālis* < *mēnstruus,* menstrual < *mēnsis,* month. See **mē-**[2*].]

men•stru•ate (mĕn′strōō-āt′) *intr.v.* **-at•ed, -at•ing, -ates.** To undergo menstruation. [LLat. *mēnstruāre, mēnstruāt-* < Lat. *mēnstrua,* menses < neut. pl. of *mēnstruus,* menstrual. See MENSTRUAL.]

men•stru•a•tion (mĕn′strōō-ā′shən) *n.* The process or an instance of discharging the menses.

men•stru•um (mĕn′strōō-əm) *n., pl.* **-stru•ums** or **-stru•a** (-strōō-ə). A solvent, esp. one used in extracting compounds from plant and animal tissues and preparing drugs. [ME, menstruation < Med.Lat. *mēnstruum,* sing. of Lat. *mēnstrua,* menses. See MENSTRUATE.]

men•su•ra•ble (mĕn′sər-ə-bəl, -shər-) *adj.* **1.** That can be measured. **2.** Having fixed rhythm and measure; mensural. **— men′su•ra•bil′i•ty, men′su•ra•ble•ness** *n.*

men•su•ral (mĕn′sər-əl, -shər-) *adj.* **1.** Of or relating to measure. **2.** *Mus.* Having notes of fixed rhythmic value. [LLat. *mēnsūrālis* < Lat. *mēnsūra,* measure. See MEASURE.]

men•su•ra•tion (mĕn′sə-rā′shən, -shə-) *n.* **1.** The act, process, or art of measuring. **2.** Measurement of geometric quantities. [LLat. *mēnsūrātiō, mēnsūrātiōn-* < *mēnsūrātus,* p.part. of *mēnsūrāre,* to measure < Lat. *mēnsūra,* measure. See MEASURE.] **— men′su•ra′tive** *adj.*

mens•wear also **men's wear** (mĕnz′wâr′) *n.* Clothing for men.

–ment *suff.* **1.** Action; process: *appeasement.* **2.** Result of an action or process: *advancement.* **3.** Means, instrument, or agent of an action or process: *adornment.* [ME < OFr. < Lat. *-mentum,* n. suff.]

men•tal[1] (mĕn′tl) *adj.* **1.** Of or relating to the mind; intellectual. **2.** Executed or performed by the mind; existing in the mind. **3.** Of, relating to, or affected by a disorder of the mind. **4.** Intended for treatment of people affected with disorders of the mind. **5.** Of or relating to telepathy or mind reading. **6.** *Slang.* **a.** Emotionally upset; crazed. **b.** *Offensive Slang.* Mentally or psychologically disturbed. [ME < OFr. < LLat. *mentālis* < Lat. *mēns, ment-,* mind. See **men-**[1*].] **— men′tal•ly** *adv.*

men•tal[2] (mĕn′tl) *adj.* Of or relating to the chin. [< Lat. *mentum,* chin. See **men-**[2*].]

mental age *n.* A measure of mental development as determined by intelligence tests, usu. restricted to children and expressed as the age at which that level is typically attained.

mental deficiency *n.* See **mental retardation.**

mental hospital *n.* See **psychiatric hospital.**

men•tal•ism (mĕn′tl-ĭz′əm) *n.* **1.** Parapsychological activities. **2.** The belief that some mental phenomena are inexplicable by physical laws. **— men′tal•ist** *n.* **— men′tal•is′tic** *adj.*

men•tal•i•ty (mĕn-tăl′ĭ-tē) *n., pl.* **-ties. 1.** Cast or turn of mind: *a vindictive mentality.* **2.** The sum of a person's intellectual capabilities or endowment.

mental retardation *n.* Subnormal intellectual development or functioning due to congenital causes, brain injury, or disease and characterized by any of various deficiencies, ranging from impaired learning ability to social and vocational inadequacy.

mental telepathy *n.* Telepathy.

men•ta•tion (mĕn-tā′shən) *n.* Mental activity; thinking. [< Lat. *mēns, ment-,* mind. See MENTAL[1].]

men•thol (mĕn′thôl′) *n.* A white crystalline organic compound, $CH_3C_6H_9(C_3H_7)OH$, found in peppermint oil and used in perfumes, in cigarettes, and as a mint flavoring. [Ger. < Lat. *mentha,* mint.] **— men′tho•lat′ed** *adj.*

men•tion (mĕn′shən) *tr.v.* **-tioned, -tion•ing, -tions.** To refer to, esp. incidentally. *— n.* **1.a.** The act of referring to something briefly or casually. **b.** An incidental reference or allusion. **2.** Honorable mention. [< ME *mencioun,* reference < OFr. < Lat. *mentiō, mentiōn-.* See **men-**[1*].] **— men′tion•a•ble** *adj.*

men•tor (mĕn′tôr′, -tər) *n.* **1.** A wise and trusted counselor or teacher. **2. Mentor.** *Gk. Myth.* Odysseus's trusted counselor, under whose disguise Athena became the guardian and teacher of Telemachus. [Fr. *Mentor,* Mentor < Lat. *Mentōr* < Gk. See **men-**[1*].] **— men′tor** *v.*

Men•tor (mĕn′tər). A city of NE OH, a suburb of Cleveland on Lake Erie. Pop. 47,358.

men•u (mĕn′yōō, mā′nyōō) *n.* **1.** A list of the dishes served or available for a meal. **2.** The dishes served or available at a meal. **3.a.** *Comp. Sci.* A list, displayed on a monitor, of options for a computer user. **b.** A list of options. [Fr., small, minute, menu < OFr. *menut,* small < Lat. *minūtus,* p.part. of *minuere,* to diminish. See **mei-**[2*].]

Men•u•hin (mĕn′yōō-ĭn), **Yehudi.** b. 1916. Amer. violinist considered among the great virtuosos of his time.

Men•zies (mĕn′zēz), Sir **Robert Gordon.** 1894–1978. Australian prime minister (1939–41 and 1949–66).

Me•o (mē-ou′) *n.* Var. of **Miao.**

me•ow (mē-ou′) *n.* **1.** *Informal.* The cry of a cat. **2.** *Informal.* A malicious, spiteful comment. *— intr.v.* **-owed, -ow•ing, -ows.** To make the crying sound of a cat. [Imit.]

me•per•i•dine (mə-pĕr′ĭ-dēn′) *n.* A synthetic narcotic compound, $C_{15}H_{21}NO_2$, used in its hydrochloride form as an analgesic and a sedative. [ME(THYL) + (PI)PERIDINE.]

Meph•i•stoph•e•les (mĕf′ĭ-stŏf′ə-lēz′) *n.* The devil in the Faust legend to whom Faust sold his soul. **— Me•phis′to•phe′le•an, Me•phis′to•phe′li•an** (mə-fĭs′tō-fē′lē-ən, -fēl′yən, mĕf′ĭ-stō-) *adj.*

me•phit•ic (mə-fĭt′ĭk) also **me•phit•i•cal** (-ĭ-kəl) *adj.* Of, relating to, or resembling mephitis; poisonous or foul-smelling.

me•phi•tis (mə-fī′tĭs) *n.* **1.** A foul smell. **2.** A poisonous or foul-smelling gas emitted from the earth. [Lat. *mephītis.*]

mep•ro•bam•ate (mĕp′rō-băm′āt′, mĕ-prō′bə-) *n.* A bitter white powder, $C_9H_{18}N_2O_4$, used as a tranquilizer and an anticonvulsant. [ME(THYL) + PRO(PYL) + (CAR)BAMATE.]

Meq•uon (mĕk′wŏn′). A city of SE WI, a suburb of Milwaukee. Pop. 18,885.

meniscus
View of a flexed knee

menorah

ă pat	oi boy
ā pay	ou out
âr care	ŏŏ took
ä father	ōō boot
ĕ pet	ŭ cut
ē be	ûr urge
ĭ pit	th thin
ī pie	*th* this
îr pier	hw which
ŏ pot	zh vision
ō toe	ə about, item
ô paw	

Stress marks:
′ (primary);
′ (secondary), as in
dictionary (dĭk′shə-nĕr′ē)

mer. *abbr.* Meridian.
mer– *pref.* Var. of **mero–**.
–mer *suff.* Var. of **–mere.**
mer•bro•min (mər-brō′mĭn) *n.* A green crystalline organic compound, $C_{20}H_8Br_2HgNa_2O_6$, that forms a red aqueous solution, used as a germicide and an antiseptic. [MER(CURIC) + (ACETATE) + (DI)BROM(IDE) + (FLUORESCE)IN.]
mer•can•tile (mûr′kən-tēl′, -tīl′, -tĭl) *adj.* **1.** Of or relating to merchants or trade. **2.** Of or relating to mercantilism. [Fr. < Ital. < *mercante*, merchant < Lat. *mercāns, mercant-* < pr.part. of *mercārī*, to trade < *merx, merc-*, merchandise, goods.]
mer•can•til•ism (mûr′kən-tē-lĭz′əm, -tī-) *n.* **1.** The theory and system of political economy prevailing in Europe after feudalism, based on national policies of accumulating bullion, establishing colonies and a merchant marine, and developing industry and a favorable balance of trade. **2.** The practice, methods, or spirit of merchants; commercialism. **—mer′can•til•ist** *adj. & n.* **—mer′can•til•is′tic** *adj.*
mer•cap•tan (mər-kăp′tăn′) *n.* A sulfur-containing organic compound, RSH, where R is any radical, esp. ethyl mercaptan, C_2H_5SH. [Ger. < Dan. < Med.Lat. *(corpus) mercurium captāns*, (substance) seizing mercury : *mercurium*, accusative of *mercurius*, mercury; see MERCURY + Lat. *captāns*, pr.part. of *captāre*, freq. of *capere*, to seize; see CAPTURE.]
mercapto– *pref.* Containing the univalent radical –SH: *mercaptopurine.* [< MERCAPTAN.]
mer•cap•to•pu•rine (mər-kăp′tō-pyo͝or′ēn) *n.* A purine analogue, $C_5H_4N_4S$, that acts as an antimetabolite by interfering with purine synthesis, used in the treatment of acute leukemia.
Mer•ca•tor (mər-kā′tər, mĕr-kä′tôr), **Gerhardus.** 1512–94. Flemish cartographer who developed the Mercator projection (1568).
Mercator projection *n.* A cylindrical map projection in which the meridians and parallels of latitude appear as lines crossing at right angles and in which areas appear greater farther from the equator. [After Gerhardus MERCATOR.]
Mer•ced (mər-sĕd′). A city of central CA in the San Joaquin Valley NW of Fresno. Pop. 56,216.
Mer•ce•da•rio (mĕr′sə-där′ē-ō, -sĕ-*thä*′ryô). A mountain, 6,774.4 m (22,211 ft), in the Andes of W Argentina.
mer•ce•nar•y (mûr′sə-nĕr′ē) *adj.* **1.** Motivated solely by a desire for monetary or material gain. **2.** Hired for service in a foreign army. —*n., pl.* **-ies. 1.** One who serves or works merely for monetary gain; a hireling. **2.** A professional soldier hired for service in a foreign army. [ME *mercenarie*, a mercenary < OFr. *mercenaire* < Lat. *mercēnārius* < *mercēs*, wages, price.] **—mer′ce•nar′i•ly** *adv.* **—mer′ce•nar′i•ness** *n.*
mer•cer (mûr′sər) *n. Chiefly British.* A dealer in textiles, esp. silks. [ME < OFr. *mercier*, trader < *merz*, merchandise < Lat. *merx, merc-*, merchandise.]
Mer•cer Island (mûr′sər). A city of W-central WA, coextensive with **Mercer Island** in Lake Washington near Seattle. Pop. 20,816.
mer•cer•ize (mûr′sə-rīz′) *tr.v.* **-ized, -iz•ing, -iz•es.** To treat (cotton thread) with sodium hydroxide so as to shrink the fiber and increase its luster and affinity for dye. [After John *Mercer* (1791–1866), British calico printer.]
mer•chan•dise (mûr′chən-dīz′, -dīs′) *n.* Goods bought and sold in business; commercial wares. —*v.* (-dīz′) also **mer•chan•dize. -dised, -dis•ing, -dis•es** also **-dized, -diz•ing, -diz•es.** —*tr.* **1.** To buy and sell (goods). **2.** To promote the sale of, as by advertising. —*intr.* To buy and sell goods; trade commercially. [ME *merchaundise* < OFr. *marchandise*, trade < *marcheant, marchand*, merchant. See MERCHANT.] **—mer′chan•dis′a•ble** *adj.* **—mer′chan•dis′er** *n.*
mer•chan•dis•ing also **mer•chan•diz•ing** (mûr′chən-dī′zĭng) *n.* The promotion of merchandise sales, as by coordinating production and marketing.
mer•chant (mûr′chənt) *n.* **1.** One who buys goods wholesale and sells them retail for profit. **2.** One who runs a retail business; a shopkeeper. —*adj.* **1.** Of or relating to merchants, merchandise, or commercial trade. **2.** Of or relating to the merchant marine. [ME *merchaunt* < OFr. *marcheant* < VLat. **mercātāns*, pr.part. of **mercātāre*, freq. of Lat. *mercārī*, to trade < *merx, merc-*, merchandise.]
mer•chant•a•ble (mûr′chən-tə-bəl) *adj.* Suitable for buying and selling; marketable. **—mer′chant•a•bil′i•ty** *n.*
mer•chant•man (mûr′chənt-mən) *n.* **1.** *Naut.* A ship used in commerce. **2.** *Archaic.* A merchant.
merchant marine *n.* **1.** A nation's commercial ships. **2.** The personnel of a nation's commercial ships.
Mer•ci•a (mûr′shē-ə, -shə). An Anglo-Saxon kingdom of central England; settled by Angles c. A.D. 500.
Mer•ci•an (mûr′shē-ən, -shən) *adj.* Of or relating to Mercia or its people, dialect, or culture. —*n.* **1.** A native or inhabitant of Mercia. **2.** The Old English dialect of Mercia.
mer•ci•ful (mûr′sĭ-fəl) *adj.* Full of mercy; compassionate: *merciful treatment of captives.* See Syns at **humane. —mer′ci•ful•ly** *adv.* **—mer′ci•ful•ness** *n.*
mer•ci•less (mûr′sĭ-lĭs) *adj.* Having no mercy; cruel. **—mer′ci•less•ly** *adv.* **—mer′ci•less•ness** *n.*

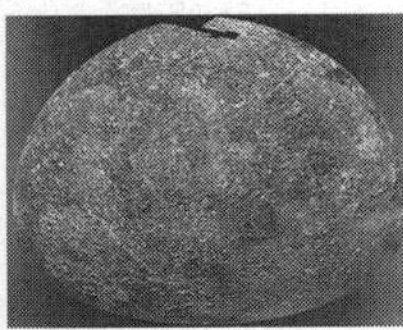

Mercury
Top: 1793 American post office sign
Bottom: Mercury's South Pole, photographed by Mariner 10 on December 1, 1975

merganser
Male hooded merganser
Mergus cucullatus

mer•cu•rate (mûr′kyə-rāt′) *tr.v.* **-rat•ed, -rat•ing, -rates.** To treat or combine with mercury or a mercury compound. **—mer′cu•ra′tion** *n.*
mer•cu•ri•al (mər-kyo͝or′ē-əl) *adj.* **1.** Often **Mercurial. a.** *Rom. Myth.* Of or relating to the god Mercury. **b.** *Astron.* Of or relating to the planet Mercury. **2.** Having the characteristics of eloquence, shrewdness, swiftness, and thievishness attributed to the god Mercury. **3.** Containing or caused by the action of the element mercury. **4.** Quick and changeable in temperament; volatile: *a mercurial nature.* —*n.* A pharmacological or chemical preparation containing mercury. [ME, of the planet Mercury < Lat. *mercuriālis* of the god or planet Mercury < *Mercurius*, Mercury.] **—mer•cu′ri•al•ly** *adv.*
mer•cu•ri•al•ism (mər-kyo͝or′ē-ə-lĭz′əm) *n. Pathol.* Poisoning caused by mercury or a compound containing mercury.
mer•cu•ric (mər-kyo͝or′ĭk) *adj.* Relating to or containing mercury, esp. with valence 2.
mercuric chloride *n.* A poisonous white crystalline compound, $HgCl_2$, used as an antiseptic and a disinfectant, in insecticides, preservatives, and batteries, and in photography.
mercuric sulfide *n.* A poisonous compound, HgS, having two forms, both used as pigments: **a.** Black mercuric sulfide, a black powder obtained from mercury salts or by the reaction of mercury with sulfur. **b.** Red mercuric sulfide, a bright scarlet powder derived from heating mercury with sulfur.
mercuro– or **mercur–** *pref.* Mercury: *mercurous.* [< MERCURY.]
Mer•cu•ro•chrome (mər-kyo͝or′ə-krōm′). A trademark used for a solution of merbromin.
mer•cu•rous (mər-kyo͝or′əs, mûr′kyər-əs) *adj.* Relating to or containing mercury, esp. with valence 1.
mercurous chloride *n.* See **calomel.**
mer•cu•ry (mûr′kyə-rē) *n.* **1.** *Symbol* **Hg** A silvery-white poisonous metallic element, liquid at room temperature and used in thermometers, barometers, and batteries. Atomic number 80; atomic weight 200.59; melting point −38.87°C; boiling point 356.58°C; specific gravity 13.546 (at 20°C); valence 1, 2. See table at **element. 2.** Temperature. **3.** A weedy plant of the genus *Mercurialis* or *Acalypha.* [ME *mercurie* < Med.Lat. *mercurius* < Lat. *Mercurius*, Mercury.]
Mer•cu•ry (mûr′kyə-rē) *n.* **1.** *Rom. Myth.* The messenger of the gods, himself the god of commerce, travel, and thievery. **2.** The smallest of the planets and the one nearest the sun, having a sidereal period of revolution about the sun of 88.0 days at a mean distance of 58.3 million kilometers (36.2 million miles) and a mean radius of approx. 2,414 kilometers (1,500 miles). [ME *Mercurie* < OFr. < Lat. *Mercurius.*]
mer•cu•ry-va•por lamp (mûr′kyə-rē-vā′pər) *n.* A lamp in which ultraviolet and yellowish-green to blue visible light is produced by an electric discharge through mercury vapor.
mer•cy (mûr′sē) *n., pl.* **-cies. 1.** Compassionate treatment, esp. of those under one's power; clemency. **2.** A disposition to be kind and forgiving. **3.** Something for which to be thankful; a blessing. **4.** Alleviation of distress; relief. —***idiom.* at the mercy of.** Without any protection against; helpless before. [ME < OFr. *merci* < Med.Lat. *mercēs* < Lat., reward.]
Syns: *mercy, leniency, lenity, clemency, charity.* These nouns mean humane and kind, forgiving, or sympathetic treatment of or disposition toward others. *Mercy* is compassionate forbearance: *"We hand folks over to God's mercy, and show none ourselves"* (George Eliot). *Leniency* and *lenity* imply mildness, gentleness, and often a tendency to reduce punishment: *"When you have gone too far to recede, do not sue* [appeal] *to me for leniency"* (Charles Dickens). *"His Majesty gave many marks of his great lenity, often . . . endeavoring to extenuate your crimes"* (Jonathan Swift). *Clemency* is mercy shown especially by one in a position of judicial authority or power: *The judge believed in clemency. Charity* is goodwill and benevolence, especially in judging others: *"But how shall we expect charity towards others, when we are uncharitable to ourselves?"* (Thomas Browne).
mercy killing *n.* Euthanasia.
mercy seat *n.* **1.** The golden covering of the ark of the covenant, regarded as the resting place of God. **2.** The throne of God.
mere¹ (mîr) *adj.* Superl. **mer•est. 1.** Being nothing more than what is specified. **2.** Considered apart from anything else. **3.** Small; slight. **4.** *Obsolete.* Pure; unadulterated. [ME, absolute, pure < OFr. *mier*, pure < Lat. *merus.*]
mere² (mîr) *n.* A small lake, pond, or marsh. [ME < OE. See **mori-*.**]
mere³ (mîr) *n. Archaic.* A boundary. [ME < OE *mǣre.*]
–mere or **–mer** *suff.* Part; segment: *blastomere.* [Fr. < Gk. *meros*, part. See **(s)mer-²*.**]
Mer•e•dith (mĕr′ĭ-dĭth), **George.** 1828–1909. British writer whose works include *The Ordeal of Richard Feverel* (1859).
Meredith, James Howard. b. 1933. Amer. civil rights advocate who was the first Black student to register (1963) at the traditionally segregated University of Mississippi.
mere•ly (mîr′lē) *adv.* And nothing else or more; only.
me•ren•gue (mə-rĕng′gā) *n.* **1.** A ballroom dance of Dominican and Haitian folk origin, characterized by a sliding step.

2. Music for this dance, in rapid 2/4 time. [Am.Sp. < Sp., meringue < Fr. *méringue*.]

mer•e•tri•cious (mĕr′ĭ-trĭsh′əs) *adj.* **1.a.** Attracting attention in a vulgar manner. **b.** Plausible but false or insincere; specious. **2.** Of or relating to prostitutes or prostitution. [Lat. *meretrīcius*, of prostitutes < *meretrīx, meretrīc-*, prostitute < *merēre*, to earn money. See **(s)mer-[2]***.] — **mer′e•tri′cious•ly** *adv.* — **mer′e•tri′cious•ness** *n.*

mer•gan•ser (mər-găn′sər) *n.* Any of various fish-eating diving ducks of the genus *Mergus* or related genera, having a slim hooked bill. [NLat. : Lat. *mergus*, diver (< *mergere*, to plunge) + Lat. *ānser*, goose; see **ghans-***.]

merge (mûrj) *v.* **merged, merg•ing, merg•es.** — *tr.* **1.** To cause to be absorbed, esp. in gradual stages. **2.** To combine or unite: *merging two sets of data.* — *intr.* **1.** To blend together, esp. in gradual stages. **2.** To become combined or united. [Lat. *mergere*, to plunge.] — **mer′gence** *n.*

Mer•gen•thal•er (mûr′gən-thô′lər, mĕr′gən-tä′-), **Ottmar.** 1854–99. German-born Amer. inventor of the Linotype typesetting machine (patented 1884).

merg•er (mûr′jər) *n.* **1.** The act or an instance of merging; union. **2.** The union of two or more commercial interests or corporations. **3.** *Law.* The absorption of a lesser estate, liability, right, action, or offense into a greater one.

Mé•ri•da (mĕr′ĭ-də, mĕ′rē-*th*ä). A city of SE Mexico on the Yucatán Peninsula; founded 1542. Pop. 59,479.

Mer•i•den (mĕr′ĭ-dən). A city of S-central CT NNE of New Haven; settled in 1661. Pop. 59,479.

me•rid•i•an (mə-rĭd′ē-ən) *n.* **1.a.** An imaginary great circle on the earth's surface passing through the North and South geographic poles. **b.** Either half of such a great circle from pole to pole. **2.** *Astron.* A great circle passing through the two poles of the celestial sphere and the zenith of an observer. **3.** *Math.* **a.** A curve on a surface of revolution, formed by the intersection of the surface with a plane containing the axis of revolution. **b.** A plane section of a surface of revolution containing the axis of revolution. **4.** Any of the longitudinal lines or pathways on the body along which the acupuncture points are distributed. **5.** *Archaic.* **a.** The highest point in the sky reached by the sun or another celestial body; a zenith. **b.** Noon. **6.** The highest point or stage of development; peak. **7.** *Upper Midwest.* See **median strip.** See Regional Note at **neutral ground.** — *adj.* **1.** Of or relating to a meridian; meridional. **2.** Of or at midday: *the meridian hour.* **3.** Of, relating to, or constituting the highest point, as of development or power. [ME < OFr., midday < Lat. *merīdiānus*, of midday < *merīdiēs*, midday < *merīdiē*, at midday < OLat. **mediei diē* : **mediei*, dative (locative) of *medius*, middle; see **medhyo-*** + *diē*, dative of *diēs*, day; see **deiw-***.]

Me•rid•i•an (mə-rĭd′ē-ən). A city of E MS near the AL border E of Jackson. Pop. 41,036.

me•rid•i•o•nal (mə-rĭd′ē-ə-nəl) *adj.* **1.** Of or relating to meridians or a meridian. **2.** Located in the south; southern. **3.** Of or characteristic of southern areas or people. — *n.* An inhabitant of a southern region, esp. the south of France. [ME, pertaining to the sun's position at noon < OFr. *meridionel*, southern < LLat. *merīdiōnālis* < Lat. *merīdiānus*, of midday, southern. See MERIDIAN.]

Mé•ri•mée (mĕr′ə-mā′, mā-rē-mā′), **Prosper.** 1803–70. French writer of romantic works such as *Carmen* (1846).

me•ringue (mə-răng′) *n.* **1.** A topping for pastry or pies made of stiffly beaten baked egg whites and sugar. **2.** A small pastry shell or cake made of meringue. [Fr. *méringue*.]

me•ri•no (mə-rē′nō) *n., pl.* **-nos. 1.a.** Any of a breed of sheep, originally from Spain, having long fine wool. **b.** The wool of this sheep. **2.** A soft lightweight fabric made originally of merino wool but now of any fine wool. **3.a.** A fine wool and cotton yarn used esp. for knitting underwear and hosiery. **b.** A knitted fabric made from this yarn. [Sp., perh. < Berber *Benī Merīn*, name of the tribe that developed the breed, or < Sp. *merino*, local magistrate (< Lat. *māiōrīnus*, larger < *māior*; see MAJOR).] — **me•ri′no** *adj.*

mer•i•stem (mĕr′ĭ-stĕm′) *n.* The undifferentiated plant tissue from which new cells are formed, as that at the tip of a stem or root. [Gk. *meristos*, divided (< *merizein*, to divide < *meris*, division; see **(s)mer-[2]***) + *-em* (as in *xylem* and *phloem*).] — **mer′i•ste•mat′ic** (-stə-măt′ĭk) *adj.*

me•ris•tic (mə-rĭs′tĭk) *adj. Biol.* **1.** Having or composed of segments; segmented. **2.** Relating to a change in the number or placement of body parts or segments: *meristic variation.* [< Gk. *meristos*, divided. See MERISTEM.] — **me•ris′ti•cal•ly** *adv.*

mer•it (mĕr′ĭt) *n.* **1.a.** Superior quality or worth; excellence. **b.** A quality deserving praise or approval; virtue. **2.** Demonstrated ability or achievement. **3.** An aspect of character or behavior deserving approval or disapproval. Often used in the plural. **4.** *Theol.* Spiritual credit granted for good works. **5. merits. a.** *Law.* A party's strict legal rights, excluding jurisdictional, personal, or technical aspects. **b.** The factual content of a matter, apart from emotional, contextual, or formal considerations. — *v.* **-it•ed, -it•ing, -its.** — *tr.* To earn; deserve. See Syns at **earn[1]**. — *intr.* To be worthy or deserving. [ME < OFr. *merite*, reward or punishment < Lat. *meritum* < neut. p.part. of *merēre*, to deserve. See **(s)mer-[2]***.]

mer•i•toc•ra•cy (mĕr′ĭ-tŏk′rə-sē) *n., pl.* **-cies. 1.** A system in which advancement is based on ability or achievement. **2.a.** A group of leaders or officeholders selected for individual ability or achievement. **b.** Leadership by such a group. — **mer′it•o•crat′** (-ĭ-tə-krăt′) *n.* — **mer′it•o•crat′ic** *adj.*

mer•i•to•ri•ous (mĕr′ĭ-tôr′ē-əs, -tōr′-) *adj.* Deserving reward or praise; having merit. [ME < Lat. *meritōrius*, earning money < *meritus*, p.part. of *merēre*, to earn. See MERIT.] — **mer′i•to′ri•ous•ly** *adv.* — **mer′i•to′ri•ous•ness** *n.*

merit system *n.* The system of appointing and promoting civil service personnel for merit rather than politically.

merle also **merl** (mûrl) *n.* See **blackbird** 2. [ME < OFr. < Lat. *merulus, merula.*]

mer•lin (mûr′lĭn) *n.* A small falcon *(Falco columbarius)* of northern regions having dark plumage and a black-striped tail. [ME < AN *merilun* < OFr. *esmerillon*, dim. of *esmeril*, of Gmc. orig.]

Mer•lin (mûr′lĭn) *n.* In Arthurian legend, a magician and prophet who served as counselor to King Arthur.

Mer•lo (mĕr′lō). A city of E Argentina, a suburb of Buenos Aires. Pop. 293,059.

mer•lon (mûr′lən) *n.* A solid portion of a crenelated wall between two open spaces. [Fr. < Ital. *merlone*, aug. of *merlo*, battlement, perh. < Med.Lat. *merulus* < Lat., merle (< their imagined similarity to blackbirds sitting on a wall).]

mer•lot or **Mer•lot** (mər-lō′, mĕr-) *n.* A dry red wine made from a grape originating in southern France and Italy. [Fr., dim. of *merle*, blackbird < OFr. See MERLE.]

mer•maid (mûr′măd′) *n.* A legendary sea creature having the head and upper body of a woman and the tail of a fish. [ME : *mere*, sea, lake; see MERE[2] + *maid*, maid; see MAID.]

mer•man (mûr′măn′, -mən) *n.* A legendary sea creature having the head and upper body of a man and the tail of a fish.

mero– or **mer–** *pref.* **1.** Part; segment: *merozoite.* **2.** Partial; partially: *meropia.* [< Gk. *meros*, part. See **(s)mer-[2]***.]

mer•o•blas•tic (mĕr′ə-blăs′tĭk) *adj. Embryol.* Undergoing partial cleavage. Used of a fertilized egg.

mer•o•crine (mĕr′ə-krĭn, -krīn′, -krēn′) *adj.* Of or relating to a gland whose secretory cells remain undamaged during secretion. [MERO– + Gk. *krinein*, to separate; see ENDOCRINE.]

Mer•o•ë also **Mer•o•we** (mĕr′ō-ē′). An ancient city of N Sudan on the Nile R. N of Khartoum; cap. of a Cush dynasty from 530 B.C. to A.D. 350.

mer•o•my•o•sin (mĕr′ə-mī′ə-sĭn) *n.* Either of two protein subunits of a myosin molecule, obtained esp. through the digestive action of trypsin.

me•ro•pi•a (mə-rō′pē-ə) *n.* Partial blindness. — **me•ro′pic** (-rō′pĭk, -rŏp′ĭk) *adj.*

mer•o•plank•ton (mĕr′ə-plăngk′tən) *n.* Any of various organisms that spend part of their life cycle, usu. the larval or egg stages, as plankton.

–merous *suff.* Having a specified kind or number of parts: *isomerous.* [< NLat. *-merus* < Gk. *-meros* < *meros*, part. See **(s)mer-[2]***.]

Mer•o•vin•gi•an (mĕr′ə-vĭn′jē-ən, -jən). A Frankish ruling dynasty (c. A.D. 450–751). — **Mer′o•vin′gi•an** *adj.*

mer•o•zo•ite (mĕr′ə-zō′īt) *n.* A protozoan cell that arises from the schizogony of a parent sporozoan and may enter either the asexual or sexual phase of the life cycle.

Mer•rill•ville (mĕr′əl-vĭl′). A town of NW IN, a suburb of Gary. Pop. 27,257.

Mer•ri•mack River (mĕr′ə-măk′). A river rising in S-central NH and flowing c. 177 km (110 mi) to the Atlantic Ocean.

mer•ri•ment (mĕr′ĭ-mənt) *n.* High-spirited fun and enjoyment; hilarity.

Mer•ritt Island (mĕr′ĭt). A city of E-central FL on **Merritt Island** between the mainland and Cape Canaveral. Pop. 32,886.

mer•ry (mĕr′ē) *adj.* **-ri•er, -ri•est. 1.** Full of high-spirited gaiety; jolly. **2.** Marked by or offering fun and gaiety; festive. **3.** Brisk: *a merry pace.* **4.** *Archaic.* Delightful; entertaining. [ME *merri* < OE *mirige*, pleasant. See **mregh-u-***.] — **mer′ri•ly** *adv.* — **mer′ri•ness** *n.*

mer•ry-an•drew (mĕr′ē-ăn′drōō) *n.* A clown; a buffoon. [MERRY + the name *Andrew*.]

mer•ry-bells (mĕr′ē-bĕlz′) *pl.n. (used with a sing. or pl. v.)* See **bellwort.**

mer•ry-go-round (mĕr′ē-gō-round′) *n.* **1.** A revolving circular platform with seats, ridden for amusement. **2.** A toy consisting of a small circular platform that revolves when pushed or pedaled. **3.** A busy round; a whirl.

mer•ry•mak•ing (mĕr′ē-mā′kĭng) *n.* **1.** Participation in festive activities. **2.a.** A festivity; a revelry. **b.** Festive activities. — **mer′ry•mak′er** *n.*

mer•ry•thought (mĕr′ē-thôt′) *n. Chiefly British.* A wishbone.

Mer•sey (mûr′zē). A river of NW England flowing c. 113 km (70 mi) to the Irish Sea at Liverpool.

Mer•sin (mĕr-sēn′). A city of S Turkey on the Mediterranean Sea WSW of Adana. Pop. 216,308.

Mer•thi•o•late (mər-thī′ə-lāt′). A trademark used for thimerosal.

meridian
Terrestrial meridians

merlon

ă pat	oi boy
ā pay	ou out
âr care	ŏŏ took
ä father	ōō boot
ĕ pet	ŭ cut
ē be	ûr urge
ĭ pit	th thin
ī pie	*th* this
îr pier	hw which
ŏ pot	zh vision
ō toe	ə about, item
ô paw	

Stress marks:
′ (primary);
′ (secondary), as in
dictionary (dĭk′shə-nĕr′ē)

ductors of heat and electricity, and can be melted or fused, hammered into thin sheets, or drawn into wires. **2.** An alloy of two or more metallic elements. **3.** An object made of metal. **4.** Basic character; mettle. **5.** Broken stones used for road surfaces or railroad beds. **6.** Molten glass, esp. when used in glassmaking. **7.** Molten cast iron. **8.** *Print.* Type made of metal. — *tr.v.* **-aled, -al•ing, -als** also **-alled, -al•ling, -als.** To cover or surface with broken stones. [ME < OFr. < Lat. *metallum* < Gk. *metallon,* mine, mineral, metal.]

metal. *abbr.* **1.** Metallurgic. **2.** Metallurgy.

met•a•lin•guis•tics (mĕt′ə-lĭng-gwĭs′tĭks) *n.* *(used with a sing. v.)* The study of the interrelationship between language and other cultural behavior.

metall. *abbr.* **1.** Metallurgic. **2.** Metallurgy.

me•tal•lic (mə-tăl′ĭk) *adj.* **1.** Of, relating to, or having the characteristics of a metal. **2.** Containing a metal. **3.** Having a quality suggesting or associated with metal, esp.: **a.** Lustrous; sparkling: *metallic colors.* **b.** Sharp-tasting. **4.** Harshly resonant. — *n.* **1.** A yarn or fiber made of or containing metal. **2.** A fabric, typically shiny or iridescent, made of such yarn or fiber. — **me•tal′li•cal•ly** *adv.*

metallic bond *n.* The chemical bond characteristic of metals, in which mobile valence electrons are shared among atoms in a usu. stable crystalline structure.

met•al•lif•er•ous (mĕt′l-ĭf′ər-əs) *adj.* Containing metal. Used of a mineral deposit or an ore. [< Lat. *metallifer* : *metallum,* metal; see METAL + *-fer,* -fer.]

met•al•line (mĕt′l-ĭn, -īn′) *adj.* **1.** Of, resembling, or having the properties of a metal. **2.** Containing metal ions.

metallo– or **metall–** or **metalli–** *pref.* Metal: *metallography.* [< Lat. *metallum,* metal. See METAL.]

met•al•log•ra•phy (mĕt′l-ŏg′rə-fē) *n.* The study of the structure of metals and alloys, esp. by optical and electron microscopy and x-ray diffraction. — **met′al•log′ra•pher** *n.* — **me•tal′lo•graph′ic** (mə-tăl′ə-grăf′ĭk) *adj.*

met•al•loid (mĕt′l-oid′) *n.* **1.** A nonmetallic element, such as arsenic, that has some of the chemical properties of a metal. **2.** A nonmetallic element, such as carbon, that can form an alloy with metals. — *adj.* (mĕt′l-oid′l) also **met•al•loi•dal.** **1.** Relating to or having the properties of a metalloid. **2.** Having the appearance of a metal.

met•al•lur•gy (mĕt′l-ûr′jē) *n.* The science and technology that studies metals, esp. the processes used in extracting metals from their ores. [NLat. *metallurgia* < Gk. *metallourgos,* miner, worker in metals : *metallon,* a mine, metal + *-ourgos,* -worker (< *ergon,* work; see **werg-***).] — **met′al•lur′gic, met′al•lur′gi•cal** *adj.* — **met′al•lur′gi•cal•ly** *adv.* — **met′al•lur′gist** *n.*

met•al•mark (mĕt′l-märk′) *n.* Any of several small, darkly colored butterflies of the family Riodinidae of mainly tropical regions, having iridescent lines or spots on the wings.

met•al•work (mĕt′l-wûrk′) *n.* Work done in metal.

met•al•work•ing (mĕt′l-wûr′kĭng) *n.* The process or art of shaping things out of metal. — **met′al•work′er** *n.*

met•a•math•e•mat•ics (mĕt′ə-măth′ə-măt′ĭks) *n.* *(used with a sing. v.)* The branch of mathematics that deals with the logic and consistency of mathematical proofs, formulas, and equations. — **met′a•math′e•mat′i•cal** *adj.*

met•a•mere (mĕt′ə-mîr′) *n.* *Zool.* Any of the homologous segments, lying in a longitudinal series, that compose the body of certain animals, such as earthworms. — **met′a•mer′ic** (-mĕr′ĭk, -mîr′-) *adj.* — **met′a•mer′i•cal•ly** *adv.*

me•tam•er•ism (mə-tăm′ə-rĭz′əm) *n.* The condition of having the body divided into metameres, exhibited in most animals only in the early embryonic stages of development.

met•a•mor•phic (mĕt′ə-môr′fĭk) *adj.* **1.** Also **met•a•mor•phous** (-fəs). Of, relating to, or characterized by metamorphosis. **2.** *Geol.* Changed in structure or composition as a result of metamorphism. Used of rock.

met•a•mor•phism (mĕt′ə-môr′fĭz′əm) *n.* *Geol.* The process by which rocks are altered in composition, texture, or internal structure by extreme heat, pressure, and the introduction of new chemical substances. [METAMORPH(IC) + –ISM.]

met•a•mor•phose (mĕt′ə-môr′fōz′, -fōs′) *v.* **-phosed, -phos•ing, -phos•es.** — *tr.* **1.** To change into a wholly different form or appearance; transform. **2.** To subject to metamorphosis or metamorphism. — *intr.* To be changed or transformed by or as if by metamorphosis or metamorphism. [Fr. *métamorphoser* < OFr. < *metamorphose,* metamorphosis < Lat. *metamorphōsis.* See METAMORPHOSIS.]

met•a•mor•pho•sis (mĕt′ə-môr′fə-sĭs) *n., pl.* **-ses** (-sēz′). **1.** A transformation, as by magic or sorcery. **2.** A marked change in appearance, character, condition, or function. **3.** *Biol.* A change in the form and often habits of an animal during normal development after the embryonic stage. **4.** *Pathol.* A usu. degenerative change in the structure of a particular body tissue. [Lat. *metamorphōsis* < Gk. < *metamorphoun,* to transform : *meta-,* meta- + *morphē,* form.]

met•a•neph•ros (mĕt′ə-nĕf′rōs′) *n.* The third and final excretory organ that develops in a vertebrate embryo, replacing the mesonephros as the excretory organ and developing into the adult kidney. [META– + Gk. *nephros,* kidney.]

metamorphosis
Of a monarch butterfly
Danaus plexippus

metaph. *abbr.* **1.** Metaphor. **2.** Metaphoric. **3.** Metaphysics.

met•a•phase (mĕt′ə-fāz′) *n.* The stage of mitosis and meiosis, following prophase and preceding anaphase, during which the chromosomes are aligned along the metaphase plate.

metaphase plate *n.* An imaginary plane perpendicular to the spindle fibers of a dividing cell, along which chromosomes align during metaphase.

met•a•phor (mĕt′ə-fôr′, -fər) *n.* **1.** A figure of speech in which a word or phrase that designates one thing is applied to another in an implicit comparison, as in *"All the world's a stage"* (Shakespeare). **2.** One thing conceived as representing another; a symbol. [ME *methaphor* < OFr. *metaphore* < Lat. *metaphora* < Gk., transference, metaphor < *metapherein,* to transfer : *meta-,* meta- + *pherein,* to carry; see **bher-**[1]*.] — **met′a•phor′ic** (-fôr′ĭk, -fŏr′-), **met′a•phor′i•cal** *adj.* — **met′a•phor′i•cal•ly** *adv.*

met•a•phos•phate (mĕt′ə-fŏs′fāt′) *n.* A salt or an ester of metaphosphoric acid.

met•a•phos•phor•ic acid (mĕt′ə-fŏs-fôr′ĭk, -fŏr′-) *n.* An inorganic compound, HPO_3, used as a dehydrating agent.

met•a•phrase (mĕt′ə-frāz′) *n.* A word-for-word translation. — *tr.v.* **-phrased, -phras•ing, -phras•es. 1.** To translate, esp. literally. **2.** To alter the wording of (a text). [NLat. *metaphrasis* < Gk., translation, paraphrase < *metaphrazein,* to translate : *meta-,* meta- + *phrazein,* to tell, show; see **g^whren-***.] — **met′a•phras′tic** (-frăs′tĭk) *adj.*

met•a•phrast (mĕt′ə-frăst′) *n.* One who changes the form of a text, as by recasting prose in verse. [Med.Gk. *metaphrastēs* < Gk. *metaphrazein,* to translate. See METAPHRASE.]

met•a•phys•ic (mĕt′ə-fĭz′ĭk) *n.* **1.a.** Metaphysics. **b.** A system of metaphysics. **2.** An underlying philosophical or theoretical principle: *luck, the metaphysic of the gambler.* [ME *methaphisik, metaphisik.* See METAPHYSICS.]

met•a•phys•i•cal (mĕt′ə-fĭz′ĭ-kəl) *adj.* **1.** Of or relating to metaphysics. **2.** Based on speculative or abstract reasoning. **3.** Highly abstract or theoretical; abstruse. **4.a.** Immaterial; incorporeal. **b.** Supernatural. **5.** Often **Metaphysical.** Of or relating to the poetry of certain 17th-century English poets whose verse is marked by conceits. [ME *metaphisicalle* < Med.Lat. *metaphysicālis* < *metaphysica,* metaphysics. See METAPHYSICS.] — **met′a•phys′i•cal•ly** *adv.*

met•a•phy•si•cian (mĕt′ə-fĭ-zĭsh′ən) *n.* One who specializes or is skilled in metaphysics.

met•a•phys•ics (mĕt′ə-fĭz′ĭks) *n.* **1.** *(used with a sing. v.)* *Philos.* The branch of philosophy that addresses questions about the ultimate composition of reality, including the relationship between mind and matter, substance and attribute, fact and value. **2.** *(used with a pl. v.)* The theoretical or first principles of a particular discipline. **3.** *(used with a sing. v.)* A priori speculation upon questions that are unanswerable to scientific observation, analysis, or experiment. **4.** *(used with a sing. v.)* Excessively subtle or recondite reasoning. [Pl. of ME *methaphisik* < Med.Lat. *metaphysica* < Med.Gk. *(ta) metaphusika* < Gk. *(Ta) meta (ta) phusika,* (the things) after the physics, the title of Aristotle's treatise on first principles (following his work on physics) : *meta,* after; see META– + *phusika,* physics; see PHYSICS.]

met•a•pla•sia (mĕt′ə-plā′zhə, -zhē-ə) *n.* **1.** Normal transformation of tissue from one type to another. **2.** Transformation of cells from a normal to an abnormal state. — **met′a•plas′tic** (-plăs′tĭk) *adj.*

met•a•plasm[1] (mĕt′ə-plăz′əm) *n.* *Gram.* Alteration of a word by the addition, omission, or transposition of sounds or syllables or the letters that represent them. [Ult. < Gk. *metaplasmos,* remodeling < *metaplassein,* to remold : *meta-,* meta- + *plassein,* to mold; see **pelə-**[2]*.] — **met′a•plas′tic** (-plăs′tĭk), **met′a•plas′mic** (-plăz′mĭk) *adj.*

met•a•plasm[2] (mĕt′ə-plăz′əm) *n.* *Biol.* Nonliving material in the protoplasm of a cell, such as pigment granules or nutritive substances. — **met′a•plas′mic** (-plăz′mĭk) *adj.*

Met•a•pon•tum (mĕt′ə-pŏn′təm). An ancient city of SE Italy on the Gulf of Taranto; settled by Greeks c. 700 B.C.

met•a•pro•tein (mĕt′ə-prō′tēn′, -prō′tē-ĭn) *n.* Any of various protein derivatives that result from the action of an acid or alkali and are soluble in weak acids or alkalis.

met•a•psy•chol•o•gy (mĕt′ə-sī-kŏl′ə-jē) *n.* Philosophical inquiry supplementing the empirical science of psychology.

met•a•so•ma•tism (mĕt′ə-sō′mə-tĭz′əm) also **met•a•so•ma•to•sis** (-sō′mə-tō′sĭs) *n.* The process by which the chemical composition of a rock is changed by interaction with fluids; replacement of one mineral by another without melting. — **met′a•so•mat′ic** (-măt′ĭk) *adj.*

met•a•sta•ble (mĕt′ə-stā′bəl) *adj.* Of, relating to, or being a relatively stable but transient state of a chemical or physical system, as of an excited atom. — **met′a•sta•bil′i•ty** (-stə-bĭl′ĭ-tē) *n.*

me•tas•ta•sis (mə-tăs′tə-sĭs) *n., pl.* **-ses** (-sēz′). **1.** *Pathol.* Transmission of pathogenic microorganisms or cancerous cells from an original site to one or more sites elsewhere in the body. **2.** A secondary cancerous growth formed by transmission of cancerous cells from a primary growth located elsewhere in the body. [Gk. < *methistanai,* to change : *meta-,*

meta- + *histanai*, to cause to stand, place; see **stā-***.] —**met′a·stat′ic** (mĕt′ə-stăt′ĭk) *adj.* —**met′a·stat′i·cal·ly** *adv.*

me·tas·ta·size (mə-tăs′tə-sīz′) *intr.v.* **-sized, -siz·ing, -siz·es.** To be transmitted or transferred by or as if by metastasis.

met·a·tar·sal (mĕt′ə-tär′səl) *adj.* Of or relating to the metatarsus. —*n.* Any of the bones of the metatarsus.

met·a·tar·sus (mĕt′ə-tär′səs) *n., pl.* **-si** (-sī, -sē). **1.** The middle part of the human foot that forms the instep and includes the five bones between the toes and the ankle. **2.** The corresponding part of the quadruped hind foot or the bird foot.

me·ta·te (mə-tä′tē, mĕ-tä′tĕ) *n.* A stone block with a shallow concave surface, used with a mano for grinding corn or other grains. [Am.Sp. < Nahuatl *metlatl.*]

me·tath·e·sis (mĭ-tăth′ĭ-sĭs) *n., pl.* **-ses** (-sēz′). **1.** *Ling.* Transposition within a word of letters, sounds, or syllables, as in the change from Old English *brid* to modern English *bird.* **2.** *Chem.* Double decomposition. [LLat. < Gk. < *metatithenai*, to transpose : *meta-*, meta- + *tithenai*, to place; see **dhē-***.] —**met′a·thet′ic** (mĕt′ə-thĕt′ĭk), **met′a·thet′i·cal** *adj.* —**met′a·thet′i·cal·ly** *adv.*

me·tath·e·size (mĭ-tăth′ĭ-sīz′) *tr. & intr.v.* **-sized, -siz·ing, -siz·es.** To subject to or undergo metathesis.

met·a·tho·rax (mĕt′ə-thôr′ăks′, -thōr′-) *n., pl.* **-tho·rax·es** or **-tho·ra·ces** (-thôr′ə-sēz′, -thōr′-). The hindmost of the three divisions of the thorax of an insect, bearing the third pair of legs and the second pair of wings. —**met′a·tho·rac′ic** (-thô-răs′ĭk, -thō-) *adj.*

met·a·zo·an (mĕt′ə-zō′ən) *n.* A multicellular animal of the subkingdom Metazoa. [< NLat. *Metazoa*, a subdivision of the animal kingdom : META- + *-zoa*, pl. of *-zoon*, animal; see -ZOON.] —**met′a·zo′al, met′a·zo′an, met′a·zo′ic** *adj.*

Metch·ni·koff also **Metch·ni·kov** (mĕch′nĭ-kôf′, myĕch′nĭ-kəf), **Elie.** 1845–1916. Russian zoologist who shared a 1908 Nobel Prize.

mete[1] (mēt) *tr.v.* **met·ed, met·ing, metes. 1.** To distribute by or as if by measure; allot: *mete out punishment.* **2.** *Archaic.* To measure. [ME *meten* < OE *metan.* See **med-***.]

mete[2] (mēt) *n.* A boundary line; a limit: *metes and bounds.* [ME < AN < Lat. *mēta*, turning post, boundary.]

me·tem·psy·cho·sis (mə-tĕm′sĭ-kō′sĭs, mĕt′əm-sī-) *n., pl.* **-ses** (-sēz). Reincarnation. [LLat. *metempsȳchōsis* < Gk. *metempsukhōsis* < *metempsukhousthai*, to transmigrate : *meta-*, meta- + *empsukhos*, animate (*en*, in; see EN-[2] + *psukhē*, soul; see **bhes-***).]

met·en·ceph·a·lon (mĕt′ĕn-sĕf′ə-lŏn′) *n., pl.* **-la** (-lə). The anterior part of the embryonic hindbrain, giving rise to the cerebellum and pons. —**met′en·ce·phal′ic** (-sə-făl′ĭk) *adj.*

me·te·or (mē′tē-ər, -ôr′) *n.* A bright trail or streak that appears in the sky when a meteoroid is heated to incandescence by friction with the earth's atmosphere. [ME *metheour*, atmospheric phenomenon < OFr. *meteore* < Med.Lat. *meteōrum* < Gk. *meteōron*, astronomical phenomenon < neut. of *meteōros*, high in the air : *meta-*, meta- + *-aoros*, lifted; akin to *aeirein*, to lift up; see AORTA.]

meteor. *abbr.* **1.** Meteorological. **2.** Meteorology.

me·te·or·ic (mē′tē-ôr′ĭk, -ŏr′-) *adj.* **1.** Of, relating to, or formed by a meteoroid. **2.** Of or relating to the earth's atmosphere. **3.** Similar to a meteor in speed, brilliance, or brevity: *a meteoric rise to fame.* —**me′te·or′i·cal·ly** *adv.*

me·te·or·ite (mē′tē-ə-rīt′) *n.* A stony or metallic mass of matter that has fallen to the earth's surface from outer space. —**me′te·or·it′ic** (-ə-rĭt′ĭk), **me′te·or·it′i·cal** *adj.*

me·te·or·oid (mē′tē-ə-roid′) *n.* A solid body, moving in space, that is smaller than an asteroid and at least as large as a speck of dust.

me·te·or·ol·o·gist (mē′tē-ə-rŏl′ə-jĭst) *n.* **1.** One who studies meteorology. **2.** One who reports and forecasts weather conditions, as on television.

me·te·or·ol·o·gy (mē′tē-ə-rŏl′ə-jē) *n.* The science that deals with the phenomena of the atmosphere, esp. weather. [Ult. < Gk. *meteōrologia*, discussion of astronomical phenomena : *meteōron*, astronomical phenomenon; see METEOR + *-logia*, -logy.] —**me′te·or·o·log′i·cal** (-ər-ə-lŏj′ĭ-kəl), **me′te·or·o·log′ic** *adj.* —**me′te·or·o·log′i·cal·ly** *adv.*

meteor shower *n.* A large number of meteors that appear together and seem to come from the same area in the sky.

me·ter[1] (mē′tər) *n.* **1.a.** The measured arrangement of words in poetry, as by accentual rhythm. **b.** A particular arrangement of words in poetry, such as iambic pentameter, determined by the kind and number of metrical units in a line. **c.** The rhythmic pattern of a stanza, determined by the kind and number of lines. **2.** *Mus.* **a.** Division into measures or bars. **b.** A specific rhythm determined by the number of beats and the time value assigned to each note in a measure. [ME < OE *meter* and < OFr. *metre*, both < Lat. *metrum* < Gk. *metron*, measure, poetic meter. See **mē-**[2]*.]

me·ter[2] (mē′tər) *n.* The International System unit of length, equal to the distance traveled by light in a vacuum in 1/299,792,458 of a second and approx. equal to 39.37 inches. See table at **measurement.** [Fr. *mètre* < Gk. *metron*, measure. See **mē-**[2]*.]

me·ter[3] (mē′tər) *n.* **1.** Any of various devices designed to measure time, distance, speed, or intensity or indicate and record or regulate the amount or volume, as of an electric current. **2.** A postage meter. **3.** A parking meter. —*tr.v.* **-tered, -ter·ing, -ters. 1.** To measure with a meter. **2.** To supply in a measured or regulated amount. **3.** To imprint with revenue stamps by means of a postage meter or similar device. **4.** To provide with a parking meter or parking meters. [< -METER.]

-meter *suff.* Measuring device: *anemometer.* [Fr. *-mètre* < Gk. *metron*, measure. See **mē-**[2]*.]

me·ter-kil·o·gram-sec·ond (mē′tər-kĭl′ə-grăm-sĕk′ənd) *adj.* Of, relating to, or being a system of units for mechanics, using the meter, the kilogram, and the second as basic units of length, mass, and time.

meter maid *n.* A woman member of a police traffic control department who issues tickets for parking violations.

me·tes·trus (mĕ-tĕs′trəs) *n.* The period of sexual inactivity that follows estrus. —**me·tes′trous** (-trəs) *adj.*

meth (mĕth) *n. Slang.* Methamphetamine.

meth- *pref.* Methyl: *methane.* [< METHYL.]

meth·ac·ry·late (mĕth-ăk′rə-lāt′) *n.* **1.** An ester of methacrylic acid, CH_2:C(CH_3)COOR, R being an organic radical. **2.** A resin derived from methacrylic acid.

meth·a·cryl·ic acid (mĕth′ə-krĭl′ĭk) *n.* A colorless liquid, CH_2:C(CH_3)COOH, used in the manufacture of resins and plastics.

meth·a·done (mĕth′ə-dōn′) *n.* A potent synthetic narcotic drug, $C_{21}H_{27}NO$, that is less addictive than morphine or heroin and is used as a substitute for these drugs in addiction treatment programs. [Short for *methadone hydrochloride* : (DI)METH(YL) + A(MINO) + D(IPHENYL) + *(heptan)one*, a ketone.]

meth·am·phet·a·mine (mĕth′ăm-fĕt′ə-mēn′, -mĭn) *n.* An amine derivative of amphetamine, $C_{10}H_{15}N$, used in the form of its crystalline hydrochloride as a stimulant.

meth·ane (mĕth′ān′) *n.* An odorless colorless flammable gas, CH_4, the major constituent of natural gas, that is used as a fuel and as a source of hydrogen and organic compounds.

methane series *n. Chem.* See **alkane series.**

meth·a·nol (mĕth′ə-nôl′, -nōl′, -nŏl′) *n.* A colorless toxic flammable liquid, CH_3OH, used as an antifreeze, a solvent, a fuel, and a denaturant for ethyl alcohol. [METHAN(E) + -OL[1].]

meth·a·qua·lone (mĕth′ə-kwā′lōn′) *n.* A potentially habit-forming drug, $C_{16}H_{14}N_2O$, used as a sedative and hypnotic. [Blend of METH- and *quinazolinon*, a derivative of quinoline.]

Meth·e·drine (mĕth′ĭ-drēn′, -drĭn). A trademark used for methamphetamine.

me·theg·lin (mə-thĕg′lĭn) *n.* A beverage typically made of fermented honey and water; mead. [Welsh *meddyglyn* : *meddyg*, medicinal (< Lat. *medicus* < *medērī*, to heal; see **med-***) + *llyn*, liquor.]

met·he·mo·glo·bin (mĕt-hē′mə-glō′bĭn) *n.* A brownish-red crystalline organic compound formed in the blood when hemoglobin is oxidated. [MET(A)- + HEMOGLOBIN.]

me·the·na·mine (mə-thē′nə-mēn′, -mĭn) *n.* An organic compound, $(CH_2)_6N_4$, used as a urinary tract antiseptic and in rubber vulcanizing. [METH- + -EN(E) + AMINE.]

meth·i·cil·lin (mĕth′ĭ-sĭl′ĭn) *n.* A synthetic antibiotic, $C_{17}H_{19}N_2O_6NaS$, related to penicillin. [METH- + (PEN)ICILLIN.]

me·thinks (mĭ-thĭngks′) *intr.v.* P.t. **me·thought** (-thôt′). *Archaic.* It seems to me. [ME *me thinkes* < OE *mē thyncth* : *mē*, to me; see ME + *thyncth*, it seems; see **tong-***.]

me·thi·o·nine (mə-thī′ə-nēn′) *n.* A sulfur-containing essential amino acid, $C_5H_{11}NO_2S$, obtained from various proteins or prepared synthetically and used as a dietary supplement and in pharmaceuticals. [ME(TH)- + THION- + -INE[2].]

meth·od (mĕth′əd) *n.* **1.** A means or manner of procedure, esp. a regular and systematic way of accomplishing something. See Usage Note at **methodology. 2.** Orderly arrangement of parts or steps to accomplish an end. **3.** The procedures and techniques characteristic of a particular discipline or field of knowledge: *archaeological method.* **4. Method.** A technique of acting in which the actor recalls emotions and reactions from past experience and uses them in portraying a character. [ME, medical procedure < Lat. *methodus*, method < Gk. *methodos*, pursuit, method : *meta-*, beyond, after; see META- + *hodos*, way, journey.]

Syns: *method, system, routine, manner, mode, fashion, way.* These nouns refer to the plans or procedures followed to accomplish a task or attain a goal. *Method* implies a detailed, logically ordered plan: *"I do not know of a better method for choosing a presidential nominee"* (Harry S. Truman). *System* suggests order, regularity, and coordination of methods: *"Of generalship, of strategic system . . . there was little or none"* (John Morley). A *routine* is a habitual, often tiresome method: *"The common business of the nation . . . is carried on in a constant routine by the clerks of the different offices"* (Tobias Smollett). *Manner* and *fashion* emphasize a personal or distinctive behavior: *She has a precise manner of speaking. The chief of staff gave orders in an arbitrary fashion. Mode* often denotes a manner influenced by or arising from tradition or custom: *a nomadic mode of life. Way* is the least

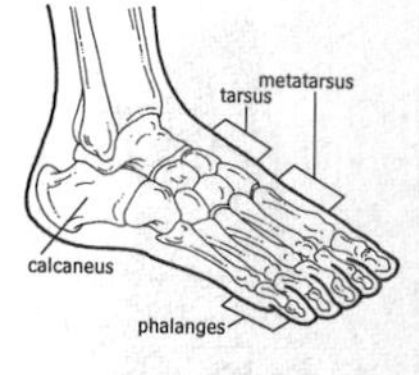

metatarsus

metate
Grinding meal

ă pat	oi boy
ā pay	ou out
âr care	ŏŏ took
ä father	ōō boot
ĕ pet	ŭ cut
ē be	ûr urge
ĭ pit	th thin
ī pie	*th* this
îr pier	hw which
ŏ pot	zh vision
ō toe	ə about, item
ô paw	

Stress marks:
′ (primary);
′ (secondary), as in
dictionary (dĭk′shə-nĕr′ē)

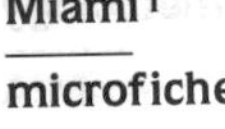

Mi•am•i¹ (mī-ăm′ē, -ăm′ə) *n., pl.* **Miami** or **-is. 1.** A member of a Native American people originally of the Green Bay area of Wisconsin, with present-day populations inhabiting parts of northern Indiana and northeast Oklahoma. **2.** The variety of Illinois spoken by the Miami.

Mi•am•i² (mī-ăm′ē, -ăm′ə). A city of SE FL on Biscayne Bay S of Fort Lauderdale; settled in the 1870's. Pop. 358,548.

Miami Beach. A city of SE FL across from Miami on an island between Biscayne Bay and the Atlantic. Pop. 92,639.

Miami River or **Great Miami River.** A river rising in W OH and flowing c. 257 km (160 mi) to the Ohio R. at the IN border.

Miao (myou′) also **Me•o** (mē-ou′) *n., pl.* **Miao** or **Miaos** also **Meo** or **Me•os.** See **Hmong.**

Miao-Yao (myou′ you′) *n.* A small group of languages of uncertain affinity, including Hmong and Yao, spoken in southern China, northern Laos, Thailand, and Vietnam.

mi•as•ma (mī-ăz′mə, mē-) *n., pl.* **-mas** or **-ma•ta** (-mə-tə). **1.** A noxious atmosphere or influence. **2.a.** A poisonous atmosphere once thought to rise from swamps and putrid matter and cause disease. **b.** A vaporous atmosphere or emanation. [Gk., pollution, stain < *miainein*, to pollute.] **—mi•as′mal, mi′as•mat′ic** (mī′əz-măt′ĭk), **mi•as′mic** *adj.*

Mic *abbr. Bible.* Micah.

mi•ca (mī′kə) *n.* Any of a group of chemically and physically related aluminum silicate minerals, characteristically splitting into flexible sheets used in insulation and electrical equipment. [Lat. *mīca*, grain.] **—mi•ca′ceous** (-kā′shəs) *adj.*

Mi•cah (mī′kə) also **Mi•che•as** (mī-kē′əs) *n. Bible.* **1.** A Hebrew prophet of the 8th cent. B.C. **2.** See table at **Bible.**

Mic•co•su•kee (mĭk′ə-so͞o′kē) *n.* Var. of **Mikasuki.**

mice (mīs) *n.* Pl. of **mouse.**

mi•celle (mī-sĕl′) *n.* **1.** A submicroscopic aggregation of molecules, as a droplet in a colloidal system. **2.** A coherent strand or structure in fibers. **3.** A submicroscopic structural unit of protoplasm, composed of a cluster of molecules. [NLat. *mīcella* < Lat. *mīca*, grain.] **—mi•cel′lar** (-sĕl′ər) *adj.*

Mich. *abbr.* Michigan.

Mi•chael (mī′kəl) *n.* The guardian archangel of the Jews in the Bible.

Mich•ael•mas (mĭk′əl-məs) *n.* A Christian feast observed on September 29 in honor of the archangel Michael. [ME *mychelmesse* < OE *(Sanct) Michaeles mæsse*, (St.) Michael's mass.]

Michaelmas daisy *n.* Any of several North American species of asters that have leafy stems and flower in the fall.

Mi•che•as (mī-kē′əs) *n. Bible.* Var. of **Micah.**

Michelangelo
Portrait by
Daniele de Volterra
(1509–1566)

Mi•chel•an•ge•lo Buo•nar•ro•ti (mī′kəl-ăn′jə-lō′ bwôn′ə-rô′tē, mĭk′əl-, mē′kĕl-än′jĕ-lô). 1475–1564. Italian sculptor, painter, architect, and poet whose works include the marble sculpture *David* (1501), the paintings on the ceiling of the Sistine Chapel (1508–12), and the plans for St. Peter's Church in Rome.

Mi•che•let (mēsh-ə-lā′, mēsh-lā′), **Jules.** 1798–1874. French historian noted for his *Histoire de France* (1833–67).

Mi•chel•son (mī′kəl-sən), **Albert Abraham.** 1852–1931. German-born Amer. physicist who won a 1907 Nobel Prize.

Mich•i•gan (mĭsh′ĭ-gən). A state of the N-central U.S.; admitted as the 26th state in 1837. Cap. Lansing. Pop. 9,328,784. **—Mich′i•gan′der** (-găn′dər) *adj. & n.*

Michigan, Lake. The third largest of the Great Lakes, between WI and MI, linked with the Atlantic Ocean by the St. Lawrence Seaway.

Michigan City. A city of NW IN on Lake Michigan NE of Gary. Pop. 33,822.

mick (mĭk) *n. Offensive Slang.* Used as a disparaging term for an Irish person. [Prob. the name *Mick*, nickname for *Michael*.]

mick•ey (mĭk′ē) *n., pl.* **-eys. 1.** *Informal.* A roasted potato. **2.** *Canadian.* A small bottle of liquor, shaped to fit in a pocket. **3.** *Chiefly British.* Self-assurance. [Perh. < MICK.]

Mick•ey Finn (mĭk′ē fĭn′) *n. Slang.* An alcoholic beverage surreptitiously altered to be incapacitating. [?]

Mickey Mouse *adj.* **1.a.** *Slang.* Unimportant; trivial. **b.** *Slang.* Irritatingly petty. **2.** *Slang.* Intellectually unchallenging; simple. [After *Mickey Mouse*, created by Walt Disney.]

mick•le (mĭk′əl) *Scots.* —*adj.* Great. —*adv.* Greatly. [ME *mikel* < OE *micel* and < ON *mikill*; see **meg-*.**]

Mic•mac (mĭk′măk′) *n., pl.* **Micmac** or **-macs. 1.** A member of a Native American people inhabiting Nova Scotia, New Brunswick, Prince Edward Island, and the Gaspé Peninsula of Quebec. **2.** The Algonquian language of the Micmac.

MICR *abbr.* Magnetic ink character recognition.

mi•cra (mī′krə) *n.* Pl. of **micron.**

mi•cro (mī′krō) *adj.* Basic or small-scale: *the economy at the micro level.* —*n., pl.* **-cros. 1.** *Comp. Sci.* **a.** A microcomputer. **2.** A microwave oven. [< MICRO-.]

micro– or **micr–** *pref.* **1.a.** Small: *microcircuit.* **b.** Abnormally small: *microcephaly.* **c.** Requiring or involving microscopy: *microsurgery.* **2.** One-millionth (10^{-6}): *microampere.* [Gk. *mikro-* < *mikros*, small.]

mi•cro•am•pere (mī′krō-ăm′pîr) *n.* A unit of electric current equal to one millionth of an ampere.

micrometer¹

mi•cro•a•nal•y•sis (mī′krō-ə-năl′ĭ-sĭs) *n.* The chemical identification and analysis of extremely small quantities of matter. **—mi′cro•an′a•lyst** (-ăn′ə-lĭst) *n.* **—mi′cro•an′a•lyt′ic** (-ăn′ə-lĭt′ĭk), **mi′cro•an′a•lyt′i•cal** *adj.*

mi•cro•a•nat•o•my (mī′krō-ə-năt′ə-mē) *n.* Histology. **—mi′cro•an′a•tom′i•cal** (-ăn′ə-tŏm′ĭ-kəl) *adj.*

mi•cro•bal•ance (mī′krō-băl′əns) *n.* A balance designed to weigh very small loads, up to 0.1 gram.

mic•ro•bar•o•graph (mī′krō-băr′ə-grăf′) *n.* An instrument used to record very small changes in atmospheric pressure.

mi•crobe (mī′krōb′) *n.* A minute life form; a microorganism, esp. a bacterium that causes disease. Not in technical use. [Fr. : Gk. *mikro-*, micro- + Gk. *bios*, life; see **gʷei-*.**]

mi•cro•bi•ol•o•gy (mī′krō-bī-ŏl′ə-jē) *n.* The branch of biology that deals with microorganisms and their effects on other living organisms. **—mi′cro•bi′o•log′i•cal** (-bī′ə-lŏj′ĭ-kəl), **mi′cro•bi′o•log′ic** *adj.* **—mi′cro•bi•ol′o•gist** *n.*

mi•cro•burst (mī′krō-bûrst′) *n.* A sudden violent downdraft of air over a small area that is hazardous to airplanes during landing or taking off.

mi•cro•bus (mī′krō-bŭs′) *n., pl.* **-bus•es** or **-bus•ses.** A station wagon in the shape of a small bus.

mi•cro•cap•sule (mī′krō-kăp′səl, -so͞ol) *n.* A small, sometimes microscopic capsule designed to release its contents when broken by pressure, dissolved, or melted.

mi•cro•ceph•a•ly (mī′krō-sĕf′ə-lē) *n., pl.* **-lies.** Abnormal smallness of the head. **—mi′cro•ce•phal′ic** (-sə-făl′ĭk) *adj. & n.* **—mi′cro•ceph′a•lous** (-sĕf′ə-ləs) *adj.*

mi•cro•chem•is•try (mī′krō-kĕm′ĭ-strē) *n.* Chemistry that deals with minute quantities of materials, frequently less than one milligram in mass or one milliliter in volume. **—mi′cro•chem′i•cal** (-ĭ-kəl) *adj.* **—mi′cro•chem′ist** *n.*

mi•cro•chip (mī′krə-chĭp′) *n. Comp. Sci.* See **chip¹** 4a.

mi•cro•cir•cuit (mī′krō-sûr′kĭt) *n.* An electric circuit of miniaturized components. **—mi′cro•cir′cuit•ry** (-kĭ-trē) *n.*

mi•cro•cli•mate (mī′krō-klī′mĭt) *n.* The climate of a small specific place within an area. **—mi′cro•cli•mat′ic** (-măt′ĭk) *adj.* **—mi′cro•cli′ma•to•log′ic** (-mə-tə-lŏj′ĭk), **mi′cro•cli′ma•to•log′i•cal** *adj.* **—mi′cro•cli′ma•tol′o•gy** (-tŏl′ə-jē) *n.*

mi•cro•cline (mī′krō-klīn′) *n.* A mineral of the feldspar group, chiefly $KAlSi_3O_8$, used in making glass and porcelain. [Gk. *mikro-*, micro- (< the fact that its cleavage angle is not exactly equal to 90°) + Gk. *klinein*, to lean; see CLINE.]

mi•cro•coc•cus (mī′krō-kŏk′əs) *n., pl.* **-coc•ci** (-kŏk′sī′, -kŏk′ī′). A spherical aerobic gram-positive bacterium of the genus *Micrococcus*, usu. occurring in irregular clusters. **—mi′cro•coc′cal** (-kŏk′əl) *adj.*

mi•cro•com•put•er (mī′krō-kəm-pyo͞o′tər) *n. Comp. Sci.* A very small computer built around a microprocessor and designed to be used by one person at a time.

mi•cro•cop•y (mī′krō-kŏp′ē) *n., pl.* **-ies.** A greatly reduced photographic copy, usu. reproduced by projection.

mi•cro•cosm (mī′krə-kŏz′əm) *n.* A small representative system having analogies to a larger system in constitution, configuration, or development. [ME *microcosme*, man as a little world < OFr. < LLat. *mīcrocosmus* < Gk. *mikros kosmos* : *mikros*, small + *kosmos*, world, order.] **—mi′cro•cos′mic** (-kŏz′mĭk), **mi′cro•cos′mi•cal** (-mĭ-kəl) *adj.* **—mi′cro•cos′mi•cal•ly** *adv.*

microcosmic salt *n.* A white crystalline salt of phosphorus, $HNaNH_4PO_4{\cdot}4H_2O$, used in blowpipe analysis of minerals to test for the presence of certain metals.

mi•cro•crys•tal•line (mī′krō-krĭs′tə-lĭn) *adj.* Having a crystalline structure visible only under a microscope. **—mi′cro•crys′tal** *n.*

mi•cro•cyte (mī′krə-sīt′) *n.* An abnormally small red blood cell that may occur in certain forms of anemia. [MICRO- + (ERYTHRO)CYTE.] **—mi′cro•cyt′ic** (-sĭt′ĭk) *adj.*

mi•cro•dot (mī′krə-dŏt′) *n.* A copy or photograph that has been reduced to an extremely small size.

mi•cro•ec•o•nom•ics (mī′krō-ĕk′ə-nŏm′ĭks, -ē′kə-) *n.* *(used with a sing. v.)* The study of the operations of the components of a national economy, such as individual firms, households, and consumers. **—mi′cro•ec′o•nom′ic** *adj.*

mi•cro•e•lec•tron•ics (mī′krō-ĭ-lĕk-trŏn′ĭks) *n. (used with a sing. v.)* The branch of electronics that deals with miniature components. **—mi′cro•e•lec•tron′ic** *adj.*

mi•cro•en•cap•su•late (mī′krō-ĕn-kăp′sə-lāt′) *tr.v.* **-lat•ed, -lat•ing, -lates.** To enclose in microcapsules.

mi•cro•en•vi•ron•ment (mī′krō-ĕn-vī′rən-mənt, -vī′ərn-) *n.* The environment of a very small specific area.

mi•cro•ev•o•lu•tion (mī′krō-ĕv′ə-lo͞o′shən, -ē′və-) *n.* Evolution resulting from a succession of relatively small genetic variations that often cause the formation of new subspecies. **—mi′cro•ev′o•lu′tion•ar′y** *adj.*

mi•cro•far•ad (mī′krō-făr′əd, -ăd) *n.* A unit of capacitance equal to one millionth (10^{-6}) of a farad.

mi•cro•fiche (mī′krō-fēsh′) *n., pl.* **microfiche** or **-fich•es.** A card or sheet of microfilm capable of preserving printed text in reduced form. [Fr. : Gk. *mikro-*, micro- + Fr. *fiche*, peg, slip of paper, index card (< OFr., peg < *fichier*, to drive in, fasten < VLat. **fīgicāre* < Lat. *fīgere*; see **dhīgʷ-***).]

mi·cro·fil·a·ment (mī′krō-fĭl′ə-mənt) *n.* Any of the minute fibers throughout the cytoplasm of a cell, functioning primarily in maintaining its structural integrity.

mi·cro·fi·lar·i·a (mī′krə-fə-lâr′ē-ə) *n., pl.* **-i·ae** (-ē-ē′). The minute larval form of a filarial worm.

mi·cro·film (mī′krə-fĭlm′) *n.* **1.** A film on which printed materials are photographed at greatly reduced size for ease of storage. **2.** A reproduction on this kind of film. — *tr.v.* **-filmed, -film·ing, -films.** To reproduce (documents, for example) on microfilm.

mi·cro·flop·py (mī′krō-flŏp′ē) *n., pl.* **-pies.** *Comp. Sci.* A computer disk 3½ inches in diameter and encased in a hard protective covering.

mi·cro·form (mī′krə-fôrm′) *n.* An arrangement of images reduced in size, as on microfilm or microfiche.

mi·cro·fos·sil (mī′krō-fŏs′əl) *n.* A microscopic fossil, as of a pollen grain or unicellular organism.

mi·cro·gam·ete (mī′krō-găm′ēt′, -gə-mēt′) *n.* The smaller of a pair of conjugating gametes, usu. the male, in an organism that reproduces by heterogamy.

mi·cro·graph (mī′krə-grăf′) *n.* **1.** A drawing or photograph of an object as viewed through a microscope. **2.** An instrument used to make tiny writing or engraving. — **mi′cro·graph′ic** *adj.* — **mi·crog′ra·phy** (mī-krŏg′rə-fē) *n.*

mi·cro·hab·i·tat (mī′krō-hăb′ĭ-tăt′) *n.* A very small specialized habitat, such as a clump of grass.

mi·cro·in·jec·tion (mī′krō-ĭn-jĕk′shən) *n.* Injection of minute amounts of a substance into a microscopic structure.

mi·cro·in·struc·tion (mī′krō-ĭn-strŭk′shən) *n. Comp. Sci.* A small specific instruction, used in microprogramming.

mi·cro·mere (mī′krō-mîr′) *n.* A very small blastomere.

mi·cro·me·te·or·ite (mī′krō-mē′tē-ə-rīt′) *n.* A tiny particle of meteoric dust.

mi·cro·me·te·or·oid (mī′krō-mē′tē-ə-roid′) *n.* A very small, often dust-sized meteoroid.

mi·cro·me·te·or·ol·o·gy (mī′krō-mē′tē-ə-rŏl′ə-jē) *n.* The study of weather conditions on a small scale, such as the area immediately around a mountain, that can affect meteorological conditions. — **mi′cro·me′te·or′o·log′i·cal** (-ôr′ə-lŏj′ĭ-kəl, -ər-ə-) *adj.* — **mi′cro·me′te·or·ol′o·gist** *n.*

mi·crom·e·ter¹ (mī-krŏm′ĭ-tər) *n.* A device for measuring very small distances, objects, or angles, esp. one based on the rotation of a finely threaded screw.

mi·cro·me·ter² (mī′krō-mē′tər) *n.* A unit of length equal to one thousandth (10^{-3}) of a millimeter or one millionth (10^{-6}) of a meter.

mi·crom·e·try (mī-krŏm′ĭ-trē) *n.* Measurement of minute objects with a micrometer. — **mi′cro·met′ric** (mī′krō-mĕt′rĭk), **mi′cro·met′ri·cal** (-rĭ-kəl) *adj.*

mi·cro·min·i·a·tur·ize (mī′krō-mĭn′ē-chə-rīz′, -mĭn′ə-) *tr.v.* **-ized, -iz·ing, -iz·es.** To construct (devices) on an extremely small scale. Used esp. of electronic circuitry.

mi·cron (mī′krŏn′) *n., pl.* **-crons** or **-cra** (-krə). A micrometer (unit of length). No longer in technical use. [Gk. *mikron*, neut. of *mikros*, small.]

Mi·cro·ne·si·a (mī′krō-nē′zhə, -shə). A division of Oceania in the W Pacific E of the Philippines and N of the equator.

Micronesia, Federated States of. A group of associated islands in the Caroline Is. of the W Pacific; self-governing under a compact of free association with the U.S. Cap. Kolonia, on Pohnpei (Ponape) I. Pop. 104,937.

Mi·cro·ne·sian (mī′krə-nē′zhən, -shən) *adj.* Of or relating to Micronesia or its peoples, languages, or cultures. — *n.* **1.** A member of any of the peoples inhabiting Micronesia. **2.** A subfamily of the Austronesian language family that includes the languages of Micronesia.

mi·cron·ize (mī′krə-nīz′) *tr.v.* **-ized, -iz·ing, -iz·es.** To reduce to particles that are only a few micrometers in diameter.

mi·cro·nu·cle·us (mī′krō-no͞o′klē-əs, -nyo͞o′-) *n., pl.* **-cle·i** (-klē-ī′) or **-cle·us·es.** The smaller of two nuclei in ciliate protozoans that contains genetic material and functions in reproduction. — **mi′cro·nu′cle·ar** *adj.*

mi·cro·nu·tri·ent (mī′krō-no͞o′trē-ənt, -nyo͞o′-) *n.* A substance, such as a vitamin or mineral, that is essential in minute amounts for the proper growth of a living organism.

mi·cro·or·gan·ism (mī′krō-ôr′gə-nĭz′əm) *n.* An organism of microscopic size, esp. a bacterium or protozoan.

mi·cro·pa·le·on·tol·o·gy (mī′krō-pā′lē-ŏn-tŏl′ə-jē, -ən-) *n.* The branch of paleontology that deals with microfossils. — **mi′cro·pa′le·on′to·log′ic** (-ŏn′tl-ŏj′ĭk), **mi′cro·pa′le·on′to·log′i·cal** *adj.* — **mi′cro·pa′le·on·tol′o·gist** *n.*

mi·cro·phage (mī′krə-fāj′) *n.* A small phagocyte.

mi·cro·phone (mī′krə-fōn′) *n.* An instrument that converts sound waves into an electric current, usu. fed into an amplifier, a recorder, or a transmitter. — **mi′cro·phon′ic** (-fŏn′ĭk) *adj.*

mi·cro·pho·to·graph (mī′krō-fō′tə-grăf′) *n.* **1.** A photograph requiring magnification for viewing. **2.** A photograph on microfilm. **3.** See **photomicrograph.** — **mi′cro·pho′to·graph′ic** *adj.* — **mi′cro·pho·tog′ra·pher** (-fə-tŏg′rə-fər) *n.* — **mi′cro·pho·tog′ra·phy** (-rə-fē) *n.*

mi·cro·phyte (mī′krə-fīt′) *n.* A plant of microscopic size.

mi·cro·pi·pette (mī′krō-pī-pĕt′) *n.* **1.** A very small pipette used in microinjection. **2.** A pipette used to measure very small volumes of liquids.

mi·cro·print (mī′krə-prĭnt′) *n.* The printed or positive reproduction of a microphotograph.

mi·cro·proc·es·sor (mī′krō-prŏs′ĕs-ər) *n. Comp. Sci.* An integrated circuit that contains the entire central processing unit of a computer on a single chip.

mi·cro·pro·gram·ming (mī′krō-prō′grăm-ĭng, -grə-mĭng) *n. Comp. Sci.* A method of operating the control unit of a computer by breaking down the control instructions into a sequence of small steps.

mi·cro·pyle (mī′krə-pīl′) *n.* **1.** *Bot.* A minute opening in the ovule of a seed plant through which the pollen tube usu. enters. **2.** *Zool.* A pore in the membrane covering the ovum of some animals through which a spermatozoon can enter. [MICRO– + Gk. *pulē*, gate.] — **mi′cro·py′lar** *adj.*

mi·cro·ra·di·o·graph (mī′krō-rā′dē-ō-grăf′) *n.* An enlarged x-ray photograph, used to study small details. — **mi′cro·ra′di·og′ra·phy** (-ŏg′rə-fē) *n.*

mi·cro·read·er (mī′krō-rē′dər) *n.* A device for reading materials in microform, such as microfilm and microfiche.

microreader

mi·cro·scope (mī′krə-skōp′) *n.* **1.** An optical instrument that uses a lens or a combination of lenses to produce magnified images of objects too small to be seen by the unaided eye. **2.** An instrument that uses electronic or other processes to magnify objects.

mi·cro·scop·ic (mī′krə-skŏp′ĭk) also **mi·cro·scop·i·cal** (-ĭ-kəl) *adj.* **1.a.** Too small to be seen by the unaided eye but large enough to be studied under a microscope. **b.** Of, relating to, or concerned with a microscope. **2.** Exceedingly small; minute. **3.** Characterized by or done with extreme attention to detail. — **mi′cro·scop′i·cal·ly** *adv.*

Mi·cro·sco·pi·um (mī′krə-skō′pē-əm) *n.* A constellation in the Southern Hemisphere. [NLat. *Mīcroscopium*, microscope, Microscopium : MICRO– + *-scopium*, -scope.]

mi·cros·co·py (mī-krŏs′kə-pē) *n., pl.* **-pies. 1.a.** The study of microscopes. **b.** The use of microscopes. **2.** Investigation employing a microscope. — **mi·cros′co·pist** *n.*

mi·cro·seism (mī′krə-sī′zəm) *n.* A faint earth tremor caused by natural phenomena, such as winds and strong ocean waves. — **mi′cro·seis′mic** (-sīz′mĭk, -sīs′-) *adj.*

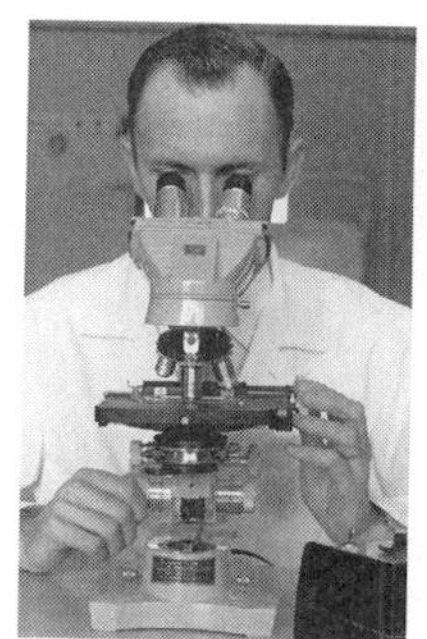

microscope

mi·cro·some (mī′krə-sōm′) *n.* A small particle in the cytoplasm of a cell, typically consisting of fragmented endoplasmic reticulum to which ribosomes are attached. — **mi′cro·so′mal** (-sō′məl), **mi′cro·so′mic** (-sō′mĭk) *adj.*

mi·cro·spo·ran·gi·um (mī′krō-spə-răn′jē-əm) *n., pl.* **-gi·a** (-jē-ə). *Bot.* A structure in which microspores are formed. — **mi′cro·spo·ran′gi·ate** (-jē-ĭt) *adj.*

mi·cro·spore (mī′krə-spôr′, -spōr′) *n. Bot.* The smaller of two types of spores that give rise to a male gametophyte. — **mi′cro·spo′ric, mi′cro·spo′rous** (mī′krə-spôr′əs, -spōr′-, mī-krŏs′pər-əs) *adj.*

mi·cro·spo·ro·cyte (mī′krə-spôr′ə-sīt′, -spōr′-) *n. Bot.* A cell that undergoes meiosis to produce four microspores.

mi·cro·spo·ro·phyll (mī′krə-spôr′ə-fĭl′, -spōr′-) *n. Bot.* A leaflike structure that bears microsporangia.

mi·cro·state (mī′krō-stāt′) *n.* An independent country that is very small in area and population.

mi·cro·struc·ture (mī′krō-strŭk′chər) *n.* The structure of an organism or object as revealed through microscopy.

mi·cro·sur·ger·y (mī′krō-sûr′jə-rē) *n., pl.* **-ies.** Surgery on minute body structures or cells performed with the aid of a microscope and other specialized instruments. — **mi′cro·sur′gi·cal** (-jĭ-kəl) *adj.*

mi·cro·tome (mī′krə-tōm′) *n.* An instrument used to cut a specimen into thin sections for microscopic examination.

mi·crot·o·my (mī-krŏt′ə-mē) *n., pl.* **-mies.** The preparation of specimens with a microtome. — **mi′cro·tom′ic** (mī′krə-tŏm′ĭk) *adj.*

mi·cro·tone (mī′krə-tōn′) *n. Mus.* An interval smaller than a semitone. — **mi′cro·ton′al** (-tō′nəl) *adj.* — **mi′cro·to·nal′i·ty** (-tō-năl′ĭ-tē) *n.* — **mi′cro·ton′al·ly** *adv.*

mi·cro·tu·bule (mī′krō-to͞o′byo͞ol, -tyo͞o-) *n.* Any of the proteinaceous cylindrical structures found throughout the cytoplasm of eukaryotic cells, providing structural support and assisting in cellular locomotion and transport.

mi·cro·vil·lus (mī′krō-vĭl′əs) *n., pl.* **-vil·li** (-vĭl′ī′). Any of the minute hairlike structures projecting from the surface of certain types of epithelial cells, esp. of the small intestine.

mi·cro·volt (mī′krə-vōlt′) *n.* A unit of electric potential equal to one millionth (10^{-6}) of a volt.

mi·cro·watt (mī′krō-wŏt′) *n.* A unit of power equal to one millionth (10^{-6}) of a watt.

mi·cro·wave (mī′krə-wāv′, -krō-) *n.* **1.** A high-frequency electromagnetic wave, one millimeter to one meter in wavelength, intermediate between infrared and short-wave radio wavelengths. **2.** *Informal.* A microwave oven. — *tr.v.* **-waved, -wav·ing, -waves.** To cook or heat (food) in a microwave oven. — **mi′cro·wav′a·ble, mi′cro·wave′a·ble** *adj.*

microwave oven *n.* An oven using microwaves to cook.

ă **pat**	oi **boy**
ā **pay**	ou **out**
âr **care**	o͝o **took**
ä **father**	o͞o **boot**
ĕ **pet**	ŭ **cut**
ē **be**	ûr **urge**
ĭ **pit**	th **thin**
ī **pie**	*th* **this**
îr **pier**	hw **which**
ŏ **pot**	zh **vision**
ō **toe**	ə **about, item**
ô **paw**	

Stress marks:
′ (primary);
′ (secondary), as in **dictionary** (dĭk′shə-nĕr′ē)

mihrab

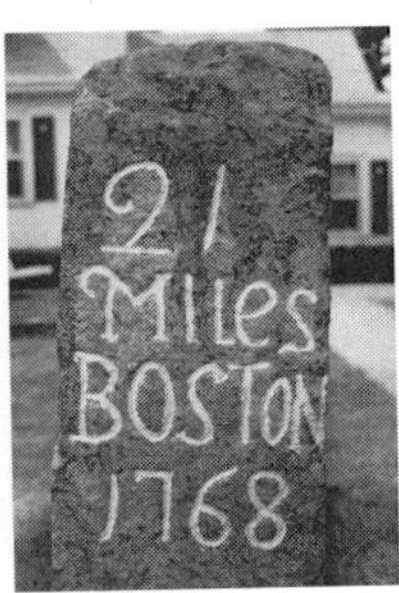

milestone

milkweed

2. Of or relating to a migration. **3.** Roving; nomadic.

mih·rab (mîr′əb) *n. Islam.* **1.** A niche in the wall of a mosque or a mosque room that indicates the direction of Mecca. **2.** An undecorated oblong space in the middle of a prayer rug, pointed toward Mecca. [Ar. *miḥrāb.*]

mi·ka·do (mĭ-kä′dō) *n., pl.* **-dos.** An emperor of Japan. [J. : *mi,* honorific pref. + *kado,* gate.]

Mik·a·su·ki also **Mic·co·su·kee** (mĭk′ə-so͞o′kē) *n., pl.* **Mik·asuki** or **-kis** also **Miccosukee** or **-kees. 1.** A member of a Native American people formerly inhabiting northwest Florida, now forming part of the Seminole people of southern Florida. **2.** The Muskogean language of the Mikasuki.

mike (mīk) *Informal.* —*n.* A microphone. —*tr.v.* **miked, mik·ing, mikes.** To supply with or transmit through a microphone.

Mí·ko·nos (mē′kô-nôs′). See **Mykonos.**

Mi·koy·an (mē′kō-yän′, myĭ-kə-), **Anastas Ivanovich.** 1895–1978. Soviet politician who was chairman of the presidium of the Supreme Soviet (1964–65).

mik·vah (mĭk′və, mēk-vä′) *n., pl.* **-voth** or **-vot** (-vōt′) or **-vos** (-vōs). **1.** A ritual bath taken by Jews for purification on certain occasions, as before the Sabbath or after menstruation. **2.** A building, room, or fixture in which this bath takes place. [Heb. *miqwāh.*]

mil (mĭl) *n.* **1.** A unit of length equal to one thousandth (10^{-3}) of an inch (0.0254 millimeter), used, for example, to specify the diameter of wire. **2.** A milliliter; one cubic centimeter. **3.** A unit of angular measurement used in artillery and equal to 1⁄6400 of a complete revolution. [Short for Lat. *mīllēsimus,* thousandth < *mīlle,* thousand. See **gheslo-*.**]

mil. *abbr.* Military; militia.

mi·la·dy (mĭ-lā′dē) *n., pl.* **-dies. 1.** An English noblewoman or gentlewoman. **2.** Used as a form of address for such a woman. **3.** A chic or fashionable woman. [Fr. < E., my lady.]

Mi·lan (mĭ-lăn′, -län′). A city of N Italy NE of Genoa; probably of Celtic origin. Pop. 1,634,638. —**Mil′a·nese′** (mĭl′ə-nēz′, -nēs′) *adj. & n.*

milch (mĭlch) *adj.* Giving milk. [ME *milche* < OE *-milce,* in *thrimilce,* May (when milking is thrice a day). See **melg-*.**]

mil·chig (mĭl′KHĭk) *adj.* Derived from or made of milk or dairy products. [Yiddish *milkhik* < *milkh,* milk < MHGer. < OHGer. *miluh.* See **melg-*.**]

mild (mīld) *adj.* **mild·er, mild·est. 1.** Gentle or kind in disposition or behavior. **2.a.** Moderate in type, degree, effect, or force. **b.** Not extreme. **c.** Warm and full of sunshine; pleasant. **3.** Not severe or acute. **4.** Easily molded, shaped, or worked; malleable. [ME < OE *milde.* See **mel-[1]*.**] —**mild′ly** *adv.* —**mild′ness** *n.*

mil·dew (mĭl′do͞o′, -dyo͞o′) *n.* **1.** Any of various fungi that form a superficial, usu. whitish growth on plants and various organic materials. **2.** A superficial coating or discoloration, as of paper or leather, caused by fungi. **3.** A plant disease caused by such fungi. —*tr. & intr.v.* **-dewed, -dew·ing, -dews.** To affect or become affected with mildew. [ME < OE *mildēaw,* honeydew, nectar. See **melit-*.**] —**mil′dew′y** *adj.*

mile (mīl) *n.* **1.** A unit of length equal to 5,280 feet or 1,760 yards (1,609 meters), used in the United States and other English-speaking countries. See table at **measurement. 2.** A nautical mile. **3.** An air mile. **4.** *Sports.* A race that is one mile long. **5.** A relatively great distance. [ME < OE *mīl* < Lat. *mīlia (passuum),* a thousand (double paces), a Roman mile, pl. of *mīlle,* thousand. See **gheslo-*.**]

mile·age also **mil·age** (mī′lĭj) *n.* **1.** Total length, extent, or distance measured or expressed in miles. **2.** Total miles covered or traveled in a given time. **3.** The amount of service, use, or wear estimated by miles used or traveled. **4.** The number of miles traveled by a motor vehicle on a given quantity of fuel. **5.a.** An allowance for travel expenses established at a specified rate per mile. **b.** Expense per mile, as for the use of a car. **6.** *Informal.* The amount of service something has yielded or may yield in the future; usefulness.

mile·post (mīl′pōst′) *n.* A post set up to indicate distance in miles, as along a highway.

mil·er (mī′lər) *n. Sports.* One that competes in races one mile long.

mi·les glo·ri·o·sus (mē′lās glôr′ē-ō′səs, glōr′-) *n., pl.* **mi·li·tes glo·ri·o·si** (mē′lĭ-tās glôr′ē-ō′sē, glōr′-). A bragging and often cowardly soldier, esp. as a stock character in comedy. [Lat. *mīles glōriōsus,* after *Mīles Glōriōsus* by Plautus.]

Mi·le·sian[1] (mī-lē′zhən, -shən) *adj.* Of or relating to Miletus or its inhabitants. —*n.* A native or inhabitant of Miletus. [< Lat. *Mīlēsius* < Gk. *Milēsios* < *Milētos,* Miletus.]

Mi·le·sian[2] (mĭ-lē′zhən, -shən) *n.* **1.** *Myth.* A member of a people who invaded Ireland and became the ancestors of the Irish. **2.** A native or inhabitant of Ireland. [After *Milesius,* legendary ancestor of the Irish people.] —**mi·le′sian** *adj.*

mile·stone (mīl′stōn′) *n.* **1.** A stone marker set up on a roadside to indicate the distance in miles from a given point. **2.** An important event, as in the history of a nation; a turning point.

Mi·let·us (mī-lē′təs). An ancient Ionian city of W Asia Minor in present-day Turkey; occupied by Greeks c. 1000 B.C.

mil·foil (mĭl′foil′) *n.* **1.** See **yarrow. 2.** Water milfoil. [ME < OFr. < Lat. *mīlifolium* : *mīlle,* thousand; see **gheslo-*** + *folium,* leaf; see **bhel-[3]*.**]

Mil·ford (mĭl′fərd). **1.** A city of SW CT on Long Island Sound SW of New Haven; founded 1639. Pop. 48,168. **2.** A city of S-central MA SE of Worcester. Pop. 25,355.

Mil·haud (mē-yō′), **Darius.** 1892–1974. French composer who experimented with polytonality and jazz styles.

mil·i·a (mĭl′ē-ə) *n.* Pl. of **milium.**

mil·i·ar·i·a (mĭl′ē-âr′ē-ə) *n.* See **heat rash.** [NLat. *(fēbris) miliāria,* miliary (fever), fem. of Lat. *miliārius,* of millet. See MILIARY.] —**mil′i·ar′i·al** *adj.*

mil·i·ar·y (mĭl′ē-ĕr′ē) *adj.* **1.** Having the appearance of millet seeds. **2.** *Pathol.* Characterized by the presence of small miliary skin lesions. [< ME *miliaris, miliari,* miliary skin disease < Med.Lat. *miliāris* < Lat. *miliārius,* of millet < *milium,* millet. See MILLET.]

mi·lieu (mĭl-yo͞o′, mē-lyœ′) *n., pl.* **-lieus** or **-lieux** (-lyœ′). An environment or a setting. [Fr. < OFr., center : *mi,* middle (< Lat. *medius;* see **medhyo-***) + *lieu,* place (< Lat. *locus*).]

Mi·li·la·ni Town (mē′lē-lä′nē). A community of S-central Oahu, HI, a suburb of Honolulu. Pop 29,359.

mil·i·tant (mĭl′ĭ-tənt) *adj.* **1.** Fighting or warring. **2.** Having a combative character; aggressive, esp. on behalf of a cause. —*n.* A militant person or party. [ME < OFr. < Lat. *mīlitāns, mīlitant-,* pr.part. of *mīlitāre,* to serve as a soldier. See MILITATE.] —**mil′i·tance, mil′i·tan·cy** *n.* —**mil′i·tant·ly** *adv.*

mil·i·tar·i·a (mĭl′ĭ-târ′ē-ə) *pl.n.* Objects of historical interest related to warfare or military service that are collected. [MILITARY + -IA[2].]

mil·i·ta·rism (mĭl′ĭ-tə-rĭz′əm) *n.* **1.** Glorification of the ideals of a professional military class. **2.** Predominance of the armed forces in the administration or policy of the state. **3.** A policy in which military preparedness is of primary importance to a state. —**mil′i·ta·rist** *n.* —**mil′i·ta·ris′tic** (-rĭs′tĭk) *adj.* —**mil′i·ta·ris′ti·cal·ly** *adv.*

mil·i·ta·rize (mĭl′ĭ-tə-rīz′) *tr.v.* **-rized, -riz·ing, -riz·es. 1.** To equip or train for war. **2.** To imbue with militarism. **3.** To adopt for use by or in the military. —**mil′i·ta·ri·za′tion** (-tər-ĭ-zā′shən) *n.*

mil·i·tar·y (mĭl′ĭ-tĕr′ē) *adj.* **1.** Of, relating to, or characteristic of members of the armed forces. **2.** Performed or supported by the armed forces: *military service.* **3.** Of or relating to war: *military operations.* **4.** Of or relating to land forces. —*n., pl.* **military** also **-ies. 1.** Armed forces. **2.** Members, esp. officers, of an armed force. [ME < Lat. *mīlitāris* < *mīles, mīlit-,* soldier.] —**mil′i·tar′i·ly** (-târ′ə-lē) *adv.*

military law *n.* The statutes, codes, and traditions concerned with the discipline and trial of military personnel.

military police *n.* The branch of an armed force assigned to perform law enforcement duties, as on a military installation.

military science *n.* The principles of military conflict and of warfare.

mil·i·tate (mĭl′ĭ-tāt′) *intr.v.* **-tat·ed, -tat·ing, -tates.** To have force or influence; bring about an effect or a change. [Lat. *mīlitāre, mīlitāt-,* to be a soldier < *mīles, mīlit-,* soldier.]

mi·li·tes glo·ri·o·si (mē′lĭ-tās glôr′ē-ō′sē, glōr′-) *n.* Pl. of **miles gloriosus.**

mi·li·tia (mə-lĭsh′ə) *n.* **1.** An army of ordinary citizens. **2.** A military force that is not part of a regular army, subject to call for emergency service. **3.** The body of physically fit civilians legally eligible for military service. [Lat. *mīlitia,* warfare, military service < *mīles, mīlit-,* soldier.]

mi·li·tia·man (mə-lĭsh′ə-mən) *n.* A male militia member.

mil·i·um (mĭl′ē-əm) *n., pl.* **-i·a** (-ē-ə). A small white or yellowish cyst on the skin, caused by retention of sebaceous gland secretions. [ME, millet < Lat. See **melə-*.**]

milk (mĭlk) *n.* **1.** A whitish liquid containing proteins, fats, lactose, vitamins, and minerals produced by the mammary glands of female mammals to nourish their young. **2.** The milk of cows, goats, or other animals, used as food by human beings. **3.** A liquid, such as coconut milk, or various medical emulsions, with a milklike appearance. —*v.* **milked, milk·ing, milks.** —*tr.* **1.a.** To draw milk from the teat or udder of (a female mammal). **b.** To draw or extract a liquid from. **2.** To press out, drain off, or remove by or as if by milking. **3.** *Informal.* **a.** To draw out or extract something from, as if by milking. **b.** To obtain money or benefits from, in order to achieve personal gain; exploit. —*intr.* **1.** To yield or supply milk. **2.** To draw milk from a female mammal. [ME < OE *milc.* See **melg-*.**] —**milk′er** *n.*

milk chocolate *n.* Sweetened chocolate made with milk.

milk fever *n.* **1.** A mild fever, usu. occurring at the beginning of lactation, associated with infection. **2.** A disease affecting dairy cows, esp. soon after giving birth.

milk·fish (mĭlk′fĭsh′) *n., pl.* **milkfish** or **-fish·es.** A large silvery fish *(Chanos chanos)* of the South Pacific and Indian oceans, widely used for food. [< its color.]

milk glass *n.* An opaque or translucent whitish glass.

milk leg *n.* A painful swelling of the leg occurring in women after childbirth as a result of clotting of the femoral veins.

milk·maid (mĭlk′mād′) *n.* A girl or woman who milks cows.

milk·man (mĭlk′măn′) *n.* A man who sells or delivers milk.

milk of magnesia *n.* A white aqueous suspension of magnesium hydroxide, $Mg(OH)_2$, used as an antacid and a laxative.

Milk River (mĭlk). A river rising in the Rocky Mts. of NW MT and flowing c. 1,006 km (625 mi) to S Alberta then back to N MT, where it joins the Missouri R.

milk run *n. Slang.* A routine trip with stops at many places.

milk shake *n.* **1.** A beverage made of milk, flavoring, and ice cream, shaken or whipped until foamy. Also called regionally *cabinet, frappé, velvet.* **2.** *New England.* A beverage made of milk and flavored syrup, whipped until foamy.

Regional Note: To most Americans, a milk shake naturally includes ice cream. To a person living in Rhode Island or the adjoining part of Massachussetts, a milk shake consists of milk shaken up with flavored syrup; if ice cream is included, the drink is called a *cabinet,* possibly, says food writer John F. Mariani in *The Dictionary of American Food and Drink,* named after the square wooden cabinet in which the mixer was encased. Farther north in New England the same drink is called a *velvet* or a *frappé* (from French *frapper,* "to ice").

milk sickness *n.* **1.** A disease characterized by vomiting and intestinal pain caused by eating dairy products or meat from a cow that has fed on white snakeroot. **2.** See **tremble** 3b.

milk snake *n.* Any of various nonvenomous king snakes of the species *Lampropeltis triangulum* of the southeast and central United States and Mexico, often having red, yellow, and black markings. [< the claim that it sucks milk from cows.]

milk•sop (mĭlk′sŏp′) *n.* A man lacking courage and other qualities deemed manly. **— milk′sop′py** *adj.*

milk sugar *n.* See **lactose.**

milk toast *n.* Toast, usu. buttered, served in warm milk, often with sugar or seasonings.

milk tooth *n.* Any of the deciduous teeth of a young mammal.

milk vetch *n.* Any of various plants of the genus *Astragalus,* having compound leaves and purple, white, or yellowish flowers. [< the belief that it increases the milk yield of goats.]

milk•weed (mĭlk′wēd′) *n.* Any of numerous plants of the genus *Asclepias,* having milky juice, usu. opposite leaves, and pods that split open to release seeds with downy tufts.

milk•wort (mĭlk′wûrt′, -wôrt′) *n.* Any of various plants of the genus *Polygala,* having variously colored flowers with two petaloid sepals. [Thought to increase human lactation.]

milk•y (mĭl′kē) *adj.* **-i•er, -i•est. 1.** Resembling milk in color or consistency. **2.** Filled with, consisting of, or yielding milk or a fluid resembling milk. **3.** Meek; timid. **— milk′i•ness** *n.*

milky disease *n.* A bacterial disease of scarabaeid grubs that eventually turns them a milky white color.

Milk•y Way (mĭl′kē) *n.* The galaxy containing our solar system, visible as a broad band of faint light in the night sky. [ME, transl. of Lat. *via lactea* : *via,* way + *lactea,* milky.]

mill¹ (mĭl) *n.* **1.a.** A building equipped with machinery for grinding grain into flour or meal. **b.** A device or mechanism that grinds grain. **2.** A machine or device that reduces a solid or coarse substance into pulp or minute grains by crushing, grinding, or pressing: *a pepper mill.* **3.** A machine that releases the juice of fruits and vegetables by pressing or grinding: *a cider mill.* **4.a.** A machine, such as one for stamping coins, that produces something by the repetition of a simple process. **b.** A steel roller bearing a raised design, used for making a die or a printing plate by pressure. **c.** Any of various machines for shaping, cutting, polishing, or dressing metal surfaces. **5.a.** A building or group of buildings equipped with machinery for processing raw materials into finished or industrial products: *a textile mill.* **b.** A building or collection of buildings that has machinery for manufacture; a factory. **6.** A process, an agency, or an institution that operates in a routine way or turns out products in the manner of a factory: *a diploma mill.* **7.** A slow or laborious process. **—** *v.* **milled, mill•ing, mills. —** *tr.* **1.** To grind, pulverize, or break down into smaller particles in a mill. **2.** To transform or process mechanically in a mill. **3.** To shape, polish, dress, or finish in a mill or with a milling tool. **4.a.** To produce a ridge around the edge of (a coin). **b.** To groove or flute the rim of (a coin or other metal object). **5.** To agitate or stir until foamy. **6.** *Western U.S.* To halt (a cattle stampede) by turning the lead animals in a wide arc so that they form the center of a gradually tightening spiral. **—** *intr.* **1.** To move around in churning confusion. **2.** *Slang.* To fight with the fists; box. **3.** To undergo milling. [ME *milne, mille* < OE *mylen* < LLat. *molīna, molīnum* < fem. and neut. of *molīnus,* of a mill < Lat. *mola,* millstone < *molere,* to grind. See **melə-*.**]

mill² (mĭl) *n.* A monetary unit equal to 1/1000 of a U.S. dollar or 1/10 of a cent. [Short for Lat. *millēsimus,* thousandth. See MIL.]

Mill (mĭl), **James.** 1773–1836. Scottish philosopher and economist who was a founder of utilitarianism.

Mill, John Stuart. 1806–73. British philosopher known esp. for his interpretations of empiricism and utilitarianism in works such as *Principles of Political Economy* (1848).

mill•age (mĭl′ĭj) *n.* A tax rate on property, expressed in mills per dollar of value of the property.

Mil•lais (mĭ-lā′), Sir **John Everett.** 1829–96. British painter and a founder of the Pre-Raphaelite Brotherhood (1848).

Mil•lay (mĭ-lā′), **Edna Saint Vincent.** 1892–1950. Amer. poet who wrote *The Harp Weaver and Other Poems* (1923).

Edna Saint Vincent Millay
Photographed in 1933

mill•board (mĭl′bôrd′, -bōrd′) *n.* A stiff heavy paperboard used primarily for book covers. [Alteration of *milled board.*]

Mill•brae (mĭl′brā′). A city of W CA S of San Francisco. Pop. 20,412.

Mill•burn (mĭl′bərn). A community of NE NJ, a suburb W of Newark. Pop. 18,630.

mill•dam (mĭl′dăm′) *n.* A dam constructed across a stream to raise the water level so that the overflow will have sufficient power to turn a mill wheel.

mil•le•nar•i•an (mĭl′ə-nâr′ē-ən) *adj.* **1.** Of or relating to a thousand, esp. to a thousand years. **2.** Of, relating to, or believing in the doctrine of the millennium. **—** *n.* One who believes the millennium will occur. **— mil′le•nar′i•an•ism** *n.*

mil•le•nar•y (mĭl′ə-nĕr′ē, mə-lĕn′ə-rē) *adj.* **1.** Of or relating to a thousand, esp. to a thousand years; millenarian. **2.a.** Of or relating to the doctrine of the millennium; millenarian. **b.** Of or relating to millenarians. **—** *n., pl.* **-ies. 1.** A sum or total of one thousand, esp. a thousand years. **2.** A millenarian. [Lat. *millēnārius* < *millēnī,* a thousand each < *mīlle,* thousand. See **gheslo-*.**]

mil•len•ni•um (mə-lĕn′ē-əm) *n., pl.* **-len•ni•ums** or **-len•ni•a** (-lĕn′ē-ə). **1.** A span of one thousand years. **2.** A thousand-year period of holiness mentioned in Revelation 20, during which Jesus and his followers are to rule on earth. **3.** A hoped-for period of joy, prosperity, and justice. **4.** A thousandth anniversary. [NLat. : Lat. *mīlle,* thousand; see **gheslo-*** + Lat. *annus,* year; see **at-*.**] **— mil•len′ni•al** (-əl) *adj.* **— mil•len′ni•al•ism** *n.* **— mil•len′ni•al•ist** *n.*

mil•le•pede (mĭl′ə-pēd′) *n.* Var. of **millipede.**

mil•le•pore (mĭl′ə-pôr′, -pōr′) *n.* Any of various reef-building organisms of the order Milleporina of tropical marine waters, forming white or yellowish calcareous structures and resembling the true corals of the class Anthozoa. [Ital. *millepora* : *mille,* thousand (< Lat. *mīlle;* see **gheslo-***) + *-pora* (alteration of *poro,* tufa, pore; see MADREPORE).]

mill•er (mĭl′ər) *n.* **1.** One who works in, operates, or owns a mill, esp. a grain mill. **2.** A milling machine. **3.** Any of various moths whose wings and bodies have a powdery appearance.

Mil•ler (mĭl′ər), **Arthur.** b. 1915. Amer. playwright whose works include *Death of a Salesman* (1949).

Miller, Glenn. 1909–44. Amer. bandleader and composer from the Big Band era.

Glenn Miller
Photographed in 1940

Miller, Henry Valentine. 1891–1980. Amer. writer noted for *Tropic of Cancer* (1934) and *Tropic of Capricorn* (1939).

Miller, Joaquin. Cincinnatus Hiner Miller. 1837–1913. Amer. poet whose work is based on his adventures in the West.

Miller, Samuel Freeman. 1816–90. Amer. jurist; associate justice of the U.S. Supreme Court (1862–90).

mil•ler•ite (mĭl′ə-rīt′) *n.* A nickel sulfide mineral, NiS, usu. occurring in long hairlike crystals and used as a nickel ore. [After William H. *Miller* (1801–80), British mineralogist.]

mill•er's thumb (mĭl′ərz) *n.* Any of several small freshwater sculpins of the genus *Cottus,* esp. *C. gobio,* having a large spiny head and spiny fins. [< its thumblike shape.]

mil•les•i•mal (mə-lĕs′ə-məl) *adj.* **1.** Thousandth. **2.** Consisting of a thousandth. **3.** Relating to thousandths. **—** *n.* A thousandth. [< Lat. *millēsimus* < *mīlle,* thousand. See **gheslo-*.**]

mil•let (mĭl′ĭt) *n.* **1.a.** An annual grass *(Panicum milaiceum)* cultivated in Eurasia for its grains and in North America for hay. **b.** The grains of this plant. **2.** Any of several similar or related grasses. [ME *milet* < OFr., dim. of *mil,* millet < Lat. *milium.* See **melə-*.**]

Mil•let (mĭ-lā′, mē-), **Jean François.** 1814–75. French painter whose works include *The Gleaners* (1857).

Mil•lett (mĭl′ĭt), **Kate.** b. 1934. Amer. feminist leader who wrote *Sexual Politics* (1970).

milli– *pref.* One thousandth (10^{-3}): *millisecond.* [Lat. *mīlli-* < *mīlle,* thousand. See **gheslo-*.**]

mil•li•am•pere (mĭl′ē-ăm′pîr) *n.* A unit of current equal to one thousandth (10^{-3}) of an ampere.

mil•liard (mĭl′yərd, -yärd′, mĭl′ē-ärd′) *n. Chiefly British.* The cardinal number equal to 10^9. [Fr. < OFr. *milliart* < *milion,* million. See MILLION.]

mil•li•ar•y (mĭl′ē-ĕr′ē) *adj.* Relating to or marking the distance of an ancient Roman mile, equal to 1,000 paces. [Lat. *milliārius,* of a thousand, one mile long < *mīlle (passuum),* a thousand (double paces), a Roman mile. See **gheslo-*.**]

mil•li•bar (mĭl′ə-bär′) *n.* A unit of atmospheric pressure equal to one thousandth (10^{-3}) of a bar.

mil•li•cur•ie (mĭl′ĭ-kyo͝or′ē, -kyo͝o-rē′) *n.* A unit of radioactivity equal to one thousandth (10^{-3}) of a curie.

mil•li•gram (mĭl′ĭ-grăm′) *n.* A unit of mass equal to one thousandth (10^{-3}) of a gram. See table at **measurement.**

mil•li•hen•ry (mĭl′ə-hĕn′rē) *n., pl.* **-rys** or **-ries.** A unit of inductance equal to one thousandth (10^{-3}) of a henry.

Mil•li•kan (mĭl′ĭ-kən), **Robert Andrews.** 1868–1953. Amer. physicist who won a 1923 Nobel Prize.

mil•li•lam•bert (mĭl′ə-lăm′bərt) *n.* A unit of luminance equal to one thousandth (10^{-3}) of a lambert.

mil•li•li•ter (mĭl′ə-lē′tər) *n.* A unit of volume equal to one thousandth (10^{-3}) of a liter. See table at **measurement.**

ă pat	oi boy
ā pay	ou out
âr care	o͝o took
ä father	o͞o boot
ĕ pet	ŭ cut
ē be	ûr urge
ĭ pit	th thin
ī pie	*th* this
îr pier	hw which
ŏ pot	zh vision
ō toe	ə about, item
ô paw	

Stress marks:
′ (primary);
′ (secondary), as in dictionary (dĭk′shə-nĕr′ē)

Ming (mĭng). A Chinese dynasty (1368–1644) noted esp. for its development of the arts. — **Ming** *adj.*

min•gle (mĭng′gəl) *v.* **-gled, -gling, -gles.** — *tr.* **1.** To mix or bring together in combination, usu. without loss of individual characteristics. **2.** To mix so that the components become united; merge. — *intr.* **1.** To be or become mixed or united. **2.** To join or take part with others. [ME *menglen,* freq. of *mengen,* to mix < OE *mengan.* See **mag-*.**] — **min′gler** *n.*

min•gy (mĭn′jē) *adj.* **-gi•er, -gi•est.** *Informal.* **1.** Small in quantity; meager: *mingy wages.* **2.** Mean and stingy. [Perh. < M(EAN)[2] + (ST)INGY.]

Mi•nho (mē′nyo͞o) or **Mi•ño** (-nyô). A river flowing c. 338 km (210 mi) from NW Spain to the Atlantic Ocean.

min•i (mĭn′ē) *n., pl.* **min•is. 1.** Something distinctively smaller than others of its type. **2.** A miniskirt. — **min′i** *adj.*

mini– *pref.* Small; miniature: *minibike.* [< MINIATURE and MINIMUM.]

min•i•a•ture (mĭn′ē-ə-cho͝or′, -chər, mĭn′ə-) *n.* **1.a.** A copy or model that represents or reproduces something in a greatly reduced size. **b.** Something small of its class. **2.a.** A small painting executed with great detail. **b.** A small portrait, picture, or decorative letter on an illuminated manuscript. **c.** The art of painting miniatures. — *adj.* Being on a small or greatly reduced scale. See Syns at **small.** [Ital. *miniatura,* illumination of manuscripts < *miniare,* to illuminate < Lat. *miniāre,* to color red < *minium,* red lead.] — **min′i•a•tur′ist** *n.*

miniature golf *n. Games.* A version of golf played with a putter on a miniature course having obstacles.

min•i•a•tur•ize (mĭn′ē-ə-chə-rīz′, mĭn′ə-) *tr.v.* **-ized, -iz•ing, -iz•es.** To plan or make on a greatly reduced scale. — **min′i•a•tur′i•za′tion** (-chər-ĭ-zā′shən) *n.*

min•i•bike (mĭn′ē-bīk′) *n.* A small motorbike having a low frame, small wheels, and elevated handlebars. [Originally a trademark.] — **min′i•bik′er** *n.*

min•i•bus (mĭn′ē-bŭs′) *n., pl.* **-bus•es** or **-bus•ses.** A small bus typically used for short trips.

min•i•cam (mĭn′ē-kăm′) *n.* A small portable television camera used esp. for on-the-scene videotaping.

min•i•car (mĭn′ē-kär′) *n.* A very small car, esp. a subcompact.

min•i•com•put•er (mĭn′ē-kəm-pyo͞o′tər) *n. Comp. Sci.* A small computer that has more memory and a higher execution speed than a microcomputer.

Min•i•con•jou also **Min•ne•con•jou** (mĭn′ĭ-kŏn′jo͞o) *n., pl.* **Miniconjou** or **-jous** also **Minneconjou** or **-jous.** A member of a Native American people constituting a subdivision of the Teton Sioux, once inhabiting an area from the Black Hills to the Platte River and presently in South Dakota.

Mi•ni•coy Island (mĭn′ĭ-koi′). An island in the Arabian Sea off the SW coast of India.

min•ié ball (mĭn′ē, mĭn′ē-ā′) *n.* A conical rifle bullet used in the 19th century, having a hollow base that expanded when fired. [After C.E. *Minié* (1814?–79), French army officer.]

min•i•fy (mĭn′ə-fī′) *tr.v.* **-fied, -fy•ing, -fies.** To make smaller or less significant; reduce. [MIN(IMUM) + (MAGN)IFY.]

min•i•kin (mĭn′ĭ-kĭn) *n. Archaic.* A very small delicate creature. [Obsolete Du. *minneken,* darling < MDu., dim. of *minne,* love. See **men-[1]*.**]

min•im (mĭn′əm) *n.* **1.** A unit of fluid measure, as: **a.** In the United States, 1/60 of a fluid dram (0.0616 milliliters). **b.** In Great Britain, 1/20 of a scruple (0.0592 milliliters). **2.** *Mus.* A half note. **3.** An insignificantly small portion or thing. **4.** A downward vertical stroke in handwriting. [ME, half note < Med.Lat. *minimus,* least < Lat.]

min•i•mal (mĭn′ə-məl) *adj.* **1.a.** Smallest in amount or degree. **b.** Small in amount or degree. **c.** Only barely adequate. **2.** Often **Minimal.** Of, relating to, or being minimalism. — **min′i•mal′i•ty** (-măl′ĭ-tē) *n.* — **min′i•mal•ly** *adv.*

minimal art *n.* See **minimalism** 1. — **minimal artist** *n.*

min•i•mal•ism (mĭn′ə-mə-lĭz′əm) *n.* **1.** A school of abstract art that emphasizes simplification of form, as by the use of basic shapes. **2.** Use of the fewest and barest essentials or elements, as in literature or design. **3.** *Mus.* A school or mode of contemporary music marked by simplified rhythms and patterns and prolonged chordal or melodic repetitions.

min•i•mal•ist (mĭn′ə-mə-lĭst) *n.* **1.** One who advocates a moderate or conservative approach, action, or policy, as in a political organization. **2.** A practitioner of minimalism. — *adj.* **1.** Of, relating to, characteristic of, or in the style of minimalism. **2.** Being or providing the bare minimum.

min•i•mal•ize (mĭn′ə-mə-līz′) *tr.v.* **-ized, -iz•ing, -iz•es.** To make minimal. — **min′i•mal•i•za′tion** (-mə-lĭ-zā′shən) *n.*

min•i•mize (mĭn′ə-mīz′) *tr.v.* **-mized, -miz•ing, -miz•es. 1.a.** To reduce to the smallest possible amount, extent, size, or degree. **b.** To reduce. **2.** To represent as having the least degree of importance, value, or size. [< MINIMUM.] — **min′i•mi•za′tion** (-mĭ-zā′shən) *n.* — **min′i•miz′er** *n.*

min•i•mum (mĭn′ə-məm) *n., pl.* **-mums** or **-ma** (-mə). **1.a.** The least possible quantity or degree. **b.** The lowest degree or amount reached or recorded; the lower limit of variation. **2.** A lower limit permitted by law or other authority. **3.** A sum of money set by a nightclub or restaurant as the least amount each patron must spend. **4.** *Math.* **a.** The smallest number in a finite set of numbers. **b.** A value of a function that is less than any other value of the function over a specific interval. — *adj.* Of, consisting of, or representing the lowest possible amount or degree permissible or attainable. [Lat. < neut. of *minimus,* least. See **mei-[2]*.**]

minimum wage *n.* **1.** The lowest wage, determined by law or contract, that an employer may pay an employee for a specified job. **2.** See **living wage.**

min•ing (mī′nĭng) *n.* The process or business of extracting ore or minerals from the ground.

min•ion (mĭn′yən) *n.* **1.** An obsequious follower or dependent; a sycophant. **2.** A subordinate official. **3.** One highly esteemed or favored; a darling. [Fr. *mignon,* darling < OFr.]

min•is•cule (mĭn′ĭ-skyo͞ol′) *adj.* Var. of **minuscule.**

min•i•se•ries (mĭn′ē-sîr′ēz) *n., pl.* **miniseries.** A televised production, as of a novel, shown in a number of episodes.

min•i•skirt (mĭn′ē-skûrt′) *n.* A short skirt with a hemline that falls above the knee. — **min′i•skirt′ed** *adj.*

min•i•state (mĭn′ē-stāt′) *n.* See **microstate.**

min•is•ter (mĭn′ĭ-stər) *n.* **1.a.** One who is authorized to perform religious functions in a Christian church, esp. a Protestant church. **b.** *Rom. Cath. Ch.* The superior in certain orders. **2.** A high officer of state appointed to head an executive or administrative department of government. **3.** An authorized diplomatic representative of a government, usu. ranking next below an ambassador. **4.** A person serving as an agent for another by carrying out specified orders or functions. — *v.* **-tered, -ter•ing, -ters.** — *intr.* **1.** To attend to others' wants and needs. See Syns at **tend[2]. 2.** To perform the functions of a cleric. — *tr.* To administer or dispense, as a sacrament. [ME < OFr. *ministre* < Lat. *minister,* servant. See **mei-[2]*.**]

min•is•te•ri•al (mĭn′ĭ-stîr′ē-əl) *adj.* **1.** Of, relating to, or characteristic of a minister of religion or of the ministry. **2.** Of or relating to administrative and executive duties and functions of government. **3.** *Law.* Of, relating to, or being a mandatory act or duty admitting of no personal discretion or judgment in its performance. **4.** Acting or serving as an agent; instrumental. — **min′is•te′ri•al•ly** *adv.*

minister plenipotentiary *n., pl.* **ministers plenipotentiary.** A diplomatic representative ranking below an ambassador but having full governmental power and authority.

minister resident *n., pl.* **ministers resident.** A diplomatic agent ranking below a minister plenipotentiary.

min•is•trant (mĭn′ĭ-strənt) *n.* One who ministers. — *adj. Archaic.* Serving attendance on someone.

min•is•tra•tion (mĭn′ĭ-strā′shən) *n.* **1.** The act or process of serving or aiding. **2.** The act of performing the duties of a cleric. [ME < OFr. < Lat. *ministrātiō, ministrātiōn-* < *ministrātus,* p.part. of *ministrāre,* to serve < *minister,* servant. See MINISTER.] — **min′is•tra′tive** *adj.*

min•is•try (mĭn′ĭ-strē) *n., pl.* **-tries. 1.a.** The act of serving; ministration. **b.** One that serves as a means; an instrumentality. **2.a.** The profession, duties, and services of a minister. **b.** The Christian clergy. **c.** The period of service of a minister. **3.a.** A governmental department presided over by a minister. **b.** The building in which such a department is housed. **c.** The duties, functions, or term of a governmental minister. **d.** Often **Ministry.** Governmental ministers considered as a group. [ME *ministerie* < OFr. *ministere* < Lat. *ministerium* < *minister,* servant. See **mei-[2]*.**]

min•i•track (mĭn′ē-trăk′) *n.* An electronic system designed to follow the course of satellites and rockets and correlate radio signals received by a network of ground stations.

min•i•um (mĭn′ē-əm) *n.* Red lead. [Lat.]

min•i•van (mĭn′ē-văn′) *n.* A small passenger van having a boxlike shape and typically removable rear seats for cargo.

min•i•ver (mĭn′ə-vər) *n.* A white or light gray fur used as a trim on medieval robes and on ceremonial robes of state. [ME *meniver* < OFr. *menu vair,* small vair : *menu,* small; see MINUET + *vair,* vair; see VAIR.]

mink (mĭngk) *n., pl.* **mink** or **minks. 1.** Any of various semiaquatic carnivores of the genus *Mustela,* esp. *M. vison* of North America having short ears, a pointed snout, and short legs. **2.a.** The fur of the mink. **b.** A coat, stole, or hat made of mink. [ME, mink fur, poss. of Scand. orig.]

min•ke whale (mĭng′kē) *n.* See **piked whale.** [Partial transl. of Norw. *minkehval* : *minke* (perh. after *Meincke,* member of a 19th-cent. Norwegian whaling crew) + *hval,* whale.]

Minn. *abbr.* Minnesota.

Min•nan (mĭ-nän′) *n.* The dialect of Chinese spoken on most of Taiwan, in southern Fujian province, and in parts of Guangzhou and Hainan. [Chin. (Mandarin) *mĭn nán* : *mĭn,* Fujian province + *nán,* south.]

Min•ne•ap•o•lis (mĭn′ē-ăp′ə-lĭs). A city of SE MN on the Mississippi R. adjacent to St. Paul. Pop. 368,383.

Min•ne•con•jou (mĭn′ĭ-kŏn′jo͞o) *n.* Var. of **Miniconjou.**

min•ne•sing•er (mĭn′ĭ-sĭng′ər, -zĭng′-) *n.* One of the German lyric poets and singers in the troubadour tradition who flourished from the 12th to the 14th century. [Ger. < MHGer. : *minne,* love (< OHGer. *minna*; see **men-[1]***) + *singer,* singer (< *singen,* to sing < OHGer. *singan*; see **seng^{wh}-***).]

miniature
c. 1590 portrait of George Clifford, Third Earl of Cumberland, by Nicolas Hilliard; approximately 2 3/4" × 2 3/16"

miniature golf

Min•ne•so•ta (mĭn′ĭ-sō′tə). A state of the N U.S. bordering on Lake Superior and on Manitoba and Ontario, Canada; admitted as the 32nd state in 1858. Cap. St. Paul. Pop. 4,387,029. — **Min′ne•so′tan** *adj. & n.*

Minnesota River. A river of S MN flowing c. 534 km (332 mi) to the Mississippi R. near St. Paul.

Min•ne•ton•ka (mĭn′ĭ-tŏng′kə). A city of SE MN, a suburb of Minneapolis. Pop. 48,370.

Min•ne•wit (mĭn′ə-wĭt), **Peter.** See Peter **Minuit.**

min•now (mĭn′ō) *n., pl.* **minnow** or **-nows. 1.** Any of a large group of small freshwater fishes of the family Cyprinidae, widely used as live bait. **2.** Any of various other small, often silver-colored fishes. [ME *meneu.* See **men-**[4]*.]

Mi•ño (mē′nyô). See **Minho.**

Mi•no•an (mĭ-nō′ən) *adj.* Of or relating to the advanced Bronze Age culture that flourished in Crete from about 3000 to 1100 B.C. — *n.* A native or inhabitant of ancient Crete. [< Lat. *Mīnōus,* of Minos < Gk. *Minōios* < *Minōs,* Minos.]

mi•nor (mī′nər) *adj.* **1.** Lesser or smaller in amount, extent, or size. **2.** Lesser in importance, rank, or stature. **3.** Lesser in seriousness or danger. **4.** *Law.* Being under legal age; not yet a legal adult. **5.** *Chiefly British.* Relating to or being the junior or younger of two pupils with the same surname. **6.** Of or relating to a secondary area of academic specialization. **7.** *Logic.* Dealing with a more restricted category. **8.** *Mus.* **a.** Relating to or being a minor scale. **b.** Less in distance by a half step than the corresponding major interval. **c.** Based on a minor scale. — *n.* **1.** One that is lesser in comparison with others of the same class. **2.** *Law.* One who has not reached full legal age. **3.a.** A minor area of academic study. **b.** One studying a minor field. **4.** *Logic.* **a.** A minor premise. **b.** A minor term. **5.** *Mus.* A minor key, scale, or interval. **6.** *Sports.* The minor leagues of a sport, esp. baseball. — *intr.v.* **-nored, -nor•ing, -nors.** To pursue academic studies in a minor field. [ME < Lat. See **mei-**[2]*.]

Mi•nor•ca[1] (mĭ-nôr′kə) also **Me•nor•ca** (mə-nôr′kə, mĕ-nôr′kä). A Spanish island in the Balearics of the W Mediterranean. — **Mi•nor′can** *adj. & n.*

Mi•nor•ca[2] (mĭ-nôr′kə) *n.* A domestic fowl of a breed originating in the Mediterranean region and having white or black plumage. [After MINORCA[1].]

Mi•nor•ite (mī′nə-rīt′) *n.* A Franciscan friar. [< Med.Lat. *(Frātrēs) Minōrēs,* minor (friars) < Lat. *minōrēs,* pl. of *minor,* lesser. See MINOR.]

mi•nor•i•ty (mə-nôr′ĭ-tē, -nŏr′-, mī-) *n., pl.* **-ties. 1.a.** The smaller in number of two groups forming a whole. **b.** A group or party having fewer than a controlling number of votes. **2.a.** A racial, religious, or other group regarded as different from the group of which it is part. **b.** A member of such a group. See Usage Note at **color. 3.** The state or period of being under legal age: *still in her minority.*

minority leader *n.* The head of the minority party in a legislative body.

minor league *n. Sports.* A league of professional sports clubs, esp. baseball, not belonging to the major leagues. — **mi′nor-league′** (mī′nər-lēg′) *adj.* — **mi′nor-leagu′er** *n.*

minor order *n. Eccles.* One of the lower grades of the priesthood or ministry in some Christian churches. Often used in the plural.

minor planet *n.* See **asteroid** 1.

minor premise *n. Logic.* The premise in a syllogism containing the minor term, which will form the subject of the conclusion.

Mi•nor Prophets (mī′nər) *pl.n.* The Hebrew prophets Hosea, Joel, Amos, Obadiah, Jonah, Micah, Nahum, Habakkuk, Zephaniah, Haggai, Zechariah, and Malachi.

minor scale *n. Mus.* A diatonic scale having an interval of a minor third between the first and third tones and several forms with different intervals above the fifth.

minor suit *n. Games.* The suit of clubs or of diamonds in bridge.

minor term *n. Logic.* The term in a syllogism that is stated in the minor premise and forms the subject of the conclusion.

Mi•nos (mī′nəs, -nŏs′) *n. Gk. Myth.* A king of Crete who was made one of the three judges in the underworld.

Mi•not (mī′nŏt′). A city of NW-central ND NNW of Bismarck. Pop. 34,544.

Min•o•taur (mĭn′ə-tôr′, mī′nə-) *n. Gk. Myth.* A monster who was half man and half bull, to whom young Athenian men and women were sacrificed in the Cretan labyrinth.

Minsk (mĭnsk, myĕnsk). The cap. of Belorussia, in the central part; ruled since the 13th cent. by various powers, including Lithuania, Russia, Poland, and Sweden. Pop. 1,472,000.

min•ster (mĭn′stər) *n. Chiefly British.* A monastery church. [ME < OE *mynster* < VLat. **monistērium* < LLat. *monastērium,* monastery. See MONASTERY.]

min•strel (mĭn′strəl) *n.* **1.** A medieval entertainer who traveled from place to place, esp. to sing and recite poetry. **2.a.** A lyric poet. **b.** A musician. **3.a.** One of a troupe of entertainers in blackface presenting a comic variety show. **b.** A performance of such a show. [ME *minstral* < OFr. *menestrel,* servant, entertainer < LLat. *ministeriālis,* imperial household official < Lat. *ministerium,* ministry. See MINISTRY.]

minstrel show *n.* A comic variety show featuring minstrels.

min•strel•sy (mĭn′strəl-sē) *n., pl.* **-sies. 1.** The art or profession of a minstrel. **2.** A troupe of minstrels. **3.** Ballads and lyrics sung by minstrels. [ME *minstralsie* < AN *menestralsie* < OFr. *menestrel,* entertainer. See MINSTREL.]

mint[1] (mĭnt) *n.* **1.** A place where the coins of a country are manufactured by authority of the government. **2.** A place or source of manufacture or invention. **3.** An abundant amount, esp. of money. — *tr.v.* **mint•ed, mint•ing, mints. 1.** To produce (money) by stamping metal; coin. **2.** To invent or fabricate. — *adj.* Undamaged as if freshly minted. [ME < OE *mynet,* coin < Lat. *monēta.* See MONEY.] — **mint′er** *n.*

mint[2] (mĭnt) *n.* **1.** A member of the mint family. **2.a.** Any of various plants of the genus *Mentha,* some of which are cultivated for their aromatic oil and used for flavoring. **b.** The fresh or dried aromatic foliage of some of these plants. **3.** Any of various similar or related plants. **4.** A candy flavored with mint. [ME *minte* < OE < Gmc. **minta* < Lat. *menta,* poss. < Gk. *minthē.*] — **mint′y** *adj.*

mint•age (mĭn′tĭj) *n.* **1.** The act or process of minting coins. **2.** Coins manufactured in a mint. **3.** The fee paid to a mint by a government. **4.** The impression stamped on a coin.

mint family *n.* A large family of aromatic herbs, the Labiatae (or Lamiaceae), characterized by opposite leaves, square stems, and bilaterally symmetrical flowers.

mint julep *n.* A drink of bourbon, sugar, and mint leaves.

Min•ton (mĭn′tən), **Sherman.** 1890–1965. Amer. jurist; associate justice of the U.S. Supreme Court (1949–56).

min•u•end (mĭn′yo͞o-ĕnd′) *n. Math.* The quantity from which another quantity, the subtrahend, is to be subtracted. [Lat. *minuendum,* thing to be diminished, neut. gerundive of *minuere,* to lessen. See **mei-**[2]*.]

min•u•et (mĭn′yo͞o-ĕt′) *n.* **1.** A slow stately pattern dance in 3/4 time for groups of couples, originating in 17th-century France. **2.** The music for or in the rhythm of the minuet. [Fr. *menuet* < OFr., small, dainty (< its small steps), dim. of *menu,* small < Lat. *minūtus.* See MINUTE[2].]

Min•u•it (mĭn′yo͞o-ĭt) also **Min•ne•wit** (-ə-wĭt), **Peter.** 1580–1638. Dutch colonial administrator who purchased Manhattan from Native Americans for the equivalent of $24.

mi•nus (mī′nəs) *prep.* **1.** *Math.* Reduced by the subtraction of; less: *Nine minus three is six.* **2.** *Informal.* Without: *minus my briefcase.* — *adj.* **1.** *Math.* Negative or on the negative part of a scale. **2.** Ranking on the lower end of a designated scale. — *n.* **1.** *Math.* **a.** The minus sign (−). **b.** A negative quantity. **2.** A deficiency or defect. [ME < Lat. *minus,* neut. of *minor,* less. See **mei-**[2]*.]

min•us•cule (mĭn′ə-skyo͞ol′, mĭ-nŭs′kyo͞ol′) also **min•is•cule** (mĭn′ĭ-skyo͞ol′) — *adj.* **1.** Very small; tiny. See Syns at **small. 2.** Of, relating to, or written in miniscule. — *n.* **1.** A small cursive script developed from uncial and used in medieval manuscripts. **2.** A letter written in minuscule. **3.** A lowercase letter. [Fr. < Lat. *minusculus,* rather small, dim. of *minus,* neut. of *minor,* smaller. See **mei-**[2]*.] — **mi•nus′cu•lar** (mĭ-nŭs′kyə-lər) *adj.*

minus sign *n. Math.* The symbol −, as in 4 − 2 = 2, that is used to indicate subtraction or a negative quantity.

min•ute[1] (mĭn′ĭt) *n.* **1.** A unit of time equal to one sixtieth of an hour, or 60 seconds. **2.** A unit of angular measurement equal to one sixtieth of a degree, or 60 seconds. **3.** A measure of the distance one can cover in a minute. **4.** A short interval of time; moment. **5.** A specific point in time. **6.** A note or summary covering points to be remembered; a memorandum. **7. minutes.** An official record of the proceedings at a meeting. — *tr.v.* **-ut•ed, -ut•ing, -utes.** To record in a memorandum or the minutes of a meeting. [ME < OFr. < Med.Lat. *(pars) minūta (prīma),* (first) minute (part) < Lat. *minūta,* fem. of *minūtus,* small. See MINUTE[2].]

mi•nute[2] (mī-no͞ot′, -nyo͞ot′, mĭ-) *adj.* **1.** Exceptionally small; tiny. See Syns at **small. 2.** Beneath notice; insignificant. **3.** Characterized by careful scrutiny and close examination. See Syns at **detailed.** [ME < Lat. *minūtus,* p.part. of *minuere,* to lessen. See **mei-**[2]*.] — **mi•nute′ness** *n.*

min•ute hand (mĭn′it) *n.* The long hand on a clock or watch that indicates minutes.

mi•nute•ly[1] (mī-no͞ot′lē, -nyo͞ot′-, mĭ-) *adv.* **1.** With attention to small details. **2.** On a very small scale. **3.** Into tiny pieces.

min•ute•ly[2] (mĭn′ĭt-lē) *adj. Archaic.* On a minute-by-minute basis.

min•ute•man (mĭn′ĭt-măn′) *n.* An armed man pledged to be ready to fight on a minute's notice just before and during the Revolutionary War in the United States.

min•ute of arc (mĭn′ĭt) *n.* See **minute**[1] 2.

min•ute steak (mĭn′ĭt) *n.* A small thin steak, often scored or cubed, that can be cooked quickly.

mi•nu•ti•a (mĭ-no͞o′shē-ə, -shə, -nyo͞o′-) *n., pl.* **-ti•ae** (-shē-ē′). A small or trivial detail. [< LLat. *minūtiae,* petty details < Lat. *minūtia,* smallness < *minūtus,* small. See MINUTE[2].]

minx (mĭngks) *n.* **1.** A girl or young woman considered pert, flirtatious, or impudent. **2.** *Obsolete.* A promiscuous woman. [?] — **minx′ish** *adj.*

min•yan (mĭn′yən, mēn-yän′) *n., pl.* **min•ya•nim** (mēn-yä-

minor scale

minuteman
Statue of Capt. John Parker (1729–1775) in Lexington, Massachusetts, by Henry Kitson (1865–1947)

ă pat	oi boy
ā pay	ou out
âr care	o͝o took
ä father	o͞o boot
ĕ pet	ŭ cut
ē be	ûr urge
ĭ pit	th thin
ī pie	*th* this
îr pier	hw which
ŏ pot	zh vision
ō toe	ə about, item
ô paw	

Stress marks:
′ (primary);
′ (secondary), as in dictionary (dĭk′shə-nĕr′ē)

mis•hap (mĭs′hăp′, mĭs-hăp′) *n.* **1.** Bad luck. **2.** An unfortunate accident.

Mish•a•wa•ka (mĭsh′ə-wô′kə, -wŏk′ə). A city of N IN, a suburb of South Bend. Pop. 42,608.

mish•e•gaas or **mish•e•goss** (mĭsh′ə-gäs′) *n. Slang.* Var. of **meshugaas.**

mis•hit (mĭs-hĭt′) *tr.v.* **-hit, -hit•ting, -hits.** To hit (a tennis or cricket ball, for example) incorrectly or badly. **—mis′hit′** *n.*

mish•mash (mĭsh′măsh′, -mäsh′) *n.* A collection or mixture of unrelated things; a hodgepodge. [ME *misse-masche,* prob. redup. of *mash,* soft mixture. See MASH.]

Mish•nah also **Mish•na** (mĭsh′nə) *n. Judaism.* **1.** The first section of the Talmud, being a collection of early oral interpretations of the scriptures as compiled about A.D. 200. **2.** A paragraph from this section of the Talmud. **3.** The teaching of a rabbi or other authority on Jewish laws. [Rabbinical Heb. *mišnâ,* repetition, instruction < *šānâ,* to repeat.] **—Mish•na′ic** (mĭsh-nā′ĭk) *adj.*

Mishnaic Hebrew *n.* The Hebrew language as used from the fifth century B.C. to the late seventh century A.D.

mis•in•ter•pret (mĭs′ĭn-tûr′prĭt) *tr.v.* **-pret•ed, -pret•ing, -prets. 1.** To interpret inaccurately. **2.** To explain inaccurately. **—mis′in•ter′pre•ta′tion** *n.* **—mis′in•ter′pret•er** *n.*

mis•join•der (mĭs-join′dər) *n. Law.* Improper joining of different causes of action or of different parties to a lawsuit.

Mis•ki•to (mĭ-skē′tō) *n., pl.* **Miskito** or **-tos. 1.** A member of an American Indian people inhabiting the Caribbean coast of northeast Nicaragua and southeast Honduras. **2.** The language of the Miskito.

mis•know (mĭs-nō′) *tr.v.* **-knew** (-no͞o′, -nyo͞o′), **-known** (-nōn′), **-know•ing, -knows.** To misunderstand. **—mis•knowl′edge** (-nŏl′ĭj) *n.*

Mis•kolc (mĭsh′kôlts′). A city of NE Hungary NE of Budapest. Pop. 211,645.

mis•lay (mĭs-lā′) *tr.v.* **-laid** (-lād′), **-lay•ing, -lays. 1.** To put in a place that is afterward forgotten. **2.** To place or put down incorrectly: *They mislaid the linoleum.* **—mis•lay′er** *n.*

mis•lead (mĭs-lēd′) *tr.v.* **-led** (-lĕd′), **-lead•ing, -leads. 1.** To lead in the wrong direction. **2.** To lead into error of thought or action, esp. by intentionally deceiving. See Syns at **deceive.** **—mis•lead′er** *n.*

mis•lead•ing (mĭs-lē′dĭng) *adj.* Tending to mislead.

mis•like (mĭs-līk′) *tr.v.* **-liked, -lik•ing, -likes. 1.** To disapprove of; dislike. **2.** *Archaic.* To displease. **—***n.* Disapproval; dislike. [ME *misliken* < OE *mislīcian* : *mis-,* ill; see MIS-[1] + *līcian,* to please; see LIKE[1].]

mis•no•mer (mĭs-nō′mər) *n.* **1.** An error in naming a person or place. **2.a.** Application of a wrong name. **b.** A name wrongly or unsuitably applied to a person or an object. [ME *misnoumer* < OFr. *mesnomer,* to misname : *mes-,* wrongly; see MIS-[1] + *nommer,* to name (< Lat. *nōmināre* < *nōmen,* name; see **nō-men-***).] **—mis•no′mered** *adj.*

mi•so (mē′sō) *n., pl.* **-sos.** A thick fermented paste made by grinding together cooked soybeans, rice or barley, and salt and used esp. in making soups and sauces. [J.]

miso– or **mis–** *pref.* Hatred: *misogamy.* [Gk. < *misein,* to hate and *misos,* hatred.]

mi•sog•a•my (mĭ-sŏg′ə-mē) *n.* Hatred of marriage. **—mis′o•gam′ic** (mĭs′ə-găm′ĭk) *adj.* **—mis•og′a•mist** *n.*

mi•sog•y•nist (mĭ-sŏj′ə-nĭst) *n.* One who hates women. **—***adj.* Of or characterized by a hatred of women. **—mi•sog′y•nis′tic, mi•sog′y•nous** *adj.*

mi•sog•y•ny (mĭ-sŏj′ə-nē) *n.* Hatred of women. [Gk. *misogunia* : *miso-,* miso- + *gunē,* woman; see -GYNY.] **—mis′o•gyn′ic** (mĭs′ə-jĭn′ĭk, -gī′nĭk) *adj.*

mi•sol•o•gy (mĭ-sŏl′ə-jē) *n.* Hatred of reason, argument, or enlightenment. **—mi•sol′o•gist** *n.*

mis•o•ne•ism (mĭs′ə-nē′ĭz′əm) *n.* Hatred or fear of change or innovation. [Ital. *misoneismo* : Gk. *miso-,* miso- + Gk. *neos,* new; see **newo-***.] **—mis′o•ne′ist** *n.*

mis•o•ri•ent (mĭs-ôr′ē-ənt, -ĕnt′, -ōr′-) *tr.v.* **-ent•ed, -ent•ing, -ents.** To orient incorrectly or inappropriately. **—mis•o′ri•en•ta′tion** *n.*

mis•pick•el (mĭs′pĭk′əl) *n.* See **arsenopyrite.** [Ger.]

mis•place (mĭs-plās′) *tr.v.* **-placed, -plac•ing, -plac•es. 1.a.** To put into a wrong place. **b.** To mislay. **2.** To bestow (confidence, for example) on an improper, unsuitable, or unworthy person or idea. **—mis•place′ment** *n.*

mis•placed modifier (mĭs′plāst′) *n.* A modifying clause or phrase placed so awkwardly as to create ambiguity or misunderstanding, as in *Streaking through the sky, we watched the rocket reenter the atmosphere.*

mis•play (mĭs-plā′, mĭs′plā′) *n. Sports & Games.* A mistaken play. **—***tr.v.* (mĭs-plā′) **-played, -play•ing, -plays.** To make a misplay of.

mis•print (mĭs-prĭnt′) *tr.v.* **-print•ed, -print•ing, -prints.** To print incorrectly. **—***n.* (mĭs′prĭnt′, mĭs-prĭnt′). An error in printing.

mis•pri•sion[1] (mĭs-prĭzh′ən) *n. Law.* **1.** Maladministration of public office. **2.** Neglect in preventing or reporting a felony or treason by one not an accessory. **3.** An act of sedition against a government or the courts. [ME < AN, var. of OFr. *mesprison* < *mespris,* p.part. of *mesprendre,* to make a mistake : *mes-,* wrongly; see MIS-[1] + *prendre,* to take, seize (< Lat. *prehendere, prendere*; see **ghend-***).]

mis•pri•sion[2] (mĭs-prĭzh′ən) *n.* Contempt; disdain. [*mispris(e)* (var. of MISPRIZE) + -ION.]

mis•prize (mĭs-prīz′) *tr.v.* **-prized, -priz•ing, -priz•es. 1.** To despise. **2.** To undervalue. **—mis•priz′er** *n.*

mis•read (mĭs-rēd′) *tr.v.* **-read** (-rĕd′), **-read•ing, -reads. 1.** To read inaccurately. **2.** To misinterpret or misunderstand.

mis•rep•re•sent (mĭs-rĕp′rĭ-zĕnt′) *tr.v.* **-sent•ed, -sent•ing, -sents. 1.** To give an incorrect or misleading representation of. **2.** To serve incorrectly or dishonestly as an official representative of. **—mis•rep′re•sen•ta′tion** *n.* **—mis•rep′re•sen′ta•tive** (-zĕn′tə-tĭv) *adj.* **—mis•rep′re•sent′er** *n.*

mis•rule (mĭs-ro͞ol′) *n.* **1.** Disorder or lawless confusion. **2.** Inept or unwise rule; misgovernment. **—***tr.v.* **-ruled, -rul•ing, -rules.** To rule ineptly, unjustly, or unwisely; misgovern.

miss[1] (mĭs) *v.* **missed, miss•ing, miss•es. —***tr.* **1.** To fail to hit, reach, catch, meet, or otherwise make contact with. **2.** To fail to perceive, achieve, understand, or experience. **3.** To fail to accomplish, achieve, or attain (a goal). **4.** To fail to attend or perform. **5.a.** To leave out; omit. **b.** To let go by; let slip. **6.** To escape or avoid. **7.** To discover the absence or loss of. **8.** To feel the lack or loss of. **—***intr.* **1.** To fail to hit or otherwise make contact with something. **2.a.** To be unsuccessful; fail. **b.** To misfire, as an internal-combustion engine. **—***n.* **1.** A failure to hit, succeed, or find. **2.** The misfiring of an engine. **—*idioms.* miss fire. 1.** To fail to discharge. Used of a firearm. **2.** To fail to achieve the anticipated result. **miss out on.** To lose a chance for. **miss the boat.** *Informal.* **1.** To fail to avail oneself of an opportunity. **2.** To fail to understand. [ME *missen* < OE *missan.* See **mei-**[1]*.]

miss[2] (mĭs) *n.* **1. Miss.** Used as a courtesy title before the surname or full name of a girl or an unmarried woman. See Usage Note at **Ms. 2.** Used as a form of polite address for a girl or young woman: *Thanks, miss.* **3.** A young unmarried woman. **4. Miss.** Used as a prefix to the name of that which a usu. young woman is held to represent: *Miss Personality.* **5. mis•ses.** A series of clothing sizes for women and girls of average height and proportions. [Short for MISTRESS.]

Miss. *abbr.* Mississippi.

mis•sa cantata (mĭs′ə) *n.* A Mass in which certain parts are sung but which is less elaborate than a High Mass. [NLat. *missa cantāta* : LLat. *missa,* Mass + Lat. *cantāta,* sung.]

mis•sal (mĭs′əl) *n.* **1.** *Rom. Cath. Ch.* A book containing all the prayers and responses necessary for celebrating the Mass throughout the year. **2.** A prayer book. [ME *messel* < OFr. < Med.Lat. *missāle* < neut. of *missālis,* of the Mass < LLat. *missa,* Mass. See MASS.]

mis•sel thrush (mĭs′əl) *n.* Var. of **mistle thrush.**

mis•sense (mĭs′sĕns′) *n. Genet.* A section within a strand of messenger RNA containing a codon altered through mutation so that it codes for a different amino acid.

missense mutation *n. Genet.* A mutation that changes a codon for one amino acid into a codon for a different amino acid. [MIS-[1] + (NON)SENSE.]

mis•shape (mĭs-shāp′) *tr.v.* **-shaped** or **-shap•en** (-shā′pən), **-shap•ing, -shapes.** To shape badly; deform. **—mis•shap′en•ly** *adv.* **—mis•shap′er** *n.*

mis•sile (mĭs′əl, -īl′) *n.* **1.** An object or a weapon that is fired, thrown, dropped, or otherwise projected at a target; a projectile. **2.** A guided missile. **3.** A ballistic missile. [Lat. < neut. of *missilis,* able to be thrown < *missus,* p.part. of *mittere,* to let go, throw.]

mis•sile•ry also **mis•sil•ry** (mĭs′əl-rē) *n.* **1.** The science and technology of making and using guided or ballistic missiles. **2.** Missiles considered as a group.

miss•ing (mĭs′ĭng) *adj.* **1.a.** Not present; absent. **b.** Lost: *a missing person.* **2.** Lacking; wanting.

missing link *n.* **1.** A primate postulated to bridge the evolutionary gap between the anthropoid apes and human beings. **2.** Something lacking that is needed to complete a series.

mis•sion (mĭsh′ən) *n.* **1.a.** A body of persons sent to conduct negotiations or establish relations with a foreign country. **b.** The business with which such a body of persons is charged. **c.** A permanent diplomatic office abroad. **d.** A body of experts or dignitaries sent to a foreign country. **2.a.** A body of persons sent to a foreign land by a religious organization, to spread its faith and provide assistance. **b.** A mission established abroad. **c.** The district assigned to a mission worker. **d.** A building or compound housing a mission. **e.** An organization for carrying on missionary work in a territory. **f. missions.** Missionary duty or work. **3.** A Christian church or congregation with no cleric of its own that depends for support on a larger religious organization. **4.** A series of special Christian services for purposes of proselytizing. **5.** A welfare or educational organization established for the needy people of a district. **6.a.** A special assignment given to a person or group. **b.** A combat operation assigned to a person or military unit. **c.** An aerospace operation intended to carry out specific program objectives. **7.** An inner calling to pursue an activity or perform a service; a vocation. **—***tr.v.* **-sioned, -sion•ing,**

mission
San Xavier del Bac Mission, founded in 1700, near Tucson, Arizona

-sions. 1. To send on a mission. **2.** To organize or establish a religious mission among or in. *— adj.* **1.** Of or relating to a mission. **2.** Of or relating to a style of architecture or furniture used in the early Spanish missions of California. **3.** Often **Mission.** Of, relating to, or having the distinctive qualities of an early 20th-century style of plain heavy dark-stained wood furniture. [Fr. < OFr. < Lat. *missiō, missiōn-* < *missus,* p.part. of *mittere,* to send off.] **— mis′sion•al** *adj.*

Mission. A city of S TX near the Rio Grande WNW of Brownsville. Pop. 28,653.

mis•sion•ar•y (mĭsh′ə-nĕr′ē) *n., pl.* **-ies. 1.** One sent on a mission, esp. to do religious or charitable work in a territory or foreign country. **2.** One who attempts to persuade or convert others, as to a doctrine; a propagandist. *— adj.* **1.** Of or relating to missions or missionaries. **2.** Engaged in the activities of a mission or missionary. **3.** Tending to propagandize or use insistent persuasion.

missionary position *n.* A position for sexual intercourse in which a woman and man lie facing each other, with the woman on the bottom and the man on the top.

Mis•sion•ar•y Ridge (mĭsh′ə-nĕr′ē). A range of hills in SE TN and NW GA; site of an important Union victory (Nov. 25, 1863) in the Civil War.

mis•sion•er (mĭsh′ə-nər) *n.* A missionary.

mis•sion•ize (mĭsh′ə-nīz′) *v.* **-ized, -iz•ing, -iz•es.** *— intr.* To do missionary work. *— tr.* **1.** To perform missionary work in or among. **2.** To bring under the influence or control of a mission.

Mission Vi•e•jo (vē-ā′hō). A community of S CA SE of Irvine. Pop. 72,820.

mis•sis or **mis•sus** (mĭs′ĭz, -ĭs) *n. Informal.* **1.** The mistress of a household. **2.** Used as a term of reference by a man of his wife. [Alteration of MISTRESS.]

Mis•sis•sau•ga (mĭs′ĭ-sô′gə). A town of S Ontario, Canada, a suburb of Toronto on Lake Ontario. Pop. 315,056.

Mis•sis•sip•pi (mĭs′ĭ-sĭp′ē). A state of the SE U.S.; admitted as the 20th state in 1817. The **Mississippi Territory,** organized in 1798 and enlarged in 1804 and 1813, also included the present state of AL. Cap. Jackson. Pop. 2,586,443.

Mis•sis•sip•pi•an (mĭs′ĭ-sĭp′ē-ən) *adj.* **1.** Of or relating to the state or residents of Mississippi or the Mississippi River. **2.** Of, belonging to, or being the fifth period of the Paleozoic Era, characterized by the submergence of extensive land areas under shallow seas. See table at **geologic time.** *— n.* **1.** A native or resident of Mississippi. **2.** The Mississippian Period or its deposits.

Mississippi River. The chief river of the U.S., rising in the lake region of N MN and flowing c. 3,781 km (2,350 mi) to enter the Gulf of Mexico through a huge delta in SE LA. La Salle claimed the entire region for France after he descended to the river's mouth in 1682.

mis•sive (mĭs′ĭv) *n.* A written message; a letter. [< ME *(letter) missive,* (letter) sent (by superior authority) < Med.Lat. *(litterae) missīve,* fem. pl. of *missīvus,* sent < Lat. *missus,* p.part. of *mittere,* to send.]

Mis•sou•la (mĭ-zo͞o′lə). A city of W MT WNW of Helena. Pop. 42,918.

Mis•sou•ri[1] (mĭ-zo͝or′ē) *n., pl.* **Missouri** or **-ris. 1.** A member of a Native American people formerly inhabiting north-central Missouri, with present-day descendants in north-central Oklahoma. **2.** Their Siouan language. [Fr. < Illinois *ouemessourita,* those that have dugout canoes.]

Mis•sou•ri[2] (mĭ-zo͝or′ē, -zo͝or′ə). A state of the central U.S.; admitted as the 24th state in 1821. Its application for admission as a slaveholding state in 1817 sparked a bitter controversy over the question of allowing slavery in new territories. By the Missouri Compromise (1820) ME was admitted as a free state and MO as a slave state. Cap. Jefferson City. Pop. 5,137,804. **— Mis•sou′ri•an** *adj. & n.*

Missouri City. A city of SE TX, a suburb of Houston. Pop. 36,176.

Missouri River. A river of the U.S. rising in the Rocky Mts. as various headstreams that join to form the Missouri proper in SW MT. The longest river in the U.S., it flows c. 4,127 km (2,565 mi) to the Mississippi R. N of St. Louis MO.

mis•speak (mĭs-spēk′) *v.* **-spoke** (-spōk′), **-spo•ken** (-spō′kən), **-speak•ing, -speaks.** *— tr.* To speak or pronounce incorrectly. *— intr.* To speak mistakenly or inappropriately.

mis•spell (mĭs-spĕl′) *tr.v.* **-spelled** or **-spelt** (-spĕlt′), **-spell•ing, -spells.** To spell incorrectly.

mis•spell•ing (mĭs-spĕl′ĭng) *n.* **1.** The act or an instance of spelling incorrectly. **2.** A word spelled incorrectly.

mis•step (mĭs-stĕp′) *n.* **1.** A misplaced or awkward step. **2.** An instance of wrong or improper conduct; a blunder.

mis•sus (mĭs′ĭz, -ĭs) *n.* Var. of **missis.**

miss•y (mĭs′ē) *n., pl.* **-ies.** *Informal.* Used as a familiar term of address for a young woman or girl.

mist (mĭst) *n.* **1.** A mass of fine droplets of water in the atmosphere near or in contact with the earth. **2.** Water vapor condensed on and clouding the appearance of a surface. **3.** Fine drops of a liquid, such as water, perfume, or medication, sprayed into the air. **4.** A suspension of fine drops of a liquid in a gas. **5.** Something that dims or conceals. **6.** A haze before the eyes that blurs the vision. **7.** Something that produces or gives the impression of dimness or obscurity. **8.** A drink of liquor over cracked ice. *— v.* **mist•ed, mist•ing, mists.** *— intr.* **1.** To be or become obscured by or as if by mist. **2.** To rain in a fine shower. *— tr.* **1.** To conceal or veil with or as if with mist. **2.** To moisturize (plants, for example) with a fine spray of water. [ME < OE. See **meigh-*.**]

mis•tak•a•ble (mĭ-stā′kə-bəl) *adj.* Capable of being mistaken or misunderstood: *mistakable signals.* **— mis•tak′a•bly** *adv.*

mis•take (mĭ-stāk′) *n.* **1.** An error or a fault resulting from defective judgment, deficient knowledge, or carelessness. **2.** A misconception or misunderstanding. See Syns at **error.** *— v.* **mis•took** (mĭ-sto͝ok′), **mis•tak•en** (mĭ-stā′kən), **mis•tak•ing, mis•takes.** *— tr.* **1.** To understand wrongly; misinterpret. **2.** To recognize or identify incorrectly. *— intr.* To make a mistake; err. [< ME *mistaken,* to misunderstand < ON *mistaka,* to take in error : *mis-,* wrongly; see **mei-**[1]* + *taka,* to take.] **— mis•tak′er** *n.*

mis•tak•en (mĭ-stā′kən) *adj.* **1.** Wrong or incorrect in opinion, understanding, or perception. **2.** Based on error; wrong: *a mistaken view of the situation.* **— mis•tak′en•ly** *adv.*

Mis•tas•si•ni (mĭs′tə-sē′nē), **Lake.** A lake of S-central Quebec, Canada, draining into James Bay via the Rupert R.

Mis•ter (mĭs′tər) *n.* **1.** Used as a courtesy title before the surname, full name, or professional title of a man, usu. written in its abbreviated form: *Mr. Jones.* **2.** Used as the official term of address for certain U.S. military personnel, such as warrant officers. **3. mister.** *Informal.* Used as a form of address for a man: *Thanks, mister.* **4.** *Informal.* Used by a woman to refer to her husband. [Alteration of MASTER.]

Mister Char•lie (chär′lē) *n. Offensive Slang.* Var. of **Mr. Charlie.**

mist•flow•er (mĭst′flou′ər) *n.* A perennial plant *(Eupatorium coelestinum)* of the southeast and central United States having corymbs of small blue flowers.

Mis•ti (mē′stē), **El.** See **El Misti.**

mis•tle thrush also **mis•sel thrush** (mĭs′əl) *n.* A European thrush *(Turdus viscivorus)* that feeds on berries, esp. those of mistletoe. [< obsolete *missel,* mistletoe < ME *mistel* < OE. See MISTLETOE.]

mistletoe

mis•tle•toe (mĭs′əl-tō′) *n.* **1.** A Eurasian parasitic shrub *(Viscum album)* having leathery evergreen leaves and waxy white berries. **2.** Any of several American parasitic shrubs, such as *Phoradendron flavescens* of eastern North America. **3.** A sprig of mistletoe, often used as a Christmas decoration. [ME *mistelto,* back-formation < OE *misteltān* (*tān,* taken for pl. of *tā,* toe) : *mistel,* mistletoe; see **meigh-*** + *tān,* twig.]

mis•tral (mĭs′trəl, mĭ-sträl′) *n.* A dry cold northerly wind that blows in squalls toward the Mediterranean coast of southern France. [Fr. < Prov. *maestral* < OProv. < LLat. *magistrālis,* of a master < Lat. *magister,* master. See **meg-*.**]

Mis•tral (mĭ-sträl′, mē-), **Frédéric.** 1830–1914. French Provençal writer who shared the 1904 Nobel Prize for literature.

Mistral, Gabriela. 1889–1957. Chilean poet who won the 1945 Nobel Prize for literature.

mis•treat (mĭs-trēt′) *tr.v.* **-treat•ed, -treat•ing, -treats.** To treat roughly or wrongly; abuse. See Syns at **abuse.** **— mis•treat′ment** *n.*

mis•tress (mĭs′trĭs) *n.* **1.** A woman in a position of authority, control, or ownership, as the head of a household. **2.** A woman owner of an animal or a slave. **3.** A woman with ultimate control over something. **4.a.** A nation or country that has supremacy over others. **b.** Something personified as female that directs or reigns. **5.** A woman who has expertise in a skill or a branch of learning. **6.** A woman who has a continuing sexual relationship with and receives financial support from a usu. married man. **7. Mistress.** Used formerly as a courtesy title when speaking to or of a woman. **8.** *Chiefly British.* A woman schoolteacher. [ME *maistresse* < OFr., fem. of *maistre,* master < Lat. *magister.* See MASTER.]

mis•tri•al (mĭs-trī′əl, -trīl′) *n. Law.* **1.** A trial that becomes invalid because of basic prejudicial error in procedure. **2.** An inconclusive trial, as one in which the jurors fail to agree.

mis•trust (mĭs-trŭst′) *n.* Lack of trust or confidence arising from suspicion. See Syns at **uncertainty.** *— v.* **-trust•ed, -trust•ing, -trusts.** *— tr.* To regard with mistrust. *— intr.* To be wary, suspicious, or doubtful. **— mis•trust′ful** *adj.* **— mis•trust′ful•ly** *adv.* **— mis•trust′ful•ness** *n.*

mist•y (mĭs′tē) *adj.* **-i•er, -i•est. 1.** Consisting of or marked by mist: *a misty rain.* **2.** Obscured or clouded by or as if by mist. **3.a.** Vague; hazy: *a misty recollection.* **b.** Full of tender emotion; sentimental. **— mist′i•ly** *adv.* **— mist′i•ness** *n.*

mist•y-eyed (mĭs′tē-īd′) *adj.* **1.** Having the eyes blurred, as with tears. **2.** Having a sentimental or dreamy quality.

mis•un•der•stand (mĭs′ŭn-dər-stănd′) *tr.v.* **-stood** (-sto͝od′), **-stand•ing, -stands.** To understand incorrectly.

mis•un•der•stand•ing (mĭs′ŭn-dər-stăn′dĭng) *n.* **1.** A failure to understand or interpret correctly. **2.** A disagreement or quarrel.

mis•un•der•stood (mĭs′ŭn-dər-sto͝od′) *adj.* **1.** Incorrectly understood or interpreted. **2.** Not appreciated or given sympa-

ă pat	oi boy
ā pay	ou out
âr care	o͝o took
ä father	o͞o boot
ĕ pet	ŭ cut
ē be	ûr urge
ĭ pit	th thin
ī pie	*th* this
îr pier	hw which
ŏ pot	zh vision
ō toe	ə about,
ô paw	item

Stress marks:
′ (primary);
′ (secondary), as in dictionary (dĭk′shə-nĕr′ē)

lesque of the heroic manner or style. —**mock′-he•ro′ic** *adj.* —**mock′-he•ro′i•cal•ly** *adv.*

mock•ing•bird (mŏk′ĭng-bûrd′) *n.* Any of several species of New World birds of the family Mimidae, esp. *Mimus polyglottos,* a gray and white bird of the southern and eastern United States, noted for the ability to mimic other birds.

mock moon *n.* A paraselene.

mock orange *n.* **1.** Any of numerous deciduous shrubs of the genus *Philadelphus,* having opposite simple leaves and white, usu. fragrant flowers with four petals and numerous stamens. **2.** Any of various similar or related shrubs or trees.

mock sun *n.* A parhelion.

mock turtle soup *n.* Soup made from calf's head, veal, or other meat and spiced to taste like green turtle soup.

mock•up also **mock-up** (mŏk′ŭp′) *n.* **1.** A usu. full-sized scale model of a structure. **2.** A layout of printed matter.

mod[1] (mŏd) *n.* An unconventionally modern style of fashionable dress originating in England in the 1960's. —*adj.* **1.** In or characteristic of this style. **2.** Fashionably up-to-date, esp. in style, design, or dress. [After *the Mods,* name of several gangs of English youths in the 1960's, short for MODERN.]

mod[2] *abbr. Math.* Modulus.

mod. *abbr.* **1.** Moderate. **2.** *Mus.* Moderato. **3.** Modern.

mod•a•cryl•ic (mŏd′ə-krĭl′ĭk) *n.* One of several synthetic, long-chain polymer textile fibers containing 35–85 percent acrylonitrile. [*mod(ified) acrylic.*]

mod•al (mōd′l) *adj.* **1.** Of, relating to, or characteristic of a mode. **2.** *Gram.* Of, relating to, or expressing the mood of a verb. **3.** *Mus.* Of, relating to, characteristic of, or composed in any of the modes typical of medieval church music. **4.** *Philos.* Of or relating to mode without referring to substance. **5.** *Logic.* Expressing or characterized by modality. **6.** *Statistics.* Of or relating to a statistical mode or modes. [Med.Lat. *modālis* < Lat. *modus,* measure. See **med-***.] —**mod′al•ly** *adv.*

modal auxiliary *n.* One of a set of English verbs, including *can, may, must, ought, shall, should, will,* and *would,* that are usu. used with other verbs to express mood or tense.

mo•dal•i•ty (mō-dăl′ĭ-tē) *n., pl.* **-ties. 1.** The fact, state, or quality of being modal. **2.** A tendency to conform to a pattern or belong to a group or category. **3.** *Logic.* The classification of propositions based on whether they assert or deny the possibility, impossibility, contingency, or necessity of their content. **4. modalities.** The ceremonial forms, protocols, or conditions that surround formal agreements or negotiations. **5.** *Medic.* A therapeutic method or agent, such as surgery, that involves the physical treatment of a disorder. **6.** *Physiol.* Any of the various types of sensation, such as vision.

mode (mōd) *n.* **1.a.** A manner, way, or method of doing or acting. See Syns at **method. b.** A particular form, variety, or manner: *a mode of expression.* **c.** A given condition of functioning; a status. **2.** The current or customary fashion or style. **3.** *Mus.* **a.** Any of certain fixed arrangements of the diatonic tones of an octave. **b.** A patterned arrangement, as the one characteristic of the music of classical Greece. **4.** *Philos.* The particular appearance, form, or manner in which an underlying substance or a permanent aspect or attribute of it is manifested. **5.** *Logic.* **a.** See **modality** 3. **b.** The arrangement or order of the propositions in a syllogism according to both quality and quantity. **6.** *Statistics.* The value or item occurring most frequently in a series of observations or statistical data. **7.** *Math.* The number or range of numbers in a set that occurs most frequently. **8.** *Geol.* The mineral composition of a sample of igneous rock. **9.** *Phys.* Any of numerous patterns of wave motion. **10.** *Gram.* Mood. [ME, tune < Lat. *modus,* manner, tune. Sense 2, Fr. < OFr., fashion, manner < Lat. *modus.* See **med-***.]

mod•el (mŏd′l) *n.* **1.** A small object, usu. built to scale, that represents in detail another, often larger object. **2.a.** A preliminary work or construction that serves as a plan from which to make a final product. **b.** Such a work or construction used in testing or perfecting a final product. **3.** A schematic description of a system, theory, or phenomenon that accounts for its properties and may be used for further study of its characteristics. **4.** A style or design of an item. **5.** One serving as an example to be imitated or compared. **6.** One that serves as the subject for an artist, esp. a person employed to pose. **7.** A person employed to display merchandise, such as clothing. **8.** *Zool.* An animal whose appearance is copied by a mimic. —*v.* **-eled, -el•ing, -els** also **-elled, -el•ling, -els.** —*tr.* **1.** To make or construct a model of. **2.** To plan, construct, or fashion according to a model. **3.** To make conform to a standard. **4.** To make by shaping a plastic substance. **5.** To display by wearing or posing. **6.** In painting, drawing, and photography, to give a three-dimensional appearance to, as by shading or highlighting. —*intr.* **1.** To make a model. **2.** To serve as a model. —*adj.* **1.** Being, serving as, or used as a model. **2.** Worthy of imitation. [Fr. *modèle* < Ital. *modello,* dim. of *modo,* form < Lat. *modus,* measure, standard. See **med-***.] —**mod′el•er** *n.*

mod•el•ing (mŏd′l-ĭng) *n.* **1.** The act or art of sculpturing or forming in a pliable material, such as clay. **2.a.** Representation of depth and solidity in painting, drawing, or photography. **b.** Visual shape and texture of something regarded aesthetically. **3.** The act or profession of being a model.

mo•dem (mō′dĕm′) *n. Comp. Sci.* A device that converts data from one form into another, as from one form usable in data processing to another form usable in telephonic transmission. [MO(DULATOR) + DEM(ODULATOR).]

Mo•de•na (môd′n-ə, mô′dĕ-nä). A city of N Italy WNW of Bologna; orig. settled by Etruscans. Pop. 179,933.

mod•er•ate (mŏd′ər-ĭt) *adj.* **1.** Being within reasonable limits; not excessive or extreme. **2.** Not violent or subject to extremes; mild or calm; temperate. **3.a.** Of medium or average quantity or extent. **b.** Of limited or average quality; mediocre. **4.** Opposed to radical or extreme views or measures, esp. in politics or religion. —*n.* One who holds or champions moderate views or opinions. —*v.* (mŏd′ə-rāt′) **-at•ed, -at•ing, -ates.** —*tr.* **1.** To lessen the violence, severity, or extremeness of. **2.** To preside over. —*intr.* **1.** To become less violent, severe, or extreme; abate. **2.** To act as a moderator. [ME *moderat* < Lat. *moderātus,* p.part. of *moderārī,* to moderate. See **med-***.] —**mod′er•ate•ly** *adv.* —**mod′er•ate•ness** *n.* —**mod′er•a′tion** *n.*

mod•e•ra•to (mŏd′ə-rä′tō) *adv. & adj. Mus.* In moderate tempo that is slower than allegretto but faster than andante. [Ital. < Lat. *moderātus,* moderate. See MODERATE.]

mod•er•a•tor (mŏd′ə-rā′tər) *n.* **1.** One that moderates, as: **a.** One that arbitrates or mediates. **b.** One who presides over a meeting, forum, or debate. **2.** The officer who presides over a synod or general assembly of the Presbyterian Church. **3.** *Phys.* A substance used in a nuclear reactor to slow down fast neutrons and increase the likelihood of fission.

mod•ern (mŏd′ərn) *adj.* **1.a.** Of or relating to recent times or the present: *modern history.* **b.** Characteristic or expressive of recent times or the present; contemporary or up-to-date. **2.a.** Of or relating to a recently developed or advanced style, technique, or technology: *modern art.* **b.** Avant-garde; experimental. **3. Modern.** *Ling.* Of, relating to, or being a living language or group of languages: *Modern Italian.* —*n.* **1.** One who lives in modern times. **2.** One who has modern ideas, standards, or beliefs. **3.** *Print.* Any of a variety of typefaces characterized by strongly contrasted heavy and thin parts. [Fr. *moderne* < OFr. < LLat. *modernus* < Lat. *modo,* in a certain manner, just now < *modō,* ablative of *modus,* manner. See **med-***.] —**mod′ern•ly** *adv.* —**mod′ern•ness** *n.*

modern dance *n.* A style of theatrical dance that originally favored movement as the expression of inner feeling.

mo•derne (mō-dârn′) *adj.* Striving to be modern in appearance or style but lacking taste or refinement; pretentious. [Fr., modern < OFr. See MODERN.]

Modern English *n.* English since about 1500.

Modern Greek *n.* Greek since the early 16th century.

Modern Hebrew *n.* **1.** The Hebrew language as used from 1948 to the present. **2.** See **New Hebrew.**

mod•ern•ism (mŏd′ər-nĭz′əm) *n.* **1.a.** Modern thought, character, or practice. **b.** Sympathy with or conformity to modern ideas, practices, or standards. **2.** A usage or style, as of a word, peculiar to modern times. **3.** Often **Modernism.** The use of nontraditional innovative forms of expression characteristic of many styles in the arts and literature of the 20th century. **4.** Often **Modernism.** A Roman Catholic movement that examined traditional belief according to contemporary philosophy, criticism, and historiography. —**mod′ern•ist** *n.* —**mod′ern•is′tic** *adj.*

mo•der•ni•ty (mŏ-dûr′nĭ-tē, mō-) *n., pl.* **-ties.** The state or quality of being modern.

mod•ern•ize (mŏd′ər-nīz′) *v.* **-ized, -iz•ing, -iz•es.** —*tr.* To make modern in appearance, style, or character; update. —*intr.* To accept or adopt modern ways, ideas, or style. —**mod′ern•i•za′tion** (-nĭ-zā′shən) *n.* —**mod′ern•iz′er** *n.*

modern pentathlon *n. Sports.* An athletic contest in which each participant competes in five events: running, swimming, horseback riding, fencing, and pistol shooting.

mod•est (mŏd′ĭst) *adj.* **1.** Having or showing a moderate estimation of one's talents, abilities, and value. **2.** Having or proceeding from a disinclination to call attention to oneself; retiring or diffident. See Syns at **shy**[1]. **3.** Observing conventional proprieties in speech, behavior, or dress. **4.** Free from showiness or ostentation; unpretentious. **5.** Moderate or limited in size, quantity, or range; not extreme. [Lat. *modestus.* See **med-***.] —**mod′est•ly** *adv.*

Mo•des•to (mə-dĕs′tō). A city of central CA SE of Stockton; founded 1870. Pop. 164,730.

mod•es•ty (mŏd′ĭ-stē) *n.* **1.** The state or quality of being modest. **2.** Reserve or propriety in speech, dress, or behavior. **3.** Lack of pretentiousness; simplicity.

mod•i•cum (mŏd′ĭ-kəm) *n., pl.* **-cums** or **-ca** (-kə). A small, moderate, or token amount. [ME < Lat. < neut. of *modicus,* moderate < *modus,* measure. See **med-***.]

mod•i•fi•ca•tion (mŏd′ə-fĭ-kā′shən) *n.* **1.** The act of modifying or the condition of being modified. **2.** A result of modifying. **3.** A small alteration, adjustment, or limitation. **4.** *Biol.* Any of the changes in an organism caused by environment or activity and not genetically transmissable to offspring. **5.** *Ling.* **a.** A change undergone by a word borrowed from another language. **b.** A phonological change undergone by a word or morpheme when used in a construction, as the change of *will* to *'ll* in *they'll.* **—mod′i•fi•ca′tor** *n.* **—mod′i•fi•ca′to•ry** (-kā′tə-rē), **mod′i•fi•ca′tive** *adj.*

mod•i•fi•er (mŏd′ə-fī′ər) *n. Gram.* A word, phrase, or clause that modifies another word or word group.

mod•i•fy (mŏd′ə-fī′) *v.* **-fied, -fy•ing, -fies.** *—tr.* **1.** To change in form or character; alter. **2.** To make less extreme, severe, or strong. **3.** *Gram.* To qualify or limit the meaning of. **4.** *Ling.* To change (a vowel) by umlaut. *—intr.* To be or become modified; change. [ME *modifien* < OFr. *modifier* < Lat. *modificāre*, to measure, limit : *modus*, measure; see **med-*** + *-ficāre*, -fy.] **—mod′i•fi′a•bil′i•ty** *n.* **—mod′i•fi′a•ble** *adj.*

Mo•di•glia•ni (mō-dē′lē-ä′nē, mô′dē-lyä′nē), **Amedeo.** 1884–1920. Italian painter and sculptor noted for graceful elongated lines in works such as *Reclining Nude* (1917).

mo•dil•lion (mō-dĭl′yən) *n. Archit.* An ornamental bracket used in series under a cornice, esp. a cornice of the Corinthian, Composite, or Ionic orders. [Ital. *modiglione* < VLat. **mutiliō, mutiliōn-* < Lat. *mūtulus*, perh. of Etruscan orig.]

mo•di•o•lus (mō-dī′ə-ləs) *n., pl.* **-li** (-lī′). The central conical bony core of the cochlea. [Lat., socket, hub, dim. of *modius*, a measure of grain, measuring vessel. See **med-***.]

mod•ish (mō′dĭsh) *adj.* Being in or conforming to the prevailing or current fashion; stylish. **—mod′ish•ly** *adv.* **—mod′ish•ness** *n.*

mo•diste (mō-dēst′) *n.* One that produces, designs, or deals in women's fashions. [Fr. < *mode*, fashion. See MODE.]

Mo•doc (mō′dŏk) *n., pl.* **Modoc** or **-docs. 1.** A member of a Native American people inhabiting an area of the Cascade Range in south-central Oregon and northern California. **2.** The dialect of Klamath spoken by the Modoc.

mod•u•lar (mŏj′ə-lər) *adj.* **1.** Of, relating to, or based on a module or modulus. **2.** Designed with standardized units or dimensions, as for easy assembly and repair. **—mod′u•lar** *n.* **—mod′u•lar′i•ty** (-lăr′ĭ-tē) *n.* **—mod′u•lar•ly** *adv.*

modular home *n.* A house built of prefabricated standardized sections.

mod•u•lar•ized (mŏj′ə-lə-rīzd′) *adj.* Having or made up of modules: *modularized housing.*

mod•u•late (mŏj′ə-lāt′) *v.* **-lat•ed, -lat•ing, -lates.** *—tr.* **1.** To adjust or adapt to a certain proportion; regulate or temper. **2.** To change the pitch, intensity, or tone of (one's voice, for example). **3.** *Electron.* **a.** To vary the frequency, amplitude, phase, or other characteristic of (electromagnetic waves). **b.** To vary (electron velocity) in an electron beam. *—intr. Mus.* **1.** To pass from one key or tonality to another by a regular melodic or chord progression. **2.** To sing or play with modulation. [Lat. *modulārī, modulāt-*, to measure off, to regulate < *modulus*, dim. of *modus*, measure. See **med-***.] **—mod′u•la•bil′i•ty** *n.* **—mod′u•la′tive, mod′u•la•to′ry** (-lə-tôr′ē, -tōr′ē) *adj.*

mod•u•la•tion (mŏj′ə-lā′shən) *n.* **1.** The act or process of modulating. **2.** The state of being modulated. **3.** *Mus.* A passing from one key or tonality to another by means of a regular melodic or chord progression. **4.a.** A change in stress, pitch, loudness, or tone of the voice. **b.** An instance of such a change. **5.** The harmonious use of language, as in poetry or prose. **6.** *Electron.* The variation of a property of an electromagnetic wave or signal, such as its frequency or phase.

mod•u•la•tor (mŏj′ə-lā′tər) *n. Electron.* A device used to modulate an electromagnetic wave.

mod•ule (mŏj′o͞ol) *n.* **1.** A standard or unit of measurement. **2.** *Archit.* The dimensions of a structural component, such as the base of a column, used in determining the proportions of the rest of the construction. **3.** A standardized, often interchangeable component of a system or construction designed for easy assembly or flexible use. **4.** *Electron.* A self-contained assembly of electronic components and circuitry installed as a unit. **5.** *Comp. Sci.* A portion of a program that carries out a specific function and may be used alone or combined with other modules of the same program. **6.** A self-contained unit of a spacecraft that performs a specific task or class of tasks in support of the major function of the craft. **7.** A unit of education or instruction with a relatively high teacher-to-student ratio in which a single topic is studied. [Lat. *modulus*, dim. of *modus*, measure. See **med-***.]

mod•u•lo (mŏj′ə-lō) *prep. Math.* With respect to a specified modulus. [Lat. *modulō*, ablative of *modulus*, dim. of *modus*, measure. See MODE.]

mod•u•lus (mŏj′ə-ləs) *n., pl.* **-li** (-lī′). **1.** *Phys.* A quantity that expresses the degree to which a substance possesses a property, such as elasticity. **2.a.** *Math.* The absolute value of a complex number. **b.** A number by which two given numbers can be divided and produce the same remainder; for example, 18 and 42 leave 6 as a remainder when divided by 12. **c.** The number by which a logarithm in one system must be multiplied to obtain the corresponding logarithm in another system. [Lat., dim. of *modus*, measure. See **med-***.]

mo•dus op•er•an•di (mō′dəs ŏp′ə-răn′dē, -dī′) *n., pl.* **mo•di operandi** (mō′dē, -dī). **1.** A method of operating or functioning. **2.** A person's manner of working. [NLat. *modus operandī* : Lat. *modus*, mode + Lat. *operandī*, genitive sing. gerund of *operārī*, to work.]

modus vi•ven•di (vĭ-vĕn′dē, -dī′) *n., pl.* **modi vivendi. 1.** A manner of living; a way of life. **2.** A temporary agreement between contending parties pending a final settlement. [NLat. *modus vīvendī* : Lat. *modus*, mode + Lat. *vīvendī*, genitive sing. gerund of *vīvere*, to live.]

Moers also **Mörs** (mœrs). A city of W-central Germany W of Essen; chartered 1300. Pop. 97,753.

Moe•sia (mē′shə, -shē-ə). An ancient region of SE Europe S of the Danube R. in what is now Serbia and N Bulgaria; orig. inhabited by Thracians.

mo•fette also **mof•fette** (mō-fĕt′) *n.* **1.** An opening in the earth from which carbon dioxide and other gases escape, usu. marking the last stage of volcanic activity. **2.** The gases escaping from such an opening. [Fr., gaseous exhalation < Ital. *moffetta*, dim. of *muffa*, mold, moldy smell, prob. of Gmc. orig.]

Mog•a•dish•u (mŏg′ə-dĭsh′o͞o, -dē′sho͞o). The cap. of Somalia, on the Indian Ocean; settled by Arab colonists in the 9th or 10th century. Pop. 400,000.

Mo•gen Da•vid (mō′gən dô′vĭd, dā′vĭd, mä-gĕn′ dä-vēd′) *n.* Var. of **Magen David.**

Mo•gi•lev (mŏg′ə-lĕf′, mə-gĭ-lyôf′). A city of E-central Belorussia on the Dnieper R. E of Minsk; founded around a castle built in 1267. Pop. 343,000.

Mo•gol•lon (mō′gə-yōn′) *n.* A Native American culture flourishing from the 2nd century B.C. to the 13th century A.D. in southeast Arizona and southwest New Mexico, esp. noted for its development of pottery. [After the MOGOLLON (PLATEAU).]

Mogollon Plateau. A tableland, 2,135–2,440 m (7,000–8,000 ft), of E-central AZ. Its S edge is the rugged escarpment **Mogollon Rim.**

mo•gul (mō′gəl) *n. Sports.* A small hard mound or bump on a ski slope. [Prob. of Scand. orig.; akin to ON *mūgi*, heap.]

Mo•gul (mō′gəl, mō-gŭl′) *n.* **1.** Also **Mo•ghul** (mo͝o-gŭl′). **a.** A member of the force that under Baber conquered India in 1526. **b.** A member of the Muslim dynasty founded by Baber that ruled India until 1857. **2.** A Mongol or Mongolian. **3. mogul.** A very rich or powerful person; a magnate. [Pers. and Ar. *muġul* < Mongolian *Moṅgul.*] **—Mo′gul** *adj.*

mo•hair (mō′hâr′) *n.* **1.** The long silky hair of the Angora goat. **2.** Fabric made with yarn from this hair. [Alteration of obsolete Ital. *mocaiaro* < Ar. *muḫayyar.*]

Mo•ham•med (mō-hăm′ĭd, -hä′mĭd, mo͝o-). See **Muhammad.**

Mo•ham•med II (mō-hăm′ĭd, -hä′mĭd, mo͝o-) also **Mu•ham•mad II** (mo͝o-). 1429?–81. Sultan of Turkey (1451–81) and founder of the Ottoman Empire who conquered Constantinople in 1453.

Mohammed A•li (ä-lē′) also **Me•he•met Ali** (mĭ-hĕm′ĕt, mä′mĕt). 1769–1849. Turkish soldier and viceroy of Egypt (1805–48) who wrested control of Egypt from the Ottoman Empire (1811).

Mo•ham•med•an (mō-hăm′ĭ-dən) also **Mu•ham•mad•an** or **Mu•ham•med•an** (mo͝o-) *—adj.* **1.** Of or relating to Muhammad. **2.** *Offensive.* Of or relating to Islam. *—n. Offensive.* A Muslim.

Mo•ham•med•an•ism (mō-hăm′ĭ-də-nĭz′əm) also **Mu•ham•mad•an•ism** (mo͝o-) *n. Offensive.* Islam.

Mo•har•ram (mō-hăr′əm) *n.* Var. of **Muharram.**

Mo•ha•ve also **Mo•ja•ve** (mō-hä′vē) *n., pl.* **Mohave** or **-ves** also **Mojave** or **-ves. 1.** A member of a Native American people inhabiting lands along the lower Colorado River on the Arizona-California border. **2.** The Yuman language of the Mohave. [Mohave *hàmakhháav.*]

Mohave Desert. See **Mojave Desert.**

Mo•hawk[1] (mō′hôk′) *n., pl.* **Mohawk** or **-hawks. 1.** A member of a Native American people formerly inhabiting northeast New York, with present-day populations chiefly in southern Ontario and extreme northern New York. **2.** The Iroquoian language of the Mohawk. [Narragansett *Mohowaúg.*]

Mo•hawk[2] (mō′hôk′) *n., pl.* **-hawks.** A hairstyle in which the scalp is shaved except for a strip of hair that runs from the forehead to the nape of the neck. [After MOHAWK[1].]

Mohawk River. A river of E-central NY flowing c. 225 km (140 mi) to the Hudson R.

Mo•he•gan (mō-hē′gən) *n., pl.* **Mohegan** or **-gans. 1.** A member of a Native American people formerly inhabiting eastern Connecticut, with present-day descendants in southeast Connecticut and Wisconsin. **2.** Their Algonquian language.

Mo•hen•jo-Da•ro (mō-hĕn′jō-där′ō). A ruined prehistoric city of Pakistan in the Indus R. valley NE of Karachi.

Mo•hi•can (mō-hē′kən, mə-) *n.* Var. of **Mahican.**

Mo•ho (mō′hō′) *n. Geol.* The Mohorovičić discontinuity.

Mo•ho•ro•vi•čić discontinuity (mō′hə-rō′və-chĭch) *n. Geol.* The boundary between the earth's crust and the underlying mantle, averaging 8 kilometers (5 miles) in depth under the

modular
Habitat housing complex in Montreal, Canada, designed by Moshe Safdie (born 1938)

ă pat	oi boy
ā pay	ou out
âr care	o͝o took
ä father	o͞o boot
ĕ pet	ŭ cut
ē be	ûr urge
ĭ pit	th thin
ī pie	*th* this
îr pier	hw which
ŏ pot	zh vision
ō toe	ə about,
ô paw	item

Stress marks:
′ (primary);
′ (secondary), as in
dictionary (dĭk′shə-nĕr′ē)

genus *Monas.* **3.** *Chem.* An atom or a radical with valence 1. [Lat. *monas, monad-*, unit < Gk. < *monos*, single. See **men-**[4]***.**] — **mo·nad′ic** (mə-năd′ĭk), **mo·nad′i·cal** *adj.* — **mo·nad′i·cal·ly** *adv.* — **mo′nad·ism** *n.*

mon·a·del·phous (mŏn′ə-dĕl′fəs, mō′nə-) *adj. Bot.* Related to or being stamens with all the filaments united into a single tubelike group.

mo·nad·nock (mə-năd′nŏk′) *n.* A mountain or rocky mass that has resisted erosion and stands isolated in an essentially level area. [After Mt. *Monadnock*, a peak of SW NH.]

mo·nan·drous (mə-năn′drəs) *adj.* **1.** *Bot.* Having flowers bearing a single stamen, as in the poinsettia. **2.** Of, relating to, or characterized by monandry.

mo·nan·dry (mə-năn′drē) *n.* **1.** The state or practice of having one husband at a time. **2.** *Bot.* The condition of being monandrous.

monarch butterfly
Danaus plexippus

mo·nan·thous (mə-năn′thəs) *adj. Bot.* Bearing one flower.

Mo·na Passage (mō′nə). A strait between Puerto Rico and the Dominican Republic connecting the N Atlantic with the Caribbean Sea.

mon·arch (mŏn′ərk, -ärk′) *n.* **1.** One who reigns over a state or territory, usu. for life and by hereditary right, esp.: **a.** A sole and absolute ruler. **b.** A sovereign, such as a king or an empress, often with constitutionally limited authority. **2.** One that commands or rules. **3.** One that surpasses others in power or preeminence. **4.** A monarch butterfly. [ME *monarke* < OFr. *monarque* < LLat. *monarcha* < Gk. *monarkhos* : *mono-*, mono- + *arkhein*, to rule.] — **mo·nar′chal** (mə-när′kəl), **mo·nar′chic** (-kĭk), **mo·nar′chi·cal** (-kĭ-kəl) *adj.* — **mo·nar′chal·ly, mo·nar′chi·cal·ly** *adv.*

monarch butterfly *n.* A large migratory American butterfly *(Danaus plexippus)* having light brown wings with black veins and noted for its brightly striped caterpillars.

Mon·ar·chi·an·ism (mə-när′kē-ə-nĭz′əm) *n.* Any of several Christological heresies of the second and third centuries A.D. that denied the independent hypostasis of God the Son. [< Lat. *Monarchiānī*, the Monarchians < *monarchia*, monarchy. See MONARCHY.] — **Mo·nar′chi·an** *n.*

mon·ar·chism (mŏn′ər-kĭz′əm, -är′-) *n.* **1.** The system or principles of monarchy. **2.** Belief in or advocacy of monarchy. — **mon′ar·chist** (-kĭst) *n.* — **mon′ar·chis′tic** *adj.*

mon·ar·chy (mŏn′ər-kē, -är′-) *n., pl.* **-chies. 1.** Government by a monarch. **2.** A state ruled or headed by a monarch. [ME *monarchie* < OFr. < Lat. *monarchia* < Gk. *monarkhia* < *monarkhos*, monarch. See MONARCH.] — **mo·nar′chi·al** (mə-när′kē-əl) *adj.*

Mongolia

mo·nar·da (mə-när′də) *n.* Any of various aromatic plants of the genus *Monarda* in the mint family, such as the bee balm. [NLat. *Monarda*, genus name, after Nicolas *Monardes* (1493–1588), Spanish botanist.]

mon·as·ter·y (mŏn′ə-stĕr′ē) *n., pl.* **-ries. 1.** A community, esp. of monks, bound by vows to an often secluded religious life. **2.** The dwelling place of such a community. [ME *monasterie* < OFr. *monastere* < LLat. *monastērium* < LGk. *monastērion* < Gk. *monazein*, to live alone < *monos*, alone. See **men-**[4]***.**] — **mon′as·te′ri·al** (-stîr′ē-əl, -stĕr′-) *adj.*

mo·nas·tic (mə-năs′tĭk) *adj.* **1.** Of, relating to, or characteristic of a monastery. **2.** Resembling life in a monastery, esp.: **a.** Secluded and contemplative. **b.** Strictly disciplined or regimented. **c.** Self-abnegating; austere. — *n.* A monk. [Ult. < LGk. *monastikos* < Gk. *monazein*, to live alone. See MONASTERY.] — **mo·nas′ti·cal·ly** *adv.*

mo·nas·ti·cism (mə-năs′tĭ-sĭz′əm) *n.* The monastic life or system, esp. as practiced in a monastery.

mon·a·tom·ic (mŏn′ə-tŏm′ĭk) *adj.* **1.** Occurring as single atoms: *Helium is a monatomic gas.* **2.** Having one replaceable atom or radical. **3.** Univalent. — **mon′a·tom′ic·al·ly** *adv.*

mon·au·ral (mŏn-ôr′əl) *adj.* **1.** Of, relating to, or being sound reception by one ear. **2.** *Electron.* Relating to a system of transmitting, recording, or reproducing sound in which one or more sources are connected to a single channel; monophonic. — **mon·au′ral·ly** *adv.*

mon·ax·i·al (mŏn-ăk′sē-əl) *adj.* Uniaxial.

mon·a·zite (mŏn′ə-zīt′) *n.* A reddish-brown phosphate mineral containing rare-earth metals, $(Ce, La, Y, Th)PO_4$, important as a source of cerium and thorium. [Gk. *monazein*, to live alone; see MONASTERY + -ITE[1].]

Mön·chen·glad·bach (mŭn′kən-glät′bäk, mœn′KHən-glät′-bäKH). A city of W-central Germany WSW of Düsseldorf; chartered 1336. Pop. 255,085.

Thelonious Monk
Photographed in 1949

Monck or **Monk** (mŭngk), **George.** 1st Duke of Albemarle. 1608–70. English general who was instrumental in the restoration of Charles II (1660).

Monc·ton (mŭngk′tən). A city of SE New Brunswick, Canada, NE of Saint John. Pop. 54,743.

Mon·dale (mŏn′dāl′), **Walter Frederick.** b. 1928. Vice President of the U.S. (1977–81) who ran unsuccessfully for President in 1984.

Mon·day (mŭn′dē, -dā′) *n.* The second day of the week. [ME < OE *Mōnandæg* : *mōnan*, genitive of *mōna*, moon; see MOON + *dæg*, day; see DAY.]

Monday morning quarterback *n. Informal.* One who criticizes or passes judgment from a position of hindsight.

Mon·dri·an (môn′drē-än′, mŏn′-), **Piet.** 1872–1944. Dutch painter whose artworks and writings, notably *Neoplasticism* (1920), profoundly influenced abstract art.

mo·ne·cious (mə-nē′shəs) *adj.* Var. of **monoecious.**

Mo·né·gasque (mô-nā-găsk′) *n.* A native or inhabitant of Monaco; a Monacan. [Fr. < Prov. *mounegasc* < *Mounegue*, Monaco.] — **Mo·né·gasque′** *adj.*

Mo·nel (mō-nĕl′). A trademark used for an alloy of nickel, copper, iron, and manganese.

mo·ne·ran (mə-nîr′ən) *n.* A member of the kingdom Monera (or Prokaryotae), comprising the prokaryotes and including all bacteria. [< NLat. *Monēra*, kingdom name < Gk. *monērēs*, solitary < *monos*, single, alone. See MONAD.] — **mo·ne′ran** *adj.*

mon·es·trous (mŏn-ĕs′trəs) *adj.* Having one estrous cycle per year. Used of certain mammals.

Mo·net (mō-nā′, mô-), **Claude.** 1840–1926. French painter whose works include *Water Lilies* (1899–1925).

Mo·ne·ta (mō-nā′tə, mô-nĕ′tä), **Ernesto Teodoro.** 1833–1918. Italian journalist who shared the 1907 Nobel Peace Prize.

mon·e·ta·rism (mŏn′ĭ-tə-rĭz′əm, mŭn′-) *n.* **1.** A theory holding that economic variations within a given system are usu. caused by fluctuations in the money supply. **2.** A policy that seeks to regulate an economy by altering the domestic money supply, esp. by increasing it in a moderate but steady manner. — **mon′e·ta·rist** *adj.* & *n.*

mon·e·tar·y (mŏn′ĭ-tĕr′ē, mŭn′-) *adj.* **1.** Of or relating to money. **2.** Of or relating to a nation's currency or coinage. See Syns at **financial.** [LLat. *monētārius* < Lat. *monēta*, money, mint. See MONEY.] — **mon′e·tar′i·ly** *adv.*

mon·e·tize (mŏn′ĭ-tīz′, mŭn′-) *tr.v.* **-tized, -tiz·ing, -tiz·es. 1.** To establish as legal tender. **2.** To coin (money). **3.** To convert (government debt) from securities into currency that can be used to purchase goods and services. [< Lat. *monēta*, money. See MONEY.] — **mon′e·ti·za′tion** (-tĭ-zā′shən) *n.*

mon·ey (mŭn′ē) *n., pl.* **-eys** or **-ies. 1.** A commodity, such as gold, or an officially issued coin or paper note legally established as an exchangeable equivalent of all other commodities and used as a measure of their comparative values. **2.** The official currency, coins, and negotiable paper notes issued by a government. **3.** Assets and property considered in terms of monetary value; wealth. **4.a.** Pecuniary profit or loss. **b.** One's salary; pay. **5.** An amount of cash or credit. **6.** A sum of money, esp. of a specified nature. Often used in the plural: *state tax moneys.* **7.** A wealthy person, family, or group. — ***idioms.* for (one's) money.** According to one's opinion, choice, or preference. **in the money. 1.** *Slang.* Rich; affluent. **2.** *Sports & Games.* Taking first, second, or third place in a contest on which a bet has been placed, such as a horserace. **on the money.** Exact; precise. **put money on.** *Sports & Games.* To place a bet on. **put (one's) money where (one's) mouth is.** *Slang.* To live up to one's words; act according to one's own advice. [ME *moneie* < OFr. < Lat. *monēta*, mint, coinage < *Monēta*, epithet of Juno, temple of Juno at Rome where money was coined.]

mon·ey·bag (mŭn′ē-băg′) *n.* **1.** A bag for holding money. **2. moneybags.** *(used with a sing. or pl. v.)* Wealth. **3. moneybags.** *(used with a sing. v.)* A rich, often extravagant person.

mon·ey·chang·er (mŭn′ē-chān′jər) *n.* **1.** One that exchanges money, as from one currency to another. **2.** A machine that holds and dispenses coins.

mon·eyed also **mon·ied** (mŭn′ēd) *adj.* **1.** Having a great deal of money: *the moneyed classes.* **2.** Representing or arising from the possession of money or wealth.

mon·ey·grub·ber (mŭn′ē-grŭb′ər) *n.* One intent on accumulating money. — **mon′ey·grub′bing** *adj.* & *n.*

mon·ey·lend·er (mŭn′ē-lĕn′dər) *n.* One that lends money at an interest rate.

mon·ey·mak·ing (mŭn′ē-mā′kĭng) *n.* Acquisition of wealth. — *adj.* **1.** Engaged or successful in acquiring wealth. **2.** Actually or potentially profitable. — **mon′ey·mak′er** *n.*

money market *n. Econ.* **1.** The trade in short-term low-risk securities, such as U.S. Treasury notes. **2.** A mutual fund that sells shares to purchase short-term securities.

money of account *n.* A monetary unit in which accounts are kept and that may or may not correspond to actual current denominations.

money order *n.* An order for the payment of an amount of money, usu. issued and payable at a bank or post office.

money plant *n.* See **honesty** 4.

money shell *n.* See **butter clam.**

money supply *n.* The amount of money in the economy, measured according to varying methods or principles.

mon·ey·wort (mŭn′ē-wûrt′, -wôrt′) *n.* A European creeping plant *(Lysimachia nummularia)* having rounded opposite leaves and single, axillary yellow flowers.

mon·ger (mŭng′gər, mŏng′-) *n.* **1.** A dealer in a specific commodity. Often used in combination: *an ironmonger.* **2.** A person promoting something undesirable or discreditable. Often used in combination: *a warmonger.* —*tr.v.* **-gered, -ger•ing, -gers.** To peddle. [ME *mongere* < OE *mangere* < Lat. *mangō,* prob. of Gk. orig.]

mon•go (mŏng′gō) *n., pl.* **mongo.** See table at **currency.** [Mongolian.]

Mon•gol (mŏng′gəl, -gōl′, mŏn′-) *n.* **1.** A member of any of the traditionally nomadic peoples of Mongolia. **2.** See **Mongolian** 4. **3.** *Anthro.* A member of the Mongoloid racial division. No longer in scientific use. —*adj.* **1.** Of or relating to Mongolia, the Mongols, or their language or culture. **2.** *Anthro.* Of or relating to the Mongoloid racial division. No longer in scientific use. [Mongolian *Mangqol.*]

Mon•go•li•a (mŏng-gō′lē-ə, -gōl′yə, mŏn-). **1.** An ancient region of E-central Asia comprising modern-day Nei Monggol (Inner Mongolia) and the country of Mongolia; center of a great empire forged by Genghis Khan in the 13th cent. **2.** Formerly **Out•er Mongolia** (out′ər). A country of N-central Asia between Russia and China; under Chinese control (1691–1911 and 1919–21) until it formed a separate state under the protection of the U.S.S.R. Cap. Ulan Bator. Pop. 1,866,300.

Mon•go•li•an (mŏng-gō′lē-ən, -gōl′yən, mŏn-) *adj.* **1.** Of or relating to Mongolia, the Mongols, or their language or culture. **2.** Also **mongolian.** *Offensive.* Of or relating to Down syndrome. —*n.* **1.** A native or inhabitant of Mongolia. **2.** A member of the Mongol people. **3.** *Anthro.* A member of the Mongoloid racial division. No longer in scientific use. **4.a.** A subfamily of the Altaic language family, including Mongolian and Kalmyk. **b.** Any of the various dialects and languages of the Mongols living in Mongolia and China.

Mongolian fold *n.* The epicanthic fold.

Mon•gol•ic (mŏng-gŏl′ĭk, mŏn-) *adj. Anthro.* Of or relating to the Mongoloid racial division. No longer in scientific use.

mon•gol•ism also **Mon•gol•ism** (mŏng′gə-lĭz′əm, mŏn′-) *n. Offensive.* Down syndrome. [< MONGOLIAN, term used in a system of classification for mentally retarded people, devised by John L.H. Down (1828–96), British physician.]

Mon•gol•oid (mŏng′gə-loid′, mŏn′-) *adj.* **1.** *Anthro.* Of or relating to a purported human racial classification distinguished by yellowish-brown skin and straight black hair and including peoples indigenous to central and eastern Asia. No longer in scientific use. **2.** Characteristic of or resembling a Mongol. **3.** Also **mongoloid.** *Offensive.* Of or relating to Down syndrome. —*n.* **1.** *Anthro.* A member of the Mongoloid racial division. No longer in scientific use. **2.** Also **mongoloid.** *Offensive.* A person affected with Down syndrome.

mon•goose (mŏng′go͞os′, mŏn′-) *n., pl.* **-goos•es.** Any of various Old World carnivorous mammals of the genus *Herpestes* and related genera, having a slender agile body and a long tail and noted for the ability to seize and kill venomous snakes. [Marathi *mangūs,* of Dravidian orig.]

mon•grel (mŭng′grəl, mŏng′-) *n.* **1.** An animal or a plant resulting from various interbreedings, esp. a dog of mixed or undetermined breed. **2.** A cross between different breeds, groups, or varieties, esp. a mixture that is or appears to be incongruous. —*adj.* Of mixed origin or character. [Prob. < ME *mong,* mixture < OE *gemang.* See **mag-***.] —**mon•grel′ism** *n.* —**mon′grel•ly** *adv.*

mon•grel•ize (mŭng′grə-līz′, mŏng′-) *tr.v.* **-ized, -iz•ing, -iz•es.** To make mongrel in race, nature, or character. —**mon′grel•i•za′tion** (-grə-lĭ-zā′shən) *n.*

mon•ied (mŭn′ēd) *adj.* Var. of **moneyed.**

mon•ies (mŭn′ēz) *n.* Pl. of **money.**

mon•i•ker or **mon•ick•er** (mŏn′ĭ-kər) *n. Slang.* A personal name or nickname. [Prob. < Shelta *munik,* name, poss. alteration of Ir.Gael. *ainm* < OIr. See **nō-men-***.]

mo•ni•li•a•sis (mō′nə-lī′ə-sĭs, mŏn′ə-) *n.* See **candidiasis.** [NLat. *Monīlia,* type genus (< Lat. *monīle,* necklace) + -IASIS.]

mo•nil•i•form (mō-nĭl′ə-fôrm′) *adj.* Resembling a string of beads, as the antennae of certain insects. [Lat. *monīle,* necklace + -FORM.] —**mo•nil′i•form′ly** *adv.*

mon•ish (mŏn′ĭsh) *tr.v.* **-ished, -ish•ing, -ish•es.** To admonish; warn. [ME *monesten, monishe* < OFr. *monester* < VLat. **monestāre,* alteration of Lat. *monēre,* to warn. See **men-**[1]*.]

mo•nism (mō′nĭz′əm, mŏn′ĭz′əm) *n. Philos.* **1.** The view in metaphysics that reality is a whole and that all existing things can be ascribed to or described by a single concept or system. **2.** The doctrine that mind and matter are formed from or reducible to the same substance or principle of being. —**mo′nist** *n.* —**mo•nis′tic** (mō-nĭs′tĭk, mŏ-) *adj.* —**mo•nis′ti•cal•ly** *adv.*

mo•ni•tion (mō-nĭsh′ən, mə-) *n.* **1.** A warning or an intimation of something imminent, esp. danger. **2.** Cautionary advice or counsel; an admonition. **3.** A formal order from a bishop or an ecclesiastical court to stop a specified offense. **4.** A summons or citation in civil or admiralty law. [ME *monicioun* < OFr. *monicion* < Lat. *monitiō, monitiōn-* < *monitus,* p.part. of *monēre,* to warn. See **men-**[1]*.]

mon•i•tor (mŏn′ĭ-tər) *n.* **1.** One that admonishes, cautions, or reminds, esp. with respect to matters of conduct. **2.** A pupil who assists a teacher in routine duties. **3.a.** A usu. electronic device used to record, regulate, or control a process or system. **b.** A receiver, such as a screen, used to check the quality or content of an electronic transmission. **c.** *Comp. Sci.* A device that accepts video signals from a computer and displays information on a screen. **4.** *Comp. Sci.* A program that observes, supervises, or controls the activities of other programs. **5.** An articulated device with a rotating nozzle that regulates a jet of water, used in mining and firefighting. **6.a.** A heavily ironclad warship of the 19th century with a low flat deck and one or more gun turrets. **b.** A modern warship designed for coastal bombardment. **7.** *Biol.* Any of various tropical carnivorous lizards of the family *Varanidae,* ranging in length from several centimeters to 3 meters (10 feet). —*v.* **-tored, -tor•ing, -tors.** —*tr.* **1.** To check the quality or content of (an electronic audio or visual signal) by means of a receiver. **2.** To check by means of an electronic receiver for significant content, such as illegal activity. **3.** To keep track of systematically with a view to collecting information. **4.a.** To test or sample on a regular or ongoing basis. **b.** To test (air or an object's surface, for example) for radiation intensity. **5.** To keep close watch over; supervise. **6.** To direct. —*intr.* To act as a monitor. [Lat. < *monēre,* to warn. See **men-**[1]*.] —**mon′i•tor•ship′** *n.*

mon•i•to•ri•al (mŏn′ĭ-tôr′ē-əl, -tōr′-) *adj.* **1.** Of or relating to monitors. **2.** Monitory. —**mon′i•to′ri•al•ly** *adv.*

mon•i•to•ry (mŏn′ĭ-tôr′ē, -tōr′ē) *adj.* Conveying an admonition or a warning. —*n., pl.* **-ries.** A letter of admonition, such as one from a bishop or an ecclesiastical court. [Ult. < Med.Lat. *monitōria,* admonition < fem. of Lat. *monitōrius,* monitory < *monitor,* monitor. See MONITOR.]

monk (mŭngk) *n.* A member of a brotherhood living in a monastery and devoted to a discipline prescribed by his order. [ME *munk* < OE *munuc* < LLat. *monachus* < LGk. *monakhos* < Gk., single < *monos.* See **men-**[4]*.]

Monk (mŭngk), **George.** See George Monck.

Monk, Thelonious Sphere. 1917–82. Amer. jazz pianist and composer noted for his unusual harmonic style.

monk•er•y (mŭng′kə-rē) *n., pl.* **-ies. 1.** Monastic life or practices. **2.** Monks considered as a group. **3.** A monastery.

mon•key (mŭng′kē) *n., pl.* **-keys. 1.** Any of various long-tailed medium-sized members of the order Primates, including the macaques and baboons. **2.** One that behaves in a way suggestive of a monkey, as a mischievous child. **3.** The iron block of a pile driver. **4.** *Slang.* A person who is mocked, duped, or made to appear a fool. **5.** *Slang.* Drug addiction. —*v.* **-keyed, -key•ing, -keys.** —*intr. Informal.* **1.** To play, trifle, or tamper with something. **2.** To behave in a mischievous or apish manner. —*tr.* To imitate or mimic; ape. [?]

monkey bars *pl.n.* A jungle gym.

monkey bread *n.* The hanging gourdlike fruit of the baobab.

monkey business *n. Slang.* Silly, mischievous, or deceitful acts or behavior.

mon•key-faced owl (mŭng′kē-fāst′) *n.* See **barn owl.**

monkey flower *n.* Any of various herbs or shrubs of the genus *Mimulus,* having variously colored two-lipped flowers.

monkey jacket *n.* **1.** A short tight-fitting jacket traditionally worn by sailors. **2.** See **mess jacket.**

monkey pot *n.* **1.a.** Any of various tropical American trees of the genus *Lecythis,* having a large woody urn-shaped pod that dehisces by a lid. **b.** The fruit of this tree. **2.** A cylindrical or barrel-shaped melting pot used in making flint glass.

mon•key-puz•zle (mŭng′kē-pŭz′əl) *n.* A coniferous evergreen tree *(Araucaria araucana)* native to Chile and having intricately ramifying branches covered with overlapping, leathery, lanceolate prickle-tipped leaves.

mon•key•shine (mŭng′kē-shīn′) *n. Slang.* A mischievous or playful trick; a prank. Often used in the plural.

monkey wrench *n.* **1.** A hand tool with adjustable jaws for turning nuts of varying sizes. **2.** *Informal.* Something that disrupts. [?]

monk•fish (mŭngk′fĭsh′) *n., pl.* **monkfish** or **-fish•es.** See **goosefish.** [Perh. < cowled appearance of its head.]

Mon-Khmer (mōn′kmĕr′) *n.* A subfamily of the Austro-Asiatic language family that includes Mon and Khmer.

monk•hood (mŭngk′ho͝od′) *n.* **1.** The character, condition, or profession of a monk. **2.** Monks considered as a group.

monk•ish (mŭng′kĭsh) *adj.* **1.** Of, relating to, or characteristic of monks or monasticism. **2.** Inclined to self-denial; ascetic. —**monk′ish•ly** *adv.* —**monk′ish•ness** *n.*

monk's cloth (mŭngks) *n.* A heavy cotton cloth in a coarse basket weave, now used chiefly for draperies.

monks•hood (mŭngks′ho͝od′) *n.* **1.** See **aconite. 2.** A poisonous perennial herb *(Aconitum napellus)* native to northern Europe, whose dried leaves and roots yield aconite.

Mon•mouth (mŏn′məth), Duke of. James Scott. 1649–85. English pretender to the throne who led a rebellion after the succession of the Catholic James II.

mon•o[1] (mŏn′ō) *n. Informal.* Infectious mononucleosis.

mon•o[2] (mŏn′ō) *adj. Informal.* Monaural; monophonic.

mono– or **mon–** *pref.* **1.** One; single; alone: *monomorphic.* **2.** Containing a single atom, radical, or group: *monobasic.* **3.** Monomolecular; monatomic: *monolayer.* [ME < OFr. < Lat. < Gk. < *monos,* single, alone. See **men-**[4]*.]

monkey bars

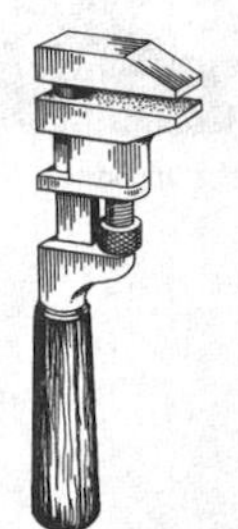

monkey wrench

ă **pat**	oi **boy**
ā **pay**	ou **out**
âr **care**	o͝o **took**
ä **father**	o͞o **boot**
ĕ **pet**	ŭ **cut**
ē **be**	ûr **urge**
ĭ **pit**	th **thin**
ī **pie**	*th* **this**
îr **pier**	hw **which**
ŏ **pot**	zh **vision**
ō **toe**	ə **about,**
ô **paw**	**item**

Stress marks:
′ (primary);
′ (secondary), as in **dictionary** (dĭk′shə-nĕr′ē)

mon•o•ac•id (mŏn′ō-ăs′ĭd) *n.* An acid having one replaceable hydrogen atom. —*adj.* also **mon•o•a•cid•ic** (-ə-sĭd′ĭk). Having only one hydroxyl group to react with acids.

mon•o•am•ine (mŏn′ō-ăm′ēn, -ə-mēn′) *n.* An amine compound containing one amino group, esp. a compound that functions as a neurotransmitter.

monoamine oxidase *n.* An enzyme in the cells of most tissues that catalyzes the oxidation of monoamines such as norepinephrine and serotonin.

mon•o•ba•sic (mŏn′ə-bā′sĭk) *adj.* **1.** Having only one hydrogen ion to donate to a base in an acid-base reaction; monoprotic. **2.** Having only one metal ion or positive radical.

mon•o•carp (mŏn′ə-kärp′) *n.* A monocarpic plant.

mon•o•car•pel•lar•y (mŏn′ə-kär′pə-lĕr′ē) *adj. Bot.* Consisting of only one carpel.

mon•o•car•pic (mŏn′ə-kär′pĭk) also **mon•o•car•pous** (-kär′pəs) *adj. Bot.* Flowering and bearing fruit only once.

mon•o•ce•phal•ic (mŏn′ō-sə-făl′ĭk) *adj. Bot.* Bearing one flower head, as in the scape of a dandelion.

Mo•noc•er•os (mə-nŏs′ər-əs) *n.* A constellation near Canis Major and Canis Minor. [Ult. < Gk. *monokerōs*, having one horn : *mono-*, mono- + *keras*, horn; see **ker-**[1]*.]

mon•o•cha•si•um (mŏn′ə-kā′zē-əm, -zhē-) *n., pl.* **-si•a** (-zē-ə, -zhē-ə, -zhə). *Bot.* A cyme having a single flower on each axis. [MONO- + (DI)CHASIUM.] —**mon′o•cha′si•al** *adj.*

mon•o•chord (mŏn′ə-kôrd′) *n. Mus.* An acoustic instrument consisting of a sounding box with one string and a movable bridge, used to study musical tones. [Ult. < Gk. *monokhordon* : *mono-*, mono- + *khordē*, string; see CORD.]

mon•o•chro•mat (mŏn′ə-krō′măt) *n.* A person with monochromatism.

mon•o•chro•mat•ic (mŏn′ə-krō-măt′ĭk) *adj.* **1.** Having or appearing to have only one color. **2.** Of or composed of radiation of only one wavelength: *monochromatic light.* **3.** Done in monochrome: *monochromatic prints.* **4.** Of or exhibiting monochromatism. —**mon′o•chro•mat′i•cal•ly** *adv.* —**mon′o•chro′ma•tic′i•ty** (-mə-tĭs′ĭ-tē) *n.*

mon•o•chro•ma•tism (mŏn′ə-krō′mə-tĭz′əm) *n.* The condition of being completely colorblind.

mon•o•chrome (mŏn′ə-krōm′) *n.* **1.a.** A picture, esp. a painting, done in different shades of a single color. **b.** The art or technique of executing such a picture. **2.** The state of being in a single color. **3.** A black-and-white image, as in photography or cinematography. [Med.Lat. *monochrōma* < fem. of Gk. *monokhrōmos*, of one color : *mono-*, mono- + *khrōma*, color.] —**mon′o•chrome′**, **mon′o•chro′mic** (-krō′mĭk) *adj.*

monocle

mon•o•cle (mŏn′ə-kəl) *n.* An eyeglass for one eye. [Fr. < LLat. *monoculus*, having one eye : Gk. *mono-*, mono- + Lat. *oculus*, eye; see **okʷ-***.] —**mon′o•cled** (-kəld) *adj.*

mon•o•cline (mŏn′ə-klīn′) *n.* A geologic structure having all layers inclined in the same direction. —**mon′o•cli′nal** *adj.*

mon•o•clin•ic (mŏn′ə-klĭn′ĭk) *adj.* Of or relating to three unequal crystal axes, two of which intersect obliquely and are perpendicular to the third.

mon•o•cli•nous (mŏn′ə-klī′nəs) *adj. Bot.* Having pistils and stamens in the same flower. [NLat. *monoclinus* : MONO- + Gk. *klinē*, bed; see **klei-***.]

mon•o•clo•nal (mŏn′ə-klō′nəl) *adj.* Of, forming, or derived from a single clone: *a monoclonal population of tumor cells.*

monoclonal antibody *n.* Any of a class of highly specific antibodies produced by the clones of a single hybrid cell formed by the fusion of a B cell with a tumor cell.

mon•o•coque (mŏn′ə-kōk′, -kŏk′) *n.* A metal structure, such as an aircraft, in which the skin absorbs all or most of the stresses to which the body is subjected. [Fr. : *mono-*, mono- + *coque*, shell (< OFr. < Lat. *coccum*, berry < Gk. *kokkos*).]

mon•o•cot (mŏn′ə-kŏt′) *n.* A monocotyledon.

mon•o•cot•y•le•don (mŏn′ə-kŏt′l-ēd′n) *n.* Any of various flowering plants, such as grasses and lilies, having a single cotyledon in the seed. —**mon′o•cot′y•le′don•ous** *adj.*

mo•noc•ra•cy (mō-nŏk′rə-sē, mə-) *n., pl.* **-cies.** Government or rule by a single person; autocracy. —**mon′o•crat′** (mŏn′ə-krăt′) *n.* —**mon′o•crat′ic** *adj.*

mo•noc•u•lar (mŏ-nŏk′yə-lər, mə-) *adj.* **1.** Having or relating to one eye. **2.** Of, relating to, or intended for use by only one eye: *a monocular microscope.* [< LLat. *monoculus*, having one eye. See MONOCLE.] —**mo•noc′u•lar•ly** *adv.*

mon•o•cul•ture (mŏn′ə-kŭl′chər) *n.* **1.** The cultivation of a single crop on a farm or in a region or country. **2.** A single homogeneous culture without diversity or dissension. —**mon′o•cul′tur•al** *adj.*

mon•o•cy•cle (mŏn′ə-sī′kəl) *n.* A unicycle.

mon•o•cy•clic (mŏn′ə-sī′klĭk, -sĭk′lĭk) *adj.* **1.** Having a single cycle, as of development. **2.** *Biol.* Having a single whorl. **3.** *Chem.* Having a molecular structure with only one ring.

mon•o•cyte (mŏn′ə-sīt′) *n.* A large circulating phagocytic white blood cell having a single well-defined nucleus and very fine granulation in the cytoplasm.

mon•o•cy•to•sis (mŏn′ə-sī-tō′sĭs) *n., pl.* **-ses** (-sēz). An abnormal increase of monocytes in the blood.

Mo•nod (mô-nō′), **Jacques Lucien.** 1910–76. French biochemist who shared a 1965 Nobel Prize.

monolith

mon•o•dac•tyl (mŏn′ə-dăk′təl) *n.* An animal having one digit or claw on each extremity. —**mon′o•dac′ty•lous** *adj.*

mon•o•dra•ma (mŏn′ə-drä′mə, -drăm′ə) *n.* A dramatic composition written for one performer. —**mon′o•dra•mat′ic** (-drə-măt′ĭk) *adj.*

mon•o•dy (mŏn′ə-dē) *n., pl.* **-dies. 1.** An ode for one voice or actor, as in Greek drama. **2.** A poem in which the poet or speaker mourns another's death. **3.** *Mus.* **a.** A style of composition having or dominated by a single melodic line; monophony. **b.** A composition in this style. [LLat. *monōdia* < Gk. *monōidia* : *mono-*, mono- + *ōidē*, song; see **wed-**[2]*.] —**mo•nod′ic** (mə-nŏd′ĭk), **mo•nod′i•cal** (-ĭ-kəl) *adj.* —**mo•nod′i•cal•ly** *adv.* —**mon′o•dist** (mŏn′ə-dĭst) *n.*

mo•noe•cious also **mo•ne•cious** (mə-nē′shəs) *adj.* **1.** *Bot.* Having unisexual reproductive organs or flowers, with the organs or flowers of both sexes on a single plant, as in corn. **2.** *Zool.* Hermaphroditic. [NLat. *Monoecia*, class name : MONO- + Gk. *oikia*, dwelling; see **weik-**[1]*.] —**mo•noe′cious•ly** *adv.* —**mo•noe′cism** (mə-nē′sĭz′əm) *n.*

mon•o•es•ter (mŏn′ō-ĕs′tər) *n.* An ester having only one ester group.

mon•o•fil•a•ment (mŏn′ə-fĭl′ə-mənt) *n.* A strand of untwisted synthetic fiber used esp. for fishing line.

mo•nog•a•my (mə-nŏg′ə-mē) *n.* **1.** The practice or condition of being married to only one person at a time. **2.** The practice of marrying only once in a lifetime. **3.** *Zool.* The condition of having only one mate. —**mo•nog′a•mist** *n.* —**mo•nog′a•mous** *adj.* —**mo•nog′a•mous•ly** *adv.*

mon•o•gen•e•sis (mŏn′ə-jĕn′ĭ-sĭs) *n.* **1.** The theory that all living organisms are descended from a single cell or organism. **2.** Asexual reproduction, as by sporulation. —**mo•nog′e•nous** (mə-nŏj′ə-nəs) *adj.*

mon•o•ge•net•ic (mŏn′ə-jə-nĕt′ĭk) *adj.* **1.** Relating to or exhibiting monogenesis. **2.** Having a single host through the course of the life cycle. **3.** Produced under a single set of continuing conditions. Used of soil.

mon•o•gen•ic (mŏn′ə-jĕn′ĭk) *adj.* **1.a.** Of or relating to monogenesis; monogenetic. **b.** Relating to monogenism. **2.** Of or regulated by one gene or one of a pair of allelic genes. **3.** Producing offspring of only one sex, as some species of aphids. —**mon′o•gen′i•cal•ly** *adv.*

mo•nog•e•nism (mə-nŏj′ə-nĭz′əm) *n.* The theory that all human beings are descended from a single pair of ancestors.

mon•o•glot (mŏn′ə-glŏt′) *n.* A person who knows only one language. [MONO- + (POLY)GLOT.] —**mon′o•glot′** *adj.*

mon•o•gram (mŏn′ə-grăm′) *n.* A design composed of one or more letters, typically the initials of a name, used as an identifying mark. —*tr.v.* **-grammed, -gram•ming, -grams** also **-gramed, -gram•ing, -grams.** To mark with a monogram. —**mon′o•gram•mat′ic** (-grə-măt′ĭk) *adj.*

mon•o•graph (mŏn′ə-grăf′) *n.* A piece of scholarly writing of essay or book length on a specific, often limited subject. —**mon′o•graph′** *v.* —**mo•nog′ra•pher** (mə-nŏg′rə-fər) *n.* —**mon′o•graph′ic** *adj.* —**mon′o•graph′i•cal•ly** *adv.*

mo•nog•y•ny (mə-nŏj′ə-nē) *n.* The practice or condition of having only one wife at a time. —**mo•nog′y•nist** *n.* —**mo•nog′y•nous** *adj.*

mon•o•hy•drate (mŏn′ō-hī′drāt′) *n.* A crystalline compound that contains one molecule of water.

mo•noi•cous (mə-noi′kəs) *adj. Bot.* Having archegonia and antheridia on the same plant; bisexual. [Alteration of MONOECIOUS.]

mon•o•lay•er (mŏn′ō-lā′ər) *n.* **1.** A film or layer of a compound one molecule thick. **2.** A layer of cells one cell thick, grown in a culture.

mon•o•lin•gual (mŏn′ə-lĭng′gwəl) *adj.* Using only one language. —**mon′o•lin′gual** *n.* —**mon′o•lin′gual•ism** *n.*

mon•o•lith (mŏn′ə-lĭth′) *n.* **1.** A large block of stone, esp. one used in architecture or sculpture. **2.** Something, such as a column or monument, made from a large block of stone. **3.** Something suggestive of a large block of stone, as in massiveness or uniformity.

mon•o•lith•ic (mŏn′ə-lĭth′ĭk) *adj.* **1.** Constituting a monolith. **2.** Massive, solid, and uniform. **3.** Constituting or acting as a single, often rigid uniform whole. —**mon′o•lith′i•cal•ly** *adv.*

mon•o•logue also **mon•o•log** (mŏn′ə-lôg′, -lŏg′) —*n.* **1.a.** A dramatic soliloquy. **b.** A literary composition in such form. **2.** A series of jokes delivered by one comedian. **3.** A long speech made by one person, often monopolizing a conversation. —*v.* **-logued, -logu•ing, -logues** also **-logged, -log•ging, -logs.** —*intr.* To give or perform a monologue. —*tr.* To address a monologue to. [Fr. : Gk. *mono-*, mono- + Gk. *-logos*, -logue.] —**mon′o•log′ic** (-lŏj′ĭk), **mon′o•log′i•cal** (-ĭ-kəl) *adj.* —**mon′o•logu′ist** (mŏn′ə-lôg′ĭst, -lŏg′-), **mo•nol′o•gist** (mə-nŏl′ə-jĭst, mŏn′ə-lôg′ĭst, -lŏg′-) *n.*

mon•o•ma•ni•a (mŏn′ə-mā′nē-ə, -mān′yə) *n.* **1.** Pathological obsession with one idea or subject, as in paranoia. **2.** Intent concentration on or exaggerated enthusiasm for one subject or idea. —**mon′o•ma′ni•ac′** *n.* —**mon′o•ma•ni′a•cal** (-mə-nī′ə-kəl) *adj.* —**mon′o•ma•ni′a•cal•ly** *adv.*

mon•o•mer (mŏn′ə-mər) *n.* A molecule that can combine

with others to form a polymer. [MONO– + (POLY)MER.] — **mon′o·mer′ic** (-mĕr′ĭk) *adj.*

mon·o·me·tal·lic (mŏn′ō-mə-tăl′ĭk) *adj.* **1.** Consisting of or containing one metal. **2.** Of, advocating, or practicing monometallism.

mon·o·met·al·lism (mŏn′ō-mĕt′l-ĭz′əm) *n.* The economic theory or practice of using only one metal as a monetary standard. — **mon′o·met′al·list** *n.*

mo·nom·e·ter (mə-nŏm′ĭ-tər) *n.* A verse consisting of a single metrical foot or one dipody.

mo·no·mi·al (mŏ-nō′mē-əl, mə-) *n.* **1.** *Math.* An algebraic expression consisting of only one term. **2.** *Biol.* A taxonomic name consisting of a single word. [MON(O)– + (BIN)OMIAL.] — **mo·no′mi·al** *adj.*

mon·o·mo·lec·u·lar (mŏn′ō-mə-lĕk′yə-lər) *adj.* **1.** Of or relating to a single molecule. **2.** Of or consisting of a layer one molecule thick. — **mon′o·mo·lec′u·lar·ly** *adv.*

mon·o·mor·phic (mŏn′ō-môr′fĭk) also **mon·o·mor·phous** (-fəs) *adj.* **1.** *Chem.* Having only one form, such as one crystal form. **2.** *Zool.* Having one or the same genotype, form, or structure through a series of developmental changes. — **mon′o·mor′phism** *n.*

Mo·non·ga·he·la River (mə-nŏng′gə-hē′lə). A river rising in N WV and flowing c. 206 km (128 mi) into SW PA, where it joins the Allegheny R. to form the Ohio R.

mon·o·nu·cle·ar (mŏn′ō-nōō′klē-ər, -nyōō′-) *adj.* **1.** Having only one nucleus. **2.** *Chem.* Monocyclic.

mon·o·nu·cle·o·sis (mŏn′ō-nōō′klē-ō′sĭs, -nyōō-) *n.* **1.** The presence of an abnormally large number of white blood cells with single nuclei in the bloodstream. **2.** Infectious mononucleosis. [MONO– + NUCLE(US) + –OSIS.]

mon·o·nu·cle·o·tide (mŏn′ō-nōō′klē-ə-tīd′, -nyōō′-) *n.* A nucleotide consisting of one molecule each of a phosphoric acid, a sugar, and either a purine or a pyrimidine base.

mo·noph·a·gous (mə-nŏf′ə-gəs) *adj.* Eating only one kind of food. — **mo·noph′a·gy** (-ə-jē) *n.*

mon·o·pho·bi·a (mŏn′ō-fō′bē-ə) *n.* An abnormal fear of being alone. — **mon′o·pho′bic** (-fō′bĭk) *adj.*

mon·o·phon·ic (mŏn′ə-fŏn′ĭk) *adj.* **1.** *Mus.* Having a single melodic line; monodic. **2.** *Electron.* Monaural. — **mon′o·phon′i·cal·ly** *adv.*

mo·noph·o·ny (mə-nŏf′ə-nē) *n.*, *pl.* **-nies.** *Mus.* Music consisting of a single melodic line. [MONO– + (POLY)PHONY.]

mon·oph·thong (mŏn′əf-thông′, -thŏng′) *n.* *Ling.* **1.** A single vowel articulated without change in quality throughout the course of a syllable, as the vowel of English *bed.* **2.** Two written vowels representing a single sound, as *oa* in *boat.* [LGk. *monophthongos* : Gk. *mono-*, mono- + Gk. *phthongos*, sound.] — **mon′oph·thon′gal** *adj.*

mon·o·phy·let·ic (mŏn′ō-fī-lĕt′ĭk) *adj.* **1.** Of or concerning a single taxon of animals. **2.** Relating to or derived from one stock or source. — **mon′o·phy·let′ic·al·ly** *adv.*

Mo·noph·y·site (mə-nŏf′ə-sīt′) *n.* *Theol.* An adherent of the doctrine that in the person of Jesus there was but a single divine nature. [LLat. *monophysita* < LGk. *monophusitēs* : Gk. *mono-*, mono- + Gk. *phusis*, nature; see **bheuə-***.] — **Mo·noph′y·site, Mo·noph′y·sit′ic** (-sĭt′ĭk) *adj.* — **Mo·noph′y·sit′ism** *n.*

mon·o·plane (mŏn′ə-plān′) *n.* An airplane with only one pair of wings.

mon·o·ple·gi·a (mŏn′ə-plē′jē-ə, -plē′jə) *n.* Complete paralysis of a single limb, muscle, or muscle group. — **mon′o·ple′gic** (-plē′jĭk) *adj.*

mon·o·ploid (mŏn′ə-ploid′) *adj.* Having a single set of chromosomes; haploid. — *n.* A monoploid cell or organism.

mon·o·pod (mŏn′ə-pŏd′) *n.* A single-legged support for a camera or other hand-held device.

mon·o·pode (mŏn′ə-pōd′) *n.* **1.** A creature having only one foot. **2.** *Bot.* A monopodium. [LLat. *monopodius*, one-footed. See MONOPODIUM.]

mon·o·po·di·um (mŏn′ə-pō′dē-əm) *n.*, *pl.* **-di·a** (-dē-ə). A main axis of a plant that maintains a single line of growth, giving off lateral branches. [NLat. < LLat. *monopodius*, one-footed < Gk. *monopous* : *mono-*, mono- + *pous*, *pod-*, foot; see **ped-***.] — **mon′o·po′di·al** (-dē-əl) *adj.*

mon·o·pole (mŏn′ə-pōl′) *n.* A magnetic monopole.

mo·nop·o·lize (mə-nŏp′ə-līz′) *tr.v.* **-lized, -liz·ing, -liz·es. 1.** To acquire or maintain a monopoly of. **2.** To dominate by excluding others: *monopolized the conversation.* — **mo·nop′o·li·za′tion** (-lĭ-zā′shən) *n.* — **mo·nop′o·liz′er** *n.*

mo·nop·o·ly (mə-nŏp′ə-lē) *n.*, *pl.* **-lies. 1.** Exclusive control by one group of the means of producing or selling a commodity or service. **2.** *Law.* A right granted by a government giving exclusive control over a specified commercial activity to a single party. **3.a.** A company or group having exclusive control over a commercial activity. **b.** A commodity or service so controlled. **4.a.** Exclusive possession or control. **b.** Something that is exclusively possessed or controlled. [Lat. *monopōlium* < Gk. *monopōlion* : *mono-*, mono- + *pōlein*, to sell; see **pel-⁴***.] — **mo·nop′o·lism** *n.* — **mo·nop′o·list** *n.* — **mo·nop′o·lis′tic** *adj.* — **mo·nop′o·lis′ti·cal·ly** *adv.*

mon·o·pro·pel·lant (mŏn′ō-prə-pĕl′ənt) *n.* A rocket propellant containing both fuel and oxidizer in a single substance.

mon·o·pro·tic (mŏn′ə-prō′tĭk) *adj.* Monobasic. [MONO– + PROT(ON) + –IC.]

mo·nop·so·ny (mə-nŏp′sə-nē) *n.*, *pl.* **-nies.** A market in which the product or service of several sellers is sought by only one buyer. [MON(O)– + Gk. *opsōnia*, purchase of food (< *opsōnein*, to buy food : *opson*, cooked food + *ōnē*, buying < *ōneisthai*, to buy; see **wes-³***).] — **mo·nop′so·nist** *n.* — **mo·nop′so·nis′tic** *adj.*

mon·o·rail (mŏn′ə-rāl′) *n.* **1.** A single rail serving as a track for wheeled vehicles traveling on it or suspended from it. **2.** A railway system using a single rail.

mon·o·sac·cha·ride (mŏn′ə-săk′ə-rīd′, -rĭd) *n.* A carbohydrate that cannot be decomposed by hydrolysis, esp. one of the hexoses, having the general formula $C_6H_{12}O_6$.

mon·o·so·di·um glu·ta·mate (mŏn′ə-sō′dē-əm glōō′tə-māt′) *n.* A white crystalline compound, $COOH(CH_2)_2CH(NH_2)COONa$, used as a flavor enhancer. [MONO– + SODIUM + GLUTAM(IC ACID) + –ATE².]

mon·o·some (mŏn′ə-sōm′) *n.* **1.** A chromosome with no homologue, esp. an unpaired X-chromosome. **2.** A single ribosome, esp. one combined with a molecule of messenger RNA. — **mon′o·so′mic** *adj.* — **mon′o·so′my** *n.*

mon·o·stich (mŏn′ə-stĭk′) *n.* **1.** A poem consisting of a single line. **2.** A single line of poetry.

mon·o·syl·lab·ic (mŏn′ə-sĭ-lăb′ĭk) *adj.* *Ling.* **1.** Having only one syllable. **2.** Characterized by or consisting of monosyllables. — **mon′o·syl·lab′ic·al·ly** *adv.*

mon·o·syl·la·ble (mŏn′ə-sĭl′ə-bəl) *n.* *Ling.* A word or an utterance of one syllable.

mon·o·the·ism (mŏn′ə-thē-ĭz′əm) *n.* The doctrine or belief that there is only one diety. — **mon′o·the′ist** *n.* — **mon′o·the·is′tic** *adj.* — **mon′o·the·is′ti·cal·ly** *adv.*

mon·o·the·mat·ic (mŏn′ə-thē-măt′ĭk) *adj.* Having only one theme.

mon·o·tint (mŏn′ə-tĭnt′) *n.* A monochrome painting or print.

mon·o·tone (mŏn′ə-tōn′) *n.* **1.** A succession of sounds or words uttered in a single tone of voice. **2.** *Mus.* **a.** A single tone repeated with different words or time values, as in plainsong. **b.** A chant in a single tone. **3.** Sameness or dull repetition in sound, style, manner, or color. — *adj.* **1.** Characterized by or uttered in a monotone. **2.** Of or having a single color. **3.** *Math.* Of or being a sequence, the successive members of which either consistently increase or decrease but do not oscillate in relative value. — **mon′o·ton′ic** (-tŏn′ĭk) *adj.* — **mon′o·ton′i·cal·ly** *adv.*

mo·not·o·nous (mə-nŏt′n-əs) *adj.* **1.** Sounded or spoken in an unvarying tone. **2.** Tediously repetitious or lacking in variety. See Syns at **boring.** — **mo·not′o·nous·ly** *adv.*

mo·not·o·ny (mə-nŏt′n-ē) *n.*, *pl.* **-nies. 1.** Uniformity or lack of variation in pitch, intonation, or inflection. **2.** Tedious sameness or repetitiousness.

mon·o·treme (mŏn′ə-trēm′) *n.* A member of the Monotremata, an order of primitive egg-laying mammals restricted to Australia and New Guinea and consisting of only the platypus and the echidna. [< NLat. *Monotremata*, order name : MONO– + Gk. *trēma*, perforation; see **terə-¹***.] — **mon′o·trem′a·tous** (-trĕm′ə-təs) *adj.*

mo·not·ri·chous (mə-nŏt′rĭ-kəs) also **mon·o·trich·ic** (mŏn′ə-trĭk′ĭk) or **mo·not·ri·chate** (mə-nŏt′rĭ-kĭt) *adj.* Having one flagellum at only one pole or end.

mon·o·type (mŏn′ə-tīp′) *n.* **1.** *Biol.* The sole member of its group, such as a single species that constitutes a genus. **2.** A unique print made by pressing paper against a painted or inked surface. — **mon′o·typ′ic** (-tĭp′ĭk) *adj.*

Mon·o·type (mŏn′ə-tīp′). A trademark used for a typesetting machine operated from a keyboard that activates a unit that casts and sets individual characters.

mon·o·un·sat·u·rat·ed (mŏn′ō-ŭn-săch′ə-rā′tĭd) *adj.* Of, relating to, or being an unsaturated fat composed mostly of fatty acids having only one double bond in the carbon chain.

mon·o·va·lent (mŏn′ə-vā′lənt) *adj.* **1.** *Chem.* Having a valence of 1; univalent. **2.** *Immunol.* **a.** Containing antigens from a single strain of a microorganism: *a monovalent serum.* **b.** Having only one site of attachment. Used of an antibody or antigen. — **mon′o·va′lence, mon′o·va′len·cy** *n.*

mon·ox·ide (mə-nŏk′sīd′) *n.* An oxide with each molecule containing one oxygen atom.

mon·o·zy·got·ic (mŏn′ō-zī-gŏt′ĭk) *adj.* Derived from a single fertilized ovum or embryonic cell mass. Used esp. of identical twins.

Mon·roe (mən-rō′). **1.** A city of NE-central LA E of Shreveport; founded 1785. Pop. 54,909. **2.** A city of SE MI on Lake Erie SW of Detroit; settled c. 1778. Pop. 22,902.

Monroe, James. 1758–1831. The fifth President of the U.S. (1817–25), whose administration was marked by the Monroe Doctrine (1823), which declared U.S. opposition to European interference in the Americas.

Monroe, Marilyn. Orig. Norma Jean Baker. 1926–62. Amer. actress whose films include *Some Like It Hot* (1959).

Mon·roe·ville (mən-rō′vĭl′). A borough of SW PA, a suburb of Pittsburgh. Pop. 29,169.

James Monroe
Detail of an 1817 portrait by Gilbert Stuart

ă pat	oi boy
ā pay	ou out
âr care	ŏŏ took
ä father	ōō boot
ĕ pet	ŭ cut
ē be	ûr urge
ĭ pit	th thin
ī pie	*th* this
îr pier	hw which
ŏ pot	zh vision
ō toe	ə about, item
ô paw	

Stress marks:
′ (primary);
′ (secondary), as in **dictionary** (dĭk′shə-nĕr′ē)

Mon•ro•vi•a (mən-rō′vē-ə). **1.** The cap. of Liberia, in the NW part on the Atlantic; founded 1822 as a haven for freed slaves. Pop. 243,243. **2.** A city of S CA, a suburb of Los Angeles in the foothills of the San Gabriel Mts. Pop. 35,761.

mons (mŏnz) *n., pl.* **mon•tes** (mŏn′tēz). A protuberance of the human body, esp. that formed by the pubic bones. [Lat. *mōns*, mountain. See **men-**[2]*.]

Mons (mōNs). A city of SW Belgium near the French border SW of Brussels. Pop. 91,868.

Mon•sei•gneur (môN-sĕ-nyœr′) *n., pl.* **Mes•sei•gneurs** (mā-sĕ-nyœr′). Used as an honorific in French-speaking areas, esp. for princes and prelates. [Fr. < OFr. : *mon*, my; see MONSIEUR + *seigneur*, lord, sir; see SEIGNIOR.]

Mon•sieur (mə-syœ′) *n., pl.* **Mes•sieurs** (mā-syœ′, mĕs′ərz). **1.** Used as a courtesy title before the surname, full name, or professional title of a man in a French-speaking area: *Monsieur Cartier; Monsieur Jacques Cartier.* **2. monsieur.** Used as a form of polite address for a man in a French-speaking area. [Fr. < OFr. : *mon*, my (< Lat. *meum*, accusative of *meus*; see **me-**[1]*) + *sieur*, lord, sir; see SEIGNIOR.]

monstrance
Late 16th- to early 17th-century Spanish

Mon•si•gnor also **mon•si•gnor** (mŏn-sēn′yər) *n. Rom. Cath. Ch.* **1.** A title conferred on a cleric by a pope. **2.** Used as a form of address prefixed to the name of such a cleric. [Ital. < Fr. *Monseigneur.* See MONSEIGNEUR.] **—Mon′si•gnor′i•al** (mŏn′sēn-yôr′ē-əl, -yōr′-) *adj.*

mon•soon (mŏn-so͞on′) *n.* **1.** A wind system that influences large climatic regions and reverses direction seasonally. **2.a.** A wind from the southwest or south that brings heavy rainfall to southern Asia in the summer. **b.** The rain that accompanies this wind. [Obsolete Du. *monssoen* < Port. *monção* < Ar. *mawsim*, season.] **—mon•soon′al** *adj.*

mons pubis *n., pl.* **montes pubis.** A rounded fleshy protuberance situated over the pubic bones that becomes covered with hair during puberty. [NLat. *mōns pūbis* : Lat. *mōns*, mount + Lat. *pūbis*, genitive of *pūbēs*, pubis.]

mon•ster (mŏn′stər) *n.* **1.a.** An imaginary or legendary creature, such as a centaur, that combines parts from various animal or human forms. **b.** A creature having a strange or frightening appearance. **2.** An animal, a plant, or other organism having structural defects or deformities. **3.** *Pathol.* A fetus or an infant that is grotesquely abnormal and usu. not viable. **4.** A very large animal, plant, or object. **5.** One who inspires horror or disgust. [ME *monstre* < OFr. < Lat. *mōnstrum*, portent, monster < *monēre*, to warn. See **men-**[1]*.]

Montezuma II

mon•strance (mŏn′strəns) *n. Rom. Cath. Ch.* A receptacle in which the host is held. [ME < OFr. < Med.Lat. *mōnstrantia* < Lat. *mōnstrāns*, *mōnstrant-*, pr.part. of *mōnstrāre*, to show < *mōnstrum*, portent, monster. See MONSTER.]

mon•stros•i•ty (mŏn-strŏs′ĭ-tē) *n., pl.* **-ties. 1.** One that is monstrous. **2.** The quality or character of being monstrous. [ME *monstruosite* < OFr. < LLat. *mōnstrōsitās* < Lat. *mōnstruōsus*, monstrous. See MONSTROUS.]

mon•strous (mŏn′strəs) *adj.* **1.** Shockingly hideous or frightful. **2.** Exceptionally large; enormous. **3.** Deviating greatly from the norm in appearance or structure; abnormal. **4.** Of or resembling a fabulous monster. [ME < OFr. *monstruos* < Lat. *mōnstruōsus* < *mōnstrum*, portent, monster. See MONSTER.] **—mon′strous•ly** *adv.* **—mon′strous•ness** *n.*

mons ve•ne•ris (vĕn′ər-ĭs) *n., pl.* **montes veneris.** The female mons pubis. [NLat. *mōns veneris* : Lat. *mōns*, mount + Lat. *Veneris*, genitive of *Venus*, Venus.]

Mont. *abbr.* Montana.

mon•tage (mŏn-täzh′, môN-) *n.* **1.a.** A single pictorial composition made by juxtaposing or superimposing many pictures or designs. **b.** The art or process of making such a composition. **2.a.** A rapid succession of different images or shots in a movie. **b.** The use of such successive images as a cinematic technique. **c.** Film editing. **3.** A composite of closely juxtaposed elements: *a montage of voices on an audiotape.* —*tr.v.* **-taged, -tag•ing, -tag•es.** To use or incorporate in a montage. [Fr. < *monter*, to mount < OFr. See MOUNT[1].]

monument
Washington Monument, Washington DC, designed by Robert Mills

Mon•tag•nais (mŏn′tən-yā′) *n., pl.* **Montagnais. 1.** A member of a Native American people inhabiting an extensive area in Quebec and Labrador. **2.** The Algonquian language of the Montagnais and Naskapi. [Canadian Fr. < Fr. *montagne*, mountain. See MONTAGNARD.]

Mon•ta•gnard also **mon•ta•gnard** (mŏn′tən-yärd′) *n.* A member of a people inhabiting the highlands of southern Vietnam near the border of Cambodia. [Fr., mountaineer < *montagne*, mountain < OFr. *montaigne.* See MOUNTAIN.]

Mon•ta•gu (mŏn′tə-gyo͞o′), **Ashley.** b. 1905. British-born Amer. anthropologist whose books include *The Natural Superiority of Women* (1953).

Montagu, Lady **Mary Wortley.** 1689–1762. English writer noted for her letters, travel writing, and social commentary.

Mon•taigne (mŏn-tān′, môN-tĕn′yə), **Michel Eyquem de.** 1533–92. French writer known for his essays.

Mon•ta•le (mōn-tä′lā, -lĕ), **Eugenio.** 1896–1981. Italian poet who won the 1975 Nobel Prize for literature.

Mon•tan•a (mŏn-tăn′ə). A state of the NW U.S. bordering on Canada; admitted as the 41st state in 1889. Cap. Helena. Pop. 803,655. **—Mon•tan′an** *adj. & n.*

mon•tane (mŏn-tān′, mŏn′tān′) *adj.* Of, growing in, or inhabiting mountain areas. [Lat. *montānus* < *mōns*, *mont-*, mountain. See **men-**[2]*.]

mon•tan wax (mŏn′tən, -tăn′) *n.* A hard white wax obtained from lignite and used in the manufacture of polishes, paints, and phonograph records. [< Lat. *montānus*, montane. See MONTANE.]

Mon•tauk (mŏn′tôk′) *n., pl.* **Montauk** or **-tauks. 1.** A member of a Native American people formerly inhabiting the eastern end of Long Island in New York. **2.** The Algonquian language of the Montauk. **3.** A member of any of various Algonquian peoples of eastern and central Long Island connected with the Montauk. [< a place name of Montauk orig.]

Montauk Point. The eastern extremity of Long I., in SE NY.

Mont Blanc (mônt blăngk, môN bläN′). See Mont **Blanc.**

Mont•calm de Saint-Ve•ran (mŏnt-käm′ də săN′vā-räN′, môN-kälm′), Marquis **Louis Joseph de.** 1712–59. French commander in Canada during the French and Indian War who repelled a British attack on Fort Ticonderoga (1758).

Mont•clair (mŏnt-klâr′). **1.** A city of S CA NE of Pomona. Pop. 28,434. **2.** A town of NE NJ, a suburb of New York City. Pop. 37,729.

mon•te (mŏn′tē) *n. Games.* A card game in which two cards are chosen from four laid out faceup and a player bets that one of the two will be matched in suit by the dealer before the other one. [Sp., mountain, pile, monte < Ital. < Lat. *mōns*, *mont-*, mountain. See **men-**[2]*.]

Mon•te Al•bán (môn′tĕ äl-bän′). A ruined Zapotec city of S Mexico near Oaxaca; site of an advanced culture that flourished c. 200 B.C.

Mon•te•bel•lo (mŏn′tə-bĕl′ō). A city of S CA, a suburb of Los Angeles. Pop. 59,564.

Mon•te Car•lo[1] (mŏn′tē kär′lō). A resort town of Monaco on the French Riviera. Pop. 11,599.

Mon•te Car•lo[2] (mŏn′tē kär′lō) *adj.* Of a problem-solving technique using statistical methods to solve mathematical or physical problems. [After MONTE CARLO[1].]

Mon•te•go Bay (mŏn-tē′gō). A town of NW Jamaica on the Caribbean Sea; visited by Columbus in 1494. Pop. 70,285.

Mon•te•ne•gro (mŏn′tə-nē′grō, -nĕg′rō). A region of the W Balkan Peninsula on the Adriatic Sea; joined (1918) the Kingdom of the Serbs, Croats, and Slovenes, which became Yugoslavia after 1929 and with Serbia formed present-day Yugoslavia in 1992. Cap. Titograd. Pop. 502,207.

Mon•te•rey (mŏn′tə-rā′). A city of W CA S of San Francisco on **Monterey Bay,** an inlet of the Pacific; a Spanish colonial cap. for much of the time from 1774 to 1846. Pop. 31,954.

Monterey Park. A city of S CA, a suburb of Los Angeles. Pop. 60,738.

mon•te•ro (mŏn-târ′ō) *n., pl.* **-ros.** A hunter's cap with side flaps. [Sp., hunter < *monte*, mountain < Lat. *mōns*, *mont-*. See MOUNTAIN.]

Mon•ter•rey (mŏn′tə-rā′, môn′tĕ-). A city of NE Mexico E of Matamoros; founded 1579. Pop. 1,090,099.

mon•tes (mŏn′tēz) *n.* Pl. of **mons.**

Mon•tes•quieu (mŏn′tə-skyo͞o′, môN-tĕ-skyœ′). Baron de la Brede et de Montesquieu. Charles de Secondat. 1689–1755. French philosopher and jurist whose works include *The Spirit of the Laws* (1748).

Mon•tes•so•ri (mŏn′tĭ-sôr′ē, -sōr′ē), **Maria.** 1870–1952. Italian physician and educator known for her reforms of methods for teaching young children.

Montessori method *n.* A method of educating young children that stresses development of a child's own initiative and natural abilities, esp. through practical play.

Mon•teux (mŏn-to͞o′, môN-tœ′), **Pierre.** 1875–1964. French-born Amer. conductor noted as an interpreter of 20th-cent. music.

Mon•te•ver•di (mŏn′tə-vâr′dē, môn′tĕ-), **Claudio.** 1567–1643. Italian composer who wrote the opera *Orfeo* (1607).

Mon•te•vi•de•o (mŏn′tə-vĭ-dā′ō, -vĭd′ē-ō′, môn′tĕ-vē-thĕ′ô). The cap. of Uruguay, in the S part on the Río de la Plata estuary; founded by the Spanish c. 1726 on the site of a captured Portuguese fort. Pop. 1,237,227.

Mon•te•zu•ma II (mŏn′tĭ-zo͞o′mə). 1466?–1520. Last Aztec emperor in Mexico (1502–20); overthrown by Cortés.

Mont•fer•rat (mŏnt-fə-rät′). A historical region of NW Italy S of the Po R.; awarded to Savoy in 1713.

Mont•fort (mŏnt′fərt, môN-fôr′), **Simon de.** Earl of Leicester. 1208?–65. French-born English nobleman who defeated Henry III at Lewes in SE England (1264) and became the virtual ruler of England.

Mont•gom•er•y (mŏnt-gŭm′ə-rē, -gŭm′rē). The cap. of AL, in the SE-central part SSE of Birmingham; first cap. (Feb.–May 1861) of the Confederacy. Pop. 187,106.

Montgomery, Sir **Bernard Law.** 1st Viscount Montgomery of Alamein. 1887–1976. British army officer who commanded the British victories over German forces in North Africa (1942) and the Allied advance through Normandy (1944).

month (mŭnth) *n.* **1.** A unit of time corresponding approx. to one cycle of the moon's phases, or about 30 days or 4 weeks. **2.** One of the 12 divisions of a year as determined by a calendar, esp. the Gregorian calendar. **3.** A period extending from a date in one calendar month to the corresponding date in the following month. **4.** A sidereal month. **5.** A lunar month. **6.** A solar month. **—*idiom.* month of Sundays.** *Informal.* An indefinitely long period of time. [ME *moneth* < OE *mōnath.* See **mē-**[2]*.]

Usage Note: The singular *month,* preceded by a numeral (or number) and a hyphen, is used as a compound attributive: *a three-month vacation.* The plural possessive form without a hyphen is also possible: *a three months' vacation.*

month•ly (mŭnth′lē) *adj.* **1.** Occurring, appearing, or coming due every month: *a monthly meeting.* **2.** Continuing or lasting for a month. —*adv.* Once a month; every month. —*n., pl.* **-lies. 1.** A periodical publication appearing once each month. **2. monthlies.** *Informal.* The menses.

Mon•ti•cel•lo (mŏn′tĭ-chĕl′ō, -sĕl′ō). An estate of central VA SE of Charlottesville; designed by Thomas Jefferson.

mon•ti•cule (mŏn′tĭ-kyo͞ol′) *n.* A minor cone of a volcano. [Fr. < LLat. *monticulus,* dim. of Lat. *mōns, mont-,* mountain. See **men-**[2]*.]

Mont•mar•tre (mōɴ-mär′trə). A hill and district of N Paris, France, on the Right Bank; noted for its nightlife and its associations with artists such as Toulouse-Lautrec.

Mont•par•nasse (mōɴ-pär-näs′). A district of S-central Paris, France, on the Left Bank; famous for its cafés patronized by artists, writers, and intellectuals.

Mont•pel•ier (mŏnt-pēl′yər). The cap. of VT, in the N-central part; founded 1780. Pop. 8,247.

Mont•pel•lier (mōɴ-pĕl-yā′). A city of S France near the Mediterranean Sea WNW of Marseilles; founded in the 8th cent. and later an important Huguenot center. Pop. 197,231.

Mon•tre•al (mŏn′trē-ôl′) or **Mont•ré•al** (môɴ′rā-äl′). A city of S Quebec, Canada, on **Montreal Island** in the St. Lawrence R.; founded by the French in 1642 and captured by the English in 1760. Pop. 980,354.

Montreal North or **Mont•ré•al-Nord** (môɴ′rā-äl-nôr′). A town of S Quebec, Canada, on Montreal I. Pop. 94,914.

Mon•treuil (môɴ-trœ′yə). A town of N-central France, a suburb of Paris. Pop. 93,368.

Mont Roy•al (môɴ rwä-yäl′) or **Mount Roy•al** (roi′əl). A town of S Quebec, Canada, on Montreal I. Pop. 19,247.

Mont-Saint-Mi•chel (môɴ-săɴ-mē-shĕl′). A small island off the coast of NW France in an arm of the English Channel; crowned by an abbey founded c. 708.

Mont•ser•rat (mŏnt′sə-răt′). An island in the Leeward Is. of the British West Indies NW of Guadaloupe; colonized by the English after 1632 but held by the French at various periods before 1783.

Mont•ville (mŏnt′vĭl′). A town of SE CT on the Thames R. NNW of New London; settled in 1670. Pop. 16,673.

mon•u•ment (mŏn′yə-mənt) *n.* **1.** A structure, such as a sculpture, erected as a memorial. **2.** An inscribed marker placed at a grave; a tombstone. **3.** Something venerated for its enduring historic significance or association with a notable past person or thing. **4.a.** An outstanding enduring achievement. **b.** An exceptional example. **5.** An object, such as a post or stone, fixed in the ground to mark a boundary or position. **6.** A written document, esp. a legal one. [ME < Lat. *monumentum,* memorial < *monēre,* to remind. See **men-**[1]*.]

mon•u•men•tal (mŏn′yə-mĕn′tl) *adj.* **1.** Of, resembling, or serving as a monument. **2.** Impressively large, sturdy, and enduring. **3.** Of outstanding significance. **4.** Astounding. **—mon′u•men•tal′i•ty** (-mĕn-tăl′ĭ-tē) *n.* **—mon′u•men′tal•ly** *adv.*

mon•u•men•tal•ize (mŏn′yə-mĕn′tl-īz′) *tr.v.* **-ized, -iz•ing, -iz•es.** To memorialize with a monument.

mon•u•ron (mŏn′yə-rŏn′) *n.* A crystalline compound, $C_9H_{11}ClN_2O$, used as a herbicide for grasses and broad-leaved weeds. [MON(O)- + UR(EA) + -ON[3].]

Mon•za (mōn′zə, môn′tsä). A city of N Italy NNE of Milan; an ancient cap. of Lombardy. Pop. 122,103.

mon•zo•nite (mŏn-zō′nīt′, mŏn′zə-nīt′) *n.* An igneous rock composed chiefly of plagioclase and orthoclase, with small amounts of other minerals. [Fr., after Mt. *Monzoni* in NE Italy.] **—mon′zo•nit′ic** (mŏn′zə-nĭt′ĭk) *adj.*

moo (mo͞o) *intr.v.* **mooed, moo•ing, moos.** To emit the deep bellowing sound made by a cow; low. —*n., pl.* **moos.** The lowing of a cow or a similar sound. [Imit.]

mooch (mo͞och) *v.* **mooched, mooch•ing, mooch•es.** —*tr.* **1.** To obtain or try to obtain by begging; cadge. **2.** To steal; filch. —*intr.* **1.** To get or try to get something free of charge; sponge. **2.** To wander about aimlessly. **3.** To skulk around; sneak. [ME *mowchen,* prob. < OFr. *muchier,* to hide, skulk.] **—mooch′er** *n.*

mood[1] (mo͞od) *n.* **1.** A state of mind or emotion. **2.** A pervading impression of an observer. **3.** An incidence of sulking or angry behavior. **4.** Inclination; disposition. [ME *mod* < OE *mōd,* disposition. See **mē-**[1]*.]

Syns: *mood, humor, temper.* These nouns refer to a temporary state of mind or feeling. *Mood* is the most inclusive term: *"I was in no mood to laugh"* (Mary Wollstonecraft Shelley). *Humor* often implies a state of mind resulting from one's characteristic disposition or temperament and sometimes suggests fitfulness or variability: *"All which had been done . . . was the effect not of humor, but of system"* (Edmund Burke). *Temper* most often refers to irritability or intense anger: *"The nation was in such a temper that the smallest spark might raise a flame"* (Macaulay).

mood[2] (mo͞od) *n.* **1.** *Gram.* A set of verb forms used to indicate the speaker's attitude toward the factuality or likelihood of the action or condition expressed. In English the indicative mood is used to state facts, the subjunctive mood to indicate doubt or unlikelihood, and the imperative mood to express a command. **2.** *Logic.* The arrangement or form of a syllogism. [Alteration of MODE.]

mood•y (mo͞o′dē) *adj.* **-i•er, -i•est. 1.** Given to frequent changes of mood; temperamental. **2.** Subject to periods of depression; sulky. **3.** Expressive of a mood, esp. a sullen or gloomy mood. **—mood′i•ly** *adv.* **—mood′i•ness** *n.*

Moo•dy (mo͞o′dē), **William Henry.** 1853–1917. Amer. jurist; associate justice of the U.S. Supreme Court (1906–10).

moo goo gai pan (mo͞o′ go͞o′ gī′ păn′) *n.* A Cantonese dish of chicken, mushrooms, vegetables, and spices sautéed together. [Cantonese, corresponding to Mandarin *mú gū jī piàn* : *mú gū,* mushroom + *jī,* chicken + *piàn,* slice.]

moo•la or **moo•lah** (mo͞o′lə) *n. Slang.* Money. [?]

moon (mo͞on) *n.* **1.** The natural satellite of Earth, having a slightly elliptical orbit, approx. 356,000 kilometers (221,600 miles) distant at perigee and 406,997 kilometers (252,950 miles) at apogee; its mean diameter is 3,475 kilometers (2,160 miles), and its average period of revolution around Earth 29 days, 12 hours, 44 minutes. **2.** A natural satellite revolving around a planet. **3.** The moon as it appears at a particular time in its cycle of phases. **4.** A month, esp. a lunar month. **5.** A disk, globe, or crescent resembling the natural satellite of Earth. **6.** Moonlight. **7.** *Slang.* The bared buttocks. —*v.* **mooned, moon•ing, moons.** —*intr.* **1.** To wander about or pass time languidly and aimlessly. **2.** To yearn or pine as if infatuated. [ME *moone* < OE *mōna.* See **mē-**[2]*.]

moon•beam (mo͞on′bēm′) *n.* A ray of moonlight.

moon•blind (mo͞on′blīnd′) *adj.* Affected with moon blindness.

moon blindness *n.* Recurrent inflammation of a horse's eyes, often ending in blindness.

moon•calf (mo͞on′kăf′, -käf′) *n.* **1.** A fool. **2.** A freak.

moon•child (mo͞on′chīld′) *n.* One born under the sign of Cancer. [< Cancer's astrological tie with the moon.]

moon dog *n.* A paraselene.

moon•eye (mo͞on′ī′) *n.* **1.** A silvery freshwater fish of the family Hiodontidae, esp. *Hiodon tergisus* of eastern North America. **2.** See **moon blindness.**

moon•eyed (mo͞on′īd′) *adj.* Moonblind.

moon-faced (mo͞on′fāst′) *adj.* Having a round face.

moon•fish (mo͞on′fĭsh′) *n., pl.* **moonfish** or **-fish•es. 1.** Any of several marine fishes of the family Carangidae, found in warm American coastal waters and having short compressed bodies and a silvery color. **2.** See **opah.**

moon•flow•er (mo͞on′flou′ər) *n.* Any of several night-blooming vines related to the morning glories.

moon•light (mo͞on′līt′) *n.* The light reflected from the surface of the moon. —*intr.v.* **-light•ed, -light•ing, -lights.** *Informal.* To work at another job, often at night, in addition to one's full-time job. **—moon′light′er** *n.*

moon•lit (mo͞on′lĭt′) *adj.* Lighted by moonlight.

moon•quake (mo͞on′kwāk′) *n.* A quake on the moon similar to an earthquake but usu. of very low magnitude.

moon•rise (mo͞on′rīz′) *n.* The event or time of the appearance of the moon above the eastern horizon.

moon•scape (mo͞on′skāp′) *n.* **1.** A view or picture of the surface of the moon. **2.** A desolate landscape.

moon•seed (mo͞on′sēd′) *n.* Any of several dioecious vines of the closely related genera *Cocculus* and *Menispermum,* having inconspicuous flowers and red or blackish fruit.

moon•set (mo͞on′sĕt′) *n.* The event or time of the disappearance of the moon below the western horizon.

moon shell *n.* Any of various marine gastropod mollusks of the family Naticidae, having a smooth rounded shell.

moon•shine (mo͞on′shīn′) *n.* **1.** Moonlight. **2.** *Informal.* Foolish talk or thought; nonsense. **3.** Illegally distilled whiskey. Also called regionally *white lightning.* —*intr.v.* **-shined, -shin•ing, -shines.** To distill and sell liquor illegally. **—moon′shin′er** *n.*

moon•stone (mo͞on′stōn′) *n.* A variety of feldspar valued as a gem for its pearly translucence.

moon•struck (mo͞on′strŭk′) also **moon•strick•en** (-strĭk′ən) *adj.* **1.** Romantically dazed or distracted. **2.** Affected by insanity; crazed. [< the belief that the moon caused lunacy.]

moon•walk (mo͞on′wôk′) *n.* A walk on the moon's surface by an astronaut. **—moon′walk′** *v.* **—moon′walk′er** *n.*

moon•ward (mo͞on′wərd) *adv.* & *adj.* Toward the moon.

moon•wort (mo͞on′wûrt′, -wôrt′) *n.* See **grape fern.**

moon•y (mo͞o′nē) *adj.* **-i•er, -i•est. 1.** Of or suggestive of the moon or moonlight. **2.** Moonlit. **3.** Dreamy in mood or nature; absent-minded.

moor[1] (mo͝or) *v.* **moored, moor•ing, moors.** —*tr.* **1.** To make

moon
Top: 4th day of new moon
Center: Full moon
Bottom: 24th day of new moon

ă **pat**	oi **boy**
ā **pay**	ou **out**
âr **care**	o͝o **took**
ä **father**	o͞o **boot**
ĕ **pet**	ŭ **cut**
ē **be**	ûr **urge**
ĭ **pit**	th **thin**
ī **pie**	*th* **this**
îr **pier**	hw **which**
ŏ **pot**	zh **vision**
ō **toe**	ə **about,**
ô **paw**	**item**

Stress marks:
′ (primary);
′ (secondary), as in
dictionary (dĭk′shə-nĕr′ē)

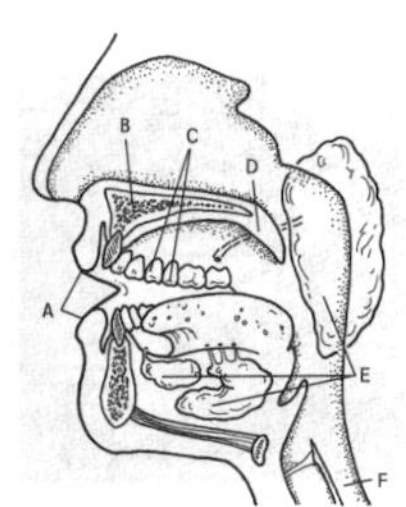

mouth
A. Lips
B. Hard palate
C. Teeth
D. Soft palate
E. Salivary glands
F. Esophagus

minished oxygen pressure at mountain elevations.

moun•tain•side (moun′tən-sīd′) *n.* The side of a mountain.

Mountain Standard Time *n.* Standard time in the seventh time zone west of Greenwich, England, reckoned at 105° west and used in the Rocky Mountain states of the United States.

moun•tain•top (moun′tən-tŏp′) *n.* A mountain summit.

Mountain View. A city of W CA on San Francisco Bay NW of San Jose. Pop. 67,460.

Mount Ath•os (mount ăth′ŏs, ā′thŏs, ä′thôs). See **Athos.**

Mount•bat•ten (mount-băt′n), **Louis.** 1st Earl Mountbatten of Burma. 1900–79. British naval officer who was Allied commander in SE Asia (1943–46) and the last viceroy and governor-general of India (1947).

Mount Clem•ens (klĕm′ənz). A city of SE MI NNE of Detroit. Pop. 18,405.

Mount Des•ert Island (dĕz′ərt). A resort island in the Atlantic Ocean off the S coast of ME.

moun•te•bank (moun′tə-băngk′) *n.* **1.** A hawker of quack medicines who attracts customers with stories, jokes, or tricks. **2.** A flamboyant charlatan. — *v.* **-banked, -bank•ing, -banks.** — *intr.* To act as a mountebank. — *tr. Archaic.* To ensnare or prevail over with trickery. [Ital. *montambanco* < the phrase *monta im banco*, one gets up onto the bench.]

Mount•ie also **Mount•y** (moun′tē) *n., pl.* **-ies.** *Informal.* A member of the Royal Canadian Mounted Police.

mount•ing (moun′tĭng) *n.* Something that serves as a support, setting, or backing.

Mount•lake Terrace (mount′lāk′). A city of NW WA S of Everett. Pop. 19,320.

Mount Leb•a•non (lĕb′ə-nən, -nŏn′). A community of SW PA, a suburb of Pittsburgh. Pop. 33,362.

Mount Pleas•ant (plĕz′ənt). A city of central MI WNW of Saginaw. Pop. 23,285.

Mount Pros•pect (prŏs′pĕkt′). A village of NE IL, a suburb of Chicago. Pop. 53,170.

Mount Roy•al (roi′əl). See **Mont Royal.**

Mount Ver•non[1] (vûr′nən). An estate of NE VA on the Potomac R. near Washington DC; built in 1743 and the home of George Washington from 1752 until his death in 1799.

Mount Ver•non[2] (vûr′nən). **1.** A city of S-central IL ESE of East St. Louis. Pop. 16,988. **2.** A city of SE NY adjacent to the Bronx; laid out in the 1850's. Pop. 67,153.

mourn (môrn, mōrn) *v.* **mourned, mourn•ing, mourns.** — *intr.* **1.** To feel or express grief or sorrow. See Syns at **grieve. 2.** To show grief for a death by conventional signs, as by wearing black. **3.** To make a low, indistinct mournful sound. Used esp. of a dove. — *tr.* **1.** To feel or express deep regret for. **2.** To grieve over (the dead). **3.** To utter sorrowfully. [ME *mournen* < OE *murnan.* See **(s)mer-**[1]***.**] — **mourn′er** *n.* — **mourn′ing•ly** *adv.*

mourn•ful (môrn′fəl, mōrn′-) *adj.* **1.** Feeling or expressing sorrow or grief; sorrowful. **2.** Causing or suggesting sadness or melancholy. — **mourn′ful•ly** *adv.* — **mourn′ful•ness** *n.*

mourn•ing (môr′nĭng, mōr′-) *n.* **1.** The actions or expressions of one who has suffered a bereavement. **2.** Conventional outward signs of grief for the dead, such as a black armband. **3.** The period during which a death is mourned.

mourning cloak *n.* A large butterfly *(Nymphalis antiopa)* of Europe and North America having purplish-brown wings with a broad yellow border.

mourning dove *n.* A grayish-brown wild dove *(Zenaidura macroura)* of North America noted for its mournful call.

mourning warbler *n.* A yellow and olive warbler *(Oporornis philadelphia)* of eastern North America having a bluish gray hood set off by a black band on its breast.

mouse (mous) *n., pl.* **mice** (mīs). **1.a.** Any of numerous small rodents of the families Muridae and Cricetidae, such as the common house mouse *(Mus musculus),* characteristically having a pointed snout, small rounded ears, and a long tail. **b.** Any of various similar or related animals, such as the jumping mouse or the vole. **2.** A cowardly or timid person. **3.** *Informal.* A discolored swelling under the eye caused by a blow; a black eye. **4.** *pl.* **mice** or **mous•es** (mous′ĭz). *Comp. Sci.* A hand-held button-activated input device that when rolled along a flat surface directs an indicator to move correspondingly about a computer screen. — *intr.v.* (mouz) **moused, mous•ing, mous•es. 1.** To hunt mice. **2.** To search furtively for something; prowl. [ME *mous* < OE *mūs.* See **mūs-*.**]

mouse deer *n.* See **chevrotain.** [Prob. alteration of MUSK DEER.]

mouse-ear chickweed (mous′îr′) *n.* Any of numerous herbs of the genus *Cerastium,* having opposite leaves and cylindrical capsules with ten toothlike projections.

mous•er (mou′zər) *n.* An animal, esp. a cat, that catches mice.

mouse-tail (mous′tāl′) *n.* A plant of the genus *Myosurus,* esp. *M. minimus,* having a taillike flower spike.

mouse•trap (mous′trăp′) *n.* A trap for catching mice. — *tr.v.* **-trapped, -trap•ping, -traps.** To trap or ensnare.

mous•ing (mou′zĭng) *n. Naut.* A binding or metal shackle around the point and shank of a hook to prevent it from slipping from an eye. [< MOUSE, mouselike rope knot.]

mous•sa•ka (mōō-sä′kə, mōō′sä-kä′) *n.* A Greek dish consisting of layers of ground lamb or beef and sliced eggplant topped with a cheese sauce and baked. [Serbo-Croatian < Turk. *mussakka* < Ar. *musakka.*]

mousse (mōōs) *n.* **1.** A chilled dessert made with flavored whipped cream, gelatin, and eggs. **2.** A molded dish containing meat, fish, or shellfish combined with whipped cream and gelatin. **3.** An aerosol foam used to style the hair. — *tr.v.* **moussed, mouss•ing, mouss•es.** To apply a mousse to (the hair). [Fr., foam, mousse < OFr., moss, foam, partly of Gmc. orig. and partly < Lat. *mulsa,* hydromel < fem. of *mulsus,* honey-sweet; see **melit-*.**]

mousse•line (mōōs-lēn′) *n.* **1.** A fine sheer fabric resembling muslin, originally made in Mosul, Iraq. **2.** A hollandaise sauce or an aspic containing whipped cream. [Fr. See MUSLIN.]

mousseline de soie (də swä′) *n., pl.* **mousselines de soie.** A fine crisp fabric made of silk or rayon. [Fr. : *mousseline,* muslin + *de,* of + *soie,* silk.]

mous•tache (mŭs′tăsh′, mə-stăsh′) *n.* Var. of **mustache.**

Mous•te•ri•an (mōō-stîr′ē-ən) *adj. Archaeol.* Of or being a Middle Paleolithic culture marked by the use of flaked tools. [Fr. *moustérien,* after *Le Moustier,* cave in SW France.]

mous•y also **mous•ey** (mou′sē, -zē) *adj.* **-i•er, -i•est. 1.** Resembling a mouse, esp.: **a.** Having a drab pale brown color: *mousy hair.* **b.** Having small sharp features: *a mousy face.* **c.** Quiet; timid; shy. **2.** Infested with mice.

mouth (mouth) *n., pl.* **mouths** (mouthz). **1.a.** The body opening through which an animal takes in food. **b.** The cavity lying at the upper end of the alimentary canal, bounded on the outside by the lips and inside by the oropharynx and containing in higher vertebrates the tongue, gums, and teeth. **c.** This cavity regarded as the source of sounds and speech. **d.** The opening to any cavity or canal in an organ or a body part. **2.** The part of the lips visible on the human face. **3.** A person viewed as a consumer of food. **4.** A pout, grimace, or similar expression. **5.a.** Utterance; voice. **b.** A tendency to talk excessively or unwisely. **c.** Impudent or vulgar talk. **6.** A spokesperson: a mouthpiece. **7.** A natural opening, as the entrance to a harbor or canyon. **8.** The opening through which a container is filled or emptied. **9.** The opening between the jaws of a vise or other holding or gripping tool. **10.** *Mus.* **a.** An opening in the pipe of an organ. **b.** The opening in the mouthpiece of a flute across which the player blows. — *v.* (mouth) **mouthed, mouth•ing, mouths.** — *tr.* **1.** To speak or pronounce, esp.: **a.** To declare in a pompous manner; declaim. **b.** To utter without conviction or understanding. **c.** To form soundlessly. **d.** To utter indistinctly; mumble. **2.** To take or move around in the mouth. — *intr.* **1.** To orate affectedly; declaim. **2.** To grimace. — ***phrasal verb.* mouth off.** *Slang.* **1.** To express one's opinions or complaints in a loud, indiscreet manner. **2.** To speak impudently; talk back. [ME < OE *mūth.* See **men-**[2]***.**]

mouth•breed•er (mouth′brē′dər) *n.* Any of various fishes, esp. of the genera *Haplochromis* and *Tilapia,* that carry their eggs and young in the mouth.

mouth•ful (mouth′fŏŏl′) *n.* **1.** The amount of food or other material that can be held in the mouth at one time. **2.** A small amount to be tasted or eaten. **3.** A long word, name, or phrase that is difficult to pronounce. **4.** An important or perceptive remark.

mouth organ *n. Mus.* **1.** See **harmonica** 1. **2.** See **panpipe.**

mouth•part (mouth′pärt′) *n.* Any of the parts of the mouth of an insect or other arthropod, esp. a part for feeding.

mouth•piece (mouth′pēs′) *n.* **1.** A part, as of a musical instrument or a telephone, that functions in or near the mouth. **2.** *Sports.* A protective rubber device worn over the teeth, as by boxers. **3.** *Informal.* One through which views are expressed. **4.** *Slang.* A defense lawyer.

mouth-to-mouth resuscitation (mouth′tə-mouth′) *n.* A technique used to resuscitate a person who has stopped breathing, in which the rescuer forces air into the lungs at intervals of several seconds.

mouth•wash (mouth′wŏsh′, -wôsh′) *n.* A flavored, usu. antiseptic solution for cleaning the mouth and freshening the breath.

mouth•wa•ter•ing or **mouth-wa•ter•ing** (mouth′wô′tər-ĭng) *adj.* Appealing to the sense of taste; appetizing.

mouth•y (mou′thē, -thē) *adj.* **-i•er, -i•est. 1.** Annoyingly talkative. **2.** Given to ranting or bombast. — **mouth′i•ness** *n.*

mou•ton (mōō′tŏn′) *n.* Sheepskin sheared and processed to resemble beaver or seal. [Fr., sheep < OFr. See MUTTON.]

mou•ton•née (mōō′tə-nā′) also **mou•ton•néed** (-nād′) *adj. Geol.* Rounded by glacial action into a shape likened to a sheep's back. Used of a rock formation. [Short for Fr. *roche moutonnée* : *roche,* rock + *moutonnée,* fleecy, p.part. of *moutonner,* to make fleecy (< *mouton,* sheep; see MOUTON).]

mov•a•ble also **move•a•ble** (mōō′və-bəl) — *adj.* **1.** Possible to move. **2.** Varying in date from year to year. — *n.* Something, esp. a piece of furniture, that can be moved. — **mov′a•bil′i•ty, mov′a•ble•ness** *n.* — **mov′a•bly** *adv.*

movable feast *n.* A religious holiday, such as Easter, that changes in date from year to year.

movable type *n. Print.* Type in which each character is cast on a separate piece of metal.

move (mo͞ov) *v.* **moved, mov•ing, moves.** —*intr.* **1.** To change in position from one point to another. **2.** To progress in sequence; go forward. **3.** To follow a specified course. **4.** To progress toward a particular state or condition. **5.** To go from one residence or location to another; relocate. **6.** To start off; depart. **7.** To be disposed of by sale. **8.** To change posture or position; stir. **9.** *Games.* To change the position of a piece in a board game. **10.** To be put in motion or to turn according to a prescribed motion. Used of machinery. **11.** To exhibit great activity or energy. **12.** To initiate an action; act. **13.** To be active in a particular environment: *moves in diplomatic circles.* **14.** To stir the emotions. **15.** To make a formal motion in parliamentary procedure. **16.** To evacuate. Used of the bowels. —*tr.* **1.** To change the place or position of. **2.** To cause to go from one place to another. **3.** *Games.* To change (a piece) from one position to another in a board game. **4.** To change the course of. **5.** To dislodge from a fixed point of view, as by persuasion. **6.** To prompt to an action; rouse. **7.a.** To set or keep in motion. **b.** To cause to function. **c.** To cause to progress or advance. **8.a.** To arouse the emotions of; affect. **b.** To excite or provoke to the expression of an emotion. **9.a.** To propose or request in formal parliamentary procedure. **b.** To make formal application to (a court, for example). **10.** To dispose of by sale. **11.** To cause (the bowels) to evacuate. —*n.* **1.a.** The act or an instance of moving. **b.** A particular manner of moving. **2.** A change of residence or location. **3.** *Games.* **a.** An act of transferring a piece from one position to another in board games. **b.** The prescribed manner in which a piece may be played. **c.** A participant's turn to make a play. **4.** An action taken to achieve an objective; a maneuver. —***phrasal verb.*** **move in.** To begin to occupy a residence or place of business. —***idioms.*** **get a move on.** *Informal.* To get started; get going. **move in on. 1.** To make intrusive advances toward; intrude on. **2.** To attempt to seize control of. **on the move. 1.** Busily moving about; active. **2.** Going from one place to another. **3.** Making progress; advancing. [ME *moven* < OFr. *movoir* < Lat. *movēre.* See **meuə-*.**]

move•ment (mo͞ov′mənt) *n.* **1.a.** The act or an instance of moving; a change in place or position. **b.** A particular manner of moving. **2.** A change in the location of troops, ships, or aircraft for tactical or strategic purposes. **3.a.** A series of actions and events that foster a principle or policy. **b.** An organized effort by supporters of a common goal. **4.** A tendency or trend. **5.** A change in the market price of a security or commodity. **6.a.** An evacuation of the bowels. **b.** The matter so evacuated. **7.** The suggestion or illusion of motion in a painting, sculpture, or design. **8.** The progression of events in the development of a literary plot. **9.** The rhythmic or metrical structure of a poetic composition. **10.** *Mus.* A self-contained section of a composition. **11.** A mechanism, such as the works of a watch, that produces or transmits motion.

mov•er (mo͞o′vər) *n.* **1.** One that moves. **2.** One that transports household or office goods as an occupation.

mover and shaker *n., pl.* **movers and shakers.** One who wields power and influence in a sphere of activity.

mov•ie (mo͞o′vē) *n.* **1.a.** A sequence of images projected onto a screen with sufficient rapidity to create the illusion of motion and continuity. **b.** A cinematic narrative represented in this form. **2.** A theater that shows movies. **3. movies. a.** A showing of a movie. Often used with *the.* **b.** The movie industry. [Shortening and alteration of MOVING PICTURE.]

mov•ie•dom (mo͞o′vē-dəm) *n.* See **filmdom.**

mov•ie•go•er (mo͞o′vē-gō′ər) *n.* One who goes to see movies. —**mov′ie•go′ing** *adj. & n.*

mov•ie•mak•er (mo͞o′vē-mā′kər) *n.* One that makes movies, esp. professionally. —**mov′ie•mak′ing** *adj. & n.*

mov•ing (mo͞o′vĭng) *adj.* **1.** Changing or capable of changing position. **2.** Of or involved in a transfer of furnishings from one location to another. **3.** Causing or producing motion. **4.** Involving a motor vehicle in motion. **5.** Arousing or capable of arousing deep emotion. —**mov′ing•ly** *adv.*

moving picture *n.* A movie.

mow[1] (mou) *n.* **1.** The place in a barn where hay, grain, or other feed is stored. **2.** A stack of hay or other feed stored in a barn. [ME, stack of hay < OE *mūga.*]

mow[2] (mō) *v.* **mowed, mowed** or **mown** (mōn), **mow•ing, mows.** —*tr.* **1.** To cut down (grass or grain) with a scythe or a mechanical device. **2.** To cut (grass or grain) from: *mow the lawn.* —*intr.* To cut down grass or other growth. —***phrasal verb.*** **mow down. 1.** To destroy in great numbers as if cutting down, as in battle. **2.** To overwhelm. [ME *mowen* < OE *māwan.* See **mē-[4]*.**] —**mow′er** (mō′ər) *n.*

mox•ie (mŏk′sē) *n. Slang.* **1.** The ability to face difficulty with spirit and courage. **2.** Aggressive energy; initiative. **3.** Skill; know-how. [< *Moxie*, trademark for a soft drink.]

moyen âge (mwä-yĕ näzh′) *n.* The Middle Ages. [Fr. : *moyen*, middle + *âge*, age.]

Mo•zam•bique (mō′zəm-bēk′, -zăm-). A country of SE Africa; colonized by the Portuguese after 1505 and an overseas province from 1951 to 1975. Cap. Maputo. Pop. 12,130,000. —**Mo′zam•bi′can** (-bē′kən) *adj. & n.*

Mozambique Channel. An arm of the Indian Ocean between Madagascar and the mainland of SE Africa.

Moz•ar•ab (mō-zăr′əb) *n.* One of a group of Spanish Christians who adopted certain aspects of Arab culture under Muslim rule but practiced a modified form of Christian worship. [Sp. *Mozárabe* < Ar. *musta'rib*, would-be Arab < *'arab*, Arab.] —**Moz•ar′a•bic** *adj.*

Mo•zart (mōt′särt), **Wolfgang Amadeus.** 1756–91. Austrian composer whose works include *Don Giovanni* (1787).

mo•zo (mō′zō) *n., pl.* **-zos.** *Southwestern U.S.* **1.** A man who helps with a pack train or serves as a porter. **2.** An assistant. [Sp., boy, servant, mozo < OSp. *moço.*]

moz•za•rel•la (mŏt′sə-rĕl′ə, mōt′-) *n.* A mild white Italian cheese with a rubbery texture, often eaten melted, as on pizza. [Ital., dim. of *mozza* < *mozzare*, to cut off < *mozzo*, mutilated < VLat. **mutius* < Lat. *mutilis.*]

moz•zet•ta or **mo•zet•ta** (mō-zĕt′ə, mōt-sĕt′tä) *n. Rom. Cath. Ch.* A short hooded cape worn over the rochet, as by the pope. [Ital. < Med.Lat. *almutia.*]

mp or **m.p.** *abbr.* **1.** Melting point. **2.** *Mus.* Mezzo piano.

MP or **M.P.** *abbr.* **1.** Member of Parliament. **2.** Military police. **3.** Military police officer. **4.** Mounted police.

M.P.A. *abbr.* **1.** Master of Public Administration. **2.** Master of Public Accounting.

M.P.E. *abbr.* Master of Public Education.

mpg or **m.p.g.** *abbr.* Miles per gallon.

mph or **m.p.h.** *abbr.* Miles per hour.

M.P.H. *abbr.* Master of Public Health.

Mr. (mĭs′tər) *n., pl.* **Messrs.** (mĕs′ərz). Used as a courtesy title before the surname or full name of a man. See Usage Note at **Ms.** [ME, abbreviation of *maister*, master. See MASTER.]

Mr. Char•lie or **Mister Char•lie** (chär′lē) *n. Offensive Slang.* A white person or white people considered as a group. [< the name *Charlie*, nickname for *Charles.*]

MRI *abbr.* Magnetic resonance imaging.

mRNA *abbr.* Messenger RNA.

Mrs. (mĭs′ĭz) *n., pl.* **Mmes.** (mā-däm′, -dăm′). **1.** Used as a courtesy title for a married or widowed woman before the surname or full name of her husband: *Mrs. Doe; Mrs. John Doe.* **2.** Used as a courtesy title for a married, widowed, or divorced woman before her own surname or full name: *Mrs. Doe; Mrs. Jane Doe.* See Usage Note at **Ms.** [Abbreviation of MISTRESS.]

Mrs. Grun•dy (grŭn′dē) *n.* A very conventional or priggish person. [After *Mrs. Grundy*, character alluded to in the play *Speed the Plough* by Thomas Morton (1764–1838).]

ms *abbr.* Millisecond.

MS *abbr.* **1.** Mississippi. **2.** Multiple sclerosis.

Ms. also **Ms** (mĭz) *n., pl.* **Mses.** also **Mses** also **Mss.** or **Mss** (mĭz′ĭz). Used as a courtesy title before the surname or full name of a woman or girl: *Ms. Doe; Ms. Jane Doe.* [Blend of MISS and MRS.]

Usage Note: *Ms.* has come to be widely used in both professional and social contexts. Many women prefer it to *Miss* or *Mrs.* because they feel that information about their marital status is often inappropriate to the contexts in which such titles are used. Many people also find *Ms.* convenient, since information about an addressee's marital status is not always available. But there are also many women who continue to prefer *Miss* or *Mrs.*, and practices vary widely.

MS. or **MS** also **ms.** or **ms** *abbr.* Manuscript.

M.S. *abbr. Lat.* Magister Scientiae (Master of Science).

M.Sc. *abbr. Lat.* Magister Scientiae (Master of Science).

MS-DOS (ĕm′ĕs-dôs′, -dŏs′). A trademark for a microcomputer operating system.

msec *abbr.* Millisecond.

MSG *abbr.* Monosodium glutamate.

msg. *abbr.* Message.

Msgr. *abbr.* **1.** Monseigneur. **2.** Monsignor.

M.Sgt. or **MSGT** *abbr.* Master sergeant.

MSH *abbr.* Melanocyte-stimulating hormone.

M.S. in L.S. *abbr.* Master of Science in Library Science.

m.s.l. or **M.S.L.** *abbr.* Mean sea level.

M.S.N. *abbr.* Master of Science in Nursing.

MSS. or **MSS** also **mss.** or **mss** *abbr.* Manuscripts.

MST or **M.S.T.** *abbr.* Mountain Standard Time.

M.S.T.S. *abbr.* Military Sea Transportation Service.

M.S.W. *abbr.* **1.** Master of Social Welfare. **2.** Master of Social Work.

Mt *abbr. Bible.* Matthew.

MT *abbr.* **1.** Machine translation. **2.** Megaton. **3.** Montana.

mt. or **Mt.** *abbr.* Mount; mountain.

m.t. or **M.T.** *abbr.* Metric ton.

mtg. *abbr.* **1.** Meeting. **2.** Mortgage.

mtge. *abbr.* Mortgage.

mtn. or **Mtn.** *abbr.* Mountain.

mts. or **Mts.** *abbr.* Mountains.

mu (myo͞o, mo͞o) *n.* The 12th letter of the Greek alphabet. [Gk., of Phoenician orig.; akin to Heb. *mēm.*]

Mu•bar•ak (mo͞o-bär′ək), **Hosni.** b. 1929. Egyptian politician who was appointed president after the assassination of Anwar el-Sadat (1981).

Mozambique

Wolfgang Amadeus Mozart

ă pat	oi boy
ā pay	ou out
âr care	o͝o to͝ok
ä father	o͞o bo͞ot
ĕ pet	ŭ cut
ē be	ûr urge
ĭ pit	th thin
ī pie	*th* this
îr pier	hw which
ŏ pot	zh vision
ō toe	ə about, item
ô paw	

Stress marks:
′ (primary);
′ (secondary), as in **dictionary** (dĭk′shə-nĕr′ē)

muc– *pref.* Var. of **muco–.**
much (mŭch) *adj.* **more** (môr, mōr), **most** (mōst). Great in quantity, degree, or extent: *not much rain; much affection.* —*n.* **1.** A large quantity or amount: *Much has been written.* **2.** Something great or remarkable: *not much to look at.* —*adv.* **more, most. 1.** To a great degree or extent: *much smarter.* **2.** Just about; almost: *much the same.* **3.** Frequently; often: *doesn't get out much.* [ME *muche*, short for *muchel* < OE *mycel.* See **meg-*.**]
much as *conj.* However much.
much•ness (mŭch′nĭs) *n.* Greatness of quantity, degree, or extent.
mu•cic acid (myo͞o′sĭk) *n.* An organic acid, HOOC-$(CHOH)_4$COOH, often derived from milk sugar.
mu•cif•er•ous (myo͞o-sĭf′ər-əs) *adj.* Secreting, producing, or containing mucus.
mu•ci•lage (myo͞o′sə-lĭj) *n.* **1.** A sticky substance used as an adhesive. **2.** A gummy substance obtained from certain plants. [ME *muscilage*, gelatinous plant substance < OFr. *mucilage* < LLat. *mūcilāgō, mūcilāgin-* < Lat. *mūcēre*, to be musty < *mūcus*, mucus.]
mu•ci•lag•i•nous (myo͞o′sə-lăj′ə-nəs) *adj.* **1.** Resembling mucilage; moist and sticky. **2.** Of or secreting mucilage.
mu•cin (myo͞o′sĭn) *n.* Any of a group of glycoproteins produced esp. by mucous membranes. —**mu′cin•ous** *adj.*
muck (mŭk) *n.* **1.** A moist sticky mixture, esp. of mud and filth. **2.** Moist farmyard dung; manure. **3.** Dark fertile soil containing decaying vegetable matter. **4.** Something filthy or disgusting. **5.** Earth, rocks, or clay excavated in mining. —*tr.v.* **mucked, muck•ing, mucks. 1.** To fertilize with manure or compost. **2.** To make dirty with or as if with muck. **3.** To remove muck or dirt from (a mine, for example). —***phrasal verbs.* muck about.** *Chiefly British.* To spend time idly; putter. **muck up.** *Informal.* To bungle, damage, or ruin. [ME *muk*, of Scand. orig.] —**muck′i•ly** *adv.* —**muck′y** *adj.*
muck•a•muck (mŭk′ə-mŭk′) *n. Slang.* A high muckamuck.
muck•rake (mŭk′rāk′) *intr.v.* **-raked, -rak•ing, -rakes.** To search for and expose misconduct in public life. [< a character in *Pilgrim's Progress* by John Bunyan.] —**muck′rak′er** *n.*
muck•worm (mŭk′wûrm′) *n.* Any wormlike insect larva, as of certain beetles, that lives and grows in manure.
muco– or **muci–** or **muc–** *pref.* **1.** Mucus: *mucoprotein.* **2.** Mucosa: *mucin.* [< Lat. *mūcus*, mucus.]
mu•coid (myo͞o′koid′) *n.* Any of various glycoproteins similar to the mucins. —*adj.* Of, relating to, or resembling mucus.
mu•co•lyt•ic (myo͞o′kə-lĭt′ĭk) *adj.* Breaking down or hydrolyzing mucus or glycosaminoglycans.
mu•co•pol•y•sac•cha•ride (myo͞o′kō-pŏl′ē-săk′ə-rīd′) *n.* See **glycosaminoglycan.**
mu•co•pro•tein (myo͞o′kō-prō′tēn′, -prō′tē-ĭn) *n.* Any of a group of organic compounds, such as the mucins, that consist of a complex of proteins and glycosaminoglycans.
mu•co•pu•ru•lent (myo͞o′kō-pyo͝or′ə-lənt, -yə-lənt) *adj.* Containing mucus and pus.
mu•co•sa (myo͞o-kō′sə) *n., pl.* **-sae** (-sē) or **-sas.** See **mucous membrane.** [< Lat. *mūcōsa*, fem. of *mūcōsus*, mucous. See MUCOUS.] —**mu•co′sal** *adj.*
mu•cous (myo͞o′kəs) *adj.* **1.** Containing, producing, or secreting mucus. **2.** Relating to, consisting of, or resembling mucus. [Lat. *mūcōsus* < *mūcus*, mucus.]
mucous membrane *n.* A mucus-secreting membrane lining all body passages that communicate with the air.
mu•cro (myo͞o′krō) *n., pl.* **mu•cro•nes** (myo͞o-krō′nēz). A sharp, pointed part or organ, esp. a sharp terminal point, as of a leaf or shell. [Lat. *mūcrō, mūcrōn-*, sharp point.]
mu•cro•nate (myo͞o′krə-nāt′) *adj.* Of or having a mucro; ending abruptly in a sharp point. —**mu′cro•na′tion** *n.*
mu•cus (myo͞o′kəs) *n.* The viscous slippery substance that consists chiefly of mucin, water, cells, and inorganic salts and is secreted as a protective lubricant coating by cells and glands of the mucous membranes. [Lat. *mūcus.*]
mud (mŭd) *n.* **1.** Wet sticky soft earth. **2.** *Slang.* Wet plaster, mortar, or cement. **3.** Slanderous or defamatory charges or comments. —*tr.v.* **mud•ded, mud•ding, muds.** To cover or spatter with or as if with mud. [ME *mudde*, prob. < MLGer. and MDu. *modde.*]
mud•bug (mŭd′bŭg′) *n.* See **crayfish** 1.
mud cat *n. Chiefly Southern U.S.* See **catfish.**
mud dauber *n. Midland U.S.* See **mud wasp** 1.
mud•der (mŭd′ər) *n.* A racehorse that runs well on a wet or muddy track.
mud•dle (mŭd′l) *v.* **-dled, -dling, -dles.** —*tr.* **1.** To make turbid or muddy. **2.** To mix confusedly; jumble. **3.** To confuse or befuddle (the mind). See Syns at **confuse. 4.** To mismanage or bungle. **5.** To stir or mix (a drink) gently. —*intr.* To think, act, or proceed in a confused or aimless manner. —*n.* **1.** A disordered condition; a mess or jumble. **2.** Mental confusion. —***phrasal verb.* muddle through.** To push on to a favorable outcome in a disorganized way. [Poss. < obsolete Du. *moddelen*, to make water muddy < MDu., freq. of **modden*, to make muddy < *modde*, mud.] —**mud′dler** *n.*

muff²

mud•dle•head•ed (mŭd′l-hĕd′ĭd) *adj.* **1.** Mentally confused. **2.** Inept; blundering. —**mud′dle•head′ed•ness** *n.*
mud•dy (mŭd′ē) *adj.* **-di•er, -di•est. 1.** Full of or covered with mud. **2.a.** Not bright or pure: *a muddy color.* **b.** Not clear; cloudy, as with sediment. **3.** Lacking luster; dull. **4.** Confused or vague. —*tr.v.* **-died, -dy•ing, -dies. 1.** To make dirty or muddy. **2.** To make dull or cloudy. **3.** To make obscure or confused. —**mud′di•ly** *adv.* —**mud′di•ness** *n.*
mud eel *n.* A small eellike amphibian *(Siren lacertina)* of the southeast United States having only front legs that are partially concealed by external gills.
Mu•dé•jar (mo͞o-thĕ′här) *n., pl.* **Mu•dé•ja•res** (-hä-rĕs′). A Muslim who remained in Spain after its Christian reconquest in the Middle Ages. —*adj.* Of or relating to a style of Spanish architecture of the 13th to the 16th century, combining Moorish and Gothic forms. [Sp., poss. < Ar. *dajana*, to stay.]
mud•fish (mŭd′fĭsh′) *n., pl.* **mudfish** or **-fish•es.** See **bowfin.**
mud flat *n.* Low-lying muddy land that is covered at high tide and exposed at low tide.
mud•flow (mŭd′flō′) *n.* A downhill movement of soft wet earth and debris, made fluid by rain or melted snow and often building up great speed.
mud•guard (mŭd′gärd′) *n.* A shield over or behind a vehicle's wheel to limit splashing of mud or water.
mud hen *n.* Any of various birds, such as the coot or rail, inhabiting marshy or coastal regions
mud minnow *n.* Any of various very small fishes of the family Umbridae, esp. of the genus *Umbra*, living in the muddy areas of North American lakes and ponds and often used as bait.
mud puppy also **mud•pup•py** (mŭd′pŭp′ē) *n., pl.* **mud puppies** also **mud•pup•pies. 1.** Any of several large North American salamanders of the genus *Necturus*, esp. *N. maculosus*, living in lakes and streams and having conspicuous clusters of dark red external gills. **2.** *Northern U.S.* See **catfish.**
mu•dra (mə-drä′) *n.* A series of symbolic body postures and hand movements used in East Indian classical dancing. [Skt. *mudrā*, seal, mystery, mudra.]
mud•room (mŭd′ro͞om′, -ro͝om′) *n.* A small room or entryway in a house where wet or muddy clothing can be removed.
mud•sill (mŭd′sĭl′) *n.* The lowest sill, block, or timber supporting a building, located at or below ground level.
mud•skip•per (mŭd′skĭp′ər) *n.* Any of several tropical African and Indo-Pacific fishes of the family Gobiidae, esp. of the genus *Periophthalmus*, able to survive on land.
mud•slide (mŭd′slīd′) *n.* A mudflow, esp. a slow-moving one.
mud•sling•er (mŭd′slĭng′ər) *n.* One who makes malicious charges and otherwise attempts to discredit an opponent, as in a political campaign. —**mud′sling′ing** *n.*
mud snake *n.* A burrowing snake *(Farancia abacura)* of swamps and lowlands of the southeast United States, having black scales with reddish markings.
mud•stone (mŭd′stōn′) *n.* A dark gray fine-grained sedimentary rock, similar to shale but without laminations.
mud turtle *n.* Any of various small turtles of the genus *Kinosternon*, having hinged lobes on the ventral part of the shell and found in fresh waters of the Western Hemisphere.
mud wasp *n.* **1.** *Northeastern U.S.* Any of various wasps that build nests of mud. Also called regionally *mud dauber.* **2.** See **potter wasp.**
Muen•ster or **Mun•ster** (mŭn′stər, mo͞on′-) *n.* A semisoft creamy cheese of mild flavor. [After *Munster* in NE France.]
mues•li (myo͞oz′lē) *n.* A mixture of usu. untoasted rolled oats and dried fruit, often used as a breakfast cereal. [Ger. dial., dim. of Ger. *Mus*, mush < MHGer. *muos*, a meal, mushlike food < OHGer.]
mu•ez•zin (myo͞o-ĕz′ĭn, mo͞o-) *n. Islam.* The crier who calls the faithful to prayer five times a day. [Ottoman Turk. *müezzin* or Pers. *muazzin* < Ar. *mu'aḏḏin*, active part. of *'aḏḏana*, to cause to listen < *'udn*, ear.]
muff¹ (mŭf) *v.* **muffed, muff•ing, muffs.** —*tr.* **1.** To perform or handle clumsily; bungle. See Syns at **botch. 2.** *Sports.* To fail to make (a catch). —*intr.* To perform an act clumsily. —*n.* **1.** A clumsy or bungled action. **2.** *Sports.* A failure to make a catch. [?]
muff² (mŭf) *n.* **1.** A small cylindrical fur or cloth cover, open at both ends, in which the hands are placed for warmth. **2.** A cluster of feathers on the face of certain breeds of fowl. [Du. *mof* < MDu. *moffel* < OFr. *moufle*, mitten < Med.Lat. *muffula*, perh. of Gmc. orig.]
muf•fin (mŭf′ĭn) *n.* **1.** A small cup-shaped quick bread, often sweetened and usu. served warm. **2.** An English muffin. [Poss. < LGer. *Muffen*, pl. of *Muffe*, small cake < MLGer.]
muf•fle¹ (mŭf′əl) *tr.v.* **-fled, -fling, -fles. 1.a.** To wrap up, as in a blanket or shawl, for warmth, protection, or secrecy. **b.** To wrap or pad in order to deaden the sound. **c.** To deaden (a sound). **2.** To make vague or obscure. **3.** To repress; stifle. —*n.* **1.** Something that muffles. **2.** A kiln or part of a kiln in which pottery can be fired without being exposed to direct flame. [ME *muflen*, poss. < OFr. *mofler*, to stuff < *moufle, mofle*, glove. See MUFF².]
muf•fle² (mŭf′əl) *n.* The fleshy hairless snout of certain mammals, such as ruminants. [Fr. *mufle*, perh. blend of *moufle*,

mitten, chubby face (< OFr.; see MUFF[2]) and *museau*, muzzle (< OFr. *musel*; see MUZZLE).]

muf•fler (mŭf′lər) *n.* **1.** A heavy scarf worn around the neck for warmth. **2.** A device that absorbs noise, esp. one used with an internal-combustion engine.

muf•fu•let•ta (mo͞o′fə-lĕt′ə) *n. New Orleans.* A sandwich made with a round loaf of Italian bread filled with layers of hard salami, ham, provolone, and olive salad. [Ital. dial., bread with a filling < Ital. *muffa*, mold, prob. of Gmc. orig.]

muf•ti[1] (mŭf′tē, mo͝of′-) *n., pl.* **-tis.** A Muslim scholar who interprets the shari'a. [Ar. *muftī* < *'aftā*, to decide by legal opinion.]

muf•ti[2] (mŭf′tē) *n., pl.* **-tis.** Civilian dress, esp. when worn by one who normally wears a uniform. [Prob. < MUFTI[1].]

mug[1] (mŭg) *n.* **1.** A cylindrical drinking cup usu. having a handle. **2.** The amount that a mug can hold. [Perh. of Scand. orig.]

mug[2] (mŭg) *n.* **1.** *Informal.* **a.** The human face. **b.** The area of the human mouth, chin, and jaw. **c.** A grimace. **d.** A mug shot. **2.** A thug; a hoodlum. **3.** *Chiefly British.* A victim or dupe. — *v.* **mugged, mug•ging, mugs.** — *tr.* **1.** *Informal.* To photograph (a person's face) for police files. **2.** To threaten or assault (a person) with the intent to rob. — *intr.* To make exaggerated facial expressions, esp. for humorous effect. [Prob. < MUG[1] (poss. in allusion to mugs decorated with grotesque faces).]

Mu•ga•be (mo͞o-gä′bē), **Robert Gabriel.** b. 1924. Zimbabwean politician who led the Black nationalists in Rhodesia.

mug•ger[1] (mŭg′ər) *n.* **1.** One who commits a mugging. **2.** One who makes exaggerated faces, as in performing.

mug•ger[2] (mŭg′ər) *n.* A large crocodile *(Crocodilus palustris)* of southwest Asia having a very broad wrinkled snout. [Hindi *magar* < Skt. *makaraḥ*, crocodile, of Dravidian orig.]

mug•ging (mŭg′ĭng) *n.* An assault upon a person esp. with the intent to rob.

mug•gy (mŭg′ē) *adj.* **-gi•er, -gi•est.** Warm and extremely humid. [Prob. < ME *mugen*, to drizzle; akin to ON *mugga*, a drizzle.] — **mug′gi•ness** *n.*

mu•gho pine or **mu•go pine** (myo͞o′gō, mo͞o′-) *n.* A shrubby European pine *(Pinus mugo).* [Fr. < Ital. *mugo.*]

mug shot *n. Informal.* A photograph of a person's face, esp. one made for police files.

mug•wump (mŭg′wŭmp′) *n.* **1.** A person who acts independently or remains neutral, esp. in politics. **2.** Often **Mugwump.** A Republican who bolted the party in 1884, refusing to support presidential candidate James G. Blaine. [Massachusett *mugguomp, mummugguomp*, war leader.]

Mu•ham•mad (mo͝o-hăm′ĭd, -hä′mĭd). Arab prophet of Islam who began to preach as God's prophet of the true religion at the age of 40.

Muhammad II. See **Mohammed II.**

Muhammad, Elijah. Orig. Elijah Poole. 1897–1975. Amer. activist and leader of the Black Muslims (1934–75).

Mu•ham•mad•an or **Mu•ham•med•an** (mo͝o-hăm′ĭ-dən) *adj. & n.* Var. of **Mohammedan.**

Mu•ham•mad•an•ism (mo͝o-hăm′ĭ-də-nĭz′əm) *n.* Var. of **Mohammedanism.**

Mu•har•ram (mo͞o-hăr′əm) also **Mo•har•ram** (mō-) or **Mu•har•rum** (mo͞o-) *n.* **1.** The first month of the Muslim calendar. **2.** A Shiite festival held during the first ten days of this month. [Ar. *Muḥarram* < p.part. of *ḥarrama*, to forbid.]

Muir (myo͝or), **John.** 1838–1914. British-born Amer. naturalist who promoted the creation of national parks.

mu•ja•hi•deen also **mu•ja•he•deen** or **mu•ja•hi•din** (mo͞o-jä′hē-dēn′) *pl.n.* Muslim guerrilla warriors engaged in a jihad. [Ar. or Pers. *mujāhidīn*, pl. of *mujāhid*, one who fights in a jihad < *jihād*, jihad.]

mu•jik (mo͞o-zhēk′, -zhĭk′) *n.* Var. of **muzhik.**

Muk•den (mo͝ok′dən, -dĕn′, mo͞ok′-). See **Shenyang.**

muk•luk (mŭk′lŭk′) *n.* **1.** A soft boot made of reindeer skin or sealskin and worn by Eskimos. **2.** A slipper with a soft sole resembling this boot. [Yupik Eskimo *maklak*, bearded seal.]

mu•lat•to (mo͝o-lăt′ō, -lä′tō, myo͝o-) *n., pl.* **-tos** or **-toes.** **1.** A person having one white and one Black parent. **2.** A person of mixed white and Black ancestry. [Sp. < Ar. *muwallad*, person of mixed race < *walada*, give birth.]

mul•ber•ry (mŭl′bĕr′ē, -bə-rē) *n.* **1.a.** Any of several deciduous trees of the genus *Morus*, having unisexual flowers in drooping catkins and edible multiple fruit. **b.** The sweet fruit of any of these trees. **2.** Any of several similar or related trees. **3.** *Color.* A grayish to dark purple. [ME *mulberrie* < OE *mōrberie* and MLGer. *mūlberi, mūrberi* : both < Lat. *mōrum* + OE *berie*, berry, or OHGer. *beri*, berry; see **bhā-[1]***.]

mulch (mŭlch) *n.* A protective covering, usu. of organic matter such as leaves, placed around plants to prevent the evaporation of moisture, the freezing of roots, and the growth of weeds. — *tr.v.* **mulched, mulch•ing, mulch•es.** To cover or surround with mulch. [Prob. < ME *melsche, molsh*, soft < OE *melsc*, mellow, mild. See **mel-[1]***.]

mulct (mŭlkt) *n.* A penalty such as a fine. — *tr.v.* **mulct•ed, mulct•ing, mulcts.** **1.** To penalize by fining or demanding forfeiture. **2.** To acquire by trickery or deception. **3.** To defraud or swindle. [< ME *multen*, to fine < Lat. *multāre, mulctāre* < *mulcta*, fine.]

mule[1] (myo͞ol) *n.* **1.** The sterile hybrid offspring of a male donkey and a female horse, having long ears and a short mane. **2.** A sterile hybrid, as between birds or plants. **3.** *Informal.* A stubborn person. **4.** A spinning machine that makes thread or yarn from fibers. **5.** A small, usu. electric tractor or locomotive used for hauling over short distances. **6.** *Slang.* A person who serves as a courier of illegal drugs. [ME < OFr. *mul* and < OE *mūl*, both < Lat. *mūlus.*]

mule[2] (myo͞ol) *n.* A slipper that has no counter or strap to fit around the heel. [Prob. Fr., slipper, poss. < MDu. *muil*, ult. < Lat. *mulleus (calceus)*, reddish-purple (ceremonial shoe).]

mule deer *n.* A brownish-gray deer *(Odocoileus hemionus)* of western North America having long mulelike ears, large branching antlers in the male, and a black-tipped tail.

mule•skin•ner (myo͞ol′skĭn′ər) *n. Informal.* A driver of mules.

mu•le•ta (mo͞o-lā′tə, -lĕt′ə) *n.* A short red cape used by a matador during the final passes before a kill. [Sp., dim. of *mula*, she-mule < Lat. *mūla*, fem. of *mūlus*, mule.]

mu•le•teer (myo͞o′lə-tîr′) *n.* A driver of mules. [Fr. *muletier* < OFr. < *mulet*, dim. of *mul*, mule. See MULE[1].]

mu•ley (myo͞o′lē, mo͞ol′ē, mo͞o′lē) *adj.* Having no horns. — *n., pl.* **-leys.** An animal without horns, esp. a cow. [< Ir. Gael. *maol* (< OIr. *mael*) or < Welsh *moel*, bald, hornless.]

Mul•ha•cén (mo͞o′lä-sän′, -thĕn′). A mountain, 3,480.4 m (11,411 ft), of S Spain in the Sierra Nevada E of Granada.

Mül•heim (mo͞ol′hīm, myo͞ol′-, mül′-). A city of W-central Germany on the Ruhr R. E of Duisburg. Pop. 173,190.

Mul•house (mə-lo͞oz′, mü-). A city of NE France SW of Strasbourg; dating from at least 803. Pop. 112,157.

mu•li•eb•ri•ty (myo͞o′lē-ĕb′rĭ-tē) *n.* **1.** The state of being a woman. **2.** Femininity. [Lat. *muliēbritās*, state of womanhood < *muliēbris*, womanly < *mulier*, woman.]

mul•ish (myo͞o′lĭsh) *adj.* Stubborn and intractable; recalcitrant. See Syns at **obstinate.** — **mul′ish•ly** *adv.* — **mul′ish•ness** *n.*

mull[1] (mŭl) *tr.v.* **mulled, mull•ing, mulls.** To heat and spice (wine, for example). [?]

mull[2] (mŭl) *v.* **mulled, -ing, mulls.** — *tr.* To go over extensively in the mind; ponder. — *intr.* To ruminate; ponder. [Prob. ME *moillen, mullen*, to moisten, crumble. See MOIL.]

mull[3] (mŭl) *n.* A soft thin muslin used in dresses and for trimmings. [Short for *mulmull* < Hindi *malmal.*]

Mull (mŭl). An island of W Scotland in the Inner Hebrides, separated from the mainland on the NE by the **Sound of Mull.**

mul•lah also **mul•la** (mŭl′ə, mo͝ol′ə) *n. Islam.* **1.** A religious teacher or leader, usu. male. **2.** Used as a form of address for such a person. [Urdu *mullā* < Pers. < Ar. *mawlā*, master.]

mul•lein (mŭl′ən) *n.* Any of various Eurasian plants of the genus *Verbascum*, esp. *V. thapsus*, a tall plant having leaves covered with dense woolly down. [ME *moleine* < AN, prob. < *mol*, soft < Lat. *mollis.* See MOIL.]

mullein pink *n.* See **rose campion.**

mul•ler (mŭl′ər) *n.* An implement of stone or other hard substance used as a pestle to grind paints or drugs. [ME *molour*, prob. < *mullen*, to grind. See MULL[2].]

Mul•ler (mŭl′ər), **Hermann Joseph.** 1890–1967. Amer. geneticist who won a 1946 Nobel Prize.

Mül•ler (mŭl′ər, myo͞o′lər, mü′-), **(Friedrich) Max.** 1823–1900. German-born British philologist and Orientalist noted for his studies of Sanskrit language and literature.

Müller, Johann. Known as **Re•gi•o•mon•ta•nus** (rē′jē-ō-mŏn-tā′nəs, -tä′-, rĕj′ē-). 1436–76. German mathematician and astronomer who contributed to the revival of astronomy during the Renaissance.

Mül•le•ri•an mimicry (myo͞o-lîr′ē-ən, mə-, mĭ-) *n.* A form of protective mimicry in which two or more distasteful or harmful species, esp. of insects, closely resemble each other and are therefore avoided equally by all their natural predators. [After Fritz *Müller* (1821–97), Brazilian zoologist.]

mul•let (mŭl′ĭt) *n., pl.* **mullet** or **-lets.** **1.** Any of various stout-bodied edible fishes of the family Mugilidae. **2.** The red mullet. [ME *molet* < Med.Lat. *mulettus*, prob. < OFr. *mulet* < *mul* < Lat. *mullus* < Gk. *mullos.*]

mul•li•gan stew (mŭl′ĭ-gən) *n.* A stew made of bits of various meats and vegetables. [Prob. < the name *Mulligan.*]

mul•li•ga•taw•ny (mŭl′ĭ-gə-tô′nē) *n., pl.* **-nies.** An East Indian soup having a meat or chicken base and curry seasoning. [Tamil *miḷagutaṇṇī* : *miḷagu*, pepper + *taṇṇīr*, cool water (*taṇ*, cool + *ṇīr*, water).]

Mul•li•kan (mŭl′ĭ-kən), **Robert Sanderson.** 1896–1986. Amer. chemist and physicist who won a 1966 Nobel Prize.

mul•lion (mŭl′yən) *n.* A vertical strip dividing the panes of a window. [Alteration of ME *moniel* < AN *moynel*, perh. < *moienel*, middle < *moien* < Lat. *mediānus* < *medius.* See **medhyo-***.] — **mul′lioned** *adj.*

Mul•ro•ney (mŭl-rō′nē, -ro͞o′-), **(Martin) Brian.** b. 1939. Canadian politician who served as prime minister (1984–93).

Mul•tan (mo͝ol-tän′). A city of E-central Pakistan SW of Lahore. Pop. 694,000.

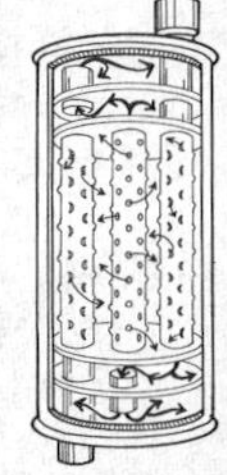
muffler
Reverse-flow muffler

mule[1]

ă pat | oi boy
ā pay | ou out
âr care | o͝o took
ä father | o͞o boot
ĕ pet | ŭ cut
ē be | ûr urge
ĭ pit | th thin
ī pie | *th* this
îr pier | hw which
ŏ pot | zh vision
ō toe | ə about, item
ô paw

Stress marks:
′ (primary);
′ (secondary), as in
dictionary (dĭk′shə-nĕr′ē)

multi– *pref.* **1.** Many; much; multiple: *multicolor.* **2.a.** More than one: *multiparous.* **b.** More than two: *multilateral.* [ME < OFr. < Lat. < *multus*, much, many. See **mel-**[2]*.]

mul•ti•cel•lu•lar (mŭl′tē-sĕl′yə-lər, -tī-) *adj.* Having or consisting of many cells. **—mul′ti•cel′lu•lar′i•ty** (-lăr′ĭ-tē) *n.*

mul•ti•col•or (mŭl′tĭ-kŭl′ər) also **mul•ti•col•ored** (-kŭl′ərd) *adj.* **1.** Having many colors. **2.** *Print.* Capable of printing in two or more colors simultaneously.

mul•ti•cul•tur•al (mŭl′tē-kŭl′chər-əl, -tī-) *adj.* Of, relating to, or including several cultures.

mul•ti•di•men•sion•al (mŭl′tĭ-dĭ-mĕn′shə-nəl) *adj.* Of, relating to, or having several dimensions. **—mul′ti•di•men′sion•al′i•ty** (-shə-năl′ĭ-tē) *n.*

mul•ti•di•rec•tion•al (mŭl′tē-dĭ-rĕk′shə-nəl, -dī-, -tī-) *adj.* **1.** Reaching out in several directions. **2.** Operating or functioning in more than one direction.

mul•ti•dis•ci•pli•nar•y (mŭl′tē-dĭs′ə-plə-nĕr′ē, -tī-) *adj.* Of, relating to, or making use of several disciplines at once.

mul•ti•eth•nic (mŭl′tē-ĕth′nĭk, -tī-) *adj.* Of, relating to, or including several ethnic groups.

mul•ti•fac•et•ed (mŭl′tē-făs′ĭ-tĭd, -tī-) *adj.* Having many facets or aspects.

mul•ti•fac•to•ri•al (mŭl′tĭ-făk-tôr′ē-əl, -tōr′-) *adj.* Involving, dependent on, or controlled by several factors.

mul•ti•far•i•ous (mŭl′tə-fâr′ē-əs) *adj.* Having great variety; diverse. [< Lat. *multifāriam*, in many places : *multi-*, multi- + *-fāriam*, adv. suff.; see **dhē-***.] **—mul′ti•far′i•ous•ly** *adv.* **—mul′ti•far′i•ous•ness** *n.*

mummer
Parading in Philadelphia

mul•ti•fid (mŭl′tə-fĭd′) *adj. Biol.* Having many clefts forming lobes.

mul•ti•flo•ra rose (mŭl′tə-flôr′ə, -flōr′ə) *n.* A climbing or sprawling shrub *(Rosa multiflora)* of eastern Asia having clusters of small fragrant flowers. [Partial transl. of NLat. *Rosa multiflōra*, species name : Lat. *rosa*, rose + LLat. *multiflōra*, fem. of *multiflōrus*, multiflorous (Lat. *multi-*, multi- + Lat. *flōs, flōr-*, flower; see FLORA).]

mul•ti•foil (mŭl′tə-foil′) *n. Archit.* A flat object or opening with scalloped edges or ornaments.

mul•ti•fold (mŭl′tə-fōld′) *adj.* Numerous and varied; manifold.

mul•ti•form (mŭl′tə-fôrm′) *adj.* Occurring in or having many forms or shapes. **—mul′ti•for′mi•ty** (-fôr′mĭ-tē) *n.*

mul•ti•lat•er•al (mŭl′tĭ-lăt′ər-əl) *adj.* **1.** Having many sides. **2.** Involving more than two nations or parties: *multilateral trade agreements.* **—mul′ti•lat′er•al•ly** *adv.*

mul•ti•lin•gual (mŭl′tē-lĭng′gwəl, -tī-) *adj.* **1.** Of, including, or expressed in several languages. **2.** Using or having the ability to use several languages. **—mul′ti•lin′gual•ism** *n.*

mul•ti•loc•u•lar (mŭl′tĭ-lŏk′yə-lər) *adj.* Having or consisting of many small compartments or cavities.

mul•ti•me•di•a (mŭl′tē-mē′dē-ə, -tī-) *pl.n. (used with a sing. v.)* **1.** The combined use of several media, esp. for the purpose of education or entertainment. **2.** The use of several mass media, esp. for the purpose of advertising or publicity.

mul•ti•mil•lion•aire (mŭl′tē-mĭl′yə-nâr′, -tī-) *n.* One whose financial assets are worth several million dollars.

mul•ti•na•tion•al (mŭl′tē-năsh′ə-nəl, -năsh′nəl, -tī-) *adj.* **1.** Having operations, subsidiaries, or investments in more than two countries. **2.** Of or involving more than two countries. —*n.* A multinational company or corporation. **—mul′ti•na′tion•al•ism** *n.*

mul•ti•no•mi•al (mŭl′tĭ-nō′mē-əl) *n. Math.* See **polynomial** 2. [MULTI– + (BI)NOMIAL.] **—mul′ti•no′mi•al** *adj.*

multinomial theorem *n. Math.* The theorem that establishes the rule for forming the terms of a polynomial expansion.

mul•ti•nu•cle•ar (mŭl′tē-no͞o′klē-ər, -nyo͞o′-, -tī-) *adj.* Multinucleate.

mul•ti•nu•cle•ate (mŭl′tē-no͞o′klē-ət, -nyo͞o′-, -tī-) also **mul•ti•nu•cle•at•ed** (-ā′tĭd) *adj.* Having two or more nuclei.

mul•tip•a•ra (mŭl-tĭp′ər-ə) *n., pl.* **-ras** also **-rae** (-rē). A woman who has given birth two or more times.

mul•tip•a•rous (mŭl-tĭp′ər-əs) *adj.* **1.** Having given birth two or more times. **2.** Giving birth to more than one offspring at a time. **—mul′ti•par′i•ty** (mŭl′tĭ-păr′ĭ-tē) *n.*

mul•ti•par•tite (mŭl′tĭ-pär′tīt′) *adj.* **1.** Divided into many parts. **2.** Involving more than two nations or parties.

mul•ti•par•ty (mŭl′tə-pär′tē) *adj.* Of, relating to, or involving more than two political parties.

mul•ti•ped (mŭl′tə-pĕd′) also **mul•ti•pede** (-pēd′) —*adj.* Having many feet. —*n.* An animal with many feet.

mul•ti•ple (mŭl′tə-pəl) *adj.* Of, having, or consisting of more than one individual, part, or other component; manifold. —*n. Math.* A number that is divisible by another number with no remainder. [Fr. < OFr. < LLat. *multiplum*, a multiple : Lat. *multi-*, multi- + Lat. *-plus*, -fold; see **pel-**[2]*.]

multiple allele *n.* Any of a set of three or more alleles, only two of which can be present in a diploid organism.

mul•ti•ple-choice (mŭl′tə-pəl-chois′) *adj.* **1.** Offering several answers from which the correct one is to be chosen. **2.** Consisting of questions of this type.

multiple factor *n.* See **polygene.**

multiple fruit *n.* A fruit, such as a fig, derived from several flowers that are combined into a single structure.

multiple myeloma *n.* A malignant proliferation of plasma cells in bone marrow causing numerous tumors and characterized by the presence of abnormal proteins in the blood.

multiple personality *n.* A psychological disorder in which a person exhibits two or more disassociated personalities, each functioning as a distinct entity.

multiple sclerosis *n.* A chronic degenerative disease of the central nervous system in which gradual destruction of myelin in patches throughout the brain or spinal cord or both interferes with the nerve pathways and causes muscular weakness, loss of coordination, and speech and visual disturbances.

multiple star *n.* A group of three or more stars, usu. with a common gravitational center, that appear as one to the unaided eye.

multiple store *n. Chiefly British.* A chain store.

mul•ti•plet (mŭl′tə-plĕt′, -plĭt) *n. Phys.* **1.** A spectral line split into more than one component, representing the energy states characteristic of an atom. **2.** Any of several groupings of subatomic particles, each of whose members have the same quantum numbers except for electric charge. [MULTIPL(E) + (DOUBL)ET.]

mul•ti•plex (mŭl′tə-plĕks′) *adj.* **1.** Relating to, having, or consisting of multiple elements or parts. **2.** Relating to or being a system of simultaneous communication of two or more messages on the same wire or radio channel. —*n.* A building, esp. a movie theater or dwelling, with multiple separate units. [ME, a multiple < Lat., various, complicated : *multi-*, multi- + *-plex*, -fold; see **plek-***.]

mul•ti•pli•a•ble (mŭl′tə-plī′ə-bəl) also **mul•ti•plic•a•ble** (-plĭk′ə-bəl) *adj.* That can be multiplied.

mul•ti•pli•cand (mŭl′tə-plĭ-kănd′) *n. Math.* The number that is or is to be multiplied by another, such as 32 in 8 × 32. [Lat. *multiplicandum*, neut. gerundive of *multiplicāre*, to multiply. See MULTIPLY[1].]

mul•tip•li•cate (mŭl-tĭp′lĭ-kĭt) *adj.* **1.** Having more than one layer or fold, as some shells. **2.** Multiple. [ME < Lat. *multiplicātus*, p.part. of *multiplicāre*, to multiply. See MULTIPLY[1].]

mul•ti•pli•ca•tion (mŭl′tə-plĭ-kā′shən) *n.* **1.** The act or process of multiplying or the condition of being multiplied. **2.** Propagation of plants and animals; procreation. **3.** *Math.* **a.** The operation that for integers consists of adding a number (the multiplicand) to itself a certain number of times and is extended to other real numbers according to the rules governing the multiplication of integers. **b.** Any of certain analogous algebraic operations. **—mul′ti•pli•ca′tion•al** *adj.*

multiplication sign *n. Math.* The sign that indicates multiplication, either a times sign (×) or a raised dot (·).

multiplication table *n. Math.* A table, used as an aid in memorization, that lists the products of certain numbers multiplied together, typically the numbers 1 to 12.

mul•ti•pli•ca•tive (mŭl′tə-plĭ-kā′tĭv, mŭl′tə-plĭk′ə-tĭv) *adj.* **1.** Tending to multiply or capable of multiplying or increasing. **2.** Having to do with multiplication.

multiplicative inverse *n. Math.* See **inverse** 2a.

mul•ti•plic•i•ty (mŭl′tə-plĭs′ĭ-tē) *n., pl.* **-ties. 1.** The state of being various or manifold. **2.** A large number: *a multiplicity of ideas.* [ME < OFr. *multiplicite* < LLat. *multiplicitās* < *multiplex*, various. See MULTIPLEX.]

mul•ti•pli•er (mŭl′tə-plī′ər) *n.* **1.** One that multiplies. **2.** *Math.* The number by which another number is multiplied, such as 8 in 8 × 32. **3.** *Phys.* A device, such as a phototube, used to enhance or increase an effect.

mul•ti•ply[1] (mŭl′tə-plī′) *v.* **-plied, -ply•ing, -plies.** —*tr.* **1.** To increase the amount, number, or degree of. **2.** *Math.* To perform multiplication on. —*intr.* **1.** To grow in amount, number, or degree. See Syns at **increase. 2.** To breed or propagate. **3.** *Math.* To perform multiplication. [ME *multiplien* < OFr. *multiplier* < Lat. *multiplicāre* < *multiplex*, multiplex. See MULTIPLEX.]

mul•ti•ply[2] (mŭl′tə-plē′) *adv.* In many or multiple ways.

mul•ti•po•lar (mŭl′tĭ-pō′lər) *adj.* Having or conceiving multiple centers of power or influence: *a multipolar world.*

mul•ti•port (mŭl′tĭ-pôrt′, -pōrt′) *adj.* Having, relating to, or being a system of multiple ports for injecting fuel separately into each cylinder of an engine.

mul•ti•pronged (mŭl′tĭ-prôngd′, -prŏngd′) *adj.* **1.** Having many prongs. **2.** Involving several different directions, aspects, or elements: *a multipronged attack.*

mul•ti•stage (mŭl′tĭ-stāj′) *adj.* **1.** Functioning in more than one stage: *a multistage design project.* **2.** Relating to or composed of two or more propulsion units.

mul•ti•tude (mŭl′tĭ-to͞od′, -tyo͞od′) *n.* **1.** The condition or quality of being numerous. **2.** A very great number. **3.** The masses; the populace: *the concerns of the multitude.* [ME < OFr. < Lat. *multitūdō* < *multus*, many. See **mel-**[2]*.]

mul•ti•tu•di•nous (mŭl′tĭ-to͞od′n-əs, -tyo͞od′-) *adj.* **1.** Very numerous; existing in great numbers. **2.** Consisting of many parts. **3.** Populous; crowded. [< Lat. *multitūdō, multitūdin-*, multitude. See MULTITUDE.] **—mul′ti•tu′di•nous•ly** *adv.* **—mul′ti•tud′in•ous•ness** *n.*

mul•ti•va•lent (mŭl′tĭ-vā′lənt, mŭl-tĭv′ə-lənt) *adj.* **1.** *Chem.* Polyvalent. **2.** *Genet.* Of or relating to the association of three or more homologous chromosomes during the first division of meiosis. **3.** *Immunol.* Having several sites of attachment for an antibody or antigen. **4.** Having various meanings or values: *multivalent allegory.* —**mul′ti•va′lence** *n.*

mul•ti•ver•si•ty (mŭl′tĭ-vûr′sĭ-tē) *n., pl.* **-ties.** A university that has numerous constituent and affiliated institutions, such as separate colleges, campuses, and research centers.

mul•ti•vi•ta•min (mŭl′tə-vī′tə-mĭn) *adj.* Containing many vitamins. —*n.* A preparation containing many vitamins.

mum[1] (mŭm) *adj.* Not verbalizing; silent. —*interj.* Used as a command to stop speaking. —***idiom.* mum's the word.** Say nothing of the secret you know. [ME.]

mum[2] (mŭm) *intr.v.* **mummed, mum•ming, mums. 1.** To act or play in a pantomime. **2.** To go merrymaking in a mask or disguise esp. during a festival. [ME *mummen* < OFr. *momer,* to wear a mask.]

mum[3] (mŭm) *n. Chiefly British.* Mother. [Short for MUMMY[2].]

mum[4] (mŭm) *n.* A chrysanthemum.

mum[5] (mŭm) *n.* A strong beer originally brewed in Brunswick, Germany. [Ger. *Mumme.*]

mum•ble (mŭm′bəl) *v.* **-bled, -bling, -bles.** —*tr.* **1.** To utter indistinctly by lowering the voice or partially closing the mouth. **2.** To chew slowly or ineffectively, as from being without teeth. —*intr.* **1.** To mumble words. **2.** To mumble food. —*n.* A low indistinct sound or utterance. [ME *momelen* < MDu. *mommelen.*] —**mum′bler** *n.* —**mum′bly** *adj.*

mum•ble•ty-peg (mŭm′bəl-tē-pĕg′, mŭm′blē-pĕg′) also **mum•ble-the-peg** (mŭm′bəl-*thə*-pĕg′) *n. Games.* A game in which players toss a jackknife in prescribed ways in order to make it stick into the ground. [< *mumble the peg,* the loser originally having to pull up a peg with the teeth.]

mum•bo jum•bo or **mum•bo-jum•bo** (mŭm′bō-jŭm′bō) *n., pl.* **-bos. 1.** Unintelligible language; gibberish. **2.** Language or ritualistic activity intended to confuse. **3.** A complicated or obscure ritual. **4.** An object believed to have supernatural powers; a fetish. [Perh. of Mandingo origin.]

Mum•ford (mŭm′fərd), **Lewis.** 1895–1990. Amer. social critic whose works include *The Culture of Cities* (1938).

mum•mer (mŭm′ər) *n.* **1.** A masked or costumed merrymaker. **2.a.** One who mums in a pantomime. **b.** An actor. [ME < OFr. *momeur* < *momer,* to wear a mask, pantomime.]

mum•mer•y (mŭm′ə-rē) *n., pl.* **-ies. 1.** A performance by mummers. **2.** A pretentious or hypocritical show or ceremony.

mum•mi•chog (mŭm′ĭ-chŏg′) *n.* A stout-bodied killifish *(Fundulus heteroclitus)* of the Atlantic coast south of the Gulf of St. Lawrence, valued as bait. [Narragansett *moamitteaũg.*]

mum•mi•fy (mŭm′ə-fī′) *v.* **-fied, -fy•ing, -fies.** —*tr.* **1.** To make into a mummy by embalming and drying. **2.** To cause to shrivel and dry up. —*intr.* To shrivel or dry up like a mummy. —**mum′mi•fi•ca′tion** (-fĭ-kā′shən) *n.*

mum•my[1] (mŭm′ē) *n., pl.* **-mies. 1.** The dead body of a human being or an animal that has been embalmed and prepared for burial, as according to ancient Egyptian practice. **2.** A withered, shrunken, or well-preserved body that resembles a mummy. [ME *mummie,* medicinal material from embalmed corpses < OFr. *momie* < Med.Lat. *mumia* < Ar. *mūmiyā'* < *mūm,* wax.]

mum•my[2] (mŭm′ē) *n., pl.* **-mies.** *Informal.* Mother. [Alteration of MAMMY.]

mumps (mŭmps) *pl.n. (used with a sing. or pl. v.)* An acute, inflammatory contagious disease caused by a paramyxovirus and marked by swollen salivary glands and sometimes pancreas, ovaries, or testes. [< pl. of dial. *mump,* grimace.]

munch (mŭnch) *v.* **munched, munch•ing, munch•es.** —*intr.* **1.** To chew food audibly or with a steady working of the jaws. **2.** To eat with pleasure. —*tr.* To chew or eat (food) audibly or with pleasure. [ME *monchen.*] —**munch′er** *n.*

Munch (mo͝ongk), **Edvard.** 1863–1944. Norwegian artist whose works include *The Scream* (1893).

Munch•hau•sen also **Mun•chau•sen** (mŭn′chou′zən, mŭnch′hou′-, münKH′hou′-), Baron **Karl Friedrich Hieronymus von.** 1720–97. German soldier and raconteur known for his fantastic stories about his adventures.

munch•ies (mŭn′chēz) *pl.n. Slang.* **1.** Food for snacking. **2.** A craving for snack food.

munch•kin (mŭnch′kĭn) *n.* **1.** A very small person, esp. one with an elflike appearance. **2.** *Informal.* A child. **3.** *Informal.* A minor official. [After the *Munchkins,* characters in *The Wonderful Wizard of Oz* by L. Frank Baum.]

Mun•cie (mŭn′sē). A city of E-central IN NE of Indianapolis; the setting for Robert and Helen Lynd's pioneering sociological study *Middletown* (1929). Pop. 71,035.

mun•dane (mŭn-dān′, mŭn′dān′) *adj.* **1.** Of, relating to, or typical of this world; secular. **2.** Relating to, characteristic of, or concerned with commonplaces; ordinary. [ME *mondeine* < OFr. *mondain* < Lat. *mundānus* < *mundus,* world.] —**mun•dane′ly** *adv.* —**mun•dane′ness** *n.*

Mun•de•lein (mŭn′dl-īn′). A village of NE IL SW of Waukegan. Pop. 21,215.

mung bean (mŭng) *n.* **1.** An Asian plant *(Vigna radiata)* in the pea family, cultivated for its edible seeds, pods, and sprouts. **2.** The seeds or pods of this plant. [Hindi *mũg* < Skt. *mudgaḥ.*]

Mu•nich (myo͞o′nĭk). A city of SE Germany near the Bavarian Alps SE of Augsburg; founded 1158. Pop. 1,267,451.

mu•nic•i•pal (myo͞o-nĭs′ə-pəl) *adj.* **1.a.** Of, relating to, or typical of a municipality. **b.** Having local self-government. **c.** Issued on the authority of a local or state government. **2.** Of or relating to the internal affairs of a nation. —*n.* A municipal bond. [Lat. *mūnicipālis* < *mūnicipium,* town < *mūniceps,* citizen : *mūnus,* public office, duty; see **mei-**[1]* + *capere,* to take; see **kap-***.] —**mu•nic′i•pal•ly** *adv.*

municipal bond *n.* An often tax-exempt bond issued by a city, county, state, or other government to finance public projects.

mu•nic•i•pal•i•ty (myo͞o-nĭs′ə-păl′ĭ-tē) *n., pl.* **-ties. 1.** A political unit, such as a city, incorporated for local self-government. **2.** A body of officials appointed to manage the affairs of a local political unit.

mu•nic•i•pal•ize (myo͞o-nĭs′ə-pə-līz′) *tr.v.* **-ized, -iz•ing, -iz•es. 1.** To place under municipal ownership. **2.** To make into a municipality. —**mu•nic′i•pal•i•za′tion** (-pə-lĭ-zā′shən) *n.*

mu•nif•i•cent (myo͞o-nĭf′ĭ-sənt) *adj.* **1.** Very liberal in giving; generous. **2.** Showing great generosity: *a munificent gift.* See Syns at **liberal.** [Lat. *mūnificēns, mūnificent-* < *mūnificus* : *mūnus,* gift; see **mei-**[1]* + *facere,* to make; see FACT.] —**mu•nif′i•cence** *n.* —**mu•nif′i•cent•ly** *adv.*

mu•ni•ment (myo͞o′nə-mənt) *n.* **1. muniments.** *Law.* Documentary evidence by which one can defend a title to property or a claim to rights. **2.** *Archaic.* A means of defense or protection. [ME < OFr. < Med.Lat. *mūnīmentum* < Lat., defense, protection < *mūnīre,* to fortify.]

mu•ni•tion (myo͞o-nĭsh′ən) *n.* War materiel, esp. weapons and ammunition. Often used in the plural. —*tr.v.* **-tioned, -tion•ing, -tions.** To supply with munitions. [ME *municion,* privilege supported by a document < OFr., fortification < Lat. *mūnītiō, mūnītiōn-* < *mūnītus,* p.part. of *mūnīre,* to defend.]

Mu•ñoz Ma•rín (mo͞o-nyōs′ mä-rēn′), **Luis.** 1898–1980. Puerto Rican journalist and politician who served as the first elected governor of Puerto Rico (1948–64).

Mun•ro (mən-rō′), **Alice.** b. 1931. Canadian writer noted for vivid novels and short stories of life in rural Ontario.

Munro, Hector Hugh. Saki. 1870–1916. British writer known for his witty and sometimes bitter short stories.

Mun•see (mŭn′sē) *n.* **1.** One of the two Algonquian languages of the Delaware peoples, spoken in New Jersey and New York State. **2.** A speaker of this language.

Mun•ster[1] (mŭn′stər). **1.** A historical region and province of SW Ireland; one of the kingdoms of ancient Ireland. **2.** A town of NW IN, a suburb of Gary. Pop. 19,949.

Mun•ster[2] (mŭn′stər, mo͝on′-) *n.* Var. of **Muenster.**

Mün•ster (mo͝on′stər, mŭn′-, mün′-). A city of W-central Germany NNE of Cologne; founded c. 800 as a Carolingian episcopal see. Pop. 272,626.

mun•tin (mŭn′tən) *n.* A strip of wood or metal separating and holding panes of glass in a window. [ME *mountaunt,* upright post or stud < OFr. *montant* < pr.part. of *monter,* to mount. See MOUNT[1].]

munt•jac also **munt•jak** (mŭnt′jăk′) *n.* Any of several small deer of the genus *Muntiacus* of southeast Asia and the East Indies. [Malay *mênjangan,* deer.]

mu•on (myo͞o′ŏn′) *n. Phys.* An elementary particle in the lepton family, having a mass 209 times that of the electron, a negative electric charge, and a mean lifetime of 2.2×10^{-6} second. See table at **subatomic particle.** [Short for *mu meson.*]

muon neutrino *n. Phys.* A stable elementary particle in the lepton family having a mass less than 0.49 times that of the electron and no charge. See table at **subatomic particle.**

Mur (mo͝or) also **Mu•ra** (mo͝or′ə). A river of S-central Austria, E Slovenia, and N Croatia flowing c. 483 km (300 mi) to the Drava R.

mu•ral (myo͝or′əl) *n.* A very large image, such as a painting, applied directly to a wall or ceiling. —*adj.* **1.** Of or resembling a wall. **2.** Painted on or applied to a wall. [ME, of a wall < OFr. < Lat. *mūrālis* < *mūrus,* wall.] —**mu′ral•ist** *n.*

mu•raled also **mu•ralled** (myo͝or′əld) *adj.* Decorated with murals or a mural: *muraled halls.*

mu•ram•ic acid (myo͞o-răm′ĭk) *n.* An amino sugar, $C_9H_{17}NO_7$, found in the cell walls of many bacteria. [Lat. *mūrus,* wall + AM(IDE) + -IC.]

Mu•ra•sa•ki Shi•ki•bu (mo͞o′rä-sä′kē shē′kē-bo͞o′), Baroness. 978?–1031? Japanese writer noted for *The Tale of Genji.*

Mu•rat (myo͞o-rä′, mü-), **Joachim.** 1767?–1815. French marshal who aided Napoleon's coup d'état (1799) and was appointed king of Naples (1808).

Mur•chi•son River (mûr′chĭ-sən). An intermittent river of W Australia flowing c. 708 km (440 mi) to the Indian Ocean.

Mur•cia (mûr′shə, -shē-ə, mo͞or′thyä). **1.** A region and former kingdom of SE Spain on the Mediterranean Sea; an independent Moorish kingdom from the 11th to the 13th cent. **2.** A city of SE Spain NNW of Cartagena; cap. of the ancient kingdom of Murcia. Pop. 200,300.

Edvard Munch
1895 self-portrait

mural

ă pat	oi boy
ā pay	ou out
âr care	o͝o took
ä father	o͞o boot
ĕ pet	ŭ cut
ē be	ûr urge
ĭ pit	th thin
ī pie	*th* this
îr pier	hw which
ŏ pot	zh vision
ō toe	ə about, item
ô paw	

Stress marks:
′ (primary);
′ (secondary), as in **dictionary** (dĭk′shə-nĕr′ē)

mur•der (mûr′dər) *n.* **1.** The unlawful killing of one human being by another, esp. when premeditated. **2.** *Slang.* Something that is very uncomfortable, difficult, or hazardous. —*v.* **-dered, -der•ing, -ders.** —*tr.* **1.** To kill (another human being) unlawfully. **2.** To kill brutally or inhumanly. **3.** To put an end to; destroy. **4.** To spoil by ineptness; mutilate. **5.** *Slang.* To defeat decisively; trounce. —*intr.* To commit murder. —***idioms.*** **get away with murder.** *Informal.* To escape punishment for or detection of an egregiously blameworthy act. **murder will out.** Secrets or misdeeds will eventually be disclosed. [ME *murther* < OE *morthor.* See **mer-***.] —**mur′der•er** *n.* —**mur′der•ess** *n.*

mur•der•ous (mûr′dər-əs) *adj.* **1.** Capable of, guilty of, or intending murder: *murderous thugs.* **2.** Characteristic of or giving rise to murder or bloodshed: *murderous mistrust.* **3.** *Informal.* Capable of devastating or overwhelming. —**mur′der•ous•ly** *adv.* —**mur′der•ous•ness** *n.*

Mur•doch (mûr′dŏk′), **(Jean) Iris.** b. 1919. Irish-born writer whose intricate novels include *Under the Net* (1954).

Mu•re•şul (mo͝or′ə-so͞ol′, mo͞o′rĕ-sho͞ol′) or **Mu•reş** (mo͞o′rĕsh). A river rising in the Carpathian Mts. of N-central Romania and flowing c. 756 km (470 mi) into S Hungary.

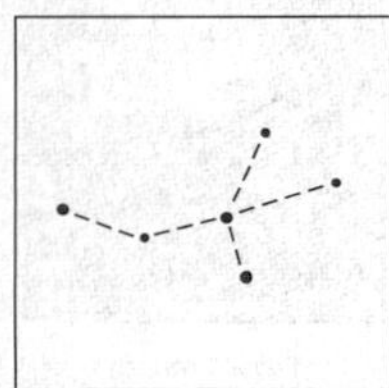

Musca

mu•rex (myo͝or′ĕks) *n., pl.* **mu•ri•ces** (myo͝or′ĭ-sēz′) or **mu•rex•es.** Any of various marine gastropods of the genus *Murex,* common in tropical seas and having rough spiny shells, esp. *M. trunculus,* the source of Tyrian purple. [NLat. *Mūrex,* genus name < Lat. *mūrex,* purple-fish.]

Mur•frees•bor•o (mûr′frēz-bûr′ō, -bŭr′ō). A city of central TN SE of Nashville. Pop. 44,922.

Mur•gab also **Mur•ghab** (mo͝or-găb′). A river rising in NE Afghanistan and flowing c. 853 km (530 mi) to the Kara Kum Desert.

mu•ri•at•ic acid (myo͝or′ē-ăt′ĭk) *n.* Hydrochloric acid. [Lat. *muriāticus,* pickled < *muria,* brine.]

mu•ri•cate (myo͝or′ĭ-kāt′) also **mu•ri•cat•ed** (-kā′tĭd) *adj.* Covered with many short spines. [Lat. *mūricātus,* shaped like a murex, pointed < *mūrex,* murex.]

Mu•ril•lo (myo͞o-rĭl′ō, mo͞o-rē′lyô), **Bartolomé Esteban.** 1617–82. Spanish painter of genre scenes, portraits, and religious subjects, such as *Immaculate Conception* (1668).

mu•rine (myo͝or′īn′) *adj.* **1.** Of or relating to a member of the rodent family Muridae, including mice. **2.** Caused, transmitted, or affected by murines. —*n.* A murine rodent. [Lat. *mūrīnus,* of mice < *mūs, mūr-,* mouse. See **mūs-***.]

murk also **mirk** (mûrk) —*n.* Partial or total darkness; gloom. —*adj. Archaic.* Partially or totally dark; gloomy. [ME *mirke* < ON *myrkr* or OE *mirce.*]

murk•y also **mirk•y** (mûr′kē) *adj.* **-i•er, -i•est. 1.** Dark, dim, or gloomy. See Syns at **dark. 2.a.** Heavy and thick with smoke, mist, or fog; hazy. **b.** Darkened or clouded with sediment. **3.** Lacking clarity or distinctness; cloudy or obscure. —**murk′i•ly** *adv.* —**murk′i•ness** *n.*

Mur•mansk (mo͝or-mänsk′, mo͝or′mənsk). A city of NW Russia on the N Kola Peninsula. Pop. 419,000.

mur•mur (mûr′mər) *n.* **1.** A low indistinct continuous sound. **2.** An indistinct, whispered, or confidential complaint; a mutter. **3.** *Medic.* An abnormal sound, usu. emanating from the heart, that sometimes indicates a diseased condition. —*v.* **-mured, -mur•ing, -murs.** —*intr.* **1.** To make a murmur or succession of murmurs. **2.** To complain in low mumbling tones; grumble. —*tr.* To say in a low indistinct voice; utter indistinctly. [ME *murmure* < OFr. < Lat. *murmur,* a humming, roaring.] —**mur′mur•er** *n.* —**mur′mur•ing•ly** *adv.* —**mur′mur•ous** *adj.* —**mur′mur•ous•ly** *adv.*

Mu•rom (mo͞o′rəm). A city of W-central Russia on the Oka R. SW of Gorky. Pop. 121,000.

Mur•phy (mûr′fē), **William Francis ("Frank").** 1890–1949. Amer. jurist; associate justice of the U.S. Supreme Court (1940–49).

Murphy bed *n.* A bed that folds or swings into a closet for concealment. [After William Lawrence *Murphy* (1876–1959), Amer. inventor.]

Mur•phy's Law (mûr′fēz) *n.* Any of certain humorous axioms stating that anything that can possibly go wrong will go wrong. [< the name *Murphy.*]

mur•rain (mûr′ĭn) *n.* **1.** Any of various highly infectious diseases of cattle, as anthrax. **2.** *Obsolete.* A pestilence or dire disease. [ME *moreine* < OFr. *morine* < Med.Lat. *morina* < Lat. *morī,* to die. See **mer-***.]

Mur•ray (mûr′ē). A city of N-central UT, a suburb of Salt Lake City. Pop. 31,282.

Murray, (George) Gilbert (Aimé). 1866–1957. Australian-born British classical scholar and pacifist.

Murray, Sir **James Augustus Henry.** 1837–1915. British philologist and the original lexicographer (1879–1915) of the *Oxford English Dictionary.*

Murray, Lindley. 1745–1826. Amer. grammarian whose works include *Grammar of the English Language* (1795).

Murray River. A river of SE Australia flowing c. 2,589 km (1,609 mi) to an arm of the Indian Ocean S of Adelaide.

murre (mûr) *n., pl.* **murre** or **murres.** Any of several auks of the genus *Uria,* with black plumage and white markings. [?]

mur•rey (mûr′ē) *n. Color.* See **mulberry** 3. [ME *murrei* < OFr. *more* < Lat. *mōrum,* mulberry, blackberry.]

Mur•row (mûr′ō, mŭr′ō), **Edward R(oscoe).** 1908–65. Amer. broadcast journalist noted for his reports from London during World War II.

Mur•rum•bidg•ee (mûr′əm-bĭj′ē). A river of SE Australia flowing c. 1,689 km (1,050 mi) to the Murray R.

Mur•rys•ville (mûr′ēz-vĭl′, mŭr′-). A borough of SW PA, a suburb of Pittsburgh. Pop. 17,240.

mur•ther (mûr′*th*ər) *n. & v. Obsolete.* Var. of **murder.**

mus. *abbr.* **1.** Museum. **2.** Music; musical; musician.

Mus.B. *abbr. Lat.* Musicae Baccalaureus (Bachelor of Music).

Mus•ca (mŭs′kə) *n.* A constellation in the polar region of the Southern Hemisphere near Apus and Carina. [Lat. *musca,* fly.]

Mus•ca•det (mŭs′kə-dā′) *n.* A dry white wine made from grapes originating in the Loire River valley. [Fr. < OFr. < *musc,* musky odor. See MUSK.]

mus•ca•dine (mŭs′kə-dīn′, -dĭn) *n.* A woody vine *(Vitis rotundifolia)* of the southeast United States bearing a musky grape used to make wine. [Alteration of MUSCATEL.]

mus•ca•rine (mŭs′kə-rēn′) *n.* A highly toxic alkaloid, $C_9H_{20}NO_2$, related to the cholines, derived from the mushroom *Amanita muscaria* and found in decaying animal tissue. [NLat. *muscaria,* Amanita species (< Lat. *muscārius,* of flies < *musca,* fly) + -INE[2].] —**mus′ca•rin′ic** (-rĭn′ĭk) *adj.*

mus•cat (mŭs′kăt′, -kət) *n.* **1.** Any of various sweet white grapes used for making wine or raisins. **2.** Muscatel wine. [Fr. < OFr. < OProv. **muscat* < *musc,* musk < LLat. *muscus.* See MUSK.]

Mus•cat (mŭs′kăt′, -kət, mŭs-kăt′). The cap. of Oman, in the N part on the Gulf of Oman. Pop. 50,000.

Muscat and O•man (ō-män′). See **Oman.**

mus•ca•tel (mŭs′kə-tĕl′) *n.* **1.** A rich sweet wine made from muscat grapes. **2.** A muscat grape or raisin. [ME *muscadelle,* partly < Med.Lat. *muscātellum* (< *muscātus,* nutmeg, musky < LLat. *muscus,* musk; see MUSK) and partly < OFr. *muscadel* (< OProv., dim. of **muscat,* muscat; see MUSCAT).]

Mus•ca•tine (mŭs′kə-tēn′). A city of SE IA on the Mississippi R. WSW of Davenport; founded 1833. Pop. 22,881.

mus•cid (mŭs′ĭd) *n.* A fly of the family Muscidae, including the housefly. [< NLat. *Muscidae,* family name < *Musca,* type genus < Lat. *musca,* fly.] —**mus′cid** *adj.*

mus•cle (mŭs′əl) *n.* **1.** A tissue composed of fibers capable of contracting to effect bodily movement. **2.** A contractile organ consisting of a special bundle of muscle tissue, which moves a particular bone, part, or substance of the body. **3.** Muscular strength. **4.** *Informal.* Power or authority. —*v.* **-cled, -cling, -cles.** —*intr. Informal.* To make one's way by or as if by force. [ME < OFr. < Lat. *mūsculus,* dim. of *mūs,* mouse. See **mūs-***.] —**mus′cly** *adj.*

mus•cle•bound also **mus•cle-bound** (mŭs′əl-bound′) *adj.* **1.** Having inelastic overdeveloped muscles, usu. as the result of excessive exercise. **2.a.** Hindered by or as if by overdeveloped muscles. **b.** Characterized by inflexibility; rigid.

muscle fiber *n.* A cylindrical multinucleate cell composed of numerous myofibrils that contracts when stimulated.

mus•cle•man also **mus•cle man** (mŭs′əl-măn′) *n. Informal.* **1.** A physically powerful man, esp. with well-developed muscles. **2.** A strong man hired as a bodyguard or thug.

mus•co•vite (mŭs′kə-vīt′) *n.* A potassium aluminum silicate mineral, $KAl_2(AlSi_3O_{10})(OH)_2$, the most common form of mica, which has a pearly luster and is used as an insulator. [*Muscovy glass,* its former name + -ITE[1].]

Mus•co•vite (mŭs′kə-vīt′) *n.* A native or resident of Moscow or Muscovy. —*adj.* Of or relating to Moscow, Muscovy, or the Muscovites.

Mus•co•vy (mŭs′kə-vē). A former principality in W-central Russia; founded c. 1280 and nucleus of the Russian empire.

Muscovy duck *n.* A gooselike duck *(Cairina moschata)* found wild from Mexico to northern Argentina and widely domesticated for food. [Alteration of *musk duck.*]

mus•cu•lar (mŭs′kyə-lər) *adj.* **1.** Of, relating to, or consisting of muscle: *muscular contraction.* **2.** Having well-developed muscles. **3.** Having or suggesting great power; forceful or vigorous. [< Lat. *mūsculus,* muscle. See MUSCLE.] —**mus′cu•lar′i•ty** (-lăr′ĭ-tē) *n.* —**mus′cu•lar•ly** *adv.*

Syns: *muscular, athletic, brawny, burly, sinewy.* The central meaning shared by these adjectives is "strong and powerfully built": *a muscular skater; an athletic dancer; brawny arms; a burly stevedore; a lean and sinewy frame.*

muscular dystrophy *n.* **1.** Any of a group of progressive muscle disorders caused by a defect in one or more genes that control muscle function and marked by gradual irreversible wasting of skeletal muscle. **2.** Duchenne's muscular dystrophy.

mus•cu•la•ture (mŭs′kyə-lə-cho͝or′) *n.* The system or arrangement of muscles in a body or a body part. [Fr. < Lat. *mūsculus,* muscle. See MUSCLE.]

mus•cu•lo•skel•e•tal (mŭs′kyə-lō-skĕl′ĭ-tl) *adj.* Relating to or involving the muscles and the skeleton. [Lat. *mūsculus,* muscle; see MUSCLE + SKELETAL.]

Mus.D. *abbr. Lat.* Musicae Doctor (Doctor of Music).

Mus.Dr. *abbr. Lat.* Musicae Doctor (Doctor of Music).

muse (myo͞oz) *v.* **mused, mus•ing, mus•es.** *— intr.* To be absorbed in one's thoughts; engage in meditation. *— tr.* To consider or say thoughtfully. *—n.* A state of meditation. [ME *musen* < OFr. *muser* (poss. < *mus,* snout < Med.Lat. *mūsum*) or of Germanic origin.] **— mus′ing•ly** *adv.*

Muse (myo͞oz) *n.* **1.** *Gk. Myth.* Any of the nine daughters of Mnemosyne and Zeus, each of whom presided over a different art or science. **2. muse. a.** A guiding spirit. **b.** A source of inspiration. **3. muse.** A poet. [ME < OFr. < Lat. *Mūsa* < Gk. *Mousa.* See **men-**[1]*.]

mu•se•ol•o•gy (myo͞o′zē-ŏl′ə-jē) *n.* The discipline of museum design, organization, and management. **— mu′se•o•log′i•cal** (-ə-lŏj′ĭ-kəl) *adj.* **— mu′se•ol′o•gist** *n.*

mu•sette (myo͞o-zĕt′) *n.* **1.** *Mus.* **a.** A small French bagpipe operated with a bellows and having a soft sound. **b.** A soft pastoral air that imitates bagpipe music. **2.** A musette bag. [ME < OFr., dim. of *muse* < *muser,* to play the musette, muse. See MUSE.]

musette bag *n.* A small canvas or leather bag with a shoulder strap, as one used by soldiers or travelers.

mu•se•um (myo͞o-zē′əm) *n.* A building, place, or institution devoted to the acquisition, conservation, study, and exhibition of objects having scientific, historical, or artistic value. [Lat. *Mūsēum* < Gk. *Mouseion,* shrine of the Muses < *Mouseios,* of the Muses < *Mousa,* Muse. See **men-**[1]*.]

mu•se•um•go•er (myo͞o-zē′əm-gō′ər) *n.* **1.** A visitor to a museum. **2.** One who visits museums frequently.

mush[1] (mŭsh) *n.* **1.** A thick porridge or pudding of cornmeal boiled in water or milk. **2.** Something thick, soft, and pulpy. **3.** *Informal.* Mawkish sentimentality, affection, or amorousness. *— tr.v.* **mushed, mush•ing, mush•es.** To reduce to mush; mash or crush. [Prob. alteration of MASH.]

mush[2] (mŭsh) *v.* **mushed, mush•ing, mush•es.** *— intr.* To travel, esp. over snow with a dogsled. *— tr.* To drive (a dogsled or team of dogs). *—n.* A journey, esp. by dogsled. *— interj.* Used to order a dog team to begin or speed up. [Poss. alteration of Fr. *marchons,* first pers. pl. imper. of *marchier,* to walk, go < OFr. See MARCH[1].] **— mush′er** *n.*

mush bread *n. Midland & Lower Southern U.S.* See **johnnycake.** See Regional Note at **johnnycake.**

mush•room (mŭsh′ro͞om′, -ro͝om′) *n.* **1.** Any of various fleshy fungi of the class Basidiomycota, having an umbrella-shaped cap borne on a stalk, esp. any of the edible kinds. **2.** Something shaped like one of these fungi. *— v.* **-roomed, -room•ing, -rooms.** *— intr.* **1.** To multiply, grow, or expand rapidly. **2.** To swell or spread out into a shape similar to a mushroom. *— adj.* **1.** Relating to, consisting of, or containing mushrooms. **2.** Resembling a mushroom in shape. **3.** Resembling mushrooms in rapidity of growth or evanescence. [ME *musheron* < AN *musherum* < OFr. *mousseron* < Med.Lat. *musariō, musariōn-.*]

mush•y (mŭsh′ē, mo͝osh′ē) *adj.* **-i•er, -i•est. 1.** Resembling mush in consistency; soft. **2.** *Informal.* **a.** Excessively sentimental. **b.** Given to or displaying mawkish affection. **— mush′i•ly** *adv.* **— mush′i•ness** *n.*

mu•sic (myo͞o′zĭk) *n.* **1.** The art of arranging sounds in time so as to produce a continuous, unified, and evocative composition, as through melody, rhythm, and timbre. **2.** Vocal or instrumental sounds possessing a degree of melody, harmony, or rhythm. **3.a.** A musical composition. **b.** The written or printed score for such a composition. **c.** Such scores considered as a group. **4.** A musical accompaniment. **5.** A particular category or kind of music. **6.** An aesthetically pleasing or harmonious sound or combination of sounds: *the music of the wind.* [ME < OFr. *musique* < Lat. *mūsica* < Gk. *(hē) mousikē (tekhnē),* (art) of the Muses, fem. of *mousikos,* of the Muses < *Mousa,* Muse. See **men-**[1]*.]

mu•si•cal (myo͞o′zĭ-kəl) *adj.* **1.** Of, relating to, or capable of producing music: *musical instruments.* **2.** Characteristic of or resembling music; melodious: *a musical voice.* **3.** Set to or accompanied by music. **4.** Devoted to or skilled in music. *—n.* **1.** A play or movie in which dialogue is interspersed with songs. **2.** *Archaic.* A musicale. **— mu′si•cal•ly** *adv.*

musical chairs *pl.n. (used with a sing. v.)* **1.** *Games.* A game in which players walk to music around a group of chairs containing one chair fewer than the number of players and vie for seats when the music stops. **2.** *Informal.* A rearrangement having little practical influence or significance.

musical comedy *n.* A play or movie with songs; a musical.

mu•si•cale (myo͞o′zĭ-kăl′) *n.* A program of music performed at a party or social gathering. [Fr. < *(soirée) musicale,* musical (evening) < *musique,* music. See MUSIC.]

mu•si•cal•i•ty (myo͞o′zĭ-kăl′ĭ-tē) *n.* **1.** The quality or condition of being musical. **2.** Musical sensitivity or talent.

mu•si•cal•ize (myo͞o′zĭ-kə-līz′) *tr.v.* **-ized, -iz•ing, -iz•es.** To adapt for performance with singing and musical accompaniment; set to music. **— mu′si•cal•i•za′tion** (-lĭ-zā′shən) *n.*

musical saw *n. Mus.* A handsaw on which varying musical tones are produced by flexing the blade and stroking it with a violin bow or striking it with a hammer.

music box *n. Mus.* A music-making device consisting of a housing or box enclosing a sounding mechanism, esp. one in which pins set in a revolving cylinder pluck tuned steel teeth.

music drama *n. Mus.* An opera in which the continuity is not interrupted by arias, recitatives, or ensembles and in which the music reflects or embodies the action of the drama.

music hall *n.* **1.** An auditorium for musical performances. **2.** *Chiefly British.* **a.** A vaudeville theater. **b.** Vaudeville.

mu•si•cian (myo͞o-zĭsh′ən) *n.* One who composes, conducts, or performs music, esp. instrumental music. [ME *musicien* < OFr. < Lat. *mūsica,* music. See MUSIC.] **— mu•si′cian•ly** *adj.* **— mu•si′cian•ship′** *n.*

music of the spheres *n.* A perfectly harmonious music, inaudible on Earth, thought by Pythagoras and certain later philosophers to be produced by the movement of celestial bodies.

mu•si•col•o•gy (myo͞o′zĭ-kŏl′ə-jē) *n.* The historical and scientific study of music. **— mu′si•co•log′i•cal** (-kə-lŏj′ĭ-kəl) *adj.* **— mu′si•co•log′i•cal•ly** *adv.* **— mu′si•col′o•gist** *n.*

music video *n.* A filmed or videotaped rendition of a song.

mu•sique con•crète (mo͞o-zēk′ kŏn-krĕt′, mü-zēk kôN-krĕt′) *n. Mus.* Electronic music composed of instrumental and natural sounds often altered or distorted in recording. [Fr.]

musk (mŭsk) *n.* **1.a.** A greasy secretion with a powerful odor, produced in a glandular sac beneath the skin of the abdomen of the male musk deer and used in making perfumes. **b.** A similar secretion of other animals, such as the otter. **c.** A synthetic chemical like natural musk in odor or use. **2.a.** The odor of musk. **b.** An odor similar to musk. **3.** A musk deer. [ME < OFr. *musc* < LLat. *muscus* < Gk. *moskhos* < Pers. *mušk,* prob. < Skt. *muṣkaḥ,* testicle.]

musk deer *n.* An antlerless deer *(Moschus moschiferus)* of central and northeast Asia, the male of which secretes musk.

musk duck *n.* **1.** See **Muscovy duck. 2.** A waterfowl *(Biziura lobata)* of Australia, the male of which has a leathery chin lobe and emits a musky odor during the breeding season.

mus•keg (mŭs′kĕg′) also **mas•keg** (măs′-) *n.* A swamp or bog formed by an accumulation of sphagnum moss, leaves, and decayed matter resembling peat. [Cree *maskek.*]

Mus•ke•gon (mŭ-skē′gən). A city of SW MI WNW of Grand Rapids at the mouth of the **Muskegon River,** flowing c. 365 km (227 mi) to Lake Michigan. Pop. 40,283.

mus•kel•lunge or **mus•ke•lunge** (mŭs′kə-lŭnj′) also **mas•ki•nonge** (măs′kə-nŏng′, -nŏnj′) *n., pl.* **muskellunge** or **-lung•es** or **muskelunge** or **-lung•es** also **maskinonge** or **-nong•es.** A large food and game fish *(Esox masquinongy)* of the pike family, found in lakes and rivers of North America. [Canadian Fr. *maskinongé* < Ojibwa *maashkinoozhe.*]

mus•ket (mŭs′kĭt) *n.* A smoothbore shoulder gun used from the late 16th through the 18th century. [Fr. *mousquet* < Ital. *moschetto,* dim. of *mosca,* fly < Lat. *musca.*]

mus•ket•eer (mŭs′kĭ-tîr′) *n.* **1.** A soldier armed with a musket. **2.** A member of the French royal household bodyguard in the 17th and 18th centuries. [Fr. *mousquetaire* < *mousquet,* musket. See MUSKET.]

mus•ket•ry (mŭs′kĭ-trē) *n.* **1.** The technique of using small arms. **2.** Muskets considered as a group. **3.** Musketeers considered as a group.

mus•kie or **mus•ky** (mŭs′kē) *n., pl.* **-kies.** The muskellunge.

musk mallow *n.* **1.** See **abelmosk. 2.** A European and North African herb *(Malva moschata).*

musk•mel•on (mŭsk′mĕl′ən) *n.* **1.** Any of several varieties of the melon *Cucumis melo,* such as the cantaloupe, having fruit characterized by a netted rind and edible flesh with a musky aroma. **2.** The fruit of any of these plants.

Mus•ko•ge•an also **Mus•kho•ge•an** (mŭs-kō′gē-ən) *n.* A family of Native American languages of the southeast United States that includes Choctaw, Chickasaw, and Creek.

Mus•ko•gee[1] (mŭs-kō′gē) *n.* See **Creek.** [Creek *maaskóoki.*]

Mus•ko•gee[2] (mə-skō′gē). A city of E OK on the Arkansas R. SE of Tulsa; founded 1872. Pop. 37,708.

musk ox or **musk•ox** (mŭsk′ŏks′) *n., pl.* **musk oxen** or **-ox•en** (-ŏk′sən). A large stocky ox *(Ovibos moschatus)* of northern Canada and Greenland having broad flat horns with curved tips, a shaggy dark coat, and a musky odor.

musk ox
Musk ox bull
Ovibos moschatus

musk•rat (mŭs′krăt′) *n., pl.* **muskrat** or **-rats. 1.** A large aquatic rodent *(Ondatra zibethica)* of North America related to the lemming and having a dense brown coat and musk glands under a broad flat tail. **2.** The fur of this rodent.

musk•root (mŭsk′ro͞ot′, -ro͝ot′) *n.* See **moschatel.**

musk rose *n.* A prickly Mediterranean shrub *(Rosa moschata)* cultivated for its clustered musk-scented white flowers.

musk turtle *n.* Any of several small freshwater turtles of the genus *Sternotherus* of the eastern United States and Canada that emit a musky odor when disturbed.

musk•y[1] (mŭs′kē) *adj.* **-i•er, -i•est.** Of, relating to, or having the odor of musk. **— musk′i•ness** *n.*

mus•ky[2] (mŭs′kē) *n.* Var. of **muskie.**

Mus•lim (mŭz′ləm, mo͝oz′-, mŭs′-, mo͝os′-) *n.* **1.** Also **Moslem** (mŏz′ləm, mŏs-). A believer in or an adherent of Islam. **2.** A Black Muslim. [Ar. *muslim,* one who surrenders, active part. of *'aslama,* to surrender < Syriac *'ašlem.*] **— Mus′lim** *adj.*

ă pat	oi boy
ā pay	ou out
âr care	o͝o took
ä father	o͞o boot
ĕ pet	ŭ cut
ē be	ûr urge
ĭ pit	th thin
ī pie	*th* this
îr pier	hw which
ŏ pot	zh vision
ō toe	ə about, item
ô paw	

Stress marks:
′ (primary);
′ (secondary), as in
dictionary (dĭk′shə-nĕr′ē)

Muslim calendar *n.* The lunar calendar used by Muslims reckoned from the year of the Hegira in A.D. 622.
mus•lin (mŭz′lĭn) *n.* Any of various sturdy cotton fabrics of plain weave, used esp. for sheets. [Fr. *mousseline* < Ital. *mussolina* < *Mussolo*, Mosul, Iraq < Ar. *Al-Mawṣil*.]
Mus.M. *abbr. Lat.* Musicae Magister (Master of Music).
mus•quash (mŭs′kwŏsh′, -kwôsh′) *n.* See **muskrat** 1. [Perh. of Massachusett origin; akin to Western Abenaki *mòskwas*.]
muss (mŭs) *tr.v.* **mussed, muss•ing, muss•es.** To make messy or untidy; rumple. —*n.* A state of disorder; a mess. [Prob. alteration of MESS.] —**muss′i•ly** *adv.* —**muss′i•ness** *n.* —**muss′y** *adj.*
mus•sel (mŭs′əl) *n.* **1.** Any of several marine bivalve mollusks, esp. the edible members of the family Mytilidae and in particular *Mytilus edulis*, a species raised commercially in Europe. **2.** Any of several freshwater bivalve mollusks of the genera *Anodonta* and *Unio*, found in the central United States, that burrow in the sand or mud of lakes and streams. [Alteration of ME *muscle* < OE *muscelle* < Med.Lat. *mūscula* < Lat. *mūsculus*, sea mussel. See MUSCLE.]
Mus•sel•shell (mŭs′əl-shĕl′). A river of central MT flowing c. 483 km (300 mi) to the Missouri R.
Mus•set (mo͞o-sā′, mü-), **(Louis Charles) Alfred de.** 1810–57. French writer whose comedies include *Lorenzaccio* (1834).
Mus•so•li•ni (mo͞o′sə-lē′nē, mo͝os′ə-, mo͞os′sô-), **Benito.** "Il Duce." 1883–1945. Italian Fascist dictator and prime minister (1922–43) who brought Italy into World War II (1940).
Mus•sorg•sky (mə-zôrg′skē, -sôrg′-, mo͞o′sərg-), **Modest Petrovich.** 1839–81. Russian composer whose works include the piano suite *Pictures at an Exhibition* (1874).
Mus•sul•man (mŭs′əl-mən) *n., pl.* **-men** or **-mans.** *Archaic.* A Muslim. [Turk. *musulmān*, prob. alteration of Ar. *muslim*, Muslim. See MUSLIM.]

Benito Mussolini

must¹ (mŭst) *v.* —*aux.* **1.** To be obliged or required by morality, law, or custom: *I must register my car.* **2.** To be compelled, as by a physical necessity or requirement: *Plants must have oxygen.* **3.** Used to express a command or an admonition: *You must be careful.* **4.** To be determined to; have as a fixed resolve: *If you must leave, do it quietly.* **5.a.** Used to indicate inevitability or certainty: *We all must die.* **b.** Used to indicate logical probability or presumptive certainty: *If the lights were on, they must have been at home.* —*intr. Archaic.* To be required or obliged to go. —*n.* Something that is absolutely required or indispensable. [ME *moste* < OE *mōste*, p.t. of *mōtan*, to be allowed. See **med-***.]
must² (mŭst) *n.* The quality or condition of being stale or musty. [Prob. back-formation < MUSTY.]
must³ (mŭst) *n.* The juice expressed from fruit, esp. grapes. [ME < OE < Lat. *mustum* < neut. of *mustus*, new, fresh.]
must⁴ (mŭst) *n.* Var. of **musth.**
must⁵ (mŭst) *n.* Musk. [Sc. < OFr., var. of *musc.* See MUSK.]

mute
On a trumpet

mus•tache also **mous•tache** (mŭs′tăsh′, mə-stăsh′) *n.* **1.** The hair on the human upper lip, esp. when groomed on a man. **2.** Something like a groomed mustache, as: **a.** A group of bristles or hairs about the mouth of an animal. **b.** Distinctive coloring or feathers near the beak of a bird. **c.** Food or drink sticking conspicuously to the upper lip. [Fr. *moustache* < Ital. dial. *mustaccio* < Med.Gk. *moustakion* < Gk. *mustax*.]
mus•ta•chio (mə-stăsh′ō, -stăsh′ē-ō′, -stä′shō, -shē-ō′) *n., pl.* **-chios.** A mustache, esp. a luxuriant one. [Ult. < Ital. dial. *mustaccio*, mustache. See MUSTACHE.]
mus•ta•chioed also **mous•ta•chioed** (mə-stăsh′ōd, -stăsh′ē-ōd′, -stä′shōd, -shē-ōd′) or **mus•tached** (mŭs′tăsht) *adj.* Having or wearing a mustache.
mus•tang (mŭs′tăng′) *n.* A small wild horse of the North American plains, descended from horses brought to the New World by Spanish explorers. [Am.Sp. *mesteño, mestengo*, stray animal < OSp. < *mesta*, association of livestock owners < Med.Lat. *(animalia) mixta*, assorted (animals) < Lat., neut. pl. p.part. of *miscēre*, to mix. See **meik-***.]
mus•tard (mŭs′tərd) *n.* **1.a.** Any of various Eurasian plants of the genus *Brassica*, esp. *B. nigra* and *B. juncea* cultivated for their pungent seeds. **b.** A condiment made from these seeds. **2.** A member of the mustard family. **3.** *Color.* A dark yellow to light olive brown. —***idiom.* cut the mustard.** To perform up to expectations or to a required standard. [ME < OFr. *mustarde* < Lat. *mustum*, must, unfermented wine. See MUST³.] —**mus′tard•y** *adj.*
mustard family *n.* A large family of herbs, the Cruciferae (Brassicaceae), characterized by pungent juice and four-petaled flowers in a cross and including broccoli and kale.
mustard gas *n.* An oily volatile liquid, $(ClCH_2CH_2)_2S$, corrosive to the skin and mucous membranes and causing severe respiratory damage, introduced in World War I as a chemical weapon. [< its smell.]
mustard oil *n.* An oil obtained from mustard seeds that is used in making soap.
mustard plaster *n.* A medicinal plaster made with a pastelike mixture of powdered black mustard, flour, and water, used esp. as a counterirritant.
mus•te•line (mŭs′tə-līn′, -lĭn) *adj.* Of, relating to, or belonging to Mustelidae, the family of fur-bearing mammals that includes the badger and weasel. [Lat. *mūstēlīnus*, of a weasel < *mūstēla*, weasel, prob. < *mūs*, mouse. See **mūs-***.]
mus•ter (mŭs′tər) *v.* **-tered, -ter•ing, -ters.** —*tr.* **1.** To call (troops) together, as for inspection. **2.** To cause to come together; gather. **3.** To call forth; summon up: *mustering up her strength.* —*intr.* To assemble or gather. —*n.* **1.a.** A gathering, esp. of troops, as for service or inspection. **b.** The persons assembled for such a gathering. **2.** A muster roll. **3.** A gathering or collection. **4.** A flock of peacocks. —***phrasal verbs.* muster in.** To enlist in military service. **muster out.** To leave or be discharged from military service. [ME *mustren* < OFr. *moustrer* < Lat. *mōnstrāre*, to show < *mōnstrum*, sign < *monēre*, to warn. See **men-¹***.]
muster roll *n.* **1.** The official roll of persons in a military or naval unit. **2.** An inventory; a roster.
musth also **must** (mŭst) *n.* An annual period of heightened aggressiveness and sexual activity in male elephants, during which violent frenzies occur. [Urdu *mast* < Pers., drunk.]
must•n't (mŭs′ənt). Must not.
must•y (mŭs′tē) *adj.* **-i•er, -i•est. 1.** Stale or moldy in odor or taste. **2.a.** Hackneyed or trite; dull. **b.** Out of date; antiquated. **c.** Out of use or practice; rusty. [Alteration of obsolete *moisty* < MOIST.] —**must′i•ly** *adv.* —**must′i•ness** *n.*
mu•ta•ble (myo͞o′tə-bəl) *adj.* **1.a.** Capable of or subject to change or alteration. **b.** Prone to frequent change; inconstant: *mutable weather.* **2.** Tending to undergo genetic mutation. —**mu′ta•bil′i•ty, mu′ta•ble•ness** *n.* —**mu′ta•bly** *adv.*
mu•ta•gen (myo͞o′tə-jən, -jĕn′) *n.* An agent, such as ultraviolet light, that can induce or increase the frequency of mutation in an organism. —**mu′ta•gen′ic** *adj.* —**mu′ta•gen′i•cal•ly** *adv.* —**mu′ta•ge•nic′i•ty** (-jə-nĭs′ĭ-tē) *n.*
mu•ta•gen•e•sis (myo͞o′tə-jĕn′ĭ-sĭs) *n., pl.* **-ses** (-sēz′). Formation or development of a mutation.
mu•ta•gen•ize (myo͞o′tə-jĕ-nīz′) *tr.v.* **-ized, -iz•ing, -iz•es.** To cause or induce mutation in (a cell or an organism).
mu•tant (myo͞ot′nt) *n.* An individual, an organism, or a new genetic character arising or resulting from mutation. —*adj.* Resulting from or undergoing mutation.
mu•tase (myo͞o′tās, -tāz) *n.* Any of various enzymes that catalyze the rearrangement of atoms within a molecule, esp. one that causes the transfer of a phosphate group from one carbon atom to another. [Lat. *mūtāre*, to change, move; see MUTATE + -ASE.]
mu•tate (myo͞o′tāt, myo͞o-tāt′) *intr. & tr.v.* **-tat•ed, -tat•ing, -tates.** To undergo or cause to undergo mutation. [Lat. *mūtāre, mūtāt-*, to change. See **mei-¹***.] —**mu′ta′tive** (-tā′tĭv, -tə-tĭv) *adj.*
mu•ta•tion (myo͞o-tā′shən) *n.* **1.** The act or process of being altered or changed. **2.** An alteration or change, as in nature, form, or quality. **3.** *Genet.* **a.** A sudden structural change within a gene or chromosome of an organism resulting in the creation of a new character or trait not found in the parental type. **b.** The process by which such a sudden structural change occurs, either through an alteration in the nucleotide sequence of the DNA coding for a gene or through a change in the physical arrangement of a chromosome. **c.** A mutant. **4.** *Ling.* The change, esp. an umlaut, that is caused in a sound by its assimilation to another sound. —**mu•ta′tion•al** *adj.* —**mu•ta′tion•al•ly** *adv.*
mu•ta•tis mu•tan•dis (mo͞o-tä′tĭs mo͞o-tän′dĭs) *adv.* The necessary changes having been made. [Lat. *mūtātīs mūtandīs* : *mūtātīs*, ablative pl. p.part. of *mūtāre*, to change + *mūtandīs*, ablative pl. gerundive of *mūtāre*.]
mutch•kin (mŭch′kĭn) *n. Scots.* A unit of liquid measure equal to 0.9 U.S. pint (0.42 liter). [ME *muchekyn* < MDu. *mudseken*, dim. of *mutse*, a kind of measure < Lat. *modius*, grain measure. See **med-***.]
mute (myo͞ot) *adj.* **mut•er, mut•est. 1.** Refraining from producing speech or vocal sound. **2.a.** Unable to speak. **b.** Unable to vocalize, as certain animals. See Syns at **dumb. 3.** Expressed without speech; unspoken: *a mute appeal.* **4.** *Ling.* **a.** Not pronounced; silent, as the *e* in the word *house.* **b.** Pronounced with a temporary stoppage of breath, as the sounds (p) and (b); plosive. —*n.* **1.** *Offensive.* One who is incapable of speech. **2.** *Mus.* Any of various devices used to muffle or soften the tone of an instrument. **3.** *Ling.* **a.** A silent letter. **b.** A plosive; a stop. —*tr.v.* **mut•ed, mut•ing, mutes. 1.** To soften or muffle the sound of. **2.** To soften the tone, color, shade, or hue of. [ME *muet* < OFr. < dim. of *mu* < Lat. *mūtus*.] —**mute′ly** *adv.* —**mute′ness** *n.*
mut•ed (myo͞o′tĭd) *adj.* **1.a.** Muffled; indistinct: *a muted voice.* **b.** Subdued; softened: *muted colors.* **2.** *Mus.* Produced by or provided with a mute. —**mut′ed•ly** *adv.*
mute swan *n.* A white swan *(Cygnus olor)* of Europe and Asia having an orange bill with a black knob and being much less vocal than most swans.
mu•ti•late (myo͞ot′l-āt′) *tr.v.* **-lat•ed, -lat•ing, -lates. 1.** To deprive of a limb or an essential part; cripple. **2.** To disfigure by damaging irreparably: *mutilate a statue.* **3.** To make imperfect by excising or altering parts. [Lat. *mutilāre, mutilāt-* < *mutilus*, maimed.] —**mu′ti•la′tion** *n.* —**mu′ti•la′tive** *adj.* —**mu′ti•la′tor** *n.*

mu•ti•neer (myo͞ot′n-îr′) *n.* One who takes part in a mutiny. [Obsolete Fr. *mutinier* < OFr. *mutin*, rebellious. See MUTINY.]

mu•ti•nous (myo͞ot′n-əs) *adj.* **1.** Of, relating to, engaged in, disposed to, or being mutiny. **2.** Unruly; disaffected. **3.** Turbulent and uncontrollable. [< obsolete *mutine*, mutiny. See MUTINY.] — **mu′ti•nous•ly** *adv.* — **mu′ti•nous•ness** *n.*

mu•ti•ny (myo͞ot′n-ē) *n., pl.* **-nies.** Open rebellion against authority, esp. rebellion of sailors against superior officers. See Syns at **rebellion.** — *intr.v.* **-nied, -ny•ing, -nies.** To engage in mutiny. [Obsolete *mutine* < OFr. *mutin*, rebellious < *muete*, revolt < VLat. **movita* < Lat. *movēre*, to move. See MOVE.]

mut•ism (myo͞o′tĭz′əm) *n.* The condition of being unable to speak as a result of a physical or psychological disorder.

mu•ton (myo͞o′tŏn′) *n.* The smallest unit of DNA at which a mutation can occur; a nucleotide. [MUT(ATION) + -ON[1].]

Mu•tsu•hi•to (mo͞o′tso͞o-hē′tō). Imperial name **Mei•ji** (mā′jē′). 1852–1912. Emperor of Japan (1867–1912).

mutt (mŭt) *n. Informal.* **1.** A mongrel dog. **2.** A person regarded as stupid. [Short for MUTTONHEAD.]

mut•ter (mŭt′ər) *v.* **-tered, -ter•ing, -ters.** — *intr.* **1.** To speak indistinctly in low tones. **2.** To complain or grumble morosely. — *tr.* To utter or say in low indistinct tones. — *n.* A low grumble or indistinct utterance. [ME *muttren*, poss. < Lat. *muttīre.*] — **mut′ter•er** *n.*

mut•ton (mŭt′n) *n.* The flesh of fully grown sheep. [ME < OFr. *mouton, moton* < Med.Lat. *multō, multōn-*, of Celt. orig. See **mel-[1]*.**]

mut•ton•chops (mŭt′n-chŏps′) *pl.n.* Side whiskers that are narrow at the temple, broad along the lower cheek or jawline, and separated by a shaven chin.

mut•ton•fish (mŭt′n-fĭsh′) *n., pl.* **muttonfish** or **-fish•es. 1.** An eelpout *(Macrozoarces americanus)* of the coastal waters of northeast North America. **2.** Mutton snapper.

mut•ton•head (mŭt′n-hĕd′) *n. Informal.* A person regarded as stupid; a fool. — **mut′ton•head′ed** *adj.*

mutton snapper *n.* An olive-green snapper *(Lutjanus analis)* of warm western Atlantic waters valued as a game fish.

Mut•tra (mŭt′rə). See **Mathura.**

mu•tu•al (myo͞o′cho͞o-əl) *adj.* **1.** Having the same relationship each to the other: *mutual predators.* **2.** Directed and received in equal amount; reciprocal: *mutual respect.* **3.** Possessed in common: *mutual interests.* **4.** Of, relating to, or in the form of mutual insurance. — *n.* A mutual fund. [French *mutuel* < OFr. < Lat. *mūtuus*, borrowed. See **mei-[1]*.**] — **mu′tu•al′i•ty** (-ăl′ĭ-tē) *n.* — **mu′tu•al•ly** *adv.*

Usage Note: *Mutual* is uncontroversially used to describe a reciprocal relationship between two or more things. Thus *their mutual animosity* means "their animosity for each other" or "the animosity between them." But *mutual* is also widely used where one might expect "common," as in *The bill serves the mutual interests of management and labor.* Critics have often objected to this use, but it is well established in reputable writing. However, *mutual* in this latter sense is reserved to describe relations that hold between two or more specific parties and a third person or thing. It cannot be used as a substitute for *common* in the sense "general."

mutual fund *n.* An investment company that offers shares, buys existing shares back on demand, and invests in diversified securities. — **mu′tu•al-fund′** (myo͞o′cho͞o-əl-fŭnd′) *adj.*

mutual inductance *n.* The ratio of the electromotive force in a circuit to the corresponding change of current in a neighboring circuit.

mutual induction *n.* The production of an electromotive force in a circuit resulting from a change of current in a neighboring circuit.

mutual insurance *n.* An insurance system in which the insured persons become company members, each paying specified amounts into a common fund from which members are entitled to indemnification in case of loss.

mu•tu•al•ism (myo͞o′cho͞o-ə-lĭz′əm) *n.* An association between organisms of two different species in which each member benefits. — **mu′tu•al•is′tic** *adj.*

mu•tu•al•ize (myo͞o′cho͞o-ə-līz′) *v.* **-ized, -iz•ing, -iz•es.** — *tr.* **1.** To make mutual. **2.** To set up or reorganize (a corporation) so that the majority of common stock is owned by customers or employees. — *intr.* To become mutual. — **mu′tu•al•i•za′tion** (-ə-lĭ-zā′shən) *n.*

muu•muu (mo͞o′mo͞o′) *n.* A long loose dress that hangs free from the shoulders. [Hawaiian *mu'umu'u*, cut off, muumuu.]

Muy•bridge (mī′brĭj′), **Eadweard.** 1830–1904. British-born motion-picture pioneer noted for his motion studies.

Mu•zak (myo͞o′zăk′). A trademark used for recorded background music transmitted by wire or radio, as to places of business, on a subscription basis.

mu•zhik also **mou•jik** or **mu•jik** or **mu•zjik** (mo͞o-zhēk′, -zhĭk′) *n.* A Russian peasant. [Russ. < *muzh*, man. See **man-[1]*.**]

Muz•tag or **Muz•tagh** (mo͞os-tä′, -täg′). A mountain, 7,286.8 m (23,891 ft), in the Kunlun Range of W China.

Muz•tag•a•ta also **Muz•tagh A•ta** (mo͞os-tä′ə-tä′, mo͞os-täg′-). A mountain, 7,550.9 m (24,757 ft), of the **Muztagata Range** in W China near Tadzhikistan.

muz•zle (mŭz′əl) *n.* **1.** The forward projecting part of the head of certain animals, such as dogs, including the mouth, nose, and jaws; the snout. **2.** A leather or wire restraining appliance fitted over an animal's snout to prevent biting. **3.** The forward discharging end of the barrel of a firearm. **4.** A restraint on free movement or expression. — *tr.v.* **-zled, -zling, -zles. 1.** To put a muzzle on (an animal). **2.** To restrain from expression. [ME *mosel* < OFr. *musel* < Med.Lat. *mūsellum*, dim. of *mūsus*, snout < Lat. *mūsum.*] — **muz′zler** *n.*

muz•zle•load•er (mŭz′əl-lō′dər) *n.* A firearm loaded at the muzzle. — **muz′zle•load′ing** *adj.*

muz•zy (mŭz′ē) *adj.* **-zi•er, -zi•est. 1.** Mentally confused; muddled. **2.** Blurred; indistinct. [?] — **muz′zi•ly** *adv.* — **muz′zi•ness** *n.*

mV *abbr.* Millivolt.

MV *abbr.* **1.** Mean variation. **2.** Megavolt. **3.** Motor vessel.

MVP *abbr. Sports.* Most valuable player.

mW *abbr.* Milliwatt.

MW *abbr.* Megawatt.

Mwe•ru (mwā′ro͞o), **Lake.** A lake of central Africa on the Zaire-Zambia border W of the S end of Lake Tanganyika.

Mx *abbr.* Maxwell (measurement).

my (mī) *adj.* The possessive form of **I. 1.** Used as a modifier before a noun: *my boots.* **2.** Used preceding various forms of polite, affectionate, or familiar address: *Yes, my friend.* **3.** Used in various interjectional phrases: *My word!* — *interj.* Used as an exclamation of surprise, pleasure, or dismay: *Oh, my! What a joke.* [ME *mi* < OE *mīn.* See **me-[1]*.**]

my– *pref.* Var. of **myo–.**

my•al•gi•a (mī-ăl′jē-ə, -jə) *n.* Muscular pain or tenderness, esp. when diffuse and nonspecific. — **my•al′gic** (-jĭk) *adj.*

Myan•mar (myän-mär′). See **Burma.**

my•as•the•ni•a (mī′əs-thē′nē-ə) *n.* **1.** Abnormal muscular weakness or fatigue. **2.** Myasthenia gravis. — **my′as•then′ic** (-thĕn′ĭk) *adj.*

myasthenia gra•vis (grăv′ĭs) *n.* A disease characterized by progressive fatigue and generalized weakness of the skeletal muscles, caused by impaired transmission of nerve impulses following an autoimmune attack on acetylcholine receptors. [NLat. : MYASTHENIA + Lat. *gravis*, heavy, severe.]

myc (mĭk) *n.* Any of a group of vertebrate oncogenes whose product, a DNA binding protein, is thought to promote the growth of tumor cells. [Poss. < *my(elo)c(ytomatosis virus).*]

my•ce•li•um (mī-sē′lē-əm) *n., pl.* **-li•a** (-lē-ə). **1.** The vegetative part of a fungus, consisting of a mass of branching threadlike hyphae. **2.** A similar mass of fibers formed by certain bacteria. [NLat. : MYC(O)- + Gk. *hēlos*, wart.] — **my•ce′li•al** (-lē-əl) *adj.*

My•ce•nae (mī-sē′nē). An ancient Greek city in the NE Peloponnesus; center of an early Bronze Age civilization.

My•ce•nae•an (mī′sə-nē′ən) *adj.* **1.** Of or relating to Mycenae or its inhabitants. **2.** Of, relating to, or being the Aegean civilization that spread its influence from Mycenae to many parts of the Mediterranean region from about 1580 to 1120 B.C. **3.** Of, relating to, or being the archaic dialect of Greek written in the Linear B script. — *n.* **1.** A native or inhabitant of Mycenae. **2.** Mycenaean Greek.

–mycete *suff.* Fungus: *basidiomycete.* [NLat. *-mycētēs* < Gk. *mukēs, mukēt-*, fungus.]

my•ce•to•ma (mī′sĭ-tō′mə) *n., pl.* **-mas** or **-ma•ta** (-mə-tə). A chronic, slowly progressing bacterial or fungal infection usu. of the foot or leg, characterized by nodules that discharge an oily pus. [Gk. *mukēs, mukēt-*, fungus + -OMA.] — **my′ce•to′ma•tous** (-tō′mə-təs, -tŏm′ə-) *adj.*

–mycin *suff.* A substance derived from a bacterium in the order Actinomycetales: *neomycin.* [MYC(O)- (the original bacterial source having been mistaken for fungi) + -IN.]

myco– or **myc–** *pref.* Fungus: *mycology.* [< Gk. *mukēs*, fungus.]

my•co•bac•te•ri•um (mī′kō-băk-tîr′ē-əm) *n., pl.* **-te•ri•a** (-tîr′ē-ə). Any of various slender rod-shaped aerobic bacteria of the genus *Mycobacterium*, which includes the bacteria that cause tuberculosis and leprosy. — **my′co•bac•ter′i•al** *adj.*

mycol. *abbr.* **1.** Mycological. **2.** Mycology.

my•col•o•gy (mī-kŏl′ə-jē) *n., pl.* **-gies. 1.** The branch of botany that deals with fungi. **2.** The fungi native to a region. **3.** The composition or characteristics of a particular fungus. — **my′co•log′i•cal** (-kə-lŏj′ĭ-kəl), **my′co•log′ic** *adj.* — **my′col•og′i•cal•ly** *adv.* — **my•col′o•gist** *n.*

my•coph•a•gous (mī-kŏf′ə-gəs) *adj.* Fungivorous.

my•co•plas•ma (mī′kō-plăz′mə) *n.* Any of numerous parasitic pathogenic microorganisms of the genus *Mycoplasma*, lacking a true cell wall, gram-negative, and needing sterols such as cholesterol for growth. — **my′co•plas′mal** *adj.*

my•cor•rhi•za or **my•co•rhi•za** (mī′kə-rī′zə) *n., pl.* **-zae** (-zē) or **-zas.** *Bot.* The symbiotic association of the mycelium of a fungus with the roots of certain plants. [MYCO- + Gk. *rhiza*, root; see **wrād-*.**] — **my′cor•rhi′zal** *adj.*

my•co•sis (mī-kō′sĭs) *n., pl.* **-ses** (-sēz). **1.** A fungal infection in or on a part of the body. **2.** A disease caused by a fungus.

my•co•tox•i•co•sis (mī′kō-tŏk′sĭ-kō′sĭs) *n.* Poisoning caused by ingestion of a mycotoxin.

ă pat	oi boy
ā pay	ou out
âr care	o͝o took
ä father	o͞o boot
ĕ pet	ŭ cut
ē be	ûr urge
ĭ pit	th thin
ī pie	*th* this
îr pier	hw which
ŏ pot	zh vision
ō toe	ə about, item
ô paw	

Stress marks:
′ (primary);
′ (secondary), as in **dictionary** (dĭk′shə-nĕr′ē)

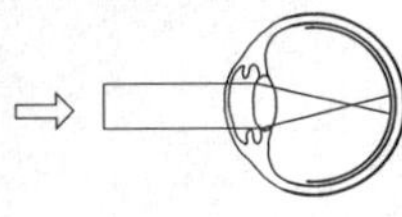

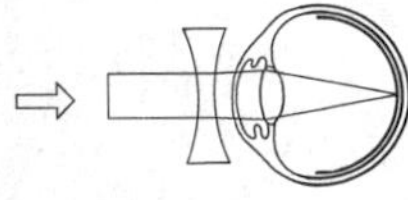

myopia
Top: Before correction
Bottom: After correction

my•co•tox•in (mī′kō-tŏk′sĭn) *n.* A toxin produced by a fungus.

my•dri•a•sis (mĭ-drī′ə-sĭs) *n.* Prolonged abnormal dilatation of the pupil of the eye caused by disease or a drug. [Lat. < Gk. *mudriasis.*]

myd•ri•at•ic (mĭd′rē-ăt′ĭk) *adj.* Causing dilatation of the pupils. —*n.* A mydriatic drug. [< MYDRIASIS.]

my•e•len•ceph•a•lon (mī′ə-lĕn-sĕf′ə-lŏn′) *n.* The posterior portion of the embryonic hindbrain, from which the medulla oblongata develops. —**my′e•len•ce•phal′ic** (-sə-făl′ĭk) *adj.*

my•e•lin (mī′ə-lĭn) also **my•e•line** (-lĭn, -lēn′) *n.* A white fatty material, composed chiefly of lipids and lipoproteins, that encloses certain axons and nerve fibers. —**my′e•lin′ic** *adj.*

my•e•li•nat•ed (mī′ə-lə-nā′tĭd) *adj.* Having a myelin sheath.

my•e•li•ni•za•tion (mī′ə-lə-nĭ-zā′shən) also **my•e•li•na•tion** (-nā′shən) *n.* The process of forming a myelin sheath.

myelin sheath *n.* The insulating envelope of myelin that surrounds the core of a nerve fiber or axon and facilitates the transmission of nerve impulses.

my•e•li•tis (mī′ə-lī′tĭs) *n.* **1.** Inflammation of the spinal column. **2.** Osteomyelitis.

myelo– or **myel–** *pref.* **1.** Spinal cord: *myelitis.* **2.** Bone marrow: *myeloma.* [NLat. < Gk. *muelos,* marrow, prob. < *mus,* muscle. See **mūs-*.**]

my•e•lo•blast (mī′ə-lə-blăst′) *n.* An immature cell of the bone marrow that is the precursor of a myelocyte.

my•e•lo•cyte (mī′ə-lə-sīt′) *n.* A large cell of the bone marrow that is a precursor of the mature granulocyte of the blood. —**my′e•lo•cyt′ic** (-sĭt′ĭk) *adj.*

my•e•lo•fi•bro•sis (mī′ə-lō-fī-brō′sĭs) *n.* Proliferation of fibroblastic cells in bone marrow, causing anemia and sometimes enlargement of the spleen and liver.

my•e•log•e•nous (mī′ə-lŏj′ə-nəs) also **my•e•lo•gen•ic** (-lə-jĕn′ĭk) *adj.* Originating in or produced by the bone marrow.

my•e•lo•gram (mī′ə-lə-grăm′) *n.* An x-ray of the spinal cord after injection of air or a radiopaque substance into the subarachnoid space. —**my′e•log′ra•phy** (-lŏg′rə-fē) *n.*

my•e•loid (mī′ə-loid′) *adj.* **1.** Of, relating to, or derived from the bone marrow. **2.** Of or relating to the spinal cord.

my•e•lo•ma (mī′ə-lō′mə) *n., pl.* **-mas** or **-ma•ta** (-mə-tə). A malignant tumor formed by the cells of the bone marrow. —**my′e•lo′ma•toid′** (-toid′) *adj.*

my•ia•sis (mī′ə-sĭs, mī-ī′ə-sĭs) *n., pl.* **my•ia•ses** (mī′ə-sēz′). **1.** Infestation of tissue by fly larvae. **2.** A disease resulting from such infestation. [Gk. *muia, mua,* fly + –IASIS.]

Myk•o•nos (mĭk′ə-nŏs′, -nōs′, mē′kô-nôs′) also **Mí•ko•nos** (mē′kô-nôs′). An island of SE Greece in the Cyclades Is.

My Lai (mē′ lī′). A village of S Vietnam where more than 300 unarmed civilians were massacred by U.S. troops (1968) during the Vietnam War.

My•lar (mī′lär′). A trademark used for a thin strong polyester film.

my•lo•nite (mī′lə-nīt′) *n.* A fine-grained laminated rock formed by the shifting of rock layers along faults. [Gk. *mulōn,* mill (< *mulē,* handmill; see **melə-***) + –ITE[1].]

my•na or **my•nah** also **mi•na** (mī′nə) *n.* Any of various starlings of southeast Asia having bluish-black or dark brown coloration and yellow bills. [Hindi *mainā,* perh. < Skt. *madanaḥ* < *madana-,* delightful, joyful < *madati,* it bubbles.]

myn•heer also **men•eer** (mə-nîr′) *n.* **1.** Often **Mynheer. a.** Used as a courtesy title before the name of a man in a Dutch-speaking area. **b.** Used as a form of polite address for a man in a Dutch-speaking area. **2.** *Informal.* A Dutchman. [Du. *mijnheer* : *mijn,* my (< MDu.; see **me-[1]***) + *heer,* lord (< MDu. *here*).]

myo– or **my–** *pref.* Muscle: *myograph.* [NLat. < Gk. *mus,* muscle. See **mūs-*.**]

myocardial infarction *n.* Necrosis of a region of the myocardium caused by an interruption in the heart's blood supply.

my•o•car•di•tis (mī′ō-kär-dī′tĭs) *n.* Inflammation of the myocardium.

my•o•car•di•um (mī′ō-kär′dē-əm) *n., pl.* **-di•a** (-dē-ə). The muscular tissue of the heart. [NLat. : MYO– + Gk. *kardia,* heart; see **kerd-*.**] —**my′o•car′di•al** *adj.*

my•oc•lo•nus (mī-ŏk′lə-nəs) *n.* A sudden twitching of muscles or parts of muscles, without any rhythm or pattern, occurring in various brain disorders.

my•o•e•lec•tric (mī′ō-ĭ-lĕk′trĭk) *adj.* Of or relating to the electrical properties of muscle tissue from which impulses may be amplified, used in the operation of prostheses.

my•o•fib•ril (mī′ə-fī′brəl, -fĭb′rəl) *n.* Any of the threadlike fibrils of the contractile part of a striated muscle fiber.

my•o•gen•ic (mī′ə-jĕn′ĭk) also **my•o•ge•net•ic** (mī′ō-jə-nĕt′ĭk) *adj.* **1.** Giving rise to or forming muscular tissue. **2.** Of muscular origin; arising from the muscles.

my•o•glo•bin (mī′ə-glō′bĭn) *n.* The form of hemoglobin found in muscle fibers, having a higher affinity for oxygen than hemoglobin of the blood.

my•o•graph (mī′ə-grăf′) *n.* An instrument for recording muscular contractions.

my•ol•o•gy (mī-ŏl′ə-jē) *n.* The scientific study of muscles. —**my′o•log′ic** (mī′ə-lŏj′ĭk) *adj.* —**my•ol′o•gist** *n.*

my•o•ma (mī-ō′mə) *n., pl.* **-mas** or **-ma•ta** (-mə-tə). A tumor composed of muscle tissue. —**my•o′ma•tous** (-ō′mə-təs, -ŏm′ə-) *adj.*

my•o•neu•ral (mī′ə-no͝or′əl, -nyo͝or′-) *adj.* Of or relating to both muscles and nerves, esp. to nerve endings in muscle.

my•op•a•thy (mī-ŏp′ə-thē) *n., pl.* **-thies.** A disease of muscle or muscle tissue. —**my′o•path′ic** (mī′ə-păth′ĭk) *adj.*

my•ope (mī′ōp′) *n.* One who is affected by myopia. [Fr. < LLat. *myops,* near-sighted < Gk. *muōps.* See MYOPIA.]

my•o•pi•a (mī-ō′pē-ə) *n.* **1.** A visual defect in which distant objects appear blurred because their images are focused in front of the retina rather than on it; nearsightedness. **2.** Lack of discernment or long-range perspective in thinking or planning. [Gk. *muōpia* < *muōps,* nearsighted : *muein,* to close the eyes + *ōps,* eye; see **okʷ-*.**] —**my•op′ic** (-ŏp′ĭk, -ō′pĭk) *adj.* —**my•op′i•cal•ly** *adv.*

my•o•sin (mī′ə-sĭn) *n.* The commonest protein in muscle cells, responsible for the elastic and contractile properties of muscle. [Gk. *muos,* genitive of *mus,* muscle; see MYO– + –*in.*]

my•o•sis (mī-ō′sĭs) *n.* Var. of **miosis.**

my•o•si•tis (mī′ə-sī′tĭs) *n.* Inflammation of a muscle, esp. a voluntary muscle, characterized by pain, tenderness, and sometimes spasm in the affected area.

my•o•so•tis (mī′ə-sō′tĭs) *n.* Any of various plants of the genus *Myosotis,* such as the forget-me-not. [NLat. *Myosōtis,* genus name < Lat. *myosōtis,* mouse-ear, a kind of plant < Gk. *muosōtis* : *muos,* genitive of *mus,* mouse; see **mūs-*** + *ous, ōt-,* ear; see **ous-*.**]

my•o•tome (mī′ə-tōm′) *n.* **1.** The segment of a somite in a vertebrate embryo that differentiates into skeletal muscle. **2.** A muscle or group of muscles derived from one somite and innervated by a single segment of a spinal nerve.

my•o•to•ni•a (mī′ə-tō′nē-ə) *n.* Tonic spasm or temporary rigidity of one or more muscles, often characteristic of various muscular disorders. —**my′o•ton′ic** (-tŏn′ĭk) *adj.*

My•ra (mī′rə). An ancient Lycian city of S Asia Minor.

Myr•dal (mür′däl′, mîr′-), **Alva.** 1902–86. Swedish sociologist and diplomat who shared the 1982 Nobel Peace Prize.

Myrdal, (Karl) Gunnar. 1898–1987. Swedish economist who shared a 1974 Nobel Prize.

myr•i•ad (mĭr′ē-əd) *adj.* **1.** Constituting a myriad; innumerable. **2.** Composed of numerous diverse elements or facets. —*n.* **1.** A vast number. **2.** *Archaic.* Ten thousand. [Gk. *murias, muriad-,* ten thousand < *murios,* countless.]

myr•i•a•pod also **myr•i•o•pod** (mĭr′ē-ə-pŏd′) *n.* Any of several arthropods, such as the centipede, having segmented bodies, one pair of antennae, and at least nine pairs of legs. [< NLat. *Myriapoda,* class name : Gk. *murias,* ten thousand; see MYRIAD + NLat. *-poda,* -pod.] —**myr′i•ap′o•dous** (-ăp′ə-dəs) *adj.*

my•ris•tic acid (mə-rĭs′tĭk, mī-) *n.* A fatty acid, $CH_3(CH_2)_{12}COOH$, occurring in animal and vegetable fats and used in the manufacture of cosmetics, soaps, perfumes, and flavorings. [Gk. *muristikos,* fragrant < *muron,* perfume.]

myrmeco– *pref.* Ant: *myrmecology.* [Gk. *murmēko-* < *murmēx,* ant.]

myr•me•col•o•gy (mûr′mĭ-kŏl′ə-jē) *n.* The branch of entomology that deals with ants. —**myr′me•col′o•gist** *n.*

myr•me•co•phile (mûr′mĭ-kə-fīl′) *n.* An organism, such as a beetle, that habitually shares the nest of an ant colony. —**myr′me•coph′i•lous** (-kŏf′ə-ləs) *adj.*

Myr•mi•don (mûr′mə-dŏn′, -dn) *n.* **1.** *Gk. Myth.* A member of a warlike Thessalian people who were ruled by Achilles and followed him on the expedition against Troy. **2. myrmidon.** A follower who carries out orders without question. [< ME *Mirmidones,* Myrmidons < Lat. *Myrmidones* < Gk. *Murmidones.*]

my•rob•a•lan (mī-rŏb′ə-lən, mə-) *n.* **1.** See **cherry plum. 2.** The fruit of this plant. [Obsolete Fr. *mirobolan* < Lat. *myrobalanum,* a fragrant oil < Gk. *murobalanos* : *muron,* perfume + *balanos,* acorn.]

myrobalan plum *n.* See **cherry plum.**

My•ron (mī′rən). 5th cent. B.C. Greek sculptor of the *Discus Thrower.*

myrrh (mûr) *n.* **1.** An aromatic gum resin obtained from several trees and shrubs of the genus *Commiphora* of India, Arabia, and eastern Africa, used in perfume and incense. **2.** See **sweet cicely** 2. [ME *mirre* < OE *myrrha* < Lat. < Gk. *murrha,* prob. of Semitic orig.]

myr•tle (mûr′tl) *n.* **1.** Any of several evergreen shrubs or trees of the genus *Myrtus,* esp. *M. communis,* an aromatic shrub of the Mediterranean region and western Asia having blue-black berries and cultivated as a hedge plant. **2.** See **periwinkle[2].** [ME *mirtille* < OFr. < Med.Lat. *myrtillus,* dim. of Lat. *myrtus* < Gk. *murtos.*]

Myr•tle Beach (mûr′tl). A city of E SC on the Atlantic E of Columbia. Pop. 24,848.

my•self (mī-sĕlf′) *pron.* **1.** That one identical with me. **a.** Used reflexively as the direct or indirect object of a verb or as the object of a preposition: *I bought myself a car.* **b.** Used for emphasis: *I myself was certain.* **c.** Used in an absolute construction: *In office myself, I helped her get a job.* **2.** My normal or healthy condition or state: *I'm myself again.* [ME *miself* < OE *mē selfum, mē selfne* : *mē*, me; see **me-**[1]* + *selfum, selfne*, dative and accusative of *self*; see SELF.]

Usage Note: The reflexive pronouns, such as *myself, ourselves, yourself, yourselves, himself,* and *herself,* are often used as emphatic forms: *Like yourself, I have no apologies to make.* The practice is particularly common in compound phrases: *Mrs. Evans or yourself will have to pick them up at the airport.* These usages have been common in the writing of reputable authors for several centuries: *"To myself, mountains are the beginning and end of all natural scenery"* (John Ruskin). The strongest criticism that can be made of these uses of reflexives is that like other emphatic devices they may easily be overused, and when the pronoun refers to the writer or speaker, the result of the emphasis may be an implication of pomposity or self-importance.

My•si•a (mĭsh′ē-ə). An ancient region of NW Asia Minor. —**My′si•an** *adj. & n.*

my•sid (mī′sĭd) *n.* Any of various small, shrimplike, chiefly marine crustaceans of the order Mysidacea, the females of which carry their eggs in a pouch beneath the thorax. [< NLat. *Mysis, Mysid-*, type genus < Gk. *musis*, a closing < *muein*, to close the lips or eyes.]

my•so•pho•bi•a (mī′sō-fō′bē-ə) *n.* An abnormal fear of dirt or contamination. [Gk. *musos*, uncleanness + -PHOBIA.]

My•sore (mī-sôr′, -sōr′). A city of S India SW of Bangalore; inhabited before the 3rd cent. B.C. and occupied by the British in 1831. Pop. 441,754.

mys•ta•gogue (mĭs′tə-gŏg′, -gôg′) *n.* **1.** One who prepares candidates for initiation into a mystery cult. **2.** One who holds or spreads mystical doctrines. [< Lat. *mystagōgus* < Gk. *mustagōgos* : *mustēs*, an initiate; see MYSTERY[1] + *agōgos*, guide, leader (< *agein*, to lead; see **ag-***).] —**mys′ta•gog′ic** (-gŏj′ĭk) *adj.* —**mys′ta•go′gy** (-gō′jē) *n.*

mys•te•ri•ous (mĭ-stîr′ē-əs) *adj.* **1.** Of, relating to, or being a mystery. **2.** Simultaneously arousing wonder and inquisitiveness and eluding explanation or comprehension. [Fr. *mystérieux* < *mystère*, secret < Lat. *mystērium.* See MYSTERY[1].] —**mys•te′ri•ous•ly** *adv.* —**mys•te′ri•ous•ness** *n.*

Syns: *mysterious, esoteric, arcane, occult, inscrutable.* These adjectives mean beyond human power to explain or understand. Something *mysterious* arouses wonder and inquisitiveness and also eludes comprehension: *"The sea lies all about us. . . . In its mysterious past it encompasses all the dim origins of life"* (Rachel Carson). What is *esoteric* is mysterious because only a small select group knows and understands it: *a compilation of esoteric philosophical theories. Arcane* applies to what is hidden from the knowledge of all but those having the key to a secret: *the arcane science of dowsing. Occult* suggests knowledge reputedly gained only by secret, magical, or supernatural means: *an occult rite.* Something that is *inscrutable* cannot be fathomed by means of investigation or scrutiny: *"It is not for me to attempt to fathom the inscrutable workings of Providence"* (Earl of Birkenhead).

mys•ter•y[1] (mĭs′tə-rē) *n., pl.* **-ies. 1.** Something not fully understood or eluding the understanding; an enigma. **2.** A mysterious character or quality. **3.** A work of fiction, drama, or film dealing with a puzzling crime. **4.** The skills, lore, or practices that are peculiar to a particular activity or group and are regarded as the special province of initiates. Often used in the plural. **5.** *Theol.* A religious truth that is incomprehensible to the reason and knowable only through divine revelation. **6.** An incident in the life of Jesus or Mary serving as a subject of meditation. **7.a.** One of the Christian sacraments, esp. the Eucharist. **b. mysteries.** The consecrated elements of the Eucharist. **8.a.** A religious cult having secret rites. **b.** A secret rite of such a cult. [ME *misterie* < Lat. *mystērium* < Gk. *mustērion*, secret rite < *mustēs*, an initiate < *muein*, to close the eyes, initiate.]

mys•ter•y[2] (mĭs′tə-rē) *n., pl.* **-ies. 1.** *Archaic.* A trade or an occupation. **2.** *Archaic.* A guild, as of artisans. **3.** A mystery play. [ME *misterie*, service, craft < Med.Lat. *misterium*, craft-guild < LLat., alteration of Lat. *ministerium*, occupation < *minister*, assistant, servant. See **mei-**[2]*.]

mystery play *n.* A medieval drama based on scriptural events esp. in the life of Jesus. [< MYSTERY[1] or MYSTERY[2].]

mys•tic (mĭs′tĭk) *adj.* **1.** Of or relating to religious mysteries or occult rites and practices. **2.** Of or relating to mysticism or mystics. **3.** Inspiring a sense of mystery and wonder. **4.a.** Mysterious; strange. **b.** Enigmatic; obscure. **5.** Mystical. —*n.* One who practices or believes in mysticism or a given form of mysticism: *medieval Christian mystics.* [ME *mystik* < Lat. *mysticus* < Gk. *mustikos* < *mustērion*, secret rite. See MYSTERY[1].]

mys•ti•cal (mĭs′tĭ-kəl) *adj.* **1.** Of or having a spiritual reality or import not apparent to the intelligence or senses. **2.** Of or stemming from direct communion with ultimate reality or God. **3.** Of or founded on subjective experience. **4.** Of or relating to mystic rites or practices. **5.** Unintelligible; cryptic. —**mys′ti•cal•ly** *adv.* —**mys′ti•cal•ness** *n.*

mys•ti•cete (mĭs′tĭ-sēt′) *n.* See **baleen whale.** [NLat. *mysticētus* < Gk. *mustikētos*, alteration of *(ho) mus to kētos*, (the) whale (called) the mouse : *mus*, mouse; see **mūs-*** + *kētos*, whale.] —**mys′ti•ce′tous** (-sē′təs) *adj.*

mys•ti•cism (mĭs′tĭ-sĭz′əm) *n.* **1.a.** Immediate consciousness of the transcendent or ultimate reality or God. **b.** The experience of mystical communion. **2.** A belief in the existence of essential realities beyond perceptual or intellectual apprehension that are accessible by subjective experience. **3.** Vague, groundless speculation.

mys•ti•fi•ca•tion (mĭs′tə-fĭ-kā′shən) *n.* **1.** The act or an instance of mystifying. **2.** The fact or condition of being mystified. **3.** Something intended to mystify.

mys•ti•fy (mĭs′tə-fī′) *tr.v.* **-fied, -fy•ing, -fies. 1.** To confuse or puzzle mentally; bewilder. **2.** To make obscure or mysterious. [Fr. *mystifier* : *mystère*, mystery (< Lat. *mystērium*; see MYSTERY[1]) + *-fier*, -fy.] —**mys′ti•fi′er** *n.* —**mys′ti•fy′ing•ly** *adv.*

mys•tique (mĭ-stēk′) *n.* An aura of heightened value, interest, or meaning surrounding something to which special power or mystery is imputed: *the cowboy mystique.* [Fr., mystical, mystique < Lat. *mysticus.* See MYSTIC.]

myth (mĭth) *n.* **1.a.** A traditional story dealing with supernatural beings, ancestors, or heroes that informs or shapes the world view of a people, as by explaining aspects of the natural world or delineating the customs or ideals of society. **b.** Such stories considered as a group. **2.** A story, a theme, an object, or a character regarded as embodying an aspect of a culture: *the pioneer myth.* **3.** A fiction or half-truth, esp. one that forms part of an ideology. **4.** A fictitious story, person, or thing. [NLat. *mȳthus* < LLat. *mȳthos* < Gk. *muthos.*]

myth. *abbr.* Mythological; mythology.

myth•i•cal (mĭth′ĭ-kəl) also **myth•ic** (-ĭk) *adj.* **1.** Of or existing in myth: *the mythical unicorn.* **2.** Imaginary; fictitious. **3.** Often **mythic.** Of, relating to, or having the nature of a myth. —**myth′i•cal•ly** *adv.*

myth•i•cize (mĭth′ĭ-sīz′) *tr.v.* **-cized, -ciz•ing, -ciz•es. 1.** To turn (a person or an event) into myth. **2.** To interpret as a myth or in terms of mythology.

myth•mak•er (mĭth′mā′kər) *n.* One that creates myths or mythical situations. —**myth′mak•ing** *n.*

my•thog•ra•pher (mĭ-thŏg′rə-fər) *n.* One who records, narrates, or comments on myths.

my•thog•ra•phy (mĭ-thŏg′rə-fē) *n., pl.* **-phies. 1.** The artistic representation of mythical subjects. **2.** A collection of myths, often with critical commentary.

mythol. *abbr.* Mythological; mythology.

myth•o•log•i•cal (mĭth′ə-lŏj′ĭ-kəl) also **myth•o•log•ic** (-ĭk) *adj.* **1.** Of, relating to, or recorded in myths or mythology. **2.** Fabulous; imaginary. —**myth′o•log′i•cal•ly** *adv.*

my•thol•o•gist (mĭ-thŏl′ə-jĭst) *n.* A student or scholar of mythology.

my•thol•o•gize (mĭ-thŏl′ə-jīz′) *v.* **-gized, -giz•ing, -giz•es.** —*tr.* To convert into myth; mythicize. —*intr.* **1.** To construct or relate a myth. **2.** To interpret or write about myths or mythology. —**my•thol′o•giz′er** *n.*

my•thol•o•gy (mĭ-thŏl′ə-jē) *n., pl.* **-gies. 1.a.** A body or collection of myths belonging to a people and addressing their history, deities, ancestors, and heroes. **b.** A body of myths concerning an individual, event, or institution. **2.** The field of scholarship dealing with myths.

myth•o•ma•ni•a (mĭth′ə-mā′nē-ə, -mān′yə) *n.* A compulsion to embroider the truth, engage in exaggeration, or tell lies. —**myth′o•ma′ni•ac′** (-ăk′) *n.*

myth•o•poe•ic or **myth•o•pe•ic** (mĭth′ə-pē′ĭk) also **myth•o•po•et•ic** (-pō-ĕt′ĭk) *adj.* **1.** Of or relating to the making of myths. **2.** Serving to create myths; productive in mythmaking. [< Gk. *muthopoios*, composer of fiction < *muthopoiein*, to relate a story : *muthos*, story + *poiein*, to make; see **k**ʷ**ei-**[2]*.] —**myth′o•poe′ia** (-pē′ə), **myth′o•po•e′sis** (-pō-ē′sĭs) *n.*

my•thos (mī′thŏs, mĭth′ŏs) *n., pl.* **my•thoi** (mī′thoi, mĭth′oi). **1.** Myth. **2.** Mythology. **3.** The pattern of basic values and attitudes of a people. [Gk. *muthos.*]

myx•a•moe•ba also **myx•a•me•ba** (mĭk′sə-mē′bə) *n., pl.* **-bas** also **-bae** (-bē). A slime mold when it is an amoebalike free-swimming cell and before it forms a plasmodium.

myx•e•de•ma or **myx•oe•de•ma** (mĭk′sĭ-dē′mə) *n.* A disease caused by decreased activity of the thyroid gland in adults and characterized by dry skin, swellings around the lips and nose, and mental deterioration. —**myx′e•dem′a•tous** (-dĕm′ə-təs, -dē′mə-), **myx′e•dem′ic** (-dĕm′ĭk) *adj.*

myxo– or **myx–** *pref.* Mucus: *myxoma.* [NLat. < Gk. *muxa*, mucus, slime.]

myx•o•ma (mĭk-sō′mə) *n., pl.* **-mas** or **-ma•ta** (-mə-tə). A benign tumor that is composed of connective tissue embedded in mucus. —**myx•o′ma•tous** (-sō′mə-təs, -sŏm′ə-) *adj.*

myx•o•ma•to•sis (mĭk-sō′mə-tō′sĭs) *n., pl.* **-ses** (-sēz). **1.** A highly infectious, usu. fatal disease of rabbits, characterized by many skin tumors similar to myxomas. **2.** A condition characterized by the growth of many myxomas.

myx•o•my•cete (mĭk′sō-mī′sēt) *n.* See **slime mold** 2.

myx•o•vi•rus (mĭk′sə-vī′rəs) *n., pl.* **-rus•es.** Any of a group of RNA-containing viruses, including those that cause influenza, typically having an affinity for certain mucins.

ă **pat**	oi **boy**
ā **pay**	ou **out**
âr **care**	o͝o **took**
ä **father**	o͞o **boot**
ĕ **pet**	ŭ **cut**
ē **be**	ûr **urge**
ĭ **pit**	th **thin**
ī **pie**	*th* **this**
îr **pier**	hw **which**
ŏ **pot**	zh **vision**
ō **toe**	ə **about,**
ô **paw**	**item**

Stress marks:
′ (primary);
′ (secondary), as in
dictionary (dĭk′shə-nĕr′ē)

IV of France and revoked in 1685 by Louis XIV. Pop. 240,539.

Nan•ti•coke[1] (năn′tĭ-kōk′) *n., pl.* **Nanticoke** or **-cokes. 1.** A member of a Native American people formerly inhabiting Delaware and eastern Maryland between Chesapeake Bay and the Atlantic coast. **2.** Their Algonquian language.

Nan•ti•coke[2] (năn′tĭ-kōk′). A city of SE Ontario, Canada, on Lake Erie SSE of Hamilton. Pop. 19,816.

Nan•tong also **Nan•tung** (nän′to͝ong′). A city of E-central China on the N bank of the Yangtze R. (Chang Jiang) estuary E of Nanjing. Pop. 300,000.

Nan•tuck•et (năn-tŭk′ĭt). An island of SE MA S of Cape Cod, from which it is separated by **Nantucket Sound**, an arm of the Atlantic Ocean. —**Nan•tuck′et•er** *n.*

Naoi•se (nē′sē, nā′-) *n.* The husband of Deidre in Irish legend.

Na•o•mi (nā-ō′mē). In the Bible, the mother-in-law of Ruth.

nap[1] (năp) *n.* A brief sleep, often during the day. —*intr.v.* **napped, nap•ping, naps. 1.** To take a nap, often during the day; doze. **2.** To be unaware of imminent danger or trouble. [ME < *nappen*, to doze < OE *hnappian*.]

nap[2] (năp) *n.* A soft or fuzzy surface on fabric or leather. —*tr.v.* **napped, nap•ping, naps.** To form or raise a nap on (fabric or leather). [Alteration of ME *noppe* < MDu.]

nap[3] (năp) *tr.v.* **napped, nap•ping, naps.** To pour or put a sauce or gravy over (a cooked dish). [Fr. *napper* < *nappe*, cover. See NAPPE.]

nap[4] (năp) *n.* **1.** *Games.* **a.** A card game that resembles whist. **b.** The highest bid in this game, announcing the intention to win five tricks, the maximum number in a hand. **2.** See **napoleon** 2. [Short for NAPOLEON.]

na•pa or **nap•pa** (năp′ə, nä′pə) *n.* See **Chinese cabbage.** [Prob. J. *nappa*, greens.]

Nap•a (năp′ə). A city of W CA N of Oakland; center of the **Napa Valley**, a region famous for its vineyards. Pop. 61,842.

NAPA *abbr.* National Association of Performing Artists.

na•palm (nā′päm′) *n.* **1.** An aluminum soap of various fatty acids that when mixed with gasoline makes a firm jelly used in some bombs and in flamethrowers. **2.** Jelly made from napalm. [*naphthenate*, salt of naphthenic acid (< NAPHTHENE) + PALM(ITATE).] —**na′palm′** *v.*

nape (nāp, năp) *n.* The back of the neck. [ME.]

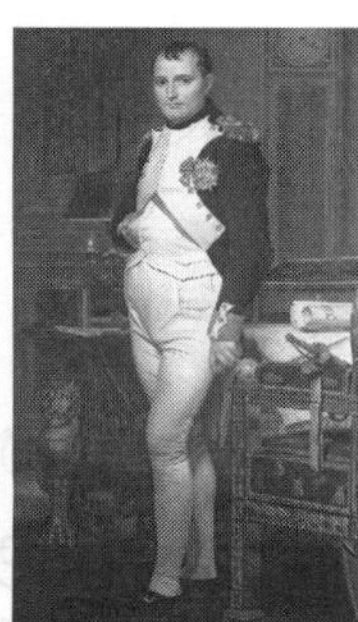

Napoleon I
Detail from *Napoleon in his Study*, 1812, by Jacques Louis David

Na•per•ville (nā′pər-vĭl′). A city of NE IL, a suburb of Chicago. Pop. 85,351.

na•per•y (nā′pə-rē) *n., pl.* **-ies.** Household linen, esp. table linen. [ME *naperie* < OFr. < *nape, nappe*, tablecloth. See NAPPE.]

Naph•ta•li (năf′tə-lī′). In the Bible, a son of Jacob and the forebear of one of the tribes of Israel.

naph•tha (năf′thə, năp′-) *n.* **1.** Any of several highly volatile flammable liquid mixtures of hydrocarbons distilled from petroleum, coal tar, and natural gas and used as fuel and solvents. **2.** *Obsolete.* Petroleum. [Lat. < Gk., liquid bitumen, of Pers. orig.] —**naph′thous** *adj.*

naph•tha•lene also **naph•tha•line** (năf′thə-lēn′, năp′-) or **naph•tha•lin** (-lĭn) *n.* A white crystalline compound, $C_{10}H_8$, derived from coal tar or petroleum and used in manufacturing dyes and moth repellents and as a solvent. [NAPHTH(A) + AL(COHOL) + -ENE.] —**naph′tha•len′ic** (-lĕn′ĭk) *adj.*

naph•thene (năf′thēn′, năp′-) *n.* Any of several cycloalkanes having the general formula C_nH_{2n} and found in various petroleums. [NAPHTH(A) + -ENE.]

naph•thol (năf′thôl′, -thōl′, -thŏl′, năp′-) also **naph•tol** (-tôl, -tōl, -tŏl) *n.* An organic compound, $C_{10}H_7OH$, occurring in two isomeric forms, alpha-naphthol and beta-naphthol. [NAPHTH(ALENE) + -OL².]

Na•pi•er (nā′pē-ər, nə-pîr′), **John.** Laird of Merchiston. 1550–1617. Scottish mathematician who introduced the use of the decimal point in writing numbers.

Na•pier•i•an logarithm (nə-pîr′ē-ən, nā-) *n. Math.* See **natural logarithm.** [After John NAPIER.]

Na•pi•er's bones (nā′pē-ərz, nə-pîrz′) *pl.n. (used with a sing. v.) Math.* A set of graduated rods used to perform multiplication quickly. [After John NAPIER.]

na•pi•form (nā′pə-fôrm′) *adj.* Shaped like a turnip: *napiform roots.* [Lat. *nāpus*, turnip + -FORM.]

nap•kin (năp′kĭn) *n.* **1.** A piece of cloth or absorbent paper used to protect the clothes or wipe the lips and fingers while eating. **2.** A cloth or towel. **3.** A sanitary napkin. **4.** *Chiefly British.* A diaper. [ME : OFr. *nape, nappe*, tablecloth; see NAPPE + *-kin*, -kin.]

Na•ples (nā′pəlz). **1.** A city of S-central Italy on the **Bay of Naples**, an arm of the Tyrrhenian Sea; formerly an independent duchy (8th cent. A.D.) and cap. of the kingdom of Naples (1282–1860). Pop. 1,210,503. **2.** A city of SW FL on the Gulf of Mexico S of Fort Myers. Pop. 19,505.

Na•po (nä′pō). A river of NE Ecuador and N Peru flowing c. 1,126 km (700 mi) to the Amazon R.

narwhal
Male and female narwhals
Monodon monoceros

na•po•le•on (nə-pō′lē-ən, -pōl′yən) *n.* **1.** A rectangular piece of pastry made with crisp flaky layers filled with custard cream. **2.** A 20-franc gold coin formerly used in France. **3.** *Games.* See **nap**⁴ 1. [After NAPOLEON I.]

Na•po•le•on I (nə-pō′lē-ən, -pōl′yən). Orig. Napoleon Bonaparte. 1769–1821. Emperor of the French (1804–14) who conquered much of Continental Europe but was forced to abdicate (1814) following a disastrous winter campaign in Russia. He escaped from exile on the island of Elba, briefly regained power, and was ultimately defeated at Waterloo (1815) and exiled to St. Helena. —**Na•po′le•on′ic** (-ŏn′ĭk) *adj.*

Napoleon II. Orig. François Charles Joseph Bonaparte. 1811–32. Titular king of Rome who succeeded his father, Napoleon I, as emperor of the French (1814).

Napoleon III. Orig. Charles Louis Napoleon Bonaparte. "Louis Napoleon." 1808–73. Emperor of the French (1852–71) who became president of the Second Republic (1848) and proclaimed himself emperor (1852).

nap•pa (năp′ə, nä′pə) *n.* Var. of **napa.**

nappe (năp) *n.* **1.** A sheet of water flowing over a dam or similar structure. **2.** *Geol.* A large sheetlike body of rock that has been moved far from its original position. **3.** *Math.* Either of the two parts into which a cone is divided by the vertex. [Fr., tablecloth, nappe < OFr., tablecloth < Lat. *mappa*, napkin. See MAP.]

nap•py[1] (năp′ē) *adj.* **-pi•er, -pi•est. 1.** Having a nap; fuzzy. **2.** Kinky; frizzy.

nap•py[2] (năp′ē) *n., pl.* **-pies.** A shallow round cooking or serving dish with a flat bottom and sloping sides. [Prob. < dial. *nap*, bowl < ME < OE *hnæp*.]

nap•py[3] (năp′ē) *n., pl.* **-pies.** *Chiefly British.* A diaper. [Alteration of NAPKIN.]

na•prox•en (nə-prŏk′sən) *n.* A drug, $C_{14}H_{14}O_3$, used to reduce inflammation and pain, esp. in the treatment of arthritis. [Shortening and alteration of *methoxynaphthylpropionic acid*, one of its chemical names.]

Na•ra (när′ə). A city of S-central Honshu, Japan, E of Osaka; first permanent cap. of Japan (710–784). Pop. 327,702.

Nar•ba•da (nər-bŭd′ə). See **Narmada.**

Nar•bonne (när-bŏn′, -bôn′). A city of S France near the Mediterranean SW of Montpellier; perhaps the first Roman colony in Transalpine Gaul (118 B.C.). Pop. 41,565.

narc or **nark** (närk) *n. Slang.* A law enforcement officer who deals with narcotics violations. [Short for *narcotics agent.*]

nar•cis•sism (när′sĭ-sĭz′əm) also **nar•cism** (-sĭz′əm) *n.* **1.** Excessive love or admiration of oneself. **2.** Erotic pleasure derived from contemplation or admiration of one's own body or self, esp. as a fixation on or a regression to an infantile stage of development. [After NARCISSUS.] —**nar′cis•sist** *n.* —**nar′cis•sis′tic** *adj.* —**nar′cis•sis′ti•cal•ly** *adv.*

nar•cis•sus (när-sĭs′əs) *n., pl.* **-cis•sus•es** or **-cis•si** (-sĭs′ī′, -sĭs′ē). Any of several bulbous plants of the genus *Narcissus*, having long narrow leaves and flowers with a cup-shaped or trumpet-shaped central crown. [Lat. < Gk. *narkissos*.]

Nar•cis•sus (när-sĭs′əs) *n. Gk. Myth.* A young man who pined away in love for his own image in a pool of water and was transformed into a narcissus.

narco– *pref.* **1.** Numbness; stupor; lethargy: *narcolepsy.* **2.** Narcotic drug: *narcoanalysis.* [Gk. *narko-* < *narkoun*, to numb < *narkē*, numbness.]

nar•co•a•nal•y•sis (när′kō-ə-năl′ĭ-sĭs) *n., pl.* **-ses** (-sēz′). Psychotherapy conducted while the patient is in a sleeplike state induced by barbiturates or other drugs, esp. as a means of releasing repressed feelings or thoughts.

nar•co•lep•sy (när′kə-lĕp′sē) *n., pl.* **-sies.** A disorder characterized by sudden and uncontrollable, though often brief attacks of deep sleep, sometimes accompanied by paralysis and hallucinations. —**nar′co•lep′tic** (-lĕp′tĭk) *adj.*

nar•co•ma (när-kō′mə) *n., pl.* **-mas** also **-ma•ta** (-mə-tə). Stupor induced by a narcotic. [NLat. *narcōma* < Gk. *narkoun*, to benumb. See NARCOSIS.]

nar•co•sis (när-kō′sĭs) *n., pl.* **-ses** (-sēz). A condition of deep stupor or unconsciousness produced by a drug or other chemical substance. [NLat. *narcōsis* < Gk. *narkōsis*, a numbing < *narkoun*, to benumb < *narkē*, numbness.]

nar•co•syn•the•sis (när′kō-sĭn′thĭ-sĭs) *n., pl.* **-ses** (-sēz′). Narcoanalysis directed toward making the patient recall repressed memories and emotional traumas.

nar•cot•ic (när-kŏt′ĭk) *n.* **1.** An addictive drug, such as opium, that reduces pain, alters mood and behavior, and usu. induces sleep or stupor. **2.** A soothing numbing agent or thing. —*adj.* **1.** Inducing sleep or stupor; causing narcosis. **2.** Of or relating to narcotics, their effects, or their use. **3.** Of, relating to, or intended for one addicted to a narcotic. [ME *narcotik* < OFr. *narcotique* < Med.Lat. *narcōticum* < Gk. *narkōtikon*, neut. of *narkōtikos*, numbing < *narkōsis*, a numbing. See NARCOSIS.] —**nar•cot′i•cal•ly** *adv.*

nar•co•tism (när′kə-tĭz′əm) *n.* **1.** Addiction to narcotics such as opium, heroin, or morphine. **2.** Narcosis.

nar•co•tize (när′kə-tīz′) *tr.v.* **-tized, -tiz•ing, -tiz•es. 1.** To place under the influence of a narcotic. **2.** To put to sleep; lull. **3.** To dull; deaden. —**nar′co•ti•za′tion** (-tĭ-zā′shən) *n.*

nard (närd) *n.* See **spikenard** 1. [ME *narde* < OFr. < Lat. *nardus* < Gk. *nardos*, prob. ult. < Skt. *naladam*, Indian spikenard.]

Na•rew also **Na•rev** (nä′rəf). A river rising in W Belorussia and flowing c. 442 km (275 mi) to the Western Bug R.

nar•ghi•le also **nar•gi•leh** (när′gə-lē′) *n.* See **hookah.** [Fr. *narghilé*, obsolete var. of *narguilé* < Pers. *nārgīleh* < *nārgīl*, coconut, of Indic orig.]

nar•is (nâr′ĭs) *n., pl.* **-es** (-ēz). An external opening in the nasal cavity of a vertebrate; a nostril. [Lat. *nāris.* See **nas-***.] — **nar′i•al** (-ē-əl) *adj.*

nark¹ (närk) *n. Slang.* Var. of **narc.**

nark² (närk) *Chiefly British.* — *n.* An informer, esp. a police informer. — *intr.v.* **narked, nark•ing, narks.** To be an informer. [Perh. < Romany *nāk*, nose. See **nas-***.]

Nar•ma•da (nər-mŭd′ə) also **Nar•ba•da** (-bŭd′ə). A river of central India flowing c. 1,247 km (775 mi) to the Gulf of Cambay.

Nar•ra•gan•sett also **Nar•ra•gan•set** (năr′ə-găn′sĭt) *n., pl.* **Narragansett** or **-setts** also **Narraganset** or **-sets. 1.a.** A member of a Native American people formerly inhabiting Rhode Island west of Narragansett Bay, with present-day descendants in the same area. **b.** The Algonquian language of the Narragansett. **2.** Any of a breed of small sturdy saddle horse developed in Rhode Island. [From a Narragansett place name.] — **Nar′ra•gan′sett** *adj.*

Narragansett Bay. A deep inlet of the Atlantic Ocean in E RI.

nar•rate (năr′āt′, nă-rāt′) *v.* **-rat•ed, -rat•ing, -rates.** — *tr.* **a.** To tell (a story, for example) in speech or writing. **b.** To give an account of (events, for example). — *intr.* **1.** To give an account or a description. **2.** To supply a running commentary for a movie or performance. [Lat. *narrāre, narrāt-* < *gnārus*, knowing. See **gnō-***.] — **nar′rat•a•bil′i•ty** *n.* — **nar′rat•a•ble** *adj.* — **nar′ra′tor, nar′rat′er** *n.*

nar•ra•tion (nă-rā′shən) *n.* **1.** The act, process, or an instance of narrating. **2.** Narrated material. — **nar•ra′tion•al** *adj.* — **nar•ra′tion•al•ly** *adv.*

nar•ra•tive (năr′ə-tĭv) *n.* **1.** A narrated account; a story. **2.** The art, technique, or process of narrating. **3.** *Comp. Sci.* A comment. — *adj.* **1.** Consisting of or characterized by the telling of a story: *narrative poetry.* **2.** Of or relating to narration: *narrative skill.* — **nar′ra•tive•ly** *adv.*

nar•row (năr′ō) *adj.* **-row•er, -row•est. 1.** Of small or limited width, esp. in comparison with length. **2.** Limited in area or scope; cramped. **3.** Lacking flexibility; rigid. **4.** Barely sufficient; close. **5.** Painstakingly thorough or attentive; meticulous. **6.** *Ling.* Tense. — *v.* **-rowed, -row•ing, -rows.** — *tr.* **1.** To reduce in width or extent; make narrower. **2.** To limit or restrict. — *intr.* To become narrower; contract. — *n.* **1.** A part of little width, such as a pass through mountains. **2. narrows.** *(used with a sing. or pl. v.)* **a.** A body of water with little width that connects two larger bodies of water. **b.** A part of a river or an ocean current that is not wide. [ME *narwe* < OE *nearu.*] — **nar′row•ish** *adj.* — **nar′row•ly** *adv.* — **nar′row•ness** *n.*

nar•row-bod•ied (năr′ō-bŏd′ēd) *adj.* Being a jet aircraft with seats for passengers on either side of a single aisle running the length of the fuselage.

nar•row•cast (năr′ō-kăst′) *intr.v.* **-cast, -cast•ing, -casts.** To transmit, as by cable, programs confined to the interests of a specific group of viewers, subscribers, or listeners.

narrow gauge *n.* **1.** A distance between the rails of a railroad track that is less than the standard width of 56½ inches (143.5 centimeters). **2.** A locomotive, car, or railway line of this gauge. — **nar′row-gauge′** (năr′ō-gāj′), **nar′row-gauged′** (-gājd′) *adj.*

nar•row-mind•ed (năr′ō-mīn′dĭd) *adj.* Lacking tolerance, breadth of view, or sympathy; petty. — **nar′row-mind′ed•ly** *adv.* — **nar′row-mind′ed•ness** *n.*

Nar•rows (năr′ōz). A strait of SE NY between Brooklyn and Staten I. in New York City.

nar•thex (när′thĕks′) *n. Archit.* **1.** A narrow portico or lobby of a basilica. **2.** An entrance hall leading to the nave of a Byzantine church. [LGk. *narthēx* < Gk., box, giant fennel, of Indic orig.]

nar•whal also **nar•wal** (när′wəl) or **nar•whale** (-hwāl′, -wāl′) *n.* An Arctic whale *(Monodon monoceros)* that has a spotted whitish pelt and is characterized in the male by a long, spirally twisted ivory tusk. [Alteration of Norw. or Dan. *narhval* < ON *nāhvalr* : *nār*, corpse (being whitish) + *hvalr*, whale.]

nar•y (nâr′ē) *adj.* Not one. [Alteration of *ne'er a.*]

NASA *abbr.* National Aeronautics and Space Administration.

na•sal (nā′zəl) *adj.* **1.** Of, in, or relating to the nose. **2.** *Ling.* Articulated by lowering the soft palate so that air resonates in the nasal cavities and passes out the nose, as in the pronunciation of (m), (n), and (ng). **3.** Characterized by or resembling a resonant sound produced through the nose: *a nasal whine.* — *n.* **1.** *Ling.* A nasal consonant. **2.** A nasal part or bone forming part of the bridge of the nose. **3.** The nosepiece of a helmet. [Poss. < ME *nasale* < Med.Lat. *nāsālis* < Lat. *nāsus*, nose. See **nas-***.] — **na•sal′i•ty** (nā-zăl′ĭ-tē) *n.* — **na′sal•ly** *adv.*

na•sal•ize (nā′zə-līz′) *tr. & intr.v.* **-ized, -iz•ing, -iz•es.** *Ling.* To make nasal or produce nasal sounds. — **na′sal•i•za′tion** (nā′zə-lĭ-zā′shən) *n.*

Nas•by (năz′bē), **Petroleum V.** See David Ross **Locke.**

NASCAR *abbr.* National Association of Stock Car Auto Racing.

nas•cence (năs′əns, nā′səns) *n.* A coming into being; birth. See Syns at **beginning.**

nas•cent (năs′ənt, nā′sənt) *adj.* Coming into existence; emerging. [Lat. *nāscēns, nāscent-*, pr.part. of *nāscī*, to be born. See **genə-***.] — **nas′cen•cy** *n.*

NASDAQ *abbr.* National Association of Securities Dealers Automated Quotation System.

nase•ber•ry (nāz′bĕr′ē) *n.* See **sapodilla.** [Alteration of Sp. *néspera* < Lat. *mespila*, medlar. See MEDLAR.]

Nase•by (nāz′bē). A village of central England near Northampton where Cromwell defeated Royalist troops in Jun. 1645.

Nash (năsh), **Ogden.** 1902–71. Amer. writer known for his droll epigrammatic verse.

Nash or **Nashe** (năsh), **Thomas.** 1567–1601. English writer noted for his witty literary criticism.

Nash•u•a (năsh′o͞o-ə). A city of S NH on the Merrimack R. S of Manchester; settled c. 1655. Pop. 79,662.

Nash•ville¹ (năsh′vĭl′). The cap. of TN, in the N-central part NE of Memphis; founded 1779. Pop. 488,374.

Nash•ville² (năsh′vĭl′) *n. Mus.* **1.** Country music. **2.** The country music industry. [After NASHVILLE¹.]

na•si•on (nā′zī-ŏn′) *n.* The point in the skull where the nasal and frontal bones unite. [NLat. *nāsion* : NAS(O)- + Gk. *-ion*, dim. suff.]

Nas•ka•pi (năs′kə-pē) *n., pl.* **Naskapi** or **-pis. 1.** A member of a Native American people inhabiting northern Quebec and Labrador. **2.** The variety of Montagnais spoken by the Naskapi. [Fr., of Montagnais orig.]

naso– *pref.* Nose: *nasopharynx.* [NLat. < Lat. *nāsus*, nose. See **nas-***.]

na•so•fron•tal (nā′zō-frŭn′təl) *adj.* Of or relating to the nasal and frontal bones.

na•so•phar•ynx (nā′zō-făr′ĭngks) *n., pl.* **-pha•ryn•ges** (-fə-rĭn′jēz) or **-phar•ynx•es.** The part of the pharynx above the soft palate that is continuous with the nasal passages. — **na′so•pha•ryn′ge•al** (-fə-rĭn′jē-əl, -jəl, -făr′ən-jē′əl) *adj.*

Nas•sau (năs′ô′). **1.** *(also* nä′sou′*).* A region and former duchy of central Germany N and E of the Main and Rhine rivers; became a duchy in 1806 and was absorbed by Prussia in 1866. **2.** The cap. of the Bahamas, on the NE coast of New Providence I. in the Atlantic E of Miami FL; settled in the 17th cent. Pop. 135,000.

Nas•ser (năs′ər, nä′sər), **Gamal Abdel.** 1918–70. Egyptian army officer and politician who served as prime minister (1954–56) and president (1956–58) of Egypt and as president of the United Arab Republic (1958–70).

Nast (năst), **Thomas.** 1840–1902. German-born Amer. editorial cartoonist whose caricatures contributed to the downfall of the Tweed Ring in New York City.

nas•tic (năs′tĭk) *adj.* Of, relating to, or characterized by the tendency in plant parts to move in a direction determined by an internal stimulus, as an increased rate of cellular growth on one side of the plant part. [Gk. *nastos*, pressed close (< *nassein*, to press) + -IC.]

nas•tur•tium (nə-stûr′shəm, nă-) *n.* **1.** Any of various New World plants of the genus *Tropaeolum*, having pungent juice and long-spurred, usu. yellow, orange, or red irregular flowers. **2.** *Color.* A brilliant orange yellow. [ME *nasturcium*, a kind of cress < Lat. *nasturtium* : perh. *nāsus*, nose; see **nas-*** + **tortāre*, freq. of *torquēre*, to twist; see **terkʷ-***.]

nas•ty (năs′tē) *adj.* **-ti•er, -ti•est. 1.a.** Disgustingly dirty. **b.** Physically repellent. **2.** Morally offensive; indecent. **3.** Malicious; spiteful. **4.** Very unpleasant or annoying. **5.** Painful or dangerous; grave. **6.** Exasperatingly difficult to solve or handle. — *n., pl.* **-ties.** One that is nasty. [ME *nasti*, poss. alteration of OFr. *nastre*, bad, short for *villenastre* : *vilein*, bad; see VILLAIN + *-astre*, pejorative suff. (< Lat. *-aster*).] — **nas′ti•ly** *adv.* — **nas′ti•ness** *n.*

–nasty *suff.* Nastic response or change: *epinasty.* [Gk. *nastos*, pressed down; see NASTIC + -Y².]

nat. *abbr.* **1.** National. **2.** Native. **3.** Natural.

na•tal (nāt′l) *adj.* **1.** Of, relating to, or accompanying birth. **2.** Of or relating to the time or place of one's birth. [ME < Lat. *nātālis* < *nātus*, p.part. of *nāscī*, to be born. See **genə-***.]

Na•tal (nə-tăl′, -täl′, -tôl′). **1.** A region of SE Africa on the Indian Ocean; a founding province of the country of South Africa (1910). **2.** A city of NE Brazil on the Atlantic Ocean N of Recife; founded in the late 1590's. Pop. 376,446.

Na•tal brown (nə-tăl′, -täl′) *n. Color.* A grayish brown.

na•tal•i•ty (nā-tăl′ĭ-tē, nə-) *n., pl.* **-ties.** See **birthrate.** [NATAL + (MORTAL)ITY.]

Na•tal plum (nə-tăl′, -täl′) *n.* A South African evergreen shrub *(Carissa grandiflora)* often cultivated as a hedge plant and having forked spines and an edible scarlet berry.

na•tant (nāt′nt) *adj.* Floating or swimming in water. [Lat. *natāns, natant-*, pr.part. of *natāre*, to swim. See **snā-***.]

na•ta•tion (nā-tā′shən, nă-) *n.* The act or skill of swimming. [Lat. *natātiō, natātiōn-* < *natātus*, p.part. of *natāre*, to swim. See **snā-***.]

Gamal Abdel Nasser

nasturtium

ă pat	oi boy
ā pay	ou out
âr care	o͝o took
ä father	o͞o boot
ĕ pet	ŭ cut
ē be	ûr urge
ĭ pit	th thin
ī pie	*th* this
îr pier	hw which
ŏ pot	zh vision
ō toe	ə about,
ô paw	item

Stress marks:
′ (primary);
′ (secondary), as in
dictionary (dĭk′shə-nĕr′ē)

na·ta·to·ri·al (nā′tə-tôr′ē-əl, -tōr′-, năt′ə-) also **na·ta·to·ry** (nā′tə-tôr′ē, -tōr′ē, năt′ə-) *adj.* Of, relating to, adapted for, or characterized by swimming: *natatorial birds.* [< LLat. *natātōrius* < Lat. *natātor*, swimmer < *natātus*, p.part. of *natāre*, to swim. See **snā-***.]

natch (năch) *adv. Slang.* Of course; naturally. [Shortening and alteration of NATURALLY.]

Natch·ez[1] (năch′ĭz) *n., pl.* **Natchez. 1.** A member of a Native American people formerly located near present-day Natchez. **2.** Their language. [Fr. < Natchez.]

Natch·ez[2] (năch′ĭz). A city of SW MS on the Mississippi R. SSW of Vicksburg; founded as a fortified settlement in 1716 and the S terminus of the **Natchez Trace,** an old road connecting the city with Nashville TN. Pop. 19,460.

Natch·i·toches (năk′ĭ-tŏsh′). A city of NW-central LA SE of Shreveport; founded c. 1714. Pop. 16,609.

NATE *abbr.* National Association of Teachers of English.

na·tes (nā′tēz) *pl.n.* The buttocks. [Lat. *natēs*, pl. of *natis*, buttock.]

Na·than (nā′thən). In the Bible, a prophet during the reigns of David and Solomon.

Nathan, George Jean. 1882–1958. Amer. critic who cofounded and edited (1924–30) the *American Mercury.*

Na·than·ael (nə-thăn′yəl). See Saint **Bartholomew.**

nathe·less (nāth′lĭs) also **nath·less** (năth′-) *adv. Archaic.* Nevertheless; notwithstanding. [ME < OE *nā thē lǣs*, not less by that : *nā*, no; see NO[1] + *thē, thȳ*, instrumental case of *se*, this, that; see **to-*** + *lǣs*, less; see LESS.]

nativity
The Nativity by Lorenzo Lotto (1480?–1556)

Na·tick[1] (nā′tĭk) *n.* The variety of Massachusett presumed to have been spoken in the mission town of Natick, Massachusetts, and used in the Massachusett Bible.

Na·tick[2] (nā′tĭk). A town of NE MA, a suburb of Boston. Pop. 30,510.

na·tion (nā′shən) *n.* **1.** A relatively large group of people organized under a single, usu. independent government; a country. **2.** The government of a sovereign state. **3.** A people who share common customs, origins, history, and frequently language; a nationality. **4.a.** A federation or a tribe, esp. one composed of Native Americans. **b.** The territory occupied by such a federation or tribe. [ME *nacioun* < OFr. *nation* < Lat. *nātiō, nātiōn-* < *nātus*, p.part. of *nāscī*, to be born. See **genə-***.] —**na′tion·hood′** *n.* —**na′tion·less** *adj.*

Na·tion (nā′shən), **Carry Amelia Moore.** 1846–1911. Amer. temperance crusader known for wielding a hatchet during her raids on saloons.

na·tion·al (năsh′ə-nəl, năsh′nəl) *adj.* **1.** Of, relating to, or belonging to a nation as an organized whole. **2.** Of or relating to nationality. **3.** Characteristic of or peculiar to the people of a nation. **4.** Of or maintained by the government of a nation. **5.** Being in the interest of one's own nation. **6.** Devoted to one's own nation or its interests; patriotic. —*n.* **1.** A citizen of a particular nation. **2.** *Sports & Games.* A contest or tournament involving participants from all parts of a nation. Often used in the plural. —**na′tion·al·ly** *adv.*

national bank *n.* **1.** A bank in a system of federally chartered privately owned banks in the United States, required by law to belong to the Federal Reserve Bank and be insured by the Federal Deposit Insurance Corporation. **2.** A bank associated with national finances and usu. owned or controlled by a government.

Na·tion·al City (năsh′ə-nəl, năsh′nəl). A city of S CA, a suburb of San Diego on San Diego Bay. Pop. 54,249.

national forest *n.* A large expanse of forest in which a government limits harvesting and hunting.

National Guard *n.* The military reserve units controlled by each state of the United States, equipped federally and subject to the call of both the federal and the state governments.

na·tion·al·ism (năsh′ə-nə-lĭz′əm, năsh′nə-) *n.* **1.** Devotion to the interests or culture of a nation. **2.** The belief that nations will benefit from acting independently rather than collectively, emphasizing national rather than international goals. **3.** Aspirations for national independence in a country under foreign domination. —**na′tion·al·ist** *n.* —**na′tion·al·is′tic** *adj.* —**na′tion·al·is′ti·cal·ly** *adv.*

na·tion·al·i·ty (năsh′ə-năl′ĭ-tē, năsh-năl′-) *n., pl.* **-ties. 1.** The status of belonging to a particular nation by origin, birth, or naturalization. **2.** A people having common origins or traditions and often constituting a nation. **3.** Existence as a politically autonomous entity; national independence. **4.** National character. **5.** Nationalism.

na·tion·al·ize (năsh′ə-nə-līz′, năsh′nə-) *tr.v.* **-ized, -iz·ing, -iz·es. 1.** To convert from private to governmental ownership and control. **2.a.** To make national in character, scope, or notoriety. **b.** To render distinctively national. —**na′tion·al·i·za′tion** (-shə-nə-lĭ-zā′shən) *n.* —**na′tion·al·iz′er** *n.*

national monument *n.* A natural landmark or a structure or site of historic interest set aside by a national government and maintained for public enjoyment or study.

national park *n.* A tract of land protected and maintained by a national government for public enjoyment or study.

national seashore *n.* A seacoast recreational area protected and maintained by a national government for public use.

National Socialism *n.* Nazism.

na·tion-state (nā′shən-stāt′) *n.* A political unit consisting of an autonomous state inhabited esp. by a predominantly homogeneous people.

na·tion·wide (nā′shən-wīd′) *adv. & adj.* Throughout a whole nation: *a speech broadcast nationwide.*

na·tive (nā′tĭv) *adj.* **1.** Existing in or belonging to one by nature; innate. **2.** Being such by birth or origin. **3.** Being one's own because of the place or circumstances of one's birth. **4.** Originating, growing, or produced in a certain place or region; indigenous. **5.** Of, belonging to, or characteristic of the original inhabitants of a particular place. **6.** Occurring in nature pure or uncombined with other substances. **7.** Natural; unaffected. **8.** *Archaic.* Closely related, as by birth or race. —*n.* **1.a.** One born in or connected with a place by birth. **b.** One of the original inhabitants or lifelong residents of a place. **2.** An animal or a plant that originated in a particular place or region. [ME < OFr. *natif* < Lat. *nātīvus* < *nātus*, p.part. of *nāscī*, to be born. See **genə-***.] —**na′tive·ly** *adv.* —**na′tive·ness** *n.*

Na·tive American (nā′tĭv) *n.* A member of any of the aboriginal peoples of the Western Hemisphere. —**Native American** *adj.*

Usage Note: The term *Indian* has always been a misnomer for the earliest inhabitants of the Americas. Certainly wherever confusion between the peoples indigenous to the Americas and the inhabitants of India might exist, *Native American* is an obvious choice. It is also preferred by many contemporary writers when emphasizing ethnic pride. However, it should not be assumed that *Indian* is necessarily offensive or out of date. On the contrary, *Indian* is firmly rooted in English in neutral terms such as *Paleo-Indian* and plant names, and in locutions of this kind there is no possibility of substitution. Furthermore, many Native Americans and others sympathetic to Native American issues continue to use *Indian* as a term of pride and respect, as in *"It was about this time that* [my mother] *began to see herself as an Indian"* (N. Scott Momaday). • The compound terms *American Indian* and the less frequent *Amerindian* offer an unambiguous and unproblematic alternative where *Native American* might seem out of place, as in certain historical contexts or in references to groups outside the boundaries of the United States. • In Canada and Alaska *Native American,* the broader term, is properly used of all aboriginal peoples, whereas *Indian* is customarily used of the northern Athabaskan and Algonquian peoples in contrast to the Eskimo and the Aleut.

na·tive-born (nā′tĭv-bôrn′) *adj.* Belonging to a place by birth.

na·tiv·ism (nā′tĭ-vĭz′əm) *n.* **1.** A sociopolitical policy, esp. in the United States in the 19th century, favoring the interests of indigenous inhabitants over those of immigrants. **2.** The reestablishment or perpetuation of native cultural traits, esp. in opposition to acculturation. **3.** *Philos.* The doctrine that the mind produces ideas that are not derived from external sources. —**na′tiv·ist** *n.* —**na′tiv·is′tic** *adj.*

na·tiv·i·ty (nə-tĭv′ĭ-tē, nā-) *n., pl.* **-ties. 1.** Birth, esp. the place, conditions, or circumstances of being born. **2. Nativity. a.** The birth of Jesus. **b.** A representation, such as a painting, of Jesus's birth. **c.** Christmas. **3.** A horoscope for the time of one's birth. [ME *nativite* < OFr. < Lat. *nātīvitās* < *nātīvus*, born. See NATIVE.]

natl. *abbr.* National.

NATO *abbr.* North Atlantic Treaty Organization.

na·tri·u·re·sis (nā′trə-yo͝o-rē′sĭs) *n.* Excretion of excessive amounts of sodium in the urine. [NLat. *natriūrēsis* : *natrium*, sodium (< Fr. *natron*, natron; see NATRON) + *ūrēsis*, urination (< Gk. *ourēsis* < *ourein*, to urinate; see URETIC).] —**na′tri·u·ret′ic** (-rĕt′ĭk) *adj.*

na·tro·lite (nā′trə-līt′) *n.* A mineral in the zeolite family, $Na_2(Al_2Si_3O_{10})\cdot 2H_2O$. [NATRO(N) + -LITE.]

na·tron (nā′trŏn′, -trən) *n.* A mineral of hydrous sodium carbonate, $Na_2CO_3\cdot 10H_2O$, often found crystallized with other salts. [Fr. < Sp. *natrón* < Ar. *naṭrūn*, niter < Gk. *nitron.* See NITER.]

Nat·ta (nä′tä), **Giulio.** 1903–79. Italian chemist who shared a 1963 Nobel Prize.

nat·ter (năt′ər) *intr.v.* **-tered, -ter·ing, -ters.** To talk idly; chatter. [Var. of *gnatter.*]

nat·ty (năt′ē) *adj.* **-ti·er, -ti·est.** Neat, trim, and smart; dapper. [Perh. var. of obsolete *netty* < *net*, elegant < ME < OFr. See NEAT[1].] —**nat′ti·ly** *adv.* —**nat′ti·ness** *n.*

nat·u·ral (năch′ər-əl, năch′rəl) *adj.* **1.** Present in or produced by nature. **2.** Of, relating to, or concerning nature. **3.** Conforming to the usual or ordinary course of nature. **4.a.** Not acquired; inherent. **b.** Having a particular character by nature. **c.** *Biol.* Not produced or changed artificially; not conditioned. **5.** Characterized by spontaneity and freedom from artificiality, affectation, or inhibitions. See Syns at **naive. 6.** Not altered, treated, or disguised. **7.** Faithfully representing nature or life. **8.** Expected and accepted. **9.** Established by moral certainty or conviction: *natural rights.* **10.** Being in a state regarded as primitive, uncivilized, or unregenerate. **11.a.** Related by blood. **b.** Born out of wedlock. **12.** *Math.* Of or relating to positive integers. **13.** *Mus.* **a.** Not sharped or flatted. **b.** Having no sharps or flats. —*n.* **1.a.** One having all the qualifications necessary for success. **b.** One suited by nature for a certain purpose or function. **2.** *Mus.* **a.** The sign (♮) placed before a note to cancel a preceding sharp or flat. **b.** A note so affected. **3.** *Color.* A yellowish gray to pale orange yellow. **4.** *Games.* A combination in certain card and dice games that wins immediately. **5.** An Afro hairstyle. [ME < OFr. < Lat. *nātūrālis* < *nātūra*, nature. See NATURE.] —**nat′u•ral•ness** *n.*

natural childbirth *n.* A method of childbirth with minimal medical intervention in which the mother often practices relaxation and breathing techniques to control pain and ease delivery.

natural food *n.* Food that does not contain any additives.

natural gas *n.* A mixture of hydrocarbon gases that occurs with petroleum deposits, chiefly methane with some ethane, propane, and butane, used widely as a fuel.

natural history *n.* **1.** The study and description of organisms and natural objects, esp. their origins, evolution, and interrelationships. **2.** A collection of facts about the development of a natural process or object: *the natural history of a fossil.*

nat•u•ral•ism (năch′ər-ə-lĭz′əm, năch′rə-) *n.* **1.** Factual or realistic representation, esp.: **a.** The practice of describing precisely the actual circumstances of human life in literature. **b.** The practice of reproducing subjects as precisely as possible in the visual arts. **2.a.** A movement or school advocating such representation. **b.** The principles and methods of such a movement or of its adherents. **3.** *Philos.* The system of thought holding that all phenomena can be explained in terms of natural causes and laws without attributing moral, spiritual, or supernatural significance to them. **4.** *Theol.* The doctrine that all religious truths are derived from nature and natural causes and not from revelation. **5.** Conduct or thought prompted by natural desires or instincts.

nat•u•ral•ist (năch′ər-ə-lĭst, năch′rə-) *n.* **1.** One versed in natural history, esp. in zoology or botany. **2.** One who believes in and follows the tenets of naturalism.

nat•u•ral•is•tic (năch′ər-ə-lĭs′tĭk, năch′rə-) *adj.* **1.** Imitating or producing the effect or appearance of nature. **2.** Of, relating to, or being in accordance with the doctrines of naturalism. —**nat′u•ral•is′ti•cal•ly** *adv.*

nat•u•ral•ize (năch′ər-ə-līz′, năch′rə-) *v.* **-ized, -iz•ing, -iz•es.** —*tr.* **1.** To grant full citizenship to (one of foreign birth). **2.** To adopt (something foreign) into general use. **3.** To adapt or acclimate (a plant or an animal) to a new environment; introduce and establish as if native. **4.** To cause to conform to nature. —*intr.* To become naturalized or acclimated; undergo adaptation. —**nat′u•ral•iz′a•ble** *adj.* —**nat′u•ral•i•za′tion** (-ĭ-zā′shən) *n.*

natural killer cell *n.* A killer cell that is activated by double-stranded RNA and fights off viral infections and tumors.

natural language *n.* A human written or spoken language as opposed to a computer language or an invented language.

natural law *n.* A law or body of laws that derives from nature and is believed to be binding upon human actions apart from or in conjunction with laws established by human authority.

natural logarithm *n. Symbol* **ln** *Math.* A logarithm in which the base is the irrational number *e* (= 2.71828 . . .).

nat•u•ral•ly (năch′ər-ə-lē, năch′rə-) *adv.* **1.** In a natural manner. **2.** By nature; inherently. **3.** Without a doubt; surely.

natural number *n. Math.* One of the set of positive whole numbers; a positive integer.

natural philosophy *n.* The study of nature and the physical universe. —**natural philosopher** *n.*

natural resource *n.* A material source of wealth, such as timber, that occurs in a natural state and has economic value.

natural science *n.* A science, such as biology, chemistry, or physics, that deals with the objects, phenomena, or laws of nature and the physical world. —**natural scientist** *n.*

natural selection *n.* The process in nature by which, according to Darwin, the organisms best adapted to their environment tend to survive and transmit their genetic characters while those less adapted tend to be eliminated.

natural theology *n.* A theology holding that knowledge of God may be acquired by human reason alone without the aid of revealed knowledge.

natural virtue *n.* Cardinal virtue.

na•ture (nā′chər) *n.* **1.** The material world and its phenomena. **2.** The forces and processes that produce and control all the phenomena of the material world. **3.** The world of living things and the outdoors. **4.** A primitive state of existence, untouched and uninfluenced by civilization or artificiality. **5.** *Theol.* Humankind's natural state as distinguished from the state of grace. **6.** A kind or sort. **7.** The essential characteristics and qualities of a person or thing. **8.** The fundamental character or disposition of a person; temperament. **9.** The natural or real aspect of a person, place, or thing. **10.** The processes and functions of the body. [ME, essential properties of a thing < OFr. < Lat. *nātūra* < *nātus*, p.part. of *nāscī*, to be born. See **genə-***.]

na•tured (nā′chərd) *adj.* Having a nature or temperament of a specified kind. Often used in combination: *mean-natured.*

nature study *n.* The study of natural objects and phenomena, esp. animal and plant life, often in school.

nature trail *n.* A trail, as through woods or by a seashore, usu. with natural features labeled esp. for study.

na•tur•ism (nā′chə-rĭz′əm) *n.* Nudism. —**na′tur•ist** *n.*

na•tur•op•a•thy (nā′chə-rŏp′ə-thē) *n., pl.* **-thies.** A system of therapy that relies on natural remedies, such as sunlight supplemented with diet and massage, to treat illness.

Nau•cra•tis (nô′krə-tĭs). An ancient city of Egypt in the Nile R. delta SE of Alexandria; probably settled by Greek colonists in the 7th cent. B.C.

Nau•ga•hyde (nô′gə-hīd′). A trademark used for an artificial leather made of vinyl-coated fabric.

Nau•ga•tuck (nô′gə-tŭk′). A town of W-central CT S of Waterbury on the **Naugatuck River.** Pop. 30,625.

naught also **nought** (nôt) —*n.* **1.** Nonexistence; nothingness. **2.** The figure 0; a cipher; a zero. —*pron.* Nothing: *All their work was for naught.* —*adj.* **1.** Nonexistent. **2.** Insignificant. [ME < OE *nāwiht* : *nā*, no; see **ne*** + *wiht*, thing; see **wekti-***.]

naugh•ty (nô′tē) *adj.* **-ti•er, -ti•est. 1.** Behaving disobediently or mischievously. **2.** Indecent; improper. **3.** *Archaic.* Wicked; immoral. —*n., pl.* **-ties.** One that is naughty. [ME *noughti*, wicked < *nought*, nothing, evil < OE *nāwiht*, nothing. See NAUGHT.] —**naugh′ti•ly** *adv.* —**naugh′ti•ness** *n.*

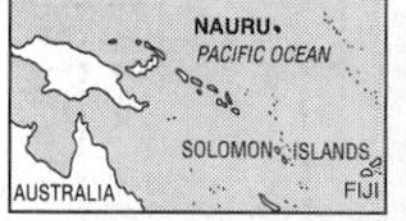

Nauru

nau•pli•us (nô′plē-əs) *n., pl.* **-pli•i** (-plē-ī′). The free-swimming first stage of the larva of certain crustaceans, having an unsegmented body with three pairs of appendages and a single median eye. [Lat., a kind of shellfish < Gk. *nauplios.*]

Na•u•ru (nä-o͞o′ro͞o). Formerly **Pleas•ant Island** (plĕz′ənt). An island country of the central Pacific S of the equator and W of Kiribati; administered by Australia from 1919 until it became independent in 1968. Cap. Yaren. Pop. 8,000. —**Na•u′ru•an** *adj. & n.*

nau•se•a (nô′zē-ə, -zhə, -sē-ə, -shə) *n.* **1.** A feeling of sickness in the stomach characterized by an urge to vomit. See Usage Note at **nauseous. 2.** Strong aversion; disgust. [ME < Lat. < Gk. *nautia, nausiē*, seasickness < *nautēs*, sailor < *naus*, ship. See **nāu-***.]

nau•se•ant (nô′zē-ənt, -zhē-, -sē-, -shē-) *adj.* Inducing nausea or vomiting. —**nau′se•ant** *n.*

nau•se•ate (nô′zē-āt′, -zhē-, -sē-, -shē-) *intr. & tr.v.* **-at•ed, -at•ing, -ates. 1.** To feel or cause to feel nausea. **2.** To feel or cause to feel loathing or disgust. See Syns at **disgust.** See Usage Note at **nauseous.** —**nau′se•at′ing•ly** *adv.* —**nau′se•a′tion** *n.*

nau•seous (nô′shəs, -zē-əs) *adj.* **1.** Causing nausea; sickening. **2.** *Usage Problem.* Affected with nausea. —**nau′seous•ly** *adv.*

Usage Note: Traditional critics have insisted that *nauseous* is appropriately used only to mean "causing nausea" and that it is incorrect to use it to mean "affected with nausea," as in *Roller coasters make me nauseous.* In this example *nauseated* is preferred by 72 percent of the Usage Panel.

nautilus
Chambered nautilus
Nautilus pompilius

Nau•sic•a•a (nô-sĭk′ē-ə, -ā-ə, nou-) *n. Gk. Myth.* In the *Odyssey*, a young woman who befriended the stranded Odysseus.

naut. *abbr.* Nautical.

nau•ti•cal (nô′tĭ-kəl) *adj.* Of, relating to, or characteristic of ships, shipping, sailors, or navigation on a body of water. [< Lat. *nauticus* < Gk. *nautikos* < *nautēs*, sailor < *naus*, ship. See **nāu-***.] —**nau′ti•cal•ly** *adv.*

Syns: *nautical, marine, maritime, naval.* The central meaning shared by these adjectives is "of or relating to the sea, ships, shipping, sailors, or navigation": *nautical charts; marine insurance; maritime law; a naval officer.*

nautical mile *n.* A unit of length used in navigation, based on the length of one minute of arc of a great circle, esp. an international and U.S. unit equal to 1,852 meters (about 6,076 feet).

nau•ti•loid (nôt′l-oid′) *n.* A mollusk of the subclass Nautiloidea, which includes the nautiluses and numerous extinct species known only from fossils. [< NLat. *Nautiloidea*, subclass name : Lat. *nautilus*, nautilus; see NAUTILUS + Gk. *-oidēs*, -oid.] —**nau′ti•loid** *adj.*

nau•ti•lus (nôt′l-əs) *n., pl.* **nau•ti•lus•es** or **nau•ti•li** (nôt′l-ī′). **1.** A cephalopod mollusk of the genus *Nautilus*, esp. *N. pompilius*, found in the Indian and Pacific oceans and having a spiral pearly-lined shell with a series of air-filled chambers. **2.** The paper nautilus. [Lat. < Gk. *nautilos*, sailor, nautilus < *nautēs*, mariner < *naus*, ship. See **nāu-***.]

nav. *abbr.* **1.** Naval. **2.** Navigable. **3.** Navigation.

Nav•a•jo also **Nav•a•ho** (năv′ə-hō′, nä′və-) *n., pl.* **Navajo** or **-jos** also **Navaho** or **-hos. 1.** A member of a Native American people inhabiting extensive reservation lands in Arizona, New Mexico, and southeast Utah. **2.** The Apachean language of the Navajo. [Am.Sp. *Navajó*, originally a place name < Tewa *navahū*, large arroyo with cultivated fields.] —**Nav′a•jo′** *adj.*

na•val (nā′vəl) *adj.* **1.** Of or relating to ships or shipping. See Syns at **nautical. 2.** Of or relating to a navy. **3.** Having a navy: *a great naval power.* [ME < OFr. < Lat. *nāvālis* < *nāvis*, ship. See **nāu-***.]

ă pat	oi boy
ā pay	ou out
âr care	o͝o took
ä father	o͞o boot
ĕ pet	ŭ cut
ē be	ûr urge
ĭ pit	th thin
ī pie	*th* this
îr pier	hw which
ŏ pot	zh vision
ō toe	ə about, item
ô paw	

Stress marks:
′ (primary);
′ (secondary), as in
dictionary (dĭk′shə-nĕr′ē)

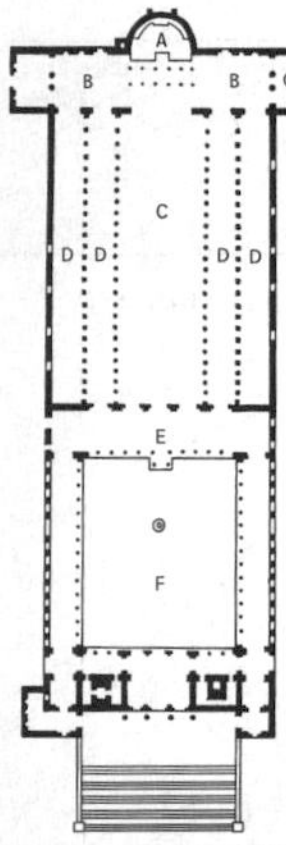

naval architect *n.* One who designs ships.
naval stores *pl.n. Naut.* Products, such as turpentine or pitch, originally used to caulk the seams of wooden ships.
Na•varre (nə-vär′, nä-). A historical region and former kingdom of SW Europe in the Pyrenees of N Spain and SW France. The S part was annexed to Spain (1512–15), and the N part became part of the French crown lands (1589).
nave[1] (nāv) *n.* The central part of a church, extending from the narthex to the chancel and flanked by aisles. [Med.Lat. *nāvis* < Lat., ship (prob. < its shape). See **nāu-***.]
nave[2] (nāv) *n.* The hub of a wheel. [ME < OE *nafu.* See **nobh-***.]
na•vel (nā′vəl) *n.* **1.** The mark on the surface of the abdomen of mammals where the umbilical cord was attached during gestation. **2.** A central point; a middle. [ME < OE *nafela.* See **nobh-***.]
navel orange *n.* A sweet, usu. seedless orange having at its apex a navellike formation enclosing an underdeveloped fruit.
na•vel•wort (nā′vəl-wûrt′, -wôrt′) *n.* **1.** See **pennywort** a. **2.** Any of various Eurasian plants of the genus *Omphalodes,* having one-sided cymes of usu. blue flowers.
na•vic•u•lar (nə-vĭk′yə-lər) *n. Anat.* **1.** A comma-shaped bone of the human wrist, located in the first row of carpals. **2.** A concave bone of the human foot, located between the talus and the metatarsals. *—adj.* Shaped like a boat; scaphoid. [< Lat. *nāvicula,* boat, dim. of *nāvis,* ship. See **nāu-***.]
nav•i•ga•ble (năv′ĭ-gə-bəl) *adj.* Sufficiently deep and wide to provide passage for vessels: *navigable waters.* **—nav′i•ga•bil′i•ty, nav′i•ga•ble•ness** *n.* **—nav′i•ga•bly** *adv.*
nav•i•gate (năv′ĭ-gāt′) *v.* **-gat•ed, -gat•ing, -gates.** *—tr.* **1.** To plan, record, and control the course and position of (a ship or an aircraft). **2.** To follow a planned course on, across, or through: *navigate a stream.* *—intr.* **1.** To control the course of a ship or an aircraft. **2.** To voyage over water in a boat or ship; sail. **3.a.** To make one's way. **b.** *Informal.* To walk. [Lat. *nāvigāre, nāvigāt-* : *nāvis,* ship; see **nāu-*** + *agere,* to drive, lead; see **ag-***.]
nav•i•ga•tion (năv′ĭ-gā′shən) *n.* **1.** The theory and practice of navigating, esp. the charting of a course for a ship or an aircraft. **2.** Travel or traffic by vessels, esp. commercial shipping. **—nav′i•ga′tion•al** *adj.*
nav•i•ga•tor (năv′ĭ-gā′tər) *n.* **1.** One who navigates. **2.** A device that directs the course of an aircraft or a missile.

nave[1]
Plan of fourth-century A.D. Saint Peter's, Rome
A. Apse
B. Transept
C. Nave
D. Aisle
E. Narthex
F. Atrium

Nav•ra•ti•lo•va (năv′rə-tĭ-lō′və, nä′vrə-), **Martina.** b. 1956. Czechoslovakian-born Amer. tennis player who won nine Wimbledon singles championships between 1978 and 1990.
nav•vy (năv′ē) *n., pl.* **-vies.** *Chiefly British.* A laborer, esp. one employed in construction or excavation projects. [Short for NAVIGATOR, canal laborer (obsolete).]
na•vy (nā′vē) *n., pl.* **-vies. 1.** All of a nation's warships. **2.** Often **Navy.** A nation's entire military organization for sea warfare and defense, including vessels, personnel, and shore establishments. **3.** A group of ships; a fleet. **4.** *Color.* Navy blue. [ME < OFr. *navie* < Lat. *nāvigia,* pl. of *nāvigium,* ship < *nāvigāre,* to sail. See NAVIGATE.]
navy bean *n.* Any of several varieties of the kidney bean, cultivated for their edible white seeds. [< its former use as a standard provision of the U.S. Navy.]
navy blue *n. Color.* A dark grayish blue. [< the color of the British naval uniform.]
Navy Cross *n.* A U.S. Navy decoration awarded for exceptional heroism.
navy gray *n. Color.* A dark gray.
navy yard *n.* A dockyard for the construction, repair, equipping, or docking of naval vessels.
na•wab (nə-wŏb′) *n.* See **nabob** 1.
Nax•os or **Náx•os** (năk′sŏs, -sōs, -səs, näk′sôs). An island of the Cyclades in SE Greece in the Aegean Sea; famous in ancient times as a center of Dionysian worship.
nay (nā) *adv.* **1.** No. **2.** And moreover: *He was ill-favored, nay, hideous.* *—n.* **1.** A denial or refusal. **2.** A negative vote or voter. [ME < ON *nei* : *ne,* not; see **ne*** + *ei,* ever; see **aiw-***.]
nay•say (nā′sā′) *tr.v.* **-said** (-sĕd′), **-say•ing, -says** (-sĕz′). To say no to; deny or oppose.
nay•say•er (nā′sā′ər) *n.* **1.** One who is assertively negative in attitude. **2.** One who critically disagrees.
Naz•a•rene (năz′ə-rēn′, năz′ə-rēn′) *n.* **1.a.** A native or inhabitant of Nazareth. **b.** Jesus. **2.** A member of a sect of early Christians of Jewish origin who retained many of the prescribed Jewish observances. **3.** A member of an American Protestant denomination, the Church of the Nazarene, that follows many of the doctrines of early Methodism. *—adj.* Of or relating to Nazareth or its inhabitants. [ME < LLat. *Nazarēnus* < Gk. *Nazarēnos* < *Nazaret,* Nazareth.]
Naz•a•reth (năz′ər-əth). A town of N Israel SE of Haifa; the boyhood home of Jesus. Pop. 46,300.
Na•zi (nät′sē, năt′-) *n., pl.* **-zis. 1.** A member of the National Socialist German Workers' Party, brought to power in Germany in 1933 under Adolf Hitler. **2.** Often **nazi.** An adherent or advocate of Nazi policies; a fascist. *—adj.* Of, relating to, controlled by, or typical of the National Socialist German Workers' Party. [Ger., short for *Nationalsozialistische deutsche Arbeiter-Partei,* National Socialist German Workers' Party.] **—Na′zi•fi•ca′tion** (-sə-fĭ-kā′shən) *n.* **—Na′zi•fy′** (-sə-fī′) *v.*
Na•zism (nät′sĭz′əm, năt′-) also **Na•zi•ism** (-sē-ĭz′əm) *n.* The ideology and practice of the Nazis, esp. the policy of racist nationalism, expansionism, and state control of the economy.
Nb The symbol for the element **niobium.**
NB also **N.B.** *abbr.* New Brunswick.
Nb. *abbr. Bible.* Numbers.
n.b. or **N.B.** *abbr.* Nota bene.
NBA also **N.B.A.** *abbr.* **1.** National Basketball Association. **2.** National Boxing Association.
NbE *abbr.* North by east.
NbW *abbr.* North by west.
NC *abbr.* **1.** No charge. **2.** No credit. **3.** Or **N.C.** North Carolina.
NC-17 (ĕn′sē-sĕv′ən-tēn′) *n.* A movie rating that admits no one under the age of 17. [*N(o) c(hildren under) 17 (admitted).*]
NCAA or **N.C.A.A.** *abbr.* National Collegiate Athletic Association.
NCC *abbr.* National Council of Churches.
NCO or **N.C.O.** *abbr.* Noncommissioned officer.
NCTE *abbr.* National Council of Teachers of English.
NCTM *abbr.* National Council of Teachers of Mathematics.
Nd *abbr.* The symbol for the element **neodymium.**
ND or **N.D.** *abbr.* North Dakota.
n.d. or **N.D.** *abbr.* No date.
N.Dak. *abbr.* North Dakota.
Nde•be•le (ən′də-bĕl′ā) *n., pl.* **Ndebele** or **-les. 1.** A member of a Zulu people of southwest Zimbabwe. **2.** The Nguni language of the Ndebele.
Ndja•me•na or **N'Dja•me•na** (ən-jä′mə-nə). Formerly **Fort-La•my** (fôr-lä-mē′). The cap. of Chad, in the SW part on the Shari R.; founded by the French in 1900. Pop. 303,000.
Ndong•o (ən-dông′gō) *n., pl.* **Ndongo** or **-os.** See **Mbundu** 3.
Ne The symbol for the element **neon** 1.
NE *abbr.* **1.** Nebraska. **2.** Or **N.E.** New England. **3.a.** Northeast. **b.** Northeastern. **4.** Not equal to.
Ne. *abbr. Bible.* Nehemiah.
NEA *abbr.* National Education Association.
Ne•an•der•thal (nē-ăn′dər-thôl′, -tôl′, nā-än′dər-täl′) *n.* **1.** Neanderthal man. **2.** *Slang.* A crude or boorish person. *—adj.* **1.** Of, having to do with, or resembling Neanderthal man. **2.** *Slang.* Crude or boorish. **—Ne•an′der•thal′oid′** (-thô′loid′, -tô′-, -tä′-) *adj.*
Neanderthal man *n.* An extinct species or race of human beings, *Homo neanderthalensis,* living during the late Pleistocene Age in the Old World and associated with Middle Paleolithic tools. [After *Neanderthal,* valley of W Germany.]
ne•an•throp•ic (nē′ən-thrŏp′ĭk) *adj.* Of or relating to members of the extant species *Homo sapiens* as compared with other, now extinct species of *Homo.*
Ne•a•pol•i•tan (nē′ə-pŏl′ĭ-tən) *adj.* Of, belonging to, or characteristic of Naples, Italy. *—n.* A native or resident of Naples, Italy. [ME < Lat. *Neapolitānus* < Gk. *neapolitēs* < *Neapolis,* Naples, Italy.]
Neapolitan ice cream *n.* Ice cream in brick form with layers of different colors and flavors.
neap tide (nēp) *n.* A tide that occurs during the first and third quarters of the moon when the difference between high and low tide is least; the lowest level of high tide. [ME *neep* < OE *nēp(flōd),* neap (tide).]
near (nîr) *adv.* **near•er, near•est. 1.** To, at, or within a short distance or interval in space or time. **2.** Just about; almost; nearly. **3.** With or in a close relationship. *—adj.* **nearer, nearest. 1.** Close in time, space, position, or degree. **2.** Closely related by kinship or association; intimate. See Syns at **close. 3.a.** Nearly occurring but not actually happening. **b.** Just barely avoided. **4.a.** Closely corresponding to or resembling an original. **b.** Closely resembling the genuine article. **5.a.** Closer of two or more: *on the near side.* **b.** Being on the left side of an animal or a vehicle. **c.** Being the animal or vehicle on the left. **6.** Short and direct. **7.** Stingy; parsimonious. *—prep.* Close to. *—v.* **neared, near•ing, nears.** *—tr.* To come close or closer to. *—intr.* To draw near or nearer; approach. [ME *ner* < OE *nēar* < comp. of *nēah,* close, near. See **nēhw-iz***.] **—near′ness** *n.*
near beer *n.* A malt liquor that does not contain enough alcohol to be considered an alcoholic beverage.
near•by (nîr′bī′) *adj.* Located a short distance away; close at hand. See Syns at **close.** *—adv.* Not far away.
Ne•arc•tic (nē-ärk′tĭk, -är′tĭk) *adj.* Of or being the biogeographic region that includes the Arctic and Temperate areas of North America and Greenland. [NE(O)- + ARCTIC.]
Near East (nîr). A region of SW Asia generally thought to include Turkey, Lebanon, Israel, Iraq, Jordan, Saudi Arabia, and the other countries of the Arabian Peninsula. **—Near East′ern** *adj.*
Near Islands. An island group of SW AK in the W Aleutians.
near•ly (nîr′lē) *adv.* **1.** Almost but not quite: *I nearly failed.* **2.** In a close manner; intimately.
near miss *n.* **1.** A narrowly avoided collision. **2.** A missile

strike that is extremely close to but not directly on target.

near point *n.* The nearest point at which an object can be seen distinctly by the eye.

near rhyme *n.* See **off rhyme.**

near•sight•ed (nîr′sī′tĭd) *adj.* Unable to see distant objects clearly; myopic. —**near′sight′ed•ly** *adv.* —**near′sight′ed•ness** *n.*

neat[1] (nēt) *adj.* **neat•er, neat•est. 1.** Orderly and clean; tidy. **2.** Orderly and precise in procedure; systematic. **3.** Marked by ingenuity and skill; adroit. **4.** Not diluted or mixed with other substances: *neat whiskey.* **5.** Left after all deductions; net: *neat profit.* **6.** *Slang.* Wonderful; terrific. [AN *neit,* clear, pure, var. of OFr. *net* < Lat. *nitidus,* elegant, gleaming < *nitēre,* to shine.] —**neat′ly** *adv.* —**neat′ness** *n.*

Syns: *neat, tidy, trim, shipshape.* These adjectives mean marked by good order and cleanliness. *Neat* is the most general: *a neat room; neat hair. Tidy* emphasizes precise arrangement and order: *"When she saw me come in tidy and well dressed, she even smiled"* (Charlotte Brontë). *Trim* stresses especially smart appearance and pleasing proportions: *"A trim little sailboat was dancing out at her moorings"* (Herman Melville). *Shipshape* evokes meticulous order: *"We'll try to make this barn a little more shipshape"* (Rudyard Kipling).

neat[2] (nēt) *n., pl.* **neat.** *Archaic.* A cow or other domestic bovine animal. [ME *net* < OE *nēat.*]

neat•en (nēt′n) *tr.v.* **-ened, -en•ing, -ens.** To put into order; make neat.

neath or **'neath** (nēth) *prep.* Beneath.

neat•herd (nēt′hûrd′) *n. Archaic.* A cowherd.

neat's-foot oil (nēts′fo͝ot′) *n.* A light yellow oil obtained from the feet and shinbones of cattle, used chiefly to dress leather.

neb (nĕb) *n.* **1.a.** A beak of a bird. **b.** A nose; a snout. **2.** A projecting part, esp. a nib. [ME < OE.]

NEB *abbr.* New English Bible.

neb•bish (nĕb′ĭsh) *n.* A person regarded as weak-willed or timid. [Yiddish *nebekh,* poor, unfortunate, of Slav. orig. See **bhag-*.**] —**neb′bish•y** *adj.*

NEbE *abbr.* Northeast by east.

NEbN *abbr.* Northeast by north.

Nebr. *abbr.* Nebraska.

Ne•bras•ka (nə-brăs′kə). A state of the central U.S. in the Great Plains; admitted as the 37th state in 1867. Cap. Lincoln. Pop. 1,584,617.

Ne•bras•kan (nə-brăs′kən) *adj.* **1.** Of or relating to Nebraska. **2.** *Geol.* Of or relating to the first glacial stage of the Pleistocene in North America. —*n.* A Nebraska native or resident.

Neb•u•chad•nez•zar II (nĕb′ə-kəd-nĕz′ər, nĕb′yə-). 630?–562 B.C. King of Babylonia (605–562) who captured (597) and destroyed (586) Jerusalem.

neb•u•la (nĕb′yə-lə) *n., pl.* **-lae** (-lē′) or **-las. 1.** *Astron.* **a.** A diffuse mass of interstellar dust or gas or both, visible as luminous patches or areas of darkness depending on the way the mass absorbs or reflects incident radiation. **b.** See **galaxy** 1a. **2.** *Pathol.* **a.** A cloudy spot on the cornea. **b.** Cloudiness in the urine. **3.** A liquid medication that is sprayed. [ME *nebule,* mist < Lat. *nebula.* See **nebh-*.**] —**neb′u•lar** *adj.*

nebular hypothesis *n.* A theory of the origin of the solar system according to which a rotating nebula cooled and contracted into the planets and the sun.

neb•u•lize (nĕb′yə-līz′) *tr.v.* **-lized, -liz•ing, -liz•es. 1.** To convert (a liquid) to a fine spray; atomize. **2.** To treat with a medicated spray. —**neb′u•li•za′tion** (-lĭ-zā′shən) *n.* —**neb′u•liz′er** *n.*

neb•u•los•i•ty (nĕb′yə-lŏs′ĭ-tē) *n., pl.* **-ties. 1.** The quality or condition of being nebulous. **2.** *Astron.* **a.** A nebula. **b.** A mass of material constituting a nebula.

neb•u•lous (nĕb′yə-ləs) *adj.* **1.** Cloudy, misty, or hazy. **2.** Lacking definite form or limits; vague: *nebulous promises.* **3.** Of, relating to, or characteristic of a nebula. [ME < Lat. *nebulōsus* < *nebula,* cloud. See **nebh-*.**] —**neb′u•lous•ly** *adv.* —**neb′u•lous•ness** *n.*

nec•es•sar•i•ly (nĕs′ĭ-sâr′ə-lē, -sĕr′-) *adv.* Of necessity; inevitably.

nec•es•sar•y (nĕs′ĭ-sĕr′ē) *adj.* **1.** Absolutely essential. See Syns at **indispensable. 2.** Needed to achieve a certain result or effect; requisite. **3.a.** Unavoidably determined by conditions or circumstances; inevitable. **b.** Logically inevitable. **4.** Required by obligation, compulsion, or convention. —*n., pl.* **-ies.** Something indispensable. [ME *necessarie* < OFr. *necessaire* < Lat. *necessārius* < *necesse.* See **ked-*.**]

ne•ces•si•tar•i•an•ism (nə-sĕs′ĭ-târ′ē-ə-nĭz′əm) *n. Philos.* The doctrine holding that events are inevitably determined by preceding causes. —**ne•ces′si•tar′i•an** *adj. & n.*

ne•ces•si•tate (nə-sĕs′ĭ-tāt′) *tr.v.* **-tat•ed, -tat•ing, -tates. 1.** To make necessary or unavoidable. **2.** To require or compel. [Med.Lat. *necessitāre, necessitāt-* < Lat. *necessitās,* necessity. See NECESSITY.] —**ne•ces′si•ta′tion** *n.* —**ne•ces′si•ta′tive** *adj.*

ne•ces•si•tous (nə-sĕs′ĭ-təs) *adj.* **1.** Needy; indigent. **2.** Compelling; urgent. [Fr. *nécessiteux* < OFr., necessary < *necessite,* necessity. See NECESSITY.] —**ne•ces′si•tous•ly** *adv.*

ne•ces•si•ty (nə-sĕs′ĭ-tē) *n., pl.* **-ties. 1.a.** The condition or quality of being necessary. **b.** Something necessary. **2.a.** Something dictated by invariable physical laws. **b.** The force exerted by circumstance. **3.** The state or fact of being in need. **4.** Pressing or urgent need, esp. that arising from poverty. —***idiom.* of necessity.** As an inevitable consequence; necessarily. [ME *necessite* < OFr. < Lat. *necessitās* < *necesse,* necessary. See NECESSARY.]

Ne•chak•o (nə-chăk′ō). A river of central British Columbia, Canada, flowing c. 462 km (287 mi) to the Fraser R.

Nech•es (nĕch′ĭz). A river of E TX flowing c. 669 km (416 mi) to Sabine Lake.

neck (nĕk) *n.* **1.** The part of the body joining the head to the shoulders or trunk. **2.** The part of a garment around or near the neck. **3.** *Anat.* **a.** A narrow or constricted part of a structure, as of a bone, that joins its parts; a cervix. **b.** The part of a tooth between the crown and the root. **4.** A relatively narrow elongation, projection, or connecting part. **5.** *Mus.* The narrow part along which the strings of an instrument extend to the pegs. **6.** *Geol.* Solidified lava filling the vent of an extinct volcano. **7.** The siphon of a bivalve mollusk, such as a clam. **8.** A narrow margin. —*v.* **necked, neck•ing, necks.** —*intr. Informal.* To kiss and caress amorously. —*tr.* To strangle or decapitate (a fowl). [ME *nekke* < OE *hnecca.*]

neck and neck *adv. & adj.* Nip and tuck, as in a race.

Neck•ar (nĕk′ər, -är). A river of SW Germany rising in the Black Forest and flowing c. 337 km (228 mi) to the Rhine R.

neck•band (nĕk′bănd′) *n.* The band around the collar of a garment.

necked (nĕkt) *adj.* Having a neck or neckline of a specified kind. Often used in combination: *a long-necked bird.*

Neck•er (nĕk′ər, nĕ-kĕr′), **Jacques.** 1732–1804. French financier and politician who advocated the formation of the States-General to effect financial reform.

neck•er•chief (nĕk′ər-chĭf, -chēf′) *n.* A kerchief worn around the neck.

neck•ing (nĕk′ĭng) *n.* **1.** *Archit.* A molding between the upper part of a column and the projecting part of the capital. **2.** *Informal.* The act of amorously kissing and caressing.

neck•lace (nĕk′lĭs) *n.* An ornament worn around the neck.

neck•line (nĕk′līn′) *n.* The line formed by the edge of a garment at or near the neck.

neck of the woods *n., pl.* **necks of the woods.** *Informal.* A region; a neighborhood.

neck•piece (nĕk′pēs′) *n.* A scarf, often of fur.

neck•tie (nĕk′tī′) *n.* A narrow fabric band of varying length worn around the neck and tied in a knot or bow close to the throat.

neck•wear (nĕk′wâr′) *n.* Articles, such as neckties, worn around the neck.

necro– or **necr–** *pref.* **1.** Dead body; corpse: *necrophilia.* **2.** Death: *necrobiosis.* [Gk. *nekro-* < *nekros.* See **nek-**[1]***.**]

nec•ro•bi•o•sis (nĕk′rō-bī-ō′sĭs) *n.* The natural death of cells or tissues through aging, as distinguished from necrosis or pathological death. —**nec′ro•bi•ot′ic** (-ŏt′ĭk) *adj.*

ne•crol•o•gy (nə-krŏl′ə-jē, nĕ-) *n., pl.* **-gies. 1.** A list of people who have died, esp. in the recent past or during a specific period. **2.** An obituary. —**nec′ro•log′ic** (nĕk′rə-lŏj′ĭk), **nec′ro•log′i•cal** *adj.* —**ne•crol′o•gist** *n.*

nec•ro•man•cy (nĕk′rə-măn′sē) *n.* **1.** The practice of supposedly communicating with the spirits of the dead in order to predict the future. **2.** Black magic; sorcery. **3.** Magic qualities. [Ult. < LLat. *necromantia* < Gk. *nekromanteia* : *nekros,* corpse; see **nek-**[1]***** + *manteia,* divination; see -MANCY.] —**nec′ro•man′cer** *n.* —**nec′ro•man′tic** (-măn′tĭk) *adj.*

nec•ro•pha•gia (nĕk′rə-fā′jə) *n.* The act or practice of feeding on dead bodies or carrion.

ne•croph•a•gous (nə-krŏf′ə-gəs, nĕ-) *adj.* Feeding on carrion or corpses: *necrophagous organisms.*

nec•ro•phil•i•a (nĕk′rə-fĭl′ē-ə) also **nec•roph′i•lism** (nĭ-krŏf′ə-lĭz′əm, nĕ-) *n.* **1.** Obsessive fascination with death and corpses. **2.** Erotic attraction to or sexual contact with corpses. —**nec′ro•phil′i•ac′** (-ē-ăk′) *adj. & n.* —**nec′ro•phile′** (-fīl′) *n.* —**nec′ro•phil′ic** (-fĭl′ĭk) *adj.*

nec•ro•pho•bi•a (nĕk′rə-fō′bē-ə) *n.* An abnormal fear of death or corpses. —**nec′ro•pho′bic** *adj.*

ne•crop•o•lis (nə-krŏp′ə-lĭs, nĕ-) *n., pl.* **-lis•es** or **-leis** (-lās′). A cemetery, esp. a large and elaborate one belonging to an ancient city. [Gk. *nekropolis* : *nekro-,* necro- + *polis,* city; see **pelə-**[3]***.**]

nec•rop•sy (nĕk′rŏp′sē) *n., pl.* **-sies.** See **autopsy** 1. —**nec′rop′sy** *v.*

ne•crose (nĕ-krōs′, -krōz′, nĕk′rōs′, -rōz′) *intr. & tr.v.* **-crosed, -cros•ing, -cros•es.** To undergo or cause to undergo necrosis. [Back-formation < NECROSIS.]

ne•cro•sis (nə-krō′sĭs, nĕ-) *n., pl.* **-ses** (-sēz′). Death of cells or tissues through injury or disease, esp. in a localized area of the body. [LLat. *necrōsis,* a causing to die, killing < Gk. *nekrōsis,* death < *nekroun,* to make dead < *nekros,* corpse. See **nek-**[1]***.**] —**ne•crot′ic** (-krŏt′ĭk) *adj.*

nec•ro•tize (nĕk′rə-tīz′) *intr. & tr.v.* **-tized, -tiz•ing, -tiz•es.** To undergo necrosis or cause to necrose.

ne•crot•o•my (nĭ-krŏt′ə-mē, nĕ-) *n., pl.* **-mies. 1.** Surgical

nebula
Lagoon nebula in Sagittarius

neckerchief

ă pat	oi boy
ā pay	ou out
âr care	o͝o took
ä father	o͞o boot
ĕ pet	ŭ cut
ē be	ûr urge
ĭ pit	th thin
ī pie	*th* this
îr pier	hw which
ŏ pot	zh vision
ō toe	ə about, item
ô paw	

Stress marks:
′ (primary);
′ (secondary), as in dictionary (dĭk′shə-nĕr′ē)

excision of dead tissue. **2.** Dissection of a dead body.

nec•tar (nĕk′tər) *n.* **1.** A sweet liquid secreted by flowers of various plants, consumed by pollinators, such as hummingbirds, and gathered by bees for making honey. **2.** *Gk. & Rom. Myth.* The drink of the gods. **3.** A delicious or invigorating drink. [Lat. < Gk. *nektar*. See **nek-1***.] **—nec′tar•ous** *adj.*

nec•tar•ine (nĕk′tə-rēn′) *n.* A variety of aromatic peach of ancient origin, having a smooth waxy skin. [< obsolete *nectarine*, sweet as nectar < NECTAR.]

nec•ta•ry (nĕk′tə-rē) *n., pl.* **-ries.** A glandlike organ, located outside or within a flower, that secretes nectar. [NLat. *nectārium* < NECTAR.] **—nec•tar′i•al** (-târ′ē-əl) *adj.*

Ne•der•land (nē′dər-lănd′). A city of SE TX near Port Arthur; founded by Dutch settlers. Pop. 16,192.

née also **nee** (nā) *adj.* **1.** Born. Used to indicate the maiden name of a married woman. **2.** *Usage Problem.* Formerly known as. [Fr., fem. p.part. of *naître*, to be born < OFr. *naistre* < Lat. *nāscī*. See **genə-***.]

Usage Note: The traditional conventions of address dictate that *née* or *nee* be followed only by a family name: *Mrs. Mary Parks, née Case,* not *née Mary Case.*

need (nēd) *n.* **1.** A lack of something required or desirable. See Syns at **lack. 2.** Something required or wanted; a requisite. **3.** Necessity; obligation. **4.** A condition of poverty or misfortune. *—v.* **need•ed, need•ing, needs.** *—aux.* To be under the necessity of or the obligation to: *They need not come.* *—tr.* To have need of; require. *—intr.* **1.** To be in need or want. **2.** To be necessary. [ME *nede* < OE *nēod, nēd*, distress, necessity.]

need•ful (nēd′fəl) *adj.* Necessary; required. See Syns at **indispensable. —need′ful•ly** *adv.* **—need′ful•ness** *n.*

Need•ham (nē′dəm). A town of E MA, a suburb of Boston. Pop. 27,557.

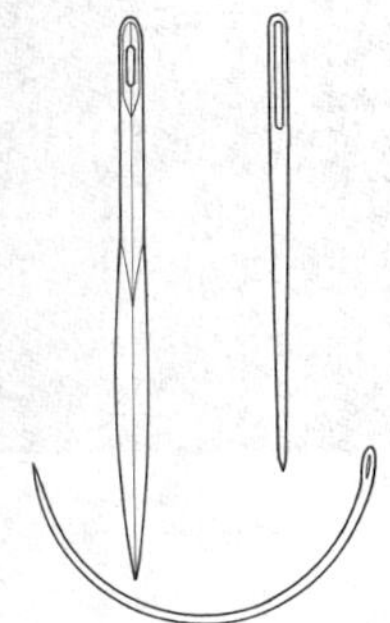

needle
Sailmaking needle (*top left*), tapestry needle (*top right*), and curved embroidery needle (*bottom*)

nee•dle (nēd′l) *n.* **1.a.** A small slender implement used for sewing or surgical suturing, made usu. of polished steel and having an eye at one end through which thread is passed and held. **b.** Any one of various other implements, such as one used in knitting or crocheting. **2.** A small pointed stylus used to transmit vibrations from the grooves of a phonograph record. **3.a.** A slender pointer or indicator on a dial, scale, or similar part of a mechanical device. **b.** A magnetic needle. **4.a.** A hypodermic needle. **b.** *Informal.* A hypodermic injection; a shot. **5.** A narrow stiff leaf, as those of conifers. **6.** A fine sharp projection, as a spine of a sea urchin. **7.** A sharp-pointed instrument used in engraving. **8.** *Informal.* A goading, provoking, or teasing remark or act. *—v.* **-dled, -dling, -dles.** *—tr.* **1.** To prick, pierce, or stitch with a needle. **2.** *Informal.* To goad, provoke, or tease. **3.** *Slang.* To increase the alcoholic content of (a beverage). *—intr.* To sew or do similar work with a needle. [ME *nedle* < OE *nǣdl*. See **(s)nē-***.] **—nee′dler** *n.*

needlepoint

nee•dle•craft (nēd′l-krăft′) *n.* The art or process of needlework.

nee•dle•fish (nēd′l-fĭsh′) *n., pl.* **needlefish** or **-fish•es. 1.** Any of several marine fishes of the family Belonidae, having slender bodies, needlelike teeth, and narrow jaws. **2.** Any of various other fishes, such as the pipefish, having projecting jaws.

nee•dle•point (nēd′l-point′) *n.* **1.** Decorative needlework on canvas, usu. in a diagonal stitch covering the entire surface of the material. **2.** A type of lace worked on paper patterns with a needle. **—nee′dle•point′** *v.*

need•less (nēd′lĭs) *adj.* Not needed or wished for; unnecessary. **—need′less•ly** *adv.* **—need′less•ness** *n.*

needle valve *n.* A valve having a slender point fitting into a conical seat, used to regulate fluid flow accurately.

nee•dle•work (nēd′l-wûrk′) *n.* Work, such as sewing or embroidery, done with a needle.

need•n't (nēd′nt). Need not.

needs (nēdz) *adv.* Of necessity; necessarily: *We must needs go.* [ME *nedes* < *nede* < OE *nēde*, genitive of *nēd*, necessity. See NEED.]

need•y (nē′dē) *adj.* **-i•er, -i•est.** Being in need; impoverished. See Syns at **poor. —need′i•ness** *n.*

Né•el (nā-ĕl′), **Louis Eugène Félix.** b. 1904. French physicist who shared a 1970 Nobel Prize.

neem (nēm) *n.* A tall, usu. evergreen East Indian tree *(Azadirachta indica)* that is widely cultivated in tropical Asia for its timber, resin, bitter bark, and aromatic seed oil. [Hindi *nīm* < Skt. *nimbaḥ*.]

Nee•nah (nē′nə). A city of E WI on Lake Winnebago NNE of Oshkosh; settled c. 1840. Pop. 23,219.

ne'er (nâr) *adv.* Never.

ne'er-do-well (nâr′do͞o-wĕl′) *n.* An idle irresponsible person. **—ne'er′-do-well′** *adj.*

ne•far•i•ous (nə-fâr′ē-əs) *adj.* Infamous by way of being extremely wicked. [< Lat. *nefārius* < *nefās*, crime, transgression : *ne-*, not; see **ne*** + *fās*, divine law; see **dhē-***.] **—ne•far′i•ous•ly** *adv.* **—ne•far′i•ous•ness** *n.*

Nef•er•ti•ti (nĕf′ər-tē′tē). 14th cent. B.C. Queen of Egypt as the wife of Akhenaton.

Ne•fud (nĕ-fo͞od′) also **Na•fud** (nă-). A desert region of N Saudi Arabia; noted for its red sand and violent winds.

neg. *abbr.* Negative.

ne•gate (nĭ-gāt′) *tr.v.* **-gat•ed, -gat•ing, -gates. 1.** To make ineffective or invalid; nullify. **2.** To rule out; deny. **3.** *Comp. Sci.* To perform the machine logic operation NOT gate. [Lat. *negāre, negāt-*, to deny. See **ne***.] **—ne•ga′tor, ne•gat′er** *n.*

ne•ga•tion (nĭ-gā′shən) *n.* **1.** The act or process of negating. **2.** A denial, contradiction, or negative statement. **3.** The opposite or absence of something regarded as actual, positive, or affirmative. **—ne•ga′tion•al** *adj.*

neg•a•tive (nĕg′ə-tĭv) *adj.* **1.a.** Expressing, containing, or consisting of a negation, refusal, or denial. **b.** Indicating opposition or resistance. **2.** Having no positive features. **3.** Marked by or exhibiting features, such as hostility, that cannot be deemed positive or constructive. **4.** *Medic.* Not indicating the presence of microorganisms, disease, or a specific condition. **5.** *Logic.* Being a proposition that denies agreement between a subject and its predicate. **6.** *Math.* **a.** Relating to or being a quantity less than zero. **b.** Relating to or being the sign (−). **c.** Relating to or being a quantity to be subtracted. **d.** Relating to or being a quantity, a number, an angle, a velocity, or a direction in a sense opposite to another indicated or understood to be positive. **7.** *Phys.* **a.** Relating to or being an electric charge of the same sign as that of an electron, symbolized by (−). **b.** Relating to or being a body having an excess of electrons. **8.** *Chem.* Of or being an ion that is attracted to a positive electrode. **9.** *Biol.* Moving or turning away from a stimulus, such as light. *—n.* **1.** A statement or an act indicating or expressing a contradiction, denial, or refusal. See Usage Note at **affirmative. 2.a.** A statement or an act that is highly critical of another or of others. **b.** Something that lacks all positive, affirmative, or encouraging features. **c.** A feature or characteristic that is not deemed positive, affirmative, or desirable. **3.** *Gram.* A word or part of a word, such as *no, not,* or *non-*, that indicates negation. See Usage Note at **double negative. 4.** The side in a debate that contradicts or opposes the question being debated. **5.a.** An image in which the light areas of the object rendered appear dark and the dark areas appear light. **b.** A film, plate, or other photographic material containing such an image. **6.** *Math.* A negative quantity. *—tr.v.* **-tived, -tiv•ing, -tives. 1.** To refuse to approve; veto. **2.** To deny; contradict. **3.** To demonstrate to be false; disprove. **4.** To counteract or neutralize. [ME < OFr. *negatif* < Lat. *negātīvus* < *negātus*, p.part. of *negāre*, to deny. See NEGATE.] **—neg′a•tive•ly** *adv.* **—neg′a•tive•ness, neg′a•tiv′i•ty** (-tĭv′ĭ-tē) *n.*

negative feedback *n.* Feedback that reduces the output of a system, as the action of heat on a thermostat to limit the output of a furnace.

negative transfer *n.* The interference of previous learning in the process of learning something new.

neg•a•tiv•ism (nĕg′ə-tĭ-vĭz′əm) *n.* **1.** A habitual attitude of skepticism or resistance to the suggestions, orders, or instructions of others. **2.** Behavior characterized by persistent refusal, without apparent or logical reasons, to act on or carry out suggestions, orders, or instructions of others. **—neg′a•tiv•ist** *n.* **—neg′a•tiv•is′tic** *adj.*

neg•a•tron (nĕg′ə-trŏn′) *n.* An electron with a negative charge, as contrasted with a positron.

Ne•gev (nĕg′ĕv) also **Ne•geb** (-ĕb). A desert region of S Israel; assigned to Israel after the partition of Palestine in 1948.

ne•glect (nĭ-glĕkt′) *tr.v.* **-glect•ed, -glect•ing, -glects. 1.** To pay little or no attention to; fail to heed; disregard. **2.** To fail to care for or attend to properly. **3.** To fail to do or carry out, as through carelessness or oversight: *neglected to return the call.* *—n.* **1.** The act or an instance of neglecting something. **2.** The state of being neglected. **3.** Habitual lack of care. [Lat. *neglegere, neglēct-* : *neg-*, not; see **ne*** + *legere*, to choose, pick up; see **leg-***.] **—ne•glect′er** *n.*

ne•glect•ful (nĭ-glĕkt′fəl) *adj.* Characterized by neglect; heedless. **—ne•glect′ful•ly** *adv.* **—ne•glect′ful•ness** *n.*

neg•li•gee also **neg•li•gée** or **neg•li•gé** (nĕg′lĭ-zhā′, nĕg′lĭ-zhā′) *n.* **1.** A woman's loose dressing gown, often of soft delicate fabric. **2.** Informal or incomplete attire. [Fr. *négligée* < fem. p.part. of *négliger*, to neglect < Lat. *neglegere*. See NEGLECT.]

neg•li•gence (nĕg′lĭ-jəns) *n.* **1.** The state or quality of being negligent. **2.** A negligent act or a failure to act. **3.** *Law.* Failure to exercise the degree of care considered reasonable under the circumstances, resulting in an unintended injury to another party.

neg•li•gent (nĕg′lĭ-jənt) *adj.* **1.** Characterized by or inclined to neglect, esp. habitually. **2.** Characterized by careless ease or informality; casual. **3.** *Law.* Guilty of negligence. [ME < OFr. < Lat. *neglegēns, neglegent-*, pr.part. of *neglegere*, to neglect. See NEGLECT.] **—neg′li•gent•ly** *adv.*

neg•li•gi•ble (nĕg′lĭ-jə-bəl) *adj.* Not significant or important enough to be worth considering; trifling. [NEGLIG(ENT) + -IBLE.] **—neg′li•gi•bil′i•ty, neg′li•gi•ble•ness** *n.* **—neg′li•gi•bly** *adv.*

ne•go•tia•ble (nĭ-gō′shə-bəl, -shē-ə-) *adj.* **1.** Easy or possible to negotiate or be negotiated. **2.** Transferable from one person to another by delivery or by delivery and endorsement. **—ne·go′tia·bil′i·ty** *n.* **—ne·go′tia·bly** *adv.*

ne·go·ti·ate (nĭ-gō′shē-āt′) *v.* **-at·ed, -at·ing, -ates.** *—intr.* To confer with another or others in order to come to terms or reach an agreement. *—tr.* **1.** To arrange or settle by discussion and mutual agreement. **2.a.** To transfer title to or ownership of (a promissory note, for example) to another party by delivery or by delivery and endorsement in return for value received. **b.** To sell or discount (securities, for example). **3.a.** To succeed in going over or coping with. **b.** To succeed in accomplishing or managing. [Lat. *negōtiārī, negōtiāt-*, to transact business < *negōtium*, business : *neg-*, not; see **ne*** + *ōtium*, leisure.] **—ne·go′ti·a′tor** *n.* **—ne·go′tia·to′ry** (-shə-tôr′ē, -tōr′ē, -shē-ə-) *adj.*

ne·go·ti·a·tion (nĭ-gō′shē-ā′shən) *n.* The act or process of negotiating: *successful negotiation of a contract.*

Ne·gress (nē′grĭs) *n. Offensive.* A Black woman or girl.

Usage Note: The word *Negress* is now widely regarded as offensive, since it seems to imply that Black women constitute a distinct racial category. Where reference to gender is relevant, the phrase *Black* (or *African-American* or *Afro-American*) *woman* should be used.

Ne·gri·to (nĭ-grē′tō) *n., pl.* **-tos** or **-toes.** A member of any of various peoples of short stature inhabiting parts of Malaysia, the Philippines, and southeast Asia. [Sp., dim. of *negro*, Black person. See NEGRO.]

ne·gri·tude or **Ne·gri·tude** (nē′grĭ-to͞od′, -tyo͞od′, nĕg′rĭ-) *n.* An aesthetic and ideological concept affirming the independent nature, quality, and validity of Black culture. [Fr. *négritude* < *nègre*, Black person < Sp. *negro*. See NEGRO.]

Ne·gro (nē′grō) *n., pl.* **-groes. 1.** A member of the Negroid racial classification. **2.** A person of Negro descent. See Usage Note at **black.** [Sp. and Port. *negro*, black, Black person < Lat. *niger, nigr-*, black.] **—Ne′gro** *adj.*

Ne·gro (nā′grō, nĕ′grō, -gro͞o), **Río. 1.** A river rising in central Argentina and flowing c. 644 km (400 mi) to the Atlantic. **2.** A river rising in S Brazil and flowing c. 805 km (500 mi) to the Uruguay R. in central Uruguay. **3.** A river of NW South America flowing c. 2,253 km (1,400 mi) from E Colombia to the Amazon R. near Manaus, Brazil.

Ne·groid (nē′groid′) *Anthro.* *—adj.* Of, relating to, or being a purported human racial classification distinguished by physical characteristics such as brown to black pigmentation and often tightly curled hair and including peoples indigenous to sub-Saharan Africa. No longer in scientific use. *—n.* A member of this racial classification. No longer in scientific use. [NEGR(O) + -OID.]

Ne·gro·phile (nē′grə-fīl′) *n.* One who admires and supports Black people and their culture. **—ne′gro·phil′ism** (nē′grə-fĭ′lĭz′əm, nĭ-grŏf′ə-) *n.*

Ne·gro·phobe (nē′grə-fōb′) *n.* One who fears or dislikes Black people. **—Ne′gro·pho′bi·a** (-fō′bē-ə) *n.*

Ne·gros (nā′grōs, nĕ′grôs). An island of the central Philippines in the Visayan Is. between Panay and Cebu.

ne·gus (nē′gəs) *n.* A beverage made of wine, hot water, lemon juice, sugar, and nutmeg. [After Francis *Negus* (d. 1732), English army officer.]

Ne·gus (nē′gəs, nĭ-go͞os′) *n.* Used formerly as a title for emperors of Ethiopia. [Amharic *negūs* < Ethiopic *nĕgūsā*, king of kings.]

Neh. *abbr. Bible.* Nehemiah.

Ne·he·mi·ah (nē′hə-mī′ə, nē′ə-) *n. Bible.* **1.** A Jewish leader in the 5th cent. B.C. **2.** See table at **Bible.**

Neh·ru (nā′ro͞o), Pandit **Motilal.** 1861–1931. Indian nationalist politician who was an influential leader in the years leading to India's independence. His son **Jawaharlal Nehru** (1889–1964) was the first prime minister of independent India (1947–64).

neigh (nā) *n.* The long high-pitched sound made by a horse. *—intr.v.* **neighed, neigh·ing, neighs.** To utter a neigh. [< ME *neighen*, to neigh < OE *hnǣgan*, prob. of imit. orig.]

neigh·bor (nā′bər) *n.* **1.** One who lives near or next to another. **2.** A person, place, or thing adjacent to or located near another. **3.** A fellow human being. **4.** Used as a form of familiar address. *—v.* **-bored, -bor·ing, -bors.** *—tr.* To lie close to or border directly on. *—intr.* To live or be situated close by. *—adj.* Situated or living near another. [ME *neighebor* < OE *nēahgebūr* : *nēah*, near; see **nēhw-iz*** + *gebūr*, dweller; see **bheuə-*.**]

neigh·bor·hood (nā′bər-ho͝od′) *n.* **1.** A district or an area with distinctive characteristics. **2.** The people who live near one another or in a particular district or area. **3.** The surrounding area; vicinity. **4.** *Informal.* Approximate amount or range: *in the neighborhood of five million dollars.* **5.** Friendliness appropriate to a neighbor. **6.** *Math.* The set of points surrounding a specified point, each of which is within a certain, usu. small distance from the specified point.

neigh·bor·ly (nā′bər-lē) *adj.* Having or exhibiting the qualities of a friendly neighbor. **—neigh′bor·li·ness** *n.*

neigh·bour (nā′bər) *n., v., & adj. Chiefly British.* Var. of **neighbor.**

Nei Mong·gol (nā′ mŏn′gōl′, mŏng′-) also **In·ner Mon·go·li·a** (ĭn′ər mŏng-gō′lē-ə, -gōl′yə, mŏn-). An autonomous region of NE China; became an integral part of China in 1911. Cap. Hohhot. Pop. 20,070,000.

Neis·se (nī′sə). A river rising in N Czech Republic and flowing c. 225 km (140 mi) to the Oder R.

nei·ther (nē′*th*ər, nī′-) *adj.* Not one or the other; not either: *Neither shoe feels comfortable.* *—pron.* Not either one; not the one or the other: *Neither of the twins is here.* *—conj.* **1.** Not either; not in either case. Used with the correlative conjunction *nor*: *I got neither the gift nor the card.* **2.** Also not: *If he won't go, neither will she.* *—adv.* Similarly not; also not: *Just as you would not, so neither would they.* [ME < OE *nāwther, nāhwæther* (influenced by *æghwæther, ægther*, either; see EITHER) : *nā*, not; see **ne*** + *hwæther*, which of two; see **kʷo-*.**]

Usage Note: According to the traditional rule, *neither* is used only to mean "not one or the other of two." To refer to "none of several," *none* is preferred: *None* (not *neither*) *of the three opposition candidates would make a better president than the incumbent.* • The traditional rule also holds that *neither* is grammatically singular: *Neither candidate is having an easy time with the press.* However, it is often used with a plural verb, especially when followed by *of* and a plural: *Neither of the candidates are really expressing their own views.* • As a conjunction *neither* is properly followed by *nor*, not *or*, in formal style: *Neither prayers nor curses did any good.* See Usage Notes at **either, every, he[1], none, nor[1], or[1].**

Nei·va (nā′və, -vä). A city of S-central Colombia on the Magdalena R. SSW of Bogotá. Pop. 179,609.

Nejd (nĕjd) also **Najd** (năjd). A vast plateau region of the central Arabian Peninsula; nucleus of modern Saudi Arabia.

nek·ton (nĕk′tən, -tŏn′) *n.* The collection of marine and freshwater organisms that can swim freely, ranging in size from microscopic organisms to whales. [Gk. *nēkton*, neut. of *nēktos*, swimming < *nēkhein*, to swim. See **snā-*.**]

nel·son (nĕl′sən) *n. Sports.* Any of several wrestling holds in which the user places an arm under the opponent's upper arm or armpit and presses the wrist or the palm of the hand against the back of the opponent's neck. [Perh. < the name *Nelson*.]

Nel·son (nĕl′sən), **Horatio.** Viscount Nelson. 1758–1805. British admiral who defeated the French and Spanish naval forces at Trafalgar (1805).

Nelson, Samuel. 1792–1873. Amer. jurist; associate justice of the U.S. Supreme Court (1845–72).

Nelson River. A river of Manitoba, Canada, flowing c. 644 km (400 mi) from Lake Winnipeg to Hudson Bay.

Nem·an (nĕm′ən, nyĕ′mən) also **Nie·men** (nē′mən, nyĕ′-). A river of W Belorussia flowing c. 933 km (580 mi) through Lithuania to the Baltic Sea.

nemato– or **nemat–** *pref.* Thread; threadlike: *nematocyst.* [NLat. *nēmato-* < Gk. *nēma, nēmat-*, thread. See **(s)nē-*.**]

nem·a·to·cide also **nem·a·ti·cide** (nĕm′ə-tĭ-sīd′, nə-măt′-ĭ-) *n.* A substance or preparation used to kill nematodes. **—nem′a·to·cid·al** (-sīd′l) *adj.*

nem·a·to·cyst (nĕm′ə-tə-sĭst′, nĭ-măt′ə-) *n.* A capsule within certain coelenterates, such as jellyfish, containing a barbed threadlike tube that delivers a paralyzing sting.

nem·a·tode (nĕm′ə-tōd′) *n.* Any of several worms of the phylum Nematoda, having unsegmented cylindrical bodies and including parasitic forms such as the hookworm. [< NLat. *Nēmatoda*, phylum name : NEMATO- + NLat. *-ōda* (alteration of Gk. *-oeidēs*, -oid).] **—nem′a·tode′** *adj.*

nem·a·tol·o·gy (nĕm′ə-tŏl′ə-jē) *n.* The branch of zoology that deals with nematodes. **—nem′a·tol′o·gist** *n.*

Nem·bu·tal (nĕm′byə-tôl′). A trademark used for the sedative pentobarbital sodium.

Ne·me·a (nē′mē-ə). A valley of N Argolis in ancient Greece; site of Nemean games after 573 B.C. **—Ne′me·an** *adj. & n.*

ne·mer·te·an (nĭ-mûr′tē-ən) also **nem·er·tine** (nĕm′ər-tīn′) *n.* Any of several velvety, usu. brightly colored worms of the phylum Nemertina (or Nemertea) that have a flat unsegmented body with an extensible proboscis and live in the sea or in the mud of the intertidal zone. [< NLat. *Nēmertēs*, type genus < Gk., name of a Nereid.] **—ne·mer′te·an** *adj.*

nem·e·sis (nĕm′ĭ-sĭs) *n., pl.* **-ses** (-sēz′). **1.** A source of harm or ruin. **2.** Retributive justice in its execution or outcome. **3.** An opponent that cannot be beaten or overcome. **4.** One that inflicts retribution or vengeance. **5. Nemesis.** *Gk. Myth.* The goddess of retributive justice or vengeance. [Gk., retribution, the goddess Nemesis < *nemein*, to allot. See **nem-*.**]

ne·ne (nā′nā) *n.* A rare wild goose *(Branta sandvicensis)* of the Hawaiian Islands having a grayish-brown body with a black face. [Hawaiian *nēnē*.]

Nen·ets (nĕn′ĕts) *n., pl.* **Nenets. 1.** A member of a reindeer-herding people of north-central Russia. **2.** The Uralic language of this people. [Nenets, human being, Nenets.]

Nen Jiang (nŭn′ jyäng′) also **Nen Chiang** (chyäng′). A river of NE China flowing c. 1,191 km (740 mi) to the Songhua Jiang.

neo– *pref.* **1.** New; recent: *Neolithic.* **2.a.** New and different: *neoimpressionism.* **b.** New and abnormal: *neoplasm.* **3.** New World: *Neotropical.* [Gk. < *neos*, new. See **newo-*.**]

Nefertiti
XVIII Dynasty limestone bust

nene
Branta sandvicensis

ă pat	oi boy
ā pay	ou out
âr care	o͝o took
ä father	o͞o boot
ĕ pet	ŭ cut
ē be	ûr urge
ĭ pit	th thin
ī pie	*th* this
îr pier	hw which
ŏ pot	zh vision
ō toe	ə about, item
ô paw	

Stress marks:
′ (primary);
′ (secondary), as in
dictionary (dĭk′shə-nĕr′ē)

ne•o•clas•si•cism also **Ne•o•clas•si•cism** (nē′ō-klăs′ĭ-sĭz′-əm) *n.* A revival of classical aesthetics and forms, esp.: **a.** A revival in literature in the late 17th and 18th centuries characterized by a regard for the classical ideas of reason, form and restraint. **b.** A revival in the 18th and 19th centuries in architecture and art, esp. in the decorative arts, characterized by order, symmetry, and simplicity of style. **c.** A movement in music in the late 19th and early 20th centuries that sought to avoid subjective emotionalism and to return to the style of the pre-Romantic composers. **—ne′o•clas′sic, ne′-o•clas′si•cal** *adj.*

ne•o•co•lo•ni•al•ism (nē′ō-kə-lō′nē-ə-lĭz′əm) *n.* A policy whereby a major power uses economic and political means to perpetuate or extend its influence over underdeveloped nations or areas. **—ne′o•co•lo′ni•al** *adj.* **—ne′o•co•lo′ni•al•ist** *n.*

ne•o•con•ser•va•tism also **ne•o-con•ser•va•tism** (nē′ō-kən-sûr′və-tĭz′əm) *n.* An intellectual and political movement in favor of political, economic, and social conservatism that arose in opposition to the perceived liberalism of the 1960's. **—ne′o•con•ser′va•tive** *adj. & n.*

ne•o•cor•tex (nē′ō-kôr′tĕks′) *n., pl.* **-ti•ces** (-tĭ-sēz′) or **-tex•es.** The dorsal region of the cerebral cortex, esp. large in higher mammals and the most recently evolved part of the brain. **—ne′o•cor′ti•cal** (-tĭ-kəl) *adj.*

Ne•o-Dar•win•ism (nē′ō-där′wə-nĭz′əm) *n.* Darwinism as modified by the findings of modern genetics. **—Ne′o-Dar•win′i•an** (-där-wĭn′ē-ən) *adj.* **—Ne′o-Dar′win•ist** *n.*

ne•o•dym•i•um (nē′ō-dĭm′ē-əm) *n. Symbol* **Nd** A rare-earth element found in monazite and bastnaesite and used for coloring glass and doping some glass lasers. Atomic number 60; atomic weight 144.24; melting point 1,024°C; boiling point 3,027°C; specific gravity 6.80 or 7.004 (depending on allotropic form); valence 3. See table at **element.** [NEO– + (DI)-DYMIUM.]

neoclassicism West Building of the National Gallery of Art in Washington DC, designed by John Russell Pope (1874–1937)

ne•o•fas•cism (nē′ō-făsh′ĭz′əm) *n.* A fringe movement inspired by the tenets and methods of fascism or Nazism. **—ne′o•fas′cist** *adj. & n.*

Ne•o-Freud•i•an (nē′ō-froi′dē-ən) *adj.* Of, relating to, or characterizing any psychoanalytic system based on but modifying Freudian doctrine by emphasizing social factors, interpersonal relations, or other cultural influences in personality development or causation of the neuroses. **—Ne′o-Freud′i•an** *n.*

Ne•o•gae•a also **Ne•o•ge•a** (nē′ə-jē′ə) *n.* A region that is coextensive with the Neotropical region and is considered one of the primary biogeographic realms. [NLat. : NEO– + Gk. *gaia*, earth.] **—Ne′o•gae′an** *adj.*

ne•o•gen•e•sis (nē′ō-jĕn′ĭ-sĭs) *n.* **1.** *Biol.* Regeneration of tissue. **2.** *Mineral.* The formation of new minerals. **—ne′o•ge•net′ic** (-jə-nĕt′ĭk) *adj.*

ne•o•im•pres•sion•ism or **ne•o-im•pres•sion•ism** (nē′ō-ĭm-prĕsh′ə-nĭz′əm) *n.* A movement in late 19th-century painting led by Georges Seurat that was stricter and more formal than impressionism in composition and employed pointillism. **—ne′o•im•pres′sion•ist** *adj. & n.*

ne•o•lib•er•al•ism (nē′ō-lĭb′ər-ə-lĭz′əm, -lĭb′rə-) *n.* A political movement beginning in the 1960's that blends traditional liberal concerns for social justice with an emphasis on economic growth. **—ne′o•lib′er•al** *adj. & n.*

ne•o•lith (nē′ə-lĭth′) *n.* A stone implement of the Neolithic Period. [Back-formation < NEOLITHIC.]

Ne•o•lith•ic (nē′ə-lĭth′ĭk) *adj. Archaeol.* Of or relating to the cultural period beginning around 10,000 B.C. in the Middle East and later elsewhere and marked by the development of agriculture and the making of polished stone implements.

ne•ol•o•gism (nē-ŏl′ə-jĭz′əm) *n.* **1.** A new word, expression, or usage. **2.** The creation or use of new words or senses. **3.** *Psychiat.* A meaningless word used by a psychotic. **4.** A new doctrine or interpretation of scripture. **—ne•ol′o•gist** *n.* **—ne•ol′o•gis′tic, ne•ol′o•gis′ti•cal** *adj.*

ne•ol•o•gize (nē-ŏl′ə-jīz′) *intr.v.* **-gized, -giz•ing, -giz•es.** To coin or use neologisms.

ne•ol•o•gy (nē-ŏl′ə-jē) *n., pl.* **-gies.** Neologism. **—ne′o•log′i•cal** (nē′ə-lŏj′ĭ-kəl) *adj.* **—ne′o•log′i•cal•ly** *adv.*

Ne•o-Mal•thu•sian•ism (nē′ō-măl-thōō′zhə-nĭz′əm, -môl-) *n.* A doctrine advocating control of population growth. **—Ne′o-Mal•thu′sian** *adj. & n.*

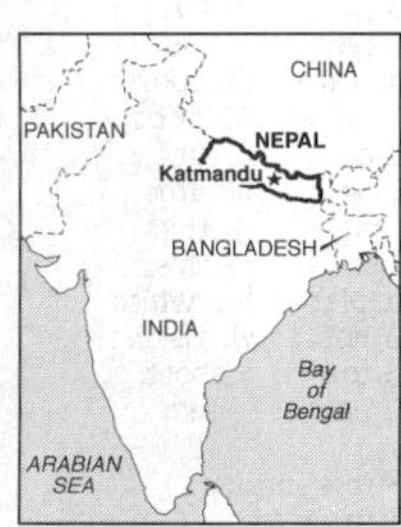

Nepal

ne•o•my•cin (nē′ə-mī′sĭn) *n.* A broad-spectrum antibiotic produced from strains of the actinomycete *Streptomyces fradiae* and used esp. in the form of its sulfate.

ne•on (nē′ŏn′) *n.* **1.** *Symbol* **Ne** A rare inert colorless gaseous element that occurs in air, glows reddish orange in an electric discharge, and is used in display and television tubes. Atomic number 10; atomic weight 20.183; melting point −248.67°C; boiling point −245.95°C. See table at **element. 2.** Neon tetra. [Gk., neut. of *neos*, new. See **newo-*.**]

ne•o•na•tal (nē′ō-nāt′l) *adj.* Of or relating to newborn infants or an infant. **—ne′o•na′tal•ly** *adv.*

ne•o•nate (nē′ə-nāt′) *n.* A newborn infant, esp. one less than four weeks old. [NEO– + Lat. *nātus*, p.part. of *nāscī*, to be born; see **genə-*.**]

ne•o•na•tol•o•gy (nē′ō-nā-tŏl′ə-jē) *n.* The branch of pediatrics that deals with the diseases and care of newborn infants. **—ne′o•na•tol′o•gist** *n.*

ne•o-Na•zi (nē′ō-nät′sē, -năt′-) *n.* A member of a fringe group inspired by Adolf Hitler's Nazis. **—ne′o-Na′zism** *n.*

neon tetra *n.* A small tropical freshwater fish *(Hyphessobrycon innesi)* of the Amazon River having blue and red markings.

ne•o-or•tho•dox•y (nē′ō-ôr′thə-dŏk′sē) *n.* A Protestant movement arising during World War I that opposes liberalism and favors Calvinism. **—ne′o-or′tho•dox′** *adj.*

ne•o•phyte (nē′ə-fīt′) *n.* **1.** A recent convert to a belief; a proselyte. **2.** A beginner or novice. **3.a.** *Rom. Cath. Ch.* A newly ordained priest. **b.** A novice of a religious order or congregation. [ME < LLat. *neophytus* < Gk. *neophutos* : *neo-*, neo- + *-phutos*, planted (< *phuein*, to bring forth; see **bheuə-*).**]

ne•o•pla•sia (nē′ō-plā′zhə, -zhē-ə) *n.* **1.** Formation of new tissue. **2.** Formation of a neoplasm or neoplasms.

ne•o•plasm (nē′ə-plăz′əm) *n.* An abnormal new growth of tissue; a tumor. **—ne′o•plas′tic** (-plăs′tĭk) *adj.*

Ne•o-Pla•to•nism also **Ne•o•pla•to•nism** (nē′ō-plāt′n-ĭz′-əm) *n.* **1.** A philosophical system developed in the third century A.D. that is based on Platonism with elements of mysticism and some Judaic and Christian concepts and posits a single source from which all existence emanates and with which an individual soul can be mystically united. **2.** A revival of Neo-Platonism or a system derived from it, as in the Middle Ages. **—Ne′o-Pla•ton′ic** (-plə-tŏn′ĭk) *adj.* **—Ne′o-Pla′to•nist** *n.*

ne•o•prene (nē′ə-prēn′) *n.* A synthetic rubber produced by polymerization of chloroprene and used in weather-resistant products, adhesives, shoe soles, paints, and rocket fuels. [NEO– + (CHLORO)PRENE.]

Ne•o-Scho•las•ti•cism (nē′ō-skə-lăs′tĭ-sĭz′əm) *n.* A chiefly Roman Catholic intellectual movement that arose in the late 19th century and seeks to revive medieval Scholasticism by infusing it with modern concepts. **—Ne′o-Scho•las′tic** (-lăs′tĭk) *adj.*

Ne•o•sho (nē-ō′shō, -shə). A river rising in E-central KS and flowing c. 740 km (460 mi) to the Arkansas R. in E OK.

ne•o•stig•mine (nē′ō-stĭg′mēn, -mĭn) *n.* Either of two related white, crystalline cholinergic compounds, $C_{12}H_{19}BrN_2O_2$ or $C_{13}H_{22}N_2O_6S$, used in the treatment of glaucoma and myasthenia gravis. [NEO– + (PHYSO)STIGMINE.]

ne•ot•e•ny (nē-ŏt′n-ē) *n.* **1.** Retention of juvenile characteristics in the adults of a species. **2.** The attainment of sexual maturity by an organism still in its larval stage. [NLat. *neotenia* : NEO– + Gk. *teinein*, *ten-*, to extend; see TENESMUS.] **—ne′o•ten′ic** (nē′ə-tĕn′ĭk, -tē′nĭk), **ne•ot′e•nous** (-ŏt′-n-əs) *adj.*

ne•o•ter•ic (nē′ə-tĕr′ĭk) *adj.* Of recent origin; modern. **—***n.* A modern writer or philosopher. [LLat. *neōtericus* < Gk. *neōterikos* < *neōteros*, younger, comp. of *neos*, new. See **newo-*.**]

Ne•o•trop•i•cal (nē′ō-trŏp′ĭ-kəl) *adj.* Of or being the biogeographic region stretching southward from the Tropic of Cancer and including southern Mexico, Central and South America, and the West Indies.

ne•o•type (nē′ə-tīp′) *n.* A new specimen selected to replace a holotype that has been lost or destroyed.

NEP or **N.E.P.** *abbr.* **1.** New Economic Policy. **2. N.E.P.** Non-English proficient.

Nep. *abbr.* Nep.

Ne•pal (nə-pôl′, -päl′, -păl′, nā-). A country of central Asia in the Himalaya Mts. between India and SW China. Cap. Katmandu. Pop. 15,022,839.

Nep•al•ese (nĕp′ə-lēz′, -lēs′) *n., pl.* **Nepalese. 1.** A native or inhabitant of Nepal. **2.** The Nepali language. **—***adj.* Of or relating to Nepal or its people, language, or culture.

Ne•pal•i (nə-pô′lē, -pä′-, -păl′ē) *n., pl.* **-is. 1.** A native or inhabitant of Nepal. **2.** The Indic language of Nepal, closely related to Hindi. **—Ne•pal′i** *adj.*

Ne•pe•an (nə-pē′ən). A city of SE Ontario, Canada, a suburb of Ottawa. Pop. 84,361.

ne•pen•the (nĭ-pĕn′thē) *n.* **1.** A drug mentioned in the *Odyssey* as a remedy for grief. **2.** Something that induces forgetfulness of sorrow or eases pain. [Alteration of Lat. *nēpenthes* < Gk. *nēpenthes (pharmakon)*, grief-banishing (drug), nepenthe : *nē-*, not; see **ne*** + *penthos*, grief; see **kʷent(h)-*.**] **—ne•pen′the•an** (-thē-ən) *adj.*

neph•e•line (nĕf′ə-lēn′, -lĭn) also **neph•e•lite** (-līt′) *n.* A mineral of sodium-potassium aluminum silicate, occurring in igneous rocks and used in the manufacture of glass. [< Greek *nephelē*, cloud (its fragments becoming cloudy when in nitric acid). See **nebh-*.**] **—neph′e•lin′ic** (-lĭn′ĭk) *adj.*

neph•e•lin•ite (nĕf′ə-lĭ-nīt′) *n.* An igneous rock consisting chiefly of pyroxene and nepheline.

neph•e•lom•e•ter (nĕf′ə-lŏm′ĭ-tər) *n.* An apparatus used to measure the size and concentration of particles in a liquid by analysis of light scattered by the liquid. [Gk. *nephelē*, cloud; see **nebh-*** + -METER.] **—neph′e•lo•met′ric** (-lō-mĕt′rĭk) *adj.* **—neph′e•lom′e•try** *n.*

neph•ew (nĕf′yo͞o) *n.* **1.** A son of one's brother or sister or of one's spouse's brother or sister. **2.** The illegitimate son of an ecclesiastic who has taken a vow of celibacy. [ME *neveu, nepheu* < OFr. *nevo, neveu* < Lat. *nepōs.* See **nepōt-***.]

ne•phrec•to•my (nə-frĕk′tə-mē) *n., pl.* **-mies.** Surgical removal of a kidney.

neph•ric (nĕf′rĭk) *adj.* Relating to or connected with a kidney.

ne•phrid•i•um (nə-frĭd′ē-əm) *n., pl.* **-i•a** (-ē-ə). **1.** A tubular excretory organ in many invertebrates, such as mollusks and earthworms. **2.** The excretory organ of a vertebrate embryo from which the kidney develops. [NEPHR(O)- + NLat. *-idium,* dim. suff. (< Gk. *-idion*).] — **ne•phrid′i•al** *adj.*

neph•rite (nĕf′rīt′) *n.* A white to dark green variety of jade, chiefly a metasilicate of iron, calcium, and magnesium. [Greek *nephros,* kidney (believed to cure kidney diseases) + -ITE[1].]

ne•phrit•ic (nə-frĭt′ĭk) *adj.* **1.** Of or relating to the kidneys; renal. **2.** Of, relating to, or affected with nephritis.

ne•phri•tis (nə-frī′tĭs) *n., pl.* **-phrit•i•des** (-frĭt′ĭ-dēz′) or **-phri•tis•es.** Any of various acute or chronic inflammations of the kidneys, such as Bright's disease.

nephro- or **nephr-** *pref.* Kidney; kidneylike structure: *nephrotomy.* [< Gk. *nephros,* kidney.]

ne•phrog•e•nous (nə-frŏj′ə-nəs) or **neph•ro•gen•ic** (nĕf′rə-jĕn′ĭk) *adj.* **1.** Originating in the kidney. **2.** Able to develop into kidney tissue.

ne•phrol•o•gy (nə-frŏl′ə-jē) *n.* The science that deals with the function and diseases of the kidneys. — **ne•phrol′o•gist** *n.*

neph•ron (nĕf′rŏn) *n.* Any of the numerous filtering units of the vertebrate kidney that remove waste matter from the blood. [Ger. < Gk. *nephros,* kidney.]

ne•phrop•a•thy (nə-frŏp′ə-thē) *n., pl.* **-thies.** A disease or an abnormality of the kidney. — **neph′ro•path′ic** (nĕf′rə-păth′ĭk) *adj.*

ne•phro•sis (nə-frō′sĭs) *n., pl.* **-ses** (-sēz). A disease of the kidneys marked by degenerative lesions. — **ne•phrot′ic** (-frŏt′ĭk) *adj.*

neph•ro•stome (nĕf′rə-stōm′) *n.* The ciliated funnel-shaped inner opening of a nephridium into the coelom in some invertebrates and lower vertebrates. [NEPHRO- + Gk. *stoma,* mouth.]

ne•phrot•o•my (nə-frŏt′ə-mē) *n., pl.* **-mies.** Surgical incision into the kidney.

ne plus ul•tra (nē′ plŭs ŭl′trə, nā′ plo͝os o͝ol′trä) *n.* **1.** The highest point, as of excellence or achievement; the ultimate. **2.** The most profound degree, as of a condition or quality. [Lat. *nē plūs ultrā,* (go) no more beyond (this point) : *nē,* no + *plūs,* more + *ultrā,* beyond.]

nep•o•tism (nĕp′ə-tĭz′əm) *n.* Favoritism shown or patronage granted to relatives. [Fr. *népotisme* < Ital. *nepotismo* < *nepote,* nephew < Lat. *nepōs, nepōt-.* See **nepōt-***.] — **nep′o•tist** *n.* — **nep′o•tis′tic, nep′o•tis′ti•cal** *adj.*

Nep•tune[1] (nĕp′to͞on′, -tyo͞on′) *n.* **1.a.** *Rom. Myth.* The god of the sea. **b.** The sea. **2.** The eighth planet from the sun, having a sidereal period of revolution around the sun of 164.8 years at a mean distance of 4.5 billion kilometers (2.8 billion miles) and a mean radius of 24,000 kilometers (15,000 miles). [Lat. *Neptūnus.*] — **Nep•tu′ni•an** (-to͞o′nē-ən, -tyo͞o′-) *adj.*

Nep•tune[2] (nĕp′to͞on′, -tyo͞on′). A community of E-central NJ S of Asbury Park. Pop. 28,366.

nep•tu•ni•um (nĕp-to͞o′nē-əm, -tyo͞o′-) *n. Symbol* **Np** A metallic radioactive element found in trace quantities in uranium ores or synthesized; its longest-lived isotope is Np 237 with a half-life of 2.1 million years. Atomic number 93. See table at **element.** [After the planet NEPTUNE[1] (< the fact that it follows uranium in the periodic table).]

nerd also **nurd** (nûrd) *n. Slang.* A person regarded as stupid, socially inept, or unattractive. [Perh. after *Nerd,* a character in *If I Ran the Zoo,* by Theodor Seuss Geisel.] — **nerd′y** *adj.*

Word History: The word *nerd* first appears in 1950 in Dr. Seuss's *If I Ran the Zoo*: "And then, just to show them, I'll sail to Ka-Troo And Bring Back an It-Kutch a Preep and a Proo a Nerkle a Nerd and a Seersucker, too!" (The nerd itself is a small humanoid creature looking comically angry, like a thin, cross Chester A. Arthur.) *Nerd* next appears, with a gloss, in the February 10, 1957, issue of the Glasgow, Scotland, *Sunday Mail* in a column entitled "ABC for SQUARES": "Nerd — a square, any explanation needed?" Authorities disagree whether Dr. Seuss's *nerd* and the Glaswegian *nerd* are the same word. Some claim there is no semantic connection and the identity of the words is fortuitous. Others maintain that Dr. Seuss is the true originator of *nerd* and that the word was picked up by the five- and six-year-olds of 1950 and passed on to their older siblings, who by 1957, as teenagers, had applied *nerd* to the most comically obnoxious creature of their own class, a "square."

Ne•re•id (nîr′ē-ĭd) *n.* **1.** *Gk. Myth.* Any of the sea nymphs, the 50 daughters of Nereus. **2.** A satellite of Neptune. [Lat. *Nērēïs, Nērēïd-* < Gk. < *Nēreus,* Nereus.]

ne•re•is (nîr′ē-ĭs) *n., pl.* **ne•re•i•des** (nə-rē′ĭ-dēz′). See **clamworm.** [Lat. *Nērēïs,* Nereid. See NEREID.]

Ne•re•us (nîr′ē-əs, nîr′yo͞os′) *n. Gk. Myth.* A sea god, son of Oceanus and Gaea and father of the Nereids.

Ne•ri (nā′rē), Saint **Philip.** 1515–95. Italian ecclesiastic who founded (1564) the Fathers of the Oratory.

ne•rit•ic (nə-rĭt′ĭk) *adj.* Of, relating to, or inhabiting the ocean waters between the low tide mark and a depth of about a hundred fathoms (200 meters). [Ger. *neritisch,* perh. ult. < *Nēreus,* Nereus.]

Nernst (nĕrnst), **Walther Hermann.** 1864–1941. German physicist and chemist who won a 1920 Nobel Prize.

Ne•ro (nîr′ō, nē′rō). A.D. 37–68. Emperor of Rome (54–68) noted for his cruelty who may have set the Great Fire of Rome (64). — **Ne•ro′ni•an** (nĭ-rō′nē-ən) *adj.*

ne•rol (nîr′ôl, -ŏl, -ōl, nĕr′-) *n. Chem.* A colorless liquid, $C_9H_{17}COH$, derived from orange blossoms and used in perfumery. [NER(OLI OIL) + -OL[1].]

ner•o•li oil (nĕr′ə-lē) *n.* An essential oil distilled from orange flowers and used in perfumery. [Fr. *néroli* < Ital. *neroli,* after Anna Maria de la Trémoille, 17th-cent. princess of *Nerola.*]

nerts (nûrts) *interj. Slang.* Used to express disgust, contempt, or refusal. [Alteration of NUTS.]

Ne•ru•da (nĕ-ro͞o′də, -*th*ä), **Pablo.** 1904–73. Chilean poet and diplomat who won the 1971 Nobel Prize for literature.

ner•vate (nûr′vāt′) *adj. Bot.* Having veins. Used of leaves.

ner•va•tion (nûr-vā′shən) *n.* A pattern of veins or nerves; venation.

nerve (nûrv) *n.* **1.** Any of the cordlike bundles of fibers made up of neurons through which sensory stimuli and motor impulses pass between the brain or other parts of the central nervous system and the eyes, glands, muscles, and other parts of the body. **2.** The sensitive tissue in the pulp of a tooth. **3.** A sore point or sensitive subject. **4.a.** Courage and control under pressure. **b.** Fortitude; stamina. **c.** Forceful quality; boldness. **d.** Brazen boldness; effrontery. **5. nerves.** Nervous agitation caused by fear, anxiety, or stress. **6.** A vein or rib in the wing of an insect. **7.** The midrib and larger veins in a leaf. — *tr.v.* **nerved, nerv•ing, nerves.** To give strength or courage to. — ***idioms.*** **get on (someone's) nerves.** To irritate or exasperate. **strain every nerve.** To make every effort. [ME, sinew, nerve < OFr. *nerf* < Med.Lat. *nervus* < Lat. See **(s)neəu-***.]

nerve cell *n.* **1.** See **neuron. 2.** The body of a neuron without its axon and dendrites.

nerve center *n.* **1.** A group of closely connected nerve cells that perform a specific function. **2.** A source of power or control.

nerve fiber *n.* A threadlike process of a neuron, esp. the prolonged axon that conducts nerve impulses.

nerve gas *n.* Any of various poisonous gases that interfere with the functioning of nerves by inhibiting cholinesterase.

nerve growth factor *n.* A protein that stimulates the growth of sympathetic and sensory nerve cells.

nerve impulse *n.* A wave of physical and chemical excitation along a nerve fiber in response to a stimulus.

nerve•less (nûrv′lĭs) *adj.* **1.** Lacking strength or energy; spiritless; weak. **2.** Lacking courage; spineless or cowardly. **3.** Calm and controlled in trying circumstances; cool. — **nerve′less•ly** *adv.* — **nerve′less•ness** *n.*

nerve net *n.* A diffuse network of cells that conducts impulses in all directions, forming a primitive nervous system in ctenophores, coelenterates, and certain other organisms.

nerve-rack•ing or **nerve-wrack•ing** (nûrv′răk′ĭng) *adj.* Intensely distressing or irritating to the nerves.

nerve trunk *n.* The main stem of a nerve, consisting of a bundle of nerve fibers bound together by connective tissue.

ner•vos•i•ty (nûr-vŏs′ĭ-tē) *n.* The quality or state of being nervous. [Lat. *nervōsitās,* sinewy strength < *nervōsus,* sinewy. See NERVOUS.]

nerv•ous (nûr′vəs) *adj.* **1.a.** Of or relating to the nerves or nervous system. **b.** Stemming from or affecting the nerves or nervous system: *a nervous disorder.* **2.** Easily agitated or distressed; high-strung or jumpy. **3.** Marked by or having a feeling of unease or apprehension. **4.** Vigorous in style or feeling; spirited. **5.** *Archaic.* Strong; sinewy. [ME, sinewy, containing nerves < Lat. *nervōsus,* sinewy < *nervus,* sinew. See NERVE.] — **nerv′ous•ly** *adv.* — **nerv′ous•ness** *n.*

nervous breakdown *n.* A severe or incapacitating emotional disorder marked by depression.

nervous Nel•lie or **nervous Nel•ly** (nĕl′ē) *n., pl.* **-lies.** *Informal.* An unduly timid or anxious person.

nervous system *n. Anat.* The system of cells, tissues, and organs that in vertebrates consists of the brain, spinal cord, nerves, ganglia, and parts of the receptor and effector organs and regulates the body's responses to stimuli.

ner•vure (nûr′vyər) *n.* **1.** *Bot.* See **vein** 2. **2.** *Zool.* See **vein** 3. [Fr. < OFr. *nerveure,* strap < *nerf,* sinew < Lat. *nervus.* See NERVE.]

nerv•y (nûr′vē) *adj.* **-i•er, -i•est. 1.** Arrogantly impudent; brazen. **2.** Showing or requiring courage and fortitude; bold. **3.** *Chiefly British.* Jumpy; nervous. **4.** *Archaic.* Full of muscular force; sinewy. — **nerv′i•ness** *n.*

n.e.s. or **N.E.S.** *abbr.* Not elsewhere specified.

nes•cience (nĕsh′əns, nĕsh′ē-əns, nēsh′-, nĕs′ē-əns, nē′sē-) *n.* **1.** Absence of knowledge or awareness; ignorance. **2.** Agnosticism. [LLat. *nescientia* < Lat. *nesciēns, nescient-,* pr.part. of

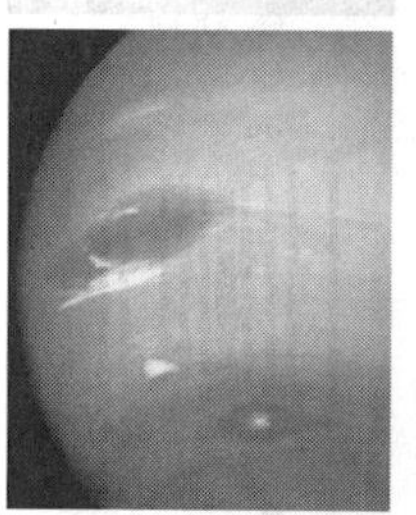

Neptune[1]
Top: Roman god
Bottom: Neptune's Great Dark Spot, photographed by Voyager 2 in August 1989

ă pat	oi boy
ā pay	ou out
âr care	o͝o to͝ok
ä father	o͞o bo͞ot
ĕ pet	ŭ cut
ē be	ûr urge
ĭ pit	th thin
ī pie	*th* this
îr pier	hw which
ŏ pot	zh vision
ō toe	ə about, item
ô paw	

Stress marks:
′ (primary);
′ (secondary), as in dictionary (dĭk′shə-nĕr′ē)

neutral; neutrality. **2.** A political policy or advocacy of nonalignment or noninvolvement in conflicting alliances and of attempting to mediate or conciliate in conflicts between states. — **neu′tral•ist** *adj. & n.* — **neu′tral•is′tic** *adj.*

neu•tral•i•ty (no͞o-trăl′ĭ-tē, nyo͞o-) *n.* The state or policy of being neutral, esp. nonparticipation in war.

neu•tral•i•za•tion (no͞o′trə-lĭ-zā′shən, nyo͞o′-) *n.* **1.a.** The act or process of neutralizing. **b.** The state or quality of being neutralized. **2.** *Chem.* A reaction between an acid and a base that yields a salt and water.

neu•tral•ize (no͞o′trə-līz′, nyo͞o′-) *tr.v.* **-ized, -iz•ing, -iz•es. 1.** To make neutral. **2.** To counterbalance or counteract the effect of; render ineffective. **3.** To declare neutral and therefore inviolable during a war. **4.** *Chem.* **a.** To make (a solution) neutral. **b.** To cause (an acid or a base) to undergo neutralization. **5.** *Medic.* To counteract the effect of (a drug or toxin). **6.** *Slang.* To remove as a threat, esp. by killing. — **neu′tral•iz′er** *n.*

neutral spirits *pl.n.* *(used with a sing. or pl. v.)* Ethyl alcohol distilled at or above 190 proof and used frequently in blended alcoholic beverages.

neu•tri•no (no͞o-trē′nō, nyo͞o-) *n., pl.* **-nos.** Any of three electrically neutral subatomic particles in the lepton family. See table at **subatomic particle.** [Ital. < *neutro*, neuter < Lat. *neuter, neutr-*. See NEUTER.]

neu•tron (no͞o′trŏn′, nyo͞o′-) *n.* A neutral subatomic particle in the baryon family, having a mass 1,839 times that of the electron, stable when bound in an atomic nucleus, and having a mean lifetime of approx. 1.0×10^3 seconds as a free particle. See table at **subatomic particle.** [NEUTR(AL) + -ON[1].]

neutron bomb *n.* A nuclear bomb that would produce great numbers of neutrons but little blast and thus destroy life but spare property.

neutron star *n.* A star in a terminal stage of stellar evolution, essentially consisting of a superdense mass of neutrons and having a powerful gravitational attraction from which only neutrinos and high-energy photons can escape.

neu•tro•phil (no͞o′trə-fĭl′, nyo͞o′-) *adj.* Stained readily by neutral dyes. Used esp. of white blood cells. — *n.* A neutrophil cell, esp. a type of granular white blood cell that is highly destructive of microorganisms. [NEUTR(AL) + -PHIL(E).] — **neu′tro•phile′** (-fīl′), **neu′tro•phil′ic** (-fĭl′ĭk) *adj.*

Nev. *abbr.* Nevada.

Ne•va (nē′və, nyĭ-vä′). A river of NW Russia flowing c. 74 km (46 mi) from Lake Ladoga to the Gulf of Finland.

Ne•vad•a (nə-văd′ə, -vä′də). A state of the W U.S.; admitted as the 36th state in 1864. It became a territory in 1861 after the discovery (1859) of the Comstock Lode. Cap. Carson City. Pop. 1,206,152. — **Ne•vad′an, Ne•vad′i•an** *adj. & n.*

né•vé (nā-vā′) *n.* **1.** The upper part of a glacier where the snow turns into ice. **2.a.** A snow field at the head of a glacier. **b.** The granular snow typically found in such a field. [Fr. < Fr. dial. *névi* < VLat. **nivātum* < neut. of Lat. *nivātus*, cooled by snow < *nix, niv-*, snow.]

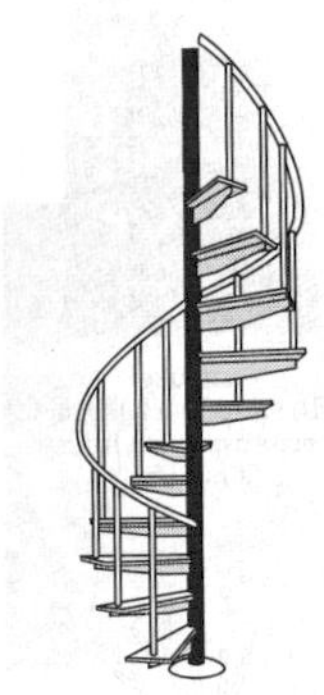

newel
Top: Of a circular staircase
Bottom: At the landing of a staircase

Nev•el•son (nĕv′əl-sən), **Louise.** 1899–1988. Russian-born Amer. sculptor known for her massive abstract works.

nev•er (nĕv′ər) *adv.* **1.** Not ever; on no occasion; at no time: *had never been there before.* **2.** Not at all; in no way; absolutely not: *That will never do.* [ME < OE *nǣfre* : *ne*, not; see **ne*** + *ǣfre*, ever; see **aiw-***.]

nev•er-end•ing (nĕv′ər-ĕn′dĭng) *adj.* Having no foreseeable end.

nev•er•more (nĕv′ər-môr′, -mōr′) *adv.* Never again.

nev•er-nev•er land (nĕv′ər-nĕv′ər) *n.* An imaginary and wonderful place; a fantasy land. [After *Never-Never Land*, fictional setting used in the play *Peter Pan* by J.M. Barrie.]

nev•er•the•less (nĕv′ər-*th*ə-lĕs′) *adv.* In spite of that; nonetheless; however.

Ne•vis (nē′vĭs, nĕv′ĭs). One of the Leeward Is. of the E West Indies in the Caribbean Sea; colonized by the English after 1628 and now part of St. Christopher-Nevis.

ne•vus (nē′vəs) *n., pl.* **-vi** (-vī′). A congenital growth or mark on the skin, such as a birthmark. [Lat. *naevus.*] — **ne′void′** (-void′) *adj.*

new (no͞o, nyo͞o) *adj.* **new•er, new•est. 1.** Having been made or come into being only a short time ago; recent. **2.a.** Still fresh. **b.** Never used or worn before now. **3.** Just found, discovered, or learned. **4.** Not previously experienced or encountered; novel or unfamiliar. **5.** Different from the former or the old. **6.** Recently obtained or acquired. **7.** Additional; further. **8.** Recently arrived or established in a place, position, or relationship. **9.** Changed for the better; rejuvenated. **10.** Being the later or latest in a sequence. **11.** Currently fashionable. **12. New.** In the most recent form, period, or development. **13.** Inexperienced or unaccustomed. — *adv.* Freshly; recently. Often used in combination: *new-mown.* [ME *newe* < OE *nīwe, nēowe.* See **newo-*.**] — **new′ness** *n.*

Syns: *new, fresh, novel, newfangled, original.* These adjectives describe what has existed for only a short time, has only lately come into use, or has only recently arrived at a state or position, as of prominence. *New* is the most general: *"It is time for a new generation of leadership"* (John F. Kennedy). Something *fresh* has qualities of newness such as briskness, brightness, or purity: *fresh footprints; fresh hope. Novel* applies to the new and strikingly unusual: *a novel solution. Newfangled* suggests that something is needlessly novel: *"the newfangled doctrine of utility"* (John Galt). Something that is *original* is novel and the first of its kind: *"The science of pure mathematics, in its modern development, may claim to be the most original creation of the human spirit"* (Alfred North Whitehead).

New Age *adj.* Of or relating to a complex of spiritual and consciousness-raising movements of the 1980's, including belief in spiritualism and reincarnation and holistic approaches to health and ecology. — *n. Mus.* Modern music marked by soft tones on instruments such as acoustic piano, guitar, or synthesizer. — **New Ager** *n.*

New Al•ba•ny (ôl′bə-nē). A city of S IN on the Ohio R. opposite Louisville KY. Pop. 36,322.

New Am•ster•dam (ăm′stər-dăm′). A settlement estab. in 1624 by the Dutch at the mouth of the Hudson R. on the S end of Manhattan I.; cap. of New Netherland (1626–64).

New•ark (no͞o′ərk, nyo͞o′-). **1.** A city of W CA SSE of Oakland. Pop. 37,861. **2.** (*also* -ärk′). A city of NW DE WSW of Wilmington; settled c. 1694. Pop. 25,098. **3.** A city of NE NJ on **Newark Bay,** an inlet of the Atlantic; settled in 1666. Pop. 275,221. **4.** A city of central OH E of Columbus; near the site of Mound Builder earthworks. Pop. 44,389.

New Bed•ford (bĕd′fərd). A city of SE MA on Buzzards Bay ESE of Fall River; settled in the mid-1600's. Pop. 99,922.

New Ber•lin (bûr-lĭn′). A city of SE WI, a suburb of Milwaukee. Pop. 33,592.

New Bern (bûrn). A city of E NC on the Neuse R. SE of Raleigh; settled in 1710. Pop. 17,363.

new blood *n.* New people considered as a revitalizing force, as in an organization.

new•born (no͞o′bôrn′, nyo͞o′-) *adj.* **1.** Very recently born. **2.** Born anew: *newborn courage.* — *n.* A neonate.

New Braun•fels (broun′fəlz). A city of S-central TX NE of San Antonio; founded by German immigrants. Pop. 27,334.

New Brigh•ton (brīt′n). A city of SE MN, a suburb of Minneapolis–St. Paul. Pop. 22,207.

New Brit•ain[1] (brĭt′n). A volcanic island of Papua New Guinea in the SW Pacific; controlled by Germany after 1884 and by Australia from 1920 until 1975.

New Brit•ain[2] (brĭt′n). A city of central CT SSW of Hartford. Pop. 75,491.

New Bruns•wick (brŭnz′wĭk). **1.** A province of E Canada on the Gulf of St. Lawrence; joined Nova Scotia, Quebec, and Ontario to form the confederated Dominion of Canada in 1867. Cap. Fredericton. Pop. 696,711. **2.** A city of central NJ SW of Newark; settled in 1681. Pop. 41,711.

New•burg also **New•burgh** (no͞o′bûrg′, nyo͞o′-) *adj.* Served in a sauce made of cream, egg yolks, butter, and sherry. [?]

Newburgh. A city of SE NY on the Hudson R. SSW of Poughkeepsie; founded c. 1709. Pop. 26,454.

New•bur•y•port (no͞o′bə-rē-pôrt′, -pōrt′, nyo͞o′-). A city of NE MA ENE of Lawrence; settled in 1635. Pop. 16,317.

New Cal•e•do•ni•a (kăl′ĭ-dō′nē-ə, -dōn′yə). A French overseas territory in the SW Pacific consisting of the island of **New Caledonia** and several smaller islands; annexed by France in 1853. Cap. Nouméa. Pop. 145,368.

New Ca•naan (kā′nən). A town of SW CT NNE of Stamford. Pop. 17,864.

New Cas•tile (kăs-tēl′). A historical region of central Spain that combined with the N region of Old Castile to form the kingdom of Castile; united with Aragon after the marriage of Ferdinand and Isabella (1479).

New•cas•tle (no͞o′kăs′əl, nyo͞o′-). **1.** A town of S Ontario, Canada, on Lake Ontario E of Toronto. Pop. 32,229. **2.** Or **New•cas•tle-un•der-Lyme** (-ŭn′dər-līm′). A municipal borough of W-central England SSW of Stoke. Pop. 74,200. **3.** Or **Newcastle upon Tyne** (tīn). A borough of NE England on the Tyne R. N of Leeds. Pop. 285,300.

New Cas•tle (kăs′əl). **1.** A city of E-central IN S of Muncie. Pop. 17,753. **2.** A city of W PA NNW of Pittsburgh. Pop. 28,334.

new-col•lar (no͞o′kŏl′ər, nyo͞o′-) *adj.* Relating to a class of workers who hold primarily service and clerical jobs.

New•comb (no͞o′kəm, nyo͞o′-), **Simon.** 1835–1909. Amer. astronomer who updated the tables indicating the position of the moon, planets, and important stars.

new•com•er (no͞o′kŭm′ər, nyo͞o′-) *n.* One who has only recently arrived.

New Criticism *n.* A method of close textual literary criticism chiefly of the mid-20th century that pays little regard to biographical or historical information. — **New Critic** *n.*

New Deal *n.* **1.** The programs and policies of economic recovery and social reform introduced in the 1930's by Franklin D. Roosevelt. **2.** The period of development of the New Deal. — **New Dealer** *n.*

New Del•hi (dĕl′ē). The cap. of India, in the N-central part S of Delhi; constructed between 1912 and 1929 and officially inaugurated in 1931. Pop. 273,036.

new•el (no͞o′əl, nyo͞o′-) *n.* **1.** A vertical support at the center of a circular staircase. **2.** A post that supports a handrail at the bottom or at the landing of a staircase. [ME *nouel, niewel* < OFr. *noiel* < VLat. **nōdellus*, little knot, dim. of Lat. *nōdulus*, dim. of *nōdus*, knot. See NODE.]
New Eng•land (ĭng′glənd). A region of the NE U.S. comprising the modern-day states of ME, NH, VT, MA, CT, and RI. — **New Eng′land•er** *n.*
New England boiled dinner *n.* A dish consisting of meat simmered with carrots, potatoes, and cabbage.
New England clam chowder *n.* A thick soup made with clams, onions, potatoes, milk, and sometimes salt pork.
New English *n.* See **Modern English.**
New English Bible *n.* A modern translation of the Bible by a British interdenominational team published in 1970.
Newf. *abbr.* Newfoundland.
new•fan•gled (no͞o′făng′gəld, nyo͞o′-) *adj.* **1.** New and often needlessly novel. See Syns at **new. 2.** Fond of novelty. [ME *newfanglyd*, fond of novelty, alteration of *neufangel* : *new*, new; see NEW + *-*fangel*, taken; see **pag-***.] — **new′fan′gled•ness** *n.*
new-fash•ioned (no͞o′făsh′ənd, nyo͞o′-) *adj.* **1.** Up-to-date; current. **2.** Created in a new form or fashion.
New For•est (fôr′ĭst, fŏr′-). A region of S England set aside as a hunting ground by William the Conqueror in 1079.
new•found (no͞o′found′, nyo͞o′-) *adj.* Recently discovered.
New•found•land[1] (no͞o′fən-lənd, -lănd′, -fənd-, nyo͞o′-). A province of E Canada including the island of **Newfoundland** and nearby islands and the mainland area of Labrador with its adjacent islands; joined the confederation in 1949. The province of Quebec claimed Labrador until 1927. Cap. St. John's. Pop. 567,681. — **New′found•land•er** *n.*
New•found•land[2] (no͞o′fən-lənd, nyo͞o′-) *n.* Any of a breed of large strong dog developed in Newfoundland and having a thick, usu. black coat.
New France (frăns). The possessions of France in North America from the 16th cent. until the Treaty of Paris (1763), when the French holdings were awarded to Great Britain and Spain.
New Geor•gia Island (jôr′jə). An island of the Solomon Is. in the SW Pacific.
New Gra•na•da (grə-nä′də). A former Spanish colony (c. 1530–1819) of N South America including present-day Colombia, Ecuador, Panama, and Venezuela.
New Greek *n.* See **Modern Greek.**
New Guin•ea (gĭn′ē). An island in the SW Pacific N of Australia; divided between Indonesia and Papua New Guinea. — **New Guin′e•an** *adj. & n.*
New Guinea, Trust Territory of. A former trust territory of Australia consisting of NE New Guinea, the Bismarck Archipelago, and Bougainville in the Solomon Is.
New Hamp•shire (hămp′shər, -shîr′, hăm′-). A state of the NE U.S. between VT and ME; admitted as one of the original Thirteen Colonies in 1788. Cap. Concord. Pop. 1,113,915. — **New Hamp′shir•ite′** *n.*
New Har•mo•ny (här′mə-nē). A village of SW IN on the Wabash R. WNW of Evansville; founded in 1814 by the Harmony Society led by George Rapp and the site (1825–28) of a utopian community estab. by Robert Owen.
New Ha•ven (hā′vən). A city of S CT on Long Island Sound NE of Bridgeport; settled 1637–38. Pop. 130,474.
New Hebrew *n.* The Hebrew language as used from the mid-18th century until 1948.
New Heb•ri•des (hĕb′rĭ-dēz′). See **Vanuatu.**
New Hope (hōp). A city of SE MN, a suburb of Minneapolis. Pop. 21,853.
New I•be•ri•a (ī-bîr′ē-ə). A city of S LA SW of Baton Rouge; settled by Acadians after c. 1765. Pop. 31,828.
New•ing•ton (no͞o′ĭng-tən, nyo͞o′-). A town of N-central CT SW of Hartford. Pop. 29,208.
New Ire•land (īr′lənd). A volcanic island of the SW Pacific in the Bismarck Archipelago; a German protectorate from 1884 to 1914 and now part of Papua New Guinea.
new•ish (no͞o′ĭsh, nyo͞o′-) *adj.* Fairly new.
New Jer•sey (jûr′zē). A state of the E-central U.S. on the Atlantic Ocean; admitted as one of the original Thirteen Colonies in 1787. Cap. Trenton. Pop. 7,748,634. — **New Jer′sey•ite′** *n.*
New Je•ru•sa•lem (jə-ro͞o′sə-ləm, -zə-) *n.* **1.** *Theol.* The final resting place of souls redeemed by Jesus. **2.** An ideal community on earth.
New Journalism *n.* Journalism that is characterized by the reporter's subjective interpretations and often features fictional dramatized elements. — **New Journalist** *n.*
New Kingdom. Ancient Egypt during the XVIII–XX Dynasties, from c. 1580 to 1090 B.C.; noted as a period of territorial expansion and flourishing art and architecture.
New Latin *n.* Latin as used since about 1500.
New Left *n.* A political movement originating in the United States in the 1960's, marked by active advocacy of radical changes in government, politics, and society. — **New Leftist** *n.*
New Lon•don (lŭn′dən). A city of SE CT on the Thames R. near Long Island Sound; laid out in 1654. Pop. 28,540.
new•ly (no͞o′lē, nyo͞o′-) *adv.* **1.** Not long ago; recently: *newly baked bread.* **2.** Once more; anew: *a newly painted room.* **3.** In a new or different way; freshly.
new•ly•wed (no͞o′lē-wĕd′, nyo͞o′-) *n.* A person recently married.
New•man (no͞o′mən, nyo͞o′-), **John Henry.** 1801–90. British prelate who converted to Roman Catholicism (1845) and was made a cardinal (1879).
New•mar•ket (no͞o′mär′kĭt, nyo͞o′-). **1.** A town of SE Ontario, Canada, N of Toronto. Pop. 29,753. **2.** An urban district of E England E of Cambridge; a center for horseracing since the early 17th cent. Pop. 16,235.
new math *n.* Mathematics taught in elementary and secondary schools that uses set theory.
New Mex•i•co (mĕk′sĭ-kō′). A state of the SW U.S. on the Mexican border; admitted as the 47th state in 1912. The region was ceded to the U.S. by the Treaty of Guadelupe Hidalgo (1848). Cap. Sante Fe. Pop. 1,521,779. — **New Mex′i•can** *adj. & n.*
New Mil•ford (mĭl′fərd). A town of W CT on the Housatonic R. NNE of Danbury. Pop. 23,629.
new moon *n.* **1.** The phase of the moon occurring when it passes between the earth and the sun and is invisible or visible only as a narrow crescent at sunset. **2.** The crescent moon.
New Neth•er•land (nĕ*th*′ər-lənd). A Dutch colony (after 1624) in North America along the Hudson and lower Delaware rivers; renamed New York by the English in 1664.
New Norwegian *n.* A Norwegian national standard language based on the spoken, esp. rural dialects, devised in 1853 and recognized as a second national language in 1885.
New Or•leans (ôr′lē-ənz, ôr′lənz, ôr-lēnz′). A city of SE LA between the Mississippi R. and Lake Pontchartrain; founded 1718. Pop. 496,938. — **New Or•lea′ni•an** (ôr-lē′nē-ən, -lēn′yən) *n.*
new penny *n.* See **penny** 3a.
New•port (no͞o′pôrt′, -pōrt′, nyo͞o′-). **1.** A municipal borough of S England, the administrative center of the Isle of Wight. Pop. 23,570. **2.** A city of N KY on the Ohio R. opposite Cincinnati OH; laid out in 1791. Pop. 18,871. **3.** A city of SE RI SSE of Providence; settled in 1639. Pop. 28,227. **4.** A borough of SE Wales NE of Cardiff. Pop. 134,200.
Newport Beach. A resort city of S CA on the Pacific Ocean S of Santa Ana. Pop. 66,643.
Newport News. An independent city of SE VA at the mouth of the James R. off Hampton Roads NNW of Norfolk; settled c. 1620. Pop. 170,045.
New Prov•i•dence (prŏv′ĭ-dəns). An island of the Bahamas in the West Indies.
New River. A river of the SE U.S. flowing c. 515 km (320 mi) from the Blue Ridge in NW NC to the Allegheny Plateau in S-central WV.
New Ro•chelle (rə-shĕl′, rō-). A city of SE NY on Long Island Sound E of Mount Vernon; settled in 1688. Pop. 67,265.
news (no͞oz, nyo͞oz) *pl.n.* *(used with a sing. v.)* **1.a.** Information about recent events or happenings, esp. as reported by the newspapers, periodicals, radio, or television. **b.** A presentation of such information, as in a newspaper. **2.** New information of any kind. **3.** Newsworthy material. [ME *newes*, new things, tidings, pl. of *newe*, new thing, new. See NEW.]
news agency *n.* An organization that provides news coverage to subscribers, as to newspapers or periodicals.
news•boy (no͞oz′boi′, nyo͞oz′-) *n.* A boy who sells or delivers newspapers.
news•break (no͞oz′brāk′, nyo͞oz′-) *n.* **1.** An urgent or immediate item of news. **2.** The act or an instance of interrupting a broadcast in order to report a newsworthy event or story.
news•cast (no͞oz′kăst′, nyo͞oz′-) *n.* A radio or television news broadcast. [NEWS + (BROAD)CAST.] — **news′cast′er** *n.*
news conference *n.* See **press conference.**
news flash *n.* See **newsbreak.**
news•girl (no͞oz′gûrl′, nyo͞oz′-) *n.* A girl who sells or delivers newspapers.
New Si•be•ri•an Islands (sī-bîr′ē-ən). An archipelago of NE Russia in the Arctic Ocean between the Laptev and East Siberian seas; discovered in the 1770's.
news•let•ter (no͞oz′lĕt′ər, nyo͞oz′-) *n.* A printed report giving news or information of interest to a special group.
news•mag•a•zine (no͞oz′măg′ə-zēn′, nyo͞oz′-) *n.* A magazine that contains reports and analyses of current events.
news•mak•er (no͞oz′mā′kər, nyo͞oz′-) *n.* One that is newsworthy.
news•man (no͞oz′măn′, -mən, nyo͞oz′-) *n.* A man who gathers, reports, or edits news.
news•mon•ger (no͞oz′mŭng′gər, -mŏng′-, nyo͞oz′-) *n.* One who spreads news, esp. a gossip.
New Spain (spān). **1.** A former Spanish viceroyalty (1521–1821) in North America, including the SW U.S., Mexico, Central America N of Panama, some West Indian islands, and the Philippines. **2.** The former Spanish possessions in the New World, including South America (except Brazil), Central America, Mexico, the West Indies, Florida, and much of the land W of the Mississippi R.

Newfoundland[2]

ă pat	oi boy
ā pay	ou out
âr care	o͝o took
ä father	o͞o boot
ĕ pet	ŭ cut
ē be	ûr urge
ĭ pit	th thin
ī pie	*th* this
îr pier	hw which
ŏ pot	zh vision
ō toe	ə about, item
ô paw	

Stress marks:
′ (primary);
′ (secondary), as in dictionary (dĭk′shə-nĕr′ē)

Niebuhr, Reinhold. 1892–1971. Amer. theologian who wrote primarily about morality and social concerns.

niece (nēs) *n.* **1.** The daughter of one's brother or sister or of the brother or sister of one's spouse. **2.** The illegitimate daughter of an ecclesiastic who has taken a vow of celibacy. [ME *nece* < OFr. < VLat. **neptia* < Lat. *neptis.* See **nepōt-*.**]

ni•el•lo (nē-ĕl′ō) *n., pl.* **-el•li** (-ĕl′ē) or **-el•los. 1.** Any of several black metallic alloys of sulfur with copper, silver, or lead, used to fill an incised design on the surface of another metal. **2.** A surface or an object decorated with niello. **3.** The art or process of ornamenting metal surfaces with niello. —*tr.v.* **-loed, -lo•ing, -los.** To decorate or inlay with niello. [Ital. < Med.Lat. *nigellum* < neut. of Lat. *nigellus,* dim. of *niger,* black.] —**ni•el′list** *n.*

niels•bohr•i•um (nēlz-bôr′ē-əm, -bōr′-) *n.* Element 105. [After Niels Henrik David Bohr.]

Niel•sen (nēl′sən), **Carl August.** 1865–1931. Danish composer whose works include the opera *Saul and David* (1903).

Nie•men (nē′mən, nyĕ′-). See **Neman.**

Nie•mey•er Soa•res Fil•ho (nē′mī′ər swä′rĕsh fēl′yō), **Oscar.** b. 1907. Brazilian architect who directed the creation of Brazil's capital, Brasília (1950–60).

Nie•tzsche (nē′chə, -chē), **Friedrich Wilhelm.** 1844–1900. German philosopher whose works include *Thus Spake Zarathustra* (1883–92). —**Nie′tzsche•an** *adj. & n.*

Friedrich Nietzsche

Nif•l•heim (nĭv′əl-hām′) *n. Myth.* The realm of the dead in Norse myth. [ON *niflheimr* : *nifl-,* mist, dark; see **nebh-*** + *heimr,* home; see **tkei-*.**]

nif•ty (nĭf′tē) *Slang.* —*adj.* **-ti•er, -ti•est.** First-rate; great. —*n., pl.* **-ties.** A nifty person or thing, esp. a clever joke. [?] —**nif′ti•ly** *adv.* —**nif′ti•ness** *n.*

Ni•ger (nī′jər, nē-zhâr′). A country of W-central Africa; gained its independence from France in 1960. Cap. Niamey. Pop. 5,772,000.

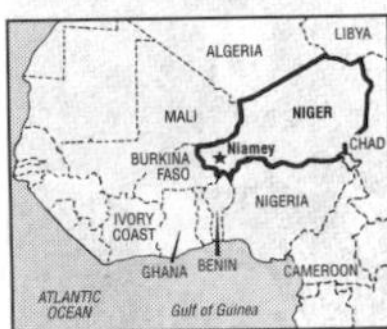

Niger

Ni•ger-Con•go (nī′jər-kŏng′gō) *n.* A large, widely dispersed language family of sub-Saharan Africa including the Mande, West Atlantic, and Central Niger-Congo branches.

Ni•ge•ri•a (nī-jîr′ē-ə). A country of W Africa on the Gulf of Guinea; gained independence from Great Britain in 1960. Cap. Lagos. Pop. 89,117,500. —**Ni•ge′ri•an** *adj. & n.*

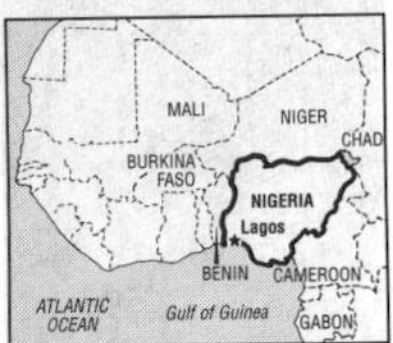

Nigeria

Ni•ger-Kor•do•fan•i•an (nī′jər-kôr′də-făn′ē-ən, -făn′yən) *n.* The largest language family of sub-Saharan Africa, consisting of the Niger-Congo and Kordofanian branches.

Niger River. A river of W Africa rising in Guinea and flowing c. 4,183 km (2,600 mi) to the Gulf of Guinea.

nig•gard (nĭg′ərd) *n.* A stingy, grasping person; a miser. —*adj.* Stingy; miserly. [ME *nigard,* perh. < *nig,* stingy person, of Scand. orig.]

nig•gard•ly (nĭg′ərd-lē) *adj.* **1.** Grudging and petty in giving or spending. **2.** Meanly small; scanty or meager. —**nig′gard•li•ness** *n.* —**nig′gard•ly** *adv.*

nig•ger (nĭg′ər) *n. Offensive Slang.* **1.a.** Used as a disparaging term for a Black person. **b.** Used as a disparaging term for a member of any dark-skinned people. **2.** Used as a disparaging term for a member of any socially, economically, or politically deprived group of people. [Alteration of dial. *neger,* black person < Fr. *nègre* < Sp. *negro.* See Negro.]

nig•gle (nĭg′əl) *intr.v.* **-gled, -gling, -gles. 1.** To be preoccupied with trifles or petty details. **2.** To find fault constantly and trivially; carp. [Perh. of Scand. orig.] —**nig′gler** *n.*

nig•gling (nĭg′lĭng) *adj.* **1.** Petty, esp. in a nagging or annoying way; trifling. **2.** Overconcerned with details; exacting and fussy. —**nig′gling** *n.* —**nig′gling•ly** *adv.*

nigh (nī) *adv.* **nigh•er, nigh•est. 1.** Near in time, place, or relationship. **2.** Nearly; almost. —*adj.* **nigher, nighest. 1.** Being near in time, place, or relationship; close. See Syns at **close. 2.a.** Being on the left side of an animal or a vehicle. **b.** Being the animal or vehicle on the left. —*prep.* Not far from; near. —*tr. & intr.v.* **nighed, nigh•ing, nighs.** To come near to or draw near. [ME *neigh* < OE *nēah, nēh.* See **nēhw-iz*.**]

night (nīt) *n.* **1.a.** The period between sunset and sunrise, esp. the hours of darkness. **b.** This period considered as a unit of time: *for two nights running.* **c.** This period considered in terms of its conditions: *a rainy night.* **2.** The period between dusk and midnight of a given day. **3.a.** The period between evening and bedtime. **b.** This period considered in terms of its activities: *a night at the opera.* **c.** This period set aside for a specific purpose: *Parents' Night at school.* **4.a.** The period between bedtime and morning. **b.** One's sleep during this period: *a restless night.* **5.** Nightfall. **6.** Darkness: *vanished into the night.* **7.a.** A time or condition of gloom, obscurity, ignorance, or despair. **b.** A time or condition marked by absence of moral or ethical values. —*adj.* **1.** Of or relating to the night. **2.** Intended for use at night. **3.** Working during the night. **4.** Active chiefly at night. **5.** Occurring after dark. [ME < OE *niht.* See **nek^w-t-*.**]

night-blind (nīt′blīnd′) *adj.* Affected with night blindness.

night blindness *n.* A condition of the eyes in which vision is normal in daylight or other strong light but is abnormally weak or completely lost at night or in dim light.

Florence Nightingale
Photographed c. 1857

night-bloom•ing cereus (nīt′blo͞o′mĭng) *n.* Any of various night-blooming cacti of the genera *Hylocereus, Nyctocereus, Peniocereus,* and *Selenicereus,* having large fragrant flowers.

night•cap (nīt′kăp′) *n.* **1.** A usu. alcoholic drink taken just before bedtime. **2.** *Sports & Games.* The last event in a day's competition, esp. the final game in a baseball double-header. **3.** A cloth cap worn esp. in bed.

night•clothes (nīt′klōz′, -klōthz′) *pl.n.* Clothes, such as pajamas or a nightgown, worn in bed.

night•club (nīt′klŭb′) *n.* An establishment that stays open late at night and provides food, drink, entertainment, and music for dancing. —**night′club′ber** *n.* —**night′club′by** *adj.*

night court *n. Law.* A criminal court holding sessions at night for routine disposition of charges and granting of bail.

night crawler *n.* Any of various large earthworms that crawl out from the ground at night and are often used as fish bait.

night•dress (nīt′drĕs′) *n.* **1.** See **nightgown. 2.** See **nightclothes.**

night•fall (nīt′fôl′) *n.* The approach of darkness; dusk.

night•glow (nīt′glō′) *n.* Airglow occurring at night.

night•gown (nīt′goun′) *n.* A loose garment worn in bed by women and girls.

night•hawk (nīt′hôk′) *n.* **1.a.** Any of several chiefly nocturnal birds of the genus *Chordeiles,* esp. *C. minor,* having mottled grayish-brown plumage. **b.** The European nightjar. **2.** *Informal.* A night owl.

night heron *n.* Any of several nocturnal or crepuscular herons of the genus *Nycticorax,* esp. the black-crowned heron *(N. nycticorax).*

night•ie or **night•y** (nī′tē) *n., pl.* **-ies.** *Informal.* A nightgown.

night•in•gale (nīt′n-gāl′, nī′tĭng-) *n.* **1.** A European songbird *(Luscinia megarhynchos)* with reddish-brown plumage, noted for the melodious song of the male at night during the breeding season. **2.** Any of various other nocturnal songbirds of the genus *Luscinia.* [ME < OE *nihtegale* : *niht,* night; see night + *galan,* to sing; see **ghel-[1]*.**]

Night•in•gale (nīt′n-gāl′, nī′tĭng-), **Florence.** "the Lady with the Lamp." 1820–1910. British nurse who is considered the founder of modern nursing.

night•jar (nīt′jär′) *n.* A goatsucker, esp. *Caprimulgus europaeus* of Europe, having gray and brown mottled plumage. [night + jar[2] (< its harsh call).]

night latch *n.* A spring lock that can be opened from the inside by turning a knob but from the outside only with a key.

night letter *n.* A telegram sent at night at a reduced rate for delivery the next morning.

night•life (nīt′līf′) *n.* Social activities or entertainment available or pursued in the evening.

night-light (nīt′līt′) *n.* A small dim light left on all night.

night•long (nīt′lông′, -lŏng′) *adj.* Lasting through the night. —*adv.* Through the night; all night.

night•ly (nīt′lē) *adj.* **1.** Of or occurring during the night; nocturnal. **2.** Happening or done every night. —**night′ly** *adv.*

night•mare (nīt′mâr′) *n.* **1.** A dream arousing feelings of intense fear, horror, and distress. **2.** An event or experience that is intensely distressing. **3.** A demon or spirit once thought to plague sleeping people. [ME, a female demon that afflicts sleeping people : *night,* night; see night + *mare,* goblin (< OE; see **mer-***).] —**night′mar′ish** *adj.* —**night′mar′ish•ly** *adv.* —**night′mar′ish•ness** *n.*

night owl *n. Informal.* A person who habitually stays up and is active late into the night.

night•rid•er (nīt′rī′dər) *n.* One of a secret band of mounted, usu. masked white men who engaged in nocturnal terrorism in the southern United States esp. during Reconstruction.

night school *n.* A school that holds classes in the evening.

night•shade (nīt′shād′) *n.* **1.** Any of several plants of the genus *Solanum,* most of which have a poisonous juice. **2.** Any of various similar or related plants, such as belladonna.

night shift or **night•shift** (nīt′shĭft′) *n.* **1.** A group of employees working during the night in a factory or business. **2.** The period of time for such work.

night•shirt (nīt′shûrt′) *n.* A long loose shirt worn in bed, esp. by men.

night soil *n.* Human excrement collected for use as fertilizer.

night•spot (nīt′spŏt′) *n.* See **nightclub.**

night•stand (nīt′stănd′) *n.* See **night table.**

night•stick (nīt′stĭk′) *n.* A club carried by a police officer.

night table *n.* A small table or stand placed at a bedside.

night terror *n.* A state of intense fear and agitation sometimes experienced, esp. by children, on awakening from a stage of sleep characterized by extremely vivid hallucinations.

night•time (nīt′tīm′) *n.* The time between sunset and sunrise. —*adj.* Occurring in or appropriate for use during the night.

night•walk•er (nīt′wô′kər) *n.* **1.** One, esp. a robber or prostitute, who walks the streets at night. **2.** See **night crawler.**

night watch *n.* **1.** A watch or guard kept during the night. **2.** The person or persons on such a watch.

night watchman *n.* A man who serves as a guard at night.

night•wear (nīt′wâr′) *n.* See **nightclothes.**

night•y (nī′tē) *n.* Var. of **nightie.**

ni•gres•cence (nī-grĕs′əns) *n.* **1.** The process of becoming black or dark. **2.** Blackness or darkness, as of complexion. [< *nigrescent*, blackish < Lat. *nigrēscēns, nigrēscent-*, pr.part. of *nigrēscere*, to become black < *niger, nigr-*, black.] **— ni•gres′cent** *adj.*

ni•gro•sine (nī′grə-sēn′, -sĭn) *n.* Any of a class of dyes, varying from blue to black, used in the manufacture of inks and for dyeing wood. [Lat. *niger, nigr-*, black + -OS(E)² + -INE².]

NIH *abbr.* National Institutes of Health.

ni•hil•ism (nī′ə-lĭz′əm, nē′-) *n.* **1.** *Philos.* **a.** An extreme form of skepticism that denies all existence. **b.** A doctrine holding that all values are baseless and that nothing can be known or communicated. **2.** Rejection of all distinctions in moral or religious value and a willingness to repudiate all previous theories of morality or religious belief. **3.** The belief that destruction of existing political or social institutions is necessary for future improvement. **4.** Also **Nihilism.** A movement of mid 19th-century Russia that believed in radical societal and governmental change through terrorism and assassination. **5.** *Psychiat.* A delusion that the world or one's mind, body, or self does not exist. [Lat. *nihil*, nothing; see **ne*** + -ISM.] **— ni′hil•ist** *n.* **— ni′hil•is′tic** *adj.* **— ni′hil•is′ti•cal•ly** *adv.*

ni•hil•i•ty (nī-hĭl′ĭ-tē, nē-) *n.* Nonexistence; nothingness. [Fr. *nihilité* < OFr. < Med.Lat. *nihilitās* < Lat. *nihil*, nothing. See NIHILISM.]

ni•hil ob•stat (nī′hĭl ŏb′stät′, -stăt′, nē′-) *n.* **1.** *Rom. Cath. Ch.* An attestation by a church censor that a book contains nothing damaging to faith or morals. **2.** Official approval, as of an artistic work. [Lat., nothing hinders : *nihil*, nothing + *obstat*, third pers. sing. pr.t. of *obstāre*, to hinder.]

Ni•i•ga•ta (nē′ē-gä′tə, -tä). A city of NW Honshu, Japan, on the Sea of Japan NNW of Tokyo. Pop. 475,633.

Ni•i•ha•u (nē′ē-hou′, nē′hou′). An island of NW HI W of Kauai I.

Ni•jin•sky (nĭ-zhĭn′skē, -jĭn′-), **Vaslav** or **Waslaw.** 1890–1950. Russian-born dancer and choreographer noted for his leading roles with Diaghilev's Ballets Russes in Paris.

Nij•me•gen (nī′mā′gən, -KHən). A city of E Netherlands on the Waal R. near the German border. Pop. 147,102.

-nik *suff.* One associated with or characterized by: *beatnik; peacenik.* [Yiddish and Russ. (Yiddish < Russ.), of Slav. orig.]

Ni•ke (nī′kē) *n. Gk. Myth.* The goddess of victory.

Nik•ko (nĭk′ō, nē′kō). A town of central Honshu, Japan, N of Tokyo. Pop. 21,705.

Ni•ko•la•yev (nĭk′ə-lä′yəf, nyĭ-kə-). A city of S Ukraine at the mouth of the Western Bug R. NE of Odessa; founded c. 1784 as a fortress. Pop. 486,000.

nil (nĭl) *n.* Nothing; zero. [Lat. *nīl*, contraction of *nihil.* See **ne*.**] **— nil** *adj.*

Nile (nīl). A river of NE Africa flowing c. 6,677 km (4,150 mi) from its sources in Burundi to a delta on the Mediterranean in NE Egypt. The main headstreams, the **Blue Nile** and the **White Nile,** join at Khartoum to form the Nile proper.

Nile blue *n. Color.* A light greenish blue.

Nile crocodile *n.* A large crocodile *(Crocodylus niloticus)* common in most parts of Africa.

Nile green *n. Color.* A moderate yellow green to vivid light green.

Niles (nīlz). **1.** A village of NE IL, a suburb of Chicago on the Chicago R. Pop. 28,284. **2.** A city of NE OH NNW of Youngstown. Pop. 21,128.

nil•gai (nĭl′gī) *n., pl.* **-gais** or **nilgai.** A large long-legged antelope *(Boselaphus tragocamelus)* of India, the male of which has short sturdy horns and a tuft of long hair under the chin. [Hindi *nīlgāī*, fem. of *nīlgāw* : Skt. *nīla-*, dark blue + Skt. *gauḥ*, ox, cow; see GAYAL.]

nill (nĭl) *v.* **nilled, nill•ing, nills.** *— tr.* Not to will; not to wish. *— intr.* To be unwilling; will not. [ME *nilen* < OE *nyllan* : *ne*, not; see **ne*** + *willan*, to desire; see **wel-¹*.**]

Ni•lo-Sa•har•an (nī′lō-sə-hăr′ən, -hä′rən) *n.* A language family of sub-Saharan Africa spoken from Nigeria to Kenya and including Kanuri, Nubian, and the Nilotic languages.

Ni•lot•ic (nī-lŏt′ĭk) *adj.* **1.** Of the Nile or the Nile Valley. **2.** Of or relating to the peoples who speak Nilotic languages. *—n.* A large group of Nilo-Saharan languages, spoken in southern Sudan, Uganda, Kenya, and northern Tanzania. [Lat. *Nīlōticus* < *Nīlōtis* < Gk. *Neilōtis* < *Neilos*, Nile.]

nil•po•tent (nĭl-pōt′nt, nĭl′pōt′nt) *n. Math.* An algebraic quantity that when raised to a certain power equals zero. [NIL + Lat. *potēns, potent-*, having power; see POTENT.] **— nil•po′ten•cy** *n.*

nim¹ (nĭm) *tr. & intr.v.* **nimmed, nim•ming, nims.** *Archaic.* To steal; pilfer. [ME *nimen*, to take < OE *niman.* See **nem-*.**]

nim² (nĭm) *n. Games.* A game in which players in turn remove small objects from a collection, such as matchsticks arranged in rows, and attempt to take, or avoid taking, the last one. [Perh. < Ger. *nimm*, third pers. sing. imper. of *nehmen*, to take < MHGer. *nemen* < OHGer. *neman.* See **nem-*.**]

nim•ble (nĭm′bəl) *adj.* **-bler, -blest. 1.** Quick, light, or agile in movement or action; deft. **2.** Quick, clever, and acute in devising or understanding. See Syns at **dexterous.** [ME *nemel* < OE *nǣmel*, quick to seize, and *numol*, quick at learning; see **nem-*.**] **— nim′ble•ness** *n.* **— nim′bly** *adv.*

nim•bo•stra•tus (nĭm′bō-strā′təs, -străt′əs) *n., pl.* **-stra•ti** (-strā′tī, -străt′ī). A low, gray, often dark cloud that precipitates rain, snow, or sleet. [NIMB(US) + STRATUS.]

nim•bus (nĭm′bəs) *n., pl.* **-bi** (-bī′) or **-bus•es. 1.** A cloudy radiance said to surround a classical deity when on earth. **2.** A radiant light that appears usu. in the form of a circle or halo about or over the head in the representation of a god, saint, or sacred person. **3.** A splendid atmosphere or aura, as of glamour, that surrounds a person or thing. **4.** A rain cloud, esp. a nimbostratus. [Lat., cloud. See **nebh-*.**]

NIM•BY also **nim•by** (nĭm′bē) *n., pl.* **NIM•BYs** also **nim•bys.** *Slang.* One who objects to having institutions or projects, such as prisons or incinerators, in close proximity. [*N(ot) i(n) m(y) b(ack) y(ard).*] **— nim′by•ness** *n.*

Nîmes (nēm). A city of S France NE of Montpellier; a leading city of Roman Gaul. Pop. 124,220.

ni•mi•e•ty (nĭ-mī′ĭ-tē) *n.* Superfluity; excess. [LLat. *nimietās* < Lat. *nimius*, excessive < *nimis*, excessively. See **ne*.**]

nim•i•ny-pim•i•ny (nĭm′ə-nē-pĭm′ə-nē) *adj.* Affectedly delicate or refined; mincing. [Perh. alteration of NAMBY-PAMBY.] **— nim′i•ny-pim′i•ny** *n.*

Nim•itz (nĭm′ĭts), **Chester William.** 1885–1966. Amer. admiral of the Pacific fleet during World War II.

nim•rod also **Nim•rod** (nĭm′rŏd′) *n.* A hunter.

Nimrod. In the Bible, a hunter and king of Shinar who was a grandson of Ham and a great-grandson of Noah.

Nin (nēn, nĭn), **Anaïs.** 1903–77. French-born Amer. writer best known for her diaries (published 1966–80).

nin•com•poop (nĭn′kəm-po͞op′, nĭng′-) *n.* A person regarded as silly, foolish, or stupid. [?] **— nin′com•poop′er•y** *n.*

nine (nīn) *n.* **1.** The cardinal number equal to 8 + 1. **2.** The ninth in a set or sequence. **3.** Something having nine parts, units, or members. **4.** *Games.* A playing card marked with nine pips. **5.** A set of nine persons or things, esp.: **a.** *Baseball.* The nine players on a team. **b. Nine.** *Gk. Myth.* The nine Muses. **6.** A size, as in clothing or shoes, designated as nine. **7.** *Sports.* The first or second 9 holes of an 18-hole golf course. **— *idiom.* to the nines.** *Informal.* To the highest degree. [ME < OE *nigon.* See **newn̥*.**] **— nine** *adj. & pron.*

nine-band•ed armadillo (nīn′băn′dĭd) *n.* The most common species of armadillo, *Dasypus novemcinctus*, usu. having nine jointed bands of bony plates.

nine days' wonder (dāz) *n.* A thing or an event that creates a brief sensation.

nine•pin (nīn′pĭn′) *n. Sports.* **1. ninepins.** *(used with a sing. or pl. v.)* A bowling game in which nine wooden pins are the target. **2.** A wooden pin used in the game of ninepins.

nine•teen (nīn-tēn′) *n.* **1.** The cardinal number equal to 18 + 1. **2.** The 19th in a set or sequence. [ME *nintene* < OE *nigontēne.* See **newn̥*.**] **— nine•teen′** *adj. & pron.*

nine•teenth (nīn-tēnth′) *n.* **1.** The ordinal number matching the number 19 in a series. **2.** One of 19 equal parts. **— nine•teenth′** *adv. & adj.*

nine•ti•eth (nīn′tē-ĭth) *n.* **1.** The ordinal number matching the number 90 in a series. **2.** One of 90 equal parts. **— nine′ti•eth** *adv. & adj.*

nine-to-fiv•er (nīn′tə-fī′vər) *n.* One who works regular daytime hours, as in an office.

nine•ty (nīn′tē) *n., pl.* **-ties. 1.** The cardinal number equal to 9 × 10. **2. nineties. a.** Often **Nineties.** The decade from 90 to 99 in a century. **b.** A decade or the numbers from 90 to 99: *The temperature stayed in the nineties.* [ME *ninti* < OE *nigontig.* See **newn̥*.**] **— nine′ty** *adj. & pron.*

Nin•e•veh (nĭn′ə-və). An ancient city of Assyria on the Tigris R. opposite the site of present-day Mosul, Iraq; captured and destroyed by Babylonia and its allies in 612 B.C.

Ning•bo (nĭng′bō′) also **Ning•po** (-pō′). A city of E China ESE of Hangzhou on Hangzhou Bay; built on a site occupied since the 8th cent. Pop. 350,000.

Ning•xia Hui•zu (nĭng′shyä′ hwē′dzo͞o′) also **Ning•sia Hui** (hwē′). An autonomous region of N China. Cap. Yinchuan. Pop. 4,150,000.

nin•ja (nĭn′jə) *n., pl.* **ninja** or **-jas.** A member of a class of 14th-century Japanese mercenary agents who were trained in the martial arts and hired for covert operations such as assassination and sabotage. [J. : *nin*, to endure + *ja*, person.]

nin•ny (nĭn′ē) *n., pl.* **-nies.** A fool; a simpleton. [Perh. alteration of INNOCENT.]

Ni•ño (nēn′yō) *n.* El Niño.

ni•non (nē′nŏn′) *n.* A sheer fabric of silk, rayon, or nylon made in a variety of tight smooth weaves or open lacy patterns. [Prob. < Fr. *Ninon*, nickname for *Anne.*]

ninth (nīnth) *n.* **1.** The ordinal number matching the number nine in a series. **2.** One of nine equal parts. **3.** *Mus.* **a.** A harmonic or melodic interval of an octave and a second. **b.** The tone at the upper limit of such an interval. **c.** A chord consisting of a root with its third, seventh, and ninth. [ME *ninthe* < OE *nigonthe* < *nigon*, nine. See **newn̥*.**] **— ninth** *adv. & adj.*

Ni•o•be (nī′ə-bē) *n. Gk. Myth.* The daughter of Tantalus who turned to stone while bewailing the loss of her children.

ni•o•bite (nī′ə-bīt′) *n.* Columbite. [NIOB(IUM) + -ITE¹.]

Nike
Detail from a fifth-century B.C. Greek bell krater

nimbostratus
Nimbostratus clouds releasing rain

ă **pat**	oi **boy**
ā **pay**	ou **out**
âr **care**	o͝o **took**
ä **father**	o͞o **boot**
ĕ **pet**	ŭ **cut**
ē **be**	ûr **urge**
ĭ **pit**	th **thin**
ī **pie**	*th* **this**
îr **pier**	hw **which**
ŏ **pot**	zh **vision**
ō **toe**	ə **about,**
ô **paw**	**item**

Stress marks:
′ (primary);
′ (secondary), as in
dictionary (dĭk′shə-nĕr′ē)

ni•o•bi•um (nī-ō′bē-əm) *n. Symbol* **Nb** A soft ductile metallic element that occurs chiefly in columbite-tantalite and is used in steel alloys and superconductors. Atomic number 41; atomic weight 92.906; melting point 2,468°C; boiling point 4,927°C; specific gravity 8.57; valence 2, 3, 5. See table at **element.** [After NIOBE (because extracted from tantalite).]

Ni•o•brar•a (nī′ə-brâr′ə). A river rising in E WY and flowing c. 692 km (430 mi) to the Missouri R. in NE NE.

Niort (nyôr). A city of W France SE of Nantes; a Huguenot stronghold in the 16th and 17th cent. Pop. 58,203.

nip¹ (nĭp) *v.* **nipped, nip•ping, nips.** *—tr.* **1.** To seize and pinch or bite. **2.** To remove or sever by pinching or snipping: *nipped off the plant leaf.* **3.** To bite or sting with the cold; chill. **4.** To check or cut off the growth or development of. **5.** *Slang.* **a.** To snatch up hastily. **b.** To take (the property of another) unlawfully; steal. *—intr. Chiefly British.* To move quickly; dart. *—n.* **1.** The act or an instance of seizing, pinching, or biting. **2.a.** A pinch or snip that cuts off or removes a small part. **b.** The small bit or portion so removed. **3.a.** A sharp stinging quality, as of frosty air. **b.** Severely sharp cold or frost. **4.** A cutting remark. **5.** A sharp biting flavor; a tang. [ME *nippen,* perh. < MDu. *nipen.*]

nip² (nĭp) *Informal. —n.* A small amount of liquor. *—v.* **nipped, nip•ping, nips.** *—tr.* To sip (alcoholic liquor) in small amounts. *—intr.* To take a sip or sips of alcoholic liquor. [Prob. short for *nipperkin,* of Du. or LGer. orig.]

ni•pa (nē′pə) *n.* **1.** A large palm *(Nipa frutescens)* of the Philippines and Australia having long leaves often used for thatching. **2.** An alcoholic beverage made from the sap of this plant. [NLat. < Malay *nipah.*]

Pat Nixon

nip and tuck *adv. & adj.* So close that the advantage or lead is virtually indeterminable; neck and neck.

Nip•i•gon (nĭp′ĭ-gŏn′), **Lake.** A lake of SW-central Ontario, Canada, N of Lake Superior.

Nip•is•sing (nĭp′ĭ-sĭng′), **Lake.** A lake of SE Ontario, Canada, between the Ottawa R. and Georgian Bay.

nip•per (nĭp′ər) *n.* **1.** A tool, such as pliers, used for squeezing or nipping. Often used in the plural. **2.** A pincerlike part, such as a large crustacean claw. **3.** *Chiefly British.* A small boy.

nip•ping (nĭp′ĭng) *adj.* **1.** Sharp and biting, as the cold. **2.** Bitingly sarcastic. **—nip′ping•ly** *adv.*

nip•ple (nĭp′əl) *n.* **1.** The small projection near the center of the mammary gland containing the outlets of the milk ducts through which young mammals obtain milk from the adult female; a teat. **2.a.** The rubber cap on a bottle from which a baby nurses. **b.** A pacifier for an infant. **3.** Any of various devices functioning like or resembling a nipple, esp.: **a.** A regulated opening for discharging a liquid, as in a small stopcock. **b.** A pipe coupling threaded on both ends. **c.** A small projection through which grease can be forced into a bearing. **4.** A natural or geographic projection resembling a nipple, as a mountain crest. [< obsolete *neble,* dim. of NEB.]

Nip•pon (nĭ-pŏn′, nĭp′ŏn, nē-pôn′). Japan. The name was derived from the Chinese characters for "the place where the sun comes from," or the Land of the Rising Sun.

Nip•pon•ese (nĭp′ə-nēz′, -nēs′) *adj. & n.* Japanese.

Nip•pur (nĭ-po͝or′). An ancient city of Babylonia on the Euphrates R. SE of Babylon; an important religious center in Sumerian times.

nip•py (nĭp′ē) *adj.* **-pi•er, -pi•est. 1.** Tending to nip: *An exuberant, nippy puppy.* **2.** Sharp or biting: *nippy cheese.* **3.** Bitingly cold: *a nippy day.* **—nip′pi•ly** *adv.* **—nip′pi•ness** *n.*

nip-up (nĭp′ŭp′) *n. Sports.* An acrobatic spring from a supine to an upright position.

N.Ire. *abbr.* Northern Ireland.

nir•va•na (nîr-vä′nə, nər-) *n.* **1.** Often **Nirvana. a.** *Buddhism.* The state in which one has attained disinterested wisdom and compassion. **b.** *Hinduism.* Emancipation from ignorance and the extinction of all attachment. **2.** An ideal condition of rest, harmony, or joy. [Skt. *nirvāṇam,* a blowing out, extinction, nirvana : *nis-, nir-,* out, away + *vāti,* it blows; see **wē-*.**]

Niš also **Nish** (nĭsh). A city of SW Serbia near the Bulgarian border; birthplace of Constantine the Great. Pop. 151,600.

Ni•san (nĭs′ən, nē-sän′) *n.* The seventh month of the year in the Jewish calendar. [Heb. *nîsān* < Akkadian *nissanu,* the first month of the year < Sumerian *nisag,* first fruits.]

Ni•sei (nē-sā′, nē′sā′) *n., pl.* **Nisei** or **-seis.** A person born in America of parents who emigrated from Japan. [J. : *ni,* second + *sei,* generation.]

Ni•shi•no•mi•ya (nĭsh′ə-nō′mē-ä, nē′shē-nô′mē-yä′). A city of S Honshu, Japan, on Osaka Bay E of Kobe. Pop. 421,267.

Richard M. Nixon
Photographed in 1969

ni•si (nī′sī′) *adj. Law.* Taking effect at a specified date unless cause is shown for modification or nullification: *a decree nisi.* [Lat. *nisī,* unless. See **ne*.**]

Nis•sen hut (nĭs′ən) *n.* A prefabricated building of corrugated steel in the shape of a half cylinder. [After Peter Norman *Nissen* (1871–1930), British mining engineer.]

ni•sus (nī′səs) *n., pl.* **nisus.** An effort or endeavor to realize an aim. [Lat. *nīsus* < p.part. of *nītī,* to strive.]

nit¹ (nĭt) *n.* The egg or young of a parasitic insect, such as a louse. [ME < OE *hnitu.*] **—nit′ty** *adj.*

nit² (nĭt) *n.* A unit of illuminative brightness equal to one candela per square meter, measured perpendicular to the rays of the source. [< Lat. *nitor,* brightness < *nitēre,* to shine.]

NIT *abbr.* **1.** National Intelligence Test. **2.** *Sports.* National Invitational Tournament.

ni•ter (nī′tər) *n.* A white, gray, or colorless mineral of potassium nitrate, KNO_3, used in making gunpowder. [ME *nitre,* sodium carbonate, natron < OFr. < Lat. *nitrum* < Gk. *nitron* < Egypt. *ntr.*]

Ni•te•rói (nē′tə-roi′). A city of SE Brazil on Guanabara Bay opposite Rio de Janeiro; founded 1671. Pop. 382,736.

nit•pick (nĭt′pĭk′) *intr.v.* **-picked, -pick•ing, -picks.** To be concerned with or find fault with insignificant details. **—nit′pick′er** *n.*

nit•pick•ing (nĭt′pĭk′ĭng) *n.* Minute, trivial, unnecessary, and unjustified criticism or faultfinding.

nitr– *pref.* Var. of **nitro–.**

Ni•tra (nē′trə). A city of W Slovakia on the **Nitra River,** a tributary of the Danube. Pop. 83,338.

ni•trate (nī′trāt′, -trĭt) *n.* **1.** The univalent radical NO_3 or a compound containing it, as a salt or an ester of nitric acid. **2.** Fertilizer consisting of sodium nitrate or potassium nitrate. *—tr.v.* **-trat•ed, -trat•ing, -trates.** To treat or combine with nitric acid or a nitrate, usu. to change into a nitrate. **—ni•tra′tion** *n.* **—ni′tra′tor** *n.*

ni•tre (nī′tər) *n. Chiefly British.* Var. of **niter.**

ni•tric (nī′trĭk) *adj.* Of, derived from, or containing nitrogen, esp. in a valence state higher than that in a comparable nitrous compound.

nitric acid *n.* A fuming corrosive liquid, HNO_3, a highly reactive oxidizing agent used in the production of fertilizers and explosives and in a wide variety of metallurgical processes.

nitric oxide *n.* A colorless poisonous gas, NO, produced as an intermediate during the manufacture of nitric acid from ammonia or atmospheric nitrogen.

ni•tride (nī′trīd′) *n.* A compound containing nitrogen with another more electropositive element, such as phosphorus.

ni•tri•fy (nī′trə-fī′) *tr.v.* **-fied, -fy•ing, -fies. 1.** To oxidize (an ammonia compound) into nitric acid, nitrous acid, or any nitrate or nitrite, esp. by the action of nitrobacteria. **2.** To treat or combine with nitrogen or compounds containing nitrogen. **—ni′tri•fi•ca′tion** (-fĭ-kā′shən) *n.* **—ni′tri•fi′er** *n.*

ni•trile also **ni•tril** (nī′trəl) *n.* An organic cyanide containing a CN group. [NITR(O)– + *-ile,* chemical suff. (prob. var. of –YL).]

ni•trite (nī′trīt′) *n.* The univalent radical NO_2 or a compound containing it, such as a salt or an ester of nitrous acid.

nitro– or **nitr–** *pref.* **1.** Nitrate; niter: *nitrobacterium.* **2.a.** Nitrogen: *nitrile.* **b.** Containing the univalent group NO_2: *nitromethane.* [NLat. < Lat. *nitrum,* natron. See NITER.]

ni•tro•bac•te•ri•um (nī′trō-băk-tîr′ē-əm) *n., pl.* **-te•ri•a** (-tîr′ē-ə). Any of various soil bacteria that take part in the nitrogen cycle, oxidizing ammonium compounds into nitrites or nitrites into nitrates.

ni•tro•ben•zene (nī′trō-bĕn′zēn′, -bĕn-zēn′) *n.* A poisonous organic compound, $C_6H_5NO_2$, an oily liquid having the odor of almonds and used in the manufacture of aniline.

ni•tro•cel•lu•lose (nī′trō-sĕl′yə-lōs′, -lōz′) *n.* A pulpy or cottonlike polymer derived from cellulose treated with sulfuric and nitric acids and used in the manufacture of explosives, collodion, plastics, and solid monopropellants.

ni•tro•chlo•ro•form (nī′trō-klôr′ə-fôrm′, -klōr′-) *n.* See **chloropicrin.**

ni•tro•fu•ran (nī′trō-fyo͝or′ăn′, -fyo͝o-răn′) *n.* Any of several drugs derived from furan that are used to inhibit bacterial growth.

ni•tro•gen (nī′trə-jən) *n. Symbol* **N** A nonmetallic element that constitutes nearly four fifths of the air by volume, occurring as a colorless, odorless, almost inert diatomic gas, N_2, in various minerals and in all proteins and used in a wide variety of important manufactures, including ammonia, nitric acid, TNT, and fertilizers. Atomic number 7; atomic weight 14.0067; melting point −209.86°C; boiling point −195.8°C; valence 3, 5. See table at **element.** [Fr. *nitrogène* : *nitro-,* nitric acid (< NLat.; see NITRO–) + *-gène,* -gen.] **—ni•trog′e•nous** (nī-trŏj′ə-nəs) *adj.*

ni•trog•e•nase (nī-trŏj′ə-nās′, -nāz′, nī′trə-jə-) *n.* An enzyme of nitrogen-fixing bacteria that activates the conversion of nitrogen to ammonia.

nitrogen balance *n.* The difference between the amount of nitrogen taken into the body or the soil and the amount excreted or lost.

nitrogen cycle *n.* **1.** *Ecol.* The circulation of nitrogen in nature, consisting of a cycle in which atmospheric nitrogen is compounded, dissolved in rain, and deposited in the soil, where it is assimilated by bacteria and plants, eventually returning to the atmosphere by bacterial decomposition of organic matter. **2.** *Phys.* See **carbon-nitrogen cycle.**

nitrogen dioxide *n.* A poisonous brown gas, NO_2, often found in smog and automobile exhaust fumes and synthesized for use as a nitrating agent, a catalyst, and an oxidizing agent.

nitrogen fixation *n.* **1.** The conversion of atmospheric nitrogen into compounds, such as ammonia, by natural agencies or industrial processes. **2.** The conversion by certain soil microorganisms, such as rhizobia, of atmospheric nitrogen into compounds that plants and other organisms can assimilate. —**ni′tro·gen-fix′er** (nī′trə-jən-fĭk′sər) *n.* —**ni′tro·gen-fix′ing** *adj.*

ni·trog·en·ize (nī-trŏj′ə-nīz′, nī′trə-jə-) *tr.v.* **-ized, -iz·ing, -iz·es.** To combine or treat with nitrogen or a nitrogen compound.

nitrogen narcosis *n.* A condition of confusion or stupor resulting from increased levels of dissolved nitrogen in the blood.

ni·tro·glyc·er·in also **ni·tro·glyc·er·ine** (nī′trō-glĭs′ər-ĭn, -trə-) *n.* An explosive liquid, $CH_2NO_3CHNO_3CH_2NO_3$, that is used in the production of dynamite and blasting gelatin and as a vasodilator in medicine.

ni·tro·hy·dro·chlo·ric acid (nī′trō-hī′drə-klôr′ĭk, -klōr′-) *n.* See **aqua regia.**

ni·tro·meth·ane (nī′trō-mĕth′ān′) *n.* A colorless oily liquid, CH_3NO_2, used in making dyes and resins, in organic synthesis, and as a rocket propellant.

ni·tro·par·af·fin (nī′trō-păr′ə-fĭn) *n.* Any of a group of compounds formed by replacing one or more of the hydrogen atoms of a paraffin hydrocarbon with the univalent group, NO_2.

ni·tros·a·mine (nī-trō′sə-mēn′, nī′trōs-ăm′ēn) *n.* Any of a class of compounds with the general formula R_2NNO, present in various cooked foods and carcinogenic in laboratory animals. [Lat. *nitrōsus*, full of natron (< *nitrum*, natron; see NITER) + AMINE.]

ni·tro·starch (nī′trə-stärch′) *n.* An explosive powder, $C_{12}H_{12}(NO_2)_8O_{10}$, derived from starch and used for demolition.

ni·trous (nī′trəs) *adj.* Of, derived from, or containing nitrogen, esp. in a valence state lower than that in a comparable nitric compound.

nitrous acid *n.* A weak inorganic acid, HNO_2, existing only in solution or in the form of its salts.

nitrous oxide *n.* A colorless sweet-tasting gas, N_2O, used as a mild anesthetic in dentistry and surgery.

nit·ty-grit·ty (nĭt′ē-grĭt′ē) *n. Informal.* The specific or practical details; the heart of a matter. [?]

nit·wit (nĭt′wĭt′) *n.* A person regarded as stupid or silly. [Prob. obsolete *nit*, nothing (< Ger. dial. < MHGer. *niht, nit*; see NIX[2]) + WIT[1].]

Ni·u·e (nē-ōō′ā). An island dependency of New Zealand in the S-central Pacific E of Tonga; became internally self-governing in 1974. Cap. Alofi. Pop. 3,578.

ni·val (nī′vəl) *adj.* Of, relating to, or growing in or under snow: *nival species of plants.* [Lat. *nivālis* < *nix, niv-*, snow.]

niv·e·ous (nĭv′ē-əs) *adj.* Resembling snow; snowy. [< Lat. *niveus* < *nix, niv-*, snow.]

Ni·ver·nais (nĭv′ər-nā′, nē-vĕr-nĕ′). A historical region and former province of central France; became part of the royal domain in 1669.

nix[1] (nĭks) *n. Myth.* A water sprite of German mythology, usu. in human form or half-human and half-fish. [Ger. < MHGer. *nickes* < OHGer. *nihhus.*]

nix[2] (nĭks) *Slang.* —*n.* Nothing. —*adv.* Not so; no. —*tr.v.* **nixed, nix·ing, nix·es.** To forbid, refuse, or veto. [Ger. dial. < MHGer. *nihtes*, genitive of *niht* < OHGer. *niwiht* : *ni*, not, no; see **ne*** + *wiht*, thing; see **wekti-***.]

nix·ie also **nix·y** (nĭk′sē) *n., pl.* **-ies.** *Slang.* A misaddressed or illegible piece of mail, therefore undeliverable. [< NIX[2].]

Nix·on (nĭk′sən), **Richard Milhous.** b. 1913. The 37th President of the U.S. (1969–74). When Congress recommended three articles of impeachment for Nixon's involvement in the Watergate scandal, he resigned from office (Aug. 9, 1974).

Nixon, Thelma Catherine Ryan ("Pat"). b. 1912. First Lady of the U.S. (1969–74) who worked to make the White House more accessible for disabled and sightless people.

Ni·zam (nĭ-zäm′, -zăm′, nī-) *n.* **1.** Used formerly as a title for rulers of Hyderabad, India. **2. nizam,** *pl.* **nizam.** A Turkish soldier, esp. in the 19th century. [Urdu *nizām(-almulk)*, governor (of the empire) < Ar. *niẓām*, order, arrangement < *naẓama*, to arrange.]

Nizh·ne·var·tovsk (nĭzh′nə-vär-tôfsk′, nyĭzh-). A city of central Russia on the Ob R. Pop. 190,000.

Nizh·niy Ta·gil (nĭzh′nē tə-gēl′, nyē′zhnē tə-gyēl′). A city of central Russia in the E-central Ural Mts. Pop. 419,000.

Nizh·ny Nov·go·rod (nĭzh′nē nŏv′gə-rŏd′, nyē′zhnē nôv′-gə-rət). See **Gorky.**

NJ or **N.J.** *abbr.* New Jersey.

Nkru·mah (ən-krōō′mə, əng-), **Kwame.** 1909–72. Ghanaian politician who served as president (1960–66).

NKVD or **N.K.V.D.** *abbr.* Narodny Kommissariat Vnutrennikh Del (Peoples' Commissariat of Internal Affairs).

NL or **N.L.** *abbr.* **1.** *Baseball.* National League. **2.** Also **n.l.** New line. **3.** New Latin. **4.** *Lat.* Non licet (not permitted). **5.** *Lat.* Non liquet (not clear).

NLRB or **N.L.R.B.** *abbr.* National Labor Relations Board.

nm *abbr.* **1.** Nanometer. **2.** Nuclear magneton. **3.** Also **n.m.** or **NM** Nautical mile.

NM or **N.M.** *abbr.* New Mexico.

N.Mex. *abbr.* New Mexico.

NMR *abbr.* Nuclear magnetic resonance.

NNE *abbr.* North-northeast.

NNW *abbr.* North-northwest.

no[1] (nō) *adv.* **1.** Used to express refusal, denial, disbelief, emphasis, or disagreement: *No, I'm not going. No, you're wrong.* **2.** Not at all; not by any degree. Often used with the comparative: *no better; no more.* **3.** Not: *whether or no.* —*n., pl.* **noes** (nōz). **1.** A negative response; a denial or refusal: *The proposal produced only noes.* **2.** A negative vote or voter. [ME < OE *nā* : *ne*, not; see **ne*** + *ā*, ever; see **aiw-***.]

no[2] (nō) *adj.* **1.** Not any; not one; not a: *No cookies are left.* **2.** Not at all; not close to being: *He is no child.* **3.** Hardly any: *got there in no time.* See Usage Note at **nor[1]**. [ME, var. of *non* < OE *nān*, none : *ne*, not; see **ne*** + *ān*, one; see ONE.]

No[1] also **Noh** (nō) *n., pl.* **No** also **Noh.** The classical drama of Japan, with music and dance performed in a highly stylized manner by elaborately dressed performers on an almost bare stage. [J. *nō*, talent, ability, No < Chin. *néng.*]

No[1]

No[2] The symbol for the element **nobelium.**

No (nō), **Lake.** A lake of S-central Sudan formed by the flood waters of the White Nile.

no. or **No.** *abbr.* **1.** North; northern. **2.** Number.

NOAA *abbr.* National Oceanic and Aeronautic Administration.

no-ac·count (nō′ə-kount′) *adj. Informal.* Worthless.

No·a·chi·an (nō-ā′kē-ən) also **No·ach·ic** (-ăk′ĭk) or **No·ach·i·cal** (-ĭ-kəl) *adj.* **1.** *Bible.* Of or relating to Noah or his time. **2.** Antiquated; ancient; long obsolete.

No·ah (nō′ə). In the Bible, the patriarch who was chosen by God to build an ark, in which he, his family, and a pair of every animal were saved from the Flood.

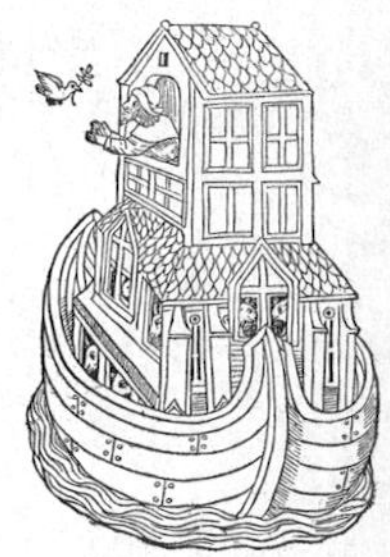

Noah
15th-century French rendering of Noah in his ark, from *La Mer des Histoires*

No·a·tak (nō-ā′tək, -tăk). A river of NW AK flowing c. 644 km (400 mi) to Kotzebue Sound.

nob[1] (nŏb) *n.* **1.** *Slang.* The human head. **2.** *Games.* The jack of the suit turned up by the dealer in cribbage, scoring one point for the holder: *one for his nob.* [Perh. var. of KNOB.]

nob[2] (nŏb) *n. Chiefly British.* A person of wealth or social standing. [Poss. < NOB[1] or KNOB.]

nob·ble (nŏb′əl) *tr.v.* **-bled, -bling, -bles.** *Chiefly British.* **1.** To disable (a racehorse), esp. by drugging. **2.** To win (a person) over. **3.** To outdo or get the better of by devious means. **4.** To filch or steal. **5.** To kidnap. [?] —**nob′bler** *n.*

nob·by (nŏb′ē) *adj.* **-bi·er, -bi·est.** Fashionable; stylish.

No·bel (nō-bĕl′), **Alfred Bernhard.** 1833–96. Swedish chemist and engineer who invented dynamite (1866) and bequeathed his fortune to institute the Nobel Prizes.

No·bel·ist (nō-bĕl′ĭst) *n.* A recipient of a Nobel prize.

no·bel·i·um (nō-bĕl′ē-əm) *n. Symbol* **No** A radioactive synthetic element in the actinide series; its longest-lived isotope is No 255 with a half-life of 3 minutes. Atomic number 102. See table at **element.** [After Alfred Bernhard NOBEL.]

Nobel Prize *n.* Any of the six international prizes awarded annually by the Nobel Foundation for outstanding achievements in the fields of physics, chemistry, physiology or medicine, literature, and economics and for the promotion of world peace. [After Alfred Bernhard NOBEL.]

no·bil·i·ar·y (nō-bĭl′ē-ĕr′ē, -bĭl′yə-rē) *adj.* Of or relating to the nobility. [Fr. *nobiliaire* < Lat. *nōbilis*, noble. See NOBLE.]

nobiliary particle *n.* A preposition used as a mark of noble rank before a title or surname, as German *van* in *Ludwig van Beethoven* and French *de* in *Simone de Beauvoir.*

no·bil·i·ty (nō-bĭl′ĭ-tē) *n., pl.* **-ties. 1.** A class of persons distinguished by high birth or rank. **2.** Noble rank or status: *titles of nobility.* **3.** The state or quality of being exalted in character. [ME *nobilite*, the quality of being noble < OFr. < Lat. *nōbilitās* < *nōbilis*, noble. See NOBLE.]

no·ble (nō′bəl) *adj.* **-bler, -blest. 1.** Possessing high rank, often hereditary, in a political system or social class derived from a feudalistic stage of a country's development. **2.a.** Having or showing qualities of high moral character, such as courage, generosity, or honor. **b.** Proceeding from or indicative of such a character; showing magnanimity. **3.** Grand and stately in appearance; majestic. **4.** *Chem.* Inactive or inert. —*n.* **1.** A member of the nobility. **2.** A gold coin formerly used in England, worth half of a mark. [ME < OFr. < Lat. *nōbilis.* See **gnō-***.] —**no′ble·ness** *n.* —**no′bly** *adv.*

noble gas *n.* Any of the elements in Group O of the periodic table, including helium, neon, argon, krypton, xenon, and radon, that are monatomic and largely chemically inert.

no·ble·man (nō′bəl-mən) *n.* A man of noble rank.

noble metal *n.* A metal or an alloy, such as gold, that is highly resistant to oxidation and corrosion.

no·blesse (nō-blĕs′) *n.* **1.** Noble birth or condition. **2.** The members of the nobility, esp. the French nobility. [ME < OFr. < *noble*, noble < Lat. *nōbilis.* See NOBLE.]

noblesse o·blige (ō-blēzh′) *n.* Benevolent honorable behavior considered to be the responsibility of persons of high birth or rank. [Fr., nobility is an obligation : *noblesse*, nobility + *oblige*, third pers. sing. pr.t. of *obliger*, to obligate.]

no·ble·wom·an (nō′bəl-wōōm′ən) *n.* A woman of noble rank.

ă pat	oi boy
ā pay	ou out
âr care	ōō took
ä father	ōō boot
ĕ pet	ŭ cut
ē be	ûr urge
ĭ pit	th thin
ī pie	*th* this
îr pier	hw which
ŏ pot	zh vision
ō toe	ə about, item
ô paw	

Stress marks:
′ (primary);
′ (secondary), as in
dictionary (dĭk′shə-nĕr′ē)

no•bod•y (nō′bŏd′ē, -bŭd′ē, -bə-dē) *pron.* No person; not anyone. — *n., pl.* **-ies.** An unimportant or uninfluential person.

no•cent (nō′sənt) *adj.* Causing injury; harmful. [ME *nocent,* guilty < Lat. *nocēns, nocent-,* pr.part. of *nocēre,* to harm. See **nek-[1]*.**]

no•ci•cep•tive (nō′sĭ-sĕp′tĭv) *adj.* **1.** Causing pain. Used of a stimulus. **2.** Caused by or responding to a painful stimulus: *a nociceptive spinal reflex.* [< NOCICEPTOR.]

no•ci•cep•tor (nō′sĭ-sĕp′tər) *n.* A sensory receptor that responds to pain. [Lat. *nocēre,* to hurt; see NOCENT + (RE)CEPTOR.]

nock (nŏk) *n.* **1.** The groove at either end of a bow for holding the bowstring. **2.** The notch in the end of an arrow that fits on the bowstring. — *tr.v.* **nocked, nock•ing, nocks. 1.** To put a nock in (a bow or an arrow). **2.** To fit (an arrow) to a bowstring. [ME *nokke.*]

noc•tam•bu•lism (nŏk-tăm′byə-lĭz′əm) also **noc•tam•bu•la•tion** (-tăm′byə-lā′shən) *n.* See **sleepwalking.** [NOCT(I)– + Lat. *ambulāre,* to walk + –ISM.] — **noc•tam′bu•list** *n.*

nocti– or **noct–** *pref.* Night: *noctilucent.* [NLat. < Lat. *nox, noct-,* night. See **nek^w-t-*.**]

noc•ti•lu•ca (nŏk′tə-lo͞o′kə) *n.* Any of various bioluminescent dinoflagellates of the genus *Noctiluca* that when grouped in large numbers make the sea phosphorescent. [NLat. *Noctilūca,* genus name < Lat. *noctilūca,* lantern, moon : *nocti-,* nocti- + *lūcēre,* to shine; see **leuk-*.**]

noc•ti•lu•cent (nŏk′tə-lo͞o′sənt) *adj.* Luminous at night. Used esp. of certain high clouds.

noc•tu•id (nŏk′cho͞o-ĭd) *n.* Any of numerous night-flying moths of the family Noctuidae, having a proboscis for sucking nectar and larvae that are destructive, as to young trees. [< NLat. *Noctuidae,* family name < *Noctua,* type genus < Lat. *noctua,* night owl. See **nek^w-t-*.**] — **noc′tu•id** *adj.*

noc•tule (nŏk′cho͞ol′) *n.* A large insectivorous bat of the genus *Nyctalus,* found in Eurasia, Indonesia, and the Philippines. [Fr. < Ital. *nottola,* bat, owl < LLat. *noctula* < Lat., dim. of *noctua,* night owl. See **nek^w-t-*.**]

noc•turn (nŏk′tûrn′) *n.* Any of the three canonical divisions of the office of matins. [ME *nocturne* < Med.Lat. *nocturna* < Lat., fem. of *nocturnus,* of the night. See NOCTURNAL.]

noc•tur•nal (nŏk-tûr′nəl) *adj.* **1.** Of, relating to, or occurring in the night: *nocturnal stillness.* **2.** *Bot.* Having flowers that open during the night. **3.** *Zool.* Most active at night. [ME < OFr. < LLat. *nocturnālis* < Lat. *nocturnus* < *nox, noct-,* night. See **nek^w-t-*.**] — **noc•tur′nal•ly** *adv.*

noc•turne (nŏk′tûrn′) *n.* **1.** A painting of a night scene. **2.** *Mus.* A pensive, dreamy instrumental composition. [Fr. < OFr., nocturnal < Lat. *nocturnus.* See NOCTURNAL.]

noc•u•ous (nŏk′yo͞o-əs) *adj.* Harmful; noxious. [< Lat. *nocuus* < *nocēre,* to harm. See **nek-[1]*.**] — **noc′u•ous•ly** *adv.*

nod (nŏd) *v.* **nod•ded, nod•ding, nods.** — *intr.* **1.** To lower and raise the head quickly, as in agreement. **2.** To let the head fall forward when sleepy; doze momentarily. **3.** To be careless or momentarily inattentive as if sleepy; lapse. **4.** To sway, move up and down, or droop, as flowers in the wind. — *tr.* **1.** To lower and raise (the head) quickly in agreement or acknowledgment. **2.** To express by lowering and raising the head. **3.** To summon, guide, or send by nodding the head. — *n.* **1.** A forward or up-and-down movement of the head, usu. expressive of drowsiness or agreement. **2.** An indication of approval or assent. [ME *nodden;* perh. akin to MHGer. *notten.*] — **nod′der** *n.*

nod•al (nōd′l) *adj.* Of, relating to, resembling, being, or situated near or at a node. — **nod′al•ly** *adv.*

nod•dle (nŏd′l) *n.* The head. [ME *noddel,* back of the head, perh. < Lat. *nōdulus,* lump, knob. See NODULE.]

nod•dy (nŏd′ē) *n., pl.* **-dies. 1.** A dunce or fool; a simpleton. **2.** Any of several terns of the genera *Anous* and *Micranous,* found in tropical waters and having a dark brown or black color with a white or gray head. [Perh. < obsolete *noddy,* foolish, poss. < NOD.]

node (nōd) *n.* **1.** A knob, knot, protuberance, or swelling. **2.a.** *Bot.* The point on a stem where a leaf is attached or has been attached; a joint. **b.** See **knot[1]** 7. **3.** *Phys.* A point or region of virtually zero amplitude in a periodic system. **4.** *Math.* The point at which a continuous curve crosses itself. **5.** *Comp. Sci.* A terminal in a computer network. **6.** *Astron.* **a.** Either of two points at which the orbit of a planet intersects the ecliptic. **b.** Either of two points at which the orbit of a satellite intersects the orbital plane of a planet. [ME, lump in the flesh < Lat. *nōdus,* knot. See **ned-*.**]

node of Ran•vier (rän′vyā, rän-vyā′, räN-) *n., pl.* **nodes of Ranvier.** A constriction in the myelin sheath, occurring at varying intervals along the length of a nerve fiber. [After Louis Antoine *Ranvier* (1835–1922), French histologist.]

no•dose (nō′dōs′) *adj.* Characterized by or having many nodes or protuberances; jointed or knobby at intervals. — **no•dos′i•ty** (-dŏs′ĭ-tē) *n.*

nod•ule (nŏj′o͞ol) *n.* **1.** A small knotlike protuberance. **2.** *Anat.* A small mass of tissue or aggregation of cells. **3.** *Bot.* A small knoblike outgrowth, as those found on the roots of many leguminous plants. **4.** *Mineral.* A small rounded lump of a mineral or mixture of minerals, usu. harder than the surrounding rock or sediment. [ME < Lat. *nōdulus,* dim. of *nōdus,* knot. See **ned-*.**] — **nod′u•lar** (nŏj′ə-lər), **nod′u•lose′** (-lōs′), **nod′u•lous** (-ləs) *adj.*

no•dus (nō′dəs) *n., pl.* **-di** (-dī). A difficult situation or problem; a complication. [Lat. *nōdus,* knot. See **ned-*.**]

No•ël also **No•el** (nō-ĕl′) *n.* **1.** Christmas. **2. noël.** A Christmas carol. [ME *noel* < OFr., var. of *nael* < Lat. *nātālis (diēs),* (day) of birth < *nātus,* p.part. of *nāscī,* to be born. See **genə-*.**]

No•el-Ba•ker (nō′əl-bā′kər), **Philip John.** 1889–1982. British politician who won the 1959 Nobel Peace Prize.

noes (nōz) *n.* Pl. of **no[1]**.

no•e•sis (nō-ē′sĭs) *n. Psychol.* The cognitive process; cognition. [Gk. *noēsis,* understanding < *noein,* to perceive < *nous,* mind.]

no•et•ic (nō-ĕt′ĭk) *adj.* Of, relating to, originating in, or apprehended by the intellect.

no-fault (nō′fôlt′) *adj.* **1.** Of, indicating, or being a system of motor vehicle insurance in which accident victims are compensated by their insurance companies without assignment of blame. **2.** *Law.* Of, indicating, or being a type of divorce in which blame is assigned to neither party.

no-frills (nō′frĭlz′) *adj. Informal.* Marked by the absence of extra or special features; basic: *no-frills airline service.*

nog[1] (nŏg) *n.* **1.** A wooden block built into a masonry wall to hold nails that support joinery structures. **2.** A wooden peg or pin. [?]

nog[2] (nŏg) *n.* Eggnog.

No•gal•es (nō-găl′ĭs, -gä′lĭs). A city of S AZ S of Tucson on the Mexican border adjacent to **Nogales,** Mexico. Pop. in AZ, 19,489; in Mexico, 14,254.

nog•gin (nŏg′ĭn) *n.* **1.** A small mug or cup. **2.** A unit of liquid measure equal to one quarter of a pint. **3.** *Slang.* The human head. [?]

no-go (nō′gō′) *adj.* Not proceeding or functioning properly.

no-good (no′go͝od′) *adj.* Having no value, use, merit, or virtue. — *n.* One that is worthless.

No•gu•chi (nō-go͞o′chē), **Hideyo.** 1876–1928. Japanese-born Amer. bacteriologist who discovered the cause of syphilis and yellow fever.

Noguchi, Isamu. b. 1904. Amer. sculptor noted for his abstract works of bronze, stone, and terra cotta.

Noh (nō) *n.* Var. of **No[1]**.

no-hit (nō′hĭt′) *adj. Baseball.* Of, relating to, or being a no-hitter.

no-hit•ter (nō′hĭt′ər) *n. Baseball.* A game in which one pitcher allows the opposing team no hits.

no-holds-barred (nō′hōldz′bärd′) *adj. Informal.* Open and unrestrained.

no•how (nō′hou′) *adv. Non-Standard.* In no way; not at all.

noil (noil) *n.* A short fiber combed from long fibers during the preparation of textile yarns. [Perh. < ME **noil* < OFr. *noel* < Med.Lat. *nōdellus* < Lat., dim. of *nōdus,* knot. See NODE.]

noise (noiz) *n.* **1.a.** Sound or a sound that is loud, unpleasant, unexpected, or undesired. **b.** Sound or a sound of any kind. **2.** A loud outcry or commotion. **3.** *Phys.* A disturbance, esp. a random and persistent disturbance, that obscures or reduces the clarity of a signal. **4.** *Comp. Sci.* Irrelevant or meaningless data generated by a computer along with desired data. **5.** *Informal.* **a.** A complaint or protest. **b.** Rumor; talk. **c. noises.** Remarks or actions intended to convey a specific impression or to attract attention. — *v.* **noised, nois•ing, nois•es.** — *tr.* To spread the rumor or report of. — *intr.* **1.** To talk much or volubly. **2.** To be noisy; make noise. [ME < OFr., perh. < VLat. **nausea,* discomfort < Lat. *nausea,* seasickness. See NAUSEA.]

Syns: *noise, din, racket, pandemonium, uproar, hullabaloo, hubbub, clamor, babel.* These nouns refer to loud, confused, or disagreeable sound or sounds. *Noise* is the least specific: *the noise of cannon fire.* A *din* is a jumble of loud, usually discordant sounds: *the din in the factory. Racket* is loud, distressing noise: *the racket of trucks rolling along cobblestone streets. Pandemonium, uproar,* and *hullabaloo* imply disorderly tumult together with loud, bewildering sound: *"a pandemonium of dancing and whooping, drumming and feasting"* (Francis Parkman). *"The evening uproar of the howling monkeys burst out"* (W.H. Hudson). *The speech created a tremendous hullabaloo in the audience. Hubbub* emphasizes turbulent activity and concomitant din: *the hubbub of bettors. Clamor* is loud, usually sustained noise, as of a public outcry of dissatisfaction: *"not in the clamor of the crowded street"* (Henry Wadsworth Longfellow). *Babel* stresses confusion of vocal sounds arising from simultaneous utterance and random mixture of languages: *guests chattering in a babel of tongues at the reception.*

noise•mak•er (noiz′mā′kər) *n.* One that makes noise, esp. a horn or rattle used to make noise at a party. — **noise′mak′ing** *n.*

noise pollution *n.* Environmental noise that is annoying, distracting, or physically harmful.

noi•sette (nwä-zĕt′) *n.* A small round piece of meat. —*adj.* Made or flavored with hazelnuts. [Fr. < OFr., dim. of *nois,* nut < Lat. *nux.*]

noi•some (noi′səm) *adj.* **1.** Offensive to the point of arousing disgust; foul: *a noisome odor.* **2.** Harmful or dangerous: *noisome exhaust fumes.* [ME *noiesom* : *noie,* harm (short for *anoi,* annoyance < OFr. < *anoier,* to annoy; see ANNOY) + *-som,* adj. suff.; see -SOME[1].] —**noi′some•ly** *adv.* —**noi′some•ness** *n.*

nois•y (noi′zē) *adj.* **-i•er, -i•est. 1.** Making noise: *a small, noisy dog.* **2.** Full of, characterized by, or accompanied by noise: *a noisy cafeteria.* —**nois′i•ly** *adv.* —**nois′i•ness** *n.*

no•lens vo•lens (nō′lĕnz vō′lĕnz, nō′lĕns wō′lĕns) *adv.* Whether willing or unwilling. [Lat. *nōlēns volēns* : *nōlēns,* pr.part. of *nolle,* to be unwilling + *volēns,* pr.part. of *velle,* to wish, be willing.]

no•li-me-tan•ge•re (nō′lē-mē-tăn′jə-rē, nō′lī-) *n.* **1.** A warning or prohibition against touching or interfering. **2.** A representation of Jesus appearing to Mary Magdalen after his resurrection. [LLat. *nōlī mē tangere,* do not touch me (Jesus's words to Mary Magdalene, John 20:17).]

nol•le pros•e•qui (nŏl′ē prŏs′ĭ-kwī′, -kwē′) *n. Law.* A declaration that the plaintiff in a civil case or the prosecutor in a criminal case will drop prosecution of all or part of a suit or an indictment. [Lat. *nolle prōsequī,* to be unwilling to pursue : *nolle,* to be unwilling + *prōsequī,* to pursue.]

no•lo (nō′lō) *n., pl.* **-los.** *Law.* Nolo contendere.

no-load (nō′lōd′) *adj. Bus.* Sold directly to customers at net asset value without a sales commission.

no•lo con•ten•de•re (nō′lō kən-tĕn′də-rē) *n. Law.* A plea made by the defendant in a criminal action that is substantially but not technically an admission of guilt and subjects the defendant to punishment but permits denial of the alleged facts in other proceedings. [Lat. *nōlō contendere,* I do not wish to contend : *nōlō,* first pers. sing. pr.t. of *nolle,* to be unwilling + *contendere,* to contend.]

no-lose (nō′lo͞oz′) *adj. Slang.* Certain to end happily or successfully.

nol-pros (nŏl′prŏs′) *tr.v.* **-prossed, -pros•sing, -pros•ses.** *Law.* To drop prosecution of by entering a nolle prosequi in court records.

nol. pros. *abbr. Law.* Nolle prosequi.

nom. *abbr.* Nominative.

no•ma (nō′mə) *n.* A severe, often gangrenous inflammation of the mouth or genitals, occurring usu. after an infectious disease and found most often in children in poor hygienic or malnourished condition. [Lat. *nomē,* ulcer < Gk. See **nem-***.]

no•mad (nō′măd′) *n.* **1.** A member of a group of people who have no fixed home and move according to the seasons from place to place in search of food, water, and grazing land. **2.** A person with no fixed residence who roams about; a wanderer. [Fr. *nomade* < Lat. *nomas, nomad-* < Gk. *nomas,* wandering in search of pasture. See **nem-***.] —**no•mad′ic** *adj.* —**no•mad′i•cal•ly** *adv.* —**no′mad′ism** *n.*

no man's land (mănz) *n.* **1.** Land disputed by two parties, esp. land between two armies. **2.** An area of uncertainty or ambiguity. **3.** An unclaimed or unowned piece of land.

nom•ar•chy (nŏm′är′kē) *n., pl.* **-chies.** Any of the administrative provinces of the modern Greek state. [Mod.Gk. *nomarkhia* < Gk., district : *nomos,* district; see NOME + *-arkhia,* -archy.]

nom•bril (nŏm′brəl) *n. Her.* The point on an escutcheon between the fess point and the base point; the midpoint in the lower half of the escutcheon. [Fr. < OFr. < *(un) ombril,* (a) navel < VLat. **umbilīculus* < Lat., dim. of *umbilīcus.* See **nobh-***.]

nom de guerre (nŏm′ də gâr′) *n., pl.* **noms de guerre** (nŏm′). A fictitious name; a pseudonym. [Fr. : *nom,* name + *de,* of + *guerre,* war.]

nom de plume (nŏm′ də plo͞om′) *n., pl.* **noms de plume** (nŏm′). See **pen name.** [Fr. : *nom,* name + *de,* of + *plume,* pen.]

nome (nōm) *n.* **1.** A province of Pharaonic, Hellenistic, and Roman Egypt. **2.** A nomarchy. [Gk. *nomos,* district, custom. See **nem-***.]

Nome (nōm). A city of W AK on Norton Sound and the S coast of Seward Peninsula; founded as a gold-mining camp in 1896. Pop. 3,500.

no•men•cla•tor (nō′mən-klā′tər) *n.* One who assigns names, as in scientific classification. [Lat. *nōmenclātor,* a slave who accompanied his master to tell him the names of people he met, var. of *nōmenculātor* : *nōmen,* name; see **nō̆-men-*** + *calātor,* servant, crier (< *calāre,* to call; see **kelə-**[2]*).]

no•men•cla•to•ri•al (nō′mən-klə-tôr′ē-əl, -tōr′-) *adj.* Of or relating to nomenclature.

no•men•cla•ture (nō′mən-klā′chər, nō-mĕn′klə-) *n.* **1.** A system of names used in an art or a science. **2.** The procedure of assigning names to organisms listed in a taxonomic classification. [Lat. *nōmenclātūra* < *nōmenclātor,* nomenclator. See NOMENCLATOR.]

no•men•kla•tu•ra (nō′mən-klä-to͞or′ə, nô′myĕn-klä-to͞or′ä) *n.* (*used with a sing. or pl. v.*) The privileged class of bureaucrats appointed by the government in the former Soviet Union and certain other countries. [Russ. < Lat. *nōmenclātūra,* list of names. See NOMENCLATURE.]

nom•i•nal (nŏm′ə-nəl) *adj.* **1.a.** Of, resembling, relating to, or consisting of a name or names. **b.** Assigned to or bearing a person's name: *nominal shares.* **2.** Existing in name only. **3.** *Philos.* Of or relating to nominalism. **4.** Insignificantly small; trifling: *a nominal sum.* **5.** *Bus.* **a.** Of, relating to, or being the amount or face value of a sum of money or a stock certificate, for example, and not the purchasing power or market value. **b.** Of, relating to, or being the rate of interest or return without adjustment for compounding or inflation. **6.** *Gram.* Of or relating to a noun or word group that functions as a noun. **7.** *Aerospace & Engineering.* According to plan or design: *a nominal flight check.* —*n. Gram.* A word or group of words functioning as a noun. [ME *nominalle,* of nouns < Lat. *nōminālis,* of names < *nōmen, nōmin-,* name. See **nō̆-men-***.] —**nom′i•nal•ly** *adv.*

nom•i•nal•ism (nŏm′ə-nə-lĭz′əm) *n. Philos.* The doctrine holding that abstract concepts, general terms, or universals have no objective reference but exist only as names. —**nom′i•nal•ist** *n.* —**nom′i•nal•is′tic** *adj.*

nominal value *n.* See **par value.**

nominal wages *pl.n.* Wages measured in terms of money paid, not in terms of purchasing power.

nom•i•nate (nŏm′ə-nāt′) *tr.v.* **-nat•ed, -nat•ing, -nates. 1.** To propose by name as a candidate, esp. for election. **2.** To designate or appoint to an office, a responsibility, or an honor. [Lat. *nōmināre, nōmināt-,* to name < *nōmen, nōmin-,* name. See **nō̆-men-***.] —**nom′i•na′tor** *n.*

nom•i•na•tion (nŏm′ə-nā′shən) *n.* **1.** The act or an instance of appointing a person to office. **2.** The act or an instance of submitting a name for candidacy or appointment. **3.** The state of being nominated.

nom•i•na•tive (nŏm′ə-nā′tĭv) *adj.* **1.a.** Appointed to office. **b.** Nominated as a candidate for office. **2.** Having or bearing a person's name. **3.** (-nə-tĭv). *Gram.* Of, relating to, or belonging to a case of the subject of a finite verb and of words identified with the subject of a copula, such as a predicate nominative. —*n.* (-nə-tĭv). *Gram.* The nominative case.

nom•i•nee (nŏm′ə-nē′) *n.* **1.** One who has been nominated to an office or for a candidacy. **2.** A person or an organization in whose name a security is registered though true ownership is held by another party. [NOMIN(ATE) + -EE[1].]

nom•o•graph (nŏm′ə-grăf′, nō′mə-) or **nom•o•gram** (-grăm′) *n.* **1.** A graph consisting of three coplanar curves, each graduated for a different variable so that a straight line cutting all three curves intersects the related values of each variable. **2.** A chart representing numerical relationships. [Gk. *nomos,* law; see **nem-*** + -GRAPH.] —**nom′o•graph′ic** *adj.* —**no•mog′ra•phy** (nō-mŏg′rə-fē) *n.*

no•mol•o•gy (nō-mŏl′ə-jē) *n.* The study and discovery of general physical and logical laws. [Gk. *nomos,* law; see **nem-*** + -LOGY.] —**nom′o•log′ic** (nŏm′ə-lŏj′ĭk, nō′mə-), **nom′o•log′i•cal** (-ĭ-kəl) *adj.* —**nom′o•log′i•cal•ly** *adv.* —**no•mol′o•gist** *n.*

nom•o•thet•ic (nŏm′ə-thĕt′ĭk) or **nom•o•thet•ic•al** (-ĭk-əl) *adj.* **1.** Of or relating to lawmaking; legislative. **2.** Based on a system of law. **3.** Of or relating to the philosophy of law. **4.** Of or relating to the study or discovery of general scientific laws. [Gk. *nomothetikos* : *nomos,* law; see **nem-*** + *thetikos,* thetic; see THETIC.] —**nom•o•thet′i•cal•ly** *adv.*

-nomy *suff.* A system of laws governing or a body of knowledge about a specified field: *aeronomy.* [Gk. *-nomia* < *nomos,* law. See **nem-***.]

non- *pref.* Not: *noncombatant.* [ME < OFr. < Lat. *nōn,* not. See **ne***.]

nona- *pref.* Ninth; nine: *nonagon.* [< Lat. *nōnus,* ninth. See **newn̥***.]

non•age (nŏn′ĭj, nō′nĭj) *n.* **1.** The period during which one is legally underage. **2.** A period of immaturity. [ME *nounage* < AN, var. of OFr. *nonaage* : *non-,* non- + *aage,* age; see AGE.]

non•a•ge•nar•i•an (nŏn′ə-jə-nâr′ē-ən, nō′nə-) *n.* A person 90 years old or between 90 and 100 years old. [< Lat. *nōnāgēnārius* < *nōnāgēnī,* ninety each < *nōnāgintā,* ninety : *nōnus,* ninth; see NONA- + *-gintā,* ten times; see **dekm̥***.] —**non′a•ge•nar′i•an** *adj.*

non•a•gon (nŏn′ə-gŏn′, nō′nə-) *n.* A polygon with nine sides.

non•al•co•hol•ic (nŏn′ăl-kə-hô′lĭk, -hŏl′ĭk) *n.* A beverage usu. containing less than 0.5 percent alcohol by volume. —*adj.* **1.** Of, relating to, or being a beverage whose alcohol content is very low or negligible. **2.** Containing no alcohol: *nonalcoholic medication.* **3.** Dealcoholized.

non•a•ligned (nŏn′ə-līnd′) *adj.* Not allied with any other nation or bloc; neutral. —**non′a•lign′ment** *n.*

non•ap•pear•ance (nŏn′ə-pîr′əns) *n. Law.* Failure of a witness or party to appear in response to a subpoena or notice.

non•as•sess•a•ble (nŏn′ə-sĕs′ə-bəl) *adj.* **1.** Impossible to estimate, set, or determine: *nonassessable damages.* **2.** Of or relating to capital stock for which owners cannot be assessed additional funds to cover liabilities of the firm and therefore cannot lose more than their original investments.

ă pat	oi boy
ā pay	ou out
âr care	o͝o took
ä father	o͞o boot
ĕ pet	ŭ cut
ē be	ûr urge
ĭ pit	th thin
ī pie	*th* this
îr pier	hw which
ŏ pot	zh vision
ō toe	ə about, item
ô paw	

Stress marks:
′ (primary);
′ (secondary), as in **dictionary** (dĭk′shə-nĕr′ē)

noon•day (no͞on′dā′) *n.* Midday; noon.
no one *pron.* No person; nobody.
noon•tide (no͞on′tīd′) *n.* See **noon** 1.
noon•time (no͞on′tīm′) *n.* See **noon** 1.
noose (no͞os) *n.* **1.** A loop formed in a rope by a slipknot so that it binds tighter as the rope is pulled. **2.** A snare or trap. —*tr.v.* **noosed, noos•ing, noos•es. 1.** To capture or hold by or as if by a noose. **2.** To make a noose of or in. [ME *nose,* prob. < OFr. *nos, nous,* knot < Lat. *nōdus.* See NODE.]
Noot•ka (no͞ot′kə, no͝ot′-) *n., pl.* **Nootka** or **-kas. 1.** A member of a Native American people inhabiting Vancouver Island in British Columbia and Cape Flattery in northwest Washington. **2.** The Wakashan language of the Nootka.
Nootka Sound. An inlet of the Pacific Ocean on the W coast of Vancouver I. in SW British Columbia, Canada.
no•pal (nō′pəl, nō-päl′, -păl′) *n.* Any of several cacti of the genus *Nopalea,* esp. *N. cochenillifera,* found chiefly in Mexico and having reddish flowers. [Am.Sp. < Nahuatl *nopalli.*]
no-par (nō′pär′) *adj.* Being without face value; having no par value: *a no-par stock certificate.*
nope (nōp) *adv. Informal.* No. [Alteration of NO[1].]
nor[1] (nôr; nər *when unstressed*) *conj.* And not; or not; not either: *neither plants nor animals.* [ME, blend of *ne,* no; see NO[1], and *or,* or; see OR[1].]
Usage Note: The traditional rule requires that *nor* be used following *neither* in expressions in which the negation is carried over to the second element: *neither able nor* (not *or*) *willing. Nor* is likewise required when a negation is carried over into the second of two independent clauses, in which case it also triggers inversion of the subject and the auxiliary verb in the second clause: *Jane will never compromise with Bill, nor will Bill compromise with Jane.* When the first negative is expressed by *not* or *never,* however, and when the second conjoined element is a verb phrase, the use of *nor* is often optional: *He will not permit the change, or* (or *nor*) *even consider it.* When a noun phrase of the type *no this or that* is introduced by *no, or* is more common than *nor: He has no experience or interest* (less frequently *nor interest*) *in math. Or* is also more common when such a noun phrase, adjective phrase, or adverb phrase is introduced by *not: We were not rich or happy.* See Usage Notes at **neither, or**[1].
nor[2] (nôr, nər *when unstressed*) *conj. Regional.* Than. [ME, perh. ult. < *nor,* nor. See NOR[1].]
Nor. *abbr.* **1.** Norman. **2.** North. **3.** Norway; Norwegian.
nor– *pref.* An unaltered parent compound: *norepinephrine.* [Short for NORMAL.]
NORAD *abbr.* North American Air Defense Command.
nor•a•dren•a•lin (nôr′ə-drĕn′ə-lĭn) *n.* See **norepinephrine.**
nor•ad•ren•er•gic (nôr′ăd-rə-nûr′jĭk) *adj.* Stimulated by or releasing norepinephrine. —**nor′ad•ren•er′gi•cal•ly** *adv.*
Noraid or **NORAID** *abbr.* Irish Northern Aid Committee.
Nor•co (nôr′kō, nōr′-). A city of S CA WSW of Riverside. Pop. 23,302.
Nor•dau (nôr′dou′), **Max Simon.** 1849–1923. Hungarian-born Zionist leader in Europe (1895–1923).
Nor•den•skjöld (nôr′dn-shōld′, -shəld, no͝or′dən-shœld′), Baron **Nils Adolf Erik.** 1832–1901. Finnish-born Swedish explorer and geologist who was the first to navigate the Northeast Passage (1878–80).
Nor•dic (nôr′dĭk) *adj.* **1.** Of, relating to, or characteristic of Scandinavia or its peoples, languages, or cultures. **2.** Of or relating to a human physical type exemplified esp. by the tall, narrow-headed, light-skinned blond-haired peoples of Scandinavia. **3.** *Sports.* Of or relating to ski competition featuring ski jumping and cross-country racing. —*n.* A person of the Nordic physical type. [Fr. *nordique* < *nord,* north < OFr. *nort* < OE *north.* See **ner-**[1]*.]
Nord•kyn (nôr′kən, -kün), **Cape.** The N point of the European mainland, in N Norway.
Nord•mann fir (nôrd′mən) *n.* A widely planted evergreen tree *(Abies nordmanniana)* native to Greece, Turkey, and the Caucasus and having erect reddish-brown cones. [After Alexander von *Nordmann* (1803–66), Finnish naturalist.]
Nord-Ost•see Ka•nal (nört-ôst′zā kä-näl′). See **Kiel Canal.**
nor'east•er (nôr-ē′stər) *n.* A northeaster.
nor•ep•i•neph•rine (nôr′ĕp-ə-nĕf′rĭn) *n.* A substance, $C_8H_{11}NO_3$, both a hormone and neurotransmitter, secreted by the adrenal medulla and the nerve endings of the sympathetic nervous system and used to cause vasoconstriction.
Nor•folk (nôr′fək, -fōk). **1.** A historical region of E England bordering on the North Sea; settled in prehistoric times and part of the Anglo-Saxon kingdom of East Anglia. **2.** A city of NE NE NW of Omaha. Pop. 21,476. **3.** An independent city of SE VA on Hampton Roads SE of Richmond; founded 1682. Pop. 261,229.
Norfolk Island. An island territory of Australia in the S Pacific NE of Sydney; formerly a British penal colony.
Norfolk Island pine *n.* An evergreen tree *(Araucaria heterophylla)* with incurved decurrent needles, native to Norfolk Island and grown as an indoor plant.

Norfolk Island pine
Araucaria heterophylla

Norfolk jacket *n.* A belted jacket with two box pleats in front and back. [After NORFOLK, England.]
Norfolk terrier *n.* Any of an English breed of small sturdy short-legged terrier identical with the Norwich terrier except for ears that bend forward. [After NORFOLK, England.]
NOR gate (nôr) *n. Comp. Sci.* A logic circuit that produces an output inverse to that of an OR gate. [N(OT) + **OR** GATE.]
Nor•gay (nôr′gā), **Tenzing.** 1914–86. Sherpa guide who with Sir Edmund Hillary first climbed Mt. Everest (1953).
no•ri (nôr′ē) *n., pl.* **-ris.** An edible dried preparation of red algae of the genus *Porphyra.* [J.]
no•ri•a (nôr′ē-ə, nōr′-) *n.* A water wheel with buckets attached to its rim, used to raise water from a stream, esp. for transfer to an irrigation channel. [Sp. < Ar. *nā'ūrah.*]
Nor•i•cum (nôr′ĭ-kəm, nŏr′-). An ancient country and province of the Roman Empire S of the Danube R. in present-day Austria W of Vienna.
No•rilsk (nə-rēlsk′). A city of N-central Russia; founded 1935. Pop. 180,000.
nor•ite (nôr′īt) *n.* See **gabbro.** [Norw. *Norge,* Norway + -ITE[1].] —**nor•it′ic** (nô-rĭt′ĭk) *adj.*
norm (nôrm) *n.* **1.** A standard, model, or pattern regarded as typical: *social norms.* **2.** *Math.* **a.** A mode. **b.** An average. **c.** The length of a vector. [Fr. *norme* < OFr. < Lat. *norma,* carpenter's square, norm. See **gnō-***.]
norm. *abbr.* Normal.
Norm. *abbr.* Norman.
Nor•ma (nôr′mə) *n.* A constellation in the Southern Hemisphere within the Milky Way near Lupus and Ara. [Lat. *norma,* carpenter's square. See **gnō-***.]
nor•mal (nôr′məl) *adj.* **1.** Conforming with, adhering to, or constituting a norm, standard, pattern, level, or type; typical: *normal room temperature.* **2.** *Biol.* Functioning or occurring in a natural way; lacking observable abnormalities or deficiencies. **3.** *Chem.* **a.** Having one gram equivalent weight of solute per liter. Used of a solution. **b.** Having a straight unbranched chain of carbon atoms. Used of an aliphatic hydrocarbon. **4.** *Math.* Being at right angles; perpendicular. **5.a.** Relating to or characterized by average intelligence or development. **b.** Free from emotional disorder. —*n.* **1.** Something normal; the standard: *scored close to the normal.* **2.** The usual or expected state, form, amount, or degree. **3.a.** Correspondence to a norm. **b.** An average. **4.** *Math.* A perpendicular, esp. a perpendicular to a line tangent to a plane curve or a plane tangent to a space curve. [ME < LLat. *normālis* < Lat., made according to the square < *norma,* carpenter's square. See **gnō-***.] —**nor′mal•ly** *adv.*
Nor•mal (nôr′məl). A town of central IL NNE of Bloomington. Pop. 40,023.
nor•mal•cy (nôr′məl-sē) *n.* Normality.
normal distribution *n.* A theoretical frequency distribution for a set of variable data, usu. represented by a bell-shaped curve symmetrical about the mean.
nor•mal•i•ty (nôr-măl′ĭ-tē) *n.* **1.** The state or fact of being normal. **2.** *Chem.* The concentration of a solution, expressed in gram equivalent weights of solute per liter.
nor•mal•ize (nôr′mə-līz′) *tr.v.* **-ized, -iz•ing, -iz•es. 1.** To make normal, esp. to cause to conform to a standard or norm: *normalizing relations with a former enemy.* **2.** To make (a text or language) regular and consistent, esp. in spelling or style. **3.** To remove strains and reduce coarse crystalline structures in (metal), esp. by heating and cooling. —**nor′mal•i•za′tion** (-mə-lĭ-zā′shən) *n.* —**nor′mal•iz′er** *n.*
normal school *n.* A school that trains teachers, chiefly for the elementary grades. [Transl. of Fr. *école normale* (so called because the first school so named was intended as a model).]
Nor•man[1] (nôr′mən) *n.* **1.a.** A member of a Scandinavian people who settled in northern France in the tenth century. **b.** A descendant of this people, esp. one ruling or inhabiting England from the time of the Norman Conquest. **2.** A native or inhabitant of Normandy. —*adj.* **1.** Of or relating to Normandy, the Normans, their culture, or their language. **2.** Of or being a style of Romanesque architecture that was introduced from Normandy into England before 1066 and flourished until about 1200. [ME < OFr. *Normant* < ON *Nordhmadhr* (*nordhr,* north + *madhr,* man) and < OE *Norman* (var. of *Northman* : *north,* north; see **ner-**[1]* + *man,* man; see **man-**[1]*).]
Nor•man[2] (nôr′mən). A city of central OK S of Oklahoma City. Pop. 80,071.
Norman Conquest *n.* The conquest of England by the Normans under William the Conqueror, esp. the Battle of Hastings in 1066.
Nor•man•dy (nôr′mən-dē). A historical region and former province of NW France on the English Channel. Its beaches were the focal point of Allied landings on D-day (Jun. 6, 1944) in World War II.
Norman French *n.* The dialect of Old French used in medieval Normandy.
nor•ma•tive (nôr′mə-tĭv) *adj.* Of, relating to, or prescribing a norm or standard: *normative grammar.* —**nor′ma•tive•ly** *adv.* —**nor′ma•tive•ness** *n.*
nor•mo•cyte (nôr′mə-sīt′) *n.* A red blood cell having normal size, shape, or color. [Lat. *norma,* norm; see NORM + -CYTE.]

nor•mo•ten•sive (nôr′mō-tĕn′sĭv) *adj.* Having normal blood pressure; not hypertensive or hypotensive. [Lat. *norma*, norm; see NORM + (HYPER)TENSIVE.] — **nor′mo•ten′sive** *n.*

nor•mo•ther•mi•a (nôr′mō-thûr′mē-ə) *n.* A condition of normal body temperature. [Lat. *norma*, norm; see NORM + THERM(O)- + -IA[1].] — **nor′mo•ther′mic** *adj.*

Norn (nôrn) *n. Myth.* Any of the three goddesses of fate in Norse myth.

Nor•ris (nôr′ĭs, nŏr′-), **Benjamin Franklin Jr. ("Frank").** 1870–1902. Amer. writer noted for *McTeague* (1899).

Norris, George William. 1861–1944. Amer. politician from NE who drafted the 20th Amendment to the U.S. Constitution, which limits the President to two full terms.

Nor•rish (nôr′ĭsh, nŏr′-), **Ronald George Wreyford.** 1897–1978. British chemist who shared a 1967 Nobel Prize.

Nor•ris•town (nôr′ĭs-toun′, nŏr′-). A borough of SE PA on the Schuylkill R. NW of Philadelphia; settled in the early 1700's. Pop. 30,749.

Norr•kö•ping (nôr′chœ′pĭng). A city of SE Sweden on **Norrköping Bay**, an inlet of the Baltic Sea SW of Stockholm; chartered 1384. Pop. 118,451.

Norse (nôrs) *adj.* **1.** Of or relating to medieval Scandinavia or its peoples, languages, or cultures. **2.** Of or relating to Norway or its people, language, or culture. **3.** Of, relating to, or being the branch of the North Germanic languages that includes Norwegian, Icelandic, and Faeroese. — *n.* **1.a.** The people of Scandinavia. **b.** The people of Norway; the Norwegians. **c.** Speakers of Norwegian, Icelandic, and Faeroese. **2.a.** See **North Germanic. b.** Any of the West Scandinavian languages, esp. Norwegian. [Prob. Du. *Noorsch*, Scandinavian < MDu. *Noortsch* < *nort*, north. See **ner-**[1]*.]

Norse•man (nôrs′mən) *n.* A member of any of the peoples of medieval Scandinavia.

north (nôrth) *n.* **1.a.** The direction along a meridian 90° counterclockwise from east; the direction to the left of sunrise. **b.** The cardinal point on the compass located at 0°. **2.** An area or a region lying in the north. **3.** Often **North. a.** The northern part of the earth. **b.** The northern part of a region or country. **4. North.** The northern part of the United States, esp. the states that fought for the Union in the Civil War. — *adj.* **1.** To, toward, of, facing, or in the north. **2.** Originating in or coming from the north: *a cold north wind.* — *adv.* In, from, or toward the north. [ME < OE. See **ner-**[1]*.]

North, Frederick. 2nd Earl of Guilford. "Lord North." 1732–92. British politician who served as prime minister (1770–82) under George III.

North Ad•ams (ăd′əmz). A city of NW MA NNE of Pittsfield; settled c. 1737. Pop. 16,797.

North Af•ri•ca (ăf′rĭ-kə). A region of N Africa generally considered to include the modern-day countries of Morocco, Algeria, Tunisia, and Libya. — **North Af′ri•can** *adj. & n.*

North A•mer•i•ca (ə-mĕr′ĭ-kə). The N continent of the Western Hemisphere, extending N from the Colombia-Panama border and including Central America, Mexico, the islands of the Caribbean Sea, the U.S., Canada, the Arctic Archipelago, and Greenland. — **North A•mer′i•can** *adj. & n.*

North•amp•ton (nôr-thămp′tən, nôrth-hămp′-). **1.** A borough of central England NNW of London. Pop. 158,900. **2.** A city of W-central MA on the Connecticut R. N of Springfield; seat of Smith College (founded 1875). Pop. 29,289.

North An•do•ver (ăn′dō′vər). A town of NE MA on the Merrimack R. ENE of Lowell. Pop. 22,792.

North At•lan•tic Ocean (ăt-lăn′tĭk). The N part of the Atlantic, extending N from the equator to the Arctic Ocean.

North At•tle•bor•o (ăt′l-bûr′ō, -bŭr′ō). A town of SE MA NNE of Providence RI; settled in 1669. Pop. 16,178.

North Bay. A city of SE Ontario, Canada, on Lake Nipissing ESE of Sudbury. Pop. 51,268.

North Ber•gen (bûr′gən). A community of NE NJ N of Jersey City. Pop. 48,414.

north•bound (nôrth′bound′) *adj.* Going toward the north.

North•brook (nôrth′brŏŏk′). A village of NE IL, a suburb of Chicago. Pop. 32,308.

North Bruns•wick (brŭnz′wĭk). A community of central NJ SW of New Brunswick. Pop. 31,287.

north by east *n.* The direction or compass point halfway between due north and north-northeast, or 11°15′ east of due north. — *adv. & adj.* Toward or from north by east.

north by west *n.* The direction or compass point halfway between due north and north-northwest, or 11°15′ west of due north. — *adv. & adj.* Toward or from north by west.

North Ca•na•di•an River (kə-nā′dē-ən). A river rising in NE NM and flowing c. 1,223 km (760 mi) to the Canadian R.

North Car•o•li•na (kăr′ə-lī′nə). A state of the SE U.S. bordering on the Atlantic Ocean; admitted as one of the original Thirteen Colonies in 1789. It was part of the province of Carolina until 1691. Cap. Raleigh. Pop. 6,657,630. — **North Car•o•lin′i•an** (-lĭn′ē-ən) *adj. & n.*

North Channel. A strait between Scotland and Northern Ireland connecting the Atlantic Ocean with the Irish Sea.

North Charles•ton (chärl′stən). A city of SE SC, a suburb of Charleston. Pop. 70,218.

North Chi•ca•go (shĭ-kä′gō, -kô′-). A city of NE IL, a suburb of Waukegan on Lake Michigan. Pop. 34,978.

North•cliffe (nôrth′klĭf′), Viscount. See Alfred Charles William **Harmsworth.**

North Da•ko•ta (də-kō′tə). A state of the N-central U.S. bordering on Canada; admitted as the 39th state in 1889. Cap. Bismarck. Pop. 641,364. — **North Da•ko′tan** *adj. & n.*

North Downs (dounz). See **Downs.**

north•east (nôrth-ēst′, nôr-ēst′) *n.* **1.** The direction or compass point halfway between due north and due east, or 45° east of due north. **2.** An area or a region lying in the northeast. **3. Northeast.** A region of the northeast United States, generally including the New England states, New York, and sometimes Pennsylvania and New Jersey. — *adj.* **1.** To, toward, of, facing, or in the northeast. **2.** Originating in or coming from the northeast: *a northeast wind.* — *adv.* In, from, or toward the northeast. — **north•east′ern** *adj.*

northeast by east *n.* The direction or compass point halfway between northeast and east-northeast, or 56°15′ east of due north. — *adv. & adj.* Toward or from northeast by east.

northeast by north *n.* The direction or compass point halfway between northeast and north-northeast, or 33°45′ east of due north. — *adv. & adj.* Toward or from northeast by north.

north•east•er (nôrth-ē′stər, nôr-ē′-) *n.* A storm or gale blowing from the northeast.

north•east•er•ly (nôrth-ē′stər-lē, nôr-ē′-) *adj.* **1.** Situated toward the northeast. **2.** Coming or being from the northeast. — **north•east′er•ly** *adv.*

Northeast Passage. A water route along the N coast of Europe and Asia between the Atlantic and Pacific oceans.

north•east•ward (nôrth-ēst′wərd, nôr-ēst′-) *adv. & adj.* Toward, to, or in the northeast. — *n.* A northeastward direction, point, or region. — **north•east′ward•ly** *adv. & adj.* — **north•east′wards** *adv.*

north•er (nôr′*th*ər) *n.* A sudden cold gale coming from the north.

north•er•ly (nôr′*th*ər-lē) *adj.* **1.** Situated toward the north. **2.** Coming or being from the north. — *n., pl.* **-lies.** A storm or wind coming from the north. — **north′er•ly** *adv.*

north•ern (nôr′*th*ərn) *adj.* **1.** Situated in, toward, or facing the north. **2.** Coming from the north: *northern breezes.* **3.** Native to or growing in the north. **4.** Often **Northern.** Of, relating to, or characteristic of northern regions or the North. **5.** Being north of the equator. [ME *northerne* < OE. See **ner-**[1]*.] — **north′ern•ness′** *n.*

Northern Cross *n.* See **Cygnus.**

Northern Crown *n.* See **Corona Borealis.**

Northern Dvi•na (dvē-nä′). See **Dvina** 1.

north•ern•er also **North•ern•er** (nôr′*th*ər-nər) *n.* A native or inhabitant of the north, esp. the northern United States.

northern harrier *n.* A slim-bodied hawk *(Circus cyaneus)* found in marshy areas of northern North America and Eurasia and having an owllike face and a white patch on the tail.

Northern Hemisphere *n.* **1.** The half of the earth north of the equator. **2.** *Astron.* The half of the celestial sphere north of the celestial equator.

Northern Ire•land (īr′lənd). A division of the United Kingdom in the NE section of the island of Ireland occupying much of the ancient Irish kingdom of Ulster and often known by that name; colonized by the British in the 17th cent. and a part of the United Kingdom since 1920. Cap. Belfast. Pop. 1,488,077.

Northern Kingdom. See **Israel**[2].

northern lights *pl.n.* See **aurora borealis.**

Northern Mar•i•an•a Islands (măr′ē-ăn′ə, mâr′-, mä′rē-ä′nä). See **Mariana Islands.**

north•ern•most (nôr′*th*ərn-mōst′) *adj.* Farthest north.

northern oriole *n.* A species of American songbird *(Icterus galbula)* composed of two subspecies, the Baltimore and Bullock's orioles.

Northern Paiute *n.* **1.** See **Paiute** 1. **2.** The Uto-Aztecan language of the Northern Paiute.

northern pike *n.* See **pike**[2] 1.

Northern Shoshone *n.* See **Shoshone** 1a.

Northern Spy *n.* A large yellowish-red late-ripening apple. [?]

North Fort My•ers (mī′ərz). A community of SW FL on the Caloosahatchee R. opposite Fort Myers. Pop. 30,027.

North Frig•id Zone (frĭj′ĭd). See **Frigid Zone.**

North Fri•sian Islands (frĭzh′ən, frē′zhən). See **Frisian Islands.**

North Germanic *n.* A subdivision of the Germanic languages including Norwegian, Icelandic, Swedish, and Danish.

North•glenn (nôrth-glĕn′). A city of N-central Colorado, a suburb of Denver. Pop. 27,195.

North Ha•ven (hā′vən). A town of S CT NNE of New Haven; settled c.1650. Pop. 22,249.

north•ing (nôr′thĭng, -*th*ĭng) *n.* **1.** The difference in latitude between two positions as a result of a movement to the north. **2.** Progress toward the north.

North Island. An island of New Zealand separated from South I. by Cook Strait.

North Kar•roo (kə-rōō′). See **Karroo.**

noria

ă pat	oi boy
ā pay	ou out
âr care	ŏŏ took
ä father	ōō boot
ĕ pet	ŭ cut
ē be	ûr urge
ĭ pit	th thin
ī pie	*th* this
îr pier	hw which
ŏ pot	zh vision
ō toe	ə about, item
ô paw	

Stress marks:
′ (primary);
′ (secondary), as in dictionary (dĭk′shə-nĕr′ē)

noth•ing•ness (nŭth′ĭng-nĭs) *n.* **1.** The condition or quality of being nothing; nonexistence. **2.** Empty space; a void. **3.** Lack of consequence; insignificance. **4.** Something inconsequential or insignificant.

no•tice (nō′tĭs) *n.* **1.** The act of noting or observing; perception or attention. **2.** Respectful attention or consideration. **3.** A written or printed announcement. **4.a.** A formal announcement, notification, or warning, esp. an announcement of one's intention to withdraw from an agreement or leave a job. **b.** The condition of being formally warned or notified. **5.** A printed critical review, as of a play or book. —*tr.v.* **-ticed, -tic•ing, -tic•es. 1.** To take notice of; observe. See Syns at **see**[1]. **2.** To perceive with the mind; detect. **3.** To comment on; mention. **4.** To treat with courteous attention. **5.** To give or file a notice of. [ME, knowledge < OFr. < Lat. *nōtitia* < *nōtus*, known, p.part. of *nōscere*, to get to know. See **gnō-***.]

no•tice•a•ble (nō′tĭ-sə-bəl) *adj.* **1.** Evident; observable. See Syns at **perceptible. 2.** Worthy of notice; significant. —**no′tice•a•bil′i•ty** *n.* —**no′tice•a•bly** *adv.*

no•ti•fi•ca•tion (nō′tə-fĭ-kā′shən) *n.* **1.** The act or an instance of notifying. **2.** Something, such as a letter, by which notice is given.

no•ti•fy (nō′tə-fī′) *tr.v.* **-fied, -fy•ing, -fies. 1.** To give notice to; inform: *notified them of the curfew.* **2.** *Chiefly British.* To give notice of; make known. [ME *notifien* < OFr. *notifier* < Lat. *nōtificāre* : *notus*, known, p.part. of *nōscere*, to get to know; see **gnō-*** + *-ficāre*, -fy.] —**no′ti•fi′er** *n.*

no•tion (nō′shən) *n.* **1.** A belief or opinion. **2.** A mental image or representation; an idea or conception. **3.** A fanciful impulse; a whim. See Syns at **idea. 4. notions.** Small lightweight items for household use, such as needles and buttons. [ME *nocioun*, concept < Lat. *nōtiō*, *nōtiōn-* < *nōtus*, known, p.part. of *nōscere*, to get to know. See **gnō-***.]

no•tion•al (nō′shə-nəl) *adj.* **1.** Of, containing, or being a notion; mental or imaginary. **2.** Speculative or theoretical. **3.** *Ling.* Conveying an idea of a thing or an action; having full lexical meaning as distinguished from relational meaning. The word *did* is notional in *We did the work* and relational in *We did not agree.* —**no′tion•al•ly** *adv.*

no•to•chord (nō′tə-kôrd′) *n.* **1.** A flexible rodlike structure that forms the main support of the body in the lowest chordates; a primitive backbone. **2.** A similar structure in embryos of higher vertebrates, from which the spinal column develops. [Gk. *nōton*, back + CHORD[2].] —**no′to•chord′al** *adj.*

No•to•gae•a or **No•to•ge•a** (nō′tə-jē′ə) *n.* A zoogeographic region including Australia, New Zealand, and the islands of the SW Pacific Ocean.

no•to•ri•e•ty (nō′tə-rī′ĭ-tē) *n.* The quality or condition of being notorious; ill fame.

no•to•ri•ous (nō-tôr′ē-əs, -tōr′-) *adj.* Known widely and usu. unfavorably; infamous: *a notorious gangster.* [< Med.Lat. *nōtōrius*, well-known < Lat. *nōtus*, known, p.part. of *nōscere*, to get to know. See **gnō-***.] —**no•to′ri•ous•ly** *adv.*

no•tor•nis (nō-tôr′nĭs) *n., pl.* **notornis.** Any of several flightless New Zealand birds, now rare, of the genus *Notornis.* [NLat. *Notornis*, genus name : Gk. *notos*, south + Gk. *ornis*, bird; see **or-***.]

no-trump (nō′trŭmp′) *n. Games.* **1.** A declaration to play a hand without a trump suit in bridge and other card games. **2.** A hand played without a trump suit. —**no′-trump′** *adj.*

Not•ta•way (nŏt′ə-wā′). A river of SW Quebec, Canada, flowing c. 644 km (400 mi) into James Bay.

Not•ting•ham (nŏt′ĭng-əm). A borough of central England N of Leicester. Charles I raised his standard here in 1642, marking the beginning of the English Civil War. Pop. 277,500.

no•tum (nō′təm) *n., pl.* **-ta** (-tə). The dorsal part of the thoracic segment of an insect. [NLat. *nōtum* < Gk. *nōton*, back.]

not•with•stand•ing (nŏt′wĭth-stăn′dĭng, -wĭth-) *prep.* In spite of: *We walked, notwithstanding the rain.* —*adv.* All the same; nevertheless: *We proceeded, notwithstanding.* —*conj.* In spite of the fact that; although. [ME *notwithstandinge* : *not*, not; see NOT + *withstanding*, pr.part. of *withstanden*, to resist; see WITHSTAND.]

Nouak•chott (nwäk-shŏt′). The cap. of Mauritania, in the W part on the Atlantic Ocean. Pop. 150,000.

nou•gat (no͞o′gət) *n.* A confection made from a sugar or honey paste into which nuts are mixed. [Fr. < Prov. < *nougo*, nut < OProv. *noga* < VLat. **nuca* < Lat. *nux*, *nuc-*, nut.]

nought (nôt) *n., pron., & adj.* Var. of **naught.**

Nou•mé•a (no͞o-mā′ə). The cap. of New Caledonia, on the SW coast of the island of New Caledonia in the SW Pacific Ocean. Pop. 60,112.

nou•me•non (no͞o′mə-nŏn′) *n., pl.* **-na** (-nə). *Philos.* **1.** An object that can be intuited only by the intellect and not perceived by the senses. **2.** An object independent of intellectual intuition of it or of sensuous perception of it. **3.** In the philosophy of Kant, an object, such as the soul, that cannot be known through perception, although its existence can be demonstrated. [Ger. < Gk. *noumenon* < neut. pr. middle part. of *noein*, to perceive by thought < *nous*, mind.] —**nou′men•al** (-mə-nəl) *adj.*

noun (noun) *n. Gram.* A word that is used to name a person, place, thing, quality, or action and can function as the subject or object of a verb, the object of a preposition, or an appositive. [ME, name, noun < AN < Lat. *nōmen*, *nōmin-*. See **nō-men-***.]

nour•ish (nûr′ĭsh, nŭr′-) *tr.v.* **-ished, -ish•ing, -ish•es. 1.** To provide with food or other substances necessary for life and growth; feed. **2.** To foster the development of; promote. **3.** To keep alive; maintain: *nourish a hope.* [ME *norishen* < OFr. *norrir*, *norriss-* < VLat. **nutrīre* < Lat. *nūtrīre*. See **(s)nāu-***.] —**nour′ish•er** *n.*

nour•ish•ment (nûr′ĭsh-mənt, nŭr′-) *n.* **1.a.** The act of nourishing. **b.** The state of being nourished. **2.** Something that nourishes; food.

nous (no͞os, nous) *n.* **1.** *Philos.* **a.** Reason and knowledge as opposed to sense perception. **b.** The rational part of the individual human soul. **c.** The principle of the cosmic mind or soul responsible for the rational order of the cosmos. **d.** In Stoicism, the equivalent of Logos. **e.** In Neo-Platonism, the image of the absolute good, containing the cosmos of intelligible beings. **2.** *Chiefly British.* Good sense; shrewdness. [Gk.]

nou•veau riche (no͞o′vō rēsh′) *n., pl.* **nou•veaux riches** (no͞o′vō rēsh′). One who has recently become rich, esp. one who flaunts newly acquired wealth. [Fr.]

nou•velle cuisine (no͞o-vĕl′) *n.* A school of French cooking that uses light low-calorie sauces and stocks. [Fr. : *nouvelle*, new + *cuisine*, cuisine.]

nouvelle vague (väg′) *n.* See **new wave** 1. [Fr.]

Nov. or **Nov** *abbr.* November.

no•va (nō′və) *n., pl.* **-vae** (-vē) or **-vas.** A star that suddenly becomes much brighter and then gradually returns to its original brightness over a period of weeks to years. [NLat. (*stēlla*) *nova*, new (star), nova, fem. of Lat. *novus*, new. See **newo-***.]

no•vac•u•lite (nō-văk′yə-līt′) *n.* A very hard, dense, even-textured, silica-bearing sedimentary rock used in whetstones. [Lat. *novācula*, razor + -ITE[1].]

No•va I•gua•çu (nô′vä ē′gwä-so͞o′). A city of SE Brazil, a suburb of Rio de Janeiro. Pop. 491,766.

No•va•ra (nō-vär′ə, -vä′rä). A city of NW Italy W of Milan. Pop. 101,635.

No•va Sco•tia (nō′və skō′shə). A province of E Canada comprising a mainland peninsula and the adjacent Cape Breton I.; joined the confederation in 1867. France and Great Britain contested the area, part of Acadia, until 1763. Cap. Halifax. Pop. 847,442. —**No′va Sco′tian** *adj. & n.*

no•va•tion (nō-vā′shən) *n. Law.* Substitution of a new obligation for an old one. [LLat. *novātiō*, *novātiōn-* < Lat., a renewing < *novātus*, p.part. of *novāre*, to make new < *novus*, new. See **newo-***.]

No•va•to (nə-vä′tō). A city of W CA N of San Rafael. Pop. 47,585.

No•va•ya Zem•lya (nō′və-yə zĕm′lē-ä′, zĭm-lyä′). An archipelago of N-central Russia in the Arctic Ocean between the Barents and Kara seas.

nov•el[1] (nŏv′əl) *n.* **1.** A fictional prose narrative of considerable length, typically having a plot that is unfolded by the actions, speech, and thoughts of the characters. **2.** The literary genre represented by novels. [Ult. < Ital. *novella* < OItal., piece of news, chit-chat, tale < VLat. **novella* < neut. pl. of Lat. *novellus*, dim. of *novus*, new. See **newo-***.]

nov•el[2] (nŏv′əl) *adj.* Strikingly new, unusual, or different. See Syns at **new.** [ME < OFr. < Lat. *novellus*, dim. of *novus*. See **newo-***.] —**nov′el•ly** *adv.*

nov•el•ette (nŏv′ə-lĕt′) *n.* A short novel.

nov•el•ist (nŏv′ə-lĭst) *n.* A writer of novels.

nov•el•is•tic (nŏv′ə-lĭs′tĭk) *adj.* Of, relating to, or characteristic of novels. —**nov′el•is′ti•cal•ly** *adv.*

nov•el•ize (nŏv′ə-līz′) *tr.v.* **-ized, -iz•ing, -iz•es. 1.** To write a novel based on. **2.** To turn into fiction; fictionalize. —**nov′el•i•za′tion** (-ə-lĭ-zā′shən) *n.* —**nov′el•iz′er** *n.*

no•vel•la (nō-vĕl′ə) *n., pl.* **-vel•las** or **-vel•le** (-vĕl′ē, -vĕl′ā). **1.** A short prose tale often characterized by moral teaching or satire. **2.** A short novel. [Ital. See NOVEL[1].]

nov•el•ty (nŏv′əl-tē) *n., pl.* **-ties. 1.** The quality of being novel; newness. **2.** Something new and unusual; an innovation. **3.** A small mass-produced article, such as a toy or trinket.

No•vem•ber (nō-vĕm′bər) *n.* The 11th month of the year in the Gregorian calendar. [ME *Novembre* < OFr. < Lat. *November*, ninth month < *novem*, nine. See **newn̥***.]

no•ve•na (nō-vē′nə) *n., pl.* **-nas** or **-nae** (-nē). In some western Christian churches, a nine-day period of prayer and devotion. [Med.Lat. *novēna* < fem. of Lat. *novēnus*, nine each < *novem*, nine. See **newn̥***.]

no•ver•cal (nō-vûr′kəl) *adj.* Of, relating to, or characteristic of a stepmother. [Lat. *novercālis* < *noverca*, stepmother. See **newo-***.]

Nov•go•rod (nŏv′gə-rŏd′, nôv′gə-rət). A city of NW Russia SSE of St. Petersburg. Pop. 220,000.

No•vi (nō′vī′). A village of SE MI NW of Detroit. Pop. 32,998.

nov•ice (nŏv′ĭs) *n.* **1.** A person new to a field or activity; a beginner. **2.** A person who has entered a religious order but has not yet taken vows. [ME < OFr. < Med.Lat. *novīcius* < Lat., recently entered into a condition < Lat. *novus*, new. See **newo-***.]

No•vi Sad (nō′vē säd′). A city of N Serbia on the Danube R. NW of Belgrade. Pop. 170,800.

no•vi•ti•ate also **no•vi•ci•ate** (nō-vĭsh′ē-ĭt, -āt′) *n.* **1.** The period of being a novice. **2.** A place where novices live. **3.** See **novice** 2. [Med.Lat. *novīciātus* < *novīcius*, novice. See NOVICE.]

no•vo•bi•o•cin (nō′və-bī′ə-sĭn) *n.* An antibiotic, $C_{31}H_{36}N_2O_{11}$, produced by the actinomycete *Streptomyces nivens* and used to treat infections by gram-positive bacteria. [Prob. Lat. *novus*, new; see NOVICE + (ANTI)BIO(TIC) + -IN.]

No•vo•cain (nō′və-kān′). A trademark used for an anesthetic preparation of procaine.

No•vo•cher•kassk (nō′və-chər-käsk′, nə-və-chĭr-). A city of SW Russia NE of Rostov; founded 1805. Pop. 186,000.

No•vo Ham•bur•go (nô′vo͝o äNm-bo͝or′go͞o). A city of S Brazil N of Pôrto Alegre; founded by German immigrants in the 19th cent. Pop. 133,221.

No•vo•kuz•netsk (nō′və-ko͞oz-nĕtsk′, nə-və-ko͞oz-nyĕtsk′). A city of S-central Russia SE of Novosibirsk; founded by Cossacks in 1617. Pop. 577,000.

No•vo•ros•siysk (nō′və-rə-sēsk′, nə-və-). A city of SW Russia on the Black Sea SSW of Rostov. Pop. 175,000.

No•vo•si•birsk (nō′və-sə-bîrsk′, nə-və-sĭ-). A city of S-central Russia on the Ob R. E of Omsk. Pop. 1,393,000.

now (nou) *adv.* **1.** At the present time: *goods now on sale.* **2.** At once; immediately: *Stop now.* **3.** In the immediate past; very recently: *left the room just now.* **4.** At this point in the series of events; then: *The ship was now listing to port.* **5.** Nowadays. **6.** In these circumstances; as things are: *Now we won't be able to stay.* **7.a.** Used to introduce a command, reproof, or request: *Now pay attention.* **b.** Used to indicate a change of subject or to preface a remark: *Now, let's get down to work.* —*conj.* Seeing that; since: *Now that it's spring, we can travel.* —*n.* The present time or moment: *wouldn't work up to now.* —*adj.* **1.** Of the present time; current: *our now governor.* **2.** *Slang.* Currently fashionable; trendy: *the now sound.* —***idiom.*** **now and again (**or **then).** Occasionally. [ME < OE *nū*. See **nu-***.] —**now′ness** *n.*

NOW *abbr.* National Organization for Women.

NOW account (nou) *n.* An interest-bearing savings account against which drafts may be written. [*n(egotiable) o(rder of) w(ithdrawal).*]

now•a•days (nou′ə-dāz′) *adv.* During the present time; now. [ME *nouadaies* : *nou*, now; see NOW + *a* (var. of *on*, on; see ON) + *daies*, genitive of *dai*, day; see DAY.]

no•way (nō′wā′) *adv.* also **no•ways** (-wāz′). In no way or degree; nowise. —*interj.* also **no way.** *Informal.* Used to express emphatic negation.

no•where (nō′hwâr′, -wâr′) *adv.* **1.** Not anywhere. **2.** To no place or result. —*n.* A remote or unknown place.

no•wheres (nō′hwârz′, -wârz′) *adv. Non-Standard.* Nowhere.

no•whith•er (nō′hwĭth′ər, -wĭth′-) *adv.* In no definite direction.

no-win (nō′wĭn′) *adj. Informal.* Certain to end in failure or disappointment.

no•wise (nō′wīz′) *adv.* In no way or degree; not at all.

nox•ious (nŏk′shəs) *adj.* **1.** Harmful to living things; injurious to health. **2.** Harmful to the mind or morals; corrupting: *noxious ideas.* [ME *noxius* < Lat. < *noxa*, damage. See **nek-**[1]*.] —**nox′ious•ly** *adv.* —**nox′ious•ness** *n.*

Noyes (noiz), **Alfred.** 1880–1958. British poet who also wrote plays and short stories.

Noyes, John Humphrey. 1811–86. Amer. religious leader who founded (1848) an experimental community at Oneida NY.

noz•zle (nŏz′əl) *n.* **1.** A projecting part with an opening, as at the end of a hose, for regulating and directing a flow of fluid. **2.** *Slang.* The human nose. [ME *noselle*, socket on a candlestick, dim. of *nose*. See NOSE.]

Np The symbol for the element **neptunium.**

NP *abbr.* **1.** Neuropsychiatry. **2.** *Gram.* Noun phrase. **3.** Nurse practitioner.

N.P. *abbr.* Notary public.

NPN *abbr.* Nonprotein nitrogen.

NPR *abbr.* National Public Radio.

nr *abbr.* Near.

NRA *abbr.* **1.** National Recovery Administration. **2.** National Rifle Association. **3.** Naval Reserve Association.

NRC *abbr.* **1.** National Research Council. **2.** Nuclear Regulatory Commission.

ns *abbr.* Nanosecond.

NS *abbr.* **1.** Also **N.S.** Nova Scotia. **2.** Nuclear ship.

n.s. *abbr.* **1.** New series. **2.** Not specified.

N.S. *abbr.* New Style.

n/s *abbr.* Not sufficient.

NSA *abbr.* National Security Agency.

NSC *abbr.* National Security Council.

nsec *abbr.* Nanosecond.

NSF *abbr.* National Science Foundation.

n.s.f. or **N.S.F.** *abbr.* Not sufficient funds.

N.S.P.C.A. *abbr.* National Society for the Prevention of Cruelty to Animals.

NT *abbr.* **1.** Also **N.T.** *Bible.* New Testament. **2.** Northwest Territories.

-n't Not.

nth (ĕnth) *adj.* **1.** Relating to an indefinitely large ordinal number: *ten to the nth power.* **2.** Highest; utmost: *delighted to the nth degree.* [N[2], indefinite number + -TH[3].]

nth root *n. Math.* See **root**[1] 9a.

n.t.p. or **N.T.P.** *abbr.* Normal temperature and pressure.

nt.wt. *abbr.* Net weight.

nu (no͞o, nyo͞o) *n.* The 13th letter of the Greek alphabet. [Gk., of Semitic orig.; akin to Heb. *nûn*, nun.]

nu•ance (no͞o′äns′, nyo͞o′-, no͞o-äns′, nyo͞o-) *n.* **1.** A subtle or slight degree of difference, as in meaning; a gradation. **2.** Expression or appreciation of nuances: *a performance full of nuance.* [Fr. < OFr. < *nuer*, to shade, cloud < *nue*, cloud < VLat. **nūba* < Lat. *nūbēs*.] —**nu•anced′** *adj.*

nub (nŭb) *n.* **1.** A protuberance or knob. **2.** A small lump. **3.** The essence; the core. [Var. of *knub*, prob. < LGer. *knubbe* < MLGer., var. of *knobbe*.] —**nub′by** *adj.*

Nu•ba (no͞o′bə, nyo͞o′-) *n., pl.* **Nuba.** **1.** A member of any of several peoples inhabiting the hills of south-central Sudan. **2.** See **Nubian** 2.

Nu•bi•a (no͞o′bē-ə, nyo͞o′-). A desert region and ancient kingdom in the Nile R. valley of S Egypt and N Sudan.

Nu•bi•an (no͞o′bē-ən, nyo͞o′-) *adj.* Of or relating to Nubia or its peoples, languages, or cultures. —*n.* **1.** A native or inhabitant of Nubia. **2.** Any of a group of closely related Nilo-Saharan languages spoken in the Sudan.

Nubian Desert. A desert region of NE Sudan extending E of the Nile R. to the Red Sea.

nu•bile (no͞o′bĭl, -bīl′, nyo͞o′-) *adj.* **1.** Ready for marriage; of a marriageable age or condition. Used of young women. **2.** Sexually mature and attractive. Used of young women. [Lat. *nūbilis* < *nūbere*, to take a husband.] —**nu•bil′i•ty** (no͞o-bĭl′ĭ-tē, nyo͞o-) *n.*

nu•cel•lus (no͞o-sĕl′əs, nyo͞o-) *n., pl.* **-cel•li** (-sĕl′ī). *Bot.* The central portion of an ovule containing the embryo. [NLat. < *nux*, *nuc-*, nut.] —**nu•cel′lar** *adj.*

nu•cha (no͞o′kə, nyo͞o′-) *n.* The nape of the neck. [ME, spinal cord < Med.Lat. < Ar. *nuḫḫ*, marrow.] —**nu′chal** *adj.*

nucle– *pref.* Var. of **nucleo–.**

nu•cle•ar (no͞o′klē-ər, nyo͞o′-) *adj.* **1.** *Biol.* Of, relating to, or forming a nucleus: *a nuclear membrane.* **2.** *Phys.* Of or relating to atomic nuclei. **3.** Using or derived from the energy of atomic nuclei; atomic. **4.** Of, using, or possessing atomic or hydrogen bombs: *nuclear war.* [< NUCLEUS.]

nuclear age *n.* The atomic age.

nuclear emulsion *n. Phys.* Any of several photographic emulsions used to detect and visually display the paths of charged subatomic particles, esp. of charged cosmic ray particles.

nuclear energy *n.* **1.** The energy released by a nuclear reaction, esp. by fission or fusion. **2.** Nuclear energy regarded as a source of power.

nuclear family *n.* A family unit consisting of a mother and father and their children.

nuclear force *n. Phys.* The strong interaction.

nu•cle•ar-free zone (no͞o′klē-ər-frē′, nyo͞o′-) *n.* An area in which the siting of nuclear weapons or reactors is banned.

nu•cle•ar•ize (no͞o′klē-ə-rīz′, nyo͞o′-) *tr.v.* **-ized, -iz•ing, -iz•es.** To equip with nuclear weapons. —**nu′cle•ar•i•za′tion** (-ər-ĭ-zā′shən) *n.*

nuclear magnetic resonance *n.* The absorption of electromagnetic radiation of a specific frequency by an atomic nucleus in a strong magnetic field, used esp. in spectroscopy and in medicine to measure rates of metabolism.

nuclear magneton *n. Phys.* A unit of the magnetic moment of a nucleon.

nuclear medicine *n.* The branch of medicine that deals with the use of radionuclides in the diagnosis and treatment of disease.

nuclear membrane *n.* The double-layered membrane enclosing the nucleus of a cell.

nuclear physics *n. (used with a sing. v.)* The study of the forces, reactions, and internal structures of atomic nuclei.

nuclear power *n.* Power, esp. electricity, the source of which is nuclear fission or fusion.

nuclear reaction *n.* A reaction, as in fission, that alters the energy, composition, or structure of an atomic nucleus.

nuclear reactor *n.* Any of several devices in which a chain reaction is initiated and controlled, with the resulting heat typically used for power generation.

nuclear weapon *n.* A device, such as a bomb, whose great explosive power derives from the release of nuclear energy.

nuclear winter *n.* A darkening and cooling of the atmosphere with consequent devastation of surviving life, considered to be a possible outcome of large-scale nuclear war.

nu•cle•ase (no͞o′klē-ās′, -āz′, nyo͞o′-) *n.* Any of several enzymes, such as endonucleases, that hydrolize nucleic acids.

nu•cle•ate (no͞o′klē-ĭt, nyo͞o′-) *adj.* Nucleated. —*v.* (-āt′) **-at•ed, -at•ing, -ates.** —*tr.* **1.** To bring together into a nu-

ă pat	oi boy
ā pay	ou out
âr care	o͝o took
ä father	o͞o boot
ĕ pet	ŭ cut
ē be	ûr urge
ĭ pit	th thin
ī pie	*th* this
îr pier	hw which
ŏ pot	zh vision
ō toe	ə about, item
ô paw	

Stress marks:
′ (primary);
′ (secondary), as in
dictionary (dĭk′shə-nĕr′ē)

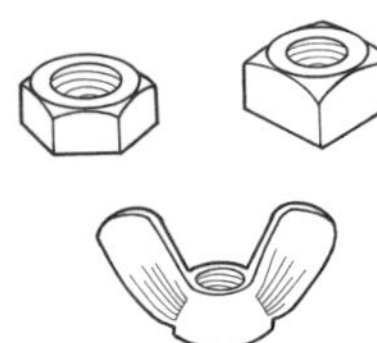

nut
Hexagonal (*top left*), square (*top right*), and wing (*bottom*)

nuthatch
White-breasted nuthatch
Sitta carolinensis

nutmeg
Myristica fragrans

carefully; look after with care; foster. See Syns at **nurture. 6.** To bear privately in the mind. **7.** To consume slowly, esp. in order to conserve. — *intr.* **1.** To serve as a nurse. **2.** To take nourishment from the breast; suckle. [ME *norice, nurse*, wet nurse < OFr. *norrice* < VLat. **nutrīcia* < LLat. *nūtrīcia* < fem. of Lat. *nūtrīcius*, that suckles < *nūtrīx, nūtrīc-*, wet nurse. See **(s)nāu-***.] — **nurs′er** *n.*

nurse•maid (nûrs′mād′) *n.* A woman employed to take care of children.

nurse practitioner *n.* A registered nurse with special training for providing primary health care, including many tasks customarily performed by a physician.

nurs•er•y (nûr′sə-rē, nûrs′rē) *n., pl.* **-ies. 1.** A room or area in a household set apart for children. **2.a.** A place for the temporary care of children in the absence of their parents. **b.** A nursery school. **3.** A place where plants are grown for sale, transplanting, or experimentation. **4.** A place in which something is produced, fostered, or developed. [ME *noricerie*, prob. < OFr. *norricerie* < *norrice*, nursemaid. See NURSE.]

nursery rhyme *n.* A short rhymed poem or tale for children.

nursery school *n.* A school for children, usu. between the ages of three and five, who are not old enough to attend kindergarten. — **nursery schooler** *n.*

nurse's aide (nûr′sĭz) *n., pl.* **nurses' aides.** A person who assists nurses at a hospital or other medical facility.

nurs•ing (nûr′sĭng) *n.* **1.** The profession of a nurse. **2.** The tasks or care of a nurse.

nursing home *n.* A private establishment that provides living quarters and care for the elderly or the chronically ill.

nurs•ling (nûrs′lĭng) *n.* **1.** A nursing infant or young animal. **2.** A carefully nurtured person or thing.

nur•tur•ance (nûr′chər-əns) *n.* The providing of loving care and attention. — **nur′tur•ant** *adj.*

nur•ture (nûr′chər) *n.* **1.** Something that nourishes; sustenance. **2.** The act of bringing up. **3.** *Biol.* The sum of environmental influences and conditions acting on an organism. — *tr.v.* **-tured, -tur•ing, -tures. 1.** To nourish; feed. **2.** To educate; train. **3.** To help grow or develop; cultivate: *nurture talent.* [ME < OFr. < LLat. *nūtrītūra*, act of suckling < Lat. *nūtrītus*, p.part. of *nūtrīre*, to suckle. See **(s)nāu-***.] — **nur′tur•er** *n.*

Syns: nurture, cultivate, foster, nurse. The central meaning shared by these verbs is "to promote and sustain the growth and development of": *nurturing hopes; cultivating tolerance; foster friendly relations; nursed the business.*

nut (nŭt) *n.* **1.a.** An indehiscent hard-shelled one-seeded fruit, such as an acorn. **b.** A seed borne within a fruit having a hard shell, as in the almond. **c.** The kernel of any of these. **2.** *Slang.* **a.** A crazy or eccentric person. **b.** An enthusiast; a buff: *a movie nut.* **3.** *Informal.* A difficult endeavor or problem. **4.** *Slang.* The human head. **5.** *Mus.* **a.** A ridge of wood at the top of the fingerboard or neck of a stringed instrument, over which the strings pass. **b.** A device on the bow of a stringed instrument for tightening the hairs. **6.** A small block of metal or wood with a central threaded hole that is designed to fit around and secure a bolt or screw. **7.** *Slang.* **a.** The cost of launching a business venture. **b.** The operating expenses of a theater, theatrical production, or similar enterprise. **8. nuts.** *Vulgar Slang.* The testicles. — *intr.v.* **nut•ted, nut•ting, nuts.** To gather or hunt for nuts. [ME *nute* < OE *hnutu.*] — **nut′ter** *n.*

nu•ta•tion (nōō-tā′shən, nyōō-) *n.* **1.** The act or an instance of nodding the head. **2.** A wobble in a spinning gyroscope or other rotating body. **3.** *Astron.* A small periodic motion of the celestial pole of Earth with respect to the pole of the ecliptic. **4.** *Bot.* A slight curving or circular growth in a stem, as of a twining plant. [Lat. *nūtātiō, nūtātiōn-* < *nūtātus*, p.part. of *nūtāre*, freq. of *-nuere*, to nod.] — **nu•ta′tion•al** *adj.*

nut case *n. Slang.* A person regarded as eccentric or crazy.

nut•crack•er (nŭt′krăk′ər) *n.* **1.** An implement used to crack nuts, typically consisting of two hinged metal levers between which the nut is squeezed. **2.a.** Any of various birds of the genus *Nucifraga* that are related to the crow and feed chiefly on the seeds of pine cones. **b.** See **nuthatch.**

nut•gall (nŭt′gôl′) *n.* A nutlike swelling produced on an oak or other tree by certain parasitic wasps.

nut•hatch (nŭt′hăch′) *n.* Any of several small short-tailed birds of the family Sittidae, having a long sharp bill and known for climbing down trees headfirst. [ME *notehache* : *note*, nut; see NUT + *hache*, hatchet < OFr., perh. of Gmc. orig. (< its wedging nuts in bark and hacking them open).]

nut house *n. Slang.* A mental health facility.

nut•let (nŭt′lĭt) *n.* **1.** A small nut. **2.** The stone or pit of certain fruits such as the peach or cherry.

Nut•ley (nŭt′lē). A town of NE NJ, a suburb of Newark. Pop. 27,099.

nut•meat (nŭt′mēt′) *n.* The edible kernel of a nut.

nut•meg (nŭt′mĕg′) *n.* **1.** An evergreen tree *(Myristica fragrans)* native to the East Indies and cultivated for its spicy seeds. **2.** The hard aromatic seed of this tree, used as a spice when grated or ground. **3.** *Color.* A grayish to moderate brown. [ME *notemuge*, prob. ult. < OFr. *nois mugede*, alteration of *nois muscade*, nut smelling like musk < OProv. *notz muscada* : *notz*, nut (< Lat. *nux, nuc-*, nut) + *muscada*, smelling like musk (< *musc*, musk < LLat. *muscus*; see MUSK).]

nut pick also **nut•pick** (nŭt′pĭk′) *n.* A small sharp-pointed tool used for digging the meat from nuts.

nut pine *n.* See **piñon.**

nu•tri•a (nōō′trē-ə, nyōō′-) *n.* **1.** See **coypu. 2.** The light brown fur of the coypu. [Sp. < VLat. **nutria*, var. of Lat. *lutra*. See **wed-¹***.]

nu•tri•ent (nōō′trē-ənt, nyōō′-) *n.* A source of nourishment, esp. a nourishing ingredient in a food. — *adj.* Providing nourishment. [Lat. *nūtriēns, nutrient-*, pr.part. of *nūtrīre*, to suckle. See **(s)nāu-***.]

nu•tri•ment (nōō′trə-mənt, nyōō′-) *n.* **1.** A source of nourishment; food. **2.** An agent that promotes growth or development. [ME < Lat. *nūtrīmentum* < *nūtrīre*, to suckle. See **(s)nāu-***.] — **nu′tri•men′tal** (-mĕn′tl) *adj.*

nu•tri•tion (nōō-trĭsh′ən, nyōō-) *n.* **1.** The process of nourishing or being nourished, esp. the process by which a living organism assimilates food and uses it for growth and for maintenance of tissues. **2.** The science or study that deals with food and nourishment, esp. in human beings. **3.** A source of nourishment; food. [ME *nutricion* < OFr. *nutrition* < LLat. *nūtrītiō, nūtrītiōn-* < Lat. *nūtrītus*, p.part. of *nūtrīre*, to suckle. See **(s)nāu-***.] — **nu•tri′tion•al** *adj.* — **nu•tri′tion•al•ly** *adv.*

nu•tri•tion•ist (nōō-trĭsh′ə-nĭst, nyōō-) *n.* One who is trained or an expert in the field of nutrition.

nu•tri•tion•ist's calorie (nōō-trĭsh′ə-nĭsts, nyōō-) *n.* See **calorie** 3b.

nu•tri•tious (nōō-trĭsh′əs, nyōō-) *adj.* Providing nourishment; nourishing. [< Lat. *nūtrītius* < *nūtrīx, nūtrīc-*, nurse. See **(s)nāu-***.] — **nu•tri′tious•ly** *adv.* — **nu•tri′tious•ness** *n.*

nu•tri•tive (nōō′trĭ-tĭv, nyōō′-) *adj.* **1.** Nutritious; nourishing. **2.** Of or relating to nutrition. [ME *nutritif* < OFr. < LLat. *nūtrītīvus* < Lat. *nūtrītus*, p.part. of *nūtrīre*, to suckle. See **(s)nāu-***.] — **nu′tri•tive•ly** *adv.*

nuts (nŭts) *Slang.* — *adj.* **1.** Crazy; insane. **2.** Extremely enthusiastic: *I'm nuts about opera.* — *interj.* Used to express contempt, disappointment, or refusal. [< NUT.]

nuts and bolts *pl.n. Slang.* The basic working components or practical aspects. — **nuts′-and-bolts′** (nŭts′ən-bōlts′) *adj.*

nut sedge *n.* Either of two Old World sedges *(Cyperus esculentus* or *C. rotundus)* having aromatic tubers.

nut•shell (nŭt′shĕl′) *n.* The shell enclosing the meat of a nut. — *idiom.* **in a nutshell.** In a few words; concisely.

nut•ty (nŭt′ē) *adj.* **-ti•er, -ti•est. 1.** Containing or producing nuts: *nutty trees.* **2.** Having a flavor like that of nuts. **3.** *Slang.* Crazy; idiotic. — **nut′ti•ly** *adv.* — **nut′ti•ness** *n.*

nux vom•i•ca (nŭks vŏm′ĭ-kə) *n.* A tree *(Strychnos nux-vomica)* native to southeast Asia and having poisonous seeds that are the source of the medicinal alkaloids strychnine and brucine. [Med.Lat. : Lat. *nux*, nut + Med.Lat. *vomica*, fem. of *vomicus*, emetic (< Lat. *vomere*, to vomit; see **wemə-***).]

nuz•zle (nŭz′əl) *v.* **-zled, -zling, -zles.** — *tr.* **1.** To rub or push against gently with or as if with the nose or snout: *nuzzled the kitten.* **2.** To root or move with the snout. — *intr.* **1.** To make rubbing or pressing motions with or as if with the nose or snout. **2.** To nestle together. [ME *noselen*, to bend down, perh. back-formation < *noselyng*, on the face, prostrate < *nose*, nose. See NOSE.] — **nuz′zler** *n.*

NV *abbr.* **1.** Nevada. **2.** Not voting.

NW *abbr.* **1.** Northwest. **2.** Northwestern.

NWbN *abbr.* Northwest by north.

NWbW *abbr.* Northwest by west.

NWT or **N.W.T.** *abbr.* Northwest Territories.

n.wt. *abbr.* Net weight.

NY or **N.Y.** *abbr.* New York.

nya•la (nyä′lə) *n., pl.* **nyala** or **-las.** Any of several African antelopes of the genus *Tragelaphus*, having vertical stripes on the sides of the body. [Prob. of Bantu orig.]

Nyan•ja (nyăn′jə) *n.* A Bantu language closely related to Chewa and spoken in Malawi.

Ny•as•a (nī-ăs′ə, nyä′sä), **Lake.** Also **Lake Ma•la•wi** (mə-lä′wē). A lake of SE-central Africa between Tanzania, Mozambique, and Malawi.

Ny•as•a•land (nī-ăs′ə-lănd′, nyä′sä-). See **Malawi.**

NYC or **N.Y.C.** *abbr.* New York City.

nyc•ta•lo•pi•a (nĭk′tə-lō′pē-ə) *n.* See **night blindness.** [LLat. *nyctalōpia* < Gk. *nuktalōps*, night-blind : *nux, nukt-*, night; see **nekʷ-t-*** + *alaos*, blind + *ōps, ōp-*, eye; see **okʷ-***.] — **nyc′ta•lo′pic** (-lō′pĭk, -lŏp′ĭk) *adj.*

nyc•tit•ro•pism (nĭk-tĭt′rə-pĭz′əm) *n. Bot.* The tendency of the leaves of some plants to change their position at nightfall. [Gk. *nux, nukt-*, night; see **nekʷ-t-*** + -TROPISM.] — **nyc′ti•tro′pic** (-tĭ-trō′pĭk, -trŏp′ĭk) *adj.*

nyc•to•pho•bi•a (nĭk′tə-fō′bē-ə) *n.* An abnormal fear of the night or darkness. [Gk. *nux, nukt-*, night; see NYCTALOPIA + -PHOBIA.]

Nye (nī), **Edgar Wilson ("Bill").** 1850–96. Amer. humorist noted for his anecdotes.

Nyí•regy•há•za (nē′rĕj-hä′zô, nyē′rĕd-yə-). A city of NE Hungary north of Debrecen; inhabited since the 13th cent. Pop. 90,200.

ny•lon (nī′lŏn′) *n.* **1.a.** Any of a family of high-strength, resilient synthetic polymers containing recurring amide groups. **b.** Cloth or yarn made from one of these synthetic materials. **2. nylons.** Stockings made of one of these synthetic materials. [Coined by E.I. Du Pont de Nemours and Co.]

nymph (nĭmf) *n.* **1.** *Gk. & Rom. Myth.* Any of numerous minor deities represented as beautiful young women inhabiting and sometimes personifying features of nature such as trees. **2.** A girl, esp. a beautiful one. **3.** The larval form of certain insects, such as silverfish, usu. resembling the adult form but smaller and lacking fully developed wings. [ME *nimphe* < OFr. < Lat. *nympha* < Gk. *numphē.*] — **nymph′al** (nĭm′fəl) *adj.*

nym•pha (nĭm′fə) *n., pl.* **-phae** (-fē). **1.** See **nymph** 3. **2. nymphae.** The labia minora. [Lat. < Gk. *numphē.*]

nym•pha•lid (nĭm′fə-lĭd) *n.* Any of various cosmopolitan butterflies of the family Nymphalidae, characterized by vestigial forelegs and often brilliant coloring. [< NLat. *Nymphălidae*, family name < *Nymphălis*, type genus, ult. < Lat. *nympha*, nymph < Gk. *numphē.*]

nym•phet (nĭm-fĕt′, nĭm′fĭt) *n.* A pubescent girl regarded as sexually desirable.

nym•pho•lep•sy (nĭm′fə-lĕp′sē) *n., pl.* **-sies. 1.** A frenzy supposed by ancient peoples to have been induced by nymphs. **2.** An emotional frenzy. [< NYMPHOLEPT.]

nym•pho•lept (nĭm′fə-lĕpt′) *n.* One who is in a state of nympholepsy. [Gk. *numpholēptos*, caught by nymphs, frenzied : *numphē*, nymph + *lēptos*, seized (< *lambanein, lēp-*, to seize).] — **nym′pho•lep′tic** *adj.*

nym•pho•ma•ni•a (nĭm′fə-mā′nē-ə, -mān′yə) *n.* Excessive sexual desire in a female. [NLat. : Gk. *numphē*, nymph + -MANIA.] — **nym′pho•ma′ni•ac′** (-nē-ăk′) *adj. & n.* — **nym′pho•ma•ni′a•cal** (-mə-nī′ə-kəl) *adj.*

Ny•norsk (no͞o-nôrsk′, nü′nôshk′) *n.* See **New Norwegian.** [Norw. : *ny*, new (< ON *nýr*; see SPAN-NEW) + *norsk*, Norwegian (< **noregsk* < ON *Nōregr*, Norway).]

NYP *abbr.* Not yet published.

NYSE *abbr.* New York Stock Exchange.

nys•tag•mus (nĭ-stăg′məs) *n.* A rapid, involuntary oscillatory motion of the eyeball. [NLat. < Gk. *nustagmos*, drowsiness.] — **nys•tag′mic** (-mĭk) *adj.*

nys•ta•tin (nĭs′tə-tĭn) *n.* An antibiotic, $C_{46}H_{77}NO_{19}$, produced by the actinomycete *Streptomyces noursei* and used esp. in the treatment of fungal infections. [*N(ew) Y(ork) Stat(e)* + -IN.]

N.Z. *abbr.* New Zealand.

O o

o¹ or **O** (ō) *n., pl.* **o's** or **O's. 1.** The 15th letter of the modern English alphabet. **2.** Any of the speech sounds represented by the letter *o.* **3.** The 15th in a series. **4.** Something shaped like the letter O. **5.** A zero. **6. O.** One of four types of blood in the ABO system.

o² *abbr.* **1. O** or **O.** *Print.* Octavo. **2.** Ohm.

O¹ (ō) *interj.* **1.** Used before the name of or a pronoun referring to a person or thing being formally addressed. **2.** Used to express surprise or strong emotion.

O² The symbol for the element **oxygen.**

O³ *abbr.* **1.** Or **O.** Ocean. **2.** Also **o.** Old. **3.** Also **O.** or **o.** Order. **4.** *Baseball.* Out.

o. *abbr. Lat.* Octarius (pint).

O. *abbr.* Ohio.

-o *suff.* Used to form an informal, abbreviated, or slang word or variant: *ammo.* [Perh. < OH.]

-o-. Used as a connective to join word elements: *acidophilic.* [ME < OFr. < Lat. < Gk., thematic vowel of nouns and adjectives used in combination.]

o/a *abbr.* On or about.

oaf (ōf) *n.* A stupid or clumsy person. [ON *alfr*, elf, silly person. See **albho-*.**] — **oaf′ish** *adj.* — **oaf′ish•ly** *adv.* — **oaf′ish•ness** *n.*

O•a•hu (ō-ä′ho͞o). An island of central HI between Molokai and Kauai; the chief island of the state.

oak (ōk) *n.* **1.a.** Any of numerous monoecious deciduous or evergreen trees or shrubs of the genus *Quercus,* bearing acorns as fruit. **b.** The durable wood of an oak. **c.** Something made of oak. **2.** Any of various similar trees or shrubs. **3.** *Color.* Any of various brown shades resembling the wood of an oak in color. [ME *ok* < OE *āc.*] — **oak′en** (ō′kən) *adj.*

oak apple *n.* An insect gall on oak trees.

Oak Creek (ōk). A city of SE WI, a suburb of Milwaukee on Lake Michigan. Pop. 19,513.

Oak Forest. A city of NE IL, a suburb of Chicago. Pop. 26,203.

Oak•land (ōk′lənd). A city of W CA on San Francisco Bay opposite San Francisco; founded on a site settled by Spanish colonists in 1820. Pop. 372,242.

Oakland Park. A city of SE FL on the Atlantic N of Fort Lauderdale. Pop. 23,035.

Oak Lawn. A village of NE IL, a suburb of Chicago. Pop. 56,182.

oak leaf cluster *n.* A decoration of bronze or silver oak leaves and acorns given to holders of various U.S. military medals who earn another award of the same medal.

Oak•ley (ōk′lē), **Annie.** 1860–1926. Amer. sharpshooter who was the star of Buffalo Bill's Wild West Show.

Oak Park. 1. A village of NE IL, a suburb of Chicago. Pop. 53,648. **2.** A city of SE MI, a suburb of Detroit. Pop. 30,462.

Oak Ridge. A city of E TN W of Knoxville; founded in 1942 as an atomic research facility. Pop. 27,310.

oa•kum (ō′kəm) *n.* Loose hemp or jute fiber, sometimes treated with tar, creosote, or asphalt, used for caulking seams in wooden ships and packing pipe joints. [ME *okom* < OE *ācumba.* See **gembh-*.**]

Oak•ville (ōk′vĭl′). A town of SE Ontario, Canada, on Lake Ontario SW of Toronto. Pop. 75,773.

oak wilt *n.* A disease of oak trees caused by the fungus *Chalara quercina* and often resulting in wilting and dropping of leaves.

oar (ôr, ōr) *n. Naut.* **1.** A long, usu. wooden pole with a blade at one end, used to row or steer a boat. **2.** A person who rows a boat. — *v.* **oared, oar•ing, oars.** — *tr.* **1.** To propel with or as if with oars or an oar. **2.** To traverse with or as if with oars or an oar. — *intr.* To move forward by or as if by rowing. [ME *or* < OE *ār.*] — **oared** *adj.* — **oar′less** *adj.*

oar•fish (ôr′fĭsh′, ōr′-) *n., pl.* **oarfish** or **-fish•es.** A widespread marine fish *(Regalecus glesne)* having a slender body, a red dorsal fin, and an undulating motion.

oar•lock (ôr′lŏk′, ōr′-) *n. Naut.* A device, usu. a U-shaped metal hoop on a swivel in the gunwale, used to hold an oar in place and as a fulcrum in rowing.

oars•man (ôrz′mən, ōrz′-) *n. Naut.* A man who rows.

oars•wom•an (ôrz′wo͝om′ən) *n. Naut.* A woman who rows.

OAS *abbr.* Organization of American States.

o•a•sis (ō-ā′sĭs) *n., pl.* **-ses** (-sēz). **1.** A fertile or green spot in a desert or wasteland, made so by the presence of water. **2.** A situation or place preserved from surrounding unpleasantness; a refuge. [LLat. < Gk., prob. of Egypt. orig.]

oasis

oast (ōst) *n.* A kiln for drying hops or malt or drying and curing tobacco. [ME *ost* < OE *āst.*]

oat (ōt) *n.* **1.a.** Any of various grasses of the genus *Avena,* esp. *A. sativa.* **b.** The grain of any of these plants, used as food and fodder. In both senses often used in the plural with a singular or plural verb. **2.** *Archaic.* A musical pipe made of an oat straw. [ME *ote* < OE *āte.*]

oat•cake (ōt′kāk′) *n.* A flattened cake of baked oatmeal.

oat•en (ōt′n) *adj.* Of, made of, or containing oats, oatmeal, or oat straw: *oaten fodder.*

oat•er (ō′tər) *n. Slang.* A western movie. [From the prominence of horses in such films.]

Oates (ōts), **Joyce Carol.** b. 1938. Amer. writer whose novels include *Bellefleur* (1980).

Oates, Titus. 1649–1705. English conspirator who forged evidence of a Jesuit plot to assassinate Charles II (1678).

oat grass *n.* **1.** Any of various grasses of the genera *Arrhenatherum* and *Danthonia.* **2.** Any of several oatlike grasses.

oath (ōth) *n., pl.* **oaths** (ōthz, ōths). **1.a.** A solemn formal declaration or promise, often calling on God or a sacred object as witness. **b.** The words or formula of an oath. **c.** Something declared or promised. **2.** An irreverent or blasphemous use of the name of God or something held sacred. **3.** An imprecation; a curse. [ME *oth* < OE *āth.*]

oat•meal (ōt′mēl′) *n.* **1.** Meal made from oats; rolled or ground oats. **2.** A porridge made from rolled or ground oats.

Oa•xa•ca (wə-hä′kə). A city of SE Mexico S of Orizaba; probably founded in 1486 by the Aztecs. Pop. 154,223.

Ob (ŏb, ôb, ôp). A river of central Russia flowing c. 3,700 km (2,300 mi) to the **Gulf of Ob,** an arm of the Arctic Ocean.

OB or **Ob.** also **ob.** *abbr.* Obstetric; obstetrician; obstetrics.

ob. *abbr.* **1.** *Lat.* Obiit (he or she died). **2.** *Lat.* Obiter (incidentally). **3.** *Mus.* Oboe.

Ob. *abbr. Bible.* Obadiah.

ob- *pref.* Inverse; inversely: *obcordate.* [NLat., short for *obversē*, obversely < Lat. *obversus*, p.part. of *obvertere*, to turn

ă pat	oi boy
ā pay	ou out
âr care	o͝o took
ä father	o͞o boot
ĕ pet	ŭ cut
ē be	ûr urge
ĭ pit	th thin
ī pie	*th* this
îr pier	hw which
ŏ pot	zh vision
ō toe	ə about, item
ô paw	

Stress marks:
′ (primary);
′ (secondary), as in dictionary (dĭk′shə-nĕr′ē)

ob•scure (ŏb-skyo͝or′, əb-) *adj.* **-scur•er, -scur•est. 1.** Deficient in light; dark. **2.a.** So faintly perceptible as to lack clear delineation; indistinct. See Syns at **dark. b.** Indistinctly heard; faint. **c.** *Ling.* Having the reduced, neutral sound represented by schwa (ə). **3.a.** Far from centers of human population. **b.** Out of sight; hidden: *an obscure retreat.* **4.** Not readily noticed or seen; inconspicuous: *an obscure flaw.* **5.** Of undistinguished or humble station or reputation. **6.** Not clearly understood or expressed; ambiguous or vague. See Syns at **ambiguous.** —*tr.v.* **-scured, -scur•ing, -scures. 1.** To make dim or indistinct. See Syns at **block. 2.** To conceal in obscurity; hide. **3.** *Ling.* To reduce (a vowel) to the neutral sound represented by schwa (ə). —*n.* Something obscure or unknown. [ME < OFr. *obscur* < Lat. *obscūrus.* See **(s)keu-*.**] —**ob•scure′ly** *adv.* —**ob•scure′ness** *n.*

ob•scu•ri•ty (ŏb-skyo͝or′ĭ-tē, əb-) *n., pl.* **-ties. 1.** Deficiency or absence of light; darkness. **2.a.** The quality or state of being unknown. **b.** One that is unknown. **3.a.** The quality or state of being imperfectly known or difficult to understand. **b.** An instance of such obscurity.

ob•se•qui•ous (ŏb-sē′kwē-əs, əb-) *adj.* Full of or exhibiting servile compliance; fawning. [ME < Lat. *obsequiōsus* < *obsequium,* compliance < *obsequī,* to comply : *ob-,* to; see OB- + *sequī,* to follow; see **sek^{w}-[1]*.**] —**ob•se′qui•ous•ly** *adv.* —**ob•se′qui•ous•ness** *n.*

ob•se•quy (ŏb′sĭ-kwē) *n., pl.* **-quies.** A funeral rite or ceremony. Often used in the plural. [ME *obsequi* < OFr. *obseque* < Med.Lat. *obsequiae,* alteration of Lat. *obsequia,* pl. of *obsequium,* dutiful service. See OBSEQUIOUS.]

ob•serv•a•ble (əb-zûr′və-bəl) *adj.* **1.** Possible to observe. **2.** Deserving or worthy of note; noteworthy. —*n. Phys.* A physical property, such as weight, that can be observed or measured directly. —**ob•serv′a•bly** *adv.*

ob•ser•vance (əb-zûr′vəns) *n.* **1.** The act or practice of observing or complying with a law, custom, command, or rule. **2.** The act or custom of keeping or celebrating a holiday or other ritual occasion. **3.** A customary rite or ceremony. **4.** The act of watching; observation. **5.** *Rom. Cath. Ch.* The rule governing a religious order.

ob•ser•vant (əb-zûr′vənt) *adj.* **1.** Quick to perceive or apprehend; alert. See Syns at **careful. 2.** Diligent in observing a law, custom, duty, or principle. —**ob•ser′vant•ly** *adv.*

ob•ser•va•tion (ŏb′zər-vā′shən) *n.* **1.a.** The act or faculty of observing. **b.** The fact of being observed. **2.a.** The act of noting and recording something with instruments. **b.** The result or record of such notation. **3.** A comment or remark. See Syns at **comment. 4.** An inference or a judgment that is acquired from or based on observing. —**ob′ser•va′tion•al** *adj.*

observatory
U.S. Naval Observatory in Washington DC

ob•ser•va•to•ry (əb-zûr′və-tôr′ē, -tōr′ē) *n., pl.* **-ries. 1.** A building, a place, or an institution designed and equipped for making observations of astronomical, meteorological, or other natural phenomena. **2.** A structure overlooking an extensive view. [Fr. *observatoire* (influenced by CONSERVATORY) < *observer,* to observe < OFr. See OBSERVE.]

ob•serve (əb-zûrv′) *v.* **-served, -serv•ing, -serves.** —*tr.* **1.** To be or become aware of, esp. through careful and directed attention; notice. See Syns at **see[1]. 2.** To watch attentively. **3.** To make a systematic or scientific observation of. **4.** To say casually; remark. **5.** To adhere to or abide by. **6.** To keep or celebrate (a holiday, for example). —*intr.* **1.** To take notice. **2.** To say something; make a comment or remark. **3.** To watch or be present without participating actively. [ME *observen,* to conform to < OFr. *observer* < Lat. *observāre,* to abide by, watch : *ob-,* over; see OB- + *servāre,* to keep, watch; see **ser-[1]*.**]

ob•serv•er (əb-zûr′vər) *n.* **1.** One that observes. **2.** A delegate sent to observe and report on the proceedings of an assembly or a meeting. **3.a.** A crew member on a military aircraft who makes observations. **b.** A member of an armed force who watches and reports from an observation post.

ob•sess (əb-sĕs′, ŏb-) *v.* **-sessed, -sess•ing, -sess•es.** —*tr.* To preoccupy the mind of excessively. —*intr.* To have the mind excessively preoccupied with a single emotion or topic. [Lat. *obsidēre, obsess-,* to beset, occupy : *ob-,* on; see OB- + *sedēre,* to sit; see **sed-*.**] —**ob•ses′sor** *n.*

ob•ses•sion (əb-sĕsh′ən, ŏb-) *n.* **1.** Compulsive preoccupation with a fixed idea or an unwanted feeling or emotion, often accompanied by symptoms of anxiety. **2.** A compulsive, often unreasonable idea or emotion. —**ob•ses′sion•al** *adj.* —**ob•ses′sion•al•ly** *adv.*

ob•ses•sive (əb-sĕs′ĭv, ŏb-) *adj.* **1.** Of, relating to, characteristic of, or causing an obsession. **2.** Excessive in degree or nature. —**ob•ses′sive** *n.* —**ob•ses′sive•ly** *adv.* —**ob•ses′sive•ness** *n.*

ob•ses•sive-com•pul•sive (əb-sĕs′ĭv-kəm-pŭl′sĭv, ŏb-) *adj.* Relating to or characterized by a tendency to dwell on unwanted thoughts or ideas or perform certain repetitious rituals, esp. as a defense against anxiety from unconscious conflicts. —*n.* An obsessive-compulsive person.

ob•sid•i•an (ŏb-sĭd′ē-ən) *n.* A usu. black or banded hard volcanic glass that displays shiny curved surfaces when fractured and is formed by rapid cooling of lava. [Lat. *obsidiānus,* misreading of *obsiānus (lapis),* Obsian (stone), obsidian, after *Obsius,* Roman who may have discovered it.]

ob•so•lesce (ŏb′sə-lĕs′) *intr.v.* **-lesced, -lesc•ing, -lesc•es.** To undergo the process of becoming obsolete. [Lat. *obsolēscere.* See OBSOLESCENT.]

ob•so•les•cent (ŏb′sə-lĕs′ənt) *adj.* **1.** Being in the process of passing out of use or usefulness; becoming obsolete. **2.** *Biol.* Gradually disappearing; imperfectly or only slightly developed. Used of a part of an organism. [Lat. *obsolēscēns, obsolēscent-,* pr.part. of *obsolēscere,* to fall into disuse : *ob-,* away; see OB- + *solēre,* to be accustomed to.] —**ob′so•les′cence** *n.* —**ob′so•les′cent•ly** *adv.*

ob•so•lete (ŏb′sə-lēt′, ŏb′sə-lēt′) *adj.* **1.** No longer in use. See Syns at **old. 2.** Outmoded in design, style, or construction. **3.** *Biol.* Vestigial or imperfectly developed, esp. in comparison with other individuals or related species. Used of a part of an organism. —*tr.v.* **-let•ed, -let•ing, -letes.** To cause to become obsolete. [Lat. *obsolētus,* p.part. of *obsolēscere,* to fall into disuse. See OBSOLESCENT.] —**ob′so•lete′ly** *adv.* —**ob′so•lete′ness** *n.* —**ob′so•let′ism** *n.*

ob•sta•cle (ŏb′stə-kəl) *n.* One that opposes, stands in the way of, or holds up progress. [ME < OFr. < Lat. *obstāculum* < *obstāre,* to hinder : *ob-,* against; see OB- + *stāre,* to stand; see **stā-*.**]

obstacle course *n.* **1.** A training course with obstacles that must be negotiated speedily, as by troops in training. **2.** A situation full of obstacles that must be overcome.

obstet. *abbr.* Obstetric; obstetrics.

ob•stet•ric (ŏb-stĕt′rĭk, əb-) also **ob•stet•ri•cal** (-rĭ-kəl) *adj.* Of or relating to the profession of obstetrics or the care of women during and after pregnancy. [Lat. *obstetrīcius,* pertaining to a midwife < *obstetrix, obstetric-,* midwife < *obstāre,* to stand opposite to : *ob-,* opposite to; see OB- + *stāre,* to stand; see **stā-*.**] —**ob•stet′ri•cal•ly** *adv.*

ob•ste•tri•cian (ŏb′stĭ-trĭsh′ən) *n.* A physician who specializes in obstetrics.

ob•stet•rics (ŏb-stĕt′rĭks, əb-) *n.* *(used with a sing. or pl. v.)* The branch of medicine that deals with the care of women during pregnancy and during and following childbirth.

ob•sti•na•cy (ŏb′stə-nə-sē) *n., pl.* **-cies. 1.** The state or quality of being stubborn or refractory. **2.** The act or an instance of being stubborn or refractory.

ob•sti•nate (ŏb′stə-nĭt) *adj.* **1.** Stubbornly adhering to an attitude, an opinion, or a course of action; obdurate. **2.** Difficult to manage, control, or subdue; refractory. **3.** Difficult to alleviate or cure. [ME *obstinat* < Lat. *obstinātus,* p.part. of *obstināre,* to persist. See **stā-*.**] —**ob′sti•nate•ly** *adv.* —**ob′sti•nate•ness** *n.*

Syns: *obstinate, stubborn, headstrong, stiff-necked, bullheaded, pigheaded, mulish, dogged, pertinacious.* These adjectives refer to tenacious unwillingness to yield. *Obstinate* implies unreasonable rigidity: *"Mr. Quincy labored hard with the governor to obtain his assent, but he was obstinate"* (Benjamin Franklin). *Stubborn* pertains to innate, often perverse resoluteness or unyieldingness: *"She was very stubborn when her mind was made up"* (Samuel Butler). One who is *headstrong* is stubbornly, often recklessly willful: *The headstrong teenager ignored school policy. Stiff-necked* implies stubbornness combined with arrogance or aloofness: *the stiff-necked family patriarch. Bullheaded* suggests foolish or irrational obstinacy, and *pigheaded,* stupid obstinacy: *Don't be bullheaded; see a doctor. "It's a pity pious folks are so apt to be pigheaded"* (Harriet Beecher Stowe). *Mulish* implies obstinacy and intractability: *"Obstinate is no word for it, for she is mulish"* (Ouida). *Dogged* emphasizes stubborn perseverance: *"two warring ideals in one dark body, whose dogged strength alone keeps it from being torn asunder"* (W.E.B. Du Bois). *Pertinacious* stresses a tenacity, as of purpose, that is sometimes vexatious: *pertinacious critics.*

ob•strep•er•ous (ŏb-strĕp′ər-əs, əb-) *adj.* **1.** Noisily and stubbornly defiant. **2.** Aggressively boisterous. [< Lat. *obstreperus,* noisy < *obstrepere,* to make a noise against : *ob-,* against; see OB- + *strepere,* to make a noise (of imit. orig.).] —**ob•strep′er•ous•ly** *adv.* —**ob•strep′er•ous•ness** *n.*

ob•struct (əb-strŭkt′, ŏb-) *tr.v.* **-struct•ed, -struct•ing, -structs. 1.** To block or fill (a passage) with obstacles or an obstacle. See Syns at **block. 2.** To impede, retard, or interfere with; hinder. **3.** To get in the way of so as to hide from sight. [Lat. *obstruere, obstrūct-* : *ob-,* against; see OB- + *struere,* to pile up; see **ster-[2]*.**] —**ob•struct′er, ob•struc′tor** *n.* —**ob•struc′tive** *adj.* —**ob•struc′tive•ly** *adv.* —**ob•struc′tive•ness** *n.*

ob•struc•tion (əb-strŭk′shən, ŏb-) *n.* **1.** One that obstructs; an obstacle. **2.a.** The act or an instance of obstructing. **b.** The condition of being obstructed. **3.** The act of causing a delay or an attempt to cause a delay in the conduct of business, esp. in a legislative body. **4.** *Sports.* The act of impeding another player in a match or race.

ob•struc•tion•ist (əb-strŭk′shə-nĭst, ŏb-) *n.* One who systematically blocks or interrupts a process, esp. one who attempts to impede passage of legislation by the use of delaying tactics. —**ob•struc′tion•ism** *n.* —**ob•struc′tion•is′tic** *adj.*

obstruction of justice *n. Law.* The criminal offense, under common law and according to the statutes of many jurisdictions, of obstructing the administration and due process of law.

ob•stru•ent (ŏb′stro͞o-ənt) *adj.* Obstructing or closing natural openings or passages of the body. — *n.* **1.** An obstruent medicine or agent. **2.** *Ling.* A sound, such as an affricate, produced with complete blockage or at least partial constriction of the airflow through the nose or mouth. [Lat. *obstruēns, obstruent-*, pr.part. of *obstruere*, to obstruct. See OBSTRUCT.]

ob•tain (əb-tān′, ŏb-) *v.* **-tained, -tain•ing, -tains.** — *tr.* To succeed in gaining possession of as the result of planning or endeavor; acquire. — *intr.* **1.** To be established, accepted, or customary. **2.** *Archaic.* To succeed. [ME *obteinen* < OFr. *obtenir* < Lat. *obtinēre* : *ob-*, intensive pref.; see OB- + *tenēre*, to hold; see **ten-***.] — **ob•tain′a•ble** *adj.* — **ob•tain′er** *n.*

ob•tect (ŏb-tĕkt′) also **ob•tect•ed** (-tĕk′tĭd) *adj.* Having the wings and appendages enclosed or covered by a secretion that forms a hard shell or horny case, as the pupae of most butterflies and moths. [Lat. *obtēctus*, p.part. of *obtegere*, to cover over : *ob-*, over; see OB- + *tegere*, to cover; see **(s)teg-***.]

ob•test (ŏb-tĕst′) *tr.v.* **-test•ed, -test•ing, -tests.** To supplicate; entreat. [Lat. *obtestārī* : *ob-*, to; see OB- + *testārī*, to call as a witness (< *testis*, witness; see **trei-***).] — **ob′tes•ta′tion** *n.*

ob•trude (ŏb-tro͞od′, əb-) *v.* **-trud•ed, -trud•ing, -trudes.** — *tr.* **1.** To impose (oneself or one's ideas) on others with undue insistence or without invitation. **2.** To thrust out; push forward. — *intr.* To impose oneself on others. [Lat. *obtrūdere* : *ob-*, against; see OB- + *trūdere*, to thrust; see **treud-***.] — **ob•trud′er** *n.* — **ob•tru′sion** (-tro͞o′zhən) *n.*

ob•tru•sive (ŏb-tro͞o′sĭv, -zĭv, əb-) *adj.* **1.** Thrusting out; protruding. **2.** Tending to push self-assertively forward; brash: *obtrusive behavior.* **3.** Undesirably noticeable: *an obtrusive scar.* [< Lat. *obtrūsus*, p.part. of *obtrūdere*, to obtrude. See OBTRUDE.] — **ob•tru′sive•ly** *adv.* — **ob•tru′sive•ness** *n.*

ob•tund (ŏb-tŭnd′) *tr.v.* **-tund•ed, -tund•ing, -tunds.** To make less intense; dull or deaden. [ME *obtunden* < Lat. *obtundere* : *ob-*, against; see OB- + *tundere*, to beat.] — **ob•tund′ent** *adj.* — **ob•tun′di•ty** *n.*

ob•tu•rate (ŏb′tə-rāt′, -tyə-) *tr.v.* **-rat•ed, -rat•ing, -rates.** To close or obstruct. [Lat. *obtūrāre, obtūrāt-* : *ob-*, ob- + *-tūrāre*, to stop up; see **teuə-***.] — **ob′tu•ra′tion** *n.*

ob•tu•ra•tor (ŏb′tə-rā′tər, -tyə-) *n.* **1.** An organic structure, such as the soft palate, that closes an opening in the body. **2.** A prosthetic device serving to close an opening in the body.

ob•tuse (ŏb-to͞os′, -tyo͞os′, əb-) *adj.* **-tus•er, -tus•est.** **1.** Lacking quickness of perception or intellect. **2.a.** Not sharp, pointed, or acute in form; blunt. **b.** *Bot.* Having a blunt or rounded tip: *an obtuse leaf.* [ME < OFr. < Lat. *obtūsus*, p.part. of *obtundere*, to blunt. See OBTUND.] — **ob•tuse′ly** *adv.* — **ob•tuse′ness** *n.*

obtuse angle *n. Math.* An angle between 90° and 180°.

ob•verse (ŏb-vûrs′, əb-, ŏb′vûrs′) *adj.* **1.** Facing or turned toward the observer. **2.** Serving as a counterpart or complement. — *n.* (ŏb′vûrs′, ŏb-vûrs′, əb-). **1.** The side of a coin, medal, or badge that bears the principal stamp or design. **2.** The more conspicuous of two possible alternatives, cases, or sides. **3.** *Logic.* The counterpart of a proposition obtained by exchanging the affirmative for the negative quality of the whole proposition and then negating the predicate: *The obverse of "Every act is predictable" is "No act is unpredictable."* [Lat. *obversus*, p.part. of *obvertere*, to turn toward. See OBVERT.] — **ob•verse′ly** *adv.*

ob•ver•sion (ŏb-vûr′zhən, -shən, əb-) *n.* **1.** The process of obverting or the condition so resulting. **2.** *Logic.* Inference of the obverse of a proposition.

ob•vert (ŏb-vûrt′, əb-) *tr.v.* **-vert•ed, -vert•ing, -verts.** **1.** To turn (something) so as to present another side or aspect to view. **2.** To alter the appearance of. **3.** *Logic.* To subject (a proposition) to obversion. [Lat. *obvertere*, to turn toward : *ob-*, toward; see OB- + *vertere*, to turn; see **wer-²***.]

ob•vi•ate (ŏb′vē-āt′) *tr.v.* **-at•ed, -at•ing, -ates.** To anticipate and dispose of effectively; render unnecessary. [Lat. *obviāre, obviāt-*, to hinder < *obvius*, in the way. See OBVIOUS.] — **ob′vi•a′tion** *n.* — **ob′vi•a′tor** *n.*

ob•vi•ous (ŏb′vē-əs) *adj.* **1.** Easily perceived or understood. See Syns at **apparent.** **2.** Easily seen through because of a lack of subtlety. **3.** *Archaic.* Standing in the way or in front. [< Lat. *obvius* < *obviam*, in the way, within reach : *ob-*, against; see OB- + *viam*, accusative sing. of *via*, way; see **wegh-***.] — **ob′vi•ous•ly** *adv.* — **ob′vi•ous•ness** *n.*

oc. or **Oc.** *abbr.* Ocean.

o.c. *abbr. Lat.* Opere citato (in the work cited).

O.C. *abbr.* **1.** Officer Commanding. **2.** Old Catholic.

o/c *abbr.* Overcharge.

o•ca (ō′kə) *n.* **1.** A perennial plant *(Oxalis tuberosa)* of the high Andes. **2.** The edible tuber of this plant. [Sp., poss. < Quechua *oqa.*]

O•cal•a (ō-kăl′ə). A city of N-central FL SSE of Gainesville. Pop. 42,045.

oc•a•ri•na (ŏk′ə-rē′nə) *n. Mus.* A small wind instrument with finger holes, a mouthpiece, and an elongated ovoid shape. [Ital. < dial. *ucarenna*, dim. of Ital. *oca*, goose < VLat. **auca* < **avica* < Lat. *avis*, bird. See **awi-***.]

OCAS *abbr.* Organization of Central American States.

O'Ca•sey (ō-kā′sē), **Sean.** 1880–1964. Irish playwright whose dramas include *Juno and the Paycock* (1924).

occ. *abbr.* **1.** Occident; occidental. **2.** Occupation.

Oc•cam (ŏk′əm), **William of.** See William of **Ockham.**

Oc•cam's razor (ŏk′əmz) *n.* Var. of **Ockham's razor.**

occas. *abbr.* Occasional; occasionally.

oc•ca•sion (ə-kā′zhən) *n.* **1.a.** An event or a happening; an incident. **b.** The time at which an event occurs. **2.** A significant event. **3.** A favorable or appropriate time or juncture; an opportunity. **4.** Something that brings on or precipitates an action, a condition, or an event, esp. the immediate cause. **5.** Something that provides a reason or justification; a ground. **6.** A need created by a particular circumstance. **7.** A large or important social gathering. **8. occasions.** *Archaic.* Personal requirements or necessities. — *tr.v.* **-sioned, -sion•ing, -sions.** To provide occasion for; cause. — ***idiom.* on occasion.** From time to time; now and then. [ME < OFr. < Lat. *occāsiō, occāsiōn-* < *occāsus*, p.part. of *occidere*, to fall : *ob-*, down; see OB- + *cadere*, to fall; see **kad-***.]

oc•ca•sion•al (ə-kā′zhə-nəl) *adj.* **1.a.** Occurring from time to time. See Syns at **periodic. b.** Not habitual; infrequent. **2.** Created for a special occasion. **3.** Intended for use as the occasion requires. **4.** Acting as a cause. **5.** Acting in a specified capacity from time to time.

oc•ca•sion•al•ly (ə-kā′zhə-nə-lē) *adv.* Now and then; from time to time.

oc•ci•dent (ŏk′sĭ-dənt, -dĕnt′) *n.* **1.** Western lands or regions; the west. **2. Occident.** The countries of Europe and the Western Hemisphere. [ME < OFr. < Lat. *occidēns, occident-* < pr.part. of *occidere*, to set (used of the sun). See OCCASION.]

oc•ci•den•tal or **Oc•ci•den•tal** (ŏk′sĭ-dĕn′tl) — *adj.* Of or relating to the Occident or its peoples or cultures; western. — *n.* A native or inhabitant of an Occidental country.

Oc•ci•den•tal•ism (ŏk′sĭ-dĕn′tl-ĭz′əm) *n.* The characteristic traits or customs of Occidental peoples.

oc•ci•den•tal•ize or **Oc•ci•den•tal•ize** (ŏk′sĭ-dĕn′tl-īz′) *tr.v.* **-ized, -iz•ing, -iz•es.** To make Occidental, as in character or way of life. — **oc′ci•den′tal•i•za′tion** (-ĭ-zā′shən) *n.*

oc•cip•i•tal (ŏk-sĭp′ĭ-tl) *adj.* Of or relating to the occiput or to the occipital bone: *an occipital fracture.* — *n.* The occipital bone. — **oc•cip′i•tal•ly** *adv.*

occipital bone *n.* A curved trapezoid compound bone that forms the lower posterior part of the skull; the occipital.

occipital lobe *n.* The posterior lobe of each cerebral hemisphere, having the shape of a three-sided pyramid.

oc•ci•put (ŏk′sə-pŭt′, -pət) *n., pl.* **oc•cip•i•ta** (ŏk-sĭp′ĭ-tə) or **oc•ci•puts.** The back part of the head or skull. [ME < Lat. *occiput, occipit-* : *ob-*, against; see OB- + *caput*, head; see **kaput-***.]

oc•clude (ə-klo͞od′) *v.* **-clud•ed, -clud•ing, -cludes.** — *tr.* **1.** To cause to become closed; obstruct. **2.** To prevent the passage of. **3.** *Chem.* To absorb or adsorb and retain (a substance). **4.** *Meteorol.* To force (air) upward, as when a cold front overtakes and undercuts a warm front. **5.** *Dentistry.* To bring together (the upper and lower teeth) in proper alignment. — *intr. Dentistry.* To close so that the cusps fit together. [Lat. *occlūdere* : *ob-*, intensive pref.; see OB- + *claudere*, to close.] — **oc•clud′ent** *adj.*

oc•clud•ed front (ə-klo͞o′dĭd) *n. Meteorol.* The front formed when a cold front occludes a warm front.

oc•clu•sal (ə-klo͞o′zəl, -səl) *adj.* Of or relating to occlusions of the teeth, esp. the chewing or biting surfaces: *occlusal wear.*

oc•clu•sion (ə-klo͞o′zhən) *n.* **1.a.** The process of occluding. **b.** Something that occludes. **2.** *Medic.* An obstruction or a closure of a passageway or vessel. **3.** *Dentistry.* The alignment of the upper and lower teeth when brought together. **4.** *Meteorol.* An occluded front. **5.** *Ling.* Closure at some point in the vocal tract that blocks the flow of air in producing an oral or a nasal stop. [< Lat. *occlūsus*, p.part. of *occlūdere*, to occlude. See OCCLUDE.]

oc•clu•sive (ə-klo͞o′sĭv, -zĭv) *adj.* Occluding or tending to occlude. — *n. Ling.* An oral or a nasal stop.

oc•cult (ə-kŭlt′, ŏk′ŭlt′) *adj.* **1.** Of, relating to, or dealing with supernatural influences, agencies, or phenomena. **2.** Beyond the realm of human comprehension; inscrutable. **3.** Available only to the initiate; secret. See Syns at **mysterious.** **4.** Hidden from view; concealed. **5.a.** *Medic.* Detectable only by microscopic examination or chemical analysis. **b.** Not accompanied by readily detectable signs or symptoms: *occult carcinoma.* — *n.* Occult practices or techniques. — *v.* (ə-kŭlt′) **-cult•ed, -cult•ing, -cults.** — *tr.* **1.** To conceal or cause to disappear from view. **2.** *Astron.* To conceal by occultation. — *intr.* To become concealed or extinguished at regular intervals. [Lat. *occultus*, secret, p.part. of *occulere*, to cover over. See **kel-¹***.] — **oc•cult′ly** *adv.* — **oc•cult′ness** *n.*

oc•cul•ta•tion (ŏk′ŭl-tā′shən) *n.* **1.** The act of occulting or the state of being occulted. **2.** *Astron.* **a.** The passage of a

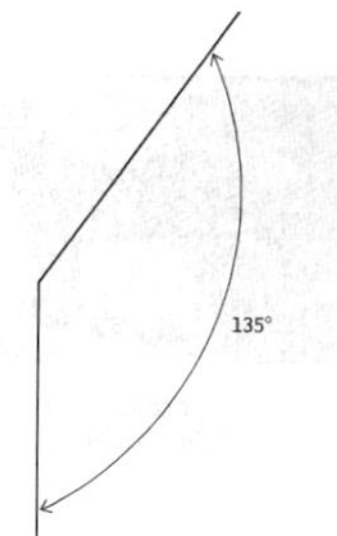

obtuse angle

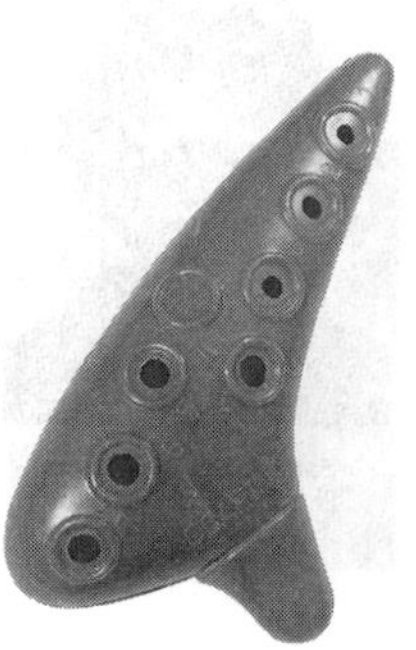

ocarina

ă pat	oi boy
ā pay	ou out
âr care	o͝o took
ä father	o͞o boot
ĕ pet	ŭ cut
ē be	ûr urge
ĭ pit	th thin
ī pie	*th* this
îr pier	hw which
ŏ pot	zh vision
ō toe	ə about, item
ô paw	

Stress marks:
′ (primary);
′ (secondary), as in dictionary (dĭk′shə-nĕr′ē)

o•de•um (ō-dē′əm, ō′dē-) *n., pl.* **o•de•a** (ō-dē′ə, ō′dē-ə). **1.** A small building of ancient Greece and Rome used for public performances. **2.** A contemporary theater or concert hall. [Lat. *ōdēum* < Gk. *ōideion* < *aoidē*, *ōidē*, song. See ODE.]

O•din (ō′dĭn) *n. Myth.* The Norse god of wisdom and war, who created the cosmos. [ON *Ódhinn*. See **wet-**[1]***.**]

o•di•ous (ō′dē-əs) *adj.* Arousing or meriting strong dislike, aversion, or intense displeasure. [ME < OFr. *odieus* < Lat. *odiōsus* < *odium*, hatred. See ODIUM.] **—o′di•ous•ly** *adv.* **—o′di•ous•ness** *n.*

o•di•um (ō′dē-əm) *n.* **1.** The state or quality of being odious. **2.** Strong dislike, contempt, or aversion. **3.** A state of disgrace resulting from detestable conduct. [Lat., hatred. See **od-*.**]

O•do•a•cer (ō′dō-ā′sər) also **O•do•va•car** or **O•do•va•kar** (-vā′kər). A.D. 434?–493. Germanic tribal leader who deposed Romulus Augustulus (reigned 475–476), bringing the Western Roman Empire to an end.

o•do•graph (ō′də-grăf′) *n.* An instrument for recording the distance and course traveled by a vehicle. [Gk. *hodos*, journey + -GRAPH.]

o•dom•e•ter (ō-dŏm′ĭ-tər) *n.* An instrument that indicates distance traveled by a vehicle. [Fr. *odomètre* < Gk. *hodometron* : *hodos*, journey + *metron*, measure; see -METER.] **—o•dom′e•try** *n.*

-odon *suff.* An animal having a specified kind of teeth: *sphenodon.* [NLat. < Gk. *odōn*, tooth. See **dent-*.**]

o•do•nate (ōd′n-āt′, ō-dŏn′-) *n.* Any of the insects of the order Odonata, including the dragonflies, having two pairs of wings and compound eyes. [< NLat. *Odōnata*, order name < Gk. *odōn*, tooth. See -ODON.] **—o′do•nate′** *adj.*

-odont *suff.* Having teeth of a specified kind: *pleurodont.* [< Gk. *odous*, *odont-*, tooth. See **dent-*.**]

o•don•tal•gia (ō′dŏn-tăl′jə, -jē-ə) *n.* A toothache.

-odontia *suff.* The form of, condition of, or manner of treating the teeth: *orthodontia.*

odonto- or **odont-** *pref.* Tooth: *odontophore.* [Gk. < *odous*, *odont-*, tooth. See **dent-*.**]

o•don•to•blast (ō-dŏn′tə-blăst′) *n.* One of the dentin-forming cells of the outer surface of dental pulp.

o•don•toid (ō-dŏn′toid′) *adj.* **1.** Resembling a tooth. **2.** Of or relating to the odontoid process: *the odontoid ligaments.*

odontoid process *n.* A small projection from the second vertebra of the neck around which the first vertebra rotates.

o•don•tol•o•gy (ō′dŏn-tŏl′ə-jē) *n.* The study of the structure, development, and abnormalities of the teeth. **—o•don′to•log′i•cal** (-tə-lŏj′ĭ-kəl) *adj.* **—o′don•tol′o•gist** *n.*

o•don•to•phore (ō-dŏn′tə-fôr′, -fōr′) *n.* A structure at the base of the mouth of most mollusks over which the radula is drawn back and forth in breaking up food.

o•dor (ō′dər) *n.* **1.** The property or quality of a thing that affects, stimulates, or is perceived by the sense of smell. See Syns at **smell. 2.** A sensation, stimulation, or perception of the sense of smell. **3.** A strong, pervasive quality. **4.** Esteem; repute. [ME *odour* < OFr. < Lat. *odor*.]

o•dor•if•er•ous (ō′də-rĭf′ər-əs) *adj.* Having or giving off an odor. **—o′dor•if′er•ous•ness** *n.*

o•dor•ous (ō′dər-əs) *adj.* Having a distinctive odor: *odorous jasmine flowers.* **—o′dor•ous•ly** *adv.* **—o′dor•ous•ness** *n.*

o•dour (ō′dər) *n. Chiefly British.* Var. of **odor.**

O•do•va•car or **O•do•va•kar** (ō′dō-vā′kər). See **Odoacer.**

O•dys•seus (ō-dĭs′yo͞os′, ō-dĭs′ē-əs) *n. Gk. Myth.* The king of Ithaca, a leader of the Greeks in the Trojan War, who reached home after ten years of wandering.

od•ys•sey (ŏd′ĭ-sē) *n., pl.* **-seys. 1.** A long adventurous voyage or trip. **2.** An intellectual or spiritual quest. [After the *Odyssey*, a Homeric epic about Odysseus's wanderings after Troy's fall < Gk. *Odusseia* < *Odusseus*, Odysseus.]

Oe *abbr.* Oersted.

OE also **O.E.** *abbr.* Old English.

OECD *abbr.* Organization for Economic Cooperation and Development.

oe•de•ma (ĭ-dē′mə) *n. Pathol. & Bot.* Var. of **edema.**

oed•i•pal also **Oed•i•pal** (ĕd′ə-pəl, ē′də-) *adj.* Of or relating to the Oedipus complex. **—oed′i•pal•ly** *adv.*

Oed•i•pus (ĕd′ə-pəs, ē′də-) *n. Gk. Myth.* A son of Laius and Jocasta, who unwittingly killed his father and then married his mother. [Lat. < Gk. *Oidipous* : *oidein*, to swell + *pous*, foot; see OCTOPUS.]

Oedipus
With the sphinx

Oedipus complex *n.* In psychoanalysis, a subconscious sexual desire in a child, esp. a male child, for the parent of the opposite sex, which may result in neurosis in adulthood.

OEM *abbr.* Original equipment manufacturer.

oe•nol•o•gy (ē-nŏl′ə-jē) *n.* Var. of **enology.** [Gk. *oinos*, wine + -LOGY.]

oe•no•mel (ē′nə-mĕl′) *n.* An ancient Greek beverage of wine and honey. [LLat. *oenomeli* < Gk. *oinomeli* : *oinos*, wine + *meli*, honey; see **melit-*.**]

OEO *abbr.* Office of Economic Opportunity.

o'er (ôr, ōr) *prep. & adv.* Over.

oer•sted (ûr′stĕd′) *n.* The centimeter-gram-second electromagnetic unit of magnetic field strength. [After Hans Christian *Oersted* (1777–1851), Danish physicist.]

oe•soph•a•gus (ĭ-sŏf′ə-gəs) *n.* Var. of **esophagus.**

oes•tro•gen (ĕs′trə-jən) *n.* Var. of **estrogen.**

oes•trus (ĕs′trəs) *n.* Var. of **estrus.**

oeu•vre (œ′vrə) *n., pl.* **oeu•vres** (œ′vrə). **1.** A work of art. **2.** The sum of the lifework of an artist, a writer, or a composer. [Fr. < OFr. *uevre*, work < Lat. *opera* < pl. of *opus*, work. See OPUS.]

of (ŭv, ŏv; əv *when unstressed*) *prep.* **1.** Derived or coming from; originating at or from: *men of the north.* **2.** Caused by; resulting from: *a death of flu.* **3.** Away from; at a distance from: *a mile east of here.* **4.** So as to be separated or relieved from: *cured of distemper.* **5.** From the total or group comprising: *most of the cases.* **6.** Composed or made from: *a dress of silk.* **7.** Associated with or adhering to: *a man of your religion.* **8.** Belonging or connected to: *the rungs of a ladder.* **9.a.** Possessing; having: *a person of honor.* **b.** On one's part: *nice of you.* **10.** Containing or carrying: *a bag of food.* **11.** Specified as; named or called: *the Garden of Eden.* **12.** Centering on; directed toward: *a love of horses.* **13.** Produced by; issuing from: *products of the vine.* **14.** Characterized or identified by: *a year of famine.* **15.a.** With reference to; about: *will speak of it later.* **b.** In respect to: *slow of speech.* **16.** Set aside for; taken up by: *a day of rest.* **17.** Before; until: *five minutes of two.* **18.** During or on a specified time: *of recent years.* **19.** By: *beloved of the family.* **20.** Used to indicate an appositive: *that idiot of a driver.* **21.** *Archaic.* On. [ME < OE. See **apo-*.**]

Usage Note: Grammarians have sometimes condemned the so-called double genitive construction, as in *a friend of my father's; a book of mine.* However, this useful construction is well supported by literary precedent.

OF *abbr. Baseball.* Outfield; outfielder.

O'Fao•lain (ō-făl′ən, ō-fā′lən), **Sean.** 1900–91. Irish writer best known for his short stories.

o•fay (ō′fā′) *n. Offensive Slang.* Used as a disparaging term for a white person. [Poss. of West African orig.]

off (ôf, ŏf) *adv.* **1.** From a place or position: *drove off.* **2.a.** At a certain distance in space or time: *a week off.* **b.** From a given course or route; aside: *off the road.* **c.** Into a state of unconsciousness: *dozed off.* **3.a.** So as to be no longer on, attached, or connected: *shaved off his beard.* **b.** So as to be divided: *marked off the field.* **4.** So as to be no longer continuing, operating, or functioning: *switched off the TV.* **5.** So as to be completely removed, finished, or eliminated: *kill off the mice.* **6.** So as to be smaller, fewer, or less: *Sales dropped off.* **7.** So as to be away from work or duty: *a day off.* **8.** Offstage. *—adj.* **1.a.** Distant or removed; farther: *the off side.* **b.** Remote; slim: *an off chance.* **2.** Not on, attached, or connected: *with his shoes off.* **3.** Not operating or operational: *The oven is off.* **4.** No longer taking place; canceled: *The trip is off.* **5.** Slack: *Sales are off.* **6.a.** Not up to standard; below a normal or satisfactory level. **b.** Not accurate; incorrect: *Your results are off.* **c.** Somewhat crazy; eccentric. **7.** Started on the way; going: *I'm off to school.* **8.a.** Absent or away from work or duty. **b.** Spent away from work or duty: *an off day.* **9.a.** Being on the right side of an animal or a vehicle. **b.** Being the animal or vehicle on the right. **10.** *Sports.* Toward or being the side of the field facing the batsman in cricket. **11.** Off-color. *—prep.* **1.** So as to be removed or distant from: *off the branch.* **2.** Away or relieved from: *off duty.* **3.a.** By consuming: *living off milk.* **b.** With the means provided by: *living off my pension.* **c.** *Informal.* From. **4.** Extending or branching out from: *an artery off the heart.* **5.** Not up to the usual standard of: *off his game.* **6.** So as to abstain from: *off narcotics.* **7.** *Naut.* To seaward of. *—v.* **offed, off•ing, offs.** *—intr.* To go away; leave. *—tr. Slang.* To murder. [Var. of ME *of* < OE. See **apo-*.**]

Usage Note: In Modern English the compound preposition *off of* is best avoided in formal speech and writing: *He stepped off* (not *off of*) *the platform. Off* is informal as well in its use to indicate a source: formal style requires *I borrowed it from* (not *off*) *my brother.*

off. *abbr.* Office; officer; official.

Of•fa (ô′fə). d. 796. King of Mercia (757–796) who signed the first recorded English commercial treaty (796).

off-air (ôf′âr′, ŏf′-) *adj.* Spoken, occurring, or used not during broadcasting or not while being recorded for broadcasting.

of•fal (ô′fəl, ŏf′əl) *n.* **1.** Waste parts, esp. of a butchered animal. **2.** Refuse; rubbish. [ME : *of-*, off (< OE < *of*; see **apo-***) + *fal*, fall.]

off and on *adv.* In an intermittent manner.

off•beat (ôf′bēt′, ŏf′-) *n. Mus.* An unaccented beat in a measure. *—adj.* (ôf′bēt′, ŏf′-). *Slang.* Not conforming to an ordinary type or pattern; unconventional: *offbeat humor.*

off-Broad•way (ôf′brôd′wā′, ŏf′-) *n.* Theatrical work, often experimental, presented outside the Broadway entertainment district of New York City. *—adj.* **1.** Of, relating to, or being such theatrical activity. **2.** Located outside the Broadway entertainment district. **—off′-Broad′way′** *adv.*

off-col•or (ôf′kŭl′ər, ŏf′-) *adj.* **1.** Exhibiting bad taste: *an off-color joke.* **2.** Varying from the usual, expected, or required color. **3.** Not in good health or spirits.

Of•fen•bach (ôf′ən-bäk′, -bäKH′). A city of central Germany NNE of Mannheim on the Main R. Pop. 107,378.

Of•fen•bach (ô′fən-bäk′, ŏf′ən-, ô-fĕn-bäk′), **Jacques.** 1819–80. French composer noted for the opera *Tales of Hoffman* (first performed 1881).

of•fence (ə-fĕns′) *n. Chiefly British.* Var. of **offense.**

of•fend (ə-fĕnd′) *v.* **-fend•ed, -fend•ing, -fends.** —*tr.* **1.** To cause displeasure, anger, resentment, or wounded feelings in. **2.** To be displeasing or disagreeable to. **3.a.** To transgress; violate: *offend all laws of humanity.* **b.** To cause to sin. —*intr.* **1.** To result in displeasure. **2.a.** To violate a moral or divine law; sin. **b.** To violate a rule or law. [ME *offenden* < OFr. *offendre* < Lat. *offendere.* See **gʷhen-*.**]

of•fend•er (ə-fĕn′dər) *n.* One that offends, esp. one that breaks a public law: *youthful offenders.*

of•fense (ə-fĕns′) *n.* **1.a.** The act of causing anger, resentment, displeasure, or affront. **b.** The state of being offended. **2.a.** A violation or an infraction of a moral or social code; a transgression or a sin. **b.** A transgression of law; a crime. **3.** Something that outrages moral sensibilities. **4.** (ŏf′ĕns′). The act of attacking or assaulting. **5.** (ŏf′ĕns′). *Sports.* **a.** A team in possession of the ball or puck. **b.** Scoring ability or potential. **c.** The means used in an attempt to score points. [ME < OFr. *ofense* < Lat. *offēnsa* < fem. p.part. of *offendere,* to offend. See OFFEND.]

of•fen•sive (ə-fĕn′sĭv) *adj.* **1.** Disagreeable to the senses. **2.** Causing anger, displeasure, resentment, or affront. **3.a.** Making an attack: *offensive troops.* **b.** Of, relating to, or designed for attack. **4.** (ŏf′ĕn-). *Sports.* Of or relating to a team having possession of a ball or puck. —*n.* **1.** An attitude or a position of attack. **2.** An attack or assault. —**of•fen′sive•ly** *adv.* —**of•fen′sive•ness** *n.*

of•fer (ô′fər, ŏf′ər) *v.* **-fered, -fer•ing, -fers.** —*tr.* **1.** To present for acceptance or rejection; proffer. **2.a.** To put forward for consideration; propose. **b.** To present in order to meet a need or satisfy a requirement. **3.a.** To present for sale. **b.** To provide; furnish. **4.** To propose as payment; bid. **5.** To present as an act of worship. **6.** To exhibit readiness or desire to do; volunteer. **7.** To put up; mount. **8.** To threaten. **9.** To produce or introduce on the stage. —*intr.* **1.** To present an offering in worship or devotion. **2.** To make an offer or a proposal, esp. of marriage. **3.** To present itself. —*n.* **1.** The act of offering. **2.** Something, such as a suggestion, proposal, or bid, that is offered. **3.** *Law.* A proposal that if accepted constitutes a legally binding contract. **4.** The condition of being offered, esp. for sale. **5.a.** An attempt; a try. **b.** A show of intention. [ME *offren* < OE *offrian,* to offer in worship, and < OFr. *offrir,* to propose, present, both < Lat. *offerre,* to offer : *ob-,* to; see OB- + *ferre,* to bring; see **bher-[1]*.**] —**of′fer•er, of′fer•or** *n.*

Syns: *offer, proffer, tender, present.* These verbs are compared as they mean to put before another for acceptance or rejection. *Offer* is the general term in this group: *"She offered no response"* (Arnold Bennett). *Proffer* implies voluntary action motivated especially by courtesy or generosity: *"Mr. van der Luyden . . . proffered to Newland low-voiced congratulations"* (Edith Wharton). To *tender* is to offer formally: *tendered her respects. Present* suggests formality and often ceremony: *"A footman entered, and presented . . . some mail on a silver tray"* (Winston Churchill).

of•fer•ing (ô′fər-ĭng, ŏf′ər-) *n.* **1.** The act of making an offer. **2.** Something that is offered. **3.** A presentation made to a deity as an act of religious worship or sacrifice; an oblation. **4.** A contribution or gift, esp. one made at a religious service.

of•fer•to•ry (ô′fər-tôr′ē, -tōr′ē, ŏf′ər-) *n., pl.* **-ries. 1.** Often **Offertory. a.** One of the principal parts of the Eucharistic liturgy at which the celebrant offers bread and wine to God. **b.** A musical setting for this part of the liturgy. **2.** A collection of offerings at a religious service. [ME *offertori* < LLat. *offertōrium* < Lat. *offerre,* to offer. See OFFER.]

off•hand (ôf′hănd′, ŏf′-) *adv.* Without preparation or forethought; extemporaneously. —*adj.* also **off•hand•ed** (-hăn′dĭd). Extemporaneous. —**off′hand′ed•ly** *adv.* —**off′hand′ed•ness** *n.*

off-hour (ôf′our′, ŏf′-) *n.* A period of time during which motor vehicular and pedestrian traffic is light.

of•fice (ô′fĭs, ŏf′ĭs) *n.* **1.a.** A place in which business, clerical, or professional activities are conducted. **b.** The administrative personnel, executives, or staff working in such a place. **2.** A duty or function assigned to or assumed by someone. See Syns at **function. 3.** A position of authority, duty, or trust given to a person, as in a government or corporation. **4.** A subdivision of a governmental department. **5.** A major executive division of a government. **6.** A public position. **7. offices.** *Chiefly British.* The parts of a house, such as the kitchen, in which servants carry out household work. **8.** A usu. beneficial act performed for another. Often used in the plural. **9.** *Eccles.* A ceremony, rite, or service, usu. prescribed by liturgy, esp.: **a.** The canonical hours. **b.** A prayer service in the Anglican Church, such as Evening Prayer. **c.** A ceremony, rite, or service for a special purpose, esp. a rite for the dead. [ME < OFr., duty < Lat. *officium.* See **dhē-*.**]

office boy *n.* A boy or young man employed in a business office to do odd jobs.

office girl *n.* A girl or young woman employed in a business office to do odd jobs.

of•fice•hold•er (ô′fĭs-hōl′dər, ŏf′ĭs-) *n.* One who holds public office.

of•fi•cer (ô′fĭ-sər, ŏf′ĭ-) *n.* **1.** One who holds an office of authority or trust in an organization. **2.** One who holds a commission in the armed forces. **3.** A person licensed in the merchant marine as master, mate, chief engineer, or assistant engineer. **4.** A police officer. [ME < OFr. *officier* < Med.Lat. *officārius* < Lat. *officium,* service, duty. See OFFICE.]

officer of the day *n., pl.* **officers of the day.** A military officer who, for a given day, assumes responsibility for security, order, and supervision of the guard.

officer of the deck *n., pl.* **officers of the deck.** A naval officer assigned to represent the commanding officer of a vessel or an installation for a specified period.

of•fi•cial (ə-fĭsh′əl) *adj.* **1.** Of or relating to an office or a post of authority. **2.** Authorized by a proper authority; authoritative. **3.** Holding office or serving in a public capacity. **4.** Characteristic of or befitting a person of authority; formal. **5.** Authorized by or contained in the U.S. Pharmacopoeia or National Formulary. Used of drugs. —*n.* **1.** One who holds an office or a position, esp. one who acts in a subordinate capacity for an institution. **2.** *Sports.* A referee or an umpire. [< ME, ecclesiastical officer < OFr. < Lat. *officiālis,* an attendant of an office < *officium,* duty, service. See OFFICE.] —**of•fi′cial•dom** *n.* —**of•fi′cial•ly** *adv.*

of•fi•cial•ese (ə-fĭsh′ə-lēz′, -lēs′) *n.* Language characteristic of official documents or statements, esp. when obscure, pretentiously wordy, or excessively formal.

of•fi•cial•ism (ə-fĭsh′ə-lĭz′əm) *n.* Rigid adherence to official regulations, forms, and procedures.

of•fi•ci•ant (ə-fĭsh′ē-ənt) *n.* One who performs a religious rite or presides over a religious service or ceremony.

of•fi•ci•ar•y (ə-fĭsh′ē-ĕr′ē) *n., pl.* **-ies. 1.** A body of officials or officers. **2.** An official or officer. —*adj.* **1.** Attached to or resulting from an office held. Used of a title. **2.** Having a title resulting from the holding of an office. Used of a dignitary.

of•fi•ci•ate (ə-fĭsh′ē-āt′) *intr.v.* **-at•ed, -at•ing, -ates. 1.** To perform the duties and functions of an office or a position of authority. **2.** To serve as an officiant. **3.** *Sports.* To serve as a referee or an umpire. [Med.Lat. *officiāre, officiāt-,* to conduct < Lat. *officium,* service, duty. See OFFICE.] —**of•fi′ci•a′tion** *n.* —**of•fi′ci•a′tor** *n.*

of•fic•i•nal (ə-fĭs′ə-nəl, ô′fĭ-sī′nəl, ŏf′ĭ-) *adj.* **1.** Readily available in pharmacies; not requiring special preparation. **2.** Recognized by a pharmacopoeia: *an officinal herb.* —*n.* An officinal drug. [Fr. < Med.Lat. *officīnālis,* of a storeroom or workshop < Lat. *officīna,* workshop, alteration of *opificīna* < *opifex, opific-,* workman : *opus,* work; see **op-*** + *facere,* to do; see **dhē-*.**] —**of•fic′i•nal•ly** *adv.*

of•fi•cious (ə-fĭsh′əs) *adj.* **1.** Marked by excessive eagerness in offering unwanted services or advice to others. **2.** Informal; unofficial. **3.** *Archaic.* Eager to render services or help others. [Lat. *officiōsus,* obliging, dutiful < *officium,* duty. See OFFICE.] —**of•fi′cious•ly** *adv.* —**of•fi′cious•ness** *n.*

off•ing (ô′fĭng, ŏf′ĭng) *n. Naut.* The part of the sea visible from shore that is very distant or beyond anchoring ground. —***idiom.* in the offing. 1.** In the near or immediate future; soon to come. **2.** Nearby; at hand.

off•ish (ô′fĭsh, ŏf′ĭsh) *adj.* Inclined to be distant and reserved; aloof. —**off′ish•ly** *adv.* —**off′ish•ness** *n.*

off-key (ôf′kē′, ŏf′-) *adj.* **1.** *Mus.* Pitched higher or lower than the correct notes of a melody. **2.** Being out of accord with what is considered normal or appropriate. —**off′key′** *adv.*

off-lim•its (ôf-lĭm′ĭts, ŏf-) *adj.* Not to be entered or frequented by a designated group.

off-line (ôf′līn′, ŏf′-) *adj. Comp. Sci.* **1.** Not under the control of a central computer, as in a manufacturing process. **2.** Not connected to a computer or computer network.

off•load or **off-load** (ôf′lōd′, ŏf′-) —*v.* **-load•ed, -load•ing, -loads.** —*tr.* **1.** To unload (a vehicle or container). **2.** *Comp. Sci.* To transfer (data) to a peripheral device. —*intr.* To unload a vehicle or container.

off of *prep. Informal.* Off. See Usage Note at **off.**

off-off-Broad•way also **Off-Off-Broad•way** (ôf′ôf-brôd′wā′, ŏf′ŏf-) *n.* The avant-garde or experimental theatrical productions of New York City, typically performed in small or multipurpose venues. —**off′-off-Broad′way** *adv. & adj.*

off-peak (ôf′pēk′, ŏf′-) *adj.* Not in the period of most frequent or heaviest use: *off-peak airfares.*

off-price (ôf′prīs′, ŏf′-) *adj.* **1.** Of, relating to, or being a retail store that sells merchandise at prices lower than usual. **2.** For sale at prices lower than usual.

off•print (ôf′prĭnt′, ŏf′-) *Print.* —*n.* A reproduction of or an excerpt from an article originally contained in a larger publication. —*tr.v.* **-print•ed, -print•ing, -prints.** To reproduce or reprint (an article or excerpt).

off-put•ting (ôf′po͝ot′ĭng, ŏf′-) *adj.* Tending to disconcert or repel.

ă pat	oi boy
ā pay	ou out
âr care	o͝o took
ä father	o͞o boot
ĕ pet	ŭ cut
ē be	ûr urge
ĭ pit	th thin
ī pie	*th* this
îr pier	hw which
ŏ pot	zh vision
ō toe	ə about, item
ô paw	

Stress marks:
′ (primary);
′ (secondary), as in
dictionary (dĭk′shə-nĕr′ē)

Old English sheepdog

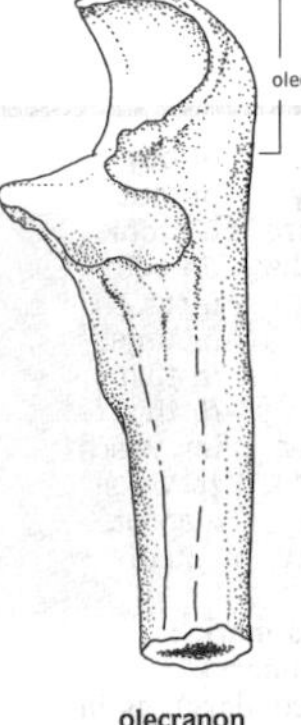

olecranon

Old Bulgarian *n.* See **Old Church Slavonic.**
Old Cas•tile (kăs-tēl′). A historical region of N-central Spain that combined with the S region of New Castile to form the kingdom of Castile; united with Aragon after the marriage of Ferdinand and Isabella (1479).
Old Catholic *n.* A member of a group of German Roman Catholics who refused to accept papal infallibility.
Old Church Slavonic *n.* The medieval Slavic language used by Cyril and Methodius in their translation of the Bible and still used as a liturgical language by several Byzantine churches.
old country *n.* The native country of an immigrant.
Old Danish *n.* The Danish language from the beginning of the 12th to the end of the 14th century.
Old Dutch *n.* The Dutch language from the beginning of the 12th to the middle of the 13th century.
old•en (ōl′dən) *adj.* Of, relating to, or belonging to time long past; old or ancient: *olden days.*
Ol•den•burg (ōl′dən-bûrg′, -bŏŏrk′). A city of NW Germany W of Bremen; chartered 1345. Pop. 138,469.
Oldenburg, Claes Thure. b. 1929. Swedish-born Amer. sculptor best known for his "soft sculptures" of household objects.
Old English *n.* **1.** The English language from the middle of the 5th to the beginning of the 12th century. **2.** *Print.* See **black letter.**
Old English sheepdog *n.* Any of an English breed of sturdy dog, having a docked tail and a thick, shaggy, bluish-gray and white coat with fur that hangs over the eyes.
Old Faith•ful (fāth′fəl). A geyser in Yellowstone National Park in NW WY known for its eruptions lasting c. 4 minutes.
old-fash•ioned (ōld′făsh′ənd) *adj.* **1.** Of a style or method formerly in vogue; outdated. **2.** Attached to or favoring methods, ideas, or customs of an earlier time. —*n.* A cocktail made of whiskey, bitters, sugar, and fruit.
old-field (ōld′fēld′) *n. Virginia.* An overcultivated field allowed to lie fallow.
old-field colt *n. Virginia.* An illegitimate child. Also called regionally *catch colt, woods colt.*
Old French *n.* The French language from the 9th to the early 16th century.
Old Frisian *n.* The Frisian language until about 1575.
old girl *n. Chiefly British.* A graduate of a public school for girls.
old-girl network (ōld′gûrl′) *n.* An informal system of mutual assistance through which women of a particular group exchange favors and connections, as in politics or business.
Old Glory *n.* The flag of the United States.
old gold *n. Color.* A dark yellow, from light olive or olive brown to deep or strong yellow.
old growth *n.* Forest or woodland having a mature ecosystem characterized by old woody plants and the wildlife and plants associated with them. —**old′-growth′** (ōld′grōth′) *adj.*
old guard also **Old Guard** *n.* A conservative, often reactionary element of a class, society, or political group.
Old•ham (ōl′dəm). A borough of NW England NE of Manchester. Pop. 221,800.
old hand *n.* One who is experienced; a veteran.
old hat *adj.* **1.** Old-fashioned. **2.** Overused; trite.
Old High German *n.* High German from the middle of the 9th to the end of the 11th century.
Old Icelandic *n.* Icelandic from the middle of the 12th to the middle of the 16th century.
old•ie (ōl′dē) *n.* Something old, esp. a once popular song.
Old Iranian *n.* Any of the Iranian languages in use before the beginning of the Christian era.
Old Irish *n.* The Irish language from 725 to about 950.
Old Italian *n.* The Italian language until the middle of the 16th century.
Old Kingdom. Ancient Egypt during the III–VI Dynasties, from c. 2980 to 2475 B.C.; noted as "the Age of the Pyramids," with monuments built by rulers such as Cheops.
old lady *n. Slang.* **1.** One's mother. **2.a.** One's wife. **b.** One's girlfriend, esp. a lover with whom one lives.
Old Latin *n.* The earliest recorded Latin, dating from the beginning of the sixth century B.C. until the middle of the first century B.C.
old-line (ōld′līn′) *adj.* **1.** Adhering to conservative or reactionary principles. **2.** Long established: *an old-line family.*
old maid *n.* **1.** *Offensive.* Used as a disparaging term for a woman, esp. an older unmarried woman. **2.** *Informal.* A person regarded as being primly fastidious. **3.** *Games.* **a.** A card game in which the player who holds a designated card at the end is the loser. **b.** The loser of this game. **4.** *Chiefly Southern U.S.* See **zinnia.** —**old-maid′ish** (ōld′mā′dĭsh) *adj.*
old maid flower *n. Chiefly Southern U.S.* See **zinnia.**
old man *n.* **1.** *Slang.* One's father. **2.** *Slang.* **a.** One's husband. **b.** One's boyfriend, esp. a lover with whom one lives. **3.** *Informal.* **a.** A man in authority; a boss. **b.** Often **Old Man.** The commanding officer, esp. of a U.S. naval vessel. **4.** See **southernwood.**
old-man-and-wom•an (ōld′măn′ənd-wŏŏm′ən) *n., pl.* **old-man-and-wom•ans** (-wŏŏm′ənz). See **houseleek.**
old-man cactus (ōld′măn′) *n.* A treelike central Mexican cactus *(Cephalocereus senilis)* having rose-colored flowers and tufts of long white hair on the tips of its branches.
old-man's-beard (ōld′mănz-bîrd′) *n.* **1.** Any of various plants having parts suggestive of a beard, as Spanish moss. **2.** See **fringe tree. 3.** See **virgin's bower.**
old master *n.* **1.** A distinguished European artist of the period from about 1500 to the early 1700's, esp. one of the great painters. **2.** A work created by one of these artists.
old money *n.* **1.** The inherited wealth of established upper-class families. **2.** A person, family, or lineage with old money.
old moon *n.* The waning moon.
Old Nick (nĭk) *n.* The Devil; Satan.
Old Norse *n.* **1.** The North Germanic languages until the middle of the 14th century. **2.a.** Old Icelandic. **b.** Old Norwegian.
Old North French *n.* The dialects of Old French spoken in northern France, esp. in Normandy and Picardy.
Old Northwest. See **Northwest Territory.**
Old Norwegian *n.* The Norwegian language from the middle of the 12th to the end of the 14th century.
Old Persian *n.* An Old Iranian language attested in cuneiform inscriptions dating from the sixth to the fifth century B.C.
Old Portuguese *n.* The Portuguese language until the middle of the 16th century.
Old Provençal *n.* The Provençal language before the middle of the 16th century.
Old Prussian *n.* The Baltic language of eastern Prussia that became extinct in the 18th century.
old rose *n. Color.* A dark pink to grayish or moderate red.
Old Russian *n.* The Russian language as used in documents from the middle of the 11th to the end of the 16th century.
Old Saxon *n.* The Low German language of the continental Saxons until the 12th century.
old school *n.* A group committed to traditional ideas or practices: *a diplomat of the old school.*
old-school tie (ōld′skōōl′) *n.* **1.** A necktie that has the colors of a British public school. **2.** The upper-middle-class exclusive solidarity attributed to alumni of such schools. **3.** The narrow clannish attitudes of the members of a clique.
Old Scratch *n. Chiefly Southern U.S.* The Devil; Satan. [Prob. alteration of *scrat* < ME, hermaphrodite goblin < ON *skratte,* wizard, goblin.]
old snow *n.* See **firn.**
Old Spanish *n.* Spanish before the middle of the 16th century.
old•squaw (ōld′skwô′) *n.* A marine duck *(Clangula hyemalis)* that is black with a white breast and found in Arctic and North Temperate regions.
old•ster (ōld′stər) *n. Informal.* An elderly person.
Old Stone Age *n.* The Paleolithic Age.
old style *n.* **1.** *Print.* A style of type originating in the 18th century and characterized by slight contrast between light and heavy strokes and slanting serifs. **2. Old Style.** The method of reckoning dates according to the Julian calendar.
Old Swedish *n.* Swedish from the early 13th to the late 14th century.
Old Testament *n.* **1.** *Bible.* The first of the two main divisions of the Christian Bible, corresponding to the Hebrew Bible. See table at **Bible. 2.** The covenant of God with Israel as distinguished in Christianity from the dispensation of Jesus constituting the New Testament.
old-time (ōld′tīm′) *adj.* Of, relating to, or characteristic of a time in the past.
old-tim•er (ōld′tī′mər) *n. Informal.* **1.a.** An elderly person. **b.** A person with considerable tenure or experience in a given place or activity. **2.** Something very old or antiquated.
Old Turkic *n.* The language of the oldest texts of the Turkic dialects, dating from the 7th to the 12th century.
Ol•du•vai Gorge (ōl′də-vī′, ôl′dōō-). A ravine in N Tanzania W of Mt. Kilimanjaro containing archaeological sites rich in fossils and Paleolithic implements.
Old Welsh *n.* The Welsh language before the 12th century.
old•wife (ōld′wīf′) *n., pl.* **-wives** (-wīvz′). **1.** See **oldsquaw. 2.** Any of various fishes such as the alewife and the menhaden.
old wives' tale (wīvz) *n.* A superstitious belief or story belonging to traditional folklore.
Old World (wûrld). The Eastern Hemisphere. The term is often used to refer specifically to Europe.
ole– *pref.* Var. of **oleo–.**
–ole or **–ol** *suff.* **1.** A usu. heterocyclic chemical compound containing a five-membered ring: *pyrrole.* **2.** A chemical compound, esp. an ether, that does not contain hydroxyl: *eucalyptol.* [Fr. < Lat. *oleum,* oil. See OIL.]
o•lé (ō-lā′) *interj.* Used to express excited approval. —*n.* A cry of "olé." [Sp., perh. < Ar. *wāllah,* by God!]
o•le•a (ō′lē-ə) *n.* Pl. of **oleum.**
o•le•ag•i•nous (ō′lē-ăj′ə-nəs) *adj.* **1.** Of or relating to oil. **2.** Falsely or smugly earnest; unctuous. [< ME *oliaginose* and < Fr. *oléagineux* (< OFr.), both < Lat. *oleāginus,* of the olive tree < *olea,* olive tree, alteration of *olīva.* See OLIVE.] —**o′le•ag′i•nous•ly** *adv.* —**o′le•ag′i•nous•ness** *n.*
O•le•an (ō′lē-ăn′, ō′lē-ăn′). A city of W NY on the Allegheny R. near the PA border. Pop. 16,946.

o•le•an•der (ō′lē-ăn′dər, ō′lē-ăn′dər) *n.* A poisonous Eurasian evergreen shrub *(Nerium oleander)* having fragrant white, rose, or purple flowers and whorled leaves. [Med.Lat., prob. alteration of LLat. *lorandrum,* alteration of Lat. *rhododendron.* See RHODODENDRON.]

o•le•as•ter (ō′lē-ăs′tər) *n.* **1.** A small Eurasian tree *(Elaeagnus angustifolia)* having oblong silvery leaves, fragrant greenish flowers, and olivelike fruit. **2.** The fruit of this tree. [ME < Lat. < *olea,* olive tree. See OLEAGINOUS.]

o•le•ate (ō′lē-āt′) *n.* An ester or a salt of oleic acid.

o•lec•ra•non (ō-lĕk′rə-nŏn′) *n.* The large process on the upper end of the ulna that projects behind the elbow joint and forms the point of the elbow. [Gk. *ōlekranon* : *ōlenē,* elbow; see **el-*** + *kranion,* skull, head; see **ker-**[1]*.] —**o•lec′ra•nal** (-nəl), **o′le•cra′ni•al** (ō′lĭ-krā′nē-əl) *adj.*

o•le•fin (ō′lə-fĭn) *n.* Any of a class of unsaturated open-chain hydrocarbons, such as ethylene, having the general formula C_nH_{2n}; an alkene with only one carbon-carbon double bond. [Fr. *(gaz) oléfiant,* oil-forming (gas), ethylene : Lat. *oleum,* oil; see OIL + Fr. *-fiant,* pr.part. of *-fier,* -fy.] —**o′le•fin′ic** *adj.*

o•le•ic (ō-lē′ĭk) *adj. Chem.* **1.** Of, relating to, or derived from oil. **2.** Of or relating to oleic acid.

oleic acid *n.* An oily liquid, $C_{17}H_{33}COOH$, occurring in animal and vegetable oils and used in making soap.

o•le•in (ō′lē-ĭn) also **o•le•ine** (-ĭn, -ēn′) *n.* An oily yellow liquid, $(C_{17}H_{33}COO)_3C_3H_5$, occurring naturally in most fats and oils and used as a textile lubricant.

O•lek•ma (ŏ-lĕk′mə). A river of E Russia flowing c. 1,319 km (820 mi) to the Lena R.

O•le•nek (ŏl′ən-yôk′, ə-lə-nyôk′). A river of NE Russia flowing c. 2,172 km (1,350 mi) to the Laptev Sea.

o•le•o (ō′lē-ō′) *n., pl.* **-os.** Margarine.

oleo– or **ole–** *pref.* Oil: *oleoresin.* [Fr. *oléo-* < *oléine,* olein < Lat. *oleum,* oil. See OIL.]

o•le•o•graph (ō′lē-ə-grăf′) *n.* A chromolithograph printed with oil paint on canvas in imitation of an oil painting. —**o′le•og′ra•pher** (-ŏg′rə-fər) *n.* —**o′le•og′ra•phy** *n.*

o•le•o•mar•ga•rine (ō′lē-ō-mär′jə-rĭn, -rēn′) *n.* Margarine.

o•le•o•res•in (ō′lē-ō-rĕz′ĭn) *n.* A naturally occurring mixture of an oil and a resin extracted from various plants, such as pine or balsam fir. —**o′le•o•res′in•ous** *adj.*

o•le•um (ō′lē-əm) *n., pl.* **o•le•a** (ō′lē-ə) or **o•le•ums.** A corrosive solution of sulfur trioxide in sulfuric acid. [Lat., olive oil. See OIL.]

O level *n. Chiefly British.* **1.** The earlier of two standardized tests in a secondary school subject. **2.** The educational background and skills required to pass this test. [O(RDINARY) LEVEL.]

ol•fac•tion (ŏl-făk′shən, ōl-) *n.* **1.** The sense of smell. **2.** The act or process of smelling. [Lat. *olfactus,* p.part. of *olfacere,* to smell; see OLFACTORY + -ION.]

ol•fac•tom•e•ter (ŏl′făk-tŏm′ĭ-tər, ōl′-) *n.* An apparatus for measuring the acuity of the sense of smell. —**ol•fac′to•met′ric** (-tə-mĕt′rĭk) *adj.* —**ol′fac•tom′e•try** *n.*

ol•fac•to•ry (ŏl-făk′tə-rē, -trē, ōl-) *adj.* Of, relating to, or contributing to the sense of smell. [Lat. *olfactōrius,* used to sniff at < *olfactus,* p.part. of *olfacere,* to smell : *olēre,* to smell + *facere,* to do; see FACT.]

olfactory bulb *n.* The bulblike distal end of the olfactory lobe, where the olfactory nerves terminate.

olfactory lobe *n.* A projection of the lower anterior portion of each cerebral hemisphere, functioning in the sense of smell.

olfactory nerve *n.* Either of the first pair of cranial nerves that conduct impulses from the nose to the olfactory bulb.

ol•i•cook (ō′lĭ-ko͝ok′, ŏl′ĭ-) *n. Hudson Valley.* See **doughnut** 1. [Du. *oliekoek* : *olie,* oil (< MDu. < Lat. *oleum, olium*; see OIL) + *koeke,* cake.]

Regional Note: Originally brought to the Hudson Valley of New York by settlers from the Netherlands, a few items of Dutch vocabulary have survived there from colonial times until the present. The word *olicook,* meaning "doughnut," comes from Dutch *oliekoek*—literally, "oil cake." And the Dutch word *kill* for a small running stream is used throughout New York State. *Stoop,* "a small porch," from Dutch *stoep,* is now in general use in the Northeast and beyond.

ol•i•garch (ŏl′ĭ-gärk′, ō′lĭ-) *n.* A member of a small governing faction. [Gk. *oligarkhēs* : *oligos,* few + *-arkhēs,* -arch.]

ol•i•gar•chy (ŏl′ĭ-gär′kē, ō′lĭ-) *n., pl.* **-chies. 1.a.** Government by a few, esp. by a small faction of persons or families. **b.** Those making up such a government. **2.** A state governed by an oligarchy. —**ol′i•gar′chic, ol′i•gar′chi•cal** *adj.*

oligo– or **olig–** *pref.* Few: *oligosaccharide.* [Gk. < *oligos,* little, few.]

Ol•i•go•cene (ŏl′ĭ-gō-sēn′, ō′lĭ-) *Geol.* —*adj.* Of, relating to, or being the geologic time and deposits of the epoch in the Tertiary Period of the Cenozoic Era, extending from the Eocene Epoch to the Miocene Epoch. See table at **geologic time.** —*n.* The Oligocene Epoch or its deposits.

ol•i•go•chaete or **ol•i•go•chete** (ŏl′ĭ-gō-kēt′, ō′lĭ-) *n.* Any of various annelid worms of the class Oligochaeta, including the earthworms and a few small freshwater forms. [< NLat. *Oligochaeta,* class name : OLIGO- + CHAETA.] —**ol′i•go•chae′tous** (-kē′təs) *adj.*

ol•i•go•clase (ŏl′ĭ-gō-klās′, -klāz′, ō′lĭ-) *n. Geol.* See **plagioclase.** [OLIGO- + Gk. *klasis,* cleavage; see PLAGIOCLASE.]

ol•i•go•den•dro•cyte (ŏl′ĭ-gō-dĕn′drə-sīt′, ō′lĭ-) *n.* One of the cells comprising the oligodendroglia.

ol•i•go•den•drog•li•a (ŏl′ĭ-gō-dĕn-drŏg′lē-ə, ō′lĭ-) *n.* Neuroglia consisting of cells found in the central nervous system and associated with the formation of myelin. [OLIGO- + DENDRO- + (NEURO)GLIA.]

o•lig•o•mer (ə-lĭg′ə-mər) *n.* A polymer that consists of two, three, or four monomers. —**o•lig′o•mer′ic** (-mĕr′ĭk) *adj.* —**o•lig′o•mer′i•za′tion** *n.*

ol•i•go•nu•cle•o•tide (ŏl′ĭ-gō-no͞o′klē-ə-tīd, -nyo͞o′-, ō′lĭ-) *n.* A short polymeric chain of two to ten nucleotides.

ol•i•goph•a•gous (ŏl′ĭ-gŏf′ə-gəs, ō′lĭ-) *adj.* Feeding on a restricted range of food substances, esp. a limited number of plants. Used chiefly of insects. —**ol′i•goph′a•gy** (-jē) *n.*

ol•i•gop•o•ly (ŏl′ĭ-gŏp′ə-lē, ō′lĭ-) *n., pl.* **-lies.** A market in which sellers are so few that the actions of any one of them will affect price and their competitors. [OLIGO- + (MONO)POLY.] —**ol′i•gop′o•lis′tic** (-lĭs′tĭk) *adj.*

ol•i•gop•so•ny (ŏl′ĭ-gŏp′sə-nē, ō′lĭ-) *n., pl.* **-nies.** A market in which purchasers are so few that the actions of one can affect price and the costs that competitors must pay. [OLIG(O)- + (MON)OPSONY.] —**ol′i•gop′so•nis′tic** (-nĭs′tĭk) *adj.*

ol•i•go•sac•cha•ride (ŏl′ĭ-gō-săk′ə-rīd′, ō′lĭ-) *n.* A carbohydrate that consists of a relatively small number of monosaccharides.

ol•i•go•tro•phic (ŏl′ĭ-gō-trō′fĭk, -trŏf′ĭk, ō′lĭ-) *adj.* Lacking in plant nutrients and having a large amount of dissolved oxygen throughout. Used of a pond or lake. —**ol′i•got′ro•phy** (-gŏt′rə-fē) *n.*

O•lin•da (ō-lĭn′də, o͞o-lēN′dä). A city of NE Brazil, a suburb of Recife; founded 1537. Pop. 266,751.

o•lin•go (ō-lĭng′gō) *n., pl.* **-gos.** A small nocturnal, chiefly arboreal mammal of the genus *Bassaricyon,* native to Central and South America and resembling the kinkajou but having a nonprehensile tail. [Am.Sp., howler monkey.]

o•li•o (ō′lē-ō′) *n., pl.* **-os. 1.** A spicy stew of meat, vegetables, and chickpeas. **2.a.** A mixture or medley; a hodgepodge. **b.** A collection of various artistic or literary works or musical pieces; a miscellany. **3.** Vaudeville or musical entertainment presented between the acts of a burlesque or minstrel show. [Alteration of Sp. *olla,* pot. See OLLA.]

ol•i•va•ceous (ŏl′ə-vā′shəs) *adj. Color.* Olive-green.

ol•ive (ŏl′ĭv) *n.* **1.** A Mediterranean evergreen tree *(Olea europaea)* having fragrant white flowers, usu. lance-shaped leathery leaves, and edible drupes. **2.** The small ovoid fruit of this tree, an important food and source of oil. **3.** *Color.* Olive green. [ME < Lat. *olīva* < Gk. *elaia, elaiwā.*] —**ol′ive** *adj.*

ol•ive-backed thrush (ŏl′ĭv-băkt′) *n.* A North American thrush *(Hylocichla ustulata)* having a dark olive-brown back and common in spruce and fir forests.

olive branch *n.* **1.** A branch of an olive tree regarded as an emblem of peace. **2.** An offer of peace.

olive drab *n.* **1.** *Color.* A grayish olive to dark olive brown or olive gray. **2.a.** Cloth of this color, often used in military uniforms. **b.** A uniform made from cloth of this color. Also used in the plural.

olive green *n. Color.* A green-yellow hue of low to medium lightness and low to moderate saturation.

olive oil *n.* Oil pressed from olives, used in salad dressings, for cooking, as an ingredient in soaps, and as an emollient.

Ol•ives (ŏl′ĭvz), **Mount of.** Also **Ol•i•vet** (ŏl′ə-vĕt′). A ridge of hills in the West Bank E of Jerusalem. At its W foot is the biblical site of the Garden of Gethsemane.

ol•ive•wood (ŏl′ĭv-wo͝od′) *n.* An evergreen tree *(Cassine laneana)* native to Bermuda and having oblanceolate leaves, unisexual flowers, and creamy-white fruit.

O•liv•i•er (ō-lĭv′ē-ā′), Sir **Laurence Kerr.** Baron Olivier of Brighton. 1907–89. British actor and director best known for his interpretations of Shakespeare's Othello and Richard III.

ol•i•vine (ŏl′ə-vēn′) *n.* A mineral silicate of iron and magnesium, $(Mg, Fe)_2SiO_4$, found in igneous and metamorphic rocks and used in refractories. [OLIVE (< its color) + -INE[1].]

ol•la (ŏl′ə, ô′yä) *n.* **1.** *South Texas.* An earthenware crock. **2.** An olla podrida. [Sp. < OSp. < Lat., var. of *aula, aulla,* pot, jar.]

Regional Note: The unglazed earthenware *olla,* a large crock or jar, was used for generations in parts of the United States where Spanish culture predominates, particularly in South Texas and California. Usually used to store water on a patio, it was wrapped in burlap to keep the water cool.

olla po•dri•da (pə-drē′də, pô-*th*rē′*th*ä) *n., pl.* **ol•la po•dri•das** also **ol•las po•dri•das. 1.** A spicy stew of meat and vegetables. **2.** An assorted mixture; a miscellany. [Sp. : *olla,* olla; see OLLA + *podrida,* fem. of *podrido,* rotten (< Lat. *putridus*; see PUTRID).]

Ol•mec (ŏl′mĕk, ōl′-) *n., pl.* **Olmec** or **-mecs. 1.** An early Mesoamerican Indian civilization centered in the Veracruz region of southeast Mexico that flourished before the Maya and had a widespread cultural influence. **2.** A member of any of various peoples who contributed to the Olmec civilization.

Laurence Olivier
Photographed in 1958

olla
c. 1885 olla

ă pat	oi boy
ā pay	ou out
âr care	o͝o took
ä father	o͞o boot
ĕ pet	ŭ cut
ē be	ûr urge
ĭ pit	th thin
ī pie	*th* this
îr pier	hw which
ŏ pot	zh vision
ō toe	ə about,
ô paw	item

Stress marks:
′ (primary);
′ (secondary), as in
dictionary (dĭk′shə-nĕr′ē)

one another *pron.* Used to indicate a reciprocal relationship or reciprocal actions among the members of the set referred to by the antecedent, often with the implication that the actions are temporally ordered: *The students help one another.*

one-armed bandit (wŭn′ärmd′) *n. Games.* A slot machine for gambling operated by pulling a lever on the side.

one-base hit (wŭn′bās′) *n. Baseball.* A base hit by which a batter can reach first base safely.

one-di•men•sion•al (wŭn′dĭ-mĕn′shə-nəl, -dī-) *adj.* **1.** Having or existing in one dimension only. **2.** Lacking depth; superficial.

O•ne•ga (ō-nē′gə, ə-nyĕ′-), **Lake.** A lake of NW Russia between Lake Ladoga and the White Sea.

Onega Bay. An arm of the White Sea in NW Russia that receives the **Onega River,** c. 418 km (260 mi).

one-hand•ed (wŭn′hăn′dĭd) *adj.* **1.** Having or making use of only one hand. **2.** Calling for or brought about by the use of only one hand. **—one′-hand′ed** *adv.*

one-horse (wŭn′hôrs′) *adj.* **1.** Drawn by or using only one horse. **2.** Very small or insignificant: *a one-horse town.*

Eugene O'Neill

O•nei•da[1] (ō-nī′də) *n., pl.* **Oneida** or **-das. 1.** A member of a Native American people formerly inhabiting central New York, with present-day populations in Wisconsin, New York, and Ontario. **2.** The Iroquoian language of the Oneida. [Oneida *one·nyóte′*, erected stone, a village name.]

O•nei•da[2] (ō-nī′də). A city of central NY ENE of Syracuse; site of the Oneida Community, a Utopian society estab. in 1848 by John Humphrey Noyes. Pop. 10,850.

Oneida Lake. A lake of central NY NE of Syracuse; part of the New York State Barge Canal system.

O'Neill (ō-nēl′), **Eugene Gladstone.** 1888–1953. Amer. playwright whose works include *Long Day's Journey into Night* (produced 1956). He won the 1936 Nobel Prize for literature.

o•nei•ric (ō-nī′rĭk) *adj.* Of, relating to, or suggestive of dreams. [Gk. *oneiros*, dream + -IC.]

o•nei•ro•man•cy (ō-nī′rə-măn′sē) *n.* The practice of predicting the future through interpretation of dreams. [Gk. *oneiros*, dream + -MANCY.] **—o•nei′ro•man′cer** *n.*

one-lin•er (wŭn′lī′nər) *n.* A short joke or witticism.

one-man (wŭn′măn′) *adj.* **1.** Consisting of a single man: *a one-man business.* **2.** Designed for or restricted to one person.

one•ness (wŭn′nĭs) *n.* **1.** The quality or state of being one; singleness. **2.** Singularity; uniqueness. **3.** The condition of being undivided; wholeness. **4.** Sameness of character: *the oneness of roadside landscapes.* **5.** Unison; agreement.

one-night stand (wŭn′nīt′) *n.* **1.a.** A performance by a musical or dramatic performer or group in one place on one night only. **b.** The place at which such a performance is given. **2.** *Slang.* A sexual encounter limited to only one occasion.

one-on-one (wŭn′ŏn-wŭn′, -ôn-) *adj.* **1.** Relating to or being direct exchange between two people: *one-on-one instruction.* **2.** *Sports.* Man-to-man. **—one′-on-one′** *adv.*

one-per•son (wŭn′pûr′sən) *adj.* **1.** Consisting of a single person. **2.** Designed for or restricted to one person.

one-piece (wŭn′pēs′) *adj.* Consisting of or fashioned in a single whole piece: *a one-piece swimsuit.*

on•er•ous (ŏn′ər-əs, ō′nər-) *adj.* **1.** Troublesome or oppressive; burdensome. **2.** *Law.* Entailing obligations that exceed advantages. [ME < OFr. *onereus* < Lat. *onerōsus* < *onus*, *oner-*, burden.] **—on′er•ous•ly** *adv.* **—on′er•ous•ness** *n.*

one•self (wŭn-sĕlf′) also **one's self** (wŭn sĕlf′, wŭnz sĕlf′) *pron.* **1.** One's own self: **a.** Used reflexively as the direct or indirect object of a verb or the object of a preposition: *congratulate oneself on one's victories.* **b.** Used in an absolute construction: *When in charge oneself, one may make decisions.* **2.** One's normal or healthy condition or state.

one-shot (wŭn′shŏt′) *adj. Informal.* **1.** Becoming effective after only one attempt: *a one-shot solution.* **2.** Being the only one and unlikely to be repeated.

one-sid•ed (wŭn′sī′dĭd) *adj.* **1.** Favoring one side or group; partial or biased. **2.** Larger or more developed on one side. **3.** Existing or occurring on one side only. **—one′-sid′ed•ly** *adv.* **—one′-sid′ed•ness** *n.*

one-step (wŭn′stĕp′) *n.* **1.** A ballroom dance consisting of a series of unbroken rapid steps in 2/4 time. **2.** A piece of music for this dance. **—one′-step′** *v.*

onion
Allium cepa

one•time (wŭn′tīm′) *adj.* Former: *a onetime champion.*

one-time (wŭn′tīm′) *adj.* Only once: *a one-time winner.*

one-to-one (wŭn′tə-wŭn′) *adj.* **1.** Allowing the pairing of each member of a class uniquely with a member of another class. **2.** *Math.* Relating to or being a mapping that assigns to each member of a given set a unique member of another set.

one-track (wŭn′trăk′) *adj.* Obsessively limited to a single idea or purpose: *a one-track mind.*

one-two (wŭn′to͞o′) *n.* A one-two punch.

one-two punch *n.* **1.** *Sports.* A combination of two blows delivered in rapid succession in boxing, esp. a left lead followed by a right cross. **2.** *Informal.* An esp. forceful or effective combination or sequence of two things.

one-up (wŭn′ŭp′) *tr.v.* **-upped, -up•ping, -ups.** *Informal.* To keep one step ahead of (a competitor, for example).

one-up•man•ship (wŭn-ŭp′mən-shĭp′) *n. Informal.* The art of outdoing or showing up a rival or competitor.

one-way (wŭn′wā′) *adj.* **1.** Moving or permitting movement in one direction only. **2.** Providing for travel in one direction only: *a one-way ticket.*

one-wom•an (wŭn′wo͝om′ən) *adj.* Consisting of a single woman: *a one-woman business empire.*

on•go•ing (ŏn′gō′ĭng, ôn′-) *adj.* **1.** Currently taking place: *an ongoing festival.* **2.** In progress or evolving.

ONI *abbr.* Office of Naval Intelligence.

on•ion (ŭn′yən) *n.* **1.** A bulbous plant *(Allium cepa)* cultivated worldwide as a vegetable. **2.** The rounded edible bulb of this plant, composed of fleshy tight concentric leaf bases having a pungent odor and taste. [ME *oinyon* < OFr. *oignon* < Lat. *uniō, uniōn-*.]

On•ions (ŭn′yənz), **Charles Talbut.** 1873–1965. British lexicographer who was coeditor (1914–33) of the *Oxford English Dictionary.*

on•ion•skin (ŭn′yən-skĭn′) *n.* A thin strong translucent paper.

on•lay (ŏn′lā′, ôn′-) *n.* **1.** Something laid or applied over something else, as to add relief to a surface. **2.** *Medic.* A graft applied to the surface of the recipient organ or structure. **3.** *Dentistry.* A cast, usu. of gold, attached to the occlusal surface of a tooth.

on-line (ŏn′līn′, ôn′-) *adj.* **1.** *Comp. Sci.* **a.** Under the control of a central computer, as in an experiment. **b.** Connected to a computer network. **c.** Accessible via a computer or computer network. **2.** In progress; ongoing.

on•load (ŏn′lōd′, ôn′-) *v.* **-load•ed, -load•ing, -loads.** —*tr.* To load (a vehicle or container). —*intr.* To load a vehicle or container.

on•look•er (ŏn′lo͝ok′ər, ôn′-) *n.* One that looks on; a spectator.

on•ly (ōn′lē) *adj.* **1.** Alone in kind or class; sole. **2.** Standing alone by reason of superiority or excellence. —*adv.* **1.** Without anyone or anything else; alone: *room for only one passenger.* **2.a.** At the very least: *If you would only come home.* **b.** And nothing else or more: *I only work here.* **3.** Exclusively; solely: *known only to us.* **4.a.** In the last analysis or final outcome: *will only make things worse.* **b.** With the final result; nevertheless: *hired only to be laid off.* **5.a.** As recently as: *only last month.* **b.** In the immediate past: *only just saw her.* —*conj.* **1.** Were it not that; except. **2.a.** With the restriction that; but: *You may go, only be careful.* **b.** However; and yet: *It's good, only we can't use it.* [ME < OE *ānlīc* : *ān*, one; see ONE + *-līc*, having the form of; see -LY[1].]

Usage Note: When used as an adverb, *only* should be placed with care to avoid ambiguity. Generally this means having *only* adjoin the word or words that it limits. Variation in the placement of *only* can change the meaning of the sentence, as the following example shows: *Dictators respect only force; they are not moved by words. Dictators only respect force; they do not worship it.* See Usage Note at **not.**

on•o•mas•tic (ŏn′ə-măs′tĭk) *adj.* **1.** Of, relating to, or explaining a name or names. **2.** Of or relating to onomastics. [Fr. *onomastique* < Gk. *onomastikos* < *onomazein*, to name < *onoma*, name. See **nō-men-*.**]

on•o•mas•tics (ŏn′ə-măs′tĭks) *n. (used with a sing. or pl. v.)* **1.a.** The study of the origins and forms of proper names. **b.** The study of the origins and forms of terms used in specialized fields. **2.** The system that underlies the formation and use of proper names or terms used in specialized fields.

on•o•mat•o•poe•ia (ŏn′ə-măt′ə-pē′ə, -mä′tə-) *n.* The formation or use of words such as *buzz* that imitate the sounds associated with the objects or actions they refer to. [LLat. < Gk. *onomatopoiia* < *onomatopoios*, coiner of names : *onoma, onomat-*, name; see **nō-men-*** + *poiein*, to make; see **kʷei-[2]*.**] **—on′o•mat′o•poe′ic, on′o•mat′o•po•et′ic** (-pō-ĕt′ĭk) *adj.* **—on′o•mat′o•poe′i•cal•ly, on′o•mat′o•po•et′i•cal•ly** *adv.*

On•on•da•ga (ŏn′ən-dô′gə, -dä′-, -dā′-) *n., pl.* **Onondaga** or **-gas. 1.** A member of a Native American people formerly inhabiting the eastern Finger Lakes region of west-central New York, with present-day populations in this same area and in southeast Ontario. **2.** The Iroquoian language of the Onondaga. [Onondaga *onó·ntà′ke*, on the hill, a village name.] **—On′on•da′gan** *adj.*

on•rush (ŏn′rŭsh′, ôn′-) *n.* **1.** A forward rush or flow. **2.** A violent physical or verbal attack. **—on′rush′ing** *adj.*

On•sa•ger (ôn′sä′gər), **Lars.** 1903–76. Norwegian-born Amer. chemist who won a 1968 Nobel Prize.

on-screen or **on•screen** (ŏn′skrēn′, ôn′-) *adj. & adv.* **1.** Within sight of the viewer of a movie or television screen. **2.** Within public view; in public.

on•set (ŏn′sĕt′, ôn′-) *n.* **1.** An onslaught; an assault. **2.** A beginning; a start: *the onset of a cold.*

on•shore (ŏn′shôr′, -shōr′, ôn′-) *adj.* **1.** Moving or directed toward the shore: *an onshore wind.* **2.** Located on the shore: *an onshore beacon.* —*adv.* Toward the shore.

on•side (ŏn′sīd′, ôn′-) *adv. & adj. Sports.* In such a position as to be able to play or receive a ball or puck legally.

on-site (ŏn′sīt′, ôn′-) *adj.* Done or located at the site, as of a particular activity: *an on-site filming.* **—on′-site′** *adv.*

on•slaught (ŏn′slôt′, ôn′-) *n.* **1.** A violent attack. **2.** An overwhelming outpouring. [Alteration (influenced by obsolete *slaughte*, slaughter) of Du. *aanslag*, a striking at < MDu. *aenslach* : *aen*, on; see **an-*** + *slach*, a striking.]

on-stage or **on•stage** (ŏn-stāj′, ôn-) —*adj.* Situated or taking place in the area of a stage visible to the audience. —*adv.* In or into the area of a stage visible to the audience.

Ont. *abbr.* Ontario.

-ont *suff.* Cell; organism: *-biont.* [< Gk. *ōn*, *ont-*, pr.part. of *einai*, to be. See **es-***.]

On•tar•i•o (ŏn-târ′ē-ō′). **1.** A province of E-central Canada; joined the confederation in 1867. First visited by French explorers in the early 1600's, it passed to the British in 1763. Cap. Toronto. Pop. 8,625,107. **2.** A city of S CA E of Los Angeles. Pop. 133,179.

Ontario, Lake. The smallest of the Great Lakes, between SE Ontario, Canada, and NW NY.

on-the-job (ŏn′*th*ə-jŏb′, ôn′-) *adj.* Acquired or learned while working at a job: *on-the-job training.*

on•tic (ŏn′tĭk) *adj. Philos.* Relating to or possessing real existence.

on•to (ŏn′to͞o′, -tə, ôn′-) *prep.* **1.** On top of; to a position on; upon. See Usage Note at **on. 2.** *Informal.* Fully aware of; informed about. —*adj. Math.* Of, relating to, or being a mapping such that every element of the set referred to is the image of an element in another.

onto- or **ont-** *pref.* **1.** Existence; being: *ontology.* **2.** Organism: *ontogeny.* [LGk. < Gk. *ōn*, *ont-*, pr.part. of *einai*, to be. See **es-***.]

on•to•gen•e•sis (ŏn′tō-jĕn′ĭ-sĭs) *n.*, *pl.* **-ses** (-sēz′). See **ontogeny.**

on•tog•e•ny (ŏn-tŏj′ə-nē) *n.*, *pl.* **-nies.** The development of an individual organism from embryo to adult. —**on′to•ge•net′ic** (ŏn′tō-jə-nĕt′ĭk) *adj.* —**on′to•ge•net′i•cal•ly** *adv.*

on•tol•o•gy (ŏn-tŏl′ə-jē) *n.* The branch of metaphysics that deals with the nature of being. —**on′to•log′i•cal** (ŏn′tə-lŏj′ĭ-kəl) *adj.* —**on′to•log′i•cal•ly** *adv.* —**on•tol′o•gist** *n.*

o•nus (ō′nəs) *n.* **1.** A difficult or disagreeable responsibility or necessity; a burden or an obligation. **2.a.** A stigma. **b.** Blame. **3.** The burden of proof. [Lat.]

on•ward (ŏn′wərd, ôn′-) *adj.* Moving or tending forward. —*adv.* also **on•wards** (-wərdz). In a direction or toward a position that is ahead in space or time; forward.

-onym *suff.* Word; name: *acronym.* [Gk. *-ōnumon*, neut. of *-ōnumos*, having a specified kind of name < *onuma*, name. See **nō̆-men-***.]

-onymy *suff.* A set of names; the study of a kind of names: *toponymy.* [Gk. *-ōnumia* < *-ōnumos*, having a specified kind of name < *onuma*, name. See **nō̆-men-***.]

on•yx (ŏn′ĭks) *n.* A chalcedony that occurs in bands of different colors and is used as a gemstone, esp. in cameos and intaglios. [ME *onix* < OFr. < Lat. *onyx* < Gk. *onux*, nail, onyx. See **nogh-***.]

oo- *pref.* Egg; ovum: *oogenesis.* [Gk. *ōio-* < *ōion*, egg. See **awi-***.]

o•o•cyst (ō′ə-sĭst′) *n.* A thick-walled structure in which sporozoan zygotes develop.

o•o•cyte (ō′ə-sīt′) *n.* A cell from which an egg or ovum develops by meiosis; a female gametocyte.

O.O.D. *abbr.* Officer of the deck.

O'o•dham (ō′ə-däm) *n.*, *pl.* **O'odham** or **-dhams.** See **Papago.**

oo•dles (o͞od′lz) *pl.n. Informal.* A great amount or number: *oodles of fun.* [?]

o•o•ga•mete (ō′ə-găm′ēt′, -gə-mēt′) *n.* A female gamete, esp. the larger of two gametes produced by an oogamous species.

o•og•a•mous (ō-ŏg′ə-məs) *adj.* Characterized by or having small motile male gametes and large nonmotile female gametes. —**o•og′a•my** *n.*

o•o•gen•e•sis (ō′ə-jĕn′ĭ-sĭs) *n.* The formation, development, and maturation of an ovum. —**o′o•ge•net′ic** (-jə-nĕt′ĭk) *adj.*

o•o•go•ni•um (ō′ə-gō′nē-əm) *n.*, *pl.* **-ni•a** (-nē-ə) or **-ni•ums. 1.** A descendant of a primordial germ cell that differentiates into an oocyte. **2.** A female reproductive structure in certain thallophytes, usu. a rounded cell or sac containing one or more oospheres. [OO- + NLat. *gonium*, cell (< Gk. *gonos*, seed; see GONO-).] —**o′o•go′ni•al** (-nē-əl) *adj.*

ooh (o͞o) *interj.* Used to express pleasure, satisfaction, surprise, or great joy. —*intr.v.* **oohed, ooh•ing, oohs.** To exclaim in pleasure, satisfaction, surprise, or great joy. —**ooh** *n.*

o•o•lite (ō′ə-līt′) also **o•o•lith** (-lĭth′) *n.* **1.** A small round calcareous grain found in sedimentary rock. **2.** Rock, usu. limestone, composed of oolites. —**o′o•lit′ic** (-lĭt′ĭk) *adj.*

o•ol•o•gy (ō-ŏl′ə-jē) *n.* The branch of zoology that deals with the study of eggs. —**o′o•log′ic** (ō′ə-lŏj′ĭk), **o′o•log′i•cal** (-ĭ-kəl) *adj.* —**o′o•log′i•cal•ly** *adv.* —**o•ol′o•gist** *n.*

oo•long (o͞o′lông′, -lŏng′) *n.* A dark Chinese tea that has been partially fermented before drying. [Chin. (Mandarin) *wū lóng* : *wū*, dark, black + *lóng*, dragon.]

oo•mi•ak (o͞o′mē-ăk′) *n.* Var. of **umiak.**

oom•pah (o͞om′pä, o͝om′-) also **oom•pah-pah** (o͞om′pä-pä′) *n. Mus.* A rhythmic sound made by a tuba or other brass instrument. [Imit.]

oomph (o͝omf) *n. Slang.* **1.** Spirited vigor. **2.** Physical or sexual attractiveness. [Expressive of exertion.]

o•o•pho•rec•to•my (ō′ə-fə-rĕk′tə-mē) *n.*, *pl.* **-mies.** See **ovariectomy.**

o•o•pho•ri•tis (ō′ə-fə-rī′tĭs) *n.* Inflammation of an ovary.

Oort cloud (ôrt, ōrt) *n.* A swarm of comets orbiting the sun at a distance of one to two light-years. [After Jan Hendrix *Oort* (b. 1900), Dutch astronomer.]

o•o•sphere (ō′ə-sfîr′) *n.* A large nonmotile female gamete or egg cell, formed in an oogonium and ready for fertilization.

o•o•spore (ō′ə-spôr′, -spōr′) *n.* A fertilized female cell or zygote, esp. one with thick chitinous walls, developed from a fertilized oosphere.

Oost•en•de (ō-stĕn′də). See **Ostend.**

o•o•the•ca (ō′ə-thē′kə) *n.*, *pl.* **-cae** (-sē). The egg case of certain insects and mollusks. —**o′o•the′cal** *adj.*

o•o•tid (ō′ə-tĭd′) *n.* A haploid cell that results from the meiotic division of an oocyte and becomes a female gamete or an ovum. [OO- + (SPERMA)TID.]

ooze¹ (o͞oz) *v.* **oozed, ooz•ing, ooz•es.** —*intr.* **1.** To flow or leak out slowly, as through small openings. **2.** To disappear or ebb slowly: *His courage oozed away.* **3.** To progress slowly but steadily. **4.** To exude moisture. **5.** To emit a particular essence or quality. —*tr.* **1.** To give off; exude. **2.** To emit or radiate in abundance: *She oozes confidence.* —*n.* **1.** The act of oozing. **2.** Something that oozes. **3.** An infusion of vegetable matter, as from oak bark, used in tanning. [ME *wosen* < *wose*, juice < OE *wōs*.]

ooze² (o͞oz) *n.* **1.** Soft mud or slime. **2.** A layer of mudlike sediment on the floor of oceans and lakes, composed chiefly of remains of microscopic sea animals. **3.** Muddy ground. [ME *wose* < OE *wāse*.]

ooz•y¹ (o͞o′zē) *adj.* **-i•er, -i•est.** Exuding moisture. —**ooz′i•ly** *adv.* —**ooz′i•ness** *n.*

ooz•y² (o͞o′zē) *adj.* **-i•er, -i•est.** Of, resembling, or containing ooze: *soft oozy ground.* —**ooz′i•ly** *adv.* —**ooz′i•ness** *n.*

OP *abbr.* **1.** Observation post. **2.** Out of print.

op. or **Op.** *abbr.* **1.** Operation. **2.** Opus.

O.P. *abbr. Rom. Cath. Ch.* Order of Preachers (Dominican).

o•pac•i•fi•er (ō-păs′ə-fī′ər) *n.* A chemical agent added to a material to make it opaque.

o•pac•i•ty (ō-păs′ĭ-tē) *n.*, *pl.* **-ties. 1.** The quality or state of being opaque. **2.** Something opaque. **3.a.** Obscurity; impenetrability. **b.** Dullness of mind. [Fr. *opacité* < OFr. < Lat. *opācitās* < *opācus*, dark.]

o•pah (ō′pə) *n.* A large, oval-shaped, vividly colored marine fish *(Lampris regius)* having edible red flesh. [Of West African orig.; akin to Ibo *uba*.]

o•pal (ō′pəl) *n.* A translucent mineral of hydrated silica, often used as a gem. [ME *opalus* < Lat., alteration of Gk. *opallios*, prob. < Skt. *upalaḥ* < *upara-*, lower < *upa*, below. See **upo***.] —**o′pal•ine′** (ō′pə-līn′, -lēn′) *adj.*

o•pal•esce (ō′pə-lĕs′) *intr.v.* **-esced, -esc•ing, -esc•es.** To exhibit an iridescent shimmer of colors.

o•pal•es•cent (ō′pə-lĕs′ənt) *adj.* Exhibiting a milky iridescence like that of an opal. —**o′pal•es′cence** *n.*

o•paque (ō-pāk′) *adj.* **1.a.** Impenetrable by light; neither transparent nor translucent. **b.** Not reflecting light; having no luster. **2.** Impenetrable by a form of radiant energy other than visible light. **3.a.** So obscure as to be unintelligible. **b.** Obtuse of mind; dense. —*n.* Something that is opaque, esp. an opaque pigment used to darken parts of a photographic print or negative. [ME *opake*, shady, and Fr. *opaque*, opaque (< OFr., shady), both < Lat. *opācus*.] —**o•paque′ly** *adv.* —**o•paque′ness** *n.*

op art also **Op Art** (ŏp) *n.* A school of abstract art characterized by the use of geometric shapes and brilliant colors to create optical illusions, as of motion, and free the art of all but visual associations. [OP(TICAL) ART.]

op. cit. *abbr. Lat.* Opere citato (in the work cited).

OPEC (ō′pĕk′) *n.* Organization of Petroleum Exporting Countries.

op-ed page or **Op-Ed page** (ŏp′ĕd′) *n.* A newspaper page, usu. opposite the editorial page, that features articles expressing personal viewpoints. [OP(POSITE) + ED(ITORIAL).]

O•pe•li•ka (ō′pə-lī′kə). A city of E AL ENE of Montgomery. Pop. 22,122.

Op•e•lou•sas (ŏp′ə-lo͞o′səs). A city of S-central LA WNW of Baton Rouge; founded c. 1756. Pop. 18,151.

o•pen (ō′pən) *adj.* **1.a.** Affording unobstructed entrance and exit; not shut or closed. **b.** Affording unobstructed passage or view: *open waters.* **2.a.** Having no protecting or concealing cover: *an open wound.* **b.** Completely obvious; blatant. **c.** Carried on in full view: *open warfare.* **3.a.** Not sealed or tied. **b.** Spread out; unfolded: *an open book.* **4.** Having interspersed gaps, spaces, or intervals: *an open weave.* **5.a.** Accessible to all; unrestricted as to participants. **b.** Free from limitations, boundaries, or restrictions. **c.** Enterable by registered voters regardless of political affiliation. **6.a.** Lacking effective regulation. **b.** Not legally repressed: *open drug traf-*

ă pat	oi boy
ā pay	ou out
âr care	o͝o took
ä father	o͞o boot
ĕ pet	ŭ cut
ē be	ûr urge
ĭ pit	th thin
ī pie	*th* this
îr pier	hw which
ŏ pot	zh vision
ō toe	ə about,
ô paw	item

Stress marks:
′ (primary);
′ (secondary), as in
dictionary (dĭk′shə-nĕr′ē)

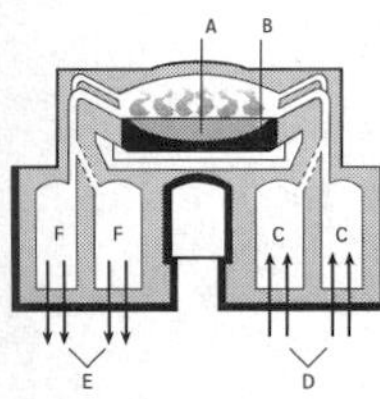

open-hearth
Open-hearth furnace
A. Molten pig iron
B. Hearth
C. Heating chamber (hot)
D. Preheated gas and air entry
E. Gas and air escape
F. Heating chamber (cold)

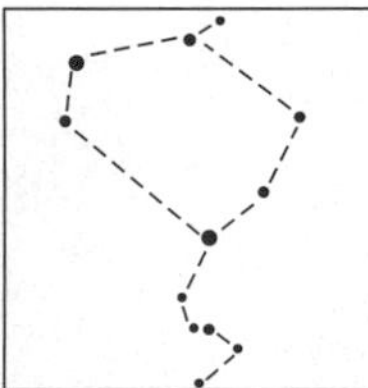

Ophiuchus

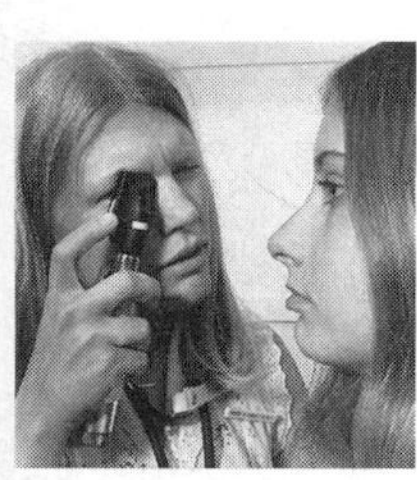

ophthalmoscope

ficking. **7.a.** Susceptible; vulnerable: *open to interpretation.* **b.** Willing to consider or deal with: *open to suggestions.* **8.a.** Available; obtainable: *The job is still open.* **b.** Available for use: *an open account.* **9.** Ready to transact business. **10.** Not engaged or filled: *an open hour for the meeting.* **11.** Not yet decided; subject to further thought. **12.a.** Characterized by lack of pretense or reserve; candid. See Syns at **frank**[1]. **b.** Free of prejudice; receptive to new ideas and arguments. **c.** Generous. **13.** *Print.* **a.** Widely spaced or leaded. Used of typeset or other printed matter. **b.** Having constituent elements separated by a space in writing or printing: *The word* sea gull *is an open compound.* **14.** *Mus.* **a.** Not stopped by a finger. Used of a string or hole of an instrument. **b.** Produced by an unstopped string or hole or without the use of slides, valves, or keys. **c.** Played without a mute. **15.a.** Articulated with the tongue in a low position, as the vowel in *far.* **b.** Ending in a vowel or diphthong. **16.** Being a method of punctuation in which commas and other marks are used sparingly. **17.** Being in operation; live: *an open microphone.* **18.** *New England.* Clear. Used of weather. See Regional Note at **fair**[1]. **19.** *Elect.* Containing a gap across which electricity cannot pass. **20.** *Math.* **a.** Of, relating to, or being a set such that at least one neighborhood of every point in the set is within the set. **b.** Of, relating to, or being a set that is the complement of a closed set. — *v.* **o•pened, o•pen•ing, o•pens.** — *tr.* **1.** To release from a closed or fastened position. **2.** To remove obstructions from; clear. **3.** To make or force an opening in. **4.** To form spaces or gaps between. **5.a.** To remove the cover, cork, or lid from. **b.** To remove the wrapping from; undo. **6.** To unfold so that the inner parts are displayed; spread out. **7.a.** To get (something) going; initiate. **b.** To commence the operation of: *open a new business.* **8.** *Games.* To begin (the action in a game of cards) by making the first bid, placing the first bet, or playing the first lead. **9.** To make available for use. **10.** To make more responsive or understanding. **11.** To reveal the secrets of; bare. — *intr.* **1.** To become open: *The door opened.* **2.** To draw apart; separate: *The wound opened.* **3.** To spread apart; unfold. **4.** To come into view; become revealed. **5.** To become receptive or understanding. **6.a.** To begin; commence. **b.** To begin business or operation. **7.** To give the first public performance. **8.** *Games.* To make a bid, bet, or lead in starting a game of cards. **9.** To give access: *The room opens onto a terrace.* — *n.* **1.** An unobstructed area of land or water. **2.** The outdoors. **3.** An undisguised or unconcealed state. **4.** *Sports & Games.* A tournament or contest in which both professional and amateur players may participate. — ***phrasal verb.*** **open up. 1.** To spread out; unfold. **2.a.** To begin operation. **b.** To begin firing. **3.** *Informal.* To speak freely and candidly. **4.** To make an opening in by cutting. **5.** To make available or accessible. **6.** *Informal.* To accelerate. Used of a motor vehicle. — ***idioms.*** **open fire.** To begin firing on. **open (one's) eyes.** To become aware of the truth of a situation. [ME < OE. See **upo*.**] — **o′pen•ly** *adv.* — **o′pen•ness** *n.*

open admissions *pl.n. (used with a sing. or pl. v.)* A policy that permits enrollment of a student in a college or university regardless of academic qualifications or financial situation.

o•pen-air (ō′pən-âr′) *adj.* Outdoor: *an open-air concert.*

o•pen-and-shut (ō′pən-ən-shŭt′) *adj.* So obvious as to present no difficulties; easily settled or determined.

open chain *n.* An arrangement of atoms, as in aliphatic hydrocarbons, that does not form a ring.

open city *n.* A city that is declared demilitarized during a war, thus gaining immunity from attack under international law.

open door *n.* **1.** Unhindered opportunity; free access. **2.** Admission to all on equal terms. **3.** A policy whereby a nation trades with all other nations on equal terms. — **o′pen-door′** (ō′pən-dôr′, -dōr′) *adj.*

o•pen-end (ō′pən-ĕnd′) *adj.* **1.** Having no definite limit of duration or amount. **2.** Permitting the borrowing of additional funds under existing terms: *an open-end mortgage.*

o•pen-end•ed (ō′pən-ĕn′dĭd) *adj.* **1.** Not restrained by definite limits, restrictions, or structure. **2.** Allowing for or adaptable to change. **3.** Inconclusive or indefinite. **4.** Allowing for a spontaneous unstructured response.

open enrollment *n.* See **open admissions.**

o•pen•er (ō′pə-nər) *n.* **1.** One that opens, esp. a device to open cans or bottles. **2.** *Games.* **a.** The player who opens in a game of cards. **b. openers.** Cards of sufficient value to enable the holder to open the betting. **3.** The first act in a theatrical variety show. **4.** *Sports.* The first game in a series. — ***idiom.*** **for openers.** *Informal.* To begin with.

o•pen-eyed (ō′pən-īd′) *adj.* **1.** Having the eyes wide open, as in surprise. **2.** Watchful and alert.

o•pen-faced (ō′pən-fāst′) *adj.* **1.** Having a face that seems to exhibit honesty and sincerity. **2.** Having a side uncovered.

o•pen•hand•ed (ō′pən-hăn′dĭd) *adj.* Giving freely; generous. See Syns at **liberal.** — **o′pen•hand′ed•ly** *adv.* — **o′pen•hand′ed•ness** *n.*

o•pen•heart•ed (ō′pən-här′tĭd) *adj.* **1.** Frank. **2.** Kindly. — **o′pen•heart′ed•ly** *adv.* — **o′pen•heart′ed•ness** *n.*

o•pen-hearth (ō′pən-härth′) *adj.* **1.** Of or being a reverberatory furnace used in the production of high-quality steel. **2.** Of or relating to the steel produced in such a furnace.

o•pen-heart surgery (ō′pən-härt′) *adj.* Surgery in which the thoracic cavity is opened to expose the heart and the blood is recirculated and oxygenated by a heart-lung machine.

open house *n.* **1.** A social event in which hospitality is extended to all. **2.** An occasion when a school or an institution is open for visiting by the public. **3.a.** A period of time during which a house or an apartment for sale is open for public viewing. **b.** A house or an apartment open for such viewing.

o•pen•ing (ō′pə-nĭng) *n.* **1.** The act or an instance of becoming open or being made to open. **2.** An open space serving as a passage or gap. **3.** A breach or an aperture. **4.** A clearing in the woods. **5.** The first part or stage, as of a book. **6.** The first performance: *the opening of a play.* **7.** A formal commencement of operation. **8.** *Games.* A specific pattern or series of beginning moves in certain games, esp. chess. **9.** An opportunity affording a chance of success. **10.** An unfilled job or position; a vacancy.

open interval *n. Math.* See **interval** 5.

open letter *n.* A letter of general interest, addressed to a person but published for general readership.

open loop *n. Engineering.* A control system that is not self-correcting.

open market *n.* A freely competitive market operating without restrictions.

open marriage *n.* A marriage in which the partners agree that each is free to engage in extramarital relationships.

o•pen-mind•ed (ō′pən-mīn′dĭd) *adj.* Having or showing receptiveness to new and different ideas or the opinions of others. See Syns at **broad-minded.** — **o′pen-mind′ed•ly** *adv.* — **o′pen-mind′ed•ness** *n.*

o•pen-mouthed (ō′pən-mouthd′, -moutht′) *adj.* **1.** Having the mouth open. **2.** Gaping in astonishment or wonder. **3.** Loudly insistent. — **o′pen-mouth′ed•ly** *adv.* — **o′pen-mouth′ed•ness** *n.*

open season *n.* **1.** The period during which it is legal to hunt or catch game or fish. **2.** *Informal.* A time of unrestrained harassment, criticism, or attack.

open secret *n.* Something supposedly secret but in fact generally known.

open sesame *n.* A means of attaining a goal that has been repeatedly successful. [< *Open Sesame,* used by Ali Baba in the *Arabian Nights* to open the robbers' cave door.]

open shop *n.* A business or factory in which workers are employed without regard to union membership.

open stock *n.* Merchandise kept in stock so as to enable customers to replace or supplement articles purchased in sets.

o•pen•work (ō′pən-wûrk′) *n.* Ornamental or structural work, as of embroidery or metal, containing numerous openings, usu. in set patterns.

op•er•a[1] (ŏp′ər-ə, ŏp′rə) *n. Mus.* **1.** A theatrical presentation in which a dramatic performance is set to music. **2.** The score of such a work. **3.** A theater designed primarily for operas. [Ital., work, opera < Lat., work, service. See **op-*.**]

o•pe•ra[2] (ō′pər-ə, ŏp′ər-ə) *n.* Pl. of **opus.**

op•er•a•ble (ŏp′ər-ə-bəl, ŏp′rə-) *adj.* **1.** Being such that use or operation is possible. **2.** Possible to put into practice; practicable. **3.** Treatable by surgery with a reasonable chance of success. — **op′er•a•bil′i•ty** *n.* — **op′er•a•bly** *adv.*

o•pé•ra bouffe (ŏp′ər-ə bo͞of′, ŏp′rə, ô-pā-rä bo͞of′) *n. Mus.* A comic, often farcical opera. [Fr. < Ital. *opera buffa.* See OPERA BUFFA.]

o•pe•ra buf•fa (ŏp′ər-ə bo͞o′fə, ŏp′rə, ô′pĕ-rä bo͞of′fä) *n. Mus.* A comic opera of the 18th century. [Ital. : *opera,* opera + *buffa,* fem. of *buffo,* comic.]

o•pé•ra co•mique (ŏp′ər-ə kŏ-mēk′, ŏp′rə, ô-pā-rä kô-mēk′) *n. Mus.* See **comic opera.** [Fr.]

op•er•a glass (ŏp′ər-ə, ŏp′rə) *n.* A pair of small low-powered binoculars for use esp. at a theatrical performance. Often used in the plural.

opera house *n.* A theater designed chiefly for the performance of operas.

op•er•and (ŏp′ər-ənd) *n. Math.* A quantity on which an operation is performed. [< Lat. *operandum,* neut. gerundive of *operārī,* to operate. See OPERATE.]

op•er•ant (ŏp′ər-ənt) *adj.* **1.** Operating to produce effects; effective. **2.** *Psychol.* Of, relating to, or being a response that occurs spontaneously and is identified by its reinforcing or inhibiting effects. — *n.* **1.** One that operates. **2.** *Psychol.* An element of operant behavior. — **op′er•ant•ly** *adv.*

operant conditioning *n. Psychol.* A process of behavior modification in which a subject is encouraged to behave in a desired manner through positive or negative reinforcement.

op•er•ate (ŏp′ə-rāt′) *v.* **-at•ed, -at•ing, -ates.** — *intr.* **1.** To perform a function; work. **2.** To perform surgery. **3.a.** To exert an influence: *forces operating on the economy.* **b.** To produce a desired or proper effect. **4.** To carry on a military or naval action or campaign. **5.** *Informal.* To conduct business in an irregular or devious manner. — *tr.* **1.** To control the functioning of; run. **2.** To conduct the affairs of; manage. [Lat. *operārī, operāt-* < *opera,* work. See **op-*.**]

op•er•at•ic (ŏp′ə-răt′ĭk) *adj. Mus.* Of, relating to, or typical of the opera. [< OPERA[1].] —**op′er•at′i•cal•ly** *adv.*

op•er•at•ics (ŏp′ə-răt′ĭks) *n. (used with a sing. or pl. v.)* Exaggerated behavior of a type associated with grand opera.

op•er•at•ing room (ŏp′ə-rā′tĭng) *n.* A room equipped for performing surgical operations.

operating system *n. Comp. Sci.* Software that controls the hardware and application programs of a specific system.

op•er•a•tion (ŏp′ə-rā′shən) *n.* **1.** The act or process of operating or functioning. **2.** The state of being operative or functional. **3.** A process or series of acts involved in a particular form of work. **4.** An instance or a method of efficient, productive activity. **5.** An unethical or illegal business. **6.** *Medic.* A surgical procedure for remedying an injury, an ailment, a defect, or a dysfunction. **7.** *Math.* A process or an action, such as addition or differentiation, performed according to specific rules. **8.** *Comp. Sci.* An action resulting from a single instruction. **9.a.** A military or naval action, campaign, or mission. **b. operations.** The headquarters or center from which a military action or other activities are controlled. **10. operations.** The division of an organization that carries out the major planning and operating functions.

op•er•a•tion•al (ŏp′ə-rā′shə-nəl) *adj.* **1.** Of or relating to an operation or a series of operations. **2.** Of, intended for, or involved in military operations. **3.** Fit for proper functioning; ready for use. **4.** Being in effect or operation. —**op′er•a′tion•al•ly** *adv.*

op•er•a•tion•al•ism (ŏp′ə-rā′shə-nə-lĭz′əm) *n. Philos.* The view that all theoretical terms in science are to be defined in terms of experimental procedures or operations with no reference to unobservable entities or processes. —**op′er•a′tion•al•ist** *n.*

op•er•a•tions research (ŏp′ə-rā′shənz) *n.* Mathematical analysis of a process or an operation, used in making decisions.

op•er•a•tive (ŏp′ər-ə-tĭv, -ə-rā′tĭv, ŏp′rə-) *adj.* **1.** Being in effect; having force; operating. **2.** Functioning effectively; efficient. **3.** Engaged in or concerned with physical or mechanical activity. **4.** Of or relating to a surgical operation. —*n.* **1.** A skilled worker, esp. in industry. **2.a.** A secret agent; a spy. **b.** A private detective. —**op′er•a•tive•ly** *adv.*

op•er•a•tor (ŏp′ə-rā′tər) *n.* **1.** One who operates a machine or device. **2.** The owner or manager of a business or an industrial enterprise. **3.** One who deals aggressively in stocks or commodities. **4.** *Informal.* A person who accomplishes goals through shrewd or unscrupulous maneuvers. **5.** *Math.* A symbol, such as a plus sign, that represents an operation. **6.** A chromosomal segment of DNA that regulates the activity of the structural genes of an operon by interacting with a specific repressor.

o•per•cu•late (ō-pûr′kyə-lĭt) also **o•per•cu•lat•ed** (-lā′tĭd) *adj. Biol.* Having an operculum.

o•per•cu•lum (ō-pûr′kyə-ləm) *n., pl.* **-la** (-lə) or **-lums.** *Biol.* A lid or flap covering an aperture, such as the gill cover in some fishes. [Lat., lid < *operīre*, to cover. See **wer-**[4]*.] —**o•per′cu•lar** (-lər) *adj.* —**o•per′cu•lar•ly** *adv.*

op•e•ret•ta (ŏp′ə-rĕt′ə) *n. Mus.* A theatrical production that has many of the musical elements of opera but is lighter and more popular in subject and style and contains spoken dialogue. [Ital., dim. of *opera*, opera. See OPERA[1].]

op•er•on (ŏp′ə-rŏn′) *n.* A unit of gene activity consisting of a sequence of genetic material that functions in a coordinated manner by means of an operator, a promoter, and one or more structural genes. [OPER(ATOR) + -ON[1].]

op•er•ose (ŏp′ə-rōs′) *adj.* **1.** Involving great labor; laborious. **2.** Industrious; diligent. [Lat. *operōsus* < *opus*, *oper-*, work. See **op-***.] —**op′er•ose′ly** *adv.* —**op′er•ose′ness** *n.*

o•phid•i•an (ō-fĭd′ē-ən) *adj.* Of or resembling snakes. —*n.* A member of the suborder Ophidia or Serpentes; a snake. [< NLat. *Ophidia*, suborder name < Gk. *ophis*, snake.]

oph•i•ol•o•gy (ŏf′ē-ŏl′ə-jē, ō′fē-) *n.* The branch of herpetology that deals with snakes. [Gk. *ophis*, snake + -LOGY.] —**oph′i•o•log′i•cal** (-ə-lŏj′ĭ-kəl) *adj.* —**oph′i•ol′o•gist** *n.*

oph•ite (ŏf′īt′, ō′fīt′) *n.* **1.** A mottled green rock composed of diabase. **2.** Any of various green rocks, such as serpentine. [ME *ophites* < Lat. *ophītēs* < Gk. *ophitēs (lithos)*, serpentlike (stone) < *ophis*, serpent.]

o•phit•ic (ŏ-fĭt′ĭk, ō-fĭt′-) *adj.* **1.** Of or relating to ophite. **2.** Having a texture composed of lath-shaped plagioclase crystals in a matrix of pyroxene crystals.

Oph•i•u•chus (ŏf′ē-yo͞o′kəs, ō′fē-) *n.* A constellation in the equatorial region near Scorpius. [Lat. *Ophiūchus* < Gk. *ophioukhos* : *ophis*, serpent + *okhos*, holder (< *ekhein*, to hold; see **segh-***).]

oph•thal•mi•a (ŏf-thăl′mē-ə, ŏp-) *n.* Inflammation of the eye, esp. of the conjunctiva. [Ult. < LLat. < Gk. < *ophthalmos*, eye. See OPHTHALMO-.]

oph•thal•mic (ŏf-thăl′mĭk, ŏp-) *adj.* Of or relating to the eye.

ophthalmo- or **ophthalm-** *pref.* Eye; eyeball: *ophthalmoscope.* [Gk. < *ophthalmos*, eye. See **okʷ-***.]

oph•thal•mol•o•gist (ŏf′thəl-mŏl′ə-jĭst, -thăl-, ŏp′-) *n.* A physician who specializes in ophthalmology.

oph•thal•mol•o•gy (ŏf′thəl-mŏl′ə-jē, -thăl-, ŏp′-) *n.* The branch of medicine that deals with the anatomy, functions, pathology, and treatment of the eye. —**oph•thal′mo•log′ic** (-thăl′mə-lŏj′ĭk), **oph•thal′mo•log′i•cal** (-ĭ-kəl) *adj.* —**oph•thal′mo•log′i•cal•ly** *adv.*

oph•thal•mo•scope (ŏf-thăl′mə-skōp′, ŏp-) *n.* An instrument for examining the interior structures of the eye, esp. the retina, consisting of a mirror that reflects light into the eye and a central hole through which the eye is examined. —**oph•thal′mo•scop′ic** (-skŏp′ĭk), **oph•thal′mo•scop′i•cal** *adj.* —**oph′thal•mos′co•py** (ŏf′thăl-mŏs′kə-pē, ŏp′-) *n.*

-opia *suff.* A visual condition or defect of a specified kind: *anisometropia.* [Gk. *-ōpia* < *ōps*, *ōp-*, eye. See PELOPS.]

o•pi•ate (ō′pē-ĭt, -āt′) *n.* **1.** Any of various sedative narcotics containing opium or one or more of its derivatives. **2.** A drug or other substance having effects similar to those containing opium or its derivatives. **3.** Something that dulls the senses and induces relaxation or torpor. —*adj.* **1.a.** Containing opium or any of its derivatives. **b.** Resembling opium or its derivatives in activity. **2.** Inducing sleep or sedation; soporific. **3.** Causing dullness or apathy; deadening. —*tr.v.* (-āt′) **-at•ed, -at•ing, -ates. 1.** To subject to the action of an opiate. **2.** To dull or deaden as if with a narcotic drug. [ME < Med. Lat. *opiātum* < Lat. *opium*, opium. See OPIUM.]

o•pine (ō-pīn′) *tr.v.* **o•pined, o•pin•ing, o•pines.** To hold or state as an opinion. [ME *opinen* < OFr. *opiner* < Lat. *opīnārī*, to suppose.]

o•pin•ion (ə-pĭn′yən) *n.* **1.** A belief or conclusion held with confidence but not substantiated by positive knowledge or proof. **2.** A judgment based on special knowledge and given by an expert. **3.** A judgment or an estimation of the merit of a person or thing. **4.** The prevailing view. **5.** *Law.* A formal statement by a court or other adjudicative body of the legal reasons and principles for the conclusions of the court. [ME < OFr. < Lat. *opīniō*, *opīniōn-*.]

o•pin•ion•at•ed (ə-pĭn′yə-nā′tĭd) *adj.* Holding stubbornly and often unreasonably to one's own opinions. [Prob. < obsolete *opinionate* : OPINION + -ATE[1].] —**o•pin′ion•at′ed•ly** *adv.* —**o•pin′ion•at′ed•ness** *n.*

o•pin•ion•a•tive (ə-pĭn′yə-nā′tĭv) *adj.* **1.** Of, based on, or of the nature of an opinion. **2.** Opinionated. —**o•pin′ion•a′tive•ly** *adv.*

o•pi•oid (ō′pē-oid′) *n.* See **opiate** 2. —*adj.* Opiate.

o•pis•tho•branch (ə-pĭs′thə-brăngk′) *n., pl.* **-branchs.** Any of various marine gastropod mollusks of the subclass or order Opisthobranchia, characterized by gills, a reduced or absent shell, and two pairs of tentacles. [< NLat. *Opisthobranchia*, order name : Gk. *opistho-*, behind (< *opisthen*; see **epi***) + Gk. *brankhia*, pl. of *brankhion*, gill.]

op•is•thog•na•thous (ŏp′ĭs-thŏg′nə-thəs) *adj.* Having receding jaws. [Gk. *opistho-*, behind (< *opisthen*; see **epi***) + -GNATHOUS.] —**op′is•thog′na•thism** *n.*

o•pi•um (ō′pē-əm) *n.* **1.** A bitter, strongly addictive narcotic drug prepared from the dried juice of unripe pods of the opium poppy. **2.** Something that numbs or stupefies. [ME < Lat. < Gk. *opion*, dim. of *opos*, vegetable juice.]

opium poppy *n.* An annual plant *(Papaver somniferum)* native to Turkey and adjacent areas and having grayish-green leaves and variously colored flowers.

opium poppy
Papaver somniferum

O•po•le (ô-pô′lə). A city of S Poland on the Oder R. SE of Wroclaw; orig. a Slavic settlement. Pop. 124,000.

O•por•to (ō-pôr′tō, ō-pōr′-) also **Por•to** or **Pôr•to** (pôr′to͝o). A city of NW Portugal near the mouth of the Douro R. N of Lisbon; probably of pre-Roman origin. Pop. 327,368.

o•pos•sum (ə-pŏs′əm, pŏs′əm) *n., pl.* **opossum** or **-sums. 1.** Any of various nocturnal, usu. arboreal marsupials of the family Didelphidae, esp. *Didelphis marsupialis* of the Western Hemisphere, having a thick coat of hair, a long snout, and a long prehensile tail. See Regional Note at **possum. 2.** Any of several similar marsupials of Australia belonging to the family Phalangeridae. [Virginia Algonquian.]

opossum

opp. *abbr.* Opposite.

Op•pen•hei•mer (ŏp′ən-hī′mər), **J(ulius) Robert.** 1902–67. Amer. physicist who directed the Los Alamos NM laboratory during the development of the first atomic bomb (1942–45).

op•po•nent (ə-pō′nənt) *n.* One that opposes another or others, as in a battle, contest, or debate. See Syns at **enemy.** —*adj.* **1.** Acting against an antagonist or opposing force. **2.** Located in front. [Lat. *oppōnēns*, *oppōnent-*, pr.part. of *oppōnere*, to oppose. See OPPOSE.] —**op•po′nen•cy** *n.*

op•por•tune (ŏp′ər-to͞on′, -tyo͞on′) *adj.* **1.** Suited or right for a particular purpose. **2.** Occurring at a fitting or advantageous time. [ME < OFr. *opportun* < Lat. *opportūnus* < *ob portum (veniēns)*, (coming) toward port : *ob*, to; see OB- + *portum*, accusative of *portus*, harbor; see **per-**[2]*.] —**op′por•tune′ly** *adv.* —**op′por•tune′ness** *n.*

op•por•tun•ist (ŏp′ər-to͞o′nĭst, -tyo͞o′-) *n.* One who takes advantage of any opportunity to achieve an end, often regardless of principles or consequences. —**op′por•tun′ism** *n.*

op•por•tun•is•tic (ŏp′ər-to͞o-nĭs′tĭk, -tyo͞o-) *adj.* Taking immediate advantage, often unethically, of any circumstance of possible benefit.

ă pat	oi boy
ā pay	ou out
âr care	o͝o took
ä father	o͞o boot
ĕ pet	ŭ cut
ē be	ûr urge
ĭ pit	th thin
ī pie	*th* this
îr pier	hw which
ŏ pot	zh vision
ō toe	ə about, item
ô paw	

Stress marks:
′ (primary);
′ (secondary), as in dictionary (dĭk′shə-nĕr′ē)

opportunistic infection *n.* An infection by a microorganism that normally does not cause disease but becomes pathogenic when the body's immune system is impaired and unable to fight off infection, as in AIDS and certain other diseases.

op•por•tu•ni•ty (ŏp′ər-to͞o′nĭ-tē, -tyo͞o′-) *n., pl.* **-ties. 1.a.** A favorable or advantageous circumstance or combination of circumstances. **b.** A favorable or suitable occasion or time. **2.** A chance for progress or advancement.

op•pos•a•ble (ə-pō′zə-bəl) *adj.* **1.** Possible to oppose or resist. **2.** That can be placed opposite something else: *The thumb is an opposable digit.* **—op•pos′a•bil′i•ty** *n.*

op•pose (ə-pōz′) *v.* **-posed, -pos•ing, -pos•es.** *—tr.* **1.** To be in contention or conflict with. **2.** To be resistant to: *opposes new ideas.* **3.** To place opposite in contrast or counterbalance. **4.** To place so as to be opposite something else. *—intr.* To act or be in opposition. [ME *opposen,* to question, interrogate < OFr. *opposer,* alteration (influenced by *poser,* to place; see POSE[1]) of Lat. *oppōnere,* to oppose (*ob-,* against; see OB- + *pōnere,* to put; see **apo-***).] **—op•pos′er** *n.*

***Syns:** oppose, fight, combat, resist, withstand, contest.* These verbs mean to set someone or something in opposition to another. *Oppose* has the fewest connotations: *"The idea is inconsistent with our constitutional theory and has been stubbornly opposed . . . since the early days of the Republic"* (E.B. White). *Fight* and *combat* suggest vigor and aggressiveness: *"All my life I have fought against prejudice and intolerance"* (Harry S. Truman). *"We are not afraid . . . to tolerate any error so long as reason is left free to combat it"* (Thomas Jefferson). To *resist* is to strive to fend off or offset the actions, effects, or force of: *"Pardon was freely extended to all who had resisted the invasion"* (John R. Green). *Withstand* often implies successful resistance: *"Neither the southern provinces, nor Sicily, could have withstood his power"* (Henry Hallam). To *contest* is to call something into question and take an active stand against it: *contested his right to sell the land.*

op•po•site (ŏp′ə-zĭt) *adj.* **1.** Placed or located directly across from something else or from each other. **2.** Facing the other way; moving or tending away from each other: *opposite directions.* **3.** Altogether different, as in nature, quality, or significance. **4.** *Bot.* Growing in pairs on either side of a stem. *—n.* **1.** One that is opposite or contrary to another. **2.** An opponent or antagonist. **3.** An antonym. *—adv.* In an opposite position. *—prep.* **1.** Across from or facing. **2.** In a complementary dramatic role to. [ME < OFr. < Lat. *oppositus,* p.part. of *oppōnere,* oppose. See OPPOSE.] **—op′po•site•ly** *adv.* **—op′po•site•ness** *n.*

opposite number *n.* A person who holds a position in an organization or a system that corresponds to that of a person in another organization or system; a counterpart.

op•po•si•tion (ŏp′ə-zĭsh′ən) *n.* **1.a.** The act of opposing or resisting. **b.** The condition of being in conflict; antagonism. **2.** Placement opposite to or in contrast with another. **3.** Something that serves as an obstacle. **4.** Often **Opposition.** A political party or an organized group opposed to the group, party, or government in power. **5.** *Astron.* **a.** A configuration in which the earth lies on a straight line between the sun and a superior planet or the moon. **b.** The position of the superior planet or the moon in this configuration. **6.** *Logic.* The relation existing between two propositions having an identical subject and predicate but differing in quantity, quality, or both. **7.** *Ling.* Contrast in a language between two phonemes or other linguistically important elements. **—op′po•si′tion•al** *adj.*

op•po•si•tion•ist (ŏp′ə-zĭsh′ə-nĭst) *n.* A member of an opposition. **—op′po•si′tion•ist** *adj.*

op•press (ə-prĕs′) *tr.v.* **-pressed, -press•ing, -press•es. 1.** To keep down by severe and unjust use of force or authority. **2.** To weigh heavily on: *Poverty oppresses the spirit.* **3.** *Obsolete.* To overwhelm or crush. [Ult. < Lat. *oppressus,* p.part. of *opprimere,* to press against : *ob-,* against; see OB- + *premere,* to press; see **per-**[4]*.] **—op•pres′sor** *n.*

op•pres•sion (ə-prĕsh′ən) *n.* **1.a.** The act of oppressing; arbitrary and cruel exercise of power. **b.** The state of being oppressed. **2.** Something that oppresses. **3.** A feeling of being heavily weighed down in mind or body.

op•pres•sive (ə-prĕs′ĭv) *adj.* **1.** Difficult to bear; burdensome: *oppressive laws.* **2.** Exercising power arbitrarily and often unjustly; tyrannical. **3.** Weighing heavily on the senses or spirit. **—op•pres′sive•ly** *adv.* **—op•pres′sive•ness** *n.*

op•pro•bri•ous (ə-prō′brē-əs) *adj.* **1.** Expressing contemptuous reproach; scornful or abusive. **2.** Bringing disgrace; shameful or infamous. **—op•pro′bri•ous•ly** *adv.*

op•pro•bri•um (ə-prō′brē-əm) *n.* **1.** Disgrace arising from exceedingly shameful conduct; ignominy. **2.** Scornful reproach or contempt. **3.** A cause of shame or disgrace. [Lat. < *opprobrāre,* to reproach : *ob-,* against; see OB- + *probum,* reproach; see **bher-**[1]*.]

op•pugn (ə-pyo͞on′) *tr.v.* **-pugned, -pugn•ing, -pugns.** To oppose, contradict, or call into question. [ME *oppugnen* < Lat. *oppugnāre,* to attack : *ob-,* against; see OB- + *pugnāre,* to fight with the fist; see **peuk-***.] **—op•pugn′er** *n.*

op•sin (ŏp′sĭn) *n.* A protein of the retina, esp. the protein constituent of rhodopsin, that makes up one of the visual pigments. [Prob. back-formation < RHODOPSIN.]

-opsis *suff.* Something resembling a specified thing: *caryopsis.* [Gk., sight, seeing, like < *opsis,* sight, appearance. See **okʷ-***.]

op•so•nin (ŏp′sə-nĭn) *n.* An antibody in blood serum that causes bacteria or other foreign cells to become more susceptible to the action of phagocytes. [Lat. *opsōnāre,* to buy provisions (< Gk. *opsōnein* < *opson,* condiment, delicacy) + -IN.] **—op•son′ic** (ŏp-sŏn′ĭk) *adj.*

op•so•nize (ŏp′sə-nīz′) *tr.v.* **-nized, -niz•ing, -niz•es.** To make (bacteria or other cells) more susceptible to the action of phagocytes. [< OPSONIN.] **—op′so•ni•za′tion** (-nĭ-zā′shən) *n.*

-opsy *suff.* Examination: *biopsy.* [Gk. *-opsia,* sight, seeing < *opsis.* See **okʷ-***.]

opt (ŏpt) *intr.v.* **opt•ed, opt•ing, opts.** To make a choice or decision. ***—phrasal verb.* opt out.** *Slang.* To choose not to participate in something. [Fr. *opter* < OFr. < Lat. *optāre.*]

opt. *abbr.* **1.** *Gram.* Optative. **2.** Optical; optician; optics. **3.** Optimum. **4.** Optional.

op•ta•tive (ŏp′tə-tĭv) *adj.* **1.** Expressing a wish or choice. **2.** *Gram.* **a.** Of, relating to, or being a mood of verbs in some languages, such as Greek, used to express a wish. **b.** Of, relating to, or being a statement using a verb in the subjunctive mood to indicate a wish or desire, as in *Were it possible, I would do it.* *—n. Gram.* **1.** The optative mood. **2.** A verb or an expression in the optative mood. [ME *optatif* < OFr. < LLat. *optātīvus* < Lat. *optātus,* p.part. of *optāre,* to wish.] **—op′ta•tive•ly** *adv.*

op•tic (ŏp′tĭk) *adj.* **1.** Of or relating to the eye or vision. **2.** Of or relating to the science of optics or optical equipment. *—n.* **1.** An eye. **2.** Any of the lenses, prisms, or mirrors of an optical instrument. [ME *optik* < OFr. *optique* < Med.Lat. *opticus* < Gk. *optikos* < *optos,* visible. See **okʷ-***.]

op•ti•cal (ŏp′tĭ-kəl) *adj.* **1.** Of or relating to sight; visual. **2.** Designed to assist sight. **3.** Of or relating to optics. **4.** Relating to or using visible light: *optical astronomy.* **5.** Using light-sensitive devices. **—op′ti•cal•ly** *adv.*

optical activity *n. Chem.* A property caused by asymmetrical molecular structure that enables a substance to rotate the plane of incident polarized light.

optical art *n.* Op art.

optical character reader *n. Comp. Sci.* A device used for optical character recognition.

optical character recognition *n. Comp. Sci.* The use of light-sensitive devices to identify and encode printed or handwritten characters.

optical disk or **optical disc** *n. Comp. Sci.* A plastic-coated disk that stores digital data, such as music or text, as tiny pits etched into the surface and is read with a laser.

optical fiber *n.* A flexible optically transparent fiber, usu. glass or plastic, through which light can be transmitted by successive internal reflections.

optical illusion *n.* A visually perceived image that is deceptive or misleading.

optic axis *n.* An optical path through a crystal along which a ray of light can pass without undergoing double refraction.

optic chiasma *n.* The partial intersection or crossing of the optic nerve fibers on the underside of the hypothalamus.

optic disk *n. Anat.* See **blind spot** 1.

op•ti•cian (ŏp-tĭsh′ən) *n.* **1.** One that makes lenses and eyeglasses. **2.** One that sells lenses, eyeglasses, and other optical instruments.

optic nerve *n.* Either of the second pair of cranial nerves that carry visual information from the retina to the brain.

op•tics (ŏp′tĭks) *n.* *(used with a sing. v.)* The branch of physics that deals with visible light, vision, and usu. ultraviolet and infrared electromagnetic radiation.

op•ti•mal (ŏp′tə-məl) *adj.* Most favorable or desirable; optimum. **—op′ti•mal•ly** *adv.*

op•ti•mism (ŏp′tə-mĭz′əm) *n.* **1.** A tendency to expect the best possible outcome or dwell on the most hopeful aspects of a situation. **2.** *Philos.* **a.** The doctrine, asserted by Leibnitz, that this world is the best of all possible worlds. **b.** The belief that the universe is improving and that good will ultimately triumph over evil. [Fr. *optimisme* < NLat. *optimum,* the greatest good. See OPTIMUM.]

op•ti•mist (ŏp′tə-mĭst) *n.* **1.** One who usu. expects a favorable outcome. **2.** A believer in philosophical optimism. **—op′ti•mis′tic** *adj.* **—op′ti•mis′ti•cal•ly** *adv.*

op•ti•mi•za•tion (ŏp′tə-mĭ-zā′shən) *n.* The procedure or procedures used to make a system or design most effective or functional, esp. the mathematical techniques involved.

op•ti•mize (ŏp′tə-mīz′) *tr.v.* **-mized, -miz•ing, -miz•es. 1.** To make most perfect or effective. **2.** To make the most of.

op•ti•mum (ŏp′tə-məm) *n., pl.* **-ma** (-mə) or **-mums. 1.** The point at which the condition, degree, or amount of something is the most favorable. **2.** *Biol.* The most favorable condition for growth and reproduction. *—adj.* Most favorable or advantageous; best. [Lat., neut. sing. of *optimus,* best. See **op-***.]

op•tion (ŏp′shən) *n.* **1.** The act of choosing; choice. See Syns at **choice. 2.** The power or freedom to choose. **3.a.** The exclusive right, usu. obtained for a fee, to buy or sell something within a specified time at a set price. **b.** The privilege of demanding fulfillment of a contract at a specified time. **c.** A right to buy or sell specific securities or commodities at a stated price within a specified time. **d.** The right of the holder of an insurance policy to specify how payments are to be made or credited to the policyholder. **4.** Something chosen or available as a choice. **5.** An item or a feature that may be chosen to replace or enhance standard equipment, as in a car. **6.** *Football.* An offensive play in which a back can pass or run with the ball. — *tr.v.* **-tioned, -tion•ing, -tions.** To acquire or grant an option on. [Lat. *optiō, optiōn-.*]

op•tion•al (ŏp′shə-nəl) *adj.* Left to choice; not compulsory or automatic. — **op′tion•al•ly** *adv.*

op•tom•e•trist (ŏp-tŏm′ĭ-trĭst) *n.* A person who is professionally trained and licensed to examine the eyes for visual defects, diagnose problems or impairments, and prescribe corrective lenses or provide other types of treatment.

op•tom•e•try (ŏp-tŏm′ĭ-trē) *n.* The practice or profession of an optometrist. [Gk. *optos,* visible; see **okʷ-*** + -METRY.] — **op′to•met′ric** (ŏp′tə-mĕt′rĭk), **op′to•met′ri•cal** *adj.*

op•u•lence (ŏp′yə-ləns) also **op•u•len•cy** (-lən-sē) *n.* **1.** Wealth; affluence. **2.** Great abundance; profusion.

op•u•lent (ŏp′yə-lənt) *adj.* **1.** Possessing or exhibiting great wealth; affluent. **2.** Characterized by rich abundance; luxuriant. [Lat. *opulentus.* See **op-***.] — **op′u•lent•ly** *adv.*

o•pun•ti•a (ō-pŭn′shē-ə, -shə) *n.* Any of various cacti of the genus *Opuntia,* esp. the prickly pear. [Lat. *(herba) Opuntia,* Opuntian (herb), after *Opūs, Opunt-,* ancient town of E-central Greece.]

o•pus (ō′pəs) *n., pl.* **o•pe•ra** (ō′pər-ə, ŏp′ər-ə) or **o•pus•es.** A creative work, esp. a musical piece numbered by its place in the order of a composer's works. [Lat. See **op-***.]

o•pus•cule (ō-pŭs′kyo͞ol) *n.* A small minor work. [Lat. *opusculum,* dim. of *opus,* work. See OPUS.]

or[1] (ôr; ər *when unstressed*) *conj.* **1.a.** Used to indicate an alternative, usu. only before the last term of a series: *this, that, or the other.* **b.** Used to indicate the second of two alternatives, the first being preceded by *either* or *whether*: *whether to laugh or cry.* **c.** *Archaic.* Used to indicate the first of two alternatives, with the force of *either* or *whether.* **2.** Used to indicate a synonymous or equivalent expression: *acrophobia, or fear of great heights.* **3.** Used to indicate uncertainty or indefiniteness: *two or three.* [ME < *other,* or (< OE < *oththe*) and < *outher* (< OE *āhwæther, āther*; see EITHER).]

Usage Note: When all the elements in a series connected by *or* are singular, the verb they govern is singular: *Beer, ale, or wine is included in the charge.* When all the elements are plural, the verb is plural. When the elements do not agree in number, some grammarians have suggested that the verb be governed by the element to which it is nearer: *Tom or his sisters are coming.* Other grammarians, however, have argued that such constructions must be avoided and that substitutes be found in which the problem of agreement does not arise: *Either Tom is coming or his sisters are.* See Usage Notes at **and/or, either, neither, nor**[1].

or[2] (ôr) *Archaic.* — *conj.* Before. Followed by *ever* or *ere*: *"dead or ere I come"* (Shakespeare). — *prep.* Before. [ME, var. of *er* < OE *ǣr,* soon, early, and < ON *ār*; see **ayer-***.]

or[3] (ôr) *n. Her.* Gold, represented in heraldic engraving by a white field with small dots. [ME < OFr. < Lat. *aurum.*]

OR *abbr.* **1.** Or **O.R.** Operating room. **2.** Operations research. **3.** Oregon. **4.** Owner's risk.

-or[1] *suff.* One that performs a specified action: *accelerator.* [ME *-or, -our* < OFr. *-eor, -eur* and AN *-our, -ur,* all < Lat. *-or, -ōr-.*]

-or[2] *suff.* State; quality; activity: *valor.* [ME *-our* < OFr. *-eur* < Lat. *-or, -ōr-.*]

o•ra (ôr′ə, ōr′ə) *n.* Pl. of **os**[1].

or•ach also **or•ache** (ôr′ĭch, ŏr′-) *n.* Any of various plants of the genus *Atriplex,* esp. *A. hortensis* having edible spinachlike leaves. [ME *orage,* arage < OFr. *arrache* < VLat. **ātripica* < Lat. *ātriplex, ātriplic-* < Gk. *atraphaxus.*]

or•a•cle (ôr′ə-kəl, ŏr′-) *n.* **1.a.** A shrine consecrated to the worship and consultation of a prophetic deity, as that of Apollo at Delphi. **b.** A person, such as a priestess, through whom a deity is held to respond when consulted. **c.** The response given through such a medium, often an enigmatic statement or allegory. **2.a.** A person considered a source of wise counsel or prophetic opinions. **b.** An authoritative or wise statement or prediction. **3.** *Theol.* A command or revelation from God. **4.** In the Bible, the sanctuary of the Temple. [ME < OFr. < Lat. *ōrāculum* < *ōrāre,* to speak.]

o•rac•u•lar (ô-răk′yə-lər, ō-răk′-) *adj.* **1.** Of, relating to, or being an oracle. **2.a.** Solemnly prophetic. **b.** Enigmatic; obscure. [< Lat. *ōrāculum,* oracle < *ōrāre,* to speak.] — **o•rac′u•lar′i•ty** (-lăr′ĭ-tē) *n.* — **o•rac′u•lar•ly** *adv.*

O•ra•dea (ô-räd′yä). A city of NW Romania near the Hungarian border; ceded to Romania by Hungary in 1919 and again after World War II. Pop. 206,206.

o•ral (ôr′əl, ōr′-) *adj.* **1.** Spoken rather than written. See Usage Note at **verbal. 2.** Of or relating to the mouth: *oral surgery.* **3.** Used in or taken through the mouth: *an oral vaccine.* **4.** Consisting of or using speech: *oral instruction.* **5.** *Ling.* Articulated through the mouth only, with the nasal passages closed. **6.** *Psychol.* In psychoanalytic theory, of or relating to the first stage of psychosexual development, during which the mouth is the chief focus of exploration and pleasure. — *n.* An academic examination in which questions and answers are spoken rather than written. Often used in the plural. [LLat. *ōrālis* < Lat. *ōs, ōr-,* mouth. See **ōs-***.] — **o′ral•ly** *adv.*

oral contraceptive *n.* A pill, usu. containing estrogen or progesterone, that inhibits ovulation and prevents conception.

o•ral-for•mu•la•ic (ôr′əl-fôr′myə-lā′ĭk, ōr′-) *adj.* Of or relating to poetry in which traditional material is improvised at each performance by using verbal formulas to aid memory.

oral history *n.* **1.** Historical information, usu. tape-recorded, obtained in interviews with persons having firsthand knowledge. **2.** An audiotape or a written account of such an interview or interviews.

oral sex *n.* Sexual activity involving oral stimulation of one's partner's sex organs.

O•ran (ō-rän′, ô-räɴ′). A city of NW Algeria on the **Gulf of Oran,** an inlet of the Mediterranean Sea WSW of Algiers; held by Vichy France during World War II. Pop. 409,788.

o•rang (ō-răng′, ô′răng) *n. Informal.* An orangutan.

or•ange (ôr′ĭnj, ŏr′-) *n.* **1.a.** Any of several southeast Asian evergreen trees of the genus *Citrus,* having fragrant white flowers and round fruit with a yellowish or reddish rind and a sectioned pulpy interior. **b.** The fruit of any of these trees, having a sweetish acidic juice. **2.** Any of several similar plants, such as the mock orange. **3.** *Color.* The hue of that portion of the visible spectrum lying between red and yellow, with wavelengths of approx. 590 to 630 nanometers; any of a group of colors between red and yellow in hue, of medium lightness and moderate saturation. [ME < OFr. *pume orenge,* transl. and alteration (influenced by *Orenge,* Orange, a town in France) of OItal. *melarancio* : *mela,* fruit + *arancio,* orange tree (alteration of Ar. *nāranj* < Pers. *nārang* < Skt. *nāraṅgaḥ,* poss. of Dravidian orig.).] — **or′ange** *adj.*

Word History: Oranges originated in China, then were introduced to India, and traveled on to the Middle East, into Europe, and finally to the New World. The history of the word *orange* keeps step with this journey only part of the way. The word is possibly of Dravidian origin, that is, it comes from a language or languages in a large non-Indo-European family of languages that are spoken in southern India and northern Sri Lanka. The Dravidian word or words were adopted into the Indo-European language Sanskrit with the form *nāraṅgaḥ.* As the fruit passed westward, so did the word, as evidenced by Persian *nārang* and Arabic *nāranj.* The important word for the development of our term is Old Italian *melarancio,* derived from *mela,* "fruit," and *arancio,* "orange tree," from Arabic *nāranj.* Old Italian *melarancio* was translated into Old French as *pume orenge,* the *o* replacing the *a* because of the influence of the name of the town of Orange, from which oranges reached northern France. The final stage of the odyssey of the word was its borrowing into English from the Old French form *orenge.* Our word is first recorded in Middle English in a text probably composed around 1380.

Or•ange[1] (ôr′ĭnj, ŏr′-). Princely family of Europe ruling continously in the Netherlands since 1815.

Or•ange[2] (ôr′ĭnj, ŏr′-). **1.** A city of S CA NNE of Santa Ana. Pop. 110,658. **2.** A city of NE NJ, a suburb of Newark and New York City. Pop. 29,925. **3.** A city of SE TX E of Beaumont. Pop. 19,381.

or•ange•ade (ôr′ĭn-jād′, ŏr′-) *n.* A beverage of orange juice, sugar, and water.

Orange Free State. A province and historical region of E-central South Africa; a Boer republic (1854–1900) later controlled by Great Britain as the **Orange River Colony** (1900–07). The renamed Orange Free State became a founding province of South Africa in 1910.

orange hawkweed *n.* A European perennial weed *(Hieracium aurantiacum)* with hairy leaves and orange-red flower heads.

Or•ange•man (ôr′ĭnj-mən, ŏr′-) *n.* **1.** A member of a secret society founded in Northern Ireland in 1795 to maintain the political and religious ascendancy of Protestantism. **2.** An Irish Protestant. [After William, Prince of ORANGE[1].]

orange pekoe *n.* A grade of black tea consisting of the end buds of the shoot or their surrounding two full leaves. [< the orange color of its infusion.]

Orange River. A river of Lesotho, South Africa, and Namibia flowing c. 2,092 km (1,300 mi) to the Atlantic Ocean.

or•ange•ry (ôr′ĭnj-rē, ŏr′-) *n., pl.* **-ries.** A sheltered place, esp. a greenhouse, used for growing orange trees in cool climates.

orange stick *n.* A stick of orangewood with tapered ends, used in manicuring.

or•ange•wood (ôr′ĭnj-wo͝od′, ŏr′-) *n.* The fine-grained wood of the orange tree, used in fine woodwork.

o•rang•u•tan (ô-răng′ə-tăn′, ō-răng′-, ə-răng′-) also **o•rang•ou•tang** (-ə-tăng′) *n.* An arboreal anthropoid ape *(Pongo pygmaeus)* of Borneo and Sumatra having a shaggy

orach
Atriplex patula

orangutan
Pongo pygmaeus

ă **pat**	oi **boy**
ā **pay**	ou **out**
âr **care**	o͝o **took**
ä **father**	o͞o **boot**
ĕ **pet**	ŭ **cut**
ē **be**	ûr **urge**
ĭ **pit**	th **thin**
ī **pie**	*th* **this**
îr **pier**	hw **which**
ŏ **pot**	zh **vision**
ō **toe**	ə **about,**
ô **paw**	**item**

Stress marks:
′ (primary);
′ (secondary), as in
dictionary (dĭk′shə-nĕr′ē)

reddish-brown coat, very long arms, and no tail. [Malay *ōrang hūtan* : *ōrang*, man + *hūtan*, wilderness, jungle.]

o•rate (ô-rāt′, ō-rāt′, ôr′āt′, ōr′-) *intr.v.* **o•rat•ed, o•rat•ing, o•rates.** To speak in a formal pompous manner. [Lat. *ōrāre, ōrāt-*, to pray, speak publicly.]

o•ra•tion (ô-rā′shən, ō-rā′-) *n.* **1.** A formal speech, esp. one given on a ceremonial occasion. **2.** A speech delivered in a high-flown or pompous manner. [ME *oracion*, prayer < LLat. *ōrātiō, ōrātiōn-* < Lat., discourse < *ōrātus*, p.part. of *ōrāre*, to speak.]

or•a•tor (ôr′ə-tər, ŏr′-) *n.* **1.** One who gives an oration. **2.** An eloquent and skilled public speaker. —**or′a•tor•ship′** *n.*

Or•a•to•ri•an (ôr′ə-tôr′ē-ən, -tōr′-) *n. Rom. Cath. Ch.* A member of an Oratory.

or•a•tor•i•cal (ôr′ə-tôr′ĭ-kəl, ŏr′ə-tŏr′-) *adj.* Of or relating to oratory or an orator. —**or′a•tor′i•cal•ly** *adv.*

or•a•to•ri•o (ôr′ə-tôr′ē-ō′, -tōr′-, ŏr′-) *n., pl.* **-os.** *Mus.* A composition for voices and orchestra, telling a sacred story without costumes, scenery, or dramatic action. [Ital., after *Oratorio*, the Oratory of St. Philip Neri at Rome, where famous musical services were held in the 16th cent.]

or•a•to•ry[1] (ôr′ə-tôr′ē, -tōr′ē, ŏr′-) *n.* **1.** The art of public speaking. **2.** Eloquence or skill in making speeches to the public. **3.** Public speaking marked by the use of overblown rhetoric. [Lat. *(ars) ōrātōria*, (art) of speaking, fem. sing. of *ōrātōrius*, oratorical < *ōrātor*, speaker < *ōrāre*, to speak.]

or•a•to•ry[2] (ôr′ə-tôr′ē, -tōr′ē, ŏr′-) *n., pl.* **-ries. 1.** A place for prayer, such as a chapel. **2.** Also **Oratory. a.** A Roman Catholic religious society of secular priests founded in 1575 by Saint Philip Neri. **b.** A branch or church of this society. [ME *oratorie* < OFr. < LLat. *ōrātōrium*, place of prayer < Lat., neut. of *ōrātōrius*, for praying < *ōrāre*, to pray.]

orb

orb (ôrb) *n.* **1.** A sphere or spherical object. **2.a.** A celestial body, such as the sun or moon. **b.** *Archaic.* The planet Earth. **3.** One of a series of concentric transparent spheres thought by ancient and medieval astronomers to revolve about Earth and carry the celestial bodies. **4.** A globe surmounted by a cross, used as a symbol of monarchial power and justice. **5.** An eye or eyeball. **6.** *Archaic.* Something of circular form; a circle or an orbit. **7.** *Archaic.* A range of endeavor or activity; a province. —*v.* **orbed, orb•ing, orbs.** —*tr.* **1.** To shape into a circle or sphere. **2.** *Archaic.* To encircle; enclose. —*intr. Archaic.* To move in an orbit. [ME *orbe*, orbit < OFr. < Lat. *orbis*, circle, disk, orbit.]

or•bic•u•lar (ôr-bĭk′yə-lər) *adj.* Circular or spherical. [ME *orbiculer* < OFr. *orbiculaire* < LLat. *orbiculāris* < Lat. *orbiculus*, dim. of *orbis*, circle, disk.] —**or•bic′u•lar′i•ty** (-lăr′ĭ-tē) *n.* —**or•bic′u•lar•ly** *adv.*

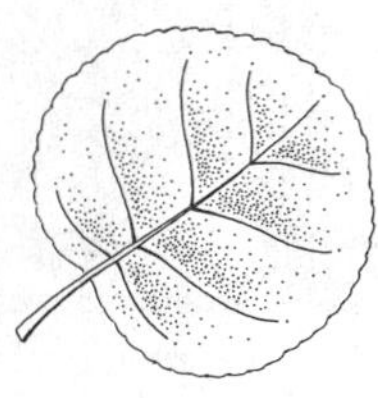
orbicular
Orbicular leaf

or•bic•u•late (ôr-bĭk′yə-lĭt, -lāt′) also **or•bic•u•lat•ed** (-lā′tĭd) *adj.* Orbicular. [Lat. *orbiculātus* < *orbiculus*, dim. of *orbis*, circle, disk.] —**or•bic′u•late•ly** *adv.*

Or•bi•son (ôr′bĭ-sən), **Roy.** 1936–88. Amer. singer and songwriter noted for his smooth tenor voice and haunting ballads.

or•bit (ôr′bĭt) *n.* **1.a.** The path of a celestial body or an artificial satellite as it revolves around another body. **b.** One complete revolution of such a body. **2.** The path of a body in a field of force surrounding another body; for example, the movement of an atomic electron in relation to a nucleus. **3.a.** A range of activity, experience, or knowledge. **b.** A range of control or influence. **4.** Either of two bony cavities in the skull containing an eye and its external structures; an eye socket. —*v.* **-bit•ed, -bit•ing, -bits.** —*tr.* **1.** To put into an orbit. **2.** To revolve around (a center of attraction). —*intr.* To move in an orbit. [ME *orbite*, eye socket < OFr. < Lat. *orbita*, orbit, prob. < *orbis*.]

or•bit•al (ôr′bĭ-tl) *adj.* Of or relating to an orbit. —*n.* The wave function of an electron in an atom or molecule, indicating the electron's probable location.

or•bit•er (ôr′bĭ-tər) *n.* Something that orbits, esp. a spacecraft that orbits a planet or moon without landing on it.

or•ca (ôr′kə) *n.* See **killer whale.** [Lat. *ōrca*, whale, prob. alteration of Gk. *orux, orug-*, pickax, a kind of large fish or whale, perh. < *orussein*, to dig.]

orch. *abbr. Mus.* Orchestra.

or•chard (ôr′chərd) *n.* **1.** An area of land devoted to the cultivation of fruit or nut trees. **2.** The trees cultivated in such an area. [ME < OE *orceard*, alteration of *ortgeard* : perh. *wyrt, wort*, plant; see WORT[1] + *geard*, yard; see **gher-**[1]*.]

orchard grass *n.* A Eurasian grass *(Dactylis glomerata)* widely planted in pastures.

or•char•dist (ôr′chər-dĭst) *n.* One who owns or cultivates an orchard.

or•ches•tra (ôr′kĭ-strə, -kĕs′trə) *n.* **1.** *Mus.* **a.** A large group of musicians who play together on various instruments, usu. including strings, woodwinds, and brass and percussion instruments. **b.** The instruments played by such a group. **2.** The area in a theater or concert hall where the musicians sit, immediately in front of and below the stage. **3.a.** The front section of seats nearest the stage in a theater. **b.** The entire main floor of a theater. **4.** A semicircular space in front of the stage used by the chorus in ancient Greek theaters. [Lat. *orchēstra*, orchestra in Greek theaters < Gk. *orkhēstra* < *orkheisthai*, to dance.] —**or•ches′tral** (ôr-kĕs′trəl) *adj.* —**or•ches′tral•ly** *adv.*

or•ches•trate (ôr′kĭ-strāt′) *tr.v.* **-trat•ed, -trat•ing, -trates. 1.** *Mus.* To compose or arrange (music) for performance by an orchestra. **2.** To arrange or control the elements of, as to achieve a desired overall effect. —**or′ches•tra′tor** *n.*

or•ches•tra•tion (ôr′kĭ-strā′shən) *n.* **1.** *Mus.* **a.** A composition that has been orchestrated. **b.** Arrangement of music for performance by an orchestra. **2.** Arrangement or control.

or•chid (ôr′kĭd) *n.* **1.a.** A member of the orchid family. **b.** The flower of any of these plants, esp. one cultivated for ornament. **2.** *Color.* A pale to light purple, from grayish to purplish pink to strong reddish purple. [< NLat. *Orchideae*, family name < Lat. *orchis*, orchid < Gk. *orkhis*, testicle, orchid (< the slope of its root).] —**or′chid** *adj.*

or•chi•da•ceous (ôr′kĭ-dā′shəs) *adj.* **1.** Of, relating to, or characteristic of the orchid family. **2.** Suggesting ostentatious luxury; showy. [< NLat. *Orchidaceae*, family name < Lat. *orchis*, orchid. See ORCHID.]

orchid family *n.* A large family of epiphytic or terrestial perennial herbs, the Orchidaceae, found chiefly in the tropics and subtropics and characterized by bilaterally symmetrical showy flowers with an inferior ovary and dustlike seeds.

or•chi•ec•to•my (ôr′kē-ĕk′tə-mē) or **or•chi•dec•to•my** (-kĭ-dĕk′-) *n., pl.* **-mies.** Surgical removal of one or both testes. [Gk. *orkhis, orkhi-*, testicle + -ECTOMY.]

or•chil (ôr′kĭl, -chĭl) also **ar•chil** (är′-) *n.* **1.** Any of several lichens, chiefly of the genera *Roccella* and *Lecanora*, from which a dye is obtained. **2.** The reddish dyestuff obtained from any of these organisms. [ME *orchell*, ult. < Old Catalan *orxella* < Mozarabic *'urĝâla*.]

or•chis (ôr′kĭs) *n.* Any of numerous orchids of the genus *Orchis*, having magenta, white, or magenta-spotted flowers. [Lat., orchid. See ORCHID.]

Or•cus (ôr′kəs) *n. Rom. Myth.* **1.** The world of the dead; Hades. **2.** Pluto, the god of the underworld.

ord. *abbr.* **1.** Order. **2.** Ordinal. **3.** Ordinance. **4.** Ordnance.

or•dain (ôr-dān′) *tr.v.* **-dained, -dain•ing, -dains. 1.a.** To invest with ministerial or priestly authority; confer holy orders on. **b.** To authorize as a rabbi. **2.** To order by virtue of superior authority; decree or enact. **3.** To prearrange unalterably; predestine: *by fate ordained.* See Syns at **dictate.** [ME *ordeinen* < OFr. *ordener, ordein-* < Lat. *ōrdināre*, to organize, appoint to office < *ōrdō, ōrdin-*, order. See **ar-***.] —**or•dain′er** *n.* —**or•dain′ment** *n.*

or•deal (ôr-dēl′) *n.* **1.** A difficult or painful experience, esp. one that severely tests character or endurance. **2.** A method of trial in which the accused is subjected to physically painful or dangerous tests, the result being regarded as a divine judgment of guilt or innocence. [Alteration (influenced by DEAL[1]) of ME *ordal*, trial by ordeal < OE *ordāl*. See **dail-***.]

or•der (ôr′dər) *n.* **1.** A condition of logical or comprehensible arrangement among the separate elements of a group. **2.a.** A condition of methodical or prescribed arrangement among component parts such that proper functioning or appearance is achieved. **b.** Condition or state in general: *in good order.* **3.a.** The established system of social organization. **b.** A condition in which freedom from disorder or disruption is maintained through respect for established authority. **4.** A sequence or an arrangement of successive things. **5.** The prescribed form or customary procedure: *the order of worship.* **6.** An authoritative indication to be obeyed; a command or direction. **7.a.** A command given by a superior military officer requiring obedience, as in the execution of a task. **b. orders.** Formal written instructions to report for military duty at a specified time and place. **8.a.** A commission or an instruction to buy, sell, or supply something. **b.** That which is supplied, bought, or sold. **9.a.** A request made by a customer at a restaurant for a portion of food. **b.** The food requested. **10.** *Law.* A direction or command delivered by a court or other adjudicative body and entered into the record but not necessarily included in the final judgment or verdict. **11.** *Eccles.* **a.** Any of several grades of the Christian ministry: *the order of priesthood.* **b.** The rank of an ordained Christian minister or priest. Often used in the plural. **c.** The sacrament or rite of ordination. Often used in the plural. **12.** Any of the nine grades or choirs of angels. **13.** A group of persons living under a religious rule: *Order of Saint Benedict.* **14.** An organization of people united by a common fraternal bond or social aim. **15.a.** A group of people upon whom a government or sovereign has formally conferred honor for unusual service or merit, entitling them to wear a special insignia: *the Order of the Garter.* **b.** The insignia worn by such people. **16.** A social class. Often used in the plural: *the lower orders.* **17.** A class defined by the common attributes of its members; a kind. **18.** Degree of quality or importance; rank: *poetry of a high order.* **19.** *Archit.* **a.** Any of several styles of classical architecture characterized by type of column. **b.** A style of building: *a cathedral of the Gothic order.* **20.** *Biol.* A taxonomic category of organisms ranking above a family and below a class. See table at **taxonomy. 21.** *Math.* **a.** The sum of the exponents to which the variables in a term are raised;

degree. **b.** The number of successive differentiations to be performed. **c.** The number of elements in a finite group. **d.** The number of rows or columns in a determinant or matrix. *—v.* **-dered, -der•ing, -ders.** *—tr.* **1.** To issue a command or an instruction to. **2.** To give a command or an instruction for. **3.** To direct to proceed as specified. **4.** To give an order for; request to be supplied with. **5.** To put into a methodical, systematic arrangement. See Syns at **arrange. 6.** To predestine; ordain. *—intr.* To give an order or orders; request that something be done or supplied. ***—idioms.*** **in order that.** So that. **in order to.** For the purpose of. **in short order.** With no delay; quickly. **on order.** Requested but not yet delivered. **on the order of. 1.** Of a kind or fashion similar to; like. **2.** Approximately; about. **to order.** According to the buyer's specifications. [ME *ordre* < OFr., var. of *ordene* < Lat. *ōrdō, ōrdin-*. See **ar-*.**] **—or′der•er** *n.*

order arms *n.* **1.** A position in the military manual of arms in which the rifle is held vertically by the right leg, its butt resting on the ground. **2.** A command to assume order arms.

or•der•ly (ôr′dər-lē) *adj.* **1.a.** Free from disorder; neat. **b.** Having a systematic arrangement. **2.** Marked by or adhering to method or system. **3.** Devoid of violence or disruption; peaceful. *—n., pl.* **-lies. 1.** An attendant who does routine nonmedical work in a hospital. **2.** A soldier assigned to attend a superior officer. *—adv.* Systematically; regularly. **—or′der•li•ness** *n.*

Syns: *orderly, methodical, systematic.* These adjectives mean proceeding in or observant of a prescribed pattern or arrangement. *Orderly* especially implies correct or customary procedure or proper or harmonious arrangement: *the orderly evacuation of the building. Methodical* stresses adherence to a logically and carefully planned succession of steps: *methodical instructions for assembly. Systematic* emphasizes observance of a coordinated and orderly set of procedures that is part of a complex whole: *systematic research.*

order of battle *n., pl.* **orders of battle.** The identification, command structure, strength, and disposition of personnel, equipment, and units of an armed force.

order of business *n., pl.* **orders of business.** A matter, such as a task, that must be addressed.

order of magnitude *n., pl.* **orders of magnitude. 1.** An estimate of size or magnitude expressed as a power of ten. **2.** A range of values between a designated lower value and an upper value ten times as large.

order of the day *n., pl.* **orders of the day. 1.** The business to be considered or done by a legislature or other body on a particular day. Often used in the plural. **2.** The characteristic or most significant aspect or activity.

or•di•nal (ôr′dn-əl) *adj.* **1.** Being of a specified position in a numbered series: *an ordinal rank of seventh.* **2.** Of or relating to a taxonomic order. *—n.* **1.** An ordinal number. **2.** *Eccles.* **a.** A book of instructions for daily services. **b.** A book of forms for ordination. [ME *ordinel,* orderly, regular < LLat. *ōrdinālis,* ordinal < Lat. *ōrdō, ōrdin-,* order. See **ar-*.**]

ordinal number *n.* A number indicating position in a series or order, such as first (1st), second (2nd), and third (3rd).

or•di•nance (ôr′dn-əns) *n.* **1.** An authoritative command or order. **2.** A custom or practice established by long usage. **3.** A Christian rite, esp. the Eucharist. **4.** A statute or regulation, esp. one enacted by a city government. [ME *ordinaunce* < OFr. *ordenance* < Med.Lat. *ōrdinantia* < Lat. *ōrdināns, ōrdinant-,* pr.part. of *ōrdināre,* to ordain < *ōrdō, ōrdin-,* order. See **ar-*.**]

or•di•nar•i•ly (ôr′dn-âr′ə-lē, ôr′dn-ĕr′-) *adv.* **1.** As a general rule; usually. **2.** In the common or usual manner. **3.** To the usual extent or degree: *an ordinarily small profit.*

or•di•nar•y (ôr′dn-ĕr′ē) *adj.* **1.** Commonly encountered; usual. **2.a.** Of no exceptional ability, degree, or quality; average. **b.** Of inferior quality; second-rate. **3.** Having immediate rather than delegated jurisdiction, as a judge. **4.** *Math.* Being a differential equation containing no more than two variables and derivatives of one with respect to the other. *—n., pl.* **-ies. 1.** The usual or normal condition or course of events. **2.** *Law.* **a.** The judge of a probate court in some states of the United States. **3.** Often **Ordinary.** *Eccles.* **a.** The part of the Mass that remains unchanged from day to day. **b.** A division of the Roman Breviary containing the unchangeable parts of the office other than the Psalms. **c.** A cleric, such as the residential bishop of a diocese, with ordinary jurisdiction over a specified territory. **4.** *Her.* One of the simplest and commonest charges, such as the bend and the cross. **5.** *Chiefly British.* **a.** A complete meal provided at a fixed price. **b.** A tavern or an inn providing such a meal. [ME *ordinarie* < OFr. < Lat. *ōrdinārius* < *ōrdō, ōrdin-,* order. See **ar-*.**] **—or′di•nar′i•ness** *n.*

Ordinary level *n. Chiefly British.* O level.

ordinary seaman *n.* A seaman of the lowest grade in the merchant marine.

or•di•nate (ôr′dn-ĭt, -āt′) *adj.* Arranged in regular rows, as the spots on the wings of an insect. *—n. Symbol* **y** *Math.* The plane Cartesian coordinate representing the distance from a specified point to the *x*-axis, measured parallel to the *y*-axis. [ME, properly ordered < Lat. *ōrdinātus,* p.part. of *ōrdināre,* to set in order < *ōrdō, ōrdin-,* order. See **ar-*.**]

or•di•na•tion (ôr′dn-ā′shən) *n.* **1.** The act of ordaining or the state of being ordained. **2.** *Eccles.* The ceremony of consecration to the ministry. **3.** An arrangement or ordering.

ordn. *abbr.* Ordnance.

ord•nance (ôrd′nəns) *n.* **1.** Military materiel, such as weapons, ammunition, combat vehicles, and equipment. **2.** The branch of an armed force that procures, maintains, and issues such materiel. **3.** Cannon; artillery. [ME *ordnaunce,* var. of *ordinaunce,* order, military provision. See ORDINANCE.]

or•do (ôr′dō) *n., pl.* **-di•nes** (-də-nēz′) or **-dos.** *Rom. Cath. Ch.* An annual calendar containing instructions for the Mass and office to be celebrated on each day of the year. [Med.Lat. *ōrdō* < Lat., order. See **ar-*.**]

or•don•nance (ôr′dn-əns, ôr′dô-näns′) *n.* The arrangement of elements in a literary or artistic work or an architectural plan. [Fr., var. of OFr. *ordenance,* an arranging. See ORDINANCE.]

Or•do•vi•cian (ôr′də-vĭsh′ən) *adj.* Of, relating to, or being the geologic time of the second period of the Paleozoic Era, characterized by the appearance of primitive fishes. See table at **geologic time.** *—n.* The Ordovician Period or its deposits. [< Lat. *Ordovicēs,* an ancient Celtic tribe of Wales < Celt. *Ordovices.* See **weik-3*.**]

or•dure (ôr′jər) *n.* **1.** Excrement; dung. **2.** Something morally offensive; filth. [ME < OFr. < *ord,* filthy < Lat. *horridus,* frightful < *horrēre,* to shudder.]

Or•dzho•ni•kid•ze (ôr′jŏn-ĭ-kĭd′zə, ər-jə-nyĭ-kyē′dzĭ). A city of SW Russia at the foot of the Caucasus Mts. NNW of Tbilisi; founded 1784. Pop. 303,000.

ore (ôr, ōr) *n.* A mineral or an aggregate of minerals from which a valuable constituent, esp. a metal, can be profitably mined or extracted. [ME < OE *ōra* and < OE *ār,* brass, copper, bronze.]

Ore. *abbr.* Oregon.

ö•re (œ′rə) *n., pl.* **öre.** See table at **currency.** [Dan. and Norw. *ore* and Swed. *öre,* all < Lat. *aureus,* gold coin < *aurum,* gold.]

o•re•ad (ôr′ē-ăd′, ōr′-) *n. Gk. Myth.* Any of a group of mountain nymphs. [Lat. *Orēas, Orēad-* < Gk. *Oreias* < *oreios,* of a mountain < *oros,* mountain.]

Ör•e•bro (œ′rə-brōō′). A city of S-central Sweden W of Stockholm. Pop. 117,569.

o•reg•a•no (ə-rĕg′ə-nō′, ô-rĕg′-) *n.* A perennial Eurasian herb *(Origanum vulgare)* of the mint family, having aromatic leaves used as a seasoning. [Sp. *orégano,* wild marjoram < Lat. *orīganum* < Gk. *origanon,* prob. of North African orig.]

Or•e•gon (ôr′ĭ-gən, -gŏn′, ŏr′-). **1.** A state of the NW U.S. in the Pacific Northwest; admitted as the 33rd state in 1859. The **Oregon Country,** a region stretching from Alaska to California and the Pacific Ocean to the Rocky Mts., was held jointly by Great Britain and the U.S. from 1818 until 1846. In 1848 the **Oregon Territory** was created, including present-day WA and ID. Cap. Salem. Pop. 2,853,733. **2.** A city of NW OH, a suburb of Toledo on Lake Erie. Pop. 18,334. **—Or′e•go′ni•an** (-gō′nē-ən) *adj. & n.*

Oregon grape *n.* Any of various evergreen shrubs of the genus *Mahonia,* esp. *M. aquifolium* of northwest North America, having compound leaves and black berries with blue bloom.

Oregon Trail. A historical overland route to the W U.S. extending from various cities on the Missouri R. to the Pacific Northwest; opened in 1842 and abandoned in the 1870's.

O•rel (ô-rĕl′, ō-rĕl′, ôr-yôl′). A city of W Russia on the Oka R. S of Moscow; founded 1564. Pop. 328,000.

O•rem (ôr′əm, ōr′-). A city of N-central UT NNW of Provo. Pop. 67,561.

O•ren•burg (ôr′ən-bûrg′, ōr′-, ə-rĭn-bŏŏrk′). Formerly (1938–57) **Chka•lov** (chə-kä′ləf, chkä′-). A city of W Russia on the Ural R.; founded as a fortress in 1735. Pop. 519,000.

O•ren•se (ô-rĕn′sĕ). A city of NW Spain E of Vigo; noted for its hot sulfur springs. Pop. 85,500.

O•res•tes (ô-rĕs′tēz) *n. Gk. Myth.* The son of Agamemnon and Clytemnestra, who with his sister Electra avenged the murder of his father by killing his mother and her lover.

O•re•sund or **Ø•re•sund** (œ′rə-sŭn′, -sŏŏnd′). A narrow strait between S Sweden and E Denmark connecting the Baltic Sea with the Kattegat.

Orff (ôrf), **Carl.** 1895–1982. German composer and educator who developed a system of music instruction for children.

or•fray (ôr′frā′) *n.* Var. of **orphrey.**

org. *abbr.* **1.** Organic. **2.a.** Organization. **b.** Organized.

or•gan (ôr′gən) *n.* **1.** *Mus.* **a.** An instrument consisting of a number of pipes that sound tones when supplied with air and a keyboard that operates a mechanism controlling the flow of air to the pipes. **b.** Any of various other instruments that resemble a pipe organ in mechanism or sound. **2.** *Biol.* A differentiated part of an organism, such as an eye or a leaf, with a specific function. **3.** An instrument or agency dedicated to the performance of specified functions. **4.** An instrument or a means of communication, esp. a periodical issued by a political party, business firm, or other group. [ME < OFr. *or-*

organ
Pipes and console

ă pat	oi boy
ā pay	ou out
âr care	ŏŏ took
ä father	ōō boot
ĕ pet	ŭ cut
ē be	ûr urge
ĭ pit	th thin
ī pie	*th* this
îr pier	hw which
ŏ pot	zh vision
ō toe	ə about, item
ô paw	

Stress marks:
′ (primary);
′ (secondary), as in **dictionary** (dĭk′shə-nĕr′ē)

José Orozco

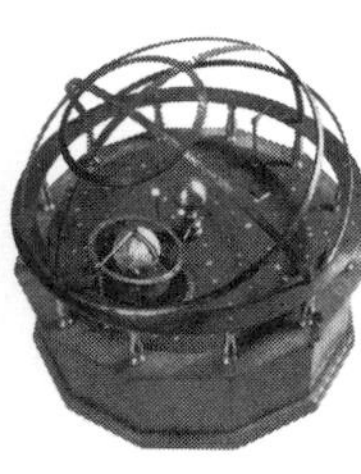
orrery
c. 1800 miniature orrery by Edward Troughton

José Ortega y Gasset

or•nate (ôr-nāt′) *adj.* **1.** Elaborately, heavily, and often excessively ornamented. **2.** Flashy, showy, or florid in style or manner; flowery. [ME < Lat. *ōrnātus*, p.part. of *ōrnāre*, to embellish. See **ar-***.] **—or•nate′ly** *adv.* **—or•nate′ness** *n.*

or•ner•y (ôr′nə-rē) *adj.* **-i•er, -i•est.** Mean-spirited and disagreeable; cantankerous. [Alteration of ORDINARY.] **—or′ner•i•ness′** *n.*

ornith. *abbr.* **1.** Ornithologic; ornithological. **2.** Ornithology.

or•nith•ic (ôr-nĭth′ĭk) *adj.* Of or relating to birds.

or•ni•thine (ôr′nə-thēn′) *n.* An amino acid, $C_5H_{12}N_2O_2$, formed by hydrolyzing arginine and important in the formation of urea. [*ornithuric acid*, an acid found in birds' urine (ORNITH(O)- + URIC ACID) + -INE[2].]

or•nith•is•chi•an (ôr′nə-thĭs′kē-ən) *n.* A dinosaur of the order Ornithischia, having a pelvic structure like that of a bird. [< NLat. *Ornithischia*, order name : ORNITH(O)- + Gk. *iskhion*, hip joint.] **—or′nith•is′chi•an** *adj.*

ornitho– or **ornith–** *pref.* Bird: *ornithosis.* [NLat. < Gk. < *ornis, ornith-*, bird. See **or-***.]

or•ni•thol•o•gy (ôr′nə-thŏl′ə-jē) *n.* The branch of zoology that deals with the study of birds. **—or′ni•tho•log′ic** (-thə-lŏj′ĭk), **or′ni•tho•log′i•cal** (-ĭ-kəl) *adj.* **—or′ni•tho•log′i•cal•ly** *adv.* **—or′ni•thol′o•gist** *n.*

or•ni•thop•ter (ôr′nə-thŏp′tər) *n.* A machine shaped like an aircraft that is held aloft and propelled by wing movements.

or•ni•tho•sis (ôr′nə-thō′sĭs) *n.* Psittacosis, esp. as contracted from birds by human beings.

oro– *pref.* Mountain: *orogeny.* [Gk. < *oros*, mountain.]

o•rog•e•ny (ô-rŏj′ə-nē) also **or•o•gen•e•sis** (ôr′ə-jĕn′ĭ-sĭs, ŏr′-) *n.* The process of mountain formation, esp. by crustal folding and faulting. **—or′o•gen′ic** (ôr′ə-jĕn′ĭk, ŏr′-) *adj.*

o•rog•ra•phy (ô-rŏg′rə-fē) *n.* The study of the physical geography of mountains. **—or′o•graph′ic** (ôr′ə-grăf′ĭk, ŏr′-), **or′o•graph′i•cal** (-ĭ-kəl) *adj.* **—or′o•graph′i•cal•ly** *adv.*

o•ro•ide (ôr′ō-īd′, ŏr′-) *n.* An alloy of copper, zinc, and tin, used in imitation gold jewelry. [Alteration of Fr. *oréide* : *or*, gold; see OR[3] + *-éide*, resembling (< Gk. *-oeidēs*, -oid).]

o•rol•o•gy (ô-rŏl′ə-jē) *n.* The study of mountains. **—o′ro•log′i•cal** (ôr′ə-lŏj′ĭ-kəl, ŏr′-) *adj.* **—o′ro•log′i•cal•ly** *adv.* **—o•rol′o•gist** *n.*

O•ro•mo (ô-rō′mō) *n., pl.* **Oromo** or **-mos. 1.** A member of a widely acculturated people of southern and central Ethiopia and northern Kenya. **2.** The Cushitic language of the Oromo.

O•ron•tes (ô-rŏn′tēz). A river, c. 402 km (250 mi), flowing through Lebanon, Syria, and S Turkey to the Mediterranean.

o•ro•phar•ynx (ôr′ō-făr′ĭngks, ŏr′-) *n., pl.* **-pha•ryn•ges** (-fə-rĭn′jēz) or **-phar•ynx•es.** The part of the pharynx between the soft palate and the epiglottis. [Lat. *ōs, ōr-*, mouth; see OS[1] + PHARYNX.] **—o′ro•pha•ryn′ge•al** (-fə-rĭn′jē-əl, -făr′ən-jē′əl) *adj.*

o•ro•tund (ôr′ə-tŭnd′, ŏr′-) *adj.* **1.** Pompous and bombastic: *orotund talk.* **2.** Full in sound; sonorous: *orotund tones.* [< alteration of Lat. *ōre rotundō*, with a round mouth : *ōre*, ablative of *ōs*, mouth; see **ōs-*** + *rotundō*, ablative of *rotundus*, round; see ROTUND.] **—o′ro•tun′di•ty** (-tŭn′dĭ-tē) *n.*

O•roz•co (ō-rôs′kō), **José Clemente.** 1883–1949. Mexican painter best known for his murals.

or•phan (ôr′fən) *n.* **1.a.** A child whose parents are dead. **b.** A child who has been deprived of parental care and has not been adopted. **2.** A young animal without a mother. **3.** One that lacks support, supervision, or care. —*adj.* **1.** Deprived of parents. **2.** Intended for orphans: *an orphan home.* **3.** Lacking support or supervision; abandoned. —*tr.v.* **-phaned, -phan•ing, -phans.** To deprive (a child) of one parent or both parents. [ME < LLat. *orphanus* < Gk. *orphanos*, orphaned. See **orbh-***.] **—or′phan•hood′** *n.*

or•phan•age (ôr′fə-nĭj) *n.* **1.** A public institution for the care and protection of children without parents. **2.** The condition of being a child without parents.

Or•phe•us (ôr′fē-əs, -fyo͞os′) *n. Gk. Myth.* A legendary Thracian poet and musician who almost succeeded in rescuing his wife Eurydice from Hades. [Gk.] **—Or•phe′an** (ôr-fē′ən, ôr′fē-ən) *adj.*

Or•phic (ôr′fĭk) *adj.* **1.** *Gk. Myth.* Of or ascribed to Orpheus: *the Orphic poems.* **2.** Of, relating to, or characteristic of the dogmas, mysteries, and philosophies in the poems ascribed to Orpheus. **3.** Capable of casting a charm or spell; entrancing. **4.** Often **orphic.** Mystic or occult. [Gk. *Orphikos* < *Orpheus*, Orpheus.] **—Or′phi•cal•ly** *adv.*

Or•phism (ôr′fĭz′əm) *n.* **1.** An ancient Greek mystery religion, a synthesis of pre-Hellenic beliefs, the Thracian cult of Zagreus, the Eleusinian mysteries, and Pythagoreanism. **2.** Often **orphism.** A movement in early 20th-century painting, derived from cubism but marked by a lyrical style and bold color. [Fr. *orphisme* < *Orphée*, Orpheus < Gk. *Orpheus*.] **—Or′phist** *n.*

or•phrey (ôr′frē) also **or•fray** (-frā′) *n., pl.* **-phreys** also **-frays. 1.** A band of elaborate embroidery on certain ecclesiastical vestments. **2.** Elaborate embroidery, esp. when made of gold. [ME *orfrey*, alteration of *orfreis* < OFr. < Med.Lat. *aurifrigium* : Lat. *aurum*, gold + Lat. *Phrygius*, Phrygian.]

or•pi•ment (ôr′pə-mənt) *n.* Arsenic trisulfide, As_2S_3, a yellow mineral used as a pigment. [ME < OFr. < Lat. *auripigmentum* : *aurum*, gold + *pigmentum*, pigment; see PIGMENT.]

or•pine (ôr′pĭn) *n.* Any of several succulent plants of the genus *Sedum*, esp. the Eurasian species *S. telephium* having clusters of reddish-purple flowers. [ME *orpin* < OFr. < *orpiment*, orpiment. See ORPIMENT.]

Or•ping•ton (ôr′pĭng-tən) *n.* Any of a breed of large white-skinned fowls with a single comb and unfeathered legs, originally bred in England. [After *Orpington*, SE England.]

or•re•ry (ôr′ə-rē, ŏr′-) *n., pl.* **-ries.** A mechanical model of the solar system. [After Charles Boyle, 4th Earl of *Orrery* (1676–1731), for whom one was made.]

or•ris (ôr′ĭs, ŏr′-) *n.* **1.** Any of several species of iris having a fragrant rootstock, esp. a variety of the hybrid *Iris germanica.* **2.** The fragrant rootstock of the orris, used in perfumes and cosmetics. [Prob. alteration of ME *yreos* < Med.Lat., alteration of Lat. *īris.* See IRIS.]

or•ris•root (ôr′ĭs-ro͞ot′, -ro͝ot′, ŏr′-) *n.* See **orris** 2.

Orsk (ôrsk). A city of W Russia on the Ural R. ESE of Orenburg. Pop. 266,000.

ort (ôrt) *n.* **1.** A small scrap or leaving of food after a meal is completed. Often used in the plural. **2.** A scrap; a bit. [ME *orte*, food left by animals, prob. < MDu. : *oor*, out; see **ud-*** + *eten*, to eat; see **ed-***.]

Or•te•ga (ôr-tā′gə, -tĕ′gä), **Daniel.** b. 1945. Nicaraguan revolutionary leader who served as president (1984–90).

Or•te•ga y Gas•set (ôr-tā′gə ē gä-sĕt′), **José.** 1883–1955. Spanish philosopher whose works include *The Revolt of the Masses* (1929).

orth. *abbr.* **1.** Orthopedic. **2.** Orthopedics.

or•thi•con (ôr′thĭ-kŏn′) *n.* A television camera pickup tube, more sensitive than the iconoscope, that scans a photoactive mosaic with a low-velocity electron beam. [ORTH(O)- + ICON(OSCOPE).]

or•tho (ôr′thō) *adj.* Orthochromatic. [< ORTHO-.]

ortho– or **orth–** *pref.* **1.** Straight; upright; vertical: *orthotropous.* **2.** Perpendicular: *orthorhombic.* **3.** Correct; correction: *orthopsychiatry.* **4.** The most fully hydrated form of an acid: *orthoboric acid.* **5.** Diatomic molecules in which the nuclei have the same spin direction: *orthohydrogen.* **6.** Of or relating to an isomer of a benzene ring with chemical groups attached to two adjacent carbon atoms: ortho-*dibromobenzene.* [ME < OFr. < Lat. < Gk. < *orthos*, straight, correct, right.]

or•tho•cen•ter (ôr′thō-sĕn′tər) *n.* The point of intersection of the three altitudes of a triangle.

or•tho•chro•mat•ic (ôr′thō-krō-măt′ĭk) *adj.* **1.** Of, having, or accurately reproducing the colors of nature, esp. in photography. **2.** In photography, being sensitive to all colors except red. **—or′tho•chro′ma•tism** (-krō′mə-tĭz′əm) *n.*

or•tho•clase (ôr′thə-klās′, -klāz′) *n.* A monoclinic variety of feldspar, potassium aluminum silicate, $KAlSi_3O_8$, commonly found in many igneous rocks. [Gk. *ortho-*, ortho- + Gk. *klasis*, a breaking (< *klan*, to break).]

or•tho•don•tia (ôr′thə-dŏn′shə) or **or•tho•don•ture** (-dŏn′chər) *n.* Orthodontics.

or•tho•don•tics (ôr′thə-dŏn′tĭks) *n.* (*used with a sing. v.*) The dental specialty and practice of preventing and correcting irregularities of the teeth, as with braces. **—or′tho•don′tic** *adj.* **—or′tho•don′ti•cal•ly** *adv.* **—or′tho•don′tist** *n.*

or•tho•dox (ôr′thə-dŏks′) *adj.* **1.** Adhering to the accepted or traditional and established faith, esp. in religion. **2.** Adhering to the Christian faith as expressed in the early Christian ecumenical creeds. **3. Orthodox. a.** Of or relating to any of the churches or rites of the Eastern Orthodox Church. **b.** Of or relating to Orthodox Judaism. **4.** Adhering to what is commonly accepted, customary, or traditional. —*n.* **1.** One that is orthodox. **2. Orthodox.** A member of an Eastern Orthodox church. [ME *orthodoxe* < OFr. < LLat. *orthodoxus* < LGk. *orthodoxos* : Gk. *ortho-*, ortho- + Gk. *doxa*, opinion (< *dokein*, to think; see **dek-***).] **—or′tho•dox′ly** *adv.*

Orthodox Church *n.* The Eastern Orthodox Church.

Orthodox Judaism *n.* The branch of Judaism that is governed by adherence to the Torah as interpreted in the Talmud.

orthodox sleep *n.* Sleep characterized by a slow alpha rhythm and the absence of REM.

or•tho•dox•y (ôr′thə-dŏk′sē) *n., pl.* **-ies. 1.** The quality or state of being orthodox. **2.** Orthodox practice, custom, or belief. **3. Orthodoxy. a.** The beliefs and practices of the Eastern Orthodox Church. **b.** Orthodox Judaism.

or•tho•e•py (ôr-thō′ə-pē, ôr′thō-ĕp′ē) *n. Ling.* **1.** The study of the pronunciation of words. **2.** The customary pronunciation of words. [Gk. *orthoepeia*, correctness of diction : *ortho-*, ortho- + *epos, epe-*, word; see **wek^w-***.] **—or′tho•ep′ic** (-ĕp′ĭk), **or′tho•ep′i•cal** *adj.* **—or•tho′e•pist** *n.*

or•tho•gen•e•sis (ôr′thō-jĕn′ĭ-sĭs) *n.* **1.** *Biol.* The theory that the evolution of a species is influenced by internal factors and not by external forces of natural selection. **2.** The theory that all cultures pass through sequential periods in the same order. **—or′tho•ge•net′ic** (-jə-nĕt′ĭk) *adj.* **—or′tho•ge•net′i•cal•ly** *adv.*

or•thog•o•nal (ôr-thŏg′ə-nəl) *adj. Math.* Relating to or composed of right angles. [< Gk. *orthogōnios* : *ortho-*, ortho- +

gōnia, angle; see **genu-**[1]***.**] —**or·thog′o·nal·ly** *adv.*

orthogonal projection *n.* The two-dimensional graphic representation of an object by the perpendicular intersections of lines drawn from points on the object to a plane of projection.

or·tho·graph·ic (ôr′thə-grăf′ĭk) also **or·tho·graph·i·cal** (-ĭ-kəl) *adj.* **1.** Of or relating to orthography. **2.** Spelled correctly. **3.** *Math.* Having perpendicular lines.

orthographic projection *n.* See **orthogonal projection.**

or·thog·ra·phy (ôr-thŏg′rə-fē) *n., pl.* **-phies. 1.** The art or study of standard spelling. **2.** The aspect of language study concerned with letters and spelling. **3.** A method of representing the sounds of language or a language by letters and diacritics; spelling. —**or·thog′ra·pher, or·thog′ra·phist** *n.*

or·tho·mo·lec·u·lar (ôr′thō-mə-lĕk′yə-lər) *adj.* Of, relating to, or being a theory holding that mental diseases or abnormalities can be cured by restoring proper levels of chemical substances, such as vitamins and minerals, in the body.

or·tho·pe·dics also **or·tho·pae·dics** (ôr′thə-pē′dĭks) *n.* *(used with a sing. v.)* The branch of medicine that treats injuries or disorders of the skeletal system and associated muscles, joints, and ligaments. [< *orthopedic* < Fr. *orthopédique* < *orthopédie*, orthopedic surgery : Gk. *ortho-*, ortho- + Gk. *paideia*, child-rearing (< *pais, paid-*, child; see **pau-***).] —**or′tho·pe′dic** *adj.* —**or′tho·pe′di·cal·ly** *adv.* —**or′tho·pe′dist** *n.*

or·tho·psy·chi·a·try (ôr′thō-sĭ-kī′ə-trē, -sī-) *n.* The psychiatric study, treatment, and prevention of emotional and behavioral problems, esp. of those that arise during early development. —**or′tho·psy′chi·at′ric** (-sī′kē-ăt′rĭk), **or′tho·psy′chi·at′ri·cal** (-rĭ-kəl) *adj.* —**or′tho·psy·chi′a·trist** *n.*

or·thop·ter·an (ôr-thŏp′tər-ən) also **or·thop·ter·on** (-tə-rŏn′, -tər-ən) *n.* An insect of the order Orthoptera, characterized by folded membranous hind wings covered by narrow leathery forewings and including the locusts and cockroaches. [< NLat. *Orthoptera*, order name : Gk. *ortho-*, ortho- + Gk. *ptera*, neut. pl. of *pteron*, wing; see **pet-***.] —**or·thop′ter·an, or·thop′ter·ous, or·thop′ter·al** *adj.*

or·tho·rhom·bic (ôr′thō-rŏm′bĭk) *adj.* Of or relating to a crystalline structure of three mutually perpendicular axes of different length.

or·tho·scop·ic (ôr′thə-skŏp′ĭk) *adj.* **1.** Having normal vision; free from visual distortion. **2.** Giving an undistorted image. Used of an optical instrument.

or·tho·stat·ic (ôr′thə-stăt′ĭk) *adj.* Relating to or caused by standing upright: *orthostatic hypotension.* [ORTHO- + Gk. *statos*, standing; see STATIC + -IC.]

or·thot·ics (ôr-thŏt′ĭks) *n.* *(used with a sing. v.)* The science that deals with the use of specialized mechanical devices to support or supplement weakened or abnormal joints or limbs. [< NLat. *orthōsis, orthōt-*, artificial support, brace < Gk., a straightening < *orthoun*, to straighten < *orthos*, straight.] —**or·thot′ic** *adj. & n.* —**or·thot′ist** (ôr-thŏt′ĭst, ôr′thə-tĭst) *n.*

or·tho·trop·ic (ôr′thə-trŏp′ĭk, -trō′pĭk) *adj.* **1.** Tending to grow or form along a vertical axis. **2.** Of or relating to a bridge deck consisting of steel plates supported by ribs underneath. —**or′tho·trop′i·cal·ly** *adv.* —**or·thot′ro·pism** (ôr-thŏt′rə-pĭz′əm) *n.*

or·thot·ro·pous (ôr-thŏt′rə-pəs) *adj. Bot.* Growing straight, so that the micropyle is opposite the stalk. Used of an ovule.

Ort·les (ôrt′lās) also **Ort·ler** (-lər). A range of the Alps in N Italy rising to 3,901.6 m (12,792 ft) at **Ortles** peak.

or·to·lan (ôr′tl-ən) *n.* **1.** A small brownish Old World bunting *(Emberiza hortulana)*, eaten as a delicacy. **2.** Any of several New World birds, such as the bobolink and the sora. [Fr. < Prov., gardener, ortolan < Lat. *hortulānus* < *hortulus*, dim. of *hortus*, garden. See **gher-**[1]***.**]

O·ru·ro (ô-rōō′rô). A city of W Bolivia SE of La Paz. Pop. 178,393.

ORV *abbr.* Off-road vehicle.

Or·well (ôr′wĕl′, -wəl), **George.** Eric Arthur Blair. 1903–50. British writer whose works include *Animal Farm* (1945) and *1984* (1949). —**Or·well′i·an** *adj.*

-ory *suff.* **1.** Of, relating to, or characterized by: *advisory.* **2.** A place or thing used for or connected with: *crematory.* [ME *-orie* < ONFr. and AN < Lat. *-ōrius*, adj. suff., and *-ōrium*, n. suff.]

o·ryx (ôr′ĭks, ōr′-, ŏr′-) *n., pl.* **oryx** or **o·ryx·es.** Any of several African antelopes of the genus *Oryx*, including the gemsbok, having long straight or slightly curved horns and a hump above the shoulders. [Lat. < Gk. *orux*, pickax, gazelle (< its sharp horns), perh. < *orussein*, to dig.]

or·zo (ôr′zō) *n.* A kind of pasta shaped like pearls of barley. [Ital., barley, orzo < Lat. *hordeum.*]

os[1] (ŏs) *n., pl.* **o·ra** (ôr′ə, ōr′ə). A mouth or an opening. [Lat. *ōs*, mouth. See **ōs-***.]

os[2] (ŏs) *n., pl.* **os·sa** (ŏs′ə). A bone. [Lat., bone. See **ost-***.]

os[3] (ōs) *n., pl.* **os·ar** (ō′sär′). See **esker.** [Swed. *ås*, ridge < ON *āss.*]

Os The symbol for the element **osmium.**

o.s. *abbr.* **1.** *Lat.* Oculus sinister (left eye). **2.** Old series. **3.** Or **o/s** Out of stock.

O.S. *abbr.* **1.** Or **O/S** Old Style. **2.** Ordinary seaman.

O·sage (ō′sāj′, ō-sāj′) *n., pl.* **Osage** or **O·sag·es. 1.** A member of a Native American people formerly inhabiting western Missouri and southeast Kansas, with a present-day population in Oklahoma. **2.** The Siouan language of the Osage. [Fr. < Osage *wazházhe*, tribal name.] —**O′sage′** *adj.*

Osage orange *n.* A dioecious spiny tree *(Maclura pomifera)* native to Arkansas and Texas and having pulpy, inedible, orangelike multiple fruit.

Osage River. A river of central MO flowing c. 579 km (360 mi) through the Lake of the Ozarks to the Missouri R.

O·sa·ka (ō-sä′kə, ô′sä-kä′). A city of S Honshu, Japan, on **Osaka Bay**, an inlet of the Pacific. Pop. 2,636,260.

O·sas·co (ōō-säs′kōō). A city of SE Brazil, a suburb of São Paulo. Pop. 474,543.

Os·born (ŏz′bərn, -bôrn′), **Henry Fairfield.** 1857–1935. Amer. paleontologist who was president (1908–35) of the American Museum of Natural History in New York City.

Os·borne (ŏz′bərn, -bôrn′, -bōrn′), **John James.** b. 1929. British playwright noted for *Look Back in Anger* (1956).

Osborne, Thomas Mott. 1859–1926. Amer. prison reformer who was warden of Sing Sing state prison (1914–16).

Os·can (ŏs′kən) *n.* **1.** A member of an ancient people of Campania. **2.** The Italic language of the Oscans. —**Os′can** *adj.*

Os·car (ŏs′kər) *n.* Any of the golden statuettes awarded annually by the Academy of Motion Picture Arts and Sciences for achievement in movies.

Oscar II also **Os·kar II** (ôs′kär). 1829–1907. King of Sweden from 1872 to 1907 and of Norway from 1872 to 1905.

Os·ce·o·la (ŏs′ē-ō′lə, ō′sē-). 1804?–38. Seminole leader who resisted the removal of his people from Florida.

os·cil·late (ŏs′ə-lāt′) *intr.v.* **-lat·ed, -lat·ing, -lates. 1.** To swing back and forth with a steady uninterrupted rhythm. **2.** To waver, as between conflicting opinions or courses of action; vacillate. **3.** *Phys.* To vary between alternate extremes, usu. within a definable period of time. [Lat. *ōscillāre, ōscillāt-* < *ōscillum*, swing, prob. < *ōscillum*, small mask of Bacchus, dim. of *ōs*, mouth. See **ōs-***.] —**os′cil·la′tor** *n.* —**os′cil·la·to′ry** (-lə-tôr′ē, -tōr′ē) *adj.*

os·cil·la·tion (ŏs′ə-lā′shən) *n.* **1.** The act or state of oscillating. **2.** A single oscillatory cycle. —**os′cil·la′tion·al** *adj.*

os·cil·lo·gram (ə-sĭl′ə-grăm′) *n.* **1.** The graph traced by an oscillograph. **2.** An instantaneous oscilloscope trace or photograph. [OSCILLO(GRAPH) + -GRAM.]

os·cil·lo·graph (ə-sĭl′ə-grăf′) *n.* A device that records oscillations, as of an electric current and voltage. [OSCILL(ATION) + -GRAPH.] —**os·cil′lo·graph′ic** *adj.* —**os·cil′lo·graph′i·cal·ly** *adv.* —**os′cil·log′ra·phy** (ŏs′ə-lŏg′rə-fē) *n.*

os·cil·lo·scope (ə-sĭl′ə-skōp′) *n.* An electronic instrument that produces an instantaneous trace on the screen of a cathode-ray tube corresponding to oscillations of voltage and current. —**os·cil′lo·scop′ic** (-skŏp′ĭk) *adj.*

os·cine (ŏs′īn′) *adj.* Of, relating to, or belonging to the Oscines, a suborder of passerine birds that includes most songbirds. [< NLat. *Oscinēs*, suborder name < Lat. *oscinēs*, pl. of *oscen*, bird used in augury. See **kan-***.] —**os′cine′** *n.*

os·ci·tance (ŏs′ĭ-təns) *n.* Oscitancy.

os·ci·tan·cy (ŏs′ĭ-tən-sē) *n., pl.* **-cies. 1.** The act of yawning. **2.** The state of being drowsy or inattentive; dullness. [< *oscitant*, yawning < Lat. *ōscitāns, ōscitant-*, pr.part. of *ōscitāre*, to yawn : *ōs*, mouth; see **ōs-*** + *citāre*, to move; see **kei-**[2]***.**]

Os·co-Um·bri·an (ŏs′kō-ŭm′brē-ən) *n.* A subdivision of the Italic languages that consists of Oscan and Umbrian.

os·cu·lant (ŏs′kyə-lənt) *adj.* **1.** *Biol.* Intermediate in characteristics between two similar or related taxonomic groups. **2.** Closely adhering or joined; embracing. [Lat. *ōsculāns, ōsculant-*, pr.part. of *ōsculārī*, to kiss. See OSCULATE.]

os·cu·late (ŏs′kyə-lāt′) *v.* **-lat·ed, -lat·ing, -lates.** —*tr.* **1.** To kiss. **2.** *Math.* To have three or more points coincident with. —*intr.* To come together; contact. [Lat. *ōsculārī, ōsculāt-* < *ōsculum*, kiss, dim. of *ōs*, mouth. See **ōs-***.]

os·cu·la·tion (ŏs′kyə-lā′shən) *n.* **1.a.** The act of kissing. **b.** A kiss. **2.** *Math.* A contact, as between two curves or surfaces, at three or more common points.

os·cu·lum (ŏs′kyə-ləm) also **os·cule** (-kyōōl′) *n., pl.* **-cu·la** (-kyə-lə) also **-cules.** The mouthlike opening in a sponge, used to expel water. [Lat. *ōsculum*, dim. of *ōs*, mouth. See **ōs-***.]

-ose[1] *suff.* Possessing; having the characteristics of; full of: *cymose.* [ME, var. of *-ous* < Lat. *-ōsus.*]

-ose[2] *suff.* **1.** Carbohydrate: *fructose.* **2.** Product of protein hydrolysis: *proteose.* [Fr. < *glucose*, glucose. See GLUCOSE.]

OSHA (ō′shə) *n.* Occupational Safety and Health Administration.

Osh·a·wa (ŏsh′ə-wä′, -wə). A city of SE Ontario, Canada, on Lake Ontario ENE of Toronto. Pop. 117,519.

Osh·kosh (ŏsh′kŏsh). A city of E WI on Lake Winnebago NNW of Fond du Lac. Pop. 55,006.

O·shog·bo (ō-shŏg′bō). A city of SW Nigeria NE of Ibadan. Pop. 336,000.

o·sier (ō′zhər) *n.* **1.a.** Any of several willows having long rodlike twigs used in basketry, esp. the Eurasian *Salix viminalis* and *S. purpurea.* **b.** A twig of one of these trees. **2.** Any of

George Orwell

ă pat	oi boy
ā pay	ou out
âr care	ŏŏ took
ä father	ōō boot
ĕ pet	ŭ cut
ē be	ûr urge
ĭ pit	th thin
ī pie	*th* this
îr pier	hw which
ŏ pot	zh vision
ō toe	ə about, item
ô paw	

Stress marks:
′ (primary);
′ (secondary), as in **dictionary** (dĭk′shə-nĕr′ē)

various similar or related trees. [ME < OE *oser* and OFr. *osier*, both < Med.Lat. *osera, osiera*.]

O•si•jek (ô′sē-ĕk, -yĕk′). A city of E Croatia on the Drava R. ESE of Zagreb; under Turkish rule from 1526 to 1687. Pop. 103,600.

O•si•ris (ō-sī′rĭs) *n. Myth.* The ancient Egyptian god whose annual death and resurrection personified the self-renewing vitality and fertility of nature.

Osiris

–osis *suff.* **1.** Condition; process; action: *osmosis.* **2.** Diseased or abnormal condition: *neurosis.* **3.** Increase; formation: *leukocytosis.* [Lat. *-ōsis* < Gk., n. suff.]

Os•kar II (ôs′kär). See **Oscar II.**

Os•lo (ŏz′lō, ŏs′-). Formerly (1624–1925) **Chris•ti•a•ni•a** (krĭs′tē-ăn′ē-ə, -än′-, krĭs′chē-). The cap. of Norway, in the SE part at the head of the **Oslo Fjord**, a deep inlet of the Skagerrak; founded c. 1050 and rebuilt and renamed in 1624 by Christian IV (1577–1648). Pop. 448,747.

Os•man I (ŏz′mən, ôs′-, ŏs-män′) also **Oth•man I** (ŏth′mən, o͞oth-män′). 1258–1326? Founder of the Ottoman dynasty that controlled most of NW Asia Minor.

Os•man•li (ŏz-măn′lē, ŏs-) *n., pl.* **-lis. 1.** An Ottoman Turk. **2.** Ottoman Turkish. —*adj.* Ottoman. [Turk. *osmānli* : OSMAN (I) + *-li*, adj. suff.]

os•mat•ic (ŏz-măt′ĭk) *adj.* Having or characterized by a well-developed sense of smell. [< Gk. *osmē*, smell.]

os•mic[1] (ŏz′mĭk) *adj.* Of, relating to, or containing osmium, esp. in a compound with valence 4 or a valence higher than that in a comparable osmous compound. [OSM(IUM) + –IC.]

os•mic[2] (ŏz′mĭk) *adj.* Of or relating to odors or the sense of smell. [Gk. *osmē*, smell + –IC.] —**os′mi•cal•ly** *adv.*

osmic acid *n.* See **osmium tetroxide.**

os•mics (ŏz′mĭks) *n.* (*used with a sing. v.*) The science that deals with smells and the olfactory sense.

os•mi•rid•i•um (ŏz′mə-rĭd′ē-əm) *n.* A mineral that is a natural alloy of osmium and iridium with small inclusions of platinum, rhodium, and other metals. [OSM(IUM) + IRIDIUM.]

os•mi•um (ŏz′mē-əm) *n. Symbol* **Os** A hard metallic element, found in small amounts in osmiridium and platinum ores and used as a platinum hardener and in making pen points and instrument pivots. Atomic number 76; atomic weight 190.2; melting point 3,000°C; boiling point 5,000°C; specific gravity 22.57; valence 2, 3, 4, 8. See table at **element.** [< Gk. *osmē*, smell (< the odor of osmium tetroxide).]

osmium tetroxide *n.* A poisonous compound, OsO_4, with a pungent smell, used as a stain and a tissue fixative.

os•mom•e•ter (ŏz-mŏm′ĭ-tər, ŏs-) *n.* A device for measuring osmotic pressure. [OSMO(SIS) + –METER.] —**os′mo•met′ric** (ŏz′mə-mĕt′rĭk, ŏs′-) *adj.* —**os•mom′e•try** *n.*

os•mo•reg•u•la•tion (ŏz′mə-rĕg′yə-lā′shən, ŏs′-) *n. Physiol.* Maintenance of an optimal constant osmotic pressure in the body of a living organism. [OSMO(SIS) + REGULATION.]

os•mose (ŏz′mōs′, ŏs′-) *intr. & tr.v.* **-mosed, -mos•ing, -mos•es.** To diffuse or cause to diffuse by osmosis.

osprey
Pandion haliaetus

os•mo•sis (ŏz-mō′sĭs, ŏs-) *n., pl.* **-ses** (-sēz). **1.a.** Diffusion of fluid through a semipermeable membrane until there is an equal concentration of fluid on both sides of the membrane. **b.** The tendency of fluids to diffuse in such a manner. **2.** A gradual, often unconscious process of absorption or learning. [< *osmose* < earlier *endosmose* < Fr. : Gk. *endo-*, endo- + Gk. *ōsmos*, thrust, push (< *ōthein*, to push).] —**os•mot′ic** (-mŏt′ĭk) *adj.* —**os•mot′i•cal•ly** *adv.*

osmotic pressure *n.* The pressure exerted by the flow of water through a semipermeable membrane separating two solutions with different concentrations of solute.

osmotic shock *n.* The rupture of bacterial or other cells in a solution following a sudden reduction in osmotic pressure.

os•mous (ŏz′məs) also **os•mi•ous** (-mē-əs) *adj.* Of, relating to, or containing osmium in a compound with a valence lower than that in a comparable osmic compound.

os•mun•da (ŏz-mŭn′də) also **os•mund** (ŏz′mənd) *n.* Any of several ferns of the genus *Osmunda*, having bipinnately compound fronds and edible crosiers. [NLat. *Osmunda*, genus name < ME *osmunde*, a fern < OFr. *osmonde*.]

Os•na•brück (ŏz′nə-bro͝ok′, ôs′nä-brük′). A city of NW Germany NE of Münster. Pop. 153,587.

os•na•burg (ŏz′nə-bûrg′) *n.* A heavy coarse cotton fabric, used for grain sacks, upholstery, and draperies. [After *Osnaburg* (Osnabrück).]

os•prey (ŏs′prē, -prā) *n., pl.* **-preys. 1.** A fish-eating hawk (*Pandion haliaetus*) having plumage that is dark on the back and white below. **2.** A plume formerly used to trim women's hats. [ME *osprai* < AN *ospreit* < Med.Lat. *avis prede*, bird of prey : Lat. *avis*, bird; see **awi-*** + Lat. *praedae*, genitive of *praeda*, booty, prey; see **ghend-*.**]

OSS *abbr.* Office of Strategic Services.

os•sa (ŏs′ə) *n.* Pl. of **os[2].**

Os•sa (ŏs′ə), **Mount.** A peak, 1,979.1 m (6,489 ft), of the Olympus Mts. in N Greece.

os•sa•ture (ŏs′ə-cho͝or′, -chər) *n.* A framework or skeleton, as for a building. [Fr. < Lat. *os, oss-*, bone. See os[2].]

os•se•in (ŏs′ē-ĭn) *n.* The collagen component of bone. [OSSE(OUS) + –IN.]

os•se•ous (ŏs′ē-əs) *adj.* Composed of, containing, or resembling bone; bony. [< Lat. *osseus* < *os, oss-*, bone. See **ost-*.**] —**os′se•ous•ly** *adv.*

Os•set (ŏs′ĭt, ŏ-sĕt′) also **Os•sete** (ŏs′ēt′, ŏ-sēt′) *n.* A member of a people of mixed Iranian and Caucasian origin inhabiting Ossetia.

Os•se•tia (ō-sē′shə, ə-syĕ′tĭ-yə). A region of the central Caucasus in Georgia and SW Russia; annexed by Russia between 1801 and 1806. —**Os•se′tian** *adj. & n.*

Os•set•ic (ŏ-sĕt′ĭk) *adj.* Of or relating to Ossetia, the Ossets, or their language or culture. —*n.* Their Iranian language.

os•si•a (ō-sē′ə) *conj. Mus.* Or else. Used to designate an alternate section or passage. [Ital. < *o sia*, or let it be : *o*, or (< Lat. *aut*) + *sia*, third pers. sing. pr. subjunctive of *essere*, to be (< Lat. *esse*; see **es-***).]

Os•sian (ŏsh′ən, ŏs′ē-ən) *n.* A legendary Gaelic hero and bard of the third century A.D.

os•si•cle (ŏs′ĭ-kəl) *n.* A small bone, esp. of the middle ear. [Lat. *ossiculum*, dim. of *os*, bone. See **ost-*.**] —**os•sic′u•lar** (ŏ-sĭk′yə-lər), **os•sic′u•late** (-lĭt) *adj.*

Os•si•etz•ky (ŏs′ē-ĕt′skē ô′sē-), **Carl von.** 1889–1938. German journalist who won the 1935 Nobel Peace Prize.

os•si•fi•ca•tion (ŏs′ə-fĭ-kā′shən) *n.* **1.** The natural process of bone formation. **2.a.** The hardening or calcification of soft tissue into a bonelike material. **b.** A mass or deposit of such material. **3.a.** The process of becoming set in a rigid conventionalism, as of behavior. **b.** Rigid unimaginative convention.

os•si•frage (ŏs′ə-frĭj, -frāj′) *n.* **1.** See **lammergeier. 2.** *Archaic.* An osprey. [Lat. *ossifraga* < *ossifragus*, bone-breaking : *os, oss-*, bone; see **ost-*** + *frangere*, to break; see **bhreg-*.**]

os•si•fy (ŏs′ə-fī′) *v.* **-fied, -fy•ing, -fies.** —*intr.* **1.** To change into bone; become bony. **2.** To become set in a rigid conventionalism. —*tr.* **1.** To convert (a membrane or cartilage, for example) into bone. **2.** To mold into a rigidly conventional pattern. [Lat. *os, oss-*, bone; see **ost-*** + –FY.] —**os•sif′ic** (ŏ-sĭf′ĭk) *adj.*

Os•si•ning (ŏs′ə-nĭng′). A village of SE NY on the Hudson R. N of White Plains; site of Sing Sing state prison (estab. 1824). Pop. 22,582.

os•so bu•co (ō′sō bo͞o′kō, ŏs′sō) *n., pl.* **osso bu•cos.** An Italian dish consisting of braised veal shanks in white wine. [Ital. *ossobuco*, marrowbone : *osso*, bone + *buco*, hole.]

os•su•ar•y (ŏsh′o͞o-ĕr′ē, ŏs′yo͞o-) *n., pl.* **-ies.** A container or receptacle for the bones of the dead. [LLat. *ossuārium* < neut. of Lat. *ossuārius*, of bones < *os, oss-*, bone. See **ost-*.**]

os•te•al (ŏs′tē-əl) *adj.* **1.** Bony; osseous. **2.** Relating to bone or to the skeleton.

os•te•i•tis (ŏs′tē-ī′tĭs) *n.* Inflammation of bone or bony tissue.

Ost•end (ŏs-tĕnd′, ŏs′tĕnd′) also **Oost•en•de** (ō-stĕn′də). A city of NW Belgium WSW of Bruges. Pop. 69,129.

os•ten•si•ble (ŏ-stĕn′sə-bəl) *adj.* Represented or appearing as such; professed. [Fr. < Med.Lat. *ostēnsibilis* < Lat. *ostēnsus*, p.part. of *ostendere*, to show : *ob-*, ob- + *tendere*, to stretch; see **ten-*.**] —**os•ten′si•bly** *adv.*

os•ten•sive (ŏ-stĕn′sĭv) *adj.* Seeming or professed; ostensible. —**os•ten′sive•ly** *adv.*

os•ten•so•ri•um (ŏs′tən-sôr′ē-əm, -sōr′-) also **os•ten•so•ry** (ŏ-stĕn′sə-rē) *n., pl.* **-so•ri•a** (-sôr′ē-ə, -sōr′-) also **-so•ries.** *Rom. Cath. Ch.* See **monstrance.** [Med.Lat. *ostēnsōrium* < Lat. *ostēnsus*, p.part. of *ostendere*, to show. See OSTENSIBLE.]

os•ten•ta•tion (ŏs′tĕn-tā′shən, -tən-) *n.* **1.** Pretentious display meant to impress others; boastful showiness. **2.** *Archaic.* The act or an instance of showing; an exhibition. [ME *ostentacioun* < OFr. *ostentacion* < Lat. *ostentātiō, ostentātiōn-* < *ostentāre*, freq. of *ostendere*, to show. See OSTENSIBLE.]

os•ten•ta•tious (ŏs′tĕn-tā′shəs, -tən-) *adj.* Characterized by or given to ostentation; pretentious. See Syns at **showy.** —**os′ten•ta′tious•ly** *adv.*

osteo– or **oste–** *pref.* Bone: *osteoarthritis.* [Gk. < *osteon*, bone. See **ost-*.**]

os•te•o•ar•thri•tis (ŏs′tē-ō-är-thrī′tĭs) *n.* A form of arthritis, occurring mainly in older persons, that is characterized by chronic degeneration of the cartilage of the joints. —**os′te•o•ar•thrit′ic** (-thrĭt′ĭk) *adj.*

os•te•o•blast (ŏs′tē-ə-blăst′) *n.* A cell from which bone develops; a bone-forming cell. —**os′te•o•blas′tic** *adj.*

os•te•oc•la•sis (ŏs′tē-ŏk′lə-sĭs) *n., pl.* **-ses** (-sēz′). **1.** The process of dissolution and resorption of bony tissue. **2.** Surgical fracture of a bone, performed to correct a deformity. [OSTEO– + Gk. *klasis*, breakage (< *klan*, to break).]

os•te•o•clast (ŏs′tē-ə-klăst′) *n.* **1.** A large multinucleate cell found in growing bone that resorbs bony tissue, as in the formation of cavities. **2.** An instrument used in surgical osteoclasis. [OSTEO– + Med.Lat. *-clastēs*, breaker (< LGk. *-klastēs* < Gk. *klastos*, broken < *klan*, to break).]

os•te•o•cyte (ŏs′tē-ə-sīt′) *n.* A branched cell embedded in the matrix of bone tissue.

os•te•o•gen•e•sis (ŏs′tē-ə-jĕn′ĭ-sĭs) *n., pl.* **-ses** (-sēz′). The formation and development of bony tissue. —**os′te•o•ge•net′ic** (-ō-jə-nĕt′ĭk), **os′te•og′e•nous** (-ŏj′ə-nəs) *adj.*

os•te•o•gen•ic (ŏs′tē-ə-jĕn′ĭk) *adj.* **1.** Derived from or composed of bone-forming tissue. **2.** Of osteogenesis.

os•te•oid (ŏs′tē-oid′) *adj.* Resembling bone. —*n.* The bone matrix, esp. before calcification.

os•te•ol•o•gy (ŏs′tē-ŏl′ə-jē) *n., pl.* **-gies. 1.** The anatomical study of bones. **2.** The bone structure or system of an animal. —**os′te•o•log′i•cal** (-ə-lŏj′ĭ-kəl) *adj.* —**os′te•o•log′i•cal•ly** *adv.* —**os′te•ol′o•gist** *n.*

os•te•o•ma (ŏs′tē-ō′mə) *n., pl.* **-mas** or **-ma•ta** (-mə-tə). A benign tumor of bony tissue, often developing on the skull.

os•te•o•ma•la•cia (ŏs′tē-ō-mə-lā′shə, -shē-ə) *n.* A disease occurring mostly in adult women as a result of a deficiency in vitamin D or calcium and characterized by a softening of the bones, pain, and weakness. [NLat. : OSTEO- + Gk. *malakia,* softness (< *malakos,* soft; see **mel-**[1]*).]

os•te•o•my•e•li•tis (ŏs′tē-ō-mī′ə-lī′tĭs) *n.* Inflammation of bone and bone marrow.

os•te•o•path (ŏs′tē-ə-păth′) also **os•te•op•a•thist** (ŏs′tē-ŏp′ə-thĭst) *n.* A physician who practices osteopathy.

os•te•op•a•thy (ŏs′tē-ŏp′ə-thē) *n.* A system of medicine based on the theory that disturbances in the musculoskeletal system affect other bodily parts, causing disorders that can be corrected by various manipulative techniques in conjunction with conventional therapeutic procedures. —**os′te•o•path′ic** (-ə-păth′ĭk) *adj.* —**os′te•o•path′i•cal•ly** *adv.*

os•te•o•phyte (ŏs′tē-ə-fīt′) *n.* A small abnormal bony outgrowth. —**os′te•o•phyt′ic** (-fĭt′ĭk) *adj.*

os•te•o•plas•tic (ŏs′tē-ə-plăs′tĭk) *adj.* **1.** Of or relating to osteoplasty. **2.** Relating to or functioning in bone formation.

os•te•o•plas•ty (ŏs′tē-ə-plăs′tē) *n., pl.* **-ties.** Surgical repair or alteration of bone.

os•te•o•po•ro•sis (ŏs′tē-ō-pə-rō′sĭs) *n., pl.* **-ses** (-sēz). A disease in which the bones become extremely porous, are subject to fracture, and heal slowly, occurring esp. in women after menopause and often leading to curvature of the spine. [NLat. : OSTEO- + Gk. *poros,* passage, pore; see FORE[2] + -OSIS.] —**os′te•o•po•rot′ic** (-rŏt′ĭk) *adj.*

os•te•o•sar•co•ma (ŏs′tē-ō-sär-kō′mə) *n., pl.* **-ma•ta** (-mə-tə) or **-mas.** A malignant bone tumor.

os•te•ot•o•my (ŏs′tē-ŏt′ə-mē) *n., pl.* **-mies.** Surgical division or sectioning of bone. —**os′te•ot′o•mist** *n.*

Os•ti•a (ŏs′tē-ə, ô′styä). An ancient city of W-central Italy at the mouth of the Tiber R.; developed as a port after the 1st cent. B.C.

Os•ti•ak (ŏs′tē-ăk′) *n.* Var. of **Ostyak.**

os•ti•na•to (ŏs′tĭ-nä′tō) *n., pl.* **-tos.** *Mus.* A short melody or phrase that is constantly repeated, usu. the same part at the same pitch. [Ital. < Lat. *obstinātus,* stubborn, p.part. of *obstināre,* to persist. See OBSTINATE.]

os•ti•ole (ŏs′tē-ōl′) *n.* A small opening or pore, as of a fruiting body. [Lat. *ōstiolum,* dim. of *ōstium,* opening. See OSTIUM.] —**os′ti•o′lar** (ŏs′tē-ō′lər, ŏ-stī′ə-) *adj.*

os•ti•um (ŏs′tē-əm) *n., pl.* **-ti•a** (-tē-ə). **1.** A small orifice, as in a body organ. **2.** Any of the small pores in a sponge. [Lat. *ōstium,* door, opening < *ōs,* mouth. See **ōs-***.]

os•tler (ŏs′lər) *n.* Var. of **hostler.**

ost•mark (ôst′märk′, ŏst′-) *n.* A former monetary unit of East Germany worth 100 pfennigs. [Ger. : *Ost,* east (< MHGer. *ōst, ōsten* < OHGer. *ōstan;* see **aus-***) + *Mark,* mark (< MHGer. *marke, marc;* see MARK[2]).]

os•to•mate (ŏs′tə-māt′) *n.* One who has undergone an ostomy.

os•to•my (ŏs′tə-mē) *n., pl.* **-mies.** Surgical construction of an artificial excretory opening. [< (COL)OSTOMY.]

os•tra•cism (ŏs′trə-sĭz′əm) *n.* **1.a.** The act of banishing or excluding. **b.** Banishment or exclusion from a group; disgrace. **2.** In ancient Greece, the temporary banishment by popular vote of one deemed a threat to the state.

os•tra•cize (ŏs′trə-sīz′) *tr.v.* **-cized, -ciz•ing, -ciz•es. 1.** To exclude from a group. **2.** To banish by ostracism. [Gk. *ostrakizein* < *ostrakon,* shell, potsherd (< the potsherds used as ballots in voting for ostracism). See **ost-***.]

os•tra•cod (ŏs′trə-kŏd′) *n.* Any of various minute, chiefly freshwater crustaceans of the subclass Ostracoda, having a bivalve carapace. [NLat. *Ostracōda,* subclass name < Gk. *ostrakōdēs,* testaceous < *ostrakon,* shell. See **ost-***.]

Os•tra•va (ô′strä-vä). A city of NE Czech Republic near the Oder R. Pop. 325,431.

os•trich (ŏs′trĭch, ô′-) *n., pl.* **ostrich** or **-trich•es. 1.a.** A large swift-running flightless bird *(Struthio camelus)* of Africa having a long bare neck, small head, and two-toed feet. **b.** A rhea. **2.** One who tries to avoid disagreeable situations by refusing to face them. [ME < OFr. *ostrusce, ostrice* and Med. Lat. *ostrica,* both < VLat. **avis strūthiō* : Lat. *avis,* bird; see **awi-*** + LLat. *strūthiō,* ostrich; see STRUTHIOUS.]

ostrich fern *n.* A fern *(Matteuccia struthiopteris)* of northern temperate regions having long fronds that form a crown.

Os•tro•goth (ŏs′trə-gŏth′) *n.* One of a tribe of eastern Goths that conquered and ruled Italy from A.D. 493 to 555. [< ME *Ostrogotes,* Ostrogoths < LLat. *Ostrogothī* : *ostro-,* eastern (of Gmc. orig.; see **aus-***) + *Gothī,* Goths (of Gmc. orig.).]

Ost•wald (ōst′wôld′, ôst′vält), **Wilhelm.** 1853–1932. German chemist who won a 1909 Nobel Prize.

Os•ty•ak also **Os•ti•ak** (ŏs′tē-ăk′) *n.* **1.** A member of a Finno-Ugric people inhabiting western Siberia. **2.** The Ugric language of this people. [Russ. < Ostyak *āsyakh,* pl. of *āskho,* person from the Ob R. < *Ās,* the Ob R.]

Os•wald (ŏz′wôld′), **Lee Harvey.** 1939–63. Amer. alleged assassin of President John F. Kennedy (Nov. 22, 1963) who was shot while under arrest (Nov. 24).

Os•we•go (ŏs-wē′gō). A city of N-central NY at the mouth of the **Oswego River,** c. 37 km (23 mi), on Lake Ontario NW of Syracuse. Pop. 19,195.

Oś•wię•cim (ôsh-vyĕn′chēm). Formerly **Ausch•witz** (oush′vĭts′). A city of S Poland W of Cracow; site of the largest Nazi concentration camp. Pop. 45,700.

OT[1] also **O.T.** *abbr. Bible.* Old Testament.

OT[2] *abbr.* **1.** Occupational therapy. **2.** also **o.t.** or **O.T.** Overtime.

ot– *pref.* Var. of **oto–.**

O•ta•hei•te orange (ō′tə-hē′tē, -hā′-) *n.* A widely cultivated house plant, considered a hybrid between *Citrus limon* and *C. reticulata,* having lemon-shaped insipid fruit. [After *Otaheite* (Tahiti).]

o•tal•gi•a (ō-tăl′jē-ə, -jə) *n.* Pain in the ear; earache. —**o•tal′gic** *adj.*

OTB *abbr. Sports & Games.* Off-track betting.

OTC also **O.T.C.** *abbr.* **1.** Officers' Training Corps. **2.** Over-the-counter.

oth•er (ŭ*th*′ər) *adj.* **1.a.** Being the remaining one of two or more: *the other ear.* **b.** Being the remaining ones of several: *His other books are packed.* **2.** Different from that or those implied or specified: *Any other person would go.* **3.** Of a different character or quality. **4.** Of a different time or era either future or past: *other centuries.* **5.** Additional; extra: *I have no other shoes.* **6.** Opposite or contrary; reverse: *the other side.* **7.** Alternate; second: *every other day.* **8.** Of the recent past: *just the other day.* —*n.* **1.a.** The remaining one of two or more: *One wept, and the other giggled.* **b. others.** The remaining ones of several: *After she left the others sighed.* **2.a.** A different person or thing: *one hurricane after the other.* **b.** An additional person or thing: *How many others will come?* —*pron.* **1.** A different or an additional person or thing: *someone or other.* **2. others.** People aside from oneself: *what others think.* —*adv.* In another way; otherwise; differently: *other than perfectly.* [ME < OE *ōther.* See **al-**[1]*.]

oth•er•ness (ŭ*th*′ər-nĭs) *n.* The quality or condition of being or seeming other or different, esp. if exotic or strange.

oth•er•wise (ŭ*th*′ər-wīz′) *adv.* **1.** In another way; differently. **2.** Under other circumstances: *Otherwise I might go.* **3.** In other respects: *an otherwise logical mind.* —*adj.* Other than supposed; different: *The evidence is otherwise.* [ME < OE *(on) ōthere wīsan,* (in) another manner : *ōthre,* dative of *ōther,* other + *wīsan,* dative of *wīse,* manner; see WISE[2].]

oth•er•world (ŭ*th*′ər-wûrld′) *n.* A world or existence beyond earthly reality.

oth•er•world•ly (ŭ*th*′ər-wûrld′lē) *adj.* **1.** Of or relating to another world, esp. a mystical or transcendental one. **2.** Devoted to the world of the mind and intellectual or imaginative things. **3.** Concerned with an afterlife, esp. when inattentive to the present. —**oth′er•world′li•ness** *n.*

Oth•man (ŏth′mən) *n., pl.* **-mans.** *Archaic.* An Ottoman Turk; a Turk. [After *Othman,* variant of OSMAN (I).]

Oth•man I (ŏth′mən, o͝oth-män′). See **Osman I.**

O•tho I (ō′thō, ō′tō). See **Otto I.**

o•tic (ō′tĭk, ŏt′ĭk) *adj.* Of, relating to, or located near the ear; auricular. [Gk. *ōtikos* < *ous, ōt-,* ear. See **ous-***.]

–otic *suff.* **1.** Of, relating to, or characterized by a specified condition or process: *anabiotic.* **2.** Having a specified disease or abnormal condition: *epizootic.* **3.** Characterized by an increase or formation of a specified kind: *leukocytotic.* [Fr. *-otique* < Lat. *-ōticus* < Gk. *-ōtikos,* adj. suff.]

o•ti•ose (ō′shē-ōs′, ō′tē-) *adj.* **1.** Lazy; indolent. **2.** Of no use. **3.** Ineffective; futile. [Lat. *ōtiōsus,* idle < *ōtium,* leisure.] —**o′ti•ose′ly** *adv.* —**o′ti•os′i•ty** (-ŏs′ĭ-tē) *n.*

O•tis (ō′tĭs), **Elisha Graves.** 1811–61. Amer. inventor of the first passenger elevator (installed 1857).

Otis, James. 1725–83. Amer. Revolutionary politician who influenced sentiment against the British.

o•ti•tis (ō-tī′tĭs) *n.* Inflammation of the ear. —**o•tit′ic** (ō-tĭt′ĭk) *adj.*

otitis media *n.* Inflammation of the middle ear, common in children and often causing pain and temporary hearing loss. [NLat. : OTITIS + Lat. *media,* fem. of *medius,* middle.]

O•to (ō′tō) *n., pl.* **Oto** or **O•tos. 1.** A member of a Native American people formerly inhabiting eastern Nebraska along the Platte River, with present-day descendants in north-central Oklahoma. **2.** The Siouan language of the Oto.

oto– or **ot–** *pref.* Ear: *otology.* [NLat. < Gk. *ous, ōt-,* ear. See **ous-***.]

o•to•cyst (ō′tə-sĭst′) *n.* **1.** The structure formed by invagination of the embryonic ectodermal tissue that develops into the inner ear. **2.** See **statocyst.** —**o′to•cys′tic** *adj.*

otol. *abbr.* Otology.

o•to•lar•yn•gol•o•gy (ō′tō-lăr′ĭng-gŏl′ə-jē) *n.* The branch

ostrich
Male Masai ostrich
Struthio camelus massaicus

ostrich fern
Matteuccia struthiopteris

ă pat	oi boy
ā pay	ou out
âr care	o͝o took
ä father	o͞o boot
ĕ pet	ŭ cut
ē be	ûr urge
ĭ pit	th thin
ī pie	*th* this
îr pier	hw which
ŏ pot	zh vision
ō toe	ə about,
ô paw	item

Stress marks:
′ (primary);
′ (secondary), as in
dictionary (dĭk′shə-nĕr′ē)

of medicine that deals with diagnosis and treatment of diseases of the ear, nose, and throat. — **o′to•lar•yn′go•log′i•cal** (-lə-rĭng′gə-lŏj′ĭ-kəl) *adj.* — **o′to•lar′yn•gol′o•gist** *n.*

o•to•lith (ō′tə-lĭth′) *n.* One of many minute calcareous particles found in the inner ear of certain lower vertebrates and in the statocysts of many invertebrates. — **o′to•lith′ic** *adj.*

o•tol•o•gy (ō-tŏl′ə-jē) *n.* The branch of medicine that deals with the structure, function, and pathology of the ear. — **o′to•log′i•cal** (ō′tə-lŏj′ĭ-kəl) *adj.* — **o•tol′o•gist** *n.*

o•to•rhi•no•lar•yn•gol•o•gy (ō′tō-rī′nō-lăr′ĭng-gŏl′ə-jē) *n.* See **otolaryngology.** — **o′to•rhi′no•la•ryn′go•log′i•cal** (-lə-rĭng′gə-lŏj′ĭ-kəl) *adj.* — **o′to•rhi′no•lar′yn•gol′o•gist** *n.*

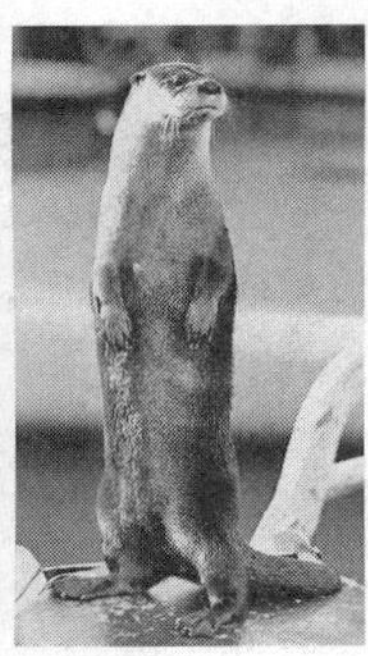

otter
North American river otter
Lutra canadensis

o•to•scle•ro•sis (ō′tō-sklə-rō′sĭs) *n.* A disease of the ear in which abnormal deposits of spongy bone in the inner ear cause a progressive loss of hearing. — **o′to•scle•rot′ic** (-rŏt′ĭk) *adj.*

o•to•scope (ō′tə-skōp′) *n.* An instrument for examining the interior of the ear, esp. the eardrum, consisting essentially of a magnifying lens and a light.

o•to•tox•ic (ō′tə-tŏk′sĭk) *adj.* Having a toxic effect on the structures of the ear, esp. on its nerve supply.

O•tran•to (ō-trän′tō), **Strait of.** A passage between SE Italy and W Albania connecting the Adriatic with the Ionian Sea.

OTS also **O.T.S.** *abbr.* Officers' Training School.

ot•tar (ŏt′ər) *n.* Var. of **attar.**

ot•ta•va (ō-tä′və) *adv.* & *adj. Mus.* At an octave higher or lower than the notes written. [Ital. *(all')ottava,* (at the) octave < Med.Lat. *octāva* < Lat., fem. of *octāvus,* eighth. See OCTAVE.]

ottava ri•ma (rē′mə) *n.* A stanza of verse consisting of eight lines in iambic pentameter rhyming *abababcc.* [Ital. : *ottava,* fem. of *ottavo,* eighth + *rima,* rhyme.]

Ot•ta•wa¹ (ŏt′ə-wə, -wä′, -wô′) *n., pl.* **Ottawa** or **-was. 1.** A member of a Native American people formerly inhabiting the northern shore of Lake Huron, with present-day populations mainly in southern Ontario, northern Michigan, and Oklahoma. **2.** Their Ojibwa dialect. [Ojibwa *odaawaa.*]

Ot•ta•wa² (ŏt′ə-wə). **1.** The cap. of Canada, in SE Ontario at the confluence of the Ottawa R. and the Rideau Canal; founded as Bytown during the construction of the Rideau Canal and renamed Ottawa in 1854. Pop. 295,163. **2.** A city of N-central IL SW of Chicago. Pop. 17,451.

ottoman
c. 1882 American ottoman
by the Herter brothers
(fl. 1865–1908)

Ottawa River. A river rising in the Laurentian Plateau of SW Quebec, Canada, and flowing c. 1,126 km (700 mi) to the St. Lawrence R. near Montreal.

ot•ter (ŏt′ər) *n., pl.* **otter** or **-ters. 1.** Any of various aquatic carnivorous mammals of the genus *Lutra* and allied genera, having webbed feet and dense, dark brown fur. **2.** The fur of this mammal. [ME *oter* < OE *otor.* See **wed-¹*.**]

otter hound *n.* Any of a breed of hardy dog developed in England for hunting otters, having slightly webbed feet and a thick coarse coat with an oily undercoat.

ot•to (ŏt′ō) *n.* Var. of **attar.**

Ot•to I (ŏt′ō, ôt′ō) also **O•tho I** (ō′thō, ō′tō). "Otto the Great." 912–973. King of Germany (936–973) and first Holy Roman emperor (962–973).

ot•to•man (ŏt′ə-mən) *n., pl.* **-mans. 1.a.** An upholstered sofa or divan without arms or a back. **b.** An upholstered low seat or cushioned footstool. **2.** A heavy silk or rayon fabric with a corded texture, usu. used for coats and trimmings. [Fr. *ottomane,* fem. of *ottoman,* Ottoman. See OTTOMAN.]

Ot•to•man (ŏt′ə-mən) *n., pl.* **-mans.** A Turk, esp. a member of the family or tribe of Osman I. — *adj.* **1.** Of or relating to the Ottoman Empire or its people, language, or culture. **2.** Ottoman Turkish. [Fr. < Ital. *ottomano* < Ar. *'uṯmānī,* of Uthman < *'Uṯman,* Osman I.]

Ottoman Empire. Also called **Turk•ish Empire** (tûr′kĭsh). A vast Turkish sultanate of SW Asia, NE Africa, and SE Europe; founded in the 13th cent. by Osman I and dissolved after World War I.

Ottoman Turkish *n.* The Turkic language spoken in Turkey, the Balkan Peninsula, Cyprus, Germany, and elsewhere.

Ot•tum•wa (ə-tŭm′wə, ō-tŭm′-). A city of SE IA SE of Des Moines. Pop. 24,488.

oua•ba•in (wä-bā′ĭn) *n.* A poisonous glycoside, $C_{29}H_{44}O_{12}·8H_2O$, extracted from the seeds of the African trees *Strophanthus gratus* and *Acokanthera ouabaio* and used as a heart stimulant. [< Fr. *ouabaïo* < Somali *wabayo.*]

Ouach•i•ta Mountains (wŏsh′ĭ-tô′). A mountain range extending c. 322 km (200 mi) from central AR to SE OK and rising to 839.7 m (2,753 ft).

Ouachita River. A river rising in the Ouachita Mts. of W AR and flowing c. 965 km (600 mi) into E LA.

Oua•ga•dou•gou (wä′gə-dōō′gōō). The cap. of Burkina Faso, in the central part. Pop. 345,150.

ou•bli•ette (ōō′blē-ĕt′) *n.* A dungeon with a trap door in the ceiling as its only means of entrance or exit. [Fr. < *oublier,* to forget < OFr. *oblider* < VLat. **oblītāre* < Lat. *oblītus,* p.part. of *oblīvīscī.* See **lei-*.**]

ouch¹ (ouch) *interj.* Used to express sudden pain or displeasure.

ouch² (ouch) *n.* **1.** A setting for a precious stone. **2.** A brooch or buckle set with jewels. **3.** *Obsolete.* A clasp; a brooch. [ME *ouche* < AN, alteration of *(une) nouche,* (a) brooch, of Gmc. orig. See **ned-*.**]

oud (ōōd) *n. Mus.* An instrument of northern Africa and southwest Asia resembling a lute. [Ar. *'ūd.*]

Oudh (oud). A historical region of N-central India dating from at least the 4th cent. A.D.; ruled by the Moguls after the 16th cent. and annexed by Great Britain in 1856.

ought¹ (ôt) *aux.v.* **1.** Used to indicate obligation or duty: *You ought to help.* **2.** Used to indicate advisability or prudence: *You ought to wear a raincoat.* **3.** Used to indicate desirability: *You ought to have been there; it was great fun.* **4.** Used to indicate probability or likelihood: *She ought to finish by next week.* [ME *oughten,* to be obliged to < *oughte,* owned < OE *āhte,* p.t. of *āgan,* to possess. See **ēik-*.**]

Usage Note: *Ought to* is sometimes used without a following verb if the meaning is clear: *Should we begin soon? Yes, we ought to.* In questions and negative sentences, especially with contractions, *to* is sometimes omitted: *Oughtn't we be going?* Although the omission of *to* was formerly possible in English, it is now considered nonstandard.

ought² (ôt) *pron.* & *adv.* Var. of **aught¹.**

ought³ (ôt) *n.* Var. of **aught².**

ought⁴ (ôt) *v. Obsolete.* A p.part. of **owe.**

ou•gui•ya (ōō-gē′yə) *n.* See table at **currency.** [Native word in Mauritania.]

Oui•ja (wē′jə, -jē). A trademark used for a board with the alphabet and other symbols on it and a planchette that is thought, when touched with the fingers, to move so as to spell spiritualistic and telepathic messages on the board.

Ouj•da (ōōj-dä′). A city of NE Morocco near the Algerian border; founded 944. Pop. 260,082.

Ou•lu (ō′lōō, ou′-). A city of W-central Finland on the Gulf of Bothnia; chartered 1610. Pop. 96,525.

ounce¹ (ouns) *n.* **1.a.** A unit of weight in the U.S. Customary System, an avoirdupois unit equal to 437.5 grains (28.35 grams). **b.** A unit of apothecary weight, equal to 480 grains (31.10 grams). See table at **measurement. 2.** A fluid ounce. See table at **measurement. 3.** A tiny bit: *not an ounce of sympathy.* [ME *unce* < OFr. < Lat. *uncia.* See **oi-no-*.**]

ounce² (ouns) *n.* See **snow leopard.** [ME *unce* < OFr. *once,* alteration of *lonce* < VLat. **luncea* < Lat. *lynx, lync-,* lynx < Gk. *lunx.* See **leuk-*.**]

our (our) *adj.* The possessive form of **we.** Used as a modifier before a noun: *our street.* [ME < OE *ūre.* See **nes-²*.**]

Our Father (our) *n.* See **Lord's Prayer.**

Our Lady *n.* The Virgin Mary.

ours (ourz) *pron. (used with a sing. or pl. v.)* Used to indicate the one or ones belonging to us: *This notebook is ours.* [ME *oures* < *oure,* our < OE *ūre.* See **nes-²*.**]

our•self (our-sĕlf′, är-) *pron.* Myself. Used as a reflexive when *we* is used instead of *I* by a singular speaker or author, as in an editorial. See Usage Note at **myself.**

our•selves (our-sĕlvz′, är-) *pron.* **1.** Those ones identical with us. **a.** Used reflexively as the object of a verb or the object of a preposition: *We bought ourselves lunch.* **b.** Used for emphasis: *We ourselves were certain.* **c.** Used in an absolute construction: *Feeling chilly ourselves, we went indoors.* **2.** Our normal or healthy condition or state: *We're feeling ourselves again after our colds.* See Usage Note at **myself.**

-ous *suff.* **1.** Possessing; full of; characterized by: *joyous.* **2.** Having a valence lower than that of a specified element in compounds or ions named with adjectives ending in *-ic*: *ferrous.* [ME < OFr. *-ous, -eus, -eux* < Lat. *-ōsus* and *-us,* adj. suff.]

ou•sel (ōō′zəl) *n.* Var. of **ouzel.**

Ouse River (ōōz). **1.** Also **Great Ouse River.** A river, c. 249 km (155 mi), flowing from S-central England to the Wash, an inlet of the North Sea. **2.** A river, c. 97 km (60 mi), of NE England joining the Trent R. to form the Humber R.

oust (oust) *tr.v.* **oust•ed, oust•ing, ousts. 1.** To eject from a position or place; force out: *ousted him from power.* See Syns at **eject. 2.** To take the place of, esp. by force; supplant. [ME *ousten* < AN *ouster* < Lat. *obstāre,* to hinder. See OBSTACLE.]

oust•er (ous′tər) *n.* **1.a.** The act of ousting. **b.** The state of being ousted. **2.** One that ousts. **3.** *Law.* The act of forcing one out of possession or occupancy of material property to which that one is entitled; illegal or wrongful dispossession. [AN, to oust, ouster. See OUST.]

out (out) *adv.* **1.** In a direction away from the inside: *go out.* **2.** Away from the center or middle: *They fanned out.* **3.a.** Away from a usual place: *went out for the evening.* **b.** Out of normal position: *threw his back out.* **4.a.** From inside a building or shelter into the open air; outside: *went out to play.* **b.** In the open air; outside: *Is it snowing out?* **5.a.** From within a container or source: *drained the water out.* **b.** From among others: *picked out the thief in the crowd.* **6.a.** To exhaustion or depletion: *Supplies ran out.* **b.** Into extinction or imperceptibility: *The fire has gone out.* **c.** To a finish or conclusion: *Play the game out.* **d.** To the fullest extent or degree: *all decked out for the dance.* **e.** In or into competition or directed effort: *went out for golf.* **7.a.** Into being or evident existence: *The new car models have come out.* **b.** Into public circulation: *The paper came out early today.* **8.** Into view: *The moon came out.* **9.** Without inhibition; boldly: *Speak out.* **10.** Into possession of another or others; into distribution: *giving out free passes.* **11.a.** Into disuse or an unfashionable status: *Narrow ties have gone out.* **b.** Into a state of deprivation or loss: *voted the governor out.* **c.** Out of consideration: *A taxi is out, because of the money.* **12.** In the time following; afterward: *six months out.* **13.** *Baseball.* So as to be retired, or counted as an out: *He grounded out.* — *adj.* **1.** Exterior; external: *the out surface.* **2.** Directed away from a place or center; outgoing: *the out door.* **3.** No longer fashionable. **4.** *Baseball.* Not allowed to continue to bat or run; retired. — *prep.* **1.** Forth from; through: *He fell out the window.* **2.** Beyond or outside of: *Out this door is the garage.* — *n.* **1.** One that is out, esp. one who is out of power. **2.** *Informal.* A means of escape. **3.** *Baseball.* **a.** A play in which a batter or base runner is retired. **b.** The player retired in such a play. **4.** *Sports.* A serve or return that falls out of bounds in a court game. **5.** *Print.* A word or other part of a manuscript omitted from the printed copy. — *v.* **out•ed, out•ing, outs.** — *intr.* To be disclosed or revealed; come out. — *tr.* **1.** *Sports.* To send (a tennis ball, for example) outside the court or playing area. **2.** *Chiefly British.* To knock unconscious. — *idiom.* **on the outs.** *Informal.* Not on friendly terms; disagreeing. — *interj.* Used in a two-way radio to indicate that a transmission is complete and no reply is expected. [ME < OE *ūt.* See **ud-***.]

out– *pref.* In a way that surpasses, exceeds, or goes beyond: *outdistance.* [< OUT.]

out•age (ou′tĭj) *n.* **1.** A quantity or portion of something lacking after delivery or storage. **2.** A temporary suspension of operation, esp. of electric power.

out and away *adv.* By far: *She's out and away the best.*

out-and-out (out′n-out′) *adj.* Complete; thoroughgoing.

out-and-out•er (out′ən-ou′tər) *n.* One given to extremes.

out•back (out′băk′) *adv.* Out to or in the outback. — *n.* (out′băk′). The remote rural part of a country, esp. of Australia or New Zealand. — **out′back′er** *n.*

out•bal•ance (out-băl′əns) *tr.v.* **-anced, -anc•ing, -anc•es.** To exceed in influence or significance; outweigh.

out•bid (out-bĭd′) *tr.v.* **-bid, -bid•den** (-bĭd′n) or **-bid, -bid•ding, -bids.** To bid higher than: *We outbid our rivals.*

out•board (out′bôrd′, -bōrd′) *adj.* **1.** *Naut.* **a.** Situated or positioned outside the hull of a vessel. **b.** Being in a position that is away from the center line of a ship. **2.** Situated or positioned toward the end of an aircraft wing. — *n.* **1.** An outboard motor. **2.** A boat with an outboard motor. — **out′board′** *adv.*

outboard motor *n. Naut.* A detachable engine mounted on outboard brackets or on the transom of a boat.

out•bound (out′bound′) *adj.* Outward bound; headed away.

out•break (out′brāk′) *n.* **1.** A sudden increase: *a flu outbreak.* **2.** A sudden eruption; an outburst: *a violent outbreak.*

out•breed (out′brēd′) *tr.v.* **-bred** (-brĕd′), **-breed•ing, -breeds.** To subject to outbreeding.

out•breed•ing (out′brē′dĭng) *n.* **1.** The breeding of distantly related or unrelated individuals, often producing a superior hybrid. **2.** *Anthro.* The mating of persons from different groups, often as a result of marriage taboos within the group.

out•build•ing (out′bĭl′dĭng) *n.* A building separate from but associated with a main building.

out•burst (out′bûrst′) *n.* A sudden violent display, as of activity or emotion: *an outburst of indignation.*

out•call (out′kôl′) *n.* A visit by a professional person to a client or patient's home; a house call.

out•cast (out′kăst′) *n.* One that has been excluded from a society or system. — **out′cast′** *adj.*

out•caste (out′kăst′) *n.* In India, one who has been expelled from or has abandoned a caste.

out•class (out-klăs′) *tr.v.* **-classed, -class•ing, -class•es.** To surpass decisively, so as to appear of a higher class.

out•come (out′kŭm′) *n.* A natural result; a consequence. See Syns at **effect.**

out•crop (out′krŏp′) *n.* A portion of bedrock or other stratum protruding through the soil level. — *intr.v.* (out-krŏp′) **-cropped, -crop•ping, -crops.** To protrude above the soil.

out•cross (out′krôs′, -krŏs′) *tr.v.* **-crossed, -cross•ing, -cross•es.** To cross (animals or plants) by breeding individuals of different strains but usu. of the same breed. — *n.* **1.** The process of outcrossing. **2.** Offspring thus produced.

out•cry (out′krī′) *n., pl.* **-cries. 1.** A loud cry or clamor. **2.** A strong protest or objection: *public outcry over prices.*

out•date (out-dāt′) *tr.v.* **-dat•ed, -dat•ing, -dates.** To replace or make obsolete or old-fashioned.

out•dat•ed (out-dā′tĭd) *adj.* Out-of-date; old-fashioned.

out•dis•tance (out-dĭs′təns) *tr.v.* **-tanced, -tanc•ing, -tanc•es. 1.** To outrun, esp. in a long-distance race. **2.** To surpass by a wide margin, esp. through superior skill or endurance.

out•do (out-do͞o′) *tr.v.* **-did** (-dĭd′), **-done** (-dŭn′), **-do•ing, -does** (-dŭz′). To do more or better than.

out•door (out′dôr′, -dōr′) also **out-of-door** (out′əv-dôr′, -dōr′) *adj.* Located in, done in, or suited to the open air.

out•doors (out-dôrz′, -dōrz′) also **out-of-doors** (out′əv-dôrz′, -dōrz′) — *adv.* In or into the open; outside. — *n.* **1.** The open air. **2.** An area away from human settlements.

out•doors•man (out-dôrz′mən, -dōrz′-) *n.* A man who spends considerable time in outdoor pursuits.

out•doors•wo•man (out-dôrz′wo͝om′ən, -dōrz′-) *n.* A woman who spends considerable time in outdoor pursuits.

out•door•sy (out-dôr′zē, -dōr′-) *adj. Informal.* **1.** Associated with the outdoors. **2.** Showing a liking for the outdoors.

out•er (ou′tər) *adj.* **1.** Located on the outside; external. **2.** Farther than another from the center or middle. **3.** Relating to the body or its appearance rather than the mind or spirit.

outer ear *n.* See **external ear.**

Out•er Heb•ri•des (out′ər hĕb′rĭ-dēz′). See **Hebrides.**

Outer Mon•go•li•a (mŏng-gō′lē-ə, -gōl′yə, mŏn-). See **Mongolia** 2.

out•er•most (ou′tər-mōst′) *adj.* Most distant from the center or inside; outmost.

outer planet *n.* Any of the five planets, Jupiter, Saturn, Uranus, Neptune, and Pluto, with orbits outside that of Mars.

outer space *n.* **1.** The region of space immediately beyond Earth's atmosphere. **2.** Interplanetary or interstellar space.

out•er•wear (ou′tər-wâr′) *n.* Clothing, such as hats, coats, and gloves, for use outdoors.

out•face (out-fās′) *tr.v.* **-faced, -fac•ing, -fac•es. 1.** To overcome with a bold or self-assured look; stare down. **2.** To defy or resist.

out•fall (out′fôl′) *n.* The place where a sewer, drain, or stream discharges.

out•field (out′fēld′) *n. Baseball.* **1.** The playing area extending outward from the diamond, divided into left, center, and right field. **2.** The position played by an outfielder. **3.** The members of a team playing in the outfield.

out•field•er (out′fēl′dər) *n. Baseball.* A player who defends left, center, or right field.

out•fit (out′fĭt′) *n.* **1.** A set of tools or equipment for a specialized purpose. **2.** A set of clothing. **3.** *Informal.* An association of persons, esp. a military or business group. **4.** The act of equipping. — *tr.v.* **-fit•ted, -fit•ting, -fits.** To provide with necessary equipment. — **out′fit′ter** *n.*

out•flank (out-flăngk′) *tr.v.* **-flanked, -flank•ing, -flanks. 1.** To maneuver around and behind the flank of (an opposing force). **2.** To gain a tactical advantage over.

out•flow (out′flō′) *n.* **1.** The act or the process of flowing out. **2.a.** Something that flows out. **b.** The amount flowing out: *a heavy outflow of cash.* — *intr.v.* **-flowed, -flow•ing, -flows.** To issue or stream out, in or as if in a flow.

out•fox (out-fŏks′) *tr.v.* **-foxed, -fox•ing, -fox•es.** To surpass (another) in cleverness or cunning; outsmart.

out-front (out′frŭnt′) *adj. Informal.* Straightforward; frank.

out•gas (out′găs′) *v.* **-gassed, -gas•sing, -gas•ses.** — *tr.* To remove embedded gas from (a solid), as by heating or reducing the pressure. — *intr.* To lose gas, as from a solid.

out•gen•er•al (out-jĕn′ər-əl) *tr.v.* **-aled, -al•ing, -als.** To surpass (another, esp. an opponent) in leadership.

out•giv•ing (out′gĭv′ĭng) *adj.* Friendly and responsive; outgoing.

out•go (out-gō′) *tr.v.* **-went** (-wĕnt′), **-gone** (-gôn′, -gŏn′), **-go•ing, -goes** (-gōz′). To go beyond; exceed or surpass. — *n.* (out′gō′), *pl.* **-goes. 1.** Something that goes out, esp. an expenditure or a cost. **2.** The act or process of going out.

out•go•ing (out′gō′ĭng) *adj.* **1.a.** Going out or away; departing. **b.** Retiring from or relinquishing a place, a position, or an office. **c.** Addressed for sending: *outgoing mail.* **2.** Sociable and responsive to others; friendly. **3.** Intended to be taken out, as from a restaurant. — **out•go′ing•ness** *n.*

out-group (out′gro͞op′) *n.* A group of people excluded from or not belonging to one's own group, esp. when viewed as subordinate or contemptibly different.

out•grow (out-grō′) *tr.v.* **-grew** (-gro͞o′), **-grown** (-grōn′), **-grow•ing, -grows. 1.** To grow too large for. **2.** To lose or discard in the course of maturation. **3.** To surpass in growth.

out•growth (out′grōth′) *n.* **1.** The act or process of growing out. **2.** A product of growing out; an offshoot. **3.** A result or consequence.

out•guess (out-gĕs′) *tr.v.* **-guessed, -guess•ing, -guess•es. 1.** To anticipate correctly the actions of. **2.** To gain the advantage over (another) by cleverness or forethought; outwit.

out•gun (out′gŭn′) *tr.v.* **-gunned, -gun•ning, -guns. 1.** To surpass in military force. **2.** To overwhelm or defeat.

out•haul (out′hôl′) *n. Naut.* A line used to extend a sail along a spar or boom.

out•house (out′hous′) *n.* **1.** An enclosed structure having a seat with one or two holes over a pit and serving as an outdoor toilet. **2.** An outbuilding, as on a farm.

out•ing (ou′tĭng) *n.* **1.** An excursion, typically a pleasure trip. **2.** A walk outdoors.

outing flannel *n.* A soft lightweight cotton fabric, usu. with a short nap on both sides.

out•land (out′lănd′, -lənd) *n.* **1.** A foreign land. **2. outlands.** A country's outlying areas; the provinces. — **out′land′** *adj.*

outboard motor

ă pat	oi boy
ā pay	ou out
âr care	o͝o took
ä father	o͞o boot
ĕ pet	ŭ cut
ē be	ûr urge
ĭ pit	th thin
ī pie	*th* this
îr pier	hw which
ŏ pot	zh vision
ō toe	ə about, item
ô paw	

Stress marks:
′ (primary);
′ (secondary), as in
dictionary (dĭk′shə-nĕr′ē)

located in the White House. **2.** The office, authority, or executive power of the U.S. President; the presidency.

oval window *n.* The oval opening in the middle ear to which the base of the stapes is connected and through which the ossicles of the ear transmit sound vibrations to the cochlea.

o•var•i•ec•to•my (ō-vâr′ē-ĕk′tə-mē) *n., pl.* **-mies.** Surgical removal of one ovary or both.

o•var•i•ot•o•my (ō-vâr′ē-ŏt′ə-mē) *n., pl.* **-mies. 1.** An ovariectomy. **2.** Surgical incision into an ovary.

o•va•ri•tis (ō′və-rī′tĭs) *n.* See **oophoritis.**

o•va•ry (ō′və-rē) *n., pl.* **-ries. 1.** The usu. paired female or hermaphroditic reproductive organ that produces ova and in vertebrates estrogen and progesterone. **2.** *Bot.* The ovule-bearing lower part of a pistil that ripens into a fruit. [NLat. *ōvārium* < Lat. *ōvum,* egg. See **awi-*.**] **—o•var′i•an** (ō-vâr′ē-ən), **o•var′i•al** (-ē-əl) *adj.*

o•vate (ō′vāt′) *adj.* **1.** Shaped like an egg; oval. **2.** *Bot.* Broad and rounded at the base and tapering toward the end. [Lat. *ōvātus* < *ōvum,* egg. See **awi-*.**] **—o′vate′ly** *adv.*

o•va•tion (ō-vā′shən) *n.* **1.** Prolonged enthusiastic applause. **2.** A show of public homage or welcome. **3.** An ancient Roman victory ceremony of somewhat less importance than a triumph. [Lat. *ovātiō, ovātiōn-,* a Roman victory ceremony < *ovātus,* p.part. of *ovāre,* to rejoice.] **—o•va′tion•al** *adj.*

overalls

ov•en (ŭv′ən) *n.* A chamber or enclosed compartment for heating, baking, or roasting food, as in a stove, or for firing, baking, or drying objects, as in a kiln. [ME < OE *ofen.*]

ov•en•bird (ŭv′ən-bûrd′) *n.* **1.** A thrushlike North American warbler *(Seiurus aurocapillus)* having a shrill call and building a domed oven-shaped nest on the ground. **2.** Any of various South American birds of the family Furnariidae, esp. of the genus *Furnarius.*

ov•en•proof (ŭv′ən-prōōf′) *adj.* Capable of resisting the heat produced in a kitchen oven: *an ovenproof casserole dish.*

ov•en•ware (ŭv′ən-wâr′) *n.* Heat-resistant baking dishes.

o•ver (ō′vər) *prep.* **1.** In or at a position above or higher than: *a sign over the door.* **2.a.** Above and across from one end or side to the other: *a jump over the fence.* **b.** To the other side of; across: *strolled over the bridge.* **c.** Across the edge of and down: *fell over the cliff.* **3.** On the other side of: *over the border.* **4.a.** Upon the surface of: *varnish over the woodwork.* **b.** On top of or down upon: *tripped over the toys.* **5.a.** Through the extent of; all through: *walked over the grounds.* **b.** Through the medium of; via: *spoke over the phone.* **6.** So as to cover: *a shawl over her shoulders.* **7.** Up to or higher than the level or height of: *The water was over my shoulders.* **8.a.** Through the period or duration of: *records maintained over two years.* **b.** Until or beyond the end of: *stayed over the holidays.* **9.** More than in degree, quantity, or extent: *over ten miles.* **10.a.** In superiority to: *a victory over her rival.* **b.** In preference to: *selected over the others.* **11.** In a position to rule or control: *presiding over the meeting.* **12.** So as to have an effect or influence on: *the change that came over you.* **13.** While occupied with or engaged in: *a chat over coffee.* **14.** With reference to; concerning: *an argument over methods.* —*adv.* **1.** Above the top or surface: *climbed up and peered over.* **2.a.** Across to another or opposite side: *stopped at the curb, then crossed over.* **b.** Across the edge, brink, or brim: *The coffee spilled over.* **c.** Across an intervening space: *Throw the ball over.* **3.a.** Across a distance in a particular direction or at a location: *lives over in England.* **b.** To another often specified place or position: *Move over.* **c.** To one's place of residence or business: *invited us over.* **4.** Throughout an entire area or region: *wandered all over.* **5.a.** To a different opinion or allegiance: *win someone over.* **b.** So as to be comprehensible, acceptable, or effective; across: *got my point over.* **6.** To a different person, condition, or title: *sign the property over.* **7.** So as to be completely enclosed or covered: *The river froze over.* **8.** Completely through; from beginning to end: *Think it over.* **9.a.** From an upright position: *kicked the stool over.* **b.** From an upward position to an inverted or reversed position: *turn the paper over.* **10.** Another time; again: *had to do it over.* **11.** In repetition: *said it over.* **12.** In addition or excess; in surplus: *food left over.* **13.** Beyond or until a specified time: *stay a day over.* **14.** At an end: *Fall is over.* —*adj.* **1.** External; outer. **2.** Excessive; extreme. **3.a.** Not yet used up; remaining. **b.** Extra; surplus. —*n. Sports.* A series of six balls bowled from one end of a cricket pitch. —*tr.v.* **o•vered, o•ver•ing, o•vers.** To jump over. —*interj.* Used in two-way radio to indicate that a transmission is complete and a reply is awaited. —***idioms.* over against.** As opposed to; contrasted with. **over with.** Completely finished; done. [ME < OE *ofer.* See **uper*.**]

o•ver•a•bun•dance (ō′vər-ə-bŭn′dəns) *n.* A going or being beyond what is needed, desired, or appropriate; an excess. **—o′ver•a•bun′dant** *adj.* **—o′ver•a•bun′dant•ly** *adv.*

o•ver•a•chieve (ō′vər-ə-chēv′) *intr.v.* **-chieved, -chiev•ing, -chieves.** To perform better or achieve more success than expected. **—o′ver•a•chieve′ment** *n.* **—o′ver•a•chiev′er** *n.*

o•ver•act (ō′vər-ăkt′) *v.* **-act•ed, -act•ing, -acts.** —*tr.* To act (a dramatic role) with unnecessary exaggeration. —*intr.* **1.** To exaggerate a role; overplay. **2.** To act over and above what is required; overdo in acting. **—o′ver•ac′tion** *n.*

o•ver•ac•tive (ō′vər-ăk′tĭv) *adj.* Active to an excessive or abnormal degree: *an overactive child.* **—o′ver•ac•tiv′i•ty** *n.*

o•ver•age¹ (ō′vər-ĭj) *n.* **1.** An amount, as of money or goods, that is actually on hand and exceeds the listed amount in records or books. **2.** A surplus; an excess.

o•ver•age² (ō′vər-āj′) *adj.* **1.** Beyond the proper or required age. **2.** Older than usual for a particular position or activity. **3.** Too old to be of use or service: *an overage vehicle.*

o•ver•all (ō′vər-ôl′) *adj.* **1.** From one end to the other. **2.** Including everything; comprehensive. **3.** Regarded as a whole; general. —*adv.* (ō′vər-ôl′). On the whole; generally. —*n.* **1.** *Chiefly British.* A loose-fitting protective outer garment; a smock. **2. overalls.** Loose-fitting trousers, usu. of strong fabric, with a bib front and shoulder straps, often worn over regular clothing as protection from dirt.

over and above *prep.* In addition to.

over and over *adv.* Again and again; repeatedly.

o•ver•arch (ō′vər-ärch′) *tr.v.* **-arched, -arch•ing, -arch•es.** To form an arch over: *Grape vines overarched the garden path.*

o•ver•arch•ing (ō′vər-är′chĭng) *adj.* **1.** Forming an arch overhead or above. **2.** Extending over or throughout: *overarching enthusiasm.* **—o′ver•arch′ing•ly** *adv.*

o•ver•arm¹ (ō′vər-ärm′) *adj. Sports.* **1.** Executed with the arm raised above the shoulder; overhand: *an overarm throw.* **2.** Of, relating to, or being a stroke in swimming that is begun with the arm lifted and stretched forward over the shoulder.

o•ver•arm² (ō′vər-ärm′) *tr.v.* **-armed, -arm•ing, -arms.** To supply with an excess of weaponry, esp. nuclear missiles.

o•ver•awe (ō′vər-ô′) *tr.v.* **-awed, -aw•ing, -awes.** To control or subdue by inspiring awe.

o•ver•bal•ance (ō′vər-băl′əns) *v.* **-anced, -anc•ing, -anc•es.** —*tr.* **1.** To have greater weight or importance than. **2.** To throw off balance. —*intr.* To lose one's balance. —*n.* (ō′vər-băl′əns). **1.** An excess in weight or quantity. **2.** Something that overbalances or more than equals something else.

o•ver•bear (ō′vər-bâr′) *v.* **-bore** (-bôr′, -bōr′), **-borne** (-bôrn′), **-bear•ing, -bears.** —*tr.* **1.** To crush or press down on with physical force. **2.** To prevail over, as if by superior weight or force; dominate. **3.** To be more important than;

o′ver•ag•gres′sive *adj.*
o′ver•ag•gres′sive•ly *adv.*
o′ver•ag•gres′sive•ness *n.*
o′ver•am•bi′tion *n.*
o′ver•am•bi′tious *adj.*
o′ver•am•bi′tious•ly *adv.*
o′ver•am•bi′tious•ness *n.*
o′ver•anx•i′e•ty *n.*
o′ver•anx′ious *adj.*
o′ver•anx′ious•ly *adv.*
o′ver•anx′ious•ness *n.*
o′ver•as•sess′ *tr.v.*
o′ver•as•sess′ment *n.*
o′ver•cau′tious *adj.*
o′ver•cau′tious•ly *adv.*
o′ver•cau′tious•ness *n.*
o′ver•con′fi•dence *n.*
o′ver•con′fi•dent *adj.*
o′ver•con′fi•dent•ly *adv.*
o′ver•crit′i•cal *adj.*
o′ver•crit′i•cal•ly *adv.*
o′ver•crit′i•cal•ness *n.*
o′ver•crowd′ *tr. & intr.v.*
o′ver•dose′ *n., tr.v., & intr.v.*
o′ver•ea′ger *adj.*
o′ver•ea′ger•ly *adv.*
o′ver•ea′ger•ness *n.*
o′ver•eat′ *intr.v.*
o′ver•eat′er *n.*
o′ver•em′pha•size′ *tr. & intr.v.*
o′ver•fa•tigue′ *n.*
o′ver•feed′ *tr. & intr.v.*
o′ver•fill′ *tr. & intr.v.*
o′ver•in•dulge′ *tr. & intr.v.*
o′ver•in•dul′gence *n.*
o′ver•in•dul′gent *adj.*
o′ver•in•dul′gent•ly *adv.*
o′ver•long′ *adj. & adv.*
o′ver•med′i•cate′ *tr.v.*
o′ver•med′i•ca′tion *n.*
o′ver•op′ti•mism *n.*
o′ver•op′ti•mis′tic *adj.*
o′ver•op′ti•mis′ti•cal•ly *adv.*
o′ver•pay′ *tr. & intr.v.*
o′ver•pay′ment *n.*
o′ver•praise′ *tr.v.*
o′ver•pre•scribe′ *tr. & intr.v.*
o′ver•pre•scrip′tion *n.*
o′ver•price′ *tr.v.*
o′ver•priv′i•leged *adj. & n.*
o′ver•prize′ *tr.v.*
o′ver•pro•duce′ *tr.v.*
o′ver•pro•duc′er *n.*
o′ver•pro•duc′tion *n.*
o′ver•pro•tect′ *tr.v.*
o′ver•pro•tec′tion *n.*
o′ver•pro•tec′tive *adj.*
o′ver•pro•tec′tive•ness *n.*
o′ver•rate′ *tr.v.*
o′ver•re•fine′ *tr.v.*
o′ver•re•fined′ *adj.*
o′ver•re•fine′ment *n.*
o′ver•reg′u•late′ *tr.v.*
o′ver•reg′u•la′tion *n.*
o′ver•sen′si•tive *adj.*
o′ver•sen′si•tive•ness *n.*
o′ver•sen′si•tiv′i•ty *n.*
o′ver•sim′ple *adj.*
o′ver•sim′pli•fi•ca′tion *n.*
o′ver•sim′pli•fi′er *n.*
o′ver•sim′pli•fy′ *tr. & intr.v.*
o′ver•sim′ply *adv.*
o′ver•spe′cial•i•za′tion *n.*
o′ver•spe′cial•ize′ *intr.v.*
o′ver•spe′cial•ized′ *adj.*
o′ver•staff′ *tr.v.*
o′ver•tax′ *tr.v.*
o′ver•tax•a′tion *n.*
o′ver•trade′ *tr. & intr.v.*
o′ver•use′ *tr.v. & n.*
o′ver•val′u•a′tion *n.*
o′ver•val′ue *tr.v.*
o′ver•wear′ *tr.v.*
o′ver•wea′ry *adj. & tr.v.*
o′ver•wind′ *tr.v.*
o′ver•zeal′ous *adj.*
o′ver•zeal′ous•ly *adv.*
o′ver•zeal′ous•ness *n.*

outweigh. — *intr.* To bear an overabundance of fruit or offspring.

o•ver•bear•ing (ō′vər-bâr′ĭng) *adj.* **1.** Domineering in manner; arrogant: *an overbearing person.* **2.** Overwhelming in power or significance; predominant. **— o′ver•bear′ing•ly** *adv.* **— o′ver•bear′ing•ness** *n.*

o•ver•bid (ō′vər-bĭd′) *v.* **-bid, -bid•den** (-bĭd′n) or **-bid, -bid•ding, -bids.** — *tr.* **1.** To outbid (a person) for something, as at an auction. **2.** *Games.* To bid more than the value of (one's hand in bridge, for example). — *intr.* To bid higher than the actual value of something. — *n.* (ō′vər-bĭd′). A bid higher than another bid. **— o′ver•bid′der** *n.*

o•ver•bite (ō′vər-bīt′) *n.* A malocclusion in which the front upper incisor and canine teeth project over the lower.

o•ver•blouse (ō′vər-blous′, -blouz′) *n.* A blouse fashioned for wearing outside the waistband of a skirt or slacks.

o•ver•blow (ō′vər-blō′) *tr.v.* **-blew** (-blo͞o′), **-blown** (-blōn′), **-blow•ing, -blows.** To blow (a wind instrument) so as to produce an overtone instead of a fundamental tone.

o•ver•blown (ō′vər-blōn′) *adj.* **1.a.** Done to excess; overdone. **b.** Full of empty or pretentious language; bombastic. **2.** Past the stage of full bloom. **3.** Very fat; obese. **4.** Having been blown down or over.

o•ver•board (ō′vər-bôrd′, -bōrd′) *adv.* Over or as if over the side of a boat or ship. — ***idiom.*** **go overboard.** To go to extremes, esp. as a result of enthusiasm.

o•ver•book (ō′vər-bo͝ok′) *v.* **-booked, -book•ing, -books.** — *tr.* To take reservations for (a restaurant, for example) beyond the capacity for accommodation. — *intr.* To take reservations beyond the capacity for accommodation. **— o′ver•book′ing** *n.*

o•ver•borne (ō′vər-bôrn′) *adj.* Overpowered or overcome.

o•ver•bought (ō′vər-bôt′) *adj.* Characterized by excessively high prices owing to prior heavy buying.

o•ver•build (ō′vər-bĭld′) *v.* **-built** (-bĭlt′), **-build•ing, -builds.** — *tr.* **1.** To build over or on top of. **2.** To construct more buildings in (an area) than necessary. **3.** To build with excessive size or elaboration. — *intr.* To overbuild an area.

o•ver•bur•den (ō′vər-bûr′dn) *tr.v.* **-dened, -den•ing, -dens.** **1.** To burden with too much weight; overload. **2.** To subject to an excessive burden or strain; overtax. — *n.* (ō′vər-bûr′dn). **1.** An excessive burden; an overload. **2.** *Geol.* **a.** Material overlying a useful mineral deposit. **b.** Sedimentary rock covering older crystalline layers. **3.** *Archaeol.* A sterile stratum overlying a stratum with traces of the culture under study.

o•ver•buy (ō′vər-bī′) *v.* **-bought** (-bôt′), **-buy•ing, -buys.** — *tr.* **1.** To buy in excess. **2.** To buy (stock) on margin in excess of one's ability to provide further security if prices drop. — *intr.* To buy goods beyond one's means or needs.

o•ver•call (ō′vər-kôl′) *v.* **-called, -call•ing, -calls.** — *tr.* To bid beyond or in excess of (a previous bid or player) in a game of cards. — *intr.* To bid higher than one's opponent when one's partner has not bid in bridge. — *n.* (ō′vər-kôl′). *Games.* **a.** An overbid. **b.** An instance of overcalling in bridge.

o•ver•ca•pac•i•ty (ō′vər-kə-păs′ĭ-tē) *n.* Too great a capacity for production of commodities or delivery of services in relation to actual need.

o•ver•cap•i•tal•ize (ō′vər-kăp′ĭ-tl-īz′) *tr.v.* **-ized, -iz•ing, -iz•es.** **1.** To provide excess capital for (a business enterprise). **2.** To overestimate the value of (property). **3.** To put an unlawfully or unreasonably high value on the nominal capital of (a corporation). **— o′ver•cap′i•tal•i•za′tion** (-ĭ-zā′shən) *n.*

o•ver•cast (ō′vər-kăst′, ō′vər-kăst′) *adj.* **1.a.** Covered or obscured, as with mist. **b.** Clouded over. **2.** Gloomy; melancholy. **3.** Sewn with long overlying stitches to prevent raveling, as of the raw edges of fabric. — *n.* (ō′vər-kăst′). **1.** A covering, as of mist or clouds. **2.** An arch or a support for one passage over another in a mine. **3.** An overcast stitch or seam. — *v.* (ō′vər-kăst′, ō′vər-kăst′) **-cast, -cast•ing, -casts.** — *tr.* **1.** To make cloudy or gloomy. **2.** To sew with long overlying stitches. — *intr.* To become cloudy or gloomy.

o•ver•cast•ing (ō′vər-kăs′tĭng) *n.* **1.a.** The act of overcasting raw edges of fabric. **b.** Overcast stitching. **2.** An overcast stitch.

o•ver•charge (ō′vər-chärj′) *v.* **-charged, -charg•ing, -charg•es.** — *tr.* **1.** To charge (a party) an overcharge. **2.** To fill too full; overload. **3.** To overstate or exaggerate. — *intr.* To charge too much. — *n.* (ō′vər-chärj′). **1.** An excessive charge or price. **2.** A load or burden that is too full or heavy.

o•ver•cloud (ō′vər-kloud′) *v.* **-cloud•ed, -cloud•ing, -clouds.** — *tr.* **1.** To cover with clouds. **2.** To make dark and gloomy. — *intr.* To become cloudy.

o•ver•coat (ō′vər-kōt′) *n.* **1.** A heavy winter coat worn over clothing. **2.** An additional protective coating, as of paint.

o•ver•coat•ing (ō′vər-kō′tĭng) *n.* An overcoat, as of paint.

o•ver•come (ō′vər-kŭm′) *v.* **-came** (-kām′), **-come, -com•ing, -comes.** — *tr.* **1.** To defeat (another) in competition or conflict; conquer. See Syns at **defeat.** **2.** To prevail over; surmount. **3.** To overpower, as with emotion; affect deeply. — *intr.* To surmount opposition; be victorious.

o•ver•com•mit (ō′vər-kə-mĭt′) *v.* **-mit•ted, -mit•ting, -mits.** — *tr.* **1.** To bind or obligate (oneself, for example) beyond the capacity for realization. **2.** To allocate or apportion (money, goods, or resources) in amounts incapable of replacement. — *intr.* To be or become overcommitted. **— o′ver•com•mit′ment** *n.*

o•ver•com•pen•sate (ō′vər-kŏm′pən-sāt′) *v.* **-sat•ed, -sat•ing, -sates.** — *intr.* To engage in overcompensation. — *tr.* To pay (someone) too much; compensate excessively. **— o′ver•com•pen′sa•to′ry** (-kəm-pĕn′sə-tôr′ē, -tōr′ē) *adj.*

o•ver•com•pen•sa•tion (ō′vər-kŏm′pən-sā′shən) *n.* Excessive compensation, esp. for a physical or psychological characteristic or defect.

o•ver•cor•rect (ō′vər-kə-rĕkt′) *v.* **-rect•ed, -rect•ing, -rects.** — *tr.* To correct beyond what is needed, appropriate, or usual, esp. when causing a mistake. — *intr.* To correct something to an excessive or unusual degree. **— o′ver•cor•rec′tion** *n.*

o•ver•crop (ō′vər-krŏp′) *tr.v.* **-cropped, -crop•ping, -crops.** To exhaust the fertility of by continuous cultivation of crops.

o•ver•de•vel•op (ō′vər-dĭ-vĕl′əp) *tr.v.* **-oped, -op•ing, -ops.** **1.** To develop to excess: *overdeveloped muscles.* **2.** To process (a photographic plate or film) too long or in too concentrated a solution. **— o′ver•de•vel′op•ment** *n.*

o•ver•do (ō′vər-do͞o′) *v.* **-did** (-dĭd′), **-done** (-dŭn′), **-do•ing, -does** (-dŭz′). — *tr.* **1.a.** To do, use, or stress to excess; carry (something) too far. **b.** To exaggerate. **2.** To wear out the strength of; overtax. **3.** To cook (food) too long. — *intr.* To do too much; go to extremes. **— o′ver•do′er** *n.*

o•ver•dog (ō′vər-dôg′, -dŏg′) *n.* *Informal.* One that has a significant advantage. [OVER + (UNDER)DOG.]

o•ver•draft (ō′vər-drăft′) *n.* **1.a.** The act of overdrawing a bank account. **b.** The amount overdrawn. **c.** The maximum amount of credit extended to a customer. **2.** Also **o•ver•draught** (-drăft′). **a.** A current of air made to pass over the ignited fuel in a furnace. **b.** A series of flues in a brick kiln designed to force air down from the top. **c.** The air so forced.

o•ver•draw (ō′vər-drô′) *v.* **-drew** (-dro͞o′), **-drawn** (-drôn′), **-draw•ing, -draws.** — *tr.* **1.** To draw against (a bank account) in excess of credit. **2.** To pull back too far: *overdraw a bow.* **3.** To spoil the effect of by exaggeration in telling or describing. — *intr.* To make an overdraft.

o•ver•dress (ō′vər-drĕs′) *v.* **-dressed, -dress•ing, -dress•es.** — *intr.* To overdress oneself. — *tr.* To dress (oneself) more formally or elaborately than appropriate or desirable. — *n.* (ō′vər-drĕs′). A skirted garment worn over outer clothing.

o•ver•drive (ō′vər-drīv′) *n.* **1.** A gearing mechanism of a motor vehicle engine that reduces the power output required to maintain driving speed in a specific range by lowering the gear ratio. **2.** *Informal.* A state of heightened activity or concentration. — *tr.v.* (ō′vər-drīv′) **-drove** (-drōv′), **-driv•en** (-drĭv′ən), **-driv•ing, -drives.** **1.** To drive (a vehicle) too far or too long. **2.** To push (oneself) too far, as with tasks.

o•ver•dub (ō′vər-dŭb′) *tr.v.* **-dubbed, -dub•bing, -dubs.** To add (an overdub) to a previously taped musical recording esp. in order to heighten the effect. — *n.* Additional recorded sound blended into a musical recording.

o•ver•due (ō′vər-do͞o′, -dyo͞o′) *adj.* **1.** Being unpaid when due. **2.** Coming or arriving after the scheduled or expected time. **3.a.** Expected or required but not yet having occurred. **b.** Being something that should have occurred earlier.

o•ver•es•ti•mate (ō′vər-ĕs′tə-māt′) *tr.v.* **-mat•ed, -mat•ing, -mates.** **1.** To estimate too highly. **2.** To esteem too greatly. **— o′ver•es′ti•mate** (-mĭt) *n.* **— o′ver•es′ti•ma′tion** *n.*

o•ver•ex•ert (ō′vər-ĭg-zûrt′) *tr.v.* **-ert•ed, -ert•ing, -erts.** To exert (oneself) too much; overtax. **— o′ver•ex•er′tion** *n.*

o•ver•ex•pose (ō′vər-ĭk-spōz′) *tr.v.* **-posed, -pos•ing, -pos•es.** **1.** To expose too long or too much: *overexposed to TV.* **2.** To expose (a photographic film or plate) too long or to too much light. **— o′ver•ex•po′sure** (-ĭk-spō′zhər) *n.*

o•ver•ex•tend (ō′vər-ĭk-stĕnd′) *tr.v.* **-tend•ed, -tend•ing, -tends.** **1.** To expand or disperse beyond a safe or reasonable limit: *overextended their defenses.* **2.** To obligate (oneself) beyond a limit, esp. a financial one. **— o′ver•ex•ten′sion** *n.*

o•ver•fa•mil•iar (ō′vər-fə-mĭl′yər) *adj.* Too familiar, as: **a.** Exceedingly common or ordinary. **b.** Unduly forward or brash; offensively presumptuous: *overfamiliar behavior.* **— o′ver•fa•mil′iar′i•ty** (-mĭl′yăr′ĭ-tē, -mĭl′ē-ăr′-) *n.*

o•ver•fish (ō′vər-fĭsh′) *v.* **-fished, -fish•ing, -fish•es.** — *tr.* To fish (a body of water) to such a degree as to upset the ecological balance or cause depletion of living creatures. — *intr.* To overfish a body of water.

o•ver•flight (ō′vər-flīt′) *n.* An aircraft flight over a particular area, esp. over foreign territory.

o•ver•flow (ō′vər-flō′) *v.* **-flowed, -flow•ing, -flows.** — *intr.* **1.** To flow or run over the top, brim, or banks. **2.** To be filled beyond capacity, as a container. **3.** To have a boundless supply. See Syns at **teem**[1]. — *tr.* **1.** To flow over the top, brim, or banks of. **2.** To spread or cover over; flood. **3.** To cause to fill beyond capacity. — *n.* (ō′vər-flō′). **1.** The act of overflowing. **2.** Something that flows over; an excess. **3.** An outlet or a vent through which excess liquid may escape. **4.** *Comp. Sci.* A condition in which the result of a calculation is too large to be stored in the allotted location.

o•ver•fly (ō′vər-flī′) *tr.v.* **-flew** (-flo͞o′), **-flown** (-flōn′), **-fly•**

ă pat	oi boy
ā pay	ou out
âr care	o͝o took
ä father	o͞o boot
ĕ pet	ŭ cut
ē be	ûr urge
ĭ pit	th thin
ī pie	*th* this
îr pier	hw which
ŏ pot	zh vision
ō toe	ə about, item
ô paw	

Stress marks:
′ (primary);
′ (secondary), as in
dictionary (dĭk′shə-nĕr′ē)

kən), **-tak•ing, -takes. 1.a.** To catch up with; draw even or level with. **b.** To pass after catching up with. **2.** To come upon unexpectedly; take by surprise.

o•ver-the-air (ō′vər-thē-âr′) *adj.* Of, relating to, or being a medium of broadcast transmission, such as radio.

o•ver-the-count•er (ō′vər-*thə*-koun′tər) *adj.* **1.** Not listed or available on an officially recognized stock exchange but traded directly between buyers and sellers. **2.** That can be sold legally without a prescription.

o•ver-the-hill (ō′vər-*thə*-hĭl′) *adj. Informal.* **1.** Past one's peak of youthful vigor and freshness. **2.** Far along in life; old.

o•ver•throw (ō′vər-thrō′) *tr.v.* **-threw** (-thro͞o′), **-thrown** (-thrōn′), **-throw•ing, -throws. 1.** To throw over; overturn. **2.** To cause the downfall or destruction of, esp. by force or concerted action. **3.** *Sports.* To throw an object over and beyond (an intended mark). — *n.* (ō′vər-thrō′). **1.** An instance of overthrowing, esp. one that results in downfall or destruction. **2.** *Sports.* The overthrowing of a ball.

Syns: *overthrow, overturn, subvert, topple, upset.* The central meaning shared by these verbs is "to cause the downfall, destruction, abolition, or undoing of": *overthrow an empire; overturn existing institutions; subverting civil order; toppled the government; unable to upset the will.*

o•ver•thrust fault (ō′vər-thrŭst′) *n. Geol.* A fault in which one section of crust has ridden up over another.

o•ver•time (ō′vər-tīm′) *n.* **1.** Time beyond an established limit, as: **a.** Working hours in addition to those of a regular schedule. **b.** *Sports.* A period of playing time added after the expiration of the set time limit. **2.** Payment for work done overtime. — *adv.* Beyond the established time limit, esp. that of the normal working day. — *tr.v.* (ō′vər-tīm′) **-timed, -tim•ing, -times.** To exceed the desired timing for.

o•ver•tone (ō′vər-tōn′) *n.* **1.** An ulterior, usu. implicit meaning or quality; an implication or a hint. Often used in the plural. **2.** See **harmonic** 1.

Jesse Owens
Photographed at the 1936 Summer Olympics in Berlin, Germany

o•ver•top (ō′vər-tŏp′) *tr.v.* **-topped, -top•ping, -tops. 1.** To extend or rise above or beyond; tower over. **2.** To take precedence over; override. **3.** To be greater or better than; surpass.

o•ver•trick (ō′vər-trĭk′) *n. Games.* A card trick won in excess of game or of contract, as in bridge.

o•ver•trump (ō′vər-trŭmp′, ō′vər-trŭmp′) *v.* **-trumped, -trump•ing, -trumps.** — *intr.* To overtrump a card. — *tr.* To trump with a higher trump card than one previously played on a trick.

o•ver•ture (ō′vər-cho͝or′) *n.* **1.** *Mus.* **a.** An instrumental composition intended esp. as an introduction to an extended work. **b.** A similar orchestral work, such as a concert piece. **2.** An introductory section or part, as of a poem; a prelude. **3.** An act, an offer, or a proposal indicating readiness for a course of action or a relationship. — *tr.v.* **-tured, -tur•ing, -tures. 1.** To present as an introduction or a proposal. **2.** To present an offer or a proposal to. [ME, opening < OFr. < VLat. **ōpertūra*, alteration of Lat. *apertūra* < *apertus*, p.part. of *aperīre*, to open. See **wer-**[4]***.**]

o•ver•turn (ō′vər-tûrn′) *v.* **-turned, -turn•ing, -turns.** — *tr.* **1.** To cause to turn over or capsize; upset. **2.a.** To cause the ruin or destruction of. See Syns at **overthrow. b.** *Law.* To invalidate or reverse (a decision) by legal means. — *intr.* To turn over or capsize. — *n.* (ō′vər-tûrn′). **1.** The act or process of overturning. **2.** The state of having been overturned.

o•ver•view (ō′vər-vyo͞o′) *n.* **1.** A broad comprehensive view; a survey. **2.** A summary or review.

o•ver•ween•ing (ō′vər-wē′nĭng) *adj.* **1.** Presumptuously arrogant; overbearing: *overweening manners.* **2.** Excessive; immoderate: *overweening ambition.* **—o′ver•ween′ing•ly** *adv.*

o•ver•weigh (ō′vər-wā′) *tr.v.* **-weighed, -weigh•ing, -weighs. 1.** To have more weight than. **2.** To weigh down excessively; overburden or oppress.

o•ver•weight (ō′vər-wāt′) *adj.* Weighing more than is normal, necessary, or allowed, esp. having more body weight than is considered normal or healthy for one's age or build. — *n.* (ō′vər-wāt′). **1.** More weight than is normal, necessary, or allowed. **2.** Greater weight or importance; preponderance. — *tr.v.* (ō′vər-wāt′) **-weight•ed, -weight•ing, -weights. 1.** To weigh down too heavily; overload. **2.** To give too much emphasis, importance, or consideration to.

o•ver•whelm (ō′vər-hwĕlm′, -wĕlm′) *tr.v.* **-whelmed, -whelm•ing, -whelms. 1.** To surge over and submerge; engulf. **2.a.** To defeat completely and decisively. **b.** To affect deeply in mind or emotion. **3.** To present with an excessive amount. **4.** To turn over; upset.

o•ver•whelm•ing (ō′vər-hwĕl′mĭng, -wĕl′-) *adj.* Overpowering in effect or strength. **—o′ver•whelm′ing•ly** *adv.*

o•ver•win•ter (ō′vər-wĭn′tər) *intr.v.* **-tered, -ter•ing, -ters. 1.** To remain alive through the winter: *sheep that overwintered on the steppe.* **2.** To pass or spend the winter. — *adj.* (ō′vər-wĭn′tər). Occurring during the period of winter.

o•ver•with•hold (ō′vər-wĭth-hōld′, -wĭ*th*-) *v.* **-held** (-hĕld′), **-hold•ing, -holds.** — *tr.* **1.** To deduct (an amount in withholding tax) beyond the tax owed. **2.** To subject to overwithholding. — *intr.* To deduct too much withholding tax.

o•ver•work (ō′vər-wûrk′) *v.* **-worked, -work•ing, -works.** — *tr.* **1.** To force to work too hard or too long. **2.a.** To rework to excess. **b.** To use too often: *overworked clichés.* **3.** To decorate the entire surface of. — *intr.* To work too long or too hard. — *n.* (ō′vər-wûrk′). Excessive work.

o•ver•write (ō′vər-rīt′) *v.* **-wrote** (-rōt′), **-writ•ten** (-rĭt′n), **-writ•ing, -writes.** — *tr.* **1.** To cover (something) with writing. **2.** To write about in an artificial or an excessively elaborate, wordy style. — *intr.* To write artificial, excessively elaborate, or wordy prose.

o•ver•wrought (ō′vər-rôt′) *adj.* **1.** Excessively nervous or excited; agitated. **2.** Extremely elaborate or ornate; overdone.

ovi– or **ovo–** or **ov–** *pref.* Egg; ovum: *oviferous.* [Lat. *ōvi-* < *ōvum*, egg. See **awi-*.**]

o•vi•cide (ō′vĭ-sīd′) *n.* A chemical agent that kills eggs, esp. the eggs of insects. **—o′vi•cid′al** (-sīd′l) *adj.*

Ov•id (ŏv′ĭd). 43 B.C.–A.D. 17. Roman poet known for his explorations of love, esp. in *Metamorphoses* (c. A.D. 8). **—O•vid′i•an** (ō-vĭd′ē-ən) *adj.*

o•vi•duct (ō′vĭ-dŭkt′) *n.* A tube through which ova pass from the ovary to the uterus or to the outside. **—o′vi•duc′tal** *adj.*

O•vie•do (ō-vyā′dō, ô-vyĕ′*th*ô). A city of NW Spain near the Cantabrian Mts.; founded c. 760 and the cap. of Asturian kings until 910. Pop. 189,376.

o•vif•er•ous (ō-vĭf′ər-əs) *adj.* Bearing or producing ova.

o•vi•form (ō′və-fôrm′) *adj.* Shaped like an egg; ovoid.

O•vim•bun•du (ō′vĭm-bo͝on′do͞o) *n., pl.* **Ovimbundu** or **-dus.** See **Mbundu** 1.

o•vine (ō′vīn′) *adj.* Of, relating to, or characteristic of sheep; sheeplike. — *n.* An ovine animal. [LLat. *ovīnus* < Lat. *ovis*, sheep. See **owi-*.**]

o•vip•a•rous (ō-vĭp′ər-əs) *adj.* Producing eggs that hatch outside the body. **—o′vi•par′i•ty** (ō′və-păr′ĭ-tē) *n.* **—o•vip′a•rous•ly** *adv.*

o•vi•pos•it (ō′və-pŏz′ĭt) *intr.v.* **-it•ed, -it•ing, -its.** To lay eggs, esp. by means of an ovipositor. **—o′vi•po•si′tion** (-pə-zĭsh′ən) *n.* **—o′vi•po•si′tion•al** *adj.*

o•vi•pos•i•tor (ō′və-pŏz′ĭ-tər) *n.* **1.** A tubular structure, usu. concealed, with which many female insects deposit eggs. **2.** A similar organ of certain fishes.

o•vi•sac (ō′vĭ-săk′) *n.* An egg-containing capsule, such as an ootheca or a Graafian follicle.

ovo– *pref.* Var. of **ovi–.**

o•void (ō′void′) also **o•voi•dal** (ō-void′l) — *adj.* Shaped like an egg; ovate. — *n.* Something that is shaped like an egg.

o•vo•lac•to•veg•e•tar•i•an (ō′vō-lăk′tō-vĕj′ĭ-târ′ē-ən) *n.* A vegetarian whose diet includes eggs and dairy products.

o•vo•lo (ō′və-lō′) *n., pl.* **-li** (-lī′). *Archit.* A rounded convex molding, often a quarter section of a circle or an ellipse. [Obsolete Ital., dim. of *uovo, ovo*, egg < Lat. *ōvum.* See **awi-*.**]

o•von•ic (ō-vŏn′ĭk) *adj.* Of or relating to a device whose operation is based on the Ovshinsky effect. [OV(SHINSKY EFFECT) + (ELECTR)ONIC.]

o•vo•tes•tis (ō′vō-tĕs′tĭs) *n., pl.* **-tes** (-tēz′). A hermaphroditic reproductive organ that produces both sperm and eggs, found in certain gastropods.

o•vo•vi•vip•a•rous (ō′vō-vī-vĭp′ər-əs) *adj.* Producing eggs that hatch within the female's body without obtaining nourishment from it. Used of certain fishes and reptiles and many invertebrates. **—o′vo•vi′vi•par′i•ty** (-vī′və-păr′ĭ-tē), **o′vo•vi•vip′a•rous•ness** (-vĭp′ər-əs-nĭs) *n.* **—o′vo•vi•vip′a•rous•ly** *adv.*

Ov•shin•sky effect (ŏv-shĭn′skē, ôv-) *n.* The effect by which a specific glassy thin film switches from a nonconductor to a semiconductor upon application of a minimum voltage. [After Stanford R. *Ovshinsky* (b. 1922), Amer. inventor.]

o•vu•late (ō′vyə-lāt′, ŏv′yə-) *intr.v.* **-lat•ed, -lat•ing, -lates.** To produce ova; discharge eggs from the ovary. [< OVULE.] **—o′vu•la′tion** *n.* **—o′vu•la•to′ry** (-lə-tôr′ē, -tōr′ē) *adj.*

o•vule (ō′vyo͞ol, ŏv′yo͞ol) *n.* **1.** *Bot.* A minute structure in seed plants, containing the embryo sac and surrounded by the nucellus, that develops into a seed after fertilization. **2.** *Zool.* A small or immature ovum. [NLat. *ōvulum*, dim. of Lat. *ōvum*, egg. See **awi-*.**] **—o′vu•lar** (ō′vyə-lər, ŏv′yə-), **o′vu•lar′y** (-lĕr′ē) *adj.*

o•vum (ō′vəm) *n., pl.* **o•va** (ō′və). The female reproductive cell or gamete of animals; egg. [Lat. *ōvum*, egg. See **awi-*.**]

ow (ou) *interj.* Used esp. in response to sudden pain.

O•wa•ton•na (ō′wə-tŏn′ə). A city of SE MN S of Minneapolis. Pop. 19,386.

owe (ō) *v.* **owed, ow•ing, owes.** — *tr.* **1.** To be indebted to the amount of. **2.** To have a moral obligation to render or offer. **3.** To be in debt to. **4.** To be indebted or obliged for. **5.** To bear (a certain feeling) toward someone. **6.** *Archaic.* To have as a possession; own. — *intr.* To be in debt. [ME *owen* < OE *āgan*, to possess. See **ēik-*.**]

Ow•en (ō′ĭn), **Robert.** 1771–1858. Welsh-born British manufacturer and social reformer who attempted to establish a cooperative community at New Harmony in IN (1825–28).

Owen, Wilfred. 1893–1918. British poet whose work reflects his experiences in World War I.

Ow•ens (ō′ĭnz), **Jesse.** 1913–80. Amer. track star who won four gold medals at the 1936 Olympics.

O•wens•bor•o (ō′ĭnz-bûr′ō, -bŭr′ō). A city of NW KY on the Ohio R. WSW of Louisville; settled c. 1800. Pop. 53,549.

Owen Sound. A city of SE Ontario, Canada, on **Owen Sound,** an inlet of Georgian Bay. Pop. 19,883.

Owens River. A river of E CA rising in the Sierra Nevada and flowing c. 193 km (120 mi) via aqueduct to Los Angeles.

Owen Stan•ley Range (stăn′lē). A mountain range extending c. 483 km (300 mi) SE on New Guinea I. in Papua New Guinea and rising to 4,075.7 m (13,363 ft).

ow•ing (ō′ĭng) *adj.* Still to be paid; due.

owing to *prep.* Because of; on account of.

owl (oul) *n.* **1.** Any of various often nocturnal birds of prey of the order Strigiformes, having hooked talons, large heads with short hooked beaks, and large eyes set forward. **2.** Any of a breed of domestic pigeons resembling owls. [ME *owle* < OE *ūle*, of imit. orig.]

owl•et (ou′lĭt) *n.* A small or young owl.

owlet moth *n.* See **noctuid.**

owl•ish (ou′lĭsh) *adj.* Resembling or characteristic of an owl. — **owl′ish•ly** *adv.* — **owl′ish•ness** *n.*

owl's clover (oulz) *n.* Any of various New World plants of the genus *Orthocarpus,* having bracteate spikes, variously colored flowers, and tubular bilabiate corolla.

own (ōn) *adj.* Of or belonging to oneself or itself: *her own clothes.* — *n.* That which belongs to one: *It is my own.* — *v.* **owned, own•ing, owns.** — *tr.* **1.a.** To have or possess as property. **b.** To have control over. **2.** To admit as being in accordance with fact, truth, or a claim; acknowledge. — *intr.* To make a full confession or acknowledgment: *The thief owned up.* — ***idioms.* of one's own.** Belonging completely to oneself. **on (one's) own. 1.** By one's own efforts. **2.** Responsible for oneself; independent of outside help or control. [ME *owen* < OE *āgen.* See **ēik-*.**] — **own′er** *n.*

own•er•ship (ō′nər-shĭp′) *n.* **1.** The state or fact of being an owner. **2.** Legal right to the possession of a thing.

O•wos•so (ō-wŏs′ō). A city of central MI W of Flint. Pop. 16,322.

O•wy•hee (ō-wī′ē, -hē). A river, c. 483 km (300 mi), of SW ID, N NV, and SE OR emptying into the Snake R.

ox (ŏks) *n., pl.* **ox•en** (ŏk′sən). **1.** An adult castrated bull of the genus *Bos,* esp. *B. taurus,* used chiefly as a draft animal. **2.** A bovine mammal. [ME < OE *oxa.*]

ox– *pref.* Var. of **oxo–.**

ox•a•cil•lin (ŏk′sə-sĭl′ĭn) *n.* A semisynthetic penicillin effective against penicillin-resistant infections, esp. those of staphylococci. [OX(O)– + A(ZOLE) + (PENI)CILLIN.]

ox•a•late (ŏk′sə-lāt′) *n.* A salt or an ester of oxalic acid. — *tr.v.* **-lat•ed, -lat•ing, -lates.** To treat (a specimen) with an oxalate or oxalic acid. [OXAL(IC ACID) + –ATE[2].]

ox•al•ic acid (ŏk-săl′ĭk) *n.* A poisonous crystalline organic acid, $H_2C_2O_4 \cdot 2H_2O$, found in many plants, such as spinach, and used as a bleach and rust remover. [Lat. *oxalis*, wood sorrel; see OXALIS + –IC.]

ox•a•lis (ŏk′sə-lĭs, ŏk-săl′ĭs) *n.* Any of numerous plants of the genus *Oxalis,* having often cloverlike compound leaves with three leaflets and flowers that are usu. clustered in umbels. [Lat. *oxalis,* wood sorrel < Gk. < *oxus,* sour. See **ak-*.**]

ox•a•lo•ac•e•tate (ŏk′sə-lō-ăs′ĭ-tāt′) or **ox•al•ac•e•tate** (-ăs′ĭ-tāt′) *n.* A salt or an ester of oxaloacetic acid. [OXAL(IC ACID) + ACET(IC ACID) + –ATE[2].]

ox•a•lo•a•ce•tic acid (ŏk′sə-lō-ə-sē′tĭk, ŏk-săl′ō-) or **ox•al•a•ce•tic acid** (ŏk-sĕl′ə-sē′tĭk, ŏk′sə-lə-) *n.* A colorless crystalline dicarboxylic acid, $C_4H_4O_5$, that is formed by oxidation of malic acid in the Krebs cycle and is an intermediate in the metabolism of carbohydrates. [OXAL(IC ACID) + ACETIC ACID.]

ox•blood red (ŏks′blŭd′) *n. Color.* A dark or deep red to medium reddish brown.

ox•bow (ŏks′bō′) *n.* **1.** A U-shaped piece of wood that fits under and around the neck of an ox, with its upper ends attached to the bar of the yoke. **2.a.** A U-shaped bend in a river. **b.** The land within an oxbow. — **ox′bow′** *adj.*

oxbow lake *n.* A crescent-shaped lake formed when a meander of a river or stream is cut off from the main channel.

Ox•bridge (ŏks′brĭj′) *n. Chiefly British.* Oxford and Cambridge universities. — *adj.* Of or relating to Oxbridge.

ox•en (ŏk′sən) *n.* Pl. of **ox.**

ox•eye (ŏks′ī′) *n.* **1.** Either of two Eurasian plants of the genus *Buphthalum,* having flowers with yellow rays and dark centers. **2.** Any of various New World plants of the genus *Heliopsis,* having similar flowers. **3.** A round or oval dormer window.

oxeye daisy *n.* See **daisy** 1.

ox•ford (ŏks′fərd) *n.* **1.** A low sturdy shoe that laces over the instep. **2.** A cotton cloth of a tight basket weave, used primarily for shirts. [After OXFORD, England.]

Ox•ford (ŏks′fərd). **1.** A borough of S-central England on the Thames R. WNW of London; chartered 1605. Oxford University was founded in the 12th cent. and still dominates the center of the city. Pop. 114,400. **2.** A village of SW OH NW of Hamilton near the IN border. Pop. 18,937.

oxford gray *n. Color.* A dark gray. [After OXFORD, England.]

Oxford movement *n.* A 19th-century Anglican movement, originating in Oxford, England, for restoration of High-Church ideals.

ox•heart (ŏks′härt′) *n.* A variety of cultivated cherry having sweet juicy fruit. [< its shape.]

ox•i•dant (ŏk′sĭ-dənt) *n.* See **oxidizer.** [Fr. *oxidant,* pr.part. of *oxider,* to oxidize < *oxide,* oxide. See OXIDE.]

ox•i•dase (ŏk′sĭ-dās′, -dāz′) *n.* Any of a group of enzymes that catalyze oxidation, esp. one that reacts with molecular oxygen to catalyze the oxidation of a substrate. [OXID(ATION) + –ASE.] — **ox′i•da′sic** *adj.*

ox•i•da•tion (ŏk′sĭ-dā′shən) *n.* **1.** The combination of a substance with oxygen. **2.** A reaction in which the atoms in an element lose electrons and the valence of the element is correspondingly increased. [Fr. < *oxider,* to oxidize < *oxide,* oxide. See OXIDE.] — **ox′i•da′tive** *adj.*

ox•i•da•tion-re•duc•tion (ŏk′sĭ-dā′shən-rĭ-dŭk′shən) *n.* A chemical reaction in which an atom or ion loses electrons to another atom or ion.

oxidative phosphorylation *n.* The process in cell metabolism by which respiratory enzymes in the mitochondria synthesize ATP from ADP during the oxidation of reduced NAD by molecular oxygen.

ox•ide (ŏk′sīd′) *n.* A binary compound of an element or a radical with oxygen. [Fr. : *ox(ygène),* oxygen; see OXYGEN + *(ac)ide,* acid (< Lat. *acidus,* tart, acid; see ACID).] — **ox•id′ic** (ŏk-sĭd′ĭk) *adj.*

ox•i•dize (ŏk′sĭ-dīz′) *v.* **-dized, -diz•ing, -diz•es.** — *tr.* **1.** To combine with oxygen; make into an oxide. **2.** To increase the positive charge or valence of (an element) by removing electrons. **3.** To coat with oxide. — *intr.* To become oxidized. — **ox′i•diz′a•ble** *adj.* — **ox′i•di•za′tion** (-dĭ-zā′shən) *n.*

ox•i•diz•er (ŏk′sĭ-dī′zər) *n.* A substance that oxidizes another substance; an oxidizing agent.

ox•i•do•re•duc•tase (ŏk′sĭ-dō-rĭ-dŭk′tās′, -tāz′) *n.* An enzyme that catalyzes an oxidation-reduction reaction. [OXID(ATION) + REDUCT(ION) + –ASE.]

ox•ime (ŏk′sēm) *n.* Any of a group of compounds containing a CNOH group, formed by treating aldehydes or ketones with hydroxylamine. [OX(O)– + IM(ID)E.]

ox•lip (ŏks′lĭp′) *n.* A Eurasian primrose *(Primula elatior)* having yellow flowers clustered in a one-sided umbel. [ME *oxeslippe* < OE *oxanslyppe* : *oxan,* genitive sing. of *oxa,* ox + *slyppe,* slimy substance; see **sleubh-*.**]

Ox•nard (ŏks′närd′). A city of S CA WNW of Los Angeles on the Pacific coast. Pop. 142,216.

oxo– or **ox–** *pref.* Oxygen: *oxime.* [< OXYGEN.]

Ox•on Hill (ŏk′sŏn, -sən). A community of central MD, a suburb of Washington DC. Pop. 35,794.

Ox•o•ni•an (ŏk-sō′nē-ən) *adj.* Of or relating to Oxford, England, or Oxford University. — *n.* **1.** A native or inhabitant of Oxford, England. **2.** One who studies or has studied at Oxford University. [< Med.Lat. *Oxōnia,* Oxford < OE *Oxnaford* : *oxena,* genitive pl. of *oxa,* ox + *ford,* ford; see FORD.]

ox•peck•er (ŏks′pĕk′ər) *n.* Either of two African starlings *(Buphagus africanus* or *B. erythrorhyncus)* that eat ticks on the hides of large wild or domestic animals.

ox•tail (ŏks′tāl′) *n.* The tail of an ox, esp. when used for food.

Ox•us (ŏk′səs). See **Amu Darya.**

oxy– *pref.* Oxygen, esp. additional oxygen: *oxyacetylene.* [< OXYGEN.]

ox•y•a•cet•y•lene (ŏk′sē-ə-sĕt′l-ĭn, -ēn′) *adj.* Of or using a mixture of acetylene and oxygen: *an oxyacetylene torch.*

ox•y•ac•id (ŏk′sē-ăs′ĭd) *n.* An oxygen-containing acid.

ox•y•ceph•a•ly (ŏk′sē-sĕf′ə-lē) *n., pl.* **-lies.** A congenital abnormality of the skull in which the top of the head assumes a conical or pointed shape. [< Gk. *oxukephalos,* sharp-headed : *oxus,* sharp; see OXYGEN + *–kephalos,* -cephalous.] — **ox′y•ce•phal′ic** (-sə-făl′ĭk), **ox′y•ceph′a•lous** *adj.*

ox•y•co•done (ŏk′sĭ-kō′dōn′) *n.* A narcotic alkaloid, $C_{18}H_{21}NO_4$, related to codeine and used as an analgesic and a sedative chiefly in the form of its hydrochloride salt. [< chemical name *(dihydrohydr)oxycod(ein)one.*]

ox•y•gen (ŏk′sĭ-jən) *n. Symbol* **O** An element constituting 21 percent of the atmosphere by volume that occurs as a diatomic gas, O_2, combines with most elements, is essential for plant and animal respiration, and is required for nearly all combustion. Atomic number 8; atomic weight 15.9994; melting point −218.4°C; boiling point −183.0°C; gas density at 0°C 1.429 grams per liter; valence 2. See table at **element.** [Fr. *oxygène* : Gk. *oxus,* sharp, acid; see **ak-*** + Fr. *-gène,* -gen.] — **ox′y•gen′ic** (-jĕn′ĭk) *adj.* — **ox′y•gen′i•cal•ly** *adv.* — **ox•yg′e•nous** (ŏk-sĭj′ə-nəs) *adj.*

ox•y•gen•ase (ŏk′sĭ-jə-nās′, -nāz′) *n.* An oxidoreductase that catalyzes the incorporation of molecular oxygen into its substrate.

ox•y•gen•ate (ŏk′sĭ-jə-nāt′) also **ox•y•gen•ize** (-jə-nīz′) *tr.v.* **-at•ed, -at•ing, -ates** also **-ized, -iz•ing, -iz•es.** To treat, combine, or infuse with oxygen. — **ox′y•gen•a′tion** *n.* — **ox′y•gen•a′tor** *n.*

oxygen debt *n.* The amount of extra oxygen required by muscle tissue during recovery from vigorous exercise.

oxygen mask *n.* A device placed over the mouth and nose,

owl
Snowy owl
Nyctea scandiaca

ox
Bos grunniens

ă **pat**	oi **boy**
ā **pay**	ou **out**
âr **care**	ŏŏ **took**
ä **father**	ōō **boot**
ĕ **pet**	ŭ **cut**
ē **be**	ûr **urge**
ĭ **pit**	th **thin**
ī **pie**	*th* **this**
îr **pier**	hw **which**
ŏ **pot**	zh **vision**
ō **toe**	ə **about,**
ô **paw**	**item**

Stress marks:
′ (primary);
′ (secondary), as in
dictionary (dĭk′shə-nĕr′ē)

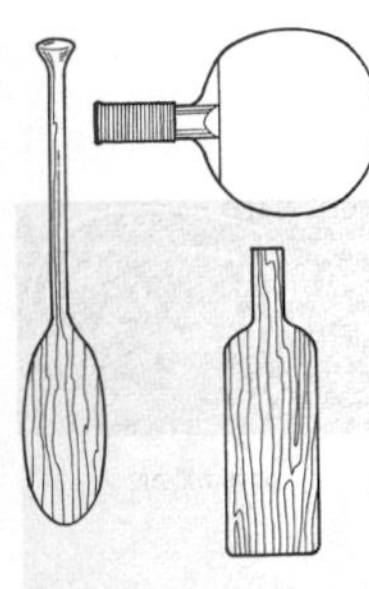
paddle[1]
Canoe (*left*), table tennis (*top right*), and pottery (*bottom right*)

paddy
Rice paddies in Java

other material into a body cavity or wound for therapeutic purposes. **b.** The material so used; a pack.
pack•ing•house (păk′ĭng-hous′) *n.* **1.** A firm that slaughters livestock and processes and packs meat and meat products. **2.** A firm that processes and packs other food products.
pack•man (păk′măn′, -mən) *n.* A peddler.
pack rat *n.* **1.** Any of various small North American rodents of the genus *Neotoma* that collect a great variety of small objects in or around their nests. **2.** *Western U.S.* A petty thief. **3.** *Slang.* A collector of miscellaneous objects.
pack•sack (păk′săk′) *n.* A canvas or leather traveling bag designed to be carried while strapped to the shoulders.
pack•sad•dle (păk′săd′l) *n.* A saddle on which loads can be secured.
pack•thread (păk′thrĕd′) *n.* A strong two-ply or three-ply twine for sewing or tying packages or bundles.
pack train *n.* A line of animals, such as horses or mules, loaded with supplies for an expedition.
pact (păkt) *n.* **1.** A formal agreement, as between nations; a treaty. **2.** A compact; a bargain. [Ult. < Lat. *pactum* < neut. sing. p.part. of *pacīscī*, to agree. See **pag-***.]
pad[1] (păd) *n.* **1.** A thin cushionlike mass of soft material used to fill, give shape, or protect against jarring, scraping, or other injury. **2.** A flexible saddle without a frame. **3.** An ink-soaked cushion used to ink a rubber stamp. **4.** A number of sheets of paper of the same size stacked one on top of the other and glued together at one end; a tablet. **5.** The broad floating leaf of an aquatic plant such as the water lily. **6.a.** The cushionlike flesh on the underpart of the toes and feet of many animals. **b.** The foot of such an animal. **7.** The fleshy underside of the end of a finger or toe. **8.a.** A launch pad. **b.** A helipad. **9.** A keypad. **10.** *Slang.* One's apartment or room. —*tr.v.* **pad•ded, pad•ding, pads. 1.** To line or stuff with soft material. **2.** To lengthen (something written or spoken) with extraneous material. —***idiom.* on the pad.** *Slang.* Taking bribes. [?]
pad[2] (păd) *v.* **pad•ded, pad•ding, pads.** —*intr.* **1.** To go about on foot. **2.** To move about quietly. —*tr.* To go along (a route) on foot. —*n.* **1.** A muffled sound like soft footsteps. **2.** A horse with a plodding gait. [Prob. of LGer. orig.; akin to *path*.] —**pad′der** *n.*
Pa•dang (pä′däng′, pä-däng′). A city of W Indonesia on the W-central coast of Sumatra. Pop. 296,680.
pa•dauk (pə-dôk′) also **pa•douk** (-do͝ok′) *n.* **1.** A southeast Asian tree *(Pterocarpus indicus)* having reddish wood with a black grain. **2.** The wood of this tree. [Burmese.]
pad•ding (păd′ĭng) *n.* **1.** The act of stuffing, filling, or lining. **2.** A soft material used to make pads or a pad. **3.** Extraneous material added to written work to make it longer.
pad•dle[1] (păd′l) *n.* **1.** *Naut.* A wooden implement having a blade at one or both ends, used without an oarlock to propel a canoe or small boat. **2.** Any of various implements resembling the paddle of a boat or canoe, as: **a.** An iron tool for stirring molten ore in a furnace. **b.** A tool with a shovellike blade used to mix materials in glassmaking. **c.** A potter's pallet. **d.** A narrow board used to beat clothes in laundering by hand. **e.** A flat board for administering physical punishment. **f.** *Sports.* A light racket for playing table tennis. **3.** A board on a paddle wheel. **4.** A flipper or flat appendage of certain animals. **5.** The act of paddling. —*v.* **-dled, -dling, -dles.** —*intr.* **1.** *Naut.* **a.** To propel a watercraft with paddles or a paddle. **b.** To row slowly and gently. **2.** To move through water by repeated short strokes of the limbs. —*tr.* **1.** *Naut.* **a.** To propel (a watercraft) with paddles or a paddle. **b.** To convey in a watercraft propelled by paddles. **2.** To spank with a paddle, esp. as a punishment. **3.** To stir or shape (material) with a paddle. [ME *padell*, implement used for cleaning a plowshare, perh. < Med.Lat. *padela*.] —**pad′dler** *n.*
pad•dle[2] (păd′l) *intr.v.* **-dled, -dling, -dles. 1.** To dabble about in shallow water; splash gently with the hands or feet. **2.** To move with a waddling motion; toddle. [Perh. of LGer. orig.]
pad•dle•ball (păd′l-bôl′) *n. Sports.* **1.** A game for two to four participants played with a wooden or plastic paddle and a ball similar to a tennis ball on a court having one, three, or four walls. **2.** The ball used in this game.
pad•dle•board (păd′l-bôrd′, -bōrd′) *n. Sports.* A long narrow floatable board used esp. in surfing.
pad•dle•boat (păd′l-bōt′) *n. Naut.* A boat, esp. a steamship, propelled through the water by paddle wheels on each side or by one paddle wheel astern.
pad•dle•fish (păd′l-fĭsh′) *n., pl.* **paddlefish** or **-fish•es.** A fish of the family Polyodontidae, having a long paddle-shaped snout, esp. *Polyodon spathula* of the Mississippi River basin.
paddle wheel *n. Naut.* A wheel with boards or paddles affixed around its circumference, usu. driven by steam to propel a ship. —**pad′dle-wheel′** (păd′l-hwēl′, -wēl′) *adj.*
paddle wheeler *n. Naut.* See **paddleboat.**
pad•dling (păd′lĭng, păd′l-ĭng) *n.* **1.** *Naut.* Moving a boat with a paddle. **2.** A beating or spanking with a paddle.
pad•dock (păd′ək) *n.* **1.** A fenced area, usu. near a stable, used chiefly for grazing horses. **2.** *Sports.* **a.** An enclosure at a racetrack where the horses are assembled, saddled, and paraded before each race. **b.** An area of an automobile racetrack where cars are prepared. **3.** *Australian.* A piece of fenced-in land. —*tr.v.* **-docked, -dock•ing, -docks.** To confine in a paddock. [Alteration of ME *parrok* < OE *pearroc*.]
pad•dy (păd′ē) *n., pl.* **-dies. 1.** Rice, esp. in the husk, whether gathered or still in the field. **2.** A specially irrigated or flooded field where rice is grown. [Malay *padi*.]
Pad•dy (păd′ē) *n. Offensive Slang.* Used as a disparaging term for an Irishman. [Nickname for Ir.Gael. *Pádraig*, Patrick.]
paddy field *n.* A rice paddy.
paddy wagon *n. Slang.* A van used by police for taking suspects into custody. [?]
Pa•der•born (pä′dər-bôrn′). A city of W-central Germany NW of Kassel; joined the Hanseatic League in the 13th cent. Pop. 109,514.
Pa•de•rew•ski (păd′ə-rĕf′skē, -rĕv′-, pä′də-), **Ignace Jan.** 1860–1941. Polish pianist and prime minister (1919–20) who led (1940–41) the exiled Polish government.
Pa•di•shah (pä′dĭ-shä′) *n.* **1.** Used formerly as a title for the monarch of Iran. **2.** Used formerly as a title for the sultan of Turkey. [Pers. *pādshāh* : OPers. *pati-*, master; see **poti-*** + Pers. *shāh*, king.]
pad•lock (păd′lŏk′) *n.* A detachable lock with a U-shaped bar hinged at one end, designed to be passed through the staple of a hasp or a link in a chain and then snapped shut. —*tr.v.* **-locked, -lock•ing, -locks.** To lock up with or as if with a padlock. [ME *padlok* : *pad-*, of unknown meaning + *lok*, lock; see LOCK[1].]
pa•douk (pə-do͞ok′) *n.* Var. of **padauk.**
pa•dre (pä′drā, -drē) *n.* **1.** Father. Used as a form of address for a priest in Italy, Spain, Portugal, and Latin America. **2.** *Informal.* A military chaplain. **3.** *Chiefly British.* A parson. [Sp., Ital., or Port., all < Lat. *pater, patr-*, father. See **pəter-***.]
pa•dro•ne (pə-drō′nē, -nā) *n., pl.* **-nes** (-nēz, -nāz) or **-ni** (-nē). **1.** An owner or a manager, esp. of an inn; a proprietor. **2.** A man who exploitatively employs or finds work for Italian immigrants in America. [Ital. < Lat. *patrōnus*, patron. See PATRON.] —**pa•dro′nism** *n.*
Pad•u•a (păj′o͞o-ə, păd′yo͞o-ə). A city of NE Italy W of Venice; an important cultural center during the Middle Ages. Pop. 231,337. —**Pad′u•an** *adj. & n.*
pad•u•a•soy (păj′o͞o-ə-soi′) *n.* **1.** A rich heavy silk fabric with a corded effect. **2.** A hanging or garment made of this fabric. [Alteration of Fr. *pou-de-soie* < OFr. *pout-de-soie* : *pout* + *de*, of (< Lat. *dē*, of; see DE–) + *soie*, silk (< VLat. **sēta* < LLat. *saeta*, raw silk < Lat., bristle).]
Pa•du•cah (pə-do͞o′kə, -dyo͞o′-). A city of W KY on the Ohio R. and the IL border. Pop. 27,256.
pae•an also **pe•an** (pē′ən) *n.* **1.** *Mus.* A song of joyful praise or exultation. **2.** A fervent expression of joy or praise. **3.** An ancient Greek hymn of thanksgiving or invocation, esp. to Apollo. [Lat. *paeān*, Greek paean < Gk. *paian* < *Paian*, a title of Apollo.] —**pae′an•is′tic** (-ĭs′tĭk) *adj.*
paed– or **paedo–** *pref.* Var. of **pedo–**[2].
pae•do•gen•e•sis also **pe•do•gen•e•sis** (pē′dō-jĕn′ĭ-sĭs) *n.* Reproduction of young during the larval or preadult stage, esp. in insects. —**pae′do•ge•net′ic** (-jə-nĕt′ĭk) *adj.*
paed•o•mor•phism also **ped•o•mor•phism** (pĕd′ə-môr′fĭz′əm, pē′də-) *n.* Retention of juvenile characteristics in the adult, occurring in mammals. —**paed′o•mor′phic** (-fĭk) *adj.*
pa•el•la (pä-ĕl′ə, pä-ā′lyä, -ā′yä) *n.* A Spanish dish made with rice, vegetables, meat, chicken, and seafood and spiced with saffron. [Catalan, frying pan, paella < OFr. *paelle*, frying pan, pot < Lat. *patella*, dim. of *patina*, pan. See PATEN.]
pae•on (pē′ən, -ŏn′) *n.* In quantitative verse, a foot of one long syllable and three short syllables occurring in any order. [Lat. *paeōn* < Gk. *paiōn* < *paian, paiōn*, paean. See PAEAN.]
Paes•tum (pĕs′təm, pē′stəm). An ancient city of S Italy on the Gulf of Salerno; founded as a Greek colony before 600 B.C.
pa•gan (pā′gən) *n.* **1.** One who is not a Christian, Muslim, or Jew; a heathen. **2.** One who has no religion. **3.** A non-Christian. **4.** A hedonist. —*adj.* **1.** Not Christian, Muslim, or Jewish. **2.** Professing no religion; heathen. [ME < LLat. *pāgānus* < Lat., country dweller, civilian < *pāgus*, country, rural district. See **pag-***.] —**pa′gan•dom** (-dəm) *n.* —**pa′gan•ish** *adj.* —**pa′gan•ism** *n.* —**pa′gan•ize′** *v.* —**pa′gan•i•za′tion** (-gə-nĭ-zā′shən) *n.*
Pa•ga•ni•ni (păg′ə-nē′nē, pä′gä-), **Nicolò.** 1782–1840. Italian violinist and composer whose works include six violin concertos.
page[1] (pāj) *n.* **1.a.** One side of a leaf, as of a book, letter, newspaper, or manuscript, esp. the entire leaf. **b.** The writing or printing on one side of a leaf. **c.** The type set for printing one side of a leaf. **2.** A noteworthy or memorable event. **3.** *Comp. Sci.* A quantity, usu. fixed for a given system, of data or program coding that can be transferred between a computer's main memory and an auxiliary memory. **4. pages.** A source or record of knowledge. —*tr.v.* **paged, pag•ing, pag•es. 1.** To number the pages of; paginate. **2.** To turn the pages of. [Fr., alteration of OFr. *pagine* < Lat. *pāgina*. See **pag-***.] —**page′ful′** *n.*
page[2] (pāj) *n.* **1.** A boy who acted as a knight's attendant as the first stage of training for knighthood. **2.** A youth in ceremo-

nial employment or attendance at court. **3.a.** One employed to run errands, carry messages, or act as a guide in a hotel, theater, or club. **b.** One similarly employed in the U.S. Congress or another legislature. **4.** A boy who holds the bride's train at a wedding. —*tr.v.* **paged, pag•ing, pag•es. 1.** To summon or call (a person) by name. **2.** To summon or call (a person) by means of a beeper. **3.** To attend as a page. [ME < OFr., poss. < Ital. *paggio*, perh. ult. < Gk. *paidion*, dim. of *pais, paid-*, child. See **pau-***.]

Page (pāj), **Thomas Nelson.** 1853–1922. Amer. writer and diplomat remembered for his works about the Old South.

Page, Walter Hines. 1855–1918. Amer. journalist who served as U.S. ambassador to Great Britain (1913–18).

pag•eant (păj′ənt) *n.* **1.** An elaborate public dramatic presentation, usu. of a historical or traditional event. **2.** A spectacular procession or celebration. **3.** Colorful showy display; pageantry or pomp. [ME *pagin, pagent*, mystery play, alteration of Med.Lat. *pāgina*, prob. < Lat., page. See **pag-***.]

pag•eant•ry (păj′ən-trē) *n., pl.* **-ries. 1.** Pageants and their presentation. **2.a.** Grand display; pomp. **b.** Empty pomp or show; flashy display.

page•boy (pāj′boi′) *n.* **1.** One, usu. a boy, who acts or serves as a page. **2.** A hairstyle, usu. shoulder-length, with the ends of the hair curled under smoothly in a loose roll.

pag•er (pā′jər) *n.* See **beeper** 2.

Pag•et (păj′ĭt), Sir **James.** 1814–99. British surgeon and pathologist who discovered (1834) the cause of trichinosis.

Pag•et's disease (păj′ĭts) *n.* **1.** A disease, occurring chiefly in old age, in which the bones become enlarged and weakened, often resulting in fracture or deformation. **2.** A form of breast cancer affecting the areola and nipple. [After Sir James PAGET.]

pag•i•nal (păj′ə-nəl) *adj.* **1.** Of, relating to, or consisting of pages. **2.** Page for page: *a paginal facsimile.* [LLat. *pāginālis* < Lat. *pāgina*, page. See PAGE[1].]

pag•i•nate (păj′ə-nāt′) *tr.v.* **-nat•ed, -nat•ing, -nates.** To number the pages of; page. [< Lat. *pāgina*, page. See PAGE[1].]

pag•i•na•tion (păj′ə-nā′shən) *n.* **1.** The system by which pages are numbered. **2.** The arrangement and number of pages in a book, as noted in a catalog or bibliography.

pa•go•da (pə-gō′də) *n.* **1.** A religious building of the Far East, esp. a many-storied Buddhist tower, erected as a memorial or shrine. **2.** A structure, such as a garden pavilion, built in imitation of such a tower. [Port. *pagode*, perh. < Tamil *pagavadi* < Skt. *bhagavatī*, goddess < *bhagavant-*, blessed < *bhagaḥ*, good fortune. See **bhag-***.]

Pa•go Pa•go (päng′ō päng′ō, păng′gō păng′gō, päng′gō päng′gō, pä′gō pä′gō, pä′gō pä′gō) also **Pan•go Pan•go** (päng′ō päng′ō, păng′gō păng′gō, päng′gō päng′gō). The cap. of American Samoa, on Tutuila I. Pop. 3,075.

pah (pä) *interj.* Used to express disgust or irritation.

pah•la•vi (pä′lə-vē′) *n., pl.* **-vis.** A gold coin formerly used in Iran. [Pers. *pahlawī*, after Reza Shah *Pahlavi* (1878–1944), Shah of Iran.]

Pah•la•vi (pä′lə-vē′) also **Peh•le•vi** (pā′-) *n.* An Iranian language used in Persia during the reign of the Sassanids. [Pers. *pahlawī* < *Pahlav*, Parthia < OPers. *Parthava-*.]

Pahlavi, Mohammed Reza. 1919–80. Shah of Iran from 1941 to 1979, when he was deposed by Islamic fundamentalists.

paid[1] (pād) *v.* P.t. and p.part. of **pay**[1].

paid[2] (pād) *v. Naut.* A p.t. and p.part. of **pay**[2].

Paige (pāj), **Leroy Robert ("Satchel").** 1906–82. Amer. baseball player who became the first Black pitcher in the American League (1948).

pail (pāl) *n.* **1.** A watertight cylindrical vessel, open at the top and fitted with a handle; a bucket. **2.** The amount that a pail can hold. [ME *paile* prob. < OFr. *paele*, warming pan, perh. < Lat. *patella*, small pan. See PAELLA.] —**pail′ful′** *n.*

pail•lard (pī-yär′) *n.* A slice of veal, chicken, or beef pounded very thin and quickly grilled, broiled, or sautéed. [?]

pail•lasse also **pal•liasse** (păl-yăs′, păl′yăs′) *n.* A thin mattress filled with straw or sawdust. [Fr. < OFr. < *paille*, straw < LLat. *palea* < Lat., chaff.]

pail•lette (pä-yĕt′, pā-, pă-lĕt′) *n.* **1.** A small piece of metal or foil used in painting with enamel. **2.** A spangle used to ornament a dress or costume. [Fr. < OFr., dim. of *paille*, straw. See PAILLASSE.] —**pail•let′ted** *adj.*

pain (pān) *n.* **1.** An unpleasant sensation varying in severity, resulting from injury, disease, or emotional disorder. **2.** Suffering or distress. **3. pains.** The pangs of childbirth. **4. pains.** Great care or effort. **5.** *Informal.* A source of annoyance; a nuisance. —*v.* **pained, pain•ing, pains.** —*tr.* To cause pain to; hurt or injure. —*intr.* To be the cause of pain. —***idiom.* on** (or **under**) **pain of.** Subject to the penalty of a specified punishment. [ME < OFr. *peine* < Lat. *poena*, penalty, pain < Gk. *poinē*, penalty. See **k^{w}ei-[1]***.]

Paine (pān), **Robert Treat.** 1731–1814. Amer. Revolutionary leader and jurist who signed the Declaration of Independence.

Paine, Thomas. 1737–1809. British-born Amer. writer and Revolutionary leader who wrote *Common Sense* (1776) and *The Rights of Man* (1791–92).

pain•ful (pān′fəl) *adj.* **1.** Causing pain. **2.** Full of pain. **3.** Requiring care and labor; irksome: *a painful task.* **4.** *Archaic.* Diligent; careful. —**pain′ful•ly** *adv.* —**pain′ful•ness** *n.*

pain•kill•er (pān′kĭl′ər) *n.* An agent, such as an analgesic drug, that relieves pain. —**pain′kill′ing** *adj.*

pains•tak•ing (pānz′tā′kĭng) *adj.* Marked by or requiring great pains; careful and diligent. —*n.* Careful and diligent work or effort. —**pains′tak′ing•ly** *adv.*

paint (pānt) *n.* **1.a.** A liquid mixture, usu. of a solid pigment in a liquid vehicle, used as a decorative or protective coating. **b.** The thin dry film formed by such a mixture applied to a surface. **c.** The solid pigment before it is mixed with a vehicle. **2.** A cosmetic, such as rouge, used to give color to the face; makeup. **3.** See **pinto.** —*v.* **paint•ed, paint•ing, paints.** —*tr.* **1.** To make (a picture) with paints. **2.a.** To represent in a picture with paints. **b.** To depict vividly in words. **3.** To coat or decorate with paint. **4.** To apply cosmetics to. **5.** To apply medicine to; swab. —*intr.* **1.** To practice the art of painting pictures. **2.** To cover something with paint. **3.** To apply cosmetics to oneself. **4.** To serve as a surface to be coated with paint. —***idiom.* paint the town red.** *Slang.* To go on a spree. [< ME *painten*, to paint < OFr. *peintier* < *peint*, p.part. of *peindre* < Lat. *pingere.* See **peig-***.] —**paint′a•bil′i•ty** *n.* —**paint′a•ble** *adj.*

paint•brush (pānt′brŭsh′) *n.* **1.** A brush for applying paint. **2.** The Indian paintbrush.

paint•ed (pān′tĭd) *adj.* **1.** Represented in paint. **2.a.** Covered or decorated with paint. **b.** Brightly colored; gaudy. **3.** Excessively or improperly made up with cosmetics.

painted bunting *n.* A small finch *(Passerina ciris)* of the southern United States and Mexico, the male of which has brilliant multicolored plumage.

painted cup *n.* See **Indian paintbrush.**

Paint•ed Desert (pān′tĭd). A plateau region of N-central AZ E of the Colorado and Little Colorado rivers. Eroded layers of sediment and clay have left striking bands of color.

pagoda

painted lady *n.* A widely distributed butterfly *(Vanessa cardui)* having brown, black, and orange markings.

paint•er[1] (pān′tər) *n.* One who paints, either as an artist or a worker.

pain•ter[2] (pān′tər) *n. Naut.* A rope attached to the bow of a boat, esp. a small boat or dinghy, used for tying up, as when docking or towing. [ME *peintour*, prob. < OFr. *pentoir*, strong rope < *pendre*, to hang < VLat. **pendere* < Lat. *pendēre.* See **(s)pen-***.]

pain•ter[3] (pān′tər) *n. Chiefly Upper Southern U.S.* See **mountain lion.** [Alteration of PANTHER.]

paint•er•ly (pān′tər-lē) *adj.* **1.** Of, relating to, or characteristic of a painter; artistic. **2.a.** Having qualities unique to the art of painting. **b.** Of, relating to, or being a style of painting marked by openness of form, with shapes distinguished by variations of color rather than by outline or contour.

paint•er's colic (pān′tərz) *n.* Chronic intestinal pains and constipation caused by lead poisoning. [So called because the disease is often caused by exposure to lead-base paint.]

Mohammed Reza Pahlavi

paint•ing (pān′tĭng) *n.* **1.** The process, art, or occupation of coating surfaces with paint for a utilitarian or an artistic effect. **2.** A picture or design in paint.

pair (pâr) *n., pl.* **pair** or **pairs. 1.** Two corresponding persons or items, similar in form or function and matched or associated. **2.** One object composed of two joined similar parts dependent upon each other: *a pair of pliers.* **3.a.** Two persons joined in marriage or engaged. **b.** Two persons who have something in common and are considered together. **c.** Two mated animals. **d.** Two animals joined together in work. **4.** *Games.* Two playing cards of the same denomination. **5.** Two members of a deliberative body in opposition on a given issue who offset each other's vote by abstention. **6.** *Chem.* An electron pair. —*v.* **paired, pair•ing, pairs.** —*tr.* **1.** To arrange in sets of two; couple. **2.** To join in a pair; mate. **3.** To provide a partner for. —*intr.* **1.** To form pairs or a pair. **2.** To join in marriage; mate. [ME < OFr. *paire* < Lat. *paria*, equals, pl. of *pār*, a pair < *pār*, equal. See **perə-[2]***.]

Usage Note: *Pair* as a noun can be followed by a singular or plural verb. The singular is always used when *pair* denotes the set taken as a single entity: *This pair of shoes is on sale.* A plural verb is used when the members are considered as individuals: *The pair are working together.* After a number other than one, *pair* can be either singular or plural, but the plural is now more common: *She bought six pairs* (or *pair*) *of stockings.*

pair bond *n.* The association formed between a female and male animal during courtship and mating. —**pair bonding** *n.*

pair of compasses *n.* See **compass** 2.

pair of virginals *n. Mus.* See **virginal**[2].

pair production *n.* The simultaneous creation of a positron and an electron from a gamma ray photon in a strong electric field, such as that near a nucleus.

pai•sa (pī-sä′) *n., pl.* **-se** (-sā′) or **-sas** (-säs′). See table at **currency.** [Hindi *paisā*, perh. < *pā'ī*, unit of currency. See PIE[3].]

pai•sa•no (pī-zä′nō) also **pai•san** (-zän′) *n., pl.* **-sa•nos** also **-sans. 1.** A countryman; a compatriot. **2.** *Slang.* A friend; a pal. [Sp. < Fr. *paysan* < OFr. *paisant*, peasant. See PEASANT.]

ă pat	oi boy
ā pay	ou out
âr care	o͝o took
ä father	o͞o boot
ĕ pet	ŭ cut
ē be	ûr urge
ĭ pit	th thin
ī pie	*th* this
îr pier	hw which
ŏ pot	zh vision
ō toe	ə about, item
ô paw	

Stress marks:
′ (primary);
′ (secondary), as in
dictionary (dĭk′shə-nĕr′ē)

pais•ley (pāz′lē) *adj.* **1.** Made of a soft wool fabric with a colorful, woven or printed swirled pattern of abstract curved shapes. **2.** Marked with this pattern. — *n., pl.* **-leys.** An article of clothing made of paisley fabric. [After Paisley.]

Pais•ley (pāz′lē). A burgh of SW Scotland W of Glasgow; became famous in the 19th cent. for its colorful patterned shawls. Pop. 86,100.

Pai•ute also **Pi•ute** (pī′yo͞ot′) *n., pl.* **Paiute** or **-utes** also **Piute** or **-utes. 1.** A member of a Native American people occupying eastern Oregon, western Nevada, and adjacent areas of northeast California. **2.** A member of a Native American people occupying southern Utah and Nevada, northern Arizona, and adjacent areas of southeast California.

paisley

pa•ja•ma (pə-jä′mə, -jăm′ə) *n.* **1.** A loose-fitting garment consisting of trousers and a jacket, worn for sleeping or lounging. Often used in the plural. **2.** Loose-fitting trousers worn in the Far East by men and women. Often used in the plural. [Hindi *pāijāma*, loose-fitting trousers : Pers. *pāī*, leg (< MPers.; see **ped-***) + Pers. *jāmah*, garment.]

Pak. *abbr.* Pakistan.

pak choi (bŏk′ choi′) *n.* Var. of **bok choy.**

Pak•i•stan (păk′ĭ-stăn′, pä′kĭ-stän′). A country of S Asia; home of a prehistoric Indus Valley civilization that flourished until overrun by Aryans c. 1500 B.C. Pakistan passed to the British as part of India and became a separate Muslim state in 1947. Cap. Islamabad. Pop. 83,782,000. — **Pak′i•stan′i** (-stăn′ē, -stä′nē) *adj. & n.*

pal (păl) *Informal.* — *n.* A friend; a chum. — *intr.v.* **palled, pal•ling, pals.** To associate as friends or chums. Often used with *around.* [Romany *phral, phal*; akin to Skt. *bhrātā*, brother. See **bhrāter-***.] — **pal′ly** *adj.*

Pal. *abbr.* Palestine.

pal•ace (păl′ĭs) *n.* **1.** An official royal residence. **2.** *Chiefly British.* The official residence of a high dignitary, such as a bishop. **3.a.** A large or splendid residence. **b.** A large, often gaudy building used for entertainment or exhibitions. [ME < OFr. *palais* < *Palātium*, Palatine, imperial residence.]

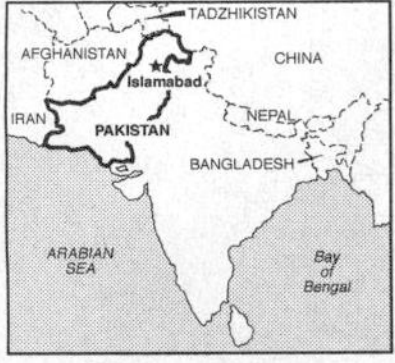

Pakistan

pal•a•din (păl′ə-dĭn) *n.* **1.** A paragon of chivalry; a heroic champion. **2.** A strong supporter or defender of a cause. **3.** Any of the 12 peers of Charlemagne's court. [Fr. < Ital. *paladino* < LLat. *palātīnus*, palatine. See palatine[1].]

palae– or **palaeo–** *pref.* Var. of **paleo–.**

pa•laes•tra (pə-lĕs′trə) *n.* Var. of **palestra.**

pal•an•quin also **pal•an•keen** (păl′ən-kēn′) *n.* A covered litter carried on poles on the shoulders of two or four men, formerly used in eastern Asia. [Port. *palanquim* < Javanese *pĕlangki* < Pali *pallaṅko* < Skt. *palyaṅkaḥ*, bed.]

pa•la•pa (pə-lä′pə) *n.* An open-sided dwelling or structure with a thatched roof of dried palm leaves. [Perh. < Am.Sp., a palm tree.]

palapa
Meetinghouse, Saleaula Village, Savaii Island

pal•at•a•ble (păl′ə-tə-bəl) *adj.* **1.** Acceptable to the taste; sufficiently agreeable in flavor to be eaten. **2.** Acceptable or agreeable to the mind or sensibilities. — **pal′at•a•bil′i•ty, pal′at•a•ble•ness** *n.* — **pal′at•a•bly** *adv.*

pal•a•tal (păl′ə-təl) *adj.* **1.** Of or relating to the palate. **2.** *Ling.* **a.** Produced with the front of the tongue near or against the hard palate, as the (y) in English *young.* **b.** Produced with the blade of the tongue near the hard palate, as the (ch) in English *chin.* **c.** Produced with the front of the tongue in a forward position. Used of a vowel. — *n. Ling.* A palatal sound. — **pal′a•tal•ly** *adv.*

pal•a•tal•ize (păl′ə-tə-līz′) *tr.v.* **-ized, -iz•ing, -iz•es.** *Ling.* To pronounce as or alter to a palatal sound. — **pal′a•tal•i•za′tion** (-tə-lĭ-zā′shən) *n.*

pal•ate (păl′ĭt) *n.* **1.** The roof of the mouth in vertebrates having separate oral and nasal cavities and consisting of the hard palate and the soft palate. **2.** The sense of taste. [ME < OFr. *palat* < Lat. *palātum*, perh. of Etruscan origin.]

pa•la•tial (pə-lā′shəl) *adj.* **1.** Of or suitable for a palace: *palatial furnishings.* **2.** Of the nature of a palace, as in spaciousness: *a palatial yacht.* [< Lat. *Palātium*, imperial residence. See palace.] — **pa•la′tial•ly** *adv.* — **pa•la′tial•ness** *n.*

pa•lat•i•nate (pə-lăt′n-āt′, -ĭt) *n.* The office, powers, or territory of a palatine.

Pa•lat•i•nate (pə-lăt′n-ĭt). Either of two historical districts and former states of S Germany: the **Lower Palatinate** in SW Germany between Luxembourg and the Rhine R. and the **Upper Palatinate** in E Bavaria.

pale[1]

pal•a•tine[1] (păl′ə-tīn′) *n.* **1.a.** A soldier of the imperial palace guard formed under Diocletian. **b.** A Roman soldier in the time of Constantine I. **2.** Used as a title for various administrative officials of the late Roman and Byzantine empires. **3.** A feudal lord exercising sovereign power over his lands. — *adj.* **1.** Belonging to or fit for a palace. **2.** Of or relating to a palatine or palatinate. [< ME, ruled by an independent lord < OFr. *palatin* < LLat. *palātīnus*, palace official < Lat. *palātīnus* < *Palātium*, imperial residence. See palace.]

pal•a•tine[2] (păl′ə-tīn′) *adj.* **1.** Of or relating to the palate. **2.** Of or relating to either of two bones that make up the hard palate. — *n.* Either of the palatine bones.

Pal•a•tine[1] (păl′ə-tīn′). The most important of the seven hills of ancient Rome; traditionally the earliest to be settled and later the site of many imperial palaces. — **Pal′a•tine** *adj.*

Pal•a•tine[2] (păl′ə-tīn′). A village of NE IL, a suburb of Chicago. Pop. 39,253.

Pa•lau (pä-lou′, pə-). See **Belau.**

pa•lav•er (pə-lăv′ər, -lä′vər) *n.* **1.a.** Idle chatter. **b.** Talk intended to charm or beguile. **2.** *Obsolete.* A parley between European explorers and representatives of local populations, esp. in Africa. — *v.* **-ered, -er•ing, -ers.** — *tr.* To flatter or cajole. — *intr.* To chatter idly. [Port. *palavra*, speech, alteration of LLat. *parabola*, speech, parable. See parable.]

Pa•la•wan (pə-lä′wən, pä-lä′wän). A long narrow island of the SW Philippines N of Borneo between the Sulu Sea and the **Palawan Passage** of the South China Sea.

pa•laz•zo (pə-lät′sō) *n., pl.* **-zi** (-sē) or **-zos.** A large splendid residence or public building, such as a palace or museum. [Ital. < Lat. *Palātium*, imperial residence. See palace.]

pale[1] (pāl) *n.* **1.** A stake or pointed stick; a picket. **2.** A fence enclosing an area. **3.** The area enclosed by a fence or boundary. **4.** *Her.* A wide vertical band in the center of an escutcheon. **5. Pale.** The medieval English dominions in Ireland. — *tr.v.* **paled, pal•ing, pales.** To enclose with pales; fence in. — ***idiom.* beyond the pale.** Irrevocably unacceptable or unreasonable. [ME < OFr. *pal* < Lat. *pālus.* See **pag-***.]

pale[2] (pāl) *adj.* **pal•er, pal•est. 1.** Whitish in complexion; pallid. **2.** *Color.* **a.** Of a low intensity of color; light. **b.** Having high lightness and low saturation. **3.** Of a low intensity of light; dim or faint. **4.** Feeble; weak: *a pale rendition of the aria.* — *v.* **paled, pal•ing, pales.** — *tr.* To cause to turn pale. — *intr.* **1.** To become pale; blanch. **2.** To decrease in relative importance. [ME < OFr. < Lat. *pallidus* < *pallēre*, to be pale. See **pel-[1]***.] — **pale′ly** *adv.* — **pale′ness** *n.*

pale– *pref.* Var. of **paleo–.**

pa•le•a (pā′lē-ə) *n., pl.* **-le•ae** (-lē-ē′). **1.** A small chafflike bract enclosing the flower of a grass. **2.** The chaffy scales on the receptacle of a flower head in a plant of the composite family, such as the sunflower. [Lat., chaff.]

Pa•le•arc•tic (pā′lē-ärk′tĭk, -är′tĭk) *adj.* Of or relating to the biogeographic region that includes Europe, the northwest coast of Africa, and Asia north of the Himalaya Mountains, esp. with respect to distribution of animals.

pale-dry (pāl′drī′) *adj.* Light in color and dry in flavor.

pa•le•eth•nol•o•gy (pā′lē-ĕth-nŏl′ə-jē) *n., pl.* **-gies.** The ethnology of early human beings. — **pa′le•eth′no•log′ic** (-ĕth′nə-lŏj′ĭk), **pa′le•eth′no•log′i•cal** (-ĭ-kəl) *adj.*

pale•face (pāl′fās′) *n. Offensive Slang.* A white person.

Pa•lem•bang (pä′ləm-bäng′, -lĕm-). A city of Indonesia on SE Sumatra; center of a powerful Hindu kingdom in the 7th and 8th centuries. Pop. 787,187.

Pa•len•que (pä-lĕng′kĕ). An ancient Mayan city of S Mexico SE of Villahermosa; noted for its Temple of Inscriptions.

paleo– or **pale–** or **palaeo–** or **palae–** *pref.* **1.** Ancient; prehistoric; old: *paleobotany.* **2.** Early; primitive: *paleoanthropology.* [Gk. *palaio-* < *palaios*, ancient < *palai*, long ago. See **k^wel-[2]***.]

pa•le•o•an•throp•ic (pā′lē-ō-ăn-thrŏp′ĭk) *adj.* Of or relating to extinct members of the genus *Homo.*

pa•le•o•an•thro•pol•o•gy (pā′lē-ō-ăn′thrə-pŏl′ə-jē) *n.* The study of humanlike creatures more primitive than *Homo sapiens.* — **pa′le•o•an′thro•po•log′ic** (-pə-lŏj′ĭk), **pa′le•o•an′thro•po•log′i•cal** (-ĭ-kəl) *adj.* — **pa′le•o•an′thro•pol′o•gist** *n.*

pa•le•o•bi•o•chem•is•try (pā′lē-ō-bī′ō-kĕm′ĭ-strē) *n., pl.* **-tries. 1.** The biochemistry of fossil organisms. **2.** The study of the development and evolution of biochemicals and biochemical processes. — **pa′le•o•bi′o•chem′i•cal** (-ĭ-kəl) *adj.*

pa•le•o•bi•o•ge•og•ra•phy (pā′lē-ō-bī′ō-jē-ŏg′rə-fē) *n.* The study of the geographic distribution of fossil organisms. — **pa′le•o•bi′o•ge′o•graph′ic** (-jē′ə-grăf′ĭk), **pa′le•o•bi′o•ge′o•graph′i•cal** (-ĭ-kəl) *adj.*

pa•le•o•bot•a•ny (pā′lē-ō-bŏt′n-ē) *n.* The paleontology of plant fossils and ancient vegetation. — **pa′le•o•bo•tan′ic** (-bə-tăn′ĭk), **pa′le•o•bo•tan′i•cal** (-ĭ-kəl) *adj.* — **pa′le•o•bo•tan′i•cal•ly** *adv.* — **pa′le•o•bot′a•nist** *n.*

Pa•le•o•cene (pā′lē-ə-sēn′) *adj.* Of, belonging to, or being the geologic time of the earliest epoch of the Tertiary Period, characterized by the appearance of placental mammals. See table at **geologic time.** — *n.* The Paleocene Epoch or its deposits.

pa•le•o•e•col•o•gy (pā′lē-ō-ĭ-kŏl′ə-jē) *n.* The branch of ecology that deals with the interaction between ancient or prehistoric organisms and their environment. — **pa′le•o•ec′o•log′i•cal** (-ĕk′ə-lŏj′ĭ-kəl, -ē′kə-), **pa′le•o•ec′o•log′ic** (-lŏj′ĭk) *adj.* — **pa′le•o•e•col′o•gist** *n.*

pa•le•og•ra•phy (pā′lē-ŏg′rə-fē) *n.* **1.** The study and scholarly interpretation of ancient documents. **2.** The documents so studied. — **pa′le•og′ra•pher** *n.* — **pa′le•o•graph′ic** (-ə-grăf′ĭk), **pa′le•o•graph′i•cal** (-ĭ-kəl) *adj.*

Pa•le•o-In•di•an (pā′lē-ō-ĭn′dē-ən) *adj.* Of or relating to prehistoric human culture in the Western Hemisphere from the earliest habitation to around 5000 B.C. — **Pa′le•o-In′di•an** *n.*

pa•le•o•lith (pā′lē-ə-lĭth′) *n.* A stone implement of the Paleolithic Age. [Back-formation < Paleolithic.]

Pa·le·o·lith·ic (pā′lē-ə-lĭth′ĭk) *adj.* Of, belonging to, or being the cultural period from the earliest chipped stone tools, about 750,000 years ago, to the beginning of the Mesolithic, about 15,000 years ago. —*n.* The Paleolithic Age.

pa·le·on·tol·o·gy (pā′lē-ŏn-tŏl′ə-jē) *n.* The study of the forms of life existing in prehistoric or geologic times. —**pa′le·on′to·log′ic** (-ŏn′tə-lŏj′ĭk), **pa′le·on′to·log′i·cal** (-ĭ-kəl) *adj.* —**pa′le·on·tol′o·gist** *n.*

Pa·le·o·zo·ic (pā′lē-ə-zō′ĭk) *adj.* Of, belonging to, or being the era of geologic time that extends from the Cambrian through the Permian periods, characterized by the appearance of marine invertebrates, primitive fishes and reptiles, and land plants. See table at **geologic time.** —*n.* The Paleozoic Era.

pa·le·o·zo·ol·o·gy (pā′lē-ō-zō-ŏl′ə-jē) *n.* The paleontology of animal fossils and ancient animal life. —**pa′le·o·zo′o·log′i·cal** (-zō′ə-lŏj′ĭ-kəl) *adj.* —**pa′le·o·zo·ol′o·gist** *n.*

Pa·ler·mo (pə-lûr′mō, -lâr′-, pä-lĕr′mô). A city of NW Sicily, Italy, on the Tyrrhenian Sea; founded by Phoenicians c. 8th cent. B.C. and cap. of the kingdom of Sicily (1072–1194). Pop. 699,691.

Pal·es·tine¹ (păl′ĭ-stīn′). Often called "the Holy Land." A historical region of SW Asia between the E Mediterranean shore and the Jordan R. roughly coextensive with modern Israel and the West Bank. —**Pal′es·tin′i·an** (-stĭn′ē-ən) *adj. & n.*

pa·les·tra also **pa·laes·tra** (pə-lĕs′trə) *n., pl.* **-trae** (-trē) or **-tras.** A public place in ancient Greece for training and practice in wrestling and other athletics. [ME *palestre* < OFr. < Lat. *palaestra* < Gk. *palaistra* < *palaiein*, to wrestle.] —**pa·les′tral, pa·les′tri·an** *adj.*

Pa·le·stri·na (păl′ĭ-strē′nə, pä′lĕ-strē′nä), **Giovanni Pierluigi da.** 1526?–94. Italian composer known for his Masses.

pal·ette (păl′ĭt) *n.* **1.** A board, usu. with a hole for the thumb, that an artist can hold while painting and on which the artist mixes colors. **2.a.** The range of colors used in a particular painting or by a particular artist: *a limited palette.* **b.** The range of qualities inherent in nongraphic art forms such as music and literature. [Fr. < OFr., small potter's shovel, dim. of *pale*, shovel, spade < Lat. *pāla*. See **pag-*.**]

palette knife *n.* A knife with a thin flexible blade, used by artists for mixing, scraping, or applying paint.

Pa·ley (pā′lē), **William.** 1743–1805. British theologian and utilitarian philosopher whose works include *The Principles of Moral and Political Philosophy* (1785).

pal·frey (pôl′frē) *n., pl.* **-freys.** *Archaic.* A saddle horse, esp. one for a woman to ride. [ME < OFr. *palefrei* < Med.Lat. *palafrēdus*, alteration of LLat. *paraverēdus*, post horse for secondary routes, extra horse : Gk. *para*, extra, beyond; see **per¹*** + Lat. *verēdus*, post horse, of Celt. orig. See **reidh-*.**]

Pal·grave (păl′grāv′, pôl′-), **Francis Turner.** 1824–97. British poet known for his *Golden Treasury of the Best Songs and Lyrical Poems in the English Language* (1861).

Pa·li (pä′lē) *n.* An early Prakit language that is one of the canonical languages of Buddhism. [Short for Skt. *pālibhāṣā*, language of the row, series of Buddhist sacred texts < *pāliḥ*, row, perh. of Dravidian orig.]

pal·i·mo·ny (păl′ə-mō′nē) *n. Informal.* An allowance for support made under court order and given usu. by one person to a former lover or live-in companion after separation.

pal·imp·sest (păl′ĭmp-sĕst′) *n.* **1.** A manuscript, usu. of papyrus or parchment, written on more than once, with the earlier writing incompletely erased and often legible. **2.** An object, place, or area that reflects its history. [Lat. *palimpsēstum* < Gk. *palimpsēston*, neut. of *palimpsēstos*, scraped again : *palin*, again; see **kʷel-¹*** + *psēn*, to scrape.]

pal·in·drome (păl′ĭn-drōm′) *n.* A word, phrase, verse, or sentence that reads the same backward or forward; for example, *Madam, I'm Adam.* [< Gk. *palindromos*, running back again, recurring : *palin*, again; see **kʷel-¹*** + *dromos*, a running.] —**pal′in·dro′mic** (-drō′mĭk, -drŏm′ĭk) *adj.*

pal·ing (pā′lĭng) *n.* **1.** One of a row of upright pointed sticks forming a fence; a pale. **2.** Pointed sticks used in making fences; pales. **3.** A fence made of pales or pickets.

pal·in·gen·e·sis (păl′ĭn-jĕn′ĭ-sĭs) *n., pl.* **-ses** (-sēz′). **1.** The doctrine of transmigration of souls; metempsychosis. **2.** *Biol.* The repetition by a single organism of various stages in the evolution of its species during embryonic development. [Gk. *palin*, again; see **kʷel-¹*** + -GENESIS.] —**pal′in·ge·net′ic** (-jə-nĕt′ĭk) *adj.* —**pal′in·ge·net′i·cal·ly** *adv.*

pal·i·node (păl′ə-nōd′) *n.* **1.** A poem in which the author retracts something said in a previous poem. **2.** A formal statement of retraction. [< LLat. *palinōdia* < Gk. *palinōidia* : *palin*, again; see **kʷel-¹*** + *ōidē*, song; see PARODY.]

pal·i·sade (păl′ĭ-sād′) *n.* **1.a.** A fence of pales forming a defense barrier or fortification. **b.** A pale of such a fence. **2. palisades.** A line of lofty steep cliffs, usu. by a river. —*tr.v.* **-sad·ed, -sad·ing, -sades.** To equip or fortify with palisades or a palisade. [Fr. *palissade* < OFr. < OProv. *palissada* < *palissa*, stake < VLat. **pālīcea* < Lat. *pālus*. See **pag-*.**]

palisade parenchyma *n. Bot.* A leaf tissue composed of columnar cells containing numerous chloroplasts in which the long axis of each cell is perpendicular to the leaf surface.

Pal·i·sades (păl′ĭ-sādz′). A row of cliffs in NE NJ along the W bank of the Hudson R.

pal·ish (pā′lĭsh) *adj.* Slightly pale.

Palk Strait (pôk, pôlk). A waterway between SE India and N Sri Lanka.

pall¹ (pôl) *n.* **1.** A cover for a coffin, bier, or tomb, often made of black, purple, or white velvet. **2.** A coffin, esp. one being carried to a grave or tomb. **3.a.** A covering that darkens or obscures. **b.** A gloomy effect or atmosphere. **4.** *Eccles.* **a.** A linen cloth or a square of cardboard faced with cloth used to cover the chalice. **b.** See **pallium** 2. —*tr.v.* **palled, pall·ing, palls.** To cover with or as if with a pall. [ME *pal* < OE *pæll*, cloak, covering < Lat. *pallium*.]

pall² (pôl) *v.* **palled, pall·ing, palls.** —*intr.* **1.** To become insipid, boring, or wearisome. **2.** To have a dulling, wearisome, or boring effect. **3.** To become cloyed or satiated. —*tr.* **1.** To cloy; satiate. **2.** To make vapid or wearisome. [ME *pallen*, to grow feeble, prob. short for *appallen*. See APPALL.]

Pal·la·di·an¹ (pə-lā′dē-ən) *adj.* **1.** *Gk. Myth.* Of, relating to, or characteristic of Athena. **2.** Of, relating to, or characterized by wisdom or study. [< Lat. *Palladius* < Gk. *Palladios* < *Pallas, Pallad-*, Pallas Athena.]

Pal·la·di·an² (pə-lā′dē-ən) *adj.* **1.** Of or characteristic of the Renaissance architectural style of Palladio. **2.** Of or characteristic of an architectural style of the mid-18th century derived from that of Palladio, esp. in Britain.

pal·la·dic (pə-lā′dĭk, -lăd′ĭk) *adj.* Of or being compounds that contain palladium, esp. with valence 4.

Pal·la·dio (pə-lä′dē-ō, pä-lä′dyô), **Andrea.** 1508–80. Italian architect whose style was based on the classicism of ancient Rome.

pal·la·di·um¹ (pə-lā′dē-əm) *n. Symbol* **Pd** A soft ductile metallic element occurring naturally with platinum, esp. in gold, nickel, and copper ores, used as a catalyst in hydrogenation and alloyed for use in electric contacts, jewelry, nonmagnetic watch parts, and surgical instruments. Atomic number 46; atomic weight 106.4; melting point 1,552°C; boiling point 3,140°C; specific gravity 12.02 (20°C); valence 2, 3, 4. See table at **element.** [< PALLAS, (discovered at the same time).]

pal·la·di·um² (pə-lā′dē-əm) *n., pl.* **-di·a** (-dē-ə) or **-di·ums.** **1.** A safeguard, esp. of the integrity of social institutions. **2.** A sacred object having the power to preserve a city or state possessing it. [ME *Palladion*, a statue of Pallas Athena believed to protect Troy < OFr. *palladion* < Lat. *Palladium* < Gk. *Palladion* < *Pallas, Pallad-*, Pallas Athena.]

pal·la·dous (pə-lā′dəs, păl′ə-dəs) *adj.* Of or being compounds that contain palladium, esp. with valence 2.

Pal·las (păl′əs) *n.* **1.** A large asteroid, the second to be discovered. **2.** *Gk. Myth.* Athena. [After PALLAS (ATHENA).]

Pallas A·the·na (ə-thē′nə) also **Pallas A·the·ne** (-nē) *n. Gk. Myth.* Athena.

pall·bear·er (pôl′bâr′ər) *n.* One of the persons carrying or attending a coffin at a funeral.

pal·let¹ (păl′ĭt) *n.* **1.** A projection on a machine part that engages the teeth of a ratchet wheel to convert reciprocating motion to rotary motion or vice versa. **2.** A wooden shovellike potter's tool for working clay. **3.** A metal tool for printing on book bindings. **4.** A fine brush for taking up and applying gold leaf. **5.** A portable platform for storing or moving cargo or freight. **6.** A painter's palette. [ME *palet*, tongue depressor < OFr. *palete*, small potter's shovel. See PALETTE.]

pal·let² (păl′ĭt) *n.* **1.** A narrow hard bed or straw-filled mattress. **2.** *Chiefly Southern U.S.* A temporary bed made from bedding arranged on the floor. [ME *paillet* < AN, bundle of straw < *paille*, straw < LLat. *palea*. See PAILLASSE.]

pal·li·al (păl′ē-əl) *adj.* **1.** Of or relating to the cerebral cortex. **2.** Of the mantle of a mollusk, brachiopod, or bird.

pal·liasse (păl-yăs′, păl′yăs′) *n.* Var. of **paillasse.**

pal·li·ate (păl′ē-āt′) *tr.v.* **-at·ed, -at·ing, -ates.** **1.** To make (an offense or crime) seem less serious; extenuate. **2.** To make less severe or intense; mitigate. See Syns at **relieve. 3.** To relieve the symptoms of a disease or disorder. [ME *palliaten* < LLat. *palliāre, palliāt-*, to cloak, palliate < Lat. *pallium*, cloak.] —**pal′li·a′tion** *n.* —**pal′li·a′tor** *n.*

pal·li·a·tive (păl′ē-ā′tĭv, -ē-ə-tĭv) *adj.* **1.** Tending or serving to palliate. **2.** Relieving or soothing the symptoms of a disease or disorder without effecting a cure. —*n.* One that palliates, esp. a palliative drug or medicine. —**pal′li·a′tive·ly** *adv.*

pal·lid (păl′ĭd) *adj.* **1.** Having an abnormally pale or wan complexion. **2.** Lacking intensity of color or luminousness. **3.** Lacking in radiance or vitality; dull: *pallid prose.* [Lat. *pallidus* < *pallēre*, to be pale. See **pel-¹*.**] —**pal′lid·ly** *adv.* —**pal′lid·ness** *n.*

pal·li·um (păl′ē-əm) *n., pl.* **pal·li·ums** or **pal·li·a** (ē-ə). **1.** A cloak or mantle worn by the ancient Greeks and Romans. **2.** *Eccles.* A vestment worn by the pope and conferred by him on archbishops and sometimes on bishops. **3.a.** The mantle of gray matter forming the cerebral cortex. **b.** The mantle of a mollusk, brachiopod, or bird. [Lat.]

pall-mall (pĕl′mĕl′, păl′măl′, pôl′môl′) *n. Games.* **1.** A 17th-century game in which a ball was struck with a mallet to drive it through an iron ring suspended at the end of an alley.

palette

Palladian²
The Basilica, Venice, Italy

pallet¹
Unloading cargo stacked on a pallet; unused pallets appear in the background

ă pat	oi boy
ā pay	ou out
âr care	o͝o took
ä father	o͞o boot
ĕ pet	ŭ cut
ē be	ûr urge
ĭ pit	th thin
ī pie	*th* this
îr pier	hw which
ŏ pot	zh vision
ō toe	ə about, item
ô paw	

Stress marks:
′ (primary);
′ (secondary), as in **dictionary** (dĭk′shə-nĕr′ē)

2. This alley. [Obsolete Fr. *pallemaille* < Ital. *pallamaglio* : *palla*, ball (of Gmc. orig.; see **bhel-²***) + *maglio*, mallet (< Lat. *malleus*; see **melə-***).]

pal•lor (păl′ər) *n.* Extreme or unnatural paleness. [ME *pallour* < OFr. *palor* < Lat. *pallor* < *pallēre*, to be pale. See **pel-¹***.]

palm¹ (päm) *n.* **1.a.** The inner surface of the hand that extends from the wrist to the base of the fingers. **b.** The similar part of the forefoot of a quadruped. **2.** A unit of length equal to either the width or the length of the hand. **3.** The part of a glove or mitten that covers the palm of the hand. **4.** *Naut.* A leather shield worn by sailmakers over the palm of the hand and used to force a needle through heavy canvas. **5.** *Naut.* The blade of an oar or a paddle. **6.** The flattened part of the antlers of certain animals, such as the moose. — *tr.v.* **palmed, palm•ing, palms. 1.** To conceal (something) in the palm of the hand, as in a sleight-of-hand trick. **2.** To pick up furtively. **3.** *Basketball.* To commit a violation by letting (the ball) rest momentarily in the palm of the hand while dribbling. —***phrasal verb.* palm off.** To dispose of or pass off by deception. [ME *paume* < OFr. < Lat. *palma*, palm tree, palm of the hand. See **pelə-²***.] —**palm′ful′** *n.*

palm² (päm) *n.* **1.** Any of various chiefly tropical evergreen trees, shrubs, or woody vines of the family Palmae (or Arecaceae), having unbranched trunks with a crown of large pinnate or palmate leaves having conspicuous parallel venation. **2.** A leaf of a palm tree, carried as an emblem of victory, success, or joy. **3.** Triumph; victory. **4.** A small metallic representation of a palm leaf added to a military decoration awarded more than one time. [ME < OE and < OFr. *palme*, both < Lat. *palma*, palm, palm tree. See **pelə-²***.]

Pal•ma (päl′mä) also **Palma de Mal•lor•ca** (də mä-yôr′kä, *thĕ* mä-lyôr′kä). A city of W Majorca I., Spain, on the **Bay of Palma**, an inlet of the Mediterranean Sea. Pop. 311,197.

palmate
Top: Compound palmate leaf
Bottom: Digitately compound palmate leaf

pal•mar (păl′mər, päl′-, pä′mər) *adj.* Of, relating to, or corresponding to the palm of the hand or an animal's paw.

pal•ma•ry (păl′mə-rē, päl′-, pä′mə-) *adj.* Outstanding; great.

pal•mate (păl′māt′, päl′-, pä′māt′) also **pal•mat•ed** (-mā′tĭd) *adj.* **1.** Having a shape similar to that of a hand with the fingers extended. **2.** *Bot.* Having three or more veins, leaflets, or lobes radiating from one point; digitate. **3.** *Zool.* Having webbed toes. —**pal′mate′ly** *adv.*

Olaf Palme
Photographed in 1980

Palm Bay (päm). A city of E FL on the Indian R. lagoon SE of Orlando. Pop. 62,632.

Palm Beach. A city of SE FL on a barrier beach of the Atlantic Ocean N of Fort Lauderdale. Pop. 9,814.

Pal•me (päl′mə), **Olaf.** 1927–86. Swedish politician who served as premier (1969–76 and 1982–86).

palm•er (pä′mər) *n.* A medieval European pilgrim who carried a palm branch as a token of having visited the Holy Land.

Pal•mer (pä′mər, päl′-), **Alice Elvira Freeman.** 1855–1902. Amer. educator who was president of Wellesley College (1882–88).

Palmer, Arnold. b. 1929. Amer. golfer who was the first to win four Masters championships (1958, 1960, 1962, and 1964).

Palmer, Daniel David. 1845–1913. Canadian-born Amer. founder of chiropractic.

Palmer Archipelago. Formerly **Ant•arc•tic Archipelago** (ănt-ärk′tĭk, -är′tĭk). An island group between the S tip of South America and the NW coast of the Antarctic Peninsula.

Palmer Peninsula. See **Antarctic Peninsula.**

palmette
Detail from the frieze of the Erechtheum in Athens, Greece, showing two palmettes and one anthemion

Pal•mer•ston (pä′mər-stən, päl′-), 3rd Viscount. Henry John Temple. 1784–1865. British politician and prime minister (1855–58 and 1859–65).

palm•er•worm (pä′mər-wûrm′) *n.* Any of several caterpillars that injure fruit trees by feeding on their leaves, esp. the small green caterpillar of the North American moth *Dichomeris ligulella.* [< appearing like a throng of pilgrims.]

pal•mette (păl-mĕt′) *n.* A stylized palm leaf used as a decorative element, notably in Persian rugs and in classical moldings, reliefs, frescoes, and vase paintings. [Fr., dim. of *palme*, palm < OFr. < Lat. *palma.* See PALM².]

pal•met•to (păl-mĕt′ō) *n., pl.* **-tos** or **-toes. 1.** Any of several small tropical palms with fan-shaped leaves, esp. one of the genus *Sabal,* such as *S. palmetto* of the southeast United States. **2.** Leaf strips of any of these plants, used in weaving. [Sp. *palmito*, dim. of *palma*, palm < Lat. See PALM².]

Pal•mi•ra (päl-mîr′ə, -mē′rä). A city of W Colombia SW of Bogotá on the Pan-American Highway. Pop. 174,425.

Pan

palm•ist (pä′mĭst) also **palm•is•ter** (-mĭ-stər) *n.* One who practices palmistry. [Prob. back-formation < PALMISTRY.]

palm•is•try (pä′mĭ-strē) *n.* The practice or art of telling fortunes from the lines, marks, and patterns on the palms of the hands. [ME *palmestrie* < *palme, paume*, palm. See PALM¹.]

pal•mi•tate (păl′mĭ-tāt′, päl′-, pä′mĭ-) *n.* An ester or salt of palmitic acid. [PALMIT(IC) ACID + -ATE².]

pal•mit•ic acid (păl-mĭt′ĭk, päl-, pä-mĭt′-) *n.* A fatty acid, $C_{15}H_{31}COOH$, occurring in many natural oils and fats and used in making soaps. [Fr. *palmitique* < *palmite*, pith of the palm tree. See PALMITIN.]

pal•mi•tin (păl′mĭ-tĭn, päl′-, pä′mĭ-) *n.* The glyceryl ester, $C_3H_5(OOC_{16}H_{31})_3$, of palmitic acid, found in palm oil and animal fats and used to manufacture soap. [Fr. *palmitine*, perh. < *palmite*, pith of the palm tree < Port. *palmito*, dim. of *palma*, palm < Lat. *palma.* See PALM².]

palm oil *n.* A yellowish fatty oil obtained esp. from the crushed nuts of an African palm *(Elaeis guineensis)* and used in the manufacture of soaps, chocolates, cosmetics, and candles.

Palm Springs. A resort city of SE CA ESE of Riverside. Pop. 40,181.

palm sugar *n.* Sugar made from the sap of various palm trees.

Palm Sunday *n.* The Sunday before Easter, observed by Christians in commemoration of Jesus's entry into Jerusalem, when palm fronds were strewn before him.

palm•y (pä′mē) *adj.* **-i•er, -i•est. 1.** Of or relating to palm trees. **2.** Covered with palm trees. **3.** Prosperous; flourishing.

pal•my•ra (păl-mī′rə) *n.* A tall dioecious palm *(Borassus flabellifer)* of tropical Africa and Asia having large fanlike leaves. [Alteration (influenced by PALMYRA) of Port. *palmeira* < *palma*, palm tree < Lat. See PALM².]

Pal•my•ra (păl-mī′rə). An ancient city of central Syria NE of Damascus; said to have been built by Solomon.

Pal•o Al•to (păl′ō ăl′tō). A city of W CA NW of San Jose. Pop. 55,900.

Pal•o•mar (păl′ə-mär′), **Mount.** A peak, 1,868.4 m (6,126 ft), of S CA NE of San Diego; site of an observatory with one of the world's largest reflecting telescopes.

pal•o•mi•no (păl′ə-mē′nō) *n., pl.* **-nos.** A horse with a golden or tan coat and a white or cream-colored mane and tail. [Am. Sp. < Sp., young dove, perh. < Ital. *palombino*, dove-colored < Lat. *palumbīnus*, pertaining to ringdoves < *palumbēs*, ringdove. See **pel-¹***.]

pa•loo•ka (pə-lo͞o′kə) *n.* **1.** *Sports.* An incompetent or easily defeated athlete, esp. a prizefighter. **2.** *Slang.* A stupid or clumsy person. [?]

Pa•los Hills (pā′ləs). A city of NE IL, a suburb of Chicago. Pop. 17,803.

Pa•louse (pə-lo͞os′) *n., pl.* **Palouse** or **Pa•louses.** A member of a Sahaptin-speaking Native American people formerly inhabiting an area of southeast Washington and northwest Idaho, with present-day descendants in northeast Washington.

Palouse River. A river rising in NW ID and flowing c. 225 km (140 mi) to the Snake R. in SE WA.

pa•lo ver•de (păl′ō vûr′dē, vûrd′) *n.* **1.** A spiny, nearly leafless bushy tree *(Cercidium floridum)* of the southwest United States having yellow flowers and blue-green bark. **2.** Any of several similar shrubs. [Am.Sp. : Sp. *palo*, tree (< Lat. *pālus*, stake; see PALE¹) + Sp. *verde*, green (< Lat. *viridis*).]

palp (pălp) *n. Zool.* An elongated, often segmented appendage usu. near the mouth in invertebrate organisms such as insects, used for sensation, locomotion, or feeding. [Fr. *palpe* < NLat. *palpus* < Lat., a touching. See **pōl-***.]

pal•pa•ble (păl′pə-bəl) *adj.* **1.** Capable of being handled, touched, or felt. **2.** Easily perceived; obvious. See Syns at **perceptible. 3.** *Medic.* That can be felt by palpating. [ME < OFr. < LLat. *palpābilis* < Lat. *palpāre*, to touch gently. See **pōl-***.] —**pal′pa•bil′i•ty** *n.* —**pal′pa•bly** *adv.*

pal•pal (păl′pəl) *adj.* Of, relating to, or characteristic of a palp.

pal•pate¹ (păl′pāt′) *tr.v.* **-pat•ed, -pat•ing, -pates.** To examine or explore by touching (an organ or area of the body), usu. as a diagnostic aid. [Lat. *palpāre, palpāt-*, to touch gently. See **pōl-***.] —**pal•pa′tion** *n.* —**pal′pa′tor** *n.* —**pal′pa•tor′y** (-pə-tôr′ē, -tōr′ē) *adj.*

pal•pate² (păl′pāt′) *adj.* Having a palp or palps.

pal•pe•bra (păl′pə-brə, păl-pē′-) *n., pl.* **-pe•brae** (-pə-brē′, -pē′brē) also **-pe•bras.** *Anat.* An eyelid. [Lat. See **pōl-***.] —**pal′pe•bral** (păl′pə-brəl, păl-pē′brəl, -pĕb′rəl) *adj.*

pal•pi•tant (păl′pĭ-tənt) *adj.* **1.** Shaking; trembling. **2.** Undergoing pulsation; pulsating. [Lat. *palpitāns, palpitant-*, pr.part. of *palpitāre*, to palpitate. See PALPITATE.]

pal•pi•tate (păl′pĭ-tāt′) *intr.v.* **-tat•ed, -tat•ing, -tates. 1.** To move with a slight tremulous motion; tremble, shake, or quiver. **2.** To beat with excessive rapidity; throb. [Lat. *palpitāre, palpitāt-*, freq. of *palpāre*, to touch gently. See **pōl-***.] —**pal′pi•tat′ing•ly** *adv.*

pal•pi•ta•tion (păl′pĭ-tā′shən) *n.* **1.** A trembling or shaking. **2.** Irregular rapid beating or pulsation of the heart.

pal•pus (păl′pəs) *n., pl.* **-pi** (-pī). *Zool.* See **palp.** [Lat., a toweling, the soft palm of the hand. See PALP.]

pals•grave (pôlz′grāv′) *n.* See **palatine¹** 3. [Obsolete Du. *paltsgrave* < MDu. *palsgrēve, palsgrave* : *pals*, palatine (< VLat. **palantia*, palace < Lat. *palātia*, pl. of *Palātium*, imperial palace; see PALACE) + MDu. *grēve, grave*, count.]

pal•sied (pôl′zēd) *adj.* **1.** Affected with palsy. **2.** Trembling or shaking.

pal•sy (pôl′zē) *n., pl.* **-sies. 1.** Complete or partial muscle paralysis, often accompanied by loss of sensation and uncontrollable body movements or tremors. **2.a.** A weakening or debilitating influence. **b.** An enfeebled condition or debilitated state thought to result from such an influence. **3.** A fit of strong emotion marked by the inability to act. — *tr.v.* **-sied, -sy•ing, -sies. 1.a.** To paralyze. **b.** To deprive of strength. **2.** To make helpless, as with fear. [ME *palsie*, alteration of OFr. *paralisie*, alteration of Lat. *paralysis.* See PARALYSIS.]

pal•sy-wal•sy (păl′zē-wăl′zē) *adj. Slang.* Having or appearing to have a close friendly relationship. [Redup. of *palsy*, alteration of PALLY.]

pal•ter (pôl′tər) *intr.v.* **-tered, -ter•ing, -ters. 1.** To talk or act insincerely or misleadingly; equivocate. **2.** To be capricious. **3.** To quibble, esp. in bargaining. [?] **—pal′ter•er** *n.*

pal•try (pôl′trē) *adj.* **-tri•er, -tri•est. 1.** Lacking in importance or worth; trivial. **2.** Wretched or contemptible. [Prob. < obsolete and dial. *paltry*, trash, perh. < LGer. *paltrig*, ragged < *palte*, rag.] **—pal′tri•ly** *adv.* **—pal′tri•ness** *n.*

pa•lu•dal (pə-lo͞od′l, păl′yə-dəl) *adj.* Of or relating to a swamp; marshy. [< Lat. *palūs*, *palūd-*, marsh. See **pelə-1***.]

pal•u•dism (păl′yə-dĭz′əm) *n.* See **malaria** 1. [< Lat. *palūs*, *palūd-*, marsh. See **pelə-1***.]

pal•y1 (pā′lē) *adj.* **-i•er, -i•est.** *Archaic.* Pale.

pal•y2 (pā′lē) *adj. Her.* Divided into several equal parts by perpendicular lines. Used of a field. [ME < OFr. *pale* < *pal*, stake. See PALE1.]

pal•y•nol•o•gy (păl′ə-nŏl′ə-jē) *n.* The scientific study of spores and pollen. [Gk. *palunein*, to sprinkle + -LOGY.] **—pal′y•no•log′i•cal** (-nə-lŏj′ĭ-kəl), **pal′y•no•log′ic** *adj.* **—pal′y•no•log′i•cal•ly** *adv.* **—pal′y•nol′o•gist** *n.*

pam (păm) *n. Games.* The jack of clubs and highest trump in certain variations of loo. [Prob. ultimately < the Greek name *Pamphilos.*]

pam. *abbr.* Pamphlet.

Pa•mir (pə-mîr′, pä-). A mountainous region of S-central Asia mostly in Tadzhikistan with extensions in N Afghanistan, N Kashmir, and W China and rising to 7,500 m (24,590 ft).

Pam•li•co Sound (păm′lĭ-kō′). An inlet of the Atlantic Ocean between the E coast of NC and a row of sandy barrier islands.

pam•pa (păm′pə) *n., pl.* **-pas** (-pəz, -pəs). In South America, a treeless grassland area. [Am.Sp. < Quechua, flat field.]

Pam•pa (păm′pə). A city of NW TX in the Panhandle ENE of Amarillo. Pop. 19,959.

Pam•pas (păm′pəz, -pəs). A vast plain of S-central South America from the lower Paraná R. to S-central Argentina.

pam•pas grass (păm′pəs) *n.* A grass *(Cortaderia selloana)* of southern South America having silvery plumes and growing in large clumps more than three meters (ten feet) tall.

pam•pe•an also **Pam•pe•an** (păm′pē-ən, păm-pē′ən) *adj.* Of or relating to a pampa or the Pampas or their inhabitants.

pam•per (păm′pər) *tr.v.* **-pered, -per•ing, -pers. 1.** To treat with excessive indulgence. **2.** To give in to; gratify. **3.** *Archaic.* To indulge with rich food; glut. [ME *pamperen*, prob. of LGer. orig.] **—pam′per•er** *n.*

pam•pe•ro (păm-pâr′ō, päm-) *n., pl.* **-ros.** A strong, cold southwest wind that blows across the Pampas. [Am.Sp. < *pampa*, pampa. See PAMPA.]

pam•phlet (păm′flĭt) *n.* **1.** An unbound printed work, usu. with a paper cover. **2.** A short essay or treatise, usu. on a current topic, published without a binding. [ME *pamflet* < Med.Lat. *pamfletus* < *Pamphiletus*, dim. of *Pamphilus*, a short amatory Latin poem of the 12th cent. < Gk. *pamphilos*, beloved by all : *pan-*, pan- + *philos*, beloved.] **—pam′phlet•ar′y** (păm′flĭ-tĕr′ē) *adj.*

pam•phlet•eer (păm′flĭ-tîr′) *n.* A partisan writer of pamphlets or other short works. **—pam′phlet•eer′** *v.*

Pam•plo•na (păm-plō′nə, päm-plô′nä). A city of N Spain ESE of Bilbao; an ancient Basque city and cap. of the kingdom of Navarre (824–1512). Pop. 181,688.

pam•pro•dac•ty•lous (păm′prō-dăk′tə-ləs) *adj.* Having all toes pointing forwards. Used of certain birds. [PAN- + PRO-2 + DACTYL(O)- + -OUS.]

pan1 (păn) *n.* **1.** A shallow wide open container, usu. of metal and without a lid, for cooking and other domestic purposes. **2.** A vessel similar to a pan, esp.: **a.** An open metal dish for separating gold or other metal from gravel or waste by washing. **b.** Either of the receptacles on a balance or pair of scales. **c.** A vessel for boiling and evaporating liquids. **3.a.** A basin or depression in the earth, often containing mud or water. **b.** A basin for obtaining salt by evaporating brine. **c.** Hardpan. **4.** A freely floating piece of ice that has broken off a larger floe. **5.** The small cavity in the lock of a flintlock used to hold powder. **6.** *Slang.* The face. **7.** *Informal.* Severe criticism, esp. a negative review. **—*v.*** **panned, pan•ning, pans. —*tr.*** **1.** To wash (gravel, for example) in a pan for gold or other precious metal. **2.** To cook (food) in a pan. **3.** *Informal.* To criticize or review harshly. **—*intr.*** **1.** To wash gravel, sand, or other sediment in a pan. **2.** To yield gold as a result of washing in a pan. **—*phrasal verb.*** **pan out.** To turn out well; be successful. [ME < OE *panne* < West Gmc. **panna*, prob. < VLat. **patna* < Lat. *patina*, shallow pan, platter < Gk. *patanē*. See **petə-***.]

pan2 (pän) *n.* **1.** A leaf of the betel vine. **2.** A chewing preparation of this leaf with betel nuts, spices, and lime. [Hindi *pān* < Skt. *parṇam*, feather, betel leaf. See **per-2***.]

pan3 (păn) *v.* **panned, pan•ning, pans. —*intr.*** To pan a movie or television camera. **—*tr.*** To move (a camera) to follow an object or create a panoramic effect.

Pan (păn) *n. Gk. Myth.* The god of woods, fields, and flocks, having a man's torso and head with a goat's legs, horns, and ears. [ME < Lat. *Pān* < Gk. *Pan.*]

Pan. *abbr.* Panama.

pan– *pref.* **1.** All: *panorama.* **2. Pan–.** Involving all of or the union of a specified group: *Pan-Hellenic.* **3.** General; whole: *panleukopenia.* [Gk. < *pan*, neut. of *pas*, *pant-*, all. See **pant-***.]

pan•a•ce•a (păn′ə-sē′ə) *n.* A remedy for all diseases, evils, or difficulties; a cure-all. [Lat. *panacēa* < Gk. *panakeia* < *panakēs*, all-healing : *pan-*, pan- + *akos*, cure.] **—pan′a•ce′an** *adj.*

pa•nache (pə-năsh′, -näsh′) *n.* **1.** Dash; verve. **2.** A bunch of feathers or a plume, esp. on a helmet. [Fr., plume, verve < Ital. *pinnacchio*, plume < LLat. *pinnāculum*, dim. of Lat. *pinna*, feather, wing. See **pet-***.]

pa•na•da (pə-nä′də) *n.* A paste or gruel of bread crumbs, toast, or flour combined with milk, stock, or water and used for making soups, binding forcemeats, or thickening sauces. [Sp. < *pan*, bread < Lat. *pānis*. See **pā-***.]

Pan•a•ma (păn′ə-mä′, -mô′). **1.** A country of SE Central America; gained independence in 1903. Cap. Panama. Pop. 1,795,012. **2.** Also **Panama City.** The cap. of Panama, in the central part on the Gulf of Panama. Pop. 389,172. **—Pan′a•ma′ni•an** (-mā′nē-ən) *adj. & n.*

Panama, Gulf of. A wide inlet of the Pacific Ocean on the S coast of Panama.

Panama, Isthmus of. Formerly **Isthmus of Da•ri•én** (dâr′ē-ĕn′, där-yĕn′). An isthmus of Central America connecting North and South America and separating the Pacific Ocean from the Caribbean Sea; first crossed by Balboa in 1513.

Panama Canal. A ship canal, c. 82 km (51 mi), crossing the Isthmus of Panama in the Canal Zone and connecting the Caribbean Sea with the Pacific Ocean; opened to traffic on Aug. 15, 1914. A 1977 treaty stipulated that Panama gain full rights of sovereignty over the canal on Dec. 31, 1999.

Panama Canal Zone. See **Canal Zone.**

Panama City. A city of NW FL on the Gulf of Mexico ESE of Pensacola. Pop. 34,378.

Panama hat *n.* A natural-colored hand-plaited hat made from leaves of the jipijapa plant of South and Central America.

Pan-A•mer•i•can (păn′ə-mĕr′ĭ-kən) *adj.* Of or relating to North, South, and Central America.

Pan-American Highway. A system of roadways, about 25,744 km (16,000 mi) long, extending from AK to Chile and linking the nations of the Western Hemisphere.

Pan•a•mint Range (păn′ə-mĭnt′). A range of E CA between Death Valley and the **Panamint Valley** rising to 3,370 m (11,049 ft).

pan•a•tel•a (păn′ə-tĕl′ə) also **pan•e•tel•a** or **pan•e•tel•la** (păn′ĭ-) *n.* A long slender cigar. [Sp., biscuit, cigar < Am.Sp., long thin biscuit < Ital. *panatella*, dim. of *panata*, panada < *pane*, bread < Lat. *pānis*. See **pā-***.]

Pa•nay (pə-nī′, pä-). An island of the central Philippines in the Visayan Is. NW of Negros.

pan-broil (păn′broil′) *tr.v.* **-broiled, -broil•ing, -broils.** To cook (steak, for example) over direct heat in an uncovered, usu. ungreased skillet.

pan•cake (păn′kāk′) *n.* A thin cake made of batter that is poured onto a hot greased surface and cooked until brown. Also called regionally *battercake*

Pan-Cake (păn′kāk′). A trademark used for a semisolid cosmetic or theatrical makeup pressed into a flat cake and usu. applied with a damp sponge.

pancake landing *n.* An irregular or emergency landing in which an aircraft drops flat to the ground from a low altitude.

pan•cet•ta (păn-chĕt′ə) *n.* Italian bacon that has been cured in salt and spices and then air-dried. [Ital., dim. of *pancia*, belly < Lat. *pantex*, *pantic-*.]

pan•chax (păn′chăks′) *n.* Any of various small, brightly colored Old World tropical fishes of the genus *Aplocheilus* and related genera, often kept in home aquariums. [NLat., former genus name.]

Pan•chen La•ma (pän′chən lä′mə) *n.* One of Tibet's two grand lamas, the other being the Dalai Lama. [Tibetan : *panchen*, great scholar (Skt. *paṇḍitaḥ*, scholar; see PUNDIT + Tibetan *chen-po*, great) + Tibetan *bla-ma*, monk.]

pan•chro•mat•ic (păn′krō-măt′ĭk) *adj.* Sensitive to all colors. **—pan•chro′ma•tism** (-krō′mə-tĭz′əm) *n.*

pan•cra•ti•um (păn-krā′shē-əm) *n.* An athletic contest in ancient Greece that involved boxing and wrestling. [Lat. < Gk. *pankration* : *pan-*, all (< neut. of *pas*, *pant-*; see **pant-***) + *kratos*, strength; see -CRACY.]

pan•cre•as (păng′krē-əs, păn′-) *n.* A long, irregularly shaped gland in vertebrates, lying behind the stomach, that secretes pancreatic juice into the duodenum and insulin, glucagon, and somatostatin into the bloodstream. [Gk. *pankreas* : *pan-*, all (< neut. of *pas*, *pant-*; see **pant-***) + *kreas*, flesh; see **kreuə-***.] **—pan′cre•at′ic** (păng′krē-ăt′ĭk, păn′-) *adj.*

pancreat– *pref.* Var. of **pancreato–.**

pan•cre•a•tec•to•my (păng′krē-ə-tĕk′tə-mē, păn′-) *n., pl.* **-mies.** Surgical removal of all or part of the pancreas.

pancreatic juice *n.* A clear alkaline secretion of the pancreas containing enzymes that aid in the digestion of proteins, carbohydrates, and fats.

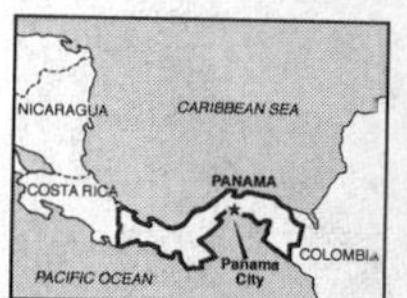

Panama

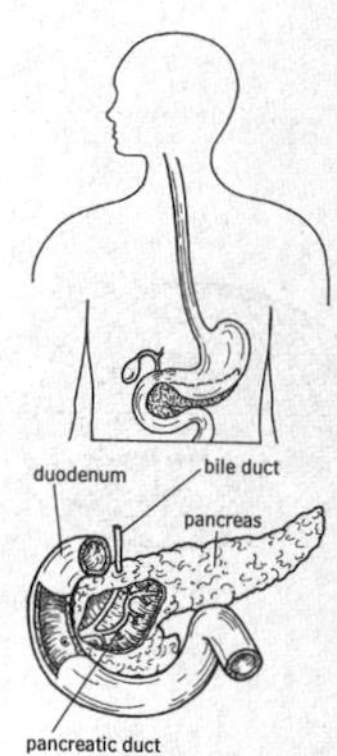

pancreas

ă pat · ā pay · âr care · ä father · ĕ pet · ē be · ĭ pit · ī pie · îr pier · ŏ pot · ō toe · ô paw · oi boy · ou out · o͝o took · o͞o boot · ŭ cut · ûr urge · th thin · *th* this · hw which · zh vision · ə about, item

Stress marks:
′ (primary);
′ (secondary), as in
dictionary (dĭk′shə-nĕr′ē)

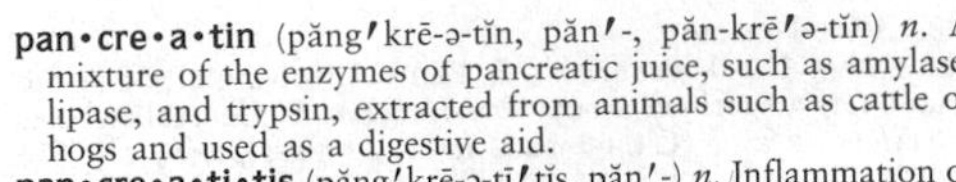

pan•cre•a•tin (păng′krē-ə-tĭn, păn′-, păn-krē′ə-tĭn) *n.* A mixture of the enzymes of pancreatic juice, such as amylase, lipase, and trypsin, extracted from animals such as cattle or hogs and used as a digestive aid.

pan•cre•a•ti•tis (păng′krē-ə-tī′tĭs, păn′-) *n.* Inflammation of the pancreas.

pancreato– or **pancreat–** *pref.* Pancreas: *pancreatin.* [< Gk. *pankreas, pankreat-,* pancreas. See PANCREAS.]

pan•cre•o•zy•min (păng′krē-ō-zī′mĭn, păn′-) *n.* See **cholecystokinin.** [PANCRE(AS) + ZYM(O)– + –IN.]

pan•cy•to•pe•ni•a (păn′sī-tə-pē′nē-ə) *n.* See **aplastic anemia.**

panda
Giant panda
Ailuropoda melanoleuca

pan•da (păn′də) *n.* **1.** A rare bearlike mammal *(Ailuropoda melanoleuca)* of the mountains of China and Tibet (Xizang) having woolly fur with distinctive black and white markings. **2.** A small raccoonlike mammal *(Ailurus fulgens)* of northeast Asia having reddish fur, white face markings, and a long ringed tail. [Fr., perh. of Nepalese origin.]

pan•da•nus (păn-dā′nəs, -dăn′əs) *n.* Any of numerous palmlike trees and shrubs of the genus *Pandanus* of the Old World tropics, having large prop roots and narrow spiny leaves that yield a fiber used in weaving mats and similar articles. [NLat. *Pandanus,* genus name < Malay *pandan,* screw pine.] **— pan′da•na′ceous** (păn′də-nā′shəs) *adj.*

Pan•da•rus (păn′dər-əs) also **Pan•dar** (-dər) *n.* **1.** The leader of the Lycians, slain by Diomedes in the *Iliad.* **2.** The procurer of Cressida for Troilus in medieval romance.

Pan•de•an pipe (păn-dē′ən) *n. Mus.* See **panpipe.** [< PAN.]

pan•dect (păn′dĕkt′) *n.* **1.** A comprehensive digest or complete treatise. **2. pandects.** A complete body of laws; a legal code. **3. Pandects.** A digest of Roman civil law, compiled for the emperor Justinian in the sixth century A.D. and part of the Corpus Juris Civilis. [Lat. *pandectēs,* encyclopedia < Gk. *pandektēs,* all-receiving : *pan-,* pan- + *dektēs,* receiver (< *dekhesthai,* to receive, accept; see **dek-***).]

pan•dem•ic (păn-dĕm′ĭk) *adj.* **1.** Widespread; general. **2.** *Medic.* Epidemic over a wide geographic area: *pandemic influenza.* —*n.* A pandemic disease. [< LLat. *pandēmus* < Gk. *pandēmos,* of all the people : *pan-,* pan- + *dēmos,* people; see **dā-***.]

pan•de•mo•ni•um also **pan•dae•mo•ni•um** (păn′də-mō′nē-əm) *n.* **1.** A very noisy place. **2.** Wild uproar or noise. See Syns at **noise.** [< *Pandæmonium,* capital of Hell in *Paradise Lost* by John Milton : Gk. *pan-,* pan- + LLat. *daemonium,* demon (< Gk. *daimonion* < *daimōn,* lesser god, demon; see DEMON).] **— pan′de•mo′ni•ac** (-nē-ăk′) *adj.*

Pangaea

pan•der (păn′dər) *intr.v.* **-dered, -der•ing, -ders. 1.** To act as a go-between in sexual intrigues; function as a procurer. **2.** To cater to the lower tastes and desires of others or exploit their weaknesses. [Ult. < Gk. *Pandaros,* Pandarus.] **— pan′der** *n.*

pan•der•er (păn′dər-ər) *n.* **1.** A sexual procurer. **2.** One who caters to or exploits the lower tastes and desires of others.

pan•dit (păn′dĭt) or **pun•dit** (pŭn′-) *n.* **1.** A Brahman scholar or learned man. **2.** Used as a title of respect for a learned man in India. [Hindi *paṇḍit* < Skt. *paṇḍitaḥ.* See PUNDIT.]

Pan•do•ra (păn-dôr′ə, -dōr′ə) *n. Gk. Myth.* The first woman, who was bestowed upon humankind as punishment for Prometheus's theft of fire and who out of curiosity opened a box containing all human ills and released them.

pan•dore (păn′dôr′, -dōr′) *n. Mus.* See **bandore.** [Ult. Gk. *pandoura.*]

pan•dow•dy (păn-dou′dē) *n., pl.* **-dies.** Sliced fruit with sugar, spices, and a thick top crust, in a deep dish. [Perh. < obsolete dial. *pandoulde,* custard : PAN[1] + dial. *dowl,* to mix dough in a hurry (prob. var. of DOUGH).]

pane (pān) *n.* **1.a.** One of the glass-filled divisions of a window or door. **b.** The glass used in such a division. **2.** A panel, as of a door or wall. **3.** One of the flat surfaces or facets of an object, such as a bolt, having many sides. [ME, section, pane of glass < OFr. *pan,* piece of cloth, panel < Lat. *pannus,* cloth. See **pan-***.]

paned (pānd) *adj.* Having a specified kind or number of panes. Often used in combination: *clear-paned windows.*

pan•e•gyr•ic (păn′ə-jĭr′ĭk, -jī′rĭk) *n.* **1.** A formal public eulogy. **2.** Elaborate praise or laudation. [Lat. *panēgyricus* < Gk. *panēgurikos (logos),* (speech) at a public assembly, panegyric < *panēguris,* public assembly : *pan-,* pan- + *aguris,* assembly, marketplace; see **ger-***.] **— pan′e•gyr′i•cal** *adj.*

pan•e•gyr•ist (păn′ə-jĭr′ĭst, -jī′rĭst) *n.* One who writes or delivers panegyrics; a eulogist. **— pan′e•gy•rize′** (-jə-rīz′) *v.*

pan•el (păn′əl) *n.* **1.** A flat, usu. rectangular piece forming a raised, recessed, or framed part of the surface in which it is set. **2.** The space or section in a fence or railing between two posts. **3.** A vertical section of fabric; a gore. **4.a.** A thin wooden board, used as a surface for an oil painting. **b.** A painting on such a board. **5.a.** A board having switches or buttons to control an electric device. **b.** An instrument panel. **6.** A section of a telephone switchboard. **7.** *Law.* **a.** The complete list of persons summoned for jury duty. **b.** Those persons selected from this list to compose a jury. **c.** A jury. **8.a.** A group of people gathered to plan or discuss an issue, judge a contest, or act as a team on a quiz program. **b.** A discussion by such a group. —*tr.v.* **-eled, -el•ing, -els** or **-elled, -el•ling, -els. 1.** To cover or furnish with panels. **2.** To decorate with panels. **3.** To separate into panels. **4.** *Law.* To select or impanel (a jury). [ME, piece of cloth < OFr., prob. < VLat. **pannellus,* dim. of Lat. *pannus,* cloth. See **pan-***.]

panel discussion *n.* A discussion of a subject of public interest by a panel of persons, often before an audience.

pan•el•ing (păn′ə-lĭng) *n.* A section of panels or paneled wall.

pan•el•ist (păn′ə-lĭst) *n.* A member of a panel.

pan•el•ized (păn′ə-līzd′) *adj.* Consisting of or characterized by prefabricated wall, floor, and roof sections.

panel truck *n.* A small truck with a fully enclosed body.

pan•en•ceph•a•li•tis (păn′ĕn-sĕf′ə-lī′tĭs) *n.* **1.** Encephalitis that affects both the gray and the white matter of the brain, resulting in progressive loss of mental and motor functions. **2.** Subacute sclerosing panencephalitis.

pan•e•tel•a or **pan•e•tel•la** (păn′ĭ-tĕl′ə) *n.* Var. of **panatela.**

pan•et•to•ne (păn′ĭ-tō′nē) *n., pl.* **-nes** or **-ni** (-nē). An Italian yeast cake made with candied fruit peels and raisins. [Ital., aug. of *panetto,* a small loaf, dim. of *pane,* bread < Lat. *pānis.* See PANADA.]

pan fish *n.* A fish small enough to be fried whole in a pan.

pan-fry also **pan•fry** (păn′frī′) *tr.v.* **-fried, -fry•ing, -fries.** To fry in a frying pan or skillet with a small amount of fat.

pan•ful (păn′fo͝ol′) *n.* The amount that a pan can hold.

pang (păng) *n.* **1.** A sudden sharp spasm of pain. **2.** A sudden sharp feeling of emotional distress. —*tr.v.* **panged, pang•ing, pangs.** To cause to feel pangs; distress acutely. [?]

Pan•gae•a also **Pan•ge•a** (păn-jē′ə) *n.* A hypothetical supercontinent that included all the landmasses of the earth before the Triassic Period. [PAN– + Gk. *gaia,* earth.]

pan•gen•e•sis (păn-jĕn′ĭ-sĭs) *n.* A theory of heredity proposed by Charles Darwin in which gemmules of hereditary information from every part of the body coalesce in the gonads and are incorporated into the reproductive cells.

Pan•gloss•i•an (păn-glŏs′ē-ən, -glôs′-, păng-) *adj.* Blindly or naively optimistic. [After *Pangloss,* in *Candide* by Voltaire.]

pan•go•lin (păng′gə-lĭn, păn′-) *n.* Any of several long-tailed scale-covered mammals of the order Pholidota of tropical Africa and Asia, having a long snout and a sticky tongue. [Malay *pêngguling* : *pêng-,* pref. + *guling,* to roll over.]

Pango Pango. See **Pago Pago.**

pan•gram (păn′grăm′, -grəm, păng′-) *n.* A sentence that uses all the letters of the alphabet.

pan•han•dle[1] (păn′hăn′dl) *v.* **-dled, -dling, -dles.** —*intr.* To approach strangers and beg for money or food. —*tr.* **1.** To approach and beg from (a stranger). **2.** To obtain by panhandling. [Back-formation < *panhandler,* beggar : perh. PAN[1] + HANDLER.] **— pan′han′dler** *n.*

pan•han•dle[2] (păn′hăn′dl) *n.* **1.** The handle of a pan. **2.** Often **Panhandle.** A narrow strip of territory projecting from a larger, broader area, as in Alaska or Texas.

Pan-Hel•len•ic also **Pan•hel•len•ic** (păn′hə-lĕn′ĭk) *adj.* **1.** Of or relating to all Greek peoples or a movement to unify them. **2.** Of or relating to all Greek-letter fraternities and sororities.

pan•hu•man (păn-hyo͞o′mən) *adj.* Of or relating to all humanity.

pan•ic (păn′ĭk) *n.* **1.** A sudden overpowering terror, often affecting many people at once. See Syns at **fear. 2.** A sudden widespread alarm concerning finances, often resulting in a rush to sell. **3.** *Slang.* One that is uproariously funny. —*adj.* **1.** Of, relating to, or resulting from sudden overwhelming terror. **2.** Of or resulting from a financial panic. **3.** Often **Panic.** *Myth.* Of or relating to Pan. —*tr. & intr.v.* **-icked, -ick•ing, -ics.** To affect or be affected with panic. [< Fr. *panique,* terrified < Gk. *Panikos,* of Pan (a source of terror, as in flocks), groundless (used of fear) < *Pan,* Pan. See PAN.] **— pan′ick•y** *adj.*

panic disorder *n.* A psychological disorder characterized by the occurrence of intense attacks of anxiety in specific circumstances and situations.

panic grass *n.* Any of numerous grasses of the genus *Panicum,* many of which are grown for grain and fodder. [ME *panik* < OFr. < Lat. *pānicum.*]

pan•i•cle (păn′ĭ-kəl) *n. Bot.* A branched cluster of flowers in which the branches are racemes. [Lat. *pānicula,* fem. dim. of *pānus,* a swelling, main stalk of a panicle.] **— pan′i•cled** *adj.*

pan•ic-strick•en (păn′ĭk-strĭk′ən) also **pan•ic-struck** (-strŭk′) *adj.* Overcome by panic; terrified.

pa•nic•u•late (pə-nĭk′yə-lĭt, -lāt′) also **pa•nic•u•lat•ed** (-lā′tĭd) *adj. Bot.* Growing or arranged in a panicle. [NLat. *pāniculātus* < Lat. *pānicula,* panicle. See PANICLE.] **— pa•nic′u•late•ly** *adv.*

Pa•ni•ni (pä-nē′nē). fl. 400 B.C. Indian grammarian whose *Ashtadhyayi* describes grammatical rules for Sanskrit.

Pan•ja•bi (pŭn-jä′bē, -jăb′ē) *n. & adj.* Var. of **Punjabi.**

pan•jan•drum (păn-jăn′drəm) *n.* An important or self-important person. [After the Grand *Panjandrum,* a character in a nonsense farrago by Samuel Foote (1720–77).]

Pank•hurst (păngk′hûrst′), **Emmeline Goulden.** 1858–1928. British suffrage leader who with her daughters **Christabel Pankhurst** (1880–1958) and **Sylvia Pankhurst** (1882–1960) founded (1903) the Women's Social and Political Union.

pan•leu•ko•pe•ni•a also **pan•leu•co•pe•ni•a** (păn′lo͞o-kə-pē′nē-ə) *n.* See **distemper**[1] 1b.

pan•mic•tic (păn-mĭk′tĭk) *adj.* Relating to panmixia. [< PAN– + Gk. *miktos*, mixed (< *mignunai*, to mix; see **meik-***).]

pan•mix•i•a (păn-mĭk′sē-ə) also **pan•mix•is** (-mĭk′sĭs) *n.* Random mating within a breeding population. [< PAN– + Gk. *mixis*, act of mingling (< *mignunai*, to mix; see **meik-***).]

Pan•mun•jom (pän′mo͞on′jŭm′). A village of NW South Korea just S of the 38th parallel where the truce ending the Korean War was officially signed on Jul. 27, 1953.

panne (păn) *n.* A special finish for velvet and satin that produces a high luster. [Fr., a soft cloth < OFr. *penne, pane*, fur lining < Lat. *pinna, penna*, feather. See PENNA.]

pan•nier (păn′yər, păn′ē-ər) *n.* **1.** A large wicker basket, esp.: **a.** One of a pair of baskets carried on either side of a pack animal. **b.** A basket carried on a person's back. **2.** A basket or pack that fastens to the rack of a bicycle. **3.a.** A framework of wire, bone, or other material formerly used to expand a woman's skirt at the hips. **b.** A skirt or an overskirt puffed out at the hips. [ME *panier* < OFr. < Lat. *pānārium*, breadbasket < *pānis*, bread. See **pā-***.] — **pan′niered** *adj.*

Pan•no•ni•a (pə-nō′nē-ə). An ancient Roman province of central Europe including present-day W Hungary and the NW Balkan Peninsula. — **Pan•no′ni•an** *adj. & n.*

pa•no•cha (pə-nō′chə) also **pa•no•che** (-chē) *n.* **1.** A coarse grade of Mexican sugar. **2.** Var. of **penuche.** [Am.Sp., prob. < Sp. *panoja, panocha*, ear of grain, panicle < Lat. *pānicula*. See PANICLE.]

pan•o•ply (păn′ə-plē) *n., pl.* **-plies. 1.** A splendid or striking array. **2.** Ceremonial attire with all accessories. **3.** Something that covers and protects. **4.** The complete arms and armor of a warrior. [Gk. *panoplia* : *pan-*, pan- + *hopla*, arms, armor, pl. of *hoplon*, weapon.]

pan•op•tic (păn-ŏp′tĭk) also **pan•op•ti•cal** (-tĭ-kəl) *adj.* Including everything visible in one view. [< Gk. *panoptos*, fully visible : *pan-*, pan- + *optos*, visible; see **okʷ-***.]

pan•o•ram•a (păn′ə-răm′ə, -rä′mə) *n.* **1.** An unbroken view of an entire surrounding area. **2.** A comprehensive presentation; a survey. **3.** A picture or series of pictures representing a continuous scene. **4.** A mental vision of a series of events. [PAN– + Gk. *horama*, sight (< *horan*, to see; see **wer-³***).] — **pan′o•ram′ic** (-răm′ĭk) *adj.* — **pan′o•ram′i•cal•ly** *adv.*

pan•pipe (păn′pīp′) *n. Mus.* A primitive wind instrument consisting of a series of pipes or reeds of graduated length bound together, played by blowing across the top open ends. Often used in the plural. [PAN + PIPE.]

pan•sex•u•al (păn-sĕk′sho͞o-əl) *adj.* Exhibiting or suggesting a sexuality that has many different forms. — **pan′sex•u•al′i•ty** (-ăl′ĭ-tē) *n.*

pan•sy (păn′zē) *n., pl.* **-sies. 1.** Any of various plants of the genera *Achimenes* or *Viola*, having flowers with velvety petals of various colors. **2.** *Color.* A deep to strong violet. **3.** *Offensive Slang.* **a.** Used as a disparaging term for a man or boy who is considered effeminate. **b.** Used as a disparaging term for a gay or homosexual man. [ME *pancy* < OFr. *pensee* < fem. p.part. of *penser*, to think. See PENSIVE.]

pant[1] (pănt) *v.* **pant•ed, pant•ing, pants.** —*intr.* **1.** To breathe rapidly in short gasps, as after exertion. **2.** To beat loudly or heavily; throb or pulsate. **3.** To give off loud puffs, esp. while moving. **4.** To long demonstratively; yearn. —*tr.* To utter hurriedly or breathlessly. —*n.* **1.** A short labored breath; a gasp. **2.** A throb; a pulsation. **3.** A short loud puff. [ME *panten*, perh. alteration of OFr. *pantaisier* < VLat. **pantasiāre* < Gk. *phantasioun*, to form images < *phantasia*, appearance. See FANTASY.] — **pant′ing•ly** *adv.*

pant[2] (pănt) *n.* **1.** Trousers. Often used in the plural. **2.** Underpants. Often used in the plural. —***idiom.* with (one's) pants down.** *Slang.* In an embarrassing position. [Short for *pantaloon*.]

pan•ta•let also **pan•ta•lette** (păn′tə-lĕt′) *n.* **1.** Long underpants trimmed with ruffles extending below the skirt, worn by women in the mid-19th century. Often used in the plural. **2.** A frill attached to the leg of underpants. Often used in the plural. [< PANTALOON.]

pan•ta•loon (păn′tə-lo͞on′) *n.* **1.a.** Men's wide breeches extending from waist to ankle, worn esp. in England in the late 17th century. Often used in the plural. **b.** Tight trousers extending from waist to ankle with straps passing under the instep, worn esp. in the 19th century. Often used in the plural. **2.** Trousers; pants. Often used in the plural. [Fr. *pantalon*, a kind of trouser < *Pantalon*, Pantaloon. See PANTALOON.]

Pan•ta•loon (păn′tə-lo͞on′) *n.* **1.** Often **Pan•ta•lo•ne** (păn′tə-lō′nā, pän′tä-lô′nĕ). A character in the commedia dell'arte, portrayed as a foolish old man in tight trousers and slippers. **2.** A stock character in modern pantomime, the butt of a clown's jokes. [Fr. *Pantalon* < Ital. *Pantalone*, after San *Pantalone*, or St. Pantaleon (d. A.D. 303), Roman martyr.]

pan•the•ism (păn′thē-ĭz′əm) *n.* **1.** A doctrine identifying the Deity with the universe and its phenomena. **2.** Belief in and worship of all gods. — **pan′the•ist** *n.* — **pan′the•is′tic, pan′the•is′ti•cal** *adj.* — **pan′the•is′ti•cal•ly** *adv.*

pan•the•on (păn′thē-ŏn′, -ən) *n.* **1. Pantheon.** A circular temple in Rome, completed in 27 B.C. and dedicated to all the gods. **2.** A temple dedicated to all gods. **3.** All the gods of a people. **4.** A public building commemorating and dedicated to the heroes and heroines of a nation. **5.** A group of persons who have contributed greatly to a field or an endeavor. [ME *Panteon*, Pantheon < Lat. *Pantheon* < Gk. *Pantheion*, shrine of all the gods < neut. sing. of *pantheios*, of all the gods : *pan-*, pan- + *theos*, god; see **dhēs-***.]

pan•ther (păn′thər) *n.* **1.** The leopard, esp. in its black unspotted form. **2.** See **mountain lion.** [ME *pantere* < OFr. and < OE *panthera*, both < Lat. *panthēra* < Gk. *panthēr*.]

pant•ie or **pant•y** (păn′tē) *n., pl.* **pant•ies.** Short underpants for women or children. Often used in the plural. [Dim. of PANT².]

pan•tile (păn′tīl′) *n.* A roofing tile with an S-shaped profile, laid so that the down curve of one tile overlaps the up curve of the next one. [PAN¹ + TILE.] — **pan′tiled′** *adj.*

pan•tof•fle also **pan•to•fle** (păn-tŏf′əl, -tō′fəl, -to͞o′fəl, păn′tə-fəl) *n.* A slipper. [ME *pantufle* < OFr. *pantoufle*.]

pan•to•graph (păn′tə-grăf′) *n.* **1.** An instrument for copying a plane figure to a desired scale, consisting of styluses mounted on four jointed rods in the form of a parallelogram with extended sides. **2.** A similarly jointed framework, such as an extensible telephone arm. [Gk. *panto-*, all (< *pas, pant-*; see PAN–) + –GRAPH.] — **pan′to•graph′ic** *adj.*

pan•to•mime (păn′tə-mīm′) *n.* **1.** Communication by means of gesture and facial expression. **2.a.** The telling of a story without words, by means of bodily movements and facial expressions. **b.** A theatrical performance characterized by such storytelling. **c.** An ancient Roman theatrical performance in which one actor played all the parts by means of gesture and movement, accompanied by a narrative chorus. **d.** Such an actor. **3.** A British light musical comedy for children at Christmas time, usu. based on nursery tales and featuring audience participation. —*v.* **-mimed, -mim•ing, -mimes.** —*tr.* To represent or express by pantomime. —*intr.* To express oneself in pantomime. [Lat. *pantomīmus*, a pantomimic actor < Gk. *pantomimos* : *panto-*, all (< *pas, pant-*; see PAN–) + *mimos*, mime.] — **pan′to•mim′ic** (-mĭm′ĭk) *adj.* — **pan′to•mim′ist** (-mī′mĭst) *n.*

pan•to•then•ate (păn′tə-thĕn′āt′, păn-tŏth′ə-nāt′) *n.* A salt or an ester of pantothenic acid. [PANTOTHEN(IC ACID) + –ATE².]

pan•to•then•ic acid (păn′tə-thĕn′ĭk) *n.* A yellow oily acid, $C_9H_{17}NO_5$, found widely in plant and animal tissues. [< Gk. *pantothen*, from all sides : *panto-*, all (< *pas, pant-*; see PAN–) + *-othen*, adverbial suff. (for motion from).]

pan•trop•ic (păn-trŏp′ĭk, -trō′pĭk) *adj.* Having an affinity for or indiscriminately affecting many kinds of tissue.

pan•try (păn′trē) *n., pl.* **-tries. 1.** A small room or closet, usu. off a kitchen, where food, tableware, and similar items are stored. **2.** A small room where cold foods are prepared. [ME *pantrie* < OFr. *paneterie*, bread closet < *panetier*, pantry servant < *pan*, bread < Lat. *pānis*. See **pā-***.]

pant•suit also **pants suit** (pănt′so͞ot′) *n.* A woman's suit having trousers and a jacket. — **pant′suit′ed** *adj.*

pant•y•hose or **pant•y hose** (păn′tē-hōz′) *pl.n.* A woman's one-piece undergarment consisting of underpants and stretchable stockings.

pant•y•waist (păn′tē-wāst′) *n.* **1.** A child's undergarment consisting of a shirt and pants buttoned together at the waist. **2.** *Slang.* A boy or man who is considered weak or effeminate. — **pant′y•waist′** *adj.*

pan•zer (păn′zər, pänt′sər) *n.* A German armored vehicle, such as a tank, esp. of the type used during World War II. —*adj.* **1.** Of or equipped with armored vehicles. **2.** Of or relating to an armored division. [Ger., short for *Panzerdivision*, armored unit < *Panzer*, tank < MHGer. *panzier*, armor < OFr. *pancier*, belly armor < *pance*, belly. See PAUNCH.]

Pao•ting (bou′dĭng′). See **Baoding.**

Pao•tow (bou′tō′). See **Baotou.**

pap[1] (păp) *n.* **1.** *Midland U.S.* A teat or nipple. **2.** Something resembling a nipple. [ME *pappe*, prob. < Lat. *papilla*. See PAPILLA.]

pap[2] (păp) *n.* **1.** Soft or semiliquid food, as for infants. **2.** Material lacking real value or substance. **3.** *Slang.* Money and favors obtained as political patronage. [ME < OFr. *papa* < Lat., children's word for food.]

pa•pa (pä′pə, pə-pä′) also **pop•pa** (pä′pə) *n. Informal.* Father. [Fr. See **papa***.]

pa•pa•cy (pā′pə-sē) *n., pl.* **-cies. 1.** The office and jurisdiction of a pope. **2.** The period of time during which a pope is in office. **3.** A succession or line of popes: *the Medici papacy.* **4. Papacy.** *Rom. Cath. Ch.* The system of church government headed by the pope. [ME *papacie* < Med.Lat. *pāpātia* < LLat. *pāpa*, pope. See POPE.]

Pa•pa•go (păp′ə-gō′, pä′pə-) *n., pl.* **Papago** or **-gos. 1.** A member of a Native American people inhabiting desert regions of southern Arizona and northwest Mexico. **2.** The Uto-Aztecan language of this people.

pa•pa•in (pə-pā′ĭn, -pī′ĭn) *n.* An enzyme capable of digesting protein, obtained from unripe papaya fruit and used as a meat

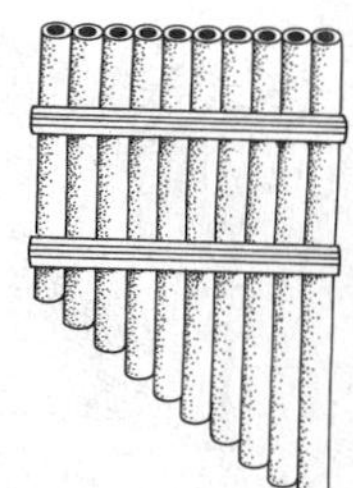

panpipe

Pantheon
Rome, Italy

ă pat	oi boy
ā pay	ou out
âr care	o͝o took
ä father	o͞o boot
ĕ pet	ŭ cut
ē be	ûr urge
ĭ pit	th thin
ī pie	*th* this
îr pier	hw which
ŏ pot	zh vision
ō toe	ə about, item
ô paw	

Stress marks:
′ (primary);
′ (secondary), as in
dictionary (dĭk′shə-nĕr′ē)

tenderizer and in medicine as a digestive aid. [PAPA(YA) + -IN.]

pa•pal (pā′pəl) *adj.* **1.** Of, relating to, or issued by a pope: *a papal bull.* **2.** Of or relating to the Roman Catholic Church. [ME < OFr. < Med.Lat. *pāpālis* < LLat. *pāpa*, pope. See POPE.] **— pa′pal•ly** *adv.*

papal infallibility *n.* In Christian churches in communion with Rome, the doctrine that the pope is unable to err in his definition that a dogma concerning faith or morals is part of the deposit of divine revelation handed down in apostolic tradition.

Pa•pal States (pā′pəl). A group of territories in central Italy ruled by the popes from 754 until 1870; orig. given to the papacy by Pepin the Short.

Pap•an•dre•ou (păp′ən-drā′o͞o, pä′pän-drĕ′-), **Andreas George.** b. 1919. Greek politician and premier (1981–89).

Pa•pa•ni•co•laou test (pä′pə-nē′kə-lou′, păp′ə-nĭk′ə-lou′) *n.* A Pap smear.

pa•pa•raz•zo (pä′pə-rät′sō) *n.*, *pl.* **-zi** (-sē). A freelance photographer who pursues celebrities to take candid pictures for sale to magazines and newspapers. [After Signor *Paparazzo*, a character in *La Dolce Vita*, a film by Federico Fellini.]

pa•pav•er•ine (pə-păv′ə-rēn′, -ər-ĭn) *n.* A nonaddictive opium derivative, $C_{20}H_{21}NO_4$, used medicinally to relieve spasms of smooth muscle. [Lat. *papāver*, poppy + -INE[2].]

pa•paw also **paw•paw** (pô′pô′) *n.* **1.** A deciduous tree *(Asimina triloba)* of the eastern and southeast United States having flowers with three sepals and three petals and fleshy edible fruit. **2.** The fruit of this tree. **3.** See **papaya.** [Ult. < Sp. and obsolete Port. *papaya*, papaya; see PAPAYA.]

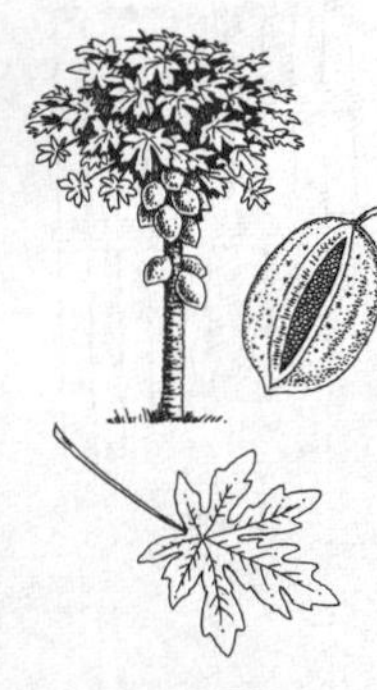

papaya
Carica papaya

pa•pa•ya (pə-pä′yə) *n.* **1.** An evergreen tropical American tree *(Carica papaya)* having a crown of palmately divided leaves and large edible yellow fruit. **2.** The fruit of this tree. [Sp. and Port., both of Cariban orig.]

Pa•pe•e•te (pä′pē-ā′tā, pə-pē′tē). The cap. of the overseas territory of French Polynesia, a port on the NW coast of Tahiti in the Society Is. of the S Pacific. Pop. 23,496.

Pa•pen (pä′pən), **Franz von.** 1879–1969. German politician and diplomat who served as vice chancellor (1933–34).

pa•per (pā′pər) *n.* **1.** A material made of cellulose pulp, derived mainly from wood and rags, processed into flexible sheets or rolls by deposit from an aqueous suspension, and used for writing, printing, drawing, wrapping, and covering walls. **2.** A single sheet of this material. **3.** One or more sheets of paper bearing writing or printing, esp.: **a.** A formal written composition intended to be published or read aloud; a scholarly essay or treatise. **b.** A piece of written work for school; a report or theme. **c.** An official document, esp. one establishing the identity of the bearer. Often used in the plural. **4. papers.** A collection of letters, diaries, and other writings, esp. by one person. **5.** Commercial documents that represent value and have transferable ownership; negotiable instruments considered as a group. **6.** A newspaper. **7.** Wallpaper. **8.** A wrapper made of paper, often with its contents. **9.** *Slang.* **a.** A free pass to a theater. **b.** The audience admitted with free passes. — *tr.v.* **-pered, -per•ing, -pers. 1.** To cover, wrap, or line with paper. **2.** To cover with wallpaper. **3.** To supply with paper. **4.** *Slang.* To issue free passes for (a theater, for example). — *adj.* **1.** Made of paper. **2.** Resembling paper, as in flimsiness. **3.** Of or relating to clerical work. **4.a.** Existing only in printed or written form. **b.** Planned but not realized; theoretical. ***—phrasal verb.*** **paper over. 1.** To put or keep out of sight; conceal: *paper over a deficit.* **2.** To downplay or gloss over (differences, for example). ***—idiom.*** **on paper. 1.** In writing or print. **2.** In theory, as opposed to actual performance or fact. [ME < OFr. *papier* < Lat. *papȳrus*, papyrus plant, papyrus paper < Gk. *papuros.*] **— pa′per•er** *n.*

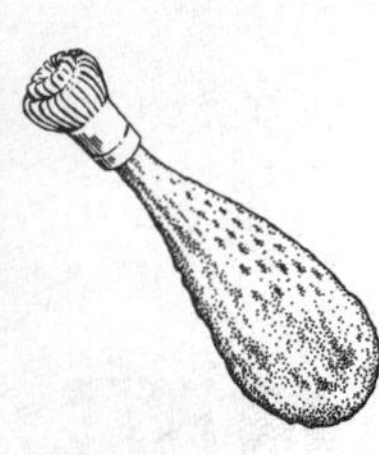

papillote

pa•per•back (pā′pər-băk′) *n.* A book having a flexible paper binding. **— pa′per•back′, pa′per•backed′** *adj.*

paper birch *n.* A North American birch tree *(Betula papyrifera)* having paperlike white bark.

pa•per•board (pā′pər-bôrd′, -bōrd′) *n.* Cardboard; pasteboard.

pa•per•bound (pā′pər-bound′) *adj.* Bound in paper; paperback.

pa•per•boy (pā′pər-boi′) *n.* A boy who sells or delivers newspapers.

paper clip also **pa•per•clip** (pā′pər-klĭp′) *n.* A wire or plastic clip for papers. Also called regionally *gem clip.*

paper cutter *n.* A device for trimming paper, typically a ruled board with a long pivoted cutting knife attached to one side.

pa•per•girl (pā′pər-gûrl′) *n.* A girl who sells or delivers newspapers.

pa•per•hang•er (pā′pər-hăng′ər) *n.* **1.** One whose occupation is covering or decorating walls with wallpaper; a paperer. **2.** *Slang.* One who passes bad checks. **— pa′per•hang′ing** *n.*

pa•per•knife (pā′pər-nīf′) *n.* A thin dull knife used for opening sealed envelopes and slitting uncut pages of books.

pa•per•mak•ing (pā′pər-mā′kĭng) *n.* The process or craft of making paper. **— pa′per•mak′er** *n.*

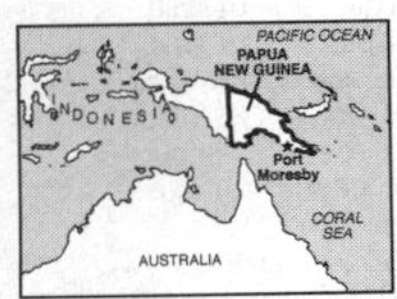

Papua New Guinea

paper money *n.* Currency in the form of government notes and bank notes.

paper mulberry *n.* An eastern Asian ornamental deciduous tree *(Broussonetia papyrifera)* having bark that can be processed into a paperlike fabric.

paper nautilus *n.* A cephalopod mollusk *(Argonauta argo)* with eight tentacles, the female of which inhabits a paper-thin shell that later acts as an egg case.

paper plant *n.* See **papyrus** 1.

paper tiger *n.* One only seemingly dangerous and powerful.

paper trail *n.* *Informal.* Documentary evidence, as of crime.

pa•per-train (pā′pər-trān′) *tr.v.* **-trained, -train•ing, -trains.** To train (a pet) to urinate and defecate on paper.

paper wasp *n.* Any of various social wasps, such as the hornet, that builds papery nests from chewed wood pulp.

pa•per•weight (pā′pər-wāt′) *n.* A small, heavy, often decorative object placed on loose papers to hold them down.

pa•per•work also **pa•per work** (pā′pər-wûrk′) *n.* Work involving the handling of reports, letters, and forms.

pa•per•y (pā′pə-rē) *adj.* Resembling paper, as in thickness or texture. **— pa′per•i•ness** *n.*

pap•e•terie (păp′ĭ-trē, păp-trē′) *n.* A box used to hold stationery and other writing materials. [Fr. < OFr. *papetier*, papermaking < *papier*, paper. See PAPER.]

Pa•pia•men•tu (pä′pyə-mĕn′to͞o) also **Pa•pia•men•to** (-tō) *n.* A creole of the Netherlands Antilles based on Portuguese and pidgin Spanish. [< Papiamentu *papia*, talk, prob. < Port. *papaguear, papear*, to chatter < *papagaio*, parrot.]

pa•pier-mâ•ché (pā′pər-mə-shā′, pă-pyā′-) *n.* A material, made from paper pulp or shreds mixed with glue or paste, that can be molded when wet and becomes hard and suitable for painting and varnishing when dry. [Fr. : *papier*, paper; see PAPER + *mâché*, p.part. of *mâcher*, to chew (< OFr. *maschier* < Lat. *masticāre*; see MASTICATE).] **— pa′pier-mâ•ché′** *adj.*

pa•pil•i•o•na•ceous (pə-pĭl′ē-ə-nā′shəs) *adj.* Having a bilaterally symmetrical corolla somewhat resembling a butterfly, characteristic of most plants of the pea family. [Lat. *pāpiliō*, *pāpiliōn-*, butterfly; see PAVILION + -ACEOUS.]

pa•pil•la (pə-pĭl′ə) *n.*, *pl.* **-pil•lae** (-pĭl′ē). **1.** A small nipplelike projection, such as a protuberance at the root of a hair. **2.** One of the small protuberances on the top of the tongue that contain taste buds. **3.** A pimple or pustule. **4.** *Bot.* A minute projection on the surface of a stigma, petal, or leaf. [Lat., nipple, dim. of *papula*, swelling, pimple.] **— pap′il•lar′y** (păp′ə-lĕr′ē, pə-pĭl′ə-rē) *adj.* **— pap′il•late′** (păp′ə-lāt′, pə-pĭl′ĭt) *adj.* **— pap•il•lose** (păp′ə-lōs′, pə-pĭl′ōs′) *adj.*

pap•il•lo•ma (păp′ə-lō′mə) *n.*, *pl.* **-mas** or **-ma•ta** (-mə-tə). A small benign epithelial tumor, such as a wart, consisting of an overgrowth of cells on a core of smooth connective tissue. **— pap′il•lo′ma•tous** *adj.*

pap•il•lon (păp′ə-lŏn′, pä′pē-yôN) *n.* Any of a breed of small dog related to the spaniel, having a long silky coat and large ears shaped like the wings of a butterfly. [Fr. < OFr., butterfly < Lat. *pāpiliō, pāpiliōn-*. See PAVILION.]

pap•il•lote (pä′pē-yōt′, păp′ē-) *n.* **1.** A paper frill used to decorate a bone end, as on a rack of lamb. **2.** An oiled paper or foil wrapper in which certain foods are baked. [Fr. < OFr., ornament for the hair < fem. of *papillot*, dim. of *papillon*, butterfly < Lat. *pāpiliō, pāpiliōn-*. See PAVILION.]

pa•pist (pā′pĭst) *n.* *Offensive.* Used as a disparaging term for a Roman Catholic. [NLat. *pāpista* < LLat. *pāpa*. See POPE.] **— pa′pist, pa•pis′tic** (pə-pĭs′tĭk) *adj.* **— pa′pist•ry** *n.*

pa•poose (pă-po͞os′, pə-) *n.* A Native American infant or very young child. [Narragansett *papoòs*, child.]

pa•po•va•vi•rus (pə-pō′və-vī′rəs) *n.*, *pl.* **-rus•es.** Any of a group of DNA-containing viruses associated with or causing papillomas or polyomas in animals. [PA(PILLOMA) + PO(LYOMA VIRUS) + VA(CUOLATION) + VIRUS.]

Papp (păp), **Joseph.** 1921–91. Amer. producer and director best known for *Hair* (1967), *A Chorus Line* (1975), and the New York Shakespeare Festival.

pap•pa•ta•ci fever (pä′pə-tä′chē) *n.* See **sandfly fever.** [Ital. *pappataci*, sandfly : *pappare*, to eat (< Lat. *pappāre* < *pappa*, food) + *-taci*, silently (< *tacito*, p.part. of *tacere*, to be silent < Lat. *tacēre*).]

pap•pus (păp′əs) *n.*, *pl.* **pap•pi** (păp′ī). A modified calyx, composed of scales, bristles, or fine hairs, in plants of the composite family. [Lat., old man, seed down < Gk. *pappos*. See **papa***.] **— pap′pose** (-ōs), **pap′pous** (-əs) *adj.*

pap•py[1] (păp′ē) *adj.* **-pi•er, -pi•est.** Paplike; mushy.

pap•py[2] (păp′ē) *n.*, *pl.* **-pies.** *Informal.* Father. [Dim. of PAPA.]

pa•pri•ka (pă-prē′kə, pə-, păp′rĭ-kə) *n.* **1.** A mild powdered seasoning made from sweet red peppers. **2.** *Color.* A dark to deep or vivid reddish orange. [Hung. < Serbian < *papar*, ground pepper < Slav. **pipru* < Lat. *piper*. See PEPPER.]

Pap smear (păp) *n.* A test for cancer, esp. of the female genital tract, in which a smear of exfoliated cells is specially stained and examined under a microscope for pathological changes. [After George *Papanicolaou* (1883–1962), Amer. anatomist.]

Pap•u•a (păp′yo͞o-ə, pä′po͞o-ä′), **Gulf of.** A large inlet of the Coral Sea on the SE coast of New Guinea.

Pap•u•an (păp′yo͞o-ən) *adj.* **1.** Of or relating to the peoples, languages, or cultures of Papua New Guinea or New Guinea.

2. Of or relating to the Papuan language. — *n.* **1.** A native or inhabitant of Papua New Guinea or New Guinea. **2.** A member of any of the indigenous peoples of New Guinea and neighboring islands. **3.** Any of the indigenous languages of New Guinea, New Britain, and the Solomon Islands.

Papua New Guin•ea (gĭn′ē). An island country of the SW Pacific comprising the E half of New Guinea, the Bismarck Archipelago, the W Solomons, and adjacent islands; became fully independent from Australia in 1975. Cap. Port Moresby. Pop. 3,010,727. — **Pap′u•a New Guin′e•an** *adj. & n.*

pap•ule (păp′yo͞ol) also **pap•u•la** (-yə-lə) *n., pl.* **-ules** also **-u•lae** (-yə-lē′). A small, solid, usu. inflammatory elevation of the skin that does not contain pus. [Lat. *papula.*] — **pap′u•lar** (-yə-lər) *adj.*

pap•y•rol•o•gy (păp′ə-rŏl′ə-jē) *n.* The study of papyrus manuscripts. — **pap′y•ro•log′ic** (păp′ər-ə-lŏj′ĭk, pə-pī′rə-), **pap′y•ro•log′i•cal** (-ĭ-kəl) *adj.*

pa•py•rus (pə-pī′rəs) *n., pl.* **-rus•es** or **-ri** (-rī′). **1.** A tall aquatic Mediterranean sedge *(Cyperus papyrus)* having numerous drooping rays grouped in umbels. **2.a.** A material on which to write made from the pith or the stems of this sedge, used esp. by the ancient Egyptians, Greeks, and Romans. **b.** A document written on this material. [ME *papirus* < Lat. *papȳrus* < Gk. *papuros.*]

par (pär) *n.* **1.** An amount or a level considered to be average; a standard. **2.** An equality of status, level, or value; equal footing. **3.** The established value of a monetary unit expressed in terms of a monetary unit of another country using the same metal standard. **4.** The face value of a stock, bond, or other negotiable instrument. **5.** *Sports.* The number of golf strokes considered necessary to complete a hole or course in expert play. — *tr.v.* **parred, par•ring, pars.** *Sports.* To score par on (a hole or course) in golf. — *adj.* **1.** Equal to the standard; normal. **2.** Of or relating to monetary face value. [< Lat. *pār,* equal, that which is equal. See **perə-²*.**]

par. *abbr.* **1.** Paragraph. **2.** Parallel. **3.** Parenthesis. **4.** Parish.

Par. *abbr.* Paraguay.

pa•ra (pä-rä′, pä′rä) *n.* See table at **currency.** [Serbo-Croatian < Turk. < Pers. *parāh,* piece, para.]

para–¹ or **par–** *pref.* **1.** Beside; near; alongside: *parathyroid.* **2.** Beyond: *paranormal.* **3.** Incorrect; abnormal: *paresthesia.* **4.** Similar to; resembling: *paratyphoid fever.* **5.** Subsidiary; assistant: *paraprofessional.* **6.** Isomeric; polymeric: *paraldehyde.* **7.** A diatomic molecule in which the nuclei have opposite spin directions: *parahydrogen.* **8.** Of or relating to an isomer of a benzene ring in which the two carbon atoms with attached groups are separated by two unsubstituted carbon atoms: para-*bromoiodobenzene.* [Gk. < *para,* beside. See **per¹*.**]

para–² *pref.* Parachute; parachutist: *paratroops.* [< PARACHUTE.]

–para *suff.* A woman who has given birth to a specified number of children: *multipara.* [Lat. < *parere,* to give birth. See **perə-¹*.**]

Pa•rá (pə-rä′). See **Belém.**

par•a-a•mi•no•ben•zo•ic acid (păr′ə-ə-mē′nō-bĕn-zō′ĭk, -ăm′ə-) *n.* PABA.

par•a•bi•o•sis (păr′ə-bī-ō′sĭs) *n., pl.* **-ses** (-sēz). **1.** The union of anatomical parts of two organisms, usu. involving exchange of blood, as in Siamese twins or certain transplant operations. **2.** A temporary suspension of conductivity or excitability in a nerve. — **par′a•bi•ot′ic** (-ŏt′ĭk) *adj.*

par•a•blast (păr′ə-blăst′) *n.* The nutritive yolk of a meroblastic egg. — **par′a•blas′tic** *adj.*

par•a•ble (păr′ə-bəl) *n.* A simple story illustrating a moral or religious lesson. [ME < OFr. < LLat. *parabola* < Gk. *parabolē* < *paraballein,* to compare : *para-,* beside; see PARA–¹ + *ballein,* to throw; see **gʷelə-*.**]

pa•rab•o•la (pə-răb′ə-lə) *n.* **1.** A plane curve formed by the intersection of a right circular cone and a plane parallel to an element of the cone. **2.** A plane curve formed by the locus of points equidistant from a fixed line and a fixed point not on the line. [NLat. < Gk. *parabolē,* comparison, application, parabola (< the relationship between the line joining the vertices of a conic and the line through its focus and parallel to its directrix) < *paraballein,* to compare. See PARABLE.]

par•a•bol•ic (păr′ə-bŏl′ĭk) also **par•a•bol•i•cal** (-ĭ-kəl) *adj.* **1.** Of or similar to a parable. **2.** Of or having the form of a parabola or paraboloid. [Ult. < Gk. *parabolē,* comparison. See PARABLE. Sense 2 < PARABOLA.] — **par′a•bol′i•cal•ly** *adv.*

pa•rab•o•loid (pə-răb′ə-loid′) *n.* A surface having parabolic sections parallel to a coordinate axis and elliptic sections perpendicular to that axis. — **pa•rab′o•loi′dal** (-loid′l) *adj.*

Par•a•cel•sus (păr′ə-sĕl′səs), **Philippus Aureolus.** 1493–1541. German-Swiss alchemist and physician who introduced the concept of disease to medicine.

par•a•chute (păr′ə-sho͞ot′) *n.* **1.** An apparatus used to retard free fall from an aircraft, consisting of a usu. hemispherical canopy attached to a harness. **2.** Any of various similar unpowered devices used to retard free-speeding or free-falling motion. **3.** See **patagium** 1. — *v.* **-chut•ed, -chut•ing, -chutes.** — *tr.* To drop by means of a parachute. — *intr.* To descend by means of a parachute. [Fr. : *para(sol),* parasol; see PARASOL + *chute,* fall; see CHUTE.] — **par′a•chut′ic** *adj.* — **par′a•chut′ist, par′a•chut′er** *n.*

parachute spinnaker *n. Naut.* An oversize spinnaker used on racing yachts.

Par•a•clete (păr′ə-klēt′) *n.* The Holy Spirit. [ME *Paraclit* < OFr. *Paraclet* < Lat. *Paraclētus* < Gk. *Paraklētos* < *parakalein,* to invoke : *para-,* to the side of; see PARA–¹ + *kalein, klē-,* to call; see **kelə-²*.**]

pa•rade (pə-rād′) *n.* **1.a.** An organized public procession on a festive or ceremonial occasion. **b.** The participants in such a procession. **2.a.** A place where troops are reviewed. **b.** A ceremonial review of troops. **3.** A line or extended group of moving persons or things. **4.** An extended, usu. showy succession. **5.** An ostentatious show; an exhibition. **6.** A public square or promenade. — *v.* **-rad•ed, -rad•ing, -rades.** — *intr.* **1.** To take part in a parade; march in a public procession. **2.** To assemble for a military parade. **3.** To stroll in public, esp. so as to be seen; promenade. **4.** To behave so as to attract attention; show off. — *tr.* **1.** To cause to take part in a parade. **2.** To assemble (troops) for a parade. **3.** To march or walk through or around. **4.** To exhibit ostentatiously; flaunt. [Prob. Fr. < OFr., exhibition < *parer,* to embellish < Lat. *parāre,* to prepare. See **perə-¹*.**] — **pa•rad′er** *n.*

par•a•di•chlo•ro•ben•zene (păr′ə-dī-klôr′ə-bĕn′zēn′, -bĕn-zēn′, -klōr′-) *n.* A white crystalline compound, $C_6H_4Cl_2$, used as a germicide and an insecticide.

par•a•did•dle (păr′ə-dĭd′l) *n. Mus.* A pattern of drumbeats characterized by four basic beats and alternating left-handed and right-handed strokes on the successive primary beats. [Prob. imit.]

par•a•digm (păr′ə-dīm′, -dĭm′) *n.* **1.** An example that serves as pattern or model. **2.** The conceptual framework that permits the explanation and investigation of phenomena or the objects of study in a field of inquiry. **3.** A list of all the inflectional forms of a word used to illustrate the conjugation or declension to which it belongs. [ME, example < LLat. *paradīgma* < Gk. *paradeigma* < *paradeiknunai,* to compare : *para-,* alongside; see PARA–¹ + *deiknunai,* to show; see **deik-*.**] — **par′a•dig•mat′ic** (-dĭg-măt′ĭk) *adj.*

par•a•dise (păr′ə-dīs′, -dīz′) *n.* **1.** Often **Paradise.** The Garden of Eden. **2.** *Theol.* **a.** The abode of the righteous after death; heaven. **b.** An intermediate resting place for righteous souls awaiting the Resurrection. **3.** A place of ideal beauty or loveliness. **4.** A state of delight. [ME *paradis* < OFr. < LLat. *paradīsus* < Gk. *paradeisos,* garden, enclosed park, paradise < Avestan *pairi-daēza-,* enclosure, park : *pairi-,* around; see **per¹*** + *daēza-,* wall; see **dheigh-*.**] — **par′a•di•si′a•cal** (-dĭ-sī′ə-kəl, -zī′-), **par′a•di•si′ac** (-ăk), **par′a•di•sa′i•cal** (-dĭ-sā′ĭ-kəl, -zā′-), **par′a•di•sa′ic** (-ĭk), **par′a•dis′al** (-dī′səl, -zəl) *adj.* — **par′a•di•si′a•cal•ly, par′a•di•sa′i•cal•ly, par′a•dis′al•ly** *adv.*

par•a•dor (păr′ə-dôr′, pä′rä-*th*ôr′) *n., pl.* **-dors** or **-dor•es** (-*th*ô′rĕs). A government-run country hotel in Spain or Latin America. [Sp. < *parar,* to stop < Lat. *parāre,* to prepare. See PARADE.]

par•a•dox (păr′ə-dŏks′) *n.* **1.** A seemingly contradictory statement that may nonetheless be true. **2.** One exhibiting inexplicable or contradictory aspects. **3.** An assertion that is essentially self-contradictory, though based on a valid deduction from acceptable premises. **4.** A statement contrary to received opinion. [Lat. *paradoxum* < Gk. *paradoxon* < neut. sing. of *paradoxos,* conflicting with expectation : *para-,* beyond; see PARA–¹ + *doxa,* opinion (< *dokein,* to think; see **dek-***).] — **par′a•dox′i•cal** *adj.* — **par′a•dox′i•cal•ly** *adv.* — **par′a•dox′i•cal•ness** *n.*

paradoxical sleep *n.* See **REM sleep.**

par•a•drop (păr′ə-drŏp′) *n.* Delivery of supplies to a place by parachute. — **par′a•drop′** *v.*

par•aes•the•sia (păr′ĭs-thē′zhə) *n.* Var. of **paresthesia.**

par•af•fin (păr′ə-fĭn) *n.* **1.** A waxy solid hydrocarbon mixture used to make candles, wax paper, lubricants, and sealing materials. **2.** *Chem.* A member of the alkane series. **3.** *Chiefly British.* Kerosene. — *tr.v.* **-fined, -fin•ing, -fins.** To saturate, impregnate, or coat with paraffin. [Ger. : Lat. *parum,* little; see **pau-*** + Lat. *affīnis,* associated with (< its lack of affinity with other materials); see AFFINED.] — **par′af•fin′ic** *adj.*

paraffin series *n. Chem.* See **alkane series.**

paraffin wax *n.* See **paraffin** 1.

par•a•for•mal•de•hyde (păr′ə-fôr-măl′də-hīd′) *n.* A solid polymer of formaldehyde, $(HCHO)_n$, where n is at least 6, used as a disinfectant, fumigant, and fungicide.

par•a•gen•e•sis (păr′ə-jĕn′ĭ-sĭs) also **par•a•ge•ne•sia** (-jə-nē′zhə, -zhē-ə) *n.* The order of formation of associated minerals in a rock or vein. — **par′a•ge•net′ic** (-jə-nĕt′ĭk) *adj.*

par•a•gon (păr′ə-gŏn′, -gən) *n.* **1.** A model of excellence or perfection of a kind; a peerless example. **2.a.** An unflawed diamond weighing at least 100 carats. **b.** A very large spherical pearl. **3.** *Print.* A type size of 20 points. — *tr.v.* **-goned, -gon•ing, -gons. 1.** To compare; parallel. **2.** To equal; match. [Obsolete Fr. < OFr. < OItal. *paragone* < *paragonare,* to test on a touchstone, perh. < Gk. *parakonan,* to sharpen : *para-,* alongside; see PARA–¹ + *akonē,* whetstone; see **ak-*.**]

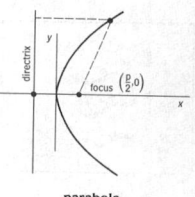

directrix y focus $(\frac{p}{2},0)$ x

parabola
$y^2 = 2px$

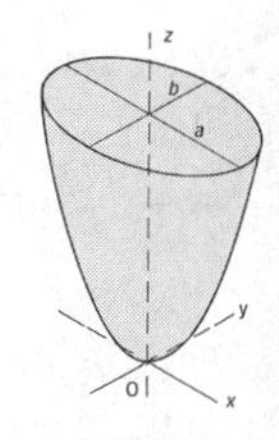

paraboloid
$z = \frac{x^2}{a^2} + \frac{y^2}{b^2}$

parachute

ă pat	oi boy
ā pay	ou out
âr care	o͝o took
ä father	o͞o boot
ĕ pet	ŭ cut
ē be	ûr urge
ĭ pit	th thin
ī pie	*th* this
îr pier	hw which
ŏ pot	zh vision
ō toe	ə about, item
ô paw	

Stress marks:
′ (primary);
′ (secondary), as in
dictionary (dĭk′shə-nĕr′ē)

Paraguay

Par•a•gould (păr′ə-go͞old′). A city of NE AR NE of Jonesboro. Pop. 18,540.

par•a•graph (păr′ə-grăf′) *n.* **1.** A division of written or printed matter that begins on a new, usu. indented line, has one or more sentences, and typically deals with one topic or quotes one speaker's continuous words. **2.** A mark (¶) used to indicate where a new paragraph should begin or serve as a reference mark. **3.** A brief article, notice, or announcement, as in a newspaper. —*tr.v.* **-graphed, -graph•ing, -graphs.** To divide or arrange into paragraphs. [ME *paragraf* < OFr. *paragrafe* < Med.Lat. *paragraphus* < Gk. *paragraphos*, line showing a break in sense or a change of speakers in a dialogue < *paragraphein*, to write beside : *para-*, beside; see PARA-[1] + *graphein*, to write; see **gerbh-***.] —**par′a•graph′ic, par′a•graph′i•cal** *adj.*

Par•a•guay (păr′ə-gwī′, -gwā′). A country of S-central South America; achieved independence from Spain in 1811. Cap. Asunción. Pop. 3,026,165. —**Par′a•guay′an** *adj. & n.*

Paraguay River. A river rising in SW Brazil and flowing c. 2,574 km (1,600 mi) to the Paraná R. in SW Paraguay.

Paraguay tea *n.* See **maté** 2.

Pa•ra•í•ba (păr′ə-ē′bə, pä′rä-ē′bä) also **Paraíba do Sul** (do͞o so͞ol′). A river, c. 1,046 km (650 mi), of SE Brazil emptying into the Atlantic Ocean.

par•a•in•flu•en•za (păr′ə-ĭn′flo͞o-ĕn′zə) *adj.* Of, relating to, or being any of a group of paramyxoviruses that are similar to the influenza viruses and cause respiratory infections.

par•a•jour•nal•ism (păr′ə-jûr′nə-lĭz′əm) *n.* Subjective journalism that uses some of the techniques or license of fiction.

par•a•keet (păr′ə-kēt′) *n.* Any of various small slender parrots, usu. having long tapering tails and often kept as pets. [Sp. *periquito*, prob. dim. of *Perico*, dim. of *Pedro*, Peter.]

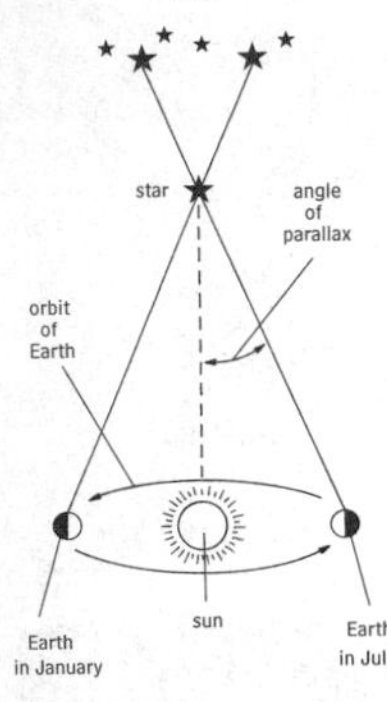

parallax

par•al•de•hyde (pə-răl′də-hīd′) *n.* A colorless liquid polymer, $C_6H_{12}O_3$, of acetaldehyde, used as a solvent and a sedative.

par•a•le•gal (păr′ə-lē′gəl) *adj. Law.* Of, relating to, or being a person with specialized training who assists an attorney. —**par′a•le′gal** *n.*

par•al•lax (păr′ə-lăks′) *n.* An apparent change in the direction of an object, caused by a change in observational position that provides a new line of sight. [Fr. *parallaxe* < Gk. *parallaxis* < *parallassein*, to change : *para-*, among; see PARA-[1] + *allassein*, to exchange (< *allos*, other; see **al-**[1]*).] —**par′al•lac′tic** (-lăk′tĭk) *adj.*

par•al•lel (păr′ə-lĕl′) *adj.* **1.** Being an equal distance apart everywhere. **2.** *Math.* Of, relating to, or being lines, curves, or surfaces that are everywhere equidistantly apart, such as nonintersecting coplanar lines or nonintersecting planes. **3.a.** Having comparable parts, analogous aspects, or readily recognized similarities. See Usage Note at **unique. b.** Having the same tendency or direction. **4.** *Gram.* Having identical or equivalent syntactic constructions in corresponding clauses or phrases. **5.** *Mus.* Moving consistently by the same intervals: *parallel voices.* **6.** *Electron.* Of or being a circuit or part of a circuit connected in parallel. **7.** *Comp. Sci.* **a.** Of or relating to the simultaneous transmission of all the bits of a byte over separate wires: *a parallel printer.* **b.** Of or relating to the simultaneous performance of multiple operations: *parallel processing.* —*adv.* In a parallel relationship or manner. —*n.* **1.** *Math.* One of a set of parallel geometric figures, such as lines or planes. **2.a.** One that closely resembles or is analogous to another. **b.** A comparison indicating likeness; an analogy. **3.** The condition of being parallel; near similarity or exact agreement in particulars; parallelism. **4.** Any of the imaginary lines representing degrees of latitude that encircle the earth parallel to the plane of the equator. **5.** *Print.* A sign indicating material referred to in a note or reference. **6.** *Electron.* An arrangement of components in a circuit that splits the current into two or more paths. —*tr.v.* **-leled, -lel•ing, -lels** also **-lelled, -lel•ling, -lels. 1.** To make or place parallel to something else. **2.** To be or extend parallel to. **3.** To be similar or analogous to. **4.** To be or provide an equal for; match. **5.** To show to be analogous; compare or liken. [Lat. *parallēlus* < Gk. *parallēlos* : *para*, beside; see PARA-[1] + *allēlōn*, of one another (< *allos*, other; see **al-**[1]*).]

parallel bars *pl.n. Sports.* An apparatus for gymnastic exercises consisting of two horizontal bars set parallel to each other in adjustable upright supports.

parallel cousin *n.* A cousin who is the child of one's mother's sister or one's father's brother.

par•al•lel•e•pi•ped (păr′ə-lĕl′ə-pī′pĭd, -pĭp′ĭd) *n.* A solid with six faces, each a parallelogram and each being parallel to the opposite face. [Gk. *parallēlepipedon* : *parallēlos*, parallel; see PARALLEL + *epipedon*, plane surface < neut. sing. of *epipedos*, level (*epi-*, epi- + *pedon*, ground; see **ped-***).]

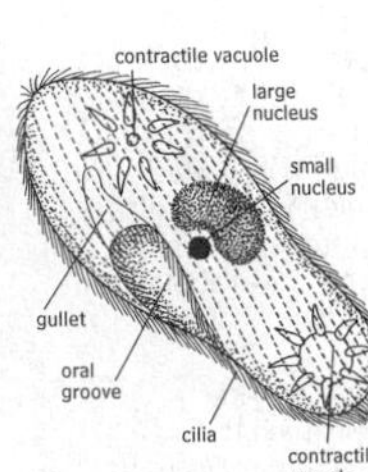

paramecium

par•al•lel•ism (păr′ə-lĕl-ĭz′əm) *n.* **1.** The quality or condition of being parallel. **2.** Likeness, correspondence, or similarity in aspect, course, or tendency. **3.** *Gram.* The use of parallel syntactic constructions. **4.** *Philos.* The doctrine that to every mental change there corresponds a concomitant but causally unconnected physical alteration.

par•al•lel•o•gram (păr′ə-lĕl′ə-grăm′) *n.* A four-sided plane figure with opposite sides parallel. [LLat. *parallēlogrammum* < Gk. *parallēlogrammon* < neut. sing. of *parallēlogrammos*, bounded by parallel lines : *parallēlos*, parallel; see PARALLEL + *grammē*, line; see **gerbh-***.]

pa•ral•o•gism (pə-răl′ə-jĭz′əm) *n.* A fallacious or illogical argument or conclusion. [LLat. *paralogismus* < Gk. *paralogismos* < *paralogos*, unreasonable : *para-*, beyond; see PARA-[1] + *logos*, reason; see **leg-***.] —**pa•ral′o•gist** *n.* —**pa•ral′o•gis′tic** *adj.*

par•a•lyse (păr′ə-līz′) *v. Chiefly British.* Var. of **paralyze.**

pa•ral•y•sis (pə-răl′ĭ-sĭs) *n., pl.* **-ses** (-sēz′). **1.a.** Loss or impairment of the ability to move a body part, usu. as a result of damage to its nerve supply. **b.** Loss of sensation over a region of the body. **2.** Inability to move or function; total stoppage or severe impairment of activity. [Lat. < Gk. *paralusis* < *paraluein*, to disable, loosen : *para-*, on one side; see PARA-[1] + *luein*, to release; see **leu-***.]

paralysis ag•i•tans (ăj′ĭ-tănz′) *n.* See **Parkinson's disease.** [NLat. *paralysis agitāns* : Lat. *paralysis*, palsy + Lat. *agitāns*, pr.part. of *agitāre*, to shake.]

par•a•lyt•ic (păr′ə-lĭt′ĭk) *adj.* **1.** Of or relating to paralysis. **2.** Characteristic of or resembling paralysis. **3.** Affected with paralysis; paralyzed. —*n.* One affected with paralysis. —**par′a•lyt′i•cal•ly** *adv.*

par•a•lyze (păr′ə-līz′) *tr.v.* **-lyzed, -lyz•ing, -lyz•es. 1.** To affect with paralysis; make paralytic. **2.** To make unable to move or act. **3.** To impair the progress or functioning of; make inoperative or powerless. [Fr. *paralyser* < *paralysie*, paralysis < OFr. < Lat. *paralysis.* See PARALYSIS.] —**par′a•ly•za′tion** (-lĭ-zā′shən) *n.* —**par′a•lyz′er** *n.* —**par′a•lyz′ing•ly** *adv.*

par•a•mag•net (păr′ə-măg′nĭt) *n.* A paramagnetic substance.

par•a•mag•net•ic (păr′ə-măg-nĕt′ĭk) *adj.* Relating to or being a substance in which an induced magnetic field is parallel and proportional to the magnetizing field but is much weaker than in ferromagnetic materials. —**par′a•mag•net′i•cal•ly** *adv.* —**par′a•mag′net•ism** (-măg′nĭ-tĭz′əm) *n.*

Par•a•mar•i•bo (păr′ə-măr′ə-bō′). The cap. of Suriname, on the Suriname R.; under Dutch rule after 1815. Pop. 67,905.

par•a•mat•ta or **par•ra•mat•ta** (păr′ə-măt′ə) *n.* A fine, lightweight, silk and wool or cotton and wool dress fabric. [After PARRAMATTA.]

par•a•me•ci•um (păr′ə-mē′shē-əm, -sē-əm) *n., pl.* **-ci•a** (-shē-ə, -sē-ə) or **-ci•ums.** Any of various freshwater ciliate protozoans of the genus *Paramecium*, usu. oval and having an oral groove for feeding. [NLat. *Paramēcium*, genus name < Gk. *paramēkēs*, oblong in shape : *para-*, alongside; see PARA-[1] + *mēkos*, length; see **māk-***.]

par•a•med•ic (păr′ə-mĕd′ĭk) *n.* A person who is trained to give emergency medical treatment or assist medical professionals. —**par′a•med′i•cal** (-ĭ-kəl) *adj.*

par•a•ment (păr′ə-mənt) *n., pl.* **-ments** or **-men•ta** (-mĕn′tə). An ecclesiastical vestment or hanging. [< ME *paramentes*, adornments < OFr. *parement*, ornament < Med.Lat. *parāmentum* < *parāre*, to decorate < Lat., to ready. See PARE.]

pa•ram•e•ter (pə-răm′ĭ-tər) *n.* **1.** *Math.* **a.** A constant in an equation that varies in other equations of the same general form, esp. in the equation of a curve or surface that can be varied to represent a family of curves or surfaces. **b.** One of a set of independent variables that express the coordinates of a point. **2.a.** One of a set of measurable factors, such as temperature, that define a system and determine its behavior and are varied in an experiment. **b.** A factor that restricts what is possible or what results. **c.** A factor that determines a range of variations; a boundary. **3.** *Statistics.* A quantity, such as a mean, that is calculated from data and describes a population. **4.** A distinguishing characteristic or feature. [NLat. *parametrum*, a line through the focus and parallel to the directrix of a conic : Gk. *para-*, beside; see PARA-[1] + Gk. *metron*, measure; see -METER.] —**par′a•met′ric** (păr′ə-mĕt′rĭk), **par′a•met′ri•cal** *adj.* —**par′a•met′ri•cal•ly** *adv.*

par•a•mil•i•tar•y (păr′ə-mĭl′ĭ-tĕr′ē) *adj.* Of, relating to, or being a group of civilians organized in a military fashion, esp. to operate in place of or assist regular army troops. —*n., pl.* **-ies.** A member of a paramilitary force.

par•am•ne•sia (păr′ăm-nē′zhə) *n.* **1.** A distortion of memory in which fantasy and objective experience are confused. **2.** An inability to recall the meanings of common words.

pa•ra•mo (pä′rə-mō′, păr′ə-) *n., pl.* **-mos.** A treeless alpine plateau of the Andes and tropical South America. [Am.Sp. *páramo* < Sp., wasteland.]

par•a•morph (păr′ə-môrf′) *n.* A mineral crystal formed or affected by paramorphism.

par•a•mor•phine (păr′ə-môr′fēn′) *n.* See **thebaine.**

par•a•mor•phism (păr′ə-môr′fĭz′əm) *n.* Structural alteration of a mineral without change of chemical composition. —**par′a•mor′phic** (-fĭk), **par′a•mor′phous** (-fəs) *adj.*

par•a•mount (păr′ə-mount′) *adj.* **1.** Of chief concern or importance. **2.** Supreme in rank, power, or authority. —*n.* One that has the highest rank, power, or authority. [AN *paramont*, above : *par*, by (< Lat. *per*; see **per**[1]*) + *amont*, above, upward; see AMOUNT.] —**par′a•mount′cy** *n.* —**par′a•mount′ly** *adv.*

Par•a•mount (păr′ə-mount′). A city of S CA SE of Los Angeles. Pop. 47,669.

par•a•mour (păr′ə-mo͝or′) *n.* A lover, esp. one in an adulterous relationship. [ME < *par amour*, by way of love, passionately < AN : *par*, by (< Lat. *per*; see **per**[1]*) + *amour*, love (< Lat. *amor* < *amāre*, to love).]

Pa•ram•us (pə-răm′əs). A borough of NE NJ NE of Paterson. Pop. 25,067.

par•a•myx•o•vi•rus (păr′ə-mĭk′sə-vī′rəs) *n., pl.* **-rus•es.** Any of a group of viruses that contain RNA, are related to the myxoviruses, and include the parainfluenza viruses.

Pa•ra•ná (păr′ə-nä′, pä′rä-). A city of NE Argentina on the Paraná R. N of Rosario. Pop. 161,638.

Pa•ra•na•í•ba (păr′ə-nə-ē′bə, pä′rä-nä-ē′bä). A river of S-central Brazil flowing c. 805 km (500 mi) to the Paraná R.

Paraná River. A river of central South America rising in E-central Brazil and flowing c. 2,896 km (1,800 mi) to the Río de la Plata estuary in E Argentina.

pa•rang (pä′răng′) *n.* A short heavy straight-edged knife used in Malaysia and Indonesia as a tool and weapon. [Malay.]

par•a•noi•a (păr′ə-noi′ə) *n.* **1.** A psychotic disorder characterized by delusions of persecution or grandeur, often strenuously rationalized. **2.** Extreme irrational distrust of others. [Gk., madness < *paranoos*, demented : *para-*, beyond; see PARA–[1] + *nous, noos*, mind.]

par•a•noi•ac (păr′ə-noi′ăk′, -noi′ĭk) *n.* A paranoid. — *adj.* Of, relating to, or resembling paranoia.

par•a•noid (păr′ə-noid′) *adj.* **1.** Relating to or affected with paranoia. **2.** Exhibiting or characterized by extreme fear or distrust of others. — *n.* One affected with paranoia.

par•a•nor•mal (păr′ə-nôr′məl) *adj.* Beyond the range of normal experience or scientific explanation. — **par′a•nor•mal′i•ty** (-nôr-măl′ĭ-tē) *n.* — **par′a•nor′mal•ly** *adv.*

par•a•pa•re•sis (păr′ə-pə-rē′sĭs, -păr′ĭ-sĭs) *n., pl.* **-ses** (-sēz). Partial paralysis of the lower extremities.

par•a•pet (păr′ə-pĭt, -pĕt′) *n.* **1.** A low protective wall or railing along the edge of a raised structure such as a roof. **2.** An earthen or stone embankment protecting soldiers from enemy fire. [Fr. < Ital. *parapetto* : *parare*, to shield; see PARASOL + *petto*, chest (< Lat. *pectus*).]

par•aph (păr′əf, pə-răf′) *n.* A flourish made after or below a signature, originally to prevent forgery. [Fr. *paraphe* < OFr. *paraffe*, abbreviated signature < Med.Lat. *paraphus*, paragraph sign, short for *paragraphus*. See PARAGRAPH.]

par•a•pher•na•lia (păr′ə-fər-nāl′yə, -fə-nāl′yə) *pl.n.* *(used with a sing. or pl. v.)* **1.** Personal belongings. **2.** The articles used in a particular activity; equipment. **3.** *Law.* A married woman's personal property exclusive of her dowry, according to common law. [Med.Lat. *paraphernālia*, neut. pl. of *paraphernālis*, of legal paraphernalia < LLat. *parapherna*, legal paraphernalia < Gk. : *para-*, beyond; see PARA–[1] + *phernē*, dowry; see **bher-**[1]*.]

par•a•phrase (păr′ə-frāz′) *n.* **1.** A restatement of a text or passage in another form or other words. **2.** The restatement of texts in other words as a studying or teaching device. — *v.* **-phrased, -phras•ing, -phras•es.** — *tr.* To restate in a paraphrase. — *intr.* To compose a paraphrase. [Fr. < Lat. *paraphrasis* < Gk. < *paraphrazein*, to paraphrase : *para-*, alongside; see PARA–[1] + *phrazein*, to show, explain; see **gʷhren-***.] — **par′a•phras′a•ble** *adj.* — **par′a•phras′er** *n.*

par•a•phras•tic (păr′ə-frăs′tĭk) or **par•a•phras•ti•cal** (-tĭ-kəl) *adj.* Of, relating to, or having the nature of paraphrase. [Med.Lat. *paraphrasticus* < Gk. *paraphrastikos* < *paraphrazein*, to paraphrase. See PARAPHRASE.]

pa•raph•y•sis (pə-răf′ĭ-sĭs) *n., pl.* **-ses** (-sēz′). One of the erect sterile filaments often occurring among the reproductive organs of certain fungi, algae, and mosses. [NLat. : PARA–[1] + Gk. *phusis*, nature, growth; see PHYSIC.]

par•a•ple•gi•a (păr′ə-plē′jē-ə, -jə) *n.* Complete paralysis of the lower half of the body, usu. caused by damage to the spinal cord. [Gk. *paraplēgiē*, hemiplegia < *paraplēssesthai*, to be paralyzed < *paraplēssein*, to strike on one side : *para-*, beside; see PARA–[1] + *plēssein*, to strike; see **plāk-**[2]*.] — **par′a•ple′gic** (-plē′jĭk) *adj. & n.*

par•a•po•di•um (păr′ə-pō′dē-əm) *n., pl.* **-di•a** (-dē-ə). One of the fleshy paired appendages of polychete annelids that function in locomotion and breathing.

par•a•prax•is (păr′ə-prăk′sĭs) *n., pl.* **-prax•es** (-prăk′sēz). *Psychol.* A minor error, such as a slip of the tongue, thought to reveal a subconscious motive. [PARA–[1] + Gk. *praxis*, act, action; see PRAXIS.]

par•a•pro•fes•sion•al (păr′ə-prə-fĕsh′ə-nəl) *n.* A worker trained to assist a professional. — *adj.* Of, relating to, or performing the work of a paraprofessional.

par•a•psy•chol•o•gy (păr′ə-sī-kŏl′ə-jē) *n.* The study of the evidence for psychological phenomena, such as telepathy, that are inexplicable by science. — **par′a•psy′cho•log′i•cal** (-sī′kə-lŏj′ĭ-kəl) *adj.* — **par′a•psy•chol′o•gist** *n.*

par•a•quat (păr′ə-kwŏt′) *n.* A yellow compound, $C_{12}H_{14}N_2{\cdot}2CH_3SO_4$, used as a herbicide. [PARA–[1] + QUAT(ERNARY).]

Pa•rá rubber (pə-rä′, păr′ə) *n.* Rubber obtained from various tropical South American trees of the genus *Hevea*, esp. *H. brasiliensis*. [After *Pará*, a state of N Brazil.]

par•a•sail (păr′ə-sāl′) *n.* A parachute that lifts a rider in its harness up and through the air when towed by an automobile or a motorboat. — **par′a•sail′** *v.* — **par′a•sail′er** *n.*

par•a•sang (păr′ə-săng′) *n.* An ancient Persian unit of distance, usu. estimated at 3.5 miles (5.6 kilometers). [Lat. *parasanga* < Gk. *parasangēs*, of Iran. orig.]

par•a•se•le•ne (păr′ə-sĭ-lē′nē) *n., pl.* **-nae** (-nē). A luminous spot on a lunar halo. [PARA–[1] + Gk. *selēnē*, moon.]

par•a•sen•so•ry (păr′ə-sĕn′sə-rē) *adj.* Extrasensory. — **par′a•sen•so′ri•ly** (-sôr′ə-lē, -sōr′-) *adv.*

par•a•sex•u•al (păr′ə-sĕk′sho͞o-əl) *adj.* Of, relating to, or involving a form of reproduction in which recombination of genes from different individuals occurs without meiosis and fertilization. — **par′a•sex′u•al′i•ty** (-ăl′ĭ-tē) *n.*

par•a•site (păr′ə-sīt′) *n.* **1.** *Biol.* An organism that grows, feeds, and lives on or in another organism to whose survival it contributes nothing. **2.a.** One who habitually takes advantage of generosity without making any useful return. **b.** One who lives off and flatters the rich; a sycophant. **3.** A professional dinner guest, esp. in ancient Greece. [Lat. *parasītus*, a person who lives by amusing the rich < Gk. *parasitos*, person who eats at someone else's table, parasite : *para-*, beside; see PARA–[1] + *sitos*, grain, food.]

par•a•sit•ic (păr′ə-sĭt′ĭk) also **par•a•sit•i•cal** (-ĭ-kəl) *adj.* **1.** Of, relating to, or characteristic of a parasite. **2.** Caused by a parasite: *parasitic diseases.* — **par′a•sit′i•cal•ly** *adv.*

par•a•sit•i•cide (păr′ə-sĭt′ĭ-sīd′) *n.* An agent or a preparation used to destroy parasites. — *adj.* Destructive to parasites. — **par′a•sit′i•ci′dal** (-sīd′l) *adj.*

par•a•sit•ism (păr′ə-sĭ-tĭz′əm, -sī-) *n.* **1.** The characteristic behavior or mode of existence of a parasite or parasitic population. **2.** Parasitosis.

par•a•sit•ize (păr′ə-sĭ-tīz′, -sī-) *tr.v.* **-ized, -iz•ing, -iz•es.** To live on or in (a host) as a parasite.

par•a•sit•oid (păr′ə-sĭ-toid′, -sī′toid) *n.* Any of various insects whose parasitic larvae eventually kill their hosts. — *adj.* Of or relating to a parasitic insect of this kind.

par•a•si•tol•o•gy (păr′ə-sĭ-tŏl′ə-jē, -sī-) *n.* The scientific study of parasitism. — **par′a•si′to•log′ic** (-sī′tə-lŏj′ĭk), **par′a•si′to•log′i•cal** (-ĭ-kəl) *adj.* — **par′a•si•tol′o•gist** *n.*

par•a•si•to•sis (păr′ə-sĭ-tō′sĭs, -sī-) *n., pl.* **-ses** (-sēz). A disease resulting from parasitic infestation.

par•a•sol (păr′ə-sôl′, -sŏl′) *n.* A light, usu. small umbrella carried as protection from the sun. [Fr. < Ital. *parasole* : *parare*, to shield (< Lat. *parāre*, to prepare; see **perə-**[1]*) + *sole*, sun (< Lat. *sōl*; see **sāwel-***).] — **par′a•soled′** *adj.*

parasol

par•a•som•ni•a (păr′ə-sŏm′nē-ə) *n.* Any of several disorders that may interfere with sleep, occurring esp. in children and including bed-wetting. [Prob. PARA–[1] + (IN)SOMNIA.]

par•a•sym•pa•thet•ic (păr′ə-sĭm′pə-thĕt′ĭk) *adj.* Of, relating to, or affecting the parasympathetic nervous system. — *n.* **1.** The parasympathetic nervous system. **2.** Any of the nerves of this system. — **par′a•sym′pa•thet′i•cal•ly** *adv.*

parasympathetic nervous system *n.* The part of the autonomic nervous system originating in the brain stem and the lower part of the spinal cord that in general inhibits or opposes the physiological effects of the sympathetic nervous system, as in tending to slow the heart and dilate blood vessels.

par•a•sym•pa•tho•mi•met•ic (păr′əsĭm′pə-thō-mĭ-mĕt′ĭk, -mī-) *adj.* Producing effects similar to those produced by a parasympathetic nerve. — *n.* A drug or an agent that produces such effects.

par•a•syn•the•sis (păr′ə-sĭn′thĭ-sĭs) *n., pl.* **-ses** (-sēz′). The formation of words by both compounding and adding an affix, as in *downhearted*, formed from *down* plus *heart* plus *-ed*, not *down* plus *hearted*. — **par′a•syn•thet′ic** (-thĕt′ĭk) *adj.*

par•a•tax•is (păr′ə-tăk′sĭs) *n.* The juxtaposition of clauses or phrases without conjunctions, as *It was cold; it snowed.* [Gk., a placing side by side < *paratassein*, to arrange side by side : *para-*, beside; see PARA–[1] + *tassein*, *tag-*, to arrange.] — **par′a•tac′tic** (-tăk′tĭk), **par′a•tac′ti•cal** (-tĭ-kəl) *adj.* — **par′a•tac′ti•cal•ly** *adv.*

par•a•thi•on (păr′ə-thī′ŏn) *n.* A liquid agricultural insecticide, $(C_2H_5O)_2P(S)OC_6H_4NO_2$. [PARA–[1] + *thio(phosphate)*, phosphoric acid salt (THIO– + PHOSPHATE) + –ON[3].]

par•a•thy•roid (păr′ə-thī′roid) *adj.* Of, relating to, or obtained from the parathyroid glands. — *n.* **1.** The parathyroid gland. **2.** A parathyroid hormone.

parathyroid gland *n.* Any of usu. four small kidney-shaped glands that lie in pairs near or within the posterior surface of the thyroid gland and secrete parathyroid hormone.

parathyroid hormone *n.* A hormone produced by the parathyroid glands that regulates calcium metabolism.

par•a•troop•er (păr′ə-tro͞o′pər) *n.* A member of the paratroops.

par•a•troops (păr′ə-tro͞ops′) *pl.n.* Infantry trained and equipped to parachute. — **par′a•troop′** *adj.*

par•a•ty•phoid fever (păr′ə-tī′foid′) *n.* An acute intestinal disease, similar to typhoid fever but less severe, caused by certain bacteria of the genus *Salmonella*.

ă pat	oi boy
ā pay	ou out
âr care	o͝o took
ä father	o͞o boot
ĕ pet	ŭ cut
ē be	ûr urge
ĭ pit	th thin
ī pie	*th* this
îr pier	hw which
ŏ pot	zh vision
ō toe	ə about,
ô paw	item

Stress marks:
′ (primary);
′ (secondary), as in
dictionary (dĭk′shə-nĕr′ē)

par•a•vane (păr′ə-vān′) *n.* A device equipped with sharp teeth and towed alongside a ship to cut the mooring cables of submerged mines.

par•boil (pär′boil′) *tr.v.* **-boiled, -boil•ing, -boils. 1.** To cook partially by boiling for a brief period. **2.** To subject to intense, often uncomfortable heat. [ME *parboilen,* to boil partly, to boil thoroughly (influenced by *part,* part) < OFr. *parboillir,* to boil thoroughly < LLat. *perbullīre* : Lat. *per-,* thoroughly; see PER– + Lat. *bullīre,* to boil.]

par•buck•le (pär′bŭk′əl) *n.* **1.** A rope sling for rolling cylindrical objects up or down an inclined plane. **2.** A sling for raising or lowering an object vertically. —*tr.v.* **-led, -ling, -les.** To raise or lower with such a sling. [Alteration (influenced by BUCKLE) of *parbunkel.*]

parbuckle

Par•cae (pär′sē) *pl.n. Rom. Myth.* The Fates. [Lat. See **perə-**[1]*.]

par•cel (pär′səl) *n.* **1.** Something wrapped up or packaged; a package. **2.** A plot of land, usu. a division of a larger area. **3.** A quantity of merchandise offered for sale. **4.** A group or company; a pack. —*tr.v.* **-celed, -cel•ing, -cels** also **-celled, -cel•ling, -cels. 1.** To divide into parts and distribute. **2.** To make into a parcel; package. **3.** *Naut.* To wind protective strips of canvas around (rope). [ME < OFr., portion < VLat. *particella, dim. of Lat. *particula,* dim. of *pars, part-,* part. See **perə-**[2]*.]

parcel post *n.* A postal service or department that handles and delivers packages.

par•ce•ner (pär′sə-nər) *n. Law.* See **coparcener.** [ME < AN < *parcen,* portion, division < VLat. **partiō, partiōn-* < Lat. *partitiō, partitiōn-.* See PARTITION.]

parch (pärch) *v.* **parched, parch•ing, parch•es.** —*tr.* **1.** To make extremely dry, esp. by exposure to heat. **2.** To make thirsty. **3.** To dry or roast (corn, for example) by exposing to heat. —*intr.* **1.** To become very dry. **2.** To become thirsty. [ME *parchen.*]

Par•chee•si (pär-chē′zē). A trademark used for a board game based on the ancient game of pachisi.

parch•ment (pärch′mənt) *n.* **1.** The skin of a sheep or goat prepared as a material on which to write or paint. **2.** A written text or drawing on parchment. **3.** Paper made in imitation of this material. [ME *parchemin, parchement* < OFr. *parchemin* < LLat. *pergamīna,* var. of Lat. *pergamēna,* parchment < fem. of *Pergamēnus,* of Pergamum < Gk. *Pergamēnos,* after *Pergamon* (Pergamum).]

pard (pärd) *n.* A leopard or other large cat. [ME *parde* < OFr. < Lat. *pardus* < Gk. *pardos,* prob. of Iran. orig.]

pard•ner (pärd′nər) *n. Regional.* A partner, companion, or friend. [Var. of PARTNER.]

par•don (pär′dn) *tr.v.* **-doned, -don•ing, -dons. 1.** To release (a person) from punishment; exempt from penalty. **2.** To let (an offense) pass without punishment. **3.** To make courteous allowance for; excuse: *Pardon me.* See Syns at **forgive.** —*n.* **1.** The act of pardoning. **2.** *Law.* **a.** Exemption of a convicted person from the penalties of an offense or a crime by the power of the executor of the laws. **b.** An official document or warrant declaring such an exemption. **3.** Allowance or forgiveness for an offense or a discourtesy. [ME *pardonen* < OFr. *pardoner* < VLat. **perdōnāre,* to give wholeheartedly : Lat. *per-,* intensive pref.; see PER– + Lat. *dōnāre,* to give, forgive (< *dōnum,* gift; see **dō-***).] —**par′don•a•ble** *adj.* —**par′don•a•ble•ness** *n.* —**par′don•a•bly** *adv.*

parget
Framing a painting

par•don•er (pär′dn-ər) *n.* **1.** One that pardons. **2.** A medieval cleric authorized to grant papal indulgences to contributors.

Par•du•bi•ce (pär′dōō-bĭ′tsə). A city of N-central Czech Republic on the Elbe R. E of Prague. Pop. 93,822.

pare (pâr) *tr.v.* **pared, par•ing, pares. 1.** To remove the outer covering or skin of with a knife or similar instrument. **2.** To remove by or as if by cutting, clipping, or shaving: *pared off the excess dough.* **3.** To reduce as if by cutting off outer parts; trim. [ME *paren* < OFr. *parer,* to prepare, trim < Lat. *parāre,* to prepare. See **perə-**[1]*.] —**par′er** *n.*

par•e•gor•ic (păr′ə-gôr′ĭk, -gŏr′-) *n.* A camphorated tincture of opium, taken internally for the relief of diarrhea and intestinal pain. [LLat. *parēgoricus,* soothing < Gk. *parēgorikos* < *parēgorein,* to talk over, soothe < *parēgoros,* consoling : *para-,* beside; see PARA–[1] + *agora,* agora; see AGORA[1].]

paren. *abbr.* Parenthesis.

pa•ren•chy•ma (pə-rĕng′kə-mə) *n.* **1.** *Anat.* The tissue characteristic of an organ, as distinguished from associated connective or supporting tissues. **2.** *Bot.* The primary tissue of higher plants, composed of thin-walled cells and forming the greater part of leaves, roots, the pulp of fruit, and the pith of stems. [NLat. < Gk. *parenkhuma,* visceral flesh < *parenkhein,* to pour in beside : *para-,* beside; see PARA–[1] + *en-,* in; see **en*** + *khein,* to pour; see **gheu-***.] —**pa•ren′chy•mal, par′en•chym′a•tous** (păr′ĕn-kĭm′ə-təs) *adj.*

par•ent (pâr′ənt, păr′-) *n.* **1.** One who begets, gives birth to, or nurtures and raises a child; a father or a mother. **2.** An ancestor; a progenitor. **3.** An organism that produces or generates offspring. **4.** A guardian; a protector. **5.** A source or cause; an origin: *the parent of rebellion.* —*v.* **-ent•ed, -ent•ing, -ents.** —*tr.* **1.** *Usage Problem.* To act as a parent to; raise and nurture. **2.** To cause to come into existence; originate. —*intr. Usage Problem.* To act as a parent. [ME < OFr. < Lat. *parēns, parent-* < pr.part. of *parere,* to give birth. See **perə-**[1]*.] —**par′ent•hood′** *n.*

Usage Note: A majority, albeit a smaller majority, of the Usage Panel continues to find the verb *parent* unacceptable. In 1968 it was acceptable to only 19 percent of the Panel; in the most recent survey 45 percent accepted it in the sentence *In looking for foster homes, we give preference first to relatives and second to families with prior experience in parenting.*

par•ent•age (pâr′ən-tĭj, păr′-) *n.* **1.** Descent from parents; lineage: *of humble parentage.* **2.** The state or relationship of being a parent. **3.** Derivation from a source; origin.

pa•ren•tal (pə-rĕn′tl) *adj.* **1.** Of, relating to, or characteristic of a parent. **2.** *Genet.* Of or being the generation from which hybrid offspring are produced. —**pa•ren′tal•ly** *adv.*

par•en•ter•al (pă-rĕn′tər-əl) *adj.* **1.** *Physiol.* Located outside the alimentary canal. **2.** *Medic.* Taken into the body or administered in a manner other than through the digestive tract, as by intravenous injection. —**par•en′ter•al•ly** *adv.*

pa•ren•the•sis (pə-rĕn′thĭ-sĭs) *n., pl.* **-ses** (-sēz′). **1.** Either or both of the upright curved lines, ( ), used to mark off explanatory or qualifying remarks in writing or printing or enclose a sum, product, or other expression treated as a collective entity in a mathematical operation. **2.a.** A qualifying or amplifying word, phrase, or sentence inserted within written matter so as to be independent of the surrounding grammatical structure. **b.** A comment departing from the theme of discourse; a digression. **3.** An interruption of continuity; an interval. [LLat., insertion of a letter or syllable in a word < Gk. < *parentithenai,* to insert : *para-,* beside; see PARA–[1] + *en-,* in; see **en*** + *tithenai,* to put; see **dhē-***.]

par•en•thet•i•cal (păr′ən-thĕt′ĭ-kəl) also **par•en•thet•ic** (-ĭk) *adj.* **1.** Set off within or as if within parentheses; qualifying or explanatory: *a parenthetical remark.* **2.** Using or containing parentheses. —**par′en•thet′i•cal•ly** *adv.*

parent language *n.* A language from which a later language is derived: *Latin is the parent language of Italian and French.*

pa•re•sis (pə-rē′sĭs, păr′ĭ-sĭs) *n.* **1.** Slight or partial paralysis. **2.** General paresis. [Gk., act of letting go, paralysis < *parienai,* to let fall : *para-,* beside; see PARA–[1] + *hienai,* to throw; see **yē-***.] —**pa•ret′ic** (pə-rĕt′ĭk) *adj. & n.*

par•es•the•sia also **par•aes•the•sia** (păr′ĭs-thē′zhə) *n.* A skin sensation, such as burning or tingling, with no apparent physical cause. [NLat. : PARA–[1] + Gk. *aisthēsis,* feeling; see ANESTHESIA + –IA[1].] —**par′es•thet′ic** (-thĕt′ĭk) *adj.*

Pa•re•to (pə-rā′tō, pä-rĕ′tô), **Vilfredo.** 1848–1923. Italian economist and sociologist whose theories influenced the development of fascism.

pa•re•u (pä′rā-ōō′) *n.* A rectangular piece of cloth worn esp. in Polynesia as a wraparound skirt or loincloth. [Tahitian.]

pa•re•ve (pä′rə-və) also **par•ve** (pär′və) *adj. Judaism.* Prepared without meat, milk, or their derivatives and therefore permissible to be eaten with both meat and dairy dishes according to dietary laws. [Yiddish *páreve.*]

par ex•cel•lence (pär ĕk-sə-läns′) *adj.* Being the best or truest of a kind; quintessential. [Fr. : *par,* by + *excellence,* preeminence.]

par•fait (pär-fā′) *n.* **1.** A dessert made of cream, eggs, sugar, and flavoring frozen together and served in a tall glass. **2.** A dessert made of several layers of different flavors of ice cream or ices served in a tall glass. [Fr. < OFr., perfect < Lat. *perfectus.* See PERFECT.]

parfait glass *n.* A tall slender glass with a short stem.

par•fleche (pär′flĕsh′) *n.* **1.** An untanned animal hide soaked in lye and water to remove the hair and then dried on a stretcher. **2.** An article, such as a shield, made of this hide. [Canadian Fr. *parflèche* : Fr. *parer,* to parry, defend; see PARRY + Fr. *flèche,* arrow; see FLÈCHE.]

par•get (pär′jĭt) *n.* **1.** A mixture, such as plaster, used to coat walls and line chimneys. **2.** Ornamental work in plaster. **3.** A cement mixture used to waterproof outer walls. —*tr.v.* **-get•ed, -get•ing, -gets** also **-get•ted, -get•ting, -gets.** To cover or adorn with parget. [ME, prob. < *pargetten,* to parget < OFr. *pargeter, parjeter,* to throw about (*par-,* intensive pref. < Lat. *per;* see **per**[1]* + *jeter,* to throw < Lat. *iactāre,* freq. of *iacere;* see **yē-***) and < OFr. *porgeter,* to roughcast a wall (*por-,* forward, ult. < Lat. *porrō;* see **per**[1]* + *iactāre,* to throw).] —**par′get•ing** *n.*

par•he•lic circle (pär-hē′lĭk) *n.* A luminous halo visible at the height of the sun and parallel to the horizon, caused by the sun's rays reflecting off atmospheric ice crystals.

par•he•li•on (pär-hē′lē-ən, -hēl′yən) *n., pl.* **-he•li•a** (-hē′lē-ə, -hēl′yə). A bright spot sometimes appearing on either side of the sun, often on a luminous ring or halo. [Lat. *parēlion* < Gk. : *para-,* beside; see PARA–[1] + *hēlios,* sun; see **sāwel-***.] —**par•he′lic** (-hē′lĭk) *adj.*

pa•ri•ah (pə-rī′ə) *n.* **1.** A social outcast. **2.** A member of a low caste of agricultural and domestic workers in southern India and Burma. [Tamil *paṛaiyar,* pl. of *paṛaiyan,* pariah caste < *paṛai,* festival drum.]

Par•i•an (pâr′ē-ən, păr′-) *adj.* **1.** Of or relating to the island of Páros or its inhabitants. **2.** Of or being a type of white semitranslucent marble quarried at Páros and highly valued in ancient times for making sculptures. **3.** Of or being a fine white porcelain. —*n.* **1.** A native or inhabitant of Páros. **2.** Parian marble. **3.** Parian porcelain.

Pa•ri•cu•tin (pä-rē′ko͞o-tēn′). A volcano, 2,272.3 m (7,450 ft), of W-central Mexico W of Mexico City; first erupted in Feb. 1943.

pa•ri•es (pâr′ē-ēz′) *n., pl.* **pa•ri•e•tes** (pə-rī′ĭ-tēz′). A wall of a body part, organ, or cavity. Often used in the plural. [Lat. *pariēs*, wall.]

pa•ri•e•tal (pə-rī′ĭ-təl) *adj.* **1.** Relating to or forming the wall of a body part, organ, or cavity. **2.** Of or relating to either of the parietal bones. **3.** *Bot.* Borne on the inside of the ovary wall. Used of the ovules or placentas in flowering plants. **4.** Dwelling within or having authority within the walls or buildings of a college. —*n.* **1.** A parietal part, such as a wall or bone. **2. parietals.** The rules governing visits from members of the opposite sex in college or university dormitories. [ME < LLat. *parietālis*, of a wall < Lat. *pariēs, pariet-*, wall.]

parietal bone *n.* Either of two large, irregularly quadrilateral bones between the frontal and occipital bones that together form the sides and top of the skull.

parietal lobe *n.* The division of each hemisphere of the brain that lies beneath each parietal bone.

par•i•mu•tu•el (păr′ĭ-myo͞o′cho͞o-əl) *n. Sports & Games.* **1.** A system of betting on races whereby winnings are divided in proportion to the sums individually wagered. **2.** A machine that records such bets and computes the payoffs. [Fr. *pari-mutuel* : *pari*, wager (< *parier*, to wager < Lat. *pariāre*, to settle a debt < *pār, par-*, equal; see **perə-²***) + *mutuel*, mutual (< OFr.; see MUTUAL).]

par•ing (pâr′ĭng) *n.* Something pared off, such as a peel.

paring knife *n.* A small knife for paring fruits and vegetables.

pa•ri pas•su (păr′ē păs′o͞o, păr′ī, păr′ē) *adv.* At an equal pace; side by side. [Lat. *parī passū* : *parī*, ablative of *pār*, equal + *passū*, ablative of *passus*, step.]

par•i•pin•nate (păr′ĭ-pĭn′āt, -ĭt) *adj. Bot.* Pinnately compound with two terminal leaflets: *paripinnate leaves.* [Lat. *pār, par-*, equal, a pair + PINNATE.]

Par•is¹ (păr′ĭs) *n. Gk. Myth.* The prince of Troy whose abduction of Helen provoked the Trojan War.

Par•is² (păr′ĭs). **1.** The cap. of France, in the N-central part on the Seine R.; founded as a fishing village on the Île de la Cité and estab. as the cap. of France by Hugh Capet in 987. Pop. 2,149,900. **2.** A city of NE TX NE of Dallas. Pop. 24,699.

Paris, Matthew. 1200?–59. English monk known for his *Chronica Majora.*

Paris daisy *n.* See **marguerite** 1.

Paris green *n.* A poisonous emerald-green powder, $(CuO)_3As_2O_3 \cdot Cu(C_2H_3O_2)_2$, formerly used as an insecticide.

par•ish (păr′ĭsh) *n.* **1.a.** An administrative part of a diocese with its own church in the Anglican, Roman Catholic, and some other churches. **b.** The members of such a parish. **2.** A political subdivision of a British county, usu. corresponding to parish boundaries. **3.** An administrative subdivision in Louisiana that corresponds to a county in other U.S. states. [ME < OFr. *parroche* < LLat. *parochia*, diocese, alteration of *paroecia* < LGk. *paroikia* < Gk., a sojourning < *paroikos*, neighboring, neighbor, sojourner : *para-*, near; see PARA-¹ + *oikos*, house; see **weik-¹***.]

pa•rish•ion•er (pə-rĭsh′ə-nər) *n.* A member of a parish. [ME < *parishon*, parishioner < OFr. *parochien* < *parroche*, parish. See PARISH.]

par•i•ty¹ (păr′ĭ-tē) *n., pl.* **-ties. 1.** Equality, as in amount, status, or value. **2.** Functional equivalence, as in the military strength of adversaries. **3.** The equivalent in value of a sum of money expressed in terms of a different currency at a fixed official rate of exchange. **4.** Equality of prices of goods or securities in two different markets. **5.** A level for farm-product prices maintained by governmental support in order to give farmers the same purchasing power they had during a chosen base period. **6.** *Math.* The even or odd quality of an integer; for example, 1 and 7 have the same parity, but 3 and 4 do not. **7.** *Phys.* **a.** An intrinsic symmetry property of a wave function that determines its behavior under reflection through the origin of spatial coordinates. **b.** A quantum number, either +1 (even) or −1 (odd), that describes this property. **8.** *Comp. Sci.* **a.** The even or odd quality of the number of 1's or 0's in a binary code, often used to check the integrity of data esp. after transmission. **b.** A bit added to a binary code that indicates parity. [Fr. *parité* < OFr. *parite* < LLat. *paritās* < *pār, par-*, equal. See PAIR.]

par•i•ty² (păr′ĭ-tē) *n. Medic.* **1.** The condition of having given birth. **2.** The number of children borne by one woman. [Lat. *parere*, to give birth, bring forth; see **perə-¹*** + -ITY.]

park (pärk) *n.* **1.** An area of land set aside for public use, as: **a.** A piece of land with few or no buildings within or adjoining a town, maintained for recreational and ornamental purposes. **b.** A landscaped city square. **c.** A large tract of rural land kept in its natural state and usu. reserved for the enjoyment and recreation of visitors. **2.** A broad, fairly level valley between mountain ranges. **3.** A tract of land attached to a country house, esp. when including extensive gardens, woods, pastures, or a game preserve. **4.** *Sports.* A stadium or an enclosed playing field. **5.a.** An area where military vehicles or artillery are stored and serviced. **b.** The materiel kept in such an area. **6.** An area in or near a town designed and usu. zoned for a certain purpose. **7.** See **parking lot.** —*v.* **parked, park•ing, parks.** —*tr.* **1.** To put or leave (a vehicle) for a time in a certain location. **2.** *Aerospace.* To place (a spacecraft or satellite) in a usu. temporary orbit. **3.** *Informal.* To place or leave temporarily. **4.** To assemble (artillery or other equipment) in a military park. —*intr.* **1.** To park a motor vehicle. **2.** *Slang.* To engage in kissing or caressing in a vehicle stopped in a secluded spot. [ME, enclosed tract of land < OFr. *parc*, of Gmc. orig.] —**park′er** *n.*

Park (pärk), **Mungo.** 1771–1806. Scottish explorer known for his expeditions on the Niger R. (1795–96 and 1805).

par•ka (pär′kə) *n.* **1.** A hooded fur pullover outer garment worn in the Arctic. **2.** A coat or jacket with a hood and usu. a warm lining for cold-weather wear. [Alaskan Russ., pelt, ult. of Nenets orig.]

Park Avenue. A wide thoroughfare extending N to S on the East Side of Manhattan I..

Par•ker (pär′kər), **Charlie.** "Bird." 1920–55. Amer. musician and composer best remembered for his improvisations.

Parker, Dorothy Rothschild. 1893–1967. Amer. writer noted for her satirical wit in poems such as "Resumé" (1926).

Parker, Sir **(Horatio) Gilbert (George).** 1862–1932. Canadian writer whose works include *The Seats of the Mighty* (1896).

Parker, Matthew. 1504–1575. English prelate who helped establish ecclesiastical forms for the Anglican Church.

Parker, Theodore. 1810–60. Amer. cleric and social reformer known for his abolitionist activities.

Par•kers•burg (pär′kərz-bûrg′). A city of NW WV at the confluence of the Little Kanawha and Ohio rivers N of Charleston. Pop. 33,862.

Park Forest. A village of NE IL, a suburb of Chicago. Pop. 24,656.

park•ing (pär′kĭng) *n.* **1.** The act or practice of parking a vehicle. **2.** Space in which to park vehicles or a vehicle: *can't find parking.* **3.** *Upper Midwest.* The grass strip, often planted with shade trees, between a sidewalk and a street.

Regional Note: *Parking* is an Upper Midwestern term for the grass strip, often planted with shade trees, between a sidewalk and a street. The presence of this word also in Western states attests to the close linguistic connection, owing to settlement patterns, between the Upper Midwest and the West.

parking lot *n.* An area for parking motor vehicles.

parking meter *n.* A coin-operated device that registers the amount of time purchased for the parking of a motor vehicle, at the expiration of which the driver is liable for a fine.

Par•kin•son•ism (pär′kĭn-sə-nĭz′əm) *n.* **1.** Any of a group of nervous disorders similar to Parkinson's disease, marked by muscular rigidity, tremor, and impaired motor control and often having a specific cause, such as frequent exposure to toxic chemicals. **2.** Parkinson's disease. [< PARKINSON'S DISEASE.]

Par•kin•son's disease (pär′kĭn-sənz) *n.* A progressive nervous disease usu. occurring after the age of 50, associated with the destruction of brain cells that produce dopamine and characterized by muscular tremor, slowing of movement, partial facial paralysis, and weakness. [After James *Parkinson* (1755–1824), British physician.]

Parkinson's Law *n.* Any of several satirical observations propounded as economic laws, esp. "Work expands to fill the time available for its completion." [After Cyril Northcote *Parkinson* (1909–93), British historian.]

Parkinson's syndrome *n.* See **Parkinsonism** 1.

park•land (pärk′lănd′) *n.* **1.** Land within or suitable for public parks. **2.** Grassland with scattered clusters of trees or shrubs.

Park•land (pärk′lənd). A community of W-central Washington, a suburb of Tacoma. Pop. 20,882.

Park•man (pärk′mən), **Francis.** 1823–93. Amer. historian who wrote *The California and Oregon Trail* (1849).

Park Range. A range of the Rocky Mts. in N-central CO and S WY rising to 4,357.2 m (14,286 ft).

Park Ridge. A city of NE IL, a suburb of Chicago. Pop. 36,175.

Parks (pärks), **Rosa.** b. 1913. Amer. civil rights leader whose refusal to give up her seat on a bus to a white man in Montgomery AL stirred the civil rights movement across the nation.

park•way (pärk′wā′) *n.* A broad landscaped highway, often divided by a planted median strip.

parl. *abbr.* **1.** Also **Parl.** Parliament. **2.** Parliamentary.

par•lance (pär′ləns) *n.* **1.** A particular manner of speaking; idiom: *legal parlance.* **2.** Speech, esp. a conversation or parley. [OFr. < *parler*, to speak. See PARLEY.]

par•lan•do (pär-län′dō) also **par•lan•te** (-tā) *adv. & adj. Mus.* To be sung in a style suggestive of speech. [Ital., pr.part. of *parlare*, to speak < VLat. **parabolāre*. See PARLEY.]

par•lay (pär′lā′, -lē) *tr.v.* **-layed, -lay•ing, -lays. 1.** *Games.* To bet (an original wager and its winnings) on a subsequent event. **2.** To maneuver (an asset) to great advantage. —*n. Games.* A bet comprising the sum of a prior wager plus its

Rosa Parks

ă pat	oi boy
ā pay	ou out
âr care	o͝o took
ä father	o͞o boot
ĕ pet	ŭ cut
ē be	ûr urge
ĭ pit	th thin
ī pie	*th* this
îr pier	hw which
ŏ pot	zh vision
ō toe	ə about, item
ô paw	

Stress marks:
′ (primary);
′ (secondary), as in
dictionary (dĭk′shə-nĕr′ē)

winnings or a series of such bets. [Alteration of *paroli*, staking of double a prior stake in faro < Fr. < obsolete Ital., prob. < Ital. *parare*, to place a bet < Lat. *parāre*, to prepare. See PARE.]

par•ley (pär′lē) *n.*, *pl.* **-leys.** A discussion or conference, esp. one between enemies over terms of truce or other matters. — *intr.v.* **-leyed, -ley•ing, -leys.** To have a discussion, esp. with an enemy. [ME < OFr. *parlee* < fem. p.part. of *parler*, to talk < VLat. **paraulāre* < LLat. *parabolāre* < LLat. *parabola*, discourse. See PARABLE.]

par•lia•ment (pär′lə-mənt) *n.* **1.** A national representative body having supreme state legislative powers. **2. Parliament.** The national legislature of various countries, esp. that of the United Kingdom. [ME, a meeting about national concerns < OFr. *parlement* < *parler*, to talk. See PARLEY.]

par•lia•men•tar•i•an (pär′lə-mĕn-târ′ē-ən) *n.* **1.** One who is expert in parliamentary procedures, rules, or debate. **2.** A member of a parliament. **3. Parliamentarian.** A Roundhead.

par•lia•men•ta•ry (pär′lə-mĕn′tə-rē, -mĕn′trē) *adj.* **1.** Of, relating to, or resembling a parliament. **2.** Enacted or decreed by a parliament. **3.** Being in accord with the rules and customs of a parliament. **4.a.** Having a parliament. **b.** Characterized by an executive consisting of cabinet ministers selected from and responsible to the parliament.

parliamentary law *n.* A body of rules governing procedure in legislative and deliberative assemblies.

parquetry
Parquet floor

par•lor (pär′lər) *n.* **1.** A room in a private home set apart for the entertainment of visitors. **2.** A small lounge or sitting room affording limited privacy, as at a tavern. **3.** A room equipped and furnished for a special function or business. [ME *parlur* < OFr. < *parler*, to talk. See PARLEY.]

parlor car *n.* A railroad car for day travel fitted with individual reserved seats.

parlor game *n.* *Games.* A game that can be played indoors.

par•lour (pär′lər) *n.* *Chiefly British.* Var. of **parlor.**

par•lous (pär′ləs) *adj.* **1.** Perilous; dangerous: *a parlous journey.* **2.** *Obsolete.* Dangerously cunning. [ME, var. of *perilous*, perilous < *peril*, peril. See PERIL.] — **par′lous•ly** *adv.*

Par•ma (pär′mə). **1.** A city of N-central Italy SE of Milan; founded by Romans in 183 B.C. Pop. 176,750. **2.** A city of NE OH, a suburb of Cleveland. Pop. 87,876.

Parma Heights. A city of NE OH, a suburb of Cleveland. Pop. 21,448.

Par•men•i•des (pär-mĕn′ĭ-dēz′). b. 515? B.C. Greek philosopher and a founder of the Eleatic school.

Par•me•san (pär′mə-zän′, -zăn′, -zən) *n.* A sharp dry hard Italian cheese made from skim milk and usu. served grated as a garnish. [Fr. < OFr. *permigean*, of Parma < OItal. *parmigiano.* See PARMIGIANA.]

par•mi•gia•na (pär′mĭ-zhä′nə, -jä′-) *adj.* Made or covered with Parmesan cheese: *eggplant parmigiana.* [Ital., fem. of *parmigiano*, of Parma, after PARMA, Italy.]

Par•mi•gia•ni•no (pär′mĭ-jä-nē′nō, -mē-) or **Par•mi•gia•no** (-jä′nō), **Il.** 1503–40. Italian Mannerist painter.

Par•na•í•ba (pär′nə-ē′bə, -nä-ē′bä). A river of NE Brazil flowing c. 1,287 km (800 mi) to the Atlantic.

Par•nas•si•an (pär-năs′ē-ən) *adj.* Of or relating to poetry. — *n.* A member of a school of late 19th-century French poets whose work is characterized by detachment and emphasis on metrical form. [< Lat. *Parnassius*, of Parnassus < Gk. *parnasios*, after *Parnasos* (Parnassus), sacred to Apollo and the Muses.] — **Par•nas′si•an** *adj.*

Catherine Parr
c. 1545 portrait by an unknown artist

Par•nas•sus (pär-năs′əs) also **Par•nas•sós** (-nä-sôs′). A mountain, c. 2,458 m (8,060 ft), of central Greece N of the Gulf of Corinth.

Par•nell (pär-nĕl′, pär′nəl), **Charles Stewart.** 1846–91. Irish politician who led the Home Rule Movement.

pa•ro•chi•al (pə-rō′kē-əl) *adj.* **1.** Of, relating to, supported by, or located in a parish. **2.** Of or relating to a parochial school. **3.** Narrowly restricted in scope or outlook; provincial: *parochial attitudes.* [ME < OFr. < LLat. *parochiālis* < *parochia*, diocese. See PARISH.] — **pa•ro′chi•al•ism** *n.* — **pa•ro′chi•al•ist** *n.* — **pa•ro′chi•al•ly** *adv.*

parochial school *n.* A school supported by a church parish.

par•o•dy (păr′ə-dē) *n.* **-dies. 1.a.** A literary or artistic work that imitates the characteristic style of an author or a work for comic effect or ridicule. **b.** The genre of literature comprising such works. **2.** Something so bad as to be equivalent to intentional mockery; a travesty. — *tr.v.* **-died, -dy•ing, -dies.** To make a parody of. See Syns at **imitate.** [Lat. *parōdia* < Gk. *parōidia* : *para-*, subsidiary to; see PARA-[1] + *ōidē*, song; see **wed-**[2]***.**] — **pa•rod′ic** (pə-rŏd′ĭk), **pa•rod′i•cal** (-ĭ-kəl) *adj.* — **par′o•dist** *n.* — **par′o•dis′tic** *adj.*

parsnip
Pastinaca sativa

pa•rol (pə-rōl′, păr′əl) *Law.* — *n.* An oral statement or utterance. — *adj.* Expressed or evidenced by word of mouth; not written. [ME *parole* < AN < VLat. **paraula.* See PAROLE.]

pa•role (pə-rōl′) *n.* **1.** *Law.* **a.** The release of a prisoner whose term has not expired on condition of sustained lawful behavior that is subject to monitoring by an officer of the law for a set period of time. **b.** The duration of such conditional release. **2.** A password used by an officer of the day, an officer on guard, or the personnel commanded by such an officer. **3.** Word of honor, esp. that of a prisoner of war who is granted freedom only after promising to lay down arms. **4.** *Ling.* The act of speaking; a particular utterance or word. — *tr.v.* **-roled, -rol•ing, -roles.** To release (a prisoner) on parole. [Fr., promise, word < VLat. **paraula* < Lat. *parabola*, discourse. See PARABLE.]

pa•rol•ee (pə-rō′lē′) *n.* One who is released on parole.

par•o•no•ma•sia (păr′ə-nō-mā′zhə, -zhē-ə) *n.* **1.** Word play; punning. **2.** A pun. [Lat. < Gk. < *paronomazein*, to call by a different name : *para-*, beside; see PARA-[1] + *onomazein*, to name; see ONOMASTIC.] — **par′o•no•mas′tic** (-măs′tĭk), **par′o•no•ma′sial** (-mā′zhəl, -zhē-əl) *adj.*

par•o•nych•i•a (păr′ə-nĭk′ē-ə) *n.* *Medic.* Inflammation of the tissue surrounding a nail. [Lat. *parōnychia* < Gk. *parōnukhia* : *para-*, around; see PARA-[1] + *onux*, *onukh-*, nail; see **nogh-*.**] — **par′o•nych′i•al** *adj.*

par•o•nym (păr′ə-nĭm′) *n.* A paronymous word. [Gk. *parōnumon* < neut. sing. of *parōnumos*, derivative. See PARONYMOUS.] — **par′o•nym′ic** *adj.*

pa•ron•y•mous (pə-rŏn′ə-məs) *adj.* Allied by derivation from the same root; having the same stem; for example, *beautiful* and *beauteous.* [Gk. *parōnumos*, derivative : *para-*, beside; see PARA-[1] + *onuma*, name; see **nō-men-*.**]

Pá•ros also **Par•os** (pâr′ŏs, pä′rôs). An island in the Cyclades of SE Greece in the Aegean Sea; settled by Ionians and held by the Ottoman Turks from 1537 to 1832

pa•ros•mi•a (pə-rŏz′mē-ə) *n.* A distortion of the sense of smell, as in smelling odors that are not present. [PAR(A)-[1] + Gk. *osmē*, smell + -IA[1].]

pa•rot•id (pə-rŏt′ĭd) *n.* A parotid gland. — *adj.* **1.** Situated near the ear. **2.** Of or relating to a parotid gland.

parotid gland *n.* Either of the pair of salivary glands situated below and in front of each ear. [NLat. *parōtis*, *parōtid-* < Lat., tumor near the ear < Gk. : *para-*, beside; see PARA-[1] + *ous*, *ōt-*, ear; see **ous-*.**]

par•o•ti•tis (păr′ə-tī′tĭs) also **pa•rot•i•di•tis** (pə-rŏt′ĭ-dī′tĭs) *n.* Inflammation of the parotid glands, as in mumps.

par•ous (păr′əs, pâr′-) *adj.* Having given birth one or more times. [< -PAROUS.]

-parous *suff.* Giving birth to; producing: *multiparous.* [< Lat. *-parus* < *parere*, to give birth. See **perə-**[1]***.**]

Par•ou•si•a (pär′o͞o-sē′ə, pə-ro͞o′zē-ə) *n.* The Second Coming. [Gk. < fem. pr.part. of *pareinai*, to be present : *para-*, beside; see PARA-[1] + *einai*, to be; see **es-*.**]

par•ox•ysm (păr′ək-sĭz′əm) *n.* **1.** A sudden outburst of emotion or action. **2.** *Medic.* **a.** A sudden attack, recurrence, or intensification of a disease. **b.** A spasm or fit; a convulsion. [ME *paroxism*, periodic attack of a disease < Med.Lat. *paroxysmus* < Gk. *paroxusmos* < *paroxunein*, to stimulate, irritate : *para-*, intensive pref.; see PARA-[1] + *oxunein*, to goad, sharpen (< *oxus*, sharp; see **ak-***).] — **par′ox•ys′mal** (-ək-sĭz′məl) *adj.* — **par′ox•ys′mal•ly** *adv.*

par•ox•y•tone (pă-rŏk′sĭ-tōn′) *adj.* Having an acute accent on the next to last syllable. Used of some words in Greek and certain Romance languages. — *n.* A paroxytone word. [Gk. *paroxutonos* : *para-*, beside; see PARA-[1] + *oxutonos*, oxytone; see OXYTONE.]

par•quet (pär-kā′) *n.* **1.** A floor made of parquetry. **2.** The art or process of making parquetry. **3.a.** The part of the main floor of a theater between the orchestra pit and the parquet circle. **b.** The entire main floor of a theater. — *tr.v.* **-queted** (-kād′), **-quet•ing** (-kā′ĭng), **-quets** (-kāz′). **1.** To furnish with a floor of parquetry. **2.** To make (a floor, for example) of parquetry. [Fr., parquetry < OFr., dim. of *parc*, enclosure. See PARK.]

parquet circle *n.* The part of the main floor of a theater that lies under the balcony section.

par•quet•ry (pär′kĭ-trē) *n.*, *pl.* **-ries.** Inlay of wood in a geometric pattern or mosaic, used esp. for floors. [Fr. *parqueterie* < *parquet.* See PARQUET.]

parr (pär) *n.*, *pl.* **parr** or **parrs. 1.** A young salmon during its first two years of life, when it lives in fresh water. **2.** The young of various other fishes. [?]

Parr (pär), **Catherine.** 1512–48. Queen of England as the sixth and last wife of Henry VIII.

par•ra•mat•ta (păr′ə-măt′ə) *n.* Var. of **paramatta.**

Par•ra•mat•ta (păr′ə-măt′ə). A city of SE Australia, a suburb of Sydney; founded 1788. Pop. 131,800.

par•rel also **par•ral** (păr′əl) *n.* *Naut.* A sliding loop of rope or metal by which a running yard or gaff is connected to, while still being able to move vertically along, the mast. [ME *perel*, *parrail*, short for *appareil*, apparel, rigging. See APPAREL.]

par•ri•cide (păr′ĭ-sīd′) *n.* **1.** The murdering of one's father, mother, or other near relative. **2.** One who commits such a murder. [Lat. *parricīda* and *parricīdium* : *pāri-*, *parri-*, kin + *-cīda*, *-cīdium*, -cide.] — **par′ri•cid′al** (-sīd′l) *adj.*

Par•ring•ton (păr′ĭng-tən), **Vernon Louis.** 1871–1929. Amer. literary historian known esp. for his *Main Currents in American Thought* (1927–30).

Par•rish (păr′ĭsh), **Anne.** 1760–1800. Amer. philanthropist who founded (1795) the first charitable institution for women in the U.S.

Parrish, Maxfield Frederick. 1870–1966. Amer. artist noted for his murals, magazine covers, and book illustrations.

Par•ris Island (părʹĭs). An island of the Sea Is. off S SC.

par•rot (părʹət) *n.* **1.** Any of numerous tropical and semitropical birds of the order Psittaciformes, characterized by a short hooked bill, brightly colored plumage, and in some species the ability to mimic human speech. **2.** One who imitates the words or actions of another, esp. without understanding them. —*tr.v.* **-rot•ed, -rot•ing, -rots.** To repeat or imitate, esp. without understanding. [Prob. < Fr. dial. *Perrot,* dim. of *Pierre,* Peter.] —**parʹrot•er** *n.*

parrot fever *n.* See **psittacosis.**

par•rot•fish (părʹət-fĭshʹ) *n., pl.* **parrotfish** or **-fish•es.** Any of various tropical marine fishes, esp. of the family Scaridae, having fused teeth resembling a parrot's beak.

par•ry (părʹē) *v.* **-ried, -ry•ing, -ries.** —*tr.* **1.** To deflect or ward off (a fencing thrust, for example). **2.** To deflect, evade, or avoid. —*intr.* To parry a thrust or blow. —*n., pl.* **-ries. 1.** The parrying of a thrust or blow. **2.** An evasive answer or action. [Prob. < Fr. *parez,* imper. of *parer,* to defend < Ital. *parare* < Lat. *parāre,* to prepare. See **perə-[1]*.**]

Par•ry (părʹē), Sir **William Edward.** 1790–1855. British navigator who commanded three expeditions in search of the Northwest Passage between 1819 and 1825.

parse (pärs) *v.* **parsed, pars•ing, pars•es.** —*tr.* **1.** To break (a sentence) down into its component parts of speech with an explanation of the form, function, and syntactical relationship of each part. **2.** To describe (a word) by stating its part of speech, form, and syntactical relationships in a sentence. **3.** To examine closely or subject to detailed analysis, esp. by breaking into components. **4.** *Comp. Sci.* To analyze or separate (input, for example) into more easily processed components. Used of software. —*intr.* To admit of being parsed. [Prob. < ME *pars,* part of speech < Lat. *pars (ōrātiōnis),* part (of speech). See **perə-[2]*.**] —**parsʹer** *n.*

par•sec (pärʹsĕkʹ) *n.* A unit of astronomical length based on the distance from Earth at which stellar parallax is one second of arc and equal to 3.258 light-years, 3.086×10^{13} kilometers, or 1.918×10^{13} miles. [PAR(ALLAX) + SEC(OND)[1].]

Par•see also **Par•si** (pärʹsē, pär-sēʹ) *n., pl.* **-sees** also **-sis. 1.** A member of a Zoroastrian religious sect in India, descended from Persians. **2.** The Iranian dialect used in the religious literature of the Parsees. [Pers. *Pārsī* < *Pārs,* Persia < OPers. *Pārsā.*] —**Parʹsee'ism** *n.*

par•si•mo•ni•ous (pärʹsə-mōʹnē-əs) *adj.* Excessively sparing or frugal. —**parʹsi•moʹni•ous•ly** *adv.* —**parʹsi•moʹni•ous•ness** *n.*

par•si•mo•ny (pärʹsə-mōʹnē) *n.* **1.** Unusual or excessive frugality; stinginess. **2.** Adoption of the simplest assumption, as in the formulation of a theory. [ME *parcimony* < Lat. *parsimōnia* < *parsus,* p.part. of *parcere,* to spare.]

pars•ley (pärsʹlē) *n., pl.* **-leys. 1.** A member of the parsley family. **2.** A Eurasian herb *(Petroselinum crispum)* having flat or curled, ternately compound leaves that are used for seasoning or as a garnish. [ME *persely* < OE *petersilie* and OFr. *persil,* both ult. < LLat. *petrosillum,* alteration of Lat. *petroselīnum* < Gk. *petroselinon* : *petra,* rock + *selinon,* celery.]

pars•leyed (pärʹslēd) *adj.* Prepared or garnished with parsley.

parsley family *n.* A large family of aromatic herbs, the Umbelliferae (Apiaceae), having compound leaves and small flowers grouped in umbels and including vegetables such as carrots, celery, and parsley and spices such as cumin.

pars•nip (pärsʹnĭp) *n.* **1.** A strong-scented plant *(Pastinaca sativa)* cultivated for its white edible root. **2.** The root of this plant. [ME *pasnepe,* alteration of OFr. *pasnaie* < Lat. *pastināca* < *pastinum,* a kind of two-pronged dibble.]

par•son (pärʹsən) *n.* **1.** An Anglican cleric with full legal control of a parish under ecclesiastical law; a rector. **2.** A member of the clergy, esp. a Protestant minister. [ME, parish priest < OFr. *persone* < Med.Lat. *persōna* < Lat., character. See PERSON.]

par•son•age (pärʹsə-nĭj) *n.* The official residence usu. provided by a church for its parson; a rectory.

parson bird *n.* See **tui.**

Par•sons (pärʹsənz), **Talcott.** 1902–79. Amer. sociologist noted for developing the structural-functional approach to studying social systems. —**Par•sonʹi•an** (pär-sōʹnē-ən) *adj.*

par•son's nose (pärʹsənz) *n. Informal.* See **pope's nose.**

Parsons table *n.* A usu. rectangular table with straight legs that are equal in thickness to the top of the table and form its four corners. [After the *Parsons* School of Design in New York.]

part (pärt) *n.* **1.** A portion, division, piece, or segment of a whole. **2.** Any of several equal portions or fractions that can constitute a whole or into which a whole can be divided. **3.** A division of a literary work. **4.a.** An organ, a member, or another division of an organism. **b. parts.** The external genitalia. **5.** A component that can be separated from or attached to a system; a detachable piece. **6.** A role: *part in the play.* **7.** One's responsibility, duty, or obligation; share. **8.** Individual endowment or ability; talent. Often used in the plural. **9.** A region, area, land, or territory. Often used in the plural. **10.** The line where the hair on the head is parted. **11.** *Mus.* **a.** The music or score for a particular instrument, as in an orchestra. **b.** One of the melodic divisions or voices of a contrapuntal composition. —*v.* **part•ed, part•ing, parts.** —*tr.* **1.** To divide or break into separate parts. **2.** To break up by separating the elements involved. **3.** To put or keep apart. See Syns at **separate. 4.** To comb (hair, for example) away from a dividing line, as on the scalp. **5.** *Archaic.* To divide into shares or portions. —*intr.* **1.** To become divided or separated. **2.** To go apart from one another; separate. **3.** To separate or divide into ways going in different directions. **4.** To go away; depart. **5.** To disagree by factions. **6.** *Archaic.* To die. —*adv.* Partially; in part. —*adj.* Not full or complete; partial. —***phrasal verb.*** **part with.** To give up or let go of; relinquish. —***idioms.*** **for (one's) part.** So far as one is concerned. **for the most part.** To the greater extent; generally or mostly. **in good part.** Good-naturedly or with good grace. **in part.** To some extent; partly. **on the part of.** Regarding or with respect to. **part and parcel.** A basic or essential part. **take part.** To join in; participate. **take (someone's) part.** To side with in a disagreement; support. [ME < OFr. < Lat. *pars, part-.* See **perə-[2]*.**]

part. *abbr.* **1.** Particle. **2.** Particular.

par•take (pär-tākʹ) *v.* **-took** (-to͝okʹ), **-tak•en** (-tāʹkən), **-tak•ing, -takes.** —*intr.* **1.** To take or have a part or share; participate. **2.** To take or be given part or portion. **3.** To have part of the quality, nature, or character of something. —*tr.* To take or have a part in; share in. [Back-formation < *partaker,* one who partakes < ME *part-taker.*] —**par•takʹer** *n.*

part•ed (pärʹtĭd) *adj.* **1.** Separated or divided into parts. **2.** Being or kept apart; separated. **3.** *Bot.* Cleft almost to the base, so as to have distinct divisions or lobes. **4.** *Archaic.* Deceased.

par•terre (pär-târʹ) *n.* **1.** An ornamental flower garden having the beds and paths arranged to form a pattern. **2.** See **parquet circle.** [Fr. < OFr., ornamental garden < *par terre,* on the ground : *par,* over, on; see PARAMOUNT + *terre,* ground (< OFr. < Lat. *terra,* earth; see **ters-***).]

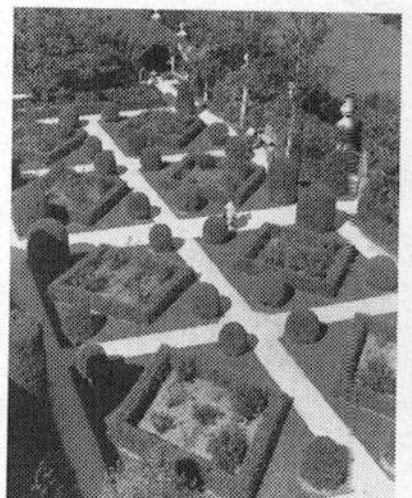

parterre
Garden at the Governor's Palace in Colonial Williamsburg, Virginia

par•the•no•car•py (pärʹthə-nō-kärʹpē) *n.* The production of fruit without fertilization. [Gk. *parthenos,* virgin + Gk. *karpos,* fruit; see -CARP + -Y[2].] —**parʹthe•no•carʹpic** *adj.*

par•the•no•gen•e•sis (pärʹthə-nō-jĕnʹĭ-sĭs) *n.* A form of reproduction in which an unfertilized egg develops into a new individual, occurring commonly among insects and certain other arthropods. [NLat. : Gk. *parthenos,* virgin + GENESIS.] —**parʹthe•no•ge•netʹic** (-jə-nĕtʹĭk) *adj.* —**parʹthe•no•ge•netʹi•cal•ly** *adv.*

Par•the•non (pärʹthə-nŏnʹ, -nən) *n.* The chief temple of the goddess Athena built on the acropolis at Athens between 447 and 432 B.C. and considered a supreme example of Doric architecture. [Lat. *Parthenōn* < Gk. < *parthenos,* virgin.]

Parthenon
On the Acropolis, Athens, Greece

Par•thi•a (pärʹthē-ə). An ancient country and kingdom of SW Asia corresponding to modern NE Iran; reached the height of its influence at the beginning of the 1st cent. B.C.

Par•thi•an (pärʹthē-ən) *adj.* **1.** Of or relating to Parthia or its people, language, or culture. **2.** Delivered in or as if in retreat. —*n.* **1.** A native or inhabitant of Parthia. **2.** The Iranian language of the Parthians.

par•tial (pärʹshəl) *adj.* **1.** Of, relating to, being, or affecting only a part; not total; incomplete. **2.** Favoring one person or side over another or others; biased or prejudiced. **3.** Having a particular liking or fondness for something or someone: *partial to jazz.* —*n.* **1.** *Mus.* See **harmonic** 1. **2.** *Math.* A partial derivative. [ME *parcial* < OFr. < LLat. *partiālis* < Lat. *pars, part-,* part. See PART.] —**parʹtial•ness** *n.*

partial derivative *n. Math.* The derivative with respect to a single variable of a function of two or more variables, regarding other variables as constants.

partial differential equation *n. Math.* A differential equation containing at least one partial derivative.

partial differentiation *n. Math.* Differentiation with respect to a single variable in a function of several variables, regarding other variables as constants.

partial fraction *n.* One of a set of fractions having an algebraic sum equal to a specified fraction.

par•ti•al•i•ty (pärʹshē-ălʹĭ-tē, pär-shălʹ-) *n., pl.* **-ties. 1.** The state of being partial. **2.** Favorable prejudice or bias. **3.** A special fondness; a predilection. See Syns at **predilection.**

par•tial•ly (pärʹshə-lē) *adv.* To a degree; not totally.

partial pressure *n.* The pressure that one component of a mixture of gases would exert if it were alone in a container.

partial tone *n. Mus.* See **harmonic** 1.

par•ti•ble (pärʹtə-bəl) *adj.* That can be parted, divided, or separated; divisible: *a partible estate.*

par•tic•i•pant (pär-tĭsʹə-pənt) *n.* One that participates, shares, or takes part in something. —*adj.* Sharing in or taking part; participating. —**par•ticʹi•pance** *n.*

par•tic•i•pate (pär-tĭsʹə-pātʹ) *v.* **-pat•ed, -pat•ing, -pates.** —*intr.* **1.** To take part in something. **2.** To share in something. —*tr. Archaic.* To partake of. [Lat. *participāre, participāt-* < *particeps, particip-,* partaker : *pars, part-,* part; see PART + *capere,* to take; see **kap-*.**] —**par•ticʹi•paʹtive** *adj.* —**par•ticʹi•paʹtor** *n.*

ă pat	oi boy
ā pay	ou out
âr care	o͝o took
ä father	o͞o boot
ĕ pet	ŭ cut
ē be	ûr urge
ĭ pit	th thin
ī pie	*th* this
îr pier	hw which
ŏ pot	zh vision
ō toe	ə about, item
ô paw	

Stress marks:
ʹ (primary);
ʹ (secondary), as in dictionary (dĭkʹshə-nĕrʹē)

par•tic•i•pa•tion (pär-tĭs′ə-pā′shən) *n.* The act of taking part or sharing in something. **—par•tic′i•pa′tion•al** *adj.*

par•tic•i•pa•to•ry (pär-tĭs′ə-pə-tôr′ē, -tōr′ē) *adj.* Marked by, requiring, or involving participation, esp. individually.

par•ti•cip•i•al (pär′tĭ-sĭp′ē-əl) *Gram.* —*adj.* Of, relating to, consisting of, or formed with a participle. —*n.* A participle. [Lat. *participiālis* < *participium*, part. See PARTICIPLE.] **—par′ti•cip′i•al•ly** *adv.*

par•ti•ci•ple (pär′tĭ-sĭp′əl) *n. Gram.* A form of a verb that in some languages, such as English, can function independently as an adjective, as *baked* in *We had some baked beans,* and is used with an auxiliary verb to indicate tense, aspect, or voice, as *baked* in *The beans were baked too long.* [ME < OFr., var. of *participe* < Lat. *participium* < *particeps, particip-*, partaker. See PARTICIPATE.]

Usage Note: The use of the "dangling participle" in writing can lead to unintentional absurdities, as in *He went to watch his horse take a turn around the track carrying a copy of the breeders' guide under his arm.* Even when the construction occasions no ambiguity, it is likely to distract the reader, who will ordinarily be operating on the assumption that a participle or other modifying phrase will be associated with the noun phrase that is immediately adjacent to it. • A number of expressions originally derived from active participles are now well established as prepositions of a kind, and these may be used freely to introduce phrases that are not associated with the immediately adjacent noun phrase. Such expressions include *concerning, considering, failing, granting, judging by,* and *speaking of.* Thus one may write *Speaking of politics, the elections have been postponed* or *Considering the hour, it is surprising that he arrived at all.*

par•ti•cle (pär′tĭ-kəl) *n.* **1.** A very small piece or part; a tiny portion or speck. **2.** A very small or the smallest possible amount or degree: *a particle of doubt.* **3.** *Phys.* **a.** A body whose spatial extent and internal motion and structure, if any, are irrelevant in a specific problem. **b.** An elementary particle. **c.** A subatomic particle. See table at **subatomic particle.** **4.** *Gram. & Ling.* **a.** An uninflected item that has grammatical function but does not clearly belong to one of the major parts of speech, such as *to* in English infinitives. **b.** In some systems of grammatical analysis, any short function word, including articles, prepositions, and conjunctions. **5.** *Rom. Cath. Ch.* **a.** A small piece of a consecrated host. **b.** One of the smaller, individual hosts. **6.** *Archaic.* A small division or section of something written, such as a clause of a document. [ME < Lat. *particula*, dim. of *pars, part-*, part. See PART.]

par•ti•cle•board (pär′tĭ-kəl-bôrd′, -bōrd′) *n.* A structural material made of wood fragments that are mechanically pressed into sheet form and bonded together with resin.

particle physics *n.* The branch of physics that deals with subatomic particles.

par•ti-col•ored (pär′tē-kŭl′ərd) *adj.* Having parts, sections, or areas colored differently from each other; pied. [< Obsolete *party*, variegated < ME *parti* < OFr., divided, striped, p.part. of *partir*, to divide. See PARTY.]

par•tic•u•lar (pər-tĭk′yə-lər, pə-tĭk′-) *adj.* **1.** Of, belonging to, or associated with a specific person, group, thing, or category; not general or universal. **2.** Separate and distinct from others of the same group, category, or nature. **3.** Worthy of note; exceptional. **4.a.** Of, relating to, or providing details: *a particular description.* See Syns at **detailed. b.** Attentive to or concerned with details or niceties, often excessively so; meticulous or fussy. **5.** *Logic.* Encompassing some but not all of the members of a class or group. Used of a proposition. —*n.* **1.** An individual item, fact, or detail. See Syns at **item. 2.** An item or a detail of information or news. Often used in the plural. **3.** A separate case or an individual thing or instance, esp. one that can be distinguished from a larger category or class. Often used in the plural. **4.** *Logic.* A particular proposition. **—*idiom.* in particular.** Particularly; especially. [ME *particuler* < OFr. < LLat. *particulāris* < Lat. *particula*, dim. of *pars, part-*, part. See PART.]

par•tic•u•lar•ism (pər-tĭk′yə-lə-rĭz′əm, pə-tĭk-) *n.* **1.** Exclusive adherence to or interest in one's own group, party, sect, or nation. **2.** A principle of allowing each state in a nation or federation to act independently of the central authority. **3.** *Theol.* The belief that a person can gain salvation only by God's free choice. **—par•tic′u•lar•ist** *n.* **—par•tic′u•lar•is′tic** *adj.*

par•tic•u•lar•i•ty (pər-tĭk′yə-lăr′ĭ-tē, pə-tĭk′-) *n., pl.* **-ties. 1.** The quality or state of being particular rather than general. **2.** Exactitude of detail, esp. in description. **3.** Attention to or concern with detail; fastidiousness. **4.** A specific point or detail; a particular. **5.** An individual characteristic; a peculiarity.

par•tic•u•lar•ize (pər-tĭk′yə-lə-rīz′, pə-tĭk-) *v.* **-ized, -iz•ing, -iz•es.** —*tr.* **1.** To mention, describe, or treat individually; itemize or specify. **2.** To make particular as opposed to general or universal. —*intr.* To go into or give details or particulars. **—par•tic′u•lar•i•za′tion** (-lər-ĭ-zā′shən) *n.* **—par•tic′u•lar•iz′er** *n.*

par•tic•u•lar•ly (pər-tĭk′yə-lər-lē, pə-tĭk′-) *adv.* **1.** To a great degree. **2.** With particular reference or emphasis; individually or specifically. **3.** With regard to particulars; in detail.

par•tic•u•late (pər-tĭk′yə-lĭt, -lāt′, pär-) *adj.* Of, relating to, or formed of separate particles. —*n.* A particulate substance. [< Lat. *particula*, a small part. See PARTICLE.]

part•ing (pär′tĭng) *n.* **1.a.** The act or process of separating or dividing. **b.** The state of being separated or divided. **2.** A departure or leave-taking. —*adj.* Given, received, or done on departing or separating: *a parting gift.* **—*idiom.* parting of the ways.** A point of divergence, esp. an important one.

parting shot *n.* An act of aggression or retaliation, such as a retort or threat, that is made upon one's departure or at the end of a heated discussion. [Perh. alteration of PARTHIAN.]

par•ti pris (pär′tē prē′) *n., pl.* **par•tis pris** (pär′tē). An inclination for or against something or someone that affects judgment; bias. [Fr. : *parti*, decision, side + *pris*, taken.]

par•ti•san¹ (pär′tĭ-zən) *n.* **1.** A fervent, sometimes militant supporter or proponent of a party, cause, person, or idea. **2.** A member of an organized body of fighters who attack or harass an enemy; a guerrilla. —*adj.* **1.** Of, relating to, or characteristic of a partisan or partisans. **2.** Devoted to or biased in support of a party, group, or cause. [Fr. < OFr. < OItal. dial. *partisano*, var. of OItal. *partigiano* < *parte*, part < Lat. *pars, part-*. See PART.] **—par′ti•san•ship′** *n.*

par•ti•san² also **par•ti•zan** (pär′tĭ-zən) *n.* A weapon having a blade with lateral projections mounted on the end of a long shaft, used chiefly in the 16th and 17th centuries. [Fr. *partizane* < Ital. dial. **(arma) partisana*, partisan (weapon), fem. sing. of *partisano*, supporter. See PARTISAN¹.]

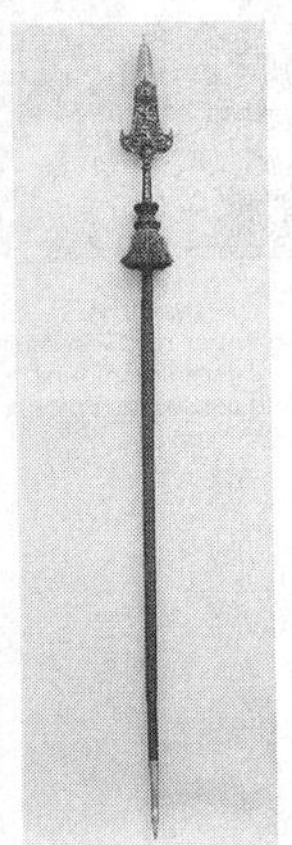

partisan²
Late 17th-century French; designed for the guard of Louis XIV

par•ti•ta (pär-tē′tə) *n. Mus.* **1.** An instrumental piece, such as a suite, composed of a series of variations. **2.** One of the variations contained in such a piece. [Ital. < fem. p.part. of *partire*, divide < Lat. *partīre*. See PARTITE.]

par•tite (pär′tīt′) *adj.* Divided into parts. [Lat. *partītus*, p.part. of *partīre*, to divide < *pars, part-*, part. See PART.]

par•ti•tion (pär-tĭsh′ən) *n.* **1.a.** The act or process of dividing something into parts. **b.** The state of being so divided. **2.a.** Something that divides or separates, as a wall dividing one room or cubicle from another. **b.** A wall, septum, or other separating membrane in an organism. **3.** A part or section into which something has been divided. **4.** Division of a country into separate autonomous nations. **5.** *Math.* **a.** An expression of a positive integer as a sum of positive integers. **b.** The decomposition of a set into a family of mutually exclusive sets. **6.** *Comp. Sci.* A location in memory assigned to a program. **7.** *Law.* Division of property, esp. real estate. —*tr.v.* **-tioned, -tion•ing, -tions. 1.** To divide into parts, pieces, or sections. **2.** To divide or separate by means of a partition. **3.** To divide (a country) into separate autonomous nations. [ME *particioun* < OFr. *partition* < Lat. *partītiō, partītiōn-* < *partītus*, p.part. of *partīre*, to divide < *pars, part-*, part. See PART.] **—par•ti′tion•er** *n.* **—par•ti′tion•ment** *n.*

par•ti•tion•ist (pär-tĭsh′ə-nĭst) *n.* One who advocates partition of a country.

par•ti•tive (pär′tĭ-tĭv) *adj.* **1.** Dividing or serving to divide something into parts; marked by division. **2.** *Gram.* Indicating a part as distinct from a whole, as *some of the coffee* in the sentence *She drank some of the coffee.* —*n. Gram.* **1.** A partitive word, such as *many* or *less.* **2.** A partitive construction or case. [ME < OFr. *partitif* < Med.Lat. *partītīvus* < Lat. *partītus*, p.part. of *partīre*, to divide. See PARTITE.]

part•let (pärt′lĭt) *n.* A collared, usu. ruffled covering for the neck and shoulders, popular in 16th-century Europe and worn esp. by women. [Alteration of ME *patelet* < OFr. *patelete*, band of cloth, dim. of *pate*, paw. See PATOIS.]

part•ly (pärt′lē) *adv.* In part or in some degree; not completely.

part•ner (pärt′nər) *n.* **1.** One that is united or associated with another or others in an activity or a sphere of common interest, esp.: **a.** A member of a business partnership. **b.** A spouse. **c.** Either of two persons dancing together. **d.** *Sports & Games.* One of a pair or team in a sport or game, such as tennis or bridge. **2.** *Naut.* A wooden framework used to strengthen a ship's deck at the point where a mast or other structure passes through it. Often used in the plural. —*v.* **-nered, -ner•ing, -ners.** —*tr.* **1.** To make a partner of. **2.** To bring together as partners. **3.** To be the partner of. —*intr.* To work or perform as a partner. [ME *partener*, alteration (influenced by *part*, part) of *parcener*, parcener. See PARCENER.]

Syns: *partner, colleague, ally, confederate.* These nouns all denote one who is united or associated with another, as in a relationship. A *partner* participates in a relationship in which each member has equal status: *a partner in a firm.* A *colleague* is an associate in an occupation or profession: *a colleague and fellow professor.* An *ally* is one who associates with another, at least temporarily, in a common cause: *countries that were allies.* A *confederate* is a member of a confederacy, a league, or an alliance or sometimes a collaborator in a suspicious venture: *The burglar's confederate got away.*

part•ner•ship (pärt′nər-shĭp′) *n.* **1.** The state of being a partner. **2.a.** A legal contract entered into by two or more persons in which each agrees to furnish a part of the capital and labor for a business enterprise, and by which each shares a fixed proportion of profits and losses. **b.** The persons bound by such a contract. **3.** A relationship of individuals or groups marked by mutual cooperation and responsibility.

part of speech *n., pl.* **parts of speech. 1.** One of a group of traditional classifications of words according to their functions in context, including the noun, pronoun, verb, adjective, adverb, preposition, conjunction, and interjection and sometimes the article. **2.** A word considered as a part of speech.

par•ton (pär′tŏn′) *n.* A hypothetical elementary particle believed to be a constituent of hadrons. [PART(ICLE) + -ON[1].]

par•took (pär-to͝ok′) *v.* P.t. of **partake.**

par•tridge (pär′trĭj) *n., pl.* **partridge** or **-tridg•es. 1.** Any of several plump-bodied Old World game birds, esp. of the genera *Perdix* and *Alectoris,* related to the pheasants and grouse. **2.** Any of several birds, such as the bobwhite, similar or related to the partridge. [ME *partrich* < OFr. *perdriz,* alteration of *perdis* < Lat. *perdix* < Gk. *perdix.* See **perd-*.**]

par•tridge•ber•ry (pär′trĭj-bĕr′ē) *n.* A creeping evergreen perennial plant *(Mitchella repens)* of eastern North America having small white flowers and scarlet berries.

part song *n. Mus.* **1.** A homophonic choral composition, esp. of the 19th century. **2.** A polyphonic song of the premadrigal period.

part-time (pärt′tīm′) *adj.* For or during less than the customary or standard time: *a part-time job.* **—part′-time′** *adv.* **—part′-tim′er** *n.*

par•tu•ri•ent (pär-to͝or′ē-ənt, -tyo͝or′-) *adj.* **1.** About to bring forth young; being in labor. **2.** Of or relating to giving birth. **3.** About to produce or come forth with something, such as an idea. [Lat. *parturiēns, parturient-,* pr.part. of *parturīre,* to be in labor < *partus,* p.part. of *parere,* to give birth. See **perə-[1]*.**] **—par•tu′ri•en•cy** *n.*

par•tu•ri•fa•cient (pär-to͝or′ə-fā′shənt, -tyo͝or′-) *adj.* Inducing or facilitating childbirth. **—** *n.* A parturifacient drug. [Lat. *parturīre,* to be in labor; see PARTURIENT + -FACIENT.]

par•tu•ri•tion (pär′tyo͝o-rĭsh′ən, -to͝o-, pär′chə-) *n.* The act or process of giving birth; childbirth. [LLat. *parturītiō, parturītiōn-* < Lat. *parturītus,* p.part. of *parturīre,* to be in labor. See PARTURIENT.]

part•way (pärt′wā′) *adv. Informal.* To a certain degree or distance; in part.

par•ty (pär′tē) *n., pl.* **-ties. 1.a.** A social gathering esp. for pleasure or amusement. **b.** A group of people who have gathered to participate in an activity. **2.** An established political group organized to promote and support its principles and candidates for public office. **3.a.** A person or group involved in an enterprise; a participant or an accessory. **b.** *Law.* A person or group involved in a legal proceeding as a litigant. **4.a.** A subscriber to a telephone party line. **b.** A person using a telephone. **5.** A person. **6.** A selected group of soldiers. **7.** *Slang.* **a.** An act of sexual intercourse. **b.** An orgy. **—** *adj.* **1.** Of, relating to, or participating in an established political organization. **2.** Suitable for use at a social gathering. **3.** Characteristic of a pleasurable social gathering. **—** *intr.v.* **-tied, -ty•ing, -ties.** *Informal.* To celebrate or carouse at or as if at a party. [ME *partie,* group < OFr. < fem. p.part. of *partir,* to divide < Lat. *partīre* < *pars, part-,* part. See PART.]

Usage Note: *Party* is unexceptionable when used to refer to a participant in a social arrangement, as in *She was not named as a party in the conspiracy.* It is this sense that underlies the legal use of the term, as when one speaks of the *parties to a contract.* But *party* is also widely used as a general substitute for *person,* as in *Would all parties who left packages at the desk please reclaim their property.* This use of *party* may have been reinforced by its modern adoption by telephone operators. In other contexts, when used in earnest, it may be perceived as a superfluous variant for *person.*

par•ty•go•er (pär′tē-gō′ər) *n.* One who attends parties or a party.

party line *n.* **1.** A telephone circuit connecting subscribers with the same exchange. **2.** One or more of the policies or principles of a political party to which members are expected to adhere. **—party liner, par′ty-lin′er** (pär′tē-lī′nər) *n.*

par•ty poop•er also **par•ty-poop•er** (pär′tē-po͞o′pər) *n. Slang.* One who declines to participate with enthusiasm, esp. in the recreational activities of a group.

party wall *n. Law.* A wall built on the boundary line of adjoining properties and shared by both owners. [Obsolete *party,* shared, divided < OFr. *parti.* See PARTI-COLORED.]

pa•rure (pə-ro͝or′) *n.* A set of matched jewelry or other ornaments. [Fr. < OFr., adornment < *parer,* to adorn. See PARE.]

par value *n.* The value imprinted on a security, such as a stock certificate or bond, used to calculate a payment, such as a dividend or interest; face value.

par•ve (pär′və) *adj. Judaism.* Var. of **pareve.**

par•ve•nu (pär′və-no͞o′, -nyo͞o′) *n.* A person who has suddenly risen to a higher social and economic class and has not yet gained social acceptance in that class. [Fr. < p.part. of *parvenir,* to arrive < Lat. *pervenīre* : *per,* through; see **per[1]*** + *venīre,* to come; see **gʷā-*.**] **—par′ve•nu′** *adj.*

par•vis (pär′vĭs) *n.* **1.** An enclosed courtyard or space at the entrance to a building, esp. a cathedral, that is sometimes surrounded by porticoes or colonnades. **2.** Such a portico or colonnade. [ME < OFr., alteration of *pareis,* paradise < LLat. *paradīsus,* garden, paradise. See PARADISE.]

par•vo (pär′vō) *n., pl.* **-vos.** A parvovirus.

par•vo•vi•rus (pär′vō-vī′rəs) *n., pl.* **-rus•es.** Any of a group of small viruses that contain DNA in an icosahedral protein shell and cause disease in many vertebrates, esp. mammals. [Lat. *parvus,* small; see **pau-*** + VIRUS.]

pas (pä) *n., pl.* **pas** (pä). **1.** A step or dance. **2.** The right of precedence. [Fr. < OFr. < Lat. *passus,* step. See PACE[1].]

Pas•a•de•na (păs′ə-dē′nə). **1.** A city of S CA NE of Los Angeles; noted for its annual Tournament of Roses parade. Pop. 131,591. **2.** A city of SE TX, a suburb of Houston. Pop. 119,363.

Pa•sar•ga•dae (pə-sär′gə-dē′). A ruined city of ancient Persia NE of Persepolis; said to have been founded by Cyrus the Great in 550 B.C.

Pas•ca•gou•la (păs′kə-go͞o′lə). A city of extreme SE MS E of Biloxi on Mississippi Sound. Pop. 25,899.

pas•cal (pă-skăl′, pä-skäl′) *n.* **1.** A unit of pressure equal to one newton per square meter. See table at **measurement. 2. Pascal** or **PASCAL.** A high-level computer programming language for support of structured programming, used in applications and systems programming. [After PASCAL.]

Pas•cal (pă-skăl′, pä-skäl′), **Blaise.** 1623–62. French mathematician who developed the modern theory of probability.

Blaise Pascal
Detail of a portrait by Philippe de Champaigne (1602–1674)

pas•cal celery also **Pas•chal celery** (păs′kəl) *n.* Any of several types of celery having unblanched green stalks. [?]

Pasch (păsk) *n.* **1.** Passover. **2.** Easter. [ME < OFr. *pasche* < LLat. *pascha,* Passover, Easter < LGk. *paskha* < Aram. *pasḥā,* passover; akin to Heb. *pesaḥ,* Pesach. See PESACH.] **—Pas′chal, pas′chal** *adj.*

paschal lamb *n.* **1.** The lamb sacrificed at the first Passover. **2. Paschal Lamb.** Jesus. **3. Paschal Lamb.** See **Agnus Dei** 1.

Pas•co (păs′kō). A city of SE WA on the Columbia R. near its confluence with the Snake and Yakima rivers. Pop. 20,337.

pas de bour•rée (pä də bo͞o-rā′, bo͞o-) *n., pl.* **pas de bourrée.** A short stepping movement in ballet, usu. executed on pointe. [Fr. : *pas,* step + *de,* of + *bourrée,* bourrée.]

Pas de Ca•lais (pä də kă-lā′, kăl′ā, kä-lĕ′). The Strait of Dover.

pas de chat (shä) *n., pl.* **pas de chat.** A ballet jump in which the feet are lifted, one after the other, to the level of the opposite knee. [Fr. : *pas,* step + *de,* of + *chat,* cat.]

pas de deux (dœ) *n., pl.* **pas de deux. 1.** A dance for two, esp. in ballet. **2.** A close relationship between two people or things, as during an activity. [Fr. : *pas,* step + *de,* of, for + *deux,* two.]

pas de quat•re (kăt′rə) *n., pl.* **pas de quatre.** A dance for four. [Fr. : *pas,* step + *de,* of, for + *quatre,* four.]

pas de trois (trwä) *n., pl.* **pas de trois.** A dance for three. [Fr. : *pas,* step + *de,* of, for + *trois,* three.]

pa•se (pä′sā) *n.* One of several usu. one-handed maneuvers in bullfighting in which the matador presents and moves the cape to attract a close passing charge of the bull. [Sp. < *pasar,* to pass < VLat. **passāre.* See PASS.]

pa•se•o (pä-sā′ō) *n., pl.* **-os. 1.** A slow easy stroll or walk outdoors. **2.** The street, series of streets, or walkway along which such a walk is taken. **3.** In bullfighting, the formal procession into the ring of the players, including the matadors, banderilleros, and horses, that occurs just before the first bull is fought. [Sp. < *pasear,* to take a stroll, freq. of *pasar,* to go, pass. See PASE.]

pash (păsh) *n. Slang.* **a.** A romantic infatuation. **b.** The object of such an infatuation. [Short for PASSION.]

pa•sha also **pa•cha** (pä′shə, păsh′ə, pə-shä′) *n.* Used formerly as a title for military and civil officers, esp. in Turkey and northern Africa. [Turk. *paşa.*]

Pash•to (pŭsh′tō) also **Push•tu** (pŭsh′to͞o) *n.* An Iranian language that is the principal vernacular language of Afghanistan and parts of western Pakistan. [Pers. *pashtu* < Pashto.]

Pa•siph•a•ë (pə-sĭf′ə-ē′) *n. Gk. Myth.* The wife of Minos and mother, by a white bull, of the Minotaur.

pa•so do•ble also **pa•so•do•ble** (pä′sō-dō′blā, -dô′vlĕ) *n., pl.* **paso do•bles** also **pa•so•do•bles** (-blāz, -vlĕs). **1.** A lively Spanish dance. **2.** Music for or in the rhythm of this dance, set in march time and often played at bullfights. [Sp. : *paso,* step + *doble,* double.]

pasque•flow•er (păsk′flou′ər) *n.* Any of several plants of the genus *Anemone,* esp. *A. patens,* having large blue, purple, or white flowers. [Alteration (influenced by *pasque,* Easter, < their flowering in April) of obsolete *passeflower* < Fr. *passefleur* : *passer,* to pass; see PASS + *fleur,* flower; see FLOWER.]

pas•qui•nade (păs′kwə-nād′) *n.* A satire or lampoon, esp. one that ridicules a specific person, traditionally written and posted in a public place. [Fr. < Ital. *pasquinata,* after *Pasquino,* nickname of a Roman statue used for lampoons.] **—pas′qui•nade′** *v.* **—pas′qui•nad′er** *n.*

pass (păs) *v.* **passed, pass•ing, pass•es.** **—** *intr.* **1.** To move on or ahead; proceed. **2.** To extend; run: *The river passes through our land.* **3.a.** To move by: *The band passed our spot.* **b.** To move past another vehicle. **4.** To gain passage despite obstacles. **5.** To move past in time; elapse. **6.a.** To be

ă **pat**	oi **boy**
ā **pay**	ou **out**
âr **care**	o͝o **took**
ä **father**	o͞o **boot**
ĕ **pet**	ŭ **cut**
ē **be**	ûr **urge**
ĭ **pit**	th **thin**
ī **pie**	*th* **this**
îr **pier**	hw **which**
ŏ **pot**	zh **vision**
ō **toe**	ə **about,**
ô **paw**	**item**

Stress marks:
′ (primary);
′ (secondary), as in
dictionary (dĭk′shə-nĕr′ē)

transferred from one to another; circulate. **b.** *Sports.* To transfer a ball or puck to a teammate. **7.** To be communicated or exchanged between persons. **8.** To be transferred or conveyed to another by will or deed. **9.** To undergo transition from one condition, form, quality, or characteristic to another. **10.** To come to an end. **11.** To cease to exist; die. **12.** To happen; take place. **13.a.** To be allowed to happen without notice or challenge. **b.** *Games.* To decline one's turn to play or bid. **14.** To undergo an examination or a trial with favorable results. **15.a.** To serve as a barely acceptable substitute. **b.** To be accepted as a member of a group by denying one's own ancestry or background. **16.** To be approved or adopted. **17.** *Law.* **a.** To pronounce an opinion, a judgment, or a sentence. **b.** To sit in adjudication. **18.** To be voided. **19.** *Sports.* To thrust or lunge in fencing. — *tr.* **1.** To go by without stopping; leave behind. **2.a.** To go by without paying attention to; disregard or ignore. **b.** To fail to pay (a dividend). **3.** To go beyond; surpass. **4.** To go across; go through: *We passed the border.* **5.a.** To undergo (a trial or an examination) with favorable results. **b.** To cause or allow to go through a trial, a test, or an examination successfully. **6.a.** To cause to move: *We passed our hands over the fabric.* **b.** To cause to move into a certain position. **c.** To cause to move as part of a process: *pass liquid through a filter.* **d.** To cause to go by. **e.** *Baseball.* To walk (a batter). **7.** To allow to go by or elapse; spend. **8.a.** To cause to be transferred from one to another; circulate. **b.** To hand over to someone else. **c.** *Sports.* To transfer (a ball, for example) to a teammate, as by throwing. **d.** To cause to be accepted; circulate fraudulently. **9.** To discharge (body waste, for example); void. **10.a.** To approve; adopt. **b.** To be sanctioned, ratified, or approved by. **11.** To pronounce; utter. — *n.* **1.** The act of passing; passage. **2.** A way or means of passage, as through a barrier. See Syns at **way. 3.a.** A permit, a ticket, or an authorization to come and go at will. **b.** A free ticket entitling one to transportation or admisssion. **c.** Written leave of absence from military duty. **4.a.** A sweep or run by an aircraft over an area or a target. **b.** A single complete cycle of operations, as by a computer program. **5.** A condition or situation, often critical in nature; a predicament. **6.** A sexual invitation or overture. **7.** A motion of the hand or the waving of a wand. **8.a.** *Sports.* A transfer of a ball or puck between teammates. **b.** *Sports.* A lunge or thrust in fencing. **c.** *Baseball.* A base on balls. **9.** *Games.* **a.** A refusal to bid, draw, bet, or play. **b.** A winning throw of the dice in craps. **10.** A pase. — ***phrasal verbs.*** **pass away. 1.** To pass out of existence; end. **2.** To die. **pass for.** To be accepted as or believed to be. **pass off.** To offer, sell, or put into circulation (an imitation) as genuine. **pass out.** To lose consciousness. **pass over.** To leave out; disregard. **pass up.** *Informal.* To let go by; reject. — ***idioms.*** **bring to pass.** To cause to happen. **come to pass.** To occur. **pass muster.** To pass an examination or inspection; measure up to a given standard. **pass (one's) lips. 1.** To be eaten or drunk. **2.** To issue or be spoken. **pass the buck.** *Slang.* To shift responsibility or blame to another. **pass the time of day.** To exchange greetings or engage in pleasantries. [ME *passen* < OFr. *passer* < VLat. *passāre* < Lat. *passus*, step. See PACE[1].] — **pass′er** *n.*

passant

pass. *abbr.* **1.** Passage; passenger. **2.** *Gram.* Passive.

pass•a•ble (păs′ə-bəl) *adj.* **1.** That can be passed, traversed, or crossed; navigable. **2.** Acceptable for general circulation. **3.** Satisfactory but not outstanding; adequate. **4.** That can be legislated. — **pass′a•ble•ness** *n.* — **pass′a•bly** *adv.*

pas•sa•ca•glia (pä′sə-käl′yə, păs′ə-käl′yə) *n.* **1.** *Mus.* A musical form of the 17th and 18th centuries consisting of continuous variations on a ground bass in 3/4 time and similar to the chaconne. **2.** A courtly dance of the period performed to such music. [Ital. < Sp. *pasacalle* : *pasar*, to pass, step; see PASE + *calle*, street (< Lat. *callis, call-*, path).]

pas•sade (pə-säd′) *n.* **1.** A dressage technique in which the horse is made to course repeatedly over the same spot. **2.** A passing flirtation or romance. [Fr., passado, passade < Ital. *passata* < *passare*, to pass. See PASSAGE[2].]

pas•sa•do (pə-sä′dō) *n., pl.* **-dos** or **-does.** A fencing maneuver in which the foil is thrust forward and one foot advanced at the same time. [Alteration of French *passade.* See PASSADE.]

pas•sage[1] (păs′ĭj) *n.* **1.** The act or process of passing, esp.: **a.** A movement from one place to another, as by going by or across; transit or migration. **b.** The process of elapsing: *the passage of time.* **c.** The process of passing from one condition or stage to another; transition. **d.** Enactment into law of a legislative measure. **2.** A journey, esp. one by air or water. **3.** The right to travel as a passenger, esp. on a ship. **4.** The right, permission, or power to come and go freely. **5.a.** A path, channel, or duct through, over, or along which something may pass. **b.** A corridor. See Syns at **way. 6.a.** An occurrence or event. **b.** Something, such as an exchange of words, that occurs between two persons. **7.a.** A segment of a written work or speech. **b.** *Mus.* A segment of a composition. **c.** A section of a painting or other piece of artwork; a detail. **8.** *Physiol.* An act of emptying, as of the bowels. **9.** *Biol.* The process of passing or maintaining a group of microorganisms or cells through a series of hosts or cultures. **10.** *Obsolete.* Death. [ME < OFr. < *passer*, to pass. See PASS.]

pas•sage[2] (păs′ĭj, pə-säzh′) *n.* A slow cadenced trot in which the horse raises and returns to the ground first one diagonal pair of feet, then the other. — *v.* **-saged, -sag•ing, -sag•es.** — *intr.* To execute a passage. — *tr.* To cause (a horse) to execute a passage. [Fr. < *passager*, to passage, alteration of *passéger* < Ital. *passeggiare* < *passare*, to pass < VLat. **passāre* < Lat. *passus*, step. See PACE[1].]

pas•sage•way (păs′ĭj-wā′) *n.* A way allowing passage, esp. a corridor.

pas•sage•work (păs′ĭj-wûrk′) *n. Mus.* **1.** A portion of a composition that permits a performer to make a display of technique. **2.** A musician's performance of a passagework.

Pas•sa•ic (pə-sā′ĭk). A city of NE NJ S of Paterson on the **Passaic River,** c. 129 km (80 mi); settled in 1678. Pop. 58,041.

pass-a•long also **pass•a•long** (păs′ə-lông′, -lŏng′) *n.* The policy, practice, or act of paying for an increased cost by raising the price charged to one's customers or clients.

Pas•sa•ma•quod•dy (păs′ə-mə-kwŏd′ē) *n., pl.* **Passamaquoddy** or **-dies. 1.** A member of a Native American people formerly inhabiting parts of coastal Maine and New Brunswick, with present-day descendants in eastern Maine. **2.** Their Algonquian language. [Of Micmac orig.]

Passamaquoddy Bay. An arm of the Bay of Fundy between S New Brunswick, Canada, and E ME.

pas•sant (păs′ənt) *adj. Her.* Being a beast facing and walking toward the viewer's right with one front leg raised. [ME < OFr., pr.part. of *passer*, to pass. See PASS.]

pass•book (păs′bŏŏk′) *n.* **1.** See **bankbook. 2.** A book in which a merchant records credit sales.

pas•sé (pă-sā′) *adj.* **1.** No longer current or in fashion; out-of-date. **2.** Past the prime; faded or aged. [Fr., p.part. of *passer*, to pass < OFr. See PASS.]

passed ball (păst) *n. Baseball.* A pitch that the catcher should field but misses, allowing a runner to advance a base or more.

pas•sel (păs′əl) *n. Informal.* A large quantity or group. [Alteration of PARCEL.]

passe•men•terie (păs-mĕn′trē) *n.* Trimming, such as braid or lace, for a garment. [Fr. < *passement*, braid, cloth < OFr., a passing < *passer*, to pass. See PASS.]

pas•sen•ger (păs′ən-jər) *n.* **1.** A person who travels in a conveyance, such as a car or train, without participating in its operation. **2.** *Informal.* One that participates only passively in an activity. **3.** A wayfarer or traveler. [ME *passinger*, alteration of *passager* < OFr. *passageor* < *passager*, passing < *passage*, passage. See PASSAGE[1].]

passenger pigeon *n.* An extinct migratory bird *(Ectopistes migratorius)* abundant in eastern North America until the latter part of the 19th century.

passe-par•tout (păs-pär-to͞o′) *n.* **1.** Something, such as a master key, that permits one to pass or go at will. **2.a.** A border, such as a mat, that is used to frame or mount a picture. **b.** An adhesive tape or a gummed paper used for a similar purpose. [Fr. : *passer*, to pass + *partout*, everywhere.]

passe•pied (päs-pyā′) *n.* **1.** A spirited court dance, popular in France and England in the 17th and 18th centuries, resembling a minuet but faster. **2.** Music for or in the rhythm of this dance. [Fr. : *passer*, to pass; see PASS + *pied*, foot (< OFr. < Lat. *pēs, ped-*; see PEDAL).]

pas•ser•by also **pas•ser-by** (păs′ər-bī′, -bī′) *n., pl.* **pas•sers•by** also **pas•sers-by** (păs′ərz-). A person who passes by.

pas•ser•ine (păs′ə-rīn′) *adj.* Of or relating to birds of the order Passeriformes, which includes perching birds and songbirds such as the finches and sparrows. [Lat. *passerīnus*, of sparrows < *passer*, sparrow.] — **pas′ser•rine′** *n.*

pas seul (pä sœl′) *n., pl.* **pas seuls** (pä sœl′). A dance for one person. [Fr. : *pas*, step + *seul*, solo.]

pass-fail (păs′fāl′) *adj.* Of, relating to, or being a system of grading in which a student passes or fails instead of receiving a letter grade. — *n.* This kind of a grading system.

pas•si•ble (păs′ə-bəl) *adj.* Capable of feeling or suffering; sensitive. [ME < OFr. < Lat. *passibilis* < Lat. *passus*, p.part. of *patī*, to suffer. See **pē(i)-***.] — **pas′si•bil′i•ty** *n.*

pas•sim (păs′ĭm) *adv.* Throughout or frequently; here and there. Used in textual annotation to indicate that something occurs frequently in the work cited. [Lat. < *passus*, p.part. of *pandere*, to scatter, spread out. See **petə-***.]

pass•ing (păs′ĭng) *adj.* **1.** Moving by; going past. **2.** Of brief duration; transitory. **3.** Cursory or superficial; casual. **4.** Allowing one to pass something such as a test or an inspection; satisfactory. **5.** *Archaic.* Very or great; surpassing. — *adv.* Very; surpassingly. — *n.* **1.** The act of one that passes or the fact of having passed. **2.** A place where or a means by which one can pass. **3.** Death. — ***idiom.*** **in passing.** While going by; incidentally. — **pass′ing•ly** *adv.*

passing note *n. Mus.* A note placed between two chords to provide a smooth melodic transition from one to the other.

passing shot *n. Sports.* A forceful shot, as in tennis, that travels to one side out of the reach of one's opponent.

passing tone *n. Mus.* See **passing note.**

pas•sion (păsh′ən) *n.* **1.** A powerful emotion, such as love, joy, hatred, or anger. See Syns at **feeling. 2.a.** Ardent love. **b.** Strong sexual desire; lust. **c.** The object of such love or desire. **3.a.** Boundless enthusiasm. **b.** The object of such enthusiasm. **4.** An abandoned display of emotion, esp. of anger. **5. Passion. a.** The sufferings of Jesus in the period following the Last Supper and including the Crucifixion. **b.** A narrative, musical setting, or pictorial representation of Jesus's sufferings. **6.** *Archaic.* Martyrdom. **7.** *Archaic.* Passivity. [ME < OFr. < Med.Lat. *passiō, passiōn-*, sufferings of Jesus < LLat., physical suffering, sinful desire < Lat., an undergoing < *passus*, p.part. of *patī*, to suffer. See **pē(i)-*.**]

pas•sion•al (păsh′ə-nəl) *adj.* Of, relating to, or filled with passion. —*n.* A book of the sufferings of saints and martyrs.

pas•sion•ate (păsh′ə-nĭt) *adj.* **1.** Capable of, having, or dominated by powerful emotions. **2.** Wrathful by temperament; choleric. **3.** Marked by strong sexual desire; amorous or lustful. **4.** Showing or expressing strong emotion; ardent. **5.** Arising from or marked by passion. —**pas′sion•ate•ly** *adv.* —**pas′sion•ate•ness** *n.*

pas•sion•flow•er (păsh′ən-flou′ər) *n.* Any of various climbing, chiefly tropical American vines of the genus *Passiflora,* having showy flowers with a fringelike crown and a conspicuous stalk that bears the stamens and pistil. [< the resemblance of its parts to the instruments of the Passion.]

passion fruit *n.* The edible fruit of the passionflower.

pas•sion•less (păsh′ən-lĭs) *adj.* **1.** Lacking strong emotion or feeling. **2.** Unbiased or impartial; detached.

Passion play *n.* A dramatic performance of medieval origin that represents the events associated with the Passion of Jesus.

Passion Sunday *n.* The second Sunday before Easter.

Pas•sion•tide (păsh′ən-tīd′) *n.* The two weeks between Passion Sunday and Easter.

Passion Week *n.* The week between Passion Sunday and Palm Sunday.

pas•si•vate (păs′ə-vāt′) *v.* **-vat•ed, -vat•ing, -vates.** —*tr.* **1.** To treat or coat (a metal) in order to reduce the chemical reactivity of its surface. **2.** To coat (a semiconductor, for example) with an oxide layer to protect against contamination and increase electrical stability. —**pas′si•va′tion** *n.* —**pas′si•va•tor** *n.*

pas•sive (păs′ĭv) *adj.* **1.** Receiving or subjected to an action without responding or initiating an action in return. **2.** Accepting or submitting without objection or resistance; compliant. **3.** Not participating, acting, or operating; inert. See Syns at **inactive. 4.** Of, relating to, or being certain bonds or shares that do not bear financial interest. **5.** Of, relating to, or being a solar heating or cooling system that uses no external mechanical power. **6.** *Gram.* Of, relating to, or being a verb form or voice used to indicate that the grammatical subject is the object of the action or the effect of the verb. For example, in *They were impressed by his manner, were impressed* is in the passive voice. **7.** *Chem.* Unreactive except under special or extreme conditions; inert. **8.** *Electron.* Exhibiting no gain or contributing no energy. **9.** *Psychol.* Relating to or characteristic of an inactive or submissive role in a relationship. —*n.* **1.** *Gram.* **a.** The passive voice. **b.** A verb or construction in the passive voice. **2.** One that is submissive or inactive. Often used in the plural. [ME < OFr. *passif* < Lat. *passīvus*, capable of suffering < *passus*, p.part. of *patī*, to suffer. See **pē(i)-*.**] —**pas′sive•ly** *adv.* —**pas′sive•ness** *n.*

passive immunity *n.* Immunity acquired by the transfer of antibodies from another individual, as through injection or placental transfer to a fetus. —**passive immunization** *n.*

passive resistance *n.* Resistance by nonviolent methods to a government, an occupying power, or specific laws, as refusing to comply or demonstrating in protest. —**passive resister** *n.*

passive restraint *n.* An automatic safety device, such as an air bag, in a motor vehicle that protects a person during a crash.

passive smoking *n.* The involuntary inhalation of tobacco smoke by a person who occupies an area with a smoker.

pas•siv•ism (păs′ə-vĭz′əm) *n.* Passive character, attitude, quality, or behavior. —**pas′siv•ist** *n.*

pas•siv•i•ty (pă-sĭv′ĭ-tē) *n.* The condition or quality of being passive; inactivity, quiescence, or submissiveness.

pass•key (păs′kē′) *n.* **1.** See **master key. 2.** See **skeleton key.**

Pass•o•ver (păs′ō′vər) *n. Judaism.* A holiday beginning on the 14th of Nisan and continuing for eight days or seven days, commemorating the exodus of the Jews from Egypt. [Transl. of Heb. *pesaḥ*, Pesach. See PESACH.]

pass•port (păs′pôrt′, -pōrt′) *n.* **1.** An official government document that certifies one's identity and citizenship and permits a citizen to travel abroad. **2.** An official permit issued by a foreign country allowing one to transport goods or travel through that country. **3.** An official document issued by an allied foreign government to a ship, esp. a neutral merchant ship in time of war, authorizing it to enter and travel through certain waters freely. **4.** Something that gives one the right or privilege of passage, entry, or acceptance. [Fr. *passeport* < OFr. : *passer*, to pass; see PASS + *port*, port; see PORT[1].]

pass-through (păs′thro͞o′) *n.* **1.** An opening between two rooms, esp. a shelved space between a kitchen and dining room that is used for passing food. **2.** A route through which something is permitted to pass. **3.** A security that passes through payments made by debtors, thus providing investors with regular returns. **4.** See **pass-along.** —**pass-through** *adj.*

pass•word (păs′wûrd′) *n.* **1.** A secret word or phrase giving admittance or access to information. **2.** *Comp. Sci.* A sequence of characters giving access to a computer system.

Pas•sy (pă-sē′, pä-), **Frédéric.** 1822–1912. French economist who shared the first Nobel Peace Prize (1901).

Passy, Paul Édouard. 1859–1940. French philologist who founded the International Phonetic Association (1894).

past (păst) *adj.* **1.** No longer current; gone by; over. **2.** Having existed or occurred in an earlier time; bygone. **3.a.** Earlier than the present time; ago: *40 years past.* **b.** Just gone by or elapsed. **4.** Having served formerly in a given capacity, esp. an official one. **5.** *Gram.* Of, relating to, or being a verb tense or form used to express an action or a condition prior to the time it is expressed. —*n.* **1.** The time before the present. **2.a.** Previous background, career, experiences, and activities. **b.** A former period of someone's life kept secret or thought to be shameful. **3.** *Gram.* **a.** The past tense. **b.** A verb form in the past tense. —*adv.* So as to pass by or go beyond. —*prep.* **1.** Beyond in time; later than or after: *a quarter past two.* **2.** Beyond in position; farther than. **3.a.** Beyond the power, scope, extent, or influence of. **b.** Beyond in development or appropriateness. **4.** Beyond the number or amount of. [ME < p.part. of *passen*, to pass. See PASS.]

passionflower

pas•ta (päs′tə) *n.* **1.** Paste or dough made of flour, eggs, and water, often formed into shapes and dried and used in a variety of recipes after being boiled. **2.** A prepared dish containing pasta. [Ital. < LLat., paste, pastry cake. See PASTE[1].]

paste[1] (pāst) *n.* **1.** A smooth viscous mixture, as of starch and water, used as an adhesive for joining light materials, such as paper. **2.** A soft, smooth, thick mixture, as: **a.** A smooth dough of water, flour, and butter or other shortening, used in making pastry. **b.** A food that has been pounded until it is reduced to a smooth creamy mass. **c.** A sweet doughy candy or confection. **3.** The moist clay or clay mixture used in making porcelain or pottery. **4.a.** A hard brilliant lead-containing glass used in making artificial gems. **b.** A gem made of this glass. —*tr.v.* **past•ed, past•ing, pastes. 1.** To cause to adhere by or as if by applying paste. **2.** To cover with something by or as if by pasting. [ME < OFr. < LLat. *pasta* < Gk., barley porridge < neut. pl. of *pastos*, sprinkled, salted < *passein*, to sprinkle. See **kwēt-*.**]

paste[2] (pāst) *tr.v.* **past•ed, past•ing, pastes.** *Slang.* To punch or strike. —*n.* A hard blow. [Prob. alteration of BASTE[3].]

paste•board (pāst′bôrd′, -bōrd′) *n.* **1.** A thin firm board made of sheets of paper pasted together or of pressed paper pulp. **2.** A card, esp.: **a.** A ticket. **b.** *Games.* A playing card. **c.** A visiting card. —*adj.* **1.** Made of pasteboard. **2.** Of inferior quality; flimsy or unsubstantial.

pas•tel (pă-stĕl′) *n.* **1.a.** A drawing medium of dried paste made of ground pigments and a water-based binder that is manufactured in crayon form. **b.** A crayon of this material. **2.a.** A picture or sketch drawn with this type of crayon. **b.** The art or process of drawing with pastels. **3.** A soft delicate hue; a pale color. **4.** A sketchy or brief prose work. —*adj.* **1.** Of, relating to, or made of pastel. **2.** Pale and soft in color. [Fr. < Ital. *pastello*, material made into a paste < LLat. *pastellus*, woad dye, dim. of *pasta*, paste. See PASTE[1].] —**pas•tel′ist, pas•tel′list** *n.*

Louis Pasteur

past•er (pā′stər) *n.* **1.** One that applies or covers with paste. **2.** A paper sticker.

pas•tern (păs′tərn) *n.* **1.** The part of a horse's foot between the fetlock and hoof. **2.** An analogous part of the leg of a dog or other quadruped. [Alteration of ME *pastron*, hobble, pastern < OFr. *pasturon*, dim. of *pasture*, pasture, tether, alteration of **pastoire* < Lat. *pāstōria*, fem. sing. of *pāstōrius*, of herdsmen < *pāstor*, shepherd. See PASTOR.]

Pas•ter•nak (păs′tər-năk′, pə-styĭr-näk′), **Boris Leonidovich.** 1890–1960. Russian writer, best known for *Doctor Zhivago* (1957), who was forced to refuse the 1958 Nobel Prize for literature.

paste-up (pāst′ŭp′) *n.* **1.** A composition of light flat objects pasted onto a sheet of paper, board, or other backing. **2.** The art or process of making such a composition.

Pas•teur (păs-tûr′, pä-stœr′), **Louis.** 1822–95. French chemist who invented the process of pasteurization and developed vaccines for anthrax and rabies. —**Pas•teur′i•an** *adj.*

Pasteur effect *n.* The inhibiting effect of oxygen on the process of fermentation. [After Louis PASTEUR.]

pas•teur•i•za•tion (păs′chər-ĭ-zā′shən, păs′tər-) *n.* **1.** The act or process of heating a beverage or other food, such as milk or beer, to a specific temperature for a specific period of time in order to kill microorganisms that could cause disease, spoilage, or undesired fermentation. **2.** The act or process of destroying most microorganisms in certain foods by irradiating them to prevent spoilage. [After Louis PASTEUR.]

pas•teur•ize (păs′chə-rīz′, păs′tə-) *tr.v.* **-ized, -iz•ing, -iz•es.** To subject (a beverage or other food) to pasteurization. —**pas′teur•iz′er** *n.*

Pasteur treatment *n.* A treatment for rabies in which a series

ă **pat**	oi **boy**
ā **pay**	ou **out**
âr **care**	o͝o **took**
ä **father**	o͞o **boot**
ĕ **pet**	ŭ **cut**
ē **be**	ûr **urge**
ĭ **pit**	th **thin**
ī **pie**	*th* **this**
îr **pier**	hw **which**
ŏ **pot**	zh **vision**
ō **toe**	ə **a**bout,
ô **paw**	it**e**m

Stress marks:
′ (primary);
′ (secondary), as in
dictionary (dĭk′shə-nĕr′ē)

pasture

patchwork
Detail of a patchwork quilt

of increasingly strong inoculations with attenuated virus is given to stimulate antibody production during the incubation period of the disease. [After Louis PASTEUR.]

pas•tic•cio (pă-stē′chō, -chē-ō, pä-) *n., pl.* **-ci** (-chē). A work or style produced by borrowing fragments, ingredients, or motifs from various sources; a potpourri. [Ital. < VLat. *pasticium, pasty. See PATISSERIE.]

pas•tiche (pă-stēsh′, pä-) *n.* **1.** A dramatic, literary, or musical piece openly imitating the previous works of other artists, often with satirical intent. **2.** A pasticcio of incongruous parts; a hodgepodge. [Fr. < Ital. *pasticcio*. See PASTICCIO.]

past•ies (pā′stēz′) *pl.n.* A pair of adhesive patches that conceal a woman's nipples, worn usu. by erotic dancers.

pas•tille (pă-stēl′) also **pas•til** (păs′tĭl) *n.* **1.** A small medicated or flavored tablet; a troche. **2.** A tablet containing aromatic substances that is burned to fumigate or deodorize the air. **3.** A pastel paste or crayon. [Fr. < Sp. *pastilla*, perfume pellet, and Ital. *pastillo*, pastille, both < Lat. *pastillus*, little loaf, medicine tablet, dim. of *pānis*, bread. See **pā-*.**]

pas•time (păs′tīm′) *n.* An activity that occupies one's spare time pleasantly. [ME *passe tyme*, transl. of Fr. *passe temps* : *passer*, to pass + *temps*, time.]

pas•ti•na (pă-stē′nə) *n.* Tiny pieces of pasta, often cooked in soup. [Ital., dim. of *pasta*, pasta. See PASTA.]

pas•tis (pă-stēs′) *n.* A French licorice-flavored liqueur, usu. drunk as an apéritif. [Fr., muddle, pastis < OProv. *pastitz*, paste, pasty < VLat. *pasticium. See PATISSERIE.]

past master *n.* **1.** One who has formerly held the position of master in an organization, esp. a social one. **2.** One who is experienced and skilled in a particular craft or activity.

past•ness (păst′nĭs) *n.* **1.** The quality or condition of being past. **2.** The emotion or feeling evoked by memory.

Pas•to (päs′tō). A city of SW Colombia near the Ecuadorian border; founded 1539. Pop. 196,800.

pas•tor (păs′tər) *n.* **1.** A Christian minister or priest having spiritual charge over a congregation or other group. **2.** A layperson having spiritual charge over a person or group. **3.** A shepherd. *—tr.v.* **-tored, -tor•ing, -tors.** To serve or act as pastor of. [ME < OFr. < Lat. *pāstor*, shepherd. See **pā-*.**] **—pas′tor•ship′** *n.*

pas•tor•al (păs′tər-əl) *adj.* **1.a.** Of or relating to shepherds or herders. **b.** Of or used for animal husbandry. **2.a.** Of or relating to the country or country life; rural. **b.** Charmingly simple and serene; idyllic. **3.** Of, relating to, or being a literary or other artistic work that portrays or evokes rural life, usu. in an idealized manner. **4.** Of or relating to a pastor or a pastor's duties. *—n.* **1.** A pastoral literary or other artistic work. **2.** *Mus.* A pastorale. [ME < OFr. < Lat. *pāstōrālis* < *pāstor*, shepherd. See PASTOR.] **—pas′tor•al•ly** *adv.*

pas•to•rale (păs′tə-räl′, -răl′, -rä′lē, pä′stə-) *n., pl.* **-ra•li** (-rä′lē) or **-rales. 1.** *Mus.* An instrumental or vocal composition with a tender melody in a moderately slow rhythm, suggestive of traditional shepherds' music and rural life. **2.** A dramatic performance or opera, popular in the 16th and 17th centuries, based on a rural theme or subject. [Ital. < Lat. *pāstōrālis*, of herdsmen. See PASTORAL.]

Pas•tor•al Epistles (păs′tər-əl) *n. Bible.* The three New Testament Epistles, two addressed to Timothy and one to Titus, that are attributed to Saint Paul and concerned with the duties of ministers and certain issues of Church doctrine.

pas•tor•al•ism (păs′tər-ə-lĭz′əm, pä′stər-) *n.* **1.** The quality or state of being pastoral. **2.** A social and economic system based on raising livestock. **—pas′tor•al•ist** *n.*

pas•tor•ate (păs′tər-ĭt) *n.* **1.** The office, rank, or jurisdiction of a pastor. **2.** A pastor's term of office with one congregation. **3.** A body of pastors.

pas•to•ri•um (pă-stôr′ē-əm, -stōr′-) *n., pl.* **-ums.** *Chiefly Southern U.S.* The residence of a pastor; a parsonage. [PAST(OR) + Lat. *-orium*, n. suff.; see -ORY.]

past participle *n. Gram.* A verb form indicating past or completed action or time that is used as a verbal adjective in phrases such as *baked beans* and with auxiliaries to form the passive voice or perfect and pluperfect tenses in constructions such as *She had baked the beans* and *The work was finished.*

past perfect *n. Gram.* See **pluperfect** 1.

pas•tra•mi (pə-strä′mē) *n., pl.* **-mis.** A highly seasoned smoked cut of beef, usu. taken from the shoulder. [Yiddish *pastrame* < Romanian *pastramă*.]

pas•try (pā′strē) *n., pl.* **-tries. 1.** Dough or paste consisting primarily of flour, water, and shortening that is baked and often used as a crust for foods such as pies and tarts. **2.a.** Baked sweet foods made with pastry. **b.** One of these baked foods. [ME *pastree* < *paste*, dough. See PASTE[1].]

past tense *n. Gram.* A verb tense used to express an action or a condition that occurred in or during the past.

pas•tur•age (păs′chər-ĭj) *n.* **1.** The grass or other vegetation eaten by grazing animals. **2.** Land covered with vegetation suitable for grazing animals. **3.** The business of grazing cattle.

pas•ture (păs′chər) *n.* **1.a.** Grass or other vegetation eaten as food by grazing animals. **b.** Ground on which such vegetation grows, esp. that used by domestic grazing animals. **2.** The feeding or grazing of animals. *—v.* **-tured, -tur•ing, -tures.** *—tr.* **1.** To herd (animals) into a pasture to graze. **2.** To provide (animals) with pasturage. Used of land. **3.a.** To graze on (land or vegetation). **b.** To use (land) as pasture. *—intr.* To graze in a pasture. **—*idiom.* put out to pasture. 1.** To herd (grazing animals) into pasturable land. **2.** *Informal.* To retire or compel to retire from work or a full workload. [ME < OFr. < LLat. *pāstūra* < Lat. *pāstus*, p.part. of *pāscere*, to feed. See **pā-*.**] **—pas′tur•a•ble** *adj.* **—pas′tur•er** *n.*

pas•ture•land (păs′chər-lănd′) *n.* Land suitable for grazing.

past•y[1] (pā′stē) *adj.* **-i•er, -i•est. 1.** Resembling paste in consistency. **2.** Having a pale lifeless appearance; pallid: *an unhealthy pasty complexion.* **—past′i•ness** *n.*

pas•ty[2] (păs′tē) *n., pl.* **-ties.** *Chiefly British.* A pie or turnover, esp. one filled with seasoned meat or fish. [ME *pastey* < OFr. *paste* < VLat. *pastātum < LLat. *pasta*, paste. See PASTE[1].]

PA system (pē′ā′) *n.* A public-address system.

pat[1] (păt) *v.* **pat•ted, pat•ting, pats.** *—tr.* **1.a.** To tap gently with the open hand or with something flat. **b.** To stroke lightly as a gesture of affection. **2.** To mold by tapping gently with the hands or a flat implement. *—intr.* **1.** To run or walk with a tapping sound. **2.** To hit something or against something gently or lightly. *—n.* **1.** A light gentle stroke or tap. **2.** The sound made by a light stroke or tap or by light footsteps. **3.** A small mass shaped by or as if by patting: *a pat of butter.* **—*idiom.* pat on the back.** A word or gesture of praise or approval. [< ME, a blow, perh. of imit. orig.]

pat[2] (păt) *adj.* **1.** Trite or glib; superficially complete or satisfactory. **2.a.** Timely or opportune. **b.** Suitable; fitting. **3.** *Games.* Being a poker hand that is strong enough to make drawing cards unlikely to improve it. *—adv. Informal.* Completely, exactly, or perfectly. [< PAT[1].] **—pat′ly** *adv.* **—pat′ness** *n.*

pat. *abbr.* Patent.

pa•ta•ca (pə-tä′kə) *n.* See table at **currency.** [Port. < Ar. *'abū ṭāqah*.]

pa•ta•gi•um (pə-tā′jē-əm) *n., pl.* **-gi•a** (-jē-ə). **1.** A thin membrane extending between the body and a limb to form a wing or winglike extension, as in bats. **2.** An expandable membranous fold of skin between the wing and body of a bird. [Lat. *patagium*, gold tunic edging, perh. < Gk. *patageion < *patagos*, clatter, of imit. origin.] **—pa•ta′gi•al** (-jē-əl) *adj.*

Pat•a•go•ni•a (păt′ə-gō′nē-ə, -gōn′yə). A tableland region of South America in S Argentina and Chile extending from the Colorado R. to the Straits of Magellan and the Andes to the Atlantic Ocean. **—Pat′a•go′ni•an** *adj. & n.*

Patagonian hare *n.* See **mara.**

pa•ta•phys•ics (pä′tə-fĭz′ĭks) *n.* (*used with a sing. v.*) The French absurdist concept of a philosophy or science dedicated to studying what lies beyond the realm of metaphysics, often expressed in nonsensical language. [Fr. *pataphysique*, alteration of Gk. *ta epi ta metaphusika*, things after the metaphysics : *epi*, after; see EPI- + *metaphusika*, metaphysics; see METAPHYSICS.]

patch[1] (păch) *n.* **1.a.** A small piece of material affixed to another larger piece to conceal, reinforce, or repair a worn area, hole, or tear. **b.** A small piece of cloth used for patchwork. **2.** A small cloth badge affixed to a garment as a decoration or an insignia, as of a military unit. **3.a.** A dressing or covering applied to protect a wound or sore. **b.** A pad or shield of cloth worn over an eye socket or an injured eye. **c.** A transdermal patch. **4.** A beauty spot applied to the skin. **5.a.** A small piece, part, or section, esp. that which differs from or contrasts with the whole. **b.** A small plot or piece of land, esp. one that produces specific vegetation. **6.** A temporary, removable electronic connection, as one between two components in a communications system. *—v.* **patched, patch•ing, patch•es.** *—tr.* **1.** To put a patch or patches on. **2.** To make by sewing scraps of material together: *patch a quilt.* **3.** To mend, repair, or put together, esp. hastily, clumsily, or poorly: *patched up their friendship.* **4.** To connect (electronic components) temporarily, as with a patch cord. *—intr. Electron.* To be connected temporarily. [ME *pacche*, perh. alteration of *pece*, *pieche*, piece. See PIECE.] **—patch′a•ble** *adj.* **—patch′er** *n.*

patch[2] (păch) *n.* A fool or clown; a dolt. [Perh. < Ital. dial. *paccio* < OItal.]

patch cord *n.* A conductor with a plug at each end that is used to temporarily connect components of an electronic system.

patch•ou•li also **patch•ou•ly** or **pach•ou•li** (pə-cho͞o′lē, păch′o͞o-lē) *n., pl.* **-lis** also **-lies** or **-lis. 1.** A small southeast Asian shrub (*Pogostemon cablin*) in the mint family, having leaves that yield a fragrant oil. **2.** A perfume made from this oil. [Tamil *paccuḷi*.]

patch pocket *n.* A flat pocket on the outside of a garment.

patch test *n.* A test for allergic sensitivity in which a suspected allergen is applied to the skin on a small surgical pad.

patch•work (păch′wûrk′) *n.* **1.** Needlework consisting of varicolored patches of material sewn together, as in a quilt. **2.** A collection of miscellaneous or incongruous parts; a jumble.

patch•y (păch′ē) *adj.* **-i•er, -i•est. 1.** Made up of or marked by patches: *patchy trousers.* **2.** Uneven in quality or performance. **—patch′i•ly** *adv.* **—patch′i•ness** *n.*

patd. *abbr.* Patented.

pate (pāt) *n.* **1.** The human head, esp. the top of the head. **2.** The intellect; one's brains. [ME.] —**pat′ed** *adj*

pâte (pät) *n.* See **paste**[1] 3. [Fr. < OFr. *paste*, paste. See PASTE[1].]

pâ•té (pä-tā′) *n.* **1.** A meat paste, such as pâté de foie gras. **2.** A small pastry filled with meat or fish. [Fr. < OFr. *paste*, paste, pâté. See PASTE[1].]

pâ•té de foie gras (pä-tā′ də fwä grä′) *n., pl.* **pâtés de foie gras** (pä-tā′). A paste made from goose liver, pork fat, onions, mushrooms, and often truffles. [Fr. : *pâté*, pâté + *de*, of + *foie*, liver + *gras*, fat.]

pa•tel•la (pə-tĕl′ə) *n., pl.* **-tel•lae** (-tĕl′ē). **1.a.** A flat triangular bone located at the front of the knee joint. **b.** A dish-shaped anatomical formation. **2.** A pan or dish in ancient Rome. [Lat., dim. of *patina*, plate, pan. See PATEN.] —**pa•tel′lar, pa•tel′late** (-tĕl′ĭt, -āt′) *adj.*

pa•tel•li•form (pə-tĕl′ə-fôrm′) *adj.* Shaped like a pan, dish, or cup. [Lat. *patella*, small plate, pan; see PATELLA + -FORM.]

pat•en also **pat•in** (păt′n) *n.* **1.** A plate, usu. of gold or silver, that is used to hold the host during the celebration of the Eucharist. **2.** A plate or shallow dish, esp. an artifact from an ancient civilization. **3.** A thin disk of or resembling metal. [ME < OFr. *patene* < Med.Lat. *patina* < Lat., pan < Gk. *patanē*, platter. See **petə-***.]

pa•ten•cy (pāt′n-sē) *n.* **1.** The state or quality of being obvious. **2.** *Biol.* The state or quality of being open, expanded, or unblocked.

pat•ent (păt′nt) *n.* **1.a.** A grant made by a government that confers upon the creator of an invention the sole right to make, use, and sell that invention for a set period of time. **b.** Letters patent. **c.** An invention protected by such a grant. **2.a.** A grant made by a government that confers on an individual fee-simple title to public lands. **b.** The official document of such a grant. **c.** The land so granted. **3.** An exclusive right or title. —*adj.* **1.a.** Protected or conferred by a patent or letters patent. **b.** Of, relating to, or dealing in patents: *patent law.* **2.** (*also* pāt′nt). Obvious; plain. See Syns at **apparent. 3.** (păt′nt). *Biol.* **a.** Not blocked; open. **b.** Spreading open; expanded. **4.** Of, relating to, or being a nonprescription drug or other medical preparation that is often protected by a trademark. **5.** Of high quality. Used of flour. **6.** (*also* pāt′-nt). *Archaic.* Open to general inspection. Used esp. of documents. —*tr.v.* **-ent•ed, -ent•ing, -ents. 1.** To obtain a patent on or for (an invention, for example). **2.** To invent, originate, or be the proprietor of (an idea, for example). **3.** To grant a patent to or for. [ME, document granting a right, short for *(lettre) patent*, open (letter) < OFr. *(lettre) patente* < Lat. *patēns, patent-*, open, pr.part. of *patēre*, to be open. See **petə-***.] —**pat′ent•a•bil′i•ty** *n.* —**pat′ent•a•ble** *adj.*

pat•ent•ed (păt′n-tĭd) *adj.* **1.** Characteristic of, unique to, or originated by a particular person or group. **2.** Protected or conferred by a patent or letters patent.

pat•ent•ee (păt′n-tē′) *n.* The party that possesses or has been granted a patent.

patent leather *n.* Black leather finished to a hard glossy surface and used esp. for shoes and clothing accessories.

patent log *n. Naut.* A torpedo-shaped instrument with rotary fins that is dragged from the stern of a vessel to measure the speed or distance traveled.

pat•ent•ly (păt′nt-lē, pāt′-) *adv.* In a patent manner.

patent office *n.* A government bureau that studies claims for, grants, and maintains records of patents.

pat•en•tor (păt′n-tər, păt′n-tôr′) *n.* One that grants a patent.

pa•ter (pā′tər) *n. Chiefly British.* Father. [Lat. See **pəter-***.]

Pa•ter (pā′tər), **Walter Horatio.** 1839–94. British writer of *Studies in the History of the Renaissance* (1873).

pa•ter•fa•mil•i•as (pā′tər-fə-mĭl′ē-əs, pä′-, păt′ər-) *n., pl.* **pa•tres•fa•mil•i•as** (pā′trēz-fə-mĭl′ē-əs, pä′-, păt′rēz-). A man who is the head of a household or the father of a family. [Lat. *paterfamiliās* : *pater*, father; see PATER + *familiās*, archaic genitive of *familia*, family; see FAMILY.]

pa•ter•nal (pə-tûr′nəl) *adj.* **1.** Relating to or characteristic of a father or fatherhood; fatherly. **2.** Received or inherited from a father: *a paternal trait.* **3.** Related through one's father: *my paternal aunt.* [ME < OFr. < LLat. *paternālis* < Lat. *paternus* < *pater*, father. See **pəter-***.] —**pa•ter′nal•ly** *adv.*

pa•ter•nal•ism (pə-tûr′nə-lĭz′əm) *n.* A policy or practice of treating or governing people in a fatherly way, esp. by providing for them without giving them rights or responsibilities. —**pa•ter′nal•ist** *adj. & n.* —**pa•ter′nal•is′tic** *adj.*

pa•ter•ni•ty (pə-tûr′nĭ-tē) *n., pl.* **-ties. 1.** The state of being a father; fatherhood. **2.** Descent on a father's side; paternal descent. **3.** Authorship; origin. —*adj.* Of or relating to a lawsuit brought by a woman attempting to establish that a particular man is the father of her child and so must provide the child with financial support. [ME *paternite* < OFr. < LLat. *paternitās* < Lat. *paternus*, paternal. See PATERNAL.]

paternity leave *n.* A leave of absence from work granted to a father to care for an infant.

paternity test *n.* A test using blood group identification of a mother, child, and putative father to establish the probability of paternity. —**paternity testing** *n.*

pa•ter•nos•ter (pā′tər-nŏs′tər, pä′-, păt′ər-) *n.* **1.** Often **Paternoster.** The Lord's Prayer. **2.** One of the large beads on a rosary on which the Lord's Prayer is said. **3.** A sequence of words spoken as a prayer or a magic formula. **4.** An elevator constructed of a series of doorless compartments hung on chains that move slowly and continuously, allowing passengers to step on and off at will. [ME < OE < LLat. : Lat. *pater*, father; see PATER + Lat. *noster*, our; see **nes-**[2]***.]

Pat•er•son (păt′ər-sən). A city of NE NJ at the falls of the Passaic R. N of Newark; founded 1791. Pop. 140,891.

Paterson, William. 1745–1806. Irish-born jurist; associate justice of the U.S. Supreme Court (1793–1806).

path (păth, päth) *n., pl.* **paths** (păthz, päthz, păths, päths). **1.** A trodden track or way. **2.** A road, way, or track made for a particular purpose. **3.** The route or course along which something travels or moves. **4.** A course of action or conduct: *the path of righteousness.* [ME < OE *pæth*. See **pent-***.]

path. or **pathol.** *abbr.* **1.** Pathological. **2.** Pathology.

-path *suff.* **1.** A practitioner of a specified kind of medical treatment: *naturopath.* **2.** One affected by a specified kind of disorder: *sociopath.* [Back-formation < -PATHY.]

Pa•than (pə-tän′) *n.* A member of a Pashto-speaking people of eastern Afghanistan and northwest Pakistan, constituting the majority population of Afghanistan. [Hindi *Paṭhān* < Pashto *Pĕṣtana*, pl. of *Pĕṣtūn*, an Afghan < *paṣtu*, Pashto.]

pa•thet•ic (pə-thĕt′ĭk) also **pa•thet•i•cal** (-ĭ-kəl) *adj.* **1.** Arousing or capable of arousing sympathetic sadness and compassion. **2.** Arousing or capable of arousing scornful pity. [Fr. *pathétique* < LLat. *pathēticus* < Gk. *pathētikos*, sensitive < *pathētos*, liable to suffer < *pathos*, suffering. See **k^{w}ent(h)-***.] —**pa•thet′i•cal•ly** *adv.*

pathetic fallacy *n.* The attribution of human emotions or characteristics to inanimate objects or to nature.

path•find•er (păth′fīn′dər, päth′-) *n.* One that discovers a new course or way, esp. through or into unexplored regions.

patho- or **path-** *pref.* Disease; suffering: *pathogen.* [NLat. < Gk. < *pathos*, suffering. See **k^{w}ent(h)-***.]

path•o•bi•ol•o•gy (păth′ō-bī-ŏl′ə-jē) *n.* See **pathology** 1.

path•o•gen (păth′ə-jən) *n.* An agent that causes disease, esp. a living microorganism such as a bacterium or fungus.

path•o•gen•e•sis (păth′ə-jĕn′ĭ-sĭs) also **pa•thog•e•ny** (pă-thŏj′ə-nē) *n.* The development of a diseased condition.

path•o•gen•ic (păth′ə-jĕn′ĭk) also **path•o•ge•net•ic** (-jə-nĕt′ĭk) *adj.* **1.** Capable of causing disease. **2.** Originating or producing disease. **3.** Of or relating to pathogenesis. —**path′o•gen′i•cal•ly** *adv.* —**path′o•ge•nic′i•ty** (-jə-nĭs′ĭ-tē) *n.*

pa•thog•no•mon•ic (pə-thŏg′nə-mŏn′ĭk, păth′əg-nō-) *adj.* Characteristic or symptomatic of a particular disease or condition. [Gk. *pathognōmonikos* : *patho-*, patho- + *gnōmonikos*, able to judge (< *gnōmōn*, interpreter; see **gnō-***).]

path•o•log•i•cal (păth′ə-lŏj′ĭ-kəl) also **path•o•log•ic** (-ĭk) *adj.* **1.** Of or relating to pathology. **2.** Relating to or caused by disease. **3.** Of, relating to, or manifesting behavior that is habitual and compulsive. —**path′o•log′i•cal•ly** *adv.*

pa•thol•o•gy (pă-thŏl′ə-jē) *n., pl.* **-gies. 1.** The scientific study of the nature of disease and its causes. **2.** The anatomic or functional manifestations of a disease: *the pathology of cancer.* **3.** A departure or deviation from a normal condition. —**pa•thol′o•gist** *n.*

path•o•phys•i•ol•o•gy (păth′ō-fĭz′ē-ŏl′ə-jē) *n.* **1.** The functional changes associated with or resulting from disease or injury. **2.** The scientific study of such changes. —**path′o•phys′i•o•log′ic** (-ə-lŏj′ĭk), **path′o•phys′i•o•log′i•cal** (-ĭ-kəl) *adj.* —**path′o•phys′i•ol′o•gist** *n.*

pa•thos (pā′thŏs′, -thôs′) *n.* **1.** A quality, as of an experience or a work of art, that arouses feelings of pity, sympathy, tenderness, or sorrow. **2.** The feeling, as of sympathy or pity, so aroused. [Gk., suffering. See **k^{w}ent(h)-***.]

path•way (păth′wā′, päth′-) *n.* **1.** A path. **2.** *Physiol.* **a.** A course usu. followed by a body part. **b.** A chain of nerve fibers along which impulses normally travel. **c.** A sequence of enzymatic or other reactions by which one biological material is converted to another.

-pathy *suff.* **1.** Feeling; suffering; perception: *telepathy.* **2.a.** Disease: *neuropathy.* **b.** A system of treating disease: *homeopathy.* [Gk. *-patheia* < *pathos*. See **k^{w}ent(h)-***.]

pa•tience (pā′shəns) *n.* **1.** The capacity, quality, or fact of being patient. **2.** *Chiefly British.* The game solitaire.

Syns: *patience, long-suffering, resignation, forbearance.* These nouns all denote the capacity to endure hardship, difficulty, or inconvenience without complaint. *Patience* emphasizes calmness, self-control, and the willingness or ability to tolerate delay: *"Our patience will achieve more than our force"* (Edmund Burke). *Long-suffering* is long and patient endurance, as of wrong or provocation: *The general, a man not known for docility and long-suffering, flew into a rage. Resignation* implies acceptance of or submission to something trying, as out of despair or necessity: *undertook the job with an air of resignation. Forbearance* denotes restraint, as in retaliating, demanding what is due, or voicing disapproval: *"It is the mutual duty of all to practice Christian forbearance,*

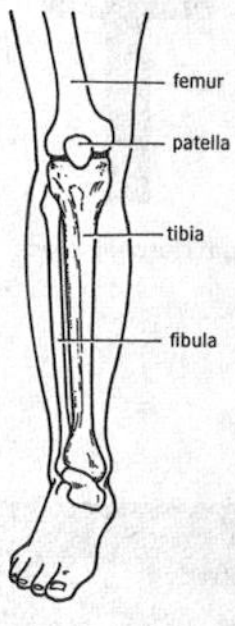

femur
patella
tibia
fibula

patella

ă pat	oi boy
ā pay	ou out
âr care	o͝o took
ä father	o͞o boot
ĕ pet	ŭ cut
ē be	ûr urge
ĭ pit	th thin
ī pie	*th* this
îr pier	hw which
ŏ pot	zh vision
ō toe	ə about,
ô paw	item

Stress marks:
′ (primary);
′ (secondary), as in
dictionary (dĭk′shə-nĕr′ē)

love, and charity towards each other" (Patrick Henry).

pa•tient (pā′shənt) *adj.* **1.** Bearing or enduring pain, difficulty, provocation, or annoyance with calmness. **2.** Marked by or exhibiting calm endurance of pain, difficulty, provocation, or annoyance. **3.** Tolerant; understanding. **4.** Persevering; constant. **5.** Capable of calmly awaiting an outcome or a result; not hasty or impulsive. **6.** Capable of patience. — *n.* **1.** One who receives medical attention, care, or treatment. **2.** *Archaic.* One who suffers. [ME *pacient* < OFr. < Lat. *patiēns, patient-*, pr.part. of *patī*, to endure. See **pē(i)-*.**] — **pa′tient•ly** *adv.*

pat•in (păt′n) *n.* Var. of **paten.**

patriarchal cross

pat•i•na[1] (păt′n-ə) *n., pl.* **pat•i•nae** (păt′n-ē). See **paten** 1. [Med.Lat. < Lat., plate. See PATEN.]

pat•i•na[2] (păt′n-ə, pə-tē′nə) also **pa•tine** (pă-tēn′) *n.* **1.** A thin greenish layer, usu. basic copper sulfate, that forms on copper or copper alloys, such as bronze, as a result of corrosion. **2.** The sheen on any surface, produced by age and use. **3.** A change in appearance produced by long-standing behavior, practice, or use. [Ital. < Lat., plate. See PATEN.]

pat•i•naed (păt′n-ĭd, pə-tē′nĭd) *adj.* Having a coating, covering, or sheen; patinated.

pat•i•nate (păt′n-āt′) *v.* **-nat•ed, -nat•ing, -nates.** — *tr.* To furnish with a patina. — *intr.* To acquire a patina.

pa•tine (pă-tēn′) *tr.v.* **-tined, -tin•ing, -tines.** To coat with a patina. [Fr. *patiner* < *patine*, patina < Ital. *patina.* See PATINA[2].]

pat•i•o (păt′ē-ō′, pä′tē-ō′) *n., pl.* **-os. 1.** An outdoor space for dining or recreation that adjoins a residence and is often paved. **2.** A roofless inner courtyard, typically found in Spanish and Spanish-style dwellings. [Sp. < OSp., poss. < OProv. *patu, pati*, pasture, perh. < Lat. *pactum*, agreement. See PACT.]

pa•tis•se•rie (pə-tĭs′ə-rē, pä-tēs-rē′) *n.* A bakery specializing in French pastry. [Fr. *pâtisserie* < OFr. *pastiserie* < *pasticier*, to make pastry < **pastitz*, pastry < VLat. **pastīcium* < LLat. *pasta*, dough. See PASTE[1].]

Linus Pauling
Photographed in 1962

Pát•mos also **Pat•mos** (păt′mŏs, -məs, pät′môs). An island of SE Greece in the Dodecanese Is. of the Aegean Sea.

Pat•na (pŭt′nə). A city of NE India on the Ganges R. NW of Calcutta; Asoka's cap. in the 3rd cent. B.C. Pop. 776,371.

pat•ois (păt′wä′, pă-twä′) *n., pl.* **pat•ois** (păt′wäz′, pă-twä′). **1.** A regional dialect, esp. one without a literary tradition. **2.a.** A creole. **b.** Nonstandard speech. **3.** The special jargon of a group; cant. [Fr. < OFr., poss. < *pate*, paw < VLat. **patta*, perh. of imit. orig.]

Pa•ton (pāt′n), **Alan Stewart.** 1903–88. South African writer noted for *Cry, the Beloved Country* (1948).

Pa•tos (păt′əs, pä′to͞os), **Lagoa dos.** A shallow tidal lagoon of SE Brazil separated from the Atlantic by a wide sandbar.

Pá•trai (pä′trē) also **Pa•tras** (pə-trăs′, păt′rəs). A city of S Greece in the NW Peloponnesus on the **Gulf of Pátrai,** or **Gulf of Patras,** an inlet of the Ionian Sea. Pop. 142,163.

Luciano Pavarotti

pa•tres•fa•mil•i•as (pā′trēz-fə-mĭl′ē-əs, pä′-, păt′rēz-) *n.* Pl. of **paterfamilias.**

patri– or **patr–** *pref.* Father, paternal: *patrilineal.* [Lat. (< *pater, patr-*, father) and Gk. (< *patēr, patr-*, father; see **pəter-***).]

pa•tri•arch (pā′trē-ärk′) *n.* **1.** A man who rules a family, clan, or tribe. **2.** In the Bible: **a.** One of the progenitors of the human race, from Adam to Noah. **b.** Abraham, Isaac, Jacob, or any of Jacob's 12 sons, the eponymous progenitors of the 12 tribes of Israel. **3.** Used formerly as a title for the bishops of Rome, Constantinople, Jerusalem, Antioch, and Alexandria. **4.** *Rom. Cath. Ch.* A bishop who holds the highest episcopal rank after the pope. **5.** *Eastern Orthodox Ch.* Any one of the bishops of the sees of Constantinople, Antioch, Alexandria, Moscow, and Jerusalem who has authority over other bishops. **6.** *Judaism.* The head of the Sanhedrin in Syrian Palestine from about 180 B.C. to A.D. 429. **7.** *Mormon Ch.* A high dignitary of the priesthood empowered to invoke blessings. **8.** One who is regarded as the founder or original head of an enterprise, an organization, or a tradition. **9.** A very old, venerable man; an elder. **10.** The oldest member of a group. [ME *patriarche* < OFr. < LLat. *patriarcha* < Gk. *patriarkhēs* : *patria*, lineage (< *patēr, patr-*, father; see **pəter-***) + *-arkhēs*, -arch.]

pavis
15th-century German

pa•tri•ar•chal (pā′trē-är′kəl) also **pa•tri•ar•chic** (-är′kĭk) *adj.* **1.** Of, relating to, or characteristic of a patriarch. **2.** Of or relating to a patriarchy. **3.** Ruled by a patriarch. — **pa′tri•ar′chal•ism** *n.* — **pa′tri•ar′chal•ly** *adv.*

patriarchal cross *n.* A Latin cross having two horizontal bars, of which the upper is the shorter.

pa•tri•ar•chate (pā′trē-är′kĭt, -kāt′) *n.* **1.** The territory, rule, or rank of a patriarch. **2.** See **patriarchy.**

pa•tri•ar•chy (pā′trē-är′kē) *n., pl.* **-chies. 1.** A social system in which the father heads the family and descent is traced through the father's side of the family. **2.** A family, community, or society based on this system or governed by men.

pa•tri•cian (pə-trĭsh′ən) *n.* **1.** A person of refined upbringing, manners, and tastes. **2.** A member of an aristocracy; an aristocrat. **3.** A member of one of the noble families of the ancient Roman Republic, which before the third century B.C. had exclusive rights to the Senate and the magistracies. **4.** Used as a title for members of a class of honorary nobility appointed by the Byzantine emperors. **5.** A member of the hereditary ruling class in the medieval free cities of Italy and Germany. [ME *patricion* < OFr. *patricien* < Lat. *patricius* < *patrēs (cōnscrīptī)*, enrolled fathers, senators, pl. of *pater, patr-*, father (see **pəter-***).] — **pa•tri′cian** *adj.* — **pa•tri′cian•ly** *adv.*

pa•tri•ci•ate (pə-trĭsh′ē-ĭt, -āt′) *n.* **1.** Nobility or aristocracy. **2.** The rank, position, or term of office of a patrician. [Lat. *patriciātus* < *patricius*, patrician. See PATRICIAN.]

pat•ri•cide (păt′rĭ-sīd′) *n.* **1.** The act of murdering one's father. **2.** One who murders one's father. [LLat. *patricīdium* and *patricīda* : Lat. *patri-*, patri- + *-cīdium, -cīda*, -cide.]

Pat•rick (păt′rĭk), Saint. A.D. 389?–461? Christian missionary and patron saint of Ireland.

pat•ri•lin•e•age (păt′rə-lĭn′ē-ĭj) *n.* The line of descent as traced through the paternal side of a family.

pat•ri•lin•e•al (păt′rə-lĭn′ē-əl) *adj.* Relating to, based on, or tracing ancestral descent through the paternal line.

pat•ri•lo•cal (păt′rə-lō′kəl) *adj. Anthro.* Of or relating to the residence of a husband's kin group or clan.

pat•ri•mo•ny (păt′rə-mō′nē) *n., pl.* **-nies. 1.a.** An inheritance from a father or other ancestor. **b.** An inheritance or a legacy; heritage. **2.** An endowment or estate of an institution, esp. a church. [ME < OFr. *patrimoine* < Lat. *patrimōnium* < *pater, patr-*, father. See **pəter-***.] — **pat′ri•mo′ni•al** *adj.*

pa•tri•ot (pā′trē-ət, -ŏt′) *n.* One who loves, supports, and defends one's country. [Fr. *patriote* < OFr., compatriot < LLat. *patriōta* < Gk. *patriōtēs* < *patrios*, of one's fathers < *patēr, patr-*, father. See **pəter-***.]

pa•tri•ot•ic (pā′trē-ŏt′ĭk) *adj.* Feeling, expressing, or inspired by love for one's country. — **pa′tri•ot′i•cal•ly** *adv.*

pa•tri•ot•ism (pā′trē-ə-tĭz′əm) *n.* Love of and devotion to one's country.

Pa•tri•ots' Day (pā′trē-əts, -ŏts′) *n.* The third Monday in April, a holiday in Maine and Massachusetts commemorating the battles of Lexington and Concord in 1775.

pa•tris•tic (pə-trĭs′tĭk) also **pa•tris•ti•cal** (-tĭ-kəl) *adj.* Of or relating to the fathers of the early Christian church or their writings. — **pa•tris′ti•cal•ly** *adv.*

pa•tris•tics (pə-trĭs′tĭks) *n.* *(used with a sing. v.)* **1.** The study of the lives, writings, and doctrines of the Church fathers. **2.** The writings of the Church fathers.

Pa•tro•clus (pə-trō′kləs) *n. Gk. Myth.* A Greek warrior and friend to Achilles, killed by Hector in the Trojan War.

pa•trol (pə-trōl′) *n.* **1.** The act of moving about an area esp. by an authorized and trained person or group, for purposes of observation, inspection, or security. **2.** A person or group of persons who perform such an act. **3.a.** A military unit sent out on a reconnaissance or combat mission. **b.** One or more military vehicles, boats, ships, or aircraft assigned to guard or reconnoiter a given area. **4.** A division of a Boy Scout troop consisting of between six and eight boys. — *v.* **-trolled, -trol•ling, -trols.** — *tr.* To engage in a patrol of. — *intr.* To engage in a patrol. [Fr. *patrouille* < *patrouiller*, to patrol, alteration of OFr. *patouiller*, to paddle about in mud, patrol, prob. < *pate*, paw. See PATOIS.] — **pa•trol′ler** *n.*

patrol car *n.* See **squad car.**

pa•trol•man (pə-trōl′mən) *n.* **1.** A policeman who patrols or polices an assigned area. **2.** One who patrols an assigned area.

patrol wagon *n.* An enclosed police truck for prisoners.

pa•trol•wom•an (pə-trōl′wo͝om′ən) *n.* A policewoman who patrols or polices an assigned area.

pa•tron (pā′trən) *n.* **1.** One that supports or champions someone or something; a sponsor or benefactor: *a patron of the arts.* **2.** A customer, esp. a regular customer. **3.** (*also* pä-trōn′). The owner or manager of an establishment, esp. a French or Spanish restaurant or inn. **4.a.** A noble or wealthy person in ancient Rome who granted favor and protection to someone in exchange for certain services. **b.** A slave owner in ancient Rome who freed a slave without relinquishing all legal claim to him. **5.** One who possesses the right to grant an ecclesiastical benefice to a member of the clergy. **6.** A patron saint. **7.** *Naut.* The captain or master of a ship, esp. a barge. [ME < OFr. < Med.Lat. *patrōnus* < Lat. < *pater, patr-*, father. See **pəter-***.] — **pa′tron•al** (pā′trə-nəl) *adj.*

pa•tron•age (pā′trə-nĭj, păt′rə-) *n.* **1.** Support, encouragement, or championship, as of a person or a cause, from a patron. **2.** Support or encouragement proffered in a condescending manner. **3.** The trade given to a commercial establishment by its customers. **4.** Customers or patrons considered as a group; clientele. **5.a.** The power to distribute or appoint people to governmental or political positions. **b.** The act of distributing or appointing people to such positions. **c.** The positions so distributed or filled. **6.** The right to grant an ecclesiastical benefice to a member of the clergy.

pa•tron•ess (pā′trə-nĭs) *n.* **1.** A woman who supports, protects, or champions someone or something; a sponsor or benefactor. **2.** A woman who possesses the right to grant an ecclesiastical benefice to a member of the clergy.

pa•tron•ize (pā′trə-nīz′, păt′rə-) *tr.v.* **-ized, -iz•ing, -iz•es. 1.** To act as a patron to; support or sponsor. **2.** To go to as a customer, esp. on a regular basis. **3.** To treat in a condescending manner. **— pa′tron·i·za′tion** (-trə-nĭ-zā′shən) *n.*

patron saint *n.* A saint who is regarded as the intercessor and advocate in heaven of a nation, place, craft, class, or person.

pat·ro·nym·ic (păt′rə-nĭm′ĭk) *adj.* Of, relating to, or derived from the name of one's father or a paternal ancestor. *—n.* A name so derived. [LLat. *patrōnymicus* < Gk. *patrōnumikos* < *patrōnumos*, named after one's father : *patēr, patr-*, father + *onuma*, name; see **nō-men-***.] **— pat′ro·nym′i·cal·ly** *adv.*

pa·troon (pə-tro͞on′) *n.* A landholder in New Netherland who, under Dutch colonial rule, was granted proprietary and manorial rights to a large tract of land in exchange for bringing 50 new settlers to the colony. [Du. < Fr. *patron*, patron, master < OFr. See PATRON.]

pat·sy (păt′sē) *n., pl.* **-sies.** *Slang.* A person easily taken advantage of, cheated, blamed, or ridiculed. [Perh. < Ital. *pazzo*, fool < OItal. *paccio*.]

pat·ten (păt′n) *n.* Any one of various types of wooden-soled footwear, such as a sandal or clog, worn to increase one's height or keep one's feet out of the mud. [ME *patin* < OFr., perh. < *pate*, paw, hoof. See PATOIS.]

pat·ter[1] (păt′ər) *v.* **-tered, -ter·ing, -ters.** *—intr.* **1.** To make a quick series of light soft tapping sounds. **2.** To move with quick, light, softly audible steps. *—tr.* To cause to patter. *—n.* A quick succession of pattering sounds. [Freq. of PAT[1].]

pat·ter[2] (păt′ər) *v.* **-tered, -ter·ing, -ters.** *—intr.* **1.** To speak or chatter glibly and rapidly. **2.** To mumble prayers in a mechanical manner. *—tr.* To utter in a pattering manner. *—n.* **1.** The jargon of a particular group; cant. **2.** Glib rapid speech, as of a salesperson. **3.** Meaningless talk; chatter. [ME *patren* < *paternoster*, paternoster (< its sometimes pattering recitation). See PATERNOSTER.] **— pat′ter·er** *n.*

pat·tern (păt′ərn) *n.* **1.a.** A model or an original used as an archetype. **b.** A person or thing considered worthy of imitation. **2.** A plan, diagram, or model to be followed in making things. **3.** A representative sample; a specimen. **4.a.** An artistic or decorative design. **b.** A design of natural or accidental origin. **5.** A consistent characteristic form, style, or method, as: **a.** A composite of traits or features characteristic of an individual or a group. **b.** Form and style in an artistic work or body of artistic works. **6.a.** The configuration of gunshots upon a target that is used as an indication of skill in shooting. **b.** The distribution and spread, around a targeted region, of spent shrapnel, bomb fragments, or shot from a shotgun. **7.** Enough material to make a complete garment. **8.** A test pattern. **9.** The flight path of an aircraft about to land. *—v.* **-terned, -tern·ing, -terns.** *—tr.* **1.** To make, mold, or design by following a pattern. **2.** To cover or ornament with a design or pattern. *—intr.* To make a pattern. [ME *patron* < OFr. See PATRON.]

pat·tern·ing (păt′ər-nĭng) *n.* **1.** Design, structure, or configuration of a form, style, or method. **2.** Physical therapy in which a pattern of exercises is imposed to stimulate weak or paralyzed nerves and muscles to act on their own.

pat·tern·mak·er also **pattern maker** (păt′ərn-mā′kər) *n.* One who makes patterns, as for sewing, carpentry, or industrial machinery. **— pat′tern·mak′ing** *n.*

Pat·ti (păt′ē, pä′tē), **Adelina.** 1843–1919. Spanish-born Italian coloratura soprano.

Pat·ton (păt′n), **George Smith, Jr.** 1885–1945. Amer. general who led the Allied armies into Germany (1944–45).

pat·ty (păt′ē) *n., pl.* **-ties. 1.** A small rounded flattened cake of food, esp. one made from ground ingredients. **2.** A patty shell. **3.** A small pie; a pasty. [Fr. *pâté*, pâté < OFr. *paste*, paste. See PASTY[2].]

pat·ty·pan squash (păt′ē-păn′) *n.* A variety of squash *(Cucurbita Pepo)* having a wheel-shaped fruit, ribbed white skin, and creamy white flesh.

patty shell *n.* An edible shell of baked puff pastry that is made to be filled with other food, such as creamed meat.

pat·u·lous (păch′ə-ləs) also **pat·u·lent** (-lənt) *adj. Bot.* Spreading or expanded. [< Lat. *patulus* < *patēre*, to be open. See **petə-***.] **— pat′u·lous·ness** *n.*

pat·zer (păt′sər, pät′-) *n. Slang.* A poor or amateurish chess player. [Prob. < Ger., bungler < *patzen*, to bungle.]

Pau (pō). A city of SW France in the foothills of the Pyrenees S of Bordeaux. Pop. 83,790.

PAU also **P.A.U.** *abbr.* Pan American Union.

pau·ci·ty (pô′sĭ-tē) *n.* **1.** Smallness of number; fewness. **2.** Scarcity; dearth. [ME *paucite* < OFr. < Lat. *paucitās* < *paucus*, few. See **pau-***.]

Paul (pôl), Saint. A.D. 5?–67? Apostle to the Gentiles whose life and teachings appear in the Acts of the Apostles. **— Paul′ine** (-īn, -ēn) *adj.*

Paul I[1]. 1754–1801. Russian czar (1796–1801) who led military campaigns against France (1798–1800).

Paul I[2]. 1901–64. King of Greece (1947–64) who took refuge in South Africa during World War II.

Paul III. 1468–1549. Pope (1534–49) who initiated the Catholic Reformation.

Paul VI. 1897–1978. Pope (1963–78) noted for easing regulations on fasting and interfaith marriages.

Paul, Alice. 1885–1977. Amer. feminist who wrote (1923) the first equal rights amendment considered by Congress.

Paul Bun·yan (bŭn′yən) *n.* A giant lumberjack noted for superhuman acts in American folklore.

Pau·li (pou′lē), **Wolfgang.** 1900–58. Austrian-born Amer. physicist who won a 1945 Nobel Prize.

Pau·li exclusion principle (pô′lē, pou′-) *n.* See **exclusion principle.** [After Wolfgang PAULI.]

Pau·ling (pô′lĭng), **Linus Carl.** b. 1901. Amer. chemist who won a 1954 Nobel Prize and the 1962 Nobel Peace Prize.

Paul·ist (pô′lĭst) *n.* A member of the Roman Catholic Missionary Society of Saint Paul the Apostle, founded in New York in 1858.

pau·low·ni·a (pô-lō′nē-ə) *n.* Any of several Chinese deciduous trees of the genus *Paulownia*, having large heart-shaped opposite leaves and pyramidal flower panicles. [NLat., genus name, after Anna *Paulovna* (1795–1865), Russian princess.]

paunch (pônch, pänch) *n.* **1.** The belly, esp. a potbelly. **2.** See **rumen.** [ME *paunche* < OFr. *panche* < Lat. *pantex*.]

paunch·y (pôn′chē, pän′-) *adj.* **-i·er, -i·est.** Having a potbelly. **— paunch′i·ness** *n.*

pau·per (pô′pər) *n.* **1.** One who is extremely poor. **2.** One living on or eligible for public charity. [< Lat., poor. See **pau-***.] **— pau′per·ism** *n.*

pau·per·ize (pô′pə-rīz′) *tr.v.* **-ized, -iz·ing, -iz·es.** To make a pauper of. **— pau′per·i·za′tion** (-pər-ĭ-zā′shən) *n.*

pau·piette (pō-pyĕt′) *n.* A thin slice of meat or fish wrapped around a forcemeat or vegetable filling. [Fr., prob. < obsolete *poulpe*, fleshy part < OFr. *polpe* < Lat. *pulpa*.]

Pau·sa·ni·as (pô-sā′nē-əs). fl. 2nd cent. A.D. Greek geographer and historian who wrote *Periegesis of Greece*.

pause (pôz) *intr.v.* **paused, paus·ing, paus·es. 1.** To cease or suspend an action temporarily. **2.** To linger; tarry. **3.** To hesitate. *—n.* **1.** A temporary cessation. **2.** A delay or suspended reaction, as from uncertainty; a hesitation. **3.** A break, stop, or rest, often for a calculated purpose or effect. **4.a.** *Mus.* A sign indicating that a note or rest is to be held. **b.** A caesura in poetry. **5.** Reason for hesitation. [< ME, pause < OFr. < Lat. *pausa* < Gk. *pausis* < *pauein*, to stop.]

Syns: *pause, intermission, recess, respite, suspension.* The central meaning shared by these nouns is "a temporary stop, as in activity": *a short pause in the conversation; a concert with the usual 15-minute intermission; the legislature's summer recess; toiling without respite; a suspension of work.*

pa·vane also **pa·van** (pə-vän′, -văn′) *n.* **1.** A slow, stately court dance of the 16th and 17th centuries. **2.** Its music. [Fr. *pavane* < Ital. *pavana* < fem. of *pavano*, of Padua < dial. *pavàn* < *Pava*, dialectal var. of *Padova*, Padua.]

Pav·a·rot·ti (păv′ə-rŏt′ē, pä′vä-rôt′tē), **Luciano.** b. 1935. Italian-born operatic tenor.

pave (pāv) *tr.v.* **paved, pav·ing, paves. 1.** To cover with a pavement. **2.** To cover uniformly, as if with pavement. **3.** To be or compose the pavement of. **—*idiom.* pave the way.** To make progress or development easier. [ME *paven* < OFr. *paver* < Lat. *pavīre*, to beat, tread down. See **peu-***.] **— pav′er** *n.*

pa·vé (pă-vā′, păv′ā) *n.* A setting of precious stones placed together so closely that no metal shows: *diamonds in pavé.* [Fr. < p.part. of *paver*, to pave < OFr. See PAVE.] **— pa·vé** *adj.*

pave·ment (pāv′mənt) *n.* **1.a.** A hard smooth surface, esp. of a public area or way, that will bear travel. **b.** Material for making such a surface. **2.** *Chiefly British.* A sidewalk.

Pa·vi·a (pə-vē′ə, pä-vē′ä). A city of NW Italy S of Milan; orig. a Roman stronghold known as Ticinum. Pop. 85,056.

pav·id (păv′ĭd) *adj.* Exhibiting or experiencing fear; timid. [Lat. *pavidus* < *pavēre*, to fear. See **peu-***.]

pa·vil·ion (pə-vĭl′yən) *n.* **1.** An ornate tent. **2.a.** A light roofed structure for amusement or shelter, as at parks. **b.** A usu. temporary structure housing an exhibition at a fair or show. **c.** A large structure housing sports or entertainment facilities; an arena. **3.** A structure or building connected to a larger building; an annex. **4.** One of the buildings in a complex. **5.** The lower surface of a brilliant-cut gem, slanting outward from the culet to the girdle. *—tr.v.* **-ioned, -ion·ing, -ions. 1.** To cover or furnish with or as if with a pavilion. **2.** To put in or as if in a pavilion. [ME *pavilon* < OFr. *pavillon* < Lat. *pāpiliō, pāpiliōn-*, butterfly, tent.]

pav·ing (pā′vĭng) *n.* **1.** The act or technique of laying pavement. **2.** A pavement. **3.** Material used for pavement.

pav·is also **pav·isse** (păv′ĭs) *n.* A medieval shield large enough to protect the whole body. [ME < OFr. *pavais* < OItal. *pavese* < PAVIA.]

Pav·lo·dar (păv′lə-där′, pə-vlə-). A town of NE Kazakhstan on the Irtysh R. SE of Omsk. Pop. 315,000.

Pav·lov (păv′lôf′, -lôv′, päv′ləf), **Ivan Petrovich.** 1849–1936. Russian physiologist who won a 1904 Nobel Prize. **— Pav·lo′vi·an** (păv-lō′vē-ən, -lô′-) *adj.*

Pav·lo·va (păv-lō′və, päv-, păv′lə-, päv′-), **Anna.** 1882–1931. Russian ballerina famous for her role in *Swan Lake.*

Pavlovian conditioning *n.* Classical conditioning.

Pa·vo (pā′vō) *n.* A constellation in the Southern Hemisphere near Apus and Indus. [Lat. *pāvō*, peacock.]

pav·o·nine (păv′ə-nīn′) *adj.* **1.** Of or resembling a peacock.

Anna Pavlova
In character for
The Dying Swan

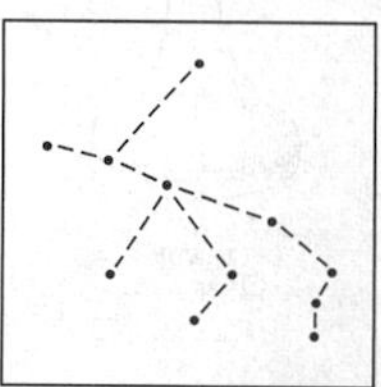

Pavo

ă pat	oi boy
ā pay	ou out
âr care	o͝o took
ä father	o͞o boot
ĕ pet	ŭ cut
ē be	ûr urge
ĭ pit	th thin
ī pie	*th* this
îr pier	hw which
ŏ pot	zh vision
ō toe	ə about, item
ô paw	

Stress marks:
′ (primary);
′ (secondary), as in
dictionary (dĭk′shə-nĕr′ē)

2. Resembling a peacock's tail in color, design, or iridescence. [Lat. *pāvōnīnus* < *pāvō*, peacock.]

paw (pô) *n.* **1.** The nailed or clawed foot of an animal, esp. of a quadruped. **2.** *Informal.* A human hand, esp. a large clumsy one. —*v.* **pawed, paw•ing, paws.** —*tr.* **1.** To strike with the paw or paws. **2.** To strike or scrape with a beating motion. **3.** To handle clumsily, rudely, or with too much familiarity. —*intr.* **1.** To scrape the ground with the forefeet. **2.** To paw someone or something as in rudeness. [ME *pawe* < OFr. *powe.*] —**paw′er** *n.*

pawk•y (pô′ke) *adj.* **-i•er, -i•est.** *Chiefly British.* Shrewd and cunning, often humorously. [< E. dial. *pawk*, a trick.]

pawl (pôl) *n.* A hinged or pivoted device that fits into a notch of a ratchet wheel to impart forward motion or prevent backward motion. [Prob. < Du. *pal* < Lat. *pālus*, stake. See **pag-***.]

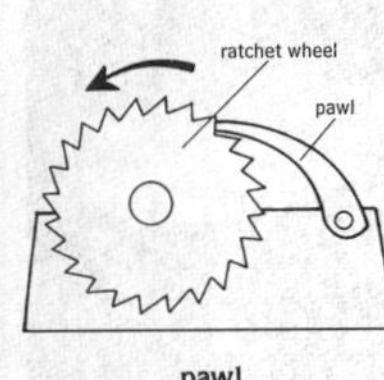

pawl

pawn[1] (pôn) *n.* **1.** Something given as security for a loan; a pledge or guaranty. **2.** The condition of being held as a pawn: *jewels in pawn.* **3.** A person serving as security; a hostage. **4.** The act of pawning. —*tr.v.* **pawned, pawn•ing, pawns. 1.** To give or deposit (property) as security for the payment of money borrowed. **2.** To risk; hazard: *pawn one's honor.* [ME *paun* < OFr. *pan*, of Germanic origin.] —**pawn′a•ble** *adj.* —**pawn′age** *n.* —**pawn′er** (pô′nər), **paw′nor′** (-nôr′) *n.*

pawn[2] (pôn) *n.* **1.** *Games.* A chess piece of the lowest value. **2.** A person or an entity used to further the purposes of another: *treated as a political pawn.* [ME < OFr. *pedon, paon* < Med.Lat. *pedō, pedōn-*, foot soldier < LLat., one who has wide feet < Lat. *pēs, ped-*, foot. See **ped-***.]

pawn[2]
Chess piece

pawn•bro•ker (pôn′brō′kər) *n.* One that lends money at interest in exchange for personal property deposited as security. —**pawn′bro′king** *n.*

Paw•nee (pô-nē′) *n., pl.* **Pawnee** or **-nees. 1.** A member of a Native American people formerly inhabiting the Platte River valley in south-central Nebraska and northern Kansas, with a present-day population in north-central Oklahoma. **2.** The Caddoan language of the Pawnee. [N.Amer.Fr. *Pani*, of Illinois orig., ult. of Siouan orig.]

pawn•shop (pôn′shŏp′) *n.* The shop of a pawnbroker.

pawn ticket *n.* A receipt for goods pawned.

paw•paw (pô′pô) *n.* Var. of **papaw.**

Paw•tuck•et (pô-tŭk′ĭt, pə-). A city of NE RI, a suburb of Providence. Pop. 72,644.

pay[1] (pā) *v.* **paid** (pād), **pay•ing, pays.** —*tr.* **1.** To give money to in return for goods or services rendered. **2.** To give (money) in exchange for goods or services. **3.** To discharge or settle (a debt or an obligation). **4.a.** To give recompense for; requite: *pay back a kindness.* **b.** To give recompense to; reward or punish: *paid him back for his insult.* **5.** To bear (a cost or penalty, for example) in recompense. **6.** To yield as a return: *paid 12 percent.* **7.** To afford an advantage to; profit. **8.** To give or bestow. **9.** To make (a visit or call). **10.** *P.t. and p.part.* **paid** or **payed** (pād). To let out (a line or cable) by slackening. —*intr.* **1.** To give money in exchange for goods or services. **2.** To discharge a debt or an obligation. **3.** To bear a cost or penalty in recompense. **4.** To be profitable or worthwhile. —*adj.* **1.** Of, relating to, giving, or receiving payments. **2.** Requiring payment to use or operate. **3.** Yielding valuable metal in mining. —*n.* **1.** The act of paying or state of being paid. **2.** Money given in return for work done; salary; wages. **3.a.** Recompense or reward. **b.** Retribution or punishment. **4.** Paid employment. **5.** One considered with regard to one's credit or reliability in discharging debts. —***phrasal verbs.*** **pay off. 1.** To pay the full amount on (a debt). **2.** To effect profit. **3.** To get revenge for or on; requite. **4.** To pay the wages due to (an employee) upon discharge. **5.** *Informal.* To bribe. **pay out. 1.** To give (money) out; spend. **2.** To let out (a line or rope) by slackening. **pay up.** To give over the full monetary amount demanded. —***idioms.*** **pay (one's) dues.** To earn a position through hard work, long-term experience, or suffering. **pay (one's) way.** To contribute one's own share; pay for oneself. **pay the piper.** To bear the consequences of something. **pay through the nose.** *Informal.* To pay excessively. [ME *paien* < OFr. *paiier* < LLat., to appease < Lat. *pācāre*, to pacify < *pāx, pāc-*, peace. See **pag-***.]

pay[2] (pā) *tr.v.* **payed** or **paid** (pād), **pay•ing, pays.** *Naut.* To coat or cover (seams of a ship, for example) with waterproof material such as tar or asphalt. [Obsolete Fr. *peier* < OFr. < Lat. *picāre* < *pix, pic-*, pitch.]

pay•a•ble (pā′ə-bəl) *adj.* **1.** Requiring payment on a certain date; due. **2.** Requiring payment to a particular person or entity. **3.** Capable of producing profit: *a payable business.* —*n.* Money owed to a creditor. Often used in the plural.

pay-as-you-go also **pay as you go** (pā′əz-yo͞o-gō′) *n.* The system or practice of paying debts as they are incurred. —**pay′-as-you-go′** *adj.*

pay•back (pā′băk′) *n.* **1.a.** The return gained from or paid on an investment. **b.** The return on an investment equal to the amount invested. **2.** A benefit gained as the result of a previous action. **3.** The act or process of paying back.

pay•check (pā′chĕk′) *n.* **1.** A check issued to an employee in payment of salary or wages. **2.** Salary or wages.

pay•day (pā′dā′) *n.* The day on which employees' salaries or wages are paid.

pay dirt *n.* **1.** Earth, ore, or gravel that is profitable to mine. **2.** *Informal.* A useful or profitable discovery or venture.

pay•ee (pā-ē′) *n.* One to whom money is paid.

pay equity *n.* Comparable worth.

pay•er (pā′ər) *n.* **1.** One that pays: *a prompt payer of bills.* **2.** One named responsible for paying a bill or note.

pay•load (pā′lōd′) *n.* **1.** The revenue-producing part of a cargo. **2.a.** The total weight of passengers and cargo that an aircraft carries or can carry. **b.** The total weight of the instruments, crew, and life-support systems that a spacecraft carries or can carry. **c.** The passengers, crew, instruments, or equipment carried by an aircraft, a spacecraft, or a rocket. **3.** The explosive charge carried in the warhead of a missile.

pay•mas•ter (pā′măs′tər) *n.* A person in charge of paying wages and salaries.

pay•ment (pā′mənt) *n.* **1.** The act of paying or the state of being paid. **2.** An amount paid: *received a large payment.* **3.** One's due, reward, or punishment; requital.

pay•nim (pā′nĭm) *n. Archaic.* **1.** A non-Christian, esp. a Muslim. **2.** A pagan or heathen. [ME *painim* < OFr. *paienime*, heathendom < LLat. *pāgānismus* < *pāgānus*, pagan. See PAGAN.]

pay•off (pā′ôf′, -ŏf′) *n.* **1.a.** Full payment of a salary or wages. **b.** The time of such payment. **2.** *Informal.* **a.** A final settlement or reckoning. **b.** The climax of a narrative or sequence of events. **3.** Final retribution or revenge. **4.** *Informal.* A bribe.

pay•o•la (pā-ō′lə) *n.* **1.** Bribery, esp. the bribing of disc jockeys to promote records. **2.** A bribe, esp. one given to a disc jockey. [Prob. PAY(OFF) + *(Victr)ola*, a phonograph.]

pay•out (pā′out′) *n.* **1.** The act or an instance of paying out. **2.** A percentage of corporate earnings that is paid as dividends to shareholders.

pay•roll also **pay roll** (pā′rōl′) *n.* **1.** A list of employees receiving wages or salaries, with the amounts due to each. **2.** The total amount paid to employees in a given period.

payt. *abbr.* Payment.

pay-TV (pā′tē-vē′) *n.* A system for receiving television broadcasts by making subscription payments, as by renting a device that unscrambles the broadcaster's scrambled signal.

Paz (päz, päs), **Octavio.** b. 1914. Mexican writer who won the 1990 Nobel Prize for literature.

Pb The symbol for the element **lead[2]** 1. [Lat. *plumbum*, lead.]

PBS *abbr.* Public Broadcasting Service.

PBX also **P.B.X.** *abbr.* Private branch exchange.

PC *abbr.* **1.** *Comp. Sci.* Personal computer. **2.** Or **p.c. a.** Politically correct. **b.** Political correctness.

p.c. *abbr.* **1.** Percent. **2.** Post card. **3.** *Lat.* Post cibum (after meals).

P.C. *abbr.* **1.** Past Commander. **2.** Police constable. **3.** Post commander. **4.** Privy Council.

p/c or **P/C** *abbr.* **1.** Also **p.c.** Petty cash. **2.** Prices current.

PCB (pē′sē-bē′) *n.* Any of a family of industrial chemical compounds produced by chlorination of biphenyl, noted as an environmental pollutant that accumulates in animal tissue with resultant pathogenic and teratogenic effects. [P(OLY)C(HLORINATED) B(IPHENYL).]

PCP[1] (pē′sē-pē′) *n.* Phencyclidine. [< the chemical name *p(henyl)c(yclohexyl)p(iperidine).*]

PCP[2] *abbr.* Pneumocystis pneumonia.

PCR *abbr.* Polymerase chain reaction.

pct. *abbr.* Percent.

Pd The symbol for the element **palladium[1]**.

pd. *abbr.* Paid.

p.d. or **P.D.** *abbr.* Per diem.

P.D. *abbr.* **1.** Police Department. **2.** Postal district. **3.** Potential difference.

PDT or **P.D.T.** *abbr.* Pacific Daylight Time.

pe[1] (pā) *n.* The 17th letter of the Hebrew alphabet. [Heb. *pê*, mouth, pe.]

pe[2] also **p.e.** *abbr.* Printer's error.

PE *abbr.* Prince Edward Island.

P.E. *abbr.* **1.** Physical Education. **2.** *Statistics.* Probable error. **3.** Professional Engineer.

pea (pē) *n.* **1.** A member of the pea family. **2.** A Eurasian climbing annual vine *(Pisum sativum)* cultivated in temperate zones and having compound leaves with terminal leaflets modified into tendrils and globose edible seeds enclosed in a green pod. **3.** The seed of this plant, used as a vegetable. **4.** The unopened pod of this plant. Also used in the plural. **5.** Any of several plants of the genus *Lathyrus,* such as the sweet pea. [Back-formation < ME *pease* (mistaken for pl.) < OE *pise, piose* < LLat. *pīsa*, var. of Lat. *pīsum* < Gk. *pison.*]

pea bean *n.* The navy bean.

Pea•bod•y (pē′bŏd′ē, -bə-dē). A city of NE MA W of Salem; settled c. 1633. Pop. 47,039.

Peabody, Elizabeth Palmer. 1804–94. Amer. educator who founded the first kindergarten in the U.S. (1860).

Peabody, George. 1795–1869. Amer. merchant and philanthropist who endowed the Peabody Institute of Baltimore.

pea•bod•y bird (pē′bŏd′ē, -bə-dē) *n.* The white-throated sparrow. [Prob. imit. of its song.]

peace (pēs) *n.* **1.** The absence of war or other hostilities. **2.** An agreement or a treaty to end hostilities. **3.** Freedom from quarrels and disagreement; harmonious relations. **4.** Public security and order. **5.** Inner contentment; serenity. —*interj.* Used as a greeting or farewell and as a request for silence. —***idioms.* at peace. 1.** In a state of tranquillity; serene. **2.** Free from strife. **keep (or hold) one's peace.** To be silent. **keep the peace.** To maintain or observe law and order. [ME *pes* < OFr. *pais, pes* < Lat. *pāx, pāc-*. See **pag-***.]

peace•a•ble (pē′sə-bəl) *adj.* **1.** Inclined or disposed to peace; promoting calm: *They met in a peaceable spirit.* **2.** Peaceful; undisturbed. —**peace′a•ble•ness** *n.* —**peace′a•bly** *adv.*

Peace Corps (pēs) *n.* A U.S. government organization that sends volunteers to work on technological, agricultural, and educational projects in developing countries.

peace•ful (pēs′fəl) *adj.* **1.** Undisturbed by strife, turmoil, or disagreement; tranquil. See Syns at **calm. 2.** Inclined or disposed to peace; peaceable. **3.** Of or characteristic of a condition of peace. —**peace′ful•ly** *adv.* —**peace′ful•ness** *n.*

peace•keep•er (pēs′kē′pər) *n.* **1.** One that preserves or promotes peace. **2.** A member of a military force engaged in peacekeeping, often under international sanction.

peace•keep•ing (pēs′kē′pĭng) *adj.* Of or relating to the preservation of peace, esp. the supervision by international forces of a truce between hostile nations. —**peace′keep′ing** *n.*

peace•mak•er (pēs′mā′kər) *n.* One that makes peace, esp. by settling disputes. —**peace′mak′ing** *adj. & n.*

peace•nik (pēs′nĭk) *n. Informal.* A person against war or the proliferation of weapons; a pacifist.

peace offering *n.* An offering made to an adversary in the interests of peace or reconciliation.

peace officer *n.* A law enforcement officer, such as a sheriff, who is responsible for maintaining civil peace.

peace pipe *n.* A calumet.

Peace River. A river, c. 1,521 km (945 mi), rising in central British Columbia, Canada, and flowing E to Alberta then NE to the Slave River near Lake Athabasca.

peace sign *n.* A hand sign made with the palm forward and the middle and index fingers forming a V to express peace.

peace•time (pēs′tīm′) *n.* A time free from war. —**peace′-time′** *adj.*

peach[1] (pēch) *n.* **1.a.** A small Chinese tree *(Prunus persica)* widely cultivated in temperate regions and having pink flowers and edible fruit. **b.** The soft juicy fruit of this tree, having yellow flesh, downy red-tinted yellow skin, and a stone containing a single seed. **2.** *Color.* A light yellowish pink to light orange. **3.** *Informal.* A particularly admirable or pleasing person or thing. [ME *peche* < OFr., a peach < Lat. *persica*, peach tree, ult. < *persicus*, Persian < PERSIA.]

peach[2] (pēch) *v.* **peached, peach•ing, peach•es.** —*intr.* To inform on someone; turn informer. —*tr.* To inform against. [ME *pechen* < *apechen*, to accuse (prob. < AN **anpecher* < LLat. *impedicāre*, to entangle; see IMPEACH) and < *empechen*, to accuse; see IMPEACH.]

peach palm *n.* A densely spiny, widely cultivated Amazonian palm *(Bactris gasipaes)* having an edible heart and a highly nutritious, mealy fruit wall.

peach•y (pē′chē) *adj.* **-i•er, -i•est. 1.** Resembling a peach, esp. in color or texture. **2.** *Informal.* Splendid; fine. —**peach′i•ness** *n.*

pea coat *n.* See **pea jacket.**

pea•cock (pē′kŏk′) *n.* **1.a.** A male peafowl, distinguished by its crested head, brilliant blue or green plumage, and long modified back feathers that are marked with iridescent eyelike spots and can be spread in a fanlike form. **b.** A peafowl, either male or female. **2.** A vain person; a dandy. —*intr.v.* **-cocked, -cock•ing, -cocks.** To strut about like a peacock; exhibit oneself vainly. [ME *pocock, pecok* : *po*, peacock (< OE *pawa, pēa*, peafowl < Lat. *pāvō*, peacock) + ME *cok*; see COCK[1].] —**pea′cock′ish, pea′cock′y** *adj.*

Pea•cock (pē′kŏk′), **Thomas Love.** 1785–1866. British writer whose satirical novels include *Nightmare Abbey* (1818).

peacock blue *n. Color.* A moderate to dark or strong greenish blue. —**pea′cock-blue′** (pē′kŏk-blo͞o′) *adj.*

peacock orchid *n.* See **acidanthera.**

pea family *n.* A large and widespread family of plants, the Leguminosae (Fabaceae), characterized by stipulate, usu. compound leaves, often bilaterally symmetrical flowers, and legume fruits and including such food plants as beans and peas.

pea•fowl (pē′foul′) *n., pl.* **peafowl** or **-fowls.** Either of two large pheasants, *Pavo cristatus* of India and Sri Lanka or *P. muticus* of southeast Asia. [PEA(COCK) + FOWL.]

peag also **peage** (pēg) *n.* See **wampum** 1. [Short for WAMPUMPEAG.]

pea green *n. Color.* A moderate, strong, or brilliant yellow green. —**pea′-green′** (pē′grēn′) *adj.*

pea•hen (pē′hĕn′) *n.* A female peafowl. [ME *pohen, pehenne* : *po*, peacock; see PEACOCK + *hen*, female bird; see HEN.]

pea jacket *n.* A short double-breasted coat of heavy wool, worn esp. by sailors. [Prob. transl. of Du. *pijjekker* : *pij*, a kind of coarse cloth (< MDu. *pīe*) + *jekker*, jacket.]

peak[1] (pēk) *n.* **1.** A tapering, projecting point; a pointed extremity. **2.a.** The pointed summit of a mountain. **b.** The mountain itself. **3.a.** The point of a beard. **b.** A widow's peak. **4.** The point of greatest development, value, or intensity. **5.** *Phys.* The highest value attained by a varying quantity. **6.** *Naut.* **a.** The narrow portion of a ship's hull at the bow or stern. **b.** The upper after corner of a gaff-headed sail. **c.** The outermost end of a gaff. —*v.* **peaked, peak•ing, peaks.** —*tr.* **1.** *Naut.* To raise (a gaff) above the horizontal. **2.** To bring to a maximum of development, value, or intensity. —*intr.* **1.** To be formed into a peak or peaks. **2.** To achieve a maximum of development, value, or intensity. —*adj.* Approaching or constituting the maximum. [Prob. ME *pike, peke*. See PIKE[5].]

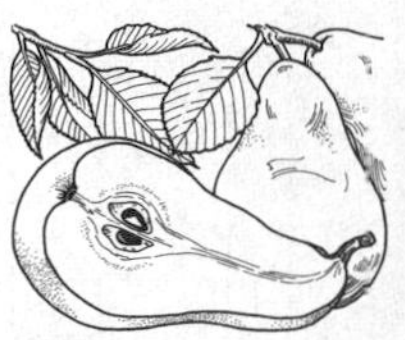

peacock
Blue peacock
Pavo cristatus

peak[2] (pēk) *intr.v.* **peaked, peak•ing, peaks.** To become sickly, emaciated, or pale. [?]

peaked[1] (pēkt, pē′kĭd) *adj.* Ending in a peak; pointed.

peak•ed[2] (pē′kĭd) *adj.* Having a sickly appearance.

peal (pēl) *n.* **1.** A ringing of a set of bells, esp. a change or set of changes rung on bells. **2.** A set of bells tuned to each other; a chime. **3.** A loud burst of noise. —*v.* **pealed, peal•ing, peals.** —*intr.* To sound in a peal; ring. —*tr.* To sound loudly and sonorously. [ME *pele*, a bell peal, esp. as a summons to church, short for *apel*, appeal. See APPEAL.]

Peale (pēl). Amer. family of painters, including **Charles Willson Peale** (1741–1827) and his brother **James** (1749–1831). Four of Charles's children became painters: **Raphael** (1774–1825), **Rembrandt** (1778–1860), **Rubens** (1784–1865), and **Titian** (1799–1885).

pe•an (pē′ən) *n.* Var. of **paean.**

pea•nut (pē′nŭt′) *n.* **1.** A prostrate southern Brazilian plant *(Arachis hypogaea)* widely cultivated in warm regions and having yellow flowers on stalks that bend over so that the seed pods ripen underground. **2.** The edible, nutlike oily seed of this plant, used for food and as a source of oil. Also called regionally *goober, goober pea.* **3.** *Slang.* **a.** A person small in stature. **b.** An insignificant person. **4. peanuts.** *Informal.* A very small amount of money; a trifling sum. —*adj. Slang.* Of no importance; insignificant.

peanut brittle *n.* A hard toffee containing peanuts.

peanut butter *n.* A paste made from ground roasted peanuts.

peanut oil *n.* The oil pressed from peanuts, used for cooking, in soaps, and as a solvent for pharmaceutical preparations.

pear (pâr) *n.* **1.** A widely cultivated tree *(Pyrus communis)* in the rose family, having glossy leaves, white flowers grouped in a corymb, and edible fruit. **2.** The fruit of this tree, spherical at the base and tapering toward the stalk. [ME *pere* < OE *peru*, a pear, ult. < VLat. **pira* < Lat., pl. of *pirum*.]

pear
Pyrus communis

pearl[1] (pûrl) *n.* **1.** A smooth, lustrous, variously colored deposit, chiefly calcium carbonate, formed around a grain of sand or other foreign matter in the shells of certain mollusks and valued as a gem. **2.** Mother-of-pearl; nacre. **3.** One that is prized for beauty or value. **4.** *Print.* A type size measuring approximately five points. **5.** *Color.* A yellowish white. —*v.* **pearled, pearl•ing, pearls.** —*tr.* **1.** To decorate or cover with or as if with pearls. **2.** To make into the shape or color of pearls. —*intr.* **1.** To dive or fish for pearls or pearl-bearing mollusks. **2.** To form beads resembling pearls. [ME *perle* < OFr. < Lat. **pernula*, dim. of *perna*, ham, seashell.]

pearl[2] (pûrl) *v. & n.* Var. of **purl[2].**

Pearl (pûrl). A city of central MS, a suburb of Jackson. Pop. 19,588.

pearl ash *n.* An impure form of potassium carbonate.

Pearl City. A village of HI on Pearl Harbor in S Oahu. Pop. 30,993.

pearl danio *n.* A slender freshwater tropical fish *(Brachydanio albolineatus)* having silvery scales, common in aquariums.

pearl•er (pûr′lər) *n.* **1.** One who dives for pearls. **2.** A boat engaged in seeking or trading pearls.

pearl•es•cent (pûr-lĕs′ənt) *adj.* Having a luster resembling that of pearls.

pearl gray *n. Color.* A light gray, from yellowish to light bluish gray. —**pearl′-gray′** (pûrl′grā′) *adj.*

Pearl Harbor[1]. An inlet of the Pacific Ocean on the S coast of Oahu HI W of Honolulu; site of a naval base that was attacked by the Japanese on Dec. 7, 1941.

Pearl Harbor[2] *n.* A swift, usu. very destructive surprise attack. [After PEARL HARBOR[1].]

pearl•ite (pûr′līt′) *n.* **1.** A mixture of ferrite and cementite forming distinct layers or bands in slowly cooled carbon steels. **2.** Var. of **perlite.**

pearl millet *n.* A tropical Old World grass *(Pennisetum americanum)* having long dense flowering panicles and whitish grains that are used as food.

pearl oyster *n.* Any of several bivalve marine mollusks of the genus *Pinctada* and related genera of tropical waters, esp. *P. margaritifera*, a major commercial source of pearls.

Pearl River[1]. A river of central and S MS flowing c. 780 km (485 mi) generally S to the Gulf of Mexico.

pearl•y (pûr′lē) *adj.* **-i•er, -i•est. 1.** Resembling pearls. **2.** Covered or decorated with pearls or mother-of-pearl.

ă pat	oi boy
ā pay	ou out
âr care	o͝o took
ä father	o͞o boot
ĕ pet	ŭ cut
ē be	ûr urge
ĭ pit	th thin
ī pie	*th* this
îr pier	hw which
ŏ pot	zh vision
ō toe	ə about,
ô paw	item

Stress marks:
′ (primary);
′ (secondary), as in
dictionary (dĭk′shə-nĕr′ē)

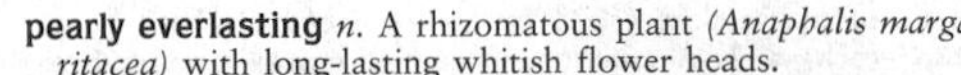

pearly everlasting *n.* A rhizomatous plant *(Anaphalis margaritacea)* with long-lasting whitish flower heads.
pearly nautilus *n.* See **nautilus** 1.
pear psylla *n.* A small plant louse *(Psylla pyricola)* that is a destructive pest of pear trees.
Pear•son (pîr′sən), **Lester Bowles.** 1897–1972. Canadian politician who served as prime minister (1963–68) and won the 1957 Nobel Peace Prize.
Pea•ry (pîr′ē), **Robert Edwin.** 1856–1920. Amer. naval officer who led the expedition credited with first reaching the North Pole (1909).

Robert E. Peary
c. 1896 photograph by George N. Rockwood (1833–1911)

peas•ant (pĕz′ənt) *n.* **1.** A member of the class comprising small farmers and tenants, sharecroppers, and laborers on the land where they form the main agricultural labor force. **2.** A country person; a rustic. **3.** An uncouth, crude, or ill-bred person; a boor. [ME *paissaunt* < OFr. *paisant* < *pais*, country < LLat. *pāgēnsis*, inhabitant of a district < Lat. *pāgus*, district. See **pag-***.]
peas•ant•ry (pĕz′ən-trē) *n.* **1.** The social class comprising peasants. **2.** The condition, rank, or conduct of a peasant.
pease (pēz) *n., pl.* **pease** or **peas•en** (pē′zən). *Archaic.* A pea. [ME. See PEA.]
pease•cod also **peas•cod** (pēz′kŏd′) *n.* The pod of the pea.
pea•shoot•er (pē′sho͞o′tər) *n.* A toy consisting of a small tube through which dried peas or other pellets are blown.
pea soup *n.* **1.** A purée or soup made of cooked dried peas. **2.** *Slang.* Dense fog.
peat (pēt) *n.* Partially carbonized vegetable matter, usu. mosses, found in bogs and used as fertilizer and fuel. [ME *pete*, perh. < Med.Lat. *peta.*] —**peat′y** *adj.*
peat bog *n.* See **bog** 1.
peat moss *n.* **1.** Any of various mosses of the genus *Sphagnum*, growing in very wet places. **2.** The partly carbonized remains of these plants, used as a mulch and plant food.
peau de soie (pō′ də-swä′) *n.* A silk fabric of satin weave having a dull finish. [Fr. : *peau*, skin + *de*, of + *soie*, silk.]
pea•vey also **pea•vy** (pē′vē) *n., pl.* **-veys** also **-vies.** An implement consisting of a wooden shaft with a metal point and a hinged hook near the end, used to handle logs. [After Joseph *Peavey* (fl. 1875), Amer. inventor.]

peavey

peb•ble (pĕb′əl) *n.* **1.** A small stone, esp. one worn smooth by erosion. **2.a.** Clear colorless quartz; rock crystal. **b.** A lens made of such quartz. **3.** *Geol.* A rock fragment between 4 and 64 millimeters in diameter, esp. one that has been naturally rounded. **4.** An irregularly rough grainy surface, as on leather or paper. —*tr.v.* **-bled, -bling, -bles. 1.** To pave with pebbles. **2.** To impart an irregularly rough grainy surface to (leather or paper). **3.** To pelt with pebbles. [ME *pobble, pibel, pebul* < OE *papol-*, as in *papolstān*, pebblestone.] —**peb′bly** *adj.*
pebble plant *n.* See **fig marigold.**
pe•can (pĭ-kän′, -kăn′, pē′kăn) *n.* **1.** A deciduous tree *(Carya illinoinensis)* of southern North America having deeply furrowed bark, pinnately compound leaves, and edible nuts. **2.** The smooth thin-shelled oval nut of this tree. [N.Amer.Fr. *pacane* < Illinois *pakani.*]
pec•ca•ble (pĕk′ə-bəl) *adj.* Liable to sin. [Med.Lat. *peccābilis* < Lat. *peccāre*, to sin. See **ped-***.] —**pec′ca•bil′i•ty** *n.*
pec•ca•dil•lo (pĕk′ə-dĭl′ō) *n., pl.* **-loes** or **-los.** A small sin or fault. [Sp. *pecadillo*, dim. of *pecado*, sin, and Ital. *peccadiglio*, dim. of *peccato*, sin, both < Lat. *peccātum* < neut. of *peccātus*, p.part. of *peccāre*, to sin. See **ped-***.]
pec•cant (pĕk′ənt) *adj.* **1.** Sinful; guilty. **2.** Violating a rule or an accepted practice; erring. [Lat. *peccāns, peccant-*, pr.part. of *peccāre*, to sin. See **ped-***.] —**pec′can•cy** *n.*
pec•ca•ry (pĕk′ə-rē) *n., pl.* **-ries.** Any of several piglike hoofed mammals of the family Tayassuidae, found in the Americas and having long dark dense bristles. [Ult. < Carib *pakira.*]

peccary
Collared peccary
Tayassu tajacu

pec•ca•vi (pĕ-kä′wē, -vē, -kā′vī′) *n., pl.* **-vis.** A confession of sin. [Lat. *peccāvi*, I have sinned, first pers. sing. perfect t. of *peccāre*, to sin. See PECCABLE.]
Pe•cho•ra (pə-chôr′ə, -chōr′ə, pyĭ-). A river of N-central Russia flowing c. 1,802 km (1,120 mi) N to **Pechora Bay,** an arm of the Barents Sea.
peck[1] (pĕk) *v.* **pecked, peck•ing, pecks.** —*tr.* **1.** To strike with the beak or a pointed instrument. **2.** To make (a hole, for example) by striking repeatedly with the beak or a pointed instrument. **3.** To grasp and pick up with the beak. **4.** *Informal.* To kiss briefly and casually. —*intr.* **1.** To make strokes with the beak or a pointed instrument. **2.** To eat in sparing bits; nibble: *pecked at dinner.* **3.** To criticize repeatedly; carp. —*n.* **1.a.** A stroke or light blow with the beak or a pointed instrument. **b.** A mark or hole made by such a stroke. **2.** *Informal.* A light quick kiss. [ME *pecken*, prob. var. of *piken*, to peck (perh. influenced by MLGer. *pekken*). See PICK[1].]
peck[2] (pĕk) *n.* **1.a.** A unit of dry volume or capacity in the U.S. Customary System equal to 8 quarts or approx. 537.6 cubic inches. **b.** A unit of dry volume or capacity in the British Imperial System equal to 8 quarts or approx. 554.8 cubic inches. See table at **measurement. 2.** A container holding or measuring a peck. **3.** *Informal.* A large quantity; a lot. [ME.]
peck•er (pĕk′ər) *n.* **1.** One that pecks, as a beak. **2.** *Chiefly British Slang.* Courage; pluck. **3.** *Vulgar Slang.* The penis.
peck•er•wood (pĕk′ər-wo͝od′) *n. Chiefly Southern U.S.* See **woodpecker.** See Regional Note at **everwhere.**
Peck•ham (pĕk′əm), **Rufus Wheeler.** 1838–1909. Amer. jurist; associate justice of the U.S. Supreme Court (1896–1909).
peck•ing order (pĕk′ĭng) *n.* **1.** A hierarchy among a group, as of people, classes, or nations. **2.** The social hierarchy in a flock of domestic fowl in which each bird pecks subordinate birds and submits to being pecked by dominant birds.
peck•ish (pĕk′ĭsh) *adj.* **1.** Ill-tempered; irritable. **2.** *Chiefly British.* Somewhat hungry. [< PECK[1], to eat.]
Peck's bad boy (pĕks) *n.* A person whose bad behavior embarrasses and annoys others. [After *Peck's Bad Boy and His Pa*, by George Wilbur Peck (1840–1916), Amer. writer.]
Peck•sniff•i•an (pĕk-snĭf′ē-ən) *adj.* Hypocritically benevolent; sanctimonious. [After Seth *Pecksniff*, a character in *Martin Chuzzlewit*, a novel by Charles Dickens.]
pe•co•ri•no (pĕk′ə-rē′nō) *n., pl.* **-nos.** An Italian cheese, esp. Romano, made from ewe's milk. [Ital. < *pecora*, ewe, sheep < Lat., cattle, pl. of *pecus, pecor-*. See **peku-***.]
Pe•cos (pā′kəs). A river of E NM and W TX flowing c. 1,490 km (926 mi) to the Rio Grande.
Pécs (pāch). A city of SW Hungary near the Croatian border SSW of Budapest; orig. a Celtic settlement. Pop. 175,477.
pec•tase (pĕk′tās′, -tāz′) *n.* See **pectinesterase.** [PECT(IN) + -ASE.]
pec•tate (pĕk′tāt′) *n.* A salt or an ester of pectic acid. [PECT(IC ACID).]
pec•ten (pĕk′tən) *n., pl.* **-tens** or **-ti•nes** (-tə-nēz′). **1.** A body structure or an organ resembling a comb. **2.** A scallop of the genus *Pecten.* [Lat. *pecten, pectin-*, comb.]
pec•tic acid (pĕk′tĭk) *n.* A transparent gelatinous acid, $C_{17}H_{24}O_{16}$, insoluble in water and formed by the hydrolysis of certain esters of pectin. [Fr. *pectique*, related to pectin < Gk. *pēktikos*, coagulating < *pēktos*, coagulated. See PECTIN.]
pec•tin (pĕk′tĭn) *n.* Any of a group of water-soluble colloidal carbohydrates of high molecular weight found in ripe fruits and used to jell various foods, drugs, and cosmetics. [Fr. *pectine* < Gk. *pēktos*, coagulated < *pēgnunai*, to coagulate. See **pag-***.] —**pec′tic, pec′tin•ous** *adj.*
pec•ti•nate (pĕk′tə-nāt′) also **pec•ti•nat•ed** (-nā′tĭd) *adj.* Having projections resembling the teeth of a comb; comblike. —**pec′ti•na′tion** *n.*
pec•tin•es•ter•ase (pĕk′tə-nĕs′tə-rās′, -rāz′) *n.* An enzyme found in certain plants, bacteria, and fungi that catalyzes the hydrolysis of pectin to pectic acid and methanol.
pec•to•ral (pĕk′tər-əl) *adj.* **1.** Relating to or situated in the breast or chest. **2.** Useful in relieving disorders of the chest or respiratory tract. **3.** Worn on the chest or breast. —*n.* **1.** A muscle or an organ of the chest. **2.** A pectoral fin. **3.** A pectoral medicine. **4.** An ornament or a decoration worn on the chest. [Prob. Lat. *pectorālis* < *pectus, pector-*, breast.]
pectoral arch *n.* See **pectoral girdle.**
pectoral fin *n.* Either of the anterior pair of fins attached to the pectoral girdle of fishes.
pectoral girdle *n.* A bony or cartilaginous structure in vertebrates, attached to and supporting the forelimbs or anterior fins.
pectoral sandpiper *n.* A New World sandpiper *(Calidris melanotos)* with brownish streaks on the upper breast.
pec•u•late (pĕk′yə-lāt′) *tr. & intr.v.* **-lat•ed, -lat•ing, -lates.** To embezzle (funds) or engage in embezzlement. [Lat. *peculārī, peculāt-* < *pecūlium*, private property. See **peku-***.] —**pec′u•la′tion** *n.* —**pec′u•la′tor** *n.*
pe•cu•liar (pĭ-kyo͞ol′yər) *adj.* **1.** Unusual or eccentric; odd. **2.** Distinct from all others. See Syns at **strange. 3.** Belonging distinctively or primarily to one person, group, or kind; special or unique: *rights peculiar to the rich.* —*n.* **1.** One's exclusive privilege or property. **2.** *Chiefly British.* A church or parish under the jurisdiction of a diocese different from that in which it lies. [ME *peculier*, personal < Lat. *pecūliāris* < *pecūlium*, private property. See **peku-***.] —**pe•cu′liar•ly** *adv.*
pe•cu•li•ar•i•ty (pĭ-kyo͞o′lē-ăr′ĭ-tē, -kyo͞ol-yăr′-) *n., pl.* **-ties. 1.** The quality or state of being peculiar. **2.** A notable or distinctive feature or characteristic. **3.** An eccentricity; an idiosyncrasy.
pe•cu•ni•ar•y (pĭ-kyo͞o′nē-ĕr′ē) *adj.* **1.** Of or relating to money. See Syns at **financial. 2.** Requiring payment of money. [Latin *pecūniārius* < *pecūnia*, wealth. See **peku-***.]
ped–[1] *pref.* Var. of **pedo–[1].**
ped–[2] *pref.* Var. of **pedo–[2].**
–ped or **–pede** *suff.* Foot: *maxilliped.* [< Lat. *pēs, ped-*, foot. See **ped-***.]
ped•a•gog•ic (pĕd′ə-gŏj′ĭk, -gō′jĭk) also **ped•a•gog•i•cal** (-gŏj′ĭ-kəl, -gō′jĭ-) *adj.* **1.** Of, relating to, or characteristic of pedagogy. **2.** Characterized by pedantic formality.
ped•a•gog•ics (pĕd′ə-gŏj′ĭks, -gō′jĭks) *n. (used with a sing. v.)* The art of teaching; pedagogy.
ped•a•gogue (pĕd′ə-gŏg′, -gôg′) *n.* **1.** A schoolteacher; an educator. **2.** One who instructs in a pedantic or dogmatic manner. [ME *pedagoge* < OFr. < Lat. *paedagōgus*, slave who supervised children, including taking them to and from school

< Gk. *paidagōgos* : *paido-*, boy; see PEDO–[1] + *agōgos*, leader (< *agein*, to lead; see **ag-***).] —**ped'a·gogu'ish** *adj.*

ped·a·go·gy (pĕd'ə-gō'jē, -gŏj'ē) *n.* **1.** The art or profession of teaching. **2.** Training or instruction. [Fr. *pédagogie* < OFr. < Gk. *paidagōgia* < *paidagōgos*, slave who took children to and from school. See PEDAGOGUE.]

ped·al (pĕd'l) *n.* **1.a.** A foot-operated lever used for actuating or controlling a mechanism, as in a loom or a piano. **b.** A similar foot-operated part attached to a crank and used for powering various devices, such as a bicycle. **2.** *Mus.* **a.** A pedal point. **b.** A pedal keyboard. —*adj.* **1.** Of or relating to a pedal. **2.** (*also* pēd'l). Of or relating to a foot or footlike part. —*v.* **-aled, -al·ing, -als** or **-alled, -al·ling, -als.** —*intr.* **1.** To use or operate a pedal or pedals. **2.** To ride a bicycle. —*tr.* To operate the pedals of. [Fr. *pédale* < Ital. *pedale* < Lat. *pedālis*, one foot long < *pēs*, *ped-*, foot. See **ped-***.]

ped·al·er also **ped·al·ler** (pĕd'l-ər) *n.* One who rides a pedal-driven vehicle, such as a bicycle.

pe·dal·fer (pĭ-dăl'fər) *n.* Soil rich in alumina and iron and deficient in carbonates, found in and characteristic of humid regions. [PED(O)–[1] + AL(UMINUM) + Lat. *ferrum*, iron.]

pedal keyboard *n. Mus.* A keyboard of pedals in an instrument such as a pipe organ.

pedal piano *n. Mus.* A piano with a pedal keyboard.

pedal point *n. Mus.* A note, usu. in the bass and on the tonic or dominant, sustained through harmonic changes in the other parts. [POINT, musical note.]

pedal pushers *pl.n.* Calf-length slacks worn by women and girls. [< their originally being worn by bicyclists.]

pedal steel *n. Mus.* An electronically amplified guitar mounted on legs, with up to ten strings whose pitch can be altered by sliding a steel bar or by depressing pedals.

ped·ant (pĕd'nt) *n.* **1.** One who pays undue attention to book learning and formal rules. **2.** One who exhibits learning or scholarship ostentatiously. **3.** *Obsolete.* A schoolmaster. [Fr. *pédant* or Ital. *pedante* (Fr. < Ital.), poss. < VLat. **paedēns*, **paedent-*, pr.part. of **paedere*, to instruct, prob. < Gk. *paidein* < *pais*, *paid-*, child. See PEDO–[2].]

pe·dan·tic (pə-dăn'tĭk) *adj.* Characterized by a narrow, often ostentatious concern for book learning and formal rules: *a pedantic attention to details.* —**pe·dan'ti·cal·ly** *adv.*

ped·ant·ry (pĕd'n-trē) *n., pl.* **-ries. 1.** Pedantic attention to detail or rules. **2.** An instance of pedantic behavior. **3.** The habit of mind or manner characteristic of a pedant.

ped·ate (pĕd'āt') *adj.* **1.** Resembling or functioning as a foot: *pedate appendages.* **2.** *Zool.* Having feet: *pedate larvae.* **3.** *Bot.* Having palmately divided lobes with the lateral lobes cleft or divided. [Lat. *pedātus*, p.part. of *pedāre*, to furnish with feet < *pēs*, *ped-*, foot. See **ped-***.]

ped·dle (pĕd'l) *v.* **-dled, -dling, -dles.** —*tr.* **1.a.** To travel about selling (wares). **b.** To sell (narcotics) illicitly. **2.** *Informal.* To seek to disseminate; give out. —*intr.* **1.** To peddle wares. **2.** To occupy oneself with trifles. [Back-formation < PEDDLER. V., intr., sense 2, prob. influenced by PIDDLE.]

ped·dler (pĕd'lər) *n.* One who peddles for a living; a hawker. [ME *pedlere*, prob. alteration of *peddere* < Med.Lat. *pedārius*, crozier bearer < Lat. *pēs*, *ped-*, foot. See PEDI–.]

–pede *suff.* Var. of **–ped.**

ped·er·ast (pĕd'ə-răst') *n.* A man who has sexual relations with a boy. [Gk. *paiderastēs* : *pais*, *paid-*, child; see PEDO–[2] + *erastēs*, lover (< *erasthai*, to love).] —**ped'er·as'ty** *n.*

pe·des (pĕd'ās') *n.* Pl. of **pes.**

ped·es·tal (pĕd'ĭ-stəl) *n.* **1.** An architectural support or base, as for a column. **2.** A support or foundation. **3.** A position of high regard or adoration. —*tr.v.* **-taled, -tal·ing, -tals** or **-talled, -tal·ling, -tals.** To place on or provide with a pedestal. [Obsolete Fr. *pedestal* < Ital. *piedestallo* : *piede*, foot (< Lat. *pēs*; see PEDI–) + *di*, of (< Lat. *dē*; see DE–) + *stallo*, stall (of Gmc. orig.; see **stel-***).]

pe·des·tri·an (pə-dĕs'trē-ən) *n.* One who travels on foot; a walker. —*adj.* **1.** Of, relating to, or made for pedestrians. **2.** Going or performed on foot. **3.** Undistinguished; ordinary: *pedestrian prose.* [< Lat. *pedester*, *pedestr-*, going on foot < *pedes*, a pedestrian < *pēs*, *ped-*, foot. See **ped-***.] —**pe·des'tri·an·ism** *n.*

pedi– *pref.* Foot: *pediform.* [Lat. < *pēs*, *ped-*, foot. See **ped-***.]

pe·di·a·tri·cian (pē'dē-ə-trĭsh'ən) also **pe·di·at·rist** (-ăt'rĭst) *n.* A physician who specializes in pediatrics.

pe·di·at·rics (pē'dē-ăt'rĭks) *n.* (*used with a sing. v.*) The branch of medicine that deals with the care and treatment of infants and children. —**pe'di·at'ric** *adj.*

ped·i·cab (pĕd'ĭ-kăb') *n.* A small three-wheeled vehicle having a seat, pedals, and handlebars in front for the operator and a usu. hooded cab in back for passengers.

ped·i·cel (pĕd'ĭ-səl, -sĕl') *n.* **1.** *Biol.* A small stalk, part, or organ, esp. serving as a support. **2.** *Bot.* **a.** A stalk bearing one flower in an inflorescence. **b.** A support for a fern sporangium or moss capsule. [NLat. *pedicellus*, dim. of Lat. *pediculus*, dim. of *pēs*, *ped-*, foot. See **ped-***.]

ped·i·cel·late (pĕd'ĭ-sĕl'ĭt, -āt') *adj. Biol.* Having or supported by a pedicel.

ped·i·cle (pĕd'ĭ-kəl) *n.* **1.** See **pedicel. 2.** A slender footlike or stemlike part, as at the base of a tumor. [Lat. *pediculus*, dim. of *pēs*, *ped-*, foot. See PEDICEL.]

pe·dic·u·lar (pə-dĭk'yə-lər) *adj.* Of or caused by lice. [Lat. *pēdiculāris* < *pēdiculus*, dim. of *pēdis*, louse. See **pezd-***.]

pe·dic·u·late (pə-dĭk'yə-lĭt, -lāt') *adj.* Of, relating to, or being the marine teleost fishes of the order Pediculati, characterized by pectoral fins extending from an armlike process and a dorsal fin ray that serves as a lure for prey. [< NLat. *Pediculātī*, order name < Lat. *pediculus*, dim. of *pēs*, *ped-*, foot. See PEDI–.] —**pe·dic'u·late'** *n.*

pe·dic·u·lo·sis (pə-dĭk'yə-lō'sĭs) *n.* Infestation with lice. [Lat. *pēdiculus*, dim. of *pēdis*, louse; see PEDICULAR + –OSIS.] —**pe·dic'u·lous** (-ləs) *adj.*

ped·i·cure (pĕd'ĭ-kyo͝or') *n.* **1.** Cosmetic care or a cosmetic treatment of the feet and toenails. **2.** A podiatrist. [Fr. *pédicure* : Lat. *pēs*, *ped-*, foot; see PEDI– + Lat. *cūra*, care; see CURE.] —**ped'i·cure'** *v.* —**ped'i·cur'ist** *n.*

ped·i·form (pĕd'ə-fôrm') *adj.* Shaped like a foot.

ped·i·gree (pĕd'ĭ-grē') *n.* **1.a.** A line of ancestors; a lineage. **b.** A list of ancestors; a family tree. **2.** A chart of an individual's ancestors used in human genetics to analyze Mendelian inheritance, esp. of familial diseases. **3.** A list of the ancestors of a purebred animal. [ME *pedegru* < AN *pe de grue* : *pe*, foot (< Lat. *pēs*; see PEDI–) + *de*, of (< Lat. *dē*; see DE–) + *grue*, crane (< the resemblance of a crane's foot to the lines of succession on a genealogical chart) (< VLat. **grūa* < Lat. *grūs*, *gru-*; see **gerə-[2]***).] —**ped'i·greed'** *adj.*

ped·i·ment (pĕd'ə-mənt) *n.* **1.a.** A wide low-pitched gable surmounting the façade of a building in the Grecian style. **b.** A similar triangular element, used in architecture and decoration. **2.** *Geol.* A broad, gently sloping rock surface at the base of a steeper slope, often covered with alluvium and formed primarily by erosion. [Alteration of Lat., of earlier *perement*, prob. alteration of PYRAMID.] —**ped'i·men'tal** (-mĕn'tl) *adj.* —**ped'i·ment'ed** *adj.*

ped·i·palp (pĕd'ə-pălp') *n.* One of the second pair of appendages near the mouth of an arachnid that are modified for various reproductive, predatory, or sensory functions.

ped·lar (pĕd'lər) *n. Chiefly British.* Var. of **peddler.**

pedo–[1] or **ped–** *pref.* Soil: *pedocal.* [< Gk. *pedon*, soil, earth. See **ped-***.]

pedo–[2] or **ped–** or **paed–** or **paedo–** *pref.* Child; children: *pedodontics.* [Gk. *paido-* < *pais*, *paid-*, child. See **pau-***.]

ped·o·cal (pĕd'ə-kăl') *n.* A soil of semiarid and arid regions that is rich in calcium carbonate and lime. [PEDO–[1] + CAL(CIUM).] —**ped'o·cal'ic** *adj.*

pe·do·don·tia (pē'də-dŏn'shə) *n.* Pedodontics.

pe·do·don·tics (pē'də-dŏn'tĭks) *n.* (*used with a sing. v.*) The branch of dentistry that deals with the care and treatment of children's teeth. —**pe'do·don'tist** (-dŏn'tĭst) *n.*

ped·o·gen·e·sis[1] (pĕd'ə-jĕn'ĭ-sĭs) *n.* The process of soil formation.

pe·do·gen·e·sis[2] (pē'dō-jĕn'ĭ-sĭs) *n.* Var. of **paedogenesis.**

pe·dol·o·gy[1] (pē-dŏl'ə-jē) *n.* The study of the physical and mental development and characteristics of children. —**pe'do·log'ic** (-də-lŏj'ĭk), **pe'do·log'i·cal** (-ĭ-kəl) *adj.* —**pe'do·log'i·cal·ly** *adv.* —**pe·dol'o·gist** *n.*

pe·dol·o·gy[2] (pĭ-dŏl'ə-jē, pĕ-) *n.* The scientific study of soils, including their origins, characteristics, and uses. —**ped'o·log'ic** (pĕd'l-ŏj'ĭk), **ped'o·log'i·cal** (-ĭ-kəl) *adj.* —**ped'o·log'i·cal·ly** *adv.* —**pe·dol'o·gist** *n.*

pe·dom·e·ter (pĭ-dŏm'ĭ-tər) *n.* An instrument that gauges the distance traveled on foot by counting the steps taken.

pe·do·mor·phism (pĕd'ə-môr'fĭz'əm, pē'də-) *n.* Var. of **paedomorphism.**

ped·o·phil·i·a (pĕd'ə-fĭl'ē-ə, pē'də-) *n.* Sexual attraction felt by an adult toward a child. —**ped'o·phile'** (-fīl') *n.* —**ped'o·phil'i·ac** *adj. & n.* —**ped'o·phil'ic** *adj.*

Pe·dro I (pā'drō, pĕ'dro͞o). 1798–1834. Brazilian political leader who was the country's first emperor (1822–31).

Pedro II. 1825–91. Brazilian emperor (1831–89) who abolished slavery.

pe·dun·cle (pĭ-dŭng'kəl, pē'dŭng'kəl) *n.* **1.** *Bot.* The stalk of an inflorescence or a stalk bearing a solitary flower. **2.** *Zool.* A stalklike structure in invertebrate animals, usu. serving as an attachment for a larger part or structure. **3.** *Anat.* A stalklike bundle of nerve fibers connecting different parts of the brain. **4.** *Medic.* The stalklike base to which a polyp or tumor is attached. [NLat. *pedunculus*, dim. of Lat. *pēs*, *ped-*, foot. See **ped-***.] —**pe·dun'cu·lar** (pĭ-dŭng'kyə-lər) *adj.*

pe·dun·cu·late (pĭ-dŭng'kyə-lĭt, -lāt') also **pe·dun·cu·lat·ed** (-lā'tĭd) *adj.* Having or supported on a peduncle.

pee[1] (pē) *n.* The letter *p.*

pee[2] (pē) *Slang.* —*intr.v.* **peed, pee·ing, pees.** To urinate. —*n.* **1.** Urine. **2.** An act of urination. [< the first letter of PISS.]

Pee Dee (pē' dē') also **Great Pee Dee** (grāt). A river, c. 375 km (233 mi), of S-central NC and NE SC.

peek (pēk) *intr.v.* **peeked, peek·ing, peeks. 1.** To glance quickly. **2.** To look or peer furtively, as from a place of concealment. **3.** To be only partially visible, as if peering or emerging from hiding. —*n.* A brief or furtive look. [ME *piken*, perh. alteration of MDu. *kieken*, var. of *kīken*.]

ă pat	oi boy
ā pay	ou out
âr care	o͝o took
ä father	o͞o boot
ĕ pet	ŭ cut
ē be	ûr urge
ĭ pit	th thin
ī pie	*th* this
îr pier	hw which
ŏ pot	zh vision
ō toe	ə about, item
ô paw	

Stress marks:
' (primary);
' (secondary), as in
dictionary (dĭk'shə-nĕr'ē)

peek•a•boo (pēk′ə-bo͞o′) *n.* A game for amusing a small child, in which one covers one's face or hides and then returns to view saying "Peekaboo!" —*adj.* **1.** Decorated with embroidered holes or eyelets. **2.** Made of a sheer or transparent fabric. [PEEK + BOO[1].]

Peeks•kill (pēk′skĭl′). A city of SE NY on the Hudson R. N of White Plains. Pop. 19,536.

peel[1] (pēl) *n.* The skin or rind of certain fruits and vegetables. —*v.* **peeled, peel•ing, peels.** —*tr.* **1.** To strip or cut away the skin, rind, or bark from; pare. **2.** To strip away; pull off. —*intr.* **1.** To lose or shed skin, bark, or other covering. **2.** To come off in thin strips or pieces, as bark, skin, or paint. **3.** *Slang.* To remove one's clothes; undress. —***phrasal verb.*** **peel off. 1.** To leave flight formation in order to land or make a dive. Used of an aircraft. **2.** To leave or depart. [< ME *pilen, pelen,* to peel < OFr. *peler* and OE *pilian* (both < Lat. *pilāre,* to deprive of hair < *pilus,* hair) and < OFr. *pillier,* to tug, pull, plunder (< Lat. *pilleum,* felt cap).]

peel[2] (pēl) *n.* **1.** A long-handled shovellike tool used by bakers to move bread or pastries into and out of an oven. **2.** *Print.* A T-shaped pole used for hanging up freshly printed sheets of paper to dry. [ME < OFr. *pele* < Lat. *pāla,* spade, peel. See **pag-***.]

peel[3] (pēl) *n.* A fortified house or tower of a kind constructed in the borderland of Scotland and England in the 16th century. [ME *pel,* stake, small castle < AN, stockade, var. of OFr., stake < Lat. *pālus.* See **pag-***.]

Peel (pēl), Sir **Robert.** 1788–1850. British politician who served as prime minister (1834–35 and 1841–46).

peel•a•ble (pē′lə-bəl) *adj.* **1.** Having a peel or rind that can be peeled off. **2.** That can be removed and used again.

peel•er[1] (pē′lər) *n.* **1.** One that peels, esp. a kitchen implement for peeling fruits and vegetables. **2.** *Slang.* A stripteaser.

peel•er[2] (pē′lər) *n. Chiefly British.* A police officer. [After Sir Robert PEEL.]

peel•ing (pē′lĭng) *n.* A peeled piece or strip, as of a fruit rind.

Peel River. A river of N Yukon Terr. and W Northwest Terrs., Canada, flowing c. 644 km (400 mi) to the Mackenzie R.

peen (pēn) *n.* The end of a hammerhead opposite the flat striking surface, used for chipping, indenting, and metalworking. —*tr.v.* **peened, peen•ing, peens.** To hammer, bend, or shape with a peen. [Prob. of Scand. orig.]

peep[1] (pēp) *intr.v.* **peeped, peep•ing, peeps. 1.** To utter short high-pitched sounds, like those of a baby bird; cheep. **2.** To speak in a hesitant, thin, high-pitched voice. —*n.* **1.** A peeping sound or utterance. **2.** A slight sound or utterance. **3.** Any of various small North American sandpipers. [ME **pepen,* prob. alteration of *pipen* < OE *pīpian,* to pipe < *pīpe,* tube, musical instrument, and < Lat. *pīpāre,* to peep; see PIPE.]

peep[2] (pēp) *v.* **peeped, peep•ing, peeps.** —*intr.* **1.** To peek furtively; steal a quick glance. **2.** To peer through a small aperture or from behind something. **3.** To appear as though emerging from a hiding place. —*tr.* To cause to emerge or become partly visible. —*n.* **1.** A quick or furtive look or glance. **2.** A first glimpse or appearance: *the peep of dawn.* [ME *pepen,* perh. alteration of *piken,* to peek. See PEEK.]

peep•er[1] (pē′pər) *n.* A creature that makes short high-pitched sounds, esp. a frog.

peep•er[2] (pē′pər) *n.* **1.** One who peeks furtively. **2.** *Slang.* An eye.

peep•hole (pēp′hōl′) *n.* A small hole or crevice for peeping.

peep•ing Tom (pē′pĭng tŏm) *n.* A person who gets pleasure, esp. sexual pleasure, from secretly watching others; a voyeur. [After the legendary *Peeping Tom* of Coventry, England, who was the only person to see the naked Lady Godiva.]

peep•show also **peep show** (pēp′shō′) *n.* **1.** An exhibit viewed through a small hole or magnifying glass. **2.** A short pornographic film seen usu. in a coin-operated booth.

peep sight *n.* A rear sight of a firearm consisting of an adjustable eyepiece with a small opening through which the front sight and the target are aligned.

pee•pul also **pi•pal** (pē′pəl) *n.* A fig tree *(Ficus religiosa)* native to India, having broadly ovate leaves and sacred to Buddhists. [Hindi *pīpal* < Skt. *pippalam.*]

peer[1] (pîr) *intr.v.* **peered, peer•ing, peers. 1.** To look intently, searchingly, or with difficulty. **2.** To be partially visible; show: *Stars peered through the clouds.* [ME *piren* (prob. < Frisian *piren*) and *peren* (short for *aperen,* to appear; see APPEAR).]

peer[2] (pîr) *n.* **1.** One who has equal standing with another or others, as in rank, class, or age: *influenced by their peers.* **2.a.** A nobleman. **b.** A man who holds a peerage by descent or appointment. **3.** *Archaic.* A companion; comrade. [ME < OFr. *per,* equal, peer < Lat. *pār.* See **perə-[2]***.]

peer•age (pîr′ĭj) *n.* **1.** The rank, title, or jurisdiction of a noble; a duchy, marquisate, county, viscountcy, or barony. **2.** Nobles considered as a group. **3.** A listing of nobles and their families.

peer•ess (pîr′ĭs) *n.* **1.a.** A noblewoman. **b.** A woman who holds a peerage by descent or appointment. **2.** A woman who holds a title by association, as the wife or widow of a peer.

peer•less (pîr′lĭs) *adj.* Being such as to have no match; incomparable. —**peer′less•ly** *adv.* —**peer′less•ness** *n.*

Pegasus
Fourth-century B.C.
Greek coin

pelican
Brown pelican
Pelecanus occidentalis

peeve (pēv) *tr.v.* **peeved, peev•ing, peeves.** To cause to be annoyed or resentful. —*n.* **1.** A vexation; a grievance. **2.** A resentful mood: *in a peeve.* [Back-formation < PEEVISH.]

pee•vish (pē′vĭsh) *adj.* **1.a.** Querulous or discontented. **b.** Ill-tempered. **2.** Contrary; fractious. [ME *pevish,* poss. < Lat. *perversus,* p.part. of *perversus.* See PERVERSE.] —**pee′vish•ly** *adv.* —**pee′vish•ness** *n.*

pee•wee[1] (pē′wē) *n. Informal.* One, such as a child, that is notably small. [Prob. redup. of WEE.] —**pee′wee** *adj.*

pee•wee[2] (pē′wē) *n.* Var. of **pewee.**

pee•wit (pē′wĭt′, pyo͞o′ĭt) *n.* Var. of **pewit.**

peg (pĕg) *n.* **1.a.** A small cylindrical or tapered pin, as of wood, used to fasten things or plug a hole. **b.** A similar pin forming a projection that may be used as a support or boundary marker. **2.** *Mus.* One of the pins of a stringed instrument that are turned to tighten or slacken the strings so as to regulate their pitch. **3.** A degree or notch, as in estimation. **4.** *Chiefly British.* A drink of liquor. **5.** *Baseball.* A low and fast throw made to put a base runner out. **6.** *Informal.* A leg, esp. a wooden one. —*v.* **pegged, peg•ging, pegs.** —*tr.* **1.** To fasten or plug with a peg or pegs. **2.** To designate or mark by means of a peg or pegs. **3.** To fix (a price) at a certain level or within a certain range. **4.** *Informal.* To classify; categorize. **5.** *Informal.* To throw. —*intr.* To work steadily; persist: *pegged away in school.* —***idiom.*** **take (someone) down a peg.** To reduce the pride of; humble. [ME *pegge* < MDu.]

Peg•a•sus (pĕg′ə-səs) *n.* **1.** *Gk. Myth.* A winged horse that with a stroke of his hoof caused the fountain Hippocrene to spring forth from Mount Helicon. **2.** A constellation in the Northern Hemisphere near Aquarius and Andromeda. [ME < Lat. *Pēgasus* < Gk. *Pēgasos.*]

peg•board (pĕg′bôrd′, -bōrd′) *n.* **1.** *Games.* **a.** A game board perforated with a pattern of holes into which pegs can be fitted. **b.** A game played by fitting pegs into such holes. **2.** A board fitted with pegs for hanging clothing.

Peg-Board (pĕg′bôrd′, -bōrd′). A trademark used for a type of hardboard with rows of regularly spaced holes into which hooks may be inserted for storing or displaying objects.

peg leg *n. Informal.* An artificial leg.

peg•ma•tite (pĕg′mə-tīt′) *n.* A coarse-grained granite, sometimes rich in rare elements such as uranium and tungsten. [Gk. *pēgma, pēgmat-,* something fastened together (< *pēgnunai,* to fasten; see **pag-***) + -ITE[1].]

Peh•le•vi (pā′lə-vē′) *n.* Var. of **Pahlavi.**

Pei (pā), **I(eoh) M(ing).** b. 1917. Chinese-born Amer. architect who designed Place Ville Marie in Montreal.

P.E.I. *abbr.* Prince Edward Island.

pei•gnoir (pān-wär′, pĕn-) *n.* A woman's loose-fitting dressing gown. [Fr. < OFr. *peignouer,* linen covering used while combing oneself < *peigner,* to comb the hair < Lat. *pectināre* < *pecten, pectin-,* comb.]

Pei•ping (pā′pĭng′). See **Beijing.**

Pei•pus (pī′pəs), **Lake.** A lake bordering on E Estonia amd NW Russia.

Peirce (pîrs, pûrs), **Charles Sanders.** 1839–1914. Amer. philosopher and scientist who cofounded pragmatism.

Pei•sis•tra•tus (pī-sĭs′trə-təs, pĭ-). See **Pisistratus.**

pej•o•ra•tion (pĕj′ə-rā′shən, pē′jə-) *n.* **1.** The process or condition of worsening or degenerating. **2.** *Ling.* The process by which the meaning of a word becomes negative or less elevated over time. [Med.Lat. *pēiōrātiō, pēiōrātiōn-* < LLat. *pēiōrātus,* p.part. of *pēiōrāre,* to make worse < Lat. *pēior,* worse. See **ped-***.]

pe•jor•a•tive (pĭ-jôr′ə-tĭv, -jŏr′-, pĕj′ə-rā′tĭv, pē′jə-) *adj.* **1.** Tending to make or become worse. **2.** Disparaging; belittling. —*n.* A pejorative word or expression. —**pe•jor′a•tive•ly** *adv.*

pek•an (pĕk′ən) *n.* See **fisher** 2a. [Canadian Fr. *pékan* < Eastern Abenaki *pékané.*]

pe•kin (pē′kĭn′) *n.* **1.** A striped or figured silk fabric. **2.** Also **Pekin.** A large white duck of a Chinese breed, widely raised for food. [Fr. *pékin,* after *Pékin* (Beijing), China.]

Pe•kin (pē′kĭn). A city of central Illinois, a suburb of Peoria on the Illinois R. Pop. 32,254.

Pe•king (pē′kĭng′, pā′-). See **Beijing.**

Peking duck *n.* A Chinese dish of roast duck with crispy skin.

Pe•king•ese (pē′kĭng-ēz′, -ēs′) also **Pe•kin•ese** (pē′kə-nēz′, -nēs′) *n., pl.* **Pekingese** also **Pekinese. 1.** A native or resident of Peking (Beijing). **2.** The Chinese dialect of Peking. **3.** (pē′kə-nēz′, -nēs′). Any of a breed of small dog developed in China having a flat nose, a long-haired coat, and a tail that curls over its back. —**Pe′king•ese′** *adj.*

Peking man *n.* An early member of an extinct species of human beings, considered a subspecies of *Homo erectus* and known from Pleistocene fossils. [After *Peking* (Beijing), China.]

pe•koe (pē′kō) *n.* A grade of black tea consisting of the leaves around the buds. [Chin. (Amoy) *pek ho* : *pek,* white + *ho,* down, fine feathers.]

pel•age (pĕl′ĭj) *n.* **1.** The coat of a mammal, consisting of hair, fur, wool, or other soft covering, as distinct from bare skin. **2.** Something resembling the coat of a mammal. [Fr. < OFr. < *peil, pel,* hair < Lat. *pilus.*]

Pe·la·gi·an·ism (pə-lāʹjē-ə-nĭzʹəm) *n. Theol.* The doctrine of Pelagius, a British monk, denying original sin and affirming the exercise of free will to achieve righteousness, condemned as heresy by the Roman Catholic Church in A.D. 416. —**Pe·laʹgi·an** *adj. & n.*

pe·lag·ic (pə-lăjʹĭk) *adj.* Of, relating to, or living in open oceans or seas rather than waters adjacent to land or inland waters: *pelagic birds.* [Lat. *pelagicus* < Gk. *pelagikos* < *pelagos*, sea. See **plāk-**[1]*.]

pel·ar·go·ni·um (pĕlʹär-gōʹnē-əm) *n.* Any of various herbs and shrubs of the genus *Pelargonium,* including the geraniums. [NLat. *Pelargonium*, genus name < Gk. *pelargos*, stork (its capsules being like a stork's bill). See **pel-**[1]*.]

Pe·las·gi·an (pə-lăzʹjē-ən) *n.* A member of a people living in the region of the Aegean Sea before the Greeks. [ME < Lat. *Pelasgus* < Gk. *Pelasgos.*] —**Pe·lasʹgi·an, Pe·lasʹgic** (-jĭk) *adj.*

pe·lec·y·pod (pə-lĕsʹə-pŏdʹ) *n.* See **lamellibranch.** [< NLat. *Pelecypoda*, class name : Gk. *pelekus*, ax + NLat. *-poda*, -pod.]

Pe·lée (pə-lāʹ), **Mount.** A volcano, c. 1,373 m (4,500 ft), on N Martinique; erupted violently in 1902, killing 40,000 people.

pel·er·ine (pĕlʹə-rēnʹ, pĕlʹər-ĭn) *n.* A woman's cape, usu. short, with points in front. [Fr. *pèlerine* < fem. of *pèlerin*, pilgrim < LLat. *pelegrīnus*. See PILGRIM.]

Pe·le·us (pēʹlē-əs, pēlʹyōōsʹ) *n. Gk. Myth.* A king of the Myrmidons and the father of Achilles.

pelf (pĕlf) *n.* Wealth or riches, esp. when dishonestly acquired. [ME < Med.Lat. *pelfra, pelfa*, prob. < OFr. *pelfre*.]

pel·i·can (pĕlʹĭ-kən) *n.* Any of various large web-footed birds of the genus *Pelecanus* of warm regions, having a pouch of skin hanging from a long bill for catching and holding fish. [ME < OE *pellican* and < OFr. *pelican*, both < LLat. *pelicānus* < Gk. *pelekan*.]

Pe·li·on (pēʹlē-ən, -ônʹ), **Mount.** A peak, 1,601.9 m (5,252 ft), of NE Greece; legendary home of the centaurs.

pe·lisse (pə-lēsʹ) *n.* **1.** A long cloak or outer robe, usu. of fur or with a fur lining. **2.** A woman's loose light cloak, often with arm holes. [Fr. < OFr. *pelice* < LLat. *pellīcia* < Lat., fem. of *pellīcius*, made of skin < *pellis*, skin. See **pel-**[3]*.]

pe·lite (pēʹlītʹ) *n.* Sedimentary rock composed of fine fragments, as of clay or mud. [Gk. *pēlos*, clay + -ITE[1].] —**pe·litʹic** (pĭ-lĭtʹĭk) *adj.*

Pel·la (pĕlʹə). An ancient city of Greek Macedonia; cap. of Macedonia from the 4th cent. to 168 B.C.

pel·lag·ra (pə-lăgʹrə, -lāʹ-, -lăʹgrə) *n.* A disease caused by a dietary deficiency of niacin and protein and characterized by skin eruptions, digestive and nervous system disturbances, and mental deterioration. [Ital. : *pelle*, skin (< Lat. *pellis*; see **pel-**[3]*) + *-agra*, a seizure (< Lat. < Gk. < *agra*, a seizing; see **ag-***).] —**pel·lagʹrous** *adj.*

pel·lag·rin (pə-lăgʹrĭn, -lāʹ-, -lăʹgrĭn) *n.* A person affected with pellagra. [< PELLAGRA.]

pel·let (pĕlʹĭt) *n.* **1.** A small solid or densely packed ball or mass, as of food. **2.a.** A bullet or piece of small shot. **b.** A stone ball used as a catapult missile or a primitive cannonball. —*tr.v.* **-let·ed, -let·ing, -lets. 1.** To make or form into pellets. **2.** To strike with pellets. [ME *pelet* < OFr. *pelote* < VLat. **pilotta*, dim. of Lat. *pila*, ball.]

pel·li·cle (pĕlʹĭ-kəl) *n.* A thin skin or film, such as an organic membrane or a liquid film. [Fr. < Lat. *pellicula*, husk, dim. of *pellis*, skin. See **pel-**[3]*.] —**pel·licʹu·lar** (pə-lĭkʹyə-lər) *adj.*

pel·li·to·ry (pĕlʹĭ-tôrʹē, -tōrʹē) *n., pl.* **-ries. 1.** A small Mediterranean plant *(Anacyclus pyrethrum)* containing a volatile oil that relieves toothache and facial neuralgia. **2.** Any of various monoecious plants of the genus *Parietaria*, having long narrow leaves with hairy tufts at the base and apetalous flowers. [ME *peletre, peletori* < OFr. *piretre, peletre* < Lat. *pyrethrum*. See PYRETHRUM.]

pell-mell also **pell·mell** (pĕlʹmĕlʹ) *adv.* **1.** In a jumbled, confused manner; helter-skelter. **2.** In frantic, disorderly haste; headlong. [Fr. *pêle-mêle* < OFr. *pesle mesle*, prob. redup. of *mesle*, imper. of *mesler*, to mix. See MEDDLE.] —**pellʹ-mellʹ** *adj. & n.*

pel·lu·cid (pə-lōōʹsĭd) *adj.* **1.** Admitting the passage of light; transparent or translucent. **2.** Transparently clear in style or meaning. [Lat. *pellūcidus* < *pellūcēre*, to shine through : *per-*, through; see PER– + *lūcēre*, to shine; see **leuk-***.] —**pel·lu·cidʹi·ty, pel·luʹcid·ness** *n.* —**pel·luʹcid·ly** *adv.*

Pel·ly (pĕlʹē). A river of central Yukon Terr., Canada, flowing c. 531 km (330 mi) generally NW to the Yukon R.

Pe·lop·i·das (pə-lŏpʹĭ-dəs). d. 364 B.C. Theban general who helped liberate Thebes from the Spartans (379).

Pel·o·pon·ne·sus or **Pel·o·pon·ne·sos** (pĕlʹə-pə-nēʹsəs) also **Pel·o·pon·nese** (pĕlʹə-pə-nēzʹ, -nēsʹ). A peninsula forming the S part of Greece S of the Gulf of Corinth; dominated by Sparta until the 4th cent. B.C. —**Pelʹo·pon·neʹsian** (-nēʹzhən, -shən) *adj. & n.*

Pe·lops (pēʹlŏpsʹ) *n. Gk. Myth.* The son of Tantalus and father of Atreus. [Lat. < Gk. : *pelios*, dark; see **pel-**[1]* + *ōps*, face, eye; see **okw-***.]

pe·lo·ri·a (pə-lôrʹē-ə, -lōrʹ-) *n.* Regularity in form of a normally irregular flower. [NLat. < Gk. *pelōros*, monstrous < *pelōr*, monster. See **kwer-***.] —**pe·lorʹic** (-lôrʹĭk, -lŏrʹ-) *adj.*

pe·lo·rus (pə-lôrʹəs, -lōrʹ-) *n., pl.* **-rus·es.** *Naut.* A fixed compass card on which bearings relative to a ship's heading are taken. [?]

pe·lo·ta (pə-lōʹtə) *n. Sports.* **1.** Jai alai. **2.** The ball used in jai alai. [Sp. < OFr. *pelote*, pellet. See PELLET.]

Pe·lo·tas (pə-lōʹtəs, pĭ-lôʹtäs). A city of SE Brazil on a lagoon SSW of Pôrto Alegre. Pop. 196,919.

pelt[1] (pĕlt) *n.* **1.** The skin of an animal with the fur or hair still on it. **2.** A stripped animal skin ready for tanning. [ME, prob. < OFr. *pelete*, dim. of *pel*, skin < Lat. *pellis*. See **pel-**[3]*.]

pelt[2] (pĕlt) *v.* **pelt·ed, pelt·ing, pelts.** —*tr.* **1.** To strike or assail repeatedly with or as if with blows or missiles; bombard. **2.** To cast, hurl, or throw (missiles). **3.** To strike repeatedly. —*intr.* **1.** To beat or strike heavily and repeatedly. **2.** To move at a vigorous gait. —*n.* **1.** A sharp blow; a whack. **2.** A rapid pace. [ME *pelten*, var. of *pilten*, perh. ult. < Lat. *pultāre*, to beat, var. of *pulsāre*, freq. of *pellere*, to strike. See **pel-**[5]*.] —**peltʹer** *n.*

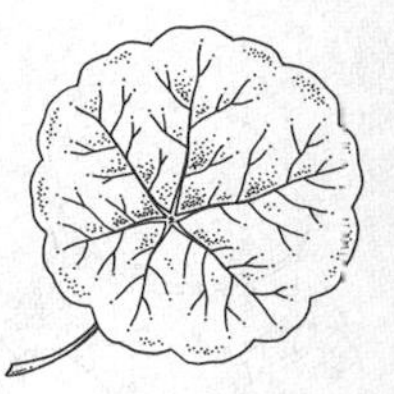

peltate
Peltate leaf

pel·tate (pĕlʹtātʹ) *adj.* Having a flat circular structure attached to a stalk near the center rather than the margin: *a peltate leaf.* [Lat. *peltātus*, armed with a small shield < Lat. *pelta*, small shield < Gk. *peltē*. See **pel-**[3]*.]

pelt·ing (pĕlʹtĭng) *adj. Archaic.* Paltry; petty. [Perh. < dial. *pelt*, trash.]

pel·try (pĕlʹtrē) *n.* Undressed pelts considered as a group. [ME < OFr. *peleterie* < *peletier*, furrier < *pel*, skin < Lat. *pellis*. See PELT[1].]

pel·vic (pĕlʹvĭk) *adj.* Of, in, near, or relating to the pelvis.

pelvic arch *n.* See **pelvic girdle.**

pelvic fin *n.* Either of a pair of lateral hind fins of fishes, attached to the pelvic girdle.

pelvic girdle *n.* A bony or cartilaginous structure in vertebrates, attached to and supporting the hind limbs or fins.

pelvic inflammatory disease *n.* Inflammation of the female genital tract, esp. of the fallopian tubes, caused by any of several microorganisms, chiefly chlamydia and gonococci, and marked by abdominal pain, fever, and vaginal discharge.

pel·vis (pĕlʹvĭs) *n., pl.* **-vis·es** or **-ves** (-vēz). **1.a.** A basin-shaped structure of the vertebrate skeleton, composed of the innominate bones on the sides, the pubis in front, and the sacrum and coccyx behind and resting on the lower limbs and supporting the spinal column. **b.** The cavity formed by this structure. **2.** The funnel in the outlet of the kidney, through which urine passes to the ureter. [Lat. *pēlvis*, basin.]

Pem·ba (pĕmʹbə). An island of Tanzania in the Indian Ocean N of Zanzibar; under British control after 1890.

Pem·broke Pines (pĕmʹbrŏŏkʹ, -brōkʹ). A city of SE FL, a suburb of Fort Lauderdale. Pop. 65,452.

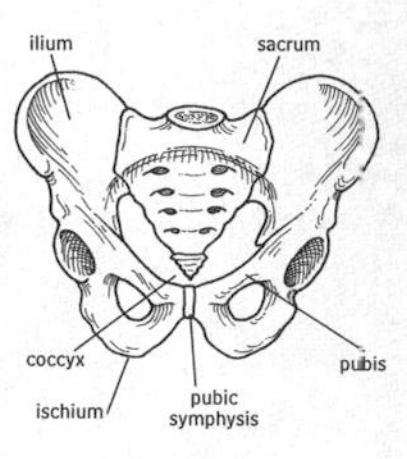

pelvis

pem·mi·can also **pem·i·can** (pĕmʹĭ-kən) *n.* **1.** A Native American food prepared from lean dried strips of meat pounded into paste, mixed with fat and berries, and pressed into small cakes. **2.** A food made from beef, dried fruit, and suet and used as emergency rations. [Cree *pimihkaam*.]

pem·o·line (pĕmʹə-lēnʹ) *n.* A crystalline synthetic compound, $C_9H_8N_2O_2$, used as a mild stimulant of the central nervous system, usu. with magnesium hydroxide, esp. to treat depression. [< *p(h)e(nyli)m(inooxooxaz)ol(id)ine*, its chemical name.]

pem·phi·gus (pĕmʹfĭ-gəs, pĕm-fīʹgəs) *n.* Any of several skin diseases characterized by itching blisters. [NLat. < Gk. *pemphix, pemphig-*, pustule.] —**pemʹphi·gous** *adj.*

pen[1] (pĕn) *n.* **1.** An instrument for writing or drawing with ink or similar fluid, esp.: **a.** A ballpoint pen. **b.** A fountain pen. **c.** A pen point. **d.** A penholder and its pen point. **e.** A quill. **2.** An instrument for writing regarded as a means of expression. **3.** A writer or an author. **4.** A style of writing: *a witty pen.* **5. pens.** Pinions. **6.** The chitinous internal shell of a squid. —*tr.v.* **penned, pen·ning, pens.** To write or compose with or as if with a pen. [ME *penne* < OFr. < LLat. *penna* < Lat., feather. See **pet-***.] —**penʹner** *n.*

pen[2] (pĕn) *n.* **1.a.** A fenced enclosure for animals. **b.** The animals kept in a pen. **c.** Any of various enclosures, such as a bullpen or playpen. **2.** A repair dock for submarines. —*tr.v.* **penned** or **pent** (pĕnt), **pen·ning, pens.** To confine in or as if in a pen. [ME < OE *penn*.]

pen[3] (pĕn) *n.* A female swan. [?]

pen[4] (pĕn) *n. Informal.* A penitentiary; a prison.

pen. *abbr.* Peninsula.

pe·nal (pēʹnəl) *adj.* **1.** Of, relating to, or prescribing punishment, as for breaking the law. **2.** Subject to punishment; legally punishable: *a penal offense.* **3.** Serving as or constituting a means or place of punishment: *a penal colony.* [ME < OFr. *peinal* and < Med.Lat. *pēnālis*, both < Lat. *poenālis* < *poena*, penalty < Gk. *poinē*. See **kwei-**[1]*.] —**peʹnal·ly** *adv.*

penal code *n. Law.* A body of laws relating to crimes and offenses and the penalties for their commission.

pe·nal·ize (pēʹnə-līzʹ, pĕnʹə-) *tr.v.* **-ized, -iz·ing, -iz·es. 1.** To subject to a penalty, esp. for infringement of a law or regulation. **2.** To impose a handicap on; place at a disadvantage. —**peʹnal·i·zaʹtion** (-nə-lĭ-zāʹshən) *n.*

ă pat	oi boy
ā pay	ou out
âr care	ŏŏ took
ä father	ōō boot
ĕ pet	ŭ cut
ē be	ûr urge
ĭ pit	th thin
ī pie	*th* this
îr pier	hw which
ŏ pot	zh vision
ō toe	ə about, item
ô paw	

Stress marks:
ʹ (primary);
ʹ (secondary), as in
dictionary (dĭkʹshə-nĕrʹē)

pen•al•ty (pĕn′əl-tē) *n., pl.* **-ties. 1.** A punishment established by law or authority for an offense. **2.** Something, esp. a sum of money, required as a forfeit for an offense. **3.** The disadvantage or painful consequences resulting from an action or a condition: *rarely slept and paid the penalty.* **4.** *Sports.* A punishment, handicap, or loss of advantage imposed on a team or competitor for infraction of a rule. **5.** *Games.* Points scored in contract bridge by the opponents when the declarer fails to make a bid. [ME *penalte* < OFr. *penalite* < Med.Lat. *poenālitās* < Lat. *poenālis*, penal. See PENAL.]

penalty box *n. Sports.* An area to the side of an ice hockey rink where penalized players wait out their penalties.

pen•ance (pĕn′əns) *n.* **1.** A voluntary act of self-mortification or devotion expressing sorrow for sin. **2.** A sacrament in some Christian churches that includes contrition, confession to a priest, acceptance of punishment, and absolution. —*tr.v.* **-anced, -anc•ing, -anc•es.** To impose penance upon. [ME < OFr. < Lat. *paenitentia*, penitence < *paenitēns, paenitent-*, penitent. See PENITENT.]

Pe•nang (pə-năng′, pē′năng′). See **George Town** 1.

Pe•na•tes (pə-nā′tēz, -nä′-) *pl.n. Rom. Myth.* The household deities whose cult was connected with that of the Lares. [Lat. *Penātēs* < *penus*, foodstuff, interior of a house.]

pence (pĕns) *n. Chiefly British.* Pl. of **penny** 3.

pen•cel also **pen•sil** (pĕn′səl) *n.* A narrow flag, streamer, or pennon, esp. one carried at the top of a lance or spear. [ME < OFr. *penoncel*, dim. of *penon*, pennon. See PENNON.]

pen•chant (pĕn′chənt) *n.* A definite liking; a strong inclination. See Syns at **predilection.** [Fr. < pr.part. of *pencher*, to incline < OFr. < VLat. **pendicāre* < Lat. *pendēre*, to hang. See **(s)pen-*.**]

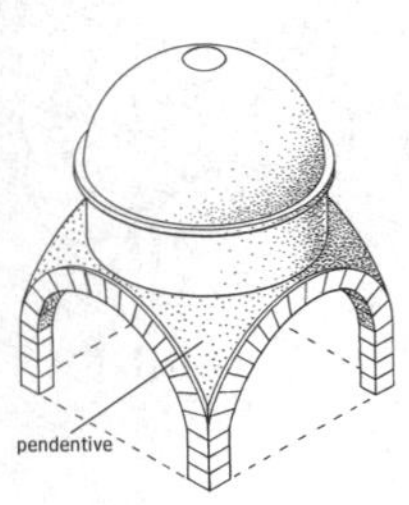

pendentive

pen•cil (pĕn′səl) *n.* **1.** A narrow, usu. cylindrical implement for writing, drawing, or marking, consisting of a thin rod of graphite, colored wax, or similar substance encased in wood or held in a mechanical holder. **2.** Something shaped or used like a pencil, esp. a narrow medicated or cosmetic stick: *an eyebrow pencil.* **3.a.** Style, technique, or skill in drawing, delineating, or describing. **b.** An artist's brush, esp. a fine one. **4.** *Phys.* A beam of radiant energy in the form of a narrow cone or cylinder. **5.** *Math.* A family of geometric objects that have a common property, such as all lines passing through a given point. —*tr.v.* **-ciled, -cil•ing, -cils** also **-cilled, -cil•ling, -cils. 1.** To write or produce by using a pencil. **2.** To mark or color with or as if with a pencil. [ME *pencel*, artist's brush < OFr. *pincel, peincel* < VLat. **pēnicellus*, alteration of Lat. *pēnicillus*, dim. of *pēniculus*, dim. of *pēnis*, tail, brush. See **pes-*.**] —**pen′cil•er, pen′cil•ler** *n.*

pencil pusher *n. Informal.* One whose job involves paperwork.

pen•dant[1] also **pen•dent** (pĕn′dənt) *n.* **1.** Something suspended from something else, esp. an ornament or a piece of jewelry attached to a necklace or bracelet. **2.** A hanging lamp or chandelier. **3.** A sculptured ornament suspended from a vaulted Gothic roof or ceiling. **4.** One of a matched pair; a companion piece. [ME *pendaunt* < OFr. *pendant* < pr.part. of *pendre*, to hang < VLat. **pendere* < Lat. *pendēre*. See **(s)pen-*.**]

pen•dant[2] (pĕn′dənt) *adj.* Var. of **pendent**[1].

Pen•del•i•kón (pĕn-dĕl′ĭ-kŏn′, pĕn′dĕ-lē-kôn′). A mountain, c. 1,119 m (3,670 ft), of E-central Greece NE of Athens.

pen•dent[1] also **pen•dant** (pĕn′dənt) *adj.* **1.** Hanging down; dangling; suspended. **2.** Projecting; overhanging. **3.** Awaiting settlement; pending. [ME *pendant* (influenced by Lat. *pendēns, pendent-*, pr.part. of *pendēre*, to hang) < OFr. See PENDANT[1].] —**pen′dent•ly** *adv.*

pen•dent[2] (pĕn′dənt) *n.* Var. of **pendant**[1].

pen•den•tive (pĕn-dĕn′tĭv) *n. Archit.* A triangular section of vaulting between the rim of a dome and each adjacent pair of the arches that support it. [Fr. *pendentif* < Lat. *pendēns, pendent-*, hanging, pr.part. of *pendēre*, to hang. See **(s)pen-*.**]

pend•ing (pĕn′dĭng) *adj.* **1.** Not yet decided or settled; awaiting conclusion or confirmation. **2.** Impending; imminent. —*prep.* **1.** While in the process of; during. **2.** While awaiting; until. [Fr. *pendant*, pendant, pending (< OFr.; see PENDENT[1]) + -ING[1].]

Pend O•reille (pŏn′də-rā′). A river rising in **Pend Oreille Lake** in N ID and flowing c. 161 km (100 mi) to the Columbia R. just N of the British Columbia, Canada, border.

pen•du•lar (pĕn′jə-lər, pĕn′dyə-, -də-) *adj.* Of or resembling the motion of a pendulum; swinging back and forth.

pen•du•lous (pĕn′jə-ləs, pĕn′dyə-, -də-) *adj.* **1.** Hanging loosely; suspended so as to swing or sway. **2.** Wavering; undecided. [< Lat. *pendulus* < *pendēre*, to hang. See **(s)pen-*.**] —**pen′du•lous•ly** *adv.* —**pen′du•lous•ness** *n.*

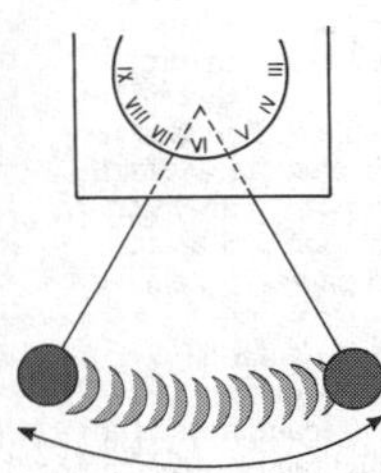
pendulum

pen•du•lum (pĕn′jə-ləm, pĕn′dyə-, pĕn′də-) *n.* **1.** A body suspended from a fixed support so that it swings freely back and forth under the influence of gravity, used to regulate various devices, esp. clocks. **2.** Something that swings back and forth from one course, opinion, or condition to another. [NLat., prob. < Ital. *pendolo*, pendulous, pendulum < Lat. *pendulus*, hanging. See PENDULOUS.]

Pe•nel•o•pe (pə-nĕl′ə-pē) *n. Gk. Myth.* The wife of Odysseus and mother of Telemachus.

pe•ne•plain also **pe•ne•plane** (pē′nə-plān′) *n. Geol.* A nearly flat land surface representing an advanced stage of erosion. [Lat. *paene, pēne*, almost + PLAIN.]

pe•nes (pē′nēz) *n. Anat.* Pl. of **penis.**

pen•e•tra•ble (pĕn′ĭ-trə-bəl) *adj.* Capable of being penetrated. —**pen′e•tra•bil′i•ty** *n.* —**pen′e•tra•bly** *adv.*

pen•e•tra•li•a (pĕn′ĭ-trā′lē-ə) *pl.n.* **1.** The innermost parts of a building, esp. the sanctuary of a temple. **2.** The most private or secret parts; recesses. [Lat. *penetrālia* < neut. pl. of *penetrālis*, inner < *penetrāre*, to penetrate. See PENETRATE.]

pen•e•trance (pĕn′ĭ-trəns) *n.* The frequency, under given environmental conditions, with which a specific genotype is expressed by those individuals that possess it.

pen•e•trant (pĕn′ĭ-trənt) *adj.* Penetrating; piercing. —*n.* Something that penetrates or is capable of penetrating.

pen•e•trate (pĕn′ĭ-trāt′) *v.* **-trat•ed, -trat•ing, -trates.** —*tr.* **1.** To enter or force a way into; pierce. **2.a.** To enter into and permeate. **b.** To cause to be permeated or diffused; steep. **3.** To insert the penis into the vagina or anus of. **4.** To enter (an organization, for example), usu. surreptitiously, so as to gain influence or information; infiltrate. **5.** To enter and gain a share of (a market). **6.** To grasp the inner significance of; understand. **7.** To see through. **8.** To affect deeply, as by piercing the consciousness or emotions. —*intr.* **1.** To pierce, enter into, or make a way in or through something. **2.** To gain admittance or access. **3.** To gain insight. [Lat. *penetrāre, penetrāt-* < *penitus*, deeply.] —**pen′e•tra′tor** *n.*

pen•e•trat•ing (pĕn′ĭ-trā′tĭng) *adj.* **1.** Capable of penetrating or seeming to penetrate. **2.** Keenly perceptive or understanding; acute. —**pen′e•trat′ing•ly** *adv.*

pen•e•tra•tion (pĕn′ĭ-trā′shən) *n.* **1.** The act or process of piercing or penetrating something, esp.: **a.** The act of entering a country or an organization so as to establish influence or gain information. **b.** An attack that penetrates enemy territory or a military front. **c.** Insertion of the penis into the vagina or anus. **2.** The power or ability to penetrate. **3.** The depth reached by a projectile after hitting its target. **4.a.** The degree to which something is sold or recognized in a particular market. **b.** The influence that one culture or nation has in another. **5.** The capacity or action of understanding; insight.

pen•e•tra•tive (pĕn′ĭ-trā′tĭv) *adj.* **1.** Tending to penetrate; penetrant. **2.** Displaying keen insight; acute.

pen•e•trom•e•ter (pĕn′ĭ-trŏm′ĭ-tər) also **pen•e•tram•e•ter** (-trăm′ĭ-tər) *n.* **1.** A device for measuring the penetrating power of radiation, esp. x-rays. **2.** A device for measuring the penetrability of semisolids.

Peng•hu (pŭng′ho͞o′). See **Pescadores.**

Peng•pu (pŭng′po͞o′). See **Bengbu.**

pen•guin (pĕng′gwĭn, pĕn′-) *n.* **1.** Any of various flightless marine birds of the family Spheniscidae, native to cool regions of the Southern Hemisphere and having flipperlike wings and webbed feet adapted for swimming and diving. **2.** *Obsolete.* The great auk. [Poss. < Welsh *pen gwyn*, White Head (name of an island in Newfoundland), great auk : *pen*, chief, head + *gwynn*, white; see **weid-*.**]

pen•hold•er (pĕn′hōl′dər) *n.* **1.** A holder for a pen point. **2.** A rack or cup for holding a pen or pens.

-penia *suff.* Lack; deficiency: *leukopenia.* [NLat. < Gk. *penia*, poverty, lack. See **(s)pen-*.**]

pen•i•cil•la•mine (pĕn′ĭ-sĭl′ə-mēn′) *n* A degradation product of penicillin, $C_5H_{11}NO_2S$, used as a chelating agent and in the treatment of rheumatoid arthritis and copper poisoning. [PENICILL(IN) + -AMINE.]

pen•i•cil•late (pĕn′ĭ-sĭl′ĭt, -āt′) *adj.* Having or resembling a tuft or brush of fine hairs, as those on caterpillars and certain grasses. [Lat. *pēnicillus*, brush; see PENCIL + -ATE[2].]

pen•i•cil•lin (pĕn′ĭ-sĭl′ĭn) *n.* Any of a group of broad-spectrum antibiotic drugs obtained from penicillium molds or produced synthetically and used in the treatment of various infections and diseases. [PENICILL(IUM) + -IN.]

pen•i•cil•li•um (pĕn′ĭ-sĭl′ē-əm) *n., pl.* **-cil•li•ums** or **-cil•li•a** (-sĭl′ē-ə). Any of various characteristically bluish-green fungi of the genus *Penicillium* that are used in the production of penicillin and in making cheese. [NLat. *Pēnicillium*, genus name < Lat. *pēnicillus*, brush. See PENCIL.]

pe•nile (pē′nīl′, -nəl) *adj.* Of or relating to the penis.

pen•in•su•la (pə-nĭn′syə-lə, -sə-lə) *n.* A piece of land that projects into a body of water and is connected with the mainland by an isthmus. [Lat. *paenīnsula* : *paene*, almost + *īnsula*, island.] —**pen•in′su•lar** *adj.*

pe•nis (pē′nĭs) *n., pl.* **-nis•es** or **-nes** (-nēz). *Anat.* **1.** The male organ of copulation in higher vertebrates that in mammals also serves as the male organ of urinary excretion. **2.** Any of various copulatory organs in males of lower animals. [Lat. *pēnis.* See **pes-*.**]

penis envy *n. Psychol.* The wish of a girl or woman to have a penis, postulated by Sigmund Freud as a cause of feelings of inferiority and neurotic behavior.

pen•i•tence (pĕn′ĭ-təns) *n.* The condition or quality of being penitent; regret for wrongdoing.

pen•i•tent (pĕn′ĭ-tənt) *adj.* Feeling or expressing remorse for one's misdeeds or sins. —*n.* **1.** One who is penitent. **2.** A person performing penance under the direction of a confessor.

[ME < OFr. < Med.Lat. *pēnitēns, pēnitent-* < Lat. *paenitēns,* pr.part. of *paenitēre,* to repent.] — **pen′i•tent•ly** *adv.*

pen•i•ten•tial (pĕn′ĭ-tĕn′shəl) *adj.* **1.** Of, relating to, or expressing penitence. **2.** Of or relating to penance. — *n.* **1.** A book or set of church rules concerning the sacrament of penance. **2.** A penitent. — **pen′i•ten′tial•ly** *adv.*

pen•i•ten•tia•ry (pĕn′ĭ-tĕn′shə-rē) *n., pl.* **-ries. 1.** A prison for those convicted of major crimes. **2.** *Rom. Cath. Ch.* **a.** A tribunal of the Roman Curia having jurisdiction in matters relating to penance, dispensations, and papal absolutions. **b.** A priest whose special function is the administration of the sacrament of penance in a particular church or diocese. — *adj.* **1.** Of or for the purpose of penance; penitential. **2.** Relating to or used for punishment or reform of criminals or wrongdoers. **3.** Resulting in or punishable by imprisonment in a penitentiary. [ME *penitenciarie,* penance officer, episcopal prison < Med.Lat. *pēnitentiāria,* fem. of *pēnitentiārius* < Lat. *paenitentia,* penitence < *paenitēns,* penitent. See PENITENT.]

Pen•ki (bŭn′jē′). See **Benxi.**

pen•knife (pĕn′nīf′) *n.* A small pocketknife.

pen•light (pĕn′līt′) *n.* A small flashlight having the size and shape of a fountain pen.

pen•man (pĕn′mən) *n.* **1.** A copyist; a scribe. **2.** An expert in penmanship. **3.** An author; a writer.

pen•man•ship (pĕn′mən-shĭp′) *n.* The art, skill, style, or manner of handwriting; calligraphy.

Penn (pĕn), **William.** 1644–1718. English Quaker colonizer in America who founded Pennsylvania in 1681.

Penn, Sir **William.** 1621–70. English admiral who led the English fleet during the Dutch War (1665–67).

Penn. *abbr.* Pennsylvania.

pen•na (pĕn′ə) *n., pl.* **pen•nae** (pĕn′ē). A contour feather of a bird, as distinguished from a down feather or a plume. [Lat., feather. See **pet-***.] — **pen•na′ceous** (pĕ-nā′shəs) *adj.*

Penna. *abbr.* Pennsylvania.

pen name also **pen•name** (pĕn′nām′) *n.* A pseudonym.

pen•nant (pĕn′ənt) *n.* **1.** *Naut.* A long, usu. triangular flag, used on ships for signaling or identification. **2.** A flag or an emblem similar in shape to a ship's pennant. **3.** *Sports.* **a.** A flag that symbolizes the championship of a league, esp. in professional baseball. **b.** The championship so symbolized. [Blend of PENDANT[1] and PENNON.]

pen•nate (pĕn′āt′) also **pen•nat•ed** (pĕn′ā′tĭd) *adj.* **1.** Having feathers or wings. **2.** *Bot.* Pinnate. **3.** Of diatoms of the class Pennales, distinguished by bilaterally symmetrical form. [Lat. *pennātus* < *penna,* feather. See **pet-***.]

pen•ne (pĕn′ā) *n., pl.* **penne.** Short tubular pasta with diagonally cut ends. [Ital., pl. of *penna,* quill pen < Lat. See PENNA.]

Pen•nell (pĕn′əl, pə-nĕl′), **Joseph.** 1857–1956. Amer. illustrator known for *Lithography and Lithographers* (1898).

Penn Hills. A community of SW PA, a suburb of Pittsburgh. Pop. 51,430.

pen•ni (pĕn′ē) *n., pl.* **pen•nis** or **pen•ni•a** (pĕn′ē-ə). See table at **currency.** [Finn., poss. < Swed. *penning.*]

pen•ni•less (pĕn′ē-lĭs, pĕn′ə-) *adj.* **1.** Entirely without money. **2.** Very poor. See Syns at **poor.** — **pen′ni•less•ness** *n.*

Pen•nine Alps (pĕn′īn′). A range of the Alps along the Swiss-Italian border rising to 4,636.9 m (15,203 ft).

Pen•nines (pĕn′īnz′) also **Pennine Chain.** A range of hills extending c. 257 km (160 mi) from the Scottish border to central England and rising to 893.7 m (2,930 ft).

pen•non (pĕn′ən) *n.* **1.** A long narrow banner borne upon a lance. **2.** A pennant, banner, or flag. **3.** A pinion; a wing. [ME < OFr. *penon,* streamer, feather of an arrow, aug. of *penne,* feather < Lat. *penna.* See **pet-***.] — **pen′noned** *adj.*

pen•non•cel also **pen•on•cel** or **pen•non•celle** (pĕn′ən-sĕl′) *n.* A small pennon or flag borne on a lance. [ME *penoncel* < OFr., dim. of *penon,* pennon. See PENNON.]

Penn•sau•ken (pĕn-sô′kĭn). A community of SW NJ, a suburb of Camden and Philadelphia PA. Pop. 34,733.

Penn•syl•va•nia (pĕn′səl-vān′yə, -vā′nē-ə). A state of the E U.S.; admitted as one of the original Thirteen Colonies in 1787. Cap. Harrisburg. Pop. 11,924,710.

Pennsylvania Dutch *n.* **1.** The descendants of German and Swiss immigrants who settled in Pennsylvania in the 17th and 18th centuries. **2.** The dialect of High German spoken by the Pennsylvania Dutch. **3.** The style of folk art and decorative arts developed by the Pennsylvania Dutch. [Alteration of Ger. *Deutsch,* German. See PLATTDEUTSCH.]

Penn•syl•va•nian (pĕn′səl-vān′yən, -vā′nē-ən) *adj.* **1.** Of or relating to Pennsylvania. **2.** *Geol.* Of, belonging to, or being the geologic time of the sixth period of the Paleozoic Era, characterized by the deposition of coal-bearing rock. See table at **geologic time.** — *n.* **1.** A native or resident of Pennsylvania. **2.** *Geol.* The Pennsylvanian Period or its deposits.

pen•ny (pĕn′ē) *n., pl.* **-nies. 1.** See table at **currency. 2.** In the United States and Canada, the coin worth one cent. **3.** *pl.* **pence** (pĕns). **a.** A coin used in Great Britain since 1971, worth 1/100 of a pound. **b.** A coin formerly used in Great Britain, worth 1/240 of a pound. **4.** Any of various coins of small denomination. **5.** A sum of money. — *idiom.* **pretty penny.** A large sum of money. [ME, a coin < OE *penig.*]

penny ante *n.* **1.** *Games.* A poker game in which the highest bet is limited to a penny or another small sum. **2.** *Informal.* A business transaction on a trivial scale. — **pen′ny-an′te** (pĕn′ē-ăn′tē) *adj.*

pen•ny•cress (pĕn′ē-krĕs′) *n.* Any of several plants of the genus *Thlaspi,* having small flattened seed pods with winglike margins, esp. the Eurasian species *T. arvense.*

penny pincher *n. Informal.* A very stingy person.

pen•ny-pinch•ing (pĕn′ē-pĭn′chĭng) *adj.* Giving or spending money grudgingly; niggardly. — **pen′ny-pinch′ing** *n.*

pen•ny•roy•al (pĕn′ē-roi′əl) *n.* **1.** A Eurasian mint *(Mentha pulegium)* having ovate or nearly orbicular leaves that yield a useful aromatic oil. **2.** An aromatic plant *(Hedeoma pulegioides)* of eastern North America having glabrous leaves that yield an oil used as an insect repellent. [Prob. by folk ety. < ME *puliol real* < AN : *puliol,* thyme (< Lat. *pūlegium*) + *real,* royal (< Lat. *rēgālis;* see REGAL).]

pen•ny•weight (pĕn′ē-wāt′) *n.* A unit of troy weight equal to 24 grains, 1/20 of a troy ounce or approx. 1.555 grams.

pen•ny•whis•tle also **pen•ny whis•tle** (pĕn′ē-hwĭs′əl, -wĭs′-) *n. Mus.* An inexpensive fipple flute, usu. having a plastic mouthpiece and a tin body.

pen•ny-wise or **pen•ny•wise** (pĕn′ē-wīz′) *adj.* Careful in dealing with small sums of money or small matters.

pen•ny•wort (pĕn′ē-wûrt′, -wôrt′) *n.* Any of several plants having rounded leaves suggestive of pennies, as: **a.** A Eurasian plant (Umbilicus rupestris) having thick peltate leaves and yellowish-green flowers. **b.** A North American plant *(Obolaria virginica)* having small white or purplish flowers.

pen•ny•worth (pĕn′ē-wûrth′) *n.* **1.** As much as a penny will buy. **2.** A small amount; a modicum. **3.** A bargain.

Pe•nob•scot (pə-nŏb′skət, -skŏt′) *n., pl.* **Penobscot** or **-scots. 1.** A member of a Native American people inhabiting Penobscot Bay and the Penobscot River valley in Maine. **2.** The Algonquian language of the Penobscot, a dialect of Eastern Abenaki. [< a Penobscot place name.]

Penobscot River. A river rising in several lakes and tributaries in W and central ME and flowing c. 563 km (350 mi) to **Penobscot Bay,** an inlet of the Atlantic Ocean.

pe•nol•o•gy also **poe•nol•o•gy** (pē-nŏl′ə-jē) *n.* The study, theory, and practice of prison management and criminal rehabilitation. [Lat. *poena,* penalty (< Gk. *poinē;* see **kʷei-[1]***) + -LOGY.] — **pe′no•log′i•cal** (pē′nə-lŏj′ĭ-kəl) *adj.* — **pe′no•log′i•cal•ly** *adv.* — **pe•nol′o•gist** *n.*

pen•on•cel (pĕn′ən-sĕl′) *n.* Var. of **pennoncel.**

pen pal *n.* A person with whom one becomes acquainted through regular correspondence.

pen point *n.* **1.** A tapering metal device with a split point that fits into a holder and is used for writing; a nib. **2.** The point or tip of a pen.

Pen•sa•co•la (pĕn′sə-kō′lə). A city of extreme NW Florida on **Pensacola Bay,** an inlet of the Gulf of Mexico; settled by the Spanish in 1559. Pop. 58,165.

pen•sil (pĕn′səl) *n.* Var. of **pencel.**

pen•sile (pĕn′sīl′) *adj.* **1.** Hanging loosely; suspended. **2.** Having or building a hanging nest. Used of birds. [Lat. *pēnsilis* < *pēnsus,* p.part. of *pendere,* to hang. See **(s)pen-***.]

pen•sion[1] (pĕn′shən) *n.* A sum of money paid regularly as a retirement benefit or by way of patronage. — *tr.v.* **-sioned, -sion•ing, -sions. 1.** To grant a pension to. **2.** To retire or dismiss with a pension. [ME *pensioun,* payment < OFr. *pension* < Lat. *pēnsiō, pēnsiōn-* < *pēnsus,* p.part. of *pendere,* to weigh, pay. See **(s)pen-***.] — **pen′sion•a•ble** *adj.*

pen•sion[2] (pän-syôɴ′) *n.* **1.** A boarding house or small hotel in Europe. **2.** Accommodations or the payment for accommodations, esp. at a pension. **3.** Room and board. [Fr. < OFr., payment. See PENSION[1].]

pen•sion•ar•y (pĕn′shə-nĕr′ē) *adj.* **1.** Constituting a pension. **2.** Mercenary. — *n., pl.* **-ies. 1.** A pensioner. **2.** A hireling.

pen•sion•er (pĕn′shə-nər) *n.* **1.** One who receives a pension. **2.** One who is dependent on the bounty of another. **3.** *Obsolete.* **a.** A gentleman-at-arms. **b.** An attendant; a retainer.

pen•sive (pĕn′sĭv) *adj.* **1.** Deeply, often wistfully or dreamily thoughtful. **2.** Suggestive or expressive of melancholy thoughtfulness. [ME *pensif* < OFr. < *penser,* to think < Lat. *pēnsāre,* freq. of *pendere,* to weigh. See **(s)pen-***.] — **pen′sive•ly** *adv.* — **pen′sive•ness** *n.*

Syns: *pensive, contemplative, reflective, meditative, thoughtful.* These adjectives mean characterized by or disposed to thought, especially serious or deep thought. *Pensive* often connotes a wistful, dreamy, or sad quality: *"while pensive poets painful vigils keep"* (Alexander Pope). *Contemplative* implies slow, directed consideration, often with conscious intent of achieving better understanding or spiritual or aesthetic enrichment: *"The Contemplative Atheist is rare . . . And yet they seem to be more than they are"* (Francis Bacon). *Reflective* suggests careful, analytical deliberation, as in reappraising past experience: *"Cromwell was of the active, not the reflective temper"* (John Morley). *Meditative* implies earnest, sustained thought: *the meditative scholar. Thoughtful* can refer to absorption in thought or to the habit of reflection and circumspection: *thoughtful voters.*

William Penn
c. 1700 chalk portrait
by Francis Place
(1647–1728)

ă pat	oi boy
ā pay	ou out
âr care	ŏŏ took
ä father	ōō boot
ĕ pet	ŭ cut
ē be	ûr urge
ĭ pit	th thin
ī pie	*th* this
îr pier	hw which
ŏ pot	zh vision
ō toe	ə about, item
ô paw	

Stress marks:
′ (primary);
′ (secondary), as in
dictionary (dĭk′shə-nĕr′ē)

pen·ste·mon (pĕn-stē′mən, pĕn′stə-mən) *n.* Any of numerous plants of the genus *Penstemon* of North America and eastern Asia, having flowers with a usu. two-lipped, variously colored corolla. [NLat. *Pēnstēmōn*, genus name : Gk. *pente*, five; see **penkʷe*** + Gk. *stēmōn*, thread; see **stā-***.]

pen·stock (pĕn′stŏk′) *n.* **1.** A sluice or gate used to control a flow of water. **2.** A pipe or conduit used to carry water to a water wheel or turbine.

pent (pĕnt) *v.* A p.t. and p.part. of **pen²**. —*adj.* Penned or shut up; closely confined.

penta– or **pent–** *pref.* Five: *pentamerous.* [Gk. < *pente*, five. See **penkʷe***.]

pen·ta·chlo·ro·phe·nol (pĕn′tə-klôr′ə-fē′nōl′, -nôl′, -nŏl′, -klōr′-) *n.* A toxic white crystalline compound, C_6Cl_5OH, used in solution as a fungicide and wood preservative.

pen·ta·cle (pĕn′tə-kəl) *n.* A five-pointed star formed by five straight lines connecting the vertices of a pentagon and enclosing another pentagon in the completed figure. [Med.Lat. **pentaculum* : Gk. *penta-*, penta- + Lat. *-culum*, dim. suff.]

pen·tad (pĕn′tăd′) *n.* A group of five. [Gk. *pentas, pentad-*, group of five < *pente*, five. See **penkʷe***.]

pen·ta·dac·tyl (pĕn′tə-dăk′təl) also **pen·ta·dac·ty·late** (-tə-lĭt, -lāt′) *adj.* Having five fingers or toes on each hand or foot. [Lat. *pentadactylus* < Gk. *pentadaktulos* : *penta-*, penta- + *daktulos*, finger.] —**pen′ta·dac′tyl·ism** *n.*

pen·ta·gon (pĕn′tə-gŏn′) *n.* **1.** A polygon having five sides and five interior angles. **2. Pentagon.** The United States military establishment. Used with *the.* —**pen·tag′o·nal** (pĕn-tăg′ə-nəl) *adj.* —**pen·tag′o·nal·ly** *adv.*

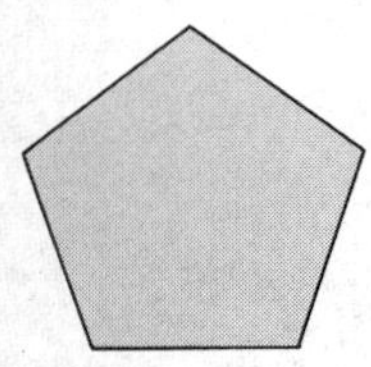

pentagon
Top: Polygonal figure
Bottom: The Pentagon, Arlington, Virginia

pen·ta·gram (pĕn′tə-grăm′) *n.* See **pentacle.**

pen·ta·he·dron (pĕn′tə-hē′drən) *n., pl.* **-drons** or **-dra** (-drə). A solid having five plane faces. —**pen′ta·he′dral** (-drəl) *adj.*

pen·tam·er·ous (pĕn-tăm′ər-əs) *adj.* **1.** Having five similar parts. **2.** Having flower parts, such as petals and stamens, in sets of five, as in the geranium. —**pen·tam′er·ism** *n.*

pen·tam·e·ter (pĕn-tăm′ĭ-tər) *n.* **1.** A line of verse consisting of five metrical feet. **2.** English verse composed in iambic pentameter. [Lat. < Gk. *pentametros* : *penta-*, penta- + *metron*, measure; see METER¹.]

pen·tane (pĕn′tān′) *n.* Any of three colorless flammable isomeric hydrocarbons, C_5H_{12}, derived from petroleum and used as solvents.

pen·tan·gu·lar (pĕn-tăng′gyə-lər) *adj.* Having five angles.

pen·ta·ploid (pĕn′tə-ploid′) *adj.* Having five haploid sets of chromosomes. —*n.* A pentaploid individual.

pen·tar·chy (pĕn′tär′kē) *n., pl.* **-chies. 1.** Government by five rulers. **2.** A body of five joint rulers. **3.** An association or federation of five governments, each ruled by a different leader. —**pen·tar′chi·cal** (pĕn-tär′kĭ-kəl) *adj.*

pen·ta·stich (pĕn′tə-stĭk′) *n.* A poem or stanza having five lines. [< LGk. *pentastikhos*, of five lines : *penta-*, penta- + *stikhos*, line; see **steigh-***.]

Pen·ta·teuch (pĕn′tə-to͞ok′, -tyo͞ok′) *n.* The first five books of the Hebrew Bible. [ME *Pentateuke* < LLat. *Pentateuchus* < Gk. *Pentateukhos* : *penta-*, penta- + *teukhos*, implement, vessel, scroll case; see **dheugh-***.] —**Pen′ta·teuch′al** *adj.*

pen·tath·lete (pĕn-tăth′lēt) *n. Sports.* An athlete who participates in a pentathlon.

pen·tath·lon (pĕn-tăth′lən, -lŏn′) *n. Sports.* **1.** An athletic contest made up of five track-and-field events. **2.** The modern pentathlon. [Gk. : *penta-*, penta- + *athlon*, contest.]

pen·ta·ton·ic (pĕn′tə-tŏn′ĭk) *adj. Mus.* Of or using only five tones, esp. the first, second, third, fifth, and sixth tones of a diatonic scale.

pen·ta·va·lent (pĕn′tə-vā′lənt) *adj.* Having valence 5.

pen·taz·o·cine (pĕn-tăz′ə-sēn′) *n.* A synthetic narcotic drug, $C_{19}H_{27}NO$, used as a nonaddictive analgesic, often in place of morphine. [PENT(A)– + AZO– + –INE².]

Pen·te·cost (pĕn′tĭ-kôst′, -kŏst′) *n.* **1.** The seventh Sunday after Easter, commemorating the descent of the Holy Spirit upon the disciples. **2.** *Judaism.* See **Shavuot.** [ME *pentecoste* < OE *Pentecosten* < LLat. *Pentēcostē* < Gk. *pentēkostē (hēmera)*, fiftieth (day), fem. of *pentēkostos*, fiftieth < *pentēkonta*, fifty. See **penkʷe***.]

Pen·te·cos·tal (pĕn′tĭ-kŏs′təl, -kô′stəl) *adj.* **1.** Of, relating to, or occurring at Pentecost. **2.** Of, relating to, or being any of various Christian congregations whose members seek to be filled with the Holy Spirit, in emulation of the Apostles at Pentecost. —*n.* A member of a Pentecostal congregation. —**Pen′te·cos′tal·ism** *n.* —**Pen′te·cos′tal·ist** *adj. & n.*

pent·house (pĕnt′hous′) *n.* **1.a.** An apartment or dwelling situated on the roof of a building. **b.** A residence, often with a terrace, on the top floor or floors of a building. **c.** A structure housing machinery on the roof of a building. **2.** A shed or sloping roof attached to the side of a building or wall. [Alteration of ME *pentis, pentace*, a shed attached to a wall of a building < AN *pentiz*, penthouses < OFr. *apentiz*, penthouse < *apent*, p.part. of *apendre*, to belong, depend < Med. Lat. *appendere* < Lat., to hang, suspend. See APPEND.]

Pen·tic·ton (pĕn-tĭk′tən). A city of S British Columbia, Canada, E of Vancouver on Okanagan Lake. Pop. 23,181.

pen·ti·men·to (pĕn′tə-mĕn′tō) *n., pl.* **-ti** (-tē). An underlying image in a painting, as an earlier painting, a part of a painting, or an original draft, that shows through, usu. when the top layer of paint has become transparent with age. [Ital., correction, pentimento < *pentire*, to repent < Lat. *paenitēre*.]

Pent·land Firth (pĕnt′lənd). A narrow channel between NE Scotland and the Orkney Is.

pent·land·ite (pĕnt′lən-dīt′) *n.* A yellowish-brown nickel iron sulfide that is the principal ore of nickel. [Fr., after Joseph B. *Pentland* (1797–1873), Irish scientist.]

pen·to·bar·bi·tal sodium (pĕn′tə-bär′bĭ-tôl′, -tăl′) *n.* A white crystalline or powdery barbiturate, $C_{11}H_{17}N_2O_3Na$, used as a hypnotic, a sedative, and an anticonvulsive drug.

pen·to·san (pĕn′tə-săn′) *n.* Any of a group of polysaccharides found with cellulose in many woody plants and yielding pentoses on hydrolysis.

pen·tose (pĕn′tōs′, -tōz′) *n.* Any of a class of monosaccharides having five carbon atoms per molecule and including ribose and several other sugars.

Pen·to·thal (pĕn′tə-thôl′). A trademark used for thiopental sodium.

pent·ox·ide (pĕnt-ŏk′sīd′) *n.* A compound having five atoms of oxygen combined with another element or radical.

pent-up (pĕnt′ŭp′) *adj.* Not given expression; repressed.

pen·tyl (pĕn′təl) *n.* See **amyl.**

pe·nu·che also **pe·nu·chi** (pə-no͞o′chē) or **pa·no·cha** (-nō′-chə) or **pa·no·che** (-chē) *n.* A fudgelike confection of brown sugar, cream or milk, and chopped nuts. [Var. of PANOCHA.]

pe·nuch·le or **pe·nuck·le** (pē′nŭk′əl) *n.* Var. of **pinochle.**

pe·nult (pē′nŭlt′, pĭ-nŭlt′) also **pe·nul·ti·ma** (pĭ-nŭl′tə-mə) *n.* **1.** The next to the last item in a series. **2.** The next to the last syllable in a word. [Short for *penultima* < Lat. *paenultima*, fem. of *paenultimus*, next to last : *paene*, almost + *ultimus*, last; see ULTIMATE.]

pe·nul·ti·mate (pĭ-nŭl′tə-mĭt) *adj.* **1.** Next to last. **2.** Of or relating to the penult of a word. —*n.* The next to the last. [< Lat. *paenultimus*. See PENULT.] —**pe·nul′ti·mate·ly** *adv.*

pe·num·bra (pĭ-nŭm′brə) *n., pl.* **-brae** (-brē) or **-bras. 1.** A partial shadow, as in an eclipse, between regions of complete shadow and complete illumination. **2.** The grayish outer part of a sunspot. **3.** An area in which something exists to a lesser or an uncertain degree. **4.** An outlying surrounding region; a periphery. [NLat. : Lat. *paene*, almost + Lat. *umbra*, shadow.] —**pe·num′bral, pe·num′brous** *adj.*

pe·nu·ri·ous (pə-no͝or′ē-əs, -nyo͝or′-) *adj.* **1.** Ungenerously or pettily unwilling to spend money. **2.** Yielding little; barren. **3.** Poverty-stricken; destitute. [< Med.Lat. *pēnūriōsus* < Lat. *pēnūria*, want.] —**pe·nu′ri·ous·ness** *n.*

pen·u·ry (pĕn′yə-rē) *n.* **1.** Extreme want or poverty; destitution. **2.** Extreme dearth; barrenness or insufficiency. [ME *penurie* < Lat. *pēnūria*, want.]

Pe·nu·ti·an (pə-no͞o′tē-ən, -shən) *n.* A proposed stock of North American Indian languages spoken in Pacific coastal areas from California into British Columbia.

Pen·za (pĕn′zə, pyĕn′-). A city of W-central Russia SSW of Kazan; founded 1666. Pop. 527,000.

Pen·zance (pĕn-zăns′). A municipal borough of SW England WSW of Plymouth. Pop. 19,521.

Pen·zi·as (pĕnt′sē-əs), **Arno Allan.** b. 1933. German-born Amer. physicist who shared a 1978 Nobel Prize.

pe·on (pē′ŏn′, pē′ən) *n.* **1.a.** An unskilled laborer or farm worker of Latin America or the southwest United States. **b.** Such a worker bound in servitude to a landlord creditor. **2.** A menial worker; a drudge. **3.** (also pyo͞on). An Indian or Ceylonese messenger, servant, or foot soldier. [Sp., day laborer < Med.Lat. *pedō, pedōn-*, foot soldier. See PIONEER.]

pe·on·age (pē′ə-nĭj) *n.* **1.** The condition of being a peon. **2.** A system by which debtors are bound in servitude to their creditors until their debts are paid.

pe·o·ny (pē′ə-nē) *n., pl.* **-nies.** Any of various plants of the genus *Paeonia*, having large, variously colored flowers with numerous stamens and several pistils. [ME *pione*, ult. < Med. Lat. *peōnia* < Lat. *paeōnia* < Gk. *paiōnia*, perh. < *Paiōn*, Apollo, physician of the gods.]

peo·ple (pē′pəl) *n., pl.* **people. 1.** Human beings considered as a group or in indefinite numbers. **2.** A body of persons living in the same country under one national government; a nationality. **3.** *pl.* **peo·ples.** A body of persons sharing a religion, culture, language, or inherited condition of life. **4.** Persons with regard to their residence, class, profession, or group. **5.** The mass of ordinary persons; the populace. **6.** The citizens of a political unit, such as a nation or a state; the electorate. **7.** Persons subordinate to or loyal to a ruler, a superior, or an employer. **8.** Family, relatives, or ancestors. **9.** *Informal.* Animals or other beings distinct from human beings. —*tr.v.* **-pled, -pling, -ples.** To furnish with or as if with people; populate. [ME *peple* < OFr. *pueple* < Lat. *populus*, of Etruscan orig.] —**peo′pler** *n.*

Usage Note: Used as a plural *people* is a form with no exactly corresponding singular. In the past, grammarians have sometimes insisted that *people* is a collective noun that should not be used as a substitute for *persons* when referring to a specific number of individuals, as in *Six people were arrested.*

This distinction is now so widely ignored in general writing that it seems pedantic to insist on it. *Persons* is still preferred in quasilegal contexts, however, as in *Vehicles containing fewer than three persons may not use the left lane during rush hours.* See Usage Note at **man.**

people mover *n.* A means of mass transit, such as a monorail, used to transport people, usu. along a fixed route.

Peo•ple's Party (pē′pəlz) *n.* See **Populist Party.**

People's Republic *n.* A political organization founded and controlled by a national Communist party.

Pe•or•i•a[1] (pē-ôr′ē-ə, -ōr′-) *n., pl.* **Peoria** or **-as.** A member of a Native American people in the Illinois confederacy.

Pe•or•i•a[2] (pē-ôr′ē-ə, -ōr′-). A city of NW-central IL on the Illinois R. N of Springfield; founded on the site of a French fort estab. by La Salle in 1680. Pop. 113,504.

pep (pĕp) *Informal.* — *n.* Energy and high spirits; vim. — *tr.v.* **pepped, pep•ping, peps.** To bring energy or liveliness to; invigorate. [Short for PEPPER.]

pep•er•o•mi•a (pĕp′ə-rō′mē-ə) *n.* Any of numerous succulent tropical herbs of the genus *Peperomia,* having palmately veined leaves and minute flowers densely grouped in cylindrical spikes. [NLat. *Peperomia,* genus name : < Gk. *peperi,* pepper; see PEPPER + Gk. *homos,* same; see HOMO–.]

Pep•in the Short (pĕp′ĭn). Also **Pepin III.** 714?–768. King of the Franks (751–768) who established the Papal States.

pep•los (pĕp′ləs, -lŏs′) also **pep•lus** (-ləs) *n., pl.* **-los•es** also **-lus•es.** A loose outer robe worn by women in ancient Greece. [Gk.]

pep•lum (pĕp′ləm) *n., pl.* **-lums. 1.** A short overskirt or ruffle attached at the waistline of a jacket, blouse, or dress. **2.** See **peplos.** [Lat., robe of state < Gk. *peplon,* neut. of *peplos,* peplos.] — **pep′lumed** *adj.*

pe•po (pē′pō) *n., pl.* **-pos.** The fruit of any of various related plants, such as the watermelon, cucumber, squash, and melon, having a hard or leathery rind, fleshy pulp, and flattened seeds. [Lat., a kind of melon < Gk. *pepōn,* ripe. See **pek^{w}-*.**]

pep•per (pĕp′ər) *n.* **1.** Black pepper. **2.** Any of several plants of the genus *Piper,* such as cubeb, betel, and kava. **3.a.** Any of several tropical American cultivated forms of *Capsicum frutescens* or *C. annuum* having podlike many-seeded berries. **b.** The podlike fruit of any of these plants, varying in size, shape, and degree of pungency. **4.** Any of various condiments made from the more pungent varieties of *Capsicum frutescens,* such as cayenne pepper or chili. **5.** *Baseball.* A warm-up exercise in which players standing a short distance from a batter field the ball and toss it to the batter, who hits each toss back to the fielders. — *tr.v.* **-pered, -per•ing, -pers. 1.** To season or sprinkle with pepper. **2.** To sprinkle liberally; dot. **3.** To shower with or as if with small missiles. **4.** To make (a speech, for example) lively and vivid with wit or invective. [ME *peper* < OE *pipor* < Lat. *piper* < Gk. *peperi* < Skt. *pippalī* < *pippalam,* pepper tree.]

pep•per-and-salt (pĕp′ər-ən-sôlt′) *adj.* Having a close mixture of black and white: *a pepper-and-salt beard.*

pep•per•box (pĕp′ər-bŏks′) *n.* See **peppershaker.**

pep•per•bush (pĕp′ər-bo͝osh′) *n. Bot.* Sweet pepperbush.

pep•per•corn (pĕp′ər-kôrn′) *n.* **1.** A dried berry of the pepper vine *Piper nigrum.* **2.** A small or insignificant thing.

pep•per•cress (pĕp′ər-krĕs′) *n.* See **peppergrass.**

pep•per•grass (pĕp′ər-grăs′) *n.* Any of several plants of the genus *Lepidium,* esp. the North American species *L. virginicum,* having white flowers and pungent foliage and seeds.

pep•per•idge (pĕp′ər-ĭj) *n.* See **sour gum.** [?]

pepper mill *n.* A utensil for grinding peppercorns.

pep•per•mint (pĕp′ər-mĭnt′) *n.* **1.** A plant *(Mentha piperita)* having downy leaves that yield a pungent oil. **2.** The oil from this plant or a preparation made from it, used as a flavoring. **3.** A candy or lozenge flavored with this oil.

pep•per•o•ni (pĕp′ə-rō′nē) *n., pl.* **-nis. 1.** A highly spiced pork and beef sausage. **2.** A slice of this type of sausage. [Ital. *peperoni,* pl. of *peperone,* pimento, red pepper, aug. of *pepe,* pepper < Lat. *piper.* See PEPPER.]

pepper pot *n.* **1.** A soup made with vegetables and tripe or other meat, seasoned with pepper and often containing dumplings. **2.** A thick West Indian stew of meat or fish, vegetables, and regional condiments. **3.** See **peppershaker.**

pep•per•shak•er (pĕp′ər-shā′kər) *n.* A container with small holes in the top for sprinkling ground pepper.

pepper tree also **pep•per•tree** (pĕp′ər-trē′) *n.* Any of several evergreen trees of the genus *Schinus,* esp. *S. molle* of South America, having compound leaves, yellowish-white flowers, and small rose-colored drupes.

pep•per•wood (pĕp′ər-wo͝od′) *n.* See **Hercules' club** 2.

pep•per•wort (pĕp′ər-wûrt′, -wôrt′) *n.* **1.** Any of various aquatic or marsh ferns of the genus *Marsilea,* having floating, four-parted palmate leaves. **2.** See **peppergrass.**

pep•per•y (pĕp′ə-rē) *adj.* **1.** Of, containing, or resembling pepper; sharp or pungent in flavor. **2.** Vigorously sharp-tempered. **3.** Sharp and stinging in style or content; vivid or fiery: *peppery criticism.* — **pep′per•i•ness** *n.*

pep pill *n. Slang.* A tablet or capsule containing a stimulant drug, esp. an amphetamine.

pep•py (pĕp′ē) *adj.* **-i•er, -i•est.** *Informal.* Full of or characterized by energy and high spirits; lively. — **pep′pi•ly** *adv.* — **pep′pi•ness** *n.*

pep•sin also **pep•sine** (pĕp′sĭn) *n.* **1.** A digestive enzyme found in gastric juice that catalyzes the breakdown of protein to peptides. **2.** A substance containing pepsin, found in hog and calf stomachs and used as a digestive aid. [Gk. *pepsis,* digestion (< *peptein,* to digest; see **pek^{w}-***) + –IN.]

pep talk *n. Informal.* A speech of exhortation, as to a team or staff, meant to instill enthusiasm or bolster morale.

pep•tic (pĕp′tĭk) *adj.* **1.a.** Of, relating to, or assisting digestion. **b.** Induced by or associated with the action of digestive secretions. **2.** Of, relating to, or involving pepsin. **3.** Capable of digesting. — *n.* A digestive agent. [Lat. *pepticus* < Gk. *peptikos,* digested < *peptos* < *peptein,* to digest. See **pek^{w}-*.**]

pep•ti•dase (pĕp′tĭ-dās′, -dāz′) *n.* An enzyme that hydrolyzes peptides into amino acids.

pep•tide (pĕp′tīd′) *n.* Any of various natural or synthetic compounds containing two or more amino acids linked by the carboxyl group of one amino acid and the amino group of another. [PEPT(ONE) + –IDE.] — **pep•tid′ic** (-tĭd′ĭk) *adj.*

peptide bond *n.* The chemical bond formed between the carboxyl groups and amino groups of neighboring amino acids, constituting the primary linkage of all protein structures.

pep•tize (pĕp′tīz′) *tr.v.* **-tized, -tiz•ing, -tiz•es.** To disperse (a precipitate) to form a colloid. [Gk. *peptein,* to digest; see **pek^{w}-*** + –IZE.] — **pep′ti•za′tion** (-tĭ-zā′shən) *n.* — **pep′tiz′er** *n.*

pep•tone (pĕp′tōn′) *n.* Any of various compounds obtained by acid or enzyme hydrolysis of natural protein and used as nutrients in culture media. [Ger. *Pepton* < Gk. *peptos,* digested < *peptein,* to digest. See **pek^{w}-*.**] — **pep•ton′ic** (-tŏn′ĭk) *adj.*

pep•to•nize (pĕp′tə-nīz′) *tr.v.* **-nized, -niz•ing, -niz•es. 1.** To convert (protein) into a peptone. **2.** To dissolve (food) by means of a proteolytic enzyme. **3.** To combine with peptone. — **pep′to•ni•za′tion** (-nĭ-zā′shən) *n.*

Pepys (pēps, pĕp′ĭs), **Samuel.** 1633–1703. English civil servant whose diary includes descriptions of the Great Fire of London (1665) and the Great Plague (1666). — **Pepys′i•an** *adj.*

Pe•quot (pē′kwŏt′) *n., pl.* **Pequot** or **-quots. 1.** A member of a Native American people formerly inhabiting eastern Connecticut, with present-day descendants in the same area. **2.** The Algonquian language of the Pequot.

per (pûr) *prep.* **1.** To, for, or by each; for every: *40 cents per gallon.* **2.** *Usage Problem.* According to; by: *changes made per instructions.* **3.** By means of; through. — *adv. Informal.* **1.** For each one; apiece: *cookies for one dollar per.* **2.** Per hour: *driving at 60 miles per.* [Lat. See **per[1]*.**]

Usage Note: *Per* is appropriately used in the description of ratios (*five miles per day; 20 dollars per person*). In its more general use to mean "according to" (as in *per our discussion*), it is best reserved for business and legal communications, unless the writer seeks a tone of jocular formality.

per. *abbr.* **1.** Period. **2.** Person.

per– *pref.* **1.** Thoroughly; completely; intensely: *perfervid.* **2.** Containing an element in its highest oxidation state: *perchloric acid.* **3.** Containing a large or the largest possible proportion of an element: *peroxide.* **4.** Containing the peroxy group: *peracid.* [Lat. < *per,* through. See **per[1]*.**]

per•ac•id (pûr′ăs′ĭd) *n.* **1.** Any of various acids containing the peroxy group. **2.** An inorganic acid containing the largest proportion of oxygen in a series of related acids.

per•ad•ven•ture (pûr′əd-vĕn′chər, pĕr′-) *adv. Archaic.* Perhaps; perchance. — *n.* Chance or uncertainty; doubt. [ME *per aventure* < OFr., by chance : *per,* through (< Lat.; see PER) + *aventure,* chance; see ADVENTURE.]

per•am•bu•late (pə-răm′byə-lāt′) *v.* **-lat•ed, -lat•ing, -lates.** — *tr.* **1.** To walk through. **2.** To inspect (an area) on foot. — *intr.* To walk about; roam or stroll. [Lat. *perambulāre, perambulāt-* : *per-,* per- + *ambulāre,* to walk.] — **per•am′bu•la′tion** *n.* — **per•am′bu•la•to′ry** (-lə-tôr′ē, -tōr′ē) *adj.*

per•am•bu•la•tor (pə-răm′byə-lā′tər) *n. Chiefly British.* A baby carriage.

per an•num (pər ăn′əm) *adv.* By the year; annually. [Lat.]

per•bo•rate (pər-bôr′āt′, -bōr′-) *n.* A salt containing the radical BO_3, formed from a borate and hydrogen peroxide.

per•cale (pər-kāl′) *n.* A closely woven cotton fabric used for sheets and clothing. [Fr. < Pers. *pargālah,* rag.]

per•ca•line (pûr′kə-lēn′) *n.* A fine cotton fabric, usu. glazed, used esp. for linings and in the bindings of books. [Fr., dim. of *percale,* percale. See PERCALE.]

per cap•i•ta (pər kăp′ĭ-tə) *adv. & adj.* **1.** Per unit of population. **2.** Equally to each individual. [Med.Lat., by heads : Lat. *per,* per + Lat. *capita,* heads.]

per•ceive (pər-sēv′) *tr.v.* **-ceived, -ceiv•ing, -ceives. 1.** To become aware of directly through any of the senses, esp. sight or hearing. **2.** To achieve understanding of; apprehend. See Syns at **see[1].** [ME *perceiven* < OFr. *perceivre* < Lat. *percipere* : *per-,* per- + *capere,* to seize; see **kap-*.**] — **per•ceiv′a•ble** *adj.* — **per•ceiv′a•bly** *adv.* — **per•ceiv′er** *n.*

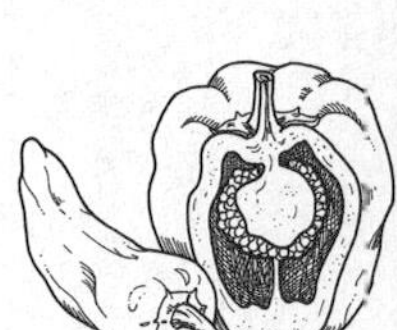

pepper

peppermint
Mentha piperita

ă pat	oi boy
ā pay	ou out
âr care	o͝o took
ä father	o͞o boot
ĕ pet	ŭ cut
ē be	ûr urge
ĭ pit	th thin
ī pie	*th* this
îr pier	hw which
ŏ pot	zh vision
ō toe	ə about, item
ô paw	

Stress marks:
′ (primary);
′ (secondary), as in
dictionary (dĭk′shə-nĕr′ē)

per•cent also **per cent** (pər-sĕnt′) —*adv.* Out of each hundred; per hundred. —*n.* **1.** *pl.* **percent.** One part in a hundred: *fifty percent of the alumni.* **2.** *pl.* **percents.** A percentage or portion. **3. percents.** *Chiefly British.* Public securities yielding interest at a specified percentage. —*adj.* Paying or demanding interest at a specified percentage. [< *per cent.*, abbreviation of *per centum*, by the hundred : *per*, per; see PER + *centum*, hundred; see **dekm̥*.**]

Usage Note: Statistically speaking, a quantity can be increased by any percentage but cannot be decreased by more than 100 percent. In defiance of this logic, however, advertisers sometimes refer to *a new dental rinse that reduces plaque on teeth by over 300 percent.* Presumably the rinse is three times as effective as some other tooth-cleaning procedure, but the phrasing serves mostly to obscure the fact that the standard of comparison has not been made explicit. This phrase was unacceptable to 66 percent of the Usage Panel.

per•cent•age (pər-sĕn′tĭj) *n.* **1.a.** A fraction or ratio with 100 understood as the denominator; for example, 0.98 equals a percentage of 98. **b.** The result obtained by multiplying a quantity by a percent. **2.** A proportion or share in relation to a whole; a part: *a small percentage of the audience.* **3.** An amount, such as a commission, that varies in proportion to a larger sum, such as total sales. **4.** *Informal.* Advantage; gain.

Usage Note: *Percentage,* when preceded by *the,* takes a singular verb: *The percentage of unskilled workers is small.* When preceded by *a,* it takes either a singular or plural verb, depending on the number of the noun in the prepositional phrase that follows: *A small percentage of the workers are unskilled. A large percentage of the crop has spoiled.*

per•cen•tile (pər-sĕn′tīl′) *n.* One of a set of points on a scale arrived at by dividing a group into parts in order of magnitude. For example, a score higher than 97 percent of those attained on an examination is in the 97th percentile.

per cen•tum (pər sĕn′təm) *n.* See **percent** 1. [Lat. See PERCENT.]

per•cept (pûr′sĕpt′) *n.* **1.** The object of perception. **2.** A mental impression of something perceived by the senses, viewed as the basic component in the formation of concepts; a sense datum. [< Lat. *perceptum*, neut. p.part. of *percipere*, to perceive. See PERCEIVE.]

per•cep•ti•ble (pər-sĕp′tə-bəl) *adj.* Capable of being perceived by the senses or the mind. —**per•cep′ti•bil′i•ty** *n.* —**per•cep′ti•bly** *adv.*

Syns: *perceptible, palpable, appreciable, noticeable, discernible.* These adjectives apply to what is capable of being apprehended with the mind or through the senses as being real. *Perceptible* is the least specific: *a perceptible pause in his speech. Palpable* applies both to what is perceptible by means of the sense of touch and to what is readily perceived by the mind: *"I felt as if my soul were grappling with a palpable enemy"* (Mary Wollstonecraft Shelley). What is *appreciable* is capable of being estimated or measured: *dumping appreciable amounts of waste. Noticeable* means easily observed: *noticeable shadows. Discernible* means distinguishable, especially by vision or intellect: *no discernible progress.*

per•cep•tion (pər-sĕp′shən) *n.* **1.** The process, act, or faculty of perceiving. **2.** The effect or product of perceiving. **3.** *Psychol.* **a.** Recognition and interpretation of sensory stimuli based chiefly on memory. **b.** The neurological processes by which such recognition and interpretation are effected. **4.a.** Insight, intuition, or knowledge gained by perceiving. **b.** The capacity for such insight. [ME *percepcioun* < OFr. *percepcion* < Lat. *perceptiō, perceptiōn-* < *perceptus*, p.part. of *percipere*, to perceive. See PERCEIVE.] —**per•cep′tion•al** *adj.*

per•cep•tive (pər-sĕp′tĭv) *adj.* **1.** Of or relating to perception: *perceptive faculties.* **2.a.** Having the ability to perceive; keen in discernment. **b.** Marked by discernment and understanding; sensitive. —**per•cep′tive•ly** *adv.* —**per′cep•tiv′i•ty** (pûr′sĕp-tĭv′ĭ-tē), **per•cep′tive•ness** (pər-sĕp′tĭv-nĭs) *n.*

per•cep•tu•al (pər-sĕp′cho͞o-əl) *adj.* Of, based on, or involving perception. —**per•cep′tu•al•ly** *adv.*

perch¹ (pûrch) *n.* **1.** A rod or branch serving as a roost for a bird. **2.a.** An elevated place for resting or sitting. **b.** A position that is secure, advantageous, or prominent. **3.** A pole, stick, or rod. **4.** *Chiefly British.* **a.** A linear measure equal to 5.50 yards or 16.5 feet (5.03 meters); a rod. **b.** One square rod of land. **5.** A unit of cubic measure used in stonework, usu. 16.5 feet by 1.0 foot by 1.5 feet, or 24.75 cubic feet (0.70 cubic meter). **6.** A frame on which cloth is laid for examination of quality. —*v.* **perched, perch•ing, perch•es.** —*intr.* **1.** To alight or rest on a perch; roost. **2.** To stand, sit, or rest on an elevated place or position. —*tr.* **1.** To place on or as if on a perch. **2.** To lay (cloth) on a perch in order to examine it. [ME *perche* < OFr. < Lat. *pertica*, stick, pole.]

perch² (pûrch) *n., pl.* **perch** or **perch•es. 1.** Any of various spiny-finned freshwater fishes of the genus *Perca*, esp. *P. flavescens* of North America and *P. fluviatilis* of Europe. **2.** Any of various similar or related fishes, such as the pike perch. [ME *perche* < OFr. < Lat. *perca* < Gk. *perkē*.]

per•chance (pər-chăns′) *adv.* Perhaps; possibly.

perch•er (pûr′chər) *n.* **1.** One that perches. **2.** A bird whose feet are adapted for perching.

Per•che•ron (pûr′chə-rŏn′, -shə-) *n.* Any of a breed of gray or black draft horse originally used in France. [Fr. < *Perche*, a historical region of NW France.]

per•chlo•rate (pər-klôr′āt′, -klōr′-) *n.* An ester or a salt of perchloric acid.

per•chlo•ric acid (pər-klôr′ĭk, -klōr′-) *n.* A clear colorless liquid, $HClO_4$, explosively unstable under some conditions, that is a powerful oxidant used as a catalyst and in explosives.

per•chlo•ride (pər-klôr′īd′, -klōr′-) also **per•chlo•rid** (-klôr′ĭd, -klōr′-) *n.* A chloride having more chlorine than other chlorides of the same element.

per•chlor•o•eth•yl•ene (pər-klôr′ō-ĕth′ə-lēn′, -klōr′-) *n.* A colorless nonflammable organic solvent, $Cl_2C{:}CCl_2$, used in dry-cleaning solutions and as an industrial solvent.

per•cip•i•ent (pər-sĭp′ē-ənt) *adj.* Having the power of perceiving, esp. keenly and readily. —*n.* One that perceives. [Lat. *percipiēns, percipient-*, pr.part. of *percipere*, to perceive. See PERCEIVE.] —**per•cip′i•ence, per•cip′i•en•cy** *n.*

per•coid (pûr′koid′) also **per•coi•de•an** (pər-koi′dē-ən) *adj.* Of or relating to the Percoidea, a large suborder of spiny-finned fishes that includes the perches, sunfishes, and groupers. [< NLat. *Percoidea*, suborder name : Lat. *perca*, perch; see PERCH² + NLat. *-oidea*, pl. of *-oidēs*, resembling (< Gk. *-oeidēs*; see -OID).] —**per′coid′** *n.*

per•co•late (pûr′kə-lāt′) *v.* **-lat•ed, -lat•ing, -lates.** —*tr.* **1.** To cause (liquid, for example) to pass through a porous substance or small holes; filter. **2.** To pass or ooze through. **3.** To make (coffee) in a percolator. —*intr.* **1.** To drain or seep through a porous material or filter. **2.** *Informal.* To become lively or active. —*n.* (-lĭt, -lāt′). A liquid that has been percolated. [Lat. *percōlāre, percōlāt-* : *per-*, per- + *cōlāre*, to filter (< *cōlum*, sieve).] —**per′co•la′tion** *n.*

per•co•la•tor (pûr′kə-lā′tər) *n.* A coffeepot in which boiling water is forced repeatedly up through a central tube to filter back down through a basket of ground coffee beans.

per con•tra (pər kŏn′trə) *adv.* **1.** On the contrary. **2.** By way of contrast. [Lat. *per contrā* : *per*, per + *contrā*, against.]

per•cuss (pər-kŭs′) *tr.v.* **-cussed, -cuss•ing, -cuss•es.** To strike or tap firmly. [Lat. *percutere, percuss-*, to strike hard : *per-*, per- + *quatere*, to strike; see **kwēt-*.**]

per•cus•sion (pər-kŭsh′ən) *n.* **1.** The striking together of two bodies, esp. when noise is produced. **2.** The sound, vibration, or shock caused by the striking together of two bodies. **3.** The act of detonating a percussion cap in a firearm. **4.** A method of medical diagnosis in which various areas of the body, esp. the chest, back, and abdomen, are tapped to determine by resonance the condition of internal organs. **5.** *Mus.* **a.** The section of a band or an orchestra composed of percussion instruments. **b.** Percussion instruments or their players considered as a group. [Lat. *percussiō, percussiōn-* < *percussus*, p.part. of *percutere*, to percuss. See PERCUSS.]

percussion cap *n.* A thin metal cap containing gunpowder or another detonator that explodes on being struck.

percussion instrument *n. Mus.* An instrument, such as a drum, xylophone, piano, or maraca, in which sound is produced by one object striking another.

per•cus•sion•ist (pər-kŭsh′ə-nĭst) *n. Mus.* One who plays percussion instruments.

per•cus•sive (pər-kŭs′ĭv) *adj.* Of, relating to, or marked by percussion. —**per•cus′sive•ly** *adv.* —**per•cus′sive•ness** *n.*

per•cu•ta•ne•ous (pûr′kyo͞o-tā′nē-əs) *adj. Medic.* Passed, done, or effected through the skin.

Per•cy (pûr′sē), Sir **Henry.** "Hotspur." 1364–1403. English soldier killed leading an uprising against Henry IV (1403).

Percy, Thomas. 1729–1811. English prelate, antiquary, and poet who edited *Reliques of Ancient English Poetry* (1765).

per di•em (pər dē′əm, dī′əm) *adv.* By the day; per day. —*adj.* **1.** Reckoned on a daily basis; daily. **2.** Paid by the day. —*n., pl.* **per diems.** An allowance for daily expenses. [Lat.]

per•di•tion (pər-dĭsh′ən) *n.* **1.a.** Loss of the soul; eternal damnation. **b.** Hell. **2.** *Archaic.* Utter ruin. [ME *perdicion* < OFr. < LLat. *perditiō, perditiōn-* < Lat. *perditus*, p.part. of *perdere*, to lose : *per-*, per- + *dare*, to give; see **dō-*.**]

per•du or **per•due** (pər-do͞o′, -dyo͞o′) *n. Obsolete.* A soldier sent on an especially dangerous mission. [< Fr. *sentinelle perdue*, forward sentry : *sentinelle*, sentinel + *perdu*, p.part. of *perdre*, to lose (< Lat. *perdere*; see PERDITION).]

per•du•ra•ble (pər-do͝or′ə-bəl, -dyo͝or′-) *adj.* Extremely durable; permanent. [ME < OFr. < LLat. *perdūrābilis* < Lat. *perdūrāre*, to endure : *per-*, per- + *dūrāre*, to last; see **deuə-*.**] —**per•du′ra•bil′i•ty** *n.* —**per•du′ra•bly** *adv.*

per•dure (pər-do͝or′, -dyo͝or′) *intr.v.* **-dured, -dur•ing, -dures.** To last permanently; endure. [ME *perduren* < OFr. *pardurer* < Lat. *perdūrāre*. See PERDURABLE.]

père (pĕr) *n.* **1.** Used after a father's surname to distinguish him from his son. **2. Père.** *Rom. Cath. Ch.* Used as a title for some priests. [Fr. < OFr. *pedre* < Lat. *pater*. See **pəter-*.**]

per•e•gri•nate (pĕr′ĭ-grə-nāt′) *v.* **-nat•ed, -nat•ing, -nates.** —*intr.* To journey or travel from place to place, esp. on foot. —*tr.* To travel through or over; traverse. [Lat. *peregrīnārī, peregrīnāt-* < *peregrīnus*, foreigner. See PEREGRINE.] —**per′e•gri•na′tion** *n.* —**per′e•gri•na′tor** *n.*

per•e•grine (pĕr′ə-grĭn, -grēn′) *adj.* **1.** Foreign; alien. **2.** Roving or wandering; migratory. —*n.* A peregrine falcon. [ME < OFr. < Med.Lat. *peregrīnus*, wandering, pilgrim < Lat., foreigner < *pereger*, being abroad : *per*, through; see PER + *ager*, land; see **agro-***.]

peregrine falcon *n.* A widely distributed swift-flying bird of prey *(Falco peregrinus)* having gray and white plumage and much used in falconry. [ME, transl. of Med.Lat. *falcō peregrīnus* (so called because they were caught in passage).]

Pe•rei•ra (pə-rĕr′ə, pĕ-rā′rä). A city of W-central Colombia W of Bogotá. Pop. 232,311.

Per•el•man (pĕr′əl-mən), **S(idney) J(oseph).** 1904–79. Amer. writer known for his satirical pieces in the *New Yorker*.

per•emp•to•ry (pə-rĕmp′tə-rē) *adj.* **1.** Putting an end to all debate or action. **2.** Not allowing contradiction or refusal; imperative. **3.** Having the nature of or expressing a command; urgent: *a peremptory tone.* **4.** Offensively self-assured; dictatorial. [Lat. *peremptōrius* < *peremptus*, p.part. of *perimere*, to take away : *per-*, per- + *emere*, to obtain; see **em-***.] —**per•emp′to•ri•ly** *adv.* —**per•emp′to•ri•ness** *n.*

per•en•nate (pĕr′ə-nāt′, pə-rĕn′āt) *intr.v.* **-nat•ed, -nat•ing, -nates.** To survive from one growing season to the next, often with a period of reduced or arrested growth between seasons. [Lat. *perennāre*, *perennāt-*, to last many years < *perennis*, lasting for years. See PERENNIAL.] —**per′en•na′tion** *n.*

per•en•ni•al (pə-rĕn′ē-əl) *adj.* **1.** Lasting or active through the year or through many years. **2.a.** Lasting an indefinitely long time; enduring. **b.** Appearing again and again; recurrent. See Syns at **continual. 3.** *Bot.* Living three or more years. —*n.* **1.** *Bot.* A perennial plant. **2.** Something that recurs or seems to recur yearly or continually. [Lat. *perennis* (*per-*, throughout; see PER + *annus*, year; see **at-***) + -AL[1].] —**per•en′ni•al•ly** *adv.*

per•e•stroi•ka (pĕr′ĭ-stroi′kə, pyĕ-ryĭ-stroi′kä) *n.* **1.** The organizational restructuring of the Soviet economy and bureaucracy that was begun in the mid 1980's. **2.** An economic and bureaucratic restructuring. [Russ. *perestroĭka* : *pere-*, around, again (< ORuss.; see **per[1]***) + *stroĭka*, construction (< *stroit'*, to build < ORuss. *stroiti* < *strojĭ*, order; see **ster-[2]***).]

Pé•rez de Cuél•lar (pĕr′əz də kwā′yär, pĕ′rĕs dĕ kwĕ′yär), **Javier.** b. 1920. Peruvian diplomat who served as secretary-general of the United Nations (1982–91).

Pe•rez Es•qui•vel (pĕr′əs ĕs′kē-vĕl′, pĕr′ĕs), **Adolfo.** b. 1932. Argentine civil rights leader who won the 1980 Nobel Peace Prize.

per•fect (pûr′fĭkt) *adj.* **1.** Lacking nothing essential to the whole; complete of its nature or kind. See Usage Notes at **complete, unique. 2.** Being without defect or blemish. **3.** Thoroughly skilled or talented in a certain field or area; proficient. **4.** Completely suited for a particular purpose or situation. **5.a.** Completely corresponding to a description, standard, or type. **b.** Accurately reproducing an original. **6.** Complete; thorough; utter. **7.** Pure; undiluted; unmixed. **8.** Excellent and delightful in all respects. **9.** *Bot.* Having both stamens and pistils in the same flower; monoclinous. **10.** *Gram.* Of, relating to, or constituting a verb form expressing action completed prior to a fixed point of reference in time. **11.** *Mus.* **a.** Being the three basic intervals of the octave, fourth, and fifth. **b.** Being a cadence or chord progression from the dominant to the tonic at the end of a phrase or piece of music. —*n.* **1.** *Gram.* The perfect tense. **2.** A verb or verb form in the perfect tense. —*tr.v.* (pər-fĕkt′) **-fect•ed, -fect•ing, -fects.** To bring to perfection or completion. [ME *perfit* < OFr. *parfit* < Lat. *perfectus*, p.part. of *perficere*, to finish : *per-*, per- + *facere*, to do; see **dhē-***.] —**per•fect′er** *n.* —**per′fect•ness** *n.*

Syns: perfect, consummate, faultless, flawless, impeccable. The central meaning shared by these adjectives is "being wholly without flaw": *a perfect diamond; a consummate performer; faultless logic; a flawless instrumental technique; speaks impeccable French.* **Ant:** *imperfect.*

per•fec•ta (pər-fĕk′tə) *n. Sports & Games.* See **exacta.** [< Am.Sp. *(quiniela) perfecta*, perfect (quinella), fem. of *perfecto*, perfect < Lat. *perfectus*. See PERFECT.]

perfect game *n.* **1.** *Baseball.* A complete game in which no opposing batter reaches first base. **2.** *Sports.* A game in bowling in which a player bowls 12 successive strikes.

per•fect•i•ble (pər-fĕk′tə-bəl) *adj.* Capable of becoming perfect or being made perfect. —**per•fect′i•bil′i•ty** *n.*

per•fec•tion (pər-fĕk′shən) *n.* **1.** The quality or condition of being perfect. **2.** The act or process of perfecting. **3.** A person or thing considered to be perfect. **4.** An instance of excellence.

per•fec•tion•ism (pər-fĕk′shə-nĭz′əm) *n.* **1.** A propensity for being displeased with anything that is not perfect or does not meet extremely high standards. **2.** A belief that moral or spiritual perfection can be achieved by people in this life. —**per•fec′tion•ist** *adj. & n.* —**per•fec′tion•ist′ic** *adj.*

per•fec•tive (pər-fĕk′tĭv) *adj.* **1.** Tending toward perfection. **2.** *Gram.* Of or being the aspect of a verb that expresses a completed action as distinct from a continuing or not necessarily completed action. —*n. Gram.* **1.** The perfective aspect. **2.** A verb in the perfective aspect. —**per•fec′tive•ly** *adv.* —**per•fec′tive•ness, per′fec•tiv′i•ty** (pûr′fĕk-tĭv′ĭ-tē) *n.*

per•fect•ly (pûr′fĭkt-lē) *adv.* **1.** In a perfect manner or to a perfect degree. **2.** To a complete or full degree or extent.

perfect number *n. Math.* A positive integer that is equal to the sum of its integral factors, including 1 but excluding itself.

per•fec•to (pər-fĕk′tō) *n., pl.* **-tos.** A cigar of standard length, thick in the center and tapered at each end. [< Sp., perfect < Lat. *perfectus*. See PERFECT.]

perfect participle *n. Gram.* See **past participle.**

perfect pitch *n. Mus.* See **absolute pitch** 2.

perfect rhyme *n.* **1.** Rhyme in which the final accented vowel and all succeeding consonants or syllables are identical, while the preceding consonants are different, for example, *rider, beside her.* **2.** Rime riche.

perfect square *n. Math.* An integer that is the square of an integer.

per•fer•vid (pər-fûr′vĭd) *adj.* Extremely eager; impassioned or zealous. —**per•fer′vid•ly** *adv.* —**per•fer′vid•ness** *n.*

per•fid•i•ous (pər-fĭd′ē-əs) *adj.* Of, relating to, or marked by perfidy; treacherous. —**per•fid′i•ous•ly** *adv.*

per•fi•dy (pûr′fĭ-dē) *n., pl.* **-dies. 1.** Deliberate breach of faith; calculated violation of trust; treachery. **2.** The act or an instance of treachery. [Lat. *perfidia* < *perfidus*, treacherous : *per*, through; see PER + *fidēs*, faith; see **bheidh-***.]

per•fo•li•ate (pər-fō′lē-ĭt) *adj.* Of or relating to a sessile leaf or bract that completely clasps the stem and is apparently pierced by it. [NLat. *perfoliātus* : Lat. *per*, through; see PER + Lat. *foliātus*, bearing leaves (< *folium*, leaf; see **bhel-[3]***).] —**per•fo′li•a′tion** *n.*

per•fo•rate (pûr′fə-rāt′) *v.* **-rat•ed, -rat•ing, -rates.** —*tr.* **1.** To pierce, punch, or bore a hole or holes in; penetrate. **2.** To pierce or stamp with rows of holes, as those between postage stamps, to allow easy separation. —*intr.* To pass into or through something. —*adj.* (pûr′fər-ĭt, -fə-rāt′). Having been perforated. [Lat. *perforāre*, *perforāt-* : *per-*, per- + *forāre*, to bore.] —**per′fo•ra•ble** (-fər-ə-bəl) *adj.* —**per′fo•ra′tive** *adj.* —**per′fo•ra′tor** *n.*

per•fo•ra•ted (pûr′fə-rā′tĭd) *adj.* Having a hole or holes, esp. a row of small holes.

per•fo•ra•tion (pûr′fə-rā′shən) *n.* **1.** A hole or series of holes punched or bored through something, esp. a hole in a series, separating sections in a sheet or roll. **2.a.** The act of perforating. **b.** The state of being perforated.

per•force (pər-fôrs′, -fōrs′) *adv.* By necessity; by force of circumstance. [ME *par force* < OFr. : *par*, by (< Lat. *per*; see PER) + *force*, force; see FORCE.]

per•form (pər-fôrm′) *v.* **-formed, -form•ing, -forms.** —*tr.* **1.** To begin and carry through to completion; do. **2.** To take action in accordance with the requirements of; fulfill. **3.a.** To enact (a feat or role) before an audience. **b.** To give a public presentation of; present. —*intr.* **1.** To carry on; function. **2.** To fulfill an obligation or requirement; accomplish something as promised or expected. **3.** To portray a role or demonstrate a skill before an audience. **4.** To present a dramatic or musical work or other entertainment before an audience. [ME *performen* < AN *performer* < OFr. *parfornir* : *par-*, intensive pref. (< Lat. *per-*, per-) + *fournir*, to furnish; see FURNISH.] —**per•form′a•ble** *adj.* —**per•form′er** *n.*

per•form•ance (pər-fôr′məns) *n.* **1.** The act of performing or the state of being performed. **2.** The act or style of performing a work or role before an audience. **3.** The way in which someone or something functions. **4.** A presentation before an audience. **5.** Something performed; an accomplishment.

performance art *n.* A form of art in which thematically related works in a variety of media are presented simultaneously or successively to an audience. —**performance artist** *n.*

per•form•ing arts (pər-fôr′mĭng) *pl.n.* Arts, such as dance, drama, and music, that are performed before an audience.

per•fume (pûr′fyo͞om′, pər-fyo͞om′) *n.* **1.** A substance that emits and diffuses a fragrant odor, esp. a volatile liquid distilled from flowers or prepared synthetically. **2.** A pleasing, agreeable scent or odor. —*tr.v.* (pər-fyo͞om′) **-fumed, -fum•ing, -fumes.** To impregnate with fragrance; impart a pleasant odor to. [Fr. *parfum* < OItal. *parfumo* < *parfumare*, to fill with smoke : *par-*, intensive pref. (< Lat. *per-*, per-) + *fumare*, to smoke (< Lat. *fūmāre* < *fūmus*, smoke).]

per•fum•er (pər-fyo͞o′mər) *n.* A maker or seller of perfumes.

per•fum•er•y (pər-fyo͞o′mə-rē) *n., pl.* **-ies. 1.** Perfumes. **2.** An establishment that makes or sells perfume. **3.** The art of making perfume.

per•func•to•ry (pər-fŭngk′tə-rē) *adj.* **1.** Done routinely and with little interest or care. **2.** Showing little interest or care. [LLat. *perfūnctōrius* < Lat. *perfūnctus*, p.part. of *perfungī*, to get through with : *per-*, per- + *fungī*, to perform.] —**per•func′to•ri•ly** *adv.* —**per•func′to•ri•ness** *n.*

per•fuse (pər-fyo͞oz′) *tr.v.* **-fused, -fus•ing, -fus•es. 1.** To coat or permeate with liquid, color, or light; suffuse. **2.** To pour or diffuse (a liquid, for example) over or through something. [Lat. *perfundere*, *perfūs-*, to pour over : *per-*, per- + *fundere*, to pour; see **gheu-***.] —**per•fu′sive** (pər-fyo͞o′sĭv, -zĭv) *adj.*

per•fu•sion (pər-fyo͞o′zhən) *n.* **1.** The act of perfusing. **2.** The

peregrine falcon
Continental peregrine falcon
Falco peregrinus

ă **pat**	oi **boy**
ā **pay**	ou **out**
âr **care**	o͝o **took**
ä **father**	o͞o **boot**
ĕ **pet**	ŭ **cut**
ē **be**	ûr **urge**
ĭ **pit**	th **thin**
ī **pie**	*th* **this**
îr **pier**	hw **which**
ŏ **pot**	zh **vision**
ō **toe**	ə **a**bout,
ô **paw**	it**e**m

Stress marks:
′ (primary);
′ (secondary), as in
dictionary (dĭk′shə-nĕr′ē)

injection of fluid into a blood vessel in order to reach an organ or tissues, usu. to supply nutrients and oxygen.

Per•ga•mum (pûr′gə-məm). An ancient Greek city and kingdom of W Asia Minor in modern-day W Turkey; noted for its library, which Mark Antony gave to Cleopatra.

per•go•la (pûr′gə-lə) *n.* An arbor or a passageway of columns supporting a roof of trelliswork on which climbing plants are trained to grow. [Ital. < Lat. *pergula.*]

Per•go•le•si (pĕr′gə-lā′zē, -gô-lĕ′-), **Giovanni Battista.** 1710–36. Italian composer known for his comic operas.

per•haps (pər-hăps′) *adv.* Maybe; possibly. [< ME *perhap* : *per*, by (< Lat.; see PER) + *hap*, chance; see HAP.]

peri– *pref.* **1.** Around; about; enclosing: *perimysium.* **2.** Near: *perinatal.* [Gk. < *peri.* See **per**[1]*.]

pergola

per•i•anth (pĕr′ē-ănth′) *n.* The outer envelope of a flower, consisting of either the calyx or the corolla or both. [Fr. *périanthe* < NLat. *perianthum* : Gk. *peri-*, peri- + Gk. *anthos*, flower.]

per•i•apt (pĕr′ē-ăpt′) *n.* A charm worn as protection against mischief and disease; an amulet. [Fr. *périapte* < Gk. *periapton* < *periaptos*, hung around : *peri-*, peri- + *haptos*, fastened (< *haptein*, to fasten).]

Per•i•bon•ca (pĕr′ə-bŏng′kə). A river of central Quebec, Canada, flowing c. 451 km (280 mi) through **Peribonca Lake** to Lake St. John.

per•i•car•di•tis (pĕr′ĭ-kär-dī′tĭs) *n.* Inflammation of the pericardium.

per•i•car•di•um (pĕr′ĭ-kär′dē-əm) *n., pl.* **-di•a** (-dē-ə). The membranous sac filled with serous fluid that encloses the heart and the roots of the aorta and other large blood vessels. [NLat. < Gk. *perikardion* < *perikardios*, around the heart : *peri-*, peri- + *kardia*, heart; see **kerd-***.] **—per′i•car′di•al** (-dē-əl), **per′i•car′di•ac′** (-dē-ăk′) *adj.*

per•i•carp (pĕr′ĭ-kärp′) *n.* **1.** *Bot.* The wall of a ripened ovary; fruit wall. **2.** A membranous structure surrounding the cystocarp of red algae. **—per′i•car′pi•al** *adj.*

per•i•chon•dri•um (pĕr′ĭ-kŏn′drē-əm) *n., pl.* **-dri•a** (-drē-ə). The fibrous membrane of connective tissue covering the surface of cartilage except at joint endings. [NLat. : PERI– + Gk. *khondrion*, dim. of *khondros*, cartilage; see CHONDRO–.] **—per′i•chon′dri•al** (-drē-əl) *adj.*

Pericles
Copy of a mid fifth-century B.C. herma attributed to Cresilas (fl. 450–430 B.C.)

Per•i•cles (pĕr′ĭ-klēz′). d. 429 B.C. Athenian leader noted for advancing democracy. **—Per′i•cle′an** (-klē′ən) *adj.*

per•i•cy•cle (pĕr′ĭ-sī′kəl) *n.* A plant tissue characteristic of the roots, located between the endodermis and phloem. [Fr. *péricycle* < Gk. *perikuklos*, spherical : *peri-*, peri- + *kuklos*, circle; see CYCLE.] **—per′i•cy′clic** (-sī′klĭk, -sĭk′lĭk) *adj.*

per•i•derm (pĕr′ĭ-dûrm′) *n.* The outer layers of tissue of woody roots and stems, consisting of the cork cambium and the tissues produced by it. **—per′i•der′mal, per′i•der′mic**

pe•rid•i•um (pə-rĭd′ē-əm) *n., pl.* **-i•a** (-ē-ə). The covering of the spore-bearing organ in many fungi. [NLat. *pēridium* < Gk. *pēridion*, dim. of *pēra*, leather pouch.] **—pe•rid′i•al** (-ē-əl) *adj.*

per•i•dot (pĕr′ĭ-dŏt′, -dō′) *n.* A yellowish-green variety of olivine used as a gem. [ME < OFr.]

per•i•do•tite (pĕr′ĭ-dō-tīt′, pə-rĭd′ə-) *n.* Any of a group of igneous rocks composed mainly of olivine and various pyroxenes and having a granitelike texture.

per•i•gee (pĕr′ə-jē) *n.* **1.** The point nearest the earth's center in the orbit of the moon or a satellite. **2.** The point in any orbit nearest to the body being orbited. [Fr. *périgée* < Med. Lat. *perigēum* < LGk. *perigeion* : Gk. *peri-*, peri- + Gk. *gē*, earth.] **—per′i•ge′al** (-jē′əl), **per′i•ge′an** (-jē′ən) *adj.*

periodical cicada

pe•rig•y•nous (pə-rĭj′ə-nəs) *adj. Bot.* **1.** Having sepals, petals, and stamens around the edge of a cuplike receptacle containing the ovary, as in flowers of the rose or cherry. **2.** Of or being perigynous flower parts. **—pe•rig′y•ny** (-ə-nē) *n.*

per•i•he•li•on (pĕr′ə-hē′lē-ən, -hēl′yən) *n., pl.* **-he•li•a** (-hē′lē-ə, -hēl′yə). The point nearest the sun in the orbit of a planet or other celestial body. [Alteration of NLat. *perihēlium* : PERI– + Gk. *hēlios*, sun; see **sāwel-***.] **—per′i•he′li•al** (-hē′lē-əl, -hēl′yəl) *adj.*

per•i•kar•y•on (pĕr′ĭ-kăr′ē-ŏn′, -ən) *n., pl.* **-kar•y•a** (-kăr′ē-ə). The cell body of a neuron, containing the nucleus and organelles. [PERI– + Gk. *karuon*, nut; see KARYO–.] **—per′i•kar′y•al** (-ē-əl) *adj.*

per•il (pĕr′əl) *n.* **1.a.** Imminent danger. **b.** Exposure to the risk of harm or loss. **2.** Something that endangers or involves risk. —*tr.v.* **-iled, -il•ing, -ils** also **-illed, -il•ling, -ils.** To expose to danger or the chance of injury; imperil. [ME < OFr. < Lat. *perīculum.* See **per-**[3]*.]

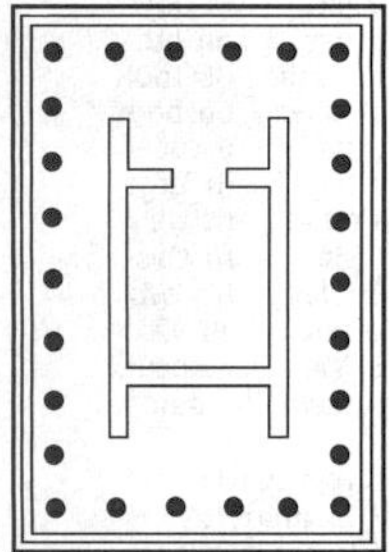

peristyle
Plan of a Greek temple

pe•ril•la (pə-rĭl′ə) *n.* **1.** An annual Asian plant *(Perilla frutescens)* having opposite leaves and flowers with a white tubular corolla. **2.** The oil from the seeds of this plant, used in the manufacture of paint, varnish, and artificial leather and as a substitute for linseed oil. [NLat., genus name.]

per•il•ous (pĕr′ə-ləs) *adj.* Full of or involving peril; dangerous. **—per′il•ous•ly** *adv.* **—per′il•ous•ness** *n.*

per•i•lymph (pĕr′ə-lĭmf′) *n.* The fluid in the space between the membranous and bony labyrinths of the inner ear.

pe•rim•e•ter (pə-rĭm′ĭ-tər) *n.* **1.** *Math.* **a.** A closed curve bounding a plane area. **b.** The length of such a boundary. **2.** The outer limits of an area. See Syns at **circumference. 3.** A fortified strip or boundary usu. protecting a military position. [ME *perimetre* < Lat. *perimetros* < Gk. : *peri-*, peri- + *metron*, measure; see METER[2].] **—per′i•met′ric** (pĕr′ə-mĕt′rĭk), **per′i•met′ri•cal** (-rĭ-kəl) *adj.*

per•i•morph (pĕr′ə-môrf′) *n.* A mineral that encloses a different mineral. **—per′i•mor′phic, per′i•mor′phous** *adj.* **—per′i•mor′phism** *n.*

per•i•my•si•um (pĕr′ə-mĭzh′ē-əm, -mĭz′ē-əm) *n., pl.* **-my•si•a** (-mĭzh′ē-ə, -mĭz′ē-ə). The sheath of connective tissue enveloping bundles of muscle fibers. [NLat. : PERI– + Gk. *mus*, muscle; see **mūs-***.]

per•i•na•tal (pĕr′ə-nāt′l) *adj.* Of, relating to, or being the period around childbirth, esp. the five months before and one month after birth. **—per′i•na′tal•ly** *adv.*

per•i•ne•um (pĕr′ə-nē′əm) *n., pl.* **-ne•a** (-nē′ə). **1.** The portion of the body in the pelvis occupied by urogenital passages and the rectum, bounded in front by the pubic arch, in the back by the coccyx, and laterally by part of the hipbone. **2.** The region between the scrotum and the anus in males and between the posterior vulva junction and the anus in females. [ME < Med.Lat. *perinaeon* < Gk. *perinaion* : *peri-*, peri- + *inan*, to excrete.] **—per′i•ne′al** (-nē′əl) *adj.*

per•i•neu•ri•um (pĕr′ə-no͝or′ē-əm, -nyo͝or′-) *n., pl.* **-neu•ri•a** (-no͝or′ē-ə, -nyo͝or′-). The sheath of connective tissue enclosing a bundle of nerve fibers. [NLat. : PERI– + Gk. *neuron*, nerve; see NEURON.] **—per′i•neu′ri•al** *adj.*

pe•ri•od (pîr′ē-əd) *n.* **1.** An interval of time characterized by the occurrence of a certain condition, event, or phenomenon. **2.** An interval of time characterized by the prevalence of a specified culture, ideology, or technology. **3.** An interval regarded as a distinct evolutionary or developmental phase. **4.** *Geol.* A unit of time, longer than an epoch and shorter than an era. **5.** Any of various arbitrary units of time, esp.: **a.** Any of the divisions of the academic day. **b.** *Sports & Games.* A division of the playing time of a game. **6.** *Phys. & Astron.* The time interval between two successive occurrences of a recurrent event or phases of an event; a cycle. **7.** An instance or occurrence of menstruation. **8.** A point or portion of time at which something is ended; a completion or conclusion. **9.** The full pause at the end of a spoken sentence. **10.** A punctuation mark (.) indicating a full stop, placed at the end of declarative sentences and other statements thought to be complete and after many abbreviations. **11.** A sentence of several carefully balanced clauses in formal writing. **12.a.** A metrical unit of quantitative verse consisting of two or more cola. **b.** An analogous unit or division of classical Greek or Latin prose. **13.** *Mus.* A group of two or more phrases within a composition, made up of 8 or 16 measures and terminating with a cadence. **14.** *Math.* **a.** The least interval in the range of the independent variable of a periodic function of a real variable in which all possible values of the dependent variable are assumed. **b.** A group of digits separated by commas in a written number. **c.** The number of digits that repeat in a repeating decimal. For example, 1/7 = 0.142857142857 . . . has a six-digit period. **15.** *Chem.* A sequence of elements arranged in order of increasing atomic number and forming one of the horizontal rows in the periodic table. —*adj.* Of, belonging to, or representing a certain historical age or time. [ME *periode* < OFr. < Med.Lat. *periodus* < Lat. *perihodos*, rhetorical period < Gk. *periodos*, circuit : *peri-*, peri- + *hodos*, way.]

pe•ri•od•ic (pîr′ē-ŏd′ĭk) *adj.* **1.** Having or marked by repeated cycles. **2.** Happening or appearing at regular intervals. **3.** Recurring or reappearing from time to time. **4.** Characterized by periodic sentences. **—pe′ri•od′i•cal•ly** *adv.*

Syns: *periodic, sporadic, intermittent, occasional, fitful.* These adjectives all mean recurring now and then. Something *periodic* occurs at regular or at least generally predictable intervals: *periodic anxiety. Sporadic* implies scattered, irregular, unpredictable, or isolated instances: *sporadic bombings. Intermittent* describes something that stops and starts at intervals: *intermittent rain.* What is *occasional* happens at random and irregularly: *occasional anger.* Something *fitful* occurs in spells and often abruptly: *fitful activity.*

per•i•od•ic acid (pûr′ī-ŏd′ĭk) *n.* A white crystalline inorganic acid, $HIO_4{\cdot}2H_2O$, used as an oxidizer.

pe•ri•od•i•cal (pîr′ē-ŏd′ĭ-kəl) *adj.* **1.** Periodic. **2.a.** Published at regular intervals of more than one day. **b.** Of a publication issued at such intervals. —*n.* A periodical publication.

periodical cicada *n.* A cicada of the genus *Magicicada* of the eastern United States whose 17-year or 13-year life cycle consists almost entirely of a nymphal stage spent underground.

pe•ri•o•dic•i•ty (pîr′ē-ə-dĭs′ĭ-tē) *n., pl.* **-ties. 1.** The quality or state of being periodic; recurrence at regular intervals. **2.** The tendency of chemical elements with similar positions in the periodic table to have similar properties. **3.** The position of an element in the periodic table.

pe•ri•od•ic law (pîr′ē-ŏd′ĭk) *n. Chem.* The principle that the properties of the elements recur periodically as their atomic numbers increase.

periodic sentence *n.* A sentence in which the main clause or its predicate is withheld until the end; for example, *Despite heavy winds and ground fog, we landed.*

periodic table *n. Chem.* A tabular arrangement of the elements in rows according to their atomic numbers so that elements with similar properties are in the same column. See table at **element.**

per•i•o•don•tal (pĕr′ē-ə-dŏn′tl) *adj.* **1.** Surrounding or encasing a tooth. **2.** Relating to or affecting periodontal tissue and structures. — **per′i•o•don′tal•ly** *adv.*

per•i•o•don•tia (pĕr′ē-ə-dŏn′shə) *n.* Periodontics.

per•i•o•don•tics (pĕr′ē-ə-dŏn′tĭks) *n. (used with a sing. v.)* The branch of dentistry that deals with the study and treatment of periodontal disease. — **per′i•o•don′tic, per′i•o•don′ti•cal** *adj.* — **per′i•o•don′tist** *n.*

per•i•o•nych•i•um (pĕr′ē-ō-nĭk′ē-əm) *n., pl.* **-i•a** (-ē-ə). The border of epidermal tissue surrounding a fingernail or toenail. [NLat. : PERI- + Gk. *onux,* nail; see **nogh-*.**]

per•i•os•te•um (pĕr′ē-ŏs′tē-əm) *n., pl.* **-te•a** (-tē-ə). The dense fibrous membrane covering the surface of bones except at the joints and serving as an attachment for muscles and tendons. [NLat. < LLat. *periosteon* < Gk. < *periosteos,* around the bone : *peri-,* peri- + *osteon,* bone; see **ost-*.**] — **per′i•os′te•al** (-tē-əl), **per′i•os′te•ous** (-tē-əs) *adj.*

per•i•os•ti•tis (pĕr′ē-ŏs-tī′tĭs) *n.* Inflammation of the periosteum. — **per′i•os•tit′ic** (-tĭt′ĭk) *adj.*

per•i•o•tic (pĕr′ē-ō′tĭk) *adj.* **1.** Situated around the ear. **2.** Of or relating to the bones immediately around the inner ear.

per•i•pa•tet•ic (pĕr′ə-pə-tĕt′ĭk) *adj.* **1.** Walking about or from place to place; traveling on foot. **2. Peripatetic.** Of or relating to the philosophy of Aristotle, who conducted discussions while walking about in the Lyceum of ancient Athens. — *n.* **1.** One who walks from place to place; an itinerant. **2. Peripatetic.** A follower of the philosophy of Aristotle. [ME *peripatetik* < Lat. *peripatēticus* < Gk. *peripatētikos* < *peripatein,* to walk about : *peri-,* peri- + *patein,* to walk; see **pent-*.**]

per•i•pe•te•ia also **per•i•pe•ti•a** (pĕr′ə-pə-tē′ə, -tī′ə) *n.* A sudden change of events or reversal of circumstances, esp. in a literary work. [Gk. < *peripiptein,* to change suddenly : *peri-,* peri- + *piptein,* to fall; see **pet-*.**]

pe•rip•e•ty (pə-rĭp′ĭ-tē) *n.* Peripeteia. [Fr. *péripétie* < Gk. *peripeteia.* See PERIPETEIA.]

pe•riph•er•al (pə-rĭf′ər-əl) *adj.* **1.** Relating to, located in, or constituting an outer boundary or periphery. **2.** Perceived or perceiving near the outer edges of the retina. **3.** *Anat.* **a.** Of the surface or outer part of a body or organ; external. **b.** Of or relating to the peripheral nervous system. **4.** Of minor relevance or importance. **5.** Auxiliary. — *n. Comp. Sci.* An auxiliary device, such as a modem, that works in conjunction with a computer. — **pe•riph′er•al•ly** *adv.*

peripheral nervous system *n.* The part of the vertebrate nervous system constituting the nerves outside the central nervous system and including the cranial nerves, the spinal nerves, and the sympathetic and parasympathetic nervous systems.

pe•riph•er•y (pə-rĭf′ə-rē) *n., pl.* **-ies. 1.** A line that forms the boundary of an area; a perimeter. See Syns at **circumference. 2.** The surface of a solid. **3.a.** The outermost part or region within a precise boundary. **b.** A zone constituting an imprecise boundary. [ME *periferie* < Med.Lat. *periferia* < LLat. *periphería* < Gk. *periphereia* < *peripherēs,* carrying around : *peri-,* peri- + *pherein,* to carry; see **bher-[1]*.**]

pe•riph•ra•sis (pə-rĭf′rə-sĭs) *n., pl.* **-ses** (-sēz′). **1.** The use of circumlocution. **2.** A circumlocution. [Lat. < Gk. < *periphrazein,* to express periphrastically : *peri-,* peri- + *phrazein,* to say; see **g^{w}hren-*.**]

per•i•phras•tic (pĕr′ə-frăs′tĭk) *adj.* **1.** Having the nature of or characterized by periphrasis. **2.** *Gram.* Constructed by using an auxiliary word rather than an inflected form; for example, *did say* is the periphrastic past tense of *say,* but *said* is the inflected past tense. — **per′i•phras′ti•cal•ly** *adv.*

pe•riph•y•ton (pə-rĭf′ĭ-tŏn′) *n.* Sessile organisms, such as algae and small crustaceans, that live attached to surfaces projecting from the bottom of a freshwater aquatic environment. [NLat. < Gk. *periphuton* < neut. sing. of *periphutos,* planted all over < *periphuein,* to grow around, cling to : *peri-,* peri- + *phuein,* to grow; see **bheuə-*.**]

pe•rip•ter•al (pə-rĭp′tər-əl) *adj. Archit.* Having a single row of columns on all sides. [< Lat. *peripteros* < Gk. : *peri-,* peri- + *pteron,* wing; see **pet-*.**]

pe•rique (pə-rēk′) *n.* A strongly flavored black tobacco grown in Louisiana and used in blends. [Louisiana Fr., perh. from *Périque,* nickname of *Pierre Chenet,* a LA tobacco grower.]

per•i•sarc (pĕr′ĭ-särk′) *n.* A horny external covering that encloses the polyp colonies of certain hydrozoans. [PERI- + Gk. *sarx, sark-,* flesh.] — **per′i•sar′cal, per′i•sar′cous** *adj.*

per•i•scope (pĕr′ĭ-skōp′) *n.* Any of various tubular optical instruments that contain reflecting elements, such as mirrors and prisms, to permit observation from a position displaced from a direct line of sight. — **per′i•scop′ic** (-skŏp′ĭk), **per′i•scop′i•cal** (-ĭ-kəl) *adj.*

per•ish (pĕr′ĭsh) *v.* **-ished, -ish•ing, -ish•es.** — *intr.* **1.** To die or be destroyed, esp. in a violent or untimely manner. **2.** To pass from existence; disappear gradually. **3.** *Chiefly British.* To spoil or deteriorate. — *tr.* To bring to destruction; destroy. — ***idiom.*** **perish the thought.** Used to express the wish that one not even think about something. [ME *perishen* < OFr. *perir, periss-,* to perish < Lat. *perīre* : *per-,* per- + *īre,* to go; see **ei-*.**]

per•ish•a•ble (pĕr′ĭ-shə-bəl) *adj.* Subject to decay, spoilage, or destruction. — *n.* Something, esp. food, subject to decay or spoilage. Often used in the plural. — **per′ish•a•bil′i•ty, per′ish•a•ble•ness** *n.* — **per′ish•a•bly** *adv.*

pe•ris•so•dac•tyl (pə-rĭs′ō-dăk′təl) *adj. Zool.* **1.** Having an uneven number of toes. **2.** Of or relating to certain hoofed mammals, such as horses and rhinoceroses, of the order Perissodactyla, having an uneven number of toes. [NLat. *perissodactylus* < Gk. *perissodaktulos* : *perissos,* irregular, uneven (< *peri,* beyond; see **per[1]***) + *daktulos,* finger.] — **pe•ris′so•dac′tyl** *n.* — **pe•ris′so•dac′ty•lous** (-dăk′tə-ləs) *adj.*

per•i•stal•sis (pĕr′ĭ-stôl′sĭs, -stăl′-) *n., pl.* **-ses** (-sēz). The wavelike muscular contractions of the alimentary canal or other tubular structures by which contents are forced onward toward the opening. [NLat. < Gk. *peristaltikos,* peristaltic < *peristellein,* to wrap around : *peri-,* peri- + *stellein,* to place; see **stel-*.**] — **per′i•stal′tic** (-stôl′tĭk, -stăl′-) *adj.* — **per′i•stal′ti•cal•ly** *adv.*

per•i•stome (pĕr′ĭ-stōm′) *n.* **1.** *Bot.* A fringe of toothlike appendages around the mouth of a moss capsule. **2.** *Zool.* The area or parts around the mouth in some invertebrates. — **per′i•sto′mal** (-stō′məl), **per′i•sto′mi•al** *adj.*

per•i•style (pĕr′ĭ-stīl′) *n. Archit.* **1.** A series of columns surrounding a building or enclosing a court. **2.** A court enclosed by columns. [Fr. *péristyle* < Lat. *peristȳlum* < Gk. *peristulon* < neut. of *peristulos,* surrounded by columns : *peri-,* peri- + *stulos,* pillar; see **stā-*.**] — **per′i•sty′lar** (-stī′lər) *adj.*

per•i•the•ci•um (pĕr′ə-thē′shē-əm, -sē-əm) *n., pl.* **-ci•a** (-shē-ə, -sē-ə). A small flask-shaped fruiting body in ascomycetous fungi that contains the ascospores. [NLat. : PERI- + Gk. *thēkion,* dim. of *thēkē,* case; see **dhē-*.**]

per•i•to•ne•um also **per•i•to•nae•um** (pĕr′ĭ-tn-ē′əm) *n., pl.* **-to•ne•a** also **-to•nae•a** (-tn-ē′ə). The serous membrane that lines the walls of the abdominal cavity and folds inward to enclose the viscera. [ME < LLat. *peritonaeum* < Gk. *peritonaion* : ult. *peri-,* peri- + *teinein,* to stretch; see **ten-*.**] — **per′i•to•ne′al** *adj.* — **per′i•to•ne′al•ly** *adv.*

per•i•to•ni•tis (pĕr′ĭ-tn-ī′tĭs) *n.* Inflammation of the peritoneum.

per•i•trich (pĕr′ĭ-trĭk′) *n., pl.* **pe•rit•richs** also **pe•rit•ri•cha** (pə-rĭt′rĭ-kə). Any of various protozoans, such as the vorticella, having a wide oral opening surrounded by cilia. [< NLat. *Peritrichida,* former order name : PERI- + Gk. *thrix, trikh-,* hair.]

pe•rit•ri•chous (pə-rĭt′rĭ-kəs) *adj.* **1.** Having flagella uniformly distributed over the body surface, as certain bacteria. **2.** Having a band of cilia around the mouth, as certain protozoans. — **pe•rit′ri•chous•ly** *adv.*

per•i•wig (pĕr′ĭ-wĭg′) *n.* A wig, esp. a peruke. [Alteration of OFr. *perruque.* See PERUKE.]

per•i•win•kle[1] (pĕr′ĭ-wĭng′kəl) *n.* **1.** Any of several small, often edible marine snails, esp. of the genus *Littorina,* having thick, cone-shaped whorled shells. **2.** Their shell. [ME **periwinkle,* prob. alteration of OE *pīnewincle* : Lat. *pīna,* mussel (< Gk. *pinē*) + OE *-wincel,* snail shell.]

periwinkle[2]
Common periwinkle
Vinca minor

per•i•win•kle[2] (pĕr′ĭ-wĭng′kəl) *n.* Any of several shrubby, trailing evergreen plants of the genus *Vinca,* esp. *V. minor,* having dark green opposite leaves and flowers with a blue funnel-shaped corolla. [ME *pervinkle,* dim. of *pervinke* < OE *pervince* < Lat. *(vinca) pervinca* < *pervincīre,* to wind about.]

per•jure (pûr′jər) *tr.v.* **-jured, -jur•ing, -jures.** *Law.* To render (oneself) guilty of perjury by deliberately testifying falsely under oath. [ME *perjuren* < OFr. *perjurer* < Lat. *periūrāre* : *per-,* per- + *iūrāre,* to swear; see **yewes-*.**] — **per′jur•er** *n.*

per•ju•ry (pûr′jə-rē) *n., pl.* **-ries. 1.** *Law.* The deliberate, willful giving of false, misleading, or incomplete testimony under oath. **2.** The breach of an oath or a promise. [ME *periurie* < AN < Lat. *periūrium* < *periūrāre,* to perjure. See PERJURE.] — **per•ju′ri•ous** (pər-jŏŏr′ē-əs) *adj.* — **per•ju′ri•ous•ly** *adv.*

perk[1] (pûrk) *v.* **perked, perk•ing, perks.** — *intr.* **1.** To stick up or jut out. **2.** To carry oneself in a lively and jaunty manner. — *tr.* To cause to stick up quickly. — *adj.* Perky. — ***phrasal verb.*** **perk up. 1.** To regain or cause to regain one's good spirits or liveliness. **2.** To refresh the appearance of. [Poss. ME *perken,* to perch < *perk,* rod, perch, prob. < Med.Lat. *perca* and < OFr. *perche, perce,* both < Lat. *pertica,* rod. See PERCH[1].]

perk[2] (pûrk) *n. Informal.* A perquisite.

perk[3] (pûrk) *intr.v.* **perked, perk•ing, perks.** *Informal.* To percolate: *The coffee was perking on the stove.*

Frances Perkins

Per•kins (pûr′kĭnz), **Frances.** 1882–1965. Amer. social reformer who served as U.S. secretary of labor (1933–45).

Perkins, Maxwell Evarts. 1884–1946. Amer. editor who helped writers such as F. Scott Fitzgerald.

ă pat | oi boy
ā pay | ou out
âr care | ŏŏ took
ä father | ōō boot
ĕ pet | ŭ cut
ē be | ûr urge
ĭ pit | th thin
ī pie | *th* this
îr pier | hw which
ŏ pot | zh vision
ō toe | ə about, item
ô paw |

Stress marks:
′ (primary);
′ (secondary), as in **dictionary** (dĭk′shə-nĕr′ē)

per•ky (pûr**′**kē) *adj.* **-i•er, -i•est. 1.** Having a buoyant or self-confident air; briskly cheerful. **2.** Jaunty; sprightly. **—perk′i•ly** *adv.* **—perk′i•ness** *n.*

per•lite also **pearl•ite** (pûr**′**līt′) *n.* A volcanic glass having distinctive concentric cracks and a relatively high water content, used in a heat-expanded form as a lightweight aggregate in insulation and potting soil. [Fr. (< *perle*, pearl < OFr.; see PEARL[1]) or Ger. *Perlite* (< *Perle*, pearl, ult. < VLat. **pernula*).]

perm (pûrm) *Informal.* —*n.* A permanent. —*tr.v.* **permed, perm•ing, perms.** To give (hair) a permanent.

Perm (pěrm, pyěrm). A city of W-central Russia on the Kama R. in the foothills of the Ural Mts. Pop. 1,056,000.

perm. *abbr.* Permanent.

per•ma•frost (pûr**′**mə-frôst′, -frŏst′) *n.* Permanently frozen subsoil, occurring throughout the Polar Regions and locally in perennially frigid areas. [PERMA(NENT) + FROST.]

Perm•al•loy (pûr**′**mə-loi′, pûrm-ăl**′**oi′). A trademark used for any of several alloys of nickel and iron having high magnetic permeability.

per•ma•nence (pûr**′**mə-nəns) *n.* The quality or condition of being permanent.

per•ma•nen•cy (pûr**′**mə-nən-sē) *n.* Permanence.

per•ma•nent (pûr**′**mə-nənt) *adj.* **1.** Lasting or remaining without essential change. **2.** Not expected to change in status, condition, or place. —*n.* A long-lasting hair wave produced chemically and with heat. [ME < OFr. < Lat. *permanēns*, *permanent-*, pr.part. of *permanēre*, to endure : *per-*, throughout; see PER- + *manēre*, to remain; see **men-[3]***.] **—per′ma•nent•ly** *adv.* **—per′ma•nent•ness** *n.*

permanent magnet *n.* A piece of magnetic material that retains its magnetism after it is removed from a magnetic field.

permanent press *n.* **1.** A chemical process in which fabrics are permanently shaped and treated for wrinkle resistance. **2.** A fabric treated by permanent press. **—per′ma•nent-press′** (pûr**′**mə-nənt-prĕs**′**) *adj.*

permanent tooth *n.* One of the second set of teeth in mammals. Human beings have 32 permanent teeth.

permanent wave *n.* See **permanent.**

per•man•ga•nate (pər-măng**′**gə-nāt′) *n.* Any of the salts of permanganic acid, all of which are strong oxidizing agents.

per•man•gan•ic acid (pûr′măn-găn**′**ĭk, -măng-) *n.* An unstable inorganic acid, $HMnO_4$, existing only in dilute solution.

per•me•a•bil•i•ty (pûr′mē-ə-bĭl**′**ĭ-tē) *n.*, *pl.* **-ties. 1.** The property or condition of being permeable. **2.** The rate of flow of a liquid or gas through a porous material.

per•me•a•ble (pûr**′**mē-ə-bəl) *adj.* That can be permeated or penetrated, esp. by liquids or gases.

per•me•ance (pûr**′**mē-əns) *n.* A measure of the ability of a magnetic circuit to conduct magnetic flux; the reciprocal of reluctance. [< Lat. *permeāre*, to penetrate. See PERMEATE.]

per•me•ase (pûr**′**mē-ās′) *n.* An enzyme that promotes the passage of a substance across a cell membrane.

per•me•ate (pûr**′**mē-āt′) *v.* **-at•ed, -at•ing, -ates.** —*tr.* **1.** To spread or flow throughout; pervade. **2.** To pass through the openings or interstices of: *liquid permeating a membrane.* —*intr.* To spread through or penetrate something. [Lat. *permeāre*, *permeāt-*, to penetrate : *per-*, through; see PER- + *meāre*, to pass; see **mei-[1]***.] **—per′me•ant** (-ənt), **per′me•a′tive** (-ā′tĭv) *adj.* **—per′me•a′tion** *n.*

Per•mi•an (pûr**′**mē-ən, pĕr**′**-) *Geol.* —*adj.* Of, belonging to, or being the geologic time of the seventh and last period of the Paleozoic Era. See table at **geologic time.** —*n.* The Permian Period or its deposits. [After *Perm* in W-central Russia.]

per•mis•si•ble (pər-mĭs**′**ə-bəl) *adj.* Permitted; allowable: *permissible tax deductions.* **—per•mis′si•bil′i•ty, per•mis′si•ble•ness** *n.* **—per•mis′si•bly** *adv.*

per•mis•sion (pər-mĭsh**′**ən) *n.* **1.** The act of permitting. **2.** Consent, esp. formal consent; authorization. [ME < OFr. < Lat. *permissiō*, *permissiōn-* < *permissus*, p.part. of *permittere*, to permit. See PERMIT.]

per•mis•sive (pər-mĭs**′**ĭv) *adj.* **1.** Granting or inclined to grant permission; tolerant or lenient. **2.** Permitting discretion; optional. **3.** *Archaic.* Not forbidden; permitted. **—per•mis′sive•ly** *adv.* **—per•mis′sive•ness** *n.*

per•mit (pər-mĭt**′**) *v.* **-mit•ted, -mit•ting, -mits.** —*tr.* **1.** To allow the doing of (something); consent to. **2.** To grant leave or consent to (someone); authorize. **3.** To afford opportunity or possibility for. —*intr.* To afford opportunity; allow. —*n.* (pûr**′**mĭt, pər-mĭt**′**). **1.** Permission, esp. in written form. **2.** A document or certificate giving permission to do something; a license or warrant. [ME *permitten* < Lat. *permittere* : *per-*, through; see PER- + *mittere*, to let go.] **—per′mit•tee′** (pûr′mĭ-tē**′**) *n.* **—per•mit′ter** *n.*

Usage Note: In the sense "to allow for, be consistent with," *permit* is often accompanied by *of* when its subject is inanimate: *The wording permits of several interpretations.* But *permit of* should not be used in the sense "to give permission": *The law permits* (not *permits of*) *camping.*

per•mit•tiv•i•ty (pûr′mĭ-tĭv**′**ĭ-tē) *n.*, *pl.* **-ties.** *Phys.* A measure of the ability of a material to resist the formation of an electric field within it.

per•mu•ta•tion (pûr′myŏŏ-tā**′**shən) *n.* **1.** A complete change; a transformation. **2.** The act of altering a given set of objects in a group. **3.** *Math.* **a.** An ordered arrangement of the elements of a set. **b.** An operation that rearranges the elements of a set. **—per′mu•ta′tion•al** *adj.*

per•mute (pər-myōōt**′**) *tr.v.* **-mut•ed, -mut•ing, -mutes. 1.** To change the order of. **2.** *Math.* To subject to permutation. [ME *permuten* < OFr. *permuter* < Lat. *permūtāre* : *per-*, per- + *mūtāre*, to change; see **mei-[1]***.] **—per•mut′a•bil′i•ty** *n.* **—per•mut′a•ble** *adj.* **—per•mut′a•bly** *adv.*

per•ni•cious (pər-nĭsh**′**əs) *adj.* **1.a.** Tending to cause death or serious injury; deadly: *a pernicious virus.* **b.** Causing great harm; destructive: *pernicious rumors.* **2.** *Archaic.* Evil; wicked. [ME < OFr. *pernicios* < Lat. *perniciōsus* < *perniciēs*, destruction : *per-*, per- + *nex*, *nec-*, violent death; see **nek-[1]***.] **—per•ni′cious•ly** *adv.* **—per•ni′cious•ness** *n.*

pernicious anemia *n.* A severe anemia caused by failure of the stomach to absorb vitamin B_{12} and characterized by abnormally large red blood cells and gastrointestinal disturbances.

per•nick•e•ty (pər-nĭk**′**ĭ-tē) *adj.* Persnickety. [?]

Pe•rón (pə-rōn**′**, pě-rôn**′**), **Juan Domingo.** 1895–1974. Argentine soldier who served as president (1946–55 and 1973–74). His second wife, **(Maria) Eva Duarte de Perón** (1919–52), "Evita," was popular for her charitable works. Perón was succeeded by his third wife, **Maria Estela Martínez de Perón** (b. 1931), "Isabelita," who was ousted in 1976.

per•o•ne•al (pĕr′ə-nē**′**əl) *adj.* Of or relating to the fibula or to the outer portion of the leg. [< Gk. *peronē*, pin of a brooch, fibula. See **per-[2]***.]

per•o•ral (pər-ôr**′**əl, -ōr**′**-) *adj.* Through or by way of the mouth: *a peroral infection.* **—per•o′ral•ly** *adv.*

per•o•rate (pĕr**′**ə-rāt′) *intr.v.* **-rat•ed, -rat•ing, -rates. 1.** To conclude a speech with a formal recapitulation. **2.** To speak at great length, often in a grandiloquent manner; declaim. [Lat. *perōrāre*, *perōrāt-* : *per-*, per- + *ōrāre*, to speak.] **—per′o•ra′tion** *n.* **—per′o•ra′tion•al** *adj.*

per•ox•i•dase (pə-rŏk**′**sĭ-dās′, -dāz′) *n.* Any of a group of enzymes that occur esp. in plant cells and catalyze the oxidation of a substance by a peroxide.

per•ox•ide (pə-rŏk**′**sīd′) *n.* **1.** A compound, such as sodium peroxide, Na_2O_2, that contains a peroxyl group and yields hydrogen peroxide when treated with an acid. **2.** Hydrogen peroxide. —*tr.v.* **-id•ed, -id•ing, -ides. 1.** To treat with peroxide. **2.** To bleach (hair) with hydrogen peroxide. **—per•ox′ide′** *adj.* **—per′ox•id′ic** (pûr′ŏk-sĭd**′**ĭk) *adj.*

per•ox•i•some (pə-rŏk**′**sĭ-sōm′) *n.* A cell organelle containing enzymes, such as catalase and oxidase, that catalyze the production and breakdown of hydrogen peroxide.

peroxy– *pref.* Containing the bivalent group O_2: *peroxybenzoic acid.* [PER- + OXY-.]

perp (pûrp) *n. Slang.* One who perpetrates a crime.

perp. *abbr.* Perpendicular.

per•pend (pər-pĕnd**′**) *v.* **-pend•ed, -pend•ing, -pends.** —*tr.* To consider carefully; ponder. —*intr.* To be attentive; reflect. [Lat. *perpendere* : *per-*, per- + *pendere*, to weigh; see **(s)pen-***.]

per•pen•dic•u•lar (pûr′pən-dĭk**′**yə-lər) *adj.* **1.** *Math.* Intersecting at or forming right angles. **2.** Being at right angles to the horizontal; vertical. **3.** Often **Perpendicular.** Of or relating to a style of English Gothic architecture of the 14th and 15th centuries characterized by emphasis of the vertical element. —*n.* **1.** *Math.* A line or plane perpendicular to a given line or plane. **2.** A perpendicular position. **3.** A device, such as a plumb line, used in marking the vertical from a given point. **4.** A vertical or nearly vertical line or plane. [ME *perpendiculer* < OFr. < Lat. *perpendiculāris* < *perpendiculum*, plumb line < *perpendere*, to weigh carefully : *per-*, per- + *pendere*, to weigh; see **(s)pen-***.] **—per′pen•dic′u•lar′i•ty** (-lăr**′**ĭ-tē) *n.* **—per′pen•dic′u•lar•ly** *adv.*

per•pe•trate (pûr**′**pĭ-trāt′) *tr.v.* **-trat•ed, -trat•ing, -trates.** To be responsible for; commit. [Lat. *perpetrāre*, *perpetrāt-*, to accomplish : *per-*, per- + *patrāre*, to bring about (< *pater*, father; see **pəter-***).] **—per′pe•tra′tion** *n.* **—per′pe•tra′tor** *n.*

per•pet•u•al (pər-pĕch**′**ōō-əl) *adj.* **1.** Lasting for eternity. **2.** Continuing or lasting for an indefinitely long time. **3.** Instituted to be in effect or have tenure for an unlimited duration: *perpetual friendship.* **4.** Continuing without interruption. See Syns at **continual. 5.** Flowering throughout the growing season. [ME *perpetuel* < OFr. < Lat. *perpetuālis* < *perpetuus*, continuous : *per-*, per- + *petere*, to go toward; see **pet-***.] **—per•pet′u•al•ly** *adv.*

perpetual calendar *n.* A chart or device that indicates the day of the week corresponding to a date over a period of years.

perpetual motion *n.* The hypothetical continuous operation of an isolated mechanical device or other closed system without a sustaining energy source.

per•pet•u•ate (pər-pĕch**′**ōō-āt′) *tr.v.* **-at•ed, -at•ing, -ates. 1.** To cause to continue indefinitely; make perpetual. **2.** To prolong the existence of; cause to be remembered. [Lat. *perpetuāre*, *perpetuāt-* < *perpetuus*, continuous. See PERPETUAL.] **—per•pet′u•ance, per•pet′u•a′tion** *n.* **—per•pet′u•a′tor** *n.*

per•pe•tu•i•ty (pûr′pĭ-to͞o′ĭ-tē, -tyo͞o′-) *n., pl.* **-ties. 1.** The quality or condition of being perpetual. **2.** Time without end; eternity. **3.** *Law.* A property interest granted contingent upon the fulfillment of a condition that may not be fulfilled until more than 21 years after the death of a person alive at the time of the creation of the interest, thus void under the classic rule against perpetuities. **—*idiom.* in perpetuity.** For an indefinite period of time; forever.

per•phen•a•zine (pər-fĕn′ə-zēn′) *n.* A crystalline compound, $C_{21}H_{26}ClN_3OS$, used as a tranquilizer and in treating nausea and vomiting. [Shortening and rearrangement of chemical name *(chloro)phen(othiazinpropylpi)perazine(ethanol)*.]

Per•pi•gnan (pĕr-pē-nyäN′). A city of S France near the Spanish border and the Mediterranean Sea; probably founded in the 10th cent. Pop. 111,669.

per•plex (pər-plĕks′) *tr.v.* **-plexed, -plex•ing, -plex•es. 1.** To confuse or trouble with uncertainty or doubt. **2.** To make confusedly intricate; complicate. **—per•plex′ing•ly** *adv.*

per•plexed (pər-plĕkst′) *adj.* **1.** Filled with confusion or bewilderment; puzzled. **2.** Full of complications or difficulty; involved. [ME < *perplex*, confused < OFr. *perplexe* < Lat. *perplexus* : *per-*, per- + *plexus*, p.part. of *plectere*, to entwine; see **plek-***.] **—per•plex′ed•ly** (-plĕk′sĭd-lē) *adv.*

per•plex•i•ty (pər-plĕk′sĭ-tē) *n., pl.* **-ties. 1.** The state of being perplexed or puzzled. **2.** The state of being intricate or complicated. **3.** Something that perplexes.

per•qui•site (pûr′kwĭ-zĭt) *n.* **1.** A payment or profit received in addition to a regular wage or salary, esp. a benefit expected as one's due. See Syns at **right. 2.** A tip; a gratuity. **3.** Something claimed as an exclusive right. [< ME *perquisites*, property acquired otherwise than by inheritance < Med.Lat. *perquīsītum*, acquisition < Lat., neut. p.part. of *perquīrere*, to search diligently for : *per-*, per- + *quaerere*, to seek.]

Per•rault (pə-rō′, pĕ-), **Charles.** 1628–1703. French writer best known for his *Contes de ma Mère l'Oye* (c. 1697), a collection of retold fairy tales including "Sleeping Beauty."

Per•rin (pĕ-răN′), **Jean Baptiste.** 1870–1942. French physicist and chemist who won a 1926 Nobel Prize.

per•ry (pĕr′ē) *n., pl.* **-ries.** A fermented, often effervescent beverage made from pears. [ME *pere* < OFr. *pere* < VLat. **pirātum* < Lat. *pirum*, pear.]

Per•ry (pĕr′ē), **Matthew Calbraith.** 1794–1858. Amer. naval officer who opened diplomatic relations with Japan (1854).

Perry, Oliver Hazard. 1785–1819. Amer. naval officer who led the fleet that defeated the British in the Battle of Lake Erie (1813) during the War of 1812.

Perry, Ralph Barton. 1876–1957. Amer. philosopher who wrote *Thought and Character of William James* (1935).

pers. *abbr.* **1.** Person. **2.** Personal.

Pers. *abbr.* Persia; Persian.

perse (pûrs) *adj. Color.* Dark grayish blue or purple. [ME *pers* < OFr. < Med.Lat. *persus*, back-formation < Lat. *Persicus*, Persian < *Persa*, a Persian.]

per se (pər sā′, sē′) *adv.* Of, in, or by itself or oneself; intrinsically. [Lat. *per sē* : *per*, per + *sē*, itself.]

Perse (pĕrs, pûrs), **Saint-John.** See Alexis Saint-Léger **Léger.**

per•se•cute (pûr′sĭ-kyo͞ot′) *tr.v.* **-cut•ed, -cut•ing, -cutes. 1.** To oppress or harass with ill-treatment, as because of race. **2.** To annoy persistently; bother. [Ult. < LLat. *persecūtus*, p.part. of *persequī*, to persecute < Lat., to pursue : *per-*, per- + *sequī*, to follow; see **sek^{w}-^{1}***.] **—per′se•cu•tee′** (-kyo͞o-tē′) *n.* **—per′se•cu′tive, per′se•cu•to′ry** (-kyo͞o-tôr′ē, -tōr′ē, -kyo͞o′tə-rē) *adj.* **—per′se•cu′tor** *n.*

per•se•cu•tion (pûr′sĭ-kyo͞o′shən) *n.* **1.** The act or practice of persecuting, as on the basis of race or religion. **2.** The condition of being persecuted. **—per′se•cu′tion•al** *adj.*

Per•se•id (pûr′sē-ĭd) *n., pl.* **Per•se•ids** or **Per•se•i•des** (pər-sē′ĭ-dēz′). One of a shower of meteors that appears to originate in the vicinity of the constellation Perseus during the second week of August. [< Lat. *Perseus*, the constellation Perseus; see PERSEUS or < Gk. *Persēides*, pl. of *Persēis*, offspring of Perseus (< *Perseus*, Perseus).]

Per•seph•o•ne (pər-sĕf′ə-nē) *n. Gk. Myth.* The daughter of Demeter and Zeus who was abducted by Hades but was rescued by her mother and thereafter spent six months of the year on earth and six in the underworld.

Per•sep•o•lis (pər-sĕp′ə-lĭs). An ancient city of Persia NE of modern Shiraz in SW Iran; ceremonial cap. of Darius I and his successors.

Per•se•us (pûr′sē-əs, -syo͞os′) *n.* **1.** *Gk. Myth.* Andromeda's husband, who killed Medusa. **2.** A constellation in the Northern Hemisphere near Andromeda and Auriga. [Lat. < Gk.]

per•se•ver•ance (pûr′sə-vîr′əns) *n.* **1.** Steady persistence in adhering to a course of action, a belief, or a purpose; steadfastness. **2.** *Theol.* The Calvinistic doctrine that God's chosen will continue in a state of grace to the end and will be saved.

per•sev•er•ate (pər-sĕv′ə-rāt′) *intr.v.* **-at•ed, -at•ing, -ates.** *Psychol.* To manifest or experience perseveration. [Back-formation < PERSEVERATION.] **—per•sev′er•a′tive** *adj.*

per•sev•er•a•tion (pər-sĕv′ə-rā′shən) *n.* **1.** *Psychol.* **a.** Uncontrollable repetition of a particular response, such as a word or gesture, despite the absence of a stimulus, usu. caused by an organic disorder. **b.** The tendency to continue or repeat an act or activity after the cessation of the original stimulus. **2.** The act or an instance of persevering; perseverance.

per•se•vere (pûr′sə-vîr′) *intr.v.* **-vered, -ver•ing, -veres.** To persist in a purpose, an idea, or a task in the face of obstacles or discouragement. [ME *perseveren* < OFr. *perseverer* < Lat. *persevērāre* < *persevērus*, very serious : *per-*, per- + *sevērus*, severe; see **wēro-***.] **—per′se•ver′ing•ly** *adv.*

Per•shing (pûr′shĭng, -zhĭng), **John Joseph.** "Black Jack." 1860–1948. Amer. general who commanded the American Expeditionary Force in Europe during World War I.

Per•sia (pûr′zhə, -shə). **1.** Also **Per•sian Empire** (-zhən, -shən). A vast empire of SW Asia founded by Cyrus II after 546 B.C., brought to its height by Darius I and his son Xerxes, and conquered by Alexander the Great in 334 B.C. **2.** See **Iran.**

Per•sian (pûr′zhən, -shən) *adj.* Of Persia or Iran or their peoples, languages, or cultures. **—*n.* 1.** A native or inhabitant of Persia or Iran. **2.** Any of the western Iranian dialects or languages of ancient or medieval Persia and modern Iran.

Persian cat

Persian cat *n.* A stocky domestic cat having long silky fur, short legs, and a broad round head with small ears.

Persian Gulf also **A•ra•bi•an Gulf** (ə-rā′bē-ən). An arm of the Arabian Sea between the Arabian Peninsula and SW Iran.

Persian lamb *n.* **1.** The lamb of the karakul sheep of Asia. **2.** The pelt of a Persian lamb, having glossy, tightly curled fur.

Persian melon *n.* A variety of melon *(Cucumis melo)* having a netted unridged rind and musky orange-colored flesh.

per•si•flage (pûr′sə-fläzh′) *n.* **1.** Light good-natured talk; banter. **2.** A light or frivolous manner of discussing a subject. [Fr. < *persifler*, to banter : *per-*, intensive pref. (< Lat.; see PER–) + *siffler*, to whistle (< OFr. < LLat. *sīfilāre*, alteration of Lat. *sībilāre*).]

per•sim•mon (pər-sĭm′ən) *n.* **1.** Any of various chiefly tropical trees of the genus *Diospyros*, having orange-red fruit that is edible only when completely ripe. **2.** The fruit of any of these trees. [Of Virginia Algonquian orig.]

per•sist (pər-sĭst′, -zĭst′) *intr.v.* **-sist•ed, -sist•ing, -sists. 1.** To be obstinately repetitious, insistent, or tenacious. **2.** To hold firmly and steadfastly to a purpose, a state, or an undertaking despite obstacles, warnings, or setbacks. **3.** To continue in existence; last. [Lat. *persistere* : *per-*, per- + *sistere*, to stand; see **stā-***.] **—per•sis′ter** *n.*

per•sist•ence (pər-sĭs′təns, -zĭs′-) *n.* **1.** The act of persisting. **2.** The state or quality of being persistent; persistency. **3.** Continuance of an effect after the cause is removed. **—per•sist′en•cy** *n.*

per•sist•ent (pər-sĭs′tənt, -zĭs′-) *adj.* **1.** Refusing to give up or let go; persevering obstinately. **2.** Insistently repetitive or continuous. **3.** Existing or remaining in the same state for an indefinitely long time; enduring: *persistent rumors.* **4.** *Bot.* Lasting past maturity without being shed. **5.** *Zool.* Retained permanently, rather than disappearing in an early stage of development. **—per•sist′ent•ly** *adv.*

persimmon

per•snick•e•ty (pər-snĭk′ĭ-tē) *adj.* **1.a.** Overparticular about trivial details; fastidious. **b.** Snobbish; pretentious. **2.** Requiring strict attention to detail; demanding. [Alteration of *pernickety*. See PERNICKETY.] **—per•snick′e•ti•ness** *n.*

per•son (pûr′sən) *n.* **1.** A living human being. Often used in combination: *chairperson; spokesperson; salesperson.* See Usage Note at **man. 2.** An individual of specified character. **3.** The composite of characteristics that make up an individual personality; the self. **4.** The living body of a human being. **5.** Physique and general appearance. **6.** *Law.* A human being or an organization with legal rights and duties. **7.** *Theol.* The separate individualities of the Father, Son, and Holy Spirit. **8.** *Gram.* **a.** Any of three groups of pronoun forms with corresponding verb inflections that distinguish the speaker (first person), the individual addressed (second person), and the individual or thing spoken of (third person). **b.** Any of the different forms or inflections expressing these distinctions. **9.** A character or role, as in a play; a guise. **—*idiom.* in person.** In one's physical presence; personally. [ME < OFr. *persone* < Lat. *persōna*, prob. < Etruscan *phersu*, mask.]

per•so•na (pər-sō′nə) *n.* **1.** *pl.* **-nas** or **-nae** (-nē). A voice or character representing the speaker in a literary work. **2. personae.** The characters in a dramatic or literary work. **3.** *pl.* **personas.** The role that one assumes in public. [Lat. See PERSON.]

per•son•a•ble (pûr′sə-nə-bəl) *adj.* Pleasing in personality or appearance. **—per′son•a•ble•ness** *n.* **—per′son•a•bly** *adv.*

per•son•age (pûr′sə-nĭj) *n.* **1.** A character in a literary work. **2.a.** A person. **b.** A person of distinction. [ME, person < OFr. < *persone*. See PERSON.]

persona gra•ta (grä′tə, grăt′ə) *adj.* Fully acceptable or welcome, esp. to a foreign government. [Lat. *persōna*, person + *grata*, acceptable.]

per•son•al (pûr′sə-nəl) *adj.* **1.** Of or relating to a particular person; private. **2.a.** Done, made, or performed in person. **b.** Done to or for or directed toward a particular person. **3.** Concerning a particular person and his or her private business, interests, or activities; intimate. **4.a.** Aimed pointedly at

ă pat	oi boy
ā pay	ou out
âr care	o͝o took
ä father	o͞o boot
ĕ pet	ŭ cut
ē be	ûr urge
ĭ pit	th thin
ī pie	*th* this
îr pier	hw which
ŏ pot	zh vision
ō toe	ə about, item
ô paw	

Stress marks:
′ (primary);
′ (secondary), as in
dictionary (dĭk′shə-nĕr′ē)

the most intimate aspects of a person, esp. in a critical or hostile manner. **b.** Tending to make remarks, or be unduly questioning, about another's affairs. **5.** Of or relating to the body or physical being. **6.** Relating to or having the nature of a person or self-conscious being. **7.** *Law.* Relating to a person's movable property. **8.** *Gram.* Indicating grammatical person. —*n.* **1.** A personal item or notice in a newspaper. **2. personals.** A column in a newspaper or magazine featuring personal notices.

personal computer *n. Comp. Sci.* A microcomputer for use by an individual, as in an office or at home.

personal effects *pl.n.* Privately owned items, such as a wallet, regularly worn on one's person.

personal equation *n. Psychol.* **1.** Personal characteristics that cause variation in observation, judgment, and reasoning. **2.** An allowance or adjustment made for such variation.

personal foul *n. Sports.* A foul in a game that usu. involves bodily contact with or willful roughing of an opponent.

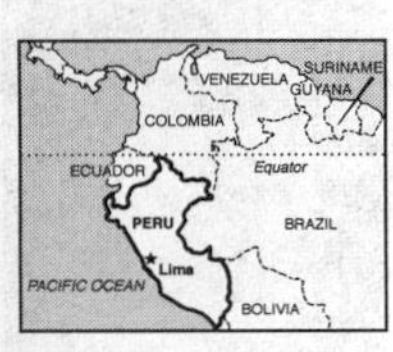

Peru

per•son•a•li•a (pûr′sə-nā′lē-ə, -nāl′yə) *pl.n.* **1.** Personal allusions or references. **2.** Personal belongings or affairs. [Lat. *persōnālia*, neut. pl. of *persōnālis*, relating to a person. See PERSONALITY.]

per•son•al•ism (pûr′sə-nə-lĭz′əm) *n.* **1.** The quality of being characterized by purely personal modes of expression or behavior; idiosyncrasy. **2.** *Philos.* Any of various theories of subjective idealism regarding personality as the key to the interpretation of reality. —**per′son•al•ist** *adj. & n.* —**per′son•al•is′tic** *adj.*

per•son•al•i•ty (pûr′sə-năl′ĭ-tē) *n., pl.* **-ties. 1.** The quality or condition of being a person. **2.** The totality of qualities and traits, as of character or behavior, peculiar to a specific person. **3.** The pattern of collective character, behavioral, temperamental, emotional, and mental traits of a person. **4.** Distinctive qualities of a person, esp. those distinguishing personal characteristics that make one socially appealing. **5.a.** A person as the embodiment of distinctive traits of mind and behavior. **b.** *Usage Problem.* A person of prominence or notoriety: *television personalities.* **6.** An offensively personal remark. Often used in the plural: *Let's not engage in personalities.* **7.** The distinctive characteristics of a place or situation. [ME *personalite* < OFr. < LLat. *persōnālitās* < Lat. *persōnālis*, personal < *persōna*, person. See PERSON.]

Usage Note: *Personality* is often used to mean "celebrity," particularly in popular journalism. This usage may fit those best known simply for who they are rather than what they have done. It is slighting, however, when used of people whose renown is based on substantive achievements. Perhaps for this reason, the word was unacceptable to 57 percent of the Usage Panel in an earlier survey.

per•son•al•ize (pûr′sə-nə-līz′) *tr.v.* **-ized, -iz•ing, -iz•es. 1.** To take (a general remark) in a personal manner. **2.** To attribute human or personal qualities to; personify. **3.** To have printed, engraved, or monogrammed with one's name or initials. —**per′son•al•i•za′tion** (-sə-nə-lĭ-zā′shən) *n.*

per•son•al•ly (pûr′sə-nə-lē) *adv.* **1.** Without the intervention of another; in person. **2.** As far as oneself is concerned. **3.** As a person. **4.** In a personal manner: *took it personally.*

personal pronoun *n. Gram.* A pronoun designating the person speaking (*I, me, we, us*), the person spoken to (*you*), or the person or thing spoken about (*he, she, it, they, him, her, them*).

personal property *n. Law.* Temporary or movable property.

per•son•al•ty (pûr′sə-nəl-tē) *n., pl.* **-ties.** *Law.* Personal property; chattels. [AN *personalte* < LLat. *persōnālitās*, personality. See PERSONALITY.]

persona non gra•ta (nŏn grä′tə, grăt′ə) *adj.* Fully unacceptable or unwelcome, esp. to a foreign government. [Lat. : Lat. *persōna*, person + *nōn*, not + *grata*, acceptable.]

per•son•ate[1] (pûr′sə-nāt′) *tr.v.* **-at•ed, -at•ing, -ates. 1.** To play the role or portray the part of (a character); impersonate. **2.** To endow with personal qualities; personify. **3.** *Law.* To assume the identity of, with intent to deceive. [LLat. *persōnāre*, *persōnāt-*, to bear the character of, represent < Lat. *persōna*, person. See PERSON.] —**per′son•a′tion** *n.* —**per′son•a′tive** *adj.* —**per′son•a′tor** *n.*

per•son•ate[2] (pûr′sə-nĭt) *adj. Bot.* Having two lips, with the throat closed by a prominent palate. [Lat. *persōnātus*, masked < *persōna*, mask. See PERSON.]

per•son•i•fi•ca•tion (pər-sŏn′ə-fĭ-kā′shən) *n.* **1.** The act of personifying. **2.** A person or thing typifying a certain quality or idea; an embodiment. **3.** A figure of speech in which inanimate objects or abstractions are represented with human qualities or form. **4.** Artistic representation of an abstract quality or idea as a person.

per•son•i•fy (pər-sŏn′ə-fī′) *tr.v.* **-fied, -fy•ing, -fies. 1.** To think of or represent (an inanimate object or abstraction) as having personality or the qualities, thoughts, or movements of a living being. **2.** To represent (an object or abstraction) by a human figure. **3.** To represent (an abstract quality or idea). **4.** To be the embodiment or perfect example of. [Fr. *personnifier* < *personne*, person < OFr. *persone*. See PERSON.] —**per•son′i•fi′er** *n.*

per•son•nel (pûr′sə-nĕl′) *n.* **1.a.** The people employed by or active in an organization. **b.** (*used with a pl. v.*) Persons. **2.** An administrative division of an organization concerned with its personnel. [Fr. < OFr., personal < Lat. *persōnālis*. See PERSONALITY.]

per•son-to-per•son (pûr′sən-tə-pûr′sən) *adj.* **1.** Of or relating to a telephone call chargeable only when an indicated person is reached. **2.** Involving direct communication or contact between persons. —**per′son-to-per′son** *adv.*

per•spec•tive (pər-spĕk′tĭv) *n.* **1.** The technique of representing three-dimensional objects and depth relationships on a two-dimensional surface. **2.a.** A view or vista. **b.** A mental view or outlook. **3.** The appearance of objects in depth as perceived by normal binocular vision. **4.a.** The relationship of aspects of a subject to each other and to a whole. **b.** Subjective evaluation of relative significance; a point of view. **c.** The ability to perceive things in their actual interrelations or comparative importance. —*adj.* Of, seen, or represented in perspective. [ME, science of optics (influenced by Fr. *perspective*, perspective, alteration of Ital. *prospettiva* < *prospetto*, new < Lat. *prōspectus*; see PROSPECT) < Med.Lat. *perspectīva (ars)*, fem. of *perspectīvus*, optical < *perspectus*, p.part. of *perspicere*, to inspect : *per-*, per- + *specere*, to look; see **spek-***.] —**per•spec′tiv•al** *adj.* —**per•spec′tive•ly** *adv.*

per•spi•ca•cious (pûr′spĭ-kā′shəs) *adj.* Having or showing penetrating mental discernment; clear-sighted. [< Lat. *perspicāx*, *perspicāc-* < *perspicere*, to look through. See PERSPECTIVE.] —**per′spi•ca′cious•ly** *adv.* —**per′spi•ca′cious•ness** *n.*

per•spi•cac•i•ty (pûr′spĭ-kăs′ĭ-tē) *n.* Acuteness of perception, discernment, or understanding.

per•spi•cu•i•ty (pûr′spĭ-kyōō′ĭ-tē) *n.* **1.** The quality of being perspicuous; clearness and lucidity. **2.** Perspicacity.

per•spic•u•ous (pər-spĭk′yōō-əs) *adj.* Clearly expressed or presented; easy to understand. [< Lat. *perspicuus* < *perspicere*, to see through. See PERSPICACIOUS.] —**per•spic′u•ous•ly** *adv.* —**per•spic′u•ous•ness** *n.*

per•spi•ra•tion (pûr′spə-rā′shən) *n.* **1.** The fluid, consisting of water with small amounts of urea and salts, excreted through the pores of the skin by the sweat glands; sweat. **2.** The act or process of perspiring. —**per•spir′a•to′ry** (pər-spīr′ə-tôr′ē, -tōr′ē, pûr′spər-ə-) *adj.*

per•spire (pər-spīr′) *v.* **-spired, -spir•ing, -spires.** —*intr.* To excrete perspiration through the pores of the skin. —*tr.* To expel through external pores; exude. [Lat. *perspīrāre*, to blow steadily : *per-*, through; see PER- + *spīrāre*, to breathe.]

per•suade (pər-swād′) *tr.v.* **-suad•ed, -suad•ing, -suades.** To induce to undertake a course of action or embrace a point of view by means of argument, reasoning, or entreaty. [Lat. *persuādēre* : *per-*, per- + *suādēre*, to urge; see **swād-***.] —**per•suad′a•ble** *adj.* —**per•suad′er** *n.*

per•sua•si•ble (pər-swā′zə-bəl, -sə-bəl) *adj.* Capable of being persuaded. —**per•sua′si•bil′i•ty, per•sua′si•ble•ness** *n.*

per•sua•sion (pər-swā′zhən) *n.* **1.** The act of persuading or the state of being persuaded. **2.** The ability or power to persuade. **3.** A strongly held opinion; a conviction. **4.a.** A body of religious beliefs; a religion. **b.** A party, faction, or group holding to a particular set of ideas or beliefs. **5.** *Informal.* Kind; sort. [ME < OFr. < Lat. *persuāsiō*, *persuāsiōn-* < *persuāsus*, p.part. of *persuādēre*, to persuade. See PERSUADE.]

per•sua•sive (pər-swā′sĭv, -zĭv) *adj.* Tending or having the power to persuade. —**per•sua′sive•ness** *n.*

pert (pûrt) *adj.* **pert•er, pert•est. 1.** Trim and stylish in appearance; jaunty. **2.** High-spirited; vivacious. **3.** Impudently bold; saucy. [ME, unconcealed, bold, short for *apert*, obvious, frank < OFr. < Lat. *apertus*, open, p.part. of *aperīre*, to open. See **wer-**[4]***.] —**pert′ly** *adv.* —**pert′ness** *n.*

pert. *abbr.* Pertaining.

per•tain (pər-tān′) *intr.v.* **-tained, -tain•ing, -tains. 1.** To have reference; relate: *evidence that pertains to the accident.* **2.** To belong as an adjunct, part, holding, or quality. **3.** To be fitting or suitable. [ME *pertenen*, *pertainen* < OFr. *partenir* < Lat. *pertinēre* : *per-*, per- + *tenēre*, to hold; see **ten-***.]

Perth (pûrth). **1.** A city of SW Australia near the Indian Ocean; founded 1829. Pop. 82,600. **2.** A burgh of central Scotland on the Tay R. NNW of Edinburgh; cap. of Scotland from the 11th to the mid-15th cent. Pop. 42,000.

Perth Am•boy (ăm′boi′). A city of E-central NJ on Raritan Bay; settled in the late 17th cent. Pop. 41,967.

per•ti•na•cious (pûr′tn-ā′shəs) *adj.* **1.** Holding tenaciously to a purpose, belief, opinion, or course of action. **2.** Stubbornly or perversely persistent. See Syns at **obstinate.** [< Lat. *pertināx*, *pertināc-* : *per-*, per- + *tenāx*, tenacious (< *tenēre*, to hold; see **ten-***).] —**per′ti•na′cious•ly** *adv.* —**per′ti•na′cious•ness** *n.*

per•ti•nac•i•ty (pûr′tn-ăs′ĭ-tē) *n.* The quality or state of being pertinacious.

per•ti•nent (pûr′tn-ənt) *adj.* Having precise logical relevance to the matter at hand. [ME < OFr. < Lat. *pertinēns*, *pertinent-*, pr.part. of *pertinēre*, to pertain. See PERTAIN.] —**per′ti•nence, per′ti•nen•cy** *n.* —**per′ti•nent•ly** *adv.*

per•turb (pər-tûrb′) *tr.v.* **-turbed, -turb•ing, -turbs. 1.** To disturb greatly; make uneasy or anxious. **2.** To throw into great confusion. **3.** *Phys. & Astron.* To cause perturbation, as of a celestial orbit. [ME *perturben* < OFr. *perturber* < Lat. *perturbāre* : *per-*, per- + *turbāre*, to throw into disorder (< *turba*, confusion, perh. < Gk. *turbē*).] **— per•turb′a•ble** *adj.*

per•tur•ba•tion (pûr′tər-bā′shən) *n.* **1.a.** The act of perturbing. **b.** The state of being perturbed; agitation. **2.a.** A small change in a physical system. **b.** *Phys. & Astron.* Variation in a designated orbit, as of a planet, resulting from the influence of one or more external bodies. **— per′tur•ba′tion•al** *adj.*

per•tus•sis (pər-tŭs′ĭs) *n.* See **whooping cough. — per•tus′sal** *adj.*

Pe•ru (pə-ro͞o′). A country of W South America on the Pacific; inhabited since at least the 9th millennium B.C. and the center of an Incan empire established after the 12th cent. A.D. The Spanish under Pizarro conquered the empire in 1533. Peru achieved full independence in 1824. Cap. Lima. Pop. 17,031,221. **— Pe•ru′vi•an** (-vē-ən) *adj. & n.*

Peru Current *n.* See **Humboldt Current.**

Pe•ru•gia (pə-ro͞o′jə, -jē-ə, pĕ-ro͞o′jä). A city of central Italy on a hill overlooking the Tiber R. N of Rome; orig. an Etruscan settlement. Pop. 142,522. **— Pe•ru′gian** *adj. & n.*

Pe•ru•gi•no (pĕr′ə-jē′nō, pĕ′ro͞o-), **Il.** 1445–1523? Italian painter known for his religious frescoes.

pe•ruke (pə-ro͞ok′) *n.* A wig, esp. one worn by men in the 17th and 18th centuries; a periwig. [Fr. *perruque* < OFr., head of hair < OItal. *perrucca.*]

pe•ruse (pə-ro͞oz′) *tr.v.* **-rused, -rus•ing, -rus•es.** To read or examine, typically with great care. [ME *perusen*, to use up : Lat. *per-*, per- + ME *usen*, to use; see USE.] **— pe•rus′a•ble** *adj.* **— pe•rus′al** *n.* **— pe•rus′er** *n.*

Usage Note: *Peruse* has long meant "to read thoroughly" and is often used loosely when one could use the word *read* instead. The worst that can be said about the latter use is that it is excessively literary or precious. However, common misuse of the word in the sense "to glance over, skim," as in *I only had a moment to peruse the manual quickly,* was unacceptable to 66 percent of the Usage Panel.

Per•utz (pə-ro͞ots′, pĕr′əts), **Max Ferdinand.** b. 1914. Austrian-born biochemist who shared a 1962 Nobel Prize.

Peruvian balsam *n.* Balsam of Peru.

Peruvian bark *n.* See **cinchona** 2.

Pe•ruz•zi (pə-ro͞ot′sē, pĕ-), **Baldassare.** 1481–1536. Italian artist who became architect for St. Peter's in Rome in 1520.

per•vade (pər-vād′) *tr.v.* **-vad•ed, -vad•ing, -vades.** To be present throughout; permeate. [Lat. *pervādere* : *per-*, through; see PER- + *vādere*, to go.] **— per•vad′er** *n.* **— per•va′sion** (-vā′zhən) *n.*

per•va•sive (pər-vā′sĭv, -zĭv) *adj.* Having the quality or tendency to pervade or permeate: *the pervasive odor of garlic.* [< Lat. *pervāsus*, p.part. of *pervādere*, to pervade. See PERVADE.] **— per•va′sive•ly** *adv.* **— per•va′sive•ness** *n.*

per•verse (pər-vûrs′, pûr′vûrs′) *adj.* **1.** Directed away from what is right or good; perverted. **2.** Obstinately persisting in an error or a fault. **3.a.** Marked by a disposition to oppose and contradict. **b.** Arising from such a disposition. **4.** Cranky; peevish. [ME *pervers* < OFr. < Lat. *perversus*, p.part. of *pervertere*, to pervert. See PERVERT.] **— per•verse′ly** *adv.* **— per•verse′ness** *n.*

per•ver•sion (pər-vûr′zhən, -shən) *n.* **1.a.** The act of perverting. **b.** The state of being perverted. **2.** A sexual practice or act considered deviant. **— per•ver′sive** (-sĭv, -zĭv) *adj.*

per•ver•si•ty (pər-vûr′sĭ-tē) *n., pl.* **-ties. 1.** The quality or state of being perverse. **2.** An instance of being perverse.

per•vert (pər-vûrt′) *tr.v.* **-vert•ed, -vert•ing, -verts. 1.** To cause to turn away from what is right, proper, or good; corrupt. **2.** To bring to a bad or worse condition; debase. **3.** To put to a wrong or improper use; misuse. **4.** To interpret incorrectly; misconstrue or distort. — *n.* (pûr′vûrt′). One who practices sexual perversion. [ME *perverten* < OFr. *pervertir* < Lat. *pervertere* : *per-*, per- + *vertere*, to turn; see **wer-**[2]***.**] **— per•vert′er** *n.* **— per•vert′i•ble** *adj.*

per•vert•ed (pər-vûr′tĭd) *adj.* **1.** Deviating from what is considered right and correct. **2.** Of, relating to, or practicing sexual perversion. **3.** Marked by misinterpretation or distortion. **— per•vert′ed•ly** *adv.* **— per•vert′ed•ness** *n.*

per•vi•ous (pûr′vē-əs) *adj.* **1.** Open to passage or entrance; permeable. **2.** Open to arguments, ideas, or change; approachable. [< Lat. *pervius* : *per-*, through; see PER- + *via*, way; see **wegh-*.**] **— per′vi•ous•ness** *n.*

pes (pās) *n., pl.* **pe•des** (pĕd′ās′). A foot or footlike part, esp. the foot of a four-footed vertebrate. [Lat. *pēs.* See **ped-*.**]

Pe•sach (pā′säKH′, pĕ′-) *n. Judaism.* Passover. [Heb. *pesaḥ* < *pāsaḥ*, to pass over.]

pe•sade (pə-säd′, -zäd′) *n.* The act or position of a horse when rearing on its hind legs with its forelegs in the air. [Fr., alteration of obsolete *posade* < OItal. *posata*, a pause < *posare*, to pause < LLat. *pausāre*. See POSE[1].]

Pe•sa•ro (pā′zə-rō′, pĕ′zä-rô). A city of N-central Italy on the Adriatic Sea W of Florence. Pop. 90,147.

Pes•ca•do•res (pĕs′kə-dôr′ēz, -ĭs, -dōr′-). In Pinyin **Peng•hu** (pŭng′ho͞o′). An island group of Taiwan in Taiwan Strait between the W coast of Taiwan and SW China; ceded to Japan in 1895 and returned to China after World War II.

Pes•ca•ra (pə-skär′ə, pĕ-skä′rä). A city of central Italy on the Adriatic Sea ENE of Rome. Pop. 131,345.

pe•se•ta (pə-sā′tə) *n.* See table at **currency.** [Sp., dim. of *peso*, peso. See PESO.]

pe•se•wa (pā-sā′wä) *n., pl.* **pesewa** or **-was.** See table at **currency.** [< Akan *pésewabo*, dark blue seed of a plant, formerly used as the smallest gold weight.]

Pe•sha•war (pə-shä′wər). A city of NW Pakistan NW of Lahore near the Khyber Pass. Pop. 500,000.

pes•ky (pĕs′kē) *adj.* **-ki•er, -ki•est.** *Informal.* Troublesome; annoying: *a pesky mosquito.* [Prob. alteration of PEST.] **— pes′ki•ly** *adv.* **— pes′ki•ness** *n.*

pe•so (pā′sō) *n., pl.* **-sos.** See table at **currency.** [Sp. < Lat. *pēnsum*, something weighed < neut. p.part. of *pendere*, to weigh. See **(s)pen-*.**]

pes•sa•ry (pĕs′ə-rē) *n., pl.* **-ries. 1.** A device worn in the vagina to support or correct the position of the uterus or rectum. **2.** A contraceptive diaphragm. **3.** A medicated vaginal suppository. [ME *pessarie* < LLat. *pessārium* < *pessus*, *pessum* < Gk. *pessos*, oval-shaped stone, pessary.]

pes•si•mism (pĕs′ə-mĭz′əm) *n.* **1.** A tendency to stress the negative or take the gloomiest possible view. **2.** The doctrine or belief that this is the worst of all possible worlds and that all things ultimately tend toward evil. **3.** The doctrine or belief that the evil in the world outweighs the good. [Fr. *pessimisme* (as Fr. *optimisme*, optimism) < Lat. *pessimus*, worst. See **ped-*.**] **— pes′si•mist** *n.* **— pes′si•mis′tic** *adj.* **— pes′si•mis′ti•cal•ly** *adv.*

peruke
Portrait of a Man by Jeremiah Theus (1716–1774)

pest (pĕst) *n.* **1.** An annoying person or thing; a nuisance. **2.** An injurious plant or animal, esp. one harmful to human beings. **3.** A deadly epidemic disease; a pestilence. [Fr. *peste*, pestilence < OFr. < Lat. *pestis.*]

Pest (pĕst, pĕsht). A former town of N-central Hungary on the left bank of the Danube R.; part of Budapest since 1873.

Pes•ta•loz•zi (pĕs′tə-lŏt′sē, -tä-lôt′-), **Johann Heinrich.** 1746–1827. Swiss educational reformer whose teaching theories are based on respect and attention to the individual.

pes•ter (pĕs′tər) *tr.v.* **-tered, -ter•ing, -ters.** To harass with petty annoyances; bother. See Syns at **harass.** [Prob. short for Fr. *empestrer*, to constrain, embarrass < OFr. < VLat. **impāstōriāre* : Lat. *in-*, in; see IN-[2] + VLat. **pastōria*, a hobble < Lat., fem. of *pāstōrius*, of a herdsman < Lat. *pāstor*, herdsman. See **pā-*.**] **— pes′ter•er** *n.*

pest•hole (pĕst′hōl′) *n.* A place that is considered a breeding ground for epidemic disease.

pest house *n.* A hospital for people affected with plague or other infectious disease.

pes•ti•cide (pĕs′tĭ-sīd′) *n.* A chemical used to kill pests, esp. insects. **— pes′ti•cid′al** (-sīd′l) *adj.*

pes•tif•er•ous (pĕ-stĭf′ər-əs) *adj.* **1.a.** Producing or breeding infectious disease. **b.** Infected with or contaminated by an epidemic disease. **2.** Morally evil or deadly; pernicious. **3.** Bothersome; annoying. [ME < Lat. *pestiferus*, var. of *pestifer* : *pestis*, pestilence; see PEST + *-fer*, -fer.] **— pes•tif′er•ous•ly** *adv.* **— pes•tif′er•ous•ness** *n.*

pes•ti•lence (pĕs′tə-ləns) *n.* **1.a.** A usu. fatal epidemic disease, esp. bubonic plague. **b.** An epidemic of such a disease. **2.** A pernicious, evil influence or agent.

pes•ti•lent (pĕs′tə-lənt) *adj.* **1.** Tending to cause death; deadly. **2.** Likely to cause an epidemic disease. **3.** Infected or contaminated with a contagious disease. **4.** Morally, socially, or politically harmful; pernicious. **5.** Causing annoyance or disapproval. [ME < OFr. < Lat. *pestilēns*, *pestilent-* < *pestis*, pestilence. See PEST.]

pestle
In a mortar

pes•ti•len•tial (pĕs′tə-lĕn′shəl) *adj.* Pestilent. **— pes′ti•len′tial•ly** *adv.*

pes•tle (pĕs′əl, pĕs′təl) *n.* **1.** A club-shaped tool for grinding or mashing substances in a mortar. **2.** A large bar moved vertically to stamp or pound, as in a mill. — *v.* **-tled, -tling, -tles.** — *tr.* To pound, grind, or mash with or as if with a pestle. — *intr.* To use a pestle. [ME *pestel* < OFr. < Lat. *pistillum.*]

pes•to (pĕs′tō) *n.* A sauce consisting of usu. fresh basil, garlic, pine nuts, olive oil, and grated cheese. [Ital. < p.part. of *pistare, pestare*, to pound. See PISTON.]

pet[1] (pĕt) *n.* **1.** An animal kept for amusement or companionship. **2.** An object of the affections. **3.** A person esp. loved or indulged; a favorite: *the teacher's pet.* — *adj.* **1.** Kept as a pet: *a pet cat.* **2.a.** Particularly cherished or indulged. **b.** Expressing or showing affection. **3.** Being a favorite. — *v.* **pet•ted, pet•ting, pets.** — *tr.* To stroke or caress gently; pat. — *intr. Informal.* To make love by fondling and caressing. [Sc.Gael. *peata*, tame animal, pet < OIr.] **— pet′ter** *n.*

pet[2] (pĕt) *n.* A fit of bad temper or pique. — *intr.v.* **pet•ted, pet•ting, pets.** To be sulky and peevish. [?]

PET *abbr.* Positron emission tomography.

pet. *abbr.* Petroleum.

Pet. *abbr. Bible.* Peter.

Pe•tah Tiq•wa (pĕt′ə tĭk′və, -vä, pĕ′täKH). A city of central Israel E of Tel Aviv–Jaffa; founded 1878. Pop. 128,300.

Pé•tain (pā-tăN′), **Henri Philippe.** 1856–1951. French soldier

ă pat	oi boy
ā pay	ou out
âr care	o͝o took
ä father	o͞o boot
ĕ pet	ŭ cut
ē be	ûr urge
ĭ pit	th thin
ī pie	*th* this
îr pier	hw which
ŏ pot	zh vision
ō toe	ə about, item
ô paw	

Stress marks:
′ (primary);
′ (secondary), as in **dictionary** (dĭk′shə-nĕr′ē)

Peter the Great

Petrarch

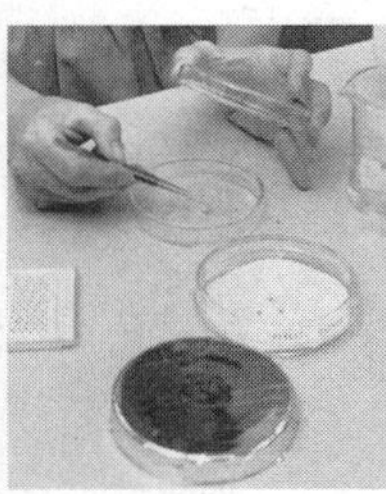

petri dish

petroglyph
Newspaper Rock
at Indian Creek, Utah

who led the government of Vichy France (1940–44).

pet·al (pĕt′l) *n.* A unit of a corolla, usu. showy and colored. [NLat. *petalum* < Gk. *petalon*, leaf. See **petə-***.] **—pet′aled, pet′alled** *adj.*

–petal *suff.* Moving toward: *basipetal.* [< NLat. *-petus* < Lat. *petere*, to seek. See **pet-***.]

pet·al·oid (pĕt′l-oid′) *adj.* Resembling a petal.

pet·al·ous (pĕt′l-əs) *adj.* Having petals.

Pet·a·lu·ma (pĕt′l-o͞o′mə). A city of W CA NNW of San Rafael; founded 1833. Pop. 43,184.

pe·tard (pĭ-tärd′) *n.* **1.** A small bell-shaped bomb used to breach a gate or wall. **2.** A loud firecracker. [Fr. *pétard* < OFr. < *peter*, to break wind < *pet*, a breaking of wind < Lat. *pēditum* < neut. p.part. of *pēdere*, to break wind. See **pezd-***.]

pet·a·sos or **pet·a·sus** (pĕt′ə-səs) *n.* **1.** A wide-brimmed hat worn by ancient Greeks and Romans. **2.** *Gk. Myth.* The winged hat of Hermes. [Gk. See **petə-***.]

pet·cock (pĕt′kŏk′) *n.* A small valve or faucet used to drain or reduce pressure, as from a boiler. [Perh. PET^1 + COCK^1.]

pe·te·chi·a (pə-tē′kē-ə) *n., pl.* **-chi·ae** (-kē-ī′). A small purplish spot on a body surface, such as the skin, caused by a minute hemorrhage and often seen in typhus. [NLat. < Ital. *petecchie*, pl. of *petecchia*, spot on skin, perh. ult. < Lat. *impetīx*, *impetīc-*, var. of *impetīgo*. See IMPETIGO.]

pe·ter^1 (pē′tər) *intr.v.* **-tered, -ter·ing, -ters. 1.** To diminish slowly and come to an end; dwindle. Often used with *out: My strength petered out.* **2.** To become exhausted. Used with *out.* [Perh. < Fr. *peter*, to break wind < OFr. See PETARD.]

pe·ter^2 (pē′tər) *n. Vulgar Slang.* The penis. [< the name *Peter.*]

Pe·ter (pē′tər) *n.* See table at **Bible.**

Peter, Saint. d. c. A.D. 67. The chief of the 12 Apostles who is traditionally regarded as the first bishop of Rome.

Peter I. "Peter the Great." 1672–1725. Russian czar (1682–1725) who extended his territory around the Baltic and Caspian shores and reformed the administration of the state.

Peter II. 1923–70. Yugoslavian king (1934–45) who was forced to abdicate by the Communist government.

Pe·ter·bor·ough (pē′tər-bûr′ə, -bər-ə, -bŭr′ō). **1.** A city of SE Ontario, Canada, NE of Toronto; settled in the 1820's. Pop. 60,620. **2.** A municipal borough of E-central England E of Leicester. Pop. 126,200.

Peter Pan collar *n.* A small, close-fitting, usu. flat collar with rounded ends. [After *Peter Pan*, in the play of the same name by J.M. Barrie.]

Peter Principle *n.* The theory that employees within an organization will advance to and remain at their level of incompetence. [After Laurence Johnston *Peter* (1919–90).]

Pe·ters·burg (pē′tərz-bûrg′). An independent city of SE VA S of Richmond; site of a prolonged siege (Jun. 15, 1864–Apr. 3, 1865) during the Civil War. Pop. 38,386.

Pe·ter's pence (pē′tərz) *n. Rom. Cath. Ch.* **1.** A tax of one penny per household paid in medieval England to the Papal See. **2.** An annual voluntary contribution made toward the expenses of the Holy See. [ME *Peteres pens*, pl. of *Peteres peni* : *Peteres*, Saint Peter's + *peni*, penny; see PENNY.]

pet·i·o·lar (pĕt′ē-ō′lər) *adj.* Of, relating to, or growing on a petiole: *a petiolar sheath.*

pet·i·o·late (pĕt′ē-ə-lāt′, pĕt′ē-ō′lĭt) *adj.* Having a petiole.

pet·i·ole (pĕt′ē-ōl′) *n.* **1.** *Bot.* The stalk by which a leaf is attached to a stem. **2.** *Zool.* A slender stalklike part. [Lat. *petiolus*, var. of *peciolus*, little foot, fruit stalk, prob. < **pediciolus*, dim. of *pediculus*. See PEDICEL.] **—pet′i·oled′** *adj.*

pet·i·o·lule (pĕt′ē-ō-lo͞ol′, pĕt′ē-ŏl′yo͞ol) *n.* The stalk of a leaflet in a compound leaf.

pet·it also **pet·ty** (pĕt′ē) *adj. Law.* Lesser; minor. [ME < OFr.]

pet·it bourgeois (pĕt′ē, pə-tē′) *n.* A member of the petite bourgeoisie. [Fr. *petit-bourgeois* : *petit*, small + *bourgeois*, bourgeois.] **—pet·it′-bour·geois′** *adj.*

pe·tite (pə-tēt′) *adj.* Small and slender. Used of a girl or woman. See Syns at **small.** *—n.* A clothing size for women 5′4″ and under. [Fr., fem. of *petit*. See PETIT.] **—pe·tite′ness** *n.*

petite bourgeoisie *n.* The lower middle class, including small businesspeople, tradespeople, and craftworkers. [Fr. *petite-bourgeoisie* : *petite*, small + *bourgeoisie*, bourgeoisie.]

pet·it four (pĕt′ē fôr′, fōr′) *n., pl.* **pe·tits fours** or **pet·it fours** (pĕt′ē fôrz′, fōrz′). A small, square-cut, frosted and decorated piece of cake. [Fr. : *petit*, little + *four*, oven.]

pe·ti·tion (pə-tĭsh′ən) *n.* **1.** A supplication or request to a superior authority; an entreaty. **2.** A formal document requesting a right or benefit from an authority. **3.** *Law.* **a.** A formal written application requesting a court for a specific judicial action. **b.** The judicial action asked for in any such request. **4.** Something requested or entreated. *—v.* **-tioned, -tion·ing, -tions.** *—tr.* **1.** To address a petition to. **2.** To ask for by petition; request formally. *—intr.* To make a request, esp. formally. [ME *peticion* < OFr. *petition* < Lat. *petītiō*, *petītiōn-* < *petītus*, p.part. of *petere*, to request. See **pet-***.] **—pe·ti′tion·ar′y** (pə-tĭsh′ə-nĕr′ē) *adj.* **—pe·ti′tion·er** *n.*

pe·ti·ti·o prin·ci·pi·i (pə-tĭsh′ē-ō′ prĭn-sĭp′ē-ē′, -ē-ī′) *n. Logic.* The fallacy of assuming in the premise of an argument that which one wishes to prove in the conclusion; a begging of the question. [Med.Lat. *petītiō prīncipiī* : Lat. *petītiō*, request + Lat. *prīncipiī*, genitive of *prīncipium*, beginning.]

pet·it jury also **pet·ty jury** (pĕt′ē) *n. Law.* A jury that sits at civil and criminal trials.

pet·it larceny also **pet·ty larceny** (pĕt′ē) *n. Law.* The theft of objects whose value is below a certain arbitrary standard.

pet·it mal (pĕt′ē mäl′, măl′) *n.* A form of epilepsy, occurring most often in adolescents and children, characterized by frequent but transient lapses of consciousness and only rare spasms or falling. [Fr. : *petit*, small + *mal*, illness.]

pet·it point (pĕt′ē point′) *n.* **1.** A small stitch used in needlepoint. **2.** Needlepoint done with a small stitch. [Fr.]

pet·nap·ping (pĕt′năp′ĭng) *n.* The stealing of a pet, such as a dog or cat. [PET^1 + (KID)NAP.] **—pet′nap′per** *n.*

Pe·tö·fi (pĕt′ə-fē, pĕ′tœ-), **Sándor.** 1823–49. Hungarian poet best known for the epic *Janos the Hero* (1845).

petr– *pref.* Var. of **petro–.**

Pe·tra (pē′trə, pĕt′rə). An ancient ruined city of Edom in present-day SW Jordan; captured by Muslims in the 7th cent. and by Crusaders in the 12th cent.

Pe·trarch (pē′trärk′, pĕt′rärk′) or **Pe·trar·ca** (pĕ-trär′kä), **Francesco.** 1304–74. Italian poet, scholar, and humanist famous for his love lyrics. **—Pe·trarch′an** (pĭ-trär′kən) *adj.*

Petrarchan sonnet *n.* A sonnet containing an octave with the rhyme pattern *abbaabba* and a sestet of various rhyme patterns such as *cdecde* or *cdcdcd.* [After Francesco PETRARCH.]

pet·rel (pĕt′rəl) *n.* Any of numerous black, gray, or white sea birds of the order Procellariiformes, esp. the storm petrel. [Perh. alteration of earlier *pitteral.*]

pe·tri dish (pē′trē) *n.* A shallow circular dish with a loose-fitting cover, used to culture microorganisms. [After Julius R. *Petri* (1852–1921), German bacteriologist.]

Pe·trie (pē′trē), Sir **(William Matthew) Flinders.** 1853–1942. British Egyptologist who excavated at Memphis and Thebes.

pet·ri·fac·tion (pĕt′rə-făk′shən) also **pet·ri·fi·ca·tion** (-fĭ-kā′shən) *n.* **1.** A process of fossilization in which dissolved minerals replace organic matter. **2.** The state of being stunned or paralyzed with fear.

Pet·ri·fied Forest (pĕt′rə-fīd′). A section of the Painted Desert in E AZ reserved for its fossilized trees dating from the Triassic Period.

pet·ri·fy (pĕt′rə-fī′) *v.* **-fied, -fy·ing, -fies.** *—tr.* **1.** To convert (wood or other organic matter) into a stony replica by petrifaction. **2.** To cause to become stiff or stonelike; deaden. **3.** To stun or paralyze with terror; daze. *—intr.* To become stony, esp. by petrifaction. [ME *petrifien*, to harden < OFr. *petrifier* : Lat. *petra*, rock (< Gk.) + OFr. *-fier*, -fy.]

Pe·trine (pē′trīn′) *adj.* Of or relating to Saint Peter. [LLat. *Petrus*, St. Peter + -INE^1.]

petro– or **petri–** or **petr–** *pref.* **1.** Rock; stone: *petroglyph.* **2.** Petroleum: *petrochemistry.* [Gk. < *petros*, stone.]

pet·ro·chem·i·cal (pĕt′rō-kĕm′ĭ-kəl) *n.* A chemical derived from petroleum or natural gas. **—pet′ro·chem′i·cal** *adj.*

pet·ro·chem·is·try (pĕt′rō-kĕm′ĭ-strē) *n.* **1.** The chemistry of petroleum and its derivatives. **2.** The branch of geochemistry that deals with the chemical composition of rocks.

pet·ro·dol·lars (pĕt′rō-dŏl′ərz) *pl.n.* Money paid to oil-producing countries that is then deposited in Western banks.

pet·ro·gen·e·sis (pĕt′rō-jĕn′ĭ-sĭs) *n.* The branch of petrology that deals with the origin of rocks, esp. igneous rocks. **—pet′ro·ge·net′ic** (-jə-nĕt′ĭk) *adj.*

pet·ro·glyph (pĕt′rə-glĭf′) *n. Archaeol.* A carving or line drawing on rock, esp. one made by prehistoric people. **—pet′ro·glyph′ic** *adj.*

Pet·ro·grad (pĕt′rə-grăd′, pyĭ-trə-grät′). See **Saint Petersburg.**

pe·trog·ra·phy (pə-trŏg′rə-fē) *n.* The description and classification of rocks. **—pe·trog′ra·pher** *n.* **—pet′ro·graph′ic** (pĕt′rə-grăf′ĭk), **pet′ro·graph′i·cal** (-ĭ-kəl) *adj.*

pet·rol (pĕt′rəl) *n. Chiefly British.* Gasoline. [Fr. *(essence de) pétrole*, (essence of) petroleum, gasoline < OFr. *petrole*, petroleum < Med.Lat. *petrōleum.* See PETROLEUM.]

pet·ro·la·tum (pĕt′rə-lā′təm, -lä′təm) *n.* See **petroleum jelly.** [< PETROL.]

pe·tro·le·um (pə-trō′lē-əm) *n.* A thick, flammable, yellow to black mixture of gaseous, liquid, and solid hydrocarbons that occurs naturally beneath the earth's surface, can be separated into fractions including natural gas, gasoline, fuel and lubricating oils, paraffin, and asphalt, and is used as raw material for many derivative products. [ME < Med.Lat. *petrōleum* : Lat. *petra*, rock (< Gk.) + Lat. *ōleum*, oil; see OIL.]

petroleum jelly *n.* A semisolid mixture of hydrocarbons obtained from petroleum, used in lubricants and ointments.

pe·trol·ic (pə-trŏl′ĭk) *adj.* Of or relating to petroleum.

pe·trol·o·gy (pə-trŏl′ə-jē) *n.* The branch of geology that deals with the origin, composition, structure, and alteration of rocks. **—pet′ro·log′ic** (pĕt′rə-lŏj′ĭk), **pet′ro·log′i·cal** (-ĭ-kəl) *adj.* **—pet′ro·log′i·cal·ly** *adv.* **—pe·trol′o·gist** *n.*

Pe·tro·ni·us (pĭ-trō′nē-əs), **Gaius.** "Petronius Arbiter." d. A.D. 66. Roman courtier credited with writing the *Satyricon.*

Pet·ro·pav·lovsk (pĕt′rə-păv′lôfsk′, pyĭ-trə-päv′ləfsk). **1.** A city of N-central Kazakhstan W of Novosibirsk; founded 1752. Pop. 226,000. **2.** Or **Pet•ro•pav•lovsk-Kam•chat•ski** (-kăm-chät′skē, -kə-chyät′-). A city of E Russia on the Pacific coast of the Kamchatka Peninsula. Pop. 245,000.

Pe•tróp•o•lis (pə-trŏp′ə-lĭs, pĭ-trô′po͞o-). A city of SE Brazil N of Rio de Janeiro. Pop. 150,249.

pe•tro•sal (pə-trō′səl) *adj.* Relating to or located near the petrous portion of the temporal bone. [< Lat. *petrōsus*, rocky. See PETROUS.]

pet•rous (pĕt′rəs) *adj.* **1.** Of, relating to, or resembling rock, esp. in hardness; stony. **2.** Of or relating to the very dense hard portion of the temporal bone that forms a protective case for the inner ear. [ME < OFr. *petros* < Lat. *petrōsus*, rocky < *petra*, rock < Gk.]

Pet•ro•za•vodsk (pĕt′rə-zə-vŏtsk′, pyĭ-trə-zə-vôtsk′). A city of NW Russia NE of St. Petersburg. Pop. 255,000.

pe-tsai (bā′tsī′) *n.* See **Chinese cabbage.** [Alteration of Chin. (Mandarin) *bái cài*. See BOK CHOY.]

PET scan (pĕt) *n.* A cross-sectional image produced by a PET scanner.

PET scanner *n.* A device that produces cross-sectional x-rays of metabolic processes by means of positron emission tomography. [P(OSITRON) E(MISSION) T(OMOGRAPHY).]

PET scanning *n.* The act or process of using a PET scanner.

pet•ti•coat (pĕt′ē-kōt′) *n.* **1.** A woman's slip or underskirt, often full and trimmed with ruffles or lace. **2.** Something, such as a valance, that resembles a woman's underskirt. **3.** *Offensive Slang.* A woman or girl. —*adj. Offensive Slang.* **1.** Female; feminine. **2.** Of, relating to, or carried out by women. [ME *peticote* : *peti*, small; see PETTY + *cote*, coat; see COAT.]

pet•ti•fog (pĕt′ē-fŏg′, -fôg′) *intr.v.* **-fogged, -fog•ging, -fogs.** To act like a pettifogger.

pet•ti•fog•ger (pĕt′ē-fŏg′ər, -fô′gər) *n.* **1.** A petty, quibbling, unscrupulous lawyer. **2.** One who quibbles over trivia. [Prob. PETTY + obsolete *fogger*, pettifogger.] —**pet′ti•fog′ger•y** *n.*

pet•ting (pĕt′ĭng) *n. Informal.* The act or practice of amorously embracing, kissing, and caressing one's partner.

petting zoo *n.* A collection of farm and docile wild animals, such as goats and deer, for children to feed and pet.

pet•tish (pĕt′ĭsh) *adj.* Ill-tempered; peevish. [Prob. < PET[2].] —**pet′tish•ly** *adv.* —**pet′tish•ness** *n.*

pet•ti•skirt (pĕt′ē-skûrt′) *n.* See **petticoat** 1.

pet•ti•toes (pĕt′ē-tōz′) *pl.n.* **1.** The feet of a pig used as food. **2.** Human feet or toes, esp. those of a child. [Poss. < earlier *pettytoe*, offal, poss. < OFr. *petite oye*, giblets of a goose : *petite*, small + *oye*, goose (< LLat. *auca*; see OCARINA).]

pet•ty (pĕt′ē) *adj.* **-ti•er, -ti•est. 1.** Of small importance; trivial. **2.** Marked by narrowness of mind, ideas, or views. **3.** Marked by meanness or lack of generosity, esp. in trifling matters. **4.** Secondary in importance or rank; subordinate. **5.** *Law.* Var. of **petit.** [ME *peti* < OFr., var. of *petit*. See PETIT.] —**pet′ti•ly** *adv.* —**pet′ti•ness** *n.*

petty cash *n.* A small fund of money for incidental expenses.

petty jury *n. Law.* Var. of **petit jury.**

petty larceny *n. Law.* Var. of **petit larceny.**

petty officer *n.* A noncommissioned naval officer ranking between enlisted personnel and commissioned officers.

pet•u•lant (pĕch′ə-lənt) *adj.* **1.** Unreasonably irritable or ill-tempered; peevish. **2.** Contemptuous in speech or behavior. [Lat. *petulāns*, *petulant-*, insolent < *petere*, to assail. See **pet-***.] —**pet′u•lance, pet′u•lan•cy** *n.*

pe•tu•nia (pĭ-to͞on′yə, -tyo͞on′-) *n.* **1.** Any of various widely cultivated South American plants of the genus *Petunia*, having funnel-shaped white to purple flowers. **2.** *Color.* A moderate to dark purple. [NLat. *Petunia*, genus name < obsolete Fr. *pétun*, tobacco < Port. *petum*, of Tupi-Guarani orig.]

pe•tun•tze or **pe•tun•tse** (pə-to͝on′tsĕ) *n.* A variety of feldspar sometimes mixed with kaolin and used in Chinese porcelain. [Chin. (Mandarin) *bāi dūnzi* : *bāi*, white + *dūnzi*, block of stone.]

Pevs•ner (pĕvz′nər, pyĕf′snĭr), **Antoine.** 1886–1962. Russian artist who was a founder of constructivism.

pew (pyo͞o) *n.* **1.** One of the long fixed benches with backs used as seats in a church. **2.** An enclosed compartment in a church that provides seating for a number of people. [ME *pewe*, prob. < OFr. *puie*, balcony < Lat. *podia*, pl. of *podium*, balcony. See PODIUM.]

pe•wee also **pee•wee** (pē′wē) *n.* Any of various small olive-gray North American flycatchers of the genus *Contopus.* [Imit. of its call.]

pe•wit also **pee•wit** (pē′wĭt′, pyo͞o′ĭt) *n.* See **lapwing.** [Imit. of its call.]

pew•ter (pyo͞o′tər) *n.* **1.** Any of numerous silver-gray alloys of tin with various amounts of antimony, copper, and sometimes lead, used widely for fine kitchen utensils and tableware. **2.** Pewter articles considered as a group. [ME *pewtre* < OFr. *peutre* < VLat. **peltrum*.] —**pew′ter** *adj.*

pe•yo•te (pā-ō′tē) also **pe•yo•tl** (-ōt′l) *n.* **1.** A spineless dome-shaped cactus *(Lophophora williamsii)* native to Mexico and the southwest United States and having buttonlike tubercles that can be chewed as a hallucinogenic drug. **2.** See **mescal button. 3.** See **mescaline.** [Am.Sp. < Nahuatl *peyotl*.]

pf. *abbr.* **1.** Preferred. **2.** Pfennig.

PFC also **Pfc** *abbr.* Private first class.

pfd. *abbr.* Preferred.

pfen•nig (fĕn′ĭg) *n., pl.* **pfen•nigs** or **pfen•ni•ge** (fĕn′ĭ-gə). See table at **currency.** [Ger. < MHGer. *pfennic* < OHGer. *pfenning*.]

pfft (ft, pft) *interj.* Used to express or indicate a usu. sudden disappearance or ending.

pfg. *abbr.* Pfennig.

Pforz•heim (fôrts′hīm, fŏrts′-, pfôrts′-). A city of SW Germany WNW of Stuttgart; chartered c. 1195. Pop. 104,023.

PG (pē′jē′) *n.* A movie rating that admits all ages but suggests parental guidance of children. [P(ARENTAL) + G(UIDANCE).]

pg. *abbr.* Page.

Pg. *abbr.* Portuguese.

PG-13 (pē′jē′thûr-tēn′) *n.* A movie rating that admits all ages but suggests parental guidance of children under age 13.

P.G. *abbr.* **1.** Paying guest. **2.** Postgraduate.

PGA *abbr.* Professional Golfers' Association.

pH (pē′āch′) *n. Chem.* A measure of the acidity or alkalinity of a solution, equal to 7 for neutral solutions and increasing to 14 with increasing alkalinity and decreasing to 0 with increasing acidity. [*p(otential of) h(ydrogen)*.]

Ph *abbr. Bible.* Philippians.

PH also **P.H.** *abbr.* **1.** Public Health. **2.** Purple Heart.

ph. *abbr.* Phase.

PHA *abbr.* Public Housing Administration.

phac•o•e•mul•si•fi•ca•tion (făk′ō-ĭ-mŭl′sə-fĭ-kā′shən) *n.* Removal of a cataract by emulsifying the lens ultrasonically. [Gk. *phakos*, lentil, lentil-shaped object; see **bha-bhā-*** + EMULSIFICATION.]

Phae•dra (fē′drə, fĕd′rə) *n. Gk. Myth.* The wife of Theseus who killed herself after accusing Hippolytus of rape.

Phae•drus (fē′drəs, fĕd′rəs). fl. 1st cent. A.D. Roman fabulist who wrote fables based on those attributed to Aesop.

Pha•ë•thon (fā′ə-thŏn′, -thən) *n. Gk. Myth.* A son of Helios who was killed while driving his father's chariot across the sky. [Lat. *Phaëtōn*, *Phaethōn* < Gk. *Phaethōn*.]

pha•e•ton (fā′ĭ-tn) *n.* **1.** A light four-wheeled open carriage, usu. drawn by a pair of horses. **2.** A touring car. [Fr. *phaéton* < *Phaeton*, Phaethon < OFr. < Lat. *Phaethōn*. See PHAETHON.]

phage (fāj) *n.* A bacteriophage.

–phage *suff.* One that eats: *macrophage.* [< Gk. *-phagos*, eating < *phagein*, to eat. See **bhag-***.]

–phagia or **–phagy** *suff.* The eating of a specified substance or eating in a specified manner: *dysphagia.* [Gk. < *phagein*, to eat. See **bhag-***.]

phago– *pref.* Eating; consuming: *phagocyte.* [Gk. < *phagein*, to eat. See **bhag-***.]

phag•o•cyte (făg′ə-sīt′) *n.* A cell, such as a white blood cell, that engulfs and absorbs foreign bodies in the bloodstream and tissues. —**phag′o•cyt′ic** (-sĭt′ĭk) *adj.*

phagocytic index *n.* The average number of bacteria ingested by each phagocyte in an individual's blood as observed in a mixture of the blood serum, bacteria, and phagocytes.

phag•o•cy•tize (făg′ə-sĭ-tīz′, -sī′-) *tr.v.* **-tized, -tiz•ing, -tiz•es.** To ingest by phagocytosis.

phag•o•cy•to•sis (făg′ə-sī-tō′sĭs) *n.* The engulfing and ingestion of bacteria or other foreign bodies by phagocytes. —**phag′o•cy•tot′ic** (-tŏt′ĭk) *adj.*

–phagous *suff.* Eating; feeding on: *ichthyophagous.* [< Lat. *-phagus* < Gk. *-phagos* < *phagein*, to eat. See **bhag-***.]

pha•lange (fā′lănj′, fə-lănj′) *n.* See **phalanx** 3. [Ult. < Gk. *phalanx*, *phalang-*, log, battle array, bone between the finger and toe joints. See PHALANX.]

pha•lan•ge•al (fə-lăn′jē-əl, fā-) also **pha•lan•gal** (fə-lăng′gəl, fā-) or **pha•lan•ge•an** (fə-lăn′jē-ən, fā-) *adj. Anat.* Of or relating to a phalanx or phalanges.

pha•lan•ger (fə-lăn′jər) *n.* Any of various small arboreal marsupials of the family Phalangeridae of Australia, having a long tail and dense woolly fur. [NLat. < Gk. *phalanx*, *phalang-*, toe bone (< its fused hind toes). See PHALANX.]

phal•an•ster•y (făl′ən-stĕr′ē) *n.* **-ies. 1.a.** A self-sustaining cooperative community of the followers of Fourierism. **b.** The buildings in such a community. **2.** An association resembling a Fourierist phalanstery. [Fr. *phalanstère* : *phalange*, phalanx (< Lat. *phalanx*, *phalang-*; see PHALANX) + *monastère*, monastery (< LLat. *monastērium*; see MONASTERY).]

pha•lanx (fā′lăngks′, făl′ăngks′) *n., pl.* **pha•lanx•es** or **pha•lan•ges** (fə-lăn′jēz, fā-). **1.** A compact or close-knit body of people. **2.** A formation of infantry carrying overlapping shields and long spears, used in classical Greece. **3.** *pl.* **phalanges.** *Anat.* A bone of a finger or toe. **4.** See **phalanstery** 1a. [Lat. *phalanx*, *phalang-* < Gk.]

phal•a•rope (făl′ə-rōp′) *n.* Any of several small wading birds of the family Phalaropodidae, resembling sandpipers but having lobed toes that enable them to swim. [Fr. < NLat. *phalaropus* : Gk. *phalaris*, coot (< *phalaros*, having a white spot; see **bhel-**[1]*) + Gk. *pous*, foot; see **ped-***.]

phal•lic (făl′ĭk) *adj.* **1.** Of, relating to, or resembling a phallus. **2.** Of or relating to the cult of the phallus as an embodiment

pew

phaeton

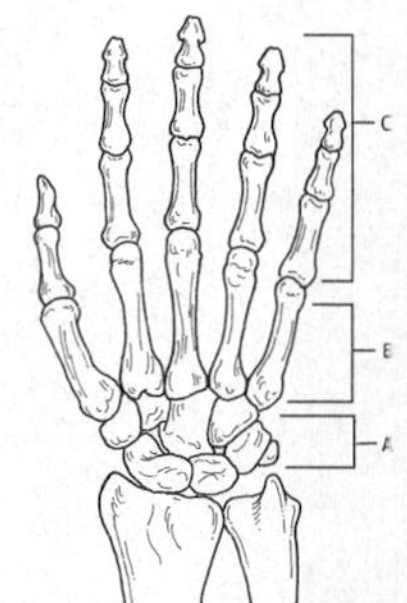

phalanx
A. Carpus
B. Metacarpus
C. Phalanges

ă pat	oi boy
ā pay	ou out
âr care	o͝o took
ä father	o͞o boot
ĕ pet	ŭ cut
ē be	ûr urge
ĭ pit	th thin
ī pie	*th* this
îr pier	hw which
ŏ pot	zh vision
ō toe	ə about,
ô paw	item

Stress marks:
′ (primary);
′ (secondary), as in
dictionary (dĭk′shə-nĕr′ē)

of generative power. **3.** In psychoanalytic theory, of or relating to the third stage of psychosexual development during which the genital organs first become the focus of sexual feeling. [Gk. *phallikos* < *phallos*, phallus. See PHALLUS.] —**phal′li•cal•ly** *adv.*

phal•lus (făl′əs) *n.*, *pl.* **phal•li** (făl′ī′) or **phal•lus•es. 1.** *Anat.* **a.** The penis. **b.** The sexually undifferentiated tissue in an embryo that becomes the penis or clitoris. **2.** A representation of the penis and testes as an embodiment of generative power. **3.** The immature penis considered in psychoanalysis as the libidinal object of infantile sexuality in the male. [LLat. < Gk. *phallos*. See **bhel-**[2]*.]

–phane or **–phan** *suff.* A substance resembling something specified: *tryptophan.* [< Gk. *-phanēs*, appearing < *phainesthai*, to appear. See **bhā-**[1]*.]

phan•er•o•gam (făn′ər-ə-găm′, fə-nâr′ə-) *n.* A plant that produces seeds. [NLat. *phanerogamus* : Gk. *phaneros*, visible (< *phainein*, to cause to appear; see **bhā-**[1]*) + Gk. *gamos*, marriage; see -GAMOUS.] —**phan′er•o•gam′ic, phan′er•og′a•mous** (făn′ə-rŏg′ə-məs) *adj.*

phan•tasm (făn′tăz′əm) *n.* **1.** Something apparently seen but having no physical reality; a phantom or an apparition. **2.** An illusory mental image. **3.** In Platonic philosophy, objective reality as perceived and distorted by the five senses. [Ult. < Gk. *phantazein*, to make visible < *phantos*, visible < *phainein*, to show. See **bhā-**[1]*.] —**phan•tas′mal** (făn-tăz′-məl), **phan•tas′mic** (-tăz′mĭk) *adj.*

phan•tas•ma (făn-tăz′mə) *n.*, *pl.* **-ma•ta** (-mə-tə). See **phantasm** 1, 2. [Ult. < Gk. See PHANTASM.]

phan•tas•ma•go•ri•a (făn-tăz′mə-gôr′ē-ə, -gōr′-) also **phan•tas•ma•go•ry** (făn-tăz′mə-gôr′ē, -gōr′ē) *n.* **1.a.** A fantastic sequence of haphazardly associative imagery, as seen in dreams or fever. **b.** A constantly changing scene composed of numerous elements. **2.** Fantastic imagery as represented in art. [Alteration of obsolete Fr. *phantasmagorie*, art of creating supernatural illusions : perh. *fantasme*, illusion (< OFr., ult. < Gk. *phantasma*; see PHANTASM) + *allégorie*, allegory, allegorical visual representation (< OFr., allegory < Lat. *allēgoria*; see ALLEGORY).] —**phan•tas′ma•gor′ic** (-gôr′ĭk, -gŏr′-) *adj.*

phan•tom also **fan•tom** (făn′təm) —*n.* **1.a.** Something apparently seen, heard, or sensed but having no physical reality; a ghost or an apparition. **b.** Something elusive or delusive. **2.** An image that appears only in the mind; an illusion. **3.** Something dreaded or despised. —*adj.* **1.** Resembling, characteristic of, or being a phantom; illusive. **2.** Fictitious; nonexistent: *phantom employees on the payroll.* [ME *fantom* < OFr. *fantosme*, prob. < VLat. **phantauma* < Gk. dial. **phantagma* < Gk. *phantasma*. See PHANTASM.]

phantom limb pain *n.* Pain or discomfort felt by an amputee in the area of the missing limb.

phar. or **Phar.** *abbr.* **1.** Pharmaceutical. **2.** Pharmacist. **3.** Pharmacopoeia. **4.** Pharmacy.

Phar•aoh also **phar•aoh** (fâr′ō, fā′rō) *n.* **1.** A king of ancient Egypt. **2.** A tyrant. [ME *Pharao* < LLat. *Pharaō* < Gk. < Heb. *Par'ōh* < Egypt. *pr-'o* : *pr*, house + *'o*, great.] —**Phar′a•on′ic** (fâr′ā-ŏn′ĭk) *adj.*

pharaoh ant *n.* A tiny yellowish-red ant *(Monomorium pharaonis)* that infests human dwellings throughout the world.

phar•i•sa•ic (făr′ĭ-sā′ĭk) also **phar•i•sa•i•cal** (-sā′ĭ-kəl) *adj.* **1. Pharisaic.** Of, relating to, or characteristic of the Pharisees. **2.** Hypocritically self-righteous and condemnatory. —**phar′i•sa′i•cal•ly** *adv.* —**phar′i•sa′i•cal•ness** *n.*

phar•i•sa•ism (făr′ĭ-sā-ĭz′əm) also **phar•i•see•ism** (-sē-ĭz′-əm) *n.* **1. Pharisaism.** The doctrines and practices of the Pharisees. **2.** Hypocritical observance of the letter of religious or moral law without regard for the spirit.

phar•i•see (făr′ĭ-sē) *n.* **1. Pharisee.** A member of an ancient Jewish sect that emphasized strict interpretation and observance of the Mosaic law. **2.** A hypocritically self-righteous person. [ME *pharise* < OE *fariseus* and < OFr. *pharise*, both < LLat. *pharīsaeus* < Gk. *pharisaios* < Aram. *pĕrīšayyā.*]

pharm. or **Pharm.** *abbr.* **1.** Pharmaceutical. **2.** Pharmacist. **3.** Pharmacopoeia. **4.** Pharmacy.

phar•ma•ceu•ti•cal (făr′mə-so͞o′tĭ-kəl) also **phar•ma•ceu•tic** (-tĭk) —*adj.* Of or relating to pharmacy or pharmacists. —*n.* A pharmaceutical product or preparation. [< LLat. *pharmaceuticus* < Gk. *pharmakeutikos* < *pharmakeutēs*, preparer of drugs, var. of *pharmakeus* < *pharmakon*, drug.] —**phar′ma•ceu′ti•cal•ly** *adv.*

phar•ma•ceu•tics (făr′mə-so͞o′tĭks) *n.* **1.** *(used with a sing. v.)* The science of preparing and dispensing drugs. **2.** *(used with a pl. v.)* Pharmaceutical preparations; medicinal drugs.

phar•ma•cist (făr′mə-sĭst) *n.* One trained in pharmacy.

pharmaco– *pref.* Drug; medicine: *pharmacognosy.* [Gk. < *pharmakon*, poison, drug.]

phar•ma•co•dy•nam•ics (făr′mə-kō′dī-năm′ĭks) *n.* *(used with a sing. v.)* The study of the action or effects of drugs on living organisms. —**phar′ma•co′dy•nam′ic** *adj.* —**phar′ma•co′dy•nam′i•cal•ly** *adv.*

phar•ma•cog•no•sy (făr′mə-kŏg′nə-sē) *n.* The branch of pharmacology that deals with drugs in their crude or natural state. [PHARMACO– + Gk. *gnōsis*, knowledge; see GNOSIS.] —**phar′ma•cog•nos′tic** (-kŏg-nŏs′tĭk) *adj.*

phar•ma•co•ki•net•ics (făr′mə-kō-kĭ-nĕt′ĭks, -kī-) *n.* *(used with a sing. v.)* **1.** The process by which a drug is absorbed, distributed, metabolized, and eliminated by the body. **2.** The study of this process. —**phar′ma•co•ki•net′ic** *adj.*

phar•ma•col•o•gy (făr′mə-kŏl′ə-jē) *n.* **1.** The science of drugs, including their composition, uses, and effects. **2.** The characteristics or properties of a drug, esp. those that make it medically effective. —**phar′ma•co•log′ic** (-kə-lŏj′ĭk), **phar′ma•co•log′i•cal** (-ĭ-kəl) *adj.* —**phar′ma•co•log′i•cal•ly** *adv.* —**phar′ma•col′o•gist** *n.*

phar•ma•co•poe•ia also **phar•ma•co•pe•ia** (făr′mə-kə-pē′ə) *n.* **1.** A book containing an official list of medicinal drugs together with articles on their preparation and use. **2.** A collection or stock of drugs. [NLat. < Gk. *pharmakopoiia*, preparation of drugs < *pharmakopoios*, preparing drugs : *pharmako-*, pharmaco- + *-poios*, preparing (< *poiein*, to make; see **k**ʷ**ei-**[2]*).] —**phar′ma•co•poe′ial** (-pē′əl) *adj.*

phar•ma•co•ther•a•py (făr′mə-kō-thĕr′ə-pē) *n.*, *pl.* **-pies.** Treatment of disease through the use of drugs.

phar•ma•cy (făr′mə-sē) *n.*, *pl.* **-cies. 1.** The art of preparing and dispensing drugs. **2.** A place where drugs are sold; a drugstore. [Ult. < Med.Lat. *pharmacīa*, a medicine < Gk. *pharmakeia*, use of drugs < *pharmakon*, drug.]

pha•ros (fâr′ŏs′) *n.* A lighthouse. [Lat. < Gk., after *Pharos*, near Alexandria, Egypt, site of an ancient lighthouse.]

Pharr (făr). A city of extreme S TX WNW of Brownsville. Pop. 32,921.

Phar•sa•lus (făr-sā′ləs) or **Phar•sa•la** (făr′sä-lä). An ancient city of Thessaly in NE Greece; site of Julius Caesar's defeat of Pompey (48 B.C.).

pha•ryn•ge•al (fə-rĭn′jē-əl, -jəl, făr′ĭn-jē′əl) also **pha•ryn•gal** (fə-rĭng′gəl) —*adj.* Of, relating to, located in, or coming from the pharynx. —*n.* *Ling.* A speech sound produced in the pharynx. [< NLat. *pharyngeus* < *pharynx*, *pharyng-*, pharynx. See PHARYNX.]

phar•yn•gi•tis (făr′ĭn-jī′tĭs) *n.* Inflammation of the pharynx.

pharyngo– or **pharyng–** *pref.* Pharynx: *pharyngoscope.* [NLat. < Gk. *pharungo-* < *pharunx*, *pharung-*. See PHARYNX.]

pha•ryn•go•scope (fə-rĭng′gə-skōp′) *n.* An instrument used in examining the pharynx. —**phar′yn•gos′co•py** (făr′ĭn-gŏs′kə-pē, făr′ĭng-) *n.*

phar•ynx (făr′ĭngks) *n.*, *pl.* **pha•ryn•ges** (fə-rĭn′jēz) or **phar•ynx•es.** The section of the alimentary canal that extends from the mouth and nasal cavities to the larynx, where it joins the esophagus. [NLat. *pharynx*, *pharyng-* < Gk. *pharunx*.]

phase (fāz) *n.* **1.** A distinct stage of development. **2.** A temporary manner, attitude, or pattern of behavior. **3.** An aspect; a part. **4.** *Astron.* One of the cyclically recurring apparent forms of the moon or a planet. **5.** *Phys.* **a.** A stage in a periodic process or phenomenon. **b.** The fraction of a complete cycle elapsed as measured from a reference point and often expressed as an angle. **6.** *Chem.* **a.** Any of the forms or states, solid, liquid, gas, or plasma, in which matter can exist, depending on temperature and pressure. **b.** A discrete homogeneous part of a material system that is separable from the rest, as ice is from water. **7.** *Biol.* A characteristic form, appearance, or stage of development that occurs in a cycle or distinguishes some individuals of a group. —*tr.v.* **phased, phas•ing, phas•es. 1.** To plan or carry out systematically by phases. **2.** To set or regulate so as to be synchronized. —***phrasal verbs.*** **phase in.** To introduce one stage at a time. **phase out.** To bring or come to an end one stage at a time. —***idioms.*** **in phase.** In a correlated or synchronized way. **out of phase.** In an unsynchronized or uncorrelated way. [Backformation < NLat. *phasēs*, phases of the moon < Gk., pl. of *phasis*, appearance < *phainein*, to show. See **bhā-**[1]*.] —**pha′sic** (fā′zĭk) *adj.*

phase contrast microscope *n.* A microscope that uses the differences in the phase of light transmitted or reflected by a specimen to form distinct, contrasting images of the specimen.

phased array (fāzd) *n.* An arrangement of dipoles on a radar antenna, in which the phase of each dipole is controlled by a computer so that the beam can scan very rapidly.

phase modulation *n.* A type of modulation in which the phase of a carrier wave is varied in proportion to the amplitude of the signal.

–phasia *suff.* A speech disorder of a specified kind: *dysphasia.* [Gk., speech < *phasis*, utterance < *phanai*, to say, speak. See **bhā-**[2]*.]

phas•mid (făz′mĭd) *n.* Any of various insects of the order Phasmida, including the leaf insects and walking sticks, common esp. in tropical areas and resembling foliage in color and form. [< NLat. *Phasmida*, order name < *Phasma*, type genus < Gk. *phasma*, apparition < *phainein*, to show. See PHASE.]

phat•ic (făt′ĭk) *adj.* Of, relating to, or being speech used to share feelings or establish a mood of sociability rather than communicate information or ideas. [< Gk. *phatos*, spoken < *phanai*, to speak. See -PHASIA.] —**phat′i•cal•ly** *adv.*

Ph.B. *abbr.* *Lat.* Philosophiae Baccalaureus (Bachelor of Philosophy).

Ph.C. *abbr.* Pharmaceutical Chemist.

Ph.D. *abbr. Lat.* Philosophiae Doctor (Doctor of Philosophy).

pheas•ant (fĕz′ənt) *n., pl.* **pheas•ants** or **pheasant. 1.** Any of various Old World birds of the family Phasianidae, esp. the ring-necked pheasant, having long tails and in the males of many species brilliantly colored plumage. **2.** Any of several birds that resemble the pheasant, such as the partridge. [ME *fesaunt* < OFr. *fesan* < Lat. *phāsiānus* < Gk. *phasianos (ornis)*, (bird) of the Phasis R., pheasant < *Phasis*, Georgia.]

phel•lem (fĕl′əm, -ĕm′) *n. Bot.* See **cork** 4. [Ger. : Gk. *phellos*, cork; see **bhel-**[2*] + *-em* (as in *Phloëm*, phloem; see PHLOEM).]

phel•lo•derm (fĕl′ə-dûrm′) *n.* A tissue produced inwardly by the cork cambium. [Gk. *phellos*, cork; see **bhel-**[2*] + -DERM.]

phel•lo•gen (fĕl′ə-jən) *n.* See **cork cambium.** [Gk. *phellos*, cork; see **bhel-**[2*] + -GEN.]

phen– *pref.* Var. of **pheno–.**

phe•na•caine (fē′nə-kān′, fĕn′ə-) *n.* A white crystalline compound, $C_{18}H_{22}N_2O_2$, used in the form of its hydrochloride as a local anesthetic. [PHEN(O)– + A(CETO–) + –CAINE.]

phe•nac•e•tin (fə-năs′ĭ-tĭn) *n.* See **acetophenetidin.** [Rearrangement of chemical name ACETOPHENETIDIN.]

phen•a•cite (fĕn′ə-sīt′) or **phen•a•kite** (-kīt′) *n.* A natural beryllium silicate, Be_2SiO_4, occurring as vitreous crystals used as gems. [Gk. *phenax*, *phenak-*, impostor + –ITE[1].]

phe•nan•threne (fə-năn′thrēn′) *n.* A colorless crystalline hydrocarbon, $C_{14}H_{10}$, obtained by fractional distillation of coal tar oils and used in dyes, drugs, and explosives. [PHEN(O)– + ANTHR(AC)ENE.]

phen•a•zine (fĕn′ə-zēn′) also **phen•a•zin** (-zĭn) *n.* A crystalline compound, $C_6H_4N_2C_6H_4$, used in making dyes.

phen•cy•cli•dine (fĕn-sī′klĭ-dēn′, -dĭn, -sĭk′lĭ-) *n.* A drug, $C_{17}H_{25}N$, used as a hallucinogen and in veterinary medicine as an anesthetic; PCP. [PHEN(O)– + CYCL(O)– + –ID(E) + –INE[2].]

phe•net•ic (fĭ-nĕt′ĭk) *adj.* Of, relating to, or being a system of classification of organisms based on overall or observable similarities rather than on phylogenetic or evolutionary relationships. [PHEN(OTYPE) + –ETIC.] **—phe•net′i•cal•ly** *adv.*

phe•net•ics (fĭ-nĕt′ĭks) *n. (used with a sing. v.)* The phenetic system of taxonomic classification.

phe•nix (fē′nĭks) *n.* Var. of **phoenix.**

Phe•nix City (fē′nĭks). A city of E AL on the Chattahoochee R. across from Columbus GA. Pop. 25,312.

pheno– or **phen–** *pref.* **1.** Showing; displaying: *phenotype.* **2.a.** Related to or derived from benzene: *phenol.* **b.** Containing phenyl: *phenothiazine.* [Gk. *phaino-* < *phainein*, to show. See **bhā-**[1*].]

phe•no•bar•bi•tal (fē′nō-bär′bĭ-tôl′, -tăl′) *n.* A crystalline barbiturate, $C_{12}H_{12}N_2O_3$, used medicinally as a sedative, a hypnotic, and an anticonvulsant.

phe•no•bar•bi•tone (fē′nō-bär′bĭ-tōn′) *n. Chiefly British.* Phenobarbital.

phe•no•cop•y (fē′nə-kŏp′ē) *n., pl.* **-ies.** An environmentally induced, nonhereditary variation in an organism, closely resembling a genetically determined trait. [PHENO(TYPE) + COPY.]

phe•no•cryst (fē′nə-krĭst′) *n.* A conspicuous, usu. large crystal embedded in porphyritic igneous rock. [PHENO– + CRYST(AL).] **—phe′no•crys′tic** *adj.*

phe•nol (fē′nôl′, -nōl′, -nŏl′) *n.* **1.** A caustic poisonous crystalline compound, C_6H_5OH, derived from benzene and used in resins, plastics, and pharmaceuticals. **2.** Any of a class of aromatic organic compounds having at least one hydroxyl group attached directly to the benzene ring.

phe•no•late (fē′nə-lāt′) *n.* A salt of phenol.

phe•no•lic (fĭ-nō′lĭk, -nŏl′ĭk) *adj.* Of, relating to, containing, or derived from phenol. —*n.* Any of various synthetic thermosetting resins, obtained by the reaction of phenols with simple aldehydes and used in molded products and coatings.

phe•nol•o•gy (fĭ-nŏl′ə-jē) *n.* **1.** The relationship between a periodic biological phenomenon and climatic conditions. **2.** The scientific study of phenology. [PHENO(MENON) + –LOGY.] **—phe′no•log′i•cal** (fē′nə-lŏj′ĭ-kəl) *adj.*

phe•nol•phthal•ein (fē′nōl-thăl′ēn′, -thăl′ē-ĭn, -thā′lēn′, -thā′lē-ĭn) *n.* A crystalline powder, $C_{20}H_{14}O_4$, used as an acid-base indicator, in making dyes, and as a laxative.

phenol red *n.* A red water-soluble dye, $C_{19}H_{14}O_5S$, used as an acid-base indicator and in medicine to test kidney function.

phe•nom (fĭ-nŏm′) *n. Slang.* A phenomenon, esp. a remarkable or outstanding person.

phe•nom•e•nal (fĭ-nŏm′ə-nəl) *adj.* **1.** Of, relating to, or constituting phenomena or a phenomenon. **2.** Extraordinary; outstanding. **3.** *Philos.* Known or derived through the senses rather than through the mind. **—phe•nom′e•nal•ly** *adv.*

phe•nom•e•nal•ism (fĭ-nŏm′ə-nə-lĭz′əm) *n. Philos.* The doctrine, set forth esp. by David Hume, that percepts and concepts present in the mind constitute the sole object of knowledge, whereas the objects of perception, their origin outside the mind, and the nature of the mind remain forever beyond inquiry. **—phe•nom′e•nal•ist** *n.* **—phe•nom′e•nal•is′tic** *adj.* **—phe•nom′e•nal•is′ti•cal•ly** *adv.*

phe•nom•e•nol•o•gy (fĭ-nŏm′ə-nŏl′ə-jē) *n. Philos.* **1.** The study of all possible appearances in human experience, during which considerations of objective reality and of purely subjective response are temporarily left out of account. **2.** A movement based on this study, originated about 1905 by Edmund Husserl. **—phe•nom′e•no•log′i•cal** (-nə-lŏj′ĭ-kəl) *adj.* **—phe•nom′e•no•log′i•cal•ly** *adv.* **—phe•nom′e•nol′o•gist** *n.*

phe•nom•e•non (fĭ-nŏm′ə-nŏn′, -nən) *n., pl.* **-na** (-nə). **1.** An occurrence, a circumstance, or a fact that is perceptible by the senses. **2.** *pl.* **-nons. a.** An unusual, significant, or unaccountable fact or occurrence; a marvel. **b.** A remarkable or outstanding person; a paragon. See Syns at **wonder. 3.** *Philos.* **a.** That which appears real to the mind, regardless of whether its existence is proved or its nature understood. **b.** In Kantian philosophy, the appearance of an object to the mind as opposed to its existence independent of the mind. **4.** *Phys.* An observable event. [LLat. *phaenomenon* < Gk. *phainomenon* < neut. pr.part. of *phainesthai*, to appear. See **bhā-**[1*].]

Usage Note: *Phenomenon* is the only singular form of this noun; *phenomena* is the usual plural. *Phenomenons* may also be used as the plural in nonscientific writing when the meaning is "extraordinary things, occurrences, or persons."

phe•no•thi•a•zine (fē′nō-thī′ə-zēn′, -nə-) *n.* **1.** An organic compound, $C_{12}H_9NS$, used in insecticides, livestock anthelmintics, and dyes. **2.** Any of a group of drugs derived from this compound and used as major tranquilizers.

phe•no•type (fē′nə-tīp′) *n.* **1.a.** The observable physical or biochemical traits of an organism, as determined by both genetics and environment. **b.** The expression of a given trait based on phenotype. **2.** An individual or group of organisms with a particular phenotype. **—phe′no•typ′ic** (-tĭp′ĭk), **phe′no•typ′i•cal** (-ĭ-kəl) *adj.* **—phe′no•typ′i•cal•ly** *adv.*

phe•nox•ide (fĭ-nŏk′sīd′) *n.* See **phenolate.**

phen•yl (fĕn′əl, fē′nəl) *n.* The univalent organic radical C_6H_5, derived from benzene by removal of one hydrogen atom. **—phe•nyl′ic** (fĭ-nĭl′ĭk) *adj.*

phen•yl•al•a•nine (fĕn′əl-ăl′ə-nēn′, fē′nəl-) *n.* An essential amino acid, $C_6H_5CH_2CH(NH_2)COOH$, that occurs as a constituent of many proteins.

phen•yl•bu•ta•zone (fĕn′əl-byōō′tə-zōn′) *n.* A compound, $C_{19}H_{20}N_2O_2$, used as an anti-inflammatory and analgesic drug. [PHENYL + BUT– + AZO– + –ONE.]

phen•yl•ene (fĕn′ə-lēn′, fē′nə-) *n.* A bivalent organic radical, C_6H_4, derived from benzene by removal of two hydrogen atoms.

phen•yl•eph•rine (fĕn′əl-ĕf′rēn, fē′nəl-) *n.* An adrenergic drug, $C_9H_{13}NO_2$, that is a powerful vasoconstrictor and is used to relieve nasal congestion, dilate the pupils, and maintain blood pressure during anesthesia. [PHENYL + (EPIN)EPHRINE.]

phen•yl•ke•to•nur•i•a (fĕn′əl-kēt′n-ŏŏr′ē-ə, -yŏŏr′-, fē′nəl-) *n.* A genetic disorder in which the body lacks the enzyme necessary to metabolize phenylalanine, causing possible brain damage and progressive mental retardation. **—phen′yl•ke′to•nur′ic** *adj. & n.*

phen•yl•pro•pa•nol•a•mine (fĕn′əl-prō′pə-nŏl′ə-mēn′, fē′nəl-) *n.* An adrenergic drug, $C_9H_{13}NO$, that acts as a vasoconstrictor and is used as a nasal decongestant, a bronchodilator, an appetite suppressant, and a mild stimulant.

phen•yl•thi•o•car•ba•mide (fĕn′əl-thī′ō-kär′bə-mīd′, -kär-băm′īd, fē′nəl-) *n.* A crystalline compound, $C_6H_5NHCSNH_2$, that tastes bitter to people with a specific dominant gene, used to test for the presence of the gene.

phen•yl•thi•o•u•re•a (fĕn′əl-thī′ō-yŏŏ-rē′ə, fē′nəl-) *n.* See **phenylthiocarbamide.**

phen•y•to•in (fĕn′ĭ-tō′ĭn, fə-nĭt′ō-) *n.* An anticonvulsant drug, $C_{15}H_{12}N_2O_2$, chemically related to the barbiturates and used in the treatment of epilepsy. [(DI)PHENY(LHYDAN)TOIN.]

phe•re•sis (fə-rē′sĭs, fĕr′ə-) *n. Informal.* Apheresis.

pher•o•mone (fĕr′ə-mōn′) *n.* A chemical secreted by an animal, esp. an insect, that influences the behavior or development of others of the same species. [Gk. *pherein*, to carry; see **bher-**[1*] + (HOR)MONE.] **—pher′o•mon′al** *adj.*

phew (fyōō) *interj.* Used to express relief, fatigue, surprise, or disgust.

Ph.G. *abbr.* Graduate in Pharmacy.

phi (fī) *n.* The 21st letter of the Greek alphabet. [LGk. < Gk. *phei.*]

phi•al (fī′əl) *n.* A vial. [ME *fiole* < OFr. < LLat. *fiola*, shallow vessel, alteration of Lat. *phiala* < Gk. *phialē.*]

Phi Be•ta Kap•pa (fī′ bā′tə kăp′ə, bē′tə) *n.* **1.** An honorary society of college students and graduates chosen on the basis of high academic standing. **2.** A member of this society. [< the initials of the society's motto in Gk. *philosophia biou kubernētēs*, philosophy the guide of life.]

Phid•i•as (fĭd′ē-əs) fl. 5th cent. B.C. Athenian sculptor whose Olympian Zeus was one of the Seven Wonders of the World.

phil. *abbr.* Philosopher; philosophical; philosophy.

Phil. *abbr.* **1.** *Bible.* Philippians. **2.** Philippines.

phil– *pref.* Var. of **philo–.**

–phil *suff.* Var. of **–phile.**

Phil•a•del•phi•a (fĭl′ə-dĕl′fē-ə). **1.** An ancient city of Asia Minor NE of the Dead Sea in modern-day Jordan; chief city of the Ammonites. **2.** A city of SE PA on the Delaware R.;

pheasant
Phasianus colchicus

ă pat	oi boy
ā pay	ou out
âr care	ŏŏ took
ä father	ōō boot
ĕ pet	ŭ cut
ē be	ûr urge
ĭ pit	th thin
ī pie	*th* this
îr pier	hw which
ŏ pot	zh vision
ō toe	ə about,
ô paw	item

Stress marks:
′ (primary);
′ (secondary), as in
dictionary (dĭk′shə-nĕr′ē)

founded in 1681 and the second cap. of the U.S. (1790–1800). Pop. 1,585,577. — **Phil′a•del′phi•an** *adj. & n.*

Philadelphia lawyer *n.* An attorney adept at the discovery and manipulation of legal technicalities.

Philadelphia pepper pot *n.* See **pepper pot** 1.

Phi•lae (fī′lē). A former island in the Nile R. of SE Egypt; noted for its temple dedicated to Isis.

phi•lan•der (fĭ-lăn′dər) *intr.v.* **-dered, -der•ing, -ders.** To carry on a sexual affair or many affairs, esp. with a frivolous or casual attitude. Used of a man. [< *philander*, lover, ult. < Gk. *philandros*, loving men : *phil-*, *philo-*, philo- + *anēr*, *andr-*, man; see **ner-**[2]***.**] — **phi•lan′der•er** *n.*

phil•an•throp•ic (fĭl′ən-thrŏp′ĭk) also **phil•an•throp•i•cal** (-ĭ-kəl) *adj.* **1.** Of, relating to, or marked by philanthropy; humanitarian. **2.** Organized to provide humanitarian or charitable assistance. — **phil′an•throp′i•cal•ly** *adv.*

Prince Philip
Photographed in 1985

phi•lan•thro•py (fĭ-lăn′thrə-pē) *n., pl.* **-pies. 1.** The effort or inclination to increase human well-being, as by charitable aid. **2.** Love of humankind in general. **3.** Something intended to promote human welfare. [LLat. *philanthrōpia* < Gk. < *philanthrōpos*, humane, benevolent : *phil-*, *philo-*, philo- + *anthrōpos*, man, mankind.] — **phi•lan′thro•pist** *n.*

phi•lat•e•ly (fĭ-lăt′l-ē) *n.* The collection and study of postage stamps, postmarks, and related materials; stamp collecting. [Fr. *philatélie* : Gk. *phil-*, *philo-*, philo- + Gk. *ateleia*, exemption from payment (*a-*, without; see A-[1] + *telos*, tax, charge; see **telə-***).] — **phil′a•tel′ic** (fĭl′ə-tĕl′ĭk), **phil′a•tel′i•cal** (-ĭ-kəl) *adj.* — **phi•lat′e•list** *n.*

–phile or **–phil** *suff.* **1.** One that loves or has a strong affinity or preference for: *audiophile.* **2.** Loving; having a strong affinity or preference for: *Francophile.* [NLat. *-philus* < Gk. *-philos*, beloved, dear < *philos*, beloved, loving.]

Phi•le•mon (fĭ-lē′mən, fī-) *n.* **1.** See table at **Bible. 2.** *Gk. Myth.* The husband of Baucis.

phil•har•mon•ic (fĭl′här-mŏn′ĭk, fĭl′ər-) *Mus.* — *adj.* **1.** Devoted to or appreciative of music. **2.** Relating to a symphony orchestra. — *n.* also **Philharmonic.** A symphony orchestra or the group that supports it. [Fr. *philharmonique* < Ital. *filarmonico* : Gk. *phil-*, *philo-*, philo- + Gk. *harmonika*, theory of music < neut. pl. of *harmonikos*, musical; see HARMONIC.]

phil•hel•lene (fĭl-hĕl′ēn′) also **phil•hel•len•ist** (-hĕl′ə-nĭst) *n.* One who admires Greece or the Greeks. [Gk. *philellēn* : *phil-*, philo- + *Hellēn*, Gk.] — **phil′hel•len′ic** (fĭl′hĕ-lĕn′ĭk) *adj.* — **phil•hel′len•ism** *n.*

Phil. I. *abbr.* Philippine Islands.

–philia *suff.* **1.** Tendency toward: *hemophilia.* **2.** Abnormal attraction to: *necrophilia.* [NLat. < Gk. *philia*, friendship < *philos*, loving.]

–philiac *suff.* **1.** One that has a tendency toward: *hemophiliac.* **2.** One that has an abnormal attraction to: *coprophiliac.* [–PHILIA + –AC.]

–philic *suff.* Var. of **–philous.**

Phil•ip (fĭl′ĭp). d. 1676. Wampanoag leader who waged King Philip's War (1675–76) against New England colonists who had encroached on Native American territory.

Philip, Prince. Duke of Edinburgh. b. 1921. Husband of Elizabeth II of Great Britain; given the title Prince in 1957.

Philip, Saint. fl. 1st cent. A.D. One of the 12 Apostles, who was present at the feeding of the 5,000.

Philip II[1]**.** 382–336 B.C. King of Macedon (359–336) whose army defeated a Greek coalition at Chaeronea (338).

Philip II[2] or **Philip Au•gus•tus** (ô-gŭs′təs). 1165–1223. King of France (1180–1223) whose reign was marked by an expansion of royal territories.

Philip II[3]**.** 1527–98. King of Spain (1556–98), of Naples and Sicily (1554–98), and of Portugal (1580–98) as Philip I. In 1588 he launched the Spanish Armada.

Philip IV. "Philip the Fair." 1268–1314. King of France (1285–1314) and of Navarre (1284–1305) as the husband of Joan I (1273–1305).

Philip V. 238–179 B.C. King of Macedon (221–179) who won the First Macedonian War with Rome (205) but was defeated in the Second Macedonian War (197).

Philip VI. 1293–1350. King of France (1328–50) whose reign was dominated by the Hundred Years' War.

Phi•lip•pi (fĭ-lĭp′ī). An ancient town of N-central Macedonia; site of Antony and Octavian's defeat of Brutus and Cassius in 42 B.C. — **Phi•lip′pi•an** (-lĭp′ē-ən) *adj. & n.*

Phi•lip•pi•ans (fĭ-lĭp′ē-ənz) *pl.n. (used with a sing. v.)* See table at **Bible.**

Phi•lip•pic (fĭ-lĭp′ĭk) *n.* **1.** Any of the orations of Demosthenes against Philip of Macedon in the fourth century B.C. **2.** Any of the orations of Cicero against Antony in 44 B.C. **3. philippic.** A harsh, often insulting verbal denunciation; a tirade.

Philippine mahogany *n.* **1.** Any of various southeast Asian hardwood trees of the genus *Shorea* and related genera. **2.** The wood of any of these trees.

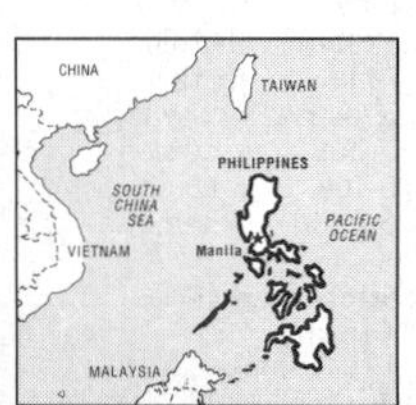

Philippines

Phil•ip•pines (fĭl′ə-pēnz′, fĭl′ə-pēnz′). A country of E Asia consisting of the **Philippine Islands,** an archipelago in the W Pacific Ocean SE of China; came under U.S. control in 1898 after the Spanish-American War and achieved independence in 1946. Cap. Manila. Pop. 48,098,460. — **Phil′ip•pine** *adj.*

Philippine Sea. A section of the W Pacific Ocean E of the Philippines and W of the Marianas.

Phil•ips (fĭl′ĭps), **Ambrose.** "Namby Pamby." 1674–1749. British poet known esp. for his collection *Pastorals* (1709).

Phi•lis•ti•a (fĭ-lĭs′tē-ə). An ancient region of SW Palestine; strategically important in biblical times.

Phil•is•tine (fĭl′ĭ-stēn′, fĭ-lĭs′tĭn, -tēn′) *n.* **1.** A member of an Aegean people who settled ancient Philistia around the 12th century B.C. **2.a.** A smug, ignorant, esp. middle-class person seen as indifferent or antagonistic to artistic and cultural values. **b.** One who lacks knowledge in a given area. — *adj.* **1.** Of ancient Philistia. **2.** Often **philistine.** Boorish; barbarous. [< ME *Philistines*, Philistines < LLat. *Philistīnī* < Gk. *Philistinoi* < Heb. *Pělištîm* < *Pěléšet*, Philistia.]

Phil•is•tin•ism also **phi•lis•tin•ism** (fĭl′ĭ-stē-nĭz′əm, fĭ-lĭs′tə-nĭz′əm, -tē-nĭz′əm) *n.* An attitude of smug ignorance and conventionalism, esp. toward artistic and cultural values.

Phil•lips (fĭl′ĭps). A trademark used for a screw with a head having two intersecting perpendicular slots and for a screwdriver with a tip shaped to fit into these slots.

Phillips, Wendell. 1811–84. Amer. abolitionist who was president of the American Antislavery Society (1865–70).

Phil•lips•burg (fĭl′ĭps-bûrg′). A town of NW NJ NW of Trenton; settled in the early 1700's. Pop. 15,757.

phil•lu•men•ist (fə-lo͞o′mə-nĭst) *n.* One who collects matchbooks or matchboxes. [PHIL(O)- + Lat. *lūmen*, light; see **leuk-*** + –IST.]

philo– or **phil–** *pref.* Having a strong affinity or preference for; loving: *philoprogenitive.* [Gk. < *philos*, beloved, loving.]

phil•o•den•dron (fĭl′ə-dĕn′drən) *n., pl.* **-drons** or **-dra** (-drə). Any of various climbing tropical American plants of the genus *Philodendron*, many of which are cultivated as houseplants. [< Gk., neut. of *philodendros*, fond of trees : *philo-*, philo- + *dendron*, tree; see **deru-*.**]

Phi•lo Ju•dae•us (fī′lō jo͞o-dē′əs, -dā′-). Philo of Alexandria. 30? B.C.–A.D. 45? Alexandrian Jewish philosopher who attempted to reconcile faith and philosophical reason.

phi•lol•o•gy (fĭ-lŏl′ə-jē) *n.* **1.** Literary study or classical scholarship. **2.** See **historical linguistics.** [ME *philologie* < Lat. *philologia*, love of learning < Gk. < *philologos*, fond of learning or of words : *philo-*, philo- + *logos*, reason, speech; see –LOGY.] — **phi•lol′o•ger, phi•lol′o•gist** *n.* — **phil′o•log′ic** (fĭl′ə-lŏj′ĭk), **phil′o•log′i•cal** (-ĭ-kəl) *adj.* — **phil′o•log′i•cal•ly** *adv.*

phil•o•mel (fĭl′ə-mĕl′) *n.* A nightingale. [Alteration of ME *phylomene* < Med.Lat. *philomēna* < Lat. *Philomēla*, Philomela. See PHILOMELA.]

Phil•o•me•la (fĭl′ə-mē′lə) *n. Gk. Myth.* A princess of Athens who, after being raped by her brother-in-law Tereus, was avenged by her sister Procne and was later turned into a swallow or nightingale. [Lat. *Philomēla* < Gk. *Philomēlē.*]

phil•o•pro•gen•i•tive (fĭl′ō-prō-jĕn′ĭ-tĭv) *adj.* **1.** Producing many offspring; prolific. **2.** Loving children or one's own children. **3.** Of or relating to love of children. — **phil′o•pro•gen′i•tive•ly** *adv.* — **phil′o•pro•gen′i•tive•ness** *n.*

philos. *abbr.* Philosopher; philosophical; philosophy.

phi•lo•sophe (fĭl′ə-sŏf′, fē′lô-zôf′) *n.* Any of the philosophical, political, and social writers of the 18th-century French Enlightenment. [Fr. < OFr., philosopher. See PHILOSOPHER.]

phi•los•o•pher (fĭ-lŏs′ə-fər) *n.* **1.** A student of or specialist in philosophy. **2.** One who lives and thinks according to a particular philosophy. **3.** One who is invariably calm and rational. [ME *philosophre* < OFr. *philosophe* < Lat. *philosophus* < Gk. *philosophos*, lover of wisdom, philosopher : *philo-*, philo- + *sophia*, knowledge, learning.]

phi•los•o•phers' stone also **phi•los•o•pher's stone** (fĭ-lŏs′ə-fərz) *n.* A substance that was believed to have the power of transmuting base metal into gold.

phil•o•soph•i•cal (fĭl′ə-sŏf′ĭ-kəl) also **phil•o•soph•ic** (-ĭk) *adj.* **1.** Of, relating to, or based on a system of philosophy. **2.** Characteristic of a philosopher, as in equanimity, enlightenment, and wisdom. — **phil′o•soph′i•cal•ly** *adv.*

phi•los•o•phize (fĭ-lŏs′ə-fīz′) *v.* **-phized, -phiz•ing, -phiz•es.** — *intr.* **1.** To speculate in a philosophical manner. **2.** To set forth or express a moralistic, often superficial philosophy. — *tr.* To consider (a matter) from a philosophical standpoint. — **phi•los′o•phiz′er** *n.*

phi•los•o•phy (fĭ-lŏs′ə-fē) *n., pl.* **-phies. 1.a.** Love and pursuit of wisdom. **b.** The investigation of causes and laws underlying reality. **c.** A system of philosophical inquiry or demonstration. **2.** Inquiry into the nature of things based on logical reasoning rather than empirical methods. **3.** The critique and analysis of fundamental beliefs as they come to be conceptualized and formulated. **4.** The synthesis of all learning. **5.** All the disciplines presented in university curriculums of science and the liberal arts, except medicine, law, and theology. **6.** The science comprising logic, ethics, aesthetics, metaphysics, and epistemology. **7.** A system of motivating concepts or principles. **8.** A basic theory; a viewpoint: *a philosophy of advertising.* **9.** The system of values by which one lives. [ME *philosophie* < OFr. < Lat. *philosophia* < Gk. < *philosophos*, lover of wisdom, philosopher. See PHILOSOPHER.]

–philous or **–philic** *suff.* Having a strong affinity or preference for; loving: *anemophilous.* [< NLat. *-philus* < Gk. *philos,* beloved, loving.]

phil•ter also **phil•tre** (fĭl′tər) —*n.* **1.** A love potion. **2.** A magic potion or charm. —*tr.v.* **-tered, -ter•ing, -ters** also **-tred, -tring, -tres.** To enchant with or as if with a philter. [Fr. *philtre* < OFr. < Lat. *philtrum* < Gk. *philtron* : *philein,* to love (< *philos,* beloved, loving) + *-tron,* instrumental suff.]

phi•mo•sis (fī-mō′sĭs, fĭ-) *n., pl.* **-ses** (-sēz). An abnormal constriction of the foreskin of the penis that prevents it from being drawn back to uncover the glans. [NLat. *phimōsis* < Gk. < *phimoun,* to muzzle < *phimos,* muzzle.]

phle•bi•tis (flĭ-bī′tĭs) *n.* Inflammation of a vein. —**phle•bit′ic** (-bĭt′ĭk) *adj.*

phlebo– or **phleb–** *pref.* Vein: *phlebology.* [Gk. < *phleps, phleb-,* blood vessel, vein.]

phle•bog•ra•phy (flĭ-bŏg′rə-fē) *n.* See **venography.** —**phle′bo•gram** (flē′bə-grăm′) *n.*

phle•bol•o•gy (flĭ-bŏl′ə-jē) *n.* The branch of medicine that deals with veins and their diseases.

phleb•o•scle•ro•sis (flĕb′ō-sklə-rō′sĭs) *n.* The thickening or hardening of the walls of veins.

phle•bot•o•mist (flə-bŏt′ə-mĭst) *n.* **1.** One who practices phlebotomy. **2.** One who draws blood for analysis or transfusion.

phle•bot•o•mus fever (flə-bŏt′ə-məs) *n.* See **sandfly fever.** [NLat. *Phlebotomus,* sand fly genus (< LLat. *phlebotomus,* lancet < Gk. *phlebotomos,* opening a vein; see PHLEBOTOMY).]

phle•bot•o•my (flĭ-bŏt′ə-mē) *n., pl.* **-mies.** The act or practice of opening a vein by incision or puncture to remove blood as a therapeutic treatment. [ME *flebotomie* < OFr. *flebothomie* < LLat. *phlebotomia* < Gk. < *phlebotomos,* opening a vein : *phlebo-,* phlebo- + *-tomos,* cutting; see -TOME.] —**phleb′o•tom′ic** (flĕb′ə-tŏm′ĭk), **phleb′o•tom′i•cal** (-ĭ-kəl) *adj.* —**phle•bot′o•mize′** *v.*

Phleg•e•thon (flĕg′ə-thŏn′) *n. Gk. Myth.* A river of fire, one of the five rivers of Hades. [ME *Flegeton* < Lat. *Phlegethōn* < Gk. < the pr.part. of *phlegethein,* to blaze, var. of *phlegein,* to burn. See **bhel-**[1]*.]

phlegm (flĕm) *n.* **1.** Thick, sticky, stringy mucus secreted by the mucous membrane of the respiratory tract, as during a cold. **2.** One of the four humors of ancient physiology, described as cold and moist and thought to cause sluggishness, apathy, and evenness of temper. **3.** Sluggishness of temperament. **4.** Calm self-possession; equanimity. [ME *fleume,* mucous discharge, the humor phlegm < OFr. < Med.Lat. *phlegma, flegma* < LLat. *phlegma,* the humor phlegm < Gk., heat, the humor phlegm < *phlegein,* to burn. See **bhel-**[1]*.] —**phlegm′y** *adj.*

phleg•mat•ic (flĕg-măt′ĭk) also **phleg•mat•i•cal** (-ĭ-kəl) *adj.* **1.** Of or relating to phlegm. **2.** Having or suggesting a calm sluggish temperament; unemotional. [ME *fleumatik* < OFr. *fleumatique* < LLat. *phlegmaticus,* full of phlegm < Gk. *phlegmatikos* < *phlegma, phlegmat-,* heat, the humor phlegm < *phlegein,* to burn. See **bhel-**[1]*.] —**phleg•mat′i•cal•ly** *adv.*

phlo•em (flō′ĕm′) *n.* The food-conducting tissue of vascular plants, consisting of sieve tubes, fibers, parenchyma, and sclereids. [Ger. < Gk. *phloios,* bark. See **bhleu-***.]

phlo•gis•tic (flō-jĭs′tĭk) *adj.* **1.** Of or relating to phlogiston. **2.** *Medic.* Of, relating to, or inducing inflammation or fever.

phlo•gis•ton (flō-jĭs′tŏn′, -tən) *n.* A hypothetical substance formerly thought to be a volatile constituent of all combustible substances, released as flame in combustion. [< Gk., neut. of *phlogistos,* inflammable < *phlogizein,* to set on fire < *phlox, phlog-,* flame. See **bhel-**[1]*.]

phlog•o•pite (flŏg′ə-pīt′) *n.* A yellow to dark brown mica, $K(Mg,Fe)_3AlSi_3O_{10}(OH)_2$, used in insulation. [Gk. *phlogōpos,* fiery-looking (*phlox, phlog-,* flame; see **bhel-**[1]* + *ōps,* eye, face; see **ok**ʷ**-***) + -ITE[1].]

phlox (flŏks) *n., pl.* **phlox** or **phlox•es.** Any of various North American plants of the genus *Phlox,* having opposite leaves and a salverform corolla. [Lat., a kind of flame-colored flower < Gk., flame, wallflower. See **bhel-**[1]*.]

phlyc•te•na also **phlyc•tae•na** (flĭk-tē′nə) *n., pl.* **-nae** (-nē). A small blister or vesicle, esp. from a mild burn. [NLat. < Gk. *phluktaina,* blister < *phluzein,* to boil over. See **bhleu-***.]

Phm *abbr. Bible.* Philemon.

Phnom Penh (pə-nôm′ pĕn′, nŏm′). The cap. of Cambodia, in the SW part on the Mekong R.; founded in the 14th cent. and the cap. of Cambodia after 1867. Pop. 400,000.

–phobe *suff.* One that fears or is averse to a specified thing: *ailurophobe.* [Fr. < Lat. *-phobus* < Gk. *-phobos,* fearing < *phobos,* fear. See **bheg**ʷ**-***.]

pho•bi•a (fō′bē-ə) *n.* **1.** A persistent, abnormal, or irrational fear of a specific thing or situation that compels one to avoid the feared stimulus. **2.** A strong fear, dislike, or aversion. [< LLat. *-phobia,* -phobia.]

–phobia *suff.* An intense, abnormal, or illogical fear of a specified thing: *xenophobia.* [LLat. < Gk. < *phobos,* fear. See **bheg**ʷ**-***.]

pho•bic (fō′bĭk) *adj.* Of, relating to, arising from, or having a phobia. —*n.* One who has a phobia.

–phobic or **–phobous** *suff.* **1.** Having a fear of or an aversion for: *xenophobic.* **2.** Lacking an affinity for: *lyophobic.* [LLat. *-phobicus* < Gk. *-phobikos* < *-phobia,* -phobia.]

Pho•bos (fō′bəs) *n.* One of the two satellites of Mars. [Gk., fear, deity of fear < *phobos,* fear. See -PHOBE.]

Pho•cae•a (fō-sē′ə). An ancient Ionian Greek city of W Asia Minor on the Aegean Sea in present-day Turkey; an important maritime state c. 1000 to 600 B.C.

pho•cine (fō′sīn) *adj. Zool.* Of, relating to, or resembling seals. [< Lat. *phōca,* seal < Gk. *phōkē.*]

Pho•cis (fō′sĭs). A region of ancient Greece N of the Gulf of Corinth; controlled the oracle at Delphi before 590 B.C.

phoe•be (fē′bē) *n.* Any of several medium-sized birds of the genus *Sayornis* of North America, noted for the flicking motion of the tail. [Imit. of its song.]

Phoe•be (fē′bē) *n.* **1.** *Gk. Myth.* Artemis. **2.** The moon. **3.** A satellite of Saturn. [ME *phebe* < Lat. *Phoebē* < Gk. *Phoibē* < fem. of *phoibos,* shining.]

Phoe•bus (fē′bəs) *n.* **1.** *Gk. Myth.* Apollo. **2.** The sun. [ME *phebus* < Lat. *Phoebus* < Gk. *phoibos,* shining, Apollo.]

Phoe•ni•cia (fĭ-nĭsh′ə, -nē′shə). An ancient country of city-states of SW Asia along the E Mediterranean Sea in present-day Syria and Lebanon. Its people became the foremost navigators and traders of the Mediterranean by 1250 B.C.

Phoe•ni•cian (fĭ-nĭsh′ən, -nē′shən) *adj.* Of or relating to ancient Phoenicia or its people, language, or culture. —*n.* **1.** A native or inhabitant of ancient Phoenicia. **2.** The Semitic language of ancient Phoenicia. [ME *Phenicien* < Lat. *Phoenīcia,* fem. of *Phoenīcius* < *Phoenīcē,* Phoenicia.]

phoe•nix also **phe•nix** (fē′nĭks) *n.* **1.** *Myth.* A bird in Egyptian mythology that lived in the desert for 500 years and then consumed itself by fire, later to rise renewed from its ashes. **2.** A person or thing of unsurpassed excellence or beauty; a paragon. **3. Phoenix.** A constellation in the Southern Hemisphere near Tucana and Sculptor. [ME *fenix* < OE and < OFr., both < Med.Lat. *fēnix* < Lat. *phoenix* < Gk. *phoinix.*]

Phoenix. The cap. of AZ, in the S-central part NW of Tucson; settled c. 1868 and territorial cap. from 1889 to 1912. Pop. 983,403.

Phoenix Islands. A group of eight small islands of Kiribati in the central Pacific N of Samoa.

phon (fŏn) *n.* A unit of apparent loudness, equal in number to the intensity in decibels of a 1,000-hertz tone judged to be as loud as the sound being measured. [Ger. < Gk. *phōnē,* sound. See PHONE[1].]

phon. *abbr.* **1.** Phonetic; phonetics. **2.** Phonology.

pho•nate (fō′nāt′) *intr.v.* **-nat•ed, -nat•ing, -nates.** To utter speech sounds; vocalize. —**pho•na′tion** *n.*

phone[1] (fōn) *Informal.* —*n.* **1.** A telephone. **2.** An earphone. —*v.* **phoned, phon•ing, phones.** —*intr.* To telephone. —*tr.* **1.** To get in touch with by telephone. **2.** To impart (news, for example) by telephone. [Short for TELEPHONE.]

phone[2] (fōn) *n. Ling.* A speech sound considered without reference to its status as a phoneme or an allophone in a language. [Gk. *phōnē,* sound, voice. See **bhā-**[2]*.]

–phone *suff.* **1.** Sound: *homophone.* **2.** Device that receives or emits sound: *geophone.* **3.** Speaker of a language: *Anglophone.* [< Gk. *phōnē,* sound, voice. See **bhā-**[2]*.]

phone book *n. Informal.* A telephone book.

phone booth *n. Informal.* A telephone booth.

pho•ne•mat•ic (fō′nĭ-măt′ĭk) *adj. Ling.* Phonemic.

pho•neme (fō′nēm′) *n. Ling.* The smallest phonetic unit in a language capable of conveying a distinction in meaning, as the *m* of *mat* and the *b* of *bat.* [Fr. *phonème* < Gk. *phōnēma, phōnēmat-,* utterance, sound produced < *phōnein,* to produce a sound < *phōnē,* sound, voice. See **bhā-**[2]*.]

pho•ne•mic (fə-nē′mĭk, fō-) *adj. Ling.* **1.** Of or relating to phonemes. **2.** Of or relating to phonemics. **3.** Serving to distinguish phonemes or distinctive features. —**pho•ne′mi•cal•ly** *adv.*

pho•ne•mics (fə-nē′mĭks, fō-) *n.* (*used with a sing. v.*) *Ling.* The study and establishment of the phonemes of a language. —**pho•ne′mi•cist** (-mĭ-sĭst) *n.*

pho•net•ic (fə-nĕt′ĭk) *adj. Ling.* **1.** Of or relating to phonetics. **2.** Representing the sounds of speech with a set of distinct symbols for every sound: *phonetic spelling.* **3.** Of, relating to, or being features of pronunciation that are not phonemically distinctive in a language, as aspiration of consonants in English. [NLat. *phōnēticus,* representing speech sounds < Gk. *phōnētikos,* vocal < *phōnētos,* to be spoken < *phōnein,* to produce a sound < *phōnē,* sound, voice. See **bhā-**[2]*.] —**pho•net′i•cal** *adj.* —**pho•net′i•cal•ly** *adv.*

phonetic alphabet *n.* **1.** *Ling.* A standardized set of symbols used in phonetic transcription. **2.** Any of various systems of code words for identifying letters in voice communication.

pho•ne•ti•cian (fō′nĭ-tĭsh′ən) also **pho•net•i•cist** (fə-nĕt′ĭ-sĭst) *n. Ling.* An expert in phonetics.

pho•net•ics (fə-nĕt′ĭks) *n.* (*used with a sing. v.*) *Ling.* **1.** The branch of linguistics dealing with speech sounds and their production, combination, description, and representation by written symbols. **2.** The system of sounds of a given language.

pho•ney (fō′nē) *adj. & n.* Var. of **phony.**

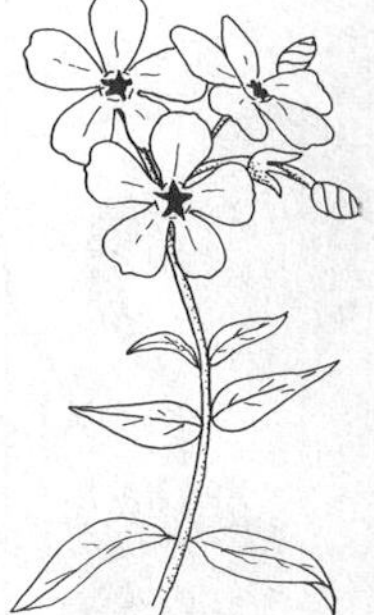
phlox
Blue phlox
Phlox divaricata

phoenix
On its funeral pyre

ă pat	oi boy
ā pay	ou out
âr care	ŏŏ took
ä father	ōō boot
ĕ pet	ŭ cut
ē be	ûr urge
ĭ pit	th thin
ī pie	*th* this
îr pier	hw which
ŏ pot	zh vision
ō toe	ə about, item
ô paw	

Stress marks:
′ (primary);
′ (secondary), as in
dictionary (dĭk′shə-nĕr′ē)

phon•ic (fŏn′ĭk) *adj. Ling.* Of, relating to, or having the nature of sound, esp. speech sounds. —**phon′i•cal•ly** *adv.*

phon•ics (fŏn′ĭks) *n.* *(used with a sing. v.)* **1.** A method of teaching elementary reading and spelling based on the phonetic interpretation of ordinary spelling. **2.** Phonetics.

pho•no (fō′nō) *n., pl.* **-nos.** *Informal.* A phonograph.

phono– or **phon–** *pref.* Sound; voice; speech: *phonology.* [Gk. *phōno-* < *phōnē*, sound, voice. See **bhā-**[2]*.]

pho•no•car•di•o•gram (fō′nə-kär′dē-ə-grăm′) *n.* A graphic record of heart sounds and murmurs that is produced by a phonocardiograph.

pho•no•car•di•o•graph (fō′nə-kär′dē-ə-grăf′) *n.* An instrument consisting of microphones and recording equipment used to make phonocardiograms. —**pho′no•car′di•o•graph′ic** *adj.* —**pho′no•car′di•og′ra•phy** (-ŏg′rə-fē) *n.*

pho•no•gram (fō′nə-grăm′) *n. Ling.* A character or symbol, as in a phonetic alphabet, representing a word or phoneme in speech. —**pho′no•gram′ic, pho′no•gram′mic** *adj.*

phonograph
c. 1910 Edison phonograph

pho•no•graph (fō′nə-grăf′) *n.* A machine that reproduces sound by a stylus in contact with a grooved rotating disk. —**pho′no•graph′ic** *adj.* —**pho′no•graph′i•cal•ly** *adv.*

pho•nog•ra•phy (fə-nŏg′rə-fē, fō-) *n.* **1.** *Ling.* The science or practice of transcribing speech by means of symbols representing elements of sound; phonetic transcription. **2.** A system of shorthand based on phonetic transcription. —**pho•nog′ra•pher, pho•nog′ra•phist** *n.*

pho•no•lite (fō′nə-līt′) *n.* A light-colored volcanic rock composed largely of feldspars. —**pho′no•lit′ic** (-lĭt′ĭk) *adj.*

pho•nol•o•gy (fə-nŏl′ə-jē, fō-) *n., pl.* **-gies.** *Ling.* **1.** The study of speech sounds in language or a language with reference to their distribution and patterning and to pronunciation rules. **2.** The sound system of a language: *the phonology of English.* —**pho•no•log′ic** (fō′nə-lŏj′ĭk), **pho′no•log′i•cal** (-ĭ-kəl) *adj.* —**pho′no•log′i•cal•ly** *adv.* —**pho•nol′o•gist** *n.*

pho•non (fō′nŏn′) *n. Phys.* The quantum of acoustic or vibrational energy, considered a discrete particle and used esp. in mathematical models to calculate thermal and vibrational properties of solids.

pho•no•re•cep•tion (fō′nō-rĭ-sĕp′shən) *n.* Perception of or response to sound waves. —**pho′no•re•cep′tor** (-tər) *n.*

pho•no•scope (fō′nə-skōp′) *n.* A device that produces a visible display of the mechanical properties of a sounding body.

pho•no•type (fō′nə-tīp′) *n.* **1.** A phonetic symbol used in printing. **2.** Text printed in phonetic symbols. —**pho′no•typ′ic** (fō′nə-tĭp′ĭk), **pho′no•typ′i•cal** (-ĭ-kəl) *adj.*

pho•no•typ•y (fō′nə-tī′pē) *n. Ling.* The practice of transcribing speech sounds by means of phonetic symbols. —**pho′no•typ′ist** *n.*

pho•ny also **pho•ney** (fō′nē) —*adj.* **-ni•er, -ni•est. 1.a.** Not genuine or real; counterfeit. **b.** False; spurious. **2.** Not honest or truthful; deceptive. **3.a.** Insincere or hypocritical. **b.** Giving a false impression of truth or authenticity; specious. —*n., pl.* **-nies** also **-neys. 1.** Something not genuine; a fake. **2.a.** One who is insincere or pretentious. **b.** An impostor; a hypocrite. [Alteration of *fawney*, swindler's ring < Ir.Gael. *fáinne*, ring < OIr.] —**pho′ni•ly** *adv.* —**pho′ni•ness** *n.*

–phony *suff.* Sound: *telephony.* [Gk. *-phōnia* < *phōnē*, sound, voice. See **bhā-**[2]*.]

phoo•ey (fo͞o′ē) *interj.* Used to express disgust, disbelief, or contempt.

pho•rate (fôr′āt′, fōr′-) *n.* A toxic liquid, $C_7H_{17}O_2PS_3$, used as an insecticide esp. in soil treatment. [< chemical name *(phos)phor(odithio)ate* : PHOSPHORUS + *dithioate* (DI–[1] + THIO– + –ATE[2]).]

–phore *suff.* Bearer; carrier: *chromatophore.* [< Gk. *-phoros*, bearing < *pherein*, to carry. See **bher-**[1]*.]

–phoresis *suff.* Transmission: *electrophoresis.* [< Gk. *phorēsis*, a carrying < *phorein*, freq. of *pherein*, to bear. See **bher-**[1]*.]

phor•e•sy (fôr′ĭ-sē) *n.* A symbiotic relationship, esp. among arthropods and some fishes, in which one organism transports another organism of a different species. [NLat. *phorēsia* < Gk. *phorēsis*, a carrying. See –PHORESIS.]

–phorous *suff.* Bearing: *gonophorous.* [< Gk. *-phoros* < *pherein*, to carry. See **bher-**[1]*.]

phos– *pref.* Light: *phosgene.* [< Gk. *phōs*, light. See **bhā-**[1]*.]

phos•gene (fŏs′jēn′, fŏz′-) *n.* A volatile liquid or gas, $COCl_2$, used as a poison gas in World War I and in making plastics.

phosph– *pref.* Var. of **phospho–.**

phos•pham•i•don (fŏs-făm′ĭ-dŏn′) *n.* An insecticide, $C_{10}H_{19}ClNO_5P$, used to control mites and other plant pests. [PHOSPH(ATE) + AMID(E) + –ON[3].]

phos•pha•tase (fŏs′fə-tās′, -tāz′) *n.* Any of numerous enzymes that catalyze the hydrolysis of esters of phosphoric acid. [PHOSPHAT(E) + –ASE.]

phos•phate (fŏs′fāt′) *n.* **1.** A salt or an ester of phosphoric acid. **2.** A fertilizer containing phosphorus compounds. **3.** *Chicago.* A soda fountain drink made from carbonated water and flavored syrup. —**phos•phat′ic** (fŏs-făt′ĭk) *adj.*

phosphate rock *n.* Any of various rocks composed largely of phosphate minerals, esp. apatite, used as fertilizer and as a source of phosphorous compounds.

phos•pha•tide (fŏs′fə-tīd′) *n.* See **phospholipid.**

phos•pha•tize (fŏs′fə-tīz′) *tr.v.* **-tized, -tiz•ing, -tiz•es. 1.** To change into phosphates or a phosphate. **2.** To treat with phosphate or phosphoric acid. —**phos′pha•ti•za′tion** (-tĭ-zā′shən) *n.*

phos•pha•tu•ri•a (fŏs′fə-to͝or′ē-ə, -tyo͝or′-) *n.* An excess of phosphates in the urine.

phos•phene (fŏs′fēn′) *n.* A sensation of light caused by excitation of the retina by mechanical or electrical means rather than by light, as when the eyeballs are pressed through closed lids. [Fr. *phosphène* : Gk. *phōs*, light; see PHOS– + Gk. *phainein*, to cause to appear, to show; see **bhā-**[1]*.]

phos•phide (fŏs′fīd′) also **phos•phid** (-fĭd) *n.* A compound of phosphorus and a more electropositive element or radical.

phos•phine (fŏs′fēn′) also **phos•phin** (-fĭn) *n.* **1.** A spontaneously flammable poisonous gas, PH_3, used as a doping agent for solid-state components. **2.** Any of several analogues of an amine with phosphorus in place of nitrogen.

phos•phite (fŏs′fīt′) *n.* A salt or an ester of phosphorous acid.

phospho– or **phosph–** *pref.* **1.** Phosphorus: *phosphine.* **2.** Phosphate: *phospholipid.* [< PHOSPHORUS.]

phos•pho•cre•a•tine (fŏs′fō-krē′ə-tēn′) also **phos•pho•cre•a•tin** (-tĭn) *n.* An organic compound, $C_4H_{10}N_3O_5P$, found in muscle tissue and capable of storing and providing energy for muscular contraction.

phos•pho•lip•id (fŏs′fō-lĭp′ĭd) *n.* A phosphorous-containing lipid composed mainly of fatty acids, a phosphate group, and a simple organic molecule.

phos•pho•ni•um (fŏs-fō′nē-əm) *n.* A univalent radical, PH_4, derived from phosphine. [PHOSPH(O)– – (AMM)ONIUM.]

phos•pho•pro•tein (fŏs′fō-prō′tēn′, -tē-ĭn) *n.* Any of a group of proteins with chemically bound phosphoric acid.

phos•phor (fŏs′fər, -fôr′) *n.* **1.** A substance that exhibits phosphorescence. **2.** The phosphorescent coating on the inside of the screen of a cathode-ray tube. [Lat. *Phōsphorus*, the morning star. See PHOSPHORUS.]

phosphor bronze *n.* A hard corrosion-resistant bronze containing tin and some phosphorus, used in machine parts.

phos•pho•resce (fŏs′fə-rĕs′) *intr.v.* **-resced, -resc•ing, -resc•es.** To persist in emitting light, unaccompanied by sensible heat or combustion, after exposure to and removal of a source of radiation. [Prob. back-formation < PHOSPHORESCENT.]

phos•pho•res•cence (fŏs′fə-rĕs′əns) *n.* **1.** Persistent emission of light following exposure to and removal of incident radiation. **2.** Emission of light with no burning or very slow burning without appreciable heat. —**phos′pho•res′cent** *adj.* —**phos′pho•res′cent•ly** *adv.*

phos•phor•ic (fŏs-fôr′ĭk, -fŏr′-) *adj.* Of, relating to, or containing phosphorus, esp. with valence 5 or a valence higher than that of a comparable phosphorous compound.

phosphoric acid *n.* A clear colorless liquid, H_3PO_4, used in fertilizers, detergents, food flavoring, and pharmaceuticals.

phos•pho•rism (fŏs′fə-rĭz′əm) *n.* Chronic phosphorus poisoning.

phos•pho•rite (fŏs′fə-rīt′) *n.* A sedimentary rock consisting predominantly of apatite and other phosphates.

phos•pho•rous (fŏs′fər-əs, fŏs-fôr′əs, -fōr′-) *adj.* Of, relating to, or containing phosphorus, esp. with valence 3 or a valence lower than that of a comparable phosphoric compound.

phosphorous acid *n.* A hygroscopic crystalline solid, H_3PO_3, used as a reducing agent and to produce phosphite salts.

phos•pho•rus (fŏs′fər-əs) *n.* **1.** *Symbol* **P** A highly reactive poisonous nonmetallic element occurring naturally in phosphates, esp. apatite, and existing in three allotropic forms, white, red, and black. An essential constituent of protoplasm, it is used in safety matches, pyrotechnics, incendiary shells, and fertilizers. Atomic number 15; atomic weight 30.9738; melting point (white) 44.1°C; boiling point 280°C; specific gravity (white) 1.82; valence 3, 5. See table at **element. 2.** A phosphorescent substance. [Lat. *Phōsphorus*, morning star < Gk. : *phōs*, light; see **bhā-**[1]* + *-phoros*, -phorous.]

phos•pho•ryl•ase (fŏs′fər-ə-lās′, -lāz′) *n.* An enzyme that catalyzes the production of glucose phosphate from glycogen and inorganic phosphate.

phos•pho•ryl•ate (fŏs′fər-ə-lāt′) *tr.v.* **-at•ed, -at•ing, -ates.** To add a phosphate group to (an organic molecule). —**phos′pho•ryl•a′tion** *n.* —**phos′pho•ryl•a′tive** *adj.*

phot (fŏt) *n. Phys.* A unit of illumination equal to one lumen per square centimeter. [Gk. *phōs*, *phōt-*, light. See **bhā-**[1]*.]

pho•tic (fō′tĭk) *adj.* **1.** Of or relating to light. **2.** Penetrated by or receiving light. **3.** Being or relating to the layer of a body of water that receives sufficient sunlight for photosynthesis.

pho•to (fō′tō) *Informal.* —*n., pl.* **-tos.** A photograph. —*tr. & intr.v.* **-toed, -to•ing, -tos.** To photograph or take photographs.

photo– or **phot–** *pref.* **1.** Light; radiant energy: *photosynthesis.* **2.** Photographic: *photomontage.* **3.** Photoelectric: *photoemission.* [Gk. *phōto-* < *phōs*, *phōt-*. See **bhā-**[1]*.]

pho•to•ac•tive (fō′tō-ăk′tĭv) *adj.* **1.** Capable of responding to light photoelectrically. **2.** Capable of responding to sunlight or ultraviolet radiation by chemical reaction.

pho•to•au•to•troph (fō′tō-ô′tə-trŏf′, -trōf′) *n.* An organism, such as a green plant, that can synthesize its own food from inorganic substances using light as an energy source. —**pho′to·au′to·troph′ic** *adj.*

pho·to·bi·ol·o·gy (fō′tō-bī-ŏl′ə-jē) *n.* The study of the effects of light on living organisms. —**pho′to·bi′o·log′ic** (-bī′ə-lŏj′ĭk), **pho′to·bi′o·log′i·cal** (-ĭ-kəl) *adj.*

pho·to·bi·ot·ic (fō′tō-bī-ŏt′ĭk) *adj. Biol.* Depending on light for life and growth.

pho·to·cell (fō′tō-sĕl′) *n.* A photoelectric cell.

photochemical smog *n.* Air pollution produced by the action of sunlight on hydrocarbons and other pollutants.

pho·to·chem·is·try (fō′tō-kĕm′ĭ-strē) *n.* The chemistry of the effects of light on chemical systems. —**pho′to·chem′i·cal** (-ĭ-kəl) *adj.* —**pho′to·chem′i·cal·ly** *adv.*

pho·to·co·ag·u·la·tion (fō′tō-kō-ăg′yə-lā′shən) *n.* Surgical coagulation of tissue by means of intense light energy, such as a laser beam, so as to destroy abnormal tissues or form adhesive scars, esp. in ophthalmology. —**pho′to·co·ag′u·late** *v.*

pho·to·com·pose (fō′tō-kəm-pōz′) *tr.v.* **-posed, -pos·ing, -pos·es.** *Print.* To prepare (written matter) for printing by photocomposition. —**pho′to·com·pos′er** *n.*

pho·to·com·po·si·tion (fō′tō-kŏm′pə-zĭsh′ən) *n. Print.* The preparation of manuscript for printing by the projection of type characters on photographic film, from which printing plates are made.

pho·to·con·duc·tiv·i·ty (fō′tō-kŏn′dŭk-tĭv′ĭ-tē) *n., pl.* **-ties.** Electrical conductivity enhanced by exposure to light. —**pho′to·con·duc′tion** *n.* —**pho′to·con·duc′tive** *adj.*

pho·to·cop·i·er (fō′tə-kŏp′ē-ər) *n.* A machine used for photocopying.

pho·to·cop·y (fō′tə-kŏp′ē) *tr.v.* **-cop·ied, -cop·y·ing, -cop·ies.** To make a photographic reproduction of (written, printed, or graphic material), esp. by xerography. —*n., pl.* **-cop·ies.** A photographic or xerographic reproduction.

pho·to·cur·rent (fō′tō-kûr′ənt, -kŭr′-) *n.* An electric current produced by illumination of a photoelectric material.

pho·to·de·com·po·si·tion (fō′tō-dē-kŏm′pə-zĭsh′ən) *n.* Chemical breakdown caused by radiant energy.

pho·to·de·grad·a·ble (fō′tō-dĭ-grā′də-bəl) *adj.* Capable of being chemically broken down by light.

pho·to·dis·in·te·gra·tion (fō′tō-dĭs-ĭn′tĭ-grā′shən) *n.* Nuclear disintegration or transformation caused by absorption of high-energy radiation, as of gamma rays.

pho·to·dra·ma (fō′tə-drä′mə, -drăm′ə) *n.* See **photoplay.**

pho·to·dy·nam·ic (fō′tō-dī-năm′ĭk) *adj.* **1.** Of or relating to the energy of light. **2.** Enhancing the effects of or inducing a toxic reaction to light, esp. to ultraviolet light.

pho·to·dy·nam·ics (fō′tō-dī-năm′ĭks) *n.* *(used with a sing. v.)* The science that deals with the activating effects of light on living organisms.

pho·to·e·lec·tric (fō′tō-ĭ-lĕk′trĭk) also **pho·to·e·lec·tri·cal** (-trĭ-kəl) *adj.* Of or relating to the electric effects of light, esp. the ejection of electrons from a substance by incident electromagnetic radiation. —**pho′to·e·lec′tri·cal·ly** *adv.*

photoelectric cell *n.* An electronic device having an electrical output that varies in response to incident radiation, esp. to visible light.

pho·to·e·lec·tron (fō′tō-ĭ-lĕk′trŏn′) *n.* An electron released or ejected from a substance by photoelectric effect.

pho·to·e·mis·sion (fō′tō-ĭ-mĭsh′ən) *n.* Emission of photoelectrons, esp. from metallic surfaces.

pho·to·en·grave (fō′tō-ĕn-grāv′) *tr.v.* **-graved, -grav·ing, -graves.** To reproduce by photoengraving; make a photoengraving of. —**pho′to·en·grav′er** *n.*

pho·to·en·grav·ing (fō′tō-ĕn-grā′vĭng) *n.* **1.** The process of reproducing graphic material by transferring the image photographically to a plate or another surface, which is then etched for printing. **2.** A plate prepared by this process. **3.** A reproduction made by this process.

pho·to-es·say also **pho·to es·say** (fō′tō-ĕs′ā′) *n.* A story told chiefly through photographs usu. supplemented by a written commentary. —**pho′to-es′say·ist** *n.*

photo finish *n.* **1.** *Sports.* A race in which the leading contestants finish so close together that the winner must be determined by a photograph. **2.** *Informal.* An extremely close competition.

pho·to·fin·ish·ing (fō′tō-fĭn′ĭ-shĭng) *n.* The act or business of developing camera films and printing photographs for customers. —**pho′to·fin′ish·er** *n.*

pho·to·flash (fō′tō-flăsh′) *n.* See **flashbulb.**

pho·to·flood (fō′tō-flŭd′) *n.* An electric lamp that produces a bright light for photographic illumination.

pho·to·fluor·o·gram (fō′tə-flo͝or′ə-grăm′, -flôr′-, -flōr′-) *n.* A photograph made by photofluorography.

pho·to·fluor·og·ra·phy (fō′tō-flo͝o-rŏg′rə-fē, -flô-, -flō-) *n.* The photographic record of x-ray images from a fluoroscope.

pho·tog (fə-tŏg′) *n. Informal.* A photographer.

photog. *abbr.* Photograph; photographic; photography.

pho·to·gel·a·tin process (fō′tō-jĕl′ə-tĭn) *n.* See **collotype** 1.

pho·to·gene (fō′tə-jēn′) *n.* See **afterimage.**

pho·to·gen·ic (fō′tə-jĕn′ĭk) *adj.* **1.** Attractive as a subject for photography. **2.** *Biol.* Producing or emitting light; phosphorescent. **3.** Caused or produced by light. —**pho′to·gen′i·cal·ly** *adv.*

pho·to·gram (fō′tə-grăm′) *n.* An image made by placing an object on photosensitive paper and exposing it to light.

pho·to·gram·me·try (fō′tə-grăm′ĭ-trē) *n.* **1.** The process of making maps or scale drawings from photographs, esp. aerial photographs. **2.** The process of making precise measurements by means of photography. —**pho′to·gram·met′ric** (-grə-mĕt′rĭk) *adj.* —**pho′to·gram′me·trist** *n.*

pho·to·graph (fō′tə-grăf′) *n.* An image, esp. a positive print, recorded by a camera and reproduced on a photosensitive surface. —*v.* **-graphed, -graph·ing, -graphs.** —*tr.* To take a photograph of. —*intr.* **1.** To practice photography. **2.** To be the subject for photographs: *She photographs well.* —**pho′to·graph′a·ble** *adj.* —**pho·tog′ra·pher** (fə-tŏg′rə-fər) *n.*

pho·to·graph·ic (fō′tə-grăf′ĭk) also **pho·to·graph·i·cal** (-ĭ-kəl) *adj.* **1.** Of, relating to, or consisting of photography or a photograph. **2.** Used in photography. **3.** Resembling a photograph, esp. representing or simulating something with great accuracy and fidelity of detail. **4.** Capable of retaining accurate visual impressions. —**pho′to·graph′i·cal·ly** *adv.*

pho·tog·ra·phy (fə-tŏg′rə-fē) *n.* **1.** The art or process of producing photographs. **2.** The art, practice, or occupation of taking and printing photographs. **3.** A body of photographs.

pho·to·gra·vure (fō′tə-grə-vyo͝or′) *n.* The process of printing from an intaglio plate, etched according to a photographic image.

pho·to·he·li·o·graph (fō′tō-hē′lē-ə-grăf′) *n.* A telescope equipped to photograph the sun.

pho·to·jour·nal·ism (fō′tō-jûr′nə-lĭz′əm) *n.* Journalism in which photographs supplemented by texts present a story.

pho·to·ki·ne·sis (fō′tō-kĭ-nē′sĭs, -kī-) *n.* Movement as a response to light. —**pho′to·ki·net′ic** (-nĕt′ĭk) *adj.*

pho·to·lith·o·graph (fō′tō-lĭth′ə-grăf′) *n.* A picture made by photolithography. —*tr.v.* **-graphed, -graph·ing, -graphs.** To reproduce by means of photolithography; make a photolithograph of. —**pho′to·li·thog′ra·pher** (-lĭ-thŏg′rə-fər) *n.*

pho·to·li·thog·ra·phy (fō′tō-lĭ-thŏg′rə-fē) *n.* A planographic printing process using plates made according to a photographic image. —**pho′to·lith′o·graph′ic** (-lĭth′ə-grăf′ĭk) *adj.* —**pho′to·lith′o·graph′i·cal·ly** *adv.*

pho·tol·y·sis (fō-tŏl′ĭ-sĭs) *n.* Chemical decomposition induced by light or other radiant energy. —**pho′to·lyt′ic** (fō′tə-lĭt′ĭk) *adj.* —**pho′to·lyt′i·cal·ly** *adv.*

pho·to·map (fō′tə-măp′) *n.* A map made by superimposing orienting data and markings on an aerial photograph. —**pho′to·map′** *v.*

pho·to·me·chan·i·cal (fō′tō-mĭ-kăn′ĭ-kəl) *adj.* Of, relating to, or involving any of various methods by which plates are prepared for printing by means of photography. —**pho′to·me·chan′i·cal·ly** *adv.*

pho·tom·e·ter (fō-tŏm′ĭ-tər) *n.* An instrument for measuring a property of light, esp. luminous intensity or flux.

pho·tom·e·try (fō-tŏm′ĭ-trē) *n. Phys.* Measurement of the properties of light, esp. luminous intensity. —**pho′to·met′ric** (fō′tə-mĕt′rĭk), **pho′to·met′ri·cal** (-rĭ-kəl) *adj.* —**pho′to·met′ri·cal·ly** *adv.* —**pho·tom′e·trist** *n.*

pho·to·mi·cro·graph (fō′tō-mī′krə-grăf′) *n.* A photograph made through a microscope. —*tr.v.* **-graphed, -graph·ing, -graphs.** To photograph (an object) through a microscope. —**pho′to·mi·crog′ra·pher** (-mī-krŏg′rə-fər) *n.* —**pho′to·mi′cro·graph′ic** *adj.* —**pho′to·mi·crog′ra·phy** *n.*

pho·to·mon·tage (fō′tō-mŏn-täzh′, -môn-) *n.* **1.** The technique of combining photographs in a montage. **2.** The picture produced by this technique.

pho·ton (fō′tŏn′) *n.* **1.** The quantum of electromagnetic energy, generally regarded as a discrete particle having zero mass, no electric charge, and an indefinitely long lifetime. See table at **subatomic particle. 2.** A unit of retinal illumination, equal to the amount of light that reaches the retina through 1 square millimeter of pupil area from a surface having a brightness of 1 candela per square meter. —**pho·ton′ic** *adj.*

pho·to·neg·a·tive (fō′tō-nĕg′ə-tĭv) *adj. Biol.* Exhibiting a negative phototactic or phototropic response.

pho·to·nu·cle·ar (fō′tō-no͞o′klē-ər, -nyo͞o′-) *adj.* Of or relating to a nuclear reaction induced by photons.

pho·to-off·set (fō′tō-ôf′sĕt′, -ŏf′-) *n.* A method of offset printing using photomechanical plates.

photo opportunity *n.* A brief period reserved for the press to photograph the participants in a newsworthy event.

pho·to·pe·ri·od (fō′tō-pĭr′ē-əd) *n.* The duration of an organism's daily exposure to light, considered esp. with regard to its effect on growth and development. —**pho′to·pe′ri·od′ic** (-ŏd′ĭk), **pho′to·pe′ri·od′i·cal** (-ĭ-kəl) *adj.*

pho·to·pe·ri·od·ism (fō′tō-pîr′ē-ə-dĭz′əm) also **pho·to·pe·ri·o·dic·i·ty** (-dĭs′ĭ-tē) *n., pl.* **-isms** also **-i·ties.** The response of an organism to changes in its photoperiod, esp. as indicated by vital processes.

pho·to·phil·ic (fō′tə-fĭl′ĭk) also **pho·toph·i·lous** (fō-tŏf′ə-ləs) *adj. Biol.* Growing or functioning best in strong light.

pho·to·pho·bi·a (fō′tə-fō′bē-ə) *n.* **1.** An abnormal sensitivity to or intolerance of light, esp. by the eyes, as may be

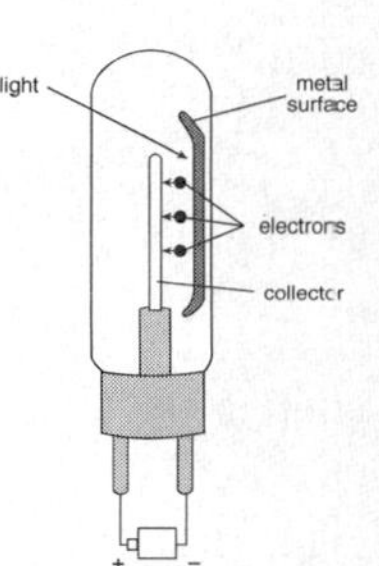

photoelectric cell

ă pat	oi boy
ā pay	ou out
âr care	o͝o took
ä father	o͞o boot
ĕ pet	ŭ cut
ē be	ûr urge
ĭ pit	th thin
ī pie	*th* this
îr pier	hw which
ŏ pot	zh vision
ō toe	ə about, item
ô paw	

Stress marks:
′ (primary);
′ (secondary), as in
dictionary (dĭk′shə-nĕr′ē)

caused by eye inflammation, lack of pigmentation in the iris, or various diseases. **2.** An abnormal or irrational fear of light.

pho•to•pho•bic (fō′tə-fō′bĭk) *adj.* **1.** Exhibiting photophobia. **2.** Avoiding light. **3.** Growing best in the absence of light; photonegative.

pho•to•phore (fō′tə-fôr′, -fōr′) *n.* A light-producing organ found esp. in marine fishes that emits light from specialized structures or derives light from luminescent bacteria.

pho•to•phos•phor•y•la•tion (fō′tō-fŏs′fôr-ə-lā′shən, -fər-) *n.* Phosphorylation induced by radiant energy in photosynthesis.

pho•to•pi•a (fō-tō′pē-ə) *n.* Vision in bright light, mediated by cone cells of the retina; daylight vision. **—pho•to′pic** (-tō′pĭk, -tŏp′ĭk) *adj.*

pho•to•play (fō′tə-plā′) *n.* A play filmed as a movie.

pho•to•pos•i•tive (fō′tō-pŏz′ĭ-tĭv) *adj. Biol.* Drawn to light; exhibiting a positive phototactic or phototropic response.

pho•to-re•al•ism (fō′tō-rē′ə-lĭz′əm) *n.* A style of painting that is like photography in its attention to realistic detail. **—pho′to-re′al•ist** *adj. & n.* **—pho′to•re′al•is′tic** *adj.*

pho•to•re•cep•tion (fō′tō-rĭ-sĕp′shən) *n.* The detection, absorption, and use of light, as for vision in animals or photosynthesis in plants. **—pho′to•re•cep′tive** *adj.*

pho•to•re•cep•tor (fō′tō-rĭ-sĕp′tər) *n.* A nerve ending, cell, or group of cells specialized to sense or receive light.

pho•to•re•con•nais•sance (fō′tō-rĭ-kŏn′ə-səns, -zəns) *n.* Photographic aerial reconnaissance esp. of military targets.

pho•to•res•pi•ra•tion (fō′tō-rĕs′pə-rā′shən) *n.* Oxidation of carbohydrates in plants with the release of carbon dioxide during photosynthesis.

pho•to•sen•si•tive (fō′tō-sĕn′sĭ-tĭv) *adj.* **1.** Sensitive or responsive to light or other radiant energy. **2.** *Medic.* Abnormally sensitive or reactive to light.

pho•to•sen•si•tiv•i•ty (fō′tō-sĕn′sĭ-tĭv′ĭ-tē) *n., pl.* **-ties. 1.** Sensitivity or responsiveness to light. **2.** *Medic.* An abnormally heightened response, esp. of the skin, to sunlight or ultraviolet radiation, caused by certain disorders or chemicals.

pho•to•sen•si•ti•za•tion (fō′tō-sĕn′sĭ-tĭ-zā′shən) *n.* The act or process of inducing photosensitivity.

pho•to•sen•si•tize (fō′tō-sĕn′sĭ-tīz′) *tr.v.* **-tized, -tiz•ing, -tiz•es.** To make (an organism, for example) photosensitive.

pho•to•set (fō′tō-sĕt′) *tr.v.* **-set, -set•ting, -sets.** *Print.* To photocompose. **—pho′to•set′ter** *n.*

pho•to•sphere (fō′tə-sfîr′) *n.* The visible outer layer of a star, esp. of the sun. **—pho′to•spher′ic** (-sfîr′ĭk, -sfĕr′ĭk) *adj.*

Pho•to•stat (fō′tə-stăt′). A trademark used for a photographic device for making positive or negative copies of graphic matter.

pho•to•syn•the•sis (fō′tō-sĭn′thĭ-sĭs) *n.* The process by which green plants and certain other organisms synthesize carbohydrates from carbon dioxide and water using light as an energy source and usu. releasing oxygen as a byproduct. **—pho′to•syn′the•size′** (-sīz′) *v.* **—pho′to•syn•thet′ic** (-sĭn-thĕt′ĭk) *adj.* **—pho′to•syn•thet′i•cal•ly** *adv.*

pho•to•tax•is (fō′tō-tăk′sĭs) *n. Biol.* The movement of an organism or a cell toward or away from a source of light. **—pho′to•tac′tic** (-tăk′tĭk) *adj.*

pho•to•tox•ic (fō′tō-tŏk′sĭk) *adj.* Making the skin susceptible to damage by light. **—pho′to•tox•ic′i•ty** (-tŏk-sĭs′ĭ-tē) *n.*

pho•to•tran•sis•tor (fō′tō-trăn-zĭs′tər) *n.* A transistor having highly photosensitive electrical characteristics.

pho•tot•ro•pism (fō-tŏt′rə-pĭz′əm) *n.* Growth or movement of a sessile organism toward or away from a source of light. **—pho′to•tro′pic** (fō′tə-trō′pĭk, -trŏp′ĭk) *adj.* **—pho′to•tro′pi•cal•ly** *adv.*

pho•to•tube (fō′tō-to͞ob′, -tyo͞ob′) *n.* An electron tube with a photosensitive cathode.

pho•to•type•set•ter (fō′tō-tīp′sĕt′ər) *n. Print.* **1.** Any of various machines used in photocomposition. **2.** The operator of one of these machines.

pho•to•type•set•ting (fō′tō-tīp′sĕt′ĭng) *n. Print.* See **photocomposition.**

pho•to•ty•pog•ra•phy (fō′tō-tī-pŏg′rə-fē) *n. Print.* Photomechanical printing that resembles metal typography. **—pho′to•ty′po•graph′ic** (-tī′pə-grăf′ĭk), **pho′to•ty′po•graph′i•cal** (-ĭ-kəl) *adj.*

pho•to•vol•ta•ic (fō′tō-vŏl-tā′ĭk, -vōl-) *adj.* Capable of producing a voltage when exposed to radiant energy, esp. light. **—pho′to•vol•ta′ic** *n.*

photovoltaic cell *n.* See **solar cell.**

phr. *abbr.* Phrase.

phrag•mi•tes (frăg-mī′tēz) *n.* Any of several perennial long-stemmed reeds of the genus *Phragmites* in the grass family, found in wetlands. [Lat. *phragmitēs*, a hedge reed < Gk., fencing in < *phragma*, fence < *phrassein*, to fence in.]

phrasal verb *n.* An English verb complex consisting of a verb and one or more following particles that act as a complete syntactic and semantic unit, as *go on* in *What's going on?*

phrase (frāz) *n.* **1.** A meaningful sequence of words. **2.a.** A characteristic way or mode of expression. **b.** A brief, apt, and cogent expression. **3.** A word or group of words read or spoken as a unit and separated by pauses or other junctures. **4.** *Gram.* Two or more words in sequence forming a syntactic unit that is less than a complete sentence. **5.** *Mus.* A segment of a composition, usu. consisting of four or eight measures. **6.** A series of dance movements forming a unit in a choreographic pattern. **—***v.* **phrased, phras•ing, phras•es.** **—***tr.* **1.** To express orally or in writing: *clearly phrased prose.* **2.** To pace or mark off (something read aloud or spoken) by pauses. **3.** *Mus.* **a.** To divide (a passage) into phrases. **b.** To combine (notes) in a phrase. **—***intr.* **1.** To make or render phrases, as in reading aloud. **2.** *Mus.* To perform a passage with the correct phrasing. [Lat. *phrasis*, diction < Gk., speech, diction, phrase < *phrazein*, to point out, show. See **gʷhren-*.**] **—phras′al** *adj.* **—phras′al•ly** *adv.*

phrase book *n.* A book of foreign language expressions and their translations.

phra•se•o•gram (frā′zē-ə-grăm′) *n.* A symbol, such as one used in shorthand, that designates a particular phrase.

phra•se•o•graph (frā′zē-ə-grăf′) *n.* A phrase represented by a phraseogram. **—phra′se•o•graph′ic** *adj.*

phra•se•ol•o•gy (frā′zē-ŏl′ə-jē) *n., pl.* **-gies. 1.** The way in which words and phrases are used in speech or writing; style. **2.** A set of expressions used by a particular person or group: *nautical phraseology.* **—phra′se•o•log′i•cal** (-ə-lŏj′ĭ-kəl) *adj.* **—phra′se•ol′o•gist** *n.*

phras•ing (frā′zĭng) *n.* **1.** The act of making phrases. **2.** The manner in which an expression is phrased. **3.** *Mus.* The manner in which a phrase is rendered.

phra•try (frā′trē) *n., pl.* **-tries. 1.** A kinship group among the ancient Greeks of several patrilinear clans. **2.** *Anthro.* An exogamous subdivision of the tribe, constituting two or more related clans. [Gk. *phratria* < *phratēr*, *phratr-*, fellow member of a clan. See **bhrāter-*.**] **—phra′tric** *adj.*

phre•at•ic (frē-ăt′ĭk) *adj.* Of or relating to ground water. [< Gk. *phrear*, *phreat-*, well, spring. See **bhreu-*.**]

phre•at•o•phyte (frē-ăt′ə-fīt′) *n.* A deep-rooted plant that obtains water from a permanent ground supply or from the water table. [Gk. *phrear*, *phreat-*, well, spring + -PHYTE.] **—phre•at′o•phyt′ic** (-fĭt′ĭk) *adj.*

phren. *abbr.* Phrenology.

phre•net•ic (frə-nĕt′ĭk) or **phre•net•i•cal** (-ĭ-kəl) *adj.* Var. of **frenetic.**

-phrenia *suff.* Mental disorder: *schizophrenia.* [< Gk. *phrēn*, mind. See **gʷhren-*.**]

phren•ic (frĕn′ĭk, frē′nĭk) *adj.* **1.** Of or relating to the mind. **2.** *Anat.* Of or relating to the diaphragm: *the phrenic nerve.*

phre•ni•tis (frĭ-nī′tĭs) *n.* **1.** Inflammation of the diaphragm. **2.** Encephalitis. No longer in scientific use.

phreno- or **phren-** *pref.* **1.** Mind: *phrenology.* **2.** Diaphragm: *phrenic.* [Gk. < *phrēn*, *phren-*, diaphragm, midriff, heart, mind. See **gʷhren-*.**]

phre•nol•o•gy (frĭ-nŏl′ə-jē) *n.* The study of the shape and protuberances of the skull, based on the now discredited belief that they reveal character and mental capacity. **—phren′o•log′ic** (frĕn′ə-lŏj′ĭk, frē′nə-), **phren′o•log′i•cal** (-ĭ-kəl) *adj.* **—phre•nol′o•gist** *n.*

phren•sy (frĕn′zē) *n. & v. Archaic.* Var. of **frenzy.**

Phryg•i•a (frĭj′ē-ə). An ancient region of central Asia Minor in modern-day central Turkey; settled c. 1200 B.C. and flourished from the 8th to the 6th cent.

Phryg•i•an (frĭj′ē-ən) *adj.* Of or relating to Phrygia or its people, language, or culture. **—***n.* **1.** A native or inhabitant of Phrygia. **2.** The Indo-European language of the Phrygians.

Phrygian cap *n.* See **liberty cap.**

PHS *abbr.* Public Health Service.

phthal•ein also **phthal•eine** (thăl′ēn′, thăl′ē-ĭn, thā′lēn′, thā′lē-ĭn, fthăl′-) *n.* Any of a group of chemical compounds formed by a reaction of phthalic anhydride with a phenol, from which certain synthetic dyes are derived.

phthal•ic (thăl′ĭk, fthăl′-) *adj.* **1.** Of, relating to, or derived from naphthalene. **2.** Relating to phthalic acid. [Short for *naphthalic acid* : NAPHTHAL(ENE) + -IC.]

phthalic acid *n.* A colorless crystalline organic acid, $C_6H_4(COOH)_2$, prepared from naphthalene and used in the synthesis of dyes, perfumes, and other organic compounds.

phthalic anhydride *n.* A crystalline compound, $C_6H_4(CO)_2O$, prepared by oxidizing naphthalene and used in the manufacture of dyes, resins, plasticizers, and insecticides.

phthal•in (thăl′ĭn, fthăl′-) *n.* Any of various colorless compounds derived from the reduction of phthaleins.

phthal•o•cy•a•nine (thăl′ō-sī′ə-nēn′, fthăl′-) *n.* Any of several stable light-fast blue or green organic pigments derived from the basic compound $(C_6H_4C_2N)_4N_4$ and used in enamels, inks, linoleum, and plastics. [PHTHAL(IC) + CYANINE.]

phthi•ri•a•sis (thĭ-rī′ə-sĭs, thī-) *n.* Infestation with lice, esp. crab lice; pediculosis. [Lat. *phthīriāsis* < Gk. *phtheiriasis* < *phtheirian*, to be lousy < *phtheir*, louse.]

phthis•ic (tĭz′ĭk, thĭz′-) *n.* **1.** Var. of **phthisis. 2.** *Archaic.* Any illness of the lungs or throat, such as asthma or a cough. [ME *ptisike* < OFr. *ptisique* < *phthisicus*, consumptive < Gk. *phthisikos* < *phthisis*, wasting away, consumption. See PHTHISIS.] **—phthis′ic, phthis′i•cal** *adj.*

phthi•sis (thī′sĭs, tī′-) also **phthis•ic** (tĭz′ĭk, thĭz′-) *n.* **1.** A disease marked by the wasting away or atrophy of the body or a body part. **2.** Tuberculosis of the lungs. No longer in scientific use. [Lat. < Gk. < *phthinein*, to waste away.]

phyco– *pref.* Seaweed; algae: *phycology.* [Gk. *phuko-* < *phukos*, seaweed.]

phy•co•cy•a•nin (fī′kō-sī′ə-nĭn) *n.* A blue protein pigment occurring esp. in the cells of cyanobacteria.

phy•co•er•y•thrin (fī′kō-ĕr′ĭ-thrĭn) *n.* A red protein pigment occurring esp. in the cells of red algae.

phy•col•o•gy (fī-kŏl′ə-jē) *n.* The branch of botany that deals with algae. **—phy′co•log′i•cal** (fī′kə-lŏj′ĭ-kəl) *adj.* **—phy•col′o•gist** *n.*

phy•co•my•cete (fī′kō-mī′sēt′, -mī-sēt′) *n.* Any of various fungi that resemble algae, including certain molds and mildews. [< NLat. *Phycomycetes*, class name : PHYCO– + –MYCETE.] **—phy′co•my•ce′tous** *adj.*

Phyfe (fīf), **Duncan.** 1768?–1854. Scottish-born Amer. cabinetmaker who pioneered factory methods of construction.

phy•la (fī′lə) *n.* Pl. of **phylum.**

phy•lac•ter•y (fĭ-lăk′tə-rē) *n., pl.* **-ies. 1.** *Judaism.* Either of the two boxes comprising tefillin. **2.a.** An amulet. **b.** A reminder. [Ult. < LLat. *phylactērium* < Gk. *phulaktērion* < *phulaktēr*, guard < *phulax*, *phulak-*.]

phy•le (fī′lē) *n., pl.* **-lae** (-lē). A large citizens' organization based on kinship, constituting the largest political subdivision of an ancient Greek city-state. [Gk. *phulē*, tribe, phyle. See **bheuə-*.**] **—phy′lic** *adj.*

phy•let•ic (fī-lĕt′ĭk) *adj.* Of or relating to the evolutionary descent and development of a species or group of organisms; phylogenetic. [< Gk. *phuletikos*, of a tribesman < *phuletēs*, tribesman < *phulē*, tribe. See **bheuə-*.**] **—phy•let′i•cal•ly** *adv.*

–phyll *suff.* Leaf: *chlorophyll; sporophyll.* [< Gk. *phullon*, leaf. See PHYLLO–.]

phyl•lite (fĭl′īt′) *n.* A green, gray, or red metamorphic rock, similar to slate but often having a wavy surface and a distinctive micaceous luster. **—phyl•lit′ic** (fĭ-lĭt′ĭk) *adj.*

phyl•lo (fē′lō) *n.* Very thin sheets of pastry dough used esp. in Greek dishes. [Mod.Gk. *phullon* < Gk., leaf. See PHYLLO–.]

phyllo– or **phyll–** *pref.* Leaf: *phylloid.* [Gk. < *phullon*, leaf. See **bhel-3*.**]

phyl•lo•clade (fĭl′ə-klād′) also **phyl•lo•clad** (-klăd′) *n.* A flattened branch or stem that performs the function of or resembles a leaf, as in the Christmas cactus. [NLat. *phyllocladium* : PHYLLO– + Gk. *klados*, branch.]

phyl•lode (fĭl′ōd) also **phyl•lo•di•um** (fĭ-lō′dē-əm) *n., pl.* **-lodes** also **-lo•di•a** (-lō′dē-ə). A flattened leafstalk that functions as a leaf, as in an acacia. [NLat. *phyllōdium* < Gk. *phullōdēs*, leaflike : *phullon*, leaf; see PHYLLO– + *-ōdēs*, var. of *-oeidēs*, -oid.] **—phyl•lo′di•al** *adj.*

phyl•loid (fĭl′oid′) *adj.* Resembling a leaf; leaflike.

phyl•lome (fĭl′ōm′) *n.* A leaf or a plant part that evolved from a leaf. **—phyl•lo′mic** (fĭ-lō′mĭk, -lŏm′ĭk) *adj.*

phyl•loph•a•gous (fĭ-lŏf′ə-gəs) *adj.* Feeding on leaves.

phyl•lo•pod (fĭl′ə-pŏd′) *n.* Any of various branchiopod crustaceans having phylloid swimming and respiratory appendages. — *adj.* also **phyl•lop•o•dous** (fĭ-lŏp′ə-dəs). Of or relating to the phyllopods. **—phyl•lop′o•dan** (fĭ-lŏp′ə-dən) *adj. & n.*

phyl•lo•tax•y (fĭl′ə-tăk′sē) also **phyl•lo•tax•is** (fĭl′ə-tăk′sĭs) *n., pl.* **-tax•ies** also **-tax•es. 1.** The arrangement of leaves on a stem. **2.** The principles governing leaf arrangement. **—phyl′lo•tac′tic** (-tăk′tĭk), **phyl′lo•tac′ti•cal** *adj.*

–phyllous *suff.* Having a specified kind or number of leaves: *gamophyllous.* [< NLat. *-phyllus* < Gk. *-phullos* < *phullon*, leaf. See **bhel-3*.**]

phyl•lox•e•ra (fĭl′ŏk-sîr′ə, fĭ-lŏk′sər-ə) *n., pl.* **-rae** (-rē). Any of several small insects of the genus *Phylloxera* related to aphids, esp. *P. vitifoliae,* a widely distributed species harmful to grape crops. [NLat. *Phylloxera*, genus name : Gk. *phullo-*, phyllo- + Gk. *xēros*, dry.] **—phyl′lox•e′ran** *adj. & n.*

phy•lo•gen•e•sis (fī′lō-jĕn′ĭ-sĭs) *n.* See **phylogeny** 1.

phy•lo•ge•net•ic (fī′lō-jə-nĕt′ĭk) *adj.* **1.** Of phylogeny or phylogenetics. **2.** Relating to or based on evolutionary development or history. **—phy′lo•ge•net′i•cal•ly** *adv.*

phy•lo•ge•net•ics (fī′lō-jə-nĕt′ĭks) *n.* (*used with a sing. v.*) The study of phylogeny.

phy•log•e•ny (fī-lŏj′ə-nē) *n., pl.* **-nies. 1.** The evolutionary development and history of a species or higher taxonomic grouping of organisms. **2.** The evolutionary development of an organ or other part of an organism. **3.** The historical development of a tribe or racial group. [Gk. *phulon*, race, class; see **bheuə-*** + –GENY.] **—phy′lo•gen′ic** (-jĕn′ĭk) *adj.*

phy•lum (fī′ləm) *n., pl.* **-la** (-lə). **1.** *Biol.* A primary division of a kingdom, as of the animal kingdom, ranking next above a class in size. See table at **taxonomy. 2.** *Ling.* A large group of possibly related languages or language families. [NLat. < Gk. *phulon*, class. See **bheuə-*.**]

phys. *abbr.* **1.** Physical. **2.** Physician. **3.** Physicist; physics. **4.** Physiological; physiology.

phys– *pref.* Var. of **physio–.**

phys. ed. or **phys ed** *abbr.* Physical education.

physi– *pref.* Var. of **physio–.**

phys•i•at•rics (fĭz′ē-ăt′rĭks) *n.* (*used with a sing. v.*) **1.** See **physical medicine. 2.** Physical therapy.

phys•i•at•rist (fĭz′ē-ăt′rĭst, fĭ-zī′ə-trĭst) *n.* **1.** A physician specializing in physical medicine. **2.** A physical therapist.

phys•i•at•ry (fĭz′ē-ăt′rē, fĭ-zī′ə-trē) *n.* **1.** See **physical medicine. 2.** Physical therapy.

phys•ic (fĭz′ĭk) *n.* **1.** A medicine or drug, esp. a cathartic. **2.** *Archaic.* The art or profession of medicine. — *tr.v.* **-icked, -ick•ing, -ics. 1.** To act on as a cathartic. **2.** To cure or heal. **3.** To treat with or as if with medicine. [ME *phisik* < OFr. *fisique*, medical science, natural science < Lat., natural science < Gk. *phusikē*, fem. of *phusikos*, of nature < *phusis*, nature. See **bheuə-*.**]

phys•i•cal (fĭz′ĭ-kəl) *adj.* **1.a.** Of or relating to the body as distinguished from the mind or spirit. See Syns at **bodily. b.** Involving or marked by vigorous bodily activity. **c.** *Slang.* Involving or characterized by violence. **2.** Of or relating to material things: *our physical environment.* **3.** Of or relating to matter and energy or the sciences dealing with them, esp. physics. — *n.* A physical examination. [ME *phisical*, medical < Med.Lat. *physicālis* < Lat. *physica*, physics. See PHYSICS.] **—phys′i•cal′i•ty** (-kăl′ĭ-tē) *n.* **—phys′i•cal•ly** *adv.*

physical anthropology *n.* The branch of anthropology that deals with human evolutionary biology, racial variation, and classification. **—physical anthropologist** *n.*

physical chemistry *n.* Scientific analysis of the properties and behavior of chemical systems primarily by physical theory and technique.

physical education *n.* Education in the care and development of the human body, stressing athletics and including hygiene.

physical examination *n.* A medical examination to determine the condition of a person's health or physical fitness.

physical geography *n.* The study of the natural features of the earth's surface, esp. in its current aspects, including land formation, climate, currents, and distribution of flora and fauna.

phys•i•cal•ism (fĭz′ĭ-kə-lĭz′əm) *n.* *Philos.* The doctrine that all phenomena can be described in spatiotemporal terms and consequently that any descriptive scientific statement can in principle be reduced to an empirically verifiable physical statement. **—phys′i•cal•ist** *n.* **—phys′i•cal•is′tic** *adj.*

physical medicine *n.* The branch of medicine that deals with the treatment, prevention, and diagnosis of disease by essentially physical means, including manipulation and exercise.

physical science *n.* Any of the sciences, such as physics, chemistry, astronomy, and geology, that analyze the nature and properties of energy and nonliving matter.

physical therapy *n.* The treatment of physical dysfunction or injury by the use of therapeutic exercise and the application of modalities, intended to restore or facilitate normal function or development. **—physical therapist** *n.*

phy•si•cian (fĭ-zĭsh′ən) *n.* **1.** A person licensed to practice medicine; a medical doctor. **2.** A person who practices general medicine as distinct from surgery. **3.** A person who heals or exerts a healing influence. [ME *fisicien* < OFr. < *fisique*, medical science. See PHYSIC.]

phy•si•cian's assistant (fĭ-zĭsh′ənz) *n., pl.* **physicians' assistants.** A person trained to provide basic medical services, usu. under the supervision of a physician.

phys•i•cist (fĭz′ĭ-sĭst) *n.* A scientist who specializes in physics.

phys•i•co•chem•i•cal (fĭz′ĭ-kō-kĕm′ĭ-kəl) *adj.* **1.** Relating to both physical and chemical properties. **2.** Relating to physical chemistry.

phys•ics (fĭz′ĭks) *n.* **1.** (*used with a sing. v.*) The science of matter and energy and of interactions between the two, grouped in traditional fields such as acoustics, optics, mechanics, and thermodynamics, as well as in modern extensions including atomic and nuclear physics, cryogenics, and particle physics. **2.** (*used with a pl. v.*) Physical properties, interactions, processes, or laws: *the physics of supersonic flight.* **3.** (*used with a sing. v.*) *Archaic.* The study of the natural or material world and phenomena; natural philosophy. [< Lat. *physica* < Gk. (*ta*) *phusika* < neut. pl. of *phusikos*, of nature < *phusis*, nature. See **bheuə-*.**]

physio– or **physi–** or **phys–** *pref.* **1.** Nature; natural: *physiography.* **2.** Physical: *physiotherapy.* [Gk. *phusio-* < *phusis*, nature. See **bheuə-*.**]

phys•i•og•no•my (fĭz′ē-ŏg′nə-mē, -ŏn′ə-mē) *n., pl.* **-mies. 1.a.** The art of judging human character from facial features. **b.** Divination based on this art. **2.a.** Facial features, esp. when seen as revealing character. **b.** Aspect and character of an inanimate or abstract entity. [Ult. < LLat. *physiognōmia* < Gk. *phusiognōmia*, var. of *phusiognōmonia* : *phusio-*, physio- + *gnōmōn*, *gnōmon-*, interpreter; see **gnō-*.**] **—phys′i•og•nom′ic** (-ŏg-nŏm′ĭk, -ə-nŏm′ĭk), **phys′i•og•nom′i•cal** (-ĭ-kəl) *adj.* **—phys′i•og′no•mist** *n.*

phys•i•og•ra•phy (fĭz′ē-ŏg′rə-fē) *n.* See **physical geography. —phys′i•og′ra•pher** *n.* **—phys′i•o•graph′ic** (-ə-grăf′ĭk), **phys′i•o•graph′i•cal** (-ĭ-kəl) *adj.*

physiol. *abbr.* Physiological; physiology.

phys•i•o•log•i•cal (fĭz′ē-ə-lŏj′ĭ-kəl) also **phys•i•o•log•ic** (-ĭk) *adj.* **1.** Of or relating to physiology. **2.** Consistent with

phylactery
Phylacteries strapped to the forehead and left arm

ă pat	oi boy
ā pay	ou out
âr care	ŏŏ took
ä father	ōō boot
ĕ pet	ŭ cut
ē be	ûr urge
ĭ pit	th thin
ī pie	*th* this
îr pier	hw which
ŏ pot	zh vision
ō toe	ə about,
ô paw	item

Stress marks:
′ (primary);
′ (secondary), as in
dictionary (dĭk′shə-nĕr′ē)

or characteristic of the normal functioning of a living organism. **3.** *Color.* Of or being an additive primary color. —**phys′i•o•log′i•cal•ly** *adv.*

physiological psychology *n.* See **psychophysiology.** —**physiological psychologist** *n.*

physiological saline *n.* A sterile solution of sodium chloride that is isotonic to body fluids, used to maintain living tissue temporarily and as a solvent for parenterally administered drugs.

phys•i•ol•o•gy (fĭz′ē-ŏl′ə-jē) *n.* **1.** The biological study of the functions of living organisms and their parts. **2.** All the functions of a living organism or any of its parts. —**phys′i•ol′o•gist** *n.*

phys•i•o•pa•thol•o•gy (fĭz′ē-ō-pə-thŏl′ə-jē) *n.* See **pathophysiology.** —**phys′i•o•path′o•log′ic** (-păth′ə-lŏj′ĭk), **phys′i•o•path′o•log′i•cal** (-ĭ-kəl) *adj.* —**phys′i•o•pa•thol′o•gist** *n.*

phys•i•o•ther•a•py (fĭz′ē-ō-thĕr′ə-pē) *n.* See **physical therapy.** —**phys′i•o•ther′a•peu′tic** (-thĕr′ə-pyo͞o′tĭk) *adj.* —**phys′i•o•ther′a•pist** *n.*

phy•sique (fĭ-zēk′) *n.* The body considered with reference to its proportions, muscular development, and appearance. [Fr., physical, physique < Lat. *physicus,* of nature < Gk. *phusikos* < *phusis,* nature. See **bheuə-*.**] —**phy•siqued′** *adj.*

Syns: *physique, build, constitution.* The central meaning shared by these nouns is "bodily structure or development": *a delicate physique; a stocky build; a robust constitution.*

phy•so•stig•mine (fī′sō-stĭg′mēn′) also **phy•so•stig•min** (-mĭn) *n.* A crystalline alkaloid, $C_{15}H_{21}N_3O_2$, extracted from the Calabar bean and used in medicine as a miotic and cholinergic agent and to enhance memory in patients with Alzheimer's disease. [NLat. *Physostigma,* genus name of the Calabar bean (Gk. *phusa,* bellows + STIGMA) + -INE[2].]

phy•sos•to•mous (fī-sŏs′tə-məs) *adj.* Having a connecting tube between the air bladder and a part of the alimentary canal. [< Gk. *phusa,* bladder + Gk. *stoma,* mouth.]

–phyte *suff.* **1.** A plant with a specified character or habitat: *halophyte.* **2.** A pathological growth: *osteophyte.* [< Gk. *phuton,* plant < *phuein,* to make grow. See **bheuə-*.**]

phyto– or **phyt–** *pref.* Plant: *phytogenesis.* [NLat. < Gk. *phuto-* < *phuton,* plant < *phuein,* to make grow. See **bheuə-*.**]

phy•to•chem•is•try (fī′tō-kĕm′ĭ-strē) *n.* The chemistry of plants. —**phy′to•chem′i•cal** (-ĭ-kəl) *adj.* —**phy′to•chem′i•cal•ly** *adv.* —**phy′to•chem′ist** *n.*

phy•to•chrome (fī′tə-krōm′) *n.* A cytoplasmic pigment of green plants that absorbs light and regulates dormancy, seed germination, and flowering.

phy•to•gen•e•sis (fī′tō-jĕn′ĭ-sĭs) also **phy•tog•e•ny** (fī-tŏj′ə-nē) *n.* The origin and evolutionary development of plants. —**phy′to•ge•net′ic** (-jə-nĕt′ĭk), **phy′to•ge•net′i•cal** (-ĭ-kəl) *adj.* —**phy′to•ge•net′i•cal•ly** *adv.*

phy•to•gen•ic (fī′tō-jĕn′ĭk) also **phy•tog•e•nous** (fī-tŏj′ə-nəs) *adj.* Having a plant origin, as coal.

phy•to•ge•og•ra•phy (fī′tō-jē-ŏg′rə-fē) *n.* The study of the geographic distribution of plants. —**phy′to•ge•og′ra•pher** *n.* —**phy′to•ge′o•graph′i•cal** (-jē′ə-grăf′ĭ-kəl), **phy′to•ge′o•graph′ic** (-grăf′ĭk) *adj.*

phy•tog•ra•phy (fī-tŏg′rə-fē) *n.* The science of plant description; descriptive botany.

phy•to•he•mag•glu•ti•nin (fī′tō-hē′mə-glo͞ot′n-ĭn) *n.* A hemagglutinin extracted from a plant.

phy•to•hor•mone (fī′tō-hôr′mōn′) *n.* See **plant hormone.**

phy•tol•o•gy (fī-tŏl′ə-jē) *n.* The study of plants; botany. —**phy′to•log′ic** (fī′tə-lŏj′ĭk), **phy′to•log′i•cal** (-ĭ-kəl) *adj.*

phy•ton (fī′tŏn′) *n.* The smallest unit of plant structure. [NLat. < Gk. *phuton,* plant. See PHYTO–.] —**phy•ton′ic** *adj.*

phy•to•pa•thol•o•gy (fī′tō-pə-thŏl′ə-jē) *n.* The science of plant diseases. —**phy′to•path′o•log′ic** (-păth′ə-lŏj′ĭk), **phy′to•path′o•log′i•cal** (-ĭ-kəl) *adj.*

phy•toph•a•gous (fī-tŏf′ə-gəs) *adj.* Feeding on plants, including shrubs and trees. Used esp. of certain insects.

phy•to•plank•ton (fī′tō-plăngk′tən) *n.* Minute free-floating aquatic plants. —**phy′to•plank•ton′ic** (-plăngk-tŏn′ĭk) *adj.*

phy•to•so•ci•ol•o•gy (fī′tō-sō′sē-ŏl′ə-jē, -shē-) *n.* The branch of ecology that deals with the traits, classification, relationships, and distribution of plant communities.

phy•to•tox•ic (fī′tō-tŏk′sĭk) *adj.* Poisonous to plants. —**phy′to•tox•ic′i•ty** (-tŏk-sĭs′ĭ-tē) *n.*

pi[1] (pī) *n., pl.* **pis. 1.** The 16th letter of the Greek alphabet. **2.** *Math.* A transcendental number, approx. 3.14159, represented by the symbol π, that expresses the ratio of the circumference to the diameter of a circle and appears as a constant in many mathematical expressions. [Med.Gk. < Gk. *pei,* of Phoenician orig.; akin to Heb. *pē.*]

pi[2] also **pie** (pī) *Print.* —*n., pl.* **pis** also **pies.** An amount of type that has been jumbled or thrown together at random. —*v.* **pied** (pīd) , **pi•ing, pies** also **pied, pie•ing, pies.** —*tr.* To jumble or mix up (type). —*intr.* To become jumbled. [?]

pi•a (pī′ə, pē′ə) *n.* The pia mater. —**pi′al** *adj.*

Pia•cen•za (pyä-chĕn′zə, -tsä). A town of N Italy on the Po R. SE of Milan; founded as Placentia in 218 B.C. Pop. 108,177.

pi•ac•u•lar (pī-ăk′yə-lər) *adj.* **1.** Making expiation or atonement for a sacrilege: *piacular sacrifice.* **2.** Requiring expiation; wicked or blameworthy. [Lat. *piāculāris* < *piāculum,* propitiatory sacrifice < *piāre,* to appease < *pius,* dutiful.]

Pi•af (pē-äf′, pē′äf′), **Edith.** 1915–63. French cabaret singer whose songs include *Non, Je Ne Regrette Rien.*

Edith Piaf

piaffe (pyăf) *intr.v.* **piaffed, piaf•fing, piaffes.** To perform the piaffer. [Fr. *piaffer.*]

piaf•fer (pyăf′ər) *n.* A movement in which a horse trots in place with high action of the legs. [Fr. < *piaffer,* to strut, piaffe.]

Pia•get (pē′ə-zhā′, pyä-), **Jean.** 1896–1980. Swiss psychologist noted for his studies of mental development in children.

pia ma•ter (mā′tər, mä′tər) *n.* The fine vascular membrane that closely envelops the brain and spinal cord under the arachnoid and the dura mater. [ME < Med.Lat. *pia māter* : Lat. *pia,* tender + Lat. *māter,* mother.]

pi•an•ism (pē-ăn′ĭz′əm, pē′ə-nĭz′əm) *n. Mus.* The technique or execution of piano playing.

pi•a•nis•si•mo (pē′ə-nĭs′ə-mō′) *Mus.* —*adv. & adj.* In a very soft or quiet tone. —*n., pl.* **-mos.** A part of a composition played very softly or quietly. [Ital., superl. of *piano,* soft. See PIANO[2].]

pi•an•ist (pē-ăn′ĭst, pē′ə-nĭst) *n. Mus.* One who plays the piano.

pi•a•nis•tic (pē′ə-nĭs′tĭk) *adj. Mus.* **1.** Of or relating to the piano. **2.** Well suited to the piano. —**pi′a•nis′ti•cal•ly** *adv.*

piano[1]

pi•an•o[1] (pē-ăn′ō, pyăn′ō) *n., pl.* **-os.** *Mus.* An instrument with a manual keyboard actuating hammers that strike wire strings, creating sounds that may be softened or sustained by means of pedals. [Ital., short for *pianoforte.* See PIANOFORTE.]

pi•a•no[2] (pē-ä′nō, pyä′-) *Mus.* —*adv. & adj.* In a soft or quiet tone. —*n., pl.* **-nos.** A passage to be played softly or quietly. [Ital. < LLat. *plānus,* smooth, graceful < Lat., flat. See **pelə-**[2]***.**]

pi•an•o•for•te (pē-ăn′ō-fôr′tā, -fôr′tē, pē-ăn′ō-fôrt′) *n. Mus.* See **piano**[1]**.** [Ital. < *(clavicembalo con) piano (e) forte,* (harpsichord with) soft (and) loud.]

piano hinge *n.* A long narrow hinge with a pin running the entire length of its joint.

pi•as•sa•va (pē′ə-sä′və) also **pi•as•sa•ba** (-sä′bə) *n.* **1.** Either of two South American palm trees, *Attalea funifera* or *Leopoldinia piassaba,* from which a strong coarse fiber is obtained. **2.** The fiber of either of these plants, used for making ropes, brushes, and brooms. [Port. < Tupi *plaçaba.*]

pi•as•ter also **pi•as•tre** (pē-ăs′tər, -ä′stər) *n.* **1.** See table at **currency. 2.** Piece of eight. [Fr. *piastre* < Ital. *piastra,* thin metal plate < Lat. *emplastrum,* medical dressing. See PLASTER.]

pi•az•za (pē-ăz′ə, -ä′zə) *n., pl.* **-zas. 1.** (*also* pē-ät′sə, pyät′sä). *pl.* **pi•az•ze** (pē-ät′sə, pyät′sĕ). A public square in an Italian town. **2.** A roofed and arcaded passageway; a colonnade. **3.** A verandah. [Ital. < Lat. *platēa,* street < Gk. *plateia (hodos),* broad (way), fem. of *platus,* broad. See **plat-*.**]

pi•broch (pē′brŏkн′) *n. Mus.* A series of variations on a traditional dirge or martial theme for the highland bagpipes. [Sc. Gael. *piobaireachd,* pipe music < *piobair,* piper < *piob,* pipe < MIr. *píp* < Med.Lat. *pīpa* < VLat. See PIPE.]

pic (pĭk) *n., pl.* **pics** or **pix** (pĭks). *Slang.* **1.** A photograph. **2.** A movie. [Short for PICTURE.]

pi•ca[1] (pī′kə) *n. Print.* **1.a.** A printer's unit of type size, equal to 12 points or about ⅙ of an inch. **b.** An equivalent unit of composition measurement used to determine the dimensions of lines, illustrations, or printed pages. **2.** A type size for typewriters, providing ten characters to the inch. [Prob. < Med. Lat. *pīca,* list of church services.]

pi•ca[2] (pī′kə) *n.* An abnormal craving or appetite for nonfood substances, such as dirt, paint, or clay. [NLat. *pīca* < Lat., magpie (< its omnivorous nature).]

pic•a•dor (pĭk′ə-dôr′, pē′kä-thôr′) *n., pl.* **pic•a•dors** or **pic•a•do•res** (pĭk′ə-dôr′ās, pē′kä-thô′rĕs). A horseman in a bullfight who lances the bull's neck muscles so that it will tend to keep its head low for the subsequent stages of the fight. [Sp. < *picar,* to prick. See PICARO.]

pi•can•te (pĭ-kän′tā) *adj.* Prepared so as to be spicy, esp. having a spicy sauce. [Sp., pr.part. of *picar,* to bite, prick. See PICARO.]

pi•ca•ra (pē′kä-rä′) *n., pl.* **-ras** (-räz′, -räs′). A woman who is a picaro. [Sp. *pícara,* fem. of *pícaro,* rogue. See PICARO.]

Pi•card (pē-kär′), **Jean.** 1620–82. French astronomer who calculated the circumference of the earth (1668–70).

Pic•ar•dy (pĭk′ər-dē). A historical region of N France bordering on the English Channel; became part of the French crown lands in 1477.

pic•a•resque (pĭk′ə-rĕsk′, pē′kə-) *adj.* **1.** Of or involving clever rogues or adventurers. **2.** Of or relating to a genre of prose fiction that originated in Spain and depicts in realistic detail the adventures of a rogue, often with satiric or humorous effects. —*n.* One that is picaresque. [Fr. < Sp. *picaresco* < *pícaro,* picaro. See PICARO.]

Pablo Picasso
Photographed c. 1953

pi•ca•ro (pē′kä-rō) *n., pl.* **-ros** (-rōz′, -rōs′). A bohemian adventurer; a rogue. [Sp. *pícaro,* perh. < *picar,* to prick < VLat. **piccāre.* See PIQUE.]

pic•a•roon (pĭk′ə-ro͞on′) *n.* **1.a.** A pirate. **b.** A pirate ship. **2.** See **picaro.** — *intr.v.* **-rooned, -roon•ing, -roons.** To act as a pirate. [Sp. *picarón,* aug. of *pícaro,* picaro. See PICARO.]

Pi•cas•so (pĭ-kä′sō, -kăs′ō), **Pablo.** 1881–1973. Spanish artist who cofounded cubism (1906–25) and introduced collage.

pic•a•yune (pĭk′ə-yo͞on′) *adj.* **1.** Of little value or importance; paltry. **2.** Petty; mean. — *n.* **1.** A Spanish-American half-real piece formerly used in parts of the southern United States. **2.** A five-cent piece. **3.** Something of very little value; a trifle. [Louisiana Fr. *picaillon,* small coin < Fr. < Prov. *picaioun* < *picaio,* money, perh. < OProv. *piquar,* to jingle, clink < VLat. **piccāre,* to pierce. See PIQUE.] — **pic′a•yun′ish** *adj.*

Pic•ca•dil•ly Circus (pĭk′ə-dĭl′ē). A traffic junction and meeting place in W London, England, noted for the statue *Eros.*

pic•ca•lil•li (pĭk′ə-lĭl′ē) *n., pl.* **-lis.** A pickled relish made of various chopped vegetables. [Prob. alteration of PICKLE.]

Pic•card (pē-kärd′, -kär′), **Auguste.** 1884–1962. Swiss physicist noted for extreme altitude and depth experiments.

Piccard, Jean Felix. 1884–1963. Swiss-born Amer. chemist and aeronautical engineer.

pic•ca•ta (pĭ-kä′tə) *adj.* Sliced, sautéed, and served in a sauce containing lemon, butter, and spices. Used of meat or fish. [Ital., fem. of *piccato,* larded < Fr. *piqué,* p.part. of *piquer,* to prick, lard. See PIQUE.]

pic•co•lo[1] (pĭk′ə-lō′) *n., pl.* **-los.** *Mus.* A small flute pitched an octave above a regular flute. [Fr. < Ital., short for *(flauto) piccolo,* small (flute).] — **pic′co•lo′ist** *n.*

pic•co•lo[2] (pĭk′ə-lō′) *adj. Mus.* Of or being an instrument considerably smaller than the usual size. [Ital., small.]

pice (pīs) *n., pl.* **pice.** A monetary unit worth 1/64 of a rupee, formerly used in India. [Hindi *paisā.* See PAISA.]

pi•ce•ous (pī′sē-əs) *adj.* **1.** *Bot.* Of or relating to pitch. **2.** *Color.* Glossy black. [< Lat. *piceus* < *pix, pic-,* pitch.]

pick[1] (pĭk) *v.* **picked, pick•ing, picks.** — *tr.* **1.a.** To select from a group. **b.** To select or cull. **2.a.** To gather in; harvest. **b.** To gather the harvest from. **3.a.** To remove the outer covering of; pluck. **b.** To tear off bit by bit. **4.** To remove extraneous matter from (the teeth). **5.** To poke and pull at (something) with the fingers. **6.** To break up, separate, or detach by means of a sharp pointed instrument. **7.** To pierce or make (a hole) with a sharp pointed instrument. **8.** To take up (food) with the beak; peck. **9.** To steal the contents of. **10.** To open (a lock) without the use of a key. **11.** To provoke: *pick a fight.* **12.** *Mus.* **a.** To pluck (the strings of an instrument). **b.** To play (a tune) by plucking strings. — *intr.* **1.** To decide with care or forethought. **2.** To work with a pick. **3.** To find fault or make petty criticisms; carp. **4.** To be harvested or gathered. — *n.* **1.** The act of picking, esp. with a sharp pointed instrument. **2.** The act of selecting or choosing; choice. **3.** Something selected as the most desirable; the best or choicest part. **4.** The amount or quantity of a crop that is picked by hand. **5.** *Basketball.* The positioning of an offensive player to impede or obstruct a defender. — ***phrasal verbs.*** **pick apart.** To refute or find flaws in by close examination. **pick at. 1.** To pluck or pull at, esp. with the fingers. **2.** To eat sparingly or without appetite. **3.** *Informal.* To nag. **pick off. 1.** To shoot after singling out. **2.** *Baseball.* To catch (a base runner) off base and put out with a quick throw, as from the pitcher or catcher. **3.** *Sports.* To intercept, as a football pass. **pick on.** To tease or bully. **pick out. 1.** To choose or select. **2.** To discern from the surroundings; distinguish. **pick over.** To sort out or examine item by item. **pick up. 1.a.** To take up (something) by hand. **b.** To collect or gather. **c.** To tidy up. **2.** To take on (passengers or freight, for example). **3.** *Informal.* **a.** To acquire casually or by accident. **b.** To acquire (knowledge) by learning or experience. **c.** To claim: *picked up her shoes.* **d.** To buy. **e.** To accept (a bill or charge) in order to pay it. **f.** To come down with (a disease). **g.** To gain. **4.** *Informal.* To take into custody. **5.** *Slang.* To make casual acquaintance with, usu. in anticipation of sexual relations. **6.a.** To come upon and follow. **b.** To come upon and observe. **7.** To continue after a break. **8.** *Informal.* To improve in condition or activity. **9.** *Slang.* To pack one's belongings. — ***idioms.*** **pick and choose.** To select with great care. **pick holes in.** To seek and discover flaws or a flaw in. **pick (one's) way.** To find passage and make careful progress through it. **pick (someone) to pieces.** To criticize sharply. **pick up on.** *Informal.* **1.** To take into the mind and understand, typically with speed. **2.** To notice. [ME *piken,* to prick < OE **pīcian,* to prick, and < OFr. *piquer,* to pierce (< VLat. **piccāre;* see PIQUE).] — **pick′er** *n.*

pick[2] (pĭk) *n.* **1.** A tool for breaking hard surfaces, consisting of a curved bar sharpened at both ends and fitted to a long handle. **2.a.** A tool for picking, such as an ice pick or a toothpick. **b.** A long-toothed comb, usu. designed for curly hair. **c.** *Sports.* A pointed projection on the front of the blade of a figure skate. **3.** *Mus.* A plectrum. [ME *pik,* var. of *pike,* sharp point. See PIKE[5].]

pick[3] (pĭk) *n.* **1.** A weft thread. **2.** A throw of the shuttle in a loom. — *tr.v.* **picked, pick•ing, picks. 1.** To throw (a shuttle) across a loom. **2.** *Archaic.* To cast; pitch. [Dial. < *pick,* to pitch, thrust, var. of PITCH[2].]

pick•a•nin•ny (pĭk′ə-nĭn′ē) *n., pl.* **-nies.** *Offensive.* Used as a disparaging term for a young Black child. [Poss. < Sp. *pequeño,* small + *niño,* child, or Port. *pequenino,* dim. of *pequeno,* small.]

pick•ax or **pick•axe** (pĭk′ăks′) *n.* A pick, esp. with one end of the head pointed and the other end with a chisel edge for cutting through roots. [ME *picax,* alteration (influenced by *ax,* ax) of *picas* < OFr. *picois* (< *pic,* pick) and < Med.Lat. *pīcōsa,* both prob. < Lat. *pīcus,* woodpecker.] — **pick′ax′** *v.*

picked[1] (pĭkt) *adj.* **1.** Chosen by careful selection. **2.** Gathered, harvested, or plucked: *picked berries.*

picked[2] (pĭkt) *adj. Regional.* Pointed: *a picked cap.* [< PICK[2].]

pick•er•el (pĭk′ər-əl, pĭk′rəl) *n., pl.* **pickerel** or **-els. 1.** Any of several small North American freshwater game and food fishes of the genus *Esox,* esp. *E. reticulatus* of the eastern and southern United States. **2.** Any of various fishes, such as the walleye, similar to the pickerel. **3.** *Chiefly British.* A young pike. [ME *pikerel,* dim. of *pike,* pike. See PIKE[2].]

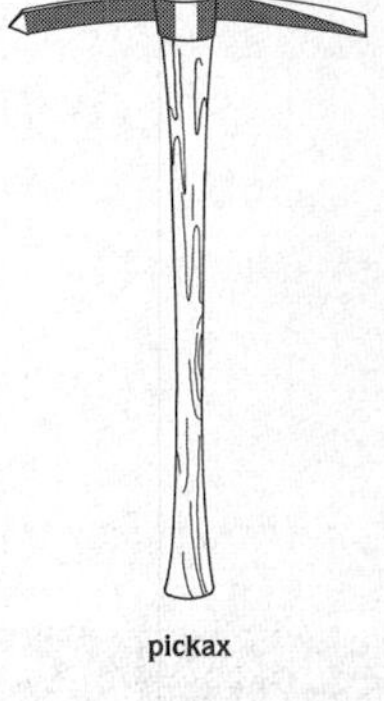

pickax

pick•er•el•weed (pĭk′ər-əl-wēd′, pĭk′rəl-) *n.* A freshwater plant *(Pontederia cordata)* of eastern North America having heart-shaped leaves with spikes of violet-blue flowers.

Pick•er•ing (pĭk′ər-ĭng). A town of S Ontario, Canada, a suburb of Toronto on Lake Ontario. Pop. 37,754.

Pickering, Edward Charles. 1846–1919. Amer. astronomer noted for his work on photometry. His brother **William Henry** (1858–1938) discovered the ninth moon of Saturn (1899).

pick•et (pĭk′ĭt) *n.* **1.** A pointed stake often driven into the ground to support a fence, secure a tent, tether animals, mark points in surveying, or, when pointed at the top, serve as a defense. **2.** A military detachment held in readiness or advanced to warn of an enemy's approach. **3.a.** A person or group of persons stationed outside a place of employment, usu. during a strike, to express grievance or protest and discourage entry by customers or nonstriking employees. **b.** A person or group of persons present outside a building to protest. — *v.* **-et•ed, -et•ing, -ets.** — *tr.* **1.** To enclose, secure, tether, mark out, or fortify with pickets. **2.a.** To post as a picket. **b.** To guard with a picket. **3.** To post a picket or pickets during a strike or demonstration. — *intr.* To act or serve as a picket. [Fr. *piquet* < OFr. < *piquer,* to prick. See PIQUE.] — **pick′et•er** *n.*

picket fence *n.* A fence of upright pointed pickets.

picket line *n.* A line or procession of picketing protesters.

Pick•ett (pĭk′ĭt), **George Edward.** 1825–75. Amer. Confederate general known for leading Pickett's Charge at Gettysburg (1863), in which three fourths of his troops were lost.

Pick•ford (pĭk′fərd), **Mary.** 1893–1979. Canadian-born American actress who appeared in numerous silent films.

Mary Pickford

pick•ing (pĭk′ĭng) *n.* **1.** The act of one that picks. **2. pickings.** Something or a group of things that are or may be picked. **3.a.** Leftovers. **b.** A share of spoils. In both senses often used in the plural.

pick•le (pĭk′əl) *n.* **1.** An edible product, esp. a cucumber, that has been preserved and flavored in a solution of brine or vinegar. **2.** A solution of brine or vinegar for preserving and flavoring food. **3.** A chemical solution, such as an acid, used as a bath to remove scale and oxides from the surface of metals before plating or finishing. **4.** *Informal.* A disagreeable or troublesome situation; a plight. — *tr.v.* **-led, -ling, -les. 1.** To preserve or flavor (food) in a brine or vinegar solution. **2.** To treat (metal) in a chemical bath. [ME *pikle,* highly seasoned sauce, prob. < MDu. *pekel,* pickle, brine.]

Word History: Trade with the Low Countries across the North Sea was important to England in the later Middle Ages, and it is perhaps because of this trade that we have the word *pickle.* Middle English *pikel,* the ancestor of our word, is first recorded around 1400 with the meaning "a spicy sauce or gravy served with meat or fowl." This sense is somewhat related to our word's possible Middle Dutch source *pekel,* a solution, such as spiced brine, for preserving and flavoring food. After coming into English the word *pickle* expanded its sense range in several ways. It was applied, as in Middle Dutch, to a pickling solution. Later *pickle* was used to refer to something so treated, such as a cucumber.

pick•led (pĭk′əld) *adj.* **1.** Preserved in or treated with pickle. **2.** *Slang.* Intoxicated; drunk.

pick•le•worm (pĭk′əl-wûrm′) *n.* The larva of a pyralid moth *(Diaphania nitidalis)* of southern North America that feeds destructively on cucumbers and gourds.

pick•lock (pĭk′lŏk′) *n.* **1.** A person who picks locks, esp. a thief. **2.** An instrument for picking a lock.

pick-me-up (pĭk′mē-ŭp′) *n. Informal.* A drink, often an alcoholic beverage, taken as a stimulant or a cure for a hangover.

pick•off (pĭk′ôf′, -ŏf′) *n.* **1.** *Baseball.* A play in which a runner is caught off base and is put out by a throw, as from the pitcher. **2.** *Sports.* An interception, as in football.

pick•pock•et (pĭk′pŏk′ĭt) *n.* One who steals from pockets.

pick•up (pĭk′ŭp′) *n.* **1.a.** The act or process of picking up. **b.** *Sports.* The act of striking or fielding a ball after it has touched the ground. **c.** Capacity for acceleration. **d.** *Informal.* An improvement in condition or activity. **e.** *Slang.* An arrest by a law enforcement officer. **2.** One that is picked up, esp.:

ă pat	oi boy
ā pay	ou out
âr care	o͝o took
ä father	o͞o boot
ĕ pet	ŭ cut
ē be	ûr urge
ĭ pit	th thin
ī pie	*th* this
îr pier	hw which
ŏ pot	zh vision
ō toe	ə about, item
ô paw	

Stress marks:
′ (primary);
′ (secondary), as in
dictionary (dĭk′shə-nĕr′ē)

a. Passengers or freight. b. *Informal.* A hitchhiker. c. *Slang.* A stranger with whom casual acquaintance is made, usu. in anticipation of sexual relations. 3. *Accounting.* A balance brought forward. 4. Previous journalistic copy to which succeeding copy is added. 5. *Mus.* The unstressed note or notes introductory to a phrase or composition. 6. One that picks up, esp.: a. A pickup truck. b. The rotary rake on a piece of machinery, such as a harvester, that picks up windrowed hay or straw. 7. *Electron.* a. A device that converts the oscillations of a phonograph needle into electrical impulses for subsequent conversion into sound. b. The tone arm of a record player. 8.a. The reception of light or sound waves for conversion to electrical impulses. b. The apparatus used for such reception. c. A telecast from outside a studio. d. The apparatus for transmitting a broadcast from an outside place to the broadcasting station. —*adj.* Being, relating to, or involving people assembled informally for a temporary purpose.

pickup truck *n.* A light truck with an open body and low sides.

pick•y (pĭk′ē) *adj.* **-i•er, -i•est.** Overmeticulous; fussy.

pic•lo•ram (pĭk′lə-răm′, pī′klə-) *n.* A compound, $C_6H_3Cl_3N_2O_2$, used as a herbicide. [PIC(OLINE) + (CH)LOR(O)- + AM(INE).]

pic•nic (pĭk′nĭk) *n.* 1. A meal eaten outdoors, as on an outing. 2. *Slang.* An easy task or a pleasant experience. 3. A boned section of a pork shoulder. —*intr.v.* **-nicked, -nick•ing, -nics.** To go on or hold a picnic. [Fr. *piquenique*, prob. redup. of *piquer*, to pick. See PIQUE.] —**pic′nick•er** *n.*

pico– *pref.* 1. One-trillionth (10^{-12}): *picosecond.* 2. Very small: *picornavirus.* [Sp. *pico*, beak, small quantity < Lat. *beccus*, beak, of Celt. orig.,. See PICARO.]

Pi•co del•la Mi•ran•do•la (pē′kō dĕl′ə mə-răn′də-lə, dĕl′lä mē-rän′dô-lä), Count **Giovanni.** 1463–94. Italian philosopher famous for his 900 theses (1486).

pi•co•far•ad (pē′kə-făr′əd, -ăd, pī′-) *n.* One trillionth (10^{-12}) of a farad.

pic•o•line (pĭk′ə-lēn′, pī′kə-) *n.* Any of three isomeric liquids, $C_5H_4N(CH_3)$, found in coal tar, tobacco smoke, and bone oil and used as a solvent. [Lat. *pix, pic-*, pitch + -OL[1] + -INE[2].]

Pico Ri•ve•ra (rə-vîr′ə). A city of S CA, a suburb of Los Angeles. Pop. 59,177.

pi•cor•na•vi•rus (pē-kôr′nə-vī′rəs, pī-) *n., pl.* **-rus•es.** Any of a group of small viruses that infect animals and consist of RNA surrounded by an icosahedral protein shell. [PICO- + RNA + VIRUS.]

pi•co•sec•ond (pē′kə-sĕk′ənd, pī′-) *n.* One trillionth (10^{-12}) of a second.

pi•cot (pē′kō, pē-kō′) *n.* A small embroidered loop forming an ornamental edging on some ribbon and lace. —*tr.v.* **-coted** (-kōd), **-cot•ing** (-kō-ĭng), **-cots** (-kōz). To trim with picots. [Fr. < OFr. < *pic*, point < *piquer*, to prick. See PIQUE.]

pic•o•tee (pĭk′ə-tē′) *n.* A carnation having pale petals bordered by a darker color. [Fr. *picoté*, p.part. of *picoter*, to mark with points < *picot*, point, picot. See PICOT.]

pi•co•wave (pē′kə-wāv′, pī′-) *tr.v.* **-waved, -wav•ing, -waves.** To irradiate (food) with gamma rays in order to kill insects or worms.

pic•quet (pĭ-kā′) *n.* Var. of **piquet.**

pic•rate (pĭk′rāt′) *n.* A salt or an ester of picric acid.

pic•ric acid (pĭk′rĭk) *n.* A poisonous, explosive crystalline solid, $C_6H_2(NO_2)_3OH$, used in explosives, dyes, and antiseptics.

picro– or **picr–** *pref.* 1. Bitter: *picrotoxin.* 2. Picric acid: *picrate.* [Gk. *pikro-* < *pikros*, bitter. See **peig-*.**]

pic•ro•tox•in (pĭk′rə-tŏk′sĭn) *n.* A bitter crystalline compound, $C_{30}H_{34}O_{13}$, derived from the seed of an East Indian woody vine *(Animirta cocculus)* and used as a stimulant, esp. in treating barbiturate poisoning. —**pic′ro•tox′ic** *adj.*

Pict (pĭkt) *n.* One of an ancient people of northern Britain who in the ninth century joined with the Scots to form a kingdom that later became Scotland. [< ME *Pictes*, Picts < LLat. *Pictī* < Lat. *pictī*, pl. of *pictus*, painted. See PICTURE.]

Pict•ish (pĭk′tĭsh) *adj.* Of or relating to the Picts or their language or culture. —*n.* The language of the Picts, of uncertain affiliation and extinct by the tenth century.

pic•to•gram (pĭk′tə-grăm′) *n.* See **pictograph.** [Lat. *pictus*, p.part. of *pingere*, to paint; see PICTOGRAPH + -GRAM.]

pic•to•graph (pĭk′tə-grăf′) *n.* 1. A picture representing a word or idea; a hieroglyph. 2. A record in hieroglyphic symbols. 3. A pictorial representation of numerical data, esp. a graph, in which a given value is represented by a picture. [Lat. *pictus*, p.part. of *pingere*, to paint; see **peig-*** + -GRAPH.] —**pic′to•graph′ic** *adj.* —**pic′to•graph′i•cal•ly** *adv.* —**pic•tog′ra•phy** (pĭk-tŏg′rə-fē) *n.*

Pic•tor (pĭk′tər) *n.* A constellation in the Southern Hemisphere near Columba and Dorado. [Lat. *pictor*, painter < *pingere*, to paint. See **peig-*.**]

pic•to•ri•al (pĭk-tôr′ē-əl, -tōr′-) *adj.* 1. Relating to, characterized by, or composed of pictures. 2. Represented as if in a picture. 3. Illustrated by pictures. —*n.* An illustrated periodical. [< Lat. *pictōrius* < *pictor*, painter. See PICTOR.] —**pic•to′•ri•al′i•ty** (-ăl′ĭ-tē), **pic•to′ri•al•ness** (-əl-nĭs) *n.* —**pic•to′ri•al•i•za′tion** (-ə-lĭ-zā′shən) *n.* —**pic•to′ri•al•ize′** (-ə-līz′) *v.* —**pic•to′ri•al•ly** *adv.*

pier
Top: Fishing pier
Bottom: Piers supporting a bridge

pic•ture (pĭk′chər) *n.* 1. A visual representation or image drawn, photographed, or otherwise rendered on a flat surface. 2. A visible image, esp. one on a flat surface: *the picture reflected in the lake.* 3.a. A vivid or realistic verbal description. b. A vivid mental image. 4. A person or an object bearing a marked resemblance to another. 5. A person or an object that typifies or embodies an emotion or a state of mind. 6. The chief circumstances of an event or time; a situation. 7. A movie. 8. A tableau vivant. —*tr.v.* **-tured, -tur•ing, -tures.** 1. To make a visible representation of. 2. To form a mental image of; visualize. 3. To describe vividly; make a verbal picture of. [ME < Lat. *pictūra* < *pictus*, painted, p.part. of *pingere*, to paint. See **peig-*.**]

picture card *n. Games.* See **face card.**

picture hat *n.* A decorated broad-brimmed hat for women.

picture puzzle *n. Games.* See **jigsaw puzzle.**

pic•tur•esque (pĭk′chə-rĕsk′) *adj.* 1. Of, suggesting, or suitable for a picture. 2. Striking or interesting in an unusual way; irregularly or quaintly attractive. 3. Strikingly expressive or vivid. [Alteration of Fr. *pittoresque* < Ital. *pittoresco* < *pittore*, painter < Lat. *pictor* < *pingere*, to paint. See **peig-*.**] —**pic′tur•esque′ness** *n.*

picture tube *n.* A cathode-ray tube in a television receiver that translates electrical signals into a picture on a luminescent screen.

picture window *n.* A large, usu. single-paned window that provides a broad outside view.

pic•ul (pĭk′əl) *n.* Any of various units of weight used in southeast Asia and China and equal to 100 catties. [Malay *pikul*, to carry the heaviest load a man can carry.]

PID *abbr.* Pelvic inflammatory disease.

pid•dle (pĭd′l) *v.* **-dled, -dling, -dles.** —*tr.* To use triflingly; squander: *piddle away one's time.* —*intr.* 1. To spend time aimlessly; diddle. 2. *Informal.* To urinate. [?]

pid•dling (pĭd′lĭng) *adj.* Trifling; trivial.

pid•dock (pĭd′ək) *n.* A marine bivalve mollusk of the family Pholadidae, having a long shell with which it bores into wood, rock, and clay, often destroying wharf pilings. [?]

pidg•in (pĭj′ən) *n.* A simplified form of speech that is usu. a mixture of two or more languages, has a rudimentary grammar and vocabulary, is used for communication between speakers of different languages, and is no one's native language. [< PIDGIN ENGLISH.] —**pidg′in•i•za′tion** *n.* —**pidg′in•ize′** *v.*

Pid•gin English also **pid•gin English** (pĭj′ən) *n.* Any of several pidgins based on English and now spoken mostly on the Pacific islands and in West Africa. [Alteration of *pigeon English* < Pidgin E. *pigeon*, business, perh. < the Chinese pronunciation of E. BUSINESS.]

pi-dog (pī′dôg′, -dŏg′) *n.* Var. of **pye-dog.**

pie[1] (pī) *n.* 1. A baked food composed of a shell of pastry that is filled with fruit, meat, or other ingredients and often covered with a pastry crust. 2. A layer cake having cream, custard, or jelly filling. 3. A whole that can be shared. —*idiom.* **pie in the sky.** n e mpty wish or promise. [ME.]

pie[2] (pī) *n.* See **magpie** 1. [ME < OFr. < Lat. *pica.*]

pie[3] (pī) *n.* A monetary unit formerly used in India and Pakistan. [Hindi *pā′ī* < Skt. *pādikā*, quarter < *pāt, pād-*, foot, leg. See **ped-*.**]

pie[4] (pī) *n.* An almanac of services used in the English church before the Reformation. [Med.Lat. *pīca.*]

pie[5] (pī) *n. & v. Print.* Var. of **pi**[2].

PIE *abbr.* Proto-Indo-European.

pie•bald (pī′bôld′) *adj.* Spotted or patched, esp. in black and white. —*n.* A piebald animal, esp. a horse. [PIE[2] + BALD.]

piece (pēs) *n.* 1. A thing considered as a unit or an element of a larger thing, quantity, or class; a portion. 2. A portion or part separated from a whole. 3. An object that is one member of a group or class: *a piece of furniture.* 4. An artistic, musical, or literary work or composition. 5. An instance; a specimen. 6. A declaration of one's opinions or findings. 7. A coin. 8. *Games.* a. One of the counters or figures used in various board games. b. Any one of the chess figures other than a pawn. 9. *Slang.* A firearm, esp. a rifle. 10. *Informal.* A given distance. 11. *Vulgar Slang.* A sexually attractive person. —*tr.v.* **pieced, piec•ing, piec•es.** 1. To mend by adding pieces or a piece to. 2. To join or unite the pieces of: *pieced together the vase.* —*idioms.* **a piece of (one's) mind.** Frank and severe criticism; censure. **of a piece.** Belonging to the same class or kind. **piece by piece.** In stages. **piece of the action.** *Slang.* A share of an activity or of profits. [ME *pece* < OFr. < VLat. **pettia*, prob. of Celt. orig.]

pièce de ré•sis•tance (pyĕs də rā-zē-stäns′) *n., pl.* **pièces de ré•sis•tance** (pyĕs). 1. An outstanding accomplishment. 2. The principal dish of a meal. [Fr. : *pièce*, piece + *de*, of, with + *résistance*, staying power, lastingness.]

piece goods *pl.n.* Fabrics made and sold in standard lengths.

piece•meal (pēs′mēl′) *adv.* 1. By a small amount at a time; in stages: *articles acquired piecemeal.* 2. In pieces; apart. —*adj.* Accomplished or made in stages. [ME *pecemeale* : *pece*, piece; see PIECE + *-mele*, by a fixed measure (< OE *-mǣlum*, at a time < dative pl. of *mǣl*, appointed time; see **mē-**[2]*).]

piece of cake *n. Informal.* Something very easy to do.

piece of eight *n., pl.* **pieces of eight.** An old Spanish silver coin. [< its original value of eight reals.]

piece•work (pēs′wûrk′) *n.* Work paid for according to the number of units turned out. — **piece′work′er** *n.*

pie chart *n.* A circular graph having radii dividing the circle into sectors proportional in angle and area to the relative size of the quantities represented.

pied[1] (pīd) *adj.* Patchy in color; splotched or piebald. [ME < *pie*, magpie. See PIE[2].]

pied[2] (pīd) *v. Print.* P.t. and p.part. of **pi**[2].

pied-à-terre (pyā-dä-târ′) *n., pl.* **pieds-à-terre** (pyā-dä-târ′). A secondary or temporary place of lodging. [Fr. : *pied*, foot + *à*, to, on + *terre*, ground.]

pied-billed grebe (pīd′bĭld′) *n.* A small brown North American diving bird *(Podilymbus podiceps)* found in freshwater ponds and having a short heavy whitish bill.

pied•mont (pēd′mŏnt′) *n.* An area of land formed or lying at the foot of a mountain or mountain range. [After PIEDMONT.]

Pied•mont (pēd′mŏnt′). **1.** A historical region of NW Italy bordering on France and Switzerland; occupied by Rome in the 1st cent. B.C. **2.** A plateau region of the E U.S. from NY to AL between the Appalachian Mts. and the Atlantic coastal plain. — **Pied′mon•tese′** (-tēz′, -tēs′) *adj. & n.*

pied piper *n.* **1.** A person who offers others strong yet delusive enticements. **2.** One who makes irresponsible promises. [After *The Pied Piper of Hamelin*, a poem by Robert Browning.]

pie-eyed (pī′īd′) *adj. Slang.* Intoxicated; drunk.

Pie•gan (pē-găn′) *n., pl.* **Piegan** or **-gans.** A member of the southernmost tribe of the Blackfoot confederacy, inhabiting northwest Montana and southern Alberta.

pie plant *n.* See **rhubarb** 1.

pier (pîr) *n.* **1.a.** A platform extending from a shore over water and supported by piles or pillars, used to secure, protect, and provide access to ships or boats. **b.** Such a platform used esp. for entertainment. **2.** A supporting structure at the junction of connecting spans of a bridge. **3.** *Archit.* Any of various vertical supporting structures, esp.: **a.** A pillar, rectangular in cross section, supporting an arch or roof. **b.** The portion of a wall between windows. **c.** A reinforcing structure that projects from a wall; a buttress. [ME *per*, bridge support, partly < Norman Fr. *pere, piere* (< OFr. *puiere*, a support < *puie*, support < *puier*, to support < VLat. **podiāre* < Lat. *podium*, platform; see PODIUM) and partly < Med.Lat. *pera* (< ONFr. *pire, piere*, breakwater, poss. < Lat. *petra*, rock < Gk.).]

pierce (pîrs) *v.* **pierced, pierc•ing, pierc•es.** — *tr.* **1.** To cut or pass through with or as if with a sharp instrument; stab or penetrate. **2.** To make a hole or opening in; perforate. **3.** To make a way through: *The path pierced the woods.* **4.** To sound sharply through: *Shouts pierced the din.* **5.** To succeed in penetrating (something) with the eyes or the intellect. — *intr.* To penetrate into or through something. [ME *percen* < OFr. *percer*, prob. < VLat **pertūsiāre* < Lat. *pertūsus*, p.part. of *pertundere*, to bore through : *per-*, per- + *tundere*, to beat.] — **pierc′er** *n.* — **pierc′ing** *adj.* — **pierc′ing•ly** *adv.*

Pierce (pîrs), **Franklin.** 1804–69. The 14th President of the U.S. (1853–57), who failed to resolve the issue of slavery.

Pi•e•ri•a (pī-îr′ē-ə). A region of ancient Macedonia including Mt. Olympus and Mt. Pierus.

Pi•e•ri•an Spring (pī-îr′ē-ən) *n.* **1.** *Gk. Myth.* A spring in Macedonia, sacred to the Muses. **2.** A source of inspiration. [< Lat. *Pierius*, sacred to the Muses < Gk. *Pieria*, Pieria. See **peiə-*.**]

Pie•ro del•la Fran•ce•sca (pyâr′ō dĕl′ə frăn-chĕs′kə, frän-). 1420?–92. Italian painter whose works show a mastery of geometric perspective.

Pierre (pîr). The capital of SD, in the central part on the Missouri R.; chosen as state cap. in 1889. Pop. 12,906.

Pierre•fonds (pē-ĕr-fôN′, pyĕr-). A city of S Quebec, Canada, on Montreal Island W of Montreal. Pop. 38,390.

Pier•rot (pē′ə-rō′, pyĕ-rō′) *n.* A character in French pantomime, dressed in a floppy white outfit. [Fr., dim. of the name *Pierre*, Peter < OFr. < Lat. *Petrus*.]

pie•tà also **Pie•tà** (pyā-tä′) *n.* A painting or sculpture of the Virgin Mary holding and mourning over the dead body of Jesus. [Ital., pity, a pietà < Lat. *pietās, pietās*. See PIETY.]

pi•e•tism (pī′ĭ-tĭz′əm) *n.* **1.** Stress on the emotional and personal aspects of religion. **2.** Affected or exaggerated piety. **3. Pietism.** A 17th- and 18th-century reform movement in the German Lutheran Church. [Ger. *Pietismus* < Lat. *pietās, pietās*, piety. See PIETY.] — **pi′e•tist** *n.* — **pi′e•tis′tic, pi′e•tis′ti•cal** *adj.* — **pi′e•tis′ti•cal•ly** *adv.*

pi•e•ty (pī′ĭ-tē) *n., pl.* **-ties. 1.** The state or quality of being pious, esp.: **a.** Religious devotion and reverence to God. **b.** Devotion and reverence to parents and family. **2.** A devout act, thought, or statement. **3.** A conventional or hypocritical position or statement. [ME *piete*, mercy, pity < OFr. < Lat. *pietās, pietās*, dutiful conduct < *pius, pius*, dutiful.]

piezo– *pref.* Pressure: *piezoelectricity.* [< Gk. *piezein*, to press tight, squeeze. See **sed-*.**]

pi•e•zo•e•lec•tric•i•ty (pī-ē′zō-ĭ-lĕk-trĭs′ĭ-tē, -ē′lĕk-, pē-ā′zō-) *n.* The generation of electricity or of electric polarity in dielectric crystals subjected to mechanical stress or the generation of stress in such crystals subjected to an applied voltage. — **pi•e′zo•e•lec′tric, pi•e′zo•e•lec′tri•cal** *adj.*

pi•e•zom•e•ter (pī′ĭ-zŏm′ĭ-tər, pē′ĭ-) *n.* An instrument for measuring pressure, esp. high pressure. — **pi•e′zo•met′ric** (pī-ē′zə-mĕt′rĭk, pē-ā′zə-), **pi′e′zo•met′ri•cal** (-rĭ-kəl) *adj.* — **pi•e′zom′e•try** *n.*

pif•fle (pĭf′əl) *intr.v.* **-fled, -fling, -fles.** To talk or act in a feeble or futile way. — *n.* Foolish or futile talk or ideas. [?]

pig (pĭg) *n.* **1.a.** Any of several mammals of the family Suidae, having short legs, cloven hoofs, bristly hair, and a cartilaginous snout used for digging. **b.** The edible parts of one of these mammals. **2.** *Informal.* A person considered piglike, greedy, or gross. **3.a.** A crude block of metal, chiefly iron or lead, poured from a smelting furnace. **b.** A mold in which such metal is cast. **c.** Pig iron. **4.** *Offensive Slang.* Used as a disparaging term for a police officer. **5.** *Slang.* A person holding sexist or racist views. — *intr.v.* **pigged, pig•ging, pigs.** To give birth to pigs; farrow. — ***phrasal verb.* pig out.** *Slang.* To eat ravenously; gorge oneself. — ***idioms.* in a pig's eye.** *Slang.* Under no condition; never. **pig in a poke.** Something that is offered in a manner that conceals its true nature or value. [ME *pigge*, young pig, prob. < OE **picga*.]

pig bed *n.* A bed of sand in which pigs of iron are cast.

pig•boat (pĭg′bōt′) *n. Slang.* A submarine.

pi•geon (pĭj′ən) *n.* **1.** Any of various birds of the widely distributed family Columbidae, typically having plump bodies, small heads, and short legs, esp. the rock dove. **2.** *Slang.* One who is easily swindled; a dupe. [ME < OFr. *pijon*, prob. < VLat. **pībiō, pībiōn-*, alteration of LLat. *pīpiō*, young chirping bird, squab < *pīpīre*, to chirp.]

pigeon breast *n.* A chest deformity marked by a projecting sternum, often occurring as a result of infantile rickets.

pigeon hawk *n.* See **merlin.**

pi•geon•hole (pĭj′ən-hōl′) *n.* **1.** A small compartment or recess, as in a desk, for papers. **2.** A specific, often oversimplified category. **3.** The hole or holes in a pigeon loft for nesting. — *tr.v.* **-holed, -hol•ing, -holes. 1.** To place or file in a pigeonhole. **2.** To classify mentally. **3.** To put aside and ignore.

pigeon pea *n.* See **cajan pea.**

pi•geon-toed (pĭj′ən-tōd′) *adj.* Having the toes turned inward.

pig•fish (pĭg′fĭsh′) *n., pl.* **pigfish** or **-fish•es.** A North American grunt *(Orthopristis chrysoptera)* with a piglike mouth, found along the Atlantic and Gulf coasts and important as a food fish. [< the grunting sound it makes.]

pig•ger•y (pĭg′ə-rē) *n., pl.* **-ies. 1.** A place where pigs are raised or kept. **2.** Piggish conduct.

pig•gish (pĭg′ĭsh) *adj.* **1.** Greedy: *a piggish appetite.* **2.** Stubborn; pigheaded. — **pig′gish•ly** *adv.* — **pig′gish•ness** *n.*

pig•gy (pĭg′ē) *n., pl.* **-gies.** *Informal.* A little pig.

pig•gy•back (pĭg′ē-băk′) *adv. & adj.* **1.** On the shoulders or back. **2.** By or relating to a method of transportation, such as one by which truck trailers are carried on trains. **3.** In connection with something larger or more important. — *n.* The act of transporting piggyback. — *v.* **-backed, -back•ing, -backs.** — *tr.* To cause to be aligned with an issue, for example, that is larger or more important. — *intr.* To function as if carried on the back of another. [Alteration of dial. *pig back*, alteration of *pickaback, pickback, pick pack* : prob. dial. *pick*, to throw (var. of PITCH[2]) + BACK[1] or PACK[1].]

piggy bank *n.* A child's coin bank, often shaped like a pig.

pig•head•ed (pĭg′hĕd′ĭd) *adj.* Stupidly obstinate. See Syns at **obstinate.** — **pig′head′ed•ly** *adv.* — **pig′head′ed•ness** *n.*

pig iron *n.* Crude iron cast in blocks.

pig Latin *n.* A code language formed by the transposition of the initial consonant to the end of the word and the suffixation of the vowel ā, as *igpay atinlay* for *pig Latin.*

pig lead (lĕd) *n.* Crude lead cast in blocks.

pig•let (pĭg′lĭt) *n.* A young pig.

pig•ment (pĭg′mənt) *n.* **1.** A substance used as coloring. **2.** Dry coloring matter, usu. an insoluble powder, that is mixed with water, oil, or another base to produce paint and similar products. **3.** A substance, such as chlorophyll or melanin, that produces a characteristic color in plant or animal tissue. — *tr.v.* **-ment•ed, -ment•ing, -ments.** To color with pigment. [ME, spice, red dye < Lat. *pigmentum* < *pingere*, to paint. See **peig-*.**] — **pig′men•tar′y** (pĭg′mən-tĕr′ē) *adj.*

pig•men•ta•tion (pĭg′mən-tā′shən) *n. Biol.* **1.** Coloration of tissues by pigment. **2.** Deposition of pigment by cells.

pigment cell *n. Biol.* See **chromatophore** 1.

Pig•my (pĭg′mē) *n. & adj.* Var. of **Pygmy.**

pigmy hippopotamus *n.* A small hippopotamus *(Choeropsis liberiensis)* of Liberia and the Ivory Coast.

pig•nut (pĭg′nŭt′) *n.* **1.** Either of two deciduous trees *(Carya glabra* or *C. ovalis)* of the eastern United States having pinnately compound leaves and nuts with somewhat bitter kernels. **2.** The nut of a pignut. **3.** The wood of a pignut.

pig-out (pĭg′out′) *n. Slang.* The act or an instance of voracious eating.

pig•pen (pĭg′pĕn′) *n.* **1.** A pen for pigs. **2.** *Slang.* A dirty or very untidy place.

Franklin Pierce

pietà
Pietà by Michelangelo, Saint Peter's Cathedral, Rome

ă pat	oi boy
ā pay	ou out
âr care	ŏŏ took
ä father	ōō boot
ĕ pet	ŭ cut
ē be	ûr urge
ĭ pit	th thin
ī pie	*th* this
îr pier	hw which
ŏ pot	zh vision
ō toe	ə about, item
ô paw	

Stress marks:
′ (primary);
′ (secondary), as in
dictionary (dĭk′shə-nĕr′ē)

Pigs (pĭgz), **Bay of.** An inlet of the Caribbean on the S coast of W Cuba; site of an ill-fated invasion by U.S.-trained guerrilla troops on Apr. 17, 1961.

pig•skin (pĭg′skĭn′) *n.* **1.** The skin of a pig. **2.** Leather made from pigskin. **3.** *Sports.* A football. **4.** *Informal.* A saddle.

pigs•ney (pĭgz′nē) *n., pl.* **-neys.** *Obsolete.* **1.** A darling. **2.** An eye. [ME *piggesnye* : *pigges*, genitive of *pigge*, pig; see PIG + *nye* (< *an eye*, an eye; see EYE).]

pig•sty (pĭg′stī′) *n., pl.* **-sties. 1.** A shelter where pigs are kept. **2.** *Slang.* A dirty or very untidy place.

pig•tail (pĭg′tāl′) *n.* **1.** A plait of braided hair. **2.** A twisted roll of tobacco. **— pig′tailed′** *adj.*

pig•weed (pĭg′wēd′) *n.* **1.** A common weed *(Chenopodium album)* having leaves with a mealy surface and small green flowers. **2.** A coarse cosmopolitan weed *(Amaranthus retroflexus)* with hairy leaves and spikes of green flowers.

pi•ka (pī′kə, pē′-) *n.* Any of several small tailless furry mammals of the genus *Ochotona* of North America and Eurasia. [Tungus *piika*, perh. < Russ. *pikat′*, to squeak.]

pike[2]
Northern pike
Esox lucius

pike[1] (pīk) *n.* A long spear formerly used by infantry. *— tr.v.* **piked, pik•ing, pikes.** To attack or pierce with a pike. [Fr. *pique* < OFr. < *piquer*, to prick. See PIQUE.] **— piked** *adj.*

pike[2] (pīk) *n., pl.* **pike** or **pikes. 1.** A freshwater game and food fish *(Esox lucius)* of the Northern Hemisphere that has a long snout and attains a length of over 1.2 meters (4 feet). **2.** Any of various similar or related fishes. [ME, perh. < OE *pīc*, sharp point (< its shape).]

pike[3] (pīk) *n.* **1.** A turnpike. **2.a.** A tollgate on a turnpike. **b.** A toll paid. *— intr.v.* **piked, pik•ing, pikes.** To move quickly. ***— idiom.* come down the pike.** *Slang.* To become prominent. [Short for TURNPIKE.]

pike[4] (pīk) *n. Chiefly British.* A hill with a pointed summit. [ME, poss. of Scand. orig.]

pike[5] (pīk) *n.* A spike or sharp point, as on the tip of a spear. [ME < OE *pīc.*]

pike[6] (pīk) *n.* A mid-air position in sports such as diving and gymnastics in which the contestant bends to touch the toes or grab the calves while keeping the legs straight. [?]

Pike (pīk), **Zebulon Montgomery.** 1779–1813. Amer. explorer noted for his expedition to the Rocky Mts. (1806–07).

piked whale (pīkt) *n.* A small dark gray whale *(Balaenoptera acutorostrata)* having a white underside.

pike•perch (pīk′pûrch′) *n., pl.* **pikeperch** or **-perch•es.** A fish that is related to the perch and resembles the pike.

pik•er (pī′kər) *n. Slang.* **1.** A cautious gambler. **2.** A person regarded as petty or stingy. [Poss. < *Piker*, a poor migrant to CA, after *Pike* County in E MO.]

Pikes Peak (pīks). A mountain, 4,303.6 m (14,110 ft), of the Rocky Mts. in central CO; named after Zebulon M. Pike.

pike•staff (pīk′stăf′) *n.* **1.** The shaft of a pike. **2.** A walking stick tipped with a metal spike.

pi•laf or **pi•laff** (pĭ-läf′, pē′läf′) also **pi•lau** (pĭ-läf′, -lô′, -lou′, pē′läf′, -lô′, -lou′) *n.* A steamed rice dish often with meat, shellfish, or vegetables. [Pers. *pilāw* < Turk. *pilâv.*]

pilaster

pi•lar (pī′lər) *adj.* Of, relating to, or covered with hair. [NLat. *pilāris* < Lat. *pilus*, hair.]

pi•las•ter (pĭ-lăs′tər) *n. Archit.* A rectangular column with a capital and base, set into a wall as an ornamental motif. [Fr. *pilastre* < OFr. < OItal. *pilastro* < Med.Lat. *pīlaster* : Lat. *pīla*, pillar + Lat. *-aster*, n. suff., or blend of Lat. *pīla*, pillar, and LLat. *parastatēs*, pilaster (< Gk., stay, supporter : *para-*, beside; see PARA-[1] + *-statēs*, -stat).]

Pi•late (pī′lət), **Pontius.** fl. 1st cent. A.D. Roman governor of Judea who ordered Jesus's crucifixion.

Pi•la•tus (pĭ-lä′təs, pē-lä′to͞os). A peak, 2,121.3 m (6,955 ft), in the Alps of central Switzerland; so named supposedly because Pontius Pilate's body was thrown into a lake here.

pil•chard (pĭl′chərd) *n.* Any of various small marine fishes related to the herrings, esp. the edible species *Sardina pilchardus* of European waters. [?]

Pil•co•ma•yo (pĭl′kō-mä′yō, pēl′-). A river of central South America rising in central Bolivia and flowing c. 1,609 km (1,000 mi) SE to the Paraguay R.

pillory
At Colonial Williamsburg, Virginia

pile[1] (pīl) *n.* **1.** A quantity of objects stacked or thrown together in a heap. **2.** *Informal.* A large accumulation or quantity. **3.** *Slang.* A large sum of money; a fortune. **4.** A funeral pyre. **5.** A very large building or complex of buildings. **6.** A voltaic pile. *— v.* **piled, pil•ing, piles.** *— tr.* **1.a.** To place or lay in or as if in a pile or heap. **b.** To load (something) with a heap or pile. **2.** To heap (something) in abundance. *— intr.* **1.** To form a heap or pile. **2.** To move in, out, or forward in a disorderly mass or group: *pile into a bus.* ***— phrasal verb.* pile up. 1.** To accumulate. **2.** *Informal.* To undergo a serious vehicular collision. [ME < OFr. < Lat. *pīla*, pillar.]

pile[2] (pīl) *n.* **1.** A heavy beam of timber, concrete, or steel, driven into the earth as a foundation or support for a structure. **2.** *Her.* A wedge-shaped charge pointing downward. **3.** A Roman javelin. *— tr.v.* **piled, pil•ing, piles. 1.** To drive piles into. **2.** To support with piles. [ME < OE *pīl*, shaft, stake < Lat. *pīlum*, spear, pestle.]

pile[3] (pīl) *n.* **1.a.** Cut or uncut loops of yarn forming the surface of certain fabrics, such as velvet and carpeting. **b.** The surface so formed. **2.** Soft fine hair, fur, or wool. [< ME *piles*, hair, plumage, prob. < MDu. *pijl*, fine hair, and MLGer. *pile*, downy plumage, both < Lat. *pilus*, hair.] **— piled** *adj.*

pi•le•at•ed (pī′lē-ā′tĭd) also **pi•le•ate** (-ĭt) *adj.* **1.** *Bot.* Having a pileus. **2.** Having a crest covering the pileum. Used of a bird. [< Lat. *pīleātus*, wearing a pileus < *pīleus*, felt cap.]

pileated woodpecker *n.* A large North American woodpecker *(Dryocopus pileatus)* having black and white plumage and a bright red crest.

pile driver *n.* A machine that drives a pile by raising a weight between guideposts and dropping it on the head of the pile.

piles (pīlz) *pl.n.* See **hemorrhoid** 2. [ME *piles* < Med.Lat. *pilī* < Lat. *pila*, ball.]

pi•le•um (pī′lē-əm) *n., pl.* **-le•a** (-lē-ə). The top of a bird's head, extending from the base of the bill to the nape. [NLat. *pīleum* < Lat. *pīleus*, felt cap.]

pile•up or **pile-up** (pīl′ŭp′) *n.* **1.** *Informal.* A serious collision usu. involving several motor vehicles. **2.** An accumulation.

pi•le•us (pī′lē-əs) *n., pl.* **-le•i** (-lē-ī′). **1.** *Bot.* The umbrellalike fruiting structure forming the top of a stalked fleshy fungus; the cap. **2.** A brimless skullcap worn by ancient Romans. **3.** See **caul** 1. [NLat. *pīleus* < Lat., cap.]

pile•wort (pīl′wûrt′, -wôrt′) *n.* Any of several plants, such as the lesser celandine and the fireweed, reputed to be effective in treating hemorrhoids. [< its use in treating piles.]

pil•fer (pĭl′fər) *v.* **-fered, -fer•ing, -fers.** *— tr.* To steal (a small amount or item). *— intr.* To steal or filch. [< ME *pilfre*, spoils < OFr. *pelfre.*] **— pil′fer•age** (-ĭj) *n.* **— pil′fer•er** *n.*

pil•grim (pĭl′grəm) *n.* **1.** A religious devotee who journeys to a shrine or sacred place. **2.** One who embarks on a quest for something held sacred. **3.** A traveler. **4. Pilgrim.** One of the English separatists who founded Plymouth Colony in 1620. [ME < OFr. *peligrin* < LLat. *pelegrīnus*, alteration of Lat. *peregrīnus*, foreigner. See PEREGRINE.]

pil•grim•age (pĭl′grə-mĭj) *n.* **1.** A journey to a sacred place or shrine. **2.** A long journey or search, esp. one of exalted purpose or moral significance. **— pil′grim•age** *v.*

pilgrim bottle *n.* A costrel.

pi•li (pī′lī′) *n.* Pl. of **pilus.**

pi•lif•er•ous (pī-lĭf′ər-əs) *adj.* Bearing or producing hair. [Lat. *pilus*, hair + -FEROUS.]

pil•i•form (pĭl′ə-fôrm′) *adj.* Having the form of a hair. [Lat. *pilus*, hair + -FORM.]

pil•ing (pī′lĭng) *n.* **1.** The act of driving piles. **2.** Piles considered as a group. **3.** A structure composed of piles.

Pil•i•pi•no (pĭl′ə-pē′nō) *n.* The Filipino language. [Tagalog < *pilipino*, Filipino < Sp. *filipino* < *Filipinas*, the Philippines.]

pill[1] (pĭl) *n.* **1.** A small, often coated pellet or tablet of medicine, taken by swallowing or by chewing. **2.** *Informal.* An oral contraceptive. **3.** *Slang.* Something, such as a baseball, that resembles a medicinal pill. **4.** Something distasteful but necessary. **5.** *Slang.* An insipid or ill-natured person. *— v.* **pilled, pil•ling, pills.** *— tr.* **1.** To dose with pills. **2.** To make into pills. **3.** *Slang.* To blackball. *— intr.* To form small balls resembling pills. [ME *pille* < MDu. or MLGer. *pille* and OFr. *pile*, all < Lat. *pilula*, dim. of *pila*, ball.]

pill[2] (pĭl) *v.* **pilled, pil•ling, pills.** *— intr. Chiefly British.* To come off, as in flakes or scales. *— tr. Archaic.* To subject to extortion. [ME *pillen*, to plunder, peel < OE *pilian*; see PEEL[1], and < OFr. *piller*, to plunder; see PILLAGE.]

pil•lage (pĭl′ĭj) *v.* **-laged, -lag•ing, -lag•es.** *— tr.* **1.** To rob of goods by force, esp. in wartime; plunder. **2.** To take as spoils. *— intr.* To take spoils by force. *— n.* **1.** The act of pillaging. **2.** Something pillaged; spoils. [< ME, booty < OFr. < *piller*, to plunder < VLat. **pīliāre* and *peille*, rag (prob. < Lat. *pilleus*, *pīleus*, felt cap).] **— pil′lag•er** *n.*

pil•lar (pĭl′ər) *n.* **1.a.** A slender freestanding vertical support; a column. **b.** Such a structure or one like it used for decoration. **2.** One who occupies a central or responsible position: *a pillar of the state.* *— tr.v.* **-lared, -lar•ing, -lars.** To support or decorate with pillars or a pillar. ***— idiom.* from pillar to post.** From one place to another; hither and thither. [ME < OFr. *pilier* < Med.Lat. *pīlāre* < Lat. *pīla.*]

Pil•lars of Her•cu•les (pĭl′ərz; hûr′kyə-lēz′). Two promontories at the E end of the Strait of Gibraltar and the entrance to the Mediterranean; usu. identified as Gibraltar in Europe and Jebel Musa in North Africa.

pill•box (pĭl′bŏks′) *n.* **1.** A small box for pills. **2.** A woman's small hat with upright sides and a flat crown. **3.** A low-roofed concrete emplacement for a machine gun or antitank gun.

pill bug *n.* A small terrestrial isopod crustacean of the genus *Armadillidium*, related to the sow bug and having a convex segmented body enabling it to curl up when disturbed.

pil•lion (pĭl′yən) *n.* **1.** A pad or cushion for an extra rider behind the saddle on a horse or motorcycle. **2.** A bicycle or motorcycle saddle. [Prob. < Sc.Gael., *pillean*, dim. of *peall*, rug, or Ir.Gael. *pillín*, dim. of *pell*, rug, both < OIr. *pell* < Lat. *pellis*, animal skin. See **pel-**[3]*.]

pil•lo•ry (pĭl′ə-rē) *n., pl.* **-ries.** A wooden framework on a post, with holes for the head and hands, in which offenders were formerly locked to be exposed to public scorn as punishment. *— tr.v.* **-ried, -ry•ing, -ries. 1.** To ridicule and abuse.

2. To put in a pillory as punishment. [ME < OFr. *pilori*, prob. < Lat. *pīla*, pillar.]

pil•low (pĭl′ō) *n.* **1.** A cloth case, stuffed with something soft, such as down, used to cushion the head, esp. during sleep. **2.** A decorative cushion. **3.** The pad on which bobbin lace is made. — *v.* **-lowed, -low•ing, -lows.** — *tr.* **1.** To rest (one's head) on or as if on a pillow. **2.** To serve as a pillow for: *Grass pillowed my head.* — *intr.* **1.** To rest on or as if on a pillow. **2.** To assume the shape of a pillow. [ME < OE *pyle* < West Gmc. **pulwī* < Lat. *pulvīnus*.] —**pil′low•y** *adj.*

pillow block *n.* A block that encloses and supports a journal or shaft; a bearing.

pil•low•case (pĭl′ō-kās′) *n.* A removable pillow covering.

pillow lace *n.* See **bobbin lace.**

pillow sham *n.* A decorative covering for a pillow on a bed.

pil•low•slip (pĭl′ō-slĭp′) *n.* See **pillowcase.**

pillow talk *n.* Intimate conversation between lovers in bed.

pi•lo•car•pine (pī′lō-kär′pēn′) *n.* A poisonous compound, $C_{11}H_{16}N_2O_2$, obtained from the jaborandi and used to induce sweating, promote salivation, and treat glaucoma. [NLat. *Pilocarpus*, jaborandi genus (Gk. *pilos*, wool, felt + Gk. *karpos*, fruit; see -CARP) + -INE2.]

pi•lose (pī′lōs) also **pi•lous** (-ləs) *adj.* Covered with fine soft hair. [Lat. *pilōsus* < *pilus*, hair.] —**pi•los′i•ty** (-lŏs′ĭ-tē) *n.*

pi•lot (pī′lət) *n.* **1.** One who operates or is licensed to operate an aircraft in flight. **2.** *Naut.* **a.** One licensed to conduct a ship into and out of port or through dangerous waters. **b.** The helmsman of a ship. **3.** One who guides or directs others. **4.** The part of a tool, device, or machine that leads or guides the whole. **5.** A pilot light, as in a stove. **6.** A television program produced as a prototype of a series under consideration. — *tr.v.* **-lot•ed, -lot•ing, -lots. 1.** To serve as the pilot of. **2.** To steer or control the course of. — *adj.* **1.** Serving as a tentative model for future experiment or development. **2.** Serving or leading as guide. [Obsolete Fr., helmsman < OFr. < OItal. *pilota*, alteration of *pedota*, prob. < Med.Gk. **pēdōtēs* < Gk. *pēdon*, steering oar. See **ped-*.**]

Word History: The pilot of a flying aircraft has a foot on the ground not literally but etymologically. The word *pilot* goes back to the Indo-European root *ped–*, meaning "foot." From the lengthened-grade suffixed form *pēdo–* came the Greek word *pēdon*, "blade of an oar," and in the plural, "rudder." The assumed Medieval Greek derivative *pēdōtēs*, "steersman," passed into Old Italian, acquiring the forms *pedota* and *pilota*, the source of Old French *pilot*. English borrowed the word from French, and as *pilot* it was first recorded in 1848 with reference to an airborne pilot — a balloonist.

pi•lot•age (pī′lə-tĭj) *n.* **1.** *Naut.* **a.** The technique or act of piloting. **b.** The fee paid to a pilot. **2.** Aerial navigation by visual identification of landmarks.

pilot balloon *n.* A balloon for determining wind velocity.

pilot burner *n.* **1.** A small service burner, as in a boiler system, kept lighted to ignite main fires. **2.** See **pilot light** 1.

pilot engine *n.* A locomotive sent ahead of a train to check the track for safety and clearance.

pilot fish *n.* A small slender marine fish *(Naucrates ductor)* that often swims with larger fishes, esp. sharks and mantas.

pi•lot•house (pī′lət-hous′) *n.* *Naut.* An enclosed area, usu. on a vessel's bridge, from which the vessel is controlled.

pi•lot•ing (pī′lə-tĭng) *n.* **1.** The occupation or service of a pilot. **2.** *Naut.* Coastal navigation, as by reference to buoys.

pilot lamp *n.* A small electric lamp used to indicate that an electric circuit is energized.

pilot light *n.* **1.** A small jet of gas that is kept burning in order to ignite a gas burner, as in a stove. **2.** See **pilot lamp.**

pilot whale *n.* Any of several large, usu. black dolphins of the genus *Globicephala,* having an outward-curving globular forehead and noted for their occasional mass strandings.

pi•lous (pī′ləs) *adj.* **1.** Var. of **pilose. 2.** Of the nature of hair; consisting of hair; hairlike. [< Lat. *pilōsus*. See PILOSE.]

Pil•sud•ski (pĭl-so͝ot′skē), **Jozef.** 1867–1935. Polish politician and first president (1918–22) of independent Poland.

Pilt•down man (pĭlt′doun′) *n.* A supposed early species of human being postulated from a skull allegedly found in a gravel bed in about 1912 but determined in 1953 to be a fake. [After *Piltdown* Common in SE England.]

pil•ule (pĭl′yo͞ol) *n.* A small pill or pellet. [Fr. < OFr. *pillule* < Lat. *pilula*. See PILL1.] —**pil′u•lar** (pĭl′yə-lər) *adj.*

pi•lus (pī′ləs) *n., pl.* **-li** (-lī′). A hair or hairlike structure, esp. on the surface of a cell or microorganism. [Lat.]

Pi•ma (pē′mə) *n., pl.* **Pima** or **-mas. 1.** A member of a Native American people inhabiting south-central Arizona. **2.** The Uto-Aztecan language of the Pima. [< Am.Sp. *Pimahitos*, Pimas < obsolete Pima *pimahaitu*, nothing.] —**Pi′man** *adj.*

pi•ma cotton (pē′mə) *n.* A very strong high-grade cotton of medium staple developed from Egyptian cottons in the southwest United States. [After *Pima* County in S AZ.]

pi•men•to (pĭ-mĕn′tō) *n., pl.* **-tos. 1.** See **allspice. 2.** Var. of **pimiento.** [Sp. *pimiento*, red or green pepper, pepper plant < *pimienta*, black pepper, pepper fruit < LLat. *pigmenta*, pl. of *pigmentum*, vegetable juice, condiment, pigment < Lat., pigment < *pingere*, to paint. See **peig-*.**]

pi meson *n.* *Phys.* See **pion.**

pi•mien•to (pĭ-mĕn′tō, -myĕn′tō) also **pi•men•to** (-mĕn′tō) *n., pl.* **-tos. 1.** A garden pepper *(Capsicum annuum)* having a mild red fruit. **2.** The fruit of this plant, used in cookery, salad, and as stuffing for green olives. [Sp. See PIMENTO.]

pimp (pĭmp) *n.* One who finds customers for a prostitute; a procurer. [?] —**pimp** *v.*

pim•per•nel (pĭm′pər-nĕl′, -nəl) *n.* Any of various plants of the genus *Anagallis*, esp. the scarlet pimpernel *(A. arvensis),* having opposite entire leaves and small red flowers. [ME *pimpernelle* < OFr., alteration of *piprenelle* < LLat. *pimpinella*, perh. < Lat. *piper*, pepper. See PEPPER.]

pim•ple (pĭm′pəl) *n.* A small red swelling of the skin, usu. caused by acne; a papule or pustule. [ME.] —**pim′pled, pim′ply** *adj.*

pin (pĭn) *n.* **1.a.** A short, straight, stiff piece of wire with a blunt head and a sharp point, used esp. for fastening. **b.** Something, such as a safety pin, that resembles such a piece of wire in shape or use. **c.** A whit; a jot. **2.** A slender, usu. cylindrical piece of wood or metal for holding or fastening parts together or serving as a support for suspending one thing from another, as: **a.** A thin rod for securing the ends of fractured bones. **b.** A peg for fixing the crown to the root of a tooth. **c.** A cotter pin. **d.** The part of a key stem entering a lock. **e.** *Mus.* One of the pegs securing the strings and regulating their tension on a stringed instrument. **f.** *Naut.* A belaying pin. **g.** *Naut.* A thole pin. **3.** An ornament fastened to clothing by means of a clasp. **4.** A rolling pin. **5.** *Sports.* **a.** One of the wooden clubs at which the ball is aimed in bowling. **b.** A flagstick. **c.** See **fall** 14a. **6. pins.** *Informal.* The legs. **7.** *Electron.* A lead on a device that plugs into a socket to connect the device to a system. **8.** *Comp. Sci.* **a.** Any of the pegs on the platen of a printer that engage holes at the edges of paper. **b.** Any of the styluses that form a dot matrix on a printer. — *tr.v.* **pinned, pin•ning, pins. 1.** To fasten or secure with or as if with a pin or pins. **2.** To transfix. **3.** To place in a position of trusting dependence. **4.a.** To hold fast; immobilize. **b.** *Sports.* To win a fall from in wrestling. — *adj.* Having a grain suggestive of the heads of pins. Used of leather. —***phrasal verbs.*** **pin down. 1.** To fix or establish clearly. **2.** To force (someone) to give firm opinions or precise information. **pin on.** To attribute (a wrongdoing or crime) to. [ME < OE *pinn*, perh. < Lat. *pinna*, feather. See **pet-*.**]

pi•ña cloth (pēn′yə) *n.* A soft sheer fabric made from the fibers of pineapple leaves. [Sp. *piña*, pine cone, pineapple < Lat. *pīnea*, pine cone < *pīnus*, pine. See **peiə-*.**]

pi•ña co•la•da (pēn′yə kō-lä′də, kə-, pĭn′-) *n.* A drink made of rum, coconut cream, and unsweetened pineapple juice. [Sp., strained pineapple : *piña*, pineapple + *colada*, strained.]

pin•a•fore (pĭn′ə-fôr′, -fōr′) *n.* A sleeveless garment similar to an apron, worn esp. by girls as a dress or an overdress. [PIN + AFORE (formerly pinned to the front of the dress).]

Pi•nang (pə-năng′, pē′näng′). See **George Town** 1.

pi•nas•ter (pī-năs′tər) *n.* A Mediterranean pine tree *(Pinus pinaster)* having a characteristic pyramidal form and needles in fascicles of two. [Lat., wild pine < *pīnus*, pine. See PINE1.]

pi•ña•ta (pēn-yä′tə) *n.* *Games.* A decorated container filled with candy and toys and suspended from a height, intended to be broken by blindfolded players with sticks in a game of Latin-American origin. [Sp. < Ital. *pignatta*, a pot, prob. < dial. *pigna*, pine cone < Lat. *pīnea*. See PINEAL.]

pin•ball (pĭn′bôl′) *n.* *Games.* A game in which the player operates a plunger to shoot a ball through a box past obstacles.

pince-nez (păns′nā′, pĭns′-) *n., pl.* **pince-nez** (-nāz′, -nā′). Eyeglasses clipped to the bridge of the nose. [Fr. : *pincer*, to pinch (< OFr. *pincier*; see PINCH) + *nez*, nose (< Lat. *nāsus*; see **nas-***).]

pin•cer (pĭn′sər) *n.* **1.** An object resembling one of the grasping parts of a set of pincers. **2.** A maneuver in which an enemy force is attacked from two flanks and the front.

pin•cers (pĭn′sərz) also **pinch•ers** (pĭn′chərz) *pl.n. (used with a sing. or pl. v.)* **1.** A grasping tool having a pair of jaws and handles pivoted together to work in opposition. **2.** The prehensile claws of certain arthropods, such as the lobster. [ME *pinsours* < OFr. *pinceure* < OFr. *pincier*, to pinch. See PINCH.]

pinch (pĭnch) *v.* **pinched, pinch•ing, pinch•es.** — *tr.* **1.** To squeeze between the thumb and a finger, the jaws of a tool, or other edges. **2.** To squeeze or bind (a part of the body) so as to cause discomfort or pain. **3.** To nip, wither, or shrivel. **4.** To straiten. **5.** *Slang.* To take (money or property) unlawfully; steal. **6.** *Slang.* To take into custody; arrest. **7.** To move (something) by means of a pinch bar. **8.** *Naut.* To point (a boat) so close to the wind as to cause the sails to stall. — *intr.* **1.** To press, squeeze, or bind painfully. **2.** To be miserly. **3.** *Naut.* To drag an oar at the end of a stroke. — *n.* **1.** The act or an instance of pinching. **2.** An amount that can be held between thumb and forefinger. **3.** A painful, difficult, or straitened circumstance. **4.** An emergency situation. **5.** A narrowing of a mineral deposit, as in a mine. **6.** *Informal.* A theft. **7.** *Slang.* An arrest by a law enforcement officer. — *adj.* *Baseball.* Relating to pinch-hitting or pinch runners. —***idiom.*** **pinch pennies.** *Informal.* To be thrifty or miserly.

piñata

pince-nez
Worn by Theodore Roosevelt

ă **pat**	oi **boy**
ā **pay**	ou **out**
âr **care**	o͝o **took**
ä **father**	o͞o **boot**
ĕ **pet**	ŭ **cut**
ē **be**	ûr **urge**
ĭ **pit**	th **thin**
ī **pie**	*th* **this**
îr **pier**	hw **which**
ŏ **pot**	zh **vision**
ō **toe**	ə **about,**
ô **paw**	**item**

Stress marks:
′ (primary);
′ (secondary), as in
dictionary (dĭk′shə-nĕr′ē)

[ME *pinchen* < ONFr. **pinchier*, var. of OFr. *pincier*, perh. < VLat. **pīnctiāre*.]

pinch bar *n.* A crowbar with a pointed projection at one end.

pinch•beck (pĭnch′bĕk′) *n.* **1.** An alloy of zinc and copper used as imitation gold. **2.** A cheap imitation. —*adj.* **1.** Made of pinchbeck. **2.** Imitation; spurious. [After Christopher *Pinchbeck* (1670?–1732), English watchmaker.]

pinch•cock (pĭnch′kŏk′) *n.* A clamp used to regulate or close a flexible tube, esp. in laboratory apparatus.

pinch effect *n. Phys.* Radial constriction of flowing plasma or other matter carrying an electric current, caused by the magnetic field that is produced by the current.

pinch-hit (pĭnch′hĭt′) *intr.v.* **-hit, -hit•ting, -hits. 1.** *Baseball.* To bat in place of the scheduled batter, esp. when a hit is needed. **2.** *Informal.* To substitute for another in a time of need. —**pinch hitter** *n.*

pinch•pen•ny (pĭnch′pĕn′ē) *adj.* **1.** Miserly; penny-pinching. **2.** Marked by scarcity of money. —**pinch′pen′ny** *n.*

pinch runner *n. Baseball.* A substitute base runner.

Pinck•ney (pĭngk′nē), **Charles Cotesworth.** 1746–1825. Amer. minister to France (1797) who refused to bribe French negotiators, causing the conflict known as the XYZ Affair.

pin clover *n.* See **alfilaria.**

pin curl *n.* A usu. damp coiled strand of hair secured with a bobby pin or clip and combed into a wave or curl when dry.

pin•cush•ion (pĭn′ko͝osh′ən) *n.* A small firm cushion into which pins are stuck when not in use.

Pin•dar (pĭn′dər). 522?–443? B.C. Greek lyric poet remembered esp. for his *Odes.*

Pin•dar•ic (pĭn-dăr′ĭk) *adj.* **1.** Relating to or characteristic of the poetic style of Pindar. **2.** Of or characteristic of a Pindaric ode. —*n.* A Pindaric ode.

Pindaric ode *n.* An ode in the form used by Pindar, consisting of a series of triads in which the strophe and antistrophe have the same stanza form and the epode has a different form.

Pin•dus Mountains (pĭn′dəs). A range of mountains extending c. 161 km (100 mi) S from S Albania to NW Greece and rising to 2,638.3 m (8,650 ft).

pine[1] (pīn) *n.* **1.** Any of various evergreen trees of the genus *Pinus,* having fascicles of needle-shaped leaves and producing woody seed-bearing cones. **2.** Any of various other coniferous trees, such as the Norfolk Island pine. **3.** The wood of any of these trees. [ME < OE *pīn-* (as in *pīntreow,* pine tree) < Lat. *pīnus.* See **peiə-*.**]

pine[2] (pīn) *v.* **pined, pin•ing, pines.** —*intr.* **1.** To feel a lingering, often nostalgic desire. **2.** To wither or waste away from longing or grief: *pined away.* —*tr. Archaic.* To grieve or mourn for. —*n. Archaic.* Intense longing or grief. [ME *pinen* < OE *pīnian,* to cause to suffer < **pīne,* pain < VLat. **pēna,* penalty, var. of Lat. *poena* < Gk. *poinē.* See **kʷei-[1]*.**]

pin•e•al (pĭn′ē-əl, pī′nē-) *adj.* **1.** Having the form of a pine cone. **2.** Of or relating to the pineal gland. [Fr. *pinéal* < Lat. *pīnea,* pine cone < fem. of *pīneus,* of pine < *pīnus,* pine tree. See **peiə-*.**]

pineal body *n.* See **pineal gland.**

pineal gland *n.* A small cone-shaped organ in the brain of most vertebrates that secretes the hormone melatonin.

pine•ap•ple (pīn′ăp′əl) *n.* **1.a.** A tropical American plant *(Ananas comosus)* having large swordlike leaves and a large edible multiple fruit with a terminal tuft of leaves. **b.** Its fruit. **2.** *Slang.* A hand grenade. [ME *pinappel,* pine cone : *pine,* pine; see PINE[1] + *appel,* apple; see APPLE.]

pineapple weed *n.* A western North American plant *(Matricaria matricarioides)* having greenish-yellow discoid flower heads and an odor of pineapple when crushed.

Pine Bar•rens (pīn băr′ənz). A coastal plain region of SE-central and S NJ.

Pine Bluff (blŭf′). A city of SE-central AR SSE of Little Rock; founded c. 1820. Pop. 57,140.

pine•drops (pīn′drŏps′) *pl.n. (used with a sing. or pl. v.)* A purplish-brown, leafless North American plant *(Pterospora andromedea)* living as a parasite on roots and having reddish or white flowers arranged in a terminal raceme.

pine finch *n.* See **pine siskin.**

Pine Hills. A community of central FL, a suburb of Orlando. Pop. 35,322.

pine•land (pīn′lănd′, lənd) *n.* A forested area in which pine trees predominate. Also used in the plural.

Pi•nel•las Park (pī-nĕl′əs). A city of W-central FL, a suburb of St. Petersburg. Pop. 43,426.

pine mouse *n.* Any of various voles of the genus *Pitymys,* esp. *P. pinetorum* of eastern North America.

pi•nene (pī′nēn′) *n.* Either of two isomeric terpene liquids, $C_{10}H_{16}$, used as solvents and in making resins.

pine nut *n.* The edible seed of certain pines, such as the piñon.

Pi•ne•ro (pə-nîr′ō), Sir **Arthur Wing.** 1855–1934. British playwright whose farces include *Dandy Dick* (1887).

pin•er•y (pī′nə-rē) *n., pl.* **-ies. 1.** A hothouse or plantation where pineapples are grown. **2.** A forest of pine trees.

pine•sap (pīn′săp′) *n.* A white or reddish plant *(Monotropa hypopithys)* growing as a saprophyte or parasite on tree roots and having racemes with drooping flowers.

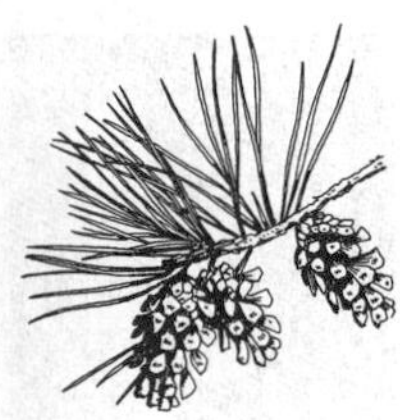

pine[1]
Scotch pine
Pinus sylvestris

pineapple
Ananas comosus

pinnace

pintail
Male pintail
Anas acuta

pine siskin *n.* A North American finch *(Carduelis pinus)* having streaked brownish plumage.

pine snake *n.* Any of various bull snakes common in pine woods, esp. *Pituophis melanoleucus* of the eastern United States.

pine straw *n. Chiefly Southern U.S.* Dead fallen pine needles.

pine tar *n.* A viscous or semisolid brown-to-black substance produced by the destructive distillation of pine wood and used in roofing compositions and as an expectorant and antiseptic.

pi•ne•tum (pī-nē′təm) *n., pl.* **-ta** (-tə). An area planted with pine trees or related conifers, esp. for botanical study. [Lat. *pīnētum,* pine grove < *pīnus,* pine. See PINE[1].]

pine vole *n.* See **pine mouse.**

pine warbler *n.* A small yellow-breasted songbird *(Dendroica pinus)* found in pine forests of the eastern United States.

pine•wood (pīn′wo͝od′) *n.* **1.** The wood of the pine tree. **2.** A forest of pines. Often used in the plural.

pine•y (pī′nē) *adj.* Var. of **piny.**

pin•feath•er (pĭn′fĕth′ər) *n.* A growing feather still enclosed in its horny sheath, esp. one just emerging through the skin.

pin•fish (pĭn′fĭsh′) *n., pl.* **pinfish** or **-fish•es.** A small spiny-finned fish *(Lagodon rhomboides)* found along the southeast coast of the United States.

pin•fold (pĭn′fōld′) *n.* An enclosure where stray animals are confined. [ME *pynfold,* alteration of OE *pundfald* : *pund-,* enclosure + *fald,* fold.] —**pin′fold′** *v.*

ping (pĭng) *n.* **1.** A sharp high-pitched sound, as that made by a bullet striking metal. **2.** See **knock** 3. —*intr.v.* **pinged, ping•ing, pings.** To make a ping. [Imit.]

Ping (pĭng). A river, c. 563 km (350 mi), of W Thailand, a major tributary of the Chao Phraya.

ping•er (pĭng′ər) *n.* A device used underwater to produce pulses of sound, as for an echo sounder.

pin•go (pĭng′gō) *n., pl.* **-gos** or **-goes.** An Arctic mound or conical hill consisting of an outer layer of soil covering a core of solid ice. [Inupiaq or Inuit *pinguq.*]

Ping-Pong (pĭng′pông′, -pŏng′). A trademark used for table tennis and associated equipment.

pin•guid (pĭn′gwĭd) *adj.* Fat; oily. [Lat. *pinguis* + *-id* (as in LIQUID).]

pin•head (pĭn′hĕd′) *n.* **1.** The head of a pin. **2.** Something very small or insignificant. **3.** *Slang.* A person regarded as stupid. —**pin′head′ed** *adj.* —**pin′head′ed•ness** *n.*

pin•hole (pĭn′hōl′) *n.* A puncture made by or as if by a pin.

pin•ion[1] (pĭn′yən) *n.* **1.** The wing of a bird. **2.** The outer rear edge of the wing of a bird, containing the primary feathers. **3.** A primary feather of a bird. —*tr.v.* **-ioned, -ion•ing, -ions. 1.a.** To remove or bind the wing feathers of (a bird) to prevent flight. **b.** To cut or bind (the wings of a bird). **2.a.** To restrain (a person) by binding the arms. **b.** To bind (a person's arms). **3.** To bind fast or hold down; shackle. [ME < OFr. *pignon* < VLat. **pinniō, pinniōn-* < Lat. *pinna,* feather. See PINNA.]

pin•ion[2] (pĭn′yən) *n.* A small cogwheel that engages or is engaged by a larger cogwheel or a rack. [Fr. *pignon* < OFr. *peignon,* prob. < *peigne,* comb < Lat. *pecten* < *pectere,* to comb.]

pink[1] (pĭngk) *n.* **1.** *Color.* Any of a group of colors reddish in hue, of medium to high lightness, and of low to moderate saturation. **2.a.** Any of various plants of the genus *Dianthus,* such as the carnation, having fragrant showy flowers. **b.** Any of various other plants, such as the wild pink. **c.** A flower of any of these plants. **3.** The highest or best degree. **4. pinks. a.** Light-colored trousers formerly worn as part of the winter semidress uniform by U.S. Army officers. **b.** The scarlet coat worn by fox hunters. **5.** *Slang.* A pinko. —*adj.* **pink•er, pink•est. 1.** *Color.* Of the color pink. **2.** *Slang.* Having moderately leftist political opinions. [?] —**pink′ness** *n.*

pink[2] (pĭngk) *tr.v.* **pinked, pink•ing, pinks. 1.** To stab lightly with a pointed weapon; prick. **2.** To decorate with a perforated pattern. **3.** To cut with pinking shears. [ME *pinken.*]

pink[3] (pĭngk) also **pink•ie** or **pink•y** (pĭng′kē) *n., pl.* **pinks** also **pink•ies.** *Naut.* A sailing vessel with a narrow overhanging stern. [ME < MDu. *pinke.*]

pink bollworm *n.* The pinkish larva of a moth *(Pectinophora gossypiella)* that is destructive to the cotton plant.

pink-col•lar (pĭngk′kŏl′ər) *adj.* Of or relating to a class of jobs, such as typist, once traditionally filled by women.

Pin•ker•ton (pĭng′kər-tən), **Allan.** 1819–84. Scottish-born detective whose agency was notorious for strikebreaking.

pink•eye (pĭngk′ī′) *n.* An acute contagious conjunctivitis, caused by the hemophilic bacterium *Hemophilus aegyptius* and characterized by inflammation of the eyelids and eyeballs.

pink•ie[1] also **pink•y** (pĭng′kē) *n., pl.* **-ies.** *Informal.* The little finger. [Prob. < Du. *pinkje,* dim. of *pink,* little finger.]

pink•ie[2] (pĭng′kē) *n. Naut.* Var. of **pink**[3].

pink•ing shears (pĭng′kĭng) *pl.n.* Shears with notched blades, used to finish edges of cloth with a zigzag cut.

pink•ish (pĭng′kĭsh) *adj. Color.* Somewhat pink.

pink lady *n.* A cocktail of gin, brandy, lemon or lime juice, egg white, and grenadine, shaken with cracked ice and strained.

pink•o (pĭng′kō) *n., pl.* **-os.** *Slang.* A person who holds moderately leftist political views; a pink.

pink•root (pĭngk′ro͞ot′, -ro͝ot′) *n.* A perennial plant *(Spigelia marilandica)* of the southeast United States, having flowers with a tubular corolla that is red outside and yellow inside.

pink root *n.* A disease of onions and related bulbous plants caused by a fungus *(Pyrenochaeta terrestris)* and resulting in stunted growth and shriveled pink roots.

pink salmon *n.* A small salmon *(Oncorhynchus gorbuscha)* of Pacific waters, the male of which has a pink color and a conspicuous dorsal hump during the spawning season.

pink slip *n. Informal.* A notice of termination of employment. — **pink′-slip′** (pĭngk′slĭp′) *v.*

Pink•ster also **Pinx•ter** (pĭngk′stər) *n. Regional.* Whitsunday or Whitsuntide. [Du. < MDu. *pinxter,* ult. < Goth. *paintekuste* < Gk. *pentēkostē,* fiftieth. See PENTECOST.]

pink•ster flower (pĭngk′stər) *n.* Var. of **pinxter flower.**

pink•y[1] (pĭng′kē) *n.* Var. of **pinkie**[1].

pink•y[2] (pĭng′kē) *n. Naut.* Var. of **pink**[3].

pin money *n.* Money for incidental expenses.

pin•na (pĭn′ə) *n., pl.* **pin•nae** (pĭn′ē) or **pin•nas. 1.** *Bot.* A leaflet or primary division of a pinnately compound leaf. **2.** *Zool.* A feather, wing, fin, or similar appendage. **3.** *Anat.* See **auricle** 1a. [Lat., feather. See **pet-*.**] — **pin′nal** *adj.*

pin•nace (pĭn′ĭs) *n. Naut.* **1.** A small sailing boat formerly used as a tender for merchant and war vessels. **2.** A small ship or ship's boat. [Fr. *pinace* < OFr., prob. < OSp. *pinaza* < *pino,* pine tree, boat < Lat. *pīnus.* See **peiə-*.**]

pin•na•cle (pĭn′ə-kəl) *n.* **1.** *Archit.* A small turret or spire on a roof or buttress. **2.** A tall pointed formation, such as a mountain peak. **3.** The highest point; the culmination. — *tr.v.* **-cled, -cling, -cles. 1.** To furnish with a pinnacle. **2.** To place on or as if on a pinnacle. [ME < OFr. < LLat. *pinnāculum,* dim. of Lat. *pinna,* feather. See **pet-*.**]

pin•nate (pĭn′āt′) also **pin•nat•ed** (-ā′tĭd) *adj.* Resembling a feather; having parts or branches arranged on each side of a common axis: *pinnate leaves.* [Lat. *pinnātus,* feathered < *pinna,* feather. See **pet-*.**] — **pin′nate′ly** *adv.*

pinnati– *pref.* Resembling a feather: *pinnatifid.* [< Lat. *pinnātus,* feathered. See PINNATE.]

pin•nat•i•fid (pĭ-năt′ə-fĭd) *adj.* Divided or cleft in a pinnate fashion. Used of certain leaves. — **pin•nat′i•fid•ly** *adv.*

pin•nat•i•sect (pĭ-năt′ĭ-sĕkt′) *adj.* Divided pinnately nearly to the midrib. Used of certain leaves.

pin•ni•ped (pĭn′ə-pĕd′) *adj.* Of or belonging to the Pinnipedia, a suborder of carnivorous aquatic mammals that includes the seals, walruses, and similar animals having finlike flippers for locomotion. [< NLat. *Pinnipedia,* order name : Lat. *pinna,* feather; see PINNA + Lat. *pēs, ped-,* foot; see -PED.] — **pin′ni•ped′** *n.*

pin•nule (pĭn′yo͞ol) also **pin•nu•la** (pĭn′yə-lə) *n., pl.* **pin•nules** also **pin•nu•lae** (pĭn′yə-lē′). **1.** *Bot.* Any of the ultimate leaflets of a bipinnately compound leaf. **2.** *Zool.* A featherlike or plumelike organ or part. [Lat. *pinnula,* dim. of *pinna,* feather. See **pet-*.**] — **pin′nu•lar** *adj.*

pi•noch•le or **pi•noc•le** (pē′nŭk′əl, -nŏk′əl) also **pe•nuch•le** or **pe•nuck•le** (pē′nŭk′əl) *n. Games.* **1.** A game of cards for two to four persons, played with a special deck of 48 cards, with points being scored by taking tricks and forming certain combinations. **2.** The combination of the queen of spades and jack of diamonds in this game. [Perh. < Ger. dial. *Binokel,* beziquelike card game < Fr. dial. *binocle,* spectacles < NLat. *binoculus,* the two eyes : BI-[1] + Lat. *oculus,* eye; see **ok^w-*.**]

pin•o•cy•to•sis (pĭn′ə-sī-tō′sĭs, -sī-, pī′nə-) *n.* Introduction of fluids into a cell by the formation of vesicles in the cell membrane. [Gk. *pinein,* to drink; see **pō(i)-*** + CYT(O)- + -OSIS.] — **pin′o•cy•tot′ic** (-tŏt′ĭk) *adj.*

pi•no•le (pĭ-nō′lē) *n.* Meal made of ground corn or wheat and mesquite beans. [Am.Sp. < Nahuatl *pinolli,* mixture of vanilla powder, spices, and ground toasted chocolate beans.]

pi•ñon also **pin•yon** (pĭn′yōn′, -yən) *n., pl.* **pi•ñons** or **pi•ño•nes** (pĭn-yō′nēz) also **pin•yons.** Any of several pine trees bearing edible nutlike seeds, esp. *Pinus edulis* of the western United States and Mexico. [Sp. *piñón,* pine nut, pine cone, aug. of *piña* < Lat. *pīnea* < fem. of *pīneus,* of pine < *pīnus,* pine tree. See **peiə-*.**]

piñon jay also **pinyon jay** *n.* A small, dull blue uncrested jay *(Gymnorhinus cyanocephala)* of western North America.

pi•not (pē′nō, pē-nō′) *n.* **1.** Any of several related white or red grapes chiefly grown in California and France and used for making wine. **2.** A white or red pinot wine. [Fr., var. of *pineau,* dim. of *pin,* pine tree < Lat. *pīnus.* See **peiə-*.**]

pin•point (pĭn′point′) *n.* **1.** Something extremely small or trifling. **2.** A very small or sharp point. **3.** A point on a map marking a precise location or target. — *tr.v.* **-point•ed, -point•ing, -points. 1.** To locate or identify with precision. **2.** To take precise aim at. **3.** To direct attention to. — *adj.* **1.** Meticulously precise. **2.** Extremely small; minuscule.

pin•prick (pĭn′prĭk′) *n.* **1.** A small puncture made by or as if by a pin. **2.** A slight wound. **3.** A minor annoyance. — **pin′prick′** *v.*

pins and needles (pĭnz) *pl.n.* A tingling sensation felt in a part of the body numbed from lack of circulation. — *idiom.* **on pins and needles.** In a state of tense anticipation.

pin•scher (pĭn′shər) *n.* A Doberman pinscher.

pin•set•ter (pĭn′sĕt′ər) *n.* An employee or a mechanical apparatus that sets up pins in a bowling alley.

Pinsk (pĭnsk, pyĕnsk). A city of SW Belorussia SSW of Minsk; cap. of the Pinsk duchy in the 13th cent. Pop. 109,000.

pin•stripe also **pin stripe** (pĭn′strīp′) *n.* **1.** A very thin stripe, esp. on a fabric. **2.a.** A fabric with very thin stripes, often used for suits. **b.** A suit made of such fabric. Often used in the plural. — **pin′striped′** *adj.*

pint (pīnt) *n.* **1.a.** A unit of volume or capacity in the U.S. Customary System, used in liquid measure, equal to 1/8 gallon or 16 ounces (0.473 liter). **b.** A unit of volume or capacity in the U.S. Customary System, used in dry measure, equal to 1/16 peck or 1/2 quart (0.551 liter). **c.** A unit of volume or capacity in the British Imperial System, used in dry and liquid measure, equal to 0.568 liter. See table at **measurement. 2.a.** A container with a pint capacity. **b.** The amount that can be held in such a container. [ME *pinte,* a unit of volume < OFr. < VLat. **pīncta,* mark on a container < fem. of **pīnctus,* p.part. of Lat. *pingere,* to paint. See **peig-*.**]

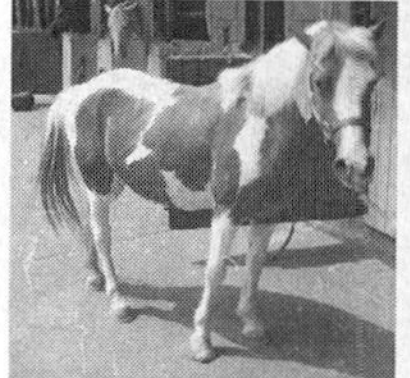
pinto

pin•ta (pĭn′tə, pēn′tä) *n.* A contagious tropical American skin disease caused by a spirochete *(Treponema carateum)* and marked by extreme thickening and spotty discoloration of the skin. [Sp., colored spot < VLat. **pīncta.* See PINT.]

pin•tail (pĭn′tāl′) *n., pl.* **pintail** or **-tails.** A duck *(Anas acuta)* of the Northern Hemisphere having gray, brown, and white plumage and a sharply pointed tail.

pin•ta•no (pĭn-tä′nō) *n., pl.* **pintano** or **-nos.** Any of various brilliantly colored damselfishes of the genus *Abudefduf,* esp. the sergeant major. [Am.Sp.]

Pin•ter (pĭn′tər), **Harold.** b. 1930. British playwright whose works include *The Dumbwaiter* (1957) and *Birthday Party* (1958). — **Pin′ter•esque′** (-ĕsk′) *adj.*

pin•tle (pĭn′tl) *n.* **1.** A pin or a bolt on which another part pivots. **2.** *Naut.* The pin on which a rudder turns. **3.** The pin on which a gun carriage revolves. **4.** A hook or a bolt on the rear of a towing vehicle for attaching a gun or trailer. [ME *pintel* < OE, penis.]

pin•to (pĭn′tō) *n., pl.* **-tos** or **-toes.** A horse with patchy markings of white and another color. — *adj.* Mottled; pied. [Sp., piebald, spotted < VLat. **pīnctus,* p.part. of Lat. *pingere,* to paint. See **peig-*.**]

pinto bean *n.* A form of the string bean that has mottled seeds and is grown esp. in the southwest United States.

pint•size (pīnt′sīz′) also **pint•sized** (-sīzd′) *adj. Informal.* Of small dimensions; diminutive.

pin•up (pĭn′ŭp′) *n.* **1.a.** A picture, esp. of a sexually attractive person, that is displayed on a wall. **b.** A person considered a suitable model for such a picture. **2.** Something intended to be affixed to a wall. — **pin′up′** *adj.*

pin•wale (pĭn′wāl′) *adj.* Made with narrow wales.

pin•weed (pĭn′wēd′) *n.* Any of various North American perennial plants of the genus *Lechea,* having narrow leaves and numerous small flowers.

piolet

pin•wheel (pĭn′hwēl′, -wēl′) *n.* **1.** A toy consisting of vanes of colored paper or plastic pinned to a stick so that they revolve when blown on. **2.** A firework that forms a rotating wheel of colored flames. **3.** A wheel with a circle of pins at right angles to its face, used as a tripping device.

pin•work (pĭn′wûrk′) *n.* Fine stitches raised from the surface of the design in the embroidery of needlepoint lace.

pin•worm (pĭn′wûrm′) *n.* Any of various small nematode worms of the family Oxyuridae that are parasitic on mammals, esp. *Enterobius vermicularis,* a species that infests the human intestines and rectum.

pin•wrench (pĭn′rĕnch′) *n.* A wrench having a projection designed to fit a hole in the object to be turned.

pinx. *abbr. Lat.* Pinxit (He or she painted it).

Pinx•ter (pĭngk′stər) *n. Regional.* Var. of **Pinkster.**

pinx•ter flower also **pink•ster flower** (pĭngk′stər) *n.* A deciduous shrub *(Rhododendron periclymenoides)* of the southeast United States having a funnel-shaped pink or purple corolla and flowers that bloom before the leaves appear.

pin•y also **pine•y** (pī′nē) *adj.* **-i•er, -i•est.** Relating to, suggestive of, or abounding in pines.

Pin•yin or **pin•yin** (pĭn′yĭn′, -yĭn) *n.* A system for transliterating Chinese ideograms into the Roman alphabet, officially adopted by China in 1979. [Chin. (Mandarin) *pīn yīn,* to combine sounds into syllables : *pīn,* to combine + *yīn,* sound.]

pin•yon (pĭn′yōn′, -yən) *n.* Var. of **piñon.**

pinyon jay *n.* Var. of **piñon jay.**

Pin•zón (pĭn-zōn′, pēn-thôn′), **Martín Alonso.** 1440?–93. Spanish navigator who commanded the *Pinta* on Christopher Columbus's first voyage to America (1492–93). His brother **Vicente Yáñez Pinzón** (1460?–1524) was the first European explorer of the Amazon R. (1500).

pi•o•let (pē′ə-lā′) *n.* An ice ax used in mountain climbing. [Fr. < Fr. dial., dim. of *piola,* small axe < OFr. **piola* < OProv., dim. of *apcha, apia,* of Gmc. orig.]

pi•on (pī′ŏn′) *n. Phys.* A meson produced either in a neutral form with a mean lifetime of 8.4×10^{-17} second or in a

ă pat	oi boy
ā pay	ou out
âr care	o͝o took
ä father	o͞o boot
ĕ pet	ŭ cut
ē be	ûr urge
ĭ pit	th thin
ī pie	*th* this
îr pier	hw which
ŏ pot	zh vision
ō toe	ə about, item
ô paw	

Stress marks:
′ (primary);
′ (secondary), as in **dictionary** (dĭk′shə-nĕr′ē)

positively charged form with a mean lifetime of 2.6×10^{-8} second. See table at **subatomic particle.** [Contraction of PI MESON.]

pi•o•neer (pī′ə-nîr′) *n.* **1.** One who goes into unknown or unclaimed territory to settle. **2.** One who opens up new areas of thought, research, or development. **3.** A soldier who does construction and demolition work in the field to facilitate troop movements. **4.** *Ecol.* An animal or plant species that establishes itself in a previously barren environment. — *adj.* **1.** Of or characteristic of early settlers. **2.** Leading the way; trailblazing. — *v.* **-neered, -neer•ing, -neers.** — *tr.* **1.a.** To open up (an area) or prepare (a way). **b.** To settle (a region). **2.** To initiate or participate in the development of. — *intr.* To act as a pioneer. [Fr. *pionnier* < OFr. *peonier*, foot soldier < *peon* < Med.Lat. *pedō, pedōn-* < LLat., one with broad feet < Lat. *pēs, ped-*, foot. See **ped-*.**]

pipeline
Section of the Trans-Alaska Pipeline

pi•os•i•ty (pī-ŏs′ĭ-tē) *n., pl.* **-ties.** An exaggerated display of piety. [< PIOUS.]

pi•ous (pī′əs) *adj.* **1.** Having or exhibiting religious reverence; earnestly compliant in the observance of religion; devout. **2.a.** Marked by conspicuous devoutness. **b.** Marked by false devoutness; solemnly hypocritical. **3.** Devotional. **4.** Professing or exhibiting a strict, traditional sense of virtue and morality; high-minded. **5.** Commendable; worthy. [< Lat. *pius*, dutiful.] — **pi′ous•ly** *adv.* — **pi′ous•ness** *n.*

Pioz•zi (pyôt′sē), **Hester Lynch.** "Mrs. Thrale." 1741–1821. British writer whose works include *Anecdotes of the Late Samuel Johnson* (1786).

pip[1] (pĭp) *n.* The small seed of a fruit. [Short for PIPPIN.]

pip[2] (pĭp) *tr.v.* **pipped, pip•ping, pips.** *Chiefly British.* **1.** To wound or kill with a bullet. **2.** To get the better of; defeat. **3.** To blackball. [Poss. < PIP[3].]

pip[3] (pĭp) *n.* **1.** *Games.* **a.** A dot indicating a unit of numerical value on dice or dominoes. **b.** A mark indicating the suit or numerical value of a playing card. **2.** A spot or a speck. **3.** A rootstock of certain flowering plants, esp. the lily of the valley. **4.** Any of the segments of the surface of a pineapple. **5.** *Informal.* A shoulder insignia indicating the rank of certain officers, as in the British Army. **6.** See **blip** 1. [?]

pipkin
c. 1810 pipkin by Hugh Wishart (fl. 1793–1837)

pip[4] (pĭp) *v.* **pipped, pip•ping, pips.** — *tr.* To break through (the shell) in hatching. Used of a chick. — *intr.* To peep or chirp, as a chick does. — *n.* A short high-pitched radio signal. [Var. of PEEP[1] and PEEP[2].]

pip[5] (pĭp) *n.* **1.a.** A disease of birds, characterized by a thick mucous discharge that forms a crust in the mouth and throat. **b.** The crust symptomatic of this disease. **2.** *Slang.* A minor unspecified human ailment. [ME *pippe* < MDu., phlegm, pip < Med.Lat. **pippīta*, alteration of Lat. *pītuīta.* See **peiə-*.**]

pi•pal (pē′pəl) *n.* Var. of **peepul.**

piranha

pipe (pīp) *n.* **1.a.** A hollow cylinder or tube used to conduct a liquid, gas, or finely divided solid. **b.** A section or piece of such a tube. **2.a.** A device for smoking, consisting of a tube of wood, clay, or other material with a small bowl at one end. **b.** An amount of smoking material, such as tobacco, needed to fill the bowl of a pipe; a pipeful. **3.** *Informal.* **a.** A tubular part or organ of the body. **b. pipes.** The passages of the human respiratory system. **4.a.** A wine cask having a capacity of 126 gallons or 2 hogsheads (478 liters). **b.** This volume as a unit of liquid measure. **5.** *Mus.* **a.** A tubular wind instrument, such as a flute. **b.** Any of the tubes in an organ. **c. pipes.** A small wind instrument, consisting of tubes of different lengths bound together. **d. pipes.** A bagpipe. **6. pipes.** *Informal.* The vocal cords; the voice, esp. as used in singing. **7.** A birdcall. **8.** *Naut.* A whistle used for signaling crew members. **9.** *Geol.* **a.** A vertical cylindrical vein of ore. **b.** One of the vertical veins of eruptive origin in which diamonds are found in South Africa. **10.** *Geol.* An eruptive passageway opening into the crater of a volcano. **11.** *Metall.* A cone-shaped cavity in an ingot, formed during cooling by escaping gases. — *v.* **piped, pip•ing, pipes.** — *tr.* **1.a.** To convey (liquid or gas) by means of pipes. **b.** To convey as if by pipes, esp. to transmit by wire or cable: *piped music.* **2.** To provide with pipes or connect with pipes. **3.a.** To play (a tune) on a pipe or pipes. **b.** To lead by playing on pipes. **4.** *Naut.* **a.** To signal (crew members) with a boatswain's pipe. **b.** To receive aboard or mark the departure of by sounding a boatswain's pipe. **5.** To utter in a shrill reedy tone. **6.** To furnish (a garment or fabric) with piping. **7.** To force through a pastry tube, as frosting onto a cake. **8.** *Slang.* To take a look at; notice. — *intr.* **1.** To play on a pipe. **2.** To speak shrilly; make a shrill sound. **3.** To chirp or whistle, as a bird does. **4.** *Naut.* To signal the crew with a boatswain's pipe. **5.** *Metall.* To develop pipes during solidification. — ***phrasal verbs.* pipe down.** *Slang.* To stop talking; be quiet. **pipe up.** To speak up. [ME < OE *pīpe* < VLat. **pīpa* < Lat. *pīpāre*, to chirp.]

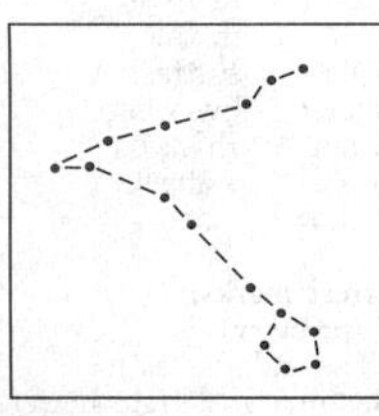

Pisces

pipe bomb *n.* An explosive device contained in a metal pipe.

pipe clay *n.* A fine white clay used in making tobacco pipes and pottery and in whitening leather.

pipe cleaner *n.* A pliant tufted narrow rod used for cleaning the stem of a tobacco pipe.

pipe dream *n.* A fantastic notion or vain hope.

pipe•fish (pīp′fĭsh′) *n., pl.* **pipefish** or **-fish•es.** Any of various slim elongated fishes of the family Syngnathidae, living in temperate and warm seas and characterized by a tubelike snout and an external covering of bony plates.

pipe fitter *n.* One that installs and repairs piping systems.

pipe•fit•ting (pīp′fĭt′ĭng) *n.* **1.** The act of connecting pipes. **2.** A trade that installs and repairs piping systems. **3.** A section of pipe used to connect two or more pipes.

pipe•ful (pīp′fo͝ol′) *n.* The amount of smoking material that a pipe can hold.

pipe•line (pīp′līn′) *n.* **1.** A conduit of pipe, esp. one used to convey water, gas, or petroleum products. **2.** A direct channel by which information is privately transmitted. **3.** A system through which something is conducted, esp. as a means of supply. — *tr.v.* **-lined, -lin•ing, -lines. 1.** To convey by or as if by piping. **2.** To lay piping through.

pipe organ *n. Mus.* See **organ** 1a.

pip•er (pī′pər) *n. Mus.* **1.** One who plays on a pipe. **2.** One who plays the bagpipe.

pi•per•a•zine (pī-pĕr′ə-zēn′, pĭ-) *n.* A crystalline compound, $C_4H_{10}N_2$, used as a hardener for epoxy resins, an antihistamine, and an anthelmintic. [PIPER(INE) + AZ(O)- + -INE[2].]

pi•per•i•dine (pī-pĕr′ĭ-dēn′, pĭ-) *n.* A strongly basic liquid, $C_5H_{10}NH$, used in the manufacture of rubber and as a curing agent in epoxy resins. [PIPER(INE) + -ID(E) + -INE[2].]

pip•er•ine (pĭp′ə-rēn′) *n.* A crystalline solid, $C_{17}H_{19}NO_3$, extracted from black pepper and used as flavoring and as an insecticide. [Lat. *piper*, pepper; see PEPPER + -INE[2].]

pi•per•o•nal (pī-pĕr′ə-năl′, pĭ-) *n.* A powder, $C_8H_6O_3$, used as flavoring and in perfume. [PIPER(INE) + -ON(E) + -AL[3].]

pipe•stone (pīp′stōn′) *n.* A heat-hardened compacted red clay stone used in Native American tobacco pipes.

pi•pette also **pi•pet** (pī-pĕt′) *n.* A narrow, usu. calibrated glass tube into which small amounts of liquid are suctioned for transfer or measurement. [Fr. < OFr., tube, dim. of *pipe*, pipe < VLat. **pīpa.* See PIPE.] — **pi•pette′** *v.*

pipe vine *n.* A deciduous woody vine *(Aristolochia durior)* of the eastern United States having greenish brown-mottled flowers shaped like a curved pipe.

pipe wrench *n.* A wrench with two serrated jaws, one adjustable, for gripping and turning pipe.

pip•ing (pī′pĭng) *n.* **1.** A system of pipes, such as those used in plumbing. **2.** *Mus.* **a.** The act of playing on a pipe. **b.** The music produced by a pipe when played. **3.** A shrill high-pitched sound. **4.** A narrow tube of fabric, sometimes enclosing a cord, used for trimming seams and edges, as of slipcovers. **5.** A tubular ribbon of icing on a pastry. — *adj.* **1.** *Mus.* Playing on a pipe. **2.** Having a high-pitched sound. **3.** Tranquil; peaceful. — ***idiom.* piping hot.** Very hot: *piping hot tea.*

pip•i•strelle also **pip•i•strel** (pĭp′ĭ-strĕl′, pĭp′ĭ-strĕl′) *n.* Any of various very small insectivorous cosmopolitan bats of the genus *Pipistrellus.* [Fr. < Ital. *pipistrello*, bat, alteration of OItal. *vipistrello* < Lat. *vespertiliō.* See VESPERTILIONID.]

pip•it (pĭp′ĭt) *n.* Any of various widely distributed songbirds of the genus *Anthus*, characteristically having brownish upper plumage and a streaked breast. [Imit. of its call.]

pip•kin (pĭp′kĭn) *n.* A small earthenware or metal cooking pot. [Poss. PIP(E), cask + -KIN.]

pip•pin (pĭp′ĭn) *n.* **1.** Any of several varieties of apple. **2.** The seed of a fleshy fruit; a pip. **3.** *Informal.* A person or thing that is admired. [ME *pipin* < OFr. *pepin.*]

pip•sis•se•wa (pĭp-sĭs′ə-wô′, -wə) *n.* Any of several evergreen plants of the genus *Chimaphila*, esp. the Eurasian species *C. umbellata*, having a terminal corymb of white or pinkish flowers. [Perh. Eastern Abenaki *kpi-pskwáhsawe.*]

pip-squeak (pĭp′skwēk′) *n. Informal.* One that is small or insignificant.

Piq•ua (pĭk′wā′, -wə). A city of W-central OH N of Dayton. Pop. 20,612.

pi•quant (pē′kənt, -känt′, pē-känt′) *adj.* **1.** Pleasantly pungent or tart in taste; spicy. **2.a.** Appealingly provocative: *a piquant wit.* **b.** Charming, interesting, or attractive. **3.** *Archaic.* Causing hurt feelings; stinging. [Fr. < OFr., pr.part. of *piquer*, to prick. See PIQUE.] — **pi′quan•cy, pi′quant•ness** *n.* — **pi′quant•ly** *adv.*

pique (pēk) *n.* A state of vexation caused by a perceived slight or indignity; a feeling of wounded pride. — *tr.v.* **piqued, piqu•ing, piques. 1.** To cause to feel resentment or indignation. **2.** To provoke; arouse: *piqued her curiosity.* **3.** To pride (oneself). [Fr., a prick, irritation < OFr. < *piquer*, to prick < VLat. **piccāre*, ult. of imit. orig.]

pi•qué (pĭ-kā′, pē-) *n.* A tightly woven fabric with raised patterns, produced esp. by a double warp. [Fr., p.part. of *piquer*, to quilt < OFr., to backstitch, prick. See PIQUE.]

pi•quet also **pic•quet** (pĭ-kā′) *n. Games.* A card game for two people, played with a deck from which all cards below the seven, aces being high, are omitted. [Fr.]

Pi•ra•ci•ca•ba (pĭr′ə-sĭ-kä′bə, pē′rä-sĭ-kä′bä). A city of SE Brazil NW of São Paulo. Pop. 179,380.

pi•ra•cy (pī′rə-sē) *n., pl.* **-cies. 1.a.** Robbery committed at sea. **b.** A similar act of robbery, as the hijacking of an airplane. **2.** The unauthorized use or reproduction of copyrighted or patented material. **3.** The operation of an unlicensed, illegal radio or television station. [Med.Lat. *pīrātia* < LGk. *peirateia* < Gk. *peiratēs*, pirate. See PIRATE.]

Pi•rae•us (pī-rē′əs, pī-rā′-). A city of E-central Greece on the Saronic Gulf SW of Athens. Pop. 196,389.

pi•ra•gua (pĭ-rä′gwə) *n. Naut.* **1.** A canoe made by hollowing out a tree trunk; a dugout. **2.** A flatbottom sailing boat with two masts. [Sp. < Carib.]

Pi•ran•del•lo (pîr′ən-dĕl′ō, pē′rän-dĕl′lô), **Luigi.** 1867–1936. Italian writer of *Six Characters in Search of an Author* (1921) who won the 1934 Nobel Prize for literature.

Pi•ra•ne•si (pîr′ə-nā′zē, pē′rä-nĕ′-), **Giambattista.** 1720–78. Italian architect and artist whose etchings of Roman ruins aided the revival of neoclassicism. **— Pi′ra•ne′si•an** *adj.*

pi•ra•nha also **pi•ra•ña** (pĭ-rän′yə, -răn′yə, -rä′nə, -răn′ə) *n.* Any of several aggressive, voraciously carnivorous tropical American freshwater fishes of the genus *Serrasalmus*. [Port. < Tupi : *pirá*, fish + *ánha*, to cut.]

pi•ra•ru•cu (pĭ-rär′ə-ko͞o′) *n.* See **arapaima.** [Port. *pirarucú* < Tupi *pirá-rucú* : *pirá*, fish + *urucú*, red.]

pi•rate (pī′rĭt) *n.* **1.a.** One who robs at sea or plunders the land from the sea without commission from a sovereign nation. **b.** A ship used for this purpose. **2.** One who preys on others; a plunderer. **3.** One who makes use of or reproduces the work of another without authorization. **4.** One that operates an unlicensed illegal television or radio station. *— v.* **-rat•ed, -rat•ing, -rates.** *— tr.* **1.** To attack and rob (a ship at sea). **2.** To take (something) by piracy. **3.** To make use of or reproduce (another's work) without authorization. *— intr.* To act as a pirate; practice piracy. [ME < OFr. < Lat. *pīrāta* < Gk. *peiratēs* < *peiran*, to attempt < *peira*, trial. See **per-**[3]*.] **— pi•rat′ic** (pī-răt′ĭk), **pi•rat′i•cal** (-ĭ-kəl) *adj.*

pirate perch *n.* A small North American freshwater fish *(Aphredoderus sayanus)* that has its anal opening near the throat.

Pire (pîr), **Dominique Georges.** 1910–69. Belgian priest who won the 1958 Nobel Peace Prize.

pi•rog (pĭ-rōg′) *n., pl.* **-ro•ghi** or **-ro•gi** (-rō′gē). A large flat pastry filled with finely chopped meat or cabbage often mixed with chopped hard-boiled eggs. [Russ., prob. < *pir*, feast < Old Church Slavonic *pirŭ*. See **pō(i)-***.]

pi•rogue (pĭ-rōg′) *n. Naut.* A canoe made from a hollowed tree trunk; a piragua. [Fr. < Sp. *piragua*. See PIRAGUA.]

pir•o•plasm (pĭr′ə-plăz′əm) *n.* See **babesia.** [NLat. *Piroplasma*, genus name : Lat. *pirum*, pear + Gk. *plasma*, image; see PLASMA.]

pir•o•plas•mo•sis (pĭr′ə-plăz-mō′sĭs) *n.* See **babesiosis.**

pir•ou•ette (pĭr′o͞o-ĕt′) *n.* A turn of the body on the point of the toe or the ball of the foot in ballet. [Fr. < OFr. *pirouet*, spinning top.] **— pir′ou•ette′** *v.*

pi•rozh•ki also **pi•rosh•ki** (pĭ-rôsh′kē, -rŏsh′-) *pl.n.* Small pastries filled with finely chopped meat or cabbage, baked or fried. [Russ., pl. of *pirozhok*, dim. of *pirog*, pirog. See PIROG.]

Pi•sa (pē′zə, -zä). A city of W Italy on the Arno R. near the Tyrrhenian Sea; noted for the campanile known as the Leaning Tower of Pisa. Pop. 104,334. **— Pi′san** *adj. & n.*

pis al•ler (pē zä-lā′) *n.* The final recourse or expedient; the last resort. [Fr. : *pis*, worse + *aller*, to go.]

Pi•sa•no (pē-zä′nō), **Nicola** or **Niccolò.** 1220–84? Italian sculptor whose works include the hexagonal pulpit of the Baptistry in Pisa. Nicola's son **Giovanni** (1245?–1314?) designed the Church of the Franciscans in Naples (1268).

pis•ca•ry (pĭs′kə-rē) *n., pl.* **-ries.** A fishery. [Med.Lat. *piscārium* : Lat. *piscis*, fish + Lat. *-ārium*, -arium.]

Pis•cat•a•way (pĭs-kăt′ə-wā′). A community of N-central NJ N of New Brunswick; founded before 1693. Pop. 42,223.

pis•ca•to•ri•al (pĭs′kə-tôr′ē-əl, -tōr′-) or **pis•ca•to•ry** (pĭs′kə-tôr′ē, -tōr′ē) *adj.* **1.** Of or relating to fish or fishing. **2.** Involved in or dependent on fishing. [< Lat. *piscātōrius* < *piscātor*, fisherman < *piscārī*, to fish < *piscis*, fish.]

Pi•sces (pī′sēz) *pl.n. (used with a sing. v.)* **1.** A constellation in the Northern Hemisphere near Aries and Pegasus. **2.a.** The 12th sign of the zodiac in astrology. **b.** One born under this sign. [Ult. < Lat. *piscēs*, pl. of *piscis*, fish.]

pisci– *pref.* Fish: *piscivorous.* [< Lat. *piscis*, fish.]

pi•sci•cul•ture (pī′sĭ-kŭl′chər, pĭs′ĭ-) *n.* The breeding, hatching, and rearing of fish under controlled conditions. **— pi′sci•cul′tur•al** *adj.* **— pi′sci•cul′tur•ist** *n.*

pi•sci•form (pī′sĭ-fôrm′, pĭs′ĭ-) *adj.* Shaped like a fish.

pi•sci•na (pĭ-sē′nə, -sī′nə, -shē′nə) *n., pl.* **-nae** (-nē). *Eccles.* A stone basin with a drain for carrying away the water used in ceremonial ablutions. [ME *piscine* < Med.Lat. *piscīna* < Lat., fishpond, pool < *piscis*, fish.] **— pis′ci•nal** (pĭs′ə-nəl) *adj.*

pi•scine (pī′sēn′, pĭs′īn′) *adj.* Of, relating to, or characteristic of a fish or fishes. [Med.Lat. *piscīnus* < Lat. *piscis*, fish.]

Pi•scis Aus•tri•nus (pī′sĭs ô-strī′nəs) *n.* A constellation in the Southern Hemisphere near Aquarius and Grus. [NLat. : Lat. *piscis*, fish + Lat. *austrinus*, southern.]

pi•sciv•o•rous (pĭ-sĭv′ər-əs, pī-) *adj.* Fish-eating.

pish (pĭsh) *interj.* Used to express disdain.

pi•shogue also **pi•shoge** (pĭ-shōg′) *n. Irish.* **1.** Black magic; sorcery. **2.** An evil spell; an incantation. [Ir.Gael. *piseog* < MIr. *pisóc, piseóc.*]

pi•si•form (pī′sə-fôrm′) *adj.* Resembling a pea in size or shape. *— n. Anat.* A small bone at the junction of the ulna and the carpus. [Lat. *pīsum*, pea; see PEA + -FORM.]

Pi•sis•tra•tus or **Pei•sis•tra•tus** (pī-sĭs′trə-təs, pĭ-). d. 527 B.C. Athenian tyrant (560–527) remembered for encouraging athletic contests and literary efforts.

pis•mire (pĭs′mīr′, pĭz′-) *n.* An ant. [ME *pissemyre* : *pisse*, urine (< the smell of the formic acid that ants secrete); see PISS + *mire*, ant (prob. of Scand. orig.; akin to Dan. *myre*).]

pis•mo clam (pĭz′mō) *n.* A large thick-shelled edible marine clam *(Tivela stultorum)* of the southern Pacific coast of North America. [After *Pismo* Beach, a city of SW CA.]

pi•so•lite (pī′sə-līt′) *n. Geol.* **1.** Rock, usu. limestone, composed of pisoliths. **2.** See **pisolith.** [Gk. *pisos*, pea + -LITE.] **— pi′so•lit′ic** (-lĭt′ĭk) *adj.*

pi•so•lith (pī′sə-lĭth′, -zə-, pĭs′ə-, pĭz′ə-) *n. Geol.* A small rounded accretionary mass, usu. of calcium carbonate, larger and less regular than an oolite. [Gk. *pisos*, pea + -LITH.]

piss (pĭs) *Vulgar Slang. — v.* **pissed, piss•ing, piss•es.** *— intr.* To urinate. *— tr.* **1.** To urinate on or in. **2.** To discharge (blood, for example) in the urine. *— n.* **1.** Urine. **2.** The act or an instance of urinating. ***— phrasal verb.* piss off.** To make or become angry. [ME *pissen* < OFr. *pissier* < VLat. **pissiāre*, of imit. orig.]

piss•ant also **piss-ant** or **piss ant** (pĭs′ănt′) *Slang. n.* A stickler for petty details. **— piss′ant** *adj.*

Pis•sar•ro (pĭ-sär′ō, pē-), **Camille.** 1830–1903. French painter whose works include *Orchard in Blossom* (1877).

pissed (pĭst) *adj. Vulgar Slang.* **1.** Angry. **2.** Drunk.

piss•er (pĭs′ər) *n. Vulgar Slang.* **1.** One that is extremely disagreeable. **2.** One that is extraordinary or remarkable.

pis•soir (pē-swär′) *n.* A public urinal located on the street in some European countries. [Fr. < OFr. < *pissier*, to urinate. See PISS.]

pis•ta•chi•o (pĭ-stăsh′ē-ō′, -stä′shē-ō′) *n., pl.* **-os. 1.a.** A deciduous Asian tree *(Pistacia vera)* having pinnately compound leaves and nutlike fruits. **b.** The fruit of this tree, having an edible oily green or yellow kernel. **2.** The flavor of these nuts. [Ital. *pistacchio* < Lat. *pistacium*, pistachio nut < Gk. *pistakion* < *pistakē*, pistachio tree, perh. < MPers. **pistak*.]

pistachio green *n. Color.* A moderate to light yellowish or yellow green.

pis•ta•reen (pĭs′tə-rēn′) *n.* A small silver coin used in America and the West Indies during the 18th century. [Prob. alteration of Sp. *peseta*, peseta. See PESETA.]

piste (pēst) *n. Sports.* A ski trail densely packed with snow. [Fr. < Ital. *pista* < obsolete *pistare*, to trample down, var. of *pestare*. See PISTON.]

pis•til (pĭs′təl) *n.* The female ovule-bearing organ of a flower, including the stigma, style, and ovary. [Fr. < NLat. *pistillum* < Lat., pestle (< its shape).]

pis•til•late (pĭs′tə-lāt′, -lĭt) *adj.* **1.** Having one or more pistils. **2.** Having pistils but no stamens: *pistillate flowers.*

Pis•to•ia (pĭ-stoi′ə, pē stō′yä). A city of N-central Italy NW of Florence; settled in the 6th cent. B.C. Pop. 83,600.

pis•tol (pĭs′təl) *n.* A firearm held and fired with one hand. *— tr.v.* **-toled, -tol•ing, -tols.** To shoot with such a handgun. [Fr. *pistole* < Ger. < MHGer. *pischulle* < Czech *pištala*, pipe, whistle, firearm < *pištěti*, to whistle, of imit. orig.]

pis•tole (pĭ-stōl′) *n.* **1.** A gold coin equal to two escudos, formerly used in Spain. **2.** Any of several gold coins used in various European countries until the late 19th century. [Fr., back-formation < *pistolet*, dim. of *pistole*, pistol. See PISTOL.]

pistol grip *n.* **1.a.** The grip of a pistol, shaped to fit the hand. **b.** A similar grip sometimes used on another firearm. **2.** A grip used on certain tools shaped to fit the hand.

pis•tol-whip (pĭs′təl-hwĭp′, -wĭp′) *tr.v.* **-whipped, -whip•ping, -whips.** To beat with a pistol.

pis•ton (pĭs′tən) *n.* **1.** A cylinder or disk that fits into a larger cylinder and moves under fluid pressure, as in a reciprocating engine, or displaces or compresses fluids, as in a pump. **2.** *Mus.* A valve mechanism in brass instruments for altering the pitch. [Fr. < Ital. *pistone, pestone*, large pestle < *pestare*, to pound < LLat. *pistāre*, freq. of Lat. *pīnsere, pīnsāre*.]

piston ring *n.* An adjustable split metal ring that fits around a piston to seal the gap between it and the cylinder wall.

piston rod *n.* A connecting rod that transmits power to or is powered by a piston.

pis•tou (pē-sto͞o′) *n.* A sauce made of garlic, basil, tomato, Parmesan, and olive oil. [Fr. < Prov. < *pestar*, to crush < OProv. < LLat. *pistāre*. See PISTON.]

pit[1] (pĭt) *n.* **1.** A natural or artificial hole or cavity in the ground. **2.a.** An excavation for the removal of mineral deposits; a mine. **b.** The shaft of a mine. **3.** A concealed hole in the ground used as a trap; a pitfall. **4.a.** Hell. **b.** A miserable or depressing place or situation. **c. pits.** *Slang.* The worst. **5.** A small indentation in a surface. **6.a.** A natural hollow or depression in the body or an organ. **b.** A small indented scar left in the skin by smallpox or other eruptive disease; a pockmark. **c.** *Informal.* An armpit. Often used in the plural. **7.** An enclosed, usu. sunken area in which animals, such as dogs or gamecocks, are placed for fighting. **8.a.** The section directly in front of and below the stage of a theater, in which the mu-

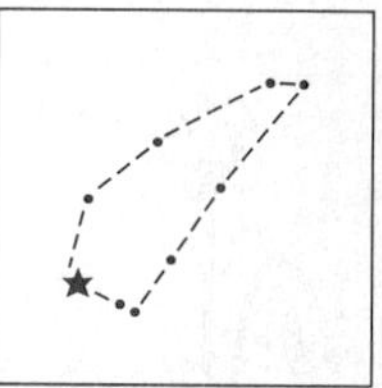

Piscis Austrinus

pistachio
Pistacia vera

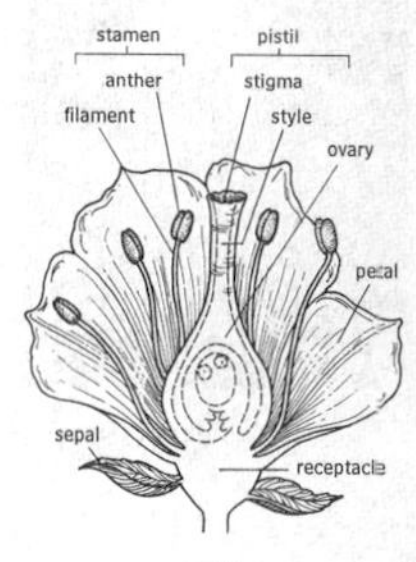

pistil

ă pat	oi boy
ā pay	ou out
âr care	o͝o took
ä father	o͞o boot
ĕ pet	ŭ cut
ē be	ûr urge
ĭ pit	th thin
ī pie	*th* this
îr pier	hw which
ŏ pot	zh vision
ō toe	ə about, item
ô paw	

Stress marks:
′ (primary);
′ (secondary), as in
dictionary (dĭk′shə-nĕr′ē)

sicians sit. **b.** *Chiefly British.* The ground floor of a theater behind the stalls. **9.a.** The section of an exchange where trading in a specific commodity is carried on. **b.** The gambling area of a casino. **10.a.** A sunken area in a garage floor from which mechanics may work on cars. **b.** *Sports.* An area beside an auto racecourse where cars may be refueled or serviced during a race. Often used in the plural. **11.** *Football.* The middle areas of the defensive and offensive lines. **12.** *Bot.* A cavity in the wall of a plant cell where there is no secondary wall, as in fibers, tracheids, and vessels. *—v.* **pit•ted, pit•ting, pits.** *—tr.* **1.** To mark with cavities, depressions, or scars. **2.** To set in direct opposition or competition. **3.** To place, bury, or store in a pit. *—intr.* **1.** To become marked with pits. **2.** To retain an impression after being indented. Used of the skin. **3.** To stop at a refueling area during an auto race. [ME < OE *pytt*, ult. < Lat. *puteus*, well. See **peu-***.]

pit[2] (pĭt) *n.* The single, central kernel or stone of certain fruits, such as a peach or cherry. *—tr.v.* **pit•ted, pit•ting, pits.** To extract the pit from (a fruit). [Du. < MDu.]

pi•ta[1] (pē′tə) *n.* A round flat bread that can be opened into a pocket for filling. [Mod.Gk. *pētta, pita*, pie, cake, bread.]

pi•ta[2] (pē′tə) *n.* **1.** Any of several plants of the genus *Agave* that yield strong leaf fibers. **2.** This fiber, used in making cordage and paper. [Sp. < Quechua, to complicate.]

pit•a•pat (pĭt′ə-păt′) *intr.v.* **-pat•ted, -pat•ting, -pats. 1.** To move with a series of quick tapping steps. **2.** To make a repeated tapping sound. *—n.* A series of quick steps, taps, or beats. *—adv.* With a rapid tapping sound. [Imit.]

pit boss *n.* One who supervises the gambling in a casino.

pit bull *n.* See **American Staffordshire terrier.**

pit-bull (pĭt′bo͝ol′) *adj. Slang.* Marked by or exhibiting great aggression, ruthlessness, and often bitterness.

pit bull terrier *n.* See **American Staffordshire terrier.**

Pit•cairn Island (pĭt′kârn′). A volcanic island of the S Pacific ESE of Tahiti; settled in 1790 by mutineers from H.M.S. *Bounty* and administered by the British since 1839.

pitch[1] (pĭch) *n.* **1.** Any of various thick, dark, sticky substances obtained from the distillation residue of coal tar, wood tar, or petroleum and used for waterproofing, roofing, caulking, and paving. **2.** Any of various natural bitumens, such as mineral pitch or asphalt. **3.** A resin derived from the sap of various coniferous trees. *—tr.v.* **pitched, pitch•ing, pitch•es.** To smear or cover with or as if with pitch. [ME *pich* < OE *pic* and < AN *piche*, both < Lat. *pix, pic-*.]

pitch[2] (pĭch) *v.* **pitched, pitch•ing, pitch•es.** *—tr.* **1.a.** To throw, usually with careful aim. See Syns at **throw. b.** To discard by throwing. **2.** *Baseball.* **a.** To throw (the ball) from the mound to the batter. **b.** To play (a game) as pitcher. **c.** To assign as pitcher. **3.** To erect or establish; set up. **4.** To set firmly; implant; embed. **5.** To set at a specified downward slant. **6.a.** To set at a particular level, degree, or quality. **b.** *Mus.* To set the pitch or key of. **c.** To adapt so as to be applicable; direct. **7.** *Informal.* To attempt to promote or sell, often in a high-pressure manner. **8.** *Sports.* To pitch a golf ball. *—intr.* **1.** To throw or toss something, such as a ball, horseshoe, or bale. **2.** *Baseball.* To play in the position of pitcher. **3.** To plunge headlong. **4.a.** To stumble around; lurch. **b.** To buck, as a horse. **5.a.** *Naut.* To dip bow and stern alternately. **b.** To oscillate about a lateral axis so that the nose lifts or descends in relation to the tail. Used of an aircraft. **6.** To slope downward. **7.** To set up living quarters; encamp; settle. **8.** *Sports.* To hit a golf ball in a high arc with backspin so that it does not roll very far after striking the ground. *—n.* **1.** The act or an instance of pitching. **2.** *Baseball.* **a.** A throw of the ball by the pitcher to the batter. **b.** A ball so thrown. **3.** *Sports.* The rectangular area between the wickets in cricket, 22 yards (20.1 meters) by 10 feet (3.1 meters). **4.a.** *Naut.* The pitching of a ship. **b.** The pitching of an airplane. **5.a.** A steep downward slope. **b.** The degree of such a slope. **6.** *Archit.* **a.** The angle of a roof. **b.** The highest point of a structure: *the pitch of an arch.* **7.** A level or degree, as of intensity. **8.a.** *Acoustics.* The quality of highness or lowness of a sound, dependent primarily on the frequency of the sound waves produced by its source. **b.** *Mus.* The relative position of a tone within a range of musical sounds, as determined by pitch. **c.** *Mus.* Any of various standards for pitch associating each tone with a particular frequency. **9.a.** The distance traveled by a machine screw in one revolution. **b.** The distance between two corresponding points on adjacent screw threads or gear teeth. **c.** The distance between two corresponding points on a helix. **10.** The distance that a propeller would travel in an ideal medium during one revolution, measured parallel to its shaft. **11.** *Informal.* **a.** A line of talk designed to persuade. **b.** An advertisement. **12.** *Chiefly British.* The stand of a vendor or hawker. **13.** *Games.* See **seven-up. 14.** *Print.* The density of characters in a printed line, usu. expressed as characters per inch. ***—phrasal verbs.*** **pitch in.** *Informal.* **1.** To set to work vigorously. **2.** To join forces with others; help or cooperate. **pitch into.** *Informal.* To attack verbally or physically; assault. **pitch on** (or **upon**). *Informal.* To succeed in choosing or achieving, usu. quickly. [ME *pichen*, prob. < OE **piccean*, causative of **pīcian*, to prick.]

pitcher plant
Sarracenia purpurea

pith helmet

pitch accent *n. Ling.* See **tonic accent.**

pitch-black (pĭch′blăk′) *adj. Color.* Extremely dark.

pitch•blende (pĭch′blĕnd′) *n.* A massive variety of the mineral uraninite. [Partial transl. of Ger. *Pechblende* : *Pech*, pitch + *Blende*, blende; see BLENDE.]

pitch-dark (pĭch′därk′) *adj.* Extremely dark.

pitched battle (pĭcht) *n.* **1.** An intense battle fought in close contact by troops in a predetermined formation. **2.** A fiercely waged battle or struggle between opposing forces.

pitch•er[1] (pĭch′ər) *n.* **1.** One that pitches. **2.** *Baseball.* The player who throws the ball from the mound to the batter. **3.** *Sports.* A seven iron used in golf.

pitch•er[2] (pĭch′ər) *n.* **1.** A container for liquids, usu. having a handle and a lip or spout for pouring. **2.** *Bot.* A pitcherlike part, such as the leaf of a pitcher plant. [ME *picher* < OFr. *pichier*, alteration of *bichier* < Med.Lat. *bicārium*, drinking cup, prob. < Gk. *bikos*, jar, poss. < Egypt. *bik*, oil vessel.]

Pitch•er (pĭch′ər), **Molly.** See Mary Ludwig Hays **McCauley.**

pitcher plant *n.* Any of various insectivorous plants of the genera *Sarracenia, Nepenthes,* or *Darlingtonia,* having pitcherlike leaves that attract and trap insects.

pitch•fork (pĭch′fôrk′) *n.* A large long-handled fork with sharp, widely spaced prongs for lifting and pitching hay. [Alteration (influenced by *pichen*, to throw) of ME *pikforke* : *pik*, pick; see PICK[2], or *pik*, spike; see PIKE[5] + *forke*, fork; see FORK.] **—pitch′fork′** *v.*

pitch•man (pĭch′mən) *n.* **1.** A hawker of small wares, as on the streets or at a carnival. **2.** One who makes aggressive selling or promotional efforts. **3.** One who delivers commercials on radio or television.

pitch•out (pĭch′out′) *n.* **1.** *Baseball.* A pitch deliberately thrown high and away from the batter to make it easier for the catcher to throw out a base runner who is standing off a base or attempting to steal. **2.** *Football.* A lateral pass from the back receiving the snap from the center to another back behind the line of scrimmage.

pitch pine *n.* An eastern North American pine tree *(Pinus rigida)* that yields pitch or turpentine.

pitch pipe *n. Mus.* A small pipe that, when sounded, gives the standard pitch for a piece of music or for tuning.

pitch•stone (pĭch′stōn′) *n.* Any of various volcanic glasses distinguished by their dull pitchlike luster.

pitch•y (pĭch′ē) *adj.* **-i•er, -i•est. 1.** Full of or covered with pitch. **2.** Resembling pitch in consistency. **3.** Extremely dark; black. **—pitch′i•ness** *n.*

pit•e•ous (pĭt′ē-əs) *adj.* **1.** Demanding or arousing pity. **2.** *Archaic.* Pitying; compassionate. [ME < OFr. *piteus* < LLat. *pietōsus*, *pietōsus*, merciful < Lat. *pietās, pietās*, compassion. See PIETY.] **—pit′e•ous•ly** *adv.* **—pit′e•ous•ness** *n.*

pit•fall (pĭt′fôl′) *n.* **1.** An unapparent source of trouble or danger; a hidden hazard. **2.** A concealed hole in the ground that serves as a trap.

pith (pĭth) *n.* **1.** *Bot.* The soft spongy parenchymatous center of the stems of most flowering plants. **2.** *Zool.* The soft inner substance of a feather or hair. **3.** The essential or central part; the heart or essence. **4.** Strength; vigor; mettle. **5.** Significance; importance. **6.** *Archaic.* Spinal cord or bone marrow. *—tr.v.* **pithed, pith•ing, piths. 1.** To remove the pith from (a plant stem). **2.** To sever or destroy the spinal cord of, usu. by a needle inserted into the vertebral canal. **3.** To kill (cattle) by cutting the spinal cord. [ME < OE *pitha.*]

pith•e•can•thro•pus (pĭth′ĭ-kăn′thrə-pəs, -kăn-thrō′pəs) *n.* An extinct primate postulated from bones found in Java in 1891, now classified as *Homo erectus.* [NLat., genus name : Gk. *pithēkos*, ape + Gk. *anthrōpos*, man.] **—pith′e•can•throp′ic** (-kən-thrŏp′ĭk) *adj.* **—pith′e•can′thro•pine** (-kăn′thrə-pīn′) *adj.*

pith•e•coid (pĭth′ĭ-koid′, pĭ-thē′koid) *adj.* **1.** Resembling or relating to the apes, esp. the anthropoid apes. **2.** Of or belonging to a genus *(Pithecia)* of small slender South American monkeys related to the titi. [Gk. *pithēkos*, ape + -OID.]

pith helmet *n.* A lightweight hat made from dried pith and worn in tropical countries for protection from the sun.

pith ray *n.* The parenchymatous tissue that extends between the vascular bundles of a stem or root.

pith•y (pĭth′ē) *adj.* **-i•er, -i•est. 1.** Precisely meaningful; forceful and brief: *a pithy comment.* **2.** Consisting of or resembling pith. **—pith′i•ly** *adv.* **—pith′i•ness** *n.*

pit•i•a•ble (pĭt′ē-ə-bəl) *adj.* **1.** Arousing or deserving of pity or compassion; lamentable. **2.** Arousing disdainful pity. **—pit′i•a•ble•ness** *n.* **—pit′i•a•bly** *adv.*

pit•i•ful (pĭt′ĭ-fəl) *adj.* **1.** Inspiring or deserving pity. **2.** Arousing contemptuous pity, as through ineptitude or inadequacy. **3.** *Archaic.* Filled with pity or compassion. **—pit′i•ful•ly** *adv.* **—pit′i•ful•ness** *n.*

pit•i•less (pĭt′ĭ-lĭs) *adj.* Having no pity; merciless. **—pit′i•less•ly** *adv.* **—pit′i•less•ness** *n.*

pit•man (pĭt′mən) *n.* **1.** *pl.* **pit•men** (-mĕn). A worker employed inside a pit in various industrial operations, as in a coal mine. **2.** *pl.* **pit•mans** (-mənz). See **connecting rod.**

Pit•man (pĭt′mən), Sir **Isaac.** 1813–97. British educator and inventor (1837) of a system of shorthand.

Pit•ney (pĭt′nē), **Mahlon.** 1858–1924. Amer. jurist; associate justice of the U.S. Supreme Court (1912–22).

pi•ton (pē′tŏn′) *n. Sports.* A metal spike fitted at one end with an eye for securing a rope and driven into rock or ice as a support in mountain climbing. [Fr. < OFr., nail.]

Pi•tot-stat•ic tube (pē′tō-stăt′ĭk, pē-tō′-) *n.* A device consisting of a Pitot tube and a static tube, used in aircraft to determine relative wind speed.

Pi•tot tube (pē′tō, pē-tō′) *n.* A tube set parallel to the direction of fluid-stream movement and attached to a manometer, used to measure the total pressure of a fluid stream. [After Henri *Pitot* (1695–1771), French physicist.]

Pit River[1] (pĭt) *n.* See **Achomawi.**

Pit River[2] (pĭt). A river of N CA flowing c. 322 km (200 mi) to the Sacramento R.

pit•saw also **pit saw** (pĭt′sô′) *n.* A large saw for cutting logs, operated jointly by a person standing above the log and another in a pit underneath.

pit stop *n. Sports.* **1.** A stop at a pit for refueling or service during an automobile race. **2.** *Informal.* **a.** A brief stop for rest and refreshment, esp. during an automobile trip. **b.** A place where such a stop is made.

Pitt (pĭt), **William**[1]. 1st Earl of Chatham. "the Elder." 1708–78. British politician who directed his country's military effort during the Seven Years' War (1756–63).

Pitt (pĭt), **William**[2]. 2nd Earl of Chatham. "the Younger." 1759–1806. British prime minister (1783–1801 and 1804–06) who secured the Act of Union between Ireland and Great Britain (1800).

pit•ta (pĭt′ə) *n.* Any of several brightly colored perching birds of the family Pittidae of Asia, Australia, and Africa, having a strong bill, short tail, and long legs. [Telugu *piṭṭa*, bird.]

pit•tance (pĭt′ns) *n.* **1.** A meager monetary allowance, wage, or remuneration. **2.** A very small amount. [ME *pitance* < OFr., allowance of food < Med.Lat. *pietantia*, ult. < Lat. *pietās, pietās*, piety. See PITY.]

pit•ted (pĭt′ĭd) *adj.* **1.** Marked by pits. **2.** Having the pit removed: *pitted dates.*

pit•ter-pat•ter (pĭt′ər-păt′ər) *n.* A rapid series of light tapping sounds. [Imit.] **—pit′ter-pat′ter** *v.*

pit•tos•po•rum (pĭ-tŏs′pər-əm, pĭt′ə-spôr′əm, -spōr′-) *n.* Any of various Old World evergreen shrubs or plants of the genus *Pittosporum.* [NLat., genus name : Gk. *pissa, pitta*, pitch + NLat. *spora*, spore; see SPORE.]

Pitts•burg (pĭts′bûrg′). **1.** A city of W CA at the junction of the Sacramento and San Joaquin rivers NE of Oakland. Pop. 47,564. **2.** A city of SE KS near the MO border; founded 1876. Pop. 17,775.

Pitts•burgh (pĭts′bûrg′). A city of SW PA at the point where the confluence of the Allegheny and Monongahela rivers forms the Ohio R. Pop. 369,879.

Pitts•field (pĭts′fēld′). A city of W MA NW of Springfield near the NY border. Pop. 48,622.

pi•tu•i•tar•y (pĭ-to͞o′ĭ-tĕr′ē, -tyo͞o′-) *n., pl.* **-ies. 1.** The pituitary gland. **2.** *Medic.* An extract of the pituitary gland, prepared for therapeutic use. *—adj.* **1.** Of or relating to the pituitary gland. **2.** Of or secreting phlegm or mucus; mucous. [< Lat. *pītuītārius*, of phlegm (< the early belief that it produced mucus) < *pītuīta*, phlegm. See **peiə-*.**]

pituitary gland *n.* A small oval endocrine gland attached to the base of the vertebrate brain and consisting of an anterior and a posterior lobe, the secretions of which control the other endocrine glands and influence growth, metabolism, and maturation.

pit viper *n.* Any of various venomous snakes of the family Crotalidae, such as a copperhead, rattlesnake, or fer-de-lance, characterized by a small sensory pit below each eye.

pit•y (pĭt′ē) *n., pl.* **-ies. 1.** Sympathy and sorrow aroused by the misfortune or suffering of another. **2.** A matter of regret. *—v.* **-ied, -y•ing, -ies.** *—tr.* To feel pity for. *—intr.* To feel pity. ***—idiom.* have (or take) pity on.** To show compassion for. [ME *pite* < OFr. < Lat. *pietās*, piety, compassion < *pius*, dutiful.] **—pit′y•ing•ly** *adv.*

pit•y•ri•a•sis (pĭt′ĭ-rī′ə-sĭs) *n., pl.* **-ses** (-sēz′). Any of various skin diseases characterized by shedding of flaky epidermal scales. [Gk. *pituriasis* < *pituron*, grain husk, dandruff.]

più (pyo͞o) *adv. Mus.* More. [Ital. < Lat. *plūs.* See **pelə-[1]*.**]

Pi•us II (pī′əs). 1405–64. Pope (1458–64) noted for his unsuccessful attempt to lead a crusade against the Turks.

Pius V, Saint. 1504–72. Pope (1566–72) who excommunicated Elizabeth I of England.

Pius VII. 1742–1823. Pope (1800–23) who was forced to crown Napoleon emperor in 1804.

Pius IX. 1792–1878. Pope (1846–78) who summoned the First Vatican Council (1869–70).

Pius X, Saint. 1835–1914. Pope (1903–14) who was strongly opposed to religious modernism.

Pius XI. 1857–1939. Pope (1922–39) who signed a treaty with Benito Mussolini granting papal sovereignty over the Vatican City.

Pius XII. 1876–1958. Pope (1939–58) who maintained neutrality during World War II and was later criticized for not taking forceful measures to aid European Jews.

Pi•ute (pī′yo͞ot′) *n.* Var. of **Paiute.**

piv•ot (pĭv′ət) *n.* **1.** A short rod or shaft on which a related part rotates or swings. **2.** A person or thing on which something depends or turns; the central or crucial factor. **3.** The act of turning on or as if on a pivot. *—v.* **-ot•ed, -ot•ing, -ots.** *—tr.* **1.** To mount on, attach by, or provide with a pivot or pivots. **2.** To cause to rotate, revolve, or turn. *—intr.* To turn on or as if on a pivot. [Fr. < OFr.] **—piv′ot•a•ble** *adj.*

piv•ot•al (pĭv′ə-tl) *adj.* **1.** Of, relating to, or serving as a pivot. **2.** Being of vital importance; crucial. **—piv′ot•al•ly** *adv.*

pivot joint *n.* A joint in which a bone rotates around another.

pix[1] (pĭks) *n.* Pl. of **pic.**

pix[2] (pĭks) *n. Eccles.* Var. of **pyx.**

pix•el (pĭk′səl, -sĕl′) *n. Comp. Sci.* The smallest image-forming unit of a video display. [PIX[1] + EL(EMENT).]

pix•i•lat•ed or **pix•il•lat•ed** (pĭk′sə-lā′tĭd) *adj.* **1.** Behaving as if mentally unstable; eccentric. **2.** Whimsical; prankish. **3.** *Slang.* Intoxicated; drunk. [< PIXY.] **—pix′i•la′tion** *n.*

pix•y or **pix•ie** (pĭk′sē) *—n., pl.* **-ies.** A fairylike or elfin creature, esp. one that is mischievous; a playful sprite. *—adj.* Playfully mischievous. [?] **—pix′y•ish** *adj.*

Francisco Pizarro
c. 1760 painting by an unknown artist

Pi•zar•ro (pĭ-zär′ō, pē-thär′ō, -sär′), **Francisco.** 1475?–1541. Spanish explorer and conqueror of Peru (1531–33).

piz•za (pēt′sə) *n.* A baked pie of Italian origin consisting of a shallow breadlike crust covered with tomato sauce, cheese, and often other toppings. [Ital., pie, tart, pizza.]

piz•zazz or **piz•zaz** (pĭ-zăz′) *n. Slang.* **1.** Dazzling style; flamboyance; flair. **2.** Vigorous spirit; energy or excitement. [?]

piz•ze•ri•a (pēt′sə-rē′ə) *n.* A place where pizzas are made and sold. [Ital. < *pizza*, pie, pizza.]

piz•zi•ca•to (pĭt′sĭ-kä′tō) *Mus. —adj.* Played by plucking rather than bowing the strings. *—n., pl.* **-ti** (-tē). A pizzicato note or passage. [Ital., p.part. of *pizzicare*, to pluck < *pizzare*, to prick < *pizzo*, point.] **—piz′zi•ca′to** *adv.*

piz•zle (pĭz′əl) *n.* **1.** The penis of an animal, esp. a bull. **2.** A whip made from a bull's penis. [Poss. < LGer. *pēsel*, dim. of MLGer. *pese*, penis, tendon.]

pk. *abbr.* **1.** Pack. **2.** Park. **3.** Peak. **4.** Peck.

pkg. *abbr.* Package.

pkt. *abbr.* Packet.

PKU *abbr.* Phenylketonuria.

pkwy *abbr.* Parkway.

pky *abbr.* Parkway.

pl. *abbr.* **1.** Or **Pl.** Place. **2.** *Print. & Photography.* Plate. **3.** Plural.

placard

plac•a•ble (plăk′ə-bəl, plā′kə-) *adj.* Easily calmed or pacified; tolerant. [ME, agreeable < OFr. < Lat. *plācābilis* < *plācāre*, to calm. See **plāk-[1]*.**] **—plac′a•bil′i•ty** *n.* **—plac′a•bly** *adv.*

plac•ard (plăk′ärd′, -ərd) *n.* **1.** A sign or notice for display in a public place. **2.** A small card or plaque, such as a nameplate on a door. *—tr.v.* **-ard•ed, -ard•ing, -ards. 1.** To announce or advertise by means of placards. **2.** To post placards on or in. **3.** To display as a placard. [ME, official document < OFr. < *plaquier*, to plaster, piece together < MDu. *placken*, to patch.] **—plac′ard′er** *n.*

pla•cate (plā′kāt′, plăk′āt′) *tr.v.* **-cat•ed, -cat•ing, -cates.** To allay the anger of, esp. by making concessions; appease. See Syns at **pacify.** [Lat. *plācāre, plācāt-*, to calm. See **plāk-[1]*.**] **—pla′cat′er** *n.* **—pla•ca′tion** (plā-kā′shən) *n.* **—pla′ca•to′ry** (-tôr′ē, -tōr′ē), **pla′ca′tive** (-kā′tĭv) *adj.*

place (plās) *n.* **1.a.** A bounded area; a portion of space. **b.** Room or space, esp. adequate space. **2.a.** The given portion of space occupied by or allocated to a person or thing. **b.** A building or an area set aside for a specified purpose. **3.a.** A dwelling; a house. **b.** A business establishment or office. **c.** A locality, such as a town or a city. **4.** Often **Place.** A public square or street with houses in a town. **5.a.** A space in which one person, such as a passenger, can sit or stand. **b.** A setting for one person at a table. **6.** A position regarded as belonging to someone or something else; stead. **7.** A particular point reached, as in a book. **8.** A particular spot, as on the body. **9.a.** The proper or designated role or function. **b.** The proper or customary position or order. **c.** A suitable setting or occasion. **d.** The appropriate right or duty. **10.** Social station. **11.** A particular situation or circumstance. **12.** High rank or status. **13.** A job, post, or position. **14.** Relative position in a series; standing. **15.** *Games.* Second position for betting purposes, as in a horserace. **16.** The specified stage in a list of points to be made, as in an argument: *in the first place.* **17.** *Math.* The position of a figure in a numeral or series. *—v.* **placed, plac•ing, plac•es.** *—tr.* **1.** To put in or as if in a particular place or position; set. **2.** To put in a specified relation or order. **3.** To offer for consideration. **4.** To find accommodation or employment for. **5.** To put into a particular condition. **6.** To arrange for the publication or display of. **7.** To appoint to a post. **8.a.** To rank in an order or a sequence. **b.** To estimate. **9.** To identify or classify in a particular context. **10.a.** To give an order for: *place a bet.* **b.** To apply or arrange for: *place an order.* **11.** To adjust (one's voice) for the best effects. *—intr. Sports & Games.* To arrive among the first three finishers in a race, esp. to finish second.

ă pat	oi boy
ā pay	ou out
âr care	o͝o took
ä father	o͞o boot
ĕ pet	ŭ cut
ē be	ûr urge
ĭ pit	th thin
ī pie	*th* this
îr pier	hw which
ŏ pot	zh vision
ō toe	ə about, item
ô paw	

Stress marks:
′ (primary);
′ (secondary), as in
dictionary (dĭk′shə-nĕr′ē)

— **idioms. in place. 1.** In the appropriate or usual position or order. **2.** In the same spot; without moving forward or backward. **in place of.** Instead of. **keep (or know) (one's) place.** To recognize one's social position and act accordingly. **put in (someone's) place.** To lower the dignity of (someone); humble. **place in the sun.** A dominant or favorable position or situation. [ME < OE *plæce* and < OFr. *place*, open space (< Med.Lat. *placea* < VLat. **plattea*), both < Lat. *platēa*, broad street < Gk. *plateia (hodos)*, broad (street), fem. of *platus*. See **plat-***.] — **place′a•ble** *adj.* — **plac′er** *n.*

pla•ce•bo (plə-sē′bō) *n., pl.* **-bos** or **-boes. 1.a.** *Medic.* A substance containing no medication and given to reinforce a patient's expectation to get well. **b.** An inactive substance used as a control in an experiment or test to determine the effectiveness of a medicinal drug. **2.** Something of no intrinsic remedial value that is used to appease or reassure another. **3.** (plä-chā′bō). *Rom. Cath. Ch.* The service or office of vespers for the dead. [ME, vespers for the dead < LLat. *placēbō*, I will please, first pers. sing. fut. t. of Lat. *placēre*, to please. See **plāk-[1]*.**]

placebo effect *n.* A beneficial effect in a patient following a treatment that arises from the patient's expectations concerning the treatment rather than from the treatment itself.

plaid

place•hold•er (plās′hōl′dər) *n.* **1.** One who holds an office or a place, esp.: **a.** One who acts as a deputy or a proxy. **b.** One who holds an appointed office in a government. **2.** A mathematical or logical symbol that may be replaced by the name of any element of a set. **3.** A nonsignificant digit in a decimal number.

place kick *n. Football.* A kick, as for a field goal, for which the ball is held or propped up in a fixed position on the ground. — **place′kick′** (plās′kĭk′) *v.* — **place′-kick′er** *n.*

place•man (plās′mən) *n. Chiefly British.* One who has a political appointment in the government.

place mat *n.* A protective table mat for a single place setting.

place•ment (plās′mənt) *n.* **1.a.** The act of placing or arranging. **b.** The state of being placed or arranged. **2.a.** The finding of suitable accommodation or employment for applicants. **b.** Assignment of students to appropriate classes or programs. **3.** *Football.* **a.** The setting of the ball in position for a place kick. **b.** A place kick.

pla•cen•ta (plə-sĕn′tə) *n., pl.* **-tas** or **-tae** (-tē). **1.a.** A membranous vascular organ that develops in female mammals during pregnancy, lining the uterine wall and partially enveloping the fetus, to which it is attached by the umbilical cord. **b.** An organ with similar functions in some nonmammals, such as certain sharks and reptiles. **2.** *Bot.* The part within the ovary of a flowering plant to which the ovules are attached. [NLat. < Lat., flat cake, alteration of Gk. *plakoenta* < accusative of *plakoeis*, flat < *plax*, *plak-*, flat land, surface. See **plāk-[1]*.**] — **pla•cen′tal** *adj.*

plac•en•ta•tion (plăs′ən-tā′shən) *n.* **1.a.** Formation of a placenta in the uterus. **b.** The type or structure of a placenta. **2.** *Bot.* Arrangement of placentas within the ovary.

Pla•cen•tia (plə-sĕn′chə, -shə). A city of S CA ENE of Long Beach. Pop. 41,259.

plac•er (plăs′ər) *n.* **1.** A glacial or alluvial deposit of sand or gravel containing eroded particles of valuable minerals. **2.** A place where a placer deposit is washed to extract its mineral content. [Sp., shoal, placer < Catalan, shoal < *plassa*, place < Med.Lat. *placea*. See PLACE.]

place setting *n.* A table service for one person.

plac•id (plăs′ĭd) *adj.* **1.** Undisturbed by tumult or disorder; calm or quiet. See Syns at **calm. 2.** Satisfied; complacent. [Lat. *placidus* < *placēre*, to please. See **plāk-[1]*.**] — **pla•cid′i•ty** (plə-sĭd′ĭ-tē), **plac′id•ness** (plăs′ĭd-nĭs) *n.* — **plac′id•ly** *adv.*

Plac•id (plăs′ĭd), **Lake.** A lake of NE NY in the Adirondack Mts.

plack•et (plăk′ĭt) *n.* **1.** A slit in a dress, blouse, or skirt. **2.** A pocket, esp. in a woman's skirt. [?]

plac•oid (plăk′oid) *adj.* Platelike, as the hard toothlike scales of sharks, skates, and rays. [Gk. *plax*, *plak-*, flat land, surface; see **plāk-[1]*** + -OID.]

pla•fond (plə-fŏn′, plä-fôN′) *n.* A decorated ceiling. [Fr. : *plat*, flat; see PLATE + *fond*, base, bottom; see FOND[2].]

pla•gal (plā′gəl) *adj. Mus.* **1.** Of or being a medieval mode having a range from the fourth below to the fifth above its final tone. **2.** Of or being a cadence with the subdominant chord immediately preceding the tonic chord. [Med.Lat. *plagālis* < *plaga*, plagal mode < *plagius*, plagal < Med.Gk. *plagios (ēkhos)*, plagal (mode) < Gk., oblique < *plagos*, side. See **plāk-[1]*.**]

plage (plăzh) *n.* **1.** A sandy beach at a seaside resort. **2.** A bright and intensely hot area in the sun's chromosphere, usu. associated with a sunspot. [Fr. < Ital. *piaggia*, ult. < Gk. *plagia*, neut. pl. of *plagios*, oblique, slanting. See PLAGAL.]

pla•gia•rism (plā′jə-rĭz′əm) *n.* **1.** The act of plagiarizing. **2.** Something plagiarized. [< PLAGIARY.] — **pla′gia•rist** *n.* — **pla′gia•ris′tic** *adj.*

pla•gia•rize (plā′jə-rīz′) *v.* **-rized, -riz•ing, -riz•es.** — *tr.* **1.** To use and pass off as one's own (the ideas or writings of another). **2.** To appropriate for use as one's own passages or ideas from (another). — *intr.* To plagiarize the ideas or words of another. — **pla′gia•riz′er** *n.*

pla•gia•ry (plā′jə-rē) *n., pl.* **-ries. 1.** Plagiarism. **2.** *Archaic.* One who plagiarizes. [Lat. *plagiārius*, kidnapper, plagiarist < *plagium*, kidnapping < *plaga*, net. See **plāk-[1]*.**]

plagio– *pref.* Slanting; inclining: *plagiotropism.* [Gk., oblique < *plagios* < *plagos*, side. See **plāk-[1]*.**]

pla•gi•o•clase (plā′jē-ə-klās′, -klāz′, plăj′ē-) *n.* Any of a common rock-forming series of triclinic feldspars, consisting of mixtures of sodium and calcium aluminum silicates. [Gk. *plagio-*, plagio- + Gk. *klasis*, breaking (< *klan*, to break).]

pla•gi•ot•ro•pism (plā′jē-ŏt′rə-pĭz′əm) *n. Bot.* The tendency to grow at an oblique or horizontal angle, as roots or branches. — **pla′gi•o•tro′pic** (-ə-trō′pĭk, -trŏp′ĭk) *adj.*

plague (plāg) *n.* **1.** A widespread affliction or calamity, esp. one seen as divine retribution. **2.** A sudden destructive influx or injurious outbreak: *a plague of accidents.* **3.** A cause of annoyance; a nuisance. **4.** A highly infectious, usu. fatal epidemic disease, esp. bubonic plague. — *tr.v.* **plagued, plagu•ing, plagues. 1.** To pester or annoy persistently or incessantly. See Syns at **harass. 2.** To afflict with or as if with a disease or calamity. [ME *plage*, blow, calamity, plague < LLat. *plāga* < Lat., blow, wound. See **plāk-[2]*.**] — **plagu′er** *n.*

pla•guy also **pla•guey** (plā′gē) *adj.* Vexatious; bothersome. — **pla′guy, pla′gui•ly** *adv.*

plaice (plās) *n., pl.* **plaice** or **plaic•es. 1.** A large edible marine flatfish *(Pleuronectes platessa)* of western European waters. **2.** Any of various flatfishes, such as *Hippoglossoides platessoides* of North American Atlantic waters, related to the plaice. [ME < OFr. *plais* < VLat. **platīx*, alteration of LLat. *platessa*, prob. ult. < Gk. *platus*, broad. See **plat-***.]

plaid (plăd) *n.* **1.** A rectangular woolen scarf of a tartan pattern worn over the left shoulder by Scottish Highlanders. **2.a.** Cloth with a tartan or checked pattern. **b.** A pattern of this kind. [Sc.Gael. *plaide.*] — **plaid** *adj.*

plaid•ed (plăd′ĭd) *adj.* **1.** Made of plaid or having a plaid pattern. **2.** Wearing a plaid.

plain (plān) *adj.* **plain•er, plain•est. 1.** Free from obstructions; open; clear. **2.** Obvious to the mind; evident. See Syns at **apparent. 3.** Not elaborate or complicated; simple. **4.** Straightforward; frank or candid. **5.** Not mixed with other substances; pure. **6.** Common in rank or station; average; ordinary. **7.** Not pretentious; unaffected. **8.** Marked by little or no ornamentation or decoration. **9.** Not dyed, twilled, or patterned. **10.** Lacking beauty or distinction. **11.** Sheer; utter; unqualified. **12.** *Archaic.* Having no visible elevation or depression; flat; level. — *n.* **1.a.** An extensive, level, usu. treeless area of land. **b.** A broad level expanse, as a part of the sea floor or a lunar mare. **2.** Something free of ornamentation or extraneous matter. — *adv. Informal.* Clearly; simply: *plain stubborn.* [ME < OFr. < Lat. *plānus.* See **pelə-[2]*.**] — **plain′ly** *adv.* — **plain′ness** *n.*

plain•chant (plān′chănt′) *n. Rom. Cath. Ch.* See **plainsong** 2. [Fr. *plain-chant* (transl. of Med.Lat. *cantus plānus*) : *plain*, plain; see PLAIN + *chant*, song; see CHANT.]

plain•clothes man or **plain•clothes•man** (plān′klōz′mən, -klōthz′-) *n.* A member of a police force, esp. a detective, who wears civilian clothes on duty.

Plain•field (plān′fēld′). A city of NE NJ SW of Newark; settled in 1684. Pop. 46,567.

plain-Jane (plān′jān′) *adj.* Lacking adornment or pretension; basic or simple.

plain-laid (plān′lād′) *adj.* Made of three strands laid together with a right-hand twist. Used of a rope.

Plain People (plān) *pl.n.* Members of the Mennonites, Amish, or Dunkers, noted for their plain dress and simple style of life.

plain sailing *n. Informal.* Easy progress over a smooth and direct course.

Plains Indian (plānz) *n.* A member of any of the Native American peoples inhabiting the Great Plains.

plains•man (plānz′mən) *n.* An inhabitant or a settler of the plains, esp. of the prairie regions of the United States.

plain•song (plān′sông′, -sŏng′) *n. Rom. Cath. Ch.* **1.a.** A Gregorian chant. **b.** A melody to which contrapuntal voices are added in Gregorian chant. **2.** Any medieval liturgical music without strict meter and sung without accompaniment. [Transl. of Med.Lat. *cantus plānus*.]

plain•spo•ken (plān′spō′kən) *adj.* Frank; straightforward; blunt. — **plain′spo′ken•ness** *n.*

plaint (plānt) *n.* **1.** A complaint. **2.** A lamentation. [ME < OFr. *plainte* < Lat. *plānctus*, lament < p.part. of *plangere*, to strike one's breast, lament. See **plāk-[2]*.**]

plain text or **plain•text** (plān′tĕkst′) *n.* The original form of a message as opposed to the encrypted form.

plain•tiff (plān′tĭf) *n. Law.* The party that institutes a suit in a court. [ME *plaintif* < AN *pleintif* < OFr. *plaintif*, aggrieved. See PLAINTIVE.]

plain•tive (plān′tĭv) *adj.* Expressing sorrow; mournful or melancholy. [ME *plaintif* < OFr., lamenting < *plaint*, complaint. See PLAINT.] — **plain′tive•ly** *adv.* — **plain′tive•ness** *n.*

Plain•view (plān′vyo͞o′). A city of NW TX S of Amarillo. Pop. 21,700.

Plain•ville (plān′vĭl′). A town of central CT SW of Hartford. Pop. 17,392.

plain weave *n.* A weave in which the filling threads and the warp threads interlace alternately, forming a checkerboard pattern.

plain-wo•ven (plān′wō′vən) *adj.* Made in plain weave.

plait (plāt, plăt) *n.* **1.** A braid, esp. of hair. **2.** A pleat. —*tr.v.* **plait•ed, plait•ing, plaits. 1.** To braid. **2.** To pleat. **3.** To make by braiding. [ME *pleit,* fold, braid, poss. < *pleiten,* to fold, braid, alteration (influenced by OFr. *pleit,* fold) of OFr. *plier, pleiir* < Lat. *plicāre,* to fold. See **plek-*.**] —**plait′er** *n.*

plan (plăn) *n.* **1.** A scheme, program, or method worked out beforehand to accomplish an objective. **2.** A tentative project or course of action. **3.** A systematic arrangement of parts; an outline or a sketch. **4.** A drawing or diagram made to scale showing the structure or arrangement of something. **5.** In perspective rendering, one of several imaginary planes perpendicular to the line of vision between the viewer and the object being depicted. —*v.* **planned, plan•ning, plans.** —*tr.* **1.** To form a scheme or program for the accomplishment or attainment of. **2.** To have as a specific aim or purpose; intend. **3.** To draw or make a graphic representation of. —*intr.* To make plans. [Fr., alteration of *plant,* ground plan, map < *planter,* to plant < Lat. *plantāre* < *planta,* sole of the foot. See **plat-*.**] —**plan′ner** *n.*

Syns: plan, blueprint, design, project, scheme, strategy. The central meaning shared by these nouns is "a method or program in accordance with which something is to be done or accomplished": *has no plans; a blueprint for reorganization; social conventions of human design; an urban-renewal project; a scheme for conservation; a strategy for survival.*

plan– *pref.* Var. of **plano–.**

pla•nar (plā′nər, -när′) *adj.* **1.** Of, relating to, or situated in a plane. **2.** Flat: *a planar surface.* **3.** Having a two-dimensional quality. [LLat. *plānāris,* flat < Lat. *plānus.* See PLAIN.] —**pla•nar′i•ty** (plā-năr′ĭ-tē) *n.*

pla•nar•i•an (plə-nâr′ē-ən) *n.* Any of various small, chiefly freshwater turbellarian flatworms of the order Tricladida, having soft broad ciliated bodies. [< NLat. *Plānāria,* genus name < fem. of LLat. *plānārius,* on level ground < *plānus,* flat. See **pelə-[2]*.**]

pla•na•tion (plā-nā′shən) *n.* The process of erosion and deposition in which a level surface is produced, as by streams or wind. [Lat. *plānum,* flat surface; see PLANE[1] + –ATION.]

planch•et (plăn′chĭt) *n.* **1.** A flat disk of metal ready for stamping as a coin; a coin blank. **2.** A small shallow metal container in which a radioactive substance is deposited for measurement of its activity. [Dim. of *planch,* flat plate, slab < ME *plaunche,* plank < OFr. *planche* < LLat. *planca* < fem. of Lat. *plancus,* flat. See **plāk-[1]*.**]

plan•chette (plăn-shĕt′) *n.* A small triangular board supported by two casters and a vertical pencil that, when lightly touched by the fingertips, is said to spell out subconscious or supernatural messages. [Fr. < OFr., dim. of *planche,* board. See PLANCHET.]

Planck (plängk), **Max Karl Ernst Ludwig.** 1858–1947. German physicist who won a 1918 Nobel Prize.

Planck's constant (plängks) *n. Symbol* **h** The constant of proportionality relating the energy of a photon to its frequency, equal to approx. 6.626×10^{-34} joule-second. [After Max Karl Ernst Ludwig PLANCK.]

plane[1] (plān) *n.* **1.** *Math.* A surface containing all the straight lines that connect any two points on it. **2.** A flat or level surface. **3.** A level of development, existence, or achievement. **4.** An airplane or a hydroplane. **5.** A supporting surface of an airplane; an airfoil or a wing. —*adj.* **1.** *Math.* Of or being a figure lying in a plane: *a plane curve.* **2.** Flat; level. [Lat. *plānum,* flat surface < neut. of *plānus,* flat. See **pelə-[2]*.** N., sense 4, short for AEROPLANE.] —**plane′ness** *n.*

plane[2] (plān) *n.* **1.** A carpenter's tool with an adjustable blade for smoothing and leveling wood. **2.** A trowel-shaped tool for smoothing the surface of clay, sand, or plaster in a mold. —*v.* **planed, plan•ing, planes.** —*tr.* **1.** To smooth or finish with or as if with a plane. **2.** To remove with a plane. —*intr.* **1.** To work with a plane. **2.** To act as a plane. [ME < OFr. < LLat. *plāna* < *plānāre,* to plane < *plānus,* flat. See **pelə-[2]*.**]

plane[3] (plān) *intr.v.* **planed, plan•ing, planes. 1.** To rise partly out of the water, as a boat does at high speeds. **2.** To soar or glide. **3.** To travel by airplane. [ME *planen,* to glide, soar < OFr. *planer* < *plain,* flat, level < Lat. *plānus.* See **pelə-[2]*.**]

plane[4] (plān) *n.* The plane tree. [ME < OFr. < Lat. *platanus* < Gk. *platanos,* perh. < *platus,* broad. See **plat-*.**]

plane angle *n. Math.* An angle formed by two straight lines in the same plane.

plane geometry *n. Math.* The geometry of planar figures.

plane•load (plān′lōd′) *n.* The load an airplane can carry.

plan•er (plā′nər) *n.* **1.** One that planes, esp. a machine tool that is used to smooth or finish the surfaces of wood or metal. **2.** *Print.* A smooth block of wood used to level a form of type.

pla•ner tree (plā′nər) *n.* A small, deciduous elmlike swamp tree *(Planera aquatica)* of the southern United States, having small ribbed nutlike fruit. [After Johann Jacob *Planer* (1743–89), German botanist.]

plane•side (plān′sīd′) *n.* The area adjacent to an airplane.

plan•et (plăn′ĭt) *n.* **1.** A nonluminous celestial body larger than an asteroid or a comet that revolves around a star, such as the sun. **2.** One of the seven celestial bodies, Mercury, Venus, the moon, the sun, Mars, Jupiter, and Saturn, thought by ancient astronomers to revolve in the heavens about a fixed Earth and among fixed stars. **3.** One of the seven revolving astrological celestial bodies that in conjunction with the stars are believed to influence human affairs. [ME < OFr. *planete* < LLat. *planēta* < Gk. *planētēs,* var. of *planēs, planēt-* < *planasthai,* to wander. See **pelə-[2]*.**]

plane table *n.* A portable surveying instrument consisting essentially of a drawing board and a ruler mounted on a tripod and used to sight and map topographic details.

plan•e•tar•i•um (plăn′ĭ-târ′ē-əm) *n., pl.* **-i•ums** or **-i•a** (-ē-ə). **1.** An apparatus or a model representing the solar system. **2.a.** An optical device for projecting images of celestial bodies and other astronomical phenomena onto the inner surface of a hemispherical dome. **b.** A building or room containing a planetarium, with seats for an audience.

plan•e•tar•y (plăn′ĭ-tĕr′ē) *adj.* **1.** Of, relating to, or resembling the physical or orbital characteristics of a planet or the planets. **2.a.** Of or relating to the earth; terrestrial or earthly. **b.** Of or affecting the entire world; global. **3.** Wandering; erratic. **4.** Being or relating to a gear train having a central gear with an internal ring gear and one or more pinions.

planetary nebula *n.* A nebula consisting of a hot blue-white central star surrounded by an envelope of expanding gas.

plan•e•tes•i•mal (plăn′ĭ-tĕs′ə-məl) *n.* Any of innumerable small bodies thought to have orbited the sun and aggregated into the planets. [PLANET + (INFINIT)ESIMAL.]

plan•e•toid (plăn′ĭ-toid′) *n. Astron.* See **asteroid** 1. —**plan′e•toi′dal** (-toid′l) *adj.*

plan•e•tol•o•gy (plăn′ĭ-tŏl′ə-jē) *n.* The branch of astronomy that deals with the planets, satellites, and meteors of the solar system. —**plan′e•to•log′i•cal** (plăn′ĭ-tl-ŏj′ĭ-kəl) *adj.* —**plan′e•tol′o•gist** *n.*

plane tree *n.* Any of several trees of the genus *Platanus,* having ball-shaped fruit clusters and usu. outer bark that flakes off in patches.

planet wheel *n.* A small gear wheel in an epicyclic train.

plan•gent (plăn′jənt) *adj.* **1.** Loud and resounding: *plangent bells.* **2.** Expressing or suggesting sadness; plaintive. [Lat. *plangēns, plangent-,* pr.part. of *plangere,* to strike, lament. See **plāk-[2]*.**] —**plan′gen•cy** *n.* —**plan′gent•ly** *adv.*

pla•nim•e•ter (plə-nĭm′ĭ-tər, plā-) *n.* An instrument that measures the area of a plane figure as a mechanically coupled pointer traverses the perimeter of the figure. —**pla′ni•met′ric** (plā′nə-mĕt′rĭk), **pla′ni•met′ri•cal** (-rĭ-kəl) *adj.* —**pla′ni•met′ri•cal•ly** *adv.* —**pla•nim′e•try** *n.*

plan•ish (plăn′ĭsh) *tr.v.* **-ished, -ish•ing, -ish•es.** To smooth (metal) by rolling or hammering. [ME **planishen* < OFr. *planir, planiss-,* to make smooth < *plan,* level < Lat. *plānus.* See **pelə-[2]*.**] —**plan′ish•er** *n.*

pla•ni•sphere (plā′nĭ-sfîr′) *n.* **1.** A representation of a sphere or part of a sphere on a plane surface. **2.** *Astron.* A polar projection of half or more of the celestial sphere on a chart with an adjustable overlay to show the stars visible at a given time and place. —**pla′ni•spher′ic** (-sfîr′ĭk, -sfĕr′-), **pla′ni•spher′i•cal** (-ĭ-kəl) *adj.*

plank (plăngk) *n.* **1.a.** A piece of lumber cut thicker than a board. **b.** Planking. **2.** A foundation; a support. **3.** One of the articles of a political platform. —*tr.v.* **planked, plank•ing, planks. 1.** To furnish or cover with planks. **2.** To bake or broil and serve (fish or meat) on a plank. **3.** To put or set down, often emphatically or with force. [ME < ONFr. *planke* < LLat. *planca* < *plancus,* flat. See **plāk-[1]*.**]

plank•ing (plăng′kĭng) *n.* **1.** Planks considered as a group; plank. **2.** An object or a structure made of planks.

plank•ter (plăngk′tər) *n.* One of the minute organisms that collectively constitute plankton. [Gk. *planktēr,* wanderer < *planktos,* wandering. See PLANKTON.]

plank•ton (plăngk′tən) *n.* The collection of small or microscopic organisms, including algae, that float or drift in great numbers in fresh or salt water, esp. at or near the surface, and serve as food for larger organisms. [Ger. < Gk., neut. of *planktos,* wandering < *plazein,* to turn aside. See **plāk-[2]*.**] —**plank•ton′ic** (-tŏn′ĭk) *adj.*

Planned Parenthood (plănd). A service mark used for an organization that provides family planning services.

Pla•no (plā′nō). A city of NE TX, a suburb of Dallas. Pop. 128,713.

plano– or **plani–** or **plan–** *pref.* Flat: *planoconvex.* [< Lat. *plānus,* flat. See **pelə-[2]*.**]

plan•o•blast (plăn′ə-blăst′) *n.* The medusa of certain hydrozoans. [Gk. *planos,* wandering (< *planasthai,* to wander; see PLANET) + –BLAST.]

pla•no•con•cave (plā′nō-kŏn-kāv′, -kŏn′kāv′) *adj.* Flat on one side and concave on the other: *a planoconcave lens.*

pla•no•con•vex (plā′nō-kŏn-vĕks′, -kŏn′vĕks′) *adj.* Flat on

plane[2]
Bench plane

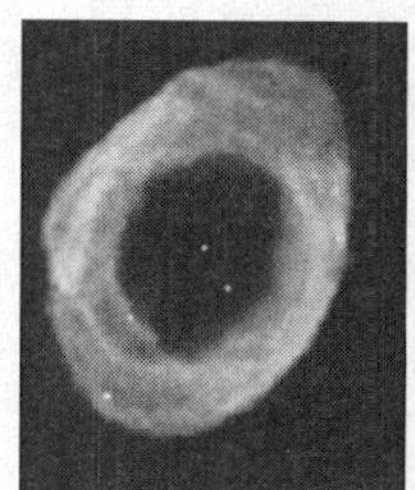
planetary nebula

ă pat	oi boy
ā pay	ou out
âr care	o͝o took
ä father	o͞o boot
ĕ pet	ŭ cut
ē be	ûr urge
ĭ pit	th thin
ī pie	*th* this
îr pier	hw which
ŏ pot	zh vision
ō toe	ə about, item
ô paw	

Stress marks:
′ (primary);
′ (secondary), as in dictionary (dĭk′shə-nĕr′ē)

one side and convex on the other: *a planoconvex lens.*

plan•o•gam•ete (plăn′ō-găm′ēt, -gə-mēt′) *n.* A motile gamete, esp. one having undulipodia. [Gk. *planos,* wandering; see PLANOBLAST + GAMETE.]

pla•nog•ra•phy (plə-nŏg′rə-fē, plā-) *n.* A process for printing from a smooth surface, as lithography or offset. — **pla′no•graph′ic** (plā′nə-grăf′ĭk) *adj.* — **pla′no•graph′i•cal•ly** *adv.*

pla•nom•e•ter (plə-nŏm′ĭ-tər, plā-) *n.* A flat metal plate for gauging the accuracy of a plane surface in precision metalworking. — **pla•nom′e•try** *n.*

plant (plănt) *n.* **1.** *Bot.* **a.** Any of various photosynthetic, eukaryotic multicellular organisms of the kingdom Plantae, characteristically producing embryos, containing chloroplasts, having cellulose cell walls, and lacking locomotion. **b.** A plant having no permanent woody stem; an herb. **2.a.** A building or group of buildings for manufacture; a factory. **b.** The equipment, including machinery, tools, and fixtures and the buildings containing them, necessary for an industrial or manufacturing operation. **3.** The buildings, equipment, and fixtures of an institution. **4.** A person or thing put into place in order to mislead or function secretly, esp.: **a.** A person placed in a group of spectators to influence behavior. **b.** A spy or an observer stationed in a given location. **c.** A misleading piece of evidence placed so as to be discovered. **d.** A remark or an action in a play or narrative that becomes important later. **5.** *Slang.* A scheming trick; a swindle. —*tr.v.* **plant•ed, plant•ing, plants. 1.a.** To place or set (seeds, for example) in the ground to grow. **b.** To place seeds or young plants in (land); sow. **2.a.** To place (spawn or young fish) in water or an underwater bed for cultivation. **b.** To stock with spawn or fish. **3.** To introduce (an animal) into an area. **4.** To set firmly in position; fix. **5.** To establish; found. **6.** To fix firmly in the mind; implant. **7.a.** To station (a person) for the purpose of functioning in secret, as by spying. **b.** To place so as to be discovered and to mislead. **8.** *Slang.* To conceal; hide. **9.** *Slang.* To deliver (a blow or punch). [ME *plante* < OE and OFr., both < Lat. *planta,* shoot, sole of the foot. See **plat-***.]

Plan•tag•e•net (plăn-tăj′ə-nĭt). Royal house of English kings from Henry II to Richard III (1154–1485).

plan•tain[1] (plăn′tən) *n.* Any of various plants of the genus *Plantago* that produce dense spikes of small greenish flowers, esp. either of two Eurasian weeds, *P. major* or *P. lanceolata.* [ME < OFr. < Lat. *plantāgō, plantāgin-* < *planta,* sole of the foot (< its broad leaves). See **plat-***.]

plan•tain[2] (plăn′tən) *n.* **1.** A large southeast Asian treelike herb *(Musa paradisiaca)* resembling the banana and bearing similar fruit. **2.** The fruit of this plant, used as a staple food. [Sp. *plátano, plántano,* plane tree, plantain < Lat. *platanus.* See PLANE[4].]

plantain lily *n.* Any of several eastern Asian plants of the genus *Hosta,* cultivated for their large white, blue, or lilac flowers borne in a terminal scapose one-sided raceme.

plan•tar (plăn′tər, -tär′) *adj.* Of or occurring on the sole of the foot. [Lat. *plantāris* < *planta,* sole. See **plat-***.]

plan•ta•tion (plăn-tā′shən) *n.* **1.** An area under cultivation. **2.** A group of cultivated trees or plants. **3.** A large estate or farm on which crops are raised, often by resident workers. **4.** A newly established settlement; a colony.

Plan•ta•tion (plăn-tā′shən). A city of SE FL, a suburb of Fort Lauderdale. Pop. 48,501.

plant bug *n.* An insect of the order Hemiptera, having mouthparts adapted for piercing plants and sucking their juices.

Plant City (plănt). A city of W-central FL E of Tampa. Pop. 22,754.

plant•er (plăn′tər) *n.* **1.a.** One who plants. **b.** A machine or tool for planting seeds. **2.** The owner or manager of a plantation. **3.** An early settler or colonist. **4.** A decorative container for a plant or small tree.

plant•er's punch (plăn′tərz) *n.* A drink of rum with lemon or lime juice, sugar syrup, water or soda, bitters, and grenadine.

plant hormone *n.* Any of various hormones produced by plants that control or regulate physiological activities.

plan•ti•grade (plăn′tĭ-grād′) *adj.* Walking with the entire sole of the foot on the ground. —*n.* A plantigrade animal. [Fr. : Lat. *planta,* sole of the foot; see **plat-*** + Lat. *-gradus,* going (< *gradī,* to walk, go; see **ghredh-***).]

plant•let (plănt′lĭt) *n.* A young or small plant.

plant louse *n.* See **aphid.**

plan•u•la (plăn′yə-lə) *n., pl.* **-lae** (-lē′). The flat free-swimming ciliated larva of a coelenterate. [NLat. < Lat., fem. dim. of *plānus,* flat (from its shape). See **pelə-**[2]*.]

plaque (plăk) *n.* **1.** A flat plate, slab, or disk ornamented or engraved for mounting, as on a wall for decoration. **2.** A small pin or brooch worn as an ornament or a membership badge. **3.a.** *Pathol.* A small disk-shaped formation or growth; a patch. **b.** A deposit of fatty material on the inner lining of an arterial wall, characteristic of atherosclerosis. **c.** A scaly patch formed on the skin by psoriasis. **d.** A film of mucus and bacteria on a tooth surface. **e.** A clear patch of lysed cells in an otherwise opaque layer of a bacteria or cell culture. [Fr. < OFr., metal plate, perh. < MDu. *placke,* disk, patch.]

plash (plăsh) *n.* **1.** A light splash. **2.** The sound of a light splash. —*v.* **plashed, plash•ing, plash•es.** —*tr.* To spatter (liquid) about; splash. —*intr.* To cause a light splash. [Poss. < ME *plashe,* pool of water < OE *plæsc.*]

-plasia or **-plasy** *suff.* Growth; development: *achondroplasia.* [NLat. < Gk. *plasis,* molding < *plassein,* to mold. See **pelə-**[2]*.]

plasm (plăz′əm) *n.* See **germ plasm** 3.

plasm- *pref.* Var. of **plasmo-.**

-plasm *suff.* Material forming cells or tissue: *cytoplasm.* [< PLASMA.]

plas•ma (plăz′mə) also **plasm** (plăz′əm) *n.* **1.a.** The clear yellowish fluid portion of blood, lymph, or intramuscular fluid in which cells are suspended. **b.** Blood plasma. **2.** *Medic.* Cell-free sterilized blood plasma, used in transfusions. **3.** Protoplasm or cytoplasm. **4.** The fluid portion of milk from which the curd is separated by coagulation; whey. **5.** *Phys.* A highly ionized gas containing nearly equal numbers of positive ions and electrons. [NLat. < LLat., image, figure < Gk. < *plassein,* to mold. See **pelə-**[2]*.] — **plas•mat′ic** (plăz-măt′ĭk), **plas′mic** (-mĭk) *adj.*

plasma cell *n.* An antibody-producing cell found in lymphoid tissue and derived from a B cell upon reaction with a specific antigen.

plas•ma•cyte (plăz′mə-sīt′) *n.* See **plasma cell.**

plas•ma•gel (plăz′mə-jĕl′) *n.* A jellylike state of cytoplasm, characteristically occurring in the pseudopod of the amoeba.

plas•ma•gene (plăz′mə-jēn′) *n.* A self-replicating hereditary structure thought to exist in cytoplasm and function in a manner analogous to but independent of chromosomal genes.

plas•ma•lem•ma (plăz′mə-lĕm′ə) *n.* See **cell membrane.** [PLASMA + Gk. *lemma,* husk; see LEMMA[2].]

plasma membrane *n.* See **cell membrane.**

plas•ma•pher•e•sis (plăz′mə-fĕr′ĭ-sĭs, -fə-rē′-) *n.* A process in which plasma is taken from donated blood and the remaining components are returned to the donor. [PLASM(A) + Gk. *aphairesis,* removal; see APHAERESIS.]

plas•ma•sol (plăz′mə-sôl′, -sŏl′, -sōl′) *n.* A state of cytoplasm that is more liquid than plasmagel.

plas•mid (plăz′mĭd) *n.* A circular double-stranded unit of DNA that replicates within a cell independently of the chromosomal DNA and is most often found in bacteria.

plas•min (plăz′mĭn) *n.* A proteolytic enzyme in plasma that dissolves fibrin and other blood clotting factors.

plas•min•o•gen (plăz-mĭn′-ə-jən) *n.* The inactive precursor to plasmin that is found in body fluids and blood plasma.

plasmo- or **plasm-** *pref.* Plasma: *plasmin.* [< PLASMA.]

plas•mo•des•ma (plăz′mə-dĕz′mə) also **plas•mo•desm** (plăz′mə-dĕz′əm) *n., pl.* **-ma•ta** (-mə-tə) or **-mas** also **-desms.** *Bot.* A strand of cytoplasm that passes through openings in cell walls and connects the protoplasts of adjacent living plant cells. [PLASMO- + Gk. *desma,* bond (< *dein,* to bind).]

plas•mo•di•um (plăz-mō′dē-əm) *n., pl.* **-di•a** (-dē-ə). **1.** A multinucleate mass of cytoplasm formed by the fusion of a number of amoeboid cells. **2.** A protozoan of the genus *Plasmodium,* which includes the parasites that cause malaria. [NLat. *Plasmodium,* genus name : PLASM(O)- + *-odium,* resembling (< Gk. *-ōdēs,* var. of *-oeidēs,* -oid).] — **plas•mo′di•al** (-dē-əl) *adj.*

plas•mol•y•sis (plăz-mŏl′ĭ-sĭs) *n., pl.* **-ses** (-sēz′). Shrinkage or contraction of the protoplasm away from the wall of a living plant or bacterial cell, caused by water loss. — **plas′mo•lyt′ic** (plăz′mə-lĭt′ĭk) *adj.* — **plas′mo•lyt′i•cal•ly** *adv.* — **plas′mo•lyze′** (-mə-līz′) *v.*

-plast *suff.* A small body, structure, particle, or granule, esp. of living matter; cell: *chloroplast.* [< Gk. *plastos,* molded < *plassein,* to mold. See **pelə-**[2]*.]

plas•ter (plăs′tər) *n.* **1.** A mixture of lime or gypsum, sand, and water that hardens to a smooth solid, used for coating walls and ceilings. **2.** Plaster of Paris. **3.** A pastelike mixture applied to a part of the body for healing or cosmetic purposes. **4.** *Chiefly British.* An adhesive bandage. —*v.* **-tered, -ter•ing, -ters.** —*tr.* **1.** To cover, coat, or repair with plaster. **2.** To cover or hide with or as if with a coat of plaster: *plastered over differences.* **3.** To apply a plaster to. **4.a.** To cover conspicuously, as with things pasted on; overspread. **b.** To affix conspicuously, usu. with a paste. **5.** To make smooth by applying a sticky substance. **6.** To make adhere to another surface. **7.** *Informal.* **a.** To inflict heavy damage or injury on. **b.** To defeat decisively. —*intr.* To apply plaster. [ME < OE, medical dressing, and < OFr. *plastre,* cementing material, both < Lat. *emplastrum,* dressing < Gk. *emplastron* < *emplassein,* to plaster on : *en-,* in, on; see EN-[2] + *plassein,* to mold; see **pelə-**[2]*.] — **plas′ter•er** *n.* — **plas′ter•y** *adj.*

plas•ter•board (plăs′tər-bôrd′, -bōrd′) *n.* A board of layers of fiberboard or paper bonded to a gypsum plaster core, used instead of plaster or wood panels for walls.

plaster cast *n.* **1.** A sculptured mold or cast in plaster of Paris. **2.** See **cast** 11.

plas•tered (plăs′tərd) *adj. Slang.* Intoxicated; drunk.

plas•ter•ing (plăs′tər-ĭng) *n.* **1.** A layer or coating of plaster. **2.** *Informal.* A resounding defeat; a beating.

plaster of Par•is (păr′ĭs) *n.* Any of a group of gypsum cements, made up essentially of hemihydrated calcium sulfate, $CaSO_4 \cdot \frac{1}{2}H_2O$, a powder that forms a paste when mixed with water and hardens into a solid, used in making casts, molds, and sculpture. [ME, after PARIS², France.]

plas•ter•work (plăs′tər-wûrk′) *n.* Construction or ornamental work done with plaster.

plas•tic (plăs′tĭk) *adj.* **1.** Capable of being shaped or formed. **2.** Relating to or dealing with shaping or modeling. **3.** Having the qualities of sculpture; well-formed. **4.** Giving form or shape to a substance. **5.** Easily influenced; impressionable. **6.** Made of a plastic or plastics. **7.** *Phys.* Capable of undergoing continuous deformation without rupture or relaxation. **8.** *Biol.* Capable of building tissue; formative. **9.** Marked by artificiality or superficiality; synthetic. **10.** *Informal.* Of or obtained by means of credit cards. —*n.* **1.** Any of various organic compounds produced by polymerization and capable of being molded, extruded, cast into shapes and films, or drawn into filaments used as textile fibers. **2.** An object or objects made of plastic. **3.** *Informal.* A credit card or credit cards. [Lat. *plasticus* < Gk. *plastikos* < *plastos*, molded < *plassein*, to mold. See **pelə-²***.] —**plas′ti•cal•ly** *adv.* —**plas•tic′i•ty** (plă-stĭs′ĭ-tē) *n.*

–plastic *suff.* Forming; growing; changing; developing: *metaplastic.* [Gk. *plastikos*, fit for molding. See PLASTIC.]

plastic explosive *n.* A moldable explosive substance used in bombs detonated by fuse or electrical impulse.

plas•ti•cize (plăs′tĭ-sīz′) *tr. & intr. v.* **-cized, -ciz•ing, -ciz•es.** To make or become plastic. —**plas′ti•ci•za′tion** (-sĭ-zā′shən) *n.*

plas•ti•ciz•er (plăs′tĭ-sī′zər) *n.* Any of various substances added, as to plastics, for softness or pliability.

plastic surgery *n.* Surgery to remodel, repair, or restore body parts, esp. by the transfer of tissue. —**plastic surgeon** *n.*

plas•tid (plăs′tĭd) *n.* Any of several pigmented cytoplasmic organelles found in plant cells and other organisms and having various functions such as food synthesis and storage. [< Gk. *plastis, plastid-*, fem. of *plastēs*, molder < *plastos*, molded. See PLASTIC.] —**plas•tid′i•al** (plă-stĭd′ē-əl) *adj.*

plas•tron (plăs′trən) *n.* **1.** A metal breastplate worn under a coat of mail. **2.** A quilted pad worn by fencers to protect the torso and side. **3.** A trimming on a bodice. **4.** The front of a man's dress shirt. **5.** *Zool.* The ventral part of the shell of a turtle or tortoise. [Fr. < OFr. < OItal. *piastrone*, aug. of *piastra*, thin metal plate. See PIASTER.] —**plas′tral** (-trəl) *adj.*

–plasty *suff.* Molding or forming surgically; plastic surgery: *dermatoplasty.* [Gk. *-plastia* < *plastos*, molded < *plassein*, to mold. See **pelə-²***.]

–plasy *suff.* Var. of **–plasia.**

plat¹ (plăt) *tr.v.* **plat•ted, plat•ting, plats.** To plait or braid. —*n.* A braid. [ME *platen*, alteration of *plaiten*, to fold, braid. See PLAIT.]

plat² (plăt) *n.* **1.** A piece of land; a plot. **2.** A map showing actual or planned features, such as streets. —*tr.v.* **plat•ted, plat•ting, plats.** To make a plat of. [ME, prob. alteration (influenced by *plat*, something flat) of *plot*. See PLOT.]

plat. *abbr.* **1.** Plateau. **2.** Platform. **3.** Platoon.

Pla•ta (plä′tə, -tä), **Río de la.** A wide estuary of SE South America between Argentina and Uruguay formed by the Paraná and Uruguay rivers and opening on the Atlantic.

Pla•tae•a (plə-tē′ə). An ancient city of Greece SW of Thebes; site of a Greek victory over the Persians in 479 B.C.

plat du jour (plä′ də zho͝or′) *n., pl.* **plats du jour** (plä′ də zho͝or′). A featured dish of the day at a restaurant. [Fr. : *plat*, plate + *du*, of the + *jour*, day.]

plate (plāt) *n.* **1.** A smooth, flat, thin, rigid body of uniform thickness. **2.a.** A sheet of hammered, rolled, or cast metal. **b.** A very thin applied or deposited coat of metal. **3.a.** A flat piece of metal forming part of a machine: *a boiler plate.* **b.** A flat piece of metal on which something is engraved. **4.a.** A thin piece of metal used for armor. **b.** Armor made of such pieces. **5.** *Print.* **a.** A sheet of metal, rubber, or other material prepared for use as a printing surface, such as an electrotype. **b.** A print of a woodcut or other engraved material, esp. when reproduced in a book. **c.** A full-page book illustration, often in color and printed on paper different from that used on the text pages. **6.** *Photography.* A light-sensitive sheet of glass or metal on which a photographic image can be recorded. **7.** *Dentistry.* A thin metallic or plastic support fitted to the gums to anchor artificial teeth. **8.** *Archit.* In wood-frame construction, a horizontal member, capping the exterior wall studs, upon which the roof rafters rest. **9.** *Baseball.* Home plate. **10.a.** A shallow dish for food. **b.** The contents of such a dish. **c.** A whole course served on such a dish. **11.** Service and food for one person at a meal. **12.** Household articles, such as holloware, covered with a precious metal, such as gold. **13.** A dish passed, as in a congregation, for offerings. **14.** *Sports.* **a.** A dish or other article of silver or gold offered as a prize. **b.** A contest, esp. a horserace, offering such a prize. **15.** A thin cut of beef from the brisket. **16.** *Anat. & Zool.* **a.** A thin flat layer or scale, as that of a fish. **b.** A platelike part, organ, or structure, such as that covering some reptiles. **17.** *Elect.* **a.** An electrode, as in a storage battery or capacitor. **b.** The anode in an electron tube. **18.** *Geol.* In the theory of plate tectonics, one of the sections into which the earth's crust is divided that are in constant motion relative to each other. —*tr.v.* **plat•ed, plat•ing, plates. 1.** To coat or cover with a thin layer of metal. **2.** To cover with armor plate. **3.** *Print.* To make a plate from. **4.** To give a glossy finish to (paper) by pressing between metal sheets or rollers. [ME < OFr. < fem. of *plat*, flat < VLat. **plattus* < Gk. *platus*. See **plat-***.] —**plat′er** *n.*

pla•teau (plă-tō′) *n., pl.* **-teaus** or **-teaux** (-tōz′). **1.** An elevated, relatively level expanse of land; a tableland. **2.** A relatively stable level, period, or state. —*intr.v.* **-teaued, -teau•ing, -teaus.** To reach a stable level; level off. [Fr. < OFr. *platel*, platter < *plat*, flat. See PLATE.]

plat•ed (plā′tĭd) *adj.* **1.** Coated with a thin adherent layer of metal. Often used in combination: *a gold-plated pen.* **2.** Covered with protective plates or sheets of metal. Often used in combination: *a steel-plated safe.* **3.** Knitted with two kinds of yarn, one on the face and one on the back.

plate•ful (plāt′fo͝ol′) *n., pl.* **-fuls. 1.** The amount that a plate can hold. **2.** A generous portion of food.

plate glass *n.* A strong rolled and polished glass containing few impurities, used for mirrors and large windows.

plate•let (plāt′lĭt) *n.* A minute disklike cytoplasmic body in the blood plasma of mammals that promotes blood clotting.

plat•en (plăt′n) *n.* **1.** The roller in a typewriter that serves as the backing for the paper against which the type bars strike. **2.** *Comp. Sci.* The roller in a computer printer against which the print head strikes. **3.** A flat plate or rolling cylinder in a printing press that positions the paper and holds it against the inked type. [ME *plateine*, paten < OFr. *platine*, metal plate < *plat*, flat. See PLATE.]

plate proof *n. Print.* A proof taken from a master plate.

plate tectonics *n.* **1.** *(used with a sing. v.)* A theory of global dynamics holding that the movement of a small number of semirigid sections of the earth's crust, at whose margins seismic activity and volcanism occur, causes continental drift and changes the shape and size of ocean basins and continents. **2.** *(used with a sing. or pl. v.)* The dynamics of plate movement. —**plate′-tec•ton′ic** (plāt′tĕk-tŏn′ĭk) *adj.*

plat•form (plăt′fôrm′) *n.* **1.a.** A horizontal surface raised above the level of the adjacent area, as a stage for public speaking. **b.** A vessel, such as a submarine, from which weapons can be deployed. **c.** An oil platform. **2.** A place, a means, or an opportunity for public expression of opinion. **3.** A vestibule at the end of a railway car. **4.** A formal declaration of the principles on which a group makes its appeal to the public. **5.a.** A thick layer, as of cork, between the inner and outer soles of a shoe, giving added height. **b.** A shoe having such a construction. [Fr. *plate-forme*, diagram < OFr. : *plat*, flat; see PLATE + *forme*, form (< Lat. *forma*).]

platform bed *n.* A bed consisting of a mattress on a platform supported by legs, with available space on the floor beneath.

platform scale *n.* An industrial weighing instrument consisting of a platform coupled to an automatic system of levers and adjustable weights, used to weigh large or heavy objects.

platform tennis *n. Sports.* An outdoor court game played with paddles and a rubber ball on a raised and fenced wooden floor that is smaller than a tennis court.

Plath (plăth), **Sylvia.** 1932–63. Amer. writer whose poems are noted for their images of alienation.

pla•ti•na (plə-tē′nə) *n.* Platinum, esp. as found naturally in impure form. [Sp., dim. of *plata*, silver, plate < VLat. **plattus*. See PLATE.]

plat•ing (plā′tĭng) *n.* **1.** A thin layer of metal deposited on or applied to a surface. **2.** A coating of metal sheets or plates.

pla•tin•ic (plə-tĭn′ĭk) *adj.* Of, relating to, or containing platinum, esp. with valence 4.

plat•i•nize (plăt′n-īz′) *tr.v.* **-nized, -niz•ing, -niz•es.** To electroplate with platinum.

platino– or **platini–** or **platin–** *pref.* Platinum: *platinotype.* [< PLATINUM.]

plat•i•no•cy•a•nide (plăt′n-ō-sī′ə-nīd′) *n.* A double salt of platinous cyanide and another cyanide.

plat•i•noid (plăt′n-oid′) *adj.* Resembling platinum. —*n.* **1.** An alloy of copper, nickel, tungsten, and zinc, formerly used in electric coils. **2.** A metal chemically resembling platinum, esp. osmium, iridium, or palladium.

plat•i•no•type (plăt′n-ō-tīp′) *n.* **1.** A process formerly used for making photographic prints, using a platinum salt and an iron salt in the sensitizing solution to produce prints in platinum black. **2.** A print produced by platinotype.

plat•i•nous (plăt′n-əs) *adj.* Of, relating to, or containing platinum, esp. with valence 2.

plat•i•num (plăt′n-əm) *n.* **1.** *Symbol* **Pt** A ductile malleable metallic element usu. occurring mixed with other metals such as iridium, osmium, or nickel and used as a catalyst and in electrical components, jewelry, dentistry, and electroplating. Atomic number 78; atomic weight 195.09; melting point 1,772°C; boiling point 3,827°C; specific gravity 21.45; valence 2, 3, 4. See table at **element. 2.** *Color.* A medium to

plastron
Fencer wearing a plastron

Sylvia Plath
Photographed in 1955

ă **pat**	oi **boy**
ā **pay**	ou **out**
âr **care**	o͝o **took**
ä **father**	o͞o **boot**
ĕ **pet**	ŭ **cut**
ē **be**	ûr **urge**
ĭ **pit**	th **thin**
ī **pie**	*th* **this**
îr **pier**	hw **which**
ŏ **pot**	zh **vision**
ō **toe**	ə **about, item**
ô **paw**	

Stress marks:
′ (primary);
′ (secondary), as in
dictionary (dĭk′shə-nĕr′ē)

Plato
Copy of a mid fourth-century B.C. herma attributed to Silanion (fl. 360–330 B.C.)

platypus
Ornithorhynchus anatinus

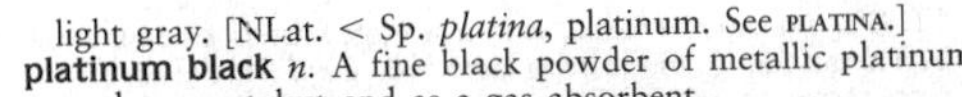

light gray. [NLat. < Sp. *platina*, platinum. See PLATINA.]

platinum black *n.* A fine black powder of metallic platinum, used as a catalyst and as a gas absorbent.

platinum blond *n.* **1.** A very light silver-blond hair color, esp. when artificially produced. **2.** One with hair of this color.

plat•i•tude (plăt′ĭ-to͞od′, -tyo͞od′) *n.* **1.** A trite or banal remark or statement, esp. one expressed as if it were original or significant. **2.** Lack of originality; triteness. [Fr. < *plat*, flat < OFr. See PLATE.] **— plat′i•tu′di•nous** (-to͞od′n-əs, -tyo͞od′-), **plat′i•tu′di•nal** (-to͞od′n-əl, -tyo͞od′-) *adj.* **— plat′i•tu′di•nous•ly** *adv.*

plat•i•tu•di•nar•i•an (plăt′ĭ-to͞od′n-âr′ē-ən, -tyo͞od′-) *n.* One who habitually uses platitudes.

plat•i•tu•di•nize (plăt′ĭ-to͞od′n-īz′, -tyo͞od′-) *intr.v.* **-nized, -niz•ing, -niz•es.** To speak or write with platitudes.

Pla•to (plā′tō). 427?–347? B.C. Greek philosopher who presented his ideas in dramatic dialogues, as in *The Republic.*

Pla•ton•ic (plə-tŏn′ĭk, plā-) *adj.* **1.** Often **Pla•ton•i•cal** (-ĭ-kəl). Of, relating to, or characteristic of Plato or his philosophy. **2.** Often **platonic.** Transcending physical desire and tending toward the purely spiritual or ideal. **3.** Often **platonic.** Speculative or theoretical. **— Pla•ton′i•cal•ly** *adv.*

Pla•to•nism (plāt′n-ĭz′əm) *n. Philos.* The philosophy of Plato, esp. insofar as it asserts ideal forms as an absolute reality of which the phenomena of the world are an imperfect and transitory reflection. **— Pla′to•nist** *n.* **— Pla′to•nis′tic** *adj.*

pla•toon (plə-to͞on′) *n.* **1.** A subdivision of a company of troops consisting of two or more sections and usu. commanded by a lieutenant. **2.** A group of people working, traveling, or assembled together: *a platoon of firefighters.* **3.** *Sports.* A group of players within a team, esp. a football team, that is trained and sent into or withdrawn from play as a unit. *— tr.v.* **-tooned, -toon•ing, -toons.** *Sports.* To play (a player) in alternation with another player in the same position. [Fr. *peloton* < OFr., dim. of *pelote*, ball. See PELLET.]

platoon sergeant *n.* The senior noncommissioned officer in an army platoon or comparable unit.

Platt•deutsch (plät′doich′) *n.* See **Low German** 1. [Ger. (partial transl. of Du. *Platduits*, Low German) : Du. *plat*, low, flat (< MDu. < OFr.; see PLATE) + Ger. *Deutsch*, Ger. (< MHGer. *diutsch* < OHGer. *diutisc*, of the people; see **teutā-***).]

Platte (plăt). A river of central NE flowing c. 499 km (310 mi) to the Missouri R. at the IA border.

plat•ter (plăt′ər) *n.* **1.** A large shallow dish or plate, used esp. for serving food. **2.** A meal or course served on a platter. **3.** *Slang.* A phonograph record. **— *idiom.* on a platter.** Without exertion; effortlessly. [ME *plater* < AN < OFr. *plate*, plate. See PLATE.]

Platts•burgh (plăts′bûrg′). A city of extreme NE NY on Lake Champlain; site of a major naval battle during the War of 1812. Pop. 21,255.

plat•y[1] (plā′tē) *adj.* **-i•er, -i•est.** Relating to or being soil or minerals occurring in flaky layers.

plat•y[2] (plăt′ē) *n., pl.* **-ys** or **-ies.** Any of several small freshwater live-bearing fishes of the genus *Xiphophorus* of southern North America, popular in aquariums for their bright and variable colors. [Short for NLat. *Platypoecilus*, former genus name : PLATY– + Gk. *poikilos*, many-colored; see **peig-***.]

platy– *pref.* Flat: *platyhelminth.* [Gk. *platu-* < *platus.* See **plat-***.]

plat•y•fish (plăt′ē-fĭsh′) *n., pl.* **platyfish** or **plat•y•fish•es.** See **platy**[2].

plat•y•hel•minth (plăt′ĭ-hĕl′mĭnth) *n.* See **flatworm.** [< NLat. *Platyhelminthes*, phylum name : PLATY– + Gk. *helmis, helminth-*, parasitic worm; see **wel-**[2]*****.] **— plat′y•hel•min′thic** *adj.*

plat•y•pus (plăt′ĭ-pəs) *n., pl.* **-pus•es.** A semiaquatic egg-laying mammal *(Ornithorhynchus anatinus)* of Australia and Tasmania having a broad flat tail, webbed feet, and a snout resembling a duck's bill. [NLat. < Gk. *platupous*, flat-footed : *platu-*, platy- + *pous*, foot; see **ped-***.]

plat•yr•rhine (plăt′ĭ-rīn′) also **plat•yr•rhin•i•an** (plăt′ĭ-rĭn′ē-ən) *— adj.* **1.** Having a broad flat nose. **2.** Of or being the New World monkeys, distinguished from the Old World monkeys by widely separated nostrils that generally open to the side. *— n.* **1.** A platyrrhine person. **2.** A platyrrhine monkey. [NLat. *Platyrrhina*, group name < Gk. *platurrhis*, broad-nosed : *platu-*, platy- + *rhis, rhin-*, nose.]

plau•dit (plô′dĭt) *n.* Enthusiastic praise or approval. [Short for Lat. *plaudite*, pl. imper. of *plaudere*, to applaud.]

Plau•en (plou′ən). A city of E-central Germany SSW of Leipzig; founded in the 12th cent. Pop. 78,797.

plau•si•ble (plô′zə-bəl) *adj.* **1.** Seemingly or apparently valid, likely, or acceptable; credible: *a plausible excuse.* **2.** Giving a deceptive impression of truth, acceptability, or reliability; specious. [Lat. *plausibilis*, deserving applause < *plausus*, p.part. of *plaudere*, to applaud.] **— plau′si•bil′i•ty, plau′si•ble•ness** *n.* **— plau′si•bly** *adv.*

Syns: *plausible, believable, colorable, credible.* The central meaning shared by these adjectives is "appearing to merit belief or acceptance": *a plausible clue; a believable excuse; a colorable story; a credible hint.* **Ant:** *implausible.*

plau•sive (plô′zĭv, -sĭv) *adj.* **1.** Showing or expressing praise or approbation; applauding. **2.** *Obsolete.* Plausible. [< Lat. *plaudere, plaus-*, to applaud.]

Plau•tus (plô′təs), **Titus Maccius.** 254?–184 B.C. Roman comic playwright whose works influenced Shakespeare.

play (plā) *v.* **played, play•ing, plays.** *— intr.* **1.** To occupy oneself in amusement, sport, or other recreation. **2.a.** *Games.* To take part in a game. **b.** To participate in betting; gamble. **3.** To act in jest or sport. **4.** To deal or behave carelessly or indifferently; toy. **5.** To behave or converse in a sportive or playful way. **6.** To act or conduct oneself in a specified way. **7.** To act, esp. in a dramatic production. **8.** *Mus.* **a.** To perform on an instrument. **b.** To emit sound or be sounded in performance. **9.** To be performed, as in a theater. **10.** To be received or accepted. **11.** To move or seem to move quickly, lightly, or irregularly. **12.** To function or discharge uninterruptedly: *The fountains played in the courtyard.* **13.** To move or operate freely within a bounded space, as machine parts do. *— tr.* **1.a.** To perform or act (a role or part) in a dramatic performance. **b.** To assume the role of; act as. **2.** To perform (a theatrical work) on or as if on the stage. **3.** To present a theatrical performance in (a given place). **4.** To pretend to be; mimic the activities of. **5.** *Sports & Games.* **a.** To engage in (a game or sport). **b.** To compete against in a game or sport. **c.** To occupy or work at (a position) in a game. **d.** To employ (a player) in a game or position. **e.** To use or move (a card, piece, or ball) in a game or sport. **f.** To make (a shot or stroke), as in tennis. **6.** *Games.* **a.** To bet; wager. **b.** To make bets on. **7.** To perform or put into effect, esp. as a jest or deception. **8.** To handle; manage. **9.** To use or manipulate, esp. for one's own interests. **10.** *Mus.* **a.** To perform on (an instrument). **b.** To perform (a piece) on instruments or an instrument. **11.** To cause (a phonograph, for example) to emit recorded sounds. **12.** To discharge or direct in or as if in a continuous stream. **13.** To cause to move rapidly, lightly, or irregularly: *play lights over the floor.* **14.** To exhaust (a hooked fish) by allowing it to pull on the line. *— n.* **1.a.** A literary work written for performance on the stage; a drama. **b.** The performance of such a work. **2.** Activity engaged in for enjoyment or recreation. **3.** Fun or jesting. **4.** *Sports & Games.* **a.** The act or manner of engaging in a game or sport. **b.** The act or manner of using a card, piece, or ball in a game or sport. **c.** A move or an action in a game. **5.** *Games.* Participation in betting; gambling. **6.** Manner of dealing with others; conduct. **7.** An attempt to obtain something; a bid. **8.a.** Action, motion, or use. **b.** Freedom or occasion for action; scope. **9.** Movement or space for movement, as of mechanical parts. **10.** Quick, often irregular movement or action, esp. of light or color. **— *phrasal verbs.* play along.** *Informal.* To cooperate or pretend to cooperate. **play at. 1.** To participate in; engage in. **2.** To do or take part in half-heartedly. **play back.** To replay (a recently recorded tape, for example). **play down.** To minimize the importance of; make little of. **play off. 1.** *Sports.* **a.** To establish the winner of (a tie) by playing in an additional game or series of games. **b.** To participate in a playoff. **2.** To set (one individual or party) in opposition to another so as to advance one's own interests. **play on** (or **upon**). To take advantage of (another's attitudes or feelings) for one's own interests. **play out.** To use up; exhaust. **play up.** To emphasize or publicize. **— *idioms.* in play. 1.** *Sports.* In a position to be legally or feasibly played. **2.** In a position or rumored to be in a position of possible corporate takeover. **out of play.** *Sports.* Not in a position to be legally or feasibly played. **play ball.** *Slang.* To cooperate. **play both ends against the middle.** To set opposing parties or interests against one another so as to advance one's own goals. **play fast and loose.** To behave in a recklessly irresponsible or deceitful manner. **play for time.** To use delaying tactics; temporize. **play games.** *Slang.* To be evasive or deceptive. **play into the hands of.** To act or behave so as to give an advantage to (an opponent). **play (one's) cards.** *Informal.* To use the resources or strategies at one's disposal. **play possum.** To pretend to be sleeping or dead. **play the field.** To date more than one person. **play the game.** *Informal.* To behave according to the accepted customs or standards. **play up to.** To curry favor with. **play with fire.** To take part in a dangerous or risky undertaking. **play with (oneself).** *Vulgar Slang.* To masturbate. [ME *playen* < OE *plegian.*] **— play′a•bil′i•ty** *n.* **— play′a•ble** *adj.*

pla•ya (plī′ə) *n.* A nearly level area at the bottom of an undrained desert basin, sometimes temporarily covered with water. [Sp. < LLat. *plagia*, shoreline, prob. < Gk., sides < neut. pl. of *plagios*, oblique < *plagos*, side. See **plāk-**[1]*****.]

play-act (plā′ăkt′) *intr.v.* **-act•ed, -act•ing, -acts. 1.** To play a role in a dramatic performance. **2.** To play a pretended role; make believe. **3.** To behave overdramatically or artificially.

play•back (plā′băk′) *n.* **1.** The act or process of replaying a record or tape. **2.** A method of or an apparatus for reproducing sound recordings.

play•bill (plā′bĭl′) *n.* A poster announcing a theatrical performance.

play•book (plā′bo͝ok′) *n.* **1.** A book containing the scripts of dramatic plays. **2.** *Sports.* A notebook containing descriptions and diagrams of the plays of a team, esp. a football team.

play•boy (plā′boi′) *n.* A man given to sexual promiscuity and the pursuit of pleasure.

play-by-play (plā′bī-plā′) *adj.* Being or giving a detailed running account of the action of an event, esp. a sports event, as it occurs. — *n.* A play-by-play account of an event.

play•er (plā′ər) *n.* **1.** One that plays, esp.: **a.** *Sports & Games.* A participant in a game or sport. **b.** A gambler. **c.** One who performs in theatrical roles. **d.** *Mus.* One who plays an instrument. **2.** An active participant. **3.** *Mus.* The mechanism actuating a player piano. **4.** A phonograph.

player piano *n. Mus.* A mechanically operated piano that uses a perforated paper roll to actuate the keys.

play•ful (plā′fəl) *adj.* **1.** Full of fun and high spirits; frolicsome or sportive: *a playful kitten.* **2.** Humorous; jesting. — **play′ful•ly** *adv.* — **play′ful•ness** *n.*

play•girl (plā′gûrl′) *n.* A woman given to sexual promiscuity and the pursuit of pleasure.

play•go•er (plā′gō′ər) *n.* One who attends the theater. — **play′go′ing** *n.*

play•ground (plā′ground′) *n.* **1.** An outdoor area for recreation and play, esp. one having items such as swings. **2.** A field or sphere of unrestricted pleasurable activity.

play•house (plā′hous′) *n., pl.* **-hous•es** (-hou′zĭz, -sĭz). **1.** A theater. **2.** A small house for children to play in. **3.** A child's toy house; a dollhouse.

play•ing card (plā′ĭng) *n. Games.* A card marked with its rank and suit and belonging to any of several decks used in games.

playing field *n. Sports.* A field for games such as soccer.

play•let (plā′lĭt) *n.* A short play.

play•mak•er (plā′mā′kər) *n. Sports.* A player, esp. a guard in basketball, who calls the signals for and initiates offensive plays. — **play′mak′ing** *n.*

play•mate (plā′māt′) *n.* A companion in play or recreation.

play•off also **play-off** (plā′ôf′, -ŏf′) *n. Sports.* **1.** A final game or series of games played to break a tie. **2.** A series of games played to determine a championship.

play•pen (plā′pĕn′) *n.* A portable enclosure in which a baby or young child can be safely left to play.

play•room (plā′ro͞om′, -ro͝om′) *n.* A room designed or set aside for recreation or playing.

play•suit (plā′so͞ot′) *n.* A woman's or child's play outfit usu. consisting of shorts and a blouse, sometimes in one piece.

play therapy *n.* A form of psychotherapy used with children that makes use of dolls, toys, and other playthings under the guidance of a therapist. — **play therapist** *n.*

play•thing (plā′thĭng′) *n.* **1.** Something to play with; a toy. **2.** One treated as a toy: *a plaything of fate.*

play•wear (plā′wâr′) *n.* Garments suitable for recreation.

play•wright (plā′rīt′) *n.* One who writes plays; a dramatist.

pla•za (plä′zə, plăz′ə) *n.* **1.** A public square or similar open area in a town or city. **2.a.** A widened roadway forming the approach to tollbooths on a highway. **b.** A parking or service area next to a highway. **3.** A shopping center. [Sp. < VLat. *plattea < Lat. *platea*, broad street. See PLACE.]

plea (plē) *n.* **1.** An earnest request; an appeal. **2.** An excuse; a pretext. **3.** *Law.* **a.** An allegation offered in pleading a case. **b.** A defendant's answer to the plaintiff's declaration in a civil action. **c.** The answer of the accused to a criminal charge or indictment. **d.** A special answer depending on or demonstrating one or more reasons for delaying, dismissing, or barring a suit in equity law. **e.** An action or a suit. [ME *plai*, lawsuit < OFr. *plai, plaid* < LLat. *placitum*, decree < Lat. < neut. p.part. of *placēre*, to please. See **plāk-¹***.]

plea-bar•gain (plē′bär′gən) *intr.v.* **-gained, -gain•ing, -gains.** *Law.* To make an agreement in which a defendant pleads guilty to a lesser charge and the prosecutor in return drops more serious charges. — **plea′-bar′gain•ing** *n.*

pleach (plēch, plāch) *tr.v.* **pleached, pleach•ing, pleach•es. 1.** To plait or interlace (vines, for example), esp. in making a hedge or an arbor. **2.** To shade or border with interlaced branches or vines. [ME *plechen* < ONFr. *plechier*, prob. < Lat. *plectere.* See **plek-***.]

plead (plēd) *v.* **plead•ed** or **pled** (plĕd), **plead•ing, pleads.** — *intr.* **1.** To appeal earnestly; beg. **2.** To offer reasons for or against something; argue earnestly. **3.** To provide an argument or appeal. **4.** *Law.* **a.** To put forward a plea of a specific nature in court. **b.** To make or answer an allegation in a legal proceeding. **c.** To address a court as a lawyer or an advocate. — *tr.* **1.** To assert as defense, vindication, or excuse; claim as a plea. **2.** *Law.* **a.** To present as an answer to a charge, an indictment, or a declaration made against one. **b.** To argue or present (a case) in a court or similar tribunal. [ME *pleden* < OFr. *plaidier* < Med.Lat. *placitāre*, to appeal to the law < LLat. *placitum*, decree, opinion. See PLEA.] — **plead′a•ble** *adj.* — **plead′er** *n.* — **plead′ing•ly** *adv.*

plead•ing (plē′dĭng) *n.* **1.** A plea; an entreaty. **2.** *Law.* Advocacy of causes in court. **3.** *Law.* **a.** A formal statement, generally written, propounding the cause of action or the defense in a case. **b. pleadings.** The consecutive statements, allegations, and counterallegations made in turn by plaintiff and defendant, or prosecutor and accused, in a legal proceeding.

pleas•ance (plĕz′əns) *n.* **1.** A secluded garden or landscaped area. **2.** *Archaic.* Pleasure or a source of pleasure.

pleas•ant (plĕz′ənt) *adj.* **-er, -est. 1.** Giving or affording pleasure or enjoyment; agreeable: *a pleasant scene.* **2.** Pleasing in manner, behavior, or appearance. **3.** Fair and comfortable: *pleasant weather.* **4.** Merry; lively. [ME *plesaunt* < OFr. *plaisant*, pr.part. of *plaisir*, to please < Lat. *placēre.* See **plāk-¹***.] — **pleas′ant•ly** *adv.* — **pleas′ant•ness** *n.*

Pleas•ant Hill (plĕz′ənt). A city of W CA NE of Berkeley. Pop. 31,585.

Pleasant Island. See **Nauru.**

Pleas•an•ton (plĕz′ən-tən). A city of W CA SE of Oakland. Pop. 50,553.

pleas•ant•ry (plĕz′ən-trē) *n., pl.* **-ries. 1.** A humorous remark or act; a jest. **2.** A polite social utterance; a civility: *exchanged pleasantries.* **3.** A good-humored or playful manner in conversation or social relations. [Fr. *plaisanterie* < OFr. *plesanterie* < *plaisant*, pleasant. See PLEASANT.]

please (plēz) *v.* **pleased, pleas•ing, pleas•es.** — *tr.* **1.** To give enjoyment, pleasure, or satisfaction to; make glad or contented. **2.** To be the will or desire of: *May it please the court to admit this evidence.* — *intr.* **1.** To give satisfaction or pleasure; be agreeable: *We aim to please.* **2.** To have the will or desire; wish: *Do as you please.* — *adv.* **1.** If it is your desire or pleasure; if you please. Used in polite requests: *Please stand back.* **2.** Yes. Used in polite affirmative replies to offers: *May I help you? Please.* [ME *plesen* < OFr. *plaisir* < Lat. *placēre.* See **plāk-¹***.] — **pleas′er** *n.*

Syns: *please, delight, gladden, gratify, tickle.* The central meaning shared by these verbs is "to give pleasure to": *was pleased by the song; a gift to delight a child; praise that gladdens the spirit; progress that gratified them; compliments that tickle their vanity.* ***Ant:*** *displease.*

pleas•ing (plē′zĭng) *adj.* Giving pleasure or enjoyment; agreeable. — **pleas′ing•ly** *adv.* — **pleas′ing•ness** *n.*

pleas•ur•a•ble (plĕzh′ər-ə-bəl) *adj.* Agreeable; gratifying. — **pleas′ur•a•bil′i•ty, pleas′ur•a•ble•ness** *n.* — **pleas′ur•a•bly** *adv.*

pleas•ure (plĕzh′ər) *n.* **1.** The state or feeling of being pleased or gratified. **2.** A source of enjoyment or delight. **3.** Amusement, diversion, or worldly enjoyment. **4.** Sensual gratification or indulgence. **5.** One's preference or wish. — *v.* **-ured, -ur•ing, -ures.** — *tr.* To give pleasure or enjoyment to; gratify. — *intr.* **1.** To take pleasure; delight. **2.** To go in search of pleasure or enjoyment. [ME < OFr. *plaisir* < *plaisir*, to please. See PLEASE.] — **pleas′ure•less** *adj.*

pleasure principle *n.* In psychoanalysis, the tendency or drive to achieve pleasure and avoid pain as the chief motivating force in behavior.

pleat (plēt) *n.* A fold in cloth made by doubling the material upon itself and then pressing or stitching it into place. — *tr.v.* **pleat•ed, pleat•ing, pleats.** To press or arrange in pleats. [ME *plet*, var. of *plait*, pleat, fold. See PLAIT.] — **pleat′er** *n.*

pleb (plĕb) *n.* **1.** A commoner; a plebeian. **2.** A freshman; a plebe. [Short for PLEBEIAN, or perh. < PLEBS (taken as pl.).]

plebe (plēb) also **pleb** (plĕb) *n.* A first-year student at the U.S. Military or Naval Academy. [Prob. short for PLEBEIAN.]

ple•be•ian (plĭ-bē′ən) *adj.* **1.** Of or relating to the common people of ancient Rome. **2.** Of, belonging to, or characteristic of commoners. **3.** Unrefined or coarse in nature or manner. — *n.* **1.** One of the common people of ancient Rome. **2.** A member of the lower classes. **3.** A vulgar or coarse person. [< Lat. *plēbius* < *plēbs, plēb-*, the common people. See **pelə-¹***.] — **ple•be′ian•ism** *n.* — **ple•be′ian•ly** *adv.*

pleb•i•scite (plĕb′ĭ-sīt′, -sĭt) *n.* **1.** A direct vote in which the entire electorate is invited to accept or refuse a proposal. **2.** A vote in which a population exercises the right of national self-determination. [Fr. *plébiscite* < Lat. *plēbiscītum* : *plēbis*, genitive of *plēbs*, the people; see **pelə-¹*** + *scītum*, decree < neut. p.part. of *scīscere*, to vote for, inchoative of *scīre*, to know; see **skei-***.] — **ple•bis′ci•tar′y** (plə-bĭs′ĭ-tĕr′ē, plĕb′ĭ-sīt′ə-rē) *adj.*

plebs (plĕbz) *n., pl.* **ple•bes** (plē′bēz). **1.** The common people of ancient Rome: *the plebs and the patricians.* **2.** The common people; the populace. [Lat. *plēbs.* See **pelə-¹***.]

ple•cop•ter•an (plĭ-kŏp′tər-ən) *n.* See **stonefly.** [< NLat. *Plecoptera*, order name : Gk. *plekein*, to plait, twist; see **plek-*** + Gk. *pteron*, wing; see **pet-***.] — **ple•cop′ter•an** *adj.*

plec•tog•nath (plĕk′tŏg-năth′) *n.* Any of various tropical marine fishes of the order Tetraodontiformes or Plectognathi, which includes the puffers. [< NLat. *Plectognathī*, order name : Gk. *plektos*, twisted; see **plek-*** + Gk. *gnathos*, jaw; see -GNATHOUS.] — **plec′tog•nath′** *adj.*

plec•trum (plĕk′trəm) *n., pl.* **-trums** or **-tra** (-trə). *Mus.* A small device used to pluck the strings of certain instruments, such as the guitar or lute. [Lat. *plēctrum* < Gk. *plēktron* < *plēssein, plēg-*, to strike. See **plāk-²***.]

pled (plĕd) *v.* A p.t. and p.part. of **plead.**

pledge (plĕj) *n.* **1.** A solemn binding promise to do, give, or refrain from doing something. **2.a.** Something given or held as

player piano

ă pat	oi boy
ā pay	ou out
âr care	o͝o took
ä father	o͞o boot
ĕ pet	ŭ cut
ē be	ûr urge
ĭ pit	th thin
ī pie	*th* this
îr pier	hw which
ŏ pot	zh vision
ō toe	ə about, item
ô paw	

Stress marks:
′ (primary);
′ (secondary), as in dictionary (dĭk′shə-nĕr′ē)

security to guarantee payment of a debt or fulfillment of an obligation. **b.** The condition of something thus given or held. **3.** *Law.* **a.** Delivery of goods or personal property as security for a debt or an obligation. **b.** The contract by which such delivery is made. **4.** A token or sign. **5.** A person about to join a fraternity, sorority, or similar organization. **6.** The act of drinking in honor of someone; a toast. **7.** A vow to abstain from alcoholic liquor. —*v.* **pledged, pledg•ing, pledg•es.** —*tr.* **1.** To offer or guarantee by a solemn binding promise. **2.** To bind or secure by or as if by a pledge. **3.** To deposit as security; pawn. **4.a.** To promise to join (a fraternity or similar organization). **b.** To accept as a prospective member of such an organization. **5.** To drink a toast to. —*intr.* **1.** To make a solemn binding promise; swear. **2.** To drink a toast. [ME < OFr. *plege*, prob. < LLat. *plevium*, a security, of Gmc. orig.]

Pleiades
Pleiades cluster

pledg•ee (plĕj-ē′) *n.* **1.** A person to whom something is pledged. **2.** A person with whom a pledge is deposited.

pledg•er (plĕj′ər) *n.* One who makes or gives a pledge.

pled•get (plĕj′ĭt) *n.* A small flat absorbent pad used to medicate, drain, or protect a wound or sore. [?]

pledg•or also **pledge•or** (plĕj′ər, plĕj-ôr′) *n. Law.* A person who deposits property as a pledge.

–plegia *suff.* Complete paralysis: *monoplegia.* [Gk. *-plēgia* < *plēgē*, a blow < *plēssein, plēg-*, to strike. See **plāk-**[2]*.]

Ple•iad (plē′əd, -ăd′, plī′-) *n., pl.* **Ple•ia•des** (plē′ə-dēz′, plī′-). **1.** One of the Pleiades. **2.** Often **pleiad.** A group of seven illustrious persons. [Back-formation < PLEIADES.]

Ple•ia•des (plē′ə-dēz′, plī′-) *pl.n.* **1.** *Gk. Myth.* The seven daughters of Atlas who were metamorphosed into stars. **2.** An open star cluster in the constellation Taurus, consisting of several hundred stars, of which six are visible to the naked eye. [ME *Pliades* < Lat. *Plēïades* < Gk. *Pleiades.*]

pleio– *pref.* Var. of **pleo–.**

plei•o•tax•y (plī′ə-tăk′sē) *n. Bot.* An increase in the number of whorls in an inflorescence. [Gk. *pleiōn*, more; see **pelə-**[1]* + -TAXY.]

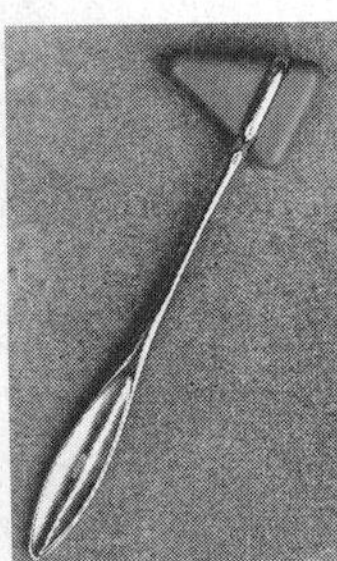
plexor

plei•ot•ro•pism (plī-ŏt′rə-pĭz′əm) also **plei•ot•ro•py** (-pē) *n.* The control by a single gene of several distinct and seemingly unrelated phenotypic effects. [Gk. *pleiōn*, more; see **pelə-**[1]* + -TROPISM.] —**plei′o•tro′pic** (plī′ə-trō′pĭk, -trŏp′ĭk) *adj.* —**plei′o•tro′pi•cal•ly** *adv.*

Pleis•to•cene (plī′stə-sēn′) *adj.* Of, belonging to, or being the geologic time of the earlier epoch of the Quaternary Period, characterized by a succession of northern glaciations and the appearance of human beings. See table at **geologic time.** —*n.* The Pleistocene Epoch or its deposits. [Gk. *pleistos*, most; see **pelə-**[1]* + -CENE.]

ple•na•ry (plē′nə-rē, plĕn′ə-) *adj.* **1.** Complete in all respects; unlimited or full: *plenary powers.* **2.** Fully attended by all qualified members. [LLat. *plēnārius* < Lat. *plēnus*, full. See **pelə-**[1]*.] —**ple′na•ri•ly** *adv.* —**ple′na•ri•ness** *n.*

plenary indulgence *n. Rom. Cath. Ch.* An indulgence that remits the full temporal punishment incurred by a sinner.

plen•i•po•ten•ti•ar•y (plĕn′ə-pə-tĕn′shē-ĕr′ē, -shə-rē) *adj.* Invested with or conferring full powers: *a plenipotentiary deputy.* —*n., pl.* **-ies.** A diplomat with full authority. [Med. Lat. *plēnipotentiārius* < LLat. *plēnipotēns, plēnipotent-*, invested with full power : Lat. *plēnus*, full; see **pelə-**[1]* + Lat. *potēns*, powerful; see POTENT.]

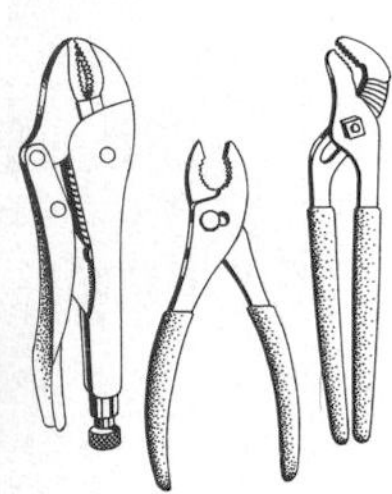
pliers
Left to right: Locking-grip, slip-joint, and multiple-joint pliers

plen•i•tude (plĕn′ĭ-to͞od′, -tyo͞od′) *n.* **1.** An ample amount or quantity; an abundance. **2.** The condition of being full, ample, or complete: *granaries filled to plenitude.* [ME < OFr. < Lat. *plēnitūdō* < *plēnus*, full. See **pelə-**[1]*.] —**plen′i•tu′di•nous** (-to͞od′n-əs, -tyo͞od′-) *adj.*

plen•te•ous (plĕn′tē-əs) *adj.* **1.** Abundant; copious. **2.** Producing or yielding in abundance. [ME, alteration of *plentivous* < OFr. *plentiveus* < *plentif* < *plente*, plenty. See PLENTY.] —**plen′te•ous•ly** *adv.* —**plen′te•ous•ness** *n.*

plen•ti•ful (plĕn′tĭ-fəl) *adj.* **1.** Existing in great quantity or ample supply. **2.** Providing or producing an abundance. —**plen′ti•ful•ly** *adv.* —**plen′ti•ful•ness** *n.*

plen•ty (plĕn′tē) *n.* **1.** A full or completely adequate amount or supply. **2.** A large quantity or amount; an abundance. **3.** A condition of general abundance or prosperity. —*adj.* Plentiful; abundant. —*adv. Informal.* Sufficiently; very. [ME < OFr. *plente* < Lat. *plēnitās* < *plēnus*, full. See **pelə-**[1]*.]

ple•num (plē′nəm, plĕn′əm) *n., pl.* **ple•nums** or **ple•na** (plē′nə, plĕn′ə). **1.** An assembly or a meeting with all members present. **2.** A condition, space, or enclosure in which air or other gas is at a pressure greater than that of the outside atmosphere. **3.** The condition of being full; fullness. **4.** A space completely filled with matter. [Lat. *plēnum (spatium)*, full (space), neut. of *plēnus.* See **pelə-**[1]*.]

plinth

pleo– or **pleio–** or **plio–** *pref.* More: *pleopod.* [< Gk. *pleiōn, pleōn*, more. See **pelə-**[1]*.]

ple•och•ro•ism (plē-ŏk′rō-ĭz′əm) *n.* The property possessed by some crystals of exhibiting different colors, esp. three different colors, when viewed along different axes. [PLEO– + Gk. *khrōs*, color + -ISM.] —**ple′o•chro′ic** (plē′ə-krō′ĭk) *adj.*

ple•o•mor•phism (plē′ə-môr′fĭz′əm) *n.* **1.** *Chem.* See **polymorphism** 2. **2.** *Biol.* The occurrence of two or more structural forms during a life cycle. —**ple′o•mor′phic** *adj.*

ple•o•nasm (plē′ə-năz′əm) *n.* **1.a.** The use of more words than are required to express an idea; redundancy. **b.** An instance of pleonasm. **2.** A superfluous word or phrase. [LLat. *pleonasmus* < Gk. *pleonasmos* < *pleonazein*, to be excessive < *pleōn*, more. See **pelə-**[1]*.] —**ple′o•nas′tic** (-năs′tĭk) *adj.* —**ple′o•nas′ti•cal•ly** *adv.*

ple•o•pod (plē′ə-pŏd′) *n.* See **swimmeret.**

ple•ro•cer•coid (plîr′ō-sûr′koid′) *n.* The infective larva of some tapeworms, characterized by its solid elongated body. [Gk. *plērēs*, full, infected; see **pelə-**[1]* + *kerkos*, tail + -OID.]

ple•si•o•saur (plē′sē-ə-sôr′, plē′zē-) also **ple•si•o•sau•rus** (plē′sē-ə-sôr′əs, plē′zē-) *n., pl.* **-saurs** also **-saur•i** (-sôr′ī). *Paleont.* A large extinct marine reptile having paddlelike limbs that was common in Europe and North America during the Mesozoic Era. [NLat. *Plesiosaurus*, type genus : Gk. *plēsios*, near; see **pel-**[5]* + NLat. *saurus*, lizard; see SAURIAN.]

ples•sim•e•ter (plĕ-sĭm′ĭ-tər) *n.* See **pleximeter.** [Gk. *plēssein*, to strike; see PLEXOR + -METER.]

ples•sor (plĕs′ər) *n.* Var. of **plexor.**

pleth•o•ra (plĕth′ər-ə) *n.* **1.** A superabundance; an excess. **2.** An excess of blood in the circulatory system or in one organ or area. [LLat. *plēthōra* < Gk. < *plēthein*, to be full. See **pelə-**[1]*.]

ple•thor•ic (plĕ-thôr′ĭk, -thŏr′-, plĕth′ə-rĭk) *adj.* **1.a.** Excessive in quantity; superabundant. **b.** Excessive in style; turgid: *plethoric prose.* **2.** Characterized by an overabundance of blood. —**ple•thor′i•cal•ly** *adv.*

ple•thys•mo•gram (plĕ-thĭz′mə-grăm′, plə-) *n.* A record or tracing produced by a plethysmograph.

ple•thys•mo•graph (plĕ-thĭz′mə-grăf′, plə-) *n.* An instrument that measures variations in the size of an organ or body part on the basis of the amount of blood passing through or present in the part. [Gk. *plēthusmos*, increase (< *plēthunein*, to increase < *plēthus*, quantity < *plēthein*, to be full; see **pelə-**[1]*) + -GRAPH.] —**ple•thys′mo•graph′ic** *adj.* —**pleth′ys•mog′ra•phy** (plĕth′ĭz-mŏg′rə-fē) *n.*

pleu•ra[1] (plo͝or′ə) *n., pl.* **pleu•rae** (plo͝or′ē). A thin serous membrane in mammals that envelops each lung and folds back to make a lining for the chest cavity. [ME < Med.Lat. < Gk., side, rib.] —**pleu′ral** *adj.*

pleu•ra[2] (plo͝or′ə) *n.* Pl. of **pleuron.**

pleu•ri•sy (plo͝or′ĭ-sē) *n.* Inflammation of the pleura, usu. occurring as a complication of a disease such as pneumonia, accompanied by accumulation of fluid in the pleural cavity, chills, fever, and painful breathing and coughing. [ME *pluresy* < OFr. *pleuresie* < LLat. *pleurisis*, alteration of Lat. *pleurītis* < Gk. *pleuritis* : *pleura*, side + *-itis*, -itis.] —**pleu•rit′ic** (plo͞o-rĭt′ĭk) *adj.*

pleurisy root *n.* See **butterfly weed.**

pleuro– or **pleur–** *pref.* **1.** Side; lateral: *pleurodont.* **2.** Pleura; pleural: *pleurotomy.* [Gk. < *pleura*, side, rib.]

pleu•ro•dont (plo͝or′ə-dŏnt′) *adj.* Having the teeth attached by their sides to the inner side of the jaw, as in some lizards. —*n.* A lizard with pleurodont teeth.

pleu•ro•dyn•i•a (plo͝or′ə-dĭn′ē-ə) *n.* **1.** Paroxysmal pain and soreness of the muscles between the ribs. **2.** A disease caused by a coxsackievirus, characterized by paroxysmal pain in the lower chest, fever, headache, and malaise. [NLat. : PLEUR(O)– + Gk. *odunē*, pain; see **ed-*** + -IA[1].]

pleu•ron (plo͝or′ŏn′) *n., pl.* **pleu•ra** (plo͝or′ə). An external lateral plate of the body segments of arthropods. [NLat. < Gk., side, rib.]

pleu•ro•pneu•mo•nia (plo͝or′ō-no͞o-mōn′yə, -nyo͞o-) *n.* **1.** Pneumonia aggravated by pleurisy. **2.** An infectious febrile disease of cattle, caused by a mycoplasma and characterized by inflammation of the pleura and lungs.

pleu•ro•pneu•mo•nia-like organism (plo͝or′ō-no͞o-mōn′yə-līk′, -nyo͞o-) *n.* See **mycoplasma.**

pleu•rot•o•my (plo͞o-rŏt′ə-mē) *n., pl.* **-mies.** Surgical incision of the pleura.

pleus•ton (plo͞o′stən, -stŏn′) *n.* Plants that float on the surface of bodies of fresh water. [Gk. *pleusis*, sailing; see **pleu-*** + (PLANK)TON.] —**pleus•ton′ic** (plo͞o-stŏn′ĭk) *adj.*

Plev•en (plĕv′ən, -ĕn) or **Plev•na** (-nə, -nä). A city of N Bulgaria NE of Sofia; orig. settled by Thracians. Pop. 144,000.

plex•i•form (plĕk′sə-fôrm′) *adj.* Similar to or having the form of a plexus. [PLEX(US) + -FORM.]

Plex•i•glas (plĕk′sĭ-glăs′). A trademark used for a light transparent weather-resistant thermoplastic.

plex•im•e•ter (plĕk-sĭm′ĭ-tər) *n.* A small thin plate held against the body and struck with a plexor in diagnosis by percussion. [Gk. *plēxis*, a blow; see PLEXOR + -METER.] —**plex′i•met′ric** (plĕk′sə-mĕt′rĭk) *adj.* —**plex•im′e•try** *n.*

plex•or (plĕk′sər) also **ples•sor** (plĕs′ər) *n.* A small rubber-headed hammer used in examination or diagnosis by percussion. [< Gk. *plēxis*, a blow < *plēssein, plēg-*, to strike. See **plāk-**[2]*.]

plex•us (plĕk′səs) *n., pl.* **plexus** or **-us•es.** **1.** A structure in the form of a network, esp. of nerves, blood vessels, or lymphatics. **2.** A combination of interlaced parts; a network. [NLat. < Lat., braid < p.part. of *plectere*, to plait. See **plek-***.]

pli•a•ble (plī′ə-bəl) *adj.* **1.** Easily bent or shaped. **2.** Receptive to change; adaptable. **3.** Easily influenced, persuaded, or swayed; tractable. [ME < OFr. < *plier*, to bend. See PLIANT.] —**pli′a·bil′i·ty, pli′a·ble·ness** *n.* —**pli′a·bly** *adv.*

pli·ant (plī′ənt) *adj.* **1.** Easily bent or flexed; pliable. **2.** Easily altered or modified to fit conditions; adaptable. **3.** Yielding readily to influence or domination; compliant. [ME < OFr., pr.part. of *plier*, to fold, bend < Lat. *plicāre*. See **plek-***.] —**pli′an·cy, pli′ant·ness** *n.* —**pli′ant·ly** *adv.*

pli·ca (plī′kə) *n., pl.* **pli·cae** (plī′sē, -kē). A fold or ridge, as of skin, membrane, or shell. [Med.Lat., fold < Lat. *plicāre*, to fold. See **plek-***.] —**pli′cal** *adj.*

pli·cate (plī′kāt′) also **pli·cat·ed** (-kā′tĭd) *adj.* Arranged in folds like those of a fan; pleated. [Lat. *plicātus*, p.part. of *plicāre*, to fold. See **plek-***.] —**pli′cate′ly** *adv.*

pli·ca·tion (plī-kā′shən) also **plic·a·ture** (plĭk′ə-cho͝or′) *n.* **1.a.** The act or process of folding. **b.** The state of being folded. **2.** A fold.

pli·é (plē-ā′) *n.* A movement in ballet in which the knees are bent while the back is held straight. [Fr. < p.part. of *plier*, to fold, bend < OFr. See PLIANT.]

plied[1] (plīd) *v.* P.t. and p.part. of **ply[1]**.

plied[2] (plīd) *v.* P.t. and p.part. of **ply[2]**.

pli·er also **ply·er** (plī′ər) *n.* **1.** One who plies a trade. **2. pliers.** A variously shaped hand tool having a pair of pivoted jaws, used for holding, bending, or cutting.

plies[1] (plīz) *v.* Third pers. sing. pr.t. of **ply[1]**. —*n.* Pl. of **ply[1]**.

plies[2] (plīz) *v.* Third pers. sing. pr.t. of **ply[2]**.

plight[1] (plīt) *n.* A situation, esp. a bad or unfortunate one. [ME, alteration of *plit*, fold, wrinkle, situation < AN < Lat. *plicitum*, neut. p.part. of *plicāre*, to fold. See **plek-***.]

plight[2] (plīt) *tr.v.* **plight·ed, plight·ing, plights. 1.** To promise or bind by a solemn pledge, esp. to betroth. **2.** To give or pledge (one's word or oath, for example). —*n.* A solemn pledge, as of faith. —***idiom.* plight (one's) troth. 1.** To become engaged to marry. **2.** To give one's solemn oath. [ME *plighten* < OE *plihtan*, to endanger, put at risk < *pliht*, danger, risk.] —**plight′er** *n.*

plim·soll (plĭm′səl, -sôl′) also **plim·sol** or **plim·sole** (-sōl′) *n.* *Chiefly British.* A rubber-soled cloth shoe; a sneaker. [Prob. < the resemblance of its mudguard to a PLIMSOLL MARK.]

Plim·soll (plĭm′səl, -sôl′), **Samuel.** 1824–98. British merchant who introduced the Merchant Shipping Act of 1876.

Plimsoll line *n.* See **Plimsoll mark.**

Plimsoll mark *n.* *Naut.* Any of a set of lines on the hull of a merchant ship that indicate the depth to which it may be legally loaded under specified conditions. [After Samuel PLIMSOLL.]

plink (plĭngk) *v.* **plinked, plink·ing, plinks.** —*tr.* **1.** To cause to make a soft sharp metallic sound; clink. **2.** To shoot at casually. —*intr.* **1.** To make a soft sharp metallic sound. **2.** To shoot casually at random targets. [Imit.]

plinth (plĭnth) *n.* **1.** *Archit.* A block or slab on which a pedestal, column, or statue is placed. **2.** The base block at the intersection of the baseboard and the vertical trim around an opening. **3.** A continuous course of stones supporting a wall. **4.** A square base, as for a vase. [Fr. *plinthe* < Lat. *plinthus* < Gk. *plinthos*, tile, plinth.]

Plin·y[1] (plĭn′ē). "the Elder." A.D. 23–79. Roman scholar who wrote the 37-volume *Historia Naturalis.*

Plin·y[2] (plĭn′ē). "the Younger." A.D. 62?–113? Roman consul noted for his letters describing Roman life.

plio– *pref.* Var. of **pleo–.**

Pli·o·cene (plī′ə-sēn′) *Geol.* —*adj.* Of, belonging to, or being the geologic time of the last epoch of the Tertiary Period, characterized by the appearance of distinctly modern animals. See table at **geologic time.** —*n.* The Pliocene Epoch or its deposits. [Gk. *pleiōn*, more; see **pelə-[1]*** + –CENE.]

plis·sé also **plis·se** (plĭ-sā′) *n.* **1.** A puckered finish given to fabric by treating it with a caustic soda. **2.** Fabric with a plissé. [Fr. < p.part. of *plisser*, to pleat < OFr. < *pli*, fold < *plier*, to fold < Lat. *plicāre*. See **plek-***.]

PLO *abbr.* Palestine Liberation Organization.

Plock (pwôtsk). A city of Poland on the Vistula R. WSW of Warsaw; known since the 10th cent. Pop. 114,500.

plod (plŏd) *v.* **plod·ded, plod·ding, plods.** —*intr.* **1.** To move or walk heavily or laboriously; trudge. **2.** To work or act perseveringly or monotonously; drudge: *plodding through paperwork.* —*tr.* To trudge along or over. —*n.* **1.** The act of moving or walking heavily and slowly. **2.** The sound made by a heavy step. [Perh. imit.] —**plod′der** *n.* —**plod′ding·ly** *adv.*

–ploid *suff.* Having a number of chromosomes that has a specified relationship to or is a multiple of the basic number of chromosomes of a group: *heteroploid.* [< DIPLOID and HAPLOID.]

ploi·dy (ploi′dē) *n.* A multiple of the basic number of chromosomes in a cell. [< DIPLOIDY and HAPLOIDY.]

Plo·ieş·ti or **Plo·eş·ti** (plô-yĕsht′, -yĕsh′tē). A city of SE-central Romania N of Bucharest. Pop. 229,915.

plonk[1] (plŏngk, plŭngk) *v., n., & adv.* Var. of **plunk.**

plonk[2] (plŏngk) *n.* *Chiefly British.* Cheap or inferior wine. [Short for earlier *plink-plonk*, perh. alteration of Fr. *vin blanc*, white wine : *vin*, wine (< OFr.; see VINEGAR) + *blanc*, white (< OFr.; see BLANK).]

plop (plŏp) *v.* **plopped, plop·ping, plops.** —*intr.* **1.** To fall with a sound like that of an object falling into water without splashing. **2.** To let the body drop heavily. —*tr.* To drop or set heavily, with or as if with a plop. —*n.* A plopping sound or movement. [Imit.] —**plop** *adv.*

plo·sion (plō′zhən) *n.* *Ling.* **1.** The articulation of a plosive sound. **2.** The sudden release of occluded air characteristic of plosives. [< EXPLOSION.]

plo·sive (plō′sĭv, -zĭv) *Ling.* —*adj.* Of or being a speech sound produced by complete closure of the oral passage and subsequent release with a burst of air, as in the sound (p) in *pit.* —*n.* A plosive speech sound. [< EXPLOSIVE.]

plot (plŏt) *n.* **1.a.** A small piece of ground, generally used for a specific purpose. **b.** A measured area of land; a lot. **2.** A ground plan, as for a building; a diagram. **3.** See **graph[1]** 1. **4.** The pattern of events or main story in a narrative or drama. **5.** A secret plan to accomplish a hostile or illegal purpose; a scheme. —*v.* **plot·ted, plot·ting, plots.** —*tr.* **1.** To represent graphically, as on a chart. **2.** *Math.* **a.** To locate (points or other figures) on a graph by means of coordinates. **b.** To draw (a curve) connecting points on a graph. **3.** To conceive and arrange the action and incidents of. **4.** To form a plot for; prearrange secretly or deviously. —*intr.* **1.** To be located by means of coordinates, as on a chart or with data. **2.** To form or take part in a plot; scheme. [ME < OE.]

Plo·ti·nus (plō-tī′nəs). A.D. 205–270. Egyptian-born Roman philosopher and writer who founded Neo-Platonism.

plot line or **plot·line** (plŏt′līn′) *n.* **1.** A literary or dramatic plot; a story line. **2.** Dialogue essential to the development of a plot in a drama. Often used in the plural.

plot·tage (plŏt′ĭj) *n.* The area of land in a plot or group of plots.

plot·ter (plŏt′ər) *n.* *Comp. Sci.* A computer output device that draws graphs or pictures, usu. by moving a pen.

Plov·div (plôv′dĭf′). A city of S-central Bulgaria on the Maritsa R. SE of Sofia; orig. built by Thracians. Pop. 378,000.

plov·er (plŭv′ər, plō′vər) *n., pl.* **plover** or **-ers. 1.** Any of various widely distributed wading birds of the family Charadriidae, having rounded bodies, short tails, and short bills. **2.** Any of various similar or related birds. [ME < AN < VLat. *_pluviārius_ < Lat. *pluvia*, rain. See PLUVIAL.]

plow also **plough** (plou) —*n.* **1.** A farm implement consisting of a heavy blade at the end of a beam, usu. hitched to a draft team or motor vehicle and used for breaking up soil and cutting furrows in preparation for sowing. **2.** An implement of similar function, such as a snowplow. —*v.* **plowed, plow·ing, plows** also **ploughed, plough·ing, ploughs.** —*tr.* **1.a.** To break and turn over (earth) with a plow. **b.** To form (a furrow, for example) with a plow. **c.** To form furrows in with or as if with a plow. **2.** To make or form with driving force. **3.** To cut through (water). —*intr.* **1.** To break and turn up earth with a plow. **2.** To admit of plowing. **3.** To move or progress with driving force. **4.** To proceed laboriously; plod. —***phrasal verbs.* plow back.** To reinvest (earnings or profits) in one's business. **plow into.** *Informal.* **1.** To strike with force. **2.** To undertake (a task, for example) with eagerness and vigor. **plow under. 1.** To cause to vanish under something piled up. **2.** To overwhelm, as with burdens. [ME *plough, plouw* < OE *plōh, plōg*, plow, plowland.] —**plow′a·ble** *adj.* —**plow′er** *n.*

Plow (plou) *n.* See **Big Dipper.**

plow·back (plou′băk′) *n.* **1.** The plowing back of profits. **2.** An amount of profits plowed back.

plow·boy (plou′boi′) *n.* **1.** A boy who leads or guides a team of animals in plowing. **2.** A country boy.

plow·man (plou′mən) *n.* **1.** A man who plows. **2.** A farmer or rustic.

plow·share (plou′shâr′) *n.* The cutting blade of a plow.

plow steel *n.* A high-strength steel having a carbon content of 0.5 to 0.95 percent and used primarily to make wire rope.

ploy (ploi) *n.* An action calculated to frustrate an opponent or gain an advantage indirectly or deviously; a maneuver. [Perh. < EMPLOY, employment (obsolete).]

PLSS *abbr.* Portable life-support system.

plu. *abbr.* Plural.

pluck (plŭk) *v.* **plucked, pluck·ing, plucks.** —*tr.* **1.** To remove or detach by grasping and pulling abruptly with the fingers; pick. **2.** To pull out the hair or feathers of. **3.** To remove abruptly or forcibly. **4.** To give an abrupt pull to; tug at. **5.** *Mus.* To sound (the strings of an instrument) by pulling and releasing them. —*intr.* To give an abrupt pull; tug. —*n.* **1.** The act or an instance of plucking. **2.** Resourceful courage and daring in the face of difficulties; spirit. **3.** The heart, liver, windpipe, and lungs of a slaughtered animal. [ME *plukken* < OE *pluccian*, prob. < VLat. *_piluccāre_, ult. < Lat. *pilāre* < *pilus*, hair.] —**pluck′er** *n.*

pluck·y (plŭk′ē) *adj.* **-i·er, -i·est.** Having or showing courage and spirit in trying circumstances. See Syns at **brave.** —**pluck′i·ly** *adv.* —**pluck′i·ness** *n.*

plug (plŭg) *n.* **1.** An object, such as a cork, used to fill a hole tightly; a stopper. **2.** A dense mass of material that obstructs a passage. **3.** A usu. cylindrical or conic piece cut from some-

plover
Great thick-knee plover
Esacus recuvirostris

plow
Top: Moldboard plow
Bottom: Chisel plow

ă pat	oi boy
ā pay	ou out
âr care	o͝o took
ä father	o͞o boot
ĕ pet	ŭ cut
ē be	ûr urge
ĭ pit	th thin
ī pie	*th* this
îr pier	hw which
ŏ pot	zh vision
ō toe	ə about,
ô paw	item

Stress marks:
′ (primary);
′ (secondary), as in
dictionary (dĭk′shə-nĕr′ē)

thing larger, often as a sample. **4.** *Elect.* **a.** A fitting, commonly with two metal prongs for insertion in a fixed socket, used to connect an appliance to a power supply. **b.** A spark plug. **5.** A hydrant. **6.a.** A flat cake of pressed or twisted tobacco. **b.** A piece of chewing tobacco. **7.** *Geol.* A mass of igneous rock filling the vent of a volcano. **8.** *Informal.* A favorable public mention of a commercial product, business, or performance, esp. when broadcast. **9.** *Slang.* Something inferior, useless, or defective, esp. an old horse. **10.** *Slang.* A gunshot or bullet. **11.** *Sports.* A lure to which hooks are attached, used esp. in angling. — *v.* **plugged, plug•ging, plugs.** — *tr.* **1.** To fill (a hole) tightly with or as if with a plug; stop up. **2.** To insert (something) as a plug. **3.** *Slang.* **a.** To hit with a bullet; shoot. **b.** To hit with the fist; punch. **4.** *Informal.* To publicize (a product, for example) favorably, as by mentioning on a broadcast. — *intr.* **1.** To become stopped up or obstructed. **2.** *Informal.* To work doggedly and persistently. — ***phrasal verbs.*** **plug in. 1.** To connect (an appliance) to an electrical outlet. **2.** To function by being connected to an electrical outlet. **plug into. 1.** To connect or be connected to in the manner of an electrical appliance. **2.** *Slang.* To cause to be closely attuned or responsive to. [Du. < MDu. *plugge.*] — **plug′ger** *n.*

plug board *n.* **1.** A control panel or wiring panel. **2.** *Comp. Sci.* A removable panel in a computing device that may be rewired at will to sort data by a prescribed pattern.

plug-com•pat•i•ble (plŭg′kəm-păt′ə-bəl) *adj. Comp. Sci.* Capable of being connected peripherally to a computer without modification. Used of hardware.

plug-ug•ly (plŭg′ŭg′lē) *n., pl.* **-lies.** *Slang.* A gangster or ruffian. [< the *Plug Uglies,* an East Coast gang in the 1850's.]

plum[1] (plŭm) *n.* **1.a.** Any of several shrubs or small trees of the genus *Prunus,* bearing smooth-skinned fleshy edible fruit with a single hard-shelled stone that encloses the seed. **b.** The fruit of any of these trees. **2.a.** Any of several trees bearing plumlike fruit. **b.** The fruit of such a tree. **3.** A raisin, when added to a pudding or cake. **4.** A sugarplum. **5.** *Color.* A dark purple to deep reddish purple. **6.** An esp. desirable position, assignment, or reward. [ME < OE *plūme* < VLat. **prūna* < neut. pl. of Lat. *prūnum.*]

plum[2] (plŭm) *Informal.* — *adv.* Var. of **plumb** 3. — *adj.* Var. of **plumb** 2.

Plum (plŭm). A borough of SW PA, a suburb of Pittsburgh. Pop. 25,609.

plum•age (plo͞o′mĭj) *n.* **1.** The covering of feathers on a bird. **2.** Feathers used ornamentally. **3.** Elaborate dress; finery. [ME < OFr. < *plume,* plume < Lat. *plūma.*] — **plum′aged** *adj.*

plu•mate (plo͞o′māt′) *adj.* Resembling a plume or feather. [Lat. *plūmātus,* feathered < *plūma,* feather.]

plumb (plŭm) *n.* **1.** A weight on the end of a line, used to determine water depth. **2.** A weight on the end of a line, used esp. by masons and carpenters to establish a vertical. — *adv.* **1.** In a vertical or perpendicular line. **2.** *Informal.* Directly; squarely. **3.** Also **plum.** *Informal.* Utterly; completely. — *adj.* **1.** Exactly vertical. **2.** Also **plum.** *Informal.* Utter; absolute; sheer. — *v.* **plumbed, plumb•ing, plumbs.** — *tr.* **1.** To determine the depth of with a plumb; sound. **2.** To test the verticality or alignment of with a plumb. **3.** To straighten or make perpendicular: *plumb up the wall.* **4.** To examine closely or deeply; probe. **5.** To seal with lead. — *intr.* To work as a plumber. — ***idiom.*** **out of** (or **off**) **plumb.** Not vertical. [ME, lead, a plumb < OFr. *plomb* < Lat. *plumbum,* lead.] — **plumb′a•ble** *adj.*

plum•ba•go (plŭm-bā′gō) *n., pl.* **-gos. 1.** See **graphite. 2.** Any of various plants of the genus *Plumbago;* leadwort. [Lat. *plumbāgō,* lead ore < *plumbum,* lead.]

plumb bob *n.* A weight attached to the end of a plumb line.

plumb•er (plŭm′ər) *n.* **1.** One that installs and repairs pipes and plumbing. **2.** *Slang.* One assigned to investigate and stop leaks of sensitive information. [ME *plummer* < OFr. *plomier* < Lat. *plumbārius,* lead worker < Lat. *plumbum,* lead.]

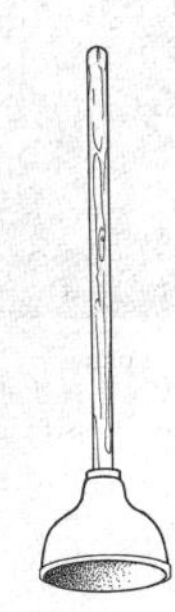

plunger

plumb•er's helper (plŭm′ərz) *n.* See **plunger** 2.

plumber's snake *n.* See **snake** 3.

plumb•er•y (plŭm′ə-rē) *n., pl.* **-ies. 1.** A plumber's workshop or place of business. **2.** A plumber's work; plumbing.

plum•bif•er•ous (plŭm-bĭf′ər-əs) *adj.* Containing lead. [Lat. *plumbum,* lead + -FEROUS.]

plumb•ing (plŭm′ĭng) *n.* **1.** The pipes, fixtures, and other apparatus of a water, gas, or sewage system in a building. **2.** The work or trade of a plumber.

plum•bism (plŭm′bĭz′əm) *n.* Chronic lead poisoning. [< Lat. *plumbum,* lead.]

plumb line *n.* **1.** A line from which a weight is suspended to determine verticality or depth. **2.** A line regarded as directed exactly toward the earth's center of gravity.

plumb rule *n.* A narrow strip of wood with a plumb line and bob attached, used to test verticality.

plume (plo͞om) *n.* **1.** A feather, esp. a large and showy one. **2.** A large feather or cluster of feathers worn as an ornament or symbol of rank. **3.** A token of honor or achievement. **4.** A structure or form that is like a long feather. **5.** *Ecol.* A space in air, water, or soil containing pollutants released from a point source. **6.** *Geol.* An upwelling of molten material from the earth's mantle. — *tr.v.* **plumed, plum•ing, plumes. 1.** To decorate, cover, or supply with or as if with plumes. **2.** To smooth (feathers); preen. **3.** To congratulate (oneself) in a self-satisfied way. [ME < OFr. < Lat. *plūma.*]

plume•let (plo͞om′lĭt) *n.* A small plume.

plum•met (plŭm′ĭt) *n.* **1.** A plumb bob. **2.** Something that weighs down or oppresses; a burden. — *intr.v.* **-met•ed, -met•ing, -mets. 1.** To fall straight down; plunge. **2.** To decline suddenly and steeply. [ME *plomet* < OFr., ball of lead, dim. of *plom, plomb,* sounding lead < Lat. *plumbum.*]

plum•my (plŭm′ē) *adj.* **-mi•er, -mi•est. 1.a.** Filled with plums. **b.** Smelling or tasting of plums. **2.** Choice; desirable. **3.** Exceedingly or affectedly mellow and rich.

plu•mose (plo͞o′mōs′) *adj.* **1.** Having feathers or featherlike growths; feathered. **2.** Resembling a plume; feathery. [Lat. *plūmōsus* < *plūma,* feather.] — **plu′mose′ly** *adv.* — **plu•mos′i•ty** (-mŏs′ĭ-tē) *n.*

plump[1] (plŭmp) *adj.* **plump•er, plump•est. 1.** Well-rounded and full in form; chubby. See Syns at **fat. 2.** Abundant; ample: *a plump reward.* — *v.* **plumped, plump•ing, plumps.** — *tr.* To make well-rounded or full in form: *plumped up the pillows.* — *intr.* To become well-rounded, chubby, or full in form. [ME, dull, prob. < MLGer. *plomp,* blunt, thick.] — **plump′ish** *adj.* — **plump′ly** *adv.* — **plump′ness** *n.*

plump[2] (plŭmp) *v.* **plumped, plump•ing, plumps.** — *intr.* **1.** To drop abruptly or heavily. **2.** To give full support or praise. — *tr.* To throw down or drop (something) abruptly or heavily. — *n.* **1.** A heavy or abrupt fall or collision. **2.** The sound of a heavy fall or collision. — *adj.* Blunt; direct. — *adv.* **1.** With a heavy or abrupt drop. **2.** Straight down. **3.** Without qualification; bluntly. [ME *plumpen,* to immerse quickly, perh. < MLGer., prob. of imit. orig.]

plum pudding *n.* A rich boiled or steamed pudding made with flour, suet, raisins, currants, citron, and spices.

plu•mule (plo͞om′yo͞ol) *n.* **1.** A down feather. **2.** *Bot.* The rudimentary bud of a plant embryo. [Lat. *plūmula,* dim. of *plūma,* feather.] — **plu′mu•lose′** (plo͞om′yə-lōs′) *adj.*

plum•y (plo͞o′mē) *adj.* **-i•er, -i•est. 1.** Consisting of or covered with feathers. **2.** Resembling a feather or plume.

plun•der (plŭn′dər) *v.* **-dered, -der•ing, -ders.** — *tr.* **1.** To rob of goods by force, esp. in time of war; pillage. **2.** To seize wrongfully or by force; steal. — *intr.* To take booty; rob. — *n.* **1.** The act or practice of plundering. **2.** Property stolen by fraud or force; booty. [Ger. *plündern* < MHGer. *plundern* < MLGer. *plunder,* household goods.] — **plun′der•a•ble** *adj.* — **plun′der•er** *n.* — **plun′der•ous** *adj.*

plunge (plŭnj) *v.* **plunged, plung•ing, plung•es.** — *tr.* **1.** To thrust or throw forcefully into a substance or place. **2.** To cast suddenly, violently, or deeply into a given state or situation. — *intr.* **1.** To fall or throw oneself into a substance or place. **2.** To throw oneself earnestly or wholeheartedly into an activity or a situation. **3.** To enter or move headlong through something. **4.** To descend steeply; fall precipitously. **5.** To move forward and downward violently. **6.** To speculate or gamble extravagantly. — *n.* **1.** The act or an instance of plunging. **2.a.** A place or an area, such as a swimming pool, for diving or plunging. **b.** A swim; a dip. — ***idiom.*** **take the plunge.** *Informal.* To begin an unfamiliar venture, esp. after hesitating. [ME *plungen* < OFr. *plongier* < VLat. **plumbicāre,* to heave a sounding lead < Lat. *plumbum,* lead.]

plung•er (plŭn′jər) *n.* **1.** One who plunges or dives. **2.** A device consisting of a rubber suction cup attached to a stick, used to clean out clogged drains and pipes. **3.** A machine part that operates with a thrusting or plunging movement.

plunk (plŭngk) also **plonk** (plŏngk, plŭngk) — *v.* **plunked, plunk•ing, plunks** also **plonked, plonk•ing, plonks.** — *tr.* **1.** To throw or place heavily or abruptly: *plunked the money down.* **2.** *Mus.* To strum or pluck (a stringed instrument). — *intr.* **1.** To drop or fall abruptly or heavily; plump. **2.** To emit a hollow twanging sound. — *n.* **1.** *Informal.* A heavy blow or stroke. **2.** A short hollow twanging sound. — *adv.* *Informal.* **1.** With a short hollow thud. **2.** Exactly; precisely. [Imit.] — **plunk′er** *n.* — **plunk′y** *adj.*

plu•per•fect (plo͞o-pûr′fĭkt) *adj.* **1.** *Gram.* Of, relating to, or being a verb tense used to express action completed before a specified or implied past time. **2.** More than perfect; ideal. — *n. Gram.* **1.** The pluperfect tense, formed in English with the past participle of a verb and the auxiliary *had,* as *had learned* in the sentence *He had learned to type by that time.* **2.** A verb or form in the pluperfect tense. [ME *pluperfyth,* alteration of Lat. *plūs quam perfectum,* more than perfect : *plūs,* more; see **pelə-[1]*** + *quam,* than + *perfectum,* neut. p.part. of *perficere,* to complete; see PERFECT.]

plu•ral (plo͝or′əl) *adj.* **1.** Relating to or composed of more than one member, set, or kind. **2.** *Gram.* Of, relating to, or being a grammatical form that designates more than one of the things specified. — *n. Gram.* **1.** The plural number or form. **2.** A word or term in the plural form. [Ult. < Lat. *plūrālis* < *plūs, plūr-,* more. See **pelə-[1]*.**] — **plu′ral•ly** *adv.*

plu•ral•ism (plo͝or′ə-lĭz′əm) *n.* **1.** The condition of being plural. **2.** A condition of society in which numerous ethnic, religious, or cultural groups coexist within one nation. **3.** *Eccles.* The holding by one person of two or more positions or offices, esp. two or more ecclesiastical benefices, at the same time. **4.** *Philos.* **a.** The doctrine that reality is composed of many ultimate substances. **b.** The belief that no single explanatory system or view of reality can account for all the phenomena of life.

plu•ral•ist (plŏŏr′ə-lĭst) *n.* **1.** *Eccles.* A person who holds two or more offices, esp. two or more benefices, at the same time. **2.** *Philos.* One who adheres to pluralism. **—plu′ral•is′tic** *adj.* **—plu′ral•is′ti•cal•ly** *adv.*

plu•ral•i•ty (plŏŏ-răl′ĭ-tē) *n., pl.* **-ties. 1.** The state or fact of being plural. **2.** A large number or amount; a multitude. **3.** *Eccles.* **a.** Pluralism. **b.** The offices or benefices held by a pluralist. **4.a.** In a contest of more than two choices, the number of votes cast for the winning choice if this number is not more than one half of the total votes cast. **b.** The number by which the vote of the winning choice in such a contest exceeds that of the closest opponent. **5.** The larger or greater part.

plu•ral•ize (plŏŏr′ə-līz′) *v.* **-ized, -iz•ing, -iz•es.** *—tr.* **1.** To make plural. **2.** *Gram.* To express in the plural. *—intr.* **1.** To become plural. **2.** *Eccles.* To engage in pluralism. **—plu′ral•i•za′tion** (plŏŏr′ə-lĭ-zā′shən) *n.*

plus (plŭs) *conj.* **1.** *Math.* Increased by the addition of: *Two plus two is four.* **2.** Added to; along with. **3.** *Usage Problem.* And. *—adj.* **1.** Positive or on the positive part of a scale: *a plus value.* **2.** Added or extra. **3.** *Informal.* Increased to a further degree or number. **4.** Ranking on the higher end of a designated scale: *a grade of C plus.* **5.** *Phys.* Positive. *—n., pl.* **plus•es** or **plus•ses. 1.** *Math.* The plus sign (+). **2.** A positive quantity. **3.** A favorable factor. [Lat. *plūs*, more. See **pelə-**[1]***.**]

Usage Note: When mathematical equations involving the + sign are pronounced as English sentences, the verb is usually in the singular: *Two plus two* is (or *equals*) *four.* By the same token, subjects containing two noun phrases joined by *plus* are usually construed as singular: *The construction slowdown plus the bad weather has made for a weak market.* • The usage of *plus* in *The construction industry has seen a rise in rates. Plus which, bad weather has affected it* is not well established in formal writing, nor is the use of *plus* introducing an independent clause, as in *She has a great deal of talent, plus she works hard.*

plus fours *pl.n.* Loose knickers bagging below the knees, worn formerly for sports. [< the fact that they were four inches longer than ordinary knickers.]

plush (plŭsh) *n.* A fabric, as of silk, having a thick deep pile. *—adj.* **plush•er, plush•est. 1.** Made of or covered with plush. **2.** Luxurious. [Fr. *pluche*, var. of *peluche* < *pelucher*, to become fluffy, shed < OFr. *peluchier*, to pluck, prob. < VLat. **piluccāre.* See PLUCK.] **—plush′ly** *adv.* **—plush′ness** *n.*

plush•y (plŭsh′ē) *adj.* **-i•er, -i•est. 1.** Resembling plush in texture. **2.** *Informal.* Ostentatiously luxurious: *a plushy office.* **—plush′i•ly** *adv.* **—plush′i•ness** *n.*

plus sign *n. Math.* The symbol (+), as in $2 + 2 = 4$, that is used to indicate addition or a positive quantity.

Plu•tarch (plōō′tärk′). A.D. 46?–120? Greek biographer who wrote *Parallel Lives.* **—Plu•tarch′an** (-tär′kən), **Plu•tarch′i•an** (-tär′kē-ən) *adj.*

Plu•to (plōō′tō) *n.* **1.** *Rom. Myth.* The god of the dead and the ruler of the underworld. **2.** The ninth and usu. farthest planet from the sun, having a sidereal period of revolution about the sun of 248.4 years, 4.5 billion kilometers (2.8 billion miles) distant at perihelion and 7.4 billion kilometers (4.6 billion miles) at aphelion, and a diameter less than half Earth's. [Lat. *Plūtō, Plūtōn-* < Gk. *Ploutōn* < *ploutos*, wealth. See **pleu-*.**]

plu•toc•ra•cy (plōō-tŏk′rə-sē) *n., pl.* **-cies. 1.** Government by the wealthy. **2.** A wealthy class that controls a government. **3.** A government or state in which the wealthy rule. [Gk. *ploutokratia* : *ploutos*, wealth; see **pleu-*** + *-kratia*, -cracy.] **—plu′to•crat′** (plōō′tə-krăt′) *n.* **—plu′to•crat′ic, plu′to•crat′i•cal** *adj.* **—plu′to•crat′i•cal•ly** *adv.*

plu•ton (plōō′tŏn′) *n.* A body of igneous rock formed beneath the surface of the earth by consolidation of magma. [Ger., back-formation < *plutonisch*, plutonic < Lat. *Plūtō, Plūtōn-*, Pluto. See PLUTO.]

Plu•to•ni•an (plōō-tō′nē-ən) also **Plu•ton•ic** (-tŏn′ĭk) *adj.* **1.** Of or relating to the god Pluto or the underworld; infernal. **2.** Of or relating to the planet Pluto.

plu•ton•ic (plōō-tŏn′ĭk) *adj.* Of deep igneous or magmatic origin. [< Lat. *Plūtō, Plūtōn-*, Pluto. See PLUTO.]

plu•to•ni•um (plōō-tō′nē-əm) *n. Symbol* **Pu** A naturally radioactive, metallic transuranic element, occurring in uranium ores or produced artificially by neutron bombardment of uranium and used, esp. the highly fissionable isotope Pu 239, as a reactor fuel and in nuclear weapons. Its longest-lived isotope is Pu 244 with a half-life of 76 million years. Atomic number 94; melting point 640°C; boiling point 3,235°C; specific gravity 19.84; valence 3, 4, 5, 6. See table at **element.** [After the planet PLUTO (following neptunium in the periodic table).]

plu•vi•al (plōō′vē-əl) *adj.* **1.** Of or relating to rain; rainy. **2.** *Geol.* Caused by rain. [Lat. *pluviālis* < *pluvia*, rain. See PLUVIOUS.]

plu•vi•ous (plōō′vē-əs) also **plu•vi•ose** (-ōs′) *adj.* Characterized by heavy rainfall; rainy. [Ult. < Lat. *pluviōsus* < *(aqua) pluvia*, rain (water), fem. of *pluvius*, of rain < *pluere*, to rain. See **pleu-*.**] **—plu′vi•os′i•ty** (-ŏs′ĭ-tē) *n.*

ply[1] (plī) *tr.v.* **plied** (plīd), **ply•ing, plies** (plīz). **1.** To join together, as by molding or twisting. **2.** To double over (cloth, for example). *—n., pl.* **plies** (plīz). **1.** A layer, as of paperboard. **2.** One of the sheets of wood glued together to form plywood. **3.** One of the strands twisted together to make yarn, rope, or thread. Often used in combination: *three-ply cord.* **4.** A bias; an inclination. [ME *plien* < OFr. *plier*, alteration of *pleier* < Lat. *plicāre*, to fold. See **plek-*.**]

ply[2] (plī) *v.* **plied** (plīd), **ply•ing, plies** (plīz). *—tr.* **1.** To use diligently; wield. **2.** To engage in diligently; practice. **3.** To traverse or sail over regularly. **4.** To continue supplying or offering to. **5.** To assail vigorously. *—intr.* **1.** To traverse a route or course regularly. **2.** To perform or work diligently or regularly. **3.** *Naut.* To work against the wind by a zigzag course; tack. [ME *plien* < *applien*, to apply. See APPLY.]

Plym•outh (plĭm′əth). **1.** A borough of SW England on **Plymouth Sound,** an inlet of the English Channel. Pop. 250,300. **2.** A town of SE MA on **Plymouth Bay,** an inlet of the Atlantic SE of Boston; founded 1620 by Pilgrims, who supposedly set foot on **Plymouth Rock** when disembarking from the *Mayflower*, and the center of **Plymouth Colony,** absorbed by Massachusetts in 1691. Pop. 45,608. **3.** A city of SE MN, a suburb of Minneapolis–St. Paul. Pop. 50,889.

Plymouth Rock *n.* Any of an American breed of medium-sized chicken raised for both meat and eggs.

ply•wood (plī′wŏŏd′) *n.* A structural material made of layers of wood glued together, usu. with the grains of adjoining layers at right angles to each other. [PLY[1] + WOOD[1].]

Plzeň (pəl′zĕn′, -zĕn′yə). A city of W Czech Republic WSW of Prague; famed for its beer. Pop. 174,555.

pm also **p-m** *abbr.* Phase modulation.

Pm The symbol for the element **promethium.**

PM or **P.M.** *abbr.* **1.** Past master. **2.** Police magistrate. **3.a.** Postmaster. **b.** Postmistress. **4.** Prime minister. **5.** Provost marshal.

pm. *abbr.* Premium.

p.m. also **P.M.** *abbr.* Postmortem.

P.M. also **p.m.** or P.M. *abbr.* Post meridiem. See Usage Note at **ante meridiem.**

P.M.G. *abbr.* Postmaster general.

pmk. *abbr.* Postmark.

PMS *abbr.* Premenstrual syndrome.

pmt. *abbr.* Payment.

p.n. or **P/N** *abbr.* Promissory note.

pneu•ma (nōō′mə, nyōō′-) *n.* The soul or vital spirit. [Gk. See **pneu-*.**]

pneu•mat•ic (nōō-măt′ĭk, nyōō-) also **pneu•mat•i•cal** (-ĭ-kəl) *adj.* **1.** Of or relating to air or other gases. **2.** Of or relating to pneumatics. **3.a.** Run by or using compressed air. **b.** Filled with air, esp. compressed air. **4.** *Zool.* Having cavities filled with air, as the bones of certain birds. **5.** *Theol.* Of or relating to the pneuma; spiritual. [Fr. *pneumatique* < Lat. *pneumaticus* < Gk. *pneumatikos* < *pneuma, pneumat-*, wind. See **pneu-*.**] **—pneu•mat′i•cal•ly** *adv.* **—pneu′ma•tic′i•ty** (nōō′mə-tĭs′ĭ-tē, nyōō′-) *n.*

pneu•mat•ics (nōō-măt′ĭks, nyōō-) *n. (used with a sing. v.)* The study of the mechanical properties of air and other gases.

pneumato– or **pneumat–** *pref.* **1.** Air; gas: *pneumatolysis.* **2.** Breath; respiration: *pneumatophore.* [< Gk. *pneuma, pneumat-*, wind, breath. See **pneu-*.**]

pneu•ma•tol•o•gy (nōō′mə-tŏl′ə-jē, nyōō′-) *n.* **1.** The doctrine or study of spiritual beings and phenomena, esp. the belief in spirits intervening between human beings and God. **2.** The Christian doctrine of the Holy Ghost. **—pneu′ma•to•log′ic** (-tə-lŏj′ĭk), **pneu′ma•to•log′i•cal** (-ĭ-kəl) *adj.* **—pneu′ma•tol′o•gist** *n.*

pneu•ma•tol•y•sis (nōō′mə-tŏl′ĭ-sĭs, nyōō′-) *n.* A process of rock alteration or mineral formation brought about by the action of gases emitted from solidifying magma. **—pneu′ma•to•lyt′ic** (-tə-lĭt′ĭk) *adj.*

pneu•mat•o•phore (nōō-măt′ə-fôr′, -fōr′, nyōō-, nōō′mə-tə-, nyōō′-) *n.* **1.** A gas-filled sac serving as a float in some colonial marine hydrozoans, such as the Portuguese man-of-war. **2.** *Bot.* A specialized respiratory root structure in certain aquatic plants, such as the bald cypress.

pneumo– or **pneum–** *pref.* **1.** Air; gas: *pneumothorax.* **2.** Lung; pulmonary: *pneumoconiosis.* **3.** Respiration: *pneumograph.* **4.** Pneumonia: *pneumococcus.* [< Gk. *pneuma*, wind, breath; see **pneu-*,** and < Gk. *pneumōn*, alteration (influenced by *pneuma*) of *pleumōn*, lung. See **pleu-*.**]

pneu•mo•ba•cil•lus (nōō′mō-bə-sĭl′əs, nyōō′-) *n., pl.* **-cil•li** (-sĭl′ī′). A nonmotile gram-negative bacterium *(Klebsiella pneumoniae)* that causes a severe form of pneumonia and is associated with other respiratory infections.

pneu•mo•coc•cus (nōō′mə-kŏk′əs, nyōō′-) *n., pl.* **-coc•ci** (-kŏk′sī′, -kŏk′ī′). A nonmotile gram-positive bacterium *(Streptococcus pneumoniae)* that is the most common cause of bacterial pneumonia. **—pneu′mo•coc′cal** (-kŏk′əl) *adj.*

pneu•mo•co•ni•o•sis (nōō′mō-kō′nē-ō′sĭs, nyōō′-) *n.* A

plus fours

Plymouth Rock
Rooster

ă pat	oi boy
ā pay	ou out
âr care	ŏŏ took
ä father	ōō boot
ĕ pet	ŭ cut
ē be	ûr urge
ĭ pit	th thin
ī pie	*th* this
îr pier	hw which
ŏ pot	zh vision
ō toe	ə about, item
ô paw	

Stress marks:
′ (primary);
′ (secondary), as in
dictionary (dĭk′shə-nĕr′ē)

disease of the lungs, such as asbestosis or silicosis, caused by long-continued inhalation of dusts, esp. mineral or metallic dusts. [PNEUMO– + Gk. *konis, konia,* dust + –OSIS.] — **pneu′mo·co′ni·ot′ic** (-ŏt′ĭk) *adj. & n.*

pneu·mo·cys·tis (nōō′mə-sĭs′tĭs, nyōō′-) *n.* A severe lung infection caused by the parasitic protozoan *Pneumocystis pneumonia* and affecting primarily individuals with an immunodeficiency disease, such as AIDS. [< NLat. *Pneumocystis,* genus name : PNEUMO– + NLat. *cystis,* cyst; see CYST.]

pneu·mo·graph (nōō′mə-grăf′, nyōō′-) also **pneu·mat·o·graph** (nōō-măt′ə-grăf′, nyōō-) *n.* A device for recording the force and speed of chest movements during respiration. — **pneu′mo·graph′ic** *adj.*

pneu·mo·nec·to·my (nōō′mə-nĕk′tə-mē, nyōō′-) also **pneu·mec·to·my** (nōō-mĕk′tə-mē, nyōō-) *n., pl.* **-mies.** Surgical removal of all or part of a lung. [Gk. *pneumōn,* lung; see PNEUMONIC + –ECTOMY.]

Pocahontas
Portrait based on a 1616 engraving by Simon de Passe (1595?–1647)

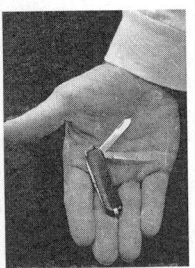

pneu·mo·nia (nōō-mōn′yə, nyōō-) *n.* An acute or chronic disease marked by inflammation of the lungs and caused by viruses, bacteria, or other microorganisms and sometimes by physical and chemical irritants. [NLat. < Gk., lung disease, alteration (influenced by *pneuma,* breath) of *pleumonia* < *pleumōn,* lung. See **pleu-***.]

pneu·mon·ic (nōō-mŏn′ĭk, nyōō-) *adj.* **1.** Of, affecting, or relating to the lungs; pulmonary. **2.** Relating to, affected by, or similar to pneumonia. [NLat. *pneumonicus* < Gk. *pneumonikos,* of the lungs < *pneumōn,* lung. See **pleu-***.]

pneu·mo·tho·rax (nōō′mō-thôr′ăks′, -thōr′-, nyōō′-) *n.* Accumulation of air or gas in the pleural cavity, occurring as a result of disease or injury or sometimes induced to collapse the lung in the treatment of lung diseases.

po or **p.o.** *abbr. Baseball.* Putout.

Po[1] (pō). A river of N Italy flowing c. 652 km (405 mi) to the Adriatic Sea.

Po[2] The symbol for the element **polonium.**

PO or **P.O.** *abbr.* **1.** Personnel officer. **2.** Petty officer. **3.** Postal order. **4.** Also **p.o.** Post office.

poach[1] (pōch) *tr.v.* **poached, poach·ing, poach·es.** To cook in a boiling or simmering liquid. [Back-formation < ME *poched,* poached < *poche,* dish of poached eggs < OFr. < p.part. of *pochier,* to poach eggs < *poche,* pocket, bag (< their appearance), of Gmc. orig.] — **poach′a·ble** *adj.*

poach[2] (pōch) *v.* **poached, poach·ing, poach·es.** — *tr.* **1.** To trespass on (another's property) for fishing or hunting. **2.** To take (fish or game) illegally. **3.** To make (land) muddy or broken up by trampling. **4.** To take or appropriate unfairly or illegally. — *intr.* **1.** To poach another's property. **2.** To poach fish or game. **3.** To become poached. Used of land. **4.** To sink into soft earth when walking. **5.** To poach something. [Obsolete Fr. *pocher,* to poke, thrust, intrude < OFr. *pochier,* to poke, gouge, of Gmc. orig.] — **poach′a·ble** *adj.*

pocketknife

poach·er[1] (pō′chər) *n.* A vessel or dish designed for the poaching of food, such as eggs or fish.

poach·er[2] (pō′chər) *n.* **1.** One who hunts or fishes illegally on the property of another. **2.** Any of various elongated marine fishes of the family Agonidae, chiefly of northern Pacific waters and having an external covering of bony plates.

Po·be·da Peak (pō-bĕd′ə, pə-byĕ′də). A mountain, 7,443.8 m (24,406 ft), of the Tien Shan on the border between E Kirghiz and W China.

Po·ca·hon·tas (pō′kə-hŏn′təs). 1595?–1617. Powhatan princess who befriended the English colonists at Jamestown and is said to have saved Capt. John Smith from execution.

Po·ca·tel·lo (pō′kə-tĕl′ō, -tĕl′ə). A city of SE ID SSW of Idaho Falls. Pop. 46,080.

po·chard (pō′chərd) *n.* Any of various diving ducks of the genus *Aythya,* esp. *A. ferina* of Europe and Asia, having gray and black plumage and a reddish head. [?]

pock (pŏk) *n.* **1.** A pustule caused by smallpox or a similar eruptive disease. **2.** A mark or scar left in the skin by such a pustule; a pockmark. — *tr.v.* **pocked, pock·ing, pocks.** To mark with pocks; pit. [ME *pokke* < OE *pocc.*] — **pock′y** *adj.*

podium
Mother Teresa speaking at commencement exercises

pock·et (pŏk′ĭt) *n.* **1.** A small baglike attachment forming part of a garment and used to carry small articles, as a flat pouch sewn inside a pair of pants or a piece of material sewn on its sides and bottom to the outside of a shirt. **2.** A small sack or bag. **3.** A receptacle, a cavity, or an opening. **4.** Financial means; money supply. **5.a.** A small cavity in the earth, esp. one containing ore. **b.** A small body or accumulation of ore. **6.** A pouch in an animal body, such as the cheek pouch of a rodent or the abdominal pouch of a marsupial. **7.** *Games.* One of the pouchlike receptacles at the corners and sides of a billiard or pool table. **8.** *Sports.* A racing position in which a contestant has no room to pass a group of contestants. **9.** A small, isolated, or protected area or group. **10.** An air pocket. **11.** A bin for storing ore, grain, or other materials. — *adj.* **1.** Suitable for or capable of being carried in one's pocket. **2.** Small; miniature. — *tr.v.* **-et·ed, -et·ing, -ets. 1.** To place in or as if in a pocket. **2.** To take possession of for oneself, esp. dishonestly. **3.a.** To accept or tolerate (an insult, for example). **b.** To conceal or suppress. **4.** To prevent (a bill) from becoming law by failing to sign until the adjournment of the legislature. **5.** *Sports.* To hem in (a competitor) in a race. **6.** *Games.* To hit (a ball) into a pocket of a pool or billiard table. — ***idioms.* in (one's) pocket.** In one's power, influence, or possession. **in pocket. 1.** Having funds. **2.** Having gained or retained funds of a specified amount. **line (one's) pockets.** To make a profit, esp. by illegitimate means. [ME, pouch, small bag < AN *pokete,* dim. of ONFr. *poke,* bag, of Gmc. orig.] — **pock′et·a·ble** *adj.* — **pock′et·less** *adj.*

pocket billiards *pl.n.* (*used with a sing. or pl. v.*) *Games.* See **pool**[2] 7.

pock·et·book (pŏk′ĭt-bŏŏk′) *n.* **1.** A pocket-sized folder or case used to hold money and papers; a billfold. **2.** A purse; a handbag. **3.** Financial resources; money supply. **4.** Often **pocket book.** A pocket-sized, usu. paperbound book.

pocket borough *n.* A borough in England, before the parliamentary reform of 1832, whose representation was controlled by a single person or family.

pocket edition *n.* See **pocketbook** 4.

pock·et·ful (pŏk′ĭt-fŏŏl′) *n., pl.* **pock·et·fuls** or **pock·ets·ful** (pŏk′ĭts-fŏŏl′). The amount that a pocket can hold.

pocket gopher *n.* See **gopher** 1.

pock·et·knife (pŏk′ĭt-nīf′) *n.* A small knife with blades or a blade that can fold into the handle when not in use.

pocket money *n.* Money for incidental or minor expenses.

pocket mouse *n.* Any of various small nocturnal North American burrowing rodents of the genus *Perognathus,* having fur-lined external cheek pouches, small ears, and a very long tail.

pock·et-sized (pŏk′ĭt-sīzd′) or **pock·et-size** (-sīz′) *adj.* **1.** Of a size suitable to be carried in a pocket. **2.** Small.

pocket veto *n.* **1.** The President's indirect veto of a bill that has been presented within ten days of adjournment, by the retention of the bill unsigned until Congress adjourns. **2.** A similar action exercised by a state governor or other chief executive. — **pock′et-ve′to** (pŏk′ĭt-vē′tō) *v.*

pock·mark (pŏk′märk′) *n.* **1.** A pitlike scar left on the skin by smallpox or another eruptive disease. **2.** A small pit on a surface. — **pock′mark′** *v.* — **pock′marked′** *adj.*

po·co (pō′kō) *adv. Mus.* To a slight degree or amount; somewhat. [Ital. < Lat. *paucus.* See **pau-***.]

po·co a po·co (pō′kō ä pō′kō) *adv. Mus.* Little by little; gradually. [Ital. : *poco,* little + *a,* by + *poco,* little.]

po·co·cu·ran·te (pō′kō-kōō-răn′tē, -rän′tē) *adj.* Indifferent; apathetic. — *n.* One who does not care. [Ital. : *poco,* little; see POCO + *curante,* pr.part. of *curare,* to care for (< Lat. *cūrāre* < *cūra,* care).] — **po′co·cu·ran′tism** *n.*

Po·co·no Mountains (pō′kə-nō′). A range of the Appalachian system in NE PA rising to c. 488 m (1,600 ft).

po·co·sin (pə-kō′sĭn) *n. Chiefly South Atlantic U.S.* A swamp in an upland coastal region. Also called regionally *dismal.* [Poss. of Virginia Algonquian orig.]

pod[1] (pŏd) *n.* **1.** *Bot.* **a.** A dehiscent fruit of a leguminous plant such as the pea. **b.** A dry several-seeded dehiscent fruit. **2.** *Zool.* A protective covering that encases the eggs of some insects and fish. **3.** A casing or housing forming part of a vehicle, as: **a.** A streamlined external housing that encloses engines, machine guns, or fuel. **b.** *Aerospace.* A detachable compartment on a spacecraft for carrying personnel or instrumentation. **4.** Something resembling a pod, as in compactness. — *v.* **pod·ded, pod·ding, pods.** — *intr.* **1.** To bear or produce pods. **2.** To expand or swell like a pod. — *tr.* To remove (seeds) from a pod. [?]

pod[2] (pŏd) *n.* A school of marine mammals, such as seals, whales, or dolphins. [?]

pod[3] (pŏd) *n.* **1.** The lengthwise groove in boring tools such as augers. **2.** The socket for holding the bit in a boring tool. [?]

–pod or **–pode** *suff.* Foot; footlike part: *pleopod.* [< NLat. *-podium* (< Gk. *podion;* see PODIUM) and < NLat. *-poda* (< Gk., pl. of *pous, pod-,* foot; see **ped-***).]

po·dag·ra (pə-dăg′rə) *n.* Gout, esp. of the big toe. [ME < Lat. < Gk. : *pous, pod-,* foot; see **ped-*** + *agra,* trap, seizing; see **ag-***.] — **po·dag′ral, po·dag′ric** *adj.*

po·des·ta (pō-dĕs′tə, pō′dĕ-stä′) *n.* The chief magistrate of a republic in medieval Italy. [Ital. *podestà* < OItal. *podestate* < Lat. *potestās,* power < *potis,* powerful, able. See **poti-***.]

Pod·gor·ny (pŏd-gôr′nē), **Nikolai Viktorovich.** 1903–83. Soviet politician who was president of the U.S.S.R. (1965–77).

po·di·a·try (pə-dī′ə-trē) *n.* The branch of medicine that deals with the diagnosis, treatment, and prevention of diseases of the human foot. [Gk. *pous, pod-,* foot; see **ped-*** + –IATRY.] — **po′di·at′ric** (pō′dē-ăt′rĭk) *adj.* — **po·di′a·trist** *n.*

pod·ite (pŏd′īt′) *n.* A segment of the limb of an arthropod. [Gk. *pous, pod-,* foot; see **ped-*** + –ITE[1].]

po·di·um (pō′dē-əm) *n., pl.* **-di·a** (-dē-ə) or **-di·ums. 1.** An elevated platform, as for a public speaker. **2.** A stand for holding the notes of a public speaker; a lectern. **3.** *Archit.* **a.** A low wall serving as a foundation. **b.** A wall circling the arena of an ancient amphitheater. **4.** *Biol.* A structure resembling or functioning as a foot. [Lat. < Gk. *podion,* base, dim. of *pous, pod-,* foot. See **ped-***.]

Po·dolsk (pə-dôlsk′). A city of W-central Russia S of Moscow. Pop. 208,000.

pod·o·phyl·lin (pŏd′ə-fĭl′ĭn) *n.* A bitter-tasting resin obtained from the dried root of the May apple and used as a cathartic and caustic. [< NLat. *Podophyllum*, genus name : Gk. *pous, pod-*, foot; see **ped-*** + Gk. *phullon*, leaf; see **bhel-³*** + -IN.]

-podous *suff.* Having a specified kind or number of feet or footlike parts: *polypodous*.

Po·dunk (pō′dŭngk′) *n. Slang.* A small isolated town, region, or place regarded as unimportant. [After *Podunk*, name of two New England towns.]

pod·zol (pŏd′zôl′) also **pod·sol** (-sôl′) *n.* A leached soil formed mainly in cool humid climates. [Russ. : *pod*, under; see **ped-*** + *zola*, ashes; see **ghel-²***.] — **pod·zol′ic** *adj.*

pod·zol·i·za·tion (pŏd′zô-lĭ-zā′shən) also **pod·sol·i·za·tion** (pŏd′sô-) *n.* **1.** The process by which soils are depleted of bases and become acidic. **2.** The development of a podzol.

Poe (pō), **Edgar Allan.** 1809–49. Amer. writer whose works include "The Gold Bug" (1843) and "The Raven" (1845).

POE or **P.O.E.** *abbr.* Port of entry.

po·em (pō′əm) *n.* **1.** A verbal composition designed to convey experiences, ideas, or emotions, characterized by the use of condensed language chosen for its sound and suggestive power and by the use of literary techniques such as meter, metaphor, and rhyme. **2.** A composition in verse rather than in prose. **3.** A literary composition written with an intensity or beauty of language more characteristic of poetry than of prose. **4.** A creation, an object, or an experience having beauty suggestive of poetry. [Fr. *poème* < OFr. < Lat. *poēma* < Gk. *poiēma* < *poiein*, to create. See **kʷei-²***.]

poe·nol·o·gy (pē-nŏl′ə-jē) *n.* Var. of **penology.**

po·e·sy (pō′ĭ-zē, -sē) *n., pl.* **-sies. 1.** Poetical works; poetry. **2.** The art or practice of composing poems. **3.** The inspiration involved in composing poetry. [ME *poesie* < OFr. < Lat. *poēsis* < Gk. *poiēsis* < *poiein*, to create. See **kʷei-²***.]

po·et (pō′ĭt) *n.* **1.** A writer of poems. **2.** One who demonstrates great imaginative power, insight, or beauty of expression. [ME < OFr. *poete* < Lat. *poēta* < Gk. *poiētēs*, maker, composer < *poiein*, to create. See **kʷei-²***.]

poet. *abbr.* Poetic; poetical; poetry.

po·et·as·ter (pō′ĭt-ăs′tər) *n.* A writer of insignificant, meretricious, or shoddy poetry. [NLat. : Lat. *poēta*, poet; see POET + Lat. *-aster*, pejorative suff.]

po·et·ess (pō′ĭ-tĭs) *n.* A woman who writes poems.

po·et·ic (pō-ĕt′ĭk) *adj.* **1.** Of or relating to poetry. **2.** Having a quality or style characteristic of poetry. **3.** Suitable as a subject for poetry. **4.** Of, relating to, or befitting a poet: *poetic insight*. **5.** Characterized by romantic imagery. — *n.* The theory or practice of writing poetry; poetics. [Lat. *poēticus* < Gk. *poiētikos*, inventive < *poiein*, to make. See **kʷei-²***.]

po·et·i·cal (pō-ĕt′ĭ-kəl) *adj.* **1.** Poetic. **2.** Fancifully depicted or embellished; idealized. — **po·et′i·cal·ly** *adv.* — **po·et′i·cal·ness, po·et′i·cal′i·ty** (-kăl′ĭ-tē) *n.*

po·et·i·cism (pō-ĕt′ĭ-sĭz′əm) *n.* A poetic expression that is hackneyed, archaic, or excessively artificial.

po·et·i·cize (pō-ĕt′ĭ-sīz′) *v.* **-cized, -ciz·ing, -ciz·es.** — *tr.* To describe or express in poetry or in a poetic manner. — *intr.* To write poetry.

poetic justice *n.* The rewarding of virtue and the punishment of vice, often in an esp. appropriate or ironic manner.

poetic license *n.* The liberty taken by an artist or a writer in deviating from convention to achieve a desired effect.

po·et·ics (pō-ĕt′ĭks) *n. (used with a sing. or pl. v.)* **1.** Literary criticism that deals with the nature, forms, and laws of poetry. **2.** A treatise on or study of poetry or aesthetics. **3.** The practice of writing poetry; poetic composition.

po·et·ize (pō′ĭ-tīz′) *v.* **-ized, -iz·ing, -iz·es.** — *tr.* To describe or express in poetry or a poetic manner. — *intr.* To write poetry. — **po′et·iz′er** *n.*

poet laureate *n., pl.* **poets laureate** or **poet laureates. 1.** A poet appointed for life by a British monarch as a member of the royal household and formerly expected to write patriotic poems. **2.** A poet appointed to a similar honorary position or honored for artistic excellence. **3.** A poet acclaimed as the most excellent or most representative of a locality or group.

po·et·ry (pō′ĭ-trē) *n.* **1.** The art or work of a poet. **2.a.** Poems regarded as forming a division of literature. **b.** The poetic works of a given author, group, nation, or kind. **3.** A piece of literature written in meter; verse. **4.** Prose that resembles a poem in some respect, as in form or sound. **5.** The essence or characteristic quality of a poem. **6.** The quality of a poem, as possessed by an object, act, or experience. [ME *poetrie* < OFr. < Med.Lat. *poētria* < Lat. *poēta*, poet. See POET.]

pog·o·nip (pŏg′ə-nĭp′) *n.* See **ice fog.** [Shoshone *pakenappeh*.]

po·go stick (pō′gō) *n. Sports & Games.* A stick with footrests and a spring set into the bottom end, used to propel oneself along the ground by hopping. [< *Pogo*, a former trademark.]

po·grom (pə-grŏm′, pō′grəm) *n.* An organized, often officially encouraged massacre or persecution, esp. one against Jews. [Russ., outrage, havoc < *pogromit'*, to wreak havoc : *po-*, adverbial pref. (< *po*, next to; see **apo-***) + *gromit'*, wreak havoc (< *grom*, thunder).] — **po·grom′** *v.*

po·gy (pō′gē) *n., pl.* **pogy** or **-gies.** See **menhaden.** [Alteration of dial. *poghaden*, perh. of Eastern Abenaki orig.]

Po Hai (bō′ hī′). See **Bo Hai.**

poi (poi) *n.* A Hawaiian food made from taro root that is cooked, pounded to a paste, and fermented. [Hawaiian.]

-poiesis *suff.* Production; creation; formation: *hematopoiesis*. [< Gk. *poiēsis*, creation < *poiein*, to make. See **kʷei-²***.]

-poietic *suff.* Productive; formative: *galactopoietic*. [< Gk. *poiētikos*, creative < *poiētēs*, maker < *poiein*, to make. See **kʷei-²***.]

poign·ant (poin′yənt) *adj.* **1.a.** Physically painful. **b.** Keenly distressing to the mind or feelings. **c.** Profoundly moving; touching. **2.** Piercing; incisive. **3.a.** Neat, skillful, and to the point. **b.** Astute and pertinent; relevant. **4.** Agreeably intense or stimulating: *poignant delight*. **5.** *Archaic.* **a.** Sharp or sour to the taste; piquant. **b.** Sharp or pungent to the smell. [ME *poinaunt* < OFr. *poignant*, pr.part. of *poindre*, to prick < Lat. *pungere*. See **peuk-***.] — **poign′ance, poign′an·cy** *n.* — **poign′ant·ly** *adv.*

poi·kil·o·therm (poi-kĭl′ə-thûrm′) *n.* An organism, such as a fish or reptile, having a body temperature that varies with the temperature of its surroundings; an ectotherm. [Gk. *poikilos*, spotted, various; see **peig-*** + -THERM.]

poi·ki·lo·ther·mic (poi′kə-lō-thûr′mĭk) also **poi·ki·lo·ther·mal** (-məl) also **poi·ki·lo·ther·mous** (-məs) *adj.* Of or relating to an organism having a body temperature that varies with the temperature of its surroundings; cold-blooded. — **poi′ki·lo·ther′mi·a, poi′ki·lo·ther′mism** *n.*

poi·lu (pwä-lü′) *n. Slang.* A French soldier, esp. in World War I. [Fr., hairy, tough, poilu < OFr. *pelu*, hairy < VLat. **pilūtus* < Lat. *pilus*, hair.]

Poin·ca·ré (pwăɴ-kä-rā′), **Jules Henri.** 1854–1912. French mathematician and physicist who made a number of contributions to the field of celestial mechanics.

Poincaré, Raymond. 1860–1934. French president (1913–20) and premier (1912–13, 1922–23, and 1926–29).

poin·ci·an·a (poin′sē-ăn′ə, -ä′nə) *n.* See **royal poinciana.** [NLat. *Poinciana*, genus name, after M. De *Poinci*, 17th-cent. governor of the French West Indies.]

poin·set·ti·a (poin-sĕt′ē-ə, -sĕt′ə) *n.* A tropical American shrub *(Euphorbia pulcherrima)* that has showy, usu. scarlet bracts beneath the small yellow inflorescences. [NLat., after Joel Roberts *Poinsett* (1779–1851), Amer. diplomat.]

point (point) *n.* **1.** A sharp or tapered end. **2.** An object having a sharp or tapered end. **3.** A tapering extension of land projecting into water; a peninsula, cape, or promontory. **4.** A mark formed by or as if by a sharp end. **5.** A mark or dot used in printing or writing for punctuation, esp. a period. **6.** A decimal point. **7.** *Ling.* A vowel point. **8.** One of the protruding marks used in certain methods of writing and printing for the sightless. **9.** *Math.* A dimensionless geometric object having no properties except location. **10.a.** A place or locality considered with regard to its position. **b.** A narrowly particularized and localized position or place; a spot. **11.** A specified degree, condition, or limit, as in a scale or course. **12.a.** Any of the 32 equal divisions marked at the circumference of a mariner's compass card that indicate direction. **b.** The interval of 11°15′ between any two adjacent markings. **13.a.** A distinct condition or degree. **b.** The interval of time immediately before a given occurrence; the verge. **14.** A specific moment in time. **15.** An objective or a purpose to be reached or achieved, or one that is worth reaching or achieving. **16.** The major idea or essential part of a concept or narrative. **17.** A significant, outstanding, or effective idea, argument, or suggestion. **18.** A separate distinguishing item or element; a detail: *not his strong point*. **19.** A quality or characteristic that is important or distinctive, esp. a standard characteristic used to judge an animal. **20.** A single unit, as in counting, rating, or measuring. **21.a.** A unit of academic credit usu. equal to one hour of class work per week during one semester. **b.** A numerical unit of academic achievement equal to a letter grade. **22.** *Sports & Games.* A unit of scoring or counting. **23.a.** A unit equal to one dollar, used to quote or state variations in the current prices of stocks or commodities. **b.** A unit equal to one percent, used to quote or state interest rates or shares in gross profits. **24.** One percent of the total principal of a loan, paid up front to the lender and considered separately from the interest. **25.** *Mus.* A phrase, such as a fugue subject, in contrapuntal music. **26.** *Print.* A unit of type size equal to 0.01384 inch, or approx. 1/72 of an inch. **27.** A jeweler's unit of weight equal to 2 milligrams or 0.01 carat. **28.a.** The act or an instance of pointing. **b.** The stiff and attentive stance taken by a hunting dog. **29.a.** Needlepoint. **b.** See **bobbin lace. 30.a.** A reconnaissance or patrol unit that moves ahead of an advance party or guard, or that follows a rear guard. **b.** The position occupied by such a unit or guard. **31.a.** An electrical contact, esp. one in the distributor of an automobile engine. **b.** *Chiefly British.* An electrical socket or outlet. **32. points.** The extremities of an animal, such as a horse or dog. **33.a.** A movable rail, tapered at the end, such as that used in a railroad switch. **b.** The vertex of the angle created by the intersection of rails in a frog or switch. **34.** A ribbon or cord with a metal tag at the end, used to fasten

ă pat	oi boy
ā pay	ou out
âr care	o͝o took
ä father	o͞o boot
ĕ pet	ŭ cut
ē be	ûr urge
ĭ pit	th thin
ī pie	*th* this
îr pier	hw which
ŏ pot	zh vision
ō toe	ə about, item
ô paw	

Stress marks:
′ (primary);
′ (secondary), as in
dictionary (dĭk′shə-nĕr′ē)

clothing in the 16th and 17th centuries. —*v.* **point•ed, point•ing, points.** —*tr.* **1.** To direct or aim. **2.** To bring (something) to notice: *pointed out an error.* **3.** To indicate the position or direction of: *pointed them out over there.* **4.** To sharpen (a pencil, for example); provide with a point. **5.** To separate with decimal points: *pointed off the tenths place.* **6.** To mark (text) with points; punctuate. **7.** *Ling.* To mark (a consonant) with a vowel point. **8.** To give emphasis to; stress: *pointing up my error.* **9.** To indicate the presence and position of (game) by standing immobile and directing the muzzle toward it. Used of a hunting dog. **10.** To fill and finish the joints of (masonry) with cement or mortar. —*intr.* **1.** To direct attention or indicate position with or as if with the finger. **2.** To turn the mind or thought in a particular direction or to a particular conclusion: *All signs point to an early spring.* **3.** To be turned or faced in a given direction; aim. **4.** To point game. **5.** *Naut.* To sail close to the wind. —***idioms.* beside the point.** Irrelevant to the matter at hand. **in point.** Having relevance or pertinence. **in point of.** With reference to; in the matter of. **make a point of.** To consider or treat (an action or activity) as indispensable. **stretch a point.** To make an exception. **to the point.** Concerning or with relevance to the matter at hand. [ME, partly < OFr. *point*, prick, mark, moment (< VLat. **punctum* < Lat. *pūnctum* < neut. p.part. of *pungere*, to prick) and partly < OFr. *pointe*, sharp end (< VLat. **puncta* < Lat. *pūncta*, fem. p.part. of *pungere*, to prick; see **peuk-***).]

pointer
Hunting dog

point-blank (point′blăngk′) *adj.* **1.** Aimed straight at the mark or target without allowing for the drop in a projectile's course. **2.a.** So close to a target that a weapon may be aimed directly at it. **b.** Close enough so that missing the target is unlikely or impossible. **3.** Straightforward; blunt. —*adv.* **1.** With a straight aim; directly. **2.** Without hesitation, deliberation, or equivocation. [Perh. < Fr. *point (de tir)*, (firing) point, or *point (visé)*, (aiming) point (< OFr.; see POINT) + Fr. *blanc*, bullseye, target (< OFr., white; see BLANK).]

point-de•vice (point′dĭ-vīs′) *adj.* Scrupulously correct or neat; precise or meticulous. [ME *at point devis*, prob. < OFr. **a point devis* : *a*, to + *point*, point, moment + *devis*, fixed, arranged.] —**point′-de•vice′** *adv.*

pointe (pwănt) *n.* In ballet, dancing that is performed on the tips of the toes. [< Fr. *pointe (des pieds)*, point (of the feet), tiptoe. See POINT.]

pointillism
Detail of *The Channel at Gravelines, Evening,* 1890, by Georges Seurat

Pointe aux Trem•bles (pwănt ō trän′blə). A city of S Quebec, Canada, on NE Montreal I. Pop. 36,270.

Pointe Claire (point′ klâr′, pwănt). A city of S Quebec, Canada, a suburb of Montreal on SW Montreal I. Pop. 24,571.

point•ed (poin′tĭd) *adj.* **1.** Having an end coming to a point. **2.** Sharp; cutting: *a pointed critique.* **3.** Obviously directed at or making reference to a particular person or thing. **4.** Clearly evident or conspicuous; marked. **5.** Characterized by the use of a pointed crown, as in Gothic architecture. —**point′ed•ly** *adv.* —**point′ed•ness** *n.*

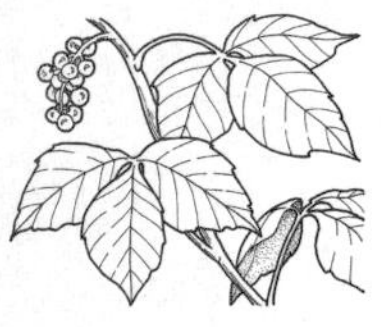

poison ivy
Rhus radicans

point•er (poin′tər) *n.* **1.** One that directs, indicates, or points. **2.** A scale indicator on a watch or other measuring instrument. **3.** A long tapered stick for indicating objects, as on a chart. **4.** Any of a breed of hunting dogs that points game, typically having a smooth short-haired coat, usu. white with dark spots. **5.a.** A piece of advice; a suggestion. **b.** A piece of indicative information. **6.** *Comp. Sci.* A word that gives the address of a core storage location. **7.** Either of the two stars in the Big Dipper that point to Polaris.

poin•til•lism (pwăn′tē-ĭz′əm, point′l-ĭz′-) *n.* A postimpressionist school of painting flourishing in late 19th-century France, characterized by the application of paint in small dots and brush strokes. [Fr. *pointillisme* < *pointiller*, to paint small dots, stipple < OFr. **pointille*, engraved with small dots < *point*, point < Lat. *pūnctum* < neut. p.part. of *pungere*, to prick. See **peuk-***.] —**poin′til•list** *adj. & n.*

poin•til•lis•tic (pwăn′tē-ĭs′tĭk, point′l-ĭs′-) *adj.* **1.** Of or relating to pointillism. **2.** Minutely particularized.

point lace *n.* See **needlepoint** 2.

point•less (point′lĭs) *adj.* **1.** Lacking meaning; senseless. **2.** Ineffectual. —**point′less•ly** *adv.* —**point′less•ness** *n.*

point man *n.* **1.** A soldier assigned to a position some distance ahead of a patrol as a lookout. **2.** A man who has a crucial, often hazardous role in the forefront of an enterprise.

point of accumulation *n. Math.* See **limit** 6.

point of honor *n., pl.* **points of honor.** A matter that affects one's honor or reputation.

Poland

point of no return *n.* **1.** The point in a course of action when it cannot be reversed. **2.** The point in an aircraft flight when the fuel amount precludes return to the starting point.

point of order *n., pl.* **points of order.** A question as to whether the present proceedings are in order or allowed by the rules of parliamentary procedure.

point of view *n., pl.* **points of view. 1.** A manner of viewing things; an attitude. **2.a.** A position from which something is observed or considered. **b.** The attitude or outlook of a narrator or character, as in a piece of literature or a movie.

Point Pleas•ant (point plĕz′ənt). A borough of E NJ near the Atlantic S of Asbury Park. Pop. 18,177.

point source *n.* A source, esp. of pollution or radiation, occupying a very small area and having a concentrated output.

Point Suc•cess (sək-sĕs′). A peak, 4,318.2 m (14,158 ft), in the Cascade Range of W-central WA near Mt. Rainier.

point system *n.* **1.** A system of evaluating academic achievement based on grade points. **2.** Any of various systems of printing or writing for sightless people that use an alphabet of raised symbols or dots. **3.** *Print.* A system of graduating sizes of type in multiples of the point. **4.** A system of assigning points to drivers for each type of traffic violation and revoking a license for a certain number of points.

point woman *n.* A woman who has a crucial, often hazardous role in the forefront of an enterprise.

point•y (poin′tē) *adj.* **-i•er, -i•est.** Having an end tapering to a point.

poise[1] (poiz) *v.* **poised, pois•ing, pois•es.** —*tr.* To carry or hold in equilibrium; balance. —*intr.* To be balanced or held in suspension; hover. —*n.* **1.** A state of balance or equilibrium; stability. **2.** Freedom from affectation or embarrassment; composure. **3.** The bearing or deportment of the head or body; mien. **4.** A state or condition of hovering or being suspended. [ME *poisen*, to balance, weigh < OFr. *peser, pois-* < VLat. **pēsāre* < Lat. *pēnsāre*. See **(s)pen-***.]

poise[2] (pwäz) *n.* A centimeter-gram-second unit of dynamic viscosity equal to one dyne-second per square centimeter. [Fr., after Jean Louis Marie *Poiseuille* (1799–1869), French physician and physiologist.]

poi•son (poi′zən) *n.* **1.** A substance that causes injury, illness, or death, esp. by chemical means. **2.** Something destructive or fatal. **3.** *Chem. & Phys.* A substance that inhibits another substance or a reaction. —*tr.v.* **-soned, -son•ing, -sons. 1.** To kill or harm with poison. **2.** To put poison on or into. **3.a.** To pollute. **b.** To have a harmful influence on; corrupt: *Jealousy poisoned the friendship.* **4.** *Chem. & Phys.* To inhibit (a substance or reaction). —*adj.* Poisonous. [ME < OFr. < Lat. *pōtiō, pōtiōn-*, drink. See **pō(i)-***.] —**poi′son•er** *n.*

poison gas *n.* A gas or vapor used esp. in chemical warfare to injure, disable, or kill upon inhalation or contact.

poison hemlock *n.* A deadly poisonous European plant *(Conium maculatum)* having bipinnately compound leaves and compound umbels of small white flowers.

poison ivy *n.* A North American shrub or vine *(Rhus radicans)* that has compound leaves with three leaflets, small green flowers, and whitish berries and causes a rash on contact.

poison oak *n.* **1.** Either of two shrubs, *Rhus toxicodendron* of the southeast United States or *R. diversiloba* of western North America, related to poison ivy and causing a rash on contact. **2.** See **poison ivy.**

poi•son•ous (poi′zə-nəs) *adj.* **1.** Having the capability of harming or killing by or as if by poison; toxic or venomous. **2.** Containing a poison. **3.** Marked by apparent ill will. —**poi′son•ous•ly** *adv.* —**poi′son•ous•ness** *n.*

poi•son-pen letter (poi′zən-pĕn′) *n.* A usu. anonymous letter or note containing abusive or malicious statements or accusations about the recipient or a third party.

poison sumac *n.* A swamp shrub *(Rhus vernix)* of the southeast United States, having compound leaves and greenish-white berries and causing a skin rash on contact.

Pois•son distribution (pwä-sôN′) *n.* A probability distribution that can be applied to distributions that are not continuous. [After Siméon Denis *Poisson* (1781–1840), French mathematician.]

Poi•tiers (pwä-tyā′). A city of W France ESE of Nantes; settled by a Gallic people. Pop. 79,350.

Poi•tou (pwä-to͞o′). A historical region of W-central France bordering on the Bay of Biscay; frequently contested by France and England until the end of the Hundred Years' War.

poke[1] (pōk) *v.* **poked, pok•ing, pokes.** —*tr.* **1.** To push or jab at, as with a finger or an arm; prod. **2.** To make (a hole or pathway, for example) by or as if by prodding, elbowing, or jabbing. **3.** To push; thrust. **4.** To stir (a fire) by prodding the wood or coal with a poker or stick. **5.** *Slang.* To strike; punch. —*intr.* **1.** To make thrusts or jabs, as with a stick or poker. **2.** To pry or meddle; intrude. **3.** To search or look curiously in a desultory manner. **4.** To proceed in a slow or lazy manner; putter. **5.** To thrust forward; appear. —*n.* **1.** A push, thrust, or jab. **2.** *Slang.* A punch or blow with the fist. **3.** One who moves slowly or aimlessly; a dawdler. —***idiom.* poke fun at.** To ridicule in a mischievous manner; tease. [ME *poken*, prob. < MLGer. or MDu.]

poke[2] (pōk) *n.* **1.** A projecting brim at the front of a bonnet. **2.** A large bonnet having a projecting brim. [< POKE[1].]

poke[3] (pōk) *n. Chiefly Southern U.S.* A sack; a bag. [ME, prob. < ONFr. See POCKET.]

Regional Note: The noun *poke* — meaning a bag or sack — dates from the 14th century in English. In many parts of Scotland *poke* means a little paper bag for carrying purchases or a cone-shaped piece of paper for an ice-cream cone.

poke[4] (pōk) *n.* Pokeweed. [Short for dial. *pocan*, of Virginia Algonquian orig.; akin to *puccoon*.]

poke•ber•ry (pōk′bĕr′ē) *n.* **1.** The blackish-red berry of the pokeweed. **2.** See **pokeweed.**

pok•er1 (pō′kər) *n.* One that pokes, esp. a metal rod used to stir a fire.

pok•er2 (pō′kər) *n. Games.* Any of various card games played by two or more who bet on the value of their hands. [?]

poker face *n.* A face lacking any expression, as that of an expert poker player. **—pok′er•faced′** (pō′kər-fāst′) *adj.*

poke sal•lit (săl′ĭt) *n. Chiefly Southern U.S.* Greens of the wild pokeweed eaten boiled. [Var. of *poke salad.*]

poke•weed (pōk′wēd′) *n.* A tall North American plant *(Phytolacca americana)* having small white flowers, blackish-red berries, and a poisonous root. [POKE4 + WEED1.]

po•key1 also **po•ky** (pō′kē) *n., pl.* **-keys** also **-kies.** *Slang.* A jail or prison. [?]

poke•y2 (pō′kē) *adj. Informal.* Var. of **poky1**.

pok•y1 also **poke•y** (pō′kē) *adj.* **pok•i•er, pok•i•est.** *Informal.* **1.** Dawdling; slow. **2.** Frumpish; shabby. **3.** Small and cramped. [< POKE1.] **—pok′i•ly** *adv.* **—pok′i•ness** *n.*

po•ky2 (pō′kē) *n. Slang.* Var. of **pokey1**.

pol (pôl) *n. Informal.* A politician.

pol. *abbr.* Political; politics.

Pol. *abbr.* Poland; Polish.

Po•lack (pō′lŏk′, -lăk′) *n.* **1.** *Offensive Slang.* Used as a disparaging term for a person of Polish birth or descent. **2.** *Obsolete.* A Pole. [Pol. *Polak* < Slav. *polje,* field. See **pelə-2*.**]

Po•land (pō′lənd). A country of central Europe bordering on the Baltic Sea; unified as a kingdom in the 10th cent., carved up among other states in three partitions (1772, 1793, and 1795), and reconstituted as a republic in 1918. Cap. Warsaw. Pop. 37,063,000.

Poland China *n.* Any of a breed of large black-and-white hogs developed in North America.

Poland China
Sow

po•lar (pō′lər) *adj.* **1.a.** Of or relating to a pole. **b.** Measured from or referred to a pole. **2.** Relating to or located near the North Pole or South Pole. **3.a.** Passing over a planet's north and south poles: *a polar orbit.* **b.** Traveling in a polar orbit. **4.** Serving as a guide or polestar. **5.** Occupying or marked by opposite extremes. **6.** Central or pivotal. **7.** *Chem.* Having to do with or characterized by a dipole.

polar angle *n. Math.* The angle formed by the polar axis and the radius vector in a polar coordinate system.

polar axis *n. Math.* The fixed reference axis from which the polar angle is measured in a polar coordinate system.

polar bear *n.* A large white-furred bear *(Ursus maritimus* or *Thalarctos maritimus)* living in Arctic regions.

polar bear
Ursus maritimus

polar body *n.* A minute cell produced and ultimately discarded in the development of an oocyte, containing one of the nuclei derived from the first or second meiotic division.

polar cap *n.* **1.a.** Either of the regions around the poles of the earth that are permanently covered with ice. **b.** A high-altitude icecap. **2.** *Astron.* Either of the polar regions of Mars covered with frozen carbon dioxide and water.

polar circle *n.* **1.** The Arctic Circle. **2.** The Antarctic Circle.

polar coordinate *n. Math.* Either of two coordinates, the radius vector or the polar angle, that together specify the position of a point in a plane.

po•lar•im•e•ter (pō′lə-rĭm′ĭ-tər) *n.* An instrument used to measure the rotation of the plane of polarization of polarized light passing through an optical structure or sample. **—po′lar•i•met′ric** (-lər-ə-mĕt′rĭk) *adj.* **—po′lar•im′e•try** *n.*

Po•lar•is (pə-lăr′ĭs) *n.* A star of the second magnitude, at the end of the handle of the Little Dipper and almost at the north celestial pole. [NLat. *(Stella) Polāris,* polar (star) < Lat. *polus,* pole. See POLE1.]

po•lar•i•scope (pō-lăr′ĭ-skōp′) *n.* Any of several instruments for studying the interactions of polarized light with optically transparent media.

po•lar•i•ty (pō-lăr′ĭ-tē, pə-) *n., pl.* **-ties. 1.** Intrinsic polar separation, alignment, or orientation, esp. of a physical property: *magnetic polarity.* **2.** An indicated polar extreme: *an electric terminal with positive polarity.* **3.** The possession or manifestation of two opposing attributes, tendencies, or principles.

po•lar•i•za•tion (pō′lər-ĭ-zā′shən) *n.* **1.** The production or condition of polarity, as: **a.** A process or state in which rays of light exhibit different properties in different directions, esp. the state in which all the vibration takes place in one plane. **b.** *Chem. & Phys.* The partial or complete polar separation of positive and negative electric charge in a nuclear, atomic, molecular, or chemical system. **2.** A concentration, as of groups, about two conflicting or contrasting positions.

po•lar•ize (pō′lə-rīz′) *v.* **-ized, -iz•ing, -iz•es.** *—tr.* **1.** To induce polarization in; impart polarity to. **2.** To cause to concentrate about two conflicting or contrasting positions. *—intr.* **1.** To acquire polarity. **2.** To cause polarization of light. **—po′lar•iz′a•ble** *adj.* **—po′lar•iz′er** *n.*

polar nucleus *n. Bot.* Either of two nuclei in a flowering plant embryo sac that fuse to form the endosperm nucleus.

po•lar•og•ra•phy (pō′lə-rŏg′rə-fē) *n. Chem.* An electrochemical method of quantitative or qualitative analysis based on measuring a current passing through the solution being analyzed as an applied voltage is increased. [POLAR(IZATION) + -GRAPHY.] **—po•lar′o•graph′ic** (-lăr′ə-grăf′ĭk) *adj.*

Po•lar•oid (pō′lə-roid′). **1.** A trademark used for a specially treated transparent plastic capable of polarizing light passing through it, used in glare-reducing optical devices. **2.** A trademark used for a camera and film that produce instant photographs.

Po•lar Regions (pō′lər). The various lands and waters surrounding the North Pole and the South Pole, known respectively as the **North Polar Region** and the **South Polar Region.**

polar star *n.* See **Polaris.**

pol•der (pōl′dər) *n.* An area of low-lying land, esp. in the Netherlands, that has been reclaimed from a body of water and is protected by dikes. [Du. < MDu.]

pole1 (pōl) *n.* **1.** Either extremity of an axis through a sphere. **2.** *Geog.* Either of the regions contiguous to the extremities of the earth's rotational axis, the North Pole or the South Pole. **3.** *Phys.* A magnetic pole. **4.** Either of two oppositely charged terminals, as in an electric cell or battery. **5.** *Astron.* A celestial pole. **6.** *Biol.* **a.** Either extremity of the main axis of a nucleus, a cell, or an organism. **b.** Either end of the spindle formed in a cell during mitosis. **c.** The point on a cell where a process originates, such as a flagellum. **7.** Either of two antithetical ideas, propensities, forces, or positions. **8.** A fixed point of reference. **9.** *Math.* The origin in a polar coordinate system; the vertex of a polar angle. [ME < OFr. < Lat. *polus* < Gk. *polos,* axis, sky. See **kʷel-1*.**]

pole2 (pōl) *n.* **1.** A long, relatively slender, generally rounded piece of wood or other material. **2.** The long tapering wooden shaft extending up from the front axle of a vehicle to the collars of the animals drawing it; a tongue. **3.a.** See **rod** 6a. **b.** A unit of area equal to a square rod. **4.** *Sports.* The inside position on the starting line of a racetrack. *—v.* **poled, pol•ing, poles.** *—tr.* **1.a.** *Naut.* To propel with a pole. **b.** To propel (oneself) or make (one's way) by the use of ski poles. **2.** To support (plants) with a pole. **3.** To strike, poke, or stir with a pole. *—intr.* **1.** *Naut.* To propel a boat or raft with a pole. **2.** *Sports.* To use ski poles to maintain or gain speed. [ME < OE *pāl* < Lat. *pālus,* stake. See **pag-*.**]

Pole (pōl) *n.* **1.** A native or inhabitant of Poland. **2.** A person of Polish descent.

Pole, Reginald. 1500–58. English prelate who was the last Roman Catholic archbishop of Canterbury (1556).

pole•ax or **pole•axe** (pōl′ăks′) *—n.* **1.** An ax having a hammer face opposite the blade, used to slaughter cattle. **2.** A battle-ax used in the Middle Ages, consisting of a long shaft topped with an ax or a combination of an ax, a hammer, and a pick. *—tr.v.* **-axed, -ax•ing, -ax•es.** To strike or fell with or as if with a poleax. [ME, alteration of *pollax* : *poll,* head; see POLL + *ax,* ax; see AX.]

pole bean *n.* Any of various cultivated climbing beans that grow on poles or supports.

pole•cat (pōl′kăt′) *n.* **1.a.** A chiefly nocturnal European carnivorous mammal *(Mustela putorius)* of the weasel family that ejects a malodorous fluid to mark its territory and ward off enemies. **b.** Any of various related mammals of Asia, esp. *Mustela eversmanni* of central Asia. **2.** See **skunk** 1a. [ME *polcat* : poss. OFr. *poll, poule,* fowl, hen; see PULLET + *cat,* cat; see CAT.]

pole vault

pole horse *n.* A horse harnessed to the pole of a vehicle.

po•leis (pō′lās′) *n.* Pl. of **polis.**

po•lem•ic (pə-lĕm′ĭk) *n.* **1.** A controversial argument, esp. one refuting or attacking an opinion or a doctrine. **2.** One engaged in or inclined to polemical matters. *—adj.* also **po•lem•i•cal** (-ĭ-kəl). Of or relating to a controversy, an argument, or a refutation. [Fr. *polémique* < Gk. *polemikos,* hostile < *polemos,* war.] **—po•lem′i•cal•ly** *adv.*

po•lem•i•cist (pə-lĕm′ĭ-sĭst) also **po•lem•ist** (pə-lĕm′ĭst, pŏl′ə-mĭst) *n.* A person skilled or involved in polemics.

po•lem•i•cize (pə-lĕm′ĭ-sīz′) *intr.v.* **-cized, -ciz•ing, -ciz•es.** To write or deliver an argument; engage in controversy.

po•lem•ics (pə-lĕm′ĭks) *n. (used with a sing. or pl. v.)* **1.** The art or practice of argumentation or controversy. **2.** The practice of theological controversy to refute errors of doctrine.

po•len•ta (pō-lĕn′tə) *n.* A thick mush made of boiled cornmeal. [Ital. < Lat., crushed grain, barley meal.]

pol•er (pō′lər) *n.* **1.** One that propels, supports, conveys, or strikes with a pole. **2.** A pole horse.

pole•star (pōl′stär′) *n.* **1.** See **Polaris. 2.** A guiding principle.

pole vault *n. Sports.* **1.** A field event in which the contestant jumps or vaults over a high crossbar with the aid of a long pole. **2.** A vault made with the aid of a long pole. **—pole′-vault′** (pōl′vôlt′) *v.* **—pole′-vault′er** *n.*

po•lice (pə-lēs′) *n., pl.* **police. 1.** The governmental department charged with the regulation and control of the affairs of a community, now chiefly the department established to maintain order, enforce the law, and prevent and detect crime. **2.a.** A body of persons making up such a department. **b.** A body of persons having similar organization and function: *campus police.* **3.** *(used with a pl. v.)* Police officers considered as a group. **4.** Regulation and control of the affairs of a community, esp. with respect to maintenance of such things as order, law, health, morals, and safety. **5.a.** The cleaning of a military base or other military area. **b.** The soldiers assigned

ă pat	oi boy
ā pay	ou out
âr care	ŏŏ took
ä father	ōō boot
ĕ pet	ŭ cut
ē be	ûr urge
ĭ pit	th thin
ī pie	*th* this
îr pier	hw which
ŏ pot	zh vision
ō toe	ə about, item
ô paw	

Stress marks:
′ (primary);
′ (secondary), as in
dictionary (dĭk′shə-nĕr′ē)

to a specified maintenance duty. —*tr.v.* **-liced, -lic•ing, -lic•es. 1.** To regulate, control, or keep in order with or as if with a law enforcement agency. **2.** To make (a military area, for example) neat in appearance. [Fr. < OFr. *policie,* civil organization < LLat. *polītīa* < Lat., the State < Gk. *politeia* < *politēs,* citizen < *polis,* city. See **pelə-³*.**] —**po•lice′a•ble** *adj.* —**po•lic′er** *n.*

police action *n.* A localized military action undertaken without a formal declaration of war.

police dog *n.* **1.** A dog trained to aid the police, as in detecting controlled substances. **2.** See **German shepherd.**

police force *n.* See **police** 2.

po•lice•man (pə-lēs′mən) *n.* A man on a police force.

police officer *n.* A policeman or policewoman.

police power *n.* The inherent authority of a government to impose restrictions on private rights for the sake of public welfare, order, and security.

police state *n.* A state in which the government exercises rigid and repressive controls over the social, economic, and political life of the people, esp. by means of a secret police force.

police station *n.* The headquarters of a unit of a police force, where those under arrest are first charged.

po•lice•wom•an (pə-lēs′wo͝om′ən) *n.* A woman on a police force.

pol•i•clin•ic (pŏl′ē-klĭn′ĭk) *n.* The department of a hospital or health care facility that treats outpatients. [Ger. *Poliklinik* : Gk. *polis,* city; see **pelə-³*** + *Klinik,* clinic (< Gk. *klinikos,* of a bed; see CLINIC).]

pol•i•cy¹ (pŏl′ĭ-sē) *n., pl.* **-cies. 1.** A plan or course of action, as of a government, political party, or business, intended to influence and determine decisions, actions, and other matters. **2.a.** A course of action, guiding principle, or procedure considered expedient, prudent, or advantageous. **b.** Prudence, shrewdness, or sagacity in practical matters. [ME *policie,* art of government, civil organization < OFr. See POLICE.]

pol•i•cy² (pŏl′ĭ-sē) *n., pl.* **-cies. 1.** A written contract or certificate of insurance. **2.** A numbers game. [Obsolete *police* < Fr., contract, bill of lading < OFr. < OItal. *polizza,* alteration of Med.Lat. *apodixa,* receipt < Med.Gk. *apodeixis* < Gk., proof < *apodeiknunai,* to prove : *apo-,* intensive pref.; see APO- + *deiknunai,* to show; see **deik-*.**]

pol•i•cy•hol•der (pŏl′ĭ-sē-hōl′dər) *n.* One that holds an insurance contract or policy.

pol•i•cy•mak•ing or **pol•i•cy-mak•ing** (pŏl′ĭ-sē-mā′kĭng) *n.* High-level development of policy, esp. government policy. —**pol′i•cy•mak′er** *n.* —**pol′i•cy•mak′ing** *adj.*

po•li•o (pō′lē-ō′) *n.* Poliomyelitis.

po•li•o•my•e•li•tis (pō′lē-ō-mī′ə-lī′tĭs) *n.* A highly infectious viral disease that chiefly affects children and in its acute forms causes inflammation of motor neurons of the spinal cord and brainstem, leading to paralysis, muscular atrophy, and often deformity. [NLat. : Gk. *polios,* gray; see **pel-¹*** + MYELITIS.] —**po′li•o•my′e•lit′ic** (-lĭt′ĭk) *adj.*

po•li•o•vi•rus (pō′lē-ō-vī′rəs) *n., pl.* **-rus•es.** Any of three enteroviruses that cause poliomyelitis.

po•lis (pō′lĭs) *n., pl.* **-leis** (-lās′). A city-state of ancient Greece. [Gk. See **pelə-³*.**]

pol•ish (pŏl′ĭsh) *v.* **-ished, -ish•ing, -ish•es.** —*tr.* **1.** To make smooth and shiny by rubbing or chemical action. **2.** To remove the outer layers from (grains of rice) by rotation in drums. **3.** To free from coarseness; refine. **4.** To remove flaws from; perfect or complete. —*intr.* **1.** To become smooth or shiny by or as if by being rubbed. **2.** To become perfect or refined. —*n.* **1.** Smoothness or shininess of surface or finish. **2.** A substance containing chemical agents or abrasive particles and applied to smooth or shine a surface. **3.** The act or process of polishing. **4.** Elegance of style or manner. —***phrasal verb.* polish off.** *Informal.* To finish or dispose of quickly and easily. [ME *polisshen* < OFr. *polir, poliss-* < Lat. *polīre.* See **pel-⁵*.**] —**pol′ish•er** *n.*

Po•lish (pō′lĭsh) *adj.* Of or relating to Poland or its people, their language, or culture. —*n.* The Slavic language of the Poles.

Polish Corridor. A strip of land between the German territories of Pomerania and East Prussia awarded to Poland by the Treaty of Versailles (1919) to afford access to the Baltic Sea.

pol•ished (pŏl′ĭsht) *adj.* **1.a.** Made shiny and smooth by or as if by rubbing or chemical action. **b.** Naturally shiny and smooth. **2.** Having the husk or outer layers removed. Used of grains of rice. **3.** Refined; cultured: *a polished manner.* **4.** Having no imperfections or errors; flawless.

polit. *abbr.* Political; politics.

pol•it•bu•ro (pŏl′ĭt-byo͝or′ō, pə-lĭt′-) *n., pl.* **-ros.** The chief political and executive committee of a Communist party. [Russ., contraction of *Polit(icheskoe) Buro,* political bureau.]

po•lite (pə-līt′) *adj.* **-lit•er, -lit•est. 1.** Marked by or showing consideration for others, tact, and observance of accepted social usage. **2.** Refined; elegant: *polite society.* [ME *polit,* polished < Lat. *polītus,* p.part. of *polīre,* to polish. See POLISH.] —**po•lite′ly** *adv.* —**po•lite′ness** *n.*

Syns: *polite, mannerly, civil, courteous, genteel.* All these adjectives mean mindful of, conforming to, or marked by good manners. *Polite* and *mannerly* imply consideration for others and the adherence to conventional social standards of good behavior: *"It costs nothing to be polite"* (Winston S. Churchill). *The child was scolded for not being more mannerly. Civil* suggests only the barest observance of accepted social usages; it often means merely neither polite nor rude: *gave a civil reply to every question. Courteous* implies courtliness and dignity: *"If a man be gracious and courteous to strangers, it shows he is a citizen of the world"* (Francis Bacon). *Genteel,* which originally meant well-bred, now usually suggests excessive and affected refinement: *"A man, indeed, is not genteel when he gets drunk"* (James Boswell).

James K. Polk

pol•i•tesse (pŏl′ĭ-tĕs′, pô′lē-) *n.* Courteous formality; politeness. [Fr. < OFr., cleanliness < Ital. *pulitezza, politezza* < *pulire,* to polish, clean < Lat. *polīre.* See POLITE.]

Po•li•tian (pə-lĭsh′ən, pō-). 1454–94. Italian scholar and poet who wrote *Orfeo* (1475), the first play in Italian.

pol•i•tic (pŏl′ĭ-tĭk) *adj.* **1.** Using or marked by prudence, expedience, and shrewdness; artful. **2.** Using, displaying, or proceeding from policy; judicious: *a politic decision.* **3.** Crafty; cunning. [ME *politik* < OFr. *politique* < Lat. *polīticus,* political < Gk. *politikos* < *politēs,* citizen < *polis,* city. See **pelə-³*.**] —**pol′i•tic•ly** *adv.*

po•lit•i•cal (pə-lĭt′ĭ-kəl) *adj.* **1.** Of, relating to, or dealing with the structure or affairs of government, politics, or the state. **2.** Relating to, involving, or characteristic of politics, parties, or politicians. **3.** Having or marked by a definite or organized policy or structure with regard to government: *political pressure.* **4.** Relating to or involving acts regarded as damaging to a government or state: *political crimes.* —**po•lit′i•cal•i•za′tion** (-ĭzā′shən) *n.* —**po•lit′i•cal•ize′** (-kə-līz′) *v.* —**po•lit′i•cal•ly** *adv.*

political action committee *n.* A committee formed by special-interest groups to raise money and make contributions to the campaigns of political candidates whom they support.

political economy *n.* **1.** The social science that deals with political science and economics as one subject; the study of the interrelationships between political and economic processes. **2.** The science of economics through the 19th century.

politically correct *adj.* **1.** Of, relating to, or supporting a program of broad social, political, and educational change, esp. to redress historical injustices in matters such as race, class, gender, and sexual orientation. **2.** Being or perceived as being overconcerned with this program, often to the exclusion of other matters. —**political correctness** *n.*

political science *n.* The study of the processes, principles, and structure of government and political institutions; politics.

pol•i•ti•cian (pŏl′ĭ-tĭsh′ən) *n.* **1.a.** One who is actively involved in politics, esp. party politics. **b.** One who holds or seeks a political office. **2.** One who seeks personal or partisan gain, often by maneuvering. **3.** One who is skilled or experienced in the science or administration of government.

po•lit•i•cize (pə-lĭt′ĭ-sīz′) *v.* **-cized, -ciz•ing, -ciz•es.** —*intr.* To engage in or discuss politics. —*tr.* To make political. —**po•lit′i•ci•za′tion** (-sĭ-zā′shən) *n.*

pol•i•tick (pŏl′ĭ-tĭk) *intr.v.* **-ticked, -tick•ing, -ticks.** To engage in or discuss politics. [Back-formation < *politicking* < POLITICS.] —**pol′i•tick′er** *n.*

po•lit•i•co (pə-lĭt′ĭ-kō′) *n., pl.* **-cos.** A politician. [< Ital. or < Sp. *político,* both < Lat. *polīticus,* political. See POLITIC.]

pol•i•tics (pŏl′ĭ-tĭks) *n.* **1.** *(used with a sing. v.)* **a.** The art or science of government or governing, esp. the governing of a political entity, such as a nation, and the administration and control of its internal and external affairs. **b.** Political science. **2.** *(used with a sing. or pl. v.)* **a.** The activities or affairs engaged in by a government, politician, or political party. **b.** The methods or tactics involved in managing a state or government. **3.** *(used with a sing. or pl. v.)* Political life. **4.** *(used with a sing. or pl. v.)* Intrigue or maneuvering within a political unit or a group in order to gain control or power. **5.** *(used with a sing. or pl. v.)* Political attitudes and positions. **6.** *(used with a sing. or pl. v.)* The often internally conflicting interrelationships among people in a society.

Usage Note: *Politics,* although etymologically plural, takes a singular verb when used to refer to the art or science of governing or to political science: *Politics has been a concern of philosophers since Plato.* But in its other senses *politics* can take either a singular or plural verb. Many other nouns that end in *-ics* behave similarly, and the user is advised to consult specific entries for precise information.

pol•i•ty (pŏl′ĭ-tē) *n., pl.* **-ties. 1.** The form of government of a nation, a state, a church, or an organization. **2.** An organized society, such as a nation, having a specific form of government. [Obsolete Fr. *politie* < OFr. < LLat. *polītīa,* the Roman government. See POLICE.]

Polk (pōk), **James Knox.** 1795–1849. The 11th President of the U.S. (1845–49).

pol•ka (pōl′kə, pō′kə) *n.* **1.** A lively round dance for couples, originating in Bohemia. **2.** Music for this dance, having duple meter. —*intr.v.* **-kaed, -ka•ing, -kas.** To dance the polka. [Czech, prob. < Pol. < *Polka,* Polish woman, fem. of *Polak,* Pole < Slav. *polje,* field. See **pelə-²*.**]

pol•ka dot (pō′kə) *n.* **1.** One of a number of dots or round spots forming a pattern. **2.** A pattern or fabric with such dots.

poll (pōl) *n.* **1.** The casting and registering of votes in an election. **2.** The number of votes cast or recorded. **3.** The place where votes are cast and registered. Used with *the.* Often used in the plural. **4.** A survey of the public or of a sample of public opinion to acquire information. **5.** The head, esp. the top of the head where hair grows. **6.** The blunt or broad end of a tool such as an ax. —*v.* **polled, poll•ing, polls.** —*tr.* **1.** To receive (a given number of votes). **2.** To receive or record the votes of. **3.** To cast (a vote or ballot). **4.** To question in a survey; canvass. **5.** To cut off or trim (hair or wool, for example); clip. **6.** To trim or cut off the hair, wool, branches, or horns of. —*intr.* To vote at the polls in an election. [ME *pol,* head < MLGer. or MDu.] —**poll′er** *n.*

pol•lack also **pol•lock** (pŏl′ək) *n.* A marine food fish *(Pollachius virens)* of northern Atlantic waters, related to the cod. [Alteration of Sc. *podlok.*]

pol•lard (pŏl′ərd) *n.* **1.** A tree whose top branches have been cut back to the trunk so that it may produce a dense growth of new shoots. **2.** An animal, such as an ox, a goat, or a sheep, that no longer has its horns. —*tr.v.* **-lard•ed, -lard•ing, -lards.** To convert or make into a pollard. [< POLL.]

polled (pōld) *adj.* Having no horns; hornless.

pol•len (pŏl′ən) *n.* The fine powderlike material consisting of pollen grains produced by anthers. [Lat., fine flour.]

pollen count *n.* The average number of pollen grains, usu. of ragweed, in a cubic yard or other standard volume of air over a 24-hour period at a specified time and place.

pollen grain *n.* A microspore of seed plants, containing a male gametophyte.

pollen tube *n.* The slender tube formed by the pollen grain that penetrates an ovule and releases the male gametes.

pol•lex (pŏl′ĕks′) *n., pl.* **pol•li•ces** (pŏl′ĭ-sēz′). See **thumb** 1. [Lat., thumb, big toe.]

pol•li•nate also **pol•len•ate** (pŏl′ə-nāt′) *tr.v.* **-li•nat•ed, -li•nat•ing, -li•nates** also **-len•at•ed, -len•at•ing, -len•ates.** To transfer pollen from an anther to the stigma of (a flower). [NLat. *pollen, pollin-,* pollen (< Lat., fine flour) + -ATE[1].] —**pol′li•na′tion** *n.* —**pol′li•na′tor** *n.*

pollini– or **pollin–** *pref.* Pollen: *polliniferous.* [< NLat. *pollen, pollin-,* pollen. See POLLINATE.]

pol•li•nif•er•ous also **pol•len•if•er•ous** (pŏl′ə-nĭf′ər-əs) *adj.* **1.** Producing or yielding pollen. **2.** Adapted for carrying pollen.

pol•lin•i•um (pŏ-lĭn′ē-əm) *n., pl.* **-i•a** (-ē-ə). A mass of coherent pollen grains, found in the flowers of orchids and milkweeds. [NLat. < *pollen, pollin-,* pollen. See POLLINATE.]

pol•li•nize (pŏl′ə-nīz′) *tr.v.* **-nized, -niz•ing, -niz•es.** To pollinate. —**pol′li•ni•za′tion** (-nĭ-zā′shən) *n.* —**pol′li•niz′er** *n.*

pol•li•no•sis also **pol•len•o•sis** (pŏl′ə-nō′sĭs) *n.* See **hay fever.**

pol•li•wog also **pol•ly•wog** (pŏl′ē-wŏg′, -wôg′) *n.* See **tadpole.** [Var. of *polliwig* < ME *polwigle* : *pol,* head; see POLL + *wiglen,* to wiggle; see WIGGLE.]

pol•lock (pŏl′ək) *n.* Var. of **pollack.**

Pol•lock (pŏl′ək), **Jackson.** 1912–56. Amer. artist who was a leader of abstract expressionism.

poll•ster (pōl′stər) *n.* One that takes public-opinion surveys.

Word History: A *pollster* does not have to be a woman, despite the fact that the suffix *–ster,* originally *–estre* in Old English, was used to form feminine agent nouns. *Hoppestere,* for example, meant "female dancer." But in Old English *–estre* was occasionally applied to men, although perhaps largely or completely in the case of translations of Latin masculine nouns denoting occupations that were held by women in Anglo-Saxon society. An example is *bæcester,* "baker," glossing Latin *pistor;* it survives as the Modern English name *Baxter.* In Middle English the suffix was still largely feminine in the south of England but masculine and feminine in the north, a tendency that became general in English starting with the 16th century. In Modern English the suffix is usually derogatory. This use probably arose from the occurrence of the suffix with ambiguous verbs, such as *game,* "to play at sports, to play at sex," or with pejorative verbs, such as *rime* or *rhyme.* In some modern formations on neutral words *–ster* is not derogatory, as in *youngster* (1589), but in most cases, as with *pollster* (1939), *–ster* has pejorative force.

poll•tak•er (pōl′tā′kər) *n.* See **pollster.**

poll tax *n.* A tax levied on people rather than on property, often as a requirement for voting.

pol•lut•ant (pə-lōōt′nt) *n.* Something that pollutes, esp. a waste material that contaminates air, soil, or water.

pol•lute (pə-lōōt′) *tr.v.* **-lut•ed, -lut•ing, -lutes. 1.** To make unfit for or harmful to living things, esp. by the addition of waste matter. **2.** To make less suitable for an activity, esp. by the introduction of unwanted factors. **3.** To render impure or morally harmful; corrupt. **4.** To make ceremonially impure; profane. [ME *polluten* < Lat. *polluere, pollūt-.*] —**pol•lut′er** *n.*

pol•lu•tion (pə-lōō′shən) *n.* **1.** The act or process of polluting or the state of being polluted, esp. the contamination of soil, water, or the atmosphere by the discharge of harmful substances. **2.** Something that pollutes; a pollutant.

Pol•lux (pŏl′əks) *n. Gk. Myth.* **1.** One of the Dioscuri. **2.** A bright star in the constellation Gemini. [Latin < Gk. *Poludeukēs.*]

Pol•ly•an•na (pŏl′ē-ăn′ə) *n.* One held to be foolishly or blindly optimistic. [After the heroine of the novel *Pollyanna,* by Eleanor Hodgman Porter (1868–1920), Amer. writer.]

po•lo (pō′lō) *n. Sports.* **1.** A game played by two teams of three or four players on horseback equipped with long-handled mallets for driving a small wooden ball through the opponents' goal. **2.** Water polo. [Anglo-Indian *polo,* of Tibeto-Burman orig.] —**po′lo•ist** *n.*

Po•lo (pō′lō), **Marco.** 1254–1324. Venetian traveler who explored Asia (1271–95) and wrote the only account of the Far East available to Europeans until the 17th cent.

polo coat *n.* A loose-fitting tailored overcoat made from camel's hair or a similar material.

pol•o•naise (pŏl′ə-nāz′, pō′lə-) *n.* **1.** A stately marchlike Polish dance, primarily a promenade by couples. **2.** Music for or in the style of this dance, having triple meter. **3.** A woman's dress of the 18th century, having a fitted bodice and draped cutaway skirt and worn over an elaborate underskirt. [Fr. < fem. of *polonais,* Polish < Med.Lat. *Polōnia,* Poland.]

po•lo•ni•um (pə-lō′nē-əm) *n. Symbol* **Po** A naturally radioactive metallic element, occurring in minute quantities in uranium ores and produced by bombarding bismuth with neutrons; its most readily available isotope is Po 210, with a half-life of 138.39 days. Atomic number 84; melting point 254°C; boiling point 962°C; specific gravity 9.32; valence 2, 4. See table at **element.** [< Med.Lat. *Polōnia,* Poland.]

polo shirt *n.* A pullover sport shirt of knitted cotton.

Pol Pot (pŏl pŏt′). b. 1928. Cambodian political leader whose Khmer Rouge movement overthrew the Cambodian government in 1975.

Pol•ta•va (pəl-tä′və). A city of central Ukraine WSW of Kharkov; a Cossack stronghold in the 17th cent. Pop. 302,000.

pol•ter•geist (pōl′tər-gīst′) *n.* A ghost that makes its presence known by noises and the moving of objects. [Ger. : *poltern,* to make noises (< MHGer. *boldern*) + *Geist,* ghost (< MHGer. < OHGer.).]

pol•troon (pŏl-trōōn′) *n.* A base coward. [Fr. *poltron* < OItal. *poltrone,* coward, idler, perh. aug. of *poltro,* unbroken colt (< VLat. **pulliter* < Lat. *pullus,* young animal; see **pau-***) or < *poltro,* bed, lazy.] —**pol•troon′er•y** *n.*

pol•y (pŏl′ē) *n.* **1.** Polyester. **2.** Polyethylene.

poly– *pref.* **1.** More than one; many; much: *polyandry.* **2.** More than is usual; excessive; abnormal: *polydipsia.* **3.** Polymer; polymeric: *polyethylene.* [Gk. *polu-* < *polus,* much, many. See **pelə-**[1]*.]

pol•y•a•cryl•a•mide (pŏl′ē-ə-krĭl′ə-mīd′) *n.* A white polyamide, (=$CH_2CHCONH_2$=), related to acrylic acid. [POLY– + ACRYL(IC ACID) + AMIDE.]

pol•y•ad•e•nyl•ic acid (pŏl′ē-ăd′n-ĭl′ĭk) *n.* A polymer of adenylic acid attached to messenger RNA that stabilizes the molecule before transport from the nucleus into the cytoplasm.

pol•y•am•ide (pŏl′ē-ăm′īd′) *n.* A polymer containing repeated amide groups, as in various kinds of nylon.

pol•y•an•drous (pŏl′ē-ăn′drəs) *adj.* **1.** Relating to, characterized by, or practicing polyandry. **2.** *Bot.* Having an indefinite number of stamens.

pol•y•an•dry (pŏl′ē-ăn′drē) *n.* **1.** The condition or practice of having more than one husband at one time. **2.** *Zool.* A mating pattern in which a female mates with more than one male during a single breeding season. **3.** *Bot.* The condition of being polyandrous. —**pol′y•an′dric** *adj.*

pol•y•an•thus (pŏl′ē-ăn′thəs) *n., pl.* **-thus•es.** Any of a group of hybrid garden primroses having clusters of variously colored flowers. [NLat. < Gk. *poluanthos,* having many flowers : *polu-,* poly- + *anthos,* flower.]

polyanthus narcissus *n.* A bulbous Mediterranean plant *(Narcissus tazetta)* having fragrant white and yellow flowers.

pol•y•ba•sic (pŏl′ē-bā′sĭk) *adj.* Of or relating to an acid that has two or more hydrogen atoms that can be replaced by basic atoms or radicals.

pol•y•ba•site (pŏl′ē-bā′sīt′) *n.* A black mineral with a metallic luster, $(Ag,Cu)_{16}Sb_2S_{11}$, that is an ore of silver. [POLY– + BAS(IS) + -ITE[1].]

Po•lyb•i•us (pə-lĭb′ē-əs). 200?–118? B.C. Greek historian known for the 5 extant books of his history of Rome.

pol•y•car•bon•ate (pŏl′ē-kär′bə-nāt′) *n.* Any of a family of thermoplastics characterized by a high-impact strength, used in making unbreakable windows.

Pol•y•carp (pŏl′ē-kärp′), Saint. A.D. 69?–155? Christian martyr who was burned at the stake.

pol•y•car•pel•lar•y (pŏl′ē-kär′pə-lĕr′ē) *adj. Bot.* Having or consisting of many carpels.

pol•y•car•pous (pŏl′ē-kär′pəs) also **po•ly•car•pic** (-pĭk) *adj.* Having fruit or pistils with two or more carpels. —**pol′y•car′py** *n.*

polo

ă pat	oi boy
ā pay	ou out
âr care	ŏŏ took
ä father	ōō boot
ĕ pet	ŭ cut
ē be	ûr urge
ĭ pit	th thin
ī pie	*th* this
îr pier	hw which
ŏ pot	zh vision
ō toe	ə about, item
ô paw	

Stress marks:
′ (primary);
′ (secondary), as in dictionary (dĭk′shə-nĕr′ē)

pol•y•cen•tric (pŏl′ē-sĕn′trĭk) *adj.* **1.** Having many centers, esp. of authority or control. **2.** Having several central parts, such as centrosomes or chromatids. —*n.* A polycentric chromosome. —**pol′y•cen′trism** *n.*

pol•y•chete also **pol•y•chaete** (pŏl′ĭ-kēt′) *n.* Any of various annelid worms of the class Polychaeta, including mostly marine worms such as the lugworm and characterized by fleshy paired appendages tipped with bristles on each body segment. [NLat. *Polychaeta,* class name < Gk. *polukhaitēs,* with much hair : *polu-,* poly- + *khaitē,* long hair.] —**pol′y•chete′, pol′y•che′tous** *adj.*

pol•y•chlo•rin•at•ed biphenyl (pŏl′ē-klôr′ə-nā′tĭd, -klōr′-) *n.* PCB.

pol•y•chro•mat•ic (pŏl′ē-krō-măt′ĭk) also **pol•y•chro•mic** (-krō′mĭk) or **pol•y•chro•mous** (-krō′məs) *adj.* **1.** Having or exhibiting many colors. **2.** Of or composed of radiation of more than one wavelength: *polychromatic light.*

pol•y•chrome (pŏl′ē-krōm′) *adj.* **1.** Having many or various colors; polychromatic. **2.** Made or decorated in many or various colors. —*n.* A polychrome object or work.

pol•y•chro•my (pŏl′ē-krō′mē) *n.* The use of many colors in decoration, esp. in architecture and sculpture.

Pol•y•cli•tus or **Pol•y•clei•tus** (pŏl′ĭ-klī′təs). fl. 5th cent. B.C. Greek sculptor known for his statues of athletes.

pol•y•clone (pŏl′ē-klōn′) *n.* A clone descended from one or more small groups of cells, esp. ones of genetically different origins. —**pol′y•clo′nal** *adj.* —**pol′y•clo′nal•ly** *adv.*

pol•y•con•ic projection (pŏl′ē-kŏn′ĭk) *n.* A conic map projection having distances between meridians along every parallel equal to those distances on a globe.

pol•y•cot•y•le•don (pŏl′ē-kŏt′l-ēd′n) also **pol•y•cot** (-kŏt′) *n.* A plant whose seed contains more than two cotyledons. —**pol′y•cot′y•le′don•ous** *adj.*

pol•y•cy•clic (pŏl′ĭ-sī′klĭk, -sĭk′lĭk) *adj. Chem.* Having two or more atomic rings in a molecule.

pol•y•cy•the•mi•a (pŏl′ē-sī-thē′mē-ə) *n.* A condition marked by an abnormally large number of red blood cells.

pol•y•dac•tyl (pŏl′ē-dăk′təl) also **pol•y•dac•ty•lous** (-tə-ləs) *Biol.* —*adj.* Having more than the normal number of digits. —*n.* A polydactyl person or animal.

pol•y•dip•si•a (pŏl′ē-dĭp′sē-ə) *n.* Excessive or abnormal thirst. [POLY- + Gk. *dipsa,* thirst + -IA[1].]

pol•y•e•lec•tro•lyte (pŏl′ē-ĭ-lĕk′trə-līt′) *n.* An electrolyte, such as a polysaccharide, having a high molecular weight.

pol•y•em•bry•o•ny (pŏl′ē-ĕm′brē-ə-nē, -ĕm-brī′-) *n.* Development of more than one embryo from a single egg or ovule. —**pol′y•em′bry•on′ic** (-brē-ŏn′ĭk) *adj.*

pol•y•ene (pŏl′ē-ēn′) *n.* An organic compound containing many double bonds.

pol•y•es•ter (pŏl′ē-ĕs′tər, pŏl′ē-ĕs′tər) *n.* **1.** Any of numerous synthetic polymers produced by reaction of dibasic acids with dihydric alcohols and used as light, strong, weather-resistant resins in boat hulls, textile fibers, and molded parts. **2.** A wrinkle-resistant fabric of fibers made from any of these resins. —**pol′y•es′ter** *adj.* —**pol′y•es′ter•i•fi•ca′tion** *n.*

pol•y•es•trous (pŏl′ē-ĕs′trəs) *adj.* **1.** Having several estrous cycles during a single breeding season. **2.** Ovulating more than once a year.

pol•y•eth•yl•ene (pŏl′ē-ĕth′ə-lēn′) *n.* A polymerized ethylene resin, used esp. for containers, kitchenware, and tubing or in the form of films and sheets for packaging.

polyethylene glycol *n.* Any of a family of colorless liquids with high molecular weight that are soluble in water and in many organic solvents and are used as emulsifiers and plasticizers.

po•lyg•a•la (pə-lĭg′ə-lə) *n.* Any of various plants of the genus *Polygala,* which constitutes the milkworts. [NLat. *Polygala,* genus name < Gk. *polugalon,* milkwort : *polu-,* poly- + *gala,* milk; see **melg-***.]

po•lyg•a•mist (pə-lĭg′ə-mĭst) *n.* A practicer of polygamy.

po•lyg•a•mous (pə-lĭg′ə-məs) *adj.* **1.** Of, characterized by, or practicing polygamy. **2.** *Bot.* Having hermaphroditic and unisexual flowers on the same plant or on separate plants of the same species. —**po•lyg′a•mous•ly** *adv.*

po•lyg•a•my (pə-lĭg′ə-mē) *n.* **1.** The condition or practice of having more than one spouse at one time. **2.** *Zool.* A mating pattern in which a single individual mates with more than one individual of the opposite sex. [Fr. *polygamie* < LLat. *polygamia* < Gk. *polugamia* : *polu-,* poly- + *-gamia,* -gamy.]

pol•y•gene (pŏl′ē-jēn′) *n.* Any of a group of nonallelic genes, each having a small quantitative effect, that together produce a wide range of phenotypic variation. —**pol′y•gen′ic** *adj.*

pol•y•gen•e•sis (pŏl′ē-jĕn′ĭ-sĭs) *n.* Derivation of a species or type from more than one ancestor or germ cell. —**pol′y•gen′e•sist** *n.* —**pol′y•ge•net′ic** (-jə-nĕt′ĭk) *adj.*

pol•y•glot (pŏl′ē-glŏt′) *adj.* Speaking, writing, written in, or composed of several languages. —*n.* **1.** A person having a knowledge of several languages. **2.** A book, esp. a Bible, containing several versions of the same text in different languages. **3.** A mixture or confusion of languages. [Fr. *polyglotte* < Gk. *poluglōttos* : *polu-,* poly- + *glōtta,* tongue, language.] —**pol′y•glot′ism, pol′y•glot′tism** *n.*

pol•y•gon (pŏl′ē-gŏn′) *n.* A closed plane figure bounded by three or more line segments. —**po•lyg′o•nal** (pə-lĭg′ə-nəl) *adj.* —**po•lyg′o•nal•ly** *adv.*

po•lyg•o•num (pə-lĭg′ə-nəm) *n.* Any of numerous plants of the widely distributed genus *Polygonum,* characterized by stems with knotlike joints and conspicuous sheathlike stipules. [NLat. *Polygonum,* genus name < Gk. *polugonon,* knotgrass : *polu-,* poly- + *gonu,* knee; see **genu-1***.]

pol•y•graph (pŏl′ē-grăf′) *n.* An instrument that simultaneously records changes in physiological processes such as blood pressure and respiration, often used as a lie detector. —*tr.v.* **-graphed, -graph•ing, -graphs.** To test (a suspect, for example) with a polygraph. —**po•lyg′ra•pher** (pə-lĭg′rə-fər), **po•lyg′ra•phist** (-fĭst) *n.* —**pol′y•graph′ic** *adj.*

po•lyg•y•ny (pə-lĭj′ə-nē) *n.* **1.** The condition or practice of having more than one wife at one time. **2.** *Zool.* A mating pattern in which a male mates with more than one female in a single breeding season. —**po•lyg′y•nous** *adj.*

polyhedral angle *n. Math.* A shape formed by three or more planes intersecting at a common point.

pol•y•he•dron (pŏl′ē-hē′drən) *n., pl.* **-drons** or **-dra** (-drə). A solid bounded by polygons. —**pol′y•he′dral** *adj.*

pol•y•his•tor (pŏl′ē-hĭs′tər) *n.* A person with broad knowledge. [Lat. *Polyhistōr* < Gk. *poluistōr,* very learned : *polu-,* poly- + *histōr,* learned; see **weid-***.]

Pol•y•hym•ni•a (pŏl′ē-hĭm′nē-ə) also **Po•lym•ni•a** (pə-lĭm′nē-ə) *n. Gk. Myth.* The Muse of sacred song and oratory.

pol•y I:C (pŏl′ē ī′sē′) *n.* A synthetic chemical that resembles the RNA of infectious viruses and is used to stimulate the production of interferon by the immune system. [POLY- + *i(nosinic acid)* (Gk. *inos,* genitive of *is,* sinew; see INOSITOL + -INE[2] + -IC) + *c(ytidylic acid)* (CYTIDINE + -YL + -IC).]

pol•y•im•ide (pŏl′ē-ĭm′īd′) *n.* A synthetic polymeric resin of a class resistant to high temperatures, wear, and corrosion, used primarily as a coating or film on a substrate substance.

pol•y•math (pŏl′ē-măth′) *n.* A person of great or varied learning. [Gk. *polumathēs* : *polu-,* poly- + *manthanein, math-,* to learn; see **mendh-***.] —**pol′y•math′, pol′y•math′ic** *adj.* —**po•lym′a•thy** (pə-lĭm′ə-thē) *n.*

pol•y•mer (pŏl′ə-mər) *n.* Any of numerous natural or synthetic compounds of usu. high molecular weight consisting of repeated linked units, each a relatively light and simple molecule.

pol•y•mer•ase (pŏl′ə-mə-rās′, -rāz′) *n.* Any of various enzymes that catalyze the formation of polynucleotides of DNA or RNA using an existing strand of DNA or RNA as a template.

polymerase chain reaction *n.* A laboratory technique in which trace amounts of DNA can be amplified into large quantities by repeatedly separating paired DNA strands and using each strand as a template for a new DNA segment.

pol•y•mer•ic (pŏl′ə-mĕr′ĭk) *adj.* Of, relating to, or consisting of a polymer. —**pol′y•mer′i•cal•ly** *adv.* —**po•lym′er•ism** (pə-lĭm′ə-rĭz′əm, pŏl′ə-mə-) *n.*

po•lym•er•i•za•tion (pə-lĭm′ər-ĭ-zā′shən, pŏl′ə-mər-) *n.* **1.** The bonding of two or more monomers to form a polymer. **2.** A chemical process that effects this bonding. —**pol′y•mer•ize′** (pŏl′ə-mə-rīz′, pə-lĭm′ə-) *v.*

pol•y•morph (pŏl′ē-môrf′) *n.* **1.** *Biol.* An organism characterized by polymorphism. **2.** *Chem.* A specific crystalline form of a compound that can crystallize in different forms.

pol•y•mor•phism (pŏl′ē-môr′fĭz′əm) *n.* **1.** *Biol.* The occurrence of different forms in organisms of the same species, independent of sexual variations. **2.** *Chem.* Crystallization of a compound in at least two distinct forms. —**pol′y•mor′phic, pol′y•mor′phous** *adj.* —**pol′y•mor′phous•ly** *adv.*

pol•y•mor•pho•nu•cle•ar (pŏl′ē-môr′fə-no͞o′klē-ər, -nyo͞o′-) *adj.* Having a lobed nucleus. Used esp. of neutrophil white blood cells. —*n.* A polymorphonuclear cell.

polymorphous perverse *adj.* Characterized by or displaying sexual tendencies that have no specific direction, as in an infant or a young child.

pol•y•myx•in (pŏl′ē-mĭk′sĭn) *n.* Any of various mainly toxic antibiotics derived from strains of the soil bacterium *Bacillus polymyxa* and used to treat various infections with gram-negative bacteria. [NLat. *polymyxa,* species name (POLY- + Gk. *muxa,* slime) + -IN.]

Pol•y•ne•sia (pŏl′ə-nē′zhə, -shə). A division of Oceania including volcanic and coral islands of the central and S Pacific roughly between New Zealand, Hawaii, and Easter I.

Pol•y•ne•sian (pŏl′ə-nē′zhən, -shən) *adj.* Of or relating to Polynesia or its peoples, languages, or cultures. —*n.* **1.** A native or inhabitant of Polynesia. **2.** A subfamily of the Austronesian language family spoken in Polynesia.

Pol•y•ni•ces (pŏl′ə-nī′sēz) *n. Gk. Myth.* A son of Oedipus, for whom an expedition against Thebes was raised.

pol•y•no•mi•al (pŏl′ē-nō′mē-əl) *adj.* Of, relating to, or consisting of more than two names or terms. —*n.* **1.** A taxonomic designation consisting of more than two terms. **2.** *Math.* An algebraic expression consisting of summed terms, each term being the product of a constant and one or more variables raised to integral powers, for example, $2p^3q + y$. [POLY- + (BI)NOMIAL.]

Polyphemus
c. 150 B.C. Greek marble sculpture

pol·y·nu·cle·o·tide (pŏl′ē-no͞o′klē-ə-tīd′, -nyo͞o′-) *n.* A polymeric compound consisting of a number of nucleotides.

po·lyn·ya (pŏl′ən-yä′, pə-lĭn′yə) *n.* An area of open water surrounded by sea ice. [Russ. *polyn'ya* < *polyĭ*, open, hollow. See **pelə-²***.]

pol·y·o·ma virus (pŏl′ē-ō′mə) *n.* A papovavirus that contains DNA and causes various tumors in rodents.

pol·yp (pŏl′ĭp) *n.* **1.** A coelenterate, such as a coral, having a cylindrical body and an oral opening usu. surrounded by tentacles. **2.** A usu. nonmalignant growth or tumor protruding from the mucous lining of an organ such as the nose, often causing obstruction. [ME *polip*, nasal tumor < OFr. *polipe* < Lat. *pōlypus*, cuttlefish, nasal tumor < Gk. *polupous* (prob. by folk ety. < *polus*, many; see POLY- and *pous*, foot; see **ped-***).] — **pol′yp·oid′** *adj.*

pol·y·par·y (pŏl′ə-pĕr′ē) also **pol·y·par·i·um** (pŏl′ə-pâr′ē-əm) *n., pl.* **-ies** also **-i·a** (-ē-ə). The common supporting framework of a colony of polyps, esp. of coral.

pol·y·pep·tide (pŏl′ē-pĕp′tīd′) *n.* A peptide containing many molecules of amino acids, typically between 10 and 100.

pol·y·pet·al·ous (pŏl′ē-pĕt′l-əs) *adj.* Having separate petals, as on the corolla of a rose or carnation.

pol·y·pha·gi·a (pŏl′ē-fā′jē-ə, -jə) **po·lyph·a·gy** (pə-lĭf′ə-jē) *n.* **1.** An excessive or pathological desire to eat. **2.** *Zool.* The habit of feeding on many different kinds of food. — **pol′y·pha′gi·an** *adj.*

po·lyph·a·gous (pə-lĭf′ə-gəs) *adj.* Feeding on many different kinds of food: *polyphagous insects or birds.*

Pol·y·phe·mus (pŏl′ə-fē′məs) *n.* *Gk. Myth.* The Cyclops who confined Odysseus in a cave until Odysseus blinded him and escaped. [Lat. < Gk. *Poluphēmos.*]

pol·y·phe·mus moth (pŏl′ə-fē′məs) *n.* A large North American silkworm moth *(Antheraea polyphemus)* having an eyelike spot on each hind wing. [After POLYPHEMUS.]

pol·y·phone (pŏl′ē-fōn′) *n.* *Ling.* A written character or combination of characters having two or more phonetic values, such as the English letter *a.*

pol·y·phon·ic (pŏl′ē-fŏn′ĭk) *adj.* **1.** *Mus.* Of, relating to, or characterized by polyphony. **2.** *Ling.* Having two or more phonetic values. — **pol′y·phon′i·cal·ly** *adv.*

po·lyph·o·ny (pə-lĭf′ə-nē) *n., pl.* **-nies.** *Mus.* Music with two or more independent melodic parts sounded together. — **po·lyph′o·nous** *adj.* — **po·lyph′o·nous·ly** *adv.*

pol·y·phy·let·ic (pŏl′ē-fī-lĕt′ĭk) *adj.* Of or characterized by development from more than one ancestral type.

pol·y·ploid (pŏl′ē-ploid′) *Genet. adj.* Having one or more extra sets of chromosomes. — **pol′y·ploid′** *n.* — **pol′y·ploi′dy** *n.*

pol·yp·ne·a (pŏl′ĭp-nē′ə) *n.* Very rapid breathing; panting. [NLat. : POLY- + Gk. *pnoia*, *pnoē*, breath, breathing (< *pnein*, to breathe; see **pneu-***).] — **pol′yp·ne′ic** (-nē′ĭk) *adj.*

pol·y·pod (pŏl′ē-pŏd′) also **po·lyp·o·dous** (pə-lĭp′ə-dəs) *adj. Biol.* Having numerous feet.

pol·y·po·dy (pŏl′ē-pō′dē) *n., pl.* **-dies.** Any of various ferns of the genus *Polypodium*, having simple or compound fronds, round sori arranged in one or more rows along the midrib, and creeping rootstocks. [ME *polypodie* < Lat. *polypodium* < Gk. *polupodion* < dim. of *polupous*, many-footed : *polu-*, poly- + *pous*, *pod-*, foot; see -POD.]

pol·y·pore (pŏl′ē-pôr′, -pōr′) *n.* See **pore fungus.**

pol·y·pro·pyl·ene (pŏl′ē-prō′pə-lēn′) *n.* **1.** Any of various thermoplastic resins that are polymers of propylene and used to make molded articles and fibers. **2.** A fabric of fibers made from any of these resins. — **pol′y·pro′pyl·ene′** *adj.*

pol·yp·tych (pŏl′ĭp-tĭk′) *n.* A work consisting of four or more painted or carved panels hinged together. [< LLat. *polyptycha*, registers, account books < Gk. *poluptukha* < neut. pl. of *poluptukhos*, having many folds : *polu-*, poly- + *ptukhē*, fold; see DIPTYCH.]

pol·y·rhythm (pŏl′ē-rĭth′əm) *n.* *Mus.* The use or an instance of simultaneous contrasting rhythms. — **pol′y·rhyth′mic** *adj.*

pol·y·ri·bo·some (pŏl′ē-rī′bə-sōm′) *n.* A cluster of ribosomes connected by a strand of messenger RNA and functioning as a unit in protein synthesis.

pol·y·sac·cha·ride (pŏl′ē-săk′ə-rīd′) also **pol·y·sac·cha·rid** (-rĭd) or **pol·y·sac·cha·rose** (-rōs′, -rōz′) *n.* Any of a class of carbohydrates, such as starch and cellulose, consisting of a number of monosaccharides joined by glycosidic bonds.

pol·y·se·mous (pŏl′ē-sē′məs) *adj.* *Ling.* Having or characterized by many meanings. [< LLat. *polysēmus* < Gk. *polusēmos* : *polu-*, poly- + *sēma*, sign.] — **pol′y·se′my** (pŏl′ē-sē′mē, pə-lĭs′ə-) *n.*

pol·y·sep·al·ous (pŏl′ē-sĕp′ə-ləs) *adj. Bot.* Having separate sepals.

pol·y·some (pŏl′ē-sōm′) *n.* See **polyribosome.**

pol·y·so·mic (pŏl′ē-sō′mĭk) *Genet.* — *adj.* Having an extra copy of one or more chromosomes: *a polysomic cell.* — *n.* A polysomic organism or cell. [POLY- + (CHROMO)SOM(E) + -IC.]

po·lys·ti·chous (pə-lĭs′tĭ-kəs) *adj. Bot.* Arranged in two or more series or rows. [Gk. *polustikhos*, of many lines : < *polu-*, poly- + *stikhos*, row; see STICH.]

pol·y·sty·rene (pŏl′ē-stī′rēn) *n.* A rigid clear thermoplastic polymer that can be molded into objects or made into a foam used in insulation and packaging. — **pol′y·sty′rene** *adj.*

pol·y·sul·fide (pŏl′ē-sŭl′fīd) *n.* A sulfide compound containing at least two sulfur atoms per molecule.

pol·y·syl·lab·ic (pŏl′ē-sĭ-lăb′ĭk) *adj. Ling.* **1.** Having more than three syllables. **2.** Characterized by words having more than three syllables. — **pol′y·syl·lab′i·cal·ly** *adv.*

pol·y·syl·la·ble (pŏl′ē-sĭl′ə-bəl) *n.* *Ling.* A word of more than three syllables.

pol·y·syn·de·ton (pŏl′ē-sĭn′dĭ-tŏn′) *n.* The repetition of conjunctions in close succession for rhetorical effect, as in *here and there and everywhere.* [LGk. *polusundeton*, neut. of *polusundetos*, using many connectives : Gk. *polu-*, poly- + Gk. *sundetos*, bound together; see SYNDETIC.]

pol·y·syn·thet·ic (pŏl′ē-sĭn-thĕt′ĭk) *adj. Ling.* Of or relating to a language such as Eskimo or Mohawk, characterized by long, morphologically complex words with a large number of affixes that express syntactic relationships and meanings usu. expressed as phrases or sentences in other languages.

pol·y·tech·nic (pŏl′ē-tĕk′nĭk) *adj.* Offering, receiving, or dealing with instruction in many industrial arts and applied sciences. — *n.* A polytechnic school.

pol·y·tet·ra·fluor·o·eth·yl·ene (pŏl′ē-tĕt′rə-flo͝or′ō-ĕth′ə-lēn′, -flôr′-, -flōr′-) *n.* A thermoplastic resin, $(C_2F_4)_n$, that is resistant to heat and chemicals, has a low coefficient of friction, and is used as a coating, as on cookware.

pol·y·the·ism (pŏl′ē-thē-ĭz′əm, pŏl′ē-thē′ĭz-əm) *n.* The worship of or belief in more than one god. [Fr. *polythéisme* < Gk. *polutheos*, polytheistic : *polu-*, poly- + *theos*, god; see **dhēs-***.] — **pol′y·the′ist** *n.* — **pol′y·the·is′tic** *adj.*

pol·y·thene (pŏl′ə-thēn′) *n.* *Chiefly British.* Var. of **polyethylene.**

po·lyt·o·cous (pə-lĭt′ə-kəs) *adj.* Producing many offspring in a single birth. [Gk. *polutokos*, bearing many offspring : *polu-*, poly- + *tokos*, offspring, birth; see **tek-***.]

pol·y·to·nal·i·ty (pŏl′ē-tō-năl′ĭ-tē) *n.* *Mus.* Simultaneous use of two or more tonalities in a composition. — **pol′y·to′nal** (-tōn′əl) *adj.* — **pol′y·to′nal·ly** *adv.*

pol·y·tro·phic (pŏl′ē-trō′fĭk, -trŏf′ĭk) *adj.* Subsisting on various types of organic material. Used of certain bacteria.

pol·y·typ·ic (pŏl′ē-tĭp′ĭk) also **pol·y·typ·i·cal** (-ĭ-kəl) *adj.* Having several variant forms, esp. subspecies or varieties.

pol·y·un·sat·u·rat·ed (pŏl′ē-ŭn-săch′ə-rā′tĭd) *adj.* Relating to or being an unsaturated fat composed chiefly of fatty acids with two or more double bonds in the carbon chain.

pol·y·u·re·thane (pŏl′ē-yo͝or′ə-thān′) *n.* Any of various resins, widely varying in flexibility, used in chemical-resistant coatings, adhesives, and foams. — **pol′y·u′re·thane′** *adj.*

pol·y·u·ri·a (pŏl′ē-yo͝or′ē-ə) *n.* Excessive passage of urine, as in diabetes. — **pol′y·u′ric** *adj.*

pol·y·va·lent (pŏl′ē-vā′lənt) *adj.* **1.** Acting against or interacting with more than one kind of antigen or toxin. **2.** *Chem.* **a.** Having more than one valence. **b.** Having a valence of 3 or higher. — **pol′y·va′lence, pol′y·va′len·cy** *n.*

pol·y·vi·nyl (pŏl′ē-vī′nəl) *adj.* Designating any of a group of polymerized thermoplastic vinyls, as polyvinyl chloride.

polyvinyl chloride *n.* PVC.

pol·y·zo·an (pŏl′ē-zō′ən) *n.* See **bryozoan.** [< NLat. *Polyzoa*, phylum name : POLY- + -*zoa*, pl. of -*zoon*; see -ZOON.] — **pol′y·zo′an** *adj.*

pol·y·zo·ar·i·um (pŏl′ē-zō-âr′ē-əm) also **pol·y·zo·a·ry** (-zō′ə-rē) *n., pl.* **-ar·i·a** (-âr′ē-ə) also **-a·ries.** A bryozoan colony or its supporting skeletal structure. [NLat. : *Polyzoa*, phylum name; see POLYZOAN + -ARIUM.]

pom·ace (pŭm′ĭs, pŏm′-) *n.* **1.** The pulpy material remaining after the juice has been pressed from fruit. **2.** Pulpy material remaining after the extraction of oil from nuts, seeds, or fish. [ME *pomis* < Med.Lat. *pōmācium*, cider < VLat. **pōma*, apple, fruit. See POME.]

pomace fly *n.* See **fruit fly** 1.

po·ma·ceous (pō-mā′shəs) *adj.* Of, relating to, bearing, or characteristic of apples or pomes. [< NLat. *pōmāceus* < LLat. *pōmum*, apple, fruit. See POME.]

po·made (pō-mād′, -mäd′, pŏ-) *n.* A perfumed ointment, esp. one used to groom the hair. — *tr.v.* **-mad·ed, -mad·ing, -mades.** To anoint with pomade. [Fr. *pommade* < Ital. *pomata* < *pomo*, apple < LLat. *pōmum.* See POME.]

po·man·der (pō′măn′dər, pō-măn′-) *n.* **1.** A mixture of aromatic substances enclosed in a bag or box as a protection against odor or infection. **2.** A case, box, or bag for holding this mixture. [ME *pomendambre*, alteration of OFr. *pome d'embre*, apple of amber < Med.Lat. *pōmum dē ambrā* : *pōmum*, apple, ball (< Lat., fruit) + Lat. *dē*, of; see DE- + *ambrā*, ablative of *ambra*, amber; see AMBER.]

pome (pōm) *n.* A fleshy fruit, such as an apple, having several seed chambers and an outer fleshy part largely derived from the hypanthium. [ME < OFr., apple, fruit < VLat. **pōma* < neut. pl. of LLat. *pōmum* < Lat., fruit.]

pome·gran·ate (pŏm′grăn′ĭt, pŏm′ĭ-, pŭm′-, pŭm′ĭ-) *n.* **1.** A deciduous shrub or small tree *(Punica granatum)* native to Asia and widely cultivated for its edible fruit. **2.** The fruit

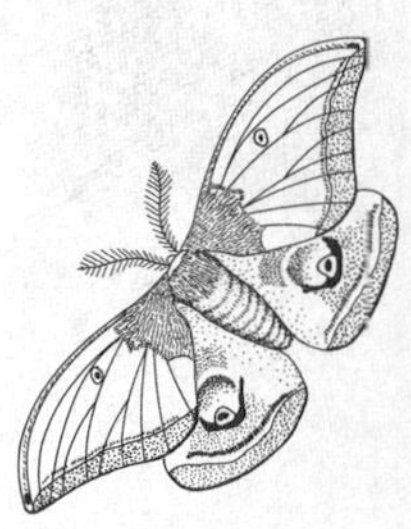
polyphemus moth
Antheraea polyphemus

pomegranate
Punica granatum

ă pat	oi boy
ā pay	ou out
âr care	o͝o took
ä father	o͞o boot
ĕ pet	ŭ cut
ē be	ûr urge
ĭ pit	th thin
ī pie	*th* this
îr pier	hw which
ŏ pot	zh vision
ō toe	ə about, item
ô paw	

Stress marks:
′ (primary);
′ (secondary), as in **dictionary** (dĭk′shə-nĕr′ē)

of this tree, having a tough reddish rind and containing many seeds, each enclosed in a juicy, mildly acidic red pulp. [ME *pome granate* < OFr. *pome grenate* : *pome*, apple; see POME + *grenate*, having many seeds (< Lat. *grānātus* < *grānum*, grain, seed; see **grə-no-***).]

pom•e•lo (pŏm′ə-lō′) *n., pl.* **-los.** See **shaddock.** [Alteration of POMPELMOUS.]

Pom•er•a•ni•a (pŏm′ə-rā′nē-ə, -rān′yə). A historical region of N-central Europe on the Baltic Sea in present-day NW Poland and NE Germany; inhabited since the 10th cent.

Pom•er•a•ni•an (pŏm′ə-rā′nē-ən, -rān′yən) *adj.* Of or relating to Pomerania or its people. — *n.* **1.** A native or inhabitant of Pomerania. **2.** Any of a breed of small dogs having long hair, a foxlike face, and a tail curling over the back.

Pomeranian

po•mif•er•ous (pō-mĭf′ər-əs) *adj.* Bearing pomes. [Lat. *pōmifer*, fruit-bearing (*pōmum*, fruit + *-fer*, -fer) + -OUS.]

pom•mel (pŭm′əl, pŏm′-) *tr.v.* **-meled, -mel•ing, -mels** also **-melled, -mel•ling, -mels.** To beat; pummel. — *n.* **1.** The upper front part of a saddle; a saddlebow. **2.** A knob on the hilt of a sword or similar weapon. [< ME *pomel*, a pommel < OFr., dim. of *pom*, ball, fruit < Lat. *pōmum*, fruit.]

pom•my or **pom•mie** (pŏm′ē) *n., pl.* **-mies.** *Australian & New Zealand.* Used as a disparaging term for a British person, esp. a recent immigrant. [Short for *pomegranate*, alteration of *Pummy Grant*, prob. alteration of *immigrant*.]

Po•mo (pō′mō) *n., pl.* **Pomo** or **-mos. 1.** A member of a group of Native American peoples inhabiting an area of the Coast Ranges of northern California. **2.** Any of the seven languages of the Pomo.

po•mol•o•gy (pō-mŏl′ə-jē) *n.* The scientific study and cultivation of fruit. [Lat. *pōmum*, fruit + -LOGY.] — **po′mo•log′i•cal** (pō′mə-lŏj′ĭ-kəl) *adj.* — **po•mol′o•gist** *n.*

Po•mo•na (pə-mō′nə). A city of S CA, a suburb of Los Angeles. Pop. 131,723.

pomp (pŏmp) *n.* **1.** Dignified or magnificent display; splendor: *the pomp of a funeral.* **2.** Vain or ostentatious display. [ME < OFr. *pompe* < Lat. *pompa*, pomp, procession < Gk. *pompē*, procession < *pempein*, to send.]

pom•pa•dour (pŏm′pə-dôr′, -dōr′) *n.* **1.** A woman's hairstyle formed by sweeping the hair up from the forehead. **2.** A man's hairstyle formed by brushing the hair up from the forehead. [After the Marquise de POMPADOUR.]

Madame de Pompadour
Portrait by François Boucher

Pom•pa•dour (pŏm′pə-dôr′, -dōr′, -do͝or′, pôN-pä-do͝or′), Marquise de. Jeanne Antoinette Poisson. "Madame de Pompadour." 1721–64. The lover of Louis XV who was blamed for establishing France's alliance with Austria, which led to the Seven Years' War (1756–63).

pom•pa•no (pŏm′pə-nō′) *n., pl.* **pompano** or **-nos.** Any of several marine food fishes of the genus *Trachinotus*, esp. *T. carolinus*, of tropical and temperate Atlantic waters, having a silvery oblong body with a bluish back. [Am.Sp. *pámpano*, a fish < Sp. < Lat. *pampinus*, vine tendril.]

Pom•pa•no Beach (pŏm′pə-nō′). A city of SE FL on the Atlantic coast N of Miami. Pop. 72,411.

Pompeian red *n. Color.* A grayish to moderate red.

Pom•pe•ii (pŏm-pā′, -pā′ē). A city of S Italy SE of Naples; founded c. 6th cent. B.C. and destroyed by an eruption of Mt. Vesuvius in A.D. 79. — **Pom•pe′ian, Pom•pei′ian** *adj. & n.*

pom•pel•mous (pŏm′pəl-mo͞os′) *n.* See **shaddock.** [Du. *pompelmoes*, prob. ult. < Tamil *pampalimāsu*.]

Pom•pey (pŏm′pē). 106–48 B.C. Roman general and politician who was defeated by Caesar and murdered in Egypt.

Pom•pi•dou (pŏm′pĭ-do͞o′, pôN-pē-do͞o′), **Georges Jean Raymond.** 1911–74. French politician who served as premier (1962–68) and president (1969–74).

pom•pon or **pom-pon** (pŏm′pŏn′) also **pom-pom** or **pom•pom** (pŏm′pŏm′) *n.* **1.** A tuft or ball of material used as a decoration, esp. on shoes, caps, and curtains. **2.** A small buttonlike flower of some chrysanthemums and dahlias. [Fr.]

pom•pous (pŏm′pəs) *adj.* **1.** Marked by excessive self-esteem or exaggerated dignity; pretentious. **2.** Full of high-sounding phrases; bombastic. **3.** Marked by pomp or stately display; ceremonious. [ME < OFr. *pompeux* < LLat. *pompōsus* < Lat. *pompa*, pomp. See POMP.] — **pom•pos′i•ty** (-pŏs′ĭ-tē), **pom′pous•ness** (-pəs-nĭs) *n.* — **pom′pous•ly** *adv.*

Pon•ca (pŏng′kə) *n., pl.* **Ponca** or **-cas. 1.** A member of a Native American people formerly inhabiting northeast Nebraska, with present-day populations also in Oklahoma. **2.** The Siouan language of the Ponca.

Ponca City. A city of N OK on the Arkansas R. NNE of Oklahoma City; founded 1893. Pop. 26,359.

Pon•ce (pôn′sā, -sĕ). A city of S Puerto Rico SW of San Juan. Pop. 161,739.

Ponce de Le•ón (pŏns′ də lē′ən, lē-ōn′, pôn′thĕ *thĕ* lĕ-ôn′, pôn′sĕ), **Juan.** 1460–1521. Spanish explorer of Florida (1513) who was searching for the Fountain of Youth.

Pon•chiel•li (pông-kyĕl′lē), **Amilcare.** 1834–86. Italian composer noted for the opera *La Gioconda* (1876).

pon•cho (pŏn′chō) *n., pl.* **-chos. 1.** A blanketlike cloak having a hole in the center for the head. **2.** A similar garment having a hood and used as a raincoat. [Am.Sp. < Sp., cape, perh. var. of *pocho*, faded, discolored.]

pond (pŏnd) *n.* A still body of water smaller than a lake, often of artificial origin. [ME *ponde* < OE *pund-*, enclosure.]

pon•der (pŏn′dər) *v.* **-dered, -der•ing, -ders.** — *tr.* To weigh in the mind with thoroughness and care. — *intr.* To reflect or consider with thoroughness and care. [ME *ponderen* < OFr. *ponderer* < Lat. *ponderāre*. See **(s)pen-***.] — **pon′der•er** *n.*

pon•der•a•ble (pŏn′dər-ə-bəl) *adj.* Considerable enough to be weighed or assessed; appreciable. — **pon′der•a•bil′i•ty** *n.*

pon•der•o•sa pine (pŏn′də-rō′sə) *n.* A tall timber tree (*Pinus ponderosa*) of western North America having long dark green needles grouped in fascicles of three. [Transl. of NLat. *Pīnus ponderōsa* : Lat. *pīnus*, pine tree + Lat. *ponderōsa*, fem. of *ponderōsus*, heavy; see PONDEROUS.]

pon•der•ous (pŏn′dər-əs) *adj.* **1.** Having great weight. **2.** Unwieldy from weight or bulk. **3.** Lacking grace or fluency; labored and dull. [Ult. < Lat. *ponderōsus* < *pondus*, *ponder-*, weight. See **(s)pen-***.] — **pon′der•ous•ly** *adv.* — **pon′der•ous•ness, pon′der•os′i•ty** (-ŏs′ĭ-tē) *n.*

Pon•di•cher•ry (pŏn′dĭ-chĕr′ē, -shĕr′ē). A city of SE India on the Bay of Bengal SSW of Madras. Pop. 162,636.

pond lily *n.* See **water lily.**

pond scum *n.* Any of various freshwater algae that form a usu. greenish film on the surface of stagnant water.

pond•weed (pŏnd′wēd′) *n.* Any of various submerged or floating aquatic plants of the genus *Potamogeton*, having inconspicuous flowers borne in small spikes.

pone (pōn) *n. Chiefly Southern U.S.* See **johnnycake.** See Regional Note at **johnnycake.** [Virginia Algonquian *poan*, *appoans*, cornbread.]

Regional Note: *Pone* is one of several Virginia Algonquian words (including *hominy* and *tomahawk*) borrowed into the English of the Atlantic seaboard. The word *pone*, usually in the compound *cornpone*, is now used mainly in the South, where it means cakes of cornbread baked on a griddle or in hot ashes.

pon•gee (pŏn-jē′, pŏn′jē) *n.* A soft thin cloth woven from Chinese or Indian raw silk or an imitation thereof. [Chin. (Mandarin) *běn zhī* : *běn*, one's own + *zhī*, to weave, spin.]

pon•gid (pŏn′jĭd) *n.* An anthropoid ape of the family Pongidae, which includes the chimpanzee, gorilla, and orangutan. [< NLat. *Pongidae*, family name < *Pongo*, type genus, of African orig.] — **pon′gid** *adj.*

pon•iard (pŏn′yərd) *n.* A dagger typically having a slender square or triangular blade. — *tr.v.* **-iard•ed, -iard•ing, -iards.** To stab with such a dagger. [Fr. *poignard* < *poing*, fist < OFr. < Lat. *pugnus*. See **peuk-***.]

pons (pŏnz) *n., pl.* **pon•tes** (pŏn′tēz). **1.** A slender tissue joining two parts of an organ. **2.** The pons Varolii. [Lat. *pōns*, bridge. See **pent-***.]

pons as•i•no•rum (pŏnz′ ăs′ə-nôr′əm, -nōr′əm) *n.* A problem that severely tests the ability of an inexperienced person. [NLat. *pōns asinōrum* : Lat. *pōns*, bridge + Lat. *asinōrum*, genitive pl. of *asinus*, ass, fool.]

Pon•selle (pŏn-sĕl′), **Rosa Melba.** 1897–1981. Amer. soprano who performed with the Metropolitan Opera.

pons Va•ro•li•i (pŏnz′ və-rō′lē-ī′) *n.* A band of nerve fibers on the ventral surface of the brain stem that links the medulla oblongata and the cerebellum with upper portions of the brain. [NLat. *pōns Varoliī*, bridge of Varoli, after Costanzo *Varolio* (1543?–75), Italian anatomist.]

Pon•ta Del•ga•da (pŏn′tə dĕl-gä′də, pôN′-). A city of SW Sao Miguel I. in the Azores. Pop. 21,187.

Pont•char•train (pŏn′chər-trān′), **Lake.** A lake of SE LA N of New Orleans.

Pon•ti•ac¹ (pŏn′tē-ăk′). 1720?–69. Ottawa leader who led a revolt against the British (1763–66).

Pon•ti•ac² (pŏn′tē-ăk′). A city of SE MI NW of Detroit. Pop. 71,166.

Pon•ti•a•nak (pŏn′tē-ä′näk). A city of W Borneo, Indonesia, at the N edge of the Kapuas R. delta. Pop. 304,778.

pon•ti•fex (pŏn′tə-fĕks′) *n., pl.* **pon•tif•i•ces** (pŏn-tĭf′ĭ-sēz′). A man on the highest council of priests in ancient Rome. [Lat. See **pent-***.]

pon•tiff (pŏn′tĭf) *n.* **1.a.** The pope. **b.** A bishop. **2.** A pontifex. [Fr. *pontife* < OFr. *pontif* < Lat. *pontifex*, pontifex. See **pent-***.]

pon•tif•i•cal (pŏn-tĭf′ĭ-kəl) *adj.* **1.** Relating to, characteristic of, or suitable for a pope or a bishop. **2.** Having the dignity, pomp, or authority of a pontiff or a bishop. **3.** Pompously dogmatic or self-important; pretentious. — *n.* **1. pontificals.** The vestments and insignia of a pontiff or a bishop. **2.** A book of forms for ceremonies performed by a bishop. [ME < OFr. < Lat. *pontificālis*, of a pontifex < *pontifex*, *pontific-*, pontifex. See PONTIFEX.] — **pon•tif′i•cal•ly** *adv.*

pon•tif•i•cate (pŏn-tĭf′ĭ-kĭt, -kāt′) *n.* The office or term of office of a pontiff. — *intr.v.* (-kāt′) **-cat•ed, -cat•ing, -cates. 1.** To express opinions or judgments in a dogmatic way. **2.** To administer the office of a pontiff. [Lat. *pontificātus* < *pontifex*, *pontific-*, pontifex. See PONTIFEX.] — **pon•tif′i•ca′tor** *n.*

pon•til (pŏn′tĭl) *n.* See **punty.** [Fr., poss. < Ital. *puntello*, dim. of *punto*, point < Lat. *pūnctum* < neut. p.part. of *pungere*, to prick. See **peuk-***.]

pon•tine (pŏn′tīn′, -tēn′) *adj.* **1.** Of or relating to bridges. **2.** Of or relating to a pons, esp. the pons Varolii. [Lat. *pōns, pont-*, bridge; see **pent-*** + -INE[1].]
Pon•tine Marshes (pŏn′tēn, -tīn). An area of central Italy between the Tyrrhenian Sea and the Apennine foothills; drained during the 1930's to produce fertile farmland.
Pon•tius Pi•late (pŏn′chəs pī′lət). See Pontius **Pilate.**
Pont l'É•vêque (pônt′ lə-vĕk′, pôN′ lā-vĕk′) *n.* A mild soft-centered French cheese made of whole milk. [After *Pont l'Évêque*, a town of NW France.]
pon•to•nier (pŏn′tə-nîr′) *n.* One who is in charge of pontoons or is engaged in the construction of pontoon bridges. [Fr. *pontonnier* < OFr. < *ponton*, pontoon. See PONTOON.]
pon•toon (pŏn-to͞on′) *n.* **1.** A floating structure, such as a flat-bottomed boat, used to support a bridge. **2.** A floating structure serving as a dock. **3.** A float on a seaplane. [Fr. *ponton* < OFr. < Lat. *pontō, pontōn-*, floating bridge < *pōns, pont-*, bridge. See **pent-***.]
pontoon bridge *n.* A temporary floating bridge that uses pontoons for support.
Pon•top•pi•dan (pŏn-tŏp′ĭ-dăn′, -dän′), **Henrik.** 1857–1943. Danish writer who shared the 1917 Nobel Prize for literature.
Pon•tus (pŏn′təs). An ancient country of NE Asia Minor along the S coast of the Black Sea. — **Pon′tic** (-tĭk) *adj.*
Pon•ty•pool (pŏn′tə-po͞ol′). An urban district of SE Wales NNE of Cardiff. Pop. 90,300.
po•ny (pō′nē) *n., pl.* **-nies. 1.** Any of several types or breeds of horses that are small in size when full grown, such as the Shetland pony. **2.a.** *Informal.* A racehorse. **b.** *Sports.* A polo horse. **3.** Something small for its kind, esp. a small glass for beer or liqueur. **4.** A word-for-word translation of a foreign language text, esp. one used secretly by students as an aid. **5.** *Chiefly British.* The sum of 25 pounds. — *tr. & intr.v.* **-nied, -ny•ing, -nies.** To study with the aid of a pony. — ***phrasal verb.* pony up.** *Slang.* To pay (money owed or due). [Prob. < obsolete Fr. *poulenet*, dim. of *poulain*, colt < LLat. *pullāmen*, young of an animal < Lat. *pullus*. See **pau-***.]
pony express *n.* A system of rapid mail transportation by relays of horses in use in the West in 1860 to 1861.
po•ny•tail (pō′nē-tāl′) *n.* A hairstyle in which the hair is held back so as to hang down like a pony's tail.
Pon•zi scheme (pŏn′zē) *n.* An investment swindle in which high profits are promised from fictitious sources and early investors are paid off with funds raised from later ones. [After Charles *Ponzi* (1882?–1949), Italian-born speculator.]
pooch (po͞och) *n. Slang.* A dog. [?]
pood (po͞od) *n.* A Russian unit of weight equivalent to about 16.4 kilograms (36.1 pounds) avoirdupois. [Russ. *pud* < ON *pund*, pound, ult. < Lat. *pondō*. See POUND[1].]
poo•dle (po͞od′l) *n.* Any of a breed of dogs originally developed in Europe as hunting dogs, having thick curly hair and classified by shoulder height into standard, miniature, and toy varieties. [Ger. *Pudel*, short for *Pudelhund* : LGer. *pudeln*, to splash about (< *pudel*, puddle) + *Hund*, dog; see DACHSHUND.]
pooh (po͞o) *interj.* Used to express disdain or disbelief.
Pooh-Bah or **pooh-bah** (po͞o′bä′) *n.* **1.** A pompous, ostentatious official, esp. one who performs none of many offices held. **2.** A person who holds high office. [After *Pooh-Bah* in *The Mikado* by W.S. Gilbert and Arthur Sullivan.]
pooh-pooh (po͞o′po͞o′) *tr.v.* **-poohed, -pooh•ing, -poohs.** *Informal.* To express contempt for or impatience about; make light of. [Redup. of POOH.]
pool[1] (po͞ol) *n.* **1.** A small body of still water. **2.** An accumulation of standing liquid, as a puddle. **3.** A deep or still place in a stream. **4.** A swimming pool. **5.** An underground accumulation of petroleum or gas in porous sedimentary rock. — *intr.v.* **pooled, pool•ing, pools. 1.** To form pools or a pool. **2.** To accumulate in a body part. [ME < OE *pōl*.]
pool[2] (po͞ol) *n.* **1.** *Games.* **a.** A game of chance, resembling a lottery, in which the contestants put staked money into a common fund that is later paid to the winner. **b.** A fund containing all the money bet in a game of chance or on the outcome of an event. **2.** A grouping of resources for the common advantage of the participants. **3.** An available supply, the use of which is shared by a group. **4.** A group of journalists who cover an event and then share their reports with participating news media. **5.** A mutual fund established by a group of stockholders for speculating in or manipulating prices of securities. **6.** An agreement between competing business concerns to establish controls over production, market, and prices for common profit. **7.** Any of several games played on a six-pocket billiard table usu. with 15 object balls and a cue ball. — *v.* **pooled, pool•ing, pools.** — *tr.* To put into a fund for use by all. — *intr.* To join or form a pool. [Fr. *poule*, hen, stakes, booty < OFr., hen, young chicken < Lat. *pullus*, young of an animal. See **pau-***.] — **pool′er** *n.*
Poole (po͞ol). A municipal borough of S England WSW of Southhampton; chartered 1248. Pop. 120,000.
pool•room (po͞ol′ro͞om′, -ro͝om′) *n. Games.* A commercial establishment or room for the playing of pool or billiards.
pool•side (po͞ol′sīd′) *n.* The area near a swimming pool.
pool table *n. Games.* A six-pocket billiards table for pool.
poon (po͞on) *n.* Any of several trees of the genus *Calophyllum* of southern Asia, having light hard wood used for masts and spars. [Singhalese *pūna*, perh. of Dravidian orig.]
Poo•na (po͞o′nə). A city of W-central India ESE of Bombay; a Maratha cap. in the 17th and 18th cent. Pop. 1,203,351.
poop[1] (po͞op) *Naut.* — *n.* **1.** A superstructure at the stern of a ship. **2.** A poop deck. — *tr.v.* **pooped, poop•ing, poops. 1.** To break over the stern of (a ship). **2.** To take (a wave) over the stern. [ME *poupe* < OFr. < Lat. *puppis*.]
poop[2] (po͞op) *tr.v.* **pooped, poop•ing, poops.** *Slang.* To cause to become fatigued; tire. — ***phrasal verb.* poop out.** *Slang.* **1.** To quit because of exhaustion: *poop out of a race.* **2.** To decide not to participate, esp. at the last moment. [?]
poop[3] (po͞op) *n. Slang.* Inside information. [Origin unknown.]
poop[4] (po͞op) *n. Slang.* A person regarded as very disagreeable. [Perh. short for NINCOMPOOP.]
poop[5] (po͞op) *Slang.* — *n.* Excrement. — *intr.v.* **pooped, poop•ing, poops.** To defecate. [Poss. < obsolete *poop*, to break wind < ME *poupen*, to blow a horn, toot, of imit. orig.]
poop deck *n. Naut.* An exposed partial deck on the stern superstructure of a ship.
poop•er-scoop•er (po͞o′pər sko͞o′pər) *n.* A scoop for picking up and removing the feces of a pet.
poor (po͝or) *adj.* **poor•er, poor•est. 1.** Having little or no wealth and few or no possessions. **2.** Lacking in a specified resource or quality. **3.** Not adequate in quality; inferior. **4.a.** Lacking in value; insufficient. **b.** Lacking in quantity. **5.** Lacking fertility: *poor soil.* **6.** Undernourished; lean. **7.** Humble. **8.** Eliciting or deserving pity; pitiable. — *n.* People with little or no wealth and possessions considered as a group. [ME *poure* < OFr. *povre* < Lat. *pauper*. See **pau-***.] — **poor′ness** *n.*

Syns: *poor, indigent, needy, impecunious, penniless, impoverished, poverty-stricken, destitute.* These adjectives mean lacking the money or the means for an adequate or comfortable life. *Poor* is the most general: *"Resolve not to be poor: whatever you have, spend less"* (Samuel Johnson). *Indigent* and *needy* refer to one in need or want: *indigent people living on the street; distributed food to needy families. Impecunious* and *penniless* mean having little or no money: *"Certainly an impecunious Subaltern was not a catch"* (Rudyard Kipling). *Poor investments left the family penniless.* One who is *impoverished* has been reduced to poverty: *an impoverished country. Poverty-stricken* means suffering from poverty and miserably poor: *poverty-stricken refugees. Destitute* means lacking any means of subsistence: *The fire left many tenants destitute.*

Usage Note: In informal speech *poor* is sometimes used as an adverb, as in *They never played poorer.* In formal usage *more poorly* would be required in this example.

poor box *n.* A box, as one in a church, for collecting alms.
poor boy *n. New Orleans.* See **submarine** 2. See Regional Note at **submarine.**
poor farm *n.* A farm that houses, supports, and employs the poor at public expense.
poor•house (po͝or′hous′) *n.* An establishment maintained at public expense as housing for the homeless.
poo•ri also **pu•ri** (po͝or′ē) *n., pl.* **-ris.** A puffy deep-fried bread of Pakistan and India. [Hindi *puri* < Skt. *pūraḥ*, cake. See **pelə-**[1]*.]
poor law *n.* A law or system of laws providing for public relief and support of the poor.
poor•ly (po͝or′lē) *adv.* In a poor manner. See Usage Note at **poor.** — *adj. Chiefly Southern U.S.* In poor health; ill: *feeling poorly.* See Usage Note at **bad**[1].
poor•mouth (po͝or′mouth′, -mouth′) *v.* **-mouthed, -mouth•ing, -mouths.** — *tr.* To speak ill of. — *intr.* To claim poverty as an excuse or a defense. — *n.* An exaggerated assertion of poverty.
poor white *n. Offensive.* Used as a disparaging term for a member of a class of low-income white farmers and laborers, esp. in the southern United States.
pop[1] (pŏp) *v.* **popped, pop•ping, pops.** — *intr.* **1.** To make a pop. **2.** To burst open with a pop. **3.** To move quickly or unexpectedly; appear abruptly. **4.** To open wide suddenly. **5.** *Baseball.* To hit a short high fly ball. **6.** To shoot a firearm, such as a pistol. — *tr.* **1.** To cause to make a sharp bursting sound. **2.** To cause to explode with a sharp bursting sound. **3.** To put or thrust suddenly or unexpectedly. **4.a.** To discharge (a firearm). **b.** To fire at; shoot. **5.** To hit or strike. **6.** *Baseball.* To hit (a ball) high in the air but not far. **7.** *Slang.* **a.** To take (drugs), esp. orally. **b.** To have (a drink). — *n.* **1.** A sudden sharp explosive sound. **2.** A shot with a firearm. **3.** *Chiefly Midwestern U.S.* See **soft drink.** See Regional Note at **tonic. 4.** *Baseball.* A pop fly. — *adv.* **1.** With a popping sound. **2.** Abruptly or unexpectedly. — ***phrasal verb.* pop off.** *Informal.* **1.** To leave abruptly or hurriedly. **2.** To die suddenly. **3.** To speak thoughtlessly in a burst of anger. — ***idiom.* pop the question.** *Informal.* To propose marriage. [ME *poppen* < *pop*, a blow, stroke, of imit. orig.]
pop[2] (pŏp) *n. Informal.* Father. [Short for PAPA.]

ă pat	oi boy
ā pay	ou out
âr care	o͝o took
ä father	o͞o boot
ĕ pet	ŭ cut
ē be	ûr urge
ĭ pit	th thin
ī pie	*th* this
îr pier	hw which
ŏ pot	zh vision
ō toe	ə about, item
ô paw	

Stress marks:
′ (primary);
′ (secondary), as in
dictionary (dĭk′shə-nĕr′ē)

pop³ (pŏp) *Informal.* —*adj.* **1.** Of or for the general public; popular or popularized: *pop culture.* **2.** Of, relating to, or specializing in popular music: *a pop singer.* **3.** Of or suggestive of pop art: *a pop style.* —*n.* **1.** Popular music. **2.** Pop art.

POP *abbr.* Proof of purchase.

pop. *abbr.* **1.** Popular. **2.** Population.

pop art *n.* A form of art that depicts everyday life and employs techniques of commercial art and popular illustration.

pop art
Campbell's Soup, 1965, by Andy Warhol.
Oil silk-screened on canvas, 36⅛" × 24". The Museum of Modern Art, New York. Philip Johnson Fund.

pop•corn (pŏp′kôrn′) *n.* **1.a.** A variety of corn, *Zea mays everta,* having hard kernels that burst to form white, irregularly shaped puffs when heated. **b.** The edible popped kernels of this variety of corn. **2.** A small piece, as of polystyrene, used in quantity to protect items in shipping. [Contraction of *popped corn.*]

pope (pōp) *n.* **1.** Often **Pope.** *Rom. Cath. Ch.* The bishop of Rome and head of the Roman Catholic Church on earth. **2.** *Eastern Orthodox Ch.* The patriarch of Alexandria. **3.** The Coptic patriarch of Alexandria. **4.** A person considered to have unquestioned authority. [ME < OE *pāpa* < LLat. < Lat., father (title of bishops) < Gk. *pappas.* See **papa*.**]

Pope, Alexander. 1688–1744. English poet whose works include *The Dunciad* (1728).

Pope, John. 1822–92. Amer. Union general who was defeated at the Second Battle of Bull Run (1862).

pop•er•y (pō′pə-rē) *n. Offensive.* The doctrines, practices, and rituals of the Roman Catholic Church.

pope's nose (pōps) *n. Informal.* The tail of a cooked fowl.

pop•eyed (pŏp′īd′) *adj.* **1.** Having bulging eyes. **2.** Amazed; astonished: *popeyed with wonder.*

pop fly *n. Baseball.* A short high fly ball.

pop•gun (pŏp′gŭn′) *n.* A toy gun that makes a popping noise.

pop•in•jay (pŏp′ĭn-jā′) *n.* A vain talkative person. [ME, parrot < OFr. *papegai* < Sp. *papagayo* or OProv. *papagai,* both < Ar. *babġā', babaġā'* < Pers. *babbaghā.*]

pop•ish (pō′pĭsh) *adj. Offensive.* Of or relating to the Roman Catholic Church. —**pop′ish•ly** *adv.* —**pop′ish•ness** *n.*

pop•lar (pŏp′lər) *n.* **1.a.** Any of several fast-growing deciduous trees of the genus *Populus,* having unisexual flowers borne in catkins. **b.** The wood of these trees. **2.** See **tulip tree.** [ME *popler* < OFr. *poplier* < *pouple* < Lat. *pōpulus.*]

Pop•lar Bluff (pŏp′lər). A city of SE MO near the AR border S of St. Louis. Pop. 16,996.

pop•lin (pŏp′lĭn) *n.* A ribbed fabric of silk, rayon, wool, or cotton, used in making clothing and upholstery. [Obsolete Fr. *papeline,* perh. < Prov. *papalino,* fem. of *papalin,* papal (so called because it was first made at the papal town of Avignon) < Med.Lat. *pāpālis* < LLat. *pāpa,* pope. See POPE.]

pop•lit•e•al (pŏp-lĭt′ē-əl, pŏp′lĭ-tē′əl) *adj.* Of or relating to the hollow part of the leg behind the knee joint. [< NLat. *popliteus* < Lat. *poples, poplit-,* ham of the knee.]

Po•po•ca•té•petl (pō′pə-kăt′ə-pĕt′l, pô′pô-kä-tĕ′pĕt′l). A volcano, 5,455.5 m (17,887 ft), of Mexico W of Puebla.

poppy
Prickly poppy
Argemone mexicana

pop•o•ver (pŏp′ō′vər) *n.* A very light hollow muffin made with eggs, milk, and flour.

pop•pa (pä′pə) *n.* Var. of **papa.**

pop•per (pŏp′ər) *n.* **1.** One that pops. **2.** A container or pan for making popcorn. **3.** *Slang.* An ampoule of amyl nitrite or butyl nitrite used as a stimulant drug.

pop•pet (pŏp′ĭt) *n.* **1.** A poppet valve. **2.** *Naut.* **a.** A small wooden strip on a gunwale that forms or supports an oarlock. **b.** One of the beams of a launching cradle supporting a ship's hull. **3.** *Chiefly British.* A darling. [ME *popet,* small child, doll, puppet. See PUPPET.]

poppet valve *n.* An intake or exhaust valve, operated by springs and cams, that opens and closes by axial motion.

pop•ple¹ (pŏp′əl) *intr.v.* **-pled, -pling, -ples.** To move in a tossing, bubbling, or rippling manner, as choppy water. —*n.* **1.** Choppy water. **2.** The motion or sound of boiling liquid. [ME *poplen,* prob. of MDu. orig.]

pop•ple² (pŏp′əl) *n. Informal.* A poplar. [ME *popel* (perh. < OE *popul-*) < Lat. *pōpulus.*]

pop•py (pŏp′ē) *n., pl.* **-pies. 1.** Any of numerous plants of the genus *Papaver,* having nodding buds with four crumpled petals, showy red, orange, or white flowers, a milky juice, and capsules that dehisce through terminal pores. **2.** Any of several similar or related plants, such as the California poppy. **3.** An extract from poppy seedpods, used in medicine and narcotics. **4.** *Color.* A vivid red to reddish orange. [ME *popi* < OE *popig,* prob. alteration of VLat. **papāvum,* alteration of Lat. *papāver.*]

pop•py•cock (pŏp′ē-kŏk′) *n.* Senseless talk; nonsense. [Du. dial. *pappekak* : *pap,* pap (< MDu. *pappe,* perh. < Lat. *pappa,* food) + *kak,* dung (< *kakken,* to defecate < MDu. *kacken* < Lat. *cacāre*; see **kakka-***).]

Pop•si•cle (pŏp′sĭ-kəl, -sĭk′əl). A trademark used for a colored, flavored ice confection with one or two flat sticks for a handle.

porcupine
African porcupine
Hystrix cristata

pop-top (pŏp′tŏp′) *adj.* Having a tab that can be pulled up or off to make an opening in a container. —**pop′-top′** *n.*

pop•u•lace (pŏp′yə-lĭs) *n.* **1.** The general public; the masses. **2.** A population. [Fr. < Ital. *popolaccio,* rabble < *popolo,* the people < Lat. *populus.* See POPULAR.]

pop•u•lar (pŏp′yə-lər) *adj.* **1.** Widely liked or appreciated. **2.** Liked by acquaintances; sought after for company. **3.** Of, representing, or carried on by the people at large. **4.** Fit for, adapted to, or reflecting the taste of the people at large. **5.** Accepted by or prevalent among the people in general. **6.** Suited to or within the means of ordinary people. **7.** Originating among the people: *popular legend.* [ME *populer* < OFr. *populaire* < Lat. *populāris,* of the people < *populus,* the people, of Etruscan orig.] —**pop′u•lar•ly** *adv.*

popular front *n.* A political coalition of leftist parties against fascism, such as that in European countries during the 1930's.

pop•u•lar•i•ty (pŏp′yə-lăr′ĭ-tē) *n.* The quality or state of being popular, esp. of being widely admired or sought after.

pop•u•lar•ize (pŏp′yə-lə-rīz′) *tr.v.* **-ized, -iz•ing, -iz•es. 1.** To make popular: *popularized the hairstyle.* **2.** To present in a widely understandable or acceptable form. —**pop′u•lar•i•za′tion** (-lər-ĭ-zā′shən) *n.* —**pop′u•lar•iz′er** *n.*

pop•u•late (pŏp′yə-lāt′) *tr.v.* **-lat•ed, -lat•ing, -lates. 1.** To supply with inhabitants, as by colonization; people. **2.** To live in; inhabit: *creatures that populate the ocean.* [Med.Lat. *populāre, populāt-* < Lat. *populus,* the people. See POPULAR.]

pop•u•la•tion (pŏp′yə-lā′shən) *n.* **1.a.** All of the people inhabiting a specified area. **b.** The total number of such people. **2.** The total number of inhabitants constituting a particular race, class, or group in a specified area. **3.** The act or process of furnishing with inhabitants. **4.** *Ecol.* All the organisms that constitute a specific group or occur in a specified habitat. **5.** *Statistics.* The set of individuals, items, or data from which a statistical sample is taken.

population explosion *n.* The geometric expansion of a biological population, esp. the unchecked growth in human population resulting from a decrease in infant mortality and an increase in longevity.

pop•u•lism (pŏp′yə-lĭz′əm) *n.* **1.a.** A political philosophy supporting the rights and power of the people in their struggle against the elite. **b.** The movement organized around this philosophy. **2. Populism.** The philosophy of the Populist Party.

pop•u•list (pŏp′yə-lĭst) *n.* **1.** A supporter of the rights and power of the people. **2. Populist.** A supporter of the Populist Party. —*adj.* **1.** Of or characteristic of populism or its advocates. **2. Populist.** Of or relating to the Populist Party.

Populist Party *n.* A U.S. political party in the 1890's that advocated free silver and a graduated federal income tax.

pop•u•lous (pŏp′yə-ləs) *adj.* Containing many people or inhabitants. [ME < Lat. *populōsus* < *populus,* the people. See POPULAR.] —**pop′u•lous•ly** *adv.* —**pop′u•lous•ness** *n.*

pop-up (pŏp′ŭp′) *adj.* Rising to form a three-dimensional structure when a page is opened. —*n.* **1.** A device or an illustration that pops up. **2.** *Baseball.* See **pop fly.**

por•bea•gle (pôr′bē′gəl) *n.* A mackeral shark *(Lamna nasus)* of temperate Atlantic waters. [Cornish *porbugel.*]

por•ce•lain (pôr′sə-lĭn, pōr′-, pôrs′lĭn, pōrs′-) *n.* **1.** A hard white translucent ceramic made by firing a pure clay and then glazing it with fusible materials; china. **2.** An object made of porcelain. [Fr. *porcelaine,* cowry shell, porcelain < OFr. < OItal. *porcellana* < fem. of *porcellano,* of a young sow (from the shell's resemblance to a pig's back) < *porcella,* young sow, dim. of *porca,* sow < Lat., fem. of *porcus,* pig. See **porko-*.**] —**por′ce•la′ne•ous** (-lā′nē-əs) *adj.*

porcelain enamel *n.* A glass coating fired on metal.

porcelain flower *n.* See **hoya.**

porch (pôrch, pōrch) *n.* **1.** A covered platform, usu. having a separate roof, at an entrance to a building. **2.** An open or enclosed gallery or room attached to the outside of a building; a veranda. **3.** *Obsolete.* A portico or covered walk. [ME *porche* < OFr. < Lat. *porticus,* portico < *porta,* gate. See **per-²*.**]

por•cine (pôr′sīn′) *adj.* Of or resembling swine or a pig. [ME < OFr. *porcin* < Lat. *porcīnus* < *porcus,* pig. See **porko-*.**]

por•cu•pine (pôr′kyə-pīn′) *n.* Any of various rodents of the Old World family Hystricidae or the New World family Erethizontidae, having long sharp erectile quills interspersed with coarse hair. [ME *porke despine* < OFr. *porc espin* : Lat. *porcus,* pig; see **porko-*** + Lat. *spīna,* thorn, spine.]

porcupine fish *n.* Any of various tropical marine fishes of the family Diodontidae, having strong spines on the body.

Por•cu•pine River (pôr′kyə-pīn′). A river rising in NW Yukon Terr., Canada, and flowing c. 721 km (448 mi) to the Yukon R. in NE AK.

pore¹ (pôr, pōr) *intr.v.* **pored, por•ing, pores. 1.** To read or study carefully and attentively: *pored over the ads.* **2.** To gaze intently. **3.** To meditate deeply; ponder. [ME *pouren.*]

pore² (pôr, pōr) *n.* **1.** A minute opening in tissue, as in the skin of an animal, serving as an outlet for perspiration, or in a plant leaf or stem, serving as a means of absorption and transpiration. **2.** A space in rock, soil, or unconsolidated sediment that is not occupied by mineral matter and allows the passage or absorption of fluids: *pores of a rock.* [ME < OFr. < LLat. *porus,* passage < Gk. *poros.* See **per-²*.**]

pore fungus *n.* Any of various basidiomycetous fungi of the families Boletaceae and Polyporaceae, whose basidia line the inside of tubes that lead to exterior pores.

por·gy (pôr′gē) *n., pl.* **porgy** or **-gies. 1.** Any of various deep-bodied marine food fishes of the family Sparidae, esp. the common species *Pagrus pagrus* of Mediterranean and Atlantic waters. **2.** Any of several fishes similar to the porgy. [Alteration of Sp. and Port. *pargo*, both alteration of Lat. *phager*, a kind of fish < Gk. *phagros*, sea bream.]

Po·ri (pôr′ē). A city of SW Finland on the Gulf of Bothnia NW of Helsinki; chartered 1564. Pop. 78,933.

po·rif·er·an (pə-rĭf′ər-ən) *n.* Any of various members of the phylum Porifera constituting the sponges. [< NLat. *Porifera*, phylum name : Lat. *porus*, passage; see PORE[2] + Lat. *-fera*, neut. pl. of *-fer*, -fer.] **—po·rif′er·al, po·rif′er·an** *adj.*

po·rif·er·ous (pə-rĭf′ər-əs) *adj.* **1.** Having pores. **2.** Of or relating to the poriferans.

pork (pôrk, pōrk) *n.* **1.** The flesh of a pig or hog used as food. **2.** *Slang.* Government funds, appointments, or benefits that are dispensed or enacted by politicians to gain favor with their constituents. [ME < OFr. *porc*, pig < Lat. *porcus*. See **porko-***.]

pork barrel *n. Slang.* A government project or appropriation that yields jobs or other benefits to a specific locale and patronage opportunities to its political representative.

pork belly *n.* A side of fresh pork.

pork·er (pôr′kər, pōr′-) *n.* A fattened young pig.

pork·pie (pôrk′pī′, pōrk′-) *n.* A man's hat having a low flat crown and a flexible brim.

por·ky (pôr′kē, pōr′-) *n., pl.* **-kies.** *Informal.* A porcupine.

porn (pôrn) also **por·no** (pôr′nō) *Slang.* —*n.* Pornography. —*adj.* Pornographic. **—porn′y** *adj.*

por·nog·ra·phy (pôr-nŏg′rə-fē) *n.* **1.** Sexually explicit material that sometimes equates sex with power and violence. **2.** The presentation or production of this material. [Fr. *pornographie* < *pornographe*, pornographer < LGk. *pornographos*, writing about prostitutes : *pornē*, prostitute; see **per-**[5]* + *graphein*, to write; see -GRAPHY.] **—por·nog′ra·pher** *n.* **—por′no·graph′ic** (pôr′nə-grăf′ĭk) *adj.* **—por′no·graph′i·cal·ly** *adv.*

po·ros·i·ty (pə-rŏs′ĭ-tē, pô-) *n., pl.* **-ties. 1.** The state or property of being porous. **2.** A structure or part that is porous. **3.** The ratio of the volume of all the pores in a material to the volume of the whole. [ME *porosite* < OFr. < Med.Lat. *porōsitās* < *porōsus*, porous. See POROUS.]

po·rous (pôr′əs, pōr′-) *adj.* **1.** Full of or having pores. **2.** Admitting the passage of gas or liquid through pores or interstices. **3.** Easily crossed or penetrated. [ME < OFr. *poreux*, *poros* < Med.Lat. *porōsus* < Lat. *porus*, passage. See PORE[2].] **—po′rous·ly** *adv.* **—po′rous·ness** *n.*

por·phyr·i·a (pôr-fîr′ē-ə) *n.* Any of several disorders of porphyrin metabolism, usu. hereditary, characterized by the presence of large amounts of porphyrins in the blood and urine. [NLat. : PORPHYR(IN) + -IA[1].] **—por·phyr′ic** *adj.*

por·phy·rin (pôr′fə-rĭn) *n.* Any of various nitrogen-containing organic compounds, derived from pyrrole and occurring in protoplasm. [Gk. *porphura*, purple; see PURPLE + -IN.]

por·phy·rit·ic (pôr′fə-rĭt′ĭk) also **por·phy·rit·i·cal** (-ĭ-kəl) *adj.* **1.** Containing relatively large isolated crystals in a mass of fine texture. **2.** Of or containing porphyry.

por·phy·roid (pôr′fə-roid′) *n.* Metamorphic rock having porphyritic texture.

por·phy·rop·sin (pôr′fə-rŏp′sĭn) *n.* A purple pigment similar to rhodopsin, found in the rods of the retinas of freshwater fishes and certain frogs. [Gk. *porphura*, purple + OPSIN.]

por·phy·ry (pôr′fə-rē) *n., pl.* **-ries.** Igneous rock having porphyritic texture. [ME *porphiri, porfurie* < OFr. *porfire* < Ital. *porfiro* < Med.Lat. *porphyrium* < Lat. *porphyrītēs* < Gk. *porphuritēs* < *porphura*, purple (< its color). See PURPLE.]

por·poise (pôr′pəs) *n., pl.* **porpoise** or **-pois·es. 1.** Any of several gregarious toothed whales of the genus *Phocœna* and related genera of oceanic waters, having a blunt snout and a triangular dorsal fin. **2.** Any of several related mammals, such as the dolphin. [ME *porpeis* < OFr. (prob. transl. of a Gmc. compound meaning sea pig) : *porc*, pig (< Lat. *porcus*; see **porko-***) + *peis*, fish (< Lat. *piscis*).]

por·rect (pə-rĕkt′, pô-) *adj. Zool.* Stretched out or forth; extended, esp. forward: *porrect mandibles.* [Lat. *porrēctus*, p.part. of *porrigere*, to stretch out : *por-*, forward, out; see **per**[1]* + *regere*, to direct, rule; see DIRECT.]

por·ridge (pôr′ĭj, pŏr′-) *n.* A soft food made by boiling oatmeal or another meal in water or milk. [Alteration of POTTAGE (influenced by obsolete *porray*, vegetable soup, ult. < Lat. *porrum*).] **—por′ridg·y** *adj.*

por·rin·ger (pôr′ĭn-jər, pŏr′-) *n.* A shallow cup or bowl with a handle. [ME, alteration of *potinger, potager* < OFr. *potager* < *potage*, soup. See POTTAGE.]

port[1] (pôrt, pōrt) *n.* **1.a.** A place on a waterway with facilities for loading and unloading ships. **b.** A city or town on a waterway with such facilities. **c.** The waterfront district of a city. **2.** A place along a coast that gives ships and boats protection; a harbor. **3.** A port of entry. [ME < OE < Lat. *portus*. See **per-**[2]*.]

port[2] (pôrt, pōrt) *Naut.* —*n.* The left-hand side of a ship or aircraft facing forward. —*adj.* Of, relating to, or on the port side. —*tr. & intr.v.* **port·ed, port·ing, ports.** To turn (a craft) or make a shift to the port side. [Prob. < *port side* < PORT[1].]

port[3] (pôrt, pōrt) *n.* **1.** *Naut.* **a.** A porthole. **b.** *Archaic.* A cover for a porthole. **2.** An opening, as in a cylinder or valve face, for the passage of steam or fluid. **3.** A hole in an armored vehicle or a fortified structure for viewing or for firing weapons. **4.** *Comp. Sci.* **a.** An entrance to or exit for a data network. **b.** A connection point for a peripheral device. **5.** *Scots.* A gateway or portal, as to a town. [ME, gate, porthole < OFr. *porte*, gate < Lat. *porta*. See **per-**[2]*.]

port[4] also **Port** (pôrt, pōrt) *n.* A rich sweet fortified wine. [After OPORTO.]

port[5] (pôrt, pōrt) *tr.v.* **port·ed, port·ing, ports.** To carry (a weapon) diagonally across the body, with the muzzle or blade near the left shoulder. —*n.* **1.** The position of a weapon when ported. **2.** The manner in which one carries oneself; bearing. [Fr. *porter*, to carry < OFr. < Lat. *portāre*. See **per-**[2]*.]

Port. *abbr.* Portugal; Portuguese.

port·a·ble (pôr′tə-bəl, pōr′-) *adj.* **1.** Carried or moved with ease. **2.** *Obsolete.* Bearable; endurable. —*n.* Something portable, such as a light typewriter. [ME < OFr. < LLat. *portābilis* < Lat. *portāre*, to carry. See **per-**[2]*.] **—port′a·bil′i·ty, port′a·ble·ness** *n.* **—port′a·bly** *adv.*

port·age (pôr′tĭj, pōr′-, pôr-täzh′) *n.* **1.a.** The act or an instance of carrying. **b.** A charge for carrying. **2.** *Naut.* **a.** The carrying of boats and supplies overland between two waterways or around an obstacle to navigation. **b.** A track or route used for such carrying. —*tr. & intr.v.* **-aged, -ag·ing, -ag·es.** *Naut.* To transport or travel by portage. [ME < OFr. < *porter*, to carry < Lat. *portāre*. See **per-**[2]*.]

Por·tage (pôr′tĭj, pōr′-). **1.** A city of NW IN, a suburb of Gary on Lake Michigan. Pop. 29,060. **2.** A city of SW MI S of Kalamazoo. Pop. 41,042.

por·tal (pôr′tl, pōr′-) *n.* **1.** A doorway, an entrance, or a gate, esp. a large and imposing one. **2.** An entrance or a means of entrance. **3.** The portal vein. —*adj.* **1.** Of or relating to the portal vein or the portal system. **2.** Of or relating to a point of entrance to an organ, esp. the transverse fissure of the liver, through which the blood vessels enter. [ME < OFr. < Med. Lat. *portāle*, city gate < neut. of *portālis*, of a gate < Lat. *porta*, gate. See **per-**[2]*. N., sense 3 and adj. < NLat. *porta (hepatis)*, transverse fissure (of the liver) < Lat., gate.]

Port Al·ber·ni (ăl-bûr′nē). A city of SW British Columbia, Canada, on SE-central Vancouver I. Pop. 19,892.

portal system *n.* A system of blood vessels that begins and ends in capillaries.

por·tal-to-por·tal (pôr′tl-tə-pôr′tl, pōr′tl-tə-pōr′tl) *adj.* Of or based on the time a worker spends on the employer's property, calculated from arrival to departure.

portal vein *n.* A vein that conducts blood from the digestive organs, spleen, pancreas, and gallbladder to the liver.

por·ta·men·to (pôr′tə-mĕn′tō, pōr′-) *n., pl.* **-ti** (-tē) or **-tos.** *Mus.* A smooth uninterrupted glide in passing from one tone to another, esp. with the voice or a bowed stringed instrument. [Ital. < *portare*, to carry < Lat. *portāre*. See **per-**[2]*.]

Port An·ge·les (ăn′jə-lĭs). A city of NW WA S of Victoria, British Columbia, Canada. Pop. 17,710.

Port Ar·thur (är′thər). A city of extreme SE TX on Sabine Lake near the LA border. Pop. 58,724.

por·ta·tive (pôr′tə-tĭv, pōr′-) *adj.* **1.** Portable. **2.** Capable of or used in carrying. [ME *portatif* < OFr. < Lat. *portāre*, to carry. See **per-**[2]*.]

Port-au-Prince (pôrt′ō-prĭns′, pōrt′-, pôr′tō-prăns′). The cap. of Haiti, in the SW part on an arm of the Caribbean; founded by French sugar planters in 1749. Pop. 684,284.

Port Ches·ter (chĕs′tər). A village of SE NY on Long Island Sound near the CT border. Pop. 24,728.

Port Col·borne (kōl′bûrn′). A city of SE Ontario, Canada, on Lake Erie W of Buffalo NY. Pop. 19,225.

Port Co·quit·lam (kō-kwĭt′ləm). A city of SW British Columbia, Canada, on the Fraser R. E of Vancouver. Pop. 27,535.

port·cul·lis (pôrt-kŭl′ĭs, pōrt-) *n.* A grating of iron or wooden bars or slats, suspended in the gateway of a fortified place and lowered to block passage. [ME *port-colice* < OFr. *porte coleice*, sliding gate : *porte*, gate (< Lat. *porta*; see **per-**[2]*) + *coleice*, fem. of *coleis*, sliding (< VLat. **cōlāticius* < Lat. *cōlātus*, p.part. of *cōlāre*, to filter, strain < *cōlum*, sieve).]

Port du Sa·lut (pôrt′ də să-lo͞o′, pōrt′, pôr′ dü să-lü′) *n.* Var. of **Port Salut.**

Porte (pôrt, pōrt) *n.* The government of the Ottoman Empire. [Fr., short for *la Sublime Porte*, the High Gate < OFr. *porte*, gate. See PORT[3].]

porte-co·chère or **porte-co·chere** (pôrt′kō-shâr′, pōrt′-) *n.* **1.** A carriage entrance leading through a building or wall into an enclosed courtyard. **2.** An enclosure over a driveway at the entrance of a building to provide shelter. [Fr. *porte cochère* : *porte*, door + *cochère*, for coaches.]

Port E·liz·a·beth (ĭ-lĭz′ə-bəth). A city of SE South Africa on an inlet of the Indian Ocean. Pop. 281,600.

por·tend (pôr-tĕnd′, pōr-) *tr.v.* **-tend·ed, -tend·ing, -tends.**

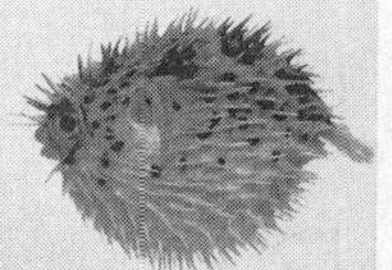
porcupine fish
Diodon hystrix

porringer
c. 1730 silver porringer by Simeon Soumaine (1685–1750)

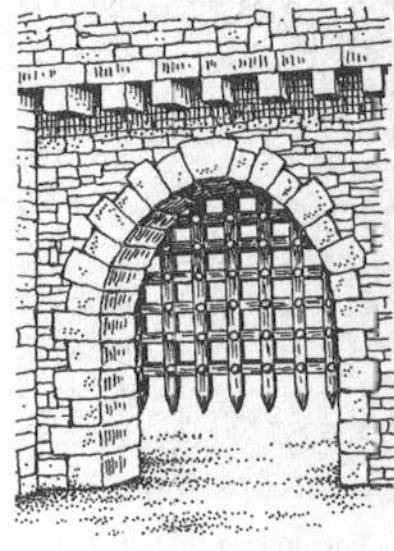
portcullis

ă **pat**	oi **boy**
ā **pay**	ou **out**
âr **care**	o͝o **took**
ä **father**	o͞o **boot**
ĕ **pet**	ŭ **cut**
ē **be**	ûr **urge**
ĭ **pit**	th **thin**
ī **pie**	*th* **this**
îr **pier**	hw **which**
ŏ **pot**	zh **vision**
ō **toe**	ə **about,**
ô **paw**	**item**

Stress marks:
′ (primary);
′ (secondary), as in
dictionary (dĭk′shə-nĕr′ē)

1. To serve as an omen or a warning of; presage: *Clouds portend a storm.* **2.** To indicate by prediction; forecast. [ME *portenden* < Lat. *portendere.* See **ten-***.]

por•tent (pôr′tĕnt′, pōr′-) *n.* **1.** A prophecy of something important or calamitous; an omen. **2.** Prophetic or threatening significance. **3.** Something amazing or marvelous; a prodigy. [Lat. *portentum* < neut. p.part. of *portendere,* to portend. See PORTEND.]

por•ten•tous (pôr-tĕn′təs, pōr-) *adj.* **1.** Of the nature of or constituting a portent; foreboding. **2.** Full of unspecifiable significance; exciting wonder and awe. **3.** Marked by pompousness; pretentiously weighty. —**por•ten′tous•ly** *adv.* —**por•ten′tous•ness** *n.*

por•ter¹ (pôr′tər, pōr′-) *n.* **1.** A person employed to carry burdens, esp. an attendant who carries baggage at a hotel or transportation station. **2.** A railroad employee who waits on passengers in a sleeping car or parlor car. **3.** A maintenance worker for a building or an institution. [ME *portour* < AN < LLat. *portātor* < Lat. *portāre,* to carry. See **per-²***.]

por•ter² (pôr′tər, pōr′-) *n. Chiefly British.* One in charge of a gate or door. [ME < AN < LLat. *portārius* < Lat. *porta,* gate. See **per-²***.]

por•ter³ (pôr′tər, pōr′-) *n.* A dark beer made from malt dried at a high temperature. [Short for *porter's ale.*]

Por•ter (pôr′tər, pōr′-), **Cole Albert.** 1891?–1964. Amer. composer and lyricist remembered for his witty scores.

Porter, Sir **George.** b. 1920. British chemist who shared a 1967 Nobel Prize.

Porter, Katherine Anne. 1890–1980. Amer. writer known for her short stories and her novel *Ship of Fools* (1962).

Porter, Rodney Robert. b. 1917. British biochemist who shared a 1972 Nobel Prize.

Porter, William Sydney. O. Henry. 1862–1910. Amer. writer whose works include *Cabbages and Kings* (1904).

por•ter•age (pôr′tər-ĭj, pōr′-) *n.* **1.** The carrying of burdens or goods as done by porters. **2.** The charge for this activity.

por•ter•ess (pôr′tər-ĭs, pōr′-) *n.* Var. of **portress.**

por•ter•house (pôr′tər-hous′, pōr′-) *n.* **1.** A cut of beef from the thick end of the short loin, having a T-shaped bone and a sizable piece of tenderloin. **2.** *Archaic.* An alehouse or a chophouse.

Por•ter•ville (pôr′tər-vĭl′, pōr′-). A city of S-central CA N of Bakersfield; founded 1859. Pop. 29,563.

port•fo•li•o (pôrt-fō′lē-ō′, pōrt-) *n., pl.* **-os. 1.a.** A portable case for holding material, such as photographs or drawings. **b.** The materials collected in such a case, esp. when representative of a person's work. **2.** The office or post of a cabinet member or minister of state. **3.** A group of investments. [Ital. *portafoglio* : *porta* (< *portare,* to carry < Lat. *portāre*; see **per-²***) + *foglio,* sheet (< Lat. *folium,* leaf; see **bhel-³***).]

port•hole (pôrt′hōl′, pōrt′-) *n.* **1.** *Naut.* A small, usu. circular window that can be opened in a ship's side. **2.** An opening in a fortified wall; an embrasure.

Port Hue•ne•me (wī-nē′mē). A town of S CA W of Los Angeles. Pop. 20,319.

Port Hu•ron (hyo͝or′ən, -ŏn′). A city of SE MI on Lake Huron NNE of Detroit; first settled in 1686. Pop. 33,694.

por•ti•co (pôr′tĭ-kō′, pōr′-) *n., pl.* **-coes** or **-cos.** A porch or walkway with a roof supported by columns, often leading to the entrance of a building. [Ital. < Lat. *porticus* < *porta,* gate. See **per-²***.] —**por′ti•coed′** *adj.*

por•tière or **por•tiere** (pôr-tyâr′, pōr-) *n.* A heavy curtain hung across a doorway. [Fr., fem. of *portier,* porter < OFr. < LLat. *portārius* < Lat. *porta,* gate. See **per-²***.]

por•tion (pôr′shən, pōr′-) *n.* **1.** A section or quantity within a larger thing; a part of a whole. **2.** A part separated from a whole. **3.** A part allotted to a person or group, as: **a.** A helping of food. **b.** The part of an estate received by an heir. **c.** A woman's dowry. **4.** A person's lot or fate. —*tr.v.* **-tioned, -tion•ing, -tions. 1.** To divide into parts for distribution; parcel. **2.** To provide with a share, inheritance, or dowry. [ME < OFr. < Lat. *portiō, portiōn-.* See **perə-²***.] —**por′tion•a•ble** *adj.* —**por′tion•er** *n.* —**por′tion•less** *adj.*

Port•land (pôrt′lənd, pōrt′-). **1.** A city of SW ME on an arm of the Gulf of Maine S of Lewiston; settled c. 1632. Pop. 64,348. **2.** A city of NW OR on the Willamette R.; founded 1845. Pop. 437,319. —**Port′land•er** *n.*

Portland cement or **port•land cement** (pôrt′lənd, pōrt′-) *n.* A hydraulic cement made by heating a mixture of limestone and clay in a kiln and pulverizing the resulting material. [After *Portland,* an urban district of S England.]

Port Lou•is (lo͞o′ĭs, lo͞o′ē, lo͞o-ē′). The cap. of Mauritius, in the NW on the Indian Ocean; founded 1735. Pop. 136,812.

port•ly (pôrt′lē, pōrt′-) *adj.* **-li•er, -li•est. 1.** Comfortably stout; corpulent. See Syns at **fat. 2.** *Archaic.* Stately; majestic; imposing. [< PORT⁵.] —**port′li•ness** *n.*

port•man•teau (pôrt-măn′tō, pōrt-, pôrt′măn-tō′, pōrt′-) *n., pl.* **-teaus** or **-teaux** (-tōz, -tōz′). A large leather suitcase with two hinged compartments. [Fr. *portemanteau* : *porte* (< *porter,* to carry < OFr.; see PORT⁵) + *manteau,* cloak (< OFr. *mantel* < Lat. *mantellum*).]

portmanteau word *n.* A word formed by merging the sounds and meanings of two different words; for example, *chortle,* from *chuckle* and *snort.*

Port Mores•by (môrz′bē, mōrz′-). The cap. of Papua New Guinea, on SE New Guinea. Pop. 123,624.

Por•to or **Pôr•to** (pôr′to͞o). See **Oporto.**

Pôrto A•le•gre (ə-lĕ′grə). A city of SE Brazil on a lagoon near the Atlantic Ocean; founded c. 1742. Pop. 1,125,477.

port of call *n., pl.* **ports of call.** A port where ships dock to load or unload cargo, obtain supplies, or undergo repairs.

port of entry *n., pl.* **ports of entry.** A place where travelers or goods may enter or leave a country under official supervision.

Port of Spain (spān) or **Port-of-Spain** (pôrt′əv-spān′, pōrt′-). The cap. of Trinidad and Tobago, on the NW coast of Trinidad on an arm of the Atlantic. Pop. 65,906.

Por•to-No•vo (pôr′tō-nō′vō, pōr′-). The cap. of Benin, in the SE part on an inlet of the Gulf of Guinea; settled as a slave-trading center in the 17th cent. Pop. 123,000.

Port Or•ange (ôr′ĭnj, ŏr′-). A city of NE FL on the Atlantic coast SSE of Daytona Beach. Pop. 35,317.

Pôrto Vel•ho (vĕl′yo͞o). A city of NW Brazil on the Madeira R. near the Bolivian border. Pop. 101,162.

Port Phil•lip Bay (fĭl′əp). A large deep-water inlet of Bass Strait on the SE coast of Australia.

por•trait (pôr′trĭt, -trāt′, pōr′-) *n.* **1.** A likeness of a person, esp. of the face. **2.** A verbal picture or description, esp. of a person. [Fr. < OFr., image < p.part. of *portraire,* to portray. See PORTRAY.]

por•trait•ist (pôr′trə-tĭst, pōr-) *n.* A person who makes portraits, esp. a painter or photographer.

por•trai•ture (pôr′trĭ-cho͝or′, pōr′-) *n.* **1.** The art or practice of making portraits. **2.** A portrait. **3.** Portraits as a group.

por•tray (pôr-trā′, pōr-) *tr.v.* **-trayed, -tray•ing, -trays. 1.** To depict or represent pictorially; make a picture of. **2.** To depict or describe in words. **3.** To represent dramatically, as on the stage. [ME *portraien* < OFr. *portraire* : *por-,* forth (< Lat. *prō-,* forth; see PRO-¹) + *traire,* to draw (< Lat. *trahere,* to drag).] —**por•tray′a•ble** *adj.* —**por•tray′er** *n.*

por•tray•al (pôr-trā′əl, pōr-) *n.* **1.** The act or process of depicting or portraying. **2.** A representation or description.

por•tress (pôr′trĭs, pōr′-) also **por•ter•ess** (-tər-ĭs) *n.* A woman doorkeeper or porter, esp. in a convent.

Port Roy•al (roi′əl). See **Annapolis Royal.**

Port Sa•id (sä-ēd′). A city of NE Egypt on the Mediterranean Sea at the N entrance to the Suez Canal; founded by the builders of the canal in 1859. Pop. 374,000.

Port Sa•lut (pôr′ să-lo͞o′, -lü′) also **Port du Sa•lut** (pôrt′ də să-lo͞o′, pōrt′, pôr dü să-lü′) *n.* A semihard fermented cheese. [After Notre Dame de *Port-du-Salut,* a Trappist abbey in NW France.]

port•side (pôrt′sīd′, pōrt′-) *adv. & adj.* **1.** On a port waterfront. **2.** *Naut.* On the port side of a ship or boat.

Ports•mouth (pôrt′sməth, pōrt′-). **1.** A borough of S England on the English Channel opposite the Isle of Wight; chartered 1194. Pop. 187,900. **2.** A city of SE NH on the Atlantic Ocean. The Treaty of Portsmouth, ending the Russo-Japanese War, was signed here in 1905. Pop. 25,925. **3.** A city of S OH on the Ohio R. S of Columbus. Pop. 22,676. **4.** An independent city of SE VA opposite Norfolk. Pop. 103,907.

Port Stan•ley (stăn′lē). See **Stanley.**

Port Su•dan (so͞o-dăn′). A city of NE Sudan on the Red Sea NE of Khartoum; estab. after 1905. Pop. 206,727.

Por•tu•gal (pôr′chə-gəl, pōr′-). A country of SW Europe on the W Iberian Peninsula, including the Madeira Is. and the Azores in the N Atlantic Ocean; an independent kingdom after 1143. Cap. Lisbon. Pop. 9,933,000.

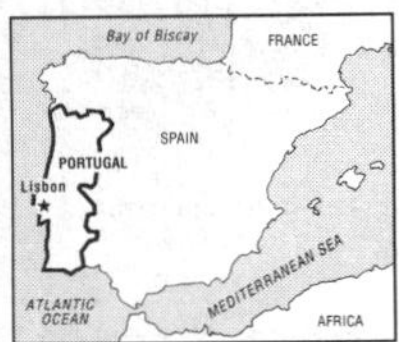

Portugal

Por•tu•guese (pôr′chə-gēz′, -gēs′, pōr′-) *adj.* Of or relating to Portugal or its people, language, or culture. —*n., pl.* **Portuguese. 1.a.** A native or inhabitant of Portugal. **b.** A person of Portuguese descent. **2.** The Romance language of Portugal and Brazil. [Port. *português* < VLat. **portugalēnsis,* ult. < LLat. *Portus Cale,* the ancient port of Gaya (Oporto).]

Portuguese man-of-war *n.* A complex colonial siphonophore of the genus *Physalia* of warm seas, having a broad saillike float from which hang numerous long stinging tentacles.

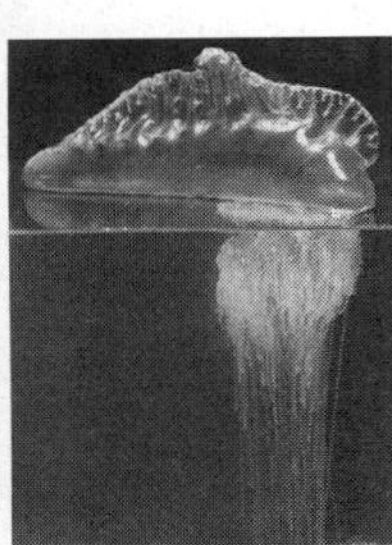
Portuguese man-of-war
Physalia physalis

por•tu•lac•a (pôr′chə-lăk′ə, pōr′-) *n.* Any of various fleshy plants of the genus *Portulaca,* esp. *P. grandiflora* of South America, having colorful flowers that open in sunlight. [ME < Lat. *portulāca,* purslane < *portula,* dim. of *porta,* gate (from the gatelike covering of the seed capsule). See **per-²***.]

pos. *abbr.* **1.** Position. **2.** Positive.

po•sa•da (pō-sä′də, pô-sä′thä) *n.* A Christmas festival originating in Latin America that dramatizes Joseph and Mary's search for lodging. [Am.Sp. < Sp., lodging < *posar,* to lodge < LLat. *pausāre,* to rest < Lat. *pausa,* pause. See PAUSE.]

pose¹ (pōz) *v.* **posed, pos•ing, pos•es.** —*intr.* **1.** To assume or hold a particular position or posture, as for a portrait. **2.** To affect a particular mental attitude. **3.** To represent oneself falsely; pretend to be other than what one is. —*tr.* **1.** To place (a model, for example) in a specific position. **2.** To set forth in words; propound: *pose a question.* **3.** To put forward; present: *pose a threat.* —*n.* **1.** A bodily attitude or position, esp. one assumed for a portrait. **2.** A studied attitude assumed for effect. See Syns at **affectation.** [ME *posen*, to place < OFr. *poser* < VLat. **pausāre* < LLat. *pausāre*, to rest < Lat. *pausa*, pause. See PAUSE.] —**pos′a•ble** *adj.*

pose² (pōz) *tr.v.* **posed, pos•ing, pos•es.** To puzzle, confuse, or baffle. [Short for *appose*, to examine closely (< ME *apposen*, alteration of *opposen*; see OPPOSE) and < Fr. *poser*, to assume (obsolete) (< OFr.; see POSE¹).]

Po•sei•don (pō-sīd′n, pə-) *n. Gk. Myth.* The brother of Zeus and god of the waters, earthquakes, and horses.

pos•er¹ (pō′zər) *n.* One who poses.

pos•er² (pō′zər) *n.* A baffling question or problem.

po•seur (pō-zœr′) *n.* One who affects a particular attitude, character, or manner to impress others. [Fr. < *poser*, to pose < OFr. See POSE¹.]

posh (pŏsh) *adj.* Smart and fashionable. [Perh. *posh*, halfpenny, money, dandy < Romany *pāšh*.] —**posh′ly** *adv.* —**posh′ness** *n.*

pos•it (pŏz′ĭt) *tr.v.* **-it•ed, -it•ing, -its. 1.** To affirm or assume the existence of; postulate. See Syns at **presume. 2.** To put forward, as for study; suggest. **3.** To place firmly in position. [< Lat. *positus*, p.part. of *pōnere*, to place. See POSITION.]

po•si•tion (pə-zĭsh′ən) *n.* **1.** A place or location. **2.a.** The right or appropriate place. **b.** An area occupied by members of a force for a strategic purpose. **3.a.** The way in which something is placed. **b.** The arrangement of body parts; posture. **4.** An advantageous place or location. **5.** A situation relative to the surrounding circumstances. **6.** A point of view or attitude on a certain question. **7.** Social standing or status; rank. **8.** A post of employment; a job. **9.a.** *Sports.* The area for which a particular player is responsible. **b.** *Games.* The arrangement of the pieces or cards at any particular time in a game. **10.a.** The act or process of positing. **b.** A principle or proposition posited. **11.a.** A commitment to buy or sell a given amount of securities or commodities. **b.** The amount of securities or commodities held by a person, firm, or institution. **c.** The ownership status of a person's or an institution's investments. —*tr.v.* **-tioned, -tion•ing, -tions. 1.** To put in place or position. **2.** To determine the position of; locate. [ME *posicioun* < OFr. *posicion* < Lat. *positiō, positiōn-* < *positus*, p.part. of *pōnere*, to place. See **apo-***.] —**po•si′tion•al** *adj.* —**po•si′tion•al•ly** *adv.* —**po•si′tion•er** *n.*

positional notation *n.* A system of writing numbers in which the value of a digit depends on its position.

position paper *n.* **1.** A detailed policy report that usu. explains, justifies, or recommends a particular course of action. **2.** See **aide-mémoire** 1.

pos•i•tive (pŏz′ĭ-tĭv) *adj.* **1.** Marked by or displaying certainty, acceptance, or affirmation: *positive criticism.* **2.** Measured or moving forward or in a direction of increase or progress. **3.** Explicitly or openly expressed or laid down. **4.** Admitting of no doubt; irrefutable. **5.a.** Very sure; confident. **b.** Overconfident; dogmatic. **6.** Formally or arbitrarily determined; prescribed. **7.** Concerned with practical rather than theoretical matters. **8.** Composed of or marked by the presence of particular qualities or attributes; real. **9.** *Philos.* **a.** Of or relating to positivism. **b.** Of or relating to laws imposed by human authority rather than by nature or reason alone. **c.** Of or relating to religion based on revelation rather than on nature or reason alone. **10.** *Informal.* Utter; absolute: *a positive darling.* **11.** *Math.* **a.** Relating to or being a quantity greater than zero. **b.** Relating to or being the sign (+). **c.** Relating to or being a quantity, number, angle, or direction opposite to another specified or understood as negative. **12.** *Phys.* Relating to or being electric charge of a sign opposite to that of an electron. **13.** *Medic.* Indicating the presence of a particular disease, condition, or organism: *positive test results.* **14.** *Biol.* Indicating or marked by response or motion toward the source of a stimulus, such as light. **15.** Having the areas of light and dark in their original and normal relationship, as in a photographic print made from a negative. **16.** *Gram.* Of, relating to, or being the simple uncompared degree of an adjective or adverb, as opposed to either the comparative or superlative. **17.** Driven by or generating power directly through intermediate machine parts having little or no play: *positive drive.* —*n.* **1.** An affirmative element or characteristic. **2.** *Philos.* Something perceptible to the senses. **3.** *Math.* A quantity greater than zero. **4.** *Phys.* A positive electric charge. **5.** A photographic image in which the lights and darks appear as in nature. **6.** *Gram.* **a.** The uncompared degree of an adjective or adverb. **b.** A word in this degree. **7.** *Mus.* A division of some pipe organs, similar in sound to the great but smaller and less powerful. [ME, having a specified quality < OFr. *positif* < Lat. *positīvus*, formally laid down < *positus*, p.part. of *pōnere*, to place. See **apo-***.] —**pos′i•tive•ly** *adv.* —**pos′i•tive•ness, pos′i•tiv′i•ty** *n.*

pos•i•tiv•ism (pŏz′ĭ-tĭ-vĭz′əm) *n.* **1.** *Philos.* **a.** A doctrine contending that sense perceptions are the only admissible basis of human knowledge and precise thought. **b.** The application of this doctrine in logic, epistemology, and ethics. **c.** The system of Auguste Comte designed to supersede theology and metaphysics and depending on a hierarchy of the sciences, beginning with mathematics and culminating in sociology. **d.** Any of several doctrines or viewpoints that stress attention to actual practice over consideration of what is ideal. **2.** The state or quality of being positive. —**pos′i•tiv•ist, pos′i•tiv•is′tic** *adj.* —**pos′i•tiv•ist** *n.*

pos•i•tron (pŏz′ĭ-trŏn′) *n.* The antiparticle of the electron.

positron emission tomography *n.* Tomography in which a computer-generated image of a biological activity within the body is produced through the detection of gamma rays that are emitted when introduced radionuclides decay and release positrons.

pos•i•tro•ni•um (pŏz′ĭ-trō′nē-əm) *n.* A short-lived association of an electron and a positron bound together in a configuration resembling the hydrogen atom.

po•sol•o•gy (pə-sŏl′ə-jē, pō-) *n.* The medical or pharmacological study of the dosages of medicines and drugs. [Gk. *posos*, what quantity + -LOGY.]

poss. *abbr.* **1.** Possession. **2.** Possessive. **3.** Possible.

pos•se (pŏs′ē) *n.* **1.** A group of people summoned by a sheriff to aid in law enforcement. **2.** A search party. [Short for *posse comitatūs* : Med.Lat. *posse*, power, body of men (< Lat., to be able; see POTENT) + *comitātūs*, genitive of *comitātus*, county.]

pos•sess (pə-zĕs′) *tr.v.* **-sessed, -sess•ing, -sess•es. 1.** To have as property; own. **2.** To have as a quality, characteristic, or other attribute. **3.** To acquire command of or have knowledge of. **4.a.** To gain or exert influence or control over; dominate. **b.** To control or maintain (one's nature) in a particular condition. **5.** To cause to own, hold, or be proficient in something, such as property or knowledge. **6.** To cause to be influenced or controlled, as by an idea or emotion. **7.** *Obsolete.* To gain or seize. [ME *possessen* < OFr. *possesser* < Lat. *possidēre, possess-* : *pos-*, as master; see **poti-*** + *sedēre*, to sit; see **sed-***.] —**pos•ses′sor** *n.*

pos•sessed (pə-zĕst′) *adj.* **1.** Owning or mastering something. Used with *of.* **2.** Controlled by or as if by a spirit or other force; obsessed. **3.** Calm; collected.

Usage Note: *Possessed* is often followed by the prepositions *of, by,* or *with.* Mere possession of a thing or an attribute is indicated by *of*: *possessed of property; possessed of a sharp tongue.* When the term indicates obsession or lack of self-control, *by* and *with* are more often used: *possessed by* (or *with*) *an urge to kill.*

pos•ses•sion (pə-zĕsh′ən) *n.* **1.a.** The act or fact of possessing. **b.** The state of being possessed. **2.** Something owned or possessed. **3. possessions.** Wealth or property. **4.** *Law.* Actual holding or occupancy with or without rightful ownership. **5.** A territory subject to foreign control. **6.** Self-control. **7.** The state of being dominated by or as if by evil spirits or by an obsession. **8.** *Sports.* **a.** Physical control of the ball or puck by a player or team. **b.** The condition of being on offense. —**pos•ses′sion•al** *adj.*

pos•ses•sive (pə-zĕs′ĭv) *adj.* **1.** Of or relating to ownership or possession. **2.** Having or demonstrating a desire to control or dominate: *a possessive parent.* **3.** *Gram.* Relating to or being a noun or pronoun case that indicates possession. —*n. Gram.* **1.** The possessive case. **2.** A possessive form or construction. —**pos•ses′sive•ly** *adv.* —**pos•ses′sive•ness** *n.*

pos•ses•so•ry (pə-zĕs′ə-rē) *adj.* **1.** Of, relating to, or having possession. **2.** *Law.* Depending on or arising from possession.

pos•set (pŏs′ĭt) *n.* A spiced drink of hot sweetened milk curdled with wine or ale. [ME *poshet, possot* : perh. OFr. **posce* (Lat. *pōsca*, drink of vinegar and water < *potāre*, to drink; see POTABLE + Lat. *esca*, food < *edere*, to eat; see EDIBLE) + ME *hot*, hot; see HOT.]

pos•si•bil•i•ty (pŏs′ə-bĭl′ĭ-tē) *n., pl.* **-ties. 1.** The fact or state of being possible. **2.** Something that is possible. **3. possibilities.** Potentiality for favorable or interesting results.

pos•si•ble (pŏs′ə-bəl) *adj.* **1.** Capable of happening, existing, or being true without contradicting facts, laws, or circumstances. **2.** Capable of occurring or being done without offense to character, nature, or custom. **3.** Capable of favorable development; potential: *a possible building site.* **4.** Of uncertain likelihood. [ME < OFr. < Lat. *possibilis* < *posse*, to be able. See **poti-***.] —**pos′si•bly** *adv.*

pos•sum (pŏs′əm) *n. Chiefly Southern U.S.* An opossum.

Regional Note: Since English is a language that stresses some syllables and not others, weakly stressed syllables are dropped at times. This process, called aphesis when it occurs at the beginning of a word, is more common in regional American dialects than in Standard English. Aphesis is most famous in the dialects of the South, where it yields pronunciations such as *count of* for *(on) account of, tater* for *potato, possum* for *opossum,* and *skeeter* for *mosquito.*

post¹ (pōst) *n.* **1.** A long piece of wood or other material set upright into the ground to serve as a marker or support. **2.** A similar vertical support or structure, as: **a.** A support for a beam in the framework of a building. **b.** A terminal of a battery. **3.** *Sports.* A goal post. **4.** The starting point at a racetrack. —*tr.v.* **post•ed, post•ing, posts. 1.a.** To display (an announcement) in a place of public view. **b.** To cover (a wall, for example) with posters. **2.** To announce by or as if by posters. **3.** To put up signs on (property) warning against

ă pat	oi boy
ā pay	ou out
âr care	ŏŏ took
ä father	ōō boot
ĕ pet	ŭ cut
ē be	ûr urge
ĭ pit	th thin
ī pie	*th* this
îr pier	hw which
ŏ pot	zh vision
ō toe	ə about, item
ô paw	

Stress marks:
′ (primary);
′ (secondary), as in
dictionary (dĭk′shə-nĕr′ē)

trespassing. **4.** To denounce publicly. **5.** To publish (a name) on a list. **6.** *Games.* To gain (points or a point) in a game or contest; score. [ME < OE < Lat. *postis.* See **stā-*.**]

post² (pōst) *n.* **1.** A military base. **2.** A local organization of military veterans. **3.** Either of two bugle calls sounded as a tattoo in the British Army. **4.** An assigned position or station, as of a guard or sentry. **5.** A position of employment, esp. an appointed public office. **6.** A place to which someone is assigned for duty. **7.** A trading post. —*tr.v.* **post•ed, post•ing, posts. 1.** To assign to a specific position or station: *post a sentry at the gate.* **2.** To appoint to a naval or military command. **3.** To put forward; present: *post bail.* [Fr. *poste* < Ital. *posto* < OItal. < VLat. **postum* < Lat. *positum*, neut. p.part. of *pōnere*, to place. See **apo-*.**]

post³ (pōst) *n.* **1.a.** A delivery of mail. **b.** The mail delivered. **2.** *Chiefly British.* **a.** A governmental system for transporting and delivering the mail. **b.** A post office. **3.a.** *Archaic.* One of a series of relay stations along a fixed route, furnishing fresh riders and horses for the delivery of mail on horseback. **b.** *Obsolete.* A rider on such a mail route; a courier. —*v.* **post•ed, post•ing, posts.** —*tr.* **1.** To mail (a letter or package). **2.** To send by mail in a system of relays on horseback. **3.** To inform of the latest news: *Keep us posted.* **4.a.** To transfer (an item) to a ledger in bookkeeping. **b.** To make the necessary entries in (a ledger). **5.** *Comp. Sci.* To enter (a unit of information) on a record or into a section of storage. —*intr.* **1.** To travel in stages or relays. **2.** To travel with speed or in haste. **3.** To bob up and down in the saddle in rhythm with a horse's trotting gait. —*adv.* **1.** By mail. **2.** With great speed; rapidly. **3.** By post horse. [Fr. *poste* < OFr., relay station for horses < OItal. *posta* < VLat. **posta*, station < Lat. *posita*, fem. p.part. of *pōnere*, to place. See **apo-*.**]

Post (pōst), **Emily Price.** 1872–1960. Amer. etiquette authority who wrote *Etiquette: The Blue Book of Social Usage* (1922).

Post, Wiley. 1899–1935. Amer. aviator who made the first solo flight around the world (1933).

post– *pref.* **1.** After; later: *postdate.* **2.** Behind; posterior to: *postaxial.* [Lat. < *post*, behind, after. See **apo-*.**]

post•age (pō′stĭj) *n.* **1.** The charge for mailing an item. **2.** The stamps, labels, or printing placed on an item to be mailed as evidence of payment of this charge.

postage meter *n.* A machine used in bulk mailing to print the correct amount of postage for each piece of mail.

postage stamp *n.* A small, usu. adhesive label issued by a government and sold in various denominations to be affixed to items of mail as evidence of the payment of postage.

post•al (pō′stəl) *adj.* Of or relating to a post office or mail service. —**post′al•ly** *adv.*

postal card *n.* A plain card printed with the image of a postage stamp, issued by a government and used for sending messages.

postal order *n.* *Chiefly British.* A money order.

postal service *n.* See **post office** 1.

post•ax•i•al (pōst-ăk′sē-əl) *adj. Anat.* Located behind an axis of the body, as the lateral aspect of the lower leg or the medial aspect of the upper arm. —**post•ax′i•al•ly** *adv.*

post•bel•lum (pōst-bĕl′əm) *adj.* Of the period after a war, esp. the U.S. Civil War. [Lat. *post*, after + *bellum*, war.]

post•box also **post box** (pōst′bŏks′) *n.* See **mailbox** 1.

post card also **post•card** (pōst′kärd′) *n.* **1.** A commercially printed card with space on one side for an address and a postage stamp, used for sending messages. **2.** See **postal card.**

post•ca•va (pōst-kā′və) *n.* A large vein that returns blood to the heart from the lower half of the body; the inferior vena cava. —**post•ca′val** *adj.*

post chaise *n.* A closed four-wheeled horse-drawn carriage, formerly used to transport mail and passengers.

post•cra•ni•al (pōst-krā′nē-əl) *adj.* **1.** Situated behind the cranium. **2.** Consisting of the parts or structures behind the cranium. —**post•cra′ni•al•ly** *adv.*

post•date (pōst-dāt′, pōst′-) *tr.v.* **-dat•ed, -dat•ing, -dates. 1.** To put a date on (a check, for example) that is later than the actual date. **2.** To occur later than; follow in time.

post•di•lu•vi•an (pōst′dĭ-lo͞o′vē-ən) also **post•di•lu•vi•al** (-əl) *Bible.* —*adj.* Existing or occurring after the Flood. —*n.* A person or thing living after the Flood. [POST– + Lat. *dīluvium*, flood; see DILUVIAL + –AN¹.]

post•doc•tor•al (pōst-dŏk′tər-əl) also **post•doc•tor•ate** (-ĭt) *adj.* Of, relating to, or engaged in academic study beyond the level of a doctoral degree.

post•er¹ (pō′stər) *n.* **1.a.** A large, usu. printed placard, bill, or announcement, often illustrated, that advertises or publicizes something. **b.** An artistic work, often a reproduction, printed on a large sheet of paper. **2.** One that posts bills or notices.

post•er² (pō′stər) *n. Archaic.* One that travels rapidly.

poster color *n.* See **tempera** 1.

poste res•tante (pōst′ rĕ-stänt′) *n.* A notation written on a letter indicating that the letter should be held at the post office until claimed by the addressee. [Fr. : *poste*, mail + *restante*, fem. pr.part. of *rester*, to remain.]

pos•te•ri•or (pŏ-stîr′ē-ər, pō-) *adj.* **1.** Located behind a part or toward the rear of a structure. **2.** Relating to the caudal end of the body in quadrupeds or the dorsal side in human beings and other primates. **3.** *Bot.* Next to or facing the main stem or axis. **4.** Coming after in order; following. **5.** Following in time; subsequent. —*n.* The buttocks. [Lat., comp. of *posterus*, coming after < *post*, afterward. See **apo-*.**] —**pos•te′ri•or•ly** *adv.*

pos•te•ri•or•i•ty (pŏ-stîr′ē-ôr′ĭ-tē, -ŏr′-, pō-) *n.* The condition of being posterior in location or time.

pos•ter•i•ty (pŏ-stĕr′ĭ-tē) *n.* **1.** Future generations. **2.** All of a person's descendants. [ME *posterite* < OFr. < Lat. *posteritās* < *posterus*, coming after. See POSTERIOR.]

pos•tern (pō′stərn, pŏs′tərn) *n.* A small rear gate, esp. one in a fort or castle. —*adj.* Situated in the back or at the side. [ME *posterne* < OFr., alteration of *posterle* < LLat. *posterula*, dim. of Lat. *posterus*, behind. See POSTERIOR.]

poster paint *n.* See **tempera** 1.

Post Exchange A service mark used for a store on a military base that sells goods to military personnel and their families or to authorized civilians.

post•ex•il•ic (pōst′ĕg-zĭl′ĭk, -ĕk-sĭl′-) also **post•ex•il•i•an** (-ĕg-zĭl′ē-ən, -zĭl′yən, -ĕk-sĭl′ē-ən, -sĭl′yən) *adj.* Of or relating to the period of Jewish history following the Babylonian captivity (after 586 B.C.).

post•fix (pōst-fĭks′) *Ling.* —*tr.v.* **-fixed, -fix•ing, -fix•es.** To suffix. —*n.* (pōst′fĭks′). A suffix. —**post•fix′al, post•fix′i•al** *adj.*

post•fron•tal (pōst-frŭn′tl) *adj.* **1.** At the back of the frontal bone; behind the forehead: *a postfrontal suture.* **2.** Toward the rear of the frontal lobe.

post•gan•gli•on•ic (pōst′găng-glē-ŏn′ĭk) *adj.* Located posterior or distal to a ganglion.

post•grad•u•ate (pōst-grăj′o͞o-ĭt, -āt′) *adj.* Of, relating to, or pursuing advanced study after graduation from high school or college. —*n.* One who is engaged in postgraduate study.

post•haste (pōst′hāst′) *adv.* With great speed; rapidly. —*n.* *Archaic.* Great speed; rapidity. [< the phrase *haste, post, haste*, a direction on letters.]

post hoc (hŏk, hōk) *adv. & adj.* In or of the form of an argument in which one event is asserted to have caused a later event simply because it happened earlier. [Lat., after this.]

post•hole (pōst′hōl′) *n.* A hole dug in the ground to hold a fence post.

post•hu•mous (pŏs′chə-məs) *adj.* **1.** Occurring or continuing after one's death. **2.** Published after the writer's death. **3.** Born after the death of the father: *a posthumous child.* [ME *posthumus* < LLat., alteration (perh. influenced by Lat. *humus*, earth or *humāre*, to bury) of *postumus*, superl. of *posterus*, coming after. See POSTERIOR.] —**post′hu•mous•ly** *adv.* —**post′hu•mous•ness** *n.*

post•hyp•not•ic suggestion (pōst′hĭp-nŏt′ĭk) *n.* A suggestion made to a hypnotized person that specifies an action to be performed after awakening, often in response to a cue.

pos•tiche (pô-stēsh′, pŏ-) *n.* **1.** Something false; a sham. **2.** A small hairpiece; a toupee. [Fr. < Ital. *posticcio* < *posto*, added (< Lat. *positus*, p.part. of *pōnere*, to place) or < VLat. **appostīcius* (alteration of Lat. *appositus*, p.part. of *appōnere*, to place by, to add : *ad-*, ad- + *pōnere*, to place; see **apo-***).]

pos•til•ion also **pos•til•lion** (pō-stĭl′yən, pŏ-) *n.* One who rides the near horse of the leaders to guide the horses drawing a coach. [Fr. *postillon* < Ital. *postiglione* < *posta*, mail < OItal., mail station. See POST³.]

post•im•pres•sion•ism (pōst′ĭm-prĕsh′ə-nĭz′əm) *n.* A school of painting in France in the late 19th century that rejected the objective naturalism of impressionism and used form and color in more personally expressive ways. —**post′im•pres′sion•ist** *n.* —**post′im•pres′sion•is′tic** *adj.*

post•in•dus•tri•al (pōst′ĭn-dŭs′trē-əl) *adj.* Of or relating to an economic period in which manufacturing lessens in importance in relation to services, information, and research.

post•lude (pōst′lo͞od′) *n.* **1.** *Mus.* **a.** An organ voluntary played at the end of a church service. **b.** A concluding piece. **2.** A final chapter or phase. [POST– + (PRE)LUDE.]

post•man (pōst′mən) *n.* See **mailman.**

post•mark (pōst′märk′) *n.* An official mark printed over a postage stamp, esp. one that cancels the stamp and records the date and place of mailing. —*tr.v.* **-marked, -mark•ing, -marks.** To stamp with such a mark.

post•mas•ter (pōst′măs′tər) *n.* A man in charge of the operations of a local post office. —**post′mas′ter•ship′** *n.*

postmaster general *n., pl.* **postmasters general.** The executive head of a national postal service.

post•me•rid•i•an (pōst′mə-rĭd′ē-ən) *adj.* Of, relating to, or taking place in the afternoon.

---

post•clas′si•cal *adj.*
post′co•lo′ni•al *adj.*
post′em•bry•on′ic *adj.*
post•gla′cial *adj.*
post′men•o•paus′al *adj.*
post•men′stru•al *adj.*
post•na′tal *adj.*
post•na′tal•ly *adv.*
post•nup′tial *adj.*
post•nup′tial•ly *adv.*
post•o′vu•la•to′ry *adj.*
post′war′ *adj.*

post me•rid•i•em (mə-rĭd′ē-əm) *adv. & adj.* After noon. Used chiefly in abbreviated form to tell time: *10:30 P.M.* See Usage Note at **ante meridiem.** [Lat. *post merīdiem* : *post*, after + *merīdiem*, accusative of *merīdiēs*, midday.]

post•mil•le•nar•i•an (pōst′mĭl-ə-nâr′ē-ən) *adj.* Of or relating to postmillennialism. — *n.* One who believes in postmillennialism.

post•mil•le•nar•i•an•ism (pōst′mĭl-ə-nâr′ē-ə-nĭz′əm) *n.* Postmillennialism.

post•mil•len•ni•al (pōst′mə-lĕn′ē-əl) also **post•mil•len•ni•an** (-ən) *adj.* Happening or existing after the millennium.

post•mil•len•ni•al•ism (pōst′mə-lĕn′ē-ə-lĭz′əm) *n.* The doctrine that Jesus's Second Coming will follow the millennium. — **post′mil•len′ni•al•ist** *n.*

post•mis•tress (pōst′mĭs′trĭs) *n.* A woman in charge of the operations of a local post office.

post•mod•ern or **post-mod•ern** (pōst-mŏd′ərn) *adj.* Of or relating to art, architecture, or literature that reacts against earlier modernist principles, as by using traditional, classical, or extreme modernist styles or practices. — **post•mod′ern•ism** *n.* — **post•mod′ern•ist** *adj.*

post•mor•tem (pōst-môr′təm) *adj.* **1.** Occurring or done after death. **2.** Of or relating to a medical examination of a dead body. — *n.* **1.** See **autopsy** 1. **2.** *Informal.* An analysis or review of a completed event. [Lat. *post mortem* : *post*, afterward; see POST– + *mortem*, accusative of *mors*, death; see **mer-***.] — **post mor′tem** *adv.*

post•na•sal drip (pōst-nā′zəl) *n.* The chronic secretion of mucus from the posterior nasal cavities, often caused by a cold or an allergy.

post•na•tal (pōst-nāt′l) *adj.* Of or occurring after birth, esp. immediately after birth. — **post•na′tal•ly** *adv.*

post office *n.* **1.** The public department responsible for the transportation and delivery of the mails. **2.** A local office where mail is received, sorted, and delivered, and where postal materials are sold. **3.** A game in which kisses are exchanged for pretended letters.

post office box *n.* A container at a central mailing location, in which incoming mail is held for one renting the container.

post•op•er•a•tive (pōst-ŏp′ər-ə-tĭv, -ŏp′rə-, -ŏp′ə-rā′-) *adj.* Happening or done after a surgical operation. — **post•op′er•a•tive•ly** *adv.*

post•or•bi•tal (pōst-ôr′bĭ-tl) *adj.* Situated behind the socket of the eye: *a postorbital bone.*

post•paid (pōst′pād′) *adj.* With the postage paid in advance.

post•par•tum (pōst-pär′təm) *adj.* Of or occurring in the period shortly after childbirth. [Lat. *post partum* : *post*, after; see POST– + *partum*, accusative of *partus*, birth < p.part. of *parere*, to beget; see **perə-[1]***.]

post-po•li•o syndrome (pōst-pō′lē-ō′) *n.* A condition affecting poliomyelitis patients several decades after the initial attack, characterized by fatigue, muscular deterioration, pain in the joints, and respiratory problems.

post•pone (pōst-pōn′, pōs-pōn′) *tr.v.* **-poned, -pon•ing, -pones. 1.** To delay until a future time; put off. **2.** To place after in importance; subordinate. [Lat. *postpōnere* : *post-*, post- + *pōnere*, to put; see POST[2].] — **post•pon′a•ble** *adj.* — **post•pone′ment** *n.* — **post•pon′er** *n.*

post•pose (pōst-pōz′) *v.* **-posed, -pos•ing, -pos•es.** — *tr.* To place (a word or phrasal constituent) after other constituents in a sentence, as the direct object noun phrase *all he had seen* in the sentence *He described to them all he had seen.* — *intr.* To become postposed.

post•po•si•tion (pōst′pə-zĭsh′ən) *n. Ling.* **1.** The placing of a word or suffixed element after the word to which it is grammatically related. **2.** A word or element placed postpositionally, as a preposition placed after its object. — **post′po•si′tion•al** *adj.* — **post′po•si′tion•al•ly** *adv.*

post•pos•i•tive (pōst-pŏz′ĭ-tĭv) *Ling.* — *adj.* Placed after or suffixed to another word. — *n.* A postpositive word or particle; a postposition. [LLat. *postpositīvus* < Lat. *postpositus*, p.part. of *postpōnere*, to put after. See POSTPONE.] — **post•pos′i•tive•ly** *adv.*

post•pran•di•al (pōst-prăn′dē-əl) *adj.* Following a meal, esp. dinner. — **post•pran′di•al•ly** *adv.*

post•pro•duc•tion (pōst′prə-dŭk′shən) *n.* A final stage in the production of a film or a television program, occurring after filming or videotaping and typically involving editing, special effects, titling, and the addition of soundtracks.

post•script (pōst′skrĭpt′, pōs′skrĭpt′) *n.* **1.** A message appended to a letter after the writer's signature. **2.** Additional information appended to the manuscript, as of a book. [Med. Lat. **postscriptum* < neut. p.part. of Lat. *postscrībere*, to write after : *post-*, post- + *scrībere*, to write; see **skrībh-***.]

post•syn•ap•tic (pōst′sĭ-năp′tĭk) *adj.* Situated behind or occurring after a synapse. — **post′syn•ap′ti•cal•ly** *adv.*

post time *n. Sports.* The time set immediately before the official start of a race after which no betting is allowed.

post•tran•scrip•tion•al (pōst′trăn-skrĭp′shə-nəl) *adj.* Occurring or formed after genetic transcription.

post•trans•fu•sion (pōst′trăns-fyo͞o′zhən) *adj.* Occurring after or as a consequence of blood transfusion.

post•trans•la•tion•al (pōst′trăns-lā′shə-nəl, -trănz-) *adj.* Occurring or formed after genetic translation.

post•trau•mat•ic (pōst′trou-măt′ĭk, -trô-) *adj.* Following injury or resulting from it: *posttraumatic amnesia.*

posttraumatic stress disorder *n.* A psychological disorder of individuals who have had profound trauma, such as torture, marked by recurrent flashbacks, nightmares, eating disorders, anxiety, fatigue, forgetfulness, and withdrawal.

pos•tu•lant (pŏs′chə-lənt) *n.* **1.** A person submitting a request or application; a petitioner. **2.** A candidate for admission into a religious order. [Fr. < OFr. < Lat. *postulāns*, *postulant-*, pr.part. of *postulāre*, to request. See POSTULATE.] — **pos′tu•lan•cy, pos′tu•lant•ship′** *n.*

pos•tu•late (pŏs′chə-lāt′) *tr.v.* **-lat•ed, -lat•ing, -lates. 1.** To make claim for; demand. **2.** To assume or assert the truth, reality, or necessity of, esp. as a basis of an argument. **3.** To assume as a premise or axiom; take for granted. See Syns at **presume.** — *n.* (pŏs′chə-lĭt, -lāt′). **1.** Something assumed without proof as being self-evident or generally accepted, esp. when used as a basis for an argument. **2.** A fundamental element; a basic principle. **3.** *Math.* An axiom. **4.** A requirement; a prerequisite. [Med.Lat. *postulāre*, *postulāt-*, to nominate to a bishopric, to assume < Lat., to request. See **prek-***.] — **pos′tu•la′tion** *n.*

pos•tu•la•tor (pŏs′chə-lā′tər) *n.* **1.** One who postulates. **2.** *Rom. Cath. Ch.* A church official who presents a plea for canonization or beatification.

pos•ture (pŏs′chər) *n.* **1.a.** A position of the body or of body parts. **b.** An attitude; a pose. **2.** A characteristic way of bearing one's body; carriage. **3.** Relative placement or arrangement. **4.** A stance or disposition with regard to something. **5.** A frame of mind affecting one's thoughts or behavior; an overall attitude. — *v.* **-tured, -tur•ing, -tures.** — *intr.* **1.** To assume an exaggerated or unnatural pose or mental attitude; attitudinize. **2.** To assume a pose. — *tr.* To put into a specific posture; pose. [Fr. < Ital. *postura* < Lat. *positūra*, position < *positus*, p.part. of *pōnere*, to place. See **apo-***.] — **pos′tur•al** *adj.* — **pos′tur•er, pos′tur•ist** *n.*

post•ver•te•bral (pōst-vûr′tə-brəl, pōst′vər-tē′-) *adj.* Situated behind the vertebrae: *postvertebral muscles.*

post•vo•cal•ic (pōst′vō-kăl′ĭk) *adj. Ling.* **1.** Being a consonant or consonantal sound directly following a vowel. **2.** Of, relating to, or being a form of a linguistic element, such as a suffix or word, that occurs only after vowels.

po•sy (pō′zē) *n., pl.* **-sies. 1.** A flower or bunch of flowers; a nosegay. **2.** *Archaic.* A brief verse or sentimental phrase, esp. one inscribed on a trinket. [Alteration of POESY, motto or line of verse (archaic).]

pot[1] (pŏt) *n.* **1.** Any of various usu. domestic containers made of pottery, metal, or glass, as: **a.** A round, fairly deep cooking vessel with a handle and often a lid. **b.** A short round container for storing or serving food: *a jam pot.* **c.** A coffeepot. **d.** A teapot. **2.a.** Such a container and its contents: *a pot of stew.* **b.** A potful. **3.a.** A large drinking cup; a tankard. **b.** A drink of liquor contained in such a cup. **4.** An artistic or decorative ceramic vessel of any shape. **5.** A flowerpot. **6.** Something, such as a chimney pot, that resembles a round cooking vessel in appearance or function. **7.** A trap for fish or crustaceans, typically a wicker or wire basket or cage. **8.** *Games.* **a.** The total amount staked by all the players in one hand at cards. See Syns at **bet. b.** The area on a card table where stakes are placed. **c.** A shot in billiards or related games intended to send a ball into a pocket. **9.** *Informal.* A common fund to which members of a group contribute. **10.** *Informal.* A large amount. Often used in the plural: *pots of money.* **11.** *Informal.* A potshot. **12.** *Informal.* A potbelly. **13.** *Informal.* A potty or toilet. **14.** See **potentiometer** 2. — *v.* **pot•ted, pot•ting, pots.** — *tr.* **1.** To place or plant in a pot. **2.** To preserve (food) in a pot. **3.** To cook in a pot. **4.** To shoot (game) for food rather than for sport. **5.** *Informal.* To shoot with a potshot. **6.** *Informal.* To win or capture; bag. **7.** *Games.* To hit (a ball) into a pocket. — *intr. Informal.* To take a potshot. [ME < OE *pott* < VLat. **pottus.*]

pot[2] (pŏt) *n. Slang.* Marijuana. [?]

pot. *abbr.* Potential.

po•ta•ble (pō′tə-bəl) *adj.* Fit to drink. — *n.* A beverage, esp. an alcoholic beverage. [ME < OFr. < LLat. *pōtābilis* < Lat. *pōtāre*, to drink < *pōtus*, a drink. See **pō(i)-***.] — **po′ta•bil′i•ty, po′ta•ble•ness** *n.*

po•tage (pō-täzh′) *n.* A thick, often creamy soup. [Fr. < OFr. See POTTAGE.]

pot•a•mo•plank•ton (pŏt′ə-mō-plăngk′tən) *n.* The plankton of rivers or streams. [Gk. *potamos*, river; see HIPPOPOTAMUS + PLANKTON.]

Po•ta•ro (pə-tär′ō, pô-tä′rô). A river, c. 161 km (100 mi), of central Guyana; site of Kaieteur Falls.

pot•ash (pŏt′ăsh′) *n.* **1.** See **potassium carbonate. 2.** See **potassium hydroxide. 3.** Any of several compounds containing potassium, esp. potassium oxide, potassium chloride, and various potassium sulfates, used chiefly in fertilizers. [Sing. of obsolete *pot ashes*, translated < obsolete Du. *potaschen* (this substance originally being obtained from wood ashes).]

ă **pat**	oi **boy**
ā **pay**	ou **out**
âr **care**	o͝o **took**
ä **father**	o͞o **boot**
ĕ **pet**	ŭ **cut**
ē **be**	ûr **urge**
ĭ **pit**	th **thin**
ī **pie**	*th* **this**
îr **pier**	hw **which**
ŏ **pot**	zh **vision**
ō **toe**	ə **a**bout,
ô **paw**	**i**tem

Stress marks:
′ (primary);
′ (secondary), as in
dictionary (dĭk′shə-nĕr′ē)

potash feldspar *n.* See **orthoclase.**

potash mu•ri•ate (myo͝or′ē-ĭt, -āt′) *n.* See **potassium chloride.**

po•tas•si•um (pə-tăs′ē-əm) *n.* *Symbol* **K** A soft, highly or explosively reactive metallic element that occurs in nature only in compounds and is found in or converted to a wide variety of salts used esp. in fertilizers and soaps. Atomic number 19; atomic weight 39.102; melting point 63.65°C; boiling point 774°C; specific gravity 0.862; valence 1. See table at **element.** [< POTASH.] — **po•tas′sic** *adj.*

po•tas•si•um-ar•gon (pə-tăs′ē-əm-är′gŏn′) *adj.* Of, relating to, or being a geologic dating method relying on the percentage of potassium that has radioactively decayed to argon in a specimen.

potato
Solanum tuberosum

potassium bicarbonate *n.* A compound, $KHCO_3$, in the form of a white powder or colorless crystals, used in baking powder and as an antacid medicine.

potassium bitartrate *n.* A white acid crystalline solid or powder, $KHC_4H_4O_6$, used in baking powder, in the tinning of metals, and as a component of laxatives.

potassium bromide *n.* A crystalline solid or powder, KBr, used as a sedative, in photography and lithography.

potassium carbonate *n.* A transparent, deliquescent granular powder, K_2CO_3, used in making glass, enamels, and soaps.

potassium chlorate *n.* A poisonous crystalline compound, $KClO_3$, used as an oxidizing agent, a bleach, and a disinfectant and in making explosives, matches, and fireworks.

potassium chloride *n.* A crystalline solid or powder, KCl, used in fertilizers and in the preparation of most potassium salts.

potassium cyanide *n.* A poisonous compound, KCN, used in the extraction of gold and silver from ores, in electroplating and photography, and as a fumigant and insecticide.

potassium dichromate *n.* A crystalline compound, $K_2Cr_2O_7$, used as an oxidizing agent and in explosives.

potassium hydroxide *n.* A caustic white solid, KOH, used as a bleach and in the manufacture of soaps, dyes, alkaline batteries, and many potassium compounds.

potassium iodide *n.* A white crystalline compound, KI, used in photography and medicine and as an analytical reagent.

potassium mu•ri•ate (myo͝or′ē-ĭt, -āt′) *n.* See **potassium chloride.**

potassium nitrate *n.* A crystalline compound, KNO_3, used to pickle meat and in the manufacture of pyrotechnics, explosives, matches, rocket propellants, and fertilizers.

potassium permanganate *n.* A dark purple crystalline compound, $KMnO_4$, used as an oxidizing agent and disinfectant and in deodorizers and dyes.

potassium sodium tartrate *n.* An efflorescent crystalline compound, $KNaC_4H_4O_6{\cdot}4H_2O$, used in making mirrors, in electronics, and as a laxative.

potassium sulfate *n.* A crystalline compound, K_2SO_4, used in glassmaking and fertilizers and as an analytical reagent.

po•ta•tion (pō-tā′shən) *n.* **1.** The act of drinking. **2.** A drink, esp. of an alcoholic beverage. [ME *potacion* < OFr. < Lat. *pōtātiō*, *pōtātiōn-*, a drinking party < *pōtātus*, p.part. of *pōtāre*, to drink < *pōtus*, a drink. See **pō(i)-*.**]

po•ta•to (pə-tā′tō) *n.*, *pl.* **-toes. 1.** A South American plant *(Solanum tuberosum)* widely cultivated for its starchy edible tubers. **2.** A tuber of this plant. **3.** A sweet potato. See Regional Note at **possum.** [Sp. *patata*, alteration (prob. influenced by Quechua *papa*, white potato) of Taino *batata*, sweet potato.]

potato beetle *n.* The Colorado potato beetle.

potato bug *n.* The Colorado potato beetle.

potato chip *n.* A thin slice of potato fried in deep fat until crisp and then salted. Often used in the plural.

po•ta•to•ry (pō′tə-tôr′ē, -tōr′ē) *adj.* Of, relating to, or given to drinking. [LLat. *pōtātōrius* < Lat. *pōtātus*, p.part. of *pōtāre*, to drink < *pōtus*, a drink. See **pō(i)-*.**]

potato skin *n.* A slice of baked potato skin topped with cheese or meat and usu. broiled or baked and served as an appetizer. Often used in the plural.

potato yam *n.* See **air potato.**

pot-au-feu (pô-tō-fœ′) *n.*, *pl.* **pot-au-feu.** A French dish of boiled meats and vegetables. [Fr. : *pot*, pot + *au*, on the + *feu*, fire.]

Pot•a•wat•o•mi (pŏt′ə-wŏt′ə-mē) *n.*, *pl.* **Potawatomi** or **-mis. 1.** A member of a Native American people formerly located in Michigan, Wisconsin, Illinois, and Indiana, with present-day populations in Oklahoma, Kansas, Michigan, and Ontario. **2.** Their Algonquian language.

potbelly stove

pot•bel•lied stove (pŏt′bĕl′ēd) *n.* See **potbelly stove.**

pot•bel•ly (pŏt′bĕl′ē) *n.*, *pl.* **-lies. 1.** A protruding abdominal region. **2.** A potbelly stove. — **pot′bel′lied** *adj.*

potbelly stove *n.* A short rounded stove in which wood or coal is burned.

pot•boil (pŏt′boil′) *intr.v.* **-boiled, -boil•ing, -boils.** To produce potboilers. [Back-formation < POTBOILER.]

pot•boil•er (pŏt′boi′lər) *n.* A literary or artistic work of poor quality, produced quickly for profit. [< the phrase *boil the pot*, to provide one's livelihood.]

pot•bound (pŏt′bound′) *adj.* Having grown too large for its container, resulting in matting or tangling of the roots.

pot•boy (pŏt′boi′) *n.* *Chiefly British.* A boy or man who works in an inn or a public house.

pot cheese *n.* See **cottage cheese.**

po•teen (pō-tēn′) *n.* Unlawfully distilled Irish whiskey. [Ir. Gael. *poitín*, small pot, poteen < *pota*, pot < POT[1].]

Po•tem•kin (pō-tĕm′kĭn, pə-, pə-tyôm′-), **Grigori Aleksandrovich.** 1739–91. Russian army officer who helped Catherine II seize power in 1762.

Potemkin village *n.* Something that appears elaborate and impressive but in actual fact lacks substance. [After Grigori Aleksandrovich POTEMKIN, who had elaborate fake villages constructed for some of Catherine the Great's tours.]

po•tence (pōt′ns) *n.* Potency.

po•ten•cy (pōt′n-sē) *n.*, *pl.* **-cies. 1.** The quality or condition of being potent. **2.** Inherent capacity for growth and development; potentiality.

po•tent (pōt′nt) *adj.* **1.** Possessing inner or physical strength; powerful. **2.a.** Exerting or capable of exerting strong physiological or chemical effects: *potent liquor.* **b.** Exerting or capable of exerting strong influence; cogent: *potent arguments.* **3.** Having great control or authority. **4.** Able to have sexual intercourse. Used of a male. [ME < Lat. *potēns*, *potent-*, pr.part. of *posse*, to be able. See **poti-*.**] — **po′tent•ly** *adv.* — **po′tent•ness** *n.*

po•ten•tate (pōt′n-tāt′) *n.* **1.** One who has the power and position to rule over others; a monarch. **2.** One who dominates or leads a group or an endeavor: *industrial potentates.* [ME *potentat* < OFr. < LLat. *potentātus* < Lat., power < *potēns*, pr.part. of *posse*, to be able. See POTENT.]

po•ten•tial (pə-tĕn′shəl) *adj.* **1.** Capable of being but not yet in existence; latent: *a potential problem.* **2.** Having possibility, capability, or power. **3.** *Gram.* Of, relating to, or being a verbal construction with auxiliaries such as *may* or *can*; for example, *It may snow.* — *n.* **1.** The inherent ability or capacity for growth, development, or realization. **2.** Something possessing the capacity for growth or development. **3.** *Gram.* A potential verb form. **4.** *Phys.* The work required to bring a unit electric charge, magnetic pole, or mass from an infinitely distant position to a designated point in a static electric, magnetic, or gravitational field, respectively. **5.** *Symbol* **V** *Elect.* The potential energy of a unit charge at any point in an electric circuit measured with respect to a specified reference point in the circuit or to ground; voltage. [ME *potencial* < OFr. *potenciel* < LLat. *potentiālis*, powerful < Lat. *potentia*, power < *potēns*, *potent-*, pr.part. of *posse*, to be able. See POTENT.] — **po•ten′tial•ly** *adv.*

potential energy *n.* The energy of a particle or system of particles derived from position or condition rather than motion.

po•ten•ti•al•i•ty (pə-tĕn′shē-ăl′ĭ-tē) *n.*, *pl.* **-ties. 1.** The state of being potential. **2.a.** Inherent capacity for growth, development, or realization. **b.** Something with such capacity.

po•ten•ti•ate (pə-tĕn′shē-āt′) *tr.v.* **-at•ed, -at•ing, -ates. 1.** To make potent or powerful. **2.** To enhance or increase the effect of (a drug). **3.** To promote or strengthen (a biochemical or physiological action or effect). [< Lat. *potentia*, power. See POTENTIAL.] — **po•ten′ti•a′tion** *n.*

po•ten•til•la (pōt′n-tĭl′ə) *n.* Any of numerous herbs or shrubs of the genus *Potentilla* of the North Temperate Zone, having compound leaves and flowers with many pistils. [Med. Lat., garden valerian < Lat. *potēns*, *potent-*, pr.part. of *posse*, to be able. See POTENT.]

po•ten•ti•om•e•ter (pə-tĕn′shē-ŏm′ĭ-tər) *n.* **1.** An instrument for measuring an unknown voltage by comparison to a standard voltage. **2.** A three-terminal resistor with an adjustable center connection, widely used for volume control in radio and television receivers. [POTENTI(AL) + -METER.] — **po•ten′ti•o•met′ric** (-ə-mĕt′rĭk) *adj.*

pot•ful (pŏt′fo͝ol′) *n.* **1.** The amount that a pot can hold. **2.** *Informal.* A large amount: *won a potful of money.*

pot•head (pŏt′hĕd′) *n.* *Slang.* A regular marijuana smoker.

poth•er (pŏ*th*′ər) *n.* **1.** A commotion; a disturbance. **2.** A state of nervous activity; a fuss. **3.** A cloud of smoke or dust that chokes or smothers. — *v.* **-ered, -er•ing, -ers.** — *tr.* To make confused; trouble; worry. — *intr.* To be overconcerned with trifles; fuss. [?]

pot•herb (pŏt′ûrb′, -hûrb′) *n.* A plant whose leaves, stems, or flowers are cooked and eaten or used as seasoning.

pot•hold•er (pŏt′hōl′dər) *n.* A small fabric pad used to handle hot cooking utensils.

pot•hole (pŏt′hōl′) *n.* **1.** A hole or pit, esp. one in a road surface. **2.** A deep round hole worn in rock by stones whirling in strong rapids or waterfalls. **3.** *Western U.S.* A place filled with mud or quicksand and hazardous to cattle.

pot•hook (pŏt′ho͝ok′) *n.* **1.** A bent or hooked piece of iron for hanging a pot or kettle over a fire. **2.** A curved iron rod with a hooked end used for lifting hot pots, irons, or stove lids. **3.** A curved S-shaped mark made in writing. **4.a.** Illegible handwriting or aimless scribbling. **b.** *Informal.* Stenographic writing. In both senses often used in the plural.

pot•house (pŏt′hous′) *n.* *Chiefly British.* A tavern.

pot•hunt•er (pŏt′hŭn′tər) *n.* **1.** One who hunts game for food, ignoring the rules of sport. **2.** One who participates in contests simply to win prizes. **3.** A nonprofessional archaeologist. — **pot′hunt′ing** *n.*

po•tiche (pô-tēsh′) *n.* A vase or jar with a round or polygonal body tapering at the neck and having a removable cover. [Fr. < *pot,* pot < OFr. < VLat. **pottus.*]

po•tion (pō′shən) *n.* A liquid dose, esp. one of medicinal, magic, or poisonous content. [ME *pocion* < OFr. < Lat. *pōtiō, pōtiōn-.* See **pō(i)-*.**]

pot•latch (pŏt′lăch′) *n.* A ceremonial feast among certain Native American peoples of the northwest Pacific coast, as for a marriage or an accession, at which the host distributes gifts according to each guest's rank or status. [Chinook Jargon < Nootka *p'achitl,* to make a potlatch gift.]

pot•luck (pŏt′lŭk′) *n.* **1.** Whatever food happens to be available, esp. when offered to a guest: *Unannounced guests got potluck.* **2.** A meal at which each guest brings food to be shared. **3.** Whatever is available at a particular time.

pot marigold *n.* See **calendula.**

pot marjoram *n.* Marjoram.

Po•to•mac (pə-tō′mək). A community of central MD, a residential suburb of Washington DC Pop. 22,800.

Potomac River. A river of the E-central U.S. rising in NE WV and flowing c. 459 km (285 mi) to Chesapeake Bay.

Po•to•sí (pō-tə-sē′, pô-tô-). A city of S-central Bolivia SW of Sucre in the Andes at an altitude of c. 4,203 m (13,780 ft); founded after silver was discovered in 1545. Pop. 113,380.

pot•pie (pŏt′pī′) *n.* **1.** A mixture of meat or poultry and vegetables covered with a pastry crust and baked in a deep dish. **2.** A meat or poultry stew with dumplings.

pot•pour•ri (pō′po͝o-rē′) *n., pl.* **-ris. 1.** An incongruous combination. **2.** A miscellaneous anthology or collection. **3.** A mixture of dried flower petals and spices used to scent the air. [Fr. *pot pourri* (transl. of Sp. *olla podrida;* see OLLA PODRIDA) : *pot,* pot; see POTICHE + *pourri,* p.part. of *pourrir,* to rot (< OFr. *purir* < VLat. **putrire* < Lat. *putrēscere;* see PUTRID).]

pot roast *n.* A cut of beef that is browned and then cooked until tender, often with vegetables, in a covered pot.

Pots•dam (pŏts′dăm′). A city of NE Germany on the Havel R. near Berlin; site of the Potsdam Conference (Jul.–Aug. 1945), at which Allied leaders drew up plans for the postwar administration of Germany. Pop. 135,922.

pot•sherd (pŏt′shûrd′) also **pot•shard** (-shärd′) *n.* A pottery fragment, esp. one found in an archaeological excavation.

pot•shot also **pot shot** (pŏt′shŏt′) *n.* **1.** A random or easy shot. **2.** A criticism made without careful thought and aimed at a handy target for attack. [< a pothunter's shots.]

pot•stone (pŏt′stōn′) *n.* A variety of steatite once used to make cooking vessels.

pot•tage (pŏt′ĭj) *n.* **1.** A thick soup or stew of vegetables and sometimes meat. **2.** *Archaic.* Porridge. [ME *potage* < OFr. < *pot,* pot. See POTICHE.]

pot•ted (pŏt′ĭd) *adj.* **1.a.** Placed in a pot. **b.** Grown in a pot. **2.** Preserved in a pot, can, or jar. **3.** *Slang.* **a.** Intoxicated; drunk. **b.** Under the influence of a hallucinogen.

pot•ter[1] (pŏt′ər) *n.* One who makes pottery.

pot•ter[2] (pŏt′ər) *v. Chiefly British.* Var. of **putter[2].**

Pot•ter (pŏt′ər), **Beatrix.** 1866–1943. British writer and illustrator of *The Tale of Peter Rabbit* (1900).

Potter, Paul or **Paulus.** 1625–54. Dutch painter noted for his animal paintings, such as *Horses at Pasture* (1649).

Pot•ter•ies (pŏt′ə-rēz). A district of W-central England in the Trent R. valley; a center for the manufacture of china and earthenware since the 16th cent.

pot•ter's clay (pŏt′ərz) *n.* A clay free of iron, suitable for making pottery or for modeling.

potter's field *n.* A place for the burial of unknown or indigent persons. [< the potter's field mentioned in Matthew 27:7.]

potter's wheel *n.* A revolving, often treadle-operated horizontal disk on which clay is shaped manually.

potter wasp *n.* Any of various small black and yellow solitary wasps of the genus *Eumenes,* characteristically building pot-shaped nests of clay. Also called regionally *dirt dauber*

pot•ter•y (pŏt′ə-rē) *n., pl.* **-ies. 1.** Ware, such as pots, shaped from moist clay and hardened by heat. **2.** The craft or work of a potter. **3.** The place where a potter works. [Fr. *poterie* < OFr. < *potier,* potter < *pot,* pot. See POTICHE.]

pot•tle (pŏt′l) *n.* **1.** A pot or drinking vessel with a capacity of 2.0 quarts (1.9 liters). **2.** The liquid contained in a pottle. **3.** An old English liquid measure equal to 2.0 quarts (1.9 liters). [ME *potel* < OFr. < *pot,* pot. See POTICHE.]

pot•to (pŏt′ō) *n., pl.* **-tos.** Any of several small nocturnal African primates of the genera *Perodicticus* and *Arctocebus,* having a pointed snout and a stumplike tail. [Of Niger-Congo orig.; perh. akin to Wolof *pata,* a tailless monkey; or Akan (Twi) *apɔsɔ,* a fierce monkeylike animal.]

Pott's disease (pŏts) *n.* Partial destruction of the vertebral bones, usu. caused by a tuberculous infection and often producing curvature of the spine. [After Percival *Pott* (1714–88), British surgeon.]

Potts•town (pŏts′toun′). A borough of SE PA on the Schuylkill R. ESE of Reading. Pop. 21,831.

Potts•ville (pŏts′vĭl′). A city of E-central PA WNW of Allentown. Pop. 16,603.

pot•ty[1] (pŏt′ē) *adj.* **-ti•er, -ti•est.** *Chiefly British.* **1.** Of little importance; trivial. **2.** Slightly intoxicated. **3.** Somewhat silly or crazy; addlebrained. [Poss. < POT[1].]

pot•ty[2] (pŏt′ē) *n., pl.* **-ties.** A small pot for use as a toilet by an infant or young child.

pot•ty-chair (pŏt′ē-châr′) *n.* A small chair with an opening in the seat and a receptacle beneath, used in toilet training.

pouch (pouch) *n.* **1.** A small bag often closing with a drawstring and used esp. for carrying loose items in one's pocket. **2.** A bag or sack used to carry mail or diplomatic dispatches. **3.** A leather bag or case for carrying powder or small-arms ammunition. **4.** A sealed plastic or foil container used in packaging frozen or dehydrated food. **5.** Something resembling a bag in shape. **6.** *Zool.* A saclike structure, such as the abdominal pocket of marsupials. **7.** *Anat.* A pocketlike space in the body. **8.** *Scots.* A pocket. **9.** *Archaic.* A purse for small coins. — *v.* **pouched, pouch•ing, pouch•es.** — *tr.* **1.** To place in or as if in a pouch; pocket. **2.** To cause to resemble a pouch. **3.** To swallow. Used of certain birds or fishes. — *intr.* To assume the form of a pouch or pouchlike cavity. [ME < OFr., of Gmc. orig.] — **pouch′y** *adj.*

pouched (poucht) *adj.* Having a pouch, as a gopher or pelican.

pouf (po͞of) *n.* **1.** A woman's hairstyle popular in the 18th century, marked by high rolled puffs. **2.** A part of a garment that is gathered into a puff. **3.** A rounded ottoman. [Fr. < OFr., interjection for a fall, of imit. orig.] — **pouf′fy** *adj.*

Pough•keep•sie (pə-kĭp′sē, pō-). A city of SE NY on the Hudson R. N of New York City; settled in 1687. Pop. 28,844.

pouil•ly-fuis•sé (po͞o-yē′fwē-sā′) *n.* A dry white Burgundy wine. [After *Solutré-Pouilly* and *Fuissé* in E-central France.]

pou•lard also **pou•larde** (po͞o-lärd′) *n.* A young hen spayed for fattening. [Fr. *poularde* < *poule,* hen < OFr. < Lat. *pulla,* fem. of *pullus,* young of an animal, chicken. See **pau-*.**]

Pou•lenc (po͞o-lăNk′), **Francis.** 1899–1963. French composer and pianist whose works include the ballet *Les Biches* (1924).

poult (pōlt) *n.* A young fowl, esp. a turkey, chicken, or pheasant. [ME *pult,* short for *polet* < OFr. *poulet,* dim. of *poule, polle,* hen. See POULARD.]

poul•ter's measure (pōl′tərz) *n.* A metrical pattern employing couplets in which the first line is in iambic hexameter and the second is in iambic heptameter. [< obsolete *poulter,* a poultry dealer (< the practice of giving a few extra eggs in the dozen) < ME *pulter* < OFr. *pouletier.* See POULTRY.]

poul•tice (pōl′tĭs) *n.* A soft moist mass of bread, meal, clay, or other adhesive substance, usu. heated, spread on cloth, and applied to warm, moisten, or stimulate an aching or inflamed part of the body. — *tr.v.* **-ticed, -tic•ing, -tic•es.** To apply a poultice to. [ME *pultes* < Med.Lat. *pultēs,* thick paste < Lat., pl. of *puls, pult-,* pottage. See PULSE[2].]

poul•try (pōl′trē) *n.* Domestic fowls, such as chickens or turkeys, raised for meat or eggs. [ME *pultrie* < OFr. *pouletrie* < *pouletier,* poulterer < *poulet,* pullet. See PULLET.]

pounce[1] (pouns) *v.* **pounced, pounc•ing, pounc•es.** — *intr.* **1.** To spring or swoop with intent to seize someone or something. **2.** To attack suddenly. **3.** To seize something swiftly and eagerly. — *tr.* To seize with or as if with talons. — *n.* **1.** The act or an instance of pouncing. **2.** The talon or claw of a bird of prey. [< ME, talon of a hawk, perh. var. of *ponson,* pointed tool. See PUNCHEON[1].] — **pounc′er** *n.*

pounce[2] (pouns) *n.* **1.** A fine powder formerly used to smooth and finish writing paper and soak up ink. **2.** A fine powder, such as pulverized charcoal, dusted over a stencil to transfer a design. — *tr.v.* **pounced, pounc•ing, pounc•es. 1.** To sprinkle, smooth, or treat with pounce. **2.** To transfer (a stenciled design) with pounce. [Fr. *ponce* < OFr. < VLat. **pōmex, pōmic-* < Lat. *pūmex,* pumice.] — **pounc′er** *n.*

pounce[3] (pouns) *tr.v.* **pounced, pounc•ing, pounc•es.** To ornament (metal, for example) by perforating from the back with a pointed implement. [ME *pouncen,* prob. < OFr. *poinssonner* < *poinson,* pointed tool. See PUNCHEON[1].]

pounce box *n.* A small box with a perforated top, formerly used to sprinkle sand or pounce on writing paper.

poun•cet box (poun′sĭt) *n.* A small perfume box with a perforated top. [Perh. alteration of **pounced-box* < POUNCE[3].]

pound[1] (pound) *n., pl.* **pound** or **pounds. 1.a.** A unit of weight equal to 16 ounces (453.592 grams). **b.** A unit of apothecary weight equal to 12 ounces (373.242 grams). See table at **measurement. 2.** A unit of weight differing in various countries and times. **3.** A British unit of force equal to the weight of a standard one-pound mass where the local acceleration of gravity is 9.817 meters (32.174 feet) per second per second. **4.a.** The basic monetary unit of the United Kingdom, worth 20 shillings or 240 old pence before the decimalization of 1971. **b.** See table at **currency. 5.** A monetary unit of Scotland before 1707. [ME < OE *pund* < West Gmc. **punda-* < Lat. *(lībra) pondō,* (a pound) by weight. See **(s)pen-*.**]

pound[2] (pound) *v.* **pound•ed, pound•ing, pounds.** — *tr.* **1.** To strike repeatedly and forcefully. **2.** To beat to a powder or pulp; pulverize or crush. **3.** To instill by persistent, emphatic repetition. **4.** To assault with heavy gunfire. — *intr.* **1.** To

potter's wheel

ă pat	oi boy
ā pay	ou out
âr care	o͝o took
ä father	o͞o boot
ĕ pet	ŭ cut
ē be	ûr urge
ĭ pit	th thin
ī pie	*th* this
îr pier	hw which
ŏ pot	zh vision
ō toe	ə about,
ô paw	item

Stress marks:
′ (primary);
′ (secondary), as in
dictionary (dĭk′shə-nĕr′ē)

strike repeated vigorous blows. **2.** To move along heavily and noisily. **3.** To pulsate rapidly and heavily; throb. **4.** To move or work laboriously. —*n.* **1.** A heavy blow. **2.** The sound of a heavy blow; a thump. **3.** The act of pounding. —*idiom.* **pound the pavement.** *Slang.* To travel the streets on foot, esp. in search of work. [ME *pounden*, alteration of *pounen* < OE *pūnian*.] —**pound′er** *n.*

pound[3] (pound) *n.* **1.** A public enclosure for stray dogs or livestock. **2.** A place in which impounded property is held. **3.** An enclosure for trapping or keeping animals or fish. **4.** A place of confinement for lawbreakers. —*tr.v.* **pound•ed, pound•ing, pounds.** To confine in or as if in a pound; impound. [ME < OE *pund-*, enclosure, as in *pundfald*, pen.]

Pound (pound), **Ezra Loomis.** 1885–1972. Amer. writer whose influential poetic works include *Cantos* (1925–60).

Pound, Roscoe. 1870–1964. Amer. jurist who wrote *The Spirit of the Common Law* (1921).

pound•age[1] (poun′dĭj) *n.* **1.** A tax or commission based on value per pound sterling. **2.** A rate or charge based on weight in pounds. **3.** Weight measured in pounds.

powder horn
1767 American

pound•age[2] (poun′dĭj) *n.* **1.** Confinement of animals in a pound. **2.** A fee charged for the redemption of impounded animals or other property.

pound•al (poun′dl) *n.* A unit of force in the foot-pound-second system of measurement, equal to the force required to accelerate a one-pound mass one foot per second per second (approx. 0.138 newton). [POUND[1] + *-al* (as in QUINTAL).]

pound cake *n.* A rich yellow cake containing a large proportion of eggs, flour, butter, and sugar. [< the original recipe, calling for a pound each of butter, sugar, and flour.]

pound-fool•ish (pound′fo͞o′lĭsh) *adj.* Unwise in dealing with large sums of money or large matters. [< the phrase *penny-wise, pound-foolish.*]

pound scots *n.* See **pound[1]** 5.

pound sterling *n.* See **pound[1]** 4a.

pour (pôr, pōr) *v.* **poured, pour•ing, pours.** —*tr.* **1.** To make (a liquid or granular solid) stream or flow, as from a container. **2.** To send forth, produce, express, or utter copiously, as if in a stream or flood: *poured out my thoughts.* —*intr.* **1.** To stream or flow continuously or profusely. **2.** To rain hard or heavily. **3.** To pass or proceed in large numbers or quantity. **4.** To serve a beverage to a gathering. —*n.* A pouring or flowing forth, esp. a downpour of rain. [ME *pouren*, prob. < ONFr. *purer*, to sift, pour out < Lat. *pūrāre*, to purify < *pūrus*, pure. See **peuə-*.**] —**pour′er** *n.*

pour•boire (po͝or-bwär′) *n.* Money given as a gratuity; a tip. [Fr. < *pour boire*, for drinking : *pour*, for (< OFr. < Lat. *prō*; see PRO-[1]) + *boire*, to drink (< OFr. *boivre* < Lat. *bibere*; see BEVERAGE).]

pour•par•ler (po͝or′pär-lā′) *n.* Conversation or discussion preliminary to negotiation. [Fr. < OFr. : *pour*, for, before (< OFr. < Lat. *prō*; see PRO-[1]) + *parler*, to talk; see PARLEY.]

pour point *n.* The lowest temperature at which an oil or other liquid will pour under given conditions.

pousse-ca•fé (po͞os′kă-fā′) *n.* **1.** A drink consisting of several liqueurs of different densities, poured to form differently colored layers. **2.** A brandy or liqueur served after dinner with coffee. [Fr. : *pousse* (< *pousser*, to push < OFr.; see POUSSETTE) + *café*, coffee; see CAFÉ.]

pous•sette (po͞o-sĕt′) *n.* A country-dance figure in which couples or a couple join hands and swing around the floor. [Fr., pushpin, dim. of obsolete *pousse*, a push < *pousser*, to push < OFr. *poulser, pousser*, to push < Lat. *pulsāre*, freq. of *pellere*, to push. See **pel-[5]*.**]

Pous•sin (po͞o-săN′), **Nicolas.** 1594–1665. French painter whose works include *Landscape with Diogenes* (1648).

pout[1] (pout) *v.* **pout•ed, pout•ing, pouts.** —*intr.* **1.** To show displeasure or disappointment; sulk. **2.** To protrude the lips in displeasure or sulkiness. **3.** To project or protrude. —*tr.* **1.** To protrude (the lips). **2.** To utter or express with a pout. —*n.* **1.** A protrusion of the lips, esp. as an expression of sullen discontent. **2.** A fit of petulant sulkiness. Often used in the plural. [ME *pouten*, perh. of Scand. orig.] —**pout′y** *adj.*

pout[2] (pout) *n.*, *pl.* **pout** or **pouts.** Any of various freshwater or marine fishes, esp. the eelpout or hornpout. [ME **poute* < OE *-pūte*, as in *ǣlepūte*, eelpout.]

pout•er (pou′tər) *n.* **1.** One that pouts. **2.** One of a breed of pigeons capable of distending the crop until the breast becomes puffed out.

pov•er•ty (pŏv′ər-tē) *n.* **1.** The state of being poor; lack of the basic material goods. **2.** Deficiency in amount; scantiness. **3.** Unproductiveness; infertility. **4.** Renunciation by a member of a religious order of the right to own property. [ME *poverte* < OFr. < Lat. *paupertās* < *pauper*, poor. See **pau-*.**]

poverty grass *n.* Any of several North American grasses that grow in poor or sandy soil.

poverty level *n.* A minimum income level below which a person is officially considered to be living in poverty.

pov•er•ty-strick•en (pŏv′ər-tē-strĭk′ən) *adj.* Suffering from poverty; miserably poor. See Syns at **poor.**

POW (pē′ō-dŭb′əl-yo͞o, -yo͝o) *n.*, *pl.* **POW's** also **POWs.** A prisoner of war.

Pow•ay (pou′ā). A community of S CA N of San Diego. Pop. 43,516.

pow•der (pou′dər) *n.* **1.** A substance of ground, pulverized, or otherwise finely dispersed solid particles. **2.** Any of various preparations in powder form, as certain medicines. **3.** An explosive mixture, such as gunpowder. **4.** Light dry snow. —*v.* **-dered, -der•ing, -ders.** —*tr.* **1.** To reduce to powder; pulverize. **2.** To dust or cover with or as if with powder. —*intr.* **1.** To become powder; be pulverized. **2.** To use powder as a cosmetic. —*idioms.* **keep (one's) powder dry.** To be ready for a challenge with little warning. **take a powder.** To make a quick departure; run away. [ME *poudre* < OFr. < Lat. *pulvis, pulver-.*] —**pow′der•er** *n.*

powder blue *n. Color.* A moderate to pale blue or purplish blue. [< the color of powdered smalt.]

powder horn *n.* An animal's horn capped at the open end, used to carry gunpowder.

powder keg *n.* **1.** A small cask for holding gunpowder or other explosives. **2.** A potentially explosive situation or thing.

powder metallurgy *n.* The technology of powdered metals, esp. as used for fabricating massive materials and shaped objects.

powder monkey *n. Slang.* One who carries or sets explosives.

powder puff *n.* A soft pad for applying powder to the skin.

Pow•der River (pou′dər). A river rising in the Bighorn Mts. of central WY and flowing c. 782 km (486 mi) into S MT.

powder room *n.* **1.** A lavatory for women. **2.** A lavatory for guests in a private home.

pow•der•y (pou′də-rē) *adj.* **1.** Composed of or similar to powder. **2.** Dusted or covered with or as if with powder. **3.** Easily made into powder; friable.

powdery mildew *n.* **1.** Any of various fungi, esp. of the family Erysiphaceae, that produce powdery conidia on the host surface. **2.** A plant disease caused by any of these fungi.

Pow•ell (pou′əl), **Adam Clayton, Jr.** 1908–72. Amer. politician from NY who was an outspoken advocate of civil rights.

Powell, Anthony. b. 1905. British writer best known for *A Dance to the Music of Time* (1951–75).

Powell, Cecil Frank. 1903–69. British physicist who won a 1950 Nobel Prize.

Powell, John Wesley. 1834–1902. Amer. geologist and ethnologist who directed the U.S. Geological Survey (1881–94) and classified many Native American languages.

Powell, Lewis Franklin, Jr. b. 1907. Amer. jurist; associate justice of the U.S. Supreme Court (1971–87).

pow•er (pou′ər) *n.* **1.** The ability or capacity to perform or act effectively. **2.** A specific capacity, faculty, or aptitude. Often used in the plural. **3.** Strength or force exerted or capable of being exerted; might. See Syns at **strength. 4.** The ability or official capacity to exercise control; authority. **5.** A person, group, or nation having great influence or control over others. **6.** The might of a nation, political organization, or similar group. **7.** Forcefulness; effectiveness. **8.** *Chiefly Upper Southern U.S.* A large number or amount. **9.a.** The energy or motive force by which a physical system or machine is operated. **b.** The capacity of a system or machine to operate. **c.** Electrical or mechanical energy, esp. as used to assist or replace human energy. **d.** Electricity supplied to a home, building, or community. **10.** *Phys.* The rate at which work is done, expressed as the amount of work per unit time and commonly measured in units such as the watt and horsepower. **11.** *Elect.* **a.** The product of applied potential difference and current in a direct-current circuit. **b.** The product of the effective values of the voltage and current with the cosine of the phase angle between current and voltage in an alternating-current circuit. **12.** *Math.* **a.** See **exponent** 3. **b.** The number of elements in a finite set. **13.** *Statistics.* The probability of rejecting the null hypothesis where it is false. **14.** A measure of the magnification of an optical instrument, such as a telescope. **15. powers.** *Theol.* The sixth of the nine orders of angels. **16.** *Archaic.* An armed force. —*adj.* **1.** Of or relating to political, social, or economic control. **2.** Operated with mechanical or electrical energy in place of bodily exertion: *a power tool.* **3.** Of or relating to the generation or transmission of electricity. **4.** *Informal.* Of or relating to influential business or professional practices. —*tr.v.* **-ered, -er•ing, -ers.** To supply with power, esp. mechanical power. —*idiom.* **powers that be.** Those who hold effective power in a system or situation. [ME < OFr. *poeir*, to be able, power < VLat. **potēre*, to be able < *potis*, able, powerful. See **poti-*.**]

pow•er•boat (pou′ər-bōt′) *n.* See **motorboat.**

power broker or **pow•er•brok•er** (pou′ər-brō′kər) *n.* A person who exerts strong political or economic influence, esp. by virtue of the individuals and votes he or she controls.

power dive *n.* A downward plunge of an aircraft accelerated by both gravity and engine power. —**pow′er-dive′** *v.*

power drill *n.* **1.** A portable electric drill. **2.** A large drilling machine having a vertical, motorized drill set in a table stand.

pow•er•ful (pou′ər-fəl) *adj.* **1.** Having or capable of exerting power. **2.** Effective or potent. **3.** *Chiefly Upper Southern U.S.* Great. —*adv. Chiefly Upper Southern U.S.* Very. —**pow′er•ful•ly** *adv.* —**pow′er•ful•ness** *n.*

pow•er•house (pou′ər-hous′) *n.* **1.** See **power plant** 2. **2.** One with great force or energy.

pow•er•less (pou′ər-lĭs) *adj.* **1.** Lacking strength or power; helpless and totally ineffectual. **2.** Lacking legal or other authority. **— pow′er•less•ly** *adv.* **— pow′er•less•ness** *n.*

power mower *n.* A lawn mower powered by a gasoline or electric motor.

power of appointment *n., pl.* **powers of appointment.** *Law.* Authority granted to one person by another to transfer property upon the death of the latter.

power of attorney *n., pl.* **powers of attorney.** *Law.* A legal instrument authorizing one to act as another's attorney or agent.

power pack *n.* A usu. compact portable device that converts supply current to direct or alternating current as required by specific equipment.

power plant *n.* **1.** All the equipment, including structural members, that constitutes a unit power source: *the power plant of a truck.* **2.** A complex of structures, machinery, and associated equipment for generating electric energy from another source of energy, such as a hydroelectric dam.

power play *n.* **1.** *Sports.* **a.** An offensive maneuver in a team game, esp. in football, using massive concentration of players in a certain area. **b.** A temporary numerical advantage of one ice hockey team because the other team has one or more players in the penalty box. **2.** A strategic maneuver, as in politics, based on the use or threatened use of power for coercion.

power politics *n. (used with a sing. or pl. v.)* International diplomacy in which each nation uses or threatens to use military or economic power to further its own interests.

Pow•ers (pou′ərz), **Hiram.** 1805–73. Amer. sculptor whose works include *Greek Slave* (1843).

power series *n. Math.* A sum of successively higher integral powers of a variable or combination of variables, each multiplied by a constant coefficient.

power shovel *n.* A large, usu. mobile earthmoving machine having a boom and a hinged bucket for excavating.

power station *n.* See **power plant** 2.

power steering *n.* A device driven by the engine of a vehicle that facilitates the turning of the steering wheel by the driver.

power structure *n.* **1.** An elite group of people in influential positions within a government, a society, or an organization. **2.** A hierarchy of managerial authority.

power takeoff *n.* A mechanism attached to a motor vehicle engine that supplies power to a nonvehicular device, such as a pump or pneumatic hammer.

power train *n.* An assembly of gears and associated parts by which power is transmitted from an engine to a driving axle.

power trip *n. Slang.* An action undertaken chiefly for the gratification of exercising power over another or others. **— pow′er-trip′** (pou′ər-trĭp′) *v.* **— power tripper** *n.*

Pow•ha•tan^{1} (pou′ə-tăn′, pou-hăt′n). Orig. Wahunsonacock. 1550?–1618. Algonquian leader and father of Pocahontas who founded the Powhatan confederacy.

Pow•ha•tan^{2} (pou′ə-tăn′, pou-hăt′n) *n., pl.* **Powhatan** or **-tans. 1.** A member of a confederacy of Native American peoples of eastern Virginia in the 16th and 17th centuries, with present-day descendants in the same area. **2.** The Algonquian language of the Powhatan. [After POWHATAN^{1}.]

pow•wow (pou′wou′) *n.* **1.** A council or meeting with or of Native Americans. **2.a.** A Native American shaman. **b.** A ceremony conducted by a shaman, as in the performance of healing or hunting rituals. **3.** *Informal.* A conference or gathering. *— intr.v.* **-wowed, -wow•ing, -wows.** *Informal.* To hold a powwow. [Narragansett *powwaw*, shaman.]

Word History: Because trances were so important to the Native American shaman, the title *powah*, literally meaning "one who has visions," was accorded him. One of the early occurrences of this word represents the Puritan attitudes to Native American religions: "The office and dutie of the Powah is to be exercised principally in calling upon the Devil; and curing diseases of the sicke or wounded." The word whose spelling was eventually settled in English as *powwow* was also used as the name for ceremonies and councils, probably because of the shaman's important role in both. Eventually the newcomers decided that they could have powwows too, the first reference to one of these being recorded in the Salem, Massachusetts, *Gazette* of 1812: "The Warriors of the Democratic Tribe will hold a powwow at Agawam on Tuesday next."

Pow•ys (pō′ĭs). Family of British writers including the brothers **John Cowper Powys** (1872–1963), whose novels, such as *Wolf Solent* (1929), glorify nature; and **Theodore Francis Powys** (1875–1953), who wrote allegorical novels, such as *Mr. Weston's Good Wine* (1927).

pox (pŏks) *n.* **1.** A disease such as smallpox, characterized by purulent skin eruptions that may leave pockmarks. **2.** Syphilis. **3.** *Archaic.* Misfortune and calamity. [Alteration of *pocks* < ME, pl. of *pocke, pokke.* See POCK.]

pox•vi•rus (pŏks′vī′rəs) *n., pl.* **-rus•es.** Any of a group of DNA-containing viruses, including those that cause smallpox, cowpox, and other poxlike diseases in vertebrates.

Po•yang (pō′yäng′). A lake of E China SE of Wuhan; connected to the Yangtze R. (Chang Jiang) by canal.

Poz•nań (pōz′năn′, -nän′, pôz′nän′yə). A city of W-central Poland W of Warsaw. Pop. 579,100.

poz•zuo•la•na (pŏt′swə-lä′nə) or **pozzolan** (-sə-län′) also **poz•zo•la•na** (-sə-lä′nə) *n.* **1.** A siliceous volcanic ash used to produce hydraulic cement. **2.** Any of various artificially produced substances resembling pozzuolana ash. [Ital. *pozzolana*, after POZZUOLI.] **— poz′zuo•la′nic** *adj.*

Poz•zuo•li (pôt-swô′lē). A city of S Italy W of Naples on the **Bay of Pozzuoli**, a section of the Bay of Naples; founded by Greek exiles c. 529 B.C. Pop. 61,300.

pp or **pp.** *abbr. Mus.* Pianissimo.

pp. *abbr.* **1.** Pages. **2.** Or **PP.** Prepaid.

p.p.^{1} *abbr. Lat.* Per procurationem (by proxy).

p.p.^{2} or **P.P.** *abbr.* **1.** Parcel post. **2.** Parish priest. **3.** Or **pp.** Past participle. **4.** Postpaid.

ppb *abbr.* Parts per billion.

ppd. *abbr.* **1.** Postpaid. **2.** Prepaid.

ppm *abbr.* Parts per million.

P.P.S. also **p.p.s.** *abbr. Lat.* Post postscriptum (additional postscript).

ppt *abbr.* **1.** Parts per thousand. **2.** Parts per trillion.

PQ *abbr.* Province of Quebec.

Pr^{1} The symbol for the element **praseodymium.**

Pr^{2} *abbr.* **1.** Propyl. **2.** *Bible.* Proverbs.

PR *abbr.* **1.** Payroll. **2.** Also **P.R.** or **p.r.** Public relations. **3.** Or **P.R.** Puerto Rico.

pr. *abbr.* **1.** Pair. **2.** *Gram.* Present. **3.** Price. **4.a.** Printed. **b.** Printing. **5.** *Gram.* Pronoun.

Pr. *abbr.* **1.** Priest. **2.** Prince.

P.R. *abbr.* Proportional representation.

praam (präm) *n. New England, Chiefly British, & Naut.* Var. of **pram^{2}.**

prac•ti•ca•ble (prăk′tĭ-kə-bəl) *adj.* **1.** Capable of being effected, done, or put into practice; feasible. **2.** Usable for a specified purpose: *a practicable way of entry.* [Med.Lat. *practicābilis*, capable of being used < *practicāre*, to practice < *prāctica*, practice < LLat. *prāctica*, practical as against contemplative life < Gk. *praktikē*, fem. of *praktikos*, practical. See PRACTICE.] **— prac′ti•ca•bil′i•ty** *n.* **— prac′ti•ca•bly** *adv.*

Usage Note: *Practicable* means "feasible" as well as "usable" and hence overlaps in meaning to some extent with *practical*, which can mean "useful." However, *practicable* does not share any other senses with *practical.*

prac•ti•cal (prăk′tĭ-kəl) *adj.* **1.** Of, relating to, governed by, or acquired through practice or action, rather than theory, speculation, or ideals. **2.** Manifested in or involving practice. **3.** Actually engaged in a specified occupation or a certain kind of work; practicing. **4.** Capable of being used or put into effect; useful. See Usage Note at **practicable. 5.** Intended to serve a purpose without elaboration. **6.** Concerned with the production or operation of something useful. **7.** Level-headed, efficient, and unspeculative. **8.** Being actually so in almost every respect; virtual. [ME *practicale* < Med.Lat. *practicālis* < LLat. *prācticus* < Gk. *praktikos* < *prassein*, to make, do.] **— prac′ti•cal′i•ty** (-kăl′ĭ-tē), **prac′ti•cal•ness** *n.*

practical joke *n.* A mischievous trick, esp. one that causes embarrassment, indignity, or discomfort. **— practical joker** *n.*

prac•ti•cal•ly (prăk′tĭk-lē) *adv.* **1.** In a practical way. **2.** For all practical purposes; virtually. **3.** All but; nearly; almost.

practical nurse *n.* **1.** A licensed practical nurse. **2.** One with practical experience but no degree in nursing.

prac•tice (prăk′tĭs) *v.* **-ticed, -tic•ing, -tic•es.** *— tr.* **1.** To do or perform habitually or customarily; make a habit of. **2.** To do or perform (something) repeatedly in order to acquire or polish a skill. **3.** To give lessons or repeated instructions to; drill. **4.** To work at, esp. as a profession: *practice law.* **5.** To carry out in action; observe. **6.** *Obsolete.* To plot (something evil). *— intr.* **1.** To do or perform something habitually or repeatedly. **2.** To do something repeatedly in order to acquire or polish a skill. **3.** To work at a profession. **4.** *Archaic.* To intrigue or plot. *— n.* **1.** A habitual or customary action or way of doing something. **2.a.** Repeated performance of an activity in order to learn or perfect a skill. **b.** *Archaic.* The skill so learned or perfected. **c.** The condition of being skilled through repeated exercise. **3.** The act or process of doing something; performance or action. **4.** Exercise of an occupation or a profession. **5.** The business of a professional person. **6.** A habitual or customary action or act. Often used in the plural. **7.** *Law.* The methods of procedure used in a court of law. **8.** *Archaic.* **a.** The act of tricking or scheming, esp. with malicious intent. **b.** A trick, a scheme, or an intrigue. [ME *practisen* < OFr. *practiser*, alteration of *practiquer* < *practique*, practice < LLat. *prāctice*, practical. See PRACTICABLE.] **— prac′tic•er** *n.*

Syns: *practice, drill, exercise, rehearse.* The central meaning shared by these verbs is "to do or cause to do again and again in order to acquire proficiency": *practice the shot put; drill pupils in the multiplication tables; exercising one's wits; an actor rehearsing a role.* See also Syns at **habit.**

prac•ticed (prăk′tĭst) *adj.* **1.** Skilled or expert; proficient.

ă **pat**	oi **boy**
ā **pay**	ou **out**
âr **care**	o͝o **took**
ä **father**	o͞o **boot**
ĕ **pet**	ŭ **cut**
ē **be**	ûr **urge**
ĭ **pit**	th **thin**
ī **pie**	*th* **this**
îr **pier**	hw **which**
ŏ **pot**	zh **vision**
ō **toe**	ə **about,** item
ô **paw**	

Stress marks:
′ (primary);
′ (secondary), as in
dictionary (dĭk′shə-nĕr′ē)

prairie dog
Black-tailed prairie dog
Cynomys ludovicianus

prayer rug
19th-century Turkish

2. Acquired or brought to perfection by practice.

practice teacher *n.* See **student teacher.** —**prac′tice-teach′** (prăk′tĭs-tēch′) *v.* —**practice teaching** *n.*

prac•tic•ing (prăk′tĭ-sĭng) *adj.* Actively engaged in or observing, esp. a given profession or religion: *a practicing attorney.*

prac•ti•cum (prăk′tĭ-kəm) *n.* A school or college course, esp. one in a specialized field, designed to give students supervised practical experience. [Ger. *Praktikum* < LLat. *prāctĭcum,* neut. of *prāctĭcus,* practical. See PRACTICAL.]

prac•tise (prăk′tĭs) *v. & n. Chiefly British.* Var. of **practice.**

prac•ti•tion•er (prăk-tĭsh′ə-nər) *n.* One who practices something, esp. an occupation, a profession, or a technique. [Alteration of *practician* < OFr. *practicien* < *practiser,* to practice. See PRACTICE.]

prae•di•al also **pre•di•al** (prē′dē-əl) *adj.* **1.** Relating to, containing, or possessing land; landed. **2.** Attached to, bound to, or arising from the land: *praedial serfs.* [ME < Med.Lat. *praediālis,* of an estate < Lat. *praedium,* estate < *praes, praed-,* surety, bondsman : *prae-,* pre- + *vas-,* guarantor.]

prae•mu•ni•re (prē′myo͝o-nī′rē) *n. Law.* **1.** The offense under English law of appealing to or obeying a foreign court or authority, thus challenging the supremacy of the Crown. **2.** The writ charging this offense. **3.** The penalty for it. [Short for ME *premunire facias,* a writ of premunire < Med.Lat. *praemūnīre faciās : praemūnīre,* to warn (< Lat., to fortify : *prae-,* pre- + *mūnīre,* to defend) + Lat. *faciās,* that you cause, second pers. sing. pr. subjunctive of *facere,* to do.]

prae•no•men (prē-nō′mən) *n., pl.* **-no•mens** or **-nom•i•na** (-nŏm′ə-nə, -nō′mə-). **1.** A first or given name. **2.** The first name of a citizen of ancient Rome, as *Gaius* in *Gaius Julius Caesar.* [Lat. *praenōmen : prae-,* pre- + *nōmen,* name; see **nō-men-***.] —**prae•nom′i•nal** (-nŏm′ə-nəl) *adj.*

prae•tor also **pre•tor** (prē′tər) *n.* An annually elected magistrate of the ancient Roman Republic, ranking below but having approximately the same functions as a consul. [ME *pretor* < OFr. < Lat. *praetor,* perh. < *praeīre,* to go before : *prae-,* pre- + *īre,* to go; see **ei-***.] —**prae•to′ri•al** (prē-tôr′ē-əl, -tōr′-) *adj.* —**prae′tor•ship′** *n.*

prae•to•ri•an also **pre•to•ri•an** (prē-tôr′ē-ən, -tōr′-) —*adj.* **1.** Of or relating to a praetor or the praetorship. **2. Praetorian.** Of or belonging to the Praetorian Guard. **3.** Venal; corruptible. —*n.* **1.** A praetor or an ex-praetor. **2. Praetorian.** A member of the Praetorian Guard.

Praetorian Guard *n.* **1.** The elite bodyguard of a Roman emperor. **2.** A member of the Praetorian Guard. [Originally the bodyguard of a praetor or a general.]

prag•mat•ic (prăg-măt′ĭk) *adj.* **1.** Concerned with facts or actual occurrences; practical. **2.** *Philos.* Of or relating to pragmatism. **3.** Relating to or being the study of cause and effect in history with emphasis on the practical lessons that they offer. **4.** *Archaic.* **a.** Active; busy. **b.** Active in an officious or meddlesome way. **c.** Dogmatic; dictatorial. —*n.* **1.** A pragmatic sanction. **2.** *Archaic.* A meddler; a busybody. [Lat. *prāgmaticus,* skilled in business < Gk. *pragmatikos* < *pragma, pragmat-,* deed < *prassein,* to do.] —**prag•mat′i•cal** *adj.* —**prag•mat′i•cal•ly** *adv.*

prag•mat•ics (prăg-măt′ĭks) *n.* (*used with a sing. v.*) *Ling.* The study of language as it is used in a given context.

pragmatic sanction *n.* An edict or a decree issued by a sovereign that becomes part of the fundamental law of the land. [Transl. of LLat. *pragmatica sanctiō,* imperial decree referring to the affairs of a community.]

prag•ma•tism (prăg′mə-tĭz′əm) *n.* **1.** *Philos.* A movement consisting of various related theories and distinguished by the doctrine that the meaning of an idea or a proposition lies in its observable practical consequences. **2.** A practical matter-of-fact way of approaching or assessing situations or of solving problems. —**prag′ma•tist** *n.* —**prag′ma•tis′tic** *adj.*

Prague (präg). The cap. of Czech Republic, in the W part on the Vltava R.; the cap. of Czechoslovakia from 1918 to 1992. Pop. 1,189,828.

pra•hu (prä′o͞o) *n. Naut.* Var. of **proa.**

Prai•a (prī′ə). The cap. of Cape Verde, on the SE coast of São Tiago I. Pop. 37,480.

prai•rie (prâr′ē) *n.* An extensive area of flat or rolling grassland, esp. the large plain of central North America. [Fr. <OFr. *praierie* < VLat. **prātāria* < Lat. *prāta,* meadow.]

prairie chicken *n.* Either of two birds *(Tympanuchus cupido* or *T. pallidicinctus)* of the grouse family, found in western North America and having mottled brownish plumage.

prairie dog *n.* Any of several burrowing rodents of the genus *Cynomys* in the squirrel family, having light brown fur and a warning call similar to a dog's bark.

prairie oyster *n.* **1.** *Slang.* A drink made from a whole raw egg yolk, Worcestershire sauce, hot sauce, salt, and pepper that is taken as a palliative for a hangover or as a cure for hiccups. **2.** *Regional.* The testis of a calf, cooked and served as food.

prairie potato *n.* See **breadroot.**

Prai•rie Provinces (prâr′ē). The Canadian provinces of Manitoba, Saskatchewan, and Alberta.

prairie schooner *n.* A covered wagon drawn by horses or oxen and used by pioneers in crossing North America.

Prairie Village. A city of NE KS, a suburb of Kansas City. Pop. 23,186.

prairie wolf *n.* See **coyote.**

praise (prāz) *n.* **1.** Expression of approval, commendation, or admiration. **2.** The extolling or exaltation of a deity, ruler, or hero. **3.** *Archaic.* A reason for praise; merit. —*tr.v.* **praised, prais•ing, prais•es. 1.** To give praise to or for. **2.** To extol or exalt; worship. [ME *preise* < *preisen,* to praise < OFr. *preisier* < LLat. *pretiāre,* to prize < Lat. *pretium,* price. See **per-**[5]***.] —**prais′er** *n.*

Syns: praise, acclaim, commend, extol, laud. These verbs mean to express approval or admiration. To *praise* is to voice approbation, commendation, or esteem: *"She was enthusiastically praising the beauties of Gothic architecture"* (Francis Marion Crawford). *Acclaim* usually implies hearty approbation warmly and publicly expressed: *a highly acclaimed film. Commend* suggests moderate or restrained approval, as from a superior: *The judge commended the jury for their hard work. Extol* suggests exaltation or glorification: *"that sign of old age, extolling the past"* (Sydney Smith). *Laud* connotes respectful, often inordinate praise: *"aspirations which are lauded up to the skies"* (Charles Kingsley).

praise•wor•thy (prāz′wûr′thē) *adj.* **-thi•er, -thi•est.** Meriting praise; highly commendable. —**praise′wor′thi•ly** *adv.* —**praise′wor′thi•ness** *n.*

Pra•krit (prä′krĭt) *n.* Any of various vernacular and literary Indic languages recorded from the third century B.C. to the fourth century A.D. [< Skt. *prākṛta-,* natural, vulgar, vernacular : *pra-,* before, forward; see **per**[1]* + *karoti,* he makes; see SANSKRIT.] —**Pra•krit′ic** *adj.*

pra•line (prä′lēn′, prā′-) *n.* A confection made of nut kernels, esp. almonds or pecans, stirred in boiling sugar syrup until crisp and brown. [Fr., after César de Choiseul, Comte du Plessis-*Praslin* (1598–1675), French army officer.]

prall•tril•ler (präl′trĭl′ər) *n. Mus.* A trill consisting of alternation between a written note and the note immediately above it. [Ger. : *prallen,* to rebound (alteration of MHGer. *prellen*) + *Triller,* trill (< Ital. *trillo* < *trillare,* to trill, prob. of imit. orig.).]

pram[1] (prăm) *n. Chiefly British.* A baby carriage. [Shortening and alteration of PERAMBULATOR.]

pram[2] also **praam** (präm) *n.* **1.** *New England & Chiefly British.* A small dinghy having a flat snub-nosed bow. **2.** *Naut.* A flat-bottomed boat used chiefly in the Baltic Sea as a barge. [Du. *praam,* flatbottom boat < MDu. *praem* < Czech *prám.* See **per**[1]***.]

prance (prăns) *v.* **pranced, pranc•ing, pranc•es.** —*intr.* **1.a.** To spring forward on the hind legs. Used of a horse. **b.** To spring or bound forward in a manner reminiscent of a spirited horse. **2.** To ride a prancing horse. **3.** To walk or move about in a spirited manner; strut. —*tr.* To cause (a horse) to prance. —*n.* The act or an instance of prancing. [ME *prauncen.*] —**pranc′er** *n.* —**pranc′ing•ly** *adv.*

pran•di•al (prăn′dē-əl) *adj.* Of or relating to a meal. [< Lat. *prandium,* late breakfast. See **ed-***.] —**pran′di•al•ly** *adv.*

prang (prăng) *tr.v.* **pranged, prang•ing, prangs.** *Chiefly British.* **1.** To crash (an airplane, for example). **2.** To damage (a car, for example) in a collision. **3.** To bomb from the air. [?]

prank[1] (prăngk) *n.* A mischievous trick or practical joke. [?]

prank[2] (prăngk) *v.* **pranked, prank•ing, pranks.** —*tr.* To dec-

---

pre′ad•o•les′cence *n.*
pre′ad•o•les′cent *adj. & n.*
pre′a•dult′ *adj.*
pre′ag•ri•cul′tur•al *adj.*
pre′ar•range′ *tr.v.*
pre′ar•range′ment *n.*
pre′built′ *adj.*
pre-Chris′tian *adj.*
pre•cook′ *tr.v.*
pre′dawn′ *n. & adj.*
pre′de•cease′ *tr.v.*
pre•des′ig•nate′ *tr.v.*
pre′des•ig•na′tion *n.*
pre•heat′ *tr.v.*
pre•heat′er *n.*
pre•hom′i•nid *n. & adj.*
pre′in•dus′tri•al *adj.*
pre•judge′ *tr.v.*
pre•judg′er *n.*
pre•judg′ment *n.*
pre′launch′ *adj.*
pre•mar′i•tal *adj.*
pre•mar′i•tal•ly *adv.*
pre′men•o•paus′al *adj.*
pre′mix′ *n. & tr.v.*
pre•mod′ern *adj.*
pre•na′tal *adj.*
pre•na′tal•ly *adv.*
pre′or•dain′ *tr.v.*
pre′or•dain′ment *n.*
pre•or′di•na′tion *n.*
pre•owned′ *adj.*
pre•pay′ *tr.v.*
pre•pay′ment *n.*
pre′pro•fes′sion•al *adj.*
pre•pro′gram′ *tr.v.*
pre•pu′ber•al *adj.*
pre•pu′ber•tal *adj.*
pre•pu′ber•ty *n.*
pre′pu•bes′cence *n.*
pre′pu•bes′cent *adj. & n.*
pre•pub′li•ca′tion *adj.*
pre′re•cord′ *tr.v.*
pre•reg′is•ter *intr.v.*
pre′reg•is•tra′tion *n.*
pre′re•tire′ment *adj. & n.*
pre′se•lect′ *tr.v.*
pre′se•lec′tion *n.*
pre•set′ *tr.v.*
pre•set′ta•ble *adj.*
pre•sig′ni•fy′ *tr.v.*
pre•treat′ *tr.v.*
pre•treat′ment *n.*
pre′war′ *adj.*

orate or dress ostentatiously or gaudily. —*intr.* To make an ostentatious display. [< ME *pranken*, to show off, perh. < MDu. *pronken* (< *pronk*, show, display) and < MLGer. *prunken* (< *prank*, display).]

prank•ish (prăng′kĭsh) *adj.* Impishly playful; mischievous. —**prank′ish•ly** *adv.* —**prank′ish•ness** *n.*

prank•ster (prăngk′stər) *n.* One who plays tricks or pranks.

pra•se•o•dym•i•um (prā′zē-ō-dĭm′ē-əm, prā′sē-) *n. Symbol* **Pr** A soft malleable ductile rare-earth element that develops a characteristic green tarnish in air, occurs naturally in monazite, and is used to color glass and ceramics yellow and in metallic alloys and the cores of carbon arcs. Atomic number 59; atomic weight 140.907; melting point 935°C; boiling point 3,127°C; specific gravity 6.8; valence 3, 4. See table at **element.** [NLat. : < Gk. *prasios*, leek-green (< *prason*, leek) + (DI)DYMIUM.]

prat (prăt) *n. Slang.* The buttocks. [?]

prate (prāt) *v.* **prat•ed, prat•ing, prates.** —*intr.* To talk idly and at length; chatter. —*tr.* To utter idly or to little purpose. —*n.* Empty, foolish, or trivial talk; idle chatter. [ME *praten* < MDu. *prāten*.] —**prat′er** *n.* —**prat′ing•ly** *adv.*

prat•fall (prăt′fôl′) *n.* **1.** A fall on the buttocks. **2.** A humiliating error, failure, or defeat.

prat•in•cole (prăt′n-kōl′, prāt′-, prăt′ĭng-, prā′tĭng-) *n.* Any of several Old World shore birds of the genus *Glareola*, having brown and black plumage, long pointed wings, a forked tail, and a tapered bill. [NLat. *prātincola* : Lat. *prātum*, meadow + Lat. *incola*, inhabitant; see k^{w}el-[1]*.]

pra•tique (pră-tēk′) *n. Naut.* Clearance granted to a ship to proceed into port after compliance with health regulations or quarantine. [Fr. < OFr. *practique* < Med.Lat. *prāctica*, ult. < Gk. *praktikē* < fem. of *praktikos*, practical. See PRACTICAL.]

Pra•to (prä′tō). A city of central Italy NW of Florence. Pop. 158,797.

prat•tle (prăt′l) *v.* **-tled, -tling, -tles.** —*intr.* To talk or chatter idly or meaninglessly; babble or prate. —*tr.* To utter or express by prattling. —*n.* **1.** Idle or meaningless chatter; babble. **2.** A sound suggestive of such chattering; a babbling noise. [Freq. of PRATE.] —**prat′tler** *n.* —**prat′tling•ly** *adv.*

Pratt•ville (prăt′vĭl′, -vəl). A city of central AL, a suburb of Montgomery. Pop. 19,587.

prau (prou) *n. Naut.* Var. of **proa.**

prawn (prôn) *n.* Any of various edible crustaceans similar to the shrimps. —*intr.v.* **prawned, prawn•ing, prawns.** To fish for prawns. [ME *praine, prane*.] —**prawn′er** *n.*

prax•e•ol•o•gy also **prax•i•ol•o•gy** (prăk′sē-ŏl′ə-jē) *n.* The study of human conduct. [PRAX(IS) + -LOGY.] —**prax′e•o•log′i•cal** *adj.*

prax•is (prăk′sĭs) *n., pl.* **prax•es** (prăk′sēz′). **1.** Practical application or exercise of a branch of learning. **2.** Habitual or established practice; custom. [Med.Lat. *prāxis* < Gk. *praxis* < *prassein*, to do.]

Prax•it•e•les (prăk′sĭt′l-ēz′). fl. 4th cent. B.C. Greek sculptor whose works include *Hermes Carrying Dionysius*.

pray (prā) *v.* **prayed, pray•ing, prays.** —*intr.* **1.** To utter a prayer or prayers. **2.** To make a fervent request or an entreaty. —*tr.* **1.** To utter or say a prayer or prayers to; address by prayer. **2.** To ask (someone) imploringly; beseech. **3.** To make a devout or earnest request for: *I pray your permission to speak.* **4.** To move or bring by prayer or entreaty. [ME *preien* < OFr. *preier* < Lat. *precārī* < **prex*, prayer. See **prek-*.**]

prayer[1] (prâr) *n.* **1.a.** A reverent petition made to God or another object of worship. **b.** The act of making such a reverent petition. **2.** An act of communion with one worshiped, as in devotion or thanksgiving. **3.** A specially worded form of address used in worship. **4. prayers.** A religious observance in which praying predominates. **5.a.** A fervent request. **b.** The thing requested. **6.** The slightest chance or hope. **7.** *Law.* **a.** The request of a complainant, as stated in a complaint or in equity, that the court grant the aid or relief solicited. **b.** The section of the complaint or bill that contains this request. [ME *preiere* < OFr. < Med.Lat. *precāria* < fem. of Lat. *precārius*, obtained by entreaty < *precārī*, to entreat < **prex*, prayer. See **prek-*.**]

pray•er[2] (prā′ər) *n.* One who prays.

prayer beads (prâr) *pl.n.* A string of beads for keeping count of the prayers one is saying.

prayer book *n.* **1.** A book containing religious prayers. **2. Prayer Book.** The Book of Common Prayer.

prayer•ful (prâr′fəl) *adj.* **1.** Inclined or given to praying frequently; devout. **2.** Typical or indicative of prayer, as a mannerism, gesture, or facial expression. —**prayer′ful•ly** *adv.* —**prayer′ful•ness** *n.*

prayer meeting *n.* An evangelical service, esp. one held on a weekday evening, in which laypersons participate by singing, praying, or testifying their faith.

prayer rug *n.* A small rug used by Muslims to kneel and prostrate themselves upon during devotions.

prayer shawl *n. Judaism.* See **tallith.**

prayer wheel *n.* A cylinder containing or inscribed with prayers or litanies that is revolved on its axis in devotions, esp. by Tibetan Buddhists.

pray•ing mantis (prā′ĭng) *n.* A green or brownish predatory insect *(Mantis religiosa)* that while at rest folds its front legs as if in prayer.

pre– *pref.* **1.a.** Earlier; before; prior to: *prehistoric.* **b.** Preparatory; preliminary: *premedical.* **c.** In advance: *prepay.* **2.** Anterior; in front of: *preaxial.* [ME < OFr. < Lat. *prae-* < *prae*, before, in front. See **per**[1]***.**]

preach (prēch) *v.* **preached, preach•ing, preach•es.** —*tr.* **1.** To proclaim or put forth in a sermon. **2.** To advocate, esp. to urge acceptance of or compliance with. **3.** To deliver (a sermon). —*intr.* **1.** To deliver a sermon. **2.** To give religious or moral instruction, esp. in a tedious manner. [ME *prechen* < OFr. *preechier* < LLat. *praedicāre* < Lat., to proclaim : *prae-*, pre- + *dicāre*, to proclaim; see **deik-*.**]

preach•er (prē′chər) *n.* **1.** One who preaches, esp. one who publicly proclaims the gospel for an occupation. **2.** *Alaska.* A submerged tree or log that creates a hazard for riverboats.

preach•i•fy (prē′chə-fī′) *intr.v.* **-fied, -fy•ing, -fies.** *Informal.* To preach tediously and didactically.

preach•ment (prēch′mənt) *n.* **1.** The act of preaching. **2.** A tiresome or unwelcome moral discourse; tedious sermonizing.

preach•y (prē′chē) *adj.* **-i•er, -i•est.** Given to tedious moralizing; didactic. —**preach′i•ly** *adv.* —**preach′i•ness** *n.*

pre•ad•ap•ta•tion (prē′ăd-ăp-tā′shən, -əp-) *n.* A characteristic evolved by an ancestral species or population that serves an adaptive though different function in a descendant one.

pre•am•ble (prē′ăm′bəl, prē-ăm′-) *n.* **1.** A preliminary statement, esp. one that explains the purpose of a formal document. **2.** An introductory occurrence or fact; a preliminary. [ME < OFr. *preambule* < Med.Lat. *preambulum* < neut. of *praeambulus*, walking in front : *prae-*, pre- + *ambulāre*, to walk; see AMBULATE.] —**pre•am′bu•lar′y** (-byə-lĕr′ē) *adj.*

pre•amp (prē′ămp) *n. Informal.* A preamplifier.

pre•am•pli•fi•er (prē-ăm′plə-fī′ər) *n.* An electronic circuit or device that detects and strengthens weak signals, as from a radio receiver, for subsequent amplification stages.

pre•a•tom•ic (prē′ə-tŏm′ĭk) *adj.* Of, relating to, or being the time preceding the use of, existence of, or capability for atomic energy or weapons.

pre•ax•i•al (prē-ăk′sē-əl) *adj. Anat.* Situated in front of or superior to the median axis of the body or a body part. —**pre•ax′i•al•ly** *adv.*

preb•end (prĕb′ənd) *n.* **1.** A stipend drawn from the endowment or revenues of an Anglican church by a presiding cleric; a benefice. **2.** The property or tithe providing the endowment for such a stipend. **3.** A prebendary. [ME *prebende* < OFr. < Med.Lat. *praebenda* < LLat., state allowance < Lat., neut. pl. gerundive of *praebēre*, to grant < *praehibēre* : *prae-*, pre- + *habēre*, to hold; see **ghabh-*.**]

preb•en•dar•y (prĕb′ən-dĕr′ē) *n., pl.* **-ies. 1.** A member of the Anglican clergy who receives a prebend. **2.** An Anglican cleric holding the honorary title of prebend without a stipend.

pre•bi•o•log•i•cal (prē′bī-ə-lŏj′ĭ-kəl) *adj.* Of, relating to, or being the time before the appearance of living things.

pre•bi•ot•ic (prē′bī-ŏt′ĭk) *adj.* Prebiological.

prec. *abbr.* Preceding.

Pre•cam•bri•an (prē-kăm′brē-ən) *adj.* Of, belonging to, or being the oldest and largest division of geologic time, preceding the Cambrian Period and characterized by the appearance of primitive forms of life. See table at **geologic time.** —*n.* The Precambrian Era or its deposits.

pre•can•cel (prē-kăn′səl) *tr.v.* **-celed, -cel•ing, -cels** or **-celled, -cel•ling, -cels.** To cancel (a postage stamp, as on an envelope) before mailing. —*n.* A precanceled stamp or envelope. —**pre′can•cel•la′tion** *n.*

pre•can•cer (prē′kăn′sər) *n.* A precancerous condition.

pre•can•cer•ous (prē-kăn′sər-əs) *adj.* Of, relating to, or being a condition that typically precedes or develops into a cancer.

pre•car•i•ous (prĭ-kâr′ē-əs) *adj.* **1.** Dangerously lacking in security or stability. **2.** Subject to chance or unknown conditions. **3.** Based on uncertain, unwarranted, or unproved premises. **4.** *Archaic.* Dependent on the will or favor of another. [< Lat. *precārius*, obtained by entreaty, uncertain < *precārī*, to entreat < **prex*, prayer. See **prek-*.**] —**pre•car′i•ous•ly** *adv.* —**pre•car′i•ous•ness** *n.*

pre•cast (prē-kăst′) *adj.* Relating to or being a structural member, esp. of concrete, that has been cast into form before being transported to its site of installation. —**pre•cast′** *v.*

prec•a•to•ry (prĕk′ə-tôr′ē, -tōr′ē) also **prec•a•tive** (-tĭv) *adj.* Relating to or expressing entreaty or supplication. [LLat. *precātōrius* < Lat. *precārī*, to entreat. See PRECARIOUS.]

pre•cau•tion (prĭ-kô′shən) *n.* **1.** An action taken in advance to protect against possible danger or failure; a safeguard. **2.** Caution practiced in advance; forethought or circumspection. [LLat. *praecautiō*, *praecautiōn-* < *praecautus*, p.part. of Lat. *praecavēre*, to guard against : *prae-*, pre- + *cavēre*, to beware.] —**pre•cau′tion•ar′y, pre•cau′tion•al** *adj.*

pre•ca•va (prē-kā′və, -kä′-) *n., pl.* **-vae** (-vē). The superior vena cava. [PRE- + (VENA) CAVA.] —**pre•ca′val** *adj.*

pre•cede (prĭ-sēd′) *v.* **-ced•ed, -ced•ing, -cedes.** —*tr.* **1.** To come, exist, or occur before in time. **2.** To come before in order or rank; surpass or outrank. **3.** To be in a position in

prayer wheel
Brass Tibetan prayer wheel

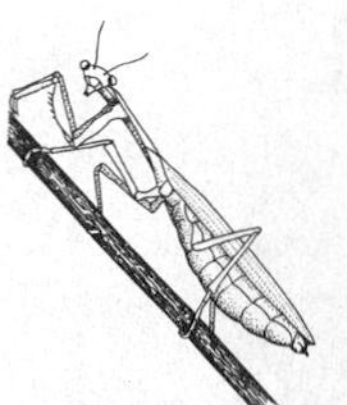

praying mantis
Mantis religiosa

ă pat	oi boy
ā pay	ou out
âr care	ŏŏ took
ä father	ōō boot
ĕ pet	ŭ cut
ē be	ûr urge
ĭ pit	th thin
ī pie	*th* this
îr pier	hw which
ŏ pot	zh vision
ō toe	ə about, item
ô paw	

Stress marks:
′ (primary);
′ (secondary), as in
dictionary (dĭk′shə-nĕr′ē)

front of; go in advance of. **4.** To preface; introduce: *He preceded his lecture with a joke.* — *intr.* To come or go before in time, order, rank, or position. [ME *preceden* < OFr. *preceder* < Lat. *praecēdere* : *prae-*, pre- + *cēdere*, to go; see **ked-***.]

prec•e•dence (prĕs′ĭ-dəns, prĭ-sēd′ns) also **prec•e•den•cy** (prĕs′ĭ-dən-sē, prĭ-sēd′n-sē) *n.* **1.** The fact, state, or right of preceding; priority. **2.** Priority claimed or received because of preeminence or superiority. **3.** A ceremonial order of rank or preference, esp. as observed on formal occasions.

prec•e•dent (prĕs′ĭ-dənt) *n.* **1.a.** An act or instance that may be used as an example in dealing with subsequent similar instances. **b.** *Law.* A judicial decision that may be used as a standard in subsequent similar cases. **2.** Convention or custom that arises from long practice. — *adj.* (prĭ-sēd′nt, prĕs′ĭ-dənt). Preceding. [ME < OFr. < Lat. *praecēdēns, praecēdent-*, pr.part. of *praecēdere*, to go before. See PRECEDE.]

prec•e•den•tial (prĕs′ĭ-dĕn′shəl) *adj.* **1.** Of, relating to, or constituting a precedent. **2.** Having precedence.

pre•ced•ing (prĭ-sē′dĭng) *adj.* Existing or coming before an other or others in time, place, rank, or sequence; previous.

pre•cen•tor (prĭ-sĕn′tər) *n.* A cleric who directs the choral services of a church or cathedral. [Lat. *praecentor* < *praecentus*, p.part. of *praecinere*, to sing before : *prae-*, pre- + *canere*, to sing; see **kan-***.] — **pre′cen•to′ri•al** (prē′sĕn-tôr′ē-əl, -tōr′-) *adj.*

pre•cept (prē′sĕpt′) *n.* A rule or principle prescribing a particular course of action or conduct. [ME < OFr. < Lat. *praeceptum* < neut. p.part. of *praecipere*, to advise, teach : *prae-*, pre- + *capere*, to take; see **kap-***.]

pre•cep•tive (prĭ-sĕp′tĭv) *adj.* **1.** Of, relating to, or expressing a precept. **2.** Instructive; didactic. — **pre•cep′tive•ly** *adv.*

pre•cep•tor (prĭ-sĕp′tər, prē′sĕp′tər) *n.* **1.** A teacher; an instructor. **2.** A specialist, such as a physician, who gives practical experience and training to a student. **3.** The head of a preceptory. [ME < Lat. *praeceptor* < *praecipere*, to teach. See PRECEPT.] — **pre′cep•to′ri•al** (prē′sĕp-tôr′ē-əl, -tōr′-) *adj.*

pre•cep•tor•ship (prĭ-sĕp′tər-shĭp′) *n.* A period of practical experience and training under a preceptor.

pre•cep•to•ry (prĭ-sĕp′tə-rē, prē′sĕp-) *n., pl.* **-ries.** A community of medieval Knights Templars located on a provincial estate and subordinate to the temples at Paris and London.

pre•cess (prē-sĕs′, prē′sĕs′) *intr.v.* **-cessed, -cess•ing, -cess•es.** *Phys. & Astron.* To move in or be subjected to precession.

pre•ces•sion (prē-sĕsh′ən) *n.* **1.** The act or state of preceding; precedence. **2.** *Phys.* The motion of the axis of a spinning body, such as the wobble of a top, due to an applied external force. **3.** *Astron.* **a.** Precession of the equinoxes. **b.** A slow gyration of Earth's axis around the pole of the ecliptic, caused mainly by the gravitational pull of the sun and moon on Earth's equatorial bulge. [LLat. *praecessiō, praecessiōn-* < Lat. *praecessus*, p.part. of *praecēdere*, to go before. See PRECEDE.] — **pre•ces′sion•al** *adj.*

precession of the equinoxes *n. Astron.* A slow westward shift of the equinoxes along the plane of the ecliptic, resulting from precession of Earth's axis of rotation and causing the equinoxes to occur earlier each sidereal year. A complete precession requires 25,800 years.

pre•cinct (prē′sĭngkt′) *n.* **1.a.** A district of a city or town under the jurisdiction of or patrolled by a specific unit of its police force. **b.** The police station situated in and having jurisdiction over a precinct. **2.** An election district of a city or town. **3.a.** A place or an enclosure marked off by definite limits. **b.** A boundary. In both senses often used in the plural. **4. precincts.** The neighborhood or surrounding area; the environs. **5. precincts.** An area of thought or action; a province or domain. [ME *precincte*, a defined district or area < Med. Lat. *praecinctum* < Lat., neut. p.part. of *praecingere*, to encircle : *prae-*, pre- + *cingere*, to gird; see **kenk-***.]

pre•ci•os•i•ty (prĕsh′ē-ŏs′ĭ-tē, prĕs′-) *n., pl.* **-ties. 1.** Extreme meticulousness or overrefinement, as in taste. **2.** An instance of preciosity. [ME *preciousite*, preciousness < OFr. *preciosite* < Lat. *pretiōsitās* < *pretiōsus*, precious < *pretium*, price. See PRECIOUS.]

pre•cious (prĕsh′əs) *adj.* **1.** Of high cost or worth; valuable. **2.** Highly esteemed; cherished. **3.** Dear; beloved. **4.** Affectedly dainty or overrefined. **5.** *Informal.* Thoroughgoing; unmitigated. — *n.* One who is dear or beloved; a darling. — *adv.* Used as an intensive: *precious little time.* [ME < OFr. *precios* < Lat. *pretiōsus* < *pretium*, price. See **per-**[5]*.] — **pre′cious•ly** *adv.* — **pre′cious•ness** *n.*

precious stone *n.* Any of several gems, such as the diamond, that are valuable because of their rarity or appearance.

prec•i•pice (prĕs′ə-pĭs) *n.* **1.** An overhanging or extremely steep mass of rock, such as a crag. **2.** The brink of a dangerous or disastrous situation. [Fr. *précipice* < Lat. *praecipitium* < *praeceps, praecipit-*, headlong. See PRECIPITATE.]

pre•cip•i•ta•ble (prĭ-sĭp′ĭ-tə-bəl) *adj. Chem.* Capable of being precipitated.

pre•cip•i•tan•cy (prĭ-sĭp′ĭ-tən-sē) also **pre•cip•i•tance** (-təns) *n.* **1.** The quality of being precipitant. **2.** Action or thought marked by impulsiveness or rash haste.

pre•cip•i•tant (prĭ-sĭp′ĭ-tənt) *adj.* **1.** Rushing or falling headlong. **2.** Acting with or marked by impulsiveness in thought or action; rash. See Usage Note at **precipitate. 3.** Abrupt or unexpected; sudden. — *n. Chem.* A substance that causes a precipitate to form when it is added to a solution. [Lat. *praecipitāns, praecipitant-*, pr.part. of *praecipitāre*, to throw headlong. See PRECIPITATE.] — **pre•cip′i•tant•ly** *adv.*

pre•cip•i•tate (prĭ-sĭp′ĭ-tāt′) *v.* **-tat•ed, -tat•ing, -tates.** — *tr.* **1.** To throw from or as if from a great height; hurl downward. **2.** To cause to happen, esp. suddenly or prematurely. **3.** *Meteorol.* To cause (water vapor) to precipitate. **4.** *Chem.* To cause (a solid substance) to be separated from a solution. — *intr.* **1.** *Meteorol.* To condense and fall from the air as rain, snow, sleet, or hail. **2.** *Chem.* To be separated from a solution as a solid. **3.** To fall or be thrown headlong. — *adj.* (-tĭt). **1.** Moving rapidly and heedlessly; speeding headlong. **2.** Acting with or marked by excessive haste and lack of due deliberation. **3.** Occurring suddenly or unexpectedly. — *n.* (-tāt′, -tĭt). **1.** *Chem.* A solid or solid phase separated from a solution. **2.** A product resulting from a process, an event, or a course of action. [Lat. *praecipitāre, praecipitāt-*, to throw headlong < *praeceps, praecipit-*, headlong : *prae-*, pre- + *caput, capit-*, head; see **kaput-***.] — **pre•cip′i•tate•ly** (-tĭt-lē) *adv.* — **pre•cip′i•tate•ness** *n.* — **pre•cip′i•ta′tive** *adj.* — **pre•cip′i•ta′tor** *n.*

Usage Note: The adjective *precipitate* and the adverb *precipitately* were once applied to physical steepness but are now used primarily of rash, headlong actions: *They made a precipitate decision. He withdrew precipitately from the race. Precipitous* currently means "steep" in both literal and figurative senses. But *precipitous* and *precipitously* are also frequently applied to abruptness and hastiness. This usage is a natural extension of the use of *precipitous* to describe a rise or fall in a quantity over time, but though well attested in the work of reputable writers, this use is still widely regarded as an error.

pre•cip•i•ta•tion (prĭ-sĭp′ĭ-tā′shən) *n.* **1.** A headlong fall or rush. **2.** Abrupt or impulsive haste. **3.** A hastening or an acceleration, esp. one that is sudden or unexpected. **4.** *Meteorol.* **a.** Any form of water, such as rain or snow, that falls to the earth's surface. **b.** The quantity of such water falling in a specific area within a specific period. **5.** *Chem.* The process of separating a substance from a solution as a solid.

pre•cip•i•tin (prĭ-sĭp′ĭ-tĭn) *n.* An antibody that reacts with a specific soluble antigen to produce a precipitate.

pre•cip•i•tin•o•gen (prĭ-sĭp′ĭ-tĭn′ə-jən) *n.* An antigen that induces the production of a precipitin.

pre•cip•i•tous (prĭ-sĭp′ĭ-təs) *adj.* **1.** Resembling a precipice; extremely steep. See Syns at **steep**[1]. **2.** Having several precipices: *a precipitous bluff.* **3.** *Usage Problem.* Extremely rapid or abrupt; precipitate. See Usage Note at **precipitate.** [Prob. < *precipitious* < Lat. *praecipitium*, precipice. See PRECIPICE.] — **pre•cip′i•tous•ly** *adv.* — **pre•cip′i•tous•ness** *n.*

pré•cis (prā′sē, prā-sē′) *n., pl.* **pré•cis** (prā′sēz, prā-sēz′). A concise summary of a book, an article, or another text; an abstract. — *tr.v.* **-cised, -cis•ing, -cis•es.** To make a précis of. [Fr. < OFr. *precis*, condensed. See PRECISE.]

pre•cise (prĭ-sīs′) *adj.* **1.** Clearly expressed or delineated; definite. **2.** Exact, as in performance or amount; accurate or correct: *a precise instrument.* **3.** Strictly distinguished from others; very. **4.** Distinct and correct in sound or meaning. **5.** Conforming strictly to rule or proper form. [ME, exact < OFr. *precis*, condensed, precisely fixed < Lat. *praecīsus*, p.part. of *praecīdere*, to shorten : *prae-*, pre- + *caedere*, to cut; see **kaə-id-***.] — **pre•cise′ness** *n.*

pre•cise•ly (prĭ-sīs′lē) *adv.* **1.** In a precise manner. **2.** Used as an intensive: *That's precisely the reason I'm angry.*

pre•ci•sian (prĭ-sĭzh′ən) *n.* **1.** One who is strict and precise in adherence to rules or standards, esp. with regard to religion or morals. **2.** A Puritan. [< PRECISE.] — **pre•ci′sian•ism** *n.*

pre•ci•sion (prĭ-sĭzh′ən) *n.* **1.** The state or quality of being precise; exactness. **2.** *Math.* The exactness with which a number is specified; the number of significant digits with which a number is expressed. — *adj.* **1.** Used or intended for accurate or exact measurement. **2.** Made so as to vary minimally from a set standard: *precision components.* **3.** Of or characterized by accurate action. [Lat. *praecīsiō, praecīsiōn-*, a cutting off < *praecīsus*, p.part. of *praecīdere*, to cut off. See PRECISE.]

pre•ci•sion•ism also **Pre•ci•sion•ism** (prĭ-sĭzh′ə-nĭz′əm) *n.* A style of early 20th-century painting in which a subject is reduced or simplified to elemental structural forms and rendered by abstractionism and realism.

pre•ci•sion•ist (prĭ-sĭzh′ə-nĭst) *n.* **1.** One who values precision; a purist. **2.** Often **Precisionist.** A painter whose work is marked by precisionism.

pre•clin•i•cal (prē-klĭn′ĭ-kəl) *adj.* Of or relating to the period of a disease before the appearance of symptoms.

pre•clude (prĭ-klo͞od′) *tr.v.* **-clud•ed, -clud•ing, -cludes. 1.** To make impossible, as by action taken in advance; prevent. **2.** To exclude or prevent (someone) from a given condition or activity. [Lat. *praeclūdere* : *prae-*, pre- + *claudere*, to close.] — **pre•clu′sion** (-klo͞o′zhən) *n.* — **pre•clu′sive** (-klo͞o′sĭv, -zĭv) *adj.* — **pre•clu′sive•ly** *adv.*

pre·co·cial (prĭ-kō′shəl) *adj.* Covered with down and capable of moving about when hatched. Used of wading birds and domestic fowl. [< NLat. *Praecocēs*, precocial birds < Lat., pl. of *praecox*, premature. See PRECOCIOUS.]

pre·co·cious (prĭ-kō′shəs) *adj.* **1.** Manifesting or characterized by unusually early development or maturity, esp. in mental aptitude. **2.** *Bot.* Blossoming before the appearance of leaves. [< Lat. *praecox*, *praecoc-*, premature < *praecoquere*, to boil before, ripen fully : *prae-*, pre- + *coquere*, to cook, ripen; see **pekʷ-***.] —**pre·co′cious·ly** *adv.* —**pre·coc′ity** (-kŏs′ĭ-tē), **pre·co′cious·ness** *n.*

pre·cog·ni·tion (prē′kŏg-nĭsh′ən) *n.* Knowledge of something in advance of its occurrence, esp. by extrasensory perception; clairvoyance. —**pre·cog′ni·tive** *adj.*

pre·co·lo·ni·al or **pre-co·lo·ni·al** (prē′kə-lō′nē-əl) *adj.* Of the period before colonization of a region or territory.

pre-Co·lum·bi·an (prē′kə-lŭm′bē-ən) *adj.* Of, relating to, or originating in the Americas before the arrival of Columbus.

pre·con·ceive (prē′kən-sēv′) *tr.v.* **-ceived, -ceiv·ing, -ceives.** To form (an opinion, for example) before possessing full or adequate knowledge or experience.

pre·con·cep·tion (prē′kən-sĕp′shən) *n.* A preconceived opinion or conception; a prejudice or bias.

pre·con·cert (prē′kən-sûrt′) *tr.v.* **-cert·ed, -cert·ing, -certs.** To agree on, settle, or arrange in advance.

pre·con·di·tion (prē′kən-dĭsh′ən) *n.* A condition that must exist or be established before something can occur or be considered; a prerequisite. —*tr.v.* **-tioned, -tion·ing, -tions.** To condition, train, or accustom in advance.

pre·con·scious (prē-kŏn′shəs) *n.* Memories or feelings of which one is not immediately aware but that are consciously recallable. —**pre·con′scious** *adj.* —**pre·con′scious·ly** *adv.*

pre·con·tract (prē-kŏn′trăkt) *n.* An existing contract that obviates the making of another contract of the same kind: *a precontract of marriage.* —**pre′con·tract′** (-kən-trăkt′) *v.*

pre·cool (prē-ko͞ol′) *tr.v.* **-cooled, -cool·ing, -cools.** To reduce the temperature of (meat, for example) by artificial means before packaging or shipping.

pre·crit·i·cal (prē-krĭt′ĭ-kəl) *adj.* Coming before a critical state or phase.

pre·cur·sive (prĭ-kûr′sĭv) *adj.* Precursory.

pre·cur·sor (prĭ-kûr′sər, prē′kûr′sər) *n.* **1.** One that indicates, suggests, or announces someone or something to come. **2.** One that precedes another; a forerunner or predecessor. **3.** A biochemical substance that gives rise to a more stable or definitive product. [ME *precursoure* < OFr. *precurseur* < Lat. *praecursor* < *praecursus*, p.part. of *praecurrere*, to run before : *prae-*, pre- + *currere*, to run; see **kers-***.]

pre·cur·so·ry (prĭ-kûr′sə-rē) *adj.* **1.** Preceding or preliminary; introductory: *a precursory statement.* **2.** Suggesting or indicating something to follow.

pre·cut (prē′kŭt′) *adj.* Cut into size or shape before being marketed, assembled, or used. —**pre·cut′** *v.*

pred. *abbr. Gram. & Logic.* Predicate.

pre·da·cious also **pre·da·ceous** (prĭ-dā′shəs) *adj.* **1.** Living by seizing or taking prey; predatory. **2.** Given to victimizing, plundering, or destroying for one's own gain. [< Lat. *praedārī*, to plunder. See PREDATORY.] —**pre·da′cious·ness, pre·da′ceous·ness, pre·dac′i·ty** (-dăs′ĭ-tē) *n.*

pre·date (prē-dāt′) *tr.v.* **-dat·ed, -dat·ing, -dates. 1.** To mark or designate with a date earlier than the actual one: *predated the check.* **2.** To precede in time; antedate.

pre·da·tion (prĭ-dā′shən) *n.* **1.** The act or practice of plundering or marauding. **2.** The capturing of prey as a means of maintaining life. [ME *predacion* < Lat. *praedātiō*, *praedātiōn-* < *praedātus*, p.part. of *praedārī*, to plunder. See PREDATORY.]

pred·a·tor (prĕd′ə-tər, -tôr′) *n.* **1.** An organism that lives by preying on other organisms. **2.** One that victimizes, plunders, or destroys, esp. for one's own gain. [Lat. *praedātor*, pillager < *praedārī*, to plunder. See PREDATORY.]

pred·a·to·ry (prĕd′ə-tôr′ē, -tōr′ē) *adj.* **1.** Living by preying on other organisms. **2.a.** Of, relating to, or marked by predation. **b.** Living by or given to victimizing or destroying others for one's own gain. [Lat. *praedātōrius*, plundering < *praedārī*, to plunder < *praeda*, booty. See **ghend-***.] —**pred′a·to′ri·ly** *adv.* —**pred′a·to′ri·ness** *n.*

pred·e·ces·sor (prĕd′ĭ-sĕs′ər, prē′dĭ-) *n.* **1.** One who precedes another in time, esp. in an office or a position. **2.** Something that has been succeeded by another. **3.** *Archaic.* An ancestor; a forebear. [ME *predecessoure* < OFr. *predecesseur* < LLat. *praedēcessor* : Lat. *prae-*, pre- + Lat. *dēcessor*, a retiring magistrate (< *dēcessus*, p.part. of *dēcēdere*, to depart : *dē-*, away; see DE- + *cēdere*, to go; see **ked-***).]

pre·des·ti·nar·i·an (prē-dĕs′tə-nâr′ē-ən) *adj.* **1.** Of or relating to predestination. **2.** Believing in or based on the doctrine of predestination. —*n.* One who believes in the doctrine of predestination. —**pre·des′ti·nar′i·an·ism** *n.*

pre·des·ti·nate (prē-dĕs′tə-nāt′) *tr.v.* **-nat·ed, -nat·ing, -nates. 1.** *Theol.* To predestine. **2.** *Archaic.* To destine or determine in advance; foreordain. —*adj.* (-nĭt, -nāt′). Foreordained; predestined. [ME *predestinaten* < LLat. *praedēstināre*, *praedēstināt-*. See PREDESTINE.]

pre·des·ti·na·tion (prē-dĕs′tə-nā′shən) *n.* **1.** The act of predestining or the condition of being predestined. **2.** *Theol.* **a.** The doctrine that God has foreordained all things, esp. salvation of certain souls. **b.** The divine decree foreordaining all souls to either salvation or damnation. **c.** The act of God foreordaining all things past and future. **3.** Destiny; fate.

pre·des·tine (prē-dĕs′tĭn) *tr.v.* **-tined, -tin·ing, -tines. 1.** To fix upon, decide, or decree in advance; foreordain. **2.** *Theol.* To foreordain or elect by divine will or decree. [ME *predestinen* < OFr. *predestiner* < LLat. *praedēstināre* : Lat. *prae-*, pre- + Lat. *dēstināre*, to determine; see DESTINE.]

pre·de·ter·mine (prē′dĭ-tûr′mĭn) *v.* **-mined, -min·ing, -mines.** —*tr.* **1.** To determine, decide, or establish in advance. **2.** To influence or sway toward an action or opinion; predispose. —*intr.* To determine or decide in advance. —**pre′de·ter′mi·nate** (-mə-nĭt) *adj.* —**pre′de·ter′mi·na′tion** *n.*

pre·de·ter·min·er (prē′dĭ-tûr′mə-nər) *n. Ling.* An adjectival word that can stand before an article, a possessive pronoun, or another determiner, as *all* in *all the flowers.*

pre·di·al (prē′dē-əl) *adj.* Var. of **praedial.**

pred·i·ca·ble (prĕd′ĭ-kə-bəl) *adj.* That can be stated or predicated: *a predicable conclusion.* —*n.* **1.** Something that can be predicated. **2.** *Logic.* One of five general attributes of a subject or class, traditionally including genus, species, property, differentia, and accident. [LLat. *praedicābilis* < *praedicāre*, to proclaim publicly, preach, predicate. See PREACH.] —**pred′i·ca·bil′i·ty, pred′i·ca·ble·ness** *n.*

pre·dic·a·ment (prĭ-dĭk′ə-mənt) *n.* **1.** A situation, esp. an unpleasant or trying one, from which extrication is difficult. See Usage Note at **dilemma. 2.** *Logic.* One of the basic Aristotelian states or classifications into which all things can be placed; a category. [ME, class, category < OFr. < LLat. *praedicāmentum* (transl. of Gk. *katēgoria*) < Lat. *praedicāre*, to proclaim publicly, predicate. See PREACH.] —**pre·dic′a·men′tal** (-mĕn′tl) *adj.* —**pre·dic′a·men′tal·ly** *adv.*

pred·i·cate (prĕd′ĭ-kāt′) *v.* **-cat·ed, -cat·ing, -cates.** —*tr.* **1.** To base or establish (an argument, for example). **2.** To state or affirm as an attribute or a quality of something. **3.** To carry the connotation of; imply. **4.** *Logic.* To make (a term or an expression) the predicate of a proposition. **5.** To proclaim or assert; declare. —*intr.* To make a statement or an assertion. —*n.* (-kĭt). **1.** *Gram.* One of the two main constituents of a sentence or clause, modifying the subject and including the verb, objects, or phrases governed by the verb, as *is red* in *The door is red.* **2.** *Logic.* That part of a proposition that is affirmed or denied about the subject, as, for example, *mortal* in the proposition *We are mortal.* —*adj.* (-kĭt). **1.** *Gram.* Of or belonging to a predicate. **2.** Stated or asserted; predicated. [LLat. *praedicāre*, *praedicāt-* < Lat., to proclaim : *prae-*, pre- + *dicāre*, to proclaim; see **deik-***.] —**pred′i·ca′tion** *n.* —**pred′i·ca′tion·al** *adj.* —**pred′i·ca′tive** *adj.* —**pred′i·ca′tive·ly** *adv.*

predicate calculus *n. Logic.* The branch of symbolic logic that deals not only with relations between propositions as a whole but also with their internal structure, esp. the relation between subject and predicate.

predicate nominative *n. Gram.* A noun or pronoun that follows a linking verb and refers back to the subject of the verb.

pred·i·ca·to·ry (prĕd′ĭ-kə-tôr′ē, -tōr′ē) *adj.* Of, relating to, or characteristic of preaching or a preacher. [LLat. *praedicātōrius*, praising < Lat. *praedicātor*, one who makes known < *praedicāre*, to proclaim. See PREACH.]

pre·dict (prĭ-dĭkt′) *v.* **-dict·ed, -dict·ing, -dicts.** —*tr.* To state, tell about, or make known in advance, esp. on the basis of special knowledge. —*intr.* To foretell something; prophesy. [Lat. *praedīcere*, *praedict-* : *prae-*, pre- + *dīcere*, to say; see **deik-***.] —**pre·dict′a·bil′i·ty** *n.* —**pre·dict′a·ble** *adj.* —**pre·dict′a·bly** *adv.* —**pre·dic′tive** *adj.* —**pre·dic′tive·ly** *adv.* —**pre·dic′tive·ness** *n.* —**pre·dic′tor** *n.*

pre·dic·tion (prĭ-dĭk′shən) *n.* **1.** The act of predicting. **2.** Something foretold or predicted; a prophecy.

pre·di·gest (prē′dī-jĕst′, -dĭ-) *tr.v.* **-gest·ed, -gest·ing, -gests. 1.** To subject (food) to partial digestion, usu. through an enzymatic or chemical process, before ingestion. **2.** To render in a simpler style or form. —**pre′di·ges′tion** *n.*

pred·i·lec·tion (prĕd′l-ĕk′shən, prēd′-) *n.* A partiality or disposition in favor of something; a preference. [Fr. *prédilection* < OFr. < Med.Lat. *predīlectus*, p.part. of *predīligere*, to prefer : Lat. *prae-*, pre- + Lat. *dīligere*, to love; see DILIGENT.]

Syns: *predilection, bias, leaning, partiality, penchant, prejudice, proclivity, propensity.* The central meaning shared by these nouns is "a predisposition to favor someone or something in particular": *a predilection for jazz; a pro-American bias; conservative leanings; a partiality for liberal friends; a penchant for exotic foods; a prejudice in favor of the poor; a proclivity for action; a propensity for lies.*

pre·dis·pose (prē′dĭ-spōz′) *tr.v.* **-posed, -pos·ing, -pos·es. 1.a.** To make (someone) inclined to something in advance. See Syns at **incline. b.** To make susceptible or liable. **2.** *Archaic.* To settle or dispose of in advance.

pre·dis·po·si·tion (prē′dĭs-pə-zĭsh′ən) *n.* The state of being predisposed; tendency, inclination, or susceptibility.

pre-Columbian
Gold pendant from west-central Colombia

ă pat	oi boy
ā pay	ou out
âr care	o͝o took
ä father	o͞o boot
ĕ pet	ŭ cut
ē be	ûr urge
ĭ pit	th thin
ī pie	*th* this
îr pier	hw which
ŏ pot	zh vision
ō toe	ə about, item
ô paw	

Stress marks:
′ (primary);
′ (secondary), as in
dictionary (dĭk′shə-nĕr′ē)

pred•nis•o•lone (prĕd-nĭsʹə-lōnʹ) *n.* A synthetic steroid, $C_{21}H_{28}O_5$, similar to hydrocortisone and used in various compounds as an anti-inflammatory, immunosuppressive, antiallergic, and anticancer drug. [Alteration of PREDNISONE.]

pred•ni•sone (prĕdʹnĭ-sōnʹ,-zōnʹ) *n.* A synthetic steroid, $C_{21}H_{26}O_5$, that is similar to cortisone and used as an anti-inflammatory, antiallergic, immunosuppressive, and anticancer drug. [*pre(gnane)*, a derivative of cholesterol + D(I–)[1] + –(E)N(E) + (CORT)ISONE.]

pre•dom•i•nance (prĭ-dŏmʹə-nəns) also **pre•dom•i•nan•cy** (-nən-sē) *n.* The state or quality of being predominant; preponderance.

pre•dom•i•nant (prĭ-dŏmʹə-nənt) *adj.* **1.** Having greatest ascendancy, importance, influence, authority, or force. **2.** Most common or conspicuous; main or prevalent. [Med.Lat. *prēdomināns, prēdominant-*, pr.part. of *prēdominārī*, to predominate. See PREDOMINATE.] — **pre•domʹi•nant•ly** *adv.*

pre•dom•i•nate (prĭ-dŏmʹə-nātʹ) *v.* **-nat•ed, -nat•ing, -nates.** —*intr.* **1.** To have or gain controlling power or influence; prevail. **2.** To be of or have greater quantity or importance; preponderate. —*tr.* To dominate or prevail over. [Med.Lat. *prēdominārī, prēdominātī-* : Lat. *prae-*, pre- + Lat. *dominārī*, to rule (< *dominus*, master; see **dem-***).] — **pre•domʹi•nate•ly** (-nĭt-lē) *adv.* — **pre•domʹi•natʹing•ly** *adv.* — **pre•domʹi•naʹtion** *n.* — **pre•domʹi•naʹtor** *n.*

pre•e•clamp•si•a (prēʹĭ-klămpʹsē-ə) *n.* A condition of hypertension occurring in pregnancy, typically accompanied by edema and proteinuria. — **preʹe•clampʹtic** (-tĭk) *adj.*

pre-em•bry•o (prē-ĕmʹbrē-ōʹ) *n., pl.* **-os.** A fertilized ovum up to 14 days old, before it becomes implanted in the uterus. — **pre-emʹbry•onʹic** (-ŏnʹĭk) *adj.*

pree•mie (prēʹmē) *n. Informal.* A prematurely born infant.

pre•em•i•nent or **pre-em•i•nent** (prē-ĕmʹə-nənt) *adj.* Superior to or notable above all others; outstanding. See Syns at **noted.** [ME < Lat. *praeēminēns*, pr.part. of *praeēminēre*, to excel : *prae-*, pre- + *ēminēre*, to stand out; see EMINENT.] — **pre•emʹi•nence** *n.* — **pre•emʹi•nent•ly** *adv.*

pre•empt or **pre-empt** (prē-ĕmptʹ) —*v.* **-empt•ed, -empt•ing, -empts.** —*tr.* **1.** To appropriate, seize, or take for oneself before others. **2.a.** To take the place of; displace. **b.** To have precedence or predominance over. **3.** To gain possession of by prior right or opportunity, esp. to settle on (public land) to obtain the right to buy first. —*intr. Games.* To make a preemptive bid in bridge. — **pre•empʹtorʹ** (-ĕmpʹtôrʹ) *n.* — **pre•empʹto•ry** (-ĕmpʹtə-rē) *adj.*

pre•emp•tion or **pre-emp•tion** (prē-ĕmpʹshən) *n.* **1.a.** The right to purchase something before others, esp. the right to purchase public land that is granted to one who has settled on that land. **b.** A purchase made by such a right. **2.** Prior seizure of, appropriation of, or claim to something, such as property. [PRE– + Lat. *ēmptiō, ēmptiōn-*, buying (< *ēmptus*, p.part. of Lat. *emere*, to buy; see **em-***).]

pre•emp•tive or **pre-emp•tive** (prē-ĕmpʹtĭv) *adj.* **1.** Of, relating to, or characteristic of preemption. **2.** Having or granted by the right of preemption. **3.a.** Relating to or constituting a military strike made so as to gain the advantage when an enemy strike is believed imminent. **b.** Initiated to deter or prevent an anticipated, usu. unpleasant situation or occurrence. **4.** Having or marked by the power to preempt or take precedence: *preemptive authority.* **5.** *Games.* Relating to or being a bid in bridge at a high level that is intended to interfere with the opponents' bidding. — **pre•empʹtive•ly** *adv.*

preemptive right *n.* The right of certain stockholders to maintain ownership of a constant percentage of a firm's stock.

preen (prēn) *v.* **preened, preen•ing, preens.** —*tr.* **1.a.** To smooth or clean (feathers) with the beak or bill. **b.** To trim or clean (fur) with the tongue, as cats do. **2.** To dress or groom (oneself) with elaborate care; primp. **3.** To take pride or satisfaction in (oneself); gloat. —*intr.* **1.** To dress up; primp. **2.** To swell with pride; gloat or exult. [ME *proinen, preinen*, blend of OFr. *proignier*, to prune; see PRUNE[2], and OFr. *poroindre*, to anoint before (*por-*, before < Lat. *prō-*; see PRO–[1] + *oindre*, to anoint < Lat. *unguere*).] — **preenʹer** *n.*

pre•en•gi•neered or **pre-en•gi•neered** (prēʹĕn-jə-nîrdʹ) *adj.* Built of or using prefabricated sections or parts.

pre•ex•il•i•an or **pre-ex•il•i•an** (prēʹĕg-zĭlʹē-ən, -zĭlʹyən, -ĕk-sĭlʹē-ən, -sĭlʹyən) also **pre•ex•il•ic** or **pre-ex•il•ic** (-ĕg-zĭlʹĭk, -ĕk-sĭlʹ-) *adj.* Relating to the history of the Jews before their exile in Babylonia in the sixth century B.C.

pre•ex•ist or **pre-ex•ist** (prēʹĭg-zĭstʹ) —*v.* **-ist•ed, -ist•ing, -ists.** —*tr.* To exist before; precede. —*intr.* To exist beforehand. — **preʹex•isʹtence** *n.* — **preʹex•isʹtent** *adj.*

pref. *abbr.* **1.** Preface. **2.** Prefatory. **3.** Preference. **4.** Preferred. **5.** Prefix.

pre•fab (prēʹfăbʹ) *Informal.* —*adj.* Prefabricated. —*n.* Something prefabricated. — **preʹfabʹ** *v.*

prefab

pre•fab•ri•cate (prē-făbʹrĭ-kātʹ) *tr.v.* **-cat•ed, -cat•ing, -cates.** **1.** To manufacture (a building, for example) in advance, esp. in sections to be shipped and assembled. **2.** To make up, construct, or develop in an artificial, unoriginal, or stereotypic manner. — **pre•fabʹri•caʹtion** *n.* — **pre•fabʹri•caʹtor** *n.*

pref•ace (prĕfʹĭs) *n.* **1.a.** An explanatory statement or essay introducing a book, usu. written by the author. **b.** An introductory section, as of a speech. **2.** Something introductory; a preliminary. **3.** Often **Preface.** The words introducing the central part of the Eucharist in several Christian churches. —*tr.v.* **-aced, -ac•ing, -ac•es.** **1.** To introduce by or provide with a preliminary statement or essay. **2.** To serve as an introduction to. [ME < OFr. < Lat. *praefātiō, praefātiōn-* < *praefātus*, p.part. of *praefārī*, to say before : *prae-*, pre- + *fārī*, to speak; see **bhā-**[2]*.] — **prefʹac•er** *n.*

pre•fad•ed (prē-fāʹdĭd) *adj.* Artificially given a faded, weathered, or aged look. Used of clothing or fabric.

pref•a•to•ry (prĕfʹə-tôrʹē, -tōrʹē) *adj.* Of or constituting a preface; introductory. [< Lat. *praefātus*, p.part. of *praefārī*, to say before. See PREFACE.] — **prefʹa•toʹri•ly** *adv.*

pre•fect (prēʹfĕktʹ) *n.* **1.** A high administrative official or chief officer, as: **a.** Any of several high officials in ancient Rome. **b.** The chief of police of Paris, France. **c.** A chief administrative official of a department of France. **d.** The administrator in charge of discipline at a Jesuit school. **2.** A student monitor or officer, esp. in a private school. [ME < OFr. < Lat. *praefectus* < p.part. of *praeficere*, to place at the head of : *prae-*, pre- + *facere*, to make; see **dhē-***.]

pre•fec•ture (prēʹfĕkʹchər) *n.* **1.** The district administered or governed by a prefect. **2.** The office or authority of a prefect. **3.** The residence or housing of a prefect. — **pre•fecʹtur•al** (prĭ-fĕkʹchər-əl) *adj.*

pre•fer (prĭ-fûrʹ) *tr.v.* **-ferred, -fer•ring, -fers.** **1.** To choose or habitually choose as more desirable or more valuable. **2.** *Law.* **a.** To give priority or precedence to (a creditor). **b.** To file, prosecute, or offer for consideration or resolution before a magistrate, court, or other legal authority. **3.** *Archaic.* To recommend for advancement or appointment; promote. [ME *preferren* < OFr. *preferer* < Lat. *praeferre* : *prae-*, pre- + *ferre*, to carry; see **bher-**[1]*.] — **pre•ferʹrer** *n.*

pref•er•a•ble (prĕfʹər-ə-bəl, prĕfʹrə-) *adj.* More desirable or worthy than another; preferred. — **prefʹer•a•bilʹi•ty, prefʹer•a•ble•ness** *n.* — **prefʹer•a•bly** *adv.*

pref•er•ence (prĕfʹər-əns, prĕfʹrəns) *n.* **1.a.** The selecting of someone or something over another or others. **b.** The right or chance to so choose. **c.** Someone or something so chosen. See Syns at **choice.** **2.** The state of being preferred. **3.** *Law.* **a.** A priority of payment given to one or more creditors by an insolvent debtor. **b.** The right of a creditor to precedence. **4.** The granting of precedence or advantage to one or more countries in international trade. [ME *preferraunce*, preferment < OFr. *preference* < *preferer*, to prefer. See PREFER.]

pref•er•en•tial (prĕfʹə-rĕnʹshəl) *adj.* **1.** Of, relating to, or giving advantage or preference. **2.** Manifesting or originating from partiality or preference. — **prefʹer•enʹtial•ism** *n.* — **prefʹer•enʹtial•ist** *n.* — **prefʹer•enʹtial•ly** *adv.*

preferential voting *n.* A system of voting in which the voter ranks candidates in order of preference.

pre•fer•ment (prĭ-fûrʹmənt) *n.* **1.** The act of advancing to a higher position or office; promotion. **2.** A position, an appointment, or a rank giving advancement, as of profit or prestige. **3.** The act of preferring or the state of being preferred.

preferred stock *n.* Stock having priority over a corporation's commonly held stock in the distribution of dividends and often of assets.

pre•fig•u•ra•tion (prē-fĭgʹyə-rāʹshən) *n.* **1.** The act of representing, suggesting, or imagining in advance. **2.** Something that prefigures; a foreshadowing.

pre•fig•ure (prē-fĭgʹyər) *tr.v.* **-ured, -ur•ing, -ures.** **1.** To suggest, indicate, or represent by an antecedent form or model; presage or foreshadow: *Cézanne prefigured cubism.* **2.** To imagine or picture to oneself in advance. [ME *prefiguren* < OFr. *prefigurer* < LLat. *praefigūrāre* : Lat. *prae-*, pre- + Lat. *figūrāre*, to shape (< *figūra*, shape; see **dheigh-***).] — **pre•figʹur•a•tive** (-fĭgʹyər-ə-tĭv) *adj.* — **pre•figʹur•a•tive•ly** *adv.* — **pre•figʹur•a•tive•ness** *n.* — **pre•figʹure•ment** *n.*

pre•fin•ished (prē-fĭnʹĭsht) *adj.* Coated or treated before being sold or distributed: *prefinished wood paneling.*

pre•fix (prēʹfĭksʹ) *tr.v.* **-fixed, -fix•ing, -fix•es.** **1.** To put or attach before or in front of. **2.** (prē-fĭksʹ). To settle or arrange in advance. **3.** *Gram.* **a.** To add as a prefix. **b.** To add a prefix to. —*n.* **1.** *Gram.* An affix, such as *dis-* in *disbelieve*, put before a word to produce a derivative or inflected form. **2.** A title placed before a person's name. [ME *prefixen* < OFr. *prefixer* : *pre-*, before (< Lat. *prae-*; see PRE–) + *fixer*, to place (< Lat. *fīxus*, p.part. of *fīgere*, to fasten). N. < NLat. *praefīxum* < neut. sing. of Lat. *praefīxus*, p.part. of *praefīgere*, to fix in front : *prae-*, pre- + *fīgere*, to fasten; see **dhīgʷ-***.] — **preʹfixʹal** *adj.* — **preʹfixʹal•ly** *adv.*

pre•flight (prēʹflītʹ) *adj.* Preparing for or occurring before flight. —*tr.v.* **-flight•ed, -flight•ing, -flights.** To check (an aircraft) for airworthiness before flight. — **preʹflightʹ** *n.*

pre•form (prēʹfôrmʹ) *tr.v.* **-formed, -form•ing, -forms.** To shape or form beforehand. — **preʹformʹ** *n.*

pre•for•ma•tion (prēʹfôr-māʹshən) *n.* **1.** The act of shaping or forming in advance; prior formation. **2.** A theory popular in the 18th century that all parts of an organism exist completely formed in the germ cell and develop only by increasing in size.

pre•fron•tal (prē-frŭn′tl) *adj.* **1.** Of, relating to, or situated in the anterior part of the frontal lobe. **2.** Situated anterior to the frontal bone.

prefrontal lobotomy *n.* A lobotomy in which the white fibers that connect the thalamus to the prefrontal and frontal lobes of the brain are severed, performed as a treatment for intense anxiety or violent behavior.

pre•gan•gli•on•ic (prē-găng′glē-ŏn′ĭk) *adj.* Of, relating to, or being the nerve fibers that supply a ganglion, esp. a ganglion of the autonomic nervous system.

preg•na•ble (prĕg′nə-bəl) *adj.* Being such that attack or capture is possible; vulnerable or assailable. [ME *preignable, pregnabul* < OFr. *pregnauble* < *prendre, pregn-*, to grasp < Lat. *prehendere.* See **ghend-***.] —**preg′na•bil′i•ty** *n.*

preg•nan•cy (prĕg′nən-sē) *n., pl.* **-cies. 1.a.** The condition of being pregnant. **b.** An instance of being pregnant. **c.** The period during which one is pregnant. **2.** Richness of significance, import, or implication. **3.** Creativity; inventiveness.

preg•nant[1] (prĕg′nənt) *adj.* **1.** Carrying developing offspring within the body. **2.a.** Weighty or significant; full of meaning. **b.** Of great or potentially great import, implication, or moment. **3.** Filled or fraught; replete. **4.** Having a profusion of ideas; creative or inventive. **5.** Producing results; fruitful. [ME < OFr. < Lat. *praegnāns, praegnant-*, var. of *praegnās.* See **genə-***.] —**preg′nant•ly** *adv.*

preg•nant[2] (prĕg′nənt) *adj. Archaic.* Convincing; cogent. Used of an argument or of a proof. [ME, prob. < OFr. *preignant*, pr.part. of *preinbre*, to press < Lat. *premere.* See **per-**[4]***.]

pre•hen•sile (prē-hĕn′səl, -sīl′) *adj.* **1.** Adapted for seizing, grasping, or holding, esp. by wrapping around an object. **2.** Having keen intellect; insightful. **3.** Greedy; grasping. [Fr. *préhensile* < Lat. *prehēnsus*, p.part. of *prehendere*, to grasp. See **ghend-***.] —**pre′hen•sil′i•ty** (-sĭl′ĭ-tē) *n.*

pre•hen•sion (prē-hĕn′shən) *n.* **1.** The act of grasping or seizing. **2.a.** Apprehension by the senses. **b.** Understanding. [Lat. *prehēnsiō, prehēnsiōn-* < *prehēnsus*, p.part. of *prehendere*, to seize. See **ghend-***.]

pre•his•tor•ic (prē′hĭ-stôr′ĭk, -stŏr′-) also **pre•his•tor•i•cal** (-ĭ-kəl) *adj.* **1.** Of, relating to, or belonging to the era before recorded history. **2.** Of or relating to a language before it is first recorded in writing. —**pre′his•tor′i•cal•ly** *adv.*

pre•his•to•ry (prē-hĭs′tə-rē) *n., pl.* **-ries. 1.** History of humankind in the period before recorded history. **2.** The circumstances or developments leading up to or surrounding a situation, event, or development; background. —**pre′his•tor′i•an** (-hĭ-stôr′ē-ən, -stŏr′-) *n.*

pre•ig•ni•tion (prē′ĭg-nĭsh′ən) *n.* The ignition of fuel in an internal-combustion engine before the spark passes through the fuel, resulting from a hot spot in the cylinder or from too great a compression ratio for the fuel.

prej•u•dice (prĕj′ə-dĭs) *n.* **1.a.** An adverse judgment or opinion formed beforehand or without knowledge or examination of the facts. **b.** A preconceived preference or idea. See Syns at **predilection. 2.** The act or state of holding unreasonable preconceived judgments or convictions. **3.** Irrational suspicion or hatred of a particular group, race, or religion. **4.** Detriment or injury caused to a person by the preconceived, unfavorable conviction of another or others. —*tr.v.* **-diced, -dic•ing, -dic•es. 1.** To cause (someone) to judge prematurely and irrationally. **2.** To affect injuriously or detrimentally by a judgment or an act. [ME < OFr. < Lat. *praeiūdicium* : *prae-*, pre- + *iūdicium*, judgment (< *iūdex, iūdic-*, judge; see **deik-***).]

prej•u•di•cial (prĕj′ə-dĭsh′əl) *adj.* **1.** Detrimental; injurious. **2.** Causing or tending to preconceived judgment or convictions. —**prej′u•di′cial•ly** *adv.* —**prej′u•di′cial•ness** *n.*

prej•u•di•cious (prĕj′ə-dĭsh′əs) *adj.* Prejudicial. —**prej′u•di′cious•ly** *adv.*

prel•a•cy (prĕl′ə-sē) *n., pl.* **-cies. 1.a.** The office or station of a prelate. **b.** Prelates considered as a group. **2.** Church government administered by prelates.

pre•lap•sar•i•an (prē′lăp-sâr′ē-ən) *adj. Theol.* Of or relating to the period before the fall of Adam and Eve. [PRE– + Lat. *lapsus*, fall; see LAPSE + –ARIAN.]

prel•ate (prĕl′ĭt) *n.* A high-ranking member of the clergy, esp. a bishop. [ME *prelat* < OFr. < Med.Lat. *praelātus* < Lat., p.part. of *praeferre*, to carry before, to prefer : *prae-*, pre- + *lātus*, brought; see **telə-***.] —**pre•lat′ic** (prĭ-lăt′ĭk) *adj.*

prel•a•ture (prĕl′ə-chər, -cho͝or′) *n.* See **prelacy** 1.

pre•law (prē′lô′) *adj. Law.* Of, relating to, or being the studies that prepare one for the study of law.

pre•lect (prĭ-lĕkt′) *intr.v.* **-lect•ed, -lect•ing, -lects.** To lecture or discourse in public. [Lat. *praelegere, praelect-* : *prae-*, pre- + *legere*, to read; see **leg-***.] —**pre•lec′tion** *n.* —**pre•lec′tor** *n.*

pre•li•ba•tion (prē′lī-bā′shən) *n.* A foretaste. [Lat. *praelībātiō, praelībātiōn-* < *praelībātus*, p.part. of *praelībāre*, to taste beforehand : *prae-*, pre- + *lībāre*, pour out, to taste.]

pre•lim (prē′lĭm′, prĭ-lĭm′) *n. Sports.* A preliminary.

pre•lim•i•nar•y (prĭ-lĭm′ə-nĕr′ē) *adj.* Prior to or preparing for the main matter, action, or business; introductory or prefatory. —*n., pl.* **-ies. 1.** Something that is preliminary. **2.** An academic test or examination preparatory to another one. **3.** *Sports.* A contest to determine the finalists in a competition. **4.** *Sports.* An event that precedes the main event of a program, esp. in boxing or wrestling. **5.** *Print.* The front matter of a book. Often used in the plural. [< NLat. *praelīmināris* : Lat. *prae-*, pre- + Lat. *līmen, līmin-*, threshold.] —**pre•lim′i•nar′i•ly** (-nâr′ə-lē) *adv.*

pre•lit•er•ate (prē-lĭt′ər-ĭt) *adj.* Of, relating to, or being a culture not having a written language. —**pre•lit′er•ate** *n.*

Pre•log (prĕl′ōg′), **Vladimir.** b. 1906. Swiss chemist born in Bosnia-Herzegovina who shared a 1975 Nobel Prize.

prel•ude (prĕl′yo͞od′, prā′lo͞od′, prē′-) *n.* **1.** An introductory performance, event, or action preceding a more important one; a preliminary or preface. **2.** *Mus.* An independent piece written for piano and usu. based on a single short thematic motif. **3.** *Mus.* A piece or movement serving as an introduction to another section or composition, esp.: **a.** A relatively long independent piece preceding a fugue. **b.** The first or opening section of a suite. **c.** The overture to an oratorio, opera, or act of an opera. **d.** An introductory voluntary. —*v.* **-ud•ed, -ud•ing, -udes.** —*tr.* **1.** To serve as a prelude to. **2.** To introduce with or as if with a prelude. —*intr.* To serve as a prelude or an introduction. [Med.Lat. *praelūdium* < Lat. *praelūdere*, to play beforehand : *prae-*, pre- + *lūdere*, to play (< *lūdus*, game; see **leid-***).] —**prel′ud′er** *n.* —**pre•lu′di•al** (prĭ-lo͞o′dē-əl) *adj.*

pre•lu•sion (prĭ-lo͞o′zhən) *n.* A prelude or an introduction. [Lat. *praelūsiō, praelūsiōn-* < *praelūsus*, p.part. of *praelūdere*, to play beforehand. See PRELUDE.]

pre•lu•sive (prĭ-lo͞o′sĭv) *adj.* Of or serving as a prelude; introductory. —**pre•lu′sive•ly** *adv.*

prem. *abbr.* Premium.

pre•ma•lig•nant (prē′mə-lĭg′nənt) *adj.* Precancerous.

pre•ma•ture (prē′mə-tyo͝or′, -to͝or′, -cho͝or′) *adj.* **1.** Occurring, growing, or existing before the customary, correct, or assigned time; uncommonly or unexpectedly early. **2.** Born after a gestation period of less than the normal time: *a premature infant.* [ME, ripe < Lat. *praemātūrus*, ripe too early : *prae-*, pre- + *mātūrus*, ripe; see **mā-**[1]***.] —**pre′ma•ture′ly** *adv.* —**pre′ma•ture′ness, pre′ma•tu′ri•ty** *n.*

pre•max•il•la (prē′măk-sĭl′ə) *n., pl.* **-max•il•lae** (-măk-sĭl′ē). Either of two bones located in front of and between the maxillary bones in the upper jaw of vertebrates. —**pre•max′il•lar′y** (-măk′sə-lĕr′ē) *adj.*

pre•med (prē′mĕd′) *Informal.* —*adj.* Premedical. —*n.* **1.** A premedical student. **2.** A premedical program of study.

pre•med•i•cal (prē-mĕd′ĭ-kəl) *adj.* Being or relating to studies that prepare one for medical school.

pre•med•i•tate (prē-mĕd′ĭ-tāt′) *v.* **-tat•ed, -tat•ing, -tates.** —*tr.* To plan, arrange, or plot (a crime, for example) in advance. —*intr.* To reflect, ponder, or deliberate beforehand. —**pre•med′i•ta′tive** *adj.* —**pre•med′i•ta′tor** *n.*

pre•med•i•tat•ed (prē-mĕd′ĭ-tā′tĭd) *adj.* Marked by deliberate purpose, previous consideration, and some degree of planning. —**pre•med′i•tat′ed•ly** *adv.*

pre•med•i•ta•tion (prē-mĕd′ĭ-tā′shən) *n.* **1.** The act of speculating, arranging, or plotting in advance. **2.** *Law.* The contemplation of a crime well enough in advance to show deliberate intent to commit the crime; forethought.

pre•men•stru•al (prē-mĕn′stro͞o-əl) *adj.* Of or occurring just before menstruation. —**pre•men′stru•al•ly** *adv.*

premenstrual syndrome *n.* A group of symptoms, including abdominal bloating, breast tenderness, headache, fatigue, irritability, and depression, that occur in many women from 2 to 14 days before the onset of menstruation.

pre•mier (prĭ-mîr′, -myîr′, prē′mîr) *adj.* **1.** First in status or importance; principal or chief. **2.** First to occur or exist; earliest. —*n.* (prĭ-mîr′). **1.** A prime minister. **2.** A chief administrative officer, as of a Canadian province. [ME *primier* < OFr. < Lat. *prīmārius* < *prīmus*, first. See **per**[1]***.] —**pre•mier′ship′** *n.*

pre•mier dan•seur (prə-myā′ dän-sœr′) *n., pl.* **pre•miers dan•seurs** (prə-myā′ dän-sœr′). A man who is the principal dancer in a ballet company. [Fr.]

pre•miere or **pre•mière** (prĭ-mîr′, -myâr′) —*n.* The first public performance, as of a movie or play. —*v.* **-miered, -mier•ing, -mieres** or **-mièred, -mièr•ing, -mières.** —*tr.* To present the premiere of. —*intr.* **1.** To have the premiere. **2.** To make a first appearance in a public performance. —*adj.* First or paramount; premier. [Fr. < fem. of *premier*, first. See PREMIER.]

Usage Note: In entertainment contexts the verb *premiere* has by now become the standard way of saying "to introduce to the public." Over the past 20 years this use has won the sometimes grudging acceptance of the Usage Panel. The example *The Philharmonic will premiere works by two young Americans* was acceptable to 51 percent of the Panelists in the most recent survey, up from 14 percent in 1969. But only 10 percent of the Panelists in the most recent survey accepted extension of the verb to nonentertainment contexts, as in *Last*

prehensile
Opossum with prehensile ta l

ă pat	oi boy
ā pay	ou out
âr care	o͝o took
ä father	o͞o boot
ĕ pet	ŭ cut
ē be	ûr urge
ĭ pit	th thin
ī pie	*th* this
îr pier	hw which
ŏ pot	zh vision
ō toe	ə about, item
ô paw	

Stress marks:
′ (primary);
′ (secondary), as in **dictionary** (dĭk′shə-nĕr′ē)

fall the school premiered several new degree programs.

pre•mière dan•seuse (prĭ-mîr′ dän-sœz′, -myâr′) *n., pl.* **pre•mières dan•seuses** (prĭ-myâr′ dän-sœz′). A woman who is the principal dancer in a ballet company. [Fr.]

pre•mil•le•nar•i•an (prē-mĭl′ə-nâr′ē-ən) *adj.* Of or relating to premillennialism. —*n.* A person who believes in premillennialism. —**pre•mil′le•nar′i•an•ism** *n.*

pre•mil•len•ni•al (prē′mĭ-lĕn′ē-əl) *adj.* Of or happening in the time before the millennium. —**pre′mil•len′ni•al•ly** *adv.*

pre•mil•len•ni•al•ism (prē′mĭ-lĕn′ē-ə-lĭz′əm) *n.* The belief that the Second Coming of Jesus will immediately precede the millennium. —**pre′mil•len′ni•al•ist** *n.*

prem•ise (prĕm′ĭs) *n.* also **prem•iss** (prĕm′ĭs). **1.** A proposition upon which an argument is based or from which a conclusion is drawn. **2.** *Logic.* **a.** One of the propositions in a deductive argument. **b.** Either the major or the minor proposition of a syllogism, from which the conclusion is drawn. **3. premises.** *Law.* The preliminary or explanatory statements or facts of a document, as in a deed. **4. premises. a.** Land and the buildings on it. **b.** A building or part of a building. —*v.* **-ised, -is•ing, -is•es.** —*tr.* **1.** To state in advance as an introduction or explanation. **2.** To state or assume as a proposition in an argument. —*intr.* To make a premise. [ME *premisse* < OFr. < Med.Lat. *praemissa (propositiō)*, (the proposition) put before, premise < Lat., fem. p.part. of *praemittere*, to set in front : *prae-*, pre- + *mittere*, to send.]

pre•mi•um (prē′mē-əm) *n.* **1.** A prize or an award. **2.** Something offered free or at a reduced price as an inducement to buy something else. **3.** A sum of money or bonus paid in addition to a regular price, salary, or other amount. **4.** The amount paid, often in addition to the interest, to obtain a loan. See Syns at **bonus. 5.** The amount paid or payable, often in installments, for an insurance policy. **6.** The amount at which something is valued above its par or nominal value, as money or securities. **7.** The amount at which a securities option is bought or sold. **8.** Payment for training in a trade or profession. **9.** An unusual or high value. —*adj.* Of superior quality or value. —***idiom.* at a premium.** More valuable than usual, as from scarcity. [Lat. *praemium*, inducement, reward : *prae-*, pre- + *emere*, to take, buy; see **em-*.**]

pre•mo•lar (prē-mō′lər) *n.* One of eight bicuspid teeth located in pairs on each side of the upper and lower jaws behind the canines and in front of the molars. —**pre•mo′lar** *adj.*

pre•mo•ni•tion (prē′mə-nĭsh′ən, prĕm′ə-) *n.* **1.** A presentiment of the future; a foreboding. **2.** A forewarning. [LLat. *praemonitiō, praemonitiōn-* < Lat. *praemonitus*, p.part. of *praemonēre*, to forewarn : *prae-*, pre- + *monēre*, to warn; see **men-[1]*.**] —**pre•mon′i•to′ri•ly** (-mŏn′ĭ-tôr′ə-lē, -tōr′-) *adv.* —**pre•mon′i•to′ry** *adj.*

pre•morse (prĭ-môrs′) *adj.* Abruptly truncated, as though bitten or broken off: *a premorse leaf.* [Lat. *praemorsus*, p.part. of *praemordēre*, to bite off in front : *prae-*, pre- + *mordēre*, to bite; see **mer-*.**]

pre•mu•ni•tion (prē′myo͞o-nĭsh′ən) *n.* Relative immunity to severe infection by a pathogen as a result of a chronic low-grade infection induced earlier by the same pathogen. [Fr. *prémunition* < Lat. *praemūnītiō, praemūnītiōn-*, fortification beforehand < *praemūnītus*, p.part. of *praemūnīre*, to fortify in advance : *prae-*, pre- + *mūnīre*, to fortify (< *moene, moenia*, town walls).] —**pre•mune′** (prē-myo͞on′) *adj.*

pre•name (prē′nām′) *n.* A forename.

pren•tice (prĕn′tĭs) *n. Archaic.* An apprentice.

pre•nup•tial (prē-nŭp′shəl, -chəl) *adj.* Before marriage or a wedding: *a prenuptial celebration.*

pre•oc•cu•pan•cy (prē-ŏk′yə-pən-sē) *n.* **1.** The act or right of occupying a place beforehand or in advance. **2.** The state of being preoccupied or engrossed; preoccupation.

pre•oc•cu•pa•tion (prē-ŏk′yə-pā′shən) *n.* **1.** The state of being preoccupied; absorption of the attention or intellect. **2.** Something that preoccupies or engrosses the mind. **3.** Occupation of a place in advance; preoccupancy.

pre•oc•cu•pied (prē-ŏk′yə-pīd′) *adj.* **1.a.** Absorbed in thought; engrossed. **b.** Excessively concerned with something; distracted. **2.** Formerly or already occupied. **3.** Already used and therefore unavailable for further use. Used of taxonomic names.

pre•oc•cu•py (prē-ŏk′yə-pī′) *tr.v.* **-pied, -py•ing, -pies. 1.** To occupy completely the mind or attention of; engross. **2.** To occupy or take possession of in advance or before another.

pre•op•er•a•tive (prē-ŏp′ər-ə-tĭv, -ŏp′rə-, -ŏp′ə-rā′-) *adj.* Occurring before surgery. —**pre•op′er•a•tive•ly** *adv.*

pre•o•ral (prē-ôr′əl, -ōr′-) *adj.* Situated in front of the mouth.

pre•or•bit•al (prē-ôr′bĭ-tl) *adj. Aerospace.* Occurring before orbit has been established.

prep (prĕp) *adj. Informal.* Preparatory. —*n.* **1.** *Informal.* A preparatory school. **2.** *Informal.* Preparation. **3.** *Chiefly British.* The preparing of lessons; homework. **4.** *Informal.* A preppy. —*v.* **prepped, prep•ping, preps.** —*intr.* **1.** To be enrolled in and attend a preparatory school. **2.** To study or train in preparation for something. —*tr.* **1.** To prepare (someone) for a medical examination or surgical procedure. **2.** To prepare or prime: *prep a surface for painting.*

prep. *abbr.* **1.** Preparation. **2.** Preparatory. **3.** Prepare. **4.** *Gram.* Preposition.

pre•pack•age (prē-păk′ĭj) *tr.v.* **-aged, -ag•ing, -ag•es.** To wrap or package (a product) before marketing.

prep•a•ra•tion (prĕp′ə-rā′shən) *n.* **1.** The act or process of preparing. **2.** The state of having been made ready beforehand; readiness. **3.** A preliminary measure that serves to make ready for something. Often used in the plural. **4.** A substance, such as a medicine, prepared for a particular purpose. **5.** *Mus.* **a.** The anticipation of a dissonant tone by means of its introduction as a consonant tone in the preceding chord. **b.** The dissonant tone so anticipated.

pre•par•a•tive (prĭ-păr′ə-tĭv, -pâr′-) *adj.* Serving or tending to prepare or make ready; preliminary. —*n.* Something that is preparative. —**pre•par′a•tive•ly** *adv.*

pre•par•a•tor (prĭ-păr′ə-tər, -pâr′-) *n.* One who prepares specimens or exhibits for scientific study or display.

pre•par•a•to•ry (prĭ-păr′ə-tôr′ē, -tōr′ē, -pâr′-, prĕp′ər-ə-) *adj.* **1.** Serving to make ready or prepare. **2.** Relating to or engaged in study or training as preparation for advanced education. —*adv.* In preparation for. Used with *to.* —**pre•par′a•to′ri•ly** *adv.*

preparatory school *n.* **1.** A usu. private secondary school that prepares students for college. **2.** A usu. private British elementary school that prepares students for public school.

pre•pare (prĭ-pâr′) *v.* **-pared, -par•ing, -pares.** —*tr.* **1.** To make ready beforehand for a specific purpose, as for an event or occasion. **2.** To put together or make by combining various elements or ingredients; manufacture or compound. **3.** To fit out; equip. **4.** *Mus.* To lead up to and soften (a dissonance or its impact) by means of preparation. —*intr.* **1.** To make things or oneself ready. **2.** To study or complete a course of study at a preparatory school. [ME *preparen* < OFr. *preparer* < Lat. *praeparāre* : *prae-*, pre- + *parāre*, prepare, equip; see **perə-[1]*.**] —**pre•par′ed•ly** (-pâr′ĭd-lē) *adv.* —**pre•par′er** *n.*

pre•par•ed•ness (prĭ-pâr′ĭd-nĭs) *n.* The state of being prepared, esp. military readiness for combat.

pre•pense (prĭ-pĕns′) *adj.* Contemplated or arranged in advance; premeditated: *malice prepense.* [< ME, p.part. of *purpensen*, to premeditate < AN *purpenser* : *pur-*, before (< Lat. *pro-*; see PRO–[1]) + *penser*, to think (< Lat. *pēnsāre*; see **(s)pen-*.**)] —**pre•pense′ly** *adv.*

pre•pon•der•ance (prĭ-pŏn′dər-əns) also **pre•pon•der•an•cy** (-ən-sē) *n.* Superiority in weight, force, importance, or influence.

pre•pon•der•ant (prĭ-pŏn′dər-ənt) *adj.* Having superior weight, force, importance, or influence. —**pre•pon′der•ant•ly** *adv.*

pre•pon•der•ate (prĭ-pŏn′də-rāt′) *intr.v.* **-at•ed, -at•ing, -ates. 1.** To exceed something else in weight. **2.** To be greater than something else, as in quantity or importance; predominate. —*adj.* (-dər-ĭt). Preponderant. [Lat. *praeponderāre, praeponderāt-* : *prae-*, pre- + *ponderāre*, to weigh; see **(s)pen-*.**] —**pre•pon′der•ate•ly** *adv.* —**pre•pon′der•a′tion** *n.*

prep•o•si•tion[1] (prĕp′ə-zĭsh′ən) *n. Gram.* **1.** In some languages, a word placed before a substantive and indicating the relation of that substantive to a verb, an adjective, or another substantive, as English *at, from,* and *with.* **2.** A word or construction similar in function to a preposition, such as *concerning.* [ME *preposicioun* < OFr. *preposicion* < Lat. *praepositiō, praepositiōn-*, a putting before, preposition (transl. of Gk. *prothesis*) < *praepositus*, p.part. of *praepōnere*, to put in front : *prae-*, pre- + *pōnere*, to put; see **apo-*.**]

Usage Note: The doctrine that a preposition may not be used to end a sentence has become one of the most venerated maxims of schoolroom grammatical lore. However, English syntax allows and sometimes requires final placement of the preposition. Such placement is the only possible one in a sentence such as *That depends on what you believe in.* • Even sticklers for the traditional rule can have no grounds for criticizing sentences such as *Where will she end up?* or *It's the most curious book I've ever run across.* In these examples, *up* and *across* are used as adverbs, not prepositions.

pre•po•si•tion[2] also **pre-po•si•tion** (prē′pə-zĭsh′ən) *tr.v.* **-tioned, -tion•ing, -tions.** To place in position in advance.

prep•o•si•tion•al (prĕp′ə-zĭsh′ə-nəl) *adj. Gram.* Relating to or used as a preposition. —**prep′o•si′tion•al•ly** *adv.*

prepositional phrase *n. Gram.* A phrase that consists of a preposition and its object and has adjectival or adverbial value, such as *in the house* in *the people in the house.*

pre•pos•i•tive (prĭ-pŏz′ĭ-tĭv) *Gram.* —*adj.* Placed before or prefixed to another word. —*n.* A prepositive word or particle. [LLat. *praepositīvus* < Lat. *praepositus*, p.part. of *praepōnere*, to put in front. See PREPOSITION[1].] —**pre•pos′i•tive•ly** *adv.*

pre•pos•sess (prē′pə-zĕs′) *tr.v.* **-sessed, -sess•ing, -sess•es. 1.** To preoccupy the mind of to the exclusion of other thoughts or feelings. **2.a.** To influence beforehand against or in favor of someone or something; prejudice. **b.** To impress favorably in advance.

pre•pos•sess•ing (prē′pə-zĕs′ĭng) *adj.* **1.** Serving to impress favorably; pleasing. **2.** *Archaic.* Causing prejudice. **—pre′pos•sess′ing•ly** *adv.* **—pre′pos•sess′ing•ness** *n.*

pre•pos•ses•sion (prē′pə-zĕsh′ən) *n.* **1.** A preconception or prejudice. **2.** The state of being preoccupied with thoughts, opinions, or feelings.

pre•pos•ter•ous (prĭ-pŏs′tər-əs) *adj.* Contrary to nature, reason, or common sense; absurd. [< Lat. *praeposterus*, inverted, unseasonable : *prae-*, pre- + *posterus*, coming behind (< *post*, behind; see **apo-***).] **—pre•pos′ter•ous•ly** *adv.* **—pre•pos′ter•ous•ness** *n.*

pre•po•ten•cy (prē-pōt′n-sē) *n.* **1.** The condition of being greater in power, influence, or force than another or others; predominance. **2.** *Genet.* The ability of one parent, variety, or strain to transmit individual traits to an offspring, apparently to the exclusion of the other parent, variety, or strain.

pre•po•tent (prē-pōt′nt) *adj.* **1.** Greater in power, influence, or force than another or others; predominant. **2.** *Genet.* Of, having, or exhibiting prepotency. [ME < Lat. *praepotēns*, *praepotent-*, pr.part. of *praeposse*, to be more powerful : *prae-*, pre- + *posse*, to be able or powerful; see **poti-***.] **—pre•po′tent•ly** *adv.*

prep•py or **prep•pie** (prĕp′ē) *n.*, *pl.* **-pies.** *Informal.* **1.** A student or former student of a preparatory school. **2.** A person whose manner and dress are deemed typical of traditional preparatory schools. **—prep′pi•ly** *adv.* **—prep′pi•ness** *n.* **—prep′py, prep′pie** *adj.*

pre•pran•di•al also **pre-pran•di•al** (prē-prăn′dē-əl) *adj.* Before a meal, esp. dinner: *a preprandial walk.*

pre•pri•mar•y (prē-prī′mĕr′ē, -mə-rē) *adj.* Relating to or taking place before a primary election.

pre•print (prē′prĭnt′) *n.* Something printed and often distributed in partial or preliminary form in advance of official publication: *a preprint of a scientific article.* —*tr.v.* (prē-prĭnt′) **-print•ed, -print•ing, -prints.** To print in advance.

pre•proc•ess (prē-prŏs′ĕs′, -prō′sĕs′) *tr.v.* **-essed, -ess•ing, -ess•es.** *Comp. Sci.* To perform conversion, formatting, or other functions on (data) before further processing. **—pre•proc′es•sor** *n.*

prep school *n. Informal.* A preparatory school.

pre•puce (prē′pyo͞os′) *n.* **1.** See **foreskin. 2.** A loose fold of skin covering the glans clitoridis. [ME < OFr. < Lat. *praepūtium* : poss. *prae-*, pre- + **pūtos*, penis.] **—pre•pu′tial** (-pyo͞o′shəl) *adj.*

pre•punch (prē-pŭnch′) *tr.v.* **-punched, -punch•ing, -punch•es.** *Comp. Sci.* To punch computer data cards or tape before an anticipated use.

pre•pu•pa (prē-pyo͞o′pə) *n.*, *pl* **-pae** (-pē) or **-pas. 1.** An inactive stage just before the pupa in the development of certain insects. **2.** The prepupal form of an insect. **—pre•pu′pal** *adj.*

pre•quel (prē′kwəl) *n.* A literary, cinematic, or dramatic work taking place in or concerned with a time before the action of a preexisting work. [PRE- + (SE)QUEL.]

Pre-Raph•a•el•ite also **pre-Raph•a•el•ite** (prē-răf′ē-ə-līt′, -rā′fē-) —*n.* A painter or writer belonging to or influenced by the Pre-Raphaelite Brotherhood, a society founded in England in 1848 to advance the style and spirit of Italian painting before Raphael. —*adj.* Of, relating to, or characteristic of the Pre-Raphaelites. **—Pre-Raph′a•el•it′ism** *n.*

pre•re•lease (prē′rĭ-lēs′) *n.* Something released before a scheduled date. **—pre′re•lease′** *adj.*

pre•req•ui•site (prē-rĕk′wĭ-zĭt) *adj.* Required or necessary as a prior condition. —*n.* Something that is prerequisite.

pre•rog•a•tive (prĭ-rŏg′ə-tĭv) *n.* **1.** An exclusive right or privilege held by a person or group, esp. a hereditary or official right. See Syns at **right. 2.** The exclusive right and power to command, decide, rule, or judge. **3.** Something, such as a natural gift or advantage, that confers superiority. —*adj.* Of, arising from, or exercising a prerogative. [ME < OFr. < Lat. *praerogātīva*, fem. of *praerogātīvus*, asked first < *praerogātus*, p.part. of *praerogāre*, to ask before : *prae-*, pre- + *rogāre*, to ask; see **reg-***.] **—pre•rog′a•tived** *adj.*

pres. *abbr.* **1.** *Gram.* Present. **2.** Also **Pres.** President.

pres•age (prĕs′ĭj) *n.* **1.** An indication or a warning of a future occurrence; an omen. **2.** A feeling or an intuition of what is going to occur; a presentiment. **3.** Prophetic significance or meaning. **4.** *Archaic.* A prediction. —*v.* **pre•sage.** (prĭ-sāj′, prĕs′ĭj) **-saged, -sag•ing, -sag•es.** —*tr.* **1.** To indicate or warn of in advance; portend. **2.** To have a presentiment of. **3.** To foretell or predict. —*intr.* To make or utter a prediction. [ME < Lat. *praesāgium* < *praesāgīre*, to perceive beforehand : *prae-*, pre- + *sāgīre*, to perceive; see **sāg-***.] **—pre•sage′ful** (prĭ-sāj′fəl) *adj.*

Presb. *abbr.* Presbyterian.

Presby. *abbr.* Presbyterian.

pres•by•ope (prĕz′bē-ōp′, prĕs′-) *n.* A person affected with presbyopia.

pres•by•o•pi•a (prĕz′bē-ō′pē-ə, prĕs′-) *n.* Inability of the eye to focus sharply on nearby objects, resulting from loss of elasticity of the crystalline lens with advancing age. [NLat. : Gk. *presbus*, old man; see **per**[1]* + -OPIA.] **—pres′by•op′ic** (-ŏp′ĭk, -ō′pĭk) *adj.*

pres•by•ter (prĕz′bĭ-tər, prĕs′-) *n.* **1.** A priest in various hierarchical churches. **2.a.** A teaching elder in the Presbyterian Church. **b.** A ruling elder in the Presbyterian Church. **3.** An elder of the congregation in the early Christian church. [LLat. < Gk. *presbuteros* < comp. of *presbus*, old man. See **per**[1]*.]

pres•byt•er•ate (prĕz-bĭt′ər-ĭt, -ə-rāt′, prĕs-) *n.* **1.** The office of a presbyter. **2.** A body or an order of presbyters.

pres•by•te•ri•al (prĕz′bĭ-tîr′ē-əl, prĕs′-) *adj.* Of or relating to a presbyter or the presbytery. **—pres′by•te′ri•al•ly** *adv.*

pres•by•te•ri•an (prĕz′bĭ-tîr′ē-ən, prĕs′-) *adj.* **1.** Of or relating to ecclesiastical government by presbyters. **2. Presbyterian.** Of or relating to a Presbyterian Church. —*n.* **Presbyterian.** A member or an adherent of a Presbyterian Church. **—pres′by•te′ri•an•ism** *n.*

Presbyterian Church *n.* Any of various Protestant churches governed by presbyters and traditionally Calvinist in doctrine.

pres•by•ter•y (prĕz′bĭ-tĕr′ē, prĕs′-) *n.*, *pl.* **-ies. 1.a.** A court composed of Presbyterian Church ministers and representative elders of a particular locality. **b.** The district represented by this court. **2.** Presbyters considered as a group. **3.** Government of a church by presbyters. **4.** The section of a church reserved for the clergy. **5.** *Rom. Cath. Ch.* The residence of a priest. [ME *presbetory*, priests' bench < LLat. *presbyterium*, council of elders < Gk. *presbuterion* < *presbuteros*, elder. See PRESBYTER.]

pre•school (prē′sko͞ol′) *adj.* Of, for, relating to, or being the early years of childhood before elementary school. —*n.* (prē′sko͞ol′). A school for preschoolers; a nursery school.

pre•school•er (prē′sko͞o′lər) *n.* **1.** A child who is not old enough to attend kindergarten. **2.** A child who is enrolled in a preschool.

pre•school•ing (prē′sko͞o′lĭng) *n.* Early childhood education, esp. when received at a preschool.

pre•sci•ence (prē′shē-əns, -shəns, prĕsh′ē-əns, prĕsh′əns) *n.* Knowledge of actions or events before they occur; foresight.

pre•sci•ent (prē′shē-ənt, -shənt, prĕsh′ē-ənt, prĕsh′ənt) *adj.* **1.** Of or relating to prescience. **2.** Possessing prescience. [Fr. < OFr. < Lat. *praesciēns*, *praescient-*, pr.part. of *praescīre*, to know beforehand : *prae-*, pre- + *scīre*, to know; see **skei-***.] **—pre′sci•ent•ly** *adv.*

pre•sci•en•tif•ic (prē-sī′ən-tĭf′ĭk) *adj.* Of, relating to, or occurring at a time before the advent of modern science and the application of its methods.

pre•scind (prĭ-sĭnd′) *v.* **-scind•ed, -scind•ing, -scinds.** —*tr.* To separate or divide in thought; consider individually. —*intr.* To withdraw one's attention. [Lat. *praescindere*, to cut off in front : *prae-*, pre- + *scindere*, to cut off, split; see **skei-***.]

Pres•cott (prĕs′kət, -kŏt′). A city of central AZ NNW of Phoenix. Pop. 26,455.

Prescott, William Hickling. 1796–1859. Amer. historian noted esp. for his *History of the Conquest of Mexico* (1843).

pre•screen (prē-skrēn′) *tr.v.* **-screened, -screen•ing, -screens. 1.** To view (a movie) before release for public showing. **2.** To examine or interview before further selection processes.

pre•scribe (prĭ-skrīb′) *v.* **-scribed, -scrib•ing, -scribes.** —*tr.* **1.** To set down as a rule or guide; enjoin. See Syns at **dictate. 2.** To order the use of (a medicine or other treatment). —*intr.* **1.** To establish rules, laws, or directions. **2.** To order a medicine or other treatment. [ME *prescriben* < Lat. *praescrībere* : *prae-*, pre- + *scrībere*, to write; see **skrībh-***.] **—pre•scrib′er** *n.*

pre•script (prē′skrĭpt′) *n.* Something prescribed, esp. a rule or regulation of conduct. —*adj.* (prē′skrĭpt′, prĭ-skrĭpt′). Having been established as a rule; prescribed. [< ME, prescribed < Lat. *praescrīptum*, neut. p.part. of *praescrībere*, to order, prescribe. See PRESCRIBE.]

pre•scrip•ti•ble (prĭ-skrĭp′tə-bəl) *adj.* **1.** That can be prescribed. **2.** Requiring or derived from prescription. **—pre•scrip′ti•bil′i•ty** *n.*

pre•scrip•tion (prĭ-skrĭp′shən) *n.* **1.a.** The act of establishing official rules, laws, or directions. **b.** Something prescribed as a rule. **2.a.** A written order, esp. by a physician, for the preparation and administration of a medicine or other treatment. **b.** A prescribed medicine or other treatment. **c.** An ophthalmologist's or optometrist's written instruction, as for the grinding of corrective lenses. **3.** A formula directing the preparation of something. **4.** *Law.* The process of acquiring title to property by reason of uninterrupted possession of specified duration. **5.** *Law.* The limitation of time beyond which an action, a debt, or a crime is no longer valid or enforceable. [ME *prescripcion*, establishment of a claim < OFr. *prescription* < Med.Lat. *praescrīptiō*, *praescrīptiōn-* < Lat., introduction, precept < *praescrīptus*, p.part. of *praescrībere*, to order. See PRESCRIBE.]

pre•scrip•tive (prĭ-skrĭp′tĭv) *adj.* **1.** Sanctioned or authorized by long-standing custom or usage. **2.** Making or giving injunctions, directions, laws, or rules. **3.** *Law.* Acquired by or based on uninterrupted possession. **—pre•scrip′tive•ly** *adv.* **—pre•scrip′tive•ness** *n.*

prescriptive grammar *n.* A grammar that attempts to establish norms or rules for correct usage and to characterize incorrect usage, as opposed to a descriptive grammar.

Pre-Raphaelite
Saint Cecilia by Edward Burne-Jones

ă pat	oi boy
ā pay	ou out
âr care	o͝o took
ä father	o͞o boot
ĕ pet	ŭ cut
ē be	ûr urge
ĭ pit	th thin
ī pie	*th* this
îr pier	hw which
ŏ pot	zh vision
ō toe	ə about, item
ô paw	

Stress marks:
′ (primary);
′ (secondary), as in **dictionary** (dĭk′shə-nĕr′ē)

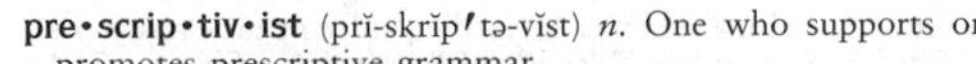

pre•scrip•tiv•ist (prĭ-skrĭp′tə-vĭst) *n.* One who supports or promotes prescriptive grammar.

pres•ence (prĕz′əns) *n.* **1.** The state or fact of being present; current existence or occurrence. **2.** Immediate proximity in time or space. **3.** The area immediately surrounding a great personage, esp. a sovereign. **4.** A person who is present. **5.a.** A person's bearing, esp. when it commands respectful attention. **b.** The quality of self-assurance and effectiveness that permits a performer to achieve a rapport with the audience: *stage presence.* **6.** A supernatural influence felt to be nearby. **7.** The diplomatic, political, or military influence of a nation in a foreign country.

presence of mind *n.* The ability to think and act calmly and efficiently, esp. in an emergency.

pres•ent[1] (prĕz′ənt) *n.* **1.** A moment or period in time perceptible as intermediate between past and future; now. **2.** *Gram.* **a.** The present tense. **b.** A verb form in the present tense. **3. presents.** *Law.* The document or instrument in question: *Be it known by these presents.* —*adj.* **1.** Existing or happening now; current. **2.a.** Being at hand or in attendance. **b.** Existing in something specified: *Oxygen is present in the bloodstream.* **3.** Now being considered; actually here or involved. **4.** *Gram.* Being a verb tense or form that expresses current time. **5.** *Archaic.* Readily available; immediate. **6.** *Obsolete.* Alert to circumstances; attentive. —*idioms.* **at present.** At the present time; right now. **for the present.** For the time being; temporarily. [ME < OFr. < Lat. *praesēns, praesent-*, pr.part. of *praeesse*, to be present : *prae-*, pre- + *esse*, to be; see **es-***.] —**pres′ent•ness** *n.*

present arms

pre•sent[2] (prĭ-zĕnt′) *tr.v.* **-sent•ed, -sent•ing, -sents. 1.a.** To introduce, esp. with formal ceremony. **b.** To introduce (a young woman) to society with conventional ceremony. **2.** To bring before the public: *present a play.* **3.a.** To make a gift or an award of. **b.** To make a gift to. **4.** To offer for observation, examination, or consideration; show or display. See Syns at **offer. 5.** To salute with (a weapon). **6.** *Eccles.* To recommend (a cleric) for a benefice. **7.** *Law.* To bring a charge or an indictment against. —*n.* **pres•ent.** (prĕz′ənt). Something presented; a gift. [ME *presenten* < OFr. *presenter* < Lat. *presentāre*, to show < *praesēns, praesent-*, pr.part. of *praeesse*, to be in front of. See PRESENT[1].] —**pre•sent′er** *n.*

pre•sent•a•ble (prĭ-zĕn′tə-bəl) *adj.* **1.** That can be given, displayed, or offered: *presentable attire.* **2.** Fit for introduction to others: *presentable relatives.* —**pre•sent′a•bil′i•ty, pre•sent′a•ble•ness** *n.* —**pre•sent′a•bly** *adv.*

pre•sent arms (prĭ-zĕnt′) *n.* **1.** A position in the military manual of arms in which the rifle is held vertically in front of the body. **2.** A command to assume present arms or give a hand salute.

pres•en•ta•tion (prĕz′ən-tā′shən, prē′zən-) *n.* **1.a.** The act of presenting. **b.** The state of being presented. **2.** A performance, as of a drama. **3.a.** Something, such as a gift, that is offered or given. **b.** Something, such as a speech, that is set forth for an audience. **4.a.** A formal introduction. **b.** A social debut. **5.** *Eccles.* The act or right of naming a cleric to a benefice. **6.** The process of offering for consideration or display. **7.** *Medic.* The position of the fetus in the uterus at birth with respect to the mouth of the uterus. —**pres′en•ta′tion•al** *adj.*

pre•sent•a•tive (prĭ-zĕn′tə-tĭv) *adj.* **1.** Having the capacity or function of bringing an idea or image to mind. **2.a.** Perceived or capable of being perceived directly rather than through association. **b.** Having the ability to so perceive. **3.** *Eccles.* Capable of naming or of being named to a benefice. —**pre•sent′a•tive•ness** *n.*

pres•ent-day (prĕz′ənt-dā′) *adj.* Now in existence or progress; current: *present-day attitudes about the family.*

pres•ent•ee (prĕz′ən-tē′, prĭ-zĕn′-) *n.* **1.** One who is presented. **2.** One to whom something is given.

pre•sen•tient (prē-sĕn′shənt, -shē-ənt) *adj.* Having a presentiment. [Lat. *praesentiēns, praesentient-*, pr.part. of *praesentīre*, to feel beforehand. See PRESENTIMENT.]

pre•sen•ti•ment (prĭ-zĕn′tə-mənt) *n.* A sense that something is about to occur; a premonition. [Obsolete Fr. < *presentir*, to feel before < Lat. *praesentīre* : *prae-*, pre- + *sentīre*, to feel; see **sent-***.] —**pre•sen′ti•men′tal** (-mĕn′tl) *adj.*

pres•ent•ly (prĕz′ənt-lē) *adv.* **1.** In a short time; soon. **2.** At this time or period; now. **3.** *Archaic.* At once.

pre•sent•ment (prĭ-zĕnt′mənt) *n.* **1.a.** The act of presenting to view or to the mind. **b.** Something expressed, presented, or exhibited. **c.** The light in which something is presented. **2.** *Law.* **a.** The act of submitting or presenting a formal statement of a legal matter to a court or an authorized person. **b.** The report written by a grand jury concerning an offense and based on the jury's knowledge and observation. **3.** The act of presenting a bill or note for payment.

Elvis Presley

pres•ent participle (prĕz′ənt) *n.* *Gram.* A participle expressing present action, formed in English by the infinitive plus *-ing* and used to express present action in relation to the time indicated by the finite verb in its clause, to form progressive tenses with the auxiliary *be,* and to function as a verbal adjective.

pres•ent per•fect (prĕz′ənt pûr′fĭkt) *n.* *Gram.* **1.** The verb tense expressing action completed at the present time, formed in English by combining the present tense of *have* with a past participle, as in *He has spoken.* **2.** A verb in the present perfect tense.

pres•ent tense (prĕz′ənt) *n.* *Gram.* The verb tense expressing action in the present time, as in *She writes; she is writing.*

pres•er•va•tion•ist (prĕz′ər-vā′shə-nĭst) *n.* One who advocates preservation, esp. of natural areas, historical sites, or endangered species. —**pres′er•va′tion•ism** *n.*

pre•ser•va•tive (prĭ-zûr′və-tĭv) *adj.* Tending to preserve or capable of preserving. —*n.* Something used to preserve, esp. a chemical added to foods to inhibit spoilage.

pre•serve (prĭ-zûrv′) *v.* **-served, -serv•ing, -serves.** —*tr.* **1.** To maintain in safety from injury, peril, or harm; protect. **2.** To keep in perfect or unaltered condition; maintain unchanged. **3.** To keep or maintain intact: *preserving family harmony.* See Syns at **defend. 4.** To prepare (food) for future use, as by canning or salting. **5.** To prevent (organic bodies) from decaying or spoiling. **6.** To keep (game or fish) for one's private hunting or fishing. —*intr.* **1.** To treat fruit or other foods so as to prevent decay. **2.** To maintain a private area stocked with game or fish. —*n.* **1.** Something that acts to preserve; a preservative. **2.** Fruit cooked with sugar to prevent decay or fermentation. Often used in the plural. **3.** An area maintained for the protection of wildlife or natural resources. **4.** Something considered as being the exclusive province of certain persons. [ME *preserven* < OFr. *preserver* < Med.Lat. *praeservāre* < LLat., to observe beforehand : Lat. *prae-*, pre- + Lat. *servāre*, to guard, preserve; see **ser-[1]***.] —**pre•serv′a•bil′i•ty** *n.* —**pre•serv′a•ble** *adj.* —**pres′er•va′tion** (prĕz′ər-vā′shən) *n.* —**pre•serv′er** *n.*

pre•shrunk also **pre-shrunk** (prē′shrŭngk′) *adj.* Of, relating to, or being fabric or a garment that has been shrunk during manufacture to minimize subsequent shrinkage.

pre•side (prĭ-zīd′) *intr.v.* **-sid•ed, -sid•ing, -sides. 1.** To hold the position of authority; act as chairperson or president. **2.** To possess or exercise authority or control. **3.** *Mus.* To be the featured instrumental performer: *presided at the keyboard.* [Fr. *présider* < OFr. < Lat. *praesidēre* : *prae-*, pre- + *sedēre*, to sit; see **sed-***.] —**pre•sid′er** *n.*

pres•i•den•cy (prĕz′ĭ-dən-sē, -dĕn′-) *n., pl.* **-cies. 1.** The office, function, or term of a president. **2.a.** Often **Presidency.** The office of president of a republic. **b. Presidency.** The office of the President of the United States. **3.** *Mormon Ch.* **a.** A governing body consisting of three men. **b.** Often **Presidency.** The chief administrative body of the church.

pres•i•dent (prĕz′ĭ-dənt, -dĕnt′) *n.* **1.** One appointed or elected to preside over an organized body of people, such as an assembly or a meeting. **2.a.** Often **President.** The chief executive of a republic. **b. President.** The chief executive of the United States, serving as both chief of state and chief political executive. **3.** The chief officer of a branch of government, a corporation, a board of trustees, a university, or a similar body. [ME < OFr. < Lat. *praesidēns, praesident-* < pr.part. of *praesidēre*, to preside. See PRESIDE.] —**pres′i•dent•ship′** *n.*

pres•i•dent-e•lect (prĕz′ĭ-dənt-ĭ-lĕkt′) *n., pl.* **pres•i•dents-e•lect** (prĕz′ĭ-dənts-). A person who has been elected president but has not yet been inducted into office.

pres•i•den•tial (prĕz′ĭ-dĕn′shəl) *adj.* **1.** Of, relating to, or befitting a president or presidency. **2.** Of or relating to a political system in which the chief officer is a president elected independently of the legislature. —**pres′i•den′tial•ly** *adv.*

president pro tem (prō tĕm′) *n., pl.* **presidents pro tem.** *Informal.* A president pro tempore.

president pro tem•po•re (prō tĕm′pə-rē) *n., pl.* **presidents pro tempore.** The senator who presides over the U.S. Senate in the absence of the Vice President.

Pres•i•dents' Day (prĕz′ĭ-dənts, -dĕnts) *n.* The third Monday in February, observed in the United States as a legal holiday in commemoration of the birthdays of George Washington and Abraham Lincoln.

pre•sid•i•al (prĭ-sĭd′ē-əl) also **pre•sid•i•ar•y** (-ĕr′ē) *adj.* Of, relating to, possessing, or being a garrison.

pre•si•di•o (prĭ-sē′dē-ō′, -sĭd′ē-ō′) *n., pl.* **-os.** A garrison, esp. a fortress of the kind established in the southwest United States by the Spanish to protect their holdings and missions. [Sp. < Lat. *praesidium*, guard, defense < *praesidēre*, to guard. See PRESIDE.]

pre•sid•i•um (prĭ-sĭd′ē-əm) *n., pl.* **-i•a** (-ē-ə) or **-i•ums.** Any of various permanent executive committees in Communist countries having power to act for a larger governing body. [Russ. *prezidium* < Lat. *praesidium*, garrison. See PRESIDIO.]

Pres•ley (prĕs′lē, prĕz′-), **Elvis Aron.** 1935–77. Amer. singer whose rock 'n' roll records and charismatic manner greatly influenced popular culture.

pre•soak (prē-sōk′) *tr.v.* **-soaked, -soak•ing, -soaks.** To soak (laundry) before washing. —*n.* (prē′sōk′). **1.** The act or an instance of presoaking. **2.** A liquid preparation in which laundry is presoaked. **3.** A cycle on an automatic washing machine for presoaking laundry.

pre-So•crat•ic (prē′sō-krăt′ĭk, -sə-) *adj.* Of or relating to the Greek philosophers or philosophical systems of thought before Socrates. — *n.* A pre-Socratic philosopher.

pre•sort (prē-sôrt′) *tr.v.* **-sort•ed, -sort•ing, -sorts.** To sort (mail) by ZIP code before delivery to a post office.

press[1] (prĕs) *v.* **pressed, press•ing, press•es.** — *tr.* **1.** To exert steady weight or force against; bear down on. **2.a.** To squeeze the juice or other contents from. **b.** To extract (juice, for example) by squeezing or compressing. **3.a.** To reshape or make compact by applying steady force; compress. **b.** To iron (clothing, for example). **4.** To clasp in fondness or politeness. **5.** To try to influence, as by insistent arguments; importune or entreat. **6.** To urge or force to action; impel. **7.** To place in trying or distressing circumstances; harass or oppress. **8.** To move (keys on a keyboard, for example) by applying pressure. **9.** To lay stress on; emphasize. **10.** To advance or carry on vigorously. **11.** To put forward importunately or insistently. **12.** To make (a phonograph record or videodisk) from a mold or matrix. **13.** *Sports.* To lift (a weight) to a position above the head without moving the legs. — *intr.* **1.** To exert force or pressure. **2.** To weigh heavily, as on the mind. **3.** To advance eagerly; push forward. **4.** To require haste; be urgent. **5.** To iron clothes or other material. **6.** To assemble closely and in large numbers; crowd. **7.** To employ urgent persuasion or entreaty. **8.** *Sports.* To raise or lift a weight in a press. **9.** *Basketball.* To employ a press. — *n.* **1.** Any of various machines or devices that apply pressure. **2.** A printing press. **3.** A place or an establishment where matter is printed. **4.** The art, method, or business of printing. **5.a.** The collecting and transmitting of news; journalism in general. **b.** The entirety of media and agencies that collect, publish, transmit, or broadcast the news. **c.** The people involved in the media, as news reporters, photographers, publishers, and broadcasters. **d.** Commentary or coverage esp. in newspapers or periodicals: *It received good press.* **6.** The act of gathering in large numbers or of pushing forward. **7.** A large gathering; a throng. **8.a.** The act of applying pressure. **b.** The state of being pressed. **9.** The haste or urgency of business or matters. **10.** The set of proper creases in a garment or fabric, formed by ironing. **11.** *Chiefly Northeastern U.S.* An upright closet or case used for storing clothing, books, or other articles. **12.** A viselike device for keeping a racket from warping. **13.** *Sports.* A lift in weightlifting in which the weight is raised to shoulder level and then steadily pushed straight overhead without movement of the legs. **14.** *Basketball.* An aggressive defense tactic in which players guard opponents closely, often over the entire court. — ***idiom.* press the flesh.** *Informal.* To shake hands and mingle with many people, esp. while campaigning for public office. [ME *pressen* < OFr. *presser* < Lat. *pressāre*, freq. of *premere*, to press. See **per-**[4]*.]

press[2] (prĕs) *tr.v.* **pressed, press•ing, press•es. 1.** To force into service in the army or navy; impress. **2.a.** To take arbitrarily or by force, esp. for public use. **b.** To use in a manner different from the usual or intended, esp. in an emergency. — *n.* **1.** Conscription, esp. into the army or navy. **2.** *Obsolete.* An official warrant for impressing men into military service. [Alteration of obsolete *prest*, to hire for military service by advance payment < ME, enlistment money, loan < OFr. < *prester*, to lend < Med.Lat. *praestāre* < Lat., to furnish < *praestō*, present, at hand.]

press agency *n.* See **news agency.**

press agent *n.* A person employed to arrange advertising and publicity, as for a performer. — **press a′gent•ry** *n.*

press•board (prĕs′bôrd′, -bōrd′) *n.* **1.** A heavy glazed paper or pasteboard used esp. to cover the platen or cylinder of a printing press. **2.** A small ironing board.

press box *n.* A section for reporters, as in a stadium.

press conference *n.* An interview held for news reporters by a political figure or a famous person.

press•er (prĕs′ər) *n.* **1.** One who presses clothes. **2.** Any of various devices that apply pressure to a product in manufacturing or canning.

press gang also **press•gang** (prĕs′găng′) *n.* A company of men under an officer detailed to force men into military or naval service.

press-gang (prĕs′găng′) *tr.v.* **-ganged, -gang•ing, -gangs. 1.** To force into military or naval service. **2.** To coerce.

press•ing (prĕs′ĭng) *adj.* **1.** Demanding immediate attention; urgent: *a pressing need.* See Syns at **urgent. 2.** Very earnest or persistent; insistent: *a pressing invitation.* — *n.* **1.** The process or an instance of applying pressure by means of a press. **2.a.** A phonograph record pressed from a master mold or matrix. **b.** A number of recordings pressed at the same time. **3.** Urgent solicitation; insistence. — **press′ing•ly** *adv.*

press kit *n.* A packaged set of promotional materials for distribution to the press.

press•man (prĕs′mən, -măn′) *n.* **1.** A man who operates a printing press. **2.** *Chiefly British.* A newspaper reporter.

press•mark (prĕs′märk′) *n.* **1.** *Print.* A notation or figure in the margin of a printed sheet indicating the press on which it was printed. **2.** *Chiefly British.* A notation in or on a book indicating where it should be placed in a library.

press of sail *n. Naut.* The greatest amount of sail that a ship can carry safely.

pres•sor (prĕs′ôr′, -ər) *adj.* Causing an increase in blood pressure. [LLat., one who presses < Lat. *premere, press-*, to press. See PRESS[1].]

press release *n.* An announcement of an event, a performance, or other newsworthy item that is issued to the press.

press•room (prĕs′ro͞om′, -ro͝om′) *n.* The room in a printing or newspaper publishing establishment for the presses.

press run or **press•run** (prĕs′rŭn′) *n.* **1.** Continuous operation of a printing press for a specific job. **2.** The number of copies printed in one such continuous operation.

press secretary *n.* One who officially manages the public affairs and press conferences of a public figure.

pres•sure (prĕsh′ər) *n.* **1.a.** The act of pressing. **b.** The condition of being pressed. **2.** The application of continuous force by one body on another that it is touching; compression. **3.** *Phys.* Force applied uniformly over a surface, measured as force per unit of area. **4.** *Meteorol.* Atmospheric pressure. **5.** A compelling or constraining influence, such as a moral force, on the mind or will. **6.** Urgent claim or demand. **7.** An oppressive condition of physical, mental, social, or economic distress. **8.** A physical sensation produced by compression of a part of the body. **9.** *Archaic.* A mark made by application of force or weight; an impression. — *tr.v.* **-sured, -sur•ing, -sures. 1.** To force, as by overpowering influence. **2.** To pressurize. **3.** To pressure-cook. [ME < OFr. < Lat. *pressūra* < *pressus*, p.part. of *premere*, to press. See **per-**[4]*.]

pressure cabin *n.* A pressurized section of an aircraft.

pres•sure-cook (prĕsh′ər-ko͝ok′) *tr.v.* **-cooked, -cook•ing, -cooks.** To cook in a pressure cooker.

pressure cooker *n.* **1.** An airtight metal pot that uses steam under pressure at high temperature to cook food quickly. **2.** *Informal.* A stressful situation or atmosphere.

pressure gauge *n.* **1.** A device for measuring the pressure of a gas or liquid. **2.** A device for measuring the pressure of explosions.

pressure group *n.* An interest group that endeavors to influence public policy and government legislation.

pressure point *n.* **1.** Any of several points on the body at which an underlying artery can be pressed against a bone to stop distal bleeding. **2.** An area on the skin that is highly sensitive to the application of pressure.

pressure suit *n.* A garment worn in high-altitude aircraft or spacecraft to compensate for low-pressure conditions.

pres•sur•ize (prĕsh′ə-rīz′) *tr.v.* **-ized, -iz•ing, -iz•es. 1.** To maintain normal air pressure in (an enclosure). **2.** To put (gas or liquid) under a greater than normal pressure. **3.** To design to resist pressure. **4.** To pressure-cook. **5.** *Informal.* To subject to excessive stress, strain, or vexation. — **pres′sur•i•za′tion** (-ər-ĭ-zā′shən) *n.* — **pres′sur•iz′er** *n.*

press•work (prĕs′wûrk′) *n.* **1.** Management or operation of a printing press. **2.** The matter printed by such a press.

Pres•ter John (prĕs′tər jŏn′) *n.* A legendary medieval Christian priest and king thought to have reigned over a Christian kingdom in the Far East or Ethiopia. [ME *prestre*, priest < OFr. < LLat. *presbyter*. See PRESBYTER.]

pre•ster•num (prē-stûr′nəm) *n.* See **manubrium** 1.

pres•ti•dig•i•ta•tion (prĕs′tĭ-dĭj′ĭ-tā′shən) *n.* Manual skill and dexterity in the execution of tricks; sleight of hand. [Fr. < *prestidigitateur*, conjurer : *preste*, nimble (< Ital. *presto*; see PRESTO) + Lat. *digitus*, finger; see DIGIT.] — **pres′ti•dig′i•ta′tor** *n.*

pres•tige (prĕ-stēzh′, -stēj′) *n.* **1.** The level of respect at which one is regarded by others; standing. **2.** A person's high standing among others; honor or esteem. **3.** Widely recognized prominence, distinction, or importance: *a position of prestige.* [Fr., illusion < Lat. *praestīgiae*, tricks, prob. alteration of **praestrīgiae* < *praestringere*, to touch, blunt, blind : *prae-*, pre- + *stringere*, to draw tight; see **streig-***.]

pres•ti•gious (prĕ-stē′jəs, -stĭj′əs) *adj.* Having prestige; esteemed. — **pres•ti′gious•ly** *adv.* — **pres•ti′gious•ness** *n.*

pres•tis•si•mo (prĕ-stĭs′ə-mō′) *Mus.* — *adv. & adj.* In as fast a tempo as possible. — *n., pl.* **-mos.** A prestissimo passage or movement. [Ital., superl. of *presto*, presto. See PRESTO.]

pres•to (prĕs′tō) *adv.* **1.** *Mus.* In a very fast tempo, usu. considered to be faster than allegro but slower than prestissimo. **2.** So suddenly that magic seems involved; right away. — *n., pl.* **-tos.** *Mus.* A passage or movement that is performed presto. [Ital. < LLat. *praestus*, quick < Lat. *praestō*, at hand.] — **pres′to** *adj.*

Pres•ton (prĕs′tən). A borough of NW England NNE of Liverpool; site of a Jacobite defeat (1715). Pop. 125,800.

pre•sum•a•ble (prĭ-zo͞o′mə-bəl) *adj.* That can be presumed or taken for granted; reasonable as a supposition: *presumable causes of the disaster.* — **pre•sum′a•bly** *adv.*

pre•sume (prĭ-zo͞om′) *v.* **-sumed, -sum•ing, -sumes.** — *tr.* **1.** To take for granted as being true in the absence of proof to the contrary. **2.** To give reasonable evidence for assuming; appear to prove. **3.** To venture without authority or permission; dare. — *intr.* **1.** To act overconfidently; take liberties. **2.** To take unwarranted advantage of something; go beyond the proper limits. **3.** To take for granted that something is true or factual; suppose. [ME *presumen* < OFr. *presumer* < LLat.

ă pat	oi boy
ā pay	ou out
âr care	o͝o took
ä father	o͞o boot
ĕ pet	ŭ cut
ē be	ûr urge
ĭ pit	th thin
ī pie	*th* this
îr pier	hw which
ŏ pot	zh vision
ō toe	ə about, item
ô paw	

Stress marks:
′ (primary);
′ (secondary), as in
dictionary (dĭk′shə-nĕr′ē)

praesūmere < Lat., to anticipate : *prae-*, pre- + *sūmere*, to take; see **em-***.] — **pre•sum′ed•ly** (-zo͞o′mĭd-lē) *adv.* — **pre•sum′er** *n.*

Syns: *presume, presuppose, postulate, posit, assume.* These verbs signify to take something for granted or as being a fact. To *presume* is to suppose that something is reasonable, justifiable, sound, or possible in the absence of proof to the contrary: *"I presume you're tired after the long ride"* (Edith Wharton). *Presuppose* can mean to believe or suppose in advance: *It is unrealistic to presuppose that kind of knowledge in a beginner. Postulate* and *posit* denote the assertion of the existence, reality, necessity, or truth of something as the basis for reasoning or argument: *"We can see individuals, but we can't see providence; we have to postulate it"* (Aldous Huxley). *Scientists posit a common ancestor for the two species.* To *assume* is to accept something as existing or being true without proof or on inconclusive grounds: *"We must never assume that which is incapable of proof"* (G.H. Lewes).

Leontyne Price

pre•sum•ing (prĭ-zo͞o′mĭng) *adj.* Having or showing excessive and arrogant self-confidence; presumptuous. — **pre•sum′ing•ly** *adv.*

pre•sump•tion (prĭ-zŭmp′shən) *n.* **1.** Arrogant or offensive behavior or language; effrontery. **2.** The act of presuming or accepting as true. **3.** Acceptance or belief based on reasonable evidence; assumption or supposition. **4.** A condition or basis for accepting or presuming. **5.** *Law.* A conclusion derived from a particular set of facts based on law, rather than probable reasoning. [ME *presumpcion* < OFr. < LLat. *praesūmptiō, praesūmptiōn-* < Lat., anticipation < *praesūmptus,* p.part. of *praesūmere,* to anticipate. See PRESUME.]

pre•sump•tive (prĭ-zŭmp′tĭv) *adj.* **1.** Providing a reasonable basis for belief or acceptance. **2.** Founded on probability or presumption. — **pre•sump′tive•ly** *adv.*

pre•sump•tu•ous (prĭ-zŭmp′cho͞o-əs) *adj.* Going beyond what is right or proper; excessively forward. [ME < OFr. *presumptueux* < LLat. *presūmptuōsus,* var. of *praesūmptiōsus* < *praesūmptiō,* presumption. See PRESUMPTION.] — **pre•sump′tu•ous•ly** *adv.* — **pre•sump′tu•ous•ness** *n.*

pre•sup•pose (prē′sə-pōz′) *tr.v.* **-posed, -pos•ing, -pos•es. 1.** To believe or suppose in advance. See Syns at **presume. 2.** To require or involve necessarily as an antecedent condition. — **pre•sup′po•si′tion** (-sŭp′ə-zĭsh′ən) *n.* — **pre•sup′po•si′tion•al** *adj.*

pre•syn•ap•tic (prē′sĭ-năp′tĭk) *adj.* Situated in front of or occurring before a synapse: *a presynaptic nerve fiber.*

pret. *abbr. Gram.* Preterit.

prêt-à-por•ter (prêt′ä-pôr-tā′, -pōr-) *n.* Ready-to-wear clothing. [Fr. : *prêt,* ready + *à,* to + *porter,* to wear.]

pre•tax (prē′tăks′) *adj.* Existing before tax deductions.

pre•teen (prē′tēn′) *adj.* **1.** Being a child esp. between the ages of 9 and 12; preadolescent. **2.** Relating to or designed for preteen children. — *n.* A preadolescent boy or girl.

pre•teen•ag•er (prē′tēn′ā′jər) *n.* A preteen.

pre•tence (prē′tĕns′, prĭ-tĕns′) *n. Chiefly British.* Var. of **pretense.**

pre•tend (prĭ-tĕnd′) *v.* **-tend•ed, -tend•ing, -tends.** — *tr.* **1.** To give a false appearance of; feign. **2.** To claim or allege insincerely or falsely; profess. **3.** To represent fictitiously in play; make believe. **4.** To take upon oneself; venture. — *intr.* **1.** To feign an action or a character, as in play. **2.** To put forward a claim. **3.** To make pretensions. — *adj. Informal.* Imitation; make-believe. [ME *pretenden* < OFr. *pretendre* < Lat. *praetendere* : *prae-,* pre- + *tendere,* to extend; see **ten-***.]

pre•tend•ed (prĭ-tĕn′dĭd) *adj.* **1.** Not genuine or sincere; feigned. **2.** Supposed; alleged. — **pre•tend′ed•ly** *adv.*

pre•tend•er (prĭ-tĕn′dər) *n.* **1.** One who simulates, pretends, or alleges falsely; a hypocrite or dissembler. **2.** One who sets forth a claim, esp. a claimant to a throne.

pre•tense (prē′tĕns′, prĭ-tĕns′) *n.* **1.** The act of pretending; a false appearance or action intended to deceive. **2.** A false or studied show; an affectation. **3.** A professed but feigned reason or excuse; a pretext. **4.** Something imagined or pretended. **5.** Mere show without reality; outward appearance. **6.** A right asserted with or without foundation; a claim. **7.** The quality or state of being pretentious; ostentation. [ME < OFr. *pretensse* < Med.Lat. **praetēnsa* < LLat., fem. of *praetēnsus,* alteration of Lat. *praetentus,* p.part. of *praetendere,* to pretend, assert. See PRETEND.]

pre•ten•sion (prĭ-tĕn′shən) *n.* **1.** A specious allegation; a pretext. **2.** A claim to something, such as a right. **3.** The advancing of a claim. **4.** Ostentatious display; pretentiousness.

pre•ten•tious (prĭ-tĕn′shəs) *adj.* **1.** Claiming or demanding a position of distinction or merit, esp. when unjustified. **2.** Outwardly extravagant; ostentatious. See Syns at **showy.** — **pre•ten′tious•ly** *adv.* — **pre•ten′tious•ness** *n.*

pret•er•it or **pret•er•ite** (prĕt′ər-ĭt) *Gram.* — *adj.* Of, relating to, or being the verb tense that describes a past action or state. — *n.* **1.** The verb form expressing or describing a past action or condition. **2.** A preterit verb. [ME < OFr. < Lat. *(tempus) praeteritum,* past (tense), neut. p.part. of *praeterīre,* to go by : *praeter,* beyond, comp. of *prae,* before; see **per**[1]* + *īre,* to go; see **ei-***.]

pret•er•i•tion (prĕt′ə-rĭsh′ən) *n.* **1.** The act of passing by, disregarding, or omitting. **2.** *Law.* Neglect of a testator to mention a legal heir in his or her will. **3.** *Theol.* The Calvinist doctrine that God neglected to designate those who would be damned, positively determining only the elect. [LLat. *praeteritiō, praeteritiōn-,* a passing over < Lat. *praeteritus,* p.part. of *praeterīre,* to go by. See PRETERIT.]

pre•term (prē′tûrm′, prē-tûrm′) *adj.* Occurring or appearing before the expected time at the end of a full-term pregnancy: *preterm labor.* — *n.* An infant born prematurely.

pre•ter•mit (prē′tər-mĭt′) *tr.v.* **-mit•ted, -mit•ting, -mits. 1.** To disregard intentionally or allow to pass unnoticed or unmentioned. **2.** To fail to do or include; omit. **3.** To interrupt or terminate. [Lat. *praetermittere* : *praeter,* beyond; see PRETERIT + *mittere,* to let go.] — **pre′ter•mis′sion** (-mĭsh′ən) *n.* — **pre′ter•mit′ter** *n.*

pre•ter•nat•u•ral (prē′tər-năch′ər-əl, -năch′rəl) *adj.* **1.** Out of or being beyond the normal course of nature; differing from the natural. **2.** Surpassing the normal or usual; extraordinary. **3.** Transcending the natural or material order; supernatural. [Med.Lat. *praeternātūrālis* < Lat. *praeter nātūrām,* beyond nature : *praeter,* beyond; see PRETERIT + *nātūra,* nature; see NATURE.] — **pre′ter•nat′u•ral•ism, pre′ter•nat′u•ral•ness** *n.* — **pre′ter•nat′u•ral•ly** *adv.*

pre•test (prē′tĕst′) *n.* **1.a.** A preliminary test given to determine whether students are sufficiently prepared for a more advanced course of studies. **b.** A test taken for practice. **2.** Advance testing, as of an idea. — *tr. & intr.v.* (prē-tĕst′) **-test•ed, -test•ing, -tests.** To subject to or conduct a pretest.

pre•text (prē′tĕkst′) *n.* **1.** An ostensible or professed purpose; an excuse. **2.** An effort or a strategy intended to conceal something. — *tr.v.* **-text•ed, -text•ing, -texts.** To allege as an excuse. [Lat. *praetextum* < neut. p.part. of *praetexere,* to disguise : *prae-,* pre- + *texere,* to weave; see **teks-***.]

pre•tor (prē′tər) *n.* Var. of **praetor.**

Pre•to•ri•a (prĭ-tôr′ē-ə, -tōr′-). The administrative cap. of South Africa, in the NE part N of Johannesburg; founded 1855. Pop. 435,100.

pre•to•ri•an (prē-tôr′ē-ən, -tōr′-) *adj.* Var. of **praetorian.**

Pre•to•ri•us (prĭ-tôr′ē-əs, -tōr′-), **Andries Wilhelmus Jacobus.** 1798–1853. Afrikaner soldier and politician who led the defeat of the Zulus (1838). His son **Marthinus Wessels Pretorius** (1819–1901) founded Pretoria.

pre•tri•al (prē-trī′əl, -trīl′) *Law.* — *n.* A proceeding held before an official trial, esp. to clarify points of law and facts. — *adj.* **1.** Of or relating to a pretrial. **2.** Existing or occurring before a trial: *pretrial hearings.*

pret•ti•fy (prĭt′ĭ-fī′) *tr.v.* **-fied, -fy•ing, -fies.** To make pretty or prettier. — **pret′ti•fi•ca′tion** (-fĭ-kā′shən) *n.* — **pret′ti•fi′er** *n.*

pret•ty (prĭt′ē) *adj.* **-ti•er, -ti•est. 1.** Pleasing or attractive in a graceful or delicate way. **2.** Clever; adroit. **3.** Very bad; terrible. **4.** Ostensibly or superficially attractive but lacking substance or conviction. **5.** *Informal.* Considerable in size or extent. — *adv.* **1.** To a fair degree; moderately. **2.** In a pretty manner; prettily or pleasingly. — *n., pl.* **-ties. 1.** One that is pretty. **2. pretties.** Delicate clothing, esp. lingerie. — *tr.v.* **-tied, -ty•ing, -ties.** To make pretty: *pretty up the house.* — ***idiom.* pretty much.** For the most part; mostly. [ME *prety,* clever, fine, handsome < OE *prættig,* cunning < *prætt,* trick.] — **pret′ti•ly** *adv.* — **pret′ti•ness** *n.*

pret•zel (prĕt′səl) *n.* A glazed brittle biscuit that is salted on the outside and usu. baked in the form of a loose knot or a stick. [Ger. *Brezel, Pretzel* < MHGer. *brēzel, prēzel* < OHGer. *brezitella* < Med.Lat. **brāchitellum,* dim. of Lat. *bracchiātus,* branched < *bracchium,* arm < Gk. *brakhiōn,* upper arm. See **mregh-u-***.]

prev. *abbr.* **1.** Previous. **2.** Previously.

pre•vail (prĭ-vāl′) *intr.v.* **-vailed, -vail•ing, -vails. 1.** To be greater in strength or influence; triumph. **2.** To be or become effective; win out. **3.** To be most common or frequent; be predominant. **4.** To be in force, use, or effect; be current. **5.** To use persuasion or inducement successfully. Often used with *on, upon,* or *with.* [ME *prevailen* < OFr. *prevaloir, prevaill-* < Lat. *praevalēre,* to be stronger : *prae-,* pre- + *valēre,* to be strong; see **wal-***.] — **pre•vail′er** *n.*

pre•vail•ing (prĭ-vā′lĭng) *adj.* **1.** Most frequent or common; predominant. **2.** Generally current; widespread. — **pre•vail′ing•ly** *adv.* — **pre•vail′ing•ness** *n.*

prev•a•lence (prĕv′ə-ləns) *n.* **1.** The condition of being prevalent. **2.** *Medic.* The total number of cases of a disease in a given population at a specific time.

prev•a•lent (prĕv′ə-lənt) *adj.* Widely or commonly occurring, existing, accepted, or practiced. [ME, very strong < Lat. *praevalēns, praevalent-,* pr.part. of *praevalēre,* to be stronger. See PREVAIL.] — **prev′a•lent•ly** *adv.*

pre•var•i•cate (prĭ-văr′ĭ-kāt′) *intr.v.* **-cat•ed, -cat•ing, -cates.** To stray from or evade the truth; equivocate. [Lat. *praevāricārī, praevāricāt-* : *prae-,* pre- + *vāricāre,* to straddle (< *vāricus,* straddling < *vārus,* bent).] — **pre•var′i•ca′tion** *n.* — **pre•var′i•ca′tor** *n.*

pre•ven•ience (prĭ-vēn′yəns) *n.* **1.** The act or state of being antecedent or prevenient. **2.** Attention to another's needs.

pre•ven•ient (prĭ-vēn′yənt) *adj.* **1.** Coming before; preceding. **2.** Expectant; anticipatory. [Lat. *praeveniēns, praevenient-*, pr.part. of *praevenīre*, to precede : *prae-*, pre- + *venīre*, to come; see **gʷā-***.] — **pre•ven′ient•ly** *adv.*

pre•vent (prĭ-vĕnt′) *v.* **-vent•ed, -vent•ing, -vents.** — *tr.* **1.** To keep from happening. **2.** To keep (someone) from doing something; impede. **3.** *Archaic.* To anticipate or counter in advance. **4.** *Archaic.* To come before; precede. — *intr.* To present an obstacle. [ME *preventen*, to anticipate < Lat. *praevenīre, praevent-* : *prae-*, pre- + *venīre*, to come; see **gʷā-***.] — **pre•vent′a•bil′i•ty, pre•vent′i•bil′i•ty** *n.* — **pre•vent′a•ble, pre•vent′i•ble** *adj.* — **pre•vent′er** *n.*

pre•ven•tion (prĭ-vĕn′shən) *n.* **1.** The act of preventing or impeding. **2.** A hindrance; an obstacle.

pre•ven•tive (prĭ-vĕn′tĭv) also **pre•ven•ta•tive** (-tə-tĭv) — *adj.* **1.** Intended or used to prevent or hinder. **2.** Carried out to deter expected aggression by hostile forces. **3.** Preventing or slowing the course of an illness or a disease; prophylactic. — *n.* **1.** Something that prevents; an obstacle. **2.** Something that prevents or slows the course of an illness or a disease. — **pre•ven′tive•ly** *adv.* — **pre•ven′tive•ness** *n.*

pre•verb (prē′vûrb′) *n. Ling.* A prefix or particle preceding the root or stem of a verb, as *for-* in *forget*. — **pre•verb′** *adj.*

pre•verb•al (prē-vûr′bəl) *adj.* **1.** *Gram.* Preceding the verb. **2.a.** Having not yet learned to speak: *preverbal children.* **b.** Marked by the absence of spoken language.

pre•view also **pre•vue** (prē′vyo͞o′) — *n.* **1.** A showing, as of art, to which a selected audience is invited before public presentation. **2.** An advance viewing or exhibition, esp. of scenes advertising a forthcoming movie; a trailer. **3.** An introductory or preliminary message, sample, or overview; a foretaste. — *tr.v.* **-viewed, -view•ing, -views** also **-vued, -vu•ing, -vues.** **1.** To view or exhibit in advance. **2.** To provide a preliminary sample or overview of.

pre•vi•ous (prē′vē-əs) *adj.* **1.** Existing or occurring before something else in time or order; prior. **2.** *Informal.* Acting, occurring, or done too soon; premature. [< Lat. *praevius*, going before : *prae-*, pre- + *via*, way; see **wegh-***.] — **pre′vi•ous•ly** *adv.* — **pre′vi•ous•ness** *n.*

previous question *n.* A parliamentary motion to take a vote on the main question being considered.

previous to *prep.* Prior to; before.

pre•vise (prĭ-vīz′) *tr.v.* **-vised, -vis•ing, -vis•es.** **1.** To know in advance; foresee. **2.** To notify in advance; forewarn. [ME *previsen* < Lat. *praevidēre, praevīs-* : *prae-*, pre- + *vidēre*, to see; see **weid-***.] — **pre•vi′sor** *n.*

pre•vi•sion (prĭ-vĭzh′ən) *n.* **1.** Prescience; foresight. **2.** A prediction. — *tr.v.* **-sioned, -sion•ing, -sions.** To foresee. — **pre•vi′sion•al, pre•vi′sion•ar′y** (-vĭzh′ə-nĕr′ē) *adj.*

pre•vo•cal•ic (prē′vō-kăl′ĭk) *adj. Ling.* **1.** Preceding a vowel. **2.** Of or relating to a form of a linguistic element, such as a prefix, that occurs only before a vowel.

pre•vo•ca•tion•al (prē′vō-kā′shə-nəl) *adj.* Of or relating to instruction given in preparation for vocational school.

Pré•vost d'Ex•iles (prā-vō′ dĕg-zēl′), **Antoine Françoise.** "Abbé Prévost." 1697–1763. French writer and cleric known for the novel *Manon Lescaut* (1731).

pre•washed (prē′wŏsht′, -wôsht′) *adj.* Washed by the manufacturer so as to impart a softer texture or faded appearance.

pre•writ•ing (prē′rī′tĭng) *n.* The creation and arrangement of ideas preliminary to writing.

prex•y (prĕk′sē) *n., pl.* **-ies.** *Slang.* A president, esp. of a college or university. [Shortening and alteration of PRESIDENT.]

prey (prā) *n.* **1.** An animal hunted or caught for food; quarry. **2.** One that is defenseless, esp. in the face of attack; a victim. **3.** The act or practice of preying. — *intr.v.* **preyed, prey•ing, preys.** **1.** To hunt, catch, or eat prey. **2.** To victimize someone or make a profit at someone else's expense. **3.** To plunder or pillage. **4.** To exert a baneful or injurious effect. [ME *preie* < OFr. < Lat. *praeda*, booty, prey. See **ghend-***.] — **prey′er** *n.*

prf. *abbr. Print.* Proof.

Pri•am (prī′əm) *n. Gk. Myth.* The father of Paris, Hector, and Cassandra and king of Troy, who was killed when his city fell to the Greeks.

pri•a•pic (prī-ā′pĭk, -ăp′ĭk) also **pri•a•pe•an** (prī′ə-pē′ən) *adj.* **1.** Of, relating to, or resembling a phallus; phallic. **2.** Relating to or overly concerned with masculinity. [< PRIAPUS.]

pri•a•pism (prī′ə-pĭz′əm) *n.* Persistent, usu. painful erection of the penis, esp. as a consequence of disease. [Fr. *priapisme* < LLat. *priāpismus* < Gk. *priapismos* < *priapizein*, to have an erection < *Priapos*, Priapus.]

pri•a•pus (prī-ā′pəs) *n.* **1. Priapus.** *Gk. & Rom. Myth.* The god of procreation, guardian of gardens and vineyards, and personification of the erect phallus. **2.** An image of this god, often used as a scarecrow in ancient gardens. **3.** A representation of a phallus. [Lat. *Priāpus* < Gk. *Priapos.*]

Prib•i•lof Islands (prĭb′ə-lôf′). A group of islands off SW AK in the Bering Sea; named by a Russian explorer in 1786.

price (prīs) *n.* **1.** The amount as of money or goods, asked for or given in exchange for something else. **2.** The cost at which something is obtained. **3.** The cost of bribing someone. **4.** A reward offered for the capture or killing of a person. **5.** *Archaic.* Value or worth. — *tr.v.* **priced, pric•ing, pric•es.** **1.** To fix or establish a price for. **2.** To find out the price of. — ***idiom.* price out of the market.** To force (oneself or one's goods or services) from commercial demand by charging too much. [ME *pris* < OFr. < Lat. *pretium.* See **per-**[5]*.] — **price′a•ble** *adj.* — **pric′er** *n.*

Price (prīs), **(Mary) Leontyne.** b. 1927. Amer. soprano who performed with the Metropolitan Opera (1961–85).

price-earn•ings ratio (prīs′ûr′nĭngz) *n.* The ratio of the market price of a common stock to its earnings per share.

price fix•ing also **price-fix•ing** (prīs′fĭk′sĭng) *n.* **1.** The setting of commodity prices by a government. **2.** The result of an unlawful agreement between manufacturers or dealers to set and maintain prices on typically competing products.

price index *n.* A number relating prices of a group of commodities to their prices during an arbitrarily chosen base period.

price•less (prīs′lĭs) *adj.* **1.** Of inestimable worth; invaluable. **2.** Highly amusing, absurd, or odd. — **price′less•ly** *adv.*

price support *n.* Maintenance of prices, as of a commodity, at a certain level usu. through government intervention.

price tag *n.* **1.** A label attached to a piece of merchandise indicating its price. **2.** The cost of something.

price war *n.* An intense competition for sales based on underselling.

pric•ey also **pric•y** (prī′sē) *adj.* **-i•er, -i•est.** *Informal.* Expensive: *a pricey restaurant.* — **pric′ey•ness** *n.* — **pric′i•ly** *adv.*

Prich•ard (prĭch′ərd). A city of SW AL, a suburb of Mobile. Pop. 34,311.

prick (prĭk) *n.* **1.a.** The act of piercing or pricking. **b.** The sensation of being pierced or pricked. **2.a.** A persistent or sharply painful feeling of sorrow or remorse. **b.** A small sharp local pain, such as that made by a needle. **3.** A small mark or puncture made by a pointed object. **4.** A pointed object, such as a goad or a thorn. **5.** A hare's track or footprint. **6.** *Vulgar Slang.* A penis. **7.** *Vulgar Slang.* A man regarded as contemptible. — *v.* **pricked, prick•ing, pricks.** — *tr.* **1.** To puncture lightly. **2.** To affect with a mental or emotional pang, as of sorrow or remorse. **3.** To impel as if with a spur; urge on. **4.** To mark or delineate on a surface by means of small punctures. **5.** *Naut.* To measure with dividers on a chart. **6.** To pierce the quick of (a horse's hoof) while shoeing. **7.** To transplant (seedlings, for example) before final planting. **8.** To cause to stand erect or point upward. — *intr.* **1.** To pierce or puncture something or cause a pricking feeling. **2.** To feel a pang or twinge from or as if from being pricked. **3.a.** To spur a horse on. **b.** To ride at a gallop. **4.** To stand erect; point upward. — ***idiom.* prick up (one's) ears.** To listen with attentive interest. [ME < OE *prica*, puncture.]

prick•er (prĭk′ər) *n.* **1.** One, such as a pricking tool, that pierces or pricks. **2.** A prickle or thorn.

prick•et (prĭk′ĭt) *n.* **1.a.** A small point or spike for holding a candle upright. **b.** A candlestick having such a spike. **2.** A buck in its second year, before the antlers branch. [ME *priket*, dim. of *prik, prick*, prick. See PRICK.]

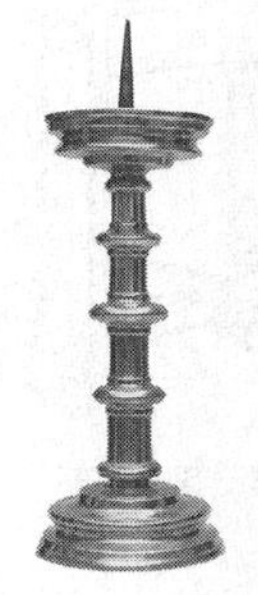

pricket
15th- or 16th-century bronze pricket

prick•le (prĭk′əl) *n.* **1.** A small sharp point, spine, or thorn. **2.** A tingling or pricking sensation. — *v.* **-led, -ling, -les.** — *tr.* **1.** To prick as if with a thorn. **2.** To cause a prickle in. — *intr.* **1.** To feel a prickle. **2.** To rise or stand up like prickles. [ME *prikel* < OE *pricel.*]

prick•ly (prĭk′lē) *adj.* **-li•er, -li•est.** **1.** Having prickles. **2.** Marked by prickling or tingling or smarting: *a prickly sensation in my foot.* **3.a.** Causing trouble or vexation; thorny: *a prickly situation.* **b.** Bristling or irritable. — **prick′li•ness** *n.*

prickly ash *n.* **1.** Any of numerous cosmopolitan deciduous or evergreen shrubs or trees of the genus *Zanthoxylum*, having alternate, mostly pinnate leaves. **2.** See **Hercules' club** 1.

prickly heat *n.* See **heat rash.**

prickly pear *n.* **1.** Any of various cacti of the genus *Opuntia*, having bristly flat or terete joints, usu. yellow flowers, and edible ovoid fruit. **2.** The fruit of any of these plants.

prickly pear
Plains prickly pear
Opuntia polyacantha

prickly poppy *n.* Any of various plants of the genus *Argemone*, chiefly of tropical America, having large yellow, lavender, or white flowers and prickly leaves, stems, and pods.

prick•y (prĭk′ē) *adj.* **-i•er, -i•est.** Prickly.

pride (prīd) *n.* **1.** A sense of one's own proper dignity or value; self-respect. **2.** Pleasure or satisfaction taken in an achievement, a possession, or an association. **3.** Arrogant or disdainful conduct or treatment; haughtiness. **4.a.** A cause or source of pleasure or satisfaction; the best of a group or class. **b.** The most successful or thriving condition; prime: *the pride of youth.* **5.** An excessively high opinion of oneself; conceit. **6.** Mettle or spirit in horses. **7.** A company of lions. **8.** A flamboyant or impressive group: *a pride of acrobats.* — *tr.v.* **prid•ed, prid•ing, prides.** To indulge (oneself) in a feeling of pleasure or satisfaction: *I pride myself on this garden.* [ME < OE *prȳde* < *prūd*, proud. See PROUD.]

Pride (prīd), **Thomas.** d. 1658. English Parliamentarian who led a regiment to Parliament and expelled those who opposed the condemnation of Charles I (1648).

pride•ful (prīd′fəl) *adj.* **1.** Arrogant; disdainful. **2.** Highly

ă pat	oi boy
ā pay	ou out
âr care	o͝o took
ä father	o͞o boot
ĕ pet	ŭ cut
ē be	ûr urge
ĭ pit	th thin
ī pie	*th* this
îr pier	hw which
ŏ pot	zh vision
ō toe	ə about, item
ô paw	

Stress marks:
′ (primary);
′ (secondary), as in
dictionary (dĭk′shə-nĕr′ē)

pleased; elated. —**pride′ful·ly** *adv.* —**pride′ful·ness** *n.*

pride of place *n.* The highest or most important position.

pried[1] (prīd) *v.* P.t. and p.part. of **pry**[1].

pried[2] (prīd) *v.* P.t. and p.part. of **pry**[2].

prie-dieu (prē-dyœ′) *n., pl.* **-dieus** or **-dieux** (-dyœz′). A desk-like kneeling bench with space above for a book, for use by a person at prayer. [Fr. *prie-Dieu* : *prier*, to pray (< OFr. < Lat. *precārī*; see PRAY) + *Dieu*, God (< OFr.; see ADIEU).]

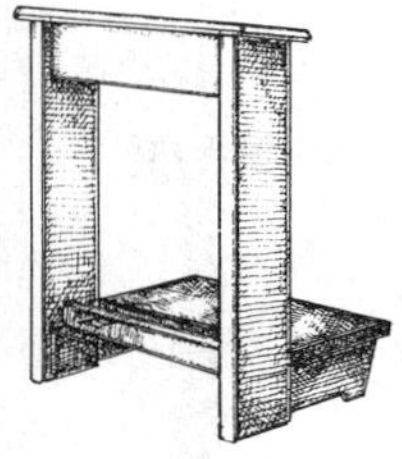

prie-dieu

pri·er also **pry·er** (prī′ər) *n.* One who pries, esp. a person who is unduly interested in the affairs of others.

pries[1] (prīz) *v.* Third pers. sing. pr.t. of **pry**[1]. —*n.* Pl. of **pry**[1].

pries[2] (prīz) *v.* Third pers. sing. pr.t. of **pry**[2]. —*n.* Pl. of **pry**[2].

priest (prēst) *n.* **1.** In many Christian churches, a member of the second grade of clergy ranking below a bishop but above a deacon and having authority to administer the sacraments. **2.** One with authority to perform and administer religious rites. —*tr.v.* **priest·ed, priest·ing, priests.** To ordain or admit to the priesthood. [ME *preost* < OE *prēost*, perh. < VLat. **prester* (< LLat. *presbyter*; see PRESBYTER) or < West Gmc. **prēvost* (< Lat. *praepositus*, superintendent; see PROVOST).]

priest·ess (prē′stĭs) *n.* A woman with the authority to perform and administer religious rites, esp. pagan ones.

priest·hood (prēst′ho͝od′) *n.* **1.** The character, office, or vocation of a priest. **2.** The clergy.

Priest·ley (prēst′lē), **J(ohn) B(oynton).** 1894–1984. British writer known for *The Good Companions* (1929).

Priestley, Joseph. 1733–1804. British chemist noted for his work on the isolation of gases and for his identification of the properties of oxygen (1774).

priest·ly (prēst′lē) *adj.* **-li·er, -li·est. 1.** Of or relating to a priest or the priesthood. **2.** Characteristic of or suitable for a priest. —**priest′li·ness** *n.*

prig (prĭg) *n.* **1.** A person who demonstrates an exaggerated conformity or propriety, esp. in an arrogant or smug manner. **2.** *Chiefly British.* A petty thief or pickpocket. **3.** *Archaic.* A conceited dandy; a fop. —*tr.v.* **prigged, prig·ging, prigs.** *Chiefly British.* To steal or pilfer. [?] —**prig′ger·y** *n.* —**prig′gish** *adj.* —**prig′gish·ly** *adv.* —**prig′gish·ness** *n.*

Pri·go·gine (prĭ-gô′zhən, -gô-zhēn′), **Ilya.** b. 1917. Russian-born Belgian chemist who won a 1977 Nobel Prize.

prim[1] (prĭm) *adj.* **prim·mer, prim·mest. 1.a.** Precise or proper to the point of affectation; excessively decorous. **b.** Straitlaced; prudish. **2.** Neat and trim: *a prim hedgerow.* —*v.* **primmed, prim·ming, prims.** —*tr.* **1.** To fix (the face or mouth) in a prim expression. **2.** To make prim, as in appearance. —*intr.* To assume a prim expression. [Poss. < obsolete *prim*, formal or demure person, perh. < OFr. *prin*, first, delicate. See PRIME.] —**prim′ly** *adv.* —**prim′ness** *n.*

prim[2] (prĭm) *n.* A privet. [Short for obsolete *primprint*, of unknown orig.]

prim. *abbr.* **1.** Primary. **2.** Primitive.

pri·ma ballerina (prē′mə) *n.* The leading woman dancer in a ballet company. [Ital.]

pri·ma·cy (prī′mə-sē) *n., pl.* **-cies. 1.** The state of being first or foremost. **2.** *Eccles.* The office, rank, or province of primate. [ME *primacie* < OFr. < Med.Lat. *prīmātia*, office of church primate < Lat. *prīmās, prīmāt-*, of first rank. See PRIMATE.]

pri·ma donna (prē′mə, prĭm′ə) *n.* **1.** The leading woman soloist in an opera company. **2.** A temperamental, conceited person. [Ital. : *prima*, fem. of *primo*, first + *donna*, lady.]

pri·ma fa·cie (prī′mə fā′shē, -shē-ē, fā′shə) *adv.* At first sight; before closer inspection. —*adj.* **1.** True, authentic, or adequate at first sight; ostensible. **2.** Evident without proof or reasoning; obvious. [ME, manifestly < Lat. *prīmā faciē* : *prīmā*, fem. ablative of *prīmus*, first + *faciē*, ablative of *faciēs*, shape, face.]

prima facie case *n. Law.* A case in which the evidence presented is sufficient for a judgment to be made unless the evidence is contested.

prima facie evidence *n. Law.* Evidence that would, if uncontested, establish a fact or raise a presumption of a fact.

pri·mal (prī′məl) *adj.* **1.** Being first in time; original; primeval. **2.** Of first importance; primary. [Med.Lat. *prīmālis* < Lat. *prīmus*, first. See **per**[1]*.] —**pri·mal′i·ty** (-măl′ĭ-tē) *n.*

primal therapy *n.* A method of psychotherapeutic treatment of neurosis by the reliving of early traumatic experiences and expression of feelings, as by angry screaming.

pri·mar·i·ly (prī-mâr′ə-lē, -mĕr′-) *adv.* **1.** Chiefly; mainly. **2.** At first; originally.

pri·mar·y (prī′mĕr′ē, -mə-rē) *adj.* **1.** First or highest in rank, quality, or importance; principal. **2.** Being or standing first in a list, series, or sequence. **3.** Occurring first in time or sequence; earliest. **4.** Being or existing as the first or earliest of a kind; primitive. **5.** *Geol.* Characteristic of or existing in a rock at the time of its formation. **6.** Serving as or being an essential component, as of a system; basic. **7.a.** Immediate; direct: *a primary effect.* **b.** Preliminary to a later stage in a continuing process. **c.** Of or relating to a primary school. **8.** *Color.* Of or relating to a primary color or colors. **9.** *Ling.* **a.** Having a word root or other linguistic element as a basis that cannot be further analyzed or broken down. **b.** Referring to present or future time. Used as a collective designation for various verb tenses. **10.** *Electron.* Of, relating to, or constituting an inducting current, circuit, or coil. **11.** Of, relating to, or being the main flight feathers projecting along the outer edge of a bird's wing. **12.** Of or relating to agriculture, forestry, the industries that extract natural materials from the earth, or the products so obtained. **13.** *Chem.* **a.** Characterized or formed by replacement of one atom or radical within a molecule. Used of a compound. **b.** Having a carbon atom attached solely to one other carbon atom in a molecule. **14.** *Biochem.* Of, relating to, or being the sequence of amino acids in a protein. —*n., pl.* **-ies. 1.a.** One that is first in time, order, or sequence. **b.** One that is first or best in degree, quality, or importance. **c.** One that is fundamental, basic, or elemental. **2.a.** A meeting of the registered voters of a political party for the purpose of nominating candidates and for choosing delegates to their party convention. **b.** A primary election. **3.** *Color.* A primary color. **4.** A primary feather. **5.** *Electron.* An inducting current, circuit, or coil, esp. the coil to which the imput voltage is applied in a transformer. **6.** *Astron.* **a.** A celestial body, esp. a star, relative to other bodies in orbit around it. **b.** The brighter of two stars that make up a double star. [ME < Lat. *prīmārius*, chief < *prīmus*, first. See **per**[1]*.]

primary accent *n. Ling.* **1.** The strongest degree of stress placed on a syllable in the pronunciation of a word. **2.** The mark (′) used to indicate the strongest degree of stress.

primary care *n.* The medical care a patient receives upon first contact with the health care system before referral.

primary cell *n.* A cell in which an irreversible chemical reaction generates electricity; a cell that cannot be recharged.

primary color *n. Color.* A color of any of three groups each of which is seen as generating all colors, the groups being: **a.** Additive, physiological, or light primaries red, green, and blue. **b.** Subtractive or colorant primaries magenta, yellow, and cyan. **c.** Psychological primaries red, yellow, green, and blue, as well as the achromatic pair black and white.

primary election *n.* A preliminary election in which voters nominate party candidates for office.

primary school *n.* **1.** A school usu. including the first three or four grades of elementary school and sometimes kindergarten. **2.** See **elementary school.**

primary tooth *n.* See **milk tooth.**

primary wall *n.* The wall layer of a plant cell deposited during cell expansion.

primary wave *n.* An earthquake wave in which rock particles vibrate parallel to the direction of wave travel.

pri·mate (prī′mĭt, -māt′) *n.* **1.** (prī′māt′). A mammal of the order Primates, which includes the anthropoids, characterized by refined development of the hands and feet, a shortened snout, and a large brain. **2.** A bishop of highest rank in a province or country. [< NLat. *Prīmātes*, order name < Lat. *prīmātēs*, pl. of *prīmās*, principal, of first rank < *prīmus*, first. See **per**[1]*. Sense 2 < ME *primat* < OFr. < Med.Lat. *prīmās, prīmāt-* < Lat.] —**pri·ma′tial** (-mā′shəl) *adj.*

pri·ma·tol·o·gy (prī′mə-tŏl′ə-jē) *n.* The branch of zoology that deals with the study of primates. —**pri′ma·to·log′i·cal** (-tl-ŏj′ĭ-kəl) *adj.* —**pri′ma·tol′o·gist** *n.*

pri·ma·ve·ra[1] or **pri·ma ve·ra** (prē′mə-vĕr′ə) *n.* **1.** A tree *(Cybistax donnellsmithii)* of Mexico and Guatemala having opposite, palmately compound leaves and close-grained light-colored wood. **2.** The wood of this tree. [Sp., spring, primavera < LLat. *prīma vēra*, early spring, pl. of *prīmum vēr* : Lat. *prīmus*, first; see **per**[1]* + Lat. *vēr*, spring; see **wes**[r]*.]

pri·ma·ve·ra[2] (prē′mə-vĕr′ə) *adj.* Made with different kinds of sliced or diced vegetables. [< Ital. *(alla) primavera*, (in the) spring (style) < LLat. *prīma vēra*. See PRIMAVERA[1].]

prime (prīm) *adj.* **1.** First in excellence, quality, or value. **2.** First in degree or rank; chief. **3.** First or early in time, order, or sequence; original. **4.** Of the highest U.S. government grade of meat. **5.** *Math.* Of, relating to, or being a prime number. —*n.* **1.** The earliest hours of the day; dawn. **2.** Spring. **3.** The age of ideal physical perfection and intellectual vigor. **4.** The period or phase of ideal or peak condition. **5.** The first position of thrust and parry in fencing. **6.** A mark (′) appended above and to the right of a character, esp.: **a.** One used to distinguish different values of the same variable in a mathematical expression. **b.** One used to represent a unit of measurement, such as feet or minutes in latitude and longitude. **7.** *Eccles.* The second of the seven canonical hours. No longer in ecclesiastical use. **8.** *Math.* A prime number. **9.** A prime rate. —*v.* **primed, prim·ing, primes.** —*tr.* **1.** To make ready; prepare. **2.** To prepare (a gun or mine) for firing by inserting a charge of gunpowder or a primer. **3.** To prepare for operation, as by pouring water into a pump. **4.** To prepare (a surface) for painting by covering with primer. **5.** To inform or instruct beforehand; coach. —*intr.* To become prepared for future action or operation. —***idiom.* prime the pump.** *Informal.* To encourage the growth or action of something. [ME, first in occurrence < OFr., fem. of *prin* < Lat. *prīmus*. See **per**[1]*.] —**prime′ly** *adv.* —**prime′ness** *n.*

prime interest rate *n.* See **prime rate.**

prime meridian *n.* The zero meridian (0°), used as a reference line from which longitude east and west is measured.

prime minister *n.* **1.** A chief minister appointed by a ruler. **2.** The head of the cabinet and often also the chief executive of a parliamentary democracy. — **prime ministerial** *adj.* — **prime ministership, prime ministry** *n.*

prime mover *n.* **1.a.** One regarded as the initial source of energy directed toward a goal. **b.** The initial force, such as wind, that engages or moves a machine. **c.** A machine or mechanism that converts natural energy into work. **2.** Any of various heavy-duty trucks or tractors. **3.** *Philos.* In Aristotelian philosophy, the self-moved being causing all motion.

prime number *n. Math.* A whole number not divisible without a remainder by any whole number other than itself and one.

prim•er[1] (prĭm′ər) *n.* **1.** An elementary textbook for teaching children to read. **2.** A book that covers the basic elements of a subject. [ME < Norman Fr. < Med.Lat. *prīmārium* < neut. of *prīmārius*, first < Lat. < *prīmus*. See PRIME.]

prim•er[2] (prī′mər) *n.* **1.** A cap or tube containing a small amount of explosive used to detonate the main explosive charge of a firearm or mine. **2.** An undercoat of paint or size applied to prepare a surface, as for painting.

prime rate *n.* The lowest rate of interest on bank loans at a given time and place, offered to preferred borrowers.

prime time *n.* The evening hours, generally between 7 and 11 P.M., when the largest television audience is available. — **prime′-time′** (prīm′tīm′) *adj.*

pri•me•val (prī-mē′vəl) *adj.* Belonging to the first or earliest age or ages; original or ancient: *a primeval forest.* [< Lat. *prīmaevus*, early in life : *prīmus*, first; see **per[1]*** + *aevum*, age; see **aiw-***.] — **pri•me′val•ly** *adv.*

prim•ing (prī′mĭng) *n.* **1.** The act of one that primes. **2.** The explosive used to ignite a charge. **3.** A preliminary coat of paint or size applied to a surface.

pri•mip•a•ra (prī-mĭp′ər-ə) *n., pl.* **-a•ras** or **-a•rae** (-ə-rē′). **1.** A woman who is pregnant for the first time. **2.** A woman who has given birth to only one child. [Lat. *prīmipara* : *prīmus*, first; see **per[1]*** + *-para*, -para.] — **pri′mi•par′i•ty** (-mī-păr′ĭ-tē) *n.* — **pri•mip′a•rous** *adj.*

prim•i•tive (prĭm′ĭ-tĭv) *adj.* **1.** Not derived from something else; primary. **2.a.** Of or relating to an earliest or original stage or state; primeval. **b.** Being little evolved from an early ancestral type. **3.** Characterized by simplicity or crudity; unsophisticated. **4.** Of or relating to a nonindustrial, often tribal culture having a simple economy. **5.** *Ling.* **a.** Serving as the basis for derived or inflected forms. **b.** Being a protolanguage: *primitive Germanic.* **6.** *Math.* An algebraic or geometric expression from which another expression is derived. **7.** Relating or belonging to forces of nature; elemental. **8.a.** Of or created by an artist without formal training; simple or naive in style. **b.** Of or relating to the work of an artist from a primitive culture. **9.** Of or relating to late medieval or pre-Renaissance European painters or sculptors. **10.** *Biol.* Occurring in or characteristic of an early stage of development or evolution. —*n.* **1.** A person belonging to a primitive society. **2.** An unsophisticated person. **3.** One that is at a low or early stage of development. **4.a.** One belonging to an early stage in the development of an artistic trend, esp. a pre-Renaissance painter. **b.** An artist having or affecting an unschooled style, as of painting. **c.** A self-taught artist. **d.** A work of art by a primitive artist. **5.** *Ling.* A primitive word or word element. **6.** *Comp. Sci.* A basic unit of machine instruction or translation. [ME < OFr. *primitif, primitive* < Lat. *prīmitīvus* < *prīmitus*, at first < *prīmus*, first. See **per[1]***.] — **prim′i•tive•ly** *adv.* — **prim′i•tive•ness, prim′i•tiv′i•ty** *n.*

prim•i•tiv•ism (prĭm′ĭ-tĭ-vĭz′əm) *n.* **1.** The condition or quality of being primitive. **2.** The style of a primitive artist. **3.a.** A belief that it is best to live simply and in a natural environment. **b.** A belief that the acquisitions of civilization are evil or that the earliest period of human history was the best. — **prim′i•tiv•ist** *adj. & n.* — **prim′i•tiv•is′tic** *adj.*

pri•mo (prē′mō) *n., pl.* **-mi** (-mē) also **-mos** (-mōz). *Mus.* The principal part in a duet or ensemble composition. —*adj.* **1.** First. **2.** *Slang.* **a.** Exceptionally good of its kind; first-class. **b.** Highly or most valuable. [Ital. < OItal., first < Lat. *prīmus*. See **per[1]***.]

Pri•mo de Ri•ve•ra y Or•ba•ne•ja (prē′mō dā rĭ-vĕr′ə, ē ôr′bə-nā′hä, *thĕ* rē-vĕ′rä ē ôr′vä-nĕ′hä), **Miguel.** Marqués de Estella. 1870–1930. Spanish general and politician who ruled as dictator (1923–30). His son **José Antonio Primo de Rivera** (1903–36) founded the Spanish Fascist Party (1933).

pri•mo•gen•i•tor (prī′mō-jĕn′ĭ-tər) *n.* **1.** The earliest ancestor. **2.** An ancestor or a forebear. [LLat. *prīmōgenitor* : Lat. *prīmō*, at first (< *prīmus*, first; see **per[1]***) + Lat. *genitor*, begetter (< *gignere*, *genit-*, to beget; see **genə-***).]

pri•mo•gen•i•ture (prī′mō-jĕn′ĭ-chŏŏr′) *n.* **1.** The state of being the first-born or eldest child of the same parents. **2.** *Law.* The right of the eldest child, esp. the eldest son, to inherit the entire estate of one or both parents. [LLat. *prīmōgenitūra* : Lat. *prīmō*, at first (< *prīmus*, first; see **per[1]***) + Lat. *genitūra*, birth (< *gignere*, *genit-*, to beget; see **genə-***).] — **pri′mo•gen′i•tar′y** (-jĕn′ĭ-tĕr′ē), **pri′mo•gen′i•tal** (-təl) *adj.*

pri•mor•di•al (prī-môr′dē-əl) *adj.* **1.** Being or happening first in sequence of time; original. **2.** Primary or fundamental: *a primordial role.* **3.** *Biol.* Belonging to or characteristic of the earliest stage of development of an organism or a part. —*n.* A basic principle. [ME < LLat. *prīmōrdiālis* < Lat. *prīmōrdium*, origin : *prīmus*, first; see **per[1]*** + *ōrdīrī*, to begin to weave; see **ar-***.] — **pri•mor′di•al•ly** *adv.*

pri•mor•di•um (prī-môr′dē-əm) *n., pl.* **-di•a** (-dē-ə). An organ or a part in its most rudimentary form or stage of development. [Lat. *prīmōrdium.* See PRIMORDIAL.]

primp (prĭmp) *v.* **primped, primp•ing, primps.** —*tr.* To dress or groom (oneself) with meticulous or excessive care. —*intr.* To primp oneself; preen. [Perh. alteration of PRIM[1].]

prim•rose (prĭm′rōz′) *n.* **1.** Any of numerous plants of the genus *Primula,* having well-developed basal leaves and tubular, variously colored flowers grouped in umbels or heads. **2.** An evening primrose. [ME *primerose* < OFr. < Med.Lat. *prīma rosa*, first rose : Lat. *prīma*, fem. of *prīmus*, first; see PRIME + Lat. *rosa*, rose.]

primrose path *n.* **1.** A way of life of worldly ease or pleasure. **2.** A course of action that seems easy and appropriate but can actually end in calamity.

pri•mum mo•bi•le (prī′məm mō′bə-lē′, prē′məm mō′bĭ-lā′) *n.* **1.** In Ptolemaic astronomy, the tenth and outermost concentric sphere of the universe, revolving around Earth from east to west in 24 hours and causing the other nine spheres to revolve with it. **2.** See **prime mover** 1. [Med.Lat. *prīmum mōbile* : *prīmum*, neut. of *prīmus*, first + *mōbile* < neut. of *mōbilis*, movable.]

pri•mus (prī′məs) *n., pl.* **-mus•es.** Often **Primus.** The first in rank of the bishops of Scotland. [Med.Lat. *prīmus* < Lat., first. See **per[1]***.]

pri•mus in•ter pa•res (prī′məs ĭn′tər pâr′ēz, prē′mŏŏs ĭn′tər pä′rĕs′) *n., pl.* **pri•mi inter pares** (-mī, -mē). The first among equals. [Lat. *prīmus inter parēs.*]

prin. *abbr.* **1.** Principal. **2.** Principle.

prince (prĭns) *n.* **1.** A male member of a royal family other than the monarch, esp. a son of the monarch. **2.a.** A man who rules a principality. **b.** A hereditary ruler, usu. a man; a king. **3.** A nobleman of varying status or rank. **4.** An outstanding man, esp. in a particular group: *a merchant prince.* [ME < OFr. < Lat. *prīnceps.* See **per[1]***.] — **prince′ship′** *n.*

Prince Al•bert[1] (prĭns ăl′bərt). A city of central Saskatchewan, Canada, NNE of Saskatoon. Pop. 31,380.

Prince Al•bert[2] (prĭns ăl′bərt) *n.* A man's long double-breasted frock coat. [After *Prince Albert* Edward, later Edward VII.]

Prince Charm•ing also **prince charm•ing** (chär′mĭng) *n.* **1.** A man who fulfills all the romantic expectations of a woman. **2.** A man who ardently seeks the company and affection of women. [After *Prince Charming*, hero of *Cinderella.*]

prince consort *n.* The husband of a sovereign queen.

prince•dom (prĭns′dəm) *n.* **1.** The territory, jurisdiction, sovereignty, rank, or estate of a prince. **2. princedoms.** *Theol.* See **principality** 3.

Prince Ed•ward Island (ĕd′wərd). A province of SE Canada consisting of **Prince Edward Island** in the S Gulf of St. Lawrence; joined the confederacy in 1873. Cap. Charlottetown. Pop. 122,506.

Prince George (jôrj). A city of central British Columbia, Canada, on the Fraser and Nechako rivers. Pop. 67,559.

prince•ling (prĭns′lĭng) *n.* A prince judged to be of minor status or importance.

prince•ly (prĭns′lē) *adj.* **-li•er, -li•est. 1.** Of or relating to a prince; royal. **2.** Befitting a prince, as: **a.** Noble. **b.** Munificent; lavish. — **prince′li•ness** *n.* — **prince′ly** *adv.*

Prince of Wales (wālz) *n.* **1.** The male heir to the British throne. **2.** Used as the title for the male heir to the British throne, conferred by the sovereign.

Prince of Wales Island. 1. An island of N Northwest Terrs., Canada, NE of Victoria I. **2.** An island of extreme SE AK in the Alexander Archipelago.

prince regent *n., pl.* **prince regents** or **princes regent.** A prince who rules during the minority, absence, or incapacity of a sovereign.

Prince Ru•pert (rōō′pərt). A city of W British Columbia, Canada, near the AK border. Pop. 16,197.

prince's feather (prĭn′sĭz) *n.* Either of two plants *(Amaranthus hybridus* var. *erythrostachys* or *A. cruentus)* having reddish foliage and dense panicles of brownish-red flowers.

prince's pine *n.* See **pipsissewa.**

prin•cess (prĭn′sĭs, -sĕs′, prĭn-sĕs′) *n.* **1.** A woman member of a royal family other than the monarch, esp. a daughter of a monarch. **2.a.** A woman who is ruler of a principality. **b.** A woman hereditary ruler; a queen. **3.** A noblewoman of varying status or rank. **4.** The wife of a prince. **5.** A woman regarded as having the status or qualities of a princess. —*adj.* Designed to hang in smooth, close-fitting unbroken lines from shoulder to flared hem: *a princess dress.* [ME *princesse* < OFr., fem. of *prince*, prince. See PRINCE.]

prin•cesse (prĭn-sĕs′) *adj.* Princess: *a gown cut on princesse lines.* [Fr. < OFr., princess. See PRINCESS.]

ă pat	oi boy
ā pay	ou out
âr care	ŏŏ took
ä father	ōō boot
ĕ pet	ŭ cut
ē be	ûr urge
ĭ pit	th thin
ī pie	*th* this
îr pier	hw which
ŏ pot	zh vision
ō toe	ə about, item
ô paw	

Stress marks:
′ (primary);
′ (secondary), as in dictionary (dĭk′shə-nĕr′ē)

princess royal *n.* **1.** The eldest daughter of a British sovereign, who has had the title conferred on her for life by the sovereign. **2.** Used as the title for such a woman.

princess tree *n.* See **paulownia.**

Prince•ton (prĭn′stən). A borough of central NJ NNE of Trenton; founded by Quakers in 1696. Pop. 12,016.

Princeton, Mount. A mountain, 4,330 m (14,197 ft), in the Sawatch Range of the Rocky Mts. in central CO.

Prince Wil•liam Sound (wĭl′yəm). An arm of the Gulf of Alaska E of the Kenai Peninsula; site of the worst oil spill in U.S. history (Mar. 1989).

prin•ci•pal (prĭn′sə-pəl) *adj.* **1.** First, highest, or foremost in importance, rank, worth, or degree; chief. **2.** Of, relating to, or being financial principal, or a principal in a financial transaction. —*n.* **1.** One who holds a position of presiding rank, esp. the head of a school. **2.** A main participant in a situation. **3.** A person having a leading or starring role. **4.a.** The capital or main body of an estate or a financial holding as distinguished from the interest or revenue from it. **b.** A sum of money owed as a debt, upon which interest is calculated. **5.** *Law.* **a.** One who empowers another to act as one's representative. **b.** One with prime responsibility for an obligation as distinguished from one who acts as surety or as an endorser. **c.** One who commits or is an accomplice to a crime. **6.** The main truss or rafter that supports and gives form to a roof. [ME < OFr. < Lat. *prīncipālis* < *prīnceps, prīncip-*, leader, emperor. See **per**[1]*.] —**prin′ci•pal•ly** *adv.* —**prin′ci•pal•ship′** *n.*

printed circuit
On a floppy disk drive

Usage Note: *Principal* and *principle* are often confused but have no meanings in common. *Principle* is only a noun, and most of its senses refer to that which is basic or to rules and standards. *Principal* is both a noun and an adjective. As a noun (aside from its specialized meanings in law and finance) it generally denotes a person who holds a high position or plays an important role. As an adjective it has the sense of "chief" or "leading."

prin•ci•pal•i•ty (prĭn′sə-păl′ĭ-tē) *n., pl.* **-ties. 1.** A territory ruled by a prince or princess from which such a title is derived. **2.** The position, authority, or jurisdiction of a prince or princess; sovereignty. **3. principalities.** *Theol.* The seventh of the nine orders of angels.

principal parts *pl.n. Gram.* **1.** In inflected languages, the verb forms traditionally considered basic, from which all other verb forms can be derived. **2.** In English, the present infinitive (*eat*), the past tense (*ate*), and the present participle (*eating*).

Prín•ci•pe (prĭn′sə-pə, prēN′sĭ-). An island of W Africa in the Gulf of Guinea, part of São Tomé and Príncipe.

prin•cip•i•um (prĭn-sĭp′ē-əm) *n., pl.* **-i•a** (-ē-ə). A principle, esp. a basic one. [Lat. *prīncipium.* See PRINCIPLE.]

prin•ci•ple (prĭn′sə-pəl) *n.* **1.** A basic truth, law, or assumption. **2.a.** A rule or standard, esp. of good behavior. **b.** The collectivity of moral or ethical standards or judgments. **3.** A fixed or predetermined policy or mode of action. **4.** A quality or an element determining intrinsic nature or characteristic behavior. **5.** A rule or law concerning the functioning of natural phenomena or mechanical processes. **6.** *Chem.* One of the elements that compose a substance, esp. one that gives some special quality or effect. **7.** A basic source. See Usage Note at **principal.** —***idioms.*** **in principle.** With regard to the basics. **on principle.** According to or because of principle. [ME, alteration of OFr. *principe* < Lat. *prīncipium* < *prīnceps, prīncip-*, leader, emperor. See **per**[1]*.]

prin•ci•pled (prĭn′sə-pəld) *adj.* Based on, marked by, or manifesting principle: *a principled decision.*

prink (prĭngk) *v.* **prinked, prink•ing, prinks.** —*tr.* To adorn (oneself) in a showy manner. —*intr.* To dress or groom oneself with elaborate care or vanity; primp. [Prob. alteration of PRANK[2].] —**prink′er** *n.*

print (prĭnt) *n.* **1.** A mark or an impression made in or on a surface by pressure. **2.a.** A device or an implement, such as a seal, used to press markings onto or into a surface. **b.** Something formed or marked by such a device. **3.a.** Lettering or other impressions produced in ink from type by a printing press or other means. **b.** Matter so produced; printed material. **c.** Printed state or form. **4.a.** A printed publication, such as a magazine or newspaper. **b.** Printed matter. **5.** A design or picture transferred from an engraved plate, wood block, or other medium. **6.** A photographic image transferred to paper or a similar surface, usu. from a negative. **7.** A copy of a film or movie. **8.a.** A fabric or garment with a dyed pattern that has been pressed onto it, usu. by engraved rollers. **b.** The pattern itself. —*v.* **print•ed, print•ing, prints.** —*tr.* **1.** To press (a mark or design, for example) onto or into a surface. **2.a.** To make an impression on or in (a surface) with a device such as a seal. **b.** To press (a stamp or similar device) onto or into a surface to leave a marking. **3.a.** To produce by means of pressed type on a paper surface, with or as if with a printing press. **b.** To offer in printed form; publish. **4.** To write (something) in characters similar to those commonly used in print. **5.** To impress firmly in the mind or memory. **6.** To produce a photographic image from (a negative, for example) by passing light through film onto a photosensitive surface, esp. sensitized paper. —*intr.* **1.a.** To work as a printer. **b.** To produce printed material. **2.** To produce something in printed form by means of a printing press or other reproduction process. **3.** To write characters similar to those commonly used in print. **4.** To produce or receive an impression, a marking, or an image. —*adj.* Of, relating to, writing for, or constituting printed publications: *print coverage.* —***phrasal verb.*** **print out.** *Comp Sci.* To print as a function; produce printout. —***idioms.*** **in print. 1.** In printed or published form. **2.** Offered for sale by a publisher. **out of print.** No longer offered for sale by a publisher. [ME *preinte* < OFr. < fem. p.part. of *preindre*, to press, alteration of *prembre* < Lat. *premere.* See **per-**[4]*.]

print•a•ble (prĭn′tə-bəl) *adj.* **1.** Capable of being printed or of producing a print: *printable negatives.* **2.** Fit for publication: *printable language.* —**print′a•bil′i•ty** *n.*

print bar *n.* A mechanism in a printing device that carries the template of the final form of the alphanumeric characters to be printed.

print•ed circuit (prĭn′tĭd) *n.* An electric circuit in which the conducting connections have been printed or otherwise deposited in predetermined patterns on an insulating base.

printed matter *n.* Printed material, such as a book, that is not considered first-class mail and has a special postal rate.

print•er (prĭn′tər) *n.* **1.** One that prints, esp. one whose occupation is printing. **2.** A device used for printing, esp. a photographic machine from which a duplicate of an original can be made. **3.** *Comp. Sci.* The part of a system that produces printed matter.

print•er's devil (prĭn′tərz) *n.* An apprentice in a printing establishment.

print head *n. Comp. Sci.* The element of a printer that applies the mark or image to the paper.

print•ing (prĭn′tĭng) *n.* **1.** The art, process, or business of producing printed material by means of inked type and a printing press or by similar means. **2.a.** The act of one that prints. **b.** Matter that is printed. **3.** All the copies of a publication, such as a book, that are printed at one time. **4.** Written characters not connected to one another and resembling those appearing in print.

printing ink *n.* Ink made esp. for use in printing.

printing office *n.* An establishment where printed material is produced, esp. one that is officially authorized.

printing press *n.* A machine that transfers lettering or images by contact with various forms of inked surface onto paper or similar material fed into it in various ways.

print•mak•ing (prĭnt′mā′kĭng) *n.* The artistic design and manufacture of prints, such as woodcuts. —**print′mak′er** *n.*

print•out (prĭnt′out′) *n. Comp. Sci.* Printed output.

print wheel *n.* A disk-shaped mechanism in a printing device that carries the template of the characters to be printed around its rim and revolves to print one character at a time.

pri•on (prē′ŏn) *n.* A microscopic protein particle similar to a virus but lacking nucleic acid, thought to be the infectious agent of certain diseases of the nervous system. [*proteinaceous* (PROTEIN + -ACEOUS) + I(NFECTIOUS) + -ON[1].]

pri•or[1] (prī′ər) *adj.* **1.** Preceding in time or order. **2.** Preceding in importance or value: *a prior consideration.* [Lat. See PRIOR[2].] —**pri′or•ly** *adv.*

pri•or[2] (prī′ər) *n.* **1.** A monastic officer in charge of a priory or ranking next below the abbot of an abbey. **2.** One of the ruling magistrates of medieval Florence. [ME *priour* < OE and OFr. *prior*, both < Med.Lat. < Lat., superior. See **per**[1]*.] —**pri′or•ate** (-ĭt), **pri′or•ship′** (-shĭp′) *n.*

Pri•or (prī′ər), **Matthew.** 1664–1721. English poet and diplomat known for his epigrams and light satirical verse.

pri•or•ess (prī′ər-ĭs) *n.* A nun in charge of a priory or ranking next below the abbess of an abbey. [ME *prioresse* < OFr., fem. of *prior*, a prior. See PRIOR[2].]

pri•or•i•tize (prī-ôr′ĭ-tīz′, -ŏr′-) *v.* **-tized, -tiz•ing, -tiz•es.** —*tr.* To arrange or deal with in order of importance. —*intr.* To put things in order of importance. [PRIORIT(Y) + -IZE.] —**pri•or′i•ti•za′tion** (-tĭ-zā′shən) *n.*

Usage Note: It can be argued that *prioritize* serves a useful function in providing a single word to mean "arrange according to priority," but like many other recent formations with *-ize*, it is widely regarded as corporate or bureaucratic jargon. In an earlier survey *prioritize* was unacceptable to the great majority of the Usage Panel. See Usage Note at **-ize.**

pri•or•i•ty (prī-ôr′ĭ-tē, -ŏr′-) *n., pl.* **-ties. 1.** Precedence, esp. established by order of importance or urgency. **2.a.** An established right to precedence. **b.** An authoritative rating that establishes such precedence. **3.** A preceding or coming earlier in time. **4.** Something afforded or deserving prior attention. [ME *priorite* < OFr. < Med.Lat. *priōritās* < Lat. *prior*, first. See PRIOR[2].]

prior to *prep.* Preceding; before.

pri•or•y (prī′ə-rē) *n., pl.* **-ies.** A monastery governed by a prior or a convent governed by a prioress.

Prip•et (prĭp′ĕt) or **Pri•pyat** (prē′pyət). A river, c. 708 km (440 mi), of N Ukraine and S Belorussia flowing generally E through the **Pripet Marshes** to the Dnieper R.

Pris•cian (prĭsh′ən, -ē-ən). fl. A.D. 500. Latin grammarian at Constantinople known for his *Institutiones Grammaticae.*

prise (prīz) *v. & n.* Var. of **prize[3]**.

prism (prĭz′əm) *n.* **1.** A solid figure whose bases or ends have the same size and shape and are parallel to one another and each of whose sides is a parallelogram. **2.** A transparent body of this form, often of glass and usu. with triangular ends, used to separate white light passed through it into a spectrum or to reflect light beams. **3.** A cut-glass object, such as a chandelier. **4.** A crystal form consisting of three or more similar faces parallel to a single axis. **5.** A medium that misrepresents whatever is seen through it. [LLat. *prīsma* < Gk. *prisma,* thing sawed off, prism < *priein, prizein,* to saw.]

pris•mat•ic (prĭz-măt′ĭk) also **pris•mat•i•cal** (-ĭ-kəl) *adj.* **1.** Of, relating to, resembling, or being a prism. **2.** Formed by refraction of light through a prism. Used of a spectrum of light. **3.** Brilliantly colored; iridescent. [Gk. *prisma, prismat-,* prism; see PRISM + -IC.] **— pris•mat′i•cal•ly** *adv.*

pris•ma•toid (prĭz′mə-toid′) *n.* A polyhedron all of whose vertices lie in one of two parallel planes. [Gk. *prisma, prismat-,* prism + -OID.] **— pris′ma•toi′dal** (-toid′l) *adj.*

pris•moid (prĭz′moid′) *n.* A prismatoid having polygons with the same number of sides as bases and faces that are parallelograms or trapezoids. **— pris•moi′dal** (-moid′l) *adj.*

pris•on (prĭz′ən) *n.* **1.** A place where persons convicted or accused of crimes are confined; a penitentiary or a jail. **2.** A place or condition of confinement or forcible restraint. **3.** A state of imprisonment or captivity. *— tr.v.* **-oned, -on•ing, -ons.** To imprison. [ME < OFr., alteration (influenced by OFr. *pris,* taken) of Lat. *prēnsiō, prēnsiōn-,* a seizing < **prehēnsiō* < *prehēnsus,* p.part. of *prehendere,* to seize. See **ghend-***.]

prison camp *n.* **1.** A camp for prisoners of war. **2.** A minimum security facility for the internment of prisoners.

pris•on•er (prĭz′ə-nər, prĭz′nər) *n.* **1.** A person held in custody, captivity, or a condition of forcible restraint, esp. while on trial or serving a prison sentence. **2.** One deprived of freedom of expression or action.

prisoner of war *n., pl.* **prisoners of war.** A person taken by or surrendering to enemy forces in wartime.

pris•on•er's base (prĭz′ə-nərz, prĭz′nərz) *n. Games.* A children's game in which two teams try to capture opposing players by tagging them and bringing them to a base.

prison fever *n.* See **typhus.**

pris•sy (prĭs′ē) *adj.* **-si•er, -si•est.** Excessively or affectedly prim and proper. [Perh. blend of PRI(M)[1] and (SI)SSY.] **— pris′si•ly** *adv.* **— pris′si•ness** *n.*

pris•tine (prĭs′tēn′, prĭ-stēn′) *adj.* **1.a.** Remaining in a pure state; uncorrupted by civilization. **b.** Remaining free from dirt or decay; clean: *pristine mountain snow.* **2.** Of, relating to, or typical of the earliest time or condition; primitive or original. [Lat. *prīstinus.* See **per[1]*.**] **— pris•tine′ly** *adv.*

prith•ee (prĭth′ē, prĭth′ē) *interj. Archaic.* Used to express a polite request. [Alteration of *(I) pray thee.*]

priv. *abbr.* **1.** Private. **2.** *Gram.* Privative.

pri•va•cy (prī′və-sē) *n.* **1.a.** The quality or condition of being secluded from the presence or view of others. **b.** The state of being free from unsanctioned intrusion: *a person's right to privacy.* **2.** The state of being concealed; secrecy.

pri•vate (prī′vĭt) *adj.* **1.a.** Secluded from the sight, presence, or intrusion of others. **b.** Designed or intended for one's exclusive use. **2.a.** Of or confined to the individual; personal. **b.** Undertaken on an individual basis. **c.** Of, relating to, or receiving special hospital services and privileges. **3.** Not available for public use, control, or participation. **4.a.** Belonging to a particular person or persons, as opposed to the public or the government. **b.** Conducted and supported primarily by private individuals or by a nongovernmental agency or corporation. **c.** Of, relating to, or derived from nongovernment sources. **5.** Not holding an official or public position. **6.a.** Not for public knowledge or disclosure; secret. **b.** Not appropriate for use or display in public; intimate. **c.** Placing a high value on personal privacy. *— n.* **1.a.** A noncommissioned officer in the U.S. Army or Marine Corps ranking below private first class. **b.** A similarly ranking officer in another military organization or in a paramilitary organization. **2. privates.** Private parts. **— *idiom.* in private.** Not in public; secretly or confidentially. [ME *privat* < Lat. *prīvātus,* not in public life, p.part. of *prīvāre,* to release, deprive < *prīvus,* single, alone. See **per[1]*.**] **— pri′vate•ly** *adv.* **— pri′vate•ness** *n.*

private detective *n.* A privately employed detective.

private enterprise *n.* **1.** Business activities not controlled or owned by any state; privately owned business. **2.** A privately owned business, esp. one operating under capitalism.

pri•va•teer (prī′və-tîr′) *n.* **1.** A ship privately owned and manned but authorized by a government during wartime to attack and capture enemy vessels. **2.** The commander or one of the crew of such a ship. *— intr.v.* **-teered, -teer•ing, -teers.** To sail as a privateer.

private eye *n.* See **private detective.**

private first class *n., pl.* **privates first class.** A noncommissioned officer in the U.S. Army ranking above private and below corporal or in the U.S. Marine Corps ranking above private and below lance corporal.

private law *n.* The branch of law that deals with the legal rights and relationships of private individuals.

private parts *pl.n.* The external organs of sex and excretion.

private school *n.* A secondary or elementary school run and supported by private individuals or a corporation rather than by a government or public agency.

pri•va•tion (prī-vā′shən) *n.* **1.a.** Lack of the basic necessities or comforts of life. **b.** The condition resulting from such lack. **2.** An act, condition, or result of deprivation or loss. [ME *privacion* < OFr. *privation* < Lat. *prīvātiō, prīvātiōn-* < *prīvātus,* p.part. of *prīvāre,* to deprive. See PRIVATE.]

pri•vat•ism (prī′və-tĭz′əm) *n.* The social position of being noncommittal to or uninvolved with anything other than one's own immediate interests. **— pri′va•tist** *adj. & n.* **— pri′va•tis′tic** *adj.*

priv•a•tive (prĭv′ə-tĭv) *adj.* **1.** Causing deprivation, lack, or loss. **2.** *Gram.* Altering the meaning of a term from positive to negative. *— n. Gram.* A privative prefix or suffix, such as *a-, non-, un-,* or *-less.* [ME *privatif* < Lat. *prīvātīvus* < *prīvātus,* p.part. of *prīvāre,* to deprive. See PRIVATE.] **— priv′a•tive•ly** *adv.*

pri•va•tize (prī′və-tīz′) *tr.v.* **-tized, -tiz•ing, -tiz•es.** *Usage Problem.* To change (an industry or a business, for example) from government or public ownership or control to private enterprise. See Usage Note at **-ize. — pri′va•ti•za′tion** (-tĭ-zā′shən) *n.*

priv•et (prĭv′ĭt) *n.* **1.** Any of several shrubs of the genus *Ligustrum,* having white flowers and widely used for hedges. **2.** Any of several similar or related plants. [?]

priv•i•lege (prĭv′ə-lĭj, prĭv′lĭj) *n.* **1.a.** A special advantage, immunity, permission, right, or benefit granted to or enjoyed by an individual, a class, or a caste. See Syns at **right. b.** Such a privilege held as a prerogative of status or rank and exercised to the exclusion or detriment of others. **2.** The principle of granting and maintaining a special right or immunity: *a society based on privilege.* **3.** *Law.* The right to privileged communication in a confidential relationship, as between patient and physician. **4.** An option to buy or sell a stock, including put, call, spread, and straddle. *— tr.v.* **-leged, -leg•ing, -leg•es. 1.** To grant a privilege to. **2.** To free or exempt. [ME < OFr. < Lat. *prīvilēgium,* a law affecting one : *prīvus,* single, alone; see **per[1]*** + *lēx, lēg-,* law; see **leg-*.**]

priv•i•leged (prĭv′ə-lĭjd, prĭv′lĭjd) *adj.* **1.** Enjoying a privilege or having privileges. **2.** Confined to an exclusive or chosen group of individuals. *— n. (used with a sing. or pl. v.)* Those enjoying a privilege or having privileges.

privileged communication *n. Law.* **1.** A confidential communication that one cannot be forced to divulge. **2.** A communication that is not subject to charges of slander or libel.

priv•i•ly (prĭv′ə-lē) *adv.* Privately or secretly.

priv•i•ty (prĭv′ĭ-tē) *n., pl.* **-ties. 1.** Knowledge of something private or secret shared between individuals, esp. with the implication of approval or consent. **2.** *Law.* **a.** A relation between parties that is held to be sufficiently close and direct to support a legal claim on behalf of or against another person with whom this relation exists. **b.** A successive or mutual interest in or relationship to the same property. [ME *privete,* secrecy, privacy < OFr. < Med.Lat. *prīvitās* < Lat. *prīvus,* single, alone. See **per[1]*.**]

priv•y (prĭv′ē) *adj.* **1.** Made a participant in knowledge of something private or secret. **2.** Belonging or proper to a person, such as a sovereign, in a private rather than official capacity. **3.** Secret; concealed. *— n., pl.* **-ies. 1.a.** An outdoor toilet; an outhouse. **b.** A toilet. **2.** *Law.* One of the parties having an interest in the same matter. [ME *prive* < OFr. < Lat. *prīvātus,* private < *prīvus,* single, alone. See **per[1]*.**]

Priv•y Council (prĭv′ē) *n.* **1.** A council of the British sovereign that until the 17th century was the supreme legislative body, now consists of cabinet ministers, and has no important function except that its Judicial Committee sometimes acts as a supreme appellate court. **2. privy council.** An advisory council to an executive. **— privy councilor** *n.*

prix fixe (prē′ fēks′) *n., pl.* **prix fixes** (prē′ fēks′). **1.** A complete meal of several courses offered by a restaurant at a fixed price. **2.** A fixed price charged for such a meal. **3.** See **table d'hôte.** [Fr. : *prix,* price + *fixe,* fixed.]

prize[1] (prīz) *n.* **1.** Something offered or won as an award for superiority or victory, as in a contest or competition. See Syns at **bonus. 2.** Something worth striving for; a highly desirable possession. *— adj.* **1.** Offered or given as a prize: *a prize cup.* **2.** Given a prize, or likely to win a prize: *a prize cow.* **3.** Worthy of a prize; first-class: *our prize azaleas.* *— tr.v.* **prized, priz•ing, priz•es. 1.** To value highly; esteem or treasure. See Syns at **appreciate. 2.** To estimate the worth of; evaluate. [Alteration of ME *pris,* value, price, reward. See PRICE.]

prize[2] (prīz) *n.* **1.** *Naut.* Something seized by force or taken as booty, esp. an enemy ship and its cargo. **2.** The act of seizing; capture. [Alteration of ME *prise* < OFr. < fem. p.part. of *prendre* < Lat. *prehendere, prendere,* to seize. See **ghend-*.**]

ă pat	oi boy
ā pay	ou out
âr care	ŏŏ took
ä father	ōō boot
ĕ pet	ŭ cut
ē be	ûr urge
ĭ pit	th thin
ī pie	*th* this
îr pier	hw which
ŏ pot	zh vision
ō toe	ə about, item
ô paw	

Stress marks:
′ (primary);
′ (secondary), as in
dictionary (dĭk′shə-nĕr′ē)

prize[3] also **prise** (prīz) —*tr.v.* **prized, priz•ing, priz•es** also **prised, pris•ing, pris•es.** To move or force with or as if with a lever; pry. —*n.* **1.** Leverage. **2.** *Chiefly Southern U.S.* Something used as a lever or for prying. [< ME *prise*, instrument for prying, prob. < *prise*, the taking of something. See PRIZE[2].]

prize•fight (prīz′fīt′) *n. Sports.* A professional boxing match for money. —**prize′fight′er** *n.* —**prize′fight′ing** *n.*

prize•win•ner (prīz′wĭn′ər) *n.* One that wins a prize.

prize•win•ning also **prize-win•ning** (prīz′wĭn′ĭng) *adj.* Having won or worthy of winning a prize: *a prizewinning wine.*

p.r.n. or **PRN** *abbr. Lat.* Pro re nata (as the situation demands).

pro[1] (prō) *n., pl.* **pros. 1.** An argument or a consideration in favor of something: *the pros and cons.* **2.** One who supports a proposal or takes the affirmative side in debate. —*adv.* In favor; affirmatively: *arguing pro and con.* —*adj.* Affirmative; supporting: *a pro vote.* [ME < Lat. *prō*, for. See **per[1]***.]

pro[2] (prō) *Informal.* —*n., pl.* **pros. 1.** A professional, esp. in sports. **2.** An expert in a field of endeavor. —*adj.* Professional.

PRO also **P.R.O.** *abbr.* Public relations officer.

pro–[1] *pref.* **1.** Acting in the place of; substituting for: *pronoun.* **2.** Supporting; favoring: *prorevolutionary.* [ME < OFr. < Lat. *pro-*, *prō-* < *prō*, for. See **per[1]***.]

pro–[2] *pref.* **1.a.** Earlier; before; prior to: *procambium.* **b.** Rudimentary: *pronucleus.* **2.** Anterior; in front of: *procephalic.* [ME < OFr. < Gk. < *pro*, before, in front. See **per[1]***.]

pro•a (prō′ə) also **prau** (prou) or **prah•u** (prä′o͞o) *n. Naut.* A swift Malayan sailboat with a triangular sail and a single outrigger. [Malay *pĕrāhū*, prob. < Marathi *paḍāv*.]

pro-a•bor•tion (prō′ə-bôr′shən) *adj.* Favoring or supporting legalized abortion. —**pro′a•bor′tion•ist** *n.*

pro•ac•tive or **pro-ac•tive** (prō-ăk′tĭv) *adj.* Acting in advance to deal with an expected difficulty; anticipatory. —**pro•ac′tion** *n.* —**pro•ac′tive•ly** *adv.*

pro-am (prō′ăm′) *Sports. n.* A sports event in which professionals and amateurs compete. —**pro′-am′** *adj.*

prob. *abbr.* **1.** Probable; probably. **2.** *Law.* Probate. **3.** Problem.

prob•a•bi•lism (prŏb′ə-bə-lĭz′əm) *n.* **1.** *Philos.* The doctrine that probability is a sufficient basis for belief and action. **2.** *Rom. Cath. Ch.* The system of casuistry that in doubtful cases allows the following of the solidly probable opinion that favors an actor's personal liberty. —**prob′a•bi•list** *adj. & n.*

proboscis
African elephant eating grass

prob•a•bil•is•tic (prŏb′ə-bə-lĭs′tĭk) *adj.* **1.** Of, relating to, or based on probabilism. **2.** Of, based on, or affected by probability, randomness, or chance.

prob•a•bil•i•ty (prŏb′ə-bĭl′ĭ-tē) *n., pl.* **-ties. 1.** The quality or condition of being probable; likelihood. **2.** A probable situation, condition, or event. **3.a.** The likelihood that a given event will occur: *a great probability of rain.* **b.** *Statistics.* The ratio of the number of actual occurrences of a specific event to the total number of possible occurrences. —*idiom.* **in all probability.** Most probably; very likely.

probability density *n. Statistics.* **1.** A function of a random variable whose integral over a given interval gives the probability that the value of the variable will fall within the interval. **2.** The calculated value of a probability density.

probability distribution *n. Statistics.* **1.** See **probability density. 2.** A function of a discrete random variable yielding the probability that the variable will have a given value.

probability theory *n.* The branch of mathematics that studies the likelihood of occurrence of random events in order to predict the behavior of defined systems.

prob•a•ble (prŏb′ə-bəl) *adj.* **1.** Likely to happen or to be true. **2.** Likely but uncertain; plausible. [ME, plausible < OFr. < Lat. *probābilis* < *probāre*, to prove. See PROVE.]

probable cause *n. Law.* Reasonable grounds for belief that an accused person may be subject to arrest or the issuance of a warrant. —**prob′a•ble-cause′** (prŏb′ə-bəl-kôz′) *adj.*

prob•a•bly (prŏb′ə-blē) *adv.* Most likely; presumably.

pro•bang (prō′băng′) *n.* A long flexible rod having a tuft or sponge at the end, used in cleaning or medicating the larynx or esophagus. [Alteration of *provang*.]

pro•bate (prō′bāt′) *Law.* —*n.* **1.** The process of legally establishing the validity of a will before a judicial authority. **2.** Judicial certification of the validity of a will. **3.** An authenticated copy of a will so certified. —*tr.v.* **-bat•ed, -bat•ing, -bates.** To establish the validity of (a will) by probate. [ME *probat* < Lat. *probātum*, neut. p.part. of *probāre*, to prove. See PROVE.]

probate court *n. Law.* A court limited to the jurisdiction of probating wills and administering estates.

pro•ba•tion (prō-bā′shən) *n.* **1.** A process or period in which a person's fitness, as for membership in a social group, is tested. **2.a.** *Law.* The act of suspending the sentence of a person convicted of a criminal offense and granting that person provisional freedom on the promise of good behavior. **b.** A discharge from commitment as an insane person on condition of continued sanity and of being recommitted upon the reappearance of insanity. **3.** A trial period in which a student is given time to try to redeem failing grades or bad conduct. **4.** The status of a person on probation. [ME *probacion*, a testing < OFr. *probation* < Lat. *probātiō*, *probātiōn-* < *probātus*, p.part. of *probāre*, to test. See PROVE.] —**pro•ba′tion•al, pro•ba′tion•ar′y** *adj.* —**pro•ba′tion•al•ly** *adv.*

pro•ba•tion•er (prō-bā′shə-nər) *n.* A person on probation.

probation officer *n. Law.* **1.** An official charged with the care of juvenile delinquents. **2.** An official charged with supervising convicts at large on suspended sentence or probation.

pro•ba•tive (prō′bə-tĭv) also **pro•ba•to•ry** (-tôr′ē, -tōr′ē) *adj.* **1.** Serving to test, try, or prove: *a probative period.* **2.** Furnishing evidence or proof.

probe (prōb) *n.* **1.** An exploratory action, expedition, or device, esp. one designed to investigate and obtain information on a remote or unknown region. **2.** A slender, flexible instrument used to explore a wound or body cavity. **3.** The act of exploring or searching with or as if with a device or an instrument. **4.** An investigation into unfamiliar matters or questionable activities. **5.** A space probe. —*v.* **probed, prob•ing, probes.** —*tr.* **1.** To explore with or as if with a probe. **2.** To delve into; investigate. —*intr.* To conduct an exploratory investigation; search. [ME, examination < Med.Lat. *proba* < LLat., proof < Lat. *probāre*, to test < *probus*, good. See **per[1]***.] —**prob′er** *n.* —**prob′ing•ly** *adv.*

pro•bi•ty (prō′bĭ-tē) *n.* Complete and confirmed integrity; uprightness. See Syns at **honesty.** [ME *probite* < OFr. < Lat. *probitās* < *probus*, upright, good. See **per[1]***.]

prob•lem (prŏb′ləm) *n.* **1.** A question to be considered, solved, or answered. **2.** A situation, matter, or person that presents perplexity or difficulty. See Usage Note at **dilemma.** —*adj.* **1.** Difficult to deal with or control. **2.** Dealing with a moral or social problem. [ME *probleme* < OFr. < Lat. *problēma*, *problēmat-* < Gk. < *proballein*, to throw before, put forward : *pro-*, before; see PRO–[2] + *ballein*, *blē-*, to throw; see **g[w]elə-***.]

prob•lem•at•ic (prŏb′lə-măt′ĭk) also **prob•lem•at•i•cal** (-ĭ-kəl) *adj.* **1.** Posing a problem; difficult to solve. **2.** Open to doubt; debatable. **3.** Not settled; unresolved or dubious: *a problematic future.* —**prob′lem•at′i•cal•ly** *adv.*

pro bo•no (prō bō′nō) *adj.* Done without compensation for the public good. [Lat. *prō bonō (publicō)*, for the (public) good : *prō*, for + *bonō*, ablative of *bonum*, the good.]

pro•bos•cid•i•an (prō′bə-sĭd′ē-ən) also **pro•bos•ci•de•an** (prō-bŏs′ĭ-dē′ən) *n.* A mammal of the order Proboscidea, such as the elephant or its extinct relatives, having a long trunk, large tusks, and a massive body. [< NLat. *Proboscidea*, order name < Lat. *proboscis*, *proboscid-*, proboscis. See PROBOSCIS.] —**pro′bos•cid′i•an** *adj.*

pro•bos•cis (prō-bŏs′ĭs) *n., pl.* **-bos•cis•es** or **-bos•ci•des** (-bŏs′ĭ-dēz′). **1.** A long flexible snout or trunk. **2.** The slender tubular feeding and sucking organ of certain invertebrates. **3.** A human nose, esp. a prominent one. [Lat. < Gk. *proboskis* : *pro-*, in front; see PRO–[2] + *boskein*, to feed.]

proc. *abbr.* **1.** Proceeding. **2.** Process.

pro•caine (prō′kān′) *n.* A white crystalline powder, $C_{13}H_{20}N_2O_2$, used chiefly in its hydrochloride form as a local anesthetic in medicine and dentistry. [PRO–[2] + (CO)CAINE.]

pro•cam•bi•um (prō-kăm′bē-əm) *n.* A type of undifferentiated plant tissue that gives rise to vascular tissue. —**pro•cam′bi•al** (-əl) *adj.*

pro•car•y•ote (prō-kăr′ē-ōt′) *n.* Var. of **prokaryote.**

pro•ce•dur•al (prə-sē′jər-əl) *adj.* Of or concerning procedure, esp. of a court of law or parliamentary body. —*n.* A police procedural. —**pro•ce′dur•al•ly** *adv.*

pro•ce•dure (prə-sē′jər) *n.* **1.** A manner of proceeding; a way of performing or effecting something. **2.** A series of steps taken to accomplish an end: *a long therapeutic procedure.* **3.** A set of established forms or methods for conducting the affairs of a business, legislative body, or court of law. [Fr. *procédure* < OFr. < *proceder*, to proceed. See PROCEED.]

pro•ceed (prō-sēd′, prə-) *intr.v.* **-ceed•ed, -ceed•ing, -ceeds. 1.** To go forward or onward, esp. after an interruption; continue. **2.** To begin to carry on an action or a process. **3.** To move on in an orderly manner. **4.** To come from a source; originate or issue. See Syns at **stem[1]. 5.** *Law.* To institute and conduct legal action. —*n.* **pro•ceeds.** (prō′sēdz′). The amount of money derived from a commercial or fundraising venture; the yield. [ME *proceden* < OFr. *proceder* < Lat. *prōcēdere* : *prō-*, forward; see PRO–[1] + *cēdere*, to go; see **ked-***.] —**pro•ceed′er** *n.*

pro•ceed•ing (prō-sē′dĭng, prə-) *n.* **1.** A course of action; a procedure. **2. proceedings.** A sequence of events occurring at a particular place or occasion. **3. proceedings.** A record of business carried on by a society or other organization; minutes. **4.** *Law.* **a.** Legal action; litigation. **b.** The instituting or conducting of legal action. In both senses, often used in the plural.

pro•ce•phal•ic (prō′sə-făl′ĭk) *adj.* Of, relating to, or located on or near the front of the head.

pro•cer•coid (prō-sûr′koid) *n.* A larval stage of certain tapeworms that typically develops in the body cavity of a copepod. [PRO–[2] + Gk. *kerkos*, tail + –OID.]

proc•ess[1] (prŏs′ĕs′, prō′sĕs′) *n., pl.* **proc•ess•es** (prŏs′ĕs′ĭz, prō′sĕs′-, prŏs′ĭ-sēz′, prō′sĭ-). **1.** A series of actions, changes, or functions bringing about a result. **2.** A series of operations performed in the making or treatment of a product. **3.** Progress; passage. **4.** *Law.* The entire course of a judicial proceeding. **5.** *Law.* **a.** A summons or writ ordering a defendant to appear in court. **b.** The total quantity of summonses or writs issued in a particular proceeding. **6.** *Biol.* An outgrowth of tissue; a projecting part. **7.** Any of various photomechanical or photoengraving methods. **8.** See **conk[3]**. —*tr.v.* **-essed, -ess•ing, -ess•es. 1.** To put through the steps of a prescribed procedure. **2.** To prepare, treat, or convert by subjecting to a special process. **3.** *Law.* **a.** To serve with a summons or writ. **b.** To institute legal proceedings against; prosecute. **4.** *Comp. Sci.* To perform operations on (data). **5.** To straighten (hair) by a chemical process; conk. —*adj.* **1.** Prepared or converted by a special process. **2.** Made by or used in any of several photomechanical or photoengraving processes. [ME *proces* < OFr., development < Lat. *prōcessus* < p.part. of *prōcēdere*, to advance. See PROCEED.]

pro•cess[2] (prə-sĕs′) *intr.v.* **-cessed, -cess•ing, -cess•es.** To move along in or as if in a procession.

pro•ces•sion (prə-sĕsh′ən) *n.* **1.** The act of moving along or forward; progression. **2.** Origination; emanation; rise. **3.a.** A group of persons, vehicles, or objects moving along in an orderly, formal manner. **b.** The movement of such a group. **4.** An orderly succession. —*intr.v.* **-sioned, -sion•ing, -sions.** To form or go in a procession. [ME < OFr. < LLat. *prōcessiō, prōcessiōn-* < Lat., an advance < *prōcessus*, p.part. of *prōcēdere*, to advance. See PROCEED.]

pro•ces•sion•al (prə-sĕsh′ə-nəl) *adj.* Of, relating to, or suitable for a procession. —*n.* **1.** A book containing the rituals observed during a religious procession. **2.** *Mus.* **a.** A piece played or sung at the entrance of the clergy in a church service. **b.** Music played or sung during a procession.

proc•es•sor (prŏs′ĕs′ər, prō′sĕs′-) *n.* **1.** One that processes, esp. an apparatus for preparing, treating, or converting material. **2.** *Comp. Sci.* **a.** A computer. **b.** A central processing unit. **c.** A program that translates another program into a form acceptable by the computer being used.

proc•ess printing (prŏs′ĕs′, prō′sĕs′) *n.* Printing from multiple halftone images, each inked with a different color such that the composite impression will reproduce the colors of the original.

pro•cès-ver•bal (prō-sā′vĕr-bäl′) *n., pl.* **-ver•baux** (-vĕr-bō′). A detailed official record of diplomatic, deliberative, or legal proceedings. [Fr. : *procès*, proceedings + *verbal*, oral.]

pro-choice (prō-chois′) *adj.* Favoring or supporting the legal right to choose whether or not to continue a pregnancy to term.

pro•claim (prō-klām′, prə-) *tr.v.* **-claimed, -claim•ing, -claims. 1.** To announce officially and publicly; declare. **2.** To indicate conspicuously; make plain. **3.** To praise; extol. [ME *proclamen, proclaimen* (influenced by *claimen*, to claim) < OFr. *proclamer* < Lat. *prōclāmāre* : *prō-*, forward; see PRO-[1] + *clāmāre*, to cry out; see **kelə-[2]***.] —**pro•claim′er** *n.* —**pro•clam′a•to′ry** (prō-klăm′ə-tôr′ē, -tōr′ē) *adj.*

proc•la•ma•tion (prŏk′lə-mā′shən) *n.* **1.** The act of proclaiming or the condition of being proclaimed. **2.** Something proclaimed, esp. an official public announcement.

pro•clit•ic (prō-klĭt′ĭk) *Ling.* —*adj.* Forming an accentual unit with the following word and thus having no independent accent. —*n.* A proclitic word. [NLat. *procliticus* : PRO-[2] + LLat. *encliticus*, enclitic; see ENCLITIC.]

pro•cliv•i•ty (prō-klĭv′ĭ-tē) *n., pl.* **-ties.** A natural propensity or inclination; predisposition. See Syns at **predilection.** [Lat. *prōclīvitās* < *prōclīvis*, inclined : *prō-*, forward; see PRO-[1] + *clīvus*, slope; see **klei-***.]

Pro•clus (prō′kləs, prŏk′ləs). A.D. 410?–485. Greek philosopher and the last major Neo-Platonic teacher.

Proc•ne (prŏk′nē) *n. Gk. Myth.* An Athenian princess who avenged the cruelty of her husband, Tereus, by killing their son and with her sister Philomela became a swallow.

pro•con•sul (prō-kŏn′səl) *n.* **1.** A provincial governor of consular rank in the Roman Republic and Roman Empire. **2.** A high administrator in a modern colonial empire. [ME < Lat. *prōcōnsul* < *prō cōnsule*, in place of the consul : *prō*, instead of; see PRO-[1] + *cōnsule*, ablative of *cōnsul*, consul; see CONSUL.] —**pro•con′su•lar** (-sə-lər) *adj.* —**pro•con′su•late** (-sə-lĭt), **pro•con′sul•ship′** *n.*

Pro•co•pi•us (prə-kō′pē-əs). fl. 6th cent. A.D. Byzantine historian who wrote about the Persian, Vandal, and Gothic wars.

pro•cras•ti•nate (prō-krăs′tə-nāt′, prə-) *v.* **-nat•ed, -nat•ing, -nates.** —*intr.* To put off doing something, esp. out of habitual carelessness or laziness. —*tr.* To postpone or delay needlessly. [Lat. *prōcrāstināre, prōcrāstināt-* : *prō-*, forward; see PRO-[1] + *crāstinus*, of tomorrow (< *crās*, tomorrow).] —**pro•cras′ti•na′tion** *n.* —**pro•cras′ti•na′tor** *n.*

pro•cre•ate (prō′krē-āt′) *v.* **-at•ed, -at•ing, -ates.** —*tr.* **1.** To beget and conceive (offspring). **2.** To produce or create; originate. —*intr.* To beget and conceive offspring. [Lat. *prōcreāre, prōcreāt-* : *prō-*, forward; see PRO-[1] + *creāre*, to create; see **ker-[2]***.] —**pro′cre•ant** (-ənt) *adj.* —**pro′cre•a′tion** *n.* —**pro′cre•a′tor** *n.*

pro•cre•a•tive (prō′krē-ā′tĭv) *adj.* **1.** Capable of reproducing; generative. **2.** Of or directed to procreation.

Pro•crus•te•an also **pro•crus•te•an** (prō-krŭs′tē-ən) *adj.* Exhibiting merciless disregard for individual differences or special circumstances. [After *Procrustes*, a mythical Greek giant who stretched or shortened captives to make them fit his beds < Lat. *Procrustēs* < Gk. *Prokroustēs* < *prokrouein*, to stretch out : *pro-*, forth; see PRO-[2] + *krouein*, to beat.]

pro•cryp•tic (prō-krĭp′tĭk) *adj. Zool.* Having a pattern or coloration adapted for natural camouflage. [Prob. PRO(TECTIVE) + CRYPTIC.]

proc•ti•tis (prŏk-tī′tĭs) *n.* Inflammation of the rectum or anus. [Gk. *prōktos*, anus + -ITIS.]

proc•tol•o•gy (prŏk-tŏl′ə-jē) *n.* The branch of medicine that deals with the diagnosis and treatment of disorders affecting the colon, rectum, and anus. [Gk. *prōktos*, anus + -LOGY.] —**proc′to•log′ic** (-tə-lŏj′ĭk), **proc′to•log′i•cal** (-ĭ-kəl) *adj.* —**proc′to•log′i•cal•ly** *adv.* —**proc•tol′o•gist** *n.*

proc•tor (prŏk′tər) *n.* A dormitory and examination supervisor in a school. —*tr.v.* **-tored, -tor•ing, -tors.** To supervise (an examination). [ME *procutor, proctour*, university officer, manager < *procuratour*. See PROCURATOR.] —**proc•to′ri•al** (-tôr′ē-əl, -tōr′-) *adj.* —**proc′tor•ship′** *n.*

proc•to•scope (prŏk′tə-skōp′) *n.* An instrument consisting of a tube or speculum equipped with a light, used to examine the rectum. [Gk. *prōktos*, anus + -SCOPE.] —**proc′to•scop′ic** (-skŏp′ĭk) *adj.* —**proc•tos′co•py** (-tŏs′kə-pē) *n.*

pro•cum•bent (prō-kŭm′bənt) *adj.* **1.** Lying face down; prone. **2.** *Bot.* Trailing along the ground but not rooting. [Lat. *prōcumbēns, prōcumbent-*, pr.part. of *prōcumbere*, to bend down : *prō-*, forward; see PRO-[1] + *-cumbere*, to lie down.]

proc•u•ra•tor (prŏk′yə-rā′tər) *n.* **1.** One authorized to manage the affairs of another; an agent. **2.** An employee of the Roman emperor in civil affairs. [ME *procuratour* < OFr. < Lat. *prōcūrātor* < *prōcūrāre*, to take care of. See PROCURE.] —**proc′u•ra•to′ri•al** (-yər-ə-tôr′ē-əl, -tōr′-) *adj.*

pro•cure (prō-kyo͝or′, prə-) *v.* **-cured, -cur•ing, -cures.** —*tr.* **1.** To get by special effort; obtain or acquire. **2.** To bring about; effect. **3.** To obtain (a person) for another for sex acts. —*intr.* To obtain sexual partners for others. [ME *procuren* < OFr. *procurer*, to take care of < Lat. *prōcūrāre* : *prō-*, for; see PRO-[1] + *cūrāre*, to care for (< *cūra*, care; see CURE).] —**pro•cur′a•ble** *adj.* —**pro•cur′ance, pro•cure′ment** *n.*

pro•cur•er (prō-kyo͝or′ər, prə-) *n.* **1.** One that procures. **2.** A pander.

Pro•cy•on (prō′sē-ŏn′) *n.* A binary star in the constellation Canis Minor. [Lat. *Procyōn* < Gk. *Prokuōn* : *pro-*, before; see PRO-[2] + *kuōn*, dog; see **kwon-***.]

prod (prŏd) *tr.v.* **prod•ded, prod•ding, prods. 1.** To jab or poke, as with a pointed object. **2.** To goad to action; incite. —*n.* **1.** A pointed object used to prod. **2.** An incitement; a stimulus. [?] —**prod′der** *n.*

prod. *abbr.* **1.** Produce. **2.** Produced. **3.** Product. **4.** Production.

prod•i•gal (prŏd′ĭ-gəl) *adj.* **1.** Rashly or wastefully extravagant. **2.** Marked by rash or wasteful extravagance: *a prodigal life.* **3.** Giving or given in abundance; lavish or profuse. —*n.* One given to wasteful luxury or extravagance. [Prob. back-formation < PRODIGALITY.] —**prod′i•gal•ly** *adv.*

prod•i•gal•i•ty (prŏd′ĭ-găl′ĭ-tē) *n., pl.* **-ties. 1.** Extravagant wastefulness. **2.** Profuse generosity. **3.** Extreme abundance; lavishness. [ME *prodigalite* < OFr. < LLat. *prōdigālitās* < **prōdigālis*, prodigal < Lat. *prōdigus*, prodigal < *prōdigere*, drive away, to squander : *prōd-, prō-*, forth; see PRO-[1] + *agere*, to drive; see **ag-***.]

pro•di•gious (prə-dĭj′əs) *adj.* **1.** Impressively great in size, force, or extent; enormous. **2.** Extraordinary; marvelous: *the pianist's prodigious talents.* **3.** *Obsolete.* Portentous; ominous. [Lat. *prōdigiōsus*, portentous, monstrous < *prōdigium*, omen.] —**pro•di′gious•ly** *adv.* —**pro•di′gious•ness** *n.*

prod•i•gy (prŏd′ə-jē) *n., pl.* **-gies. 1.** A person with exceptional talents or powers. **2.** An act or event so extraordinary or rare as to inspire wonder. See Syns at **wonder. 3.** A portentous sign or event; an omen. [ME *prodige*, portent < Lat. *prōdigium*.]

pro•drome (prō′drōm′) *n., pl.* **-dromes** or **-dro•ma•ta** (-drō′mə-tə). An early symptom indicating the onset of an attack or a disease. [Fr. < Lat. *prodromus*, precursor < Gk. *prodromos*, precursor : *pro-*, forward; see PRO-[2] + *dromos*, running.] —**pro•dro′mal, pro•drom′ic** (-drŏm′ĭk) *adj.*

pro•drug (prō′drŭg′) *n.* An inactive precursor of a drug, converted into its active form in the body by metabolic processes.

pro•duce (prə-do͞os′, -dyo͞os′, prō-) *v.* **-duced, -duc•ing, -duc•es.** —*tr.* **1.** To bring forth; yield: *produce offspring.* **2.a.** To create by physical or mental effort. **b.** To manufacture. **3.** To cause to occur or exist; give rise to. **4.** To bring forth; exhibit: *produced an eyewitness.* **5.** To supervise and finance the making and public presentation of. **6.** *Math.* To extend (an area or volume) or lengthen (a line). —*intr.* **1.** To make or yield products or a product. **2.** To manufacture or create economic goods and services. —*n.* (prŏd′o͞os, prō′do͞os). **1.** Something produced; a product. **2.** Farm products, esp. fresh fruits and vegetables. [ME *producen*, to proceed, extend < Lat. *prō-*

ă pat	oi boy
ā pay	ou out
âr care	o͝o took
ä father	o͞o boot
ĕ pet	ŭ cut
ē be	ûr urge
ĭ pit	th thin
ī pie	*th* this
îr pier	hw which
ŏ pot	zh vision
ō toe	ə about, item
ô paw	

Stress marks:
′ (primary);
′ (secondary), as in
dictionary (dĭk′shə-nĕr′ē)

dūcere, to extend, bring forth : *prō-,* forward; see PRO-[1] + *dūcere,* to lead; see **deuk-*.**] —**pro•duc′i•ble, pro•duce′a•ble** *adj.*

Syns: *produce, bear, yield.* The central meaning shared by these verbs is "to bring forth as a product": *a mine producing gold; a seed that bore fruit; a plant that yields gum.*

pro•duc•er (prə-dōō′sər, -dyōō′-, prō-) *n.* **1.** One that produces, esp. a person or an organization that produces goods or services for sale. **2.** One who finances and supervises the making and public presentation of a play, film, or similar work. **3.** A furnace that manufactures producer gas. **4.** *Ecol.* A photosynthetic green plant or chemosynthetic bacterium, constituting the first trophic level in a food chain; an autotrophic organism.

producer gas *n.* A combustible mixture of nitrogen, carbon monoxide, and hydrogen, generated by passing air with steam over burning coke or coal in a furnace and used as fuel.

producer goods *pl.n.* Goods, such as raw materials and tools, used to make consumer goods.

prod•uct (prŏd′əkt) *n.* **1.** Something produced by human or mechanical effort or by a natural process. **2.** A direct result; a consequence. **3.** *Chem.* A substance resulting from a chemical reaction. **4.** *Math.* **a.** The number or quantity obtained by multiplying two or more numbers together. **b.** A scalar product. **c.** A vector product. [ME, result of multiplication, produced < Med.Lat. *prōductum,* result of multiplication < neut. p.part. of Lat. *prōdūcere,* to bring forth. See PRODUCE.]

pro•duc•tion (prə-dŭk′shən, prō-) *n.* **1.a.** The act or process of producing: *the production of lumber.* **b.** The fact or process of being produced: *a movie in production.* **2.** The creation of value or wealth by producing goods and services. **3.** Something produced; a product. **4.** An amount or quantity produced; output. **5.a.** A work of art or literature. **b.** A work produced for the stage, screen, television, or radio. **c.** A staging or presentation of a theatrical work. **6.** An exaggerated spectacle or display. —**pro•duc′tion•al** *adj.*

production line *n.* See **assembly line** 1.

pro•duc•tive (prə-dŭk′tĭv, prō-) *adj.* **1.** Producing or capable of producing. **2.** Producing abundantly; fertile. **3.** Yielding favorable or useful results; constructive. **4.** *Econ.* Of or involved in the creation of goods and services to produce wealth or value. **5.** Effective in achieving specified results; originative. **6.** *Medic.* **a.** Producing mucus or sputum. **b.** Forming new tissue: *a productive inflammation.* **7.** *Ling.* **a.** Of or relating to the linguistic skills of speaking and writing. **b.** Of or relating to a morphological or morphophonemic element that is freely used in the creation of new derivatives. —**pro•duc′tive•ly** *adv.* —**pro•duc′tive•ness** *n.*

pro•duc•tiv•i•ty (prō′dŭk-tĭv′ĭ-tē, prŏd′ək-) *n.* **1.** The quality of being productive. **2.** *Econ.* The rate at which goods or services are produced, esp. output per unit of labor. **3.** *Ecol.* The rate at which radiant energy is used by producers to form organic substances as food for consumers.

pro•em (prō′ĕm′) *n.* An introduction; a preface. [ME *proheme* < OFr. < Lat. *prooemium* < Gk. *prooimion* : *pro-,* before; see PRO-[2] + *oimē,* song.] —**pro•e′mi•al** (prō-ē′mē-əl, -ĕm′ē-) *adj.*

pro•en•zyme (prō-ĕn′zīm′) *n.* The precursor of an enzyme, converted into an active enzyme by proteolysis.

pro•es•trus (prō-ĕs′trəs) *n.* The period immediately before estrus in most female mammals, characterized by development of the endometrium and ovarian follicles.

prof (prŏf) *n. Informal.* A professor.

prof. *abbr.* Professional.

prof•a•na•tion (prŏf′ə-nā′shən) *n.* The act or an instance of profaning; desecration.

pro•fane (prō-fān′, prə-) *adj.* **1.** Marked by contempt or irreverence for what is sacred: *profane words.* **2.** Nonreligious in subject matter, form, or use; secular. **3.** Not admitted into a body of secret knowledge or ritual; uninitiated. **4.** Vulgar; coarse. —*tr.v.* **-faned, -fan•ing, -fanes. 1.** To treat with irreverence. **2.** To put to an improper, unworthy, or degrading use; abuse. [ME *prophane* < OFr. < Lat. *profānus* < *prō fānō,* in front of the temple : *prō-,* before, outside; see PRO-[1] + *fānō,* ablative of *fānum,* temple; see **dhēs-*.**] —**pro•fan′a•to′ry** (prō-făn′ə-tôr′ē, -tōr′ē, prə-) *adj.* —**pro•fane′ly** *adv.* —**pro•fane′ness** *n.* —**pro•fan′er** *n.*

pro•fan•i•ty (prō-făn′ĭ-tē, prə-) *n., pl.* **-ties. 1.** The condition or quality of being profane. **2.a.** Abusive, vulgar, or irreverent language. **b.** The use of such language.

pro•fess (prə-fĕs′, prō-) *v.* **-fessed, -fess•ing, -fess•es.** —*tr.* **1.** To affirm openly; declare or claim. **2.** To make a pretense of; pretend. **3.** To claim skill in or knowledge of: *profess medicine.* **4.** To affirm belief in: *profess Catholicism.* **5.** To receive into a religious order or congregation. —*intr.* **1.** To make an open affirmation. **2.** To take the vows of a religious order or congregation. [ME *professen,* to take vows < OFr. *profes,* that has taken a religious vow (< Med.Lat. *professus,* avowed) and < Med.Lat. *professāre,* to administer a vow, both < Lat. *professus,* p.part. of *profitērī,* to affirm openly : *pro-,* forth; see PRO-[1] + *fatērī,* to acknowledge; see **bhā-[2]*.**] —**pro•fess′ed•ly** (-fĕs′ĭd-lē) *adv.*

profile
Portrait of Bianca Maria Sforza by Giovanni de Predis (1450?–1520?)

pro•fes•sion (prə-fĕsh′ən) *n.* **1.** An occupation requiring considerable training and specialized study: *the profession of law.* **2.** The body of qualified persons in an occupation or field. **3.** An act or instance of professing; a declaration. **4.** An avowal of faith or belief. **5.** A faith or belief.

pro•fes•sion•al (prə-fĕsh′ə-nəl) *adj.* **1.a.** Of, relating to, engaged in, or suitable for a profession: *professional training.* **b.** Conforming to the standards of a profession: *professional ethics.* **2.** Engaging in a given activity as a source of livelihood or as a career. **3.** Performed by persons receiving pay. **4.** Having or showing great skill; expert. —*n.* **1.** A person following a profession, esp. a learned profession. **2.** One who earns a living in a given or implied occupation. **3.** A skilled practitioner; an expert. —**pro•fes′sion•al•ly** *adv.*

pro•fes•sion•al•ism (prə-fĕsh′ə-nə-lĭz′əm) *n.* **1.** Professional status, methods, character, or standards. **2.** The use of professional performers, as in athletics or in the arts.

pro•fes•sion•al•ize (prə-fĕsh′ə-nə-līz′) *tr.v.* **-ized, -iz•ing, -iz•es.** To make professional. —**pro•fes′sion•al•i•za′tion** (prə-fĕsh′ə-nə-lĭ-zā′shən) *n.*

pro•fes•sor (prə-fĕs′ər) *n.* **1.a.** A college or university teacher who ranks above an associate professor. **b.** A teacher or an instructor. **2.** One who professes. [ME *professour* < OFr. *professeur* < Lat. *professor* < *professus,* p.part. of *profitērī,* to profess. See PROFESS.] —**pro′fes•so′ri•al** (prō′fĭ-sôr′ē-əl, -sōr′-, prŏf′ĭ-) *adj.* —**pro′fes•so′ri•al•ly** *adv.* —**pro•fes′sor•ship′** *n.*

pro•fes•so•ri•ate or **pro•fes•so•ri•at** (prō′fĭ-sôr′ē-ət, -sōr′-, prŏf′ĭ-) *n.* **1.** The rank or office of a professor. **2.** College or university professors considered as a group.

prof•fer (prŏf′ər) *tr.v.* **-fered, -fer•ing, -fers.** To offer for acceptance; tender. See Syns at **offer.** —*n.* The act of proffering; an offer. [ME *profren* < OFr. *poroffrir, profrir* : *por-,* forth (< Lat. *prō-*; see PRO-[1]) + *offrir,* to offer (< Lat. *offerre*; see OFFER).] —**prof′fer•er** *n.*

pro•fi•cien•cy (prə-fĭsh′ən-sē) *n., pl.* **-cies.** The state or quality of being proficient; competence.

pro•fi•cient (prə-fĭsh′ənt) *adj.* Having or marked by an advanced degree of competence, as in an art. —*n.* An expert; an adept. [Lat. *prōficiēns, prōficient-,* pr.part. of *prōficere,* to make progress. See PROFIT.] —**pro•fi′cient•ly** *adv.*

Syns: *proficient, adept, skilled, skillful, expert.* These adjectives mean having or showing knowledge, ability, or skill, as in a profession or field of study. *Proficient* implies an advanced degree of competence acquired through training: *proficient in Greek and Latin. Adept* suggests a natural aptitude improved by practice: *adept at cutting straight. Skilled* implies sound, thorough competence and often expertise, as in a craft: *a skilled potter. Skillful* adds to *skilled* the idea of natural dexterity in performance or achievement: *skillful in the use of the loom. Expert* applies to one with consummate skill and command: *expert in her playing.*

pro•file (prō′fīl′) *n.* **1.a.** A side view of an object or a structure, esp. of the human head. **b.** A representation of an object or a structure seen from the side. **2.** An outline of an object. See Syns at **outline. 3.** Degree of exposure to public notice; visibility: *kept a low profile.* **4.** A biographical essay presenting the subject's most noteworthy characteristics and achievements. **5.** A formal summary or analysis of data representing distinctive features or characteristics. **6.** *Geol.* A vertical section of soil or rock showing the sequence of the various layers. —*tr.v.* **-filed, -fil•ing, -files. 1.** To draw or shape a profile of. **2.** To produce a profile of. [Ital. *profilo* < *profilare,* to draw in outline : *pro-,* forward (< Lat. *prō-*; see PRO-[1]) + *filare,* to draw a line (< LLat. *filāre,* to spin < Lat. *fīlum,* thread; see **gʷhī-*.**)] —**pro′fil•er** *n.*

prof•it (prŏf′ĭt) *n.* **1.** An advantageous gain or return; benefit. **2.** The return on a business undertaking after all operating expenses have been met. **3.a.** The return on an investment after all charges have been paid. **b.** The rate of increase in the net worth of a business enterprise in a given accounting period. **c.** Income from investments or property. **d.** The amount received for a commodity or service in excess of the original cost. —*v.* **-it•ed, -it•ing, -its.** —*intr.* **1.** To make a gain or profit. **2.** To derive advantage; benefit. —*tr.* To be beneficial to. [ME < OFr. < Lat. *prōfectus* < p.part. of *prōficere,* make progress, to profit : *prō-,* forward; see PRO-[1] + *facere,* to make; see **dhē-*.**] —**prof′it•less** *adj.*

prof•it•a•ble (prŏf′ĭ-tə-bəl) *adj.* Yielding profit; advantageous or lucrative. See Syns at **beneficial.** —**prof′it•a•bil′i•ty, prof′it•a•ble•ness** *n.* —**prof′it•a•bly** *adv.*

profit and loss *n. Accounting.* An account showing net profit and loss over a given period.

prof•it•eer (prŏf′ĭ-tîr′) *n.* One who makes excessive profits on goods in short supply. —**prof′it•eer′** *v.*

pro•fit•er•ole (prə-fĭt′ə-rōl′) *n.* A small round cream puff. [Fr., perh. dim. of *profiter,* to profit < OFr. < *profit,* profit. See PROFIT.]

profit shar•ing (shâr′ĭng) *n.* A system by which employees receive a share of the profits of a business enterprise.

prof•li•gate (prŏf′lĭ-gĭt, -gāt′) *adj.* **1.** Given over to dissipation; dissolute. **2.** Recklessly wasteful; wildly extravagant.

—*n.* A profligate person; a wastrel. [Lat. *prōflīgātus*, p.part. of *prōflīgāre*, to ruin, cast down : *prō-*, forward; see PRO–[1] + *-flīgāre*, intensive of *flīgere*, to strike down.] —**prof′li•ga•cy** (-gə-sē) *n.* —**prof′li•gate•ly** *adv.*

pro for•ma (prō fôr′mə) *adj.* **1.** Done as a formality; perfunctory. **2.** Provided in advance so as to prescribe form or describe items. [NLat. *prō formā* : *prō*, for the sake of + *formā*, ablative of *forma*, form.]

pro•found (prə-found′, prō-) *adj.* **-er, -est. 1.** Situated at, extending to, or coming from a great depth; deep. See Syns at **deep. 2.** Coming as if from the depths of one's being: *profound contempt.* **3.** Thoroughgoing; far-reaching. **4.** Penetrating beyond what is superficial or obvious. **5.** Unqualified; absolute: *a profound silence.* [ME *profounde* < OFr. *profond* < Lat. *profundus* : *prō-*, before; see PRO–[1] + *fundus*, bottom.] —**pro•found′ly** *adv.* —**pro•found′ness** *n.*

pro•fun•di•ty (prə-fŭn′dĭ-tē, prō-) *n., pl.* **-ties. 1.** Great depth. **2.** Depth of intellect, feeling, or meaning. **3.** Something profound or abstruse. [ME *profundite* < OFr. < LLat. *profunditās* < Lat. *profundus*, deep. See PROFOUND.]

pro•fuse (prə-fyo͞os′, prō-) *adj.* **1.** Plentiful; copious. **2.** Giving or given freely and abundantly; extravagant. [ME, lavish < Lat. *profūsus*, p.part. of *profundere*, to pour forth : *pro-*, forth; see PRO–[1] + *fundere*, to pour; see **gheu-***.] —**pro•fuse′ly** *adv.* —**pro•fuse′ness** *n.*

pro•fu•sion (prə-fyo͞o′zhən, prō-) *n.* **1.** The state of being profuse; abundance. **2.** Lavish or unrestrained expense; extravagance. **3.** A profuse outpouring or quantity.

pro•gen•i•tor (prō-jĕn′ĭ-tər) *n.* **1.** A direct ancestor. See Syns at **ancestor. 2.** An originator of a line of descent; a precursor. **3.** An originator; a founder. [Ult. < Lat. *prōgenitor* < *prōgenitus*, p.part. of *prōgignere*, to beget : *prō-*, forward; see PRO–[1] + *gignere*, *gen-*, to beget; see **genə-***.]

prog•e•ny (prŏj′ə-nē) *n., pl.* **progeny** or **-nies. 1.a.** One born of, begotten by, or derived from another; an offspring or a descendant. **b.** Offspring or descendants considered as a group. **2.** A result of creative effort; a product. [ME *progeni* < OFr. *progenie* < Lat. *prōgeniēs* < *prōgignere*, to beget. See PROGENITOR.]

pro•ger•i•a (prō-jîr′ē-ə) *n.* A rare congenital disorder of childhood, characterized by rapid onset of the physical changes typical of old age, usu. resulting in death before age 20. [PRO–[2] + Gk. *gēras*, old age; see GERIATRICS + –IA[1].]

pro•ges•ta•tion•al (prō′jĕs-tā′shə-nəl) *adj.* **1.** Of or relating to the phase of the menstrual cycle immediately following ovulation, characterized by secretion of progesterone. **2.a.** Of or relating to progesterone and its actions. **b.** Having actions similar to progesterone. Used of a drug.

pro•ges•ter•one (prō-jĕs′tə-rōn′) *n.* **1.** A steroid hormone, $C_{21}H_{30}O_2$, secreted by the corpus luteum of the ovary and by the placenta, that acts to prepare the uterus for implantation of the fertilized ovum, maintain pregnancy, and promote development of the mammary glands. **2.** A drug prepared from natural or synthetic progesterone, used to prevent miscarriage and treat menstrual disorders. [PRO–[1] + GEST(ATION) + (ST)ER(OL) + –ONE.]

pro•ges•tin (prō-jĕs′tĭn) *n.* **1.** A progestational substance that mimics progesterone. **2.** A crude hormone of the corpus luteum from which progesterone can be isolated in pure form. No longer in scientific use. [PRO–[1] + GEST(ATION) + –IN.]

pro•ges•to•gen (prō-jĕs′tə-jən) *n.* Any of various substances having progestational effects; a progestin.

pro•glot•tid (prō-glŏt′ĭd) also **pro•glot•tis** (-glŏt′ĭs) *n., pl.* **-glot•tids** also **-glot•ti•des** (-glŏt′ĭ-dēz′). One of the segments of a tapeworm, containing both male and female reproductive organs. [Gk. *proglōttis*, *proglōttid-*, tip of the tongue (< its shape) : *pro-*, before; see PRO–[2] + *glōtta*, tongue.] —**pro•glot′tic, pro′glot•ti•de′an** (-glŏt-ĭ-dē′ən, -glŏ-tĭd′ē-ən) *adj.*

prog•na•thous (prŏg′nə-thəs, prŏg-nā′-) also **prog•nath•ic** (prŏg-năth′ĭk, -nā′thĭk) *adj.* Having jaws that project forward to a marked degree. —**prog′na•thism** (-nə-thĭz′əm) *n.*

prog•no•sis (prŏg-nō′sĭs) *n., pl.* **-ses** (-sēz). **1.a.** A prediction of the probable course and outcome of a disease. **b.** The likelihood of recovery from a disease. **2.** A forecast or prediction. [LLat. *prognōsis* < Gk. < *progignōskein*, to foreknow : *pro-*, before; see PRO–[2] + *gignōskein*, to know; see **gnō-***.]

prog•nos•tic (prŏg-nŏs′tĭk) *adj.* **1.** Of, relating to, or useful in prognosis. **2.** Of or relating to prediction; predictive. —*n.* **1.** A sign or symptom indicating the future course of a disease. **2.** A sign of a future happening; a portent. [ME *pronostik*, prognosticating, omen (< Med.Lat. *prognōsticus*, prognosticating) and < Lat. *prognōsticum*, omen < neut. of *prognōsticus*, both < Gk. *prognōstikos* < *prognōsis*, foreknowledge. See PROGNOSIS.]

prog•nos•ti•cate (prŏg-nŏs′tĭ-kāt′) *tr.v.* **-cat•ed, -cat•ing, -cates. 1.** To predict according to present indications or signs; foretell. **2.** To foreshadow; portend. [ME *pronosticaten* < Med.Lat. *prognōsticāre*, *prognōsticāt-* < Lat. *prognōsticum*, sign of the future < Gk. *prognōstikon* < neut. of *prognōstikos*, foreknowing. See PROGNOSTIC.] —**prog•nos′ti•ca′tion** *n.* —**prog•nos′ti•ca′tive** *adj.* —**prog•nos′ti•ca′tor** *n.*

pro•gram (prō′grăm′, -grəm) *n.* **1.a.** A listing of the order of events and other pertinent information for a public presentation. **b.** The presentation itself. **2.** A scheduled radio or television show. **3.** An ordered list of events to take place or procedures to be followed; a schedule. **4.** A system of services, opportunities, or projects, usu. designed to meet a social need. **5.a.** A course of academic study; a curriculum. **b.** A plan or system of academic and related or ancillary activities: *a work-study program.* **c.** A plan or system of nonacademic extracurricular activities. **6.** A set of coded instructions for insertion into a machine, which then performs a desired sequence of operations. **7.** *Comp. Sci.* **a.** A procedure for solving a problem that involves collection of data, processing, and presentation of results. **b.** Such a procedure coded for a computer. **8.** An instruction sequence in programmed instruction. —*tr.v.* **-grammed, -gram•ming, -grams** or **-gramed, -gram•ing, -grams. 1.** To include or schedule in a program: *program a new musical composition.* **2.** To design a program for; schedule the activities of. **3.** To provide (a machine) with a set of coded working instructions. **4.** *Comp. Sci.* To provide (a computer) with a set of instructions for solving a problem or processing data. **5.** To train to perform automatically in a desired way, as if programming a machine. **6.** To prepare an instructional sequence for (material to be taught) in programmed instruction. [LLat. *programma*, public notice < Gk. *programma*, *programmat-* < *prographein*, to write publicly : *pro-*, forth; see PRO–[2] + *graphein*, to write; see **gerbh-***.] —**pro•gram′ma•bil′i•ty** *n.* —**pro′gram′ma•ble** *adj.*

program director *n.* A radio or television station director who selects, plans, and schedules programs.

pro•gram•mat•ic (prō′grə-măt′ĭk) *adj.* **1.** Of, relating to, or having a program. **2.** Following an overall plan or schedule: *a programmatic approach.* **3.** *Mus.* Of, resembling, or constituting program music. —**pro′gram•mat′i•cal•ly** *adv.*

pro•gramme (prō′grăm′, -grəm) *n. & v. Chiefly British.* Var. of **program.**

pro•grammed instruction (prō′grămd′, -grəmd) *n.* A method of teaching in which the information to be learned is presented in discrete sequential units, with a correct response to each unit required.

pro•gram•mer or **pro•gram•er** (prō′grăm′ər) *n. Comp. Sci.* One who programs, esp. one who writes computer programs.

pro•gram•ming or **pro•gram•ing** (prō′grăm′ĭng, -grə-mĭng) *n.* The designing, scheduling, or planning of a program.

program music *n.* Music intended to depict or suggest definite incidents, scenes, or images.

program trading *n.* Large-scale computer-assisted trading of stocks or other securities according to systems in which decisions to buy and sell are triggered automatically by fluctuations in price. —**program trader** *n.*

prog•ress (prŏg′rĕs′, -rəs, prō′grĕs′) *n.* **1.** Movement, as toward a goal; advance. **2.** Development or growth. **3.** Steady improvement, as of a society or civilization. See Syns at **development. 4.** A ceremonial journey made by a sovereign through his or her realm. —*intr.v.* **pro•gress.** (prə-grĕs′) **-gressed, -gress•ing, -gress•es. 1.** To advance; proceed. **2.** To advance toward a higher or better stage; improve steadily. —***idiom.* in progress.** Going on; under way. [ME *progresse* < Lat. *prōgressus* < p.part. of *prōgredī*, to advance : *prō-*, forward; see PRO–[1] + *gradī*, to go, walk; see **ghredh-***.]

pro•gres•sion (prə-grĕsh′ən) *n.* **1.** The process of progressing; progress. **2.** Movement from one member of a continuous series to the next. **3.** A continuous series; a sequence. **4.** *Math.* A series of numbers or quantities in which there is always the same relation between each quantity and the one succeeding it. **5.** *Mus.* **a.** A succession of tones or chords. **b.** A series of repetitions of a phrase, each in a new position on the scale. —**pro•gres′sion•al** *adj.*

pro•gres•sive (prə-grĕs′ĭv) *adj.* **1.** Moving forward; advancing. **2.** Proceeding in steps; continuing steadily by increments: *progressive change.* **3.** Promoting or favoring progress toward better conditions or new policies, ideas, or methods. **4. Progressive.** Of or relating to a Progressive Party. **5.** Of or relating to progressive education. **6.** Increasing in rate as the taxable amount increases: *a progressive tax.* **7.** *Pathol.* Tending to become more severe or wider in scope. **8.** *Gram.* Relating to or being a verb form that expresses an action or condition in progress. —*n.* **1.** A person who favors or strives for progress toward better conditions, as in society or government. **2. Progressive.** A member or supporter of a Progressive Party. **3.** *Gram.* A progressive verb form. —**pro•gres′sive•ly** *adv.* —**pro•gres′sive•ness** *n.*

Pro•gres•sive-Con•ser•va•tive Party (prə-grĕs′ĭv-kən-sûr′və-tĭv) *n.* A major political party in Canada advocating economic nationalism and close ties with Great Britain and the Commonwealth.

progressive education *n.* A set of reformist educational philosophies and methods that emphasize individual instruction and informality in the classroom.

Progressive Party *n.* **1.** A U.S. political party organized by Republican insurgents in 1911. **2.** A U.S. political party organized in 1924 that was active in Wisconsin until 1946. **3.** A

ă pat	oi boy
ā pay	ou out
âr care	o͝o took
ä father	o͞o boot
ĕ pet	ŭ cut
ē be	ûr urge
ĭ pit	th thin
ī pie	*th* this
îr pier	hw which
ŏ pot	zh vision
ō toe	ə about,
ô paw	item

Stress marks:
′ (primary);
′ (secondary), as in
dictionary (dĭk′shə-nĕr′ē)

Prohibition
Federal officer destroying barrels of beer

U.S. political party formed in 1948 to support the presidential candidacy of Henry A. Wallace.

pro•gres•siv•ism (prə-grĕs′ĭ-vĭz′əm) *n.* **1.** The principles and practices of political progressives. **2.** Progressive education. — **pro•gres′siv•ist** *n.* — **pro•gres′siv•is′tic** *adj.*

pro•gres•siv•i•ty (prō′grĕ-sĭv′ĭ-tē, prŏg′rĕ-) *n., pl.* **-ties.** The quality or degree of being progressive.

pro•hib•it (prō-hĭb′ĭt) *tr.v.* **-it•ed, -it•ing, -its. 1.** To forbid by authority: *Smoking is prohibited.* See Syns at **forbid. 2.** To prevent; preclude. [ME *prohibiten* < Lat. *prohibēre, prohibit-* : *pro-*, in front; see PRO-[1] + *habēre*, to hold; see **ghabh-*.**]

pro•hi•bi•tion (prō′ə-bĭsh′ən) *n.* **1.** The act of prohibiting or the condition of being prohibited. **2.** A law, order, or decree that forbids something. **3.a.** The forbidding by law of the manufacture, transportation, sale, and possession of alcoholic beverages. **b. Prohibition.** The period (1920–1933) during which the manufacture and sale of alcoholic beverages was forbidden in the United States.

pro•hi•bi•tion•ist (prō′ə-bĭsh′ə-nĭst) *n.* **1.** One in favor of outlawing the manufacture and sale of alcoholic beverages. **2.** Often **Prohibitionist.** A member or supporter of the Prohibition Party. — **pro′hi•bi′tion•ism** *n.*

Prohibition Party *n.* A U.S. political party organized in 1869 that advocated prohibition.

pro•hib•i•tive (prō-hĭb′ĭ-tĭv) also **pro•hib•i•to•ry** (-tôr′ē, -tōr′ē) *adj.* **1.** Prohibiting; forbidding. **2.** So high or burdensome as to discourage purchase or use: *prohibitive prices.* **3.** So likely to win as to discourage competition. — **pro•hib′i•tive•ly** *adv.* — **pro•hib′i•tive•ness** *n.*

pro•in•su•lin (prō-ĭn′sə-lĭn) *n.* A single-chain polypeptide that is the precursor of insulin.

proj•ect (prŏj′ĕkt′, -ĭkt) *n.* **1.** A plan or proposal; a scheme. See Syns at **plan. 2.** An undertaking requiring concerted effort: *a cleanup project.* **3.** An extensive task undertaken by a student or group of students to apply, illustrate, or supplement classroom lessons. **4.** A housing project. — *v.* **pro•ject.** (prə-jĕkt′) **-ject•ed, -ject•ing, -jects.** — *tr.* **1.** To thrust outward or forward: *project one's jaw.* **2.** To throw forward; hurl. **3.** To send out into space; cast. **4.** To cause (an image) to appear on a surface. **5.** *Math.* To produce (a projection). **6.** To direct (one's voice) so as to be heard clearly at a distance. **7.** *Psychol.* To externalize and attribute (an emotion, for example) to someone or something else. **8.** To convey an impression of to an audience or to others. **9.** To form a plan or an intention for. **10.** To calculate, estimate, or predict (something in the future), based on present data or trends. — *intr.* **1.** To extend forward or out; jut out. **2.** To direct one's voice so as to be heard clearly at a distance. [ME *projecte* < Lat. *prōiectum*, projecting structure < neut. p.part. of *prōicere*, to throw out : *prō-*, forth; see PRO-[1] + *iacere*, to throw; see **yē-*.**] — **pro•ject′a•ble** *adj.*

pro•jec•tile (prə-jĕk′təl, -tīl′) *n.* **1.** A propelled object, such as a bullet, having no capacity for self-propulsion. **2.** A self-propelled missile, such as a rocket. — *adj.* **1.** Capable of being impelled or hurled forward. **2.** Driving forward; impelling. **3.** *Zool.* Capable of being thrust outward; protrusile. [NLat. *proiectile*, neut. of *prōiectilis*, that can be thrown < Lat. *prōiectus*, p.part. of *prōicere*, to throw out. See PROJECT.]

pro•jec•tion (prə-jĕk′shən) *n.* **1.** The act of projecting or the condition of being projected. **2.** A thing or part that extends outward beyond a prevailing line or surface. **3.** A plan for an anticipated course of action. **4.** A prediction or an estimate of something in the future, based on present data or trends. **5.a.** The process of projecting a filmed image onto a screen, for example. **b.** An image so projected. **6.** *Math.* The image of a geometric figure reproduced on a line, plane, or surface. **7.** A system of intersecting lines, such as the grid of a map, on which part or all of the globe or another spherical surface is represented as a plane surface. **8.** *Psychol.* The attribution of one's own attitudes, feelings, or desires to someone or something. — **pro•jec′tion•al** *adj.*

projection booth *n.* A booth, as in a theater, in which a movie projector is operated.

pro•jec•tion•ist (prə-jĕk′shə-nĭst) *n.* **1.** One who operates a movie or slide projector. **2.** A maker of map projections.

pro•jec•tive (prə-jĕk′tĭv) *adj.* **1.** Extending outward; projecting. **2.** Relating to or made by projection. **3.** *Math.* Relating to or being a property of a geometric figure that does not vary when the figure undergoes projection. — **pro•jec′tive•ly** *adv.*

projective geometry *n.* *Math.* The study of geometric properties that are invariant under projection.

projective test *n.* A psychological test in which responses to unstructured stimuli, such as abstract patterns or incomplete sentences, are analyzed to determine personality traits, feelings, or attitudes.

pro•jec•tor (prə-jĕk′tər) *n.* **1.** A device for projecting a beam of light. **2.** A machine for projecting an image onto a screen. **3.** One who devises plans or projects.

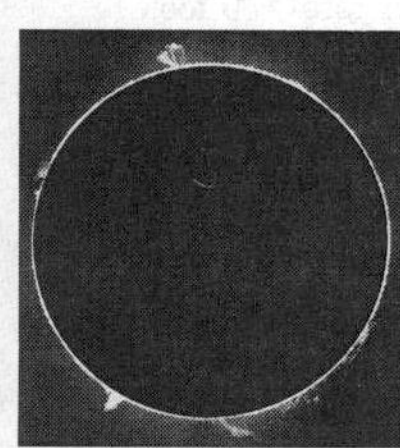
prominence
Solar prominences visible during a total eclipse

pro•kar•y•ote also **pro•car•y•ote** (prō-kăr′ē-ōt′) *n.* An organism of the kingdom Prokaryotae, constituting the bacteria and cyanobacteria, characterized by the absence of a nuclear membrane and by DNA that is not organized into chromosomes. [Fr. *procaryote* : Gk. *pro-*, before; see PRO-[2] + Gk. *karuōtos*, having nuts (< *karuon*, nut; see KARYO-).] — **pro•kar′y•ot′ic** (-ŏt′ĭk) *adj.*

Pro•kho•rov (prô′KHə-rôf′), **Aleksandr Mikhailovich.** b. 1916. Russian physicist who shared a 1964 Nobel Prize.

Pro•kof•iev (prə-kô′fē-ĕf, -əf, -kō′-, -kôf′yĭf), **Sergei Sergeyevich.** 1891–1953. Russian composer whose works include the symphonic fairy tale *Peter and the Wolf* (1936).

Pro•ko•pyevsk (prə-kôp′yəfsk). A city of S-central Russia ESE of Novosibirsk. Pop. 274,000.

pro•lac•tin (prō-lăk′tĭn) *n.* A pituitary hormone that stimulates and maintains the secretion of milk.

pro•la•mine also **pro•la•min** (prō′lə-mĭn, -mēn′) *n.* Any of a class of simple proteins found in the seeds of wheat, rye, and other grains. [PROL(INE) + AM(MONIA) + -INE[2].]

pro•lapse (prō-lăps′) *Medic.* — *intr.v.* **-lapsed, -laps•ing, -laps•es.** To fall or slip out of place. — *n.* (prō′lăps′, prō-lăps′) also **pro•lap•sus** (prō-lăp′səs). The falling down or slipping out of place of an organ or part. [Lat. *prōlābī, prōlāps-*, to fall down : *prō-*, forward; see PRO-[1] + *lābī*, to fall.]

pro•late (prō′lāt′) *adj.* **1.** Having the shape of a spheroid generated by rotating an ellipse about its longer axis. **2.** Having the polar axis longer than the equatorial diameter. [Lat. *prōlātus*, p.part. of *prōferre*, to stretch out : *prō-*, forth; see PRO-[1] + *lātus*, brought; see **telə-*.**] — **pro′late′ly** *adv.* — **pro′late′ness** *n.*

prole (prōl) *n.* A proletarian.

pro•leg (prō′lĕg′) *n.* One of the stubby limbs on the abdominal segments of caterpillars and certain other insect larvae.

pro•le•gom•e•non (prō′lĭ-gŏm′ə-nŏn′, -nən) *n., pl.* **-na** (-nə). **1.** A preliminary discussion, esp. a formal essay introducing a lengthy or complex work. **2. prolegomena.** *(used with a sing. or pl. v.)* Prefatory remarks or observations. [Gk. < neut. pr. passive part. of *prolegein*, to say beforehand : *pro-*, before; see PRO-[2] + *legein*, to speak; see **leg-*.**] — **pro′le•gom′e•nous** *adj.*

pro•lep•sis (prō-lĕp′sĭs) *n., pl.* **-ses** (-sēz). **1.** The anachronistic representation of something as existing before its proper or historical time, as in *the precolonial United States.* **2.a.** The assignment of something, such as an event or a name, to a time that precedes it, as in *If you tell the cops, you're a dead man.* **b.** The use of a descriptive word in anticipation of the act or circumstances that would make it applicable, as *dry* in *They drained the lake dry.* **3.** The anticipation and answering of an objection or argument before one's opponent has put it forward. [LLat. *prolēpsis* < Gk. < *prolambanein*, to anticipate : *pro-*, before; see PRO-[2] + *lambanein, lēp-*, to take.] — **pro•lep′tic** (-lĕp′tĭk), **pro•lep′ti•cal** (-tĭ-kəl) *adj.*

pro•le•tar•i•an (prō′lĭ-târ′ē-ən) *adj.* Of, relating to, or characteristic of the proletariat. — *n.* A member of the proletariat. [< Lat. *prōlētārius*, of the lowest class of Roman citizens (seen as contributing to the state only by having children) < *prōlēs*, offspring. See **al-[2]*.**] — **pro′le•tar′i•an•ism** *n.*

pro•le•tar•i•at (prō′lĭ-târ′ē-ĭt) *n.* **1.a.** The class of industrial wage earners who must earn their living by selling their labor. **b.** The poorest class of working people. **2.** The propertyless class of ancient Rome, constituting the lowest class of citizens. [Fr. *prolétariat* < Lat. *prōlētārius*, of the Roman proletariat. See PROLETARIAN.]

pro-life (prō-līf′) *adj.* Advocating legal protection of human embryos or fetuses, esp. by opposing legal abortion. — **pro-lif′er** *n.*

pro•lif•er•ate (prə-lĭf′ə-rāt′) *v.* **-at•ed, -at•ing, -ates.** — *intr.* **1.** To grow or multiply by rapidly producing new tissue, parts, cells, or offspring. **2.** To increase or spread at a rapid rate. — *tr.* To cause to grow or increase rapidly. [Back-formation < PROLIFERATION, the act of proliferating < Fr. *prolifération* < *prolifère*, procreative : Lat. *prōlēs, prōl-*, offspring; see PROLIFEROUS + Lat. *-fer*, -fer.] — **pro•lif′er•a′tion** *n.* — **pro•lif′er•a′tive** *adj.* — **pro•lif′er•a′tor** *n.*

pro•lif•er•ous (prə-lĭf′ər-əs) *adj.* **1.** *Zool.* Reproducing freely by means of buds and side branches, as corals do. **2.** *Bot.* Freely producing buds or offshoots, esp. from unusual places, as fruits from fruits. [< Med.Lat. *prōlifer* : Lat. *prōlēs, prōl-*, offspring; see **al-[2]*** + *-fer*, -fer.] — **pro•lif′er•ous•ly** *adv.*

pro•lif•ic (prə-lĭf′ĭk) *adj.* **1.** Producing offspring or fruit in great abundance; fertile. **2.** Producing abundant works or results. [Fr. *prolifique* < Med.Lat. *prōlificus* : Lat. *prōlēs, prōl-*, offspring; see **al-[2]*** + Lat. *-ficus*, -fic.] — **pro•lif′i•ca•cy** (-ĭ-kə-sē), **pro•lif′ic•ness** (-ĭk-nĭs) *n.* — **pro•lif′i•cal•ly** *adv.*

pro•line (prō′lēn′) *n.* An amino acid, C_4H_8NCOOH, found in most proteins and a major constituent of collagen. [Short for *pyrrolidine* : PYRROLE + -ID(E) + -INE[2].]

pro•lix (prō-lĭks′, prō′lĭks′) *adj.* **1.** Tediously prolonged; wordy. **2.** Tending to speak or write at excessive length. [ME < OFr. *prolixe* < Lat. *prōlixus*, poured forth, extended.] — **pro•lix′i•ty** (-lĭk′sĭ-tē) *n.* — **pro•lix′ly** *adv.*

Pro•log (prō′lôg′, -lŏg′) *n.* *Comp. Sci.* A programming language used for writing programs that model human thinking. [*pro(gramming in) log(ic)*.]

pro•logue also **pro•log** (prō′lôg′, -lŏg′) *n.* **1.** An introduction or a preface, esp. a poem recited to introduce a play. **2.** An introductory or introductory chapter, as to a novel. **3.** An introductory act, event, or period. [ME *prolog* < OFr. *prologue* < Lat. *prologus* < Gk. *prologos* : *pro-*, before; see PRO-[2] + *logos*, speech; see **leg-***.]

pro•long (prə-lông′, -lŏng′) *tr.v.* **-longed, -long•ing, -longs. 1.** To lengthen in duration; protract. **2.** To lengthen in extent. [Ult. < LLat. *prōlongāre* : Lat. *prō-*, forth; see PRO-[1] + Lat. *longus*, long; see **del-**[1]*.] **— pro•long′er** *n.*

pro•lon•gate (prə-lông′gāt′, -lŏng′-, prō-) *tr.v.* **-gat•ed, -gat•ing, -gates.** To prolong. **— pro′lon•ga′tion** (prō′lông-gā′shən, -lŏng-) *n.*

pro•lu•sion (prō-lo͞o′zhən) *n.* **1.** A preliminary exercise; a prelude. **2.** An essay written as a preface to a more detailed work. [Lat. *prōlūsiō, prōlūsiōn-* < *prōlūsus*, p.part. of *prōlūdere*, to practice beforehand : *prō-*, before; see PRO-[1] + *lūdere*, to play; see **leid-***.] **— pro•lu′so•ry** (-sə-rē, -zə-) *adj.*

prom (prŏm) *n.* A formal dance held for a high-school or college class typically at or near the end of the academic year. [Short for PROMENADE.]

PROM (prŏm) *n. Comp. Sci.* A memory that is programmable only once. [*p(rogrammable) r(ead-)o(nly) m(emory).*]

prom. *abbr.* Promontory.

prom•e•nade (prŏm′ə-nād′, -näd′) *n.* **1.a.** A leisurely walk, esp. one taken in a public place. **b.** A public place for such walking. **2.a.** A formal dance; a ball. **b.** A march of all the guests at the opening of a ball. **3.** A square-dance figure in which couples march counterclockwise in a circle. — *v.* **-nad•ed, -nad•ing, -nades.** — *intr.* **1.** To go on a leisurely walk. **2.** To execute a promenade. — *tr.* **1.** To take a promenade along or through. **2.** To take or display on or as if on a promenade. [Fr. < *promener*, to take for a walk < Lat. *prōmināre*, to drive forward : *prō-*, forward; see PRO-[1] + *mināre*, to drive with shouts (< *minārī*, to threaten < *minae*, threats; see **men-**[2]*).] **— prom′e•nad′er** *n.*

promenade deck *n. Naut.* The upper deck or a section of the upper deck on a ship where the passengers can promenade.

Pro•me•the•an (prə-mē′thē-ən) *adj.* **1.** *Gk. Myth.* Relating to or suggestive of Prometheus. **2.** Boldly creative; defiantly original. — *n.* One who is boldy creative or defiantly original.

Pro•me•the•us (prə-mē′thē-əs, -thyo͞os′) *n. Gk. Myth.* A Titan who stole fire from Olympus and gave it to humankind, for which Zeus chained him to a rock and sent an eagle to eat his liver, which grew back daily. [Lat. *Promētheus* < Gk.]

pro•me•thi•um (prə-mē′thē-əm) *n. Symbol* **Pm** A radioactive rare-earth element prepared by fission of uranium. Pm 147, the longest-lived isotope with a half-life of 2.5 years, is used as a source of beta rays. Atomic number 61; melting point 1,168°C; boiling point 2,460°C; valence 3. See table at **element.** [< PROMETHEUS.]

prom•i•nence (prŏm′ə-nəns) *n.* **1.** The quality or condition of being prominent. **2.** Something prominent, esp. an area of land raised above its surroundings. **3.** *Anat.* A small projection or protuberance. **4.** *Astron.* A tonguelike cloud of flaming gas rising from the sun's surface.

prom•i•nen•cy (prŏm′-ə-nən-sē) *n.* Prominence.

prom•i•nent (prŏm′ə-nənt) *adj.* **1.** Projecting outward or upward from a line or surface; protuberant. **2.** Immediately noticeable; conspicuous. **3.** Widely known; eminent. [ME < Lat. *prōminēns, prōminent-*, pr.part. of *prōminēre*, to jut out : *prō-*, forth; see PRO-[1] + *-minēre*, to jut, threaten; see **men-**[2]*.] **— prom′i•nent•ly** *adv.*

prom•is•cu•i•ty (prŏm′ĭ-skyo͞o′ĭ-tē, prō′mĭ-) *n., pl.* **-ties. 1.** The state or character of being promiscuous. **2.** Promiscuous sexual relations. **3.** A mixture of diverse or unrelated parts or individuals; a hodgepodge.

pro•mis•cu•ous (prə-mĭs′kyo͞o-əs) *adj.* **1.** Indiscriminate in the choice of sexual partners. **2.** Lacking standards of selection; indiscriminate. **3.** Casual; random. **4.** Consisting of diverse unrelated parts or individuals. [< Lat. *prōmiscuus*, possessed equally : *prō-*, intensive pref.; see PRO-[1] + *miscēre*, to mix; see **meik-***.] **— pro•mis′cu•ous•ly** *adv.* **— pro•mis′cu•ous•ness** *n.*

prom•ise (prŏm′ĭs) *n.* **1.a.** A declaration assuring that one will or will not do something; a vow. **b.** Something promised. **2.** Indication of something favorable to come; expectation. **3.** Indication of future excellence or success. — *v.* **-ised, -is•ing, -is•es.** — *tr.* **1.** To commit oneself by a promise to do or give; pledge. **2.** To afford a basis for expecting. — *intr.* **1.** To make a declaration assuring that something will or will not be done. **2.** To afford a basis for expectation. [ME *promis* < OFr. *promise* < Med.Lat. *prōmissa*, alteration of Lat. *prōmissum* < neut. p.part. of *prōmittere*, to send forth, promise : *prō-*, forth; see PRO-[1] + *mittere*, to send.] **— prom′is•er** *n.*

Prom•ised Land (prŏm′ĭst) *n. Bible.* The land of Canaan, promised to Abraham's descendants in the Old Testament.

prom•is•ee (prŏm′ĭ-sē′) *n. Law.* The party to which a promise is made.

prom•is•ing (prŏm′ĭ-sĭng) *adj.* Likely to develop in a desirable manner. **— prom′is•ing•ly** *adv.*

prom•i•sor (prŏm′ĭ-sôr′) *n. Law.* One that makes a promise.

prom•is•so•ry (prŏm′ĭ-sôr′ē, -sōr′ē) *adj.* Containing, involving, or having the nature of a promise. [Med.Lat. *prōmissōrius* < Lat. *prōmissor*, one who promises < *prōmissus*, p.part. of *prōmittere*, to promise. See PROMISE.]

promissory note *n.* A written promise to pay or repay a specified sum of money at a stated time or on demand.

pro•mo (prō′mō) *n., pl.* **-mos.** *Informal.* A promotional presentation, such as a television spot or radio announcement.

prom•on•to•ry (prŏm′ən-tôr′ē, -tōr′ē) *n., pl.* **-ries. 1.** A high ridge of land or rock jutting out into a body of water; a headland. **2.** *Anat.* A projecting part. [Lat. *prōmontorium*, alteration (influenced by *mōns, mont-*, mount; see MOUNT[2]) of *prōmunturium*, prob. < *prominēre*, to jut out. See PROMINENT.]

pro•mote (prə-mōt′) *tr.v.* **-mot•ed, -mot•ing, -motes. 1.a.** To raise to a more important or responsible job or rank. **b.** To advance (a student) to the next higher grade. **2.** To contribute to the progress or growth of; further. See Syns at **advance. 3.** To urge the adoption of; advocate. **4.** To attempt to sell or popularize by advertising or publicity. **5.** To help establish or organize (a new enterprise), as by securing financial backing. [Ult. < Lat. *prōmovēre, prōmōt-* : *prō-*, forward; see PRO-[1] + *movēre*, to move; see **meuə-***.] **— pro•mot′a•bil′i•ty** *n.* **— pro•mot′a•ble** *adj.*

pro•mot•er (prə-mō′tər) *n.* **1.** One that promotes, esp. an active supporter or advocate. **2.** A financial and publicity organizer. **3.** *Genet.* A DNA molecule to which RNA polymerase binds, initiating the transcription of messenger RNA.

pro•mo•tion (prə-mō′shən) *n.* **1.** Advancement in rank or responsibility. **2.** Encouragement of the progress, growth, or acceptance of something; furtherance. **3.** Advertising; publicity. **— pro•mo′tion•al** *adj.* **— pro•mo′tion•al•ly** *adv.*

pro•mo•tive (prə-mō′tĭv) *adj.* Tending to promote. **— pro•mo′tive•ness** *n.*

prompt (prŏmpt) *adj.* **prompt•er, prompt•est. 1.** Being on time; punctual. **2.** Carried out or performed without delay. — *tr.v.* **prompt•ed, prompt•ing, prompts. 1.** To move to act; spur; incite. **2.** To give rise to; inspire. **3.** To assist with a reminder; remind. **4.** To assist (an actor or a reciter) by providing the next words of a forgotten passage; cue. — *n.* **1.a.** The act of prompting or giving a cue. **b.** A reminder or cue. **2.** *Comp. Sci.* A symbol that appears on a monitor to indicate that the computer is ready to receive input. [ME, ready < OFr. < Lat. *prōmptus* < p.part. of *prōmere*, to bring forth : *prō-*, forth; see PRO-[1] + *emere*, to take, obtain; see **em-***.] **— prompt′er** *n.* **— promp′ti•tude′** (prŏmp′tĭ-to͞od′, -tyo͞od′), **prompt′ness** (prŏmpt′nĭs) *n.* **— prompt′ly** *adv.*

prompt•book (prŏmpt′bo͝ok′) *n.* An annotated script used by a theater prompter.

prom•ul•gate (prŏm′əl-gāt′, prō-mŭl′gāt′) *tr.v.* **-gat•ed, -gat•ing, -gates. 1.** To make known (a decree, for example) by public declaration; announce officially. **2.** To put (a law) into effect by formal public announcement. [Lat. *prōmulgāre, prōmulgāt-.*] **— prom′ul•ga′tion** (prŏm′əl-gā′shən, prō′məl-) *n.* **— prom′ul•ga′tor** *n.*

pron. *abbr.* **1.** *Gram.* Pronominal; pronoun. **2.** Pronounced. **3.** Pronunciation.

pro•na•tal•ism (prō-nāt′l-ĭz′əm) *n.* An attitude or a policy that encourages childbearing. **— pro•na′tal•ist** *n.* **— pro•na′tal•is′tic** *adj.*

pro•nate (prō′nāt′) *v.* **-nat•ed, -nat•ing, -nates.** — *tr.* **1.a.** To turn or rotate (the hand or forearm) so that the palm faces down or back. **b.** To turn or rotate (the sole of the foot) so that the inner edge of the sole bears the body's weight. **2.** To turn or rotate (a limb) so that the inner surface faces down or back. Used of a vertebrate animal. **3.** To place in a prone position. — *intr.* **1.** To become pronated. **2.** To assume a prone position. [LLat. *prōnāre, prōnāt-*, to bend forward < *prōnus*, turned forward. See PRONE.]

pro•na•tion (prō-nā′shən) *n.* **1.** The act of pronating. **2.** The condition of being pronated.

pro•na•tor (prō′nā′tər) *n.* A muscle that effects or assists in pronation.

prone (prōn) *adj.* **1.** Lying with the front or face downward. **2.** Having a tendency; inclined. — *adv.* In a prone manner. [ME, inclined, disposed < Lat. *prōnus*, leaning forward. See **per**[1]*.] **— prone′ly** *adv.* **— prone′ness** *n.*

pro•neph•ros (prō-nĕf′rəs, -rŏs′) *n., pl.* **-roi** (-roi) or **-ra** (-rə). A kidneylike organ, being either part of the most anterior pair of three pairs of organs in a vertebrate embryo or functioning as a kidney in some simple vertebrates, such as the lamprey. [PRO-[2] + Gk. *nephros*, kidney.] **— pro•neph′ric** (-rĭk) *adj.*

prong (prông, prŏng) *n.* **1.** A thin pointed projecting part. **2.** A branch; a fork. — *tr.v.* **pronged, prong•ing, prongs.** To pierce with or as if with a prong. [ME *pronge*, pointed instrument, pain < Med.Lat. *pronga*, of Gmc. orig.]

prong•horn (prông′hôrn′, prŏng′-) *n., pl.* **pronghorn** or **-horns.** A small ruminant mammal *(Antilocapra americana)* found on western North American plains, resembling an antelope and having small forked horns.

pro•no•grade (prō′nə-grād′) *adj.* Walking with the long axis of the body parallel to the ground. Used of quadrupeds. [Lat. *prōnus*, leaning forward; see PRONE + *-gradus*, walking (< *gradī*, to move; see RETROGRADE).]

promontory
In southwest Oregon

pronghorn
Male pronghorn
Antilocapra americana

ă pat	oi boy
ā pay	ou out
âr care	o͝o took
ä father	o͞o boot
ĕ pet	ŭ cut
ē be	ûr urge
ĭ pit	th thin
ī pie	*th* this
îr pier	hw which
ŏ pot	zh vision
ō toe	ə about, item
ô paw	

Stress marks:
′ (primary);
′ (secondary), as in
dictionary (dĭk′shə-nĕr′ē)

pro•nom•i•nal (prō-nŏm′ə-nəl) *adj. Gram.* **1.** Of, relating to, or functioning as a pronoun. **2.** Resembling a pronoun, as by specifying a person, place, or thing, while functioning primarily as another part of speech. *His* in *his choice* is a pronominal adjective. [LLat. *prōnōminālis* < Lat. *prōnōmen, prōnōmin-*, pronoun : *prō-*, in place of; see PRO–[1] + *nōmen*, name; see NOUN.] **—pro•nom′i•nal•ly** *adv.*

pro•noun (prō′noun′) *n. Gram.* One of a class of words that function as substitutes for nouns or noun phrases and designate persons or things asked for, previously specified, or understood from the context.

pro•nounce (prə-nouns′) *v.* **-nounced, -nounc•ing, -nounc•es.** *—tr.* **1.a.** To use the organs of speech to make heard (a word or speech sound); utter. **b.** To say clearly, correctly, or in a given manner: *pronounce French.* **2.** To represent (a word) in phonetic symbols. **3.** To declare officially or formally. *—intr.* **1.** To say words; speak. **2.** To declare one's opinion; make a pronouncement. [ME *pronouncen* < OFr. *prononcier* < Lat. *prōnūntiāre* : *prō-*, forth; see PRO–[1] + *nūntiāre*, to announce (< *nūntius*, messenger; see **neu-***).] **—pro•nounce′a•ble** *adj.* **—pro•nounc′er** *n.*

pro•nounced (prə-nounst′) *adj.* **1.** Spoken; voiced. **2.** Strongly marked; distinct: *a pronounced limp.* **—pro•nounc′ed•ly** (-noun′sĭd-lē) *adv.* **—pro•nounc′ed•ness** *n.*

pro•nounce•ment (prə-nouns′mənt) *n.* **1.** A formal expression of opinion; a judgment. **2.** An authoritative statement.

pro•nounc•ing (prə-noun′sĭng) *adj.* Relating to, designed for, or showing pronunciation: *a pronouncing dictionary.*

pron•to (prŏn′tō) *adv. Informal.* Without delay; quickly. [Sp. < Lat. *prōmptus.* See PROMPT.]

pro•nu•cle•us (prō-nōō′klē-əs, -nyōō′-) *n., pl.* **-cle•i** (-klē-ī′). The haploid nucleus of a sperm or egg before fusion of the nuclei in fertilization. **—pro•nu′cle•ar** *adj.*

pro•nun•ci•a•men•to (prō-nŭn′sē-ə-mĕn′tō) *n., pl.* **-tos** or **-toes.** An official or authoritarian declaration. [Sp. *pronunciamiento* < *pronunciar*, to pronounce < Lat. *prōnūntiāre.* See PRONOUNCE.]

pro•nun•ci•a•tion (prə-nŭn′sē-ā′shən) *n.* **1.** The act or manner of pronouncing words; utterance of speech. **2.** A way of speaking a word, esp. a way that is accepted or generally understood. **3.** A graphic representation of the way a word is spoken, using phonetic symbols. [Ult. < Lat. *prōnūntiātiō, prōnūntiātiōn-* < *prōnūntiātus*, p.part. of *prōnūntiāre*, to pronounce. See PRONOUNCE.] **—pro•nun′ci•a′tion•al** *adj.*

propeller

proof (prōōf) *n.* **1.** The evidence or argument that compels the mind to accept an assertion as true. **2.a.** The validation of a proposition by application of specified rules, as of induction or deduction, to axioms and previously derived conclusions. **b.** An argument used in such a validation. **3.** Convincing or persuasive demonstration: *proof of his identity.* **4.** Determination of the quality of something by testing; trial. **5.** *Law.* The whole body of evidence that determines the verdict or judgment in a case. **6.** The alcoholic strength of a liquor, expressed by a number that is twice the percentage by volume of alcohol present. **7.** *Print.* **a.** A trial sheet of printed material that is made to be checked and corrected. **b.** A trial impression of a plate, stone, or block taken at any of various stages in engraving. **8.a.** A trial photographic print. **b.** Any of a limited number of newly minted coins or medals struck as specimens and for collectors from a new die on a polished planchet. **9.** *Archaic.* Proven impenetrability. *—adj.* **1.** Fully or successfully resistant; impervious. Often used in combination: *waterproof watches.* **2.** Of standard alcoholic strength. **3.** Used in proving or making corrections. *—v.* **proofed, proof•ing, proofs.** *—tr.* **1.** *Print.* **a.** To make a trial impression of (printed or engraved matter). **b.** To proofread (copy). **2.a.** To activate (dormant dry yeast) by adding water. **b.** To work (dough) into proper lightness. **3.** To treat so as to make resistant: *proof a fabric against shrinkage. —intr.* **1.** *Print.* To proofread. **2.** To become properly light for cooking. [ME *prove, preve* < AN *prove* and < OFr. *prueve*, both < LLat. *proba* < Lat. *probāre*, to prove. See PROVE.] **—proof′er** *n.*

proof•read (prōōf′rēd′) *v.* **-read** (-rĕd′), **-read•ing, -reads.** *—tr.* To read (copy or proof) to find and correct errors. *—intr.* To proofread copy or proof. **—proof′read′er** *n.*

proof sheet *n. Print.* See **proof** 7a.

proof spirit *n.* An alcohol-water mixture or a beverage containing a standard amount of alcohol, the U.S. standard being 100 proof of ethyl alcohol by volume at 60°F (approx. 15.6°C).

prop[1] (prŏp) *n.* **1.** An object placed beneath or against a structure to keep it from falling or shaking; a support. **2.** One that serves as a support or stay. *—tr.v.* **propped, prop•ping, props.** To support by placing something beneath or against; shore up. [ME *proppe*, prob. < MDu.]

prop[2] (prŏp) *n.* A theatrical property.

prop[3] (prŏp) *n. Informal.* A propeller.

prop. *abbr.* **1.** Proper. **2.** Properly. **3.** Property. **4.** Proposition. **5.** Proprietary. **6.** Proprietor; proprietress.

prop– *pref.* Related to or derived from propionic acid: *propane.* [< PROPIONIC ACID.]

pro•pae•deu•tic (prō′pĭ-dōō′tĭk, -dyōō′-) *adj.* Providing introductory instruction. *—n.* Preparatory instruction. [< Gk. *propaideuein*, to teach beforehand : *pro-*, before; see PRO–[2] + *paideuein*, to teach (< *pais, paid-*, child; see PEDO–[2]).]

prop•a•gan•da (prŏp′ə-găn′də) *n.* **1.** The systematic propagation of a doctrine or cause or of information reflecting the views and interests of its propagators. **2.** Material disseminated by the advocates of a doctrine or cause: *wartime propaganda.* **3. Propaganda.** *Rom. Cath. Ch.* A division of the Roman Curia that has authority over missions. [NLat., short for *Sacra Congregātiō dē Prōpagandā Fide*, Sacred Congregation for Propagating the Faith (estab. 1622) < ablative fem. gerundive of Lat. *prōpāgāre*, to propagate. See PROPAGATE.] **—prop′a•gan′dism** *n.* **—prop′a•gan′dist** *n.* **—prop′a•gan•dis′tic** *adj.* **—prop′a•gan•dis′ti•cal•ly** *adv.*

prop•a•gan•dize (prŏp′ə-găn′dīz′) *v.* **-dized, -diz•ing, -diz•es.** *—tr.* **1.** To engage in propaganda for (a doctrine or cause). **2.** To subject (a person or group) to propaganda. *—intr.* To spread propaganda. **—prop′a•gan′diz′er** *n.*

prop•a•gate (prŏp′ə-gāt′) *v.* **-gat•ed, -gat•ing, -gates.** *—tr.* **1.** To cause (an organism) to multiply or breed. **2.** To breed (offspring). **3.** To transmit (characteristics) from one generation to another. **4.** To cause to extend to a broader area or larger number; spread: *propagate the faith.* **5.** To make widely known; publicize. **6.** *Phys.* To cause (a wave, for example) to move in some direction or through a medium; transmit. *—intr.* **1.** To have offspring; multiply. **2.** To extend to a broader area or larger number; spread. **3.** *Phys.* To move through a medium. [Lat. *prōpāgāre, prōpāgāt-.* See **pag-***.] **—prop′a•ga•ble** (-gə-bəl) *adj.* **—prop′a•ga′tive** *adj.* **—prop′a•ga′tor** *n.*

prop•a•ga•tion (prŏp′ə-gā′shən) *n.* **1.** Multiplication or increase, as by natural reproduction. **2.** The process of spreading to a larger area or greater number. **3.** *Phys.* The act or process of propagating, esp. the process by which electromagnetic or sound waves are transmitted through a medium. **—prop′a•ga′tion•al** *adj.*

prop•a•gule (prŏp′ə-gyōōl′) *n.* Any of various usu. vegetative portions of a plant, such as a bud or other offshoot, that aid in dispersal of the species and from which a new individual may develop. [NLat. *prōpāgulum*, dim. of Lat. *prōpāgō*, shoot < *prōpāgāre*, to propagate. See PROPAGATE.]

pro•pane (prō′pān′) *n.* A colorless gas, C_3H_8, found in natural gas and petroleum and widely used as a fuel.

pro•pa•no•ic acid (prō′pə-nō′ĭk) *n.* See **propionic acid.**

pro•pel (prə-pĕl′) *tr.v.* **-pelled, -pel•ling, -pels.** To cause to move forward or onward. See Syns at **push.** [ME *propellen* < Lat. *prōpellere* : *prō-*, forward; see PRO–[1] + *pellere*, to drive; see **pel-[5]***.]

pro•pel•lant also **pro•pel•lent** (prə-pĕl′ənt) *—n.* **1.** Something, such as an explosive charge or a rocket fuel, that propels or provides thrust. **2.** A compressed inert gas that acts as a vehicle for discharging the contents of an aerosol container. *—adj.* Serving to propel; propelling.

pro•pel•ler also **pro•pel•lor** (prə-pĕl′ər) *n.* A machine for propelling an aircraft or a boat, consisting of a power-driven shaft with radiating blades placed so as to thrust air or water in a desired direction when spinning.

pro•pend (prō-pĕnd′) *intr.v.* **-pend•ed, -pend•ing, -pends.** *Obsolete.* To have a propensity. [Lat. *prōpendēre* : *prō-*, forward; see PRO–[1] + *pendēre*, to hang; see **(s)pen-***.]

pro•pen•si•ty (prə-pĕn′sĭ-tē) *n., pl.* **-ties.** An innate inclination; a tendency. See Syns at **predilection.** [< *propense*, inclined < Lat. *prōpēnsus*, p.part. of *prōpendēre*, to be inclined. See PROPEND.]

prop•er (prŏp′ər) *adj.* **1.** Characterized by appropriateness or suitability; fitting. **2.** Called for by rules or conventions; correct. **3.** Strictly following rules or conventions, esp. in social behavior; seemly. **4.a.** Belonging to one; own. **b.** Characteristically belonging to the being or thing in question; peculiar. **5.** Being within the strictly limited sense, as of a term: *the township proper.* **6.** *Eccles.* For use in the liturgy of a particular feast or season of the year. **7.** *Math.* Of or relating to a subset of a given set when the set has at least one element not in the subset. **8.** Worthy of the name; true. **9.** Out-and-out; thorough. *—adv.* Thoroughly. *—n.* also **Proper.** *Eccles.* The parts of the liturgy that vary according to the feast or season. [ME *propre* < OFr. < Lat. *proprius.* See **per[1]***.] **—prop′er•ly** *adv.* **—prop′er•ness** *n.*

proper adjective *n. Gram.* An adjective formed from a proper noun.

pro•per•din (prō-pûr′dn) *n.* A natural protein in human blood serum that participates in the body's immune response by working in conjunction with the complement system. [Prob. PRO–[1] + Lat. *perdere*, to destroy; see PERDITION + –IN.]

proper fraction *n. Math.* **1.** A fraction in which the numerator is less than the denominator. **2.** A polynomial fraction in which the numerator is of a lower degree than the denominator.

proper name *n.* See **proper noun.**

proper noun *n. Gram.* A noun belonging to the class of words used as names for unique individuals, events, or places and usu. having few possibilities for modification.

prop•er•tied (prŏp′ər-tēd) *adj.* Owning land or securities as a principal source of revenue.

Pro•per•tius (prō-pûr′shəs, -shē-əs), **Sextus.** 50?–15? B.C. Roman elegiac poet whose extant works include *Cynthia.*

prop•er•ty (prŏp′ər-tē) *n., pl.* **-ties. 1.a.** Something owned; a possession. **b.** A piece of real estate. **c.** Something tangible or intangible to which its owner has legal title: *properties such as copyrights.* **d.** Possessions considered as a group. **2.** The right of ownership; title. **3.** An article, except costumes and scenery, that appears on the stage or on screen during a dramatic performance. **4.a.** A characteristic trait or peculiarity, esp. one serving to define or describe its possessor. **b.** A characteristic attribute possessed by all members of a class. **5.** A special capability or power; a virtue. [ME < OFr. *propriete* < Lat. *proprietās,* ownership < *proprius,* one's own. See **per**[1]*.] **—prop′er•ty•less** *adj.*

property tax *n.* A tax levied against the owner of real or personal property.

pro•phage (prō′fāj′) *n.* The latent form of a bacteriophage in which the viral genes are incorporated into the bacterial chromosomes without causing disruption of the bacterial cell. [Short for Fr. *probactériophage* : Gk. *pro-,* before; see PRO–[2] + NLat. *bacterium,* bacterium; see BACTERIO– + Gk. *-phagos,* -phage.]

pro•phase (prō′fāz′) *n.* **1.** The first stage of mitosis, during which the chromosomes condense and become visible, the nuclear membrane breaks down, and the spindle apparatus forms at opposite poles of the cell. **2.** The first stage of meiosis, during which DNA replicates, homologous chromosomes synapse, chiasmata form, and the chromosomes contract. **—pro•pha′sic** (-fā′zĭk) *adj.*

proph•e•cy (prŏf′ĭ-sē) *n., pl.* **-cies** (-sēz). **1.a.** An inspired utterance of a prophet, viewed as a revelation of divine will. **b.** A prediction of the future made under divine inspiration. **c.** Such an inspired message transmitted orally or in writing. **2.** The vocation or condition of a prophet. **3.** A prediction. [ME *prophecie* < OFr. < Lat. *prophētīa* < Gk. *prophēteia* < *prophētēs,* prophet. See PROPHET.]

proph•e•sy (prŏf′ĭ-sī′) *v.* **-sied** (-sīd′), **-sy•ing** (-sī′ĭng), **-sies** (-sīz′). *—tr.* **1.** To reveal by divine inspiration. **2.** To predict with certainty as if by divine inspiration. **3.** To prefigure; foreshow. *—intr.* **1.** To reveal the will or message of God. **2.** To predict the future as if by divine inspiration. **3.** To speak as a prophet. [ME *prophecien* < OFr. *prophecier* < *prophecie,* prophecy. See PROPHECY.] **—proph′e•si′er** *n.*

proph•et (prŏf′ĭt) *n.* **1.** One who speaks by divine inspiration or as the interpreter through whom the will of God or a god is expressed. **2.** One gifted with profound moral insight and exceptional powers of expression. **3.** A predictor; a soothsayer. **4.** The chief spokesperson of a movement or cause. **5. Prophets.** *(used with a sing. or pl. v.)* The second of the three divisions of the Hebrew Bible, comprising the books of Joshua, Judges, Samuel, Kings, Isaiah, Jeremiah, Ezekiel, and the Minor Prophets. See table at **Bible.** [ME *prophete* < OFr. < Lat. *prophēta* < Gk. *prophētēs* : *pro-,* before; see PRO–[2] + *-phētēs,* speaker (< *phanai,* to speak; see **bhā-**[2]*).]

proph•et•ess (prŏf′ĭ-tĭs) *n.* **1.** A woman who speaks by divine inspiration or as the interpreter through whom the will of a god is expressed. **2.** A woman predictor; a woman soothsayer. **3.** The chief spokeswoman of a movement or cause.

pro•phet•ic (prə-fĕt′ĭk) also **pro•phet•i•cal** (-ĭ-kəl) *adj.* **1.** Of, belonging to, or characteristic of a prophet or prophecy. **2.** Foretelling events as if by divine inspiration. **—pro•phet′i•cal•ly** *adv.* **—pro•phet′i•cal•ness** *n.*

pro•phy•lac•tic (prō′fə-lăk′tĭk, prŏf′ə-) *adj.* Acting to defend against or prevent something, esp. disease; protective. *—n.* **1.** A prophylactic agent, device, or measure, such as a vaccine or drug. **2.** A contraceptive device, esp. a condom. [Fr. *prophylactique* < Gk. *prophulaktikos* < *prophulassein,* to take precautions against : *pro-,* before; see PRO–[2] + *phulassein,* to protect (< *phulax,* guard).] **—pro′phy•lac′ti•cal•ly** *adv.*

pro•phy•lax•is (prō′fə-lăk′sĭs, prŏf′ə-) *n., pl.* **-lax•es** (-lăk′sēz′). Prevention of or protective treatment for disease. [NLat. < Gk. *prophulaktikos,* prophylactic. See PROPHYLACTIC.]

pro•pin•qui•ty (prə-pĭng′kwĭ-tē) *n.* **1.** Proximity; nearness. **2.** Kinship. **3.** Similarity in nature. [ME *propinquite* < OFr. < Lat. *propinquitās* < *propinquus,* near. See **per**[1]*.]

pro•pi•o•nate (prō′pē-ə-nāt′) *n.* A salt or an ester of propionic acid. [PROPION(IC ACID) + –ATE[2].]

pro•pi•on•ic acid (prō′pē-ŏn′ĭk) *n.* A liquid fatty acid, CH_3CH_2COOH, found naturally in sweat or synthesized and used in the form of its propionates to inhibit mold in baked goods. [< Gk. *pro-,* first; see PRO–[2] + Gk. *piōn,* fat (being first in order among the fatty acids); see **peiə-***.]

pro•pi•ti•ate (prō-pĭsh′ē-āt′) *tr.v.* **-at•ed, -at•ing, -ates.** To conciliate; appease. [Lat. *propitiāre, propitiāt-* < *propitius,* propitious. See PROPITIOUS.] **—pro•pi′ti•a•ble** (-pĭsh′ē-ə-bəl, -pĭsh′ə-bəl) *adj.* **—pro•pi′ti•at′ing•ly** *adv.* **—pro•pi′ti•a′tive** *adj.* **—pro•pi′ti•a′tor** *n.*

pro•pi•ti•a•tion (prō-pĭsh′ē-ā′shən) *n.* **1.** The act of propitiating. **2.** Something that propitiates, esp. a conciliatory offering to a god.

pro•pi•ti•a•to•ry (prō-pĭsh′ē-ə-tôr′ē, -tōr′ē, -pĭsh′ə-) *adj.* Of or offered in propitiation. **—pro•pi′ti•a•to′ri•ly** *adv.*

pro•pi•tious (prə-pĭsh′əs) *adj.* **1.** Presenting favorable circumstances; auspicious. See Syns at **favorable. 2.** Kindly; gracious. [ME *propicius* < OFr. *propicieux* < Lat. *propitius.* See **pet-***.] **—pro•pi′tious•ly** *adv.* **—pro•pi′tious•ness** *n.*

prop•jet (prŏp′jĕt′) *n.* See **turboprop.**

prop•o•lis (prŏp′ə-lĭs) *n.* A resinous substance collected from the buds of certain trees by bees and used in the construction of their hives. [Lat. < Gk., suburb, bee glue (originally a structure around the hive opening) : *pro-,* before; see PRO–[2] + *polis,* city; see **pelə-**[3]*.]

pro•po•nent (prə-pō′nənt) *n.* One who argues in support of something; an advocate. [Lat. *prōpōnēns, prōpōnent-,* pr.part. of *prōpōnere,* to set forth. See PROPOSE.]

pro•por•tion (prə-pôr′shən, -pōr′-) *n.* **1.** A part considered in relation to the whole. **2.** A relationship between things or parts of things with respect to comparative magnitude, quantity, or degree. **3.** A relationship between quantities such that if one varies then another varies in a manner dependent on the first. **4.** Agreeable or harmonious relation of parts within a whole; balance or symmetry. **5.** Dimensions; size. Often used in the plural. **6.** *Math.* A statement of equality between two ratios. Four quantities, *a, b, c, d,* are in proportion if $a/b = c/d$. *—tr.v.* **-tioned, -tion•ing, -tions. 1.** To adjust so that proper relations between parts are attained. **2.** To form the parts of with balance or symmetry. [Ult. < Lat. *prōportiō, prōportiōn-* < *prō portiōne,* according to (each) part : *prō,* according to; see PRO–[1] + *portiōne,* ablative of *portiō,* part; see **perə-**[2]*.] **—pro•por′tion•a•ble** *adj.* **—pro•por′tion•a•bly** *adv.* **—pro•por′tion•er** *n.* **—pro•por′tion•ment** *n.*

Syns: *proportion, harmony, symmetry, balance.* These nouns mean aesthetic arrangement marked by proper distribution of elements. *Proportion* is the agreeable or harmonious relation of parts within a whole: *a house with rooms of gracious proportion. Harmony* is the pleasing interaction or appropriate combination of elements: *the harmony of her facial features. Symmetry* and *balance* both imply an arrangement of parts and details on either side of a dividing line, but *symmetry* frequently emphasizes mirror-image correspondence of parts, while *balance* often suggests dissimilar parts that offset each other to make a harmonious and satisfying whole: *Beds of iris were set out in perfect symmetry around the pool. "In all perfectly beautiful objects, there is found the opposition of one part to another, and a reciprocal balance"* (John Ruskin).

pro•por•tion•al (prə-pôr′shə-nəl, -pōr′-) *adj.* **1.** Forming a relationship with other parts or quantities; being in proportion. **2.** Properly related in size, degree, or other measurable characteristics; corresponding. **3.** *Math.* Having the same or a constant ratio. *—n.* One of the quantities in a mathematical proportion. **—pro•por′tion•al′i•ty** (-shə-năl′ĭ-tē) *n.* **—pro•por′tion•al•ly** *adv.*

proportional representation *n.* Representation of all parties in a legislature in proportion to their popular vote.

pro•por•tion•ate (prə-pôr′shə-nĭt, -pōr′-) *adj.* Being in due proportion; proportional. *—tr.v.* (-shə-nāt′) **-at•ed, -at•ing, -ates.** To make proportionate. **—pro•por′tion•ate•ly** *adv.* **—pro•por′tion•ate•ness** *n.*

pro•pos•al (prə-pō′zəl) *n.* **1.** The act of proposing. **2.** A plan that is proposed. **3.** An offer of marriage.

pro•pose (prə-pōz′) *v.* **-posed, -pos•ing, -pos•es.** *—tr.* **1.** To put forward for consideration, discussion, or adoption; suggest. **2.** To recommend (a person) for a position, office, or membership; nominate. **3.** To offer (a toast to be drunk). **4.** To make known as one's intention; purpose or intend. *—intr.* To form or make a proposal, esp. of marriage. [ME *proposen* < OFr. *proposer,* alteration (influenced by *poser,* to put, place; see POSE[1]) of Lat. *prōpōnere* : *prō-,* forth; see PRO–[1] + *pōnere,* to put; see **apo-***.] **—pro•pos′er** *n.*

prop•o•si•tion (prŏp′ə-zĭsh′ən) *n.* **1.** A plan suggested for acceptance; a proposal. **2.** *Informal.* A matter to be dealt with; a task. **3.** *Informal.* An offer of a private bargain, esp. a request for sexual relations. **4.** A subject for discussion or analysis. **5.** *Logic.* **a.** A statement in which the subject is affirmed or denied by the predicate. **b.** Something expressed in a statement, as opposed to the way it is expressed. **c.** A statement containing only logical constants and having a fixed truth-value. *—tr.v.* **-tioned, -tion•ing, -tions.** *Informal.* To offer a proposition to. [Ult. < Lat. *prōpositiō, prōpositiōn-,* setting out in words < *prōpositus,* p.part. of *prōpōnere,* to set forth. See PROPOSE.] **—prop′o•si′tion•al** *adj.* **—prop′o•si′tion•al•ly** *adv.*

propositional calculus *n. Logic.* The branch of symbolic logic that deals with the relationships formed between propositions by connectives such as *and, or,* and *if* as opposed to their internal structure.

propositional function *n. Logic.* An expression having the form of a proposition but containing undefined symbols for the substantive elements and becoming a proposition when appropriate values are assigned to the symbols.

pro•pos•i•tus (prō-pŏz′ĭ-təs) *n., pl.* **-ti** (-tī′). The person immediately concerned about or affected by an action. [Lat.

ă pat	oi boy
ā pay	ou out
âr care	ŏŏ took
ä father	ōō boot
ĕ pet	ŭ cut
ē be	ûr urge
ĭ pit	th thin
ī pie	*th* this
îr pier	hw which
ŏ pot	zh vision
ō toe	ə about, item
ô paw	

Stress marks:
′ (primary);
′ (secondary), as in
dictionary (dĭk′shə-nĕr′ē)

prōpositus, p.part. of *prōpōnere*, to set forth. See PROPOSE.]

pro•pound (prə-pound′) *tr.v.* **-pound•ed, -pound•ing, -pounds.** To put forward for consideration; set forth. [Alteration of *propoune* < ME *proponen* < Lat. *prōpōnere*, to set forth. See PROPOSE.] — **pro•pound′er** *n.*

pro•pox•y•phene (prō-pŏk′sə-fēn′) *n.* A nonnarcotic analgesic drug, $C_{22}H_{29}NO_2$. [PROP- + OXY- + *-phene* (alteration of PHENYL).]

propr. *abbr.* Proprietor; proprietress.

pro•prae•tor (prō-prē′tər) *n.* An ancient Roman official, appointed as the chief administrator of a province after serving as praetor. [Lat. *prōpraetor* : *prō-*, for; see PRO-[1] + *praetor*, praetor; see PRAETOR.] — **pro′prae•to′ri•al** (prō′prĭ-tôr′ē-əl, -tōr′-), **pro′prae•to′ri•an** (-ən) *adj.*

pro•pri•e•tar•y (prə-prī′ĭ-tĕr′ē) *adj.* **1.** Of or relating to a proprietor or to proprietors as a group. **2.** Exclusively owned; private. **3.** Befitting an owner. **4.** Owned by a private individual or corporation under a trademark or patent. — *n.*, *pl.* **-ies. 1.** A proprietor. **2.** A group of proprietors. **3.** Ownership; proprietorship. **4.** A proprietary medicine. **5.** One granted ownership of a proprietary colony. [< ME *proprietarie*, owner of property < OFr. *proprietaire* and < Med.Lat. *proprietārius*, both < LLat., of a property owner < Lat. *proprietās*, ownership. See PROPERTY.] — **pro•pri′e•tar′i•ly** *adv.*

proprietary colony *n.* Any of certain early North American colonies, such as Pennsylvania, granted by the English Crown to one or more proprietors who had governing rights.

pro•pri•e•tor (prə-prī′ĭ-tər) *n.* **1.** One who has legal title to something; an owner. **2.** One who owns or owns and manages a business or other such establishment. [Prob. alteration of ME *proprietarie.* See PROPRIETARY.] — **pro•pri′e•to′ri•al** (-tôr′ē-əl, -tōr′-) *adj.* — **pro•pri′e•to′ri•al•ly** *adv.* — **pro•pri′e•tor•ship′** *n.*

pro•pri•e•tress (prə-prī′ĭ-trĭs) *n.* **1.** A woman who has legal title to something; an owner. **2.** A woman who owns or owns and manages a business or other such establishment.

pro•pri•e•ty (prə-prī′ĭ-tē) *n.*, *pl.* **-ties. 1.** The quality of being proper; appropriateness. **2.** Conformity to prevailing customs and usages. **3. proprieties.** The usages and customs of polite society. [ME *propriete*, ownership, particular character < OFr. See PROPERTY.]

pro•pri•o•cep•tion (prō′prē-ō-sĕp′shən) *n.* The unconscious perception of movement and spatial orientation arising from stimuli within the body itself. [Lat. *proprius*, one's own; see **per**[1]* + (RE)CEPTION.]

pro•pri•o•cep•tor (prō′prē-ō-sĕp′tər) *n.* A sensory receptor, found in muscles and the inner ear, that detects the motion or position of the body or a limb by responding to stimuli arising within the organism. [Lat. *proprius*, one's own; see **per**[1]* + (RE)CEPTOR.] — **pro′pri•o•cep′tive** *adj.*

prop root

prop root *n.* An adventitious root that arises from the stem, penetrates the soil, and helps support the stem, as in corn.

prop•to•sis (prŏp-tō′sĭs) *n.*, *pl.* **-ses** (-sēz). Forward displacement of an organ, esp. an eyeball. [LLat. *proptōsis*, prolapse < Gk. < *propiptein*, to fall forward : *pro-*, forward; see PRO-[2] + *piptein*, to fall; see **pet-***.]

pro•pul•sion (prə-pŭl′shən) *n.* **1.** The process of driving or propelling. **2.** A driving or propelling force. [Med.Lat. *prōpulsiō*, *prōpulsiōn-*, onslaught, urging on < Lat. *prōpulsus*, p.part. of *prōpellere*, to drive forward. See PROPEL.] — **pro•pul′sive, pro•pul′so•ry** (-sə-rē) *adj.*

pro•pyl (prō′pĭl) *n.* A univalent organic radical with composition C_3H_7, derived from propane. — **pro•pyl′ic** *adj.*

prop•y•lae•um (prŏp′ə-lē′əm, prō′pə-) *n.*, *pl.* **-lae•a** (-lē′ə). *Archit.* An entrance or vestibule to a temple or group of buildings. [Lat. < Gk. *propulaion* : *pro-*, before; see PRO-[2] + *pulē*, gate.]

propyl alcohol *n.* A clear colorless liquid, $CH_3CH_2CH_2OH$, used as a solvent and an antiseptic.

pro•pyl•ene (prō′pə-lēn′) *n.* A flammable gas, $CH_3CH{:}CH_2$, derived from petroleum and used in organic synthesis.

propylene glycol *n.* A viscous liquid, $CH_3CHOHCH_2OH$, used in antifreeze solutions and as a solvent.

pro ra•ta (prō rā′tə, răt′ə, rä′tə) *adv.* In proportion, according to a factor that can be calculated exactly. [Lat. *prō ratā (parte)*, according to the calculated (share).]

pro•rate (prō-rāt′, prō′rāt′) *v.* **-rat•ed, -rat•ing, -rates.** — *tr.* To divide, distribute, or assess proportionately. — *intr.* To settle affairs on the basis of proportional distribution. [< PRO RATA.] — **pro•rat′a•ble** *adj.* — **pro•ra′tion** *n.*

pro•rogue (prō-rōg′) *tr.v.* **-rogued, -rogu•ing, -rogues. 1.** To discontinue a session of (a parliament, for example). **2.** To postpone; defer. [ME *prorogen* < OFr. *proroguer*, to postpone < Lat. *prōrogāre* : *pro-*, forward; see PRO-[1] + *rogāre*, to ask; see **reg-***.] — **pro′ro•ga′tion** *n.*

pros. *abbr.* Prosody.

pros- *pref.* **1.** Near; toward: *prosenchyma.* **2.** In front of: *prosencephalon.* [Gk. < *pros*, near, at. See **per**[1]*.]

pro•sa•ic (prō-zā′ĭk) *adj.* **1.** Consisting of or characteristic of prose. **2.** Lacking in imagination; dull. [LLat. *prōsaicus* < Lat. *prōsa*, prose. See PROSE.] — **pro•sa′i•cal•ly** *adv.* — **pro•sa′ic•ness** *n.*

pro•sa•ism (prō′zā-ĭz′əm) *n.* **1.** A quality or style that is prosaic. **2.** A prosaic word, phrase, or other expression.

pro•sce•ni•um (prō-sē′nē-əm, prə-) *n.* **1.** *pl.* **-ni•ums.** The area of a modern theater located between the curtain and the orchestra. **2.** *pl.* **-ni•a** (-nē-ə). The stage of an ancient theater, located between the background and the orchestra. [Lat. *proscēnium* < Gk. *proskēnion* : *pro-*, before; see PRO-[2] + *skēnē*, buildings at the back of the stage.]

pro•sciut•to (prō-shōō′tō) *n.*, *pl.* **-ti** (-tē) or **-tos.** An aged Italian ham usu. served in thin slices. [Ital., alteration of *presciutto* < VLat. **perexsūctus*, thoroughly dried up : Lat. *per-*, per- + Lat. *exsūctus*, p.part. of *exsūgere*, to suck out (*ex-*, ex- + *sūgere*, to suck; see SUCTION).]

pro•scribe (prō-skrīb′) *tr.v.* **-scribed, -scrib•ing, -scribes. 1.** To denounce or condemn. **2.** To prohibit; forbid. See Syns at **forbid. 3.a.** To banish or outlaw (a person). **b.** To publish the name of (a person) as outlawed. [ME *proscriben* < Lat. *prōscrībere*, to put up someone's name as outlawed : *prō-*, in front; see PRO-[1] + *scrībere*, to write; see **skrībh-***.] — **pro•scrib′er** *n.*

pro•scrip•tion (prō-skrĭp′shən) *n.* **1.** The act of proscribing; prohibition. **2.** The condition of having been proscribed. [ME *proscripcion* < Lat. *prōscrīptiō*, *prōscrīptiōn-*, public notice of outlawry < *prōscrīptus*, p.part. of *prōscrībere*, to proscribe. See PROSCRIBE.] — **pro•scrip′tive** *adj.* — **pro•scrip′tive•ly** *adv.*

prose (prōz) *n.* **1.** Ordinary speech or writing, without metrical structure. **2.** Commonplace expression or quality. — *intr.v.* **prosed, pros•ing, pros•es. 1.** To write prose. **2.** To speak or write in a dull tiresome style. [ME < OFr. < Lat. *prōsa (ōrātiō)*, straightforward (discourse), fem. of *prōsus*, alteration of *prōrsus* < *prōversus*, p.part. of *prōvertere*, to turn forward : *prō-*, forward; see PRO-[1] + *vertere*, to turn; see **wer-**[2]*.]

pro•sec•tor (prō-sĕk′tər) *n.* One who dissects cadavers for anatomical instruction or pathological examination. [Lat. *prōsector*, anatomist < *prōsecāre*, to cut off or up : *prō-*, before; see PRO-[1] + *secāre*, to cut; see SECTOR.]

pros•e•cute (prŏs′ĭ-kyōōt′) *v.* **-cut•ed, -cut•ing, -cutes.** — *tr.* **1.** *Law.* **a.** To initiate civil or criminal court action against. **b.** To seek to obtain or enforce by legal action. **2.** To pursue (an undertaking, for example) until completion; follow to the very end. **3.** To carry on, engage in, or practice. — *intr. Law.* **1.** To initiate and conduct legal proceedings. **2.** To act as prosecutor. [ME *prosecuten* < Lat. *prōsequī*, *prōsecūt-* : *prō-*, forward; see PRO-[1] + *sequī*, to follow; see **sek**[w-1]*.] — **pros′e•cut′a•ble** *adj.*

pros•e•cut•ing attorney (prŏs′ĭ-kyōō′tĭng) *n. Law.* A lawyer empowered to prosecute cases on behalf of a government.

pros•e•cu•tion (prŏs′ĭ-kyōō′shən) *n.* **1.** The act of prosecuting. **2.** *Law.* The institution and conduct of a legal proceeding. **3.** *Law.* See **prosecuting attorney.**

pros•e•cu•tor (prŏs′ĭ-kyōō′tər) *n.* **1.** One that prosecutes. **2.** *Law.* One that initiates and carries out a legal action, esp. criminal proceedings. **3.** *Law.* See **prosecuting attorney.**

pros•e•cu•to•ri•al (prŏs′ĭ-kyōō-tôr′ē-əl, -tōr′-) *adj.* Of, relating to, or concerned with prosecution.

pros•e•lyte (prŏs′ə-līt′) *n.* A new convert to a doctrine or religion. — *v.* **-lyt•ed, -lyt•ing, -lytes.** — *tr.* To proselytize (a person). — *intr.* To engage in proselytization. [ME *proselite* < OFr. < LLat. *prosēlytus* < Gk. *prosēlutos*, stranger, proselyte < *prosēluth-*, aorist stem of *proserkhesthai*, to go to : *pros-*, pros- + *erkhesthai*, to go.] — **pros′e•lyt′er** *n.*

pros•e•ly•tism (prŏs′ə-lĭ-tĭz′əm, -lī-) *n.* **1.** The practice of proselytizing. **2.** The state of being a proselyte. — **pros′e•lyt′i•cal** (-lĭt′ĭ-kəl) *adj.*

pros•e•ly•tize (prŏs′ə-lĭ-tīz′) *v.* **-tized, -tiz•ing, -tiz•es.** — *intr.* **1.** To convert someone to one's own religious faith. **2.** To induce someone to join one's own political party or to espouse one's doctrine. — *tr.* To convert (a person) from one belief, doctrine, cause, or faith to another. — **pros′e•ly•ti•za′tion** (-tĭ-zā′shən) *n.* — **pros′e•ly•tiz′er** *n.*

pro•sem•i•nar (prō-sĕm′ə-när′) *n.* A course of study for graduate and advanced undergraduate students in a college or university, conducted as a seminar. [PRO-[2] + SEMINAR.]

pros•en•ceph•a•lon (prŏs′ĕn-sĕf′ə-lŏn′) *n.* The forebrain. — **pros′en•ce•phal′ic** (-sə-făl′ĭk) *adj.*

pros•en•chy•ma (prŏ-sĕng′kĭ-mə) *n.* A type of plant tissue consisting of elongated cells with tapering ends, occurring in supporting and conducting tissue. — **pros′en•chym′a•tous** (-kĭm′ə-təs) *adj.*

prose poem *n.* A prose work that has poetic characteristics such as vivid imagery and concentrated expression.

Pro•ser•pi•na (prō-sûr′pə-nə) also **Pro•ser•pi•ne** (prō-sûr′pə-nē, prŏs′ər-pīn′) *n. Rom. Myth.* The daughter of Ceres who, after being abducted by Pluto, became the goddess of the underworld.

pro•sit (prōst, prō′zĭt) or **prost** (prōst) *interj.* Used as a toast to someone's health while drinking. [Ger. < Lat., may it benefit, third pers. sing. subjunctive of *prodesse*, to benefit. See PROUD.]

pro•slav•er•y (prō-slā′və-rē, -slāv′rē) *adj.* Advocating the practice of slavery.

pros•o•dy (prŏs′ə-dē) *n., pl.* **-dies. 1.** The study of the metrical structure of verse. **2.** A particular system of versification. [ME *prosodie* < Lat. *prosōdia*, accent < Gk. *prosōidia*, song sung to music, accent : *pros-*, pros- + *ōidē*, song; see ODE.] —**pro•sod′ic** (prə-sŏd′ĭk) *adj.* —**pro•sod′i•cal•ly** *adv.* —**pros′o•dist** *n.*

pro•so•ma (prō-sō′mə) *n.* The anterior or cephalic portion of the body of certain invertebrates, such as arachnids, in which segmentation is not evident. [PRO–2 + Gk. *sōma*, body; see **teuə-***.] —**pro•so′mal** *adj.*

pros•o•pog•ra•phy (prŏs′ə-pŏg′rə-fē) *n.* A study, often using statistics, that identifies and draws relationships between various characters or people within a specific historical, social, or literary context. [Gk. *prosōpon*, character; see PROSOPOPEIA + -GRAPHY.] —**pros′o•po•graph′i•cal** (-pə-grăf′ĭ-kəl) *adj.*

pro•so•po•pe•ia also **pro•so•po•poe•ia** (prə-sō′pə-pē′ə) *n.* **1.** A figure of speech in which an absent or imaginary person is represented as speaking. **2.** See **personification** 3. [Lat. *prosōpopoeia* < Gk. *prosōpopoiia* : *prosōpon*, face, mask, dramatic character (*pros-*, pros- + *ōpon*, face < *ōps*, eye; see MYOPIA) + *poiein*, to make; see **kʷei-2***.] —**pro•so′po•pe′ial** *adj.*

pros•pect (prŏs′pĕkt′) *n.* **1.** Something expected; a possibility. **2. prospects. a.** Chances. **b.** Financial expectations, esp. of success. **3.a.** A potential customer, client, or purchaser. **b.** A candidate deemed likely to succeed. **4.** The direction in which an object, such as a building, faces; an outlook. **5.** Something presented to the eye; a scene: *a pleasant prospect.* **6.a.** The location or probable location of a mineral deposit. **b.** An actual or probable mineral deposit. **c.** The mineral yield obtained by working an ore. —*v.* **-pect•ed, -pect•ing, -pects.** —*tr.* To search for or explore (a region) for mineral deposits or oil. —*intr.* To explore for mineral deposits or oil. [ME *prospecte* < Lat. *prōspectus*, distant view < p.part. of *prōspicere*, to look out : *prō-*, forward; see PRO–1 + *specere*, to look at; see **spek-***.]

pro•spec•tive (prə-spĕk′tĭv) *adj.* **1.** Likely or expected to happen. **2.** Likely to become or be. —**pro•spec′tive•ly** *adv.*

pros•pec•tor (prŏs′pĕk′tər) *n.* One who explores an area for mineral deposits or oil.

pro•spec•tus (prə-spĕk′təs) *n.* **1.** A formal summary of a proposed venture or project. **2.** A document describing the chief features of something, esp. a stock offering or mutual fund, for prospective buyers, investors, or participants. [Lat. *prōspectus*, distant view. See PROSPECT.]

pros•per (prŏs′pər) *intr.v.* **-pered, -per•ing, -pers.** To be fortunate or successful, esp. in terms of one's finances; thrive. [ME *prosperen* < OFr. *prosperer* < Lat. *prosperāre*, to render fortunate < *prosperus*, favorable. See **spē-***.]

pros•per•i•ty (prŏ-spĕr′ĭ-tē) *n.* The condition of being prosperous.

pros•per•ous (prŏs′pər-əs) *adj.* **1.** Having success; flourishing. **2.** Well-to-do; well-off. **3.** Propitious; favorable. —**pros′per•ous•ly** *adv.* —**pros′per•ous•ness** *n.*

prost (prōst) *interj.* Var. of **prosit.**

pros•ta•glan•din (prŏs′tə-glăn′dĭn) *n.* Any of a group of hormonelike amino acid derivatives that mediate a wide range of physiological functions, such as metabolism, smooth muscle activity, and nerve transmission. [PROSTA(TE) + GLAND1 + -IN.]

pros•tate (prŏs′tāt′) *n.* The prostate gland. [NLat. *prostata* < Gk. *prostatēs (adēn)*, prostate (gland) < *proïstanai*, to set before : *pro-*, in front; see PRO–2 + *histanai*, to set, place; see **stā-***.] —**pros′tate′, pro•stat′ic** (prō-stăt′ĭk) *adj.*

pros•ta•tec•to•my (prŏs′tə-tĕk′tə-mē) *n., pl.* **-mies.** Surgical removal of all or part of the prostate gland.

prostate gland *n.* A partly muscular gland in male mammals surrounding the urethra at the base of the bladder that secretes a fluid that is a major constituent of semen.

pros•ta•tism (prŏs′tə-tĭz′əm) *n.* A disorder characterized by decreased force of urination and dysuria, usu. resulting from enlargement of the prostate gland.

pros•ta•ti•tis (prŏs′tə-tī′tĭs) *n.* Inflammation of the prostate gland.

pros•the•sis (prŏs-thē′sĭs) *n., pl.* **-ses** (-sēz). **1.** An artificial device used to replace a missing body part, such as a limb, a tooth, an eye, or a heart valve. **2.** Replacement of a missing body part with such a device. [Gk., addition < *prostithenai*, to add : *pros-*, pros- + *tithenai*, to put; see **dhē-***.]

pros•thet•ic (prŏs-thĕt′ĭk) *adj.* **1.** Serving as or relating to a prosthesis. **2.** Of or relating to prosthetics.

prosthetic group *n. Biochem.* The nonprotein component of a conjugated protein, as the heme group in hemoglobin.

pros•thet•ics (prŏs-thĕt′ĭks) *n.* *(used with a sing. v.)* The branch of medicine or surgery that deals with prostheses. —**pros′the•tist** (prŏs′thĭ-tĭst) *n.*

pros•tho•don•tia (prŏs′thə-dŏn′shə) *n.* Prosthodontics.

pros•tho•don•tics (prŏs′thə-dŏn′tĭks) *n.* *(used with a sing. v.)* The branch of dentistry that deals with the replacement of missing teeth and related mouth or jaw structures by artificial devices. [PROSTH(ESIS) + -ODONT(IA) + -ICS.] —**pros′tho•don′tic** *adj.* —**pros′tho•don′tist** *n.*

pros•ti•tute (prŏs′tĭ-to͞ot′, -tyo͞ot′) *n.* **1.** One who solicits and accepts payment for sex. **2.** One who sells one's abilities, talent, or name for an unworthy purpose. —*tr.v.* **-tut•ed, -tut•ing, -tutes. 1.** To offer (oneself or another) for sexual hire. **2.** To sell (one's talent, for example) for an unworthy purpose. [Lat. *prōstitūta* < fem. p.part. of *prōstituere*, to prostitute : *prō-*, in front; see PRO–1 + *statuere*, to cause to stand; see **stā-***.] —**pros′ti•tu′tor** *n.*

pros•ti•tu•tion (prŏs′tĭ-to͞o′shən, -tyo͞o′-) *n.* **1.** The act or practice of engaging in sex acts for hire. **2.** The act or an instance of offering or devoting one's talent unworthily.

pro•sto•mi•um (prō-stō′mē-əm) *n., pl.* **-mi•a** (-mē-ə). The portion of the head in earthworms and other annelids that is situated anterior to the mouth. [NLat. < Gk. *prostomion*, mouth, lips : Gk. *pro-*, in front of; see PRO–2 + Gk. *stomion*, dim. of *stoma*, mouth.] —**pro•sto′mi•al** (-əl) *adj.*

pros•trate (prŏs′trāt′) *tr.v.* **-trat•ed, -trat•ing, -trates. 1.** To make (oneself) bow or kneel down in humility or adoration. **2.** To throw down flat. **3.** To lay low; overcome. —*adj.* **1.** Lying face down, as in submission. **2.** Lying down at full length. **3.** Physically or emotionally incapacitated; overcome. **4.** *Bot.* Growing flat along the ground. [ME *prostraten* < *prostrat*, prostrate < Lat. *prōstrātus*, p.part. of *prōsternere*, to throw down : *pro-*, forward; see PRO–1 + *sternere*, to spread, cast down; see **ster-2***.] —**pros′tra′tor** *n.*

pros•tra•tion (prŏ-strā′shən) *n.* **1.a.** The act of prostrating oneself. **b.** The state of being prostrate. **2.** Total exhaustion or weakness; collapse.

pro•style (prō′stīl′) *adj. Archit.* Having a row of columns across the front only. [Lat. *prostȳlos* < Gk. *prostulos* : *pro-*, in front; see PRO–2 + *stulos*, pillar; see **stā-***.]

pros•y (prō′zē) *adj.* **-i•er, -i•est. 1.** Matter-of-fact and dry; prosaic. **2.** Dull; commonplace. [< PROSE.] —**pros′i•ly** *adv.* —**pros′i•ness** *n.*

Prot. *abbr.* Protestant.

prot– *pref.* Var. of **proto–.**

pro•tac•tin•i•um (prō′tăk-tĭn′ē-əm) *n. Symbol* **Pa** A rare, extremely toxic radioactive element having 13 known isotopes, the most stable of which is protactinium 231 with a half-life of 32,480 years. Atomic number 91; melting point 1,230°C; specific gravity 15.37; valence 4, 5. See table at **element.** [PROT(O)- + ACTINIUM (so called because it decays into actinium).]

pro•tag•o•nist (prō-tăg′ə-nĭst) *n.* **1.** The main character in a literary work. **2.** In ancient Greek drama, the first actor to engage in dialogue with the chorus, in later dramas playing the main character and some minor characters as well. **3.a.** A leading or principal figure. **b.** The leader of a cause; a champion. **4.** *Usage Problem.* A proponent; an advocate. [Gk. *prōtagōnistēs* : *prōto-*, proto- + *agōnistēs*, actor, combatant (< *agōnizesthai*, to contend < *agōnia*, contest < *agōn* < *agein*, to drive, lead; see **ag-***).]

Usage Note: The *protagonist* of a Greek drama was its leading actor, of whom there could be but one in any play. Thus when the members of the Usage Panel were asked "How many protagonists are there in *Othello?*" the great majority answered "One" and offered substitutes such as *antagonist, villain, principal,* and *deuteragonist* to describe Desdemona and Iago. But there is reputable precedent from the 17th century on for using *protagonist* to mean simply "important actor" or "principal party," with no implication of uniqueness. •The use of *protagonist* to refer to a proponent is likely to strike many as an error.

Pro•tag•o•ras (prō-tăg′ər-əs). fl. 5th cent. B.C. Greek philosopher who is considered the first Sophist. —**Pro•tag′o•re′an** (-ə-rē′ən) *adj.*

pro•ta•mine (prō′tə-mēn′, -mĭn) also **pro•ta•min** (-mĭn) *n.* Any of a group of simple proteins found in fish sperm that are strongly basic, are soluble in water, are not coagulated by heat, and yield chiefly arginine upon hydrolysis.

pro•ta•no•pi•a (prō′tə-nō′pē-ə) *n.* A form of colorblindness characterized by defective perception of red. [PROT(O)- + AN- + -OPIA.] —**pro′ta•nop′ic** (-nŏp′ĭk) *adj.*

prot•a•sis (prŏt′ə-sĭs) *n., pl.* **-ses** (-sēz′). **1.** *Gram.* The subordinate clause of a conditional sentence, as *if it rains* in *The game will be canceled if it rains.* **2.** The first part of an ancient Greek or Roman drama, in which the characters and subject are introduced. [LLat., proposition, first part of a play < Gk., premise of a syllogism, conditional clause < *proteinein*, to propose : *pro-*, forward; see PRO–2 + *teinein*, to stretch; see **ten-***.] —**pro•tat′ic** (prŏ-tăt′ĭk, prō-) *adj.*

prote– *pref.* Var. of **proteo–.**

pro•te•an (prō′tē-ən, prō-tē′-) *adj.* **1.** Readily taking on varied shapes, forms, or meanings. **2.** Exhibiting considerable variety or diversity. [< PROTEUS.]

pro•te•ase (prō′tē-ās′, -āz′) *n.* Any of various enzymes that catalyze the hydrolytic breakdown of proteins.

pro•tect (prə-tĕkt′) *tr.v.* **-tect•ed, -tect•ing, -tects. 1.** To keep from being damaged, attacked, stolen, or injured; guard. See Syns at **defend. 2.** To help (domestic industry) with tariffs or quotas on imported goods. **3.** To assure payment of (drafts or notes, for example) by setting aside funds. [ME *protecten* < Lat. *prōtegere*, *prōtēct-* : *prō-*, in front; see PRO–1 + *tegere*,

prospector
Panning for gold

prosthesis
Jeff Keith near the completion of his Run Across America in 1985

ă pat	oi boy
ā pay	ou out
âr care	o͝o took
ä father	o͞o boot
ĕ pet	ŭ cut
ē be	ûr urge
ĭ pit	th thin
ī pie	*th* this
îr pier	hw which
ŏ pot	zh vision
ō toe	ə about, item
ô paw	

Stress marks:
′ (primary);
′ (secondary), as in **dictionary** (dĭk′shə-nĕr′ē)

to cover; see **(s)teg-***.] — **pro·tect′ing·ly** *adv.*
pro·tec·tant (prə-tĕk′tənt) *n.* One that protects.
pro·tec·tion (prə-tĕk′shən) *n.* **1.a.** The act of protecting. **b.** The condition of being protected. **2.** One that protects. **3.** A pass guaranteeing safe-conduct to travelers. **4.** A system of tariffs or other measures protecting domestic producers from foreign competition. **5.** *Slang.* **a.** Money extorted by racketeers threatening violence for nonpayment. **b.** Bribes paid to officials by racketeers for immunity from prosecution.
pro·tec·tion·ism (prə-tĕk′shə-nĭz′əm) *n.* The advocacy, system, or theory of protecting domestic producers by impeding or limiting, as by tariffs or quotas, the importation of foreign goods and services. — **pro·tec′tion·ist** *n.*
pro·tec·tive (prə-tĕk′tĭv) *adj.* Adapted or intended to afford protection. — *n.* Something that protects. — **pro·tec′tive·ly** *adv.* — **pro·tec′tive·ness** *n.*
pro·tec·tor also **pro·tect·er** (prə-tĕk′tər) *n.* **1.** A person or a thing that protects. **2. Protector. a.** One who rules a kingdom during the minority of a sovereign. **b.** The head of the Commonwealth of England, Scotland, and Ireland from 1653 to 1659. — **pro·tec′tor·al** *adj.* — **pro·tec′tor·ship′** *n.*
pro·tec·tor·ate (prə-tĕk′tər-ĭt) *n.* **1.a.** A relationship of protection and partial control assumed by a superior power over a dependent country or region. **b.** The protected country or region. **2. Protectorate. a.** The government, office, or term of a protector. **b.** The government of England under Oliver Cromwell and his son Richard.
pro·tec·to·ry (prə-tĕk′tə-rē) *n., pl.* **-ries.** An institution providing for homeless, destitute, or delinquent children.
pro·té·gé (prō′tə-zhā′, prō′tə-zhā′) *n.* One whose welfare, training, or career is promoted by an influential person. [Fr. < p.part. of *protéger,* to protect < OFr. < Lat. *prōtegere.* See PROTECT.]
pro·té·gée (prō′tə-zhā′, prō′tə-zhā′) *n.* A woman or girl whose welfare, training, or career is promoted by an influential person. [Fr., fem. of *protégé,* protégé. See PROTÉGÉ.]
pro·te·i (prō′tē-ī′) *n.* Pl. of **proteus.**
pro·tein (prō′tēn′, -tē-ĭn) *n.* Any of a group of complex organic macromolecules that contain carbon, hydrogen, oxygen, nitrogen, and usu. sulfur, are composed of one or more chains of amino acids, and include many substances, such as enzymes, hormones, and antibodies, that are necessary for the proper functioning of an organism. [Fr. *protéine* < LGk. *prōteios,* of the first quality < Gk. *prōtos,* first. See **per**[1]*.] — **pro′tein·a′ceous** (prōt′n-ā′shəs, prō′tē-nā′-), **pro′te·in′ic** (prō′tē-ĭn′ĭk) *adj.*
pro·tein·ase (prōt′n-ās′, -āz′, prō′tē-nās′, -nāz′) *n.* A protease that hydrolyzes proteins usu. to polypeptides.
pro·tein·u·ri·a (prōt′n-o͝or′ē-ə, -yo͝or′-, prō′tē-no͝or′-, -nyo͝or′-) *n.* The presence of excessive amounts of protein in the urine.
pro tem (prō tĕm′) *adv.* Pro tempore.
pro tem·po·re (prō tĕm′pə-rē) *adv.* For the time being; temporarily. [Lat. *prō tempore* : *prō,* for + *tempore,* ablative of *tempus,* time.]
proteo– or **prote–** *pref.* Protein: *proteolysis.* [< PROTEIN.]
pro·te·ol·y·sis (prō′tē-ŏl′ĭ-sĭs) *n.* The hydrolytic breakdown of proteins into simpler soluble substances, as occurs in digestion. — **pro′te·o·lyt′ic** (-tē-ə-lĭt′ĭk) *adj.* — **pro′te·o·lyt′i·cal·ly** *adv.*
pro·te·ose (prō′tē-ōs′, -ōz′) *n.* Any of various water-soluble compounds produced by the hydrolytic breakdown of proteins during digestion.
Prot·er·o·zo·ic (prŏt′ər-ə-zō′ĭk, prō′tər-) *adj.* Of, belonging to, or being the later of two divisions of Precambrian time. — *n.* The Proterozoic Era. [Gk. *proteros,* earlier, former; see **per**[1]* + -ZOIC.]
pro·test (prə-tĕst′, prō-, prō′tĕst′) *v.* **-test·ed, -test·ing, -tests.** — *tr.* **1.** To object to, esp. in a formal statement. See Syns at **object. 2.** To promise or affirm with earnest solemnity. **3.** *Archaic.* To proclaim or make known. — *intr.* **1.** To express strong objection. **2.** To make an earnest avowal or affirmation. — *n.* (prō′tĕst′). **1.** A formal declaration of disapproval or objection issued by a concerned person, group, or organization. **2.** An individual or collective gesture or display of disapproval. [ME *protesten* < OFr. *protester* < Lat. *prōtestārī* : *prō-,* forth; see PRO–[1] + *testārī,* to testify (< *testis,* witness; see **trei-***).] — **pro·test′er** *n.*
Prot·es·tant (prŏt′ĭ-stənt) *n. Theol.* **1.** A member of a Western Christian church whose faith and practice are founded on the principles of the Protestant Reformation. **2.** One who supported the protestation presented by the German Lutheran states against the revocation of the decree of the Diet of Speyer (1529). **3. protestant** (prə-tĕs′tənt). One who makes a declaration or an avowal. [Fr. < Ger. < Lat. *prōtestāns, prōtestant-,* pr.part. of *prōtestārī,* to protest. See PROTEST.] — **Prot′es·tant** *adj.*
Protestant Episcopal Church *n.* The Episcopal Church.
Prot·es·tant·ism (prŏt′ĭ-stən-tĭz′əm) *n.* **1.** Adherence to the religion and beliefs of a Protestant church. **2.** The religion and religious beliefs fostered by the Protestant movement. **3.** Protestants considered as a group.
prot·es·ta·tion (prŏt′ĭ-stā′shən, prō′tĭ-, -tĕ-) *n.* **1.** An emphatic declaration. **2.** A strong or formal expression of dissent.
pro·te·us (prō′tē-əs) *n., pl.* **-te·i** (-tē-ī′). Any of various gram-negative rod-shaped bacteria of the genus *Proteus,* certain species of which are associated with human enteritis and urinary tract infections. [NLat. *Prōteus,* genus name < Lat., Proteus. See PROTEUS.]
Pro·te·us (prō′tē-əs, -tyo͞os′) *n. Gk. Myth.* A sea god who could change his shape at will. [Lat. *Prōteus* < Gk.]
pro·tha·la·mi·on (prō′thə-lā′mē-ən, -ŏn′) *n., pl.* **-mi·a** (-mē-ə). *Mus.* A song in celebration of a wedding. [PRO–[2] + Gk. *epithalamion,* epithalamium; see EPITHALAMIUM.]
pro·thal·lus (prō-thăl′əs) or **pro·thal·li·um** (-thăl′ē-əm) *n., pl.* **-thal·li** (-thăl′ī) or **-thal·li·a** (-thăl′ē-ə). A small flat delicate structure produced by a germinating spore of a fern and bearing sex organs. [NLat. : PRO–[2] + Gk. *thallos,* shoot (< *thallein,* to sprout).] — **pro·thal′li·al** (-lē-əl) *adj.*
proth·e·sis (prŏth′ĭ-sĭs) *n., pl.* **-ses** (-sēz′). *Ling.* The addition of a phoneme or syllable at the beginning of a word, as in Spanish *espina,* "thorn," from Latin *spina.* [Gk., prefixing < *protithenai,* to put before : *pro-,* before; see PRO–[2] + *tithenai,* to put; see **dhē-***.] — **pro·thet′ic** (prŏ-thĕt′ĭk) *adj.* — **pro·thet′i·cal·ly** *adv.*
pro·thon·o·tar·y (prō-thŏn′ə-tĕr′ē, prō′thə-nō′tə-rē) also **pro·ton·o·tar·y** (prō-tŏn′ə-tĕr′ē, prō′tə-nō′tə-rē) *n., pl.* **-ies. 1.** The principal clerk in certain courts of law. **2.** *Rom. Cath. Ch.* One of a college of 12 ecclesiastics charged with the registry of important pontifical proceedings. [ME *prothonotarie* < Med.Lat. *prōthonotārius* < LLat. *prōtonotārius* : Gk. *prōto-,* proto- + Lat. *notārius,* secretary (< *nota,* mark; see **gnō-***).]
prothonotary warbler *n.* A small North American bird *(Protonotaria citrea)* having a deep yellow head and breast and inhabiting wooded swamps.
prothoracic gland *n.* Either of a pair of glands located in the prothorax of certain insects and regulating molting.
pro·tho·rax (prō-thôr′ăks′, -thōr′-) *n., pl.* **-tho·rax·es** or **-tho·ra·ces** (-thôr′ə-sēz′, -thōr′-). The anterior division of the thorax of an insect, bearing the first pair of legs. — **pro′-tho·rac′ic** (prō′thə-răs′ĭk) *adj.*
pro·throm·bin (prō-thrŏm′bĭn) *n.* A plasma protein that is converted into thrombin during blood clotting.
pro·tist (prō′tĭst) *n.* Any of the eukaryotic unicellular organisms of the former kingdom Protista, which now belong to the kingdom Protoctista. [< NLat. *Protista,* former kingdom name < Gk. *prōtista,* neut. pl. of *prōtistos,* the very first, superl. of *prōtos,* first. See **per**[1]*.]
pro·ti·um (prō′tē-əm, prō′shē-) *n.* The most abundant isotope of hydrogen, H_1, with atomic mass 1.
proto– or **prot–** *pref.* **1.** First in time; earliest: *protolithic.* **2.** First formed; primitive; original: *protohuman.* **3. Proto–.** Being a form of a language that is the ancestor of a language or group of related languages: *Proto-Germanic.* **4.** Having the least amount of a specified element or radical: *protoporphyrin.* [Gk. *prōto-* < *prōtos.* See **per**[1]*.]
Pro·to-Al·gon·qui·an (prō′tō-ăl-gŏng′kwē-ən, -kē-ən) *n.* The reconstructed protolanguage of Algonquian.
pro·to·col (prō′tə-kôl′, -kōl′, -kŏl′) *n.* **1.a.** The forms of ceremony and etiquette observed by diplomats and heads of state. **b.** A code of correct conduct. **2.** The first copy of a treaty or other such document before its ratification. **3.** A preliminary draft or record of a transaction. **4.** The plan for a course of medical treatment or for a scientific experiment. **5.** *Comp. Sci.* A standard procedure for regulating data transmission between computers. — *intr.v.* **-coled, -col·ing, -cols** or **-colled, -col·ling, -cols.** To form or issue protocols. [Fr. *protocole* < OFr. *prothocolle,* draft of a document < Med. Lat. *prōtocollum* < LGk. *prōtokollon,* table of contents, first sheet : Gk. *prōto-,* proto- + Gk. *kollēma,* sheets of a papyrus glued together (< *kollan,* to glue together < *kolla,* glue).] — **pro′to·col′ar** (-kŏl′ər), **pro′to·col′a·ry** (-kŏl′ə-rē) *adj.*
pro·toc·tist (prə-tŏk′tĭst) *n.* Any of the unicellular protists and their descendant multicellular organisms, considered as a separate taxonomic kingdom in most modern classification systems. [< NLat. *Prōtoctista,* kingdom name : Gk. *prōto-,* proto- + Gk. *ktistos,* created (< *ktizein,* to create).]
pro·to·derm (prō′tə-dûrm′) *n. Bot.* See **dermatogen.**
Pro·to-Ger·man·ic (prō′tō-jûr-măn′ĭk) *n.* The reconstructed prehistoric ancestor of the Germanic languages.
pro·to·gy·nous (prō′tə-jī′nəs, -gī′-) *adj.* Of or relating to a flower in which the stigma is receptive before the pollen is shed from the anthers of the same flower.
pro·to·his·to·ry (prō′tō-hĭs′tə-rē, -hĭs′trē) *n.* The study of a culture just before the time of its earliest recorded history. — **pro′to·his·tor′i·an** (-hĭ-stôr′ē-ən, -stŏr′-) *n.* — **pro′to·his·tor′ic** (-hĭ-stôr′ĭk, -stŏr′-) *adj.*
pro·to·hu·man (prō′tō-hyo͞o′mən) *adj.* Of or relating to various extinct hominids or other primates that resemble modern human beings. — **pro′to·hu′man** *n.*
Pro·to-In·do-Eur·o·pe·an (prō′tō-ĭn′dō-yo͝or′ə-pē′ən) *n.* The reconstructed language that was the ancestor of the Indo-

European languages. — **Pro′to·In′do·Eur′o·pe′an** *adj.*

pro·to·lan·guage (prō′tō-lăng′gwĭj) *n.* A language that is the recorded or hypothetical ancestor of another language or group of languages.

pro·to·lith·ic (prō′tə-lĭth′ĭk) *adj.* Of, relating to, or characteristic of the very beginning of the Stone Age; Eolithic.

pro·to·mar·tyr (prō′tō-mär′tər) *n.* The first martyr in a cause. Used esp. of the first Christian martyr, Saint Stephen.

pro·ton (prō′tŏn′) *n. Phys.* A stable, positively charged subatomic particle in the baryon family having a mass 1,836 times that of the electron. See table at **subatomic particle.** [< Gk. *prōton*, neut. of *prōtos*, first. See **per[1]*.**] — **pro·ton′ic** *adj.*

pro·to·ne·ma (prō′tə-nē′mə) *n., pl.* **-ne·ma·ta** (-nē′mə-tə, -nĕm′ə-). The filamentous growth that arises from spore germination in mosses and gives rise to a mature gametophyte. [PROTO– + Gk. *nēma*, thread; see **(s)nē-*.**] — **pro′to·ne′mal** (-nē′məl), **pro′to·ne′ma·tal** (-nē′mə-təl, -nĕm′ə-) *adj.*

pro·ton·o·tar·y (prō-tŏn′ə-tĕr′ē, prō′tə-nō′tə-rē) *n.* Var. of **prothonotary.**

proton synchrotron *n. Phys.* A synchrotron that accelerates protons to energies of several hundred billion electron volts.

pro·to·path·ic (prō′tə-păth′ĭk) *adj.* Sensing stimuli in a nonspecific manner. Used esp. of certain sensory nerves. [< Med. Gk. *prōtopathēs*, affected first < Gk. *prōtopathein*, to feel first : *prōto-*, proto- + *pasthein*, to feel.]

pro·to·plasm (prō′tə-plăz′əm) *n.* The semifluid translucent substance that constitutes the living matter of plant and animal cells, is composed of proteins, fats, and other molecules suspended in water, and includes the nucleus and cytoplasm. — **pro′to·plas′mic** (-plăz′mĭk), **pro′to·plas·′mal** (-plăz′-məl), **pro′to·plas·mat′ic** (-plăz-măt′ĭk) *adj.*

pro·to·plast (prō′tə-plăst′) *n.* **1.** *Biol.* The living material of a plant or bacterial cell, including the protoplasm and plasma membrane after the cell wall has been removed. **2.** One that is the first made or formed; a prototype. [Fr. *protoplaste* < OFr., the first man < LLat. *prōtoplastus* < Gk. *prōtoplastos* : *prōto-*, proto- + *plastos*, formed, molded; see –PLAST.] — **pro′to·plas′tic** *adj.*

pro·to·por·phy·rin (prō′tō-pôr′fə-rĭn) *n.* A metal-free porphyrin, $C_{32}H_{32}N_4(COOH)_2$, that combines with iron to form the heme of hemoglobin and other iron-containing proteins.

pro·to·stele (prō′tə-stēl′, prō′tə-stē′lē) *n. Bot.* A stele that has a solid core of vascular tissue.

pro·to·tro·phic (prō′tə-trō′fĭk, -trŏf′ĭk) *adj. Microbiol.* Having the same metabolic capabilities and nutritional requirements as the wild type parent strain: *prototrophic bacteria.* — **pro′to·troph′**, **pro′to·troph′y** *n.*

pro·to·type (prō′tə-tīp′) *n.* **1.** An original type, form, or instance serving as a basis or standard for stages. **2.** An early typical example. **3.** *Biol.* A primitive or ancestral form or species. [Fr. < Gk. *prōtotupon* < neut. of *prōtotupos*, original : *prōto-*, proto- + *tupos*, model.] — **pro′to·typ′al** (-tī′-pəl), **pro′to·typ′ic** (-tĭp′ĭk), **pro′to·typ′·i·cal** (-ĭ-kəl) *adj.*

pro·to·xy·lem (prō′tə-zī′ləm) *n. Bot.* The first formed xylem that differentiates from the procambium.

pro·to·zo·an (prō′tə-zō′ən) also **pro·to·zo·on** (-ŏn′) *n., pl.* **-zo·ans** or **-zo·a** (-zō′ə) also **-zo·ons.** Any of a large group of single-celled, usu. microscopic eukaryotic organisms, such as amoebas. [< NLat. *Protozoa*, former subkingdom name : PROTO– + NLat. *-zoa*, pl. of *-zoon*, -zoon.] — **pro′to·zo′an, pro′to·zo′al, pro′to·zo′ic** *adj.*

pro·to·zo·ol·o·gy (prō′tə-zō-ŏl′ə-jē) *n.* The biological study of protozoans. — **pro′to·zo′o·log′i·cal** (-zō′ə-lŏj′ĭ-kəl) *adj.* — **pro′to·zo·ol′o·gist** *n.*

pro·tract (prō-trăkt′, prə-) *tr.v.* **-tract·ed, -tract·ing, -tracts.** **1.** To draw out or lengthen in time; prolong. **2.** *Math.* To draw to scale by means of a scale and protractor; plot. **3.** *Anat.* To extend or protrude (a body part). [Lat. *prōtrahere, prōtrāct-* : *prō-*, forth; see PRO–[1] + *trahere*, to drag.] — **pro·tract′ed·ly** (-trăk′tĭd-lē) *adv.* — **pro·tract′ed·ness** *n.* — **pro·trac′tive** *adj.*

pro·trac·tile (prō-trăk′təl, -tīl′, prə-) also **pro·tract·i·ble** (-tə-bəl) *adj.* That can be protracted; extensible: *protractile limbs and claws.* — **pro′trac·til′i·ty** (prō′trăk-tĭl′ĭ-tē) *n.*

pro·trac·tion (prō-trăk′shən, prə-) *n.* **1.a.** The act of protracting. **b.** The state of being protracted. **2.** *Ling.* The irregular lengthening of a normally short syllable.

pro·trac·tor (prō-trăk′tər, prə-) *n.* **1.** *Math.* A semicircular instrument for measuring and constructing angles. **2.** An adjustable pattern used by tailors. **3.** *Anat.* A muscle that extends a limb or other part.

pro·trude (prō-trōōd′) *v.* **-trud·ed, -trud·ing, -trudes.** — *tr.* To push or thrust outward. — *intr.* To jut out; project. [Lat. *prōtrūdere* : *prō-*, forward; see PRO–[1] + *trūdere*, to thrust; see **treud-*.**] — **pro·trud′ent** (-trōōd′nt) *adj.*

pro·tru·sile (prō-trōō′səl, -sīl′) also **pro·tru·si·ble** (-sə-bəl) *adj.* Capable of being thrust outward. [Lat. *prōtrūsus*, p.part. of *prōtrūdere*, to protrude; see PROTRUDE + –ILE[1].] — **pro′-tru·sil′i·ty** (prō′trōō-sĭl′ĭ-tē) *n.*

pro·tru·sion (prō-trōō′zhən) *n.* **1.a.** The act of protruding. **b.** The state of being protruded. **2.** Something that protrudes.

pro·tru·sive (prō-trōō′sĭv, prə-) *adj.* **1.** Tending to protrude; protruding. **2.** Unduly or disagreeably conspicuous; obtrusive. — **pro·tru′sive·ly** *adv.* — **pro·tru′sive·ness** *n.*

pro·tu·ber·ance (prō-tōō′bər-əns, -tyōō′-, prə-) *n.* **1.** Something, such as a bulge, knob, or swelling, that protrudes. **2.** The condition of being protuberant.

pro·tu·ber·an·cy (prō-tōō′bər-ən-sē, -tyōō′-, prə-) *n., pl.* **-cies.** **1.** Protuberance. **2.** Something that is protuberant.

pro·tu·ber·ant (prō-tōō′bər-ənt, -tyōō′-, prə-) *adj.* Swelling outward; bulging. — **pro·tu′ber·ant·ly** *adv.*

pro·tu·ber·ate (prō-tōō′bə-rāt′, -tyōō′-, prə-) *intr.v.* **-at·ed, -at·ing, -ates.** To swell or bulge. [LLat. *prōtūberāre, prōtūberāt-* : Lat. *prō-*, forth; see PRO–[1] + Lat. *tūber*, a swelling; see **teuə-*.**] — **pro·tu′ber·a′tion** *n.*

proud (proud) *adj.* **proud·er, proud·est.** **1.** Feeling pleasurable satisfaction over an act, a possession, a quality, or a relationship used to measure one's stature or self-worth. **2.** Occasioning or being a reason for pride. **3.** Feeling or showing justifiable self-respect. **4.** Filled with or showing excessive self-esteem. **5.** Of great dignity; honored. **6.** Majestic; magnificent. **7.** Spirited. Used of an animal. [ME < OE *prūd* < OFr. *prou, prud*, brave, virtuous, oblique case of *prouz* < VLat. **prōdis* < LLat. *prōde*, advantageous < Lat. *prōdesse*, to be good : *prōd-*, for (var. of *prō-*; see PRO–[1]) + *esse*, to be; see **es-*.**] — **proud′ly** *adv.* — **proud′ness** *n.*

Syns: *proud, arrogant, haughty, disdainful, supercilious.* These adjectives mean characterized by an inflated ego and contempt for what one considers inferior. *Proud* can suggest justifiable self-satisfaction but often implies conceit: *"I pray God to keep me from being proud"* (Samuel Pepys). One who is *arrogant* is overbearingly proud and demands excessive power or consideration: *an arrogant professor. Haughty* suggests proud superiority, as by reason of high status: *"Her laugh was satirical, and so was the habitual expression of her arched and haughty lip"* (Charlotte Brontë). *Disdainful* emphasizes scorn or contempt: *"Nor [let] grandeur hear with a disdainful smile/The short and simple annals of the poor"* (Thomas Gray). *Supercilious* implies haughty disdain and aloofness: *"His mother eyed me in silence with a supercilious air"* (Tobias Smollett).

proud flesh *n. Pathol.* The swollen flesh surrounding a healing wound. [< its swelling up.]

Prou·dhon (prōō-dôN′), **Pierre Joseph.** 1809–65. French anarchist who believed that human moral development would ultimately eliminate the need for laws and government.

Proust (prōōst), **Marcel.** 1871–1922. French writer noted for *Remembrance of Things Past* (1913–27). — **Proust′i·an** *adj.*

prov. *abbr.* **1.** Province; provincial. **2.** Provisional. **3.** Provost.

Prov. *abbr.* **1.** Provençal. **2.** *Bible.* Proverbs.

prove (prōōv) *v.* **proved** or **prov·en** (prōō′vən), **prov·ing, proves.** — *tr.* **1.** To establish the truth or validity of by presentation of argument or evidence. **2.** *Law.* To establish the authenticity of (a will). **3.** To determine the quality of by testing; try out. **4.** *Math.* **a.** To demonstrate the validity of (a hypothesis or proposition). **b.** To verify (the result of a calculation). **5.** *Print.* To make a sample impression of (type). **6.** *Archaic.* To find out or learn (something) through experience. — *intr.* To be shown to be such; turn out. [ME *proven* < OFr. *prover* < Lat. *probāre*, to test < *probus*, good. See **per[1]*.**] — **prov′a·bil′i·ty, prov′a·ble·ness** *n.* — **prov′a·ble** *adj.* — **prov′a·bly** *adv.* — **prov′er** *n.*

Usage Note: *Proved* is actually the older form of the past participle; *proven* is a Scottish variant that was first introduced into wider usage in legal contexts: *The jury ruled that the charges were not proven.* Both forms are now well established in written English as participles: *He has proved* (or *proven*) *his point.* However, *proven* is more common as an adjective before a noun: *a proven talent.*

prov·en (prōō′vən) *adj.* Having been demonstrated or verified without doubt. See Usage Note at **prove.** — **prov′en·ly** *adv.*

prov·e·nance (prŏv′ə-nəns, -näns′) *n.* **1.** Place of origin; derivation. **2.** Proof of authenticity or of past ownership. Used of art works and antiques. [Fr. < *provenant*, pr.part. of *provenir*, to originate < OFr. < Lat. *prōvenīre* : *prō-*, forth; see PRO–[1] + *venīre*, to come; see **gʷā-*.**]

Pro·ven·çal (prō′vən-säl′, -vän-, prŏv′ən-) *adj.* Of or relating to Provence or its people, language, or culture. — *n.* **1.** The Romance language of Provence. **2.** *pl.* **-çals** or **-çaux** (-sō′). A native or inhabitant of Provence. [Fr. < Lat. *prōvinciālis* < *prōvincia*, province.]

Pro·vence (prə-väns′, prô-väNs′). A historical region and former province of SE France on the Mediterranean Sea; settled c. 600 B.C. by Greeks and part of France since 1486.

prov·en·der (prŏv′ən-dər) *n.* **1.** Dry food, such as hay, used as feed for livestock. **2.** Food or provisions. [ME *provendre* < OFr., alteration of *provende* < VLat. **prōvenda*, alteration of LLat. *praebenda*. See PREBEND.]

pro·ve·nience (prə-vēn′yəns, -vē′nē-əns) *n.* A source or an origin. [Alteration of PROVENANCE.]

pro·ven·tric·u·lus (prō′vĕn-trĭk′yə-ləs) *n., pl.* **-li** (-lī′). **1.** The division of the stomach in birds that secretes digestive enzymes and passes food from the crop to the gizzard. **2.** A

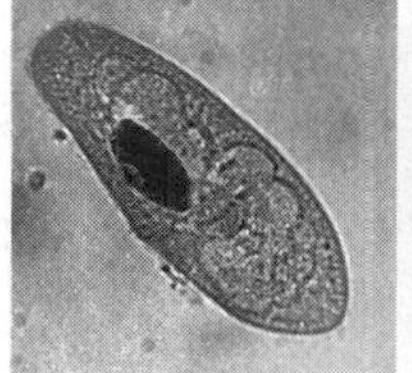

protozoan
Paramecium

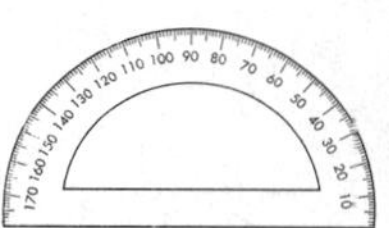

protractor
Mathematical instrument

ă pat	oi boy
ā pay	ou out
âr care	ŏŏ took
ä father	ōō boot
ĕ pet	ŭ cut
ē be	ûr urge
ĭ pit	th thin
ī pie	*th* this
îr pier	hw which
ŏ pot	zh vision
ō toe	ə about, item
ô paw	

Stress marks:
′ (primary);
′ (secondary), as in
dictionary (dĭk′shə-nĕr′ē)

similar digestive chamber in certain insects and worms. [PRO-[2] + Lat. *ventriculus*, stomach, dim. of *venter*, belly.] —**pro′ven•tric′u•lar** (-lər) *adj.*

prov•erb (prŏv′ûrb′) *n.* **1.** A short pithy saying that expresses a basic truth or practical precept. **2. Proverbs.** *(used with a sing. v.)* See table at **Bible.** [ME *proverbe* < OFr. < Lat. *prōverbium* : *prō-*, forth; see PRO-[1] + *verbum*, word; see **wer-**[5]***.**]

pro•ver•bi•al (prə-vûr′bē-əl) *adj.* **1.** Of the nature of a proverb. **2.** Expressed in a proverb. **3.** Widely referred to, as if the subject of a proverb; famous. —**pro•ver′bi•al•ly** *adv.*

pro•vide (prə-vīd′) *v.* **-vid•ed, -vid•ing, -vides.** —*tr.* **1.** To furnish; supply. **2.** To make available; afford. **3.** To set down as a stipulation. **4.** *Archaic.* To make ready ahead of time; prepare. —*intr.* **1.** To take measures in preparation. **2.** To supply means of subsistence. **3.** To make a stipulation or condition. [ME *providen* < Lat. *prōvidēre*, to provide for : *prō-*, forward; see PRO-[1] + *vidēre*, to see; see **weid-*.**]

pro•vid•ed (prə-vī′dĭd) *conj.* On the condition; if.

prov•i•dence (prŏv′ĭ-dəns, -dĕns′) *n.* **1.** Care or preparation in advance; foresight. **2.** Prudent management; economy. **3.** The care, guardianship, and control exercised by a deity; divine direction. **4. Providence.** God.

Providence. The cap. of RI, in the NE part on Narragansett Bay; founded by Roger Williams in 1636. Pop. 160,728.

prov•i•dent (prŏv′ĭ-dənt, -dĕnt′) *adj.* **1.** Providing for future needs or events. **2.** Frugal; economical. [ME < Lat. *prōvidēns*, *prōvident-*, pr.part. of *prōvidēre*, to provide for. See PROVIDE.] —**prov′i•dent•ly** *adv.*

prow
Of the *Queen Elizabeth 2*

prov•i•den•tial (prŏv′ĭ-dĕn′shəl) *adj.* **1.** Of or resulting from divine providence. **2.** Happening as if through divine intervention; opportune. —**prov′i•den′tial•ly** *adv.*

pro•vid•er (prə-vī′dər) *n.* **1.** One who supplies a means of subsistence. **2.** One that makes something available.

pro•vid•ing (prə-vī′dĭng) *conj.* On the condition; provided.

prov•ince (prŏv′ĭns) *n.* **1.** A territory governed as an administrative or political unit of a country or an empire. **2.** *Eccles.* A division of territory under the jurisdiction of an archbishop. **3. provinces.** Areas of a country situated away from the capital or population center. **4.** A comprehensive area of knowledge, activity, or interest. **5.** The range of one's proper duties and functions; scope or jurisdiction. **6.** *Ecol.* An area of land, less extensive than a region, having a characteristic plant and animal population. **7.** Any of various lands outside Italy conquered by the Romans and administered as self-contained units. [ME < OFr. < Lat. *prōvincia*.]

Prov•ince•town (prŏv′ĭns-toun′). A town of SE MA on the tip of Cape Cod. Pilgrims first landed on the site in 1620 before sailing on to Plymouth. Pop. 3,374.

pro•vin•cial (prə-vĭn′shəl) *adj.* **1.** Of or relating to a province. **2.** Of or characteristic of people from the provinces; not fashionable or sophisticated. **3.** Limited in perspective; narrow and self-centered. —*n.* **1.** A native or inhabitant of the provinces. **2.** A person who has provincial ideas or habits. —**pro•vin′cial•ism, pro•vin′ci•al′i•ty** (-shē-ăl′ĭ-tē) *n.* —**pro•vin′cial•ly** *adv.*

pro•vin•cial•ize (prə-vĭn′shə-līz′) *tr.v.* **-ized, -iz•ing, -iz•es.** To make provincial. —**pro•vin′cial•i•za′tion** (-shə-lĭ-zā′shən) *n.*

prov•ing ground (pro͞o′vĭng) *n.* A place for testing new devices, weapons, or theories.

pro•vi•rus (prō′vī′rəs, prō-vī′-) *n., pl.* **-rus•es.** The precursor or latent form of a virus that is capable of being integrated into the genetic material of a host cell and replicated with it.

pro•vi•sion (prə-vĭzh′ən) *n.* **1.** The act of supplying or fitting out. **2.** Something provided. **3.** A preparatory action or measure. **4. provisions.** A stock of necessary supplies, esp. food. **5.** A stipulation or qualification, esp. a clause in a document or an agreement. —*tr.v.* **-sioned, -sion•ing, -sions.** To supply with provisions. [ME < OFr., forethought < Lat. *prōvīsiō*, *prōvīsiōn-* < *prōvīsus*, p.part. of *prōvidēre*, to foresee, provide for. See PROVIDE.] —**pro•vi′sion•er** *n.*

pro•vi•sion•al (prə-vĭzh′ə-nəl) *adj.* Provided or serving only for the time being; temporary. —*n.* **1.** A person hired temporarily for a job, typically before having taken a qualifying examination. **2. Provisional.** A member of the extremist faction of the Irish Republican Army established in 1970. —**pro•vi′sion•al•ly** *adv.*

pro•vi•so (prə-vī′zō) *n., pl.* **-sos** or **-soes.** A clause in a document making a qualification or restriction. [ME < Med.Lat. *prōvīsō (quod)*, provided (that) < Lat. *prōvīsō*, ablative of *prōvīsus*, p.part. of *prōvidēre*, to provide. See PROVIDE.]

pro•vi•so•ry (prə-vī′zə-rē) *adj.* Depending on a proviso; conditional. [Fr. *provisoire* < OFr. < Med.Lat. *prōvīsōrius* < Lat. *prōvīsus*, p.part. of *prōvidēre*, to provide for. See PROVIDE.] —**pro•vi′so•ri•ly** *adv.*

pro•vi•ta•min (prō-vī′tə-mĭn) *n.* A vitamin precursor that is converted to its active form through normal metabolism.

Pro•vo[1] (prō′vō). A city of N-central UT SSE of Salt Lake City; settled by Mormons in 1849. Pop. 86,835.

Pro•vo[2] (prō′vō) *n., pl.* **-vos.** A Provisional.

pro•vo•ca•teur (prō-vŏk′ə-tûr′) *n.* An agent provocateur.

prov•o•ca•tion (prŏv′ə-kā′shən) *n.* **1.** The act of provoking or inciting. **2.** Something that provokes. [Ult. < Lat. *prōvocātiō*, *prōvocātiōn-*, a challenging < *prōvocātus*, p.part. of *prōvocāre*, to challenge. See PROVOKE.]

pro•voc•a•tive (prə-vŏk′ə-tĭv) *adj.* Tending to provoke. —**pro•voc′a•tive** *n.* —**pro•voc′a•tive•ly** *adv.* —**pro•voc′a•tive•ness** *n.*

pro•voke (prə-vōk′) *tr.v.* **-voked, -vok•ing, -vokes.** **1.** To incite to anger or resentment. **2.** To stir to action or feeling. **3.** To give rise to; evoke. **4.** To bring about deliberately; induce. [ME *provoken* < OFr. *provoquer* < Lat. *prōvocāre*, to challenge : *prō-*, forth; see PRO-[1] + *vocāre*, to call; see **wek**[w]**-*.**]

pro•vok•ing (prə-vō′kĭng) *adj.* Troubling the nerves or peace of mind, as by repeated vexations. —**pro•vok′ing•ly** *adv.*

pro•vo•lo•ne (prō′və-lō′nē) *n.* A hard, usu. smoked Italian cheese. [Ital., aug. of *provola*, a kind of cheese.]

pro•vost (prō′vōst′, -vəst, prŏv′əst) *n.* **1.** A university administrator of high rank. **2.** The highest official in certain cathedrals or collegiate churches. **3.** The keeper of a prison. **4.** The chief magistrate of certain Scottish cities. [ME < OE *profost* and OFr. *provost*, both < Med.Lat. *prōpositus*, alteration of Lat. *praepositus*, superintendent < p.part. of *praepōnere*, to place over : *prae-*, pre- + *pōnere*, to put; see **apo-*.**]

pro•vost marshal (prō′vō) *n.* The head of a unit of military police.

prow (prou) *n.* **1.** *Naut.* The forward part of a ship's hull; the bow. **2.** A projecting forward part, such as the front end of a ski. [Fr. *proue* < OFr. < Ital. dial. *prua* < VLat. **prōda*, alteration of Lat. *prōra* < Gk. *prōira*. See **per**[1]***.**]

prow•ess (prou′ĭs) *n.* **1.** Superior skill or ability. **2.** Superior strength, courage, or daring, esp. in battle. [ME *prowesse* < OFr. *proesse* < *prud, prou*, brave. See PROUD.]

prowl (proul) *v.* **prowled, prowl•ing, prowls.** —*tr.* To roam through stealthily, as in search of prey. —*intr.* To rove furtively or with predatory intent. —*n.* The act or an instance of prowling. —***idiom.* on the prowl.** Actively looking for something. [ME *prollen*, to move about.] —**prowl′er** *n.*

prowl car *n.* See **squad car.**

prox. *abbr.* Proximo.

prox•i•mal (prŏk′sə-məl) *adj.* **1.** Nearest; proximate. **2.** *Anat.* Nearer to a point of reference such as an origin, a point of attachment, or the midline of the body. [< Lat. *proximus*, nearest. See PROXIMATE.] —**prox′i•mal•ly** *adv.*

prox•i•mate (prŏk′sə-mĭt) *adj.* **1.** Closely related in space, time, or order; very near. See Syns at **close. 2.** Approximate. [Lat. *proximātus*, p.part. of *proximāre*, to come near < *proximus*, nearest. See **per**[1]***.**] —**prox′i•mate•ly** *adv.* —**prox′i•mate•ness** *n.*

prox•im•i•ty (prŏk-sĭm′ĭ-tē) *n.* The state, quality, sense, or fact of being near or next; closeness. See Usage Notes at **close, redundancy.** [ME < OFr. *proximite* < Lat. *proximitās* < *proximus*, nearest. See PROXIMATE.]

proximity fuze *n.* An electronic device for detonating a warhead as it approaches a target, used in antiaircraft shells.

prox•i•mo (prŏk′sə-mō′) *adv. Archaic.* Of or in the following month. [Lat. *proximō (mēnse)*, in the next (month).]

prox•y (prŏk′sē) *n., pl.* **-ies.** **1.** A person authorized to act for another; an agent or a substitute. **2.** The authority to act for another. **3.** The written authorization to act in place of another. [ME *proccy*, contraction of earlier *procracie*, annual payment to a prelate < AN *procuracie* < Med.Lat. *prōcūrātia*, alteration of Lat. *prōcūrātiō* < *prōcūrātus*, p.part. of *prōcūrāre*, to take care of. See PROCURE.]

prude (pro͞od) *n.* One who is excessively concerned with being or appearing proper, modest, or righteous. [Fr., short for *prude femme*, virtuous woman : OFr. *prude*, fem. of *prud*, virtuous; see PROUD + Fr. *femme*, woman (< Lat. *fēmina*; see FEMININE).]

pru•dence (pro͞od′ns) *n.* **1.** The state, quality, or fact of being prudent. **2.** Careful management; economy.

Syns: *prudence, discretion, foresight, forethought, circumspection.* These nouns refer to the exercise of good judgment, common sense, and even caution, especially in practical matters. *Prudence* is the most comprehensive: *"She had been forced into prudence in her youth, she learned romance as she grew older"* (Jane Austen). *Discretion* suggests wise self-restraint, as in resisting a rash impulse: *"The better part of valor is discretion"* (Shakespeare). *Foresight* implies the ability to foresee and make provision for what may happen: *the foresight to plan. Forethought* suggests advance consideration of future eventualities: *An empty refrigerator illustrates a lack of forethought. Circumspection* implies discretion, as out of concern for moral or social repercussions: *"The necessity of the times . . . calls for our utmost circumspection"* (Samuel Adams).

pru•dent (pro͞od′nt) *adj.* **1.** Wise in handling practical matters; exercising good judgment or common sense. **2.** Careful in regard to one's own interests; provident. **3.** Careful about one's conduct; circumspect. [ME < OFr. < Lat. *prūdēns*, *prūdent-*, contraction of *prōvidēns*, pr.part. of *prōvidēre*, to provide for. See PROVIDE.] —**pru′dent•ly** *adv.*

pru•den•tial (pro͞o-dĕn′shəl) *adj.* **1.** Arising from or characterized by prudence. **2.** Exercising prudence, good judgment, or common sense. —**pru•den′tial•ly** *adv.*

prud•er•y (pro͞o′də-rē) *n., pl.* **-ies. 1.** The state or quality of being prudish. **2.** An instance of prudish behavior or talk. [Fr. *pruderie* < *prude,* prude. See PRUDE.]

Prud•hoe Bay (pro͞od′hō, prŭd′-). An inlet of the Arctic Ocean on the N coast of AK E of the Colville R. delta.

prud•ish (pro͞o′dĭsh) *adj.* Marked by or exhibiting the characteristics of a prude; priggish. —**prud′ish•ly** *adv.* —**prud′ish•ness** *n.*

pru•i•nose (pro͞o′ə-nōs′) *adj. Bot.* Having a white powdery covering or bloom. [Lat. *pruīnōsus,* frosty < *pruīna,* hoarfrost. See **preus-***.]

prune1 (pro͞on) *n.* **1.a.** The partially dried fruit of any of several varieties of the common plum, *Prunus domestica.* **b.** Any kind of plum that can be dried without spoiling. **2.** *Slang.* An ill-tempered, stupid, or incompetent person. —*intr.v.* **pruned, prun•ing, prunes.** *Slang.* To make a facial expression exhibiting ill temper or disgust. [ME < OFr. < VLat. **prūna* < Lat. *prūnum,* plum.]

prune2 (pro͞on) *v.* **pruned, prun•ing, prunes.** —*tr.* **1.** To cut off or remove dead or living parts or branches of (a plant, for example) to improve shape or growth. **2.** To remove or cut out as superfluous. **3.** To reduce: *prune a budget.* —*intr.* To remove what is superfluous or undesirable. [ME *prouinen* < OFr. *proignier,* perh. < VLat. **prōretundiāre* : Lat. *prō-,* in front; see PRO-1 + Lat. *rotundus,* round (< *rota,* wheel; see **ret-***).] —**prun′er** *n.*

pru•nel•la (pro͞o-nĕl′ə) also **pru•nel•lo** (-nĕl′ō) *n., pl.* **-las** also **-los.** A heavy fabric of worsted twill, used chiefly for shoe uppers, clerical robes, and academic gowns. [Alteration of Fr. *prunelle,* sloe < OFr., dim. of *prune,* prune. See PRUNE1.]

prun•ing hook (pro͞o′nĭng) *n.* A long pole with a curved saw blade and usu. a clipping mechanism on one end, used esp. for pruning small trees.

pru•ri•ent (pro͝or′ē-ənt) *adj.* **1.** Inordinately interested in matters of sex; lascivious. **2.a.** Characterized by an inordinate interest in sex: *prurient thoughts.* **b.** Arousing or appealing to an inordinate interest in sex. [Lat. *prūriēns, prūrient-,* pr.part. of *prūrīre,* to yearn for, itch. See **preus-***.] —**pru′ri•ence, pru′ri•en•cy** *n.* —**pru′ri•ent•ly** *adv.*

pru•ri•go (pro͞o-rī′gō) *n.* A chronic skin disease having various causes, marked by the eruption of pale papules that itch severely. [Lat. *prūrīgō,* an itching < *prūrīre,* to itch. See **preus-***.] —**pru•rig′i•nous** (-rĭj′ə-nəs) *adj.*

pru•ri•tus (pro͞o-rī′təs) *n.* Severe itching, often of undamaged skin. [Lat. *prūrītus* < p.part. of *prūrīre,* to itch. See **preus-***.] —**pru•rit′ic** (-rĭt′ĭk) *adj.*

Prus•sia (prŭsh′ə). A historical region and former kingdom of N-central Europe including present-day N Germany and Poland. The kingdom of Prussia was proclaimed in 1701. It became a republic in 1918 and was formally abolished after World War II.

Prus•sian (prŭsh′ən) *adj.* **1.** Of or relating to Prussia or its Baltic or German inhabitants. **2.** Suggestive of or resembling the Junkers and the military class of Prussia. —*n.* **1.** Any of the western Balts inhabiting the region between the Vistula and Neman rivers in ancient times. **2.** A Baltic inhabitant of Prussia. **3.** A German inhabitant of Prussia.

Prussian blue *n.* **1.** An insoluble dark blue pigment and dye, ferric ferrocyanide or one of its modifications. **2.** See **iron blue. 3.** *Color.* A moderate to strong blue or deep greenish blue.

prus•si•ate (prŭs′ē-āt′) *n.* **1.** A ferrocyanide or ferricyanide. **2.** A salt of hydrocyanic acid; cyanide. [PRUSSI(C ACID) + -ATE2.]

prus•sic acid (prŭs′ĭk) *n.* See **hydrocyanic acid.** [So called because it was first obtained from Prussian blue.]

Prut (pro͞ot). A river rising in SW Ukraine and flowing c. 885 km (550 mi) to the Danube R.

pru•tah (pro͞o-tä′) *n., pl.* **-toth** or **-tot** (-tōt′). A coin formerly used in Israel, equal to one thousandth of a pound. [Mod. Heb. *pĕrūtâ.*]

pry1 (prī) *intr.v.* **pried** (prīd), **pry•ing, pries** (prīz). To look or inquire closely, curiously, or inquisitively, often in a furtive manner; snoop: *always prying into the affairs of others.* —*n., pl.* **pries** (prīz). **1.** The act of prying. **2.** An excessively inquisitive person; a snoop. [ME *prien.*] —**pry′ing•ly** *adv.*

pry2 (prī) *tr.v.* **pried** (prīd), **pry•ing, pries** (prīz). **1.** To raise, move, or force open with a lever. **2.** To obtain with effort or difficulty. —*n., pl.* **pries** (prīz). Something, such as a crowbar, that is used to apply leverage. [Alteration of PRIZE3.]

pry•er (prī′ər) *n.* Var. of **prier.**

Prynne (prĭn), **William.** 1600–69. English politician and pamphleteer whose attack on the theater, *Histrio-Mastix* (1633), resulted in his imprisonment and the amputation of his ears.

Ps or **Ps.** *abbr. Bible.* **1.** Psalm. **2.** Psalms.

p.s. *abbr.* Passenger steamer.

P.S. *abbr.* **1.** Permanent secretary. **2.** Police Sergeant. **3.** Also **PS** or **p.s.** Postscript. **4.** Public school.

psalm (säm) *n.* **1.** A sacred song; a hymn. **2. Psalms.** (*used with a sing. v.*) See table at **Bible.** —*tr.v.* **psalmed, psalm•ing, psalms.** To sing of or celebrate in psalms. [ME < OE < Lat. *psalmus* < Gk. *psalmos* < *psallein,* to play the harp. See **pōl-***.]

psalm•ist (sä′mĭst) *n.* A writer or composer of psalms.

psalm•o•dy (sä′mə-dē, săl′mə-) *n., pl.* **-dies. 1.** The act or practice of singing psalms in divine worship. **2.** The composition or arranging of psalms for singing. **3.** A collection of psalms. [ME *psalmodie* < LLat. *psalmōdia* < Gk., singing to the harp : *psalmos,* psalm; see PSALM + *ōidē, aoidē,* song; see ODE.] —**psalm′o•dist** *n.*

Psal•ter also **psal•ter** (sôl′tər) *n.* A book containing the Book of Psalms or a particular version of, musical setting for, or selection from it. [ME < OE *psaltere* and OFr. *psaultier,* both < LLat. *psaltērium* < Lat., psaltery < Gk. *psaltērion.* See PSALTERY.]

psal•te•ri•um (sôl-tîr′ē-əm) *n., pl.* **-te•ri•a** (-tîr′ē-ə). The omasum. [LLat. *psaltērium,* psalter (so called because when slit open its folds fall apart like the leaves of a book). See PSALTER.] —**psal•te′ri•al** *adj.*

psal•ter•y (sôl′tə-rē) also **psal•try** (sôl′trē) *n., pl.* **-ter•ies** also **-tries.** *Mus.* An ancient stringed instrument played by plucking the strings with the fingers or a plectrum. [ME *psalterie* < OFr. < Lat. *psaltērium* < Gk. *psaltērion* < *psallein,* to play the harp. See **pōl-***.]

p's and q's (pēz′ ən kyo͞oz′) *pl.n.* **1.** Socially correct behavior; manners. **2.** The way one acts; conduct.

PSAT *abbr.* Preliminary Scholastic Aptitude Test.

psec. *abbr.* Picosecond.

pse•phol•o•gy (sē-fŏl′ə-jē) *n.* The study of political elections. [Gk. *psēphos,* pebble, ballot + -LOGY.] —**pse′pho•log′i•cal** (sē′fə-lŏj′ĭ-kəl) *adj.* —**pse•phol′o•gist** *n.*

pseud. *abbr.* Pseudonym.

pseud•e•pig•ra•pha (so͞o′dĭ-pĭg′rə-fə) *pl.n.* **1.** Spurious writings, esp. writings falsely attributed to biblical characters or times. **2.** A body of texts written between 200 B.C. and A.D. 200 and spuriously ascribed to various prophets and kings of Hebrew Scriptures. [Gk. < neut. pl. of *pseudepigraphos,* falsely ascribed : *pseudēs,* false; see PSEUDO- + *epigraphein,* to inscribe (*epi-,* epi- + *graphein,* to write; see **gerbh-***).] —**pseud′e•pig′ra•phal** (-rə-fəl), **pseud′ep•i•graph′ic** (so͞o′dĕp-ĭ-grăf′ĭk), **pseud′ep•i•graph′i•cal** (-ĭ-kəl), **pseud′e•pig′ra•phous** (-rə-fəs) *adj.*

pseudo– or **pseud–** *pref.* **1.** False; deceptive; sham: *pseudoscience.* **2.** Apparently similar: *pseudocoel.* [Gk. < *pseudēs,* false < *pseudein,* to lie.]

pseu•do•carp (so͞o′də-kärp′) *n.* See **accessory fruit.** —**pseu′do•car′pous** *adj.*

pseu•do•coel (so͞o′də-sēl′) also **pseu•do•coe•lom** (so͞o′də-sē′ləm) *n.* An internal body cavity of some primitive invertebrates, similar to a coelom but lacking a mesodermal lining.

pseu•do•coe•lo•mate (so͞o′dō-sē′lə-māt′) *adj.* Having a pseudocoel. —*n.* An animal having a pseudocoel.

pseu•do•cy•e•sis (so͞o′dō-sī-ē′sĭs) *n.* A usu. psychosomatic condition in which physical symptoms of pregnancy are manifested without conception. [PSEUDO- + NLat. *cyēsis,* pregnancy (< Gk. *kuēsis* < *kuein,* to swell; see **keuə-***).]

pseu•do•mo•nad (so͞o′də-mō′năd′) *n.* Any of various gram-negative rod-shaped bacteria of the genus *Pseudomonas.* [< NLat. *Pseudomonas,* genus name : PSEUDO- + Lat. *monas, monad-,* unit (< Gk. < *monos,* single; see **men-4***).]

pseu•do•morph (so͞o′də-môrf′) *n.* **1.** A false, deceptive, or irregular form. **2.** *Mineral.* A mineral that has the crystalline form of another mineral rather than the form normally characteristic of its own composition. —**pseu′do•mor′phic, pseu′do•mor′phous** *adj.* —**pseu′do•mor′phism** *n.*

pseu•do•nym (so͞od′n-ĭm′) *n.* A fictitious name assumed by an author; a pen name. [Fr. *pseudonyme* < Gk. *pseudōnumon,* neut. of *pseudōnumos,* falsely named : *pseudēs,* false; see PSEUDO- + *onuma,* name; see **nō-men-***.] —**pseu•don′y•mous** (so͞o-dŏn′ə-məs) *adj.* —**pseu•don′y•mous•ly** *adv.*

pseu•do•pod (so͞o′də-pŏd′) *n.* A temporary projection of the cytoplasm of a cell, esp. an amoeba, that serves in locomotion and phagocytosis. —**pseu•dop′o•dal** (-dŏp′ə-dl), **pseu′do•po′di•al** (-pō′dē-əl) *adj.*

pseu•do•po•di•um (so͞o′də-pō′dē-əm) *n., pl.* **-po•di•a** (-pō′dē-ə). A pseudopod.

pseu•do•preg•nan•cy (so͞o′dō-prĕg′nən-sē) *n., pl.* **-cies. 1.** See **pseudocyesis. 2.** A condition resembling pregnancy that occurs in some mammals, usu. following infertile copulation. —**pseu′do•preg′nant** *adj.*

pseu•do•ran•dom (so͞o′dō-răn′dəm) *adj. Math.* Of, relating to, or being random numbers generated by a definite nonrandom computational process.

pseu•do•sci•ence (so͞o′dō-sī′əns) *n.* A theory, methodology, or practice purported to be scientific. —**pseu′do•sci′en•tif′ic** (-ən-tĭf′ĭk) *adj.* —**pseu′do•sci′en•tist** *n.*

psf. or **p.s.f.** *abbr.* Pounds per square foot.

pshaw (shô) *interj.* Used to indicate impatience, irritation, disapproval, or disbelief.

psi1 (sī, psī) *n.* The 23rd letter of the Greek alphabet. [ME < LGk. < Gk. *psei.*]

ă pat	oi boy
ā pay	ou out
âr care	o͝o took
ä father	o͞o boot
ĕ pet	ŭ cut
ē be	ûr urge
ĭ pit	th thin
ī pie	*th* this
îr pier	hw which
ŏ pot	zh vision
ō toe	ə about, item
ô paw	

Stress marks:
′ (primary);
′ (secondary), as in
dictionary (dĭk′shə-nĕr′ē)

ptarmigan
White-tailed ptarmigan
Lagopus leucurus

psi² or **p.s.i.** *abbr.* Pounds per square inch.
psil•o•cin (sĭl′ə-sĭn, sī′lə-) *n.* A hallucinogenic compound, $C_{12}H_{16}N_2O$, related to psilocybin. [PSILOC(YBIN) + -IN.]
psil•o•cy•bin (sĭl′ə-sī′bĭn, sī′lə-) *n.* A hallucinogenic compound, $C_{12}H_{17}N_2O_4P$, obtained from the mushroom *Psilocybe mexicana.* [NLat. *Psilocybe*, genus name (Gk. *psilos*, bare + Gk. *kubē*, head) + -IN.]
psi•lom•e•lane (sī-lŏm′ə-lān′) *n.* A mixture of black manganese oxide minerals. [Gk. *psilos*, bare + Gk. *melas*, *melan-*, black.]
psi particle *n.* See **J particle.**
psit•ta•cine (sĭt′ə-sīn′) *adj.* **1.** Relating to, resembling, or characteristic of parrots. **2.** Of or belonging to the family Psittacidae, which includes the parrots, macaws, and parakeets. [Lat. *psittacīnus* < *psittacus*, parrot < Gk. *psittakos.*]
psit•ta•co•sis (sĭt′ə-kō′sĭs) *n.* An infectious disease of parrots and related birds caused by the bacterium *Chlamydia psittaci* and communicable to humans, in whom it produces high fever, severe headache, and symptoms similar to pneumonia. [NLat. *psittacōsis* : Lat. *psittacus*, parrot (< Gk. *psittakos*) + -OSIS.] —**psit′ta•cot′ic** (-kŏt′ĭk, -kō′tĭk) *adj.*
Pskov (pə-skôf′, pskôf). A city of W-central Russia SSW of St. Petersburg; dating from the 8th cent. Pop. 194,000.
pso•as (sō′əs) *n.* Either of two muscles of the loin that rotate the hip joint and flex the spine. [NLat. < Gk. *psoa.*]
pso•cid (sō′sĭd, sŏs′ĭd) *n.* Any of various small, soft-bodied, sometimes winged insects of the order Psocoptera, which includes the booklice. [< NLat. *Psōcidae*, family name < *Psōcus*, type genus < Gk. *psōkhos*, dust.]
pso•ri•a•sis (sə-rī′ə-sĭs) *n.* A noncontagious inflammatory skin disease characterized by recurring scaly reddish patches. [Gk. *psōriasis*, itch, mange < *psōrian*, to have the itch < *psōra*, itch.] —**pso′ri•at′ic** (sôr′ē-ăt′ĭk, sōr′-) *adj.*
PST or **P.S.T.** *abbr.* Pacific Standard Time.
psych (sīk) *Informal.* —*n.* Psychology. —*v.* also **psyche. psyched, psych•ing, psyches.** —*tr.* **1.a.** To put into the right psychological frame of mind: *psyched up the team before the game.* **b.** To excite emotionally. **2.** To undermine the confidence of by psychological means; intimidate. **3.a.** To analyze, solve, or comprehend: *psyched out the test.* **b.** To anticipate or guess the intentions of. **4.** To psychoanalyze. —*intr.* To become confused or mentally deranged.
psych. *abbr.* Psychological; psychologist; psychology.
psych– *pref.* Var. of **psycho–.**
psy•chas•the•ni•a (sī′kəs-thē′nē-ə) *n.* A neurotic disorder characterized by phobias, obsessions, compulsions, or excessive anxiety. No longer in scientific use.
psy•che (sī′kē) *n.* **1.** The spirit or soul. **2.** *Psychiat.* The mind functioning as the center of thought, emotion, and behavior. [Lat. *psȳchē* < Gk. *psukhē*, soul. See **bhes-*.**]
Psy•che (sī′kē) *n. Gk. Myth.* A young woman who loved and was loved by Eros and who became the personification of the soul.
psy•che•de•li•a (sī′kĭ-dē′lē-ə, -dēl′yə) *n.* The subculture associated with psychedelic drugs.
psy•che•del•ic (sī′kĭ-dĕl′ĭk) *adj.* Of, characterized by, or generating hallucinations, distortions of perception, altered states of awareness, and occasionally states resembling psychosis. —*n.* A drug, such as LSD or mescaline, that produces such effects. [PSYCHE + Gk. *dēloun*, to make visible (< *dēlos*, clear, visible; see **deiw-***) + -IC.] —**psy′che•del′i•cal•ly** *adv.*
psychiatric hospital *n.* A hospital for the care and treatment of people affected with acute or chronic mental illness.
psy•chi•a•try (sĭ-kī′ə-trē, sī-) *n.* The branch of medicine that deals with mental and emotional disorders. —**psy′chi•at′ric** (sī′kē-ăt′rĭk), **psy′chi•at′ri•cal** (-rĭ-kəl) *adj.* —**psy′chi•at′ri•cal•ly** *adv.* —**psy•chi′a•trist** (-trĭst) *n.*
psy•chic (sī′kĭk) *n.* **1.** A person apparently responsive to psychic forces. **2.** See **medium** 5. —*adj.* Also **psy•chi•cal** (-kĭ-kəl). **1.** Of, relating to, affecting, or influenced by the human mind or psyche; mental. **2.a.** Capable of extraordinary mental processes, such as mental telepathy. **b.** Of or relating to such mental processes. [< Gk. *psukhikos*, of the soul < *psukhē*, soul. See **bhes-*.**] —**psy′chi•cal•ly** *adv.*
psy•cho (sī′kō) *Slang.* —*n., pl.* **-chos.** A psychopath. —*adj.* Crazy; insane.
psycho– or **psych–** *pref.* **1.a.** Mind; mental: *psychogenic.* **b.** Mental activities or processes: *psychomotor.* **2.** Psychology; psychological: *psychohistory.* [Gk. *psukho-*, soul, life < *psukhē*. See **bhes-*.**]
psy•cho•a•cous•tics (sī′kō-ə-ko͞o′stĭks) *n.* (*used with a sing. v.*) The scientific study of the perception of sound. —**psy′cho•a•cous′tic, psy′cho•a•cous′ti•cal** *adj.*
psy•cho•ac•tive (sī′kō-ăk′tĭv) *adj.* Affecting the mind or mental processes. Used of a drug.
psy•cho•a•nal•y•sis (sī′kō-ə-năl′ĭ-sĭs) *n., pl.* **-ses** (-sēz′). **1.a.** The method of psychiatric therapy originated by Sigmund Freud in which free association, dream interpretation, and analysis of resistance and transference are used to explore repressed or unconscious impulses, anxieties, and internal conflicts. **b.** The theory of personality developed by Freud that focuses on repression and unconscious forces and includes the concepts of infantile sexuality and division of the psyche into the id, ego, and superego. **2.** Psychiatric treatment incorporating this method and theory. —**psy′cho•an′a•lyst** (-ăn′ə-lĭst) *n.* —**psy′cho•an′a•lyt′ic** (-ăn′ə-lĭt′ĭk), **psy′cho•an′a•lyt′i•cal** (-ĭ-kəl) *adj.*
psy•cho•an•a•lyze (sī′kō-ăn′ə-līz′) *tr.v.* **-lyzed, -lyz•ing, -lyz•es.** To analyze and treat by psychoanalysis.
psy•cho•bab•ble (sī′kō-băb′əl) *n.* Psychological jargon, esp. that of psychotherapy. —**psy′cho•bab′bler** *n.*
psy•cho•bi•og•ra•phy (sī′kō-bī-ŏg′rə-fē, -bē-) *n., pl.* **-phies.** A biography that analyzes the psychological character of its subject. —**psy′cho•bi•og′ra•pher** *n.*
psy•cho•bi•ol•o•gy (sī′kō-bī-ŏl′ə-jē) *n.* **1.** The study of the biological foundations of the mind, emotions, and mental processes. **2.** The school of psychiatry that interprets personality, behavior, and mental illness in terms of adaptive responses to biological, social, cultural, and environmental factors. —**psy′cho•bi′o•log′ic** (-bī′ə-lŏj′ĭk), **psy′cho•bi′o•log′i•cal** (-ĭ-kəl) *adj.* —**psy′cho•bi•ol′o•gist** *n.*
psy•cho•chem•i•cal (sī′kō-kĕm′ĭ-kəl) *n.* A psychoactive drug or substance. —**psy′cho•chem′i•cal** *adj.*
psy•cho•dra•ma (sī′kə-drä′mə, -drăm′ə) *n.* **1.** A psychotherapeutic and analytic technique in which people are assigned roles to be played spontaneously within a dramatic context devised by a therapist. **2.** A dramatization in which this technique is employed. —**psy′cho•dra•mat′ic** (-drə-măt′ĭk) *adj.*
psy•cho•dy•nam•ics (sī′kō-dī-năm′ĭks, -dĭ-) *n.* **1.** (*used with a sing. or pl. v.*) The interaction of various conscious and unconscious mental or emotional processes, esp. as they influence personality and behavior. **2.** (*used with a sing. v.*) The study of personality and behavior in terms of such processes. —**psy′cho•dy•nam′ic** *adj.*
psy•cho•gen•e•sis (sī′kə-jĕn′ĭ-sĭs) *n.* **1.** The origin and development of psychological processes, personality, or behavior. **2.** Development of a physical disorder or illness resulting from psychic, rather than physiological, factors. —**psy′cho•ge•net′ic** (-jə-nĕt′ĭk) *adj.* —**psy′cho•ge•net′i•cal•ly** *adv.*
psy•cho•gen•ic (sī′kə-jĕn′ĭk) *adj.* Originating in the mind or in mental or emotional processes. Used of certain disorders. —**psy′cho•gen′i•cal•ly** *adv.*
psy•cho•graph (sī′kə-grăf′) *n.* A graphic representation or chart of personality traits. —**psy′cho•graph′ic** *adj.*
psy•cho•his•to•ry (sī′kō-hĭs′tə-rē) *n., pl.* **-ries.** A psychological or psychoanalytic interpretation or study of historical events or persons. —**psy′cho•his•tor′i•an** (-hĭ-stôr′ē-ən, -stŏr′-) *n.*
psy•cho•ki•ne•sis (sī′kō-kĭ-nē′sĭs, -kī-) *n., pl.* **-ses** (-sēz). The production or control of motion, esp. in inanimate objects, purportedly by psychic powers. —**psy′cho•ki•net′ic** (-kĭ-nĕt′ĭk, -kī-) *adj.* —**psy′cho•ki•net′i•cal•ly** *adv.*
psychol. *abbr.* Psychological; psychologist; psychology.
psy•cho•lin•guis•tics (sī′kō-lĭng-gwĭs′tĭks) *n.* (*used with a sing. v.*) The study of the influence of psychological factors on the development, use, and interpretation of language. —**psy′cho•lin′guist** *n.* —**psy′cho•lin•guis′tic** *adj.*
psy•cho•log•i•cal (sī′kə-lŏj′ĭ-kəl) also **psy•cho•log•ic** (-lŏj′ĭk) *adj.* **1.** Of or relating to psychology. **2.** Of, relating to, or arising from the mind or emotions. **3.** Influencing or intended to influence the mind or emotions. **4.** *Color.* Of or being any of certain primary colors whose mixture may be subjectively conceived as producing other colors. —**psy′cho•log′i•cal•ly** *adv.*
psychological moment *n.* The time at which the mental state of a person is most likely to produce a desired response.
psy•chol•o•gist (sī-kŏl′ə-jĭst) *n.* A person trained and educated to perform psychological research, testing, and therapy.
psy•chol•o•gize (sī-kŏl′ə-jīz′) *v.* **-gized, -giz•ing, -giz•es.** —*tr.* To explain (behavior) in psychological terms. —*intr.* To investigate, reason, or speculate in psychological terms.
psy•chol•o•gy (sī-kŏl′ə-jē) *n., pl.* **-gies. 1.** The science that deals with mental processes and behavior. **2.** The emotional and behavioral characteristics of an individual, a group, or an activity. **3.** Subtle tactical action or argument used to manipulate or influence another. **4.** *Philos.* The branch of metaphysics that studies the soul, the mind, and the relationship of life and mind to the functions of the body.
psy•cho•met•rics (sī′kə-mĕt′rĭks) *n.* (*used with a sing. v.*) The branch of psychology that deals with the design, administration, and interpretation of quantitative tests for the measurement of psychological variables such as intelligence, aptitude, and personality traits. —**psy′cho•met′ric, psy′cho•met′ri•cal** *adj.* —**psy•chom′e•tri′cian** (sī-kŏm′ĭ-trĭsh′ən), **psy•chom′e•trist** (sī-kŏm′ĭ-trĭst) *n.*
psy•chom•e•try (sī-kŏm′ĭ-trē) *n.* **1.** See **psychometrics. 2.** The ability or art of divining information about people or events associated with an object solely by touching or being near to it.
psy•cho•mo•tor (sī′kō-mō′tər) *adj.* Of or relating to movement or muscular activity associated with mental processes.
psy•cho•neu•ro•sis (sī′kō-no͞o-rō′sĭs, -nyo͞o-) *n., pl.* **-ses** (-sēz). Neurosis. —**psy′cho•neu•rot′ic** (-rŏt′ĭk) *adj.* & *n.*
psy•cho•path (sī′kə-păth′) *n.* A person with an antisocial per-

sonality disorder, esp. one manifested in aggressive, perverted, or criminal behavior. [Back-formation < PSYCHOPATHIC.]

psy•cho•path•ic (sī′kə-păth′ĭk) *adj.* **1.** Of, relating to, or characterized by psychopathy. **2.** Relating to or being a psychopath. —**psy′cho•path′i•cal•ly** *adv.*

psy•cho•pa•thol•o•gy (sī′kō-pə-thŏl′ə-jē, -pă-) *n.* The study of the origin, development, and manifestations of mental or behavioral disorders. —**psy′cho•path′o•log′i•cal** (-păth′ə-lŏj′ĭ-kəl), **psy′cho•path′o•log′ic** (-lŏj′ĭk) *adj.* —**psy′cho•pa•thol′o•gist** *n.*

psy•chop•a•thy (sī-kŏp′ə-thē) *n.* Mental disorder, esp. when manifested by antisocial behavior.

psy•cho•phar•ma•col•o•gy (sī′kō-fär′mə-kŏl′ə-jē) *n.* The branch of pharmacology that deals with the study of the actions and effects of psychoactive drugs. —**psy′cho•phar′ma•co•log′ic** (-kə-lŏj′ĭk), **psy′cho•phar′ma•co•log′i•cal** (-ĭ-kəl) *adj.* —**psy′cho•phar′ma•col′o•gist** *n.*

psy•cho•phys•ics (sī′kō-fĭz′ĭks) *n.* (*used with a sing. v.*) The branch of psychology that deals with the relationships between physical stimuli and sensory response. —**psy′cho•phys′i•cal** *adj.*

psy•cho•phys•i•ol•o•gy (sī′kō-fĭz′ē-ŏl′ə-jē) *n.* The study of correlations between the mind, behavior, and bodily mechanisms. —**psy′cho•phys′i•o•log′i•cal** (-fĭz′ē-ə-lŏj′ĭ-kəl), **psy′cho•phys′i•o•log′ic** (-lŏj′ĭk) *adj.*

psy•cho•sex•u•al (sī′kō-sĕk′shōō-əl) *adj.* Of or relating to the mental and emotional aspects of sexuality. —**psy′cho•sex′u•al′i•ty** (-ăl′ĭ-tē) *n.* —**psy′cho•sex′u•al•ly** *adv.*

psy•cho•sis (sī-kō′sĭs) *n., pl.* **-ses** (-sēz). A severe mental disorder, with or without organic damage, characterized by derangement of personality and loss of contact with reality.

psy•cho•so•cial (sī′kō-sō′shəl) *adj.* Involving aspects of social and psychological behavior. —**psy′cho•so′cial•ly** *adv.*

psy•cho•so•mat•ic (sī′kō-sō-măt′ĭk) *adj.* **1.** Of or relating to a disorder having physical symptoms but originating from mental or emotional causes. **2.** Relating to or concerned with the influence of the mind on the body, esp. with respect to disease. —**psy′cho•so•mat′i•cal•ly** *adv.*

psy•cho•sur•ger•y (sī′kō-sûr′jə-rē) *n., pl.* **-ies.** Brain surgery used to treat severe, intractable mental or behavioral disorders. —**psy′cho•sur′geon** (-sûr′jən) *n.* —**psy′cho•sur′gi•cal** (-jĭ-kəl) *adj.*

psy•cho•ther•a•peu•tics (sī′kō-thĕr′ə-pyōō′tĭks) *n.* (*used with a sing. v.*) Psychotherapy.

psy•cho•ther•a•py (sī′kō-thĕr′ə-pē) *n., pl.* **-pies.** The treatment of mental and emotional disorders through encouraging communication of conflicts and insight into problems. —**psy′cho•ther′a•peu′tic** (-pyōō′tĭk) *adj.* —**psy′cho•ther′a•pist** *n.*

psy•chot•ic (sī-kŏt′ĭk) *adj.* Of, relating to, or affected by psychosis. —*n.* A person affected by psychosis.

psy•chot•o•mi•met•ic (sī-kŏt′ō-mə-mĕt′ĭk, -mī-) *adj.* Tending to induce hallucinations, delusions, or other symptoms of a psychosis. Used of a drug. [Alteration of *psychosomimetic* : PSYCHOS(IS) + MIMETIC.] —**psy•chot′o•mi•met′ic** *n.*

psy•cho•tro•pic (sī′kə-trō′pĭk, -trŏp′ĭk) *adj.* Having an altering effect on perception or behavior. Used esp. of a drug. —*n.* A psychotropic drug or other agent.

psychro– *pref.* Cold: *psychrophilic.* [Gk. *psukhro-* < *psukhros,* cold.]

psy•chrom•e•ter (sī-krŏm′ĭ-tər) *n.* An instrument that uses the difference in readings between wet-bulb and dry-bulb thermometers to measure the relative humidity of air.

psy•chro•phil•ic (sī′krō-fĭl′ĭk) *adj. Biol.* Thriving at relatively low temperatures. Used of certain bacteria. —**psy′chro•phile′** (-fīl′) *n.*

psyl•la (sĭl′ə) also **psyl•lid** (sĭl′ĭd) *n.* Any of various jumping plant lice of the family Psyllidae, esp. of the genus *Psylla.* [NLat. *Psylla,* type genus < Gk. *psulla,* flea.]

psyl•li•um (sĭl′ē-əm) *n.* **1.** An annual Eurasian plant (*Plantago psyllium*) having opposite leaves and small flowers borne in dense spikes. **2.** The seeds of this plant, used as a mild bulk laxative. [NLat. < Gk. *psullion,* dim. of *psulla,* flea.]

Pt The symbol for the element **platinum** 1.

PT *abbr.* Patrol torpedo.

pt. *abbr.* **1.** Part. **2.** Payment. **3.** Pint. **4.** Point. **5.** Port. **6.** *Gram.* Preterit.

p.t. *abbr.* Pro tempore.

P.T. *abbr.* **1.** Physical therapy. **2.** Physical training.

PTA or **P.T.A.** *abbr.* Parent Teacher Association.

pta. *abbr.* Peseta.

ptar•mi•gan (tär′mĭ-gən) *n., pl.* **ptarmigan** or **-gans.** Any of various grouses of the genus *Lagopus* of the Northern Hemisphere having plumage that is brown or gray in summer and white in winter. [Alteration of Sc.Gael. *tàrmachan.*]

PT boat (pē-tē′) *n.* A fast, maneuverable, lightly armed vessel used to torpedo enemy shipping. [P(ATROL) + T(ORPEDO) BOAT.]

PTC *abbr.* Phenylthiocarbamide.

–pter *suff.* Wing; winglike part: *ornithopter.* [< Gk. *pteron,* feather, wing. See **pet-***.]

pter•i•dol•o•gy (tĕr′ĭ-dŏl′ə-jē) *n.* The study of ferns. [Gk. *pteris, pterid-,* fern (< *pteron,* feather, wing; see **pet-***) + -LOGY.] —**pter′i•do•log′i•cal** (-də-lŏj′ĭ-kəl) *adj.*

pte•rid•o•phyte (tə-rĭd′ə-fīt′, tĕr′ĭ-dō-) *n.* Any of various vascular plants that reproduce by means of spores, including the ferns. [< NLat. *Pteridophyta,* former division name : Gk. *pteris, pterid-,* fern; see PTERIDOLOGY + Gk. *phuton,* plant; see -PHYTE.] —**pte•rid′o•phyt′ic** (tə-rĭd′ə-fĭt′ĭk, tĕr′ĭ-dō-), **pter′i•doph′y•tous** (tĕr′ĭ-dŏf′ĭ-təs) *adj.*

pter•o•dac•tyl (tĕr′ə-dăk′təl) *n.* Any of various small, mostly tailless, extinct flying reptiles of the order Pterosauria that existed during the Jurassic and Cretaceous periods. [NLat. *Pterodactylus,* reptile genus : Gk. *pteron,* feather, wing; see -PTER + Gk. *daktulos,* finger.] —**pter′o•dac′ty•loid′** *adj.*

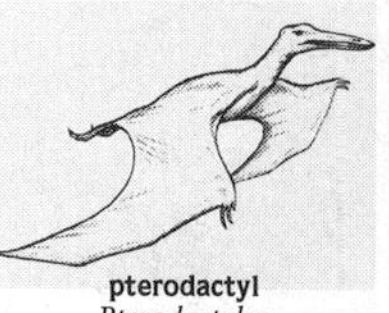
pterodactyl
Pterodactylus

pter•o•pod (tĕr′ə-pŏd′) *n.* Any of various gastropod mollusks of the subclass Opisthobranchia that have winglike lobes on the feet. [< NLat. *Pteropoda,* order name : Gk. *pteron,* feather, wing; see -PTER + NLat. *-poda,* -pod.] —**pter′o•pod′** *adj.* —**pte•rop′o•dan** (tə-rŏp′ə-dən) *adj. & n.*

pter•o•saur (tĕr′ə-sôr′) *n.* Any of various extinct flying reptiles of the order Pterosauria of the Jurassic and Cretaceous periods, characterized by wings consisting of a flap of skin supported by the very long fourth digit on each forelimb. [< NLat. *Pterosauria,* order name : Gk. *pteron,* feather, wing; see -PTER + Gk. *sauros,* lizard.]

pte•ryg•i•um (tə-rĭj′ē-əm) *n., pl.* **-i•ums** or **-i•a** (-ē-ə). An abnormal mass of tissue arising from the conjunctiva of the eye that obstructs vision by growing over the cornea. [NLat. < Gk. *pterugion,* dim. of *pterux, pterug-,* wing. See PTERYGOID.] —**pte•ryg′i•al** (-əl) *adj.*

pter•y•goid (tĕr′ĭ-goid′) *adj. Anat.* **1.** Of, relating to, or located in the region of the sphenoid bone. **2.** Resembling a wing; winglike. —*n.* Either of two processes descending from the body of the sphenoid bone. [Gk. *pterugoeidēs,* winglike : *pterux, pterug-,* wing; see **pet-*** + *-oeidēs,* -oid.]

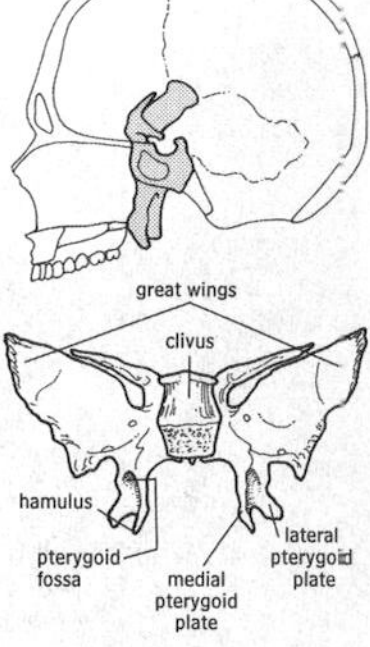

pterygoid

pter•y•la (tĕr′ə-lə) *n., pl.* **-lae** (-lē′, -lī′). An area on the skin of a bird from which feathers grow. [NLat. : Gk. *pteron,* wing, feather; see -PTER + Gk. *hulē,* forest, matter.]

ptg. *abbr.* Printing.

PTH *abbr.* Parathyroid hormone.

ptis•an (tĭz′ən, tĭ-zăn′) *n.* A medicinal infusion, such as sweetened barley water. [ME *tisane,* peeled barley, barley water < OFr. < Lat. *ptisana, tisana* < Gk. *ptisanē* < *ptissein,* to crush.]

PTO *abbr.* **1.** Parent Teacher Organization. **2.** Power takeoff.

p.t.o. or **PTO** *abbr.* Please turn over.

Ptol•e•ma•ic (tŏl′ə-mā′ĭk) *adj.* **1.** Of or relating to the astronomer Ptolemy. **2.** Of or relating to the Ptolemies or to Egypt during their rule.

Ptolemaic system *n.* The astronomical system of Ptolemy, in which Earth is at the center of the universe.

Ptol•e•my[1] (tŏl′ə-mē). An Egyptian dynasty of Macedonian kings (323–30 B.C.) including **Ptolemy I** (367?–283?), who succeeded Alexander the Great as ruler of Egypt (323–285), and **Ptolemy XV** (47–30), who ruled as coregent (44–30) with Cleopatra.

Ptol•e•my[2] (tŏl′ə-mē). fl. 2nd cent. A.D. Alexandrian astronomer and geographer who based his theories on the belief that all heavenly bodies revolve around the earth.

pto•maine (tō′mān′, tō-mān′) *n.* A nitrogenous organic compound produced by putrefaction of protein. [Ital. *ptomaina* < Gk. *ptōma,* corpse < *piptein,* to fall. See **pet-***.]

ptomaine poi•son•ing (poi′zə-nĭng) *n.* Food poisoning, erroneously believed to be the result of ptomaine ingestion. Not in scientific use.

pto•sis (tō′sĭs) *n., pl.* **-ses** (-sēz). Abnormal lowering or drooping of an organ or a part, as of the upper eyelid. [Gk. *ptōsis,* fall < *piptein,* to fall. See **pet-***.] —**pto′tic** (-tĭk) *adj.*

PTSD *abbr.* Posttraumatic stress disorder.

PTV *abbr.* **1.** Pay television. **2.** Public television.

pty. *abbr.* Proprietary.

pty•a•lin (tī′ə-lĭn) *n.* A form of amylase in the saliva of human beings and some animals that catalyzes the hydrolysis of starch into maltose and dextrin. [Gk. *ptualon,* saliva (< *ptuein,* to spit) + -IN.]

pty•a•lism (tī′ə-lĭz′əm) *n.* Excessive flow of saliva. [Gk. *ptualismos,* salivation < *ptualizein,* to salivate < *ptualon,* saliva < *ptuein,* to spit.]

Pu The symbol for the element **plutonium.**

pub (pŭb) *n.* A place of business where alcoholic beverages are sold and drunk. [Short for PUBLIC HOUSE.]

pub. *abbr.* **1.** Public. **2.** Publication. **3.** Published. **4.** Publisher.

pub-crawl (pŭb′krôl′) *intr.v.* **-crawled, -crawl•ing, -crawls.** *Slang.* To visit a series of bars.

pu•ber•ty (pyōō′bər-tē) *n.* The stage of adolescence in which an individual becomes physiologically capable of sexual reproduction. [ME *puberte* < OFr. < Lat. *pūbertās* < *pūbēs, pūber-,* adult.] —**pu′ber•tal, pu′ber•al** (-bər-əl) *adj.*

pu•ber•u•lent (pyōō-bĕr′yə-lənt, -bĕr′ə-) also **pu•ber•u•lous** (-bĕr′yə-ləs, -bĕr′ə-) *adj.* Covered with minute hairs or very fine down; finely pubescent. [Lat. *pūber,* downy, adult + *-ulentus,* abounding in.]

pu•bes (pyōō′bēz) *n., pl.* **pubes. 1.** The lower part of the abdomen, esp. the region surrounding the external genitalia.

ă **pat**	oi **boy**
ā **pay**	ou **out**
âr **care**	ŏŏ **took**
ä **father**	ōō **boot**
ĕ **pet**	ŭ **cut**
ē **be**	ûr **urge**
ĭ **pit**	th **thin**
ī **pie**	*th* **this**
îr **pier**	hw **which**
ŏ **pot**	zh **vision**
ō **toe**	ə **about,**
ô **paw**	**item**

Stress marks:
′ (primary);
′ (secondary), as in
dictionary (dĭk′shə-nĕr′ē)

2. The hair that appears on this region at puberty. [Lat. *pūbēs*.]

pu•bes•cence (pyo͞o-bĕs′əns) *n.* **1.** The state of being pubescent. **2.** The attainment or onset of puberty. **3.** A covering of soft down or short hairs, as on certain plants and insects.

pu•bes•cent (pyo͞o-bĕs′ənt) *adj.* **1.** Reaching or having reached puberty. **2.** Covered with short hairs or soft down. [Lat. *pūbēscēns, pūbēscent*, pr.part. of *pūbēscere*, to reach puberty < *pūbēs*, adult.]

pu•bic (pyo͞o′bĭk) *adj.* Of, relating to, or located in the region of the pubis or the pubes. [< PUBES and PUBIS.]

pu•bis (pyo͞o′bĭs) *n., pl.* **-bes** (-bēz). The forward portion of either of the hipbones, at the juncture forming the front arch of the pelvis. [Short for NLat. *(os) pūbis*, (bone) of the groin < Lat., genitive of *pūbēs*, groin.]

publ. *abbr.* **1.** Publication. **2.** Published. **3.** Publisher.

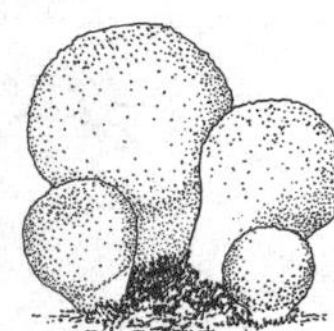

puffball
Gem puffball
Lycoperdon perlatum

pub•lic (pŭb′lĭk) *adj.* **1.** Of, concerning, or affecting the community or the people. **2.** Maintained for or used by the people or community. **3.** Capitalized in shares of stock that can be traded on the open market. **4.** Participated in or attended by the people or community. **5.** Connected with or acting on behalf of the people, community, or government. **6.** Open to the knowledge or judgment of all. —*n.* **1.** The community or the people as a whole. **2.** A group of people sharing a common interest. **3.** Admirers or followers, esp. of a famous person. See Usage Note at **collective noun.** —***idioms.* go public.** To become publicly owned by launching shares of stock onto the open market. **go public with.** *Informal.* To reveal to the public a previously unknown or secret piece of information. **in public.** In such a way as to be visible to the scrutiny of the people. [ME *publik* < OFr. *public* < Lat. *pūblicus*, alteration (influenced by *pūbēs*, adult population; see PUBERTY) of *poplicus* < *populus*, people, of Etruscan orig.] —**pub′lic•ness** *n.*

public access *n.* The availability of television or radio broadcast facilities, as provided by law, for use by the public for presentation of programs.

pub•lic-ad•dress system (pŭb′lĭk-ə-drĕs′) *n.* An electronic amplification apparatus for broadcasting in public areas.

pub•li•can (pŭb′lĭ-kən) *n.* **1.** *Chiefly British.* The keeper of a public house or tavern. **2.** A collector of public taxes or tolls in the ancient Roman Empire. **3.** A collector of taxes or tribute from the public. [ME, tax collector < OFr. < Lat. *pūblicānus* < *pūblicum*, public revenue < neut. of *pūblicus*, public. See PUBLIC.]

puffin
Horned puffin
Fratercula corniculata

public assistance *n.* Aid given to the needy, the aged, or the inhabitants of a disaster-stricken area; relief.

pub•li•ca•tion (pŭb′lĭ-kā′shən) *n.* **1.** The act or process of publishing printed matter. **2.** An issue of printed material offered for sale or distribution. **3.** Communication of information to the public. [Ult. < Lat. *pūblicātiō, pūblicātiōn-*, making public < *pūblicātus*, p.part. of *pūblicāre*, to make public < *pūblicus*, public. See PUBLIC.]

public defender *n. Law.* An attorney or a staff of attorneys, usu. publicly appointed, having responsibility for the defense of those unable to afford or obtain legal assistance.

public domain *n. Law.* **1.** Land owned and controlled by the state or federal government. **2.** The status of publications, products, and processes not protected under patent or copyright.

public health *n.* The science and practice of protecting and improving the health of a community, as by preventive medicine, health education, and sanitary measures.

public house *n. Chiefly British.* A place, such as a tavern or bar, that is licensed to sell alcoholic beverages.

public housing *n.* Housing built, operated, and owned by a government and usu. provided at nominal rent to the needy.

public interest *n.* **1.** The well-being of the general public; the commonweal. **2.** The attention of the people with respect to events or occurrences.

pub•li•cist (pŭb′lĭ-sĭst) *n.* One who publicizes, esp. a press or publicity agent.

pub•lic•i•ty (pŭ-blĭs′ĭ-tē) *n.* **1.a.** Information disseminated through various media to attract public notice, as of a person or product. **b.** Public interest, notice, or notoriety achieved by the spreading of such information. **c.** The act, process, or occupation of disseminating information to gain public interest. **2.** The condition of being public. [Fr. *publicité* < *public*, public < OFr. See PUBLIC.]

pub•li•cize (pŭb′lĭ-sīz′) *tr.v.* **-cized, -ciz•ing, -ciz•es.** To give publicity to.

public law *n.* **1.** The branch of law that deals with the state or government and its relationships with individuals or other governments. **2.** A law affecting the public.

public library *n.* A noncommercial library often supported with public funds, intended for use by the general public.

pub•lic•ly (pŭb′lĭk-lē) *adv.* **1.** In a public manner; openly. **2.** By or with consent of the public.

public offering *n.* The sale of a new securities issue to the public by way of an underwriter, a transaction that must be registered with the Securities and Exchange Commission.

public opinion *n.* Public consensus, as with respect to an issue. —**pub′lic-o•pin′ion** (pŭb′lĭk-ə-pĭn′yən) *adj.*

public policy *n.* The policy or set of policies forming the foundation of public laws, esp. when not yet formally enunciated.

public prosecutor *n. Law.* A government official who prosecutes criminal actions on behalf of the state or community.

public relations *pl.n.* **1.** *(used with a sing. v.)* The art or science of establishing and promoting a favorable relationship with the public. **2.** *(used with a pl. v.)* The methods and activities used to establish and promote such a relationship. **3.** *(used with a sing. or pl. v.)* The degree of success obtained in achieving such a relationship.

public sale *n.* An auction of property or merchandise.

public school *n.* **1.** An elementary or secondary school in the United States supported by public funds and providing free education for children of a community or district. **2.** A private boarding secondary school in Great Britain.

public servant *n.* A person who holds a government position by election or appointment.

public service *n.* **1.** Employment within a governmental system, esp. within the civil service. **2.** A service performed for the benefit of the public, esp. by a nonprofit organization. **3.** The business of supplying an essential commodity or service to the public. —**pub′lic-serv′ice** (pŭb′lĭk-sûr′vĭs) *adj.*

public-service corporation *n.* A corporation providing essential services, such as water or electricity, to the public.

public speaking *n.* The act, art, or process of making effective speeches before an audience. —**public speaker** *n.*

pub•lic-spir•it•ed (pŭb′lĭk-spĭr′ĭ-tĭd) *adj.* Motivated by or exhibiting devotion to the public welfare. —**pub′lic-spir′it•ed•ness** *n.*

public television *n.* Noncommercial television that provides programs, esp. of an educational nature, for the public.

public utility *n.* **1.** A private business organization, subject to governmental regulation, that provides an essential commodity or service to the public. **2.** Stock shares issued by such a company. Often used in the plural.

public works *pl.n.* Construction projects, such as highways or dams, financed by public funds and constructed by a government for the benefit or use of the general public.

pub•lish (pŭb′lĭsh) *v.* **-lished, -lish•ing, -lish•es.** —*tr.* **1.** To prepare and issue (printed material) for public distribution or sale. **2.** To bring to the public attention; announce. —*intr.* **1.** To issue a publication. **2.** To be the writer or author of published works or a work. [ME *publicen, publishen*, to make known publicly < OFr. *publier* < Lat. *pūblicāre*. See PUBLICATION.] —**pub′lish•a•ble** *adj.*

pub•lish•er (pŭb′lĭ-shər) *n.* One engaged in publishing printed material.

Puc•ci•ni (po͞o-chē′nē), **Giacomo.** 1858–1924. Italian composer whose operas include *Madame Butterfly* (1904).

puc•coon (pə-ko͞on′) *n.* **1.a.** Any of several North American plants of the genus *Lithospermum*, having orange or yellow flowers and roots that yield a red dye. **b.** Any of several plants, such as the bloodroot, whose roots yield a reddish dye. **2.** Any of these dyes. [Of Virginia Algonquian orig.]

puce (pyo͞os) *n. Color.* A deep red to dark grayish purple. [Fr. *(couleur) puce*, flea (color), puce < OFr., var. of *pulce*, flea < Lat. *pūlex, pūlic-*.] —**puce** *adj.*

puck (pŭk) *n. Sports.* A hard rubber disk used in ice hockey. [Perh. < dial. *puck*, to strike.]

Puck (pŭk) *n.* A mischievous sprite in English folklore. [ME *pouke*, goblin < OE *pūca*.]

puck•a (pŭk′ə) *adj.* Var. of **pukka.**

puck•er (pŭk′ər) *v.* **-ered, -er•ing, -ers.** —*tr.* To gather into small wrinkles or folds. —*intr.* To become gathered, contracted, and wrinkled. —*n.* A wrinkle or wrinkled part, as in tightly stitched cloth. [Prob. freq. of dialectal *pock*, bag, sack, var. of POKE[3].]

puck•ish (pŭk′ĭsh) *adj.* Mischievous; impish. —**puck′ish•ly** *adv.* —**puck′ish•ness** *n.*

pud•ding (po͝od′ĭng) *n.* **1.a.** A sweet dessert, usu. containing flour or a cereal product, that has been boiled, steamed, or baked. **b.** A mixture with a soft puddinglike consistency. **2.** A sausagelike preparation stuffed into a bag or skin and boiled. [ME, a kind of sausage < OFr. *boudin*.]

pud•ding•stone (po͝od′ĭng-stōn′) *n. Geol.* A conglomerate.

pud•dle (pŭd′l) *n.* **1.a.** A small pool of water, esp. rainwater. **b.** A small pool of a liquid. **2.** A tempered paste of wet clay and sand that serves as waterproofing when dry. —*v.* **-dled, -dling, -dles.** —*tr.* **1.** To make muddy. **2.** To work (clay or sand) into puddle. **3.** To process (impure metal) by puddling. —*intr.* To splash or dabble in or as if in a pool of liquid. [ME *podel*, dim. of OE *pudd*, ditch.] —**pud′dly** *adj.*

pud•dler (pŭd′lər) *n.* One that puddles iron or clay.

pud•dling (pŭd′lĭng) *n.* **1.** Purification of impure metal, esp. pig iron, by heating and stirring in an oxidizing atmosphere. **2.** Tempering of wet material, such as clay, to make puddle.

pu•den•cy (pyo͞od′n-sē) *n.* Modesty. [LLat. *pudentia* < Lat. *pudēre*, to make or be ashamed.]

pu•den•dum (pyo͞o-dĕn′dəm) *n., pl.* **-da** (-də). The human external genitalia, esp. of a woman. Often used in the plural. [Lat., neut. gerundive of *pudēre*, to make or be ashamed.] —**pu•den′dal** (-dĕn′dəl) *adj.*

pudg•y (pŭj′ē) *adj.* **-i•er, -i•est.** Short and fat; chubby: *pudgy fingers.* See Syns at **fat.** [< *pudge*, something thick and short.] **— pudg′i•ness** *n.*

Pueb•la (pwĕb′lä). A city of E-central Mexico ESE of Mexico City; founded by the Spanish in 1532. Pop. 835,759.

pueb•lo (pwĕb′lō) *n., pl.* **-los. 1. Pueblo,** *pl.* **Pueblo** or **-los.** A member of any of some 25 Native American peoples, including the Hopi, Zuñi, and Taos, living in established villages in northern and western New Mexico and northeast Arizona. **2.** A permanent village or community of any of the Pueblo peoples, typically consisting of multilevel adobe or stone apartment dwellings of terraced design around a central plaza. [Sp., people, pueblo < Lat. *populus*, people. See PUBLIC.]

Pueblo. A city of SE-central CO SSE of Colorado Springs. Pop. 98,640.

pu•er•ile (pyo͞o′ər-əl, pyo͝or′əl, -īl′) *adj.* **1.** Belonging to childhood; juvenile. **2.** Immature; childish. [Lat. *puerīlis* < *puer*, child, boy. See **pau-*.**] **— pu′er•ile•ly** *adv.* **— pu′er•il′i•ty** (-ĭl′ĭ-tē), **pu′er•ile•ness** (-əl-nĭs, -īl-) *n.*

pu•er•il•ism (pyo͞o′ər-ə-lĭz′əm, pyo͝or′ə-) *n.* Childish behavior in an adult, esp. as a symptom of mental illness.

pu•er•per•al (pyo͞o-ûr′pər-əl) *adj.* Relating to, connected with, or occurring during childbirth or the period immediately following childbirth. [< Lat. *puerper*, a woman in childbed : *puer*, child, boy; see **pau-*** + *parere*, to bear; see -PAROUS.]

puerperal fever *n.* An illness resulting from infection of the endometrium following childbirth or abortion, marked by fever and septicemia and usu. caused by unsterile technique.

pu•er•pe•ri•um (pyo͞o′ər-pîr′ē-əm) *n., pl.* **-pe•ri•a** (-pîr′ē-ə). **1.** The state of a woman during childbirth or immediately thereafter. **2.** The approximate six-week period lasting from childbirth to the return of normal uterine size. [Lat., childbirth < *puerpera*, a woman in childbed. See PUERPERAL.]

Puer•to Ca•bel•lo (pwĕr′tō kä-bā′ō, -vĕ′yô). A city of N Venezuela on the Caribbean Sea W of Caracas. Pop. 94,000.

Puer•to Ri•co (pwĕr′tə rē′kō, pôrt′ə, pōrt′ə, pwĕr′tō). A self-governing island commonwealth of the U.S. in the Caribbean Sea E of Hispaniola; colonized by the Spanish in the 16th cent. and ceded to the U.S. in 1898 after the Spanish-American War. Cap. San Juan. Pop. 3,522,037. **— Puer′to Ri′can** *adj. & n.*

Puer•to Val•lar•ta (pwĕr′tō vä-yär′tə, -tä, pwĕr′tô). A resort city of W Mexico on the Pacific Ocean. Pop. 38,645.

puff (pŭf) *n.* **1.a.** A short forceful exhalation of breath. **b.** A short sudden gust of wind. **c.** A brief sudden emission of air, vapor, or smoke. **d.** A short sibilant sound produced by a puff. **2.** An amount of vapor, smoke, or similar material released in a puff. **3.** An act of drawing in and expelling the breath, as in smoking tobacco. **4.** A swelling or rounded protuberance. **5.** Puff pastry. **6.** A light soft pad for applying powder or lotion. **7.** A gathered protruding portion of fabric. **8.** A light padded bed covering. **9.** An approving or flattering recommendation. **10.** *Genet.* A localized region of swelling in certain chromosomes indicating the active synthesis of DNA and RNA. **—** *v.* **puffed, puff•ing, puffs. —** *intr.* **1.** To blow in puffs. **2.** To come forth in puffs. **3.** To breathe forcefully and rapidly. **4.** To emit puffs. **5.** To take puffs on smoking material: *puffing on a cigar.* **6.** To swell or seem to swell, as with pride or air. Often used with *up.* **—** *tr.* **1.** To emit or give forth in puffs. **2.** To impel with puffs. **3.** To smoke (a cigar, for example). **4.** To inflate or distend. **5.** To fill with pride or conceit. **6.** To publicize with often exaggerated praise. [< ME *puffen*, to puff < OE *pyffan*, perh. of imit. orig.] **— puff′i•ly** *adv.* **— puff′i•ness** *n.* **— puff′y** *adj.*

puff adder *n.* **1.** A venomous African viper *(Bitis arietans)* having crescent-shaped yellowish markings. **2.** See **hognose snake.** [So called because it inflates its body when excited.]

puff•ball (pŭf′bôl′) *n.* **1.** Any of various fungi of the genus *Lycoperdon* and related genera, having a ball-shaped fruiting body that releases spores in puffs of dust. **2.** *Informal.* The rounded head of a dandelion that has gone to seed.

puffed-up (pŭft′ŭp′) *adj.* Displaying exaggerated dignity or self-importance; pompous.

puff•er (pŭf′ər) *n.* Any of various prickly, often poisonous, chiefly marine fishes of the family Tetraodontidae that are capable of puffing up by swallowing water or air.

puff•er•y (pŭf′ə-rē) *n.* Flattering, often exaggerated praise and publicity, esp. when used for promotional purposes.

puf•fin (pŭf′ĭn) *n.* Any of several sea birds of the genera *Fratercula* and *Lunda* of northern regions, characteristically having black and white plumage and a vertically flattened triangular bill that is brightly colored during breeding season. [ME *poffoun*, perh. < *puf*, puff. See PUFF.]

puff pastry *n.* A light flaky pastry that is formed by rolling and folding the dough in layers so that it expands when baked.

pug¹ (pŭg) *n.* **1.** A small sturdy dog of an ancient breed originating in China, having a snub nose, a wrinkled face, short smooth hair, and a curled tail. **2.** A pug nose. [?]

pug² (pŭg) *n.* **1.** Clay ground and kneaded with water into a plastic consistency for forming bricks or pottery. **2.** A machine for grinding and mixing clay. **—** *tr.v.* **pugged, pug•ging, pugs. 1.** To work or knead (clay) with water. **2.** To fill in with clay or mortar. **3.** To make soundproof by covering or packing with clay, mortar, sawdust, or felt. [?]

pug³ (pŭg) *n.* A footprint, track, or trail, esp. of an animal. [Hindi *pag*, prob. < Skt. *padakam*, footstep, foot < *padam.* See **ped-*.**]

pug⁴ (pŭg) *n. Slang.* A fighter, esp. a boxer. [Short for PUGILIST, boxer < Lat. *pugil.* See PUGILISM.]

Pu•get Sound (pyo͞o′jĭt). A deep inlet of the Pacific in W WA extending S from the Strait of Juan de Fuca through Admiralty Inlet; named by Capt. George Vancouver for his aide, Peter Puget, in 1792.

pu•gi•lism (pyo͞o′jə-lĭz′əm) *n. Sports.* The skill, practice, and sport of fighting with the fists; boxing. [< Lat. *pugil*, pugilist. See **peuk-*.**] **— pu′gi•list** *n.* **— pu′gi•lis′tic** *adj.*

Pu•glia (po͞o′lyä). See **Apulia.**

pug•mark (pŭg′märk′) *n.* The pug of an animal.

pug•na•cious (pŭg-nā′shəs) *adj.* Combative in nature; belligerent. [< Lat. *pugnāx*, *pugnāc-* < *pugnāre*, to fight < *pugnus*, fist. See **peuk-*.**] **— pug•na′cious•ly** *adv.* **— pug•na′cious•ness, pug•nac′i•ty** (-năs′ĭ-tē) *n.*

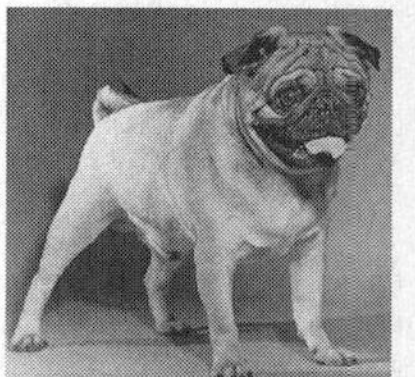
pug¹

pug nose *n.* A short nose that is somewhat flattened and turned up at the end. [< PUG¹, ape (obsolete), pug.] **— pug′-nosed′** (pŭg′nōzd′) *adj.*

puis•ne (pyo͞o′nē) *Chiefly British.* **—** *adj.* Lower in rank; junior. **—** *n.* One of lesser rank than another, esp. an associate judge. [OFr. *puisne* : *puis*, afterward (ult. < Lat. *post*; see **apo-***) + *ne*, born (< Lat. *nātus*, p.part. of *nāscī*, to be born; see **genə-***).]

puis•sance (pwĭs′əns, pyo͞o′ĭ-səns, pyo͞o-ĭs′əns) *n.* Power; might. [ME < OFr. < *poissant*, powerful, pr.part. of *pooir*, *poeir*, to be able. See POWER.] **— puis′sant** *adj.*

puke (pyo͞ok) *Slang.* **—** *intr. & tr.v.* **puked, puk•ing, pukes.** To experience vomiting or vomit (ingested matter). **—** *n.* **1.** The act of vomiting. **2.** Vomit. [Perh. imit.]

puk•ka also **puck•a** (pŭk′ə) *adj.* **1.** Genuine; authentic. **2.** Superior; first-class. [Hindi *pakkā*, cooked, ripe < Skt. *pakva-* < *pacati*, he cooks. See **pekʷ-*.**]

pul (po͞ol) *n., pl.* **puls** or **pu•li** (po͞o′lē). See table at **currency.** [Pers. *pūl*, perh. < LGk. *phollis*, bellows, money bag < Lat. *follis.* See FOOL.]

pu•la (po͞o′lä) *n.* See table at **currency.**

Pu•las•ki (po͝o-lăs′kē, pə-), **Casimir** or **Kazimierz.** 1747–79. Polish patriot and general in the Revolutionary War.

pul•chri•tude (pŭl′krĭ-to͞od′, -tyo͞od′) *n.* Great physical beauty and appeal. [ME *pulcritude* < Lat. *pulchritūdō* < *pulcher*, *pulchr-*, beautiful.]

pul•chri•tu•di•nous (pŭl′krĭ-to͞od′n-əs, -tyo͞od′-) *adj.* Characterized by or having great physical beauty and appeal.

pule (pyo͞ol) *intr.v.* **puled, pul•ing, pules.** To whine; whimper. [Perh. < Fr. *piauler*, of imit. orig.] **— pul′er** *n.*

pu•li¹ (po͝ol′ē, pyo͞o′lē) *n., pl.* **pu•lis** or **pu•lik** (po͝ol′ĕk, pyo͞o′lĕk). A longhaired sheepdog of a Hungarian breed. [Hung.]

pu•li² (po͞o′lē) *n.* Pl. of **pul.**

Joseph Pulitzer

Pu•lit•zer (po͝ol′ĭt-sər, pyo͞o′lĭt-), **Joseph.** 1847–1911. Hungarian-born Amer. journalist and publisher who established and endowed the Pulitzer Prizes.

Pulitzer Prize *n.* Any of several annual awards for accomplishment in American journalism, literature, and music.

pull (po͝ol) *v.* **pulled, pull•ing, pulls. —** *tr.* **1.** To apply force to so as to cause or tend to cause motion toward the source of the force. **2.** To remove from a fixed position; extract. **3.** To tug at; jerk or tweak. **4.** To rip or tear; rend. **5.** To stretch (taffy, for example) repeatedly. **6.** To strain (a muscle, for example) injuriously. **7.** *Informal.* To attract; draw: *pulled a large crowd.* **8.** *Slang.* To draw out (a weapon) in readiness for use. **9.** *Informal.* To remove: *pulled the engine.* **10.** *Baseball.* To hit (a ball) in the direction one is facing when the swing is carried through. **11.** *Naut.* **a.** To operate (an oar) in rowing. **b.** To transport or propel by rowing. **c.** To be rowed by. **12.** To rein in (a horse) to keep it from winning a race. **13.** *Print.* To produce (a print or an impression) from type. **—** *intr.* **1.** To exert force in moving something toward that force. **2.** To drink or inhale deeply. **3.** *Naut.* To row a boat. **4.** *Informal.* To express or feel great sympathy or empathy. **—** *n.* **1.** The act or process of pulling. **2.** Force required to overcome resistance in pulling. **3.** A sustained effort. **4.** Something, such as a knob on a drawer, that is used for pulling. **5.** A deep inhalation or draft, as of a cigarette or beverage. **6.** *Slang.* A means of gaining special advantage; influence. **7.** *Informal.* Ability to draw or attract; appeal. **— *phrasal verbs.* pull away. 1.** To move away or backward; withdraw. **2.** To move ahead, as in a race. **pull back.** To execute an orderly withdrawal, esp. of troops. **pull down. 1.** To demolish; destroy. **2.** To reduce to a lower level. **3.** To depress, as in spirits or health. **4.** *Informal.* To draw (money) as wages. **pull in. 1.** To arrive at a destination. **2.** To rein in; restrain. **3.** To arrest (a criminal suspect, for example). **pull off.** *Informal.* To perform in spite of difficulties or obstacles; bring off. **pull out. 1.** To leave or depart. **2.** To withdraw, as from a situation or commitment. **pull over. 1.** To bring a vehicle to a stop at a curb or at the side of a road. **2.** To instruct or force

ă pat	oi boy
ā pay	ou out
âr care	o͝o took
ä father	o͞o boot
ĕ pet	ŭ cut
ē be	ûr urge
ĭ pit	th thin
ī pie	*th* this
îr pier	hw which
ŏ pot	zh vision
ō toe	ə about, item
ô paw	

Stress marks:
′ (primary);
′ (secondary), as in
dictionary (dĭk′shə-nĕr′ē)

(a motorist) to pull over. **pull round.** To restore or be restored to sound health. **pull through.** To come or bring successfully through trouble or illness. **pull up. 1.** To bring or come to a halt. **2.** To move to a position or place ahead, as in a race. — ***idioms.* pull a fast one.** *Informal.* To play a trick or perpetrate a fraud. **pull (oneself) together.** To regain one's composure. **pull (one's) punch (or punches).** To refrain from deploying all the resources or force at one's disposal. **pull (one's) weight.** To do one's own share, as of work. **pull out all the stops.** *Informal.* To deploy all the resources or force at one's disposal. **pull (someone's) leg.** To play a joke on; tease. **pull strings (or wires).** *Informal.* To exert secret control or influence in order to gain an end. **pull the plug on.** *Slang.* To remove all restraints on. **pull the rug (out) from under.** *Informal.* To remove all support and assistance from, usu. suddenly. **pull the wool over (someone's) eyes.** To deceive; hoodwink. **pull together.** To make a joint effort. **pull up stakes.** To clear out; leave. [ME *pullen* < OE *pullian.*] — **pull′er** *n.*

Syns: *pull, drag, draw, haul, tow, tug.* The central meaning shared by these verbs is "to cause something to move toward the source of an applied force": *pull a sled; drag furniture; draw up a chair; hauling wood; a car towing a trailer; tugging at the oars.* ***Ant:*** *push.*

pulpit

pull•back (po͝ol′băk′) *n.* **1.** The act or process of pulling back, esp. an orderly troop withdrawal. **2.** A device for holding or drawing back.

pul•let (po͝ol′ĭt) *n.* A young domestic hen, usu. one less than one year old. [ME *pulet* < OFr. *polet, poulet,* dim. of *poul,* cock, and *poule,* hen, both < Lat. *pullus,* young fowl, young animal, chicken. See **pau-***.]

pul•ley (po͝ol′ē) *n., pl.* **-leys. 1.** A simple machine consisting essentially of a wheel with a grooved rim in which a pulled rope or chain can run to change the direction of the pull and thereby lift a load. **2.** A wheel turned by or driving a belt. [ME *poley* < OFr. *polie* and < Med.Lat. *poliva,* both ult. < Gk. *polos,* axis. See **kʷel-**[1]*.]

pull•man (po͝ol′mən) *adj.* Small, long, and narrow in architectural design. [< the resemblance to a PULLMAN[2].]

Pull•man[1] (po͝ol′mən). A city of SE WA S of Spokane; the seat of Washington State University (founded 1890). Pop. 23,478.

Pullman[2] (po͝ol′mən) *n.* **1.** A railroad parlor car or sleeping car. **2.** A large suitcase. [After George Mortimer *Pullman* (1831–97), Amer. industrialist and inventor.]

pull-on (po͝ol′ŏn′, -ôn′) *n.* A garment, such as a sweater, designed to be easily pulled on.

pul•lo•rum disease (pə-lôr′əm, -lōr′-) *n.* A contagious, often fatal diarrheal disease of young poultry, caused by the bacterium *Salmonella pullorum.* [NLat. *pullōrum,* specific epithet of *Salmonella pullōrum* < Lat., genitive plural of *pullus,* young fowl. See PULLET.]

pull•out (po͝ol′out′) *n.* **1.** A withdrawal, esp. of troops. **2.** The change from a dive to level flight. Used of an aircraft. **3.** An object designed to be pulled out.

pull•o•ver (po͝ol′ō′vər) *n.* A garment, such as a sweater, that is put on by being drawn over the head.

pul•lu•late (pŭl′yə-lāt′) *intr.v.* **-lat•ed, -lat•ing, -lates. 1.** To put forth sprouts or buds; germinate. **2.** To breed rapidly or abundantly. **3.** To teem; swarm. [Lat. *pullulāre, pullulāt-* < *pullulus,* dim. of *pullus,* young fowl. See PULLET.] — **pul′lu•la′tion** *n.* — **pul′lu•la′tive** *adj.*

pull-up (po͝ol′ŭp′) *n. Sports.* See **chin-up.**

pul•mo•nar•y (po͝ol′mə-nĕr′ē, pŭl′-) *adj.* **1.** Of, relating to, or affecting the lungs. **2.** Having lungs or lunglike organs. [Lat. *pulmōnārius* < *pulmō, pulmōn-,* lung. See **pleu-***.]

pulmonary artery *n.* An artery that carries venous blood from the right ventricle of the heart to the lungs.

pulmonary vein *n.* A vein that carries oxygenated blood from the lungs to the left atrium of the heart.

pul•mo•nate (po͝ol′mə-nāt′, pŭl′-) *adj.* **1.** Having lungs or lunglike organs. **2.** Of or belonging to the Pulmonata, a subclass of gastropods, including slugs, that are capable of breathing air through lunglike sacs. [< Lat. *pulmō, pulmōn-,* lung. See PULMONARY.] — **pul′mo•nate′** *n.*

pul•mon•ic (po͝ol-mŏn′ĭk, pŭl-) *adj.* Of or relating to the lungs; pulmonary.

pulp (pŭlp) *n.* **1.** A soft moist shapeless mass of matter. **2.** The soft moist part of fruit. **3.** A mass of pressed vegetable matter. **4.** The soft pith forming the contents of the stem of a plant. **5.** A mixture of cellulose material, such as wood, paper, and rags, ground up and moistened to make paper. **6.** The soft tissue forming the inner structure of a tooth. **7.** A mixture of crushed ore and water. **8.** A lurid publication. — *v.* **pulped, pulp•ing, pulps.** — *tr.* **1.** To reduce to pulp. **2.** To remove the pulp from. — *intr.* To be reduced to a pulpy consistency. [ME < Lat. *pulpa,* fleshy parts of the body, fruit pulp.] — **pulp′i•ness** *n.* — **pulp′ous** (pŭl′pəs), **pulp′y** *adj.*

pul•pit (po͝ol′pĭt, pŭl′-) *n.* **1.** An elevated platform, lectern, or stand used in preaching or conducting a religious service. **2.a.** Clerics considered as a group. **b.** The ministry of preaching. **3.a.** An elevated platform. **b.** *Naut.* A fixed safety railing around the bow or stern of a boat. [ME < OFr. < LLat. *pulpitum* < Lat., wooden platform.]

pulp•wood (pŭlp′wo͝od′) *n.* Soft wood, such as spruce, aspen, or pine, used in making paper.

pul•que (po͞ol′kā′, -kē, po͝ol′-) *n.* A thick fermented alcoholic beverage made in Mexico from various species of agave. [Am. Sp. < Nahuatl *poliuhqui,* decomposed, lost.]

pul•sar (pŭl′sär′) *n. Astron.* Any of a class of celestial objects believed to be rotating neutron stars, emitting intense regular bursts of radio waves. [< PULSE[1], by analogy with QUASAR.]

pul•sate (pŭl′sāt′) *intr.v.* **-sat•ed, -sat•ing, -sates. 1.** To expand and contract rhythmically; beat. **2.** To quiver; vibrate. [Lat. *pulsāre, pulsāt-,* freq. of *pellere,* to beat. See **pel-**[5]*.]

pul•sa•tile (pŭl′sə-təl, -tīl′) *adj.* Undergoing pulsation.

pul•sa•tion (pŭl-sā′shən) *n.* **1.** The act of pulsating. **2.** A single beat, throb, or vibration.

pul•sa•tor (pŭl′sā′tər, pŭl-sā′-) *n.* A pulsating device.

pul•sa•to•ry (pŭl′sə-tôr′ē, -tōr′ē) *adj.* Having rhythmical vibration or movement.

pulse[1] (pŭls) *n.* **1.** The rhythmical throbbing of arteries produced by the regular contractions of the heart, esp. as palpated at the wrist or in the neck. **2.a.** A regular or rhythmical beating. **b.** A single beat or throb. **3.** *Phys.* **a.** A brief sudden change in a normally constant quantity: *a pulse of current.* **b.** Any of a series of intermittent occurrences characterized by such a change. **4.** The perceptible emotions or sentiments of a group of people. — *intr.v.* **pulsed, puls•ing, puls•es. 1.** To pulsate; beat. **2.** *Phys.* To undergo a series of intermittent occurrences characterized by pulses. [ME < OFr. < Lat. *pulsus* < p.part. of *pellere,* to beat. See **pel-**[5]*.]

pulse[2] (pŭls) *n.* **1.** The edible seeds of certain pod-bearing plants, such as peas and beans. **2.** A plant yielding these seeds. [ME *pols* < OFr. < Lat. *puls,* pottage of meal and pulse, prob. ult. < Gk. *poltos.*]

pulse•jet (pŭls′jĕt′) *n.* A jet engine with intermittent air intake and combustion, producing rapid periodic bursts of thrust.

pulse modulation *n.* A type of modulation in which a train of pulses is varied in order to represent the signal.

pul•som•e•ter (pŭl-sŏm′ĭ-tər) *n.* A pump without pistons that operates by means of pulsed condensation of steam.

pul•ver•a•ble (pŭl′vər-ə-bəl) *adj.* That can be pulverized.

pul•ver•ize (pŭl′və-rīz′) *v.* **-ized, -iz•ing, -iz•es.** — *tr.* **1.** To pound, crush, or grind to a powder or dust. **2.** To demolish. — *intr.* To be ground or reduced to powder or dust. [ME *pulverizen* < LLat. *pulverizāre* < Lat. *pulvis, pulver-,* dust.] — **pul′ver•iz′a•ble** *adj.* — **pul′ver•i•za′tion** (-vər-ĭ-zā′shən) *n.* — **pul′ver•iz′er** *n.*

pul•ver•u•lent (pŭl-vĕr′yə-lənt, -vĕr′ə-) *adj.* **1.** Made of, covered with, or crumbling to fine powder or dust. **2.** Dusty; crumbly. [Lat. *pulverulentus* : < *pulvis, pulver-,* dust + *-ulentus,* abounding in.]

pul•vil•lus (pŭl-vĭl′əs) *n., pl.* **-vil•li** (-vĭl′ī′). A soft pad on the foot of an insect by which it clings to a surface. [Lat., short for *pulvīnulus,* dim. of *pulvīnus,* cushion.]

pul•vi•nate (pŭl′və-nāt′) also **pul•vi•nat•ed** (-nā′tĭd) *adj.* **1.** Shaped like a cushion. **2.** *Bot.* Swollen at the base. Used of a leafstalk. [Lat. *pulvīnātus* < *pulvīnus,* cushion.]

pul•vi•nus (pŭl-vī′nəs, -vē′-) *n., pl.* **-ni** (-nī′). A pulvinate swelling. [Lat. *pulvīnus,* cushion.]

pu•ma (pyo͞o′mə, po͞o′-) *n.* See **mountain lion.** [Sp. < Quechua.]

pum•e•lo (pŭm′ə-lō′) *n., pl.* **-los.** See **shaddock.** [Var. of POMELO.]

pum•ice (pŭm′ĭs) *n.* A light, porous, glassy lava, used in solid form as an abrasive and in powdered form as a polish and an abrasive. — *tr.v.* **-iced, -ic•ing, -ic•es.** To clean, polish, or smooth with pumice. [ME < AN *pomis* < LLat. *pōmex* < Lat. *pūmex,* alteration of *spūma,* foam.] — **pu•mi′ceous** (pyo͞o-mĭsh′əs, pə-) *adj.* — **pum′ic•er** *n.*

pum•mel (pŭm′əl) *tr.v.* **-meled, -mel•ing, -mels** also **-melled, -mel•ling, -mels.** To beat, as with the fists; pommel. — *n.* The act of beating, as with the fists. [Alteration of POMMEL.]

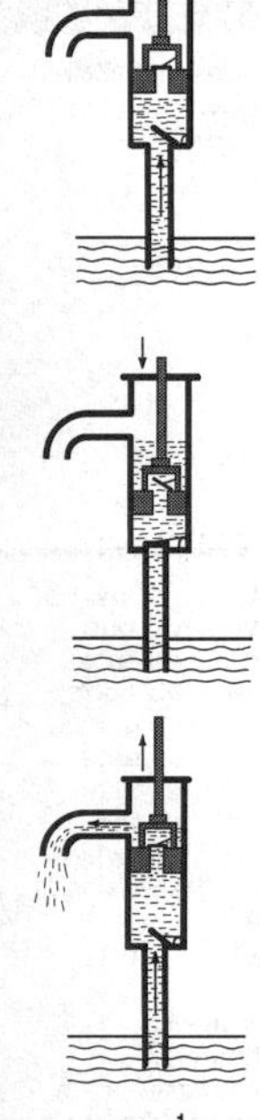

pump[1]

pump[1] (pŭmp) *n.* **1.** A machine or device for raising, compressing, or transferring fluids. **2.** *Physiol.* A molecular mechanism for the active transport of ions or molecules across a cell membrane. **3.** *Phys.* Electromagnetic radiation used to raise atoms or molecules to a higher energy level. — *v.* **pumped, pump•ing, pumps.** — *tr.* **1.** To raise or cause to flow by means of a pump. **2.** To draw, deliver, or pour forth as if with a pump. **3.** To remove the water from. **4.** To cause to move with the up-and-down motion of a pump handle. **5.** To propel, eject, or insert with or as if with a pump. **6.** *Phys.* To raise (atoms or molecules) to a higher energy level by exposing them to electromagnetic radiation at a resonant frequency. **7.** *Physiol.* To transport (ions or molecules) against a concentration gradient by the expenditure of chemically stored energy. **8.** To question closely or persistently. — *intr.* **1.** To operate a pump. **2.** To raise or move gas or liquid with a pump. **3.** To move up and down in the manner of a pump handle. — ***phrasal verb.* pump up. 1.** To inflate with gas by means of a pump. **2.** *Slang.* To fill with enthusiasm, strength, and energy. **3.** *Sports.* To be actively involved in a bodybuilding program. — ***idiom.* pump iron.** *Sports.* To lift weights. [ME *pumpe.*] — **pump′er** *n.*

pump² (pŭmp) *n.* A woman's shoe that has medium or high heels and no fastenings. [?]

pumped storage (pŭmpt) *n.* A system of generating hydroelectric power, in which electricity is generated during hours of peak consumption by using water that has been pumped into an elevated reservoir during hours of low consumption.

pum•per•nick•el (pŭm′pər-nĭk′əl) *n.* A dark sourish bread made from whole, coarsely ground rye. [Ger., prob. < dial., term of abuse : obsolete *Pumper*, breaking wind (< dial. *pumpern*, to break wind < MHGer., to knock, freq. of *pumpen*, of imit. orig.) + Ger. *Nickel*, goblin; see NICKEL.]

pump•kin (pŭmp′kĭn, pŭm′-, pŭng′-) *n.* **1.a.** A coarse trailing vine *(Cucurbita pepo)* cultivated for its fruit. **b.** The large pulpy round fruit of this plant, having a thick orange-yellow rind. **c.** Any of several other vines of the genus *Cucurbita,* esp. *C. maxima* or *C. moschata,* bearing large pumpkinlike squashes. **2.** *Color.* A moderate to strong orange. [Alteration (influenced by -KIN) of obsolete *pumpion* < obsolete Fr. *pompon, popon* < OFr. *pepon* < LLat. *pepō̆n* < Lat., watermelon or gourd < Gk., ripe, large melon. See **pekʷ-*.**]

pump•kin•seed (pŭmp′kĭn-sēd′, pŭm′-, pŭng′-) *n.* **1.** The seed of a pumpkin. **2.** A North American sunfish *(Lepomis gibbosus)* having a rounded, mostly orange body with a bright red spot on each gill cover.

pun (pŭn) *n.* A play on words, sometimes on different senses of the same word and sometimes on the similar sense or sound of different words. — *intr.v.* **punned, pun•ning, puns.** To make puns or a pun. [?] — **pun′ning•ly** *adv.*

punch¹ (pŭnch) *n.* **1.** A tool for circular or other piercing. **2.** A tool for forcing a pin, bolt, or rivet in or out of a hole. **3.** A tool for stamping a design on a surface. **4.** A tool for making a countersink. — *intr. & tr.v.* **punched, punch•ing, punch•es.** To use a punch or use a punch on. [ME *pounce, punche* < OFr. *poinçon, ponchon.* See PUNCHEON¹. V. < ME *pouncen, punchen,* to prick < OFr. *poinçoner, ponchoner,* to emboss with a punch. See PUNCH².]

punch² (pŭnch) *tr.v.* **punched, punch•ing, punch•es. 1.** To hit with a sharp blow of the fist. **2.a.** To poke or prod with a stick. **b.** *Western U.S.* To herd (cattle). **3.** To depress (a key or button, for example) in order to activate a device or perform an operation. — *n.* **1.** A blow with the fist. **2.** Vigor or drive. — ***phrasal verbs.* punch in.** To check in formally at a job upon arrival. **punch out. 1.** To check out formally at a job upon departure. **2.** *Slang.* To eject from a military aircraft. — ***idiom.* beat to the punch.** To make the first decisive move. [ME *punchen,* to thrust, prod, prick < OFr. *poinçonner, ponchonner,* to emboss with a punch < *poinçon, ponchon,* pointed tool. See PUNCHEON¹.] — **punch′less** *adj.*

punch³ (pŭnch) *n.* A beverage of fruit juices and sometimes carbonated water, often spiced and mixed with wine or liquor. [Perh. < Hindi *pañc-,* five- < Skt. *pañca,* (< the hypothesis that it was originally prepared from five ingredients). See **penkʷe*.**]

Punch (pŭnch) *n.* The quarrelsome hook-nosed husband of Judy in the comic puppet show *Punch and Judy.* — ***idiom.* pleased as Punch.** Highly pleased; gratified. [Short for PUNCHINELLO.]

punch•board (pŭnch′bord′, -bōrd′) *n. Games.* A small, usu. rectangular board that contains holes each filled with a slip of paper that, when punched out, indicates a designated prize, win, or loss.

punch bowl *n.* A large serving bowl, as for punch.

punch card also **punched card** (pŭncht) *n. Comp. Sci.* A medium for feeding data into a computer, essentially a card punched with holes or notches to represent letters and numbers or with a pattern of holes to represent related data.

punch-drunk (pŭnch′drŭngk′) *adj.* **1.** Showing signs of brain damage caused by blows to the head. Used esp. of a boxer. **2.** Behaving in a bewildered, confused, or dazed manner.

pun•cheon¹ (pŭn′chən) *n.* **1.** A short wooden upright used in structural framing. **2.** A piece of broad, heavy, roughly dressed timber with one face finished flat. **3.** A punching, perforating, or stamping tool, esp. one used by a goldsmith. [ME *punchon* < OFr. *ponçon, ponchon* < VLat. **pūnctiō, pūnctiōn-,* punch < **pūnctiāre,* to pierce < Lat. *pūnctus,* p.part. of *pungere,* to prick. See **peuk-*.**]

pun•cheon² (pŭn′chən) *n.* **1.** A cask with a capacity of from 72 to 120 gallons (273 to 454 liters). **2.** The amount of liquid contained in a puncheon. [ME *ponchon* < OFr. *poinçon, poinchon,* punch, cask. See PUNCHEON¹.]

punch•er (pŭn′chər) *n.* A cowpuncher.

Pun•chi•nel•lo (pŭn′chə-nĕl′ō) *n., pl.* **-los** or **-loes. 1.** The short fat buffoon or clown in an Italian puppet show. **2.** One who is felt to resemble a short fat clown. [Var. of *Polichinello* < Ital. dial. *Pollecinella,* dim. of *pollecena,* turkey pullet (from the resemblance between its beak and Punchinello's nose), ult. < Lat. *pullus,* young chicken. See PULLET.]

punch•ing bag (pŭn′chĭng) *n. Sports.* A stuffed or inflated leather bag that is punched with the fists for exercise.

punch line *n.* The climax of a joke or humorous story.

punch press *n.* A power press that can be fitted with various dies, as for metalworking.

punch-up (pŭnch′ŭp′) *n. Chiefly British.* A fistfight.

punch•y (pŭn′chē) *adj.* **-i•er, -i•est. 1.** Characterized by vigor or drive. **2.** Groggy or dazed from or as if from a punch or punches. — **punch′i•ly** *adv.* — **punch′i•ness** *n.*

punc•tate (pŭngk′tāt′) also **punc•tat•ed** (-tā′tĭd) *adj.* Having tiny spots, points, or depressions. [< Lat. *pūnctum,* prick mark < neut. p.part. of *pungere,* to prick. See PUNCTUATE.] — **punc•ta′tion** *n.*

punc•til•i•o (pŭngk-tĭl′ē-ō′) *n., pl.* **-os. 1.** A fine point of etiquette. **2.** Precise observance of formalities. [Obsolete Ital. *punctiglio* < Sp. *puntillo,* dim. of *punto,* point < Lat. *pūnctum* < neut. p.part. of *pungere,* to prick. See **peuk-*.**]

punc•til•i•ous (pŭngk-tĭl′ē-əs) *adj.* Strictly attentive to minute details of form in action or conduct. — **punc•til′i•ous•ly** *adv.* — **punc•til′i•ous•ness** *n.*

pumpkinseed
Lepomis gibbosus

punc•tu•al (pŭngk′cho͞o-əl) *adj.* **1.** Acting or arriving exactly at the time appointed; prompt. **2.** Paid or accomplished at or by the appointed time. **3.** Precise; exact. **4.** Confined to or having the nature of a point in space. [ME, sharp-pointed < Med.Lat. *pūnctuālis* < Lat. *pūnctum,* point < neut. p.part. of *pungere,* to prick. See **peuk-*.**] — **punc′tu•al′i•ty** (-ăl′ĭ-tē), **punc′tu•al•ness** (-əl-nĭs) *n.* — **punc′tu•al•ly** *adv.*

punc•tu•ate (pŭngk′cho͞o-āt′) *v.* **-at•ed, -at•ing, -ates.** — *tr.* **1.** To provide (a text) with punctuation marks. **2.** To interrupt periodically. **3.** To stress or emphasize. — *intr.* To use punctuation. [Med.Lat. *pūnctuāre, pūnctuāt-* < Lat. *pūnctum,* point < neut. p.part. of *pungere,* to prick. See **peuk-*.**] — **punc′tu•a′tive** *adj.* — **punc′tu•a′tor** *n.*

punc•tu•a•tion (pŭngk′cho͞o-ā′shən) *n.* **1.a.** The use of standard marks and signs in writing and printing to separate words into sentences, clauses, and phrases to clarify meaning. **b.** These marks. **2.** The act or an instance of punctuating.

punctuation mark *n.* One of a set of marks or signs, such as the comma (,) or the period (.), used to punctuate texts.

punc•ture (pŭngk′chər) *v.* **-tured, -tur•ing, -tures.** — *tr.* **1.** To pierce with a pointed object. **2.** To make (a hole) by piercing. **3.** To cause to collapse by piercing. **4.** To depreciate or deflate. — *intr.* To be pierced or punctured. — *n.* **1.** The act or an instance of puncturing. **2.** A hole or depression made by a sharp object. [< ME, a pricking < LLat. *pūnctūra* < *pūnctus,* p.part. of *pungere,* to prick. See **peuk-*.**] — **punc′tur•a•ble** *adj.*

puncture weed *n.* A prostrate weed *(Tribulus terrestris)* native to the Old World, and having opposite, pinnately compound leaves and woody fruit with stout divergent spines.

pun•dit (pŭn′dĭt) *n.* **1.** A source of opinion; a critic. **2.** A learned person. **3.** *Hinduism.* Var. of **pandit.** [Hindi *paṇḍit,* learned man < Skt. *paṇḍitaḥ,* learned; scholar, perh. of Dravidian orig.] — **pun′dit•ry** *n.*

pung (pŭng) *n. New England.* A low one-horse box sleigh. [Short for dial. *tom-pung,* from an Algonquian language.]

pun•gent (pŭn′jənt) *adj.* **1.** Affecting the organs of taste or smell with a sharp acrid sensation. **2.a.** Penetrating, biting, or caustic: *pungent satire.* **b.** To the point; sharp. **3.** Pointed: *a pungent leaf.* [Lat. *pungēns, pungent-,* pr.part. of *pungere,* to sting. See **peuk-*.**] — **pun′gen•cy** *n.* — **pun′gent•ly** *adv.*

Pu•nic (pyo͞o′nĭk) *adj.* **1.** Of or relating to ancient Carthage, its inhabitants, or their language. **2.** Having the character of treachery attributed to the Carthaginians by the Romans. — *n.* The dialect of Phoenician spoken in ancient Carthage. [Lat. *Poenicus, Pūnicus* < *Poenus,* a Carthaginian < Gk. *Phoinix,* Phoenician.]

pun•ish (pŭn′ĭsh) *v.* **-ished, -ish•ing, -ish•es.** — *tr.* **1.** To subject to a penalty for an offense, a sin, or a fault. **2.** To inflict a penalty for (an offense). **3.** To handle roughly; hurt. — *intr.* To exact or mete out punishment. [ME *punissen, punishen* < OFr. *punir, puniss-* < Lat. *poenīre, pūnīre* < *poena,* punishment < Gk. *poinē.* See **kʷei-¹*.**] — **pun′ish•a•bil′i•ty** *n.* — **pun′ish•a•ble** *adj.* — **pun′ish•er** *n.*

pun•ish•ment (pŭn′ĭsh-mənt) *n.* **1.a.** The act or an instance of punishing. **b.** The condition of being punished. **2.** A penalty for wrongdoing. **3.** Rough handling; mistreatment.

pu•ni•tive (pyo͞o′nĭ-tĭv) *adj.* Inflicting or aiming to inflict punishment; punishing. [Med.Lat. *pūnītīvus* < Lat. *poenīre, pūnīre,* to punish. See PUNISH.] — **pu′ni•tive•ly** *adv.* — **pu′ni•tive•ness** *n.*

punitive damages *pl.n. Law.* Damages awarded by a court against a defendant as a deterrent or punishment to redress an egregious wrong perpetrated by the defendant.

pu•ni•to•ry (pyo͞o′nĭ-tôr′ē, -tōr′ē) *adj.* Inflicting or intended to inflict punishment. [< Lat. *pūnītus* < p.part. of *pūnīre,* to punish. See PUNISH.]

Pun•jab (pŭn′jăb′, pŭn-jäb′). A historical region of NW India and N Pakistan bounded by the Indus and Jumna rivers. A center of the Indus Valley civilization, it was controlled by Sikhs from 1799 to 1849, when it was annexed by Great Britain, and partitioned between India and Pakistan in 1947.

Pun•ja•bi also **Pan•ja•bi** (pŭn-jä′bē, -jăb′ē) — *adj.* Of or relating to the Punjab or Punjabi. — *n., pl.* **-bis. 1.** A native or inhabitant of the Punjab. **2.** An Indic language spoken in the Punjab.

pun•ji stick (po͝on′jē, pŭn′-) *n.* A very sharp bamboo stake

ă pat	oi boy
ā pay	ou out
âr care	o͝o took
ä father	o͞o boot
ĕ pet	ŭ cut
ē be	ûr urge
ĭ pit	th thin
ī pie	*th* this
îr pier	hw which
ŏ pot	zh vision
ō toe	ə about,
ô paw	item

Stress marks:
′ (primary);
′ (secondary), as in
dictionary (dĭk′shə-nĕr′ē)

that is concealed at an angle in high grass or in deep mud, often coated with excrement, and planted to wound and infect the feet of enemy soldiers. [?]

punk (pŭngk) *n.* **1.** *Slang.* **a.** A young person, esp. a member of a rebellious counterculture group. **b.** An inexperienced young man. **2.** *Mus.* **a.** Punk rock. **b.** A punk rocker. **3.a.** *Slang.* A young man who is the sexual partner of an older man. **b.** *Archaic.* A prostitute. **4.** Dry decayed wood, used as tinder. **5.** Any of various substances that smolder when ignited, used to light fireworks. **6.** Chinese incense. —*adj. Slang.* **1.** Of or relating to the unusual style of dress worn by punk rockers. **2.** Of poor quality; worthless. **3.** Weak in spirits or health. [?] —**punk′er** *n.*

punt¹
c. 1935 American work punt

pun•ka or **pun•kah** (pŭng′kə) *n.* A fan used esp. in India, made of a palm frond or strip of cloth hung from the ceiling. [Hindi *pankhā* < Skt. *pakṣakaḥ*, fan < *pakṣaḥ*, wing.]

punk•ie also **punk•y** (pŭng′kē) *n., pl.* **-ies.** Any of various minute biting flies of the family Ceratopogonidae. [Of North American Du. orig. < Munsee (Delaware language) *pónkwəs*.]

pun•kin (pŭng′kĭn) *n. Informal.* Var. of **pumpkin.**

punk rock *n. Mus.* A form of hard-driving rock music marked by harsh lyrics and often expressing alienation and anger.

punk rocker *n. Mus.* A performer or follower of punk rock.

pun•ster (pŭn′stər) *n.* A maker of puns.

punt¹ (pŭnt) *Naut.* —*n.* An open flatbottom boat with squared ends, propelled by a long pole and used in shallow waters. —*v.* **punt•ed, punt•ing, punts.** —*tr.* **1.** To propel (a boat) with a pole. **2.** To carry in a punt. —*intr.* To go in a punt. [Prob. ME **punt* < OE *punt* < Lat. *pontō, pontōn-*, pontoon, flatbottom boat < *pōns, pont-*, bridge. See **pent-*.**] —**punt′er** *n.*

punty
Held in artisan's left hand

punt² (pŭnt) *Football.* —*n.* A kick in which the ball is dropped from the hands and kicked before it touches the ground. —*v.* **punt•ed, punt•ing, punts.** —*tr.* To propel (a ball) by means of a punt. —*intr.* To execute a punt. [Perh. < dial. *punt*, to strike, push, perh. alteration of *bunt*.] —**punt′er** *n.*

punt³ (pŭnt) *intr.v.* **punt•ed, punt•ing, punts. 1.** *Games.* To lay a bet against the bank, as in roulette. **2.** *Chiefly British.* To gamble. [Fr. *ponter* < obsolete *pont*, p.part. of *pondre*, to put (obsolete), to lay an egg < OFr., to lay an egg < Lat. *pōnere*. See **apo-*.**] —**punt′er** *n.*

punt⁴ (pŭnt) *n.* The indentation in the bottom of a champagne or wine bottle. [Perh. < PUNTY.]

Pun•ta A•re•nas (po͞on′tə ə-rĕn′əs, po͞on′tä ä-rĕ′näs). A city of S Chile on the Strait of Magellan; founded in the 1840's and the southernmost city in the world. Pop. 95,332.

pun•ty (pŭn′tē) *n., pl.* **-ties.** An iron rod on which molten glass is handled when being shaped and worked. [Prob. < Fr. *pontil* < *pointe*, point < OFr. See POINT.]

Punx•su•taw•ney (pŭngk′sə-tô′nē). A city of W-central PA NE of Pittsburgh; noted for its annual observance of Groundhog Day, Feb. 2. Pop. 6,782.

pu•ny (pyo͞o′nē) *adj.* **-ni•er, -ni•est. 1.** Of inferior size, strength, or significance; weak. **2.** *Chiefly Southern U.S.* Sickly; ill. [Var. of PUISNE.] —**pu′ni•ly** *adv.* —**pu′ni•ness** *n.*

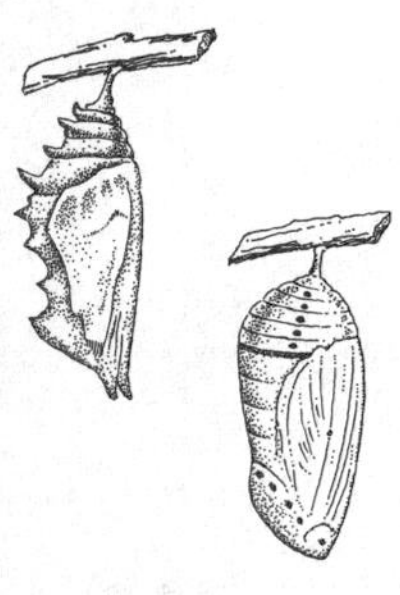

pupa
Left: Of a mourning cloak butterfly
Right: Of a monarch butterfly

pup (pŭp) *n.* **1.a.** A young dog; a puppy. **b.** The young of various other canine animals, such as the wolf. **c.** The young of certain other animals, such as the seal. **2.** An inexperienced or conceited young person. —*intr.v.* **pupped, pup•ping, pups.** To give birth to pups. [Short for PUPPY.]

pu•pa (pyo͞o′pə) *n., pl.* **-pae** (-pē) or **-pas.** The nonfeeding stage between the larva and adult in the metamorphosis of holometabolous insects, during which the larva typically undergoes complete transformation within a protective cocoon or hardened case. [Lat. *pūpa*, girl, doll.] —**pu′pal** *adj.*

pu•pate (pyo͞o′pāt′) *intr.v.* **-pat•ed, -pat•ing, -pates. 1.** To become a pupa. **2.** To go through a pupal stage. —**pu•pa′tion** *n.*

pup•fish (pŭp′fĭsh′) *n., pl.* **pupfish** or **-fish•es.** Any of various small killfishes of the genus *Cyprinodon* of Mexico and the southwest United States.

pu•pil¹ (pyo͞o′pəl) *n.* **1.** A student under the direct supervision of a teacher or professor. **2.** *Law.* A minor under the supervision of a guardian. [ME *pupille*, orphan < OFr. < Lat. *pūpillus*, dim. of *pūpus*, boy.]

pu•pil² (pyo͞o′pəl) *n.* The circular opening in the center of the iris of the eye, through which light passes to the retina. [ME < OFr. *pupille* < Lat. *pūpilla*, little doll, pupil (< the tiny image reflected in it). See PUPIL¹.] —**pu′pi•lar** *adj.*

pu•pil•age also **pu•pil•lage** (pyo͞o′pə-lĭj) *n.* The state or period of being a pupil.

pu•pil•lar•y¹ (pyo͞o′pə-lĕr′ē) *adj.* Of or relating to a student or ward.

pu•pil•lar•y² (pyo͞o′pə-lĕr′ē) *adj.* Of or affecting the pupil.

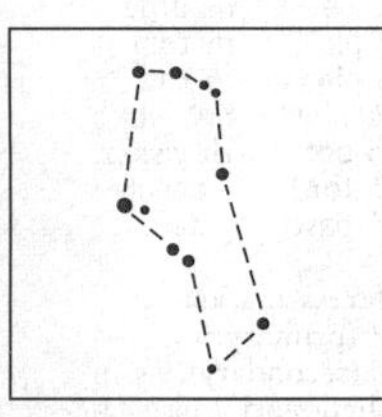

Puppis

Pu•pin (pyo͞o-pēn′, po͞o′pēn), **Michael Idvorsky.** 1858–1935. Hungarian-born Amer. physicist who worked on improvements to the telegraph, the telephone, and x-ray photography.

pu•pip•a•rous (pyo͞o-pĭp′ər-əs) *adj.* Producing well-developed young that are ready to pupate. Used of an insect.

pup•pet (pŭp′ĭt) *n.* **1.** A small figure having a hollow head and often a cloth body, designed to be fitted over and manipulated by the hand. **2.** A figure having jointed parts animated from above by strings or wires; a marionette. **3.** A toy representing a human figure; a doll. **4.** One whose behavior is determined by the will of others. [ME *poppet*, doll, poss. < AN *poppe*, doll. See PUPPY.]

pup•pet•eer (pŭp′ĭ-tîr′) *n.* One who entertains with and operates puppets or marionettes.

pup•pet•ry (pŭp′ĭ-trē) *n., pl.* **-ries. 1.** The art of making puppets and presenting puppet shows. **2.** The actions of puppets. **3.** A stilted or artificial dramatic performance.

Pup•pis (pŭp′ĭs) *n.* A constellation in the Southern Hemisphere near Canis Major and Pyxis. [Lat. *puppis*, stern, poop.]

pup•py (pŭp′ē) *n., pl.* **-pies. 1.** A young dog; a pup. **2.** An inexperienced young person; a pup. [ME *popi*, small pet dog, perh. < AN *poppe*, doll < VLat. **puppa* < Lat. *pūpa*.]

pup•py•ish (pŭp′ē-ĭsh) *adj.* Resembling a puppy.

puppy love *n.* Adolescent love or infatuation.

pup tent *n.* See **shelter tent.**

pur•blind (pûr′blīnd′) *adj.* **1.** Having poor vision; nearly or partly blind. **2.** Slow in understanding or discernment; dull. **3.** *Obsolete.* Completely blind. [ME *pur blind*, totally blind, nearsighted : *pur*, pure; see PURE + *blind*, blind; see BLIND.] —**pur′blind′ly** *adv.* —**pur′blind′ness** *n.*

Pur•cell (pûr-sĕl′), **Edward Mills.** b. 1912. Amer. physicist who shared a 1952 Nobel Prize.

Pur•cell (pûr′səl, pûr-sĕl′), **Henry.** 1659?–95. English composer known for his opera *Dido and Aeneas* (1689).

pur•chas•a•ble (pûr′chĭ-sə-bəl) *adj.* **1.** That can be bought. **2.** Capable of being bribed; venal. —**pur′chas•a•bil′i•ty** *n.*

pur•chase (pûr′chĭs) *tr.v.* **-chased, -chas•ing, -chas•es. 1.** To obtain in exchange for money or its equivalent; buy. **2.** To acquire by effort; earn. **3.** To move or hold with a mechanical device, such as a lever. —*n.* **1.a.** The act or an instance of buying. **b.** Something bought. **c.** Acquisition through the payment of money or its equivalent. **2.** A grip applied manually or mechanically to move something or prevent it from slipping. **3.** A device, such as a lever, used to obtain mechanical advantage. **4.** A position, as of a lever, affording means to move or secure a weight. **5.a.** A means of increasing power or influence. **b.** An advantage that is used in exerting one's power. [ME *purchasen*, to pursue, purchase < OFr. *purchacier* : *pur-*, forth (< Lat. *prō-*; see **per¹***) + *chacier*, to chase; see CHASE¹.] —**pur′chas•er** *n.*

pur•dah (pûr′də) *n.* **1.a.** A curtain or screen, used mainly in India to keep women separate from men or strangers. **b.** The Hindu or Muslim system of sex segregation, practiced esp. by keeping women in seclusion. **2.** Social seclusion. [Urdu *pardah*, veil < Pers. < MPers. *pardak* < OPers. **paridaka-* < *pari-dā-*, to place over : *pari*, around, over; see **per¹*** + *dā-*, to place; see **dhē-*.**]

pure (pyo͝or) *adj.* **pur•er, pur•est. 1.** Having a homogeneous or uniform composition; not mixed. **2.** Free from adulterants or impurities. **3.** Free of dirt, defilement, or pollution. **4.** Free of foreign elements. **5.** Containing nothing inappropriate or extraneous. **6.** Complete; utter. **7.** Having no faults; sinless. **8.** Chaste; virgin. **9.** Of unmixed ancestry; purebred. **10.** *Genet.* Produced by self-fertilization or continual inbreeding; homozygous. **11.** *Mus.* Free from discordant qualities. **12.** *Ling.* Articulated with a single unchanging speech sound; monophthongal: *a pure vowel.* **13.** Theoretical: *pure science.* **14.** *Philos.* Free of empirical elements: *pure reason.* [ME *pur* < OFr. < Lat. *pūrus*. See **peuə-*.**] —**pure′ly** *adv.* —**pure′ness** *n.*

Syns: pure, absolute, sheer, simple, unadulterated. The central meaning shared by these adjectives is "free of extraneous elements": *pure gold; absolute alcohol; sheer wine; a simple substance; unadulterated coffee.*

pure•blood (pyo͝or′blŭd′) also **pure•blood•ed** (-blŭd′ĭd) *adj.* Of unmixed ancestry; purebred. —**pure′blood′** *n.*

pure•bred (pyo͝or′brĕd′) *adj.* Of a recognized strain established by breeding individuals of unmixed lineage over many generations. —*n.* (pyo͝or′brĕd′). A purebred animal.

pu•rée (pyo͝o-rā′, pyo͝or′ā) *tr.v.* **-réed, -rée•ing, -rées.** To rub through a sieve or process (food) in a blender. —*n.* Food prepared by straining or blending. [< Fr., pureé < OFr. < fem. p.part. of *purer*, to strain, clean < Lat. *pūrāre*, to purify < *pūrus*, clean. See **peuə-*.**]

pur•fle (pûr′fəl) *tr.v.* **-fled, -fling, -fles.** To finish or decorate the border or edge of. —*n.* also **pur•fling** (-flĭng). An ornamental border or edging. [ME *purfilen* < OFr. *porfiler* < VLat. **prōfīlāre* : Lat. *prō-*, forth; see PRO-¹ + Lat. *fīlum*, thread; see **gʷhī-*.**]

pur•ga•tion (pûr-gā′shən) *n.* The act of purging or purifying.

pur•ga•tive (pûr′gə-tĭv) *adj.* Tending to cleanse or purge, esp. causing evacuation of the bowels. —*n.* A purgative agent or medicine; a cathartic.

Pur•ga•toire (pûr′gə-twär′, -tôr′ē, -tôr′ē). A river of SE CO flowing c. 299 km (186 mi) to the Arkansas R.

pur•ga•to•ri•al (pûr′gə-tôr′ē-əl, -tōr′-) *adj.* **1.** Serving to purify of sin; expiatory. **2.** Of or resembling purgatory.

pur•ga•to•ry (pûr′gə-tôr′ē, -tōr′ē) *n., pl.* **-ries. 1.** *Rom. Cath. Ch.* A state in which the souls of those who have died in grace must expiate their sins. **2.** A place or condition of suffering, expiation, or remorse. — *adj.* Tending to cleanse or purge. [ME *purgatorie* < OFr. *purgatoire* < Med.Lat. *pūrgātōrium* < LLat., means of purgation < neut. of *pūrgātōrius*, cleansing < Lat. *pūrgāre*, to cleanse. See PURGE.]

purge (pûrj) *v.* **purged, purg•ing, purg•es.** — *tr.* **1.a.** To free from impurities; purify. **b.** To remove (impurities and other elements) by or as if by cleansing. **2.** To rid of sin, guilt, or defilement. **3.** *Law.* To clear (a person) of a charge or an imputation. Often used with respect to contempt of court. **4.a.** To rid (a nation, for example) of people considered undesirable. **b.** To get rid of (people considered undesirable). **5.** *Medic.* **a.** To cause evacuation of (the bowels or stomach). **b.** To induce evacuation of the bowels or stomach in (an individual). — *intr.* **1.** To become pure or clean. **2.** *Medic.* To undergo or cause an emptying of the bowels or stomach. — *n.* **1.** The act or process of purging. **2.** Something that purges, esp. a medicinal purgative. [ME *purgen* < OFr. *purgier* < Lat. *pūrgāre* < *pūrus*, pure. See **peuə-***.] — **purg′er** *n.*

pu•ri (po͝or′ē) *n.* Var. of **poori.**

pu•ri•fi•ca•tion (pyo͝or′ə-fĭ-kā′shən) *n.* The act or an instance of cleansing or purifying.

pu•ri•fi•ca•tor (pyo͝or′ə-fĭ-kā′tər) *n. Eccles.* A cloth used to clean the chalice after the celebration of the Eucharist.

pu•ri•fy (pyo͝or′ə-fī′) *v.* **-fied, -fy•ing, -fies.** — *tr.* **1.** To rid of impurities; cleanse. **2.** To rid of foreign or objectionable elements. **3.** To free from sin, guilt, or other defilement. — *intr.* To become clean or pure. [ME *purifien* < OFr. *purifier* < Lat. *pūrificāre* : *pūrus*, clean; see PURE + *-ficāre*, -fy.] — **pu•rif′i•ca•to′ry** (pyo͞o-rĭf′ĭ-kə-tôr′ē, -tōr′ē) *adj.* — **pu′ri•fi′er** *n.*

Pu•rim (po͝or′ĭm, po͞o-rēm′) *n. Judaism.* The 14th of Adar, observed in celebration of the delivery by Esther of the Persian Jews from massacre. [Heb. *pûrîm*, pl. of *pûr*, lot (from the lots Haman cast to decide the day of the massacre, Esther 9:24–26) < Akkadian *pūru*, lot.]

pu•rine (pyo͝or′ēn′) *n.* **1.** A crystalline organic base, $C_5H_4N_4$, that is the parent compound of various biologically important derivatives. **2.** Any of a group of organic compounds derived from or structurally related to purine, including uric acid and the nucleic acid constituents adenine and guanine. [Ger. *Purin* : Lat. *pūrus*, clean; see PURE + NLat. *uricus, uricum*, uric (< Gk. *ouron*, urine) + *-in*, n. suff. (< Fr. *-ine*; see -IN).]

pur•ism (pyo͝or′ĭz′əm) *n.* **1.** Strict observance of or insistence on traditional correctness, esp. of language. **2.** An example of purism.

pur•ist (pyo͝or′ĭst) *n.* One who practices or urges strict correctness, esp. in the use of words. — **pu•ris′tic** (pyo͞o-rĭs′tĭk) *adj.* — **pu•ris′ti•cal•ly** *adv.*

Pu•ri•tan (pyo͝or′ĭ-tn) *n.* **1.** A member of a group of English Protestants who in the 16th and 17th centuries advocated strict religious discipline and simplification of the ceremonies and creeds of the Church of England. **2. puritan.** One who lives in accordance with strict religious or moral precepts, esp. one who regards pleasure as sinful. — *adj.* **1.** Of or relating to the Puritans or Puritanism. **2. puritan.** Characteristic of a puritan; puritanical. [< LLat. *pūritās*, purity < Lat. *pūrus*, pure. See **peuə-***.]

pu•ri•tan•i•cal (pyo͝or′ĭ-tăn′ĭ-kəl) *adj.* **1.** Rigorous in religious observance; marked by stern morality. **2. Puritanical.** Of, relating to, or characteristic of the Puritans. — **pu′ri•tan′i•cal•ly** *adv.* — **pu′ri•tan′i•cal•ness** *n.*

Pu•ri•tan•ism (pyo͝or′ĭ-tn-ĭz′əm) *n.* **1.** The practices and doctrines of the Puritans. **2. puritanism.** Scrupulous moral rigor, esp. hostility to social pleasures and indulgences.

pu•ri•ty (pyo͝or′ĭ-tē) *n.* **1.** The quality or condition of being pure. **2.** Freedom from sin or guilt; innocence; chastity. **3.** The absence in speech or writing of elements deemed inappropriate to good style. **4.** *Color.* The degree to which a color is free from being mixed with other colors.

Pur•kin•je cell (pûr-kĭn′jē) *n.* A large, drop-shaped, densely branching neuron that is the characteristic cell of the cerebellar cortex. [After Johannes Evangelista von *Purkinje* (1787–1869), Bohemian physiologist.]

Purkinje fiber *n.* One of a network of specialized cardiac muscle fibers that rapidly transmit impulses from the atrioventricular node to the ventricles.

purl¹ (pûrl) *intr.v.* **purled, purl•ing, purls.** To flow or ripple with a murmuring sound. — *n.* The sound made by rippling water. [Prob. of Scand. orig.]

purl² also **pearl** (pûrl) — *v.* **purled, purl•ing, purls** also **pearled, pearl•ing, pearls.** — *tr.* **1.** To knit (yarn) with a purl stitch. **2.** To edge or finish (a handkerchief, for example) with lace or embroidery. — *intr.* **1.** To do knitting with a purl stitch. **2.** To edge or finish with lace or embroidery. — *n.* **1.** Inversion of a knit stitch; purl stitch. **2.** A decorative edging of lace or embroidery. **3.** Gold or silver wire used in embroidery. [?]

pur•lieu (pûrl′yo͞o, pûr′lo͞o) *n.* **1.** An outlying or neighboring area. **2. purlieus.** Outskirts; the environs. **3.** A place one frequents. [ME *purlewe*, piece of land on the edge of a forest, prob. alteration of *porale, purale*, royal perambulation < OFr. *porale* < *poraler*, to traverse : *por-*, forth (< Lat. *prō-*; see PRO-¹) + *aler, aller*, to go; see ALLEY¹.]

pur•lin also **pur•line** (pûr′lĭn) *n.* One of several horizontal timbers supporting the rafters of a roof. [ME.]

pur•loin (pər-loin′, pûr′loin′) *v.* **-loined, -loin•ing, -loins.** — *tr.* To steal, often in a violation of trust. — *intr.* To commit theft. [ME *purloinen*, to remove < AN *purloigner* : *pur-*, away (< Lat. *prō-*; see PRO-¹) + *loign*, far (< Lat. *longē* < *longus*, long; see **del-¹***).] — **pur•loin′er** *n.*

purl stitch *n.* An inverted knitting stitch, often alternated with the knit stitch to produce a ribbed effect.

pu•ro•my•cin (pyo͝or′ə-mī′sĭn) *n.* An antibiotic, $C_{22}H_{29}N_7O_5$, obtained from the soil bacterium *Streptomyces alboniger* and used experimentally as an inhibitor of protein synthesis. [PUR(INE) + -MYCIN.]

pur•ple (pûr′pəl) *n.* **1.** *Color.* Any of a group of colors with a hue between that of violet and red. **2.** Cloth of a color between violet and red, once a symbol of royalty or high office. **3.** Imperial power; high rank. — *adj.* **1.** *Color.* Of the color purple. **2.** Royal or imperial; regal. **3.** Elaborate and ornate. — *tr. & intr.v.* **-pled, -pling, -ples.** To make or become purple. [ME < OE *purpul* < *purpure*, purple garment < Lat. *purpura* < Gk. *porphura*, a shellfish yielding purple dye.]

purple grackle *n.* The common grackle *(Quiscalus quiscula)* of eastern North America having iridescent blackish-purple plumage and a long keel-shaped tail.

pur•ple•heart (pûr′pəl-härt′) *n.* **1.** A tropical tree *(Peltogyne paniculata)* native to Guiana and Trinidad and having very hard durable brown wood that turns a purple color on exposure. **2.** The purplish heartwood of this tree.

Pur•ple Heart (pûr′pəl) *n.* A U.S. military decoration awarded to members of the armed forces wounded in action.

Purple Heart

purple loosestrife *n.* An Old World marsh plant *(Lythrum salicaria)* having long spikes of purple flowers.

purple martin *n.* A large North American swallow *(Progne subis)* having glossy blue-black plumage and a light-colored breast in the female.

pur•plish (pûr′plĭsh) *adj. Color.* Somewhat purple.

pur•port (pər-pôrt′, -pōrt′) *tr.v.* **-port•ed, -port•ing, -ports.** **1.** To have or present the often false appearance of being or intending; profess. **2.** To have the intention of doing; purpose. — *n.* (pûr′pôrt′, -pōrt′). **1.** Meaning presented, intended, or implied; import. **2.** Intention; purpose. [ME *purporten*, to set forth < AN *purporter* : *pur-*, forth (< Lat. *prō-*; see PRO-¹) + *porter*, to carry (< Lat. *portāre*; see **per-²***).]

pur•port•ed (pər-pôr′tĭd, -pōr′-) *adj.* Assumed to be such; supposed. — **pur•port′ed•ly** *adv.*

pur•pose (pûr′pəs) *n.* **1.** The object toward which one strives or for which something exists; an aim or a goal. **2.** A result or an effect that is intended or desired; an intention. See Syns at **intention. 3.** Determination; resolution. **4.** The matter at hand; the point at issue. — *tr.v.* **-posed, -pos•ing, -pos•es.** To intend or resolve to perform or accomplish. — ***idioms.* on purpose.** Intentionally; deliberately. **to good purpose.** With good results. **to little (or no) purpose.** With few or no results. [ME *purpos* < AN < *purposer*, to intend : *pur-*, forth (< Lat. *prō-*; see PRO-¹) + *poser*, to put; see POSE¹.]

pur•pose•ful (pûr′pəs-fəl) *adj.* **1.** Having a purpose; intentional. **2.** Having or manifesting purpose; determined. — **pur′pose•ful•ly** *adv.* — **pur′pose•ful•ness** *n.*

pur•pose•less (pûr′pəs-lĭs) *adj.* Lacking a purpose; meaningless or aimless. — **pur′pose•less•ness** *n.*

pur•pose•ly (pûr′pəs-lē) *adv.* With specific purpose.

pur•po•sive (pûr′pə-sĭv) *adj.* **1.** Having or serving a purpose. **2.** Purposeful. — **pur′po•sive•ness** *n.*

pur•pu•ra (pûr′pə-rə, -pyə-) *n.* A condition characterized by hemorrhages in the skin and mucous membranes that result in the appearance of purplish spots or patches. [Lat., purple. See PURPLE.] — **pur•pu′ric** (-pyo͝or′ĭk) *adj.*

pur•pu•rin (pûr′pyə-rĭn′) *n.* A reddish crystalline compound, $C_{14}H_5O_2(OH)_3$, used as a biological stain and commercial dye. [Lat. *purpura*, purple; see PURPLE + -IN.]

purr (pûr) *n.* **1.** The soft vibrant sound made by a cat. **2.** A sound similar to that made by a cat. — *v.* **purred, purr•ing, purrs.** — *intr.* To make or utter a purr. — *tr.* To express by a purr. [Imit.]

purse (pûrs) *n.* **1.** A woman's bag for carrying personal items; a handbag. **2.** A small bag or pouch for carrying money. **3.** Something that resembles a bag or pouch. **4.** Available wealth or resources; money. **5.** A sum of money collected as a present or offered as a prize. — *tr.v.* **pursed, purs•ing, purs•es.** To gather or contract (the lips or brow) into wrinkles or folds; pucker. [ME < OE < LLat. *bursa*. See BURSA.]

purs•er (pûr′sər) *n.* The officer in charge of money matters on a ship or commercial aircraft. [ME < *purse*, purse. See PURSE.]

purse seine *n.* A fishing seine that is drawn into the shape of a bag to enclose the catch.

purse strings or **purse•strings** (pûrs′strĭngz′) *pl.n.* Financial support or resources, or control over them.

purs•lane (pûrs′lĭn, -lān′) *n.* A trailing Asian weed *(Portulaca oleracea)* having small yellow flowers, reddish stems, and fleshy obovate edible leaves. [ME < AN **purcelane*, altera-

ă pat	oi boy
ā pay	ou out
âr care	o͝o took
ä father	o͞o boot
ĕ pet	ŭ cut
ē be	ûr urge
ĭ pit	th thin
ī pie	*th* this
îr pier	hw which
ŏ pot	zh vision
ō toe	ə about, item
ô paw	

Stress marks:
′ (primary);
′ (secondary), as in
dictionary (dĭk′shə-nĕr′ē)

tion of Lat. *portulāca, porcilāca.* See PORTULACA.]

pur•su•ance (pər-sōō′əns) *n.* A carrying out or putting into effect; prosecution.

pur•su•ant (pər-sōō′ənt) *adj.* Proceeding from and conformable to; in accordance with. — *adv.* Accordingly; consequently. [Prob. < ME *pursuant,* aspirant < AN, pr.part. of *pursure,* to pursue. See PURSUE.]

pur•sue (pər-sōō′) *v.* **-sued, -su•ing, -sues.** — *tr.* **1.** To follow in an effort to overtake or capture; chase. **2.** To strive to gain or accomplish. **3.** To proceed along the course of; follow. **4.** To carry further; advance. **5.** To be engaged in (a vocation or hobby, for example). **6.** To court. **7.** To continue to torment or afflict; haunt. — *intr.* **1.** To follow in an effort to overtake or capture; chase. **2.** To carry on; continue. [ME *pursuen* < AN *pursure* < VLat. **prōsequere* < Lat. *prōsequī.* See PROSECUTE.] — **pur•su′a•ble** *adj.* — **pur•su′er** *n.*

pur•suit (pər-sōōt′) *n.* **1.** The act or an instance of chasing or pursuing. **2.** The act of striving. **3.** An activity, such as a vocation or hobby, engaged in regularly. [ME < AN *pursuite* < *pursure,* to pursue. See PURSUE.]

pursuit plane *n.* A high-speed fighter plane designed and equipped to pursue and attack enemy aircraft.

pushup

pur•sui•vant (pûr′swĭ-vənt) *n.* **1.** An officer in the British Colleges of Heralds who ranks below a herald. **2.** A follower or an attendant. [ME *pursevant,* attendant < OFr. *poursuivant* < pr.part. of *poursuivre,* to follow < VLat. **prōsequere.* See PURSUE.]

pur•te•nance (pûr′tn-əns) *n.* An animal's viscera or internal organs, esp. the heart, liver, and lungs. [ME *pertenaunce, purtenaunce,* adjunct < OFr. *partenance, pertinence* < *partenir,* to pertain. See PERTAIN.]

pur•ty (pûr′tē) *adj. Regional.* **pretty.**

Regional Note: *Purty* is probably the most common American example of metathesis, a linguistic process in which two adjacent sounds are reversed in order. Metathesis in English often involves the consonant *r* and a vowel. For example, the word *third* used to be *thrid.* By the same process, English *pretty* often became *purty* in regional speech.

pu•ru•lence (pyŏŏr′ə-ləns, pyŏŏr′yə-) *n.* **1.** The condition of containing or discharging pus. **2.** Pus.

pu•ru•lent (pyŏŏr′ə-lənt, pyŏŏr′yə-) *adj.* Containing, discharging, or causing the production of pus. [ME *purulente* < OFr. *purulent* < Lat. *pūrulentus* < *pūs, pūr-,* pus. See **pū-*.**] — **pu′ru•lent•ly** *adv.*

Pu•rus (pə-rōōs′, pōō-). A river of E-central Peru and W Brazil flowing c. 3,379 km (2,100 mi) to the Amazon R.

pussy willow
American pussy willow
Salix discolor

pur•vey (pər-vā′, pûr′vā′) *tr.v.* **-veyed, -vey•ing, -veys. 1.** To supply (food, for example); furnish. **2.** To advertise or circulate. [ME *purveien* < AN *purveier* < Lat. *prōvidēre.* See PROVIDE.] — **pur•vey′ance** *n.*

pur•vey•or (pər-vā′ər) *n.* **1.** One that furnishes provisions, esp. food. **2.** One that promulgates something.

pur•view (pûr′vyōō′) *n.* **1.** The extent or range of function, power, or competence; scope. **2.** Range of vision, comprehension, or experience; outlook. [Alteration of ME *purveu,* proviso < AN *purveu est,* it is provided (introducing a proviso), p.part. of *purveier,* to provide. See PURVEY.]

pus (pŭs) *n.* A generally viscous yellowish-white fluid formed in infected tissue, consisting of white blood cells, cellular debris, and necrotic tissue. [Lat. *pūs.* See **pū-*.**]

Pu•san (pōō′sän′) also **Fu•san** (fōō′-). A city of SE South Korea on Korea Strait SE of Seoul. Pop. 3,517,000.

Pu•sey (pyōō′zē), **Edward Bouverie.** 1800–82. British theologian who led the Oxford movement after 1845.

Pu•sey•ism (pyōō′zē-ĭz′əm, pyōō′sē-) *n.* Tractarianism. [After Edward Bouverie PUSEY.] — **Pu′sey•ite′** (-īt′) *n.*

push (pŏŏsh) *v.* **pushed, push•ing, push•es.** — *tr.* **1.** To apply pressure against for the purpose of moving. **2.** To move (an object) by exerting force against it; thrust or shove. **3.** To force (one's way). **4.** To urge forward or urge insistently; pressure. **5.** To bear hard upon; press. **6.** To exert downward pressure on (a button or keyboard, for example); press. **7.** To extend or enlarge. **8.** *Slang.* **a.** To promote or sell (a product). **b.** To sell (a narcotic) illegally. — *intr.* **1.** To exert outward pressure or force against something. **2.** To advance despite difficulty or opposition; press forward. **3.** To expend great or vigorous effort. — *n.* **1.** The act of pushing; a thrust. **2.** A vigorous or insistent effort toward an end; a drive. **3.** A provocation to action; a stimulus. **4.** *Informal.* Persevering energy; enterprise. — ***phrasal verbs.*** **push around.** *Informal.* To treat or threaten to treat roughly; intimidate. **push off.** *Informal.* To set out; depart. **push on.** To continue or proceed along one's way. — ***idiom.*** **when** (or **if**) **push comes to shove.** At a point when or if all else has been taken into account and matters must be confronted. [ME *pusshen* < OFr. *poulser, pousser* < Lat. *pulsāre,* freq. of *pellere,* to strike, push. See **pel-⁵*.**]

Syns: *push, propel, shove, thrust.* The central meaning shared by these verbs is "to press against something in order to move it forward or aside": *push a baby carriage; wind propelling a sailboat; shove a tray across a table; thrust the stick into the ground.* ***Ant:*** *pull.*

push•ball (pŏŏsh′bôl′) *n. Sports.* **1.** A game in which two opposing teams attempt to push a heavy ball, 6 feet (5.5 meters) in diameter, across a goal. **2.** The ball used in this game.

push broom *n.* A broom having a wide brush perpendicular to the end of a long handle, designed to be pushed in sweeping.

push button or **push•but•ton** (pŏŏsh′bŭt′n) *n.* A small button that activates an electric circuit when pushed.

push-but•ton or **push•but•ton** (pŏŏsh′bŭt′n) *adj.* Equipped with or operated by a push button.

push•cart (pŏŏsh′kärt′) *n.* A light cart pushed by hand.

push•down (pŏŏsh′doun′) *n. Comp. Sci.* A set of stored data in which the first item to be retrieved is the one most recently stored.

push•er (pŏŏsh′ər) *n. Slang.* One who sells drugs illegally.

push•ful (pŏŏsh′fəl′) *adj.* Pushing. — **push′ful•ness** *n.*

push•ing (pŏŏsh′ĭng) *adj.* **1.** Energetic; enterprising. **2.** Aggressive; forward; presuming. — **push′ing•ly** *adv.*

Push•kin (pŏŏsh′kĭn, pōōsh′-), **Aleksandr Sergeyevich.** 1799–1837. Russian writer whose works include the novel *Eugene Onegin* (1831) and the play *Boris Godunov* (1831).

push•o•ver (pŏŏsh′ō′vər) *n.* **1.** One easily defeated or taken advantage of. **2.** Something easily done or attained.

push•pin (pŏŏsh′pĭn′) *n.* **1.** A tacklike pin with a large head that is easily inserted into a wall or board. **2.** *Games.* A game played by children with pins.

Push•tu (pŭsh′tōō) *n.* Var. of **Pashto.**

push•up (pŏŏsh′ŭp′) *n.* **1.** *Sports.* An exercise performed by lying face down with the palms on the floor and moving the body up and down with the arms. **2.** *Comp. Sci.* A set of stored data in which the first item to be retrieved is the one stored earliest.

push•y (pŏŏsh′ē) *adj.* **-i•er, -i•est.** Disagreeably aggressive or forward. — **push′i•ly** *adv.* — **push′i•ness** *n.*

pu•sil•la•nim•i•ty (pyōō′sə-lə-nĭm′ĭ-tē) *n.* The state or quality of being pusillanimous; cowardice.

pu•sil•lan•i•mous (pyōō′sə-lăn′ə-məs) *adj.* Lacking courage; cowardly. [ME *pusillanimus* < LLat. *pusillanimis* : Lat. *pusillus,* weak, dim. of *pullus,* young of an animal; see **pau-*** + *animus,* reason, mind; see **anə-*.**] — **pu′sil•lan′i•mous•ly** *adv.*

puss¹ (pŏŏs) *Informal. n.* **1.** A cat. **2.** A girl or young woman. [Prob. of Gmc. orig.]

puss² (pŏŏs) *n. Slang.* **1.** The mouth. **2.** The human face. [Ir. Gael. *pus,* mouth < MIr. *bus,* lip.]

puss•ley (pŭs′lē) *n.* Purslane. [Alteration of *pursley,* alteration of PURSLANE.]

puss•y¹ (pŏŏs′ē) *n., pl.* **-ies. 1.** *Informal.* A cat. **2.** *Bot.* A fuzzy catkin, esp. of the pussy willow. **3.** *Vulgar Slang.* The vulva. **4.** *Offensive Slang.* Used as a disparaging term for a woman.

pus•sy² (pŭs′ē) *adj.* **-si•er, -si•est.** Containing or resembling pus.

puss•y•cat (pŏŏs′ē-kăt′) *n.* **1.** A cat. **2.** *Informal.* One who is regarded as easygoing, mild-mannered, or amiable.

puss•y•foot (pŏŏs′ē-fŏŏt′) *intr.v.* **-foot•ed, -foot•ing, -foots. 1.** To move stealthily or cautiously. **2.** *Informal.* To act or proceed cautiously or timidly to avoid committing oneself. — **puss′y•foot′er** *n.*

puss•y•toes (pŏŏs′ē-tōz′) *pl.n. (used with a sing. or pl. v.)* Any of several low-growing perennial plants of the genus *Antennaria,* having downy leaves and clusters of white flower heads.

puss•y willow (pŏŏs′ē) *n.* **1.** A deciduous North American shrub or small tree *(Salix discolor)* having large silky catkins. **2.** Any of several willows similar to this plant.

pus•tu•lant (pŭs′chə-lənt, pŭs′tyə-) *adj.* Causing the formation of pustules. — *n.* A pustulant agent.

pus•tu•lar (pŭs′chə-lər, pŭs′tyə-) *adj.* Of, relating to, or consisting of pustules.

pus•tu•late (pŭs′chə-lāt′, pŭs′tyə-) *v.* **-lat•ed, -lat•ing, -lates.** — *tr.* To cause to form pustules. — *intr.* To form pustules. — *adj.* (*also* -lĭt). Covered with pustules. — **pus′tu•la′tion** *n.*

pus•tule (pŭs′chōōl, pŭs′tyōōl) *n.* **1.** A small inflamed elevation of the skin that is filled with pus; a pimple. **2.** A small swelling similar to a blister or pimple. **3.** Something likened to an inflamed pus-filled lesion. [ME < OFr. < Lat. *pustula,* blister.]

put (pŏŏt) *v.* **put, put•ting, puts.** — *tr.* **1.** To place in a specified location; set. **2.** To cause to be in a specified condition: *His manners put me at ease.* **3.** To cause (one) to undergo something; subject. **4.** To assign; attribute: *put a false interpretation on events.* **5.** To estimate. **6.** To impose or levy. **7.** *Games.* To wager (a stake); bet. **8.** *Sports.* To hurl with an overhand pushing motion. **9.** To bring up for consideration or judgment. **10.** To express; state. **11.** To render in a specified language or literary form. **12.** To adapt: *put lyrics to music.* **13.** To urge or force to an action. **14.** To apply: *We must put our minds to it.* — *intr.* **1.** To begin to move, esp. in a hurry. **2.** *Naut.* To proceed: *The ship put into the harbor.* — *n.* **1.** *Sports.* An act of putting the shot. **2.** An option to sell a stipulated amount of stock or securities within a specified time and at a fixed price. — *adj. Informal.* Fixed; stationary:

stay put. **—phrasal verbs. put about.** *Naut.* To change or cause to change direction; go or cause to go from one tack to another. **put across. 1.** To state so as to be understood clearly or accepted readily. **2.** To attain or carry through by deceit or trickery. **put away. 1.** To renounce; discard. **2.** *Informal.* To consume (food or drink) readily and quickly. **3.** *Informal.* To confine to a mental health facility. **4.a.** *Informal.* To kill. **b.** To bury. **put by.** To save for later use. **put down. 1.a.** To write down. **b.** To enter in a list. **2.a.** To bring to an end; repress. **b.** To render ineffective: *put down rumors.* **3.** To subject (an animal) to euthanasia. **4.** *Slang.* **a.** To criticize. **b.** To belittle; disparage. **c.** To humiliate. **5.a.** To assign to a category: *put him down as a sneak.* **b.** To attribute. **6.** To consume (food or drink) readily; put away. **put forth. 1.** To grow. **2.** To bring to bear; exert. **3.** To offer for consideration. **put forward.** To propose for consideration. **put in. 1.** To make a formal offer of. **2.** To interpose: *He put in a good word for me.* **3.** To spend (time) at a location or job. **4.** To plant: *put in 20 rows of trees.* **5.** *Naut.* To enter a port or harbor. **put off. 1.a.** To delay; postpone. **b.** To persuade to delay further action. **2.** To take off; discard. **3.** To repel or repulse, as from bad manners. **4.** To pass (money) or sell (merchandise) fraudulently. **put on. 1.** To clothe oneself with; don. **2.** To apply; activate. **3.** To assume affectedly. **4.** *Slang.* To tease or mislead (another). **5.** To add: *put on weight.* **6.** To produce; perform. **put out. 1.** To extinguish: *put out a fire.* **2.** *Naut.* To leave, as a port or harbor; depart. **3.** To expel: *put out a drunk.* **4.** To publish. **5.a.** To inconvenience. **b.** To offend or irritate. **6.** *Baseball.* To retire a runner. **7.** *Vulgar Slang.* To be sexually active. **put over. 1.** To postpone; delay. **2.** To put across, esp. in order to deceive. **put through. 1.** To bring to a successful end. **2.** To cause to undergo. **3.a.** To make a telephone connection for. **b.** To obtain a connection for (a telephone call). **put to.** *Naut.* To head for shore. **put together.** To construct; create. **put up. 1.** To erect; build. **2.** To preserve; can. **3.** To nominate. **4.** To provide (funds) in advance. **5.** To provide lodgings for. **6.** *Sports.* To startle (game animals) from cover. **7.** To offer for sale. **8.a.** To make a display or the appearance of. **b.** To engage in; carry on: *put up a good fight.* **put upon.** To impose on; overburden. **—idioms. put down roots.** To establish a permanent residence in a locale. **put it to (someone).** *Slang.* **1.** To overburden with tasks or work. **2.** To put blame on. **3.** To take unfair advantage of. **4.** To lay out the facts of a situation to (another) in a forceful, candid manner. **put (one) in mind.** To remind. **put (one's) finger on.** To identify. **put (one's) foot down.** To take a firm stand. **put (one's) foot in (one's) mouth.** To make a tactless remark. **put paid to.** *Chiefly British.* To finish off; put to rest. **put (someone) through (someone's) paces.** To cause to demonstrate ability or skill; test. **put (someone) up to.** To cause to commit a funny, mischievous, or malicious act. **put the arm** (or **bite**) or **squeeze) on.** *Slang.* To ask another for money. **put the finger on.** *Slang.* To inform on. **put the make on.** *Slang.* To make sexual advances to. **put the screws to** (or **on**). *Slang.* To pressure (another) in an extreme manner. **put the skids on.** *Slang.* To bring to a halt. **put to bed.** *Informal.* **1.** To make final preparations for the printing of (a newspaper, for example). **2.** To make final preparations for completing (a project). **put to it.** To cause extreme difficulty for: *put to it to finish the book.* **put two and two together.** To draw the proper conclusions from existing evidence or indications. **put up or shut up.** *Slang.* To have to endure (something unpleasant) without complaining or take the action necessary to remove the source of the unpleasantry. **put up with.** To endure without complaint. [ME *putten,* back-formation < OE **pūtte,* p.t. of *pȳtan,* to put out.]

pu•ta•men (pyo͞o-tā′mən) *n., pl.* **-tam•i•na** (-tăm′ə-nə). A hard shell-like covering, such as that enclosing the kernel of a peach. [Lat. *putāmen,* that which falls off in pruning, shell, husk < *putāre,* to prune. See **peu-***.] **—pu•tam′i•nous** (-tăm′ə-nəs) *adj.*

pu•ta•tive (pyo͞o′tə-tĭv) *adj.* Generally regarded as such; supposed. [ME < OFr. *putatif* < LLat. *putātīvus* < Lat. *putāre,* to prune, think. See **peu-***.] **—pu′ta•tive•ly** *adv.*

put•down or **put-down** (po͝ot′doun′) *n. Slang.* **1.** A dismissal or rejection, esp. in the form of a critical or slighting remark. **2.** A typically good-natured parody, esp. in theater.

put•log (po͝ot′lôg′, -lŏg′, pŭt′-) *n.* One of the short pieces of lumber supporting the floor of a scaffold. [Alteration (influenced by LOG[1]) of obsolete *putlock* : perh. PUT + LOCK[1].]

Put•nam (pŭt′nəm), **Israel.** 1718–90. Amer. soldier who during the Battle of Bunker Hill (Jun. 17, 1775) supposedly issued the order, "Don't one of you shoot until you see the whites of their eyes."

Putnam, Rufus. 1738–1824. Amer. Revolutionary soldier who helped force the British to evacuate Boston (1775).

put•off (po͝ot′ôf′, -ŏf′) *n.* A pretext for inaction; an excuse.

put-on (po͝ot′ŏn′, -ôn′) *adj.* Pretended; feigned. **—***n. Slang.* **1.** A deceptive outward appearance. **2.** The act of teasing or misleading someone, esp. for amusement. **3.** Something, such as a prank, intended as a hoax or joke; a spoof.

Pu•tong•hua also **Pu tong hua** (po͞o′tông′hwä′, -wä′, -tŏng′-) *n.* See **mandarin** 4. [Chin. (Mandarin) *pǔ tōnghuà* : *pǔ,* general, widespread + *tōng,* through + *huà,* words.]

put•out (po͝ot′out′) *abbr. Baseball.* A play in which a batter or base runner is retired.

put-put (pŭt′pŭt′) *n. Slang.* **1.** A small gasoline engine. **2.** A vehicle, such as a boat, that is operated by a small gasoline engine. [Imit. of a running engine.]

pu•tre•fac•tion (pyo͞o′trə-făk′shən) *n.* **1.** Decomposition of organic matter, esp. protein, by microorganisms, resulting in production of foul-smelling matter. **2.** Putrefied matter. **3.** The condition of being putrefied.

pu•tre•fac•tive (pyo͞o′trə-făk′tĭv) *adj.* **1.** Bringing about putrefaction. **2.** Of, relating to, or characterized by putrefaction.

pu•tre•fy (pyo͞o′trə-fī′) *v.* **-fied, -fy•ing, -fies. —***tr.* **1.** To cause to decay and have a foul odor. **2.** To make gangrenous. **—***intr.* **1.** To become decayed and have a foul odor. **2.** To become gangrenous. [ME *putrefien* < OFr. *putrefier* < Lat. *putrefacere* : *puter, putr-,* rotten; see **pŭ-*** + *facere,* to make; see **dhē-***.]

pu•tres•cence (pyo͞o-trĕs′əns) *n.* **1.** A putrescent character or condition. **2.** Putrid matter.

pu•tres•cent (pyo͞o-trĕs′ənt) *adj.* **1.** Becoming putrid; putrefying. **2.** Of or relating to putrefaction. [Lat. *putrēscēns, putrēscent-,* pr.part. of *putrēscere,* to rot, inchoative of *putrēre,* to be rotten < *puter, putr-,* rotten. See **pŭ-***.]

pu•tres•ci•ble (pyo͞o-trĕs′ə-bəl) *adj.* Subject to putrefaction. [Fr. < OFr. < LLat. *putrēscibilis* < Lat. *putrēscere,* to rot. See PUTRESCENT.]

pu•tres•cine (pyo͞o-trĕs′ēn) *n.* A colorless foul-smelling ptomaine, $NH_2(CH_2)_4NH_2$, produced in decaying animal tissue by the decarboxylation of ornithine. [Lat. *putrēscere,* to rot; see PUTRESCENT + -INE[2].]

pu•trid (pyo͞o′trĭd) *adj.* **1.** Decomposed and foul-smelling; rotten. **2.** Proceeding from, relating to, or exhibiting putrefaction. **3.** Morally rotten; corrupt. **4.** Extremely objectionable; vile. [ME *putred* < OFr. *putride* < Lat. *putridus* < *putrēre,* to be rotten < *puter, putr-,* rotten. See **pŭ-***.] **—pu•trid′i•ty** (-trĭd′ĭ-tē), **pu′trid•ness** (-trĭd-nĭs) *n.* **—pu′trid•ly** *adv.*

putsch also **Putsch** (po͝och) *n.* A sudden attempt by a group to overthrow a government. [Ger. < Ger. dial. < MHGer., thrust, of imit. orig.] **—putsch′ist** *n.*

putt (pŭt) *Sports.* **—***n.* A light golf stroke made on the putting green in an effort to place the ball into the hole. **—***v.* **putt•ed, putt•ing, putts. —***tr.* To hit (a golf ball) with a light stroke on the green. **—***intr.* To putt a golf ball. [Var. of PUT.]

put•tee (pŭ-tē′, pŭt′ē) *n.* **1.** A strip of cloth wound spirally around the leg from ankle to knee. Often used in the plural. **2.** A gaiter covering the lower leg. Often used in the plural. [Hindi *paṭṭī* < Skt. *paṭṭikā,* fem. of *paṭṭakaḥ,* bandage, ribbon < *paṭṭaḥ,* strip of cloth.]

put•ter[1] (pŭt′ər) *n. Sports.* **1.** A short golf club used for putting. **2.** A golfer who is putting.

put•ter[2] (pŭt′ər) *v.* **-tered, -ter•ing, -ters. —***intr.* To occupy oneself in an aimless or ineffective manner. **—***tr.* To waste (time) in idling: *puttered away the hours.* [Prob. alteration of *potter,* prob. freq. of ME *poten,* to poke, push < OE *potian.*] **—put′ter•er** *n.*

put•ty (pŭt′ē) *n., pl.* **-ties. 1.a.** A doughlike cement made by mixing whiting and linseed oil, used to fill holes in woodwork and secure panes of glass. **b.** A substance with a similar consistency or function. **2.** A fine lime cement used as a finishing coat on plaster. **3.** *Color.* A yellowish or light brownish gray to grayish yellow or light grayish brown. **—***tr.v.* **-tied, -ty•ing, -ties.** To fill, cover, or secure with putty. [Fr. *potée,* polishing powder < OFr., a potful < *pot,* pot < VLat. **pottus.*]

put•ty•root (pŭt′ē-ro͞ot′, -ro͝ot′) *n.* A North American orchid *(Aplectrum hyemale)* bearing a single leaf and yellowish-brown flowers clustered in a raceme.

Pu•tu•ma•yo (po͞o′tə-mī′ō, po͞o′to͞o-mä′yô). A river of NW South America rising in SW Colombia and flowing c. 1,609 km (1,000 mi) to the Amazon R. in NW Brazil.

put-up (po͝ot′ŭp′) *adj. Informal.* Prearranged secretly.

putz (pŭts) *n.* **1.** *Slang.* A fool; an idiot. **2.** *Vulgar Slang.* A penis. **—***intr.v.* **putzed, putz•ing, putz•es.** *Slang.* To behave in an idle manner; putter. [Yiddish *pots,* penis, fool.]

Pu•vis de Cha•vannes (pyo͞o-vē′ də shä-văn′, -vēs′, pü-vē′), **Pierre.** 1824–98. French artist noted for his decorative and allegorical murals, such as *Work* (1863).

Puy•al•lup (pyo͞o-ăl′əp). A city of W-central WA ESE of Tacoma. Pop. 23,875.

puz•zle (pŭz′əl) *v.* **-zled, -zling, -zles. —***tr.* **1.** To baffle or confuse mentally by presenting or being a difficult problem or matter. **2.** To clarify or solve (something confusing) by reasoning or study. *I puzzled it out.* **—***intr.* **1.** To be perplexed. **2.** To ponder over a problem in an effort to solve or understand it. **—***n.* **1.a.** A jigsaw puzzle. **b.** Something, such as a toy or game, that tests one's ingenuity. **2.** Something that baffles or confuses. **3.** The condition of being perplexed; bewilderment. [?] **—puz′zler** *n.*

puz•zle•ment (pŭz′əl-mənt) *n.* The state of being confused or baffled; perplexity.

ă pat	oi boy
ā pay	ou out
âr care	o͝o took
ä father	o͞o boot
ĕ pet	ŭ cut
ē be	ûr urge
ĭ pit	th thin
ī pie	*th* this
îr pier	hw which
ŏ pot	zh vision
ō toe	ə about,
ô paw	item

Stress marks:
′ (primary);
′ (secondary), as in
dictionary (dĭk′shə-nĕr′ē)

PV *abbr.* Polyvinyl.

PVC (pē′vē-sē′) *n.* A common thermoplastic resin, used in a wide variety of manufactured products, including rainwear, garden hoses, and floor tiles. [P(OLY)V(INYL) C(HLORIDE).]

PVT or **Pvt** or **pvt.** *abbr.* Private.

PWA *abbr.* **1.** Person with AIDS. **2.** Also **P.W.A.** Public Works Administration.

pwr. *abbr.* Power.

pwt. *abbr.* Pennyweight.

pxt. *abbr. Lat.* Pinxit (He, or she, painted this).

py– *pref.* Var. of **pyo–.**

py•a (pē-ä′) *n.* See table at **currency.** [Burmese.]

pyc•nid•i•um (pĭk-nĭd′ē-əm) *n., pl.* **-i•a** (-ē-ə). A flask-shaped asexual structure containing conidia, found in certain fungi. [NLat. : Gk. *puknos,* thick + Lat. *-idium,* dim. suff. (< Gk. *-idion*).] — **pyc•nid′i•al** *adj.*

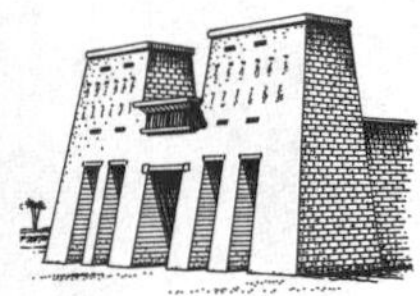
pylon

pyc•nog•o•nid (pĭk-nŏg′ə-nĭd, pĭk′nə-gŏn′ĭd) *n.* See **sea spider.** [< NLat. *Pycnogonidae,* family name < *Pycnogonum,* type genus : Gk. *puknos,* thick + Gk. *gonu,* knee; see **genu-**[1]*.]

pyc•nom•e•ter (pĭk-nŏm′ĭ-tər) *n.* A standard vessel used in measuring the density or specific gravity of materials. [Gk. *puknos,* dense + –METER.]

pye-dog also **pi-dog** (pī′dôg′, -dŏg′) *n.* A stray dog. [Perh. Hindi *pāhi,* outsider.]

py•e•li•tis (pī′ə-lī′tĭs) *n.* Acute inflammation of the pelvis of the kidney, caused by bacterial infection. [NLat. : Gk. *puelos,* basin; see **pleu-*** + –ITIS.] — **py′e•lit′ic** (-lĭt′ĭk) *adj.*

py•e•lo•gram (pī′ə-lə-grăm′) *n.* An x-ray obtained by pyelography. [Gk. *puelos,* basin; see PYELITIS + –GRAM.]

py•e•log•ra•phy (pī′ə-lŏg′rə-fē) *n.* X-ray photography of the pelvis of the kidney after injection with a radiopaque dye. [Gk. *puelos,* basin; see PYELITIS + –GRAPHY.]

py•e•lo•ne•phri•tis (pī′ə-lō-nĭ-frī′tĭs) *n.* Inflammation of the kidney and its pelvis, caused by bacterial infection. [NLat. : Gk. *puelos,* basin; see PYELITIS + NEPHRITIS.]

py•e•mi•a (pī-ē′mē-ə) *n.* Septicemia caused by pyogenic microorganisms in the blood, often resulting in the formation of multiple abscesses. — **py•e′mic** *adj.*

pyramid
The Temple of Inscriptions at Palenque, Mexico

py•gid•i•um (pī-jĭd′ē-əm) *n., pl.* **-i•a** (-ē-ə). The posterior body region or caudal segment of certain insects and other invertebrates. [NLat. < Gk. *pugidion,* dim. of *pugē,* buttocks.] — **py•gid′i•al** (-ē-əl) *adj.*

pyg•mae•an or **pyg•me•an** (pĭg-mē′ən, pĭg′mē-) *adj.* Pygmy. [< Lat. *pygmaeus,* sing. of *Pygmaeī,* the Pygmies. See PYGMY.]

Pyg•ma•lion (pĭg-māl′yən, -mā′lē-ən) *n. Gk. Myth.* A king of Cyprus who carved and then fell in love with a statue of a woman, which Aphrodite brought to life as Galatea.

Pyg•my also **Pig•my** (pĭg′mē) —*n., pl.* **-mies. 1.** *Gk. Myth.* A member of a race of dwarfs. **2.** Also **pygmy.** *Anthro.* A member of any of various peoples, esp. of equatorial Africa and parts of southeast Asia, having an average height less than 5 feet (127 centimeters). **3. pygmy. a.** An individual of unusually small size. **b.** An individual considered to be of little or no importance. —*adj.* **1.** Also **pygmy.** *Anthro.* Of or relating to the Pygmies. **2. pygmy. a.** Unusually or atypically small. **b.** Unimportant; trivial. [ME *pigmie* < Lat. *Pygmaeī,* the Pygmies < Gk. *Pugmaioi* < *pugmē,* cubit, fist. See **peuk-*.**] — **pyg′moid′** (-moid′) *adj.*

py•ja•ma (pə-jä′mə, -jăm′ə) *n. Chiefly British.* Var. of **pajama.**

pyk•nic (pĭk′nĭk) *adj.* Having a short stocky physique. [< Gk. *puknos,* compact.] — **pyk′nic** *n.*

Pyle (pīl), **Ernest ("Ernie") Taylor.** 1900–45. Amer. journalist noted for his stories about World War II soldiers.

py•lon (pī′lŏn′) *n.* **1.** A steel tower supporting high-tension wires. **2.** A tower marking a turning point in a race among aircraft. **3.** A large structure or group of structures marking an entrance or approach. **4.** A monumental gateway in the form of a pair of truncated pyramids serving as the entrance to an ancient Egyptian temple. [Gk. *pulōn,* gateway < *pulē,* gate.]

py•lo•rus (pī-lôr′əs, -lōr′-, pĭ-) *n., pl.* **-lo•ri** (-lôr′ī′, -lōr′ī′). The passage at the lower end of the stomach that opens into the duodenum. [LLat. *pylōrus* < Gk. *pulōros* : *pulē,* gate + *ouros,* guard; see **wer-**[3]*.] — **py•lo′ric** (-ĭk) *adj.*

Pym (pĭm), **John.** 1584–1643. English Parliamentarian who moved for the impeachment of the advisers to Charles I, precipitating the English Civil War.

pyrrhuloxia
Pyrrhuloxia sinuata

pyo– or **py–** *pref.* Pus: *pyoderma.* [Gk. *puo-* < *puon,* pus. See **pū-*.**]

py•o•der•ma (pī′ə-dûr′mə) *n.* A pyogenic skin disease. — **py′o•der′mic** *adj.*

py•o•gen•e•sis (pī′ə-jĕn′ĭ-sĭs) *n.* Formation of pus.

py•o•gen•ic (pī′ə-jĕn′ĭk) *adj.* **1.** Producing pus. **2.** Of, relating to, or characterized by pyogenesis.

py•oid (pī′oid) *adj.* Of or resembling pus.

Pyong•yang (pyŭng′yăng′, -yăng′, pyông′-). The cap. of North Korea, in the SW-central part; an important cultural center and Chinese colony after 108 B.C. Pop. 1,283,000.

py•or•rhe•a or **py•or•rhoe•a** (pī′ə-rē′ə) *n.* **1.** Purulent inflammation of the gums and tooth sockets, often causing loose teeth. **2.** A discharge of pus. — **py′or•rhe′al** *adj.*

py•o•sis (pī-ō′sĭs) *n.* Pyogenesis.

pyr– *pref.* Var. of **pyro–.**

py•ra•can•tha (pī′rə-kăn′thə) *n.* A shrub of the genus *Pyracantha;* the fire thorn. [Lat. < Gk. *purakantha,* a shrub : *pur,* fire; see PYRE + *akantha,* thorn.]

py•ral•id (pī-răl′ĭd, pĭr′ə-lĭd) also **py•ral•i•did** (pī-răl′ĭ-dĭd) *n.* Any of numerous small or medium-sized moths of the family Pyralidae. [< NLat. *Pyralidae,* family name < *Pyralis,* type genus < Gk. *puralis, puralid-,* an insect said to live in fire < *pur,* fire. See PYRE.] — **py•ral′id** *adj.*

pyr•a•mid (pĭr′ə-mĭd) *n.* **1.a.** A solid figure with a polygonal base and triangular faces that meet at a common point. **b.** Something shaped like this polyhedron. **2.a.** A massive monument of ancient Egypt having a rectangular base and four triangular faces culminating in a single apex, built over or around a crypt or tomb. **b.** Any of various similar constructions, esp. a four-sided Mayan temple having stepped sides and a flat top surmounted by ceremonial chambers. **3.** The transactions involved in pyramiding stock. **4.** *Anat.* A structure or part suggestive of a pyramid in shape. —*v.* **-mid•ed, -mid•ing, -mids.** —*tr.* **1.** To place or build in the shape of a pyramid. **2.** To build (an argument, for example) progressively from a basic general premise. **3.** To speculate in (stock) using paper profits as margin for buying more stock. —*intr.* **1.** To assume the shape of a pyramid. **2.** To increase rapidly and on a widening base. **3.** To pyramid stocks. [Lat. *pȳramis, pȳramid-* < Gk. *puramis,* prob. < Egypt. *pimar.*] — **py•ram′i•dal** (pĭ-răm′ĭ-dl), **pyr′a•mid′ic** (-mĭd′ĭk), **pyr′a•mid′i•cal** (-ĭ-kəl) *adj.* — **py•ram′i•dal•ly** *adv.*

pyramidal tract *n.* A major motor pathway of the central nervous system, originating in the cerebral cortex and generally descending through the brainstem to the spinal cord.

Pyr•a•mid Peak (pĭr′ə-mĭd). A mountain, 4,275.5 m (14,018 ft), in the Elk Mts. of W-central CO.

Pyr•a•mus (pĭr′ə-məs) *n. Rom. Myth.* A youth of Babylonia who committed suicide when he mistakenly thought his lover Thisbe was dead.

py•ran (pī′răn′) *n.* Either of two isomers with the formula C_5H_6O, having a ring of five carbon atoms and one oxygen atom. [*pyrone,* heterocyclic compound (PYR(O)– + –ONE) + –AN[2].]

py•rar•gy•rite (pī-rär′jə-rīt′, pĭ-) *n.* A deep red to black silver ore with composition Ag_3SbS_3. [Ger. *Pyrargyrit* : Gk. *puro-,* pyro- + Gk. *arguros,* silver; see ARGENT.]

pyre (pīr) *n.* **1.** A heap of combustibles for burning a corpse as a funeral rite. **2.** A pile of combustibles. [Lat. *pyra* < Gk. *pura* < *pur,* fire. See **pūr-*.**]

py•rene (pī′rēn′, pī-rēn′) *n.* The stone of certain fruits, such as the cherry. [NLat. *pȳrēna* < Gk. *purēn.*]

Pyr•e•nees (pîr′ə-nēz′). A mountain range of SW Europe extending from the Bay of Biscay to the Mediterranean Sea and rising to 3,406.2 m (11,168 ft). — **Pyr′e•ne′an** *adj.*

py•re•noid (pī-rē′noid′, pī′rə-) *n.* A proteinaceous structure found within the chloroplast of certain algae and hornworts that is associated with starch deposition. [NLat. *pȳrēna,* fruit stone; see PYRENE + –OID.]

py•re•thrin (pī-rē′thrĭn, -rĕth′rĭn) *n.* Either of two viscous liquid esters, $C_{21}H_{28}O_3$ or $C_{22}H_{28}O_5$, that are extracted from pyrethrum flowers and used as insecticides.

py•re•thrum (pī-rē′thrəm, -rĕth′rəm) *n.* **1.** Any of several Old World plants of the genus *Chrysanthemum* cultivated for their showy flower heads. **2.** An insecticide made from the dried flower heads of *Chrysanthemum cinerariifolium* or *C. coccineum.* [Lat., pellitory < Gk. *purethron,* feverfew < *pur,* fire (< its warming effect). See PYRETIC.]

py•ret•ic (pī-rĕt′ĭk) *adj.* Relating to, producing, or affected by fever. [NLat. *pyreticus* < Gk. *puretos,* fever < *pur,* fire. See **pūr-*.**]

Py•rex (pī′rĕks′). A trademark used for any of various types of heat-resistant and chemical-resistant glass.

py•rex•i•a (pī-rĕk′sē-ə) *n.* Fever. [NLat. < Gk. *purexis* < *puressein,* to have a fever < *puretos,* fever. See PYRETIC.] — **py•rex′i•al, py•rex′ic** *adj.*

pyr•he•li•om•e•ter (pîr′hē-lē-ŏm′ĭ-tər, pīr′-) *n.* Any of various devices that measure the intensity of solar radiation striking a surface. — **pyr′he•li•o•met′ric** (-ə-mĕt′rĭk) *adj.*

py•ric (pī′rĭk, pĭr′ĭk) *adj.* Of, relating to, or resulting from burning.

pyr•i•dine (pĭr′ĭ-dēn′) *n.* A flammable colorless or yellowish liquid base, C_5H_5N, that has a penetrating odor, serves as the parent compound of many biologically important derivatives, and is used as a solvent and waterproofing agent and in the manufacture of various drugs and vitamins. — **py•rid′ic** (pĭ-rĭd′ĭk) *adj.*

pyr•i•dox•al (pĭr′ĭ-dŏk′səl) *n.* An aldehyde, $C_8H_9NO_3$, one of several active forms of pyridoxine, important in amino acid synthesis. [PYRIDOX(INE) + –AL[3].]

pyr•i•dox•a•mine (pĭr′ĭ-dŏk′sə-mēn′) *n.* A crystalline amine, $C_8H_{12}N_2O_2$, one of several active forms of pyridoxine, important in protein metabolism. [PYRIDOX(INE) + –AMINE.]

pyr•i•dox•ine (pĭr′ĭ-dŏk′sēn, -sĭn) also **pyr•i•dox•in** (-dŏk′-

sĭn) *n.* A pyridine derivative, $C_{18}H_{11}NO_3$, occurring esp. in cereals, yeast, liver, and fish and serving as a coenzyme in amino acid synthesis. [PYRID(INE) + OX(O)– + –INE[2].]

pyr•i•form (pĭr′ə-fôrm′) *adj.* Shaped like a pear. [Med.Lat. *pyrum,* pear (alteration of Lat. *pirum*) + –FORM.]

py•rim•i•dine (pī-rĭm′ĭ-dēn′, pĭ-) *n.* **1.** A crystalline organic base, $C_4H_4N_2$, that is the parent substance of various biologically important derivatives. **2.** Any of several basic compounds derived from or structurally related to pyrimidine, esp. the nucleic acid constituents uracil, cytosine, and thymine. [Alteration of PYRIDINE.]

py•rite (pī′rīt′) *n.* A brass-colored mineral, FeS_2, used as an iron ore and in producing sulfur dioxide for sulfuric acid. [ME *perides, pirite* < OFr. *pirite* < Lat. *pyrītēs,* flint. See PYRITES.] **—py•rit′ic** (-rĭt′ĭk), **py•rit′i•cal** (-ĭ-kəl) *adj.*

py•ri•tes (pī-rī′tēz, pī′rīts′) *n., pl.* **pyrites.** Any of various natural metallic sulfide minerals, esp. of iron. [Lat. *pyrītēs* < Gk. *puritēs (lithos),* fire (stone), flint < *pur,* fire. See **pūr-***.]

pyro. *abbr.* Pyrotechnics.

pyro– or **pyr–** *pref.* **1.** Fire; heat: *pyrotechnic.* **2.** Relating to the action of fire or heat: *pyrometallurgy.* **3.** Fever: *pyrogen.* **4.** Derived from an acid by the loss of a water molecule: *pyrosulfuric acid.* [NLat. < Gk. *puro-* < *pur,* fire. See **pūr-***.]

py•ro•chem•i•cal (pī′rō-kĕm′ĭ-kəl) *adj.* Relating to or being chemical activity at elevated temperatures.

py•ro•clas•tic (pī′rō-klăs′tĭk) *adj.* Composed chiefly of rock fragments of volcanic origin.

py•ro•e•lec•tric•i•ty (pī′rō-ĭ-lĕk-trĭs′ĭ-tē, -ē′lĕk-) *n.* Generation of electric charge on a crystal by change of temperature.

py•ro•gal•lic acid (pī′rō-găl′ĭk, -gô′lĭk) *n.* See **pyrogallol.**

py•ro•gal•lol (pī′rō-găl′ôl′, -ōl′, -ŏl′, -gô′lôl′, -lōl′, -lŏl′) *n.* A toxic crystalline phenol, $C_6H_3(OH)_3$, used as a photographic developer and to treat certain skin diseases. [PYRO– + GALL(IC ACID) + –OL[1].] **—py′ro•gal′lic** (-găl′ĭk, -gô′lĭk) *adj.*

py•ro•gen (pī′rə-jən) *n.* A substance that produces fever.

py•ro•gen•ic (pī′rō-jĕn′ĭk) also **py•rog•e•nous** (pī-rŏj′ə-nəs) *adj.* **1.** Producing or produced by fever. **2.** Caused by or generating heat. **3.** Of or relating to solid rock formed from molten rock; igneous.

py•ro•lig•ne•ous (pī′rō-lĭg′nē-əs) *adj.* Made by the destructive distillation of wood.

pyroligneous acid *n.* A reddish-brown wood distillate containing acetic acid, methyl alcohol, acetone, and a tarry residue.

py•ro•lu•site (pī′rō-lo͞o′sīt) *n.* A soft black to dark gray mineral, MnO_2, the commonest and most important secondary ore of manganese. [Ger. *Pyrolusit* : Gk. *puro-,* pyro- + Gk. *lousis,* a washing (< *louein,* to wash; see **leu(ə)-***).]

py•rol•y•sis (pī-rŏl′ĭ-sĭs) *n.* Decomposition or transformation of a compound caused by heat. **—py′ro•lyt′ic** (-rə-lĭt′ĭk) *adj.* **—py′ro•lyt′i•cal•ly** *adv.*

py•ro•lyze (pī′rə-līz′) *tr.v.* **-lyzed, -lyz•ing, -lyz•es.** To subject (something) to pyrolysis.

py•ro•man•cy (pī′rə-măn′sē) *n.* Divination by fire or flames. [ME *piromance* < OFr. *pyromancie* < LLat. *pyromantia* < Gk. *puromanteia* : *puro-,* pyro- + *manteia,* divination; see –MANCY.] **—py′ro•man′tic** (-măn′tĭk) *adj.*

py•ro•ma•ni•a (pī′rō-mā′nē-ə, -mān′yə) *n. Psychiat.* An uncontrollable urge to start fires. **—py′ro•ma′ni•ac′** (-mā′nē-ăk′) *adj.* & *n.* **—py′ro•ma•ni′a•cal** (-mə-nī′ə-kəl) *adj.*

py•ro•met•al•lur•gy (pī′rō-mĕt′l-ûr′jē) *n., pl.* **-gies.** An ore-refining process, such as smelting, dependent on the action of heat. **—py′ro•met′al•lur′gi•cal** (-mĕt′l-ûr′jĭ-kəl) *adj.*

py•rom•e•ter (pī-rŏm′ĭ-tər) *n.* Any of various thermometers used for measuring high temperatures. **—py′ro•met′ric** (-rə-mĕt′rĭk), **py′ro•met′ri•cal** (-rĭ-kəl) *adj.* **—py′ro•met′ri•cal•ly** *adv.* **—py•rom′e•try** *n.*

py•ro•mor•phite (pī′rə-môr′fīt′) *n.* A green, brown, or yellow mineral, $Pb_5(PO_4)_3Cl$, a minor ore of lead. [Ger. *Pyromorphit* : Gk. *puro-,* pyro- + Gk. *morphē,* form.]

py•ro•nine (pī′rə-nēn′) *n.* Any of a group of red dyes used as a biological stain, esp. to detect the presence of RNA. [Ger. *Pyronin,* originally a trademark.]

py•rope (pī′rōp′) *n.* A deep red garnet, $Mg_3Al_2Si_3O_{12}$, used as a gem. [ME *pirope* < OFr. < Lat. *pyrōpum,* gold-bronze alloy < Gk. *purōpos,* fiery, kind of red bronze : *puro-,* pyro- + *ōps,* eye, face; see **okʷ-***.]

py•ro•phor•ic (pī′rə-fôr′ĭk, -fŏr′-) *adj.* **1.** Spontaneously igniting in air. **2.** Producing sparks by friction. [< *pyrophorus,* substance that ignites spontaneously : < Gk. *purophoros,* fire-bearing : *puro-,* pyro- + *-phoros,* -phorous.]

py•ro•phos•phate (pī′rə-fŏs′fāt′) *n.* A salt or an ester of pyrophosphoric acid. **—py′ro•phos•phat′ic** (-făt′ĭk) *adj.*

py•ro•phos•phor•ic acid (pī′rō-fŏs-fôr′ĭk, -fŏr′-) *n.* A syrupy viscous liquid, $H_4P_2O_7$, used as a catalyst and in organic chemical manufacture.

py•ro•phyl•lite (pī′rō-fĭl′īt′, pī-rŏf′ə-līt′) *n.* A silvery white or pale green aluminum silicate mineral, $Al_2Si_4O_{10}(OH)_2$, occurring naturally in soft compact masses.

py•ro•sis (pī-rō′sĭs) *n.* See **heartburn.** [NLat. < Gk. *purōsis,* a burning < *puroun,* to burn < *pur,* fire. See **pūr-***.]

py•ro•stat (pī′rə-stăt′) *n.* A high-temperature thermostat.

py•ro•sul•fate (pī′rō-sŭl′fāt′) *n.* A salt of pyrosulfuric acid.

py•ro•sul•fu•ric acid (pī′rō-sŭl-fyo͝or′ĭk) *n.* A heavy oily fuming liquid, $H_2S_2O_7$, used in petroleum refining and the manufacture of explosives.

py•ro•tech•nic (pī′rə-tĕk′nĭk) also **py•ro•tech•ni•cal** (-nĭ-kəl) *adj.* **1.** Of or relating to fireworks. **2.** Resembling fireworks; brilliant. **—py′ro•tech′ni•cal•ly** *adv.*

py•ro•tech•nics (pī′rə-tĕk′nĭks) *n.* *(used with a sing. v.)* **1.** The art of manufacturing or setting off fireworks. **2.** A fireworks display. **3.** A brilliant display, as of rhetoric or wit, or of virtuosity in the performing arts. **—py′ro•tech′nist** *n.*

py•ro•tech•ny (pī′rə-tĕk′nē) *n.* See **pyrotechnics** 1. [NLat. *pyrotechnia* : Gk. *puro-,* pyro- + Gk. *tekhnē,* craft; see TECHNIQUE.]

py•rox•ene (pī-rŏk′sēn′) *n.* Any of a group of crystalline silicate minerals common in igneous and metamorphic rocks and containing two metallic oxides, as of magnesium, iron, or calcium. [Fr. *pyroxène* : Gk. *puro-,* pyro- + Gk. *xenos,* stranger; see **ghos-ti-***.] **—py′rox•en′ic** (pī′rŏk-sē′nĭk, -sĕn′ĭk) *adj.*

py•rox•e•nite (pī-rŏk′sə-nīt′) *n.* An igneous rock consisting chiefly of pyroxenes. **—py•rox′e•nit′ic** (-nĭt′ĭk) *adj.*

py•rox•y•lin (pī-rŏk′sə-lĭn) also **py•rox•y•line** (-lēn′, -lĭn) *n.* A highly flammable nitrocellulose used in the manufacture of collodion, plastics, and lacquers.

pyr•rhic (pĭr′ĭk) *n.* A metrical foot having two short or unaccented syllables. —*adj.* Of or characterized by pyrrhics. [Lat. *pyrrhicius* < Gk. *purrikhios* < *purrikhē,* a war dance, perh. from *Purrikhos,* supposed inventor of the dance.]

Pyr•rhic victory (pĭr′ĭk) *n.* A victory that is offset by staggering losses. [After PYRRHUS.]

pyr•rho•tite (pĭr′ə-tīt′) also **pyr•rho•tine** (-tīn′) *n.* A brownish-bronze, weakly magnetic iron sulfide mineral, FeS, used as an iron ore and in making sulfuric acid. [Alteration (influenced by –ITE[1]) of Ger. *Pyrrhotin* < Gk. *purrotēs,* redness < *purros,* fiery < *pur,* fire. See **pūr-***.]

pyr•rhu•lox•i•a (pĭr′ə-lŏk′sē-ə, pĭr′yə-) *n.* A large crested finch *(Pyrrhuloxia sinuata)* of Mexico and the southwest United States having gray and red plumage and a short thick bill. [NLat. *Pyrrhuloxia,* genus name : *Pyrrhula,* finch genus (< Gk. *purroulas,* red-colored bird < *purros,* red < *pur,* fire; see PYRE) + *Loxia,* crossbill genus (< Gk. *loxos,* oblique).]

Pyr•rhus (pĭr′əs). 319–272 B.C. King of Epirus (306–302 and 297–272) who defeated the Romans at Heraclea (280) and Asculum (279) despite his own staggering losses.

pyr•role (pîr′ōl′) *n.* A five-membered heterocyclic ring compound, C_4H_5N, that has an odor similar to chloroform and is the parent compound of hemoglobin, chlorophyll, and many other biologically active substances. [Gk. *purros,* red (< *pur,* fire; see PYRE) + –OLE.] **—pyr•ro′lic** (pĭ-rō′lĭk) *adj.*

py•ru•vate (pī-ro͞o′vāt, pĭ-) *n.* A salt or an ester of pyruvic acid.

py•ru•vic acid (pī-ro͞o′vĭk, pĭ-) *n.* A colorless organic liquid, $CH_3COCOOH$, formed as a fundamental intermediate in protein and carbohydrate metabolism. [PYR(O)– + Lat. *ūva,* grape (< its being produced by the dry distillation of racemic acid, originally derived from grapes) + –IC.]

Py•thag•o•ras (pĭ-thăg′ər-əs). fl. 6th cent. B.C. Greek philosopher and mathematician who proved the universal validity of the Pythagorean theorem and is considered the first true mathematician.

Py•thag•o•re•an•ism (pĭ-thăg′ə-rē′ə-nĭz′əm) *n. Philos.* The syncretistic philosophy expounded by Pythagoras, distinguished chiefly by its description of reality in terms of arithmetical relationships. **—Py•thag′o•re′an** *adj.* & *n.*

Pythagorean theorem *n. Math.* The theorem that the sum of the squares of the lengths of the sides of a right triangle is equal to the square of the length of the hypotenuse.

Pyth•i•an (pĭth′ē-ən) also **Pyth•ic** (pĭth′ĭk) *adj.* **1.** *Gk. Myth.* Of or relating to Delphi, the temple of Apollo at Delphi, or its oracle. **2.** Of or relating to the Pythian games. [< Lat. *Pȳthius* < Gk. *Puthios* < *Puthō,* ancient name of Delphi.]

Pythian games *pl.n.* A pan-Hellenic festival of athletic games held every four years at Delphi in honor of the god Apollo.

Pyth•i•as (pĭth′ē-əs) *n.* A Greek who rescued his friend Damon, who stood bail for Pythias when he was condemned to die.

py•thon (pī′thŏn′, -thən) *n.* Any of various nonvenomous snakes of the family Pythonidae, found chiefly in Asia, Africa, and Australia, that often attain lengths of 6 meters (20 feet) or more. [Prob. Fr. < Lat. *Pȳthōn,* mythical serpent killed by Apollo near Delphi. See PYTHON.]

Py•thon (pī′thŏn′, -thən) *n. Gk. Myth.* A dragon or serpent that was the tutelary demon of the oracular cult at Delphi until killed by Apollo. [Lat. *Pȳthōn* < Gk. *Puthōn.*]

py•tho•ness (pī′thə-nĭs, pĭth′ə-) *n.* **1.** *Gk. Myth.* A priestess of Apollo at Delphi. **2.** A prophetess. [ME *phitonesse* < OFr. *phitonise* < LLat. *pythonissa* < Gk. *Puthōn,* Python.]

py•thon•ic (pī-thŏn′ĭk) *adj.* **1.** Oracular; prophetic. **2.** Of or resembling a python. **3.** Of extraordinary size and power.

py•u•ri•a (pī-yo͝or′ē-ə) *n.* The presence of pus in the urine.

pyx also **pix** (pĭks) *n.* **1.** *Eccles.* **a.** A container in which wafers for the Eucharist are kept. **b.** A container in which the Eu-

python
Ball python
Python regius

pyx
15th-century Spanish silver

ă pat	oi boy
ā pay	ou out
âr care	o͝o took
ä father	o͞o boot
ĕ pet	ŭ cut
ē be	ûr urge
ĭ pit	th thin
ī pie	*th* this
îr pier	hw which
ŏ pot	zh vision
ō toe	ə about, item
ô paw	

Stress marks:
′ (primary);
′ (secondary), as in
dictionary (dĭk′shə-nĕr′ē)

charist is carried to the sick. **2.** A chest in a mint in which specimen coins are placed to await assay. [ME *pyxe* < Lat. *pyxis*, box < Gk. *puxis*.]

pyx•id•i•um (pĭk-sĭd′ē-əm) *n., pl.* **-i•a** (-ē-ə). A pyxis. [NLat. < Gk. *puxidion*, dim. of *puxis*, box.]

pyx•ie (pĭk′sē) *n.* A creeping evergreen shrub *(Pyxidanthera barbulata)* native to pine barrens of the eastern United States and having small white or pinkish flowers. [Shortening and alteration of NLat. *Pyxidanthera*, genus name : Gk. *puxis*, *puxid-*, box + Gk. *anthera*, pollen; see ANTHER.]

pyx•is (pĭk′sĭs) *n., pl.* **pyx•i•des** (pĭk′sĭ-dēz′). *Bot.* A capsule dehiscing transversely by a lid that falls off to release the seeds. [Lat. *pyxis*, box < Gk. *puxis*.]

Pyx•is (pĭk′sĭs) *n.* A constellation in the Southern Hemisphere, near Antlia and Puppis. [NLat. *Pyxis (nautica)*, (mariner's) compass < Gk. *puxis*, box.]

Q q

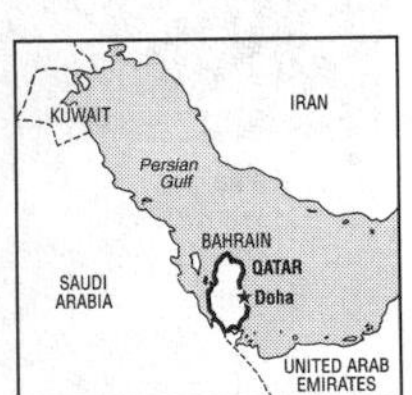

Qatar

q[1] or **Q** (kyo͞o) *n., pl.* **q's** or **Q's.** **1.** The 17th letter of the modern English alphabet. **2.** Any of the speech sounds represented by the letter *q*. **3.** The 17th in a series. **4.** Something shaped like the letter Q.

q[2] *Phys.* The symbol for **charge** 13.

Q *abbr.* **1.** *Games.* Queen (chess). **2.** Quetzal.

q. *abbr.* **1.** Quart. **2.** Quarter. **3.** Quarterly. **4.** Also **Q.** Quarto. **5.** Query. **6.** Question. **7.** Quintal. **8.** Quire.

Qad•da•fi or **Qa•dha•fi** (kə-dä′fē), **Muammar al-** or **el-.** b. 1942. Libyan political leader who seized power (1969) and imposed socialist policies and Islamic orthodoxy.

q and a *abbr.* Question and answer.

Qan•da•har (kŭn′də-här′, kän′-). See **Kandahar.**

Qa•tar (kä′tär′, kə-tär′). A country of E Arabia on the Persian Gulf; achieved independence from Great Britain in 1971. Cap. Doha. Pop. 220,000. **—Qa•tar′i** *adj. & n.*

Qaz•vin also **Kaz•vin** (kăz-vēn′). A city of NW Iran NW of Tehran; founded in the 4th cent. A.D. Pop. 244,000.

qb *abbr. Football.* Quarterback.

Q.B. *abbr. Law.* Queen's Bench.

Q.C. *abbr.* **1.** Also **QC.** Quality control. **2.** *Law.* Queen's Counsel.

Q.E.D. *abbr. Lat.* Quod erat demonstrandum (which was to be demonstrated.)

Q.E.F. *abbr. Lat.* Quod erat faciendum (which was to have been done).

QF *abbr.* Quick-firing.

Q fever *n.* An infectious disease caused by the rickettsia *Coxiella burnetii* and characterized by fever, malaise, and muscular pains. [Q(UERY) + FEVER.]

Qian•long (chyän′lo͝ong′) also **Ch'ien-lung** (chyĕn′lo͝ong′). 1711–99. Chinese emperor (1735–96) of the Qing dynasty.

q.i.d. *abbr. Lat.* Quater in die (four times a day).

Qi•lian Shan (chē′lyän′ shän′) also **Nan Shan** (nän′). A mountain range of N-central China extending NW to SE and rising to more than 6,100 m (20,000 ft).

Qin also **Ch'in** (chĭn). A Chinese dynasty (221–206 B.C.) that organized the first centralized imperial government in China.

qin•dar•ka (kĭn-där′kə) *n.* See table at **currency.** [Albanian *qindarka*, definite sing. of *qindarkë* < *qintar* < *qint, qind*, hundred < Lat. *centum*. See CENT.]

quadriga
In the center of a c. 1810 earthenware plate attributed to Josiah Spode II

Qing also **Ch'ing** (chĭng). Also called Manchu. The last Chinese dynasty (1644–1912), overthrown by nationalist revolutionaries.

Qing•dao (chĭng′dou′) also **Tsing•tao** (tsĭng′tou′). A city of E China on the Yellow Sea NNW of Shanghai; leased to Germany in 1898. Pop. 1,250,000.

Qing•hai also **Ching•hai** (chĭng′hī′) or **Tsing•hai** (tsĭng′-). A province of NW-central China, bordered on the N by the Qilian Shan. Cap. Xining. Pop. 4,070,000.

Qinghai Hu (ho͞o) also **Ko•ko Nor** (kō′kō′ nôr′, nōr′). A salt lake of N-central China S of the Qilian Shan.

Qin•huang•dao (chĭn′hwäng′dou′) also **Chin•wang•tao** (chĭn′wäng′tou′). A city of NE China on the Gulf of Bo Hai E of Beijing; formerly a treaty port. Pop. 300,000.

qin•tar (kĭn-tär′) *n.* A coin formerly used in Albania and worth one one hundredth of a lek. [Albanian. See QINDARKA.]

Qi•qi•har (chē′chē′här′) also **Tsi•tsi•har** (tsē′tsē′-). A city of NE China NW of Harbin; founded 1691. Pop. 955,200.

qi•vi•ut (kē′vē-ət, -o͞ot′) *n.* The soft wool lying beneath the long coat of the musk ox, valued for its use as a fiber. [Inupiaq.]

ql. *abbr.* Quintal.

qlty. *abbr.* Quality.

QM *abbr.* Quartermaster.

QMC *abbr.* Quartermaster Corps.

QMG *abbr.* Quartermaster General.

qn. *abbr.* Question.

Qom (kōm) also **Qum** (ko͞om). A city of W-central Iran SSW of Tehran; a Shiite Muslim center and a pilgrimage site since 17th cent. Pop. 424,000.

qoph (kôf) *n.* The 19th letter of the Hebrew alphabet. [Heb. *qôp*.]

q.p. *abbr. Lat.* Quantum placet (as much as you please).

qq. *abbr.* Questions.

qq.v. *abbr. Lat.* Quae vide (which [things] see).

qr. *abbr.* **1.** Quarter. **2.** Quarterly. **3.** Quire.

q.s. *abbr. Lat.* Quantum sufficit (as much as suffices).

qt or **qt.** *abbr.* Quart.

qt. *abbr.* Quantity.

q.t. (kyo͞o′tē′) *n. Slang.* Quiet: *spoke on the q.t.* [Short for QUIET.]

Q-Tip (kyo͞o′tĭp′). A trademark used for a cotton-tipped swab.

qto. *abbr.* Quarto.

qty. *abbr.* Quantity.

qu. *abbr.* **1.** Queen. **2.** Query. **3.** Question.

qua (kwā, kwä) *prep.* In the capacity or character of; as. [Lat. *quā*, fem. ablative sing. of *quī*, who. See **k^{w}o-***.]

Quaa•lude (kwā′lo͞od′). A trademark formerly used for methaqualone.

quack[1] (kwăk) *n.* The characteristic sound uttered by a duck. *—intr.v.* **quacked, quack•ing, quacks.** To utter a quack. [ME *quek*, of imit. orig.] **—quack′y** *adj.*

quack[2] (kwăk) *n.* **1.** An untrained person who pretends to be a physician and dispenses medical advice and treatment. **2.** A charlatan; a mountebank. *—adj.* Relating to or characteristic of a quack: *a quack cure.* *—intr.v.* **quacked, quack•ing, quacks.** To act as a quack. [Short for QUACKSALVER.] **—quack′er•y** *n.* **—quack′ish** *adj.* **—quack′ish•ly** *adv.*

quack grass *n.* See **couch grass.** [Var. of QUITCH GRASS.]

quack•sal•ver (kwăk′săl′vər) *n. Archaic.* A quack or charlatan. [Obsolete Du. : MDu. *quac-*, unguent, or *quacken*, to quack, boast + MDu. *salven*, to salve.]

quad[1] (kwŏd) *n.* A quadrangle: *the campus quad.*

quad[2] (kwŏd) *n. Print.* See **quadrat** 1.

quad[3] (kwŏd) *n.* A quadruplet.

quad[4] (kwŏd) *adj.* Quadraphonic.

quad. *abbr.* **1.** Quadrangle. **2.** Quadrant. **3.** Quadrilateral.

quadr– *pref.* Var. of **quadri–.**

quad•ran•gle (kwŏd′răng′gəl) *n.* **1.** *Math.* A plane figure consisting of four points, no three of which are collinear, connected by straight lines. **2.a.** A rectangular area surrounded on all four sides by buildings. **b.** The buildings bordering this area. **3.** The area of land shown on one atlas sheet charted by the U.S. Geological Survey. [ME < OFr. < LLat. *quadrangulum* < Lat., neut. of *quadrangulus*, four-cornered : *quadri-*, quadri- + *angulus*, angle.] **—quad•ran′gu•lar** (-răng′gyə-lər) *adj.* **—quad•ran′gu•lar•ly** *adv.* **—quad•ran′gu•lar•ness** *n.*

quad•rant (kwŏd′rənt) *n.* **1.** *Math.* **a.** A circular arc of 90°; one fourth of the circumference of a circle. **b.** The plane area bounded by such an arc and two perpendicular radii. **c.** Any of the four areas into which a plane is divided by the reference axes in a Cartesian coordinate system. **2.** A machine part or other mechanical device that is shaped like a quarter circle. **3.** An early instrument for measuring altitude of celestial bodies, consisting of a 90° graduated arc with a movable radius for measuring angles. [ME, quarter of a day < Lat. *quadrāns*, *quadrant-*, a fourth part. See **k^{w}etwer-***.]

quad•ra•phon•ic also **quad•ri•phon•ic** (kwŏd′rə-fŏn′ĭk) *adj.* Of or for a four-channel sound system in which speakers are positioned at all four corners of the listening space, reproducing signals that are independent of each other. **—qua•draph′o•ny** (kwŏ-drăf′ə-nē) *n.*

quad•ra•son•ic (kwŏd′rə-sŏn′ĭk) *adj.* Quadraphonic.

quad•rat (kwŏd′rət, -răt′) *n.* **1.** *Print.* A piece of type metal lower than the raised typeface, used for filling spaces and blank lines. **2.** *Ecol.* A rectangular plot of land designated for studying the distribution of plants or animals in an area. [ME, a square geometric instrument, rectangular area. See QUADRATE.]

quad•rate (kwŏd′rāt′, -rĭt) *n.* **1.a.** A square or cube. **b.** An approx. square or cubic area, space, or object. **2.** *Zool.* A bone or cartilaginous structure of the skull, joining the upper and lower jaws in birds, fish, reptiles, and amphibians. *—adj.* **1.** Having four sides and four angles; square or rectangular.

2. *Zool.* Being the quadrate bone or cartilage. — *intr.v.* **-rat•ed, -rat•ing, -rates.** *Archaic.* To correspond; agree. [ME *quadrat,* something square < Lat. *quadrātum* < neut. p.part. of *quadrāre,* to make square < *quadrum,* square. See **kʷetwer-*.**]

quad•rat•ic (kwŏ-drăt′ĭk) *adj. Math.* Of, relating to, or containing quantities of the second degree. [< QUADRATE.] — **quad•rat′ic** *n.* — **quad•rat′i•cal•ly** *adv.*

quadratic equation *n. Math.* An equation of the second degree having the general form $ax^2 + bx + c = 0$, where *a, b,* and *c* are constants.

quad•rat•ics (kwŏ-drăt′ĭks) *n.* *(used with a sing. v.) Math.* The algebraic study of quadratic equations.

quad•ra•ture (kwŏd′rə-cho͝or′) *n.* **1.** The process of making something square. **2.** *Math.* The process of constructing a square equal in area to a given surface. **3.** *Astron.* A configuration in which the position of one celestial body is 90° from another celestial body, as measured from a third.

quad•ren•ni•al (kwŏ-drĕn′ē-əl) *adj.* **1.** Happening once in four years. **2.** Lasting for four years. — **quad•ren′ni•al** *n.* — **quad•ren′ni•al•ly** *adv.*

quad•ren•ni•um (kwŏ-drĕn′ē-əm) *n., pl.* **quad•ren•ni•ums** or **quad•ren•ni•a** (kwŏ-drĕn′ē-ə). A period of four years. [Lat. *quadriennium* : *quadri-,* quadri- + *-ennium* (< *annus,* year; see **at-***).]

quadri– or **quadru–** or **quadr–** *pref.* **1.** Four: *quadrilateral.* **2.** Square: *quadrate.* [ME < Lat. See **kʷetwer-*.**]

quad•ric (kwŏd′rĭk) *adj. Math.* Of or relating to geometric surfaces that are defined by quadratic equations.

quad•ri•cen•ten•ni•al (kwŏd′rĭ-sĕn-tĕn′ē-əl) *n.* A 400th anniversary. — **quad′ri•cen•ten′ni•al** *adj.*

quad•ri•ceps (kwŏd′rĭ-sĕps′) *n.* The large four-part extensor muscle at the front of the thigh. [QUADRI– + (BI)CEPS.] — **quad′ri•cip′i•tal** (-sĭp′ĭ-tl) *adj.*

quad•ri•ga (kwŏd′rī-gə) *n., pl.* **-gae** (-gē). A two-wheeled chariot drawn by four horses abreast. [Lat. *quadrīga,* sing. of *quadrīgae,* team of four horses, contraction of *quadriiugae,* fem. pl. of *quadriiugus,* of a team of four : *quadri-,* quadri- + *iugum,* yoke; see JUGUM.]

quad•ri•lat•er•al (kwŏd′rə-lăt′ər-əl) *n. Math.* A plane figure with four sides and four angles. — *adj.* Having four sides.

qua•drille[1] (kwŏ-drĭl′, kwə-, kə-) *n.* **1.** A square dance of French origin composed of five figures and performed by four couples. **2.** Music for this dance in 6/8 and 2/4 time. [Fr. < *quadrille,* team, crew, one of four groups of horsemen < Sp. *cuadrilla,* prob. dim. of *cuadro,* square < Lat. *quadrum.* See **kʷetwer-*.**]

qua•drille[2] (kwŏ-drĭl′, kwə-, kə-) *n. Games.* A card game popular during the 18th century, played by four people with a deck of 40 cards. [Fr., perh. < Sp. *cuartillo,* dim. of *cuarto,* fourth < Lat. *quārtus.* See **kʷetwer-*.**]

quad•ril•lion (kwŏ-drĭl′yən) *n.* **1.** The cardinal number equal to 10^{15}. **2.** *Chiefly British.* Septillion. [QUADR(I)– + (M)ILLION.] — **quad•ril′lion** *adj.*

quad•ril•lionth (kwŏ-drĭl′yənth) *n.* **1.** The ordinal number matching the number quadrillion in a series. **2.** One of a quadrillion equal parts. — **quad•ril′lionth** *adv. & adj.*

quad•ri•par•tite (kwŏd′rə-pär′tīt′) *adj.* **1.** Consisting of or divided into four parts. **2.** Involving four participants.

quad•ri•phon•ic (kwŏd′rə-fŏn′ĭk) *adj.* Var. of **quadraphonic.** — **quad′ri•phon′y** *n.*

quad•ri•ple•gi•a (kwŏd′rə-plē′jē-ə, -jə) *n.* Total paralysis of the body from the neck down. — **quad′ri•ple′gic** *adj. & n.*

quad•ri•va•lent (kwŏd′rə-vā′lənt) *adj. Chem.* **1.** Having four valences. **2.** Having a valence of four; tetravalent. — **quad′ri•va′lence, quad′ri•va′len•cy** *n.*

quad•riv•i•um (kwŏ-drĭv′ē-əm) *n., pl.* **-i•a** (-ē-ə). The higher division of the seven liberal arts in the Middle Ages, composed of geometry, astronomy, arithmetic, and music. [LLat. < Lat., place where four roads meet : *quadri-,* quadri- + *via,* road; see VIA.]

quad•roon (kwŏ-dro͞on′) *n.* A person having one-quarter Black ancestry. [Alteration of Sp. *cuarterón* < *cuarto,* quarter < Lat. *quārtus.* See **kʷetwer-*.**]

quadru– *pref.* Var. of **quadri–.**

quad•ru•ma•nous (kwŏ-dro͞o′mə-nəs) also **quad•ru•ma•nal** (-nəl) *adj. Zool.* Having four feet with opposable first digits, as primates other than human beings. [QUADRU– + Lat. *manus,* hand; see **man-[2]*** + –OUS.]

quad•rum•vi•rate (kwŏ-drŭm′vər-ĭt) *n.* A group of four people joined in authority or office, esp. a government of four people. [QUADR(I)– + (TRI)UMVIRATE.]

quad•ru•ped (kwŏd′rə-pĕd′) *n.* A four-footed animal. — *adj.* Four-footed: *a quadruped mammal.* — **quad•ru′pe•dal** (kwŏ-dro͞o′pə-dəl, kwŏd′rə-pĕd′l) *adj.*

quad•ru•ple (kwŏ-dro͞o′pəl, -drŭp′əl, kwŏd′ro͞o-pəl) *adj.* **1.** Having four parts or members. **2.** Multiplied by four; fourfold. **3.** *Mus.* Having four beats to the measure. — *n.* A number four times as great as another. — *tr. & intr.v.* **-pled, -pling, -ples.** To multiply or be multiplied by four. [< ME *quadriple,* fourfold amount, and *quadruple,* tooth with four roots, both < OFr. *quadruple* < Lat. *quadruplum* < neut. of *quadruplus,* fourfold : *quadru-, quadri-,* quadri- + *-plus,* -fold; see **pel-[2]*.**] — **quad•ru′ply** *adv.*

quad•ru•plet (kwŏ-drŭp′lĭt, -dro͞o′plĭt, kwŏd′rə-plĭt) *n.* **1.** One of four offspring born in a single birth. **2.** A group or combination of four associated by common properties or behavior.

quad•ru•pli•cate (kwŏ-dro͞o′plĭ-kĭt) *adj.* **1.** Multiplied by four; quadruple. **2.** Fourth in a group of four identical things. — *n.* **1.** One of a group of four identical things. **2.** A set of four copies. — *tr. & intr.v.* (-kāt′) **-cat•ed, -cat•ing, -cates.** To multiply or be multiplied by four. [Lat. *quadruplicātus,* p.part. of *quadruplicāre,* to multiply by four < *quadruplex,* fourfold : *quadru-, quadri-,* quadri- + *-plex,* -fold; see DUPLEX.] — **quad•ru′pli•cate•ly** (-kĭt-lē) *adv.* — **quad•ru′pli•ca′tion** *n.*

quaes•tor (kwĕs′tər, kwē′stər) *n.* Any of various public officials in ancient Rome responsible chiefly for government and military finance. [ME *questor* < Lat. *quaestor* < *quaerere, quaest-,* to inquire.] — **quaes•to′ri•al** (kwĕ-stôr′ē-əl, -stōr′-, kwē-) *adj.* — **quaes′tor•ship′** *n.*

quaff (kwŏf, kwăf, kwôf) *v.* **quaffed, quaff•ing, quaffs.** — *tr.* To drink (a beverage) heartily. — *intr.* To drink heartily. — *n.* A hearty draft of liquid. [?] — **quaff′er** *n.*

quag (kwăg, kwŏg) *n.* A quagmire. [Perh. var. of ME *quabbe* < OE **cwabba.*]

quag•ga (kwăg′ə, kwŏg′ə) *n.* A zebralike mammal *(Equus quagga)* of southern Africa, extinct since the late 19th century. [Afr. < Nguni (Xhosa) *(i-)qwaxa,* something striped, perh. < Khoikhoin *!ua-xa.*]

quagga
Equus quagga

quag•gy (kwăg′ē, kwŏg′ē) *adj.* **-gi•er, -gi•est. 1.** Resembling a marsh; soggy. **2.** Soft and flabby.

quag•mire (kwăg′mīr′, kwŏg′-) *n.* **1.** Land with a soft muddy surface. **2.** A difficult or precarious situation; a predicament.

qua•hog also **qua•haug** (kwô′hôg′, -hŏg′, kwō′-, kō′-) *n.* An edible clam *(Venus mercenaria)* of the Atlantic coast of North America having a hard rounded shell. [Narragansett *poquaûhock.*]

quaich also **quaigh** (kwāKH) *n. Scots.* A two-handled drinking cup. [Sc.Gael. *cuach* < OIr. *cúach,* alteration of *cuäch.*]

Quai d'Or•say (kā′ dôr-sā′, kē′, kĕ dôr-sĕ′). A street paralleling the S bank of the Seine R. in Paris, France, notable for its governmental ministries.

quail[1] (kwāl) *n., pl.* **quail** or **quails. 1.** Any of various small Old World chickenlike birds of the genus *Coturnix,* esp. *C. coturnix,* having mottled brown plumage and a short tail. **2.** Any of various similar or related New World birds, such as the bobwhite. [ME *quaille* < OFr., perh. < VLat. **coacula,* of imit. orig.]

quail[1]
Male California quail
Lophortyx californicus

quail[2] (kwāl) *intr.v.* **quailed, quail•ing, quails.** To shrink back in fear; cower. [ME *quailen,* to give way, prob. < MDu. *quelen,* to suffer, be ill. See **gʷelə-*.**]

quaint (kwānt) *adj.* **quaint•er, quaint•est. 1.** Agreeably odd, esp. in an old-fashioned way. **2.** Unfamiliar or unusual in character; strange. See Syns at **strange.** [ME, clever, cunning, peculiar < OFr. *queinte, cointe* < Lat. *cognitus,* p.part. of *cognōscere,* to learn. See COGNITION.] — **quaint′ly** *adv.* — **quaint′ness** *n.*

quake (kwāk) *intr.v.* **quaked, quak•ing, quakes. 1.** To shake or tremble, as from instability or shock. **2.** To shiver, as with cold or from strong emotion. — *n.* **1.** An instance of quaking. **2.** An earthquake. [ME *quaken* < OE *cwacian.*] — **quak′y** *adj.*

quake•proof (kwāk′pro͞of′) *adj.* Designed to withstand an earthquake. — **quake′proof′** *v.*

Quak•er (kwā′kər) *n.* A member of the Society of Friends. [< QUAKE (< an early leader's admonishment to "tremble at the word of the Lord").] — **Quak′er•ism** *n.* — **Quak′er•ly** *adv. & adj.*

Quaker gun *n.* A dummy gun made of wood.

Quak•er-la•dies (kwā′kər-lā′dēz) *pl.n.* See **bluets.**

quak•ing aspen (kwā′kĭng) *n.* A North American deciduous tree *(Populus tremuloides)* having broadly ovate, finely toothed leaves with a truncate base.

qua•le (kwä′lē) *n., pl.* **-li•a** (-lē-ə). A property, such as whiteness, considered independently from things having the property. [< Lat. *quāle,* neut. of *quālis,* of what kind. See QUALITY.]

qual•i•fi•ca•tion (kwŏl′ə-fĭ-kā′shən) *n.* **1.** The act of qualifying or the condition of being qualified. **2.** A quality, an ability, or an accomplishment that makes a person suitable for a particular position or task. **3.** A condition or circumstance that must be met or complied with: *met the qualifications for residence.* **4.** A restriction or modification.

qual•i•fied (kwŏl′ə-fīd′) *adj.* **1.** Having the appropriate qualifications for an office, a position, or a task. **2.** Limited, restricted, or modified. — **qual′i•fied′ly** (-fīd′lē, -fī′ĭd-lē) *adv.*

qual•i•fi•er (kwŏl′ə-fī′ər) *n.* **1.** One that qualifies, esp. one that has or fulfills all appropriate qualifications, as for a position or task. **2.** *Gram.* A word or phrase that qualifies, limits, or modifies the meaning of another word or phrase.

qual•i•fy (kwŏl′ə-fī′) *v.* **-fied, -fy•ing, -fies.** — *tr.* **1.** To describe by enumerating the characteristics or qualities of; characterize. **2.** To make competent or eligible for an office, a

ă pat	oi boy
ā pay	ou out
âr care	o͝o took
ä father	o͞o boot
ĕ pet	ŭ cut
ē be	ûr urge
ĭ pit	th thin
ī pie	*th* this
îr pier	hw which
ŏ pot	zh vision
ō toe	ə about, item
ô paw	

Stress marks:
′ (primary);
′ (secondary), as in
dictionary (dĭk′shə-nĕr′ē)

position, or a task. **3.a.** To declare competent or capable; certify. **b.** To make legally capable; license. **4.** To modify, limit, or restrict, as by giving exceptions. **5.** To make less harsh or severe; moderate. **6.** *Gram.* To modify the meaning of (a noun, for example). — *intr.* **1.** To be or become qualified. **2.** To reach the later stages of a selection process or contest by succeeding in earlier rounds. [< Fr. *qualifier* (< OFr.) and < ME *qualifien*, to specify the time and place of a document's execution, both < Med.Lat. *quālificāre*, to attribute a quality to : Lat. *quālis*, of such a kind; see QUALITY + Lat. *-ficāre*, -fy.]

qual•i•ta•tive (kwŏl′ĭ-tā′tĭv) *adj.* Of, relating to, or concerning quality. [ME, producing a primary quality < Med.Lat. *quālitātīvus* < LLat., qualitative < Lat. *quālitās, qualitāt-*, quality. See QUALITY.] — **qual′i•ta′tive•ly** *adv.*

qualitative analysis *n.* The testing of a substance or mixture to determine its chemical constituents.

qual•i•ty (kwŏl′ĭ-tē) *n., pl.* **-ties. 1.a.** An inherent or distinguishing characteristic; a property. **b.** A personal trait, esp. a character trait. **2.** Essential character; nature: *quality of life.* **3.a.** Superiority of kind: *an intellect of quality.* **b.** Degree or grade of excellence: *goods of low quality.* **4.a.** High social position. **b.** Those in a high social position. **5.** *Mus.* Timbre, as determined by overtones: *a voice with a metallic quality.* **6.** *Ling.* The character of a vowel sound determined by the size and shape of the oral cavity and the amount of resonance with which the sound is produced. **7.** *Logic.* The positive or negative character of a proposition. — *adj.* Having a high degree of excellence. [ME *qualite* < OFr. < Lat. *quālitās, quālitāt-* < *quālis*, of what kind. See **kʷo-***.]

quality control *n.* A system for ensuring the maintenance of proper standards in manufactured goods, esp. by random inspection. — **qual′i•ty-con•trol′** (kwŏl′ĭ-tē-kən-trōl′) *adj.*

qualm (kwäm, kwôm) *n.* **1.** A sudden feeling of sickness, faintness, or nausea. **2.** A sudden disturbing feeling: *qualms of homesickness.* **3.** An uneasy feeling about the propriety or rightness of a course of action. [?] — **qualm′ish** *adj.* — **qualm′ish•ly** *adv.*

quam•ash (kwŏm′ăsh′) *n.* See **camas** 1. [NLat., species name, var. of Chinook Jargon *kamass.* See CAMAS.]

quan•da•ry (kwŏn′də-rē, -drē) *n., pl.* **-ries.** A state of uncertainty or perplexity. [?]

Quan•da•ry Peak (kwän′də-rē, -drē). A mountain, 4,350.8 m (14,265 ft), in the Park Range of the Rocky Mts. in central CO.

quan•go (kwăng′gō) *n., pl.* **-gos.** An organization or agency that is financed by a government but acts independently of it. [*qua(si) n(on-)g(overnmental) o(rganization).*]

quan•tal (kwŏn′tl) *adj.* **1.** *Phys.* **a.** Of or relating to a quantum or a quantized system. **b.** Existing in only one of two possible states. **2.** *Biol.* Of or being an all-or-none response or effect: *a quantal reaction.* — **quan′tal•ly** *adv.*

quan•tic (kwŏn′tĭk) *n. Math.* A homogeneous polynomial having two or more variables. [Lat. *quantus*, how much; see QUANTITY + -IC.]

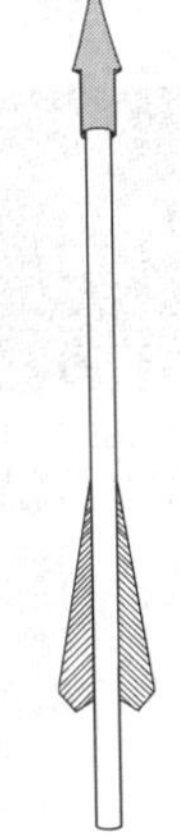

quarrel[2]

quan•ti•fy (kwŏn′tə-fī′) *tr.v.* **-fied, -fy•ing, -fies. 1.** To determine or express the quantity of. **2.** *Logic.* To limit the variables of (a proposition) by prefixing an operator such as *all* or *some.* [Med.Lat. *quantificāre* : Lat. *quantus*, how great; see QUANTITY + Lat. *-ficāre*, -fy.] — **quan′ti•fi′a•ble** *adj.* — **quan′ti•fi•ca′tion** (-fĭ-kā′shən) *n.* — **quan′ti•fi′er** *n.*

quan•ti•tate (kwŏn′tĭ-tāt′) *tr.v.* **-tat•ed, -tat•ing, -tates.** To determine or measure the quantity of. [Back-formation < QUANTITATIVE (ANALYSIS).] — **quan′ti•ta′tion** *n.*

quan•ti•ta•tive (kwŏn′tĭ-tā′tĭv) *adj.* **1.a.** Expressed or expressible as a quantity. **b.** Of, relating to, or susceptible of measurement. **c.** Of or relating to number or quantity. **2.** Of or relating to a metrical system based on the duration of syllables rather than on stress. [Med.Lat. *quantitātīvus* < Lat. *quantitās, quantitāt-*, quantity < *quantus*, how great. See QUANTITY.] — **quan′ti•ta′tive•ly** *adv.* — **quan′ti•ta′tive•ness** *n.*

quantitative analysis *n.* The testing of a substance or mixture to determine the amounts and proportions of its chemical constituents.

quantitative gene *n. Genet.* See **polygene.**

quan•ti•ty (kwŏn′tĭ-tē) *n., pl.* **-ti•ties. 1.a.** A specified or indefinite number or amount. **b.** A considerable amount or number: *sells food in quantity.* **c.** An exact amount or number. **2.** The measurable, countable, or comparable property or aspect of a thing. **3.** *Math.* Something that serves as the object of an operation. **4.a.** *Ling.* The relative amount of time needed to pronounce a vowel, consonant, or syllable. **b.** The duration of a syllable in quantitative verse. **5.** *Logic.* The exact character of a proposition in reference to its universality, singularity, or particularity. [ME *quantite* < OFr. < Lat. *quantitās, quantitāt-* < *quantus*, how great. See **kʷo-***.]

quan•tize (kwŏn′tīz′) *tr.v.* **-tized, -tiz•ing, -tiz•es.** *Phys.* **1.** To limit the possible values of (a magnitude or quantity) to a discrete set of values by quantum mechanical rules. **2.** To apply quantum mechanics or the quantum theory to. — **quan′ti•za′tion** (-tĭ-zā′shən) *n.*

quan•tum (kwŏn′təm) *n., pl.* **-ta** (-tə). **1.** A quantity or an amount. **2.** A specified portion. **3.** Something that can be counted or measured. **4.** *Phys.* **a.** The smallest amount by which certain physical quantities can change, esp. a discrete quantity of electromagnetic radiation. **b.** This amount of energy regarded as a unit. [Lat. < neut. of *quantus*, how great. See QUANTITY.]

quantum chromodynamics *Phys. n. (used with a sing. v.)* The theory of the strong interaction postulating the exchange of gluons between color-carrying quarks.

quantum electrodynamics *n. (used with a sing. v.) Phys.* The quantum theory of the interactions of electrically charged particles and the electromagnetic field.

quantum jump *n.* **1.** *Phys.* Abrupt change from one energy level to another, esp. such a change in the state of an electron with the loss or gain of a quantum of energy. **2.** A quantum leap.

quantum leap *n.* An abrupt change or advance, esp. in method, information, or knowledge.

quantum mechanics *n. (used with a sing. or pl. v.) Phys.* Quantum theory, esp. the quantum theory of the structure and behavior of atoms and molecules.

quantum number *n. Phys.* Any of a set of discrete values that individually characterize the properties and collectively specify the state of a particle or of a physical system.

quantum theory *n. Phys.* The theory that radiant energy is transmitted in the form of discrete units.

Qua•paw (kwô′pô) *n., pl.* **Quapaw** or **-paws. 1.** A member of a Native American people formerly inhabiting parts of Arkansas along the Arkansas River, with a present-day population in Oklahoma. **2.** The Siouan language of the Quapaw.

Qu'Ap•pelle (kwə-pĕl′). A river of S Saskatchewan and SW Manitoba, Canada, flowing c. 434 km (270 mi) to the Assiniboine R.

quar. *abbr.* **1.** Quarter. **2.** Quarterly.

quar•an•tine (kwôr′ən-tēn′, kwŏr′-) *n.* **1.a.** A period of time during which a vehicle, person, or material suspected of carrying a contagious disease is detained at a port of entry under enforced isolation to prevent disease from entering a country. **b.** A place for such detention. **2.** Enforced isolation or restriction of free movement imposed to prevent the spread of contagious disease. **3.** A condition of enforced isolation. **4.** A period of 40 days. — *tr.v.* **-tined, -tin•ing, -tines. 1.** To isolate in or as if in quarantine. **2.** To isolate politically or economically. [Ital. *quarantina* < *quaranta (giorni)*, forty (days) < Lat. *quadrāgintā.* See **kʷetwer-***.] — **quar′an•tin′a•ble** *adj.*

quark¹ (kwôrk, kwärk) *n.* Any of a group of elementary particles having fractional electric charges and regarded as the constituents of all hadrons. See table at **subatomic particle.** [Poss. from *Three quarks for Muster Mark!*, a line in *Finnegans Wake* by James Joyce.]

quark² (kwôrk, kwärk) *n.* A soft creamy acid-cured cheese of central Europe made from whole milk. [Ger. < MHGer. *quarc*, of Slav. orig.]

Quarles (kwärlz, kwôrlz), **Francis.** 1592–1644. English Metaphysical poet known for *Emblems, Divine and Moral* (1635).

quar•rel¹ (kwôr′əl, kwŏr′-) *n.* **1.** An angry dispute; an altercation. **2.** A cause of a dispute or an argument. — *intr.v.* **-reled, -rel•ing, -rels** or **-relled, -rel•ling, -rels. 1.** To engage in a quarrel; dispute angrily. **2.** To disagree; differ. **3.** To find fault; complain. [ME *querele* < OFr., complaint < Lat. *querella, querēla* < *querī*, to complain. See **kwes-***.] — **quar′rel•er, quar′rel•ler** *n.*

quar•rel² (kwôr′əl, kwŏr′-) *n.* **1.** A bolt for a crossbow. **2.** A tool, such as a stonemason's chisel, that has a squared head. **3.** A small diamond-shaped or square pane of glass in a latticed window. [ME *quarel* < OFr. < VLat. **quadrellus*, dim. of LLat. *quadrus*, square < Lat. *quadrum.* See **kʷetwer-***.]

quar•rel•some (kwôr′əl-səm, kwŏr′-) *adj.* **1.** Given to quarreling; contentious. See Syns at **argumentative. 2.** Marked by quarreling.

quar•ry¹ (kwôr′ē, kwŏr′ē) *n., pl.* **-ries. 1.a.** A hunted animal; a prey. **b.** Hunted animals considered as a group; game. **2.** An object of pursuit. [ME *querre*, entrails of a deer given to hounds as a reward < OFr. *cuiriee*, alteration (influenced by *cuir*, skin) of *coree* < VLat. **corāta*, viscera < Lat. *cor*, heart. See **kerd-***.]

quar•ry² (kwôr′ē, kwŏr′ē) *n., pl.* **-ries. 1.** An open excavation or pit from which stone is quarried. **2.** A rich or productive source. — *tr.v.* **-ried, -ry•ing, -ries. 1.** To obtain (stone) from a quarry, as by cutting, digging, or blasting. **2.** To extract (facts, for example) by long careful searching. **3.** To use (land) as a quarry. [ME *quarey* < Med.Lat. *quareria, quareia*, alteration of OFr. *quarriere* < **quarre*, cut stone < Lat. *quadrum*, square. See **kʷetwer-***.] — **quar′ri•er** *n.*

quar•ry³ (kwôr′ē, kwŏr′ē) *n., pl.* **-ries. 1.** A square or diamond shape. **2.** A pane of glass having this shape. [Var. of QUARREL².]

quart (kwôrt) *n.* **1.a.** A unit of volume or capacity in the U.S. Customary System, used in liquid measure, equal to ¼ gallon or 32 ounces (0.946 liter). **b.** A unit of volume or capacity in the U.S. Customary System, used in dry measure, equal to 1/8 peck or 2 pints (1.101 liters). **c.** A unit of volume or capacity in the British Imperial System, used in liquid and dry measure, equal to 1.201 U.S. liquid quarts or 1.032 U.S. dry quarts (1.136 liters). See table at **measurement. 2.a.** A container that can hold one quart. **b.** The contents of such a container. [ME < OFr. *quarte* < Lat. *quārta*, fem. of *quārtus*, fourth. See **kʷetwer-***.]

quar•tan (kwôr′tn) *adj.* Occurring every fourth day, counting inclusively, or every 72 hours. Used of a fever. — *n.* A malarial fever recurring every 72 hours. [ME *quartaine* < OFr. < Lat. *quārtāna* < *quārtānus*, of the fourth < *quārtus*, fourth. See **kʷetwer-***.]

quar•ter (kwôr′tər) *n.* **1.** One of four equal parts. **2.** A coin equal to one fourth of the dollar of the United States and Canada. **3.** One fourth of an hour; 15 minutes. **4.a.** One fourth of a year; three months. **b.** An academic term lasting approximately three months. **5.** *Astron.* **a.** One fourth of the period of the moon's revolution around Earth. **b.** One of the four phases of the moon. **6.** *Sports.* One of four equal periods of playing time into which some games, such as basketball, are divided. **7.** One fourth of a yard; nine inches. **8.** One fourth of a mile; two furlongs. **9.** One fourth of a pound; four ounces. **10.** One fourth of a ton; 500 pounds. Used as a measure of grain. **11.** *Chiefly British.* A measure of grain equal to approx. eight bushels. **12.a.** One fourth of a hundredweight; 25 pounds. **b.** One fourth of a British hundredweight; 28 pounds. **13.a.** One of the four major divisions of the compass. **b.** One fourth of the distance between any two of the 32 points of the compass. **c.** One of the four major divisions of the horizon as determined by the four major points of the compass. **d.** A region or an area of the earth thought of as falling into such a specific division of the compass. **e.** *Naut.* The general direction on either side of a ship located 45° off the stern. **14.** *Naut.* The upper portion of the after side of a ship, usu. from the mainmast or mizzen aft to the stern. **15.** *Her.* Any of four equal divisions of a shield. **16.** One leg of an animal's carcass, usu. including the adjoining parts. **17.** Either side of a horse's hoof. **18.** The part of the side of a shoe between the heel and the vamp. **19. quarters.** A place of residence, esp. for military personnel or their dependents. **20.** A proper or assigned station or place, as for officers and crew on a warship. Often used in the plural. **21.** Often **Quarter.** A specific district or section, as of a city. **22.** An unspecified person or group. Often used in the plural: *information from the highest quarters.* **23.** Mercy or clemency, esp. when displayed or given to an enemy. — *adj.* **1.** Being one of four equal or equivalent parts. **2.** Being one fourth of a standard or usual value. — *v.* **-tered, -ter•ing, -ters.** — *tr.* **1.a.** To divide into four equal or equivalent parts. **b.** To quartersaw. **2.** To divide or separate into a number of parts. **3.** To dismember (a human body) into four parts. **4.** *Her.* To divide (a shield) into four equal areas with vertical and horizontal lines. **5.a.** To mark or place (holes, for example) a fourth of a circle apart. **b.** To locate and adjust (one machine part) at right angles to its connecting part within the machine. **6.** To furnish with housing. **7.** To traverse (an area of ground) laterally back and forth while slowly advancing forward. — *intr.* **1.** To take up or be assigned lodgings. **2.** To cover an area of ground by ranging over it from side to side. [ME < OFr. *quartier* < Lat. *quārtārius* < *quārtus*, fourth. See **kʷetwer-***.]

Usage Note: When referring to the time of day, the article *a* is optional in phrases such as *(a) quarter to* (or *of, before,* or *till*) *nine; (a) quarter after* (or *past*) *ten.*

quar•ter•age (kwôr′tər-ĭj) *n.* A monetary allowance, wage, or payment made or received quarterly.

quar•ter•back (kwôr′tər-băk′) *n. Football.* The backfield player who usu. calls the signals for the plays. — *v.* **-backed, -back•ing, -backs.** — *tr.* **1.** *Football.* To direct the offense of. **2.** *Slang.* To lead or direct. — *intr. Football.* To play quarterback.

quarter day *n.* Any of the four days of the year regarded as the beginning of a new season or quarter, when most quarterly payments are due.

quar•ter•deck (kwôr′tər-dĕk′) *n. Naut.* The after part of the upper deck of a ship, usu. reserved for officers.

quar•ter•fi•nal (kwôr′tər-fī′nəl) *adj. Sports & Games.* Of or relating to one of four competitions in a tournament, whose winners go on to play in semifinal competitions. — *n.* **1. quarterfinals.** A quarterfinal round. **2.** A quarterfinal match. **— quar′ter•fi′nal•ist** *n.*

quarter horse *n.* One of a breed of strong saddle horses developed in the western United States. [< its formerly being trained for races up to a quarter mile.]

quar•ter-hour also **quar•ter hour** (kwôr′tər-our′) *n.* **1.** Fifteen minutes. **2.** The point on a clock's face marking either 15 minutes after or 15 minutes before an hour.

quar•ter•ly (kwôr′tər-lē) *adj.* **1.** Made up of four parts. **2.** Being one of four parts. **3.** Occurring or appearing at three-month intervals: *a quarterly magazine.* **4.** *Her.* Having four sections. Used of a shield. — *n., pl.* **-lies. 1.** A publication issued every three months. **2.** An examination given every three months in some colleges. — *adv.* In or by quarters.

quar•ter•mas•ter (kwôr′tər-măs′tər) *n.* **1.** An officer responsible for the food, clothing, and equipment of troops. **2.** A petty officer responsible for the navigation of a ship.

quar•tern (kwôr′tərn) *n.* **1.** One fourth of something, esp. of some weights and measures. **2.** *Chiefly British.* A loaf of bread weighing about 4 pounds (1.81 kilograms). [ME *quartron* < OFr. *quarteron* < *quartier*, quarter. See QUARTER.]

quarter note *n. Mus.* A note having one-fourth the time value of a whole note.

quar•ter-phase (kwôr′tər-fāz′) *adj. Elect.* Two-phase.

quar•ter•saw (kwôr′tər-sô′) *tr.v.* **-sawed, -sawed** or **-sawn** (-sôn′), **-saw•ing, -saws.** To saw (a log) into quarters lengthwise along its axis.

quarter section *n.* A land unit equal to a quarter of a section and measuring 1/2 of a mile on a side.

quar•ter•staff (kwôr′tər-stăf′) *n., pl.* **-staves** (-stāvz′). A long wooden staff formerly used as a weapon.

quar•ter•tone (kwôr′tər-tōn′) *n. Mus.* Half a semitone.

quar•tet also **quar•tette** (kwôr-tĕt′) *n.* **1.** *Mus.* **a.** A composition for four voices or instruments. **b.** A group of four performing musicians. **2.** A set of four persons or things. [Fr. *quartette* < Ital. *quartetto*, dim. of *quarto*, fourth < Lat. *quārtus.* See QUART.]

quar•tic (kwôr′tĭk) *adj. Math.* Of or relating to the fourth degree. [Lat. *quārtus*, fourth; see QUART + -IC.] **— quar′tic** *n.*

quar•tile (kwôr′tīl′, -tĭl) *n. Statistics.* The value of the boundary at the 25th, 50th, or 75th percentiles of a frequency distribution divided into four parts, each containing a quarter of the population. [ME, ninety degrees apart (of the relative position of two celestial bodies) < OFr. *quartil* < Med.Lat. *quārtīlis*, of a quartile < Lat. *quārtus*, fourth. See QUART.]

quar•to (kwôr′tō) *n., pl.* **-tos. 1.** The page size obtained by folding a whole sheet into four leaves. **2.** A book composed of pages of this size. [Short for ME *(in) quarto*, (in) the fourth part (of a sheet) < Med.Lat. *(in) quārtō* < Lat., ablative of *quārtus*, fourth. See **kʷetwer-***.]

quartz (kwôrts) *n.* A very hard mineral composed of silica, SiO_2, found worldwide in many different types of rocks, including sandstone and granite. [Ger. *Quarz* < MHGer. *quarc*, of Slav. orig.] **— quartz′ose′** (kwôrt′sōs′) *adj.*

quartz crystal *n.* A small crystal of quartz accurately cut along certain axes so that it can be vibrated at a particular frequency, used for its piezoelectric properties to produce an electric signal of constant known frequency.

quartz glass *n.* A clear vitreous solid, formed by melting pure quartz, that can withstand high temperatures and is extremely transparent to infrared, visible, and ultraviolet radiations.

quartz•if•er•ous (kwôrt-sĭf′ər-əs) *adj.* Containing quartz.

quartz•ite (kwôrt′sīt′) *n.* A rock formed from the metamorphism of quartz sandstone.

quartz lamp *n.* A mercury-vapor lamp enclosed by an envelope made from quartz rather than glass.

qua•sar (kwā′zär′, -sär′, -zər, -sər) *n.* A starlike object that has a large red shift and emits powerful blue light and often radio waves. [*quas(i-stell)ar (radio source).*]

quash¹ (kwŏsh) *tr.v.* **quashed, quash•ing, quash•es.** To set aside or annul, esp. by judicial action. [ME *quassen* < OFr. *casser, quasser* < Med.Lat. *quassāre*, alteration (influenced by *quassāre*, to shatter; see QUASH²) of *cassāre* < Lat. *cassus*, empty, void. See **kes-***.]

quash² (kwŏsh) *tr.v.* **quashed, quash•ing, quash•es.** To put down or suppress forcibly and completely: *quash a rebellion.* [ME *quashen* < OFr. *quasser* < Med.Lat. *quassāre*, to shatter < Lat. See SQUASH².]

qua•si (kwā′zī′, -sī′, kwä′zē, -sē) *adj.* Having a likeness to something; resembling: *a quasi success.* [ME, as if < OFr. < Lat. *quasi* : *quam*, as; see **kʷo-*** + *sī*, if; see **swo-***.]

quasi– *pref.* To some degree; in some manner: *quasi-stellar object.* [Lat. *quasi*, as if. See QUASI.]

Qua•si•mo•do (kwä′zē-mō′dō), **Salvatore.** 1901–68. Italian poet who won the 1950 Nobel Prize for literature.

qua•si-stel•lar object (kwā′zī-stĕl′ər, -sī′-, kwä′zē-, -sē-) *n.* A quasar.

quas•sia (kwŏsh′ə) *n.* **1.a.** A tropical American shrub or small tree *(Quassia amara)* yielding a fine-grained wood. **b.** The wood of this plant. **2.** A bitter substance obtained from the wood of this plant, used in medicine and as an insecticide. [NLat., after Graman *Quassi*, an 18th-cent. Surinamese.]

qua•ter•cen•ten•a•ry (kwŏt′ər-sĕn-tĕn′ə-rē, -sĕn′tə-nĕr′ē) *n., pl.* **-ries.** A quadricentennial. [Lat. *quater*, four times; see QUATERNARY + CENTENARY.]

qua•ter•nar•y (kwŏt′ər-nĕr′ē, kwə-tûr′nə-rē) *adj.* **1.** Consisting of four; in fours. **2. Quaternary.** *Geol.* Of, belonging to, or being the geologic time of the second period of the Cenozoic Era, from the end of the Tertiary Period through the present, characterized by the appearance of human beings and including the Pleistocene and Holocene epochs. See table at **geologic time. 3.** *Chem.* Relating to an atom bonded to four carbon atoms. — *n., pl.* **-nar•ies. 1.** The number four. **2.** The member of a group that is fourth in order. **3. Quaternary.** *Geol.* The Quaternary Period or its deposits. [Lat. *quaternā-*

quarter horse

ă pat	oi boy
ā pay	ou out
âr care	o͝o took
ä father	o͞o boot
ĕ pet	ŭ cut
ē be	ûr urge
ĭ pit	th thin
ī pie	*th* this
îr pier	hw which
ŏ pot	zh vision
ō toe	ə about, item
ô paw	

Stress marks:
′ (primary);
′ (secondary), as in
dictionary (dĭk′shə-nĕr′ē)

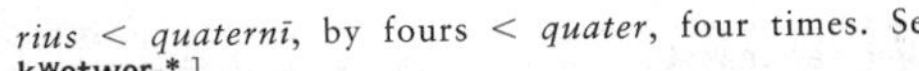

rius < *quaternī*, by fours < *quater*, four times. See **k^{w}etwer-***.]

quaternary ammonium compound *n.* Any of a group of compounds in which a central nitrogen atom is joined to four organic radicals and one acid radical, used in making plastics.

qua•ter•ni•on (kwə-tûr′nē-ən) *n.* **1.** A set of four persons or items. **2.** *Math.* An expression that is the sum of a real number and a vector and contains four terms, one real and three imaginary. [ME *quaternioun* < LLat. *quaterniō, quaterniōn-* < Lat. *quaternī*, by fours < *quater*, four times. See **k^{w}etwer-***.]

quat•rain (kwŏt′rān′, kwŏ-trān′) *n.* A stanza or poem of four lines. [Fr. < OFr. < *quatre*, four < Lat. *quattuor*. See **k^{w}etwer-***.]

quat•re•foil (kăt′ər-foil′, kăt′rə-) *n.* **1.** A representation of a flower with four petals or a leaf with four leaflets, esp. in heraldry. **2.** *Archit.* Tracery or an ornament with four foils or lobes. [ME *quaterfoile* : OFr. *quatre*, four; see QUATRAIN + OFr. *foil*, leaf; see FOIL^{2}.]

quatrefoil
Stained-glass window above an entrance to a church

quat•tro•cen•to (kwŏt′rō-chĕn′tō) *n.* The 15th-century period of Italian art and literature. [Ital., short for *(mil) quattrocento*, one thousand four hundred : *quattro*, four (< Lat. *quattuor*; see **k^{w}etwer-***) + *cento*, hundred (< Lat. *centum*; see **dekm̥***).]

qua•ver (kwā′vər) *v.* **-vered, -ver•ing, -vers.** —*intr.* **1.** To quiver, as from weakness; tremble. **2.** To speak in a quivering voice; utter a quivering sound. **3.** *Mus.* To produce a trill on an instrument or with the voice. —*tr.* To utter or sing in a trilling voice. —*n.* **1.** A quivering sound. **2.** A trill. **3.** *Chiefly British.* An eighth note. [ME *quaveren*, prob. freq. of *cwavien, quaven*, to tremble.] —**qua′ver•y** *adj.*

quay (kē, kā) *n.* A wharf or reinforced bank where ships are loaded or unloaded. [ME *keye* < ONFr. *cai*, of Celt. orig.]

quay•age (kē′ĭj) *n.* **1.** A charge for the use of a quay. **2.** A group of quays. **3.** The space available on a system of quays.

Quayle (kwāl), **James Danforth.** b. 1947. Vice President of the U.S. (1989–93).

Que. *abbr.* Quebec.

quean (kwēn) *n.* **1.** A woman regarded as being disreputable, esp. a prostitute. **2.** *Scots.* A young woman. [ME *quene* < OE *cwene*, woman. See **g^{w}en-***.]

quea•sy also **quea•zy** (kwē′zē) *adj.* **-si•er, -si•est** also **-zi•er, -zi•est. 1.** Experiencing nausea; nauseated. **2.** Easily nauseated. **3.** Causing nausea; sickening: *an airplane's queasy lurch.* **4.a.** Causing uneasiness. **b.** Uneasy; troubled. **5.a.** Easily troubled. **b.** Ill at ease; squeamish. [ME *coisy*, perh. of Scand. orig.] —**quea′si•ly** *adv.* —**quea′si•ness** *n.*

queen
Chess piece

Que•bec (kwĭ-bĕk′) or **Qué•bec** (kā-). **1.** A province of E Canada; joined the confederacy in 1867. The region was made a royal colony of France in 1663 and came under British sovereignty in 1763. Cap. Quebec. Pop. 6,438,403. **2.** Also **Quebec City** or **Québec City.** The cap. of Quebec, Canada, in the S part on the St. Lawrence R. Pop. 166,474. —**Que•beck′er, Que•bec′er** *n.*

Qué•be•cois or **Que•be•cois** (kā′bĕ-kwä′) —*adj.* Of or relating to Quebec and esp. to its French-speaking inhabitants or their culture. —*n., pl.* **Québecois** or **Quebecois.** A native or inhabitant of Quebec, esp. a French-speaking one. [Fr. *québecois* < *Québec*, Quebec.]

que•bra•cho (kā-brä′chō) *n., pl.* **-chos. 1.** Either of two South American trees, *Aspidosperma quebracho-blanco*, whose bark is used in medicine, or *Schinopsis lorentzii*, whose wood is one of the richest sources of tannin. **2.** The bark or wood of either of these trees. [Sp., alteration of *quiebrahacha* : *quebrar*, to break (< Lat. *crepāre*, to crack) + *hacha*, ax (< Fr. *hache* < OFr., of Gmc. orig.).]

Que•chan (kĕch′ən) *n.* See **Yuma^{1}.** [Yuma *k^{w}aćán*, those who descended (from the sacred mountain of creation).]

Quech•ua also **Kech•ua** (kĕch′wə, -wä′) *n., pl.* **Quechua** or **-uas** also **Kechua** or **-uas. 1.** The Quechuan language of the Inca empire, now widely spoken throughout the Andes highlands from southern Colombia to Chile. **2.a.** A member of a South American Indian people originally constituting the ruling class of the Inca empire. **b.** A speaker of the Quechua language. [Sp. < Quechua *kkechuwa*, plunderer.]

Quech•uan (kĕch′wən) *n.* A subgroup of the Quechumaran languages. —*adj.* Of or relating to the Quechua or their language or culture.

Quech•u•mar•an (kĕch′o͝o-mä-rän′) *n.* A group of languages found mostly in the Andes highlands from southern Colombia to northern Chile and Argentina, composed of the Quechuan and Aymaran languages.

Queen Anne
Mid 18th-century American side chair

queen (kwēn) *n.* **1.a.** The wife or widow of a king. **b.** A woman sovereign. **2.** Something having eminence or supremacy in a given domain and personified as a woman: *Paris is the queen of cities.* **3.** *Games.* **a.** The most powerful chess piece, able to move in any direction in a straight line. **b.** A playing card bearing the figure of a queen, ranking above the jack and below the king. **4.** The fertile, fully developed female in a colony of social bees, ants, or termites. **5.** *Offensive Slang.* Used as a disparaging term for a gay or homosexual man. —*v.* **queened, queen•ing, queens.** —*tr.* **1.** To make (a woman) a queen. **2.** *Games.* To raise (a pawn) to queen in chess. —*intr. Games.* To become a queen in chess. —***idiom.*** **queen it.** To act like a queen; domineer. [ME *quene* < OE *cwēn*. See **g^{w}en-***.]

Queen Anne (kwēn ăn′) *n.* The style in architecture and furniture typical of the reign of Queen Anne (1702–1714).

Queen Anne's lace (ănz) *n.* A widely naturalized Eurasian herb *(Daucus carota* var. *carota)* having white nonfleshy fusiform compound umbels of small white or yellowish flowers.

Queen Char•lotte Islands (shär′lət). An archipelago off the W coast of British Columbia, Canada, separated from Vancouver I. by **Queen Charlotte Sound**, an inlet of the Pacific.

queen consort *n., pl.* **queens consort.** The wife of a reigning king.

queen cup *n.* A perennial stemless plant *(Clintonia uniflora)* of Pacific North America having one white flower and a blue berry.

Queen E•liz•a•beth Islands (ĭ-lĭz′ə-bəth). A group of islands of N Northwest Terrs., Canada, in the Arctic Archipelago N of Parry Channel.

queen•ly (kwēn′lē) *adj.* **-li•er, -li•est. 1.** Having the status or rank of queen. **2.** Of, resembling, or befitting a queen; majestic and regal. —*adv.* In a royal way; regally. —**queen′li•ness** *n.*

Queen Maud Land (môd). A region of Antarctica between the Weddell Sea and Enderby Land; claimed by Norway in 1939.

Queen Maud Mountains. A mountain range of Antarctica extending c. 805 km (500 mi) near the South Pole.

queen mother *n.* A dowager queen who is the mother of a reigning monarch.

queen-of-the-prai•rie (kwēn′əv-thə-prâr′ē) *n.* A rhizomatous plant *(Filipendula rubra)* of the prairies and meadows of the eastern and central United States, having aromatic, pinnately compound leaves and showy pannicles of small pink flowers.

queen olive *n.* A large edible variety of olive not used as a source of oil.

queen post *n.* One of two upright supporting posts set vertically between the rafters and the tie beam at equal distances from the apex of a roof.

queen regnant *n., pl.* **queens regnant.** A queen reigning in her own right.

Queens (kwēnz). A borough of New York City on W Long I.; first settled in 1635. Pop. 1,951,598.

Queen's Bench (kwēnz) *n. Law.* A division of the British superior courts system that hears criminal and civil cases. Used when the sovereign is a woman.

Queens•ber•ry (kwēnz′bĕr′ē, -bə-rē), 8th Marquis of. John Sholto Douglas. 1844–1900. British aristocrat who formulated rules (1867) to govern boxing.

Queensberry rules *pl.n. Sports.* Marquis of Queensberry rules.

Queen's Counsel *n. Law.* A barrister appointed as counsel to the British crown. Used when the sovereign is a woman.

Queen's English *n.* English speech or usage that is considered standard or accepted; Received Standard English.

queen•ship (kwēn′shĭp′) *n.* **1.** The rank or state of being a queen. **2.** A noble or regal quality, as of a queen.

queen-size (kwēn′sīz′) also **queen-sized** (-sīzd′) *adj.* **1.** Extra large in size. **2.a.** Measuring about 60 inches by 80 inches (1.5 meters by 2.0 meters). Used of a bed. **b.** Being of a size that will fit such a bed: *queen-size sheets.*

queen substance *n.* A pheromone secreted by queen bees and given to worker bees to prevent them from producing more queens.

queen truss *n.* A building truss using queen posts.

queer (kwîr) *adj.* **queer•er, queer•est. 1.** Deviating from the expected or normal; strange: *a queer situation.* **2.** Odd or unconventional, as in behavior; eccentric. See Syns at **strange. 3.** Of a questionable nature or character; suspicious. **4.** *Slang.* Fake; counterfeit. **5.** Feeling slightly ill; queasy. **6.** *Offensive Slang.* Gay; homosexual. —*n. Offensive Slang.* Used as a disparaging term for a gay or homosexual person. —*tr.v.* **queered, queer•ing, queers.** *Slang.* **1.** To ruin or thwart. **2.** To put (someone) in a bad position. [Perh. < LGer., oblique, off-center < MLGer. *dwer*. See **terk^{w}-***.] —**queer′ish** *adj.* —**queer′ly** *adv.* —**queer′ness** *n.*

que•le•a (kwē′lē-ə) *n.* An African weaverbird of the genus *Quelea*, esp. *Q. quelea*, a small red-billed bird that is extremely destructive to grain crops. [NLat. *Quelea*, genus name, perh. alteration of Med.Lat. *qualea*, quail, ult. < VLat. **coacula*, of imit. orig.]

quell (kwĕl) *tr.v.* **quelled, quell•ing, quells. 1.** To put down forcibly; suppress: *quelled the riot.* **2.** To pacify; quiet. [ME *quellen*, to kill < OE *cwellan*. See **g^{w}elə-***.]

Que•moy (kĭ-moi′). In Pinyin **Jin•men** (jĭn′mœn′). An island and group of 2 islands and 12 islets off SE China in Taiwan Strait; administered by Taiwan since 1949.

quench (kwĕnch) *tr.v.* **quenched, quench•ing, quench•es. 1.** To put out (a fire, for example); extinguish. **2.** To suppress; squelch. **3.** To put an end to; destroy. **4.** To slake; satisfy: *quenched our thirst.* **5.** To cool (hot metal) by thrusting into water or other liquid. [ME *quenchen* < OE *ācwencan*.] —**quench′a•ble** *adj.* —**quench′er** *n.* —**quench′less** *adj.*

que•nelle (kə-nĕl′) *n.* A ball or dumpling of finely chopped meat or seafood bound with eggs and poached in stock or water. [Fr. < Ger. *Knödel* < MHGer., dim. of *knode*, knot, knob < OHGer. *knodo*.]

quer•ce•tin (kwûr′sĭ-tĭn) *n.* A crystalline compound, $C_5H_{15}O_2(OH)_5$, synthesized or occurring as a glycoside in the rind and bark of numerous plants and used medicinally to treat abnormal capillary fragility. [Lat. *quercētum*, oak forest (< *quercus*, oak; see **perk^{w}u-***) + -IN.]

quer•ci•tron (kwûr′sĭ-trən, -trŏn′, kwər-sĭt′rən) *n.* **1.** The bright orange inner bark of the black oak. **2.** The yellow dye obtained from this bark. [Blend of Lat. *quercus*, oak; see **perk^{w}u-*** and CITRON.]

Que•ré•ta•ro (kə-rĕt′ə-rō′, kĕ-rĕ′tä-rō′). A city of central Mexico NW of Mexico City; site of an ancient pre-Aztec settlement. Pop. 215,976.

que•rist (kwîr′ĭst) *n.* One who asks questions; an inquirer. [< obsolete *quere*, question. See QUERY.]

quern (kwûrn) *n.* A simple hand-turned grain mill. [ME *querne* < OE *cweorn*. See **g^{w}erə-[1]***.]

quer•u•lous (kwĕr′ə-ləs, kwĕr′yə-) *adj.* **1.** Given to complaining; peevish. **2.** Expressing a complaint or grievance; grumbling: *querulous comments*. [ME *querulose*, litigious, quarrelsome < OFr. *querelos* < LLat. *querulōsus*, querulous < Lat. *querulus* < *querī*, to complain. See **kwes-***.] — **quer′u•lous•ly** *adv.* — **quer′u•lous•ness** *n.*

que•ry (kwîr′ē) *n., pl.* **-ries. 1.** A question; an inquiry. **2.** A doubt in the mind; a mental reservation. **3.** A notation, usu. a question mark, calling attention to an item in order to question its validity or accuracy. — *tr.v.* **-ried, -ry•ing, -ries. 1.** To express doubt or uncertainty about; question: *query someone's motives*. **2.** To put a question to (a person). See Syns at **ask. 3.** To mark (an item) with a notation in order to question its validity or accuracy. [Alteration of obsolete *quaere*, *quere* < Lat., imper. of *quaerere*, to ask, to seek.] — **que′ri•er** *n.*

ques. *abbr.* Question.

Ques•nay (kā-nā′, kĕ-), **François.** 1694–1774. French physician and pioneer political economist.

quest (kwĕst) *n.* **1.** The act or an instance of seeking or pursuing something; a search. **2.** An expedition undertaken in medieval romance by a knight in order to perform a prescribed feat. **3.** *Archaic.* A jury of inquest. — *v.* **quest•ed, quest•ing, quests.** — *intr.* **1.** To go on a quest. **2.** To search for game. — *tr.* To search for; seek. [ME *queste* < OFr., ult. < Lat. *quaesta*, fem. p.part. of *quaerere*, to seek, ask.] — **quest′er** *n.*

ques•tion (kwĕs′chən) *n.* **1.a.** An expression of inquiry that invites or calls for a reply. **b.** An interrogative sentence, phrase, or gesture. **2.** A subject or point open to controversy; an issue. **3.** A difficult matter; a problem: *a question of ethics*. **4.** A point or subject under discussion or consideration. **5.a.** A proposition brought up for consideration by an assembly. **b.** The act of bringing a proposal to vote. **6.** Uncertainty; doubt: *no question about his competence*. — *v.* **-tioned, -tion•ing, -tions.** — *tr.* **1.** To put a question to. See Syns at **ask. 2.** To examine (a witness, for example) by questioning; interrogate. **3.** To express doubt about; dispute. **4.** To analyze; examine. — *intr.* To ask questions. — ***idiom.* out of the question.** Not worth considering; impossible. [ME < OFr., legal inquiry < Lat. *quaestiō*, *quaestiōn-* < **quaestus*, p.part. of *quaerere*, to ask, seek.] — **ques′tion•er** *n.* — **ques′tion•ing•ly** *adv.*

ques•tion•a•ble (kwĕs′chə-nə-bəl) *adj.* **1.a.** Open to doubt or challenge; problematic. **b.** Not yet determined or specified. **2.** Of dubious morality or respectability. — **ques′tion•a•ble•ness, ques′tion•a•bil′i•ty** *n.* — **ques′tion•a•bly** *adv.*

question mark *n.* A punctuation symbol (?) written at the end of a sentence or phrase to indicate a direct question.

ques•tion•naire (kwĕs′chə-nâr′) *n.* A printed form containing a set of questions often used to gather information for a statistical survey. [Fr. < *questionner*, to ask < OFr. < *question*, legal inquiry. See QUESTION.]

Quet•ta (kwĕt′ə). A city of W-central Pakistan WSW of Lahore. Pop. 243,000.

quet•zal (kĕt-säl′) *n., pl.* **-zals** or **-za•les** (-sä′lās). **1.** A Central American bird *(Pharomachrus mocino)* that has brilliant bronze-green and red plumage and long flowing tail feathers in the male. **2.** See table at **currency.** [Am.Sp. < Nahuatl *quetzalli*, large brilliant tail feather.]

Quet•zal•co•a•tl (kĕt-säl′kō-ät′l) *n. Myth.* A god of the Toltecs and Aztecs, represented as a plumed serpent.

queue (kyo͞o) *n.* **1.** A line of waiting people or vehicles. **2.** A long braid of hair at the back of the neck; a pigtail. **3.** *Comp. Sci.* A sequence of stored data or programs awaiting processing. — *intr.v.* **queued, queu•ing, queues.** To get in line: *queued up*. [Fr. < OFr. *cue*, tail < Lat. *cauda*, *cōda*.]

Que•zon City (kā′sôn′, -sōn′). A city of central Luzon, Philippines, adjoining Manila; official cap. from 1948 to 1976. Pop. 1,165,865.

Quezon y Mo•li•na (ē mə-lē′nə, mô-lē′nä), **Manuel Luis.** 1878–1944. Philippine politician who served as the first president of the Philippines (1935–44).

quib•ble (kwĭb′əl) *intr.v.* **-bled, -bling, -bles. 1.** To evade the truth of an issue with trivial distinctions and objections. **2.** To find fault or criticize for petty reasons; cavil. — *n.* **1.** A petty distinction or an irrelevant objection. **2.** *Archaic.* A pun. [Prob. dim. of obsolete *quib*, equivocation, perh. < Lat. *quibus*, dative and ablative pl. of *quī*, who, what (from its frequent use in legal documents). See **k^{w}o-***.] — **quib′bler** *n.*

quiche (kēsh) *n.* A rich unsweetened custard baked in a pastry shell often with other ingredients such as vegetables. [Fr. < Ger. dial. *Küche*, dim. of Ger. *Kuchen*, cake. See KUCHEN.]

Qui•ché (kē-chā′) *n., pl.* **Quiché** or **-chés. 1.** A member of a Mayan people of Guatemala. **2.** The Mayan language of the Quiché.

quiche Lor•raine (lə-rān′, lô-) *n.* A quiche made with cheese and pieces of bacon. [Fr., after LORRAINE.]

quick (kwĭk) *adj.* **quick•er, quick•est. 1.** Moving or functioning rapidly and energetically; speedy. **2.** Learning, thinking, or understanding with speed and dexterity; bright: *a quick mind*. **3.a.** Perceiving or responding with speed and sensitivity; keen. **b.** Reacting immediately and sharply: *a quick temper*. **4.a.** Occurring or achieved in a relatively brief period of time: *a quick promotion*. **b.** Done or occurring immediately: *a quick inspection*. See Syns at **fast[1]. 5.** Tending to react hastily: *quick to find fault*. **6.** *Archaic.* **a.** Alive. **b.** Pregnant. — *n.* **1.** Sensitive or raw exposed flesh, as under the fingernails. **2.** The most personal and sensitive aspect of the emotions. **3.** The living: *the quick and the dead*. **4.** The vital core; the essence: *the quick of the matter*. — *adv.* Quickly; promptly. [ME, alive, lively, quick < OE *cwicu*, alive. See **g^{w}ei-***.] — **quick′ly** *adv.* — **quick′ness** *n.*

Usage Note: In speech *quick* is commonly used as an adverb in phrases such as *Come quick*. In formal writing, however, *quickly* is required.

Queen Anne's lace
Daucus carota var. *carota*

quick-and-dirt•y (kwĭk′ən-dûr′tē) *adj.* Cheaply made or done; of inferior quality: *a quick-and-dirty report*.

quick assets *pl.n.* Liquid assets, including cash on hand and assets readily convertible to cash.

quick bread *n.* A bread made with a leavening agent, such as baking powder, that expands during baking and requires no leavening period beforehand.

quick•en (kwĭk′ən) *v.* **-ened, -en•ing, -ens.** — *tr.* **1.** To make more rapid; accelerate. **2.** To make alive; vitalize. **3.** To excite and stimulate; stir. **4.** To make steeper. — *intr.* **1.** To become more rapid. **2.** To come or return to life. **3.** To reach the stage of pregnancy when the fetus can be felt to move. — **quick′en•er** *n.*

quick fix *n. Slang.* A hastily contrived temporary remedy for a problem. — **quick′-fix′** (kwĭk′fĭks′) *adj.*

quick-freeze (kwĭk′frēz′) *tr.v.* **-froze** (-frōz′), **-froz•en** (-frō′zən), **-freez•ing, -freez•es.** To freeze (food) rapidly so as to retain flavor, nutritional value, or other properties.

quick•ie (kwĭk′ē) *n. Informal.* Something done rapidly.

quick•lime (kwĭk′līm′) *n.* See **lime[3]** 1b. [ME *qwike lime* : *quick*, live; see QUICK + *lime*, lime; see LIME[3].]

quick•sand (kwĭk′sănd′) *n.* **1.** A bed of loose sand and water forming a soft shifting mass that yields easily to pressure and tends to engulf any object resting on its surface. **2.** A place or situation similar to quicksand.

quick•set (kwĭk′sĕt′) *n. Chiefly British.* **1.** Cuttings or slips of a plant suitable for hedges. **2.** A hedge consisting of these plant cuttings or slips. [QUICK, alive + SET[1].]

quick•sil•ver (kwĭk′sĭl′vər) *n.* See **mercury** 1. — *adj.* Unpredictable; mercurial. [ME < OE *cwicseolfor* : *cwic*, *cwicu*, alive; see **g^{w}ei-*** + *seolfor*, silver; see SILVER.]

quick•step (kwĭk′stĕp′) *n. Mus.* A march in quick time.

quick study *n.* One who is able to memorize or understand something quickly.

quick-tem•pered (kwĭk′tĕm′pərd) *adj.* Easily angered.

quick time *n.* A marching pace of 120 steps per minute.

quick-wit•ted (kwĭk′wĭt′ĭd) *adj.* Mentally alert and sharp; keen. See Syns at **intelligent.** — **quick′-wit′ted•ly** *adv.* — **quick′-wit′ted•ness** *n.*

quetzal
Male resplendent quetzal
Pharomachrus mocino

quid[1] (kwĭd) *n.* A cut or piece, as of chewing tobacco. [ME *quide*, cud < OE *cwidu*.]

quid[2] (kwĭd) *n., pl.* **quid** or **quids.** *Chiefly British.* A pound sterling. [Poss. < Lat., something, what. See QUIDDITY.]

Quid•de (kvĭd′ə), **Ludwig.** 1858–1941. German politician who shared the 1927 Nobel Peace Prize.

quid•di•ty (kwĭd′ĭ-tē) *n., pl.* **-ties. 1.** The real nature of a thing; the essence. **2.** A hairsplitting distinction; a quibble. [Med.Lat. *quidditās* < Lat. *quid*, what. See **k^{w}o-***.]

quid•nunc (kwĭd′nŭngk′) *n.* A nosy person; a busybody. [Lat. *quid nunc?*, what now? : *quid*, what; see **k^{w}o-*** + *nunc*, now; see **nu-***.]

quid pro quo (kwĭd′ prō kwō′) *n., pl.* **quid pro quos** or **quids pro quo.** An equal exchange or substitution. [Lat. *quid prō quō* : *quid*, what? + *prō*, for + *quō*, ablative of *quid*, what?]

qui•es•cent (kwē-ĕs′ənt, kwī-) *adj.* Being quiet, still, or at rest; inactive. [Lat. *quiēscēns*, *quiēscent-*, pr.part. of *quiēscere*, to rest < *quiēs*, quiet. See QUIET.] — **qui•es′cence** *n.* — **qui•es′cent•ly** *adv.*

qui•et (kwī′ĭt) *adj.* **-et•er, -et•est. 1.** Making no noise; silent:

ă pat	oi boy
ā pay	ou out
âr care	o͝o took
ä father	o͞o boot
ĕ pet	ŭ cut
ē be	ûr urge
ĭ pit	th thin
ī pie	*th* this
îr pier	hw which
ŏ pot	zh vision
ō toe	ə about, item
ô paw	

Stress marks:
′ (primary);
′ (secondary), as in
dictionary (dĭk′shə-nĕr′ē)

a quiet baby. **2.** Free of noise; hushed: *a quiet room.* **3.** Calm and unmoving; still: *quiet waters.* **4.** Free of turmoil and agitation; untroubled. **5.** Restful; soothing: *a quiet afternoon nap.* **6.** Tranquil; serene: *a quiet manner.* **7.** Not showy or garish; restrained: *quiet colors.* — *n.* The quality or condition of being quiet. — *v.* **-et•ed, -et•ing, -ets.** — *tr.* **1.** To cause to become quiet. **2.** *Law.* To make (a title) secure by freeing from all questions or challenges. — *intr.* To become quiet: *The child wouldn't quiet down.* [ME < OFr. < Lat. *quiētus* < p.part. of *quiēscere,* to rest < *quiēs,* quiet. See **kʷeiə-*.**] — **qui′et•ly** *adv.* — **qui′et•ness** *n.*

qui•et•en (kwī′ĭ-tn) *tr. & intr.v.* **-ened, -en•ing, -ens.** To make or become quiet.

qui•et•ism (kwī′ĭ-tĭz′əm) *n.* **1.** A form of Christian mysticism enjoining passive contemplation and the beatific annihilation of the will. **2.** A state of quietness and passivity. — **qui′et•ist** *n.* — **qui′et•is′tic** *adj.*

qui•e•tude (kwī′ĭ-to͞od′, -tyo͞od′) *n.* Tranquillity. [LLat. *quiētūdō* < Lat. *quiētus,* resting < p.part. of *quiēscere,* to rest. See QUIET.]

qui•e•tus (kwī-ē′təs) *n.* **1.** Something that serves to suppress, check, or eliminate. **2.** Release from life; death. **3.** A final discharge, as of a duty. [Short for ME *quietus (est),* (he is) discharged (of an obligation) < Med.Lat. *quiētus (est)* < Lat., (he is) at rest. See QUIET.]

quiff[1] (kwĭf) *n. Chiefly British.* A tuft of hair, esp. a forelock. [?]

quiff[2] (kwĭf) *n.* A woman regarded as promiscuous. [?]

quill (kwĭl) *n.* **1.** The hollow stemlike main shaft of a feather. **2.** Any of the larger wing or tail feathers of a bird. **3.** A writing pen made from the shaft of a feather. **4.** *Mus.* **a.** A plectrum for a stringed instrument of the clavichord type. **b.** A pipe with a hollow stem. **5.** A toothpick made from the stem of a feather. **6.** One of the sharp hollow spines of a porcupine or hedgehog. **7.** A bobbin around which yarn is wound in weaving. **8.** A hollow shaft that rotates on a solid shaft when gears are engaged. — *tr.v.* **quilled, quill•ing, quills. 1.** To wind (thread or yarn) onto a quill. **2.** To make or press small ridges in (fabric). [ME *quil.*]

quill•back (kwĭl′băk′) *n., pl.* **quillback** or **-backs.** A North American freshwater fish *(Carpiodes cyprinus)* with one dorsal fin ray extending conspicuously beyond the others.

Quil•ler-Couch (kwĭl′ər-ko͞och′), Sir **Arthur Thomas.** Pen name "Q." 1863–1944. British writer and editor of *The Oxford Book of English Verse* (1900).

quill•work (kwĭl′wûrk′) *n.* Decoration, as of leather articles, with porcupine quills.

quill•wort (kwĭl′wûrt′, -wôrt′) *n.* Any of several vascular spore-bearing aquatic or marsh plants of the genus *Isoetes,* having short rhizomes and quill-like leaves.

Quil•mes (kēl′mĕs′). A city of E Argentina, a suburb of Buenos Aires on the Río de la Plata. Pop. 445,662.

quilt (kwĭlt) *n.* **1.** A coverlet or blanket made of two layers of fabric with a layer of cotton, wool, feathers, or down in between, all stitched firmly together. **2.** A thick protective cover similar to a quilt. — *v.* **quilt•ed, quilt•ing, quilts.** — *tr.* **1.** To make into a quilt by stitching (layers of fabric) together. **2.** To construct like a quilt. **3.** To pad and stitch ornamentally. — *intr.* **1.** To make a quilt. **2.** To do quilted work. [ME *quilte* < AN < Lat. *culcita,* mattress.] — **quilt′er** *n.*

quilt

quilt•ing (kwĭl′tĭng) *n.* **1.** The process of doing quilted work. **2.a.** Material used for quilts. **b.** Quilted material.

quin– *pref.* Var. of **quino–.**

quin•a•crine hydrochloride (kwĭn′ə-krēn′) *n.* A crystalline compound, $C_{23}H_{30}ClN_3O$, used primarily to treat malaria. [QUIN– + ACR(ID)INE.]

qui•nate (kwī′nāt′) *adj.* Arranged in groups of five: *quinate leaflets.* [Lat. *quīnī,* five each; see **penkʷe*** + –ATE[1].]

quince (kwĭns) *n.* **1.** A western Asian shrub or tree *(Cydonia oblonga)* having white flowers and hard applelike fruit. **2.** The many-seeded fruit of this plant, edible only when cooked. [ME *quynce,* pl. of *quyn,* quince < OFr. *cooin* < Lat. *cotōneum (mālum),* quince (fruit), prob. var. of *cydōnium* < Gk. *kudōnion (malon),* alteration (influenced by *Kudōniā,* Cydonia, an ancient city of NW Crete) of *Kodumalon.*]

quince
Cydonia oblonga

quin•cun•cial also **quin•cunx•ial** (kwĭn-kŭn′shəl) *adj.* Of, relating to, or forming a quincunx. — **quin•cun′cial•ly** *adv.*

quin•cunx (kwĭn′kŭngks′) *n.* An arrangement of five objects with one at each corner of a rectangle or square and one at the center. [Lat. *quincunx, quincunc-,* five twelfths : *quīnque,* five; see **penkʷe*** + *uncia,* twelfth part of a unit; see OUNCE[1].]

Quin•cy. 1. (kwĭn′sē). A city of W IL on a bluff above the Mississippi R. Pop. 39,681. **2.** (kwĭn′zē). A city of E MA a suburb of Boston. Pop. 84,985.

Quin•cy (kwĭn′zē, -sē), **Josiah.** 1744–75. Amer. Revolutionary patriot who traveled to England (1774–75) to present the colonists' grievances.

Josiah Quincy
1796 engraving by Charles Balthazar Julien Fevret de Saint-Memin (1770?–1852?)

quin•de•cen•ni•al (kwĭn′dĭ-sĕn′ē-əl) *adj.* **1.** Occurring once every 15 years. **2.** Lasting 15 years. — *n.* A 15th anniversary. [< Lat. *quīndecim,* fifteen; see **penkʷe*** + Lat. *-ennium* (< *annus,* year; see **at-***).]

qui•nel•la (kwĭ-nĕl′ə, kē-) also **qui•nie•la** (kēn-yĕl′ə) *n. Games.* A system of betting in which the bettor must pick the first two finishers of a race but not necessarily in the correct sequence. [Am.Sp. *quiniela,* dim. of Sp. *quina,* keno < Fr. *quine.* See KENO.]

quin•i•dine (kwĭn′ĭ-dēn′) *n.* A colorless crystalline alkaloid, $C_{20}H_{24}N_2O_2$, resembling quinine and used in treating malaria and certain heart disorders.

qui•nine (kwī′nīn′) *n.* **1.** A bitter colorless amorphous powder or crystalline alkaloid, $C_{20}H_{24}N_2O_2{\cdot}3H_2O$, derived from certain cinchona barks and used in medicine to treat malaria. **2.** Any of various compounds or salts of quinine.

quinine water *n.* A quinine-flavored carbonated beverage.

quin•nat salmon (kwĭn′ăt′) *n.* See **Chinook salmon.** [Chinook *ikwanat.*]

quino– or **quin–** *pref.* **1.** Cinchona; cinchona bark: *quinoidine.* **2.** Quinone: *quinoid.* [< Sp. *quina,* cinchona bark < Quechua *kina.*]

qui•no•a (kĭ-nō′ə, kēn′wä) *n.* A goosefoot *(Chenopodium quinoa)* native to the Andes and cultivated for its edible seeds. [Am.Sp. *quínoa* < Quechua *kinua, kinoa.*]

quin•oid (kwĭn′oid′) *n.* A substance resembling quinone in structure or physical properties.

qui•noi•dine (kwĭ-noi′dēn′, -dĭn) *n.* A brownish-black mixture of alkaloids remaining after extraction of crystalline alkaloids from cinchona bark, used as a quinine substitute.

quin•o•line (kwĭn′ə-lēn′, -lĭn) *n.* An organic base, C_9H_7N, having a tarlike odor, synthesized or obtained from coal tar, and used as a food preservative and in antiseptics and dyes.

qui•none (kwĭ-nōn′, kwĭn′ōn′) *n.* Any of a class of aromatic compounds found widely in plants, esp. the yellow form, $CO(CHCH)_2CO$, that is used in making dyes, tanning hides, and photography.

quin•o•noid (kwĭn′ə-noid′, kwĭ-nō′-) *adj.* Of or containing quinone or resembling it in structure or properties.

quin•qua•ge•nar•i•an (kwĭng′kwə-jə-nâr′ē-ən) *n.* A person 50 years old or in his or her fifties. — *adj.* Of or characteristic of a quinquagenarian. [< Lat. *quīnquāgēnārius,* containing fifty < *quīnquāgēnī,* fifty each < *quīnquāginta,* fifty. See **penkʷe*.**]

quinque– *pref.* Five: *quinquevalent.* [Lat. *quīnque-* < *quīnque,* five. See **penkʷe*.**]

quin•quen•ni•al (kwĭn-kwĕn′ē-əl, kwĭng-) *adj.* **1.** Happening once every five years. **2.** Lasting for five years. — *n.* **1.** A fifth anniversary. **2.** A period of five years. — **quin•quen′ni•al•ly** *adv.*

quin•quen•ni•um (kwĭn-kwĕn′ē-əm, kwĭng-) *n., pl.* **-quen•ni•ums** or **-quen•ni•a** (-kwĕn′ē-ə). A period of five years. [Lat. *quīnquennium* : *quīnque,* quinque- + *-ennium* (< *annus,* year; see **at-***).]

quin•que•va•lent (kwĭng′kwə-vā′lənt) *adj.* Pentavalent. — **quin′que•va′lence** *n.*

quin•sy (kwĭn′zē) *n.* Acute inflammation of the tonsils and the surrounding tissue, often leading to the formation of an abscess. [ME < Med.Lat. *quinancia* and OFr. *quinancie,* both < Gk. *kunankhē,* dog quinsy, dog collar : *kuōn, kun-,* dog; see **kwon-*** + *ankhein,* to squeeze; see **angh-*.**]

quint[1] (kwĭnt) *n. Games.* A sequence of five cards of the same suit in one hand in piquet. [Fr. *quinte* < OFr., interval of a fifth (in music), fem. of *quint,* fifth < Lat. *quīntus.* See **penkʷe*.**]

quint[2] (kwĭnt) *n.* A quintuplet.

quin•tain (kwĭn′tən) *n.* A post or an object mounted on a post, used as a target in tilting exercises. [ME *quintaine* < OFr., prob. < Lat. *quīntāna (via),* fifth (street in a Roman camp, supposedly used for military exercises) < *quīntus,* fifth. See **penkʷe*.**]

quin•tal (kwĭnt′l) *n.* **1.** A unit of mass in the metric system equal to 100 kilograms. **2.** See **hundredweight** 2. [ME, a unit of weight < OFr. < Med.Lat. *quintāle* < Ar. *qinṭār* < LGk. *kentēnarion* < LLat. *centēnārium (pondus),* hundred(weight) < Lat. *centēnārius,* of a hundred. See CENTENARY.]

Quin•te•ro (kēn-tĕ′rō), **Serafín Álvarez.** See Serafín **Álvarez Quintero.**

quin•tes•sence (kwĭn-tĕs′əns) *n.* **1.** The pure, highly concentrated essence of a thing. **2.** The purest or most typical instance: *the quintessence of evil.* **3.** In ancient and medieval philosophy, the fifth and highest essence after the four elements of earth, air, fire, and water, thought to be the substance of the heavenly bodies and latent in all things. [ME < OFr. *quinte essence,* fifth essence < Med.Lat. *quīnta essentia* : Lat. *quīnta,* fem. of *quīntus,* fifth; see **penkʷe*** + Lat. *essentia,* essence; see ESSENCE.] — **quin′tes•sen′tial** (-tə-sĕn′shəl) *adj.* — **quin′tes•sen′tial•ly** *adv.*

quin•tet also **quin•tette** (kwĭn-tĕt′) *n.* **1.** *Mus.* **a.** A composition for five voices or instruments. **b.** A group of five performing musicians. **2.** A set of five persons or things. [Prob. < Ital. *quintetto,* dim. of *quinto,* fifth < Lat. *quīntus.* See **penkʷe*.**]

quin•tile (kwĭn′tīl′, kwĭnt′l) *n.* **1.** The astrological aspect of planets distant from each other by 72° or one fifth of the zodiac. **2.** *Statistics.* The value at any of the boundaries that divide a frequency distribution into five parts, each containing one fifth of the population. [Lat. *quīntus*, fifth; see **penk^{w}e*** + *-ile*, as in QUARTILE.]

Quin•til•ian (kwĭn-tĭl′yən, -ē-ən). 1st cent. A.D. Roman rhetorician known for his *Institutio Oratorio*.

quin•til•lion (kwĭn-tĭl′yən) *n.* **1.** The cardinal number equal to 10^{18}. **2.** *Chiefly British.* The cardinal number equal to 10^{30}. [Lat. *quīntus*, fifth; see **penk^{w}e*** + (M)ILLION.] **—quin•til′lion** *adj.*

quin•til•lionth (kwĭn-tĭl′yənth) *n.* **1.** The ordinal number matching the number quintillion in a series. **2.** One of a quintillion equal parts. **—quin•til′lionth** *adj.*

quin•tu•ple (kwĭn-tōō′pəl, -tyōō′-, -tŭp′əl, kwĭn′tə-pəl) *adj.* **1.** Consisting of five parts or units. **2.** Five times as much, as many, or as large. *—n.* A fivefold amount or number. *—tr. & intr.v.* **-pled, -pling, -ples.** To multiply or be multiplied by five. [Fr. < OFr. : Lat. *quīntus*, fifth; see **penk^{w}e*** + *-ple*, -fold (< Lat. *-plus*; see **pel-[2]***).]

quin•tu•plet (kwĭn-tŭp′lĭt, -tōō′plĭt, -tyōō′-, kwĭn′tə-plĭt) *n.* **1.** One of five offspring born in a single birth. **2.** A group or combination of five associated by common properties or behavior. [< QUINTUPLE.]

quin•tu•pli•cate (kwĭn-tōō′plĭ-kĭt, -tyōō′-) *adj.* **1.** Multiplied by five; fivefold. **2.** Fifth of a group of five identical things. *—n.* **1.** One of a set of five identical things. **2.** A set of five copies. *—tr. & intr.v.* (-kāt′) **-cat•ed, -cat•ing, -cates.** To multiply or be multiplied by five. [Lat. *quīntus*, fifth; see QUINTUPLE + (QUADRU)PLICATE.]

quip (kwĭp) *n.* **1.** A clever, witty, usu. impromptu remark. **2.** A clever, often sarcastic remark; a gibe. **3.** A petty distinction or objection; a quibble. **4.** Something curious or odd. *—intr.v.* **quipped, quip•ping, quips.** To make quips or a quip. [Alteration of obsolete *quippy*, perh. < Lat. *quippe*, indeed < *quid*, what. See **k^{w}o-***.] **—quip′py** *adj.* **—quip′ster** *n.*

qui•pu (kē′pōō) *n.* A record-keeping device of the Inca empire consisting of a series of variously colored strings attached to a base rope and knotted so as to encode information, esp. accounts. [Am.Sp. < Quechua *kipu*.]

quire[1] (kwīr) *n.* **1.** A set of 24 or sometimes 25 sheets of paper of the same size and stock; one twentieth of a ream. **2.** A collection of leaves of parchment or paper, folded one within the other, in a manuscript or book. [ME *quayer*, four double sheets of paper < OFr. *quaer* < VLat. **quaternus* < Lat. *quaternī*, set of four, four each < *quater*, four times. See **k^{w}etwer-***.]

quire[2] (kwīr) *n. & v. Archaic.* Var. of **choir.**

Quir•i•nal (kwĭr′ə-nəl). One of the seven hills of ancient Rome; traditional home of the Sabines. **—Quir′i•nal** *adj.*

quirk (kwûrk) *n.* **1.** A peculiarity of behavior; an idiosyncrasy. **2.** An unpredictable or unaccountable act or event; a vagary: *a quirk of fate.* **3.** A sudden sharp turn or twist. **4.** An equivocation; a quibble. **5.** *Archit.* A lengthwise groove on a molding between the convex upper part and the soffit. [?] **—quirk′i•ly** *adv.* **—quirk′i•ness** *n.* **—quirk′y** *adj.*

quirt (kwûrt) *n.* A riding whip with a short handle and a lash of braided rawhide. [Prob. < Am.Sp. *cuarta*, whip, ult. < Lat. *quārta*, fourth. See QUART.]

quis•ling (kwĭz′lĭng) *n.* A traitor who serves as the puppet of the enemy occupying his or her country. [After Vidkun *Quisling* (1887–1945), head of Norway's government during the Nazi occupation (1940–45).]

quit (kwĭt) *v.* **quit** or **quit•ted** (kwĭt′ĭd), **quit•ting, quits.** *—tr.* **1.** To depart from; leave. **2.** To leave the company of: *quit the gathering.* **3.** To give up; relinquish: *quit a job.* **4.** To abandon or put aside; forsake: *quit smoking.* **5.** To cease or discontinue: *quit talking.* **6.a.** To rid oneself of by paying: *quit a debt.* **b.** To release from a burden or responsibility. **7.** To conduct (oneself) in a specified way: *Quit yourselves like adults.* *—intr.* **1.** To cease performing an action. See Syns at **stop. 2.** To give up, as in defeat; stop. **3.** To leave a job. *—adj.* Absolved of a duty or an obligation; free. [ME *quiten*, to release < OFr. *quiter* < Med.Lat. *quiētāre*, *quītāre* < Lat. *quiētus*, at rest. See QUIET.]

quitch grass (kwĭch) *n.* Couch grass. [ME *quich* < OE *cwice*. See **g^{w}ei-***.]

quit•claim (kwĭt′klām′) *Law.* *—n.* The transfer of a title, right, or claim to another. *—tr.v.* **-claimed, -claim•ing, -claims.** To renounce all claim to (a possession or right). [ME *quitclaime* < AN *quiteclame* < *quiteclamer*, to release : *quite*, free (< Lat. *quiētus*, freed of; see QUIET) + *clamer*, to proclaim (< Lat. *clāmāre*; see CLAIM).]

quite (kwīt) *adv.* **1.** To the greatest extent; completely: *quite alone.* **2.** Actually; really: *I'm quite positive.* **3.** To a degree; rather: *quite soon.* [ME < *quite*, clear, free < OFr. < Lat. *quiētus*, freed. See QUIET.]

Qui•to (kē′tō). The cap. of Ecuador, in the N-central part; captured by the Incas in 1487 and held by the Spanish from 1534 until 1822. Pop. 890,355.

quit•rent (kwĭt′rĕnt′) *n.* A rent paid by a freeman in lieu of the services required by feudal custom. [ME *quiterent* : *quite*, free; see QUITE + *rent*, rent; see RENT[1].]

quits (kwĭts) *adj.* On even terms with by payment or requital: *quits with the loan.* [ME, prob. alteration (influenced by Med. Lat. *quittus*, *quītus*, p.part. of *quītāre*, to free) of *quit*, rid of a debt < OFr. *quiter*. See QUIT.]

quit•tance (kwĭt′ns) *n.* **1.a.** Release from a debt, an obligation, or a penalty. **b.** A document or receipt certifying such release. **2.** Something given as requital or recompense; a repayment. [ME *quitance* < OFr. < *quiter*, to free. See QUIT.]

quit•ter (kwĭt′ər) *n.* One who gives up easily.

quit•tor (kwĭt′ər) *n.* An inflammation of the hoof cartilage of horses and other solid-hoofed animals, characterized by degeneration of hoof tissue, formation of a slough, and fistulous sores. [ME *quiture*, perh. < OFr., act of boiling < Lat. *coctūra*, boiling liquid < *coctus*, p.part. of *coquere*, to cook. See **pek^{w}-***.]

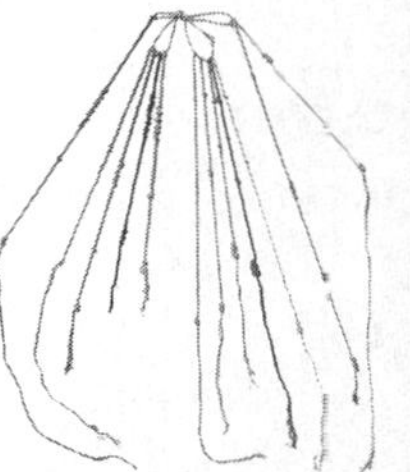
quipu
Peruvian

quiv•er[1] (kwĭv′ər) *intr.v.* **-ered, -er•ing, -ers.** To shake with a slight, rapid, tremulous movement. *—n.* The act or motion of quivering. [ME *quiveren*, perh. < *quiver*, nimble (< OE *cwifer-*; see **g^{w}ei-***).] **—quiv′er•y** *adj.*

quiv•er[2] (kwĭv′ər) *n.* **1.** A portable case for holding arrows. **2.** A case full of arrows. [ME < AN *quiveir*, var. of OFr. *cuivre* < Old Low Franconian *cocar*, prob. < Med.Lat. *cucurum*, prob. < Hunnish; akin to Mongolian *kökür*.]

qui vive (kē vēv′) *n.* A sentinel's challenge. **—*idiom.* on the qui vive.** On the alert; vigilant. [Fr., (long) live who? (a sentry's challenge to determine a person's political sympathies) : *qui*, who + *vive*, third pers. sing. pr. subjunctive of *vivre*, to live.]

quix•ot•ic (kwĭk-sŏt′ĭk) also **quix•ot•i•cal** (-ĭ-kəl) *adj.* **1.** Caught up in the pursuit of unreachable goals; idealistic without regard to practicality. **2.** Capricious; impulsive. [< E. *Quixote*, a visionary, after *Don Quixote*, hero of a romance by Miguel de Cervantes.] **—quix•ot′i•cal•ly** *adv.* **—quix′o•tism** (kwĭk′sə-tĭz′əm) *n.*

quiz (kwĭz) *tr.v.* **quizzed, quiz•zing, quiz•zes. 1.** To question closely or repeatedly; interrogate. **2.** To test the knowledge of by posing questions. See Syns at **ask. 3.** *Chiefly British.* To poke fun at; mock. *—n., pl.* **quiz•zes. 1.** A questioning or an inquiry. **2.** A short oral or written test. **3.** A practical joke. [?] **—quiz′zer** *n.*

quiver[2]
Apache

quiz show *n.* A television or radio program in which the contestants are quizzed and winners receive money or prizes.

quiz•zi•cal (kwĭz′ĭ-kəl) *adj.* **1.** Suggesting puzzlement; questioning. **2.** Teasing; mocking. **3.** Eccentric; odd. **—quiz′zi•cal′i•ty** (-kăl′ĭ-tē) *n.* **—quiz′zi•cal•ly** *adv.*

Qum (kōōm). See **Qom.**

Qum•ran (kōōm-rän′) also **Khir•bet Qumran** (kîr′bĕt). An ancient village of Palestine on the NW shore of the Dead Sea E of Jerusalem. The Dead Sea Scrolls were found here.

quod•li•bet (kwŏd′lə-bĕt′) *n.* **1.a.** A theological or philosophical issue presented for formal argument or disputation. **b.** Formal disputation of such an issue. **2.** *Mus.* A usu. humorous medley. [ME < Med.Lat. *quodlibetum* < Lat. *quod libet*, anything at all : *quod*, what; see **k^{w}o-*** + *libet*, it pleases, third pers. sing. pr.t. of *libēre*, to be pleasing; see **leubh-***.]

quoin also **coign** (koin, kwoin) *—n.* **1.a.** An exterior angle of a wall or other piece of masonry. **b.** A stone serving to form such an angle; a cornerstone. **2.** A keystone. **3.** *Print.* A wedge-shaped block used to lock type in a chase. **4.** A wedge used to raise the level of a gun. *—tr.v.* **quoined, quoin•ing, quoins** also **coigned, coign•ing, coigns.** To provide, secure, or raise with a quoin or quoins. [Var. of COIN.]

quoin

quoit (kwoit, koit) *n.* **1.** *Upper Northern U.S.* **1. quoits.** *(used with a sing. v.)* A game in which flat rings of iron or rope are pitched at a stake, with points awarded for encircling it. **2.** One of the rings used in this game. [ME *coyte*, flat stone, quoit < OFr. *coilte*, *coite* < Lat. *culcita*, cushion.]

Regional Note: The game *quoits* derives its name from *quoit*, specifically denoting a heavy iron ring slightly convex on the outside and concave inside, configured so as to give it an edge for cutting into the ground. Both the game and the term are associated almost exclusively with the Upper North (the northernmost tier of states from New York State westward to North Dakota).

quok•ka (kwŏk′ə) *n.* A small short-tailed wallaby *(Setonix brachyurus)* living in coastal areas of SW Australia. [Nyungar (Aboriginal language of SW Australia) *kwaka*.]

quon•dam (kwŏn′dəm, -dăm′) *adj.* That once was; former. [Lat. < *quom*, when. See **k^{w}o-***.]

Quon•set (kwŏn′sĭt). A trademark used for a prefabricated portable hut having a semicircular roof of corrugated metal that curves down to form walls.

quo•rum (kwôr′əm, kwōr′-) *n.* **1.** The minimal number of officers and members of a committee or an organization who must be present for valid transaction of business. **2.** A select group. [ME, quorum of justices of the peace < Lat. *quōrum*, of whom, from the wording of a commission naming certain persons as members of a body, genitive pl. of *quī*, who. See **k^{w}o-***.]

quot. *abbr.* Quotation.

quo•ta (kwō′tə) *n.* **1.** A proportional share, as of goods, assigned to a group or to each member of a group; an allotment. **2.** A production assignment. **3.** The maximum number, as of people, that may be admitted to a nation, a group, or an

ă **pat**	oi **boy**
ā **pay**	ou **out**
âr **care**	ŏŏ **took**
ä **father**	ōō **boot**
ĕ **pet**	ŭ **cut**
ē **be**	ûr **urge**
ĭ **pit**	th **thin**
ī **pie**	*th* **this**
îr **pier**	hw **which**
ŏ **pot**	zh **vision**
ō **toe**	ə **a**bout,
ô **paw**	ite**m**

Stress marks:
′ (primary);
′ (secondary), as in
dictionary (dĭk′shə-nĕr′ē)

institution. [Med.Lat. < Lat. *quota (pars)*, how large (a part), fem. of *quotus*, of what number. See QUOTE.]

quot•a•ble (kwō′tə-bəl) *adj.* Suitable for or worthy of quoting: *a quotable slogan.* —**quot′a•bil′i•ty** *n.*

quo•ta•tion (kwō-tā′shən) *n.* **1.** The act of quoting. **2.** A passage quoted. **3.** An explicit reference or allusion in an artistic work to another, usu. well-known work. **4.a.** The quoting of current prices and bids for securities and goods. **b.** The prices or bids cited. —**quo•ta′tion•al** *adj.* —**quo•ta′tion•al•ly** *adv.*

quotation mark *n.* Either element of a pair of punctuation marks (" or " or ' or ') used to mark the beginning and end of a passage attributed to another and repeated word for word.

quote (kwōt) *v.* **quot•ed, quot•ing, quotes.** —*tr.* **1.** To repeat or copy the words of (another), usu. with acknowledgment of the source. **2.** To cite or refer to for illustration or proof. **3.** To repeat a brief passage or excerpt from: *quoted a Duke Ellington melody.* **4.** To state (a price) for securities, goods, or services. —*intr.* To give a quotation, as from a book. —*n.* **1.** *Informal.* A quotation. **2.** A quotation mark. **3.** Used by a speaker to indicate the beginning of a quotation. **4.** *Usage Problem.* A dictum; a saying. [ME *coten*, to mark a book with numbers or marginal references < OFr. *coter* < Med.Lat. *quotāre*, to number chapters < Lat. *quotus*, of what number < *quot*, how many. See **kʷo-***.] —**quot′er** *n.*

Usage Note: As a transitive verb *quote* is appropriately used to describe the use of an exact wording drawn from another source. When the original source is paraphrased or alluded to, the more general term *cite* is usually preferable. • The noun *quote* is well established as a truncation of *quotation,* though many critics regard it as unduly journalistic or breezy. As such, it is best avoided in formal literary discussions. The use of the noun was acceptable to only 38 percent of the Usage Panel in the sentence *He began the chapter with a* quote *from the Bible.* But the usage is less objectionable in informal contexts or in reference to less august sources; the word was acceptable to 53 percent of the Panel in the sentence *He lightened up his talk by throwing in* quotes *from Marx Brothers movies.* • The noun *quote* is sometimes used as a synonym for "dictum, saying," as in *His career is just one more validation of Andy Warhol's* quote *that "in the future, everybody will be famous for fifteen minutes."* This example was unacceptable to 76 percent of the Usage Panel.

quoth (kwōth) *tr.v. Archaic.* Uttered; said. Used only in the first and third persons, with the subject following: *quoth I.* [ME < OE *cwæth*, third pers. sing. p.t. of *cwethan*, to say. See **gʷet-***.]

quo•tha (kwō′thə) *interj. Archaic.* Used to express surprise or sarcasm, after quoting the word or phrase of another. [Alteration of *quoth he.*]

quo•tid•i•an (kwō-tĭd′ē-ən) *adj.* **1.** Everyday; commonplace. **2.** Recurring daily. Used esp. of attacks of malaria. [ME *cotidien* < OFr. < Lat. *quōtīdiānus* < *quōtīdiē*, each day : *quot*, how many, as many as; see **kʷo-*** + *diē*, genitive and dative of *diēs*, day; see **deiw-***.]

quo•tient (kwō′shənt) *n. Math.* The number obtained by dividing one quantity by another; for example, in 45 ÷ 3 = 15, 15 is the quotient. [ME *quocient*, alteration of Lat. *quotiēns*, how many times < *quot*, how many. See **kʷo-***.]

Qur•'an (kə-rān′, -rän′, kô-, kō-) *n.* Var. of **Koran.**

q.v. *abbr. Lat.* Quod vide (which see).

QWER•TY (kwûr′tē) *adj.* Of, relating to, or being the traditional configuration of typewriter or computer keyboard keys. [< the first six letters at the upper left.]

R r

Ra[1]

r¹ or **R** (är) *n.*, *pl.* **r's** or **R's. 1.** The 18th letter of the modern English alphabet. **2.** Any of the speech sounds represented by the letter *r.* **3.** The 18th in a series.

r² *abbr.* **1.** Or **R.** *Math.* Radius. **2.** Or **R.** *Elect.* Resistance. **3.** Or **r.** *Baseball.* Run.

R¹ (är) *n.* A movie rating that admits only persons of or over a certain age, usu. 17, unless accompanied by a parent or guardian. [Short for RESTRICTED.]

R² **1.** The symbol for **gas constant. 2.** The symbol for **radical.**

R³ *abbr.* **1.** Or **R.** Réaumur (scale). **2.** Registered trademark. **3.** *Eccles.* Response. **4.** Or **r.** Roentgen. **5.** *Games.* Rook (chess).

r. *abbr.* **1.** Or **R.** Railroad; railway. **2.** Or **R.** Range. **3.** Rare. **4.** Retired. **5.** Or **R.** Right. **6.** Or **R.** River. **7.** Or **R.** Road. **8.** Rod (unit of length). **9.** *Games.* Rubber. **10.** Ruble. **11.** Or **R.** Rupee.

R. *abbr.* **1.** Rabbi. **2.** Republican. **3.** Royal.

Ra¹ (rä) also **Re** (rā) *n. Myth.* The ancient Egyptian sun god, the supreme deity represented as a man with the head of a hawk crowned with a solar disk and uraeus.

Ra² The symbol for the element **radium.**

Ra. *abbr.* Range.

R.A. *abbr.* **1.** Or **RA** Rear admiral. **2.** *Astron.* Right ascension. **3.** Royal Academy; Royal Academician.

ra•bat (răb′ē, rə-băt′) *n.* A piece of cloth fitted to the collar and covering the shirt front, worn chiefly by Roman Catholic and Anglican clergy. [Fr. < OFr. See REBATO.]

Ra•bat (rə-bät′, rä-). The cap. of Morocco, on the Atlantic NE of Casablanca. Pop. 518,616.

ra•ba•to (rə-bä′tō) *n.* Var. of **rebato.**

rab•bet (răb′ĭt) also **re•bate** (rē′bāt′, răb′ĭt) —*n.* **1.** A cut or groove along or near the edge of a piece of wood that allows another piece to fit into it to form a joint. **2.** A joint so made. —*v.* **-bet•ed, -bet•ing, -bets** also **-bat•ed, -bat•ing, -bates.** —*tr.* **1.** To cut a rabbet in. **2.** To join by a rabbet. —*intr.* To be joined by a rabbet. [ME *rabet* < OFr. *rabat*, recess in a wall < *rabattre*, to beat down again. See REBATE¹.]

rabbit

rab•bi (răb′ī) *n.*, *pl.* **-bis. 1.** A person trained in Jewish law, ritual, and tradition and ordained for leadership of a Jewish congregation. **2.** A scholar qualified to interpret Jewish law. [ME *rabi* < OFr. < LLat. *rabbī*, master < Gk. *rhabbi* < Heb. *rabbî* : *rab*, master + *-î*, my.]

rab•bin•ate (răb′ə-nāt′, -nĭt′) *n.* **1.** The office or function of a rabbi. **2.** Rabbis considered as a group.

rab•bin•i•cal (rə-bĭn′ĭ-kəl) also **rab•bin•ic** (-ĭk) *adj.* Of, relating to, or characteristic of rabbis. [< obsolete *rabbin*, rabbi < Fr. < OFr. *rabain*, prob. < Aram. *rabbīn*, pl. of *rab*, master.] —**rab•bin′i•cal•ly** *adv.*

Rab•bin•ic Hebrew (rə-bĭn′ĭk) *n.* See **Mishnaic Hebrew.**

rab•bin•ism (răb′ə-nĭz′əm) *n.* Rabbinical teachings and traditions.

rab•bit (răb′ĭt) *n.*, *pl.* **-bits** or **rabbit. 1.** Any of various long-eared short-tailed burrowing mammals of the family Leporidae, such as the commonly domesticated Old World species *Oryctolagus cuniculus.* **2.** A hare. **3.** The fur of a rabbit or hare. —*intr.v.* **-bit•ed, -bit•ing, -bits.** To hunt rabbits or hares. [ME *rabet*, young rabbit, prob. < OFr. < MDu. *robbe*, rabbit.] —**rab′bit•er** *n.*

rabbit ears *pl.n. Informal.* An indoor television antenna consisting of two usu. adjustable rods connected to a base.

rabbit fever *n.* See **tularemia.**

rabbit punch *n.* A chopping blow to the back of the neck. —**rab′bit-punch′** (răb′ĭt-pŭnch′) *v.*

rab•ble¹ (răb′əl) *n.* **1.** A tumultuous crowd; a mob. **2.** The lowest or coarsest class of people. [ME.]

rab•ble² (răb′əl) *n.* **1.** An iron bar with one end bent, used to stir and skim molten iron in puddling. **2.** Any of various similar tools used in roasting or refining furnaces. —*tr.v.* **-bled, -bling, -bles.** To stir or skim (molten iron) with an iron bar. [Fr. *râble*, fire shovel < OFr. *roable* < Med.Lat. *rotābulum* < Lat. *rutābulum* < *rutus*, p.part. of *ruere*, to rake up, tumble down.] —**rab′bler** *n.*

rab•ble-rous•er (răb′əl-rou′zər) *n.* A leader or speaker who stirs up the passions of the masses; a demagogue.

Ra•be•lais (răb′ə-lā′, răb′ə-lā′, räb-lĕ′), **François.** 1494?–1553. French humanist known for his satires, most notably *Pantagruel* (1532) and *Gargantua* (1534).

Rab•e•lai•si•an (răb′ə-lā′zē-ən, -zhən) *adj.* **1.** Of, relating to, or characteristic of Rabelais or his works. **2.** Characterized by coarse humor, exuberant learning, or bold caricature.

Ra•bi (rŭ′bē) also **Ra•bi•a** (rə-bē′ə) *n.* Either the third or the fourth month of the year in the Muslim calendar. [Ar. *rabī'*, spring.]

Ra•bi (rä′bē), **Isidor Isaac.** 1898–1988. Austrian-born Amer. physicist who studied the magnetic movement of atomic particles and won a 1944 Nobel Prize.

rab•id (răb′ĭd) *adj.* **1.** Of or affected by rabies. **2.** Raging; uncontrollable: *rabid thirst.* **3.** Extremely zealous or enthusiastic; fanatical. [Lat. *rabidus* < *rabere*, to rave.] —**ra•bid′i•ty** (rə-bĭd′ĭ-tē, ră-), **rab′id•ness** (răb′ĭd-nĭs) *n.* —**rab′id•ly** *adv.*

ra•bies (rā′bēz) *n.* An acute infectious, often fatal viral disease of most warm-blooded animals that attacks the central nervous system and is transmitted by the bite of infected animals. [Lat. *rabiēs*, rage < *rabere*, to rave.] —**ra′bi•et′ic** (-ĕt′ĭk) *adj.*

Ra•bin (rä-bēn′, rä′bēn), **Itzhak** or **Yitzhak.** b. 1922. Israeli leader who served as prime minister (1974–77).

rac•coon also **ra•coon** (ră-ko͞on′) *n., pl.* **rac•coons** or **raccoon** also **ra•coons** or **racoon. 1.** A carnivorous North American mammal *(Procyon lotor)* having grayish-brown fur, black masklike facial markings, and a black-ringed bushy tail. **2.** The fur of this mammal. **3.** Any of various similar or related animals. [Of Virginia Algonquian orig.]

race[1] (rās) *n.* **1.** A local geographic or global human population distinguished as a more or less distinct group by genetically transmitted physical characteristics. **2.** A group of people united or classified together on the basis of common history, nationality, or geographic distribution: *the Celtic race.* **3.** A genealogical line; a lineage. **4.** Human beings considered as a group. **5.** *Biol.* **a.** A population of organisms differing from others of the same species in the frequency of hereditary traits; a subspecies. **b.** A breed or strain, as of domestic animals. **6.** A distinguishing or characteristic quality, such as the flavor of a wine. [Fr. < OFr. < OItal. *razza,* race, lineage.]

race[2] (rās) *n.* **1.** *Sports.* **a.** A competition of speed, as in running. **b. races.** A series of such competitions held at a regular time and place. **2.** An extended competition similar to a race. **3.** Steady or rapid onward movement. **4.a.** A strong or swift current of water. **b.** The channel of such a current. **c.** An artificial channel built to transport water and use its energy; a raceway. **5.** A groovelike part of a machine in which a moving part slides or rolls. **6.** See **slipstream** 1. —*v.* **raced, rac•ing, rac•es.** —*intr.* **1.** *Sports.* To compete in a race. **2.** To move rapidly or at top speed. **3.** To run too rapidly because of decreased resistance or a lighter load. —*tr.* **1.** *Sports.* **a.** To compete against in a race. **b.** To cause to compete in a race; enter in a contest. **2.** To transport rapidly or at top speed; rush. **3.** To cause (an engine with the gears disengaged, for example) to run swiftly or too swiftly. [ME *ras* < ON *rās,* rush, running. See **ers-*.**]

race•course (rās′kôrs′, -kōrs′) *n. Sports.* A course for racing.

race•horse (rās′hôrs′) *n.* A horse bred and trained to race.

ra•ceme (rā-sēm′, rə-) *n. Bot.* An inflorescence having stalked flowers arranged singly along an elongated unbranched axis. [Lat. *racēmus,* a bunch of grapes.]

ra•ce•mic (rā-sē′mĭk, -sĕm′ĭk, rə-) *adj.* Of or relating to a chemical compound that contains equal quantities of dextrorotatory and levorotatory forms and therefore does not rotate the plane of incident polarized light.

racemic acid *n.* An optically inactive form of tartaric acid, $C_2H_4O_2(COOH)_2 \cdot H_2O$, that can be separated into dextrorotating and levorotating components and is found in grapes.

ra•ce•mi•form (rā-sē′mə-fôrm′) *adj. Bot.* Having the form of a raceme.

rac•e•mism (răs′ə-mĭz′əm, rā-sē′-) *n. Chem.* The condition or state of being racemic.

rac•e•mi•za•tion (răs′ə-mĭ-zā′shən) *n. Chem.* Conversion of an optically active substance to a racemic form.

rac•e•mose (răs′ə-mōs′) *adj.* **1.** *Bot.* Resembling or borne in a raceme. **2.** *Anat.* Having a structure of clustered parts. Used of glands. —**rac′e•mose′ly** *adv.*

rac•er (rā′sər) *n.* **1.** One that engages in races or is capable of great speed: *a dog bred as a racer.* **2.** Any of various fast-moving North American snakes of the genus *Coluber.*

race riot *n.* A riot caused by racial hatred or dissension.

race•run•ner (rās′rŭn′ər) *n.* Any of several fast-moving New World lizards of the genus *Cnemidophorus.*

race•track (rās′trăk′) *n. Sports.* A usu. oval, specially surfaced course on which races are held.

race walking *n.* The sport of walking for speed, the rules of which require the racer to maintain continual foot contact with the ground and keep the supporting leg straight at the knee when directly below the body. —**race walker** *n.*

race•way (rās′wā′) *n.* **1.** *Sports.* A course or track for racing, esp. harness racing. **2.** A tube that encloses and protects electric wires. **3.** A race: *the raceway beside the old mill.*

Ra•chel (rā′chəl). In the Bible, the second wife of Jacob and the mother of Joseph and Benjamin.

ra•chil•la (rə-kĭl′ə) *n., pl.* **-chil•lae** (-kĭl′ē). *Bot.* A diminutive axis of a spikelet that bears the florets, as in grasses and sedges. [NLat., dim. of RACHIS.]

ra•chis (rā′kĭs) *n., pl.* **ra•chis•es** or **rach•i•des** (răk′ĭ-dēz′, rā′kĭ-). *Biol.* A main axis or shaft, such as the main stem of an inflorescence or the spinal column. [NLat. < Gk. *rhakhis,* spine, ridge.] —**ra′chi•al** *adj.*

ra•chi•tis (rə-kī′tĭs) *n.* See **rickets.** [Gk. *rhakhis,* spine + -ITIS.] —**ra•chit′ic** (-kĭt′ĭk) *adj.*

Rach•ma•ni•noff (răk-mä′nə-nôf′, räkн-, rəкн-mä′nyĭ-nəf), **Sergei Vasilievich.** 1873–1943. Russian-born composer and pianist who interpreted the later romantic composers.

ra•cial (rā′shəl) *adj.* **1.** Of, relating to, or characteristic of race or races. **2.** Arising from or based on differences among human racial groups: *racial discrimination.* —**ra′cial•ly** *adv.*

ra•cial•ism (rā′shə-lĭz′əm) *n. Chiefly British.* Var. of **racism.** —**ra′cial•ist** *adj. & n.* —**ra′cial•is′tic** *adj.*

Ra•cine (rə-sēn′, rā-). A city of SE WI on Lake Michigan S of Milwaukee. Pop. 84,298.

Ra•cine (rə-sēn′, rä-), **Jean Baptiste.** 1639–99. French playwright whose works include *Phèdre* (1677).

rac•ing form (rā′sĭng) *n. Sports.* An information sheet about horseraces.

ra•cism (rā′sĭz′əm) *n.* **1.** The belief that race accounts for differences in human character or ability and that a particular race is superior to others. **2.** Discrimination or prejudice based on race. —**rac′ist** *adj. & n.*

rack[1] (răk) *n.* **1.a.** A framework or stand in or on which to hold, hang, or display various articles: *a laundry rack.* **b.** *Games.* A triangular frame for arranging billiard balls at the start of a game. **c.** A receptacle for livestock feed. **d.** A frame for holding bombs in an aircraft. **2.** *Slang.* A bunk; a bed. **3.** A toothed bar that meshes with a gearwheel or another toothed machine part. **4.a.** A state of intense anguish. **b.** A cause of intense anguish. **5.** An instrument of torture on which the victim's body was stretched. **6.** A pair of antlers. —*tr.v.* **racked, rack•ing, racks. 1.** *Sports.* To place (billiard balls, for example) in a rack. **2.** To cause great physical or mental suffering to: *Pain racked his body.* **3.** To torture by means of the rack. —***phrasal verb.*** **rack up.** *Informal.* To accumulate or score: *rack up points.* [ME *rakke,* prob. < MDu. *rec,* framework. See **reg-*.**] —**rack′er** *n.*

rack[2] (răk) *n.* A fast, flashy, four-beat gait of a horse in which each foot touches the ground separately and at equal intervals. —*intr.v.* **racked, rack•ing, racks.** To move in a rack. [?]

rack[3] (răk) *n.* A thin mass of wind-driven clouds. —*intr.v.* **racked, rack•ing, racks.** To be driven by the wind; scud. [ME *rak,* prob. of Scand. orig.; akin to Swed. *rak,* wreckage.]

rack[4] (răk) *n.* Var. of **wrack**[1].

rack[5] (răk) *n. & v.* Var. of **wrack**[2].

rack[6] (răk) *tr.v.* **racked, rack•ing, racks.** To drain (wine or cider) from the dregs. [ME *rakken* < OProv. *arracar* < *raca,* stems and husks of grapes.]

rack[7] (răk) *n.* **1.a.** A wholesale rib cut of lamb or veal between the shoulder and the loin. **b.** A retail rib cut of lamb or veal, prepared for roasting or for rib chops. **2.** The neck and upper spine of mutton, pork, or veal. [Prob. < RACK[1].]

rack and pinion *n.* A device for the conversion of rotary and linear motion, consisting of a pinion and a mated rack. —**rack′-and-pin′ion** (răk′ən-pĭn′yən) *adj.*

rack•et[1] also **rac•quet** (răk′ĭt) *n. Sports.* **1.** A device consisting of an oval frame with tight interlaced strings and a handle, used to strike a ball or shuttlecock. **2.** A paddle, as for table tennis. [ME *raket,* a kind of handball < OFr. *rachette,* palm of the hand, racket < Med.Lat. *rascheta,* palm < Ar. *rāḥet,* var. of *rāḥah.*]

rack•et[2] (răk′ĭt) *n.* **1.** A loud distressing noise. See Syns at **noise. 2.** A dishonest business or practice, esp. one using fraud or extortion. **3.a.** An easy, profitable means of livelihood. **b.** *Slang.* A business or an occupation. —*intr.v.* **-et•ed, -et•ing, -ets. 1.** To make or move with a loud distressing noise. **2.** To lead an active social life. [?]

rack•et•eer (răk′ĭ-tîr′) *n.* A person who commits crimes such as extortion, loansharking, bribery, and obstruction of justice in furtherance of illegal business activities. —**rack′et•eer′** *v.*

rack•et•y (răk′ĭ-tē) *adj.* Noisy; raucous.

rack railway *n.* See **cog railway.**

rack-rent (răk′rĕnt′) *n.* Exorbitant rent. —*tr.v.* **-rent•ed, -rent•ing, -rents.** To exact rack-rent for or from. [< RACK[1].] —**rack′-rent′er** *n.*

ra•clette (rä-klĕt′, ră-) *n.* **1.** A Swiss dish of cheese melted over high heat and served with boiled potatoes or bread and various garnishes. **2.** A firm cheese used in this dish. [Fr. < *racler,* to scrape < Prov. *rasclar,* to rake < OProv. < VLat. **rāsculāre* < **rāsculum,* dim. of Lat. *rāstrum,* rake. See **rēd-*.**]

rac•on•teur (răk′ŏn-tûr′) *n.* One who tells stories and anecdotes with skill and wit. [Fr. < *raconter,* to relate < OFr. : *re-,* re- + *aconter,* to count up, reckon; see ACCOUNT.]

ra•coon (ră-ko͞on′) *n.* Var. of **raccoon.**

rac•quet•ball (răk′ĭt-bôl′) *n. Sports.* A game played on a four-walled handball court by two or four players with short-handled rackets and a small hollow rubber ball.

rac•quets also **rack•ets** (răk′ĭts) *pl.n. (used with a sing. v.) Sports.* A game played on a large netless four-walled court by two or four players with long-handled rackets and a hard fast-moving ball.

rac•y (rā′sē) *adj.* **-i•er, -i•est. 1.** Having a distinctive and characteristic quality or taste. **2.** Strong and sharp in flavor or odor; piquant or pungent. **3.** Risqué; ribald. **4.** Vigorous; lively. [< RACE[1].] —**rac′i•ly** *adv.* —**rac′i•ness** *n.*

rad[1] (răd) *n. Phys.* A unit of energy absorbed from ionizing radiation, equal to 100 ergs per gram or 0.01 joule per kilogram of irradiated material. [Short for RADIATION.]

rad[2] (răd) *adj. Slang.* **1.** Radical. **2.** Wonderful; marvelous.

rad[3] *abbr. Math.* Radian.

rad. *abbr.* **1.** *Math.* Radical. **2.** Radio. **3.** *Math.* Radius. **4.** *Math.* Radix.

ra•dar (rā′där) *n.* **1.** A method of detecting distant objects and determining their position, velocity, or other characteristics by analysis of very high frequency radio waves reflected from

raccoon
Procyon lotor

Sergei Rachmaninoff

racket[1]
Top: Tennis racket
Center: Squash racket
Bottom: Badminton racket

ă pat	oi boy
ā pay	ou out
âr care	o͝o took
ä father	o͞o boot
ĕ pet	ŭ cut
ē be	ûr urge
ĭ pit	th thin
ī pie	*th* this
îr pier	hw which
ŏ pot	zh vision
ō toe	ə about, item
ô paw	

Stress marks:
′ (primary);
′ (secondary), as in
dictionary (dĭk′shə-nĕr′ē)

their surfaces. **2.** The equipment used in radar. [RA(DIO) + D(ETECTING) + A(ND) + R(ANGING).]

radar astronomy *n.* The branch of astronomy that studies bodies in the solar system by analyzing the reflections of radio waves sent from Earth.

radar beacon *n.* A fixed device that sends or receives, amplifies, alters, and returns a radar signal, permitting a distant receiver to determine its bearing and sometimes its range.

ra•dar•scope (rā′där-skōp′) *n.* The oscilloscope viewing screen of a radar receiver.

radar telescope *n.* A large radar antenna used in radar astronomy.

Rad•cliffe (răd′klĭf′), **Ann Ward.** 1764–1823. British Gothic novelist known for *The Mysteries of Udolpho* (1794).

rad•dle[1] (răd′l) *tr.v.* **-dled, -dling, -dles.** To twist together; interweave. [< dial. *raddle*, stick interwoven with others in a fence < AN *reidele*, stout pole, poss. < MHGer. *reidel*, rod. See **reidh-*.**]

rad•dle[2] (răd′l) *n. & v.* Var. of **ruddle.**

rad•dled (răd′ld) *adj.* Worn-out and broken-down. [?]

radi– *pref.* Var. of **radio–.**

ra•di•al (rā′dē-əl) *adj.* **1.a.** Of, relating to, or arranged like rays or radii. **b.** Radiating from or converging to a common center. **c.** Having or characterized by parts so arranged or so radiating. **2.** Moving or directed along a radius. **3.** *Anat.* Of, relating to, or near the radius or forearm. **4.** Developing symmetrically about a central point. —*n.* **1.** A radial part, such as a ray or radius. **2.** A radial tire. [ME < Med.Lat. *radiālis* < Lat. *radius*, ray.] —**ra′di•al•ly** *adv.*

radial engine *n.* An internal-combustion engine, formerly used in propeller-driven aircraft, with cylinders arranged radially around the crankshaft.

radially symmetrical *adj.* Having radial symmetry; actinomorphic.

radial symmetry *n.* Symmetrical arrangement of constituents, esp. of radiating parts, about a central point.

radial tire *n.* A pneumatic tire in which the ply cords extending to beads are laid at approximately right angles to the center line of the tread.

ra•di•an (rā′dē-ən) *n. Math.* A unit of angular measure equal to the angle subtended at the center of a circle by an arc equal in length to the radius of the circle, approx. 57°17′44.6″. See table at **measurement.** [RADI(US) + -AN[1].]

ra•di•ance (rā′dē-əns) also **ra•di•an•cy** (-ən-sē) *n.* **1.** The quality or state of being radiant. **2.** *Phys.* The radiant energy emitted per unit time in a specified direction by a unit area of an emitting surface.

ra•di•ant (rā′dē-ənt) *adj.* **1.** Emitting heat or light. **2.** Consisting of or emitted as radiation: *radiant heat.* **3.a.** Filled with light; bright. **b.** Glowing; beaming. See Syns at **bright.** —*n.* **1.** An object or a point from which light or heat rays are emitted. **2.** *Astron.* The apparent celestial origin of a meteoric shower. —**ra′di•ant•ly** *adv.*

radiant energy *n. Phys.* Energy transferred by radiation, esp. by an electromagnetic wave.

radiant flux *n. Phys.* The rate of flow of radiant energy.

ra•di•ate (rā′dē-āt′) *v.* **-at•ed, -at•ing, -ates.** —*intr.* **1.** To send out rays or waves. **2.** To issue or emerge in rays or waves. **3.** To extend in straight lines from or toward a center; diverge or converge like rays. **4.** *Ecol.* To spread into new habitats and thereby diverge or diversify. Used of a group of organisms. —*tr.* **1.** To emit (light, for example) in or as if in rays. **2.** To send or spread out from or as if from a center. **3.** To irradiate or illuminate (an object). **4.** To manifest in a glowing manner. —*adj.* (-ĭt). **1.** *Bot.* Having rays or raylike parts, as daisies. **2.** *Biol.* Marked by radial symmetry. **3.** Surrounded with rays. [Lat. *radiāre*, *radiāt-*, to emit beams < *radius*, ray.] —**ra′di•a′tive** *adj.*

ra•di•a•tion (rā′dē-ā′shən) *n.* **1.** The act or process of radiating: *the radiation of heat from a fire.* **2.** *Phys.* **a.** Emission and propagation of energy in the form of rays or waves. **b.** Energy radiated or transmitted in the form of rays, waves, or particles. **c.** A stream of particles or electromagnetic waves emitted by the atoms and molecules of a radioactive substance as a result of nuclear decay. **3.** *Anat.* Radial arrangement of parts, as of a group of nerve fibers connecting different areas of the brain. **4.a.** *Ecol.* The spread of a group of organisms into new habitats. **b.** Adaptive radiation.

ra•di•a•tion•al cool•ing (rā′dē-ā′shə-nəl ko͞o′lĭng) *n.* The cooling of the earth's surface and the nearby air, occurring chiefly at night and due to heat lost through terrestrial radiation.

radiation sickness *n.* Illness due to ionizing radiation, ranging in severity from vomiting, headache, and diarrhea to loss of hair and teeth, reduction in blood counts, and death.

ra•di•a•tor (rā′dē-ā′tər) *n.* **1.** A heating device consisting of connected pipes, typically inside an upright metal structure, through which steam or hot water is circulated so as to radiate heat into the surrounding space. **2.** A cooling device, as in automotive engines, through which fluid circulates as a coolant. **3.** *Phys.* A body that emits radiation. **4.** A transmitting antenna.

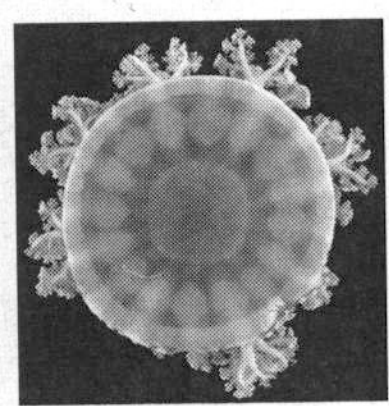

radial symmetry
Jellyfish

radiometer

radio telescope
National Radio Astronomy Observatory, Green Bank, West Virginia

radish
Raphanus sativus

rad•i•cal (răd′ĭ-kəl) *adj.* **1.** Arising from or going to a root or source; basic. **2.** Departing markedly from the usual or customary; extreme. **3.** Favoring or effecting fundamental or revolutionary changes in current practices, conditions, or institutions. **4.** *Ling.* Of or being a root: *a radical form.* **5.** *Bot.* Arising from the root or its crown. —*n.* **1.** One who advocates radical changes. **2.** *Math.* The root of a quantity as indicated by the radical sign. **3.** *Symbol* **R** An atom or a group of atoms with at least one unpaired electron. **4.** *Ling.* See **root**[1] 8. [ME, of a root < LLat. *rādīcālis*, having roots < Lat. *rādīx*, *rādīc-*, root. See **wrād-*.**] —**rad′i•cal•ly** *adv.* —**rad′i•cal•ness** *n.*

radical expression *n. Math.* An expression or form in which radical signs appear.

rad•i•cal•ism (răd′ĭ-kə-lĭz′əm) *n.* **1.** The doctrines or practices of radicals. **2.** The quality of being radical.

rad•i•cal•ize (răd′ĭ-kə-līz′) *tr.v.* **-ized, -iz•ing, -iz•es.** To make radical or more radical. —**rad′i•cal•i•za′tion** (-kə-lĭ-zā′shən) *n.*

radical sign *n. Math.* **1.** The sign $\sqrt{\ }$ placed before a quantity, indicating extraction of either the square root or the root designated by a raised integer. **2.** The radical sign together with a horizontal bar extending from its top to the end of the expression from which a root is to be extracted.

rad•i•cand (răd′ĭ-kănd′) *n. Math.* The quantity under a radical sign. For example, 3 is the radicand of $\sqrt{3}$. [Lat. *rādīcandum*, neut. gerundive of *rādīcāre*, to take root < *rādīx*, *rādīc-*, root. See RADICAL.]

ra•dic•chi•o (rə-dē′kē-ō, rä-) *n.*, *pl.* **-os.** Any of several varieties of chicory, having red or red-spotted leaves. [Ital. < OItal., chicory < VLat. **rādīculum* < Lat. *rādīcula*, dim. of *rādīx*, *rādīc-*, root. See RADISH.]

rad•i•ces (răd′ĭ-sēz′, rā′dĭ-) *n.* Pl. of **radix.**

rad•i•cle (răd′ĭ-kəl) *n.* **1.** *Bot.* The part of a plant embryo that develops into a root. **2.** *Anat.* A small structure, such as a fibril of a nerve, that resembles a root. [Lat. *rādīcula*, dim. of *rādīx*, *rādīc-*, root. See **wrād-*.**]

ra•di•i (rā′dē-ī′) *n.* Pl. of **radius.**

ra•di•o (rā′dē-ō) *n.*, *pl.* **-os. 1.** The wireless transmission through space of electromagnetic waves in the approximate frequency range from 10 kilohertz to 300,000 megahertz. **2.** Communication of audible signals encoded in electromagnetic waves. **3.** Transmission of programs for the public by radio broadcast. **4.a.** An apparatus used to transmit radio signals; a transmitter. **b.** An apparatus used to receive radio signals; a receiver. **c.** A complex of equipment capable of transmitting and receiving radio signals. **5.a.** A station for radio transmitting. **b.** A radio broadcasting organization or network of affiliated organizations. **c.** The radio broadcasting industry. **6.** A message sent by radio. —*v.* **-oed, -o•ing, -os.** —*tr.* **1.** To transmit by radio: *radio a message.* **2.** To transmit a message to by radio. —*intr.* To radio messages or a message. [Short for RADIOTELEGRAPHY.]

radio– or **radi–** *pref.* **1.** Radiation; radiant energy: *radiometer.* **2.** Radioactive: *radiochemistry.* **3.** Radio: *radiotelephone.* [< RADIATION.]

ra•di•o•ac•tive (rā′dē-ō-ăk′tĭv) *adj.* Of or exhibiting radioactivity. —**ra′di•o•ac′tive•ly** *adv.*

radioactive decay *n.* Spontaneous disintegration of a radioactive substance accompanied by emission of ionizing radiation in the form of particles and gamma rays.

radioactive series *n.* A group of isotopes representing various stages of radioactive decay in which the heavier members of the group are transformed into successively lighter ones, the lightest being stable.

ra•di•o•ac•tiv•i•ty (rā′dē-ō-ăk-tĭv′ĭ-tē) *n.* **1.** The emission of radiation, either spontaneously from unstable atomic nuclei or as a consequence of a nuclear reaction. **2.** The radiation emitted, including alpha particles, electrons, and gamma rays.

radio astronomy *n.* The branch of astronomy that deals with the detection and study of celestial sources of radio waves. —**radio astronomer** *n.*

radio beacon *n.* A fixed radio transmitter that broadcasts distinctive signals as a navigational aid.

radio beam *n.* A focused beam of radio signals transmitted by a radio beacon to guide aircraft or ships.

ra•di•o•bi•ol•o•gy (rā′dē-ō-bī-ŏl′ə-jē) *n.* **1.** The study of the effects of radiation on living organisms. **2.** The use of radioactive tracers to study biological processes. —**ra′di•o•bi′o•log′i•cal** (-ə-lŏj′ĭ-kəl) *adj.* —**ra′di•o•bi•ol′o•gist** *n.*

ra•di•o•broad•cast (rā′dē-ō-brôd′kăst′) *tr. & intr.v.* **-cast** or **-cast•ed, -cast•ing, -casts.** To broadcast or be broadcast by radio. —**ra′di•o•broad′cast′er** *n.*

ra•di•o•car•bon (rā′dē-ō-kär′bən) *n.* A radioactive isotope of carbon, esp. carbon 14.

radiocarbon dating *n.* Carbon dating.

ra•di•o•chem•is•try (rā′dē-ō-kĕm′ĭ-strē) *n.* The chemistry of radioactive materials. —**ra′di•o•chem′i•cal** (-ĭ-kəl) *adj.*

radio compass *n.* A navigational aid consisting of an automatic radio receiver that determines the transmission direction of incoming radio waves.

ra•di•o•el•e•ment (rā′dē-ō-ĕl′ə-mənt) *n.* A naturally occurring or artificially produced radioactive element.

radio frequency *n.* **1.** The frequency of the waves transmitted by a specific radio station. **2.** A frequency in the range within which radio waves may be transmitted, from about 10 kilohertz to about 300,000 megahertz.

radio galaxy *n.* A galaxy that strongly emits radio energy.

ra•di•o•ge•nic (rā′dē-ō-jĕn′ĭk) *adj.* Relating to or caused by radioactivity.

ra•di•o•gram (rā′dē-ō-grăm′) *n.* **1.** A message transmitted by wireless telegraphy. **2.** A radiograph.

ra•di•o•graph (rā′dē-ō-grăf′) *n.* An image produced on a radiosensitive surface, such as a photographic film, by radiation other than visible light, esp. by x-rays passed through an object or by photographing a fluoroscopic image. —*tr.v.* **-graphed, -graph•ing, -graphs.** To make a radiograph of. —**ra′di•og′ra•pher** (-ŏg′rə-fər) *n.* —**ra′di•o•graph′ic** *adj.*

ra•di•og•ra•phy (rā′dē-ŏg′rə-fē) *n.* The process by which radiographs are made.

ra•di•o•im•mu•no•as•say (rā′dē-ō-ĭm′yə-nō-ăs′ā, -ĭm-yo͞o′-) *n.* The immunoassay of a radiolabeled substance, such as a hormone or an enzyme.

ra•di•o•im•mu•nol•o•gy (rā′dē-ō-ĭm′yə-nŏl′ə-jē) *n.* The study of immunity, as by radiolabeling. —**ra′di•o•im′mu•no•log′i•cal** (-nə-lŏj′ĭ-kəl) *adj.*

ra•di•o•i•o•dine (rā′dē-ō-ī′ə-dīn′) *n.* A radioactive isotope of iodine widely used as a tracer in medical diagnosis.

ra•di•o•i•so•tope (rā′dē-ō-ī′sə-tōp′) *n.* A naturally or artificially produced radioactive isotope of an element.

ra•di•o•la•bel (rā′dē-ō-lā′bəl) *tr.v.* **-beled, -bel•ing, -bels** or **-belled, -bel•ling, -bels.** To tag (a hormone, an enzyme, or other substance) with a radioactive tracer. —*n.* A radioactive isotope used as a tracer; a radiotracer.

ra•di•o•lar•i•an (rā′dē-ō-lâr′ē-ən) *n.* Any of various marine protozoans of the order Radiolaria, having rigid siliceous skeletons and spicules. [< NLat. *Radiolāria*, order name < LLat. *radiolus*, dim. of Lat. *radius*, ray.]

ra•di•o•lo•ca•tion (rā′dē-ō-lō-kā′shən) *n.* Detection of distant objects, such as ships or aircraft, by radar.

ra•di•ol•o•gy (rā′dē-ŏl′ə-jē) *n.* **1.** The branch of medicine that deals with the use of radioactive substances in diagnosis and treatment of disease. **2.** The use of ionizing radiation for medical diagnosis, esp. the use of x-rays in medical radiography or fluoroscopy. **3.** The use of radiation for the scientific examination of material structures; radioscopy. —**ra′di•o•log′i•cal** (-ə-lŏj′ĭ-kəl), **ra′di•o•log′ic** (-lŏj′ĭk) *adj.* —**ra′di•o•log′i•cal•ly** *adv.* —**ra′di•ol′o•gist** *n.*

ra•di•o•lu•cent (rā′dē-ō-lo͞o′sənt) *adj.* Transparent to x-rays or other radiation; not radiopaque. —**ra′di•o•lu′cen•cy** *n.*

ra•di•ol•y•sis (rā′dē-ŏl′ĭ-sĭs) *n.*, *pl.* **-ses** (-sēz′). Molecular decomposition of a substance as a result of radiation. —**ra′di•o•lyt′ic** (-ə-lĭt′ĭk) *adj.*

ra•di•o•man (rā′dē-ō-măn′) *n.* A radio technician or operator.

ra•di•om•e•ter (rā′dē-ŏm′ĭ-tər) *n.* **1.** Any of various instruments that measure the intensity of radiant energy. **2.** Any of various instruments that detect electromagnetic radiation. —**ra′di•om′e•try** *n.*

ra•di•o•mi•met•ic (rā′dē-ō-mĭ-mĕt′ĭk) *adj.* Having effects on living tissue similar to those produced by radiation.

ra•di•o•nu•clide (rā′dē-ō-no͞o′klīd′, -nyo͞o′-) *n.* A nuclide that exhibits radioactivity.

ra•di•o•paque (rā′dē-ō-pāk′) *adj.* Not transparent to x-rays or other radiation. —**ra′di•o•pac′i•ty** (-ō-păs′ĭ-tē) *n.*

ra•di•o•phar•ma•ceu•ti•cal (rā′dē-ō-fär′mə-so͞o′tĭ-kəl) *n.* A radioactive compound used in radiotherapy or diagnosis.

ra•di•o•phone (rā′dē-ō-fōn′) *n.* A radiotelephone. —**ra′di•o•phon′ic** (-fŏn′ĭk) *adj.*

ra•di•o•pho•to (rā′dē-ō-fō′tō) *n.* A radiophotograph.

ra•di•o•pho•to•graph (rā′dē-ō-fō′tə-grăf′) *n.* A photograph transmitted by radio waves, each image point being reproduced by a received electric impulse. —**ra′di•o•pho•tog′ra•phy** (-fə-tŏg′rə-fē) *n.*

ra•di•os•co•py (rā′dē-ŏs′kə-pē) *n.* Examination of the inner structure of optically opaque objects by x-rays or other penetrating radiation; radiology. —**ra′di•o•scop′ic** (-ō-skŏp′ĭk), **ra′di•o•scop′i•cal** (-ĭ-kəl) *adj.*

ra•di•o•sen•si•tive (rā′dē-ō-sĕn′sĭ-tĭv) *adj.* Sensitive to the action of radiation. —**ra′di•o•sen′si•tiv′i•ty** *n.*

ra•di•o•sonde (rā′dē-ō-sŏnd′) *n.* An instrument carried aloft, chiefly by balloon, to gather and transmit meteorological data. [RADIO + Fr. *sonde*, sounding line (< OFr. < OE *sund(rāp)*, sounding (line) < *sund*, sea).]

radio spectrum *n.* The entire range of electromagnetic communications frequencies; the radio-frequency spectrum.

ra•di•o•tel•e•graph (rā′dē-ō-tĕl′ĭ-grăf′) *n.* Transmission of messages by radiotelegraphy. —**ra′di•o•tel′e•graph′ic** *adj.*

ra•di•o•te•leg•ra•phy (rā′dē-ō-tə-lĕg′rə-fē) *n.* Telegraphy in which messages are transmitted by radio instead of wire.

ra•di•o•tel•e•phone (rā′dē-ō-tĕl′ə-fōn′) *n.* A telephone in which audible communication is established by use of a two-way radio transmitter and receiver. —**ra′di•o•tel′e•phon′ic** (-fŏn′ĭk) *adj.* —**ra′di•o•te•leph′o•ny** (-tə-lĕf′ə-nē) *n.*

radio telescope *n.* A device for detecting and recording radio waves coming from celestial objects, consisting of a radio receiver with an antenna fixed on a wide bowl-shaped reflector.

ra•di•o•ther•a•py (rā′dē-ō-thĕr′ə-pē) *n.*, *pl.* **-pies.** Treatment of disease with radiation, esp. by selective irradiation with x-rays or other ionizing radiation and by ingestion of radioisotopes. —**ra′di•o•ther′a•pist** *n.*

ra•di•o•trac•er (rā′dē-o-trā′sər) *n.* A radioactive tracer.

radio wave *n.* An electromagnetic wave within the range of radio frequencies.

rad•ish (răd′ĭsh) *n.* **1.** A Eurasian plant *(Raphanus sativus)* having an edible root and white to purple flowers in a terminal raceme. **2.** The pungent root of this plant, eaten raw. [ME *radiche* < OE *rædic* < Lat. *rādīx*, *rādīc-*, root. See **wrād-***.]

ra•di•um (rā′dē-əm) *n.* *Symbol* **Ra** A luminescent, highly radioactive metallic element found in minute amounts in uranium ores, used as a neutron source for some research purposes, and formerly used in cancer radiotherapy and in luminescent paints; its most stable isotope is Ra 226 with a half-life of 1,622 years. Atomic number 88; melting point 700°C; boiling point 1,737°C; valence 2. See table at **element.** [Lat. *radius*, ray + -IUM.]

ra•di•us (rā′dē-əs) *n.*, *pl.* **-di•i** (-dē-ī′) or **-di•us•es. 1.** *Math.* **a.** A line segment that joins the center of a circle with any point on its circumference. **b.** A line segment that joins the center of a sphere with any point on its surface. **c.** A line segment that joins the center of a regular polygon with any of its vertices. **d.** The length of any such line segment. **2.** A circular area measured by a given radius. **3.** A bounded range of effective activity or influence: *the operating radius of a helicopter.* **4.** A radial part or structure, such as a mechanically pivoted arm or the spoke of a wheel. **5.** *Anat.* **a.** A long, prismatic, slightly curved bone, the shorter and thicker of the two forearm bones, located on the lateral side of the ulna. **b.** A similar bone in many vertebrates. [Lat., ray.]

radius vector *n.* **1.** *Math.* **a.** A line segment that joins the origin and any point in a system of polar or spherical coordinates. **b.** The length of such a line segment. **2.** *Astron.* A line connecting the center of the sun or another body with the center of a planet or another body orbiting around it.

ra•dix (rā′dĭks) *n.*, *pl.* **rad•i•ces** (răd′ĭ-sēz′, rā′dĭ-) or **ra•dix•es. 1.** *Biol.* A root or point of origin. **2.** *Math.* The base of a system of numbers, such as 10 in the decimal system. [Lat. *rādīx*, root. See **wrād-***.]

RADM or **R.Adm.** *abbr.* Rear admiral.

Ra•dom (rä′dôm). A city of E-central Poland S of Warsaw; founded in the 14th cent. Pop. 213,500.

ra•dome (rā′dōm) *n.* A domelike shell transparent to radio-frequency radiation, used to house a radar antenna.

ra•don (rā′dŏn) *n.* *Symbol* **Rn** A radioactive, largely inert gaseous element formed by the radioactive decay of radium and used as a radiation source in radiotherapy and research; its most stable isotope is Rn 222 with a half-life of 3.82 days. Atomic number 86; melting point −71°C; boiling point −61.8°C; specific gravity (solid) 4. See table at **element.** [RAD(IUM) + -ON[2].]

rad•u•la (răj′o͝o-lə) *n.*, *pl.* **-lae** (-lē′). *Zool.* A flexible tongue-like organ in certain mollusks, having rows of horny teeth on the surface. [Lat. *rādula*, scraper < *rādere*, to scrape. See **rēd-***.] —**rad′u•lar** *adj.*

Rae (rā), **John.** 1813–93. British explorer who charted much of the Canadian Arctic coast.

Rae•burn (rā′bərn), Sir **Henry.** 1756–1823. British portrait painter of Sir Walter Scott and James Boswell, among others.

RAF also **R.A.F.** *abbr.* Royal Air Force.

raf•fi•a also **raph•i•a** (răf′ē-ə) *n.* **1.** An African palm tree *(Raphia ruffia)* having large leaves. **2.** The leaf fibers of this plant, used for mats and other products. [Malagasy *rafia*.]

raf•fi•nate (răf′ə-nāt′) *n.* The portion of a liquid that remains after other components have been dissolved by a solvent. [Fr. *raffiner*, to refine; see RAFFINOSE + -ATE[2].]

raf•fi•nose (răf′ə-nōs′) *n.* A white crystalline sugar, $C_{18}H_{32}O_{16}\cdot 5H_2O$, obtained from cottonseed meal, sugar beets, and molasses. [Fr. < *raffiner*, to refine : *re-*, again (< OFr.; see RE-) + *affiner*, to refine (*a-*, to < Lat. *ad-*; see AD- + *fin*, fine < OFr.; see FINE[1]).]

raff•ish (răf′ĭsh) *adj.* **1.** Cheaply or showily vulgar in appearance or nature; tawdry. **2.** Characterized by a carefree or fun-loving unconventionality; rakish. [Prob. < dial. *raff*, rubbish < ME *raf*, perh. of Scand. orig.] —**raff′ish•ly** *adv.* —**raff′ish•ness** *n.*

raf•fle[1] (răf′əl) *Games. n.* A lottery in which chances to win a prize are sold. [ME *rafle*, a game using dice < OFr., act of seizing, dice game, perh. of Gmc. orig.] —**raf′fle** *v.* —**raf′fler** *n.*

raf•fle[2] (răf′əl) *n.* Rubbish; debris. [Prob. < Fr. *rafle*, act of seizing < OFr. See RAFFLE[1].]

Raf•fles (răf′əlz), Sir **Thomas Stamford.** 1781–1826. British colonial administrator in Singapore.

raf•fle•sia (ră-flē′zhə) *n.* Any of various parasitic plants of the genus *Rafflesia* of tropical Asia, having small brownish scale-

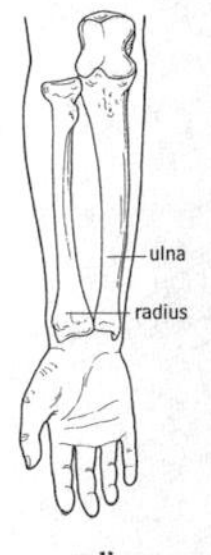

radius

radula
Magnified image of a snail's radulae

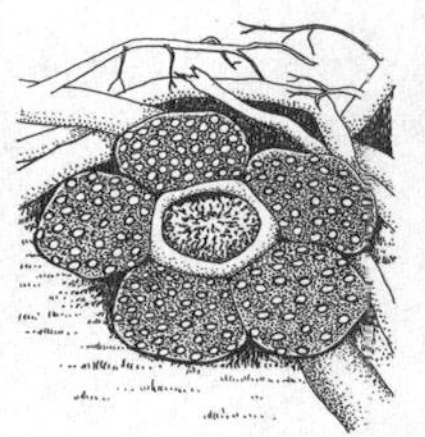
rafflesia

ă pat	oi boy
ā pay	ou out
âr care	o͝o took
ä father	o͞o boot
ĕ pet	ŭ cut
ē be	ûr urge
ĭ pit	th thin
ī pie	*th* this
îr pier	hw which
ŏ pot	zh vision
ō toe	ə about, item
ô paw	

Stress marks:
′ (primary);
′ (secondary), as in **dictionary** (dĭk′shə-nĕr′ē)

like leaves and foul-smelling fleshy apetalous flowers. [NLat., genus name, after Sir Thomas Stamford RAFFLES.]

raft[1] (răft) *n.* **1.** A flat structure, typically made of planks, logs, or barrels, that floats on water and is used for transport or as a platform for swimmers. **2.** A flatbottom inflatable craft for floating or drifting on water. —*v.* **raft•ed, raft•ing, rafts.** —*tr.* **1.** To convey on a raft. **2.** To make into a raft. —*intr.* To travel by raft. [ME < ON *raptr*, beam, rafter.]

raft[2] (răft) *n. Informal.* A great number, amount, or collection. [Alteration of dial. *raff*, rubbish. See RAFFISH.]

raft•er[1] (răf′tər) *n.* One who travels by raft.

raf•ter[2] (răf′tər) *n.* One of the sloping beams that supports a pitched roof. [ME < OE *ræfter*.] —**raf′tered** *adj.*

rag[1] (răg) *n.* **1.a.** A scrap of cloth. **b.** A piece of cloth used for cleaning, washing, or dusting. **2. rags.** Threadbare or tattered clothing. **3.** Cloth converted to pulp for making paper. **4.** A scrap; a fragment. **5.** *Slang.* A newspaper, esp. one specializing in sensationalism or gossip. **6.** The stringy central portion and membranous walls of a citrus fruit. [ME *ragge* < OE **ragg* < ON **rögg*, woven tuft of wool.]

rag[2] (răg) *tr.v.* **ragged, rag•ging, rags. 1.** *Slang.* To tease or taunt. **2.** *Slang.* To berate; scold. **3.** *Chiefly British.* To play a joke on. —*n. Chiefly British.* A practical joke; a prank. [?]

rag[3] (răg) *n.* **1.** A roofing slate with one rough surface. **2.** *Chiefly British.* A coarsely textured rock. [?]

rag[4] (răg) *Mus.* —*tr.v.* **ragged, rag•ging, rags.** To compose or play (a piece) in ragtime. —*n.* A piece written in ragtime. [Perh. < RAGGED.]

ra•ga (rä′gə) *n. Mus.* A traditional form in Hindu music, consisting of a theme that expresses religious feeling and sets forth a tonal system on which variations are improvised within a prescribed framework, as of rhythmic patterns. [Skt. *rāgaḥ*, color, musical mode.]

rag•a•muf•fin (răg′ə-mŭf′ĭn) *n.* A shabbily clothed, dirty child. [ME *Ragamuffyn*, a personal name : prob. *raggi*, ragged (< *ragge*, rag; see RAG[1]) + MDu. *moffel*, *muffe*, mitten; see MUFF[2].]

rag•bag (răg′băg′) *n.* **1.** A bag for storing rags. **2.** A motley collection; a hodgepodge.

rage (rāj) *n.* **1.a.** Violent, explosive anger. See Syns at **anger. b.** A fit of anger. **2.** Furious intensity, as of a storm or disease. **3.** A burning desire; a passion. **4.** A current, eagerly adopted fashion; a fad or craze. —*intr.v.* **raged, rag•ing, rag•es. 1.** To speak or act in violent anger. **2.** To move with great violence or intensity: *A storm raged.* **3.** To spread or prevail forcefully. [ME < OFr. < LLat. *rabia* < Lat. *rabiēs* < *rabere*, to be mad.]

rag•ged (răg′ĭd) *adj.* **1.** Tattered, frayed, or torn: *ragged clothes.* **2.** Dressed in tattered or threadbare clothes. **3.** Unkempt or shaggy. **4.** Having an irregular surface or edge; uneven or jagged in outline. **5.** Imperfect; uneven: *a ragged performance.* **6.** Harsh; rasping: *a ragged cough.* [ME < *ragge*, rag. See RAG[1].] —**rag′ged•ly** *adv.* —**rag′ged•ness** *n.*

ragged edge *n.* **1.** The edge of a cliff. **2.** A dangerous or precarious position; a brink.

ragged robin *n.* A European perennial plant *(Lychnis flos-cuculi)* with opposite clasping leaves and lobed flowers.

rag•ged•y (răg′ĭ-dē) *adj.* **-i•er, -i•est.** Tattered or worn-out; ragged.

ra•gi (răg′ē) *n., pl.* **ra•gis.** See **finger millet.** [Hindi *rāgī* < Skt., perh. of Dravidian orig.]

rag•lan (răg′lən) *adj.* Having or being a sleeve that extends in one piece to the neckline of the garment, with slanted seams from the armhole to the neck. —*n.* A garment, such as a sweater, that has raglan sleeves. [After F.J.H. Somerset (1788–1855), 1st Baron *Raglan*, British field marshal.]

rag•man (răg′măn′) *n.* A man who collects and sells rags.

ra•gout (ră-go͞o′) *n.* A well-seasoned meat or fish stew, usu. with vegetables. [Fr. *ragoût* < *ragoûter*, to revive the taste < OFr. *ragouster* : *re-*, re- + *a*, to (< Lat. *ad*; see AD-) + *gost*, taste (< Lat. *gustus*; see **geus-***).]

rag picker *n.* One who makes a living scavenging rags and other refuse.

rag•tag (răg′tăg′) *adj.* **1.** Shaggy or unkempt; ragged. **2.** Diverse and disorderly in appearance or composition.

ragtag and bobtail *n.* The lowest social class; the rabble.

rag•time (răg′tīm′) *n. Mus.* A style of jazz characterized by elaborately syncopated rhythm in the melody and a steadily accented accompaniment. [< RAG[4].]

rag•top (răg′tŏp′) *n. Slang.* A convertible automobile.

Ra•gu•sa (rə-go͞o′zə, rä-go͞o′zä). **1.** A city of SE Sicily, Italy, SSW of Messina. Pop. 53,000. **2.** See **Dubrovnik.**

rag•weed (răg′wēd′) *n.* **1.** Any of various weeds of the genus *Ambrosia*, having small greenish unisexual flower heads and producing abundant pollen that causes hay fever. **2.** *Chiefly British.* Ragwort. [< the ragged shape of its leaves.]

rag•wort (răg′wûrt′, -wôrt′) *n.* Any of several plants of the very large genus *Senecio* in the composite family, having yellow flower heads. [< the ragged shape of its leaves.]

rah (rä) *interj.* Used as an exclamation of approval or encouragement. [Short for HURRAH.]

rah-rah (rä′rä′) *adj. Informal.* Ardently enthusiastic.

Rah•way (rô′wā′). A city of NE NJ SSW of Elizabeth; settled c. 1720. Pop. 25,325.

Ra•ia•te•a (rī′ə-tā′ə). A volcanic island in the Society Is. of French Polynesia in the S Pacific WNW of Tahiti.

raid (rād) *n.* **1.** A surprise attack by a small armed force. **2.** A sudden forcible entry into a place by police. **3.** An attempt to lure away the personnel or membership of a competing organization. **4.** An attempt to seize control of a company, as by acquiring a majority of its stock. **5.** An attempt by speculators to drive stock prices down by coordinated selling. —*v.* **raid•ed, raid•ing, raids.** —*tr.* To make a raid on. —*intr.* To conduct a raid or participate in one. [Sc., raid on horseback < ME *rade* < OE *rād*, a riding, road. See **reidh-***.] —**raid′er** *n.*

Word History: *Raid* and *road* descend from the same Old English word *rād*. The *ai* in *raid* represents the standard development in the northern dialects of Old English long *a*, while the *oa* in *road* represents the standard development of Old English long *a* in the rest of the English dialects. Old English *rād* meant "the act of riding" and "the act of riding with a hostile intent; that is, a raid," senses that no longer exist for our word *road*. It was left to Sir Walter Scott to revive the Scots form *raid* with the sense "a military expedition on horseback."

rail[1] (rāl) *n.* **1.a.** A bar extending horizontally between supports, as in a fence. **b.** A structure made of such bars and supports and forming a barrier or guard; a railing. **2.** A steel bar used, usu. in pairs, as a track for railroad cars or other wheeled vehicles. **3.** The railroad as a means of transportation: *transported by rail.* **4.** A horizontal piece of wood in a door or in paneling. —*tr.v.* **railed, rail•ing, rails.** To supply or enclose with rails or a rail. [ME *raile* < OFr. *reille* < Lat. *rēgula*, straight piece of wood, ruler. See **reg-***.]

rail[2] (rāl) *n.* Any of various marsh birds of the family Rallidae, characteristically having brownish plumage and short wings adapted only for short flights. [ME *raile* < OFr. *raale*, perh. < OFr. *raler*, *racler*, to scrape < OProv. *rasclar*. See RACLETTE.]

rail[3] (rāl) *intr.v.* **railed, rail•ing, rails.** To express objections or criticisms in bitter, harsh, or abusive language. [ME *railen* < OFr. *railler*, to tease, joke < OProv. *ralhar*, to chat, joke < VLat. **ragulāre*, to bray < LLat. *ragere*.] —**rail′er** *n.*

rail•bird (rāl′bûrd′) *n. Slang.* A horseracing enthusiast, esp. one who watches races at the outer rail of the track.

rail•car (rāl′kär′) *n.* A railroad car.

rail fence *n.* A fence of split logs secured to stakes or laid across each other at an angle.

rail•head (rāl′hĕd′) *n.* **1.** The farthest point on a railroad to which rails have been laid. **2.** A place on a railroad where military supplies are unloaded.

rail•ing (rā′lĭng) *n.* **1.a.** A structure made of rails and upright members that is used as a guard or barrier or for support. **b.** The upper rail of such a structure. **2.** Rails considered as a group.

rail•ler•y (rā′lə-rē) *n., pl.* **-ies. 1.** Good-natured teasing or ridicule; banter. **2.** An instance of bantering or teasing. [Fr. *raillerie* < OFr. *railler*, to tease. See RAIL[3].]

rail•road (rāl′rōd′) *n.* **1.** A road composed of parallel steel rails supported by ties and providing a track for wheeled vehicles. **2.** A system of railroad track, together with the land, stations, and other related property under one management. —*v.* **-road•ed, -road•ing, -roads.** —*tr.* **1.** To transport by railroad. **2.** To supply (an area) with railroads. **3.** *Informal.* **a.** To rush or push (something) through quickly to prevent careful consideration and obstruction. **b.** To convict (an accused person) without a fair trial or on trumped-up charges. —*intr.* To work for a railroad company. —**rail′road′er** *n.*

railroad flat *n.* An apartment in which the rooms are connected in a line.

rail•road•ing (rāl′rō′dĭng) *n.* The construction or operation of railroads.

rail-split•ter (rāl′splĭt′ər) *n.* One that splits logs for fences.

rail•way (rāl′wā′) *n.* **1.** A railroad, esp. one operated over a limited area: *a commuter railway.* **2.** A track providing a runway for wheeled equipment.

rai•ment (rā′mənt) *n.* Clothing; garments. [ME, short for *araiment* < OFr. *areement*, array < *areer*, *arrayer*, to array. See ARRAY.]

rain (rān) *n.* **1.a.** Water condensed from atmospheric vapor and falling in drops. **b.** A fall of rain; a rainstorm. **c.** The descent of rain. **d.** Rainy weather. **e. rains.** A rainy season. **2.** A heavy or abundant fall: *a rain of insults.* —*v.* **rained, rain•ing, rains.** —*intr.* **1.** To fall in drops of water from the clouds. **2.** To fall like rain: *Praise rained down on the composer.* **3.** To release rain. —*tr.* **1.** To send or pour down. **2.** To give abundantly; shower: *rain gifts.* —***phrasal verb.*** **rain out.** To force the cancellation or postponement of (an outdoor event) because of rain. —***idiom.*** **rain cats and dogs.** *Informal.* To rain very heavily. [ME < OE *rēn*, *regn*.] —**rain′less** *adj.*

rain•bow (rān′bō′) *n.* **1.a.** An arc of all seven spectral colors appearing in the sky opposite the sun as a result of the refractive dispersion of sunlight in drops of rain or mist. **b.** A similar arc or band, as one produced by a prism. **c.** A graded display of colors. **2.** An illusory hope: *chasing the rainbow of*

overnight success. **3.** A diverse assortment or collection. [ME < OE *rēnboga* : *rēn*, rain + *boga*, bow; see BOW³.]
rainbow cactus *n.* Either of two tall spiny cylindrical varieties of cactus of the southwest United States and Mexico, *Echinocereus pectinatus* var. *neomexicanus,* having yellow flowers, or *E. pectinatus* var. *rigidissimus,* having showy magenta flowers.
rainbow trout *n.* A North American food fish *(Salmo gairdneri)* having a reddish longitudinal band and black spots.
rain check *n.* **1.** A ticket stub entitling the holder to admission to a future event if the scheduled event is rained out. **2.** An assurance to a customer that an item on sale that is sold out or out of stock may be purchased later at the sale price. **3.** A promise that an unaccepted offer will be renewed.
rain•coat (rān′kōt′) *n.* A waterproof or water-resistant coat.
rain date *n.* A second date scheduled for an outdoor event in case rain forces cancellation of the first date.
rain•drop (rān′drŏp′) *n.* A drop of rain.
Rai•ney (rā′nē), **Gertrude Pridgett.** "Ma Rainey." 1886–1939. Amer. singer considered the first great blues vocalist.
rain•fall (rān′fôl′) *n.* **1.** A shower or fall of rain. **2.** The quantity of water, expressed in inches, precipitated as rain, snow, hail, or sleet in a specified area and time interval.
rain forest *n.* A dense evergreen forest occupying a tropical region with an annual rainfall of at least 2.5 meters (100 inches).
rain gauge also **rain gage** *n.* A device for measuring rainfall.
Rai•nier III (rā-nîr′, rĕ-, rə-, rĕ-nyā′). b. 1923. Prince of Monaco (since 1949) who married Grace Kelly in 1956.
Rai•nier (rə-nîr′, rā-), **Mount.** A volcanic peak, 4,395.1 m (14,410 ft), of the Cascade Range in W-central WA.
rain•mak•er (rān′mā′kər) *n.* **1.** *Slang.* One who is known for achieving excellent results, as in business or politics. **2.** One who brings or tries to bring rain.
rain•spout (rān′spout′) *n. Chiefly Pennsylvania & New Jersey.* See **gutter** 2. See Regional Note at **gutter.**
rain•squall (rān′skwôl′) *n.* A squall accompanied by rain.
rain•storm (rān′stôrm′) *n.* A storm accompanied by rain.
rain-wash (rān′wŏsh′, -wôsh′) *Geol. n.* Rock debris transported downhill by rain. **—rain′-wash′** *v.*
rain•wat•er (rān′wô′tər, -wŏt′ər) *n.* Water that has fallen as rain and contains little dissolved mineral matter.
rain•wear (rān′wâr′) *n.* Waterproof clothing.
rain•y (rā′nē) *adj.* **-i•er, -i•est.** Characterized by, full of, or bringing rain. **—rain′i•ness** *n.*
rainy day *n.* A time of need or trouble.
Rai•pur (rī′po͝or). A city of E-central India E of Nagpur. Pop. 338,245.
raise (rāz) *v.* **raised, rais•ing, rais•es.** *—tr.* **1.** To move to a higher position; elevate. See Syns at **lift. 2.** To set in an upright or erect position. **3.** To erect or build. **4.** To cause to arise, appear, or exist: *The slap raised a welt.* **5.** To increase in size, quantity, or worth. **6.** To increase in intensity, degree, strength, or pitch. **7.** To improve in rank or dignity; promote. **8.a.** To grow, esp. in quantity; cultivate. **b.** To breed and care for to maturity. **c.** To bring up; rear. **9.** To put forward for consideration. **10.** To voice; utter. **11.a.** To awaken; arouse. **b.** To stir up; instigate. **c.** To bring about; provoke: *raised a laugh.* **12.** To make contact with by radio. **13.** To gather together; collect. **14.** To cause (dough) to puff up. **15.** To end (a siege) by withdrawing troops or forcing the enemy troops to withdraw. **16.** To remove or withdraw (an order). **17.** *Games.* **a.** To increase (a poker bet). **b.** To bet more than (a preceding bettor in poker). **c.** To increase the bid of (one's bridge partner). **18.** *Naut.* To bring into sight by approaching nearer: *raised the Cape.* **19.** To alter and increase fraudulently the written value of (a check, for example). **20.** To cough up (phlegm). **21.** *Scots.* To make angry; enrage. *—intr. Games.* To increase a poker bet or a bridge bid. *—n.* **1.** The act of raising or increasing. **2.** An increase in salary. ***—idioms.*** **raise Cain (or the devil or hell). 1.** To behave in a rowdy or disruptive fashion. **2.** To reprimand someone angrily. **raise eyebrows.** To cause surprise or mild disapproval. [ME *raisen* < ON *reisa.*] **—rais′er** *n.*
raised (rāzd) *adj.* **1.** Projecting from a flat background; in relief; embossed: *a raised design.* **2.** Made light and high by yeast or other leaven.
rai•sin (rā′zĭn) *n.* A sweet dried grape. [ME < OFr., grape < VLat. **racīmus* < Lat. *racēmus*, bunch of grapes.]
rai•son d'ê•tre (rā′zōn dĕt′rə, rĕ-zôN) *n., pl.* **rai•sons d'ê•tre** (rā′zōn, rĕ-zôN). Reason or justification for existing. [Fr. : *raison*, reason + *de*, of, for + *être*, to be.]
raj (räj) *n.* Dominion or rule, esp. the British rule over India (1757–1947). [Hindi *rāj* < Skt. *rājā*, king. See **reg-*.**]
Raj•ab (rŭj′əb) *n.* The seventh month of the year in the Muslim calendar. [Ar. *rajab.*]
Ra•ja•go•pa•la•cha•ri (rä′jə-gō-pä′lä-chär′ē), **Chakravarti.** 1879–1972. Indian governor-general (1948–50).
ra•jah or **ra•ja** (rä′jə) *n.* A prince, chief, or ruler in India or the East Indies. [Hindi *rājā* < Skt., king. See **reg-*.**]
Ra•jah•mun•dry (rä′jə-mo͞on′drē). A city of E India on the Godavari R. E of Hyderabad. Pop. 203,358.
Raj•kot (räj′kōt′). A city of W India WSW of Ahmadabad; formerly cap. of a princely state. Pop. 445,076.
Raj•put also **Raj•poot** (räj′po͝ot) *n.* A member of any of several powerful Hindu landowning and military lineages inhabiting northern and central India. [Hindi *rājpūt* < Skt. *rājaputraḥ*, king's son : *rājā*, king; see RAJAH + *putraḥ*, son.]
rake¹ (rāk) *n.* **1.** A long-handled implement with a row of projecting teeth at its head, used esp. to gather leaves or to loosen or smooth earth. **2.** A device that resembles a rake. *—v.* **raked, rak•ing, rakes.** *—tr.* **1.** To gather or move with or as if with a rake. **2.** To smooth, scrape, or loosen with a rake or similar implement. **3.** *Informal.* To gain in abundance: *raking in the money.* **4.** To search or examine thoroughly; ransack. **5.** To scrape; scratch. **6.** To aim heavy gunfire along the length of. *—intr.* **1.** To use a rake. **2.** To conduct a thorough search. ***—phrasal verb.*** **rake up.** To revive or bring to light; uncover. [ME < OE *raca.* See **reg-*.**] **—rak′er** *n.*
rake² (rāk) *n.* An immoral or dissolute person; a libertine. [Short for RAKEHELL.]
rake³ (rāk) *intr. & tr.v.* **raked, rak•ing, rakes.** To slant or cause to incline from the perpendicular: *rake a ship's mast.* *—n.* **1.** Inclination from the perpendicular. **2.** The angle between the cutting edge of a tool and a plane perpendicular to the working surface to which the tool is applied. [?]
rake•hell (rāk′hĕl′) *n.* A dissolute person; a rake. [Poss. by folk ety. < obsolete *rackle*, headstrong < ME *rakel*, perh. < *raken*, to go.]
rake-off (rāk′ôf′, -ŏf′) *n. Informal.* A percentage or share of the profits of an enterprise, esp. one given or accepted as a bribe. [< the rake used by a croupier.]
rak•i also **rak•ee** (răk′ē, rā′kē, rä′kə) *n., pl.* **-is** also **-ees.** A brandy of Turkish origin, made from grapes or plums and flavored with anise. [Turk. *rāqī* < Ar. *ʿaraq*, arrack.]
rak•ish¹ (rā′kĭsh) *adj.* **1.** *Naut.* Having a trim streamlined appearance. **2.** Dashingly or sportingly stylish; jaunty. [Prob. < RAKE³ (< the raking masts of pirate ships).]
rak•ish² (rā′kĭsh) *adj.* Of the character of a rake; dissolute.
rale also **râle** (räl) *n.* An abnormal or pathological respiratory sound. [Fr. *râle* < *râler*, to make a rattling sound in the throat < OFr. *racler*, to scrape, rattle. See RACLETTE.]
Ra•leigh (rô′lē, rä′-). The cap. of NC, in the E-central part SE of Durham; laid out in 1792. Pop. 207,951.
Raleigh or **Ra•legh** (rô′lē, rä′-), Sir **Walter.** 1552?–1618. English courtier, navigator, colonizer, and writer who colonized Virginia, introduced tobacco and the potato to Europe, and was executed for treason duing the reign of James I.
Ra•lik Chain (rä′lĭk). The W group of the Marshall Is. in the W Pacific, comprising 3 coral islands and 15 atolls.
ral•len•tan•do (răl′ən-tăn′dō, räl′lĕn-tän′dō) *Mus. —adv. & adj.* Gradually slackening in tempo; ritardando. *—n., pl.* **-dos.** A rallentando passage or movement. [Ital., pr.part. of *rallentare*, to slow down : *re-*, intensive pref. (< Lat.; see RE-) + *allentare*, to slow down (< LLat. *allentāre* : Lat. *ad-*, ad- + Lat. *lentus*, slow).]
ral•li•form (răl′ə-fôrm′) *adj.* Relating to or resembling the rail, a marsh bird. [NLat. *Rallus*, rail genus (< Fr. *râle*, rail < OFr. *raale*; see RAIL²) + -FORM.]
ral•ly¹ (răl′ē) *v.* **-lied, -ly•ing, -lies.** *—tr.* **1.** To call together for a common purpose; assemble. **2.** To reassemble and restore to order. **3.** To rouse or revive from inactivity or decline. *—intr.* **1.** To come together for a common purpose. **2.** To join in an effort for a common cause. **3.** To recover abruptly from a setback or disadvantage. **4.** To show sudden improvement in health or spirits. **5.** *Sports.* To exchange several strokes before a point is won, as in tennis. *—n., pl.* **-lies. 1.** A gathering, esp. one intended to inspire enthusiasm for a cause. **2.a.** A reassembling, as of dispersed troops. **b.** The signal ordering this reassembly. **3.** An abrupt recovery from a setback or disadvantage. **4.** A sharp improvement in health, vigor, or spirits. **5.** A notable rise in stock market prices and trading volume after a decline. **6.** *Sports.* **a.** An exchange of several strokes, before a point is won, as in tennis. **b.** An automobile competition over public roads. [Fr. *rallier* < OFr. *ralier* : *re-*, re- + *alier*, to unite, ally; see ALLY.]
ral•ly² (răl′ē) *v.* **-lied, -ly•ing, -lies.** *—tr.* To tease good-humoredly; banter. *—intr.* To engage in good-humored teasing or jesting. [Fr. *railler* < OFr., to tease. See RAIL³.]
ralph (rălf) *intr.v.* **ralphed, ralph•ing, ralphs.** *Slang.* To vomit. [Imit.]
ram (răm) *n.* **1.** A male sheep. **2.** Any of several devices used to drive, batter, or crush by forceful impact, esp.: **a.** A battering ram. **b.** The weight that drops in a pile driver or steam hammer. **c.** The plunger or piston of a force pump or hydraulic press. **3.** A hydraulic ram. **4.a.** A projection on the prow of a warship, used to batter or cut into enemy vessels. **b.** A ship having such a projection. *—tr.v.* **rammed, ram•ming, rams. 1.** To strike or drive against with a heavy impact; butt. **2.** To force or press into place. **3.** To cram; stuff. **4.** To force passage or acceptance of. [ME < OE *ramm.*] **—ram′mer** *n.*
Ram (răm) *n.* See **Aries.**
RAM *abbr.* **1.** *Comp. Sci.* Random-access memory. **2.** Also **R.A.M.** Royal Academy of Music.

rainbow trout
Salmo gairdneri

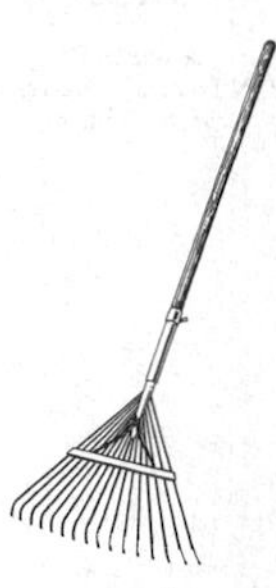
rake¹
Leaf rake

Sir Walter Raleigh

ă pat	oi boy
ā pay	ou out
âr care	o͝o took
ä father	o͞o boot
ĕ pet	ŭ cut
ē be	ûr urge
ĭ pit	th thin
ī pie	*th* this
îr pier	hw which
ŏ pot	zh vision
ō toe	ə about, item
ô paw	

Stress marks:
′ (primary);
′ (secondary), as in dictionary (dĭk′shə-nĕr′ē)

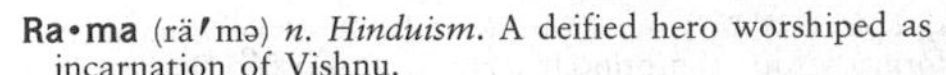

Ra•ma (räʹmə) *n. Hinduism.* A deified hero worshiped as an incarnation of Vishnu.

ra•ma•da (rə-mäʹdə) *n. Southwestern U.S.* **1.** An open porch. **2.** An openwork trellis, constructed over a walkway, onto which climbing plants are trained. [Sp. < *rama,* branch < VLat. **rāma* < Lat. *rāmus.* See RAMIFY.]

Ram•a•dan (răm′ə-dänʹ, räm′ə-dänʹ) *n.* **1.** The ninth month of the year in the Muslim calendar. **2.** A fast, held from sunrise to sunset, that is carried out during this period. [Ar. *Ramaḍān* < *ramaḍ,* dryness.]

Ra•man (räʹmən), Sir **Chandrasekhara Venkata.** 1888–1970. Indian physicist who won a 1930 Nobel Prize.

Rameses II
XIX Dynasty quartzite portrait bust

Raman effect *n. Phys.* The alteration in frequency and random alteration in phase of light passing through a transparent medium. [After Sir Chandrasekhara Venkata RAMAN.]

Ra•ma's Bridge (räʹməz). See **Adam's Bridge.**

ra•mate (rāʹmāt′) *adj.* Having branches; branched. [Lat. *rāmus,* branch; see RAMUS + -ATE[1].]

Ra•mat Gan (rə-mätʹ gän′, räʹmät). A city of W-central Israel, a suburb of Tel Aviv–Jaffa. Pop. 116,500.

ram•ble (rămʹbəl) *intr.v.* **-bled, -bling, -bles. 1.** To move about aimlessly. See Syns at **wander. 2.** To walk about casually or for pleasure. **3.** To follow an irregularly winding course of motion or growth. **4.** To speak or write at length and with many digressions. — *n.* A leisurely, sometimes lengthy walk. [Prob. < MDu. **rammelen,* to wander about in a state of sexual desire < *rammen,* to copulate with.]

ram•bler (rămʹblər) *n.* **1.** One that rambles: *ramblers about town.* **2.** A type of climbing rose having numerous red, pink, or white flowers.

ram•bling (rămʹblĭng) *adj.* **1.** Often or habitually roaming; wandering. **2.** Extended over an irregular area; sprawling. **3.** Lengthy and digressive. — **ramʹbling•ly** *adv.*

Ram•bouil•let (rămʹbo͞o-lā, räm′bo͞o-yāʹ) *n.* Any of a breed of merino sheep of French origin, raised for wool and meat. [After *Rambouillet,* a town of N-central France.]

ram•bunc•tious (răm-bŭngkʹshəs) *adj.* Boisterous and disorderly. [Prob. alteration of *robustious, rumbustious* < ROBUST.] — **ram•buncʹtious•ly** *adv.* — **ram•buncʹtious•ness** *n.*

ram•bu•tan (răm-bo͞otʹn) *n.* **1.** A tree *(Nephelium lappaceum)* of southeast Asia bearing edible oval red fruit with soft spines. **2.** This fruit. [Malay < *rambut,* hair (from its hairy covering).]

Ra•meau (rä-mōʹ), **Jean Philippe.** 1683–1764. French music theorist and composer of ballets and operas.

ram•e•kin also **ram•e•quin** (rămʹĭ-kĭn) *n.* **1.** A baked cheese preparation made with eggs and bread crumbs or unsweetened puff pastry and served in individual dishes. **2.** A small dish used for baking and serving. [Fr. *ramequin,* perh. < Du. dial. *rammeken,* toasted bread, or < LGer. *ramken,* dim. of *ram,* cream (< MLGer. *rōme*).]

ramp[1]
Airplane ramp

Ram•e•ses II also **Ram•es•ses II** (rămʹĭ-sēz′) or **Ram•ses II** (rămʹsēz′). 14th–13th cent. B.C. King of Egypt (1304–1237 B.C.) who was probably king during the Jewish exodus.

ra•met (rāʹmĭt) *n.* An individual member of a clone. [Lat. *rāmus,* branch; see RAMUS + -ET.]

ra•mi (rāʹmī′) *n. Biol. & Anat.* Pl. of **ramus.**

ram•ie (rămʹē, rāʹmē) *n.* **1.** A tropical Asian perennial herb *(Boehmeria nivea)* having broad leaves and small unisexual apetalous flowers. **2.** The flaxlike fiber from the stem of this plant, used in making fabrics and cordage. [Malay *rami.*]

ram•i•fi•ca•tion (răm′ə-fĭ-kāʹshən) *n.* **1.** A development or consequence growing out of and sometimes complicating a problem, plan, or statement. **2.a.** The act or process of branching out or dividing into branches. **b.** A subordinate part extending from a main body; a branch. **c.** An arrangement of branches or branching parts.

ram•i•form (rămʹə-fôrm′) *adj.* Branching or branchlike. [Lat. *rāmus,* branch; see RAMUS + -FORM.]

ram•i•fy (rămʹə-fī′) *v.* **-fied, -fy•ing, -fies.** — *intr.* **1.** To have complicating consequences or outgrowths. **2.** To send out branches or subordinate branchlike parts. — *tr.* To divide into or cause to extend in branches or subordinate branchlike parts. [ME *ramifien* < OFr. *ramifier* < Med.Lat. *rāmificāre* : Lat. *rāmus,* branch; see **wrād-*** + Lat. *-ficāre,* -fy.]

ram•jet (rămʹjĕt′) *n.* A jet engine that propels aircraft by igniting fuel mixed with air taken and compressed by the engine in a way that produces greater exhaust than intake velocity.

ra•mo•na (rə-mōʹnə) *n.* See **sage[2]** 1a. [Poss. after *Ramona,* heroine of a novel by Helen Hunt Jackson.]

ra•mose (rāʹmōs′, rə-mōsʹ) *adj.* Having many branches. [Lat. *rāmōsus* < *rāmus,* branch. See **wrād-*.**]

ra•mous (rāʹməs) *adj.* **1.** Of or resembling branches. **2.** Branching; ramose. [< Lat. *rāmōsus,* ramose. See RAMOSE.]

rampant
Coat of arms of the Duke of Dover

ramp[1] (rămp) *n.* **1.** An inclined surface or roadway connecting different levels. **2.** A mobile staircase for boarding and leaving an aircraft. **3.** A concave bend of a handrail where a sharp change in level or direction occurs, as at a stair landing. [Fr. *rampe* < *ramper,* to slope, rise up < OFr. See RAMP[2].]

ramp[2] (rămp) *intr.v.* **ramped, ramp•ing, ramps. 1.** To act threateningly or violently; rage. **2.** To assume a threatening stance. **3.** *Her.* To stand in the rampant position. [ME *rampen* < OFr. *ramper,* to rear, rise up, of Gmc. orig.] — **ramp** *n.*

ram•page (rămʹpāj′) *n.* A course of violent frenzied action or behavior. — *intr.v.* (*also* răm-pājʹ) **-paged, -pag•ing, -pag•es.** To move about wildly or violently. [Sc., poss. < RAMP[2].] — **ram•pagʹer** *n.*

ram•pa•geous (răm-pāʹjəs) *adj.* Raging; frenzied. — **ram•paʹgeous•ly** *adv.* — **ram•paʹgeous•ness** *n.*

ram•pant (rămʹpənt) *adj.* **1.** Extending unchecked; unrestrained. **2.** Occurring without restraint and frequently, widely, or menacingly; rife. **3.a.** Rearing on the hind legs. **b.** *Her.* Rearing on the left hind leg with the forelegs elevated, the right above the left, and usu. with the head in profile. **4.** *Archit.* Springing from a support or an abutment that is higher at one side than at the other: *a rampant arch.* [ME *rampaunt* < OFr. *rampant,* pr.part. of *ramper,* to ramp. See RAMP[2].] — **ramʹpan•cy** *n.* — **ramʹpant•ly** *adv.*

ram•part (rămʹpärt′, -pərt) *n.* **1.** A fortification consisting of an embankment, often with a parapet built on top. **2.** A means of protection or defense; a bulwark. — *tr.v.* **-part•ed, -part•ing, -parts.** To defend with a rampart. [Fr. *rempart* < OFr. < *remparer,* to fortify : *re-,* re- + *emparer,* to fortify, take possession of (< OProv. *amparar* < VLat. **ante parāre,* to prepare : Lat. *ante-,* ante- + Lat. *parāre,* to prepare; see **perə-[1]***).]

ram•pike (rămʹpīk′) *n.* A standing dead tree or tree stump, esp. one killed by fire. [?]

ram•pi•on (rămʹpē-ən) *n.* **1.** A biennial Eurasian plant *(Campanula rapunculus)* having rosette leaves with winged stalks, lilac-colored flowers, and an edible root used in salads. **2.** Any of various similar plants of the genus *Phyteuma.* [Prob. alteration of Fr. *raiponce* < OFr. *responce* < OItal. *raponzo,* prob. < *rapa,* turnip < Lat. *rāpum.*]

ram•rod (rămʹrŏd′) *n.* **1.** A rod for forcing the charge into a muzzleloading firearm. **2.** A rod for cleaning the barrel of a firearm. **3.** An overseer. — *tr.v.* **-rod•ded, -rod•ding, -rods. 1.** To control strictly; supervise closely. **2.** To force passage or acceptance of: *ramrodded the bill through Congress.*

Ram•say (rămʹzē), **Allan.** 1686–1758. Scottish poet whose works include *The Gentle Shepherd* (1725).

Ramsay, James Andrew Brown. See 10th Earl and 1st Marquis of **Dalhousie.**

Ramsay, Sir **William.** 1852–1916. British chemist who won a 1904 Nobel Prize.

Ram•ses II (rămʹsēz′). See **Rameses II.**

ram•shack•le (rămʹshăk′əl) *adj.* So poorly constructed or kept up that disintegration is likely; rickety. [Ult. < *ransackle,* to ransack, freq. of ME *ransaken,* to pillage. See RANSACK.]

ram's horn (rămz) *n. Judaism.* A shofar.

ram•son (rămʹzən, -sən) *n.* A Eurasian garlic *(Allium ursinum)* having broad, stalked, oblong to lance-shaped leaves and bulbous roots used in salads and relishes. Often used in the plural. [ME *ramsyn* < OE *hramsan,* pl. of *hramsa.*]

ram•til (rămʹtĭl) or **ram•til•la** (răm-tĭlʹə) *n.* An Ethiopian plant *(Guizotia abyssinica)* having opposite leaves and rayed yellow flower heads, grown for its oil-rich seeds. [Hindi *rāmtil* : Skt. *rāma-,* dark + Skt. *tilaḥ,* sesame.]

ram•u•lose (rămʹyə-lōs′) *adj.* Having numerous small branches. [Lat. *rāmulōsus* < *rāmulus,* dim. of *rāmus,* branch. See RAMUS.]

ra•mus (rāʹməs) *n., pl.* **-mi** (-mī′). **1.** *Biol.* A branch, as of a plant or nerve. **2.** *Anat.* A bony process extending like a branch from a larger bone, esp. the ascending part of the lower jaw that makes a joint at the temple. [Lat. *rāmus,* branch. See **wrād-*.**]

ran (răn) *v.* P.t. of **run.**

Ran (rän) *n. Myth.* The Norse goddess of the sea.

ranch (rănch) *n.* **1.** An extensive farm, esp. in the western United States, on which large herds of cattle, sheep, or horse are raised. **2.** A large specialized farm: *a mink ranch.* **3.** A house in which a rancher lives. — *intr.v.* **ranched, ranch•ing, ranch•es.** To manage or work on a ranch. [Am.Sp. *rancho,* small farm < Sp., hut, group of people who eat together < OSp. *rancharse,* to be billeted < OFr. *se ranger,* to be arranged < *renc, reng,* row, line, of Gmc. orig. See **sker-[2]*.**]

ranch•er (rănʹchər) *n.* **1.** One that owns or manages a ranch. **2.** A rectangular house of one story; a ranch house.

ran•che•ri•a (răn′chə-rēʹə) *n. Southwestern U.S.* **1.a.** A Mexican herder's hut. **b.** A village of these huts. **2.** A rural Native American settlement. [Am.Sp. *ranchería* < *rancho,* small farm. See RANCH.]

ran•che•ro (răn-chârʹō) *n., pl.* **-ros.** *Southwestern U.S.* A ranch owner; a rancher. [Am.Sp. < *rancho,* small ranch. See RANCH.]

ranch house *n.* **1.** The house of a rancher. **2.** A rectangular one-story house with a low-pitched roof.

Ran•chi (ränʹchē). A city of NE India WNW of Calcutta. Pop. 489,626.

ranch•man (rănchʹmən) *n.* The owner or manager of a ranch; a rancher.

ranch mink *n.* A mink bred in captivity from Alaskan and Labrador strains for special pelt colors and qualities.

ran•cho (rănʹchō) *n., pl.* **-chos.** *Southwestern U.S.* **1.** A hut or group of huts for housing ranch workers. **2.** A ranch. [Am. Sp., small ranch. See RANCH.]

Ran•cho Cor•do•va (răn′chō kôr-dō′və, kôr′də-). A community of N-central CA E of Sacramento. Pop. 48,731.

Rancho Cu•ca•mon•ga (ko͞o′kə-mŭng′gə, -mŏng′-). A community of SW CA W of San Bernadino. Pop. 101,409.

Rancho Pal•os Ver•des (păl′ōs vûr′dēz, păl′əs). A city of S CA on a channel W of Long Beach. Pop. 41,659.

ran•cid (răn′sĭd) *adj.* **1.** Having the disagreeable odor or taste of decomposing oils or fats; rank. **2.** Repugnant; nasty: *rancid remarks.* [Lat. *rancidus*, p.part. of *rancēre*, to stink, be rotten.] — **ran•cid′i•ty, ran′cid•ness** *n.*

ran•cor (răng′kər) *n.* Bitter long-lasting resentment; deep-seated ill will. [ME < OFr. < LLat., rancid smell < Lat. *rancēre*, to stink, be rotten.] — **ran′cor•ous** *adj.* — **ran′cor•ous•ly** *adv.* — **ran′cor•ous•ness** *n.*

ran•cour (răng′kər) *n. Chiefly British.* Var. of **rancor.**

rand (rănd, ränd) *n.* See table at **currency.** [Afr., after (WITWATERS)RAND.]

Rand (rănd). See **Witwatersrand.**

Rand, Ayn. 1905–82. Russian-born Amer. writer whose novels include *The Fountainhead* (1943).

Ran•dalls•town (răn′dlz-toun′). A community of N-central MD, a suburb of Baltimore. Pop. 26,277.

r & b or **R & B** *abbr. Mus.* Rhythm and blues.

R & D *abbr.* Research and development.

Rand•ers (rä′nərs). A city of N Denmark in the E Jutland Peninsula NNW of Århus. Pop. 61,410.

Ran•dolph (răn′dŏlf′). A town of E MA SSW of Quincy. Pop. 30,093.

Randolph, Edmund Jennings. 1753–1813. Amer. Revolutionary leader who was a member of the Constitutional Convention (1787) and served as U.S. secretary of state (1794-95).

Randolph, John. "Randolph of Roanoke." 1773–1833. Amer. politician who served as a U.S. representative (12 terms between 1799 and 1829) and senator (1825–27) from VA.

ran•dom (răn′dəm) *adj.* **1.** Having no specific pattern, purpose, or objective: *random movements.* See Syns at **chance.** **2.** *Statistics.* Of or relating to equal chances or probability of occurrence for each member of a group. — ***idiom.* at random.** Without a governing design, method, or purpose; unsystematically. [< *at random*, by chance, at great speed < ME *randon*, speed, violence < OFr. < *randir*, to run, of Gmc. orig.] — **ran′dom•ly** *adv.* — **ran′dom•ness** *n.*

ran•dom-ac•cess memory (răn′dəm-ăk′sĕs) *adj. Comp. Sci.* A memory device in which information can be accessed in any order.

ran•dom•ize (răn′də-mīz′) *tr.v.* **-ized, -iz•ing, -iz•es.** To make random in arrangement, esp. in order to control the variables in an experiment. — **ran′dom•i•za′tion** (-də-mĭ-zā′shən) *n.* — **ran′dom•iz′er** *n.*

random variable *n. Statistics.* A variable whose values are distributed according to a probability distribution.

random walk *n. Statistics.* A series of sequential movements in which the direction and size of each move is randomly determined.

R and R *abbr.* Rest and recreation.

ran•dy (răn′dē) *adj.* **-di•er, -di•est. 1.a.** Lascivious; lecherous. **b.** Of or characterized by frank uninhibited sexuality. **2.** *Scots.* Ill-mannered. [Poss. < obsolete *rand*, to rant < obsolete Du. *randen, ranten.*]

ra•nee (rä′nē) *n.* Var. of **rani.**

rang (răng) *v.* P.t. of **ring²**.

range (rānj) *n.* **1.a.** Extent of perception, knowledge, experience, or ability. **b.** The area or sphere in which an activity takes place. **c.** The full extent covered: *the range of possibilities.* **2.a.** An amount or extent of variation. **b.** *Mus.* The gamut of tones that a voice or an instrument is capable of producing. **3.a.** The maximum extent or distance limiting operation, action, or effectiveness, as of an aircraft or a sound. **b.** The maximum distance that can be covered by a vehicle with a specified payload before its fuel supply is exhausted. **c.** The distance between a projectile weapon and its target. **4.** A place equipped for practice in shooting at targets. **5.** *Aerospace.* A testing area for rockets and missiles. **6.** An extensive area of open land for livestock. **7.** The geographic region in which a plant or an animal normally lives or grows. **8.** The act of wandering or roaming over a large area. **9.** *Math.* The set of all values a given function may take on. **10.** *Statistics.* The difference or interval between the smallest and largest values in a frequency distribution. **11.** A class, a rank, or an order. **12.** An extended group or series, esp. a row or chain of mountains. **13.** One of a series of double-faced bookcases in a library stack room. **14.** A north-south strip of townships, each six miles square, numbered east and west from a specified meridian in a U.S. public land survey. **15.** A stove with spaces for cooking a number of things at the same time. — *v.* **ranged, rang•ing, rang•es.** — *tr.* **1.** To arrange or dispose in a particular order, esp. in rows or lines. **2.** To assign to a particular category; classify. **3.** To align (a gun, for example) with a target. **4.a.** To determine the distance of (a target). **b.** To be capable of reaching (a maximum distance). **5.** To pass over or through (an area or a region). **6.** To turn (livestock) onto an extensive area of open land for grazing. **7.** *Naut.* To uncoil (a line or rode) along the deck so that it will pay out smoothly. — *intr.* **1.** To vary within specified limits. **2.** To extend in a particular direction. **3.** To extend or lie in the same direction. **4.** To pass over or through an area or a region in or as if in exploration. See Syns at **wander.** **5.** To wander freely; roam. **6.** To live or grow within a particular region. [ME, row, rank < OFr. < *rangier*, to put in a row < *rang, reng*, line, of Gmc. orig. See **sker-²***.]

range finder also **range•find•er** (rānj′fīn′dər) *n.* Any of various optical, electronic, or acoustical instruments used to determine the distance of an object. — **range′find′er** *adj.*

range•land (rānj′lănd′, -lənd) *n.* An expanse of land suitable for livestock to wander and graze on.

Range•ley Lake (rānj′lē). A lake of W-central ME near the NH border.

rang•er (rān′jər) *n.* **1.** A wanderer; a rover. **2.** A member of an armed troop that patrols a given region. **3. Ranger.** A member of a group of U.S. soldiers trained to make raids. **4.a.** A warden who maintains and protects a forest or other usu. natural area. **b.** *Chiefly British.* The keeper of a royal forest or park.

Ran•goon (răn-go͞on′, răng-). Officially (since 1989) **Yan•gon** (yäɴ′gôɴ′). The cap. of Burma, in the S part on the **Rangoon River** near the Irrawaddy R. delta. Pop. 2,458,712.

rang•y (rān′jē) *adj.* **-i•er, -i•est. 1.** Having long slender limbs. **2.** Inclined to rove. **3.** Providing ample range; roomy.

ra•ni also **ra•nee** (rä′nē) *n., pl.* **-nis** also **-nees. 1.** The wife of a rajah. **2.** A reigning Hindu princess or queen. [Hindi *rānī* < Skt. *rājñī*, fem. of *rājā*, rajah. See RAJAH.]

rank¹ (răngk) *n.* **1.a.** A relative position in a society. **b.** An official position or grade. **c.** A relative position or degree of value in a graded group. **d.** High or eminent station or position. **2.** A row, line, series, or range. **3.a.** A line, as of soldiers, standing side by side in close order. **b. ranks.** The armed forces. **c. ranks.** Personnel, esp. enlisted military personnel. **4. ranks.** A body of people classed together; numbers. **5.** *Games.* Any of the horizontal lines of squares on a chessboard. — *v.* **ranked, rank•ing, ranks.** — *tr.* **1.** To place in a row or rows. **2.** To give a particular order or position to; classify. **3.** To outrank or take precedence over. — *intr.* **1.** To hold a particular rank. **2.** To form or stand in a row or rows. **3.** *Slang.* **a.** To complain. **b.** To engage in carping criticism. Often used with *on.* — ***idiom.* pull rank.** To use one's superior rank to gain an advantage. [ME, line, row < OFr. *ranc, renc*, of Gmc. orig. See **sker-²***.]

rank² (răngk) *adj.* **rank•er, rank•est. 1.** Growing profusely or with excessive vigor. **2.** Yielding a profuse, often excessive crop; highly fertile. **3.** Strong and offensive in odor or flavor. **4.** Conspicuously offensive. **5.** Absolute; complete: *a rank amateur.* [ME *ranc* < OE, strong, overbearing. See **reg-***.] — **rank′ly** *adv.* — **rank′ness** *n.*

rank and file *n.* **1.** The enlisted troops, excluding noncommissioned officers, in an army. **2.** The ordinary members of a group or an organization, excluding the leaders and officers.

rank-and-file (răngk′ən-fīl′) *adj.* **1.** Made up of or coming from the rank and file of a group. **2.** Made up of or coming from the common people.

Ran•ke (räng′kə), **Leopold von.** 1795–1886. German historian who pioneered the analysis of firsthand documentation in works such as *The History of the Popes* (1834–36).

rank•er (răng′kər) *n. Chiefly British.* **1.** An enlisted soldier. **2.** A commissioned officer who has been promoted from enlisted status.

Jeannette Rankin

Ran•kin (răng′kĭn), **Jeannette.** 1880–1973. Amer. politician who served as the first woman U.S. representative (1917–19 and 1941–43).

Ran•kine scale (răng′kĭn) *n.* A scale of absolute temperature using Fahrenheit degrees, in which the freezing point of water is 491.69° and the boiling point of water is 671.69°. [After W.J.M. *Rankine* (1820–72), Scottish physicist.]

rank•ing (răng′kĭng) *adj.* Of the highest rank; preeminent.

ran•kle (răng′kəl) *v.* **-kled, -kling, -kles.** — *intr.* **1.** To cause persistent irritation or resentment. **2.** To become sore or inflamed; fester. — *tr.* To embitter; irritate. [ME *ranclen* < OFr. *rancler*, alteration of *draoncler* < *draoncle*, festering sore < Lat. *dracunculus*, dim. of *dracō, dracōn-*, serpent. See DRAGON.]

Word History: "A little snake" is the sense of the Latin word *dracunculus* to which *rankle* can be traced, *dracunculus* being a diminutive of *dracō*, "snake." The Latin word passed into Old French, as *draoncle*, having probably already developed the sense "festering sore," because some of these sores resembled little snakes in their shape or bite. The verb *draoncler*, "to fester," was then formed in Old French. The noun and verb developed alternate forms without the *d*– that were borrowed into Middle English. Both words had literal senses having to do with festering sores. The noun is not recorded after the 16th century, but the verb went on to develop the figurative senses having to do with resentment and bitterness.

Rann of Kutch (rŭn; kŭch). A salt marsh of W India and SE

ă pat	oi boy
ā pay	ou out
âr care	o͝o took
ä father	o͞o boot
ĕ pet	ŭ cut
ē be	ûr urge
ĭ pit	th thin
ī pie	*th* this
îr pier	hw which
ŏ pot	zh vision
ō toe	ə about, item
ô paw	

Stress marks:
′ (primary);
′ (secondary), as in
dictionary (dĭk′shə-nĕr′ē)

Pakistan between the Gulf of Kutch and the Indus R. delta.

ran•sack (răn′săk′) *tr.v.* **-sacked, -sack•ing, -sacks. 1.** To search or examine thoroughly. **2.** To search carefully for plunder; pillage. [ME *ransaken* < ON *rannsaka* : *rann*, house + **saka*, to search, seek; see **sāg-***.] **— ran′sack′er** *n.*

ran•som (răn′səm) *n.* **1.a.** The release of property or a person in return for payment of a demanded price. **b.** The price or payment for such release. **2.** *Theol.* A redemption from sin and its consequences. *— tr.v.* **-somed, -som•ing, -soms. 1.a.** To obtain the release of for a certain price. **b.** To release after receiving such a payment. **2.** *Theol.* To deliver from sin and its consequences. [ME *ransome* < OFr. *rançon* < Lat. *redēmptiō, redēmptiōn-*, a buying back. See REDEMPTION.] **— ran′som•er** *n.*

rappel

Ran•som (răn′səm), **John Crowe.** 1888–1974. Amer. writer whose collections of poetry include *Chills and Fevers* (1924).

rant (rănt) *v.* **rant•ed, rant•ing, rants.** *— intr.* To speak or declaim violently, loudly, or vehemently; rave. *— tr.* To utter with violence or extravagance. *— n.* **1.** Violent, loud, or extravagant speech. **2.** *Chiefly British.* Wild or uproarious merriment. [Prob. < obsolete Du. *ranten*.] **— rant′er** *n.*

Ran•toul (răn-to͞ol′). A village of E-central IL N of Champaign. Pop. 17,212.

ran•u•la (răn′yə-lə) *n.* A cyst on the underside of the tongue caused by the obstruction of a salivary gland duct. [Lat. *rānula*, tongue swelling, dim. of *rāna*, frog. See RANUNCULUS.]

ra•nun•cu•lus (rə-nŭng′kyə-ləs) *n., pl.* **-lus•es** or **-li** (-lī′). Any of numerous plants of the genus *Ranunculus*, including the buttercups. [NLat. *Rānunculus*, genus name < Lat. *rānunculus*, a kind of medicinal plant, dim. of *rāna*, frog, perh. of imit. orig.]

rap[1] (răp) *v.* **rapped, rap•ping, raps.** *— tr.* **1.** To hit sharply and swiftly; strike. **2.** To utter sharply: *raps out an order.* **3.** To criticize or blame. *— intr.* To strike a quick light blow. *— n.* **1.** A quick light blow or knock. **2.** A knocking or tapping sound. **3.** *Slang.* **a.** A reprimand. **b.** A prison sentence. **4.** *Slang.* A negative quality or characteristic associated with a person or an object. *— **idioms.*** **beat the rap.** *Slang.* To escape punishment or be acquitted of a charge. **take the rap.** *Slang.* To accept punishment or blame for an offense or error. [ME *rappen*, poss. of imit. orig.]

rap[2] (răp) *tr.v.* **rapt** or **rapped** (răpt), **rap•ping, raps.** *Archaic.* **1.** *p.part.* **rapt.** To enchant or seize with rapture. **2.** To snatch. [Back-formation < RAPT.]

rap[3] (răp) *n. Informal.* The least bit. [< obsolete *rap*, counterfeit halfpenny < Ir.Gael., alteration of *ropaire*.]

rap[4] (răp) *n.* **1.** *Slang.* A talk or discussion. **2.** *Mus.* A form of popular music characterized by spoken or chanted rhyming lyrics with a syncopated, repetitive rhythmic accompaniment. *— intr.v.* **rap•ped, rap•ping, raps. 1.** *Slang.* To discuss freely and at length. **2.** *Mus.* To perform rap. [Poss. < RAP[1].]

ra•pa•cious (rə-pā′shəs) *adj.* **1.** Taking by force; plundering. **2.** Greedy; ravenous. **3.** Subsisting on live prey. [< Lat. *rapāx, rapāc-* < *rapere*, to seize. See **rep-***.] **— ra•pa′cious•ly** *adv.* **— ra•pac′i•ty** (rə-păs′ĭ-tē), **ra•pa′cious•ness** *n.*

Ra•pa Nu•i (rä′pə no͞o′ē). See **Easter Island.**

rape[1] (rāp) *n.* **1.** The crime of forcing another person to submit to sex acts, esp. sexual intercourse. **2.** The act of seizing and carrying off by force; abduction. **3.** Abusive or improper treatment; violation. *— tr.v.* **raped, rap•ing, rapes. 1.** To commit the crime of rape on. **2.** To seize and carry off by force. **3.** To plunder or pillage. [ME < *rapen*, to rape < OFr. *raper*, to abduct < Lat. *rapere*, to seize. See **rep-***.] **— rap′er** *n.*

rape[2] (rāp) *n.* A European plant *(Brassica napus)* of the mustard family, cultivated as fodder and for its seed. [ME < OFr. < Lat. *rāpa*, turnip.]

rape[3] (rāp) *n.* The refuse of grapes left after the extraction of the juice in winemaking. [Fr. *râpe*, grape stalk < OFr. < *rasper*, to scrape. See RASP.]

rape oil *n.* The edible oil extracted from rapeseed, also used as a lubricant and in the manufacture of various products.

rape•seed (rāp′sēd′) *n.* The seed of the rape plant.

rapeseed oil *n.* See **rape oil.**

rape shield law *n.* A law that prohibits the defense in a rape case from cross-examination regarding the plaintiff's prior sexual conduct.

Raph•a•el[1] (răf′ē-əl, rā′fē-, rä′fē-ĕl′) *n.* One of the archangels of Hebrew tradition.

Raph•a•el[2] (răf′ē-əl, rā′fē-, rä′fē-ĕl′). 1483–1520. Italian painter whose works, including religious subjects, portraits, and frescoes, exemplify the ideals of the High Renaissance.

ra•phe also **rha•phe** (rā′fē) *n., pl.* **-phae** (-fē′). **1.** *Anat.* A seamlike line or ridge between two similar parts of a body organ, as in the scrotum. **2.** *Bot.* The portion of the funiculus that is united to the ovule wall, commonly visible as a line or ridge on the seed coat. **3.** The median groove of a diatom valve. [NLat. < Gk. *rhaphē*, seam, suture < *rhaptein*, to sew. See **wer-[2]***.]

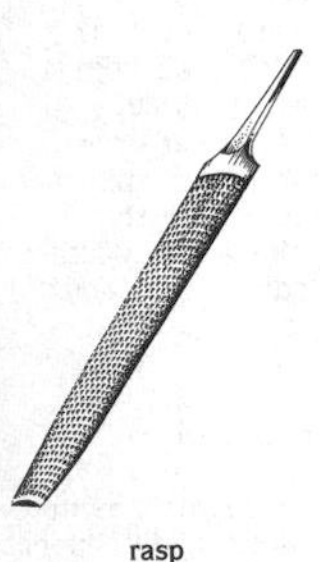

rasp
Half-rounded wood rasp

raph•i•a (răf′ē-ə) *n.* Var. of **raffia.**

ra•phide (rā′fĭd) also **ra•phis** (-fĭs) *n., pl.* **raph•i•des** (răf′ĭ-dēz′). *Bot.* One of a bundle of needlelike crystals of calcium oxalate occurring in many plant cells. [Fr., sing. of *raphides* < NLat. < Gk. *rhaphides*, pl. of *rhaphis*, needle < *rhaptein*, to sew. See **wer-[2]***.]

rap•id (răp′ĭd) *adj.* **-er, -est.** Moving, acting, or occurring with great speed; swift. See Syns at **fast[1]**. *— n.* An extremely fast-moving part of a river, caused by a steep descent in the riverbed. Often used in the plural. [Lat. *rapidus* < *rapere*, to seize. See **rep-***.] **— ra•pid′i•ty** (rə-pĭd′ĭ-tē), **rap′id•ness** (răp′ĭd-nĕs) *n.* **— rap′id•ly** *adv.*

Rap•id City (răp′ĭd). A city of SW SD WSW of Pierre in the E part of the Black Hills. Pop. 54,523.

rapid eye movement *n.* REM.

rap•id-fire (răp′ĭd-fīr′) *adj.* **1.** Designed to fire shots in rapid succession. **2.** Marked by continuous rapid occurrence.

rapid transit *n.* An urban passenger transportation system using elevated or underground trains or a combination of both.

ra•pi•er (rā′pē-ər, rāp′yər) *n.* **1.** A long slender two-edged sword with a cuplike hilt, used in the 16th and 17th centuries. **2.** A light sharp-pointed sword lacking a cutting edge and used only for thrusting. [Fr. *rapière* < OFr. *(espee) rapiere*, rapier (sword).]

rap•ine (răp′ĭn) *n.* Forcible seizure of another's property. [ME < OFr. < Lat. *rapīna* < *rapere*, to seize. See **rep-***.]

rap•ist (rā′pĭst) *n.* One who commits the crime of rape.

Rap•pa•han•nock (răp′ə-hăn′ək). A river of NE VA flowing c. 341 km (212 mi) to Chesapeake Bay.

rap•pa•ree (răp′ə-rē′) *n.* **1.** A freebooting soldier of 17th-century Ireland. **2.** A bandit or robber. [Ir.Gael. *rapaire*, var. of *ropaire*, cutpurse < *ropaid*, he stabs.]

rap•pee (ră-pē′) *n.* A strong snuff made from a coarse dark tobacco. [< Fr. *(tabac) râpé*, grated (tobacco), p.part. of *râper*, to grate < OFr. *rasper*, to scrape. See RASP.]

rap•pel (ră-pĕl′) *n.* The act or method of descending from a mountainside or cliff by means of a secured rope that is passed under one thigh and over the opposite shoulder. *— intr.v.* **-pelled, -pel•ling, -pels.** To descend from a steep height by this method. [Fr., recall, return, rappel < OFr., recall < *rapeler*, to recall : *re-*, re- + *apeler*, to summon; see APPEAL.]

rap•pen (rä′pən) *n., pl.* **rappen.** A Swiss centime. [Ger. < *Rappe*, raven (in joking reference to the eagle on the original coin) < MHGer., alteration of *raben* < OHGer. *hraban*.]

rap•per[1] (răp′ər) *n.* One that raps or strikes, esp. a door knocker.

rap•per[2] (răp′ər) *n. Mus.* One who performs rap.

rap•port (ră-pôr′, -pōr′, rə-) *n.* Relationship, esp. one of mutual trust or emotional affinity. [Fr. < OFr. < *raporter*, to bring back : *re-*, re- + *aporter*, to bring (< Lat. *apportāre* : *ad-*, ad- + *portāre*, to carry; see **per-[2]***).]

rap•por•teur (răp′ôr-tûr′, -tœr′) *n.* One who is designated to give a report, as at a meeting. [ME *raportour*, judge < OFr. *raporteur* < *raporter*, to bring back. See RAPPORT.]

rap•proche•ment (rä′prôsh-män′) *n.* **1.** A reestablishing of cordial relations, as between countries. **2.** The state of reconciliation or of cordial relations. [Fr. < *rapprocher*, to bring together : *re-*, re- + *approcher*, to approach (< OFr. *aprochier*; see APPROACH).]

rap•scal•lion (răp-skăl′yən) *n.* A rascal; a scamp. [Alteration of obsolete *rascallion* < RASCAL.]

rap session *n. Slang.* An informal discussion held esp. by a group of people with similar concerns.

rap sheet *n. Slang.* A police arrest record.

rapt (răpt) *v.* P.part. of **rap[2]**. *— adj.* **1.** Deeply moved or delighted; enraptured: *listened with rapt admiration.* **2.** Deeply absorbed; engrossed. [ME, carried away < Lat. *raptus*, p.part. of *rapere*, to seize. See **rep-***.] **— rapt•ly** *adv.*

rap•tor (răp′tər) *n.* A bird of prey. [Lat., one who seizes < *rapere*, to seize. See RAPT.]

rap•to•ri•al (răp-tôr′ē-əl, -tōr′-) *adj.* **1.** Subsisting by seizing prey; predatory. **2.** Adapted for the seizing of prey. **3.** Of, relating to, or characteristic of birds of prey.

rap•ture (răp′chər) *n.* **1.** The state of being transported by a lofty emotion; ecstasy. **2.** An expression of ecstatic feeling. Often used in the plural. **3.** The transporting of a person from one place to another, esp. to heaven. *— tr.v.* **-tured, -tur•ing, -tures.** To enrapture. [Obsolete Fr., carrying off < *rapt*, carried away < OFr. *rat* < Lat. *raptus*. See RAPT.]

rap•tur•ous (răp′chər-əs) *adj.* Filled with great joy or rapture; ecstatic. **— rap′tur•ous•ly** *adv.* **— rap′tur•ous•ness** *n.*

ra•ra a•vis (râr′ə ā′vĭs) *n., pl.* **ra•ra a•vis•es** or **ra•rae a•ves** (râr′ē ā′vēz). A rare or unique person or thing. [Lat. *rāra avis* : *rāra*, fem. of *rārus*, rare + *avis*, bird.]

rare[1] (râr) *adj.* **rar•er, rar•est. 1.** Infrequently occurring; uncommon. **2.** Excellent; extraordinary. **3.** Thin in density: rarefied. [ME < OFr. < Lat. *rārus*.] **— rare′ness** *n.*

rare[2] (râr) *adj.* **rar•er, rar•est.** Cooked a short time to retain juice and redness: *a rare steak.* [ME *rere*, lightly boiled < OE *hrēr*. See **kerə-***.] **— rare′ness** *n.*

rare•bit (râr′bĭt) *n.* Welsh rabbit. [Prob. alteration of (WELSH) RABBIT.]

rare earth *n.* **1.** Any of various oxides of the rare-earth elements. **2.** A rare-earth element.

rare-earth element (râr′ûrth′) *n.* Any of the abundant metallic elements of atomic number 57 through 71. [So called because they were originally thought to be rare.]

rar•ee show (râr′ē) *n.* **1.** See **peepshow** 1. **2.** A street show. [Alteration of RARE[1] + SHOW.]

rar•e•fac•tion (râr′ə-făk′shən) *n.* **1.** A decrease in density and pressure in a medium, such as air, caused by a sound wave. **2.** The region in which this occurs.

rar•e•fied also **rar•i•fied** (râr′ə-fīd′) *adj.* **1.** Of or reserved for an elite; esoteric. **2.** Elevated in character or style; lofty.

rar•e•fy also **rar•i•fy** (râr′ə-fī′) —*v.* **-fied, -fy•ing, -fies.** —*tr.* **1.** To make thin, less compact, or less dense. **2.** To purify or refine. —*intr.* To become thin or less compact or dense. [ME *rarefien* < OFr. *rarefier* < Med.Lat. *rārificāre*, alteration of Lat. *rārēfacere* : *rārus*, rare + *facere*, to make; see **dhē-***.] —**rar′e•fi′a•ble** *adj.*

rare•ly (râr′lē) *adv.* **1.** Not often; infrequently. **2.** In an unusual degree; exceptionally. **3.** With uncommon excellence.

Usage Note: In an earlier survey a large majority of the Usage Panel found the use of *ever* after *rarely* and *seldom,* as in *She rarely ever watches television,* unacceptable in formal writing. But *ever* has been used as an intensive with *rarely* for several hundred years, and the construction is common in informal contexts. By contrast, the constructions *rarely* (or *seldom*) *if ever* and *rarely* (or *seldom*) *or never* are unexceptionable: *She rarely if ever watches television. She rarely or never watches television.* See Usage Notes at **hardly, redundancy.**

rare•ripe (râr′rīp′) *adj.* Ripening early. —*n.* A rareripe fruit or vegetable. [Dial. *rare*, early (var. of RATHE) + RIPE.]

rar•ing (râr′ĭng) also **rar•in′** (-ĭn) *adj. Informal.* Full of eagerness; enthusiastic. [Pr.part. of dial. *rare*, to rear, var. of REAR[2].]

Rar•i•tan (răr′ĭ-tən). A river formed by the confluence of two tributaries in N-central NJ and flowing c. 129 km (80 km) to **Raritan Bay,** the W arm of Lower New York Bay.

rar•i•ty (râr′ĭ-tē) *n., pl.* **-ties. 1.** Something rare. **2.** The quality or state of being rare; infrequency of occurrence.

Rar•o•ton•ga (răr′ə-tŏng′gə). A volcanic island of the S Pacific in the SW Cook Is.

ras•bo•ra (răz-bôr′ə, -bōr′ə) *n.* Any of various brightly colored tropical fishes of the genus *Rasbora.* [NLat. *Rasbora*, genus name, from a native word in the East Indies.]

ras•cal (răs′kəl) *n.* **1.** One that is playfully mischievous. **2.** An unscrupulous, dishonest person; a scoundrel. —*adj. Archaic.* Made up of or relating to the common people. [ME *rascaile*, rabble, commoners < OFr. *rascaille*, prob. < *rasque*, mud < VLat. **rāsicāre*, to scrape. See RASH[2].] —**ras′cal•ly** *adj.*

ras•cal•i•ty (răs-kăl′ĭ-tē) *n., pl.* **-ties. 1.** Behavior or character typical of a rascal. **2.** A base or mischievous act.

rase[1] (rāz) *tr.v.* **rased, ras•ing, ras•es.** To erase. [ME *rasen*, to scrape off, erase. See RAZE.]

rase[2] (rāz) *v.* Var. of **raze.**

rash[1] (răsh) *adj.* **rash•er, rash•est. 1.** Characterized by or resulting from ill-considered haste or boldness. **2.** *Archaic.* Quick in producing a strong or marked effect. [ME *rasche*, active, perh. < OE *-raesc* (in *ligræsc*, lightning) or < MDu. or MLGer. *rasch.*] —**rash′ly** *adv.* —**rash′ness** *n.*

rash[2] (răsh) *n.* **1.** A skin eruption. **2.** An outbreak of many instances within a brief period. [Poss. < obsolete Fr. *rache*, a sore < OFr. *rasche*, scurf < *raschier*, to scrape, scratch < VLat. **rāsicāre* < Lat. *rāsus*, p.part. of *rādere*. See **rēd-***.]

rash•er (răsh′ər) *n.* **1.** A thin slice of cooked bacon. **2.** A dish or an order of rashers. [?]

Rasht (răsht) also **Resht** (rĕsht). A city of NW Iran near the Caspian Sea ESE of Tabriz. Pop. 260,000.

Rask (răsk, räsk), **Rasmus Christian.** 1787–1832. Danish philologist who was a founder of comparative linguistics.

Ras•mus•sen (răs′mə-sən, räs′mo͞os-ən), **Knud Johan Victor.** 1879–1933. Danish ethnologist and Arctic explorer who conducted extensive research on Eskimo culture and heritage.

ra•so•ri•al (rə-zôr′ē-əl, -zōr′-, -sôr′-, -sōr′-) *adj.* Characteristically scratching the ground for food. Used of chickens and similar birds. [< LLat. *rāsōr*, scraper < Lat. *rāsus*, p.part. of *rādere*, to scrape. See **rēd-***.]

rasp (răsp) *v.* **rasped, rasp•ing, rasps.** —*tr.* **1.** To file or scrape with a rasp. **2.** To utter in a grating voice. **3.** To grate on (feelings). —*intr.* **1.** To scrape harshly; grate. **2.** To make a grating sound. —*n.* **1.** A coarse file with sharp pointed projections. **2.** The act of filing with a rasp. **3.** A harsh grating sound. [ME *raspen* < MDu. *raspen* and < OFr. *rasper* (of Gmc. orig.).] —**rasp′er** *n.* —**rasp′ing•ly** *adv.*

rasp•ber•ry (răz′bĕr′ē) *n.* **1.** Any of various shrubby, usu. prickly plants of the genus *Rubus* in the rose family that bear edible fruit. **2.** The aggregate fruit of any of these plants, consisting of many small, fleshy, usu. red drupelets. **3.** *Color.* A moderate to dark or deep purplish red. **4.** *Slang.* A derisive or contemptuous sound made by vibrating the extended tongue and the lips while exhaling. [Obsolete *raspis*, raspberry + BERRY.]

Ras•pu•tin (răs-pyo͞o′tĭn, rə-spo͞o′tyĭn), **Grigori Efimovich.** 1872?–1916. Russian starets known for his influence over the court of Nicholas II.

rasp•y (răs′pē) *adj.* **-i•er, -i•est.** Rough; grating.

Ras•ta (rä′stə, răs′tə) *n.* **1.** A Rastafarian. **2.** Rastafarianism. —*adj.* Rastafarian.

Ras•ta•far•i•an (räs′tə-fär′ē-ən, răs′tə-fâr′-) *n.* An adherent of Rastafarianism. —*adj.* Of or relating to Rastafarianism or its adherents.

Ras•ta•fa•ri•an•ism (rä′stə-fär′ē-ə-nĭz′əm, răs′tə-fâr′-) *n.* A religious sect originating in Jamaica whose members worship Haile Selassie as savior and regard Africa, esp. Ethiopia, as the Promised Land. [After *Ras Tafari*, former name of Haile Selassie, : Amharic *ras*, head, prince + Amharic *tafari*, to be feared.]

rat (răt) *n.* **1.a.** Any of various long-tailed rodents resembling mice but larger, esp. one of the genus *Rattus.* **b.** Any of various similar animals. **2.** *Informal.* A despicable sneaky person, esp. one who betrays or informs upon associates. **3.** A pad of material, typically hair, worn as part of a woman's coiffure to puff out her own hair. —*intr.v.* **rat•ted, rat•ting, rats. 1.** To hunt for or catch rats, esp. with the aid of dogs. **2.** *Slang.* To desert or betray one's comrades by giving information. [ME < OE *ræt.*]

rat•a•ble (rā′tə-bəl) *adj.* **1.** That can be rated, estimated, or appraised: *ratable income.* **2.** Proportional. **3.** *Chiefly British.* Liable to assessment; taxable. —**rat′a•bil′i•ty, rat′a•ble•ness** *n.* —**rat′a•bly** *adv.*

rat•a•bles (rā′tə-bəlz) *pl.n.* **1.** Income from property taxes. **2.** Properties or buildings, esp. those used for commercial purposes, that provide tax income for local government.

rat•a•fi•a (răt′ə-fē′ə) also **rat•a•fee** (-ə-fē′) *n.* **1.** A sweet cordial flavored with fruit kernels or almonds. **2.** A biscuit flavored with ratafia. [Fr., perh. of West Indian Creole orig.]

Ra•tak Chain (rä′täk′). The E group of the Marshall Is. in the W Pacific Ocean.

rat•a•plan (răt′ə-plăn′) *n.* A tattoo, as of a drum, the hoofs of a galloping horse, or gun fire. [Fr., of imit. orig.]

rat-a-tat-tat (răt′ə-tăt′tăt′) *n.* A series of short sharp sounds, as that made by knocking on a door. [Imit.]

ra•ta•tou•ille (răt′ə-to͞o′ē, rä′tä-) *n.* A vegetable stew, usu. made of eggplant, zucchini, tomatoes, peppers, and onions. [Fr. < alteration of *toillier, touiller*, to stir, mix. See TOIL[1].]

rat-bite fever (răt′bīt′) *n.* Either of two infectious diseases contractible from a rat bite, caused by the bacterium *Streptobacillus moniliformis* or *Spirillum minus* and marked by skin inflammation, back and joint pains, and fever.

rat cheese *n.* Cheddar.

ratch•et (răch′ĭt) *n.* **1.** A mechanism consisting of a pawl that engages the sloping teeth of a wheel or bar, permitting motion in one direction only. **2.** The pawl, wheel, or bar of this mechanism. —*tr.v.* **-et•ed, -et•ing, -ets.** To increase or decrease by increments. Often used with *up, upward, down,* or *downward.* [Fr. *rochet* < OFr. *rocquet*, head of a lance (< the shape of the teeth), of Gmc. orig.]

rate[1] (rāt) *n.* **1.** A quantity measured with respect to another measured quantity: *a rate of speed of 60 miles an hour.* **2.** A measure of a part with respect to a whole; a proportion: *a tax rate.* **3.** The cost per unit of a commodity or service: *postal rates.* **4.** A charge or payment calculated in relation to a particular sum or quantity: *interest rates.* **5.** Level of quality. **6.** *Chiefly British.* A locally assessed property tax. Often used in the plural. —*v.* **rat•ed, rat•ing, rates.** —*tr.* **1.** To calculate the value of; appraise. See Syns at **estimate. 2.** To place in a particular rank or grade. **3.** To regard or account: *rated the movie excellent.* **4.** To value for purposes of taxation. **5.** To set a rate for (goods to be shipped). **6.** To specify the performance limits of. **7.** *Informal.* To merit or deserve. See Syns at **earn[1].** —*intr.* **1.** To be ranked in a particular class. **2.** *Informal.* To have status, importance, or influence. —***idiom.* at any rate. 1.** Whatever the case may be. **2.** At least. [ME < OFr. < Med.Lat. *rata*, proportion, short for Lat. *(prō) ratā (parte)*, (according to a) fixed (part) < fem. ablative p.part. of *rērī*, to consider, reckon. See **ar-***.]

rate[2] (rāt) *v.* **rat•ed, rat•ing, rates.** —*tr.* To berate. —*intr.* To express reproof. [ME *raten*, perh. of Scand. orig.]

ra•tel (rāt′l, rät′l) *n.* A carnivorous mammal *(Mellivora capensis)* of Africa and Asia having short legs and a thick coat that is dark below and whitish above. [Afr. < MDu., rattle, honeycomb (either < its cry or its taste for honey).]

rate•mak•ing (rāt′mā′kĭng) *n.* The practice of establishing rates of payment, as for public transportation or utilities.

rate of exchange *n., pl.* **rates of exchange.** The ratio at which the unit of currency of one country is or may be exchanged for the unit of currency of another country.

rate•pay•er (rāt′pā′ər) *n.* One that pays rates.

rat•er (rā′tər) *n.* **1.** One that rates, esp. one that sets a rating. **2.** One with an indicated rating. Often used in combination: *a first-rater.*

rat•fink (răt′fĭngk′) *n. Slang.* **1.** A contemptible, obnoxious, or otherwise undesirable person. **2.** An informer.

rat•fish (răt′fĭsh′) *n., pl.* **ratfish** or **-fish•es.** A fish *(Hydrolagus collei)* of Pacific waters having a long narrow tail.

rathe (rāth, răth) *adj. Archaic.* Appearing or ripening early in the year, as flowers or fruit. [ME, quick < OE *hræd, hræth.*]

Rasputin

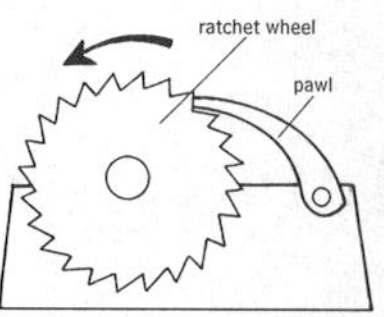

ratchet

ratel
Mellivora capensis

ă pat	oi boy
ā pay	ou out
âr care	o͝o took
ä father	o͞o boot
ĕ pet	ŭ cut
ē be	ûr urge
ĭ pit	th thin
ī pie	*th* this
îr pier	hw which
ŏ pot	zh vision
ō toe	ə about, item
ô paw	

Stress marks:
′ (primary);
′ (secondary), as in
dictionary (dĭk′shə-nĕr′ē)

rath•er (răth′ər, rä′thər) *adv.* **1.** More readily; preferably: *I'd rather go home.* **2.** With more reason or other justification. **3.** More exactly; more accurately: *He's my friend, or rather he was.* **4.** To a certain extent; somewhat: *rather cold.* **5.** On the contrary. **6.** (ră′thûr′, rä′-). *Chiefly British.* Most certainly. Used as an emphatic affirmative reply. [ME < OE *hrathor,* comp. of *hræthe,* quickly, soon < *hræth,* quick.]

Usage Note: In expressions of preference *rather* is commonly preceded by *would* or in formal style *should*: *We would rather rent the house than buy it. I should rather my daughter attended a public school.* The use of *had* in these constructions is in fact a survival of the subjunctive form *had* that appears in constructions like *had better* and *had best,* as in *We had better leave her alone.* This use of *had* shows an unbroken line of usage running back to Middle English, and traditional criticisms of these constructions are unfounded. • Before an unmodified noun only *rather a* is used: *It was rather a disaster.* When the noun is preceded by an adjective, however, both *rather a* and *a rather* are found: *It was rather a boring party. It was a rather boring party. Rather a* is the only possible choice when the adjective itself does not permit modification: *The horse was rather a long shot* (not *The horse was a rather long shot*). See Usage Notes at **better**[1], **should.**

raths•kel•ler (rät′skĕl′ər, răt′-, răth′-) *n.* A restaurant or tavern, usu. below street level, that features beer. [Obsolete Ger., city hall basement restaurant : Ger. *Rat,* council (< MHGer. *rāt* < OHGer.; see **ar-***) + Ger. *Keller,* cellar (< MHGer. < OHGer. *kellāri* < Lat. *cellārium;* see CELLAR).]

rat•i•fi•ca•tion (răt′ə-fĭ-kā′shən) *n.* The act of ratifying or the condition of being ratified.

rat•i•fy (răt′ə-fī′) *tr.v.* **-fied, -fy•ing, -fies.** To approve and give formal sanction to; confirm. See Syns at **approve.** [ME *ratifien* < OFr. *ratifier* < Med.Lat. *ratificāre* : Lat. *ratus,* fixed, p.part. of *rērī,* to reckon, consider; see RATE[1] + Lat. *-ficāre,* -fy.] **—rat′i•fi′er** *n.*

rat•i•né (răt′ə-nā′) *n.* A loosely woven fabric with a rough, nubby texture. [Fr., p.part. of *ratiner,* to adorn < *ratine,* ratteen. See RATTEEN.]

rat•ing[1] (rā′tĭng) *n.* **1.** A position assigned on a scale; a standing. **2.a.** A classification according to specialty or proficiency, as of a member of the armed forces. **b.** *Chiefly British.* An enlisted person in the navy. **3.** An evaluation of the financial status of a business or person: *a credit rating.* **4.** A specified performance limit, as of capacity, range, or operational capability: *the power rating of a light fixture.* **5.** The popularity of a television or radio program as estimated by a poll.

rat•ing[2] (rā′tĭng) *n.* A harsh scolding.

Ra•ting•en (rä′tĭng-ən). A city of W-central Germany N of Düsseldorf; chartered 1276. Pop. 87,710.

ra•tio (rā′shō, rā′shē-ō′) *n., pl.* **-tios. 1.** Relation in degree or number between two similar things. **2.** The relative value of silver and gold in a bimetallic currency. **3.** *Math.* The relation between two quantities expressed as the quotient of one divided by the other. [Lat. *ratiō,* calculation < *ratus,* p.part. of *rērī,* to reckon, consider. See **ar-*.**]

ra•ti•oc•i•nate (răsh′ē-ŏs′ə-nāt′) *intr.v.* **-nat•ed, -nat•ing, -nates.** To reason methodically and logically. [Lat. *ratiōcinārī, ratiōcināt-* < *ratiō,* calculation. See RATIO.] **—ra′ti•oc′i•na′tion** *n.* **—ra′ti•oc′i•na′tor** *n.*

ra•ti•oc•i•na•tive (răsh′ē-ŏs′ə-nā′tĭv) *adj.* Of, relating to, marked by, or skilled in methodical and logical reasoning.

ra•tion (răsh′ən, rā′shən) *n.* **1.** A fixed portion, esp. of food. **2. rations.** Food issued or available to members of a group. *—tr.v.* **-tioned, -tion•ing, -tions. 1.** To supply with rations. **2.** To distribute as rations: *rationed out flour.* See Syns at **distribute. 3.** To restrict to limited allotments, as during wartime. [Fr. < Lat. *ratiō, ratiōn-,* calculation. See RATIO.]

ra•tion•al (răsh′ə-nəl) *adj.* **1.** Having or exercising the ability to reason. **2.** Of sound mind; sane. **3.** Consistent with or based on reason; logical. **4.** *Math.* Capable of being expressed as a quotient of integers. [ME *racional* < OFr. *racionel* < Lat. *ratiōnālis* < *ratiō, ratiōn-,* reason. See REASON.] **—ra′tion•al•ly** *adv.* **—ra′tion•al•ness** *n.*

ra•tion•ale (răsh′ə-năl′) *n.* **1.** Fundamental reasons; the basis. **2.** An exposition of principles or reasons. [LLat. *ratiōnāle* < neut. of Lat. *ratiōnālis,* rational. See RATIONAL.]

rational function *n. Math.* A function that can be expressed as a quotient of polynomials.

rational horizon *n. Astron.* See **celestial horizon.**

ra•tion•al•ism (răsh′ə-nə-lĭz′əm) *n.* **1.** Reliance on reason as the best guide for belief and action. **2.** *Philos.* The theory that reason, rather than empiricism, authority, or spiritual revelation, provides the only valid basis for action or belief and that reason is the prime source of knowledge and of spiritual truth. **—ra′tion•al•ist** *n.* **—ra′tion•al•is′tic** *adj.* **—ra′tion•al•is′ti•cal•ly** *adv.*

ra•tion•al•i•ty (răsh′ə-năl′ĭ-tē) *n., pl.* **-ties. 1.** The quality or condition of being rational. **2.** A rational belief or practice.

ra•tion•al•i•za•tion (răsh′ə-nə-lĭ-zā′shən) *n.* **1.** The act or practice of rationalizing. **2.** An instance of rationalizing.

ra•tion•al•ize (răsh′ə-nə-līz′) *v.* **-ized, -iz•ing, -iz•es.** *—tr.* **1.** To make rational. **2.** To interpret rationally. **3.** To devise self-satisfying but incorrect reasons for (one's behavior). **4.** *Math.* To remove radicals without changing the value of (an expression) or roots of (an equation). **5.** *Chiefly British.* To bring modern, efficient methods to (an industry, for example). *—intr.* **1.** To think rationally or rationalistically. **2.** To devise self-satisfying but incorrect reasons for one's behavior. **—ra′tion•al•iz′er** *n.*

rattlesnake
Southwest speckled rattlesnake
Crotalus mitchellii pyrrhus

rational number *n. Math.* A number capable of being expressed as an integer or a quotient of integers, excluding zero as a denominator.

Rat Islands (răt). A group of islands in the W Aleutian Is. of SW AK.

rat•ite (răt′īt′) *adj.* Relating to or being any of a group of flightless birds having a flat breastbone with no keellike prominence. *—n.* A ratite bird, such as the emu. [< Lat. *ratītus,* marked with the figure of a raft < *ratis,* raft.]

rat•line also **rat•lin** (răt′lĭn) *n. Naut.* **1.** Any of the small ropes fastened horizontally to the shrouds of a ship and forming a ladder for going aloft. **2.** The material used for these ropes. [ME *rathelinge (line),* wattling, ratline (cord).]

ra•toon also **rat•toon** (ră-to͞on′) *—n.* A shoot sprouting from a plant base, as in the banana. *—v.* **-tooned, -toon•ing, -toons.** *—intr.* To produce or grow as a ratoon. *—tr.* To propagate (a crop) from ratoons. [Sp. *retoño,* sprout < *retoñar,* to sprout : *re-,* again (< Lat.; see RE-) + *otoñar,* to grow in autumn (< *otoño,* autumn < Lat. *autumnus;* see AUTUMN).]

rat race *n. Informal.* A difficult, tiring, often competitive activity or routine.

rats•bane (răts′bān′) *n.* **1.** Rat poison. **2.** Arsenic trioxide.

rat snake *n.* Any of several nonvenomous snakes of the genus *Elaphe* that eat rats and other rodents.

rat-tail (răt′tāl′) *n.* See **grenadier** 2. *—adj.* also **rat•tailed** (-tāld′) or **rat•tail** (răt′tāl′). Shaped like or having a part shaped like a rat's tail: *a rat-tail file.*

rattail cactus or **rat's tail cactus** (răts) *n.* A Mexican cactus *(Aporocactus flagelliformis)* having thin creeping or hanging stems and brilliant crimson-pink flowers.

rat•tan (ră-tăn′, rə-) *n.* **1.** Any of various climbing palms of the genera *Calamus, Daemonorops,* or *Plectomia* of tropical Asia, having long tough slender stems. **2.a.** The stems of any of these palms, used in wickerwork, canes, and furniture. **b.** Work made of the stems of these palms. **3.** A switch or cane made from these palms. [Malay *rōtan,* perh. < *raut,* to pare or trim for use.]

rat•teen (ră-tēn′) *n. Archaic.* A thick twilled woolen cloth. [Fr. *ratine* < OFr. *rastin* < **raster,* to scrape, ult. < Lat. *rādere.* See RASH[2].]

rat•ter (răt′ər) *n.* **1.** One that catches or kills rats: *Is the dog a ratter?* **2.** *Slang.* One who betrays or deserts another.

rat•tle[1] (răt′l) *v.* **-tled, -tling, -tles.** *—intr.* **1.a.** To make or emit a quick succession of short percussive sounds. **b.** To move with such sounds: *A train rattled by.* **2.** To talk rapidly and at length, usu. without much thought: *rattled on.* *—tr.* **1.** To cause to make a quick succession of short percussive sounds: *rattled the dishes.* **2.** To utter or perform rapidly or effortlessly: *rattled off a list of complaints.* **3.** *Informal.* To fluster; unnerve. *—n.* **1.** A rapid succession of short percussive sounds. **2.** A device, such as a baby's toy, that produces short percussive sounds. **3.** A rattling sound in the throat caused by obstructed breathing, esp. near the time of death. **4.** The series of horny structures at the end of a rattlesnake's tail. **5.** Loud or rapid talk; chatter. [ME *ratelen,* perh. < MDu., prob. of imit. orig.]

rat•tle[2] (răt′l) *tr.v.* **-tled, -tling, -tles.** *Naut.* To secure ratlines to (shrouds). [Back-formation < *rattling,* ratline, var. of RATLINE.]

rat•tle•box (răt′l-bŏks′) *n.* Any of various plants of the genus *Crotalaria,* having inflated pods containing seeds that rattle when the stem is moved.

rat•tle•brained (răt′l-brānd′) *adj.* Giddy and talkative; foolish. **—rat′tle•brain′** (-brān′) *n.*

rat•tler (răt′lər) *n.* **1.** One that rattles: *a rattler of pots and pans.* **2.** A rattlesnake. **3.** *Informal.* A freight train.

rat•tle•snake (răt′l-snāk′) *n.* Any of various venomous New World snakes of the genera *Crotalus* and *Sistrurus,* having at the end of the tail a series of loosely attached horny segments that can be vibrated to make a rattling or buzzing sound.

rattlesnake plantain *n.* Any of various rhizomatous orchids of the genus *Goodyera,* having mottled or striped leaves and spikes of small whitish flowers.

rattlesnake root *n.* Any of various plants of the genus *Prenanthes,* having bitter tuberous roots and white to purple flowers.

rattlesnake weed *n.* A North American plant *(Hieracium venosum)* having basal leaves with reddish-purple veins and yellow flower heads borne in open corymbose panicles.

rat•tle•trap (răt′l-trăp′) *n.* A rickety worn-out vehicle.

rat•tling (răt′lĭng) *adj. Informal.* Animated; brisk: *a rattling conversation.* *—adv.* Used as an intensive: *rattling good.*

rat•tly (răt′l-ē) *adj.* Rattling or likely to rattle; clattering.

rat•toon (ră-to͞on′) *n. & v.* Var. of **ratoon.**

rat•trap (răt′trăp′) *n.* **1.** A device for trapping rats. **2.** *Informal.* A dilapidated or unsanitary dwelling.

rat•ty (răt′ē) *adj.* **-ti•er, -ti•est. 1.** Of or characteristic of rats. **2.** Infested with rats. **3.** Dilapidated; shabby.

rau•cous (rô′kəs) *adj.* **1.** Rough-sounding and harsh: *raucous laughter.* **2.** Boisterous and disorderly. [< Lat. *raucus.*] **— rau′cous•ly** *adv.* **— rau′cous•ness, rau′ci•ty** (rô′sĭ-tē) *n.*

raunch (rônch,ränch) *n. Slang.* **1.** Lewdness; vulgarity; obscenity. **2.** Material or a performance that is sexual. [Back-formation < RAUNCHY.]

raun•chy (rôn′chē, rän′-) *adj.* **-chi•er, -chi•est.** *Slang.* **1.a.** Obscene, lewd, or vulgar. **b.** Sexually explicit. **c.** Exhibiting lust. **2.** Grimy; unkempt. [?] **— raun′chi•ly** *adv.* **— raun′chi•ness** *n.*

Rausch•en•berg (rou′shən-bûrg′), **Robert.** b. 1925. Amer. artist noted for his paintings that incorporate photographs and real objects.

rau•wol•fi•a (rou-wo͝ol′fē-ə, rô-) *n.* Any of various tropical trees and shrubs of the genus *Rauvolfia,* esp. *R. serpentina* of southeast Asia, the root of which is the source of tranquilizing alkaloid drugs such as reserpine. [NLat. *Rauwolfia,* genus name, after Leonhard *Rauwolf* (d. 1596), German botanist.]

rav•age (răv′ĭj) *v.* **-aged, -ag•ing, -ages.** *— tr.* **1.** To bring heavy destruction on; devastate. **2.** To pillage; sack. *— intr.* To wreak destruction. *— n.* **1.** The act or practice of pillaging, destroying, or devastating. **2.** Grievous damage; havoc: *the ravages of disease.* [Fr. *ravager* < OFr., to uproot < *ravavir,* to ravish. See RAVISH.] **— rav′ag•er**

rave (rāv) *v.* **raved, rav•ing, raves.** *— intr.* **1.** To speak wildly, irrationally, or incoherently. **2.** To roar; rage. **3.** To speak with wild enthusiasm. *— tr.* To utter in a frenzied manner. *— n.* **1.** The act or an instance of raving. **2.** *Informal.* An extravagantly enthusiastic opinion or review. *— adj. Informal.* Relating to or being such an opinion or review. [ME *raven* < ONFr. *raver,* var. of *resver,* to dream, wander, rave.]

rav•el (răv′əl) *v.* **-eled, -el•ing, -els** also **-elled, -el•ling, -els.** *— tr.* **1.** To separate the fibers or threads of (cloth, for example); unravel. **2.** To clarify by separating the aspects of. **3.** To tangle or complicate. *— intr.* **1.** To become separated into its component threads; unravel or fray. **2.** To become tangled or confused. *— n.* **1.** A raveling. **2.** A broken or discarded thread. **3.** A tangle. [Obsolete Du. *ravelen* < *ravel,* loose thread.] **— rav′el•er** *n.* **— rav′el•ment** *n.*

Ra•vel (rə-vĕl′, rä-), **Maurice Joseph.** 1875–1937. French composer whose works include *Boléro* (1928).

rav•el•ing also **rav•el•ling** (răv′ə-lĭng) *n.* A thread or fiber that has become separated from a woven material.

ra•ven[1] (rā′vən) *n.* A large bird *(Corvus corax)* having black plumage and a croaking cry. *— adj.* Black and shiny: *raven tresses.* [ME < OE *hræfn.*]

rav•en[2] (răv′ən) *v.* **-ened, -en•ing, -ens.** *— tr.* **1.** To consume greedily; devour. **2.** To seek or seize as prey or plunder. *— intr.* **1.** To seek or seize prey or plunder. **2.** To eat ravenously. [< ME *ravin, raven,* rapine, plunder, prey. See RAVIN.] **— rav′en•er** *n.*

rav•en•ing (răv′ə-nĭng) *adj.* Greedily predacious; voracious or rapacious. **— rav′en•ing•ly** *adv.*

Ra•ven•na (rə-vĕn′ə, rä-vĕn′nä). A city of NE Italy near the Adriatic Sea NE of Florence; center of Byzantine power in Italy from the late 6th cent. until c. 750. Pop. 101,000.

rav•en•ous (răv′ə-nəs) *adj.* **1.** Extremely hungry; voracious. **2.** Rapacious; predatory. **3.** Greedy for gratification. [ME < OFr. *ravineux* < *raviner,* to take by force < VLat. **rapīnāre* < Lat. *rapīna,* plunder. See RAPINE.] **— rav′en•ous•ly** *adv.* **— rav′en•ous•ness** *n.*

Ra•vi (rä′vē). A river, c. 764 km (475 mi), of NW India and NE Pakistan; one of the five rivers of the Punjab.

ra•vi•gote also **ra•vi•gotte** (ră-vē-gôt′) *n.* A vinegar sauce seasoned with onion, capers, and herbs. [Fr. < *ravigoter,* to add new vigor, alteration of obsolete *ravigorer* < OFr. : *re-,* re- + *a-,* to (< Lat. *ad-*; see AD-) + *vigeur,* vigor; see VIGOR.]

rav•in also **rav•en** (răv′ən) *n.* **1.** Voracity; rapaciousness. **2.** Something taken as prey. **3.** The act or practice of preying. [ME *ravin, raven* < OFr. *ravine,* rapine < Lat. *rapīna* < *rapere,* to seize. See **rep-***.]

ra•vine (rə-vēn′) *n.* A deep narrow valley or gorge in the earth's surface worn by running water. [Fr. < OFr., violent rush < Lat. *rapīna,* rapine. See RAVIN.]

rav•ing (rā′vĭng) *adj.* **1.** Talking or behaving irrationally; wild: *a raving maniac.* **2.** Exciting admiration: *a raving beauty.* *— n.* Delirious, irrational speech. **— rav′ing•ly** *adv.*

ra•vi•o•li (răv′ē-ō′lē, rä′vē-) *n., pl.* **ravioli** or **-lis. 1.** A small casing of pasta with fillings such as meat or cheese. **2.** A dish made with ravioli. [Ital., pl. of dial. *raviolo.*]

rav•ish (răv′ĭsh) *tr.v.* **-ished, -ish•ing, -ish•es. 1.** To seize and carry off by force. **2.** To rape; violate. **3.** To overwhelm with emotion; enrapture. [ME *ravisshen* < OFr. *ravir, raviss-,* ult. < Lat. *rapere,* to seize. See **rep-***.] **— rav′ish•er** *n.*

rav•ish•ing (răv′ĭ-shĭng) *adj.* Extremely attractive; entrancing. **— rav′ish•ing•ly** *adv.*

rav•ish•ment (răv′ĭsh-mənt) *n.* **1.** The act of seizing by force. **2.** Sexual rape. **3.** Rapture; entrancement.

raw (rô) *adj.* **raw•er, raw•est. 1.** Uncooked. **2.a.** Being in a natural condition; not processed or refined. **b.** Not finished, covered, or coated: *raw wood.* **c.** Not having been adjusted, treated, or analyzed: *raw data.* **3.** Untrained and inexperienced. **4.** Recently finished; fresh: *raw plaster.* **5.** Having subcutaneous tissue exposed. **6.** Inflamed; sore. **7.** Unpleasantly damp and chilly. **8.** Cruel and unfair. **9.** Outspoken; crude. **10.** Powerfully impressive; stark: *raw talent.* **11.** Nude; naked. **— *idiom.* in the raw. 1.** In a crude or unrefined state. **2.** Nude; naked. [ME < OE *hrēaw.* See **kreuə-***.] **— raw′ly** *adv.* **— raw′ness** *n.*

Ra•wal•pin•di (rä′wəl-pĭn′dē). A city of NE Pakistan NNW of Lahore; settled by Sikhs in 1765. Pop. 452,000.

raw•boned (rô′bōnd′) *adj.* Having a lean gaunt frame with prominent bones. See Syns at **lean[2]**.

raw•hide (rô′hīd′) *n.* **1.** The untanned hide of cattle or other animals. **2.** A whip or rope made of rawhide. *— tr.v.* **-hid•ed, -hid•ing, -hides.** To beat with a rawhide whip.

ra•win•sonde (rā′wĭn-sŏnd′) *n.* A radiosonde used to observe the velocity and direction of upper-air winds and tracked by a radio direction-finding instrument or radar. [RA(DAR) + WIN(D)[1] + (RADIO)SONDE.]

Raw•lings (rô′lĭngz), **Marjorie Kinnan.** 1896–1953. Amer. writer best known for her novel *The Yearling* (1938).

raw material *n.* **1.** An unprocessed natural product used in manufacture. **2.** Unprocessed material of any kind.

raw sienna *n.* **1.** A brownish-yellow pigment. **2.** *Color.* A brownish orange to light brown.

raw silk *n.* **1.** Untreated silk as reeled from a cocoon. **2.** Fabric or yarn made from untreated silk.

ray[1] (rā) *n.* **1.a.** A thin line or narrow beam of light or other radiant energy. **b.** A graphic or other representation of such a line. **2.** Radiance; light. **3.** A small amount; a trace: *a ray of hope.* **4.** *Math.* A straight line extending from a point. **5.** A structure or part with the form of such a straight line. **6.** Any of the bright streaks that are seen radiating from some craters on the moon. **7.** *Bot.* **a.** A ray flower or the corolla of a ray flower. **b.** A branch of an umbel. **8.** *Zool.* **a.** One of the bony spines supporting the membrane of a fish's fin. **b.** One of the arms of a starfish or other radiate animal. **9. rays.** *Slang.* Sunshine. *— tr.v.* **rayed, ray•ing, rays. 1.** To send out as rays; emit. **2.** To supply with rays or radiating lines. **3.** To cast rays on; irradiate. [ME < OFr. *rai* < Lat. *radius.*]

ray[2] (rā) *n.* Any of various marine fishes of the order Rajiformes or Batoidei, having cartilaginous skeletons, horizontally flattened bodies, and narrow tails. [ME *raye* < OFr. *raie* < Lat. *raia.*]

ray[2]

Ray (rā), **John.** 1627–1705. English naturalist who introduced "species" as the basic classification of living things.

Ray, Man. 1890–1976. Amer. artist best known for his photographs and later experiments with surrealism.

Ray (rī), **Satyajit.** 1921–92. Bengali filmmaker whose works include *The World of Apu* (1958).

ray flower *n.* A flattened flower found in members of the composite family, as the units of a flower head of the dandelion.

Ray•leigh (rā′lē), 3rd Baron. John William Strutt. 1842–1919. British physicist who won a 1904 Nobel Prize.

Rayleigh scattering *n.* The scattering of electromagnetic radiation by particles with dimensions much smaller than the wavelength of the radiation, resulting in angular separation of colors and responsible for the reddish color of sunset and the blue of the sky. [After 3rd Baron RAYLEIGH.]

ray•less (rā′lĭs) *adj.* **1.** Lacking rays. **2.** Lacking light.

Ray•mond (rā′mənd), **Henry Jarvis.** 1820–69. Amer. journalist who founded the *New York Times* (1851).

Ray•naud's phenomenon (rā-nōz′) *n.* A circulatory disorder that affects the hands and feet, causing cyanosis, numbness, pain, and in extreme cases gangrene. [After Maurice *Raynaud* (1834–81), French physician.]

ray•on (rā′ŏn) *n.* **1.** Any of several synthetic textile fibers produced by forcing a cellulose solution through fine spinnerets and solidifying the resulting filaments. **2.** A fabric so woven or knit. [Perh. < Fr. *rayon,* ray of light (< its sheen) < *rai* < OFr. See RAY[1].]

Ray•town (rā′toun′). A city of W MO, a suburb surrounded by Kansas City. Pop. 30,601.

raze also **rase** (rāz) *tr.v.* **razed, raz•ing, raz•es** also **rased, ras•ing, ras•es. 1.** To level to the ground; demolish. See Syns at **ruin. 2.** To scrape or shave off. **3.** *Archaic.* To erase. [ME *rasen,* to scrape off < OFr. *raser* < VLat. **rāsāre,* freq. of Lat. *rādere.* See RASH[2].]

ra•zor (rā′zər) *n.* **1.** A sharp-edged cutting instrument used esp. for shaving. **2.** A device for holding a razorblade, with guards to prevent cutting of the skin. **3.** An electric instrument with vibrating or rotating blades used for shaving. [ME *rasor* < OFr. < *raser,* to scrape. See RAZE.]

ra•zor•back (rā′zər-băk′) *n.* **1.** A semiwild hog of the southeast United States having a narrow body with a ridged back. **2.** See **rorqual. 3.** A sharp ridged hill.

ra•zor•bill (rā′zər-bĭl′) *n.* A razor-billed auk.

ra•zor-billed auk (rā′zər-bĭld′) *n.* A sea bird *(Alca torda)* of the northern Atlantic having black-and-white plumage and a white-ringed flattened bill.

ra•zor•blade also **ra•zor blade** (rā′zər-blād′) *n.* A thin sharp-

ă pat	oi boy
ā pay	ou out
âr care	o͝o took
ä father	o͞o boot
ĕ pet	ŭ cut
ē be	ûr urge
ĭ pit	th thin
ī pie	*th* this
îr pier	hw which
ŏ pot	zh vision
ō toe	ə about, item
ô paw	

Stress marks:
′ (primary);
′ (secondary), as in
dictionary (dĭk′shə-nĕr′ē)

edged piece of steel that can be fitted into a razor.

razor clam *n.* Any of various clams of the family Solenidae, characteristically having long narrow shells.

razor wire *n.* A sharp-edged wire used for fences and barriers.

razz (răz) *Slang.* —*n.* A raspberry sound; a Bronx cheer. —*tr.v.* **razzed, razz•ing, razz•es.** To deride, heckle, or tease. [Shortening and alteration of RASPBERRY.]

raz•zle-daz•zle (răz′əl-dăz′əl) *n. Informal.* Dazzling excitement. [Redup. of DAZZLE.]

razz•ma•tazz (răz′mə-tăz′) *n. Slang.* **1.** A flashy action or display intended to bewilder, confuse, or deceive. **2.** Ambiguous or evasive language; double talk. **3.** Ebullient energy; vim. [Perh. alteration of RAZZLE-DAZZLE.]

Rb The symbol for the element **rubidium.**

RBC or **rbc** *abbr.* **1.** Red blood cell. **2.** Red blood cell count.

RBI also **rbi** *abbr. Baseball.* Run batted in; runs batted in.

RC *abbr.* **1.** Red Cross. **2.** Roman Catholic.

RCAF also **R.C.A.F.** *abbr.* Royal Canadian Air Force.

R.C.Ch. *abbr.* Roman Catholic Church.

RCMP also **R.C.M.P.** *abbr.* Royal Canadian Mounted Police.

R.C.P. *abbr.* Royal College of Physicians.

rcpt. *abbr.* Receipt.

R.C.S. *abbr.* Royal College of Surgeons.

rct. *abbr.* Recruit.

rd *abbr.* **1.** Rod (unit of measure). **2.** Rutherford.

RD *abbr.* Rural delivery.

rd. *abbr.* **1.** Or **Rd.** Road. **2.** Round.

RDA *abbr.* Recommended daily allowance.

RDF *abbr.* Radio direction finder.

re[1] (rā) *n. Mus.* The second tone of the diatonic scale in solfeggio. [ME < Med.Lat. See GAMUT.]

re[2] (rē) *prep.* In reference to; in the case of; concerning. [Lat. *rē*, ablative of *rēs*, thing. See **rē-*.**]

Re[1] (rā) *n. Myth.* Var. of **Ra**[1].

Re[2] The symbol for the element **rhenium.**

Re. *abbr.* Rupee.

re– *pref.* **1.** Again; anew: *rebuild.* **2.** Backward; back: *react.* **3.** Used as an intensive: *refine.* [ME < OFr. < Lat. See **re-*.**]

're. Are: *They're not at home.*

re•ab•sorb (rē′əb-sôrb′, -zôrb′) *v.* **-sorbed, -sorb•ing, -sorbs.** —*tr.* **1.** To absorb again; resorb. **2.** To accommodate or accept again, as into a group or category. —*intr.* To undergo resorption; resorb. —**re′ab•sorp′tion** (-sôrp′shən, -zôrp′-) *n.*

re•ac•cred•i•ta•tion (rē′ə-krĕd′ĭ-tā′shən) *n.* **1.** The process of reviewing the accreditation of an institution. **2.** Renewal of accreditation status.

reach (rēch) *v.* **reached, reach•ing, reach•es.** —*tr.* **1.** To stretch out or put forth (a body part); extend. **2.** To touch or grasp by stretching out or extending. **3.** To arrive at; attain. **4.a.** To succeed in getting in contact with or communicating with. **b.** To succeed in having an effect on. **5.a.** To extend as far as. **b.** To project as far as: *A cry reached our ears.* **c.** To travel as far as. **6.** To aggregate or amount to. **7.** *Informal.* To grasp and hand over to another. —*intr.* **1.** To thrust out or extend something. **2.** To try to grasp or touch something. **3.a.** To have extension in space or time. **b.** To be extensive in influence or effect. **4.** To make an excessive effort, as in drawing a conclusion or making a joke; overreach. **5.** *Naut.* To sail a course between close-hauled and dead downwind. —*n.* **1.** The act or an instance of stretching or thrusting out. **2.** The extent or distance something can reach. **3.a.** Range of understanding; comprehension. **b.** Range or scope of influence or effect. **4.** An expanse: *a reach of prairie.* **5.** A pole connecting the rear axle of a vehicle with the front. **6.** *Naut.* Any course of a sailing vessel between close-hauled and dead downwind. **7.** The stretch of water visible between bends in a river or channel. [ME *rechen* < OE *rǣcan.* See **reig-*.**] —**reach′a•ble** *adj.* —**reach′er** *n.*

Syns: *reach, achieve, attain, gain, compass.* All of these verbs mean to succeed in arriving at a goal or an objective. *Reach* is the least specific: *reach an understanding. Achieve* suggests the application of skill or initiative: *achieved recognition. Attain* often implies the impelling force of ambition, principle, or ideals: *trying to attain self-confidence. Gain* connotes considerable effort in surmounting obstacles: *gained their cooperation. Compass* implies succeeding by circumventing impediments: *will compass the task.*

re•act (rē-ăkt′) *intr.v.* **-act•ed, -act•ing, -acts. 1.** To act in response to or under the influence of a stimulus or prompting: *reacted strongly to my sarcasm.* **2.** To act in opposition to a former condition or act: *reacted against romanticism.* **3.** To act reciprocally or in return. **4.** *Chem.* To undergo a reaction.

Nancy Reagan
Photographed by
Lord Snowdon
(Antony Armstrong Jones)

Ronald Reagan
Photographed in 1976

re•ac•tance (rē-ăk′təns) *n. Symbol* **X** *Elect.* Opposition to the flow of alternating current caused by the inductance and capacitance in a circuit rather than by resistance.

re•ac•tant (rē-ăk′tənt) *n.* A substance participating in a chemical reaction, esp. a directly reacting substance present at the initiation of the reaction.

re•ac•tion (rē-ăk′shən) *n.* **1.a.** A response to a stimulus. **b.** The state resulting from such a response. **2.** A reverse or opposing action. **3.a.** A tendency to revert to a former state. **b.** Opposition to progress or liberalism; extreme conservatism. **4.** *Chem.* A change or transformation in which a substance decomposes, combines with other substances, or interchanges constituents with other substances. **5.** *Phys.* A nuclear reaction. **6.** *Phys.* An equal and opposite force exerted by a body against a force acting upon it. **7.** The response of cells or tissues to an antigen. **8.** *Psychol.* A pattern of behavior constituting a mental disorder or personality type.

re•ac•tion•ar•y (rē-ăk′shə-nĕr′ē) *adj.* Characterized by political reaction, esp. opposition to progress or liberalism; extremely conservative. —**re•ac′tion•ar′y** *n.*

reaction engine *n.* An engine that develops thrust by the focused expulsion of matter, esp. ignited fuel gases.

reaction formation *n. Psychol.* A defense mechanism in which the opposite of an objectionable impulse is expressed.

reaction time *n.* The interval of time between application of a stimulus and detection of a response.

re•ac•ti•vate (rē-ăk′tə-vāt′) *tr.v.* **-vat•ed, -vat•ing, -vates. 1.** To make active again. **2.** To restore the ability to function or the effectiveness of. —**re•ac′ti•va′tion** *n.*

re•ac•tive (rē-ăk′tĭv) *adj.* **1.** Tending to be responsive or to react to a stimulus. **2.** Characterized by reaction. **3.** *Chem. & Phys.* Tending to participate readily in reactions. —**re•ac′tive•ly** *adv.* —**re•ac′tive•ness, re′ac•tiv′i•ty** *n.*

re•ac•tor (rē-ăk′tər) *n.* **1.** One that reacts to a stimulus. **2.** *Electron.* A circuit element, such as a coil, used to introduce reactance. **3.** *Phys.* A nuclear reaction.

read (rēd) *v.* **read** (rĕd), **read•ing, reads.** —*tr.* **1.** To examine and grasp the meaning of (written or printed characters, words, or sentences). **2.** To utter or render aloud (written or printed material). **3.** To have the ability to examine and grasp the meaning of (written or printed material in a given language or notation): *reads Chinese.* **4.a.** To examine and grasp the meaning of (language not in writing): *reading sign language.* **b.** To examine and grasp the meaning of (a graphic representation): *reading a map.* **5.a.** To discern and interpret the nature or significance of through close examination or sensitive observation: *read the trail for signs of deer.* **b.** To discern or anticipate through examination or observation; descry. **6.** To determine the intent or mood of: *I can read your mind.* **7.a.** To attribute a certain interpretation or meaning to: *read my words differently.* **b.** To consider (something written or printed) as having a particular meaning or significance. **8.** To foretell or predict (the future). **9.** To receive or comprehend (a radio message, for example). **10.** To study or make a study of. **11.** To learn or get knowledge of from something written or printed. **12.** To proofread. **13.** To have or use as a preferred reading in a particular passage: *For change read* charge. **14.** To indicate, register, or show: *The dial reads 32°.* **15.** *Comp. Sci.* To obtain (information) from a storage medium, such as a magnetic disk. —*intr.* **1.** To examine and grasp the meaning of printed or written characters, as of words or music. **2.** To speak aloud the words that one is reading. **3.** To learn by reading. **4.** To study. **5.** To have a particular wording: *Recite the poem exactly as it reads.* **6.** To contain a specific meaning. **7.** To indicate, register, or show a measurement or figure. **8.** To have a specified character or quality for the reader. —*n. Informal.* Something that is read: *a good read.* —*adj.* (rĕd). Informed by reading; learned. —***phrasal verbs.*** **read out.** To read aloud. **read up.** To study or learn by reading. —***idioms.*** **read a lecture** (or **lesson**). To issue a reprimand. **read between the lines.** To perceive or detect an obscure or unexpressed meaning. **read out of.** To expel by proclamation from a social, political, or other group. [ME *reden* < OE *rǣdan*, to advise. See **ar-*.**]

---

re′cal′cu•late′ *tr.v.*
re′cal•cu•la′tion *n.*
re′com•pose′ *tr.v.*
re′com•po•si′tion *n.*
re′con•firm′ *tr.v.*
re′con•fir•ma′tion *n.*
re′con•sid′er *tr. & intr.v.*
re′con•sid′er•a′tion *n.*
re′dis•trib′ute *tr.v.*
re•dis′trict *tr.v.*
re•for′est *tr.v.*
re′for•es•ta′tion *n.*
re•house′ *tr.v.*
re•in′te•grate′ *tr.v.*
re′in•te•gra′tion *n.*
re•in′te•gra′tive *adj.*
re′in•ter′pret *tr.v.*
re′in•ter′pre•ta′tion *n.*
re′in•vest′ *tr.v.*
re′in•vest′ment *n.*
re′in•vig′o•rate′ *tr.v.*
re′in•vig′o•ra′tion *n.*
re′in•vig′o•ra′tor *n.*
re•num′ber *tr.v.*
re•pack′age *tr.v.*
re•pack′ag•er *n.*
re•stock′ *tr.v.*
re′sup•ply′ *tr.v.* & *n.*
re′test′ *tr.v.* & *n.*
re•trace′ *tr.v.*
re•trace′a•ble *adj.*
re•trace′ment *n.*
re•trac′er *n.*
re•train′ *tr. & intr.v.*
re•train′a•ble *adj.*
re′train•ee′ *n.*
re•us′a•bil′i•ty *n.*
re•us′a•ble *adj.* & *n.*
re•use′ *tr.v.* & *n.*
re•val′i•date′ *tr.v.*
re•val′i•da′tion *n.*
re•wak′en *tr. & intr.v.*

Read (rēd), Sir **Herbert.** 1893–1968. British writer and critic known for his imagistic poetry.

read•a•ble (rē′də-bəl) *adj.* **1.** Easily read; legible. **2.** Pleasurable or interesting to read: *a readable story.* —**read′a•bil′i•ty, read′a•ble•ness** *n.* —**read′a•bly** *adv.*

Reade (rēd), **Charles.** 1814–84. British writer whose historical novels include *The Cloister and the Hearth* (1861).

read•er (rē′dər) *n.* **1.** One that reads. **2.** One who publicly recites literary works. **3.a.** One who reads and evaluates manuscripts for a publisher. **b.** A proofreader. **4.** A teaching assistant who reads and grades examination papers. **5.** *Chiefly British.* A university teacher, esp. one ranking next below a professor. **6.a.** A textbook of reading exercises. **b.** An anthology, esp. of literature. **7.** A layperson or minor cleric who reads lessons or prayers in church services.

read•er•ship (rē′dər-shĭp′) *n.* **1.** The readers of a publication considered as a group. **2.** *Chiefly British.* The office of a reader at a university.

read•i•ly (rĕd′ə-lē, rĕd′l-ē) *adv.* **1.** In a prompt manner. **2.** In a cooperative manner; willingly. **3.** In a manner indicating or connoting ease; easily.

read•ing (rē′dĭng) *n.* **1.** The act or activity of one that reads. **2.** The act or practice of rendering texts aloud. **3.** An official or public recitation of written material. **4.a.** The specific form of a particular passage in a text. **b.** The distinctive interpretation of a work of performing art given by the person or persons performing it. **5.** A personal interpretation or appraisal. **6.** Written or printed material. **7.** The information given by a gauge or graduated instrument.

Read•ing (rĕd′ĭng). **1.** A borough of S-central England W of London; chartered 1253. Pop. 136,200. **2.** A town of NE MA, a suburb of Boston. Pop. 22,539. **3.** A city of SE PA NW of Philadelphia; settled in 1748. Pop. 78,380.

read•ing desk (rē′dĭng) *n.* A desk or stand, usu. with a slanted top, for holding a book or papers for a standing reader.

re•ad•just (rē′ə-jŭst′) *tr.v.* **-just•ed, -just•ing, -justs.** To adjust again. —**re′ad•just′er** *n.* —**re′ad•just′ment** *n.*

read-on•ly memory (rēd′ōn′lē) *n. Comp. Sci.* A small memory that allows fast access to permanently stored data but prevents addition to or modification of the data.

read•out or **read-out** (rēd′out′) *n. Comp. Sci.* Presentation of data, usu. in digital form, from calculations or storage.

read•y (rĕd′ē) *adj.* **-i•er, -i•est. 1.** Prepared or available for service, action, or progress. **2.** Mentally disposed; willing. **3.** Likely or about to do something. **4.** Prompt in apprehending or reacting. **5.** Available: *ready money.* —*tr.v.* **read•ied, read•y•ing, read•ies.** To cause to be ready. —***idioms.* at the ready.** Available for immediate use. **make ready.** To make preparations. [ME *redy* < OE *rǣde.* See **reidh-***.] —**read′i•ness** *n.*

read•y-made or **read•y•made** (rĕd′ē-mād′) *adj.* **1.** Already made, prepared, or available. **2.** Preconceived.

read•y-mix (rĕd′ē-mĭks′) *n.* A mixture in proper proportions of two or more ingredients, as of a food, marketed for convenience; a premix. —**read′y-mix′, read′y-mixed′** *adj.*

read•y-to-wear (rĕd′ē-tə-wâr′) *adj.* **1.** Marketed in a finished condition in standard sizes. Used of clothing. **2.** Of, relating to, or doing business in ready-to-wear clothing. —*n.* Clothing marketed in a finished condition in standard sizes.

re•af•firm (rē′ə-fûrm′) *tr.v.* **-firmed, -firm•ing, -firms.** To affirm or assert again. —**re′af•fir•ma′tion** (rē′ăf-ər-mā′shən) *n.*

Rea•gan (rā′gən), **Nancy Davis.** b. 1921. First Lady of the U.S. (1981–89) who established a nationwide antidrug campaign.

Reagan, Ronald Wilson. b. 1911. The 40th President of the U.S. (1981–89) whose administration was marked by improved relations with the Soviet Union.

re•a•gent (rē-ā′jənt) *n.* A substance used in a chemical reaction to detect, analyze, or produce other substances.

re•a•gin (rē-ā′jĭn) *n.* **1.** An antibody found in the blood of individuals having a genetic predisposition to allergies such as asthma and hay fever. **2.** A substance present in the blood of individuals having a positive serological test for syphilis. [RE-AG(ENT) + -IN.] —**re′a•gin′ic** (rē′ə-jĭn′ĭk) *adj.*

re•al¹ (rē′əl, rēl) *adj.* **1.a.** Being or occurring in fact or actuality; having verifiable existence: *real objects.* **b.** True and actual; not imaginary, alleged, or ideal: *real people, not ghosts.* **c.** Of or founded on practical matters and concerns: *a recent graduate entering the real world.* **2.** Genuine and authentic; not artificial or spurious: *real mink.* See Syns at **authentic. 3.** Being no less than what is stated; worthy of the name: *a real friend.* **4.** Free of pretense, falsehood, or affectation: *real affection.* **5.** Not to be taken lightly; serious: *real trouble.* **6.** *Philos.* Existing regardless of being perceived or thought of. **7.** Relating to, being, or having value reckoned by actual purchasing power: *real income.* **8.** *Phys.* Of, relating to, or being an image formed by light rays that converge in space. **9.** *Math.* Of, relating to, or being a real number. **10.** *Law.* Of or relating to stationary or fixed property, such as land. —*adv. Informal.* Very: *I'm real sorry.* —*n.* **1.** A thing or whole having actual existence. Often used with *the.* **2.** *Math.* A real number. —***idiom.* for real.** *Slang.* Truly so in fact or actuality. [ME < OFr. < LLat. *reālis* < Lat. *rēs,* thing. See **rē-***.] —**real′ness** *n.*

re•al² (rā-äl′) *n., pl.* **-als** or **-al•es** (-ä′lĕs). A silver coin formerly used in Spain and Latin America. [Sp., royal, real < Lat. *rēgālis,* royal < *rēx, rēg-,* king. See **reg-***.]

re•al³ (rā-äl′) *n., pl.* **reals** or **reis** (rās). Either of two monetary units formerly used in Portugal and Brazil. [Port., royal, real < Lat. *rēgālis,* royal. See REAL².]

re•al estate (rē′əl, rēl) *n.* Land, including all the natural resources and permanent buildings on it. —**re′al-es•tate′** (rē′əl-ĭ-stāt′, rēl′-) *adj.*

re•al•gar (rē-ăl′gär′, -gər) *n.* A soft orange-red arsenic ore, As_2S_2, used in pyrotechnics and tanning and as a pigment. [ME < Med.Lat. < Catalan < Ar. *rahj al-ġār,* powder (of) the mine or cave : *rahj,* powder + *al,* the + *ġār,* cave.]

re•a•lign (rē′ə-līn′) *tr.v.* **-ligned, -lign•ing, -ligns. 1.** To put back into order or alignment. **2.** To make new groupings of or working arrangements between. —**re′a•lign′ment** *n.*

re•al•ism (rē′ə-lĭz′əm) *n.* **1.** An inclination toward literal truth and pragmatism. **2.** The representation in art or literature of objects, actions, or social conditions as they actually are, without idealization or presentation in abstract form. **3.** *Philos.* **a.** The scholastic doctrine, opposed to nominalism, that universals exist independently of their being thought. **b.** The modern philosophical doctrine, opposed to idealism, that physical objects exist independently of perception.

re•al•ist (rē′ə-lĭst) *n.* **1.** One who is inclined to literal truth and pragmatism. **2.** A practitioner of artistic or philosophic realism.

re•al•is•tic (rē′ə-lĭs′tĭk) *adj.* **1.** Tending to or expressing an awareness of things as they really are: *a realistic appraisal of our chances.* **2.** Of or relating to the representation of objects, actions, or social conditions as they actually are: *a realistic novel.* See Syns at **graphic.** —**re′al•is′ti•cal•ly** *adv.*

re•al•i•ty (rē-ăl′ĭ-tē) *n., pl.* **-ties. 1.** The quality or state of being actual or true. **2.** One, such as a person or an event, that is actual. **3.** The totality of all things possessing actuality, existence, or essence. **4.** That which exists objectively and in fact. **5.** *Philos.* That which has necessary and not contingent existence. —***idiom.* in reality.** In fact; actually.

reality principle *n. Psychiat.* Awareness of and adjustment to environmental demands in a manner that assures ultimate satisfaction of instinctual needs.

re•al•i•za•tion (rē′ə-lĭ-zā′shən) *n.* **1.** The act of realizing or the condition of being realized. **2.** The result of realizing.

re•al•ize (rē′ə-līz′) *v.* **-ized, -iz•ing, -iz•es.** —*tr.* **1.** To comprehend completely or correctly. **2.** To make real; fulfill. **3.** To make realistic. **4.** To obtain or achieve, as gain or profit. **5.** To bring in (a sum) as profit by sale. —*intr.* To exchange holdings or goods for money. [Fr. *réaliser* < OFr. < *real,* real. See REAL¹.] —**re′al•iz′a•ble** *adj.* —**re′al•iz′er** *n.*

re•al•ly (rē′ə-lē′, rē′lē) *adv.* **1.** In actual truth or fact: *The horseshoe crab isn't really a crab.* **2.** Truly; genuinely: *That was really fun.* **3.** Indeed: *Really, you shouldn't have done it.*

realm (rĕlm) *n.* **1.** A kingdom. **2.** A field, sphere, or province. [ME *realme* < OFr., alteration of Lat. *regimen,* government < *regere,* to rule. See **reg-***.]

re•al number (rē′əl, rēl) *n. Math.* A number that is rational or irrational, not imaginary.

re•al•po•li•tik (rā-äl′pō′lĭ-tēk′) *n.* A usu. expansionist national policy having as its sole principle advancement of the national interest. [Ger. : *real,* practical (< LLat. *reālis,* real; see REAL¹) + *Politik,* politics (< Fr. *politique,* political, policy; see POLITIC).] —**re•al′po′li•tik′er** *n.*

re•al time (rē′əl, rēl) *n. Comp. Sci.* The actual time in which a physical process under computer study or control occurs.

re•al-time (rē′əl-tīm′, rēl′-) *adj. Comp. Sci.* Of or relating to computer systems that update output at the same rate as they receive data, enabling them to direct or control a process such as an automatic pilot.

Re•al•tor (rē′əl-tər, -tôr′). A service mark used for a real-estate agent affiliated with the National Association of Realtors.

re•al•ty (rē′əl-tē) *n., pl.* **-ties.** Real estate.

ream¹ (rēm) *n.* **1.** A quantity of paper, formerly 480 sheets, now 500 sheets or, in a printer's ream, 516 sheets. **2.** A very large amount. Often used in the plural. [ME *reme* < OFr. *reime* < OSp. *resma* < Ar. *rizmah,* bundle.]

ream² (rēm) *tr.v.* **reamed, ream•ing, reams. 1.** To form, shape, taper, or enlarge (a hole) with or as if with a reamer. **2.** To remove (material) by this process. **3.** To squeeze the juice out of (fruit) with a reamer. [Poss. < ME *remen,* to make room, var. of *rimen* < OE *rȳman.* See **reuə-***.]

ream•er (rē′mər) *n.* **1.** Any of various tools used to shape or enlarge holes. **2.** A utensil with a conical ridged projection, used for extracting citrus-fruit juice.

re•an•i•mate (rē-ăn′ə-māt′) *tr.v.* **-mat•ed, -mat•ing, -mates. 1.** To give new life to: *This work reanimates the classics.* **2.** To bring to life; evoke powerfully or effectively.

reap (rēp) *v.* **reaped, reap•ing, reaps.** —*tr.* **1.** To cut (grain or pulse) for harvest with a scythe, sickle, or reaper. **2.** To harvest (a crop). **3.** To harvest a crop from. **4.** To obtain by

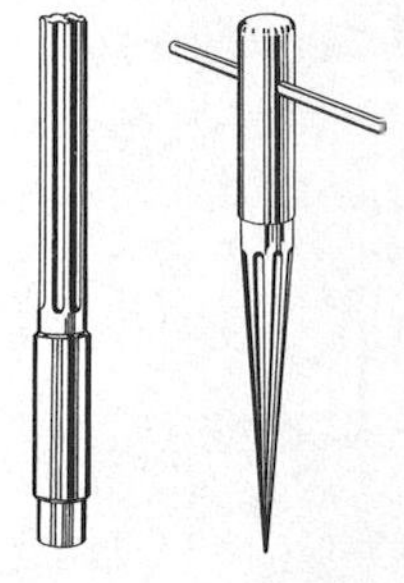

reamer
Top: Fluted (*left*) and pipe (*right*) reamers for enlarging holes
Bottom: Juice reamer

ă pat	oi boy
ā pay	ou out
âr care	ŏŏ took
ä father	ōō boot
ĕ pet	ŭ cut
ē be	ûr urge
ĭ pit	th thin
ī pie	*th* this
îr pier	hw which
ŏ pot	zh vision
ō toe	ə about, item
ô paw	

Stress marks:
′ (primary);
′ (secondary), as in **dictionary** (dĭk′shə-nĕr′ē)

effort. —*intr.* **1.** To cut or harvest grain or pulse. **2.** To obtain a return or reward. [ME *repen* < OE *rīpan.*]

reap•er (rē′pər) *n.* One that reaps, esp. a machine for harvesting grain or pulse crops.

re•ap•por•tion (rē′ə-pôr′shən) *tr.v.* **-tioned, -tion•ing, -tions.** To distribute anew.

re•ap•por•tion•ment (rē′ə-pôr′shən-mənt) *n.* **1.** The act of reapportioning or the state of being reapportioned. **2.** Redistribution of representation in a legislative body, esp. the periodic reallotment of U.S. congressional seats according to changes in the census figures as required by the Constitution.

re•ap•prais•al (rē′ə-prā′zəl) *n.* A new appraisal or evaluation.

re•ap•praise (rē′ə-prāz′) *tr.v.* **-praised, -prais•ing, -prais•es.** To make a fresh appraisal or evaluation of.

rear¹ (rîr) *n.* **1.** A hind part. **2.** The point or area farthest from the front. **3.** The part of a military deployment usu. farthest from the fighting front. **4.** *Informal.* The buttocks. —*adj.* Of, at, or located in the rear. [ME *rere,* rear of an army, short for *rerewarde,* rear guard. See REARWARD².]

rear² (rîr) *v.* **reared, rear•ing, rears.** —*tr.* **1.** To care for (children or a child) during the early stages of life; bring up. **2.** To lift upright; raise. See Syns at **lift. 3.** To build; erect. **4.** To tend (growing plants or animals). —*intr.* **1.** To rise on the hind legs, as a horse. **2.** To rise high in the air; tower. [ME *reren,* to raise < OE *rǣran.*] —**rear′er** *n.*

rear admiral *n.* A commissioned officer in the U.S. Navy or Coast Guard ranking above commodore and below vice admiral.

rear end *n.* **1.** The rear part. **2.** *Informal.* The buttocks.

rear-end (rîr′ĕnd′) *tr.v.* **-end•ed, -end•ing, -ends.** *Slang.* To run into (a motor vehicle) from behind. —**rear′-end′er** *n.*

rear guard *n.* A detachment of troops that protects the rear of a military force. [ME *reregarde* < OFr. : *rere,* backward (< Lat. *retrō;* see **re-***) + *guarde,* guard (< *guarder,* to defend; see GUARD).]

rear-guard (rîr′gärd′) *adj.* **1.** Of or relating to a rear guard. **2.** Of or relating to economic, political, or social resistance.

re•ar•gue (rē-är′gyo͞o) *tr.v.* **-gued, -gu•ing, -gues. 1.** To argue again or repeatedly. **2.** To debate again or present additional arguments for (a case, for example), esp. in a court of law.

re•arm (rē-ärm′) *v.* **-armed, -arm•ing, -arms.** —*tr.* **1.** To arm again. **2.** To equip with better weapons. —*intr.* To arm oneself again. —**re•ar′ma•ment** (rē-är′mə-mənt) *n.*

rear•most (rîr′mōst′) *adj.* Farthest in the rear; last.

re•ar•range (rē′ə-rānj′) *tr.v.* **-ranged, -rang•ing, -rang•es.** To change the arrangement of. —**re′ar•range′ment** *n.*

rear-view mirror or **rear•view mirror** also **rear view mirror** (rîr′vyo͞o′) *n.* A mirror, such as one attached to a motor vehicle, that provides a view of what is behind.

rear•ward¹ (rîr′wərd) *adv.* Toward, to, or at the rear. —*adj.* Being at or in the rear. —*n.* A rearward direction, point, or position. —**rear′wards** *adv.*

rear•ward² (rîr′wôrd′) *n.* The rear guard of an armed force. [ME *rerewarde* < AN : *rere,* behind (< Lat. *retrō;* see **re-***) + *warde,* guard (of Gmc. orig.; see **wer-³***).]

rea•son (rē′zən) *n.* **1.** The basis or motive for an action, a decision, or a conviction. See Usage Note at **why. 2.** A declaration made to explain or justify an action, a decision, or a conviction. **3.** An underlying fact or cause: *reason for doubt.* **4.** The capacity for logical, rational, and analytic thought; intelligence. **5.** Good judgment; sound sense. **6.** A normal mental state; sanity. **7.** *Logic.* A premise, usu. the minor premise, of an argument. —*v.* **-soned, -son•ing, -sons.** —*intr.* **1.** To use the faculty of reason; think logically. **2.** To talk or argue logically and persuasively. **3.** *Obsolete.* To engage in conversation or discussion. —*tr.* **1.** To determine or conclude by logical thinking: *reasoned out a solution.* **2.** To persuade or dissuade (someone) with reasons. —***idioms.* by reason of.** Because of. **in reason.** With good sense or justification; reasonably. **within reason.** Within the bounds of good sense or practicality. **with reason.** With good cause; justifiably. [ME < OFr. *raison* < Lat. *ratiō, ratiōn-* < *ratus,* p.part. of *rērī,* to consider, think. See **ar-***.] —**rea′son•er** *n.*

rea•son•a•ble (rē′zə-nə-bəl) *adj.* **1.** Capable of reasoning; rational. **2.** Governed by or being in accordance with reason or sound thinking. **3.** Being within the bounds of common sense. **4.** Not excessive or extreme; fair. —**rea′son•a•bil′i•ty, rea′son•a•ble•ness** *n.* —**rea′son•a•bly** *adv.*

rea•son•ing (rē′zə-nĭng) *n.* **1.** Use of reason, esp. to form conclusions, inferences, or judgments. **2.** Evidence or arguments used in thinking or argumentation.

re•as•sem•ble (rē′ə-sĕm′bəl) *v.* **-bled, -bling, -bles.** —*tr.* **1.** To bring or gather together again. **2.** To fit or joint the parts of (something) together again. —*intr.* To gather together again, esp. in a different place.

re•as•sign (rē′ə-sīn′) *tr.v.* **-signed, -sign•ing, -signs.** To assign to a new position, distribution, or function: *reassigned the ambassador to a new post.* —**re•as•sign′ment** *n.*

re•as•sure (rē′ə-sho͝or′) *tr.v.* **-sured, -sur•ing, -sures. 1.** To restore confidence to. **2.** To assure again. **3.** To reinsure. —**re′as•sur′ance** *n.* —**re′as•sur′ing•ly** *adv.*

re•a•ta (rē-ä′tə) *n.* Var. of **riata.**

Ré•au•mur or **Re•au•mur** (rā′ō-myo͝or′) *adj.* Relating to, being, or indicated on a thermometer scale that registers the freezing point of water as 0° and the boiling point as 80°.

Ré•au•mur (rā′ə-myo͝or′, -ō-, rā-ō-mür′), **René Antoine Ferchault de.** 1683–1757. French physicist who invented the alcohol thermometer and devised the Réaumur scale.

reave¹ (rēv) *v.* **reaved** or **reft** (rĕft), **reav•ing, reaves.** —*tr.* **1.** To seize and carry off forcibly. **2.** To deprive (one) of something. —*intr.* To rob, plunder, or pillage. [ME *reven,* to plunder < OE *rēafian.* See **reup-***.]

reave² (rēv) *tr.v.* **reaved** or **reft** (rĕft), **reav•ing, reaves.** *Archaic.* To break or tear apart. [ME *reven,* poss. alteration (influenced by *reven,* to plunder) of ON *rīfa,* to rive.]

Reb¹ also **reb** (rĕb) *n. Informal.* A Confederate soldier. [Short for REBEL.]

Reb² (rĕb) *n. Judaism.* Used with the given name as a title of respect for a man. [Yiddish < Heb. *rabbî,* my master. See RABBI.]

re•bar•ba•tive (rē-bär′bə-tĭv) *adj.* Tending to irritate; repellent. [Fr. *rébarbatif* < OFr. < *(se) rebarber,* to confront : *re-,* re- + *barbe,* beard (< Lat. *barba;* see **bhardh-ā-***).]

re•bate¹ (rē′bāt′) *n.* A deduction from or a return of part of a payment. —*tr.v.* (rē′bāt′, rĭ-bāt′) **-bat•ed, -bat•ing, -bates. 1.** To deduct or return (an amount) from a payment or bill. **2.** To lessen; diminish. [< ME *rebaten,* to deduct < OFr. *rabattre, rebattre,* to reduce, to beat down again : *re-,* re- + *abbattre,* to beat down; see ABATE.] —**re′bat•er** *n.*

re•bate² (rē′bāt′, răb′ĭt) *n.* & *v.* Var. of **rabbet.**

re•ba•to (rĭ-bä′tō) also **ra•ba•to** (rə-) *n., pl.* **-tos.** A stiff flaring collar of lace or other fabric, worn early in the 17th century. [Obsolete Fr. *rebateau,* alteration of Fr. *rabat* < OFr. < *rabattre,* to turn down again, reduce. See REBATE¹.]

reb•be (rĕb′ə, rĕb′ē) *n.* A Jewish spiritual leader or rabbi, esp. of a Hasidic sect. [Yiddish < Heb. *rabbî,* rabbi. See RABBI.]

re•bec also **re•beck** (rē′bĕk′) *n. Mus.* A pear-shaped two-stringed or three-stringed medieval instrument, played with a bow. [Fr. < OFr., alteration (influenced by *bec,* beak, < its shape) of *rebebe* < OProv. *rebeb* < Ar. *rabāb.*]

Re•bec•ca also **Re•bek•ah** (rĭ-bĕk′ə). In the Bible, the wife of Isaac and the mother of Jacob and Esau.

re•bel (rĭ-bĕl′) *intr.v.* **-belled, -bel•ling, -bels. 1.** To refuse allegiance to and oppose by force an established government or ruling authority. **2.** To resist or defy an authority or a generally accepted convention. **3.** To feel or express strong unwillingness or repugnance: *rebelled at the suggestion.* —*n.* **reb•el.** (rĕb′əl). One who rebels or is in rebellion. [ME *rebellen* < OFr. *rebeller* < Lat. *rebellāre* : *re-,* re- + *bellāre,* to make war (< *bellum,* war).]

re•bel•lion (rĭ-bĕl′yən) *n.* **1.** Open, armed, and organized resistance to a constituted government. **2.** An act or a show of defiance toward an authority or a convention. [ME < OFr. < Lat. *rebelliō, rebelliōn-* < *rebellāre,* to rebel. See REBEL.]

Syns: *rebellion, revolution, revolt, mutiny, insurrection, uprising.* These nouns denote acts of violence intended to change or overthrow an existing authority. *Rebellion* is open, armed, organized resistance to constituted political authority that often fails: *A rebellion broke out in the provinces.* A *revolution* is the overthrow of one government and its replacement with another: *Several major revolutions have altered the balance of power among nations. Revolt* is rejection of and rebellion against a prevailing state of affairs or a controlling authority: *a taxpayers' revolt. Mutiny* is revolt, esp. by sailors: *a bloody mutiny at sea. Insurrection* and *uprising* apply to popular revolts that are sometimes limited or are viewed as being the first indications of a more extensive rebellion: *mounted an insurrection against the junta. The uprising was soon quelled by military action.*

re•bel•lious (rĭ-bĕl′yəs) *adj.* **1.** Prone to or engaged in a rebellion. **2.** Of, relating to, or characteristic of a rebel or rebellion: *rebellious acts.* **3.** Resisting treatment or control; unruly. —**re•bel′lious•ly** *adv.* —**re•bel′lious•ness** *n.*

rebel yell *n. Chiefly Southern U.S.* See **wahoo⁴.**

re•bid (rē-bĭd′) *v.* **-bid, -bid•den** (-bĭd′n) or **-bid, -bid•ding, -bids.** —*tr.* **1.** *Games.* To bid (a previously bid suit) again in bridge. **2.** To offer a revised bid for (a contract). —*intr.* **1.** *Games.* To bid again in the auction in bridge. **2.** To rebid a contract. —**re′bid′** *n.*

re•bind (rē-bīnd′) *tr.v.* **-bound** (-bound′), **-bind•ing, -binds.** To bind again, esp. to put a new binding on (a book). —*n.* (rē′bīnd′). A book that has been rebound.

re•birth (rē-bûrth′, rē′bûrth′) *n.* **1.** A second or new birth; reincarnation. **2.** A renaissance; a revival.

re•book (rē-bo͝ok′) *v.* **-booked, -book•ing, -books.** —*tr.* **1.** To book again. **2.** To change a booking for (a performance or reservation). —*intr.* To make a new booking.

re•born (rē-bôrn′) *adj.* Emotionally or spiritually revived or regenerated.

re•bound¹ (rē′bound′, rĭ-) *v.* **-bound•ed, -bound•ing, -bounds.** —*intr.* **1.** To spring or bounce back after hitting or colliding with something. **2.** To recover, as from depression. **3.** To reecho; resound. **4.** *Basketball.* To retrieve and gain possession of the ball as it bounces off the backboard or rim. — *tr.* To cause to rebound. — *n.* (rē′bound′, rĭ-bound′). **1.** A springing or bounding back; a recoil. **2.a.** *Sports.* A rebounding or caroming ball or hockey puck. **b.** *Basketball.* The act or an instance of rebounding. **3.** A quick recovery from or reaction to disappointment or depression. [ME *rebounden* < OFr. *rebondir* : *re-*, re- + *bondir*, to leap; see BOUND[1].] — **re•bound′er** *n.*

re•bound[2] (rē-bound′) *v.* P.t. and p.part. of **rebind.**

re•bo•zo (rĭ-bō′sō, rĕ-bô′thô) *n., pl.* **-zos.** A long scarf worn over the head and shoulders chiefly by Mexican women. [Sp. < *rebosar*, to muffle with a shawl : *re-*, back (< Lat.; see RE-) + *bozo*, muzzle, mouth (ult. < Lat. *bucca*, cheek).]

re•broad•cast (rē-brôd′kăst′) *tr.v.* **-cast** or **-cast•ed, -cast•ing, -casts. 1.** To repeat the broadcast of (a program). **2.** To receive and send out (a broadcast) again. — *n.* A broadcast that is repeated or that is relayed from another station.

re•buff (rĭ-bŭf′) *n.* **1.** A blunt or abrupt repulse or refusal, as to an offer. **2.** A check or an abrupt setback to progress or action. — *tr.v.* **-buffed, -buff•ing, -buffs. 1.** To reject bluntly, often disdainfully; snub. See Syns at **refuse**[1]. **2.** To repel or drive back. [< obsolete Fr. *rebuffer*, to reject < Ital. *ribuffare* < *ribuffo*, reprimand : *ri-*, back (< Lat. *re-*; see RE-) + *buffo*, gust, puff (of imit. orig.).]

re•build (rē-bĭld′) *tr.v.* **-built** (-bĭlt′), **-build•ing, -builds. 1.** To build again. **2.** To make extensive structural repairs on. **3.** To remodel or make extensive changes in: *tried to rebuild society.*

re•buke (rĭ-byo͞ok′) *tr.v.* **-buked, -buk•ing, -bukes. 1.** To criticize or reprove sharply; reprimand. See Syns at **admonish. 2.** To check or repress. — *n.* A sharp reproof. [ME *rebuken* < ONFr. *rebuker* : *re-*, back (< Lat.; see RE-) + **buker*, to strike, chop wood (var. of OFr. *buschier* < *busche*, firewood, of Gmc. orig.).]

re•bus (rē′bəs) *n., pl.* **-bus•es.** A representation of words in the form of pictures or symbols, often presented as a puzzle. [Lat. *rēbus*, ablative pl. of *rēs*, thing. See **rē-*.**]

re•but (rĭ-bŭt′) *v.* **-but•ted, -but•ting, -buts.** — *tr.* **1.** To refute, esp. by offering opposing evidence or arguments. **2.** To repel. — *intr.* To present opposing evidence or arguments. [ME *reboten, rebutte*, to rebuke, repel < OFr. *rebouter* : *re-*, re- + *bouter*, to push (of Gmc. orig.; see **bhau-***).]

re•but•tal (rĭ-bŭt′l) *n.* **1.** The act of rebutting. **2.** A statement made in rebutting.

re•but•ter (rĭ-bŭt′ər) *n.* One who refutes or rebuts.

rec (rĕk) *n. Informal.* Recreation.

rec. *abbr.* **1.** Receipt. **2.** Record; recording. **3.** Recreation.

re•cal•ci•trant (rĭ-kăl′sĭ-trənt) *adj.* Marked by stubborn resistance to and defiance of authority or guidance. See Syns at **unruly.** — *n.* A recalcitrant person. [LLat. *recalcitrāns, recalcitrant-*, pr.part. of *recalcitrāre*, to be disobedient < Lat., to deny access : *re-*, re- + *calcitrāre*, to kick (< *calx, calc-*, heel).] — **re•cal′ci•trance, re•cal′ci•tran•cy** *n.*

re•ca•les•cence (rē′kə-lĕs′əns) *n.* A sudden glowing in a cooling metal caused by liberation of the latent heat of transformation. [< Lat. *recalēscēns, recalēscent-*, pr.part. of *recalēscere*, to grow warm again : *re-*, re- + *calēscere*, to become warm, inchoative of *calēre*, to be warm; see **kelə-[1]*.**] — **re′ca•les′cent** *adj.*

re•call (rĭ-kôl′) *tr.v.* **-called, -cal•ling, -calls. 1.** To ask or order to return. **2.** To summon back to awareness of or concern with the subject or situation at hand. **3.** To remember; recollect. See Syns at **remember. 4.** To cancel, take back, or revoke. **5.** To bring back; restore. **6.** To request return (of a product) to the manufacturer, as for necessary repairs or adjustments. — *n.* (*also* rē′kôl′). **1.** The act of recalling or summoning back, esp. an official order to return. **2.** A signal, such as a bugle call, used to summon troops back to their posts. **3.** The ability to remember information or experiences. **4.** The act of revoking. **5.a.** The procedure by which a public official may be removed from office by popular vote. **b.** The right to employ this procedure. **6.** The recalling of a product by its manufacturer. — **re•call′a•ble** *adj.*

Ré•ca•mi•er (rā′kəm-yā′, rā-käm-), **Jeanne Françoise Julie Adélaïde Bernard.** 1777–1849. French socialite whose Parisian salon attracted noted literary and political figures.

re•cant (rĭ-kănt′) *v.* **-cant•ed, -cant•ing, -cants.** — *tr.* To make a formal retraction or disavowal of (a previously held statement or belief). — *intr.* To recant a previously held statement or belief. [Lat. *recantāre* : *re-*, re- + *cantāre*, to sing, freq. of *canere*; see **kan-*.**] — **re′can•ta′tion** (rē′kăn-tā′shən) *n.* — **re•cant′er** *n.*

re•cap[1] (rē-kăp′) *tr.v.* **-capped, -cap•ping, -caps. 1.** To replace a cap or caplike covering on: *recapped the bottle.* **2.** To restore (a used tire of a motor vehicle) to usable condition by bonding new rubber onto the worn tread and lateral surface. — *n.* (rē′kăp′). A tire that has been recapped.

re•cap[2] (rē′kăp′) *Informal.* — *tr.v.* **-capped, -cap•ping, -caps.** To recapitulate. — *n.* A recapitulation, as of a news report.

re•cap•i•tal•ize (rē-kăp′ĭ-tl-īz′) *tr.v.* **-ized, -iz•ing, -iz•es.** To change the capital structure of (a corporation). — **re•cap′i•tal•i•za′tion** (-ĭ-zā′shən) *n.*

re•ca•pit•u•late (rē′kə-pĭch′ə-lāt′) *v.* **-lat•ed, -lat•ing, -lates.** — *tr.* **1.** To repeat in concise form. **2.** *Biol.* To appear to repeat (the evolutionary stages of the species) during the embryonic development of the individual organism. — *intr.* To make a summary. [Lat. *recapitulāre, recapitulāt-* : *re-*, re- + *capitulum*, main point, heading, dim. of *caput, capit-*, head. See **kaput-*.**] — **re•ca•pit′u•la′tive, re•ca•pit′u•la•to′ry** (-lə-tôr′ē, -tōr′ē) *adj.*

re•ca•pit•u•la•tion (rē′kə-pĭch′ə-lā′shən) *n.* **1.** The act or process of recapitulating. **2.** A summary or concise review. **3.** See **biogenesis** 4. **4.** *Mus.* Restatement of the exposition that constitutes the third section of the typical sonata form.

recapitulation theory *n.* See **biogenetic law.**

re•cap•ture (rē-kăp′chər) *n.* **1.a.** The act of retaking or recovering. **b.** The condition of having been retaken or recovered. **2.** Something recaptured. **3.** The lawful taking by a government of a fixed amount of the profits of a public-service corporation in excess of a stipulated rate of return. — *tr.v.* **-tured, -tur•ing, -tures. 1.** To capture again. **2.** To recall: *tried to recapture the past.* **3.** To acquire by the government procedure of recapture.

re•cast (rē-kăst′) *tr.v.* **-cast, -cast•ing, -casts. 1.** To mold again: *recast a bell.* **2.** To set down or present (ideas or words, for example) in a new or different arrangement. **3.** To change the cast of (a theatrical production). — *n.* (rē′kăst′). **1.** The act or process of recasting. **2.** Something made by recasting.

recd. *abbr.* Received.

re•cede (rĭ-sēd′) *intr.v.* **-ced•ed, -ced•ing, -cedes. 1.** To move back or away from a limit, point, or mark: *The flood waters receded.* **2.** To slope backward. **3.** To become or seem to become fainter or more distant: *With time, the memories receded.* **4.** To withdraw or retreat. [ME *receden* < OFr. *receder* < Lat. *recēdere* : *re-*, re- + *cēdere*, to go; see **ked-*.**]

re-cede (rē-sēd′) *tr.v.* **-ced•ed, -ced•ing, -cedes.** To yield or grant to one formerly in possession; cede (something) back.

re•ceipt (rĭ-sēt′) *n.* **1.a.** The act of receiving. **b.** The fact of being or having been received. **2.** A quantity or amount received. Often used in the plural. **3.** A written acknowledgment that a given article, sum of money, or shipment has been received. **4.** A recipe. — *v.* **-ceipt•ed, -ceipt•ing, -ceipts.** — *tr.* **1.** To mark (a bill) as having been paid. **2.** To give or write a receipt for (money, goods, or services delivered). — *intr.* To give a receipt. [ME *receite* < ONFr. < Med.Lat. *recepta*, medical prescription, money received < Lat., fem. p.part. of *recipere*, to receive. See RECEIVE.]

re•ceiv•a•ble (rĭ-sē′və-bəl) *adj.* **1.** Suitable for being received or accepted, esp. as payment. **2.** Awaiting or requiring payment; due or collectible. — *n.* A business asset due to one business from another. Often used in the plural.

re•ceive (rĭ-sēv′) *v.* **-ceived, -ceiv•ing, -ceives.** — *tr.* **1.** To take or acquire (something given, offered, or transmitted); get. **2.** To hear or see (information, for example). **3.** To have (a title, for example) bestowed on oneself. **4.** To meet with; experience. **5.** To have inflicted or imposed on oneself. **6.** To bear the weight or force of; support. **7.** To take or intercept the impact of (a blow, for example). **8.** To take in, hold, or contain. **9.** To admit: *receive new members.* **10.** To greet or welcome. **11.** To perceive or acquire mentally. **12.** To regard with approval or disapproval. **13.** To listen to and acknowledge formally and authoritatively. — *intr.* **1.** To acquire or get something; be a recipient. **2.** To admit or welcome guests or visitors. **3.** To partake of the Eucharist. **4.** *Electron.* To convert incoming electromagnetic waves into visible or audible signals. **5.** *Football.* To catch or take possession of a kicked ball. [ME *receiven* < ONFr. *receivre* < Lat. *recipere* : *re-*, re- + *capere*, to take; see **kap-*.**]

re•ceived (rĭ-sēvd′) *adj.* Accepted as true or worthy.

Re•ceived Pronunciation (rĭ-sēvd′) *n.* The prestigious pronunciation of British English based on southern English speech, at one time characteristic of the English spoken at the public schools and Oxford and Cambridge Universities and the standard form of English used in broadcasting.

Received Standard English *n.* British English characterized esp. by Received Pronunciation.

re•ceiv•er (rĭ-sē′vər) *n.* **1.** One that receives something: *a receiver of gifts.* **2.** *Electron.* A device, such as a part of a radio or telephone, that converts incoming radio or electric signals to perceptible forms, such as sound. **3.** An official appointed to receive and account for money due. **4.** *Law.* A person appointed by a court administrator to take into custody the property or funds of others, pending litigation. **5.** One who knowingly buys or receives stolen goods. **6.** A receptacle intended for a specific purpose. **7.** *Football.* A member of the offensive team eligible to catch a forward pass.

re•ceiv•er•ship (rĭ-sē′vər-shĭp′) *n. Law.* **1.** The office or functions of a receiver. **2.** The state of being held by a receiver.

re•ceiv•ing blanket (rĭ-sē′vĭng) *n.* A lightweight blanket used to wrap a baby esp. after a bath.

receiving line *n.* A line of people formed to greet arriving guests individually, as at a formal gathering.

re•cen•sion (rĭ-sĕn′shən) *n.* **1.** A critical revision of a text incorporating the most plausible elements from varying sources. **2.** A text so revised. [Lat. *recēnsiō, recēnsiōn-*, a reviewing

ă pat	oi boy
ā pay	ou out
âr care	o͝o took
ä father	o͞o boot
ĕ pet	ŭ cut
ē be	ûr urge
ĭ pit	th thin
ī pie	*th* this
îr pier	hw which
ŏ pot	zh vision
ō toe	ə about, item
ô paw	

Stress marks:
′ (primary);
′ (secondary), as in
dictionary (dĭk′shə-nĕr′ē)

< *recēnsēre*, to review : *re-*, re- + *cēnsēre*, to estimate; see **kens-***.]

re•cent (rē′sənt) *adj.* **1.** Of, belonging to, or occurring at a time immediately before the present. **2.** Modern; new. **3. Recent.** *Geol.* Of, belonging to, or being the Holocene Epoch. See table at **geologic time.** [ME, new, fresh < Lat. *recēns, recent-.* See **ken-***.] **—re′cen•cy, re′cent•ness** *n.* **—re′cent•ly** *adv.*

re•cep•ta•cle (rĭ-sĕp′tə-kəl) *n.* **1.** A container that holds items or matter. **2.** *Bot.* The expanded tip of a flower stalk or axis that bears the floral organs or the group of flowers in a head. **3.** *Electron.* A fitting connected to a power supply and equipped to receive a plug. [ME < OFr. < Lat. *receptāculum* < *receptāre*, to receive again, freq. of *recipere*, to receive. See RECEIVE.]

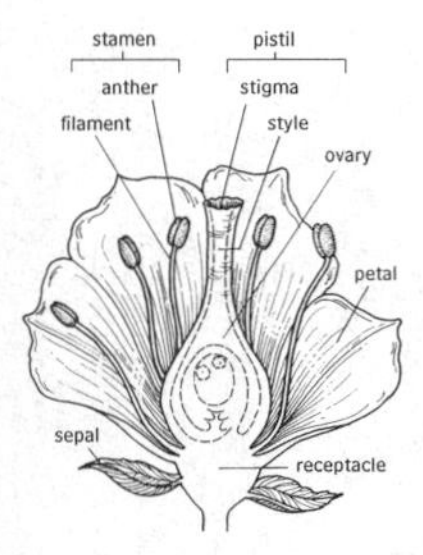

receptacle

re•cep•tion (rĭ-sĕp′shən) *n.* **1.** The act or process of receiving or of being received. **2.** A welcome, greeting, or acceptance. **3.** A social function, esp. one intended to provide a welcome or greeting. **4.** Mental approval or acceptance. **5.** *Electron.* **a.** Conversion of transmitted radio waves or electric signals into perceptible forms, such as light, by means of antennas and electronic equipment. **b.** The condition or quality of the waves or signals so received. [Ult. < Lat. *receptiō, receptiōn-* < *receptus*, p.part. of *recipere*, to receive. See RECEIVE.]

re•cep•tion•ist (rĭ-sĕp′shə-nĭst) *n.* An office worker employed chiefly to receive visitors and answer the telephone.

re•cep•tive (rĭ-sĕp′tĭv) *adj.* **1.** Capable of or qualifed for receiving. **2.** Ready or willing to receive favorably. **3.** Of or relating to the skills of listening and reading. **—re•cep′tive•ly** *adv.* **—re′cep•tiv′i•ty, re•cep′tive•ness** *n.*

re•cep•tor (rĭ-sĕp′tər) *n.* **1.** *Physiol.* A specialized cell or group of nerve endings that responds to sensory stimuli. **2.** *Biochem.* A molecular structure or site on the surface or inside a cell that binds with substances such as hormones or drugs.

re•cer•ti•fy (rē-sûr′tə-fī′) *tr.v.* **-fied, -fy•ing, -fies.** To renew the certification of, esp. certification given by a licensing board. **—re′cer•ti•fi•ca′tion** (-fĭ-kā′shən) *n.*

re•cess (rē′sĕs′, rĭ-sĕs′) *n.* **1.a.** A temporary cessation of the customary activities of an engagement, occupation, or pursuit. **b.** The period of such cessation. See Syns at **pause. 2.** A remote, secret, or secluded place. Often used in the plural. **3.a.** An indentation or small hollow. **b.** An alcove. *—v.* **-cessed, -cess•ing, -cess•es.** *—tr.* **1.** To place in a recess. **2.** To create a recess in: *recessed the wall.* **3.** To suspend for a recess: *recessed the hearings.* *—intr.* To take a recess. [Lat. *recessus*, retreat < p.part. of *recēdere*, to recede. See RECEDE.]

re•ces•sion (rĭ-sĕsh′ən) *n.* **1.** The act of withdrawing or going back. **2.** An extended decline in business, typically three consecutive quarters of falling gross national product. **3.** The withdrawal in a line or file of participants in a ceremony, esp. clerics and choir members after a church service.

re-ces•sion (rē-sĕsh′ən) *n. Law.* The act of restoring possession to a former owner.

re•ces•sion•al (rĭ-sĕsh′ə-nəl) *n.* **1.** *Mus.* A hymn that accompanies the exit of the clergy and choir after a service. **2.** A recession from a church. *—adj.* Of or relating to a recession.

re•ces•sive (rĭ-sĕs′ĭv) *adj.* **1.** Tending to go backward or recede. **2.a.** *Genet.* Of, relating to, or being an allele that does not produce a characteristic effect when present with a dominant allele. **b.** Of or relating to a trait that is expressed only when the determining allele is present in the homozygous condition. *—n. Genet.* **1.** A recessive allele or trait. **2.** An organism having a recessive trait. **—re•ces′sive•ly** *adv.* **—re•ces′sive•ness** *n.*

re•charge (rē-chärj′) *tr.v.* **-charged, -charg•ing, -charg•es.** To charge again, esp. to reenergize a storage battery. **—re′-charge′** *n.* **—re•charge′a•ble** *adj.* **—re•charg′er** *n.*

ré•chauf•fé (rā′shō-fā′) *n.* **1.** Warmed leftover food. **2.** Revised old material. [Fr., p.part. of *réchauffer*, to reheat, warm over < OFr. *rechaufer* : *re-*, re- + *echaufer*, to warm (< VLat. **excalefāre* : Lat. *ex-*, intensive pref.; see EX- + Lat. *calefacere*, to warm; see CHAFE).]

re•cher•ché (rə-shĕr′shā′) *adj.* **1.** Uncommon; rare. **2.** Exquisite; choice. **3.** Overrefined; forced. **4.** Pretentious; overblown. [Fr., p.part. of *rechercher*, to research < OFr. *recercher.* See RESEARCH.]

re•cid•i•vism (rĭ-sĭd′ə-vĭz′əm) *n.* A tendency to lapse into a previous pattern of behavior, esp. a tendency to return to criminal habits. [< RECIDIVIST < Fr. *récidiviste* < *récidiver*, to relapse < Med.Lat. *recidīvāre* < Lat. *recidīvus*, falling back < *recidere*, to fall back : *re-*, re- + *cadere*, to fall; see **kad-***.] **—re•cid′i•vist** *n.* **—re•cid′i•vis′tic, re•cid′i•vous** *adj.*

Re•ci•fe (rə-sē′fə). A city of NE Brazil on the Atlantic Ocean S of Natal; first settled in 1535. Pop. 1,203,899.

recip. *abbr.* Reciprocal; reciprocity.

rec•i•pe (rĕs′ə-pē′) *n.* **1.** A set of directions with a list of ingredients for making something, esp. food. **2.** A formula for or means to a goal. **3.** A medical prescription. [Lat., imper. of *recipere*, to take, receive. See RECEIVE.]

re•cip•i•ence (rĭ-sĭp′ē-əns) also **re•cip•i•en•cy** (-ən-sē) *n.* Capacity to receive; receptivity.

re•cip•i•ent (rĭ-sĭp′ē-ənt) *adj.* Functioning as a receiver; receptive. *—n.* **1.** One that receives or is receptive. **2.** One who receives blood, tissue, or an organ from a donor. [Lat. *recipiēns, recipient-*, pr.part. of *recipere*, to receive. See RECEIVE.]

re•cip•ro•cal (rĭ-sĭp′rə-kəl) *adj.* **1.** Concerning each of two or more persons or things. **2.** Interchanged, given, or owed to each other: *a reciprocal invitation.* **3.** Performed, experienced, or felt by both sides: *reciprocal respect.* **4.** Interchangeable; complementary: *reciprocal electric outlets.* **5.** *Gram.* Expressing mutual action or relationship. Used of some verbs and compound pronouns. **6.** *Math.* Of or relating to the reciprocal of a quantity. **7.** *Physiol.* Of or relating to a neuromuscular phenomenon in which the inhibition of one group of muscles accompanies the excitation of another. **8.** *Genet.* Of or being a pair of crosses in which the male parent in one cross is of the same genotype or phenotype as the female parent in the other cross. *—n.* **1.** Something that is reciprocal to something else. **2.** *Math.* A number related to another so that when multiplied together their product is 1. For example, the reciprocal of 7 is 1/7. [< Lat. *reciprocus*, alternating. See **per**[1]***.] **—re•cip′ro•cal′i•ty** (-kăl′ĭ-tē), **re•cip′ro•cal•ness** (-kəl-nĭs) *n.* **—re•cip′ro•cal•ly** *adv.*

reciprocal pronoun *n. Gram.* A pronoun or pronominal phrase, such as *each other,* that expresses mutual action or relationship.

re•cip•ro•cate (rĭ-sĭp′rə-kāt′) *v.* **-cat•ed, -cat•ing, -cates.** *—tr.* **1.** To give or take mutually; interchange. **2.** To show, feel, or give in return. *—intr.* **1.** To move back and forth alternately. **2.** To give and take something mutually. **3.** To make a return for something given or done. **4.** To be complementary or equivalent. [Lat. *reciprocāre, reciprocāt-*, to move back and forth < *reciprocus*, alternating. See RECIPROCAL.] **—re•cip′ro•ca′tive** *adj.* **—re•cip′ro•ca′tor** *n.*

Syns: *reciprocate, requite, return.* The central meaning shared by these verbs is "to give, take, or feel reciprocally": *doesn't reciprocate favors; service requited with favor; return a compliment.*

re•cip•ro•cat•ing engine (rĭ-sĭp′rə-kā′tĭng) *n.* An engine in which the crankshaft is turned by pistons moving up and down in a cylinder.

re•cip•ro•ca•tion (rĭ-sĭp′rə-kā′shən) *n.* **1.** An alternating back-and-forth movement. **2.** The act or fact of reciprocating.

rec•i•proc•i•ty (rĕs′ə-prŏs′ĭ-tē) *n., pl.* **-ties. 1.** A reciprocal condition or relationship. **2.** A mutual or cooperative interchange of favors or privileges, esp. the exchange of trade privileges between nations.

re•ci•sion (rĭ-sĭzh′ən) *n.* The act of rescinding; annulment or cancellation. [Obsolete Fr. < OFr., annulment of a judgment < Lat. *recīsiō, recīsiōn-* < *recīsus*, p.part. of *recīdere*, to cut back : *re-*, re- + *caedere*, to cut; see **kaə-id-***.]

re•cit•al (rĭ-sĭt′l) *n.* **1.** The act of reading or reciting before an audience. **2.** A very detailed account or report; a narration. **3.** A public music or dance performance, esp. a solo. **—re•ci′tal•ist** *n.*

rec•i•ta•tion (rĕs′ĭ-tā′shən) *n.* **1.a.** The act of reciting memorized materials in a public performance. **b.** The material so presented. **2.a.** Oral delivery of prepared lessons by a pupil. **b.** The class period within which this delivery occurs.

rec•i•ta•tive[1] (rĕs′ĭ-tā′tĭv, rĭ-sī′tə-tĭv) *adj.* Of, relating to, or having the character of a recital or recitation.

rec•i•ta•tive[2] (rĕs′ĭ-tə-tēv′) *n. Mus.* **1.** A vocal style in which a text is declaimed in the rhythm of natural speech with slight melodic variation. **2.** A passage thus rendered. [Ital. *recitativo* < *recitare*, to recite < Lat. *recitāre.* See RECITE.]

re•ci•ta•ti•vo (rĕs′ĭ-tə-tē′vō, rĕ′chē-tä-) *n., pl.* **-vi** (-vē) or **-vos** (-vōz). *Mus.* See **recitative**[2]. [Ital. See RECITATIVE[2].]

re•cite (rĭ-sīt′) *v.* **-cit•ed, -cit•ing, -cites.** *—tr.* **1.** To repeat or utter aloud (something rehearsed or memorized), esp. before an audience. **2.** To relate in detail. **3.** To list or enumerate. *—intr.* **1.** To deliver a recitation. **2.** To repeat lessons prepared or memorized. [ME *reciten* < OFr. *reciter* < Lat. *recitāre*, to read out : *re-*, re- + *citāre*, to quote; see CITE.] **—re•cit′er** *n.*

reck (rĕk) *tr. & intr.v.* **recked, reck•ing, recks.** To take heed of or to have caution. [ME *recken* < OE *reccan.* See **reg-***.]

reck•less (rĕk′lĭs) *adj.* **1.a.** Heedless or careless. **b.** Headstrong; rash. **2.** Indifferent to or disregardful of consequences: *a reckless driver.* [ME *reckeles* < OE *rēcelēas.* See **reg-***.] **—reck′less•ly** *adv.* **—reck′less•ness** *n.*

Reck•ling•hau•sen (rĕk′lĭng-hou′zən). A city of W-central Germany SW of Münster. Pop. 117,989.

reck•on (rĕk′ən) *v.* **-oned, -on•ing, -ons.** *—tr.* **1.** To count or compute: *reckon the cost.* **2.** To consider as being; regard as. **3.** *Informal.* To think or assume. *—intr.* **1.** To make a calculation; figure. **2.** To rely with confident expectancy. ***—phrasal verb.* reckon with.** To come to terms or settle accounts with. [ME *reknen* < OE *gerecenian*, to recount, arrange. See **reg-***.]

reck•on•ing (rĕk′ə-nĭng) *n.* **1.** The act of counting or computing. **2.** An itemized bill or statement of a sum due. **3.** A settlement of accounts. **4.a.** The act or process of calculating the position of a ship or an aircraft. **b.** This position.

re•claim (rĭ-klām′) *tr.v.* **-claimed, -claim•ing, -claims. 1.** To bring into or return to a suitable condition for use, as cultivation or habitation. **2.** To procure (usable substances) from refuse or waste products. **3.** To bring back, as from error, to a right or proper course; reform. **4.** To tame (a falcon, for example). [ME *reclamen*, to call back < OFr. *reclamer*, to entreat < Lat. *reclāmāre* : *re-*, re- + *clāmāre*, to cry out; see **kelə-²*.**] **—re•claim′a•ble** *adj.* **—re•claim′ant, re•claim′er** *n.*

re-claim (rē-klām′) *tr.v.* **-claimed, -claim•ing, -claims.** To demand the restoration or return of (a possession, for example); claim again or back.

rec•la•ma•tion (rĕk′lə-mā′shən) *n.* **1.** The act or process of reclaiming. **2.** A restoration, as to usefulness or morality. [ME *reclamacion* < OFr. *reclamation* < Lat. *reclāmātiō*, *reclāmātiōn-*, cry of opposition < *reclāmātus*, p.part. of *reclāmāre*, to exclaim against. See RECLAIM.]

ré•clame (rā-klăm′) *n.* **1.** Public acclaim. **2.** A taste or flair for publicity. [Fr., advertising < *réclamer*, to claim, beg for < OFr. *reclamer*, to exclaim against. See RECLAIM.]

rec•li•nate (rĕk′lə-nāt′) *adj.* *Bot.* Bent or turned downward toward the base. [Lat. *reclīnātus*, p.part. of *reclīnāre*, to recline. See RECLINE.]

re•cline (rĭ-klīn′) *v.* **-clined, -clin•ing, -clines.** *—tr.* To cause to assume a leaning or prone position. *—intr.* To lie back or down. [ME *reclinen* < OFr. *recliner* < Lat. *reclīnāre* : *re-*, re- + *-clīnāre*, to bend; see **klei-*.**] **—rec′li•na′tion** (rĕk′lə-nā′shən) *n.*

re•clin•er (rĭ-klī′nər) *n.* One that reclines, as an armchair that reclines when its back is lowered and its front raised.

re•cluse (rĕk′lo͞os′, rĭ-klo͞os′) *n.* A person who withdraws from the world to live in seclusion and often in solitude. *—adj.* Withdrawn from the world; reclusive. [ME < OFr. *reclus* < Lat. *reclūsus*, p.part. of *reclūdere*, to shut up : *re-*, re- + *claudere*, to close.]

re•clu•sion (rĭ-klo͞o′zhən) *n.* **1.** The condition of being a recluse. **2.** The state of being in solitary confinement.

re•clu•sive (rĭ-klo͞o′sĭv, -zĭv) *adj.* **1.** Seeking or preferring seclusion or isolation. **2.** Providing seclusion: *a reclusive hut.* **—re•clu′sive•ly** *adv.* **—re•clu′sive•ness** *n.*

rec•og•ni•tion (rĕk′əg-nĭsh′ən) *n.* **1.** The act of recognizing or condition of being recognized. **2.** An awareness that something perceived has been perceived before. **3.** An acceptance as true or valid, as of a claim. **4.** Attention or favorable notice. **5.** Official acceptance of the national status of a new government by another nation. **6.** *Biol.* The ability of one molecule to attach itself to another molecule having a complementary shape. [Ult. < Lat. *recognitiō*, *recognitiōn-*, act of recognizing < *recognitus*, p.part. of *recognōscere*, to recognize. See RECOGNIZE.] **—re•cog′ni•to′ry** (rĭ-kŏg′nĭ-tôr′ē, -tōr′ē), **re•cog′ni•tive** (-tĭv) *adj.*

re•cog•ni•zance (rĭ-kŏg′nĭ-zəns, -kŏn′ĭ-) *n.* **1.** *Law.* **a.** An obligation of record that is entered into before a court or magistrate, containing a condition to perform a particular act, such as appearing in court. **b.** A sum of money pledged to assure such an act. **2.** A recognition. **3.** *Archaic.* A pledge; a token. [ME *recognisanze* < OFr. *recognuissance*, alteration of *reconoissance* < *reconoistre*, *reconoiss-*, to recognize. See RECOGNIZE.] **—re•cog′ni•zant** *adj.*

rec•og•nize (rĕk′əg-nīz′) *tr.v.* **-nized, -niz•ing, -niz•es. 1.** To know to be something that has been perceived before. **2.** To know or identify from past experience or knowledge: *recognize hostility.* **3.** To perceive or show acceptance of the validity or reality of. **4.** To permit to address a meeting. **5.** To accept officially the national status of as a new government. **6.** To show awareness of; approve of or appreciate. **7.** To admit the acquaintance of, as by salutation. **8.** *Biol.* To exhibit recognition for (an antigen, for example). [ME *recognisen*, to resume possession of land, alteration (influenced by Med.Lat. *recognizāre*, to recognize) of OFr. *reconoistre*, *reconoiss-*, to know again < Lat. *recognōscere* : *re-*, re- + *cognōscere*, to get to know; see **gnō-*.**] **—rec′og•niz′a•ble** *adj.* **—rec′og•niz′a•bly** *adv.* **—rec′og•niz′er** *n.*

re•coil (rĭ-koil′) *intr.v.* **-coiled, -coil•ing, -coils. 1.** To spring back, as upon firing. **2.** To shrink back, as in fear. **3.** To fall back; return. *—n.* (*also* rē′koil′). **1.** The backward action of a firearm upon firing. **2.** The act or state of recoiling. [ME *recoilen* < OFr. *reculer* : *re-*, re- + *cul*, buttocks (< Lat. *cūlus*; see **(s)keu-***).] **—re•coil′er** *n.*

re•coil•less (rĭ-koil′lĭs, rē′koil′-) *adj.* Of or being a weapon designed to minimize the effect of recoil: *a recoilless rifle.*

rec•ol•lect (rĕk′ə-lĕkt′) *v.* **-lect•ed, -lect•ing, -lects.** *—tr.* To recall to mind. See Syns at **remember.** *—intr.* To have a recollection. [Med.Lat. *recolligere*, *recollēct-* < Lat., to gather up : *re-*, re- + *colligere*, to collect; see COLLECT¹.] **—rec′ol•lec′tive** *adj.* **—rec′ol•lec′tive•ly** *adv.*

re-col•lect (rē′kə-lĕkt′) *tr.v.* **-lect•ed, -lect•ing, -lects. 1.** To collect again. **2.** To calm or control (oneself).

rec•ol•lec•tion (rĕk′ə-lĕk′shən) *n.* **1.** The act or power of recollecting. **2.** Something recollected. See Syns at **memory.**

re•com•bi•nant (rē-kŏm′bə-nənt) *Genet.* *—n.* **1.** An organism or a cell in which genetic recombination has taken place. **2.** Genetic material produced by gene-splicing. *—adj.* **1.** Formed by or showing recombination: *a recombinant chromosome.* **2.** Of or relating to recombinant DNA.

recombinant DNA *n.* Genetically engineered DNA prepared by transplanting or splicing genes from one species into the cells of a host organism of a different species.

re•com•bi•nase (rē-kŏm′bə-nās′, -nāz′) *n.* An enzyme that catalyzes genetic recombination.

re•com•bi•na•tion (rē′kŏm-bə-nā′shən) *n.* The natural formation in offspring of genetic combinations not present in parents, by the processes of crossing over or independent assortment.

re•com•bine (rē′kəm-bīn′) *v.* **-bined, -bin•ing, -bines.** *—tr.* To combine (things) again. *—intr.* **1.** To combine again. **2.** *Genet.* To undergo or cause recombination.

rec•om•mend (rĕk′ə-mĕnd′) *v.* **-mend•ed, -mend•ing, -mends.** *—tr.* **1.** To praise or commend (one) to another as being worthy or desirable; endorse. **2.** To make (the possessor, as of an attribute) attractive or acceptable. **3.** To commit to the charge of another; entrust. **4.** To advise or counsel. *—intr.* To give advice or counsel. [ME *recomenden* < Med. Lat. *recommendāre* : Lat. *re-*, re- + Lat. *commendāre*, to entrust, commend; see COMMEND.] **—rec′om•mend′a•ble** *adj.* **—rec′om•mend′er** *n.*

rec•om•men•da•tion (rĕk′ə-mĕn-dā′shən) *n.* **1.** The act of recommending. **2.** Something that recommends, esp. a favorable statement concerning character or qualifications. **3.** Something, such as a course of action, that is recommended. See Syns at **advice.** **—rec′om•men′da•to′ry** (-də-tôr′ē, -tōr′ē) *adj.*

re•com•mit (rē′kə-mĭt′) *tr.v.* **-mit•ted, -mit•ting, -mits. 1.** To commit again. **2.** To refer (proposed bills, for example) to a committee again. **—re′com•mit′ment, re′com•mit′tal** (-mĭt′l) *n.*

rec•om•pense (rĕk′əm-pĕns′) *tr.v.* **-pensed, -pens•ing, -pens•es. 1.** To award compensation to: *recompensed those injured.* **2.** To award compensation for; make a return for. *—n.* **1.** Amends made, as for loss. **2.** Payment in return for something, such as a service. [ME *recompensen* < OFr. *recompenser* < LLat. *recompēnsāre* : Lat. *re-*, re- + Lat. *compēnsāre*, to compensate; see COMPENSATE.]

re•con¹ (rē′kŏn′) *n.* The smallest genetic unit capable of recombination. [REC(OMBINATION) + -ON¹.]

re•con² (rē′kŏn′) *n.* *Informal.* Reconnaissance.

rec•on•cil•a•ble (rĕk′ən-sī′lə-bəl, rĕk′ən-sī′-) *adj.* Capable of or qualified for reconciliation. **—rec′on•cil′a•bil′i•ty, rec′on•cil′a•ble•ness** *n.* **—rec′on•cil′a•bly** *adv.*

rec•on•cile (rĕk′ən-sīl′) *v.* **-ciled, -cil•ing, -ciles.** *—tr.* **1.** To reestablish a close relationship between. **2.** To settle or resolve. **3.** To bring (oneself) to accept. **4.** To make compatible or consistent. See Syns at **adapt.** *—intr.* **1.** To reestablish a close relationship, as in marriage. **2.** To become compatible or consistent. [ME *reconcilen* < OFr. *reconcilier* < Lat. *reconciliāre* : *re-*, re- + *conciliāre*, to conciliate; see CONCILIATE.] **—rec′on•cile′ment** *n.* **—rec′on•cil′er** *n.* **—rec′on•cil′i•a•to′ry** (-sĭl′ē-ə-tôr′ē, -tōr′ē) *adj.*

rec•on•cil•i•a•tion (rĕk′ən-sĭl′ē-ā′shən) *n.* **1.** The act of reconciling. **2.** The condition of being reconciled. **3.** See **penance** 2. [Ult. < Lat. *reconciliātiō*, *reconciliātiōn-* < *reconciliātus*, p.part. of *reconciliāre*, to reconcile. See RECONCILE.]

rec•on•dite (rĕk′ən-dīt′, rĭ-kŏn′dīt′) *adj.* **1.** Not easily understood; abstruse. See Syns at **ambiguous. 2.** Concerned with or treating something abstruse or obscure. **3.** Concealed; hidden. [Lat. *reconditus*, p.part. of *recondere*, to put away : *re-*, re- + *condere*, to put together, preserve; see **dhē-*.**] **—rec′on•dite′ly** *adv.* **—rec′on•dite′ness** *n.*

re•con•di•tion (rē′kən-dĭsh′ən) *tr.v.* **-tioned, -tion•ing, -tions.** To restore to good condition, esp. by repairing, renovating, or rebuilding.

re•con•nais•sance also **re•con•nois•sance** (rĭ-kŏn′ə-səns, -zəns) *n.* An inspection or exploration of an area, esp. one made to gather military information. [Fr. < OFr. *reconoissance*, recognition < *reconoistre*, *reconoiss-*, to recognize. See RECOGNIZE.]

re•con•noi•ter (rē′kə-noi′tər, rĕk′ə-) *v.* **-tered, -ter•ing, -ters.** *—tr.* To make a preliminary inspection of, esp. in order to gather military information. *—intr.* To make a reconnaissance. [Obsolete Fr. *reconnoître* < OFr. *reconoistre*, to recognize. See RECOGNIZE.] **—re′con•noi′ter•er** *n.*

re•con•sti•tute (rē-kŏn′stĭ-to͞ot′, -tyo͞ot′) *tr.v.* **-tut•ed, -tut•ing, -tutes. 1.** To provide with a new structure. **2.** To bring (a liquid in concentrated or powder form) to normal strength by adding water.

re•con•struct (rē′kən-strŭkt′) *tr.v.* **-struct•ed, -struct•ing, -structs. 1.** To construct again. **2.** To cause to adapt to social or economic change. **—re′con•struc′ti•ble** *adj.*

re•con•struc•tion (rē′kən-strŭk′shən) *n.* **1.** The act or result of reconstructing. **2. Reconstruction.** The period (1865–1877) when the federal government ruled the Confederate states before readmitting them to the Union. **—re′con•struc′tive** *adj.*

Re•con•struc•tion•ism (rē′kən-strŭk′shə-nĭz′əm) *n.* *Juda-*

ă pat	oi boy
ā pay	ou out
âr care	o͝o took
ä father	o͞o boot
ĕ pet	ŭ cut
ē be	ûr urge
ĭ pit	th thin
ī pie	*th* this
îr pier	hw which
ŏ pot	zh vision
ō toe	ə about, item
ô paw	

Stress marks:
′ (primary);
′ (secondary), as in
dictionary (dĭk′shə-nĕr′ē)

ism. The branch of Judaism founded in the United States in the 20th century that regards Judaism as a religious civilization and questions the doctrine that the Jews are God's chosen people. — **Re′con•struc′tion•ist** *adj. & n.*

re•con•vert (rē′kən-vûrt′) *intr. & tr.v.* **-vert•ed, -vert•ing, -verts.** To undergo or cause to undergo conversion to a previous state or condition. — **re′con•ver′sion** (-vûr′zhən, -shən) *n.*

re•con•vey (rē′kən-vā′) *tr.v.* **-veyed, -vey•ing, -veys.** To convey to a former owner or place. — **re′con•vey′ance** *n.*

re•cord (rĭ-kôrd′) *v.* **-cord•ed, -cord•ing, -cords.** — *tr.* **1.** To set down for preservation in writing or other permanent form. **2.** To register or indicate: *recorded the votes.* **3.a.** To register (sound or images) in permanent form by mechanical or electrical means for reproduction. **b.** To register the words, sound, appearance, or performance of by such means. — *intr.* To record something. — *n.* **rec•ord.** (rĕk′ərd). **1.a.** An account, as of facts, set down esp. in writing as a means of preserving knowledge. **b.** Something on which such an account is based. **c.** Something that records: *a fossil record.* **2.** Information on a particular subject collected and preserved: *the coldest day on record.* **3.** The known history of performance, activities, or achievement: *a police record.* **4.** An unsurpassed measurement. **5.** *Comp. Sci.* A collection of related, often adjacent items of data, treated as a unit. **6.** *Law.* **a.** An account officially written and preserved as evidence or testimony. **b.** An account of judicial or legislative proceedings written and preserved as evidence. **c.** The documents or volumes containing such evidence. **7.a.** A disk designed to be played on a phonograph. **b.** Something, such as magnetic tape, on which sound or visual images have been recorded. — ***idioms.*** **go on record.** To embrace a certain position publicly. **off the record.** Not for publication. **on record.** Known to have been stated or to have taken a certain position. [ME *recorden* < OFr. *recorder* < Lat. *recordārī,* to remember : *re-,* re- + *cor, cord-,* heart; see **kerd-*.**]

recorder

rec•ord changer (rĕk′ərd) *n.* A device on a phonograph that plays in turn records stacked on the spindle.

re•cord•er (rĭ-kôr′dər) *n.* **1.** One, such as a tape recorder, that makes recordings or records. **2.** *Mus.* A flute with eight finger holes and a whistlelike mouthpiece. [Sense 2, prob. < RECORD, to practice a tune, warble.]

re•cord•ing (rĭ-kôr′dĭng) *n.* **1.** Something on which sound or visual images have been recorded. **2.** A recorded sound or image or group of sounds or images.

re•cord•ist (rĭ-kôr′dĭst) *n.* One that records sound electronically, as for films or at concerts.

re•count (rĭ-kount′) *tr.v.* **-count•ed, -count•ing, -counts. 1.** To narrate the facts or particulars of. **2.** To enumerate. [ME *recounten* < OFr. *reconter* : *re-,* re- + *conter,* relate; see COUNT[1].] — **re•count′al** *n.*

re-count (rē-kount′) *tr.v.* **-count•ed, -count•ing, -counts.** To count again. — *n.* (*also* rē′kount′). An additional count, esp. a second count of votes cast in an election.

re•coup (rĭ-ko͞op′) *v.* **-couped, -coup•ing, -coups.** — *tr.* **1.** To receive an equivalent for; make up for: *recoup a loss.* See Syns at **recover. 2.** To return as an equivalent for; reimburse. **3.** *Law.* To deduct or withhold (part of something due) for an equitable reason. — *intr.* To regain a favorable position. — *n.* The act of recouping. [ME *recoupen* < OFr. *recouper,* to cut back : *re-,* re- + *couper,* to cut (< *coup,* blow; see COUP).] — **re•coup′a•ble** *adj.* — **re•coup′ment** *n.*

re•course (rē′kôrs′, -kōrs′, rĭ-kôrs′, -kōrs′) *n.* **1.** The act or an instance of turning or applying to a person or thing for aid or security. **2.** One that is turned or applied to for aid or security: *His only recourse was the police.* **3.** *Law.* The right to demand payment from the endorser of a commercial paper when the first party liable fails to pay. [ME *recours* < OFr. < Lat. *recursus,* a running back < p.part. of *recurrere,* to run back : *re-,* re- + *currere,* to run; see **kers-*.**]

re•cov•er (rĭ-kŭv′ər) *v.* **-ered, -er•ing, -ers.** — *tr.* **1.** To get back; regain. **2.** To restore (oneself) to a normal state. **3.** To compensate for: *recovered her losses.* **4.** To procure (usable substances, such as metal) from unusable substances, such as ore or waste. **5.** To bring under observation again. — *intr.* **1.** To regain a normal or usual condition, as of health. **2.** To receive a favorable judgment in a lawsuit. [ME *recoveren* < OFr. *recoverer* < Lat. *recuperāre.* See RECUPERATE.] — **re•cov′er•a•ble** *adj.* — **re•cov′er•er** *n.*

Syns: *recover, regain, recoup, retrieve.* These verbs mean to get back something lost or taken away. *Recover* is the least specific: *"In a few days Mr. Barnstaple had recovered strength of body and mind"* (H.G. Wells). *Regain* suggests success in recovering something that has been taken from one: *"hopeful to regain/Thy Love"* (John Milton). To *recoup* is to get back the equivalent of something lost: *recouped her expenses. Retrieve* pertains to the effortful recovery of something (*retrieved the ball*) or to the making good of something gone awry: *"By a brilliant coup he has retrieved . . . a rather serious loss"* (Samuel Butler).

re-cov•er (rē-kŭv′ər) *tr.v.* **-ered, -er•ing, -ers.** To cover anew: *re-cover an armchair.*

re•cov•er•y (rĭ-kŭv′ə-rē) *n., pl.* **-ies. 1.** The act, process, duration, or an instance of recovering. **2.** A return to a normal condition. **3.** Something gained or restored in recovering. **4.** The act of obtaining usable substances from unusable sources.

recovery room *n.* A hospital room equipped for the care and observation of patients immediately following surgery.

rec•re•ant (rĕk′rē-ənt) *adj.* **1.** Unfaithful or disloyal to a belief, duty, or cause. **2.** Craven or cowardly. — *n.* **1.** A faithless or disloyal person. **2.** A coward. [ME < OFr., pr.part. of *recroire,* to remember < Med.Lat. *recrēdere,* to yield, pledge : Lat. *re-,* re- + Lat. *crēdere,* to believe; see **kerd-*.**] — **rec′re•ance, rec′re•an•cy** *n.* — **rec′re•ant•ly** *adv.*

rec•re•ate (rĕk′rē-āt′) *v.* **-at•ed, -at•ing, -ates.** — *tr.* To impart fresh life to; refresh mentally or physically. — *intr.* To take recreation. [ME *recreaten* < Lat. *recreāre, recreāt-* : *re-,* re- + *creāre,* to create; see CREATE.] — **rec′re•a′tive** *adj.*

re-cre•ate (rē′krē-āt′) *tr.v.* **-at•ed, -at•ing, -ates.** To create anew.

rec•re•a•tion (rĕk′rē-ā′shən) *n.* Refreshment of one's mind or body through activity that amuses or stimulates; play. — **rec′re•a′tion•al** *adj.* — **rec′re•a′tion•al•ly** *adv.*

recreational vehicle *n.* A vehicle, such as a motor home, used for traveling and recreational activities.

recreation room *n.* A room in a house or an institution suited for games, dancing, or other kinds of recreation.

rec•re•ment (rĕk′rə-mənt) *n.* Waste matter; dross. [Lat. *recrēmentum* : *re-,* re- + *cernere, crē-,* to separate; see **krei-*.**] — **rec′re•men′tal** (-mĕn′tl) *adj.*

re•crim•i•nate (rĭ-krĭm′ə-nāt′) *v.* **-nat•ed, -nat•ing, -nates.** — *tr.* To accuse in return. — *intr.* To counter one accusation with another. [Med.Lat. *recrīminārī, recrīmināt-* : Lat. *re-,* re- + Lat. *crīmināre,* to accuse (< *crīmen, crīmin-,* accusation, crime; see **krei-***).] — **re•crim′i•na′tive, re•crim′i•na•to′ry** (-nə-tôr′ē, -tōr′ē) *adj.* — **re•crim′i•na′tor** *n.*

re•crim•i•na•tion (rĭ-krĭm′ə-nā′shən) *n.* **1.** The act of recriminating. **2.** A countercharge.

rec room (rĕk) *n. Informal.* A recreation room.

re•cru•desce (rē′kro͞o-dĕs′) *intr.v.* **-desced, -desc•ing, -desc•es.** To break out anew or come into renewed activity, as after quiescence. [Lat. *recrūdēscere,* to grow raw again : *re-,* re- + *crūdēscere,* to get worse (< *crūdus,* raw; see **kreuə-***).] — **re′cru•des′cence** *n.* — **re′cru•des′cent** *adj.*

re•cruit (rĭ-kro͞ot′) *v.* **-cruit•ed, -cruit•ing, -cruits.** — *tr.* **1.** To engage (persons) for military service. **2.** To strengthen or raise (an armed force) by enlistment. **3.** To supply with new members or employees. **4.** To enroll or seek to enroll: *colleges recruiting students.* **5.** To replenish. **6.** To renew or restore the health, vitality, or intensity of. — *intr.* **1.** To raise a military force. **2.** To obtain replacements for or new supplies of something lost, wasted, or needed. **3.** To regain lost health or strength; recover. — *n.* **1.** A newly engaged member of a military force, esp. of the lowest level. **2.** A new member of an organization or a body. [Fr. *recruter* < obsolete *recrute,* recruit, var. of *recrue* < fem. p.part. of *recroître,* to grow again < OFr. *recroistre* : *re-,* re- + *croistre,* to grow (< Lat. *crēscere;* see **ker-[2]***).] — **re•cruit′er** *n.* — **re•cruit′ment** *n.*

rec. sec. *abbr.* Recording secretary.

rect. *abbr.* **1.** Receipt. **2.** Rectangle; rectangular. **3.** Rectified.

rec•ta (rĕk′tə) *n.* Pl. of **rectum.**

rec•tal (rĕk′təl) *adj.* Of, relating to, or situated near the rectum. — **rec′tal•ly** *adv.*

rec•tan•gle (rĕk′tăng′gəl) *n.* A four-sided plane figure with four right angles. [Fr. < Med.Lat. *rēctangulum,* a right triangle < LLat. *rēctiangulum* : Lat. *rēctus,* right; see **reg-*** + Lat. *angulus,* angle.]

rec•tan•gu•lar (rĕk-tăng′gyə-lər) *adj.* **1.** Having the shape of a rectangle. **2.** Having one or more right angles. **3.** Relating to or being a geometric coordinate system with mutually perpendicular axes. — **rec•tan′gu•lar′i•ty** (-lăr′ĭ-tē) *n.* — **rec•tan′gu•lar•ly** *adv.*

rectangular coordinate *n. Math.* A coordinate in a rectangular Cartesian coordinate system.

rec•ti•fi•er (rĕk′tə-fī′ər) *n.* **1.** One that corrects errors or rights wrongs. **2.** *Electron.* A device that converts alternating current to direct current. **3.** One who rectifies alcoholic beverages.

rec•ti•fy (rĕk′tə-fī′) *tr.v.* **-fied, -fy•ing, -fies. 1.** To set right; correct. **2.** To correct by calculation or adjustment. See Syns at **correct. 3.** *Chem.* To refine or purify, esp. by distillation. **4.** *Electron.* To convert (alternating current) into direct current. **5.** To adjust (the proof of alcoholic beverages) by adding liquid. [ME *rectifien* < OFr. *rectifier* < Med.Lat. *rēctificāre* : Lat. *rēctus,* right; see **reg-*** + Lat. *-ficāre,* -fy.] — **rec′ti•fi′a•ble** *adj.* — **rec′ti•fi•ca′tion** (-fĭ-kā′shən) *n.*

rec•ti•lin•e•ar (rĕk′tə-lĭn′ē-ər) *adj.* Moving in, consisting of, bounded by, or characterized by a straight line or lines. [< LLat. *rēctilīneus* : Lat. *rēctus,* right; see **reg-*** + Lat. *līnea,* line; see LINE[1].] — **rec′ti•lin′e•ar•ly** *adv.*

rec•ti•tude (rĕk′tĭ-to͞od′, -tyo͞od′) *n.* **1.** Moral uprightness; righteousness. See Syns at **honesty. 2.** The quality or condition of judging correctly. **3.** The quality of being straight. [ME

< OFr. < LLat. *rēctitūdō* < Lat. *rēctus*, straight. See **reg-***.] **—rec′ti•tu′di•nous** *adj.*

rec•to (rĕk′tō) *n., pl.* **-tos.** *Print.* A right-hand page of a book or the front side of a leaf, on the other side of the verso. [< Lat. *(foliō) rēctō*, (the leaf) being right, ablative of *rēctus*, straight, right. See **reg-***.]

rec•tor (rĕk′tər) *n.* **1.** An Episcopalian cleric in charge of a parish. **2.** An Anglican cleric who has charge of a parish and owns the tithes from it. **3.** A Roman Catholic priest serving as managerial and spiritual head of a church or other institution. **4.** The principal of certain schools, colleges, and universities. [ME < OFr. < Lat. *rēctor*, director < *regere, rēct-*, to rule. See **reg-***.] **—rec′tor•ate** (-ĭt) *n.* **—rec•to′ri•al** (rĕk-tôr′ē-əl, -tōr′-) *adj.*

rec•to•ry (rĕk′tə-rē) *n., pl.* **-ries. 1.** The house in which a parish priest or minister lives. **2.a.** An Anglican rector's dwelling. **b.** An Anglican rector's office and benefice.

rec•trix (rĕk′trĭks) *n., pl.* **rec•tri•ces** (rĕk′trĭ-sēz′, rĕk-trī′sēz). One of the stiff main feathers of a bird's tail, used to control flight direction. [Lat. *rēctrīx*, fem. of *rēctor*, director. See RECTOR.]

rec•tum (rĕk′təm) *n., pl.* **-tums** or **-ta** (-tə). The terminal portion of the large intestine, extending from the sigmoid flexure to the anal canal. [ME < Lat. *(intestīnum) rēctum*, straight (intestine), neut. of *rēctus*. See **reg-***.]

rec•tus (rĕk′təs) *n., pl.* **-ti** (-tī′). Any of various straight muscles, as of the abdomen, eye, neck, and thigh. [NLat. *(mūsculus) rēctus* < Lat., straight (muscle). See **rector***.]

re•cum•bent (rĭ-kŭm′bənt) *adj.* **1.** Lying down, esp. for comfort or rest; reclining. **2.** Resting; idle. **3.** *Biol.* Resting on the surface from which it arises. Used of an organ or other structure. [Lat. *recumbēns, recumbent-*, pr.part. of *recumbere*, to lie down : *re-*, re- + *cumbere*, to lie.] **—re•cum′bence, re•cum′ben•cy** *n.* **—re•cum′bent•ly** *adv.*

re•cu•per•ate (rĭ-ko͞o′pə-rāt′, -kyo͞o′-) *v.* **-at•ed, -at•ing, -ates.** *—intr.* **1.** To return to health or strength; recover. **2.** To recover from financial loss. *—tr.* **1.** To restore to health or strength. **2.** To regain. [Lat. *recuperāre, recuperāt-* : *re-*, re- + *capere*, to take; see **kap-***.] **—re•cu′per•a′tion** *n.* **—re•cu′per•a′tive** (-pə-rā′tĭv, -pər-ə-tĭv), **re•cu′per•a•to′ry** (-pər-ə-tôr′ē, -tōr′ē) *adj.*

re•cur (rĭ-kûr′) *intr.v.* **-curred, -cur•ring, -curs. 1.** To happen, come up, or show up again or repeatedly. **2.** To return to one's attention or memory. **3.** To return in thought or discourse. **4.** To have recourse: *recur to force.* [Lat. *recurrere* : *re-*, re- + *currere*, to run; see **kers-***.] **—re•cur′rence** *n.*

re•cur•rent (rĭ-kûr′ənt, -kŭr′-) *adj.* **1.** Occurring or appearing again or repeatedly. **2.** *Anat.* Turning in a reverse direction. Used of blood vessels and nerves. **—re•cur′rent•ly** *adv.*

re•cur•ring decimal (rĭ-kûr′ĭng, -kŭr′-) *n. Math.* See **repeating decimal.**

re•cur•sion (rĭ-kûr′zhən) *n. Math.* **1.** An expression, such as a polynomial, each term of which is determined by application of a formula to preceding terms. **2.** A formula that generates the successive terms of a recursion. [LLat. *recursiō, recursiōn-*, a running back < Lat. *recursus*, p.part. of *recurrere*, to run back. See RECUR.] **—re•cur′sive** *adj.*

re•cur•vate (rĭ-kûr′vāt′, -vĭt) *adj.* Bent or curved backward.

re•curve (rē-kûrv′) *tr. & intr.v.* **-curved, -curv•ing, -curves.** To curve (something) backward or downward or become so curved. [Lat. *recurvāre* : *re-*, re- + *curvāre*, to curve (< *curvus*, curve; see CURVE).] **—re′cur•va′tion** (rē′kûr-vā′shən) *n.*

rec•u•sant (rĕk′yə-zənt, rĭ-kyo͞o′-) *n.* **1.** One of the Roman Catholics in England who formerly incurred legal and social penalties for refusing to attend services of the Church of England. **2.** A dissenter; a nonconformist. **—rec′u•san•cy** *n.* **—rec′u•sant** *adj.*

re•cuse (rĭ-kyo͞oz′) *tr.v.* **-cused, -cus•ing, -cus•es.** To disqualify or seek to disqualify from participation in a decision on grounds such as prejudice or personal involvement. [ME *recusen* < OFr. *recuser* < Lat. *recūsāre* : *re-*, re- + *causa*, cause.]

re•cy•cle (rē-sī′kəl) *tr.v.* **-cled, -cling, -cles. 1.** To put or pass through a cycle again, as in an industrial process. **2.** To start a different cycle in. **3.a.** To extract useful materials from (waste). **b.** To extract and esp. reprocess (materials found in waste) for reuse. **4.a.** To use again. *recycle paper.* **b.** To adapt to a new use or function. **—re•cy′cla•ble** *adj. & n.* **—re•cy′cler** *n.*

red (rĕd) *n.* **1.a.** *Color.* The hue of the long-wave end of the visible spectrum, evoked in the human observer by radiant energy with wavelengths of approx. 630 to 750 nanometers; any of a group of colors whose hue resembles that of blood; one of the additive or light primaries; one of the psychological primary hues. **b.** A pigment or dye having a red hue. **c.** Something that has a red hue. **2.a.** Often **Red.** A Communist. **b.** A revolutionary activist. *—adj.* **red•der, red•dest. 1.** *Color.* Having a color resembling that of blood. **2.** Reddish in color or having parts that are reddish in color: *a red dog.* **3.a.** Having a reddish or coppery skin color. **b.** Often **Red.** *Offensive.* Of or being a Native American. **4.** Having a ruddy or flushed complexion: *red with embarrassment.* **5.** Often **Red.** Communist. *—idiom.* **in the red.** Operating at a loss; in debt. [ME < OE *rēad*. See **reudh-***.] **—red′ly** *adv.* **—red′ness** *n.*

red. *abbr.* **1.** Reduced. **2.** Reduction.

re•dact (rĭ-dăkt′) *tr.v.* **-dact•ed, -dact•ing, -dacts. 1.** To draw up or frame (a proclamation, for example). **2.** To prepare for publication; edit or revise. [ME *redacten* < Lat. *redigere, redāct-*, to drive back : *re-, red-*, re- + *agere*, to drive; see ACT.] **—re•dac′tor** (-dăk′tər, -tôr′) *n.*

re•dac•tion (rĭ-dăk′shən) *n.* **1.** The act or process of editing or revising; preparation for publication. **2.** An edited work; a new edition or revision.

red alga *n.* Any of various predominantly marine algae of the division Rhodophyta, characteristically red or reddish in color. Often used in the plural.

red•bait (rĕd′bāt′) *tr.v.* **-bait•ed, -bait•ing, -baits.** To accuse, denounce, or attack (a person, for example) as a Communist or a Communist sympathizer. **—red′bait′er** *n.*

red•bird (rĕd′bûrd′) *n.* Any of various birds with red plumage.

red blood cell *n.* A cell in the blood of vertebrates that transports oxygen and carbon dioxide to and from the tissues.

red-blood•ed (rĕd′blŭd′ĭd) *adj.* Strong and highly spirited.

red•breast (rĕd′brĕst′) *n.* **1.** A bird, such as the robin, that has a red breast. **2.** A freshwater sunfish *(Lepomis auritus)* of the eastern United States having a reddish belly.

red•brick (rĕd′brĭk′) *adj.* Of, relating to, or being the British universities other than Oxford and Cambridge.

red•bud (rĕd′bŭd′) *n.* Any of several shrubs or small trees of the genus *Cercis*, having flat pods and pinkish flowers.

red bug also **red•bug** (rĕd′bŭg′) *n.* See **chigger** 1.

red•cap (rĕd′kăp′) *n.* A porter, usu. in a railroad station.

Red•car (rĕd′kär′). A municipal borough of NE England on the North Sea NE of Middlesbrough. Pop. 85,600.

red carpet *n.* A carpet laid down for important visitors. *—idiom.* **roll out the red carpet.** To welcome with great hospitality or ceremony.

red cedar *n.* **1.** An eastern North American evergreen coniferous tree *(Juniperus virginiana)* having purplish-black seed cones. **2.** A tall Pacific North American evergreen tree *(Thuja plicata)* having scalelike opposite leaves and ovoid seed cones. **3.** The reddish aromatic durable wood of these trees.

red cent *n. Informal.* Insignificant value: *not worth a red cent.*

Red Cloud (kloud). 1822–1909. Oglala Sioux leader of the resistance against the development of a trail through WY and MT by the U.S. government (1865–67).

Red Cloud
Photographed in 1880

Red•cloud Peak (rĕd′kloud′). A mountain, 4,280.4 m (14,034 ft), in the San Juan Mts. of SW CO.

red clover *n.* A Eurasian plant *(Trifolium pratense)* having trifoliate leaves and globular heads of rose-purple flowers, naturalized in North America and planted as a forage crop.

red•coat (rĕd′kōt′) *n.* A British soldier, esp. one serving during the American Revolution.

red corpuscle *n.* See **red blood cell.**

Red Crescent *n.* **1.** A branch of the Red Cross organization operating in a Muslim country. **2.** The crescent-shaped emblem of such a branch.

Red Cross *n.* **1.a.** An international organization that cares for the wounded, sick, and homeless in wartime and during and following natural disasters. **b.** A national branch of this organization. **2.** The emblem of this organization, a Geneva cross or a red Greek cross on a white background.

redd (rĕd) *tr.v.* **redd•ed** or **redd, redd•ing, redds.** *Chiefly Pennsylvania.* To clear: *redd the dinner table.* **—phrasal verb. redd up.** To tidy: *She redded up the front room.* [ME dial. *redden*, to clear an area (influenced by *redden*, to rescue, free from < OE *hreddan*) < ON *rydhja*. See RID.]

Regional Note: The terms *redd* and *redd up* came to the American Midlands from the Scottish immigrants who settled there. Meaning "to clear an area or make it tidy," *redd* is still used in Scotland and Northern Ireland; in the United States it is common in Pennsylvania as the phrasal verb *redd up.*

red deer *n.* **1.** A common deer *(Cervus elaphus)* of Europe and Asia having a reddish-brown coat. **2.** The summer morph of the white-tailed deer, having a reddish coat.

Red Deer (dîr). A city of S-central Alberta, Canada, on the Red Deer R. N of Calgary. Pop. 46,393.

Red Deer River. A river rising in the Rocky Mts. of SW Alberta, Canada, and flowing c. 619 km (385 mi) to the South Saskatchewan R. just across the Saskatchewan border.

red•den (rĕd′n) *tr. & intr.v.* **-dened, -den•ing, -dens.** To make or become red.

Red•ding (rĕd′ĭng). A city of N CA on the Sacramento R. SSW of Mt. Shasta. Pop. 66,462.

red•dish (rĕd′ĭsh) *adj. Color.* Mixed or tinged with red; somewhat red. **—red′dish•ness** *n.*

red•dle (rĕd′l) *n. & v.* Var. of **ruddle.**

red-dog (rĕd′dôg′, -dŏg′) *Football.* *—n.* See **blitz** 3. *—v.* **-dogged, -dog•ging, -dogs.** *—tr.* To rush (the quarterback) in a blitz. *—intr.* To carry out a blitz.

red drum *n.* A large food fish *(Sciaenops ocellata)* of the Atlantic coastal waters of North America.

rede (rēd) *tr.v.* **red•ed, red•ing, redes. 1.** To give advice to; counsel. **2.** To interpret; explain. *—n.* **1.** Advice or counsel.

ă pat	oi boy
ā pay	ou out
âr care	o͝o took
ä father	o͞o boot
ĕ pet	ŭ cut
ē be	ûr urge
ĭ pit	th thin
ī pie	*th* this
îr pier	hw which
ŏ pot	zh vision
ō toe	ə about, item
ô paw	

Stress marks:
′ (primary);
′ (secondary), as in
dictionary (dĭk′shə-nĕr′ē)

2. *Archaic.* A narration. [ME *reden* < OE *rǣdan.* See **ar-***.]
re•dec•o•rate (rē-dĕk′ə-rāt′) *v.* **-rat•ed, -rat•ing, -rates.** — *tr.* To change the appearance or furnishings of; refurbish. — *intr.* To change a decorative scheme. — **re•dec′o•ra′tion** *n.* — **re•dec′o•ra′tor** *n.*
re•deem (rĭ-dēm′) *tr.v.* **-deemed, -deem•ing, -deems. 1.** To recover ownership of by paying a specified sum. **2.** To pay off (a promissory note, for example). **3.** To turn in (coupons, for example) and receive something in exchange. **4.** To fulfill (a pledge, for example). **5.** To convert into cash: *redeem stocks.* **6.** To set free; rescue or ransom. **7.** To save from a state of sinfulness and its consequences. **8.** To make up for; compensate for. **9.** To restore the honor, worth, or reputation of. [ME *redemen* < OFr. *redimer* < Lat. *redimere* : *re-, red-,* re- + *emere,* to buy; see **em-***.] — **re•deem′a•ble** *adj.*
re•deem•er (rĭ-dē′mər) *n.* **1.** One who redeems. **2. Redeemer.** Jesus.
red eft *n.* The bright red terrestrial stage in the life cycle of the newt *(Notophthalmus viridescens)* of the eastern United States.

red fox
Vulpes fulva

re•de•liv•er (rē′dĭ-lĭv′ər) *tr.v.* **-ered, -er•ing, -ers. 1.** To deliver again. **2.** To deliver in return; give back.
re•demp•tion (rĭ-dĕmp′shən) *n.* **1.** The act of redeeming or the condition of having been redeemed. **2.** Recovery of something pawned or mortgaged. **3.** The payment of an obligation, as a government's payment of the value of its bonds. **4.** Deliverance upon payment of ransom; rescue. **5.** *Theol.* Salvation from sin through Jesus's sacrifice. [ME *redempcioun* < OFr. *redemption* < Lat. *redēmptiō, redēmptiōn-* < *redēmptus,* p.part. of *redimere,* to redeem. See REDEEM.] — **re•demp′tion•al, re•demp′tive, re•demp′to•ry** (-tə-rē) *adj.*
re•demp•tion•er (rĭ-dĕmp′shə-nər) *n.* A colonial emigrant from Europe to America who paid for the voyage by serving for a specified period as a bondservant.
Re•demp•tor•ist (rĭ-dĕmp′tər-ĭst) *n.* A member of the Congregation of the Most Holy Redeemer, a Roman Catholic order founded in 1732 by Saint Alphonsus Liguori (1696–1787). [Fr. *rédemptoriste* < LLat. *redēmptor,* redeemer < Lat., contractor < *redimere,* to buy back. See REDEEM.]
re•de•ploy (rē′dĭ-ploi′) *tr.v.* **-ployed, -ploy•ing, -ploys. 1.** To move (military forces) from one combat zone to another. **2.** To shift (something) from one place or use to another for greater effectiveness. — **re′de•ploy′ment** *n.*
re•de•sign (rē′dĭ-zīn′) *tr.v.* **-signed, -sign•ing, -signs.** To revise the appearance or function of. — **re′de•sign′** *n.*

redingote

re•de•vel•op (rē′dĭ-vĕl′əp) *v.* **-oped, -op•ing, -ops.** — *tr.* **1.** To develop (something) again. **2.** To tone or intensify (a photographic print, for example) by a second developing process. **3.** To restore (buildings or neighborhoods, for example) to a better condition. — *intr.* To develop again. — **re′de•vel′op•er** *n.* — **re′de•vel′op•ment** *n.*
red•eye (rĕd′ī′) *n.* **1.** *Informal.* A danger signal on a railroad. **2.** *Slang.* A late-night or overnight flight. **3.** Any of several fishes with red eyes. **4.** *Slang.* Inferior whiskey.
redeye gravy *n.* Gravy made from the juices of a cooked ham.
red-faced (rĕd′fāst′) *adj.* Embarrassed.
red fir *n.* **1.** An evergreen tree *(Abies magnifica)* of California and Oregon having reddish wood valued as timber. **2.** The wood of this tree.
red fire *n.* Any of various combustible compounds, esp. salts of lithium or strontium, that burn bright red and are used in flares and fireworks.
red•fish (rĕd′fĭsh′) *n., pl.* **redfish** or **-fish•es.** Any of several fishes that are reddish in color, as the red drum.
red fox *n.* A fox of the genus *Vulpes,* characteristically having reddish fur.
red giant *n.* A star of great size and brightness that has a relatively low surface temperature.
red grouse *n.* A grouse *(Lagopus lagopus* subsp. *scoticus)* of the British Isles that has chestnut plumage.
Red Guard *n.* **1.** A member of a Maoist youth movement in China, prominent during the Chinese Cultural Revolution of the late 1960's. **2.** A member of a radical political group with Maoist leanings. [Transl. of Chin. (Mandarin) *hóng wèi bīng* : *hóng,* red + *wèi bīng,* guard.]
red gum[1] *n.* Any of several Australian evergreen trees of the genus *Eucalyptus,* having lance-shaped aromatic leaves.
red gum[2] *n.* See **strophulus.**
red-hand•ed (rĕd′hăn′dĭd) *adv. & adj.* In the act of doing something wrong. — **red′-hand′ed•ly** *adv.*
red•head (rĕd′hĕd′) *n.* **1.** A person with red hair. **2.** A North American duck *(Aythya americana),* the male of which has black and gray plumage and a reddish head.
red•head•ed (rĕd′hĕd′ĭd) *adj.* **1.** Having red hair. **2.** Having a red head: *a redheaded woodpecker.*
red heat *n.* **1.** The temperature of a red-hot substance. **2.** The physical condition of a red-hot substance.
red herring *n.* **1.** A smoked herring having a reddish color. **2.** Something that draws attention away from the central issue. [Sense 2 < being used to distract hunting dogs.]
red hind *n.* A reddish-brown grouper *(Epinephelus guttatus)* of the West Indies and the Gulf of Mexico.
red-hot (rĕd′hŏt′) *adj.* **1.** Glowing hot; very hot. **2.** Heated, as with excitement, anger, or enthusiasm. **3.** Very recent; new: *red-hot information.* — *n.* **1.** See **hot dog. 2.** A small, usu. round red candy strongly flavored with cinnamon.
re•di•a (rē′dē-ə) *n., pl.* **-di•ae** (-dē-ē′). A larva of certain trematodes that is produced within the sporocyst and that can give rise to additional rediae or to cercariae. [NLat., after Francesco *Redi* (1626–97), Italian naturalist.]
re•did (rē-dĭd′) *v.* P.t. of **redo.**
re•dif•fer•en•ti•a•tion (rē′dĭf-ə-rĕn′shē-ā′shən) *n. Biol.* A process by which a group of once differentiated cells return to their original specialized form.
red•in•gote (rĕd′ĭng-gōt′) *n.* **1.** A man's long double-breasted topcoat with full skirt. **2.** A woman's full-length unlined coat or dress open down the front to show a dress or underdress. [Fr., alteration of E. *riding coat.*]
red ink *n.* **1.** A financial loss in business. **2.** The condition of showing a fiscal deficit. [< the use of red ink to record debits and losses in financial records.]
red•in•te•gra•tion (rĕd-ĭn′tĭ-grā′shən, rĭ-dĭn′-) *n. Psychol.* Evocation of a particular state of mind resulting from the recurrence of one of the elements that made up the original experience. [ME *redintegracion* < Lat. *redintegrātiō, redintegrātiōn-* < *redintegrātus,* p.part. of *redintegrāre,* to make whole again : *re-, red-,* re- + *integer,* whole, entire; see INTEGER.] — **red•in′te•gra′tive** *adj.* — **red•in′te•gra′tor** *n.*
re•di•rect (rē′dĭ-rĕkt′, -dī-) *tr.v.* **-rect•ed, -rect•ing, -rects.** To change the direction or course of. — *n.* (rē′dĭ-rĕkt′, -dī-). *Law.* A redirect examination. — **re′di•rec′tion** *n.*
redirect examination *n. Law.* Further examination of a witness after cross-examination, conducted by the party who first called the witness.
re•dis•count (rē-dĭs′kount′) *tr.v.* **-count•ed, -count•ing, -counts.** To discount again. — *n.* **1.** The act of rediscounting. **2.** Commercial paper that is discounted a second time. Often used in the plural.
re•dis•tri•bu•tion (rē′dĭs-trə-byōō′shən) *n.* **1.** The act or process of redistributing. **2.** An economic theory or policy that advocates reducing inequalities in the distribution of wealth. — **re′dis•tri•bu′tion•ist** *adj. & n.*
red•i•vi•vus (rĕd′ə-vī′vəs, -vē′-) *adj.* Come back to life; revived. [LLat. *redivīvus* < Lat., renewed : *re-, red-,* re- + *vīvus,* living; see VIVIFY.]
Red Jack•et (jăk′ĭt). 1756?–1830. Seneca leader who advocated peace with the U.S. while resisting the encroachment of settlers.
Red•lands (rĕd′ləndz). A city of S CA in the San Bernardino Valley. Pop. 60,394.
red lead (lĕd) *n.* A poisonous bright red powder, Pb_3O_4, used in paints, glass, pottery, and packing for pipe joints.
red-let•ter (rĕd′lĕt′ər) *adj.* Memorably happy. [< marking the holy days in church calendars in red.]
red light *n.* **1.** The red-colored light that signals traffic to stop. **2.** *Informal.* A command to stop.
red-light district (rĕd′līt′) *n.* A neighborhood containing many brothels.
red•line (rĕd′līn′) *v.* **-lined, -lin•ing, -lines.** — *intr.* To refuse home mortgages or home insurance to areas or neighborhoods deemed poor financial risks. — *tr.* **1.** To discriminate against by refusing to grant loans, mortgages, or insurance to. **2.** To remove from operational status because of mechanical defects or the need for scheduled maintenance.
red maple *n.* A medium-sized eastern North American maple *(Acer rubrum)* having reddish twigs and buds.
red meat *n.* Meat, esp. beef, that is red before being cooked.
Red•mond (rĕd′mənd). A city of W-central WA, a suburb of Seattle E of Lake Washington. Pop. 35,800.
red mulberry *n.* A deciduous eastern North American tree *(Morus rubra)* having irregularly lobed leaves and edible, fleshy, red to purple multiple fruit.
red mullet *n.* See **goatfish.**
red•neck (rĕd′nĕk′) *n. Offensive Slang.* **1.** Used as a disparaging term for a member of the white rural laboring class, esp. in the southern United States. **2.** One who is regarded as having a provincial, conservative, often bigoted attitude.
re•do (rē-dōō′) *tr.v.* **-did** (-dĭd′), **-done** (-dŭn′), **-do•ing, -does** (-dŭz′). **1.** To do over again. **2.** To redecorate.
red oak *n.* Either of two eastern North American deciduous trees *(Quercus rubra* or *Q. falcata)* having deeply lobed leaves and a saucer-shaped cup enclosing part of the nut.
red ocher *n.* A form of hematite used as a red pigment.
red•o•lence (rĕd′l-əns) also **red•o•len•cy** (-l-ən-sē) *n.* The quality or state of being redolent.
red•o•lent (rĕd′l-ənt) *adj.* **1.** Fragrant; aromatic. **2.** Suggestive; reminiscent: *redolent of politics.* [ME < OFr. < Lat. *redolēns, redolent-,* pr.part. of *redolēre,* to smell : *re-, red-,* re- + *olēre,* to smell.] — **red′o•lent•ly** *adv.*
Re•don (rə-dŏn′, -dôɴ′), **Odilon.** 1840–1916. French artist who was a forerunner of surrealism.
Re•don•do Beach (rĭ-dŏn′dō). A city of S CA, a suburb of Los Angeles on the Pacific Ocean. Pop. 60,167.
red osier *n.* A North American shrub *(Cornus sericea)* often

growing in dense clumps and having red branches, white flowers, and bluish-white drupes.

re•dou•ble (rē-dŭb′əl) *v.* **-bled, -bling, -bles.** — *tr.* **1.** To double. **2.** To repeat. **3.** *Games.* To double the doubling bid of (an opponent) in bridge. — *intr.* **1.** To become twice as great. **2.** *Games.* To double a double in bridge.

re•doubt (rĭ-dout′) *n.* **1.** A small, often temporary defensive fortification. **2.** A reinforcing earthwork or breastwork within a permanent rampart. **3.** A protected place of refuge or defense. [Fr. *redoute* < Ital. *ridotto* < Med.Lat. *reductus*, concealed place < Lat., p.part. of *redūcere*, to withdraw, lead back. See REDUCE.]

Re•doubt (rē′dout′), **Mount.** A volcano, 3,111 m (10,200 ft), of S AK; erupted in 1989 for the first time in 25 years.

re•doubt•a•ble (rĭ-dou′tə-bəl) *adj.* **1.** Arousing fear or awe; formidable. **2.** Worthy of respect or honor. [ME *redoubtabel* < OFr. *redoutable* < *redouter*, to dread : *re-*, re- + *douter*, to doubt, fear; see DOUBT.] — **re•doubt′a•bly** *adv.*

re•dound (rĭ-dound′) *intr.v.* **-dound•ed, -dound•ing, -dounds.** **1.** To have an effect or consequence: *deeds that redound to one's credit.* **2.** To return; recoil. **3.** To contribute; accrue. [ME *redounden*, to abound < OFr. *redonder* < Lat. *redundāre*, to overflow. See REDUNDANT.]

red•out (rĕd′out′) *n.* A sudden reddening of the visual field accompanied by severe headache and caused by engorgement of the blood vessels of the head due to negative gravity, as in stunt flying.

re•dox (rē′dŏks′) *n.* Oxidation-reduction. [RED(UCTION) + OX(IDATION).]

red panda *n.* See **panda** 2.

red pepper *n.* **1.** The pungent red podlike fruit of any of several cultivars of the pepper plants, *Capsicum frutescens* and *C. annum.* **2.** See **cayenne pepper.**

red pine *n.* An evergreen timber tree *(Pinus resinosa)* of northeast North America having long flexible glossy leaves grouped in fascicles of two.

red•poll (rĕd′pōl′) *n.* Any of several small finches of the genus *Carduelis* of northern North America and Eurasia, esp. *C. flammea,* having a red crown and black chin.

Red Poll or **Red Polled** (pōld) *n.* Any of a breed of red hornless cattle developed in England and raised for milk and meat.

red puccoon *n.* See **bloodroot.**

re•dress (rĭ-drĕs′) *tr.v.* **-dressed, -dress•ing, -dress•es.** **1.** To set right; remedy or rectify. **2.** To make amends to. **3.** To make amends for. See Syns at **correct. 4.** To adjust (a balance, for example). — *n.* (*also* rē′drĕs). **1.** Satisfaction for wrong or injury; reparation. **2.** Correction or reformation. [ME *redressen* < OFr. *redrecier* : *re-*, re- + *drecier*, to arrange; see DRESS.] — **re•dress′er, re•dres′sor** *n.*

Red River. 1. Or in China **Yu•an Jiang** (yo͞o-än′ jyäng′, yüän′) and in Vietnam **Hong Ha** (hông′ hä′) or **Song Hong** (sông′ hông′). A river of SE Asia rising in S China and flowing c. 1,175 km (730 mi) through N Vietnam to the Gulf of Tonkin. **2.** A river of the S-central U.S. rising in two branches in the Texas Panhandle and flowing c. 1,638 km (1,018 mi) to the Mississippi R. **3.** Also **Red River of the North.** A river of the N-central U.S. and S-central Canada formed by the confluence of two tributaries in W-central MN and flowing c. 499 km (310 mi) into SE Manitoba, Canada, where it empties into Lake Winnipeg.

red•root (rĕd′ro͞ot′, -ro͝ot′) *n.* **1.** An eastern North American bog plant *(Lachnanthes caroliana)* having red roots and woolly yellow flowers. **2.** See **pigweed** 2. **3.** See **ceanothus.**

red salmon *n.* See **sockeye salmon.**

Red Sea. A sea between NE Africa and Arabia linked with the Mediterranean by the Suez Canal and with the Gulf of Aden and the Arabian Sea through the Bab el Mandeb.

red•shank (rĕd′shăngk′) *n.* An Old World wading bird *(Tringa totanus)* having long red legs.

red shift *n.* An increase in the wavelength of radiation emitted by a celestial body as a consequence of the Doppler effect. [< the fact that the longer wavelengths of light are at the red end of the visible spectrum.]

red•shirt (rĕd′shûrt′) *tr.v.* **-shirt•ed, -shirt•ing, -shirts.** *Sports.* To keep (a college or school athlete) out of varsity competition for one year in order to extend the athlete's period of eligibility. [< the red jerseys worn by such athletes.] — **red′shirt′** *adj. & n.*

red•should•ered hawk (rĕd′shōl′dərd) *n.* A medium-sized North American hawk *(Buteo lineatus)* having rufous shoulder feathers and found in wet woodlands and savannas.

red•skin (rĕd′skĭn′) *n. Offensive Slang.* Used as a disparaging term for a Native American.

red snapper *n.* Any of several marine food fishes of the genus *Lutjanus* of warm waters, having red or reddish bodies.

red snow *n.* Snow on which red-pigmented algae has grown, commonly found in Arctic and Alpine regions.

red spider *n.* Any of various small red mites of the family Tetranychidae that feed on vegetation, damaging the leaves.

red-spot•ted eft (rĕd′spŏt′ĭd) *n.* See **red eft.**

red squill *n.* **1.** See **sea onion** 1. **2.** A powder prepared from the bulbs of the red squill and used as a rat poison.

red squirrel *n.* A North American squirrel *(Tamiasciurus hudsonicus)* having reddish or tawny fur.

red•start (rĕd′stärt′) *n.* **1.** A small North American bird *(Setophaga ruticilla),* the male of which has black plumage with orange patches on the wings and tail. **2.** A European bird *(Phoenicurus phoenicurus)* having grayish plumage and a rust-red breast and tail. [RED + obsolete *start*, tail (< ME *stert* < OE *steort*; see **ster-**[1]*).]

red-tailed hawk (rĕd′tāld′) *n.* A heavy-bodied North American hawk *(Buteo jamaicensis)* that feeds primarily on rodents and has a conspicuous reddish-brown tail in the male.

red tape *n.* Official forms and procedures, esp. when oppressively complex and time consuming. [< its former use in tying British official documents.]

red tide *n.* A bloom of dinoflagellates that cause reddish discoloration of coastal ocean waters and often produce toxins that kill fish and contaminate shellfish.

red•top (rĕd′tŏp′) *n.* A widely cultivated Eurasian grass *(Agrostis gigantea)* having reddish flower clusters.

red squirrel
Tamiasciurus hudsonicus

re•duce (rĭ-do͞os′, -dyo͞os′) *v.* **-duced, -duc•ing, -duc•es.** — *tr.* **1.** To bring down, as in extent, amount, or degree; diminish. See Syns at **decrease. 2.** To bring to a humbler, weaker, difficult, or forced state or condition; esp.: **a.** To gain control of; conquer. **b.** To subject to destruction: *reduced the city to rubble.* **c.** To weaken bodily. **d.** To sap the spirit or mental energy of. **e.** To compel to desperate acts. **f.** To lower in rank or grade; demote. **g.** To powder or pulverize. **h.** To thin (paint) with a solvent. **3.** To lower the price of. **4.** To put in order or arrange systematically. **5.** To separate into orderly components by analysis. **6.** *Chem.* **a.** To decrease the valence of (an atom) by adding electrons. **b.** To remove oxygen from (a compound). **c.** To add hydrogen to (a compound). **d.** To change to a metallic state by removing nonmetallic constituents; smelt. **7.** *Math.* To simplify the form of (an expression, such as a fraction) without changing the value. **8.** *Medic.* To restore (a fractured or displaced body part) to a normal condition or position. — *intr.* **1.** To become diminished. **2.** To lose weight, as by dieting. **3.** *Biol.* To undergo meiosis. [ME *reducen*, to bring back < OFr. *reducier* < Lat. *redūcere* : *re-*, re- + *dūcere*, to lead; see **deuk-***.] — **re•duc′er** *n.* — **re•duc′i•bil′i•ty** *n.* — **re•duc′i•ble** *adj.* — **re•duc′i•bly** *adv.*

re•duc•ing agent (rĭ-do͞o′sĭng, -dyo͞o′-) *n.* A substance that chemically reduces other substances, esp. by donating an electron or electrons.

re•duc•tant (rĭ-dŭk′tənt) *n.* A reducing agent.

re•duc•tase (rĭ-dŭk′tās′, -tāz′) *n.* An enzyme that promotes reduction of an organic compound. [REDUCT(ION) + -ASE.]

red-tailed hawk
Buteo jamaicensis

re•duc•ti•o ad ab•sur•dum (rĭ-dŭk′tē-ō ăd əb-sûr′dəm, -zûr′-, -shē-ō) *n., pl.* **-o•nes ad absurdum** (-ō′nēz, -nās). Disproof of a proposition by showing the absurdity of its inevitable conclusion. [Med.Lat. *reductiō ad absurdum* : Lat. *reductiō*, a bringing back, reduction + Lat. *ad*, to + Lat. *absurdum*, absurdity < neut. of *absurdus*, absurd.]

re•duc•tion (rĭ-dŭk′shən) *n.* **1.** The act or process of reducing. **2.** The result of reducing. **3.** The amount by which something is lessened or diminished. **4.** *Biol.* The first meiotic division, in which the chromosome number is reduced. **5.** *Chem.* **a.** A decrease in positive valence or an increase in negative valence by the gaining of electrons. **b.** A reaction in which hydrogen is combined with a compound. **c.** A reaction in which oxygen is removed from a compound. **6.** *Math.* **a.** The canceling of common factors in the numerator and denominator of a fraction. **b.** The converting of a fraction to its decimal equivalent. **c.** The converting of an expression or equation to its simplest form. [Ult. < Lat. *reductiō*, *reductiōn-*, restoration < *reductus*, p.part. of *redūcere*, to bring back. See REDUCE.] — **re•duc′tion•al** *adj.*

re•duc•tion•ism (rĭ-dŭk′shə-nĭz′əm) *n.* An attempt or a tendency to explain complex phenomena or structures by relatively simple principles, as by asserting that life processes or mental acts are instances of chemical and physical laws. — **re•duc′tion•ist** *adj. & n.* — **re•duc′tion•is′tic** *adj.*

re•duc•tive (rĭ-dŭk′tĭv) *adj.* **1.** Of or relating to reduction. **2.** Relating to or exhibiting reductionism. **3.** Relating to or being an instance of reductivism. — **re•duc′tive•ly** *adv.*

re•duc•tiv•ism (rĭ-dŭk′tə-vĭz′əm) *n.* See **minimalism** 1. — **re•duc′tiv•ist** *n.*

re•dun•dan•cy (rĭ-dŭn′dən-sē) *n., pl.* **-cies. 1.** The state of being redundant. **2.** A superfluity; an excess. **3.** Unnecessary repetition. **4.** *Electron.* Duplication or repetition of elements in electronic equipment to provide alternative functional channels in case of failure. **5.** Repetition of parts or all of a message to circumvent transmission errors.

Usage Note: The usages that critics have condemned as redundancies fall into several classes. In some cases, such as *consensus of opinion, close proximity, hollow tube,* and *refer back,* the use of what is regarded as an unnecessary modifier or qualifier can sometimes be justified on the grounds that it in fact makes a semantic contribution. Thus a *hollow tube* can be distinguished from one that has been blocked up with deposits, and a *consensus of opinion* can be distinguished from a consensus of judgments or practice. In other cases the use of

ă pat	oi boy
ā pay	ou out
âr care	o͝o took
ä father	o͞o boot
ĕ pet	ŭ cut
ē be	ûr urge
ĭ pit	th thin
ī pie	*th* this
îr pier	hw which
ŏ pot	zh vision
ō toe	ə about, item
ô paw	

Stress marks:
′ (primary);
′ (secondary), as in
dictionary (dĭk′shə-nĕr′ē)

the qualifier is harder to defend. Thus there is no way to *revert* without *reverting back* and no *consensus* that is not *general.* See Usage Notes at **close, cross section, rarely, refer.**

re•dun•dant (rĭ-dŭn′dənt) *adj.* **1.** Exceeding what is necessary or natural; superfluous. **2.** Needlessly repetitive; verbose. **3.** *Electron.* Of or involving redundancy in electronic equipment. **4.** Of or involving redundancy in the transmission of messages. [Lat. *redundāns, redundant-,* pr.part. of *redundāre,* to overflow : *re-, red-,* re- + *undāre,* to surge (< *unda,* wave; see **wed-**[1]*).] **— re•dun′dant•ly** *adv.*

re•du•pli•cate (rĭ-do͞o′plə-kāt′, -dyo͞o′-) *v.* **-cat•ed, -cat•ing, -cates.** *— tr.* **1.** To repeat over and over again; redouble. **2.** *Ling.* **a.** To double (the initial syllable or all of a root word) to produce an inflectional or derivational form. **b.** To form (a new word) by doubling all or part of a word. *— intr.* To be doubled. *— adj.* (-plə-kĭt). Doubled.

reed
Reed boat on Lake Titicaca

re•du•pli•ca•tion (rĭ-do͞o′plĭ-kā′shən, -dyo͞o′-) *n.* **1.** The act of reduplicating or the state of being reduplicated. **2.** The product or result of reduplicating. **3.** *Ling.* **a.** A word formed by or containing a reduplicated element. **b.** The added element in a word form that is reduplicated. **— re•du′pli•ca′tive** *adj.* **— re•du′pli•ca′tive•ly** *adv.*

re•du•vi•id (rĭ-do͞o′vē-ĭd, -dyo͞o′-) *n.* See **assassin bug.** [< NLat. *Reduviidae,* family name < *Reduvius,* type genus < Lat. *reduvia,* hangnail, fragment. See **eu-**[1]*.]

re•dux (rē-dŭks′) *adj.* Brought back; returned. Used postpositively. [Lat. : *re-,* re- + *dux,* leader; see DUKE.]

red valerian *n.* A Mediterranean perennial plant *(Centranthus ruber)* having glabrous ovate leaves and fragrant crimson to pale red flowers borne in dense terminal clusters.

red•wing (rĕd′wĭng′) *n.* **1.** See **red-winged blackbird. 2.** A European thrush *(Turdus iliacus)* having reddish feathers under the wings and a white eye stripe.

red-winged blackbird (rĕd′wĭngd′) *n.* A North American blackbird *(Agelaius phoeniceus),* the male of which has scarlet patches on the wings.

red wolf *n.* A small reddish wolf *(Canis rufus)* of the southeast United States that exists almost exclusively in captivity.

red•wood (rĕd′wo͝od′) *n.* **1.a.** A tall evergreen tree *(Sequoia sempervirens)* native to Oregon and California and having small seed-bearing cones with peltate scales and unflattened branches. **b.** The soft reddish wood of this tree. **2.** Any of various woods having a reddish color or yielding a red dye.

Red•wood City (rĕd′wo͝od′). A city of W CA NW of Palo Alto. Pop. 66,072.

re•ech•o also **re-ech•o** (rĭ-ĕk′ō) *— v.* **-oed, -o•ing, -oes.** *— intr.* To sound back or reverberate. *— tr.* To echo back; repeat.

reed (rēd) *n.* **1.a.** Any of various tall perennial grasses, esp. of the genera *Phragmites* or *Arundo,* having hollow stems, broad leaves, and large plumelike terminal panicles. **b.** The stalk of any of these plants. **c.** A collection of these stalks. **2.** *Mus.* A simple wind instrument made of a hollow reed stalk. **3.** *Mus.* **a.** A flexible strip of cane or metal set into the mouthpiece or air opening of certain instruments to produce tone by vibrating. **b.** An instrument, such as an oboe, that is fitted with a reed. **4.** A narrow frame fitted with reed or metal strips that separate the warp threads in weaving. **5.** *Archit.* A reeding. [ME *rede* < OE *hrēod.*]

Reed (rēd), **John.** 1887–1920. Amer. journalist who wrote *Ten Days That Shook the World* (1919), an account of the Russian Revolution (1917).

Reed, Stanley Forman. 1884–1980. Amer. jurist; associate justice of the U.S. Supreme Court (1938–57).

Reed, Walter. 1851–1902. Amer. physician who proved that yellow fever was transmitted by the *Aedes aegypti* mosquito.

reed•bird (rēd′bûrd′) *n.* See **bobolink.**

reed•buck (rēd′bŭk′) *n.* Any of several African antelopes of the genus *Redunca,* having long hoofs, small horns that curve forward, and a short bushy tail. [Transl. of Afr. *rietbok.*]

reed•ing (rē′dĭng) *n.* **1.** *Archit.* A convex decorative molding having parallel strips resembling thin reeds. **2.** Parallel grooves cut into the edge of a coin at right angles to the faces.

reed mace *n.* See **cattail.**

reed organ *n. Mus.* A harmonium.

reed pipe *n. Mus.* An organ pipe with a reed that vibrates and produces a tone when air is forced through it.

reed stop *n. Mus.* A stop on an organ made up of or controlling reed pipes.

re•ed•u•cate also **re-ed•u•cate** (rē-ĕj′ə-kāt′) *tr.v.* **-cat•ed, -cat•ing, -cates. 1.** To instruct again. **2.** To retrain (a person) to function effectively; rehabilitate. **— re•ed′u•ca′tion** *n.*

reed•y (rē′dē) *adj.* **-i•er, -i•est. 1.** Full of reeds. **2.** Made of reeds. **3.** Resembling a reed, esp. in being thin or fragile. **4.** *Mus.* Having a tone like that of a reed instrument. **— reed′i•ness** *n.*

reef[1] (rēf) *n.* **1.** A strip or ridge of rocks, sand, or coral that rises to or near the surface of a body of water. **2.** A vein of ore. [Obsolete Du. *rif,* poss. < ON, ridge.] **— reef′y** *adj.*

reef[2] (rēf) *Naut. — n.* A portion of a sail rolled and tied down to lessen the area exposed to the wind. *— tr.v.* **reefed, reef•ing, reefs.** To reduce the size of (a sail) by tucking in a part and tying it to or rolling it around a yard or a boom. [ME *riff* < ON *rif,* ridge, reef.]

reef•er[1] (rē′fər) *n.* **1.** A short, heavy, close-fitting double-breasted jacket. **2.** A close-fitting single-breasted or double-breasted coat. **3.** *Naut.* A person, esp. a midshipman, who reefs.

reef•er[2] (rē′fər) *n. Slang.* Marijuana, esp. a marijuana cigarette. [?]

ree•fer[3] (rē′fər) *n. Slang.* **1.** A conveyance, such as a railroad car or truck trailer, that carries cargo under refrigeration. **2.** A refrigerator. [Alteration of REFRIGERATOR.]

reef knot *n. Naut.* A square knot used in reefing sails.

reek (rēk) *v.* **reeked, reek•ing, reeks.** *— intr.* **1.** To smoke, steam, or fume. **2.** To be pervaded by something unpleasant. **3.** To give off or become permeated with a strong, unpleasant odor. *— tr.* **1.** To emit or exude (smoke, for example). **2.** To process or treat by exposing to smoke. *— n.* **1.** A strong, offensive odor; a stench. **2.** Vapor; steam. [ME *reken,* to smoke < OE *rēocan,* to emit smoke, and *rēcan,* to expose to smoke; see **reug-***.] **— reek′er** *n.* **— reek′y** *adj.*

reel[1] (rēl) *n.* **1.** A device, such as a spool, that turns on an axis and is used for winding and storing rope, film, or other flexible materials. **2.** A cylindrical device attached to a fishing rod to let out or wind up the line. **3.** The quantity of wire, film, or other material wound on one reel. **4.** A set of curved lawnmower blades that rotate around a bar parallel to the ground, cutting grass while moving against a stationary straight blade. *— tr.v.* **reeled, reel•ing, reels. 1.** To wind on or let out from a reel. **2.** To recover by winding on a reel: *reel in a fish.* ***— phrasal verb.* reel off.** To recite fluently and usu. at length: *reeled off names.* [ME < OE *hrēol.*] **— reel′a•ble** *adj.*

reel[2] (rēl) *v.* **reeled, reel•ing, reels.** *— intr.* **1.** To be thrown off balance or fall back. **2.** To stagger, lurch, or sway, as from drunkenness. **3.** To go round and round in a whirling motion. **4.** To feel dizzy. *— tr.* To cause to reel. *— n.* **1.** A staggering, swaying, or whirling movement. **2.a.** A fast dance of Scottish origin. **b.** The Virginia reel. **c.** The music for one of these dances. [ME *relen,* to whirl about, prob. < *reel,* spool. See REEL[1].] **— reel′er** *n.*

reel[3] *n. Maine.* A hand-held hammer used in a quarry for shaping granite blocks. [?]

re•e•lect also **re-e•lect** (rē′ĭ-lĕkt′) *tr.v.* **-lect•ed, -lect•ing, -lects.** To elect again. **— re′e•lec′tion** *n.*

reel•ing (rē′lĭng) *n. Maine.* Sustained noise or commotion, as from hammering: *"Hark that reeling, now, you'll wake the baby!"* (Anonymous).

reel-to-reel (rēl′tə-rēl′) *adj.* Relating to or being sound recording equipment or sound recordings using magnetic tape that must be threaded through the equipment and onto an empty reel.

re•en•act also **re-en•act** (rē′ĕn-ăkt′, -ə-năkt′) *tr.v.* **-act•ed, -act•ing, -acts. 1.** To enact again: *reenact a law.* **2.** To perform again: *reenact the scene.* **3.** To go through a second time. **— re′en•act′ment** *n.*

re•en•force or **re-en•force** (rē′ĭn-fôrs′, -fōrs′) *v.* Var. of **reinforce.**

re•en•ter also **re-en•ter** (rē-ĕn′tər) *— v.* **-tered, -ter•ing, -ters.** *— intr.* To come in or enter again. *— tr.* To record again on a list or ledger. **— re•en′trance** *n.*

re•en•trant also **re-en•trant** (rē-ĕn′trənt) *— adj.* Reentering; pointing inward. *— n.* A reentrant angle or part.

reentrant angle also **re-entrant angle** *n. Math.* In an irregular polygon, an interior angle that is greater than 180° and whose apex faces into the polygon.

re•en•try also **re-en•try** (rē-ĕn′trē) *n., pl.* **-tries. 1.** The act of reentering. **2.** *Aerospace.* The return of a missile or spacecraft into Earth's atmosphere.

reeve[1] (rēv) *n.* **1.** The elected president of a town council in some parts of Canada. **2.** Any of various minor officers of parishes or other local authorities. **3.** A bailiff or steward of a manor in the later medieval period. **4.** A high officer of local administration appointed by the Anglo-Saxon kings. [ME < OE *gerēfa.*]

reeve[2] (rēv) *tr.v.* **reeved** or **rove** (rōv), **reev•ing, reeves.** *Naut.* **1.** To pass (a line or rod) through a hole, ring, fairlead, or block. **2.** To fasten by passing through or around. [?]

reeve[3] (rēv) *n.* The female ruff. [Prob. alteration of RUFF[1].]

ref (rĕf) *n. Sports & Games.* A referee.

ref. *abbr.* **1.** Reference. **2.** Referred. **3.** Refining. **4.** Reformation; reformed. **5.** Refunding.

re•fect (rĭ-fĕkt′) *tr.v.* **-fect•ed, -fect•ing, -fects.** *Archaic.* To refresh with food and drink. [Lat. *reficere, refect-,* to refresh : *re-,* re- + *facere,* to make; see **dhē-***.]

re•fec•tion (rĭ-fĕk′shən) *n.* **1.** Refreshment with food and drink. **2.** A light meal or repast.

re•fec•to•ry (rĭ-fĕk′tə-rē) *n., pl.* **-ries.** A room where meals are served, esp. in a college or other institution.

refectory table *n.* A long table with straight heavy legs.

re•fer (rĭ-fûr′) *v.* **-ferred, -fer•ring, -fers.** *— tr.* **1.** To direct to a source for help or information. **2.** To assign or attribute to; regard as originated by. **3.** To assign to or regard as belonging within a particular kind or class. **4.** To submit (a matter in dispute) to an authority for arbitration, decision, or examination. **5.** To direct the attention of. — *intr.* **1.** To pertain; concern. **2.** To make mention or reference. **3.** To have recourse; turn. [ME *referren* < OFr. *referer* < Lat. *referre* : *re-*, re- + *ferre*, to carry; see **bher-**[1]***.**] — **ref′er•a•ble** (rĕf′ər-ə-bəl, rĭ-fûr′-) *adj.* — **re•fer′ral** *n.* — **re•fer′rer** *n.*

Usage Note: It is sometimes believed that the phrase *refer back* is redundant, since the prefix *re–* means "back," but the objection is misplaced. In fact, an expression can refer either to something that has already been mentioned or to something that is yet to be mentioned, and the distinction between *refer back* and *refer ahead* may thus be required for clarification. See Usage Notes at **allude, redundancy.**

ref•e•ree (rĕf′ə-rē′) *n.* **1.** One to whom something is referred, esp. for settlement, decision, or an opinion as to the thing's quality. **2.** *Sports & Games.* An official supervising the play; an umpire. **3.** *Law.* A person appointed by a court to make a determination of a case or investigate and make a report on it. — *v.* **-reed, -ree•ing, -rees.** — *tr.* To judge as referee. — *intr.* To act as referee.

ref•er•ence (rĕf′ər-əns, rĕf′rəns) *n.* **1.** An act of referring. **2.a.** Significance in a specified context: *Her speeches have special reference to the African situation.* **b.** Meaning or denotation. **3.** The state of being related or referred: *in reference to.* **4.** A mention of an occurrence or a situation. **5.a.** A note in a publication referring the reader to another passage or source. **b.** The passage or source so referred to. **c.** A work frequently used as a source. **d.** A mark or footnote used to direct a reader elsewhere for additional information. **6.a.** A person who is in a position to recommend another or vouch for his or her fitness, as for a job. **b.** A statement about a person's qualifications, character, and dependability. — *tr.v.* **-enced, -enc•ing, -ences. 1.** To supply references to. **2.** To mention in a reference; refer to: *He referenced her book.* See Usage Note at **allude.** — **ref′er•enc•er** *n.* — **ref′er•en′tial** (-ə-rĕn′shəl) *adj.* — **ref′er•en′tial•ly** *adv.*

reference book *n.* A book, such as a dictionary, to which one can refer for authoritative information.

ref•er•en•dum (rĕf′ə-rĕn′dəm) *n., pl.* **-dums** or **-da** (-də). **1.a.** The submission of a proposed public measure or actual statute to a direct popular vote. **b.** Such a vote. **2.** A note from a diplomat to the diplomat's government requesting instructions. [Lat., neut. gerundive of *referre*, to refer. See REFER.]

ref•er•ent (rĕf′ər-ənt, rĭ-fûr′ənt) *n.* **1.** Something that refers, esp. a word or phrase referring to an idea or object. **2.** Something referred to.

re•ferred pain (rĭ-fûrd′) *n.* Pain that is felt in a part of the body at a distance from the area of pathology.

re•fill (rē-fĭl′) *tr.v.* **-filled, -fill•ing, -fills.** To fill again. — *n.* (rē′fĭl′). **1.** A product packaged to replace the used contents of a container. **2.** A second or subsequent filling.

re•fin•ance (rē′fə-năns′, rē-fī′năns′) *intr. & tr.v.* **-nanced, -nanc•ing, -nanc•es.** To provide new financing or new financing for, as by discharging a mortgage with the proceeds from a new mortgage obtained at a lower interest rate. — **re•fi′nance′** *n.* — **re′fi•nan′cer, re′fin•an•cier′** (-fĭn-ən-sîr′, -fə-năn′-) *n.*

re•fine (rĭ-fīn′) *v.* **-fined, -fin•ing, -fines.** — *tr.* **1.** To reduce to a pure state; purify. **2.** To remove by purifying. **3.** To free from coarse, unsuitable, or immoral characteristics: *refined his manners.* — *intr.* **1.** To become free of impurities. **2.** To acquire polish or elegance. **3.** To use precise distinctions and subtlety in thought or speech. — **re•fin′er** *n.*

re•fined (rĭ-fīnd′) *adj.* **1.** Free from coarseness or vulgarity; polite. **2.** Free of impurities; purified. **3.** Highly precise.

re•fine•ment (rĭ-fīn′mənt) *n.* **1.** The act of refining. **2.** The result of refining; an improvement or elaboration. **3.** The state or quality of being refined; cultivation, as in taste. **4.** A keen or precise phrasing; a subtle distinction.

re•fin•er•y (rĭ-fī′nə-rē) *n., pl.* **-ies.** An industrial plant for purifying a crude substance, such as petroleum or sugar.

re•fin•ish (rē-fĭn′ĭsh) *tr.v.* **-ished, -ish•ing, -ish•es.** To put a new finish on (furniture). — **re•fin′ish•er** *n.*

re•fit (rē-fĭt′) *v.* **-fit•ted, -fit•ting, -fits.** — *tr.* To prepare and equip for additional use. — *intr.* To be made fit again. — *n.* (rē′fĭt′, rē-fĭt′). **1.** Repair of damage or wear. **2.** A secondary or subsequent preparation of supplies and equipment.

refl. *abbr.* **1.** Reflection; reflective. **2.** Reflex; reflexive.

re•flag (rē-flăg′) *tr.v.* **-flagged, -flag•ging, -flags.** To give a new registered nationality to (a ship or an aircraft).

re•flect (rĭ-flĕkt′) *v.* **-flect•ed, -flect•ing, -flects.** — *tr.* **1.** To throw or bend back (light, for example) from a surface. **2.** To form an image of (an object); mirror. **3.** To manifest as a result of one's actions. **4.** *Archaic.* To bend back. — *intr.* **1.** To be bent back. **2.** To give back a likeness. **3.a.** To think seriously. **b.** To express carefully considered thoughts. — ***phrasal verb.* reflect on. 1.** To form or express carefully considered thoughts about. **2.** To give evidence of the qualities of (one): *Good work reflects on you.* **3.** To give evidence that (one) has acted in a given way: *reflects well on you.* [ME *reflecten* < OFr. *reflecter* < Lat. *reflectere*, to bend back : *re-*, re- + *flectere*, to bend.]

re•flec•tance (rĭ-flĕk′təns) *n.* The ratio of the total amount of radiation, as of light, reflected by a surface to the total amount of radiation incident on the surface.

re•flect•ing telescope (rĭ-flĕk′tĭng) *n.* A telescope in which light from the object is gathered and focused by a concave mirror.

re•flec•tion (rĭ-flĕk′shən) *n.* **1.** The act of reflecting or the state of being reflected. **2.** Something, such as light, that is reflected. **3.a.** Mental concentration; careful consideration. **b.** A thought or an opinion resulting from such consideration. **4.** An indirect expression of censure or discredit. **5.** A manifestation or result. **6.** *Anat.* **a.** The folding of a membrane from the wall of a cavity over an organ. **b.** The folds so made. — **re•flec′tion•al** *adj.*

re•flec•tive (rĭ-flĕk′tĭv) *adj.* **1.a.** Of, relating to, produced by, or resulting from reflection. **b.** Capable of or producing reflection. **2.** Characterized by or given to meditation or contemplation; thoughtful. See Syns at **pensive.** — **re•flec′tive•ly** *adv.* — **re•flec′tive•ness** *n.*

re•flec•tiv•i•ty (rē′flĕk-tĭv′ĭ-tē) *n., pl.* **-ties. 1.** The quality of being reflective. **2.** The ability to reflect. **3.** *Phys.* The ratio of the intensity of a wave reflected from a surface to the energy possessed by the wave striking the surface.

re•flec•tom•e•ter (rē′flĕk-tŏm′ĭ-tər) *n.* An instrument for measuring the reflectance of a surface.

re•flec•tor (rĭ-flĕk′tər) *n.* **1.** Something, such as a surface, that reflects. **2.** A reflecting telescope.

re•flec•tor•ize (rĭ-flĕk′tə-rīz′) *tr.v.* **-ized, -iz•ing, -iz•es.** To cause (a surface, for example) to reflect light, as by chemical treatment.

re•flex (rē′flĕks′) *adj.* **1.** Bent, turned, or thrown back; reflected. **2.** *Physiol.* Being an involuntary action or response, such as a sneeze. **3.** Produced as an automatic response or reaction: *reflex opposition to change.* — *n.* **1.a.** Something, such as light, that is reflected. **b.** An image produced by reflection. **c.** A copy or reproduction. **2.** *Physiol.* An involuntary response to a stimulus. **3.** *Psychol.* An unlearned or instinctive response to a stimulus. **4.** *Ling.* A form or feature that reflects or represents an earlier, often reconstructed form or feature having undergone phonetic or other change. — *tr.v.* (rĭ-flĕks′) **-flexed, -flex•ing, -flex•es. 1.** To bend, turn back, or reflect. **2.** To cause to undergo a reflex process. [< ME *reflexen*, to refract light, bend back < Lat. *reflexus*, p.part. of *reflectere*, to bend back. See REFLECT.]

reflex angle *n. Math.* An angle between 180° and 360°.

reflex arc *n. Physiol.* The neural path of a reflex.

reflex camera *n.* A camera with a mirror that reflects the image onto a viewing screen so that focus may be evaluated.

re•flex•ion (rĭ-flĕk′shən) *n. Chiefly British.* Var. of **reflection.**

re•flex•ive (rĭ-flĕk′sĭv) *adj.* **1.** Directed back on itself. **2.** *Gram.* **a.** Of, relating to, or being a verb having an identical subject and direct object, as *dressed* in the sentence *She dressed herself.* **b.** Of, relating to, or being the pronoun used as the direct object of a reflexive verb, as *herself* in *She dressed herself.* **3.** Of or relating to a reflex. **4.** Elicited automatically; spontaneous. — *n. Gram.* A reflexive verb or pronoun. See Usage Note at **myself.** — **re•flex′ive•ly** *adv.* — **re•flex′ive•ness, re′flex•iv′i•ty** (rē′flĕk-sĭv′ĭ-tē) *n.*

re•flex•ol•o•gy (rē′flĕk-sŏl′ə-jē) *n.* **1.** The study of reflex responses, esp. as they affect behavior. **2.** A method of massage that relieves nervous tension through the application of finger pressure, esp. to the feet. — **re′flex•ol′o•gist** *n.*

ref•lu•ent (rĕf′lo͞o-ənt) *adj.* Flowing back; ebbing. [Lat. *refluēns, refluent-*, pr.part. of *refluere*, to flow back : *re-*, re- + *fluere*, to flow; see FLUENT.] — **ref′lu•ence** *n.*

re•flux (rē′flŭks′) *n.* **1.** A flowing back; ebb. **2.** *Chem.* The process of refluxing. — *v.* **-fluxed, -flux•ing, -flux•es.** — *tr. Chem.* To boil (a liquid) in a vessel attached to a condenser so that the vapors continuously condense for reboiling. — *intr.* To be boiled in such a way. [Med.Lat. *refluxus* : Lat. *re-*, re- + Lat. *fluxus*, flow < p.part. of *fluere*, to flow; see **bhleu-*.**]

re•form (rĭ-fôrm′) *v.* **-formed, -form•ing, -forms.** — *tr.* **1.** To improve by alteration, correction of error, or removal of defects; put into a better form or condition. **2.a.** To abolish abuse or malpractice in: *reform the government.* **b.** To put an end to (a wrong). See Syns at **correct. 3.** To cause (a person) to give up harmful or immoral practices; persuade to adopt a better way of life. — *intr.* To change for the better. — *n.* **1.** A change for the better; an improvement. **2.** Correction of evils, abuses, or errors. **3.** Action to improve social or economic conditions without radical or revolutionary change. — *adj.* **1.** Relating to or favoring reform. **2. Reform.** Of or relating to Reform Judaism. [ME *reformen* < OFr. *reformer* < Lat. *refōrmāre* : *re-*, re- + *fōrmāre*, to shape (< *fōrma*, form).] — **re•form′a•bil′i•ty** *n.* — **re•form′a•ble** *adj.* — **re•for′ma•tive** (-fôr′mə-tĭv) *adj.* — **re•form′er** *n.*

re-form (rē-fôrm′) *v.* **-formed, -form•ing, -forms.** — *tr.* To form again. — *intr.* To become formed again.

ref•or•ma•tion (rĕf′ər-mā′shən) *n.* **1.** The act of reforming or the state of being reformed. **2. Reformation.** A 16th-century movement in Western Europe that aimed at reforming the Roman Catholic Church and resulted in the establishment

referee

ă pat | oi boy
ā pay | ou out
âr care | o͝o took
ä father | o͞o boot
ĕ pet | ŭ cut
ē be | ûr urge
ĭ pit | th thin
ī pie | *th* this
îr pier | hw which
ŏ pot | zh vision
ō toe | ə about, item
ô paw |

Stress marks:
′ (primary);
′ (secondary), as in
dictionary (dĭk′shə-nĕr′ē)

of the Protestant churches. —**ref′or•ma′tion•al** *adj.*

re•for•ma•to•ry (rĭ-fôr′mə-tôr′ē, -tōr′ē) *n., pl.* **-ries.** A penal institution for the discipline, reformation, and training of young or first offenders. —*adj.* Reformative.

re•formed (rĭ-fôrmd′) *adj.* **1.** Improved by the removal of faults or abuses. **2.** Improved in conduct or character. **3. Reformed.** Relating to or being the Protestant churches that follow the teachings of John Calvin and Ulrich Zwingli.

re•form•ism (rĭ-fôr′mĭz′əm) *n.* A doctrine or movement of reform. —**re•form′ist** *n.*

Reform Judaism *n.* The branch of Judaism that seeks to reconcile historical Judaism with modern life and does not require strict observance of traditional religious law and ritual.

reform school *n.* See **reformatory.**

re•fract (rĭ-frăkt′) *tr.v.* **-fract•ed, -fract•ing, -fracts. 1.** To deflect (light, for example) from a straight path by refraction. **2.** To alter by viewing through a medium. **3.** *Medic.* To determine the refraction of (an eye, for example). [Lat. *refringere, refrāct-*, to break up : *re-*, re- + *frangere*, to break; see **bhreg-*.**]

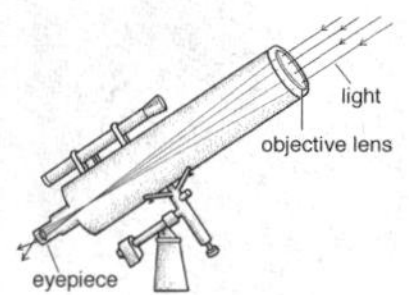

refracting telescope

re•fract•ing telescope (rĭ-frăk′tĭng) *n.* A telescope in which light from an object is gathered and focused by lenses.

re•frac•tion (rĭ-frăk′shən) *n.* **1.** The turning or bending of any wave, such as a light wave, when it passes from one medium into another of different density. **2.** *Astron.* The apparent change in position of celestial objects caused by the bending of light rays entering Earth's atmosphere. **3.** *Medic.* **a.** The ability of the eye to bend light to focus an image on the retina. **b.** Determination of the eye's refractive characteristics. —**re•frac′tion•al, re•frac′tive** *adj.* —**re•frac′tive•ly** *adv.* —**re•frac′tive•ness, re′frac•tiv′i•ty** (rē′frăk-tĭv′ĭ-tē) *n.*

refractive index *n. Phys.* See **index of refraction.**

re•frac•tom•e•ter (rē′frăk-tŏm′ĭ-tər) *n.* Any of several instruments used to measure the index of refraction of a substance.

re•frac•tor (rĭ-frăk′tər) *n.* **1.** One that refracts. **2.** A refracting telescope.

re•frac•to•ry (rĭ-frăk′tə-rē) *adj.* **1.** Obstinately resistant to authority or control. See Syns at **unruly. 2.** Difficult to melt or work; resistant to heat. **3.** Resistant to treatment. —*n., pl.* **-ries. 1.** One that is refractory. **2.** Material that has a high melting point. [Alteration of obsolete *refractary* < Lat. *refrāctārius* < *refrāctus*, p.part. of *refringere*, to break up. See REFRACT.] —**re•frac′to•ri•ly** *adv.* —**re•frac′to•ri•ness** *n.*

re•frain¹ (rĭ-frān′) *v.* **-frained, -frain•ing, -frains.** —*intr.* To hold oneself back; forbear. —*tr. Archaic.* To restrain or hold back; curb. [ME *refreinen* < OFr. *refrener*, to restrain < Lat. *refrēnāre* : *re-*, re- + *frēnāre*, to restrain (< *frēnum*, bridle < *frendere*, to grind; see **ghrendh-***).] —**re•frain′er** *n.* —**re•frain′ment** *n.*

re•frain² (rĭ-frān′) *n.* **1.a.** A phrase, verse, or group of verses repeated at intervals throughout a song or poem, esp. at the end of each stanza. **b.** Music for the refrain of a poem. **2.** A song or melody. **3.** A repeated utterance or theme. [ME *refrein* < OFr. *refrain*, alteration of *refrait*, p.part. of *refraindre*, to break off, repeat < VLat. **refrangere*, to break off, alteration of Lat. *refringere*. See REFRACT.]

re•fran•gi•ble (rĭ-frăn′jə-bəl) *adj.* That can be refracted. [< Lat. *refringere*, to refract (influenced by REFRACT).] —**re•fran′gi•bil′i•ty, re•fran′gi•ble•ness** *n.*

re•fresh (rĭ-frĕsh′) *v.* **-freshed, -fresh•ing, -fresh•es.** —*tr.* **1.** To revive with or as if with rest, food, or drink. **2.** To give new freshness or brightness to; restore. **3.** To make cool, clean, or moist; freshen up. **4.** To renew by stimulation. **5.** To fill up again; replenish. —*intr.* **1.** To take refreshment. **2.** To become fresh again; revive. [ME *refresshen* < OFr. *refreschir* : *re-*, re- + *fres, fresche*, fresh (of Gmc. orig.).]

re•fresh•er (rĭ-frĕsh′ər) *n.* **1.** One that refreshes. **2.** Instruction that serves to reacquaint one with material previously studied or to bring one's knowledge or skills up to date.

re•fresh•ing (rĭ-frĕsh′ĭng) *adj.* **1.** Serving to refresh. **2.** Pleasantly fresh and different. —**re•fresh′ing•ly** *adv.*

re•fresh•ment (rĭ-frĕsh′mənt) *n.* **1.** The act of refreshing or the state of being refreshed. **2.** Something, such as food, that refreshes. **3. refreshments.** A snack or light meal and drinks.

re•fried beans (rē′frīd′) *pl.n.* Beans that have been cooked and then mashed and fried with seasonings. [Transl. of Sp. *frijoles refritos*.]

re•frig•er•ant (rĭ-frĭj′ər-ənt) *adj.* **1.** Cooling or freezing; refrigerating. **2.** *Medic.* Reducing fever. —*n.* **1.** A substance, such as air or ammonia, used to provide cooling either as the working substance of a refrigerator or by direct absorption of heat. **2.** *Medic.* An agent used to reduce fever.

re•frig•er•ate (rĭ-frĭj′ə-rāt′) *tr.v.* **-at•ed, -at•ing, -ates. 1.** To cool or chill (a substance). **2.** To preserve (food) by chilling. [Lat. *refrīgerāre, refrīgerāt-* : *re-*, re- + *frīgerāre*, to make cool (< *frīgus, frīgor-*, coldness).] —**re•frig′er•a′tion** *n.* —**re•frig′er•a′tive, re•frig′er•a•to′ry** (-ər-ə-tôr′ē, -tōr′ē) *adj.*

re•frig•er•a•tor (rĭ-frĭj′ə-rā′tər) *n.* An appliance, a cabinet, or a room for storing substances at a low temperature.

re•frin•gence (rĭ-frĭn′jəns) *n.* Refractive power.

re•frin•gent (rĭ-frĭn′jənt) *adj.* Of, relating to, or producing refraction; refractive. [Lat. *refringēns, refringent-*, pr.part. of *refringere*, to break up. See REFRACT.]

reft¹ (rĕft) *v.* A p.t. and p.part. of **reave¹.**

reft² (rĕft) *v.* A p.t. and p.part. of **reave².**

re•fu•el (rē-fyo͞o′əl) *v.* **-eled, -el•ing, -els** also **-elled, -el•ling, -els.** —*tr.* To supply again with fuel. —*intr.* To take on a fresh supply of fuel.

ref•uge (rĕf′yo͞oj) *n.* **1.** Protection or shelter, as from danger or hardship. **2.** A place providing protection or shelter. **3.** A source of help, relief, or comfort in times of trouble. —*v.* **-uged, -ug•ing, -ug•es.** —*tr.* To give refuge to. —*intr.* To take refuge. [ME < OFr. < Lat. *refugium* < *refugere*, to run away : *re-*, re- + *fugere*, to flee.]

ref•u•gee (rĕf′yo͝o-jē′) *n.* One who flees in search of refuge, as in times of war. [Fr. *réfugié* < p.part. of *réfugier*, to take refuge < OFr. < *refuge*, refuge. See REFUGE.]

re•fu•gi•um (rĭ-fyo͞o′jē-əm) *n., pl.* **-gi•a** (-jē-ə). *Ecol.* An area that has escaped ecological changes occurring elsewhere and so provides a suitable habitat for relict species. [Lat., refuge. See REFUGE.]

re•ful•gent (rĭ-fo͝ol′jənt, -fŭl′-) *adj.* Shining radiantly; resplendent. [Lat. *refulgēns, refulgent-*, pr.part. of *refulgēre*, to flash back : *re-*, re- + *fulgēre*, to flash; see **bhel-¹*.**] —**re•ful′gence, re•ful′gen•cy** *n.* —**re•ful′gent•ly** *adv.*

re•fund (rĭ-fŭnd′, rē′fŭnd′) *v.* **-fund•ed, -fund•ing, -funds.** —*tr.* To give back, esp. money; return or repay. —*intr.* To make repayment. —*n.* (rē′fŭnd′). **1.** A repayment of funds. **2.** An amount repaid. [ME *refunden* < OFr. *refunder* < Lat. *refundere* : *re-*, re- + *fundere*, to pour; see **gheu-*.**] —**re•fund′a•ble** *adj.* —**re•fund′er** *n.* —**re•fund′ment** *n.*

re-fund (rē-fŭnd′) *tr.v.* **-fund•ed, -fund•ing, -funds. 1.** To fund anew. **2.** To pay back (a debt) with new borrowing.

re•fur•bish (rē-fûr′bĭsh) *tr.v.* **-bished, -bish•ing, -bish•es.** To make clean, bright, or fresh again; renovate. —**re•fur′bish•ment** *n.*

re•fus•al (rĭ-fyo͞o′zəl) *n.* **1.** The act or an instance of refusing. **2.** The opportunity or right to accept or reject something before it is offered elsewhere.

re•fuse¹ (rĭ-fyo͞oz′) *v.* **-fused, -fus•ing, -fus•es.** —*tr.* **1.a.** To indicate unwillingness to do, accept, give, or allow. **b.** To indicate unwillingness (to do something). **2.** To decline to jump (an obstacle). Used of a horse. —*intr.* To decline to do, accept, give, or allow something. [ME *refusen* < OFr. *refuser* < VLat. **refūsāre*, prob. Lat. *recūsāre*, to refuse; see RECUSE, and Lat. *refūtāre*; see REFUTE.] —**re•fus′er** *n.*

Syns: *refuse, decline, reject, spurn, rebuff.* These verbs all mean to be unwilling to accept, consider, or receive someone or something. *Refuse* usually implies determination and often brusqueness: *"The commander . . . refused to discuss questions of right"* (George Bancroft). To *decline* is to refuse courteously: *"Now I must decline the Pulitzer Prize"* (Sinclair Lewis). *Reject* suggests the discarding of someone or something as unsatisfactory, defective, or useless; it implies categoric refusal: *"He again offered himself for enlistment and was again rejected"* (Arthur S.M. Hutchinson). To *spurn* is to reject scornfully or contemptuously: *"The more she spurns my love/The more it grows"* (Shakespeare). *Rebuff* pertains to blunt, often disdainful rejection: *"He had . . . been rebuffed"* (Robert Louis Stevenson).

ref•use² (rĕf′yo͞os) *n.* Items or material discarded or rejected as useless or worthless; trash or rubbish. [ME < OFr. *refus*, rejection, refuse < *refuser*, to refuse. See REFUSE¹.]

re•fuse•nik (rĭ-fyo͞oz′nĭk) *n.* A Soviet citizen denied the right to emigrate.

ref•u•ta•tion (rĕf′yo͞o-tā′shən) also **re•fut•al** (rĭ-fyo͞ot′l) *n.* **1.** The act of refuting. **2.** Something, such as an argument, that refutes someone or something.

re•fute (rĭ-fyo͞ot′) *tr.v.* **-fut•ed, -fut•ing, -futes. 1.** To prove to be false or erroneous; overthrow by argument or proof. **2.** To deny the accuracy or truth of: *refuted the results of the poll.* [Lat. *refūtāre.* See **bhau-*.**] —**re•fut′a•bil′i•ty** (rĭ-fyo͞o′tə-bĭl′ĭ-tē, rĕf′yə-tə-) *n.* —**re•fut′a•ble** (rĭ-fyo͞o′tə-bəl, rĕf′yə-tə-) *adj.* —**re•fut′a•bly** *adv.* —**re•fut′er** *n.*

reg. *abbr.* **1.** Regent. **2.** Regiment. **3.** Region. **4.** Register; registered. **5.** Registrar. **6.** Registry. **7.a.** Regular. **b.** Regularly. **8.** Regulation. **9.** Regulator.

re•gain (rē-gān′) *tr.v.* **-gained, -gain•ing, -gains. 1.** To recover possession of; get back again. See Syns at **recover. 2.** To manage to reach again. —**re•gain′er** *n.*

re•gal (rē′gəl) *adj.* **1.** Of or relating to a monarch; royal. **2.** Belonging to or befitting a monarch. **3.** Magnificent; splendid. [ME < OFr. < Lat. *rēgālis* < *rēx, rēg-*, king. See **reg-*.**] —**re•gal′i•ty** (rĭ-găl′ĭ-tē) *n.* —**re′gal•ly** *adv.*

re•gale (rĭ-gāl′) *v.* **-galed, -gal•ing, -gales.** —*tr.* **1.** To provide with great enjoyment; entertain. **2.** To entertain sumptuously with food and drink; feast. —*intr.* To feast. —*n.* **1.** A great feast. **2.** A choice food; a delicacy. **3.** Refreshment. [Fr. *régaler* < OFr. *regal*, feast < *gale* < *galer*, to make merry.] —**re•gale′ment** *n.*

re•ga•lia (rĭ-gāl′yə, -gā′lē-ə) *pl.n.* *(used with a sing. or pl. v.)* **1.** The emblems and symbols of royalty. **2.** The rights and privileges of royalty. **3.** The distinguishing symbols of a rank, office, order, or society. **4.** Magnificent attire; finery. [Med. Lat. *rēgālia* < Lat., neut. pl. of *rēgālis*, regal. See REGAL.]

re•gard (rĭ-gärd′) *v.* **-gard•ed, -gard•ing, -gards.** —*tr.* **1.** To look at attentively; observe closely. **2.** To look upon or consider in a particular way. **3.** To hold in esteem or respect. **4.** To relate or refer to; concern. **5.** To take into account; consider. **6.** *Obsolete.* To take care of. —*intr.* **1.** To look or gaze. **2.** To give heed; pay attention. —*n.* **1.** A look or gaze. **2.** Careful thought or attention; heed. **3.a.** Respect, affection, or esteem. **b. regards.** Good wishes expressing such sentiment. **4.** A particular point or aspect. **5.** Basis for action; motive. **6.** *Obsolete.* Appearance or aspect. —***idioms.* as regards.** Concerning. **in (or with) regard to.** With respect to. [ME *regarden* < OFr. *regarder* : *re-*, re- + *guarder*, to guard (of Gmc. orig.; see GUARD).]

Usage Note: *Regard* is traditionally used in the singular in the phrase *in regard* (not *in regards*) *to. Regarding* and *as regards* are also standard in the sense "with reference to." In the same sense *with respect to* is acceptable, but *respecting* is not. • *Respects* is sometimes considered preferable to *regards* in the sense of "particulars": *In some respects* (not *regards*) *the books are alike.*

re•gar•dant (rĭ-gär′dnt) *adj. Her.* Looking backward in profile. [ME < OFr., pr.part. of *regarder*, to regard. See REGARD.]

re•gard•ful (rĭ-gärd′fəl) *adj.* **1.** Showing attention; heedful. **2.** Showing deference; respectful. —**re•gard′ful•ly** *adv.* —**re•gard′ful•ness** *n.*

re•gard•ing (rĭ-gär′dĭng) *prep.* In reference to; with respect to; concerning. See Usage Note at **regard.**

re•gard•less (rĭ-gärd′lĭs) *adv.* In spite of everything; anyway: *continues to work regardless.* —*adj.* Heedless; unmindful. —**re•gard′less•ly** *adv.* —**re•gard′less•ness** *n.*

regardless of *prep.* **1.** In spite of. **2.** With no heed to.

re•gat•ta (rĭ-gä′tə, -găt′ə) *n. Naut.* A boat race or a series of boat races. [Ital. dial., a contention, regatta < *regattare*, to contend, perh. < *recatare*, to sell again, compete < VLat. **recaptāre*, to contend : Lat. *re-*, re- + Lat. *captāre*, to seek to catch, freq. of *capere*, to seize; see CATCH.]

regd. *abbr.* Registered.

re•ge•la•tion (rē′jə-lā′shən) *n.* **1.** The fusion of two ice blocks by pressure. **2.** Successive melting under pressure and freezing when pressure is relaxed at the interface of two ice blocks.

re•gen•cy (rē′jən-sē) *n., pl.* **-cies. 1.** A person or group selected to govern in place of a ruler who is absent, disabled, or still in minority. **2.** The period during which a regent governs. **3.** The office, area of jurisdiction, or government of regents or a regent. —*adj.* **1. Regency.** Of, relating to, or characteristic of the style, esp. in furniture, prevalent in England during the regency (1811–1820) of George, Prince of Wales (later George IV). **2. Regency.** Of, relating to, or characteristic of the style prevalent in France during the regency (1715–1723) of Philippe, Duc d'Orléans (1674–1723). **3.** Of a regency.

re•gen•er•a•cy (rĭ-jĕn′ər-ə-sē) *n.* The state of being regenerated.

re•gen•er•ate (rĭ-jĕn′ə-rāt′) *v.* **-at•ed, -at•ing, -ates.** —*tr.* **1.** To reform spiritually or morally. **2.** To form, construct, or create anew, esp. in an improved state. **3.** To give new life or energy to; revitalize. **4.** *Biol.* To replace (an organ or part) by formation of new tissue. —*intr.* **1.** To become formed or constructed again. **2.** To undergo spiritual conversion or rebirth; reform. **3.** To effect regeneration. —*n.* (-ər-ĭt). **1.** One who is spiritually reborn. **2.** *Biol.* A regenerated organ or part. —*adj.* (-ər-ĭt). **1.** Spiritually or morally reformed. **2.** Formed or created anew. **3.** Restored to a better state; refreshed or renewed. [Lat. *regenerāre, regenerāt-*, to reproduce : *re-*, re- + *generāre*, to beget; see GENERATE.] —**re•gen′er•a•ble** (-ər-ə-bəl) *adj.* —**re•gen′er•ate•ly** *adv.* —**re•gen′er•a′tor** *n.*

re•gen•er•a•tion (rĭ-jĕn′ə-rā′shən) *n.* **1.** The act or process of regenerating or the state of being regenerated. **2.** Spiritual or moral revival or rebirth. **3.** *Biol.* Regrowth of lost or destroyed parts or organs.

re•gen•er•a•tive (rĭ-jĕn′ə-rā′tĭv, -ər-ə-tĭv) *adj.* **1.** Of, relating to, or marked by regeneration. **2.** Tending to regenerate. —**re•gen′er•a′tive•ly** *adv.*

Re•gens•burg (rā′gənz-bûrg′, -gəns-bo͝ork′). A city of SE Germany on the Danube R. NNE of Munich. Pop. 126,681.

re•gent (rē′jənt) *n.* **1.** One who rules during the minority, absence, or disability of a monarch. **2.** One acting as a ruler or governor. **3.** A member of a board that governs an institution, such as a university. [ME < OFr. < Lat. *regēns, regent-*, ruler < pr.part. of *regere*, to rule. See **reg-*.**] —**re′gent•al** (-jən-tl) *adj.*

reg•gae (rĕg′ā) *n. Mus.* Popular music of Jamaican origin having elements of calypso, soul, and rock 'n' roll. [Jamaican E., ult. < *rege-rege*, ragged clothing, prob. < RAG[1].]

Reg•gio di Ca•la•bri•a (rĕj′ē-ō dē kä-lä′brē-ä, rĕd′jō) also **Reggio** or **Reggio Calabria.** A city of extreme S Italy on the Strait of Messina opposite Sicily; founded in the late 8th cent. B.C. Pop. 171,324.

Reggio nell'E•mi•lia (nĕl′ĕ-mēl′yä) also **Reggio** or **Reggio Emilia.** A city of N-central Italy WNW of Bologna; founded by Romans in the 2nd cent. B.C. Pop. 129,893.

reg•i•cide (rĕj′ĭ-sīd′) *n.* **1.** The killing of a king. **2.** One who kills a king. [Lat. *rēx, rēg-*, king; see **reg-*** + -CIDE.] —**reg′i•cid′al** (-sīd′l) *adj.*

re•gime also **ré•gime** (rā-zhēm′, rĭ-) *n.* **1.a.** A form of government. **b.** A government in power; administration. **2.** A prevailing social system or pattern. **3.** The period during which a particular administration or system prevails. **4.** A regulated system, as of diet; a regimen. [Fr. *régime* < OFr. < Lat. *regimen* < *regere*, to rule. See **reg-*.**]

reg•i•men (rĕj′ə-mən, -mĕn′) *n.* **1.** Governmental rule or control. **2.** The systematic procedure of a natural phenomenon or process. **3.a.** A regulated system, as of diet, intended to achieve a beneficial effect. **b.** A course of intense physical training. [ME < Lat. See REGIME.]

reg•i•ment (rĕj′ə-mənt) *n.* **1.** A military unit of ground troops consisting of at least two battalions. **2.** A large group of people. —*tr.v.* (rĕj′ə-mĕnt′) **-ment•ed, -ment•ing, -ments. 1.** To form into a regiment. **2.** To put into systematic order; systematize. **3.** To subject to uniformity and rigid order. [ME, government, rule < OFr. < LLat. *regimentum*, rule < Lat. *regere*, to rule. See **reg-*.**] —**reg′i•men′tal** (-mĕn′tl) *adj.* —**reg′i•men′tal•ly** *adv.* —**reg′i•men•ta′tion** *n.*

reg•i•men•tals (rĕj′ə-mĕnt′lz) *pl.n.* **1.** The uniform and insignia of a particular regiment. **2.** Military dress.

Re•gi•na (rĭ-jī′nə). The cap. of Saskatchewan, Canada, in the S part SE of Saskatoon. Pop. 162,613.

Re•gi•o•mon•ta•nus (rē′jē-ō-mŏn-tā′nəs, -tä′-, -tăn-əs, rĕj′ē-). See Johann **Müller.**

re•gion (rē′jən) *n.* **1.** A large, usu. continuous segment of a surface or space; area. **2.** A large, indefinite portion of the earth's surface. **3.** A specified district or territory. **4.** An area of interest or activity; a sphere. **5.** *Ecol.* A part of the earth characterized by distinctive animal or plant life. **6.** An area of the body. [ME < OFr. < Lat. *regiō, regiōn-* < *regere*, to rule. See **reg-*.**]

re•gion•al (rē′jə-nəl) *adj.* **1.** Of or relating to a large geographic region. **2.** Of or relating to a particular region or district. **3.** Of or characteristic of a form of a language that is distributed in identifiable geographic areas and differs from the standard form; dialectal. —*n.* Something, such as a magazine, that serves a region. —**re′gion•al•ly** *adv.*

re•gion•al•ism (rē′jə-nə-lĭz′əm) *n.* **1.a.** Political division of an area into partially autonomous regions. **b.** Advocacy of such a political system. **2.** Loyalty to the interests of a particular region. **3.** A feature, such as an expression, that is characteristic of a geographic area. **4.** The use of regional characteristics in literature or art. —**re′gion•al•ist** *adj. & n.* —**re′gion•al•is′tic** *adj.*

re•gion•al•ize (rē′jə-nə-līz′) *tr.v.* **-ized, -iz•ing, -iz•es.** To divide into regions, esp. for administrative purposes. —**re′gion•al•i•za′tion** (rē′jə-nə-lĭ-zā′shən) *n.*

ré•gis•seur (rā′zhē-sûr′, -sœr′) *n., pl.* **-seurs** (-sûr′, -sœr′). A stage director, esp. of a ballet. [Fr. < *régir, régiss-*, to direct < OFr. *regir* < Lat. *regere.* See REGENT.]

reg•is•ter (rĕj′ĭ-stər) *n.* **1.a.** A formal or official recording of items, names, or actions. **b.** A book for such entries. **c.** An entry in such a record. **2.** The act of registering. **3.** A device that automatically records a quantity or number. **4.** *Comp. Sci.* A part of the central processing unit where groups of binary digits are stored during processing. **5.** An adjustable grill-like device through which heated or cooled air is released into a room. **6.** A state of proper alignment. **7.** *Print.* **a.** Exact alignment of the lines and margins on the opposite sides of a leaf. **b.** Proper positioning of colors. **8.** *Mus.* **a.** The range of an instrument or a voice. **b.** A part of such a range. **c.** A group of matched organ pipes; a stop. **9.** A variety of language used in a specific social setting. —*v.* **-tered, -ter•ing, -ters.** —*tr.* **1.a.** To enter in an official register. **b.** To enroll officially or formally, esp. in order to vote or attend classes. **2.** To set down in writing; record. **3.** To indicate on or as if on an instrument or a scale. **4.** To give outward signs of; express. **5.** To attain or achieve. **6.** To cause (mail) to be officially recorded and specially handled by payment of a fee. **7.** To adjust so as to be properly aligned. —*intr.* **1.** To place or cause placement of one's name in a register. **2.** To have one's name officially placed on a list of eligible voters. **3.** To enroll as a student. **4.** To be indicated on or as if on an instrument or a scale. **5.** To be shown or expressed, as on the face. **6.** To make an impression; be recorded in the mind. **7.** To be in proper alignment. [ME *registre* < OFr. < Med.Lat. *registrum*, alteration of LLat. *regesta* < Lat., neut. pl. p.part. of *regerere*, to record : *re-*, re- + *gerere*, to carry.] —**reg′is•ter•er** *n.* —**reg′is•tra•ble** (-ĭ-strə-bəl) *adj.*

reg•is•tered (rĕj′ĭ-stərd) *adj.* **1.** Having the owner's name listed in a register. **2.** Having the pedigree recorded and verified by an authorized association of breeders. **3.** Officially qualified or certified: *a registered pharmacist.*

registered mail *n.* Mail recorded by the post office when sent and at each point on its route so as to assure safe delivery.

register
Top: Hand-cranked
Bottom: Electronic

ă pat	oi boy
ā pay	ou out
âr care	o͝o took
ä father	o͞o boot
ĕ pet	ŭ cut
ē be	ûr urge
ĭ pit	th thin
ī pie	*th* this
îr pier	hw which
ŏ pot	zh vision
ō toe	ə about, item
ô paw	

Stress marks:
′ (primary);
′ (secondary), as in
dictionary (dĭk′shə-nĕr′ē)

registered nurse *n.* A graduate trained nurse who has passed a state registration examination and has been licensed to practice nursing.

reg•is•trant (rĕj′ĭ-strənt) *n.* One who registers or is registered.

reg•is•trar (rĕj′ĭ-strär′, rĕj′ĭ-strär′) *n.* **1.** One who is in charge of official records. **2.** An officer in a college or university who keeps the records of enrollment and academic standing. **3.** An officer of a corporation responsible for maintaining records of ownership of its securities. **4.** An admitting officer in a hospital. [Prob. < *registrary* < Med.Lat. *registrārius* < *registrum*, register. See REGISTER.]

reg•is•tra•tion (rĕj′ĭ-strā′shən) *n.* **1.** The act of registering. **2.** The number of persons registered; enrollment. **3.** An entry in a register. **4.** A document certifying an act of registering. **5.** *Mus.* **a.** A combination of organ stops used in playing a piece. **b.** The technique of selecting and adjusting organ stops.

reg•is•try (rĕj′ĭ-strē) *n., pl.* **-tries. 1.** The act of registering; registration. **2.** The registered nationality of a ship. **3.** A place for registering. **4.a.** A book for official records. **b.** The place where such records are kept.

re•gius professor (rē′jəs, -jē-əs) *n.* One holding a professorship established by royal subsidy at a British university. [< Lat. *rēgius*, royal < *rēx*, *rēg-*, king. See **reg-*.**]

reg•let (rĕg′lĭt) *n.* **1.** *Archit.* A narrow flat molding. **2.** *Print.* A flat piece of wood used to separate lines of type. [Fr. *réglet* < OFr., dim. of *regle*, ruler < Lat. *rēgula*, rod. See **reg-*.**]

reg•nal (rĕg′nəl) *adj.* Being a specified year of a monarch's reign calculated from the date of accession. [Med.Lat. *rēgnālis*, royal < Lat. *rēgnum*, reign. See REIGN.]

reg•nant (rĕg′nənt) *adj.* **1.** Reigning; ruling. **2.** Predominant. **3.** Widespread; prevalent. [Prob. < ME, a sovereign < OFr. < Lat. *rēgnāns*, *rēgnant-*, pr.part. of *rēgnāre*, to reign < *rēgnum*, reign. See REIGN.]

reg•o•lith (rĕg′ə-lĭth′) *n.* The layer of loose rock resting on bedrock, constituting the surface of most land. [Gk. *rhēgos*, blanket + -LITH.]

re•gorge (rē-gôrj′) *tr.v.* **-gorged, -gorg•ing, -gorg•es.** To disgorge. [Fr. *regorger* < OFr. : *re-*, re- + *gorger*, to gorge (< *gorge*, throat; see GORGE).]

re•gress (rĭ-grĕs′) *v.* **-gressed, -gress•ing, -gress•es.** —*intr.* **1.** To go back; move backward. **2.** To return to a previous, usu. worse or less developed state. **3.** To have a tendency to approach or go back to a statistical mean. —*n.* (rē′grĕs′). **1.** The act of going or coming back; return. **2.** Passage back; reentry. [Lat. *regredī*, *regress-* : *re-*, re- + *gradī*, to go; see **ghredh-*.**] —**re•gres′sor** *n.*

re•gres•sion (rĭ-grĕsh′ən) *n.* **1.** Reversion; retrogression. **2.** Relapse to a less perfect or developed state. **3.** *Psychol.* Reversion to a less mature pattern of feeling or behavior. **4.** *Biol.* The return of a population to an earlier or less complex physical type. **5.** *Statistics.* The relationship between the mean value of a random variable and the corresponding values of one or more independent variables. **6.** *Astron.* Retrograde motion of a celestial body.

re•gres•sive (rĭ-grĕs′ĭv) *adj.* **1.** Tending to return or revert. **2.** Of or characterized by regression or a tendency to regress. **3.** Decreasing proportionately as the amount taxed increases. —**re•gres′sive•ly** *adv.* —**re•gres′sive•ness** *n.*

re•gret (rĭ-grĕt′) *v.* **-gret•ted, -gret•ting, -grets.** —*tr.* **1.** To feel sorry, disappointed, or distressed about. **2.** To remember with a feeling of loss or sorrow; mourn. —*intr.* To feel regret. —*n.* **1.** A sense of loss and longing for someone or something gone. **2.** A feeling of disappointment or distress about something. **3. regrets.** A courteous expression of regret, esp. at having to decline an invitation. [ME *regretten*, to lament < OFr. *regreter* : *re-*, re- + *-greter*, to weep (perh. of Gmc. orig.).] —**re•gret′ter** *n.*

Syns: *regret, sorrow, grief, anguish, woe, heartache, heartbreak.* All of these nouns denote mental distress. *Regret* has the broadest range, from mere disappointment to a painful sense of dissatisfaction or self-reproach, as over something lost or done: *She looked back with regret on her life. Sorrow* connotes sadness caused by misfortune, affliction, or loss; it can also imply contrition: *"sorrow for his . . . children, who needed his protection, and whom he could not protect"* (James Baldwin). *Grief* is deep, acute personal sorrow, as that arising from irreplaceable loss: *"Grief fills the room up of my absent child"* (Shakespeare). *Anguish* implies agonizing, excruciating mental pain: *"I pray that our heavenly Father may assuage the anguish of your bereavement"* (Abraham Lincoln). *Woe* is intense, often prolonged wretchedness or misery: *"the deep, unutterable woe/Which none save exiles feel"* (W.E. Aytoun). *Heartache* most often applies to sustained private sorrow: *The child's difficulties are a source of heartache to the parents. Heartbreak* is overwhelming grief: *"Better a little chiding than a great deal of heartbreak"* (Shakespeare).

re•gret•ful (rĭ-grĕt′fəl) *adj.* Full of regret; sorrowful or sorry. —**re•gret′ful•ly** *adv.* —**re•gret′ful•ness** *n.*

re•gret•ta•ble (rĭ-grĕt′ə-bəl) *adj.* Eliciting or deserving regret.

re•gret•ta•bly (rĭ-grĕt′ə-blē) *adv.* **1.** To an extent deserving of regret: *regrettably brief.* **2.** As a matter of regret.

re•group (rē-gro͞op′) *v.* **-grouped, -group•ing, -groups.** —*tr.* To arrange in a new grouping. —*intr.* **1.** To come back together in a tactical formation, as after a dispersal in a retreat. **2.** To reorganize for renewed effort, as after a setback.

regt. *abbr.* **1.** Regent. **2.** Regiment.

reg•u•lar (rĕg′yə-lər) *adj.* **1.** Customary, usual, or normal. **2.** Orderly, even, or symmetrical. **3.** In conformity with a fixed procedure, principle, or discipline. **4.** Well-ordered; methodical. **5.** Occurring at fixed intervals; periodic. **6.a.** Occurring with normal or healthy frequency. **b.** Having bowel movements or menstrual periods with normal or healthy frequency. **7.** Not varying; constant. **8.** Formally correct; proper. **9.** Having the required qualifications for an occupation. **10.** *Informal.* Complete; thorough. **11.** *Informal.* Good; nice. **12.** *Bot.* Having symmetrically arranged parts of similar size and shape. **13.** *Gram.* Conforming to the usual pattern of inflection, derivation, or word formation. **14.** *Eccles.* Belonging to a religious order and bound by its rules. **15.** *Math.* **a.** Having equal sides and equal angles. Used of polygons. **b.** Having faces that are congruent regular polygons and congruent polyhedral angles. Used of polyhedrons. **16.** Belonging to or constituting the permanent army of a nation. —*n.* **1.** *Eccles.* A member of the clergy or of a religious order. **2.** A soldier belonging to a regular army. **3.** A dependable, loyal person: *a party regular.* **4.** A clothing size for persons of average height. **5.** A habitual customer. [ME *reguler*, living under religious rule < OFr. < LLat. *rēgulāris*, according to rule < Lat. *rēgula*, rod, rule. See **reg-*.**] —**reg′u•lar′i•ty** (-lăr′ĭ-tē) *n.* —**reg′u•lar•ly** *adv.*

regular army *n.* The permanent standing army of a nation or state.

reg•u•lar•ize (rĕg′yə-lə-rīz′) *tr.v.* **-ized, -iz•ing, -iz•es.** To make regular; cause to conform. —**reg′u•lar•i•za′tion** (-lər-ĭ-zā′shən) *n.* —**reg′u•lar•iz′er** *n.*

reg•u•late (rĕg′yə-lāt′) *tr.v.* **-lat•ed, -lat•ing, -lates. 1.** To control or direct according to rule, principle, or law. **2.** To adjust to a particular specification or requirement: *regulate temperature.* **3.** To adjust (a mechanism) for accurate and proper functioning. **4.** To put or maintain in order. [ME < LLat. *rēgulāre*, *rēgulāt-* < Lat. *rēgula*, rod, rule. See **reg-*.**] —**reg′u•la′tive, reg′u•la•to′ry** (-lə-tôr′ē, -tōr′ē) *adj.*

reg•u•la•tion (rĕg′yə-lā′shən) *n.* **1.** The act of regulating or the state of being regulated. **2.** A principle, rule, or law designed to control or govern conduct. **3.** A government order having the force of law. **4.** *Embryol.* The capacity of an embryo to continue normal development following injury to or alteration of a structure.

reg•u•la•tor (rĕg′yə-lā′tər) *n.* **1.** One that regulates, as: **a.** The mechanism in a watch by which its speed is governed. **b.** A clock used as a standard for timing other clocks. **c.** A device used to maintain uniform speed in a machine; a governor. **d.** A device used to control the flow of gases, liquids, or electric current. **2.** One that ensures compliance with laws and regulations.

regulator gene *n.* A gene that represses the activity of another gene in an operon.

re•gu•lus (rĕg′yə-ləs) *n., pl.* **-li** (-lī) or **-lus•es. 1.** The metallic mass that sinks to the bottom of a furnace or crucible during smelting. **2.** A relatively impure intermediate product of various ores in smelting. [Lat. *rēgulus*, dim. of *rēx*, *rēg-*, king. See **reg-*.**] —**reg′u•line** (rĕg′yə-lĭn, -līn′) *adj.*

Reg•u•lus (rĕg′yə-ləs) *n.* A bright double star in the constellation Leo. [Lat. *rēgulus*, dim. of *rēx*, *rēg-*, king. See REGULUS.]

Regulus, Marcus Atilius. d. c. 250 B.C. Roman general who while a prisoner of the Carthaginians (after 255) convinced the Romans to reject terms for a peace treaty.

re•gur•gi•tate (rē-gûr′jĭ-tāt′) *v.* **-tat•ed, -tat•ing, -tates.** —*intr.* To rush or surge back. —*tr.* To cause to pour back, esp. to cast up (partially digested food). [Med.Lat. *regurgitāre*, *regurgitāt-*, to overflow : Lat. *re-*, re- + LLat. *gurgitāre*, to engulf, flood (< Lat. *gurges*, *gurgit-*, whirlpool).] —**re•gur′gi•tant** (-tənt) *adj.* —**re•gur′gi•ta′tion** *n.* —**re•gur′gi•ta•tive** *adj.*

re•hab (rē′hăb′) *Informal.* —*n.* **1.** Rehabilitation. **2.** Something, esp. a building, that has undergone rehabilitation. —*tr.v.* **-habbed, -hab•bing, -habs.** To rehabilitate.

re•ha•bil•i•tant (rē′hə-bĭl′ĭ-tənt) *n.* One who is undergoing rehabilitation, as for a disability.

re•ha•bil•i•tate (rē′hə-bĭl′ĭ-tāt′) *tr.v.* **-tat•ed, -tat•ing, -tates. 1.** To restore to good health or useful life, as through therapy. **2.** To restore to good condition, operation, or capacity. **3.** To reinstate the good name of. **4.** To restore the former rank, privileges, or rights of. [Med.Lat. *rehabilitāre*, *rehabilitāt-*, to restore to a rank : Lat. *re-*, re- + LLat. *habilitāre*, to enable; see HABILITATE.] —**re′ha•bil′i•tat′a•ble** *adj.* —**re′ha•bil′i•ta′tion** *n.* —**re′ha•bil′i•ta′tive** *adj.*

re•hash (rē-hăsh′) *tr.v.* **-hashed, -hash•ing, -hash•es. 1.** To bring forth again in another form without significant alteration. **2.** To discuss again. —*n.* (rē′hăsh′). The act or result of rehashing.

re•hear (rē-hîr′) *tr.v.* **-heard** (-hûrd′), **-hear•ing, -hears. 1.** To hear again. **2.** *Law.* To give a new hearing to (a case) by the same court.

re•hear•ing (rē-hîr′ĭng) *n. Law.* A new hearing of a case by the same court in which it was originally heard.

re•hears•al (rĭ-hûr′səl) *n.* **1.** The act of practicing in preparation for a public performance. **2.** A session of practice for a performance. **3.** A detailed enumeration or repetition.

re•hearse (rĭ-hûrs′) *v.* **-hearsed, -hears•ing, -hears•es.** *—tr.* **1.a.** To practice (a part in a play, for example) in preparation for a public performance. **b.** To direct in rehearsal. **2.** To perfect or cause to perfect (an action) by repetition. See Syns at **practice. 3.a.** To retell or recite. **b.** To list or enumerate. *—intr.* To practice something before presenting it publicly. [ME *rehercen*, to repeat < OFr. *rehercier* : *re-*, re- + *hercier*, to harrow (< *herce*, harrow; see HEARSE).] **—re•hears′er** *n.*

Rehn•quist (rĕn′kwĭst′), **William Hubbs.** b. 1924. Amer. jurist; associate justice (1972–86) and chief justice of the U.S. Supreme Court (since 1986).

re•hy•drate (rē-hī′drāt′) *tr.v.* **-drat•ed, -drat•ing, -drates. 1.** To cause (something dehydrated) to take up fluid. **2.** To replenish the body fluids of. **—re′hy•dra′tion** *n.*

Reich (rīk, rīKH), **Wilhelm.** 1897–1957. Austrian psychoanalyst who theorized that sexual repression is the source of many psychological and social problems.

reichs•mark (rīks′märk′, rīKHs′-) *n., pl.* **reichsmark** or **-marks.** A monetary unit of Germany from 1925 to 1948. [Ger. : *Reichs*, genitive of *Reich*, realm (< MHGer. *rīch* < OHGer. *rīchi*; see **reg-***) + *Mark*, unit of currency (< MHGer. *marke*; see MARK[2]).]

re•i•fy (rē′ə-fī′, rā′-) *tr.v.* **-fied, -fy•ing, -fies.** To regard or treat (an abstraction) as if it had concrete or material existence. [Lat. *rēs*, *rē-*, thing; see **rē-*** + -FY.] **—re′i•fi•ca′tion** (-fĭ-kā′shən) *n.* **—re′i•fi′er** *n.*

Rei•gate (rī′gĭt). A municipal borough of S England, a residential suburb of London. Pop. 116,700.

reign (rān) *n.* **1.** Exercise of sovereign power. **2.** The period during which a monarch rules. **3.** Dominance or widespread influence. *—intr.v.* **reigned, reign•ing, reigns. 1.** To exercise sovereign power. **2.** To hold the title of monarch with limited authority. **3.** To be predominant or prevalent. [ME *reigne* < OFr. < Lat. *rēgnum* < *rēx*, *rēg-*, king. See **reg-***.]

Reign of Terror (rān) *n.* **1.** The period (1793–1794) of the French Revolution during which thousands of people were executed. **2. reign of terror,** *pl.* **reigns of terror.** A period of brutal suppression or intimidation by those in power.

re•im•burse (rē′ĭm-bûrs′) *tr.v.* **-bursed, -burs•ing, -burs•es. 1.** To repay (money spent); refund. **2.** To pay back or compensate (another party) for money spent or losses incurred. [RE- + *imburse*, to put in a purse, pay (< Fr. *embourser* < OFr. : *en-*, in < Lat. *in-*; see IN-[2] + *borser*, to get money < *borse*, purse < LLat. *bursa*, bag; see BURSA).] **—re′im•burs′a•ble** *adj.* **—re′im•burse′ment** *n.*

re•im•pres•sion (rē′ĭm-prĕsh′ən) *n. Print.* A second impression, as of a book, that is identical to the original; a reprint.

Reims (rēmz, răNs). See **Rheims.**

rein (rān) *n.* **1.** A long narrow leather strap attached to each end of the bit of a bridle and used by a rider or driver to control a horse or other animal. Often used in the plural. **2.** A means of restraint, check, or guidance. **3.** A means or an instrument by which power is exercised. Often used in the plural. *—v.* **reined, rein•ing, reins.** *—tr.* **1.** To check or hold back by or as if by the use of reins. Often with *in, back,* or *up.* **2.** To restrain or control. *—intr.* To control a horse, for example, with reins. ***—idioms.* draw in the reins.** To slow down or stop by or as if by pressure on the reins. **give (free** (or **full) rein to.** Allow to go unchecked. **tight rein.** Close control. [ME < OFr. *resne, reine* < VLat. **retina* < Lat. *retinēre*, to retain. See RETAIN.]

re•in•car•nate (rē′ĭn-kär′nāt) *tr.v.* **-nat•ed, -nat•ing, -nates.** To cause to be reborn in another body; incarnate again.

re•in•car•na•tion (rē′ĭn-kär-nā′shən) *n.* **1.a.** Rebirth of the soul in another body. **b.** Belief in this rebirth. **2.** A rebirth in another form; a new embodiment.

rein•deer (rān′dîr′) *n., pl.* **reindeer** or **-deers.** A large deer *(Rangifer tarandus)* of the Arctic and northern regions of Eurasia and North America, having branched antlers in both sexes. [ME *reindere* : ON *hreinn*, reindeer; see **ker-[1]*** + ME *der*, animal; see DEER.]

Rein•deer Lake (rān′dîr′). A lake of NE Saskatchewan and NW Manitoba, Canada, drained by the **Reindeer River,** flowing c. 230 km (143 mi) to the Churchill R.

reindeer moss *n.* An erect grayish branching lichen *(Cladonia rangiferina)* of Arctic regions.

re•in•fec•tion (rē′ĭn-fĕk′shən) *n.* A second infection that follows recovery from a previous infection of the same type.

re•in•force also **re•en•force** or **re-en•force** (rē′ĭn-fôrs′, -fōrs′) *tr.v.* **-forced, -forc•ing, -forc•es. 1.** To give more force or effectiveness to; strengthen. **2.** To strengthen (a military force) with additional personnel or equipment. **3.** To strengthen by adding extra support or material. **4.** To increase the number or amount of; augment. **5.** *Psychol.* **a.** To reward (an experimental subject, for example) with a reinforcer subsequent to a desired response or performance. **b.** To stimulate (a response) by means of a reinforcer. [RE- + *inforce* (var. of ENFORCE).] **—re′in•force′a•ble** *adj.*

re•in•forced concrete (rē′ĭn-fôrst′, -fōrst′) *n.* Poured concrete containing steel bars or metal netting to increase its tensile strength.

re•in•force•ment (rē′ĭn-fôrs′mənt, -fōrs′-) *n.* **1.** The act or process of reinforcing or the state of being reinforced. **2.** Something that reinforces. **3.** Additional personnel or equipment sent to support a military action. Often used in the plural. **4.** *Psychol.* An event, a circumstance, or a condition that increases the likelihood that a given response will recur in a situation like that in which the reinforcing condition originally occurred.

re•in•forc•er (rē′ĭn-fôr′sər, -fōr′-) *n. Psychol.* A stimulus, such as a reward, that in operant conditioning maintains or strengthens a desired response.

Rein•hardt (rīn′härt′), **Max.** 1873–1943. Austrian theatrical director whose productions included *Oedipus Rex.*

reins (rānz) *pl.n.* **1.** The kidneys, loins, or lower back. **2.** The seat of the affections and passions. [ME < OFr. < Lat. *rēnēs.*]

re•in•state (rē′ĭn-stāt′) *tr.v.* **-stat•ed, -stat•ing, -states. 1.** To bring back into use or existence. **2.** To restore to a previous condition or position. **—re′in•state′ment** *n.*

re•in•sure (rē′ĭn-shŏŏr′) *tr.v.* **-sured, -sur•ing, -sures.** To insure (all or part of the risk in a contract) under a new contract with another insurance agency. **—re′in•sur′ance** *n.* **—re′in•sur′er** *n.*

re•in•vent (rē′ĭn-vĕnt′) *tr.v.* **-vent•ed, -vent•ing, -vents. 1.** To make over completely. **2.** To bring back into existence or use. ***—idiom.* reinvent the wheel. 1.** To do something over again, esp. needlessly or inefficiently. **2.** To recast something familiar or old into a different form.

reindeer
Rangifer tarandus

reis (rās) *n.* Pl. of **real[3].**

re•is•sue (rē-ĭsh′ōō) *v.* **-sued, -su•ing, -sues.** *—tr.* To issue again, esp. to make available again. *—intr.* To come forth again. *—n.* **1.** A second or subsequent issue, as of a book. **2.** A reprinting of postage stamps from unchanged plates.

Rei•sters•town (rī′stərz-toun′). A community of N-central MD, a suburb of Baltimore. Pop., 19,314.

REIT *abbr.* Real estate investment trust.

re•it•er•ate (rē-ĭt′ə-rāt′) *tr.v.* **-at•ed, -at•ing, -ates.** To say or do again or repeatedly. See Syns at **repeat. —re•it′er•a′tion** *n.* **—re•it′er•a′tive** (-ə-rā′tĭv, -ər-ə-tĭv) *adj.* **—re•it′er•a′tive•ly** *adv.* **—re•it′er•a′tor** *n.*

re•ject (rĭ-jĕkt′) *tr.v.* **-ject•ed, -ject•ing, -jects. 1.** To refuse to accept, submit to, believe, or make use of. **2.** To refuse to consider or grant; deny. **3.** To refuse to recognize or give affection to (a person). See Syns at **refuse[1]. 4.** To discard as defective or useless; throw away. **5.** To spit out or vomit. **6.** *Medic.* To resist immunologically the introduction of (a transplanted organ or tissue). *—n.* (rē′jĕkt). One that has been rejected. [ME *rejecten* < Lat. *rēicere, rēiect-* : *re-*, re- + *iacere*, to throw; see **yē-***.] **—re•ject′er, re•jec′tor** *n.* **—re•jec′tive** *adj.*

re•jec•tion (rĭ-jĕk′shən) *n.* **1.** The act of rejecting or the state of being rejected. **2.** Something rejected. **3.** *Medic.* The failure of a recipient's body to accept a transplanted tissue or organ as the result of immunological incompatability.

rejection slip *n.* A printed note accompanying a manuscript rejected for publication and returned to the author.

re•jig•ger (rē-jĭg′ər) *tr.v.* **-gered, -ger•ing, -gers.** *Informal.* To readjust or rearrange.

re•joice (rĭ-jois′) *v.* **-joiced, -joic•ing, -joic•es.** *—intr.* To feel joyful; be delighted. *—tr.* To fill with joy; gladden. ***—phrasal verb.* rejoice in.** To have or possess. [ME *rejoicen* < OFr. *rejoir, rejoiss-* : *re-*, re- + *joir*, to be joyful (< VLat. **gaudīre* < Lat. *gaudēre*; see **gāu-***).] **—re•joic′er** *n.*

re•join[1] (rĭ-join′) *v.* **-joined, -join•ing, -joins.** *—tr.* To say in reply, esp. in sharp response to a reply. *—intr.* To reply. [ME *rejoinen* < OFr. *rejoindre, rejoin-* : *re-*, re- + *joindre*, to join; see JOIN.]

re•join[2] (rē-join′) *v.* **-joined, -join•ing, -joins.** *—tr.* **1.** To come again into the company of. **2.** To join together again; reunite. *—intr.* To become joined again.

re•join•der (rĭ-join′dər) *n.* An answer, esp. to a reply. [ME < OFr. *rejoindre*, to answer, rejoin. See REJOIN[1].]

re•ju•ve•nate (rĭ-jōō′və-nāt′) *tr.v.* **-nat•ed, -nat•ing, -nates. 1.** To restore to youthful vigor or appearance; make young again. **2.** To restore to an original or new condition. **3.a.** To stimulate (a stream) to renewed erosive activity, as by uplift of the land. **b.** To develop youthful topographic features in (a previously leveled area). [< RE- + Lat. *iuvenis*, young; see **yeu-***.] **—re•ju′ve•na′tion** *n.* **—re•ju′ve•na′tor** (-tər) *n.*

re•ju•ve•nes•cence (rĭ-jōō′və-nĕs′əns) *n.* A renewal of youthful appearance or character. **—re•ju′ve•nes′cent** *adj.*

re•kin•dle (rē-kĭn′dl) *tr.v.* **-dled, -dling, -dles. 1.** To relight (a fire). **2.** To revive or renew.

rel. *abbr.* **1.** Relating. **2.** Relative. **3.** Relatively. **4.** Released. **5.** Religion; religious.

re•lapse (rĭ-lăps′) *intr.v.* **-lapsed, -laps•ing, -laps•es. 1.** To fall or slide back into a former state. **2.** To regress after partial recovery from illness. **3.** To slip back into bad ways; back-

ă pat	oi boy
ā pay	ou out
âr care	ŏŏ took
ä father	ōō boot
ĕ pet	ŭ cut
ē be	ûr urge
ĭ pit	th thin
ī pie	*th* this
îr pier	hw which
ŏ pot	zh vision
ō toe	ə about,
ô paw	item

Stress marks:
′ (primary);
′ (secondary), as in
dictionary (dĭk′shə-nĕr′ē)

slide. —*n.* (rē′lăps, rĭ-lăps′). A falling back into a former state, esp. after apparent improvement. [ME *relapsen,* to forswear < Lat. *relābī, relāps-,* to fall back gradually : *re-,* re- + *lābī,* to slide.] —**re·laps′er** *n.*

re·laps·ing fever (rĭ-lăp′sĭng) *n.* Any of several infectious diseases characterized by chills and fever and caused by spirochetes transmitted by lice and ticks.

re·late (rĭ-lāt′) *v.* **-lat·ed, -lat·ing, -lates.** —*tr.* **1.** To narrate or tell. **2.** To bring into or link in logical or natural association. See Syns at **join. 3.** To establish or demonstrate a connection between. —*intr.* **1.** To have connection, relation, or reference. **2.** To have or establish a reciprocal relationship; interact. **3.** To react in response, esp. favorably: *I just can't relate to these new fashions.* [Obsolete Fr. *relater* < OFr. < Lat. *relātus,* p.part. of *referre* : *re-,* re- + *lātus,* brought; see **telə-***.] —**re·lat′a·ble** *adj.* —**re·lat′er** *n.*

relay race
Runner passing baton to a teammate

re·lat·ed (rĭ-lā′tĭd) *adj.* **1.** Being connected; associated. **2.** Connected by kinship, common origin, or marriage. **3.** *Mus.* Having a close harmonic connection. —**re·lat′ed·ly** *adv.* —**re·lat′ed·ness** *n.*

re·la·tion (rĭ-lā′shən) *n.* **1.** A logical or natural association between two or more things; connection. **2.** The connection of people by blood or marriage; kinship. **3.** A person connected to another by blood or marriage; a relative. **4.** The way in which one person or thing is connected with another: *the relation of parent to child.* **5. relations. a.** The mutual dealings or connections of persons, groups, or nations. **b.** Sexual intercourse. **6.** Reference; regard. **7.a.** The act of telling or narrating. **b.** A narrative; an account.

re·la·tion·al (rĭ-lā′shə-nəl) *adj.* **1.** Of or arising from kinship. **2.** Relating to or constituting relation. **3.** *Gram.* Of, relating to, or being a word or particle, such as a conjunction or preposition, that expresses a syntactic relation between elements in a phrase or sentence. —**re·la′tion·al·ly** *adv.*

re·la·tion·ship (rĭ-lā′shən-shĭp′) *n.* **1.** The condition or fact of being related; connection or association. **2.** Connection by blood or marriage; kinship. **3.** A particular type of connection between people related to or having dealings with each other. **4.** A romantic or sexual involvement.

rel·a·tive (rĕl′ə-tĭv) *adj.* **1.** Having pertinence or relevance; connected or related. **2.** Considered in comparison with something else. **3.** Dependent on or interconnected with something else; not absolute. **4.** *Gram.* Referring to or qualifying an antecedent, as the pronoun *who* in *the man who left.* **5.** *Mus.* Having the same key signature. Used of major and minor scales and keys. —*n.* **1.** One related by kinship, common origin, or marriage. **2.** Something having a relation or connection to something else. **3.** *Gram.* A relative pronoun. [ME < OFr. *relatif* < LLat. *relātīvus* < Lat. *relātus,* p.part. of *referre,* to relate. See RELATE.] —**rel′a·tive·ness** *n.*

relative clause *n. Gram.* A dependent clause introduced by a relative pronoun, as *which is downstairs* in *The dining room, which is downstairs, is too dark.*

relative humidity *n.* The ratio of the amount of water vapor in the air to the maximum amount that the air would hold at the same temperature, expressed as a percentage.

rel·a·tive·ly (rĕl′ə-tĭv-lē) *adv.* In a relative manner; in comparison.

relative permittivity *n. Phys.* See **permittivity.**

relative pronoun *n. Gram.* A pronoun that introduces a relative clause and has reference to an antecedent, as *who* in *the child who is wearing a hat.*

relative to *prep.* With regard to; concerning.

rel·a·tiv·ism (rĕl′ə-tĭ-vĭz′əm) *n. Philos.* A theory that conceptions of truth and moral values are not absolute but are relative to the persons or groups holding them.

relief
Top: Low relief of a ram from the Ptolemaic period
Center: Detail of a first–second century A.D. Roman half relief of a woman holding a fan
Bottom: High relief of a woman on a c. 400 B.C. Greek grave stele

rel·a·tiv·ist (rĕl′ə-tĭ-vĭst) *n.* **1.** *Philos.* A proponent of relativism. **2.** A specialist in the theories of relativity.

rel·a·tiv·is·tic (rĕl′ə-tĭ-vĭs′tĭk) *adj.* **1.** Of or relating to relativism. **2.** *Phys.* **a.** Of, relating to, or resulting from speeds approaching the speed of light. **b.** Having to do with or based on the theory of relativity.

rel·a·tiv·i·ty (rĕl′ə-tĭv′ĭ-tē) *n.* **1.** The quality or state of being relative. **2.** *Philos.* Existence dependent solely on relation to a thinking mind. **3.** A state of dependence in which the existence or significance of one entity is solely dependent on that of another. **4.** *Phys.* **a.** Special relativity. **b.** General relativity.

re·la·tor (rĭ-lā′tər) *n.* **1.** One who relates or narrates. **2.** *Law.* A beneficially interested person on whose behalf an action is maintained by a sovereign power or a state.

re·lax (rĭ-lăks′) *v.* **-laxed, -lax·ing, -lax·es.** —*tr.* **1.** To make lax or loose. **2.** To make less severe or strict. **3.** To reduce in intensity; slacken. **4.** To relieve from strain. —*intr.* **1.** To take one's ease; rest. **2.** To become lax or loose. **3.** To become less severe or strict. **4.** To become less restrained or tense. [ME *relaxen* < OFr. *relaxer* < Lat. *relaxāre* : *re-,* re- + *laxāre,* to loosen (< *laxus,* loose; see **slēg-***).] —**re·lax′a·ble** *adj.*

re·lax·ant (rĭ-lăk′sənt) *n.* Something, such as a drug, that relaxes muscular or nervous tension. —**re·lax′ant** *adj.*

re·lax·a·tion (rē′lăk-sā′shən) *n.* **1.** The act of relaxing or the state of being relaxed. **2.** Refreshment of body or mind; recreation. **3.** A loosening or slackening. **4.** A reduction in strictness or severity. **5.** *Physiol.* The lengthening of inactive muscle or muscle fibers. **6.** *Phys.* The return of a system to equilibrium following displacement or abrupt change. **7.** *Math.* A method of solving equations in which the errors resulting from an initial approximation are reduced by succeeding approximations until all errors are within specified limits.

re·laxed (rĭ-lăkst′) *adj.* **1.** Not rigorous or strict. **2.** Free from strain or tension. **3.** Easy and informal in manner.

re·lax·er (rĭ-lăk′sər) *n.* One that relaxes, as a chemical solution used on tightly curled hair to soften or loosen the curls.

re·lax·in (rĭ-lăk′sĭn) *n.* A female hormone secreted by the corpus luteum that helps soften the cervix and relax the pelvic ligaments in childbirth.

re·lay (rē′lā) *n.* **1.** An act of passing something along from one person, group, or station to another. **2.** *Sports.* **a.** A relay race. **b.** A division of a relay race. **3.** *Electron.* A device that responds to a small current or voltage change by activating switches or other devices in an electric circuit. **4.** A crew of workers who relieve another crew; a shift. **5.** A fresh team, as of horses, to relieve weary animals. —*tr.v.* (rē′lā, rĭ-lā′) **-layed, -lay·ing, -lays. 1.** To pass along by or as if by relay: *relayed the message to his boss.* **2.** To supply with fresh relays. **3.** *Electron.* To control or retransmit by means of a relay. [ME *relai,* fresh team of dogs for a hunt < OFr. < *relaier,* to relay : *re-,* re- + *laier,* to leave (of Gmc. orig.; see **leip-***).]

relay race *n. Sports.* A race between two or more teams, in which each team member runs only a set part of the race and is then relieved by another member of the team.

re·leas·a·ble (rĭ-lē′sə-bəl) *adj.* **1.** That can be released. **2.** Intended or configured to release. —**re·leas·a·bil′i·ty** *n.* —**re·leas′a·bly** *adv.*

re·lease (rĭ-lēs′) *tr.v.* **-leased, -leas·ing, -leas·es. 1.** To set free from confinement, restraint, or bondage. **2.** To free from something that binds, fastens, or holds back; let go: *released the balloons.* **3.** To dismiss, as from a job. **4.** To relieve of debt or obligation. **5.** To relieve of care and suffering. **6.a.** To issue for performance, sale, publication, or distribution. **b.** To make known or available. **7.** To relinquish (a right or claim). —*n.* **1.** A deliverance or liberation, as from confinement, restraint, or suffering. **2.** An authoritative discharge, as from an obligation or from prison. **3.** An unfastening or letting go of something caught or held fast. **4.** A device or catch for locking or releasing a mechanism. **5.a.** The act or an instance of issuing something for publication, use, or distribution. **b.** Something thus released: *a press release.* **6.** *Law.* **a.** Relinquishment to another of a right, title, or claim. **b.** The document authorizing such relinquishment. [ME *relesen* < OFr. *relaissier,* alteration of *relacher* < Lat. *relaxāre.* See RELAX.]

re·leas·er (rĭ-lē′sər) *n.* **1.** One that releases. **2.** *Zool.* A stimulus that initiates a specific behavior pattern in an animal.

re·leas·ing factor (rĭ-le′sĭng) *n.* Any of several hormones secreted by the hypothalamus that stimulate the anterior part of the pituitary gland to release certain hormones.

rel·e·gate (rĕl′ĭ-gāt′) *tr.v.* **-gat·ed, -gat·ing, -gates. 1.** To assign to an obscure place, position, or condition. **2.** To assign to a particular class or category; classify. **3.** To refer or assign (a matter or task, for example) for decision or action. **4.** To send to a place of exile; banish. [ME *relegaten,* to banish < Lat. *relēgāre, relēgāt-* : *re-,* re- + *lēgāre,* to send, depute; see **leg-***.] —**rel′e·ga′tion** *n.*

re·lent (rĭ-lĕnt′) *v.* **-lent·ed, -lent·ing, -lents.** —*intr.* To become more lenient, compassionate, or forgiving. —*tr. Obsolete.* **1.** To cause to slacken or abate. **2.** To cause to soften in attitude or temper. [ME *relenten,* to melt < AN *relenter* < *relent,* damp : Lat. *re-,* re- + Lat. *lentus,* sticky, slow.]

re·lent·less (rĭ-lĕnt′lĭs) *adj.* **1.** Unyielding in severity or strictness; unrelenting. **2.** Steady and persistent; unremitting. —**re·lent′less·ly** *adv.* —**re·lent′less·ness** *n.*

rel·e·vance (rĕl′ə-vəns) also **rel·e·van·cy** (-vən-sē) *n.* **1.** Pertinence to the matter at hand. **2.** Applicability to social issues.

rel·e·vant (rĕl′ə-vənt) *adj.* Having a bearing on or connection with the matter at hand. [Med.Lat. *relevāns, relevant-* < Lat., pr.part. of *relevāre,* to relieve, raise up. See RELIEVE.] —**rel′e·vant·ly** *adv.*

re·li·a·ble (rĭ-lī′ə-bəl) *adj.* Capable of being relied on; dependable. —**re·li′a·bil′i·ty, re·li′a·ble·ness** *n.* —**re·li′a·bly** *adv.*

re·li·ance (rĭ-lī′əns) *n.* **1.** The act of relying or the state of being reliant. **2.** The faith, confidence, or trust felt by one who relies; dependence. **3.** One relied on; a mainstay.

re·li·ant (rĭ-lī′ənt) *adj.* Having or exhibiting reliance; dependent. —**re·li′ant·ly** *adv.*

rel·ic (rĕl′ĭk) *n.* **1.** Something that has survived the passage of time, esp. an object or a custom whose original culture has disappeared. **2.** Something cherished for its age or historic interest. **3.** An object kept for its association with the past; a memento. **4.** An object of religious veneration, esp. a piece of the body or a personal item of a saint. **5.** Or **relics.** A corpse; remains. [ME *relik,* object of religious veneration < OFr. *relique* < LLat. *reliquiae,* sacred relics < Lat., remains < *reliquus,* remaining < *relinquere, reliq-,* to leave behind. See RELINQUISH.]

rel•ict (rĕl′ĭkt, rĭ-lĭkt′) *n.* **1.** *Ecol.* An organism or a species of an earlier time surviving in an environment that has undergone considerable change. **2.** Something that has survived; a remnant. **3.** A widow. —*adj. Geol.* Of or relating to something that has survived, as structures after destructive processes. [< ME *relicte,* left undisturbed < Lat. *relictus,* p.part. of *relinquere,* to leave behind. See RELINQUISH.]

re•lic•tion (rĭ-lĭk′shən) *n. Geol.* Gradual recession of water in a sea, lake, or stream, leaving permanently dry land.

re•lief (rĭ-lēf′) *n.* **1.** The easing of a burden or distress, such as pain, anxiety, or oppression. **2.** Something that alleviates pain or distress. **3.a.** Public assistance. **b.** Aid in time of danger, esp. rescue from siege. **4.a.** Release from a post or duty, as that of sentinel. **b.** One who releases another by taking over a post or duty. **5.** A pleasant or amusing change; a diversion. **6.a.** The projection of figures or forms from a flat background, as in sculpture, or such a projection that is apparent only, as in painting. **b.** A work of art featuring such projection. **7.** *Geol.* The variations in elevation of an area of the earth's surface. **8.** Distinction or prominence due to contrast. **9.** *Law.* Redress awarded by a court. **10.** A payment made by the heir of a deceased tenant to a feudal lord for the privilege of succeeding to the tenant's estate. —***idiom.* on relief.** Receiving public assistance because of need or poverty. [ME < OFr. < *relever,* to relieve. See RELIEVE. Senses 6, 7, and 8, Fr. < Ital. *rilievo.* See BAS-RELIEF.]

relief map *n.* A map that depicts land configuration, usu. with contour lines.

relief pitcher *n. Baseball.* A pitcher who replaces another during a game.

re•lieve (rĭ-lēv′) *tr.v.* **-lieved, -liev•ing, -lieves. 1.** To cause a lessening or alleviation of. **2.** To free from pain, anxiety, or distress. **3.** To furnish assistance or aid to. **4.** To rescue from siege. **5.** To release (a person) from an obligation, a restriction, or a burden, as by law. **6.** To free from a specified duty by providing or acting as a substitute. **7.** To make less tedious, monotonous, or unpleasant. **8.** To make prominent or effective by contrast; set off. **9.** *Informal.* To rob or deprive. —***idiom.* relieve oneself.** To urinate or defecate. [ME *releven* < OFr. *relever* < Lat. *relevāre* : *re-,* re- + *levāre,* to raise; see **legʷh-*.**] —**re•liev′a•ble** *adj.* —**re•liev′er** *n.*

Syns: *relieve, allay, alleviate, assuage, lighten, mitigate, palliate.* All of these verbs mean to make something less severe or more bearable. To *relieve* is to make more endurable something causing discomfort or distress: *"that misery which he strives in vain to relieve"* (Henry David Thoreau). *Allay* suggests at least temporary relief from what is burdensome or painful: *"This music crept by me upon the waters/Allaying both their fury and my passion/With its sweet air"* (Shakespeare). *Alleviate* connotes temporary lessening of distress without removal of its cause: *"No arguments shall be wanting on my part that can alleviate so severe a misfortune"* (Jane Austen). To *assuage* is to soothe or make milder: *"What shall assuage the unforgotten pain?"* (Dante Gabriel Rossetti). *Lighten* signifies to make less heavy or oppressive: *Congress endeavored to lighten the taxpayers' burden. Mitigate* and *palliate* connote moderating the force or intensity of something that causes suffering: *"I . . . prayed to the Lord to mitigate a calamity"* (John Galt). *"His ability . . . made men turn to him in the hour of distress, as of all statesmen the most fitted to palliate it"* (William E.H. Lecky).

re•lie•vo (rĭ-lē′vō) *n., pl.* **-vos.** See **relief** 6. [Ital. *rilievo.* See BAS-RELIEF.]

re•lig•ion (rĭ-lĭj′ən) *n.* **1.a.** Belief in and reverence for a supernatural power or powers regarded as creator and governor of the universe. **b.** A system grounded in such belief and worship. **2.** The life or condition of a person in a religious order. **3.** A set of beliefs, values, and practices based on the teachings of a spiritual leader. **4.** A cause, a principle, or an activity pursued with zeal or conscientious devotion. —***idiom.* get religion.** *Informal.* To accept a higher power as a controlling influence for the good in one's life. [ME *religioun* < OFr. *religion* < Lat. *religiō, religiōn-,* perh. < *religāre,* to tie fast. See RELY.]

re•lig•ion•ism (rĭ-lĭj′ə-nĭz′əm) *n.* Excessive or affected religious zeal. —**re•lig′ion•ist** *n.*

re•li•gi•ose (rĭ-lĭj′ē-ōs′) *adj.* Excessively religious, esp. in a conspicuous or sentimental manner.

re•lig•i•os•i•ty (rĭ-lĭj′ē-ŏs′ĭ-tē) *n.* **1.** The quality of being religious. **2.** Excessive or affected piety.

re•lig•ious (rĭ-lĭj′əs) *adj.* **1.** Having or showing belief in and reverence for God or a deity. **2.** Of, concerned with, or teaching religion. **3.** Extremely scrupulous or conscientious. —*n., pl.* **religious.** A member of a monastic order, esp. a nun or monk. [ME < OFr. < Lat. *religiōsus* < *religiō,* religion. See RELIGION.] —**re•lig′ious•ly** *adv.* —**re•lig′ious•ness** *n.*

re•line (rē-līn′) *tr.v.* **-lined, -lin•ing, -lines. 1.** To make new lines on. **2.** To put a new lining in.

re•lin•quish (rĭ-lĭng′kwĭsh) *tr.v.* **-quished, -quish•ing, -quish•es. 1.** To retire from; give up or abandon. **2.** To put aside or desist from (something practiced, professed, or intended). **3.** To let go; surrender. **4.** To cease holding physically; release. [ME *relinquisshen* < OFr. *relinquir, relinquiss-* < Lat. *relinquere* : *re-,* re- + *linquere,* to leave; see **leikʷ-*.**] —**re•lin′quish•er** *n.* —**re•lin′quish•ment** *n.*

Syns: *relinquish, yield, resign, abandon, surrender, cede, waive, renounce.* These verbs mean letting something go or giving something up. *Relinquish,* the least specific, sometimes connotes regret: *cannot relinquish the idea. Yield* implies giving way, as to pressure, often in the hope that such action will be temporary: *had to yield ground. Resign* suggests unresisting submission or acquiescence, as that due to hopelessness: *was forced to resign from office. Abandon* and *surrender* both imply no expectation of recovery, but *surrender* also implies the operation of compulsion or force: *abandoned all hope; surrendering control. Cede* connotes formal transfer, as of territory: *land ceded by treaty. Waive* implies a voluntary decision to dispense with something, such as a right: *waived all privileges.* To *renounce* is to relinquish formally and usually as a matter of principle: *renounced the world.*

rel•i•quar•y (rĕl′ĭ-kwĕr′ē) *n., pl.* **-ies.** A receptacle, such as a coffer or shrine, for keeping or displaying sacred relics. [Fr. *reliquaire* < OFr. < *relique,* relic < LLat. *reliquiae,* sacred relics. See RELIC.]

reliquary
15th-century German

rel•ique (rĕl′ĭk) *n. Archaic.* Var. of **relic.**

re•liq•ui•ae (rĭ-lĭk′wē-ē′) *pl.n.* Remains, as of fossil organisms. [Lat., remains. See RELIC.]

rel•ish (rĕl′ĭsh) *n.* **1.** An appetite for something; a strong appreciation or liking. **2.a.** Hearty enjoyment; zest. **b.** Something that lends pleasure or zest. **3.a.** A spicy or savory condiment or appetizer, such as chutney or olives. **b.** A condiment of chopped sweet pickle. **4.** The flavor of a food, esp. when appetizing. **5.** A trace or suggestion of a pleasurable quality. —*v.* **-ished, -ish•ing, -ish•es.** —*tr.* **1.** To take keen or zestful pleasure in. **2.** To enjoy the flavor of. **3.** To give spice or flavor to. —*intr.* To have a pleasing or distinctive taste. [Alteration of ME *reles,* taste < OFr., something remaining < *relaissier,* to leave behind. See RELEASE.]

re•live (rē-lĭv′) *v.* **-lived, -liv•ing, -lives.** —*tr.* To undergo or experience again, esp. in the imagination. —*intr.* To live again.

re•lo•cate (rē-lō′kāt) *v.* **-cat•ed, -cat•ing, -cates.** *tr. & intr.v.* To move or be moved to a new place. —**re′lo•ca′tion** *n.*

re•lu•cent (rĭ-lo͞o′sənt) *adj.* Reflecting light; shining. [Lat. *relūcēns, relūcent-,* pr.part. of *relūcēre,* to shine back : *re-,* re- + *lūcēre,* to shine; see **leuk-*.**]

re•luct (rĭ-lŭkt′) *intr.v.* **-luct•ed, -luct•ing, -lucts.** To show reluctance or repugnance. [Lat. *reluctārī* : *re-,* re- + *luctārī,* to struggle.]

re•luc•tance (rĭ-lŭk′təns) also **re•luc•tan•cy** (-tən-sē) *n.* **1.** The state of being reluctant. **2.** *Phys.* A measure of the opposition to magnetic flux, analogous to electric resistance.

re•luc•tant (rĭ-lŭk′tənt) *adj.* **1.** Unwilling; disinclined: *reluctant to help.* **2.** Exhibiting or marked by unwillingness. **3.** Offering resistance; opposing. [Lat. *reluctāns, reluctant-,* pr.part. of *reluctārī,* to reluct. See RELUCT.] —**re•luc′tant•ly** *adv.*

rel•uc•tiv•i•ty (rĕl′ək-tĭv′ĭ-tē) *n. Phys.* A measure of the resistance of a material to magnetization, equal to the ratio of the intensity of the magnetic field to the magnetic induction of the material. [RELUCT(ANCE) + (CONDUCT)IVITY.]

re•lume (rĭ-lo͞om′) *tr.v.* **-lumed, -lum•ing, -lumes.** To make bright or clear again; illuminate again. [RE- + (IL)LUME.]

re•ly (rĭ-lī′) *intr.v.* **-lied, -ly•ing, -lies. 1.** To be dependent for support, help, or supply. **2.** To place or have faith or confidence. [ME *relien,* to rally < OFr. *relier* < Lat. *religāre,* to bind fast : *re-,* re- + *ligāre,* to bind; see **leig-*.**] —**re•li′er** *n.*

rem (rĕm) *n. Phys.* **1.** The amount of ionizing radiation required to produce the same biological effect as one rad of high-penetration x-rays. **2.** A unit for measuring absorbed doses of radiation, equivalent to one roentgen of x-rays or gamma rays. [*r(oentgen) e(quivalent in) m(an).*]

REM (rĕm) *n.* The rapid periodic jerky movement of the eyes during certain stages of the sleep cycle when dreaming takes place. [R(APID) E(YE) M(OVEMENT).]

rem. *abbr.* Remittance.

re•main (rĭ-mān′) *intr.v.* **-mained, -main•ing, -mains. 1.** To continue in the same state or condition. **2.** To continue to be in the same place; stay or stay behind. **3.** To be left after the removal, loss, passage, or destruction of others. See Syns at **stay¹.** **4.** To be left as still to be dealt with. **5.** To endure or persist. [ME *remainen* < OFr. *remaneir, remaindre* < Lat. *remanēre* : *re-,* re- + *manēre,* to remain; see **men-³*.**]

re•main•der (rĭ-mān′dər) *n.* **1.** Something left over after other parts have been taken away. **2.** *Math.* **a.** The number left over when one integer is divided by another. **b.** The number obtained when one number is subtracted from another; the difference. **3.** *Law.* An estate in land that is conveyed only after the natural termination of the preceding estate created by the same document. **4.** A book that remains with a publisher after sales have fallen off, usu. sold at a reduced price. —*tr.v.* **-dered, -der•ing, -ders.** To dispose of as a remainder. [ME, second party's right of ownership < AN < *remeindre,* to remain, var. of OFr. *remaindre, remainer.* See REMAIN.]

re•mains (rĭ-mānz′) *pl.n.* **1.** All that is left after other parts

ă pat	oi boy
ā pay	ou out
âr care	o͝o took
ä father	o͞o boot
ĕ pet	ŭ cut
ē be	ûr urge
ĭ pit	th thin
ī pie	*th* this
îr pier	hw which
ŏ pot	zh vision
ō toe	ə about, item
ô paw	

Stress marks:
′ (primary);
′ (secondary), as in
dictionary (dĭk′shə-nĕr′ē)

have been taken away, used up, or destroyed. **2.** A corpse. **3.** The unpublished writings of a deceased author. **4.** Ancient ruins or fossils.

re•make (rē-māk′) *tr.v.* **-made** (-mād′), **-mak•ing, -makes.** To make again or anew. —*n.* (rē′māk′). **1.** The act of remaking. **2.** Something remade, esp. a new version of an old movie.

re•man (rē-măn′) *tr.v.* **-manned, -man•ning, -mans. 1.** To supply with new personnel. **2.** To imbue with new manliness or courage.

re•mand (rĭ-mănd′) *tr.v.* **-mand•ed, -mand•ing, -mands. 1.** To send or order back. **2.** *Law.* **a.** To send back to custody. **b.** To send back (a case) to a lower court with instructions about further proceedings. [ME *remaunden* < OFr. *remander* < LLat. *remandāre*, to send back word : Lat. *re-*, re- + Lat. *mandāre*, to order; see **man-**[2]*.] —**re•mand′, re•mand′ment** *n.*

Rembrandt
Self-portrait

rem•a•nence (rĕm′ə-nəns) *n. Phys.* The magnetic induction that remains in a material after removal of the magnetizing force. [< ME *remanent*, remaining < Lat. *remanēns, remanent-*, pr.part. of *remanēre*, to remain. See REMAIN.] —**rem′a•nent** *adj.*

re•mark (rĭ-märk′) *v.* **-marked, -mark•ing, -marks.** —*tr.* **1.** To express briefly and casually as a comment. **2.** To take notice of; observe. See Syns at **see**[1]. —*intr.* To make a comment or an observation. —*n.* **1.** The act of noticing or observing. **2.** A casual or brief expression of opinion; a comment. See Syns at **comment.** [Alteration of Fr. *remarquer* : OFr. *re-*, re- + OFr. *marquer*, to mark (ult. < *merc*, sign < ON *merki*, mark; see **merg-***).] —**re•mark′er** *n.*

re•mark•a•ble (rĭ-mär′kə-bəl) *adj.* **1.** Worthy of notice. **2.** Attracting notice as being unusual or extraordinary. —**re•mark′a•ble•ness** *n.* —**re•mark′a•bly** *adv.*

re•marque (rĭ-märk′) *n.* **1.** A small mark or sketch engraved in the margin of a plate to indicate its stage of development prior to completion. **2.** A print or proof from a plate carrying such a mark. [Fr. < *remarquer*, to remark. See REMARK.]

Frederic Remington
Photographed c. 1898

Re•marque (rə-märk′), **Erich Maria.** 1898–1970. German-born Amer. writer known for his novel *All Quiet on the Western Front* (1929).

re•match (rē-măch′, rē′măch′) *n.* A second contest between the same opponents.

Rem•brandt van Rijn or **Rem•brandt van Ryn** (rĕm′bränt′ vän rīn′, -bränt′). 1606–69. Dutch painter whose works include *The Night Watch* (1642).

re•me•di•a•ble (rĭ-mē′dē-ə-bəl) *adj.* Possible to remedy. —**re•me′di•a•ble•ness** *n.* —**re•me′di•a•bly** *adv.*

re•me•di•al (rĭ-mē′dē-əl) *adj.* **1.** Supplying a remedy. **2.** Intended to correct or improve deficient skills in a specific subject: *remedial reading.* —**re•me′di•al•ly** *adv.*

re•me•di•a•tion (rĭ-mē′dē-ā′shən) *n.* The act or process of correcting a fault or deficiency. —**re•me′di•ate′** *v.*

rem•e•dy (rĕm′ĭ-dē) *n., pl.* **-dies. 1.** Something, such as medicine, that relieves pain, cures disease, or corrects a disorder. **2.** Something that corrects an evil, a fault, or an error. **3.** *Law.* A legal order of preventing or redressing a wrong or enforcing a right. **4.** The allowance by a mint for deviation from the standard weight or quality of coins. —*tr.v.* **-died, -dy•ing, -dies. 1.** To relieve or cure (a disease or disorder). **2.** To set right; remove, rectify, or counteract. See Syns at **correct, cure.** [ME *remedie* < OFr. < Lat. *remedium* : *re-*, re- + *medērī*, to heal; see **med-***.]

re•mem•ber (rĭ-mĕm′bər) *v.* **-bered, -ber•ing, -bers.** —*tr.* **1.** To recall to the mind; think of again. **2.** To recall to the mind with effort. **3.** To retain in the memory. **4.** To keep (someone) in mind as worthy of consideration or recognition. **5.** To reward with a gift or tip. **6.** To give greetings from. **7.** *Engineering.* To return to (an original shape or form) after being deformed or altered. **8.** *Electron.* To carry out (a programmed or preset activity). **9.** *Archaic.* To remind. —*intr.* To have or use the power of memory. [ME *remembren* < OFr. *remembrer* < Lat. *rememorārī*, to remember again : *re-*, re- + *memor*, mindful; see **(s)mer-**[1]*.] —**re•mem′ber•a•bil′i•ty** *n.* —**re•mem′ber•a•ble** *adj.* —**re•mem′ber•er** *n.*

Syns: *remember, bethink, recall, recollect.* The central meaning shared by these verbs is "to bring an image or a thought back to the mind": *can't remember his name; bethought herself of her responsibilities; recalling her kindness; recollect how the accident happened.* ***Ant:*** *forget.*

re•mem•brance (rĭ-mĕm′brəns) *n.* **1.a.** The act or process of remembering. See Syns at **memory. b.** The state of being remembered: *holds him in fond rememberance.* **2.** Something serving to celebrate or honor the memory of a person or an event; a memorial. **3.** The length of time over which one's memory extends. **4.** Something remembered; a reminiscence. **5.** A souvenir. **6.** A greeting or token expressive of affection.

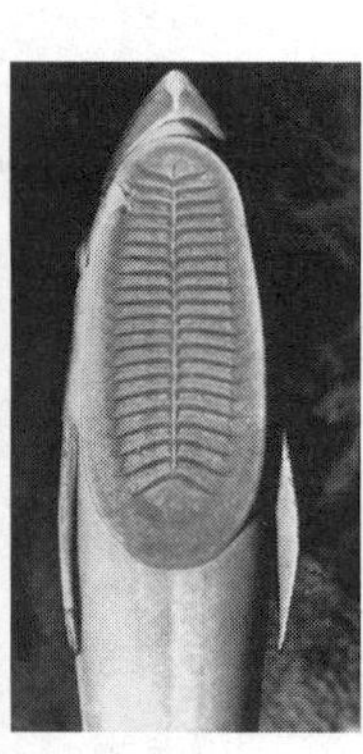
remora
Suction disk on the head of a remora

Re•mem•brance Day (rĭ-mĕm′brəns) *n.* The Sunday closest to November 11, observed in Canada and Great Britain in commemoration of those killed in the World Wars.

re•mem•branc•er (rĭ-mĕm′brən-sər) *n.* **1.** One that causes another to remember something. **2. Remembrancer. a.** An officer of the British judiciary responsible for collecting debts owed to the Crown. **b.** An official who represents the City of London.

re•mex (rē′mĕks′) *n., pl.* **rem•i•ges** (rĕm′ə-jēz′). A quill or flight feather of a bird's wing. [Lat. *rēmex*, rower : *rēmus*, oar; see **erə-*** + *agere, ēg-*, to drive; see ACT.] —**re•mig′i•al** (rĭ-mĭj′ē-əl) *adj.*

re•mind (rĭ-mīnd′) *tr.v.* **-mind•ed, -mind•ing, -minds.** To cause to remember; put in mind. —**re•mind′er** *n.*

Rem•ing•ton (rĕm′ĭng-tən), **Eliphalet.** 1793–1861. Amer. firearms manufacturer whose company was a major supplier to the U.S. government.

Remington, Frederic. 1861–1909. Amer. artist and journalist best known for his sculptures and paintings of the West.

rem•i•nisce (rĕm′ə-nĭs′) *intr.v.* **-nisced, -nisc•ing, -nisc•es.** To recollect and tell of past experiences or events. [Back-formation < REMINISCENCE.] —**rem′i•nis′cer** *n.*

rem•i•nis•cence (rĕm′ə-nĭs′əns) *n.* **1.** The act or process of recollecting past experiences or events. **2.** An experience or event recollected. See Syns at **memory. 3.** A narration of past experiences. Often used in the plural. **4.** An event that brings to mind a similar former event.

rem•i•nis•cent (rĕm′ə-nĭs′ənt) *adj.* **1.** Having the quality of or containing reminiscence. **2.** Inclined to engage in reminiscence. **3.** Tending to recall or suggest something in the past. [Lat. *reminīscēns, reminīscent-*, pr.part. of *reminīscī*, to recollect. See **men-**[1]*.] —**rem′i•nis′cent•ly** *adv.*

re•mint (rē-mĭnt′) *tr.v.* **-mint•ed, -mint•ing, -mints.** To make into new coin by melting down and reprocessing.

re•miss (rĭ-mĭs′) *adj.* **1.** Lax in attending to duty; negligent. **2.** Exhibiting carelessness or slackness. [ME < Lat. *remissus*, p.part. of *remittere*, to remit, slacken. See REMIT.] —**re•miss′ly** *adv.* —**re•miss′ness** *n.*

re•mis•si•ble (rĭ-mĭs′ə-bəl) *adj.* Being such that forgiveness is possible. —**re•mis′si•bil′i•ty** *n.* —**re•mis′si•bly** *adv.*

re•mis•sion (rĭ-mĭsh′ən) *n.* **1.a.** The act of remitting. **b.** A condition or period in which something is remitted. **2.** A lessening of intensity or degree; abatement. **3.a.** *Medic.* Abatement or subsiding of the symptoms of a disease. **b.** The period during which the symptoms of a disease abate or subside. **4.a.** Release, as from a debt. **b.** Forgiveness; pardon. [ME < OFr. < Lat. *remissiō, remissiōn-* < *remissus*, p.part. of *remittere*, to let go. See REMIT.]

re•mit (rĭ-mĭt′) *v.* **-mit•ted, -mit•ting, -mits.** —*tr.* **1.** To transmit (money) in payment. **2.a.** To refrain from exacting (a tax or penalty, for example); cancel. **b.** To pardon; forgive: *remit sins.* **3.** To restore to a former condition or position. **4.** *Law.* **a.** To refer (a case) to another court for further consideration or action. **b.** To refer (a matter) to a committee or an authority for decision. **5.** To allow to slacken. **6.** To desist from; give up. **7.** To put off; postpone. —*intr.* **1.** To transmit money. **2.** To diminish; abate. —*n.* (rĭ-mĭt′, rē′mĭt). **1.** The act of remitting, esp. the referral of a case to another court. **2.** A matter remitted for further consideration. [ME *remitten*, to send back < Lat. *remittere* : *re-*, re- + *mittere*, to send.] —**re•mit′ment** *n.* —**re•mit′ta•ble** *adj.* —**re•mit′ter** *n.*

re•mit•tal (rĭ-mĭt′l) *n.* Remission.

re•mit•tance (rĭ-mĭt′ns) *n.* **1.** The sending of money to someone at a distance. **2.** The sum of money sent.

re•mit•tent (rĭ-mĭt′nt) *adj.* Characterized by temporary abatement in severity. Used esp. of diseases. —**re•mit′tence, re•mit′ten•cy** *n.* —**re•mit′tent•ly** *adv.*

rem•nant (rĕm′nənt) *n.* **1.** Something left over; a remainder. **2.** A leftover piece of fabric remaining after the rest has been used or sold. **3.** A surviving trace or vestige. **4.** A small surviving group of people. Often used in the plural. [ME *remanant, remnant* < OFr. *remanant* < pr.part. of *remaindre*, to remain. See REMAIN.]

re•mod•el (rē-mŏd′l) *tr.v.* **-eled, -el•ing, -els** also **-elled, -el•ling, -els.** To make over in structure or style; reconstruct. —**re•mod′el•er** *n.*

re•mon•strance (rĭ-mŏn′strəns) *n.* **1.** The act of remonstrating. **2.** An expression of protest, complaint, or reproof, esp. a formal statement of grievances.

re•mon•strant (rĭ-mŏn′strənt) *adj.* Characterized by remonstrance; expostulatory. —*n.* **1.** One that remonstrates. **2. Remonstrant.** One of the Dutch Arminians who in 1610 formally stated the grounds of their dissent from strict Calvinism. —**re•mon′strant•ly** *adv.*

re•mon•strate (rĭ-mŏn′strāt′) *v.* **-strat•ed, -strat•ing, -strates.** —*tr.* To say or plead in protest, objection, or reproof. —*intr.* To reason or plead in protest; present an objection. See Syns at **object.** [Med.Lat. *remōnstrāre, remōnstrāt-*, to demonstrate : Lat. *re-*, re- + Lat. *mōnstrāre*, to show (< *mōnstrum*, portent; see MONSTER).] —**re′mon•stra′tion** (rē′mŏn-strā′shən, rĕm′ən-) *n.* —**re•mon′stra•tive** (rĭ-mŏn′strə-tĭv) *adj.* —**re•mon′stra′tor** *n.*

rem•o•ra (rĕm′ər-ə) *n.* Any of several marine fishes of the family Echeneidae, having on the head a sucking disk with which they attach themselves to sharks, whales, sea turtles, or ships. [Lat., delay < *remorārī*, to delay : *re-*, re- + *morārī*, to delay (< *mora*, delay).]

re•morse (rĭ-môrs′) *n.* **1.** Moral anguish arising from repentance for past misdeeds; bitter regret. **2.** *Obsolete.* Compassion. [ME *remors* < OFr. < Med.Lat. *remorsum* < neut. p.part. of Lat. *remordēre*, to torment : *re-*, re- + *mordēre*, to bite; see **mer-***.]

re•morse•ful (rĭ-môrs′fəl) *adj.* Marked by or filled with remorse. —**re•morse′ful•ly** *adv.* —**re•morse′ful•ness** *n.*

re•morse•less (rĭ-môrs′lĭs) *adj.* **1.** Having no pity or compassion; merciless. **2.** Unyielding; relentless. —**re•morse′less•ly** *adv.* —**re•morse′less•ness** *n.*

re•mote (rĭ-mōt′) *adj.* **-mot•er, -mot•est. 1.a.** Located far away; distant in space. **b.** Hidden away; secluded: *a remote hamlet.* **2.** Distant in time. **3.** Faint; slight: *a remote possibility.* **4.** Far removed in connection or relevance. **5.** Distantly related by blood or marriage. **6.** Distant in manner; aloof. **7.** Operating or controlled from a distance. **8.** *Comp. Sci.* Of, relating to, or being a computer device or system situated at some distance from but communicating with a central computer. —*n.* **1.** A radio or television broadcast originating from a point outside a studio. **2.** Remote control. [ME < OFr. *remot* < Lat. *remōtus*, p.part. of *removēre*, to remove. See REMOVE.] —**re•mote′ly** *adv.* —**re•mote′ness** *n.*

remote control *n.* **1.** The control of an activity, a process, or a machine from a distance, as by radioed instructions or coded signals. **2.** A device used to control an apparatus or a machine from a distance. —**re•mote′-con•trol′** (rĭ-mōt′kən-trōl′), **re•mote′-con•trolled′** (-trōld′) *adj.*

re•mo•tion (rĭ-mō′shən) *n.* **1.** The act of removing; removal. **2.** The state of being remote. **3.** *Obsolete.* Departure.

ré•mou•lade (rā′mo͞o-läd′) *n.* A piquant cold sauce made with mayonnaise, chopped pickles, capers, anchovies, and herbs. [Fr. < dial. *rémola*, large black radish < Lat. *armoracia*, wild radish.]

re•mount (rē-mount′) *tr.v.* **-mount•ed, -mount•ing, -mounts. 1.** To mount again. **2.** To supply with a fresh horse. —*n.* (rē′mount′, rē-mount′). A fresh horse.

re•mov•a•ble (rĭ-mo͞o′və-bəl) *adj.* That can be removed. —**re•mov′a•bil′i•ty, re•mov′a•ble•ness** *n.*

re•mov•al (rĭ-mo͞o′vəl) *n.* **1.a.** The act of removing. **b.** The fact of being removed. **2.** Relocation, as of a residence or business. **3.** Dismissal, as from office.

re•move (rĭ-mo͞ov′) *v.* **-moved, -mov•ing, -moves.** —*tr.* **1.** To move from a place or position occupied. **2.** To transfer or convey from one place to another. **3.** To take off. **4.** To take away; withdraw. **5.** To do away with; eliminate. **6.** To dismiss from office. —*intr.* **1.** To change one's place of residence or business; move. **2.** To go away; depart. **3.** To be removable. —*n.* **1.** The act of removing; removal. **2.** Distance or degree of separation or remoteness. [ME *removen* < OFr. *remouvoir* < Lat. *removēre* : *re-*, re- + *movēre*, to move; see MOVE.] —**re•mov′er** *n.*

re•moved (rĭ-mo͞ovd′) *adj.* **1.** Distant in space, time, or nature; remote. **2.** Separated in relationship by a given degree of descent: *a first cousin once removed.* —**re•mov′ed•ly** (-mo͞o′vĭd-lē) *adv.* —**re•mov′ed•ness** *n.*

Rem•scheid (rĕm′shīt′). A city of W-central Germany NE of Cologne. Pop. 121,830.

REM sleep *n.* A stage in the normal sleep cycle during which dreams occur as well as rapid eye movement, loss of reflexes, and increased pulse rate and brain activity.

re•mu•da (rĭ-mo͞o′də) *n. Southwestern U.S.* A herd of horses from which ranch hands select their mounts. [Am.Sp. < Sp., exchange < *remudar*, to exchange : *re-*, in return (< Lat.; see RE–) + *mudar*, to change (< Lat. *mūtāre*; see **mei-[1]***).]

re•mu•ner•ate (rĭ-myo͞o′nə-rāt′) *tr.v.* **-at•ed, -at•ing, -ates. 1.** To pay (a person) a suitable equivalent in return for goods provided, services rendered, or losses incurred; recompense. **2.** To compensate for; make payment for. [Lat. *remūnerārī, remūnerāt-* : *re-*, re- + *mūnerārī*, to give (< *mūnus, mūner-*, gift; see **mei-[1]***).] —**re•mu′ner•a•bil′i•ty** (-nər-ə-bĭl′ĭ-tē) *n.* —**re•mu′ner•a•ble** *adj.* —**re•mu′ner•a′tor** *n.*

re•mu•ner•a•tion (rĭ-myo͞o′nə-rā′shən) *n.* **1.** The act of remunerating. **2.** Something that remunerates.

re•mu•ner•a•tive (rĭ-myo͞o′nər-ə-tĭv, -nə-rā′tĭv) *adj.* **1.** Yielding recompense; profitable. **2.** Serving to remunerate. —**re•mu′ner•a•tive•ly** *adv.* —**re•mu′ner•a•tive•ness** *n.*

Re•mus (rē′məs) *n. Rom. Myth.* The twin brother of Romulus.

ren•ais•sance (rĕn′ĭ-säns′, -zäns′, rĕn′ĭ-säns′, -zäns′, rĭ-nā′səns) *n.* **1.** A rebirth or revival. **2. Renaissance. a.** The humanistic revival of classical art, architecture, literature, and learning that originated in Italy in the 14th century. **b.** The period of this revival, roughly the 14th through the 16th century, marking the transition from medieval to modern times. **3.** Often **Renaissance. a.** A revival of intellectual or artistic achievement and vigor. **b.** The period of such a revival. —*adj.* **Renaissance. 1.** Of, relating to, or characteristic of the Renaissance or its artistic and intellectual works and styles. **2.** Of or being the neoclassic style of architecture and decoration that originated in Italy in the 15th century. [Fr. < OFr. < *renaistre*, to be born again < VLat. **renāscere* < Lat. *renāscī* : *re-*, re- + *nāscī*, to be born; see **genə-***.]

Renaissance man *n.* A man who has broad intellectual interests and is accomplished in both the arts and the sciences.

Renaissance woman *n.* A woman who has broad intellectual interests and is accomplished in both the arts and the sciences.

re•nal (rē′nəl) *adj.* Of, relating to, or in the region of the kidneys. [LLat. *rēnālis* < Lat. *rēnēs*, kidneys.]

renal clearance *n. Physiol.* The volume of plasma completely cleared of a specific compound per unit time and measured as a test of kidney function.

renal corpuscle *n. Anat.* See **Malpighian corpuscle** 1.

renal pelvis *n. Anat.* See **pelvis** 2.

Re•nan (rə-näɴ′), **Joseph Ernest.** 1823–92. French philologist, philosopher, and historian who wrote the series *History of the Origins of Christianity* (1863–81).

re•nas•cence (rĭ-năs′əns, -nā′səns) *n.* **1.** A new birth or life; a rebirth. **2.** A cultural revival; a renaissance. **3. Renascence.** Renaissance.

re•nas•cent (rĭ-năs′ənt, -nā′sənt) *adj.* Coming again into being; showing renewed growth or vigor. [Lat. *renāscēns, renāscent-*, pr.part. of *renāscī*, to be born again. See RENAISSANCE.]

Re•nault (rə-nō′), **Jean Louis.** 1843–1918. French jurist who shared the 1907 Nobel Peace Prize.

ren•coun•ter (rĕn-koun′tər) *Archaic.* —*n.* **1.** An unplanned meeting. **2.** A hostile encounter or contest. —*tr.* & *intr.v.* **-tered, -ter•ing, -ters.** To meet unexpectedly or have an unexpected meeting. [Fr. *rencontre* < OFr. < *rencontrer*, to meet : *re-*, re- + *encontrer*, to meet; see ENCOUNTER.]

rend (rĕnd) *v.* **rent** (rĕnt) or **rend•ed, rend•ing, rends.** —*tr.* **1.** To tear or split apart or into pieces violently. See Syns at **tear[1]**. **2.** To tear (one's garments or hair) in anguish or rage. **3.** To tear away forcibly; wrest. **4.** To pull, split, or divide as if by tearing. **5.** To pierce or disturb with sound. **6.** To cause pain or distress to. —*intr.* To become torn or split; come apart. [ME *renden* < OE *rendan*.]

ren•der (rĕn′dər) *tr.v.* **-dered, -der•ing, -ders. 1.** To submit or present, as for consideration or payment. **2.** To give or make available; provide. **3.** To give what is due or owed. **4.** To give in return or retribution. **5.** To surrender or relinquish; yield. **6.a.** To represent in verbal form; depict. **b.** To represent in a drawing or painting, esp. in perspective. **7.** To perform an interpretation of (a musical piece, for example). **8.** To express in another language or form; translate. **9.** To deliver or pronounce formally. **10.** To cause to become; make. **11.** To reduce, convert, or melt down (fat) by heating. **12.** To coat (brick, for example) with plaster or cement. —*n.* A payment in kind, services, or cash from a tenant to a feudal lord. [ME *rendren* < OFr. *rendre*, to give back < VLat. **rendere*, alteration of Lat. *reddere* : *red-*, *re-*, re- + *dare*, to give; see **dō-***.] —**ren′der•a•ble** *adj.* —**ren′der•er** *n.*

ren•der•ing (rĕn′dər-ĭng) *n.* **1.** A depiction or an interpretation, as in painting. **2.** A drawing in perspective of a proposed structure. **3.** A translation. **4.** A coat of plaster or cement applied to a masonry surface.

ren•dez•vous (rän′dā-vo͞o′, -də-) *n., pl.* **ren•dez•vous** (-vo͞oz′). **1.** A meeting at a prearranged time and place. See Syns at **engagement. 2.** A prearranged meeting place, esp. an assembly point for troops or ships. **3.** A popular gathering place. **4.** *Aerospace.* The process of bringing two spacecraft together. —*tr.* & *intr.v.* **-voused** (-vo͞od′), **-vous•ing** (-vo͞o′ĭng), **-vous** (-vo͞oz′). To cause to assemble or to assemble at a prearranged time and place. [Fr. < the phrase *rendez vous*, present yourselves < OFr. : *rendez*, second pers. pl. imper. of *rendre*, to present; see RENDER + *vous*, yourselves, you (< Lat. *vōs*, you; see **wōs***).]

ren•di•tion (rĕn-dĭsh′ən) *n.* **1.** The act of rendering. **2.** An interpretation of a musical score or a dramatic piece. **3.** A performance of a musical or dramatic work. **4.** A translation, often interpretive. **5.** A surrender. [Obsolete Fr. < OFr. *rendre*, to give back. See RENDER.]

ren•dzi•na (rĕn-jē′nə) *n.* A dark soil that develops under grass on limestone and chalk. [Pol. *rędzina*.]

ren•e•gade (rĕn′ĭ-gād′) *n.* **1.** One who rejects a religion, a cause, an allegiance, or a group for another; a deserter. **2.** An outlaw; a rebel. —*adj.* Of, relating to, or resembling a renegade; traitorous. —*intr.v.* **-gad•ed, -gad•ing, -gades.** To become a deserter or an outlaw. [Sp. *renegado* < Med.Lat. *renegātus*, p.part. of *renegāre*, to deny : Lat. *re-*, re- + Lat. *negāre*, to deny; see **ne***.]

re•nege (rĭ-nĭg′, -nĕg′, -nēg′) *v.* **-neged, -neg•ing, -neges.** —*intr.* **1.** To fail to carry out a promise or commitment. **2.** *Games.* To fail to follow suit in cards when able and required to do so. —*tr.* To renounce; disown. —*n.* The act of reneging. [Med.Lat. *renegāre*, to deny. See RENEGADE.] —**re•neg′er** *n.*

re•ne•go•ti•ate (rē′nĭ-gō′shē-āt′) *tr.v.* **-at•ed, -at•ing, -ates. 1.** To negotiate anew. **2.** To revise the terms of (a contract) so as to limit or regain excess profits gained by the contractor. —**re′ne•go′ti•a•ble** (-shē-ə-bəl, -shə-bəl) *adj.* —**re′ne•go′ti•a′tion** *n.*

re•new (rĭ-no͞o′, -nyo͞o′) *v.* **-newed, -new•ing, -news.** —*tr.* **1.** To make new or as if new again; restore. **2.** To take up again; resume. **3.** To repeat so as to reaffirm. **4.** To regain or restore the vigor of; revive. **5.a.** To arrange for the extension

ă pat	oi boy
ā pay	ou out
âr care	o͝o took
ä father	o͞o boot
ĕ pet	ŭ cut
ē be	ûr urge
ĭ pit	th thin
ī pie	*th* this
îr pier	hw which
ŏ pot	zh vision
ō toe	ə about, item
ô paw	

Stress marks:
′ (primary);
′ (secondary), as in **dictionary** (dĭk′shə-nĕr′ē)

of. **b.** To arrange to extend the loan of. **6.** To replenish. **7.** To bring into being again; reestablish. — *intr.* **1.** To become new again. **2.** To start over. [ME *renewen* : *re-*, re- + *newen*, to renew (< *new*, new; see NEW).] — **re•new′er** *n.*

re•new•a•ble (rĭ-no͞o′ə-bəl, -nyo͞o′-) *adj.* **1.** That can be renewed: *renewable subscriptions.* **2.** Relating to or being a commodity or resource, such as solar energy, that is inexhaustible or replaceable by new growth. — **re•new′a•bil′i•ty** (-bĭl′ĭ-tē) *n.* — **re•new′a•bly** *adv.*

re•new•al (rĭ-no͞o′əl, -nyo͞o′-) *n.* **1.** The act of renewing or the state of having been renewed. **2.** Something renewed.

re•new•ed•ly (rĭ-no͞o′ĭd-lē, -nyo͞o′-) *adv.* Over again; anew.

Re•ni (rā′nē), **Guido.** 1575–1642. Italian painter whose works include the *Crucifixion of Saint Peter* (1603).

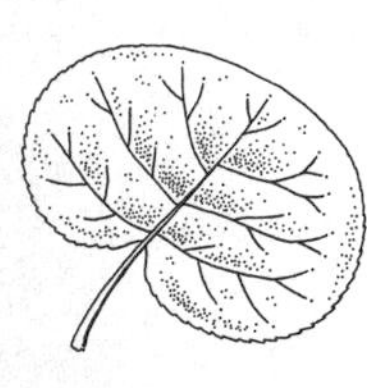

reniform

ren•i•form (rĕn′ə-fôrm′, rē′nə-) *adj.* Shaped like a kidney: *a reniform leaf.* [Lat. *rēnēs*, kidneys + -FORM.]

ren•in (rĕn′ĭn) *n.* A protein-digesting enzyme that is released by the kidney and acts to raise blood pressure by activating angiotensin. [Lat. *rēnēs*, kidneys + -IN.]

ren•i•tent (rĕn′ĭ-tənt, rĭ-nīt′nt) *adj.* **1.** Resistant to physical pressure; not pliant. **2.** Reluctant to yield or be swayed; recalcitrant. [Lat. *renītēns*, *renītent-*, pr.part. of *renītī*, to resist : *re-*, re- + *nītī*, to press forward.] — **ren′i•tence, ren′i•ten•cy** *n.*

Rennes (rĕn). A city of NW France N of Nantes; became cap. of Brittany in 1196. Pop. 117,234.

ren•net (rĕn′ĭt) *n.* **1.** The inner lining of the fourth stomach of calves and other young ruminants. **2.** A dried extract made from the stomach lining of a ruminant, used in cheesemaking to curdle milk. **3.** See **rennin.** [ME, prob. < OE **rynet.* See **rei-*.**]

ren•nin (rĕn′ĭn) *n.* A milk-coagulating enzyme found in the gastric juice of the fourth stomach of young ruminants, used in making cheeses and junkets. [RENN(ET) + -IN.]

Re•no (rē′nō′). A city of W NV near the CA border. Pop. 133,850.

re•no•gram (rē′nə-grăm′) *n.* **1.** A graphic record of the passage of radiation through the renal system after injection of a radioactive tracer. **2.** A radiograph of a kidney. [Lat. *rēnēs*, kidneys + -GRAM.] — **re′nog′ra•phy** (rē-nŏg′rə-fē) *n.*

Ren•oir (rĕn′wär′, rən-wär′), **Jean.** 1894–1979. French filmmaker whose films include *La Grande Illusion* (1937).

Renoir, Pierre Auguste. 1841–1919. French impressionist painter whose works include *Le Moulin de la Galette* (1876).

re•nom•i•nate (rē-nŏm′ə-nāt′) *tr.v.* **-nat•ed, -nat•ing, -nates.** To nominate again, esp. for a subsequent term. — **re′nom•i•na′tion** *n.*

re•nor•mal•ize (rē-nôr′mə-līz′) *tr.v.* **-ized, -iz•ing, -iz•es.** To bring into a normal or more normal state once again. — **re•nor′mal•i•za′tion** (-mə-lĭ-zā′shən) *n.*

re•nounce (rĭ-nouns′) *v.* **-nounced, -nounc•ing, -nounc•es.** — *tr.* **1.** To give up (a title, for example), esp. by formal announcement. See Syns at **relinquish. 2.** To reject; disown. — *intr. Games.* To revoke in cards. — *n. Games.* A revoke in cards. [ME *renouncen* < OFr. *renoncer* < Lat. *renūntiāre*, to report : *re-*, re- + *nūntiāre*, to announce (< *nūntius*, messenger; see **neu-***).] — **re•nounce′ment** *n.* — **re•nounc′er** *n.*

ren•o•vate (rĕn′ə-vāt′) *tr.v.* **-vat•ed, -vat•ing, -vates. 1.** To restore to an earlier condition, as by repairing or remodeling. **2.** To impart new vigor to; revive. [Lat. *renovāre*, *renovāt-* : *re-*, re- + *novāre*, to make new (< *novus*, new; see **newo-***).] — **ren′o•va′tion** *n.* — **ren′o•va′tor** *n.*

re•nown (rĭ-noun′) *n.* **1.** The quality of being widely honored and acclaimed; fame. **2.** *Obsolete.* Report; rumor. [ME *renoun* < AN < *renomer*, to make famous : *re-*, repeatedly (< Lat.; see RE-) + *nomer*, to name (< Lat. *nōmināre* < *nōmen*, *nōmin-*, name; see **nō-men-***).]

re•nowned (rĭ-nound′) *adj.* Having renown; famous. See Syns at **noted.**

rent[1] (rĕnt) *n.* **1.a.** Payment, usu. of an amount fixed by contract, made by a tenant at specified intervals in return for the right to occupy or use the property of another. **b.** A similar payment made for the use of a facility, equipment, or service provided by another. **2.** The return derived from cultivated or improved land after deduction of all production costs. **3.** The revenue yielded by a piece of land in excess of that yielded by the poorest or least favorably located land under equal market conditions. — *v.* **rent•ed, rent•ing, rents.** — *tr.* **1.** To obtain occupancy or use of (another's property) in return for regular payments. **2.** To grant temporary occupancy or use of (one's own property or a service) in return for regular payments. — *intr.* To be for rent. — ***idiom.* for rent.** Available for use or service in return for payment. [ME *rente* < OFr. < VLat. **rendita* < fem. p.part. of **rendere*, to yield, return. See RENDER.] — **rent′a•bil′i•ty** *n.* — **rent′a•ble** *adj.*

rent[2] (rĕnt) *v.* A p.t. and p.part. of **rend.** — *n.* **1.** An opening made by rending; a rip. **2.** A breach of relations; a rift.

rent-a-car (rĕnt′ə-kär′) *n.* **1.** A rented car. **2.** An agency that offers cars and vans for rent.

rent•al (rĕn′tl) *n.* **1.** An amount paid out or taken in as rent. **2.** Property available for renting. **3.** The act of renting. **4.** An agency that rents something. **5.** A list of tenants and schedule of rents. — *adj.* Of, relating to, or available for rent.

rent control *n.* Governmental control and regulation of the amounts charged for rented housing.

rent•er (rĕn′tər) *n.* **1.** One that receives payment in exchange for the use of one's property by another. **2.** One that pays rent for the use of another's property; a tenant.

rent-free (rĕnt′frē′) *adj.* Not being subject to rent. — *adv.* Without having to pay or without paying rent.

Ren•ton (rĕn′tən). A city of W-central WA, a suburb of Seattle. Pop. 41,688.

rent strike *n.* An agreement among tenants to refuse to pay rent, often in protest of poor services.

re•nun•ci•a•tion (rĭ-nŭn′sē-ā′shən) *n.* **1.** The act or an instance of renouncing: *the renunciation of earthly pleasures.* **2.** A declaration in which something is renounced. [ME < AN *renunciacion* < Lat. *renūntiātiō*, *renūntiātiōn-* < *renūntiātus*, p.part. of *renūntiāre*, to renounce. See RENOUNCE.] — **re•nun′ci•a′tive, re•nun′ci•a•to′ry** (-ə-tôr′ē, -tōr′ē) *adj.*

Ren•wick (rĕn′wĭk), **James.** 1818–95. Amer. architect who designed the Smithsonian Institution (1848).

re•o•pen (rē-ō′pən) *tr. & intr.v.* **-pened, -pen•ing, -pens. 1.** To open or be opened again. **2.** To take up again or be taken up again; resume.

re•or•der (rē-ôr′dər) *v.* **-dered, -der•ing, -ders.** — *tr.* **1.** To order (the same goods) again. **2.** To straighten out or put in order again. **3.** To rearrange. — *intr.* To order the same goods again. — *n.* A further order of goods from the same supplier.

re•or•gan•i•za•tion (rē-ôr′gə-nĭ-zā′shən) *n.* **1.** The act or process of organizing again or differently. **2.** A thorough alteration of the structure of a business corporation. — **re•or′gan•i•za′tion•al** *adj.*

re•or•gan•ize (rē-ôr′gə-nīz′) *v.* **-ized, -iz•ing, -iz•es.** — *tr.* To organize again or anew. — *intr.* To undergo or effect changes in organization. — **re•or′gan•iz′er** *n.*

re•o•vi•rus (rē′ō-vī′rəs) *n., pl.* **-rus•es.** Any of a group of viruses that contain double-stranded RNA and are associated with various diseases, including gastrointestinal infections. [R(ESPIRATORY) + E(NTERIC) + O(RPHAN) + VIRUS.]

rep[1] also **repp** (rĕp) *n.* A ribbed or corded fabric of various materials, such as cotton, wool, or silk. [Alteration of Fr. *reps* < E. *ribs*, pl. of RIB.]

rep[2] (rĕp) *n. Informal.* A representative.

rep[3] (rĕp) *n. Phys.* A unit of absorbed radiation dose, equal to the amount of ionizing radiation that will transfer 93 ergs of energy to 1 gram of water or living tissue. [R(OENTGEN) + E(QUIVALENT) + P(HYSICAL).]

rep[4] (rĕp) *n. Informal.* **1.** A repertory company. **2.** A repertory theater.

rep[5] (rĕp) *n. Informal.* Reputation.

rep. *abbr.* **1.** Repair. **2.** Repetition. **3.** Report. **4.** Reporter. **5.** Or **Rep.** Representative. **6.** Reprint. **7.** Or **Rep.** Republic.

Rep. *abbr.* Republican.

re•paid (rĭ-pād′) *v.* P.t. and p.part. of **repay.**

re•pair[1] (rĭ-pâr′) *v.* **-paired, -pair•ing, -pairs.** — *tr.* **1.** To restore to sound condition after damage or injury; fix. **2.** To set right; remedy. **3.** To renew or revitalize. **4.** To make up for or compensate for (a loss, for example). — *intr.* To make repairs. — *n.* **1.a.** The work, act, or process of repairing. **b.** An instance of repairing. **2.** General condition after use or repairing. **3.** Something that has been repaired. [ME *repairen* < OFr. *reparer* < Lat. *reparāre* : *re-*, re- + *parāre*, to prepare, put in order; see **perə-**[1]***.**] — **re•pair′a•bil′i•ty** *n.* — **re•pair′a•ble** *adj.* — **re•pair′a•bly** *adv.* — **re•pair′er** *n.*

re•pair[2] (rĭ-pâr′) *intr.v.* **-paired, -pair•ing, -pairs. 1.** To betake oneself; go. **2.** To go frequently or habitually: *repairs to the café every week.* — *n.* **1.** An act of going or sojourning. **2.** A place to which one goes frequently or habitually; a haunt. [ME *repairen*, to return < OFr. *repairier* < LLat. *repatriāre*, to return to one's country. See REPATRIATE.]

re•pair•man (rĭ-pâr′măn′, -mən) *n.* A man whose occupation is making repairs.

re•pair•per•son (rĭ-pâr′pûr′sən) *n.* A repairman or repairwoman.

re•pair•wom•an (rĭ-pâr′wo͝om′ən) *n.* A woman whose occupation is making repairs.

re•pand (rĭ-pănd′) *adj. Bot.* Having a somewhat wavy margin: *a repand leaf.* [Lat. *repandus*, bent backward : *re-*, re- + *pandus*, p.part. of *pandere*, to spread out; see **petə-*.**]

rep•a•ra•ble (rĕp′ər-ə-bəl) *adj.* Possible to repair. [Fr. *réparable* < Lat. *reparābilis* < *reparāre*, to repair. See REPAIR[1].] — **rep′a•ra•bil′i•ty** *n.* — **rep′a•ra•bly** *adv.*

rep•a•ra•tion (rĕp′ə-rā′shən) *n.* **1.** The act or process of repairing or the condition of being repaired. **2.** The act or process of making amends; expiation. **3.** Something done or paid to compensate or make amends. **4. reparations.** Compensation or remuneration required from a defeated nation as indemnity for damage or injury during a war. [ME *reparacion* < OFr. < LLat. *reparātiō*, *reparātiōn-*, restoration < Lat. *reparātus*, p.part. of *reparāre*, to repair. See REPAIR[1].]

re•par•a•tive (rĭ-păr′ə-tĭv) also **re•par•a•to•ry** (-tôr′ē, -tōr′ē) *adj.* **1.** Tending to repair. **2.** Of, relating to, or of the nature of reparations.

rep•ar•tee (rĕp′ər-tē′, -tā′, -är-) *n.* **1.** A swift witty reply. **2.** Conversation marked by the exchange of witty retorts. [Fr. *repartie* < fem. p.part. of *repartir*, to retort < OFr., to retort, to depart again : *re-*, re- + *partir*, to depart (< Lat. *partīre*, to divide < *pars, part-*, part; see **perə-**[2]*).]

re•par•ti•tion (rē′pär-tĭsh′ən) *n.* **1.** Distribution; apportionment. **2.** A partitioning again or in a different way. —*tr.v.* **-tioned, -tion•ing, -tions.** To partition again; redivide.

re•pass (rē-păs′) *v.* **-passed, -pass•ing, -pass•es.** —*tr.* **1.** To pass (something) again. **2.** To cause to pass again in the opposite direction. —*intr.* To pass again; go by again. —**re•pas′sage** (-ĭj) *n.*

re•past (rĭ-păst′) *n.* A meal or the food eaten or served at a meal. —*v.* **-past•ed, -past•ing, -pasts.** —*intr.* To eat or feast. —*tr.* *Obsolete.* To give food to. [ME < OFr. < LLat. *repāstus* < p.part. of *repāscere*, to feed : *re-*, re- + Lat. *pāscere*, to feed; see **pā-***.]

re•pa•tri•ate (rē-pā′trē-āt′) *tr.v.* **-at•ed, -at•ing, -ates.** To restore or return to the country of birth, citizenship, or origin. —*n.* (-ĭt, -āt′). One who has been repatriated. [LLat. *repatriāre, repatriāt-*, to return to one's country : Lat. *re-*, re- + Lat. *patria*, native country; see EXPATRIATE.] —**re•pa′tri•a′tion** *n.*

re•pay (rĭ-pā′) *v.* **-paid** (-pād′), **-pay•ing, -pays.** —*tr.* **1.** To pay back. **2.** To give back, either in return or in compensation. **3.** To make a return or compensation for. **4.** To make or do in return. —*intr.* To make repayment or requital. —**re•pay′a•ble** *adj.* —**re•pay′ment** *n.*

re•peal (rĭ-pēl′) *tr.v.* **-pealed, -peal•ing, -peals. 1.** To revoke or rescind, esp. by an official or formal act. **2.** *Obsolete.* To summon back or recall, esp. from exile. —*n.* The act or process of repealing. [ME *repelen, repealen* < AN *repeler*, alteration of OFr. *rapeler* : *re-*, re- + *apeler*, to appeal; see APPEAL.] —**re•peal′a•ble** *adj.* —**re•peal′er** *n.*

re•peat (rĭ-pēt′) *v.* **-peat•ed, -peat•ing, -peats.** —*tr.* **1.** To say again. **2.** To duplicate another's utterance. **3.** To recite from memory. **4.** To tell to another. **5.** To do, experience, or produce again. **6.** To express (oneself) in the same way or words. —*intr.* **1.** To do or say something again. **2.** To vote more than once in a single election. —*n.* **1.** An act of repeating. **2.** Something repeated. **3.** *Mus.* **a.** A passage or section that is repeated. **b.** A sign usu. consisting of two vertical dots that indicates a passage to be repeated. —*adj.* Of, relating to, or being something that repeats or is repeated: *a repeat offender.* [ME *repeten* < OFr. *repeter* < Lat. *repetere*, to seek again : *re-*, re- + *petere*, to seek; see **pet-***.] —**re•peat′a•bil′i•ty** *n.* —**re•peat′a•ble** *adj.*

Syns: *repeat, iterate, reiterate, restate.* The central meaning shared by these verbs is "to state again": *repeated her plea; iterate a demand; reiterating a query; restated the bid.*

re•peat•ed (rĭ-pē′tĭd) *adj.* Said, done, or occurring again and again: *repeated knocks on the door.* —**re•peat′ed•ly** *adv.*

re•peat•er (rĭ-pē′tər) *n.* **1.** One that repeats. **2.** A watch or clock with a pressure-activated mechanism that strikes the hour. **3.** A repeating firearm. **4.** A student who repeats a course, usu. one that has been failed. **5.** One who repeats in an election. **6.** One who has been convicted of wrongdoing more than once, esp. for the same offense.

re•peat•ing decimal (rĭ-pē′tĭng) *n.* *Math.* A decimal in which a pattern of one or more digits is repeated indefinitely, for example, 0.3333 . . .

repeating firearm *n.* A firearm capable of firing several times without being reloaded.

re•pel (rĭ-pĕl′) *v.* **-pelled, -pel•ling, -pels.** —*tr.* **1.** To ward off or keep away; drive back. **2.** To offer resistance to; fight against. **3.** To refuse to accept; reject. **4.** To turn away from; spurn. **5.** To cause aversion or distaste in. See Syns at **disgust.** See Usage Note at **repulse. 6.** To be resistant to; be incapable of absorbing or mixing with. **7.** *Phys.* To present an opposing force to; push back or away by a force. —*intr.* **1.** To offer a resistant force to something. **2.** To cause aversion or distaste. [ME *repellen* < OFr. *repeller* < Lat. *repellere* : *re-*, re- + *pellere*, to drive; see **pel-**[5]*.] —**re•pel′ler** *n.*

re•pel•lent also **re•pel•lant** (rĭ-pĕl′ənt) —*adj.* **1.a.** Serving or tending to repel. **b.** Able to repel. **2.** Inspiring aversion or distaste; repulsive. **3.** Resistant or impervious to a substance. Often used in combination: *water-repellent.* —*n.* **1.** One that repels. **2.a.** A substance used to repel insects. **b.** A substance or treatment for making a fabric or surface impervious or resistant to something else. —**re•pel′lence, re•pel′len•cy** *n.* —**re•pel′lent•ly** *adv.*

re•pent[1] (rĭ-pĕnt′) *v.* **-pent•ed, -pent•ing, -pents.** —*intr.* **1.** To feel remorse or self-reproach for what one has done or failed to do; be contrite. **2.** To feel such regret for past conduct as to change one's mind regarding it: *repented of poor behavior.* **3.** To make a change for the better as a result of remorse or contrition for one's sins. —*tr.* **1.** To feel regret or self-reproach for. **2.** To cause to feel remorse or regret. [ME *repenten* < OFr. *repentir* : *re-*, re- + *pentir*, to be sorry (< VLat. **paenitīre* < Lat. *paenitēre*).] —**re•pent′er** *n.*

re•pent[2] (rē′pənt) *adj.* *Biol.* Creeping along the ground; prostrate. [Lat. *rēpēns, rēpent-*, pr.part. of *rēpere*, to creep.]

re•pen•tance (rĭ-pĕn′təns) *n.* **1.** The act or process of repenting. **2.** Remorse or contrition for past conduct or sin.

re•pen•tant (rĭ-pĕn′tənt) *adj.* Characterized by or demonstrating repentance; penitent. —**re•pen′tant•ly** *adv.*

Re•pen•ti•gny (rə-päN-tē-nyē′). A town of S Quebec, Canada, a suburb of Montreal. Pop. 34,419.

re•per•cus•sion (rē′pər-kŭsh′ən, rĕp′ər-) *n.* **1.** An often indirect effect or result of an event or act. **2.** A recoil, rebounding, or reciprocal motion after impact. **3.** A reflection, esp. of sound. [Ult. < Lat. *repercussiō, repercussiōn-* < *repercussus*, p.part. of *repercutere*, to cause to rebound : *re-*, re- + *percutere*, to strike; see PERCUSS.] —**re′per•cus′sive** *adj.*

rep•er•toire (rĕp′ər-twär′) *n.* **1.** The stock of songs, plays, operas, or other pieces that a player or company is prepared to perform. **2.** The range or number of skills, aptitudes, or accomplishments of a particular person or group. [Fr. *répertoire* < OFr. < LLat. *repertōrium.* See REPERTORY.]

rep•er•to•ry (rĕp′ər-tôr′ē, -tōr′ē) *n., pl.* **-ries. 1.** A repertoire. **2.a.** A theater in which a repertory company performs. **b.** A repertory company. **3.a.** A place, such as a storehouse, where a stock of things is kept; a repository. **b.** Something stored in or as if in such a place; a stock or collection. [LLat. *repertōrium* < Lat. *repertus*, p.part. of *reperīre*, to find out : *re-*, re- + *parīre*, to get, beget; see **perə-**[1]*.] —**rep′er•to′ri•al** *adj.*

repertory company *n.* A company that presents a number of plays or other works during a season, usu. in alternation.

rep•e•tend (rĕp′ĭ-tĕnd′, rĕp′ĭ-tĕnd′) *n.* **1.** A repeated word, sound, or phrase; a refrain. **2.** *Math.* The digit or group of digits that repeats infinitely in a repeating decimal. [< Lat. *repetendum*, neut. gerundive of *repetere*, to repeat. See REPEAT.]

rep•e•ti•tion (rĕp′ĭ-tĭsh′ən) *n.* **1.** The act or process or an instance of repeating or being repeated. **2.** A recitation or recital, esp. of prepared or memorized material. [Ult. < Lat. *repetītiō, repetītiōn-* < *repetītus*, p.part. of *repetere*, to repeat. See REPEAT.] —**rep′e•ti′tion•al** *adj.*

rep•e•ti•tious (rĕp′ĭ-tĭsh′əs) *adj.* Filled with repetition, esp. needless or tedious repetition. —**rep′e•ti′tious•ly** *adv.* —**rep′e•ti′tious•ness** *n.*

re•pet•i•tive (rĭ-pĕt′ĭ-tĭv) *adj.* Given to or characterized by repetition. —**re•pet′i•tive•ly** *adv.* —**re•pet′i•tive•ness** *n.*

re•phrase (rē-frāz′) *tr.v.* **-phrased, -phras•ing, -phras•es.** To phrase again, esp. to state in a clearer or different way.

re•pine (rĭ-pīn′) *intr.v.* **-pined, -pin•ing, -pines. 1.** To be discontented or low in spirits; complain or fret. **2.** To yearn after something. [ME *repinen*, to be aggrieved : *re-*, re- + *pinen*, to yearn; see PINE[2].] —**re•pin′er** *n.*

repl. *abbr.* Replace; replacement.

re•place (rĭ-plās′) *tr.v.* **-placed, -plac•ing, -plac•es. 1.** To put back into a former position or place. **2.** To take or fill the place of. **3.** To be or provide a substitute for. **4.** To pay back or return; refund. —**re•place′a•ble** *adj.* —**re•plac′er** *n.*

Syns: *replace, supplant, supersede.* These verbs mean to turn someone or something out and place another in his, her, or its stead. To *replace* is to be or furnish an equivalent or a substitute in the place of another, especially another that has been lost, depleted, worn out, or discharged: *"A conspiracy was carefully engineered to replace the Directory by three Consuls"* (H.G. Wells). *Supplant* often, but not invariably, suggests the use of intrigue or underhand tactics to take another's place: *"The rivaling poor Jones, and supplanting him in her affections, added another spur to his pursuit"* (Henry Fielding). To *supersede* is to replace one person or thing by another held to be superior, more valuable or useful, or less antiquated: *"In our island the Latin appears never to have superseded the old Gaelic speech"* (Macaulay).

re•place•ment (rĭ-plās′mənt) *n.* **1.** The act or process of replacing or of being replaced; substitution. **2.** One that replaces, esp. a person assigned to a vacant military position.

replacement therapy *n.* Administration of a body substance to compensate for the loss, as from disease or surgery, of a gland or tissue that would normally produce the substance.

re•plant (rē-plănt′) *tr.v.* **-plant•ed, -plant•ing, -plants. 1.** To plant again or in a new place: *replanted the perennials.* **2.** To supply with new plants: *replant a window box.* **3.** To reattach (an organ, for example) surgically to the original site. —*n.* (rē′plănt′). Something replanted. —**re′plan•ta′tion** *n.*

re•play (rē-plā′) *tr.v.* **-played, -play•ing, -plays.** To play over again: *replay a tape.* —*n.* (rē′plā′). **1.** The act or process of replaying. **2.** Something replayed. **3.** An instant replay.

re•plen•ish (rĭ-plĕn′ĭsh) *v.* **-ished, -ish•ing, -ish•es.** —*tr.* **1.** To fill or make complete again; restock: *replenish the larder.* **2.** To inspire or nourish. —*intr.* To become full again. [ME *replenisshen* < OFr. *replenir, repleniss-* : *re-*, re- + *plenir*, to fill (< *plein*, full < Lat. *plēnus*; see **pelə-**[1]*).] —**re•plen′ish•er** *n.* —**re•plen′ish•ment** *n.*

re•plete (rĭ-plēt′) *adj.* **1.** Abundantly supplied; abounding: *a stream replete with trout.* **2.** Filled to satiation; gorged. **3.** *Usage Problem.* Complete. [ME < OFr. < Lat. *replētus*, p.part. of *replēre*, to refill : *re-*, re- + *plēre*, to fill; see **pelə-**[1]*.] —**re•plete′ness** *n.*

ă pat	oi boy
ā pay	ou out
âr care	o͝o took
ä father	o͞o boot
ĕ pet	ŭ cut
ē be	ûr urge
ĭ pit	th thin
ī pie	*th* this
îr pier	hw which
ŏ pot	zh vision
ō toe	ə about, item
ô paw	

Stress marks:
′ (primary);
′ (secondary), as in
dictionary (dĭk′shə-nĕr′ē)

Usage Note: *Replete* means "abundantly supplied" and is not generally accepted as a synonym for *complete.*

re•ple•tion (rĭ-plē′shən) *n.* **1.** The condition of being fully supplied or completely filled. **2.** A state of excessive fullness.

re•plev•in (rĭ-plĕv′ĭn) *Law.* —*n.* **1.** An action to recover personal property said or claimed to be unlawfully taken. **2.** The writ or procedure of such an action. —*tr.v.* **-ined, -in•ing, -ines.** To replevy. [ME < AN *replevine* < *replevir,* to give as a security : *re-,* re- + *plevir,* to pledge (< LLat. *plebere,* of Gmc. orig.).]

re•plev•y (rĭ-plĕv′ē) *Law.* —*tr.v.* **-ied, -y•ing, -ies.** To regain possession of by a writ of replevin. —*n., pl.* **-ies.** A replevin. [AN *replevir.* See REPLEVIN.]

rep•li•ca (rĕp′lĭ-kə) *n.* **1.** A copy or reproduction of a work of art, esp. one by the original artist. **2.** A copy or reproduction, esp. one smaller than the original. [Ital. < *replicare,* to repeat < LLat. *replicāre.* See REPLICATE.]

rep•li•case (rĕp′lĭ-kās′, -kāz′) *n.* An enzyme that promotes the synthesis of a complementary RNA molecule from an RNA template. [REPLIC(ATE) + -ASE.]

rep•li•cate (rĕp′lĭ-kāt′) *v.* **-cat•ed, -cat•ing, -cates.** —*tr.* **1.** To duplicate, copy, reproduce, or repeat. **2.** *Biol.* To reproduce or make an exact copy of (a cell, for example). **3.** To fold over or bend back. —*intr.* To become replicated; undergo replication. —*adj.* (-kĭt) also **rep•li•cat•ed** (-kā′tĭd). Folded over or bent back upon itself. —*n.* (-kĭt). A repetition of an experiment or a procedure. [ME *replicaten* < LLat. *replicāre, replicāt-,* to repeat < Lat., to fold back : *re-,* re- + *plicāre,* to fold; see **plek-***.] —**rep′li•ca′tive** *adj.*

rep•li•ca•tion (rĕp′lĭ-kā′shən) *n.* **1.** A fold or a folding back. **2.** A reply to an answer; a rejoinder. **3.** *Law.* The plaintiff's response to the defendant's answer or plea. **4.** An echo or a reverberation. **5.** A copy or reproduction. **6.** The act or process of duplicating or reproducing something. **7.** *Biol.* The act or process by which genetic material, a cell, or an organism reproduces or makes an exact copy of itself.

rep•li•con (rĕp′lĭ-kŏn′) *n.* A genetic element that undergoes replication as an autonomous unit. [REPLIC(ATION) + -ON[1].]

re•ply (rĭ-plī′) *v.* **-plied, -ply•ing, -plies.** —*intr.* **1.** To give an answer in speech or writing. **2.** To respond by an act or a gesture. **3.** To echo. **4.** To return gunfire or an attack. **5.** *Law.* To respond to a defendant's plea. —*tr.* To say or give as an answer: *I replied that I could.* See Syns at **answer.** —*n., pl.* **-plies. 1.** A written or spoken response. **2.** A response by action or gesture. **3.** *Law.* A plaintiff's formal response in answer to that of a defendant. [ME *replien* < OFr. *replier* < Lat. *replicāre,* to fold back. See REPLICATE.] —**re•pli′er** *n.*

re•po[1] (rē′pō′) *n., pl.* **-pos.** *Informal.* A repurchase agreement. [Shortening and alteration of REPURCHASE AGREEMENT.]

re•po[2] (rē′pō′) *n., pl.* **-pos.** *Informal.* **1.** Repossession of merchandise or property from a buyer who has defaulted on payment. **2.** Repossessed merchandise or property.

re•po•lar•i•za•tion (rē-pō′lər-ĭ-zā′shən) *n.* The restoration of a polarized state across a membrane, as in a muscle fiber following contraction.

re•po•lar•ize (rē-pō′lə-rīz′) *intr.v.* **-ized, -iz•ing, -iz•es.** To return to a polarized state; undergo repolarization.

re•port (rĭ-pôrt′ -pōrt′) *n.* **1.** An account presented usu. in detail. **2.** A formal account of the proceedings or transactions of a group. **3.** *Law.* A published collection of authoritative accounts of court cases or of judicial decisions. Often used in the plural. **4.** Common talk; rumor or gossip. **5.** Reputation; repute. **6.** An explosive noise. —*v.* **-port•ed, -port•ing, -ports.** —*tr.* **1.** To make or present an often official, formal, or regular account of. **2.** To relate or tell about; present. **3.** To write or provide an account or a summation of for publication or broadcast. **4.** To submit or relate the results of considerations concerning: *reported the bill.* **5.** To carry back and repeat to another. **6.** To complain about or denounce. —*intr.* **1.** To make a report. **2.** To serve as a reporter for a publication, broadcasting company, or other news media. **3.** To present oneself. **4.** To be accountable. —***idiom.* on report.** Subject to disciplinary action. [ME < OFr. < *reporter,* to report < Lat. *reportāre* : *re-,* re- + *portāre,* to carry; see **per-**[2]*.] —**re•port′a•ble** *adj.*

re•port•age (rĕp′ər-täzh′, rĭ-pôr′tĭj, -pōr′-) *n.* **1.** The act or process of reporting news or information. **2.** Something reported. [Fr. < *reporter,* to report < OFr. See REPORT.]

report card *n.* A report of a student's progress presented periodically to a parent or guardian.

re•port•ed•ly (rĭ-pôr′tĭd-lē, -pōr′-) *adv.* By report; supposedly.

re•port•er (rĭ-pôr′tər, -pōr′-) *n.* **1.** A writer, an investigator, or a presenter of news stories. **2.** *Law.* A person who is authorized to write and issue official accounts of judicial or legislative proceedings. —**rep′or•to′ri•al** (rĕp′ər-tôr′ē-əl, -tōr′-, rē′pər-) *adj.* —**rep′or•to′ri•al•ly** *adv.*

re•pose[1] (rĭ-pōz′) *n.* **1.** The act of resting or the state of being at rest. **2.** Freedom from worry; peace of mind. **3.** Calmness; tranquillity. —*v.* **-posed, -pos•ing, -pos•es.** —*tr.* **1.** To lay (oneself) down. **2.** To rest or relax (oneself). —*intr.* **1.** To lie at rest. **2.** To lie dead. **3.** To lie while being supported by something. [< ME *reposen,* to be at rest < OFr. *reposer* < LLat. *repausāre,* to cause to rest : Lat. *re-,* re- + LLat. *pausāre,* to rest (< Lat. *pausa,* rest; see PAUSE).] —**re•pos′al** *n.* —**re•pos′er** *n.*

re•pose[2] (rĭ-pōz′) *tr.v.* **-posed, -pos•ing, -pos•es.** To place (trust, for example) in. [ME *reposen,* to replace < Lat. *repōnere, repos-,* to put away. See REPOSIT.]

re•pose•ful (rĭ-pōz′fəl) *adj.* Marked by, conducive to, or expressing repose. —**re•pose′ful•ness** *n.*

re•pos•it (rĭ-pŏz′ĭt) *tr.v.* **-it•ed, -it•ing, -its.** To put away; store. [Lat. *repōnere, reposit-* : *re-,* re- + *pōnere,* to place; see **apo-***.] —**re′po•si′tion** (rē′pə-zĭsh′ən, rĕp′ə-) *n.*

re•pos•i•to•ry (rĭ-pŏz′ĭ-tôr′ē, -tōr′ē) *n., pl.* **-ries. 1.** A place where things may be put for safekeeping. **2.** A warehouse. **3.** A museum. **4.** A burial vault; a tomb. **5.** One that contains or is a store of something specified. **6.** One who is entrusted with secrets or confidential information.

re•pos•sess (rē′pə-zĕs′) *tr.v.* **-sessed, -sess•ing, -sess•es. 1.a.** To regain possession of. **b.** To reclaim possession of for failure to pay installments due. **2.** To give back possession to. —**re′pos•ses′sion** (-zĕsh′ən) *n.*

re•pous•sé (rə-po͞o-sā′) *adj.* **1.** Having patterns in relief formed by hammering and pressing on the reverse side. Used esp. of metal. **2.** Raised in relief. —*n.* **1.** A design in relief. **2.** The technique of hammering and pressing designs in relief. [Fr., p.part. of *repousser,* to push back < OFr. : *re-,* re- + *pousser,* to push (< Lat. *pulsāre,* to beat, freq. of *pellere,* to push; see REPEL).]

repp (rĕp) *n.* Var. of **rep**[1].

rep•re•hend (rĕp′rĭ-hĕnd′) *tr.v.* **-hend•ed, -hend•ing, -hends.** To reprove; censure. See Syns at **criticize.** [ME *reprehenden* < Lat. *reprehendere* : *re-,* re- + *prehendere,* to seize; see **ghend-***.]

rep•re•hen•si•ble (rĕp′rĭ-hĕn′sə-bəl) *adj.* Deserving rebuke or censure; blameworthy. [ME < OFr. < LLat. *reprehēnsibilis* < Lat. *reprehēnsus,* p.part. of *reprehendere,* to reprehend. See REPREHEND.] —**rep′re•hen′si•bil′i•ty, rep′re•hen′si•ble•ness** *n.* —**rep′re•hen′si•bly** *adv.*

rep•re•hen•sion (rĕp′rĭ-hĕn′shən) *n.* Reprehending.

rep•re•sent (rĕp′rĭ-zĕnt′) *tr.v.* **-sent•ed, -sent•ing, -sents. 1.a.** To stand for; symbolize. **b.** To indicate or communicate by signs or symbols. **2.a.** To depict in art; portray. **b.** To describe in words; set forth. **3.** To present clearly to the mind. **4.** To draw attention to by way of remonstrance or protest. **5.** To describe or put forward (a person or thing) as manifesting a specified quality. **6.a.** To serve as the official and authorized delegate or agent for. **b.** To act as a spokesperson for. **7.** To serve as an example of. **8.** To be the equivalent of. **9.a.** To stage (a play, for example); produce. **b.** To act the part or role of. [ME *representen* < OFr. *representer* < Lat. *repraesentāre,* to show : *re-,* re- + *praesentāre,* to present; see PRESENT[2].] —**rep′re•sent′a•bil′i•ty** *n.* —**rep′re•sent′a•ble** *adj.* —**rep′re•sent′er** *n.*

rep•re•sen•ta•tion (rĕp′rĭ-zĕn-tā′shən, -zən-) *n.* **1.** The act of representing or the state of being represented. **2.** Something that represents. **3.a.** An account or a statement, as of facts or arguments. **b.** An expostulation; a protest. **4.** A presentation or production, as of a play. **5.** The state or condition of serving as an official delegate, agent, or spokesperson. **6.** The right or privilege of being represented by delegates having a voice in a legislative body. **7.** *Law.* A statement of fact made by one party in order to induce another party to enter into a contract.

rep•re•sen•ta•tion•al (rĕp′rĭ-zĕn-tā′shə-nəl, -zən-) *adj.* Of or relating to representation, esp. to realistic graphic representation. —**rep′re•sen•ta′tion•al•ism** *n.*

rep•re•sen•ta•tive (rĕp′rĭ-zĕn′tə-tĭv) *n.* **1.** One that serves as an example or a type for others of the same classification. **2.** One that serves as a delegate or an agent for another. **3.a.** A member of a governmental body, usu. legislative, chosen by popular vote. **b.** A member of the U.S. House of Representatives or of the lower house of a state legislature. —*adj.* **1.** Representing, depicting, or portraying or able to do so. **2.** Authorized to act as an official delegate or agent. **3.** Of, relating to, or characteristic of government by representation. **4.** Like or typical of others of the same class. See Usage Note at **cross section.** —**rep′re•sen′ta•tive•ly** *adv.* —**rep′re•sen′ta•tive•ness** *n.*

re•press (rĭ-prĕs′) *v.* **-pressed, -press•ing, -press•es.** —*tr.* **1.** To hold back by an act of volition: *repressed a smirk.* **2.** To put down by force; quell. **3.** *Psychol.* To exclude (painful memories, for example) from the conscious mind. —*intr.* To take repressive action. [ME *repressen* < Lat. *reprimere, repress-* : *re-,* re- + *premere,* to press; see **per-**[4]*.] —**re•press′i•bil′i•ty** *n.* —**re•press′i•ble** *adj.*

re•pres•sion (rĭ-prĕsh′ən) *n.* **1.** The act of repressing or the state of being repressed. **2.** *Psychol.* The unconscious exclusion of painful impulses, desires, or fears from the conscious mind. —**re•pres′sion•ist** *adj.*

re•pres•sive (rĭ-prĕs′ĭv) *adj.* Causing or inclined to cause repression. —**re•pres′sive•ly** *adv.* —**re•pres′sive•ness** *n.*

re•pres•sor (rĭ-prĕs′ər) *n.* **1.** Also **re•press•er.** One that represses. 2. *Genet.* A protein that binds to an operator, blocking transcription of an operon and the enzymes for which it codes.

re•prieve (rĭ-prēv′) *tr.v.* **-prieved, -priev•ing, -prieves. 1.** To postpone or cancel the punishment of. **2.** To bring relief to. —*n.* **1.a.** Postponement or cancellation of a punishment. **b.** A warrant for such an action. **2.** Temporary relief, as from danger. [Alteration of ME *reprien*, prob. < OFr. *repris*, p.part. of *reprendre*, to take back < Lat. *reprehendere*, to hold back. See REPREHEND.] —**re•priev′a•ble** *adj.*

rep•ri•mand (rĕp′rə-mănd′) *tr.v.* **-mand•ed, -mand•ing, -mands.** To reprove severely, esp. in a formal or official way. See Syns at **admonish.** —*n.* A severe, formal, or official rebuke or censure. [Fr. *réprimander* < *réprimande*, a reprimand, alteration (influenced by *mander*, to order) of obsolete *reprimende* < Lat. *reprimenda (culpa)*, (fault) to be repressed, fem. gerundive of *reprimere*, to restrain. See REPRESS.]

re•print (rē′prĭnt′) *n.* **1.** Something that has been printed again, esp.: **a.** A printing that is identical to an original; a reimpression. **b.** A separately printed excerpt; an offprint. **2.** A facsimile of a postage stamp printed after the original has been discontinued. —*tr.v.* (rē-prĭnt′) **-print•ed, -print•ing, -prints.** To make a new copy or edition of; print again. —**re•print′er** *n.*

re•pri•sal (rĭ-prī′zəl) *n.* **1.** Retaliation for an injury with the intent of injuring at least as much in return. **2.** Forcible seizure of an enemy's goods or subjects in retaliation for injuries. **3.** The practice of using political or military force outside of war. [ME *reprisail* < OFr. *reprisaille* < OItal. *ripresaglia* < *ripreso*, p.part. of *riprendere*, to take back < Lat. *reprendere, reprehendere*, to take hold of. See REPREHEND.]

re•prise (rĭ-prēz′) *n.* **1.** *Mus.* **a.** A repetition of a phrase or verse. **b.** A return to an original theme. **2.** A recurrence or resumption of an action. —*tr.v.* **-prised, -pris•ing, -pris•es.** To repeat or resume an action; make a reprise of. [ME, act of taking back < OFr. < fem. p.part. of *reprendre*, to take back. See REPRIEVE.]

re•pro (rē′prō) *n.*, *pl.* **-pros.** *Print.* A reproduction proof.

re•proach (rĭ-prōch′) *tr.v.* **-proached, -proach•ing, -proach•es. 1.** To express disapproval of, criticism of, or disappointment in (someone). See Syns at **admonish. 2.** To bring shame upon; disgrace. —*n.* **1.** Blame; rebuke. **2.** One that causes rebuke or blame. **3.** Disgrace; shame. —***idiom.* beyond reproach.** So good as to preclude criticism. [ME *reprochen* < OFr. *reprochier* < VLat. **repropiāre* : Lat. *re-*, re- + Lat. *prope*, near; see **per**[1]***.**] —**re•proach′a•ble** *adj.* —**re•proach′a•ble•ness** *n.* —**re•proach′er** *n.*

re•proach•ful (rĭ-prōch′fəl) *adj.* Expressing reproach or blame. —**re•proach′ful•ly** *adv.* —**re•proach′ful•ness** *n.*

rep•ro•bate (rĕp′rə-bāt′) *n.* **1.** A morally unprincipled person. **2.** *Theol.* One who is predestined to damnation. —*adj.* **1.** Morally unprincipled; shameless. **2.** *Theol.* Rejected by God and without hope of salvation. —*tr.v.* **-bat•ed, -bat•ing, -bates. 1.** To disapprove of; condemn. **2.** *Theol.* To abandon to eternal damnation. [< ME, condemned < LLat. *reprobātus*, p.part. of *reprobāre*, to reprove : Lat. *re-*, opposite; see RE- + Lat. *probāre*, to approve; see PROVE.] —**rep′ro•ba′tion** *n.* —**rep′ro•ba′tive** *adj.*

re•proc•ess (rē-prŏs′ĕs′, -prō′sĕs′) *tr.v.* **-essed, -ess•ing, -ess•es.** To cause to undergo special or additional processing before reuse.

re•pro•duce (rē′prə-do͞os′, -dyo͞os′) *v.* **-duced, -duc•ing, -duc•es.** —*tr.* **1.** To produce a counterpart, an image, or a copy of. **2.** *Biol.* To generate (offspring). **3.** To produce again or anew; re-create. **4.** To bring (a memory, for example) to mind again. —*intr.* **1.** To generate offspring. **2.** To undergo copying: *graphics that reproduce well.* —**re′pro•duc′er** *n.* —**re′pro•duc′i•bil′i•ty** *n.* —**re′pro•duc′i•ble** *adj.*

re•pro•duc•tion (rē′prə-dŭk′shən) *n.* **1.** The act of reproducing or the condition or process of being reproduced. **2.** Something reproduced. **3.** *Biol.* The process by which organisms generate others of the same kind.

reproduction proof *n.* *Print.* A camera-ready proof of typeset material made through a photographic process such as photo-offset lithography.

re•pro•duc•tive (rē′prə-dŭk′tĭv) *adj.* **1.** Of or concerning reproduction. **2.** Tending to reproduce. —*n.* *Zool.* A reproductive organism, esp. a sexually mature social insect. —**re′pro•duc′tive•ly** *adv.* —**re′pro•duc′tive•ness** *n.*

re•pro•gram (rē-prō′grăm′) *tr.v.* **-grammed, -gram•ming, -grams** or **-gramed, -gram•ing, -grams.** To program again. —**re′pro•gram′ma•bil′i•ty** *n.* —**re•pro′gram•ma•ble** *adj.*

re•pro•graph•ics (rē′prə-grăf′ĭks) *n.* **1.** *(used with a sing. v.)* The technique of reprography. **2.** *(used with a sing. or pl. v.)* The materials, equipment, and processes of reprography.

re•prog•ra•phy (rĭ-prŏg′rə-fē) *n.* The process of reproducing graphic material, as by mechanical or electronic means. [RE-PRO(DUCTION) + -GRAPHY.] —**re•prog′ra•pher** *n.* —**re′pro•graph′ic** (rē′prə-grăf′ĭk, rĕp′rə-) *adj.*

re•proof (rĭ-pro͞of′) *n.* The act, an instance, or an expression of reproving; a rebuke. [ME *reprof*, var. of *reprove, repreve* < OFr. *reprueve* < *reprover*, to find fault with. See REPROVE.]

re•prove (rĭ-pro͞ov′) *tr.v.* **-proved, -prov•ing, -proves. 1.** To voice or convey disapproval of; rebuke. See Syns at **admonish. 2.** To find fault with. [ME *reproven* < AN *repruver*, var. of OFr. *reprover* < LLat. *reprobāre*, to disapprove. See REPROBATE.] —**re•prov′a•ble** *adj.* —**re•prov′al** *n.* —**re•prov′er** *n.* —**re•prov′ing•ly** *adv.*

rept. *abbr.* Report.

rep•tant (rĕp′tənt) *adj.* *Biol.* Creeping or crawling; repent. [Lat. *rēptāns, rēptant-*, pr.part. of *rēptāre*, to creep, freq. of *rēpere*.]

rep•tile (rĕp′tĭl, -tīl′) *n.* **1.** Any of various cold-blooded, usu. egg-laying vertebrates of the class Reptilia, such as a snake, turtle, or dinosaur, having an external covering of scales or horny plates and breathing by means of lungs. **2.** A person regarded as despicable or treacherous. [ME *reptil* < OFr. *reptile* < LLat. *rēptile* < neut. of Lat. *rēptilis*, creeping < *rēptus*, p.part. of *rēpere*, to creep.]

rep•til•i•an (rĕp-tĭl′ē-ən, -tĭl′yən) *adj.* **1.** Of or relating to reptiles. **2.** Resembling or characteristic of a reptile. **3.** Despicable; treacherous. —*n.* A reptile.

rep•til•i•um (rĕp-tĭl′ē-əm) *n.*, *pl.* **-i•a** (-ē-ə). A building or an enclosure housing reptiles for public display.

Repub. *abbr.* **1.** Republic. **2.** Republican.

re•pub•lic (rĭ-pŭb′lĭk) *n.* **1.a.** A political order not headed by a monarch and in modern times led usu. by a president. **b.** A nation that has such a political order. **2.a.** A political order in which the supreme power lies in a body of citizens who are entitled to vote for officers and representatives responsible to them. **b.** A nation that has such a political order. **3.** Often **Republic.** A specific republican government of a nation. **4.** An autonomous or partially autonomous political and territorial unit belonging to a sovereign federation. **5.** A group of people working as equals in the same sphere or field. [Fr. *république* < OFr. < Lat. *rēspūblica* : *rēs*, thing; see **rē-*** + *pūblica*, fem. of *pūblicus*, of the people; see PUBLIC.]

re•pub•li•can (rĭ-pŭb′lĭ-kən) *adj.* **1.** Of, relating to, or characteristic of a republic. **2.** Favoring a republican form of government. **3. Republican.** Of, relating to, typical of, or belonging to the U.S. Republican Party. —*n.* **1.** One who favors a republic as the best form of government. **2. Republican.** A member of the Republican Party. —**re•pub′li•can•ism** *n.*

re•pub•li•can•ize (rĭ-pŭb′lĭ-kə-nīz′) *tr.v.* **-ized, -iz•ing, -iz•es.** To make republican. —**re•pub′li•can•i•za′tion** (-kə-nĭ-zā′shən) *n.*

Republican Party *n.* **1.** One of the two primary political parties of the United States, organized in 1854 to oppose the extension of slavery. **2.** The Democratic-Republican Party.

Republican River. A river rising in E CO and flowing c. 676 km (420 mi) to join the Smoky Hill R. and form the Kansas R.

re•pub•li•ca•tion (rē-pŭb′lĭ-kā′shən) *n.* **1.** The act or process of republishing. **2.** Something republished.

re•pub•lish (rē-pŭb′lĭsh) *tr.v.* **-lished, -lish•ing, -lish•es.** To publish again. —**re•pub′lish•er** *n.*

re•pu•di•ate (rĭ-pyo͞o′dē-āt′) *tr.v.* **-at•ed, -at•ing, -ates. 1.** To reject the validity or authority of. **2.** To reject strongly as unfounded, false, or unjust. **3.** To refuse to recognize or pay. **4.a.** To disown (as a child). **b.** To refuse to have any dealings with. [Lat. *repudiāre, repudiāt-* < *repudium*, divorce.] —**re•pu′di•a′tive** *adj.* —**re•pu′di•a′tor** *n.*

re•pu•di•a•tion (rĭ-pyo͞o′dē-ā′shən) *n.* **1.** The act of repudiating or the state of being repudiated. **2.** The refusal, esp. by public authorities, to acknowledge a contract or debt. —**re•pu′di•a′tion•ist** *n.*

re•pugn (rĭ-pyo͞on′) *v.* **-pugned, -pugn•ing, -pugns.** —*tr.* To oppose or contend against. —*intr.* *Archaic.* To be opposed; conflict. [ME *repugnen* < OFr. *repugner* < Lat. *repugnāre*, to fight against : *re-*, re- + *pugnāre*, to fight with the fist; see **peuk-*.**]

re•pug•nance (rĭ-pŭg′nəns) *n.* **1.** Great dislike; aversion. **2.** *Logic.* The relationship of contradictory terms; inconsistency.

re•pug•nan•cy (rĭ-pŭg′nən-sē) *n.*, *pl.* **-cies.** Repugnance.

re•pug•nant (rĭ-pŭg′nənt) *adj.* **1.** Arousing disgust or aversion; repulsive: *repugnant behavior.* **2.** *Logic.* Contradictory; inconsistent. [ME, antagonistic < OFr. < Lat. *repugnāns, repugnant-*, pr.part. of *repugnāre*, to fight against. See REPUGN.] —**re•pug′nant•ly** *adv.*

re•pulse (rĭ-pŭls′) *tr.v.* **-pulsed, -puls•ing, -puls•es. 1.** To drive back; repel. **2.** To rebuff or reject with rudeness, coldness, or denial. **3.** *Usage Problem.* To cause repugnance or distaste in. —*n.* **1.** The act of repulsing or the state of being repulsed. **2.** Rejection; refusal. [ME *repulsen* < Lat. *repellere, repuls-*. See REPEL.] —**re•puls′er** *n.*

Usage Note: A number of critics have maintained that *repulse* should only be used to mean "to drive away, spurn," as in *He rudely repulsed their overtures,* and not to mean "to cause repulsion in," as in *Their hypocrisy repulsed me.* Reputable literary precedent exists for this usage, and the confusion is understandable, given that the stigmatized use of *repulse* is parallel to the unexceptionable uses of *repulsion* and *repulsive.* Still, writers who want to stay on the safe side may

ă pat	oi boy
ā pay	ou out
âr care	o͝o took
ä father	o͞o boot
ĕ pet	ŭ cut
ē be	ûr urge
ĭ pit	th thin
ī pie	*th* this
îr pier	hw which
ŏ pot	zh vision
ō toe	ə about, item
ô paw	

Stress marks:
′ (primary);
′ (secondary), as in
dictionary (dĭk′shə-nĕr′ē)

prefer to use only *repel* to mean "cause repulsion in."

re•pul•sion (rĭ-pŭl′shən) *n.* **1.** The act of repulsing or the condition of being repulsed. **2.** Aversion. **3.** *Phys.* The tendency of particles or bodies of the same electric charge or magnetic polarity to separate.

re•pul•sive (rĭ-pŭl′sĭv) *adj.* **1.** Causing repugnance or aversion; disgusting. **2.** Tending to repel or drive off. **3.** *Phys.* Opposing in direction: *a repulsive force.* **—re•pul′sive•ly** *adv.* **—re•pul′sive•ness** *n.*

re•pur•chase agreement (rē-pûr′chĭs) *n.* A contract giving the seller of an asset the right or obligation to buy back the asset at a specified price on a given date.

rep•u•ta•ble (rĕp′yə-tə-bəl) *adj.* Having a good reputation; honorable. **—rep′u•ta•bil′i•ty** *n.* **—rep′u•ta•bly** *adv.*

rep•u•ta•tion (rĕp′yə-tā′shən) *n.* **1.** The general estimation in which a person is held. **2.** The state or situation of being in high esteem. **3.** A specific characteristic or trait ascribed to a person or thing. [Ult. < Lat. *reputātiō, reputātiōn-*, a reckoning < *reputātus*, p.part. of *reputāre*, to reckon. See REPUTE.]

re•pute (rĭ-pyo͞ot′) *tr.v.* **-put•ed, -put•ing, -putes. 1.** To ascribe a particular fact or characteristic to. **2.** To consider; suppose. —*n.* **1.** Reputation. **2.** A good reputation. [ME *reputen* < OFr. *reputer* < Lat. *reputāre*, to think over : *re-*, re- + *putāre*, to think over; see **peu-***.]

re•put•ed (rĭ-pyo͞o′tĭd) *adj.* Generally supposed to be such. **—re•put′ed•ly** *adv.*

req. *abbr.* **1.** Require; required. **2.** Requisition.

reqd. *abbr.* Required.

re•quest (rĭ-kwĕst′) *tr.v.* **-quest•ed, -quest•ing, -quests. 1.** To express a desire for; ask for. **2.** To ask (a person) to do something. —*n.* **1.** The act of asking. **2.** Something asked for. —***idioms.* by request.** In response to a request. **in request.** In great demand. **on** (or **upon**) **request.** When asked for. [< ME *requeste*, the act of requesting < OFr. < VLat. **(rēs) requaesīta*, (thing) requested < Lat., fem. p.part. of *requīrere*, to ask for. See REQUIRE.] **—re•quest′er** *n.*

req•ui•em (rĕk′wē-əm, rē′kwē-) *n.* **1. Requiem.** *Rom. Cath. Ch.* **a.** A Mass for a deceased person. **b.** A musical composition for such a Mass. **2.** A hymn, composition, or service for the dead. [ME < Lat., accusative of *requiēs*, rest, first word of the Requiem : *re-*, re- + *quiēs*, quiet; see **kʷeiə-***.]

req•ui•es•cat (rĕk′wē-ĕs′kăt′, -kät′) *n.* A prayer for the repose of the souls of the dead. [Lat., third pers. sing. pr. subjunctive of *requiēscere*, to rest. See **kʷeiə-***.]

re•quire (rĭ-kwīr′) *tr.v.* **-quired, -quir•ing, -quires. 1.** To have as a requisite; need. **2.** To call for as obligatory or appropriate; demand. See Syns at **demand. 3.** To oblige; compel. [ME *requiren* < OFr. *requerre* < VLat. **requaerere*, alteration of Lat. *requīrere* : *re-*, re- + *quaerere*, to seek.] **—re•quir′a•ble** *adj.* **—re•quir′er** *n.*

re•quired (rĭ-kwīrd′) *adj.* **1.** Needed; essential. **2.** Obligatory.

re•quire•ment (rĭ-kwīr′mənt) *n.* **1.** Something that is required; a necessity. **2.** Something obligatory; a prerequisite.

req•ui•site (rĕk′wĭ-zĭt) *adj.* Required; essential. See Syns at **indispensable.** —*n.* Something that is indispensable; a requirement. [ME < Lat. *requīsītus*, p.part. of *requīrere*, to require. See REQUIRE.] **—req′ui•site•ly** *adv.* **—req′ui•site•ness** *n.*

req•ui•si•tion (rĕk′wĭ-zĭsh′ən) *n.* **1.** A formal written request for something needed. **2.** A necessity; a requirement. **3.** The state or condition of being needed or put into service. —*tr.v.* **-tioned, -tion•ing, -tions. 1.** To demand, as for military needs. **2.** To make demands of.

re•quit•al (rĭ-kwīt′l) *n.* **1.** The act of requiting. **2.** Return, as for an injury or a friendly act.

re•quite (rĭ-kwīt′) *tr.v.* **-quit•ed, -quit•ing, -quites. 1.** To make repayment or return for: *requited love.* See Syns at **reciprocate. 2.** To avenge. [ME *requiten* : *re-*, re- + *quiten*, to pay; see QUIT.] **—re•quit′a•ble** *adj.* **—re•quit′er** *n.*

re•ra•di•ate (rē-rā′dē-āt′) *tr.v.* **-at•ed, -at•ing, -ates.** To emit (radiation) following the absorption of incident radiation. **—re•ra′di•a′tion** *n.*

rere•dos (rîr′dŏs′, rîr′ĭ-, rĕr′ĭ-) *n.* **1.** A decorative screen or facing on the wall at the back of an altar; a retable. **2.** The back of an open hearth of a fireplace. [ME < AN < *areredos* : *arere*, behind (Lat. *ad-*, ad- + Lat. *retrō*, backward; see **re-***) + AN *dos*, back (< Lat. *dorsum*).]

re•re•lease (rē′rĭ-lēs′) *tr.v.* **-leased, -leas•ing, -leas•es.** To release (a movie, for example) again. **—re′re•lease′** *n.*

re•run (rē′rŭn′) *n.* The act or an instance of rebroadcasting a recorded television program. —*tr.v.* (rē-rŭn′) **-ran** (-răn′), **-run, -run•ning, -runs.** To present a rerun of.

RES *abbr.* Reticuloendothial system.

res. *abbr.* **1.** Research. **2.** Reservation. **3.** Reserve. **4.** Reservoir. **5.** Residence; resident. **6.** Resolution.

res ad•ju•di•ca•ta (rēz′ ə-jo͞o′dĭ-kä′tə, rās′) *n. Law.* Var. of **res judicata.**

re•sale (rē′sāl′, rē-sāl′) *n.* The act of selling again.

re•sched•ule (rē-skĕj′o͞ol) *tr.v.* **-uled, -ul•ing, -ules.** To schedule again or anew: *rescheduled the meeting.*

re•scind (rĭ-sĭnd′) *tr.v.* **-scind•ed, -scind•ing, -scinds.** To make void; repeal or annul. [Lat. *rescindere* : *re-*, re- + *scindere*, to split; see **skei-***.] **—re•scind′a•ble** *adj.* **—re•scind′er** *n.* **—re•scind′ment** *n.*

re•scis•sion (rĭ-sĭzh′ən) *n.* The act of rescinding. [Lat. *rescissiō, rescissiōn-* < *rescissus*, p.part. of *rescindere*, to rescind. See RESCIND.]

re•scis•so•ry (rĭ-sĭz′ə-rē, -sĭs′-) *adj.* Of, relating to, or having the power of rescission.

re•script (rē′skrĭpt′) *n.* **1.a.** The act of rewriting. **b.** Something that has been rewritten. **2.** A formal decree or edict. **3.** *Rom. Cath. Ch.* A response from an ecclesiastical superior to a question regarding discipline or doctrine. **4.** A reply from a Roman emperor to a magistrate's query about a point of law. [Lat. *rescrīptum* < neut. p.part. of *rescrībere*, to write back : *re-*, re- + *scrībere*, to write; see **skrībh-***.]

res•cue (rĕs′kyo͞o) *tr.v.* **-cued, -cu•ing, -cues.** To set free, as from danger; save. —*n.* An act of rescuing; a deliverance. [ME *rescouen* < OFr. *rescourre* : *re-*, re- + *escourre*, to shake (< Lat. *escutere* : *ex-*, ex- + *quatere*, to shake; see **kwēt-***).] **—res′cu•a•ble** *adj.* **—res′cu•er** *n.*

rescue grass *n.* A tall South American grass *(Bromus unioloides)* cultivated for hay. [Prob. alteration of FESCUE.]

re•search (rĭ-sûrch′, rē′sûrch′) *n.* **1.** Scholarly or scientific investigation or inquiry. **2.** Close careful study. —*v.* **-searched, -search•ing, -search•es.** —*intr.* To engage in or perform research. —*tr.* **1.** To study (something) thoroughly so as to present in a detailed accurate manner. **2.** To do research for. [Obsolete Fr. *recerche* < *recercher*, to search closely < OFr. : *re-*, re- + *cerchier*, to search; see SEARCH.] **—re•search′a•ble** *adj.* **—re•search′er, re•search′ist** *n.*

re•seat (rē-sēt′) *tr.v.* **-seat•ed, -seat•ing, -seats. 1.** To provide with a new or different seat. **2.** To fit (a valve, for example) in a new seating.

ré•seau or **re•seau** (rā-zō′, rĭ-) *n., pl.* **-seaus** or **-seaux** (-zōz′, -zō′). **1.** A net or mesh foundation for lace. **2.** *Astron.* A reference grid of fine lines forming uniform squares on a photographic plate or print, used to aid in measurement. **3.** A mosaic screen of fine lines of three colors, used in color photography. [Fr. < OFr. *reseuil*, dim. of *raiz*, net < Lat. *rēte*.]

re•sect (rĭ-sĕkt′) *tr.v.* **-sect•ed, -sect•ing, -sects.** To perform a resection on. [Lat. *resecāre, resect-*, to cut back : *re-*, re- + *secāre*, to cut; see **sek-***.] **—re•sect′a•bil′i•ty** *n.* **—re•sect′a•ble** *adj.*

re•sec•tion (rĭ-sĕk′shən) *n.* Surgical removal of part of an organ or a structure.

re•sec•to•scope (rĭ-sĕk′tə-skōp′) *n.* A surgical instrument for performing a resection without an opening or incision other than that made by the instrument.

re•se•da (rĭ-sē′də, -sĕd′ə) *n.* **1.** Any of various Mediterranean plants of the genus *Reseda*, including the mignonette, having flowered terminal racemes. **2.** *Color.* A grayish or dark green to yellow green or light olive. [NLat. *Resēda*, genus name < Lat. *resēda*, a plant.] **—re•se′da** *adj.*

re•sem•blance (rĭ-zĕm′bləns) *n.* **1.** The state or quality of resembling, esp. similarity in appearance or in external or superficial details. See Syns at **likeness. 2.** Something that resembles another.

re•sem•ble (rĭ-zĕm′bəl) *tr.v.* **-bled, -bling, -bles.** To exhibit similarity or likeness to. [ME *resemblen* < OFr. *resembler* : *re-*, re- + *sembler*, to appear (< Lat. *simulāre*, to imitate < *similis*, like; see **sem-**^{1}*****).] **—re•sem′bler** *n.*

re•sent (rĭ-zĕnt′) *tr.v.* **-sent•ed, -sent•ing, -sents.** To feel indignantly aggrieved at. [Fr. *ressentir*, to be angry < OFr. *resentir*, to feel strongly : *re-*, re- + *sentir*, to feel (< Lat. *sentīre*; see **sent-***).]

re•sent•ful (rĭ-zĕnt′fəl) *adj.* Full of, marked by, or inclined to resentment. **—re•sent′ful•ly** *adv.* **—re•sent′ful•ness** *n.*

re•sent•ment (rĭ-zĕnt′mənt) *n.* Indignation or ill will felt as a result of a real or imagined grievance. See Syns at **anger.**

re•ser•pine (rĭ-sûr′pēn′, -pĭn, rĕs′ər-pĭn, -pēn′, rĕz′-) *n.* A powder, $C_{33}H_{40}N_2O_9$, isolated from the roots of certain species of rauwolfia and used as a sedative and an antihypertensive. [Ger. *Reserpin* < alteration of NLat. *Rauwolfia serpentīna*, species of snakeroot : RAUWOLFIA + LLat. *serpentīna*, fem. of *serpentīnus*, serpentine; see SERPENTINE.]

res•er•va•tion (rĕz′ər-vā′shən) *n.* **1.** The act of reserving; a keeping back or withholding. **2.** Something that is kept back or withheld. **3.** A limiting qualification or exception: *reservations about the plan.* **4.** A tract of land set apart by the federal government for a special purpose, esp. one for a Native American people. **5.a.** An arrangement for securing accommodations in advance, as in a hotel. **b.** The accommodations so secured. **c.** The record or promise of such an arrangement. **—res′er•va′tion•ist** *n.*

re•serve (rĭ-zûrv′) *tr.v.* **-served, -serv•ing, -serves. 1.** To keep back, as for future use or for a special purpose. **2.** To set or cause to be set apart for a particular person or use. **3.** To keep or secure for oneself; retain. See Syns at **keep.** —*n.* **1.** Something kept back or saved for future use or a special purpose. **2.** The act of reserving. **3.** The keeping of one's feelings, thoughts, or affairs to oneself. **4.** Self-restraint in expression; reticence. **5.** Lack of enthusiasm; skeptical caution. **6.** An amount of capital held back from investment in order to meet probable or possible demands. **7.** A reservation of public land. **8.** An amount of a given resource known to exist in a particular location and to be exploitable. **9.a.** A fighting force kept uncommitted until need arises. **b.** The part of a country's armed forces not on active duty but subject to call in an emergency. In both senses, often used in the plural. — *adj.* Held in or forming a reserve. — ***idiom.* in reserve.** Kept back, set aside, or saved. [ME *reserven* < OFr. *reserver* < Lat. *reservāre*, to keep back : *re-*, re- + *servāre*, to keep; see **ser-**[1]*.] — **re•serv′a•ble** *adj.* — **re•serv′er** *n.*

reserve bank *n.* **1.** A central bank that holds the reserves of other banks. **2.** One of the 12 main banks of the U.S. Federal Reserve System.

re•served (rĭ-zûrvd′) *adj.* **1.** Held in reserve; kept back or set aside. **2.** Self-restrained and reticent. See Syns at **silent.** — **re•serv′ed•ly** (-zûr′vĭd-lē) *adv.* — **re•serv′ed•ness** *n.*

re•serv•ist (rĭ-zûr′vĭst) *n.* A member of a military reserve.

res•er•voir (rĕz′ər-vwär′, -vwôr′, -vôr′) *n.* **1.** A pond or lake used for the storage and regulation of water. **2.** A receptacle or chamber for storing a fluid. **3.** An underground accumulation of petroleum or natural gas. **4.** *Anat.* See **cisterna** 1. **5.** A large or extra supply; a reserve: *a reservoir of gratitude.* **6.** *Medic.* An organism or a population that transmits a pathogen while being virtually immune to its effects. [Fr. *réservoir* < *réserver*, to reserve < OFr. *reserver.* See RESERVE.]

re•set (rē-sĕt′) *tr.v.* **-set, -set•ting, -sets. 1.** To set again: *reset a broken bone.* **2.** To change the reading of: *reset a clock.* — *n.* (rē′sĕt′). **1.** The act of setting again. **2.** Something set again. — **re•set′ta•ble** *adj.* — **re•set′ter** *n.*

res ges•tae (rās′ gĕs′tī′, rēz′ jĕs′tē) *pl.n.* **1.** Things done; deeds. **2.** *Law.* The facts that are admissible in evidence as the surrounding circumstances of the event to be proved. [Lat. *rēs gestae* : *rēs*, pl. of *rēs*, thing + *gestae*, fem. pl. p.part. of *gerere*, to carry, show.]

resh (rĕsh) *n.* The 20th letter of the Hebrew alphabet. [Aram. *rēš*, head.]

Resht (rĕsht). See **Rasht.**

re•side (rĭ-zīd′) *intr.v.* **-sid•ed, -sid•ing, -sides. 1.** To live in a place permanently or for a long period. **2.** To be inherently present; exist. **3.** To be vested, as a power or right. [ME *residen* < OFr. *resider* < Lat. *residēre*, to remain behind, reside : *re-*, re- + *sedēre*, to sit; see **sed-***.] — **re•sid′er** *n.*

res•i•dence (rĕz′ĭ-dəns, -dĕns′) *n.* **1.** The place in which one lives; a dwelling. **2.** The act or a period of residing in a place. **3.** A medical residency. **4.** The official home or location of a corporation. — ***idiom.* in residence.** Committed to live and work in a specific place, often for a certain length of time.

res•i•den•cy (rĕz′ĭ-dən-sē, -dĕn′-) *n., pl.* **-cies. 1.** The period during which a physician receives specialized clinical training. **2.a.** The house of a colonial resident. **b.** The sphere of authority of a colonial resident. **3.** Residence.

res•i•dent (rĕz′ĭ-dənt, -dĕnt′) *n.* **1.** A physician serving a period of residency. **2.** One who resides in a particular place permanently or for an extended period. **3.a.** A diplomatic official residing in a foreign seat of government. **b.** A colonial official acting as adviser to the ruler of a protected state. **4.** A nonmigratory bird or other animal. — *adj.* **1.** Dwelling in a particular place; residing: *resident aliens.* **2.** Living somewhere in connection with duty or work. **3.** Inherently present: *resident anxieties.* **4.** Nonmigratory: *resident fauna.*

res•i•den•tial (rĕz′ĭ-dĕn′shəl) *adj.* **1.** Of, relating to, or having residence. **2.** Of, suitable for, or limited to residences: *residential zoning.* — **res′i•den′tial•ly** *adv.*

res•i•den•ti•ar•y (rĕz′ĭ-dĕn′shē-ĕr′ē, -shə-rē) *adj.* **1.** Having a residence, esp. an official one. **2.** Involving or requiring official residence. — *n., pl.* **-ies. 1.** One residing in a certain place; a resident. **2.** A cleric required to live in an official residence.

re•sid•u•al (rĭ-zĭj′o͞o-əl) *adj.* **1.** Of, relating to, or characteristic of a residue. **2.** Remaining as a residue. — *n.* **1.** The quantity left over at the end of a process; a remainder. **2.** A payment made to a performer, writer, or director for each repeat showing of a recorded television show or commercial. Often used in the plural. — **re•sid′u•al•ly** *adv.*

residual oil *n.* The low-grade oil products that remain after the distillation of petroleum, used in adhesives, roofing compounds, and asphalt manufacture.

re•sid•u•ar•y (rĭ-zĭj′o͞o-ĕr′ē) *adj.* **1.** Of, relating to, or constituting a residue. **2.** *Law.* Entitled to the residue of an estate.

res•i•due (rĕz′ĭ-do͞o′, -dyo͞o′) *n.* **1.** The remainder of something after removal of parts or a part. **2.** Matter remaining after completion of an abstractive chemical or physical process, such as evaporation, distillation, or filtration; residuum. **3.** *Law.* The remainder of a testator's estate after all claims, debts, and bequests are satisfied. [ME < OFr. *residu* < Lat. *residuum*, neut. of *residuus*, remaining < *residēre*, to remain behind. See RESIDE.]

re•sid•u•um (rĭ-zĭj′o͞o-əm) *n., pl.* **-u•a** (-o͞o-ə). **1.** Something remaining after removal of a part; a residue. **2.** *Law.* See **residue** 3. [Lat., residue. See RESIDUE.]

re•sign (rĭ-zīn′) *v.* **-signed, -sign•ing, -signs.** — *tr.* **1.** To submit (oneself) passively; accept as inevitable: *I resigned myself to a long wait.* **2.** To give up (a position, for example), esp. by formal notification. **3.** To relinquish (a privilege, right, or claim). See Syns at **relinquish.** — *intr.* To give up one's job or office; quit, esp. by formal notification. [ME *resignen* < OFr. *resigner* < Lat. *resignāre*, to unseal : *re-*, re- + *signāre*, to seal (< *signum*, mark, seal; see **sekʷ-**[1]*).] — **re•sign′er** *n.*

res•ig•na•tion (rĕz′ĭg-nā′shən) *n.* **1.** The act or an instance of resigning. **2.** An oral or written statement that one is resigning a position or an office. **3.** Unresisting acceptance of something as inescapable; submission. See Syns at **patience.**

re•signed (rĭ-zīnd′) *adj.* Feeling or marked by resignation. — **re•sign′ed•ly** (-zī′nĭd-lē) *adv.* — **re•sign′ed•ness** *n.*

re•sile (rĭ-zīl′) *intr.v.* **-siled, -sil•ing, -siles. 1.** To spring back, esp. to resume a former position or structure after being stretched or compressed. **2.** To draw back; recoil. [Obsolete Fr. *resilir* < Lat. *resilīre*, to leap back : *re-*, re- + *salīre*, to leap; see **sel-***.]

re•sil•ience (rĭ-zĭl′yəns) *n.* **1.** The ability to recover quickly from illness, change, or misfortune; buoyancy. **2.** The property of a material that enables it to resume its original shape or position after being bent, stretched, or compressed; elasticity.

re•sil•ien•cy (rĭ-zĭl′yən-sē) *n.* Resilience.

re•sil•ient (rĭ-zĭl′yənt) *adj.* **1.** Able to recover readily, as from misfortune. **2.** Having the property of resilience. [Lat. *resiliēns*, *resilient-*, pr.part. of *resilīre*, to leap back. See RESILE.] — **re•sil′ient•ly** *adv.*

res•i•lin (rĕz′ə-lĭn) *n.* An elastic substance consisting of cross-linked protein chains, found in the cuticles of many insects.

res•in (rĕz′ĭn) *n.* **1.** Any of numerous clear to translucent yellow or brown, solid or semisolid viscous substances of plant origin, such as amber, used in lacquers, varnishes, inks, and plastics. **2.** Any of numerous physically similar polymerized synthetics or chemically modified natural resins including thermoplastic materials such as polyethylene and thermosetting materials such as polyesters that are used with stabilizers and other components to form plastics. — *tr.v.* **-ined, -in•ing, -ines.** To treat or rub with resin. [ME < OFr. *resine* < Lat. *rēsīna* < Gk. dial. **rhēsina*, var. of Gk. *rhētinē.*] — **res′in•ous** (rĕz′ə-nəs) *adj.*

res•in•ate (rĕz′ə-nāt′) *tr.v.* **-at•ed, -at•ing, -ates.** To impregnate, permeate, or flavor with resin.

resin canal *n.* An intercellular tube lined with resin-secreting cells, found in the wood and leaves of many gymnosperms.

res•in•if•er•ous (rĕz′ə-nĭf′ər-əs) *adj.* Yielding resin.

res•in•oid (rĕz′ə-noid′) *adj.* Relating to, resembling, or containing resin. — *n.* A synthetic resin, esp. a thermosetting one.

re•sist (rĭ-zĭst′) *v.* **-sist•ed, -sist•ing, -sists.** — *tr.* **1.** To strive to fend off or offset the actions, effects, or force of. **2.** To remain firm against the actions, effects, or force of; withstand. **3.** To keep from giving in to or enjoying. — *intr.* To offer resistance. See Syns at **oppose.** — *n.* A substance that can cover and protect a surface, as from corrosion. [ME *resisten* < OFr. *resister* < Lat. *resistere* : *re-*, re- + *sistere*, to place; see **stā-***.] — **re•sist′er** *n.*

re•sis•tance (rĭ-zĭs′təns) *n.* **1.** The act or an instance of resisting or the capacity to resist. **2.** A force tending to oppose or retard motion. **3.** Often **Resistance.** An underground organization struggling for national liberation in a country under military or totalitarian occupation. **4.** *Psychol.* The opposition of the ego to the conscious recall of unpleasant experiences. **5.** *Biol.* **a.** The capacity of an organism to fight a disease. **b.** The capacity of an organism or a tissue to withstand the effects of a harmful environmental agent. **6.** *Elect.* The opposition of a body or substance to current passing through it, dissipating electrical energy. — **re•sis′tant** *adj.*

resistance transfer factor *n.* R factor.

Re•sis•ten•cia (rĕs′ĭ-stĕn′sē-ə, rĕ′sēs-tĕn′syä). A city of NE Argentina on the Paraná R. Pop. 220,104.

re•sist•i•ble (rĭ-zĭs′tə-bəl) *adj.* Possible to resist: *resistible impulses.* — **re•sist′i•bil′i•ty** *n.* — **re•sist′i•bly** *adv.*

re•sis•tive (rĭ-zĭs′tĭv) *adj.* Of, tending toward, or marked by resistance. — **re•sis′tive•ly** *adv.* — **re•sis′tive•ness** *n.*

re•sis•tiv•i•ty (rē′zĭs-tĭv′ĭ-tē) *n., pl.* **-ties. 1.** The capacity for or tendency toward resistance. **2.** *Elect.* The resistance per unit length of a substance with uniform cross section.

re•sist•less (rĭ-zĭst′lĭs) *adj.* **1.** Impossible to resist; irresistible. **2.** Powerless to resist; unresisting. — **re•sist′less•ness** *n.*

re•sis•tor (rĭ-zĭs′tər) *n.* A device used to control current in an electric circuit by providing resistance.

Re•şi•ta (rĕ′shē-tsä′). A city of W Romania in the W Transylvanian Alps WNW of Bucharest. Pop. 101,902.

res ju•di•ca•ta (rēz′ jo͞o′dĭ-kä′tə, rās′) also **res ad•ju•di•ca•ta** (ə-jo͞o′-) *n. Law.* An adjudicated precedent. [Lat. *rēs iūdicāta*, thing decided.]

re•sole (rē-sōl′) *tr.v.* **-soled, -sol•ing, -soles.** To put a new sole on (a shoe).

re•sol•u•ble (rĭ-zŏl′yə-bəl) *adj.* Possible to resolve; resolvable. [LLat. *resolūbilis* < Lat. *resolvere*, to resolve. See RESOLVE.] — **re•sol′u•bil′i•ty, re•sol′u•ble•ness** *n.*

res•o•lute (rĕz′ə-lo͞ot′) *adj.* Firm or determined; unwavering. [ME, dissolved, dissolute < Lat. *resolūtus*, relaxed, p.part. of

ă pat	oi boy
ā pay	ou out
âr care	o͝o took
ä father	o͞o boot
ĕ pet	ŭ cut
ē be	ûr urge
ĭ pit	th thin
ī pie	*th* this
îr pier	hw which
ŏ pot	zh vision
ō toe	ə about, item
ô paw	

Stress marks:
′ (primary);
′ (secondary), as in
dictionary (dĭk′shə-nĕr′ē)

resolvere, to relax, untie. See RESOLVE.] —**res′o•lute′ly** *adv.* —**res′o•lute′ness** *n.*

res•o•lu•tion (rĕz′ə-lo͞o′shən) *n.* **1.** The state or quality of being resolute; determination. **2.** A resolving to do something. **3.** A course of action resolved on. **4.** A formal statement of a decision or expression of opinion put before or adopted by an assembly or parliament. **5.** *Phys. & Chem.* The act or process of separating or reducing something into its constituent parts. **6.** The fineness of detail that can be distinguished in an image, as on a television. **7.** *Medic.* The subsiding or termination of an abnormal condition, such as a fever. **8.** *Law.* A court decision. **9.a.** An explanation, as of a problem; a solution. **b.** The part of a literary work in which the plot is resolved or simplified. **10.** *Mus.* **a.** The progression of a dissonant tone or chord to a consonant tone or chord. **b.** The tone or chord to which such a progression is made. **11.** The substitution of one metrical unit for another, esp. the substitution of two short syllables for one long syllable in quantitative verse.

re•solve (rĭ-zŏlv′) *v.* **-solved, -solv•ing, -solves.** —*tr.* **1.** To make a firm decision about. **2.** To cause (a person) to reach a decision. See Syns at **decide. 3.** To decide or express by formal vote. **4.** To separate (something) into constituent parts. See Syns at **analyze. 5.** To change or convert. **6.** To find a solution to; solve. See Syns at **solve. 7.** To remove or dispel (doubts). **8.** To bring to a usu. successful conclusion. **9.** *Medic.* To cause reduction of (an inflammation, for example). **10.** *Mus.* To cause (a tone or chord) to progress from dissonance to consonance. **11.** *Chem.* To separate (an optically inactive compound or mixture) into its optically active constituents. **12.** To render parts of (an image) visible and distinct. **13.** *Math.* To separate (a vector, for example) into coordinate components. **14.** To melt or dissolve (something). —*intr.* **1.** To decide or make a determination: *resolve on immediate action.* **2.** To become separated or reduced to constituents. **3.** *Mus.* To undergo resolution. —*n.* **1.** Firmness of purpose; resolution. **2.** A determination or decision; a fixed purpose. **3.** A formal resolution made by a deliberative body. [ME *resolven*, to dissolve < OFr. *resolver* < Lat. *resolvere*, to untie : *re-*, re- + *solvere*, to untie; see **leu-***.] —**re•solv′a•bil′i•ty, re•solv′a•ble•ness** *n.* —**re•solv′a•ble** *adj.* —**re•solv′ed•ly** (-zŏl′vĭd-lē) *adv.* —**re•solv′er** *n.*

re•sol•vent (rĭ-zŏl′vənt) *adj.* Causing or able to cause separation into constituents; solvent. —*n.* A resolvent substance, esp. a medicine that reduces inflammation or swelling.

res•o•nance (rĕz′ə-nəns) *n.* **1.** The quality or condition of being resonant. **2.** *Phys.* The increase in amplitude of oscillation of an electric or mechanical system due to a periodic force whose frequency is equal or very close to the natural undamped frequency of the system. **3.** *Acoustics.* Intensification and prolongation of sound, esp. of a musical tone, produced by sympathetic vibration. **4.** *Ling.* Intensification of vocal tones during articulation, as by the air cavities of the mouth and nose. **5.** *Medic.* The sound produced by diagnostic percussion of the normal chest. **6.** *Chem.* The property of a compound having simultaneously the characteristics of two or more structural forms that differ only in the distribution of electrons.

res•o•nant (rĕz′ə-nənt) *adj.* **1.a.** Strong and deep in tone; resounding. **b.** Continuing to sound in the ears or memory; echoing: *resonant words of exhortation.* **c.** Having a prolonged, subtle, or stimulating effect beyond the initial impact. **2.** Producing or exhibiting resonance: *resonant frequency excitation.* **3.** Resulting from or as if from resonance: *resonant amplification.* [Lat. *resonāns*, *resonant-*, pr.part. of *resonāre*, to resound. See RESOUND.] —**res′o•nant•ly** *adv.*

resonant circuit *n.* An electric circuit with inductance and capacitance chosen to allow the greatest flow of current at a certain frequency.

res•o•nate (rĕz′ə-nāt′) *v.* **-nat•ed, -nat•ing, -nates.** —*intr.* **1.** To exhibit or produce resonance or resonant effects. **2.** To have a profound emotional impact. —*tr.* To cause to resonate; make resonant. [Lat. *resonāre*, *resonāt-*. See RESOUND.] —**res′o•na′tion** *n.*

res•o•na•tor (rĕz′ə-nā′tər) *n.* **1.** A resonating system. **2.** A hollow chamber or cavity with dimensions chosen to permit internal resonant oscillation of electromagnetic or acoustical waves of specific frequencies. **3.** A resonant circuit.

re•sorb (rē-sôrb′, -zôrb′) *v.* **-sorbed, -sorb•ing, -sorbs.** —*tr.* **1.** To absorb again. **2.** *Biol.* To dissolve and assimilate (bone tissue, for example). —*intr.* To undergo resorption. [Lat. *resorbēre*, to suck back : *re-*, re- + *sorbēre*, to suck up.]

res•or•cin•ol (rĭ-zôr′sə-nôl′, -nōl′, -nŏl′) also **res•or•cin** (rĭ-zôr′sĭn) *n.* A white crystalline compound, $C_6H_4(OH)_2$, used to treat certain skin diseases and in dyes, resin adhesives, and pharmaceuticals. [RES(IN) + ORC(HIL) + -IN + -OL[1].]

re•sorp•tion (rē-sôrp′shən, -zôrp′-) *n.* The act or process of resorbing.

re•sort (rĭ-zôrt′) *intr.v.* **-sort•ed, -sort•ing, -sorts. 1.** To have recourse. **2.** To go customarily or frequently; repair. —*n.* **1.** A place frequented by people for relaxation or recreation. **2.** A customary or frequent going or gathering. **3.** The act of turning to for aid or relief; recourse. **4.** One turned to for aid or relief. [ME *resorten*, to return < OFr. *resortir*, to go out again : *re-*, re- + *sortir*, to go out.]

re•sort•er (rĭ-zôr′tər) *n.* One who frequents resorts for vacations or recreation.

re•sound (rĭ-zound′) *v.* **-sound•ed, -sound•ing, -sounds.** —*intr.* **1.** To be filled with sound; reverberate: *The school resounded with laughter.* **2.** To make a loud, long, or reverberating sound. **3.** To sound loudly; ring. **4.** To become famous or extolled. —*tr.* **1.** To send back (sound). **2.** To utter or emit loudly. **3.** To celebrate or praise, as in verse or song. [Alteration (influenced by SOUND[1]) of ME *resounen* < OFr. *resoner* < Lat. *resonāre* : *re-*, re- + *sonāre*, to sound; see **swen-***.] —**re•sound′ing** *adj.* —**re•sound′ing•ly** *adv.*

re•source (rē′sôrs′, -sōrs′, -zôrs′, -zōrs′, rĭ-sôrs′, -sōrs′, -zôrs′, -zōrs′) *n.* **1.** Something that can be used for support or help. **2.** An available supply that can be drawn on when needed. Often used in the plural. **3.** The ability to deal with a difficult situation effectively; initiative. **4.** Means available in a difficult situation. Often used in the plural. **5.a. resources.** The total means available for economic and political development, such as mineral wealth and labor. **b. resources.** The total means available to a company for increasing production or profit, including labor and raw material; assets. **c.** Such means considered individually. [Obsolete Fr. < OFr. < fem. p.part. of *resourdre*, to rise again < Lat. *resurgere* : *re-*, re- + *surgere*, to rise; see SURGE.]

re•source•ful (rĭ-sôrs′fəl, -sōrs′-, -zôrs′-, -zōrs′-) *adj.* Able to act effectively or imaginatively, esp. in difficult situations. —**re•source′ful•ly** *adv.* —**re•source′ful•ness** *n.*

resp. *abbr.* **1.** Respective; respectively. **2.** Respiration.

re•spect (rĭ-spĕkt′) *tr.v.* **-spect•ed, -spect•ing, -spects. 1.** To feel or show deferential regard for; esteem. **2.** To avoid violation of or interference with: *respect the law.* **3.** To relate or refer to; concern. —*n.* **1.** A feeling of appreciative, often deferential regard; esteem. **2.** The state of being regarded with honor or esteem. **3.** Willingness to show consideration or appreciation. **4. respects.** Polite expressions of consideration or deference. **5.** A particular aspect, feature, or detail. **6.** *Usage Problem.* Relation; reference. See Usage Note at **regard.** [< ME, regard < OFr. < Lat. *respectus* < p.part. of *respicere*, to look back at, regard : *re-*, re- + *specere*, to look at; see **spek-***.] —**re•spect′er** *n.*

re•spect•a•bil•i•ty (rĭ-spĕk′tə-bĭl′ĭ-tē) *n.* The quality, state, or characteristic of being respectable.

re•spect•a•ble (rĭ-spĕk′tə-bəl) *adj.* **1.** Meriting respect or esteem; worthy. **2.** Of or appropriate to good or proper behavior or conventional conduct. **3.** Of moderately good quality. **4.** Considerable in amount, number, or size. **5.** Acceptable in appearance; presentable. —**re•spect′a•bly** *adv.*

re•spect•ful (rĭ-spĕkt′fəl) *adj.* Showing or marked by proper respect. —**re•spect′ful•ly** *adv.* —**re•spect′ful•ness** *n.*

re•spect•ing (rĭ-spĕk′tĭng) *prep. Usage Problem.* With respect to; concerning. See Usage Note at **regard.**

re•spec•tive (rĭ-spĕk′tĭv) *adj.* Relating to two or more persons or things regarded individually; particular: *successful in their respective fields.* —**re•spec′tive•ness** *n.*

re•spec•tive•ly (rĭ-spĕk′tĭv-lē) *adv.* Singly in the order designated or mentioned: *I'm referring to each of you respectively.*

re•spell (rē-spĕl′) *tr.v.* **-spelled** or **-spelt** (-spĕlt′), **-spell•ing, -spells.** To spell again or in a new way, esp. phonetically.

Re•spi•ghi (rĕ-spē′gē), **Ottorino.** 1879–1936. Italian composer whose works include *Roman Festivals* (1929).

res•pi•ra•ble (rĕs′pər-ə-bəl, rĭ-spīr′-) *adj.* **1.** Fit for breathing: *respirable air.* **2.** Capable of undergoing respiration: *respirable organisms.* —**res′pi•ra•bil′i•ty** *n.*

res•pi•ra•tion (rĕs′pə-rā′shən) *n.* **1.a.** The act or process of inhaling and exhaling; breathing. **b.** The act or process by which an organism without lungs, such as a plant, exchanges gases with its environment. **2.a.** The oxidative process in living cells by which the chemical energy of organic molecules is released in metabolic steps involving the consumption of oxygen and the liberation of carbon dioxide and water. **b.** Any of various analogous metabolic processes by which certain organisms, such as fungi, obtain energy from organic molecules. —**res′pi•ra′tion•al** *adj.*

res•pi•ra•tor (rĕs′pə-rā′tər) *n.* **1.** A device supplying oxygen or a mixture of oxygen and carbon dioxide for breathing, used esp. in artificial respiration. **2.** A screenlike device worn over the mouth or nose or both to protect the respiratory tract.

res•pi•ra•to•ry (rĕs′pər-ə-tôr′ē, -tōr′ē, rĭ-spīr′ə-) *adj.* Of, relating to, used in, or affecting respiration.

respiratory distress syndrome *n.* A respiratory disease of newborn babies, esp. premature babies, characterized by distressful breathing, cyanosis, and the formation of a glassy membrane over the alveoli of the lungs.

respiratory pigment *n.* Any of various colored conjugated proteins, such as hemoglobin, that occur in living organisms and function in oxygen transfer in cellular respiration.

respiratory quotient *n.* The ratio of the volume of carbon dioxide released to the volume of oxygen consumed by a body tissue or an organism in a given period.

respiratory system *n.* The integrated system of organs involved in the intake and exchange of oxygen and carbon dioxide between an organism and the environment.

re•spire (rĭ-spīr′) *v.* **-spired, -spir•ing, -spires.** —*intr.* **1.** To breathe in and out; inhale and exhale. **2.** To undergo the metabolic process of respiration. **3.** To breathe easily again, as after a period of exertion or trouble. —*tr.* To inhale and exhale (air); breathe. [ME *respiren,* to breathe again < Lat. *respīrāre* : *re-,* re- + *spīrāre,* to breathe.]

res•pi•rom•e•ter (rĕs′pə-rŏm′ĭ-tər) *n.* An instrument for measuring the degree and nature of respiration. —**res′pi•ro•met′ric** (-rō-mĕt′rĭk) *adj.* —**res′pi•rom′e•try** *n.*

res•pite (rĕs′pĭt) *n.* **1.** A usu. short interval of rest or relief. See Syns at **pause. 2.** *Law.* Temporary suspension of a death sentence; a reprieve. —*tr.v.* **-pit•ed, -pit•ing, -pites.** To delay; postpone. [ME < OFr. *respit* < Lat. *respectus,* refuge, looking back. See RESPECT.]

re•splen•dent (rĭ-splĕn′dənt) *adj.* Splendid or dazzling in appearance; brilliant. [ME < OFr. < Lat. *resplendēns, resplendent-,* pr.part. of *resplendēre,* to shine brightly : *re-,* re- + *splendēre,* to shine.] —**re•splen′dence, re•splen′den•cy** *n.* —**re•splen′dent•ly** *adv.*

re•spond (rĭ-spŏnd′) *v.* **-spond•ed, -spond•ing, -sponds.** —*intr.* **1.** To make a reply; answer. See Syns at **answer. 2.** To act in return or in answer. **3.** To react positively or favorably: *The patient responded to the treatment.* —*tr.* To give as a reply; answer. —*n. Archit.* A pilaster supporting an arch. [ME *responden* < OFr. *respondre* < Lat. *respondēre* : *re-,* re- + *spondēre,* to promise; see **spend-***.] —**re•spond′er** *n.*

re•spon•dent (rĭ-spŏn′dənt) *adj.* **1.** Giving or given as an answer; responsive. **2.** *Law.* Being a defendant. —*n.* **1.** One who responds. **2.** *Law.* A defendant, esp. in a divorce or equity case. —**re•spon′dence, re•spon′den•cy** *n.*

re•sponse (rĭ-spŏns′) *n.* **1.** The act of responding. **2.** A reply or an answer. **3.** A reaction, as that of an organism, to a specific stimulus. **4.a.** *Eccles.* Something that is spoken or sung by a congregation or choir in answer to the officiating cleric. **b.** A responsory. [ME *respons* < OFr. < Lat. *respōnsum* < neut. p.part. of *respondēre,* to respond. See RESPOND.]

re•spon•si•bil•i•ty (rĭ-spŏn′sə-bĭl′ĭ-tē) *n., pl.* **-ties. 1.** The state, quality, or fact of being responsible. See Syns at **obligation. 2.** Something for which one is responsible; a duty, an obligation, or a burden.

re•spon•si•ble (rĭ-spŏn′sə-bəl) *adj.* **1.** Liable to be required to give account, as of one's actions. **2.** Involving personal accountability or ability to act without guidance or superior authority: *a responsible position.* **3.** Being a source or cause. **4.** Able to make moral or rational decisions and therefore answerable for one's behavior. **5.** Trustworthy or dependable; reliable. **6.** Based on or showing good judgment or sound thinking. **7.** Having the means to pay debts or fulfill obligations. **8.** Required to render account; answerable. [Obsolete Fr., corresponding to < Lat. *respōnsus,* p.part. of *respondēre,* to respond. See RESPOND.] —**re•spon′si•ble•ness** *n.* —**re•spon′si•bly** *adv.*

Syns: *responsible, answerable, liable, accountable, amenable.* These adjectives share the meaning obliged to answer, as for one's actions, to an authority that may impose a penalty for failure. *Responsible* often implies the satisfactory performance of duties or the trustworthy care for or disposition of possessions: *"I am responsible for the ship's safety"* (Robert Louis Stevenson). *Answerable* suggests a moral or legal responsibility subject to review by a higher authority: *The court held the parents answerable for their child's acts. Liable* may refer to a legal obligation or a responsibility to do something: *Wage earners are liable to income tax. Accountable* emphasizes giving an account of one's discharge of a responsibility: *"The liberal philosophy holds that enduring governments must be accountable to someone beside themselves"* (Walter Lippmann). *Amenable* implies being subject to the control of an authority and therefore the absence of complete autonomy: *"The sovereign of this country is not amenable to any form of trial"* (Letters of Junius).

re•spon•sive (rĭ-spŏn′sĭv) *adj.* **1.** Answering or replying; responding. **2.** Readily reacting to suggestions, influences, appeals, or efforts. **3.** Containing or using responses: *responsive reading.* —**re•spon′sive•ly** *adv.* —**re•spon′sive•ness** *n.*

re•spon•so•ry (rĭ-spŏn′sə-rē) *n., pl.* **-ries.** *Eccles.* A chant or an anthem recited or sung after a reading in a church service. [ME *responsorie* < LLat. *respōnsōrium* < Lat. *respōnsus,* p.part. of *respondēre,* to respond. See RESPOND.] —**re•spon•so′ri•al** (-sôr′ē-əl, -sōr′-) *adj.*

res pub•li•ca (rēz pŭb′lĭ-kə, rās po͞o′blē-kä′) *n., pl.* **-cae** (-kā, -kī). **1.** A state, republic, or commonwealth. **2.** The general public good or welfare. [Lat. *rēs pūblica.* See REPUBLIC.]

res•sen•ti•ment (rə-säN′tē-mäN′) *n.* A generalized feeling of resentment and often hostility harbored by one individual or group against another, esp. chronically and with no means of direct expression. [Fr., resentment < OFr. *ressentement* < *resentir,* to feel strongly. See RESENT.]

rest¹ (rĕst) *n.* **1.** Cessation of work, exertion, or activity. **2.** Peace, ease, or refreshment resulting from sleep or the cessation of an activity. **3.** Sleep or quiet relaxation. **4.** The repose of death. **5.** Relief or freedom from disquiet or disturbance. **6.** Mental or emotional tranquillity. **7.** Termination or absence of motion. **8.** *Mus.* **a.** An interval of silence corresponding to one of the possible time values within a measure. **b.** The mark or symbol indicating such a pause and its length. **9.** A short pause in a line of poetry; a caesura. **10.** A device used as a support: *a back rest.* **11.** *Games.* See **bridge¹** 7a. —*v.* **rest•ed, rest•ing, rests.** —*intr.* **1.** To cease motion, work, or activity. **2.** To lie down, esp. to sleep. **3.** To be at peace or ease; be tranquil. **4.** To be, become, or remain temporarily still, quiet, or inactive: *Let the issue rest.* **5.** To be supported or based; lie, lean, or sit. **6.** To be imposed or vested, as a responsibility or burden. **7.** To depend or rely: *That argument rests on a false assumption.* **8.** To be located or be in a specified place. **9.** To be fixed or directed on something: *Her eyes rested on the sunset.* **10.** To remain; linger. **11.** *Law.* To cease voluntarily the presentation of evidence in a case. —*tr.* **1.** To give rest or repose to. **2.** To place, lay, or lean for ease, support, or repose. **3.** To base or ground. **4.** To fix or direct (the gaze, for example). **5.** To bring to rest; halt. **6.** *Law.* To cease voluntarily the introduction of evidence in (a case). —***idioms.* at rest. 1.a.** Asleep. **b.** Dead. **2.** Motionless; inactive. **3.** Free from anxiety or distress. **lay** (or **put**) **to rest. 1.** To bury; inter. **2.** To settle (an issue, for example), esp. so as to be free of it. [ME < OE.] —**rest′er** *n.*

rest² (rĕst) *n.* **1.** The part that is left over after something has been removed; remainder. **2.** That or those remaining. —*intr.v.* **rest•ed, rest•ing, rests. 1.** To be or continue to be; remain: *Rest assured that I'll go.* **2.** To remain or be left over. [ME < OFr. *reste* < *rester,* to remain < Lat. *restāre,* to stay behind : *re-,* re- + *stāre,* to stand; see **stā-***.]

rest³ (rĕst) *n.* A support for a lance on the side of the breastplate of medieval armor. [ME *reste,* short for *areste,* a stopping, holding < OFr. < *arester,* to stop. See ARREST.]

rest area *n.* A designated area, usu. along a major highway, where motorists can pause to relax.

re•start (rē-stärt′) *v.* **-start•ed, -start•ing, -starts.** —*tr.* To start again or anew. —*intr.* To begin operation again. —**re′start′** *n.* —**re•start′a•ble** *adj.*

re•state (rē-stāt′) *tr.v.* **-stat•ed, -stat•ing, -states.** To state again or anew. See Syns at **repeat.** —**re•state′ment** *n.*

res•tau•rant (rĕs′tər-ənt, -tə-ränt′) *n.* A place where meals are served to the public. [Fr. < pr.part. of *restaurer,* to restore < OFr. *restorer.* See RESTORE.]

res•tau•ra•teur (rĕs′tər-ə-tûr′) also **res•tau•ran•teur** (-tə-rän-tûr′) *n.* The manager or owner of a restaurant. [Fr. < *restaurer,* to restore. See RESTAURANT.]

rest energy *n.* The energy equivalent of the rest mass of a body, equal to the rest mass multiplied by the speed of light squared.

rest•ful (rĕst′fəl) *adj.* **1.** Affording, marked by, or suggesting rest; tranquil. **2.** Being at rest; quiet. —**rest′ful•ly** *adv.* —**rest′ful•ness** *n.*

rest•har•row (rĕst′hăr′ō) *n.* Any of several Old World plants of the genus *Ononis,* having woody stems, axillary pink or purplish flowers, and trifoliate leaves. [Obsolete *rest,* to check (short for ME *aresten;* see ARREST) + HARROW¹.]

rest home *n.* An establishment where the elderly or frail are housed and cared for.

res•ti•form body (rĕs′tə-fôrm′) *n.* A large cordlike bundle of nerve fibers lying on either side of the medulla oblongata and connecting it with the cerebellum. [Lat. *restis,* rope + -FORM.]

rest•ing (rĕs′tĭng) *adj.* **1.a.** In a state of inactivity or rest. **b.** Dead. **2.** *Bot.* Dormant. Used esp. of spores that germinate after a prolonged period.

resting cell *n.* A cell that is not actively dividing.

res•ti•tute (rĕs′tĭ-to͞ot′, -tyo͞ot′) *v.* **-tut•ed, -tut•ing, -tutes.** —*tr.* **1.** To bring back to a former condition; restore. **2.** To refund. —*intr.* To undergo restitution. [Lat. *restituere, restitūt-* : *re-,* re- + *statuere,* to set up; see **stā-***.]

res•ti•tu•tion (rĕs′tĭ-to͞o′shən, -tyo͞o′-) *n.* **1.** The restoring to the rightful owner of something that has been taken away, lost, or surrendered. **2.** The act of making good or compensating for loss, damage, or injury; indemnification. **3.** A return to or restoration of a previous state or position.

res•tive (rĕs′tĭv) *adj.* **1.** Uneasily impatient under restriction, opposition, criticism, or delay. **2.** Resisting control; difficult to control. **3.** Refusing to move. Used of an animal. [ME *restif,* stationary < OFr. < *rester,* to remain < Lat. *restāre,* to keep back : *re-,* re- + *stāre,* to stand; see **stā-***.] —**res′tive•ly** *adv.* —**res′tive•ness** *n.*

rest•less (rĕst′lĭs) *adj.* **1.** Marked by a lack of quiet, repose, or rest. **2.** Not able to rest, relax, or be still. **3.** Never still or motionless. —**rest′less•ly** *adv.* —**rest′less•ness** *n.*

rest mass *n.* The physical mass of a body when it is regarded as being at rest.

Res•ton (rĕs′tən). A community of NE VA, a suburb of the Washington DC–Alexandria VA area. Pop. 48,556.

res•to•ra•tion (rĕs′tə-rā′shən) *n.* **1.a.** An act of restoring. **b.** An instance of restoring or of being restored. **c.** The state of being restored. **2.** Something, such as a renovated building, that has been restored. **3. Restoration. a.** The return of the

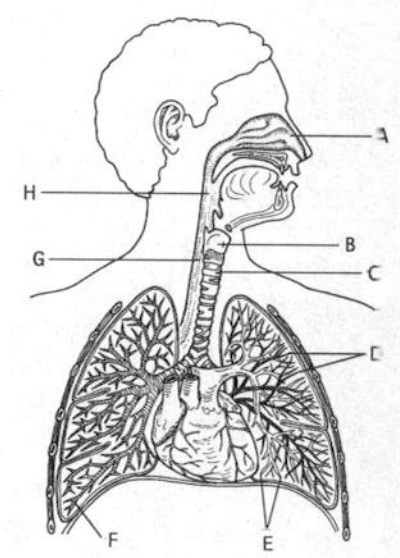

respiratory system
A. Nasal passages
B. Larynx
C. Trachea
D. Veins
E. Arteries
F. Bronchus
G. Esophagus
H. Throat

rest¹
A. Note
B. Rest

ă pat	oi boy
ā pay	ou out
âr care	o͝o to͝ok
ä father	o͞o bo͞ot
ĕ pet	ŭ cut
ē be	ûr urge
ĭ pit	th thin
ī pie	*th* this
îr pier	hw which
ŏ pot	zh vision
ō toe	ə about, item
ô paw	

Stress marks:
′ (primary);
′ (secondary), as in
dictionary (dĭk′shə-nĕr′ē)

monarchy to Great Britain in 1660 under Charles II. **b.** The period between the crowning of Charles II and the Revolution of 1688.

re•stor•a•tive (rĭ-stôr′ə-tĭv, -stōr′-) *adj.* **1.** Of or relating to restoration. **2.** Tending or having the power to restore. —*n.* **1.** Something that restores. **2.** A medicine or other agent that helps restore health, strength, or consciousness. —**re•stor′a•tive•ly** *adv.* —**re•stor′a•tive•ness** *n.*

re•store (rĭ-stôr′, -stōr′) *tr.v.* **-stored, -stor•ing, -stores. 1.** To bring back into existence or use; reestablish. **2.** To bring back to an original condition. **3.** To put (someone) back in a former position. **4.** To make restitution of; give back. [ME *restoren* < OFr. *restorer* < Lat. *restaurāre.* See **stā-*.**] —**re•stor′er** *n.*

re•strain (rĭ-strān′) *tr.v.* **-strained, -strain•ing, -strains. 1.a.** To hold back or keep in check; control: *restrained my tears.* **b.** To hold (a person) back; prevent: *restrained them from going.* **2.** To deprive of freedom or liberty. **3.** To limit or restrict. [ME *restreinen* < OFr. *restraindre, restreign-* < Lat. *restringere,* to bind back. See RESTRICT.] —**re•strain′a•ble** *adj.* —**re•strain′ed•ly** (-strā′nĭd-lē) *adv.* —**re•strain′er** *n.*

re•straint (rĭ-strānt′) *n.* **1.** The act of restraining or the condition of being restrained. **2.** Loss or abridgment of freedom. **3.** An influence that inhibits or restrains; a limitation. **4.** An instrument or a means of restraining. **5.** Control or repression of feelings; constraint. [ME *restreinte* < OFr. *restreinte* < fem. p.part. of *restraindre,* to restrain. See RESTRAIN.]

re•strict (rĭ-strĭkt′) *tr.v.* **-strict•ed, -strict•ing, -stricts.** To keep or confine within limits. [Lat. *restringere, restrict-* : *re-,* re- + *stringere,* to draw tight; see **streig-*.**] —**re•stric′tor, re•strict′er** *n.*

re•strict•ed (rĭ-strĭk′tĭd) *adj.* **1.** Kept within limits; limited: *a restricted diet.* **2.** Excluding or unavailable to certain groups: *a restricted area.* **3.** Of, relating to, or being information available only to authorized persons. —**re•strict′ed•ly** *adv.*

re•stric•tion (rĭ-strĭk′shən) *n.* **1.a.** The act of restricting. **b.** The state of being restricted. **2.** Something that restricts; a regulation or limitation.

restriction enzyme *n.* Any of a group of enzymes that cleave DNA at specific sites to produce discrete fragments, used esp. in gene-splicing.

re•stric•tion•ism (rĭ-strĭk′shə-nĭz′əm) *n.* A view or policy approving restrictions, as on trade. —**re•stric′tion•ist** *n.*

re•stric•tive (rĭ-strĭk′tĭv) *adj.* **1.a.** Of or relating to restriction. **b.** Tending or serving to restrict; limiting. **2.** *Gram.* Of or being a subordinate clause or phrase that identifies the noun, phrase, or clause it modifies and limits or restricts its meaning, as the clause *who swim* in *People who swim have fun.* —**re•stric′tive•ly** *adv.* —**re•stric′tive•ness** *n.*

re•strike (rē′strīk′) *n.* A coin or medal freshly minted from an original die at a time after the first issue. —**re•strike′** *v.*

rest•room (rĕst′ro͞om′, -ro͝om′) *n.* A room equipped with toilets and lavatories for public use.

re•struc•ture (rē-strŭk′chər) *v.* **-tured, -tur•ing, -tures.** —*tr.* **1.** To alter the makeup or pattern of. **2.** To make a basic change in (a system, for example). —*intr.* To alter the structure of something.

rest stop *n.* See **rest area.**

re•sult (rĭ-zŭlt′) *intr.v.* **-sult•ed, -sult•ing, -sults. 1.** To come about as a consequence. See Syns at **follow. 2.** To end in a particular way. —*n.* **1.a.** The consequence of a particular action, operation, or course. See Syns at **effect. b.** A favorable or concrete outcome or effect. Often used in the plural. **2.** *Math.* The quantity or expression obtained by calculation. [ME *resulten* < Med.Lat. *resultāre* < Lat., to leap back, freq. of *resilīre* : *re-,* re- + *salīre,* to leap; see **sel-*.**] —**re•sult′ful** *adj.* —**re•sult′ful•ness** *n.* —**re•sult′less** *adj.*

re•sul•tant (rĭ-zŭl′tənt) *adj.* Issuing or following as a consequence or result. —*n.* **1.** Something that results; an outcome. **2.** *Math.* A single vector that is the equivalent of a set of vectors. —**re•sul′tant•ly** *adv.*

re•sume (rĭ-zo͞om′) *v.* **-sumed, -sum•ing, -sumes.** —*tr.* **1.** To begin or take up again after interruption. **2.** To assume, take, or occupy again: *resumed his post.* **3.** To take on or take back again: *resumed my original name.* —*intr.* To begin again or continue after interruption. [ME *resumen* < OFr. *resumer* < Lat. *resūmere* : *re-,* re- + *sūmere,* to take; see **em-*.**] —**re•sum′a•ble** *adj.* —**re•sum′er** *n.*

ré•su•mé or **re•su•me** or **re•su•mé** (rĕz′o͝o-mā′, rĕz′o͝o-mā′) *n.* **1.** A brief account of one's professional or work experience and qualifications, often submitted with a job application. **2.** A summary. [Fr. < p.part. of *résumer,* to summarize < OFr. *resumer,* to resume. See RESUME.]

re•sump•tion (rĭ-zŭmp′shən) *n.* The act or an instance of resuming. [ME < OFr. < LLat. *resūmptiō, resūmptiōn-,* recovery < Lat. *resūmptus,* p.part. of *resūmere,* to resume. See RESUME.]

re•su•pi•nate (rĭ-so͞o′pə-nāt′, -nĭt) *adj. Biol.* Inverted or seemingly turned upside down, as the flowers of most orchids. [Lat. *resupīnātus,* p.part. of *resupīnāre,* to bend back : *re-,* re- + *supīnus,* supine; see SUPINE.] —**re•su′pi•na′tion** *n.*

re•su•pine (rĕs′ə-pīn′) *adj.* Lying on the back; supine. [Lat. *resupīnus* : *re-,* re- + *supīnus,* supine; see SUPINE.]

re•sur•face (rē-sûr′fəs) *v.* **-faced, -fac•ing, -fac•es.** —*tr.* To cover with a new surface. —*intr.* To come to the surface again; reappear: *The rumor resurfaced.* —**re•sur′fac•er** *n.*

re•surge (rĭ-sûrj′) *intr.v.* **-surged, -surg•ing, -surg•es.** To rise again; experience resurgence. [Lat. *resurgere* : *re-,* re- + *surgere,* to rise; see SURGE.]

re•sur•gence (rĭ-sûr′jəns) *n.* **1.** A continuing after interruption; a renewal. **2.** A restoration to use, acceptance, activity, or vigor; a revival.

re•sur•gent (rĭ-sûr′jənt) *adj.* Experiencing or tending to cause renewal or revival.

res•ur•rect (rĕz′ə-rĕkt′) *v.* **-rect•ed, -rect•ing, -rects.** —*tr.* **1.** To bring back to life; raise from the dead. **2.** To bring back into notice or use. —*intr. Theol.* To rise from the dead. [Back-formation < RESURRECTION.] —**res′ur•rec′tor** *n.*

res•ur•rec•tion (rĕz′ə-rĕk′shən) *n.* **1.** The act of rising from the dead or returning to life. **2.** The state of one who has returned to life. **3.** The act of bringing back to notice or use; revival. **4. Resurrection.** *Theol.* **a.** The rising again of Jesus after the Crucifixion. **b.** The rising again of the dead at the Last Judgment. [ME < OFr. < LLat. *resurrēctiō, resurrēctiōn-* < Lat. *resurrēctus,* p.part. of *resurgere,* to rise again. See RESURGE.] —**res′ur•rec′tion•al** *adj.*

resurrection fern *n.* An epiphytic creeping American fern *(Polypodium polypodioides)* of warm regions having fronds that curl up and appear dead in prolonged dry weather and expand under moist conditions.

res•ur•rec•tion•ist (rĕz′ə-rĕk′shə-nĭst) *n.* **1.** One who steals bodies from graves to sell for dissection; a body snatcher. **2.** One who brings something back into use or notice again.

resurrection plant *n.* See **rose of Jericho.**

re•sur•vey (rē′sər-vā′, rē-sûr′vā) *tr.v.* **-veyed, -vey•ing, -veys.** To survey or study anew. —*n.* (rē-sûr′vā). A new survey or study.

re•sus•ci•tate (rĭ-sŭs′ĭ-tāt′) *v.* **-tat•ed, -tat•ing, -tates.** —*tr.* To restore consciousness, vigor, or life to. —*intr.* To regain consciousness. [Lat. *resuscitāre, resuscitāt-* : *re-,* re- + *suscitāre,* to stir up (*sub-,* sub- + *citāre,* to move violently, freq. of *ciēre,* to set in motion; see **kei-[2]*).**] —**re•sus′ci•ta•ble** (-tə-bəl) *adj.* —**re•sus′ci•ta′tion** *n.* —**re•sus′ci•ta′tive** *adj.*

re•sus•ci•ta•tor (rĭ-sŭs′ĭ-tā′tər) *n.* One that resuscitates, as an apparatus that forces oxygen into the lungs of a person who has undergone partial asphyxiation.

ret (rĕt) *v.* **ret•ted, ret•ting, rets.** —*tr.* To moisten or soak (flax, for example) in order to soften and separate the fibers by partial rotting. —*intr.* To become so moistened or soaked. [ME *reten,* prob. < MDu. *reeten.*]

ret. *abbr.* **1.** Retain. **2.** Retired. **3.** Return.

re•ta•ble (rē′tā′bəl, rĕt′ə-) *n.* A structure forming the back of an altar, esp.: **a.** An overhanging shelf for lights and ornaments. **b.** A frame enclosing painted panels. [Fr. < Sp. *retablo* : Lat. *retro-,* retro- + Lat. *tabula,* tablet, board.]

re•tail (rē′tāl′) *n.* The sale of goods or commodities in small quantities directly to consumers. —*adj.* Of, relating to, or engaged in retail. —*adv.* **1.** In retail quantities. **2.** At a retail price. —*v.* **-tailed, -tail•ing, -tails.** —*tr.* **1.** To sell at retail. **2.** (*also* rĭ-tāl′). To tell or repeat (stories, for example) to others. —*intr.* To sell at retail. [ME < AN, var. of OFr., piece cut off < *retaillier,* to cut up : *re-,* re- + *tailler,* to cut; see TAILOR.] —**re′tail′er** *n.*

re•tain (rĭ-tān′) *tr.v.* **-tained, -tain•ing, -tains. 1.** To maintain possession of. See Syns at **keep. 2.** To keep or hold in a particular place, condition, or position. **3.** To keep in mind; remember. **4.** To hire (an attorney, for example) by the payment of a fee. **5.** To keep in one's service or pay. [ME *retainen* < OFr. *retenir* < Lat. *retinēre* : *re-,* re- + *tenēre,* to hold; see **ten-*.**] —**re•tain′a•bil′i•ty** *n.* —**re•tain′a•ble** *adj.* —**re•tain′ment** *n.*

re•tained object (rĭ-tānd′) *n. Gram.* An object in a passive construction that is identical to the object in the corresponding active construction, as *story* in *Sue was told the story by Joan.*

re•tain•er[1] (rĭ-tā′nər) *n.* **1.** One that retains, as a device, frame, or groove that restrains or guides. **2.** *Dentistry.* An appliance that holds teeth in position after orthodontic treatment. **3.a.** An employee, typically a long-term employee. **b.** A servant or an attendant, esp. in the household of a person of high rank.

re•tain•er[2] (rĭ-tā′nər) *n.* **1.** The act of engaging the services of a professional adviser, such as an attorney, a counselor, or a consultant. **2.** The fee paid to retain a professional adviser.

re•tain•ing wall (rĭ-tā′nĭng) *n.* A wall built to support or prevent the advance of a mass of earth or water.

re•take (rē-tāk′) *tr.v.* **-took** (-to͝ok′), **-tak•en** (-tā′kən), **-tak•ing, -takes. 1.** To take back or again. **2.** To recapture. **3.** To photograph, film, or record again. —*n.* (rē′tāk′). **1.** A taking again. **2.** The act or an instance of photographing, filming, or recording again.

re•tal•i•ate (rĭ-tăl′ē-āt′) *v.* **-at•ed, -at•ing, -ates.** —*intr.* To return like for like, esp. evil for evil. —*tr.* To pay back (an

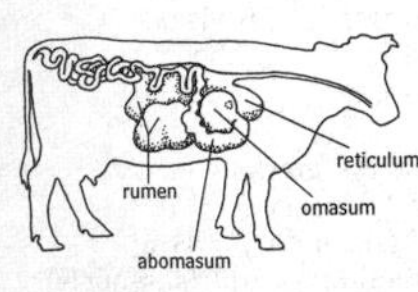

reticulum

injury) in kind. [LLat. *retāliāre, retāliāt-* : Lat. *re-*, re- + Lat. *tāliō*, punishment in kind; see **telə-*.**] — **re•tal′i•a′tion** *n.* — **re•tal′i•a′tive, re•tal′i•a•to′ry** (-ə-tôr′ē, -tōr′ē) *adj.* — **re•tal′i•a′tor** *n.*

re•tard (rĭ-tärd′) *v.* **-tard•ed, -tard•ing, -tards.** — *tr.* To cause to move or proceed slowly; delay or impede. — *intr.* To be delayed. — *n.* **1.** A slowing down or hindering of progress. **2.** *Mus.* A slackening of tempo. **3.** (rē′tärd′). *Offensive Slang.* Used as a disparaging term for a mentally retarded person. [ME *retarden* < OFr. *retarder* < Lat. *retardāre* : *re-*, re- + *tardāre*, to delay (< *tardus*, slow).] — **re•tard′er** *n.*

re•tar•dant (rĭ-tär′dnt) *adj.* Acting or tending to retard. Often used in combination. — **re•tar′dant** *n.*

re•tar•date (rĭ-tär′dāt′, -dĭt) *n.* A mentally retarded person.

re•tar•da•tion (rē′tär-dā′shən) *n.* **1.a.** The act or process of retarding. **b.** The condition of being retarded. **2.** The extent to which something is held back or delayed. **3.** Something that retards; a delay or hindrance. **4.** Mental retardation. **5.** *Mus.* A diminishing of tempo; a retard.

re•tard•ed (rĭ-tär′dĭd) *Offensive.* — *adj.* **1.** Affected with mental retardation. **2.** Relatively slow in mental, emotional, or physical development. — *n.* Persons affected with mental retardation considered as a group.

re•tar•get (rē-tär′gĭt) *tr.v.* **-get•ed, -get•ing, -gets. 1.** To direct toward a different target: *retargeting missiles.* **2.** To change the target or goal of: *funds retargeted for job training.*

retch (rĕch) *v.* **retched, retch•ing, retch•es.** — *intr.* To try to vomit. — *tr.* To vomit. [Alteration of ME *rechen* < OE *hrǣcan.*] — **retch** *n.*

re•te (rē′tē) *n., pl.* **re•ti•a** (rē′tē-ə, rē′shə). An anatomical mesh or network, as of veins or nerves. [Lat. *rēte*, net.]

re•tell (rē-tĕl′) *tr.v.* **-told** (-tōld′), **-tell•ing, -tells. 1.** To relate or tell again or in a different form. **2.** To count again.

re•tell•ing (rē-tĕl′ĭng) *n.* A new account or an adaptation of a story: *a retelling of a Roman myth.*

re•tene (rē′tēn′, rĕt′ēn′) *n.* A crystalline compound, $C_{18}H_{18}$, derived from pine tar, fossil resins, and tar oils. [< Gk. *rhētinē*, resin.]

re•ten•tion (rĭ-tĕn′shən) *n.* **1.a.** The act of retaining. **b.** The condition of being retained. **2.** Capacity or power of retaining. **3.** Memory. **4.** Something retained. **5.** *Medic.* Involuntary withholding of wastes or secretions that are normally eliminated. [ME *retencioun* < OFr. *retention* < Lat. *retentiō, retentiōn-* < *retentus*, p.part. of *retinēre*, to retain. See RETAIN.]

re•ten•tive (rĭ-tĕn′tĭv) *adj.* **1.** Having the quality, power, or capacity of retaining. **2.** Having the ability or capacity to retain knowledge or information with ease: *a retentive memory.* — **re•ten′tive•ly** *adv.* — **re•ten′tive•ness** *n.*

re•ten•tiv•i•ty (rē′tĕn-tĭv′ĭ-tē) *n.* **1.a.** The quality or state of being retentive. **b.** Capacity or power of retaining. **2.** *Phys.* The capacity for remaining magnetized after cessation of the magnetizing force.

re•think (rē-thĭngk′) *tr. & intr.v.* **-thought** (-thôt′), **-think•ing, -thinks.** To reconsider (something) or to involve oneself in reconsideration. — **re′think′** *n.* — **re•think′er** *n.*

re•ti•ar•y (rē′shē-ĕr′ē) *adj.* Of, resembling, or forming a net or web. [< Lat. *rēte*, net.]

ret•i•cence (rĕt′ĭ-səns) *n.* **1.** The state or quality of being reticent; reserve. **2.** The state or quality of being reluctant; unwillingness. **3.** An instance of being reticent.

ret•i•cent (rĕt′ĭ-sənt) *adj.* **1.** Inclined to keep one's thoughts, feelings, and personal affairs to oneself. See Syns at **silent. 2.** Restrained or reserved in style. **3.** Reluctant; unwilling. [Lat. *reticēns, reticent-*, pr.part. of *reticēre*, to keep silent : *re-*, re- + *tacēre*, to be silent.] — **ret′i•cent•ly** *adv.*

ret•i•cle (rĕt′ĭ-kəl) *n.* A grid or pattern placed in the eyepiece of an optical instrument, used to establish scale or position. [Lat. *rēticulum*, dim. of *rēte*, net.]

re•tic•u•lar (rĭ-tĭk′yə-lər) *adj.* **1.** Resembling a net in form; netlike: *reticular tissue.* **2.** Marked by complexity; intricate. [< Lat. *rēticulum*, dim. of *rēte*, net.]

reticular formation *n.* A diffuse network of nerve fibers and cells in parts of the brainstem, important in regulating consciousness or wakefulness.

re•tic•u•late (rĭ-tĭk′yə-lĭt, -lāt′) *adj.* Resembling or forming a net or network: *reticulate veins of a leaf.* — *v.* (-lāt′) **-lat•ed, -lat•ing, -lates.** — *tr.* **1.** To make a net or network of. **2.** To mark with lines resembling a network. — *intr.* To form a net or network. [Lat. *rēticulātus* < *rēticulum*, dim. of *rēte*, net.] — **re•tic′u•late•ly** *adv.* — **re•tic′u•la′tion** *n.*

ret•i•cule (rĕt′ĭ-kyo͞ol′) *n.* **1.** A woman's drawstring handbag or purse. **2.** A reticle. [Fr. *réticule* < Lat. *rēticulum*, dim. of *rēte*, net.]

re•tic•u•lo•cyte (rĭ-tĭk′yə-lō-sīt′) *n.* An immature red blood cell that contains a network of basophilic filaments. [RETICUL(UM) + -CYTE.] — **re•tic′u•lo•cyt′ic** (-sĭt′ĭk) *adj.*

re•tic•u•lo•en•do•the•li•al (rĭ-tĭk′yə-lō-ĕn′də-thē′lē-əl) *n.* Of, relating to, or being the widely diffused bodily system constituting all phagocytic cells except certain white blood cells. [RETICUL(UM) + ENDOTHELIAL.]

re•tic•u•lum (rĭ-tĭk′yə-ləm) *n., pl.* **-la** (-lə). **1.** A netlike formation or structure; a network. **2.** *Zool.* The second compartment of the stomach of a ruminant, lined with a membrane having honeycombed ridges. [Lat. *rēticulum*, dim. of *rēte*, net.]

Re•tic•u•lum (rĭ-tĭk′yə-ləm) *n.* A constellation in the Southern Hemisphere near Dorado and Horologium. [Lat. *rēticulum*, dim. of *rēte*, net.]

re•ti•form (rē′tə-fôrm′, rĕt′ə-) *adj.* Arranged like a net; reticulate. [Lat. *rēte*, net + -FORM.]

ret•i•na (rĕt′n-ə) *n., pl.* **ret•i•nas** or **ret•i•nae** (rĕt′n-ē′). A delicate light-sensitive membrane lining the inner eyeball and connected by the optic nerve to the brain. [ME < Med.Lat. *rētina* < Lat. *rēte*, net.] — **ret′i•nal** *adj.*

ret•i•nac•u•lum (rĕt′n-ăk′yə-ləm) *n., pl.* **-la** (-lə). *Biol.* A band or bandlike structure that holds a part in place. [Lat. *retināculum*, band : *retinēre*, to restrain; see RETAIN + *-culum*, suff. denoting instruments.] — **ret′i•nac′u•lar** (-lər) *adj.*

ret•i•nal (rĕt′n-ăl′, -ôl′) *n.* See **retinene.**

ret•i•nene (rĕt′n-ēn′) *n.* Either of two yellow to red retinal pigments, formed by oxidation of vitamin A alcohols.

ret•i•ni•tis (rĕt′n-ī′tĭs) *n.* Inflammation of the retina.

retinitis pig•men•to•sa (pĭg′mĕn-tō′sə, -mən-) *n.* A hereditary degenerative disease of the retina, characterized by night blindness, pigmentary changes within the retina, a narrowing of the visual field, and eventual loss of vision. [NLat. *pigmentōsa*, fem. of *pigmentōsus*, pigmented.]

retino– or **retin–** *pref.* Retina: *retinoscopy.* [< RETINA.]

ret•i•no•blas•to•ma (rĕt′n-ō-blă-stō′mə) *n., pl.* **-mas** or **-ma•ta** (-mə-tə). A hereditary retinal malignant tumor transmitted as a dominant trait.

ret•i•nol (rĕt′n-ôl′, -ōl′, -ŏl′) *n.* See **vitamin A.**

ret•i•nop•a•thy (rĕt′n-ŏp′ə-thē) *n., pl.* **-thies.** A pathological disorder of the retina. — **ret′i•no•path′ic** (-ō-păth′ĭk) *adj.*

ret•i•no•scope (rĕt′n-ə-skōp′) *n.* An optical instrument for examining refraction of light in the eye. — **ret′i•nos′co•py** (rĕt′n-ŏs′kə-pē) *n.*

retinoscope

ret•i•nue (rĕt′n-o͞o′, -yo͞o′) *n.* The retainers accompanying a high-ranking person. [ME *retenue* < OFr. < fem. p.part. of *retenir*, to retain. See RETAIN.]

re•tin•u•la (rĭ-tĭn′yə-lə) *n., pl.* **-lae** (-lē). A cluster of pigmented sensory cells in the compound eye of an arthropod. [NLat. *rētinula*, dim. of Med.Lat. *rētina*, retina. See RETINA.] — **re•tin′u•lar** *adj.*

re•tire (rĭ-tīr′) *v.* **-tired, -tir•ing, -tires.** — *intr.* **1.** To withdraw, as for rest. **2.** To go to bed. **3.** To withdraw from one's occupation, business, or office; stop working. **4.** To fall back or retreat, as from battle. **5.** To move back or away; recede. — *tr.* **1.** To cause to withdraw from one's usual field of activity. **2.** To lead (troops, for example) away from action; withdraw. **3.** To take out of circulation: *retired the bonds.* **4.** To withdraw from use or active service: *retiring an old ship.* **5.** *Baseball.* **a.** To put out (a batter). **b.** To cause (the opposing team) to end a turn at bat. [Fr. *retirer*, to retreat < OFr., to take back : *re-*, re- + *tirer*, to draw; see TIER[1].]

re•tired (rĭ-tīrd′) *adj.* **1.** Withdrawn from one's occupation; having finished one's active working life. **2.** Received by a person in retirement: *retired pay.* **3.** Withdrawn; secluded. — *n.* Retired people considered as a group. — **re•tired•ly** *adv.* — **re•tired′ness** *n.*

re•tir•ee (rĭ-tīr′ē′) *n.* One who has retired from active working life.

re•tire•ment (rĭ-tīr′mənt) *n.* **1.** The act of retiring. **2.** The state of being retired. **3.** Withdrawal from one's occupation, business, or office. **4.** Withdrawal into privacy or seclusion. **5.** A place of privacy or seclusion; a retreat.

re•tir•ing (rĭ-tīr′ĭng) *adj.* Shy and reserved; modest. — **re•tir′ing•ly** *adv.* — **re•tir′ing•ness** *n.*

re•told (rē-tōld′) *v.* P.t. and p.part. of **retell.**

re•took (rē-to͝ok′) *v.* P.t. of **retake.**

re•tool (rē-to͞ol′) *v.* **-tooled, -tool•ing, -tools.** — *tr.* **1.** To fit out (a factory, for example) with new machinery and tools for making a different product. **2.** To revise and reorganize, esp. in order to update or improve: *had to retool the city's economy.* — *intr.* To retool a factory, for example.

re•tor•sion or **re•tor•tion** (rĭ-tôr′shən) *n. Law.* An act perpetrated by one nation upon another in retaliation or reprisal for a similar act. [Prob. Fr. *rétorsion* < Lat. *retortus*, p.part. of *retorquēre*, to cast back. See RETORT[1].]

re•tort[1] (rĭ-tôrt′) *v.* **-tort•ed, -tort•ing, -torts.** — *tr.* **1.a.** To reply, esp. to answer in a quick, caustic, or witty manner. See Syns at **answer. b.** To present a counterargument to. **2.** To return in kind; pay back. — *intr.* **1.** To make a reply, esp. a quick, caustic, or witty one. **2.** To present a counterargument. **3.** To return like for like; retaliate. — *n.* **1.** A quick incisive reply, esp. one that turns the first speaker's words to his or her own disadvantage. **2.** The act or an instance of retorting. [Lat. *retorquēre, retort-*, to bend back, retort : *re-*, re- + *torquēre*, to bend, twist; see **terk^w-*.**] — **re•tort′er** *n.*

re•tort[2] (rĭ-tôrt′, rē′tôrt′) *n.* A closed laboratory vessel with an outlet tube, used for distillation, sublimation, or decomposition by heat. [Fr. *retorte* < Med.Lat. *retorta* < fem. of Lat. *retortus*, p.part. of *retorquēre*, to bend back. See RETORT[1].]

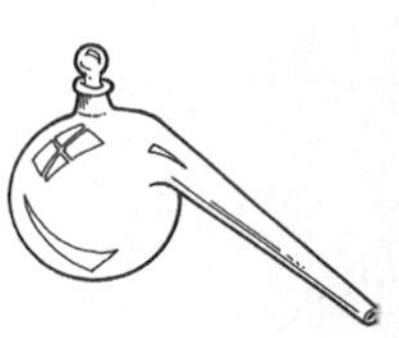

retort[2]

ă pat	oi boy
ā pay	ou out
âr care	o͝o took
ä father	o͞o boot
ĕ pet	ŭ cut
ē be	ûr urge
ĭ pit	th thin
ī pie	*th* this
îr pier	hw which
ŏ pot	zh vision
ō toe	ə about, item
ô paw	

Stress marks:
′ (primary);
′ (secondary), as in dictionary (dĭk′shə-nĕr′ē)

re•touch (rē-tŭch′) *v.* **-touched, -touch•ing, -touch•es.** — *tr.* **1.** To add new details or touches to for correction or improvement. **2.** To improve or change (a photographic negative or print), as by removing flaws. **3.** To color (recent growth of hair) to match hair that was tinted, dyed, or bleached at an earlier date. — *intr.* To give or make retouches. — *n.* (rē′-tŭch′, rē-tŭch′). The act or process or an instance of retouching. — **re•touch′er** *n.*

re•tract (rĭ-trăkt′) *v.* **-tract•ed, -tract•ing, -tracts.** — *tr.* **1.** To take back; disavow. **2.** To draw back or in. **3.** *Ling.* **a.** To utter (a sound) with the tongue drawn back. **b.** To draw back (the tongue). — *intr.* **1.** To take something back or disavow it. **2.** To draw back or in. [Lat. *retractāre*, to revoke, freq. of *retrahere*, to draw back : *re-*, re- + *trahere*, to draw. V., tr., senses 2 and 3, and v., intr., sense 2, ME *retracten* < OFr. *retracter* < Lat. *retractus*, p.part. of *retrahere*, to draw back.] — **re•tract′a•bil′i•ty, re•tract′i•bil′i•ty** *n.* — **re•tract′a•ble, re•tract′i•ble** *adj.* — **re′trac•ta′tion** (rē′trăk-tā′shən) *n.*

re•trac•tile (rĭ-trăk′tĭl, -tīl′) *adj.* That can be drawn back or in: *retractile claws.* — **re′trac•til′i•ty** (rē′trăk-tĭl′ĭ-tē) *n.*

re•trac•tion (rĭ-trăk′shən) *n.* **1.** The act of retracting or the state of being retracted. **2.a.** The act of recanting or disavowing a previously held statement or belief. **b.** A formal statement of disavowal. **c.** Something recanted or disavowed. **3.** The power of drawing back or of being drawn back.

re•trac•tive (rĭ-trăk′tĭv) *adj.* Tending or serving to retract. — **re•trac′tive•ly** *adv.* — **re•trac′tive•ness** *n.*

re•trac•tor (rĭ-trăk′tər) *n.* One that retracts, as: **a.** *Anat.* A muscle that retracts an organ or a part. **b.** *Medic.* A surgical instrument used to hold back organs, for example.

re•tral (rē′trəl, rĕt′rəl) *adj.* **1.** Situated at, located close to, or directed toward the back. **2.** Backward; reverse. [< Lat. *retrō*, back. See **re-***.] — **re′tral•ly** *adv.*

re•tread (rē-trĕd′) *tr.v.* **-tread•ed, -tread•ing, -treads. 1.** To fit (a worn automotive tire) with a new tread. **2.** To make or do over again, esp. with minimal revision; rehash: *retreading an old story.* — *n.* (rē′trĕd′). **1.** A tire that has a new tread. **2.** A revision or reworking; a remake or rehash. **3.** *Informal.* A person who has been retrained for work.

re•treat (rĭ-trēt′) *n.* **1.a.** The act or process of withdrawing, esp. from something hazardous or unpleasant. **b.** The process of receding from a position or condition gained. **2.** A place affording peace, quiet, privacy, or security. **3.a.** A period of seclusion, retirement, or solitude. **b.** A period of withdrawal for prayer, meditation, and study. **4.a.** Withdrawal of a military force from danger. **b.** The signal for such withdrawal. **c.** A bugle call or drumbeat signaling the lowering of the flag at sunset. **d.** The military ceremony of lowering the flag. — *v.* **-treat•ed, -treat•ing, -treats.** — *intr.* **1.** To fall or draw back; withdraw or retire. **2.** To slope backward. — *tr. Games.* To move (a chess piece) back. [ME *retret* < OFr. *retrait, retret* < p.part. of *retraire, retrere*, to draw back < Lat. *retrahere*. See RETRACT.] — **re•treat′er** *n.*

re•treat•ant (rĭ-trēt′nt) *n.* A participant in a religious retreat.

re•trench (rĭ-trĕnch′) *v.* **-trenched, -trench•ing, -trench•es.** — *tr.* **1.** To cut down; reduce. **2.** To remove, delete, or omit. — *intr.* To curtail expenses; economize. [Obsolete Fr. *retrencher* < OFr. *retrenchier* : *re-*, re- + *trenchier*, to cut; see TRENCH.] — **re•trench′er** *n.*

re•trench•ment (rĭ-trĕnch′mənt) *n.* **1.** A cutting down or back; reduction. **2.** A curtailment of expenses.

re•tri•al (rē-trī′əl, -trīl′, rē′trī′əl, -trīl′) *n.* A second trial, as of a legal case.

ret•ri•bu•tion (rĕt′rə-byo͞o′shən) *n.* **1.** Something deserved; recompense. **2.** Something given or demanded in repayment, esp. punishment. **3.** *Theol.* Punishment or reward in a future life based on performance in this one. [Ult. < Lat. *retribūtiō, retribūtiōn-* < *retribūtus*, p.part. of *retribuere*, to pay back : *re-*, re- + *tribuere*, to grant; see TRIBUTE.]

re•trib•u•tive (rĭ-trĭb′yə-tĭv) *adj.* Of, involving, or characterized by retribution; retributory. — **re•trib′u•tive•ly** *adv.*

re•trib•u•to•ry (rĭ-trĭb′yə-tôr′ē, -tōr′ē) *adj.* Retributive.

re•tried (rē-trīd′) *v.* P.t. and p.part. of **retry.**

re•tries (rē-trīz′) *v.* Third pers. sing. pr.t. of **retry.**

re•triev•al (rĭ-trē′vəl) *n.* **1.** The act or process of retrieving. **2.** *Comp. Sci.* The accessing of information from storage devices. **3.** The possibility of being retrieved or restored.

re•trieve (rĭ-trēv′) *v.* **-trieved, -triev•ing, -trieves.** — *tr.* **1.** To get back; regain. **2.a.** To rescue or save. **b.** *Sports.* To make a difficult but successful return of (a ball or shuttlecock). **3.** To bring back again; revive or restore. **4.** To rectify the unfavorable consequences of; remedy. See Syns at **recover. 5.** To recall to mind; remember. **6.** To find and carry back; fetch. — *intr.* To find and bring back game. — *n.* **1.** The act of retrieving; retrieval. **2.** *Sports.* A difficult but successful return of a ball or shuttlecock. [ME *retreven* < OFr. *retrover, retruev-* : *re-*, re- + *trover*, to find; see TROVER.] — **re•triev′a•bil′i•ty** *n.* — **re•triev′a•ble** *adj.* — **re•triev′a•bly** *adv.*

re•triev•er (rĭ-trē′vər) *n.* One that retrieves, esp. any one of several breeds of dog that were bred to retrieve game.

ret•ro (rĕt′rō) *adj.* **1.** Retroactive. **2.** Involving, relating to, or reminiscent of things past; retrospective. — *n.*, *pl.* **-ros.** A fashion, decor, or design reminiscent of things past.

retro– *pref.* **1.** Backward; back: *retrorocket.* **2.** Situated behind: *retrolental.* [Lat. *retrō-* < *retrō*, backward, behind. See **re-***.]

ret•ro•ac•tion (rĕt′rō-ăk′shən) *n.* **1.** An action, as of a law, that influences or applies to a prior time. **2.** An opposing or reciprocal action; a reaction. — **ret′ro•act′** *v.*

ret•ro•ac•tive (rĕt′rō-ăk′tĭv) *adj.* Influencing or applying to a period prior to enactment. [Fr. *rétroactif* < Lat. *retroāctus*, p.part. of *retroagere*, to drive back : *retrō-*, retro- + *agere*, to drive; see **ag-***.] — **ret′ro•ac′tive•ly** *adv.* — **ret′ro•ac•tiv′i•ty** *n.*

ret•ro•cede (rĕt′rō-sēd′) *v.* **-ced•ed, -ced•ing, -cedes.** — *intr.* To go back; recede. — *tr.* To cede or give back (a territory, for example); return. [Lat. *retrōcēdere* : *retrō-*, retro- + *cēdere*, to go; see **ked-***.] — **ret′ro•ces′sion** (-sĕsh′ən) *n.*

ret•ro•fire (rĕt′rō-fīr′) *v.* **-fired, -fir•ing, -fires.** — *tr.* To ignite or fire (a retrorocket). — *intr.* To become ignited or fired. Used of a retrorocket.

ret•ro•fit (rĕt′rō-fĭt′) *n.* **1.** A modification of an existing product, facility, or structure with parts, equipment, or systems not available at the time of original manufacture or construction. **2.** Something, such as a structure, so modified. — *v.* **-fit•ted, -fit•ting, -fits.** — *tr.* **1.** To provide (a product, for example) with a retrofit. **2.** To install or fit (a new device, for example) during a retrofit. — *intr.* To undergo a retrofit. [*retro(active) (re)fit.*] — **ret′ro•fit′** *adj.* — **ret′ro•fit′ta•ble** *adj.* — **ret′ro•fit′ter** *n.*

ret•ro•flex (rĕt′rə-flĕks′) *adj.* also **ret•ro•flexed** (-flĕkst′). **1.** Bent, curved, or turned backward. **2.** *Ling.* Pronounced with the tip of the tongue turned back against the roof of the mouth. — *n. Ling.* A sound pronounced with the tongue in retroflex position, as the sound (r) in some varieties of English. [Lat. **retrōflexus*, p.part. of *retrōflectere*, to bend back : *retrō*, retro- + *flectere*, to bend.] — **ret′ro•flex′ion, ret′ro•flec′tion** *n.*

ret•ro•grade (rĕt′rə-grād′) *adj.* **1.** Moving or tending backward. **2.** Opposite to the usual order; inverted or reversed. **3.** Reverting to an earlier or inferior condition. **4.** *Astron.* **a.** Of or relating to the orbital revolution or axial rotation of a planetary body that moves clockwise from east to west, in the direction opposite to most celestial bodies. **b.** Of or relating to the brief, regularly occurring, apparently backward movement of a planetary body in its orbit as viewed against the fixed stars, caused by the differing orbital velocities of Earth and the body observed. **5.** *Archaic.* Opposed; contrary. — *intr.v.* **-grad•ed, -grad•ing, -grades. 1.** To move or seem to move backward. **2.** To decline to an inferior state; degenerate. [ME < Lat. *retrōgradus* < *retrōgradī*, to go back : *retrō-*, retro- + *-gradus*, walking (< *gradī*, to go; see **ghredh-***).] — **ret′ro•gra•da′tion** (-rō-grā-dā′shən) *n.* — **ret′ro•grade′ly** *adv.*

ret•ro•gress (rĕt′rə-grĕs′, rĕt′rə-grĕs′) *intr.v.* **-gressed, -gress•ing, -gress•es. 1.** To return to an earlier, inferior, or less complex condition. **2.** To go or move backward. [Lat. *retrōgradī*, **retrōgress-* : *retrō-*, retro- + *gradī*, to go; see **ghredh-***.] — **ret′ro•gres′sive** *adj.*

ret•ro•gres•sion (rĕt′rə-grĕsh′ən) *n.* **1.** The act or process of deteriorating or declining. **2.** *Biol.* A return to a less complex or more primitive state or stage.

ret•ro•len•tal (rĕt′rō-lĕn′tl) *adj.* Situated or occurring behind a lens, as of the eye. [RETRO– + NLat. *lēns, lent-*, lens; see LENS + -AL[1].]

ret•ro•oc•u•lar (rĕt′rō-ŏk′yə-lər) *adj.* Being behind the eye.

ret•ro•per•i•to•ne•al (rĕt′rō-pĕr′ĭ-tn-ē′əl) *adj.* Situated behind the peritoneum.

ret•ro•pha•ryn•ge•al (rĕt′rō-fə-rĭn′jē-əl, -jəl, -făr′ĭn-jē′əl) *adj.* Situated or occurring behind the pharynx.

ret•ro•rock•et (rĕt′rō-rŏk′ĭt) *n.* A rocket engine used to retard, arrest, or reverse the motion of a vehicle, such as an aircraft.

re•trorse (rĭ-trôrs′, rē′trôrs′) *adj.* Directed or turned back or down. [Lat. *retrōrsus* < *retrōversus* : *retrō-*, retro- + *versus*, p.part. of *vertere*, to turn; see **wer-**[2]*.] — **re•trorse′ly** *adv.*

ret•ro•spect (rĕt′rə-spĕkt′) *n.* A review, survey, or contemplation of things in the past. — *v.* **-spect•ed, -spect•ing, -spects.** — *intr.* **1.** To contemplate the past. **2.** To refer back. — *tr.* To look back on or contemplate (things past). — ***idiom.*** **in retrospect.** Looking backward or reviewing the past. [< Lat. **retrōspectus*, p.part. of *retrōspicere*, to look back at : *retrō-*, retro- + *specere*, to look at; see **spek-***.] — **ret′ro•spec′tion** *n.*

ret•ro•spec•tive (rĕt′rə-spĕk′tĭv) *adj.* **1.** Directed to or retrospecting the past. **2.** Looking or directed backward. **3.** Applying to or influencing the past; retroactive. **4.** Of, relating to, or being a retrospective: *a retrospective exhibition.* — *n.* An extensive exhibition or performance of the work of an artist over a period of years. — **ret′ro•spec′tive•ly** *adv.*

re•trous•sé (rə-tro͞o-sā′, rĕt′ro͞o-) *adj.* Turned up at the end. Used of the nose. [Fr., p.part. of *retrousser*, to turn back < OFr. : *re-*, re- + *torser, trousser*, to tie in a bundle (prob. <

VLat. **torsāre* < **torsus*, twisted, var. of Lat. *tortus*, p.part. of *torquēre*, to twist; see TORQUE[1].]

ret•ro•ver•sion (rĕt′rō-vûr′zhən, -shən) *n.* **1.** A turning or tilting backward. **2.** The state of being turned or tilted back. [< Lat. *retrōversus*, retrorse. See RETRORSE.]

ret•ro•vi•rus (rĕt′rō-vī′rəs, rĕt′rə-vī′-) *n.*, *pl.* **-rus•es.** Any of a group of viruses that contain RNA and reverse transcriptase, including the AIDS virus. — **ret′ro•vi′ral** *adj.*

re•try (rē-trī′) *tr.v.* **-tried** (-trīd′), **-try•ing, -tries** (-trīz′). To try again.

ret•si•na (rĕt′sĭ-nə, rĕt-sē′nə) *n.* A Greek wine flavored with pine resin. [Mod.Gk., prob. < Ital. *resina*, resin < Lat. *rēsīna*. See RESIN.]

re•turn (rĭ-tûrn′) *v.* **-turned, -turn•ing, -turns.** — *intr.* **1.** To go or come back, as to an earlier condition or place. **2.** To revert in speech, thought, or practice. **3.** To revert to a former owner. **4.** To answer or respond. — *tr.* **1.** To send, put, or carry back. **2.a.** To give or send back in reciprocation. See Syns at **reciprocate. b.** To give back to the owner. **c.** To reflect or send back. **3.** To produce or yield (profit or interest) as a payment for labor, investment, or expenditure. **4.** *Law.* **a.** To submit (an official report, for example) to a judge or other person in authority. **b.** To render or deliver (a writ, for example) to the proper officer or court of law. **5.** To elect or reelect, as to a legislative body. **6.** *Games.* To respond to (a partner's lead) by leading the same suit in cards. **7.** *Archit.* To turn away from or place at an angle to the previous line of direction. **8.a.** *Sports.* To send back (a tennis ball, for example) to one's opponent. **b.** *Football.* To run with (the ball) after a kickoff, a punt, an interception, or a fumble. — *n.* **1.a.** The act or condition of going, coming, bringing, or sending back. **b.** The act of bringing or sending something back to a previous place, condition, or owner. **2.a.** Something brought or sent back. **b. returns.** Merchandise returned, as to a retailer by a consumer. **c.** Something that goes or comes back. **3.** A recurrence, as of a periodic event. **4.** Something exchanged for that received; repayment. **5.** A reply; a response. **6.a.** The profit made on an exchange of goods. **b.** A profit or yield, as from labor or investments. Often used in the plural. **c.** Output or yield per unit rather than cost per unit, as in manufacturing. **7.a.** A report, list, or set of statistics, esp. one that is formal or official. **b.** A report on the vote in an election. Often used in the plural. **c.** *Chiefly British.* An election. **8.** *Games.* A lead in certain card games that responds to the lead of one's partner. **9.** *Sports.* In tennis and certain other sports: **a.** The act of returning the ball back to one's opponent. **b.** The ball thus sent back. **10.** *Football.* **a.** The act of returning the ball. **b.** The yardage so gained. **11.** *Archit.* **a.** The extension of a molding, projection, or other part at an angle (usu. 90°) to the main part. **b.** A part of a building set at an angle to the façade. **12.a.** A turn, bend, or similar reversal of direction, as in a stream or road. **b.** A pipe or conduit for carrying something, esp. water, back to its starting point. **13.** The key or mechanism on a machine, such as a typewriter or computer, that positions the carriage, cursor, or printing element at the beginning of a new line. **14.** *Chiefly British.* A roundtrip ticket. **15.** *Law.* **a.** The bringing or sending back of a writ or other document, generally with a short written report on it, by an officer to the court from which it was issued. **b.** A certified report, as by an election official. **16.** A formal tax statement on the required official form indicating taxable income, allowed deductions, exemptions, and the computed tax that is due. — *adj.* **1.** Of, relating to, or bringing about a going or coming back to a place or situation. **2.** Given, sent, or done in reciprocation or exchange. **3.** Performed, presented, or taking place again. **4.** Used on or for returning. **5.** Returning or affording return or recirculation. **6.** Relating to or being a roundtrip ticket. **7.a.** Reversing or changing direction. **b.** Having or formed by a reversal or change in direction; returning on itself, as a bend in a road or stream. — ***idiom.* in return.** In repayment or reciprocation. [ME *retornen* < OFr. *retourner* < VLat. **retornāre* : Lat. *re-*, re- + Lat. *tornāre*, to turn in a lathe; see TURN.] — **re•turn′er** *n.*

re•turn•a•ble (rĭ-tûr′nə-bəl) *adj.* That can be returned or brought back: *returnable bottles.* — *n.* An empty beverage container that may be returned for refund of a deposit.

re•turn•ee (rĭ-tûr′nē′) *n.* **1.** One who returns, as from a journey or to school after a long absence. **2.** A person returning from military duty overseas. See Usage Note at **-ee**[1].

re•tuse (rĭ-to͞os′, -tyo͞os′) *adj. Bot.* Having a rounded or obtuse apex with a central shallow notch. [Lat. *retūsus*, p.part. of *retundere*, to beat back : *re-*, re- + *tundere*, to beat.]

Reu•ben[1] (ro͞o′bən). In the Bible, a son of Jacob and Leah and the forebear of one of the tribes of Israel.

Reu•ben[2] (ro͞o′bən) *n.* A hot sandwich consisting of corned beef, Swiss cheese, and sauerkraut usu. served on rye bread. [< the name *Reuben.*]

re•u•ni•fy (rē-yo͞o′nə-fī′) *tr.v.* **-fied, -fy•ing, -fies.** To cause (a group, party, state, or sect) to become unified again after being divided. — **re•u′ni•fi•ca′tion** (-fĭ-kā′shən) *n.*

re•un•ion (rē-yo͞on′yən) *n.* **1.a.** The act of reuniting. **b.** The state of being reunited. **2.** A gathering of the members of a group who have been separated: *a high school reunion.*

Ré•un•ion (rē-yo͞on′yən, rā-ü-nyôN′). An island of France in the W Indian Ocean SW of Mauritius; colonized in the mid-1600's and an overseas department since 1946.

re•un•ion•ist (rē-yo͞on′yə-nĭst) *n.* One who advocates reunion, as of divided parties or sects, esp. an advocate of the reunion of the Anglican Church with the Roman Catholic Church. — **re•un′ion•ism** *n.* — **re•un′ion•is′tic** *adj.*

re•u•nite (rē′yo͞o-nīt′) *tr. & intr.v.* **-nit•ed, -nit•ing, -nites.** To bring or come together again.

re-up (rē-ŭp′) *intr.v.* **-upped, -up•ping, -ups.** *Informal.* **1.** To enlist again for military service. **2.** To sign a renewed contract for employment or service.

Reus (rĕ′o͞os). A city of NE Spain near the Mediterranean Sea W of Barcelona; founded c. 13th cent. Pop. 82,354.

Reu•ter (roi′tər), Baron **Paul Julius von.** 1816–99. German-born British journalist who founded (1848) Reuter's, one of the first international news agencies.

Reu•ther (ro͞o′thər), **Walter Philip.** 1907–70. Amer. labor leader who was president of the United Auto Workers (1946–70) and the Congress of Industrial Organizations (1952–55).

Reut•ling•en (roit′lĭng-ən). A city of SW Germany S of Stuttgart; a free imperial city from 1240 to 1802. Pop. 96,337.

rev (rĕv) *Informal.* — *n.* A revolution, as of a motor. — *v.* **revved, rev•ving, revs.** — *tr.* **1.a.** To increase the speed of (a motor, for example). **b.** To accelerate or increase: *revving up output.* **2.** To make livelier or more productive: *revving ourselves up for the game.* — *intr.* **1.** To operate at an increased speed. **2.** To accelerate in quantity or activity.

rev. *abbr.* **1.** Revenue. **2.** Reverse. **3.** Reversed. **4.** Review. **5.** Reviewed. **6.** Revise; revision. **7.** Revolution.

Rev. *abbr.* **1.** *Bible.* Revelation. **2.** Reverend.

re•val•u•ate (rē-văl′yo͞o-āt′) *tr.v.* **-at•ed, -at•ing, -ates. 1.** To make a new valuation of. **2.** To increase the exchange value of (a nation's currency). — **re•val′u•a′tion** *n.*

re•val•ue (rē-văl′yo͞o) *tr.v.* **-ued, -u•ing, -ues. 1.** To revise the value of (a nation's currency). **2.** To evaluate anew; reappraise.

re•vamp (rē-vămp′) *tr.v.* **-vamped, -vamp•ing, -vamps. 1.** To patch up or restore; renovate. **2.** To revise or reconstruct (a manuscript, for example). **3.** To vamp (a shoe) anew. — *n.* The act or an instance of revamping; a complete reorganization or revision. — **re•vamp′ment** *n.*

re•vanche (rə-vänch′, -väNsh′) *n.* **1.** The act of retaliating; revenge. **2.** A usu. political policy, as of a nation, intended to regain lost territory or standing. [Fr. < OFr. *revancher*, to revenge : *re-*, re- + *vengier, vencher*, to avenge; see REVENGE.] — **re•vanch′ism** (-vän′chĭz-əm, -väN′shĭz-) *n.* — **re•vanch′ist** *adj. & n.* — **re•vanch•is′tic** *adj.*

re•veal[1] (rĭ-vēl′) *tr.v.* **-vealed, -veal•ing, -veals. 1.a.** To make known (something concealed or secret). **b.** To bring to view; show. **2.** To make known by supernatural or divine means. [ME *revelen* < OFr. *reveler* < Lat. *revēlāre* : *re-*, re- + *vēlāre*, to cover (< *vēlum*, veil).] — **re•veal′a•ble** *adj.* — **re•veal′er** *n.* — **re•veal′ment** *n.*

re•veal[2] (rĭ-vēl′) *n.* **1.a.** The part of the side of a window or door opening that is between the outer surface of a wall and the window or door frame. **b.** The whole side of such an opening; the jamb. **2.** The framework of a motor vehicle window. [< ME *revalen*, to lower < OFr. *revaler* : *re-*, re- + *avaler*, to lower (< *a val*, down : *a*, to < Lat. *ad*; see AD- + *val*, valley; see VALE[1]).]

re•veal•ing (rĭ-vē′lĭng) *adj.* Permitting an elucidating glimpse or a perception of something intimate or concealed.

re•veg•e•tate (rē-vĕj′ĭ-tāt′) *v.* **-tat•ed, -tat•ing, -tates.** — *tr.* To cause (eroded land, for example) to bear a new cover of vegetation. — *intr.* To bear a new cover of vegetation.

rev•eil•le (rĕv′ə-lē) *n.* **1.a.** The sounding of a bugle early in the morning to awaken and summon people in a camp or garrison. **b.** The first military formation of the day. **2.** A signal to get up out of bed. [Alteration of Fr. *réveillez*, second pers. pl. imper. of *réveiller*, to wake < OFr. *resveiller* : *re-*, re- + *esveiller*, to awake (< VLat. **exvigilāre* : Lat. *ex-*, ex- + Lat. *vigilāre*, to stay awake < *vigil*, awake; see **weg-***).]

rev•el (rĕv′əl) *intr.v.* **-eled, -el•ing, -els** also **-elled, -el•ling, -els. 1.** To take great pleasure or delight. **2.** To engage in uproarious festivities; make merry. — *n.* A boisterous festivity or celebration; merrymaking. Often used in the plural. [ME *revelen*, to carouse < OFr. *reveler*, to rebel, carouse < Lat. *rebellāre*, to rebel. See REBEL.] — **rev′el•ler, rev′el•er** *n.*

rev•e•la•tion (rĕv′ə-lā′shən) *n.* **1.a.** The act of revealing or disclosing. **b.** Something revealed, esp. a dramatic disclosure of something not previously known. **2.** *Theol.* A manifestation of divine will or truth. **3. Revelation.** *Bible.* See table at **Bible.** [ME *revelacion* < OFr. *revelation* < Lat. *revēlātiō*, *revēlātiōn-* < *revēlātus*, p.part. of *revēlāre*, to reveal. See REVEAL[1].]

rev•e•la•tor (rĕv′ə-lā′tər) *n.* One who reveals, esp. one who reveals divine will.

rev•e•la•to•ry (rĕv′ə-lə-tôr′ē, -tōr′ē, rĭ-vĕl′ə-) *adj.* Of, relating to, or containing a revelation.

ă pat	oi boy
ā pay	ou out
âr care	o͝o took
ä father	o͞o boot
ĕ pet	ŭ cut
ē be	ûr urge
ĭ pit	th thin
ī pie	*th* this
îr pier	hw which
ŏ pot	zh vision
ō toe	ə about, item
ô paw	

Stress marks:
′ (primary);
′ (secondary), as in
dictionary (dĭk′shə-nĕr′ē)

rev•el•ry (rĕv′əl-rē) *n., pl.* **-ries.** Boisterous merrymaking. —**rev′el•rous** (-rəs) *adj.*

rev•e•nant (rĕv′ə-nənt) *n.* **1.** One that returns after a lengthy absence. **2.** One who returns after death. [Fr. < pr.part. of *revenir*, to return < OFr. See REVENUE.]

re•venge (rĭ-vĕnj′) *tr.v.* **-venged, -veng•ing, -veng•es. 1.** To punish in return for (injury or insult). **2.** To seek or take vengeance for (someone or oneself); avenge. —*n.* **1.** The act of revenging injuries or wrongs; retaliation. **2.** Something done in vengeance; a retaliatory measure. **3.** A desire for revenge; vindictiveness. **4.** An opportunity to retaliate. [ME *revengen* < OFr. *revengier* : *re-*, re- + *vengier*, to take revenge (< Lat. *vindicāre*, to avenge < *vindex*, *vindic-*, avenger; see **deik-***).] —**re•veng′er** *n.*

re•venge•ful (rĭ-vĕnj′fəl) *adj.* Full of or given to revenge. —**re•venge′ful•ly** *adv.* —**re•venge′ful•ness** *n.*

rev•e•nue (rĕv′ə-no͞o, -nyo͞o) *n.* **1.** The income of a government from all sources appropriated for the payment of public expenses. **2.** Yield from property or investment; income. **3.** All the income from a particular source. **4.** A governmental department set up to collect public funds. [ME < OFr. < fem. p.part. of *revenir*, to return < Lat. *revenīre* : *re-*, re- + *venīre*, to come; see **g^{w}ā-***.]

revenue bond *n.* A bond issued by an agency commissioned to finance the building or improving of a public property, such as a bridge, the revenue from which will pay for the bond.

rev•e•nu•er (rĕv′ə-no͞o′ər, -nyo͞o′-) *n.* **1.** *Informal.* A government agent in charge of collecting revenue, esp. one responsible for halting the unlawful distilling or bootlegging of alcohol. **2.** *Naut.* A lightly armed motorboat used by revenuers.

revenue shar•ing (shâr′ĭng) *n.* Distribution of a portion of federal tax revenues to state and municipal governments. —**rev′e•nue-shar′ing** (rĕv′ə-no͞o-shâr′ĭng, -nyo͞o-) *adj.*

revenue stamp *n.* A stamp affixed to an item as proof that a government tax has been paid.

revenue tariff *n.* A tariff imposed chiefly to generate public revenue.

re•verb (rĭ-vûrb′) *Informal.* —*n.* **1.** A reverberative effect produced in recorded music by electronic means. **2.** A device used for producing this effect. —*intr. & tr.v.* **-verbed, -verb•ing, -verbs.** To reverberate or cause to reverberate.

re•ver•ber•ant (rĭ-vûr′bər-ənt) *adj.* **1.** Having a tendency to reverberate. **2.** Characterized by reverberation; resounding. —**re•ver′ber•ant•ly** *adv.*

re•ver•ber•ate (rĭ-vûr′bə-rāt′) *v.* **-at•ed, -at•ing, -ates.** —*intr.* **1.** To resound in or as if in a succession of echoes; reecho. **2.** To be repeatedly reflected, as sound waves, heat, or light. **3.** To be forced or driven back; recoil or rebound. —*tr.* **1.** To reecho (a sound). **2.** To reflect (heat or light) repeatedly. **3.** To drive or force back; repel. **4.** To treat (a metal, for example) in a reverberatory furnace. [Lat. *reverberāre*, *reverberāt-*, to repel : *re-*, re- + *verberāre*, to beat (< *verber*, whip; see **wer-[2]***).] —**re•ver′ber•a•tor** *n.*

re•ver•ber•a•tion (rĭ-vûr′bə-rā′shən) *n.* **1.a.** The act of reverberating. **b.** The condition of being reverberated. **2.a.** Something reverberated. **b.** An echolike force or effect; a repercussion.

re•ver•ber•a•tive (rĭ-vûr′bə-rā′tĭv, -bər-ə-) *adj.* **1.** Having the nature of reverberation. **2.** Tending to reverberate; reverberant. —**re•ver′ber•a•tive•ly** *adv.*

re•ver•ber•a•to•ry (rĭ-vûr′bər-ə-tôr′ē, -tōr′ē) *adj.* **1.** Produced or operating by reverberation, esp. deflection or diversion, as of flame or heat, onto material being treated. **2.** Of, relating to, or being a reverberatory. —*n., pl.* **-ies.** A reverberatory furnace.

reverberatory furnace *n.* A furnace or kiln in which the material is heated by a flame deflected downward from the roof.

re•vere[1] (rĭ-vîr′) *tr.v.* **-vered, -ver•ing, -veres.** To regard with awe, deference, and devotion. [Fr. *révérer* < OFr. *reverer* < Lat. *reverērī* : *re-*, re- + *verērī*, to respect; see **wer-[3]***.]

Syns: *revere, worship, venerate, adore, idolize.* These verbs all mean to regard with the deepest respect, deference, and esteem. *Revere* suggests awe coupled with profound honor: *"At least one third of the population . . . reveres every sort of holy man"* (Rudyard Kipling). *Worship* implies reverent love and homage rendered to God or a god. In a more general sense it connotes an often uncritical devotion: *"She had worshiped intellect"* (Charles Kingsley). *Venerate* connotes reverence accorded by virtue especially of dignity, character, or age: *"I venerate the memory of my grandfather"* (Horace Walpole). To *adore* is to worship with deep, often rapturous love: *a teacher adored by many students. Idolize* implies worship like that accorded an object of religious devotion: *He idolizes his wife.*

re•vere[2] (rĭ-vîr′, -vâr′) *n.* Var. of **revers.**

Re•vere (rĭ-vîr′). A city of E MA, a suburb of Boston on Massachusetts Bay. Pop. 42,786.

Revere, Paul. 1735–1818. Amer. silversmith and engraver noted for his Apr. 18, 1775, ride to warn of the British advance on Lexington and Concord.

rev•er•ence (rĕv′ər-əns) *n.* **1.** A feeling of profound awe and respect and often love; veneration. **2.** An act showing respect, esp. a bow or curtsy. **3.** The state of being revered. **4. Reverence.** Used as a form of address for certain members of the Christian clergy: *Your Reverence.* —*tr.v.* **-enced, -enc•ing, -enc•es.** To consider or treat with profound awe and respect; venerate. —**rev′er•enc•er** *n.*

rev•er•end (rĕv′ər-ənd) *adj.* **1.** Deserving reverence. **2.** Relating to or characteristic of the clergy; clerical. **3. Reverend.** Used as a title and form of address for certain clerics in many Christian churches. In formal usage, preceded by *the.* —*n. Informal.* A cleric or minister. [ME < OFr. < Lat. *reverendus*, gerundive of *reverērī*, to revere. See REVERE[1].]

rev•er•ent (rĕv′ər-ənt) *adj.* Marked by feeling, or expressing reverence. [ME < OFr. < Lat. *reverēns*, *reverent-*, pr.part. of *reverērī*, to revere. See REVERE[1].] —**rev′er•ent•ly** *adv.*

rev•er•en•tial (rĕv′ə-rĕn′shəl) *adj.* **1.** Expressing reverence; reverent. **2.** Inspiring reverence. —**rev′er•en′tial•ly** *adv.*

rev•er•ie (rĕv′ə-rē) *n.* **1.** A state of abstracted musing; daydreaming. **2.** A daydream. [ME, revelry < OFr. < *rever*, to dream, rave.]

re•vers also **re•vere** (rĭ-vîr′, -vâr′) *n., pl.* **revers** also **-veres** (-vîrz′, -vârz′). A part of a garment, such as a lapel, turned back to show the reverse side. [Fr. < OFr., reverse. See REVERSE.]

re•ver•sal (rĭ-vûr′səl) *n.* **1.a.** The act or an instance of reversing. **b.** The state of being reversed. **2.** A usu. adverse change in fortune. **3.** *Law.* The act or an instance of changing or setting aside a lower court's decision by a higher court.

re•verse (rĭ-vûrs′) *adj.* **1.a.** Turned backward in position, direction, or order. **b.** Having the back showing. **2.** Moving, acting, or organized in a manner contrary to the usual. **3.** Causing backward movement: *a reverse gear.* **4.** *Print.* Printed so that the normally colored part appears white against a colored or black background. —*n.* **1.** The opposite or contrary. **2.a.** The back or rear part. **b.** The side of a coin or medal that does not carry the principal design; the verso. **3.** A change to an opposite position, condition, or direction. **4.** A change in fortune from better to worse; a setback. **5.a.** A mechanism, such as a car gear, that is used to reverse movement. **b.** The position or operating condition of such a mechanism. **c.** Movement in an opposite direction. **6.** *Football.* An offensive play in which a back running in one direction executes a handoff to a back running in the opposite direction. —*v.* **-versed, -vers•ing, -vers•es.** —*tr.* **1.** To turn around to the opposite direction. **2.** To turn inside out or upside down. **3.** To exchange the positions of; transpose. **4.** *Law.* To revoke or annul (a decree, for example). **5.a.** To cause to adopt a contrary viewpoint. **b.** To change to the opposite. **6.** To cause (an engine or a mechanism) to function in reverse. —*intr.* **1.** To turn or move in the opposite direction. **2.** To reverse the action of an engine. —***idiom.*** **reverse (one's) field.** To turn and proceed in the opposite direction. [ME *revers* < OFr. < Lat. *reversus*, p.part. of *revertere*, to turn back. See REVERT.] —**re•verse′ly** *adv.* —**re•vers′er** *n.*

reverse discrimination *n.* Discrimination against a dominant group, esp. such discrimination resulting from policies established to correct discrimination against minority groups and women.

reverse dive *n.* A dive in which the diver leaps up facing the water and then rotates backwards.

reverse osmosis *n.* A method of producing pure water by forcing saline or waste water through a semipermeable membrane through which the salts or waste products cannot pass.

reverse transcriptase *n.* A polymerase that catalyzes the formation of DNA on an RNA template, found in oncogenic viruses containing RNA, esp. the retroviruses.

re•vers•i•ble (rĭ-vûr′sə-bəl) *adj.* **1.** That can be reversed, as: **a.** Finished so as to be usable on both sides. **b.** Wearable with either side turned outward. **2.** *Chem. & Phys.* Capable of successively assuming or producing either of two states. —*n.* A reversible fabric or garment. —**re•vers′i•bil′i•ty, re•vers′i•ble•ness** *n.* —**re•vers′i•bly** *adv.*

re•ver•sion (rĭ-vûr′zhən) *n.* **1.** A return to a former state, belief, or interest. **2.** A turning away or in the opposite direction; a reversal. **3.** *Genet.* A return to the normal phenotype, usu. by a second mutation. **4.** *Law.* **a.** The return of an estate to the grantor or to the grantor's heirs after the grant has expired. **b.** The estate thus returned. **c.** The right to succeed to an estate.

re•ver•sion•er (rĭ-vûr′zhə-nər) *n. Law.* A party entitled to receive an estate in reversion.

re•vert (rĭ-vûrt′) *intr.v.* **-vert•ed, -vert•ing, -verts. 1.** To return to a former condition, practice, subject, or belief. See Usage Note at **redundancy. 2.** *Law.* To return to the former owner or his or her heirs. Used of money or property. **3.** *Genet.* To undergo reversion. [ME *reverten* < OFr. *revertir* < VLat. **revertīre*, var. of Lat. *revertere* : *re-*, re- + *vertere*, to turn; see **wer-[2]***.] —**re•vert′er** *n.* —**re•vert′i•ble** *adj.* —**re•ver′tive** *adj.*

re•ver•tant (rĭ-vûr′tnt) *Genet.* —*adj.* Having reverted to the normal phenotype, usu. by a second mutation: *revertant cells.* —*n.* A revertant organism, cell, or strain.

re•vest (rē-vĕst′) *tr.v.* **-vest•ed, -vest•ing, -vests. 1.** To invest (someone) again with power or ownership; reinstate. **2.** To vest (power, for example) once again in a person or agency.

re•vet (rĭ-vĕt′) *v.* **-vet•ted, -vet•ting, -vets.** — *tr.* To retain (an embankment, for example) with a layer of concrete or other supporting material. — *intr.* To construct a revetment. [Fr. *revêtir* < OFr. *revestir*, to clothe again < Lat. *revestīre* : *re-*, re- + *vestīre*, to clothe (< *vestis*, garment; see **wes-**[2]*).]

re•vet•ment (rĭ-vĕt′mənt) *n.* **1.** A facing, as of masonry, used to support an embankment. **2.** A barricade against explosives.

re•view (rĭ-vyo͞o′) *v.* **-viewed, -view•ing, -views.** — *tr.* **1.** To look over, study, or examine again. **2.** To consider retrospectively; look back on. **3.** To examine critically. **4.** To write or give a critical report on (a new work, for example). **5.** *Law.* To reexamine (an action or a determination) judicially, esp. in a higher court, in order to correct possible errors. **6.** To subject to a formal inspection, esp. a military inspection. — *intr.* **1.** To go over or restudy material. **2.** To write critical reviews. — *n.* **1.** A reexamination or reconsideration. **2.** A retrospective view or survey. **3.a.** A restudying of subject matter. **b.** An exercise for use in restudying material. **4.** An inspection or examination for the purpose of evaluation. **5.a.** A report or an essay giving a critical estimate of a work or performance. **b.** A periodical devoted to current affairs, literature, or art. **6.a.** A formal military inspection. **b.** A formal military ceremony honoring a person or an occasion. **7.** *Law.* A judicial reexamination, esp. by a higher court, of an action or a determination. **8.** A revue. [Prob. < ME, inspection of military forces < OFr. *revue*, review < fem. p.part. of *reveeir*, to see again < Lat. *revidēre* : *re-*, re- + *vidēre*, to see; see **weid-***.] — **re•view′a•ble** *adj.*

re•view•er (rĭ-vyo͞o′ər) *n.* One who reviews, esp. one who writes critical reviews, as for a newspaper or magazine.

re•vile (rĭ-vīl′) *v.* **-viled, -vil•ing, -viles.** — *tr.* To assail with abusive language; vituperate. — *intr.* To use abusive language. [ME *revilen* < OFr. *reviler* : *re-*, re- + *vil*, vile; see VILE.] — **re•vile′ment** *n.* — **re•vil′er** *n.* — **re•vil′ing•ly** *adv.*

re•vis•al (rĭ-vī′zəl) *n.* The act or an instance of revising.

re•vise (rĭ-vīz′) *tr.v.* **-vised, -vis•ing, -vis•es. 1.** To prepare a newly edited version of (a text). **2.** To reconsider and change or modify: *I revised my opinion.* See Syns at **correct.** — *n.* (rē′vīz′, rĭ-vīz′). *Print.* A proof made from an earlier proof on which corrections have been made. [Lat. *revīsere*, to visit again, look at again : *re-*, re- + *vīsere*, freq. of *vidēre*, to see; see REVIEW.] — **re•vis′a•ble** *adj.* — **re•vis′er, re•vi′sor** *n.*

Re•vised Standard Version (rĭ-vīzd′) *n.* A revision of the American Standard Version of the Bible, completed in 1952 and further revised in 1991.

Revised Version *n.* A British and American revision of the King James Version of the Bible, completed in 1885.

re•vi•sion (rĭ-vĭzh′ən) *n.* **1.** The act or process of revising. **2.** A revised or new version. — **re•vi′sion•ar′y** *adj.*

re•vi•sion•ism (rĭ-vĭzh′ə-nĭz′əm) *n.* Advocacy of the revision of an accepted, usu. long-standing view, theory, or doctrine, esp. a revision of a political doctrine or a view concerning history. — **re•vi′sion•ist** *adj. & n.*

re•vis•it (rē-vĭz′ĭt) *tr.v.* **-it•ed, -it•ing, -its.** To visit again. — *n.* A second or repeated visit. — **re′vis•i•ta′tion** *n.*

re•vi•so•ry (rĭ-vī′zə-rē) *adj.* Of, relating to, effecting, or having the power of revision.

re•vi•tal•ize (rē-vīt′l-īz′) *tr.v.* **-ized, -iz•ing, -iz•es.** To impart new life or vigor to. — **re•vi′tal•i•za′tion** (-ĭ-zā′shən) *n.*

re•viv•al (rĭ-vī′vəl) *n.* **1.a.** The act or an instance of reviving. **b.** The condition of being revived. **2.** A restoration to use, acceptance, activity, or vigor after obscurity or quiescence. **3.** A new presentation of an old play, movie, opera, or similar work. **4.a.** A time of reawakened interest in religion. **b.** A meeting or series of meetings held to revive religious faith, typified by impassioned preaching and public testimony. **5.** *Law.* Renewal of validity or effect, as of a contract.

re•viv•al•ism (rĭ-vī′və-lĭz′əm) *n.* **1.** The spirit or activities characteristic of religious revivals. **2.** A desire or an inclination to revive what belongs to an earlier time.

re•viv•al•ist (rĭ-vī′və-lĭst) *n.* **1.** One who promotes or leads religious revivals. **2.** One who revives practices or ideas of an earlier time. — **re•viv′al•ist, re•viv′al•is′tic** *adj.*

re•vive (rĭ-vīv′) *v.* **-vived, -viv•ing, -vives.** — *tr.* **1.** To restore to life or consciousness; resuscitate. **2.** To impart new health, vigor, or spirit to. **3.** To restore to use, currency, activity, or notice. **4.** To restore the validity or effectiveness of. **5.** To renew in the mind; recall. **6.** To present (an old play, for example) again. — *intr.* **1.** To return to life or consciousness. **2.** To regain health, vigor, or spirit. **3.** To return to use, currency, or notice. **4.** To return to validity, effectiveness, or operative condition. [ME *reviven* < OFr. *revivre* < Lat. *revīvere*, to live again : *re-*, re- + *vīvere*, to live; see **gʷei-***.] — **re•viv′a•ble** *adj.* — **re•viv′er** *n.*

re•viv•i•fy (rē-vĭv′ə-fī′) *tr.v.* **-fied, -fy•ing, -fies.** To impart new life, energy, or spirit to. [Fr. *revivifier* < OFr., to come back to life < Lat. **revīvificāre*, to revivify : Lat. *re-*, re- + Lat. *vīvificāre*, to vivify; see VIVIFY.] — **re•viv′i•fi•ca′tion** (-fĭ-kā′shən) *n.*

rev•o•ca•ble (rĕv′ə-kə-bəl) also **re•vok•a•ble** (rĭ-vō′-) *adj.* That can be revoked: *a revocable order.*

rev•o•ca•tion (rĕv′ə-kā′shən) *n.* The act or an instance of revoking. [ME *revocacion* < OFr. < Lat. *revocātiō*, *revocātiōn-* < *revocātus*, p.part. of *revocāre*, to call back. See REVOKE.] — **rev′o•ca•to′ry** (rĕv′ə-kə-tôr′ē, -tōr′ē) *adj.*

re•voke (rĭ-vōk′) *v.* **-voked, -vok•ing, -vokes.** — *tr.* To void or annul by recalling, withdrawing, or reversing. — *intr. Games.* To fail to follow suit in cards when required and able to do so. [ME *revoken* < OFr. *revoquer* < Lat. *revocāre* : *re-*, re- + *vocāre*, to call; see **wekʷ-***.] — **re•vok′er** *n.*

re•volt (rĭ-vōlt′) *v.* **-volt•ed, -volt•ing, -volts.** — *intr.* **1.** To attempt to overthrow the authority of the state; rebel. **2.** To oppose or refuse to accept something. **3.a.** To feel disgust or repugnance. **b.** To turn away in revulsion or abhorrence. — *tr.* To fill with disgust or abhorrence; repel. See Syns at **disgust.** — *n.* **1.** An uprising, esp. against state authority; a rebellion. See Syns at **rebellion. 2.** An act of protest or rejection. **3.** The state of being in rebellion. [Fr. *revolter* < Ital. *rivoltare*, to turn round < VLat. **revolvitāre*, freq. of Lat. *revolvere*, to turn over. See REVOLVE.] — **re•volt′er** *n.*

revolver

re•volt•ing (rĭ-vōl′tĭng) *adj.* Causing abhorrence or disgust. — **re•volt′ing•ly** *adv.*

rev•o•lute (rĕv′ə-lo͞ot′) *adj. Bot.* Rolled backward from the tip or margins to the undersurface: *a revolute leaf.* [Lat. *revolūtus*, p.part. of *revolvere*, to roll back. See REVOLVE.]

rev•o•lu•tion (rĕv′ə-lo͞o′shən) *n.* **1.a.** Orbital motion about a point, esp. as distinguished from axial rotation. **b.** A turning or rotational motion about an axis. **c.** A single complete cycle of such orbital or axial motion. **2.** The overthrow and replacement of a government. See Syns at **rebellion. 3.** A sudden or momentous change in a situation. **4.** *Geol.* A time of major crustal deformation, when folds and faults are formed. [Ult. < LLat. *revolūtiō*, *revolūtiōn-* < Lat. *revolūtus*, p.part. of *revolvere*, to turn over. See REVOLVE.]

rev•o•lu•tion•ar•y (rĕv′ə-lo͞o′shə-nĕr′ē) *adj.* **1.a.** Often **Revolutionary.** Of, relating to, or being a revolution: *revolutionary war.* **b.** Bringing about or supporting a political or social revolution. **2.** Characterized by or resulting in radical change. — *n., pl.* **-ies. 1.** A militant in the struggle for revolution. **2.** A supporter of revolutionary principles. — **rev′o•lu′tion•ar′i•ly** *adv.* — **rev′o•lu′tion•ar′i•ness** *n.*

rev•o•lu•tion•ist (rĕv′ə-lo͞o′shə-nĭst) *n.* One who favors or is engaged in a revolution. — **rev′o•lu′tion•ist** *adj.*

rev•o•lu•tion•ize (rĕv′ə-lo͞o′shə-nīz′) *tr.v.* **-ized, -iz•ing, -iz•es. 1.** To bring about a radical change in. **2.** To subject to a political or social revolution. **3.** To fill with revolutionary principles. — **rev′o•lu′tion•iz′er** *n.*

re•volve (rĭ-vŏlv′) *v.* **-volved, -volv•ing, -volves.** — *intr.* **1.** To orbit a central point. **2.** To turn on an axis; rotate. **3.** To recur in cycles or periodically. **4.** To be held in the mind and considered in turn. **5.** To be centered. — *tr.* **1.** To cause to revolve. **2.** To ponder or reflect on. [ME *revolven*, to change direction < OFr. *revolver*, to reflect upon < Lat. *revolvere*, to turn over, roll back, reflect upon : *re-*, re- + *volvere*, to roll; see **wel-**[2]*.] — **re•volv′a•ble** *adj.*

revolving door

re•volv•er (rĭ-vŏl′vər) *n.* **1.** A pistol having a revolving cylinder with several cartridge chambers that may be fired in succession. **2.** One that revolves, as a part of a mechanism.

re•volv•ing (rĭ-vŏl′vĭng) *adj.* **1.** Tending to revolve or happen repeatedly. **2.** Available at regular intervals.

revolving credit *n.* Credit repeatedly available up to a specified amount as periodic repayments are made.

revolving door *n.* **1.** A door, as in the entrance of a building, usu. consisting of four rigid upright sections interconnected at right angles and rotating about a central upright pivot. **2.** *Informal.* An organization, an institution, or a place whose members or population remain only a short time. — **re•volv′ing-door′** (rĭ-vŏl′vĭng-dôr′, -dōr′) *adj.*

revolving fund *n.* A fund established for a certain purpose, such as making loans, with the stipulation that repayments to the fund may be used anew for the same purpose.

re•vue (rĭ-vyo͞o′) *n.* An often satirical musical show consisting of skits, songs, and dances. [Fr. < OFr., review. See REVIEW.]

re•vul•sion (rĭ-vŭl′shən) *n.* **1.** A sudden strong change or reaction in feeling, esp. a feeling of violent disgust or loathing. **2.** A withdrawing or turning away from something. [Lat. *revulsiō*, *revulsiōn-* < *revulsus*, p.part. of *revellere*, to tear back : *re-*, re- + *vellere*, to tear.] — **re•vul′sive** *adj.*

Rev. Ver. *abbr. Bible.* Revised Version.

re•ward (rĭ-wôrd′) *n.* **1.** Something given or received in recompense for worthy behavior or in retribution for evil acts. **2.** Money offered or given for a special service, such as the return of a lost article. See Syns at **bonus. 3.** A satisfying return or result; profit. **4.** *Psychol.* The return for performance of a desired behavior. — *tr.v.* **-ward•ed, -ward•ing, -wards. 1.** To give a reward to or for. **2.** To satisfy or gratify; recompense. [ME < AN < *rewarder*, to take notice of : *re-*, intensive pref. (< Lat.; see RE-) + *warder*, to guard, watch over (of Gmc. orig.; see **wer-**[3]*).] — **re•ward′a•ble** *adj.* — **re•ward′er** *n.*

re•ward•ing (rĭ-wôr′dĭng) *adj.* **1.** Offering or likely to offer

ă pat	oi boy
ā pay	ou out
âr care	o͝o took
ä father	o͞o boot
ĕ pet	ŭ cut
ē be	ûr urge
ĭ pit	th thin
ī pie	*th* this
îr pier	hw which
ŏ pot	zh vision
ō toe	ə about, item
ô paw	

Stress marks:
′ (primary);
′ (secondary), as in **dictionary** (dĭk′shə-nĕr′ē)

satisfaction or gratification. **2.** Affording profit; remunerative. **3.** Constituting a reward. — **re•ward′ing•ly** *adv.*

re•wind (rē-wīnd′) *tr.v.* **-wound** (-wound′), **-wind•ing, -winds. 1.** To wind again or anew. **2.** To reverse the winding of (recording tape or camera film). — *n.* (rē′wīnd′, rē-wīnd′). **1.** The act or process of rewinding. **2.** Something that rewinds or is rewound. **3.** A control mechanism for rewinding (tape or film). — **re•wind′er** *n.*

re•wire (rē-wīr′) *v.* **-wired, -wir•ing, -wires.** — *tr.* To provide with new wiring. — *intr.* To install new wiring.

re•word (rē-wûrd′) *tr.v.* **-word•ed, -word•ing, -words. 1.a.** To change the wording of. **b.** To express again in different words. **2.** To express again in the same words; repeat.

rhea
Gray rhea
Rhea americana

re•work (rē-wûrk′) *tr.v.* **-worked, -work•ing, -works. 1.** To work over again; revise. **2.** To subject to a repeated or new process. — *n.* (rē′wûrk′). Something reworked.

re•write (rē-rīt′) *v.* **-wrote** (-rōt′), **-writ•ten** (-rĭt′n), **-writ•ing, -writes.** — *tr.* **1.** To write again, esp. in a different or improved form; revise. **2.** To put (material submitted to a newspaper or magazine) in a form suitable for publishing. — *intr.* To make revisions in written material. — *n.* (rē′rīt′). **1.** The act or an instance of rewriting. **2.** Something rewritten. — **re•writ′er** *n.*

Reye's syndrome (rīz, rāz) *n.* An acute encephalopathy characterized by fever, vomiting, fatty infiltration of the liver, disorientation, and coma, occurring mainly in children and usu. following a viral infection, such as influenza. [After R.D.K. *Reye* (1912–78), Australian pediatrician.]

Rey•kja•vík (rā′kyə-vēk′, -vĭk′). The cap. of Iceland, in the SW part; traditionally founded in 874 and cap. since 1918. Pop. 88,745.

Rey•mont (rā′mŏnt′, -mônt′), **Wladyslaw Stanislaw.** 1867–1925. Polish writer who won the 1924 Nobel Prize for literature.

Rey•nard or **rey•nard** (rā′nərd, -närd′, rĕn′ərd) *n.* A fox. [ME *Renard, Reynard* < OFr. *Renart* and MDu. *Reynaert,* the name of the fox in the beast epic *Roman de Renart.*]

Reyn•olds (rĕn′əldz), Sir **Joshua.** 1723–92. British portrait painter whose subjects included the Prince of Wales (1783).

Rey•nolds•burg (rĕn′əldz-bûrg′). A city of central OH, a suburb of Columbus. Pop. 25,748.

Rey•no•sa (rā-nō′sə). A city of E Mexico on the Rio Grande ENE of Monterrey. Pop. 194,693.

re•zone (rē-zōn′) *tr.v.* **-zoned, -zon•ing, -zones.** To change the zoning classification of (a neighborhood or property, for example). — **re′zone′** *n.*

RF *abbr.* **1.** Radio frequency. **2.** Right field; right fielder.

rf. *abbr.* **1.** Reef. **2.** Refund.

R factor *n.* A genetic factor of bacteria that transmits resistance to antibiotics from one bacterium to another by conjugation. [R(ESISTANCE).]

rhesus monkey
Macaca mulatta

RFD also **R.F.D.** *abbr.* Rural free delivery.

Rh[1] (är′āch′) *adj.* Of or relating to the Rh factor.

Rh[2] The symbol for the element **rhodium.**

r.h. *abbr.* **1.** Relative humidity. **2.** Also **RH.** Right-hand.

rhab•dom (răb′dəm, -dŏm′) *n.* A transparent rod in the center of each ommatidium in the compound eye of an arthropod. [< Gk. *rhabdōma,* bundle of rods < Gk. *rhabdos,* rod. See RHABDOMANCY.]

rhab•do•man•cy (răb′də-măn′sē) *n.* Divination by means of a wand or rod, esp. for discovering underground water or ores. [LGk. *rhabdomanteia* : Gk. *rhabdos,* rod; see **wer-**[2]* + Gk. *-manteia,* -mancy.] — **rhab′do•man′cer** *n.*

rhab•do•my•o•ma (răb′dō-mī-ō′mə) *n., pl.* **-mas** or **-ma•ta** (-mə-tə). *Pathol.* A tumor in striated muscle fibers. [Gk. *rhabdos,* rod; see RHABDOMANCY + MYOMA.]

rhab•do•vi•rus (răb′də-vī′rəs) *n., pl.* **-rus•es.** Any of a group of RNA-containing plant and animal viruses, which includes the rabies virus. [Gk. *rhabdos,* rod; see **wer-**[2]* + VIRUS.]

Rhad•a•man•thine (răd′ə-măn′thĭn, -thīn′) *adj.* Strictly and uncompromisingly just. [< RHADAMANTHUS.]

Rhad•a•man•thus also **Rhad•a•man•thys** (răd′ə-măn′thəs) *n. Gk. Myth.* A son of Zeus and Europa who, in reward for his exemplary sense of justice, was made a judge of the underworld after his death. [Lat. < Gk. *Rhadamanthos.*]

Rhae•ti•a (rē′shē-ə, -shə). An ancient Roman province in present-day E Switzerland and W Austria. — **Rhae′tian** *adj.* & *n.*

Rhaetian Alps. A range of the central Alps primarily in E Switzerland rising to 4,051.6 m (13,284 ft).

Rhae•to-Ro•mance (rē′tō-rō-măns′) *n.* A group of three Romance dialects, including Romansch, spoken in southern Switzerland, northern Italy, and the Tyrol. [Lat. *Rhaetus,* of Rhaetia, a Roman province + ROMANCE.]

rhinoceros
Black rhinoceros
Diceros bicornis

rha•phe (rā′fē) *n.* Var. of **raphe.**

rhap•sod•ic (răp-sŏd′ĭk) also **rhap•sod•i•cal** (-ĭ-kəl) *adj.* **1.** Of, like, or characteristic of a rhapsody. **2.** Immoderately impassioned or enthusiastic. — **rhap•sod′i•cal•ly** *adv.*

rhap•so•dist (răp′sə-dĭst) *n.* **1.** One who uses extravagantly enthusiastic or impassioned language. **2.** One who recited epic and other poetry, esp. professionally, in ancient Greece.

rhap•so•dize (răp′sə-dīz′) *v.* **-dized, -diz•ing, -diz•es.** — *intr.* To express oneself in an immoderately enthusiastic manner. — *tr.* To recite (something) in the manner of a rhapsody.

rhap•so•dy (răp′sə-dē) *n., pl.* **-dies. 1.** Exalted or excessive enthusiasm in speech or writing. **2.** A literary work written in an impassioned or exalted style. **3.** A state of elated bliss; ecstasy. **4.** *Mus.* A composition of irregular form and often improvisatory character. **5.** An ancient Greek epic poem or a portion of one suitable for uninterrupted recitation. [Lat. *rhapsōdia,* section of an epic poem < Gk. *rhapsōidia* < *rhapsōidein,* to recite poems : *rhaptein, rhaps-,* to sew; see **wer-**[2]* + *ōidē,* song; see **wed-**[2]*.]

rhat•a•ny (răt′n-ē) *n., pl.* **-nies. 1.** Either of two South American shrubs *(Krameria lappacea* or *K. argentea)* having bilaterally symmetrical flowers, spiny globose fruits, and thick roots. **2.** The dried root of either of these plants, used as an astringent and in dental preparations, such as toothpaste. [Am. Sp. *ratania,* poss. < Quechua *ratana,* to thin, unite.]

rhe•a (rē′ə) *n.* Any of several flightless South American birds of the genus *Rhea,* resembling the ostrich but somewhat smaller and having three toes instead of two. [NLat. *Rhea,* genus name, prob. < Lat., the wife of Cronus. See RHEA.]

Rhe•a (rē′ə) *n.* **1.** *Gk. Myth.* The sister and wife of Cronus and the mother of Demeter, Hades, Hera, Hestia, Poseidon, and Zeus. **2.** *Astron.* A satellite of Saturn. [Lat. < Gk.]

Rhee (rē), **Syngman.** 1875–1965. South Korean politician who became president in 1948 and was forced into exile in 1960.

Rheims or **Reims** (rēmz, răNs). A city of NE France ENE of Paris; long the coronation site of French kings. Pop. 194,656.

Rhen•ish (rĕn′ĭsh) *adj.* Of or relating to the Rhine River or the lands bordering on it. — *n.* See **Rhine wine** 1. [Ult. < Lat. *Rhēnus,* the Rhine.]

rhe•ni•um (rē′nē-əm) *n. Symbol* **Re** A rare dense metallic element with a high melting point used for electrical contacts and with tungsten for high-temperature thermocouples. Atomic number 75; atomic weight 186.2; melting point 3,180°C; boiling point 5,627°C; specific gravity 21.02; valence 1, 2, 3, 4, 5, 6, 7. See table at **element.** [< Lat. *Rhēnus,* the Rhine.]

rheo– *pref.* Current; flow: *rheotaxis.* [< Gk. *rheos,* stream < *rhein,* to flow. See **sreu-***.]

rhe•ol•o•gy (rē-ŏl′ə-jē) *n.* The study of the deformation and flow of matter. — **rhe′o•log′i•cal** (rē′ə-lŏj′ĭ-kəl) *adj.* — **rhe′o•log′i•cal•ly** *adv.* — **rhe•ol′o•gist** *n.*

rhe•om•e•ter (rē-ŏm′ĭ-tər) *n.* An instrument for measuring the flow of viscous liquids, such as blood.

rhe•o•stat (rē′ə-stăt′) *n.* A continuously variable electrical resistor used to regulate current. — **rhe′o•stat′ic** *adj.*

rhe•o•tax•is (rē′ə-tăk′sĭs) *n.* Movement of an organism in response to a current of water or air. — **rhe′o•tac′tic** (-tăk′tĭk) *adj.*

rhe•sus (rē′səs) *n.* A rhesus monkey. [Lat. *Rhēsus,* a mythical king of Thrace < Gk. *Rhēsos.*]

Rhe•sus factor (rē′səs) *n.* Rh factor.

rhesus monkey *n.* A brownish monkey *(Macaca mulatta)* of India, used extensively in biological and medical research.

rhet. *abbr.* Rhetoric.

rhe•tor (rē′tôr′, -tər) *n.* **1.** A teacher of rhetoric. **2.** An orator. [ME *rether* < Lat. *rhētor* < Gk. *rhētōr.* See **wer-**[5]*.]

rhet•o•ric (rĕt′ər-ĭk) *n.* **1.a.** The art or study of using language effectively and persuasively. **b.** A treatise or book on this art. **2.** Skill in using language effectively and persuasively. **3.a.** A style of speaking or writing, esp. the language of a particular subject: *political rhetoric.* **b.** Language that is elaborate, pretentious, insincere, or intellectually vacuous: *His talk is mere rhetoric.* **4.** Verbal communication; discourse. [ME *rethorik* < OFr. *rethorique* < Lat. *rhētoricē, rhētorica* < Gk. *rhētorikē (tekhnē),* rhetorical (art), fem. of *rhētorikos,* rhetorical < *rhētōr, rhētor-,* rhetor. See RHETOR.]

rhe•tor•i•cal (rĭ-tôr′ĭ-kəl, -tŏr′-) *adj.* **1.** Of or relating to rhetoric. **2.** Characterized by overelaborate or bombastic rhetoric. — **rhe•tor′i•cal•ly** *adv.*

rhetorical question *n.* A question to which no answer is expected, often used for rhetorical effect.

rhet•o•ri•cian (rĕt′ə-rĭsh′ən) *n.* **1.** An expert in or teacher of rhetoric. **2.** An eloquent speaker or writer. **3.** A person given to verbal extravagance.

rheum (ro͞om) *n.* A watery or thin mucous discharge from the eyes or nose. [ME *reume* < OFr. < LLat. *rheuma* < Gk., a flowing, rheum. See **sreu-***.] — **rheum′y** *adj.*

rheu•mat•ic (ro͞o-măt′ĭk) *adj.* Of, relating to, or having rheumatism. — *n.* **1.** One who has rheumatism. **2. rheumatics.** *Informal.* Pains caused by rheumatism. [Ult. < Lat. *rheumaticus,* suffering from rheum < Gk. *rheumatikos* < *rheuma, rheumat-,* stream. See RHEUM.]

rheumatic fever *n.* A severe infectious disease occurring chiefly in children, marked by fever and painful inflammation of the joints and frequently causing permanent damage to the heart.

rheumatic heart disease *n.* Permanent damage to the heart valves caused esp. by repeated attacks of rheumatic fever.

rheu•ma•tism (ro͞o′mə-tĭz′əm) *n.* **1.** Any of several pathological conditions of the muscles, tendons, joints, bones, or nerves, characterized by discomfort and disability. **2.** Rheumatoid arthritis. [Lat. *rheumatismus*, rheum < Gk. *rheumatismos* < *rheumatizesthai*, to suffer from rheum < *rheuma*, *rheumat-*, rheum. See RHEUM.]

rheu•ma•toid (ro͞o′mə-toid′) also **rheu•ma•toi•dal** (ro͞o′-mə-toid′l) *adj.* **1.** Of or resembling rheumatism. **2.** Suffering from rheumatism. — **rheu′ma•toi′dal•ly** *adv.*

rheumatoid arthritis *n.* A chronic disease marked by stiffness and inflammation of the joints, weakness, loss of mobility, and deformity.

rheumatoid factor *n.* An immunoglobulin present in the blood serum of many individuals affected by rheumatoid arthritis, used as a means of diagnosing the disease.

rheu•ma•tol•o•gy (ro͞o′mə-tŏl′ə-jē) *n.* The medical science that deals with rheumatic diseases. — **rheu′ma•tol′o•gist** *n.*

Rh factor *n.* Any of several substances on the surface of red blood cells that induce a strong antigenic response in individuals lacking the substance. [< RH(ESUS MONKEY), from its being first detected in the blood of this animal.]

rhi•nal (rī′nəl) *adj.* Of or relating to the nose; nasal.

Rhine (rīn). A river of W Europe formed by the confluence of two tributaries in E Switzerland and flowing c. 1,319 km (820 mi) through Germany and the Netherlands to the North Sea.

Rhine•land (rīn′lănd′, -lənd). A region along the Rhine R. in W Germany; noted for its vineyards.

rhi•nen•ceph•a•lon (rī′nĕn-sĕf′ə-lŏn′, -lən) *n.*, *pl.* **-la** (-lə). The olfactory region of the brain, located in the cerebrum. — **rhi′nen•ce•phal′ic** (-sə-făl′ĭk) *adj.*

rhine•stone (rīn′stōn′) *n.* A colorless artificial gem of paste or glass, often with facets that sparkle in imitation of a diamond. [After the RHINE (transl. of Fr. *caillou du Rhin* : *caillou*, pebble + *du*, of the + *Rhin*, Rhine).] — **rhine′stoned′** *adj.*

Rhine wine *n.* **1.** Any of several dry white wines produced in the Rhine Valley. **2.** A similar light dry wine.

rhi•ni•tis (rī-nī′tĭs) *n.* Inflammation of the nasal mucous membranes.

rhi•no[1] (rī′nō) *n.*, *pl.* **-nos.** *Informal.* A rhinoceros.

rhi•no[2] (rī′nō) *n.*, *pl.* **rhino.** *Chiefly British.* Money; cash. [?]

rhino– or **rhin–** *pref.* Nose; nasal: *rhinitis.* [Gk. < *rhis*, *rhin-*, nose.]

rhi•noc•er•os (rī-nŏs′ər-əs) *n.*, *pl.* **rhinoceros** or **-os•es.** Any of several large thick-skinned herbivorous mammals of the family Rhinocerotidae of Africa and Asia, having one or two upright horns on the snout. [ME *rinoceros* < Lat. *rhīnocerōs* < Gk. *rhinokerōs* : *rhino-*, rhino- + *keras*, horn; see **ker-**[1]*.]

rhinoceros beetle *n.* Any of various large scarabaeid beetles of the genus *Dynastes* and related genera, characterized by horns on the head and thorax and found in tropical regions.

rhi•nol•o•gy (rī-nŏl′ə-jē) *n.* The anatomy, physiology, and pathology of the nose. — **rhi•nol′o•gist** *n.*

rhi•no•phar•yn•gi•tis (rī′nō-făr′ĭn-jī′tĭs) *n.* Inflammation of the nasal and pharyngeal mucous membranes.

rhi•no•plas•ty (rī′nō-plăs′tē, -nə-) *n.*, *pl.* **-ties.** Plastic surgery of the nose. — **rhi′no•plas′tic** *adj.*

rhi•nos•co•py (rī-nŏs′kə-pē) *n.*, *pl.* **-pies.** Examination of the nasal passages by means of a speculum or similar instrument.

rhi•no•vi•rus (rī′nō-vī′rəs) *n.*, *pl.* **-rus•es.** Any of a group of picornaviruses that are causative agents of disorders of the respiratory tract, such as the common cold.

rhi•zan•thous (rī-zăn′thəs) *adj. Bot.* Bearing flowers directly from the root.

rhizo– or **rhiz–** *pref.* Root: *rhizogenic.* [Greek < *rhiza*, root. See **wrād-***.]

rhi•zo•bi•um (rī-zō′bē-əm) *n.*, *pl.* **-bi•a** (-bē-ə). Any of various nitrogen-fixing bacteria of the genus *Rhizobium* that form nodules on leguminous plant roots, as of beans. [NLat. *Rhizobium*, genus name : RHIZO– + Gk. *bios*, life; see **g**[w]**ei-***.]

rhi•zo•ceph•a•lan (rī′zō-sĕf′ə-lən) *n.* Any of various small aquatic crustaceans of the order Rhizocephala that are parasitic on other crustaceans. [< NLat. *Rhizocephala*, order name : RHIZO– + Gk. *kephalē*, head; see CEPHALO–.] — **rhi′zo•ceph′a•lous** (-ləs) *adj.*

rhi•zo•gen•ic (rī′zō-jĕn′ĭk) also **rhi•zo•ge•net•ic** (-jə-nĕt′-ĭk) *adj. Bot.* Giving rise to or producing roots.

rhi•zoid (rī′zoid′) *n.* **1.** A slender rootlike filament by which mosses, liverworts, and fern gametophytes attach to the substratum and absorb nourishment. **2.** A rootlike extension of the thallus of a fungus. — **rhi′zoid′**, **rhi•zoi′dal** (-zoid′l) *adj.*

rhi•zome (rī′zōm′) *n.* A horizontal, usu. underground stem that often sends out roots and shoots from its nodes. [Gk. *rhizōma*, mass of roots < *rhizoun*, to cause to take root < *rhiza*, root. See **wrād-***.] — **rhi•zom′a•tous** (-zŏm′ə-təs, -zō′mə-) *adj.* — **rhi•zom′ic** *adj.*

rhi•zoph•a•gous (rī-zŏf′ə-gəs) *adj.* Feeding on roots.

rhi•zo•pod (rī′zō-pŏd′, -zə-) *n.* A protozoan of the phylum Rhizopoda, such as an amoeba, characteristically moving and taking in food by means of pseudopods. [< NLat. *Rhizopoda*, phylum name : RHIZO– + NLat. *-poda*, -pod.] — **rhi•zop′o•dan** (-zŏp′ə-dən) *adj. & n.* — **rhi•zop′o•dous** *adj.*

rhi•zo•pus (rī′zō-pəs, -zə-) *n.* Any of various rot-causing fungi of the genus *Rhizopus.* [NLat. *Rhizopus*, genus name : RHIZO– + Gk. *pous*, *pod-*, foot; see –POD.]

rhi•zo•sphere (rī′zə-sfîr′) *n.* The soil zone that surrounds and is influenced by the roots of plants.

rhi•zot•o•my (rī-zŏt′ə-mē) *n.*, *pl.* **-mies.** Surgical severance of spinal nerve roots to relieve pain or hypertension.

Rh-neg•a•tive (är′āch-nĕg′ə-tĭv) *adj.* Lacking an Rh factor.

rho (rō) *n.* The 17th letter of the Greek alphabet. [Gk. *rhō*, of Phoenician orig.; akin to Heb. *rēsh.*]

rhod– *pref.* Var. of **rhodo–**.

rho•da•mine (rō′də-mēn′) *n.* Any of several synthetic red to pink dyes having brilliant fluorescent qualities.

Rhode Island[1] (rōd). An island of RI at the entrance to Narragansett Bay.

Rhode Island[2] (rōd). A state of the NE U.S. on the Atlantic Ocean; admitted as one of the original Thirteen Colonies in 1790. Cap. Providence. Pop. 1,005,984. — **Rhode Is′land•er** *n.*

Rhode Island Red *n.* Any of an American breed of domestic fowls having dark reddish-brown feathers.

Rhodes (rōdz). An island of SE Greece in the Aegean Sea off SW Turkey; colonized by Dorians before 1000 B.C. The ancient city of **Rhodes**, on the NE end of the island, was founded c. 408 B.C. and was the site of the Colossus of Rhodes, one of the Seven Wonders of the World.

Rhodes, Cecil John. 1853–1902. British financier and colonizer who as prime minister of Cape Colony (1890–96) attempted to overthrow the Boer regime in the Transvaal.

Rho•de•sia (rō-dē′zhə). **1.** A region of S-central Africa S of Zaire and comprising modern-day Zambia and Zimbabwe. **2.** See **Zimbabwe**[2]. — **Rho•de′sian** *adj. & n.*

Rhodesian man *n.* A fossil human *(Homo rhodesiensis* or *Cyphanthropus rhodesiensis)* found in south-central Africa and having a large low skull with massive brow ridges and skeletal bones like those of modern human beings.

Rhodesian ridgeback (rĭj′băk′) *n.* Any of a breed of large dog developed in Africa and having short yellowish-tan hair that forms a ridge along the back.

Rhodesian ridgeback

Rhodes scholar *n.* A student who holds a scholarship established by the will of Cecil Rhodes for study at Oxford University for a period of two or three years. — **Rhodes scholarship** *n.*

rho•di•um (rō′dē-əm) *n. Symbol* **Rh** A hard durable metallic element that is used to form high-temperature alloys with platinum and produce a corrosion-resistant coating on other metals. Atomic number 45; atomic weight 102.905; melting point 1,966°C; boiling point 3,727°C; specific gravity 12.41; valence 2, 3, 4, 5, 6. See table at **element.** [Gk. *rhodo-*, rhodo- + –IUM.]

rhodo– or **rhod–** *pref.* Rose; rosy; red: *rhodochrosite; rhodolite.* [Gk. < *rhodon*, rose.]

rhododendron

rho•do•chro•site (rō′də-krō′sīt′) *n.* A mineral consisting mainly of manganese carbonate, $MnCO_3$, light pink to rose-red in color with a pearly or vitreous luster, used as a manganese ore. [Ger. *Rhodochrosit* < Gk. *rhodokhrōs*, rose-colored : *rhodo-*, rhodo- + *khrōs*, color.]

rho•do•den•dron (rō′də-dĕn′drən) *n.* Any of numerous usu. evergreen ornamental shrubs of the genus *Rhododendron* of the North Temperate Zone, having variously colored flower clusters. [Lat., oleander < Gk. : *rhodo-*, rhodo- + *dendron*, tree; see **deru-***.]

rho•do•lite (rōd′l-īt′) *n.* A rose-red or pink variety of garnet, a silicate mineral used as a gem.

rho•do•mon•tade (rŏd′ə-mŏn-tād′, -täd′, rō′də-) *n.* Var. of **rodomontade.**

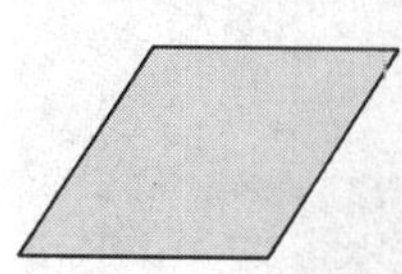

rhombus

rho•do•nite (rōd′n-īt′) *n.* A pink to rose-red mineral, essentially a glassy crystalline manganese silicate, $MnSiO_3$, used as an ornamental stone. [< Gk. *rhodon*, rose.]

Rhod•o•pe Mountains (rŏd′ə-pē, rŏ-dō′-). A range in the Balkan Peninsula of SE Europe extending SE from SW Bulgaria to NE Greece and rising to 2,926.8 m (9,596 ft).

rho•dop•sin (rō-dŏp′sĭn) *n.* The pigment sensitive to red light in the retinal rods of the eyes, consisting of opsin and retinene. [RHOD(O)– + Gk. *opsis*, sight; see –OPSIS + –IN.]

rho•do•ra (rō-dôr′ə, -dōr′ə) *n.* A deciduous shrub *(Rhododendron canadense)* of northeast North America having rose-purple two-lipped flowers that bloom before leaves appear. [Lat. *rhodōra*, var. of *rōdarum*, a plant, of Gaulish orig.]

rhom•ben•ceph•a•lon (rŏm′bĕn-sĕf′ə-lŏn′, -lən) *n.* The portion of the embryonic brain from which the metencephalon and myelencephalon develop.

rhom•bic (rŏm′bĭk) *adj.* **1.** Shaped like a rhombus. **2.** Orthorhombic.

rhombo– or **rhomb–** *pref.* Rhombus: *rhombohedron.* [Gk. < *rhombos.* See RHOMBUS.]

rhom•bo•he•dron (rŏm′bō-hē′drən) *n.*, *pl.* **-drons** or **-dra** (-drə). A prism with six faces, each a rhombus. — **rhom′bo•he′dral** (-drəl) *adj.*

rhom•boid (rŏm′boid′) *n.* A parallelogram with unequal adjacent sides. — *adj.* also **rhom•boi•dal** (-boid′l). Shaped like a rhombus or rhomboid.

rhom•bus (rŏm′bəs) *n.*, *pl.* **-bus•es** or **-bi** (-bī). An equilateral parallelogram. [LLat. < Lat., flatfish, magician's circle < Gk. *rhombos*, rhombus. See **wer-**[2]*.]

ă pat	oi boy
ā pay	ou out
âr care	o͝o took
ä father	o͞o boot
ĕ pet	ŭ cut
ē be	ûr urge
ĭ pit	th thin
ī pie	*th* this
îr pier	hw which
ŏ pot	zh vision
ō toe	ə about, item
ô paw	

Stress marks:
′ (primary);
′ (secondary), as in
dictionary (dĭk′shə-nĕr′ē)

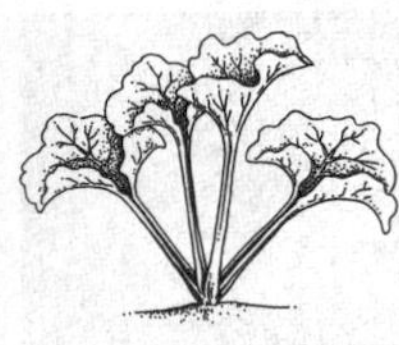
rhubarb
Rheum rhubarbarum

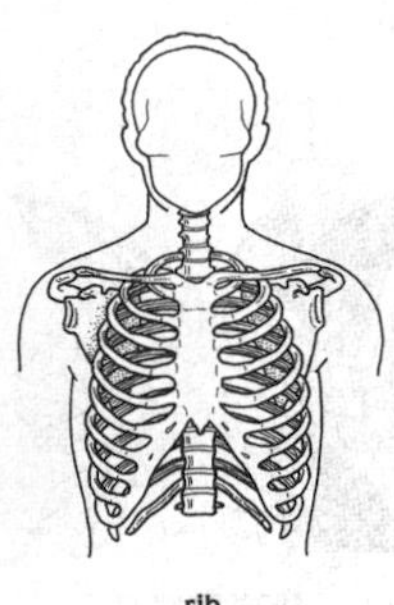
rib

Richard the Lion-Hearted
Statue near the Houses of Parliament, London, England

rhon•chus (rŏng′kəs) *n.*, *pl.* **-chi** (-kī). A coarse rattling sound somewhat like snoring, usu. caused by secretion in a bronchial tube. [Lat., a snoring < Gk. *rhonkhos, var. of *rhenkos*, *rhenkhos* < *rhenkein*, to snore.] — **rhon′chal** (-kəl), **rhon′chi•al** (-kē-əl) *adj.*

Rhon•dda (rŏn′də, hrŏn′thä). A municipal borough of S Wales NW of Cardiff. Pop. 81,700.

Rhone or **Rhône** (rōn). A river rising in S-central Switzerland and flowing c. 813 km (505 mi) to E France, where it joins the Saône R. and continues to the Mediterranean Sea.

rhp or **r.h.p.** *abbr.* Rated horsepower.

Rh-pos•i•tive (är′āch-pŏz′ĭ-tĭv) *adj.* Containing an Rh factor.

rhu•barb (ro͞o′bärb′) *n.* **1.** Any of several plants of the genus *Rheum*, esp. *R. rhubarbarum*, having edible green or reddish leafstalks. **2.** The bitter-tasting dried rhizome and roots of *Rheum palmatum* or *R. officinale* of eastern Asia, used as a laxative. **3.** *Informal.* A quarrel, fight, or heated discussion. [ME *rubarbe* < OFr. < LLat. *reubarbarum*, prob. alteration (influenced by Gk. *rhēon*) of *rhabarbarum* : *rha*, rhubarb (< Gk., perh. < *Rha*, the Volga River) + Lat. *barbarum*, neut. of *barbarus*, barbarian, foreign; see BARBAROUS.]

rhumb (rŭm, rŭmb) *n. Naut.* **1.** A rhumb line. **2.** One of the points of the compass. [Poss. < Sp. or Port. *rumbo*, course, direction, ult. < Lat. *rhombus*, rhombus. See RHOMBUS.]

rhum•ba (rŭm′bə, ro͝om′-, ro͞om′-) *n.* Var. of **rumba.**

rhumb line *n. Naut.* The path of a ship that maintains a fixed compass direction, shown on a map as a line crossing all meridians at the same angle.

rhyme also **rime** (rīm) —*n.* **1.** Correspondence of terminal sounds of words or of lines of verse. **2.a.** A poem or verse having a regular correspondence of sounds, esp. at the ends of lines. **b.** Poetry or verse of this kind. **3.** A word that corresponds with another in terminal sound, as *behold* and *cold*. —*v.* **rhymed, rhym•ing, rhymes** also **rimed, rim•ing, rimes.** —*intr.* **1.** To form a rhyme. **2.** To compose rhymes or verse. **3.** To make use of rhymes in composing verse. —*tr.* **1.** To put into rhyme or compose with rhymes. **2.** To use (a word or words) as a rhyme. [Alteration (influenced by RHYTHM) of ME *rime* < OFr., of Gmc. orig. See **ar-*.**]

rhym•er also **rim•er** (rī′mər) *n.* One who composes rhymes.

rhyme royal *n.* **1.** A form of verse having stanzas with seven lines in iambic pentameter rhyming *ababbcc*. **2.** One of these stanzas.

rhyme scheme *n.* The arrangement of rhymes in a poem or stanza.

rhyme•ster also **rime•ster** (rīm′stər) *n.* **1.** One who composes light verse. **2.** A minor or inferior poet.

rhy•ming slang (rī′mĭng) *n.* Slang in which a word is replaced by a word or phrase that rhymes with it, as *kiss* by *hit or miss*.

rhyn•cho•ce•pha•lian (rĭng′kō-sə-fāl′yən) *adj.* Of or belonging to the Rhynchocephalia, an order of mostly extinct lizardlike reptiles. [< NLat. *Rhynchocephalia*, order name : Gk. *rhunkhos*, beak + Gk. *kephalē*, head; see CEPHALIC.]

rhy•o•lite (rī′ə-līt′) *n.* A fine-grained extrusive volcanic rock, similar to granite in composition and usu. exhibiting flow lines. [< Gk. *rhuax*, stream (< *rhein*, to flow; see **sreu-***).]

Rhys (rēs), **Jean.** 1894–1979. West Indian-born British writer whose novels include *Wide Sargasso Sea* (1966).

rhythm (rĭth′əm) *n.* **1.** Movement or variation characterized by the regular recurrence or alternation of different quantities or conditions. **2.** The patterned recurring alternations of contrasting elements of sound or speech. **3.** *Mus.* **a.** A regular pattern formed by a series of notes of differing duration and stress. **b.** A specific kind of such a pattern: *a waltz rhythm*. **c.** A group of instruments supplying the rhythm in a band. **4.a.** The pattern or flow of sound created by the arrangement of stressed and unstressed syllables in accentual verse or of long and short syllables in quantitative verse. **b.** The similar but less formal sequence of sounds in prose. **c.** A specific kind of metrical pattern or flow: *iambic rhythm*. **5.a.** The sense of temporal development created in a work of literature or a film by the arrangement of formal elements such as the length of scenes, the nature and amount of dialogue, or the repetition of motifs. **b.** A regular or harmonious pattern created by lines, forms, and colors in painting, sculpture, and other visual arts. **6.** The pattern of development produced in a literary or dramatic work by repetition of elements such as words, phrases, incidents, themes, images, and symbols. **7.** Procedure or routine characterized by regularly recurring elements, activities, or factors. [Lat. *rhythmus* < Gk. *rhuthmos*. See **sreu-*.**]

rhythm and blues *pl.n.* *(used with a sing. or pl. v.) Mus.* A kind of music developed by Black Americans that combines blues and jazz, characterized by a strong backbeat and repeated variations on syncopated instrumental phrases.

rhyth•mic (rĭth′mĭk) also **rhyth•mi•cal** (-mĭ-kəl) *adj.* Of, relating to, or having rhythm; recurring with measured regularity. —**rhyth′mi•cal•ly** *adv.*

rhyth•mics (rĭth′mĭks) *n.* *(used with a sing. v.) Mus.* The study of rhythm.

rhyth•mist (rĭth′mĭst) *n.* **1.** One who is an expert in or has a keen sense of rhythm. **2.** *Mus.* One who studies or produces rhythm.

rhythm method *n.* A birth-control method dependent on abstinence during the period of ovulation

RI or **R.I.** *abbr.* Rhode Island.

ri•al[1] (rē-ôl′, -äl′) *n.* See table at **currency.** [Pers. < Ar. *riyāl* < Sp. *real*. See REAL[2].]

ri•al[2] (rē-ôl′, -äl′) *n.* Var. of **riyal.**

ri•al•to (rē-äl′tō, rā-äl′-) *n.*, *pl.* **-tos. 1.** A theatrical district. **2.** A marketplace. [After *Rialto*, an island of Venice where a market was situated.]

Ri•al•to (rē-äl′tō). A city of S CA, a suburb of San Bernardino. Pop. 72,388.

ri•a•ta also **re•a•ta** (rē-ä′tə) *n.* A lariat; a lasso. [Sp. *reata*, lasso, lariat. See LARIAT.]

Ri•au Archipelago (rē′ou). An island group of W Indonesia off the SE end of the Malay Peninsula.

rib (rĭb) *n.* **1.** *Anat.* **a.** One of a series of long curved bones occurring in 12 pairs in human beings and extending from the spine to or toward the sternum. **b.** A similar bone in most vertebrates. **2.** A part or piece similar to a rib and serving to shape or support. **3.** A cut of meat enclosing one or more rib bones. **4.** *Naut.* One of many curved members attached to a boat or ship's keel and forming the framework of the hull. **5.** One of many transverse pieces that provide an airplane wing with shape and strength. **6.** *Archit.* **a.** An arch or a projecting arched member of a vault. **b.** One of the curved pieces of an arch. **7.** A raised ridge or wale in knitted material or in cloth. **8.** *Bot.* The main vein or any of the prominent veins of a leaf or other plant organ. **9.** *Slang.* A teasing remark or action; a joke. —*tr.v.* **ribbed, rib•bing, ribs. 1.** To shape, support, or provide with a rib or ribs. **2.** To make with ridges or raised markings. **3.** *Informal.* To tease or make fun of. [ME < OE *ribb*.]

rib•ald (rĭb′əld, rī′bôld′) *adj.* Characterized by or indulging in vulgar, lewd humor. —*n.* A vulgar, lewdly funny person. [< ME *ribaud*, ribald person < OFr. < *riber*, to be wanton, of Gmc. orig. See **wer-**[2]***.**]

rib•ald•ry (rĭb′əl-drē, rī′bə-) *n.*, *pl.* **-ries.** Vulgar, lewdly humorous language or joking or an instance of it.

rib•and (rĭb′ənd) *n.* A ribbon, esp. one used as a decoration. [ME, var. of *riban*. See RIBBON.]

rib•band (rĭb′ănd, -ənd, -ən) *n. Naut.* A length of flexible wood or metal used to hold the ribs of a ship in place while the exterior planking or plating is applied. [RIB + BAND[1].]

rib•bing (rĭb′ĭng) *n.* **1.** Ribs considered as a group. **2.** An arrangement of ribs, as in a boat. **3.** *Informal.* The act or an instance of joking or teasing.

rib•bon (rĭb′ən) *n.* **1.** A narrow strip or band of fine fabric, such as satin, finished at the edges and used for trimming, tying, or finishing. **2.a.** Something, such as a tape measure, that resembles a ribbon. **b.** A long thin strip. **3. ribbons.** Tattered or ragged strips: *a dress torn to ribbons*. **4.** An inked strip of cloth used for making an impression, as in a typewriter. **5.a.** A band of colored cloth signifying membership in an order or the award of a prize. **b.** A strip of colored cloth worn on the left breast of a uniform to indicate the award of a medal or decoration. **6. ribbons.** *Informal.* Reins for driving horses. **7.** See **ledger board** 2. —*tr.v.* **-boned, -bon•ing, -bons. 1.** To decorate or tie with ribbons. **2.** To tear into ribbons or shreds. [ME *ribban*, *riban* < OFr. *ruban*, prob. of Gmc. orig. See **bhendh-*.**] —**rib′bon•y** *adj.*

rib•bon•fish (rĭb′ən-fĭsh′) *n.*, *pl.* **ribbonfish** or **-fish•es.** Any of several marine fishes, chiefly of the genus *Trachipterus*, having long, narrow, compressed bodies.

ribbon worm *n.* See **nemertean.**

rib cage *n.* The enclosing structure formed by the ribs and the bones to which they are attached.

Ri•bei•rão Prê•to (rē′bā-rouN′ prĕ′to͞o). A city of SE Brazil NNW of São Paulo. Pop. 300,828.

rib•grass (rĭb′grăs′) *n.* A weedy Eurasian plant *(Plantago lanceolata)* having ribbed lance-shaped leaves.

ri•bo•fla•vin (rī′bō-flā′vĭn, -bə-) *n.* An orange-yellow crystalline compound, $C_{17}H_{20}N_4O_6$, the principal growth-promoting factor in the vitamin B complex, naturally occurring in milk, leafy vegetables, fresh meat, and egg yolks. [RIBO(SE) + FLAVIN.]

ri•bo•nu•cle•ase (rī′bō-no͞o′klē-ās′, -āz′, -nyo͞o′-) *n.* Any of various enzymes that break down RNA.

ri•bo•nu•cle•ic acid (rī′bō-no͞o-klē′ĭk, -klā′-, -nyo͞o-) *n.* See **RNA.** [RIBO(SE) + NUCLEIC ACID.]

ri•bo•nu•cle•o•pro•tein (rī′bō-no͞o′klē-ō-prō′tēn, -tē-ĭn, -nyo͞o′-) *n.* A nucleoprotein that contains RNA.

ri•bo•nu•cle•o•side (rī′bō-no͞o′klē-ə-sīd′, -nyo͞o′-) *n.* A nucleoside that contains ribose as its sugar component.

ri•bo•nu•cle•o•tide (rī′bō-no͞oklē-ə-tīd′, -nyo͞o′-) *n.* A nucleotide that contains ribose as its sugar and is an immediate component of RNA.

ri•bose (rī′bōs′) *n.* A pentose sugar, $C_5H_{10}O_5$, occurring as a component of riboflavin, nucleotides, and nucleic acids. [Ger., alteration of E. *arabinuse*, a kind of sugar : (GUM) ARAB(IC) + -IN + -OSE[2].]

ribosomal RNA *n.* The RNA that is a permanent structural part of a ribosome.

ri•bo•some (rī′bə-sōm′) *n.* A minute round particle composed of RNA and protein found in the cytoplasm of living cells and active in the synthesis of proteins. [RIBO(SE) + -SOME[3].] — **ri•bo•so′mal** (-sō′məl) *adj.*
rib•wort (rĭb′wûrt′, -wôrt′) *n.* See **plantain[1]**.
Ri•car•do (rĭ-kär′dō), **David.** 1772–1823. British economist who wrote *Principles of Political Economy* (1817).
rice (rīs) *n.* **1.** A cereal grass *(Oryza sativa)* that is cultivated extensively in warm climates and is a staple food throughout the world. **2.** The starchy edible seed of this plant. — *tr.v.* **riced, ric•ing, ric•es.** To sieve (food) to the consistency of rice. [ME < OFr. *ris* < OItal. *riso* < Lat. *oryza* < Gk. *oruza*, of Indo-Iran. orig.]
Rice (rīs), **Elmer Leopold.** 1892–1967. Amer. playwright whose works include *The Adding Machine* (1923).
rice•bird (rīs′bûrd′) *n.* **1.** *Chiefly Southern U.S.* See **bobolink. 2.** Any of various birds that frequent rice fields.
rice paper *n.* A thin paper made chiefly from the pith of the Chinese shrub or small tree *Tetrapanax papyriferus*.
ric•er (rī′sər) *n.* A kitchen utensil used for ricing soft foods by extrusion through small holes.
rich (rĭch) *adj.* **rich•er, rich•est. 1.** Possessing great material wealth. **2.** Having great worth or value: *a rich harvest.* **3.** Magnificent; sumptuous. **4.a.** Having an abundant supply: *rich in ideas.* **b.** Abounding, esp. in natural resources. **5.** Meaningful and significant. **6.** Very productive and therefore financially profitable. **7.a.** Containing a large amount of choice ingredients, such as butter, sugar, or eggs, and therefore unusually heavy or sweet. **b.** Having or exuding a strong or pungent aroma. **8.a.** Pleasantly full and mellow: *a rich bass voice.* **b.** Warm and strong in color. **9.** Containing a large proportion of fuel to air. **10.** *Informal.* Highly amusing. — *n.* Wealthy people considered as a group. [ME *riche* < OFr. (of Gmc. orig.) and < OE *rīce*, strong, powerful; see **reg-*.**] — **rich′ly** *adv.* — **rich′ness** *n.*
Rich•ard I (rĭch′ərd). "the Lion-Hearted" or "Coeur de Lion." 1157–99. King of England (1189–99) who was a leader of the Third Crusade (1190–92).
Richard II. 1367–1400. King of England (1377–99) who quelled the Peasants' Revolt in 1381.
Richard III. 1452–85. King of England (1483–85) who claimed the throne after imprisoning the sons of his deceased brother Edward IV. Richard's death at the Battle of Bosworth Field brought an end to the Wars of the Roses.
Richard Roe (rō) *n.* A name used in legal proceedings to designate a fictitious or unidentified man.
Rich•ards (rĭch′ərdz), **I(vor) A(rmstrong).** 1893–1979. British critic who helped Charles Ogden develop Basic English.
Rich•ard•son (rĭch′ərd-sən). A city of NE TX, a suburb of Dallas. Pop. 74,840.
Richardson, Henry Hobson. 1838–86. Amer. architect whose designs include Trinity Church in Boston (1872–77).
Richardson, Samuel. 1689–1761. English writer whose epistolary novels include *Pamela* (1740).
Ri•che•lieu (rĭsh′ə-lo͞o′). A river of S Quebec, Canada, flowing c. 121 km (75 mi) to the St. Lawrence R.
Ri•che•lieu (rĭsh′ə-lo͞o′, rē-shə-lyœ′), Duc de. Armand Jean du Plessis. 1585–1642. French prelate and politician who was chief minister of Louis XIII.
rich•en (rĭch′ən) *tr.v.* **-ened, -en•ing, -ens.** To make rich.
rich•es (rĭch′ĭz) *pl.n.* **1.** Abundant wealth. **2.** Valuable or precious possessions. [ME *richesse*, wealth < OFr. < *riche*, wealthy. See RICH.]
Rich•field (rĭch′fēld′). A city of SE MN, a suburb of Minneapolis. Pop. 35,710.
Rich•land (rĭch′lənd). A city of SE WA on the Columbia R. WNW of Walla Walla; developed 1943–45 to house employees of the nearby Hanford Atomic Works. Pop. 32,315.
Rich•ler (rĭch′lər), **Mordecai.** b. 1931. Canadian writer whose novels include *The Apprenticeship of Duddy Kravitz* (1959).
Rich•mond (rĭch′mənd). **1.** A community of SW British Columbia, Canada, a suburb of Vancouver on the Strait of Georgia. Pop. 96,154. **2.** A city of W CA on an inlet of San Francisco Bay NNW of Oakland. Pop. 87,425. **3.** A city of E IN E of Indianapolis; settled by Quakers in 1806. Pop. 38,705. **4.** A city of E-central KY SSE of Lexington. Pop. 21,155. **5.** The cap. of VA, in the E-central part on the James R.; settled in the 17th cent. and the cap. of the Confederacy during the Civil War. Pop. 203,056. **6.** See **Staten Island.**
Richmond High•lands (hī′ləndz). A community of W-central WA, a suburb of Seattle. Pop. 26,037.
Richmond Hill. A city of SE Ontario, Canada, N of Toronto. Pop. 37,778.
Rich•ter (rĭk′tər), **Burton.** b. 1931. Amer. physicist who shared a 1976 Nobel Prize.
Rich•ter scale (rĭk′tər) *n.* A logarithmic scale ranging from 1 to 10, used to express the total amount of energy released by an earthquake; the largest recorded quake measured 8.9. [After Charles F. *Richter* (1900–85), Amer. seismologist.]
ri•cin (rī′sĭn, rĭs′ĭn) *n.* A poisonous protein extracted from the castor bean and used as a biochemical reagent. [< Lat. *ricinus*, castor-oil plant.]
ric•in•o•le•ic acid (rĭs′ĭn-ō-lē′ĭk) *n.* An unsaturated fatty acid, $C_{18}H_{34}O_3$, prepared from castor oil and used in making soaps and in textile finishing. [< Lat. *ricinus*, castor-oil plant.]
rick (rĭk) *n.* A stack of hay, straw, or similar material, esp. when covered or thatched for protection from the weather. — *tr.v.* **ricked, rick•ing, ricks.** To pile into ricks. [ME *reke* < OE *hrēac*.]
Rick•en•back•er (rĭk′ĭn-băk′ər), **Edward ("Eddie") Vernon.** 1890–1973. Amer. aviator who was a highly decorated combat pilot in World War I.
rick•ets (rĭk′ĭts) *n. (used with a sing. or pl. v.)* A deficiency disease resulting from a lack of vitamin D and insufficient exposure to sunlight, characterized by defective bone growth and occurring chiefly in children. [?]
rick•ett•si•a (rĭ-kĕt′sē-ə) *n., pl.* **-si•ae** (-sē-ē′). Any of various bacteria of the genus *Rickettsia*, carried as parasites by many ticks, fleas, and lice and causing diseases such as typhus, scrub typhus, and Rocky Mountain spotted fever in human beings. [NLat. *Rickettsia*, genus name, after Howard T. *Ricketts* (1871–1910), Amer. pathologist.] — **rick•ett′si•al** *adj.*
rick•et•y (rĭk′ĭ-tē) *adj.* **-i•er, -i•est. 1.** Likely to break or fall apart; shaky. **2.** Feeble with age; infirm. **3.** Of, having, or resembling rickets. [< RICKETS.] — **rick′et•i•ness** *n.*
rick•ey (rĭk′ē) *n., pl.* **-eys.** A drink of soda water, lime or lemon juice, sugar, and usu. gin. [Prob. < the name *Rickey*.]
Rick•o•ver (rĭk′ō′vər), **Hyman George.** 1900–86. Amer. admiral who advocated the development of nuclear-powered naval craft.
rick•rack (rĭk′răk′) *n.* A flat narrow braid woven in zigzag form, used to trim clothes or curtains. [Redup. of RACK[1].]
rick•sha or **rick•shaw** (rĭk′shô) *n.* A jinriksha.
RICO *abbr.* Racketeer Influenced and Corrupt Organizations Act of 1970.
ric•o•chet (rĭk′ə-shā′, rĭk′ə-shā′) *intr.v.* **-cheted** (-shād′), **-chet•ing** (-shā′ĭng), **-chets** (-shāz′). To rebound at least once from a surface. — *n.* The act or an instance of ricocheting. [Fr. < OFr., give-and-take.]
ri•cot•ta (rĭ-kŏt′ə, rē-kôt′tä) *n.* **1.** A soft Italian cheese that resembles cottage cheese. **2.** A similar soft cheese made in the United States. [Ital. < Lat. *recocta*, fem. p.part. of *recoquere*, to cook again : *re-*, re- + *coquere*, to cook; see **pekʷ-*.**]
ric•tus (rĭk′təs) *n., pl.* **rictus** or **-tus•es. 1.** The expanse of an open mouth, a bird's beak, or a similar structure. **2.** A gaping grimace. [Lat. < p.part. of *ringī*, to gape.] — **ric′tal** *adj.*
rid (rĭd) *tr.v.* **rid** or **rid•ded, rid•ding, rids.** To free from: *rid himself of all worry.* [ME *ridden* < ON *rydhja*, to clear land < *hrjōdha*, to strip, clear.] — **rid′der** *n.*
rid•dance (rĭd′ns) *n.* **1.** A deliverance from or removal of something unwanted or undesirable. **2.** The act of ridding.
rid•den (rĭd′n) *v.* P.part. of **ride.** — *adj.* Dominated, harassed, or obsessed by. Often used in combination: *disease-ridden.*
rid•dle[1] (rĭd′l) *tr.v.* **-dled, -dling, -dles. 1.** To pierce with numerous holes; perforate. **2.** To spread throughout. **3.** To put (gravel, for example) through a coarse sieve. — *n.* A coarse sieve. [ME *riddlen*, to sift < *riddil*, sieve, alteration of OE *hriddel*. See **krei-*.**] — **rid′dler** *n.*
rid•dle[2] (rĭd′l) *n.* **1.** A question or statement requiring thought to answer or understand; a conundrum. **2.** One that is perplexing; an enigma. — *v.* **-dled, -dling, -dles.** — *tr.* To solve or explain. — *intr.* **1.** To propound or solve riddles. **2.** To speak in riddles. [ME *redels* < OE *rǣdels*. See **ar-*.**] — **rid′dler** *n.*
ride (rīd) *v.* **rode** (rōd), **rid•den** (rĭd′n), **rid•ing, rides.** — *intr.* **1.** To be carried or conveyed, as in a vehicle or on horseback. **2.** To travel over a surface. **3.** To move by way of an intangible force or impetus; move as if on water. **4.** *Naut.* To lie at anchor. **5.** To seem to float. **6.** To be sustained or supported on a pivot, an axle, or another point. **7.** To be contingent; depend. **8.** To continue without interference: *Let matters ride.* **9.** To work or move from the proper place, esp. on the body: *pants that ride up.* — *tr.* **1.** To sit on and move in a given direction. **2.** To travel over, along, or through. **3.** To be supported or carried on. **4.** To take part in or do by riding: *rode his last race.* **5.** To cause to ride, esp. to cause to be carried. **6.** *Informal.* **a.** To tease or ridicule. **b.** To harass with carping and criticism. **7.** To keep partially engaged by slightly depressing a pedal with the foot. — *n.* **1.** The act or an instance of riding, as in a vehicle or on an animal. **2.** A path made for riding on horseback, esp. through woodlands. **3.** A device that one rides for pleasure or excitement. **4.** A means of transportation. — ***phrasal verb.*** **ride out.** To survive or outlast. — ***idioms.*** **ride for a fall.** To court danger or disaster. **ride herd on.** To keep watch or control over. **ride high.** To experience success. **ride roughshod over.** To act without regard for the feelings, opinions, or welfare of others. **ride shotgun. 1.** To guard a person or thing while in transit. **2.** *Slang.* To ride in the front passenger seat of a car or truck. **take for a ride.** *Slang.* **1.** To deceive or swindle. **2.** To transport to a place and kill. [ME *riden* < OE *rīdan*. See **reidh-*.**]
Ride (rīd), **Sally.** b. 1951. Amer. astronaut who in 1983 became the first U.S. woman to enter outer space.

Richard III
Portrait by an unknown artist

Duc de Richelieu
1636 portrait by Philippe de Champaigne (1602–1674)

Sally Ride
Photographed in 1983

ă pat	oi boy
ā pay	ou out
âr care	o͝o took
ä father	o͞o boot
ĕ pet	ŭ cut
ē be	ûr urge
ĭ pit	th thin
ī pie	*th* this
îr pier	hw which
ŏ pot	zh vision
ō toe	ə about, item
ô paw	

Stress marks:
′ (primary);
′ (secondary), as in **dictionary** (dĭk′shə-nĕr′ē)

rifle¹
With a telescopic sight

rig
Offshore drilling rig

rigging
Replica of the H.M.S. *Bounty* used in MGM's 1962 version of *Mutiny on the Bounty*

Ri•deau Canal (rĭ-dō′). A waterway, c. 203 km (126 mi), of SE Ontario connecting the Ottawa R. with Lake Ontario.

rid•er (rī′dər) *n.* **1.** One that rides, esp. one who rides horses. **2.a.** A clause, usu. having little relevance to the main issue, that is added to a legislative bill. **b.** An amendment or addition to a document or record. **3.** Something, such as the top rail of a fence, that rests on or is supported by something else.

rid•er•ship (rī′dər-shĭp′) *n.* The number of passengers who ride a public transport system.

ridge (rĭj) *n.* **1.** A long narrow upper section or crest. **2.** A long narrow chain of hills or mountains. **3.** A long narrow elevation on the ocean floor. **4.** *Meteorol.* An elongated zone of relatively high atmospheric pressure. **5.** A long, narrow, or crested part of the body. **6.** The horizontal line formed by the juncture of two sloping planes, esp. the line formed by the surfaces at the top of a roof. **7.** A narrow raised strip, as in cloth or on plowed ground. — *v.* **ridged, ridg•ing, ridg•es.** — *tr.* To mark with, form into, or provide with ridges. — *intr.* To form ridges. [ME *rigge* < OE *hrycg.* See **sker-²*.**]

Ridge•crest (rĭj′krĕst′). A city of S-central CA ENE of Bakersfield. Pop. 27,725.

Ridge•field (rĭj′fēld′). A town of SW CT near the NY border NNE of Stamford. Pop. 20,919.

ridge•ling also **ridg•ling** (rĭj′lĭng) *n.* A male animal with one or two undescended testicles. [< obsolete *ridgel,* perh. < RIDGE (< the belief that they remained near the back).]

ridge•pole (rĭj′pōl′) *n.* **1.** A horizontal beam at the ridge of a roof to which the rafters are attached. **2.** The horizontal pole at the top of a tent.

Ridge•wood (rĭj′wo͝od′). A village of NE NJ NNE of Paterson. Pop. 24,152.

Ridg•way (rĭj′wā′), **Matthew Bunker.** b. 1895. Amer. army officer who was commander of United Nations forces in Korea (1951–52) and NATO forces in Europe (1951–53).

ridg•y (rĭj′ē) *adj.* **-i•er, -i•est.** Having or forming ridges.

rid•i•cule (rĭd′ĭ-kyo͞ol′) *n.* Words or actions intended to evoke contemptuous laughter at or feelings toward a person or thing. — *tr.v.* **-culed, -cul•ing, -cules.** To expose to ridicule; make fun of. [Fr. < Lat. *rīdiculum,* joke < neut. of *rīdiculus,* laughable. See RIDICULOUS.] — **rid′i•cul′er** *n.*

Syns: *ridicule, mock, taunt, twit, deride, gibe.* These verbs refer to making another the butt of amusement or mirth. *Ridicule* implies purposeful disparagement: *"My father discouraged me by ridiculing my performances"* (Benjamin Franklin). To *mock* is to poke fun at someone, often by mimicry and caricature: *"Seldom he smiles, and smiles in such a sort/As if he mock'd himself, and scorn'd his spirit"* (Shakespeare). *Taunt* suggests mocking, insulting, or scornful reproach: *"taunting him with want of courage to leap into the great pit"* (Daniel Defoe). To *twit* is to taunt by calling attention to something embarrassing: *"The schoolmaster was twitted about the lady who threw him over"* (J.M. Barrie). *Deride* implies scorn and contempt: *derided his naive ideas.* To *gibe* is to make taunting, heckling, or jeering remarks: *gibed at him for his timidity.*

ri•dic•u•lous (rĭ-dĭk′yə-ləs) *adj.* Deserving or inspiring ridicule; absurd, preposterous, or silly. [< Lat. *rīdiculus,* laughable < *rīdēre,* to laugh.] — **ri•dic′u•lous•ly** *adv.* — **ri•dic′u•lous•ness** *n.*

rid•ing¹ (rī′dĭng) *n.* **1.** The act of riding. **2.** Horseback riding.

rid•ing² (rī′dĭng) *n.* **1.** An administrative division or electoral division in Canada. **2.** Any one of three former administrative divisions of Yorkshire, England. [ME, alteration of *trithing* < OE **thrithing* < ON *thridhjungr,* third part < *thridhi,* third. See **trei-*.**]

rid•ley (rĭd′lē) *n., pl.* **-leys. 1.** A marine turtle *(Lepidochelys kempii)* of the Gulf of Mexico and Atlantic coastal waters. **2.** A related species *(Lepidochelys olivaceae)* of the Pacific and Indian oceans. [?]

Rid•ley (rĭd′lē), **Nicholas.** 1500?–55. English prelate who was executed for refusing to renounce his Protestantism after the accession of the Roman Catholic Mary I.

ri•el (rē-ĕl′) *n.* See table at **currency.** [?]

Ri•el (rē-ĕl′), **Louis.** 1844–85. Canadian insurrectionist who organized métis settlers of the Red R. valley (1869) and Saskatchewan (1884–85) in uprisings over land rights.

Rie•mann (rē′mən, -män′), **Georg Friedrich Bernhard.** 1826–66. German mathematician who was a pioneer of non-Euclidean geometry.

Rie•mann•ian geometry (rē-män′ē-ən) *n. Math.* A non-Euclidean system of geometry based on the postulate that within a plane every pair of lines intersects.

Ri•en•zi (rē-ĕn′zē) or **Ri•en•zo** (-zō), **Cola di.** 1313?–54. Italian revolutionary leader who was dictator of Rome (1347).

Ries•ling (rēs′lĭng, rēz′-) *n.* A dry to sweet white wine similar to Rhine wine. [Ger., alteration of obsolete *Rüssling.*]

Rif (rĭf). See **Er Rif.**

ri•fam•pin (rĭ-făm′pĭn) also **ri•fam•pi•cin** (-pĭ-sĭn) *n.* A semisynthetic antibiotic derived from a form of rifamycin that interferes with the synthesis of RNA and is used to treat bacterial and viral diseases. [Blend of *rifam(yc)in* and P(IPERAZINE).]

rif•a•my•cin (rĭf′ə-mī′sĭn) *n.* Any of a group of antibiotics isolated from a strain of the soil microorganism *Streptomyces mediterranei,* used in the treatment of leprosy, tuberculosis, and other bacterial diseases. [Alteration of *rifomycin,* prob. < : Ital. *riformare,* to reform (*ri-,* again < Lat. *re-;* see RE- + *formare,* to form < Lat. *formāre;* see REFORM) + -MYCIN.]

rife (rīf) *adj.* **rif•er, rif•est. 1.** In widespread existence, practice, or use; increasingly prevalent. **2.** Abundant or numerous. [ME < OE *rȳfe.*]

riff (rĭf) *n.* **1.** *Mus.* A short rhythmic phrase, esp. one that is repeated in improvisation. **2.** Rapid, clever, often rhythmic speech, as by a disc jockey. — *intr.v.* **riffed, riff•ing, riffs.** *Mus.* To play riffs. [?]

Riff or **Rif** (rĭf) *n., pl.* **Riff** or **Riffs** or **Rif** or **Rifs** also **Rif•fi** (rĭf′ē). **1.** A member of any of several Berber peoples inhabiting Er Rif. **2.** The Berber language of this people. — **Rif′fi•an** *adj. & n.*

rif•fle (rĭf′əl) *n.* **1.a.** A rocky shoal or sandbar lying just below the surface of a waterway. **b.** A stretch of choppy water caused by such a shoal or sandbar; a rapid. **2.a.** In mining, the sectional stone or wood bottom lining of a sluice, arranged for trapping mineral particles, as of gold. **b.** A groove or block in such a lining. **3.** *Games.* The act or an instance of shuffling cards. — *v.* **-fled, -fling, -fles.** — *tr.* **1.** *Games.* To shuffle (playing cards) by holding part of a deck in each hand and raising up the edges before releasing them to fall alternately in one stack. **2.** To thumb through (the pages of a book, for example). — *intr.* **1.** *Games.* To shuffle cards. **2.** To become choppy, as water. [Poss. blend of RIPPLE¹ and RUFFLE¹.]

riff•raff (rĭf′răf′) *n.* **1.** People regarded as disreputable or worthless. **2.** Rubbish; trash. [ME *riffe raffe* < *rif and raf,* one and all < AN *rif et raf, rifle et rafle* : OFr. *rifler,* to rifle; see RIFLE² + OFr. *raffler,* to carry off (< *raffle,* act of seizing; see RAFFLE¹).]

ri•fle¹ (rī′fəl) *n.* **1.a.** A firearm with a rifled bore, designed to be fired from the shoulder. **b.** An artillery piece or naval gun with such spiral grooves. **2. rifles.** Troops armed with rifles. — *tr.v.* **-fled, -fling, -fles.** To cut spiral grooves within (a gun barrel, for example). [< *rifle,* to cut spiral grooves in < Fr. *rifler* < OFr., to plunder, scratch. See RIFLE².]

ri•fle² (rī′fəl) *v.* **-fled, -fling, -fles.** — *tr.* **1.** To search with intent to steal. **2.** To ransack or plunder; pillage. **3.** To rob: *rifle a safe.* — *intr.* To search vigorously. [ME *riflen,* to plunder < OFr. *rifler,* prob. of Gmc. orig.] — **ri′fler** *n.*

ri•fle•man (rī′fəl-mən) *n.* **1.** A soldier equipped with a rifle. **2.** A man who shoots a rifle skillfully.

ri•fle•ry (rī′fəl-rē) *n.* **1.** The skill and practice of shooting a gun. **2.** Rifle fire: *distant riflery.*

ri•fling (rī′flĭng) *n.* **1.** The process or operation of cutting spiral grooves in a rifle barrel. **2.** Grooves cut in a rifle barrel.

rift¹ (rĭft) *n.* **1.** A narrow fissure in rock. **2.** A break in friendly relations. — *v.* **rift•ed, rift•ing, rifts.** — *intr.* To split open; break. — *tr.* To cause to split open or break. [ME, of Scand. orig.]

rift² (rĭft) *n.* **1.** A shallow area in a waterway. **2.** The backwash of a wave that has broken upon a beach. [Prob. alteration of dial. *riff,* reef < Du. *rif, riffe.* See REEF¹.]

rift valley *n.* **1.** A deep fracture or break extending along the crest of a mid-ocean ridge. **2.** A valley that has formed along a narrow trough bounded by two or more faults.

rig (rĭg) *tr.v.* **rigged, rig•ging, rigs. 1.** To provide with a harness or equipment; fit out. **2.** *Naut.* To equip (a ship) with spars, shrouds, and sails. **3.** *Informal.* To dress, clothe, or adorn. **4.** To make or construct in haste or in a makeshift manner: *rig up a tent.* **5.** To manipulate dishonestly for personal gain. — *n.* **1.** *Naut.* The configuration of masts, spars, and sails on a sailing vessel. **2.** Special equipment or gear used for a particular purpose. **3.a.** A truck or tractor. **b.** A tractor-trailer. **c.** A vehicle with one or more horses harnessed to it. **4.** The special apparatus used for drilling oil wells. **5.** *Western U.S.* See **saddle** 1a. **6.** *Informal.* A costume or an outfit. **7.** Fishing tackle. [ME *riggen,* prob. of Scand. orig.]

Ri•ga (rē′gə). The cap. of Latvia, in the central part on the **Gulf of Riga,** an inlet of the Baltic Sea. Pop. 883,000.

rig•a•doon (rĭg′ə-do͞on′) *n.* **1.** A lively jumping quickstep for one couple. **2.** Music for this dance, usu. in rapid duple meter. [Fr. *rigaudon,* poss. < the name *Rigaud.*]

rig•a•ma•role (rĭg′ə-mə-rōl′) *n.* Var. of **rigmarole.**

rig•a•to•ni (rĭg′ə-tō′nē) *n.* Large ribbed macaroni, slightly curved and cut into short lengths. [Ital. < *rigato,* p.part. of *rigare,* to draw a line < *riga,* line, of Gmc. orig.]

Ri•gel (rī′jəl) *n.* A bright double star in the constellation Orion. [Ar. *rijl,* foot.]

rig•ger (rĭg′ər) *n.* **1.** One that rigs. **2.** *Naut.* A ship with a specific kind of rigging.

rig•ging (rĭg′ĭng) *n.* **1.** *Naut.* The system of shrouds, stays, and control lines used to support and adjust the spars and sails of a sailing vessel. **2.** The supporting material for construction work.

right (rīt) *adj.* **right•er, right•est. 1.** Conforming with or conformable to justice, law, or morality. **2.** In accordance with fact, reason, or truth; correct. **3.** Fitting, proper, or appropriate. **4.** Most favorable, desirable, or convenient: *the right* *time to act.* **5.** In or into a satisfactory state or condition: *put things right.* **6.** In good mental or physical health or order. **7.** Intended to be worn or positioned facing outward or toward an observer: *the right side of the dress.* **8.a.** Of, belonging to, located on, or being the side of the body to the south when the subject is facing east. **b.** Of, relating to, directed toward, or located on the right side. **c.** Located on the right side of a person facing downstream. **9.** Often **Right.** Of or belonging to the political or intellectual Right. **10.** *Math.* **a.** Formed by or in reference to a line or plane perpendicular to another line or plane. **b.** Having the axis perpendicular to the base: *right cone.* **11.** Straight; uncurved; direct: *a right line.* **12.** *Archaic.* Not spurious; genuine. — *n.* **1.** That which is just, good, legal, proper, or fitting. **2.a.** The direction or position on the right side. **b.** The right side. **c.** The right hand. **d.** A turn in the direction of the right hand or side. **3.** Often **Right. a.** The people and groups who advocate conservative or reactionary measures, esp. in government and politics. **b.** The opinion of those advocating such measures. **4.** *Sports.* A blow delivered by a boxer's right hand. **5.** *Baseball.* Right field. **6.** Something due to a person or community by law, tradition, or nature. **7.** A just or legal claim or title. **8.a.** A stockholder's privilege of buying additional stock in a corporation at a special price, usu. at par or at a price below the current market value. **b.** The negotiable certificate on which this privilege is indicated. **c.** A privilege of subscribing for a particular stock or bond. Often used in the plural. — *adv.* **1.** Toward or on the right. **2.** In a straight line; directly: *went right home.* **3.** In the proper or desired manner; well: *doesn't fit right.* **4.** Exactly; just: *happened right here.* **5.** Immediately: *right after dinner.* **6.** Completely; quite: *The wind blew right through me.* **7.** According to law, morality, or justice. **8.** Accurately; correctly. **9.** *Chiefly Southern U.S.* Considerably; very: *They have a right nice place.* **10.** Used as an intensive: *kept right on going.* **11.** Used in titles: *The Right Reverend Jane Smith.* — *v.* **right•ed, right•ing, rights.** — *tr.* **1.** To put in or restore to an upright or proper position. **2.** To put in order or set right; correct. **3.** To make reparation or amends for; redress. — *intr.* To regain an upright or proper position. — ***idioms.*** **by rights.** In a just or proper manner; justly. **in (one's) own right.** Through the force of one's own skills or qualifications. **right and left.** From all directions or on every side. **to rights.** In a satisfactory or orderly condition. [ME < OE *riht.* See **reg-*.**] — **right'er** *n.*

Syns: *right, privilege, prerogative, perquisite, birthright.* These nouns apply to something, such as a power or possession, to which one has an established claim. *Right* refers to a legally, morally, or traditionally just claim: *"I'm a champion for the Rights of Woman"* (Maria Edgeworth). *Privilege* usually suggests a right not enjoyed by everyone: *Use of the company jet was a privilege reserved for the top executives. Prerogative* denotes an exclusive right or privilege, as one based on custom, law, or office: *It is my prerogative to change my mind.* A *perquisite* is a privilege or advantage accorded to one by virtue of one's position or the needs of one's employment: *"The wardrobe of her niece was the perquisite of her* [maid]*"* (Tobias Smollett). A *birthright* is a right to which one is entitled by birth: *Many view gainful employment as a birthright.*

right angle *n. Math.* An angle formed by the perpendicular intersection of two straight lines; an angle of 90°. — **right'-an'gled** (rīt'ăng'gəld) *adj.*

right ascension *n. Astron.* The angular distance of a celestial body or point on the celestial sphere, measured eastward from the vernal equinox along the celestial equator to the hour circle of the body or point and expressed in degrees or hours.

right away *adv.* Without delay; at once.

Right Bank. A district of Paris on the N bank of the Seine R.

right circular cone *n. Math.* A cone with a circular directrix whose base is perpendicular to its axis.

right•eous (rī'chəs) *adj.* **1.** Morally upright; without guilt or sin. **2.** In accordance with virtue or morality. **3.** Morally justifiable: *righteous anger.* See Syns at **moral.** — *n.* Righteous people considered as a group. [ME *ryghtuous,* alteration of *rihtwise* < OE *rihtwīs* : *riht,* right; see RIGHT + *-wīse,* -wise.] — **right'eous•ly** *adv.* — **right'eous•ness** *n.*

right field *n. Baseball.* **a.** The third of the outfield that is to the right, looking from home plate. **b.** The position played by the right fielder.

right fielder *n. Baseball.* The player who defends right field.

right•ful (rīt'fəl) *adj.* **1.** Right or proper; just. **2.** Having a just or proper claim. **3.** Held or owned by just or proper claim. — **right'ful•ly** *adv.* — **right'ful•ness** *n.*

right-hand (rīt'hănd') *adj.* **1.** Of, relating to, or located on the right. **2.** Relating to, designed for, or done with the right hand. **3.** Most helpful or reliable: *my right-hand assistant.*

right-hand•ed (rīt'hăn'dĭd) *adj.* **1.a.** Using the right hand more skillfully or easily than the left. **b.** *Sports.* Swinging from the right to the left. **2.a.** Of, relating to, or done with the right hand. **b.** Intended for wear on or use by the right hand. **3.** Turning or spiraling from left to right; clockwise. — *adv.* **1.** With the right hand. **2.** *Sports.* From right to left. — **right'-hand'ed•ly** *adv.* — **right'-hand'ed•ness** *n.*

right-hand•er (rīt'hăn'dər) *n.* One who is right-handed.

right•ism also **Right•ism** (rī'tĭz'əm) *n.* **1.** The ideology of the political right. **2.** Belief in or support of the tenets of the political right. — **right'ist** *n.*

right•ly (rīt'lē) *adv.* **1.** In a correct manner; properly. **2.** With honesty; justly. **3.** *Informal.* Really: *I don't rightly know.*

right-mind•ed (rīt'mīn'dĭd) *adj.* Having ideas and views based on what is right or intended to be right. — **right'-mind'ed•ness** *n.*

right off *adv.* Right away; immediately.

right of way also **right-of-way** (rīt'əv-wā') *n., pl.* **rights of way** or **right of ways** also **rights-of-way** (rīts'-) or **right-of-ways** (-wāz'). **1.** *Law.* **a.** The right to pass over property owned by another party. **b.** The path or thoroughfare on which such passage is made. **2.** The strip of land over which facilities such as highways, railroads, or power lines are built. **3.** The customary or legal right of a person, vessel, or vehicle to pass in front of another.

right on *interj. Slang.* Used as an exclamation of encouragement, support, or enthusiastic agreement.

right-on (rīt'ŏn', -ôn') *adj. Slang.* **1.** Up-to-date and sophisticated. **2.** Absolutely right; perfectly true.

right-out (rīt'out') *adj. Chiefly Southern U.S.* Outright. See Regional Note at **everwhere.**

right-side up (rīt'sīd') *adv. & adj.* **1.a.** With the top facing upward. **b.** In or into the correct orientation. **2.** In or into a condition of order.

right-to-die (rīt'tə-dī') *adj.* Advocating or expressing, as in a living will, a person's right to refuse extraordinary life-sustaining measures.

right-to-life (rīt'tə-līf') *adj.* Pro-life. — **right-to-lif'er** *n.*

right-to-work law (rīt'tə-wûrk') *n.* A state law that prohibits required union membership of workers.

right triangle *n. Math.* A triangle containing an angle of 90°.

right•ward (rīt'wərd) *adv. & adj.* To or on the right.

right whale *n.* Any of several whales of the family Balaenidae, characterized by a large head, whalebone plates in the mouth, and absence of a dorsal fin.

right wing *n.* **1.** The conservative or reactionary faction of a group. **2.** See **right** 3a. — **right'-wing'** (rīt'wĭng') *adj.* — **right'-wing'er** *n.*

right•y (rī'tē) *Informal.* — *n., pl.* **-ies. 1.** A right-handed person. **2.** An advocate or a member of the political right. — *adv.* With the right hand or in a right-handed manner.

rig•id (rĭj'ĭd) *adj.* **1.** Not flexible or pliant; stiff. **2.** Not moving; fixed. **3.** Marked by a lack of flexibility; rigorous and exacting. **4.** Scrupulously maintained or performed. See Syns at **stiff.** [ME *rigide* < Lat. *rigidus* < *rigēre,* to be stiff. See **reig-*.**] — **rig'id•ly** *adv.* — **rig'id•ness** *n.*

ri•gid•i•ty (rĭ-jĭd'ĭ-tē) *n., pl.* **-ties. 1.** The quality or state of being rigid. **2.** An instance of being rigid.

rig•ma•role (rĭg'mə-rōl') also **rig•a•ma•role** (-ə-mə-rōl') *n.* **1.** Confused, rambling, or incoherent discourse; nonsense. **2.** A complicated petty set of procedures. [Alteration of obsolete *ragman roll,* catalog < ME *ragmane rolle,* scroll used in Ragman, a game of chance, perh. < : AN *Ragemon le bon,* Ragemon the Good, title of a set of verses about a character of this name + ME *rolle,* list (< OFr. < Lat. *rotula,* wheel; see ROLL).]

rig•or (rĭg'ər) *n.* **1.** Strictness or severity, as in temperament, action, or judgment. **2.** A harsh or trying circumstance; hardship. See Syns at **difficulty. 3.** A harsh or cruel act. **4.** *Medic.* Shivering or trembling, as caused by a chill. **5.** *Physiol.* A state of rigidity in living tissues or organs that prevents response to stimuli. **6.** *Obsolete.* Stiffness or rigidity. [ME *rigour* < OFr. < Lat. *rigor* < *rigēre,* to be stiff. See **reig-*.**]

rig•or•ism (rĭg'ə-rĭz'əm) *n.* Harshness or strictness, as in conduct or judgment. — **rig'or•ist** *n.* — **rig'or•is'tic** *adj.*

rigor mor•tis (môr'tĭs) *n.* Muscular stiffening following death. [Lat. : *rigor,* stiffness + *mortis,* genitive of *mors,* death.]

rig•or•ous (rĭg'ər-əs) *adj.* **1.** Characterized by or acting with rigor. **2.** Full of rigors; harsh. **3.** Rigidly accurate; precise. — **rig'or•ous•ly** *adv.* — **rig'or•ous•ness** *n.*

rig•our (rĭg'ər) *n. Chiefly British.* Var. of **rigor.**

Rig-Ve•da (rĭg-vā'də, -vē'də) *n.* The most ancient collection of Hindu sacred verses. [Skt. *ṛgvedaḥ* : *ṛk,* verse, sacred text + *vedaḥ,* knowledge, veda; see **weid-*.**]

Riis (rēs), **Jacob August.** 1849–1914. Danish-born Amer. journalist known for his reports on conditions in city slums.

Ri•je•ka (rē-yĕk'ə). Formerly **Fi•u•me** (fyo͞o'mā, -mĕ). A city of W Croatia on the Adriatic Sea WSW of Zagreb; formerly an independent city. Pop. 160,300.

Rijs•wijk (rīs'vīk) also **Rys•wick** (rĭz'wĭk). A city of W Netherlands, a suburb of The Hague. The Treaty of Ryswick (1697) acknowledged William of Orange as William III of England. Pop. 49,790.

Riks•mål (rĭks'môl', rēks'-) *n.* See **Dano-Norwegian.** [Norw. : *riks,* genitive of *rik,* realm (< ON *ríki*; see **reg-***) + *mål,* speech (< ON *māl*).]

rile (rīl) *tr.v.* **riled, ril•ing, riles. 1.** To stir to anger. **2.** To stir up (liquid); roil. [Var. of ROIL.]

Ri•ley (rī'lē), **James Whitcomb.** 1849–1916. Amer. poet

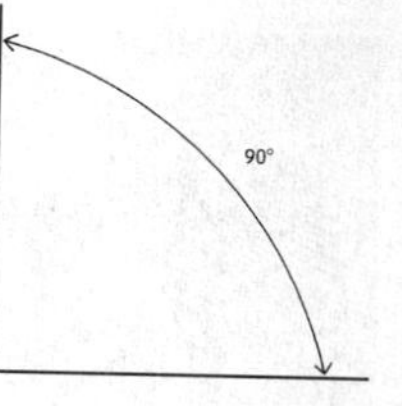

right angle

ă pat	oi boy
ā pay	ou out
âr care	o͝o took
ä father	o͞o boot
ĕ pet	ŭ cut
ē be	ûr urge
ĭ pit	th thin
ī pie	*th* this
îr pier	hw which
ŏ pot	zh vision
ō toe	ə about, item
ô paw	

Stress marks:
' (primary);
' (secondary), as in
dictionary (dĭk'shə-nĕr'ē)

whose works include "The Raggedy Man" (1890).

Ril•ke (rĭl′kə), **Rainer Maria.** 1875–1926. Austrian-born German poet who wrote *The Book of Hours* (1905).

rill also **rille** (rĭl) *n.* **1.** A small brook; a rivulet. **2.** A long, narrow, straight valley on the moon's surface. [LGer. *rille* or Du. *ril*, running stream; see **rei-*.**]

rill•et (rĭl′ĭt) *n.* A small rill.

rim (rĭm) *n.* **1.** The border, edge, or margin of an object. See Syns at **border. 2.** The circular outer part of a wheel, furthest from the axle. **3.** A circular metal structure around which a wheel tire is fitted. *—tr.v.* **rimmed, rim•ming, rims. 1.** To furnish with a rim. **2.** *Sports.* To roll around the rim of (a basket, for example) without falling in. [ME < OE *rima.*]

Rim•baud (răm-bō′, răɴ-), **Jean Nicholas Arthur.** 1854–91. French poet whose work strongly influenced the surrealists.

Charles Ringling

rime¹ (rīm) *n.* **1.** A coating of ice, as on grass and trees, formed when water droplets freeze almost instantly on a cold surface. **2.** A coating, as of mud or slime, likened to a frosty film. *—tr.v.* **rimed, rim•ing, rimes.** To cover with or as if with frost or ice. [ME *rim* < OE *hrīm.*] **—rim′y** *adj.*

rime² (rīm) *n. & v.* Var. of **rhyme.**

rim•er (rī′mər) *n.* Var. of **rhymer.**

rime riche (rēm rēsh′) *n., pl.* **rimes riches** (rēm rēsh′). Rhyme using words or parts of words that are pronounced identically but have different meanings, for example, *write-right* or *port-deport.* [Fr. : *rime*, rhyme + *riche*, rich.]

rime•ster (rīm′stər) *n.* Var. of **rhymester.**

Ri•mi•ni (rĭm′ə-nē). A city of N Italy on the Adriatic Sea SSE of Ravenna; founded by Umbrians and part of the Papal States from 1509 to 1860. Pop. 126,949.

Rim•i•ni (rĭm′ĭ-nē, rē′mē-), **Francesca da.** See **Francesca da Rimini.**

ri•mose (rī′mōs′, rī-mōs′) *adj.* Full of chinks, cracks, or crevices. [Lat. *rīmōsus* < *rīma*, fissure.] **—ri′mose•ly** *adv.* **—ri•mos′i•ty** (-mŏs′ĭ-tē) *n.*

ring-necked pheasant
Phasianus colchicus

Ri•mous•ki (rĭ-mo͞os′kē). A city of S Quebec, Canada, on the St. Lawrence R. NE of Quebec. Pop. 29,120.

Rim•ski-Kor•sa•kov or **Rim•sky-Kor•sa•kov** (rĭm′skē-kôr′sə-kôf′), **Nikolai Andreyevich.** 1844–1908. Russian composer whose works were heavily influenced by folk music.

rind (rīnd) *n.* A tough outer covering such as bark, the skin of some fruits, or the coating on cheese or bacon. [ME < OE.]

rin•der•pest (rĭn′dər-pĕst′) *n.* An acute, often fatal contagious viral disease, chiefly of cattle, characterized by ulceration of the alimentary tract and resulting in diarrhea. [Ger. : *Rinder*, genitive pl. of *Rind*, head of cattle, ox (< MHGer. *rint* < OHGer. *hrind*; see **ker-¹***) + *Pest*, plague (< Lat. *pestis*).]

Rine•hart (rīn′härt′), **Mary Roberts.** 1876–1958. Amer. writer whose mysteries include *The Circular Staircase* (1908).

ringtail
Bassariscus astutus

ring¹ (rĭng) *n.* **1.** A circular object, form, or arrangement with a vacant circular center. **2.** A small circular band, usu. made of precious metal and often set with jewels, worn on the finger. **3.** A circular band used for carrying, holding, or containing something. **4.** A circular movement or course, as in dancing. **5.** An enclosed, usu. circular area in which exhibitions, sports, or contests take place. **6.** *Sports.* **a.** A rectangular arena set off by stakes and ropes in which boxing or wrestling events are held. **b.** The sport of boxing. **7.** *Games.* **a.** An enclosed area in which bets are placed at a racetrack. **b.** Bookmakers considered as a group. **8.** An exclusive group of people acting privately or illegally to advance their own interests. **9.** A political contest; a race. **10.** *Bot.* An annual ring. **11.** *Math.* The area between two concentric circles; annulus. **12.** *Math.* A set of elements subject to the operations of addition and multiplication, in which the set is commutative under addition and associative under multiplication and in which the two operations are related by distributive laws. **13.** Any of the turns constituting a spiral or helix. **14.** *Chem.* A group of atoms linked by bonds that may be represented graphically in circular or triangular form. *—v.* **ringed, ring•ing, rings.** *—tr.* **1.** To surround with or as if with a ring; encircle. **2.** To form into a ring or rings. **3.** To ornament or supply with a ring or rings. **4.** To remove a circular strip of bark around the circumference of (a tree trunk or branch); girdle. **5.** To put a ring in the nose of (an animal). **6.** To hem in (animals) by riding in a circle around them. **7.** *Games.* To toss a ring over (a peg), as in horseshoes. *—intr.* **1.** To form a ring or rings. **2.** To move, run, or fly in a spiral or circular course. [ME < OE *hring.* See **sker-²*.**]

ring² (rĭng) *v.* **rang** (răng), **rung** (rŭng), **ring•ing, rings.** *—intr.* **1.** To give forth a clear resonant sound. **2.** To cause something to ring. **3.** To sound a bell in order to summon someone. **4.** To have a sound or character suggestive of a particular quality: *a story that rings true.* **5.** To be filled with sound; resound. **6.** To hear a persistent humming or buzzing. **7.** To be filled with talk or rumor. *—tr.* **1.** To cause (a bell, for example) to ring. **2.** To produce (a sound) by or as if by ringing. **3.** To announce, proclaim, or signal by or as if by ringing. **4.** To call (someone) on the telephone. **5.** To test (a coin, for example) for quality by the sound it produces when struck against something. *—n.* **1.** The sound created by a bell or another sonorous vibrating object. **2.** A loud sound, esp. one repeated or continued. **3.** A telephone call. **4.** A suggestion of a particular quality. **5.** A set of bells. **6.** The act or an instance of sounding a bell. ***—phrasal verb.* ring up. 1.** To record, esp. by means of a cash register. **2.** To accomplish or achieve; win. ***—idioms.* ring a bell.** *Informal.* To arouse an often indistinct memory. **ring down the curtain.** To end a performance, an event, or an action. **ring (someone's) chimes (or bells).** *Slang.* To knock (an opponent) out by force. **ring up the curtain.** To begin a performance, an event, or an action. [ME *ringen* < OE *hringan.*]

ring•bolt (rĭng′bōlt′) *n.* A bolt having a ring fitted through its eye.

ring•bone (rĭng′bōn′) *n.* A bony growth on the fetlock, pastern, or coffin bone of a horse's foot, usu. causing lameness.

ring buoy *n. Naut.* A life preserver in the shape of a ring.

ring•dove (rĭng′dŭv′) *n.* **1.** An Old World pigeon *(Streptopelia risoria)* having black markings forming a half circle on the neck. **2.** See **wood pigeon.**

ringed (rĭngd) *adj.* **1.** Wearing or marked with a ring or rings. **2.** Encircled or surrounded by bands or rings. **3.** *Zool.* Formed from segmented rings; annulate.

rin•gent (rĭn′jənt) *adj. Biol.* Having gaping liplike parts, as the corolla of some flowers. [Lat. *ringēns, ringent-*, pr.part. of *ringī*, to open the mouth wide.]

ring•er¹ (rĭng′ər) *n. Games.* A horseshoe or quoit thrown so that it encircles the peg.

ring•er² (rĭng′ər) *n.* **1.** One that rings, esp. one that sounds a bell or chime. **2.** *Slang.* A contestant entered dishonestly into a competition. **3.** *Slang.* One who bears a striking resemblance to another: *a ringer for his father.*

Ring•er's solution (rĭng′ərz) also **Ring•er solution** (-ər) *n.* An aqueous solution of the chlorides of sodium, potassium, and calcium that is isotonic to animal tissue and used topically as a physiological saline. [After Sydney *Ringer* (1835–1910), British physician.]

ring finger *n.* The third finger of the left hand.

ring•git (rĭng′gĭt) *n.* See table at **currency.** [Malay.]

ring•hals (rĭng′hăls′) *n., pl.* **-hals•es.** An African snake *(Hemachatus haemachatus)* that spits venom at the eyes of an attacker, sometimes causing blindness. [Obsolete Afr. : *ring*, ring (< MDu. *rinc*; see **sker-²***) + *hals*, neck (< MDu.; see **kʷel-¹***).]

ring•lead•er (rĭng′lē′dər) *n.* A person who leads others, esp. in illicit or informal activities.

ring•let (rĭng′lĭt) *n.* **1.** A long, spirally curled lock of hair. **2.** A small circle or ring. **—ring′let•ed** *adj.*

Ring•ling (rĭng′lĭng), **Charles.** 1863–1926. Amer. circus owner who was a founder of the Ringling Brothers and Barnum & Bailey Circus (1907).

ring•mas•ter (rĭng′măs′tər) *n.* A person, esp. a man, in charge of the performances in a circus ring.

Ring Nebula (rĭng) *n.* A planetary nebula in the constellation Lyra.

ring-necked duck (rĭng′nĕkt′) *n.* A North American duck *(Aythya collaris)* having a distinctive light ring behind the tip of the bill and in the male a light chestnut ring around the neck.

ring-necked pheasant *n.* A widely distributed bird *(Phasianus colchicus)* native to the Old World, the male of which has brightly colored plumage and a white ring around the neck.

Ring of Fire *n.* A zone of volcanic and seismic activity that coincides roughly with the borders of the Pacific Ocean.

ring•side (rĭng′sīd′) *n.* **1.** *Sports.* The area or seats immediately outside an arena or a ring, as at a prizefight. **2.** A place providing a close view of a spectacle.

ring•tail (rĭng′tāl′) *n.* A raccoonlike mammal (*Bassariscus astutus*) of the western United States.

ring-tailed (rĭng′tāld′) *adj.* **1.** Having a tail with ringlike markings. **2.** Having a tail that curls to form a ring.

ring•worm (rĭng′wûrm′) *n.* Any of a number of contagious skin diseases caused by several related fungi, characterized by ring-shaped scaly itching patches on the skin.

rink (rĭngk) *n. Sports.* **1.** An area surfaced with smooth ice for skating, hockey, or curling. **2.** A smooth floor suited for roller-skating. **3.** A building that houses a surface prepared for skating. **4.** A section of a bowling green large enough for holding a match. **5.** A team of players in quoits, bowling, or curling. [ME *renk*, racecourse < OFr. *renc*, line, of Gmc. orig. See **sker-²*.**]

rin•ky-dink (rĭng′kē-dĭngk′) *Slang. adj.* **1.** Old-fashioned; worn-out. **2.** Insignificant; unimportant. **3.** Of cheap or poor quality; makeshift. [?] **—rin′ky-dink′** *n.*

rinse (rĭns) *tr.v.* **rinsed, rins•ing, rins•es. 1.** To wash lightly with water. **2.** To remove (soap, for example) by washing lightly in water. *—n.* **1.** The act of washing lightly. **2.** A solution, such as water, used in rinsing. **3.** A solution used in coloring or conditioning the hair. [ME *rincen* < OFr. *rincier* < VLat. **recentiāre* < Lat. *recēns, recent-*, fresh. See RECENT.] **—rins′a•ble, rins′i•ble** *adj.* **—rins′er** *n.*

Rí•o or **Ri•o** (rē′ō). For names of South American rivers, see the specific element; for example, **Plata, Río de la,** or **Roosevelt, Rio.**

Ri•o•bam•ba (rē′ō-bäm′bə, -väm′bä). A city of central Ecuador in the Andes S of Quito; site of Ecuador's proclamation of independence (1830). Pop. 75,455.

Ri•o de Ja•nei•ro (rē′ō dā zhə-nâr′ō, dē-, rē′o͞o dĭ zhĭ-nā′ro͞o). A city of SE Brazil on Guanabara Bay, an arm of the Atlantic Ocean; probably first visited by Portuguese explorers in Jan. 1502. Pop. 5,090,700.

Rí•o de O•ro (rē′ō dē ôr′ō, *thē*). The southern part of Western Sahara in NW Africa.

Ri•o Grande[1] (rē′ō grănd′, grăn′dē). Or in Mexico **Rí•o Bra•vo** (rē′ō brä′vō). A river rising in SW CO and flowing c. 3,033 km (1,885 mi) to SW TX, where it forms the U.S.-Mexican border before emptying into the Gulf of Mexico.

Ri•o Gran•de[2] (rē′ō grăn′də, rē′o͞o grän′dĭ). A city of extreme SE Brazil at the S entrance of the Lagoa dos Patos; founded 1737. Pop. 130,149.

Rí•o Mu•ni (rē′ō mo͞o′nē). The mainland part of Equatorial Guinea, on the Bight of Biafra in W Africa.

ri•ot (rī′ət) *n.* **1.** A wild or turbulent disturbance created by a large number of people. **2.** *Law.* A violent disturbance of the public peace by three or more persons assembled for a common purpose. **3.** An unrestrained outbreak, as of laughter or passions. **4.** A profusion. **5.a.** Unrestrained merrymaking; revelry. **b.** Debauchery. **6.** *Slang.* An irresistibly funny person or thing. — *v.* **-ot•ed, -ot•ing, -ots.** — *intr.* **1.** To take part in a riot. **2.** To live wildly or engage in uncontrolled revelry. **3.** To exhibit profusion. — *tr.* To waste (money or time) in wild or wanton living. [ME < OFr., dispute < *rioter*, to quarrel, perh. < *ruire*, to roar < Lat. *rūgīre.*] — **ri′ot•er** *n.*

Ri•ot Act (rī′ət) *n.* An English law, enacted in 1715, providing that if 12 or more people unlawfully assemble and disturb the public peace, they must disperse upon proclamation or be considered guilty of felony. — ***idiom.* read the riot act.** To warn or reprimand energetically or forcefully.

ri•ot•ous (rī′ət-əs) *adj.* **1.** Of, relating to, or resembling a riot. **2.** Participating in or inciting to riot or uproar. **3.** Uproarious; boisterous. **4.** Dissolute; wanton. **5.** Abundant or luxuriant. — **ri′ot•ous•ly** *adv.* — **ri′ot•ous•ness** *n.*

rip[1] (rĭp) *v.* **ripped, rip•ping, rips.** — *tr.* **1.** To cut, tear apart, or tear away roughly or energetically. See Syns at **tear**[1]. **2.** To split or saw (wood) along the grain. **3.** *Informal.* To produce, display, or utter suddenly: *rips out a yell.* — *intr.* **1.** To become torn or split apart. **2.** *Informal.* To move quickly or violently. — *n.* **1.** The act of ripping. **2.** A torn or split place, esp. along a seam. **3.** A ripsaw. — ***phrasal verbs.* rip into.** To attack or criticize vehemently. **rip off.** *Slang.* **1.** To steal from. **2.** To steal. **3.** To exploit, swindle, cheat, or defraud. [ME *rippen* < Flem. See **reup-***.] — **rip′per** *n.*

rip[2] (rĭp) *n.* **1.** A stretch of water in a river, an estuary, or a tidal channel made rough by waves meeting an opposing current. **2.** A rip current. [Prob. < RIP[1].]

rip[3] (rĭp) *n.* **1.** A dissolute person. **2.** An old or worthless horse. [Poss. shortening and alteration of REPROBATE.]

R.I.P. *abbr. Lat.* Requiescat in pace (may one rest in peace).

ri•par•i•an (rĭ-pâr′ē-ən) *adj.* Of, on, or relating to the banks of a natural course of water. [< Lat. *rīpārius* < *rīpa*, bank.]

riparian right *n. Law.* The right, as to fishing or the use of a riverbed, of one who owns riparian land.

rip•cord (rĭp′kôrd′) *n.* **1.** A cord pulled to release the pack of a parachute. **2.** A cord pulled to release gas from a balloon.

rip current *n.* A strong narrow surface current that flows rapidly away from the shore.

ripe (rīp) *adj.* **rip•er, rip•est. 1.** Fully developed; mature. **2.** Resembling matured fruit, as in fullness. **3.** Sufficiently advanced in preparation or aging to be used or eaten. **4.** Thoroughly matured, as by study or experience; seasoned. **5.** Advanced in years. **6.** Fully prepared to do or undergo something; ready. **7.** Sufficiently advanced; opportune. **8.** Exhibiting overtones of or references to sex; scatological. **9.** Emitting a foul odor, esp. body odor. [ME < OE *rīpe.*] — **ripe′ly** *adv.* — **ripe′ness** *n.*

rip•en (rī′pən) *tr. & intr.v.* **-ened, -en•ing, -ens.** To make or become ripe or riper; mature. See Syns at **mature.** — **rip′en•er** *n.*

rip-off (rĭp′ôf′, -ŏf′) *n. Slang.* **1.** A theft. **2.** A thief. **3.** An act of exploitation. **4.** Something, such as a film or story, that is clearly imitative of or based on something else.

ri•poste (rĭ-pōst′) *n.* **1.** *Sports.* A quick thrust given after parrying an opponent's lunge in fencing. **2.** A retaliatory action, maneuver, or retort. — *intr.v.* **-post•ed, -post•ing, -postes. 1.** To make a return thrust. **2.** To retort quickly. [Fr., alteration of obsolete *risposte* < Ital. *risposta*, answer < fem. p.part. of *rispondere*, to answer < Lat. *respondēre.* See RESPOND.]

rip•ping (rĭp′ĭng) *adj. Informal.* Excellent; marvelous.

rip•ple[1] (rĭp′əl) *v.* **-pled, -pling, -ples.** — *intr.* **1.a.** To form or display little undulations or waves on the surface, as disturbed water does. **b.** To flow with such undulations or waves on the surface. **2.** To rise and fall gently in tone or volume. — *tr.* To cause to form small waves or undulations. — *n.* **1.** A small wave. **2.** A wavelike motion; an undulation. **3.** A sound like that made by rippling water. [ME *ripplen*, to wrinkle, crease, perh. of Scand. orig.] — **rip′pler** *n.* — **rip′pling•ly** *adv.*

rip•ple[2] (rĭp′əl) *n.* A comblike toothed instrument for removing seeds from flax and other fibers. — *tr.v.* **-pled, -pling, -ples.** To remove seeds from with a ripple. [ME < **ripelen*, to remove seeds; akin to MLGer. *repelen.*]

ripple effect *n.* A gradually spreading effect or influence.

rip•plet (rĭp′lĭt) *n.* A little wave or ripple.

rip•ply (rĭp′lē) *adj.* **-pli•er, -pli•est.** Characterized by or sounding in ripples.

rip•rap (rĭp′răp′) *n.* **1.** A loose assemblage of broken stones erected in water or on soft ground as a foundation. **2.** The broken stones used for such a foundation. — *tr.v.* **-rapped, -rap•ping, -raps. 1.** To construct a riprap in or on. **2.** To strengthen with a riprap. [Redup. of RAP[1].]

rip-roar•ing (rĭp′rôr′ĭng, -rōr′-) also **rip-roar•i•ous** (rĭp′-rôr′ē-əs, -rōr′-) *adj. Informal.* Noisy, lively, and exciting. [< RIP[1] + (UP)ROAR(IOUS).] — **rip′-roar′•ing•ly** *adv.*

rip•saw (rĭp′sô′) *n.* A coarse-toothed saw used for cutting wood along the grain.

rip•snort•er (rĭp′snôr′tər) *n. Slang.* One that is remarkable for strength, intensity, or excellence. — **rip′snort′ing** *adj.*

rip tide *n.* See **rip current.**

Rip•u•ar•i•an (rĭp′yo͞o-âr′ē-ən) *adj.* Of, relating to, or being a group of Franks who settled along the Rhine, near Cologne, in the fourth century A.D. [< Med.Lat. *Ripuārius.*] — **Rip′u•ar′i•an** *n.*

rise (rīz) *v.* **rose** (rōz), **ris•en** (rĭz′ən), **ris•ing, ris•es.** — *intr.* **1.** To assume a standing position after lying, sitting, or kneeling. **2.** To get out of bed. **3.** To move from a lower to a higher position; ascend. **4.** To increase in size, volume, or level. **5.** To increase in number, amount, or value. **6.** To increase in intensity, force, or speed. **7.** To increase in pitch or volume. **8.** To appear above the horizon. **9.** To extend upward; be prominent. **10.** To slant or slope upward. **11.** To come into existence; originate. See Syns at **stem**[1]. **12.** To be erected. **13.** To appear at the surface of the water or the earth; emerge. **14.** To puff up or become larger; swell up. **15.** To become stiff and erect. **16.** To attain a higher status. **17.** To become apparent to the mind or senses. **18.** To uplift oneself to meet a demand or challenge. **19.** To return to life. **20.** To rebel. **21.** To close a session of an official assembly; adjourn. — *tr.* To cause to rise. — *n.* **1.** The act of rising; ascent. **2.** The degree of elevation or ascent. **3.** The appearance of the sun or other celestial body above the horizon. **4.** An increase in height, as of the level of water. **5.** A gently sloped hill. **6.** A long broad elevation that slopes gently, as from the earth's surface. **7.** An origin, a beginning, or a source. See Syns at **beginning. 8.** Occasion or opportunity. **9.** The emergence of a fish seeking food or bait at the water's surface. **10.** An increase in price, worth, quantity, or degree. **11.** An increase in intensity, volume, or pitch. **12.** Elevation in status, prosperity, or importance. **13.** The height of a flight of stairs or of a single riser. **14.** *Chiefly British.* An increase in salary or wages; a raise. **15.** *Informal.* An angry or irritated reaction. [ME *risen* < OE *rīsan.*]

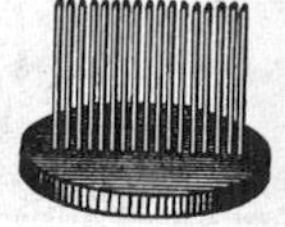

ripple[2]

ris•er (rī′zər) *n.* **1.** One who rises, esp. from sleep: *a late riser.* **2.** The vertical part of a stair step.

ris•i•bil•i•ty (rĭz′ə-bĭl′ĭ-tē) *n., pl.* **-ties. 1.** The ability or tendency to laugh. **2.** A sense of the ludicrous or amusing. Often used in the plural. **3.** Laughter; hilarity.

ris•i•ble (rĭz′ə-bəl) *adj.* **1.** Relating to laughter or used in eliciting laughter. **2.** Eliciting laughter; ludicrous. **3.** Capable of laughing or inclined to laugh. [LLat. *rīsibilis* < Lat. *rīsus*, p.part. of *rīdēre*, to laugh.] — **ris′i•bly** *adv.*

ris•ing (rī′zĭng) *adj.* **1.** Ascending, sloping upward, or advancing. **2.** Coming to maturity; emerging. — *n.* **1.** The action of one that rises. **2.** An uprising; an insurrection. **3.** A prominence or projection. **4.** The leaven or yeast used to make dough rise in baking.

rising rhythm *n.* A rhythmic pattern in which the stress falls on the last syllable of each foot, as in *"They danced by the light of the moon"* (Edward Lear).

risk (rĭsk) *n.* **1.** The possibility of suffering harm or loss; danger. **2.** A factor, thing, element, or course involving uncertain danger; a hazard. **3.a.** The danger or probability of loss to an insurer. **b.** The amount that an insurance company stands to lose. **4.a.** The variability of returns from an investment. **b.** The chance of nonpayment of a debt. **5.** One considered with respect to the possibility of loss. — *tr.v.* **risked, risk•ing, risks. 1.** To expose to a chance of loss or damage; hazard. See Syns at **endanger. 2.** To incur the risk of. [Fr. *risque* < Ital. *risco, rischio.*] — **risk′er** *n.*

risk capital *n.* See **venture capital.**

risk•y (rĭs′kē) *adj.* **-i•er, -i•est.** Accompanied by or involving risk or danger; hazardous. — **risk′i•ness** *n.*

Ri•sor•gi•men•to (rĭ-sôr′jə-mĕn′tō, rē-zôr′jē-) *n.* The period of or the movement for the liberation and political unification of Italy, beginning about 1750 and lasting until 1870. [Ital. < *risorgere*, to rise again < Lat. *resurgere.* See RESURGE.]

ri•sot•to (rĭ-sô′tō, -sŏt′ō, rē-zôt′tō) *n., pl.* **-tos.** A dish of rice cooked in broth, often with saffron, and served with grated cheese. [Ital. < *riso*, rice < OItal. See RICE.]

ă pat	oi boy
ā pay	ou out
âr care	o͝o took
ä father	o͞o boot
ĕ pet	ŭ cut
ē be	ûr urge
ĭ pit	th thin
ī pie	*th* this
îr pier	hw which
ŏ pot	zh vision
ō toe	ə about, item
ô paw	

Stress marks:
′ (primary);
′ (secondary), as in
dictionary (dĭk′shə-nĕr′ē)

ris•qué (rĭs-kā′) *adj.* Suggestive of or bordering on indelicacy or impropriety. [Fr. < p.part. of *risquer*, to risk < *risque*, risk. See RISK.]
rit. *abbr. Mus.* Ritardando.
ri•tar•dan•do (rē′tär-dän′dō) *adv. & adj. Mus.* Gradually slowing in tempo; retarding. [Ital., pr.part. of *ritardare*, to slow down < Lat. *retardāre*. See RETARD.]
rite (rīt) *n.* **1.** The prescribed or customary form for conducting a religious or other solemn ceremony. **2.** A ceremonial act or series of acts. **3. Rite.** The liturgy or practice of a branch of the Christian church. [ME < Lat. *rītus*. See **ar-*.**]
rite of passage *n., pl.* **rites of passage.** A ritual or ceremony signifying an event in a person's life indicative of a transition from one stage to another, as from adolescence to adulthood.
ri•tor•nel•lo (rē′tôr-nĕl′lō) *n., pl.* **-li** (-lē) or **-los.** *Mus.* **1.** An instrumental interlude recurring after each stanza in a vocal work. **2.** A passage for full orchestra in a baroque concerto grosso. **3.** An instrumental interlude in early 17th-century opera. **4.** The refrain of a rondo. [Ital., dim. of *ritorno*, return < *ritornare*, to return < VLat. **retornāre*. See RETURN.]
Rit•ter (rĭt′ər), **Woodward Maurice ("Tex").** 1907–74. Amer. singer who played a singing cowboy in radio shows and motion-picture Westerns.
rit•u•al (rĭch′o͞o-əl) *n.* **1.a.** The prescribed order of a religious ceremony. **b.** The body of ceremonies or rites used in a place of worship. **2.a.** The prescribed form of conducting a formal secular ceremony. **b.** The body of ceremonies used by a fraternal organization. **3.** A book of rites or ceremonial forms. **4. rituals. a.** A ceremonial act or a series of such acts. **b.** The performance of such acts. **5.a.** A detailed method of procedure faithfully or regularly followed. **b.** A state or condition characterized by the presence of established procedure or routine. [< Lat. *rītuālis*, of rites < *rītus*, rite. See RITE.] **—rit′u•al•ly** *adv.*
rit•u•al•ism (rĭch′o͞o-ə-lĭz′əm) *n.* **1.** The practice or observance of religious ritual. **2.** Insistence on or adherence to ritual.
rit•u•al•ist (rĭch′o͞o-ə-lĭst) *n.* **1.** An authority on or a student of ritual. **2.** One who practices or advocates the observance of ritual.
rit•u•al•is•tic (rĭch′o͞o-ə-lĭs′tĭk) *adj.* **1.** Relating to ritual or ritualism. **2.** Advocating or practicing ritual. **—rit′u•al•is′ti•cal•ly** *adv.*
rit•u•al•ize (rĭch′o͞o-ə-līz′) *v.* **-ized, -iz•ing, -iz•es.** *—tr.* **1.** To make a ritual of. **2.** To force a ritual on. *—intr.* To engage in ritualism. **—rit′u•al•i•za′tion** (-ə-lĭ-zā′shən) *n.*
ritual murder *n.* **1.** The murder of a person as a human sacrifice to a deity. **2.** A murder committed in such a way as to resemble a sacrifice to a deity.
ritz (rĭts) *n. Informal.* Elegant, often ostentatious display. **—*idiom.* put on the ritz.** *Informal.* To behave or live in an elegant ostentatious manner. [Back-formation < RITZY.]
ritz•y (rĭt′sē) *adj.* **-i•er, -i•est.** *Informal.* Elegant; fancy. [After the *Ritz* hotels, estab. by César Ritz (1850–1918), Swiss hotelier.]
riv. *abbr.* River.
riv•age (rĭv′ĭj) *n. Archaic.* A coast, shore, or bank. [ME < OFr. < *rive*, bank < Lat. *rīpa*.]
ri•val (rī′vəl) *n.* **1.** One who attempts to equal or surpass another or pursues the same object as another; a competitor. **2.** One that equals or almost equals another in a particular respect. **3.** *Obsolete.* A companion or an associate in a particular duty. *—v.* **-valed, -val•ing, -vals** or **-valled, -val•ling, -vals.** *—tr.* **1.** To attempt to equal or surpass. **2.** To be the equal of; match. *—intr.* To be a competitor or rival; compete. [Lat. *rīvālis*, a rival, one using the same stream as another < *rīvus*, stream. See **rei-*.**]
ri•val•rous (rī′vəl-rəs) *adj.* Characterized by or given to rivalry or competition.
ri•val•ry (rī′vəl-rē) *n., pl.* **-ries. 1.** The act of competing or emulating. **2.** The state or condition of being a rival.
rive (rīv) *v.* **rived, riv•en** (rĭv′ən) also **rived, riv•ing, rives.** *—tr.* **1.** To rend or tear apart. **2.** To break into pieces, as by a blow; cleave or split asunder. **3.** To break or distress (the spirit, for example). *—intr.* To be or become split. [ME *riven* < ON *rīfa*.]
riv•er (rĭv′ər) *n.* **1.** A large natural stream of water emptying into an ocean, a lake, or another body of water and usu. fed along its course by converging tributaries. **2.** A stream or an abundant flow. **—*idiom.* up the river.** *Slang.* In or into prison. [ME *rivere* < AN < VLat. **rīpāria* < Lat., fem. of *rīpārius*, of a bank < *rīpa*, bank.]
Ri•ve•ra (rĭ-vĕr′ə, rē-vĕ′rä), **Diego.** 1886–1957. Mexican painter noted for his murals.
Rivera y Or•ba•ne•ja (ē ôr′bä-nĕ′hä), **Miguel Primo de.** See Miguel **Primo de Rivera y Orbaneja.**
riv•er•bank (rĭv′ər-băngk′) *n.* The bank of a river.
river basin *n.* The land area drained by a river and its tributaries.
riv•er•bed (rĭv′ər-bĕd′) *n.* The area between the banks of a river ordinarily covered by water.
river blindness *n.* See **onchocerciasis.**
riv•er•boat (rĭv′ər-bōt′) *n. Naut.* A boat suitable for use on a river.
riv•er•head (rĭv′ər-hĕd′) *n.* The source of a river.
river horse *n.* See **hippopotamus** 1.
riv•er•ine (rĭv′ə-rīn′, -rēn′) *adj.* **1.** Relating to or resembling a river. **2.** Located on or inhabiting the banks of a river; riparian. **3.** Operating on or equipped to operate on rivers.
Riv•ers (rĭv′ərz), **Larry.** b. 1923. Amer. artist whose paintings combine bold brushwork and realistic images.
riv•er•side (rĭv′ər-sīd′) *n.* The bank or area alongside a river.
Riv•er•side (rĭv′ər-sīd′). A city of S CA NE of Santa Ana. Pop. 226,505.
Riv•er•ton Heights (rĭv′ər-tən). A community of W-central WA, a suburb of Seattle. Pop. 33,500.
riv•er•ward (rĭv′ər-wərd) also **riv•er•wards** (-wərdz) *adv.* Toward a river.
riv•er•weed (rĭv′ər-wēd′) *n.* An eastern North American plant *(Podostemum ceratophyllum)* having olive-green foliage resembling seaweed and growing in rapidly flowing streams.
riv•et (rĭv′ĭt) *n.* A metal bolt or pin having a head on one end, inserted through aligned holes in the pieces to be joined and then hammered on the plain end so as to form a second head. *—tr.v.* **-et•ed, -et•ing, -ets. 1.** To fasten or secure with or as if with a rivet. **2.** To hammer the headless end of so as to form a head and fasten something. **3.** To fasten or secure firmly; fix. **4.** To engross or hold (the attention, for example). [ME < OFr. *river*, to attach.] **—riv′et•er** *n.*
riv•et•ing (rĭv′ĭ-tĭng) *adj.* Wholly absorbing or engrossing one's attention; fascinating. **—riv′et•ing•ly** *adv.*
Riv•i•er•a (rĭv′ē-ĕr′ə, rē-vyĕ′rä). A narrow coastal region between the Alps and the Mediterranean Sea extending from SE France to NW Italy.
Riviera Beach. A city of SE FL on the Atlantic Ocean N of West Palm Beach. Pop. 27,639.
ri•vière (rē-vyâr′) *n.* A necklace of precious stones, usu. set in one strand. [Fr. *rivière (de diamants)*, river (of diamonds) < OFr. *rivere* < VLat. **rīpāria*. See RIVER.]
riv•u•let (rĭv′yə-lĭt) *n.* A small brook or stream; a streamlet. [Poss. < Ital. *rivoletto*, dim. of *rivolo*, small stream < Lat. *rīvulus*, dim. of *rīvus*, stream. See **rei-*.**]
Ri•yadh (rē-yäd′). The cap. of Saudi Arabia, in the E-central part ENE of Mecca. Pop. 1,250,000.
ri•yal also **ri•al** (rē-ôl′, -äl′) *n.* See table at **currency.** [Ar. *riyāl* < Sp. *real*, real. See REAL[2].]
ri•yal-o•man•i (rē-ôl′ō-mä′nē, rē-äl′-) *n., pl.* **ri•yals-o•man•i** (rē-ôlz′-, rē-älz′-). See table at **currency.** [Ar. *riyāl 'umānī* : *riyāl*, riyal + *'umānī*, of Oman.]
Ri•zal (rĭ-zäl′, rē-säl′), **José.** 1861–96. Philippine national leader and writer whose execution precipitated an insurrection against Spanish rule (1896–98).
Riz•zio (rĭt′sē-ō′, rēt′tsē-ô′), **David.** 1533?–66. Italian musician and secretary to Mary Queen of Scots.
Rm *abbr. Bible.* Romans.
RM also **Rm.** *abbr.* Reichsmark.
rm. *abbr.* **1.** Ream. **2.** Room.
rms *abbr. Math.* Root mean square.
RMS *abbr.* **1.** Railway Mail Service. **2.** Also **R.M.S.** Royal Mail Service. **3.** Also **R.M.S.** Royal Mail Steamship.
Rn The symbol for the element **radon.**
RN or **R.N.** *abbr.* **1.** Registered nurse. **2.** Royal Navy.
RNA (är′ĕn-ā′) *n.* A polymeric constituent of all living cells and many viruses, important in protein synthesis and the transmission of genetic information and consisting of a long, usu. single-stranded chain of alternating phosphate and ribose units with the bases adenine, guanine, cytosine, and uracil bonded to the ribose. [R(IBO)N(UCLEIC) A(CID).]
RNA polymerase *n.* A polymerase that catalyzes the synthesis of RNA from a DNA or RNA template.
RN•ase (är′ĕn-ās′, -āz′) also **RNA•ase** (är′ĕn-ā′ās′, -āz′) *n.* See **ribonuclease.**
RNA virus *n.* An RNA-containing virus; retrovirus.
rnd. *abbr.* Round.
roach[1] (rōch) *n., pl.* **roach** or **roach•es. 1.** A freshwater fish *(Rutilus rutilus)* of northern Europe. **2.** Any of various similar or related fishes, such as some North American sunfishes. [ME *roche* < OFr. *roce, roche*.]
roach[2] (rōch) *n., pl.* **roach•es. 1.** The cockroach. **2.** *Slang.* The butt of a marijuana cigarette.
roach[3] (rōch) *n., pl.* **roach•es. 1.** A roll of hair brushed up from the forehead or temple. **2.** A hairstyle esp. among certain Native American peoples in which the head is shaved except for a strip from front to back across the top. **3.** *Naut.* An outward curve in the leech of a fore-and-aft sail. *—v.* **roached, roach•ing, roach•es.** *—tr.* **1.** To brush (hair) in a roach. **2.** To shave (the mane of a horse) to a short bristle. [?]
road (rōd) *n.* **1.a.** An open, usu. public way for the passage of vehicles, people, and animals. **b.** The surface of a road; a roadbed. **2.** A course or path. **3.** A railroad. **4.** *Naut.* A roadstead. Often used in the plural. **—*idiom.* on the road. 1.** On tour, as a theatrical company. **2.** Traveling, esp. as a salesperson. **3.** Wandering, as a vagabond. [ME *rode, rade*, a riding, road < OE *rād*. See **reidh-*.**]

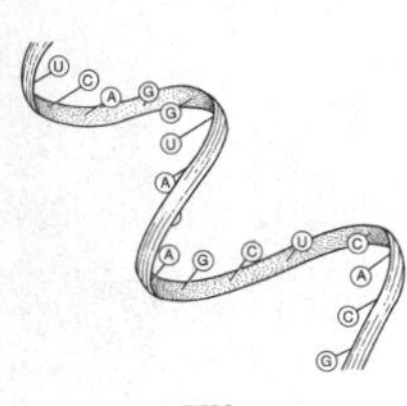

RNA

roadrunner
Geococcyx californianus

Paul Robeson

ă pat	oi boy
ā pay	ou out
âr care	o͝o took
ä father	o͞o boot
ĕ pet	ŭ cut
ē be	ûr urge
ĭ pit	th thin
ī pie	*th* this
îr pier	hw which
ŏ pot	zh vision
ō toe	ə about,
ô paw	item

Stress marks:
′ (primary);
′ (secondary), as in
dictionary (dĭk′shə-nĕr′ē)

road agent *n.* A stagecoach robber; a bandit.
road•bed (rōd′bĕd′) *n.* **1.a.** The foundation upon which the ties, rails, and ballast of a railroad are laid. **b.** A layer of ballast directly under the ties. **2.** The foundation and surface of a road.
road•block (rōd′blŏk′) *n.* **1.** A barricade or an obstruction across a road to prevent passage, as of a fugitive. **2.** An obstruction in a road, as fallen rocks. **3.** Something that prevents further progress toward an accomplishment.
road hog *n. Informal.* A motorist whose vehicle overlaps the traffic lane used by another motorist.
road•house (rōd′hous′) *n.* An inn, a restaurant, or a nightclub located on a road outside a town or city.
road•ie also **road•y** (rō′dē) *n.* A person engaged to load, unload, and set up equipment and perform errands for rock musicians on tour.
road map or **road•map** (rōd′măp′) *n.* **1.** A map, esp. one for motorists, showing and designating the roads of a region. **2.** A set of guidelines, instructions, or explanations.
road metal *n.* Crushed or broken stone, cinders, or similar material used in the construction and repair of roads and roadbeds.
road•run•ner (rōd′rŭn′ər) *n.* A swift-running crested bird *(Geococcyx californianus)* of southwest North America having streaked brownish plumage and a long tail.
road show *n.* **1.** A show presented by a troupe of theatrical performers on tour. **2.** A new movie shown at selected theaters usu. for higher ticket prices.
road•side (rōd′sīd′) *n.* The area bordering a road.
road•stead (rōd′stĕd′) *n. Naut.* A sheltered offshore anchorage area for ships. [Var. of *rodested* : RODE² + *sted*, place (var. of STEAD).]
road•ster (rōd′stər) *n.* **1.** An open automobile having a single seat in the front for two or three people and a rumble seat or luggage compartment in the back. **2.** A horse for riding on a road.
road test *n.* **1.** A test of a motor vehicle's operating capability under actual road conditions. **2.** A test of driving ability on the road required of a candidate for a driver's license. **—road′-test′** (rōd′tĕst′) *v.*
Road Town (rōd). The cap. of the British Virgin Islands, on Tortola I. in the West Indies E of Puerto Rico. Pop. 2,479.
road•way (rōd′wā′) *n.* A road, esp. the part over which vehicles travel.
road•work (rōd′wûrk′) *n.* **1.** *Sports.* Outdoor long-distance running as a form of physical exercise or conditioning. **2.** Highway construction.
road•wor•thy (rōd′wûr′*thē*) *adj.* **-thi•er, -thi•est.** Fit to be driven on the open road: *a roadworthy truck.*
roam (rōm) *v.* **roamed, roam•ing, roams.** —*intr.* To move about without purpose or plan; wander. See Syns at **wander.** —*tr.* To wander over or through. —*n.* The act or an instance of roaming. [ME *romen.*] **—roam′er** *n.*
roan (rōn) *adj.* Having a chestnut, bay, or sorrel coat thickly sprinkled with white or gray. —*n.* **1.a.** The characteristic coloring of a roan horse. **b.** A roan horse or other animal. **2.** A soft flexible sheepskin leather, often treated to resemble morocco and used in bookbinding. [Obsolete Fr. < OFr. < OSp. *roano*, prob. of Gmc. orig.]
Ro•a•noke (rō′ə-nōk′). An independent city of SW VA WSW of Richmond. Pop. 96,397.
Roanoke Island. An island of NE NC off the Atlantic coast between Albemarle and Pamlico sounds. A group of English colonists who landed on the island in Jul. 1587 vanished without a trace sometime before 1591.
Roanoke River. A river rising in SW VA and flowing c. 660 km (410 mi) to Albemarle Sound in NE NC.
roar (rôr, rōr) *v.* **roared, roar•ing, roars.** —*intr.* **1.** To utter a loud, deep, prolonged sound, esp. in distress, rage, or excitement. **2.** To laugh loudly or excitedly. **3.** To make or produce a loud noise or din. **4.** To be disorderly or rowdy. **5.** To breathe with a rasping sound. Used of a horse. —*tr.* **1.** To utter or express with a loud, deep, prolonged sound. See Syns at **shout. 2.** To put, bring, or force into a specified state by roaring. —*n.* **1.** A loud, deep, prolonged sound or cry, as of a person in distress or rage. **2.** The loud deep cry of a wild animal. **3.** A loud prolonged noise. **4.** A loud burst of laughter. [ME *roren* < OE *rārian.*] **—roar′er** *n.*
roar•ing (rôr′ĭng, rōr′-) *adj.* **1.** Very lively or successful; thriving. **2.** Used as an intensive. **—roar′ing•ly** *adv.*
roast (rōst) *v.* **roast•ed, roast•ing, roasts.** —*tr.* **1.** To cook with dry heat, as in an oven or near hot coals. **2.** To dry, brown, or parch by exposing to heat. **3.** To expose to great or excessive heat. **4.** *Metall.* To heat (ores) in a furnace in order to dehydrate, purify, or oxidize before smelting. **5.** *Informal.* To ridicule or criticize harshly. —*intr.* **1.** To cook food in an oven. **2.** To undergo roasting. —*n.* **1.a.** Something roasted. **b.** A cut of meat suitable or prepared for roasting. **2.a.** The act or process of roasting. **b.** The state of being roasted. **3.a.** Harsh ridicule or criticism. **b.** A facetious tribute, usu. in the form of a banquet, in which the honoree's friends and acquaintances alternate short speeches of praise and insult. —*adj.* Roasted. [ME *rosten* < OFr. *rostir*, of Gmc. orig.]
roast•er (rō′stər) *n.* **1.** One that roasts. **2.** A special pan or apparatus for roasting. **3.** Something, esp. a young chicken, that is fit for roasting.
rob (rŏb) *v.* **robbed, rob•bing, robs.** —*tr.* **1.** *Law.* To take property from (a person or persons) illegally by using or threatening to use violence or force; commit robbery upon. **2.** To take valuable or desired articles unlawfully from. **3.a.** To deprive unjustly of something belonging to, desired by, or legally due (someone). **b.** To deprive of something injuriously. **4.** To take as booty; steal. —*intr.* To engage in or commit robbery. **—*idioms.* rob (someone or something) blind.** To rob in an unusually deceitful or thorough way. **rob the cradle.** *Informal.* To have a romantic or sexual relationship with someone much younger than oneself. [ME *robben* < OFr. *rober*, of Gmc. orig. See **reup-*.**] **—rob′ber** *n.*
ro•ba•lo (rō-bä′lō) *n., pl.* **-los** or **robalo.** Any of various chiefly tropical marine food fishes of the family Centropomidae, such as the snook. [Sp. *róbalo*, haddock, prob. alteration of Catalan *llobarro* < *lobo*, wolf < Lat. *lupus.* See LOBO.]
Robbe-Gril•let (rôb-grē-yā′), **Alain.** b. 1922. French writer and exponent of the New Wave in French literature.
robber baron *n.* **1.** One of the American industrial or financial magnates of the latter 19th century who became wealthy by unethical means. **2.** A feudal lord who robbed travelers passing through his domain.
robber fly *n.* Any of various predatory flies of the family Asilidae, characteristically having long bristly legs.
rob•ber•y (rŏb′ə-rē) *n., pl.* **-ies.** *Law.* The act or an instance of unlawfully taking the property of another by the use of violence or intimidation.
Rob•bins (rŏb′ĭnz), **Jerome.** b. 1918. Amer. choreographer of ballets and musicals, including *West Side Story* (1957).
robe (rōb) *n.* **1.** A long, loose, flowing outer garment, esp.: **a.** An official garment worn on formal occasions to show office or rank, as by a judge or high church official. **b.** An academic gown. **c.** A dressing gown or bathrobe. **2. robes.** Clothes; apparel. **3.** A blanket or covering made of material such as fur or cloth: *a lap robe.* —*v.* **robed, rob•ing, robes.** —*tr.* To cover or dress in or as if in a robe. —*intr.* To put on robes or a robe. [ME < OFr., of Gmc. orig. See **reup-*.**]
Rob•ert I¹ (rŏb′ərt). "Robert the Devil." d. 1035. Duke of Normandy (1027–35) who named as his heir his illegitimate son William, the future William I of England.
Robert I². "Robert the Bruce." 1274–1329. King of Scotland (1306–29) who won Scottish independence from England in a battle at Bannockburn (1314).
Robert, Henry Martyn. 1837–1923. Amer. army engineer and parliamentarian who wrote *Robert's Rules of Order* (1876).
Rob•erts (rŏb′ərts), **Owen Josephus.** 1875–1955. American jurist; associate justice of the U.S. Supreme Court (1930–45).
Robe•son (rōb′sən), **Paul Bustill.** 1898–1976. Amer. singer and actor noted for his performance in *Othello.*
Robes•pierre (rōbz′pîr, -pē-âr′, rô-bĕs-pyĕr′), **Maximilien François Marie Isidore de.** 1758–94. French revolutionary leader of the Jacobins and architect of the Reign of Terror.
rob•in (rŏb′ĭn) *n.* **1.** A North American songbird *(Turdus migratorius)* having a rust-red breast and gray and black upper plumage. **2.** A small Old World bird *(Erithacus rubecula)* having an orange breast and a brown back. **3.** Any of various birds resembling a robin. [Short for *Robin Redbreast* < ME *Robin*, personal name < OFr., dim. of Robert.]
Rob•in Good•fel•low (rŏb′ĭn go͝od′fĕl′ō) *n.* Puck.
Robin Hood *n.* A legendary English outlaw of the 12th century, famous for his courage, chivalry, and practice of robbing the rich to aid the poor.
robin redbreast *n.* See **robin** 1, 2.
rob•in's-egg blue (rŏb′ĭnz-ĕg′) *n. Color.* A pale bluish green to greenish or grayish blue.
Rob•in•son (rŏb′ĭn-sən), **Edwin Arlington.** 1869–1935. Amer. poet whose works include "Miniver Cheevy" (1910).
Robinson, Jack ("Jackie") Roosevelt. 1919–72. Amer. baseball player who was the first Black player in the major leagues as a second baseman for the Brooklyn Dodgers (1947–56).
Robinson, Ray. "Sugar Ray." 1921–89. Amer. prizefighter who was world champion six times, once as a welterweight (1946–51) and five times as a middleweight (1951–60).
Robinson Cru•soe (kro͞o′sō) *n.* The hero of Daniel Defoe's novel *Robinson Crusoe* (1719), a shipwrecked English sailor who by ingenuity survives for years on a small island.
Rob•in's plantain (rŏb′ĭnz) *n.* An eastern North American plant *(Erigeron pulchellus)* having many-rayed purplish flower heads grouped in a corymb.
ro•ble (rō′blā) *n.* **1.** A Californian oak *(Quercus lobata)* having leathery leaves and slender pointed acorns. **2.** Any of various similar or related trees. [Sp. and Port., oak, both < Lat. *rōbur.* See **reudh-*.**]
rob•o•rant (rŏb′ər-ənt) *adj.* Restoring vigor or strength. —*n.* A roborant drug; a restorative or tonic. [Lat. *rōborāns, rōborant-*, pr.part. of *rōborāre*, to strengthen < *rōbur, rōbor-*, oak, strength. See **reudh-*.**]
ro•bot (rō′bət, -bŏt′) *n.* **1.** A mechanical device that may re-

Robespierre
Detail of a portrait by Louis Léopold Boilly (1761–1845)

robin
Turdus migratorius

Jackie Robinson
Photographed in the early 1950's

robot

semble a human being and is capable of performing a variety of often complex tasks on command or by being programmed in advance. **2.** A machine or device that operates automatically or by remote control. **3.** A person who works mechanically without original thought, esp. one who responds automatically to commands. [Czech < *robota*, drudgery. See **orbh-***.] — **ro•bot′ic, ro′bot•is′tic** (-bə-tĭs′tĭk) *adj.*

robot bomb *n.* A small winged missile loaded with explosives, jet-propelled and guided by a gyroscopic device.

ro•bot•ics (rō-bŏt′ĭks) *n.* *(used with a sing. v.)* The science or study of the technology associated with the design, fabrication, theory, and application of robots.

ro•bot•ize (rō′bə-tīz′) *tr.v.* **-ized, -iz•ing, -iz•es. 1.** To convert (a system, for example) to automation by the application of advanced scientific technology. **2.** To make (a person) act like a robot. — **ro′bot•i•za′tion** (-bə-tĭ-zā′shən) *n.*

robot pilot *n.* See **automatic pilot.**

rob roy (rŏb roi′) *n.* A cocktail made with Scotch whisky, sweet vermouth, and bitters. [After ROB ROY.]

Rob Roy (rŏb roi′). Orig. Robert MacGregor. 1671–1734. Scottish clan leader whose banditry is the subject of Sir Walter Scott's novel *Rob Roy* (1817).

Rob•son (rŏb′sən), **Mount.** A mountain, 3,956.5 m (12,972 ft), in the Canadian Rocky Mts. of E British Columbia, Canada, on the border with Alberta.

ro•bust (rō-bŭst′, rō′bŭst′) *adj.* **1.** Full of health and strength; vigorous. **2.** Powerfully built; sturdy. See Syns at **healthy. 3.** Requiring or suited to physical strength or endurance: *robust labor.* **4.** Rough or crude; boisterous: *a robust tale.* **5.** Marked by richness and fullness; full-bodied: *a robust wine.* [Lat. *rōbustus* < *rōbus, rōbur*, oak, strength. See **reudh-***.] — **ro•bust′ly** *adv.* — **ro•bust′ness** *n.*

ro•bus•ta coffee (rō-bŭs′tə) *n.* **1.a.** A west African tropical shrub or small tree *(Coffea canephora)* having fragrant white flowers and red fruit. **b.** The seed of this plant. **2.** The coffee brewed from the seeds of this plant. [Lat. *rōbusta*, fem. of *rōbustus*, strong. See ROBUST.]

ro•bus•tious (rō-bŭs′chəs) *adj.* **1.** Boisterous; vigorous. **2.** Rough, coarse, or crude. — **ro•bus′tious•ly** *adv.*

roc (rŏk) *n.* A mythical bird of prey having enormous size and strength. [Ar. *ruḫḫ*, prob. < Pers. *rukh*.]

Ro•ca (rō′kə, rô′-), **Cape.** A cape of W Portugal on the Atlantic Ocean WNW of Lisbon.

Norman Rockwell

roc•am•bole (rŏk′əm-bōl′) *n.* **1.** A European plant *(Allium sativum* var. *ophioscordon)* having a garliclike bulb. **2.** The bulb of this plant used as a seasoning. [Fr. < Ger. *Rockenbolle* : *Rocken*, distaff (< MHGer. *rocke* < OHGer. *rocko*) + *Bolle*, bulb (< MHGer. *bolle* < OHGer. *bolla*, ball; see **bhel-²***).]

Ro•cham•beau (rō′shăm-bō′, -shäN-), **Comte de.** Jean Baptiste Donatien de Vimeur. 1725–1807. French army officer who commanded French forces in the American Revolution, most notably in the defeat of the British at Yorktown (1781).

Roch•dale (rŏch′dāl′). A borough of NW England NNE of Manchester. Pop. 288,400.

Ro•chelle salt or **Ro•chelle salts** (rə-shĕl′, rō-) *n.* See **potassium sodium tartrate.** [After (LA) ROCHELLE.]

roche mou•ton•née (rôsh′ mo͞ot′n-ā′, mo͞o′tô-nā′) *n., pl.* **roches mou•ton•nées** (rôsh′ mo͞ot′n-ā′, -āz′, mo͞o′tô-nā′). An elongate mound of bedrock worn smooth and rounded by glacial abrasion. [Fr. : *roche*, rock + *moutonné*, fleecy.]

Roch•es•ter (rŏch′ĭ-stər, -ĕs′tər). **1.** A city of SE MN SE of St. Paul; site of the Mayo Clinic (founded 1889). Pop. 70,745. **2.** A city of SE NH NNW of Dover; settled in 1728. Pop. 25,630. **3.** A city of W NY ENE of Buffalo on the New York State Barge Canal; first settled c. 1812. Pop. 231,636.

roch•et (rŏch′ĭt) *n.* A white ceremonial vestment made of linen or lawn, worn by bishops and other church dignitaries. [ME < OFr., of Gmc. orig.]

rock¹ (rŏk) *n.* **1.** Relatively hard, naturally formed mineral or petrified matter; stone. **2.a.** A relatively small piece or fragment of such material. **b.** A relatively large body of such material, as a cliff. **3.** A naturally formed aggregate of mineral matter constituting a significant part of the earth's crust. **4.** One that is similar to or suggestive of a mass of stone, as in stability or firmness. **5. rocks.** *Slang.* Money. **6.** *Slang.* A large gem, esp. a diamond. **7.** *Slang.* Crack cocaine. **8.a.** A varicolored stick candy. **b.** Rock candy. — ***idioms.* between a rock and a hard place.** Faced with equally unpleasant alternatives and few or no opportunities to evade or circumvent them. **on the rocks. 1.** In a state of difficulty, destruction, or ruin. **2.** Without money; bankrupt. **3.** Served over ice cubes. [ME < ONFr. *roque* < VLat. *rocca.]

rock² (rŏk) *v.* **rocked, rock•ing, rocks.** — *intr.* **1.** To move back and forth or from side to side, esp. gently or rhythmically. **2.** To sway violently, as from a blow. **3.** To be washed and panned in a cradle or rocker. Used of ores. **4.** *Mus.* To play or dance to rock 'n' roll. — *tr.* **1.** To move back and forth or from side to side, esp. in order to soothe or lull to sleep. **2.** To cause to shake or sway violently. **3.** To disturb the mental or emotional equilibrium of; upset. **4.** To wash or pan (ore) in a cradle or rocker. **5.** In mezzotint engraving, to roughen (a metal plate) with a rocker or roulette. — *n.* **1.a.** A rocking motion. **b.** The act of rocking. **2.** *Mus.* Rock 'n' roll. — ***idiom.* rock the boat.** *Slang.* To disturb the balance or routine of a situation. [ME *rokken* < OE *roccian*.] — **rock′ing•ly** *adv.*

rock•a•bil•ly (rŏk′ə-bĭl′ē) *n.* *Mus.* A form of popular music combining features of rock 'n' roll and country music. [ROCK ('N' ROLL) + (HILL)BILLY.]

rock-a-bye also **rock•a•bye** or **rock•a•by** (rŏk′ə-bī′) *interj.* Used to lull an infant or a child to sleep. [ROCK² + (LULL)ABY.]

rock-and-roll (rŏk′ən-rōl′) *n.* *Mus.* Var. of **rock 'n' roll.**

rock and rye *n.* A liqueur made of whiskey blended with powdered rock candy and sometimes fruit.

rock•a•way (rŏk′ə-wā′) *n.* A four-wheeled carriage with two seats and a standing top. [Prob. after *Rockaway* in N NJ.]

rock bass (băs) *n.* **1.** A freshwater food and game fish *(Ambloplites rupestris)* of eastern and central North America. **2.** Any of various similar or related fishes.

rock bottom *n.* The lowest possible level or absolute bottom. — **rock′-bot′tom** (rŏk′bŏt′əm) *adj.*

rock•bound also **rock-bound** (rŏk′bound′) *adj.* Hemmed in by or bordered with rocks.

rock brake *n.* Any of several ferns of the genus *Crytogramma* that usu. grow in rocky ground.

rock candy *n.* A hard confection made by cooling sugar syrup into large clear crystals around a piece of string or a stick.

Rock Cornish (rŏk) *n.* A small fowl of a breed developed by crossing white Plymouth Rock and Cornish strains.

rock crab *n.* A crab found along rocky coasts, esp. one of the genus *Cancer*, whose hindmost pair of legs is adapted for running.

rock crystal *n.* Colorless transparent quartz, used in optical instruments and as a semiprecious gemstone.

rock dove *n.* The common pigeon *(Columba livia)*, native to Europe but widely distributed and having variously colored plumage with iridescent markings on the neck.

Rock•e•fel•ler (rŏk′ə-fĕl′ər). Amer. family, including **John Davison** (1839–1937), who amassed great wealth through the Standard Oil Company. His son **John Davison, Jr.** (1874–1960), was a noted philanthropist, and his grandson **Nelson Aldrich** (1908–79) served as governor of NY (1959–73) and Vice President of the U.S. (1974–77).

rock elm *n.* **1.** A deciduous eastern North American tree *(Ulmus thomasii)* having corky branches and coarsely toothed leaves. **2.** The wood of this tree.

rock•er (rŏk′ər) *n.* **1.** One that rocks, as: **a.** A rocking chair. **b.** A rocking horse. **2.** One of the two curved pieces upon which a cradle, rocking chair, or similar device rocks. **3.** A cradle used for washing or panning ores. **4.** A small curved blade with a toothed edge used in mezzotint engraving to roughen the surface of the metal plate. **5.** An ice skate with a curved blade. **6.** A curved stripe below a chevron worn by some ranks of enlisted military personnel. **7.** *Mus.* **a.** A rock 'n' roll song, singer, or musician. **b.** A fan of rock 'n' roll. — ***idiom.* off (one's) rocker.** *Slang.* Out of one's mind; crazy.

rocker arm *n.* A pivoted lever used in an internal combustion engine to transfer cam or pushrod motion to a valve stem.

rock•er•y (rŏk′ə-rē) *n., pl.* **-ies.** See **rock garden** 2.

rock•et¹ (rŏk′ĭt) *n.* **1.a.** A rocket engine. **b.** A vehicle or device propelled by one or more rocket engines, esp. such a vehicle designed to travel through space. **2.** A projectile weapon carrying a warhead that is powered and propelled by rockets. **3.** A projectile firework having a cylindrical shape and a fuse that is lit from the rear. — *v.* **-et•ed, -et•ing, -ets.** — *intr.* **1.** To move swiftly and powerfully, as a rocket. **2.** To fly swiftly straight up, as a game bird frightened from cover. **3.** To soar or rise rapidly. — *tr.* **1.** To carry by means of a rocket. **2.** To assault with rockets. [Ital. *rocchetta*, dim. of *rocca*, spindle, distaff, of Gmc. or.]

rock•et² (rŏk′ĭt) *n.* **1.** A Mediterranean plant *(Eruca vesicaria* subsp. *sativa)* having flowers with purple-veined yellowish-white petals and leaves that are sometimes used in salads. **2.** Any of several plants of the mustard family, such as the dame's rocket. [ME *rokette* < OFr. *roquette* < Ital. *rochetta*, var. of *ruchetta*, dim. of *ruca*, a cabbage < Lat. *ērūca*.]

rock•et•eer (rŏk′ĭ-tîr′) *n.* **1.** One who launches, rides in, or pilots rockets. **2.** An expert in rocketry.

rocket engine *n.* A reaction engine that operates independently of any outside substances, such as atmospheric oxygen, and thus is capable of operating in outer space.

rocket plane *n.* **1.** An aircraft powered by one or more rocket engines. **2.** An aircraft designed to carry and launch rockets.

rock•et•ry (rŏk′ĭ-trē) *n.* The science and technology of rocket design, construction, and flight.

rocket salad *n.* See **rocket²** 1.

rocket ship *n.* A spacecraft powered and propelled by rockets.

rocket sled *n.* A rocket-propelled sled that travels along rails and is used to study acceleration, deceleration, and crash survival techniques.

rock•et•sonde (rŏk′ĭt-sŏnd′) *n.* An instrument transported to the upper atmosphere by rocket, used to study meteorological conditions. [ROCKET¹ + (RADIO)SONDE.]

Rock fever *n.* See **brucellosis** 1. [After the *Rock* of Gibraltar, where it is endemic.]

rock•fish (rŏk′fĭsh′) *n., pl.* **rockfish** or **-fish•es. 1.** Any of various fishes living among rocks. **2.** Any of various fishes, chiefly of the genus *Sebastes,* of Pacific waters. **3.** See **striped bass.**

rock flour *n.* Finely ground rock particles produced by glacial abrasion.

Rock•ford (rŏk′fərd). A city of N IL WNW of Chicago; founded 1834. Pop. 139,426.

rock garden *n.* **1.** A rocky area in which plants particularly adapted to such terrain are cultivated. **2.** A garden that has a decorative scheme of rocks and cultivated plants.

Rock Hill. A city of N SC N of Columbia. Pop. 41,643.

rock hound *n. Informal.* **1.** A specialist in geology. **2.** A collecter of rocks and minerals, esp. gemstones, as a hobby. — **rock′ hound′ing, rock′hound′ing** (rŏk′hound′dĭng) *n.*

rock hyrax *n.* See **rock rabbit** 1.

Rock•ies (rŏk′ēz). See **Rocky Mountains.**

rock•ing chair (rŏk′ĭng) *n.* A chair mounted on rockers or springs.

rocking horse *n.* A toy horse mounted on rockers or springs that is large enough for a child to ride.

Rock Island. A city of NW IL on the Mississippi R. adjacent to Moline. Pop. 40,552.

rock•ling (rŏk′lĭng) *n., pl.* **rockling** or **-lings.** Any of various small marine fishes of the family Gadidae of North Atlantic coastal waters.

rock lobster *n.* See **spiny lobster.**

rock maple *n.* **1.** See **sugar maple. 2.** The tough close-grained wood of the sugar maple.

Rock•ne (rŏk′nē), **Knute Kenneth.** 1888–1931. Norwegian-born Amer. football coach at the University of Notre Dame (1918–31) who revolutionized the sport with the use of the forward pass and other offensive strategies.

rock 'n' roll or **rock-and-roll** (rŏk′ən-rōl′) *n. Mus.* A form of popular music arising from and incorporating a variety of musical styles, esp. rhythm and blues, country music, and gospel. — **rock 'n' roller, rock′-and-roll′er** *n.*

rock oil *n. Chiefly British.* Petroleum.

rock•oon (rŏ-ko͞on′) *n.* A device used for high-altitude sounding, composed of a small solid-propellant rocket that is launched from a balloon. [ROCK(ET)[1] + (BALL)OON.]

rock pigeon *n.* See **rock dove.**

rock rabbit *n.* **1.** A hyrax of the genus *Procavia* or *Dendrohyrax,* esp. the African species *P. capensis.* **2.** See **pika.**

rock-ribbed (rŏk′rĭbd′) *adj.* **1.** Having rocks or rock outcroppings; rocky. **2.** Firm and unyielding, esp. with regard to one's principles, loyalties, or beliefs: *a rock-ribbed conservative.*

Rock River. A river rising in SE WI and flowing c. 459 km (285 mi) to the Mississippi R. in NW IL.

rock•rose (rŏk′rōz′) *n.* Any of various plants of the genera *Cistus* or *Helianthemum,* having small roselike yellow, white, or reddish flowers.

rock salt *n.* Sodium chloride occurring as extensive masses or rock.

rock•shaft (rŏk′shăft′) *n.* A shaft that oscillates or rocks upon its bearings but does not revolve.

rock•slide (rŏk′slīd′) *n.* **1.** The usu. rapid downward movement of newly detached segments of bedrock. **2.** A rock mass that has undergone such a movement.

Rock Springs. A city of SW WY N of the UT border; a trading post and stagecoach station in the 1860's. Pop. 19,050.

rock squirrel *n.* A large ground squirrel *(Spermophilus variegatus)* having variegated black and white upper parts and found in Mexico and the southwest United States.

Rock•ville (rŏk′vĭl′, -vəl). A city of central MD NNW of Washington DC. Pop. 44,835.

Rockville Cen•tre (sĕn′tər). A village of SE NY on SW Long I. SSW of Hempstead. Pop. 24,727.

rock wallaby *n.* Any of several small agile wallabies, chiefly of the genus *Petrogale,* that live in rocky areas and have thick-soled feet and a slender tail.

rock•weed (rŏk′wēd′) *n.* Any of several coarse brownish seaweeds of the genera *Fucus* and *Ascophyllum* that grow on rocks in coastal areas.

Rock•well (rŏk′wĕl′), **Norman.** 1894–1978. Amer. illustrator whose works offer a nostalgic view of everyday life.

rock wool *n.* See **mineral wool.**

rock•work (rŏk′wûrk′) *n.* **1.** A natural mass or pile of rocks. **2.** Stonework imitating the irregular surface of natural rock.

rock wren *n.* **1.** Any of several wrens of the genus *Salpinctes,* esp. *S. obsoletus,* found in rocky regions of the western United States and Mexico. **2.** A small wren *(Xenicus gilviventris)* that inhabits New Zealand and feeds mostly among stones.

rock•y[1] (rŏk′ē) *adj.* **-i•er, -i•est. 1.** Consisting of, containing, or abounding in rock or rocks. **2.a.** Resembling or suggesting rock; firm or hard. **b.** Steadfast or stubborn; unyielding. **3.** Marked by obstructions. — **rock′i•ness** *n.*

rock•y[2] (rŏk′ē) *adj.* **-i•er, -i•est. 1.a.** Inclined or prone to sway or totter; unsteady or shaky. **b.** Appearing inclined to fail; discouraging or disappointing: *won the championship after a rocky start.* **2.** Weak, dizzy, or nauseated, as from excessive alcohol intake. — **rock′i•ness** *n.*

Rock•y Mount (rŏk′ē). A city of NE NC ENE of Raleigh. Pop. 48,997.

Rocky Mountain goat *n.* See **mountain goat.**

Rocky Mountains also **Rock•ies** (rŏk′ēz). A mountain system of W North America extending from NW AK to the Mexican border and rising to 4,402.1 m (14,433 ft) in central CO.

Rocky Mountain sheep *n.* See **bighorn.**

Rocky Mountain spotted fever *n.* An acute infectious disease caused by a microorganism *(Rickettsia rickettsii)* that is transmitted by ticks, characterized by muscular pains, fever, and skin eruptions and endemic throughout North America.

Rocky River. A city of NE OH, a suburb of Cleveland. Pop. 20,410.

ro•co•co (rə-kō′kō, rō′kə-kō′) *n.* **1.a.** Also **Rococo.** A style of art and architecture that originated in France in the early 18th century and is marked by elaborate ornamentation. **b.** A very ornate style of speech or writing. **2.** Also **Rococo.** *Mus.* A style of composition arising in 18th-century Europe immediately following the baroque that is characterized by a high degree of ornamentation. — *adj.* **1.** Also **Rococo.** Of or relating to the rococo. **2.** Immoderately elaborate or complicated. [Fr., prob. alteration of *rocaille,* rockwork < *roc,* rock, var. of *roche* < VLat. **rocca.*]

rococo
Doors designed by Jean François de Cuvilliés (1695?–1768?)

rod (rŏd) *n.* **1.** A thin straight piece or bar of material, such as metal, often having a particular use, as: **a.** A fishing rod. **b.** A piston rod. **c.** An often expandable horizontal bar used to suspend household items such as curtains. **d.** A leveling rod. **e.** A lightning rod. **f.** A divining rod. **g.** A measuring stick. **2.** A shoot or stem cut from or growing as part of a woody plant. **3.a.** A stick or bundle of sticks or switches used to give punishment by whipping. **b.** Punishment; correction. **4.** A scepter, staff, or wand symbolizing power or authority. **5.** Power or dominion, esp. of a tyrannical nature. **6.a.** A linear measure equal to 5.5 yards or 16.5 feet (5.03 meters). **b.** The square of this measure, equal to 30.25 square yards or 272.25 square feet (25.30 square meters). See table at **measurement. 7.** *Bible.* A line of family descent; a branch of a tribe. **8.** *Anat.* Any of various rod-shaped cells in the retina that respond to dim light. **9.** *Microbiol.* An elongated bacterium; a bacillus. **10.** *Slang.* A pistol or revolver. **11.** A portion of the undercarriage of a train, esp. the drawbar under a freight car. Often used in the plural. [ME *rodd* < OE.]

rode[1] (rōd) *v.* P.t. of **ride.**

rode[2] (rōd) *n. Naut.* A rope, esp. one attached to the anchor of a small boat. [< ME *at rode,* at an anchorage < *rode,* a riding. See ROAD.]

ro•dent (rōd′nt) *n.* Any of various mammals of the order Rodentia, such as a mouse, rat, squirrel, or beaver, characterized by large incisors adapted for gnawing or nibbling. — *adj.* **1.** Gnawing. **2.** Of or relating to rodents. [< NLat. *Rodentia,* order name < Lat. *rōdēns, rōdent-,* pr.part. of *rōdere,* to gnaw. See **rēd-*.**]

ro•den•ti•cide (rō-dĕn′tĭ-sīd′) *n.* A chemical substance used to kill rodents.

rodent ulcer *n.* A cancerous skin ulcer that derives from basal cells and usu. occurs on the face. [Lat. *rodēns, rodent-,* gnawing. See RODENT.]

ro•de•o (rō′dē-ō′, rō-dā′ō) *n., pl.* **-os. 1.** A public competition or exhibition in which skills such as riding broncos or roping calves are displayed. **2.** A cattle roundup. **3.** An enclosure for keeping cattle that have been rounded up. [Sp., corral, rodeo < *rodear,* to surround < *rueda,* wheel < Lat. *rota.* See **ret-*.**]

rodeo

Rod•gers (rŏj′ərz), **Richard.** 1902–79. Amer. composer known for his musical comedies, esp. his collaborations with Oscar Hammerstein II, including *The Sound of Music* (1959).

Ro•din (rō-dăn′, -dăɴ′), **François Auguste René.** 1840–1917. French sculptor whose works include *The Thinker* (1880).

rod•man (rŏd′mən) *n.* One who carries and employs a leveling rod under the supervision of a surveyor.

rod•o•mon•tade also **rho•do•mon•tade** (rŏd′ə-mŏn-tād′, -täd′, rō′də-) — *n.* Pretentious boasting or bragging; bluster. — *intr.v.* **-tad•ed, -tad•ing, -tades.** To boast or brag; bluster. [Fr. < Ital. *rodomontada,* from *Rodomonte,* arrogant Saracen leader of Italian Renaissance epics.] — **rod′o•mon•tade′** *adj.*

roe[1] (rō) *n.* **1.** The eggs or the egg-laden ovary of a fish. **2.** The egg mass or spawn of certain crustaceans, such as the lobster. [ME *row* < MLGer. or MDu. *roge.*]

roe[2] (rō) *n., pl.* **roe** or **roes.** The roe deer. [ME *ro* < OE *rā, rāha.*]

Roeb•ling (rō′blĭng), **John Augustus.** 1806–69. German-born Amer. engineer who designed the Brooklyn Bridge, completed (1883) by his son **Washington Augustus** (1837–1926).

roe•buck (rō′bŭk′) *n.* A male roe deer.

roe deer *n.* A small, delicately formed Eurasian deer *(Capreolus capreolus)* having short branched antlers in the male and a brownish coat.

roent•gen also **rönt•gen** (rĕnt′gən, -jən, rŭnt′-) *n.* A unit of

ă pat	oi boy
ā pay	ou out
âr care	o͝o took
ä father	o͞o boot
ĕ pet	ŭ cut
ē be	ûr urge
ĭ pit	th thin
ī pie	*th* this
îr pier	hw which
ŏ pot	zh vision
ō toe	ə about, item
ô paw	

Stress marks:
′ (primary);
′ (secondary), as in
dictionary (dĭk′shə-nĕr′ē)

radiation exposure equal to the quantity of ionizing radiation that will produce one electrostatic unit of electricity in one cubic centimeter of dry air at 0°C and standard atmospheric pressure. — **roent′gen** *adj.*

Roent•gen (rĕnt′gən, -jən, rŭnt′-) or **Rönt•gen** (rœnt′gən), **Wilhelm Konrad.** 1845–1923. German physicist who discovered x-rays and won a 1901 Nobel Prize.

roent•gen•ize (rĕnt′gə-nīz′, -jə-, rŭnt′-) *tr.v.* **-ized, -iz•ing, -iz•es.** To subject to the action of x-rays.

roentgeno– *pref.* X-ray: *roentgenography.* [< ROENTGEN.]

roent•gen•o•gram (rĕnt′gə-nə-grăm′, -jə-, rŭnt′-) *n.* A photograph made with x-rays.

roent•gen•o•graph (rĕnt′gə-nə-grăf′, -jə-, rŭnt′-) *n.* See **roentgenogram.**

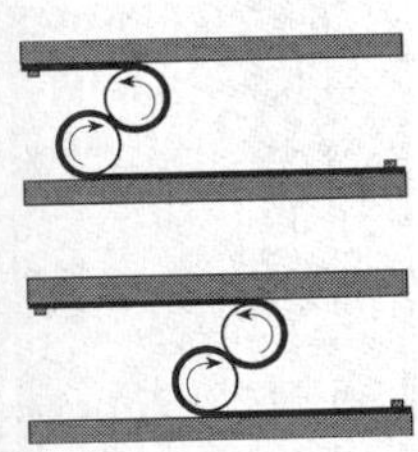
rolamite

roent•gen•og•ra•phy (rĕnt′gə-nŏg′rə-fē, -jə-, rŭnt′-) *n.* Photography with the use of x-rays. — **roent′gen•o•graph′ic** (-gə-nə-grăf′ĭk, -jə-) *adj.*

roent•gen•ol•o•gy (rĕnt′gə-nŏl′ə-jē, -jə-, rŭnt′-) *n.* Radiology that employs x-rays. — **roent′gen•o•log′ic** (-ə-lŏj′ĭk), **roent′gen•o•log′i•cal** (-ĭ-kəl) *adj.* — **roent′gen•ol′o•gist** *n.*

roent•gen•o•scope (rĕnt′gə-nə-skōp′, -jə-, rŭnt′-) *n.* See **fluoroscope.** — **roent′gen•o•scop′ic** (-skŏp′ĭk) *adj.* — **roent′gen•os′co•py** (-gə-nŏs′kə-pē, -jə-) *n.*

roent•gen•o•ther•a•py (rĕnt′gə-nə-thĕr′ə-pē, -jə-, rŭnt′-) *n., pl.* **-pies.** The therapeutic use of x-rays in treating disease.

roentgen ray *n.* See **x-ray** 1.

Roeth•ke (rĕt′kē, -kə, rĕth′-), **Theodore.** 1908–63. Amer. poet whose collections include *The Waking* (1953).

ro•ga•tion (rō-gā′shən) *n.* **1.** *Eccles.* Solemn prayer or supplication, esp. as chanted during the rites of Rogation Day. Often used in the plural. **2.a.** The formal proposal of a law in ancient Rome by a tribune or consul to the people for acceptance or rejection. **b.** A law proposed in this manner. [ME *rogacioun* < Lat. *rogātiō, rogātiōn-* < *rogātus,* p.part. of *rogāre,* to ask. See **reg-*.**]

Ro•ga•tion Day (rō-gā′shən) *n. Eccles.* One of the three days of prayer preceding Ascension Day.

ro•ga•to•ry (rō′gə-tôr′ē, -tōr′ē) *adj. Law.* Requesting information. Used esp. of a request by one court of another, often foreign court. [Fr. *rogatoire* < Med.Lat. *rogātōrius* < Lat. *rogātus,* p.part. of *rogāre,* to ask. See **reg-*.**]

rog•er (rŏj′ər) *interj.* Used esp. in radio communications to indicate receipt of a message. [< *Roger,* spoken representation of the letter *r,* short for RECEIVED.]

Rog•ers (rŏj′ərz). A city of NW AR N of Fayetteville. Pop. 24,692.

Rogers, Ginger. b. 1911. Amer. dancer and actress whose motion pictures with Fred Astaire include *Swing Time* (1936).

Rogers, Robert. 1731–95. Amer. soldier and pioneer who led (1758–63) the Rogers's Rangers on a series of missions during the French and Indian War.

Rogers, William ("Will") Penn Adair. 1879–1935. Amer. humorist noted for his wry homespun commentary on society and politics.

roller coaster

Ro•get (rō-zhā′, rō′zhā), **Peter Mark.** 1779–1869. British physician and scholar who compiled the *Thesaurus of English Words and Phrases* (1852).

rogue (rōg) *n.* **1.** An unprincipled, deceitful, and unreliable person; a scoundrel or rascal. **2.** One who is playfully mischievous; a scamp. **3.** A wandering beggar; a vagrant. **4.** A vicious and solitary animal, esp. an elephant that has separated itself from its herd. **5.** An organism, esp. a plant, that shows an undesirable variation from a standard. — *v.* **rogued, rogu•ing, rogues.** — *tr.* **1.** To defraud. **2.** To remove (diseased or abnormal specimens) from a group of plants of the same variety. — *intr.* To remove deviant plants. [?]

Rogue River (rōg). A river rising in the Cascade Range of SW OR and flowing c. 322 km (200 mi) to the Pacific Ocean.

rogu•er•y (rō′gə-rē) *n., pl.* **-ies. 1.** Behavior characteristic of a rogue. **2.** A mischievous act.

rogues' gallery (rōgz) *n.* A collection of pictures of known and suspected criminals maintained in police files and used for making identifications.

rogu•ish (rō′gĭsh) *adj.* **1.** Deceitful; unprincipled. **2.** Playfully mischievous. — **rogu′ish•ly** *adv.* — **rogu′ish•ness** *n.*

Rohn•ert Park (rō′nərt). A city of W CA, a suburb of Santa Rosa. Pop. 36,326.

roil (roil) *v.* **roiled, roil•ing, roils.** — *tr.* **1.** To make (a liquid) muddy or cloudy by stirring up sediment. **2.** To displease or disturb; vex. — *intr.* To be in a state of turbulence or agitation. [?]

roil•y (roi′lē) *adj.* **-i•er, -i•est. 1.** Full of sediment; muddy or cloudy. **2.** Turbulent; agitated.

rois•ter (roi′stər) *intr.v.* **-tered, -ter•ing, -ters. 1.** To engage in boisterous merrymaking; revel noisily. **2.** To behave in a blustering manner; swagger. [< obsolete *roister,* roisterer, prob. < OFr. *rustre,* ruffian, alteration of *ruste* < Lat. *rūsticus,* rustic. See RUSTIC.] — **rois′ter•er** *n.* — **rois′ter•ous** *adj.* — **rois′ter•ous•ly** *adv.*

ro•la•mite (rō′lə-mīt′) *n.* A mechanism consisting of two or more hard cylindrical rollers with a flexible nonstretching band looped around them, so that the rollers move against each other with very little friction. [ROL(L) + *-amite,* of unknown orig.]

Ro•land (rō′lənd, rô-läN′) *n.* A French hero in medieval chansons de geste, the nephew of Charlemagne and defender of Christianity, killed fighting the Saracens at Roncesvalles.

role also **rôle** (rōl) *n.* **1.** A character or part played by a performer. **2.** The characteristic and expected social behavior of an individual. **3.** A function or position. See Syns at **function.** [Fr. *rôle* < OFr. *rolle,* roll of parchment (on which an actor's part was written) < Lat. *rotula,* dim. of *rota,* wheel. See ROLL.]

role model *n.* A person who serves as a model in a particular behavioral or social role for another person to emulate.

role-play (rōl′plā′) *v.* **-played, -play•ing, -plays.** — *tr.* To assume deliberately the part or role of; act out. — *intr.* To assume or act out a particular role. — *n.* Role-playing.

role-play•ing (rōl′plā′ĭng) *n.* The acting out or assuming of a particular character or role, esp. as a therapeutic technique.

Rolf (rŏlf). See **Rollo.**

Rolfe (rŏlf), **John.** 1585–1622. English colonist in America and husband of Pocahontas.

roll (rōl) *v.* **rolled, roll•ing, rolls.** — *intr.* **1.** To move forward along a surface by revolving on an axis or by repeatedly turning over. **2.** To travel or be moved on wheels or rollers. **3.** To travel around; wander. **4.a.** To travel or be carried in a vehicle. **b.** To be carried on a stream. **5.a.** To start to move or operate. **b.** To work or succeed in a sustained way; gain momentum. **6.** To go by; elapse: *The days rolled along.* **7.** To recur: *Summer has rolled around again.* **8.** To move in a periodic revolution, as a planet in its orbit. **9.** To turn over and over. **10.** To shift the gaze usu. quickly and continually. **11.** To turn around or revolve on or as if on an axis. **12.** To move or advance with a rising and falling motion; undulate. **13.** To extend or appear to extend in gentle rises and falls: *The dunes roll to the sea.* **14.** To move or rock from side to side. **15.** To walk with a swaying, unsteady motion. **16.** To take the shape of a ball or cylinder: *Yarn rolls easily.* **17.** To become flattened by or as if by pressure applied by a roller. **18.** To make a deep, prolonged, surging sound: *rolling thunder.* **19.** To make a sustained trilling sound, as certain birds do. **20.** To beat a drum in a continuous series of short blows. **21.** To pour or flow in or as if in a continual stream: *tourists rolling into the city.* **22.** To enjoy ample amounts: *rolled in the money.* — *tr.* **1.** To cause to move forward along a surface by revolving on an axis or by repeatedly turning over. **2.** To move or push along on wheels or rollers. **3.** To impel or send onward in a steady swelling motion. **4.** To impart a swaying, rocking motion to. **5.** To turn around or partly turn around; rotate. **6.** To cause to begin moving or operating: *roll the presses.* **7.** To extend or lay out: *rolled out a long rope.* **8.** To pronounce or utter with a trill. **9.** To utter or emit in full, swelling tones. **10.** To beat (a drum) with a continuous series of short blows. **11.** To wrap (something) round and round upon itself or around something else: *roll up a poster.* **12.a.** To envelop or enfold in a covering: *roll laundry in a sheet.* **b.** To make by shaping into a ball or cylinder. **13.** To spread, compress, or flatten by applying pressure with a roller. **14.** *Print.* To apply ink to (type) with a roller or rollers. **15.** *Games.* To throw (dice), as in craps. **16.** *Slang.* To rob (a drunken, sleeping, or otherwise helpless person). — *n.* **1.** The act or an instance of rolling. **2.** Something rolled up. **3.** A quantity, as of cloth, rolled into a cylinder and often considered as a unit of measure. **4.** A piece of parchment or paper that may be or is rolled up; a scroll. **5.** A register or a catalog. **6.** A list of names of persons belonging to a group. **7.** A mass in cylindrical or rounded form. **8.a.** A small rounded portion of bread. **b.** A portion of food shaped like a tube with a filling. **9.** A rolling, swaying, or rocking motion. **10.** A gentle swell or undulation of a surface. **11.** A deep reverberation or rumble. **12.** A rapid succession of short sounds: *the roll of a drum.* **13.** A trill. **14.** A rhythmic resonant flow of words. **15.** A roller, esp. a cylinder on which to roll something up or with which to flatten something. **16.** A maneuver in which an airplane makes a single complete rotation about its longitudinal axis without changing direction or losing altitude. **17.** *Slang.* Money, esp. a wad of paper money. — ***phrasal verbs.* roll back. 1.** To reduce (prices or wages, for example) to a previous lower level. **2.** To cause to turn back or retreat. **roll out. 1.** To get out of bed. **2.** *Football.* To execute a rollout. **roll over. 1.** To defer or postpone payment of (an obligation). **2.** To renegotiate the terms of (a financial deal). **3.** To reinvest (funds from a maturing security) into a similar security. **roll up. 1.** To arrive in a vehicle. **2.** To accumulate; amass. — ***idioms.* on a roll.** *Informal* Undergoing or experiencing sustained, even increasing good fortune or success. **roll in the hay.** *Slang.* Sexual intercourse. **roll the bones.** *Games.* To cast dice, esp. in craps. **roll with the punches.** *Slang.* To cope with and withstand adversity, esp. by being flexible. [ME *rollen* < OFr. *roler* < VLat. **rotulāre* < Lat. *rotula,* dim. of *rota,* wheel. See **ret-*.**]

Rol•land (rô-läN′), **Romain.** 1866–1944. French writer who won the 1915 Nobel Prize for literature.

roll•a•way (rōl′ə-wā′) *adj.* Set on rollers or casters for easy moving and storing: *a rollaway bed.*
roll•back (rōl′băk′) *n.* **1.** A reduction, esp. in prices or wages, to a previous lower level. **2.** A turning back or retreat, as from a previously held position.
roll bar *n.* A sturdy metal bar built into the inside roof of a motor vehicle to prevent or reduce injury in case of a rollover.
roll call *n.* **1.** The reading aloud of a list of names of people, as in a classroom or military post, to determine who is present or absent. **2.** The time fixed for such a reading.
roll•er[1] (rō′lər) *n.* **1.** One that rolls or performs a rolling operation or activity. **2.** Any of various cylindrical or spherical devices that roll or rotate, esp.: **a.** A small spokeless wheel, such as that of a roller skate. **b.** An elongated cylinder on which something is wound. **c.** A heavy revolving cylinder that is used to level, crush, or smooth. **d.** *Print.* A cylinder, usu. of hard rubber, used to ink the type before the paper is impressed. **e.** A cylinder of wire mesh, foam rubber, or other material around which a strand of hair is wound to produce a soft curl or wave. **3.** A long rolled bandage. **4.** A heavy swelling wave that breaks on a coast. **5.** A tumbler pigeon.
rol•ler[2] (rō′lər) *n.* **1.** Any of various Old World birds of the family Coraciidae, having bright blue wings and stocky bodies and noted for rolling and twisting in flight. **2.** A canary that trills. [Ger. < *rollen*, to roll, burble. See ROLLMOPS.]
roller bearing *n.* A bearing using rollers to reduce friction between machine parts.
roller coaster *n.* **1.** A steep, sharply curving elevated railway with small open passenger cars that is operated at high speeds as a ride. **2.** Something that is marked by abrupt, extreme changes in circumstance, quality, or behavior.
roller skate *n.* A shoe or boot with two or four wheels or casters attached to its sole for skating on hard surfaces. —**roll′er-skate′** (rō′lər-skāt′) *v.* —**roller skater** *n.*
roll film *n.* Photographic film rolled on a spool and encased before being loaded into a camera.
rol•lick (rŏl′ĭk) *intr.v.* **-licked, -lick•ing, -licks.** To behave or move in a carefree, frolicsome manner; romp. [?] —**rol′lick** *n.* —**rol′lick•some, rol′lick•y** *adj.*
rol•lick•ing (rŏl′ĭ-kĭng) *adj.* Carefree and high-spirited; boisterous. —**rol′lick•ing•ly** *adv.*
Roll•ing Meadows (rō′lĭng). A city of NE IL, a suburb of Chicago. Pop. 22,591.
roll•ing mill (rō′lĭng) *n.* **1.** A factory in which metal is rolled into sheets, bars, or other forms. **2.** A machine used for rolling metal.
rolling pin *n.* A smooth cylinder, usu. of wood, with a handle at each end, used for rolling out dough.
rolling stock *n.* The equipment available for transportation, such as automotive vehicles or railroad cars, owned by a particular company or carrier.
roll•mops (rōl′mŏps′) *n.*, *pl.* **rollmops.** A marinated fillet of herring wrapped around a pickle or an onion and served as an hors d'oeuvre. [Ger. : *rollen*, to roll (< MHGer. < OFr. *roler*; see ROLL) + *Mops*, blockhead, pug dog.]
Rol•lo (rŏl′ō). Also called **Hrolf** (hrŏlf, rōlf) or **Rolf** (rŏlf). 860?–931? Norse chieftain and the first duke of Normandy.
roll-on (rōl′ŏn′, -ôn′) *adj.* Of or being a substance, such as a deodorant, that is dispensed from a container having a rolling ball at one end serving as an applicator. —**roll′-on′** *n.*
roll•out (rōl′out′) *n.* **1.** The inauguration or initial public exhibition of a new product, service, or policy. **2.** *Football.* A play in which the quarterback runs toward a sideline after receiving the snap with the intention of passing the ball.
roll•o•ver (rōl′ō′vər) *n.* **1.** The act or process of rolling over. **2.** An accident in which a motor vehicle overturns. **3.** *Econ.* Reinvestment of profits received from one often short-term security into another, similar security.
roll-top desk or **roll•top desk** (rōl′tŏp′) *n.* A desk fitted with a flexible sliding top made of parallel slats.
roll•way (rōl′wā′) *n.* A surface along which cylindrical objects or objects on rollers may be moved, esp. an inclined surface used by lumberjacks to slide logs into a waterway.
Ro•lo•dex (rō′lə-dĕks′). A trademark used for a desktop rotary file of removable cards, usu. used for names, addresses, and telephone numbers.
Röl•vaag (rōl′väg′), **Ole Edvart.** 1876–1931. Norwegian-born Amer. writer noted for *Giants in the Earth* (1927).
ro•ly-po•ly (rō′lē-pō′lē) *adj.* Short and plump; pudgy. —*n.*, *pl.* **-lies. 1.** A short plump person or thing. **2.** *Chiefly British.* A pudding made of jam or fruit rolled up in pastry dough and baked or steamed until soft. [Alteration and redup. of ROLL.]
rom also **rom.** *abbr. Print.* Roman.
ROM *abbr. Comp. Sci.* Read-only memory.
Rom. *abbr.* **1.** Roman. **2.** Romance (languages). **3.** Romania. **4.** Romanian. **5.** *Bible.* Romans.
Ro•ma•gna (rō-män′yə, rô-mä′nyä). A historical region of N-central Italy; a former center of Byzantine influence and now part of Emilia-Romagna.
Ro•ma•ic (rō-mā′ĭk) *n.* Modern Greek. [Mod.Gk. *Rhōmaikos* < Gk., Roman < *Rhōmē*, Rome < Lat. *Rōma.*] —**Ro•ma′ic** *adj.*
ro•maine (rō-mān′) *n.* A cultivar of lettuce *(Lactuca sativa)* having a slender head of oblong or obovate leaves with broad midribs. [Fr. < fem. of *Romain*, Roman < OFr. < Lat. *Rōmānus* < *Rōma*, Rome.]
Ro•mains (rō-măN′), **Jules.** 1885–1972. French writer whose works include the novel cycle *Men of Good Will* (1932–46).
ro•man (rō-mäN′) *n.* **1.** A narrative poem or a prose tale in medieval French literature. **2.** A novel. [Fr. < OFr. *romans*, romance. See ROMANCE.]
Ro•man (rō′mən) *adj.* **1.a.** Of or relating to ancient or modern Rome or its people or culture. **b.** Of or relating to the Roman Empire. **2.a.** Of, relating to, or composed in the Latin language. **b.** Of or using the Latin alphabet. **3.** Of or relating to the Roman Catholic Church. **4.** Of or being an architectural style developed by the ancient Romans and characterized by the round arch as chief structural element, the vault, concrete masonry construction, and classical ornamentation. **5. roman.** Of or being a typestyle characterized by upright letters having serifs and vertical lines thicker than horizontal lines. —*n.* **1.** A native, inhabitant, or citizen of ancient or modern Rome. **2.** The Italian language as spoken in Rome. **3.** One belonging to the Roman Catholic Church. **4. roman.** Roman print or typestyle. **5. Romans.** *(used with a sing. v.)* See table at **Bible.** [ME < OE *Rōmān* or < OFr. *romain*, both < Lat. *Rōmānus* < *Rōma*, Rome.]
ro•man à clef (rō-mäN′ ä klā′) *n.*, *pl.* **ro•mans à clef** (rōmäN′ zä klā′). A novel in which actual persons, places, or events are depicted in fictional guise. [Fr. : *roman*, novel + *à*, with + *clef*, key.]
Roman alphabet *n.* See **Latin alphabet.**
Roman calendar *n.* The lunar calendar used by the ancient Romans until the introduction of the Julian calendar in 46 B.C.
Roman candle *n.* A cylindrical firework that emits balls of fire and a shower of sparks.
Roman Catholic *adj.* Of, relating to, or being the Roman Catholic Church. —*n.* A member of the Roman Catholic Church.
Roman Catholic Church *n.* The Christian church characterized by an episcopal hierarchy with the pope as its head and belief in seven sacraments and the authority of tradition.
Roman Catholicism *n.* The doctrines, practices, and organization of the Roman Catholic Church.
ro•mance (rō-măns′, rō′măns′) *n.* **1.a.** A love affair. **b.** Ardent emotional attachment or involvement between people; love. **c.** A strong, sometimes short-lived attachment, fascination, or enthusiasm for something. **2.** A mysterious or fascinating quality or appeal. **3.a.** A long medieval narrative in prose or verse that tells of the adventures and heroic exploits of chivalric heroes. **b.** A long fictitious tale of heroes and extraordinary or mysterious events. **c.** The class of literature constituted by such tales. **4.a.** An artistic work that deals with sexual love, esp. in an idealized form. **b.** The class or style of such works. **5.** A fictitiously embellished account or explanation. **6.** *Mus.* A lyrical, tender, usu. sentimental song or short instrumental piece. **7. Romance.** The Romance languages. —*adj.* **Romance.** Of, relating to, or being any of the languages that developed from Latin, the principal ones being Italian, French, Portuguese, Romanian, and Spanish and including Catalan, Provençal, Rhaeto-Romanic, Sardinian, and Ladino. —*v.* (rō-măns′) **-manced, -manc•ing, -manc•es.** —*intr.* **1.** To invent, write, or tell romances. **2.** To think or behave in a romantic manner. —*tr. Informal.* **1.** To make love to; court or woo. **2.** To have a love affair with. [ME < OFr. *romans*, romance, work written in French < VLat. **rōmānicē (scrībere)*, (to write) in the vernacular < Lat. *Rōmānicus*, Roman < *Rōmānus*. See ROMAN.] —**ro•manc′er** *n.*
Roman Empire. Also **Rome** (rōm). An empire that succeeded the Roman Republic during the reign of Augustus (27 B.C.–A.D. 14) and at its greatest extent stretched from Britain and Germany to North Africa and the Persian Gulf. After 395 it was split into the Byzantine Empire and the Western Roman Empire, which fell to the Goths in 476.
Ro•man•esque (rō′mə-nĕsk′) *adj.* **1.** Of, relating to, or being a style of European architecture containing both Roman and Byzantine elements, prevalent esp. in the 11th and 12th centuries and characterized by thick walls, barrel vaults, and relatively simple ornamentation. **2.** Of, relating to, or being corresponding styles in painting and sculpture. —**Ro′man•esque′** *n.*
ro•man-fleuve (rō-mäN′flœv′) *n.*, *pl.* **ro•mans-fleuves** (rō-mäN′flœv′). A long novel, often in many volumes, chronicling the history of several generations of a family, community, or other group. [Fr. : *roman*, novel + *fleuve*, river.]
Roman holiday *n.* **1.** Enjoyment or satisfaction derived from the suffering of others. **2.** A violent public spectacle or disturbance. [< the bloody Roman gladiatorial contests.]
Ro•ma•ni•a (rō-mā′nē-ə, -mān′yə) or **Ru•ma•ni•a** (ro͞o-). A country of SE Europe with a short coastline on the Black Sea; independent since 1878. Cap. Bucharest. Pop. 22,533,074.
Ro•ma•ni•an (rō-mā′nē-ən, -mān′yən) also **Ru•ma•ni•an** (ro͞o-) —*adj.* Of or relating to Romania or its people, language, or culture. —*n.* **1.** A native or inhabitant of Romania. **2.** The Romance language of the Romanians.

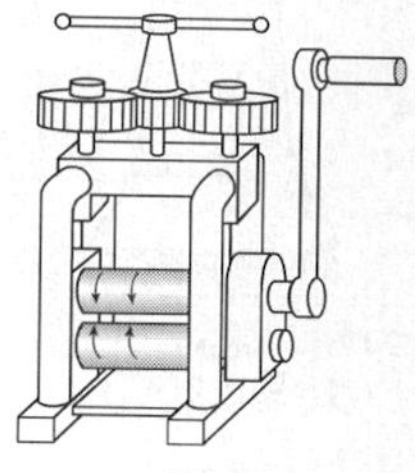
rolling mill

rolling pin

Romania

ă pat	oi boy
ā pay	ou out
âr care	o͝o took
ä father	o͞o boot
ĕ pet	ŭ cut
ē be	ûr urge
ĭ pit	th thin
ī pie	*th* this
îr pier	hw which
ŏ pot	zh vision
ō toe	ə about, item
ô paw	

Stress marks:
′ (primary);
′ (secondary), as in
dictionary (dĭk′shə-nĕr′ē)

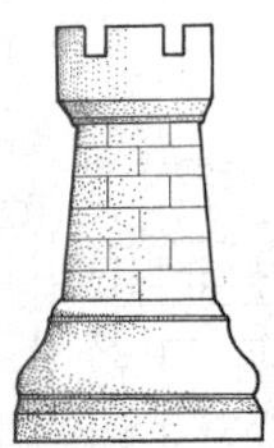

rook²
Chess piece

Ro•man•ic (rō-măn′ĭk) *adj.* **1.** Of or derived from the ancient Romans. **2.** Of or relating to the Romance languages. — **Ro•man′ic** *n.*

Ro•man•ism (rō′mə-nĭz′əm) *n. Offensive.* Roman Catholicism.

Ro•man•ist (rō′mə-nĭst) *n.* **1.** *Offensive.* One who professes Roman Catholicism. **2.** A student of or authority on ancient Roman law, culture, and institutions.

Ro•man•ize (rō′mə-nīz′) *tr.v.* **-ized, -iz•ing, -iz•es. 1.** To convert (a person) to Roman Catholicism. **2.** To make Roman in character, allegiance, or style. **3.** Often **romanize.** To write or transliterate in the Latin alphabet. — **Ro′man•i•za′tion** (-mə-nĭ-zā′shən) *n.*

Roman law *n.* The legal system of ancient Rome, which serves as the basis for modern civil law.

Roman nose *n.* A nose with a high, prominent bridge.

Roman numeral *n.* Any of the numerals in the ancient Roman system of numeration formed with the characters I, V, X, L, C, D, and M and still used in certain contexts.

Ro•ma•no (rə-mä′nō, rō-) *n.* A sharp dry hard cheese of Italian origin that is made from cow's milk and usu. served grated as a garnish. [Ital., short for *(pecorino) romano,* Roman (sheep's milk cheese) < Lat. *Rōmānus.*]

Ro•ma•nov also **Ro•ma•noff** (rō′mə-nôf′, rō-mä′nəf, rə-). Russian ruling dynasty (1613–1917) that ended with the abdication of Nicholas II during the Russian Revolution.

Ro•mansch also **Ro•mansh** (rō-mänsh′, -mănsh′) *n.* The Rhaeto-Romance dialect that is an official language of Switzerland. [Romansch *Romonsch* < Lat. *Rōmānicus,* Roman. See ROMANCE.]

ro•man•tic (rō-măn′tĭk) *adj.* **1.** Of, relating to, or characteristic of romance. **2.** Given to thoughts or feelings of romance. **3.** Displaying, expressive of, or conducive to love. **4.** Imaginative but impractical; visionary. **5.** Not based on fact; imaginary or fictitious. **6.** Often **Romantic.** Of or characteristic of romanticism in the arts. — *n.* **1.** A romantic person. **2.** Often **Romantic.** A follower or adherent of romanticism. [Fr. *romantique* < obsolete *romant,* romance < OFr. *romans, romant-,* romance. See ROMANCE.] — **ro•man′ti•cal•ly** *adv.*

Edith Roosevelt

ro•man•ti•cism (rō-măn′tĭ-sĭz′əm) *n.* **1.** Often **Romanticism.** An artistic and intellectual movement originating in Europe in the late 18th century and characterized by a heightened interest in nature, emphasis on the expression of emotion and imagination, departure from classical art forms, and rebellion against established social conventions. **2.** Romantic quality or spirit in thought, expression, or action. — **ro•man′ti•cist** *n.*

ro•man•ti•cize (rō-măn′tĭ-sīz′) *v.* **-cized, -ciz•ing, -ciz•es.** — *tr.* To view or interpret romantically; make romantic. — *intr.* To think in a romantic way. — **ro•man′ti•ci•za′tion** (-sĭ-zā′shən) *n.*

Rom•a•ny (rŏm′ə-nē, rō′mə-) *n., pl.* **-nies. 1.** A Gypsy. **2.** The Indic language of the Gypsies. — *adj.* Of or relating to the Indic language of the Gypsies or their language or culture. [Romany *romani,* fem. of *romano,* gypsy < *rom,* man < Prakrit *ḍoma,* man of a low caste, of Dravidian orig.]

ro•maunt (rō-mônt′ -mŏnt′) *n. Archaic.* A verse romance. [ME < OFr. *romans, romant-,* romance. See ROMANCE.]

Rom•berg (rŏm′bərg), **Sigmund.** 1887–1951. Hungarian-born Amer. composer noted for *The Student Prince* (1924).

Rome (rōm). **1.** The cap. of Italy, in the W-central part on the Tiber R.; traditionally founded by Romulus and Remus and cap. of the Roman Empire until A.D. 323. Pop. 2,830,569. **2.** A city of NW GA NW of Atlanta; estab. 1834. Pop. 30,326. **3.** A city of central NY on the Mohawk R. WNW of Utica. Pop. 44,350. **4.** See **Roman Empire.**

Eleanor Roosevelt
Photographed in 1949 by Clara E. Sipprell (1885–1975)

Ro•me•o (rō′mē-ō′) *n., pl.* **-os.** A man devoted to lovemaking or the pursuit of love. [After *Romeo,* the hero of Shakespeare's *Romeo and Juliet.*]

Rom•ish (rō′mĭsh) *adj. Offensive.* Of or relating to the Roman Catholic Church. — **Rom′ish•ly** *adv.* — **Rom′ish•ness** *n.*

Rom•mel (rŏm′əl), **Erwin.** "the Desert Fox." 1891–1944. German general in France, Italy, and N Africa during World War II.

Rom•ney (rŏm′nē), **George.** 1734–1802. British painter whose works include *Death of General Wolfe* (1763).

romp (rŏmp) *intr.v.* **romped, romp•ing, romps. 1.** To play or frolic boisterously. **2.** To run or advance in a rapid or easy manner. **3.** *Slang.* To win a race or game easily. — *n.* **1.a.** Lively, merry play; frolic. **b.** Lively or frolicsome play that encompasses lovemaking. **2.** One, esp. a girl, that sports and frolics. **3.** A rapid or easy pace. **4.** *Slang.* An easy win. [Alteration of RAMP².]

romp•er (rŏm′pər) *n.* **1.** One that romps. **2. rompers.** A loosely fitted one-piece garment having short bloomers that is worn esp. by small children for play.

Rom•u•lus¹ (rŏm′yə-ləs) *n. Rom. Myth.* The son of Mars and eponymous founder of Rome who with his twin brother, Remus, was reared and suckled by a wolf.

Rom•u•lus² (rŏm′yə-ləs). A city of SE MI, a suburb of Detroit. Pop. 22,897.

Ron•ces•valles (rŏn′sə-vălz′, rôn′thĕs-väl′yĕs). A mountain pass, 1,057.7 m (3,468 ft), through the W Pyrenees in N Spain; traditional site of the death of the hero Roland during the defeat of Charlemagne's army by the Saracens (778).

ron•deau (rŏn′dō, rŏn-dō′) *n., pl.* **-deaux** (-dōz, -dōz′). **1.** A lyrical poem of French origin having 13 or sometimes 10 lines with two rhymes throughout and with the opening phrase repeated twice as a refrain. **2.** *Mus.* A medieval French song, either monophonic or polyphonic in construction. [Fr., alteration of OFr. *rondel.* See RONDEL.]

ron•del (rŏn′dəl, rŏn-dĕl′) *n.* **1.** A poem similar to a rondeau, having 13 or 14 lines with two rhymes throughout, with the first and usu. second lines reappearing in the middle and at the end. **2.** Often **ron•delle** (rŏn-dĕl′). A rounded or circular object. [ME < OFr., dim. of *ronde,* circle, round. See ROUND¹.]

ron•de•let (rŏn′dl-ĕt′, -dl-ā′) *n.* A poem similar to a rondeau, usu. having seven lines and always two rhymes, with the first line repeated as lines three and seven. [Fr. < OFr., dim. of *rondel,* rondel. See RONDEL.]

ron•do (rŏn′dō, rŏn-dō′) *n., pl.* **-dos.** *Mus.* A composition having a principal theme that occurs at least three times in its original key between contrasting subordinate themes. [Ital. *rondò* < Fr. *rondeau,* rondeau. See RONDEAU.]

ron•dure (rŏn′jər, -dyŏŏr′) *n.* A circular or gracefully rounded object. [Fr. *rondeur,* roundness < OFr. < *ronde,* round. See ROUND¹.]

Ron•kon•ko•ma (rŏng-kŏng′kə-mə, rŏn-kŏn′-). A town of SE NY on central Long I. Pop. 20,391.

Ron•sard (rôN-sär′), **Pierre de.** 1524–85. French poet whose lyrical love poems include *Sonnets pour Hélène* (1578).

rönt•gen (rĕnt′gən, -jən, rŭnt′-) *n.* Var. of **roentgen.**

Rönt•gen (rœnt′gən), **Wilhelm Konrad.** See Wilhelm Konrad **Roentgen.**

rood (ro͞od) *n.* **1.a.** A crucifix symbolizing the cross on which Jesus was crucified. **b.** A large crucifix or the representation of one over the altar screen of a medieval church. **2.** *Chiefly British.* A measure of length that varies from 5½ to 8 yards (5.0 to 7.3 meters). [ME < OE *rōd.*]

rood screen *n.* An ornamented altar screen surmounted by a crucifix that separates the choir of a church from the nave.

roof (ro͞of, ro͝of) *n.* **1.a.** The exterior surface and its supporting structures on the top of a building. **b.** The upper exterior surface of a dwelling as a symbol of the home itself. **2.** The top covering of something. **3.** The upper surface of an anatomical structure, esp. one having a vaulted inner structure. **4.** The highest point or limit; the summit or ceiling. — *tr.v.* **roofed, roof•ing, roofs.** To furnish or cover with or as if with a roof. — ***idioms.* go through the roof.** *Slang.* **1.** To grow, intensify, or rise to an enormous, often unexpected degree. **2.** To become extremely angry. **raise the roof.** *Slang.* **1.** To be extremely noisy and boisterous. **2.** To complain loudly and bitterly. [ME < OE *hrōf.*]

roof•er (ro͞o′fər, ro͝of′ər) *n.* One who lays or repairs roofs.

roof garden *n.* **1.** A garden on the roof of a building. **2.** The roof or top floor of a building designed for use by the public that often contains outdoor seating or dining facilities.

roof•ing (ro͞o′fĭng, ro͝of′ĭng) *n.* **1.** Materials used in building a roof. **2.** A roof.

roof•less (ro͞of′lĭs, ro͝of′-) *adj.* **1.** Lacking a roof. **2.** Having no home or shelter; homeless or destitute.

roof•line (ro͞of′līn′, ro͝of′-) *n.* The profile of or silhouette made by a roof or series of roofs.

roof•top (ro͞of′tŏp′, ro͝of′-) *n.* A roof, esp. its outer surface.

roof•tree (ro͞of′trē′, ro͝of′-) *n.* **1.** The ridgepole of a roof. **2.** A roof.

rook¹ (ro͝ok) *n.* **1.** An Old World bird *(Corvus frugilegus)* that resembles the North American crow and nests in colonies near the tops of trees. **2.** A swindler or cheat, esp. at games. — *tr.v.* **rooked, rook•ing, rooks.** To swindle; cheat. [ME *rok* < OE *hrōc.*]

rook² (ro͝ok) *n. Games.* A chess piece that may move in a straight line over any number of empty squares in a rank or file. [ME *rok* < OFr. *roc* < Ar. *ruḫḫ* < Pers.]

rook•er•y (ro͝ok′ə-rē) *n., pl.* **-ies. 1.a.** A place where rooks nest or breed. **b.** A colony of rooks. **2.** The breeding ground of certain other birds or animals, such as penguins and seals. **3.** A crowded and dilapidated tenement.

rook•ie (ro͝ok′ē) *n.* **1.** *Slang.* **a.** An untrained or inexperienced recruit, as in the army. **b.** An inexperienced person; a novice. **2.** *Sports.* A first-year player, esp. in a professional sport. [Perh. alteration of RECRUIT.]

rook•y (ro͝ok′ē) *adj.* Of or abounding in rooks.

room (ro͞om, ro͝om) *n.* **1.** A space that is or may be occupied. **2.a.** An area separated by walls or partitions from other similar parts of the structure or building in which it is located. **b.** The people present in such an area. **3. rooms.** Living quarters; lodgings. **4.** Suitable opportunity; occasion. — *intr.v.* **roomed, room•ing, rooms.** To occupy a room; lodge. [ME *roum* < OE *rūm.* See **reuə-*.**]

room and board *n.* Lodging and meals earned, purchased for a set fee, or otherwise provided.

room•er (ro͞o′mər, ro͝om′ər) *n.* One who rents a room or rooms in which to live; a lodger.

room•ette (ro͞o-mĕt′, ro͝om-ĕt′) *n.* A small private compartment in a railroad sleeping car.

room•ful (ro͞om′fo͝ol′, ro͝om′-) *n., pl.* **-fuls.** The amount or number that a room can hold.

room•ing house (ro͞o′mĭng, ro͝om′ĭng) *n.* A house where lodgers may rent rooms.

room•mate (ro͞om′māt′, ro͝om′-) *n.* A person with whom one shares a room or rooms.

room temperature *n.* An indoor temperature of from 20 to 25°C (68 to 77°F).

room•y (ro͞o′mē, ro͝om′ē) *adj.* **-i•er, -i•est.** Having plenty of room; spacious. **—room′i•ly** *adv.* **—room′i•ness** *n.*

roor•back (ro͝or′băk′) *n.* A false or slanderous story used for political advantage. [After Baron von *Roorback,* imaginary author of *Roorback's Tour Through the Western and Southern States,* from which a passage was purportedly quoted to disparage presidential candidate James K. Polk in 1844.]

Roo•se•velt (rō′zə-vĕlt′, rōz′vĕlt′, -vəlt, ro͞o′-), **(Anna) Eleanor.** 1884–1962. Amer. diplomat, writer, and First Lady of the U.S. (1933–45) who was a delegate to the United Nations (1945–52 and 1961–62).

Roosevelt, Edith Carow. 1861–1948. First Lady of the U.S. (1901–09) who oversaw a major renovation of the White House (1902).

Roosevelt, Franklin Delano. 1882–1945. The 32nd President of the U.S. (1933–45), whose administration was marked by measures to increase employment and assist recovery from the Depression and by U.S. participation in World War II.

Roosevelt, Rio. A river, c. 644 km (400 mi), of NW Brazil; orig. known as the River of Doubt and renamed in honor of Theodore Roosevelt, who explored it in 1913.

Roosevelt, Theodore. 1858–1919. The 26th President of the U.S. (1901–09), who oversaw the building of the Panama Canal and won the 1906 Nobel Peace Prize for his role in ending the Russo-Japanese War (1904–05).

Roosevelt Island. 1. Formerly **Wel•fare Island** (wĕl′fâr′). An island in the East R. off the coast of central Manhattan. **2.** An island of Antartica in the E part of the Ross Ice Shelf.

roost (ro͞ost) *n.* **1.** A perch on which domestic fowl or other birds rest or sleep. **2.** A place with perches for fowl or other birds. **3.** A place for temporary rest or sleep. *—intr.v.* **roost•ed, roost•ing, roosts.** To rest or sleep on or as if on a perch or roost. ***—idioms.* come home to roost.** To have repercussions or aftereffects, esp. unfavorable ones. **rule the roost.** *Informal.* To be in charge; dominate. [ME *rooste* < OE *hrōst.*]

roost•er (ro͞o′stər) *n.* **1.a.** An adult male chicken. **b.** An adult male of other birds. **2.** A person regarded as cocky or pugnacious.

roost•er•fish (ro͞o′stər-fĭsh′) *n., pl.* **roosterfish** or **-fish•es.** A brightly colored food and game fish *(Nematistius pectoralis)* found from the Gulf of California to Panama.

root[1] (ro͞ot, ro͝ot) *n.* **1.** The usu. underground portion of a plant that lacks buds, leaves, or nodes and serves as support, draws minerals and water from the surrounding soil, and sometimes stores food. **2.** Any of various other underground plant parts, esp. an underground stem such as a tuber. **3.a.** The embedded part of an organ or structure such as a hair, tooth, or nerve, serving as a base or support. **b.** A base or support. **4.** An essential part or element; the basic core. **5.** A primary source; an origin. See Syns at **origin. 6.** A progenitor or an ancestor from which a person or family is descended. **7.a.** The condition of being settled and of belonging to a particular place or society. Often used in the plural. **b. roots.** The state of having or establishing an indigenous relationship with or a personal affinity for a particular culture, society, or environment: *music with African roots.* **8.** *Ling.* **a.** The element that carries the main component of meaning in a word and provides the basis from which a word is derived by adding affixes or inflectional endings or by phonetic change. **b.** Such an element reconstructed for a protolanguage. **9.** *Math.* **a.** A number that when multiplied by itself an indicated number of times equals a given product: *a fourth root of 4 is* $\sqrt{2}$. **b.** A number that reduces an equation in one variable to an identity when it is substituted for the variable. **10.** *Mus.* **a.** The note from which a chord is built. **b.** A triad or other chord that has such a note lowermost. *—v.* **root•ed, root•ing, roots.** *—intr.* **1.** To grow roots or a root. **2.** To become firmly established, settled, or entrenched. **3.** To come into existence; originate. *—tr.* **1.** To cause to put out roots and grow. **2.** To implant by or as if by the roots. **3.** To furnish a primary source or origin to. **4.** To remove by or as if by the roots. Often used with *up* or *out.* ***—idiom.* root and branch.** Utterly; completely. [ME *rot* < OE *rōt* < ON. See **wrād-*.**] **—root′er** *n.*

root[2] (ro͞ot, ro͝ot) *v.* **root•ed, root•ing, roots.** *—tr.* To dig with or as if with the snout or nose. *—intr.* **1.** To dig in the earth with or as if with the snout or nose. **2.** To rummage for something. [ME *wroten* < OE *wrōtan.*] **—root′er** *n.*

root[3] (ro͞ot, ro͝ot) *intr.v.* **root•ed, root•ing, roots. 1.** To give audible encouragement or applause to a contestant or team; cheer. **2.** To lend support to someone or something. [Poss. alteration of ROUT[3].] **—root′er** *n.*

Root (ro͞ot), **Elihu.** 1845–1937. Amer. lawyer and public official who won the 1912 Nobel Peace Prize.

Root, John Wellborn. 1850–91. Amer. architect whose designs include the Monadnock Building (1889–91) in Chicago.

root•age (ro͞o′tĭj, ro͝ot′ĭj) *n.* **1.** A system or growth of roots. **2.** Establishment by or as if by roots.

root beer *n.* A carbonated soft drink made from extracts of certain plant roots and herbs.

root canal *n.* **1.** A pulp-filled channel in a root of a tooth. **2.** A treatment in which diseased tissue from a root canal is removed and the resulting cavity filled with an inert material.

root cap *n. Bot.* A thimble-shaped mass of cells that covers and protects the root tip.

root cellar *n.* An underground pit or cellar, usu. covered with earth, used for the storage of root crops and other vegetables.

root climber *n.* A vine, such as the ivy, that clings to its support by means of adventitious roots.

root crop *n.* A crop, as of yams, grown for its edible roots.

root•ed•ness (ro͞o′tĭd-nĭs, ro͝ot′ĭd-) *n.* The quality or state of having roots, esp. of being firmly established or entrenched.

root hair *n. Bot.* A hairlike outgrowth of an epidermal cell of a plant root that absorbs water and minerals from the soil.

root•hold (ro͞ot′hōld′, ro͝ot′-) *n.* Support or stabilization of a plant in the soil through the spreading of its roots.

root knot *n.* A disease of plants characterized by protuberant enlargements on the roots caused by a nematode.

root•less (ro͞ot′lĭs, ro͝ot′-) *adj.* **1.** Having no roots. **2.** Not belonging to a place or society. **—root′less•ness** *n.*

root•let (ro͞ot′lĭt, ro͝ot′-) *n.* A small root or division of a root.

root mean square *n. Statistics.* The square root of the average of the squares of a set of numbers.

root pressure *n.* Pressure exerted in the roots of plants as the result of osmosis, causing exudation from cut stems and guttation of water from leaves.

root•stalk (ro͞ot′stôk′, ro͝ot′-) *n.* See **rhizome.**

root•stock (ro͞ot′stŏk′, ro͝ot′-) *n.* **1.** See **rhizome. 2.** A root or part of a root used as a stock for plant propagation. **3.** A source or origin.

root•worm (ro͞ot′wûrm′, ro͝ot′-) *n.* Any of several beetles of the genus *Diabrotica,* the larvae of which feed on the roots of various crop plants, esp. corn.

root•y (ro͞o′tē, ro͝ot′ē) *adj.* **-i•er, -i•est. 1.** Full or consisting of roots. **2.** Resembling roots. **—root′i•ness** *n.*

rope (rōp) *n.* **1.** A flexible heavy cord of tightly intertwined hemp or other fiber. **2.** A string of items attached in one line by or as if by twisting or braiding. **3.** A sticky glutinous formation of stringy matter in a liquid. **4.a.** A cord with a noose at one end for hanging a person. **b.** Execution or death by hanging. **5.** A lasso or lariat. **6. ropes.** *Sports.* Several cords strung between poles to enclose a boxing or wrestling ring. **7. ropes.** *Informal.* Specialized procedures or details. *—v.* **roped, rop•ing, ropes.** *—tr.* **1.** To tie or fasten with or as if with rope. **2.** To enclose, separate, or partition with or as if with a rope: *roped off the area.* **3.** To catch with a rope or lasso. **4.** *Informal.* To trick or deceive. *—intr.* To become like a cord or rope. ***—idioms.* on the ropes. 1.** *Sports.* Knocked against the ropes that enclose a boxing ring. **2.** On the verge of defeat or collapse; hopeless or powerless. **the end of (one's) rope.** The limit of one's patience, endurance, or resources. [ME < OE *rāp.*] **—rop′er** *n.*

rope tow *n.* A continuous rope conveyor used to pull skiers up a slope; a ski tow.

rope•walk (rōp′wôk′) *n.* **1.** An alley or covered pathway where strands of material, such as hemp fiber, are laid and twisted into rope. **2.** A long narrow building containing such a pathway.

rop•y also **rop•ey** (rō′pē) *adj.* **-i•er, -i•est. 1.** Resembling a rope or ropes. **2.** Forming sticky glutinous strings or threads, as some liquids. **—rop′i•ly** *adv.* **—rop′i•ness** *n.*

roque (rōk) *n. Sports.* A variation of croquet played with short-handled mallets on a hard court that is bounded by a concrete wall against which a ball may rebound and be retrieved. [Alteration of ROQUET.]

Roque•fort (rōk′fərt). A trademark used for a cheese that is made from ewes' milk and ripened in caves.

ro•que•laure (rō′kə-lôr′, -lōr′, rŏk′ə-) *n.* A knee-length cloak lined with brightly colored silk and often trimmed with fur, worn by European men in the 18th century. [After Duc de *Roquelaure* (1656–1738), French marshal.]

ro•quet (rō-kā′) *tr.v.* **-queted** (-kād′), **-quet•ing** (-kā′ĭng), **-quets** (-kāz′). *Sports.* To hit (another player's ball) in croquet. [Alteration of CROQUET.]

ro•quette (rō-kĕt′) *n. Bot.* See **rocket**[2] 1.

Ro•rem (rôr′əm, rōr′-), **Ned.** b. 1923. Amer. composer whose works include the symphony *Air Music* (1976).

ror•qual (rôr′kwəl) *n.* Any of several baleen whales of the family Balaenopteridae, having longitudinal grooves on the throat and a small pointed dorsal fin. [Fr. < Norw. *rørhval* < ON *reydharhvalr* : *reydhr,* rorqual (< *raudhr,* red; see **reudh-***) + *hvalr,* whale.]

Ror•schach test (rôr′shäk′, -shäкн′) *n. Psychol.* A projective test in which a subject's interpretations of ten standard ink-

Franklin D. Roosevelt

Theodore Roosevelt

rorqual
Piked whale
Balaenoptera acutorostrata

ă pat	oi boy
ā pay	ou out
âr care	o͝o took
ä father	o͞o boot
ĕ pet	ŭ cut
ē be	ûr urge
ĭ pit	th thin
ī pie	*th* this
îr pier	hw which
ŏ pot	zh vision
ō toe	ə about, item
ô paw	

Stress marks:
′ (primary);
′ (secondary), as in
dictionary (dĭk′shə-nĕr′ē)

blots are analyzed as a measure of emotional and intellectual functioning and integration. [After Hermann *Rorschach* (1884–1922), Swiss psychiatrist.]

Ro•sa (rō′zə, rô′zä), **Monte.** A mountain, 4,636.9 m (15,203 ft), in the Pennine Alps on the Swiss-Italian border.

ro•sa•ce•a (rō-zā′shē-ə) *n.* A chronic dermatitis of the face characterized by a red or rosy coloration and the appearance of acnelike pimples. [NLat. *(acne) rosācea*, rose-colored (acne) < Lat., fem. of *rosāceus*, made of roses. See ROSACEOUS.]

ro•sa•ceous (rō-zā′shəs) *adj.* **1.** *Bot.* Of or belonging to the rose family. **2.** Resembling the flower of a rose. [< Lat. *rosāceus*, made of roses < *rosa*, rose.]

ros•an•i•line also **ros•an•i•lin** (rō-zăn′ə-lĭn) *n.* A brownish-red crystalline aniline derivative, $C_{20}H_{21}N_3O$, used in the manufacture of dyes. [ROS(E)[1] + ANILINE.]

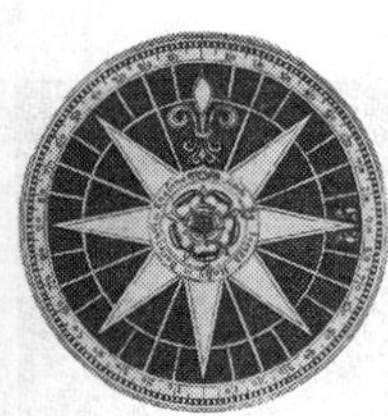
rose[1]
Compass card

ro•sar•i•an (rō-zâr′ē-ən) *n.* A person with expertise or a special interest in the cultivation of roses.

Ro•sa•ri•o (rō-zär′ē-ō′, -sär′-). A city of E-central Argentina on the Paraná R. NW of Buenos Aires. Pop. 938,120.

ro•sa•ry (rō′zə-rē) *n., pl.* **-ries. 1.** *Rom. Cath. Ch.* **a.** A form of devotion to the Virgin Mary, chiefly consisting of three sets of five decades each of the Hail Mary, each decade preceded by the Lord's Prayer and ending with a doxology. **b.** One of these sets of decades. **c.** A string of beads of 5 or 15 decades on which these prayers are counted. **2.** Similar beads used by other religious groups. [Ult. < Med.Lat. *rosārium* < Lat., rose garden < neut. of *rosārius*, of roses < *rosa*, rose.]

rosary pea *n.* A tropical woody vine *(Abrus precatorius)* widely naturalized in Florida and having scarlet and black poisonous seeds used as beads.

rose[1] (rōz) *n.* **1.** A member of the rose family. **2.a.** Any of numerous shrubs or vines of the genus *Rosa*, having prickly stems, pinnately compound leaves, and variously colored, often fragrant flowers. **b.** The flower of any of these plants. **c.** Any of various similar or related plants. **3.** *Color.* A dark pink to moderate red. **4.** An ornament, such as a decorative knot, resembling a rose in form; a rosette. **5.** A perforated nozzle for spraying water from a hose or sprinkling can. **6.a.** A form of gem cut marked by a flat base and a faceted hemispheric upper surface. **b.** A gem, esp. a diamond, cut in this manner. **7.** A rose window. **8.** A compass card or its representation, as on a map. **9. roses.** That which is marked by favor, success, or ease of execution. —*adj.* **1.** *Color.* Of the color rose. **2.** Relating to, containing, or used for roses. **3.** Scented or flavored with or as if with roses. —***idioms.* come up roses.** To result favorably or successfully. **under the rose.** Sub rosa. [ME < OE < Lat. *rosa*.]

rose[2] (rōz) *v.* P.t. of **rise.**

ro•sé (rō-zā′) *n.* A light pink wine made from red grapes from which the skins are removed during fermentation as soon as the desired color has been attained. [Fr. *(vin) rosé*, pink (wine) < OFr. < *rose*, rose. See ROSE[1].]

rosemary
Rosmarinus officinalis

rose acacia *n.* A shrub *(Robinia hispida)* of the southeast United States having bristly brittle branches and clusters of pale purple or rose flowers.

rose apple *n.* **1.** A southeast Asian evergreen tree *(Syzygium jambos)* having showy flowers and fragrant cream-yellow ovoid fruits. **2.** The fruit of this plant.

ro•se•ate (rō′zē-ĭt, -āt′) *adj.* **1.** Rose-colored. **2.** Cheerful or bright; optimistic. [< Lat. *roseus*, rosy < *rosa*, rose.] —**ro′se•ate•ly** *adv.*

roseate spoonbill *n.* A New World species of spoonbill *(Ajaia ajaja)* having rosy or pinkish plumage.

Ro•seau (rō-zō′). The cap. of Dominica, in the Windward Is. of the West Indies. Pop. 9,348.

rose•bay (rōz′bā′) *n.* **1.** Any of several shrubs of the genus *Rhododendron*, esp. *R. maximum* of the southeast United States having large glossy leaves and flowers with a rose-pink bell-shaped corolla with green spots. **2.** See **oleander. 3.** *Chiefly British.* The willow herb.

rose beetle *n.* See **rose chafer.**

rose-breast•ed grosbeak (rōz′brĕs′tĭd) *n.* A North American bird *(Pheucticus ludovicianus)*, the male of which is black and white with a rose-red patch on the breast.

rose•bud (rōz′bŭd′) *n.* The bud of a rose.

rose bug *n.* See **rose chafer.**

Rose•burg (rōz′bûrg′). A city of SW OR SSW of Eugene. Pop. 17,032.

rose•bush (rōz′bo͝osh′) *n.* A flowering rose shrub.

rose campion *n.* A Eurasian plant *(Lychnis coronaria)* having a dense cover of white woolly down and rose-red flowers.

rose window
In cathedral façade, Orvieto, Italy

rose chafer *n.* A long-legged gray North American beetle *(Macrodactylus subspinosus)* that causes damage to the roots, leaves, and blossoms of garden plants, esp. roses.

rose cold *n.* See **rose fever.**

rose-col•ored (rōz′kŭl′ərd) *adj.* **1.** *Color.* Having the color rose. **2.** Cheerful or optimistic, esp. to an excessive degree. —***idiom.* through rose-colored glasses.** With an unduly cheerful, optimistic, or favorable view of things.

Rose•crans (rōz′krănz′), **William Starke.** 1819–98. Amer. Union general who was relieved of his command after the disastrous Battle of Chickamauga (1863).

Rose•dale (rōz′dāl′). A community of N-central MD, a suburb of Baltimore. Pop. 18,703.

rose family *n.* A large family of plants, the Rosaceae, characterized by showy flowers with five separated petals and numerous stamens borne on the margin of a cuplike structure, including fruit plants such as the apple, cherry, and strawberry and ornamentals such as the rose and spirea.

rose fever *n.* A spring or early summer hay fever.

rose•fish (rōz′fĭsh′) *n., pl.* **rosefish** or **-fish•es.** A bright red marine food fish *(Sebastes marinus)* of North Atlantic waters.

rose geranium *n.* A woody plant *(Pelargonium graveolens)* having rose-pink flowers and fragrant, deeply palmately lobed leaves used for flavoring and in perfumery.

rose hip or **rose•hip** (rōz′hĭp′) *n.* The aggregate fruit of the rose plant, consisting of several dry fruitlets enclosed by an enlarged, fleshy, usu. red, flavorful floral cup.

ro•selle (rō-zĕl′) *n.* A tropical African plant *(Hibiscus sabdariffa)* having flowers with yellow petals and a persistent bright red calyx that has a pleasantly acid flavor. [?]

Ro•selle (rō-zĕl′). **1.** A city of NE IL, a suburb of Chicago. Pop. 20,819. **2.** A borough of NE NJ, a suburb in the Newark-Elizabeth area. Pop. 20,314.

rose mallow *n.* A tall marsh plant *(Hibiscus moscheutos)* of eastern North America having leaves covered with whitish down and flowers with white, pink, or rose petals.

rose•mar•y (rōz′mâr′ē) *n., pl.* **-ies.** An aromatic evergreen Mediterranean shrub *(Rosmarinus officinalis)* having light blue or pink flowers and grayish-green leaves used in cooking and perfume. [Alteration of ME *rosmarine* < Lat. *rōs marīnus*, sea dew : *rōs*, dew + *marīnus*, of the sea; see MARINE.]

Rose•mead (rōz′mēd′). A city of S CA, a suburb of Los Angeles. Pop. 51,638.

rose moss *n.* **1.** Any of the various mosses of the genus *Rhodobryum*, esp. *R. roseum*, characterized by conspicuous terminal leaf rosettes. **2.** See **portulaca.**

Ro•sen•berg (rō′zən-bûrg′). A city of SE TX on the Brazos R. WSW of Houston; founded 1883. Pop. 20,183.

Ro•sen•berg (rō′zĭn-bûrg′), **Julius.** 1918–53. Amer. spy who with his wife, **Ethel** (1915–53), was convicted of helping pass information concerning nuclear weaponry to the Soviets. Both were executed despite questions regarding the fairness of their trial.

rose of heaven *n.* A glabrous Mediterranean annual plant *(Lychnis coeli-rosa)* having opposite linear or lance-shaped leaves and large rose-pink flowers.

rose of Jer•i•cho (jĕr′ĭ-kō′) *n.* Either of two desert plants, *Anastatica hierochuntica* of the mustard family or *Selaginella lepidophylla*, that form a tight ball when dry and unfold when moistened.

rose of Shar•on (shăr′ən, shâr′-) *n.* **1.** A small eastern Asian tree or tall shrub *(Hibiscus syriacus)* having large reddish, purple, or white flowers and coarsely toothed leaves. **2.** A shrubby Eurasian evergreen plant *(Hypericum calycinum)* having oblong leaves and yellow flowers and usu. grown as a ground cover. [After the Plain of SHARON.]

ro•se•o•la (rō-zē′ə-lə, rō′zē-ō′lə) *n.* A rose-colored skin rash, sometimes occurring with diseases such as measles, syphilis, or scarlet fever. [NLat. < dim. of Lat. *roseus*, rosy < *rosa*, rose.] —**ro•se′o•lar** *adj.*

rose periwinkle *n.* See **Madagascar periwinkle.**

rose pink *n.* *Color.* A moderate to dark pink.

rose quartz *n.* A pinkish variety of the mineral quartz, used as a gemstone or an ornamental stone.

rose•root (rōz′ro͞ot′, -ro͝ot′) *n.* A perennial plant *(Sedum rosea)* of the Northern Hemisphere having fleshy leaves and greenish-yellow or purple flowers.

rose slug *n.* The larva of either of two sawflies *(Cladius isomerus* or *Endelomyia aethiops)* that feeds destructively on the leaves of roses.

Ro•set•ta stone (rō-zĕt′ə) *n.* A basalt tablet bearing inscriptions in Greek and in Egyptian hieroglyphic and demotic scripts that was discovered in 1799 near Rosetta, a town of northern Egypt in the Nile River delta, and provided the key to the decipherment of Egyptian hieroglyphics.

ro•sette (rō-zĕt′) *n.* **1.** An ornament or a badge made of ribbon or silk that is pleated or gathered to resemble a rose. **2.** A roselike marking or formation, such as one of the clusters of spots on a leopard's fur. **3.** *Archit.* A painted, carved, or sculptured ornament having a circular arrangement of parts radiating out from the center and suggesting the petals of a rose. **4.** *Bot.* A circular cluster of leaves that radiate from a center at or close to the ground. **5.** An ornamental circular band surrounding the central hole of an acoustic guitar. [Fr. < OFr., dim. of *rose*, rose. See ROSE[1].]

Rose•ville (rōz′vĭl′). **1.** A city of N-central CA NE of Sacramento in the foothills of the Sierra Nevada. Pop. 44,685. **2.** A city of SE MI, a suburb of Detroit. Pop. 51,412. **3.** A city of SE MN, a suburb of St. Paul. Pop. 33,485.

rose water *n.* A fragrant preparation made by steeping or distilling rose petals in water, used in cosmetics and in cookery.

rose window *n.* A circular window usu. of stained glass with radiating tracery suggesting the form of a rose.

rose•wood (rōz′wo͝od′) *n.* **1.** Any of various tropical or semitropical leguminous trees of the genera *Tipuana, Pterocarpus,* or *Dalbergia,* having hard reddish or dark wood with a strongly marked grain. **2.** The wood of any of these trees.

Rosh Ha•sha•nah also **Rosh Ha•sha•na** or **Rosh Ha•sho•na** or **Rosh Ha•sho•nah** (rôsh′ hə-shô′nə, -shä′-, hä-, hä-shä-nä′) *n.* The Jewish New Year, observed on the first day or the first and second days of Tishri and marked by solemnity as well as festivity. [Heb. *rō'š haššānâ* : *rō'š*, head, beginning + *ha*, the + *šānâ*, year.]

Ro•si•cru•cian (rō′zĭ-kro͞o′shən, rŏz′ĭ-) *n.* **1.** A member of an international organization devoted to the study of ancient philosophy and religion. **2.** A member of any of several secret organizations or orders of the 17th and 18th centuries devoted to mysticism. —*adj.* Of or relating to Rosicrucians or their philosophy. [< NLat. *(Frater) Rosae Crucis,* (Brother) of the Cross of the Rose, transl. of Ger. *Rosenkreutz*, surname of the traditional founder of the society.] —**Ro′si•cru′cian•ism** *n.*

ros•in (rŏz′ĭn) *n.* A translucent yellowish to dark brown resin derived from the stumps or sap of various pine trees and used to increase sliding friction and to manufacture a wide variety of products. —*tr.v.* **-ined, -in•ing, -ins.** To coat or rub with rosin. [ME, var. of *resin*. See RESIN.] —**ros′in•y** *adj.*

rosin oil *n.* A white to brown viscous liquid obtained by fractional distillation of rosin and used in lubricants, adhesives, electrical insulation, and printing inks.

ros•in•weed (rŏz′ĭn-wēd′) *n.* Any of several North American plants of the genera *Grindelia* or *Silphium,* such as the compass plant, having a resinous juice.

Ross (rôs, rŏs), **Betsy Griscom.** 1752–1836. Amer. seamstress who according to tradition made the first American flag (Jun. 1776) at the request of George Washington.

Ross, Harold Wallace. 1892–1951. Amer. publisher who founded and edited (1925–51) the *New Yorker* magazine.

Ross, Sir **James Clark.** 1800–62. British polar explorer who located the north magnetic pole (1831) and later explored Antarctica (1839–43).

Ross, John. Orig. Kooweskoowe. 1790–1866. Cherokee leader who directed the forced removal of the Cherokee from GA to the Oklahoma Terr. (1838–39) along the Trail of Tears.

Ross, Sir **John.** 1777–1856. British naval officer and Arctic explorer who led two expeditions (1818 and 1829–33) in search of the Northwest Passage.

Ross, Nellie Tayloe. 1876–1977. Amer. politician who served as governor of WY (1925–27).

Ros•set•ti (rō-zĕt′ē), **Dante Gabriel.** 1828–82. British poet and painter who was a founder (1848) of the Pre-Raphaelite Brotherhood. His sister **Christina Georgina Rossetti** (1830–94) is known for her verse collection *Goblin Market* (1862).

Ross Ice Shelf. A vast area in Antarctica bordering on **Ross Sea**, an arm of the S Pacific including **Ross Island**, site of the active volcano Mt. Erebus.

Ros•si•ni (rō-sē′nē, rô-), **Gioacchino Antonio.** 1792–1868. Italian composer whose operas include *William Tell* (1829).

Ros•tand (rôs-täN′), **Edmond.** 1868–1918. French playwright noted esp. for *Cyrano de Bergerac* (1897).

ros•tel•late (rŏs′tə-lāt′, rŏ-stĕl′ĭt) *adj.* Having a rostellum.

ros•tel•lum (rŏ-stĕl′əm) *n., pl.* **ros•tel•la** (rŏ-stĕl′ə). *Biol.* A small beaklike part. [Lat., dim. of *rōstrum*, beak. See ROSTRUM.] —**ros•tel′lar** *adj.*

ros•ter (rŏs′tər, rô′stər) *n.* **1.** A list, esp. of names. **2.** A list of the names of military officers and enlisted personnel enrolled for active duty. [Du. *rooster*, gridiron, roster (< the ruled paper used for a roster) < *roosten*, to roast.]

Ros•tock (rŏs′tŏk′, rôs′tôk′). A city of NE Germany near the Baltic Sea NNW of Berlin; chartered 1218. Pop. 241,146.

Ros•tov (rə-stôf′) also **Ros•tov-on-Don** (-ŏn-dŏn′, -dôn′, -ôn-). A city of SW Russia on the Don R. near its outlet on an arm of the Sea of Azov; chartered 1797. Pop. 986,000.

ros•trate (rŏs′trāt′, -trĭt, rô′strāt′, -strĭt) *adj.* Having a beaklike part. [Lat. *rōstrātus* < *rōstrum*, beak. See ROSTRUM.]

ros•trum (rŏs′trəm, rô′strəm) *n., pl.* **ros•trums** or **ros•tra** (rŏs′trə, rô′strə). **1.** A dais, pulpit, or other elevated platform for public speaking. **2.a.** The curved beaklike prow of an ancient Roman ship, esp. a war galley. **b.** The speaker's platform in an ancient Roman forum, which was decorated with the prows of captured enemy ships. **3.** *Biol.* A beaklike or snoutlike projection. [Lat. *rōstrum*, beak. See **rēd-***.] —**ros′tral** (-trəl) *adj.*

Ros•well (rŏz′wĕl′, -wəl). **1.** A city of NW GA, a suburb of Atlanta. Pop. 47,923. **2.** A city of SE NM SE of Albuquerque. Pop. 44,654.

ros•y (rō′zē) *adj.* **-i•er, -i•est. 1.a.** Having the characteristic pink or red color of a rose. **b.** Flushed with a healthy glow. **2.** Consisting of, decorated with, or suggestive of a rose or roses. **3.** Bright or cheerful; optimistic. —**ros′i•ly** *adv.* —**ros′i•ness** *n.*

rot (rŏt) *v.* **rot•ted, rot•ting, rots.** —*intr.* **1.** To undergo decomposition, esp. organic decomposition; decay. **2.** To become damaged, weakened, or useless because of decay. **3.** To languish; decline. **4.** To decay morally; become degenerate. —*tr.* To cause to decompose or decay. —*n.* **1.** The process of rotting or the condition of being rotten. **2.** Foot rot. **3.** See **liver fluke** 2. **4.** Any of several plant diseases characterized by the breakdown of tissue and caused by various bacteria or fungi. **5.** Pointless talk; nonsense. **6.** *Archaic.* Any disease causing the decay of flesh. —*interj.* Used to express annoyance, contempt, or impatience. [ME *roten* < OE *rotian.*]

rot. *abbr.* **1.** Rotating. **2.** Rotation.

ro•ta (rō′tə) *n.* **1.** *Chiefly British.* A roll call or roster of names. **2.** *Chiefly British.* A round or rotation of duties. **3. Rota.** *Rom. Cath. Ch.* A tribunal of prelates that serves as an ecclesiastical court. [Lat., wheel. See **ret-***.]

Ro•tar•i•an (rō-târ′ē-ən) *n.* A member of a Rotary Club, a major national and international service club.

ro•ta•ry (rō′tə-rē) *adj.* Of, relating to, causing, or characterized by rotation, esp. axial rotation. —*n., pl.* **-ries. 1.** A part or device that rotates around an axis. **2.** A traffic circle. [Med. Lat. *rotārius* < Lat. *rota*, wheel. See **ret-***.]

rotary engine *n.* An engine, such as a turbine, in which power is supplied directly to vanes or other rotary parts.

rotary plow *n.* A plow having a series of hoes arranged on a revolving power-driven shaft.

rotary press *n.* A printing press consisting of curved plates attached to a revolving cylinder that prints onto a continuous roll of paper.

rotary tiller *n.* See **rotary plow.**

ro•ta•ry-wing aircraft (rō′tə-rē-wĭng′) *n.* A rotorcraft.

ro•tate (rō′tāt) *v.* **-tat•ed, -tat•ing, -tates.** —*intr.* **1.** To turn around on an axis or center. **2.** To proceed in sequence; take turns or alternate. —*tr.* **1.** To cause to turn on an axis or center. **2.a.** To plant or grow (crops) in a fixed order of succession. **b.** To cause to alternate or proceed in sequence. —*adj.* Having radiating parts; wheel-shaped. [Lat. *rotāre, rotāt-* < *rota*, wheel. See **ret-***.] —**ro′tat′a•ble** *adj.*

ro•ta•tion (rō-tā′shən) *n.* **1.a.** The act or process of turning around a center or an axis. **b.** A single complete cycle of such motion. **2.** *Math.* A transformation of a coordinate system in which the axes are rotated through a given angle while the origin remains fixed. **3.** Regular and uniform variation in a sequence or series. **4.** *Games.* An order of shooting balls in billiards in which the ball with the lowest number on the table is always pocketed first. —**ro•ta′tion•al** *adj.*

ro•ta•tive (rō′tā′tĭv) *adj.* **1.** Of, relating to, causing, or characterized by rotation. **2.** Characterized by or occurring in alternation or succession. —**ro′ta′tive•ly** *adv.*

ro•ta•tor (rō′tā′tər) *n.* **1.** One that rotates. **2.** *pl.* **ro•ta•tor•es** (rō′tə-tôr′ēz, -tōr-). *Anat.* A muscle that serves to rotate a part of the body.

rotator cuff *n.* A set of muscles and tendons that secures the arm to the shoulder joint and permits rotation of the arm.

ro•ta•to•ry (rō′tə-tôr′ē, -tōr′ē) *adj.* **1.** Of, relating to, causing, or characterized by rotation. **2.** Occurring or proceeding in alternation or succession.

ro•ta•vi•rus (rō′tə-vī′rəs) *n., pl.* **-rus•es.** Any of a group of wheel-shaped RNA viruses that cause gastroenteritis.

ROTC *abbr.* Reserve Officers' Training Corps.

rote[1] (rōt) *n.* **1.** A memorizing process using routine or repetition, often without full attention or comprehension: *learn by rote.* **2.** Mechanical routine. [ME.] —**rote** *adj.*

rote[2] (rōt) *n.* The sound of surf breaking on the shore. [Prob. of Scand. orig.; akin to ON *rauta*, to roar.]

rote[3] (rōt) *n. Mus.* A medieval stringed instrument variably identified with a lyre, lute, or harp. [ME < OFr., prob. of Gmc. orig.]

ro•te•none (rōt′n-ōn′) *n.* A white crystalline compound, $C_{23}H_{22}O_6$, extracted from the roots of derris and cubé and used as an insecticide. [J. *rōten*, derris + -ONE.]

rot•gut (rŏt′gŭt′) *n. Slang.* Raw, inferior liquor.

Roth (rôth), **Philip Milton.** b. 1933. Amer. writer whose novels include *Portnoy's Complaint* (1969).

Roth•er•ham (rŏ*th*′ər-əm). A borough of N England NE of Sheffield. Pop. 251,900.

Roth•ko (rŏth′kō), **Mark.** 1903–70. Russian-born Amer. abstract expressionist painter whose works are characterized by horizontal bands of color with blurred edges.

Roth•schild (rŏth′chīld, rŏths′-, rôth′-, rôths′-, rōt′shĭlt′). German family, including **Mayer Amschal** (1743–1812), who founded a bank at Frankfurt am Main. His sons, esp. **Salomon** (1774–1855) and **Nathan Mayer** (1774–1836), established branches of the bank throughout Europe.

ro•ti•fer (rō′tə-fər) *n.* Any of various minute multicellular aquatic organisms of the phylum Rotifera, having at the anterior end a wheellike ring of cilia. [< NLat. *Rotifera*, phylum name : Lat. *rota*, wheel; see ROTA + Lat. *-fer*, -fer.] —**ro•tif′er•al** (-tĭf′ər-əl), **ro•tif′er•ous** (-ər-əs) *adj.*

ro•ti•form (rō′tə-fôrm′) *adj.* Shaped like a wheel. [Lat. *rota*, wheel; see **ret-*** + -FORM.]

ro•tis•se•rie (rō-tĭs′ə-rē) *n.* **1.** A cooking device equipped with a rotating spit on which meat or other food is roasted. **2.** A shop or restaurant where meats are roasted to order. [Fr. *rôtisserie* < OFr. *rostisserie* < *rostir*, to roast, of Gmc. orig.]

rot•l (rŏt′l) *n.* A unit of weight used in countries bordering on the Mediterranean and in nearby areas, varying in different

ă pat	oi boy
ā pay	ou out
âr care	o͝o took
ä father	o͞o boot
ĕ pet	ŭ cut
ē be	ûr urge
ĭ pit	th thin
ī pie	*th* this
îr pier	hw which
ŏ pot	zh vision
ō toe	ə about, item
ô paw	

Stress marks:
′ (primary);
′ (secondary), as in
dictionary (dĭk′shə-nĕr′ē)

regions from about 1 to 5 pounds (0.45 to 2.25 kilograms). [Ar. *raṭl, riṭl,* poss. < Gk. *litra.*]

ro•to•gra•vure (rō′tə-grə-vyo͝or′) *n.* **1.** An intaglio printing process in which letters and pictures are transferred from an etched copper cylinder to a web of paper, plastic, or similar material in a rotary press. **2.** Printed material produced by this process. [Lat. *rota,* wheel; see **ret-*** + GRAVURE.]

ro•tor (rō′tər) *n.* **1.** A rotating part of an electrical or mechanical device. **2.** An assembly of rotating horizontal airfoils, as that of a helicopter. [Contraction of ROTATOR.]

ro•tor•craft (rō′tər-krăft′) *n.* An aircraft, esp. a helicopter, that is kept partially or completely airborne by airfoils rotating around a vertical axis.

rotor ship *n. Naut.* A ship propelled by one or more tall cylindrical rotors operated by wind power.

rottweiler

ro•to•till (rō′tə-tĭl′) *tr.v.* **-tilled, -till•ing, -tills.** To cultivate or dig with a rototiller.

ro•to•till•er (rō′tə-tĭl′ər) *n.* A motorized rotary cultivator.

rot•ten (rŏt′n) *adj.* **-er, -est. 1.** Being in a state of putrefaction or decay; decomposed. **2.** Having a foul odor resulting from or suggestive of decay; putrid. **3.** Made weak or unsound by rot. **4.** Morally corrupt or despicable. **5.** Very bad; wretched. —*adv.* To a very great degree. [ME *roten* < ON *rotinn.*] —**rot′ten•ly** *adv.* —**rot′ten•ness** *n.*

rotten borough *n.* An election district having only a few voters but the same voting power as other more populous districts.

rot•ten•stone (rŏt′n-stōn′) *n.* A soft decomposed limestone used in powder form as a polishing material.

rot•ter (rŏt′ər) *n. Chiefly British.* A scoundrel.

Rot•ter•dam (rŏt′ər-dăm′). A city of SW Netherlands on the Rhine-Meuse delta SSE of The Hague; a major commercial power during the 16th and 17th centuries. Pop. 555,341.

rott•wei•ler (rŏt′wī′lər, rôt′vī′-) *n.* Any of a German breed of dog having a stocky body, short black fur, and tan face markings. [Ger., after *Rottweil,* a city of S Germany.]

ro•tund (rō-tŭnd′) *adj.* **1.** Rounded in figure; plump. See Syns at **fat. 2.** Having a full, rich sound; sonorous. [Lat. *rotundus.* See **ret-***.] —**ro•tun′di•ty** *n.* —**ro•tund′ly** *adv.*

ro•tun•da (rō-tŭn′də) *n.* **1.** A circular building, esp. one with a dome. **2.a.** A large area with a high ceiling, as in a hotel lobby. **b.** A large round room. [Ital. *rotonda* < fem. of *rotondo,* round < Lat. *rotundus.* See ROTUND.]

ro•tu•rier (rō-to͝or′ē-ā′, -tyo͝or′-) *n.* A commoner. [Fr. < OFr. < *roture,* newly cultivated land < Lat. *ruptūra,* action of breaking. See RUPTURE.]

rotunda
At the New York Botanical Garden

Rou•ault (ro͞o-ō′), **Georges.** 1871–1958. French artist whose paintings are characterized by brilliant colors.

Rou•baix (ro͞o-bĕ′). A city of N France NNE of Lille near the Belgian border. Pop. 101,602.

rou•ble (ro͞o′bəl) *n.* Var. of **ruble.**

rou•é (ro͞o-ā′) *n.* A lecherous, dissipated man. [Fr. < p.part. of *rouer,* to break on a wheel (from the feeling that such a person deserves that) < OFr. < Lat. *rotāre,* to rotate. See ROTATE.]

Rou•en[1] (ro͞o-än′, -äN′). A city of N France on the Seine R. WNW of Paris; of pre-Roman origin and the cap. of medieval Normandy. Pop. 101,945.

Rou•en[2] (ro͞o-än′, -äN′) *n.* Any of a breed of domestic ducks descended from and resembling the mallard. [After ROUEN[1].]

rouge (ro͞ozh) *n.* **1.** A red or pink cosmetic for coloring the cheeks or lips. **2.** A reddish powder, chiefly ferric oxide, used to polish metals or glass. —*v.* **rouged, roug•ing, roug•es.** —*tr.* To put rouge onto. —*intr.* To use rouge. [Fr. < OFr., red < Lat. *rubeus.* See **reudh-***.]

Rou•get de Lisle (ro͞o-zhā′ də lēl′), **Claude Joseph.** 1760–1836. French soldier who wrote "La Marseillaise" (1792), the French national anthem.

rough (rŭf) *adj.* **rough•er, rough•est. 1.** Having a surface marked by irregularities, protuberances, or ridges; not smooth. **2.** Coarse or shaggy to the touch. **3.a.** Difficult to travel over or through. **b.** Characterized by violent motion; turbulent. **c.** Difficult to endure or live through, esp. because of harsh or inclement weather. **d.** Unpleasant or difficult. **4.a.** Boisterous, unruly, uncouth, or rowdy. **b.** Lacking polish or finesse. **5.** Characterized by carelessness or force, as in manipulating. **6.** Harsh to the ear. **7.** Being in a natural state: *rough diamonds.* **8.** Not perfected, completed, or fully detailed. —*n.* **1.a.** Rugged overgrown terrain. **b.** *Sports.* The part of a golf course left unmowed and uncultivated. **2.** The difficult or disagreeable aspect, part, or side. **3.** Something in an unfinished or hastily worked-out state. **4.** A crude unmannered person. —*tr.v.* **roughed, rough•ing, roughs. 1.a.** To treat roughly or with physical violence: *roughed him up.* **b.** *Sports.* To treat (an opposing player) with unnecessary roughness during a sport or game. **2.** To prepare or indicate in an unfinished form: *rough out a house plan.* —*adv.* In a rough manner; roughly. —***idiom.* rough it.** To live without the usual comforts and conveniences. [ME < OE *rūh.*] —**rough′er** *n.* —**rough′ly** *adv.* —**rough′ness** *n.*

rough•age (rŭf′ĭj) *n.* See **fiber** 6.

rough-and-read•y (rŭf′ən-rĕd′ē) *adj.* Rough or crude but effective for a purpose or use.

rough-and-tum•ble (rŭf′ən-tŭm′bəl) *adj.* Characterized by roughness and disregard for order or rules. —*n.* A condition marked by rough, disorderly struggle; infighting.

rough•back (rŭf′băk′) *n.* Any of several flatfish with rough skin, esp. a species of dab *(Hippoglossoides platessoides).*

rough breathing *n. Ling.* **1.** An aspirate sound in ancient Greek like that of the sound (h) in English. **2.** The symbol (῾) written over some initial vowels and the letter rho in ancient Greek to indicate that a word begins with the sound (h). **3.** In ancient Greek, a word beginning with the sound (h) plus a vowel or diphthong.

rough•cast (rŭf′kăst′) *n.* **1.** A coarse plaster of lime, shells, and pebbles used for outside wall surfaces. **2.** A rough preliminary model or form. —*tr.v.* **-cast, -cast•ing, -casts. 1.** To plaster with roughcast. **2.** To shape or work into a rough or preliminary form. —**rough′cast′er** *n.*

rough-cut (rŭf′kŭt′) *n.* A print of a movie after assembly but before final editing.

rough•dry (rŭf′drī′) *tr.v.* **-dried, -dry•ing, -dries.** To dry (laundry) without ironing or smoothing out.

rough•en (rŭf′ən) *tr. & intr.v.* **-ened, -en•ing, -ens.** To make or become rough.

rough-hew (rŭf′hyo͞o′) *tr.v.* **-hewed, -hewed** or **-hewn** (-hyo͞on′), **-hew•ing, -hews. 1.** To hew or shape roughly, without finishing. **2.** To make in rough form.

rough•house (rŭf′hous′) *n.* Rowdy, uproarious behavior or play. —*v.* (*also* rŭf′houz′) **-housed, -hous•ing, -hous•es.** —*intr.* To engage in rowdy, uproarious behavior or play. —*tr.* To handle or treat roughly, usu. in fun.

rough-leg•ged hawk (rŭf′lĕg′ĭd) *n.* An Arctic hawk *(Buteo lagopus)* that has dark plumage and whitish feathers covering the legs and feeds mainly on small rodents.

rough•neck (rŭf′nĕk′) *n.* **1.** An uncouth person. **2.** A rowdy. **3.** A member of the crew of an oil rig other than the driller.

rough•rid•er (rŭf′rī′dər) *n.* **1.** A skilled rider of little-trained horses, esp. one who breaks horses for riding. **2. Rough Rider.** A member of the First U.S. Volunteer Cavalry regiment under Theodore Roosevelt in the Spanish-American War.

rough•shod (rŭf′shŏd′) *adj.* **1.** Shod with horseshoes having projecting nails or points to prevent slipping. **2.** Marked by brutal force. —***idiom.* ride roughshod over.** To treat with brutal force.

rough trade *n. Slang.* **1.** Violent, often brutal sex acts. **2.** One, esp. a male prostitute, who practices such acts.

rough•y (rŭf′ē) *n., pl.* **roughy** or **-ies. 1.** A perchlike food fish *(Arripis georgianus)* of Australia and New Zealand. **2.** A small fish *(Trachichthys australis)* having rough scales and found along the southeast coast of Australia. [Prob. < ROUGH.]

rou•lade (ro͞o-läd′) *n.* **1.** *Mus.* **a.** An embellishment consisting of a rapid run of several notes sung to one syllable. **b.** A roll on a drum. **2.** A slice of meat rolled around a filling and cooked. [Fr. < *rouler,* to roll < OFr. *roler.* See ROLL.]

rou•leau (ro͞o-lō′) *n., pl.* **-leaux** or **-leaus** (-lōz′). A small roll, esp. of coins wrapped in paper. [Fr. < OFr. *rolel,* dim. of *role,* roll < Lat. *rotula,* dim. of *rota,* wheel. See ROTA.]

rou•lette (ro͞o-lĕt′) *n.* **1.** *Games.* A gambling game in which the players bet on which slot of a rotating disk a small ball will come to rest in. **2.a.** A small toothed disk of tempered steel attached to a handle and used to make rows of dots, slits, or perforations, as on a sheet of postage stamps. **b.** Short consecutive incisions made between individual stamps in a sheet. —*tr.v.* **-lett•ed, -lett•ing, -lettes.** To mark or divide with a roulette. [Fr. < OFr. *ruelete,* fem. dim. of *ruele,* dim. of *roue,* wheel < Lat. *rota.* See **ret-***.]

round[1] (round) *adj.* **round•er, round•est. 1.a.** Being such that every part of the surface or the circumference is equidistant from the center: *a round ball.* **b.** Moving in or forming a circle. **c.** Shaped like a cylinder; cylindrical. **d.** Rather rounded in shape: *a round face.* **e.** Full in physique; plump. **2.a.** *Ling.* Formed or articulated with the lips in a rounded shape: *a round vowel.* **b.** Full in tone; sonorous. **3.** Whole or complete; full: *a round dozen.* **4.a.** *Math.* Expressed or designated as a whole number or integer; not fractional. **b.** Not exact; approximate: *a round estimate.* **5.** Large; considerable: *a round sum of money.* **6.** Brought to satisfactory conclusion or completion; finished. **7.a.** Outspoken; blunt: *a round scolding.* **b.** Done with full force; unrestrained. —*n.* **1.a.** Something, such as a circle, disk, globe, or ring, that is round. **b.** A circle formed of various things. **c.** Movement around a circle or about an axis. **2.** A rung or crossbar, as on a ladder. **3.** A cut of beef from the part of the thigh between the rump and the shank. **4.** An assembly of people; a group. **5.** A round dance. **6.a.** A complete course, succession, or series: *a round of negotiations.* **b.** A course of customary or prescribed actions, duties, or places. Often used in the plural: *physicians' rounds.* **7.** A complete range or extent. **8.** One drink for each person in a gathering or group. **9.** A single outburst, as of applause. **10.a.** A single shot or volley. **b.** Ammunition for a single shot or volley. **11.** A specified number of arrows shot from a specified distance to a target in archery. **12.** *Sports & Games.* An interval of play that occupies a specified time, constitutes a certain number of plays, or allows each player a turn. **13.** *Mus.* A composition for two or more voices in which each voice enters at a different time with the same melody. — *v.* **round•ed, round•ing, rounds.** — *tr.* **1.** To make round. See Syns at **bend¹**. **2.** To encompass; surround. **3.** To cause to proceed or move in a circular course. **4.** *Ling.* To pronounce with rounded lips; labialize. **5.** To fill out; make plump. **6.** To bring to completion or perfection; finish. **7.** *Math.* To express as a round number. **8.** To make a complete circuit of; go or pass around. **9.** To make a turn about or to the other side of. — *intr.* **1.** To become round. **2.** To take a circular course; complete or partially complete a circuit. **3.** To turn about, as on an axis; reverse. **4.** To become curved, filled out, or plump. **5.** To come to satisfactory completion or perfection. — *adv.* **1.** In a circular progression or movement; around. **2.** With revolutions. **3.** To a specific place or person. — *prep.* **1.** Around. **2.** From the beginning to the end of; throughout. — ***phrasal verb.*** **round up. 1.** To seek out and bring together; gather. **2.** To herd (cattle) together from various places. — ***idioms.*** **in the round. 1.** With the stage in the center of the audience. **2.** Fully shaped so as to stand free of a background. **make (or go) the rounds. 1.** To go from place to place, as on business. **2.** To be communicated or passed from person to person. [ME < AN *rounde*, var. of OFr. *rond*, ult. < VLat. **retundus* < Lat. *rotundus* < *rota*, wheel. See **ret-***.] — **round′ness** *n.*

round² (round) *tr.v.* **round•ed, round•ing, rounds.** *Archaic.* To whisper. [ME *rounden* < OE *rūnian* < *rūn*, a secret.]

round•a•bout (round′ə-bout′) *adj.* Indirect; circuitous. — *n.* **1.** A short close-fitting jacket. **2.** *Chiefly British.* A merry-go-round. **3.** *Chiefly British.* A traffic circle.

round clam *n.* See **quahog.**

round dance *n.* **1.** A folk dance performed with the dancers arranged in a circle. **2.** A ballroom dance in which couples proceed in a circular direction around the room.

round•ed (roun′dĭd) *adj.* **1.** Shaped into a circle or sphere; made round. **2.** *Ling.* Pronounced with the lips shaped ovally; labialized. **3.** Complete; balanced. — **round′ed•ness** *n.*

roun•del (roun′dəl) *n.* **1.** A curved form, esp. a semicircular panel, window, or recess. **2.a.** A rondel. **b.** A rondeau. **c.** An English variation of the rondeau consisting of three triplets with a refrain after the first and third. [ME < OFr. *rondel*, dim. of *rond*, circle, round. See ROUND¹.]

roun•de•lay (roun′də-lā′) *n.* A poem or song with a regularly recurring refrain. [ME, alteration of OFr. *rondelet*, dim. of *rondel*, roundel. See ROUNDEL.]

round•er (roun′dər) *n.* **1.** One that rounds, esp. a tool for rounding corners and edges. **2.** One, such as a security guard, who makes rounds. **3.** A dissolute person. **4.** *Sports.* **a.** A boxing match that goes on for a specified number of rounds. Often used in combination: *a five-rounder.* **b. rounders.** *(used with a sing. v.)* An English ball game similar to baseball.

round hand *n.* A style of handwriting in which the letters are rounded and full rather than angular.

Round•head (round′hĕd′) *n.* A supporter of the Parliamentarians during the English Civil War and the Commonwealth. [< the close-cropped hair of the Puritans.]

round herring *n.* Any of the mostly tropical marine fishes of the family Dussumierlidae, having a rounded abdomen.

round•house (round′hous′) *n.* **1.** A circular building for housing and switching locomotives. **2.** *Naut.* A cabin on the after part of the quarterdeck of a ship. **3.** *Games.* A meld of four kings and four queens in pinochle. **4.** *Slang.* A punch or swing delivered with a sweeping sidearm movement.

round•ish (roun′dĭsh) *adj.* Somewhat round. — **round′ish•ness** *n.*

round•let (round′lĭt) *n.* **1.** A little circle. **2.** A small circular object. [ME < OFr. *rondelet*, dim. of *rondel*, roundel. See ROUNDEL.]

round•ly (round′lē) *adv.* **1.** In the form of a circle or sphere. **2.** With full force or vigor; thoroughly: *applauded roundly.*

round robin *n.* **1.** *Sports.* A tournament in which each contestant is matched in turn against every other contestant. **2.** A petition or protest on which the signatures are arranged in a circle in order to conceal the order of signing. **3.** A letter sent among members of a group, often with comments added by each person.

round-shoul•dered (round′shōl′dərd) *adj.* Having the shoulders and upper back rounded.

rounds•man (roundz′mən) *n.* **1.** A police officer in charge of several other officers. **2.** One who makes rounds.

round steak *n.* A cut of beef from between the rump and shank.

round•ta•ble (round′tā′bəl) *n.* **1.** Often **round-ta•ble** (round′tā′bəl) or **round table.** A conference or discussion involving several participants. **2. Round Table. a.** In Arthurian legend, the circular table of King Arthur and his knights. **b.** The knights of King Arthur considered as a group.

round-the-clock (round′*thə*-klŏk′) also **a•round-the-clock** (ə-round′-) *adj.* Lasting or continuing throughout the entire 24 hours of the day; continuous.

round•trip or **round-trip** also **round trip** (round′trĭp′) *n.* A trip from one place to another and back, usu. the same way.

round•up (round′ŭp′) *n.* **1.a.** The herding together of cattle for inspection, branding, or shipping. **b.** The cattle so herded. **c.** The workers and horses employed in such herding. **2.** A gathering up, as of suspects. **3.** A summary: *a news roundup.*

round•worm (round′wûrm′) *n.* See **nematode.**

roup (ro͞op) *n.* An infectious disease of poultry and pigeons characterized by inflammation of the mouth and eyes. [?]

Rous (rous), **Francis Peyton.** 1879–1970. Amer. pathologist who shared a 1966 Nobel Prize.

rouse (rouz) *v.* **roused, rous•ing, rous•es.** — *tr.* **1.** To arouse from slumber, apathy, or depression. **2.** To excite, as to anger or action; stir up. — *intr.* **1.** To awaken. **2.** To become active. — *n.* The act or an instance of arousing. [ME *rousen*, to shake the feathers: used of a hawk, perh. < OFr. *reuser, ruser*, to repel, push back < VLat. **recūsāre* < Lat., to refuse. See RECUSE.] — **rous′er** *n.*

rous•ing (rou′zĭng) *adj.* **1.** Inducing enthusiasm or excitement; stirring. **2.** Lively; vigorous. **3.** Used as an intensive: *a rousing lie.* — **rous′ing•ly** *adv.*

Rous sarcoma *n.* A sarcoma produced in chickens by an RNA-containing virus. [After Francis Peyton ROUS.]

Rous•seau (ro͞o-sō′), **Henri.** "Le Douanier Rousseau." 1844–1910. French painter of primitive works, such as *The Snake Charmer* (1907).

Rousseau, Jean Jacques. 1712–78. French philosopher who held that humanity is essentially good but corrupted by society. His works include *The Social Contract* (1762).

Rousseau, Théodore. 1812–67. French landscape painter of the Barbizon school whose works include *Descent of the Cattle* (c. 1834).

Rous•sil•lon (ro͞o-sē-yôN′). A historical region of S France bordering on Spain and the Mediterranean Sea; orig. inhabited by Iberians and formally awarded to France by the Treaty of the Pyrenees (1659).

roust (roust) *tr.v.* **roust•ed, roust•ing, rousts.** To rout, esp. out of bed. [Prob. alteration of ROUSE.]

roust•a•bout (rous′tə-bout′) *n.* **1.** A laborer employed for temporary or unskilled jobs. **2.** A circus laborer. **3.** A deck or wharf laborer, esp. on the Mississippi River.

rout¹ (rout) *n.* **1.a.** A disorderly retreat or flight following defeat. **b.** An overwhelming defeat. **2.a.** A disorderly crowd of people; a mob. **b.** People of the lowest class; rabble. **3.** A public disturbance; a riot. **4.** A company, as of knights, that is in movement. **5.** A fashionable gathering. — *tr.v.* **rout•ed, rout•ing, routs. 1.** To put to disorderly flight or retreat. **2.** To defeat overwhelmingly. See Syns at **defeat.** [ME *route* < OFr., troop, defeat < VLat. **rupta* < fem. of Lat. *ruptus*, p.part. of *rumpere*, to break. See **reup-***.]

rout² (rout) *v.* **rout•ed, rout•ing, routs.** — *intr.* **1.** To dig with the snout; root. **2.** To poke around; rummage. — *tr.* **1.** To expose to view as if by digging; uncover. **2.** To hollow, scoop, or gouge out. **3.** To drive or force out as if by digging; eject. **4.** *Archaic.* To dig up with the snout. [Var. of ROOT².]

rout³ (rout, ro͞ot) *intr.v.* **rout•ed, rout•ing, routs.** *Chiefly British.* To bellow. Used of cattle. [ME *routen*, to roar < ON *rauta.*]

route (ro͞ot, rout) *n.* **1.a.** A road, course, or way for travel from one place to another. **b.** A highway. **2.** A customary line of travel. See Syns at **way. 3.** A fixed course or territory assigned to a salesperson or delivery person. **4.** A means of reaching a goal. — *tr.v.* **rout•ed, rout•ing, routes. 1.** To send or forward by a specific route. **2.** To schedule the order of (a sequence of procedures). [ME < OFr. < Lat. *rupta (via)*, broken (road), fem. p.part. of *rumpere*, to break. See ROUT¹.]

rout•er¹ (rou′tər) *n.* One that routs, esp. a machine tool that mills out the surface of metal or wood.

rout•er² (ro͞o′tər, rou′-) *n.* One that routes, esp. one who prepares shipments for distribution and delivery.

rou•tine (ro͞o-tēn′) *n.* **1.** A prescribed, detailed course of action to be followed regularly; a standard procedure. **2.** A set of customary procedures or activities. See Syns at **method. 3.** A set piece of entertainment, esp. in a nightclub or theater. **4.** *Slang.* A particular kind of behavior or activity. **5.** *Comp. Sci.* A set of programming instructions designed to perform a specific limited task. — *adj.* **1.** In accord with established procedure. **2.** Habitual; regular. **3.** Having no special quality; ordinary. [Fr. < *route*, route < OFr. See ROUTE.] — **rou•tine′ly** *adv.* — **rou•tin′ism** *n.* — **rou•tin′ist** *n.*

rou•tin•ize (ro͞o-tē′nīz′, ro͞ot′n-īz′) *tr.v.* **-ized, -iz•ing, -iz•es. 1.** To establish a routine for. **2.** To reduce to a routine. — **rou•tin′i•za′tion** (-ĭ-zā′shən) *n.*

roux (ro͞o) *n., pl.* **roux.** A mixture of flour and fat cooked together and used as a thickening. [Fr. *(beurre) roux*, browned (butter) < OFr. *rous*, reddish brown < Lat. *russus*, red. See **reudh-***.]

Rou•yn (ro͞o′ĭn, rwăN). A city of SW Quebec, Canada, near the Ontario border WNW of Quebec City. Pop. 17,224.

rove¹ (rōv) *v.* **roved, rov•ing, roves.** — *intr.* To wander about at random, esp. over a wide area; roam. — *tr.* To roam or wander around, over, or through. See Syns at **wander.** — *n.* An act of wandering about, over, around, or through. [ME *roven*, to shoot arrows at a mark.]

ă pat	oi boy
ā pay	ou out
âr care	o͝o took
ä father	o͞o boot
ĕ pet	ŭ cut
ē be	ûr urge
ĭ pit	th thin
ī pie	*th* this
îr pier	hw which
ŏ pot	zh vision
ō toe	ə about, item
ô paw	

Stress marks:
′ (primary);
′ (secondary), as in
dictionary (dĭk′shə-nĕr′ē)

rove[2] (rōv) *tr.v.* **roved, rov•ing, roves. 1.** To card (wool). **2.** To put (fibers) through an eye or opening. **3.** To stretch and twist (fibers) before spinning; ravel out. — *n.* A slightly twisted and extended fiber or sliver. [?]

rove[3] (rōv) *v. Naut.* A p.t. and p.part. of **reeve**[2].

rove beetle *n.* Any of numerous beetles of the family Staphylinidae, often found in decaying matter and having slender bodies and short wing covers. [Poss. < ROVE[1].]

rov•er[1] (rō′vər) *n.* **1.a.** One that roves; a wanderer. **b.** A vehicle, with or without a crew, used esp. in exploring a planet and its satellites. **2.** *Sports.* A mark in archery selected by chance.

ro•ver[2] (rō′vər) *n.* **1.** A pirate. **2.** A pirate vessel. [ME < MDu. or MLGer., robber < *roven,* to rob. See **reup-*.**]

Rov•no (rôv′nə). A city of SW Ukraine W of Kiev; held by Poland from 1921 to 1939. Pop. 221,000.

row[1] (rō) *n.* **1.** A series of objects placed next to each other, usu. in a straight line. **2.** A succession without a break or gap in time: *three years in a row.* **3.** A continuous line of buildings along a street. — *tr.v.* **rowed, row•ing, rows.** To place in a row. — ***idiom.* a tough row to hoe.** *Informal.* A difficult situation to endure. [ME < OE *rāw.*]

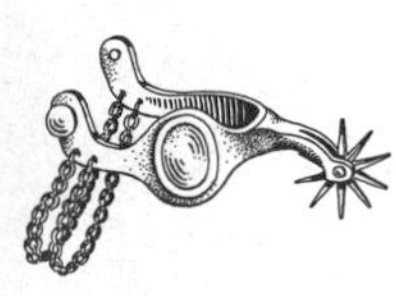

rowel

row[2] (rō) *v.* **rowed, row•ing, rows.** — *intr. Naut.* To row a boat. — *tr.* **1.** *Naut.* **a.** To propel (a boat) with or as if with oars. **b.** To carry in or on a boat propelled by oars. **c.** To use (a specified number of oars or people deploying them). **2.** To propel or convey in a manner resembling rowing of a boat. **3.** *Sports.* **a.** To pull (an oar) as part of a racing crew. **b.** To race against by rowing. — *n. Naut.* **1.** The act or an instance of rowing. **2.** A trip or an excursion in a rowboat. [ME *rowen* < OE *rōwan.* See **erə-*.**] — **row′er** *n.*

row[3] (rou) *n.* **1.** A boisterous disturbance or quarrel; a brawl. **2.** An uproar; a great noise. — *intr.v.* **rowed, row•ing, rows.** To take part in a quarrel, a brawl, or an uproar. [?]

row•an (rō′ən, rou′-) *n.* A small deciduous European tree *(Sorbus aucuparia)* of the rose family, having pinnately compound leaves, corymbs of white flowers, and orange-red berries. [Of Scand. orig. See **reudh-*.**]

row•boat (rō′bōt′) *n.* **1.** *Naut.* A small boat propelled by oars. **2.** *Sports.* A rowing machine.

row•dy (rou′dē) *n., pl.* **-dies.** A rough, disorderly person. — *adj.* **-di•er, -di•est.** Disorderly; rough. [Prob. < ROW[3].] — **row′di•ly** *adv.* — **row′di•ness** *n.* — **row′dy•ism** *n.*

row•el (rou′əl) *n.* A sharp-toothed wheel inserted into the end of the shank of a spur. [ME < OFr. *roelle,* dim. of *roue,* wheel < Lat. *rota.* See **ret-*.**] — **row′el** *v.*

row house

row•en (rou′ən) *n. New England.* A second crop, as of hay, in a season. [ME *rowein* < AN *rewain,* var. of OFr. *regain* : *re-,* re- + *gaaignier,* to till; see GAIN[1].]

row house (rō) *n.* One of a series of identical houses situated side by side and joined by common walls.

Row•land•son (rō′lənd-sən), **Thomas.** 1756–1827. British caricaturist and illustrator of works by Sterne and Swift.

row•lock (rō′lŏk′) *n. Chiefly British.* An oarlock.

Ro•xas y A•cu•ña (rô′häs ē ä-ko͞on′yə, -yä), **Manuel.** 1892–1948. Philippine politician who was the first president of the Philippines (1946–48).

Roy (roi). A city of N UT, a suburb of Ogden. Pop. 24,603.

roy•al (roi′əl) *adj.* **1.** Of or relating to a monarch. **2.** Of the rank of a monarch. **3.** Of, relating to, or in the service of a kingdom. **4.** Issued or performed by a monarch. **5.** Founded, chartered, or authorized by a monarch. **6.** Befitting royalty; stately. **7.a.** Superior, as in size or quality. **b.** Used as an intensive. — *n.* **1.** *Informal.* A member of a monarch's family. **2.** *Naut.* A sail set on a royalmast. **3.** A paper size, 20 by 25 inches for printing, 19 by 24 inches for writing. — ***idiom.* the royal road.** A way or method that presents no difficulties. [ME < OFr. < Lat. *rēgālis* < *rēx, rēg-,* king. See **reg-*.**] — **roy′al•ly** *adv.*

royal blue *n. Color.* A deep to strong blue.

royal fern *n.* A deep-rooted fern *(Osmunda regalis)* of worldwide distribution having tall, bipinnately compound fronds.

royal flush *n. Games.* A straight flush consisting of the five highest cards of one suit, ranked as the highest hand in certain games of poker.

roy•al•ism (roi′ə-lĭz′əm) *n.* Support of or adherence to the principle of rule by a monarch.

roy•al•ist (roi′ə-lĭst) *n.* **1.** A supporter of government by a monarch. **2. Royalist. a.** See **cavalier** 3. **b.** An American loyal to British rule during the American Revolution; a Tory.

royal jelly *n.* A nutritious substance secreted by the pharyngeal glands of worker bees that serves as food for all young larvae and as the only food for larvae that will become queen bees.

royal lily *n.* A western Chinese lily *(Lilium regale)* having large, fragrant, horizontal funnel-shaped flowers.

roy•al•mast also **roy•al mast** (roi′əl-măst′) *n. Naut.* A small mast immediately above a topgallant mast.

Royal Oak (ōk). A city of SE MI, a suburb of Detroit. Pop. 65,410.

royal palm *n.* Any of several tropical American palm trees of the genus *Roystonea,* having a tall naked trunk surmounted by a large tuft of pinnately compound leaves.

royal poinciana *n.* A tropical and semitropical tree *(Delonix regia)* native to Madagascar and having bipinnately compound leaves, clusters of large scarlet flowers, and long pods.

royal purple *n. Color.* A moderate or strong violet to deep purple or dark reddish purple.

roy•al•ty (roi′əl-tē) *n., pl.* **-ties. 1.a.** A person of royal rank or lineage. **b.** Monarchs and their families considered as a group. **2.** The lineage or rank of a monarch. **3.** The power, status, or authority of a monarch. **4.** Royal quality or bearing. **5.** A kingdom or possession ruled by a monarch. **6.** A right or prerogative of the crown, as that of receiving a percentage of the proceeds from mines in the royal domain. **7.a.** The granting of a right by a monarch to a corporation or an individual to exploit specified natural resources. **b.** The payment for such a right. **8.a.** A share paid to a writer or composer out of the proceeds resulting from the sale or performance of his or her work. **b.** A share in the proceeds paid to an inventor or a proprietor for the right to use his or her invention or services. **9.** A share of the profit or product reserved by the grantor, esp. of an oil or mining lease.

Royce (rois), **Josiah.** 1855–1916. Amer. philosopher known for his contributions to metaphysics, religion, and logic.

R.P. *abbr.* Received Pronunciation.

rpm or **r.p.m.** *abbr.* Revolutions per minute.

rps or **r.p.s.** *abbr.* Revolutions per second.

rpt. *abbr.* **1.** Repeat. **2.** Report.

R.Q. *abbr.* Respiratory quotient.

RR also **R.R.** *abbr.* **1.** Railroad. **2.** Rural route.

R.R. *abbr.* Right Reverend.

-rrhagia *suff.* Abnormal or excessive flow or discharge: *menorrhagia.* [Gk. *-rragia* < *rhēgnunai, rhag-,* to burst forth.]

-rrhea or **-rrhoea** *suff.* Flow; discharge: *seborrhea.* [NLat. *-rrhoea* < Gk. *-rrhoia* < *rhoia,* a flowing < *rhein,* to flow. See **sreu-*.**]

rRNA *abbr.* Ribosomal RNA.

RS *abbr.* **1.** Recording secretary. **2.** Right side. **3.** Also **R.S.** Royal Society.

RSV or **R.S.V.** *abbr. Bible.* Revised Standard Version.

R.S.V.P. or **r.s.v.p.** *abbr. Fr.* Répondez s'il vous plaît (please reply).

RT *abbr.* **1.** Radiotelephone. **2.** Room temperature.

rt. *abbr.* Right.

Rt. *abbr. Bible.* Ruth.

rte. *abbr.* Route.

Rt. Hon. *abbr.* Right Honorable.

Rt. Rev. *abbr.* Right Reverend.

RTW *abbr.* Ready-to-wear.

Ru The symbol for the element **ruthenium.**

RU 486 *n.* A drug that prevents the attachment of a fertilized ovum to the wall of the uterus by interfering with the action of progesterone. [From *R(oussel) U(CLAF),* the maker.]

Ru•an•da (ro͞o-än′də). See **Rwanda.**

Ru•an•da-U•run•di (ro͞o-än′də-o͞o-ro͞on′dē). A former colonial possession of central Africa; mandated to Belgium by the League of Nations after World War I and split into the present-day countries of Rwanda and Burundi in 1962.

rub (rŭb) *v.* **rubbed, rub•bing, rubs.** — *tr.* **1.a.** To subject to the action of something that moves back and forth with friction and pressure. **b.** To cause to move along a surface with friction and pressure. **2.** To irritate; annoy. — *intr.* **1.a.** To move along a surface with friction and pressure. **b.** To chafe with friction. **c.** To cause irritation or annoyance. **2.** To continue in a given situation, usu. with difficulty. **3.** To admit rubbing. **4.** To be transferred by contact or proximity: *wished some of her luck would rub off on me.* — *n.* **1.** The act of rubbing. **2.** The application of friction and pressure: *a back rub.* **3.** An unevenness on a surface. **4.** An act or a remark that annoys or hurts another. **5.** Difficulty. — ***phrasal verbs.* rub down.** To perform a brisk rubbing of the body, as in massage. **rub in.** To harp on (an unpleasant matter). **rub out. 1.** To obliterate by or as if by rubbing. **2.** *Slang.* To kill; murder. — ***idioms.* rub elbows** (or **shoulders**)**.** To mix or socialize closely. **rub (one's) hands.** To experience or display pleased anticipation, self-satisfaction, or glee. **rub (someone's) nose in.** *Slang.* To bring repeatedly and forcefully to another's attention. **rub (someone) the wrong way.** To annoy; irritate. [ME *rubben.*]

Rub al Kha•li (ro͝ob′ ăl kä′lē, äl KHä′lē). "the Empty Quarter." A desert region in the SE interior of Arabia.

ru•basse (ro͞o-băs′, ro͞o′băs′) *n.* A variety of quartz colored ruby red by its iron-oxide content. [Fr. *rubace* < *rubis,* ruby. See RUBY.]

ru•ba•to (ro͞o-bä′tō) *Mus. n., pl.* **-tos.** Rhythmic flexibility within a phrase or measure; a relaxation of strict time. [Ital. *(tempo) rubato,* stolen (time), rubato, p.part. of *rubare,* to rob, of Gmc. orig. See **reup-*.**] — **ru•ba′to** *adj.*

rub•ber[1] (rŭb′ər) *n.* **1.** A yellowish, amorphous elastic material obtained from the milky sap or latex of various tropical plants, esp. the rubber tree, and vulcanized and modified into products such as electric insulation, tires, and containers. **2.** Any of numerous synthetic elastic materials of varying chemical composition with properties similar to those of natural rubber. **3.** A low overshoe made of rubber. **4.** *Baseball.* The oblong piece of hard rubber on which the pitcher must stand when delivering the ball. **5.** Something made of rubber, as: **a.** An eraser. **b.** A tire. **c.** A set of tires on a vehicle. **6.** *Slang.* A condom. **7.** One that rubs, esp. one that gives a massage. [< RUB.]

rub•ber[2] (rŭb′ər) *n. Games.* **1.** A series of games of which two out of three or three out of five must be won to terminate the play. **2.** An odd game played to break a tie. [?]

rubber band *n.* An elastic loop of natural or synthetic rubber used to hold objects together. Also called regionally *gum band.*

rubber cement *n.* Nonvulcanized rubber in an organic solvent, used as an adhesive.

rubber check *n. Slang.* A check returned by a bank because of insufficient funds in the account on which it is drawn.

rub•ber•ize (rŭb′ə-rīz′) *tr.v.* **-ized, -iz•ing, -iz•es.** To coat, treat, or impregnate with rubber.

rub•ber•neck (rŭb′ər-nĕk′) *Slang.* — *intr.v.* **-necked, -neck•ing, -necks.** To look about or survey with unsophisticated wonderment or curiosity. — *n.* A rubbernecker.

rub•ber•neck•er (rŭb′ər-nĕk′ər) *n. Slang.* One who rubbernecks.

rubber plant *n.* **1.** Any of several tropical plants yielding sap that can be coagulated to form crude rubber. **2.** A small tree *(Ficus elastica)* that has large, oblong, glossy leathery leaves.

rubber stamp also **rub•ber•stamp** (rŭb′ər-stămp′) *n.* **1.** **rubber stamp.** A piece of rubber affixed to a handle and bearing raised characters used to make ink impressions. **2.** One that gives perfunctory approval or endorsement of a policy without assessing its merit. **3.** Such approval or endorsement.

rub•ber-stamp (rŭb′ər-stămp′) *tr.v.* **-stamped, -stamp•ing, -stamps.** **1.** To mark with the imprint of a rubber stamp. **2.** To endorse, vote for, or approve without question or deliberation.

rubber tree *n.* A tropical South American tree *(Hevea brasiliensis)* widely cultivated throughout the Tropics and yielding a milky juice that is a major source of commercial rubber.

rub•ber•y (rŭb′ə-rē) *adj.* **-i•er, -i•est.** Of or resembling rubber; elastic.

rub•bing (rŭb′ĭng) *n.* **1.** The act of polishing, cleaning, or drying. **2.** A representation of a textured surface made by rubbing a paper placed over the surface with a marking agent such as charcoal or chalk.

rub•bish (rŭb′ĭsh) *n.* **1.** Refuse; garbage. **2.** Worthless material. **3.** Foolish discourse; nonsense. [ME *robishe.*]

rub•bish•y (rŭb′ĭ-shē) *adj.* **1.** Littered with rubbish. **2.** Of no value; worthless.

rub•ble (rŭb′əl) *n.* **1.** A loose mass of angular fragments of rock or masonry crumbled by natural or human forces. **2.a.** Irregular fragments or pieces of rock used in masonry. **b.** The masonry made with such rocks. [ME *rubel.*] — **rub′bly** *adj.*

rub•ble•work (rŭb′əl-wûrk′) *n.* Masonry made with rubble.

rub•down (rŭb′doun′) *n.* An energetic massage of the body.

rube (ro͞ob) *n. Slang.* An unsophisticated country person. [Prob. < *Rube,* nickname for *Reuben.*]

ru•be•fa•cient (ro͞o′bə-fā′shənt) *adj.* Producing redness, as of the skin. — *n.* A substance that irritates the skin, causing redness. [Lat. *rubefaciēns, rubefacient-,* pr.part. of *rubefacere,* to make red : *rubeus,* red; see **reudh-*** + *facere,* to make; see **dhē-*.**] — **ru′be•fac′tion** (-făk′shən) *n.*

Rube Gold•berg (ro͞ob′ gōld′bûrg′) *adj.* Of, relating to, or being a contrivance that brings about by complicated means what apparently could have been accomplished simply. [After Reuben Lucius GOLDBERG.]

ru•bel•la (ro͞o-bĕl′ə) *n.* A mild, contagious, eruptive viral disease capable of producing congenital defects in infants born to mothers infected during the first three months of pregnancy. [< Lat., neut. pl. of *rubellus,* red < *ruber.* See **reudh-*.**]

ru•bel•lite (ro͞o′bə-līt′, ro͞o-bĕl′īt) *n.* The red variety of tourmaline, used as a gemstone. [Lat. *rubellus,* red; see RUBELLA + -ITE[1].]

Ru•bens (ro͞o′bənz), **Peter Paul.** 1577–1640. Flemish painter whose baroque works include *Descent from the Cross* (1611–14). — **Ru′ben•esque′** (ro͞o′bə-nĕsk′) *adj.*

ru•be•o•la (ro͞o-bē′ə-lə, ro͞o′bē-ō′lə) *n.* See **measles** 1a. [< Lat., neut. pl. dim. of *rubeus,* red. See **reudh-*.**] — **ru•be′o•lar** *adj.*

ru•bes•cent (ro͞o-bĕs′ənt) *adj.* Turning red. [Lat. *rubēscēns, rubēscent-,* pr.part. of *rubēscere,* to grow red, inchoative of *rubēre,* to be red. See **reudh-*.**] — **ru•bes′cence** *n.*

Ru•bi•con (ro͞o′bĭ-kŏn′) *n.* A limit that when passed or exceeded permits of no return. [Lat. *Rubicō, Rubicōn-,* Rubicon, a short river of N-central Italy, the crossing of which by Julius Caesar and his army in 49 B.C. began a civil war.]

ru•bi•cund (ro͞o′bĭ-kənd) *adj.* Inclined to a healthy rosiness; ruddy. [Lat. *rubicundus.* See **reudh-*.**] — **ru′bi•cun′di•ty** (-kŭn′dĭ-tē) *n.*

ru•bid•i•um (ro͞o-bĭd′ē-əm) *n. Symbol* **Rb** A soft metallic element of the alkali group that ignites spontaneously in air and reacts violently with water, used in photocells. Atomic number 37; atomic weight 85.47; melting point 38.89°C; boiling point 688°C; specific gravity (solid) 1.532; valence 1, 2, 3, 4. See table at **element.** [< Lat. *rubidus,* red. See **reudh-*.**]

ru•big•i•nous (ro͞o-bĭj′ə-nəs) also **ru•big•i•nose** (-nōs′) *adj.* Rust-colored; reddish-brown. [Lat. *rūbīginōsus* < *rūbīgo, rūbīgin-,* rust < *rōbus,* red. See **reudh-*.**]

Ru•bin•stein (ro͞o′bĭn-stīn′), **Anton Gregor.** 1829–94. Russian pianist and composer who founded the St. Petersburg Conservatory (1862).

Rubinstein, Arthur or **Artur.** 1887–1982. Polish-born Amer. pianist noted for his interpretations of the works of Chopin.

ru•bi•ous (ro͞o′bē-əs) *adj.* Of the color of a ruby; red.

ru•ble also **rou•ble** (ro͞o′bəl) *n.* See table at **currency.** [Russ. *rubl'* < ORuss. *rublĭ,* cut, piece (prob. originally a piece cut from a silver bar) < *rubiti,* to chop, hew. See **reup-*.**]

rub•out (rŭb′out′) *n. Slang.* Murder; destruction.

ru•bric (ro͞o′brĭk) *n.* **1.a.** A class or category. **b.** A title; a name. **2.** A part of a manuscript or book that appears in decorative red lettering or is otherwise distinguished from the rest of the text. **3.** A title or heading of a statute or chapter in a code of law. **4.** *Eccles.* A direction in a missal, hymnal, or other liturgical book. **5.** An authoritative rule or direction. **6.** A short commentary or explanation covering a broad subject. **7.** Red ocher. — *adj.* **1.** *Color.* Red or reddish. **2.** Written in red. [ME *rubrike* < OFr. *rubrique* < Lat. *rūbrīca,* red chalk < *ruber, rubr-,* red. See **reudh-*.**] — **ru′bri•cal** *adj.*

ru•bri•cate (ro͞o′brĭ-kāt′) *tr.v.* **-cat•ed, -cat•ing, -cates.** **1.** To arrange, write, or print as a rubric. **2.** To provide with rubrics. **3.** To establish rules for. [LLat. *rūbrīcāre, rūbrīcāt-,* to color red < Lat. *rūbrīcātus,* rubricated < *rūbrīca,* rubric. See RUBRIC.] — **ru′bri•ca′tion** *n.* — **ru′bri•ca′tor** *n.*

ru•bri•cian (ro͞o-brĭsh′ən) *n. Eccles.* A person learned in the rubrics of ritual.

ru•by (ro͞o′bē) *n., pl.* **-bies.** **1.** A deep red translucent variety of the mineral corundum, valued as a precious stone. **2.** Something, such as a watch bearing, that is made from a ruby. **3.** *Color.* A dark or deep red to deep purplish red. — *adj. Color.* Of the color ruby. [ME < OFr. *rubi* < Med.Lat. *rubīnus (lapis),* red (stone), ruby < Lat. *rubeus,* red. See **reudh-*.**]

ru•by-throat•ed hummingbird (ro͞o′bē-thrō′tĭd) *n.* A small bird *(Archilochus colubris)* of eastern North America having green upper plumage and in the male a brilliant red throat.

ruche (ro͞osh) *n.* A ruffle or pleat of fine fabric used for trimming women's garments. [Fr. < OFr. *rusche,* beehive < Med. Lat. *rūsca,* tree bark (used to make beehives), of Celt. orig.]

ruck[1] (rŭk) *n.* **1.** A multitude; a throng. **2.** The undistinguished crowd or ordinary run of persons or things. [ME *ruke,* heap, prob. of Scand. orig.]

ruck[2] (rŭk) *v.* **rucked, ruck•ing, rucks.** — *tr.* To make a fold in; crease. — *intr.* To become creased. — *n.* A crease or pucker, as in cloth. [Ult. < ON *hrukka,* wrinkle, fold. See **sker-[2]*.**]

ruck•sack (rŭk′săk′, ro͝ok′-) *n.* A knapsack. [Ger. : dialectal *Ruck,* back (< MHGer. *rück, ruck* < OHGer. *hrukki;* see **sker-[2]***) + *Sack,* sack (< MHGer. *sac* < OHGer. < Lat. *saccus;* see SACK[1]).]

ruck•us (rŭk′əs) *n.* A disturbance; a commotion. [Perh. blend of RUCTION and RUMPUS.]

ruc•tion (rŭk′shən) *n.* A riotous disturbance; a noisy quarrel. [Poss. alteration of INSURRECTION.]

Ru•da Slas•ka (ro͞o′də shlôɴ′skə). A city of S-central Poland, a suburb of Katowice. Pop. 164,600.

rudd (rŭd) *n.* A European freshwater fish *(Scardinius erythrophthalmus)* related to the carp and having a brownish body and red fins. [Prob. < *rud,* red. See RUDDLE.]

rud•der (rŭd′ər) *n.* **1.a.** *Naut.* A vertically hinged plate of metal, fiberglass, or wood mounted at the stern of a vessel for directing its course. **b.** A similar structure at the tail of an aircraft, used for effecting horizontal changes in course. **2.** A controlling agent or influence over direction; a guide. [ME *ruder* < OE *rōther,* steering oar. See **erə-*.**]

rud•der•less (rŭd′ər-lĭs) *adj.* **1.** Lacking in direction, control, or coherence. **2.** *Naut.* Lacking a rudder or a crew member at the helm.

rud•der•post (rŭd′ər-pōst′) *n.* See **rudderstock.**

rud•der•stock (rŭd′ər-stŏk′) *n.* The vertical shaft of a rudder that allows it to pivot when the tiller or steering gear is operated.

rud•dle (rŭd′l) also **red•dle** (rĕd′l) or **rad•dle** (răd′l) — *n.* Red ocherous iron ore, used in dyeing and marking. — *tr.v.* **-dled, -dling, -dles.** To dye or mark with or as if with red ocher. [Prob. dim. of *rud,* red < ME *rudde* < OE *rudu.* See **reudh-*.**]

rud•dock (rŭd′ək) *n. Chiefly British.* An Old World robin *(Erithacus rubecula)* having olive-brown upper plumage and a conspicuous orange breast. [ME *ruddok* < OE *rudduc.* See **reudh-*.**]

rud•dy (rŭd′ē) *adj.* **-di•er, -di•est.** **1.a.** Having a healthy reddish color. **b.** Reddish; rosy. **2.** *Chiefly British.* Used as an intensive: *"You ruddy liar!"* (John Galsworthy). [ME *rudi* < OE *rudig.* See **reudh-*.**] — **rud′di•ly** *adv.* — **rud′di•ness** *n.*

ruddy duck *n.* A North American duck *(Oxyura jamaicensis)*

ruddy duck
Oxyura jamaicensis

ă pat	oi boy
ā pay	ou out
âr care	o͝o took
ä father	o͞o boot
ĕ pet	ŭ cut
ē be	ûr urge
ĭ pit	th thin
ī pie	*th* this
îr pier	hw which
ŏ pot	zh vision
ō toe	ə about, item
ô paw	

Stress marks:
′ (primary);
′ (secondary), as in
dictionary (dĭk′shə-nĕr′ē)

having stiff pointed tail feathers and in the male brownish-red upper plumage and a black-and-white head.

rude (ro͞od) *adj.* **rud•er, rud•est. 1.** Relatively undeveloped; primitive. **2.a.** Being in a rough unfinished condition. **b.** Exhibiting a marked lack of skill or precision in work. **c.** In a natural raw state: *bales of rude cotton.* **3.a.** Lacking the graces and refinement of civilized life; uncouth. **b.** Lacking education or knowledge; unlearned. **c.** Ill-mannered; discourteous: *rude behavior.* **4.** Vigorous, robust, and sturdy. **5.** Abruptly and unpleasantly forceful: *a rude shock.* [ME < OFr. < Lat. *rudis.*] **—rude′ly** *adv.* **—rude′ness** *n.*

ru•der•al (ro͞o′dər-əl) *Bot.* —*adj.* Growing in rubbish, poor land, or waste. —*n.* A ruderal plant. [NLat. *rūderālis* < Lat. *rūdus, rūder-*, rubbish.]

ru•di•ment (ro͞o′də-mənt) *n.* **1.** A fundamental element, principle, or skill, as of a field of learning. Often used in the plural. **2.** Something in an incipient or undeveloped form. Often used in the plural. **3.** *Biol.* An imperfectly or incompletely developed organ or part. [Lat. *rudimentum* < *rudis*, rough, unformed.] **—ru′di•men′tal** (-mĕn′tl) *adj.*

ru•di•men•ta•ry (ro͞o′də-mĕn′tə-rē, -mĕn′trē) *adj.* **1.** Of or relating to basic facts or principles; elementary. **2.** Being in the earliest stages of development; incipient. **3.** *Biol.* Imperfectly or incompletely developed; embryonic. **—ru′di•men•tar′i•ly** (-târ′ə-lē) *adv.* **—ru′di•men′ta•ri•ness** *n.*

Ru•dolf I (ro͞o′dŏlf). 1218–91. Holy Roman emperor (1273–91) and founder of the Hapsburg dynasty.

Rudolf, Lake. See Lake **Turkana.**

Ru•dolph (ro͞o′dŏlf), **Wilma Glodean.** b. 1940. Amer. athlete who won three gold medals in track at the 1960 Olympics.

rue¹ (ro͞o) *v.* **rued, ru•ing, rues.** —*tr.* To feel regret, remorse, or sorrow for. —*intr.* To feel regret, remorse, or sorrow. —*n.* Sorrow; regret. [ME *ruen* < OE *hrēowan*, to affect with grief, and *hrēowian*, to repent.] **—ru′er** *n.*

rue² (ro͞o) *n.* Any of various aromatic southwest Asian or Mediterranean plants of the genus *Ruta,* esp. the ornamental *R. graveolens* having bipinnately compound leaves that yield an acrid volatile oil formerly used in medicine. [ME < OFr. < Lat. *rūta*, prob. < Gk. *rhutē.*]

rue anemone *n.* A small North American woodland plant *(Anemonella thalictroides)* having white or pinkish apetalous flowers grouped in umbels.

rue•ful (ro͞o′fəl) *adj.* **1.** Inspiring pity or compassion. **2.** Causing, feeling, or expressing sorrow or regret. **—rue′ful•ly** *adv.* **—rue′ful•ness** *n.*

ru•fes•cent (ro͞o-fĕs′ənt) *adj.* Tinged with red. [Lat. *rūfēscēns, rūfēscent-*, pr.part. of *rūfēscere*, to become red < *rūfus*, red, reddish. See **reudh-*.**] **—ru•fes′cence** *n.*

ruff¹ (rŭf) *n.* **1.** A stiffly starched frilled or pleated circular collar of fine fabric, worn in the 16th and 17th centuries. **2.** A distinctive collarlike projection around the neck, as of feathers on a bird. **3.** A Eurasian sandpiper *(Philomachus pugnax),* the male of which has collarlike erectile feathers around the neck during the breeding season. [Perh. short for RUFFLE¹.] **—ruffed** *adj.*

ruff² (rŭf) *Games.* —*n.* **1.** The playing of a trump card when one cannot follow suit. **2.** An old game resembling whist. —*tr. & intr.v.* **ruffed, ruff•ing, ruffs.** To trump or play a trump. [Obsolete Fr. *ronfle, roffle*, a kind of card game < OFr. *ronfle* < *renfler*, to rise : *re-*, re- + *enfler*, to cause to swell (< Lat. *inflāre*; see INFLATE).]

ruff³ (rŭf) *n.* A small European freshwater fish *(Acerina cernua)* related to the perches. [ME *ruffe*, prob. < Med.Lat. *rufus*, a kind of fish.]

ruffed grouse (rŭft) *n.* A chickenlike North American game bird *(Bonasa umbellus)* with mottled brownish plumage, the male of which makes drumming sounds with its wings.

ruf•fi•an (rŭf′ē-ən, rŭf′yən) *n.* **1.** A tough or rowdy man. **2.** A thug or gangster. [Fr., pimp < OFr. *rufien* < OProv. *rufian* < OItal. *ruffiano.*] **—ruf′fi•an•ism** *n.* **—ruf′fi•an•ly** *adj.*

ruf•fle¹ (rŭf′əl) *n.* **1.** A strip of frilled or closely pleated fabric used for trimming or decoration. **2.** A ruff on a bird. **3.a.** A ruckus or fray. **b.** Annoyance; vexation. **4.** An irregularity or a slight disturbance of a surface. —*v.* **-fled, -fling, -fles.** —*tr.* **1.** To disturb the smoothness or regularity of; ripple. **2.** To pleat or gather (fabric) into a ruffle. **3.** To erect (the feathers). Used of birds. **4.** To discompose; fluster. **5.** To flip through (the pages of a book). **6.** *Games.* To shuffle (cards). —*intr.* **1.** To become irregular or rough. **2.** To flutter. **3.** To become flustered. [< ME *ruffelen*, to roughen.]

ruf•fle² (rŭf′əl) *Mus.* —*n.* A low continuous beating of a drum that is not as loud as a roll. —*tr.v.* **-fled, -fling, -fles.** To beat a ruffle on (a drum). [Perh. < freq. of *ruff*, a drum roll, perh. of imit. orig.]

ruf•fle³ (rŭf′əl) *intr.v.* **-fled, -fling, -fles.** To behave arrogantly or roughly; swagger. [ME *ruffelen*, to quarrel.] **—ruf′fler** *n.*

ru•fi•yaa (ro͞o′fē-yä′) *n.* See table at **currency.** [Hindi *rupayā, rupiyā* < *rūpyam*, silver coin. See RUPEE.]

ru•fous (ro͞o′fəs) *adj. Color.* Strong yellowish pink to moderate orange; reddish. [< Lat. *rūfus*, red. See **reudh-*.**]

rug (rŭg) *n.* **1.** A heavy fabric used to cover a floor. **2.** An animal skin used as a floor covering. **3.** *Chiefly British.* A piece of thick warm fabric or fur used as a coverlet or lap robe. **4.** *Slang.* A toupee. [Of Scand. orig.]

ru•ga (ro͞o′gə) *n., pl.* **-gae** (-gē′, -gī′). *Biol.* A fold, crease, or wrinkle, as in the lining of the stomach. Often used in the plural. [Lat. *rūga.*] **—ru′gate′** (-gāt′) *adj.*

Rug•by¹ (rŭg′bē). A municipal borough of central England ESE of Birmingham; site of Rugby School where the game of Rugby was developed in the 19th cent. Pop. 59,564.

Rug•by² (rŭg′bē) *n. Sports.* A form of football in which players on two competing teams may kick, dribble, or run with the ball but not make a forward pass. [After *Rugby* School, England.]

Rugby shirt *n.* A knit pullover shirt typically having long sleeves, a front button closure, and bold horizontal stripes.

Rugby shirt

Rü•gen (ro͞o′gən, rü′-). An island of NE Germany in the Baltic Sea, separated from the mainland by a narrow channel.

rug•ged (rŭg′ĭd) *adj.* **1.** Having a rough irregular surface. **2.** Having strong features marked with furrows or wrinkles. **3.** Having a sturdy build or strong constitution. **4.** Tempestuous; stormy. **5.** Demanding great effort, ability, or endurance: *rugged living conditions.* **6.** Lacking culture or polish; coarse and rude: *rugged manners.* [ME, shaggy, of Scand. orig.] **—rug′ged•ly** *adv.* **—rug′ged•ness** *n.*

rug•ger (rŭg′ər) *n. Chiefly British.* Rugby.

ru•gose (ro͞o′gōs′) also **ru•gous** (-gəs) *adj.* **1.** Having many wrinkles or creases; ridged or wrinkled. **2.** *Bot.* Having a rough wrinkled surface. [Lat. *rūgōsus* < *rūga*, wrinkle.] **—ru′gose′ly** *adv.* **—ru•gos′i•ty** (-gŏs′ĭ-tē) *n.*

Ruhr (ro͝or). A region of NW Germany along and N of the **Ruhr River,** which flows c. 233 km (145 mi) W to the Rhine R.

ru•in (ro͞o′ĭn) *n.* **1.** Total destruction or disintegration, either physical, moral, social, or economic. **2.** A cause of total destruction. **3.a.** The act of destroying totally. **b.** A destroyed person, object, or building. **4.** The remains of something destroyed, disintegrated, or decayed. Often used in the plural: *the ruins of ancient Greece.* —*v.* **-ined, -in•ing, -ins.** —*tr.* **1.** To destroy completely; demolish. **2.** To harm irreparably. **3.** To reduce to poverty or bankruptcy. **4.** To deprive of chastity. —*intr.* To fall into ruin. [ME *ruine* < OFr. < Lat. *ruīna* < *ruere*, to rush, collapse.] **—ru′in•a•ble** *adj.* **—ru′in•er** *n.*

Syns: *ruin, raze, demolish, destroy, wreck.* These verbs mean to injure and deprive something — or, less often, someone — of usefulness, soundness, or value. *Ruin* usually implies irretrievable harm but not necessarily total destruction: *"You will ruin no more lives as you ruined mine"* (Arthur Conan Doyle). *Raze, demolish,* and *destroy* can all imply reduction to ruins or even complete obliteration: *Enemy forces razed the city. The prosecutor demolished the opposition's argument. "I saw the best minds of my generation destroyed by madness"* (Allen Ginsberg). To *wreck* is to ruin in or as if in a violent collision: *"The Boers had just wrecked a British military train"* (Arnold Bennett). When *wreck* is used in referring to the ruination of a person or his or her hopes or reputation, it implies irreparable shattering: *"Coleridge, poet and philosopher wrecked in a mist of opium"* (Matthew Arnold).

ru•in•ate (ro͞o′ə-nāt′) *adj.* Having been ruined. [Med.Lat. *ruinātus* < Lat. *ruīna*, ruin. See RUIN.]

ru•in•a•tion (ro͞o′ə-nā′shən) *n.* **1.** The act of ruining or the condition of being ruined. **2.** A cause of ruin.

ru•in•ous (ro͞o′ə-nəs) *adj.* **1.** Causing or apt to cause ruin; destructive. **2.** Falling to ruin; dilapidated or decayed. **—ru′in•ous•ly** *adv.* **—ru′in•ous•ness** *n.*

Ruis•dael or **Ruys•dael** (rīz′däl′, rīs′-, rois′-), **Jacob van.** 1628?–82. Dutch landscape painter whose baroque works include *Windmill at Wijk* (c. 1665).

Ru•key•ser (ro͞o′kī-zər), **Muriel.** 1913–80. Amer. writer whose collections of poetry include *The Gates* (1976).

rule (ro͞ol) *n.* **1.a.** Governing power or its possession or use; authority. **b.** The duration of such power. **2.a.** An authoritative prescribed direction for conduct. **b.** The body of regulations prescribed by the founder of a religious order for governing the conduct of its members. **3.** A usual, customary, or generalized course of action or behavior. **4.** A generalized statement that describes what is true in most or all cases. **5.** *Math.* A standard method or procedure for solving a class of problems. **6.** *Law.* **a.** A court order limited in application to a specific case. **b.** A subordinate regulation governing a particular matter. **7.** See **ruler** 2. **8.** *Print.* A thin metal strip of various widths and designs, used to print borders or lines, as between columns. —*v.* **ruled, rul•ing, rules.** —*tr.* **1.** To exercise control, dominion, or direction over; govern. **2.** To dominate by powerful influence. **3.** To decide or declare authoritatively or judicially; decree. See Syns at **decide. 4.a.** To mark with straight parallel lines. **b.** To mark (a straight line), as with a ruler. —*intr.* **1.** To be in total control or command; exercise supreme authority. **2.** To formulate and issue a decree or decision. **3.** To prevail at a particular level or rate. **—*phrasal verb.* rule out. 1.** To prevent; preclude. **2.** To remove from consideration; exclude. **—*idiom.* as a rule.** In general; for the most part. [ME *reule* < OFr. < VLat. **regula* < Lat. *rēgula*, rod, principle. See **reg-*.**] **—rul′a•ble** *adj.*

ruled surface (ro͞old) *n.* A surface, such as a cone or cylinder, generated by the motion of a straight line.

rule of the road *n., pl.* **rules of the road.** A set of customary practices, as for the operation of a motor vehicle, established to promote efficiency and safety. Often used in the plural.

rule of thumb *n., pl.* **rules of thumb.** A useful principle having wide application but not intended to be strictly accurate.

rul•er (ro͞o′lər) *n.* **1.** One, such as a monarch, that rules or governs. **2.** A straightedged strip, as of wood or metal, for drawing straight lines and measuring lengths.

rul•ing (ro͞o′lĭng) *adj.* **1.** Exercising control or authority. **2.** Predominant: *a ruling principle.* —*n.* **1.** The act of governing or controlling. **2.** An authoritative or official decision.

rum¹ (rŭm) *n.* **1.** An alcoholic liquor distilled from fermented molasses or sugar cane. **2.** Intoxicating beverages. [Prob. short for obsolete *rumbullion.*]

rum² (rŭm) *adj.* **rum•mer, rum•mest.** *Chiefly British.* **1.** Odd; strange. **2.** Presenting danger or difficulty. [?]

ru•ma•ki (rə-mä′kē) *n., pl.* **-kis.** An appetizer of Japanese origin consisting of a piece of chicken liver and a water chestnut wrapped in a slice of bacon and grilled or broiled. [?]

Ru•ma•ni•a (ro͞o-mā′nē-ə, -mān′yə). See **Romania.**

Ru•ma•ni•an (ro͞o-mā′nē-ən, -mān′yən) *adj. & n.* Var. of **Romanian.**

rum•ba also **rhum•ba** (rŭm′bə, ro͝om′-, ro͞om′-) *n.* **1.** A complex rhythmic dance that originated in Cuba. **2.** A modern ballroom adaptation of this dance. [Am.Sp. < Sp. *rumbo,* ship's course, revelry, pomp. See RHUMB.] —**rum′ba** *v.*

rum•ble (rŭm′bəl) *v.* **-bled, -bling, -bles.** —*intr.* **1.** To make a deep long rolling sound. **2.** To move or proceed with a deep long rolling sound. **3.** *Slang.* To engage in a gang fight. —*tr.* **1.** To utter with a deep long rolling sound. **2.** To polish or mix (metal parts) in a tumbling box. —*n.* **1.** A deep long rolling sound. **2.** A tumbling box. **3.** A luggage compartment or servant's seat in the rear of a carriage. **4.** *Slang.* **a.** Pervasive widespread expression of unrest or dissatisfaction. **b.** A gang fight. [ME *romblen,* perh. < MDu. *rommelen* or < Middle Low German *rummeln.*] —**rum′bler** *n.* —**rum′bly** *adj.*

rumble seat *n.* An uncovered passenger seat that opens out from the rear of an automobile.

rum•bus•tious (rŭm-bŭs′chəs) *adj.* Uncontrollably exuberant; unruly. [Prob. alteration of ROBUSTIOUS.] —**rum•bus′tious•ly** *adv.* —**rum•bus′tious•ness** *n.*

ru•men (ro͞o′mən) *n., pl.* **-mi•na** (-mə-nə) or **-mens.** The first division of the stomach of a ruminant animal, from which food is later returned to the mouth as cud. [Lat. *rūmen,* throat.] —**ru′mi•nal** *adj.*

ru•mi•nant (ro͞o′mə-nənt) *n.* Any of various hoofed, even-toed, usu. horned mammals of the suborder Ruminantia, such as cattle and sheep, characteristically having a stomach divided into four compartments and chewing a cud consisting of regurgitated, partially digested food. —*adj.* **1.** Characterized by the chewing of cud. **2.** Of or belonging to the Ruminantia. **3.** Meditative; contemplative. [< Lat. *rūminans, rūminant-,* pr.part. of *rūmināre,* to ruminate. See RUMINATE.]

ru•mi•nate (ro͞o′mə-nāt′) *v.* **-nat•ed, -nat•ing, -nates.** —*intr.* **1.** To turn a matter over and over in the mind. **2.** To chew cud. —*tr.* To reflect on again and again. [Lat. *rūmināre, rūmināt-* < *rūmen, rūmin-,* throat.] —**ru′mi•na′tive** *adj.* —**ru′mi•na′tive•ly** *adv.* —**ru′mi•na′tor** *n.*

ru•mi•na•tion (ro͞o′mə-nā′shən) *n.* **1.** The act of pondering; meditation. **2.** The act or process of chewing cud.

rum•mage (rŭm′ĭj) *v.* **-maged, -mag•ing, -mag•es.** —*tr.* **1.** To search thoroughly by handling, turning over, or disarranging the contents of. **2.** To discover by searching thoroughly. —*intr.* To make a search. —*n.* **1.** A thorough search among a number of things. **2.** A confusion of miscellaneous articles. [< earlier *romage,* act of packing cargo < Fr. *arrumage* < OFr. < *arumer,* to stow < OProv. *arumar* : *a-,* to (< Lat. *ad-*; see AD–) + perh. *run,* ship's hold (of Gmc. orig.; see **reuə-***).] —**rum′mag•er** *n.*

rummage sale *n.* **1.** A sale of assorted secondhand objects contributed by donors to raise money for a charity. **2.** A sale, esp. of unclaimed or excess goods, as at a warehouse.

rum•mer (rŭm′ər) *n.* A large drinking cup or glass. [Ger. *Römer* < Du. *roemer* < *roem,* praise < MDu.]

rum•my¹ (rŭm′ē) *n. Games.* A card game, played in many variations, in which the object is to obtain sets of three or more cards of the same rank or suit. [?]

rum•my² (rŭm′ē) *n., pl.* **-mies.** *Slang.* A drunkard.

rum•my³ (rŭm′ē) *adj.* **-mi•er, -mi•est.** *Chiefly British.* Odd, strange, or dangerous; rum.

ru•mor (ro͞o′mər) *n.* Unverified information of uncertain origin usu. spread by word of mouth; hearsay. —*tr.v.* **-mored, -mor•ing, -mors.** To spread or tell by rumor. [ME *rumour* < OFr. < Lat. *rūmor.*]

ru•mor•mon•ger (ro͞o′mər-mŭng′gər, -mŏng′-) *n.* One that spreads rumors. —*intr.v.* **-gered, -ger•ing, -gers.** To engage in the spreading of rumors.

ru•mour (ro͞o′mər) *n. & v. Chiefly British.* Var. of **rumor.**

rump (rŭmp) *n.* **1.** The fleshy hindquarters of an animal. **2.** A cut of beef or veal from the rump. **3.** The buttocks. **4.** The part of a bird's back nearest the tail. **5.** The last or inferior part. **6.** A legislature having only a small part of its original membership. [ME *rumpe,* of Scand. orig.]

rum•ple (rŭm′pəl) *v.* **-pled, -pling, -ples.** —*tr.* To wrinkle or form into folds or creases. —*intr.* To become wrinkled or creased. —*n.* An irregular or untidy crease. [Perh. Du. *rompelen* < MDu. *rumpelen.*] —**rum′ply** *adj.*

rum•pus (rŭm′pəs) *n.* A noisy clamor. [?]

rumpus room *n.* A room for play and parties.

rum•run•ner (rŭm′rŭn′ər) *n.* **1.** One who illegally transports liquor across a border. **2.** *Naut.* A boat used by rumrunners.

run (rŭn) *v.* **ran** (răn), **run, run•ning, runs.** —*intr.* **1.a.** To move swiftly on foot so that both feet leave the ground during each stride. **b.** To move at a fast gallop. Used of a horse. **2.** To retreat rapidly; flee. **3.a.** To move without hindrance or restraint. **b.** To keep company: *runs with a wild crowd.* **c.** To go or move about from place to place; roam. **4.** To migrate, esp. to move in a shoal in order to spawn. Used of fish. **5.a.** To move or go quickly; hurry. **b.** To go when in trouble or distress. **c.** To make a short, quick trip or visit. **6.a.** To take part in a race or contest. **b.** To compete in a race for elected office. **c.** To finish a race or contest in a specified position: *ran second.* **7.** To move freely, on or as if on wheels. **8.** To be in operation. **9.** To go back and forth esp. on a regular basis; ply. **10.** *Naut.* To sail directly before the wind. **11.a.** To flow, esp. in a steady stream. **b.** To emit pus, mucus, or serous fluid. **12.a.** To be wet or covered with a liquid. **b.** To melt and flow. **13.** To spread or dissolve, as dyes in fabric. **14.** To extend, stretch, or reach in a certain direction or to a particular point. **15.** To extend, spread, or climb as a result of growing. **16.** To spread rapidly: *disease that ran rampant.* **17.a.** To be valid in a given area. **b.** To be present as a valid accompaniment. **18.** To unravel along a line: *Her stocking ran.* **19.** To continue in effect or operation. **20.** To pass: *Days ran into weeks.* **21.** To tend to persist or recur. **22.a.** To accumulate or accrue: *The interest runs from the first of the month.* **b.** To become payable. **23.** To take a particular form, order, or expression: *My reasoning runs thus.* **24.** To tend or incline. **25.** To occupy or exist in a certain range: *The sizes run from small to large.* **26.** To be presented or performed for a continuous period of time. **27.** To pass into a specified condition: *We ran into debt.* —*tr.* **1.a.** To travel over on foot at a pace faster than a walk. **b.** To cause (an animal) to move quickly or rapidly. **2.** To allow to move without restraint. **3.** To do or accomplish by or as if by running: *run errands.* **4.** To hunt or pursue; chase. **5.** To bring to a given condition by or as if by running: *The toddlers ran me ragged.* **6.** To cause to move quickly. **7.a.** To cause to compete in or as if in a race. **b.** To present or nominate for elective office. **8.** To cause to move or progress freely. **9.** To cause to function; operate. **10.** To convey or transport. **11.** *Naut.* To cause to move on a course. **12.a.** To smuggle. **b.** To evade and pass through. **13.** To pass over or through: *run the rapids.* **14.** To cause to flow. **15.** To stream with. **16.** *Metall.* **a.** To melt, fuse, or smelt (metal). **b.** To mold or cast (molten metal). **17.** To cause to extend or pass: *run a rope between poles.* **18.** To mark or trace on a surface. **19.** To sew with a continuous line of stitches. **20.** To cause to unravel along a line. **21.a.** To cause to crash or collide. **b.** To cause to penetrate. **22.** To continue to present or perform. **23.** To publish in a periodical. **24.** To subject oneself or be subjected to. **25.** *Games.* **a.** To score (balls or points) consecutively in billiards. **b.** To clear (the table) in pool by consecutive scores. **26.** To conduct or perform. **27.** *Comp. Sci.* To process or execute (a program or an instruction). **28.** To control, manage, or direct. —*n.* **1.a.** A pace faster than a walk. **b.** A fast gallop. Used of a horse. **2.** An act of running. **3.a.** A distance covered by or as if by running. **b.** The time taken to cover such a distance. **4.** A quick trip or visit. **5.a.** *Sports.* A running race. **b.** A campaign for public office. **6.** *Baseball.* A point scored by advancing around the bases and reaching home plate safely. **7.** *Football.* A player's attempt to carry the ball past or through the opposing team, usu. for a specified distance. **8.a.** The migration of fish, esp. in order to spawn. **b.** A group or school of fish ascending a river in order to spawn. **9.** Unrestricted freedom or use. **10.** A stretch or period of riding, as in a race or to the hounds. **11.a.** A track or slope along or down which something can travel. **b.** *Sports.* A particular type of passage down a hill or across country, as on skis. **12.** *Sports.* The distance a golf ball rolls after hitting the ground. **13.a.** A scheduled or regular route. **b.** The territory of a news reporter. **14.a.** A continuous period of operation, as of a machine. **b.** The production achieved during such a period. **15.** A course of a sailing vessel directly before the wind. **16.a.** A movement or flow. **b.** The duration of such a flow. **c.** The amount of such a flow. **17.** A pipe or channel through which something flows. **18.** *Eastern Lower Northern U.S.* See **creek** 1. **19.** A fall or slide, as of sand or mud. **20.** Continuous length or extent. **21.** *Geol.* A vein or seam, as of ore or rock. **22.** The direction, configuration, or lie. **23.a.** A trail or way made or frequented by animals. **b.** An outdoor enclosure for domestic animals or poultry. **24.a.** A length of torn or unraveled stitches in a knit-

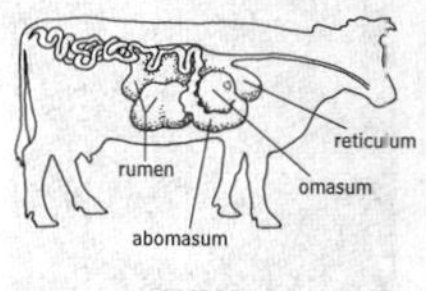

rumen

ă pat	oi boy
ā pay	ou out
âr care	o͝o took
ä father	o͞o boot
ĕ pet	ŭ cut
ē be	ûr urge
ĭ pit	th thin
ī pie	*th* this
îr pier	hw which
ŏ pot	zh vision
ō toe	ə about, item
ô paw	

Stress marks:
′ (primary);
′ (secondary), as in
dictionary (dĭk′shə-nĕr′ē)

ted fabric. **b.** A blemish caused by excessive paint flow. **25.** An unbroken series or sequence. **26.** An unbroken sequence of theatrical performances. **27.** *Mus.* A rapid sequence of notes; a roulade. **28.** A series of unexpected and urgent demands, as by customers. **29.a.** A continuous set or sequence, as of playing cards in one suit. **b.** A successful sequence of shots or points. **30.** A sustained state or condition: *a run of good luck.* **31.** A trend or tendency: *the run of events.* **32.** The average type, group, or category. **33.** *Comp. Sci.* An execution of a specific program or instruction. **34. runs.** *Slang.* Diarrhea. Often used with *the.* — *adj.* Being in a melted or molten state. — ***phrasal verbs.* run across.** To find by chance; come upon. **run after. 1.** To pursue; chase. **2.** To seek the company or attention of for purposes of courting. **run against. 1.** To encounter unexpectedly; run into. **2.** To work against; oppose. **run along.** To go away; leave. **run away. 1.** To flee; escape. **2.** To leave one's home, esp. to elope. **3.** To stampede. **run down. 1.** To stop because of lack of force or power. **2.** To become tired. **3.a.** To collide with and knock down. **b.** *Naut.* To collide with and cause to sink. **4.** To chase and capture. **5.** To trace the source of. **6.** To disparage. **7.** To go over; review. **8.** *Baseball.* To put a runner out after trapping him or her between two bases. **run in. 1.** To insert or include as something extra. **2.** *Print.* To make a solid body of text without a break. **3.** *Slang.* To take into legal custody. **4.** To go to or seek out someone's company in order to socialize; visit. **run into. 1.** To meet or find by chance. **2.** To encounter (something). **3.** To collide with. **4.** To amount to. **run off. 1.** To print, duplicate, or copy. **2.** To run away; elope. **3.** To flow off; drain away. **4.** To decide (a contest or competition) by a runoff. **5.** To force or drive off (trespassers, for example). **run on. 1.** To keep going; continue. **2.** To talk volubly, persistently, and usu. inconsequentially. **3.** To continue a text without a formal break. **run out. 1.** To become used up; be exhausted. **2.** To put out by force; compel to leave. **3.** To become void, as through the passage of time. **run over. 1.** To collide with, knock down, and often pass over. **2.** To read or review quickly. **3.** To flow over. **4.** To go beyond a limit. **run through. 1.** To pierce. **2.** To use up quickly. **3.** To rehearse quickly. **4.** To go over the salient points or facts of. **run up.** To make or become greater or larger. **run with.** To take as one's own; adopt. — ***idioms.* a run for (one's) money.** Strong competition. **in the long run.** In the final analysis or outcome. **in the short run.** In the immediate future. **on the run. 1.a.** In rapid retreat. **b.** In hiding. **2.** Hurrying busily from place to place. **run a temperature.** To have a fever. **run away with. 1.a.** To make off with hurriedly. **b.** To steal. **2.** To be greater or bigger than others in (a performance, for example). **run foul (or afoul) of. 1.** To run into; collide with. **2.** To come into conflict with. **run in place.** To go through the movements of running without leaving one's original position. **run off with.** To capture or carry off. **run (one's) eyes over.** To look at or read in a cursory manner. **run out of.** To exhaust the supply of. **run out of gas.** *Slang.* **1.** To exhaust one's energy or enthusiasm. **2.** To falter or come to a stop because of a lack of capital, support, or enthusiasm. **run out on.** To abandon. **run rings around.** To be markedly superior to. **run scared.** *Informal.* To become intimidated or frightened. **run short.** To become scanty or insufficient in supply. **run short of.** To use up so that a supply becomes insufficient or scanty. **run to earth (or ground).** To pursue and successfully capture. [ME *ernen, runnen* < OE *rinnan, eornan, earnan* and < ON *rinna.* See **rei-*.**]

Regional Note: Terms for "a small, fast-flowing stream" vary, esp. throughout the eastern United States. Speakers in Virginia, West Virginia, Delaware, Maryland, and southern Pennsylvania use the word *run.* In New York State one finds the term *kill* (a Dutch borrowing). *Brook* is used throughout the Northeast. Southerners refer to a *branch,* and throughout the northern United States the term is *crick,* a variant of *creek.*

running board

run•a•bout (rŭn′ə-bout′) *n.* **1.a.** *Naut.* A small motorboat. **b.** A light aircraft. **c.** A small open automobile or carriage. **2.** A vagabond or wanderer.

run•a•gate (rŭn′ə-gāt′) *n.* **1.** A renegade or deserter. **2.** A vagabond. [Alteration of obsolete *renegate,* renegade (influenced by RUN + *agate,* on the way < ME, straight way : ME *a,* on, var. of *on;* see ON + ON *gata,* way; see **ghē-***) < ME < Med.Lat. *renegātus.* See RENEGADE.]

run•a•round (rŭn′ə-round′) *n.* **1.** *Informal.* Deception, usu. in the form of evasive excuses. **2.** *Print.* Type set in a column narrower than the body of the text, as around a picture.

run•a•way (rŭn′ə-wā′) *n.* **1.** A person who has run away. **2.** Something that has escaped control or proper confinement. **3.** *Informal.* An easy victory. — *adj.* **1.** Escaping or having escaped restraint, captivity, or control: *runaway horses.* **2.** Out of control: *runaway inflation.* **3.** Easily won.

run•back (rŭn′băk′) *n.* *Football.* The act of returning a kickoff, a punt, or an intercepted forward pass.

run•ci•ble spoon (rŭn′sə-bəl) *n.* A three-pronged fork, such as a pickle fork, curved like a spoon and having a cutting edge. [Coined by Edward Lear, perh. alteration of *rounceval,* big woman, large pea, wart, monster, huge, from *Roncevaux* (Roncesvalles), site where giant bones were found.]

run•ci•nate (rŭn′sə-nāt′) *adj.* *Bot.* Having saw-toothed divisions directed backward: *runcinate leaves.* [Lat. *runcinātus,* p.part. of *runcināre,* to plane < *runcina,* carpenter's plane, formerly taken to mean saw, alteration (influenced by *runcāre,* to weed, pluck) of Gk. *rhukanē,* carpenter's plane.]

run•down (rŭn′doun′) *n.* **1.** A point-by-point summary. **2.** *Baseball.* A play in which a runner is trapped between bases and is pursued by fielders. — *adj.* also **run-down** (rŭn′-doun′). **1.a.** In poor physical condition; weak or exhausted. **b.** Dirty and dilapidated. **2.** Unwound and not running.

rune[1] (ro͞on) *n.* **1.a.** Any of the characters in several alphabets used by ancient Germanic peoples from the 3rd to the 13th century. **b.** A similar character in another alphabet, sometimes believed to have magic powers. **2.** A poem or an incantation of mysterious significance, esp. a magic charm. [Poss. ON or OE *rūn.*] — **run′ic** *adj.*

rune[2] (ro͞on) *n.* A Finnish poem or section of a poem. [Finn. *runo,* of Gmc. orig.]

rung[1] (rŭng) *n.* **1.** A rod or bar forming a step of a ladder. **2.** A crosspiece between the legs of a chair. **3.** The spoke in a wheel. **4.** *Naut.* One of the spokes or handles on a ship's wheel. [ME < OE *hrung.*]

rung[2] (rŭng) *v.* P.part. of **ring[2].**

run-in (rŭn′ĭn′) *n.* **1.** A quarrel or an argument. **2.** *Print.* Matter added to a text. — *adj.* *Print.* Having been added to or inserted into a text.

run•let (rŭn′lĭt) *n.* A rivulet.

run•nel (rŭn′əl) *n.* **1.** A rivulet; a brook. **2.** A narrow channel or course. [ME *rynel* < OE < *rinnan,* to run. See **rei-*.**]

run•ner (rŭn′ər) *n.* **1.** *Sports.* One who competes in a race. **2.a.** *Baseball.* One who runs the bases. **b.** *Football.* One who carries the ball. **3.** A fugitive. **4.** One who carries messages or runs errands. **5.** One who serves as an agent or a collector, as for a bank. **6.** One who solicits business, as for a hotel. **7.** A smuggler. **8.** *Naut.* A vessel engaged in smuggling. **9.** One who operates or manages something. **10.** A device in or on which something slides or moves, as: **a.** The blade of a skate. **b.** The supports on which a drawer slides. **11.** A long narrow carpet. **12.** A long narrow tablecloth. **13.** A roller towel. **14.** *Metall.* A channel along which molten metal is poured into a mold; a gate. **15.** *Bot.* **a.** A slender creeping stem that puts forth roots from nodes spaced at intervals along its length. **b.** A plant, such as the strawberry, having such a stem. **c.** A twining vine, such as the scarlet runner. **16.** Any of several marine fishes of the family Carangidae, esp. the blue runner *(Caranx crysos),* of temperate waters of the American Atlantic coast. **17.** *Sports.* See **flat[1]** 9.

run•ner-up (rŭn′ər-ŭp′) *n., pl.* **run•ners-up** (rŭn′ərz-). One that takes second place in a competition.

run•ning (rŭn′ĭng) *n.* **1.** The act or an instance of running. **2.** The power or ability to run. **3.** *Sports.* The exercise or sport of someone who runs. — *adj.* Ongoing over a period of time: *a running conversation.* — *adv.* In a consecutive way: *four years running.* — ***idioms.* in the running. 1.** Entered as a contender in a competition. **2.** Having the possibility of winning or placing well in a competition. **out of the running. 1.** Not entered as a contender in a competition. **2.** Having no possibility of winning or placing well in a competition.

running back *n.* *Football.* An offensive back, such as a fullback, who has the responsibility of advancing the ball by running with it on plays from the line of scrimmage.

running board *n.* A narrow footboard extending under and beside the doors of some automobiles and other conveyances.

running gear *n.* The working parts of an automobile, a locomotive, or other vehicle.

running hand *n.* Handwriting done rapidly without lifting the pen from the paper.

running head *n.* *Print.* A title printed at the top of every page or every other page, as in a book.

running knot *n.* See **slipknot.**

running light *n.* One of several lights on a vehicle or vessel turned on between dusk and dawn to indicate position and size.

running mate *n.* **1.** The candidate or nominee for the lesser of two closely associated political offices. **2.** A companion. **3.** A horse used to set the pace in a race for another horse.

running noose *n.* See **noose** 1.

running start *n.* See **flying start.**

running stitch *n.* One of a series of small even stitches.

running title *n.* *Print.* See **running head.**

run•ny (rŭn′ē) *adj.* **-ni•er, -ni•est.** Inclined to run or flow.

Run•ny•mede (rŭn′ē-mēd′). A meadow in SE England on the Thames R. W of London. King John accepted the Magna Carta here or on a nearby island in 1215.

run•off (rŭn′ôf′, -ŏf′) *n.* **1.** An overflow of fluid, as rainfall not absorbed by soil. **2.** Eliminated waste products from manufacturing processes. **3.** An extra competition to break a tie.

run-of-the-mill (rŭn′əv-*thə*-mĭl′) *adj.* Not special or outstanding; average.

run-on (rŭn′ŏn′, -ôn′) *n.* *Print.* Matter that is appended or added without a formal break. — **run′-on′** *adj.*

run-on sentence *n. Gram.* A sentence in which two independent clauses are not properly joined by a semicolon or conjunction.

run•out (rŭn′out′) *n.* **1.** The act or an instance of fleeing so as to evade undesirable consequences. **2.** The area where one curved surface merges with another. **3.** The act or an instance of expiring or having expired.

runt (rŭnt) *n.* **1.** An undersized animal, esp. the smallest animal of a litter. **2.** *Offensive.* A short person. [?] **— runt′i•ness** *n.* **— runt′y** *adj.*

run-through (rŭn′thro͞o′) *n.* A complete but rapid review or rehearsal of something, such as a theatrical work.

run•way (rŭn′wā′) *n.* **1.** A strip of level, usu. paved ground on which aircraft take off and land. **2.** A path, channel, or track over which something runs. **3.** The channel of a stream. **4.** A chute down which logs are skidded. **5.** A smooth ramp for wheeled vehicles. **6.** A narrow walkway extending from a stage into an auditorium.

Run•yon (rŭn′yən), **(Alfred) Damon.** 1884–1946. Amer. writer known for his stories about Broadway and the New York underworld, such as "Guys and Dolls" (1931). **— Run′yon•esque′** (rŭn′yə-nĕsk′) *adj.*

run•za (rĕn′zə) *n. Nebraska.* A pastry consisting of cabbage and usu. pork or beef encased in yeast dough. [?]

ru•pee (ro͞o-pē′, ro͞o′pē) *n.* See table at **currency.** [Hindi *rupayā, rupyā* < Skt. *rūpyam,* silver coin < *rūpya-,* silver < *rūpam,* shape.]

Ru•pert (ro͞o′pərt), Prince. 1619–82. German-born English leader of the Royalists during the English Civil War.

Rupert River. A river of W-central Quebec, Canada, rising in Lake Mistassini and flowing c. 611 km (380 mi) to James Bay.

ru•pi•ah (ro͞o-pē′ə) *n., pl.* **rupiah** or **-ahs.** See table at **currency.** [Hindi *rupayā, rupiyā.* See RUPEE.]

ru•pic•o•lous (ro͞o-pĭk′ə-ləs) *adj.* Thriving among or inhabiting rocks. [Lat. *rūpēs,* rock (< *ruptus,* p.part. of *rumpere,* to break; see **reup-***) + -COLOUS.]

rup•ture (rŭp′chər) *n.* **1.a.** The process of breaking open or bursting. **b.** The state of being broken open. **2.** A break in friendly relations. **3.** *Pathol.* **a.** A hernia, esp. of the groin or intestines. **b.** A tear in body tissue. *— v.* **-tured, -tur•ing, -tures.** *— tr.* To break open; burst. *— intr.* To undergo or suffer a rupture. [ME < OFr. < Lat. *ruptūra* < *ruptus,* p.part. of *rumpere,* to break. See **reup-***.] **— rup′tur•a•ble** *adj.*

ru•ral (ro͝or′əl) *adj.* **1.** Of, relating to, or characteristic of the country. **2.** Of or relating to people who live in the country. **3.** Of or relating to farming; agricultural. [ME < OFr. < Lat. *rūrālis* < *rūs, rūr-,* country. See **reuə-***.] **— ru′ral•ly** *adv.*

rural free delivery *n.* Free government delivery of mail in rural areas.

ru•ral•ism (ro͝or′ə-lĭz′əm) *n.* Rurality.

ru•ral•ist (ro͝or′ə-lĭst) *n.* **1.** One who resides in a rural area. **2.** An advocate of rural life.

ru•ral•i•ty (ro͞o-răl′ĭ-tē) *n., pl.* **-ties. 1.** The state or quality of being rural. **2.** A rural trait or characteristic.

ru•ral•ize (ro͝or′ə-līz′) *tr. & intr.v.* **-ized, -iz•ing, -iz•es.** To make or become rural. **— ru′ral•i•za′tion** (ro͝or′ə-lĭ-zā′shən) *n.*

rural route *n.* A rural mail route.

Ru•rik (ro͝or′ĭk, ro͞o′rĭk). d. c. 879. Scandinavian warrior and founder of the dynasty that ruled Russia until 1598.

Ru•ri•ta•ni•an (ro͝or′ĭ-tā′nē-ən) *adj.* Of, relating to, or having the characteristics of a mythical place of high, typically comic-opera romance. [After *Ruritania,* imaginary realm in the novel *The Prisoner of Zenda* by Anthony Hope.]

Rus. *abbr.* Russia; Russian.

ruse (ro͞os, ro͞oz) *n.* A crafty stratagem; a subterfuge. [ME, detour, dodging < OFr. < *ruser,* to drive back. See RUSH[1].]

Ru•se (ro͞o′sā). A city of NE Bulgaria on the Danube R. S of Bucharest; founded in the 2nd cent. A.D. Pop. 185,000.

rush[1] (rŭsh) *v.* **rushed, rush•ing, rush•es.** *— intr.* **1.** To move or act swiftly; hurry. **2.** To make a sudden or swift attack or charge. **3.** To flow or surge rapidly, often with noise. **4.** *Football.* To move the ball by running. *— tr.* **1.** To cause to move or act with unusual haste or violence. **2.** To perform with great haste. **3.** To attack swiftly and suddenly. **4.** To transport or carry hastily. **5.** To entertain or pay great attention to: *They rushed him for their fraternity.* **6.** *Football.* To charge (a quarterback or passer) in order to block or prevent a play. *— n.* **1.** A sudden forward motion. **2.a.** Surging emotion. **b.** An anxious and eager movement to get to or from a place. **c.** A sudden, very insistent, generalized demand. **3.** General haste or busyness. **4.** A sudden attack; an onslaught. **5.** A rapid, often noisy flow or passage. **6.** *Football.* **a.** An attempt to move the ball by running. **b.** An act of charging the offensive quarterback or passer in order to block or prevent a play. **7. rushes.** The dailies. **8.a.** A time of attention, usu. one in which extensive social activity occurs. **b.** A drive by a Greek society on a college campus to recruit new members. **9.a.** The intensely pleasurable sensation experienced immediately after use of a stimulant or a mind-altering drug. **b.** A sudden brief exhilaration. [ME *rushen* < AN *russher,* var. of OFr. *ruser,* to drive back < Lat. *recūsāre,* to reject : *re-,* re- + *causārī,* to give as a reason (< *causa,* cause).] **— rush′er** *n.*

rush[2] (rŭsh) *n.* **1.a.** Any of various stiff marsh plants of the genus *Juncus,* having pliant hollow or pithy stems and small flowers with scalelike perianths. **b.** Any of various similar, usu. aquatic plants. **2.** The stem of one of these plants, used in making baskets, mats, and chair seats. [ME < OE *rysc.*]

Rush (rŭsh), **Benjamin.** 1745–1813. Amer. physician and educator who signed the Declaration of Independence.

rush candle *n.* See **rushlight.**

rush hour *n.* A period of heavy traffic. **— rush′-hour′** (rŭsh′-our′) *adj.*

rush•light (rŭsh′līt′) *n.* A candle consisting of a rush wick in tallow.

Rush•more (rŭsh′môr′, -mōr′), **Mount.** A mountain, 1,708 m (5,600 ft), in the Black Hills of W SD; site of a monument with massive likenesses of Washington, Jefferson, Lincoln, and Theodore Roosevelt.

rush•y (rŭsh′ē) *adj.* **-i•er, -i•est. 1.** Resembling or characteristic of rushes; rushlike. **2.** Abounding in rushes.

rusk (rŭsk) *n.* **1.** A light, soft-textured sweetened biscuit. **2.** Sweet raised bread dried and browned in an oven. [Sp. or Port. *rosca,* coil, rusk, perh. < VLat. **rotisca,* dim. of Lat. *rota,* wheel. See ROTATE.]

Rus•ka (rŭs′kə, ro͞os′kä), **Ernst.** 1906–88. German physicist who shared a 1986 Nobel Prize.

Rus•kin (rŭs′kĭn), **John.** 1819–1900. British critic who wrote *Modern Painters* (1843–60). **— Rus′kin′i•an** *adj.*

Russ. *abbr.* Russia; Russian.

Rus•sell (rŭs′əl), **Bertrand Arthur William.** 3rd Earl Russell. 1872–1970. British philosopher, mathematician, and social critic who won the 1950 Nobel Prize for literature.

Russell, Charles Taze. 1852–1916. Amer. religious leader who founded (1884) the sect now called Jehovah's Witnesses.

Russell, George William. "A.E." 1867–1935. Irish writer and nationalist who was a leader of the Irish literary renaissance at the turn of the 20th cent.

Russell, Henry Norris. 1877–1957. Amer. astronomer who developed a theory of stellar evolution.

Russell, John. 1st Earl Russell. 1792–1878. British politician who served as prime minister (1846–52 and 1865–66).

Russell, Lillian. 1861–1922. Amer. entertainer known for her roles in comic operas.

Russell, Mount. A peak, 4,296.8 m (14,088 ft), of the Sierra Nevada in E CA.

rus•set (rŭs′ĭt) *n.* **1.** *Color.* A moderate to strong brown. **2.** A coarse reddish-brown to brown homespun cloth. **3.** A winter apple with a rough reddish-brown skin. *— adj. Color.* Moderate to strong brown. [ME < OFr. *rousset* < *rous,* red < Lat. *russus.* See **reudh-***.]

Rus•sia (rŭsh′ə). **1.** A former empire of E Europe and N Asia. Orig. settled by Slavs, the region was a conglomerate of independent principalities until Moscow gained ascendancy in the 14th, 15th, and 16th cent. and lasted until the Revolution of 1917 and the formation of the U.S.S.R. in 1922. **2.** A republic of E Europe and N Asia bordering in the W on Finland, the Baltic States, Belorussia, and Ukraine and stretching E to the Pacific. The **Russian Soviet Federated Socialist Republic,** coextensive with the region, was declared in 1917. Russia reemerged as an independent republic after the disintegration of the U.S.S.R. in 1991. Cap. Moscow. Pop. 143,093,000. **3.** The Union of Soviet Socialist Republics.

Rus•sian (rŭsh′ən) *adj.* **1.** Of or relating to Russia or its people, language, or culture. **2.** Of or relating to the former Soviet Union. *— n.* **1.a.** A native or inhabitant of Russia. **b.** A person of Russian descent. **c.** A native or inhabitant of the former Soviet Union. Often used in the plural. **2.** The Slavic language of the Russians and the official language of Russia. [Med.Lat. *Russiānus* < ORuss. *Rusĭ* < ON **rōdhsmenn,* seafarers < *rōdhr,* rowing. See **erə-***.]

Russian dressing *n.* Salad dressing, such as mayonnaise, with chili sauce or ketchup, chopped pickles, and pimientos.

Rus•sian•ize (rŭsh′ə-nīz′) *tr.v.* **-ized, -iz•ing, -iz•es.** To make Russian. **— Rus′sian•i•za′tion** (-ə-nĭ-zā′shən) *n.*

Russian olive *n.* See **oleaster.**

Russian Orthodox Church *n.* The Eastern Orthodox Church in Russia with branches outside Russia.

Russian roulette *n.* **1.** A procedure in which one spins the cylinder of a revolver loaded with only one bullet, aims the muzzle at one's head, and pulls the trigger. **2.** An act of reckless bravado.

Russian thistle *n.* A red-stemmed prickly Eurasian plant *(Salsola kali* var. *tenuifolia)* that is a troublesome weed in western North America.

Russian wolfhound *n.* See **borzoi.**

Russo– *pref.* Russia; Russian: *Russophobe.* [< RUSSIA.]

Rus•so•phile (rŭs′ə-fīl′) *n.* An admirer of Russia or its people, language, or culture. **— Rus′so•phil′i•a** (-fĭl′ē-ə) *n.*

Rus•so•phobe (rŭs′ə-fōb′) *n.* One who fears or dislikes Russia or its people or culture. **— Rus′so•pho′bi•a** *n.*

rust (rŭst) *n.* **1.** Any of various powdery or scaly reddish-brown or reddish-yellow hydrated ferric oxides formed on iron and iron-containing materials by low-temperature oxidation in the

runway
Logan Airport, Boston, Massachusetts

Mount Rushmore
Left to right: Portraits of Presidents Washington, Jefferson, Theodore Roosevelt, and Lincoln by Gutzon Borglum

ă **pat**	oi **boy**
ā **pay**	ou **out**
âr **care**	o͝o **took**
ä **father**	o͞o **boot**
ĕ **pet**	ŭ **cut**
ē **be**	ûr **urge**
ĭ **pit**	th **thin**
ī **pie**	*th* **this**
îr **pier**	hw **which**
ŏ **pot**	zh **vision**
ō **toe**	ə **about,**
ô **paw**	**item**

Stress marks:
′ (primary);
′ (secondary), as in **dictionary** (dĭk′shə-nĕr′ē)

presence of water. **2.** Any of various metallic coatings, esp. oxides, formed by corrosion. **3.** A stain or coating resembling iron rust. **4.** Deterioration, as of ability, resulting from inactivity or neglect. **5.** *Bot.* **a.** Rust fungus. **b.** A plant disease caused by a rust fungus, characterized by reddish or brownish spots on leaves, stems, and other parts. **6.** *Color.* A strong brown. —*v.* **rust•ed, rust•ing, rusts.** —*intr.* **1.** To become corroded. **2.** To deteriorate or degenerate through inactivity or neglect. **3.** To become the color of rust. **4.** *Bot.* To develop a disease caused by a rust fungus. —*tr.* **1.** To corrode or subject (a metal) to rust formation. **2.** To impair or spoil, as by misuse. **3.** To color (something) rust. [ME < OE *rūst.* See **reudh-*.**] —**rust** *adj.* —**rust′a•ble** *adj.*

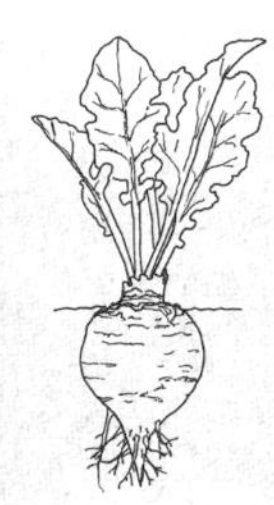

rutabaga
Brassica napus var. *napobrassica*

Rus•ta•vi (ro͞o-stä′vē, -vyĭ). A city of S Georgia SE of Tbilisi. Pop. 143,000.

rust belt or **rust•belt** also **Rust Belt** (rŭst′bĕlt′) *n.* A heavily industrialized area containing older factories, esp. those that are marginally profitable or that have been closed. —**rust′-belt′** *adj.*

rust fungus *n.* Any of various fungi of the order Uredinales that are injurious to a wide variety of plants.

rus•tic (rŭs′tĭk) *adj.* **1.** Of, relating to, or typical of country life or country people. **2.** Marked by a lack of sophistication or elegance. **3.** Appropriate for use in the country. **4.** Made of rough tree branches or roots. —*n.* **1.** A rural person. **2.** A person regarded as crude, coarse, or simple. [ME *rustik* < OFr. *rustique* < Lat. *rūsticus* < *rūs,* country. See **reuə-*.**] —**rus′ti•cal•ly** *adv.*

rus•ti•cate (rŭs′tĭ-kāt′) *v.* **-cat•ed, -cat•ing, -cates.** —*intr.* To go to or live in the country. —*tr.* **1.** To send to the country. **2.** *Chiefly British.* To suspend (a student) from a university. **3.** To construct (masonry) with conspicuous, often beveled points. [Lat. *rūsticārī, rūsticāt-* < *rūsticus,* rustic. See RUSTIC.] —**rus′ti•ca′tion** *n.* —**rus′ti•ca′tor** *n.*

rus•tic•i•ty (rŭ-stĭs′ĭ-tē) *n., pl.* **-ties. 1.** The condition of being rustic. **2.** A rustic trait or mannerism.

rus•tle (rŭs′əl) *v.* **-tled, -tling, -tles.** —*intr.* **1.** To move with soft fluttering or crackling sounds. **2.** To move or act energetically or with speed. **3.** To forage food. **4.** To rustle livestock. —*tr.* **1.** To cause to rustle. **2.** To obtain by rustling: *rustled up food.* **3.** To steal (livestock, esp. cattle). [ME *rustlen,* perh. of imit. orig.] —**rus′tler** *n.* —**rus′tling•ly** *adv.*

rust mite *n.* Any of various mites that cause a plant disease characterized by reddish or brownish spots on leaves and fruits.

Babe Ruth
Photographed in the 1930's

Rus•ton (rŭs′tən). A city of N LA W of Monroe; settled in 1884 as a railroad town. Pop. 20,027.

rust•proof (rŭst′pro͞of′) *adj.* Incapable of rusting. —**rust′-proof′** *v.*

rust•y (rŭs′tē) *adj.* **-i•er, -i•est. 1.** Covered with rust; corroded. **2.** Consisting of or produced by rust. **3.** *Color.* Of a yellowish-red or brownish-red color. **4.** Working or operating stiffly or incorrectly because of or as if because of rust. **5.** Weakened or impaired by neglect, disuse, or lack of practice. —**rust′i•ly** *adv.* —**rust′i•ness** *n.*

rut[1] (rŭt) *n.* **1.** A sunken track or groove made by the passage of vehicles. **2.** A fixed, usu. boring routine. —*tr.v.* **rut•ted, rut•ting, ruts.** To furrow. [Poss. alteration of ROUTE.]

rut[2] (rŭt) *n.* **1.** An annually recurring condition or period of sexual excitement and reproductive activity in male deer. **2.** A condition or period of mammalian sexual activity, such as estrus. —*intr.v.* **rut•ted, rut•ting, ruts.** To be in rut. [ME *rutte* < OFr. *rut* < VLat. **rūgitus* < **rūgere,* to roar < Lat. *rūgīre,* to roar.]

ru•ta•ba•ga (ro͞o′tə-bā′gə, ro͝ot′ə-, ro͞o′tə-bā′gə, ro͝ot′ə-) *n.* **1.** A European plant *(Brassica napus* var. *napobrassica)* having a thick edible bulbous root. **2.** The root of this plant. [Swed. dial. *rotabagge* : *rot,* root (< ON *rōt*; see **wrād-***) + *bagge,* bag (< ON *baggi*).]

ruth (ro͞oth) *n.* **1.** Compassion or pity for another. **2.** Sorrow or misery about one's own misdeeds or flaws. [ME *ruthe* < ON *hrygdh* (influenced by OE *hrēow,* sorrow, regret).]

Ruth (ro͞oth) *n. Bible.* **1.** A Moabite widow who converted to Judaism and moved with Naomi to Bethlehem, where she later married Boaz. **2.** See table at **Bible.**

Ruth, George Herman ("Babe"). 1895–1948. Amer. baseball player who hit 714 career home runs (1915–35) and held 54 major-league records.

Ru•the•nia (ro͞o-thēn′yə, -thē′nē-ə). A region of W Ukraine S of the Carpathian Mts.

Ru•the•ni•an (ro͞o-thē′nē-ən, -thēn′yən) *adj.* Of or relating to Ruthenia, the Ruthenians, or their language or culture. —*n.* **1.** A native or inhabitant of Ruthenia. **2.** The variety of Ukrainian used by the Ruthenians.

Rwanda

ru•then•ic (ro͞o-thĕn′ĭk, -thē′nĭk) *adj.* Relating to or containing ruthenium with a high valence.

ru•the•ni•ous (ro͞o-thē′nē-əs) *adj.* Relating to or containing ruthenium with a low valence.

ru•the•ni•um (ro͞o-thē′nē-əm) *n. Symbol* **Ru** A hard acid-resistant metallic element that is found in platinum ores and is used in nonmagnetic wear-resistant instrument pivots and electrical contacts. Atomic number 44; atomic weight 101.07; melting point 2,310°C; boiling point 3,900°C; specific gravity 12.41; valence 0, 1, 2, 3, 4, 5, 6, 7, 8. See table at **element.** [< Med.Lat. *Ruthenia,* Russia < *Rutheni,* Russians < Russ. *Rusin* < ORuss. *Rusĭ,* Russian. See RUSSIAN.]

ruth•er•ford (rŭth′ər-fərd) *n.* A unit expressing the rate of decay of radioactive material, equal to one million disintegrations per second. [After Ernest RUTHERFORD.]

Ruth•er•ford (rŭth′ər-fərd, rŭth′-). A borough of NE NJ, a suburb of New York City. Pop. 17,790.

Rutherford, Daniel. 1749–1819. British chemist and physician who is credited with the discovery of nitrogen.

Rutherford, Ernest. 1st Baron Rutherford of Nelson. 1871–1937. New Zealand-born physicist who discovered the atomic nucleus and won the 1908 Nobel Prize in chemistry.

ruth•er•ford•i•um (rŭth′ər-fôr′dē-əm, -fōr′-) *n.* Element 104. [After Ernest RUTHERFORD.]

ruth•ful (ro͞oth′fəl) *adj.* **1.** Full of sorrow; rueful. **2.** Causing sorrow or pity. —**ruth′ful•ly** *adv.* —**ruth′ful•ness** *n.*

ruth•less (ro͞oth′lĭs) *adj.* Having no compassion or pity; merciless. —**ruth′less•ly** *adv.* —**ruth′less•ness** *n.*

ru•ti•lant (ro͞ot′l-ənt) *adj.* Bright red. [ME *rutilaunt* < Lat. *rutilāns, rutilant-,* pr.part. of *rutilāre,* to make red, to be reddish < *rutilus,* red, reddish. See **reudh-*.**]

ru•tile (ro͞o′tēl′, -tīl′) *n.* A lustrous red, reddish-brown, or black mineral, TiO_2, used as a gemstone and an ore and in paints and fillers. [Fr. < Ger. *Rutil* < Lat. *rutilus,* red. See RUTILANT.]

Rut•land (rŭt′lənd). A city of central VT SSW of Montpelier. Pop. 18,230.

Rut•ledge (rŭt′lĭj), **John.** 1739–1800. Amer. jurist; associate justice (1789–91) and chief justice (1795) of the U.S. Supreme Court.

Rutledge, Wiley Blount, Jr. 1894–1949. Amer. jurist; associate justice of the U.S. Supreme Court (1943–49).

rut•tish (rŭt′ĭsh) *adj.* Lustful; libidinous. —**rut′tish•ly** *adv.* —**rut′tish•ness** *n.*

rut•ty (rŭt′ē) *adj.* **-ti•er, -ti•est.** Full of ruts. —**rut′ti•ness** *n.*

Ru•wen•zo•ri (ro͞o′wən-zôr′ē, -zōr′ē). A mountain range of E-central Africa on the Uganda-Zaire border; explored in 1889 by Henry M. Stanley.

Ruys•dael (rīz′däl′, rīs′-, rois′-), **Jacob van.** See Jacob van **Ruisdael.**

RV *abbr.* **1.** Recreational vehicle. **2.** Or **R.V.** *Bible.* Revised Version.

Rv. *abbr. Bible.* Revelations.

R-val•ue (är′văl′yo͞o) *n.* A measure of the capacity of a material, such as insulation, to impede heat flow, with increasing values indicating a greater capacity. [*r(esistance) value.*]

R.W. *abbr.* **1.** Right Worshipful. **2.** Right Worthy.

Rwan•da (ro͞o-än′də). Formerly **Ru•an•da** (ro͞o-än′də). A country of E-central Africa; part of the colonial territory of Ruanda-Urundi administered by Germany and Belgium until it achieved independence in 1962. Cap. Kigali. Pop. 5,109,000. —**Rwan′dan** *adj. & n.*

rwy. *abbr.* Railway.

Rx (är′ĕks′) *n.* **1.** A prescription for medicine or a medical appliance. **2.** A remedy, cure, or solution for a disorder or problem. [Alteration of ℞, symbol used in prescriptions, abbreviation of Lat. *recipe,* imper. of *recipere,* to take. See RECEIVE.]

ry. *abbr.* Railway.

-ry *suff.* Var. of **-ery.**

ry•a (rē′ə) *n.* **1.** A handwoven Scandinavian rug with a thick pile and usu. colorful abstract designs. **2.** The weaving pattern characteristic of such rugs. [After *Rya* in SW Sweden.]

Rya•zan (ryĭ-zän′). A city of W-central Russia on the Oka R. SE of Moscow; founded 1095 and annexed by Moscow in 1521. Pop. 494,000.

Ryb•nik (rĭb′nĭk). A town of S Poland WSW of Katowice; chartered in the 14th cent. Pop. 135,500.

Ry•der (rī′dər), **Albert Pinkham.** 1847–1917. Amer. painter whose works include *Toilers of the Sea* (c. 1884).

rye[1] (rī) *n.* **1.** A cereal grass *(Secale cereale)* widely cultivated for its grain. **2.** The grain of this plant, used in making flour and whiskey and for livestock feed. **3.** Whiskey made from the grains of this plant. [ME < OE *ryge.*]

rye[2] (rī) *n.* A Gypsy man. [Romany *rai* < Skt. *rājā,* king. See RAJAH.]

rye bread *n.* Bread made partially or entirely from rye flour.

rye grass or **rye•grass** (rī′grăs′) *n.* See **darnel.** [Alteration of *raygrass* : *ray,* darnel (< ME *rai,* perh. alteration of OFr. *ivraie* < Lat. *ēbriaca* < fem. of *ēbriācus,* drunk (< the plant's effects if ingested) < *ēbrius*; see INEBRIATE) + GRASS.]

Ryle (rīl), Sir **Martin.** 1918–84. British astronomer who shared a 1974 Nobel Prize.

Rys•wick (rĭz′wĭk). See **Rijswijk.**

Ryu•kyu Islands (rē-o͞o′kyo͞o′, ryo͞o′-kyo͞o). An island group of SW Japan extending c. 1,046 km (650 mi) between Kyushu and Taiwan; incorporated into Japan in 1879.

Rze•szów (zhĕ′sho͝of′). A city of SE Poland E of Cracow; chartered in the 14th cent. Pop. 138,000.

S s

s[1] or **S** (ĕs) *n., pl.* **s's** or **S's. 1.** The 19th letter of the modern English alphabet. **2.** Any of the speech sounds represented by the letter *s.* **3.** The 19th in a series. **4.** Something shaped like the letter S.

s[2] *abbr.* **1.** Second (unit of time). **2.** *Math.* Second (of arc). **3.** Stere. **4.** *Phys.* Strange quark.

S[1] 1. The symbol for the element **sulfur. 2.** The symbol for **entropy** 1.

S[2] *abbr.* **1.** *Bible.* Samuel. **2.** Or **s** Siemens. **3.** Also **S.** or **s** or **s.** South; southern.

s. *abbr.* **1.** Or **S.** School. **2.** Or **S.** Sea. **3.** See. **4.** Shilling. **5.** *Gram.* Singular. **6.** Sire. **7.** Sister. **8.** Small. **9.** Or **S.** Society. **10.** *Mus.* Solo. **11.** Son. **12.** Or **S.** *Mus.* Soprano. **13.** Stock. **14.** *Gram.* Substantive.

S. *abbr.* **1.** Sabbath. **2.** Saint. **3.** Saturday. **4.** Saxon. **5.** *Medic.* Signature. **6.** Signor; signore. **7.** *Gram.* Singular. **8.** Sunday.

–s[1] or **–es** *suff.* Used to form plural nouns: *letters.* [ME *-es, -s* < OE *-es, -as,* nominative and accusative pl. suff.]

–s[2] or **–es** *suff.* Used to form the third person singular present tense of all regular and most irregular verbs: *looks; holds.* [ME *-es, -s* < OE *-es, -as.*]

–s[3] *suff.* Used to form adverbs: *They were caught unawares. He works nights.* [ME *-es, -s,* genitive sing. suff. < OE *-es.*]

–'s *suff.* Used to form the possessive case of singular nouns, plural nouns that do not end in *s,* certain pronouns, and phrases that function as nouns or pronouns: *nation's; women's; another's; the girl next door's cat.* [ME *-s, -es* < OE *-es,* genitive sing. suff.]

's. 1. Is: *She's here.* **2.** Has: *He's arrived.* **3.** Does: *What's he want?* **4.** Us: *Let's go.*

SA *abbr.* Salvation Army.

s.a. *abbr. Lat.* Sine anno (without date).

S.A. *abbr.* **1.** South Africa. **2.** South America.

Saa•le (zä′lə, sä′-). A river rising in central Germany and flowing c. 426 km (265 mi) N to the Elbe R.

Saar[1] (sär, zär). A river rising in NE France and flowing c. 241 km (150 mi) NNW through the **Saar Basin** to the Moselle R. in W Germany.

Saar•brück•en (zär-brŏŏk′ən, sär-, zär-brük′-). A city of SW Germany on the Saar R. S of Bonn. Pop. 188,763.

Saa•re•maa also **Sa•re•ma** (sär′ə-mä′). An island of W Estonia in the Baltic Sea at the mouth of the Gulf of Riga.

Saa•ri•nen (sär′ə-nən, -nĕn′), **Eero.** 1910–61. Finnish-born Amer. architect whose designs include the Trans World Airlines terminal in New York City (1962).

Saar•land (sär′lănd′, zär′-, -länt′) or **Saar** (sär, zär). A region of SW Germany in the Saar R. valley. **—Saar′land′er** *n.*

Saa•ve•dra La•mas (sä-vā′drə lä′mäs, sä′ä-vĕ′thrä), **Carlos.** 1878?–1959. Argentinean diplomat who won the 1936 Nobel Peace Prize.

Sab. *abbr.* Sabbath.

Sa•ba (sā′bə, -bä). An island of the N Netherlands Antilles in the West Indies between St. Martin and St. Eustatius.

sab•a•dil•la (săb′ə-dĭl′ə, -dē′ə) *n.* **1.** A Mexican and Central American plant *(Schoenocaulon officinale)* of the lily family, having densely flowered spikelike racemes and brown seeds that are rich in veratrine. **2.** The seeds of this plant used in insecticides. [Sp. *cebadilla,* dim. of *cebada,* barley < Lat. *cibātus* < p.part. of *cibāre,* to feed < *cibus,* food.]

Sa•bah (sä′bä′). A region of Malaysia in NE Borneo; a British protectorate from the early 1800's until 1963.

sa•bal (sā′băl) *n.* See **palmetto** 1. [NLat., genus name.]

Sa•ba•tier (sä-bä-tyā′), **Paul.** 1854–1941. French chemist who shared a 1912 Nobel Prize.

sa•ba•yon (sä′bä-yôɴ′) *n.* See **zabaglione.** [Fr. < Ital. *zabaglione, zabaione.*]

sab•bat (săb′ət) *n.* Witches' Sabbath. [Fr., Sabbath, sabbat < OFr., Sabbath. See SABBATH.]

Sab•ba•tar•i•an (săb′ə-târ′ē-ən) *n.* **1.** One who observes Saturday as the Sabbath, as in Judaism. **2.** One who believes in strict observance of Sunday as the Sabbath. [< LLat. *sabbatārius* < Lat. *sabbatum,* Sabbath. See SABBATH.] **—Sab′ba•tar′i•an** *adj.* **—Sab′ba•tar′i•an•ism** *n.*

Sab•bath (săb′əth) *n.* **1.** The seventh day of the week, Saturday, observed as the day of rest and worship by Jews and some Christian groups. **2.** The first day of the week, Sunday, observed as the day of rest and worship by most Christians. [ME *sabath* < OFr. *sabbat* and OE *sabat,* both < Lat. *sabbatum* < Gk. *sabbaton* < Heb. *šabbāt* < *šābat,* to rest.]

sab•bat•i•cal (sə-băt′ĭ-kəl) also **sab•bat•ic** (-ĭk) *—adj.* **1.** Relating to a sabbatical year. **2. Sabbatical.** Relating or appropriate to the Sabbath as the day of rest. *—n.* A sabbatical year. [< LLat. *sabbaticus* < Gk. *sabbatikos* < *sabbaton,* Sabbath. See SABBATH.]

sabbatical year *n.* **1.** A leave of absence, often with pay, usu. granted every seventh year, as to a college professor, for travel, research, or rest. **2.** Often **Sabbatical year.** *Judaism.* A year during which the land of ancient Israel is left fallow, observed every seven years.

Sa•bel•li•an (sə-bĕl′ē-ən) *n.* **1.** A group of extinct Italic languages that includes Sabine. **2.** A speaker of one of these languages. [< Lat. *Sabellus,* Sabine.] **—Sa•bel′li•an** *adj.*

sa•ber (sā′bər) *n.* **1.** A heavy cavalry sword with a one-edged, slightly curved blade. **2.** A light sword having an arched guard for the hand and a tapered flexible blade with a one-sided cutting edge. *—tr.v.* **-bered, -ber•ing, -bers.** To hit, injure, or kill with a saber. [Fr. *sabre* < obsolete Ger. *sabel* < MHGer. < Hung. *száblya* < *szabni,* to cut.]

saber rattling *n.* A display of or threat to use military power.

sa•ber-toothed tiger (sā′bər-to͞otht′) *n.* Any of various extinct cats, esp. one of the larger members of the genus *Smilodon,* characterized by long upper canine teeth.

saber-toothed tiger

sa•bin (sā′bĭn) *n.* A unit of sound absorption equal to the absorption by one square foot of a surface that absorbs all incident sound. [After Wallace Clement Ware *Sabine* (1868–1919), Amer. physicist.]

Sa•bin (sā′bĭn), **Albert Bruce.** 1906–93. Amer. microbiologist who developed a live-virus vaccine against polio (1957).

Sa•bine (sā′bīn′) *n.* **1.** A member of an ancient people of central Italy, conquered and assimilated by the Romans in 290 B.C. **2.** The Italic language of the Sabines. [ME *Sabyn* < Lat. *Sabīnus.*] **—Sa′bine′** *adj.*

Sa•bine River (sə-bēn′). A river of E TX flowing c. 925 km (575 mi) and through **Sabine Lake** to the Gulf of Mexico.

Sab•ine's gull (săb′īnz, -īnz, sā′bīnz) *n.* A gull *(Xema sabini)* of Arctic regions having a forked tail. [After Sir Edward *Sabine* (1788–1883), British astronomer and explorer.]

Sabin vaccine *n.* A vaccine consisting of live attenuated polioviruses. [After Albert Bruce SABIN.]

sa•ble (sā′bəl) *n.* **1.a.** A carnivorous mammal *(Martes zibellina)* of northern Europe and Asia having soft dark fur. **b.** The pelt or fur of this animal. **c.** The similar fur of other species of martens. **2.a.** The color black, esp. in heraldry. **b. sables.** Black garments worn in mourning. **3.** *Color.* A grayish yellowish brown. **4.** A sablefish. *—adj.* **1.** *Color.* Of a grayish yellowish brown. **2.** Of the color black, as in heraldry or mourning. **3.** Dark; somber. **4.** Of the fur of the sable. [ME < OFr. < MLGer. *sabel* < ORuss. *sobol',* ult. < Pers. *samōr.*]

Sa•ble (sā′bəl), **Cape. 1.** A promontory of extreme S Nova Scotia, Canada, on an inlet S of **Sable Island. 2.** A cape at the SW tip of FL; the S extremity of the U.S. mainland.

sable antelope *n.* A large African antelope *(Hippotragus niger)* having backward-curving horns and a usu. dark coat.

sa•ble•fish (sā′bəl-fĭsh′) *n., pl.* **sablefish** or **-fish•es.** A dark-colored marine food fish *(Anoplopoma fimbria)* of North American Pacific waters.

sa•bot (să-bō′, săb′ō) *n.* **1.** A wooden shoe worn in some European countries. **2.** (săb′ət). A sandal or shoe having a band of leather or other material across the instep. **3.** A carrier in which a small projectile is centered so as to permit firing the projectile within a larger caliber weapon. [Fr. < OFr. *çabot,* alteration of *savate,* old shoe, prob. of Turk. or Ar. orig.]

sabot
A pair of sabots

sab•o•tage (săb′ə-täzh′) *n.* **1.** Destruction of property or obstruction of normal operations, as by enemy agents in war. **2.** Treacherous action to defeat or hinder a cause or an endeavor; deliberate subversion. *—tr.v.* **-taged, -tag•ing, -tag•es.** To commit sabotage against. [Fr. < *saboter,* to walk noisily, bungle, sabotage < *sabot,* sabot. See SABOT.]

sab•o•teur (săb′ə-tûr′) *n.* One that commits sabotage. [Fr. < *saboter,* to sabotage. See SABOTAGE.]

sa•bra (sä′brə) *n.* A native-born Israeli. [NHeb. *ṣābār,* sabra, prickly pear.]

sa•bre (sā′bər) *n. & v. Chiefly British.* Var. of **saber.**

sac (săk) *n.* A pouch or pouchlike structure in a plant or an animal, sometimes filled with fluid. [Fr., bag < OFr. < Lat. *saccus.* See SACK[1].]

Sac (săk, sôk) *n.* Var. of **Sauk.**

SAC *abbr.* Strategic Air Command.

Sac•a•ja•we•a (săk′ə-jə-wē′ə). 1787?–1812. Shoshone guide and interpreter who accompanied (1805–06) the Lewis and Clark expedition.

sac•a•ton (săk′ə-tōn′) *n.* A tufted perennial grass *(Sporobolus wrightii)* of the southwest United States, used for pasture and hay. [Am.Sp. *zacatón* < *zacate,* coarse grass < Nahuatl *zacatl,* grass, straw.]

sac•cade (să-käd′, sə-) *n.* A rapid intermittent eye movement, as that which occurs when the eyes fix on one point after

ă **pat**	oi **boy**
ā **pay**	ou **out**
âr **care**	ŏŏ **took**
ä **father**	o͞o **boot**
ĕ **pet**	ŭ **cut**
ē **be**	ûr **urge**
ĭ **pit**	th **thin**
ī **pie**	*th* **this**
îr **pier**	hw **which**
ŏ **pot**	zh **vision**
ō **toe**	ə **about,**
ô **paw**	**item**

Stress marks:
′ (primary);
′ (secondary), as in
dictionary (dĭk′shə-nĕr′ē)

another in the visual field. [Fr., twitch < OFr. < ONFr. *saquier*, to pull < *sac*, sack. See SAC.] —**sac·cad′ic** *adj.*

sac·cate (săk′āt′) *adj.* **1.** Shaped like a pouch or sac. **2.** Having a pouch or sac. [Lat. *saccus*, bag; see SACK[1] + -ATE[1].]

sac·cha·rase (săk′ə-rās′, -rāz′) *n.* See **invertase.**

sac·cha·rate (săk′ə-rāt′) *n.* A salt or an ester of saccharic acid. [SACCHAR(IC ACID) + -ATE[2].]

sac·char·ic acid (sə-kăr′ĭk) *n.* A white crystalline acid, $COOH(CHOH)_4COOH$, formed by the oxidation of glucose, sucrose, or starch.

sac·cha·ride (săk′ə-rīd′) *n.* Any of a series of carbohydrates in which the atoms of the latter two elements are in the ratio of 2:1, esp. those containing the group $C_6H_{10}O_5$.

sac·char·i·fy (sə-kăr′ə-fī′, să-) *tr.v.* **-fied** (-fīd′), **-fy·ing, -fies** (-fīz′). To convert (starch, for example) into sugar. —**sac·char′i·fi·ca′tion** (-fĭ-kā′shən) *n.*

sac·cha·rim·e·ter (săk′ə-rĭm′ĭ-tər) *n.* A polarimeter that indicates the concentration of sugar in a solution. —**sac′cha·rim′e·try** *n.*

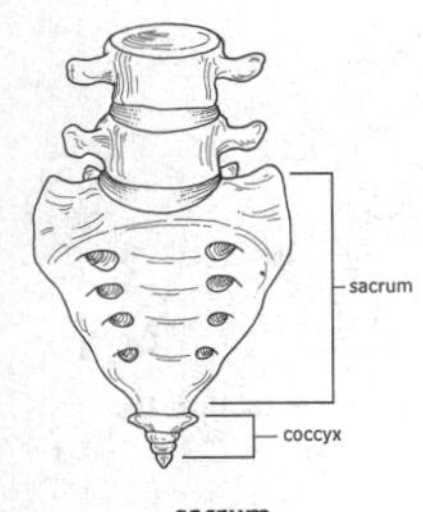

sacrum

sac·cha·rin (săk′ər-ĭn) *n.* A white crystalline powder, $C_7H_5NO_3S$, having a taste about 500 times sweeter than cane sugar and used as a calorie-free sweetener.

sac·cha·rine (săk′ər-ĭn, -ə-rēn′, -ə-rīn′) *adj.* **1.** Of or characteristic of sugar or saccharin; sweet. **2.** Cloyingly sweet in attitude, tone, or character. **3.** Excessively sentimental. —**sac′cha·rine·ly** *adv.* —**sac′cha·rin′i·ty** (-ə-rĭn′ĭ-tē) *n.*

saccharo– or **sacchar–** *pref.* Sugar: *saccharide.* [< Med.Lat. *saccharum*, sugar < Lat. *saccharon* < Gk. *sakkhar* < Pali *sakkharā* < Skt. *śarkarā.*]

sac·cha·roid (săk′ə-roid′) or **sac·cha·roi·dal** (-roid′l) *adj.* Having a texture similar to that of granulated sugar. Used of rocks and minerals.

sac·cha·rom·e·ter (săk′ə-rŏm′ĭ-tər) *n.* A hydrometer that determines the amount of sugar in a solution from density measurements.

sac·cha·ro·my·ces (săk′ə-rō-mī′sēz) *n., pl.* **saccharomyces.** Any of several single-celled yeasts belonging to the genus *Saccharomyces* that lack a true mycelium and many of which ferment sugar. [NLat. *Saccharomycēs*, genus name : SACCHARO- + Gk. *mukēs*, fungus.]

sac·cha·ro·my·cete (săk′ə-rō-mī′sēt′) *n.* A yeast of the family Saccharomycetaceae, including the saccharomyces. —**sac′cha·ro·my·ce′tic** (-mī-sē′tĭk), **sac′cha·ro·my·ce′tous** *adj.*

sac·cha·rose (săk′ə-rōs′) *n.* See **sucrose.**

Sac·co (săk′ō, säk′kō), **Nicola.** 1891–1927. Italian-born Amer. anarchist who with Bartolomeo Vanzetti was convicted of murder and sentenced to death (1921).

sac·cu·late (săk′yə-lāt′) or **sac·cu·lat·ed** (-lā′tĭd) also **sac·cu·lar** (-lər) *adj.* Formed of or divided into a series of saclike dilations or pouches.

sac·cule (săk′yo͞ol) also **sac·cu·lus** (-yə-ləs) *n., pl.* **sac·cules** also **sac·cu·li** (săk′yə-lī′). **1.** A small sac. **2.** The smaller of two membranous sacs in the vestibule of the inner ear. [Lat. *sacculus*, dim. of *saccus*, bag. See SACK[1].]

sac·er·do·tal (săs′ər-dōt′l, săk′-) *adj.* **1.** Of or relating to priests or the priesthood; priestly. **2.** Of or relating to sacerdotalism. [ME < OFr. < Lat. *sacerdōtālis* < *sacerdōs*, *sacerdōt-*, priest. See **sak-*.**] —**sac′er·do′tal·ly** *adv.*

sac·er·do·tal·ism (săs′ər-dōt′l-ĭz′əm, săk′-) *n.* The belief that priests act as mediators between God and human beings.

sac fungus *n. Bot.* See **ascomycete.**

sa·chem (sā′chəm) *n.* **1.a.** A chief of a Native American tribe or confederation, esp. an Algonquian chief. **b.** A member of the ruling council of the Iroquois confederacy. **2.** A high official of the Tammany Society, a political organization in New York City. [Of Massachusett orig.]

sa·cher torte (sä′kər tôrt′, zä′KHər tôr′tə) *n.* A rich chocolate cake filled with apricot jam and topped with chocolate icing. [Ger. *Sachertorte* : *Sacher*, surname of a family of 19th- and 20th-century hoteliers + *Torte*, torte; see TORTE.]

sa·chet (să-shā′) *n.* A small packet of perfumed powder used to scent clothes, as in trunks or closets. [Fr. < OFr., dim. of *sac*, bag < Lat. *saccus.* See SACK[1].]

Sachs (zäks, săks), **Hans.** 1494–1576. German writer noted for his dramas, poems, and songs.

Sachs, Nelly. 1891–1970. German writer who shared the 1966 Nobel Prize for literature.

sack[1] (săk) *n.* **1.a.** A large bag of strong coarse material for holding objects in bulk. **b.** A similar container of paper or plastic. **c.** The amount that a sack can hold. **2.** Also **sacque.** A short loose-fitting garment for women and children. **3.** *Slang.* Dismissal from employment: *finally got the sack.* **4.** *Informal.* A bed, mattress, or sleeping bag. **5.** *Baseball.* A base. **6.** *Football.* A successful attempt at sacking the quarterback. —*tr.v.* **sacked, sack·ing, sacks. 1.** To place into a sack. **2.** *Slang.* To discharge from employment. **3.** *Football.* To tackle (a quarterback attempting to pass the ball) behind the line of scrimmage. —***phrasal verb.* sack out.** *Slang.* To sleep. [ME < OE *sacc* < Lat. *saccus* < Gk. *sakkos*, of Semitic orig.] —**sack′er** *n.*

sack[2] (săk) *tr.v.* **sacked, sack·ing, sacks.** To rob of goods or valuables, esp. after capture. —*n.* **1.** The looting or pillaging of a captured city or town. **2.** Plunder; loot. [Prob. < Fr. *(mettre à) sac*, (to put in) a sack < OFr. *sac*, sack < Lat. *saccus*, sack, bag. See SACK[1].]

sack[3] (săk) *n.* Any of various dry light wines from Spain and the Canary Islands, imported to England in the 16th and 17th centuries. [< Fr. *(vin) sec*, dry (wine) < OFr. < Lat. *siccus*, dry.]

sack·but (săk′bŭt′) *n. Mus.* **1.** A medieval instrument resembling the trombone. **2.** An ancient triangular stringed instrument. [Fr. *saquebute* < OFr. *saqueboute* : ONFr. *saquier*, to pull; see SACCADE + OFr. *bouter*, to push (of Gmc. orig.; see **bhau-***). Sense 2, alteration of Aram. *sabbĕkā* < Gk. *sambukē.*]

sack·cloth (săk′klôth′, -klŏth′) *n.* **1.** Sacking. **2.a.** A rough cloth of camel's hair, goat hair, hemp, cotton, or flax. **b.** Garments made of this cloth, worn in mourning or as penance.

sack·ing (săk′ĭng) *n.* A coarse stout woven cloth, such as burlap or gunny, used for making sacks; sackcloth.

Sack·ville (săk′vĭl′), **Thomas.** 1st Earl of Dorset and Baron Buckhurst. 1536–1608. English poet who collaborated with Thomas Norton (1532–84) on *Gorboduc* (1561).

Sack·ville-West (săk′vĭl-wĕst′), **Victoria ("Vita") Mary.** 1892–1962. British author of *All Passion Spent* (1931).

Sa·co (sô′kō). A river rising in E-central NH and flowing c. 169 km (105 mi) SE through ME to the Atlantic Ocean.

sacr– *pref.* Var. of **sacro–.**

sa·cra (sā′krə, săk′rə) *n.* Pl. of **sacrum.**

sa·cral[1] (sā′krəl) *adj.* Of, near, or relating to the sacrum.

sa·cral[2] (sā′krəl) *adj.* Relating to sacred rites or observances. [< Lat. *sacer*, *sacr-*, sacred. See SACRED.]

sac·ra·ment (săk′rə-mənt) *n. Theol.* **1.** A visible form of invisible grace, esp.: **a.** In the Eastern, Roman Catholic, and some other Western Christian churches, any of the traditional seven rites instituted by Jesus that confer sanctifying grace. **b.** In most other Western Christian churches, the two rites, Baptism and the Eucharist, instituted by Jesus to confer sanctifying grace. **2.** Often **Sacrament. a.** The Eucharist. **b.** The consecrated elements of the Eucharist. [ME < OFr. *sacrement* < LLat. *sacrāmentum* < Lat., oath < *sacrāre*, to consecrate < *sacer*, *sacr-*, sacred. See SACRED.]

sac·ra·men·tal (săk′rə-mĕn′tl) *adj.* **1.** Of, relating to, or used in a sacrament. **2.** Consecrated or bound by or as if by a sacrament. **3.** Having the force or efficacy of a sacrament. —*n.* A rite, an act, or a sacred object used by some Christian churches in worship. —**sac′ra·men′tal·ly** *adv.*

sac·ra·men·tal·ism (săk′rə-mĕn′tl-ĭz′əm) *n.* The doctrine that observance of the sacraments is necessary for salvation and that such participation can confer grace. —**sac′ra·men′tal·ist** *n.*

Sac·ra·men·tar·i·an (săk′rə-mĕn-târ′ē-ən) *n.* One who regards the Eucharist as only the metaphorical body and blood of Jesus. —**Sac′ra·men·tar′i·an** *adj.* —**Sac′ra·men·tar′i·an·ism** *n.*

Sac·ra·men·to (săk′rə-mĕn′tō). The cap. of CA, in the N-central part NE of Oakland. Pop. 369,365.

Sacramento Mountains. A range of S-central NM extending to the TX border and rising to 3,660.9 m (12,003 ft).

Sacramento River. A river of N CA rising near Mt. Shasta and flowing c. 611 km (380 mi) to San Francisco Bay.

sa·crar·i·um (sə-krâr′ē-əm, să-, sā-) *n., pl.* **-i·a** (-ē-ə). **1.** The sanctuary or sacristy of a church. **2.** Piscina. [Med.Lat. *sacrārium* < Lat., shrine < *sacer*, *sacr-*, sacred. See SACRED.]

sa·cred (sā′krĭd) *adj.* **1.** Dedicated to or set apart for the worship of a deity. **2.** Worthy of religious veneration: *sacred teachings.* **3.** Made or declared holy: *sacred bread and wine.* **4.** Dedicated or devoted exclusively to a single use, purpose, or person. **5.** Worthy of respect; venerable. **6.** Of or relating to religious objects, rites, or practices. [ME, p.part. of *sacren*, to consecrate < OFr. *sacrer* < Lat. *sacrāre* < *sacer*, *sacr-*, sacred. See **sak-*.**] —**sa′cred·ly** *adv.* —**sa′cred·ness** *n.*

sacred baboon *n.* See **hamadryas.** [< the fact that the ancient Egyptians revered it as the god Anubis.]

sacred cow *n.* One immune from criticism, often unreasonably so. [< the veneration of the cow by Hindus.]

sac·ri·fice (săk′rə-fīs′) *n.* **1.a.** The act of offering something to a deity in propitiation or homage, esp. the ritual slaughter of an animal or a person. **b.** A victim offered in this way. **2.a.** Forfeiture of something highly valued for the sake of one considered to have a greater value or claim. **b.** Something so forfeited. **3.a.** Relinquishment of something at less than its presumed value. **b.** Something so relinquished. **c.** A loss so sustained. **4.** *Baseball.* A bunt that allows a runner to advance a base while the batter is put out. —*v.* **-ficed, -fic·ing, -fic·es.** —*tr.* **1.** To offer as a sacrifice to a deity. **2.** To forfeit (one thing) for another thing considered to be of greater value. **3.** To sell or give away at a loss. —*intr.* **1.** To make or offer a sacrifice. **2.** *Baseball.* To make a sacrifice hit. [ME < OFr. < Lat. *sacrificium* : *sacer*, sacred; see SACRED + *facere*, to make; see **dhē-*.**] —**sac′ri·fic′er** *n.*

sacrifice fly *n. Baseball.* A fly ball enabling a runner to score after it is caught by a fielder.

sac•ri•fi•cial (săk′rə-fĭsh′əl) *adj.* **1.** Of, relating to, or concerned with a sacrifice. **2.** Of or being an anode of a metal that is electrolytically decomposed while inhibiting the corrosion of another metal. **—sac′ri•fi′cial•ly** *adv.*

sac•ri•lege (săk′rə-lĭj) *n.* Desecration, profanation, misuse, or theft of something sacred. [ME < OFr. < Lat. *sacrilegium* < *sacrilegus*, one who steals sacred things : *sacer*, sacred; see SACRED + *legere*, to gather; see **leg-***.] **—sac′ri•le′gist** (săk′rə-lē′jĭst) *n.*

sac•ri•le•gious (săk′rə-lĭj′əs, -lē′jəs) *adj.* **1.** Grossly irreverent toward the sacred. **2.** Having committed sacrilege. **—sac′ri•le′gious•ly** *adv.* **—sac′ri•le′gious•ness** *n.*

Usage Note: *Sacrilegious,* the adjective of *sacrilege,* is often misspelled through confusion with *religious.*

sac•ris•tan (săk′rĭ-stən) *n.* **1.** One in charge of a sacristy. **2.** A sexton. [ME < Med.Lat. *sacristānus* < *sacrista* < Lat. *sacer*, sacred. See SACRED.]

sac•ris•ty (săk′rĭ-stē) *n., pl.* **-ties.** A room in a church housing the sacred vessels and vestments; a vestry. [ME *sacriste* < AN < Med.Lat. *sacristia* < *sacrista*, sacristan. See SACRISTAN.]

sacro– or **sacr–** *pref.* Sacrum: *sacroiliac.*

sac•ro•il•i•ac (săk′rō-ĭl′ē-ăk′, sā′krō-) *adj.* Of, relating to, or affecting the sacrum and ilium and their articulation or associated ligaments. —*n.* The sacroiliac region or cartilage.

sac•ro•sanct (săk′rō-săngkt′) *adj.* Regarded as sacred and inviolable. [Lat. *sacrōsānctus*, consecrated with religious ceremonies : *sacrum*, religious rite (< *sacer*, sacred; see SACRED) + *sānctus*, p.part. of *sancīre*, to consecrate; see **sak-***.] **—sac′ro•sanc′ti•ty** (-săngk′tĭ-tē) *n.*

sa•crum (sā′krəm, săk′rəm) *n., pl.* **sa•cra** (sā′krə, săk′rə). A triangular bone made up of five fused vertebrae and forming the posterior section of the pelvis. [NLat. < LLat. *(os) sacrum* < Lat. *sacer*, sacred. See SACRED.]

sad (săd) *adj.* **sad•der, sad•dest. 1.** Affected or characterized by sorrow or unhappiness. **2.** Expressive of sorrow or unhappiness. **3.** Causing sorrow or gloom; depressing: *sad news.* **4.** Deplorable; sorry: *a sad excuse.* **5.** Dark-hued; somber. [ME, weary, sorrowful < OE *sæd*, sated, weary. See **sā-***.] **—sad′ly** *adv.* **—sad′ness** *n.*

Syns: *sad, melancholy, sorrowful, doleful, woebegone, desolate.* These adjectives all mean affected with or marked by unhappiness, as that caused by affliction. *Sad* is the most general: *"Better by far you should forget and smile/Than that you should remember and be sad"* (Christina Rossetti). *Melancholy* can refer to a habitual state of mind marked by somberness or sadness: *a melancholy poet. Sorrowful* applies to emotional pain such as that resulting from irreparable loss: *sat through the funeral with a heavy, sorrowful heart. Doleful* describes what is mournful or morose: *wore a pathetic, doleful expression. Woebegone* suggests grief or wretchedness, especially as reflected in a person's appearance: *"His sorrow . . . made him look . . . haggard and . . . woebegone"* (George du Maurier). *Desolate* applies to one that is beyond consolation: *"No one is so accursed by fate/No one so utterly desolate/But some heart, though unknown/Responds unto his own"* (Henry Wadsworth Longfellow).

Sa•dat (sə-dăt′, -dät′), **Anwar el-.** 1918–81. Egyptian president (1970–81) who shared the 1978 Nobel Peace Prize.

sad•den (săd′n) *tr. & intr.v.* **-dened, -den•ing, -dens.** To make or become sad.

sad•dle (săd′l) *n.* **1.a.** A leather seat for a rider, secured on an animal's back by a girth. Also called regionally *rig* **b.** Similar tack used for attaching a pack to an animal. **c.** The padded part of a driving harness fitting over a horse's back. **d.** The seat of a bicycle, motorcycle, or similar vehicle. **e.** Something shaped like a saddle. **2.a.** A cut of meat consisting of part of the backbone and both loins. **b.** The lower part of a male fowl's back. **3.a.** A saddle-shaped depression in the ridge of a hill. **b.** A ridge between two peaks. —*v.* **-dled, -dling, -dles.** —*tr.* **1.** To put a saddle onto. **2.** To load or burden; encumber. —*intr.* **1.** To saddle a horse. **2.** To get into a saddle. —***idiom.* in the saddle.** In control; dominant. [ME *sadel* < OE *sadol*. See **sed-***.]

sad•dle•back (săd′l-băk′) *n.* Any of various birds, fishes, and other animals having saddle-shaped markings on the back.

sad•dle•bag (săd′l-băg′) *n.* **1.** One of a pair of pouches hanging across the back of a horse. **2.** A pouch hanging from a saddle or over the rear wheel of a motorcycle or bicycle.

sad•dle•bow (săd′l-bō′) *n.* The arched upper front part of a saddle.

sad•dle•cloth (săd′l-klôth′, -klŏth′) *n.* A cloth placed under the saddle of a racehorse and bearing its number.

saddle horse *n.* A horse bred or schooled for riding.

sad•dler (săd′lər) *n.* One that makes, repairs, or sells equipment for horses.

saddle roof *n.* A roof having a ridge and two gables.

sad•dler•y (săd′lə-rē) *n., pl.* **-ies. 1.** Equipment, such as saddles and harnesses, for horses. **2.** A shop that sells tack. **3.** The craft or business of one that makes or sells tack.

saddle shoe *n.* A flat casual shoe, usu. white, having a band of leather in a contrasting color across the instep.

saddle soap *n.* A preparation containing mild soap and neat's-foot oil, used for cleaning and softening leather.

saddle sore *n.* **1.** A sore on a horse caused by an improperly fitted saddle. **2.** A sore on a rider caused by a chafing saddle.

saddle stitch *n.* **1.** A simple overcasting stitch, usu. of a contrasting thread. **2.** A stitch used in sewing together the leaves of a book.

sad•dle•tree (săd′l-trē′) *n.* The frame of a saddle.

Sad•du•cee (săj′ə-sē′, săd′yə-) *n.* A member of a priestly Jewish sect founded in the second century B.C. that accepted only the written Mosaic law and ceased to exist after the Temple's destruction in A.D. 70. [ME *Saducee* < OE *Sadducēas*, Sadducees < LLat. *Saddūcaeī* < Gk. *Saddoukaioi* < Heb. *Ṣĕdûqî*.] **—Sad′du•ce′an** (-sē′ən) *adj.* **—Sad′du•cee′ism** *n.*

Sade (säd, săd), Comte **Donatien Alphonse François de.** "Marquis de Sade." 1740–1814. French writer of works characterized by a preoccupation with sexual violence.

sa•dhe (sä′də, tsä′-, -dē) also **tsa•de** (tsä′də, -dē) *n.* The 18th letter of the Hebrew alphabet. [Heb. *ṣādē*.]

sa•dhu (sä′do͞o) *n. Hinduism.* An ascetic holy man thought to have special powers. [< Skt. *sādhu-*, right, holy.]

sa•dism (sā′dĭz′əm, săd′ĭz′-) *n.* **1.** *Psychol.* **a.** Sexual gratification from infliction of pain on others. **b.** A psychological disorder in which sexual gratification is derived from infliction of pain on others. **2.** Delight in cruelty. **3.** Extreme cruelty. [After the Comte de SADE.] **—sa′dist** *n.* **—sa•dis′tic** (sə-dĭs′tĭk) *adj.* **—sa•dis′ti•cal•ly** *adv.*

sa•do•mas•o•chism (sā′dō-măs′ə-kĭz′əm, săd′ō-) *n. Psychol.* The derivation of sexual pleasure from simultaneous sadism and masochism. **—sa′do•mas′o•chist** *n.* **—sa′do•mas′o•chis′tic** *adj.*

sad sack *n. Informal.* A person regarded as extremely inept or clumsy. [After a cartoon character created in 1942 by George Baker (1915–75).]

Sa•far also **Sa•phar** (sə-fär′) *n.* The second month of the year in the Muslim calendar. [Ar. *ṣafar*.]

sa•fa•ri (sə-fär′ē) *n., pl.* **-ris. 1.** An overland expedition, esp. one for hunting or exploring in eastern Africa. **2.** A journey or trip. [Ar. *safarī*, journey < *safara*, to travel, set out.]

safari jacket *n.* A belted shirt jacket with large patch pockets.

safe (sāf) *adj.* **saf•er, saf•est. 1.** Secure from danger, harm, or evil. **2.** Free from danger or injury; unhurt. **3.** Free from risk; sure: *a safe bet.* **4.** Affording protection: *a safe place.* **5.** *Baseball.* Having reached a base without being put out. —*n.* **1.** A metal container usu. having a lock, used for storing valuables. **2.** A repository for protecting stored items. **3.** *Slang.* A condom. [ME *sauf* < OFr. < Lat. *salvus*, healthy. See **sol-***.] **—safe′ly** *adv.* **—safe′ness** *n.*

safe-con•duct (sāf′kŏn′dŭkt) *n.* **1.** An official document or an escort assuring unmolested passage, as through enemy territory. **2.** The protection afforded by such a document.

safe•crack•er (sāf′krăk′ər) *n.* One who breaks into safes in order to steal items from them. **—safe′crack′ing** *n.*

safe-de•pos•it box (sāf′dĭ-pŏz′ĭt) *n.* A fireproof metal box, usu. in a bank vault, for the secure storage of valuables.

safe•guard (sāf′gärd′) *n.* **1.a.** One that serves as protection or a guard. **b.** A mechanical device designed to prevent accidents. **c.** A safe-conduct. **2.a.** A protective stipulation, as in a contract. **b.** A precautionary measure. —*tr.v.* **-guard•ed, -guard•ing, -guards.** To ensure the safety of; protect. See Syns at **defend.**

safe house *n.* A house or an apartment used as a secure refuge by the members of an organization.

safe•keep•ing (sāf′kē′pĭng) *n.* The act of keeping safe or the state of being kept safe; protection.

safe•light (sāf′līt′) *n.* A lamp allowing moderate darkroom illumination without affecting photosensitive film or paper.

safe sex *n.* Sexual activity in which safeguards, such as the use of a condom, are taken to avoid acquiring or spreading a sexually transmitted disease. **—safe′-sex′** (sāf′sĕks′) *adj.*

safe•ty (sāf′tē) *n., pl.* **-ties. 1.** The condition of being safe; freedom from danger, risk, or injury. **2.** A device designed to prevent accidents, as a lock on a firearm. **3.** *Football.* **a.** A play in which a member of the offense downs the ball behind his own goal line, scoring two points for the defense. **b.** One of two defensive backs. **4.** *Slang.* A condom.

safety belt *n.* **1.** A strap or belt worn as a safety precaution by a person working at great heights. **2.** See **seat belt.**

safety glass *n.* **1.** Glass that resists shattering, esp. a composite of two sheets of glass with an intermediate layer of transparent plastic. **2.** See **wire glass. 3.** Tempered glass that breaks into rounded grains instead of jagged shards.

safety island *n.* An area marked off within a roadway from which traffic is banned, esp. to provide pedestrian safety.

safety lamp *n.* A miner's lamp with a protective wire gauze surrounding the flame to prevent ignition of flammable gases.

safety match *n.* A match that can be lighted only by being struck against a chemically prepared friction surface.

safety net *n.* **1.** A large net for catching one that falls or jumps, as from a tightrope. **2.** A guarantee, as of physical security.

safety pin *n.* **1.** A pin in the form of a clasp, having a sheath to cover and hold the point. **2.** A pin that prevents the pre-

Anwar el-Sadat
Photographed in 1974

safety net
Beneath tightrope walkers

ă pat	oi boy
ā pay	ou out
âr care	o͝o took
ä father	o͞o boot
ĕ pet	ŭ cut
ē be	ûr urge
ĭ pit	th thin
ī pie	*th* this
îr pier	hw which
ŏ pot	zh vision
ō toe	ə about, item
ô paw	

Stress marks:
′ (primary);
′ (secondary), as in
dictionary (dĭk′shə-nĕr′ē)

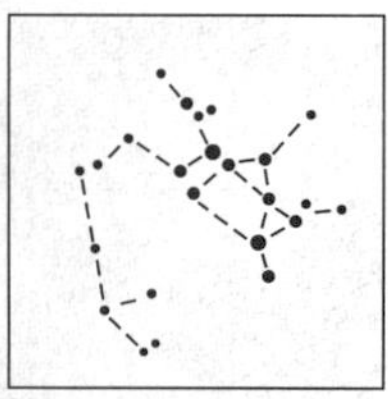
Sagittarius

saguaro
Carnegiea gigantea

saiga
Saiga tatarica

mature or accidental detonation of an explosive device.
safety razor *n.* See **razor** 2.
safety valve *n.* **1.** A valve in a pressure container, as in a steam boiler, that automatically opens when pressure reaches a dangerous level. **2.** An outlet for repressed energy or emotion.
saf•flow•er (săf′lou′ər) *n.* **1.** A thistlelike Eurasian plant *(Carthamus tinctorius)* of the composite family, having heads of orange flowers that yield a dyestuff and produce seeds containing an oil used in cooking, cosmetics, paints, and medicine. **2.** The dried flowers of this plant. [ME *saflour* < OFr. *safleur* < OItal. *saffiore* < Ar. *aṣfar*, yellow, a yellow plant.]
saf•fron (săf′rən) *n.* **1.a.** A corm-producing plant *(Crocus sativus)* native to the Old World and having purple or white flowers with orange stigmas. **b.** The dried aromatic stigmas of this plant, used in cooking and dyeing. **2.** *Color.* A moderate or strong orange yellow to moderate orange. [ME *saffran* < OFr. *safran* < Med.Lat. *safrānum* < Ar. *za'farān*.]
Sa•fi (săf′ē). A city of W Morocco on the Atlantic WNW of Marrakesh; a former Portuguese naval base. Pop. 197,309.
S.Afr. *abbr.* South Africa.
saf•ra•nine (săf′rə-nēn′, -nĭn) also **saf•ra•nin** (-nĭn) *n.* Any of a family of dyes based on phenazine, used in the textile industry and as a biological stain. [Fr. *safran*, saffron (< OFr.; see SAFFRON) + -INE[2].]
saf•role (săf′rōl′) *n.* An oily liquid, $C_{10}H_{10}O_2$, derived chiefly from oil of camphor and used in making perfume and soap. [Fr. *safran*, saffron; see SAFFRON + -OLE.]
sag (săg) *v.* **sagged, sag•ging, sags.** *—intr.* **1.** To sink, droop, or settle from pressure or weight. **2.** To lose vigor, firmness, or resilience. **3.** To decline, as in value or price: *Stock prices sagged.* **4.** *Naut.* To drift to leeward. *—tr.* To cause to sag. *—n.* **1.a.** The act or an instance of sagging. **b.** The degree or extent to which something sags. **2.** A sagging area; a depression. **3.** A temporary decline in monetary value. **4.** *Naut.* A drift to leeward. [ME *saggen*, prob. of Scandinavian origin.]
sa•ga (sä′gə) *n.* **1.a.** An Icelandic prose narrative of the 12th and 13th centuries, dealing with the families that settled Iceland, the kings of Norway, and Germanic gods and heroes. **b.** A modern prose narrative that resembles a saga. **2.** A long, detailed report. [ON. See **sek**[w]**-3***.]
sa•ga•cious (sə-gā′shəs) *adj.* Having or showing keen discernment, sound judgment, and farsightedness. [< Lat. *sagāx*, *sagāc-*, of keen perception. See **sāg-***.] **—sa•ga′cious•ly** *adv.* **—sa•ga′cious•ness** *n.*
sa•gac•i•ty (sə-găs′ĭ-tē) *n.* The quality of being discerning, sound in judgment, and farsighted; wisdom. [Fr. *sagacité* < OFr. *sagacite* < Lat. *sagācitās*, quickness of perception < *sagāx*, *sagāc-*, of keen perception. See SAGACIOUS.]
sag•a•more (săg′ə-môr′, -mōr′) *n.* A subordinate chief among the Algonquians. [Eastern Abenaki *sàkəmα*.]
Sa•gan (sā′gən), **Carl.** b. 1934. Amer. astronomer noted for research on the possibility of extraterrestrial life.
Sa•gan (sä-gäN′), **Françoise.** Françoise Quoirez. b. 1935. French writer best known for *Bonjour Tristesse* (1954).
saga novel *n.* See **roman-fleuve.**
sage[1] (sāj) *n.* One venerated for experience, judgment, and wisdom. *—adj.* **sag•er, sag•est. 1.** Having or exhibiting wisdom and calm judgment. **2.** Proceeding from or marked by wisdom and calm judgment: *sage advice.* **3.** *Archaic.* Serious; solemn. [ME < OFr. < VLat. *sapius < Lat. *sapere*, to be wise. See **sep-***.] **—sage′ly** *adv.* **—sage′ness** *n.*
sage[2] (sāj) *n.* **1.a.** Any of various plants of the genus *Salvia*, esp. *S. officinalis*, having aromatic grayish-green leaves used in cooking. **b.** The leaves of this plant. **2.** Any of various similar plants in the mint family. **3.** Sagebrush. [ME *sauge* < OFr. < Lat. *salvia* < *salvus*, healthy. See **sol-***.]
sage•brush (sāj′brŭsh′) *n.* Any of several aromatic plants of the genus *Artemisia*, esp. *A. tridentata*, a shrub of arid regions of western North America having silver-green leaves and large clusters of small white flower heads.
sage grouse *n.* A chickenlike bird *(Centrocercus urophasianus)* of western North America having long pointed tail feathers that can be spread like a fan.
sage sparrow *n.* A small brownish-gray sparrow *(Amphispiza belli)* of dry regions of the southwest United States.
sage thrasher *n.* A light grayish-brown thrasher *(Oreoscoptes montanus)* that nests in low sage and cactus bushes in dry or desert regions of the western United States.
sag•ger also **sag•gar** (săg′ər) *n.* **1.** A protective casing of fire clay in which delicate ceramic articles are fired. **2.** Clay used to make ceramic casings. [Perh. alteration of SAFEGUARD.]
Sa•gi•naw (săg′ə-nô′). A city of E-central MI on the **Saginaw River,** flowing c. 32 km (20 mi) into **Saginaw Bay,** a large inlet of Lake Huron. Pop. 69,572.
Sa•git•ta (sə-jĭt′ə) *n.* A constellation in the Northern Hemisphere near Aquila and Vulpecula. [Lat., *sagitta*, arrow.]
sag•it•tal (săj′ĭ-tl) *adj.* **1.** *Anat.* Of or relating to the suture uniting the two parietal bones of the skull. **2.** *Zool.* Of or relating to the sagittal plane. [NLat. *sagittālis* < Lat. *sagitta*, arrow.] **—sag′it•tal•ly** *adv.*
sagittal plane *n.* *Zool.* A plane that divides the body of a bilaterally symmetrical animal into right and left sections.
Sag•it•tar•i•us (săj′ĭ-târ′ē-əs) *n.* **1.** A constellation in the Southern Hemisphere near Scorpius and Capricorn. **2.a.** The ninth sign of the zodiac in astrology. **b.** One born under this sign. [ME < Lat. *Sagittārius* < *sagittārius*, archer < *sagitta*, arrow.]
sag•it•tate (săj′ĭ-tāt′) *adj.* *Biol.* Having the shape of an arrowhead: *sagittate leaves.* [Lat. *sagitta*, arrow + -ATE[1].]
sa•go (sā′gō) *n.*, *pl.* **-gos.** A starch obtained from certain sago palms and used as a food thickener and textile stiffener. [Malay *sagu*, mealy pith.]
sago palm *n.* **1.** Any of various palms of the genera *Metroxylon, Arenga,* and *Caryota* of tropical Asia. **2.** Either of two palmlike cycads *(Cycas circinalis* or *C. revoluta)* of eastern and tropical Asia.
sa•gua•ro (sə-gwär′ō, -wär′ō) also **sa•hua•ro** (sə-wär′ō) *n.*, *pl.* **-ros. 1.** A large cactus *(Carnegiea gigantea)* of the southwest United States and northern Mexico having upward-curving branches, white flowers, and edible red fruit. **2.** The fruit of this cactus. [Am.Sp., prob. of Piman orig.]
Sag•ue•nay (săg′ə-nā′). A river of S Quebec, Canada, flowing c. 201 km (125 mi) to the St. Lawrence R.
Sa•gun•to (sə-go͞on′tō, sä-). A city of E Spain NNE of Valencia. Its capture by Carthaginian forces (219–218 B.C.) precipitated the Second Punic War. Pop. 57,380.
Sa•hap•ti•an (sä-hăp′tē-ən) *n.* **1.** A North American Indian language family of Washington, Oregon, and Idaho comprising the Sahaptin and Nez Perce languages. **2.** A speaker of a Sahaptian language. **—Sa•hap′ti•an** *adj.*
Sa•hap•tin (sä-hăp′tĭn) *n.*, *pl.* **Sahaptin** or **-tins. 1.** A member of any of various Native American peoples of Idaho, Washington, and Oregon. **2.** The dialectally diverse Sahaptian language of the Sahaptin. [Southern Interior Salish *s'aptnx*.]
Sa•har•a (sə-hâr′ə, -hă′ə, -hä′rə). A vast desert of N Africa extending E from the Atlantic coast to the Nile Valley and S from the Atlas Mts. to the Sudan. **—Sa•har′an** *adj.*
Sa•hel (sə-hāl′, -hēl′). A semiarid region of N-central Africa S of the Sahara Desert. **—Sa•hel′i•an** *adj.*
sa•hib (sä′ĭb, -ēb, -hĭb) *n.* Used formerly as a form of respectful address for a European man in colonial India. [Hindi *ṣāḥib*, master < Ar., companion, master.]
said (sĕd) *v.* P.t. and p.part. of **say.** *—adj.* *Law.* Aforementioned: *Said party has denied the charges.*
Usage Note: The adjective *said* is seldom appropriate to any but legal or business writing, where it is equivalent to *aforesaid: the said tenant* (named in a lease); *said property.* In similar general contexts *said* is usually unnecessary, and *the tenant* or *the property* will suffice.
sai•ga (sī′gə) *n.* Either of two small antelopes *(Saiga tatarica* or *S. mongolia)* of the plains of northern Eurasia having a stubby snout. [Russ. *saĭga*, of Turkic orig.]
Sai•gon (sī-gŏn′). See **Ho Chi Minh City.**
sail (sāl) *n.* **1.** *Naut.* **a.** A piece of sewn fabric fitted to the spars and rigging of a vessel so as to convert the force of the wind into forward motion of the vessel. **b.** The sails of a ship or boat. **c.** The superstructure of a submarine. **2.** *pl.* **sail** or **sails.** *Naut.* A sailing vessel. **3.** *Naut.* A trip or voyage in a sailing craft. **4.** Something, such as the blade of a windmill, that resembles a sail in form or function. *—v.* **sailed, sail•ing, sails.** *—intr.* **1.** *Naut.* **a.** To move across the surface of water, esp. by means of a sailing vessel. **b.** To travel by water in a vessel. **c.** To start out on such a voyage or journey. **d.** To operate a sailing craft, esp. for sport. **2.** To move swiftly, smoothly, or effortlessly: *sailed through the exam.* *—tr.* *Naut.* **1.** To navigate or manage (a vessel). **2.** To voyage upon or across. ***—phrasal verb.*** **sail into.** To attack or criticize vigorously. [ME < OE *segl*.]
sail•board (sāl′bôrd′, -bōrd′) *Naut.* *—n.* A craft resembling a large surfboard, fitted with a mast that is held up by the operator. *—intr.v.* **-board•ed, -board•ing, -boards.** To sail a sailboard. **—sail′board′er** *n.*
sail•boat (sāl′bōt′) *n.* *Naut.* A small boat propelled by sail.
sail•cloth (sāl′klôth′, -klŏth′) *n.* A strong fabric suitable for making sails or tents.
sail•fish (sāl′fĭsh′) *n.*, *pl.* **sailfish** or **-fish•es.** Any of various large marine fishes of the genus *Istiophorus*, having a large saillike dorsal fin and a spearlike upper jaw.
sail•ing (sā′lĭng) *n.* *Naut.* **1.** The skill required to operate and navigate a vessel. **2.** The sport of operating or riding in a sailboat. **3.** Departure or time of departure from a port.
sail•or (sā′lər) *n.* **1.** *Naut.* One who serves in a navy or works on a ship. **2.** One who travels by water. **3.** A low-crowned straw hat with a flat top and flat brim.
sail•or's-choice (sā′lərz-chois′) *n.*, *pl.* **sailor's-choice.** Any of various fishes of the North American Atlantic coast, such as the pinfish or the grunt *Haemulon parrai* of southerly waters.
sail•plane (sāl′plān′) *n.* A light glider used esp. for soaring. *—intr.v.* **-planed, -plan•ing, -planes.** To fly a sailplane. **—sail′plan′er** *n.*
Sai•maa (sī′mä′), **Lake.** A lake of SE Finland; largest of the **Saimaa Lakes** in the S-central and SE part of the country.
sain•foin (sān′foin′, săn′-) *n.* A Eurasian plant *(Onobrychis viciifolia)* having pinnately compound leaves and pink or

white flowers, often grown as a forage crop. [Fr. < OFr. < Med.Lat. *sānum faenum* : Lat. *sānum*, neut. of *sānus*, healthy + Lat. *faenum*, hay; see **dhē(i)-***.]

saint (sānt) *n.* **1.a.** *Theol.* A person officially recognized as being entitled to public veneration and capable of interceding for people on earth. **b.** A person who has died and gone to heaven. **c. Saint.** A member of any of various religious groups, esp. a Latter-Day Saint. **2.** *Islam & Judaism.* An extraordinarily righteous person enjoying a special relationship with God. **3.** An extremely virtuous person. — *tr.v.* **saint•ed, saint•ing, saints.** To name, recognize, or venerate as a saint; canonize. [ME < OFr. < LLat. *sānctus* < Lat., holy, p.part. of *sancīre*, to consecrate. See **sak-***.]

Saint Ag•nes' Eve (ăg′nĭs, -nĭ-sĭz) *n.* January 20th, on which young women are said to dream of their future husbands.

Saint Al•bans (ôl′bənz). A municipal borough of SE England NNW of London; founded 793. Pop. 125,400.

Saint Al•bert (ăl′bərt). A city of central Alberta, Canada, a suburb of Edmonton. Pop. 31,996.

Saint An•drews (ăn′dro͞oz). A community of SE SC, a suburb of Charleston. Pop. 26,692.

Saint An•drew's cross (ăn′dro͞oz) *n.* **1.** A cross shaped like the letter X. **2.** A shrubby New World plant *(Hypericum hypericoides)* having four-petaled yellow flowers.

Saint An•tho•ny's cross (ăn′thə-nēz) *n.* See **tau cross.**

Saint Anthony's fire *n.* See **erysipelas.** [< the belief that St. Anthony's intercession could cure it.]

Saint Au•gus•tine (ô′gə-stēn′). A city of NE FL on the Atlantic SSE of Jacksonville; founded 1565 and the oldest permanent European settlement in the U.S. Pop. 11,692.

Saint-Bar•thél•e•my (săɴ-bär-tāl-mē′) or **Saint Bar•thol•o•mew** (sānt bär-thŏl′ə-myo͞o′). Familiarly **Saint Barts** (bärts). An island of the French overseas department of Guadeloupe in the Leeward Is. NNW of the island of Guadeloupe.

Saint Ber•nard (bər-närd′) *n.* Any of a breed of large strong dogs having a thick brown and white coat. [After the hospice at *St. Bernard* (d. c. 1081) in the Swiss Alps.]

Saint Bru•no de Mon•tar•ville or **Saint-Bru•no-de-Mon•tar•ville** (sānt bro͞o′nō də mŏn′tər-vĭl′, săɴ brü-nô′ də môɴ-tär-vēl′). A town of S Quebec, Canada, a suburb of Montreal on the E bank of the St. Lawrence R. Pop. 22,880.

Saint Cath•a•rines (sānt kăth′ə-rĭnz′, kăth′rĭnz). A city of SE Ontario, Canada, on the Welland Ship Canal ESE of Hamilton; founded 1790. Pop. 124,018.

Saint Charles (chärlz). **1.** A city of NE IL W of Chicago. Pop. 22,501. **2.** A city of E MO on the Missouri R. NW of St. Louis; settled by French traders in 1769. Pop. 54,555.

Saint Chris•to•pher-Ne•vis (krĭs′tə-fər-nē′vĭs, -nĕv′ĭs) also **Saint Kitts and Ne•vis** (kĭts; nē′vĭs, nĕv′ĭs). An island country in the Leeward Is. of the West Indies ESE of Puerto Rico comprising **Saint Christopher,** the largest island of the group, and the islands of Nevis and Sombrero; became independent from Great Britain in 1983. Cap. Basseterre. Pop. 44,404.

Saint Clair (klâr), **Lake.** A lake between SW Ontario, Canada, and SE MI connected with Lake Huron by the **Saint Clair River,** c. 64 km (40 mi).

Saint Clair Shores. A city of SE MI, a suburb of Detroit. Pop. 68,107.

Saint Cloud (kloud). A city of central MN on the Mississippi R. NW of Minneapolis. Pop. 48,812.

Saint Croix (kroi). An island of the U.S. Virgin Is. in the West Indies E of Puerto Rico; sold to the U.S. by Denmark in 1917.

Saint Croix River. 1. A river rising in NW WI and flowing c. 264 km (164 mi) to the Mississippi R. SE of St. Paul MN. **2.** A river, c. 121 km (75 mi), forming part of the boundary between E ME and SW New Brunswick, Canada.

Saint Den•is (dĕn′ĭs), **Ruth.** 1878–1968. Amer. choreographer who cofounded (1915) the Denishawn Dance School.

Saint-De•nis (săɴ-də-nē′). **1.** A city of N-central France, a suburb of Paris. Pop. 90,829. **2.** The cap. of Réunion, a port on the Indian Ocean. Pop. 84,400.

saint•dom (sānt′dəm) *n.* The condition or quality of being a saint.

Sainte Anne de Beau•pré or **Sainte-Anne-de-Beau•pré** (sānt ăn′ də bō-prā′, săɴ-tăn). A village of S Quebec, Canada, on the St. Lawrence R. NE of Quebec City; site of a shrine estab. by shipwrecked sailors in 1620.

Sainte-Beuve (săɴt-bœv′), **Charles Augustin.** 1804–69. French literary critic and historian noted for his biographical approach to literature.

saint•ed (săn′tĭd) *adj.* **1.** Having been canonized. **2.** Of saintly character; holy.

Sainte Foy or **Sainte-Foy** (sānt foi′, săɴt fwä′). A city of S Quebec, Canada, a suburb of Quebec City. Pop. 68,883.

Saint E•li•as (sānt ĭ-lī′əs), **Mount.** A peak, 5,492.4 m (18,008 ft), in the **Saint Elias Mountains,** a section of the Coast Ranges on the border between E AK and SW Yukon Terr., Canada.

Saint El•mo's fire (ĕl′mōz) *n.* A visible electric discharge on a pointed object, such as the mast of a ship or the wing of an airplane, during an electrical storm. [After *St. Elmo*, 4th-cent. A.D. patron saint of sailors.]

Sainte Thé•rèse or **Sainte-Thé•rèse** (sānt′ tə-rĕz′, săɴt tā-rĕz′). A city of S Quebec, Canada, on the St. Lawrence R. NW of Montreal. Pop. 18,750.

Saint-É•tienne (săɴ-tā-tyĕn′). A city of SE-central France SW of Lyons. Pop. 204,995.

Saint Eu•stache or **Saint-Eu•stache** (sānt′ o͞o-stăsh′, săɴ-tœ-stăsh′). A town of S Quebec, Canada, W of Montreal. Pop. 29,716.

Saint Eu•sta•ti•us (sānt yo͞o-stā′shəs, -shē-əs). An island of the Netherlands Antilles in the Leeward Is. of the West Indies NW of St. Christopher; under Dutch control after 1632.

Saint-Ex•u•pé•ry (săɴ-tĕg-zo͞o-pā-rē′, -zü-), **Antoine de.** 1900–44. French writer and aviator best known for his fairy tale *The Little Prince* (1943).

Saint Fran•cis River (frăn′sĭs). A river rising in SE MO and flowing c. 756 km (470 mi) to the Mississippi R. in E AR.

Saint Gall (sānt gôl′, gäl′, săɴ gäl′). See **Sankt Gallen.**

Saint-Gau•dens (sānt-gôd′nz), **Augustus.** 1848–1907. Irish-born Amer. sculptor noted for his heroic monuments.

Saint George's (sānt jôr′jəz). The cap. of Grenada, on the SW coast of the island in the West Indies. Pop. 7,500.

Saint George's Channel. A strait between W Wales and SE Ireland connecting the Atlantic Ocean with the Irish Sea.

Saint Gott•hard (gŏt′ərd). A range of the Lepontine Alps in S-central Switzerland; crossed by **Saint Gotthard Pass,** 2,115.2 m (6,935 ft) high.

Saint He•le•na (hə-lē′nə). A volcanic island in the S Atlantic W of Angola. With the islands of Ascension and Tristan da Cunha, it forms the British dependency of **Saint Helena.** Cap. Jamestown. Pop. 5,147.

Saint Hel•ens (hĕl′ənz). A borough of NW England ENE of Liverpool. Pop. 190,000.

Saint Helens, Mount. An active volcanic peak of the Cascade Range in SW WA. Before its violent eruption on May 18, 1980, it was 2,949.7 m (9,671 ft).

saint•hood (sānt′ho͝od′) *n.* **1.** The status, character, or condition of being a saint. **2.** Saints considered as a group.

Saint Hu•bert or **Saint-Hu•bert** (sānt′ hyo͞o′bərt, săɴ ü-bĕr′). A town of S Quebec, Canada, a suburb of Montreal E of the St. Lawrence R. Pop. 60,573.

Saint Hy•a•cinthe or **Saint-Hy•a•cinthe** (sānt′ hī′ə-sĭnth, săɴ-tyä-săɴt′). A city of S Quebec, Canada, ENE of Montreal. Pop. 38,246.

Saint Jean or **Saint-Jean** (săɴ zhäɴ′) or **Saint Johns** (sānt jŏnz′). A city of S Quebec, Canada, on the Richelieu R. SE of Montreal; founded 1666. Pop. 35,640.

Saint Jean or **Saint-Jean, Lake.** See Lake **Saint John.**

Saint Jé•rôme or **Saint-Jé•rôme** (sānt′ jə-rōm′, săɴ zhā-rōm′). A city of S Quebec, Canada, NW of Montreal. Pop. 25,123.

Saint John[1] (sānt jŏn′). An island of the U.S. Virgin Is. E of Puerto Rico; sold to the U.S. by Denmark in 1917.

Saint John[2] (sānt jŏn′). A city of S New Brunswick, Canada, at the mouth of the St. John R. on the Bay of Fundy; settled by the French in the 1630's. Pop. 80,521.

Saint John, Henry. See First Viscount **Bolingbroke.**

Saint John (sānt jŏn′) or **Saint Jean** or **Saint-Jean** (săɴ zhäɴ′), **Lake.** A lake of S-central Quebec, Canada, connected by the Saguenay R. with the St. Lawrence R.

Saint John River. A river rising in N ME and flowing c. 673 km (418 mi) to the Bay of Fundy.

Saint Johns (jŏnz). **1.** See **Saint Jean. 2.** See **Saint John's** 1.

Saint John's (jŏnz). **1.** Also **Saint Johns.** The cap. of Antigua and Barbuda, on the N coast of Antigua in the Leeward Is. of the West Indies. Pop. 24,359. **2.** The cap. of Newfoundland, Canada, on the SE coast of the island; first colonized by the English in 1583. Pop. 83,770.

Saint Johns River. A river of NE FL flowing c. 459 km (285 mi) to the Atlantic Ocean.

Saint Johns•wort (jonz′wûrt′, -wôrt′) *n.* Any of various herbs or shrubs of the genus *Hypericum,* having yellow flowers with five petals and numerous stamens.

Saint Jo•seph (jō′zəf, -səf). A city of NW MO on the Missouri R. NNW of Kansas City. Pop. 71,852.

Saint Joseph River. A river of SW MI and NW IN flowing c. 338 km (210 mi) to Lake Michigan.

Saint Kitts and Ne•vis (kĭts; nē′vĭs, nĕv′ĭs). See **Saint Christopher-Nevis.**

Saint Lam•bert or **Saint-Lam•bert** (sānt lăm′bərt, săɴ läm-bĕr′). A city of southern Quebec, Canada, a suburb of Montreal on the St. Lawrence R. Pop. 20,557.

Saint Lau•rent or **Saint-Lau•rent** (sănt′ lô-rĕnt′, săɴ lô-räɴ′). A city of S Quebec, Canada, a suburb of Montreal. Pop. 65,900.

Saint Lau•rent (săɴ lô-räɴ′), **Louis Stephen.** 1882–1973. Canadian politician who served as prime minister (1948–57).

Saint Law•rence (sānt lôr′əns, lŏr′-), **Gulf of.** An arm of the NW Atlantic off SE Canada bordered by New Brunswick, Nova Scotia, Newfoundland, and Quebec.

Saint Lawrence River. A river of SE Canada flowing c. 1,207 km (750 mi) from Lake Ontario along the Ontario–NY border and through S Quebec to the Gulf of St. Lawrence.

Saint Lawrence Seaway. A waterway, c. 3,781 km (2,350 mi),

Saint Andrew's cross

Saint Bernard

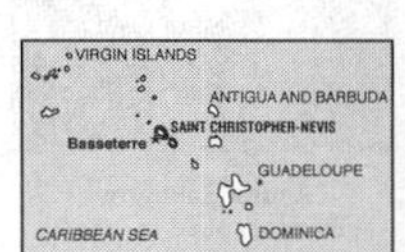

Saint Christopher-Nevis

ă pat	oi boy
ā pay	ou out
âr care	o͝o took
ä father	o͞o boot
ĕ pet	ŭ cut
ē be	ûr urge
ĭ pit	th thin
ī pie	*th* this
îr pier	hw which
ŏ pot	zh vision
ō toe	ə about, item
ô paw	

Stress marks:
′ (primary);
′ (secondary), as in
dictionary (dĭk′shə-nĕr′ē)

consisting of a system of canals, dams, and locks in the St. Lawrence R. and connecting channels through the Great Lakes; opened to navigation in 1959.

Saint Lé•o•nard or **Saint-Lé•o•nard** (sānt′ lĕn′ərd, săɴ lā-ō-när′). A city of S Quebec, Canada, a suburb of Montreal. Pop. 79,429.

Saint Lou•is (sānt lo͞o′ĭs). An independent city of E MO on the Mississippi R. just S of its confluence with the Missouri R.; settled by the French in 1763–64. Pop. 396,685.

Saint-Lou•is (săɴ-lo͞o-ē′). A city of NW Senegal at the mouth of the Senegal R.; founded c. 1658. Pop. 107,072.

Saint Lou•is encephalitis (sānt lo͞o′ĭs) *n.* A viral encephalitis occurring in parts of North America and transmitted by a culex mosquito. [After Saint Louis, MO.]

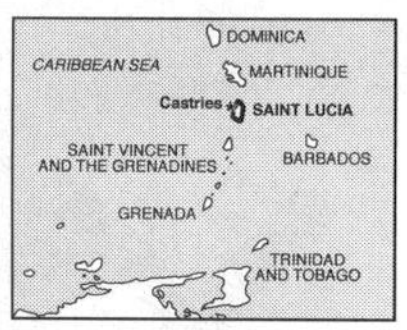

Saint Lucia

Saint Louis Park. A city of SE MN, a suburb of Minneapolis. Pop. 43,787.

Saint Lu•cia (lo͞o′shə, lo͞o-sē′ə). An island country of the West Indies S of Martinique; achieved independence from Great Britain in 1979. Cap. Castries. Pop. 134,006.

saint•ly (sānt′lē) *adj.* **-li•er, -li•est.** Of, relating to, resembling, or befitting a saint. **— saint′li•ness** *n.*

Saint-Ma•lo (săɴ-mə-lō′). A town of NW France NNW of Nantes on the **Gulf of Saint-Malo,** an inlet of the English Channel. Pop. 46,347.

Saint Mar•tin or **Saint Maar•ten** (mär′tn). An island of the West Indies in the W Leeward Is.; administered jointly by the French overseas department of Guadeloupe and the Netherlands Antilles.

Saint Mar•ys River (mâr′ēz). A river, c. 101 km (63 mi), rising in the E Upper Peninsula of MI and flowing to the N end of Lake Huron along part of the U.S.-Canadian border.

Saint Mau•rice or **Saint-Mau•rice** (sānt′ môr′ĭs, -mŏr′-, săɴ mô-rēs′). A river of S Quebec, Canada, flowing c. 523 km (325 mi) to the St. Lawrence R. at Trois Rivières.

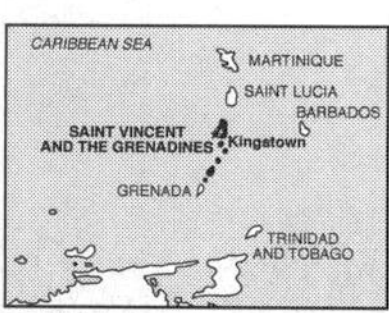

Saint Vincent and the Grenadines

Saint Mo•ritz (sānt′ mə-rĭts′, săɴ mô-rēts′). A resort city of SE Switzerland on the Inn R. SSE of Chur. Pop. 5,900.

Saint-Na•zaire (săɴ-nä-zĕr′). A city of W-central France at the mouth of the Loire R. W of Nantes. Pop. 68,348.

Saint Nich•o•las (sānt nĭk′ə-ləs) or **Saint Nick** (nĭk) *n.* Santa Claus.

Saint Pat•rick's Day (păt′rĭks) *n.* March 17, observed in honor of Saint Patrick, the patron saint of Ireland.

Saint Paul (pôl). The cap. of MN, in the SE part on the Mississippi R. adjacent to Minneapolis. Pop. 272,235.

Saint Pe•ters•burg (pē′tərz-bûrg′). **1.** Formerly (1924–91) **Len•in•grad** (lĕn′ĭn-grăd′, lyĭ-nĭn-grät′) and **Pet•ro•grad** (pĕt′rə-grăd′, pyĭ-trə-grät′). A city of NW Russia on the Neva R. at the head of the Gulf of Finland; founded by Peter the Great in 1703 and cap. of Russia from 1712 to 1918. Pop. 4,329,000. **2.** A city of W-central FL on Tampa Bay SSW of Tampa; settled in the mid-1800's. Pop. 238,629.

Andrei Sakharov
Photographed in 1988

Saint Pi•erre or **Saint-Pi•erre** (sānt′ pîr′, pē-âr′, săɴ pyĕr′). The cap. of St. Pierre and Miquelon, on St. Pierre I. in the N Atlantic. Pop. 5,371.

Saint Pierre and Mi•que•lon (sānt, săɴ; mĭk′ə-lŏn′, mē-klôɴ′). A French island group and overseas department in the N Atlantic S of Newfoundland, Canada. Cap. St. Pierre, on **Saint Pierre Island.** Pop. 6,041.

Saint-Saëns (săɴ-säɴs′, -säɴ′), **Charles Camille.** 1835–1921. French composer noted for *Danse Macabre* (1874).

saint's day (sānts) *n., pl.* **saints' days.** A day in a liturgical calendar observed in honor of a saint.

Saint-Si•mon (săɴ-sē-mōɴ′), Comte de. Claude Henri de Rouvroy. 1760–1825. French philosopher who advocated a society governed by technocrats.

Saint-Simon, Duc de. Louis de Rouvroy. 1675–1755. French diplomat known for his memoirs of the court of Louis XIV.

Saint Tho•mas[1] (sānt tŏm′əs). An island of the U.S. Virgin Is. E of Puerto Rico; sold to the U.S. by Denmark in 1917.

Saint Tho•mas[2] (sānt tŏm′əs). A city of S Ontario, Canada, near Lake Erie S of London. Pop. 28,165.

Saint-Tro•pez (săɴ-trô-pā′). A resort town of SE France on the Mediterranean coast of the French Riviera. Pop. 4,961.

Saint Val•en•tine's Day (sānt văl′ən-tīnz′) *n.* February 14, celebrated in various countries by the exchange of valentines or love tokens. [Primarily after St. Valentine.]

Saint Vin•cent (vĭn′sənt). An island of St. Vincent and the Grenadines in the central Windward Is. of the West Indies; settled by the British in the mid-1700's.

salamander
Spotted salamander
Ambystoma maculatum

Saint Vincent, Cape. A promontory SW of Portugal.

Saint Vincent and the Gren•a•dines (grĕn′ə-dēnz′). An island country in the central Windward Is. of the West Indies comprising St. Vincent I. and the N islets of the Grenadines; part of the West Indies Federation (1958–62) and independent since 1979. Cap. Kingstown. Pop. 108,704.

Saint Vi•tus' dance also **Saint Vi•tus's dance** (vītəs, -tə-sĭz) *n.* See **Sydenham's chorea.** [After *St. Vitus,* 3rd-cent. A.D. Christian martyr.]

Sai•pan (sī-păn′, -pän′, sī′păn). An island of the W Pacific in the S Mariana Is.; part of the U.S. Trust Territory of the Pacific Islands. **— Sai′pa•nese′** (-nēz′, -nēs′) *adj. & n.*

Sa•ïs (sā′ĭs). A city of ancient Egypt in the W-central region of the Nile delta; a royal residence during the XXVI Dynasty.

saith (sĕth, sā′ĭth) *v. Archaic.* A third pers. sing. pr.t. of **say.**

Sai•va (sī′və, shī′-) *n. Hinduism.* One who worships Shiva. [Skt. *śaiva-,* belonging to Shiva < *śivaḥ,* Shiva.] **— Sai′vism** *n.*

Sa•ja•ma (sə-hä′mə). A mountain, 6,574.3 m (21,555 ft), in the Andes of W Bolivia near the Chilean border.

Sa•kai (sä′kī′). A city of S Honshu, Japan, on Osaka Bay S of Osaka. Pop. 818,368.

Sak•a•ka•we•a (săk′ə-kə-wē′ə), **Lake.** A reservoir in W-central ND; a widening of the Missouri R. created in 1956 when the Garrison Dam was completed.

sake[1] (sāk) *n.* **1.** Purpose; motive. **2.** Advantage; good: *for the sake of his health.* **3.** Personal benefit or interest; welfare. [ME, lawsuit, guilt < OE *sacu.* See **sāg-*.**]

sa•ke[2] also **sa•ki** (sä′kē, -kĕ) *n.* A Japanese wine made from fermented rice. [J.]

sa•ker (sā′kər) *n.* A Eurasian falcon *(Falco cherrug)* having brown plumage. [ME *sagre* < OFr. *sacre* < Ar. *ṣaqr.*]

Sa•kha•lin (săk′ə-lēn′, -lən, să-кнə-lyēn′). An island of SE Russia in the Sea of Okhotsk N of Hokkaido, Japan; colonized by Russia and Japan in the 18th and 19th cent. and under Russian control after 1875.

Sa•kha•rov (sä′kə-rôf′, săk′ə-, sä′кнə-rəf), **Andrei Dimitrievich.** 1921–89. Soviet physicist and dissident who won the 1975 Nobel Peace Prize.

Sa•ki (sä′kē). See Hector Hugh **Munro.**

Sak•ka•ra (sə-kär′ə). See **Saqqara.**

sal (săl) *n.* Salt. [ME < OFr. < Lat. *sāl.* See **sal-*.**]

sa•laam (sə-läm′) *n.* **1.** A ceremonious act of deference or obeisance, esp. a low bow made with the right palm on the forehead. **2.** A respectful ceremonial greeting performed esp. in Islamic countries. [Ar. *salām,* peace, salaam < *salima,* to be safe.] **— sa•laam′** *v.*

sal•a•ble also **sale•a•ble** (sā′lə-bəl) *adj.* Offered or suitable for sale; marketable. **— sal′a•bil′i•ty, sal′a•ble•ness** *n.* **— sal′a•bly** *adv.*

sa•la•cious (sə-lā′shəs) *adj.* **1.** Appealing to or stimulating sexual desire. **2.** Lustful; bawdy. [< Lat. *salāx, salāc-,* fond of leaping, lustful < *salīre,* to leap. See **sel-*.**] **— sa•la′cious•ly** *adv.* **— sa•la′cious•ness, sa•lac′i•ty** (sə-lăs′ĭ-tē) *n.*

sal•ad (săl′əd) *n.* **1.a.** A dish consisting of raw green leafy vegetables, often with other raw vegetables, served with a dressing. **b.** The course of a meal consisting of this dish. **2.** A cold dish of chopped fruit, meat, fish, eggs, or other food, usu. prepared with a dressing. **3.** A green vegetable or herb used in salad, esp. lettuce. **4.** A varied mixture. [ME *salade* < OFr., poss. < OProv. *salada* < VLat. **salāta* < fem. p.part. of **salāre,* to salt < Lat. *sāl,* salt. See **sal-*.**]

Word History: The word *salad* takes its origin from the fact that salt was and is an important ingredient of salad dressings. Hence the Vulgar Latin verb **salāre,* "to salt," from Latin *sāl,* "salt," in the past participial form **salāta,* "having been salted," came to mean "salad." The Vulgar Latin word passed into languages descending from it, such as Portuguese (*salada*) and Old Provençal (*salada*). As in the case of so many culinary delights, the English borrowed the word and probably the dish from the French.

salad bar *n.* A counter in a restaurant from which customers may serve themselves salad ingredients and dressings.

salad days *pl.n.* A time of youth, innocence, and inexperience.

salad dressing *n.* A sauce, such as one made of mayonnaise or of oil and vinegar, that is served on salad.

Sal•a•din (săl′ə-dĭn). 1137?–93. Sultan of Egypt and Syria who captured (1187) Jerusalem and defended it during the Third Crusade (1189–92).

Sa•la•do (sə-lä′dō, sä-lä′*th*ō). **1.** Also **Salado del Nor•te** (dĕl nôr′tē). A river of N Argentina rising in the Andes and flowing c. 2,011 km (1,250 mi) to the Paraná R. **2.** A river, c. 1,368 km (850 mi), rising in W Argentina and flowing to the Colorado R.

sa•lal (sə-lăl′) *n.* A small evergreen shrub *(Gaultheria shallon)* native to the Pacific coast of North America and having white or pink flowers clustered in racemes and edible purple-black berries. [Chinook Jargon *sallal* < Chinook *sálal.*]

Sal•a•man•ca (săl′ə-măng′kə, sä′lä-mäng′kä). A city of W-central Spain WNW of Madrid; held by Moors from the 8th to the late 11th cent. Pop. 159,336.

sal•a•man•der (săl′ə-măn′dər) *n.* **1.** Any of various small lizardlike amphibians of the order Caudata, having porous scaleless skin and four, often weak or rudimentary legs. **2.** A mythical creature, generally resembling a lizard, believed capable of living in or withstanding fire. **3.** An object, such as a poker, used in fire or capable of withstanding heat. **4.** *Metall.* A mass of solidified material, largely metallic, left in a blast-furnace hearth. **5.** A portable stove used to heat or dry buildings under construction. [ME *salamandre* < OFr. < Lat. *salamandra* < Gk.] **— sal′a•man′drine** (-drĭn) *adj.*

sa•la•mi (sə-lä′mē) *n., pl.* **-mis.** A highly spiced and salted sausage. [Ital., pl. of *salame,* salami < VLat. **salāmen* < **salāre,* to salt < Lat. *sāl,* salt. See **sal-*.**]

Sal•a•mis[1] (săl′ə-mĭs, sä′lä-mēs′). An island of Greece in the Saronic Gulf E of Athens; site of an offshore naval battle in which the Greeks defeated the Persian fleet in 480 B.C.

Sal•a•mis² (săl′ə-mĭs, sä′lä-mēs′). An ancient city of E Cyprus; traditionally founded c. 1180 B.C.

sal ammoniac *n.* See **ammonium chloride.** [Ult. < Lat. *sāl ammōniacus*, salt of Amen : *sāl*, salt; see SAL + *ammōniacus*, of Amen; see AMMONIA.]

sal•a•ry (săl′ə-rē, săl′rē) *n., pl.* **-ries.** Fixed compensation for services, paid on a regular basis. [ME *salarie* < AN < Lat. *salārium*, money given to Roman soldiers for salt < neut. of *salārius*, of salt < *sāl*, salt. See **sal-*.**] — **sal′a•ried** *adj.*

sa•lat (sə-lät′) *n.* A Muslim prayer service.

Sa•la•zar (săl′ə-zär′, sä′lə-), **Antonio de Oliveira.** 1889–1970. Portuguese dictator (1932–68) who attempted to repress growing opposition in Portugal's African colonies.

Sal•can•tay (săl′kən-tī′, säl′kän-). The highest peak, 6,275.4 m (20,575 ft), of the Cordillera Oriental in S Peru.

sal•chow (săl′kou′) *n. Sports.* A move in figure skating in which the skater jumps from one skate, completes a full rotation, and lands on the other skate. [After Ulrich *Salchow* (1877–1949), Swedish figure skater.]

sale (sāl) *n.* **1.** The exchange of goods or services for an amount of money or its equivalent; the act of selling. **2.** An instance of selling. **3.** An opportunity for selling or being sold; demand. **4.** Availability for purchase: *pets for sale.* **5.** A selling of property to the highest bidder; an auction. **6.** A special disposal of goods at lowered prices: *coats on sale.* **7. sales. a.** Activities involved in selling goods or services. **b.** Gross receipts. [ME < OE *sala* < ON.]

sale•a•ble (sā′lə-bəl) *adj.* Var. of **salable.**

sale-lease•back (sāl′lēs′băk′) *n.* See **leaseback.**

Sa•lem (sā′ləm). **1.** A city of S India SW of Madras. Pop. 361,394. **2.** A city of NE MA NE of Boston; founded 1626 and noted as the site of witchcraft trials (1692). Pop. 38,091. **3.** A town of SE NH E of Nashua. Pop. 25,746. **4.** The cap. of OR, in the NW part on the Willamette R. SSW of Portland; founded c. 1840. Pop. 107,786. **5.** An independent city of SW VA, a suburb of Roanoke. Pop. 23,756.

sal•ep (săl′əp) *n.* A starchy meal ground from the dried roots of various Old World orchids of the genera *Orchis* and *Eulophia,* used for food and formerly as medicine. [Fr. or Sp., both < Ottoman Turk. *sālep* < Ar. *saḥlab*, a kind of orchid.]

sal•er•a•tus (săl′ə-rā′təs) *n.* Sodium or potassium bicarbonate used as a leavening agent; baking soda. [NLat. *sāl āerātus* : Lat. *sāl*, salt; see SAL + NLat. *āerātus*, aerated (< Lat. *āēr*, air; see AIR).]

Sa•ler•no (sə-lûr′nō, sä-lĕr′-). A city of S Italy on the **Gulf of Salerno,** an inlet of the Tyrrhenian Sea. Pop. 157,243.

sales check (sālz) *n.* A slip of paper given by a store to serve as a record or receipt of a purchase or sale.

sales•clerk (sālz′klûrk′) *n.* One who sells goods in a store.

sales•girl (sālz′gûrl′) *n.* A saleswoman.

sales•la•dy (sālz′lā′dē) *n.* A saleswoman.

sales•man (sālz′mən) *n.* A man who sells merchandise in a store or a designated territory. — **sales′man•ship′** *n.*

sales•per•son (sālz′pûr′sən) *n.* A salesman or a saleswoman.

sales•room (sālz′ro͞om′, -ro͝om′) *n.* A room in which items are displayed and offered for sale or auction.

sales tax *n.* A tax levied on the retail price of merchandise and collected by the retailer.

sales•wom•an (sālz′wo͝om′ən) *n.* A woman who sells merchandise in a store or a designated territory.

Sal•ford (sôl′fərd). A borough of NW England on the Manchester Ship Canal adjacent to Manchester. Pop. 247,400.

sali– *pref.* Salt: *salimeter.* [< Lat. *sāl, sal-*, salt. See **sal-*.**]

Sa•li•an (sā′lē-ən, sāl′yən) *adj.* Of or relating to a tribe of Franks who settled in the Rhine region of the Netherlands in the fourth century A.D. — *n.* A Salian Frank. [< LLat. *Salii*, the Salian Franks.]

sal•ic (săl′ĭk) *adj.* Of or relating to certain minerals, such as quartz and the feldspars, that occur in igneous rocks and are rich in silica and alumina. [S(ILICA) + AL(UMINA) + -IC.]

Sa•lic (sā′lĭk, săl′ĭk) also **Sa•lique** (sā′lĭk, săl′ĭk, să-lēk′) *adj.* **1.** Of or relating to the Salian Franks. **2.** Of or relating to the Salic law or the legal code of the Salian Franks. [Fr. *salique* < Med.Lat. *Salicus* < LLat. *Salii*, the Salian Franks.]

sal•i•cin (săl′ĭ-sĭn) *n.* A bitter glucoside, $C_{13}H_{18}O_7$, obtained mainly from the bark of poplar and willow trees and formerly used as an analgesic. [Fr. *salicine* < Lat. *salix, salic-*, willow.]

Salic law *n.* **1.** The legal code of the Salian Franks. **2.** A law, thought to derive from the code of laws of the Salian Franks, prohibiting a woman from succeeding to a throne.

sa•lic•y•late (sə-lĭs′ə-lāt′, -lĭt, săl′ə-sĭl′ĭt) *n.* A salt or an ester of salicylic acid. [SALICYL(IC ACID) + -ATE².]

sal•i•cyl•ic acid (săl′ĭ-sĭl′ĭk) *n.* A white crystalline acid, $C_6H_4(OH)(COOH)$, used in making aspirin, as a preservative, and in the treatment of skin conditions. [< Fr. *salicyle*, the radical of salicylic acid < *salicine*, salicin. See SALICIN.]

sa•li•ence (sā′lē-əns, sāl′yəns) also **sa•li•en•cy** (sā′lē-ən-sē, sāl′yən-) *n., pl.* **-en•ces** also **-en•cies. 1.** The quality or condition of being salient. **2.** A pronounced feature or part.

sa•li•ent (sā′lē-ənt, sāl′yənt) *adj.* **1.** Projecting or jutting beyond a line or surface; protruding. **2.** Strikingly conspicuous; prominent. **3.** Springing; jumping. — *n.* **1.** The area of a military defense, such as a battle line, that projects closest to the enemy. **2.** A projecting angle or part. [Lat. *saliēns, salient-*, pr.part. of *salīre*, to leap. See **sel-*.**] — **sa′li•ent•ly** *adv.* — **sa′li•ent•ness** *n.*

sa•li•en•tian (sā′lē-ĕn′shən) *n.* An amphibian of the order Salientia (formerly Anura or Batrachia), which includes the frogs and toads. [< NLat. *Salientia*, order name < Lat. *saliēns, salient-*, pr.part. of *salīre*, to leap. See SALIENT.] — **sa′li•en′tian** *adj.*

sa•lif•er•ous (sə-lĭf′ər-əs) *adj.* Containing or yielding salt.

sa•lim•e•ter (sə-lĭm′ĭ-tər) or **sa•lom•e•ter** (-lŏm′-) *n.* A hydrometer that indicates the concentration of salt in a solution. — **sal′i•met′ric** (săl′ə-mĕt′rĭk) *adj.* — **sa•lim′e•try** *n.*

sa•li•na (sə-lī′nə, -lē′-) *n.* **1.** A salt marsh, spring, pond, or lake. **2.** An area of land encrusted with salt. **3.** A saltworks. [Sp. < Lat. *salīnae*, salt pits < fem. pl. of *salīnus*, of salt. See SALINE.]

Sa•li•na (sə-lī′nə). A city of central Kansas NNW of Wichita. Pop. 42,303.

Sa•li•nas (sə-lē′nəs). A city of W CA ENE of Monterey on the **Salinas River,** c. 241 km (150 mi). Pop. 108,777.

sa•line (sā′lēn′, -līn′) *adj.* **1.** Of, relating to, or containing salt; salty. **2.** Of or relating to chemical salts. — *n.* **1.** A salt of magnesium or of the alkalis, used as a cathartic. **2.** A saline solution, esp. one that is isotonic with blood. [Lat. *salīnus* < *sāl*, salt. See **sal-*.**] — **sa•lin′i•ty** (sə-lĭn′ĭ-tē) *n.*

Sal•in•ger (săl′ĭn-jər), **J(erome) D(avid).** b. 1919. Amer. writer whose works include *The Catcher in the Rye* (1951).

J.D. Salinger

sal•i•nize (săl′ə-nīz′) *tr.v.* **-nized, -niz•ing, -niz•es.** To treat with salt. — **sal′i•ni•za′tion** (-nĭ-zā′shən) *n.*

sal•i•nom•e•ter (săl′ə-nŏm′ĭ-tər) *n.* **1.** An instrument that uses electrical conductivity to measure the concentration of salt in a solution. **2.** See **salimeter.** — **sal′i•no•met′ric** (-nə-mĕt′rĭk) *adj.* — **sal′i•nom′e•try** *n.*

Sa•lique (sā′lĭk, săl′ĭk, să-lēk′) *adj.* Var. of **Salic.**

Salis•bur•y (sôlz′bĕr′ē, -brē). **1.** A municipal borough of S England NW of Southampton on the edge of **Salisbury Plain,** the site of Stonehenge; chartered 1220. Pop. 35,700. **2.** A city of SE MD S of Dover DE. Pop. 20,592. **3.** A city of central NC SSW of Winston-Salem. Pop. 23,087. **4.** See **Harare.**

Salisbury steak *n.* A patty of ground beef mixed with eggs, milk, onions, and various seasonings and broiled, fried, or baked. [After J.H. *Salisbury* (1823–1905), Amer. physician.]

Sa•lish (sā′lĭsh) also **Sa•lish•an** (-lĭ-shən) *n.* **1.** A family of Native American languages of the northwest United States and British Columbia. **2.** The group of Native American peoples speaking languages of the Salish family. [Southern Interior Salish *se'lish*, Flatheads.] — **Sa′lish•an** *adj.*

sa•li•va (sə-lī′və) *n.* The watery mixture of secretions from the salivary and oral mucous glands that lubricates chewed food, moistens the oral walls, and contains ptyalin. [Lat. *salīva.*]

sal•i•var•y (săl′ə-vĕr′ē) *adj.* **1.** Of, relating to, or producing saliva. **2.** Of or relating to a salivary gland.

salivary gland *n.* A gland that secretes saliva, esp. any of three pairs of large glands, the parotid, submaxillary, and sublingual, that secrete into the mouth.

sallet
Late 15th-century German

sal•i•vate (săl′ə-vāt′) *v.* **-vat•ed, -vat•ing, -vates.** — *intr.* To secrete or produce saliva. — *tr.* To produce excessive salivation in. [Lat. *salīvāre, salīvāt-* < *salīva*, saliva.]

sal•i•va•tion (săl′ə-vā′shən) *n.* **1.** The act or process of secreting saliva. **2.** An abnormally abundant flow of saliva.

Salk (sôlk), **Jonas Edward.** b. 1914. Amer. microbiologist who developed the first effective killed-virus polio vaccine (1954).

Salk vaccine *n.* A polio vaccine consisting of inactivated polioviruses. [After Jonas Edward SALK.]

sal•let (săl′ĭt) *n.* A light late medieval helmet with a brim flaring in the back, sometimes fitted with a visor. [ME < OFr. *sallade* < OSp. *celada* or OItal. *celata*, both prob. < Lat. *caelāta (cassis)*, engraved (helmet), fem. p.part. of *caelāre*, to engrave < *caelum*, chisel. See CAELUM.]

sal•low¹ (săl′ō) *adj.* **-er, -est.** Of a sickly yellowish hue or complexion. — *tr.v.* **-lowed, -low•ing, -lows.** To make sallow. [ME *salowe* < OE *salo.*] — **sal′low•ly** *adv.* — **sal′low•ness** *n.*

sal•low² (săl′ō) *n.* A broad-leaved European willow *(Salix caprea)* having large catkins, which appear before the leaves, and tough wood used to make charcoal. [ME < OE *sealh.*]

Sal•lust (săl′əst). 86?–34? B.C. Roman politician and historian known for his account of the conspiracy of Catiline.

sal•ly (săl′ē) *intr.v.* **-lied, -ly•ing, -lies. 1.** To rush out or leap forth suddenly. **2.** To issue suddenly from a defensive or besieged position to attack an enemy. **3.** To set out on a trip or an excursion. — *n., pl.* **-lies. 1.** A sudden rush forward; a leap. **2.** An assault from a defensive position; a sortie. **3.** A sudden emergence into action or expression; an outburst. **4.** A sudden quick witticism; a quip. **5.** A venturing forth; a jaunt. [< Fr. *saillie*, a sally < OFr. < fem. p.part. of *salir*, to rush forward < Lat. *salīre*, to leap. See **sel-*.**]

sally lunn (lŭn′) *n.* A somewhat sweet bread leavened with yeast. [After *Sally Lunn*, 18th-cent. British baker.]

sally port *n.* A gate in a fortification designed for sorties.

ă pat	oi **boy**
ā **pay**	ou **out**
âr **care**	o͝o **took**
ä **father**	o͞o **boot**
ĕ pet	ŭ cut
ē be	ûr **urge**
ĭ pit	th **thin**
ī **pie**	*th* **this**
îr **pier**	hw **which**
ŏ pot	zh vision
ō **toe**	ə about,
ô **paw**	item

Stress marks:
′ (primary);
′ (secondary), as in
dictionary (dĭk′shə-nĕr′ē)

Sal•ma•cis (săl-mā′sĭs) *n. Gk. Myth.* A nymph who loved Hermaphroditus and was united with him in one body.

sal•ma•gun•di (săl′mə-gŭn′dē) *n., pl.* **-dis. 1.** A salad of chopped meat, anchovies, eggs, and onions, often arranged on lettuce and served with vinegar and oil. **2.** A mixture or an assortment; a potpourri. [Fr. *salmigondis* : prob. < OFr. *salemine*, salted food (< VLat. **salāmen*; see SALAMI) + OFr. *condir*, to season (< Lat. *condīre*; see CONDIMENT).]

sal•mi (săl′mē) *n., pl.* **-mis.** A highly spiced dish consisting of roasted game birds minced and stewed in wine. [Fr. *salmis*, short for *salmigondis*, salmagundi. See SALMAGUNDI.]

salm•on (săm′ən) *n., pl.* **salmon** or **-ons. 1.** Any of various large food and game fishes of the genera *Salmo* and *Oncorhynchus* of northern waters, having pink flesh. **2.** *Color.* A moderate, light, or strong yellowish pink to a moderate reddish orange or light orange. [ME < OFr. *saumon* < Lat. *salmō, salmōn-*. See **sel-***.]

saltbox

salm•on•ber•ry (săm′ən-bĕr′ē) *n.* **1.** Any of several prickly shrubs of the genus *Rubus,* esp. *R. spectabilis* of western North America, having trifoliate leaves and fragrant reddish flowers. **2.** The edible pink berrylike fruit of this plant.

sal•mo•nel•la (săl′mə-nĕl′ə) *n., pl.* **-nel•lae** (-nĕl′ē) or **-nel•las** or **salmonella.** Any of various rod-shaped bacteria of the genus *Salmonella,* many of which are pathogenic, causing food poisoning, typhoid, and paratyphoid fever in human beings. [NLat. *Salmonella*, genus name, after Daniel Elmer *Salmon* (1850–1914), Amer. pathologist.]

sal•mo•nel•lo•sis (săl′mə-nĕ-lō′sĭs) *n., pl.* **-ses** (-sēz′). Infection with salmonellae, characterized by intestinal problems and fever.

salm•o•nid (săm′ə-nĭd, săl′mə-) *adj.* Of, belonging to, or characteristic of the family Salmonidae, which includes the salmon, trout, and whitefish. [< NLat. *Salmōnidae*, family name < *Salmō*, type genus < Lat. *salmō, salmōn-*, salmon. See SALMON.] **— salm′o•nid** *n.*

salm•o•noid (săm′ə-noid′, săl′mə-) *adj.* Of, belonging to, or characteristic of the suborder Salmonoidea, which includes the salmon. **— salm′o•noid′** *n.*

Sal•mon River (săm′ən, săl′mən). A river of central ID rising in the **Salmon River Mountains** and flowing c. 684 km (425 mi) to the Snake R. The mountain range rises to 3,153.7 m (10,340 ft).

salmon trout *n.* Any of various large trouts, esp. the lake trout, the sea trout, or the steelhead.

Sa•lo•me (sə-lō′mē, săl′ə-mā′). In the Bible, the daughter of Herodias and niece of Herod Antipas, who granted her the head of John the Baptist in return for her dancing.

sa•lom•e•ter (sə-lŏm′ĭ-tər) *n.* Var. of **salimeter.**

Sal•o•mon (săl′ə-mən), **Haym.** 1740?–85. Polish-born Amer. financier who helped fund the Continental Army.

sa•lon (sə-lŏn′, săl′ŏn′, să-lôN′) *n.* **1.** A large room, such as a drawing room, used for receiving and entertaining guests. **2.** A periodic gathering of people of social or intellectual distinction. **3.** A hall or gallery for the exhibition of works of art. **4.** A commercial establishment offering a product or service related to fashion: *a beauty salon.* [Fr. < Ital. *salone*, aug. of *sala*, hall, of Gmc. orig.]

Sa•lo•ni•ka (sə-lŏn′ĭ-kə, săl′ə-nē′kə). See **Thessaloníki.**

sa•loon (sə-lo͞on′) *n.* **1.** A place where alcoholic drinks are sold and drunk; a tavern. **2.** A large room or hall for receptions, public entertainment, or exhibitions. **3.** *Naut.* **a.** The officers' dining and social room on a cargo ship. **b.** A large social lounge on a passenger ship. **4.** *Chiefly British.* A sedan automobile. [Fr. *salon*, salon. See SALON.]

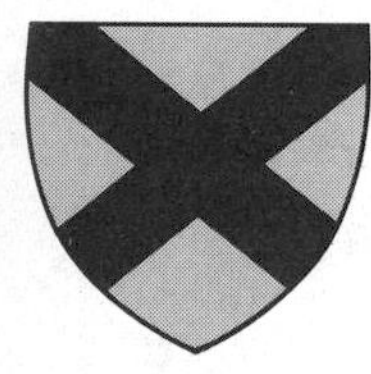

saltire

salp (sălp) also **sal•pa** (săl′pə) *n.* Any of various free-swimming chordates of the genus *Salpa* of warm seas, having a translucent, somewhat flattened keglike body. [< NLat. *Salpa*, genus name < Lat., a kind of stockfish < Gk. *salpē.*] **— sal′pi•form′** (săl′pə-fôrm′) *adj.*

salping– *pref.* Salpinx: *salpingitis.* [< Gk. *salpinx, salping-*, trumpet.]

sal•pin•gec•to•my (săl′pĭn-jĕk′tə-mē) *n., pl.* **-mies.** Surgical removal of the fallopian tube.

sal•pin•gi•tis (săl′pĭn-jī′tĭs) *n.* Inflammation of the fallopian or eustachian tube.

sal•pinx (săl′pĭngks) *n., pl.* **sal•pin•ges** (săl-pĭn′jēz). **1.** The fallopian tube. **2.** The eustachian tube. [NLat. < Gk. *salpinx*, trumpet.] **— sal•pin′gi•an** (-pĭn′jē-ən, -jən) *adj.*

sal•sa (säl′sə) *n.* **1.** A spicy sauce made of tomatoes, onions, and chili peppers, eaten with tortilla chips or served as a garnish. **2.** *Mus.* A popular form of Latin-American dance music. [Am.Sp. < Sp., sauce < OSp. < VLat. **salsa.* See SAUCE.]

sal•si•fy (săl′sə-fē, -fī′) *n., pl.* **-fies. 1.** A European plant *(Tragopogon porrifolius)* having grasslike leaves, purple flower heads, and an edible taproot. **2.** The root of this plant, eaten as a vegetable. Also called regionally *oyster plant* [Fr. *salsifis* < obsolete Ital. *(erba) salsifica.*]

sal soda *n.* A hydrated sodium carbonate used as a cleanser.

salt (sôlt) *n.* **1.** A colorless or white crystalline solid, chiefly sodium chloride, used extensively as a food seasoning and preservative. **2.** A chemical compound formed by replacing all or part of the hydrogen ions of an acid with metal ions or electropositive radicals. **3. salts.** Any of various mineral salts used as laxatives or cathartics. **4. salts.** Smelling salts. **5.** Epsom salts. Often used in the plural. **6.** An element that gives flavor or zest. **7.** Sharp, lively wit. **8.** *Informal.* A sailor, esp. when old or experienced. **9.** A saltcellar. *— adj.* **1.** Containing or filled with salt. **2.** Having a salty taste or smell. **3.** Preserved in salt or a salt solution. **4.a.** Flooded with seawater. **b.** Found in or near such a flooded area. *— tr.v.* **salt•ed, salt•ing, salts. 1.** To add, treat, season, or sprinkle with salt. **2.** To cure or preserve by treating with salt or a salt solution. **3.** To provide salt for (deer or cattle). **4.** To add zest or liveliness to. **5.** To give an appearance of value to by fraudulent means, esp. to place valuable minerals in (a mine) for the purpose of deceiving. ***— phrasal verbs.*** **salt away.** To put aside; save. **salt out.** To separate (a dissolved substance) by adding salt to the solution. ***— idiom.*** **worth (one's) salt.** Efficient and capable. [ME < OE *sealt.* See **sal-***.]

SALT *abbr.* Strategic Arms Limitation Talks.

Sal•ta (säl′tə, -tä). A city of NW Argentina NNE of Córdoba; founded 1582. Pop. 260,744.

salt-and-pep•per (sôlt′ən-pĕp′ər) *adj.* Pepper-and-salt.

sal•ta•rel•lo (săl′tə-rĕl′ō, sôl′-) *n., pl.* **-rel•los** or **-rel•li** (-rĕl′ē). A lively Italian dance with a skipping step at the beginning of each measure. [Ital. < *saltare*, to leap < Lat. *saltāre.* See SALTATION.]

sal•ta•tion (săl-tā′shən, sôl-) *n.* **1.** The act of leaping, jumping, or dancing. **2.** Discontinuous movement, transition, or development. **3.** *Genet.* A single mutation that drastically alters the phenotype. [Lat. *saltātiō, saltātiōn-* < *saltātus*, p.part. of *saltāre*, to leap, freq. of *salīre*, to jump. See SALIENT.]

sal•ta•to•ri•al (săl′tə-tôr′ē-əl, -tōr′-, sôl′-) *adj.* **1.** Of or relating to leaping or dancing. **2.** Adapted for or characterized by leaping.

sal•ta•to•ry (săl′tə-tôr′ē, -tōr′ē, sôl′-) *adj.* **1.** Of, relating to, or adapted for leaping or dancing. **2.** Proceeding by leaps rather than by smooth gradual transitions.

salt•box (sôlt′bŏks′) *n.* A frame house with two stories in front and one in back and a two-part roof with a long rear slope.

salt•bush (sôlt′bo͝osh′) *n.* Any of several salt-tolerant plants of the genus *Atriplex,* esp. *A. hortensis* of Asia, grown for greens or ornament.

salt cake *n.* Impure sodium sulfate used in making paper pulp, soaps and detergents, glass, ceramic glazes, and dyes.

salt•cel•lar (sôlt′sĕl′ər) *n.* A small dish for holding and dispensing salt. [Alteration of ME *salt saler* : *salt*, salt; see SALT + *saler*, saltcellar (< OFr. *saliere* < Med.Lat. *salāria* < Lat., fem. of *salārius*, of salt < *sāl, sal-*, salt; see **sal-***).]

salt dome *n. Geol.* An anticlinal fold with a columnar salt plug at its core.

salt•er (sôl′tər) *n.* **1.** One that manufactures or sells salt. **2.** One that treats meat, fish, or other foods with salt.

salt•ern (sôl′tərn) *n.* A saltworks. [OE *sealtærn* : *sealt*, salt; see SALT + *ærn*, house.]

salt gland *n.* A specialized gland in marine animals that excretes the excess salt taken into the body.

salt grass *n.* Any of various grasses, esp. North American perennial plants of the genus *Distichlis,* that grow in salt marshes and alkaline areas.

Sal•til•lo (säl-tē′yō). A city of NE Mexico SW of Monterrey; founded 1575. Pop. 284,937.

sal•tim•boc•ca (säl′tĭm-bō′kə) *n.* Scallops of veal, rolled and stuffed with sage, spiced ham, and cheese, sautéed and served with a wine sauce. [Ital., contraction of *salta in bocca*, it leaps into the mouth : *salta*, third pers. sing. of *saltare*, to leap (< Lat. *saltāre*, to leap; see SALTATION) + *in*, into (< Lat.; see IN-[2]) + *bocca*, mouth (< Lat. *bucca*, cheek, mouthful).]

sal•tine (sôl-tēn′) *n.* A thin crisp cracker sprinkled with salt.

sal•tire (sôl′tîr′, -tīr′, săl′-) *n. Her.* An ordinary in the shape of a Saint Andrew's cross, formed by the crossing of a bend and a bend sinister. [ME *sawtire* < OFr. *saultoir*, stile < *saulter*, to jump < Lat. *saltāre.* See SALTATION.]

salt•ish (sôl′tĭsh) *adj.* Somewhat salty.

Salt Lake City (sôlt). The cap. of UT, in the N-central part near Great Salt Lake; settled in 1847. Pop. 159,936.

salt lick *n.* **1.** A natural deposit of exposed salt that animals lick. **2.** A block of salt or an artificial medicated saline preparation set out for cattle, sheep, or deer to lick.

salt marsh *n.* Low coastal grassland frequently overflowed by the tide.

salt-marsh caterpillar (sôlt′märsh′) *n.* The larva of a common tiger moth *(Estigmene acrea)* that feeds destructively on various grasses.

Sal•ton Sea (sôl′tən). A saline lake of SE CA in the Imperial Valley, a depression known as the **Salton Sink** until 1905, when flood waters of the Colorado R. formed the lake.

salt•pe•ter (sôlt′pē′tər) *n.* **1.** See **potassium nitrate. 2.** See **sodium nitrate. 3.** See **niter.** [ME *salpetre* < OFr. < Med.Lat. *sālpetrae* : Lat. *sāl*, salt; see **sal-*** + Lat. *petrae*, genitive of *petra*, rock (< Gk.).]

Salt River. 1. A river rising in E AZ and flowing c. 322 km (200 mi) to the Gila R. near Phoenix. **2.** A river rising in NE MO and flowing c. 322 km (200 mi) to the Mississippi R.

salt•shak•er (sôlt′shā′kər) *n.* A container with a perforated top for sprinkling table salt.

salt•wa•ter or **salt-wa•ter** (sôlt′wô′tər, -wŏt′ər) *adj.* **1.** Of or containing salt water. **2.** Inhabiting or occurring in seawater or salt water. **3.** Done or used in salt water.

salt•works (sôlt′wûrks′) *pl.n.* *(used with a sing. or pl. v.)* A place where salt is produced commercially.

salt•wort (sôlt′wûrt′, -wôrt′) *n.* **1.** Any of several Old World coastal plants of the genus *Salsola,* esp. *S. kali,* having awl-shaped prickly leaves. **2.** A strong-smelling succulent New World coastal shrub *(Batis maritima)* and having unisexual flowers and thick flattened leaves.

salt•y (sôl′tē) *adj.* **-i•er, -i•est. 1.** Of, containing, or seasoned with salt. **2.** Suggestive of the sea or sailing life. **3.** Witty; pungent: *salty humor.* **—salt′i•ly** *adv.* **—salt′i•ness** *n.*

sa•lu•bri•ous (sə-lo͞o′brē-əs) *adj.* Conducive or favorable to health or well-being. [< Lat. *salūbris* < *salūs,* health. See **sol-*.**] **—sa•lu′bri•ous•ly** *adv.* **—sa•lu′bri•ous•ness, sa•lu′bri•ty** (-brĭ-tē) *n.*

sa•lu•ki (sə-lo͞o′kē) *n., pl.* **-kis.** Any of an ancient breed of tall slender dog developed in Arabia and Egypt and having a smooth, silky, variously colored coat. [Ar. *salūqīy,* of Saluq, an ancient city of S Arabia.]

sal•u•ret•ic (săl′yə-rĕt′ĭk) *n.* A saluretic drug. *—adj.* Relating to or causing excretion of salt in the urine.

sal•u•tar•y (săl′yə-tĕr′ē) *adj.* **1.** Effecting or designed to effect an improvement; remedial: *salutary advice.* **2.** Favorable to health; wholesome: *a salutary climate.* [ME < OFr. *salutaire* < Lat. *salūtāris* < *salūs, salūt-,* health. See **sol-*.**] **—sal′u•tar′i•ly** (-târ′ə-lē) *adv.* **—sal′u•tar′i•ness** *n.*

sal•u•ta•tion (săl′yə-tā′shən) *n.* **1.a.** A polite expression of greeting or goodwill. **b. salutations.** Greetings indicating respect and affection; regards. **2.** A gesture of greeting, such as a bow. **3.** A word or phrase of greeting used to begin a letter. **—sal′u•ta′tion•al** *adj.*

sa•lu•ta•to•ri•an (sə-lo͞o′tə-tôr′ē-ən, -tōr′-) *n.* The student with the second highest academic rank in a class who delivers the salutatory at graduation exercises.

sa•lu•ta•to•ry (sə-lo͞o′tə-tôr′ē, -tōr′ē) *n., pl.* **-ries.** An opening or welcoming statement, esp. one delivered at graduation exercises. *—adj.* Of, relating to, or expressing a salutation.

sa•lute (sə-lo͞ot′) *v.* **-lut•ed, -lut•ing, -lutes.** *—tr.* **1.** To greet or address with an expression of welcome, goodwill, or respect. **2.** To recognize (a superior) with a gesture prescribed by military regulations, as by raising the hand to the cap. **3.a.** To honor formally and ceremoniously. **b.** To express warm approval of; commend. **4.** To become noticeable to. *—intr.* To make a gesture of greeting or respect. *—n.* **1.** An act of greeting; a salutation. **2.a.** An act or a gesture of welcome, honor, or courteous recognition. **b.** The position of the hand or rifle or the bodily posture of a person saluting a military superior. **3.** A formal military display of honor or greeting, such as the firing of cannon. [ME *saluten* < Lat. *salūtāre* < *salūs, salūt-,* health. See **sol-*.**] **—sa•lut′er** *n.*

sal•va•ble (săl′və-bəl) *adj.* That can be salvaged or saved. [< LLat. *salvāre,* to save. See SALVAGE.]

Sal•va•dor (săl′və-dôr′, säl′və-dôr′). Formerly **Ba•hi•a** (bə-hē′ə, bä-ē′ə). A city of E Brazil on the Atlantic SSW of Recife; founded 1549. Pop. 1,501,981.

Sal•va•do•ran (săl′və-dôr′ən, -dōr′-) or **Sal•va•do•ri•an** (-dôr′ē-ən, -dōr′-) *—adj.* Of or relating to El Salvador or its people or culture. *—n.* A native or inhabitant of El Salvador.

sal•vage (săl′vĭj) *n.* **1.a.** The rescue of a ship, its crew, or its cargo from fire or shipwreck. **b.** The ship, crew, or cargo so rescued. **c.** Compensation given to those who voluntarily aid in such a rescue. **2.a.** The act of saving imperiled property from loss. **b.** The property so saved. **3.** Something saved from destruction or waste and put to further use. *—tr.v.* **-vaged, -vag•ing, -vag•es. 1.** To save from loss or destruction. **2.** To save (discarded or damaged material) for further use. [Obsolete Fr. < OFr. *salvaige,* right of salvage < LLat. *salvāre,* to save < Lat. *salvus,* safe. See **sol-*.**] **—sal′vage•a•bil′i•ty** *n.* **—sal′vage•a•ble** *adj.* **—sal′vag•er** *n.*

sal•va•tion (săl-vā′shən) *n.* **1.a.** Preservation or deliverance from destruction, difficulty, or evil. **b.** A source, means, or cause of such preservation or deliverance. **2.** *Theol.* **a.** Deliverance from the power or penalty of sin; redemption. **b.** The agent or means of such deliverance. [ME < OFr. < LLat. *salvātiō, salvātiōn-* < *salvātus,* p.part. of *salvāre,* to save. See SALVAGE.] **—sal•va′tion•al** *adj.*

Sal•va•tion Army (săl-vā′shən) *n.* An international evangelical and charitable organization founded in 1865 by William Booth as a London revival society and renamed in 1878.

sal•va•tion•ism (săl-vā′shə-nĭz′əm) *n.* Religious doctrine stressing salvation of the soul.

Sal•va•tion•ist (săl-vā′shə-nĭst) *n.* **1.** A member of the Salvation Army. **2. salvationist.** One who preaches salvation; an evangelist. **—sal•va′tion•ist** *adj.*

salve[1] (săv, säv) *n.* **1.** An analgesic or medicinal ointment. **2.** Something that soothes or heals; a balm. **3.** Flattery or commendation. *—tr.v.* **salved, salv•ing, salves. 1.** To soothe or heal with or as if with salve. **2.** To ease the distress or agitation of; assuage. [ME < OE *sealf.*]

salve[2] (sălv) *tr.v.* **salved, salv•ing, salves.** To salvage. [Back-formation < SALVAGE or SALVABLE.] **—sal′vor** *n.*

sal•ver (săl′vər) *n.* A tray for serving food or drinks. [Alteration of Fr. *salve* < Sp. *salva,* salver < *salvar,* to save, taste food to detect poison < LLat. *salvāre,* to save. See SALVAGE.]

sal•ver•form (săl′vər-fôrm′) *adj. Bot.* Of, relating to, or being a gamopetalous corolla having a slender tube and an abruptly expanded limb, as in phlox.

sal•vi•a (săl′vē-ə) *n.* Any of various plants of the genus *Salvia* in the mint family, having opposite leaves, a two-lipped corolla, and two stamens. [Lat. *salvia,* sage. See SAGE[2].]

sal•vif•ic (săl-vĭf′ĭk) *adj.* Able or intending to bring about salvation or redemption. [LLat. *salvificus* : Lat. *salvus,* safe; see SAFE + Lat. *-ficus,* -fic.] **—sal•vif′i•cal•ly** *adv.*

sal•vo[1] (săl′vō) *n., pl.* **-vos** or **-voes. 1.a.** A simultaneous discharge of firearms. **b.** The simultaneous release of a rack of bombs from an aircraft. **c.** These projectiles or bombs. **2.a.** A sudden outburst, as of cheers. **b.** A forceful oral or written assault. [Ital. *salva* < Fr. *salve* < Lat. *salvē,* hail, imper. of *salvēre,* to be in good health < *salvus,* safe. See **sol-*.**]

sal•vo[2] (săl′vō) *n., pl.* **-vos. 1.** A mental provision or reservation. **2.** An expedient for protecting one's reputation or for soothing one's conscience. [Lat. *salvō* (as in Med.Lat. *salvō jure,* saving the right), ablative of *salvus,* safe. See SAFE.]

saluki

sal vo•la•ti•le (vō-lăt′l-ē) *n.* A solution of ammonium carbonate in alcohol or ammonia water, used in smelling salts. [NLat. : Lat. *sāl,* salt + Lat. *volātile,* flying.]

Sal•ween (săl′wēn′). A river of SE Asia rising in E Tibet and flowing c. 2,816 km (1,750 mi) to the Gulf of Martaban.

Salz•burg (sôlz′bûrg′, sälz′-, zälts′bo͝ork′). A city of W-central Austria SW of Linz. Pop. 139,426.

Salz•git•ter (zälts′gĭt′ər). A city of central Germany SE of Hanover; first mentioned c. 1000. Pop. 107,023.

SAM *abbr.* Surface-to-air missile.

Sam. *abbr. Bible.* Samuel.

Sa•ma (sä′mä) *n.* An Austronesian language spoken in the Sulu Archipelago.

Sa•mal (sä-mäl′) *n.* See **Sama.**

Sa•mar (sä′mär′). An island of E-central Philippines NE of Leyte in the **Samar Sea,** an arm of the Pacific.

sam•a•ra (săm′ər-ə, sə-mâr′ə, -mär′ə) *n. Bot.* A dry indehiscent winged fruit, as of the elm or maple. [Lat., elm seed.]

Sa•mar•i•a (sə-măr′ē-ə, -mâr′-). An ancient city of central Palestine in present-day NW Jordan; founded in the 9th cent. B.C. as the cap. of the N kingdom of Israel, which was also known as **Samaria.**

Sa•mar•i•tan (sə-măr′ĭ-tn) *n.* **1.** A native or inhabitant of Samaria. **2.** Often **samaritan.** A Good Samaritan. *—adj.* Of or relating to Samaria or to Samaritans. [ME < OE < LLat. *Samaritānus* < Gk. *Samaritēs* < *Samareia,* Samaria.]

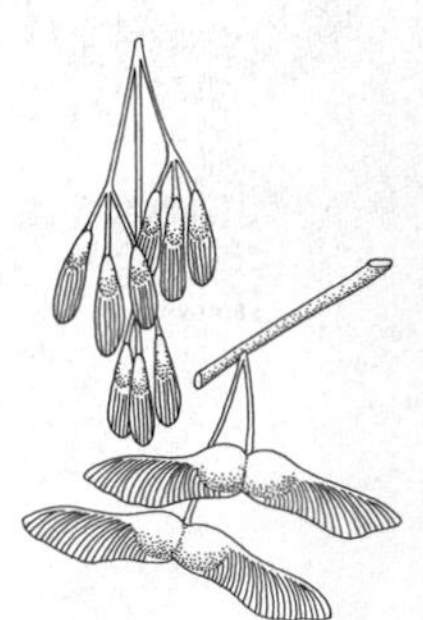

samara
Top: Field maple
Acer campestre
Bottom: Flowering ash
Fraxinus ornus

sa•mar•i•um (sə-mâr′ē-əm, -mär′-) *n. Symbol* **Sm** A metallic rare-earth element found in monazite and bastnaesite and used in ferromagnetic alloys, in infrared absorbing glass, and as a neutron absorber in certain nuclear reactors. Atomic number 62; atomic weight 150.35; melting point 1,072°C; boiling point 1,791°C; specific gravity approx. 7.50; valence 2, 3. See table at **element.** [SAMAR(SKITE) + -IUM.]

Sam•ar•kand (săm′ər-kănd′, sə-mər-känt′). A city of S Uzbekistan SE of the Aral Sea; conquered by Alexander the Great in 329 B.C., destroyed by Genghis Khan c. 1220 A.D., and Tamerlane's cap. after c. 1370. Pop. 371,000.

sa•mar•skite (sə-mär′skīt′, săm′ər-) *n.* A velvet-black mineral that is a complex mixture of several rare-earth metals with niobium and tantalum oxide. [After Col. M. von *Samarski,* 19th-cent. Russian mining official.]

sam•ba (săm′bə, säm′-) *n.* **1.** A Brazilian ballroom dance of African origin. **2.** Music in 4/4 time for performing this dance. *—intr.v.* **-baed, -ba•ing, -bas.** To perform this dance. [Port., poss. of African orig.]

sam•bal (säm′bäl) *n.* A spicy condiment or side dish of southeast Asia that is usu. seasoned with hot chili peppers. [Malay < Tamil *sambhar* < Prakrit *saṃbhārei,* he gathers < Skt. *saṃbhārayati,* he causes to be brought together : *sam,* together; see SANSKRIT + *bharati,* he carries, brings; see **bher-**[1]***.**]

sam•bar also **sam•bur** (săm′bər, säm′-) *n.* A large deer *(Cervus unicolor)* of southern Asia having three-tined antlers and a reddish-brown coat. [Hindi *sāmbar* < Skt. *śambaraḥ.*]

Sam Browne belt (săm′ broun′) *n.* A belt having a shoulder strap that runs diagonally across the chest, worn as part of a military or police uniform. [After Sir *Samuel* James *Browne* (1824–1901), British general.]

sam•bu•ca (săm-bo͞o′kə, säm-bo͞o′kä) *n.* An Italian liqueur made from elderberries and flavored with licorice. [Ital. < fem. of *sambuco,* elder < Lat. *sambūcus.*]

same (sām) *adj.* **1.** Being the very one; identical: *the same boat we rented before.* **2.** Similar in kind, quality, quantity, or degree. **3.** Conforming in every detail: *the same rules as before.* **4.** Being the one previously mentioned or indicated; aforesaid. *—adv.* In the same way. *—pron.* **1.** Someone or something identical with another. **2.** Someone or something previously

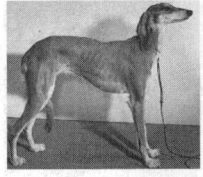

ă **pat**	oi **boy**
ā **pay**	ou **out**
âr **care**	o͝o **took**
ä **father**	o͞o **boot**
ĕ **pet**	ŭ **cut**
ē **be**	ûr **urge**
ĭ **pit**	th **thin**
ī **pie**	*th* **this**
îr **pier**	hw **which**
ŏ **pot**	zh **vision**
ō **toe**	ə **about,**
ô **paw**	**item**

Stress marks:
′ (primary);
′ (secondary), as in
dictionary (dĭk′shə-nĕr′ē)

mentioned or described. [ME < ON *samr.* See **sem-¹*.**]

Usage Note: The expressions *same* and *the same* are sometimes used in place of pronouns such as *it* or *one,* as in *When you have filled out the form, please remit same to this office.* As this example suggests, the usage is associated chiefly with commercial and legal language. But though the usage often does sound stilted, it occurs with some frequency in informal writing, particularly in the phrase *lack of same.*

sa•mekh (sä′mĕk, -məKH) *n.* The 15th letter of the Hebrew alphabet. [Heb. *sāmek.*]

same•ness (sām′nĭs) *n.* **1.** The quality or condition of being the same. **2.** A lack of variety or change; monotony.

same-sex (sām′sĕks′) *adj.* Oriented toward or occurring between members of the same sex: *same-sex relationships.*

sam hill also **Sam Hill** (săm′ hĭl′) *n. Slang.* Used as an intensive: *What in sam hill is going on?* [?]

Sa•mi (sä′mē) *n., pl.* **Sami** or **-mis.** See **Lapp** 1.

samisen

sam•i•sen (săm′ĭ-sĕn′) *n. Mus.* A Japanese instrument resembling a banjo, having a very long neck and three strings played with a plectrum. [J. : *sami,* three + *sen,* string.]

sam•ite (săm′īt′, sā′mīt′) *n.* A heavy silk fabric, often interwoven with gold or silver, worn in the Middle Ages. [ME *samit* < OFr. < Med.Lat. *examitum* < Med.Gk. *hexamiton* < Gk., neut. of *hexamitos,* of six threads : *hexa-,* hexa- + *mitos,* warp thread.]

sa•miz•dat (sä′mĭz-dät′, sə-myĭz-dät′) *n.* **1.a.** The secret publication and distribution of banned literature in the former Soviet Union. **b.** The literature thus produced. **2.** An underground press. [Russ. : *sam,* self; see **sem-¹*** + *izdatel'stvo,* publishing house (< *izdat',* to publish, on the model of *Gosizdát,* State Publishing House : *iz,* from, out of; see **eghs*** + *dat',* to give; see **dō-***).]

sam•let (săm′lĭt) *n.* A young salmon. [SA(L)M(ON) + -LET.]

Sam•ni•um (săm′nē-əm). An ancient country of central and S Italy; conquered by Rome in the Samnite Wars (343–290 B.C.). **—Sam′nite** (săm′nīt′) *adj. & n.*

Sa•mo•a (sə-mō′ə). An island group of the S Pacific ENE of Fiji, divided between **American Samoa** and **Western Samoa;** populated by Polynesians perhaps as early as 1000 B.C.

Sa•mo•an (sə-mō′ən) *adj.* Of or relating to Samoa or its people, language, or culture. —*n.* **1.** A native or inhabitant of Samoa. **2.** The Polynesian language of Samoa.

Sa•mos (sā′mŏs′, săm′ŏs, sä′môs). An island of E Greece in the Aegean Sea off the W coast of Turkey.

sa•mo•sa (sə-mō′sə, sä-mō′sä) *n.* An Indian fried turnover filled with seasoned vegetables or meat. [Urdu.]

Sam•o•set (săm′ə-sĕt′). d. c. 1653. Native American leader who was the first to sell land to the Pilgrims (1625).

Sam•o•thrace (săm′ə-thrās′) or **Sam•o•thrá•ki** (sä′mô-thrä′kē). An island of NE Greece in the NE Aegean Sea off the coast of European Turkey.

samovar

sam•o•var (săm′ə-vär′) *n.* A metal urn with a spigot, used to boil water for tea and traditionally having a chimney and heated by coals. [Russ. : *samo,* self; see **sem-¹*** + *varit',* to boil.]

Sam•o•yed also **Sam•o•yede** (săm′ə-yĕd′, -oi-ĕd′, sə-moi′ĭd) *n.* **1.** See **Nenets. 2.** Any of a breed of medium-sized dog originally developed in northern Eurasia having a thick, long, white or cream-colored coat. [Obsolete Russ. *samoyed* (*samo-,* self; see SAMOVAR + *-ed,* eater; see **ed-***), alteration of Sami *sämm emmne,* land of the Sami.] **—Sam′o•yed′, Sam′o•yed′ic** *adj.*

samp (sămp) *n. New England.* Cornmeal mush. [Narragansett *nasàump.*]

sam•pan (săm′păn′) *n. Naut.* A flatbottom Asian skiff usu. propelled by two oars. [Chin. (Mandarin) *sān bǎn* : *sān,* three + *bǎn,* board.]

sam•phire (săm′fīr′) *n.* **1.** See **glasswort. 2.** An Old World coastal plant *(Crithmum maritimum)* having fleshy compound leaves and small white flowers. [Alteration of Fr. *herbe de Saint Pierre* < *Saint Pierre,* St. Peter.]

sam•ple (săm′pəl) *n.* **1.a.** A portion, piece, or segment that is representative of a whole. **b.** An entity that is representative of a class; a specimen. **2.** *Statistics.* A set of elements drawn from and analyzed to estimate the characteristics of a population. **3.** A sound that has been recorded on a sampler. —*tr.v.* **-pled, -pling, -ples. 1.** To take a sample of, esp. to test or examine by a sample. **2.** To record a sound on a sampler. —*adj.* Serving as a representative or an example. [Partly ME (< AN) and partly short for ME *ensample* (< AN), both < Lat. *exemplum.* See EXAMPLE.]

sampan

sam•pler (săm′plər) *n.* **1.** One who is employed to take and appraise samples, as of a food product. **2.** A mechanical device that is used to obtain and analyze samples. **3.** A decorative piece of cloth embroidered with various designs displaying a variety of stitches. **4.a.** A representative collection or selection. **b.** A variety; an assortment. **5.** An electronic device that digitally records, stores, and manipulates sounds for later use in musical compositions. [Senses 3 and 4, partly ME, model (< AN **essamplur*) and partly short for ME *ensampler* (< AN *ensamplour*), both < LLat. *exemplārium,* model, copy < Lat., copy. See EXEMPLAR.]

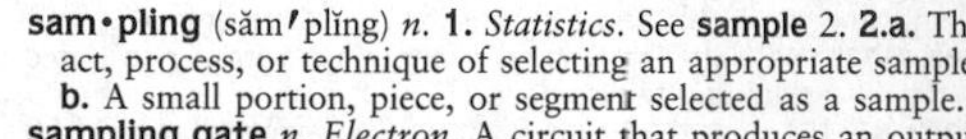

sam•pling (săm′plĭng) *n.* **1.** *Statistics.* See **sample** 2. **2.a.** The act, process, or technique of selecting an appropriate sample. **b.** A small portion, piece, or segment selected as a sample.

sampling gate *n. Electron.* A circuit that produces an output only when first activated by a preliminary pulse.

sam•sa•ra (səm-sär′ə) *n. Hinduism & Buddhism.* The eternal cycle of birth, suffering, death, and rebirth. [Skt. *saṃsāraḥ* : *sam,* together; see **sem-¹*** + *sarati,* it flows.]

Sam•son¹ (săm′sən). In the Bible, the Israelite judge and powerful warrior who was betrayed to the Philistines by Delilah.

Sam•son² (săm′sən) *n.* A man of great physical strength. **—Sam•so′ni•an** (săm-sō′nē-ən) *adj.*

Sam•sun (säm-so͞on′). A city of N Turkey NE of Ankara on **Samsun Bay,** an inlet of the Black Sea. Pop. 198,749.

Sam•u•el (săm′yo͞o-əl) *n. Bible.* **1.** Hebrew judge and prophet of the 11th cent. B.C. who anointed Saul as king. **2.** See table at **Bible.**

Sam•u•el•son (săm′yo͞o-əl-sən, -yo͝ol-sən), **Paul Anthony.** b. 1915. Amer. economist who wrote the classic textbook *Economics* (1948) and won a 1970 Nobel Prize.

sam•u•rai (săm′ə-rī′) *n., pl.* **samurai** or **-rais. 1.** The Japanese feudal military aristocracy. **2.** A professional warrior belonging to this class. [J., warrior.]

san also **-san** (sän) *n.* Used as a courtesy title in Japanese-speaking areas as a suffix to the given name, surname, or title of the person being addressed. [J. *-san.*]

San (sän) *n., pl.* **San** or **Sans. 1.** A member of a traditionally nomadic hunting people of southwest Africa. **2.** Any of the Khoisan languages of the San. [Khoikhoin (Nama) : *sa,* to pick up from the ground + *-n,* common gender pl. suff.]

Sa•na or **Sa•n'a** or **Sa•naa** (sä-nä′). The cap. of Yemen, in the W part; cap. of North Yemen from 1962 to 1990. Pop. 277,800.

San An•dre•as Fault (săn ăn-drā′əs). A major zone of fractures in the earth's crust extending along the coastline of CA from the NW part to the Gulf of California.

San An•ge•lo (ăn′jə-lō′). A city of W-central TX SSW of Abilene. Pop. 84,474.

San An•to•ni•o (ăn-tō′nē-ō′). A city of S-central TX SW of Austin on the **San Antonio River,** flowing c. 322 km (200 mi) to **San Antonio Bay** on the Gulf of Mexico. Pop. 935,933.

san•a•tive (săn′ə-tĭv) *adj.* Having the power to cure; healing or restorative. [ME *sanatif* < OFr. < LLat. *sānātīvus* < Lat. *sānātus,* p.part. of *sānāre,* to heal. See SANATORIUM.]

san•a•to•ri•um (săn′ə-tôr′ē-əm, -tōr′-) also **san•a•tar•i•um** (-târ′ē-əm) *n., pl.* **-to•ri•ums** or **-to•ri•a** (-tôr′ē-ə, -tōr′-) also **-tar•i•ums** or **-tar•i•a** (-târ′ē-ə). **1.** An institution for the treatment of chronic diseases or for medically supervised recuperation. **2.** A resort for improvement or maintenance of health. [< neut. of LLat. *sānātōrius,* curative < Lat. *sānātus,* p.part. of *sānāre,* to heal < *sānus,* healthy.]

san•be•ni•to (săn′bə-nē′tō) *n., pl.* **-tos.** A garment of sackcloth worn at an auto-da-fé of the Spanish Inquisition by those condemned as heretics. [< Sp. *sambenito, San Benito,* St. Benedict of Nursia (< its similarity to the scapular supposedly introduced by him).]

San Be•ni•to (bə-nē′tō). A city of S TX N of Brownsville. Pop. 20,125.

San Ber•nar•di•no (bûr′nə-dē′nō, -nər-). A city of S CA E of Los Angeles. Pop. 164,164.

San Bernardino Mountains. A mountain range of S CA in the Coast Ranges S of the Mojave Desert rising to 3,507.2 m (11,499 ft).

San Bernardino Pass. A pass, about 2,065 m (6,770 ft), through the Lepontine Alps in SE Switzerland.

San Blas (săn bläs′, sän bläs′), **Gulf of.** An inlet of the Caribbean Sea on the N coast of Panama E of the Panama Canal.

San Bru•no (săn bro͞o′nō). A city of W CA, a suburb of San Francisco on San Francisco Bay. Pop. 38,961.

San Car•los (kär′ləs). A city of W CA SE of San Francisco. Pop. 26,167.

San Cle•men•te (klə-mĕn′tē). A city of S CA on the Pacific SE of Long Beach. Pop. 41,100.

San Cris•tó•bal (săn krĭs-tō′bəl, sän′ krē-stô′väl). A city of extreme W Venezuela near the Colombian border SSW of Maracaibo; founded 1561. Pop. 280,000.

sanc•ti•fy (săngk′tə-fī′) *tr.v.* **-fied, -fy•ing, -fies. 1.** To set apart for sacred use; consecrate. **2.** To make holy; purify. **3.** To give religious sanction to, as with a vow. **4.** To give social or moral sanction to. **5.** To make productive of holiness or blessing. [ME *sanctifien,* alteration of *seintefien* < OFr. *saintifier* < LLat. *sānctificāre* : Lat. *sānctus,* holy < p.part. of *sancīre,* to consecrate; see **sak-*** + Lat. *-ficāre,* -fy.] **—sanc′ti•fi•ca′tion** (-fĭ-kā′shən) *n.* **—sanc′ti•fi′er** *n.*

sanc•ti•mo•ni•ous (săngk′tə-mō′nē-əs) *adj.* Feigning piety or righteousness. **—sanc′ti•mo′ni•ous•ly** *adv.* **—sanc′ti•mo′ni•ous•ness** *n.*

sanc•ti•mo•ny (săngk′tə-mō′nē) *n.* Feigned piety or righteousness; hypocritical devoutness or high-mindedness. [Obsolete Fr. *sanctimonie* < Lat. *sānctimōnia,* sacredness < *sānctus,* holy. See SANCTIFY.]

sanc•tion (săngk′shən) *n.* **1.** Authoritative permission or approval that makes a course of action valid. **2.** Support or encouragement, as from public opinion. **3.** A consideration, an influence, or a principle that dictates an ethical choice. **4.a.** A law or decree. **b.** The penalty for noncompliance specified in a law or decree. **5.** A penalty, specified or in the form of moral pressure, that acts to ensure compliance or conformity. **6.** A coercive measure adopted usu. by several nations acting together against a nation violating international law. — *tr.v.* **-tioned, -tion•ing, -tions. 1.** To give official authorization or approval to. **2.** To encourage or tolerate by indicating approval. See Syns at **approve.** [ME, enactment of a law < OFr., ecclesiastical decree < Lat. *sānctiō, sānctiōn-*, binding law, penal sanction < *sānctus*, holy. See SANCTIFY.]

sanc•ti•ty (săngk′tĭ-tē) *n., pl.* **-ties. 1.** Holiness of life or disposition; saintliness. **2.** The quality or condition of being considered sacred; inviolability. **3.** Something considered sacred. [ME *saunctite* < OFr. *sainctite* < Lat. *sānctitās* < *sānctus*, sacred. See SANCTIFY.]

sanc•tu•ar•y (săngk′cho͞o-ĕr′ē) *n., pl.* **-ies. 1.a.** A sacred place, such as a church, temple, or mosque. **b.** The holiest part of a sacred place. **2.a.** A sacred place, such as a church, where fugitives formerly were immune to arrest. **b.** Immunity to arrest afforded by a sanctuary. **3.** A place of refuge or asylum. **4.** A reserved area in which animals, esp. wild ones, are protected from molestation. [ME < OFr. *saintuarie* < LLat. *sānctuārium* < Lat. *sānctus*, sacred. See SANCTIFY.]

sanc•tum (săngk′təm) *n., pl.* **-tums** or **-ta** (-tə). **1.** A sacred or holy place. **2.** A private place where one is free from intrusion. [LLat. *sānctum* < Lat., neut. of *sānctus*, sacred. See SANCTIFY.]

sanctum sanc•to•rum (săngk-tôr′əm, -tōr′-) *n.* **1.** *Judaism.* The innermost shrine of a tabernacle and temple; the holy of holies. **2.** An inviolably private place. [LLat. *sānctum sānctōrum* : *sānctum*, holy place + *sānctōrum*, genitive pl. of *sānctum*, holy place.]

Sanc•tus (săngk′təs) *n., pl.* **-tus•es.** A hymn of praise sung at the end of the Preface in many Eucharistic liturgies. [ME < LLat. *Sānctus* < Lat. *sānctus*, holy. See SANCTIFY.]

sand (sănd) *n.* **1.a.** Small loose grains of worn or disintegrated rock. **b.** *Geol.* A sedimentary material, finer than a granule and coarser than silt, with grains between 0.06 and 2.0 millimeters in diameter. **2.** A tract of land covered with sand, as a beach. Often used in the plural. **3.a.** The sand in an hourglass. **b. sands.** Moments of allotted time or duration. **4.** *Slang.* Courage; stamina. **5.** *Color.* A light grayish brown to yellowish gray. — *tr.v.* **sand•ed, sand•ing, sands. 1.** To sprinkle or cover with or as if with sand. **2.** To polish or scrape with sand or sandpaper. **3.** To mix with sand. **4.** To fill up (a harbor) with sand. [ME < OE.]

Sand (sănd, säNd), **George.** Amandine Aurore Lucie Dupin. 1804–76. French writer whose works include *Lélia* (1833).

san•dal¹ (săn′dl) *n.* **1.** A shoe consisting of a sole fastened to the foot by thongs or straps. **2.** A low-cut shoe fastened to the foot by an ankle strap. **3.** A rubber overshoe cut very low and covering little more than the sole of the shoe. **4.** A strap or band for fastening a low shoe or slipper on the foot. [ME < OFr. *sandale* < Lat. *sandalium* < Gk. *sandalion*, dim. of *sandalon*, sandal.] — **san′daled** *adj.*

san•dal² (săn′dl) *n.* Sandalwood. [ME < OFr. *sandale* (poss. via LGk. *santalon*) < Ar. *ṣandal* < Skt. *candanam.*]

san•dal•wood (săn′dl-wo͝od′) *n.* **1.** Any of several tropical Asian trees of the genus *Santalum*, esp. *S. album*, having yellowish heartwood used in wood carving and yielding an oil used in perfumery. **2.** The wood of any of these trees. **3.** *Color.* A light to moderate or grayish brown.

san•da•rac (săn′də-răk′) *n.* **1.** A coniferous evergreen tree *(Tetraclinis articulata)* of Spain and northern Africa having scalelike leaves and bark that yields a resin used in varnishes. **2.** The resin of this tree. [ME *sandaracha* < Lat., red pigment < Gk. *sandarakē*, realgar.]

sand•bag (sănd′băg′) *n.* A bag filled with sand and used as ballast, in the formation of protective walls, or as a weapon. — *tr.v.* **-bagged, -bag•ging, -bags. 1.** To put sandbags in or around. **2.a.** To hit with or as if with a sandbag. **b.** *Slang.* To treat severely or unjustly. **c.** *Slang.* To force by crude means; coerce. — **sand′bag′ger** *n.*

sand•bank (sănd′băngk′) *n.* A ridge of sand forming a mound, shoal, or hillside.

sand•bar (sănd′bär′) *n.* A ridge of sand formed in a river or along a shore by the action of waves or currents.

sand•blast (sănd′blăst′) *n.* **1.a.** A blast of air or steam carrying sand at high velocity to etch glass or clean stone or metal surfaces. **b.** A machine used to apply such a blast. **2.** A strong wind carrying sand. — *tr.v.* **-blast•ed, -blast•ing, -blasts.** To apply a sandblast to. — **sand′blast′er** *n.*

sand-blind (sănd′blīnd′) *adj.* Having poor vision; partially blind. [ME < OE **sāmblind* : *sām-*, half; see **sēmi-*** + *blind*, blind; see BLIND.] — **sand′blind′ness** *n.*

sand•box (sănd′bŏks′) *n.* **1.** A low box filled with sand for children to play in. **2.** A litter box, esp. for a cat.

sandbox tree *n.* A tropical American tree *(Hura crepitans)* having milky juice, a spiny trunk, and large woody seed capsules that split explosively when ripe. [So called because the capsules were formerly used to hold sand for drying ink.]

sand•bur (sănd′bûr′) *n.* **1.** Any of several grasses of the genus *Cenchrus*, esp. *C. tribuloides*, found in eastern and tropical America and having a burlike envelope surrounding several one-grained spikelets. **2.** This burlike envelope.

Sand•burg (sănd′bûrg′, săn′-), **Carl.** 1878–1967. Amer. writer known esp. for his free verse celebrating American life.

sand-cast (sănd′kăst′) *tr.v.* **-cast, -cast•ing, -casts.** To make (a casting) by pouring molten metal into a sand mold.

sand casting *n.* A casting made in a mold of sand.

sand•cas•tle (sănd′kăs′əl) *n.* **1.** A castlelike structure built of wet sand. **2.** Something that lacks substance or significance.

sand crack *n.* A fissure in the side of a horse's hoof, often causing lameness.

sand dab *n.* Any of several small food fishes of the genus *Citharichthys* of Pacific waters, related to the flounders.

sand dollar *n.* Any of various thin circular echinoderms of the class Echinoidea, esp. *Echinarachnius parma*, of sandy ocean bottoms of the northern Atlantic and Pacific.

sand eel *n.* See **sand lance.**

sand•er (săn′dər) *n.* One that sands, esp.: **a.** A device that spreads sand on roads. **b.** Such a device together with the truck that carries it. **c.** A machine having a powered abrasive-covered disk or belt, used for smoothing or polishing surfaces.

sand•er•ling (săn′dər-lĭng) *n.* A small shore bird *(Crocethia alba)* related to the sandpipers and having gray and white plumage. [Perh. < SAND + -LING¹.]

sand•fish (sănd′fĭsh′) *n., pl.* **sandfish** or **-fish•es. 1.** Any of various marine fishes that live or burrow in sandy or muddy bottoms. **2.** A slender fish *(Gonorhynchus gonorhynchus)* of the Pacific and Indian oceans having an angular snout.

sand flea *n.* **1.** Any of various small crustaceans that live on sandy beaches. **2.** See **chigoe** 1.

sand fly *n.* Any of various small biting flies of the genus *Phlebotomus* of tropical areas, some of which transmit diseases.

sand•fly fever (sănd′flī′) *n.* A mild viral disease transmitted by the bite of the sand fly *(Phlebotomus papatasii)*, characterized by fever, malaise, eye pain, and headache.

sand grouse *n.* Any of various pigeonlike birds of the genus *Pterocles* and related genera of arid and semiarid regions.

san•dhi (săn′dē, sän′-) *n. Ling.* Modification of the sound of a morpheme in certain phonetic contexts, as the difference between the pronunciation of *don't* in *don't you* and in *don't we.* [Skt. *saṃdhiḥ*, union, sandhi : *sam*, together; see **sem-¹*** + *dadhāti, dhī-*, he places; see **dhē-*.**]

sand•hill crane (sănd′hĭl′) *n.* A North American crane *(Grus canadensis)* having gray plumage and a bald red forehead.

sand•hog (sănd′hôg′, -hŏg′) *n. Slang.* A laborer who works inside a caisson, as in the construction of underwater tunnels.

sand hopper *n.* See **beach flea.**

Sand•hurst (sănd′hûrst′). A village of S-central England SE of Reading; site of the Royal Military Academy.

San Di•e•go (săn dē-ā′gō). A city of S CA on **San Diego Bay,** an inlet of the Pacific Ocean. Pop. 1,110,549.

San Di•mas (dē′məs). A city of S CA E of Los Angeles. Pop. 32,397.

S & L *abbr.* Savings and loan association.

sand lance *n.* Any of several small slender marine fishes of the genus *Ammodytes* that often burrow in sand.

sand lily *n.* A low-growing plant *(Leucocrinum montanum)* of the western United States having grasslike leaves and fragrant white star-shaped flowers.

sand•lot (sănd′lŏt′) *n. Sports & Games.* A vacant lot used esp. by children for unorganized sports and games. — *adj.* Of, relating to, or played in a sandlot. — **sand′lot′ter** *n.*

S & M or **s & m** *abbr. Psychol.* Sadomasochism.

sand•man (sănd′măn′) *n.* A character in fairy tales and folklore who makes children sleep by sprinkling sand in their eyes.

sand painting *n.* **1.** A ceremonial design of the Navajo and Pueblo peoples made by trickling colored sand, pollen, or powder onto a base of neutral sand. **2.** The art of making designs with colored sand.

sand•pa•per (sănd′pā′pər) *n.* Heavy paper coated on one side with sand or other abrasive material and used for smoothing surfaces. — *tr.v.* **-pered, -per•ing, -pers.** To rub with or as if with sandpaper. — **sand′pa′per•y** *adj.*

sand pear *n.* **1.** A Chinese tree *(Pyrus pyrifolia)* of the rose family, having edible globose fruit. **2.** The fruit of this plant.

sand•pi•per (sănd′pī′pər) *n.* Any of various small wading birds of the family Scolopacidae, usu. having a long bill with which it feeds in mud and sand.

sand•pit (sănd′pĭt′) *n.* A large deep pit in sandy ground from which sand is dug.

sand shark *n.* A shark of the genus *Carcharias*, esp. *C. taurus*, of shallow temperate and tropical waters of the Atlantic.

sand•spur (sănd′spûr′) *n.* See **sandbur.**

sand•stone (sănd′stōn′) *n.* A sedimentary rock formed by the consolidation and compaction of sand and held together by a natural cement, such as silica.

sand•storm (sănd′stôrm′) *n.* A strong wind carrying clouds of sand and dust through the air.

George Sand

Carl Sandburg

sand dollar
Five-holed keyhole urchin
Mellita quinquiesperforata

ă pat	oi boy
ā pay	ou out
âr care	o͝o took
ä father	o͞o boot
ĕ pet	ŭ cut
ē be	ûr urge
ĭ pit	th thin
ī pie	*th* this
îr pier	hw which
ŏ pot	zh vision
ō toe	ə about, item
ô paw	

Stress marks:
′ (primary);
′ (secondary), as in
dictionary (dĭk′shə-nĕr′ē)

sand table *n.* **1.** A table with raised edges, used for holding sand for children's play. **2.** A table on which a sand relief model of terrain is built for the study of military maneuvers.

sand trap *n. Sports.* A hazard on a golf course consisting of a depression partly filled with sand.

San•dus•ky (sən-dŭs′kē, săn-). A city of N OH W of Cleveland on **Sandusky Bay,** an inlet of Lake Erie. The **Sandusky River,** c. 241 km (150 mi), flows into the bay. Pop. 29,764.

sand verbena *n.* Any of several herbs of the genus *Abronia* of western North America, having fragrant flowers grouped in long-stalked heads.

sand viper *n.* See **horned viper.**

sandwich board

sand•wich (sănd′wĭch, săn′-) *n.* **1.a.** Two or more slices of bread with a filling such as cheese placed between them. **b.** A partly split long or round roll with a filling. **c.** One slice of bread covered with a filling. **2.** Something resembling a sandwich. — *tr.v.* **-wiched, -wich•ing, -wich•es. 1.** To make into or as if into a sandwich. **2.** To insert (one thing) tightly between two others esp. of differing character or quality. [After John Montagu, 4th Earl of *Sandwich* (1718–92).]

Sand•wich (sănd′wĭch′, săn′-). A municipal borough of SE England N of Dover; one of the Cinque Ports. Pop. 4,227.

sandwich board *n.* Two large boards bearing placards, hinged at the top and hung over the shoulders with one board in front and the other behind, used for picketing or advertising.

Sandwich Islands. See **Hawaiian Islands.**

sandwich man *n.* A man who pickets or advertises by carrying a sandwich board.

sand•worm (sănd′wûrm′) *n.* Any of various segmented worms, esp. of the genera *Nereis* and *Arenicola,* generally inhabiting coastal mud or sand and often used as fishing bait.

sand•wort (sănd′wûrt′, -wôrt′) *n.* Any of numerous low-growing herbs of the genus *Arenaria,* having small, usu. white flowers often grouped in cymose clusters.

sand•y (săn′dē) *adj.* **-i•er, -i•est. 1.** Covered with, full of, or consisting of sand. **2.** Having characteristics similar to sand. **3.** *Color.* Of the color of sand; light yellowish brown. — **sand′i•ness** *n.*

Margaret Sanger

Sand•y or **Sand•y City** (săn′dē). A city of N-central Utah, a suburb of Salt Lake City. Pop. 75,058.

Sandy Hook. A low peninsula of E NJ at the entrance to Lower New York Bay separating **Sandy Hook Bay** from the Atlantic Ocean.

sane (sān) *adj.* **san•er, san•est. 1.** Of sound mind; mentally healthy. **2.** Having or showing sound judgment; reasonable. [Lat. *sānus,* healthy.] — **sane′ly** *adv.* — **sane′ness** *n.*

San Fer•nan•do (săn fər-năn′dō). **1.** (*also* sän′ fĕr-nän′dô). A city of S Spain, a seaport and suburb of Cádiz on the Gulf of Cádiz. Pop. 76,101. **2.** A city of S CA in the San Fernando Valley surrounded by Los Angeles. Pop. 22,580.

San Fernando Valley. A fertile valley of S CA NW of central Los Angeles; first explored by the Spanish in 1769.

San•ford (săn′fərd). A city of central FL NNE of Orlando. Pop. 32,387.

Sanford, Edward Terry. 1865–1930. Amer. jurist; associate justice of the U.S. Supreme Court (1923–30).

Sanford, Mount. A mountain, 4,952.3 m (16,237 ft), of S AK in the Wrangell Mts. NE of Anchorage.

San•for•ized (săn′fə-rīzd′). A trademark used for fabric preshrunk by a patented mechanical process.

San Marino

San Fran•cis•co (frən-sĭs′kō). A city of W CA on a peninsula between the Pacific and **San Francisco Bay,** an inlet of the Pacific; founded by the Spanish as a presidio and mission in 1776. Pop. 723,959. — **San Fran•cis′can** (-kən) *n.*

San Francisco Peaks also **San Francisco Mountains.** A group of mountains rising to 3,853.1 m (12,633 ft) in N-central AZ N of Flagstaff.

sang (săng) *v.* A p.t. of **sing.**

San Ga•bri•el (gā′brē-əl). A city of S CA, a suburb of Los Angeles. Pop. 37,120.

San Gabriel Mountains. A mountain range of S CA E and NE of Los Angeles rising to 3,074.4 m (10,080 ft).

San•ga•mon (săng′gə-mən). A river of central IL flowing c. 402 km (250 mi) SW and W to the Illinois R.

san•ga•ree (săng′gə-rē′) *n.* **1.** A sweet chilled alcoholic beverage spiced with grated nutmeg. **2.** See **sangria.** [Alteration of Sp. *sangría,* sangria. See SANGRIA.]

Sang•er (săng′ər), **Frederick.** b. 1918. British biochemist who won a 1958 Nobel Prize for determining the order of amino acids in insulin and shared a 1980 Nobel Prize for developing methods for mapping DNA.

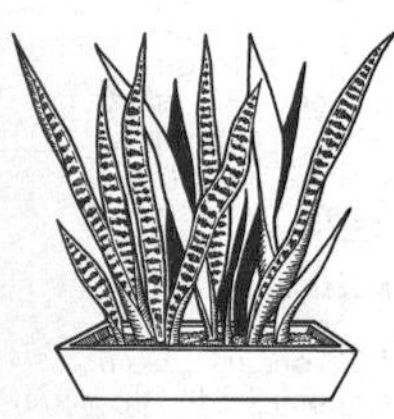
sansevieria

Sanger, Margaret Higgins. 1883–1966. Amer. nurse who founded (1929) the organization that became the Planned Parenthood Federation (1942).

sang-froid (säN-frwä′) *n.* Coolness and composure, esp. in trying circumstances. [Fr. : *sang,* blood (< OFr. < Lat. *sanguīs*) + *froid,* cold (< OFr. < VLat. **frigidus,* alteration of Lat. *frīgidus;* see FRIGID).]

San•gre de Cris•to Mountains (săng′grē dē krĭs′tō). A range of the S Rocky Mts. extending from S-central CO to N-central NM and rising to 4,375.2 m (14,345 ft).

san•gri•a (săng-grē′ə, săn-) *n.* A cold drink made of red or white wine mixed with brandy, sugar, fruit juice, and soda water. [Sp. *sangría,* act of bleeding, sangria < *sangre,* blood < Lat. *sanguīs, sanguin-.*]

san•guic•o•lous (săng-gwĭk′ə-ləs) *adj.* Living in the blood: *a sanguicolous parasite.* [Lat. *sanguīs,* blood + -COLOUS.]

san•gui•nar•i•a (săng′gwə-nâr′ē-ə) *n.* The bloodroot. [NLat. *Sanguinaria,* genus name < Lat. *(herba) sanguināria,* a plant that stanches blood, fem. of *sanguinārius,* sanguinary. See SANGUINARY.]

san•gui•nar•y (săng′gwə-nĕr′ē) *adj.* **1.** Accompanied by bloodshed. **2.** Eager for bloodshed; bloodthirsty. **3.** Consisting of blood. [Lat. *sanguinārius* < *sanguīs, sanguin-,* blood.] — **san′gui•nar′i•ly** (-nâr′ə-lē) *adv.*

san•guine (săng′gwĭn) *adj.* **1.a.** *Color.* Of the color of blood; red. **b.** Of a healthy, reddish color; ruddy: *a sanguine complexion.* **2.** *Archaic.* **a.** In medieval physiology, having blood as the dominant humor. **b.** Having the temperament and ruddy complexion once thought to be characteristic of this humor; passionate. **3.** Cheerfully confident; optimistic. [ME < OFr. *sanguin* < Lat. *sanguineus* < *sanguīs, sanguin-,* blood.] — **san′guine•ly** *adv.* — **san′guine•ness, san•guin′i•ty** *n.*

san•guin•e•ous (săng-gwĭn′ē-əs) *adj.* **1.** Relating to or involving blood or bloodshed. **2.** *Color.* Having the color of blood; blood-red.

san•guin•o•lent (săng-gwĭn′ə-lənt) *adj.* Mixed or tinged with blood. [Lat. *sanguinolentus,* full of blood : *sanguīs, sanguin-,* blood + *-olentus,* abounding in.]

San•hed•rin (săn-hĕd′rĭn, -hē′drĭn, sän-) *n.* The highest judicial and ecclesiastical council of the ancient Jewish nation, composed of from 70 to 72 members. [Heb. *sanhedhrîn* < Gk. *sunedrion,* council < *sunedros,* sitting in council : *sun-,* syn- + *hedra,* seat; see **sed-*.**]

San•i•bel Island (săn′ə-bəl). An island of SW FL in the Gulf of Mexico SW of Fort Myers.

san•i•cle (săn′ĭ-kəl) *n.* Any of various plants of the genus *Sanicula,* having usu. compound leaves and formerly used as an astringent. [ME < OFr. < Med.Lat. *sānicula,* prob. < Lat. *sānus,* healthy.]

san•i•dine (săn′ĭ-dēn′, -dĭn) *n.* A glassy variety of orthoclase feldspar, known as moonstone when translucent. [Gk. *sanis, sanid-,* board (< its flat crystals) + -INE^2.]

sa•ni•es (sā′nē-ēz′) *n., pl.* **sanies.** A thin fetid greenish fluid consisting of serum and pus discharged from a wound, an ulcer, or a fistula. [Lat. *saniēs.*] — **sa′ni•ous** (-əs) *adj.*

sanit. *abbr.* **1.** Sanitary. **2.** Sanitation.

san•i•tar•i•an (săn′ĭ-târ′ē-ən) *n.* A public health or sanitation expert.

san•i•tar•i•um (săn′ĭ-târ′ē-əm) *n., pl.* **-i•ums** or **-i•a** (-ē-ə). See **sanatorium.** [NLat. < Lat. *sānitās,* health. See SANITY.]

san•i•tar•y (săn′ĭ-tĕr′ē) *adj.* **1.** Of or relating to health. **2.** Free from elements, such as filth, that endanger health; hygienic. [Fr. *sanitaire* < Lat. *sānitās,* health. See SANITY.] — **san′i•tar′i•ly** (-târ′ə-lē) *adv.*

sanitary engineer *n.* An engineer specializing in the maintenance of urban environmental conditions conducive to the preservation of public health. — **sanitary engineering** *n.*

sanitary landfill *n.* Rehabilitated land in which garbage and trash have been buried; a landfill.

sanitary napkin *n.* A disposable pad of absorbent material worn to absorb menstrual flow.

san•i•ta•tion (săn′ĭ-tā′shən) *n.* **1.** Formulation and application of measures designed to protect public health. **2.** Disposal of sewage. [SANIT(ARY) + -ATION.]

sanitation worker *n.* A person employed, as by a municipality or private company, to collect and dispose of garbage.

san•i•tize (săn′ĭ-tīz′) *tr.v.* **-tized, -tiz•ing, -tiz•es. 1.** To make sanitary, as by disinfecting. **2.** To make more acceptable by removing unpleasant or offensive features from: *sanitized language.* — **san′i•ti•za′tion** (-tĭ-zā′shən) *n.*

san•i•ty (săn′ĭ-tē) *n.* **1.** The quality or condition of being sane; soundness of mind. **2.** Soundness of judgment or reason. [ME *sanite,* health < OFr. < Lat. *sānitās* < *sānus,* healthy.]

San Ja•cin•to (jə-sĭn′tō). A river of SE TX flowing c. 209 km (130 mi) into Galveston Bay. The final battle of the Texas Revolution was fought on its banks (Apr. 21, 1836).

San Joa•quin (wô-kēn′, wä-). A river of central CA rising in the Sierra Nevada and flowing c. 515 km (320 mi) W and NW to form a large delta with the Sacramento R. The **San Joaquin Valley** is a fertile irrigated agricultural region.

San Jo•se (hō-zā′). A city of W CA SE of San Francisco; founded 1777. Pop. 782,248.

San Jo•sé (sän′ hô-sĕ′). The cap. of Costa Rica, in the central part; settled c. 1736. Pop. 277,800.

San Jose scale *n.* A destructive scale insect *(Aspidiotus perniciosus)* that damages fruit trees and fruit-bearing plants.

San Juan (săn wän′, hwän′). **1.** A city of NW Argentina W of Córdoba; founded 1562. Pop. 310,000. **2.** The cap. of Puerto Rico, on the NE coast; first settled (1508–09) by Ponce de León. Pop. 424,600.

San Juan Cap•is•tra•no (kăp′ĭ-strä′nō). A city of S CA SE of Santa Ana; founded as a mission in 1776. Pop. 26,183.

San Juan Hill. An elevation in E Cuba near Santiago de Cuba;

captured by Cuban and U.S. forces on Jul. 1, 1898, during the Spanish-American War.

San Juan Islands. An archipelago of NW WA off the SE coast of Vancouver I. N of Puget Sound.

San Juan Mountains. A range of the Rocky Mts. in SW CO rising to 4,364.2 m (14,309 ft).

San Juan River. A river rising in S CO and flowing c. 579 km (360 mi) to the Colorado R. in SE UT.

sank (săngk) *v.* A p.t. of **sink.**

San•khya (säng′kyə) *n. Hinduism.* A system of Hindu philosophy based on a dualism involving the ultimate principles of soul and potential matter. [Skt. *sāṁkhya-*, based on enumeration, Sankhya < *saṁkhyā*, enumeration : *sam*, together; see SANDHI + *khyāti*, he tells.]

Sankt Gal•len (zängkt gä′lən) also **Saint Gall** (sānt gôl′, gäl′, săn gäl′). A city of NE Switzerland E of Zurich; developed around an abbey founded in the 7th cent. Pop. 73,500.

San•ku•ru (säng-ko͝or′o͞o). A river of S and central Zaire flowing c. 1,207 km (750 mi) WNW to the Kasai R.

San Le•an•dro (săn lē-ăn′drō). A city of W CA SE of Oakland. Pop. 68,223.

San Lu•cas (săn lo͞o′kəs, sän lo͞o′käs), **Cape.** A cape of W Mexico at the S tip of Baja California.

San Lu•is O•bis•po (săn lo͞o′ĭs ə-bĭs′pō). A city of SW CA NW of Santa Barbara; orig. founded in 1772. Pop. 41,958.

San Luis Peak. A mountain, 4,274.3 m (14,014 ft), in the San Juan Mts. of SW CO.

San Lu•is Po•to•sí (sän lo͞o-ēs′ pô′tô-sē′). A city of central Mexico NE of León. Pop. 362,371.

San Mar•cos (săn mär′kəs). **1.** A city of S CA NNW of San Diego. Pop. 38,974. **2.** A city of S-central TX NE of San Antonio. Pop. 28,743.

San Ma•ri•no (mə-rē′nō). A country in the Apennines surrounded by Italy; traditionally founded in the 4th cent. A.D. and the world's smallest republic. The city of **San Marino** (pop. 4,628) is its cap.

San Mar•tín (săn mär-tēn′, sän), **José de.** 1778–1850. Argentine revolutionary leader who played a major part in expelling the Spanish from Chile (1818) and Peru (1821).

San Ma•te•o (săn mə-tā′ō). A city of W CA SSE of San Francisco. Pop. 85,486.

San Mi•guel de Tu•cu•mán (săn′ mĭ-gĕl′ də to͞o′kə-män′, sän′ mē-gĕl′ dĕ to͞o′ko͞o-män′) or **Tucumán.** A city of N Argentina NNW of Córdoba. Pop. 392,751.

san•nup (săn′əp) *n.* A married Native American man. [Of Massachusett orig.]

sann•ya•si (sŭn-yä′sē) or **sann•ya•sin** (-sĭn) *n. Hinduism.* A wandering mendicant and ascetic who has renounced all social norms and earthly obligations. [Hindi *sannyāsī* < Skt. *saṃnyāsī* < *saṃnyasyati*, he renounces : *sam*, together; see SANSKRIT + *ni*, down + *asyati*, he throws.]

S-A node (ĕs′ā′) *n.* The sinoatrial node.

San Pab•lo (săn păb′lō). A city of W CA NNW of Oakland near **San Pablo Bay,** a N arm of San Francisco Bay. Pop. 25,158.

San Pe•dro Channel (pē′drō). A strait of S CA between the mainland and Santa Catalina I. **San Pedro Bay** is an inlet of the channel.

San Pe•dro Su•la (săn pē′drō so͞o′lə, sän pĕ′*th*rô so͞o′lä). A city of NW Honduras NW of Tegucigalpa. Pop. 344,500.

San Ra•fael (săn rə-fĕl′). A city of W CA NNW of San Francisco. Pop. 48,404.

San Re•mo (rā′mō, rē′-). A city of NW Italy on the Ligurian Sea E of Monaco. Pop. 50,200.

San River (sän). A river of SE Poland flowing c. 451 km (280 mi) from the Carpathian Mts. to the Vistula R.

sans (sănz, säN) *prep.* Without. [ME < OFr., blend of Lat. *sine* and *absentiā*, in the absence of, ablative of *absentia*, absence < *absēns*, *absent-*, pr.part. of *abesse*, to be away. See ABSENT.]

San Sal•va•dor¹ (săn săl′və-dôr′, sän säl′və-dôr′). Formerly **Wat•lings Island** (wät′lĭngz). An island of the central Bahamas in the West Indies; generally identified as the first landfall of Christopher Columbus (Oct. 12, 1492).

San Sal•va•dor² (săn săl′və-dôr′, sän säl′vä-*th*ôr′). The cap. of El Salvador, in the W-central part; founded in the 16th cent. Pop. 445,100.

sans-cu•lotte (sănz′kyo͞o-lŏt′, -ko͞o-, säN-kü-lôt′) *n.* **1.** A radical republican during the French Revolution. **2.** A revolutionary extremist. [Fr. : *sans*, without + *culotte*, breeches.] **—sans′-cu•lot′tic** (-lŏt′ĭk), **sans′-cu•lot′tish** (-lŏt′ĭsh) *adj.* **—sans′-cu•lot′tism** *n.* **—sans′-cu•lot′tist** *n.*

San Se•bas•tián (săn sə-băs′chĭn, sän′ sĕ-väs-tyän′). A city of N Spain on the Bay of Biscay near the French border E of Bilbao. Pop. 178,906.

San•sei (sän′sā′, sän-sā′) *n., pl.* **Sansei** or **-seis.** The U.S.-born grandchild of Japanese immigrants to America. [J. : *san*, three + *sei*, generation.]

san•se•vie•ri•a (săn′sə-vîr′ē-ə, -vē-ĕr′-) *n.* Any of various tropical plants of the genus *Sansevieria,* having lance-shaped leaves. [NLat. *Sanseveria*, genus name, after Raimondo di Sangro (1710–71), Prince of *San Seviero*, Italy.]

San•skrit (săn′skrĭt′) *n.* An ancient Indic language that is the language of Hinduism and the Vedas and the classical literary language of India. [Skt. *saṃskṛtam* < neut. of *saṃskṛta-*, perfected, refined : *sam*, together; see **sem-¹*** + *karoti*, he makes; see **kʷer-*.**] **—San′skrit′ist** *n.*

San•skrit•ic (săn-skrĭt′ĭk) *n.* See **Indic. —San•skrit′ic** *adj.*

sans ser•if (săn sĕr′ĭf) *n. Print.* A typeface without serifs. **—sans-ser′if** *adj.*

San•ta An•a¹ (săn′tə ăn′ə). **1.** (*also* sän′tä ä′nä). A city of W El Salvador NW of San Salvador. Pop. 132,200. **2.** A city of S CA E of Long Beach in the fertile valley of the **Santa Ana River,** c. 145 km (90 mi). Pop. 293,742.

San•ta An•a² (săn′tə ăn′ə) *n.* A strong dry hot wind blowing from the desert regions of southern California toward the Pacific, usu. in winter. [After the *Santa Ana* Canyon of S CA.]

San•ta An•na or **San•ta An•a** (săn′tä ăn′ə, sän′tə ä′nä), **Antonio López de.** 1795?–1876. Mexican military leader who failed to crush the Texan revolt and in the Mexican War lost several battles (1846–47) to Gen. Zachary Taylor.

San•ta Bar•ba•ra (săn′tə bär′bər-ə, bär′brə). A city of S CA WNW of Los Angeles. Pop. 85,571.

Santa Barbara Islands. A chain of islands and islets in the Pacific Ocean off S CA; separated from the mainland by **Santa Barbara Channel** in the N and San Pedro Channel in the S.

Santa Cat•a•li•na Island (kăt′l-ē′nə) or **Catalina Island.** An island off S CA in the S Santa Barbara Is.

Santa Cla•ra (klăr′ə, klâr′ə). **1.** (*also* sän′tä klä′rä). A city of central Cuba ESE of Havana; founded 1689. Pop. 172,652. **2.** A city of W CA NW of San Jose. Pop. 93,613.

San•ta Claus (săn′tə klôz′) *n.* The personification of the Christmas spirit, usu. represented as a jolly fat old man with a white beard and a red suit, said to bring gifts to good children on Christmas Eve. [Prob. alteration of Du. *Sinterklaas* < MDu. *Sinterclaes*, St. Nicholas : *sint*, saint (< MDu. < OFr. *saint*; see SAINT) + *heer*, lord; see MYNHEER + *claes* (short for *Niclaes*, Nicholas).]

San•ta Cruz (săn′tə kro͞oz′). **1.** (*also* sän′tä kro͞os′). A city of central Bolivia NE of Sucre; founded c. 1560. Pop. 441,717. **2.** A city of W CA SSW of San Jose. Pop. 49,040.

Santa Cruz de Te•ne•ri•fe (săn′tə kro͞oz′ də tĕn′ə-rē′fā, -rēf′, -rĭf′, sän′tä kro͞oth′ *th*ĕ tĕn′ĕ-rē′fĕ). A city of the Canary Is. on the NE coast of Tenerife I. Pop. 185,899.

San•ta Cruz Island (săn′tə kro͞oz′). An island off S CA in the N Santa Barbara Is.

Santa Cruz Islands. An island group of the SW Pacific in the SE Solomon Is.

San•ta Fe (săn′tə fā′). **1.** (*also* sän′tä fĕ′). A city of NE Argentina on the Salado R. NW of Buenos Aires; founded 1573. Pop. 291,966. **2.** The cap. of NM, in the N-central part NE of Albuquerque; estab. as a Spanish settlement c. 1609 on the site of ancient Native American ruins. Pop. 55,859.

Santa Fe Trail. A trade route to the SW U.S. extending c. 1,287 km (800 mi) W from Independence MO to Santa Fe NM; first traversed in 1821.

Santa Ger•tru•dis (gər-tro͞o′dĭs) *n., pl.* **Santa Gertrudis.** Any of a breed of large beef cattle that are highly resistant to heat and insects. [After the *Santa Gertrudis* section of the King Ranch in Kingsville TX.]

San•ta Is•a•bel (săn′tə ĭz′ə-bĕl′, sän′tä ē-sä-bĕl′). See **Malabo.**

san•ta•lol (săn′tə-lôl′, -lōl′, -lŏl′) *n.* A colorless liquid, $C_{15}H_{24}O$, obtained from sandalwood and used in perfumes. [NLat. *Santalum*, sandalwood genus (< Med.Lat. *santalum*, sandalwood; see SANDAL²) + -OL(E).]

San•ta Ma•ri•a (săn′tə mə-rē′ə). **1.** (*also* säN′tä mä-rē′ä). A city of S Brazil W of Pôrto Alegre. Pop. 151,156. **2.** A city of S CA NW of Santa Barbara. Pop. 61,284.

San•ta Mar•ta (săn′tə mär′tə, sän′tä mär′tä). A city of N Colombia on the Caribbean Sea ENE of Barranquilla; founded 1525. Pop. 193,160.

San•ta Mon•i•ca (săn′tə mŏn′ĭ-kə). A city of S CA on the Pacific Ocean W of Los Angeles. Pop. 86,905.

San•tan•der (sän′tän-dĕr′). A city of N Spain on the Bay of Biscay WNW of Bilbao. Pop. 187,057.

Santa Pau•la (pô′lə). A city of S CA E of Santa Barbara. Pop. 25,062.

San•ta•rém (săn′tə-rĕm′, säN′tä-räN′). A city of N Brazil on the Amazon R. E of Manaus; founded 1661. Pop. 102,181.

Santa Ro•sa (rō′zə). A city of W CA NNW of San Francisco. Pop. 113,313.

Santa Rosa Island. 1. An island of S CA in the NW Santa Barbara Is. separated from the mainland by the Santa Barbara Channel. **2.** A barrier island of NW FL extending c. 80 km (50 mi) along the coast of the Gulf of Mexico.

San•ta•ya•na (săn′tē-ăn′ə, sän′tä-yä′nä), **George.** 1863–1952. Spanish-born Amer. philosopher primarily known for his theories of aesthetics, morality, and the spiritual life.

San•tee¹ (săn-tē′) *n., pl.* **Santee** or **-tees.** A member of a people of the eastern branch of the Sioux, comprising the Mdewakanton, Sisseton, Wahpekute, and Wahpeton peoples, presently in Nebraska, Minnesota, the Dakotas, and Canada.

San•tee² (săn-tē′). A community of S CA, a suburb of San Diego. Pop. 52,902.

Antonio López de Santa Anna
Detail of a c. 1858 portrait by Paul L'Ouvrier

Santa Claus
Illustration from "A Visit from St. Nicholas" by Clement Clarke Moore

ă pat	oi boy
ā pay	ou out
âr care	o͝o took
ä father	o͞o boot
ĕ pet	ŭ cut
ē be	ûr urge
ĭ pit	th thin
ī pie	*th* this
îr pier	hw which
ŏ pot	zh vision
ō toe	ə about, item
ô paw	

Stress marks:
′ (primary);
′ (secondary), as in
dictionary (dĭk′shə-nĕr′ē)

Santee Dakota *n.* See **Santee¹**.
Santee River. A river of central SC flowing c. 230 km (143 mi) to the Atlantic Ocean.
Santee Sioux *n.* See **Santee¹**.
San·ti·a·go (săn′tē-ä′gō, sän′-). **1.** The cap. of Chile, in the central part ESE of Valparaiso; founded 1541. Pop. 425,924. **2.** Also **Santiago de los Ca·bal·le·ros** (dā′ lôs kä′bəl-yĕr′-ōz, *thĕ* lôs kä′vä-yĕ′rôs). A city of N Dominican Republic NW of Santo Domingo; settled c. 1500. Pop. 278,638. **3.** Also **Santiago de Com·pos·te·la** (də kŏm′pə-stĕl′ə, *thĕ* kôm′pôs-tĕ′lä). A city of NW Spain SSW of La Coruña. Pop. 62,300.
Santiago de Cu·ba (də kyōō′bə, *thĕ* kōō′vä). A city of SE Cuba on an inlet of the Caribbean Sea; founded 1514. Pop. 349,444.
Santiago del Es·te·ro (dĕl ə-stĕr′ō, *thĕl* ĕ-stĕ′rô). A city of N-central Argentina N of Córdoba; orig. founded 1553. Pop. 148,758.

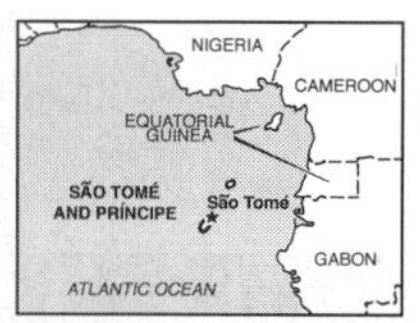

São Tomé and Príncipe

san·tir (sän′tîr′) *n. Mus.* An instrument of Persia that closely resembles a dulcimer. [Ar. *sanṭīr* < Gk. *psaltērion*, psaltery. See PSALTERY.]
San·to Do·min·go (săn′tō də-mĭng′gō, sän′tô dô-). Formerly (1936–61) **Ci·u·dad Tru·jil·lo** (sē′ōō-däd′ trōō-hē′yō, syōō-*thäth*′). The cap. of the Dominican Republic, in the SE part of the island of Hispaniola on the Caribbean Sea; founded 1496. Pop. 1,313,172.
san·ton·i·ca (săn-tŏn′ĭ-kə) *n.* **1.** A perennial or shrubby Eurasian plant *(Artemisia maritima)* having numerous flower heads that yield santonin. **2.** The dried unopened flower heads of this plant. [NLat. < Lat. *(herba) santonica* < fem. of *santonicus*, of the Santoni, a people of Aquitania.]
san·to·nin (săn′tə-nĭn) *n.* A colorless crystalline compound, $C_{15}H_{18}O_3$, obtained from species of wormwood, esp. santonica, and used as an anthelmintic. [SANTON(ICA) + –IN.]
San·to·rin (săn′tə-rēn′). See **Thíra.**
San·tos (săn′təs, sän′tōōs). A city of SE Brazil on an offshore island in the Atlantic Ocean SE of São Paulo; settled in the 1540's. Pop. 410,933.

sapsucker

São Fran·cis·co (souɴ frən-sĭs′kō, frän-sēs′kōō). A river of E Brazil flowing c. 2,896 km (1,800 mi) to the Atlantic Ocean.
São Jo·sé dos Cam·pos (zhōō-zā′ dōōs kăn′pōōs). A city of SE Brazil ENE of São Paulo. Pop. 268,034.
São Lu·is (lōō-ēs′). A city of NE Brazil on an offshore island in the Atlantic Ocean ESE of Belém; founded by the French in 1612. Pop. 182,258.
São Mi·guel (mē-gĕl′). An island of the E Azores in the Atlantic Ocean.
Saône (sōn). A river rising in the Vosges Mts. of NE France and flowing c. 431 km (268 mi) to the Rhone R. at Lyons.
São Pau·lo (pou′lō, -lōō). A city of SE Brazil WSW of Rio de Janeiro; founded by Jesuits in 1554. Pop. 8,493,226.
São To·mé (tə-mā′, tōō-mĕ′). An island of São Tomé and Príncipe in the Gulf of Guinea off W Africa. The city of **São Tomé** is on the SE coast. Its pop. is 17,380.
São Tomé and Prín·ci·pe (prĭn′sə-pə, prēɴ′sē-pə). An island country in the Gulf of Guinea off W Africa; an overseas province of Portugal from the early 16th cent. until it achieved independence in 1975. Cap. São Tomé. Pop. 73,631.
São Vi·cen·te (vē-sĕɴ′tə). A city of SE Brazil on an offshore island in the Atlantic Ocean W of Santos; founded 1532. Pop. 192,858.
sap¹ (săp) *n.* **1.a.** The watery fluid that circulates through a plant, carrying food and other substances to the various tissues. **b.** The fluid contents of a plant cell vacuole. **2.** An essential bodily fluid. **3.** Health and energy; vitality. **4.** *Slang.* A gullible person; a dupe. **5.** A leather-covered hand weapon; a blackjack. —*tr.v.* **sapped, sap·ping, saps. 1.** To drain of sap. **2.** To hit or knock out with a sap. [ME < OE *sæp.*]
sap² (săp) *n.* A covered trench or tunnel dug to a point within an enemy position. —*v.* **sapped, sap·ping, saps.** —*tr.* **1.** To undermine the foundations of (a fortification). **2.** To deplete or weaken gradually; devitalize. —*intr.* To dig a sap. [Obsolete Fr. *sappe* or Ital. *zappa*, hoe < OFr. and OItal., both < LLat. *sappa.*]
sap·a·jou (săp′ə-jōō) *n.* See **capuchin** 3. [Fr.]
Sa·phar (sə-fär′) *n.* Var. of **Safar.**
sap·head (săp′hĕd′) *n. Slang.* A person regarded as gullible or foolish. —**sap′head′ed** *adj.*
sa·phe·na (sə-fē′nə) *n., pl.* **-nae** (-nē′). Either of two main superficial veins of the leg that begin at the foot. [ME < Med.Lat. *saphēna* < Ar. *ṣāfin.*] —**sa·phe′nous** *adj.*
sap·id (săp′ĭd) *adj.* **1.a.** Perceptible to the sense of taste; having flavor. **b.** Having a strong pleasant flavor; savory. **2.** Pleasing to the mind; engaging. [Lat. *sapidus* < *sapere*, to taste. See **sep-***.] —**sa·pid′i·ty** (să-pĭd′ĭ-tē, sə-) *n.*
sa·pi·ens (sā′pē-ənz, -ĕnz) *adj.* Of, relating to, or characteristic of *Homo sapiens.* —*n.* An early or prehistoric form of *Homo sapiens.* [Lat. *sapiēns, sapient-*, pr.part. of *sapere*, to taste, be wise. See SAPIENT.]
sa·pi·ent (sā′pē-ənt) *adj.* Having great wisdom and discernment. [ME < OFr. < Lat. *sapiēns, sapient-*, pr.part. of *sapere*, to be wise. See **sep-***.] —**sa′pi·ence** *n.* —**sa′pi·ent·ly** *adv.*
Sa·pir (sə-pîr′), **Edward.** 1884–1939. Amer. anthropologist noted for his studies of Native American languages.
sap·less (săp′lĭs) *adj.* **1.** Devoid of sap; dry. **2.** Lacking spirit or energy. —**sap′less·ness** *n.*
sap·ling (săp′lĭng) *n.* **1.** A young tree. **2.** A youth.
sap·o·dil·la (săp′ə-dĭl′ə, -dē′yə) *n.* **1.** An evergreen tree *(Manilkara zapota)* of Mexico and Central America having latex that yields chicle and edible fruit with sweet yellow-brown flesh. **2.** The fruit of this plant. [Sp. *zapotillo*, dim. of *zapote*, sapodilla fruit < Nahuatl *tzapotl.*]
sap·o·na·ceous (săp′ə-nā′shəs) *adj.* Having the qualities of soap. [Lat. *sāpō, sāpōn-*, hair dye; see SAPONIN + -ACEOUS.] —**sap′o·na′ceous·ness** *n.*
sap·o·na·ted (săp′ə-nā′tĭd) *adj.* Combined or treated with a soap. [< Lat. *sāpō, sāpōn-*, hair dye. See SAPONIN.]
sa·pon·i·fi·ca·tion (sə-pŏn′ə-fĭ-kā′shən) *n.* A reaction of an ester heated with an alkali to yield an alcohol and an acid salt, esp. alkaline hydrolysis of a fat or an oil to make soap.
sa·pon·i·fy (sə-pŏn′ə-fī′) *v.* **-fied, -fy·ing, -fies.** —*tr.* **1.** To convert (an ester) by saponification. **2.** To convert (a fat or an oil) into soap. —*intr.* To undergo saponification. [Fr. *saponifier* < Lat. *sāpō, sāpōn-*, hair dye. See SAPONIN.] —**sa·pon′i·fi′a·ble** *adj.* —**sa·pon′i·fi′er** *n.*
sap·o·nin (săp′ə-nĭn, sə-pō′-) *n.* Any of various plant glucosides that form soapy lathers when mixed and agitated with water, used in detergents, foaming agents, and emulsifiers. [< Lat. *sāpō, sāpōn-*, hair dye, of Gmc. orig.]
sa·por (sā′pər, -pôr′) *n.* A quality perceptible to the sense of taste; flavor. [ME < Lat. < *sapere*, to taste. See **sep-***.] —**sa′po·rif′ic** (sā′pə-rĭf′ĭk, săp′ə-), **sa′po·rous** (sā′pər-əs, săp′ər-) *adj.*
sa·po·te (sə-pō′tē, -tā) or **sa·po·ta** (-tə) *n.* **1.** A Mexican and Central American tree *(Poulteria sapota)* having edible oval fruit. **2.** The fruit of this tree. [Sp. *zapota* < Nahuatl *tzapotl.*]
sap·pan·wood (sə-păn′wŏŏd′, săp′ăn-, -ən-) *n.* **1.** A tree *(Caesalpina sappan)* of tropical Asia having wood that yields a red dye. **2.** The wood of this tree. [Malay *sapang* + WOOD¹.]
sap·per (săp′ər) *n.* **1.** A military engineer who specializes in sapping and other field fortification activities. **2.** A military engineer who lays, detects, and disarms mines. [< SAP².]
Sap·phic (săf′ĭk) *adj.* **1.** Of or relating to the Greek poet Sappho. **2.a.** Of, relating to, or being an Aeolic verse consisting of four syllables followed by a central choriamb and a final part of three syllables. **b.** Relating to or being a stanza of three such verses followed by a verse consisting of a dactyl followed by a spondee or trochee. **c.** Relating to or being an ode made up of such stanzas. **d.** Of, relating to, or being poetry in accentual meter composed in imitation of Sapphic quantitative verse. **3.** Often **sapphic.** Of or relating to lesbianism. —*n.* A Sapphic meter, verse, stanza, or ode.
sap·phire (săf′īr′) *n.* **1.** A clear hard variety of corundum used as a gemstone that is usu. blue but may be any color except red. **2.** A corundum gem. **3.** *Color.* The blue color of a gem sapphire. —*adj.* **1.** Made of or resembling a gem sapphire. **2.** *Color.* Having the color of a blue sapphire. [ME *saphir* < OFr. *safir* < Lat. *sapphīrus* < Gk. *sappheiros* < Heb. *sappîr*, a precious stone.]
sap·phi·rine (săf′ə-rīn′, -rēn′, sə-fīr′ĭn) *adj.* Of or resembling sapphire. —*n.* A rare light blue or green aluminum-magnesium silicate mineral.
Sap·pho (săf′ō). fl. c. 600 B.C. Greek lyric poet whose works survive only in fragments.
Sap·po·ro (sə-pôr′ō, -pōr′ō). A city of SW Hokkaido, Japan, near the head of Ishikari Bay. Pop. 1,542,979.
sap·py (săp′ē) *adj.* **-pi·er, -pi·est. 1.** Full of sap; juicy. **2.** *Slang.* Excessively sentimental; mawkish. **3.** *Slang.* Silly or foolish. —**sap′pi·ly** *adv.* —**sap′pi·ness** *n.*
sa·pre·mi·a also **sa·prae·mi·a** (sə-prē′mē-ə) *n.* Blood poisoning resulting from the absorption of the products of putrefaction. —**sa·pre′mic** *adj.*
sapro– or **sapr–** *pref.* **1.** Decay; putrefaction; decomposition: *saprogenic.* **2.** Dead or decaying organic material: *saprophyte.* [Gk. < *sapros*, rotten.]
sap·robe (săp′rōb′) *n.* An organism that derives its nourishment from nonliving or decaying organic matter. [SAPRO– + Gk. *bios*, life; see **gʷei-***.] —**sap·ro′bi·al** (să-prō′bē-əl), **sap·ro′bic** (-bĭk) *adj.* —**sapro′bi·cal·ly** *adv.*
sap·ro·gen·ic (săp′rə-jĕn′ĭk) also **sa·prog·e·nous** (sə-prŏj′ə-nəs) *adj.* Of, producing, or resulting from putrefaction. —**sap′ro·ge·nic′i·ty** (-jə-nĭs′ĭ-tē) *n.*
sap·ro·lite (săp′rə-līt′) *n.* Soft, partially decomposed rock rich in clay and remaining in its original place.
sap·ro·pel (săp′rə-pĕl′) *n.* A mud rich in organic matter formed at the bottom of a body of water. [SAPRO– + Gk. *pēlos*, mud.] —**sap′ro·pel′ic** (-pĕl′ĭk, -pē′lĭk) *adj.*
sa·proph·a·gous (să-prŏf′ə-gəs) *adj.* Feeding on decaying organic matter.
sap·ro·phyte (săp′rə-fīt′) *n.* An organism, esp. a fungus or bacterium, that feeds on dead or decaying organic matter. —**sap′ro·phyt′ic** (-fĭt′ĭk) *adj.* —**sap′ro·phyt′i·cal·ly** *adv.*
sap·ro·zo·ic (săp′rə-zō′ĭk) *adj.* **1.** Obtaining nourishment by absorption of dissolved organic and inorganic materials, as in

protozoans. **2.** Feeding on dead or decaying animal matter.

sap•sa•go (săp-sā′gō, săp′sə-gō′) *n.*, *pl.* **-gos.** A hard green cheese made from skim-milk curd, colored and flavored with sweet clover. [Alteration of Ger. *Schabzieger* : *schaben*, to scrape (< MHGer. < OHGer. *skaban*) + *Zieger*, whey, whey cheese (< MHGer. *ziger*, prob. of Celt. orig.).]

sap•suck•er (săp′sŭk′ər) *n.* Any of various small American woodpeckers of the genus *Sphyrapicus* that drill holes in certain trees to drink the sap and eat insects in them.

Sa•pul•pa (sə-pŭl′pə). A city of E-central OK SSW of Tulsa. Pop. 18,074.

sap•wood (săp′wŏŏd′) *n.* Newly formed outer wood that lies just inside the cambium of a tree trunk and is more active in water conduction than the heartwood.

Saq•qa•ra also **Sak•ka•ra** (sə-kär′ə). A village of N Egypt near Cairo; site of the oldest Egyptian pyramids.

SAR *abbr.* Sons of the American Revolution.

sar•a•band also **sar•a•bande** (săr′ə-bănd′) *n.* **1.** A stately court dance of the 17th and 18th centuries, in slow triple time. **2.** The music for this dance. [Fr. *sarabande* < Sp. *zarabanda*.]

Sar•a•cen (săr′ə-sən) *n.* **1.** A member of a pre-Islamic nomadic people of the Syrian-Arabian deserts. **2.** *Archaic.* An Arab. **3.** A Muslim, esp. of the time of the Crusades. [ME < OE < LLat. *Saracēnus* < LGk. *Sarakēnos*, ult. < Ar. *šarq*, east.] **—Sar′a•cen′ic** (-sĕn′ĭk) *adj.*

Sar•a•gos•sa (săr′ə-gŏs′ə) also **Za•ra•go•za** (zăr′ə-gō′zə, thä′rä-gô′thä). A city of NE Spain NE of Madrid; held by the Moors from 713 until 1118. Pop. 601,235.

Sar•ah (sâr′ə). In the Bible, the wife of Abraham and mother of Isaac.

Sa•ra•je•vo (săr′ə-yā′vō, sär′ə-yĕ-vô′). The cap. of Bosnia-Herzegovina, in the S-central part SW of Belgrade. The assassination of Archduke Francis Ferdinand and his wife here on Jun. 28, 1914, triggered the outbreak of World War I. Pop. 374,500.

sa•ran (sə-răn′) *n.* Any of various thermoplastic resins derived from vinyl compounds and used to make packaging films, fittings, and bristles and as a fiber in various heavy fabrics. [< *Saran*, a former U.S. trademark.]

Sar•a•nac Lakes (săr′ə-năk′). A group of three lakes in the Adirondack Mts. of NE NY linked by the **Saranac River,** which flows c. 161 km (100 mi) to Lake Champlain.

Sa•ransk (sə-ränsk′). A city of W Russia W of Ulyanovsk; founded as a fort in the 1600's. Pop. 307,000.

sa•ra•pe (sə-rä′pē, -răp′ē) *n.* Var. of **serape.**

Sar•a•so•ta (săr′ə-sō′tə). A city of W-central FL on **Sarasota Bay,** an inlet of the Gulf of Mexico. Pop. 50,961.

Sar•a•to•ga (săr′ə-tō′gə). A city of W CA SW of San Jose. Pop. 28,061.

Saratoga Springs. A city of E NY in the foothills of the Adirondack Mts. N of Albany. Pop. 25,001.

Saratoga trunk *n.* A large traveling trunk having a rounded top. [After SARATOGA (SPRINGS).]

Sa•ra•tov (sə-rä′təf). A city of SW Russia on the Volga R. NNE of Volgorad; orig. founded 1590. Pop. 899,000.

Sa•ra•wak (sə-rä′wäk, -wăk, -wä). A region of Malaysia on NW Borneo; formerly a British protectorate (1888–1946) and a crown colony (1946–63).

sar•casm (sär′kăz′əm) *n.* **1.** A cutting, often ironic remark intended to wound. **2.** A form of wit that uses such remarks to make its victim the butt of contempt or ridicule. **3.** The use of sarcasm. [LLat. *sarcasmus* < Gk. *sarkasmos* < *sarkazein*, to bite the lips in rage < *sarx*, *sark-*, flesh.]

sar•cas•tic (sär-kăs′tĭk) *adj.* **1.** Expressing or marked by sarcasm. **2.** Given to using sarcasm. [SARC(ASM) + *-astic*, as in ENTHUSIASTIC.] **—sar•cas′ti•cal•ly** *adv.*

sarce•net (särs′nĭt) *n.* A fine soft silk cloth. [ME *sarsenet* < AN *sarzinett*, perh. < OFr. *Saracin*, Saracen < LLat. *Saracēnus*. See SARACEN.]

sarco– or **sarc–** *pref.* **1.** Flesh: *sarcophagic.* **2.** Striated muscle: *sarcolemma.* [Gk. *sarko-* < *sarx*, *sark-*, flesh.]

sar•co•din•i•an (sär′kə-dĭn′ē-ən) *adj.* Of or belonging to the Sarcodina, a superclass of protozoans. [NLat. *Sarcodīna*, superclass name < Gk. *sarkōdēs*, fleshy < *sarx*, *sark-*, flesh.] **—sar′co•din′i•an** *n.*

sar•coid (sär′koid′) *adj.* Relating to or resembling flesh. —*n.* **1.** See **sarcoidosis. 2.** A tumor resembling a sarcoma.

sar•coid•o•sis (sär′koi-dō′sĭs) *n.*, *pl.* **-ses** (-sēz). A disease of unknown origin marked by the formation of granulomatous lesions, esp. in the liver, lungs, skin, and lymph nodes.

sar•co•lac•tic acid (sär′kə-lăk′tĭk) *n.* An isomeric form of lactic acid produced by muscle tissue during the anaerobic metabolism of glucose.

sar•co•lem•ma (sär′kə-lĕm′ə) *n.* A thin membrane enclosing a striated muscle fiber. [SARCO– + Gk. *lemma*, husk; see LEMMA².] **—sar′co•lem′mal** *adj.*

sar•co•ma (sär-kō′mə) *n.*, *pl.* **-mas** also **-ma•ta** (-mə-tə). A malignant tumor arising from connective tissues. [NLat. < Gk. *sarkōma*, *sarkōmat-*, fleshy excrescence < *sarkoun*, to produce flesh < *sarx*, *sark-*, flesh.] **—sar•co′ma•toid′** (-mə-toid′), **sar•co′ma•tous** (-təs) *adj.*

sar•co•ma•to•sis (sär-kō′mə-tō′sĭs) *n.* Formation of numerous sarcomas in various parts of the body.

sar•co•mere (sär′kə-mîr′) *n.* One of the segments into which a fibril of striated muscle is divided.

sar•co•phag•ic (sär′kə-făj′ĭk, -fā′jĭk) also **sar•coph•a•gous** (sär-kŏf′ə-gəs) *adj.* Flesh-eating; carnivorous.

sar•coph•a•gus (sär-kŏf′ə-gəs) *n.*, *pl.* **-gi** (-jī′) or **-gus•es.** A stone coffin, often inscribed or decorated with sculpture. [Lat. < Gk. *sarkophagos*, coffin < *(lithos) sarkophagos*, limestone that consumed the flesh of corpses laid in it : *sarx*, *sark-*, flesh + *-phagos*, -phagous.]

sar•co•plasm (sär′kə-plăz′əm) *n.* The cytoplasm of a striated muscle fiber. **—sar′co•plas•mat′ic** (-plăz-măt′ĭk), **sar′co•plas′mic** (-mĭk) *adj.*

sarcoplasmic reticulum *n.* The form of endoplasmic reticulum found in striated muscle fibers.

sar•cop•tic mange (sär-kŏp′tĭk) *n.* Mange caused by the mite *Sarcoptes scabiei.* [< NLat. *Sarcoptes*, genus name : SARCO– + Gk. *koptein*, to cut.]

sar•co•some (sär′kə-sōm′) *n.* A large specialized mitrochondrion found in striated muscle. **—sar′co•so′mal** *adj.*

sar•cous (sär′kəs) *adj.* Of, relating to, or consisting of flesh or muscle tissue.

sard (särd) *n.* A clear or translucent deep orange-red to brownish-red variety of chalcedony. [ME *sarde* < OFr. < Lat. *sarda*, perh. < *Sardīs*, Sardis, ancient city of W Asia Minor.]

sar•dine (sär-dēn′) *n.* **1.** Any of various small or half-grown edible herrings or related fishes of the family Clupeidae, frequently canned, esp. the pilchard of European waters. **2.** Any of numerous small silvery edible freshwater or marine fishes unrelated to the sardine. —*tr.v.* **-dined, -din•ing, -dines.** *Slang.* To pack tightly; cram. [ME *sardin* < OFr. *sardine* < Lat. *sardīna* < *sarda*, a fish, ult. < Gk. *Sardō*, Sardinia.]

Sar•din•i•a (sär-dĭn′ē-ə, -dĭn′yə). An island of Italy in the Mediterranean Sea S of Corsica; settled by Phoenicians, Greeks, and Carthaginians before the 6th cent. B.C.

Sar•din•i•an (sär-dĭn′ē-ən, -yən) *adj.* Of Sardinia or its people, language, or culture. —*n.* **1.** A native or inhabitant of Sardinia. **2.** The Romance language of the Sardinians.

Sar•dis (sär′dĭs). An ancient city of W Asia Minor NE of Izmir, Turkey; destroyed by Tamerlane in 1402.

sar•di•us (sär′dē-əs) *n.* See **sard.** [ME < OE < Lat. < *sarda*. See SARD.]

sar•don•ic (sär-dŏn′ĭk) *adj.* Scornfully or cynically mocking. [Fr. *sardonique*, ult. < Gk. *sardanios*.] **—sar•don′i•cal•ly** *adv.* **—sar•don′i•cism** (-ĭ-sĭz′əm) *n.*

sar•don•yx (sär-dŏn′ĭks, sär′dn-ĭks′) *n.* An onyx with alternating brown and white bands of sard and other minerals. [ME *sardonix*, prob. < Lat. *sardonyx* < Gk. *sardonux* : *sardion*, sard; see SARD + *onux*, onyx, nail; see **nogh-***.]

Sar•dou (sär-dōō′), **Victorien.** 1831–1908. French playwright known esp. for his light comedies, including *Peril* (1861).

Sa•re•ma (sär′ə-mä′). See **Saaremaa.**

sar•gas•so (sär-găs′ō) *n.*, *pl.* **-sos.** See **gulfweed.** [Port. *sargaço*.]

Sar•gas•so Sea (sär-găs′ō). A part of the N Atlantic between the West Indies and the Azores.

sar•gas•sum (sär-găs′əm) *n.* See **gulfweed.** [NLat. *Sargassum*, genus name < SARGASSO.]

sargassum fish *n.* A frogfish *(Histrio histrio)* found among the drifting gulfweed of the Atlantic and western Pacific.

sarge (särj) *n. Informal.* Sergeant.

Sar•gent (sär′jənt), **John Singer.** 1856–1925. Amer. painter known esp. for his portraits and watercolor landscapes.

Sar•go•dha (sər-gō′də). A city of NE Pakistan WNW of Lahore. Pop. 235,000.

Sar•gon II (sär′gŏn′). d. 705 B.C. Assyrian king (721–705) who completed the conquest of the N Jewish kingdom of Israel, later known as Samaria.

sa•ri (sä′rē) *n.*, *pl.* **-ris.** An outer garment worn chiefly by women of India and Pakistan, consisting of lightweight cloth with one end wrapped about the waist to form a skirt and the other draped over the shoulder or head. [Hindi *sāṛī* < Prakrit *sāḍī* < Skt. *śāṭī*.]

Sark (särk). One of the Channel Is. in the English Channel E of Guernsey comprising **Great Sark** and **Little Sark,** joined by a natural causeway. **—Sark•ese′** (-ēz′, -ēs′) *adj. & n.*

Sar•ma•tia (sär-mā′shə, -shē-ə). An ancient region of E Europe NE of the Black Sea. The term is also applied to the territory between the Vistula and Volga rivers during the time of the Roman Empire. **—Sar•ma′tian** *adj. & n.*

sar•men•tose (sär-mĕn′tōs′) *adj. Bot.* Having slender prostrate stolons, as in the strawberry. [Lat. *sarmentōsus*, full of twigs < *sarmentum*, twigs.]

Sar•ni•a (sär′nē-ə). A city of SE Ontario, Canada, at the S end of Lake Huron W of London. Pop. 50,892.

sa•rod or **sa•rode** (sə-rōd′) *n. Mus.* A many-stringed lute of northern India that is usu. played with a plectrum. [Urdu < Pers. *sarūd* < MPers. *srōd* < OIran. *srauta-*. See **kleu-***.]

sa•rong (sə-rông′, -rŏng′) *n.* **1.** A skirt consisting of brightly colored cloth wrapped about the waist that is worn by men and women in Malaysia, Indonesia, and the Pacific islands.

sari

sarong

ă pat	oi boy
ā pay	ou out
âr care	ŏŏ took
ä father	ōō boot
ĕ pet	ŭ cut
ē be	ûr urge
ĭ pit	th thin
ī pie	*th* this
îr pier	hw which
ŏ pot	zh vision
ō toe	ə about, item
ô paw	

Stress marks:
′ (primary);
′ (secondary), as in **dictionary** (dĭk′shə-nĕr′ē)

2. Cloth for such skirts. [Malay *(kain) sarong,* covering (cloth), sarong.]

Sa•ron•ic Gulf (sə-rŏn′ĭk). An arm of the Aegean Sea in S Greece between Attica and the Peloponnesus E of Corinth.

Sa•ros (sâr′ŏs′, sä′rôs), **Gulf of.** An inlet of the NE Aegean Sea indenting NW European Turkey N of Gallipoli.

Sa•roy•an (sə-roi′ən), **William.** 1908–81. Amer. writer whose works include the play *The Time of Your Life* (1939).

Sar•pe•don (sär-pēd′n, -pē′dŏn) *n. Gk. Myth.* A son of Zeus and Europa who became king of Lycia and was killed by Patroclus in the Trojan War.

sar•sa (sär′sə) *n. Chiefly Southwestern U.S.* Var. of **salsa** 1.

sar•sa•pa•ril•la (săs′pə-rĭl′ə, särs′-) *n.* **1.a.** Any of several tropical American plants of the genus *Smilax.* **b.** The dried roots of any of these plants, used as a flavoring. **c.** A sweet soft drink flavored with these roots. **2.** Either of two North American plants *(Aralia hispida* or *A. nudicaulis)* having umbels of small white flowers. [Sp. *zarzaparrilla* : *zarza,* bramble (< Ar. *šaraṣ*) + *parrilla,* dim. of *parra,* vine.]

Jean Paul Sartre

Sarthe (särt). A river of NW France flowing c. 285 km (177 mi), generally S to Angers.

sar•to•ri•al (sär-tôr′ē-əl, -tōr′-) *adj.* Of or relating to a tailor, tailoring, or tailored clothing: *sartorial elegance.* [< LLat. *sartor,* tailor. See SARTORIUS.] **—sar•to′ri•al•ly** *adv.*

sar•to•ri•us (sär-tôr′ē-əs, -tōr′-) *n., pl.* **-to•ri•i** (-tôr′ē-ī, -tōr′-). A flat narrow thigh muscle crossing the front of the thigh from the hip to the inner side of the tibia. [NLat. < LLat. *sartor,* tailor (< its producing a tailor's cross-legged position < *sartus,* p.part. of *sarcīre,* to mend.]

Sar•tre (sär′trə, särt), **Jean Paul.** 1905–80. French writer and existentialist who declined the 1957 Nobel Prize for literature.

SASE *abbr.* Self-addressed stamped envelope.

sash¹ (săsh) *n.* A band or ribbon worn about the waist, as for ornament, or over the shoulder as a symbol of rank. *—tr.v.* **sashed, sash•ing, sash•es.** To put a band or ribbon about (the waist). [Ar. *šāš,* muslin.]

sash² (săsh) *n.* A frame in which window or door panes are set. *—tr.v.* **sashed, sash•ing, sash•es.** To furnish with a sash. [Alteration of Fr. *châssis,* frame (taken as pl.). See CHASSIS.]

sa•shay (să-shā′) *Informal. —intr.v.* **-shayed, -shay•ing, -shays. 1.a.** To walk or proceed, esp. easily or casually. **b.** To strut or flounce in a showy manner. **2.** To perform the chassé. **3.** To move sideways. *—n.* **1.** A chassé. **2.** An excursion; an outing. **3.** A figure in square dancing in which partners circle each other by taking sideways steps. [Alteration of CHASSÉ.]

sa•shi•mi (sä-shē′mē) *n., pl.* **-mis.** A Japanese dish consisting of bite-size slices of fresh raw fish. [J.]

Sask. *abbr.* Saskatchewan

Sas•katch•e•wan (să-skăch′ə-wän′, -wən). A province of S-central Canada; joined the Confederation in 1905. The first permanent settlement in the area was made by the Hudson's Bay Company in 1774. Cap. Regina. Pop. 968,313.

Saskatchewan River. A river of S-central Canada formed by the North and South Saskatchewan rivers and flowing c. 547 km (340 mi) to Lake Winnipeg in Manitoba.

Saturn
Photographed by Voyager 2

sas•ka•toon (săs′kə-to͞on′) *n.* **1.** A shrub *(Amelanchier alnifolia)* of northwest North America having white flowers and edible dark purple fruit. **2.** The fruit of this plant. [< Cree *misaaskwatoomin,* saskatoon berry.]

Sas•ka•toon (săs′kə-to͞on′). A city of S-central Saskatchewan, Canada, on the South Saskatchewan R. NW of Regina; settled in 1883. Pop. 154,210.

Sas•quatch (săs′kwŏch, -kwăch) *n.* See **Bigfoot.** [Halkomelem (Salish language) *sɛ́sq'əč.*]

sass (săs) *Informal. —n.* Impertinent, disrespectful speech; back talk. *—tr.v.* **sassed, sass•ing, sass•es.** To talk impudently to. [Back-formation < SASSY¹.]

sas•sa•by (săs′ə-bē) *n., pl.* **-bies.** A South African antelope *(Damaliscus lunatus)* having curved ridged horns. [Sotho (Setswana) *tshêsêbê.*]

sas•sa•fras (săs′ə-frăs′) *n.* **1.** A deciduous eastern North American tree *(Sassafras albidum)* having irregularly lobed leaves and aromatic bark, leaves, and branches. **2.** The dried root bark of this plant, used as a flavoring and a source of a volatile oil. [Sp. *sasafrás* < LLat. *saxifragia,* kind of herb, var. of *(herba) saxifraga,* saxifrage. See SAXIFRAGE.]

Sas•sa•nid (săs′ə-nĭd, sə-sä′nĭd, -săn′ĭd) also **Sas•sa•ni•an** (sə-sā′nē-ən, să-) or **Sas•sa•nide** (săs′ə-nīd′, -nĭd). A Persian dynasty (A.D. 224–651) whose rule was marked by wars against Romans, Armenians, and Huns and by the revival of Zoroastrianism. **—Sas′sa•nid** *adj.*

Sas•sa•ri (sä′sə-rē′). A city of NW Sardinia, Italy, NNW of Cagliari. Pop. 118,158.

Sas•soon (sə-so͞on′, să-), **Siegfried Lorraine.** 1886–1967. British writer known for his antiwar poems based on his combat experience in World War I.

sass•wood (săs′wo͝od′) *n.* See **sassy².** [Alteration of *sassywood* : SASSY² + WOOD¹.]

sas•sy¹ (săs′ē) *adj.* **-si•er, -si•est. 1.** Rude and disrespectful; impudent. **2.** Lively and spirited; jaunty. **3.** Stylish; chic. [Alteration of SAUCY.] **—sas′si•ly** *adv.* **—sas′si•ness** *n.*

sas•sy² (săs′ē) *n., pl.* **-sies.** A western African tree *(Erythrophleum suaveolens)* of the pea family, having bark that yields a poison. [Of West African orig.]

sas•tru•ga (să-stro͞o′gə, săs′trə-, sä′strə-) also **zas•tru•ga** (ză-stro͞o′gə, zä-) *n.* A long wavelike ridge of snow, formed by the wind and found on the polar plains. [Russ. dial. *zastruga* : *za,* beyond + *struga,* deep place; see **sreu-***.]

sat (săt) *v.* P.t. and p.part. of **sit.**

SAT (ĕs′ā-tē′). A trademark used for Scholastic Aptitude Test.

sat. *abbr.* Saturate; saturated; saturation.

Sat. *abbr.* Saturday.

Sa•tan (sāt′n) *n. Theol.* The profoundly evil adversary of God and humanity, often identified with the leader of the fallen angels; the Devil. [ME < OE < LLat. *Satān* < Gk. *Satanas, Satan* < Heb. *śāṭān,* devil, adversary < *śāṭan,* to accuse.]

sa•tang (sə-täng′) *n., pl.* **satang.** See table at **currency.** [Thai *satāṅ.*]

sa•tan•ic (sə-tăn′ĭk, sā-) or **sa•tan•i•cal** (-ĭ-kəl) *adj.* **1.** Relating to or suggestive of Satan or evil. **2.** Profoundly cruel or evil; fiendish. **—sa•tan′i•cal•ly** *adv.*

Sa•tan•ism (sāt′n-ĭz′əm) *n.* **1.** The worship of Satan characterized by a travesty of the Christian rites. **2. satanism.** Profound wickedness. **—Sa′tan•ist** *n.*

sa•tay also **sa•té** or **sa•te** (sä′tā) *n.* A dish of southeast Asia consisting of marinated meat, poultry, or seafood grilled on skewers and dipped in peanut sauce. [Malay or Indonesian.]

satch•el (săch′əl) *n.* A small bag, often having a shoulder strap. [ME *sachel* < OFr. < LLat. *saccellus* < Lat. *sacculus,* dim. of *saccus,* bag. See SACK¹.] **—satch′eled** *adj.* **—satch′el•ful′** (-fo͝ol′) *n.*

satd. *abbr.* Saturated.

sate¹ (sāt) *tr.v.* **sat•ed, sat•ing, sates. 1.** To satisfy (an appetite) fully. **2.** To satisfy to excess. [Prob. alteration of ME *saden* < OE *sadian.* See **sā-***.]

sate² (sāt, săt) *v. Archaic.* A p.t. of **sit.**

sa•teen (să-tēn′) *n.* A cotton fabric with a satinlike finish. [Alteration (influenced by VELVETEEN) of SATIN.]

sat•el•lite (săt′l-īt′) *n.* **1.** *Astron.* A celestial body that orbits a planet; a moon. **2.** *Aerospace.* An object launched to orbit Earth or another celestial body. **3.** One who attends a powerful dignitary; a minion. **4.** A subservient follower; a sycophant. **5.** A nation dominated politically and economically by another. **6.** An urban or suburban community located near a big city. **7.** *Genet.* A short segment of a chromosome separated from the rest by a constriction, typically associated with the formation of a nucleolus. **8.** *Microbiol.* A colony of microorganisms whose growth in culture medium is enhanced by certain substances produced by another nearby colony. [Fr., hanger-on, hireling < OFr. < Lat. *satelles, satellit-.*]

satellite cell *n. Anat.* Any of the cells that encapsulate the bodies of nerve cells in ganglia.

sa•tem (sä′təm) *adj.* Of, relating to, or comprising the Indo-European languages, including the Indo-Iranian, Armenian, Albanian, and Balto-Slavic subfamilies, in which original velar stops became fricatives (as *k* > *s* or *š*) and labiovelar stops became velars (as *kw* > *k*). [Avestan *satəm,* hundred (a word whose initial sound illustrates the sound change). See **dekm̥***.]

sa•ti (sŭ-tē′, sŭt′ē′) *n.* Var. of **suttee.**

sa•tia•ble (sā′shə-bəl, -shē-ə-) *adj.* Possible to satisfy or sate: *satiable thirst.* **—sa′tia•bil′i•ty** *n.* **—sa′tia•bly** *adv.*

sa•ti•ate (sā′shē-āt′) *tr.v.* **-at•ed, -at•ing, -ates. 1.** To satisfy (an appetite or a desire) fully. **2.** To satisfy to excess. *—adj.* (-ĭt). Filled to satisfaction. [ME *saciaten* < Lat. *satiāre, satiāt-* < *satis,* sufficient. See **sā-***.] **—sa′ti•a′tion** *n.*

Sa•tie (sä-tē′), **Erik.** 1866–1925. French composer whose compositions include *Socrate* (1918).

sa•ti•e•ty (sə-tī′ĭ-tē) *n.* The condition of being full or gratified beyond the point of satisfaction; surfeit. [Fr. *satiete* < OFr. *saciete* < Lat. *satietās* < *satis,* sufficient. See **sā-***.]

sat•in (săt′n) *n.* **1.** A smooth fabric, as of silk, woven with a glossy face and a dull back. **2.** A garment made of this fabric. *—adj.* **1.** Made of or covered with satin. **2.** Glossy, sleek, and smooth. [ME < OFr., prob. < Ar. *('aṭlas) zaitūnīy,* (satin) of Zaitun < *Zaitūn,* prob. Tsinkiang (Quanzhou or Chuanchow), a city of SE China.]

sat•in•et (săt′n-ĕt′) *n.* A thin inferior satin or an imitation satin, esp. one containing cotton.

satin flower *n.* **1.** A plant *(Clarkia amoena)* of coastal California having red-blotched flowers. **2.** See **honesty** 4.

satin stitch *n.* An embroidery stitch worked in close parallel lines to give a solid satinlike finish.

satin weave *n.* A basic weave construction whereby the face of the cloth shows only warp or only weft and no twill appears.

sat•in•wood (săt′n-wo͝od′) *n.* **1.** A deciduous tree *(Chloroxylon swietenia)* of India and Sri Lanka having hard yellowish close-grained wood. **2.** A West Indian tree *(Zanthoxylum flavum)* having smooth, slightly oily, lustrous wood. **3.** The wood of either of these trees.

sat•in•y (săt′n-ē) *adj.* Lustrous and smooth like satin.

sat•ire (săt′īr′) *n.* **1.a.** A literary work that attacks human vice or folly through irony, derision, or wit. **b.** The branch of literature constituting such works. **2.** Irony, sarcasm, or caustic wit used to attack or expose folly or vice. [Lat. *satira,* prob. alteration (influenced by Gk. *satur*, satyr, and *satyros*, mythical burlesque) of *(lanx) satura*, fruit (plate) mixture < fem. of *satur*, sated, well-fitted. See **sā-***.]

sa•tir•i•cal (sə-tĭr′ĭ-kəl) or **sa•tir•ic** (-ĭk) *adj.* Of, relating to, or characterized by satire. —**sa•tir′i•cal•ly** *adv.*

sat•i•rist (săt′ər-ĭst) *n.* One who is given to satire, esp. a writer of satirical works.

sat•i•rize (săt′ə-rīz′) *tr.v.* **-rized, -riz•ing, -riz•es.** To ridicule or attack by means of satire.

sat•is•fac•tion (săt′ĭs-făk′shən) *n.* **1.a.** The fulfillment or gratification of a desire, a need, or an appetite. **b.** Pleasure or contentment derived from such gratification. **c.** A source or means of gratification. **2.a.** Compensation for injury or loss; reparation. **b.** The opportunity to avenge a wrong; vindication. **3.** Assurance beyond doubt; complete conviction. [ME < OFr. < Lat. *satisfactiō*, *satisfactiōn-*, amends < *satisfactus*, p.part. of *satisfacere*, to satisfy. See SATISFY.]

sat•is•fac•to•ry (săt′ĭs-făk′tə-rē) *adj.* Giving satisfaction sufficient to meet a demand or requirement; adequate. —**sat′is•fac′to•ri•ly** *adv.* —**sat′is•fac′to•ri•ness** *n.*

sat•is•fi•a•ble (săt′ĭs-fī′ə-bəl) *adj.* Capable of being satisfied: *satisfiable needs and desires.*

sat•is•fied (săt′ĭs-fīd′) *adj.* **1.** Filled with satisfaction; content: *a very satisfied customer.* **2.** Paid or discharged in full, as a debt or an obligation. **3.** Convinced beyond a doubt.

sat•is•fy (săt′ĭs-fī′) *v.* **-fied, -fy•ing, -fies.** —*tr.* **1.** To gratify the need, desire, or expectation of. **2.** To fulfill (a need or desire). **3.a.** To free from doubt; assure. **b.** To dispel (a doubt or question). **4.a.** To discharge (a debt, for example) in full. **b.** To discharge an obligation to (a creditor). **5.** To conform to the requirements of (a standard or rule); be sufficient to (an end). **6.** To make reparation for; redress. **7.** *Math.* To make the left and right sides of (an equation) equal after substituting equivalent quantities for the unknown variables in the equation. —*intr.* **1.** To be sufficient or adequate. **2.** To give satisfaction. [ME *satisfien* < OFr. *satisfier* < Lat. *satisfacere* : *satis*, sufficient; see **sā-*** + *facere*, to make; see **dhē-***.] —**sat′is•fi′er** *n.* —**sat′is•fy′ing•ly** *adv.*

Syns: satisfy, answer, fill, fulfill, meet. The central meaning shared by these verbs is "to supply fully or completely": *satisfied all requirements; answered our needs; filling a purpose; fulfilled their aspirations; meeting her obligations.*

Sa•to (sä′tō), **Eisaku.** 1901–75. Japanese politician who won the 1974 Nobel Peace Prize.

sa•to•ri (sä-tôr′ē, -tōr′ē, sə-) *n. Buddhism.* A state of spiritual enlightenment sought in Zen Buddhism. [J.]

sa•trap (sā′trăp′, săt′răp′) *n.* **1.** A governor of a province in ancient Persia. **2.** A ruler. **3.** A subordinate bureaucrat or an official. [ME *satrape* < OFr. < Lat. *satrapēs* < Gk. < OPers. *khshathrapāvā*, protector of the province : *khshathra-*, realm, province + *pāvā*, protector; see **pā-***.]

sa•tra•py (sā′trə-pē, -trăp′ē, săt′rə-pē) *n., pl.* **-pies. 1.** The territory or sphere under the rule of a satrap. **2.** A nation, state, territory, or area controlled as if by a satrap.

sat•su•ma (săt-so͞o′mə, să-tso͞o′mä, sä′tso͞o-mä′) *n.* **1.** A tangerine native to Japan and the hardiest commercial citrus fruit. **2. Satsuma.** A Japanese porcelain. [After *Satsuma*, a peninsula of SW Kyushu, Japan.]

Sa•tu-Ma•re also **Sa•tu Ma•re** (sä′to͞o-mär′ĕ). A city of NW Romania NW of Bucharest. Pop. 124,691.

sat•u•rant (săch′ər-ənt) *adj.* Serving to saturate. —*n.* A substance used to saturate.

sat•u•rate (săch′ə-rāt′) *tr.v.* **-rat•ed, -rat•ing, -rates. 1.** To imbue or impregnate thoroughly. **2.** To soak, fill, or load to capacity. **3.** *Chem.* To cause (a substance) to unite with the greatest possible amount of another substance. —*adj.* (-rĭt). Saturated. [Lat. *saturāre*, *saturāt-*, to fill < *satur*, sated. See **sā-***.] —**sat′u•ra•ble** (-ər-ə-bəl) *adj.* —**sat′u•ra′tor** *n.*

sat•u•rat•ed (săch′ə-rā′tĭd) *adj.* **1.** Unable to hold or contain more; full. **2.** Soaked with moisture; drenched. **3.** *Chem.* **a.** Combined with or containing all the solute that can normally be dissolved at a given temperature. **b.** Relating to or being a fat, usu. of animal origin, predominantly composed of fatty acids having only single bonds in the carbon chain. **4.** *Geol.* Of or relating to minerals that can crystallize from magmas even in the presence of excess silica.

sat•u•ra•tion (săch′ə-rā′shən) *n.* **1.a.** The act or process of saturating. **b.** The condition of being saturated. **c.** The condition of being full to or beyond satisfaction; satiety. **2.** *Phys.* A state of a ferromagnetic substance in which an increase in applied magnetic field strength does not produce an increase in magnetic intensity. **3.** *Chem.* The state of a fully saturated compound or solution. **4.** *Meteorol.* A condition in which air at a specific temperature contains all the water vapor it can hold. **5.** *Color.* Vividness of hue; degree of difference from a gray of the same lightness or brightness. **6.** Intensive shelling or bombing of a target to destroy it. **7.** The flooding of a market with all of a commodity that consumers can purchase.

Sat•ur•day (săt′ər-dē, -dā′) *n.* **1.** The seventh day of the week. **2.** The Jewish Sabbath. [ME < OE *Sæternesdæg*, transl. of Lat. *Sāturnidiēs* : *Sāturnī*, genitive of *Sāturnus*, Saturn + *diēs*, day.]

Saturday night special *n. Informal.* A cheap handgun easily obtained and concealed.

Sat•urn (săt′ərn) *n.* **1.** *Rom. Myth.* The god of agriculture. **2.** The sixth planet from the sun and the second largest in the solar system, having a sidereal period of revolution about the sun of 29.5 years at a mean distance of about 1,425,000,000 kilometers (886,000,000 miles), and a mean diameter of approx. 119,000 kilometers (74,000 miles). [ME *Saturnus* < OE < Lat. *Sāturnus*, of Etruscan orig.]

sat•ur•na•li•a (săt′ər-nā′lē-ə, -nāl′yə) *pl.n.* **1. Saturnalia.** The ancient Roman seven-day festival of Saturn, which began on December 17. **2.** *(used with a sing. v.)* A celebration marked by unrestrained revelry and often licentiousness; an orgy. [Lat. *Sāturnālia* < neut. pl. of *Sāturnālis*, Saturnian < *Sāturnus*, Saturn. See SATURN.]

Sa•tur•ni•an (să-tûr′nē-ən, sə-) *adj.* **1.** Of or relating to the planet Saturn or its supposed astrological influence. **2.** *Archaic.* Of or relating to the god Saturn or his reign.

sa•tur•ni•id (să-tûr′nē-ĭd, sə-) *n.* Any of various often large colorful moths of the family Saturniidae, such as the emperor moth. [< NLat. *Sāturniidae*, family name < *Sāturnia*, type genus < Lat., Saturn's daughter < fem. of *Sāturnius*, Saturnian < *Sāturnus*. See SATURN.] —**sa•tur′ni•id** *adj.*

sat•ur•nine (săt′ər-nīn′) *adj.* **1.** Having the temperament of one born under the astrological influence of Saturn. **2.a.** Melancholy or sullen. **b.** Expressing bitterness or sardonicism. **3.** Produced by absorption of lead. —**sat′ur•nine′ly** *adv.*

sat•urn•ism (săt′ər-nĭz′əm) *n.* See **lead poisoning.** [< SATURN, lead (obsolete), associated by alchemists with the planet.]

Sa•tya•gra•ha (sə-tyä′grə-hə, sŭt′yə-grŭ′hə) *n.* The policy of nonviolent resistance initiated in India by Mahatma Gandhi to press for political reform. [Skt. *satyāgrahaḥ* : *satyam*, truth (< *sat-*, *sant-*, existing, true; see **es-***) + *āgrahaḥ*, determination, insistence (*ā-*, to + *grahaḥ*, act of seizing < *gṛhṇāti*, he seizes; see **ghrebh-¹***).]

sa•tyr (sā′tər, săt′ər) *n.* **1.** Often **Satyr.** *Gk. Myth.* A woodland creature depicted with a goat's ears, legs, and horns and a fondness for unrestrained revelry. **2.** A licentious man; a lecher. **3.** A man with satyriasis. **4.** Any of various butterflies of the family Satyridae, having brown wings with eyelike spots. [ME *satire* < OFr. < Lat. *satyrus* < Gk. *saturos.*] —**sa•tyr′ic** (sə-tîr′ĭk, sə-), **sa•tyr′i•cal** (-ĭ-kəl) *adj.*

sa•ty•ri•a•sis (sā′tə-rī′ə-sĭs, săt′ə-) *n.* Excessive, often uncontrollable sexual desire in a man. [LLat. < Gk. *saturiasis* < *saturos*, satyr.]

sa•tyr•id (sā′tər-ĭd, săt′ər-, sə-tī′rĭd) *n.* A butterfly of the family Satyridae, including the satyrs and wood nymphs. [< NLat. *Satyridae*, family name < *Satyrus*, type genus < Lat. *satyrus*, satyr. See SATYR.] —**sa′tyr•id** *adj.*

sauce (sôs) *n.* **1.** A flavorful seasoning or relish served as an accompaniment to food, esp. a liquid dressing or topping. **2.** Stewed fruit, usu. served with other foods. **3.** Something that adds zest, flavor, or piquancy. **4.** *Informal.* Impudent speech or behavior; sauciness. **5.** *Slang.* Alcoholic liquor. —*tr.v.* **sauced, sauc•ing, sauc•es. 1.** To flavor with sauce. **2.** To add piquancy or zest to. **3.** *Informal.* To be impertinent or impudent to. [ME < OFr. < VLat. **salsa* < Lat., fem. of *salsus*, p.part. of *sallere*, to salt. See **sal-***.]

sauce•box (sôs′bŏks′) *n. Informal.* An impertinent person.

sauce•pan (sôs′păn′) *n.* A deep cooking pan with a handle.

sauce•pot (sôs′pŏt′) *n.* A cooking pot having a close-fitting lid and a handle on either side.

sau•cer (sô′sər) *n.* **1.** A small shallow dish having a slight circular depression in the center for holding a cup. **2.** An object similar in shape to a saucer. [ME, sauce dish < OFr. *saussier* < *sauce*, sauce. See SAUCE.]

sauce suprême *n.* See **suprême** 1. [Fr. : *sauce*, sauce + *suprême*, suprême.]

sauc•y (sô′sē) *adj.* **-i•er, -i•est. 1.a.** Impertinent or disrespectful. **b.** Impertinent in an entertaining way; irrepressible. **2.** Piquant; pert. —**sau′ci•ly** *adv.* —**sau′ci•ness** *n.*

Sa•ud (sä-o͞od′), **Abdul Aziz ibn.** 1901?–69. Saudi Arabian king (1953–64) who was unable to deal with his country's economic problems and was replaced by his brother Faisal.

Sa•u•di A•ra•bi•a (sou′dē ə-rā′bē-ə, sô′dē, sä-o͞o′dē). A country occupying most of the Arabian Peninsula; proclaimed as a unified independent kingdom in 1932. Cap. Riyadh. Pop. 9,320,000. —**Sa•u′di, Sa•u′di A•ra′bi•an** *adj. & n.*

sau•er•bra•ten (sour′brät′n) *n.* A pot roast of beef marinated in vinegar, water, wine, and spices before being cooked. [Ger. : *sauer*, sour (< MHGer. *sūr* < OHGer.) + *Braten*, roast meat (< MHGer. *brāte*, edible meat < OHGer. *brāto*; see **bhreu-***).]

sau•er•kraut (sour′krout′) *n.* Chopped or shredded cabbage salted and fermented in its own juice. [Ger. : *sauer*, sour; see SAUERBRATEN + *Kraut*, cabbage (< MHGer. *krūt* < OHGer.).]

sau•ger (sô′gər) *n.* A small North American freshwater fish *(Stizostidion canadense)* having a spotted spiny dorsal fin. [?]

Sau•gus (sô′gəs). A town of NE MA, a suburb of Boston. Pop. 25,549.

Sauk (sôk) also **Sac** (săk, sôk) *n., pl.* **Sauk** or **Sauks** also **Sac** or **Sacs. 1.** A member of a Native American people formerly

satyr

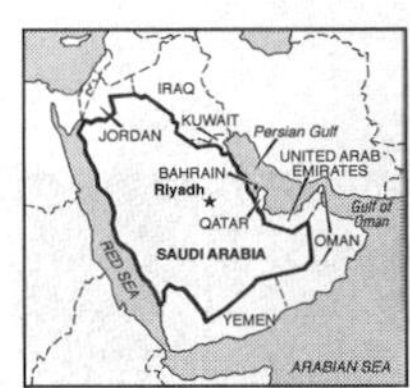

Saudi Arabia

ă pat	oi boy
ā pay	ou out
âr care	o͝o took
ä father	o͞o boot
ĕ pet	ŭ cut
ē be	ûr urge
ĭ pit	th thin
ī pie	*th* this
îr pier	hw which
ŏ pot	zh vision
ō toe	ə about, item
ô paw	

Stress marks:
′ (primary);
′ (secondary), as in dictionary (dĭk′shə-nĕr′ē)

inhabiting parts of Wisconsin, Illinois, and Iowa, with a present-day population mainly in Oklahoma. **2.** Their Algonquian language. [N.Amer.Fr. *saki* < Sauk *asaakiiha.*]

Saul (sôl). fl. 11th cent. B.C. The first king of Israel.

sault (so͞o) *n.* A waterfall or rapids. [Obsolete Fr. < OFr., leap, waterfall. See SOMERSAULT.]

Sault Sainte Ma•rie (so͞o′ sānt′ mə-rē′). A city of S Ontario, Canada, at the falls of the St. Marys R. Pop. 82,698.

Sault Sainte Marie Canals. Popularly called **Soo Canals** (so͞o). Three ship canals bypassing the rapids on the St. Marys R. between Lakes Superior and Huron.

sau•na (sô′nə, sou′-) *n.* **1.a.** A Finnish steam bath in which the steam is produced by pouring water over heated rocks. **b.** A bathhouse or room for such a bath. **2.a.** A dry heat bath. **b.** A room or an enclosure for such a bath. [Finn.]

sauropod
Brachiosaurus

saun•ter (sôn′tər) *intr.v.* **-tered, -ter•ing, -ters.** To stroll. —*n.* **1.** A leisurely pace. **2.** A stroll. [Prob. < ME *santren,* to muse.] —**saun′ter•er** *n.*

sau•rel (sôr′əl, sô-rĕl′) *n.* **1.** A marine fish of the genus *Trachurus,* characterized by bony lateral lines, esp. *T. trachurus* of eastern Atlantic waters. **2.** See **jack mackerel.** [Fr. < LLat. *saurus,* horse mackerel < Gk. *sauros.*]

sau•ri•an (sôr′ē-ən) *n.* Any of various reptiles of the suborder Sauria, which includes the lizards. [< NLat. *Sauria,* suborder name < *saurus,* lizard < Gk. *sauros.*] —**sau′ri•an** *adj.*

saur•is•chi•an (sô-rĭs′kē-ən) *n.* A dinosaur of the order Saurischia, having a pelvic girdle similar to that of modern reptiles. [< NLat. *Saurischia,* order name : *saurus,* lizard; see SAURIAN + Lat. *ischium,* hip joint (poss. of Gk. orig.).] —**saur•is′chi•an** *adj.*

sau•ro•pod (sôr′ə-pŏd′) *n.* Any of various large semiaquatic dinosaurs of the suborder Sauropoda, of the Jurassic and Cretaceous periods. [< NLat. *Sauropoda,* suborder name : *saurus,* lizard; see SAURIAN + *-poda,* -pod.] —**sau′ro•pod′, sau•rop′o•dous** (sô-rŏp′ə-dəs)

Savonarola
Portrait by Fra Bartolommeo (1472–1517)

sau•ry (sôr′ē) *n., pl.* **-ries.** Any of several offshore marine fishes of the family Scomberesocidae, related to the needlefishes. [< NLat. *saurus,* lizard < Gk. *sauros.*]

sau•sage (sô′sĭj) *n.* Finely chopped and seasoned meat, esp. pork, usu. stuffed into a casing and cooked or cured. [ME *sausige* < AN *sausiche* < VLat. *salsīcia < LLat., neut. pl. of *salsīcius,* prepared by salting < *salsus,* salted. See SAUCE.]

Sau•sa•li•to (sô′sə-lē′tō). A resort city of W CA on San Francisco Bay. Pop. 7,152.

Saus•sure (sō-so͝or′, -sür′), **Ferdinand de.** 1857–1913. Swiss linguist who founded structural linguistics.

sau•té (sō-tā′, sô-) *tr.v.* **-téed, -té•ing, -tés.** To fry lightly in fat in a shallow open pan. [Fr., sautéed < p.part. of *sauter,* to leap < OFr. < Lat. *saltāre.* See SALTATION.] —**sau•té′** *n.*

Sau•ternes or **sau•ternes** (sō-tûrn′, sô-) *n., pl.* **Sauternes** or **sauternes. 1.** A delicate sweet white wine from the Bordeaux region of France. **2.** Often **sau•terne** (-tûrn′). A sweet to moderately dry white wine from California. [Fr., after *Sauternes,* a village of SW France.]

Sa•va (sä′və, -vä). A river rising in the Julian Alps and flowing c. 933 km (580 mi), to the Danube R.

sawfish
Largetooth sawfish
Pristis pristis

sav•age (săv′ĭj) *adj.* **1.** Not domesticated or cultivated; wild. **2.** Not civilized; barbaric. **3.** Ferocious; fierce. **4.** Vicious or merciless; brutal. See Syns at **cruel. 5.** Lacking polish or manners; rude. —*n.* **1.** A primitive or uncivilized person. **2.** A brutal, fierce, or vicious person. **3.** A rude person; a boor. —*tr.v.* **-aged, -ag•ing, -ag•es. 1.** To assault ferociously. **2.** To attack without restraint or pity. [ME *sauvage* < OFr. < LLat. *salvāticus* < Lat. *silvāticus,* of the woods, wild < *silva,* forest.] —**sav′age•ly** *adv.* —**sav′age•ness** *n.*

sav•age•ry (săv′ĭj-rē) *n., pl.* **-ries. 1.** The quality or condition of being savage. **2.** An act of violent cruelty. **3.** Savage behavior or nature; barbarity.

Sa•vai•i or **Sa•vai′i** (sä-vī′ē). An island of Western Samoa in the SW Pacific.

sa•van•na also **sa•van•nah** (sə-văn′ə) *n.* A flat tropical or subtropical grassland. [Obsolete Sp. *çavana* < Taino *zabana.*]

Sa•van•nah (sə-văn′ə). A city of SE GA near the mouth of the Savannah R.; founded 1733. Pop. 137,560.

Savannah River. A river, c. 505 km (314 mi), rising in NW SC and flowing along the SC–GA border to the Atlantic Ocean.

sa•vant (să-vänt′) *n.* **1.** A learned person; a scholar. **2.** An idiot savant. [Fr. < OFr., pr.part. of *savoir,* to know < VLat. *sapēre < Lat. *sapere,* to be wise. See **sep-*.**]

sa•vate (sə-văt′, -vät′) *n. Sports.* A form of boxing in which kicking is permitted. [Fr. < OFr., old shoe.]

save[1] (sāv) *v.* **saved, sav•ing, saves.** —*tr.* **1.a.** To rescue from harm, danger, or loss. **b.** To set free from the consequences of sin; redeem. **2.** To keep in a safe condition; safeguard. **3.** To prevent the waste or loss of; conserve. **4.** To set aside for future use; store. **5.** To treat with care by avoiding fatigue, wear, or damage; spare. **6.** To make unnecessary; obviate. **7.a.** *Sports.* To prevent (a goal, score, or win by an opponent). **b.** *Baseball.* To preserve (another pitcher's win) by protecting one's team's lead during a stint of relief pitching. **8.** *Comp. Sci.* To copy (a file) from a computer's main memory to a storage medium so that it can be used again. —*intr.* **1.** To avoid waste or expense; economize. **2.** To accumulate money. **3.** To preserve a person or thing from harm or loss. —*n.* **1.** *Sports.* An act that prevents an opponent from scoring. **2.** *Baseball.* An act of saving a win. —*idiom.* **save (one's) breath.** To refrain from a futile appeal or effort. [ME *saven* < OFr. *sauver* < LLat. *salvāre* < Lat. *salvus,* safe. See **sol-*.**] —**sav′a•ble, save′a•ble** *adj.* —**sav′er** *n.*

save[2] (sāv) *prep.* With the exception of; except. —*conj.* **1.** Were it not; except. **2.** Unless. [ME < OFr. *sauf* < Lat. *salvō,* ablative sing. of *salvus,* safe. See **sol-*.**]

save-all (sāv′ôl′) *n.* **1.** Any of various devices for preventing waste, damage, or loss. **2.** A receptacle for catching the waste products of a process for further use in manufacture.

sav•e•loy (săv′ə-loi′) *n.* A highly seasoned smoked pork sausage. [Alteration of obsolete Fr. *cervelat* < Ital. *cervellato,* ult. < dial. *zervello,* brain < Lat. *cerebellum,* dim. of *cerebrum,* brain. See **ker-**[1]***.**]

sav•in or **sav•ine** (săv′ĭn) *n.* **1.** An evergreen Eurasian shrub *(Juniperus sabina)* having seed-bearing cones and yielding an oil formerly used medicinally. **2.** Any of several related plants. [ME < OE *safine* and < OFr. *savine,* both < Lat. *(herba) Sabīna,* Sabine (plant), savin, fem. of *Sabīnus.*]

sav•ing (sā′vĭng) *n.* **1.** Rescue from harm, danger, or loss. **2.** Avoidance of excess expenditure; economy. **3.** A reduction in expenditure or cost. **4.** Something saved. **5. savings.** Money saved. **6.** *Law.* An exception or reservation. —*prep.* With the exception of. —*conj.* Except; save.

sav•ings account (sā′vĭngz) *n.* A bank account with interest.

savings and loan association *n.* A financial institution that holds the funds of its members or clients in interest-bearing accounts and certificates of deposit, invests these funds esp. in home mortgage loans, and may also offer banking services.

savings bank *n.* A bank that receives and invests the savings of private depositors and pays interest on the deposits.

savings bond *n.* A nontransferable registered bond issued by the U.S. government in denominations of $50 to $10,000.

sav•ior (sāv′yər) *n.* **1.** A person who rescues another from harm, danger, or loss. **2. Savior.** Jesus. [ME *saviour* < OFr. *saveour* < LLat. *salvātor* < *salvāre,* to save. See SAVE[1].]

sav•iour (sāv′yər) *n. Chiefly British.* Var. of **savior.**

sa•voir-faire (săv′wär-fâr′) *n.* The ability to do the right or graceful thing. [Fr. : *savoir,* to know how + *faire,* to do.]

Sa•vo•na (sə-vō′nə, sä-vô′nä). A city of NW Italy on an arm of the Ligurian Sea WSW of Genoa. Pop. 75,069.

Sa•vo•na•ro•la (săv′ə-nə-rō′lə, sä′vô-nä-), **Girolamo.** 1452–98. Italian reformer who drove the Medici family out of Florence in 1494 and was later excommunicated and executed for criticizing Pope Alexander VI.

sa•vor (sā′vər) *n.* **1.** The taste or smell of something. **2.** A specific taste or smell. **3.** A distinctive quality or sensation. —*v.* **-vored, -vor•ing, -vors.** —*intr.* **1.** To have a particular taste or smell. **2.** To exhibit a specified quality or characteristic; smack. —*tr.* **1.** To impart flavor or scent to; season. **2.** To taste or smell, esp. with pleasure. **3.** To appreciate fully; enjoy or relish. [ME *savour* < OFr. < Lat. *sapor* < *sapere,* to taste. See **sep-*.**] —**sa′vor•er** *n.* —**sa′vor•ous** *adj.*

sa•vor•y[1] (sā′və-rē) *adj.* **1.** Appetizing to the taste or smell. **2.** Piquant, pungent, or salty to the taste; not sweet. **3.** Morally respectable; inoffensive. —*n., pl.* **-ies.** A dish of pungent taste. [ME *savure* < OFr. *savoure,* p.part. of *savourer,* to taste < LLat. *sapōrāre* < Lat. *sapor,* taste, smell. See SAVOR.] —**sa′vor•i•ly** *adv.* —**sa′vor•i•ness** *n.*

sa•vor•y[2] (sā′və-rē) *n., pl.* **-ies. 1.** An annual Mediterranean aromatic herb *(Satureja hortensis)* of the mint family, having flowers with a pale lavender to white corolla. **2.** A related Mediterranean aromatic herb *(Satureja montana)* having flowers in a long white or pink corolla. **3.** The leaves of either of these plants, used as seasoning. **4.** Any of several plants of the genus *Micromeria* in the mint family. [ME *saverey,* alteration of OFr. *sarree,* alteration of Lat. *saturēia.*]

sa•vour (sā′vər) *n. & v. Chiefly British.* Var. of **savor.**

sa•vour•y (sā′və-rē) *adj. & n. Chiefly British.* Var. of **savory**[1].

Sa•voy[1] (sə-voi′). A ruling house of Sardinia (1720–1861) and Italy (1861–1946).

Sa•voy[2] (sə-voi′). A historical region and former duchy of SE France, W Switzerland, and NW Italy. —**Sa•voy′ard** (sə-voi′ärd′, săv′oi-yärd′) *adj. & n.*

Savoy Alps. A range of the W Alps in SE France rising to 4,810.2 m (15,771 ft).

sav•vy (săv′ē) *Informal.* —*adj.* **-vi•er, -vi•est.** Well informed and perceptive; shrewd. —*n.* Practical understanding or shrewdness. —*tr. & intr.v.* **sav•vied** (săv′ēd), **sav•vy•ing, sav•vies** (săv′ēz). To understand. [< Sp. *sabe (usted),* (you) know < *saber,* to know < OSp. < VLat. *sapēre < Lat. *sapere,* to be wise. See **sep-*.**] —**sav′vi•ly** *adv.*

saw[1] (sô) *n.* Any of various tools having a thin metal blade or disk with a sharp, usu. toothed edge, used for cutting hard materials. —*v.* **sawed, sawed** or **sawn** (sôn), **saw•ing, saws.** —*tr.* **1.** To cut or divide with a saw. **2.** To produce or shape with a saw. **3.** To make back-and-forth motions through or on. —*intr.* **1.** To use a saw. **2.** To undergo cutting with a saw. [ME *sawe* < OE *sagu.* See **sek-*.**] —**saw′er** *n.*

saw² (sô) *n.* A familiar saying, esp. one that has become trite through repetition. [ME *sawe* < OE *sagu*, speech. See **sekʷ-³***.]
saw³ (sô) *v.* P.t. of **see¹**.
Sa•watch Range (sə-wŏch′). A range of the Rocky Mts. in central CO rising to 4,402.1 m (14,433 ft).
saw•bones (sô′bōnz′) *n., pl.* **sawbones** or **-bones•es** (-bōn′-zĭz). *Slang.* A physician, esp. a surgeon.
saw•buck (sô′bŭk′) *n.* **1.** A sawhorse, esp. one having a crossed pair of legs at each end. **2.** *Slang.* A ten-dollar bill.
saw•dust (sô′dŭst′) *n.* The small particles of material that fall from an object being sawed. **—saw′dust′y** *adj.*
sawed-off (sôd′ôf′, -ŏf′) *adj.* **1.** Having one end sawed off: *a sawed-off shotgun.* **2.** *Slang.* Short; runty.
saw•fish (sô′fĭsh′) *n., pl.* **sawfish** or **-fish•es.** Any of various marine fishes of the genus *Pristis,* related to the rays and having a bladelike snout with teeth along both sides.
saw•fly (sô′flī′) *n.* Any of various hymenopterous insects, chiefly of the family Tenthredinidae, the females of which use sawlike ovipositors to deposit their eggs in plant tissue.
saw grass *n.* A tall coastal or marshy sedge *(Cladium jamaicense)* of eastern North America, Mexico, and the West Indies, having leaves with sharp, minutely toothed margins.
saw•horse (sô′hôrs′) *n.* A frame with legs, used to support pieces of wood being sawed.
saw log *n.* A log of a size large enough to be sawed into boards.
saw•mill (sô′mĭl′) *n.* **1.** A plant where timber is sawed into boards. **2.** A large machine for sawing lumber.
sawn (sôn) *v.* A p.part. of **saw¹**.
saw palmetto *n.* A small creeping palm *(Serenoa repens)* of the southeast United States having palmately divided leaves with one-ribbed segments and black one-seeded fruit.
saw set *n.* An instrument used to give set to the teeth of a saw by bending each alternate tooth slightly outward.
saw-toothed (sô′tōōtht′) *adj.* **1.** Having teeth resembling the teeth of a saw. **2.** Often **saw•tooth** (-tōōth′). Having a jagged or zigzag pattern, outline, or course; serrate.
saw-whet owl (sô′hwĕt′, -wĕt′) *n.* A small brown and white owl *(Aegolius acadicus)* of North America.
saw•yer (sô′yər) *n.* **1.** One that is employed in sawing wood. **2.** Any of several beetles of the genus *Monochamus,* whose larvae bore holes in wood. **3.** See **snag** 1a. [ME *sauere, sawier* < *sawen,* to saw < *sawe,* saw. See SAW¹.]
sax (săks) *n. Mus.* A saxophone.
Sax. *abbr.* Saxon.
sax•a•tile (săk′sə-tĭl′, -tīl) *adj.* Saxicolous. [Lat. *saxātilis* < *saxum,* rock. See **sek-***.]
Saxe-Co•burg (săks-kō′bûrg). A British royal house (1901–10) whose only ruler was Edward VII.
sax•horn (săks′hôrn′) *n. Mus.* Any of a family of valved brass wind instruments that resemble the bugle and have a full, even tone and wide compass. [See SAXOPHONE.]
sax•ic•o•lous (săk-sĭk′ə-ləs) also **sax•ic•o•line** (-līn′) *adj.* Growing on or living among rocks: *saxicolous lichens.* [Lat. *saxum,* stone; see **sek-*** + -COLOUS.]
sax•i•frage (săk′sə-frĭj, -frāj′) *n.* Any of numerous herbs of the genus *Saxifraga,* with small flowers and leaves that often form a basal rosette. [Ult. < LLat. *(herba) saxifraga,* maidenhair fern < Lat. *saxifragus,* rock-breaking : *saxum,* rock; see **sek-*** + *frangere, frāct-,* to break; see **bhreg-***.]
sax•i•tox•in (săk′sĭ-tŏk′sĭn) *n.* A potent neurotoxin produced by certain dinoflagellates and causing food poisoning in human beings who eat shellfish that have fed on these organisms. [NLat. *Saxidomus gigantēus,* clam species (Lat. *saxum,* stone; see SAXATILE + Lat. *domus,* house; see DOME + Lat. *gigantēus,* giant) + TOXIN.]
Sax•o Gram•mat•i•cus (săk′sō grə-măt′ĭ-kəs). 1150?–1220? Danish historian whose *Gesta Danorum,* a chronicle of Danish kings, contains the story of Hamlet.
Sax•on (săk′sən) *n.* **1.** A member of a West Germanic tribal group that invaded Britain in the fifth and sixth centuries A.D. **2.** A person of English or Lowland Scots birth or descent as distinguished from one of Irish, Welsh, or Highland Scots birth or descent. **3.** A native or inhabitant of Saxony. **4.** The West Germanic language of any of the ancient Saxon peoples. **5.** The Germanic element of English as distinguished from the French and Latin elements. [ME < LLat. *Saxō, Saxon-,* of Gmc. orig. See **sek-***.] **—Sax′on** *adj.*
Sax•on•ism (săk′sə-nĭz′əm) *n.* An English word, phrase, or idiom of Anglo-Saxon origin.
sax•o•ny also **Sax•o•ny** (săk′sə-nē) *n., pl.* **-nies. 1.** A wool fabric originally made from the wool of sheep raised in Saxony. **2.** A fine woolen yarn.
Saxony. A historical region of N Germany; conquered by Charlemagne in the 8th cent. and later part of the German Empire (1871–1918).
sax•o•phone (săk′sə-fōn′) *n. Mus.* A woodwind instrument with a single-reed mouthpiece and a usu. curved conical metal tube. [After *Sax,* name of 19th-cent. Belgian instrument-making family.] **—sax′o•phon′ist** *n.*
sax•tu•ba (săks′tōō′bə, -tyōō′-) *n. Mus.* A large bass saxhorn. [SAX(HORN) + TUBA.]
say (sā) *v.* **said** (sĕd), **say•ing, says** (sĕz). *—tr.* **1.** To utter aloud; pronounce. **2.** To express in words. **3.a.** To state as one's opinion or judgment; declare. **b.** To state as a determination of fact: *say who is right.* **4.** To repeat or recite. **5.** To report or maintain; allege. **6.a.** To indicate; show: *The clock says two.* **b.** To give nonverbal expression to; signify or embody. **7.** To suppose; assume. *—intr.* To make a statement; express oneself. *—n.* **1.** A turn or chance to speak. **2.** The right or power to influence or make a decision. **3.** *Archaic.* Something said; a statement. *—adv.* **1.** Approximately. **2.** For instance. *—interj.* Used to express surprise or appeal for someone's attention. ***—idioms.*** **I say. 1.** Used preceding an utterance to call attention to it. **2.** Used as an exclamation of surprise, delight, or dismay. **that is to say.** In other words. [ME *seien* < OE *secgan.* See **sekʷ-³***.] **—say′er** *n.*
Sa•yan Mountains (sä-yän′). A range of mountains in S-central Russia W of Lake Baikal.
Say•ers (sā′ərz), **Dorothy L(eigh).** 1893–1957. British writer known for her mysteries featuring Lord Peter Wimsey.
say•ing (sā′ĭng) *n.* Something, such as an adage, that is said.
sa•yo•na•ra (sī′ə-när′ə) *interj.* Good-bye. [J.]
Say•re•ville (sā′ər-vĭl′, sâr′-). A borough of E-central NJ SSW of Perth Amboy. Pop. 34,986.
say-so (sā′sō′) *n., pl.* **-sos.** *Informal.* **1.** An unsupported statement or assurance. **2.** An authoritative expression of permission or approval. **3.** The right or authority to decide.
say•yid (sä′yĭd) *n. Islam.* **1.** Used as a title and form of address for a dignitary or saint. **2.** A descendant of Muhammad through Fatima and her son Hasan (624?–669?). [Ar.]
Sb The symbol for the element **antimony.** [Lat. *stibium.* See STIBNITE.]
sb. *abbr.* Substantive.
S.B. *abbr. Lat.* Scientiae Baccalaureus (Bachelor of Science).
SBA *abbr.* Small Business Administration.
SbE *abbr.* South by east.
'sblood (zblŭd) *interj. Archaic.* Used as an oath. [Alteration of *God's blood.*]
SBN *abbr.* Standard Book Number.
SbW *abbr.* South by west.
sc also **s.c.** *abbr. Print.* Small capital.
Sc The symbol for the element **scandium.**
SC *abbr.* **1.** Security Council. **2.** Or **S.C.** South Carolina.
sc. *abbr.* **1.** Scale. **2.** Scene. **3.** Science. **4.** Scilicet. **5.** Scruple (unit of weight).
Sc. *abbr.* **1.** Scots; Scottish. **2.** Scotch.
S.C. *abbr. Law.* Supreme Court.
scab (skăb) *n.* **1.** A crust discharged from and covering a healing wound. **2.** Scabies or mange in domestic animals or livestock, esp. sheep. **3.a.** Any of various plant diseases caused by fungi or bacteria and resulting in crustlike spots on fruit, leaves, or roots. **b.** The spots caused by such a disease. **4.** *Slang.* A person regarded as contemptible. **5.a.** A worker who refuses membership in a labor union. **b.** One who works while others are on strike. *—intr.v.* **scabbed, scab•bing, scabs. 1.** To become covered with scabs or a scab. **2.** To work or take a job as a scab. [ME < ON *skabb.*]
scab•bard (skăb′ərd) *n.* A sheath, as for a dagger or sword. *—tr.v.* **-bard•ed, -bard•ing, -bards.** To put into or furnish with such a sheath. [ME *scauberc, scabbard* < OFr. *escauberc,* poss. of Gmc. orig. See **sker-¹***.]
scab•ble (skăb′əl) *tr.v.* **-bled, -bling, -bles.** To work or dress (stone) roughly, preliminary to fine tooling. [ME *scaplen* < ONFr. *escapler,* to dress timber : *es-,* off (< Lat. *ex-*; see EX-) + *capler,* to cut (< LLat. **capulāre, cappulāre*).]
scab•by (skăb′ē) *adj.* **-bi•er, -bi•est. 1.** Having, consisting of, or covered with scabs. **2.** Affected with scab or scabies. **3.** *Informal.* Contemptible; vile. **—scab′bi•ness** *n.*
sca•bies (skā′bēz) *n., pl.* **scabies. 1.** A contagious skin disease caused by a parasitic mite *(Sarcoptes scabiei)* and characterized by intense itching. **2.** A similar disease in animals, esp. sheep. [ME < Lat. *scabiēs* < *scabere,* to scratch.]
sca•bi•et•ic (skā′bē-ĕt′ĭk) *adj.* Of or affected with scabies.
sca•bi•o•sa (skā′bē-ō′sə, -zə, skăb′ē-) *n.* See **scabious²**. [NLat. *Scabiōsa,* genus name < Med.Lat. *(herba) scabiōsa,* (herb) for scabies, scabious, fem. of Lat. *scabiōsus,* mangy < *scabiēs,* itch. See SCABIES.]
sca•bi•ous¹ (skā′bē-əs, skăb′ē-) *adj.* **1.** Of or relating to scabies. **2.** Having scabs. [< Lat. *scabiōsus,* mangy. See SCABIOSA.]
sca•bi•ous² (skā′bē-əs) *n.* Any of various plants of the genus *Scabiosa,* esp. *S. atropurpurea,* having opposite leaves and variously colored flower heads. [ME *scabiose* < Med.Lat. *(herba) scabiōsa,* (herb) for scabies, scabious. See SCABIOSA.]
scab•land (skăb′lănd′) *n.* An elevated area of barren rocky land with little soil cover, usu. crossed by dry streambeds.
scab•rous (skăb′rəs, skā′brəs) *adj.* **1.** Having or covered with scales or small projections and rough to the touch. **2.** Difficult to handle; knotty. **3.** Dealing with scandalous or salacious material. [LLat. *scabrōsus* < *scaber, scabr-,* scurfy.] **—scab′rous•ly** *adv.* **—scab′rous•ness** *n.*
scad¹ (skăd) *n., pl.* **scad** or **scads.** Any of several carangid fishes of the genus *Decapterus,* esp. *D. punctatus* of the western Atlantic. [?]

sawfly
Common sawfly
Tenthredo varipictus

sawhorse

saxophone

ă pat	oi boy
ā pay	ou out
âr care	ŏŏ took
ä father	ōō boot
ĕ pet	ŭ cut
ē be	ûr urge
ĭ pit	th thin
ī pie	*th* this
îr pier	hw which
ŏ pot	zh vision
ō toe	ə about, item
ô paw	

Stress marks:
′ (primary);
′ (secondary), as in
dictionary (dĭk′shə-nĕr′ē)

scad[2] (skăd) *n. Informal.* A large number or amount. Often used in the plural: *Scads of people are in the hall.* [?]

Sca•fell Pike (skô′fĕl′). A mountain, 979.1 m (3,210 ft), in the Cumbrian Mts. of NW England.

scaf•fold (skăf′əld, -ōld′) *n.* **1.** A temporary platform on which workers perform tasks at heights above the ground. **2.** A raised wooden framework or platform. **3.** A platform used in the execution of condemned prisoners, as by hanging or beheading. *—tr.v.* **-fold•ed, -fold•ing, -folds. 1.** To provide or support with a scaffold. **2.** To place on a scaffold. [ME < Med.Lat. *scaffaldus,* of OFr. orig.]

scaf•fold•ing (skăf′əl-dĭng, skăf′ōl′-) *n.* **1.** A scaffold or system of scaffolds. **2.** Materials used for constructing scaffolds.

scaffold

scag (skăg) *n. Slang.* Heroin. [?]

scagl•io•la (skăl-yō′lə, -yô′-) *n.* Plasterwork in imitation of marble, consisting of ground gypsum and glue colored with marble or granite dust. [Ital., dim. of *scaglia,* chip, of Gmc. orig. See **skel-[1]*.**]

scal•age (skā′lĭj) *n.* **1.** An assessed percentage of the total price or measured amount of goods being shipped or stored, used to figure a deduction from the price or amount to reflect normal shrinkage or depletion of the goods. **2.** The estimated amount of lumber in logs being scaled.

sca•lar (skā′lər, -lär′) *n.* **1.** A quantity, such as mass, length, or speed, that is completely specified by its magnitude and has no direction. **2.** A device that yields an output equal to the input multiplied by a constant, as in a linear amplifier. *—adj. Math.* Having only magnitude. Used of numbers or quantities. [Lat. *scālāris,* of a ladder < *scālae,* ladder. See SCALE[2].]

sca•la•re (skə-lâr′ē, -lär′ē) *n.* See **angelfish** 2. [Lat. *scālāre,* neut. of *scālāris,* of a ladder (from its parallel markings) < *scālae,* ladder. See SCALE[2].]

sca•lar•i•form (skə-lăr′ə-fôrm′) *adj. Biol.* Resembling the rungs of a ladder; ladderlike. Used of certain vessels and tissues. [Lat. *scālāris,* of a ladder; see SCALARE + -FORM.]

scalar product *n. Math.* The numerical product of the lengths of two vectors and the cosine of the angle between them.

scal•a•wag (skăl′ə-wăg′) also **scal•ly•wag** (skăl′ē-) *n.* **1.** *Informal.* A reprobate; a rascal. **2.** A white Southern supporter of the federal government during Reconstruction. [?]

scald[1] (skôld) *v.* **scald•ed, scald•ing, scalds.** *—tr.* **1.** To burn with or as if with hot liquid or steam. **2.** To subject to or treat with boiling water. **3.** To heat (a liquid) almost to the boiling point. **4.** To criticize harshly; excoriate. *—intr.* To become scalded. *—n.* **1.** A bodily injury caused by scalding. **2.** *Bot.* **a.** A superficial discoloration on fruit, vegetables, leaves, or tree trunks caused by sudden exposure to intense sunlight or the action of gases. **b.** A disease of some cereal grasses caused by a fungus of the genus *Rhynchosporium.* [ME *scalden* < ONFr. *escalder* < LLat. *excaldāre,* to wash in hot water : Lat. *ex-,* ex- + Lat. *calidus, caldus,* warm, hot; see **kelə-[1]*.**]

scallop
Top: Bay scallop
Pecten irradians
Bottom: Border of a c. 1752–1788 Chelsea dish

scald[2] (skôld, skäld) *n.* Var. of **skald.**

scald[3] (skôld, skäld) *n.* Var. of **scall.**

scald•ing (skôl′dĭng) *adj.* **1.** Causing a burning sensation, as from contact with hot liquid. **2.** Boiling. **3.** Scorching; searing. **4.** Harshly critical or denunciatory; scathing.

scale[1] (skāl) *n.* **1.a.** One of the many small, platelike dermal or epidermal structures that form the external covering of fishes, reptiles, and certain mammals. **b.** A similar part, such as one of the minute structures covering the wings of moths. **2.** *Pathol.* A dry thin flake of epidermis shed from the skin. **3.** A small thin piece. **4.** *Bot.* A small, thin, usu. dry plant structure, such as one that covers a tree bud. **5.a.** A scale insect. **b.** A plant disease or infestation caused by scale insects. **6.a.** A flaky oxide film formed on a metal, as on iron, that has been heated to high temperatures. **b.** A flake of rust. **7.** A hard mineral coating that forms on the inside surface of containers in which water is repeatedly heated. *—v.* **scaled, scal•ing, scales.** *—tr.* **1.** To clear or strip of scale or scales. **2.** To remove in layers or scales: *scaled off the old paint.* **3.** To cover with scales; encrust. **4.** To cause (a thin flat object) by throwing to soar through air or skip along a water surface. **5.** *Dentistry.* To remove (tartar) from tooth surfaces with a pointed instrument. **6.** *Australian.* **a.** To cheat; swindle. **b.** To ride on (a train, for example) without paying the fare. *—intr.* **1.** To come off in scales or layers; flake. **2.** To become encrusted. [ME < OFr. *escale,* of Gmc. orig. See **skel-[1]*.**]

scale[2] (skāl) *n.* **1.a.** A system of ordered marks at fixed intervals used as a reference standard in measurement. **b.** An instrument or device bearing such marks. **c.** A standard of measurement or judgment; a criterion. **2.a.** A proportion used in determining the dimensional relationship of a representation to that which it represents. **b.** A calibrated line, as on a map, indicating such a proportion. **c.** Proper proportion. **3.** A progressive classification, as of size or rank. **4.** A relative level or degree. **5.** A minimum wage fixed by contract. **6.** *Math.* A system of notation in which the values of numerical expressions are determined by their places relative to the chosen base of the system: *the decimal scale.* **7.** *Mus.* An ascending or descending series of tones proceeding by a specified scheme of intervals and varying in pitch arrangement and interval size. *—v.* **scaled, scal•ing, scales.** *—tr.* **1.** To climb up or over; ascend. **2.** To make in accord with a particular proportion or scale. **3.** To alter according to a standard or by degrees; adjust in calculated amounts. **4.** To estimate or measure the quantity of lumber in (logs or uncut trees). *—intr.* **1.** To climb; ascend. **2.** To rise in steps or stages. [ME < Lat. *scālae,* ladder. See **skand-*.**] **—scal′a•ble** *adj.*

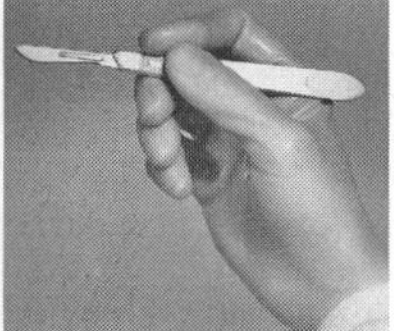
scalpel

scale[3] (skāl) *n.* **1.** An instrument or a machine for weighing. Often used in the plural. **2.** Either of the pans, trays, or dishes of a balance. *—v.* **scaled, scal•ing, scales.** *—tr.* To weigh with scales. *—intr.* To have a given weight, as determined by a scale. [ME, bowl, balance < ON *skāl.* See **skel-[1]*.**]

scale insect *n.* Any of various small homopterous insects of the superfamily Coccoidea, the females of which secrete and remain under waxy scales on plant tissue.

sca•lene (skā′lēn′, skā-lēn′) *adj. Math.* Having three unequal sides. Used of triangles. [LLat. *scalēnus* < Gk. *skalēnos* < *skallein,* to hoe, stir up. See **skel-[1]*.**]

scalene muscle *n.* Any of three muscles on each side of the neck that serve to bend and rotate the neck and assist breathing by raising or fixing the first two ribs.

sca•le•nus (skā-lē′nəs) *n., pl.* **-ni** (-nī, -nē). See **scalene muscle.** [LLat. *scalēnus,* scalene. See SCALENE.]

scal•er (skā′lər) *n.* An electronic circuit recording the aggregate of a specific number of signals that occur too rapidly to be recorded individually. [< SCALE[2].]

Scales (skālz) *pl.n. (used with a sing. v.)* See **Libra** 1, 2a.

Sca•li•a (skə-lē′ə), **Antonin.** b. 1936. Amer. jurist; associate justice of the U.S. Supreme Court (since 1986).

scall (skôl, skäl) also **scald** (skôld, skäld) *n.* A scaly eruption of the skin or scalp. [ME < ON *skalli,* a bald head. See **skel-[1]*.**]

scal•lion (skăl′yən) *n.* **1.** A young onion before it develops a bulb. **2.** Any of several onionlike plants, such as the leek. [ME *scaloun* < AN *scalun* < VLat. **escalōnia,* alteration of Lat. *(caepa) Ascalōnia,* Ascalonian (onion), shallot < *Ascalō, Ascalōn-,* Ascalon (Ashqelon).]

scal•lop (skŏl′əp, skăl′-) also **scol•lop** (skŏl′-) or **es•cal•lop** (ĭ-skŏl′-, ĭ-skăl′-) *—n.* **1.a.** Any of various free-swimming marine mollusks of the family Pectinidae, having fan-shaped bivalve shells with a fluted pattern. **b.** The edible adductor muscle of this mollusk. **c.** A shell of this mollusk or a dish in a similar shape. **2.** One of a series of curved projections forming an ornamental border. **3.** A thin boneless slice of meat. *—v.* **-loped, -lop•ing, -lops.** *—tr.* **1.** To edge (cloth, for example) with scallops. **2.** To bake in a casserole with milk or a sauce and often with bread crumbs. **3.** To cut (meat) into thin boneless slices. *—intr.* To gather scallops for eating or sale. [ME *scalop* < OFr. *escalope,* shell, of Gmc. orig.] **—scal′lop•er** *n.*

scal•ly•wag (skăl′ē-wăg′) *n.* Var. of **scalawag.**

scal•o•gram (skā′lə-grăm′) *n. Psychol.* A scale for measuring attitude or opinion in which agreement with a given item implies agreement with the items lower in rank.

sca•lop•pi•ne also **sca•lop•pi•ni** (skăl′ə-pē′nē, skä′lə-) *n.* Small, thinly sliced pieces of meat, esp. veal, dredged in flour, sautéed, and served in a sauce. [Ital., pl. of *scaloppina,* dim. of *scaloppa,* thin slice < Fr. *escalope* < OFr., shell (< the fillets being served curled like shells). See SCALLOP.]

scalp (skălp) *n.* **1.** The skin covering the top of the human head. **2.** A portion of this skin with its attached hair, cut from a body as a battle trophy or as proof in claiming a bounty. **3.** A piece of hide from the skull of certain animals, such as the fox, shown as proof to collect a bounty. **4.** A trophy of victory. *—v.* **scalped, scalp•ing, scalps.** *—tr.* **1.** To cut or tear the scalp from. **2.** *Slang.* To resell at a price higher than the established value. **3.** *Slang.* To buy and sell (securities or commodities) in order to make small quick profits. *—intr. Slang.* **1.** To engage in reselling something at a price higher than the established value. **2.** To buy and sell securities or commodities for small quick profits. [ME, top of the head, of Scand. orig. See **skel-[1]*.**] **—scalp′er** *n.*

scal•pel (skăl′pəl) *n.* A small knife with a thin blade used in surgery and dissection. [Lat. *scalpellum,* dim. of *scalper, scalprum,* knife < *scalpere,* to scratch, cut. See **skel-[1]*.**]

scalp lock *n.* A long lock of hair left on the top of the shaven head by certain Native American men.

scal•y (skā′lē) *adj.* **-i•er, -i•est. 1.** Covered or partially covered with scales. **2.** Shedding scales or flakes; flaking. **—scal′i•ness** *n.*

scaly anteater *n.* See **pangolin.**

scam (skăm) *Slang.* *—n.* A fraudulent business scheme; a swindle. *—tr.v.* **scammed, scam•ming, scams.** To defraud; swindle. [?] **—scam′mer** *n.*

scam•mo•ny (skăm′ə-nē) *n., pl.* **-nies. 1.** An eastern Mediterranean plant *(Convolvulus scammonia)* having roots that yield a resin formerly used as a cathartic. **2.** The resin from this plant. [ME *scamonie* < OE *scammōniam* and < OFr. *scamonie,* both < Lat. *scammōnea* < Gk. *skammōnia.*]

scamp[1] (skămp) *n.* **1.** A rogue; a rascal. **2.** A mischievous youngster. [Prob. < *scamp,* to go about idly, prob. < obsolete Du. *schampen,* to decamp < MDu. *ontscampen.* See SCAMPER.]

scamp[2] (skămp) *tr.v.* **scamped, scamp•ing, scamps.** To perform in a careless superficial way. [Poss. of Scand. orig.]

scam•per (skăm′pər) *intr.v.* **-pered, -per•ing, -pers.** To run or go quickly and lightly. — *n.* A quick light run or movement. [Prob. < Flem. *schampeeren*, freq. of obsolete Du. *schampen*, to run away < MDu. *ontscampen* < OFr. *escamper*, ult. < Lat. *ex campō*, out of the field : *ex-*, away; see EX– + *campō*, ablative of *campus*, field.]

scam•pi (skăm′pē, skäm′-) *n., pl.* **scampi.** Large shrimp broiled or sautéed and served in a garlic and butter sauce. [Ital., pl. of *scampo*, a kind of lobster < Gk. *kampē*, bending (< its shape), perh. < Gk. *kamptein*, to bend.]

scan (skăn) *v.* **scanned, scan•ning, scans.** — *tr.* **1.** To examine closely. **2.** To look over quickly and systematically. **3.** To look over or leaf through hastily. **4.** To analyze (verse) into metrical patterns. **5.** *Electron.* **a.** To move a beam of light or electrons in a systematic pattern over (a surface) in order to reproduce or sense and subsequently transmit an image. **b.** To move a radar beam in a systematic pattern over (a sector of sky) in search of a target. **6.** *Comp. Sci.* To search (stored data) automatically for specific data. **7.** *Medic.* To examine (a body or a body part) with a CAT scanner or similar scanning apparatus. — *intr.* **1.** To analyze verse into metrical patterns. **2.** To conform to a metrical pattern. **3.** *Electron.* To undergo electronic scanning. — *n.* **1.** The act or an instance of scanning. **2.** Scope or field of vision. **3.a.** Examination of a body part by scanning. **b.** A picture or an image produced by this means. **4.** A single sweep of the beam of electrons across a television screen. [ME *scannen*, to scan a verse < Lat. *scandere*, to climb, scan a verse. See **skand-***.] — **scan′na•ble** *adj.* — **scan′ner** *n.*

Scand. *abbr.* Scandinavia; Scandinavian.

scan•dal (skăn′dl) *n.* **1.** A publicized incident that brings about disgrace or offends the moral sensibilities of society. **2.** A person, thing, or circumstance that causes or ought to cause disgrace or outrage. **3.** Damage to reputation or character caused by disclosure of immoral or improper behavior; disgrace. **4.** Talk that is damaging to one's character; malicious gossip. [Fr. *scandale* < OFr., cause of sin < Lat. *scandalum*, trap, temptation < Gk. *skandalon*. See **skand-***.]

scan•dal•ize (skăn′dl-īz′) *tr.v.* **-ized, -iz•ing, -iz•es. 1.** To offend the morals of. **2.** *Archaic.* To dishonor; disgrace. — **scan′dal•i•za′tion** (-ĭ-zā′shən) *n.* — **scan′dal•iz′er** *n.*

scan•dal•mon•ger (skăn′dl-mŭng′gər, -mŏng′-) *n.* One who spreads malicious gossip. — **scan′dal•mon′ger•ing** *n.*

scan•dal•ous (skăn′dl-əs) *adj.* **1.** Causing scandal; shocking. **2.** Containing material damaging to reputation; defamatory. — **scan′dal•ous•ly** *adv.* — **scan′dal•ous•ness** *n.*

scandal sheet *n.* A periodical that habitually prints gossip or scandalous stories.

scan•dent (skăn′dənt) *adj. Bot.* Climbing. [Lat. *scandēns*, *scandent-*, pr.part. of *scandere*, to climb. See **skand-***.]

Scan•di•a (skăn′dē-ə). Scandinavia.

Scan•di•an (skăn′dē-ən) *adj.* Scandinavian. — *n.* A Scandinavian. [< Lat. *Scandia*, Scandinavia.]

Scan•di•na•vi•a (skăn′də-nā′vē-ə, -nāv′yə). A region of N Europe comprising Norway, Sweden, and Denmark. Finland, Iceland, and the Faeroe Islands are often included in the region.

Scan•di•na•vi•an (skăn′də-nā′vē-ən, -nāv′yən) *adj.* Of or relating to Scandinavia or to its peoples, languages, or cultures. — *n.* **1.** A native or inhabitant of Scandinavia. **2.** See **North Germanic.**

Scandinavian Peninsula. A peninsula of N Europe including Norway and Sweden.

scan•di•um (skăn′dē-əm) *n. Symbol* **Sc** A highly reactive metallic element found in various rare minerals and separated as a byproduct in the processing of certain uranium ores. Atomic number 21; atomic weight 44.956; melting point 1,540°C; boiling point 2,850°C; specific gravity 2.99; valence 3. See table at **element.** [< Lat. *Scandia*, Scandinavia.] — **scan′dic** (-dĭk) *adj.*

scan•ning electron microscope (skăn′ĭng) *n.* An electron microscope that forms a three-dimensional image on a cathode-ray tube by moving a beam of focused electrons across an object and reading both the electrons scattered by the object and the secondary electrons produced by it.

scan•sion (skăn′shən) *n.* Analysis of verse into metrical patterns. [LLat. *scānsiō*, *scānsiōn-* < Lat., act of climbing < *scānsus*, p.part. of *scandere*, to climb. See **skand-***.]

scan•so•ri•al (skăn-sôr′ē-əl, -sōr′-) *adj. Zool.* Adapted to or specialized for climbing. [< Lat. *scānsōrius* < *scānsus*, p.part. of *scandere*, to climb. See **skand-***.]

scant (skănt) *adj.* **scant•er, scant•est. 1.** Barely sufficient: *paid scant attention.* **2.** Falling short of a specific measure. **3.** Inadequately supplied; short. — *tr.v.* **scant•ed, scant•ing, scants. 1.** To give an inadequate portion or allowance to. **2.** To limit, as in amount or share; stint. **3.** To deal with or treat inadequately or neglectfully; slight. [ME < ON *skamt*, neut. of *skammr*, short.] — **scant′ly** *adv.* — **scant′ness** *n.*

scant•ling (skănt′lĭng, -lĭn) *n.* **1.** A very small amount; a modicum. **2.** A small timber used in construction. **3.** The dimensions of a building material, esp. the width and thickness of a timber. **4.** *Naut.* The dimensions of the structural parts of a vessel. Often used in the plural. [Alteration of ME *scantlon*, *scantilon*, carpenter's gauge < OFr. *escantillon*, alteration of **eschandillon* < LLat. **scandiculum*, alteration of *scandāculum*, ladder, gauge < Lat. *scandere*, to climb. See **skand-***.]

scant•y (skăn′tē) *adj.* **-i•er, -i•est. 1.** Barely sufficient or adequate. **2.** Insufficient, as in extent or degree. — **scant′i•ly** *adv.* — **scant′i•ness** *n.*

Scap•a Flow (skăp′ə). A sheltered area of water in the Orkney Is. off N Scotland; site of a naval base in both World Wars.

scape[1] (skāp) *n.* **1.** *Bot.* A leafless flower stalk growing directly from the ground, as in the tulip. **2.** *Biol.* A stalklike part, such as a feather shaft. **3.** *Archit.* The shaft of a column. [Lat. *scāpus*, stalk, perh. < Gk. *skapos.*]

scape[2] (skāp) *v. & n. Archaic.* Var. of **escape.**

scape[3] (skāp) *n.* A scene; a view. Often used in combination: *seascape; mindscape.* [< LANDSCAPE.]

scape•goat (skāp′gōt′) *n.* **1.** One that is made to bear the blame of others. **2.** *Bible.* A live goat over whose head Aaron confessed all the sins of the children of Israel on the Day of Atonement and that was then sent into the wilderness. — *tr.v.* **-goat•ed, -goat•ing, -goats.** To make a scapegoat of. [SCAPE[2] + GOAT.]

scape•grace (skāp′grās′) *n.* A scoundrel; a rascal.

scaph•oid (skăf′oid′) *adj.* Shaped like a boat. — *n. Anat.* See **navicular.** [NLat. *scaphoīdēs* < Gk. *skaphoeidēs*, like a bowl : *skaphē*, tub, boat + *-oeidēs*, -oid.]

scaph•o•pod (skăf′ə-pŏd′) *n.* See **tooth shell.** [< NLat. *Scaphopoda*, class name : Gk. *skaphē*, boat + NLat. *-poda*, -pod.]

scap•o•lite (skăp′ə-līt′) *n.* Any of a series of variously colored, often fluorescent mineral silicates of aluminum, calcium, and sodium. [Lat. *scāpus*, stalk; see SCAPE[1] + -LITE, stone (< the prismatic shape of its crystals).]

sca•pose (skā′pōs′) *adj.* Resembling or consisting of a scape.

scap•u•la (skăp′yə-lə) *n., pl.* **-las** or **-lae** (-lē′). Either of two flat triangular bones forming the back part of the shoulder. [LLat., shoulder < Lat. *scapulae*, the shoulder blades.]

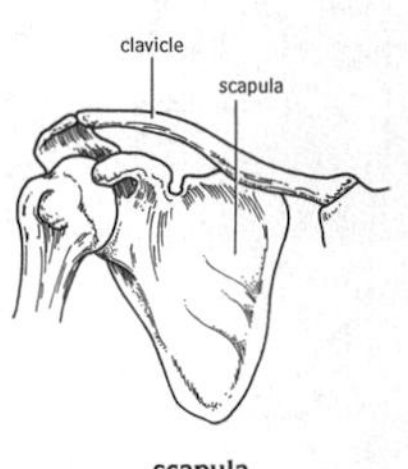

scapula

scap•u•lar (skăp′yə-lər) *n.* **1.** A monk's sleeveless outer garment that hangs from the shoulders and sometimes has a cowl. **2.** A badge worn by affiliates of certain religious orders, consisting of two pieces of cloth joined by shoulder bands and worn under the clothing on the chest and back. **3.** One of the feathers covering the shoulder of a bird. — *adj.* also **scap•u•lar•y** (-lĕr′ē). *Anat.* Of or relating to the shoulder or scapula. [ME *scapulare* < LLat. *scapulāre* < neut. of *scapulāris*, of the shoulders or scapulae < *scapula*, shoulder. See SCAPULA.]

scar[1] (skär) *n.* **1.** A mark left on the skin after a surface injury or wound has healed. **2.** A lingering sign of damage or injury, either mental or physical. **3.** *Bot.* A mark indicating a former attachment, as of a leaf to a stem. **4.** A mark, such as a dent, resulting from use or contact. — *v.* **scarred, scar•ring, scars.** — *tr.* **1.** To mark with a scar. **2.** To leave lasting signs of damage on. — *intr.* **1.** To form a scar. **2.** To become scarred. [ME, alteration of *escare* < OFr., scab < LLat. *eschara* < Gk. *eskhara*, hearth, scab caused by burning.]

scar[2] (skär) *n.* **1.** A protruding isolated rock. **2.** A bare rocky place on a mountainside or other steep slope. [ME *skerre* < ON *sker*, low reef. See **sker-**[1]*.]

scar•ab (skăr′əb) *n.* **1.** A scarabaeid beetle, esp. *Scarabaeus sacer*, regarded as sacred by the ancient Egyptians. **2.** A representation of this beetle, such as a cut gem, used in ancient Egypt as a talisman and a symbol of the soul. [Fr. *scarabée* < Lat. *scarabaeus* < Gk. *karabos*, crab, beetle.]

scar•a•bae•id (skăr′ə-bē′ĭd) *n.* Any of the numerous stout-bodied lamellicorn beetles of the family Scarabaeidae, which includes the June beetle and dung beetles. [< NLat. *Scarabaeidae*, family name < *Scarabaeus*, type genus < Lat. *scarabaeus*, beetle. See SCARAB.] — **scar′a•bae′id** *adj.*

scar•a•bae•us (skăr′ə-bē′əs) *n., pl.* **-bae•us•es** or **-bae•i** (-bē′ī′). See **scarab** 2. [Lat. See SCARAB.]

Scar•a•mouch also **Scar•a•mouche** (skăr′ə-mo͞osh′, -mo͞och′, -mouch′) *n.* A stock character in commedia dell'arte and pantomime, depicted as a boastful coward or buffoon. [Fr. *Scaramouche* < Ital. *Scaramuccia* < *scaramuccia*, skirmish, perh. of Gmc. orig.]

Scar•bor•ough (skär′bûr′ō, -bŭr′ō, -bər-ə). A municipal borough of NE England on the North Sea N of Hull; site of a Bronze Age village. Pop. 43,300.

scarce (skârs) *adj.* **scarc•er, scarc•est. 1.** Insufficient to meet a demand or requirement; short in supply. **2.** Hard to find; absent or rare. — *adv.* Barely or hardly; scarcely. — ***idiom.* make (oneself) scarce.** *Informal.* **1.** To stay away; be absent or elusive. **2.** To depart, esp. quickly or furtively; abscond. [ME *scars* < OFr. *scars* < VLat. **excarpsus*, narrow, cramped < p.part. of **excarpere*, to pluck out, alteration of Lat. *excerpere*, to pick out. See EXCERPT.] — **scarce′ness** *n.*

scarce•ly (skârs′lē) *adv.* **1.** By a small margin; barely: *We scarely made it.* **2.** Almost not; hardly: *It scarcely ever snows here.* **3.** Certainly not: *They could scarcely complain.*

Usage Note: *Scarcely* has the force of a negative and is therefore regarded as incorrectly used with another negative, as in *I couldn't scarcely believe it.* • A clause following *scarce-*

ă pat	oi boy
ā pay	ou out
âr care	o͝o took
ä father	o͞o boot
ĕ pet	ŭ cut
ē be	ûr urge
ĭ pit	th thin
ī pie	*th* this
îr pier	hw which
ŏ pot	zh vision
ō toe	ə about, item
ô paw	

Stress marks:
′ (primary);
′ (secondary), as in
dictionary (dĭk′shə-nĕr′ē)

ly is correctly introduced by *when* or *before*; the use of *than,* though common, is still unacceptable to some grammarians: *I had scarcely begun when* (or *before* but not *than*) *I was interrupted.* See Usage Notes at **double negative, hardly.**

scar•ci•ty (skâr′sĭ-tē) *n., pl.* **-ties. 1.** Insufficiency of amount or supply; shortage. **2.** Rarity of appearance or occurrence.

scare (skâr) *v.* **scared, scar•ing, scares.** *—tr.* To strike with sudden fear; alarm. *—intr.* To become frightened. *—n.* **1.** A condition or sensation of sudden fear. **2.** A general state of alarm; a panic. *—adj.* Serving or intended to frighten people. ***—phrasal verb.*** **scare up.** *Informal.* To gather or prepare with considerable effort or ingenuity. [ME *skerren, scaren* < ON *skirra* < *skjarr,* timid.] **—scar′er** *n.*

scarecrow

scare•crow (skâr′krō′) *n.* **1.** A crude image of a person set up to scare birds away from growing crops. **2.** Something frightening but not dangerous. **3.** A gaunt or haggard person.

scare•mon•ger (skâr′mŭng′gər, -mŏng′-) *n.* One who spreads frightening rumors. **—scare′mon′ger•ing** *n.*

scarf[1] (skärf) *n., pl.* **scarfs** (skärfs) or **scarves** (skärvz). **1.** A long piece of cloth worn about the head, neck, or shoulders. **2.** A decorative cloth for covering the top of a piece of furniture; a runner. **3.** A sash indicating military rank. *—tr.v.* **scarfed, scarf•ing, scarfs. 1.** To dress, cover, or decorate with or as if with a scarf. **2.** To wrap (an outer garment) around one like a scarf. [Fr. dial. *escarpe,* sash, sling < ONFr., var. of OFr. *escherpe,* pilgrim's neck bag < Frankish **skirpja,* small rush < Lat. *scirpus,* rush.]

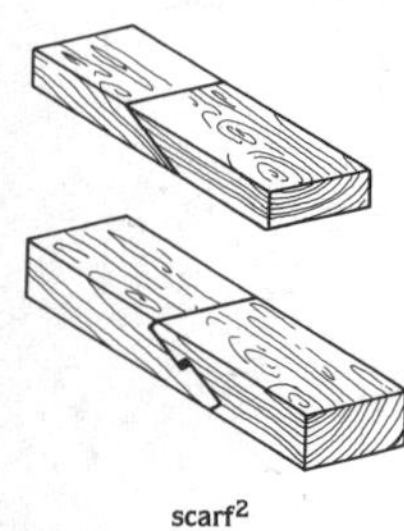

scarf[2]

scarf[2] (skärf) *n., pl.* **scarfs** (skärfs). **1.** A joint made by cutting or notching the ends of two pieces correspondingly and strapping or bolting them together. **2.** Either of the ends that form such a joint. *—tr.v.* **scarfed, scarf•ing, scarfs. 1.** To join by means of a scarf. **2.** To cut a scarf in. [ME *skarf,* prob. < ON *skarfr,* end piece of a board cut off on the bias.]

scarf[3] (skärf) *tr.v.* **scarfed, scarf•ing, scarfs.** *Slang.* To eat or drink voraciously; devour. [Var. of SCOFF[2].] **—scarf′er** *n.*

scarf joint *n.* See **scarf**[2] 1.

scarf•skin (skärf′skĭn′) *n.* The outermost layer of skin, esp. that which forms the cuticle. [SCARF[1] + SKIN.]

scar•i•fy[1] (skăr′ə-fī′) *tr.v.* **-fied, -fy•ing, -fies. 1.** To make shallow cuts in (the skin). **2.** To break up the surface of (topsoil). **3.** To distress deeply, as with severe criticism; lacerate. **4.** *Bot.* To slit or soften the outer coat of (seeds) in order to speed germination. [ME *scarifien* < OFr. *scarifier* < LLat. *scarīficāre,* alteration of Lat. *scarīfāre* < Gk. *skariphasthai,* to sketch, scratch < *skariphos,* pencil, stylus. See **skrībh-*.**] **—scar′i•fi•ca′tion** (-fĭ-kā′shən) *n.* **—scar′i•fi′er** *n.*

scar•i•fy[2] (skâr′ə-fī′) *tr.v.* **-fied, -fy•ing, -fies.** To scare.

scar•i•ous (skâr′ē-əs) also **scar•i•ose** (-ōs′) *adj.* Thin, membranous, and dry: *scarious bracts.* [NLat. *scariōsus.*]

scar•la•ti•na (skär′lə-tē′nə) *n.* See **scarlet fever.** [NLat. *(febris) scarlatina,* scarlet (fever) < Ital. *scarlattina,* fem. of *scarlattino,* scarlet, dim. of *scarlatto* < Pers. *saqirlāt.* See SCARLET.] **—scar′la•ti′nal** *adj.*

Scar•lat•ti (skär-lä′tē), **Alessandro.** 1660–1725. Italian composer who influenced the development of opera. His son **Domenico** (1685–1757) wrote harpsichord works.

scar•let (skär′lĭt) *n.* **1.** *Color.* A strong to vivid red or reddish orange. **2.** Scarlet-colored clothing or cloth. *—adj.* **1.** *Color.* Of the color scarlet. **2.** Flagrantly immoral or unchaste: *scarlet thoughts.* [ME, scarlet cloth, scarlet < OFr. *escarlate* < Med.Lat. *scarlata,* scarlet cloth < Pers. *sāqirlāt,* rich cloth, scarlet cloth, var. of *siqillāt* < Ar. *siqillāt,* perh. < Med.Gk. *sigillatos* < Lat. *sigillātus,* decorated with raised figures < *sigilla,* little figures, pl. of *sigillum,* sigil. See SIGIL.]

scarlet tanager
Piranga olivacea

scarlet fever *n.* An acute contagious disease caused by a hemolytic streptococcus, occurring predominantly in children and marked by a scarlet skin eruption and high fever.

scarlet pimpernel *n.* The pimpernel.

scarlet runner *n.* A tropical American bean plant *(Phaseolus coccineus)* having scarlet flowers and pods with edible seeds.

scarlet sage *n.* A shrubby Brazilian plant *(Salvia splendens)* having showy scarlet flowers, red bracts, and opposite leaves.

scarlet tanager *n.* A New World bird *(Piranga olivacea),* the male of which has scarlet and black plumage.

scarp (skärp) *n.* An escarpment. *—tr.v.* **scarped, scarp•ing, scarps.** To cut or make into an escarpment. [Ital. *scarpa,* slope, perh. of Gmc. orig. See **sker-**[1]***.**]

Scar•ron (skă-rōN′), **Paul.** 1610–60. French writer noted for the novel *Le Roman Comique* (1651–57).

Scars•dale (skärz′dāl′). A city of SE NY, a suburb of New York City. Pop. 16,987.

scar tissue *n.* Dense fibrous connective tissue that forms over a healed wound or cut.

scarves (skärvz) *n.* Pl. of **scarf**[1]**.**

scar•y (skâr′ē) *adj.* **-i•er, -i•est. 1.** Being the cause of fright or alarm. **2.** Easily scared; very timid. **—scar′i•ly** *adv.* **—scar′i•ness** *n.*

scat[1] (skăt) *intr.v.* **scat•ted, scat•ting, scats.** *Informal.* To go away hastily; leave at once. [?]

scat[2] (skăt) *Mus. —n.* Jazz singing in which improvised nonsense syllables are sung to a melody. *—intr.v.* **scat•ted, scat•ting, scats.** To sing scat. [?]

scat[3] (skăt) *n.* Excrement, esp. of an animal; dung. [Perh. < Gk. *skōr, skat-,* excrement. See SCATO–.]

scathe (skāth) *tr.v.* **scathed, scath•ing, scathes. 1.** To harm or injure, esp. by fire. **2.** To criticize or denounce severely. *—n.* Harm or injury. [ME *skathen* < ON *skadha.*]

scath•ing (skā′thĭng) *adj.* **1.** Bitterly denunciatory; harshly critical. **2.** Harmful or painful; injurious. **—scath′ing•ly** *adv.*

scato– *pref.* Excrement: *scatology.* [Gk. *skato-* < *skōr, skat-,* dung. See **sker-**[3]***.**]

sca•tol•o•gy (skă-tŏl′ə-jē, skə-) *n., pl.* **-gies. 1.** The study of fecal excrement, as in biology. **2.** An obsession with excrement or excretory functions. **3.** Obscene language or literature, esp. that dealing with excrement and excretory functions. **—scat′o•log′i•cal** (skăt′l-ŏj′ĭ-kəl), **scat′o•log′ic** (-ĭk) *adj.* **—sca•tol′o•gist** *n.*

scat•ter (skăt′ər) *v.* **-tered, -ter•ing, -ters.** *—tr.* **1.** To cause to scatter or disperse. **2.** To distribute loosely by or as if by sprinkling; strew. **3.** *Phys.* To deflect (radiation or particles). *—intr.* **1.** To separate and go in different directions; disperse. **2.** To occur or fall at widely spaced intervals. *—n.* **1.** The act of scattering or the condition of being scattered. **2.** Something scattered. [ME *scateren.*] **—scat′ter•er** *n.*

scat•ter•brain (skăt′ər-brān′) *n.* A person regarded as flighty, thoughtless, or disorganized. **—scat′ter•brained′** *adj.*

scat•ter•good (skăt′ər-go͝od′) *n.* A spendthrift; a wastrel.

scat•ter•ing (skăt′ər-ĭng) *n.* **1.** Something scattered, esp. a small, irregularly occurring amount or quantity. **2.** *Phys.* The dispersal of a beam of particles or of radiation into a range of directions as a result of physical interactions. *—adj.* Placed irregularly and far apart; scattered. **—scat′ter•ing•ly** *adv.*

scatter rug *n.* A small rug for covering a part of a floor.

scat•ter•shot (skăt′ər-shŏt′) *adj.* Covering a wide range in a random way; indiscriminate.

scat•ty (skăt′ē) *adj.* **-ti•er, -ti•est.** *Chiefly British.* Scatterbrained; flighty. [Prob. SCATT(ERBRAIN) + -Y[1].]

scaup (skôp) *n., pl.* **scaup** or **scaups.** Either of two diving ducks *(Aythya marila* or *A. affinis)* having predominantly black and white plumage in the male. [Perh. < Sc. *scalp, scaup,* bed of mussels (< its feeding on shellfish).]

scav•enge (skăv′ənj) *v.* **-enged, -eng•ing, -eng•es.** *—tr.* **1.** To search through for salvageable material. **2.** To collect and remove refuse from. **3.** To collect (salvageable material) by searching. **4.a.** To expel (exhaust gases) from a cylinder of an internal-combustion engine. **b.** To expel exhaust gases from (such a cylinder). **5.** *Metall.* To clean (molten metal) by chemically removing impurities. *—intr.* **1.** To scavenge refuse. **2.** To feed on dead or decaying matter.

scav•en•ger (skăv′ən-jər) *n.* **1.** One that scavenges, as a person who looks for food in refuse. **2.** An animal that feeds on dead or decaying matter. **3.** *Chem.* A substance added to a mixture to remove or inactivate impurities. [Alteration of ME *schavager,* street maintenance official < AN *scawager,* toll collector < *scawage,* tax on foreign merchants' goods < Flem. *scauwen,* to look at, show. See **keu-*.**]

Sc.B. *abbr. Lat.* Scientiae Baccalaureus (Bachelor of Science).

Sc.D. *abbr. Lat.* Scientiae Doctor (Doctor of Science).

sce•na (shā′nə) *n. Mus.* An extended operatic vocal composition for one or more voices consisting of a recitative and arias or an aria. [Ital. < Lat. *scaena,* stage. See SCENE.]

sce•nar•i•o (sĭ-nâr′ē-ō′, -när′-, -năr′-) *n., pl.* **-os. 1.** An outline of a dramatic or literary plot. **2.** A screenplay. **3.** An outline or model of an expected or supposed sequence of events. [Ital. < *scena,* scene < Lat. *scaena.* See SCENE.]

sce•nar•ist (sĭ-nâr′ĭst, -när′-, -năr′-) *n.* One who writes screenplays.

scend also **send** (sĕnd) *Naut. —intr.v.* **scend•ed, scend•ing, scends** also **send•ed, send•ing, sends.** To heave upward on a wave or swell. *—n.* The rising movement of a ship on a wave or swell. [Prob. alteration of SEND[1].]

scene (sēn) *n.* **1.** Something seen by a viewer; a view or prospect. **2.** The place where an action or event occurs. **3.** The place in which the action of a play, movie, novel, or other narrative occurs; a setting. **4.a.** A subdivision of an act in a dramatic presentation in which the setting is fixed and the time continuous. **b.** A shot or series of shots in a movie constituting a unit of continuous related action. **5.a.** The scenery and properties for a dramatic presentation. **b.** A theater stage. **6.** A real or fictitious episode, esp. when described. **7.** A public display of passion or temper. **8.a.** A sphere of activity. **b.** *Slang.* A situation or set of circumstances. ***—idiom.*** **behind the scenes. 1.** Backstage. **2.** In private. [Fr. *scène,* stage < OFr. < Lat. *scaena* < Gk. *skēnē,* tent, stage.]

scen•er•y (sē′nə-rē) *n., pl.* **-ies. 1.** A view or views of natural features, esp. in open country. **2.** Painted backdrops.

scene-steal•er (sēn′stē′lər) *n.* An actor who draws attention from or overshadows other actors in the same production.

sce•nic (sē′nĭk) *adj.* **1.** Of or relating to the stage, stage scenery, or theatrical representation: *scenic design.* **2.** Constituting or affording pleasing views of natural features. *—n.* A depiction of natural scenery. **—sce′ni•cal•ly** *adv.*

sce•nog•ra•phy (sē-nŏg′rə-fē) *n.* The art of representing objects in perspective, esp. as applied to the design of theatrical scenery. **—sce·nog′raph·er** *n.* **—sce′no·graph′ic** (-nə-grăf′ĭk) *adj.*

scent (sĕnt) *n.* **1.** A distinctive, often agreeable odor. See Syns at **smell. 2.** A perfume. **3.** An odor left by an animal. **4.** The trail of a hunted animal or fugitive. **5.** The sense of smell. **6.** A hint of something imminent; a suggestion. *—v.* **scent·ed, scent·ing, scents.** *—tr.* **1.** To perceive or identify by the sense of smell. **2.** To suspect or detect as if by smelling. **3.** To fill with a pleasant odor; perfume. *—intr.* To hunt prey by means of the sense of smell. Used of hounds. [ME *sent* < *senten,* to scent < OFr. *sentir* < Lat. *sentīre,* to feel. See **sent-***.]

scent gland *n.* A specialized apocrine gland found in many mammals that produces a strong-smelling substance.

scep·ter (sĕp′tər) *n.* **1.** A staff held by a sovereign as an emblem of authority. **2.** Ruling power or authority; sovereignty. *—tr.v.* **-tered, -ter·ing, -ters.** To invest with royal authority. [ME *sceptre* < OFr. < Lat. *scēptrum* < Gk. *skēptron.*]

scep·tic (skĕp′tĭk) *n.* Var. of **skeptic.**

scep·ti·cal (skĕp′tĭ-kəl) *adj.* Var. of **skeptical.**

scep·ti·cism (skĕp′tĭ-sĭz′əm) *n.* Var. of **skepticism.**

scep·tre (sĕp′tər) *n. & v. Chiefly British.* Var. of **scepter.**

sch. *abbr.* School.

scha·den·freu·de (shäd′n-froi′də) *n.* Pleasure derived from the misfortunes of others. [Ger. : *Schaden,* damage (< MHGer. *schade* < OHGer. *scado*) + *Freude,* joy (< MHGer. *vreude* < OHGer. *frewida* < *frō,* happy).]

Schaer·beek (skär′bāk′, SKHär′-). A city of central Belgium, a suburb of Brussels. Pop. 105,672.

Scha·pi·ro (shə-pîr′ō), **Miriam.** b. 1923. Canadian-born Amer. artist who developed "femmage," a form of collage using media such as lace and fabric.

Schaum·burg (shäm′bûrg′). A village of NE IL, a suburb of Chicago. Pop. 68,586.

sched·ule (skĕj′o͞ol, -o͞o-əl, skĕj′əl) *n.* **1.** A list of times of departures and arrivals; a timetable. **2.** A plan for performing work or achieving an objective, specifying the order and allotted time for each part. **3.** A printed or written list of items in tabular form. **4.a.** A program of events or appointments expected in a given time. **b.** A student's program of classes. **5.** A supplemental statement of details appended to a document. *—tr.v.* **-uled, -ul·ing, -ules. 1.** To enter on a schedule. **2.** To make up a schedule for. **3.** To plan or appoint for a certain time or date. [ME *sedule,* slip of parchment or paper, note < OFr. *cedule* < LLat. *schedula,* dim. of *scheda,* var. of Lat. *scida,* papyrus strip < Gk. *skhida, skhedē*; perh. akin to *skhizein,* to split. See SCHIZO-.] **—sched′u·lar** *adj.* **—sched′u·ler** *n.*

Schee·le (shā′lə), **Karl Wilhelm.** 1742–86. German-born Swedish chemist who independently discovered oxygen (c. 1772) before Joseph Priestley.

schee·lite (shā′līt′, shē′-) *n.* A variously colored mineral, $CaWO_4$, found in igneous rocks and used as an ore of tungsten.

schef·fler·a (shĕf-lîr′ə, -lĕr′ə, shĕf′lər-ə) *n.* Any of numerous evergreen shrubs or small trees of the genus *Schefflera,* having palmately compound leaves and unisexual flowers grouped in umbels. [NLat., genus name, after J.C. *Scheffler,* 18th-cent. German botanist.]

Scheldt (skĕlt). A river rising in N France and flowing c. 434 km (270 mi) to the North Sea.

Schel·ling (shĕl′ĭng), **Friedrich Wilhelm Joseph von.** 1775–1854. German idealist philosopher whose theories of the self, nature, and art influenced romanticism.

sche·ma (skē′mə) *n., pl.* **sche·ma·ta** (skē-mä′tə, skĭ-măt′ə) or **sche·mas. 1.** A diagrammatic representation; an outline or a model. **2.** *Psychol.* A pattern imposed on complex reality or experience to assist in explaining it, mediate perception, or guide response. [Lat. *schēma, schēmat-,* form. See SCHEME.]

sche·mat·ic (skē-măt′ĭk, skĭ-) *adj.* Of, relating to, or in the form of a scheme or diagram. *—n.* A structural or procedural diagram, esp. of an electrical or mechanical system. **—sche·mat′i·cal·ly** *adv.*

sche·ma·tism (skē′mə-tĭz′əm) *n.* The patterned disposition of constituents within a given system.

sche·ma·tize (skē′mə-tīz′) *tr.v.* **-tized, -tiz·ing, -tiz·es.** To express in or reduce to a scheme: *schematized the consumption of wealth.* [Gk. *skhēmatizein,* to give form to < *skhēma, skhēmat-,* form. See SCHEME.] **—sche′ma·ti·za′tion** (-tĭ-zā′shən) *n.*

scheme (skēm) *n.* **1.** A systematic plan of action. **2.** A secret or devious plan; a plot. See Syns at **plan. 3.** An impractical or unrealistic plan. **4.** An orderly combination of related parts: *an irrigation scheme.* **5.** A chart, a diagram, or an outline of a system or an object. *—v.* **schemed, schem·ing, schemes.** *—tr.* **1.** To plot. **2.** To contrive a plan or scheme for. *—intr.* To make plans, esp. secret or devious ones. [Lat. *schēma,* figure < Gk. *skhēma.* See **segh-***.] **—schem′er** *n.*

Sche·nec·ta·dy (skə-nĕk′tə-dē). A city of E NY on the Mohawk R. NW of Albany; first settled in 1661. Pop. 65,566.

scher·zan·do (skĕrt-sän′dō) *Mus. —adv. & adj.* In a light playful manner. *—n., pl.* **-dos.** A scherzando passage. [Ital., gerund of *scherzare,* to joke < OItal. See SCHERZO.]

scher·zo (skĕr′tsō) *n., pl.* **-zos** or **-zi** (-tsē). *Mus.* A lively movement, commonly in 3/4 time. [Ital., joke, scherzo < OItal. *scherzare,* to joke, perh. of Gmc. orig.]

Schia·pa·rel·li (skē-äp′ə-rĕl′ē, skăp′-, shăp′-, skyäp′ä-rĕl′-lē), **Elsa.** 1896–1973. Italian-born fashion designer noted for her use of brilliant colors and synthetic materials.

Schick test (shĭk) *n.* A test for immunity to diphtheria by injection of dilute diphtheria toxin into the skin. [After Béla *Schick* (1877–1967), Amer. pediatrician.]

Schie·dam (skē-däm′, SKHē-). A city of SW Netherlands, a suburb of Rotterdam; chartered 1275. Pop. 69,849.

schil·ler (shĭl′ər) *n.* A lustrous colored reflection from certain planes in a mineral grain. [Ger., iridescence < MHGer. *schilher,* iridescent taffeta < *schilhen,* to twinkle, squint < OHGer. *scilihen,* to squint, wink.]

Schil·ler (shĭl′ər), **Johann Christoph Friedrich von.** 1759–1805. German writer best known for his didactic poetry and historical plays, such as *Don Carlos* (1787).

schil·ling (shĭl′ĭng) *n.* See table at **currency.** [Ger. < MHGer. *schillinc* < OHGer. *skilling,* gold coin.]

schip·per·ke (skĭp′ər-kē, -kə) *n.* A small stocky dog of a Belgian breed, having dense, long black fur and small pointed ears. [Flem., dim. of *schipper,* skipper (from the dog's use as a watchdog on a boat) < MDu. See SKIPPER[1].]

schism (sĭz′əm, skĭz′-) *n.* **1.** A separation into factions. **2.a.** A formal breach of union within a Christian church. **b.** The offense of attempting to produce such a breach. **3.** Disunion; discord. [ME *scisme* < OFr. < Lat. *schisma, schismat-* < Gk. *skhisma* < *skhizein,* to split. See **skei-***.]

schis·mat·ic (sĭz-măt′ĭk, skĭz-) *adj.* Of, relating to, or engaging in schism. *—n.* One who promotes or engages in schism. **—schis·mat′i·cal·ly** *adv.*

schist (shĭst) *n.* Any of various medium-grained to coarse-grained metamorphic rocks composed of laminated, often flaky parallel layers of chiefly micaceous minerals. [Fr. *schiste* < Lat. *(lapis) schistos,* fissile (stone), a kind of iron ore < Gk. *skhistos,* split, divisible < *skhizein,* to split. See **skei-***.] **—schis′tose′** (shĭs′tōs′), **schis′tous** (-təs) *adj.*

schis·tor·rha·chis (shĭ-stôr′ə-kĭs) *n.* See **spina bifida.** [Gk. *skhistos,* split; see SCHIST + Gk. *rhakhis,* backbone.]

schis·to·some (shĭs′tə-sōm′) *n.* Any of several chiefly tropical trematode worms of the genus *Schistosoma,* many of which are parasitic in mammalian blood. [NLat. *Schistosoma,* genus name : Gk. *skhistos,* split; see SCHIST + Gk. *soma,* body; see -SOME[3].] **—schis′to·som′al** (-sō′məl) *adj.*

schis·to·so·mi·a·sis (shĭs′tə-sə-mī′ə-sĭs) *n., pl.* **-ses** (-sēz′). Any of various diseases caused by schistosomes, widespread in rural areas of Africa, Asia, and Latin America through use of contaminated water and characterized by infection and gradual destruction of the kidneys, liver, and other organs.

schiz·o (skĭt′sō) *n., pl.* **-os.** *Informal.* A schizophrenic person. **—schiz′o** *adj.*

schizo- or **schiz-** *pref.* **1.** Split; cleft: *schizocarp.* **2.** Cleavage; fission: *schizogenesis.* **3.** Schizophrenia: *schizoid.* [NLat. < Gk. *skhizo-* < *skhizein,* to split. See **skei-***.]

schiz·o·carp (skĭz′ə-kärp′, skĭt′sə-) *n.* A dry fruit that splits at maturity into two or more closed one-seeded parts, as in the carrot. **—schiz′o·car′pous, schiz′o·car′pic** *adj.*

schiz·o·gen·e·sis (skĭz′ō-jĕn′ĭ-sĭs, skĭt′sō-) *n. Biol.* Reproduction by fission.

schi·zog·o·ny (skĭ-zŏg′ə-nē, skĭt-sŏg′-) *n.* Reproduction by multiple asexual fission, characteristic of many sporozoans. **—schi·zog′o·nous** *adj.*

schiz·oid (skĭt′soid′) *adj.* **1.** Schizophrenic. **2.** Of, relating to, or having a personality marked by extreme shyness, seclusiveness, and an inability to form close relationships. *—n.* A schizoid or schizophrenic person.

schiz·ont (skĭz′ŏnt′, skĭt′sŏnt′) *n.* A sporozoan cell produced by schizogony.

schiz·o·phrene (skĭt′sə-frēn′) *n.* A person having or predisposed to schizophrenia.

schiz·o·phre·ni·a (skĭt′sə-frē′nē-ə, -frĕn′ē-ə) *n.* **1.** Any of a group of psychotic disorders usu. characterized by withdrawal from reality, illogical patterns of thinking, delusions, and hallucinations and accompanied in varying degrees by other emotional, behavioral, or intellectual disturbances. **2.** A condition that results from the coexistence of disparate or antagonistic qualities, identities, or activities.

schiz·o·phren·ic (skĭt′sə-frĕn′ĭk) *adj.* **1.** Of, relating to, or affected with schizophrenia. **2.** Of, relating to, or characterized by the coexistence of disparate or antagonistic elements. *—n.* One who is affected with schizophrenia. **—schiz′o·phren′i·cal·ly** *adv.*

schiz·o·thy·mi·a (skĭt′sə-thī′mē-ə) *n.* Behavior or characteristics resembling schizophrenia but remaining within the limits of normality. **—schiz′o·thy′mic** *adj. & n.*

schiz·y also **schiz·zy** (skĭt′sē) *adj.* **-i·er, -i·est.** *Informal.* Schizophrenic or schizoid.

Schle·gel (shlā′gəl), **August Wilhelm von.** 1767–1845. German scholar and poet who edited a literary magazine with his brother **Friedrich** (1772–1829), a poet and critic whose essays formed the basis of German romanticism.

scepter

schipperke

ă pat	oi boy
ā pay	ou out
âr care	o͝o took
ä father	o͞o boot
ĕ pet	ŭ cut
ē be	ûr urge
ĭ pit	th thin
ī pie	*th* this
îr pier	hw which
ŏ pot	zh vision
ō toe	ə about, item
ô paw	

Stress marks:
′ (primary);
′ (secondary), as in **dictionary** (dĭk′shə-nĕr′ē)

Helmut Schmidt

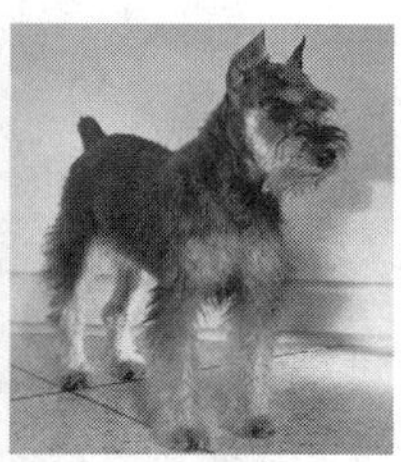
schnauzer
Miniature breed

schooner
The *Adventure*

Schlei•er•ma•cher (shlī′ər-mä′kər, -KHər), **Friedrich Ernst Daniel.** 1768–1834. German philosopher who believed that the individual must develop a personal religious attitude.

schle•miel also **shle•miel** (shlə-mēl′) *n. Slang.* A habitual bungler; a dolt. [Yiddish *shlemíl*, perh. < Heb. *šělumî'ēl*, Shelumiel, a character in the Bible (Numbers 7:36).]

schlep or **schlepp** also **shlep** (shlĕp) *Slang.* —*v.* **schlepped, schlep•ping, schleps** or **schlepped, schlepp•ing, schlepps** also **shlepped, shlep•ping, shleps.** —*tr.* To carry clumsily or with difficulty; lug. —*intr.* To move slowly or laboriously. —*n.* **1.** An arduous journey. **2.** A person regarded as clumsy or stupid. [Yiddish *shlepn*, to drag, pull < MLGer. *slēpen*. See **lei-***.] —**schlep′per, schlepp′er, shlep′per** *n.*

Schles•in•ger (shlĕs′ĭn-jər), **Arthur Meier.** 1888–1965. Amer. historian whose works include *The Rise of the City* (1933). His son **Arthur Meier, Jr.** (b. 1917), also a historian, was an adviser to President John F. Kennedy.

Schles•wig (shlĕs′wĭg, -wĭk, shlās′vĭk). A historical region and former duchy of N Germany and S Denmark in S Jutland.

Schlie•mann (shlē′män′), **Heinrich.** 1822–90. German archaeologist who discovered the ruins of ancient Troy (1871) and excavated Mycenae (1876).

schlie•ren (shlîr′ən) *pl.n.* **1.** *Geol.* Irregular streaks in plutonic igneous rock that differ in composition from the principal mass. **2.** Regions of a transparent medium that photograph as streaks when illuminated because their densities are different from that of the bulk of the medium. [Ger., pl. of *Schliere* < dial. *Shliere*, streaks < MHGer. *slier*, mud, slime < OHGer. *slierrun*, pieces, bits.]

schli•ma•zel (shlĭ-mä′zəl) *n. Slang.* An extremely unlucky or inept person. [Yiddish *shlimázl*, bad luck, unlucky person : MHGer. *slimp*, wrong + *mázl*, luck (< Heb. *mazzāl*).]

schlock also **shlock** (shlŏk) *Slang.* —*n.* Something, such as merchandise, that is inferior or shoddy. —*adj.* Of inferior quality; cheap or shoddy. [Poss. < Yiddish *shlak*, apoplexy, stroke, evil, nuisance < MHGer. *slag, slak*, stroke < *slahen*, to strike < OHGer. *slahan*.] —**schlock′y, shlock′y** *adj.*

schmaltz also **schmalz** (shmälts) *n.* **1.** *Informal.* **a.** Excessively sentimental art or music. **b.** Maudlin sentimentality. **2.** Liquid fat, esp. chicken fat. [Yiddish *shmalts*, animal fat, sentimentality < MHGer. *smalz*, animal fat < OHGer. See **mel-**[1]***.]

schmaltz•y also **schmalz•y** (shmält′sē) *adj.* **-i•er, -i•est.** *Informal.* Of, relating to, or marked by excessive or maudlin sentimentality. —**schmaltz′i•ness** *n.*

schmeer also **schmear** or **shmear** (shmîr) *n. Slang.* A number of things that go together; an aggregate: *bought the whole schmeer.* [Yiddish *shmir*, smear, smudge < *shmirn*, to smear, grease < MHGer. *smiren* < OHGer. *smirwen*.]

Schmidt (shmĭt), **Helmut.** b. 1918. German politician who served as chancellor of West Germany (1974–82).

Schmidt system *n.* A system consisting of a concave spherical mirror with a transparent plate at its center of curvature, used in reflecting telescopes to offset spherical aberration and coma. [After Bernhard Voldemar *Schmidt* (1879–1935), Estonian-b. German optical scientist.]

schmo (shmō) *n., pl.* **schmoes** or **schmos.** *Slang.* A person regarded as stupid or obnoxious. [< Yiddish *shmok*, penis, fool. See SCHMUCK.]

schmooze or **schmoose** (shmo͞oz) *Slang.* —*intr.v.* **schmoozed, schmooz•ing, schmooz•es** or **schmoosed, schmoos•ing, schmoos•es.** To talk casually; chat. —*n.* A chat. [Yiddish *shmúesn*, poss. < *shmúes*, a chat, pl. of *shmúe*, rumor; akin to Heb. *šěmû'â*, rumor.] —**schmooz′er** *n.*

schmuck also **shmuck** (shmŭk) *n. Slang.* A person regarded as clumsy or stupid; an oaf. [Yiddish *shmok*, penis, fool, prob. < Pol. *smok*, serpent, tail.]

Schna•bel (shnä′bəl), **Artur.** 1882–1951. Austrian-born Amer. pianist and composer.

schnap•per (shnăp′ər, snăp′-) *n.* A porgy *(Chrysophrys guttulatus)* of Australia, Tasmania, and New Zealand, prized as a sport fish and food fish. [Alteration of SNAPPER.]

schnapps (shnäps, shnăps) *n., pl.* **schnapps.** Any of various strong dry liquors, such as a strong Dutch gin. [Ger. *Schnaps*, mouthful, schnapps < LGer. *snaps* < *snappen*, to snap < MLGer., to snap at.]

schnau•zer (shnou′zər, shnou′tsər) *n.* Any of three German breeds of dog of a range of sizes, having a wiry pepper-and-salt or black coat and a blunt muzzle with wiry whiskers. [Ger. < *Schnauze*, snout, alteration of MLGer. *snūte*.]

schnit•zel (shnĭt′səl) *n.* A thin cutlet of veal, usu. seasoned, that is dipped in batter and fried. [Ger. < MHGer. *snitzel*, dim. of *sniz*, slice < *snitzen*, to carve, freq. of *snīden*, to cut < OHGer. *snīdan*.]

Schnitz•ler (shnĭts′lər), **Arthur.** 1862–1931. Austrian writer whose works include *La Ronde* (1896).

schnook (shno͝ok) *n. Slang.* A stupid or easily duped person. [Yiddish *shnuk*, snout, schnook < Lith. *snùkis*, mug, snout.]

schnor•rer (shnôr′ər, shnōr′-) *n. Slang.* One who habitually takes advantage of the generosity of others; a parasite. [Yiddish *shnorer* < *shnorn*, to beg < MHGer. *snurren*, to hum, whir (< a beggar's musical instrument).]

schnoz (shnŏz) also **schnoz•zle** (shnŏz′əl) *n. Slang.* The human nose. [Prob. alteration of Yiddish *snoyts*, snout, muzzle < Ger. *Schnauze*.]

schol•ar (skŏl′ər) *n.* **1.a.** A learned person. **b.** A specialist in a given branch of knowledge: *a classical scholar.* **2.** One who attends school or studies with a teacher; a student. **3.** A student holding a particular scholarship. [ME *scoler* < OFr. *escoler* and < OE *scolere*, both < Med.Lat. *scholāris* < LLat., of a school < Lat. *scola, schola*, school. See SCHOOL[1].]

schol•ar•ly (skŏl′ər-lē) *adj.* Of or characteristic of scholars or scholarship. See Syns at **learned.** —**schol′ar•li•ness** *n.*

schol•ar•ship (skŏl′ər-shĭp′) *n.* **1.** The methods, discipline, and attainments of a scholar or scholars. **2.** Knowledge resulting from study and research in a particular field. **3.** A grant of financial aid to a student.

scho•las•tic (skə-lăs′tĭk) *adj.* **1.** Of or relating to schools; academic. **2.** Often **Scholastic.** Of, relating to, or characteristic of Scholasticism. **3.** Adhering rigidly to scholarly methods; pedantic. —*n.* **1.** Often **Scholastic.** A Scholastic philosopher or theologian. **2.** A dogmatist; a pedant. [Lat. *scholasticus* < Gk. *skholastikos*, learned, studious < *skholazein*, to study < *skholē*, school. See **segh-***.] —**scho•las′ti•cal•ly** *adv.*

scho•las•ti•cism (skə-lăs′tĭ-sĭz′əm) *n.* **1.** Often **Scholasticism.** The dominant western Christian theological and philosophical school of the Middle Ages, based on the authority of the Latin Fathers and of Aristotle and his commentators. **2.** Close adherence to traditional methods or teachings.

scho•li•ast (skō′lē-ăst′) *n.* One of the ancient commentators who annotated the classical authors. [Med.Gk. *skholiastēs* < *skholiazein*, to comment on < Gk. *skholion*, scholium. See SCHOLIUM.]

scho•li•um (skō′lē-əm) *n., pl.* **-li•ums** or **-li•a** (-lē-ə). **1.** An explanatory note or commentary, as on a Greek text. **2.** A note amplifying a proof or course of reasoning, as in mathematics. [NLat. < Gk. *skholion*, dim. of *skholē*, lecture, school. See **segh-***.]

Schön•berg (shœn′bûrg, shûrn′-, shœn′bĕrk′), **Arnold.** 1874–1951. Austrian composer of *Pierrot Lunaire* (1912).

school[1] (sko͞ol) *n.* **1.** An institution for the instruction of children or people under college age. **2.** An institution for instruction in a skill or business. **3.a.** A college or university. **b.** An institution associated with a college or university that gives instruction in a specialized field and recommends candidates for degrees. **c.** A division of an educational institution constituting several grades or classes. **d.** The student body of an educational institution. **e.** The building or buildings housing an educational institution. **4.** The process of being educated formally, esp. by a planned series of courses over a number of years. **5.** A session of instruction. **6.a.** A group of people, esp. philosophers, artists, or writers, whose thought, work, or style demonstrates a common origin or influence or unifying belief. **b.** A group of people distinguished by similar manners, customs, or opinions. **7.** *Australian.* A group of people gathered together for gambling. —*tr.v.* **schooled, school•ing, schools. 1.** To educate in or as if in a school. **2.** To train or discipline. See Syns at **teach.** —*adj.* Of or relating to school or education in schools. [ME *scole* < OE *scōl* < Lat. *schola, scola* < Gk. *skholē*. See **segh-***.]

school[2] (sko͞ol) *n.* A large group of aquatic animals, esp. fish, swimming together; a shoal. —*intr.v.* **schooled, school•ing, schools.** To swim in or form into a school. [ME *scole* < MDu. See **skel-**[1]***.]

school age *n.* The age at which a child is considered old enough to attend school. —**school′-age′** (sko͞ol′āj′) *adj.*

school board *n.* A local board that oversees public schools.

school•book (sko͞ol′bo͝ok′) *n.* A book for use in school.

school•boy (sko͞ol′boi′) *n.* A boy attending school.

school bus *n.* A vehicle used for taking schoolchildren to and from school or school-related activities.

school•child also **school child** (sko͞ol′chīld′) *n.* A child attending school.

school day *n.* **1.** A day on which school is in session. **2.** The part of a day during which school is in session.

school district *n.* A geographic district, the public schools of which are administered together.

school•fel•low (sko͞ol′fĕl′ō) *n.* A schoolmate.

school•girl (sko͞ol′gûrl′) *n.* A girl attending school.

school•house (sko͞ol′hous′) *n.* A building used as a school.

school•ing (sko͞o′lĭng) *n.* **1.** Instruction or training given at school. **2.** Education from experience or exposure. **3.** The training of a horse or a horse and rider in equitation.

school•man (sko͞ol′mən) *n.* **1.** A man who is a professional educator or scholar. **2. Schoolman.** A medieval Scholastic scholar or philosopher.

school•marm (sko͞ol′märm′) also **school•ma'am** (-mäm′, -măm′) *n.* A woman teacher, esp. one regarded as strict, old-fashioned, or prudish. [SCHOOL[1] + dial. *marm* (var. of MA'AM).] —**school′marm′ish** *adj.*

school•mas•ter (sko͞ol′măs′tər) *n.* **1.** A man who is a teacher. **2.** A headmaster of a school. **3.** One that educates, guides, or instructs. **4.** A grayish-brown snapper *(Lutjanus apodus)* of the tropical Atlantic and the Gulf of Mexico. —**school′mas′ter•ish, school′mas′ter•ly** *adj.*

school•mate (sko͞ol′māt′) *n.* A companion or an associate in one's school.
school•mis•tress (sko͞ol′mĭs′trĭs) *n.* **1.** A woman who is a teacher. **2.** A headmistress of a school.
school of hard knocks *n. Informal.* The practical experiences of life that educate and temper a person.
school of thought *n., pl.* **schools of thought.** The point of view held by a particular group.
school•room (sko͞ol′ro͞om′, -ro͝om′) *n.* A classroom.
school•teach•er (sko͞ol′tē′chər) *n.* A person who teaches in a school below the college level.
school•work (sko͞ol′wûrk′) *n.* School lessons or homework.
school year *n.* The part of the year during which school is in session, typically from September to June.
schoo•ner (sko͞o′nər) *n.* **1.** *Naut.* A fore-and-aft rigged sailing vessel with at least two masts with the largest sail carried on the aftermost mast. **2.** A large beer glass, generally holding a pint or more. **3.** A prairie schooner. [?]
Scho•pen•hau•er (shō′pən-hou′ər), **Arthur.** 1788–1860. German philosopher whose works include *The World as Will and Representation* (1819).
schot•tische (shŏt′ĭsh, shŏ-tēsh′) *n.* **1.** A round dance in 2/4 time. **2.** A piece of music for this dance. [Ger. < *schottisch*, Scottish < MHGer. *schottesch* < *schotte*, a Scot < OHGer. *scotto* < LLat. *Scottus*, Irishman.]
Schou•ten Islands (skout′n). An island group of E Indonesia in the S Pacific off the N coast of New Guinea.
schrod (skrŏd) *n. New England.* Var. of **scrod.**
Schrö•ding•er (shrō′dĭng-ər, shrā′-, shrœ′-), **Erwin.** 1887–1961. Austrian physicist who shared a 1933 Nobel Prize.
schtick (shtĭk) *n.* Var. of **shtick.**
Schu•bert (sho͞o′bərt, -bĕrt′), **Franz Peter.** 1797–1828. Austrian composer who perfected the form of the German art song in his more than 600 compositions for voice and piano.
Schulz (sho͝olts), **Charles Monroe.** b. 1922. Amer. cartoonist who created the *Peanuts* comic strip.
Schu•man (sho͞o′mən), **William Howard.** 1910–92. Amer. composer whose works include *A Free Song* (1943).
Schu•mann (sho͞o′män′, -mən), **Robert.** 1810–56. German romantic composer known particularly for his song cycles.
Schu•mann-Heink (sho͞o′mən-hīngk′), **Ernestine.** 1861–1936. Amer. contralto noted for her roles in the operas of Wagner and Richard Strauss.
Schurz (sho͝orts, shûrz), **Carl.** 1829–1906. German-born Amer. army officer, politician, and newspaper editor.
schuss (sho͝os, sho͞os) *Sports.* —*intr.v.* **schussed, schuss•ing, schuss•es.** To make a schuss. —*n.* **1.** A fast straight downhill run in skiing. **2.** A straight steep skiing course. [< Ger., schuss, ult. < OHGer. *scuz*, shot. See **skeud-*.**]
schuss•boom•er (sho͝os′bo͞o′mər, sho͞os′-) *n. Sports.* A skier who schusses well.
Schuy•ler (skī′lər), **Philip John.** 1733–1804. Amer. Revolutionary general who was relieved of his command after the British capture of Fort Ticonderoga (1777).
Schuyl•kill (sko͞ol′kĭl′, sko͞o′kəl). A river of SE PA flowing c. 209 km (130 mi) to the Delaware R. at Philadelphia.
schwa (shwä) *n. Ling.* **1.** A midcentral neutral vowel, typically occurring in unstressed syllables, as the final vowel of English *sofa.* **2.** The symbol (ə) used to represent this sound and also, less often, a stressed midcentral vowel, as in *but.* [Ger. < Heb. *šěwā'*, prob. < Syriac *šěwayyā*, equal.]
Schwann (shvän), **Theodor.** 1810–82. German physiologist who described the cell as the basic structure of animal tissue.
Schwann cell (shwän, shvän) *n.* Any of the cells that cover the nerve fibers in the peripheral nervous system and form the myelin sheath. [After Theodor SCHWANN.]
Schweit•zer (shwīt′sər, shvīt′-), **Albert.** 1875–1965. French philosopher, physician, and missionary who won the 1952 Nobel Peace Prize.
Schwe•rin (shvā-rēn′). A city of N-central Germany on **Schwerin Lake** SW of Rostock; chartered c. 1160. Pop. 124,975.
sci. *abbr.* Science; scientific.
sci•ae•noid (sī-ē′noid) *adj.* Of or belonging to the Sciaenidae, a family of fishes that includes the drums. —*n.* A sciaenoid fish. [NLat. *Sciaena*, type genus (< Lat. *sciaena*, a kind of fish < Gk. *skiaina*) + -OID.] —**sci•ae′nid** (-nĭd) *adj. & n.*
sci•at•ic (sī-ăt′ĭk) *adj.* **1.** Of or relating to the ischium or the region of the hipbone in which it is located. **2.** Of or relating to sciatica. [Fr. *sciatique* < OFr. < Med.Lat. *sciaticus*, alteration of Lat. *ischiadicus* < Gk. *iskhiadikos* < *iskhias, iskhiad-*, sciatica < *iskhion*, hip.]
sci•at•i•ca (sī-ăt′ĭ-kə) *n.* Pain along the sciatic nerve radiating to the buttocks and the back of the thigh. [ME < Med.Lat. < fem. of *sciaticus*, of the hip. See SCIATIC.]
sciatic nerve *n.* A sensory and motor nerve originating in the sacral plexus and running through the pelvis and upper leg.
sci•ence (sī′əns) *n.* **1.a.** The observation, identification, description, experimental investigation, and theoretical explanation of phenomena. **b.** Such activities restricted to a class of natural phenomena. **c.** Such activities applied to an object of inquiry or study. **2.** Methodological activity, discipline, or study: *I've got it down to a science.* **3.** An activity that appears to require study and method: *the science of purchasing.* **4.** Knowledge, esp. that gained through experience. [ME, knowledge, learning < OFr. < Lat. *scientia* < *sciēns, scient-*, pr.part. of *scīre*, to know. See **skei-*.**]
science fiction *n.* A literary or cinematic genre in which the plot is typically based on speculative scientific discoveries, environmental changes, space travel, or life on other planets.
sci•en•tial (sī-ĕn′shəl) *adj.* **1.** Of or producing knowledge or science. **2.** Capable; skillful.
sci•en•tif•ic (sī′ən-tĭf′ĭk) *adj.* Of, relating to, or employing the methodology of science. [Med.Lat. *scientificus*, producing knowledge : Lat. *scientia*, knowledge; see SCIENCE + Lat. *-ficus*, -fic.] —**sci′en•tif′i•cal•ly** *adv.*
scientific method *n.* The systematic procedure for scientific investigation, generally involving the observation of phenomena, the formulation of a hypothesis concerning the phenomena, experimentation to test the hypothesis, and a conclusion that validates or modifies the hypothesis.
scientific notation *n. Math.* A method of representing a number as a decimal number between 1 and 10 multiplied by a power of 10, as 1.0492×10^4, for example, for 10,492.
sci•en•tism (sī′ən-tĭz′əm) *n.* **1.** The theory that investigational methods used in the natural sciences should be applied in all fields of inquiry. **2.** The application of quasi-scientific techniques to unsuitable subjects or topics. —**sci′en•tis′tic** *adj.*
sci•en•tist (sī′ən-tĭst) *n.* A person having expert knowledge of one or more sciences, esp. a natural or physical science.
sci-fi (sī′fī′) *n., pl.* **-fis.** *Informal.* Science fiction.
scil•i•cet (sĭl′ĭ-sĕt′, skē′lĭ-kĕt′) *adv.* That is to say; namely. [ME < Lat. *scīlicet*, contraction of *scīre licet*, it is permitted to know : *scīre*, to know; see **skei-*** + *licet*, third pers. sing. of *licēre*, to be permitted.]
Scil•ly Islands (sĭl′ē). or **Isles of Scilly.** An archipelago comprising more than 140 small islands and islets off SW England at the entrance to the English Channel WSW of Land's End.
scim•i•tar (sĭm′ĭ-tər, -tär′) *n.* A curved Asian sword with the edge on the convex side. [Fr. *cimeterre* and Ital. *scimitarra*, both perh. ult. < Pers. *šimšīr*.]
scin•coid (sĭng′koid) *adj.* Of or resembling the skinks. —*n.* A scincoid lizard. [< Lat. *scincus*, skink. See SKINK.]
scin•ti•gram (sĭn′tĭ-grăm′) *n.* A two-dimensional record of the distribution of a radioactive tracer in a tissue or organ, obtained by means of a scanning scintillation counter.
scin•ti•graph (sĭn′tĭ-grăf′) *n.* **1.** A device for producing a scintigram; a scintiscanner. **2.** See **scintigram.** —**scin′ti•graph′ic** *adj.* —**scin•ti•graph′i•cal•ly** *adv.* —**scin•tig′ra•phy** (sĭn-tĭg′rə-fē) *n.*
scin•til•la (sĭn-tĭl′ə) *n.* **1.** A minute amount; an iota or a trace. **2.** A spark; a flash. [Lat., spark.] —**scin′til•lant** *adj.*
scin•til•late (sĭn′tl-āt′) *v.* **-lat•ed, -lat•ing, -lates.** —*intr.* **1.** To throw off sparks; flash. **2.** To sparkle or shine. **3.** To be animated and brilliant. —*tr.* To give off (sparks or flashes). [Lat. *scintillāre, scintillāt-* < *scintilla*, spark.]
scin•til•la•tion (sĭn′tl-ā′shən) *n.* **1.** The act of scintillating. **2.** A spark; a flash. **3.** *Astron.* Rapid variation in the light of a celestial body caused by turbulence in Earth's atmosphere; a twinkling. **4.** *Phys.* A flash of light produced in a phosphor by absorption of an ionizing particle or photon.
scintillation counter *n.* A device for detecting and counting scintillations produced by ionizing radiation.
scin•til•la•tor (sĭn′tl-ā′tər) *n.* A substance that glows when hit by high-energy particles or photons.
scin•ti•scan (sĭn′tĭ-skăn′) *n.* See **scintigram.** [SCINTI(LLATION) + SCAN.] —**scin′ti•scan′ner** *n.*
sci•o•lism (sī′ə-lĭz′əm) *n.* A pretentious attitude of scholarliness; superficial knowledgeability. [< LLat. *sciolus*, smatterer, dim. of Lat. *scius*, knowing < *scīre*, to know. See **skei-*.**] —**sci′o•list** *n.* —**sci′o•lis′tic** *adj.*
sci•on (sī′ən) *n.* **1.** A descendant or an heir. **2.** Also **ci•on** (sī′ən). A detached shoot or twig containing buds from a woody plant, used in grafting. [ME < OFr. *cion*, poss. of Gmc. orig.]
Sci•o•to (sī-ō′tə). A river, c. 381 km (237 mi), rising in W OH and flowing E then S to the Ohio R.
Scip•io (sĭp′ē-ō′, skĭp′-), **Publius Cornelius.** "Scipio the Younger." 185?–129 B.C. Roman general and politician who led the destruction of Carthage (146) in the Third Punic War.
Scipio Af•ri•ca•nus (ăf-rĭ-kä′nəs), **Publius Cornelius.** "Scipio the Elder." 236?–183? B.C. Roman general who invaded northern Africa, conquered Carthage, and brought the Second Punic War to an end by defeating Hannibal at Zama (202).
sci•roc•co (shə-rŏk′ō, sə-) *n.* Var. of **sirocco.**
scir•rhus (skĭr′əs, sĭr′-) *n., pl.* **scir•rhi** (skĭr′ī, sĭr′ī) or **scir•rhus•es.** A hard dense cancerous growth usu. arising from connective tissue. [NLat. < Lat. *scirros* < Gk. *skiros, skirros* < *skiros*, hard.] —**scir′rhous, scir′rhoid′** *adj.*
scis•sile (sĭs′əl, -īl′) *adj.* Cut or split easily. [Fr. < Lat. *scissilis* < *scissus*, p.part. of *scindere*, to cut. See SCISSION.]
scis•sion (sĭzh′ən, sĭsh′-) *n.* The act of cutting or severing; division or fission. [ME < OFr. < LLat. *scissiō, scissiōn-* < Lat. *scissus*, p.part. of *scindere*, to cut, split. See **skei-*.**]

Franz Schubert

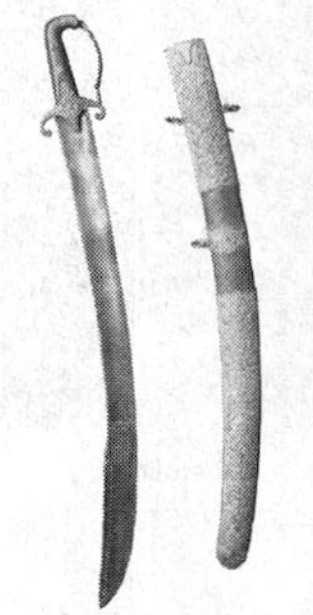
scimitar
With scabbard

ă pat · ā pay · âr care · ä father · ĕ pet · ē be · ĭ pit · ī pie · îr pier · ŏ pot · ō toe · ô paw · oi boy · ou out · o͝o took · o͞o boot · ŭ cut · ûr urge · th thin · *th* this · hw which · zh vision · ə about, item

Stress marks:
′ (primary);
′ (secondary), as in
dictionary (dĭk′shə-nĕr′ē)

scis•sor (sĭz′ər) *tr.v.* **-sored, -sor•ing, -sors.** To cut or clip with scissors or shears. — *n.* **1. scissors.** *(used with a sing. or pl. v.)* A cutting implement consisting of two blades joined by a swivel pin that allows the cutting edges to be opened and closed. **2.** Something resembling a scissors. **3. scissors.** *(used with a sing. v.) Sports.* **a.** Any of various gymnastic exercises or jumps in which the legs open and close as a scissors does. **b.** A scissors hold. [< alteration (influenced by Lat. *scissor*, cutter < *scissus*, cut; see SCISSION) of ME *sisours*, scissors < OFr. *cisoires* < VLat. **cīsōria* < LLat., pl. of *cīsōrium*, cutting instrument < Lat. *caesus, -cīsus*, p.part. of *caedere*, to cut. See **kaə-id-*.**]

scis•sors hold (sĭz′ərz) *n. Sports.* A wrestling hold in which the legs of one opponent are locked about another opponent.

scissors kick *n. Sports.* A swimming kick in which the legs are opened and closed like scissors.

scis•sor•tail (sĭz′ər-tāl′) *n.* A scissor-tailed flycatcher.

scissor-tailed flycatcher (sĭz′ər-tāld′) *n.* A flycatcher *(Muscivora forficata)* of the southwest United States, Mexico, and Central America having a long forked tail.

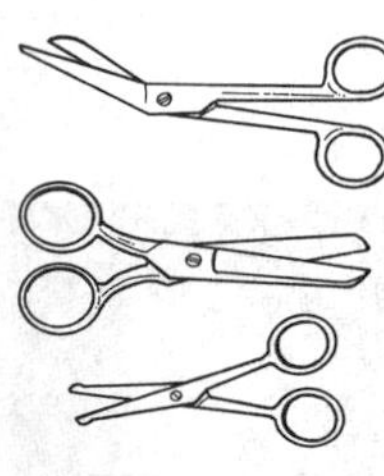

scissors
Top: Bandage scissors
Center: Safety-point scissors
Bottom: Nose and mustache scissors

scis•sure (sĭzh′ər, sĭsh′-) *n. Anat.* A split or opening in an organ or part. [ME < OFr. < Lat. *scissūra* < *scissus*, p.part. of *scindere*, to split. See SCISSION.]

Scit•u•ate (sĭch′o͞o-ĭt). A town of E MA on Massachusetts Bay SE of Boston. Pop. 16,786.

sci•u•rid (sī′yo͞o-rĭd′) *adj.* Of, belonging to, or resembling the Sciuridae, a family of rodents that includes the squirrels. [< NLat. *Sciūridae*, family name < Lat. *sciūrus*, squirrel. See SQUIRREL.] — **sci′u•rid′** *n.* — **sci′u•rine** (-rīn′) *adj.* — **sci′u•roid** (sī′yo͞o-roid′, sī-yo͝or′oid) *adj.*

sclaff (sklăf) *v.* **sclaffed, sclaff•ing, sclaffs.** — *intr.* To scrape or strike the ground with a golf club behind the ball before hitting it. — *tr.* **1.** To strike (the ground) with a golf club before hitting the ball. **2.** To hit (a ball) in this manner. [Sc., to strike with a flat surface.] — **sclaff** *n.* — **sclaff′er** *n.*

SCLC *abbr.* Southern Christian Leadership Conference.

scle•ra (sklîr′ə) *n.* The tough white fibrous outer envelope of tissue covering all of the eyeball except the cornea. [NLat. < Gk., fem. of *sklēros*, hard.] — **scle′ral** *adj.*

scle•ren•chy•ma (sklə-rĕng′kə-mə) *n.* A supportive plant tissue that consists of thick-walled, usu. lignified cells. — **scle′ren•chym′a•tous** (sklîr′ən-kĭm′ə-təs, -kī′mə-) *adj.*

scle•rite (sklîr′īt′) *n.* A chitinous or calcareous plate, spicule, or similar part of an invertebrate, esp. one of the outer plates of an arthropod.

scle•ri•tis (sklə-rī′tĭs) *n.* Inflammation of the sclera. — **scle•rit′ic** (-rĭt′ĭk) *adj.*

sclero– or **scler–** *pref.* **1.** Hard: *sclerite.* **2.** Hardness: *sclerometer.* **3.** Sclera: *scleritis.* [Gk. *sklēro-* < *sklēros*, hard.]

scle•ro•der•ma (sklîr′ə-dûr′mə) *n.* A pathological thickening and hardening of the skin.

scle•ro•der•ma•tous (sklîr′ə-dûr′mə-təs) *adj.* **1.** Of, relating to, or affected by scleroderma. **2.** *Zool.* Having an outer covering of hard plates or bony scales.

scle•roid (sklîr′oid′) *adj. Biol.* Hard or hardened.

scle•ro•ma (sklə-rō′mə) *n., pl.* **-mas** or **-ma•ta** (-mə-tə). An abnormally hard patch of body tissue. [NLat. < Gk. *sklērōma*, hardening < *sklēroun*, to harden < *sklēros*, hard.]

scle•rom•e•ter (sklə-rŏm′ĭ-tər) *n.* An instrument used to determine the relative hardness of a material by measuring the pressure required to penetrate it with a diamond stylus.

scoliosis

scle•ro•pro•tein (sklîr′ō-prō′tēn′, -tē-ĭn) *n.* Any of a class of generally insoluble proteins, such as collagen.

scle•rosed (sklə-rōzd′, -rōst′) *adj.* **1.** Affected by sclerosis; hardened. **2.** *Bot.* Lignified. [< SCLEROSIS.]

scle•ro•sis (sklə-rō′sĭs) *n., pl.* **-ses** (-sēz). **1.a.** A thickening or hardening of a body part, as of an artery. **b.** A disease characterized by this thickening or hardening. **2.** *Bot.* The hardening of cell walls by increased deposition of lignin. [ME *sclirosis* < Med.Lat. *sclīrōsis* < Gk. *sklērōsis*, hardening < *sklēroun*, to harden. See SCLEROMA.]

scle•rot•ic (sklə-rŏt′ĭk) *adj.* **1.** Affected or marked by sclerosis. **2.** *Anat.* Of or relating to the sclera. — *n.* See **sclera.**

sclerotic coat *n.* See **sclera.**

scler•o•tin (sklîr′ə-tĭn, sklĕr′-) *n.* An insoluble protein that hardens and darkens the cuticle of arthropods by a natural tanning process involving the cross-link of chitin protein molecules. [SCLERO– + *-tin* (as in KERATIN or CHITIN).]

scle•ro•ti•um (sklə-rō′shē-əm, -shəm) *n., pl.* **-ti•a** (-shē-ə, -shə). A dense mass of branched hyphae, as in certain fungi, that are capable of remaining dormant for long periods. [NLat. < Gk. *sklērotēs*, hardness < *sklēros*, hard.]

scler•o•ti•za•tion (sklĕr′ə-tĭ-zā′shən) *n.* Hardening caused by formation of sclerotin. [Gk. *sklērotēs*, hardness (< *sklēros*, hard) + -IZATION.]

scle•rot•o•my (sklə-rŏt′ə-mē) *n., pl.* **-mies.** Surgical incision of the sclera.

scle•rous (sklîr′əs, sklĕr′-) *adj.* Hardened; toughened.

scoff¹ (skŏf, skôf) *v.* **scoffed, scoff•ing, scoffs.** — *tr.* To mock at or treat with derision. — *intr.* To show or express derision or scorn. — *n.* An expression of derision or scorn. [ME *scoffen* < *scof*, mockery, prob. of Scand. orig.; akin to Dan. *skof*, jest, teasing.] — **scoff′er** *n.* — **scoff′ing•ly** *adv.*

scoreboard

scoff² (skŏf, skôf) *v.* **scoffed, scoff•ing, scoffs.** — *tr.* To eat (food) quickly and greedily. — *intr.* To eat greedily. [Alteration of obsolete *scaff*.] — **scoff′er** *n*

scoff•law (skŏf′lô′, skôf′-) *n.* One who habitually violates the law or fails to answer court summonses.

scold (skōld) *v.* **scold•ed, scold•ing, scolds.** — *tr.* To reprimand or criticize harshly and usu. angrily. — *intr.* To reprove or criticize openly. — *n.* One who persistently nags or criticizes. [ME *scolden*, to rail at < *scolde*, an abusive person, prob. of Scand. orig. See **sekʷ-³*.**] — **scold′er** *n.*

scold•ing (skōl′dĭng) *n.* A harsh or sharp reprimand.

sco•lex (skō′lĕks′) *n., pl.* **-li•ces** (-lĭ-sēz′). The knoblike anterior end of a tapeworm, having suckers or hooklike parts for attachment to the host. [NLat. < Gk. *skōlēx*, worm.]

sco•li•o•sis (skō′lē-ō′sĭs, skŏl′ē-) *n.* Abnormal lateral curvature of the spine. [Gk. *skolios*, crooked + -OSIS.] — **sco′li•ot′ic** (-ŏt′ĭk) *adj.*

scol•lop (skŏl′əp) *n. & v.* Var. of **scallop.**

scom•broid (skŏm′broid′) *adj.* Of or belonging to the suborder Scombroidei, which includes marine fishes such as the mackerel. [NLat. *Scombroidei*, suborder name < Lat. *scomber, scombr-*, mackerel < Gk. *skombros*.] — **scom′broid′** *n.*

sconce¹ (skŏns) *n.* A small defensive earthwork or fort. [Du. *schans* < Ger. *Schanze* < MHGer.]

sconce² (skŏns) *n.* **1.** A decorative wall bracket for holding candles or lights. **2.** A flattened candlestick that has a handle. **3.** *Slang.* The human head or skull. [ME < OFr. *esconse*, lantern, hiding place < Med.Lat. *scōnsa* < Lat. *absconsa*, fem. p.part. of *abscondere*, to hide away : *ab-, abs-*, away; see AB-¹ + *condere*, to preserve; see **dhē-*.**]

scone (skōn, skŏn) *n.* **1.** A small rich biscuitlike pastry or quick bread, sometimes baked on a griddle. **2.** *Utah.* Yeast bread dough, deep-fried and served with honey and butter or with a savory filling. [Perh. < Du. *schoonbrood*, fine white bread < MDu. *schoonbroot* : *schoon*, bright; see **keu-*** + *broot*, bread.]

Scone (sko͞on). A village of central Scotland NE of Perth; the coronation site of Scottish kings until 1651.

scoop (sko͞op) *n.* **1.a.** A shovellike utensil, usu. having a deep curved dish and a short handle. **b.** The amount that a scoop can hold. **2.a.** A thick-handled cuplike utensil for dispensing balls of ice cream or other semisoft food. **b.** A portion gathered with a scoop. **3.** A ladle; a dipper. **4.** An implement for bailing water from a boat. **5.** A narrow spoon-shaped instrument for surgical extraction in cavities or cysts. **6.** The bucket or shovel, as of a dredge or backhoe. **7.** A hollow area; a cavity. **8.** An opening, as on the body of a motor vehicle, by which a fluid is directed inward. **9.** A scooping movement or action. **10.** *Informal.* An exclusive news story acquired by luck or initiative before a competitor. **11.** *Informal.* Current information or details. — *tr.v.* **scooped, scoop•ing, scoops. 1.** To take up or dip into with or as if with a scoop. **2.** To hollow out by digging. **3.** To gather or collect swiftly and unceremoniously; grab: *scooped up a handful.* **4.** *Informal.* To top or outmaneuver (a competitor) in publishing an important news story. [ME *scope* < MDu. and MLGer. *schōpe*, bucket for bailing water.] — **scoop′er** *n.* — **scoop′ful′** *n.*

scoop neck *n.* A rounded, usu. low-cut neckline, as on a dress.

scoot (sko͞ot) *v.* **scoot•ed, scoot•ing, scoots.** — *intr.* To go suddenly and speedily; hurry. — *tr. Upper Southern U.S.* To squirt with water. — ***phrasal verb.* scoot over.** *Midland & Upper Southern U.S.* To move (someone or something) to the side to make room. [Sc., to squirt, prob. of Scand. orig.] — **scoot** *n.*

Regional Note: *Scoot* originally meant "to squirt with water." Two derived senses, both intransitive verbs, have become even more common: "to slide suddenly across a surface" and "to move quickly": *The mouse scooted across the floor.* In the American Midlands there is a phrasal verb *scoot over,* meaning, in its transitive sense, "to push (someone or something) to the side to make room."

scoot•er (sko͞o′tər) *n.* **1.** A child's vehicle consisting of a long footboard between two small end wheels and an upright steering handle. **2.** A motor scooter. **3.** *Naut.* A flat-bottomed sailboat with runners that can skim over water or ice.

scop (shōp) *n.* An Old English poet or bard. [OE.]

scope (skōp) *n.* **1.** The range of one's perceptions, thoughts, or actions. **2.** Breadth or opportunity to function. **3.** The area covered by a given activity or subject. **4.** The length or sweep of a mooring cable. **5.** *Informal.* A viewing instrument such as a periscope or telescope. — *tr.v.* **scoped, scop•ing, scopes.** *Slang.* To examine or study carefully and in detail. [Ital. *scopo*, aim < Gk. *skopos*, target, aim. See **spek-*.**]

–scope *suff.* An instrument for viewing or observing: *bronchoscope.* [NLat. *-scopium* < Gk. *-skopion* < *skopein*, to see. See **spek-*.**]

Scopes (skōps), **John Thomas.** 1900–70. Amer. teacher who was tried (Jul. 1925) for violating a state law by teaching the theory of evolution in a TN high school.

sco•pol•a•mine (skə-pŏl′ə-mēn′, -mĭn) *n.* A colorless alkaloid, $C_{17}H_{21}NO_4$, extracted from plants such as henbane and used as a mydriatic, sedative, and truth serum. [NLat. *Scopolia*, plant genus (after Giovanni Antonio *Scopoli* (1723–88), Italian naturalist) + -AMINE.]

scop•u•la (skŏp′yə-lə) *n., pl.* **-lae** (-lē′). A dense brushlike tuft of hairs, as on the feet of certain insects. [Lat. *scōpula*, small brush of twigs, dim. of *scōpae*, branches, broom.] **— scop′u•late′** (-lāt′) *adj.*

-scopy *suff.* Viewing; seeing; observation: *microscopy.* [Gk. *-skopia* < *skopein*, to see. See **spek-*.**]

scor•bu•tic (skôr-byo͞o′tĭk) also **scor•bu•ti•cal** (-tĭ-kəl) *adj.* Of, relating to, resembling, or affected by scurvy. [NLat. *scorbūticus* < *scorbūtus*, scurvy, perh. of Gmc. orig.] **— scor•bu′ti•cal•ly** *adv.*

scorch (skôrch) *v.* **scorched, scorch•ing, scorch•es.** *— tr.* **1.** To burn superficially so as to discolor or damage the texture of. **2.** To wither or parch with intense heat. **3.** To destroy by or as if by fire (all land and buildings in one's path) so as to leave nothing salvageable to an enemy army. **4.** To subject to severe censure; excoriate. *— intr.* **1.** To become scorched or singed. **2.** To go or move at a very fast rate. *— n.* **1.** A slight or surface burn. **2.** A discoloration caused by heat. **3.** Brown spotting on plant leaves caused by fungi, heat, or lack of water. [ME *scorchen*, poss. of Scand. orig.]

scorch•er (skôr′chər) *n.* **1.** One that scorches. **2.** *Informal.* An extremely hot day.

score (skôr, skōr) *n.* **1.** A notch or an incision, esp. one that is made to keep a tally. **2.** *Sports & Games.* **a.** A usu. numerical record of a competitive event. **b.** The total number of points made by each side in a contest, either final or at a given stage. **c.** The number of points attributed to a competitor or team. **3.** A result, usu. expressed numerically, of a test or examination. **4.a.** An amount due; a debt. **b.** A grievance that requires satisfaction. **5.** A ground; a reason. **6.** A group of 20 items. **7. scores.** Large numbers. **8.** *Mus.* **a.** The written form of a composition for orchestral or vocal parts, either complete or for a particular instrument or voice. **b.** The music for a film or a play. **9.** *Slang.* **a.** The act of securing an advantage, esp. a surprising or significant gain. **b.** The act or an instance of buying illicit drugs. **c.** A successful robbery. **d.** A sexual conquest. *— v.* **scored, scor•ing, scores.** *— tr.* **1.** To mark with lines or notches, esp. for the purpose of keeping a record. **2.** To cancel or eliminate by or as if by superimposing lines. **3.** To mark the surface of (meat, for example) with usu. parallel cuts. **4.** *Sports & Games.* **a.** To gain (a point) in a game or contest. **b.** To count or be worth as points. **5.** To achieve; win. **6.** To evaluate and assign a grade to. **7.** *Mus.* **a.** To orchestrate. **b.** To arrange for a specific instrument. **8.** To criticize cuttingly; berate. **9.** *Slang.* **a.** To succeed in acquiring. **b.** To succeed in obtaining (an illicit drug). *— intr.* **1.** *Sports & Games.* **a.** To make a point in a game or contest. **b.** To keep the score of a game or contest. **2.** *Slang.* **a.** To achieve a purpose or advantage, esp. to make a surprising gain or coup. **b.** To seduce someone sexually. **c.** To succeed in obtaining an illicit drug. [ME < OE **scoru*, twenty < ON *skor.* See **sker-**[1]***.**] **— scor′er** *n.*

score•board (skôr′bôrd′, skōr′bōrd′) *n. Sports & Games.* A large board that displays the score of a game or contest.

score•card (skôr′kärd′, skōr′-) *n. Sports & Games.* **1.** A printed program or card enabling a spectator to identify players and record the progress of a game or competition. **2.** A small card used to record one's own performance in sports such as golf.

score•keep•er (skôr′kē′pər, skōr′-) *n. Sports & Games.* An official who records the score throughout a game or competition. **— score′keep′ing** *adj. & n.*

sco•ri•a (skôr′ē-ə, skōr′-) *n., pl.* **sco•ri•ae** (skôr′ē-ē′, skōr′-). **1.** *Geol.* Porous cinderlike fragments of dark lava. **2.** *Metall.* The refuse of a smelted metal or ore; slag. [ME, dross < Lat. *scōria* < Gk. *skōria* < *skōr*, excrement, dung. See **sker-**[3]***.**] **— sco′ri•a′ceous** (-ā′shəs) *adj.*

sco•ri•fy (skôr′ə-fī′, skōr′-) *tr.v.* **-fied, -fy•ing, -fies.** To separate (an ore) into scoria and a precious metal. **— sco′ri•fi•ca′tion** (-fĭ-kā′shən) *n.* **— sco′ri•fi′er** *n.*

scorn (skôrn) *n.* **1.a.** Contempt or disdain felt toward a person or object considered despicable or unworthy. **b.** The expression of such an attitude in behavior or speech; derision. **2.** One spoken of or treated with contempt. *— v.* **scorned, scorn•ing, scorns.** *— tr.* **1.** To consider or treat as contemptible or unworthy. **2.** To reject or refuse with derision. See Syns at **despise.** *— intr.* To express contempt; scoff. [ME < OFr. *escarn*, of Gmc. orig.] **— scorn′er** *n.* **— scorn′ful** *adj.* **— scorn′ful•ly** *adv.* **— scorn′ful•ness** *n.*

scor•pae•noid (skôr-pē′noid′) *adj.* Of or belonging to the suborder Scorpaenoidei, which includes the scorpion fishes and rockfishes. *— n.* A scorpaenoid fish. [< NLat. *Scorpaenoidei*, suborder name < *Scorpaena*, type genus < Lat., a kind of fish < Gk. *skorpaina*, fem. of *skorpios*, a sea fish, scorpion.] **— scor•pae′nid** (-nĭd) *adj. & n.*

Scor•pi•o (skôr′pē-ō′) *n.* **1.** The eighth sign of the zodiac in astrology. **2.** One who is born under this sign. [ME < Lat. *Scorpiō* < *scorpiō*, scorpion. See SCORPION.]

scor•pi•oid (skôr′pē-oid′) *adj.* **1.** Of, relating to, or resembling a scorpion. **2.** *Bot.* Like the tail of a scorpion; circinate. [Gk. *skorpioeidēs*, scorpionlike : *skorpios*, scorpion + *-oeidēs*, -oid.]

scor•pi•on (skôr′pē-ən) *n.* Any of various arachnids of the order Scorpionida of warm dry regions, having an erectile tail tipped with a venomous sting. [ME < OFr. < Lat. *scorpiō*, *scorpiōn-*, alteration of *scorpius* < Gk. *skorpios.*]

Scor•pi•on (skôr′pē-ən) *n.* See **Scorpius.**

scorpion fish *n.* Any of numerous small, often brilliantly colored marine fishes of the family Scorpaenidae, most species of which have poisonous spines in the dorsal fin.

scorpion fly *n.* **1.** A mecopterous insect of the family Panorpidae, having in the male of most species a curved genital structure that resembles the sting of a scorpion. **2.** Any mecopterous insect; a mecopteran.

scorpion grass *n.* See **forget-me-not** 1.

Scor•pi•us (skôr′pē-əs) also **Scor•pi•o** (-pē-ō′) *n.* A constellation in the Southern Hemisphere near Libra and Sagittarius. [Lat. *scorpius*, scorpion, Scorpius. See SCORPION.]

scot (scŏt) *n.* Money assessed or paid. [ME, tax, partly < ON *skot* and partly < OFr. *escot* (of Gmc. orig.); see **skeud-*.**]

Scot (skŏt) *n.* **1.** A native or inhabitant of Scotland. **2.** A member of the ancient Gaelic tribe that migrated to the northern part of Britain from Ireland in about the sixth century A.D. See Usage Note at **Scottish.** [< ME *Scottes*, Scots < OE *Scottas*, Scots, Irish < LLat. *Scottī*, Irish.]

Scot. *abbr.* Scotch; Scotland; Scottish.

scot and lot *n.* A municipal tax formerly levied in Great Britain on the members of a community in proportion to their ability to pay. **— *idiom.* pay scot and lot.** To pay in full.

scotch[1] (skŏch) *tr.v.* **scotched, scotch•ing, scotch•es. 1.** To put an abrupt end to. **2.** To injure so as to render harmless. **3.** To cut or score. *— n.* **1.** A surface cut or abrasion. **2.** A line drawn on the ground, as in hopscotch. [ME *scocchen*, perh. < AN *escocher*, to notch : *es-*, intensive pref. (< Lat. *ex-*; see EX-) + OFr. *coche*, notch (prob. < Lat. *coccum*, scarlet oak berry < Gk. *kokkos*).]

scotch[2] (skŏch) *tr.v.* **scotched, scotch•ing, scotch•es.** To block (a wheel, for example) with a prop to prevent rolling or slipping. *— n.* A block or wedge used as a prop behind or under an object likely to roll. [?]

Scotch (skŏch) *n.* **1.** The people of Scotland. **2.** Scots English. **3.** Scotch whisky. *— adj.* **1.** Scottish. See Usage Note at **Scottish. 2.** Tight with money; frugal. [Contraction of SCOTTISH.]

Scotch egg *n.* A hard-boiled egg wrapped in sausage meat, coated with bread crumbs, and deep-fried.

Scotch-I•rish (skŏch′ī′rĭsh) *n.* The people of Scotland who settled in northern Ireland or their descendants, esp. those who emigrated to America. **— Scotch′-I′rish** *adj.*

Scotch•man (skŏch′mən) *n.* A Scotsman. See Usage Note at **Scottish.**

Scotch pine *n.* **1.** A Eurasian pine tree *(Pinus sylvestris)* having twisted needles arranged in fascicles of two and yellow wood that is valued as timber. **2.** The wood of this tree.

Scotch Plains. A community of NE NJ W of Elizabeth. Pop. 21,160.

Scotch terrier *n.* See **Scottish terrier.**

Scotch verdict *n.* An inconclusive judgment or pronouncement.

Scotch whisky *n.* A whiskey distilled in Scotland from malted barley.

Scotch•wom•an (skŏch′wo͝om′ən) *n.* A Scotswoman. See Usage Note at **Scottish.**

Scotch woodcock *n.* A savory dish consisting of scrambled eggs on toast with anchovies or anchovy paste.

sco•ter (skō′tər) *n.* Any of several dark-colored diving ducks of the genera *Oidemia* and *Melanitta* of northern coasts. [?]

scot-free (skŏt′frē′) *adv.* **1.** Without having to pay. **2.** Without incurring any penalty or punishment. **— scot′-free′** *adj.*

sco•tia (skō′shə) *n. Archit.* A hollow concave molding at or near the base of a column. [Lat. < Gk. *skotia* < fem. of *skotios*, shadowy (from its shadow) < *skotos*, darkness.]

Sco•tia (skō′shə). Scotland.

Scot•land (skŏt′lənd). A constituent country of the United Kingdom comprising the N part of the island of Great Britain and the Hebrides, Shetland Is., and Orkney Is. Scotland became a part of the kingdom of Great Britain by the Act of Union in 1707. Cap. Edinburgh. Pop. 5,149,500.

sco•to•ma (skə-tō′mə) *n., pl.* **-mas** or **-ma•ta** (-mə-tə). An area of diminished vision within the visual field. [NLat. *scotōma* < LLat., dim sight < Gk. *skotōma*, dizziness < *skotoun*, to darken < *skotos*, darkness.] **— sco•to′ma•tous** *adj.*

sco•to•phil (skō′tə-fĭl′) also **sco•to•phil•ic** (skō′tə-fĭl′ĭk) *adj. Biol.* Growing or functioning best in darkness. [Gk. *skotos*, darkness + -PHIL(E).]

sco•to•pi•a (skə-tō′pē-ə) *n.* The ability to see in darkness or dim light; dark-adapted vision. [Gk. *skotos*, darkness + -OPIA.] **— sco•to′pic** (-tō′pĭk, -tŏp′ĭk) *adj.*

Scots (skŏts) *adj.* Scottish. See Usage Note at **Scottish.** *— n.* The English dialect used in the Scottish Lowlands. [ME *scottis*, var. of *scottisc*, Scottish < *Scotte*, sing. of *Scottes*, Scots. See SCOT.]

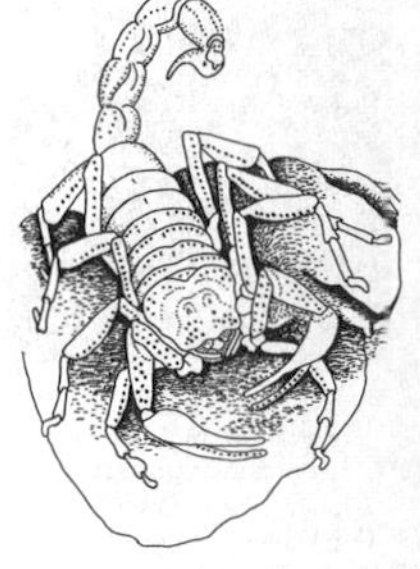

scorpion
Arizona scorpion
Centruroides sculpturatus

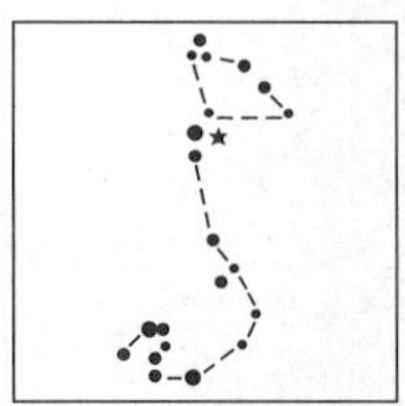

Scorpius

scotch[2]

ă pat	oi boy
ā pay	ou out
âr care	o͝o took
ä father	o͞o boot
ĕ pet	ŭ cut
ē be	ûr urge
ĭ pit	th thin
ī pie	*th* this
îr pier	hw which
ŏ pot	zh vision
ō toe	ə about, item
ô paw	

Stress marks:
′ (primary);
′ (secondary), as in **dictionary** (dĭk′shə-nĕr′ē)

Scots•man (skŏts′mən) *n.* A man who is a native or inhabitant of Scotland. See Usage Note at **Scottish.**

Scots•wom•an (skŏts′wo͝om′ən) *n.* A woman who is a native or inhabitant of Scotland. See Usage Note at **Scottish.**

Scott (skŏt), **Dred.** 1795?–1858. Amer. slave who sued for his liberty after spending four years with his master in a territory where slavery had been banned by the Missouri Compromise. The resulting decision by the U.S. Supreme Court (1857) declared the Missouri Compromise unconstitutional.

Scott, Robert Falcon. 1868–1912. British explorer who reached the South Pole in Jan. 1912, one month after Roald Amundsen.

Scott, Sir **Walter.** 1771–1832. British writer of ballads and historical novels, whose works include *Ivanhoe* (1819).

Dred Scott
Detail of an 1881 oil on canvas portrait by Louis Schultze (after an 1858 photograph)

Scott, Winfield. 1786–1866. Amer. general who was a hero of the War of 1812 and the Mexican War (1846–48).

Scot•ti•cism (skŏt′ĭ-sĭz′əm) *n.* An idiom or other expression characteristic of Scots English.

Scot•tie also **Scot•ty** (skŏt′ē) *n., pl.* **-ties.** A Scottish terrier.

Scot•tish (skŏt′ĭsh) *adj.* Of or relating to Scotland or its people, language, or culture. — *n.* **1.** Scots English. **2.** The people of Scotland. [ME *scottisc.* See SCOTS.]

Usage Note: *Scottish* is the full, original form of the adjective. *Scots* is an old Scottish variant of the form; *Scotch* is an English contraction of Scottish that at one time also came into use in Scotland but subsequently fell into disfavor. To some extent these facts can serve as a guide in choosing among the many variant forms of related words, such as *Scot, Scotsman* or *Scotswoman,* or *Scotchman* or *Scotchwoman,* for one of the people of Scotland; *Scots, (the) Scotch,* or, rarely, *(the) Scottish* for the people of Scotland; and *Scots, Scotch,* or *Scottish* for the dialect of English spoken in Scotland. The forms based on *Scotch* are English and disfavored in Scotland, while those involving the full form *Scottish* tend to be more formal. In the interest of civility, forms involving *Scotch* are best avoided in reference to people. But there is no sure rule for referring to things, since the variation in use of these words has left many expressions in which the choice is fixed, such as *Scotch whisky* and *Scots Guards.*

Scottish deerhound *n.* See **deerhound.**

Scottish Gaelic *n.* The Goidelic language of Scotland.

Scottish rite *n.* A ceremonial rite in a Masonic system.

Scottish terrier *n.* A terrier of a breed originating in Scotland, having short legs, small erect ears, and a hard wiry coat.

Scotts•dale (skŏts′dāl′). A city of S-central AZ, a suburb of Phoenix. Pop. 130,069.

scoun•drel (skoun′drəl) *n.* A villain; a rogue. [?] — **scoun′drel•ly** *adj.*

scour¹ (skour) *v.* **scoured, scour•ing, scours.** — *tr.* **1.a.** To clean, polish, or wash by scrubbing vigorously. **b.** To remove by scrubbing. **2.** To remove dirt or grease from (cloth or fibers) with a detergent. **3.** To clean (wheat) before milling. **4.** To clear (an area) by freeing of weeds or other vegetation. **5.** To clear (a channel or pipe) by flushing. — *intr.* **1.** To scrub something in order to clean or polish it. **2.** To have diarrhea. Used of livestock. — *n.* **1.** A scouring action or effect. **2.** A place that has been scoured, as by flushing with water. **3.** A cleansing agent for wool. **4. scours.** *(used with a sing. or pl. v.)* Diarrhea in livestock. [ME *scouren* < MDu. *schūren* < OFr. *escurer* < LLat. *excūrāre,* to clean out : Lat. *ex-,* ex- + LLat. *cūrāre,* to clean (< Lat., to take care of < *cūra,* care; see CURE).] — **scour′er** *n.*

scour² (skour) *v.* **scoured, scour•ing, scours.** — *tr.* **1.** To search through or over thoroughly. **2.** To range over (an area) quickly and energetically. — *intr.* **1.** To range over or about an area, esp. in a search. **2.** To move swiftly; scurry. [ME *scouren,* prob. of Scand. orig.] — **scour′er** *n.*

scourge (skûrj) *n.* **1.** A source of widespread dreadful affliction and devastation such as that of war. **2.** A means of inflicting severe suffering, vengeance, or punishment. **3.** A whip used to inflict punishment. — *tr.v.* **scourged, scourg•ing, scourg•es. 1.** To afflict with severe or widespread suffering and devastation; ravage. **2.** To chastise severely; excoriate. **3.** To flog. [ME < AN *escorge* < OFr. *escorgier,* to whip < VLat. **excorrigiāre* : Lat. *ex-,* intensive pref.; see EX- + Lat. *corrigia,* thong (prob. of Celt. orig.).] — **scourg′er** *n.*

scour•ing rush (skour′ĭng) *n.* Any of several species of horsetail, esp. *Equisetum hyemale,* having rough-ridged stems formerly used for scouring utensils.

scour•ings (skour′ĭngz) *pl.n.* **1.** The refuse that remains after scouring grain. **2.** Dregs; scum.

scouse (skous) *n.* **1.** A lobscouse. **2.a.** Also **scous•er** (skou′sər). A native or resident of Liverpool, England. **b.** Often **Scouse.** The dialect of English spoken in Liverpool.

scout¹ (skout) *v.* **scout•ed, scout•ing, scouts.** — *tr.* **1.** To spy on or explore carefully in order to obtain information; reconnoiter. **2.** To observe and evaluate (a talented person), as for possible hiring. — *intr.* **1.** To search as a scout: *scout around for some gossip.* **2.** To search for talented people. — *n.* **1.a.** One that is dispatched from a main body to gather information, esp. in preparation for military action. **b.** The act of reconnoitering. **2.** A watcher or sentinel. **3.** One who is employed to discover and recruit talented persons, esp. in the fields of sports and entertainment. **4.** *Sports.* One who is employed to observe and report on the strategies and players of rival teams. **5.** Often **Scout. a.** A member of the Boy Scouts. **b.** A member of the Girl Scouts. **6.** *Informal.* An individual; a person: *a good scout.* **7.** *Chiefly British.* A student's male servant at Oxford University. [< ME *scoute,* act of watching or spying < OFr. *escoute* < *escouter,* to listen, alteration of *ascouter* < VLat. **ascultāre,* alteration of Lat. *auscultāre.* See **ous-*.**] — **scout′er** *n.*

scout² (skout) *v.* **scout•ed, scout•ing, scouts.** — *tr.* To reject with disdain or derision. See Syns at **despise.** — *intr.* To treat another with derision; scoff. [Of Scand. orig. See **skeud-*.**]

scout•ing (skou′tĭng) *n.* **1.** The act of one that scouts. **2.** Often **Scouting.** The activities of the Boy Scouts or Girl Scouts.

scout•mas•ter (skout′măs′tər) *n.* The adult leader in charge of a troop of Boy Scouts.

scow (skou) *n. Naut.* A vessel with a flat bottom and square ends, often used for transporting freight. [Du. *schouw* < MDu. *scouwe.*]

scowl (skoul) *v.* **scowled, scowl•ing, scowls.** — *intr.* To wrinkle or contract the brow as an expression of anger or disapproval. — *tr.* To express with a frowning facial expression. — *n.* A look of anger or frowning disapproval. [ME *scoulen,* prob. of Scand. orig.] — **scowl′er** *n.*

scr. *abbr.* Scruple (unit of weight).

scrab•ble (skrăb′əl) *v.* **-bled, -bling, -bles.** — *intr.* **1.** To scrape or grope about frenetically with the hands. **2.** To struggle by or as if by scraping or groping. **3.** To climb with scrambling, disorderly haste; clamber. **4.** To make hasty, disordered markings; scribble. — *tr.* **1.** To make or obtain by scraping together hastily. **2.** To scribble on or over. — *n.* **1.** The act or an instance of scrabbling. **2.** A scribble; a doodle. [Du. *schrabbelen* < MDu., freq. of *schrabben,* to scrape. See **sker-¹*.**] — **scrab′bler** *n.* — **scrab′bly** *adj.*

scrab•bled (skrăb′əld) *adj.* Covered with sparse vegetation.

scrag (skrăg) *n.* **1.** A bony or scrawny person or animal. **2.** A piece of lean or bony meat, esp. a neck of mutton. **3.** *Slang.* The human neck. — *tr.v.* **scragged, scrag•ging, scrags.** *Slang.* To wring the neck of; strangle. [Perh. < dial. *crag,* neck < ME *cragge* < MDu. *crāghe,* throat.]

scrag•gly (skrăg′lē) *adj.* **-gli•er, -gli•est.** Ragged; unkempt.

scrag•gy (skrăg′ē) *adj.* **-gi•er, -gi•est. 1.** Jagged; rough: *scraggy cliffs.* **2.** Bony and lean: *a scraggy cat.* — **scrag′gi•ly** *adv.* — **scrag′gi•ness** *n.*

scram (skrăm) *Slang.* — *intr.v.* **scrammed, scram•ming, scrams. 1.** To leave a scene at once; go abruptly. **2.** To shut down automatically. Used of a nuclear reactor. — *n.* A rapid shutting down of a nuclear reactor. [Perh. short for SCRAMBLE.]

scram•ble (skrăm′bəl) *v.* **-bled, -bling, -bles.** — *intr.* **1.** To move or climb hurriedly, esp. on the hands and knees. **2.** To struggle or contend frantically in order to get something. **3.** To take off with all possible haste, as to intercept enemy aircraft. **4.** *Football.* To run with the ball when there is no open receiver. Used of a quarterback. — *tr.* **1.** To mix or throw together haphazardly. **2.** To gather together in a hurried or disorderly fashion. **3.** To fry (beaten eggs) until firm but with a soft consistency. **4.** *Electron.* To distort or garble (a signal) so as to render it unintelligible without a special receiver. **5.** To cause (aircraft) to scramble. — *n.* **1.** The act or an instance of scrambling. **2.** An arduous hike or climb over rough terrain. **3.** An unceremonious scuffle or struggle. **4.** A swift takeoff of military aircraft in response to an alert or an attack. [Perh. blend of obsolete *scamble,* to struggle for, and *cramble,* to crawl.]

scram•bled eggs (skrăm′bəld) *pl.n.* Eggs with the yolks and whites beaten together and fried.

scram•bler (skrăm′blər) *n.* An electronic device that scrambles telecommunication signals.

scram•jet (skrăm′jĕt′) *n.* A ramjet airplane engine designed for hypersonic flight that burns fuel in the supersonic airstream produced by the plane. [S(UPERSONIC) + C(OMBUSTION) + RAMJET.]

Scran•ton (skrăn′tən). A city of NE PA NE of Wilkes-Barre; settled in the late 1700's. Pop. 81,805.

scrap¹ (skrăp) *n.* **1.** A small piece or bit; a fragment. **2. scraps.** Leftover bits of food. **3.** Discarded waste material, esp. metal suitable for reprocessing. **4. scraps.** Crisp pieces of rendered animal fat; cracklings. — *tr.v.* **scrapped, scrap•ping, scraps. 1.** To break down into parts for disposal or salvage. **2.** To discard as worthless; junk. [ME < ON *skrap,* trifles, pieces. See **sker-¹*.**]

scrap² (skrăp) *intr.v.* **scrapped, scrap•ping, scraps.** To fight, often with the fists. — *n.* A fight or a scuffle. [Perh. var. of SCRAPE.] — **scrap′per** *n.*

scrap•book (skrăp′bo͝ok′) *n.* A book with blank pages used for the mounting of pictures, clippings, or other mementos.

scrape (skrāp) *v.* **scraped, scrap•ing, scrapes.** — *tr.* **1.** To remove (an outer layer, for example) from a surface by forceful strokes of an edged or rough instrument: *scraped the rust off.* **2.** To abrade or smooth by rubbing with a sharp or rough instrument. **3.** To rub (a surface) with considerable pressure, as with an edged instrument or a hard object. **4.** To draw (a hard or abrasive object) forcefully over a surface. **5.** To injure the surface of by rubbing against something rough or sharp. **6.** To amass or produce with difficulty: *scrape together some cash.* — *intr.* **1.** To come into sliding, abrasive contact. **2.** To rub or move with a harsh grating noise. **3.** To give forth a harsh grating noise. **4.** To economize in small amounts; scrimp. **5.** To succeed or manage with difficulty: *scraped by.* — *n.* **1.a.** The act of scraping. **b.** The sound of scraping. **2.** An abrasion on the skin. **3.a.** An embarrassing predicament. **b.** A fight; a scuffle. [ME *scrapen* < ON *skrapa.* See **sker-¹*.**]

scrap•er (skrā′pər) *n.* One that scrapes, esp. a tool for scraping off paint or other matter.

scrap•er•board (skrā′pər-bôrd′, -bōrd′) *n.* See **scratchboard.**

scrap•heap also **scrap heap** (skrăp′hēp′) *n.* **1.** A pile or heap of waste material. **2.** A place for discarding useless or worthless material.

scra•pie (skrā′pē, skrăp′ē) *n.* A usu. fatal disease of sheep and goats, marked by chronic itching and degeneration of the central nervous system. [< SCRAPE.]

scrap•ple (skrăp′əl) *n.* A boiled mush of ground pork and cornmeal set in a mold and then sliced and fried. [Dim. of SCRAP¹.]

scrap•py¹ (skrăp′ē) *adj.* **-pi•er, -pi•est.** Composed of scraps; fragmentary. — **scrap′pi•ly** *adv.* — **scrap′pi•ness** *n.*

scrap•py² (skrăp′ē) *adj.* **-pi•er, -pi•est. 1.** Quarrelsome; contentious. **2.** Full of fighting spirit. See Syns at **argumentative.** — **scrap′pi•ly** *adv.* — **scrap′pi•ness** *n.*

scratch (skrăch) *v.* **scratched, scratch•ing, scratch•es.** — *tr.* **1.** To make a thin shallow cut or mark on (a surface) with a sharp instrument. **2.** To use the nails or claws to dig or scrape at. **3.** To rub or scrape (the skin) to relieve itching. **4.** To scrape or strike on an abrasive surface. **5.** To write or draw by scraping a surface. **6.** To write or draw hurriedly: *scratched off a note.* **7.a.** To strike out or cancel (a word, for example) by or as if by drawing lines through. **b.** *Slang.* To cancel (a project, for example). **8.** *Sports & Games.* To withdraw (an entry) from a contest. — *intr.* **1.** To use the nails or claws to dig, scrape, or wound. **2.** To rub or scrape the skin to relieve itching. **3.** To make a harsh scraping sound. **4.** To gather funds or produce a living with difficulty. **5.a.** *Sports & Games.* To withdraw from a contest. **b.** *Games.* To make a shot in billiards that results in a penalty, as when the cue ball falls into a pocket. — *n.* **1.a.** A mark resembling a line produced by scratching. **b.** A slight wound. **2.** A hasty scribble. **3.** A sound made by scratching. **4.a.** *Sports.* The starting line for a race. **b.** *Sports & Games.* A contestant who has been withdrawn from a competition. **5.** *Games.* **a.** The act of scratching in billiards. **b.** A fluke or chance shot in billiards. **6.** Poultry feed. **7.** *Slang.* Money. — *adj.* **1.** Done haphazardly or by chance. **2.** Assembled hastily or at random. **3.** *Sports.* Having no golf handicap. — ***idioms.*** **from scratch.** From the very beginning. **up to scratch.** *Informal.* **1.** Meeting the requirements. **2.** In fit condition. [ME *scracchen*, prob. blend of *scratten*, to scratch, and *cracchen*, to scratch (poss. < MDu. *cratsen*).] — **scratch′er** *n.*

scratch•board (skrăch′bôrd′, -bōrd′) *n.* A drawing board covered with white clay and a black surface layer that is scraped away with a scratching tool to produce line drawings.

scratch pad *n.* **1.** A pad of paper for preliminary or hasty writing, notes, or sketches. **2.** Also **scratch•pad** (skrăch′-păd′). *Comp. Sci.* A usu. high-speed internal register used for temporary storage of preliminary data.

scratch sheet *n. Sports & Games.* A publication listing the horses withdrawn from a day's races and giving information and betting odds on the horses scheduled to race.

scratch test *n.* A test for allergy performed by scratching the skin and applying an allergen to the wound.

scratch•y (skrăch′ē) *adj.* **-i•er, -i•est. 1.** Marked by or consisting of scratches. **2.** Making a harsh, scratching noise. **3.** Harsh and irritating: *a scratchy fabric.* **4.** Irregular; uneven. — **scratch′i•ly** *adv.* — **scratch′i•ness** *n.*

scrawl (skrôl) *v.* **scrawled, scrawl•ing, scrawls.** — *tr.* To write hastily or illegibly. — *intr.* To write in a sprawling, irregular manner. — *n.* **1.** Irregular, often illegible handwriting. **2.** Something written hastily or illegibly. [Perh. < obsolete *scrawl*, to gesticulate, sprawl < ME *scrawlen*, prob. blend of *sprawlen*, to sprawl; see SPRAWL, and *craulen*, to crawl; see CRAWL¹.] — **scrawl′er** *n.* — **scrawl′y** *adj.*

scraw•ny (skrô′nē) *adj.* **-ni•er, -ni•est.** Gaunt and bony. See Syns at **lean².** [Alteration of dial. *scranny*, poss. of Scand. orig.; akin to Norw. *skran*, lean.] — **scraw′ni•ness** *n.*

screak (skrēk) *intr.v.* **screaked, screak•ing, screaks. 1.** To screech; shriek. **2.** To creak. — *n.* **1.** A screech; a shriek. **2.** A creak. [ME *skricken* < ON *skrækja.*] — **screak′y** *adj.*

scream (skrēm) *v.* **screamed, scream•ing, screams.** — *intr.* **1.** To utter a long loud piercing cry, as from pain or fear. **2.** To make a loud piercing sound. **3.** To speak or write in a heated hysterical manner. **4.** To have or produce a startling effect. — *tr.* To utter or say in or as if in a screaming voice. — *n.* **1.** A long loud piercing cry or sound. **2.** *Informal.* One that is hilariously or ridiculously funny. [ME *screamen*, poss. of Scand. orig.; akin to ON *scræma.*] — **scream′ing•ly** *adv.*

scream•er (skrē′mər) *n.* **1.** One that screams, esp. one that sings in a harsh strident manner. **2.** *Slang.* A sensational headline. **3.** *Slang.* One that evokes screams or laughter. **4.** *Slang.* An exclamation point. **5.** Any of several large aquatic birds of the family Anhimidae of South America, having a harsh resonant call.

scream•ing mee•mies (skrē′mĭng mē′mēz) *pl.n. (Used with a sing. or pl. v.) Slang.* An attack of nerves; the jitters. [Expressive of nervousness.]

scree (skrē) *n.* **1.** Loose rock debris covering a slope. **2.** A slope of loose rock debris at the base of a steep incline or cliff. [Prob. ult. < ON *skridha*, landslide < *skrīdha*, to slide.]

screech (skrēch) *n.* **1.** A high-pitched strident cry. **2.** A sound suggestive of this cry. — *v.* **screeched, screech•ing, screech•es.** — *tr.* To utter in or as if in a screech. — *intr.* **1.** To cry out in a high-pitched strident voice. **2.** To make a sound suggestive of a screech. [Alteration of obsolete *scrich* < ME *scrichen*, to screech, perh. of Scand. orig.] — **screech′er** *n.* — **screech′i•ness** *n.* — **screech′y** *adj.*

screech owl *n.* Any of various owls of the genus *Otus* of North America, esp. *O. asio*, having a quavering whistlelike call.

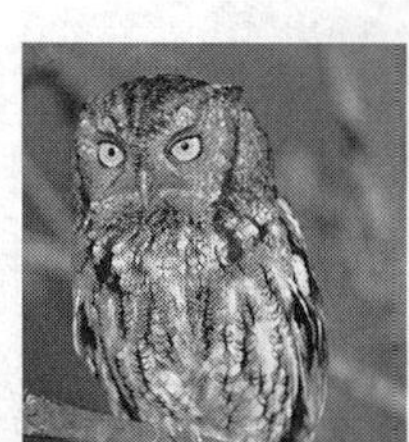

screech owl
Common screech owl
Otus asio

screed (skrēd) *n.* **1.** A long monotonous harangue or piece of writing. **2.a.** A strip of wood, plaster, or metal placed on a wall or pavement as a guide for the even application of plaster or concrete. **b.** A layer or strip of material used to level off a horizontal surface such as a floor. **c.** A smooth final surface of a substance, such as concrete, applied to a floor. [ME *screde*, fragment, strip of cloth < OE *scrēade*, shred.]

screen (skrēn) *n.* **1.** A movable device, esp. a framed construction such as a room divider or a decorative panel, designed to divide, conceal, or protect. **2.** One that serves to protect, conceal, or divide. **3.** A coarse sieve used for sifting out fine particles, as of sand, gravel, or coal. **4.** A system for preliminary appraisal and selection of personnel as to their suitability for particular jobs. **5.** A window or door insertion of framed wire or plastic mesh used to keep out insects and permit airflow. **6.a.** The white or silver surface on which a picture is projected for viewing. **b.** The movie industry. **7.a.** *Electron.* The phosphorescent surface on which an image is displayed, as on a computer monitor. **b.** *Comp. Sci.* The information or image displayed at a given time on a monitor, display, or video terminal. **8.** *Print.* A glass plate marked off with crossing lines, placed before the lens of a camera when photographing for halftone reproduction. **9.** A body of troops or ships sent to protect a larger body. **10.** *Sports.* A block, set with the body, that impedes the vision or movement of an opponent. — *tr.v.* **screened, screen•ing, screens. 1.** To provide with a screen: *screen a porch.* **2.a.** To conceal from view with or as if with a screen. See Syns at **block, hide¹. b.** To protect, guard, or shield. **3.a.** To separate or sift out (fine particles of sand, for example) by means of a sieve or screen. **b.** To examine (a job applicant, for example) systematically in order to determine suitability. **4.** To show or project (a movie, for example) on a screen. **5.** To test or examine for the presence of disease or infection. **6.** *Sports.* To block the vision or movement of (an opponent) with the body. [ME *screne* < ONFr. *escren* < MDu. *scherm*, shield, screen. See **sker-¹*.**] — **screen′a•ble** *adj.* — **screen′er** *n.*

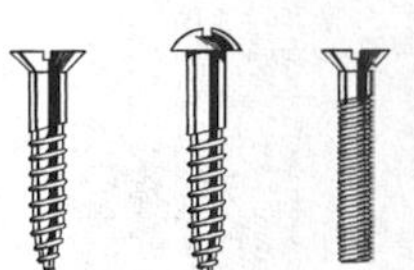

screw
Left to right: Flat head wood screw, round head wood screw, and flat head machine screw

screen•ing (skrē′nĭng) *n.* **1. screenings.** *(used with a sing. or pl. v.)* Refuse, such as waste coal, separated by a screen. **2.** The mesh material used to make door or window screens. **3.** A presentation of a movie.

screen memory *n.* A memory that is unconsciously used to repress recollection of an associated but distressing event.

screen pass *n. Football.* A short forward pass to a receiver in the flat who is protected by a formation of blockers.

screen•play (skrēn′plā′) *n.* The script for a movie, including camera directions and descriptions of scenes.

screen test *n.* A brief movie sequence filmed to test the ability of an aspiring performer. — **screen′-test′** (skrēn′tĕst′) *v.*

screen•writ•er (skrēn′rī′tər) *n.* One who writes screenplays. — **screen′writ′ing** *n.*

screw (skro͞o) *n.* **1.a.** A cylindrical rod incised with one or more helical or advancing spiral threads, as a lead screw. **b.** The tapped collar or socket that receives this rod. **2.** A metal pin with incised threads and a slotted head that can be driven as a fastener by turning with a screwdriver. **3.** A device having a helical form, such as a corkscrew. **4.** A propeller. **5.** A twist or turn of or as if of a screw. **6.** *Slang.* **a.** A prison guard. **b.** The turnkey of a jail. **7.** *Vulgar Slang.* The act or an instance of having sexual intercourse. **8.** *Chiefly British.* **a.** Salary; wages. **b.** A small paper packet, as of tobacco. **c.** An old broken-down horse. **d.** A stingy or crafty bargainer. — *v.* **screwed, screw•ing, screws.** — *tr.* **1.** To drive or tighten (a screw). **2.a.** To fasten, tighten, or attach by or as if by means of a screw. **b.** To attach (a tapped or threaded fitting or cap) by twisting into place. **c.** To rotate (a part) on a threaded axis. **3.** To contort (one's face). **4.** *Slang.* To take advantage of; cheat. **5.** *Vulgar Slang.* To have sexual intercourse with. — *intr.* **1.** To turn or twist. **2.a.** To become attached by means of the threads of a screw. **b.** To be capable of such attach-

ă **pat**	oi **boy**
ā **pay**	ou **out**
âr **care**	o͝o **took**
ä **father**	o͞o **boot**
ĕ **pet**	ŭ **cut**
ē **be**	ûr **urge**
ĭ **pit**	th **thin**
ī **pie**	*th* **this**
îr **pier**	hw **which**
ŏ **pot**	zh **vision**
ō **toe**	ə **about, item**
ô **paw**	

Stress marks:
′ (primary);
′ (secondary), as in
dictionary (dĭk′shə-nĕr′ē)

ment. **3.** *Vulgar Slang.* To have sexual intercourse. **—*phrasal verbs.* screw around. 1.** *Slang.* To act aimlessly or in a confused way and accomplish nothing. **2.** *Vulgar Slang.* To be sexually promiscuous. **screw up. 1.** To muster or summon up. **2.** *Slang.* To make a mess of (an undertaking). **3.** *Slang.* To injure; damage. **4.** *Slang.* To make neurotic or anxious. **—*idiom.* have a screw loose.** *Slang.* **1.** To behave in an eccentric manner. **2.** To be insane. [ME *skrewe* < OFr. *escrove*, female screw, nut, perh. < Med.Lat. *scrōfa* < Lat., sow. See **sker-1*.**] **—screw′a•ble** *adj.* **—screw′er** *n.*

screw•ball (skro͞o′bôl′) *n.* **1.** *Baseball.* A pitched ball that curves in the direction opposite to that of a normal curve ball. **2.** *Slang.* A person regarded as eccentric, whimsical, or irrational. —*adj. Slang.* Impulsively whimsical; eccentric.

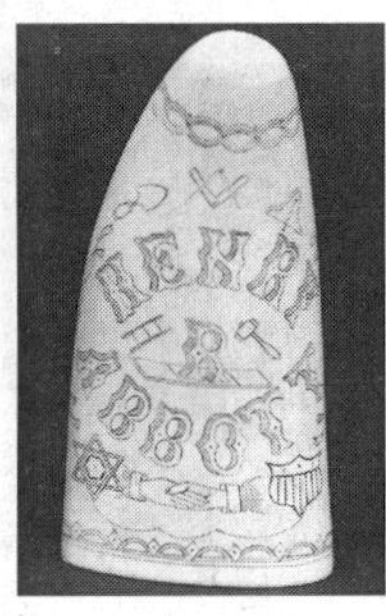

scrimshaw
Scrimshawed tooth with Masonic emblems, 1866, by Henry R. Abbott

screw bean *n.* **1.** A shrub or small tree *(Prosopis pubescens)* of southwest North America, having pinnately compound leaves and twisted pods used as fodder. **2.** The pod of this plant.

screw•driv•er (skro͞o′drī′vər) *n.* **1.** A tool used for turning screws. **2.** A cocktail made with vodka and orange juice.

screw eye *n.* A wood screw with an eyelet in place of a head.

screw jack *n.* See **jackscrew.**

screw log *n. Naut.* See **patent log.**

screw pine *n.* See **pandanus.**

screw propeller *n.* A propeller.

screw thread *n.* The continuous helical groove on a screw or the inner surface of a nut.

screw•up also **screw-up** (skro͞o′ŭp′) *n. Slang.* **1.** One that makes a mess of an undertaking; a bungler. **2.** A blunder.

screw•worm (skro͞o′wûrm′) *n.* The screwworm fly larva.

screwworm fly *n.* A bluish fly *(Cochliomyia hominivorax)* of the New World that breeds in the living tissue of mammals, having entered usu. through open wounds or the nostrils.

screw•y (skro͞o′ē) *adj.* **-i•er, -i•est.** *Slang.* **1.** Eccentric; crazy. **2.** Ludicrously odd, unlikely, or inappropriate. **—screw′i•ness** *n.*

Scri•a•bin (skrē-ä′bĭn), **Alexander Nikolayevich.** 1872–1915. Russian composer of orchestral and piano works.

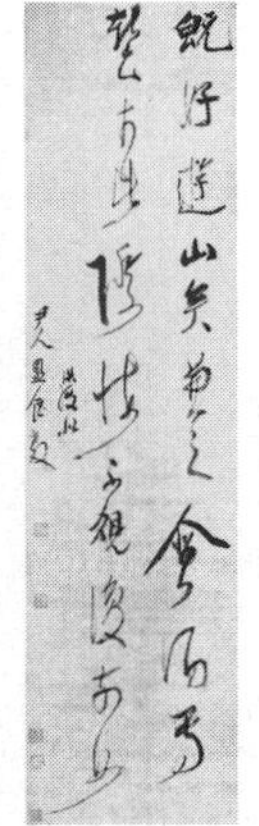

script
17th-century Chinese hanging scroll by Ch'en Hung-shou (1598–1652)

scrib•ble (skrĭb′əl) *v.* **-bled, -bling, -bles.** —*tr.* **1.** To write hurriedly without heed to legibility or style. **2.** To cover with scribbles, doodles, or meaningless marks. —*intr.* To write or draw in a hurried careless way. —*n.* **1.** Careless hurried writing. **2.** Meaningless marks and lines. [ME *scriblen*, prob. < *scriben*, to write < Lat. *scrībere*, to write. See **skrībh-*.**] **—scrib′bly** *adj.*

scrib•bler (skrĭb′lər) *n.* One who scribbles, esp. an author regarded as inferior or unimportant.

scribe (skrīb) *n.* **1.** A public clerk or secretary, esp. in ancient times. **2.** A professional copyist of manuscripts and documents. **3.** A writer or journalist. **4.** See **scriber.** —*v.* **scribed, scrib•ing, scribes.** —*tr.* **1.** To mark with a scriber. **2.** To write or inscribe. —*intr.* To work as a scribe. [ME < OFr. < LLat. *scrība* < Lat., keeper of accounts, secretary < *scrībere*, to write. See **skrībh-*.**] **—scrib′al** *adj.*

Scribe (skrēb), **Augustin Eugène.** 1791–1861. French playwright known for his comedies of manners.

scrib•er (skrī′bər) *n.* A sharply pointed tool used for marking lines, as on wood, metal, or ceramic.

scried (skrīd) *v.* P.t. and p.part. of **scry.**

scries (skrīz) *v.* Third pers. sing. pr.t. of **scry.**

scrim (skrĭm) *n.* **1.** A durable, loosely woven cotton or linen fabric used for curtains or upholstery lining or in industry. **2.** A transparent fabric used as a drop in the theater to create special effects of lights or atmosphere. [?]

scrim•mage (skrĭm′ĭj) *n.* **1.** *Football.* The contest between two teams from the time the ball is snapped until it is declared dead. **2.** *Sports.* A practice session or informal game, as between two units of the same team. **3.a.** A rough-and-tumble struggle; a tussle. **b.** A skirmish. —*intr.v.* **-maged, -mag•ing, -mag•es.** *Sports.* To engage in a scrimmage. [ME, alteration of *skirmisshe, scrimish.* See SKIRMISH.]

scrimp (skrĭmp) *v.* **scrimped, scrimp•ing, scrimps.** —*intr.* To economize severely. —*tr.* **1.** To be excessively sparing with or of. **2.** To cut or make too small or scanty. [Perh. of Scand. orig.; akin to Swed. *skrympa*, to shrink.] **—scrimp′er** *n.* **—scrimp′i•ness** *n.* **—scrimp′y** *adj.*

scrim•shand•er (skrĭm′shăn′dər) *n.* One who carves scrimshaw. [?]

scrim•shaw (skrĭm′shô′) *n., pl.* **scrimshaw** or **-shaws. 1.** The art of carving or incising intricate designs on whalebone or whale ivory. **2.** A decorative article made by this art. —*tr. & intr.v.* **-shawed, -shaw•ing, -shaws.** To decorate (whale ivory or whalebone) with intricate carvings or designs or make such designs. [Prob. < SCRIMSHANDER.]

scroll
Of a double bass

scrip1 (skrĭp) *n.* **1.** Paper money issued for temporary emergency use. **2.** A small scrap of paper, esp. with a short list or schedule written on it. [Perh. alteration of SCRIPT.]

scrip2 (skrĭp) *n.* **1.** A provisional certificate entitling the holder to a fractional share of stock or of other jointly owned property. **2.** Such certificates considered as a group. [Short for *subscription receipt*, receipt for a portion of a loan.]

scrip3 (skrĭp) *n. Archaic.* A wallet, small satchel, or bag. [ME *scrippe.*]

Scripps (skrĭps). Family of Amer. newspaper publishers, including **James Edmund** (1835–1906), who founded the *Detroit Evening News* (1873), and his half-brother **Edward Wyllis Scripps** (1854–1926), who formed (1907) the news agency that became United Press International.

script (skrĭpt) *n.* **1.a.** Handwriting. **b.** A style of writing with cursive characters. **c.** A particular system of writing: *cuneiform script.* **2.** *Print.* **a.** A style of type that imitates handwriting. **b.** The matter set in this type. **3.a.** The text of a play, broadcast, or movie. **b.** A copy of a text used by a director or performer. —*tr.v.* **script•ed, script•ing, scripts. 1.** To prepare (a text) for filming or broadcasting. **2.** To orchestrate (an event, for example) as if writing a script. [ME *skript*, a piece of writing, alteration of *scrite* < OFr. *escrit* < Lat. *scrīptum* < neut. p.part. of *scrībere*, to write. See **skrībh-*.**]

Script. *abbr.* Scriptural; Scripture.

scrip•to•ri•um (skrĭp-tôr′ē-əm, -tōr′-) *n., pl.* **-to•ri•ums** or **-to•ri•a** (-tôr′ē-ə, -tōr′-). A room in a monastery for copying, writing, or illuminating manuscripts and records. [Med. Lat. *scrīptōrium* < Lat. *scrīptus*, p.part. of *scrībere*, to write. See **skrībh-*.**]

scrip•tur•al (skrĭp′chər-əl) *adj.* **1.** Of or relating to writing; written. **2.** Often **Scriptural.** Of, relating to, based on, or contained in the Scriptures. **—scrip′tur•al•ly** *adv.*

Scrip•ture (skrĭp′chər) *n.* **1.a.** A sacred writing or book. **b.** A passage from such a writing or book. **2.** The sacred writings of the Bible. Often used in the plural. **3. scripture.** A statement regarded as authoritative. [ME < LLat. *scrīptūra* < Lat., act of writing < *scrīptus*, p.part. of *scrībere*, to write. See **skrībh-*.**]

script•writ•er (skrĭpt′rī′tər) *n.* One who writes copy to be used in a film or broadcast. **—script′writ′ing** *n.*

scriv•en•er (skrĭv′ə-nər, skrĭv′nər) *n.* **1.** A professional copyist; a scribe. **2.** A notary. [ME *scrivener* < *scrivein* < OFr. *escrivein* < VLat. **scrība, scrībān-* < Lat. *scrība*, scribe. See SCRIBE.]

scro•bic•u•late (skrō-bĭk′yə-lĭt, -lāt′) *adj. Biol.* Marked with many shallow depressions, grooves, or pits. [Lat. *scrobiculus*, dim. of *scrobis*, trench; see **sker-1*** + -ATE1.]

scrod also **schrod** (skrŏd) *n., pl.* **scrod** also **schrod.** *New England.* A young cod or haddock, esp. one split and boned for cooking. [Poss. < obsolete Du. *schrood*, slice, shred < MDu. *scrōde.*]

scrof•u•la (skrŏf′yə-lə) *n.* A form of tuberculosis affecting the lymph nodes, esp. of the neck, that is most common in children. [ME *scrophula* < LLat. *scrōfulae*, swelling of the glands, dim. of Lat. *scrōfa*, sow. See **sker-1*.**]

scrof•u•lous (skrŏf′yə-ləs) *adj.* **1.** Relating to, affected with, or resembling scrofula. **2.** Morally degenerate; corrupt. **—scrof′u•lous•ly** *adv.* **—scrof′u•lous•ness** *n.*

scroll (skrōl) *n.* **1.a.** A roll, as of parchment or papyrus, used esp. for writing a document. **b.** An ancient book or volume written on such a roll. **2.** A list or schedule of names. **3.** An ornament or ornamental design that resembles a partially rolled scroll of paper, as the volute in Ionic capitals. **4.** *Mus.* The curved head above the peg box on a stringed instrument. **5.** *Her.* A ribbon inscribed with a motto. —*v.* **scrolled, scroll•ing, scrolls.** —*tr.* **1.** To inscribe on a scroll. **2.** To roll up into a scroll. **3.** To ornament with a scroll. **4.** *Comp. Sci.* To cause (text or graphics) to move vertically or horizontally across the screen so that a new line appears for each line that moves off the screen. —*intr. Comp. Sci.* To scroll text or graphics. [ME *scrowle*, alteration of *serowe* < OFr. *escroue, escroe*, strip of parchment, scroll, of Gmc. orig.]

scroll saw *n.* A handsaw or power saw with a narrow ribbonlike blade for cutting curved or irregular shapes.

scroll•work (skrōl′wûrk′) *n.* Embellishment with a scroll motif, esp. ornamentation executed in wood with a scroll saw.

scrooch also **scrootch** (skro͞och) *intr.v.* **scrooched, scrooch•ing, scrooch•es** also **scrootched, scrootch•ing, scrootch•es.** To hunch down; crouch. [Alteration of *scrooge*, to squeeze, crowd, poss. blend of SCREW and SQUEEZE.]

Scrooge also **scrooge** (skro͞oj) *n.* A mean-spirited miserly person; a skinflint. [After Dickens's miser Ebenezer *Scrooge.*]

scro•tum (skrō′təm) *n., pl.* **-ta** (-tə) or **-tums.** The external sac of skin enclosing the testes in most mammals. [Lat. *scrōtum.*] **—scro′tal** (skrōt′l) *adj.*

scrounge (skrounj) *v.* **scrounged, scroung•ing, scroung•es.** —*tr.* **1.** To obtain (something) by begging or borrowing with no intention of reparation. **2.** To obtain by salvaging or foraging; round up. —*intr.* **1.** To seek to scrounge something, as by begging. **2.** To forage about in an effort to acquire something at no cost. [Alteration of dial. *scrunge*, to steal.] **—scroung′er** *n.*

scroung•y (skroun′jē) *adj.* **-i•er, -i•est.** *Slang.* Dirty or shabby: *a scroungy overcoat.*

scrub1 (skrŭb) *v.* **scrubbed, scrub•bing, scrubs.** —*tr.* **1.a.** To rub hard in order to clean. **b.** To remove (dirt or stains) by hard rubbing. **2.** To remove impurities from (a gas) chemically. **3.** *Slang.* To cancel or abandon; drop. —*intr.* To clean or wash something by hard rubbing. —*n.* The act or an instance of scrubbing. **—*phrasal verb.* scrub up.** To wash the hands and arms thoroughly, as before surgery. [ME *scrobben,* to currycomb a horse < MDu. *schrobben,* to clean by rubbing, scrape. See **sker-**[1]*.] **—scrub′ba•ble** *adj.*

scrub[2] (skrŭb) *n.* **1.** A straggly, stunted tree or shrub. **2.** A growth or tract of stunted vegetation. **3.** An undersized or poorly developed domestic animal. **4.** An undersized or insignificant person. **5.** *Sports.* A player not on the varsity or first team. **6.** *Australian.* Remote rural land; the bush. [ME, var. of *shrubbe.* See SHRUB[1].]

scrub•ber (skrŭb′ər) *n.* One that scrubs, esp.: **a.** One who cleans by scrubbing. **b.** A brush, appliance, or abrasive used in cleaning. **c.** An apparatus used for removing impurities from a gas.

scrub•by (skrŭb′ē) *adj.* **-bi•er, -bi•est. 1.** Covered with or consisting of scrub or underbrush. **2.** Straggly or stunted. **3.** Paltry or shabby; wretched. **—scrub′bi•ly** *adv.* **—scrub′bi•ness** *n.*

scrub fowl *n.* See **megapode.**

scrub jay *n.* A crestless blue and gray jay *(Aphelocoma coerulescens)* found in dense brush or scrub, esp. in Florida.

scrub•land (skrŭb′lănd′) *n.* An area of land that is uncultivated and covered with sparse stunted vegetation.

scrub pine *n.* **1.** A straggly pine tree *(Pinus virginiana)* of the eastern United States having prickly cones and drooping or spreading branches. **2.** See **jack pine.**

scrub typhus *n.* An infectious disease common in Asia, caused by the rickettsia *R. tsutsugamushi* and marked by fever, painful swollen lymph nodes, and skin lesions.

scrub•wom•an (skrŭb′wo͝om′ən) *n.* A woman hired to clean.

scruff (skrŭf) *n.* The back of the neck; the nape. [Alteration of dial. *scuft, scuff.*]

scruff•y (skrŭf′ē) *adj.* **-i•er, -i•est. 1.** Shabby; untidy. **2.** *Chiefly British.* Scaly; scabby. [< obsolete *scruff,* scurf, var. of *scurf.* See SCURF.] **—scruff′i•ly** *adv.* **—scruff′i•ness** *n.*

scrum (skrŭm) *Sports.* —*n.* A scrummage. —*intr.v.* **scrummed, scrum•ming, scrums.** To engage in a scrummage.

scrum•mage (skrŭm′ĭj) *Sports. n.* A Rugby formation in which the two sets of forwards mass together around the ball and, with their heads down, try to shoulder their opponents off the ball and kick it to their own team. [Alteration of SCRIMMAGE.] **—scrum′mage** *v.* **—scrum′mag•er** *n.*

scrump•tious (skrŭmp′shəs) *adj.* Splendid; delectable. [Perh. alteration of SUMPTUOUS.] **—scrump′tious•ly** *adv.* **—scrump′tious•ness** *n.*

scrunch (skrŭnch, skro͝onch) *v.* **scrunched, scrunch•ing, scrunch•es.** —*tr.* **1.** To crush or crunch. **2.** To crumple or squeeze; hunch: *scrunched up their shoulders.* —*intr.* **1.** To hunch. **2.** To move with or make a crunching sound. —*n.* A crunching sound. [Prob. alteration of CRUNCH.] **—scrunch′a•ble** *adj.*

scru•ple (skro͞o′pəl) *n.* **1.** An uneasy feeling arising from conscience or principle that tends to hinder action. **2.** A unit of apothecary weight equal to about 1.3 grams, or 20 grains. **3.** A minute part or amount. —*intr.v.* **-pled, -pling, -ples.** To hesitate as a result of conscience or principle. [ME *scrupul* < OFr. *scrupule* < Lat. *scrūpulus,* small unit of measurement, scruple, dim. of *scrūpus,* rough stone, trash.]

scru•pu•lous (skro͞o′pyə-ləs) *adj.* **1.** Conscientious and exact; painstaking. **2.** Having scruples; principled. [ME < OFr. *scrupuleux* < Lat. *scrūpulōsus* < *scrūpulus,* scruple. See SCRUPLE.] **—scru′pu•los′i•ty** (-lŏs′ĭ-tē), **scru′pu•lous•ness** (-ləs-nĭs) *n.* **—scru′pu•lous•ly** *adv.*

scru•ta•ble (skro͞o′tə-bəl) *adj.* Capable of being understood through study and observation; comprehensible. [LLat. *scrūtābilis,* searchable < Lat. *scrūtārī,* to search. See SCRUTINY.]

scru•ti•nize (skro͞ot′n-īz′) *tr.v.* **-nized, -niz•ing, -niz•es.** To examine or observe with great care; inspect critically. **—scru′ti•niz′er** *n.* **—scru′ti•niz′ing•ly** *adv.*

scru•ti•ny (skro͞ot′n-ē) *n., pl.* **-nies. 1.** A close careful examination or study. **2.** Close observation; surveillance. [ME *scrutinie,* taking of a formal vote < Lat. *scrūtinium,* inquiry, search < *scrūtārī,* to search, examine < *scrūta,* trash.]

scry (skrī) *intr.v.* **scried** (skrīd), **scry•ing, scries** (skrīz). To see or predict the future with a crystal ball. [Short for DESCRY.]

scu•ba (sko͞o′bə) *n.* A portable apparatus that contains compressed air and is used for breathing under water. [*s(elf-) c(ontained) u(nderwater) b(reathing) a(pparatus).*]

scuba diver *n.* One who uses scuba gear in underwater swimming. **—scu′ba-dive′** (sko͞o′bə-dīv′) *v.* **—scuba diving** *n.*

scud (skŭd) *intr.v.* **scud•ded, scud•ding, scuds. 1.** To run or skim along swiftly and easily: *clouds scudding by.* **2.** *Naut.* To run before a gale with little or no sail set. —*n.* **1.** The act of scudding. **2.a.** Wind-driven clouds, mist, or rain. **b.** A gust of wind. **c.** Ragged low clouds, moving rapidly beneath another cloud layer. [Poss. < ME *scut,* rabbit, rabbit's tail. See SCUT.]

scu•do (sko͞o′dō) *n., pl.* **-di** (-dē). A monetary unit and coin formerly used in Italy and Sicily. [Ital., shield, scudo < Lat. *scūtum,* shield. See **skei-***.]

scuff (skŭf) *v.* **scuffed, scuff•ing, scuffs.** —*intr.* To scrape the feet while walking; shuffle. —*tr.* **1.** To scrape with the feet. **2.** To shuffle or shift (the feet), as in embarrassment. **3.** To scrape and roughen the surface of. —*n.* **1.** The act or sound of scraping esp. with the feet. **2.** A worn or rough spot resulting from scraping. **3.** A flat backless house slipper. [Prob. of Scand. orig.; akin to ON *skūfa,* to push.] **—scuff′er** *n.*

scuf•fle[1] (skŭf′əl) *intr.v.* **-fled, -fling, -fles. 1.** To fight or struggle confusedly at close quarters. **2.** To shuffle. —*n.* A rough disorderly struggle at close quarters. [Prob. freq. of *scuff.*] **—scuf′fler** *n.*

scuf•fle[2] (skŭf′əl) *n.* A hoe that is pushed. [Du. *schoffel,* weeding hoe < MDu., hoe, shovel.]

sculch (skŭlch) *n. New England.* Var. of **culch** 3.

scull (skŭl) *Naut.* —*n.* **1.** A long oar mounted over the stern of a boat and moved from side to side to propel the boat forward. **2.** One of a pair of short-handled oars used by a single rower. **3.** A small light racing boat for one, two, or four rowers. —*v.* **sculled, scull•ing, sculls.** —*tr.* To propel (a boat) with a scull. —*intr.* To use a scull to propel a boat. [ME *sculle.*] **—scull′er** *n.*

scul•ler•y (skŭl′ə-rē) *n., pl.* **-ies.** A small room adjoining a kitchen, in which dishwashing and other kitchen chores are done. [ME < OFr. *escuelerie* < *escuelier,* keeper of dishes < *escuele,* dish < VLat. **scūtella,* alteration (influenced by *scūtum,* shield) of Lat. *scutella,* salver, dim. of *scutra,* platter.]

scul•lion (skŭl′yən) *n.* A servant employed to do menial tasks in a kitchen. [ME *sculyon,* prob. < OFr. *escouvillon,* dishcloth, dim. of *escouve,* broom < Lat. *scōpa.*]

scul•pin (skŭl′pĭn) *n., pl.* **-pins** or **sculpin. 1.** Any of various marine and freshwater fishes of the family Cottidae, having a large flattened head and spines. **2.** A scorpion fish *(Scorpaena guttata)* of California coastal waters. [?]

sculpt (skŭlpt) *v.* **sculpt•ed, sculpt•ing, sculpts.** —*tr.* **1.** To sculpture (an object). **2.** To shape, mold, or fashion esp. with artistry or precision. —*intr.* To be a sculptor. [Fr. *sculpter* < OFr. < Lat. *sculpere, sculpt-,* to carve. See SCULPTURE.]

sculp•tor (skŭlp′tər) *n.* **1.** One who produces sculptural artwork. **2.** One who shapes, molds, or fashions esp. with artistry or precision. [Lat. < *sculpere,* to carve. See SCULPTURE.]

Sculp•tor (skŭlp′tər) *n.* A constellation in the Southern Hemisphere near Cetus and Phoenix.

Sculp•tor's Workshop (skŭlp′tərz) *n.* See **Sculptor.**

sculp•tress (skŭlp′trĭs) *n. Usage Problem.* A woman who sculptures. See Usage Note at **–ess.**

sculp•ture (skŭlp′chər) *n.* **1.** The art or practice of shaping figures or designs in the round or in relief, as by chiseling marble, modeling clay, or casting in metal. **2.a.** A work of art created by sculpture. **b.** Such works of art considered as a group. **3.** Ridges, indentations, or other markings, as on a shell, formed by natural processes. —*v.* **-tured, -tur•ing, -tures.** —*tr.* **1.** To fashion (stone, for example) into a three-dimensional figure. **2.** To represent in sculpture. **3.** To ornament with sculpture. **4.** To change the shape or contour of, as by erosion. —*intr.* To make sculptures or a sculpture. [ME < Lat. *sculptūra* < *sculptus,* p.part. of *sculpere,* to carve. See **skel-**[1]*.] **—sculp′tur•al** *adj.* **—sculp′tur•al•ly** *adv.*

sculp•tur•esque (skŭlp′chə-rĕsk′) *adj.* Suggestive of or having the qualities of sculpture. **—sculp′tur•esque′ly** *adv.*

scultch (skŭlch) *n. New England.* Var. of **culch** 3.

scum (skŭm) *n.* **1.** A filmy layer of extraneous or impure matter that forms on or rises to the surface of a liquid or body of water. **2.** The refuse or dross of molten metals. **3.** Refuse or worthless matter. **4.** *Slang.* One, such as a person, that is regarded as despicable or worthless. —*v.* **scummed, scum•ming, scums.** —*tr.* To remove the scum from. —*intr.* To become covered with scum. [ME < MDu. *schūm.* See **(s)keu-***.] **—scum′mer** *n.* **—scum′mi•ly** *adv.* **—scum′mi•ness** *n.* **—scum′my** *adj.*

scum•bag (skŭm′băg′) *n. Slang.* A despicable person.

scum•ble (skŭm′bəl) *tr.v.* **-bled, -bling, -bles.** To soften the colors or outlines of (a painting or drawing) by covering with a film of opaque or semiopaque color or by rubbing. —*n.* **1.** The effect produced by scumbling. **2.** Material used for scumbling. [Poss. < SCUM.]

scun•ner (skŭn′ər) *n.* A strong dislike; an aversion. [< ME *skunner,* to shrink back in disgust < *scurnen,* to flinch.]

scup (skŭp) *n., pl.* **scup** or **scups.** A porgy *(Stenotomus chrysops)* of the northern Atlantic coastal waters, important as a food fish. [Short for Narragansett *mishcùp.*]

scup•per[1] (skŭp′ər) *n.* **1.** *Naut.* An opening in the side of a ship at deck level to allow water to run off. **2.** An opening for draining off water, as from a floor or the roof of a building. [ME *scoper;* poss. akin to *scope,* scoop. See SCOOP.]

scup•per[2] (skŭp′ər) *tr.v.* **-pered, -per•ing, -pers. 1.** *Chiefly British.* To overwhelm or massacre. **2.** To ruin or destroy. [Perh. < SCUPPER[1].]

scup•per•nong (skŭp′ər-nông′, -nŏng′) *n.* **1.** See **muscadine. 2.a.** A cultivated variety of the muscadine grape with sweet yellowish fruit. **b.** A wine made from this grape. [After the *Scuppernong* R. in NE NC.]

scurf (skûrf) *n.* **1.** Scaly or shredded dry skin, such as dandruff. **2.** A loose scaly crust coating a surface, esp. of a plant. [ME, prob. of Scand. orig. See **sker-**[1]*.] **—scurf′i•ness** *n.* **—scurf′y** *adj.*

scuba diver

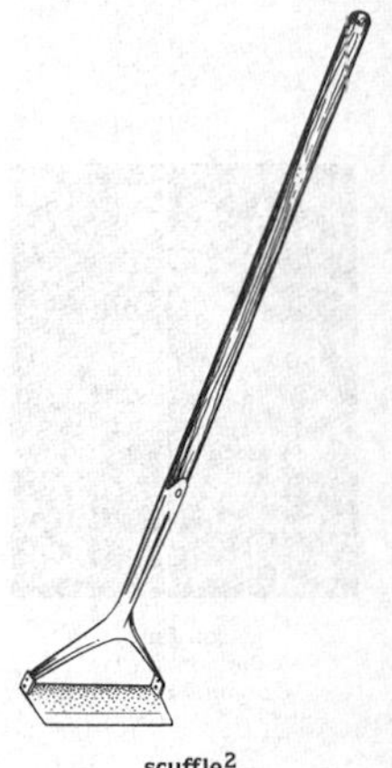

scuffle[2]

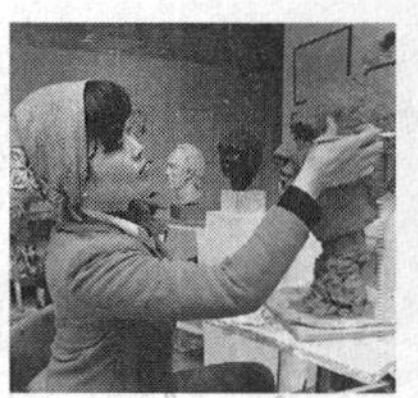

sculptor

ă pat	oi boy
ā pay	ou out
âr care	o͝o took
ä father	o͞o boot
ĕ pet	ŭ cut
ē be	ûr urge
ĭ pit	th thin
ī pie	*th* this
îr pier	hw which
ŏ pot	zh vision
ō toe	ə about,
ô paw	item

Stress marks:
′ (primary);
′ (secondary), as in
dictionary (dĭk′shə-nĕr′ē)

scur•rile also **scur•ril** (skûr′əl, skŭr′-) *adj. Archaic.* Scurrilous. [Fr. < OFr. < Lat. *scurrīlis*, jeering < *scurra*, buffoon, poss. of Etruscan orig.]

scur•ril•i•ty (skə-rĭl′ĭ-tē) *n., pl.* **-ties. 1.** The quality of being vulgar, coarse, or abusive. **2.** A vulgar, coarse, or abusive remark or passage.

scur•ri•lous (skûr′ə-ləs, skŭr′-) *adj.* **1.** Given to the use of vulgar, coarse, or abusive language; foul-mouthed. **2.** Expressed in vulgar, coarse, and abusive language. **—scur′ri•lous•ly** *adv.* **—scur′ri•lous•ness** *n.*

scur•ry (skûr′ē, skŭr′ē) *intr.v.* **-ried, -ry•ing, -ries. 1.** To go with light running steps; scamper. **2.** To flurry or swirl about. *—n., pl.* **-ries. 1.** The act of scurrying. **2.** The noise produced by scurrying. [Prob. short for HURRY-SCURRY.]

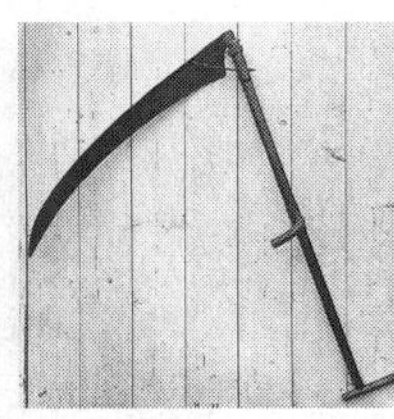
scythe

scur•vy (skûr′vē) *n.* A disease caused by deficiency of vitamin C, characterized by spongy and bleeding gums and bleeding under the skin. *—adj.* **-vi•er, -vi•est.** Mean; contemptible. [< ME *scurfy*, marked by scurf (influenced by Fr. *scorbut*, scurvy < Lat. *scorbūtus*; see SCORBUTIC) < *scurf*, scurf. See SCURF.] **—scur′vi•ly** *adv.* **—scur′vi•ness** *n.*

scurvy grass *n.* **1.** Any of various plants of the genus *Cochlearia*, esp. *C. officinalis* of northern Europe having pungent foliage and formerly used to cure scurvy. **2.** See **sea kale.**

scut (skŭt) *n.* A stubby erect tail, as of a hare. [ME, hare.]

scu•ta (skyo͞o′tə) *n.* Pl. of **scutum.**

scu•tage (skyo͞o′tĭj) *n.* A tax paid in lieu of military service in feudal times. [ME < Med.Lat. *scūtāgium* < Lat. *scūtum*, shield. See SCUTUM.]

Scu•ta•ri (sko͞o′tə-rē), **Lake.** A lake of SE Europe on the border between SE Montenegro and NW Albania.

scu•tate (skyo͞o′tāt) *adj.* **1.** *Zool.* Covered or protected by scutes. **2.** *Bot.* Shaped like a shield or buckler: *scutate leaves.* [Lat. *scūtātus*, shield-bearing < *scūtum*, shield. See SCUTUM.]

scutch (skŭch) *tr.v.* **scutched, scutch•ing, scutch•es.** To separate the valuable fibers of (flax, for example) from the woody parts by beating. *—n.* An implement used for scutching. [Obsolete Fr. *escoucher* < AN *escucher* < VLat. **excuticāre*, freq. of Lat. *excutere*, to shake out : *ex-*, ex- + *quatere*, to shake; see **kwēt-*.**] **—scutch′er** *n.*

sea fan
Common sea fan
Gorgonia ventilina

scutch•eon (skŭch′ən) *n.* **1.** An escutcheon. **2.** A shield-shaped object, such as a scute.

scutch grass *n.* See **Bermuda grass.**

scute (skyo͞ot) *n. Zool.* An external horny, chitinous, or bony plate or scale. [< Lat. *scūtum*, shield. See SCUTUM.]

scu•tel•late (skyo͞o-tĕl′ĭt, skyo͞ot′l-āt′) also **scu•tel•lat•ed** (skyo͞ot′l-ā′tĭd) *adj.* **1.** *Zool.* **a.** Covered with shieldlike bony plates or scales. **b.** Having a scutellum. **2.** *Bot.* Shaped like a shield or platter.

scu•tel•la•tion (skyo͞ot′l-ā′shən) *n.* An arrangement or a covering of scales, as on a bird's leg.

scu•tel•lum (skyo͞o-tĕl′əm) *n., pl.* **-tel•la** (-tĕl′ə). **1.** *Zool.* A shieldlike bony plate or scale, as on the thorax of some insects. **2.** *Bot.* Any of several shield-shaped structures, such as the cotyledon of a grass. [NLat. < Lat., dim. of *scūtum*, shield. See SCUTUM.] **—scu•tel′lar** (-tĕl′ər) *adj.*

scu•ti•form (skyo͞o′tə-fôrm′) *adj.* Shield-shaped: *scutiform leaves.* [Lat. *scūtum*, shield; see SCUTUM + -FORM.]

scut•ter (skŭt′ər) *intr.v.* **-tered, -ter•ing, -ters.** To move with a clattering, scurrying sound. [Alteration of SCUTTLE[3].]

scut•tle[1] (skŭt′l) *n.* **1.** A small opening or hatch with a movable lid in the deck or hull of a ship or in the roof, wall, or floor of a building. **2.** The lid or hatch of such an opening. *—tr.v.* **-tled, -tling, -tles. 1.** *Naut.* **a.** To cut or open a hole or holes in (a ship's hull). **b.** To sink (a ship) by this means. **2.** *Informal.* To scrap; discard. [ME *skottell* < OFr. *escoutille*, poss. < Sp. *escotilla*.]

scut•tle[2] (skŭt′l) *n.* **1.** A metal pail for carrying coal. **2.** A shallow open basket for carrying vegetables. [ME *scutel*, basket < OE, dish < Lat. *scutella*. See SCULLERY.]

scut•tle[3] (skŭt′l) *intr.v.* **-tled, -tling, -tles.** To run or move with short hurried movements; scurry. *—n.* A hurried run. [ME *scottlen*; poss. akin to SCUD.]

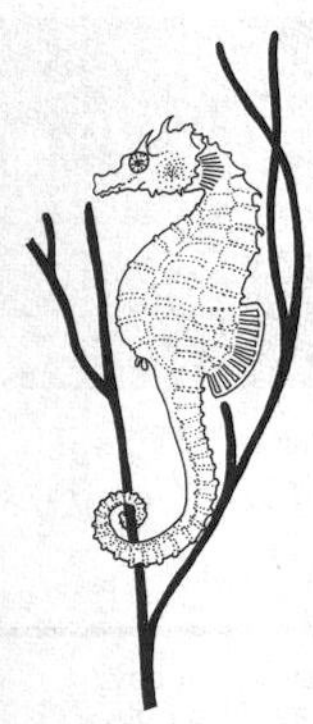
sea horse
Hippocampus hudsonius

scut•tle•butt (skŭt′l-bŭt′) *n.* **1.** *Slang.* Gossip; rumor. **2.** *Naut.* **a.** A drinking fountain on a ship. **b.** A cask on a ship for the day's supply of drinking water. [SCUTTLE[1] + BUTT[5].]

scu•tum (skyo͞o′təm) *n., pl.* **-ta** (-tə). *Zool.* See **scute.** [Lat. *scūtum*, shield. See **skei-*.**]

scut•work (skŭt′wûrk′) *n. Informal.* Monotonous work or menial tasks. [< *scut*, worthless person, perh. < SCOUT[2].]

scuz•zy (skŭz′ē) *adj.* **-zi•er, -zi•est.** *Slang.* **1.** Dirty; grimy. **2.** Disreputable; sleazy: *"ran a scuzzy operation"* (Myra MacPherson). [Poss. < blend of SCUM and FUZZ[1].]

Scyl•la (sĭl′ə) *n. Gk. Myth.* A female sea monster who lived in a cave opposite Charybdis and devoured sailors. **—*idiom.* between Scylla and Charybdis.** In a position where avoidance of one danger exposes one to another danger.

scy•phis•to•ma (sī-fĭs′tə-mə) *n., pl.* **-mae** (-mē) or **-mas.** A larva of a scyphozoan. [NLat. : Gk. *skuphos*, cup + Gk. *stoma*, mouth.]

scy•pho•zo•an (sī′fə-zō′ən) *n.* Any of various marine coelenterates of the class Scyphozoa, which includes the large jellyfishes, characterized by the absence of a true polyp stage. [< NLat. *Scyphozoa*, class name : Gk. *skuphos*, cup + Gk. *zōia*, pl. of *zōion*, -zoon.] **—scy′pho•zo′an** *adj.*

Scy•ros (skī′rəs, skē′rôs). See **Skíros.**

scythe (sīth) *n.* An implement with a long curved single-edged blade and a long bent handle, used for mowing or reaping. *—tr.v.* **scythed, scyth•ing, scythes.** To cut with or as if with a scythe. [ME *sithe* < OE, sickle. See **sek-*.**]

Scyth•i•a (sĭth′ē-ə, sĭth′-). An ancient region of Eurasia extending from the mouth of the Danube R. on the Black Sea to the territory E of the Aral Sea.

Scyth•i•an (sĭth′ē-ən, sĭth′-) *adj.* Of or relating to Scythia or its people, language, or culture. *—n.* **1.** A member of the ancient nomadic people inhabiting Scythia. **2.** The Iranian language of the Scythians.

Scyth•o-Dra•vid•i•an (sĭth′ō-drə-vĭd′ē-ən, sĭth′-) *adj.* Of or relating to an ethnic group of northwest India having Iranian and Dravidian characteristics. [SCYTH(IAN) + DRAVIDIAN.]

SD *abbr.* **1.** Sight draft. **2.** Or **S.D.** South Dakota. **3.** Special delivery. **4.** *Statistics.* Standard deviation.

sd. *abbr.* Sound (body of water).

s.d. *abbr.* Sine die.

S.Dak. *abbr.* South Dakota.

SDI or **S.D.I.** *abbr.* Strategic Defense Initiative.

SDS *abbr.* Students for a Democratic Society.

Se The symbol for the element **selenium.**

SE *abbr.* **1.a.** Southeast. **b.** Southeastern. **2.** Stock exchange.

sea (sē) *n.* **1.a.** The continuous body of salt water covering most of the earth's surface. **b.** An expanse of water within an ocean. **c.** A large body of salt water completely or partially enclosed by land. **d.** A large landlocked body of fresh water. **2.** The condition of the ocean's surface in regard to its course, flow, swell, or turbulence: *a high sea.* **3.** Something that suggests the ocean in its overwhelming sweep or vastness. **4.** Seafaring as a way of life. **5.** *Astron.* A lunar mare. **—*idiom.* at sea. 1.** On the sea, esp. a sea voyage. **2.** In confusion or perplexity. [ME *see* < OE *sǣ*.]

sea anchor *n. Naut.* A drag, usu. a canvas-covered conical frame, trailed behind a vessel to prevent drifting or to maintain a heading into the wind.

sea anemone *n.* Any of numerous flowerlike marine coelenterates of the class Anthozoa, having a flexible cylindrical body and tentacles surrounding a central mouth.

sea bass (băs) *n.* **1.** Any of various marine food fishes of the genus *Centropristes* and related genera, esp. *C. striatus*, of coastal Atlantic waters of the United States. **2.** Any of the various similar fishes of the family Serranidea.

sea•bed (sē′bĕd′) *n.* The floor of the sea or the ocean.

Sea•bee (sē′bē′) *n.* A member of one of the construction battalions in the U.S. Navy that builds naval aviation bases and facilities. [Alteration of *cee bee*, pronunciation of the initial letters of *construction battalion*.]

sea bird *n.* A bird, such as a petrel or an albatross, that frequents the ocean, esp. far from shore.

sea biscuit *n.* See **hardtack.**

sea•board (sē′bôrd′, -bōrd′) *n.* **1.** A seacoast. **2.** Land near the sea.

Sea•borg (sē′bôrg′), **Glenn Theodore.** b. 1912. Amer. chemist who shared a 1951 Nobel Prize.

sea•borne (sē′bôrn′, -bōrn′) *adj.* **1.** Conveyed by sea; transported by ship. **2.** Carried on or over the sea.

sea bread *n.* See **hardtack.**

sea bream *n.* Any of various marine food fishes of the family Sparidae or Bramidae, esp. *Archosargus rhomboidalis* of western Atlantic coastal waters.

Sea•bur•y (sē′bĕr′ē, -bə-rē), **Samuel.** 1729–96. Amer. religious leader who was the first bishop of the Protestant Episcopal Church in America (1784–96).

sea captain *n. Naut.* The captain of a ship, esp. a merchant ship.

sea change *n.* **1.** A change caused by the sea. **2.** A marked transformation.

sea chest *n.* A box or trunk suitable for use by a sailor to store personal property.

sea•coast (sē′kōst′) *n.* Land bordering the sea.

sea•cock (sē′kŏk′) *n. Naut.* A valve in the hull of a boat or ship that may be opened to let water in or out.

sea cow *n.* Any of several large cylindrical herbivorous marine mammals of the order Sirenia, having a paddlelike tail and rounded front flippers and including the manatee and dugong.

sea crayfish also **sea crawfish** *n.* See **spiny lobster.**

sea cucumber *n.* Any of various cucumber-shaped echinoderms of the class Holothuroidea.

sea devil *n.* See **manta** 2.

sea dog *n.* **1.** Any of various seals or similar marine mammals. **2.** *Naut.* A very experienced sailor. **3. sea•dog** (sē′dôg′, -dŏg′). See **fogbow.**

sea duck *n.* Any of various diving ducks, such as the eider or scoter, of coastal areas.

sea eagle *n.* Any of various fish-eating eagles or similar birds.

sea elephant *n.* See **elephant seal.**

sea fan *n.* Any of various yellowish to reddish fan-shaped corals of the genus *Gorgonia*, esp. *G. flabellum*, of warm waters.

sea·far·er (sē′fâr′ər) *n. Naut.* **1.** A sailor or mariner. **2.** One who travels by sea.
sea·far·ing (sē′fâr′ĭng) *Naut.* — *n.* A sailor's calling. — *adj.* **1.** Following a life at sea. **2.** Fit to travel on the sea; seagoing.
sea feather *n.* Any of several anthozoans of the family Pennatulidae, having an elongate shaft with paired lateral pinnules.
sea fire *n.* Bioluminescence produced by marine life.
sea floor also **sea·floor** (sē′flôr′, -flōr′) *n.* The bottom of a sea or an ocean.
sea·food (sē′fo͞od′) *n.* Edible fish or shellfish from the sea.
sea·fowl (sē′foul′) *n.* **1.** A sea bird. **2.** Sea birds considered as a group.
sea front *n.* A strip of land at the very edge of the sea, esp. land desirable for a resort.
sea·girt (sē′gûrt′) *adj.* Surrounded by the sea.
sea·go·ing (sē′gō′ĭng) *adj. Naut.* Made or used for ocean voyages; seafaring.
sea grape *n.* A small tropical American tree *(Coccolobis uvifera)* growing on sandy beaches and having large, glossy rounded leaves and grapelike clusters of purplish fruit.
sea green *n. Color.* A medium green or bluish green.
sea gull also **sea·gull** (sē′gŭl′) *n.* A gull, esp. one found near coastal areas.
sea holly *n.* A European seashore plant *(Eryngium maritimum)* having prickly bluish leaves and blue or purplish flowers.
sea horse *n.* **1.** A small marine fish of the genus *Hippocampus* that swims upright and has a prehensile tail, a horselike head, and a body covered with bony plates. **2.** See **walrus. 3.** *Myth.* An animal, half fish and half horse, ridden by Neptune and other sea gods. **4.** A large white-capped wave.
Sea Island cotton (sē) *n.* A tropical American species of cotton *(Gossypium barbadense)* widely cultivated for its fine long-staple fibers. [After the Sea Islands.]
Sea Islands. A chain of islands in the Atlantic off SC, GA, and N FL; settled by the Spanish in the 16th cent. and the English after the 17th cent.
sea kale *n.* A European seashore plant *(Crambe maritima)* of the mustard family, having edible cabbagelike leaves.
sea king *n.* A Viking pirate chief of the early Middle Ages.
seal[1] (sēl) *n.* **1.a.** A die or signet having a raised or incised emblem used to stamp an impression on a receptive substance such as wax. **b.** The impression so made. **c.** The design or emblem itself, belonging exclusively to the user. **d.** A small disk or wafer of wax, lead, or paper bearing such an imprint and affixed to a document to prove authenticity or to secure it. **2.** Something, such as a commercial hallmark, that authenticates, confirms, or attests. **3.** A substance, esp. an adhesive agent such as wax, that closes or secures something or prevents seepage of moisture or air. **4.** A device that joins two systems or elements so as to prevent leakage. **5.a.** An airtight closure. **b.** A closure, as on a package, proving that the contents have not been tampered with. **6.** A small decorative paper sticker. — *tr.v.* **sealed, seal·ing, seals. 1.** To affix a seal to in order to prove authenticity or attest to accuracy, legal weight, quality, or another standard. **2.a.** To close with or as if with a seal. **b.** To close hermetically. **c.** To make fast or fill up, as with plaster or cement. **d.** To apply a waterproof coating to. **3.** To grant, certify, or designate under seal or authority. **4.** To establish or determine irrevocably. — ***phrasal verb.*** **seal off.** To close tightly or surround with a barricade or cordon. [ME < OFr. *seel* < VLat. **sigellum* < Lat. *sigillum,* dim. of *signum,* sign, seal. See **sekʷ-¹*.**] — **seal′a·ble** *adj.*
seal[2] (sēl) *n.* **1.** Any of various aquatic carnivorous mammals of the families Phocidae and Otariidae, found chiefly in the Northern Hemisphere and having a sleek torpedo-shaped body and paddlelike flippers. **2.** The pelt or fur of one of these animals, esp. a fur seal. **3.** Leather made from the hide of one of these animals. — *intr.v.* **sealed, seal·ing, seals.** To hunt seals. [ME *sele* < OE *seolh, sēol-.*]
sea lamprey *n.* A large marine lamprey *(Petromyzon marinus)* common in the Great Lakes and parasitic to freshwater fish.
sea-lane (sē′lān′) *n. Naut.* A permanent or commonly used sea route.
seal·ant (sē′lənt) *n.* A substance, such as sealing wax, used to seal a surface.
sea lavender *n.* Any of several salt-marsh plants of the genus *Limonium,* having small lavender or pinkish flowers.
Seal Beach (sēl). A city of S CA on the Pacific Ocean SSE of Los Angeles. Pop. 25,098.
sea legs *pl.n. Naut.* The ability to walk on board ship with steadiness, esp. in rough seas.
seal·er[1] (sē′lər) *n.* **1.** One that seals, as an undercoat of paint or varnish used to size a surface. **2.** An officer who inspects, tests, and certifies weights and measures.
seal·er[2] (sē′lər) *n.* One that is engaged in the hunting of seals.
sea lettuce *n.* Any of several green algae of the genus *Ulva,* having a leaflike thallus sometimes used in salads.
sea level *n.* The level of the ocean's surface, esp. the level halfway between mean high and low tide, used as a standard in reckoning land elevation or sea depths.
sea lily *n.* Any of various marine crinoids having a flowerlike body and a long stalk usu. anchored to the ocean floor.
seal·ing wax (sē′lĭng) *n.* A resinous preparation of shellac and turpentine, soft when heated but solidifying upon cooling, used to seal letters, batteries, or jars.
sea lion *n.* Any of several large-eared Pacific seals with a relatively long neck and limbs, esp. *Zalophus californianus.*
seal ring *n.* See **signet ring.**
seal·skin (sēl′skĭn′) *n.* **1.** The pelt or fur, esp. the underfur, of a seal. **2.** A garment made of sealskin.
Sea·ly·ham terrier (sē′lē-hăm′, -lē-əm) *n.* Any of a breed of terrier originating in Wales and having a wiry white coat, a long head, powerful jaws, and short legs. [After *Sealyham,* a town of SW Wales.]
seam (sēm) *n.* **1.a.** A line of junction formed by sewing together two pieces of material along their margins. **b.** A similar line, ridge, or groove made by fitting, joining, or lapping together two sections along their edges. **c.** A suture. **d.** A scar. **2.** A line across a surface, as a crack, fissure, or wrinkle. **3.** A thin layer or stratum, as of coal or rock. — *v.* **seamed, seam·ing, seams.** — *tr.* **1.** To put together with or as if with a seam. **2.** To mark with a groove, wrinkle, scar, or other seamlike line. **3.** To form ridges in by purling. — *intr.* **1.** To become fissured or furrowed; crack open. **2.** To purl. [ME *seme* < OE *sēam.* See **syū-*.**] — **seam′er** *n.*
sea-maid·en (sē′mād′n) also **sea-maid** (-mād′) *n. Myth.* A mermaid or sea nymph.
sea·man (sē′mən) *n. Naut.* **1.** A mariner or sailor. **2.a.** A noncommissioned rank in the U.S. Navy or Coast Guard that is above seaman apprentice and below petty officer. **b.** One who holds the rank of seaman, seaman apprentice, or seaman recruit.
Sea·man (sē′mən), **Elizabeth Cochrane.** Nellie Bly. 1867–1922. Amer. journalist known for her muckraking articles.
seaman apprentice *n.* A noncommissioned officer in the U.S. Navy or Coast Guard ranking above seaman recruit and below seaman.
seaman recruit *n.* **1.** The lowest noncommissioned rank in the U.S. Navy or Coast Guard. **2.** One who holds this rank.
sea·man·ship (sē′mən-shĭp′) *n. Naut.* Skill in navigating or handling a boat or ship.
sea mew *n.* Any of various European sea gulls, esp. *Larus canus.*
seam·less (sēm′lĭs) *adj.* **1.** Having no seams. **2.** Perfectly consistent. — **seam′less·ly** *adv.* — **seam′less·ness** *n.*
sea·mount (sē′mount′) *n.* An underwater mountain rising from the ocean floor and having a submerged summit.
sea mouse *n.* Any of various large marine polychete worms of the genus *Aphrodite,* esp. *A. aculeata,* having a flattened elliptic body with overlapping scales covered by long hairs.
seam·ster (sēm′stər) *n.* A tailor. [ME *semester* < OE *sēamestre* < *sēam,* seam. See seam.]
seam·stress (sēm′strĭs) *n.* A woman who sews, esp. one who makes her living by sewing.
seam·y (sē′mē) *adj.* **-i·er, -i·est. 1.** Sordid; base. **2.** Having, marked with, or showing a seam. — **seam′i·ness** *n.*
sé·ance (sā′äns′, -äɴs′) *n.* **1.** A meeting of people to receive spiritualistic messages. **2.** A meeting, session, or sitting, as of a learned or legislative body. [Fr., a sitting < OFr. *seoir,* to sit < Lat. *sedēre.* See **sed-*.**]
sea nettle *n.* A stinging jellyfish, esp. a scyphozoan *(Dactylometra quinquecirrha)* of the tropical Atlantic.
sea oats *pl.n. (used with a sing. or pl. v.)* A tall coastal grass *(Uniola paniculata)* of southeast North America.
sea onion *n.* **1.** A Mediterranean plant *(Urginea maritima)* of the lily family, cultivated for its bulb that yields a powder used medicinally and as a rat poison. **2.** A small bulbous European plant *(Scilla verna)* having fragrant blue flowers.
sea otter *n.* A large marine otter *(Enhydra lutris)* of northern Pacific coastal waters, having soft, dark brown fur.
sea pen *n.* Any of various marine anthozoans of the families Stylatulidae and Funiculinidae, resembling and related to the sea feathers. [< its resemblance to a quill pen.]
sea·plane (sē′plān′) *n.* An aircraft equipped with floats for landing on or taking off from a body of water.
sea·port (sē′pôrt′, -pōrt′) *n.* A harbor or town having facilities for seagoing ships.
sea power *n.* **1.** A nation having significant naval strength. **2.** Naval strength.
sea purse *n.* The egg case of skates, rays, or certain sharks.
sea·quake (sē′kwāk′) *n.* An earthquake originating under the sea floor.
sear[1] (sîr) *v.* **seared, sear·ing, sears.** — *tr.* **1.** To char, scorch, or burn the surface of with or as if with a hot instrument. **2.** To cause to dry up and wither. — *intr.* To become withered or dried up. — *n.* A condition, such as a scar, produced by searing. [ME *seren* < OE *sēarian,* to wither < *sēar,* withered.]
sear[2] (sîr) *n.* The catch in a gunlock that keeps the hammer halfcocked or fully cocked. [Prob. Fr. *serre,* something that grasps < OFr., lock < *serrer,* to grasp < VLat. **serrāre* < LLat. *serāre,* to bolt < Lat. *sera,* bar, bolt. See **ser-²*.**]
sear[3] (sîr) *adj.* Var. of **sere**[1].
search (sûrch) *v.* **searched, search·ing, search·es.** — *tr.* **1.** To

seal[1]
c. 1700 official seal of Marbletown, New York, by Jacob Boelen (1657–1729)

Sealyham terrier

Elizabeth Seaman
"Nellie Bly"
Illustration from the *New York World's Correspondent,* February 2, 1890

ă pat	oi boy
ā pay	ou out
âr care	o͝o took
ä father	o͞o boot
ĕ pet	ŭ cut
ē be	ûr urge
ĭ pit	th thin
ī pie	*th* this
îr pier	hw which
ŏ pot	zh vision
ō toe	ə about, item
ô paw	

Stress marks:
′ (primary);
′ (secondary), as in
dictionary (dĭk′shə-nĕr′ē)

make a thorough examination of; look over carefully in order to find something; explore. **2.** To make a careful examination or investigation of; probe. **3.** *Law.* To make a thorough check of (a legal document); scrutinize. **4.a.** To examine in order to find something lost or concealed. **b.** To examine the person or personal effects of in order to find something lost or concealed. **5.** To come to know; learn. — *intr.* To conduct a thorough investigation; seek. — *n.* An act of searching. — ***idiom.* search me.** *Slang.* Used by a speaker to indicate lack of an answer to a question just asked. [ME *serchen* < AN *sercher*, var. of OFr. *cerchier* < Lat. *circāre*, to go around < Lat. *circus*, circle < Gk. *krikos, kirkos.* See **sker-²*.**] — **search′a•ble** *adj.* — **search′er** *n.*

search•ing (sûr′chĭng) *adj.* **1.** Examining closely or thoroughly; probing. **2.** Keenly observant. — **search′ing•ly** *adv.*

search•less (sûrch′lĭs) *adj.* Mysterious and inscrutable.

search•light (sûrch′līt′) *n.* **1.a.** An apparatus containing a light source and a reflector for projecting a high-intensity beam of light. **b.** This beam of light. **2.** A flashlight.

search warrant *n. Law.* A warrant giving legal authorization for a search.

sea robin *n.* Any of various marine fishes of the family Triglidae, having a bony head and long pectoral fins with fingerlike rays that are used as feelers over the sea bottom.

sea room *n. Naut.* Space adequate for maneuvering a vessel.

sea rover *n. Naut.* **1.** One that travels extensively by sea. **2.** A pirate. **3.** A pirate ship.

sea•scape (sē′skāp′) *n.* A view or picture of the sea.

sea scorpion *n.* See **sculpin** 2.

sea serpent *n.* A large snakelike marine animal often reported by mariners since antiquity but never positively identified.

sea•shell (sē′shĕl′) *n.* The calcareous shell of a marine mollusk or similar marine organism.

sea•shore (sē′shôr′, -shōr′) *n.* Land by the sea.

sea•sick•ness (sē′sĭk′nĭs) *n.* Motion sickness resulting from the pitching and rolling of a ship or boat in water, esp. at sea. — **sea′sick′** *adj.*

sea turtle

sea•side (sē′sīd′) *n.* The seashore.

Sea•side (sē′sīd′). A city of W CA on Monterey Bay WSW of Salinas. Pop. 38,901.

sea slug *n.* Any of various highly colorful marine gastropods of the suborder Nudibranchia, lacking a shell and gills but having fringelike projections that serve as respiratory organs.

sea snake *n.* Any of various venomous tropical snakes of the family Hydrophidae that are adapted to living in the sea, esp. in the Pacific and Indian oceans.

sea•son (sē′zən) *n.* **1.a.** One of the four natural divisions of the year, beginning astronomically at an equinox or a solstice and characterized by specific meteorological or climatic conditions; spring, summer, fall, or winter in the Temperate Zones. **b.** The two divisions of the year, rainy and dry, in some tropical regions. **2.** A recurrent period characterized by certain occurrences, occupations, festivities, or crops. **3.** A suitable, natural, or convenient time. **4.** A period of time. — *v.* **-soned, -son•ing, -sons.** — *tr.* **1.** To improve or enhance the flavor of (food), as by adding salt, spices, or herbs. **2.** To add zest, piquancy, or interest to. **3.** To treat or dry (lumber, for example) until ready for use; cure. **4.** To render competent through trial and experience. **5.** To accustom or inure; harden. **6.** To moderate; temper. — *intr.* To become usable, competent, or tempered. — ***idioms.* in season. 1.** Available or ready, as for eating. **2.** Legally permitted to be caught or hunted during a specified period. **3.** At the right moment; opportunely. **4.** In heat. Used of animals. **out of season. 1.** Not available, permitted, or ready to be eaten, caught, or hunted. **2.** Not at the right or proper moment; inopportunely. [ME < OFr. *seison* < Lat. *satiō, sation-*, sowing < *satus*, p.part. of *serere*, to plant. See **sē-*.**]

sea•son•a•ble (sē′zə-nə-bəl) *adj.* **1.** In keeping with the time or the season. **2.** Occurring or performed at the proper time; timely. See Usage Note at **seasonal.** — **sea′son•a•bly** *adv.*

sea•son•al (sē′zə-nəl) *adj.* Of or dependent on a given season. — **sea′son•al′i•ty** (-zə-năl′ĭ-tē) *n.* — **sea′son•al•ly** *adv.*

Usage Note: *Seasonal* applies to what depends on or is controlled by the season of the year: *a seasonal rise in employment. Seasonable* applies to what is appropriate to the season (*seasonable clothing*) or timely (*seasonable words).*

sea•son•er (sē′zə-nər) *n.* **1.** One that uses seasonings: *The cook is a heavy seasoner.* **2.** See **seasoning** 1.

sea•son•ing (sē′zə-nĭng) *n.* **1.** Something, such as a spice or herb, used to flavor food. **2.** The act or process by which something is seasoned.

season ticket *n.* A ticket valid for a specified period of time, as for a series of performances or games.

sea spider *n.* Any of various marine arthropods of the class Pycnogonida, having long legs and a relatively small body.

sea squirt *n.* Any of various sedentary marine animals of the class Ascidiacea, having a transparent sac-shaped body with two siphons. [< its squirting water when disturbed.]

sea star *n.* See **starfish.**

seat (sēt) *n.* **1.** Something, such as a chair or bench, that may be sat on. **2.a.** A place in which one may sit. **b.** The right to occupy such a place or a ticket indicating this right. **3.** The part on which one rests in sitting: *a bicycle seat.* **4.a.** The buttocks. **b.** The part of a garment that covers the buttocks. **5.a.** A part serving as the base of something else. **b.** The surface or part on which another part sits or rests. **6.a.** The place where something is located or based. **b.** A center of authority; a capital. See Syns at **center. 7.** A place of abode or residence, esp. a large house that is part of an estate. **8.** Membership in an organization, such as a legislative body or stock exchange, that is obtained by appointment, election, or purchase. **9.** The manner of sitting on a horse. — *v.* **seat•ed, seat•ing, seats.** — *tr.* **1.a.** To place in or on a seat. **b.** To cause or assist to sit down. **2.** To provide with a particular seat. **3.** To have or provide seats for. **4.** To install in a position of authority or eminence. **5.** To fix firmly in place. — *intr.* To rest on or fit into another part. — ***idiom.* by the seat of (one's) pants.** *Slang.* **1.** In a manner based on intuition and experience rather than method. **2.** Without the use of instruments. [ME *sete*, prob. < ON *sæti.* See **sed-*.**]

seat•back also **seat back** (sēt′băk′) *n.* The back of a chair or other type of seating.

seat belt *n.* A safety strap or harness designed to hold a person securely in a seat, as in a motor vehicle or an aircraft.

seat•ing (sē′tĭng) *n.* **1.a.** The act of providing or furnishing with a seat or seats. **b.** The seats so provided or furnished. **2.** The arrangement of seats in a room, an auditorium, or a banquet hall. **3.** The member or part on or within which another part is seated. **4.** Material for upholstering seats.

seat•mate (sēt′māt′) *n.* A person sitting next to another on a conveyance such as an airplane.

SEATO *abbr.* Southeast Asia Treaty Organization.

seat-of-the-pants (sēt′əv-*thə*-pănts′) *adj. Slang.* **1.** Based on or using intuition and experience rather than a plan or method; improvised. **2.** Performed without using instruments.

sea trout *n.* **1.** Any of several marine fishes of the genus *Cynoscion*, esp. the weakfish. **2.** Any of several trouts or similar fishes that live in the sea but migrate to fresh water to spawn.

Se•at•tle¹ (sē-ăt′l). 1786?–1866. Suquamish leader who befriended settlers of the Pacific Northwest.

Se•at•tle² (sē-ăt′l). A city of W-central WA on Puget Sound and Lake Washington; settled in the 1850's. Pop. 516,259.

sea turtle *n.* Any of various large marine turtles of the families Cheloniidae and Dermochelyidae, including the leatherback, having large flippers and usu. living in warm waters.

seat•work (sēt′wûrk′) *n.* Lessons assigned to be done by students at their desks in the classroom.

sea urchin *n.* Any of various echinoderms of the class Echinoidea, having a soft body enclosed in a symmetrical round calcareous shell covered with long spines.

sea wall also **sea•wall** (sē′wôl′) *n.* An embankment to prevent erosion of a shoreline.

sea•ward (sē′wərd) *adv. & adj.* Toward or at the sea. — *n.* A seaward place or direction. — **sea′wards** (-wərdz) *adv.*

sea•ware (sē′wâr′) *n.* Sea wrack used as fertilizer. [Poss. OE *sǣwār* : *sǣ*, sea + *wār*, seaweed; see **wei-*.**]

sea wasp *n.* Any of various jellyfishes of the class Cubozoa, having a venomous, sometimes fatal sting.

sea•wa•ter (sē′wô′tər, -wŏt′ər) *n.* The salt water in or coming from the sea or ocean.

sea•way (sē′wā′) *n. Naut.* **1.** A sea route. **2.** An inland waterway for ocean shipping. **3.** A stretch of water where waves are large enough to affect the handling of a vessel.

sea•weed (sē′wēd′) *n.* **1.** Any of numerous marine algae, such as a kelp or gulfweed. **2.** Any of various marine plants.

sea whip *n.* Any of various Atlantic gorgonian corals forming flexible colonies with few or no branches.

sea•wor•thy (sē′wûr′*thē*) *adj.* **-thi•er, -thi•est.** *Naut.* Fit to traverse the seas. — **sea′wor′thi•ness** *n.*

sea wrack *n.* Material cast ashore, esp. seaweed.

se•ba•ceous (sĭ-bā′shəs) *adj. Physiol.* **1.** Of, relating to, or resembling fat or sebum; fatty. **2.** Secreting fat or sebum. [Lat. *sēbum*, tallow + -ACEOUS.]

se•bac•ic acid (sĭ-băs′ĭk, -bā′sĭk) *n.* A crystalline acid, $COOH(CH_2)_8COOH$, used in the manufacture of certain synthetic resins, fibers, and plasticizers. [< SEBACEOUS (it being originally obtained from melted suet).]

Se•bas•to•pol (sə-băs′tə-pōl′). See **Sevastopol.**

SEbE *abbr.* Southeast by east.

sebi– or **sebo–** *pref.* Fat; sebum: *sebiferous.* [< Lat. *sēbum*, tallow.]

se•bif•er•ous (sĭ-bĭf′ər-əs) also **se•bip•a•rous** (-bĭp′-) *adj.* Producing or secreting fatty, oily, or waxy matter; sebaceous.

seb•or•rhe•a also **seb•or•rhoe•a** (sĕb′ə-rē′ə) *n.* A disease of the sebaceous glands characterized by excessive secretion of sebum or an alteration in its quality, resulting in an oily coating, crusts, or scales on the skin. — **seb′or•rhe′ic** *adj.*

SEbS *abbr.* Southeast by south.

se•bum (sē′bəm) *n.* The semifluid secretion of the sebaceous glands in the dermis of the skin, consisting chiefly of fat, keratin, and cellular material. [Lat. *sēbum*, tallow.]

sec¹ (sĕk) *adj.* Dry. Used of wines, esp. champagne. [Fr. < OFr. < Lat. *siccus.*]

sec[2] *abbr.* **1.** *Math.* Secant. **2.** Second. **3.** Secondary.

SEC *abbr.* Securities and Exchange Commission.

sec. *abbr.* **1.** Second. **2.** Secondary. **3.** Secretary. **4.** Section. **5.** Sector. **6.** *Lat.* Secundum (according to). **7.** Security.

se•cant (sē′kănt′, -kənt) *n. Math.* **1.a.** A straight line intersecting a curve at two or more points. **b.** The straight line drawn from the center through one end of a circular arc and intersecting the tangent to the other end of the arc. **c.** The ratio of the length of this line to the length of the radius of the circle. **2.** The reciprocal of the cosine of an angle. [< Lat. *secāns, secant-*, pr.part. of *secāre*, to cut. See **sek-*.**]

sec•co (sĕk′ō) *n., pl.* **-cos.** The art or an example of painting on dry plaster. —*adj. Mus.* Of or being a kind of recitative in which the words are sung rapidly to minimal melody, usu. with continuo. [Ital. < Lat. *siccus*, dry.]

se•cede (sĭ-sēd′) *intr.v.* **-ced•ed, -ced•ing, -cedes.** To withdraw formally from membership in an organization, association, or alliance. [Lat. *sēcēdere*, to withdraw : *sē-*, apart; see **s(w)e-*** + *cēdere*, to go; see **ked-*.**]

se•cern (sĭ-sûrn′) *tr.v.* **-cerned, -cern•ing, -cerns.** To discern as separate; discriminate. [Lat. *sēcernere*, to sever : *sē-*, apart; see **s(w)e-*** + *cernere*, to separate; see **krei-*.**]

se•ces•sion (sĭ-sĕsh′ən) *n.* **1.** The act of seceding. **2.** Often **Secession.** The withdrawal of 11 Southern states from the Union in 1860–1861, precipitating the U.S. Civil War. [Lat. *sēcessiō, sēcessiōn-* < *sēcessus*, p.part. of *sēcēdere*, to secede. See SECEDE.] —**se•ces′sion•al** *adj.*

se•ces•sion•ism (sĭ-sĕsh′ə-nĭz′əm) *n.* The policy of those maintaining the right of secession. —**se•ces′sion•ist** *n.*

Sech•ua•na (sĕch-wä′nə) *n.* Var. of **Setswana.**

Seck•el pear (sĕk′əl, sĭk′-) *n.* A variety of pear having small sweet reddish-brown fruit. [Perh. < *Seckle*, farmer's name.]

se•clude (sĭ-klo͞od′) *tr.v.* **-clud•ed, -clud•ing, -cludes. 1.** To set or keep apart, as from social contact. **2.** To screen from view; make private. [ME *secluden*, to shut off < Lat. *sēclūdere* : *sē-*, apart; see **s(w)e-*** + *claudere*, to shut.]

se•clud•ed (sĭ-klo͞o′dĭd) *adj.* **1.** Removed or remote from others; solitary. **2.** Screened from view; sequestered. —**se•clud′ed•ly** *adv.* —**se•clud′ed•ness** *n.*

se•clu•sion (sĭ-klo͞o′zhən) *n.* **1.a.** The act of secluding. **b.** The state of being secluded. **2.** A secluded place or abode. [Med. Lat. *sēclūsiō, sēclūsiōn-* < Lat. *sēclūsus*, p.part. of *sēclūdere*, to seclude. See SECLUDE.]

se•clu•sive (sĭ-klo͞o′sĭv, -zĭv) *adj.* Of, fond of, or seeking seclusion. —**se•clu′sive•ly** *adv.* —**se•clu′sive•ness** *n.*

sec•o•bar•bi•tal (sĕk′ō-bär′bĭ-tôl′, -tăl′) *n.* A white odorless barbiturate, $C_{12}H_{18}N_2O_3$, used in the form of its sodium salt as a sedative and hypnotic. [SECO(NDARY) + BARBITAL.]

sec•ond[1] (sĕk′ənd) *n.* **1.** A unit of time equal to one sixtieth of a minute. See table at **measurement. 2.** A brief interval of time; a moment. **3.** *Math.* A unit of angular measure equal to one sixtieth of a minute. [ME *seconde* < OFr. < Med.Lat. *(pars minūta) secunda*, second (small part), fem. of Lat. *secundus*, second, following. See SECOND[2].]

sec•ond[2] (sĕk′ənd) *adj.* **1.** Coming next after the first in order, place, rank, time, or quality. **2.a.** Repeating an initial instance. **b.** Reminiscent of one that is well known: *a second Waterloo.* **c.** Alternate; other: *every second year.* **3.** Inferior to another; subordinate. **4.** *Mus.* Being the second part, instrument, or voice in a harmonized composition. **5.** Having the second-highest ratio. Used of gears in a sequence. —*n.* **1.a.** The ordinal number matching the number 2 in a series. **b.** One of two equal parts. **2.** One that is next in order, place, time, or quality after the first. **3.** An article of merchandise of inferior quality. Often used in the plural. **4.** The official attendant of a contestant in a duel or boxing match. **5.** *Mus.* **a.** The interval between consecutive tones on the diatonic scale. **b.** A tone separated by this interval from another tone. **c.** A combination of two such tones in notation or in harmony. **d.** The second part, instrument, or voice in a harmonized composition. **6.** An utterance of endorsement, as to a parliamentary motion. **7.** The transmission gear or gear ratio used to produce forward speeds higher than those of first and lower than those of third in a motor vehicle. **8.** *Informal.* A second serving of food. Often used in the plural. **9.** *Baseball.* Second base. —*tr.v.* **-ond•ed, -ond•ing, -onds. 1.** To attend (a duelist or a boxer) as an aide or assistant. **2.** To promote or encourage; reinforce. **3.** To endorse (a motion or nomination) as a required preliminary to discussion or vote. **4.** (sĭ-kŏnd′). *Chiefly British.* To transfer (a military officer, for example) temporarily. —*adv.* **1.** In the second order, place, or rank. **2.** But for one other; save one: *my second worst tie.* [ME < OFr. < Lat. *secundus*. See **sekʷ-1*.**]

Sec•ond Advent (sĕk′ənd) *n.* See **Second Coming.**

sec•ond•ar•y (sĕk′ən-dĕr′ē) *adj.* **1.a.** Of the second rank; not primary. **b.** Inferior. **c.** Minor; lesser. **2.** Derived from what is primary or original. **3.** Of, relating to, or being the shorter flight feathers projecting along the inner edge of a bird's wing. **4.** *Elect.* Having an induced current that is generated by an inductively coupled primary. Used of a circuit or coil. **5.** *Chem.* Characterized or formed by replacement of two atoms or radicals within a molecule. Used of a compound. **6.** *Geol.* Produced from another mineral by decay or alteration. **7.** Of or relating to a secondary school. **8.** *Bot.* Of, relating to, or being growth or tissue caused by activity of the cambium and resulting in wider branches and stems: *secondary xylem.* —*n., pl.* **-ies. 1.** One that acts in an auxiliary, subordinate, or inferior capacity. **2.** One of the secondary flight feathers. **3.** *Elect.* A coil or circuit having an induced current. **4.a.** *Astron.* A celestial body that revolves around another; a satellite. **b.** The dimmer star of a binary star system. **5.** *Football.* The defensive backfield. —**sec′ond•ar′i•ly** (-dâr′ə-lē) *adv.* —**sec′ond•ar′i•ness** *n.*

secondary accent *n. Ling.* **1.** The degree of stress weaker than a primary accent placed on a syllable in the pronunciation of a word. **2.** The mark (″) used to indicate this degree of stress.

secondary battery *n. Elect.* See **storage battery.**

secondary cell *n.* A rechargeable electric cell that converts chemical energy into electrical energy.

secondary color *n. Color.* A color produced by mixing two primary colors in approximately equal proportions.

secondary electron *n.* An electron produced in secondary emission.

secondary emission *n.* Emission of electrons from the surface of a substance due to bombardment by electrons or ions.

secondary school *n.* A school that is intermediate in level between elementary school and college and usu. offers general, technical, vocational, or college-preparatory curricula.

secondary sex characteristic *n.* Any of various anatomical, physiological, or behavioral characteristics, such as abundance of facial hair or breast development, that first appear in humans at puberty but have no direct reproductive function.

secondary wave *n.* An earthquake wave in which rock particles vibrate at right angles to the direction of wave travel.

second banana *n. Slang.* **1.** One, such as an assistant or a deputy, who is subordinate to another. **2.** One who serves as the straight man in a burlesque.

second base *n. Baseball.* **1.** The base across the diamond from home plate, to be touched second by a runner. **2.** The position played by a second baseman.

second baseman *n. Baseball.* The infielder who is positioned near and to the first-base side of second base.

second best *n.* One that is next to the best. —*adv.* Next to the best. —**sec′ond-best′** (sĕk′ənd-bĕst′) *adj.*

second childhood *n.* Senility; dotage.

second class *n.* **1.** Travel accommodations ranking next below the highest or first class. **2.** Second-class mail.

sec•ond-class (sĕk′ənd-klăs′) *adj.* **1.** Of secondary status. **2.** Of or relating to travel accommodations ranking next below the highest or first class. **3.** Of a class of U.S. and Canadian mail consisting of newspapers and periodicals. —**sec′ond-class′** *adv.*

Second Coming *n. Theol.* The return of Jesus as judge for the Last Judgment.

second cousin *n.* The child of one's parents' first cousin.

sec•ond-de•gree burn (sĕk′ənd-dĭ-grē′) *n.* A burn that blisters the skin and is more severe than a first-degree burn.

Second Empire *n.* A heavily ornate style of furniture, architecture, and decoration developed in France in the mid-19th century. [After *Second Empire*, the reign of Napoleon III.]

second fiddle *n. Informal.* **1.** A secondary role. **2.** One who plays a secondary role.

second generation *n.* **1.** Persons whose parents are immigrants. **2.** Persons whose parents are citizens by birth and whose grandparents are immigrants. **3.** *Comp. Sci.* The period of computer technology distinguished by the use of solid-state circuitry. —**sec′ond-gen′er•a′tion** (sĕk′ənd-jĕn′ə-rā′shən) *adj.*

second growth *n.* Trees that cover an area after the removal of the original stand, as by cutting or fire.

sec•ond-guess (sĕk′ənd-gĕs′) *v.* **-guessed, -guess•ing, -guess•es.** —*tr.* **1.** To criticize or correct after an outcome is known. **2.a.** To outguess. **b.** To predict or anticipate. —*intr.* To criticize a decision after its outcome is known. —**sec′ond-guess′er** *n.*

sec•ond•hand (sĕk′ənd-hănd′) *adj.* **1.** Previously used by another; not new. **2.** Dealing in previously used merchandise. **3.** Obtained, derived, or borrowed from another; not original. —*adv.* In an indirect manner; indirectly.

second hand[1] *n.* The hand of a timepiece for seconds.

second hand[2] *n.* An intermediary person or source.

second lieutenant *n.* **1.** The lowest commissioned rank in the U.S. Army, Air Force, and Marine Corps. **2.** One who holds this rank.

sec•ond•ly (sĕk′ənd-lē) *adv.* In the second place; second.

second mortgage *n.* A mortgage taken out on property that already has one mortgage, with priority in settlement of claims given to the earlier mortgage.

second nature *n.* An acquired behavior or trait that is so long practiced as to seem innate.

se•con•do (sĭ-kôn′dō) *n., pl.* **-di** (-dē). *Mus.* The second part in a concert piece, esp. the lower part in a piano duet. [Ital. < Lat. *secundus*, second, following. See **sekʷ-1*.**]

second person *n. Gram.* The form of a pronoun or verb used

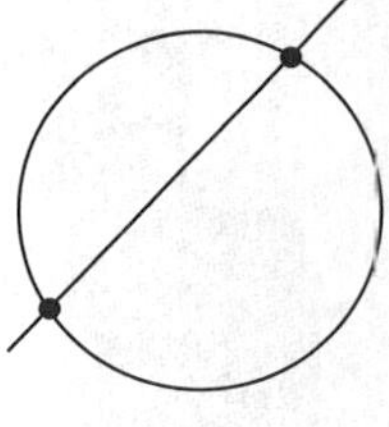

secant
Intersecting a curve

ă pat	oi boy
ā pay	ou out
âr care	o͝o took
ä father	o͞o boot
ĕ pet	ŭ cut
ē be	ûr urge
ĭ pit	th thin
ī pie	*th* this
îr pier	hw which
ŏ pot	zh vision
ō toe	ə about, item
ô paw	

Stress marks:
′ (primary);
′ (secondary), as in
dictionary (dĭk′shə-nĕr′ē)

in referring to the person addressed, as *you* and *shall* in *You shall not enter.*

sec•ond-rate (sĕk′ənd-rāt′) *adj.* Of inferior or mediocre quality or value. **—sec′ond-rate′ness** *n.* **—sec′ond-rat′er** *n.*

second sight *n.* Clairvoyance.

sec•ond•sto•ry man (sĕk′ənd-stôr′ē, -stōr′ē) *n. Informal.* A burglar adept at entering through upstairs windows.

sec•ond-string (sĕk′ənd-strĭng′) *adj.* Of, relating to, or being a substitute, as on a sports team. **—sec′ond-string′er** *n.*

second thought *n.* A reconsideration of a decision or opinion previously made.

second wind (wĭnd) *n.* **1.** The return of relative ease of breathing after the initial exhaustion that occurs during continued physical exertion. **2.** Restored energy or strength.

Second World *n.* During the Cold War, the industrialized Communist nations of the world.

Second World War *n.* World War II.

se•cre•cy (sē′krĭ-sē) *n., pl.* **-cies. 1.** The quality or condition of being secret or hidden; concealment. **2.** The ability or habit of keeping secrets; closeness. [Alteration of ME *secretee* < *secret*, secret. See SECRET.]

se•cret (sē′krĭt) *adj.* **1.** Kept hidden from knowledge or view; concealed. **2.** Dependably discreet. **3.** Operating in a hidden or confidential manner. **4.** Not expressed; inward. **5.** Not frequented; secluded. **6.** Known or shared only by the initiated. **7.** Beyond ordinary understanding; mysterious. **8.** Containing information, the unauthorized disclosure of which poses a threat to national security. *—n.* **1.** Something hidden from others or known only to oneself or to a few. **2.** Something beyond understanding or explanation; a mystery. **3.** A method or formula on which success is based. **4. Secret.** A variable prayer formerly said after the Offertory in the Mass. [ME < OFr. < Lat. *sēcrētus* < p.part. of *sēcernere*, to set aside : *sē-*, apart; see **s(w)e-*** + *cernere*, to separate; see **krei-***.] **—se′cret•ly** *adv.*

se•cre•ta•gogue (sĭ-krē′tə-gôg′, -gŏg′) *n.* A hormone or another agent that causes or stimulates secretion.

sec•re•tar•i•at (sĕk′rĭ-târ′ē-ĭt) *n.* **1.a.** The department administered by a governmental secretary, esp. for an international organization. **b.** The office occupied by such a department. **2.** The office or position of a governmental secretary. [Fr. *secrétariat* < OFr. < Med.Lat. *sēcrētāriātus* < *sēcrētārius*, secretary. See SECRETARY.]

secretary

sec•re•tar•y (sĕk′rĭ-tĕr′ē) *n., pl.* **-ies. 1.** A person employed to handle correspondence, keep files, and do clerical work for another person or an organization. **2.** An officer who keeps records, takes minutes of the meetings, and answers correspondence, as for a company. **3.** An official who presides over an administrative department of state. **4.** A desk with a small bookcase on top. [ME *secretarie* < Med.Lat. *sēcrētārius*, confidential officer, clerk < Lat. *sēcrētus*, secret. See SECRET.] **—sec′re•tar′i•al** (-târ′ē-əl) *adj.*

secretary bird
Sagittarius serpentarius

secretary bird *n.* A large African bird of prey *(Sagittarius serpentarius)* with long legs and a crest of quills on the head.

sec•re•tar•y-gen•er•al (sĕk′rĭ-tĕr′ē-jĕn′ər-əl) *n., pl.* **sec•re•tar•ies-gen•er•al** (sĕk′rĭ-tĕr′ēz-). A principal executive officer, as in governmental bodies such as the United Nations.

se•crete[1] (sĭ-krēt′) *tr.v.* **-cret•ed, -cret•ing, -cretes.** To generate and separate (a substance) from cells or bodily fluids.

se•crete[2] (sĭ-krēt′) *tr.v.* **-cret•ed, -cret•ing, -cretes. 1.** To conceal in a hiding place; cache. See Syns at **hide[1]**. **2.** To steal secretly; filch. [Prob. alteration of obsolete *secret* < SECRET.]

se•cre•tin (sĭ-krēt′n) *n.* A polypeptide hormone produced in the duodenum, esp. on contact with acid, to stimulate secretion of pancreatic juice. [SECRET(ION)[1] + -IN.]

se•cre•tion[1] (sĭ-krē′shən) *n.* **1.** The process of secreting a substance, esp. one that is not a waste, from the blood or cells. **2.** A substance, such as saliva, that is secreted. [Fr. *sécrétion* < OFr., separation < Lat. *sēcrētiō*, *sēcrētiōn-* < *sēcrētus*, p.part. of *sēcernere*, to set aside. See SECERN.] **—se•cre′tion•ar′y** (-shə-nĕr′ē) *adj.*

se•cre•tion[2] (sĭ-krē′shən) *n.* **1.** The act of concealing something in a hiding place. **2.** The act of stealing something secretly. [< SECRETE[2].]

se•cre•tive (sē′krĭ-tĭv, sĭ-krē′tĭv) *adj.* Having or marked by an inclination to secrecy; not open, forthright, or frank. **—se′cre•tive•ly** *adv.* **—se′cre•tive•ness** *n.*

se•cre•to•ry (sĭ-krē′tə-rē) *adj. Physiol.* Relating to or performing secretion.

secret partner *n.* A partner whose participation in a business partnership is hidden from the public.

secret police *n.* A police force operating largely in secret and often using terror to suppress dissent and opposition.

secret service *n.* **1.a.** Intelligence-gathering activities conducted secretly by a government agency. **b.** A government agency engaged in intelligence-gathering activities. **2. Secret Service.** A branch of the U.S. Treasury Department concerned esp. with protection of the President.

secret society *n.* An organization, such as a lodge, that requires its members to conceal certain activities, such as its rites of initiation, from outsiders.

sect (sĕkt) *n.* **1.** A group of people forming a distinct unit within a larger group by virtue of certain refinements or distinctions of belief or practice. **2.** A religious body, esp. one that has separated from a larger denomination. **3.** A faction united by common interests or beliefs. [ME *secte* < OFr. < Lat. *secta*, course, school of thought < fem. p.part. of *sequī*, to follow. See **sek^{w}-[1]***.]

sect. *abbr.* **1.** Section. **2.** Sectional.

-sect *suff.* **1.** To cut; divide: *trisect.* **2.** Cut; divided: *pinnatisect.* [< Lat. *sectus*, p.part. of *secāre*, to cut. See **sek-***.]

sec•tar•i•an (sĕk-târ′ē-ən) *adj.* **1.** Of or characteristic of a sect. **2.** Adhering or confined to the dogmatic limits of a sect or denomination; partisan. **3.** Narrow-minded; parochial. *—n.* **1.** A member of a sect. **2.** One marked by bigoted adherence to a factional viewpoint. **—sec•tar′i•an•ism** *n.*

sec•ta•ry (sĕk′tə-rē) *n., pl.* **-ries. 1.** A sectarian. **2.** A dissenter from an established church, esp. a Protestant nonconformist. [Med.Lat. *sectārius* < Lat. *secta*, sect. See SECT.]

sec•tile (sĕk′təl, -tīl′) *adj.* Of or relating to a mineral that can be cut or severed smoothly by a knife but cannot withstand pulverization. [Lat. *sectilis* < *sectus*, p.part. of *secāre*, to cut. See **sek-***.] **—sec•til′i•ty** (-tĭl′ĭ-tē) *n.*

sec•tion (sĕk′shən) *n.* **1.** One of several components; a piece. **2.** A subdivision of a written work. **3.** *Law.* A division of a statute or code. **4.** A distinct portion of a newspaper. **5.** A distinct area of a town, county, or country. **6.** A land unit equal to one square mile (2.59 square kilometers), 640 acres, or 1/36 of a township. **7.** The act or process of separating or cutting, esp. the surgical cutting or dividing of tissue. **8.** A thin slice, as of tissue, suitable for microscopic examination. **9.** A segment of a fruit, esp. a citrus fruit. **10.** Representation of a solid object as it would appear if cut by an intersecting plane, so that the internal structure is displayed. **11.** *Mus.* A group of instruments or voices in the same class considered as a division of a band, an orchestra, or a choir. **12.** A class or discussion group of students taking the same course. **13.a.** A portion of railroad track maintained by a single crew. **b.** An area in a train's sleeping car containing an upper and a lower berth. **14.** An army tactical unit smaller than a platoon and larger than a squad. **15.** A unit of vessels or aircraft within a division of armed forces. **16.** One of two or more vehicles, such as a bus or train, given the same route and schedule, often used to carry extra passengers. **17.a.** The character (§) used in printing to mark the beginning of a section. **b.** This character used as the fourth in a series of reference marks for footnotes. *—tr.v.* **-tioned, -tion•ing, -tions. 1.** To separate or divide into parts. **2.** To cut or divide (tissue) surgically. **3.** To shade or crosshatch (part of a drawing) to indicate sections. [ME *seccioun* < OFr. < Lat. *sectiō*, *sectiōn-* < *sectus*, p.part. of *secāre*, to cut. See **sek-***.]

sec•tion•al (sĕk′shə-nəl) *adj.* **1.** Of or characteristic of a particular district. **2.** Composed of or divided into component sections. *—n.* A piece of furniture made up of sections usable separately or together. **—sec′tion•al•ly** *adv.*

sec•tion•al•ism (sĕk′shə-nə-lĭz′əm) *n.* Excessive devotion to local interests and customs. **—sec′tion•al•ist** *n.*

sec•tion•al•ize (sĕk′shə-nə-līz′) *tr.v.* **-ized, -iz•ing, -iz•es.** To divide into sections, esp. into geographic sections. **—sec′tion•al•i•za′tion** (sĕk′shə-nə-lĭ-zā′shən) *n.*

Sec•tion Eight (sĕk′shən) *n.* **1.** A U.S. Army discharge based on military assessment of unfitness or character traits deemed undesirable. **2.** *Slang.* A soldier given such a discharge. [After *Section VIII* of World War II U.S. Army Regulation 615–360, which provided for such a discharge.]

section gang *n.* A work crew assigned to a railroad section.

section hand *n.* A laborer assigned to a section gang.

sec•tor (sĕk′tər, -tôr′) *n.* **1.** *Math.* **a.** The portion of a circle bounded by two radii and the included arc. **b.** A measuring instrument consisting of two graduated arms hinged together at one end. **2.a.** A division of a defensive position for which one military unit is responsible. **b.** A division of an offensive military position. **3.** A part or division, as of a city. **4.** *Comp. Sci.* A bit or a set of bits on a magnetic storage device making up the smallest addressable unit of information. *—tr.v.* **-tored, -tor•ing, -tors.** To divide (something) in sectors. [LLat. < Lat., cutter < *sectus*, p.part. of *secāre*, to cut. See **sek-***.] **—sec•to′ri•al** (-tôr′ē-əl, -tōr′-) *adj.*

sec•u•lar (sĕk′yə-lər) *adj.* **1.** Worldly rather than spiritual. **2.** Not specifically relating to religion or to a religious body. **3.** Relating to or advocating secularism. **4.** Not bound by monastic restrictions, esp. not belonging to a religious order. Used of the clergy. **5.** Occurring or observed once in an age or a century. **6.** Lasting from century to century. *—n.* **1.** A member of the secular clergy. **2.** A layperson. [ME < OFr. *seculer* < LLat. *saeculāris* < Lat., of an age < *saeculum*, generation, age.] **—sec′u•lar•ly** *adv.*

secular humanism *n.* **1.** An outlook or a philosophy that advocates human rather than religious values. **2.** Secularism. **—secular humanist** *adj. & n.*

sec•u•lar•ism (sĕk′yə-lə-rĭz′əm) *n.* **1.** Religious skepticism or indifference. **2.** The view that religious considerations should be excluded from civil affairs or public education. **—sec′u•lar•ist** *n.* **—sec′u•lar•is′tic** *adj.*

sec•u•lar•i•ty (sĕk′yə-lăr′ĭ-tē) *n.*, *pl.* **-ties. 1.** The condition or quality of being secular. **2.** Something secular.

sec•u•lar•ize (sĕk′yə-lə-rīz′) *tr.v.* **-ized, -iz•ing, -iz•es. 1.** To transfer from ecclesiastical or religious to civil or lay use or ownership. **2.** To draw away from religious orientation; make worldly. **3.** To lift the monastic restrictions from (a member of the clergy). **—sec′u•lar•i•za′tion** (-lər-ĭ-zā′shən) *n.*

se•cund (sē′kŭnd′, sĭ-kŭnd′) *adj. Bot. & Zool.* Arranged on or turned to one side of an axis. [Lat. *secundus*, following. See **sek^{w}-1*.**]

se•cure (sĭ-kyo͝or′) *adj.* **-cur•er, -cur•est. 1.** Free from danger or attack. **2.** Free from risk of loss; safe. **3.** Free from the risk of being intercepted or listened to by unauthorized persons. **4.** Free from fear, anxiety, or doubt. **5.a.** Not likely to fail or give way; stable. **b.** Firmly fastened. **6.** Reliable; dependable. **7.** Assured; certain. **8.** *Archaic.* Careless or overconfident. —*tr.v.* **-cured, -cur•ing, -cures. 1.** To guard from danger or risk of loss. **2.** To make firm or tight; fasten. **3.** To make certain; ensure. **4.a.** To guarantee payment of (a loan, for example). **b.** To guarantee payment to (a creditor). **5.** To get possession of; acquire. **6.** To capture or confine. **7.** To bring about; effect. **8.** To protect or ensure the privacy or secrecy of (a telephone line, for example). [Lat. *sēcūrus* : *sē-*, without; see **s(w)e-*** + *cūra*, care; see CURE.] **—se•cur′a•ble** *adj.* **—se•cure′ly** *adv.* **—se•cure′ment** *n.* **—se•cure′ness** *n.* **—se•cur′er** *n.*

Se•cu•ri•ties and Exchange Commission (sĭ-kyo͝or′ĭ-tēz) *n.* A U.S. government agency that supervises the exchange of securities so as to protect investors against malpractice.

se•cu•ri•ty (sĭ-kyo͝or′ĭ-tē) *n.*, *pl.* **-ties. 1.** Freedom from risk or danger; safety. **2.** Freedom from doubt, anxiety, or fear; confidence. **3.** Something that gives or assures safety, as: **a.** A group or department of private guards. **b.** Measures adopted by a government to prevent espionage, sabotage, or attack. **c.** Measures adopted, as by a business or homeowner, to prevent a crime such as burglary or assault. **d.** Measures adopted to prevent escape. **4.** *Comp. Sci.* **a.** The level to which a program or device is safe from unauthorized use. **b.** Prevention of unauthorized use of a program or device. **5.** Something deposited or given as assurance of the fulfillment of an obligation; a pledge. **6.** One who undertakes to fulfill the obligation of another; a surety. **7.** A document indicating ownership or creditorship; a stock certificate or bond. [ME *securite* < OFr. < Lat. *sēcūritās* < *sēcūrus*, secure. See SECURE.]

security blanket *n.* **1.** A blanket or toy carried by a child to reduce anxiety. **2.** *Informal.* Something that dispels anxiety.

Se•cu•ri•ty Council (sĭ-kyo͝or′ĭ-tē) *n.* The permanent peacekeeping organ of the United Nations, composed of five permanent members and ten elected members.

security guard *n.* A person hired by a private organization to guard a physical plant and maintain order.

secy. *abbr.* Secretary.

sed. *abbr.* **1.** Sediment. **2.** Sedimentation.

Se•da•lia (sĭ-dāl′yə). A city of central MO ESE of Kansas City. Pop. 19,800.

se•dan (sĭ-dăn′) *n.* **1.** A closed automobile having two or four doors and a front and rear seat. **2.** A portable enclosed chair for one person, having poles in the front and rear and carried by two other people. [?]

Se•dan (sĭ-dăn′, sə-däN′). A town of NE France on the Meuse R. near the Belgian border; site of the surrender of Napoleon III (Sep. 2, 1870) in the Franco-Prussian War. Pop. 23,477.

Se•dar•im (sĭ-där′ĭm, sĕ-dä-rēm′) *n. Judaism.* Pl. of **Seder.**

se•date[1] (sĭ-dāt′) *adj.* Serenely deliberate, composed, and dignified. [Lat. *sēdātus*, p.part. of *sēdāre*, to settle. See **sed-*.**] **—se•date′ly** *adv.* **—se•date′ness** *n.*

se•date[2] (sĭ-dāt′) *tr.v.* **-dat•ed, -dat•ing, -dates.** To administer a sedative to; calm or relieve by means of sedation.

se•da•tion (sĭ-dā′shən) *n.* **1.** Reduction of anxiety, stress, irritability, or excitement by administration of a sedative agent or drug. **2.** The state or condition induced by a sedative. [ME *sedacioun* < OFr. *sedation* < Lat. *sēdātiō*, *sēdātiōn-* < *sēdātus*, p.part. of *sēdāre*, to calm. See SEDATE[1].]

sed•a•tive (sĕd′ə-tĭv) *adj.* Having a soothing, calming, or tranquilizing effect; reducing or relieving anxiety, stress, irritability, or excitement. —*n.* A sedative agent or drug. [ME < OFr. *sedatif* < Med.Lat. *sēdātīvus* < Lat. *sēdātus*, p.part. of *sēdāre*, to calm. See SEDATE[1].]

sed•en•tar•y (sĕd′n-tĕr′ē) *adj.* **1.** Characterized by or requiring much sitting. **2.** Accustomed to sitting or to taking little exercise. **3.** Remaining or living in one area, as certain birds; not migratory. **4.** Attached to a surface and not moving freely, as a barnacle. [Fr. *sédentaire* < OFr. < Lat. *sedentārius* < *sedēns*, *sedent-*, pr.part. of *sedēre*, to sit. See **sed-*.**] **—sed′en•tar′i•ly** (-târ′ə-lē) *adv.* **—sed′en•tar′i•ness** *n.*

Se•der (sā′dər) *n.*, *pl.* **Se•ders** or **Se•dar•im** (sĭ-där′ĭm, sĕ-dä-rēm′). *Judaism.* The feast commemorating the exodus of the Jews from Egypt, celebrated on the first night or on the first two nights of Passover. [Heb. *sēder*, arrangement, Seder.]

sedge (sĕj) *n.* Any of numerous grasslike plants of the family Cyperaceae, having solid stems and leaves in three vertical rows. [ME *segge* < OE *secg*. See **sek-*.**]

Sedge•moor (sĕj′mo͝or′, -môr′, -mōr′). A marshy tract in SW England where the forces of James II defeated the Duke of Monmouth (Jun. 6, 1685).

se•di•le (sĭ-dī′lē) *n.*, *pl.* **se•di•lia** (-dĭl′yə, -dĭl′ē-ə). *Eccles.* One of a set of seats, usu. three, for the use of the presiding clergy, traditionally placed on the epistle side of the choir near the altar. [Lat. *sedīle*, seat < *sedēre*, to sit. See **sed-*.**]

sed•i•ment (sĕd′ə-mənt) *n.* **1.** Material that settles to the bottom of a liquid; lees. **2.** Solid fragments of inorganic or organic material that come from the weathering of rock and are carried and deposited by wind, water, or ice. [Lat. *sedimentum*, act of settling < *sedēre*, to sit, settle. See **sed-*.**]

sed•i•men•ta•ry (sĕd′ə-mĕn′tə-rē, -mĕn′trē) also **sed•i•men•tal** (-mĕn′tl) *adj.* **1.** Of, containing, resembling, or derived from sediment. **2.** *Geol.* Of or relating to rocks formed by the deposition of sediment.

sed•i•men•ta•tion (sĕd′ə-mən-tā′shən, -mĕn-) *n.* The act or process of depositing sediment.

sed•i•men•tol•o•gy (sĕd′ə-mən-tŏl′ə-jē, -mĕn-) *n.* The geologic study of sedimentary rock. **—sed′i•men′to•log′ic** (-mĕn′tl-ŏj′ĭk), **sed′i•men′to•log′i•cal** (-ĭ-kəl) *adj.* **—sed′i•men•tol′o•gist** *n.*

se•di•tion (sĭ-dĭsh′ən) *n.* **1.** Conduct or language inciting rebellion against the authority of a state. **2.** Insurrection; rebellion. [Ult. < Lat. *sēditiō*, *sēditiōn-*, party strife : *sēd-*, *sē-*, apart; see **s(w)e-*** + *itiō*, act of going (< *itus*, p.part. of *īre*, to go; see **ei-***).] **—se•di′tion•ist** *n.*

se•di•tious (sĭ-dĭsh′əs) *adj.* **1.** Of or having the nature of sedition. **2.** Given to or guilty of engaging in or promoting sedition. **—se•di′tious•ly** *adv.* **—se•di′tious•ness** *n.*

se•duce (sĭ-do͞os′, -dyo͞os′) *tr.v.* **-duced, -duc•ing, -duc•es. 1.** To lead away from duty, accepted principles, or proper conduct. **2.** To induce to engage in sex. **3.a.** To entice or beguile into a desired state or position. **b.** To win over; attract. [ME *seduisen* < OFr. *seduire*, *seduis-*, alteration (influenced by Med.Lat. *sēdūcere*, to lead astray < Lat., to lead away : *sē-*, apart; see **s(w)e-*** + *dūcere*, to lead) of *suduire*, to seduce < Lat. *subdūcere*, to withdraw : *sub-*, sub- + *dūcere*, to lead; see **deuk-*.**] **—se•duce′a•ble, se•duc′i•ble** *adj.* **—se•duc′er** *n.*

se•duce•ment (sĭ-do͞os′mənt, -dyo͞os′-) *n.* **1.** Seduction. **2.** Something that seduces.

se•duc•tion (sĭ-dŭk′shən) *n.* **1.a.** The act of seducing. **b.** The condition of being seduced. **2.** Something that seduces or has the qualities to seduce. [Lat. *sēductiō*, *sēductiōn-* < *sēductus*, p.part. of *sēdūcere*, to lead astray. See SEDUCE.]

Seder

se•duc•tive (sĭ-dŭk′tĭv) *adj.* Tending to seduce. **—se•duc′tive•ly** *adv.* **—se•duc′tive•ness** *n.*

se•duc•tress (sĭ-dŭk′trĭs) *n.* A woman who seduces. See Usage Note at **-ess.**

sed•u•lous (sĕj′ə-ləs) *adj.* Persevering and constant in effort or application; assiduous. [< Lat. *sēdulus* < *sēdulō*, zealously : *sē*, without; see **s(w)e-*** + *dolō*, ablative of *dolus*, trickery (prob. < Gk. *dolos*, cunning; see **del-[2]***).] **—sed′u•lous•ness, se•du′li•ty** (sĭ-do͞o′lĭ-tē, -dyo͞o′-) *n.*

se•dum (sē′dəm) *n.* Any of numerous plants of the genus *Sedum,* having thick fleshy leaves. [ME *cedum* < Lat. *sedum*, houseleek.]

see[1] (sē) *v.* **saw** (sô), **seen** (sēn), **see•ing, sees.** —*tr.* **1.** To perceive with the eye. **2.a.** To apprehend as if with the eye. **b.** To detect by means analogous to use of the eye. **3.** To have a mental image of; visualize. **4.** To understand; comprehend. **5.** To consider to be; regard. **6.** To believe possible; imagine. **7.** To foresee. **8.** To know through firsthand experience; undergo. **9.** To give rise to or be characterized by: *The nineties will see much change.* **10.** To find out; ascertain. **11.** To refer to; read. **12.** To take note of; recognize: *sees only the good aspects.* **13.** To meet or be in the company of. **14.** To share the companionship of often or regularly. **15.a.** To visit socially; call on. **b.** To visit for consultation. **16.** To admit or receive, as for consultation or a social visit: *The doctor will see you now.* **17.** To attend; view. **18.** To escort; attend. **19.** To make sure; take care. **20.** *Games.* **a.** To meet (a bet) in card games. **b.** To meet the bet of (another player). —*intr.* **1.** To have the power to perceive with or as if with the eye. **2.** To understand; comprehend. **3.** To consider. **4.a.** To go and look: *She had to see for herself.* **b.** To ascertain; find out. **5.** To have foresight. **6.** To take note. ***—phrasal verbs.*** **see about. 1.** To attend to. **2.** To investigate. **see after.** To take care of. **see off.** To take leave of (someone). **see out.** To escort (a guest) to the door. **see through. 1.** To understand the true character or nature of. **2.** To provide unstinting support, cooperation, or management in good times and bad. **see to.** To attend to. ***—idiom.*** **see red.** *Informal.* To be extremely angry. [ME *sen* < OE *sēon*. See **sek^{w}-2*.**]

Syns: *see, behold, note, notice, remark, espy, descry, observe, contemplate, survey, view, perceive, discern.* These verbs refer to being or becoming visually or mentally aware of something. *See*, the most general, can mean merely to use the faculty of sight but more often implies recognition, understanding, or appreciation: *"If I have seen further (than . . . Descartes) it is by standing upon the shoulders of Giants"*

ă pat	oi boy
ā pay	ou out
âr care	o͝o took
ä father	o͞o boot
ĕ pet	ŭ cut
ē be	ûr urge
ĭ pit	th thin
ī pie	*th* this
îr pier	hw which
ŏ pot	zh vision
ō toe	ə about, item
ô paw	

Stress marks:
′ (primary);
′ (secondary), as in dictionary (dĭk′shə-nĕr′ē)

(Isaac Newton). *Behold* implies gazing at or looking intently upon what is seen: *"My heart leaps up when I behold/A rainbow in the sky"* (William Wordsworth). *Note, notice* and *remark* suggest close, detailed observation, and *note* in particular implies making a careful, systematic mental record: *Be careful to note where the road turns left. I notice that you're out of sorts. "Their assemblies afforded me daily opportunities of remarking characters and manners"* (Samuel Johnson). *Espy* and *descry* both stress acuteness of sight that permits the detection of something distant or obscure: *"espied the misspelled Latin word in* [the] *letter"* (Los Angeles Times); *"the lighthouse, which can be descried from a distance"* (Michael Strauss). *Observe* emphasizes careful, closely directed attention: *"I saw the pots . . . and observed that they did not crack at all"* (Daniel Defoe). *Contemplate* implies looking attentively and thoughtfully: *"It is interesting to contemplate an entangled bank, clothed with many plants"* (Charles Darwin). *Survey* stresses comprehensive examination: *"Strickland looked away and idly surveyed the ceiling"* (W. Somerset Maugham). *View* usually suggests examination with a particular purpose in mind or in a special way: *The medical examiner viewed the victim's body. Perceive* and *discern* both imply not only visual recognition but also mental comprehension; *perceive* is especially associated with insight, and *discern,* with the ability to distinguish, discriminate, and make judgments: *"I plainly perceive* [that] *some objections remain"* (Edmund Burke). *We lack the musical background to discern a good musician from a bad virtuoso.*

see[2] (sē) *n.* **1.** The official seat, center of authority, jurisdiction, or office of a bishop. **2.** *Obsolete.* A cathedra. [ME < OFr. *se* < VLat. *sedem < Lat. *sēdēs,* seat. See **sed-*.**]

seed (sēd) *n., pl.* **seeds** or **seed. 1.** A ripened plant ovule containing an embryo. **2.** A propagative part of a plant, as a tuber or spore. **3.** Seeds considered as a group. **4.** The seed-bearing stage of a plant. **5.** Something that resembles a seed, as a small crystal added to a solution to start crystallization. **6.** A source or beginning; a germ. **7.** Offspring; progeny. **8.** Family stock; ancestry. **9.** Sperm; semen. **10.** A seed oyster or oysters; spat. **11.** *Sports.* A player who has been seeded for a tournament, often at a given rank. *—v.* **seed•ed, seed•ing, seeds.** *—tr.* **1.** To plant seeds in (land, for example); sow. **2.** To plant in soil. **3.** To remove the seeds from (fruit). **4.** *Meteorol.* To sprinkle (a cloud) with particles, as of silver iodide, in order to disperse it or produce rain. **5.** *Sports.* **a.** To arrange (the drawing for tournament positions) so that more skilled contestants meet in later rounds. **b.** To rank (a contestant) in this way. **6.** To help (a business, for example) in its early development. *—intr.* **1.** To sow seed. **2.** To go to seed. *—adj.* **1.** Set aside for planting a new crop. **2.** Intended to help in early stages. **—*idiom.* go (**or **run) to seed. 1.** To pass into the seed-bearing stage. **2.** To become weak or devitalized; deteriorate. [ME < OE *sǣd, sēd.* See **sē-*.**]

Andrés Segovia

seed•bed (sēd′bĕd′) *n.* **1.** A bed of soil cultivated for planting seeds. **2.** An area or source of growth or gradual manifestation.

seed cake *n.* A sweet cake or cookie containing aromatic seeds.

seed coat *n. Bot.* The outer protective covering of a seed.

seed•er (sē′dər) *n.* **1.** A machine or an implement used for planting seeds. **2.** A machine or implement used to remove the seeds from fruit. **3.** One that seeds clouds.

seed leaf *n. Bot.* See **cotyledon** 1.

seed•ling (sēd′lĭng) *n.* A young plant grown from a seed.

seed oyster *n.* A young oyster, esp. one suitable for transplanting to another bed; a spat.

seed pearl *n.* A very small, often imperfect pearl.

seed plant *n.* A seed-bearing plant.

seed•pod (sēd′pŏd′) *n.* See **pod[1]** 1.

seed stock *n.* **1.** A supply of seed for planting. **2.** A source of new entities: *a seed stock of salmon in the river.*

seed•time (sēd′tīm′) *n.* **1.** A time for planting seeds. **2.** A time of new growth or development.

seed•y (sē′dē) *adj.* **-i•er, -i•est. 1.** Having many seeds. **2.** Resembling seeds or a seed. **3.** Worn and shabby; unkempt. **4.** Tired or sick; unwell. **5.** Somewhat disreputable; squalid. **—seed′i•ly** *adv.* **—seed′i•ness** *n.*

See•ger (sē′gər), **Peter ("Pete").** b. 1919. Amer. folk singer who helped revive folk music in the 1950's and 1960's.

see•ing (sē′ĭng) *conj.* Inasmuch as; in view of the fact.

See•ing Eye (sē′ĭng). A trademark used for a dog trained to lead a blind person.

seek (sēk) *v.* **sought** (sôt), **seek•ing, seeks.** *—tr.* **1.** To try to locate or discover; search for. **2.** To endeavor to obtain or reach. **3.** To go to or toward: *Water seeks its own level.* **4.** To inquire for; request. **5.** To try; endeavor. **6.** *Obsolete.* To explore. *—intr.* To make a search or an investigation. [ME *sechen, seken* < OE *sēcan.* See **sāg-*.**]

seek•er (sē′kər) *n.* **1.** One that seeks: *a seeker of the truth.* **2.** A device used in a moving object, especially a missile, that locates a target by detecting light, heat, or other radiation.

seel (sēl) *tr.v.* **seeled, seel•ing, seels.** To stitch closed the eyes of (a falcon). [ME *silen* < OFr. *cillier* < Med.Lat. *ciliāre* < Lat. *cilium,* lower eyelid. See **kel-[1]*.**]

seem (sēm) *intr.v.* **seemed, seem•ing, seems. 1.** To give the impression of being; appear: *The child seems healthy, but the doctor is concerned.* **2.** To appear to one's own opinion or mind: *I can't seem to get it right.* **3.** To appear to be true, probable, or evident: *It seems that it will rain.* **4.** To appear to exist: *There seems no reason to stop.* [ME *semen* < ON *sœma,* to conform to < *sœmr,* fitting. See **sem-[1]*.**]

seem•ing (sē′mĭng) *adj.* Apparent; ostensible. *—n.* Outward appearance; semblance. **—seem′ing•ly** *adv.* **—seem′ing•ness** *n.*

seem•ly (sēm′lē) *adj.* **-li•er, -li•est. 1.** Conforming to standards of conduct and good taste; suitable. **2.** Of pleasing appearance; handsome. *—adv.* In a seemly manner; suitably. [ME *semely* < ON *sœmiligr* < *sœmr,* fitting. See **sem-[1]*.**] **—seem′li•ness** *n.*

seen (sēn) *v.* P.part. of **see[1].**

seep (sēp) *intr.v.* **seeped, seep•ing, seeps. 1.** To pass slowly through small openings or pores; ooze. **2.** To enter, depart, or become diffused gradually. *—n.* **1.** A spot where water or petroleum trickles out of the ground to form a pool. **2.** Seepage. [Alteration of dial. *sipe.*]

seep•age (sē′pĭj) *n.* **1.** The act or process of seeping. **2.** A quantity of something that has seeped.

seer (sîr) *n.* **1.** (sē′ər). One that sees: *an inveterate seer of sights.* **2.** A clairvoyant. **3.** A prophet.

seer•ess (sîr′ĭs) *n.* A woman prophet or clairvoyant.

seer•suck•er (sîr′sŭk′ər) *n.* A light thin fabric, usu. cotton or rayon, with a crinkled surface and a usu. striped pattern. [Hindi *śīrśakar* < Pers. *shīroshakar* : *shīr,* milk (< MPers.) + *o,* and (< MPers. *u* < OPers. *utā*) + *shakar,* sugar (< Skt. *śarkarā,* from the resemblance of its smooth and rough stripes to the smooth surface of milk and bumpy texture of sugar).]

see•saw (sē′sô′) *n.* **1.** A long plank balanced on a central fulcrum so that with a person riding on each end, one end goes up as the other goes down. Also called regionally *dandle, dandle board, teedle board, teeter, teeterboard, teeter-totter, tilt, tilting board.* See Regional Note at **teeter-totter. 2.** The act or game of riding a seesaw. **3.** A back-and-forth or up-and-down movement, as of the lead in a contest. *—intr.v.* **-sawed, -saw•ing, -saws. 1.** To play on a seesaw. **2.** To move back and forth or up and down. [Redup. of SAW[1].]

seethe (sēth) *intr.v.* **seethed, seeth•ing, seethes. 1.** To churn and foam as if boiling. **2.a.** To be in a state of turmoil or ferment. **b.** To be violently excited or agitated. See Syns at **boil[1]. 3.** *Archaic.* To come to a boil. [ME *sethen,* to boil < OE *sēothan.*] **—seethe** *n.*

see-through (sē′thro͞o′) *adj.* Transparent.

Se•fe•ri•a•des (sĕ-fē′rē-ä′thēs), **Giorgos Stylianou.** George Seferis. 1900–71. Greek poet who won the 1963 Nobel Prize for literature.

Se•gal (sē′gəl), **George.** b. 1924. Amer. sculptor known for his realistic plaster casts of people in ordinary situations.

Se•ges•ta (sĭ-jĕs′tə, sĕ-jĕs′tä). An ancient city of NW Sicily; a Carthaginian dependency after c. 400 B.C.

seg•ment (sĕg′mənt) *n.* **1.** Any of the parts into which something can be divided. **2.** *Math.* **a.** The portion of a line between any two points on the line. **b.** The area bounded by a chord and the arc of a curve subtended by the chord. **c.** The portion of a sphere cut off by two parallel planes. **3.** *Biol.* A clearly differentiated subdivision of an organism or part, such as a metamere. *—tr. & intr.v.* (sĕg-mĕnt′) **-ment•ed, -ment•ing, -ments.** To divide or become divided into segments. [Lat. *segmentum* < *secāre,* to cut. See **sek-*.**] **—seg′men•tar′y** (-mən-tĕr′ē) *adj.*

seg•men•tal (sĕg-mĕn′tl) *adj.* **1.** Of or relating to segments. **2.** Parted or arranged in segments. **—seg•men′tal•ly** *adv.*

seg•men•ta•tion (sĕg′mən-tā′shən, -mĕn-) *n.* **1.** Division into segments. **2.** *Embryol.* See **cleavage** 4a.

segmentation cavity *n.* See **blastocoel.**

se•gno (sā′nyō) *n., pl.* **-gnos.** *Mus.* A notational sign, esp. the sign marking the beginning or the end of a repeated section. [Ital. < Lat. *signum,* sign. See **sekw-[1]*.**]

se•go (sē′gō) *n., pl.* **-gos.** The succulent edible bulb of the sego lily. [Southern Paiute *sigho'o.*]

sego lily *n.* A western North American plant *(Calochortus nuttallii)* having showy, variously colored flowers.

Se•go•vi•a (sĭ-gō′vē-ə, sĕ-gô′vyä). A city of central Spain NNW of Madrid; site of a Roman aqueduct (1st or 2nd cent. A.D.) that is still in use. Pop. 53,005.

Segovia, Andrés. 1893?–1987. Spanish guitarist who spurred interest in the guitar as an instrument for classical music.

seg•re•ga•ble (sĕg′rĭ-gə-bəl) *adj.* **1.** That can be segregated. **2.** *Genet.* Able to undergo segregation.

seg•re•gant (sĕg′rĭ-gənt) *Genet. —adj.* Differing from either parent as a result of segregation. *—n.* A segregant type or organism.

seg•re•gate (sĕg′rĭ-gāt′) *v.* **-gat•ed, -gat•ing, -gates.** *—tr.* **1.** To separate or isolate from others or from a main body or group. **2.** To impose the separation of (a race or class) from society. *—intr.* **1.** To become separated from a main body or mass. **2.** To practice a policy of racial segregation. **3.** *Genet.* To undergo genetic segregation. *—adj.* (-gĭt, -gāt′). Separated; isolated. —*n.* (-gĭt, -gāt′). **1.** One that is or has been segregated. **2.** *Genet.* See **segregant.** [Lat. *sēgregāre, sēgregāt-* : *sē-*, apart; see **s(w)e-*** + *grex, greg-*, flock; see **ger-*.**] —**seg′re·ga′tive** *adj.* —**seg′re·ga′tor** *n.*

seg·re·ga·tion (sĕg′rĭ-gā′shən) *n.* **1.** The act or process of segregating or the condition of being segregated. **2.** The policy and practice of imposing the social separation of races. **3.** *Genet.* The separation of paired alleles esp. during meiosis.

seg·re·ga·tion·ist (sĕg′rĭ-gā′shə-nĭst) *n.* One that advocates or practices racial segregation. —**seg′re·ga′tion·ist** *adj.*

se·gue (sĕg′wā′, sā′gwā′) *intr.v.* **-gued, -gu·ing, -gues. 1.** *Mus.* To make a transition directly from one section or theme to another. **2.** To move smoothly and unhesitatingly from one state, condition, situation, or element to another. [< Ital., there follows, third-person sing. pr.t. of *seguire*, to follow < VLat. **sequere* < Lat. *sequī*. See **sek^{w}-^{1}*.**]

se·gui·dil·la (sĕg′ə-dē′yə, -dēl′yə, sā′gə-, sĕ′gē-*thē*′lyä) *n.* **1.** A Spanish stanza form of four to seven short verses. **2.a.** A lively Spanish dance. **b.** The music for this dance, in 3/4 time. [Sp., dim. of *seguida*, sequence < fem. p.part. of *seguir*, to follow < VLat. **sequere* < Lat. *sequī*. See **sek^{w}-^{1}*.**]

Se·guin (sĭ-gēn′). A city of S-central TX ENE of San Antonio; founded 1831. Pop. 18,853.

Se·gu·ra (sā-gŏŏr′ə, sĕ-gōō′rä). A river of southeast Spain flowing c. 322 km (200 mi), to the Mediterranean Sea.

sei (sā) *n.*, *pl.* **seis.** A sei whale. [< Norw. *seihval* : *sei*, coalfish (< ON *seidh*) + *hval*, whale (< ON *hvalr*).]

sei·cen·to (sā-chĕn′tō) *n.* The 17th century with reference to Italian literature and art. [Ital. < *(mil)seicento*, (one thousand) six hundred : *sei*, six (< Lat. *sex*; see **s(w)eks***) + *cento*, hundred (< Lat. *centum*; see **dekm̥***).]

seiche (sāsh, sĕch) *n.* A wave that oscillates in lakes, bays, or gulfs from a few minutes to a few hours as a result of seismic or atmospheric disturbances. [Fr. dial., exposed lake bottom, prob. < Fr. *sèche*, fem. of *sec*, dry. See SEC^{1}.]

sei·del (sīd′l, zīd′l) *n.* A beer mug. [Ger. < MHGer. *sīdel* < Lat. *situla*, bucket.]

Seid·litz powder (sĕd′lĭts) *n.* A mixture of tartaric acid, sodium bicarbonate, and potassium sodium tartrate, used as a mild cathartic by dissolving in water and drinking. Often used in the plural. [After *Seidlitz* (Sedlec), NW Czechoslovakia.]

Sei·fert (sī′fərt), **Jaroslav.** 1901–86. Czech poet who won the 1984 Nobel Prize for literature.

seign·eur (sān-yûr′, sĕn-) *n.* **1.** A man of rank, esp. a feudal lord in the ancien régime. **2.** In Canada, a man who owned a large estate originally granted by the king of France. **3.** Used as a form of address for such a man. [Fr. < OFr. *seignor* < VLat. **senior*. See SEIGNIOR.] —**seign·eur′i·al** *adj.*

seign·eur·y (sān′yə-rē, sĕn′-) *n.*, *pl.* **-ies.** The power, rank, or estate of a seigneur.

seign·ior (sān-yôr′, sān′yôr′) *n.* **1.** A man of rank, esp. a feudal lord. **2.** Used as a form of address for such a man. [ME *segnour* < OFr. *seignor* < VLat. **senior* < Lat., older, comp. of *senex, sen-*, old. See **sen-*.**] —**sei·gnio′ri·al** *adj.*

seign·ior·age (sān′yər-ĭj) *n.* Revenue or a profit taken from the minting of coins, usu. the difference between the value of the bullion used and the face value of the coin. [ME *seigneurage* < OFr. < *seignor*, seignior. See SEIGNIOR.]

seign·ior·y (sān′yə-rē) *n.*, *pl.* **-ies.** The power, rank, or estate of a feudal lord. [ME *seigniorie* < OFr. < *seignor*, seignior. See SEIGNIOR.]

seine (sān) *n.* A large fishing net made to hang vertically in the water by weights at the lower edge and floats at the top. —*v.* **seined, sein·ing, seines.** —*intr.* To fish with such a net. —*tr.* To fish for or catch with such a net. [ME < OE *segne* < Gmc. **sagina* < Lat. *sagēna* < Gk. *sagēnē*.] —**sein′er** *n.*

Seine (sān, sĕn). A river of N France flowing c. 772 km (480 mi) generally NW to the **Bay of the Seine,** an inlet of the English Channel, near Le Havre.

seise (sēz) *v.* Var. of **seize** 6.

sei·sin also **sei·zin** (sē′zĭn) *n.* *Law.* **1.** Legal possession of land, as a freehold estate. **2.a.** The act or an instance of taking legal possession of land. **b.** Property thus possessed. [ME *seisine* < OFr. *saisine* < *seisir*, to seize. See SEIZE.]

seism (sī′zəm) *n.* See **earthquake.** [Gk. *seismos* < *seiein*, to shake.]

seis·mic (sīz′mĭk) *adj.* **1.** Of, subject to, or caused by an earthquake or earth vibration. **2.** Earthshaking. —**seis′mi·cal·ly** *adv.* —**seis·mic′i·ty** (-mĭs′ĭ-tē) *n.*

seis·mism (sīz′mĭz′əm) *n.* The phenomena involved in earthquakes.

seismo– or **seism–** *pref.* Earthquake: *seismograph.* [Gk. < *seismos*, seism. See SEISM.]

seis·mo·gram (sīz′mə-grăm′) *n.* The record of an earth tremor made by a seismograph.

seis·mo·graph (sīz′mə-grăf′) *n.* An instrument for detecting and recording the intensity, direction, and duration of a movement of the ground, esp. of an earthquake. —**seis·mog′ra·pher** (sīz-mŏg′rə-fər) *n.* —**seis′mo·graph′ic** (-grăf′ĭk), **seis′mo·graph′i·cal** (-ĭ-kəl) *adj.* —**seis·mog′ra·phy** *n.*

seis·mol·o·gy (sīz-mŏl′ə-jē) *n.* The geophysical science of earthquakes and the mechanical properties of the earth. —**seis′mo·log′ic** (-mə-lŏj′ĭk), **seis′mo·log′i·cal** (-ĭ-kəl) *adj.* —**seis′mo·log′i·cal·ly** *adv.* —**seis·mol′o·gist** *n.*

seis·mom·e·ter (sīz-mŏm′ĭ-tər) *n.* A detecting device that receives seismic impulses. —**seis′mo·met′ric** (-mə-mĕt′rĭk), **seis′mo·met′ri·cal** (-rĭ-kəl) *adj.*

seis·mom·e·try (sīz-mŏm′ĭ-trē) *n.* The scientific study and recording of earthquakes.

seis·mo·scope (sīz′mə-skōp′) *n.* An instrument that indicates the occurrence or time of occurrence of an earthquake. —**seis′mo·scop′ic** (-skŏp′ĭk) *adj.*

sei whale *n.* A rorqual *(Balaenoptera borealis)* that is blue-black above and white below and grows up to about 55 feet (17 meters) in length. [< Norw. *seihval*. See SEI.]

seize (sēz) *v.* **seized, seiz·ing, seiz·es.** —*tr.* **1.** To grasp suddenly and forcibly; take or grab. **2.a.** To grasp with the mind; apprehend. **b.** To possess oneself of: *seize an opportunity.* **3.a.** To have a sudden overwhelming effect on. **b.** To overwhelm physically. **4.** To take into custody; capture. **5.** To take quick and forcible possession of; confiscate. **6.** Also **seise** (sēz). **a.** To put (one) into possession of something. **b.** To vest ownership of a feudal property in. **7.** *Naut.* To bind with turns of small line. —*intr.* **1.** To lay sudden or forcible hold of something. **2.a.** To cohere or fuse with another part as a result of high pressure or temperature and restrict or prevent further motion or flow. **b.** To come to a halt: *The talks seized up.* [ME *seisen* < OFr. *seisir*, to take possession, of Gmc. orig.] —**seiz′a·ble** *adj.* —**seiz′er** *n.*

sei·zin (sē′zĭn) *n.* *Law.* Var. of **seisin.**

seiz·ing (sē′zĭng) *n.* *Naut.* A binding of multiple turns of thread or light line around a rope end to keep it from unlaying.

sei·zor also **sei·sor** (sē′zər, -zôr′) *n.* *Law.* One that takes seisin.

sei·zure (sē′zhər) *n.* **1.** The act or an instance of seizing or the condition of being seized. **2.** A sudden attack, spasm, or convulsion, as in epilepsy. **3.** A sudden onset or sensation of feeling or emotion.

Sek·on·di-Ta·ko·ra·di (sĕk′ən-dē′tä-kə-rä′dē). A city of SW Ghana WSW of Accra. Pop. 93,882.

sel. *abbr.* Select; selected; selectivity.

se·la·chi·an (sĭ-lā′kē-ən) *adj.* Of or belonging to the order Selachii of elasmobranch fishes that includes the sharks and in some classifications also the rays and skates. [Prob. < NLat. *Selachiī*, order name < Gk. *selakhios*, cartilaginous < *selakhos*, cartilaginous fish.] —**se·la′chi·an** *n.*

se·lag·i·nel·la (sə-lăj′ə-nĕl′ə) *n.* Any of numerous fernlike, usu. prostrate plants of the genus *Selaginella*, having small scalelike leaves and bearing spores. [NLat. *Selāginella*, genus name < Lat. *selāgō, selāgin-*, a plant resembling the savin.]

se·lah (sē′lə, sĕl′ə) *interj.* Used to conclude a verse in the Psalms. [Heb. *selâ*.]

sel·dom (sĕl′dəm) *adv.* Not often; infrequently or rarely. See Usage Note at **rarely.** —*adj. Archaic.* Infrequent; rare. [ME < OE *seldum*, alteration of *seldan*.] —**sel′dom·ness** *n.*

se·lect (sĭ-lĕkt′) *v.* **-lect·ed, -lect·ing, -lects.** —*tr.* To take as a choice from among several; pick out. —*intr.* To make a choice or selection. —*adj.* **1.** Singled out in preference; chosen. **2.** Of special quality or value; choice. **3.** Of or relating to a lean grade of beef. —*n. (used with a sing. or pl. v.)* One preferred or chosen for special value. [Lat. *sēligere, sēlēct-* : *sē-*, apart; see **s(w)e-*** + *legere*, to choose; see **leg-*.**] —**se·lec′ta·ble** *adj.* —**se·lect′ness** *n.* —**se·lec′tor** *n.*

se·lect·ee (sĭ-lĕk′tē′) *n.* One who is selected, esp. for military service.

se·lec·tion (sĭ-lĕk′shən) *n.* **1.a.** The act or an instance of selecting or the fact of having been selected. **b.** One that is selected. **2.** A carefully chosen or representative collection of people or things. See Syns at **choice. 3.** A literary or musical text chosen for reading or performance. **4.** *Biol.* A natural or artificial process that favors or induces survival and perpetuation of one kind of organism over others.

se·lec·tion·ist (sĭ-lĕk′shə-nĭst) *adj.* also **se·lec·tion·al** (-shə-nəl). Of or relating to the view that evolution or genetic variation occurs chiefly as a result of natural selection. —**se·lec′tion·ism** *n.* —**se·lec′tion·ist** *n.*

se·lec·tive (sĭ-lĕk′tĭv) *adj.* **1.** Of or characterized by selection; discriminating. **2.** Empowered or tending to select. **3.** *Electron.* Able to reject frequencies other than the one selected or tuned. —**se·lec′tive·ly** *adv.* —**se·lec′tive·ness** *n.*

selective service *n.* A system for calling up people for compulsory military service.

selective veto *n.* See **item veto.**

se·lec·tiv·i·ty (sĭ-lĕk′tĭv′ĭ-tē, sē′lĕk-) *n.*, *pl.* **-ties. 1.** The state or quality of being selective. **2.** The degree to which an electronic receiver is selective.

se·lect·man (sĭ-lĕkt′măn′, -mən) *n.* One of a board of town officers chosen annually in New England communities to manage local affairs.

se·lect·wom·an (sĭ-lĕkt′wŏŏm′ən) *n.* A woman who is one of a board of town officers chosen annually in New England communities to manage local affairs.

ă **pat**	oi **boy**
ā **pay**	ou **out**
âr **care**	ŏŏ **took**
ä **father**	ōō **boot**
ĕ **pet**	ŭ **cut**
ē **be**	ûr **urge**
ĭ **pit**	th **thin**
ī **pie**	*th* **this**
îr **pier**	hw **which**
ŏ **pot**	zh **vision**
ō **toe**	ə **about, item**
ô **paw**	

Stress marks:
′ (primary);
′ (secondary), as in
dictionary (dĭk′shə-nĕr′ē)

sel•e•nate (sĕl′ə-nāt′) *n.* A salt or ester of selenic acid.

Se•le•ne (sə-lē′nē) *n. Gk. Myth.* The goddess of the moon.

Se•len•ga (sĕl′ĕng-gä′). A river of N Mongolia and SE Russia flowing c. 1,207 km (750 mi) to Lake Baikal.

se•le•nic (sə-lē′nĭk, -lĕn′ĭk) *adj.* Of, relating to, or containing selenium.

selenic acid *n.* A highly corrosive hygroscopic white solid acid with composition H_2SeO_4.

sel•e•nif•er•ous (sĕl′ə-nĭf′ər-əs) *adj.* Containing selenium.

sel•e•nite (sĕl′ə-nīt′, sĭ-lē′-) *n.* Gypsum in the form of colorless clear crystals. [Lat. *selēnītēs* < Gk. *selēnitēs (lithos),* moon (stone), selenite (so called because it was believed to wax and wane with the moon) < *selēnē,* moon. See SELENIUM.]

se•le•ni•um (sĭ-lē′nē-əm) *n. Symbol* **Se** A nonmetallic element, with red, black, and gray allotropic forms, resembling sulfur and obtained primarily as a byproduct of electrolytic copper refining; widely used in rectifiers, as a semiconductor, in xerography and in photocells. Atomic number 34; atomic weight 78.96; melting point (of gray selenium) 217°C; boiling point (gray) 684.9°C; specific gravity (gray) 4.79; (black) 4.28; valence 2, 4, or 6. See table at **element.** [Gk. *selēnē,* moon (< *selas,* light, brightness) + -IUM.]

selenium cell *n.* A photoconductive cell consisting of an insulated selenium strip between two suitable electrodes.

seleno– or **selen–** *pref.* **1.** Moon: *selenography.* **2.** Selenium: *selenosis.* [Gk. *selēno-* < *selēnē,* moon. See SELENIUM.]

sel•e•nog•ra•phy (sĕl′ə-nŏg′rə-fē) *n.* The study of the physical features of the moon. —**sel′e•nog′ra•pher, sel′e•nog′ra•phist** *n.* —**sel′e•no•graph′ic** (-nə-grăf′ĭk), **sel′e•no•graph′i•cal** (-ĭ-kəl) *adj.* —**sel′e•no•graph′i•cal•ly** *adv.*

sel•e•nol•o•gy (sĕl′ə-nŏl′ə-jē) *n.* The astronomical study of the moon. —**sel′e•no•log′i•cal** (-nə-lŏj′ĭ-kəl) *adj.* —**sel′e•nol′o•gist** *n.*

sel•e•no•sis (sĕl′ə-nō′sĭs) *n.* Poisoning, esp. of livestock, caused by ingesting selenium.

Se•leu•ci•a (sĭ-lo͞o′shē-ə, -shə). An ancient city of Mesopotamia on the Tigris R. SSE of Baghdad; founded c. 300 B.C.

Se•leu•cid (sĭ-lo͞o′sĭd). A Hellenistic dynasty founded by Seleucus I that ruled much of Asia Minor from 312 to 64 B.C. —**Se•leu′cid** *adj.*

Se•leu•cus I (sĭ-lo͞o′kəs). 358?–281 B.C. Macedonian general who founded and ruled (312–281) the Seleucid dynasty.

self (sĕlf) *n., pl.* **selves** (sĕlvz). **1.** The total, essential, or particular being of a person; the individual. **2.** The essential qualities distinguishing one person from another; individuality. **3.** One's consciousness of one's own being or identity; the ego. **4.** One's own interests, welfare, or advantage. **5.** *Immunol.* That which the immune system identifies as belonging to the body. —*pron.* Myself, yourself, himself, or herself. —*adj.* **1.** Of the same character throughout. **2.** Of the same material as the article with which it is used. **3.** *Obsolete.* Same or identical. [ME, selfsame < OE. See **s(w)e-*.**]

self– *pref.* **1.** Oneself; itself: *self-control.* **2.** Automatic; automatically: *self-loading.* [ME < OE < *self,* self. See SELF.]

self-a•ban•doned (sĕlf′ə-băn′dənd) *adj.* Lacking self-restraint. —**self′-a•ban′don•ment** *n.*

self-ab•ne•ga•tion (sĕlf′ăb′nĭ-gā′shən) *n.* The setting aside of self-interest for the sake of others or for a belief or principle. —**self′-ab′ne•gat′ing** *adj.*

self-a•buse (sĕlf′ə-byo͞os′) *n.* **1.** Abuse of oneself or one's abilities. **2.** Masturbation.

self-act•ing (sĕlf′ăk′tĭng) *adj.* Able to act automatically.

self-ad•dressed (sĕlf′ə-drĕst′) *adj.* Addressed to oneself.

self-ad•he•sive (sĕlf′ăd-hē′sĭv) *adj.* Having a surface coated with an adhesive and not needing any substance, such as glue, to form a bond.

self-ad•min•is•ter (sĕlf′ăd-mĭn′ĭ-stər) *tr.v.* **-tered, -ter•ing, -ters.** To administer (something) to oneself or itself. —**self′-ad•min′is•tra′tion** *n.*

self-ag•gran•dize•ment (sĕlf′ə-grăn′dĭz-mənt) *n.* The act or practice of enhancing or exaggerating one's own importance, power, or reputation. —**self′-ag•gran′diz′ing** (-ə-grăn′dī′zĭng) *adj.*

self-a•nal•y•sis (sĕlf′ə-năl′ĭ-sĭs) *n., pl.* **-ses** (-sēz′). An independent methodical attempt to study and comprehend one's own personality or emotions. —**self′-an′a•lyt′i•cal** (-ăn′ə-lĭt′ĭ-kəl), **self′-an′a•lyt′ic** (-ĭk) *adj.*

self-an•ni•hi•la•tion (sĕlf′ə-nī′ə-lā′shən) *n.* **1.** Self-destruction. **2.** Loss of self-awareness, as in a mystical state.

self-as•sert•ing (sĕlf′ə-sûr′tĭng) *adj.* **1.** Asserting oneself or one's own rights or views. **2.a.** Self-confident. **b.** Overbearing; arrogant.

self-as•ser•tion (sĕlf′ə-sûr′shən) *n.* Determined advancement of one's own personality, wishes, or views. —**self′-as•ser′tive** *adj.* —**self-as•ser′tive•ness** *n.*

self-as•sured (sĕlf′ə-sho͝ord′) *adj.* Having or showing confidence and poise. —**self′-as•sur′ance** (-sho͝or′əns) *n.*

self-bast•ing (sĕlf′bā′stĭng) *adj.* Prepared so as to remain moist while being cooked: *a self-basting turkey.*

self-care (sĕlf′kâr′) *n.* The care of oneself without medical, professional, or other assistance or oversight.

self-col•ored (sĕlf′kŭl′ərd) *adj.* **1.** Being in the natural or original color. **2.** Of only one color.

self-com•mand (sĕlf′kə-mănd′) *n.* Full presence of mind; self-confidence.

self-com•pat•i•ble (sĕlf′kəm-păt′ə-bəl) *adj. Bot.* Capable of self-fertilization. —**self′-com•pat′i•bil′i•ty** *n.*

self-con•cern (sĕlf′kən-sûrn′) *n.* Selfish or excessive concern for oneself. —**self′-con•cerned′** *adj.*

self-con•fessed (sĕlf′kən-fĕst′) *adj.* By one's own admission.

self-con•fi•dence (sĕlf′kŏn′fĭ-dəns) *n.* Confidence in oneself or one's own abilities. —**self′-con′fi•dent** *adj.*

self-con•scious (sĕlf′kŏn′shəs) *adj.* **1.** Aware of oneself as an individual or of one's own being, actions, or thoughts. **2.** Socially ill at ease. **3.** Excessively conscious of one's appearance or manner. **4.** Showing the effects of self-consciousness; stilted. —**self′-con′scious•ness** *n.*

self-con•tained (sĕlf′kən-tānd′) *adj.* **1.** Constituting a complete and independent unit in and of itself. **2.a.** Not dependent on others; self-sufficient. **b.** Keeping to oneself; reserved. —**self′-con•tain′ment** *n.*

self-con•tra•dic•tion (sĕlf′kŏn′trə-dĭk′shən) *n.* **1.** The act, state, or fact of contradicting oneself or of containing an inherent contradiction. **2.** An idea or statement containing contradictions. —**self′-con′tra•dic′to•ry** (-dĭk′tə-rē) *adj.*

self-con•trol (sĕlf′kən-trōl′) *n.* Control of one's emotions, de-

---

self′-a•base′ment *n.*
self′-ab•sorbed′ *adj.*
self′-ab•sorp′tion *n.*
self′-ac′tu•al•i•za′tion *n.*
self′-ac′tu•al•ize′ *intr.v.*
self′-ac′tu•al•iz′er *n.*
self′-ap•point′ed *adj.*
self′-a•ware′ *adj.*
self′-a•ware′ness *n.*
self′-cen′tered *adj.*
self′-cen′tered•ly *adv.*
self′-cen′tered•ness *n.*
self′-clean′ing *adj.*
self′-com•pla′cen•cy *n.*
self′-com•pla′cent *adj.*
self′-com•pla′cent•ly *adv.*
self′-con′cept *n.*
self′-con•cep′tion *n.*
self′-con•tent′ *adj. & n.*
self′con•tent′ed•ly *adv.*
self′-con•tent′ment *n.*
self′-crit′i•cal *adj.*
self′-crit′i•cal•ly *adv.*
self′-crit′i•cism *n.*
self′-de•ceit′ *n.*
self′-de•ceived′ *adj.*
self′-de•ceiv′ing *adj.*
self′-de•cep′tion *n.*
self′-de•cep′tive *adj.*
self′-de•cep′tive•ly *adv.*
self′-de•feat′ing *adj.*
self′-def′i•ni′tion *n.*
self′-dep′re•cat′ing *adj.*
self′-dep′re•cat′ing•ly *adv.*
self′-dep′re•ca•to′ry *adj.*
self′-de•struc′tive *adj.*
self′-de•struc′tive•ly *adv.*
self′-de•struc′tive•ness *n.*
self′-de•vel′op•ment *n.*
self′-di′ag•no′sis *n.*
self′-di′ag•nos′tic *adj.*
self′-di•rect′ed *adj.*
self′-di•rect′ing *adj.*
self′-di•rec′tion *n.*
self′-dis′ci•pline *n.*
self′-dis•cov′er•y *n.*
self′-dis•trust′ *n.*
self′-dis•trust′ful *adj.*
self′-doomed′ *adj.*
self′-doubt′ *n.*
self′-doubt′ing *adj.*
self′-ed′u•cat′ed *adj.*
self′-ed′u•ca′tion *n.*
self′-e•lect′ed *adj.*
self′-en•rich′ment *n.*
self′-es•teem′ *n.*
self′-e•val′u•a′tion *n.*
self′-ex′ile *n.*
self′-ex′iled *adj.*
self′fer′tile *adj.*
self′-fer′til•i•za′tion *n.*
self′-fer′til•ized′ *adj.*
self′-fer′til•iz′ing *adj.*
self′-ful•fill′ment *n.*
self′-grat′i•fi•ca′tion *n.*
self′-hate′ *n.*
self′-ha′tred *n.*
self′-help′ *n.*
self′-i•den′ti•ty *n.*
self′-im′age *n.*
self′-im•posed′ *adj.*
self′-im•prove′ment *n.*
self′-in•crim′i•nat′ing *adj.*
self′-in•crim′i•na′tion *n.*
self′-in•crim′i•na•to′ry *adj.*
self′-in•dul′gence *n.*
self′-in•dul′gent *adj.*
self′-in•dul′gent•ly *adv.*
self′-in•flict′ed *adj.*
self′-in•struct′ed *adj.*
self′-in•volved′ *adj.*
self′-in•volve′ment *n.*
self′-knowl′edge *n.*
self′-loath′ing *n.*
self′-med′i•ca′tion *n.*
self′-ob′ser•va′tion *n.*
self′-per•pet′u•at′ing *adj.*
self′-per•pet′u•a′tion *n.*
self′-pit′y *n.*
self′-pit′y•ing *adj.*
self′-pit′y•ing•ly *adv.*
self′-pol′li•nate′ *v.*
self′-pol′li•na′tion *n.*
self′-por′trait *n.*
self′-pro•mot′er *n.*
self′-pro•mo′tion *n.*
self′-pro•tec′tion *n.*
self′-pro•tec′tive *adj.*
self′-pro•tec′tive•ly *adv.*
self′-pub′lished *adj.*
self′-ref′er•ence *n.*
self′-ref′er•en′tial *adj.*
self′-ref′er•en′tial•ly *adv.*
self′-reg′u•lat′ing *adj.*
self′-reg•u•la′tion *n.*
self′-re•li′ance *n.*
self′-re•li′ant *adj.*
self′-re•li′ant•ly *adv.*
self′-rep′li•cat′ing *adj.*
self′-rep′li•ca′tion *n.*
self′-re•proach′ *n.*
self′-re•proach′ful *adj.*
self′-re•proach′ful•ly *adv.*
self′-re•spect′ *n.*
self′re•spect′ing *adj.*
self′-re•straint′ *n.*
self′-scru′ti•ny *n.*
self′-sup•port′ *n.*
self′-sup•port′ed *adj.*
self′-sup•port′ing *adj.*
self′-sus•tain′ing *adj.*
self′-sus•tain′ing•ly *adv.*
self′-taught′ *adj.*
self′-un′der•stand′ing *n.*
self′-val′i•dat′ing *adj.*

sires, or actions by one's own will. — **self′-con·trolled′** *adj.*

self-cor·rect·ing (sĕlf′kə-rĕk′tĭng) *adj.* **1.** Correcting its or one's own mistakes. **2.** Of or being a typewriter mechanism that allows for automatic correction of a typing error.

self-de·fense (sĕlf′dĭ-fĕns′) *n.* **1.** Defense of oneself when physically attacked. **2.** Defense of what belongs to oneself, as one's works. **3.** *Law.* The right to protect oneself against violence or threatened violence with whatever force or means are reasonably necessary. — **self′-de·fen′sive** *adj.*

self-de·ni·al (sĕlf′dĭ-nī′əl) *n.* Sacrifice of one's own desires or interests. — **self′-de·ny′ing** (-nī′ĭng) *adj.*

self-de·pre·ci·a·tion (sĕlf′dĭ-prē′shē-ā′shən) *n.* Disparagement or undervaluation of oneself and one's abilities.

self-de·scribed (sĕlf′dĭ-skrībd′) *adj.* **1.** As described by oneself about oneself. **2.** Self-styled. — **self′-de·scrip′tion** (-skrĭp′shən) *n.*

self-de·struct (sĕlf′dĭ-strŭkt′) *n.* A mechanism for causing a device to destroy itself. — *intr.v.* **-struct·ed, -struct·ing, -structs.** To destroy oneself or itself.

self-de·struc·tion (sĕlf′dĭ-strŭk′shən) *n.* **1.** The act or process of destroying oneself or itself. **2.** Suicide.

self-de·struc·tive (sĕlf′dĭ-strŭk′tĭv) *adj.* **1.** Tending to do harm to oneself. **2.** Marked by an impulse or tendency to harm or kill oneself. — **self′-de·struc′tive·ness** *n.*

self-de·ter·mi·na·tion (sĕlf′dĭ-tûr′mə-nā′shən) *n.* **1.** Determination of one's own fate or course of action without compulsion; free will. **2.** Freedom of the people of a given area to determine their own political status; independence.

self-de·vo·tion (sĕlf′dĭ-vō′shən) *n.* Devotion or dedication of oneself, esp. to a service or an ideal. — **self′-de·vot′ed·ly** (-vō′tĭd-lē) *adv.* — **self′-de·vot′ed·ness** *n.*

self-di·ges·tion (sĕlf′dĭ-jĕs′chən, -dī-) *n.* See **autolysis.**

self·dom (self′dəm) *n.* Selfhood.

self-ef·fac·ing (sĕlf′ĭ-fā′sĭng) *adj.* Not drawing attention to oneself; modest. — **self′-ef·face′ment** (-fās′mənt) *n.*

self-em·ployed (sĕlf′ĕm-ploid′) *adj.* Earning one's livelihood directly from one's own trade or business rather than as an employee of another. — **self′-em·ploy′ment** *n.*

self-en·forc·ing (sĕlf′ĕn-fôr′sĭng, -fōr′-) *adj.* Holding within itself the means or a guarantee of its enforcement.

self-es·teem (sĕlf′ĭ-stēm′) *n.* Pride in oneself; self-respect.

self-ev·i·dent (sĕlf′ĕv′ĭ-dənt) *adj.* Requiring no proof or explanation. — **self′-ev′i·dence** *n.* — **self′-ev′i·dent·ly** *adv.*

self-ex·am·i·na·tion (sĕlf′ĭg-zăm′ə-nā′shən) *n.* **1.** An introspective consideration of one's own thoughts or emotions. **2.** Examination of one's own body for medical reasons.

self-ex·plan·a·to·ry (sĕlf′ĭk-splăn′ə-tôr′ē, -tōr′ē) *adj.* Needing no explanation; obvious.

self-ex·pres·sion (sĕlf′ĭk-sprĕsh′ən) *n.* Expression of one's own personality, feelings, or ideas, as through speech or art. — **self′-ex·press′** *v.* — **self′-ex·pres′sive** (-sprĕs′ĭv) *adj.*

self-flag·el·la·tion (sĕlf′flăj′ə-lā′shən) *n.* **1.** The act of severely criticizing oneself. **2.** The act of punishing oneself.

self-ful·fill·ing (sĕlf′fo͝ol-fĭl′ĭng) *adj.* **1.** Achieving fulfillment as a result of having been expected or foretold: *a self-fulfilling prophecy.* **2.** Achieving self-fulfillment.

self-giv·en (sĕlf′gĭv′ən) *adj.* **1.** Originating or derived from itself. **2.** Given by oneself; self-appointed: *self-given role.*

self-giv·ing (sĕlf′gĭv′ĭng) *adj.* Characterized by self-sacrificing behavior; unselfish.

self-gov·erned (sĕlf′gŭv′ərnd) *adj.* **1.** Not controlled or swayed by others. **2.** Characterized by self-control.

self-gov·ern·ing (sĕlf′gŭv′ər-nĭng) *adj.* **1.** Exercising control or rule over oneself or itself. **2.** Having the right or power of self-government; autonomous.

self-gov·ern·ment (sĕlf′gŭv′ərn-mənt) *n.* **1.** Political independence; autonomy. **2.** Popular or representative government; democracy. **3.** Self-control.

self-hard·en·ing (sĕlf′här′dn-ĭng) *adj.* Of or relating to materials that harden without special treatment.

self-heal (sĕlf′hēl′) *n.* Any of several plants reputed to have healing powers, esp. *Prunella vulgaris,* a creeping Eurasian plant with deep violet-blue two-lipped flowers.

self·hood (sĕlf′ho͝od′) *n.* **1.** The state of having a distinct identity; individuality. **2.** The fully developed self; an achieved personality. **3.** Self-centeredness.

self-hyp·no·sis (sĕlf′hĭp-nō′sĭs) *n.* See **autohypnosis.**

self-i·den·ti·fi·ca·tion (sĕlf′ī-dĕn′tə-fĭ-kā′shən) *n.* Identification of oneself with another person or thing.

self-im·mo·la·tion (sĕlf′ĭm′ə-lā′shən) *n.* Deliberate sacrifice of oneself.

self-im·por·tance (sĕlf′ĭm-pôr′tns) *n.* Excessively high regard for one's own importance or station; conceit. — **self′-im·por′tant** *adj.* — **self′-im·por′tant·ly** *adv.*

self-in·clu·sive (sĕlf′ĭn-klo͞o′sĭv, -zĭv) *adj.* **1.** Enclosing or including itself. **2.** Whole or complete in itself.

self-in·com·pat·i·ble (sĕlf′ĭn-kəm-păt′ə-bəl) *adj. Bot.* Incapable of self-fertilization. — **self′-in′com·pat′i·bil′i·ty** *n.*

self-in·duced (sĕlf′ĭn-do͞ost′, -dyo͞ost′) *adj.* **1.** Induced by oneself or itself. **2.** *Elect.* Produced by self-induction.

self-in·duct·ance (sĕlf′ĭn-dŭk′təns) *n.* The ratio of the electromotive force produced in a circuit by self-induction to the rate of change of current producing it, stated in henries.

self-in·duc·tion (sĕlf′ĭn-dŭk′shən) *n. Elect.* The generation by a changing current of an electromotive force in the same circuit. — **self′-in·duc′tive** *adj.*

self-in·struc·tion·al (sĕlf′ĭn-strŭk′shə-nəl) *adj.* Of, relating to, or designed for independent study.

self-in·sur·ance (sĕlf′ĭn-sho͝or′əns) *n.* Insurance of oneself or one's possessions against possible loss by regularly setting aside funds. — **self′-in·sure′** *v.* — **self′-in·sured′** *adj.* — **self′-in·sur′er** *n.*

self-in·ter·est (sĕlf′ĭn′trĭst, -ĭn′tər-ĭst) *n.* **1.** Selfish or excessive regard for one's personal advantage or interest. **2.** Personal advantage or interest. — **self′-in′ter·est·ed** *adj.*

self·ish (sĕl′fĭsh) *adj.* **1.** Concerned chiefly or only with oneself. **2.** Arising from, characterized by, or showing selfishness. — **self′ish·ly** *adv.* — **self′ish·ness** *n.*

self-jus·ti·fy·ing (sĕlf′jŭs′tə-fī′ĭng) *adj.* **1.** Making excuses for oneself or one's behavior. **2.** Justifying itself automatically: *a self-justifying typewriter.* — **self′-jus′ti·fi·ca′tion** (-jŭs′tə-fĭ-kā′shən) *n.*

self·less (sĕlf′lĭs) *adj.* Having, exhibiting, or motivated by no concern for oneself; unselfish. — **self′less·ness** *n.*

self-lim·it·ed (sĕlf-lĭm′ĭ-tĭd) *adj.* **1.** Limited by its or one's own characteristics rather than by external influences. **2.** Running a definite course within a specific period; little modified by treatment. Used of a disease.

self-lim·it·ing (sĕlf-lĭm′ĭ-tĭng) *adj.* **1.** Limiting oneself or itself. **2.** Self-limited. — **self′-lim′i·ta′tion** (-tā′shən) *n.*

self-liq·ui·dat·ing (sĕlf′lĭk′wĭ-dā′tĭng) *adj.* **1.** Involving goods convertible into cash in a short time. Used of business transactions. **2.** Producing a return equal to the sum invested to create or maintain something. — **self′-liq′ui·da′tion** *n.*

self-load·ing (sĕlf′lō′dĭng) *adj.* Automatically ejecting a shell and loading the next round from the magazine; automatic or semiautomatic. Used of a firearm.

self-love (sĕlf′lŭv′) *n.* The instinct or desire to promote one's own well-being; regard for or love of one's self. — **self′-lov′ing** *adj.*

self-made (sĕlf′mād′) *adj.* **1.** Having achieved success or recognition by one's own efforts. **2.** Made by itself or oneself.

self-mail·er (sĕlf′mā′lər) *n.* A folder that can be mailed without being enclosed in an envelope. — **self′-mail′ing** *adj.*

self-mas·ter·y (sĕlf′măs′tə-rē) *n.* Self-command.

self·ness (sĕlf′nĭs) *n.* **1.** The quality or state of being self-centered; selfishness. **2.** Individuality; selfhood.

self-o·pin·ion (sĕlf′ə-pĭn′yən) *n.* An unduly high opinion of oneself.

self-o·pin·ion·at·ed (sĕlf′ə-pĭn′yə-nā′tĭd) *adj.* **1.** Obstinately insistent upon one's own opinions. **2.** Vain; conceited.

self-or·dained (sĕlf′ôr-dānd′) *adj.* Ordained by oneself rather than by others; practicing by one's own authority.

self-per·cep·tion (sĕlf′pər-sĕp′shən) *n.* An awareness of the characteristics that constitute one's self; self-knowledge.

self-poised (sĕlf′poizd′) *adj.* **1.** In command of oneself. **2.** In a state of balance without need of support.

self-pos·ses·sion (sĕlf′pə-zĕsh′ən) *n.* Full command of one's faculties, feelings, and behavior. — **self′-pos·sessed′** *adj.*

self-pres·er·va·tion (sĕlf′prĕz′ər-vā′shən) *n.* **1.** Protection of oneself from harm or destruction. **2.** The instinct for individual preservation; the innate desire to stay alive.

self-pro·claimed (sĕlf′prō-klāmd′, -prə-) *adj.* So called by oneself; self-styled.

self-pro·pelled (sĕlf′prə-pĕld′) *adj.* **1.** Containing its own means of propulsion. **2.** Fired from or mounted on a moving vehicle. — **self′-pro·pul′sion** (-pŭl′shən) *n.*

self-pu·ri·fi·ca·tion (sĕlf′pyo͝or′ə-fĭ-kā′shən) *n.* **1.** Naturally produced purification. **2.** Purification of oneself.

self-re·ac·tive (sĕlf′rē-ăk′tĭv) *adj.* Immunologically reactive to itself. Used of a cell or tissue.

self-re·al·i·za·tion (sĕlf′rē′ə-lĭ-zā′shən) *n.* Complete development or fulfillment of one's own potential.

self-re·cord·ing (sĕlf′rĭ-kôr′dĭng) *adj.* Automatically recording its own functions or operations. Used of a machine or an instrument.

self-re·crim·i·na·tion (sĕlf′rĭ-krĭm′ə-nā′shən) *n.* The act or an instance of blaming or censuring oneself.

self-ref·er·en·tial (sĕlf′rĕf′ə-rĕn′shəl) *adj.* Referring to oneself or itself: *a self-referential poem.* — **self′-ref′er·ence** *n.*

self-re·flec·tion (sĕlf′rĭ-flĕk′shən) *n.* Self-examination; introspection. — **self′-re·flec′tive** *adj.*

self-re·gard (sĕlf′rĭ-gärd′) *n.* **1.** Consideration of oneself or one's interests. **2.** Self-respect.

self-rev·e·la·tion (sĕlf′rĕv′ə-lā′shən) *n.* Revelation of one's own thoughts, emotions, or attitudes, esp. unintentionally. — **self′-re·veal′ing** (-rĭ-vē′lĭng) *adj.*

self-right·eous (sĕlf′rī′chəs) *adj.* **1.** Piously sure of one's own righteousness; moralistic. **2.** Exhibiting pious self-assurance. — **self′-right′eous·ly** *adv.* — **self′-right′eous·ness** *n.*

self-right·ing (sĕlf′rī′tĭng) *adj.* Capable of righting itself when capsized: *a self-righting boat.*

self-ris·ing flour (sĕlf′rī′zĭng) *n.* A commercially produced mixture of flour and leavening.

self-heal

ă pat	oi boy
ā pay	ou out
âr care	o͝o took
ä father	o͞o boot
ĕ pet	ŭ cut
ē be	ûr urge
ĭ pit	th thin
ī pie	*th* this
îr pier	hw which
ŏ pot	zh vision
ō toe	ə about, item
ô paw	

Stress marks:
′ (primary);
′ (secondary), as in
dictionary (dĭk′shə-nĕr′ē)

David O. Selznick

self-rule (sĕlf′ro͞ol′) *n.* Self-government.

self-sac•ri•fice (sĕlf′săk′rə-fīs′) *n.* Sacrifice of one's personal interests or well-being for the sake of others or for a cause. —**self′-sac′ri•fic′ing** *adj.*

self•same (sĕlf′sām′) *adj.* Being the very same; identical. —**self′same′ness** *n.*

self-sat•is•fac•tion (sĕlf′săt′ĭs-făk′shən) *n.* Satisfaction, esp. complacent satisfaction, with oneself or with one's accomplishments. —**self′-sat′is•fied′** (-fīd′) *adj.*

self-seal•ing (sĕlf′sē′lĭng) *adj.* **1.** Capable of sealing itself, as after being pierced: *a self-sealing tire.* **2.** Sealable without the application of moisture: *a self-sealing envelope.*

self-search•ing (sĕlf′sûr′chĭng) *n.* Careful examination of one's feelings and actions and their motivation. —**self′-search′ing** *adj.*

self-seed•ed (sĕlf′sē′dĭd) *adj. Bot.* Self-sown.

self-seek•ing (sĕlf′sē′kĭng) *adj.* **1.** Pursuing only one's own ends or interests. **2.** Exhibiting concern only with promoting one's own ends or interests. —*n.* Determined pursuit of one's own ends or interests. —**self′-seek′er** *n.*

self-se•lec•tion (sĕlf′sĭ-lĕk′shən) *n.* Selection of or by oneself. —**self′-se•lect′ed** *adj.* —**self′-se•lec′tive** *adj.*

self-serv•ice (sĕlf′sûr′vĭs) *adj.* Being a retail commercial enterprise or a service in which the customers or users help themselves. —**self′-serv′ice** *n.*

self-serv•ing (sĕlf′sûr′vĭng) *adj.* **1.** Serving one's own interests, esp. without concern for the needs or interests of others. **2.** Exhibiting concern solely for one's own interests.

self-sown (sĕlf′sōn′) *adj. Bot.* Growing from seed dispersal effected by a natural agent, such as the wind or a bird, rather than by human agency.

self-start•er (sĕlf′stär′tər) *n.* **1.** See **starter** 2. **2.** One who displays unusual initiative. —**self′-start′ing** *adj.*

self-stick (sĕlf′stĭk′) also **self-stick•ing** (-stĭk′ĭng) *adj.* Self-adhesive: *a self-stick envelope.*

self-stud•y (sĕlf′stŭd′ē) *n.* **1.** Study or examination of oneself. **2.** A form of study in which one is to a large extent responsible for one's own instruction.

self-styled (sĕlf′stīld′) *adj.* As characterized by oneself, often without right or justification: *"poets, real or self-styled"* (Constantine Fitzgibbon). See Usage Note at **so-called.**

self-suf•fi•cient (sĕlf′sə-fĭsh′ənt) *adj.* **1.** Able to provide for oneself without the help of others; independent. **2.** Having undue confidence; smug. —**self′-suf•fi′cien•cy** *n.*

self-tol•er•ance (sĕlf′tŏl′ər-əns) *n.* Tolerance by the body's immune system to its own cells and tissues.

self-treat•ment (sĕlf′trēt′mənt) *n.* Treatment of oneself without professional supervision, as to alleviate an illness.

self-trust (sĕlf′trŭst′) *n.* Self-confidence.

self-will (sĕlf′wĭl′) *n.* Willfulness, esp. in satisfying one's desires or adhering to one's opinions. —**self′-willed′** *adj.*

self-wind•ing (sĕlf′wīn′dĭng) *adj.* Designed in such a way that manual winding is unnecessary. Used of clocks and watches.

self-worth (sĕlf′wûrth′) *n.* Self-esteem; self-respect.

Sel•juk (sĕl′jo͞ok′, sĕl-jo͞ok′). A Turkish dynasty ruling in central and W Asia from the 11th to the 13th cent.

Sel•kirk Mountains (sĕl′kûrk′). A range of the Rocky Mts. in SE British Columbia, Canada, rising to 3,524.3 m (11,555 ft).

sell (sĕl) *v.* **sold** (sōld), **sell•ing, sells.** —*tr.* **1.** To exchange or deliver for money or its equivalent. **2.** To offer for sale, as for one's business or livelihood. **3.** To give up or surrender in exchange for a price or reward. **4.** To be responsible for the sale of; promote successfully. **5.** To persuade (another) to recognize the worth or desirability of something. —*intr.* **1.** To exchange ownership for money or its equivalent; engage in selling. **2.** To be sold or be on sale. **3.** To attract prospective buyers; be popular on the market. **4.** To be approved of; gain acceptance. —*n.* **1.** The activity of selling. **2.** An instance of selling. **3.** *Slang.* An item that sells in a particular way: *a difficult sell.* —***phrasal verbs.* sell off.** To get rid of by selling, often at reduced prices. **sell out. 1.** To put all of one's goods or possessions up for sale. **2.** *Slang.* To betray one's cause or colleagues. —***idioms.* sell a bill of goods.** *Informal.* To take unfair advantage of. **sell down the river.** *Informal.* To betray the true trust or faith of. **sell short. 1.** To contract for the sale of securities or commodities one expects to own at a later date and at more advantageous terms. **2.** To underestimate the true value or worth of. [ME *sellen* < OE *sellan*, to give, sell.] —**sell′a•ble** *adj.*

sell•er (sĕl′ər) *n.* **1.** One that sells; a vendor. **2.** An item that sells in a certain way: *This car is an excellent seller.*

sell•er's market also **sell•ers' market** (sĕl′ərz) *n., pl.* **sell•ers' markets.** A market condition characterized by high prices and a supply of commodities falling short of demand.

sell•ing climax (sĕl′ĭng) *n.* A sharp decline in stock prices on a heavy volume of trading followed by a rally.

selling point *n.* An aspect of a product or service that is stressed in advertising or marketing.

sell•off (sĕl′ôf′, -ŏf′) *n.* The sale or disposal of a relatively large number of stocks, bonds, or commodities that often causes a sharp decline in prices.

sell•out (sĕl′out′) *n.* **1.** The act of selling out. **2.** An event for which all the tickets are sold. **3.** *Slang.* One who has betrayed one's principles or an espoused cause.

Sel•ma (sĕl′mə). A city of S-central AL W of Montgomery; site of a voter registration drive (1965) led by Martin Luther King, Jr. Pop. 23,755.

sel•syn (sĕl′sĭn) *n. Phys.* A device by which angular movement or position in a generator is transmitted to a motor. [SEL(F) + SYN(CHRONOUS).]

selt•zer (sĕlt′sər) *n.* **1.** A natural effervescent spring water of high mineral content. **2.** See **soda water** 1a. [< Ger. *Selterser (Wasser)*, (water) of Selters, in central Germany.]

sel•va (sĕl′və) *n.* A dense tropical rain forest usu. having a cloud cover, esp. in Amazonia. [Sp., forest < Lat. *silva.*]

sel•vage also **sel•vedge** (sĕl′vĭj) *n.* **1.a.** The edge of a fabric that is woven so that it will not fray or ravel. **b.** An ornamental fringe at either end of an oriental rug. **2.** The edge plate of a lock that has a slot for a bolt. [ME (influenced by MLGer. *selfegge*) : *self*, self; see SELF + *egge*, edge; see EDGE.]

selves (sĕlvz) *n.* Pl. of **self.**

Selz•nick (sĕlz′nĭk), **David Oliver.** 1902–65. Amer. producer whose films include *Gone With the Wind* (1939).

SEM *abbr.* Scanning electron microscope.

sem. *abbr.* Seminary.

Sem. *abbr.* Semitic.

se•man•teme (sĭ-măn′tēm′) *n. Ling.* An irreducible unit of meaning. [SEMANT(IC) + -EME.]

se•man•tic (sĭ-măn′tĭk) also **se•man•ti•cal** (-tĭ-kəl) *adj.* **1.** Of or relating to meaning, esp. meaning in language. **2.** Of, relating to, or according to the science of semantics. [Fr. *sémantique* < Gk. *sēmantikos*, significant < *sēmantos*, marked < *sēmainein*, *sēman-*, to signify < *sēma*, sign.] —**se•man′ti•cal•ly** *adv.*

se•man•ti•cist (sĭ-măn′tĭ-sĭst) *n.* A specialist in semantics.

se•man•tics (sĭ-măn′tĭks) *n.* (*used with a sing. or pl. v.*) **1.** *Ling.* The study or science of meaning in language forms. **2.** *Logic.* The study of relationships between signs and symbols and what they represent.

sem•a•phore (sĕm′ə-fôr′, -fōr′) *n.* **1.** A visual signaling apparatus with flags, lights, or mechanically moving arms, as one used on a railroad. **2.** A visual system for sending information by means of two flags that are held one in each hand, using an alphabetic code based on the position of the signaler's arms. —*tr. & intr.v.* **-phored, -phor•ing, -phores.** To send (a message) or to signal by semaphore. [Gk. *sēma*, sign + -PHORE.] —**sem′a•phor′ic** *adj.*

Se•ma•rang (sə-mär′äng). A city of N Java, Indonesia, on the Java Sea E of Jakarta. Pop. 1,026,671.

se•ma•si•ol•o•gy (sĭ-mā′sē-ŏl′ə-jē, -zē-) *n. Logic.* See **semantics** 2. [Gk. *sēmasia*, meaning (< *sēmainein*, to signify; see SEMANTIC) + -LOGY.] —**se•ma′si•o•log′i•cal** (-ə-lŏj′ĭ-kəl) *adj.* —**se•ma′si•ol′o•gist** *n.*

se•mat•ic (sĭ-măt′ĭk) *adj.* Serving as a warning or signal of danger. Used esp. of the coloring of some poisonous animals. [< Gk. *sēma*, *sēmat-*, sign.]

sem•bla•ble (sĕm′blə-bəl) *adj.* **1.** Having a resemblance; resembling or like. **2.** Seeming; apparent. —*n. Archaic.* Something that closely resembles something else. [ME < OFr. < *sembler*, to resemble < Lat. *simulāre*, to simulate. See SIMULATE.] —**sem′bla•bly** *adv.*

sem•blance (sĕm′bləns) *n.* **1.** An outward or token appearance. **2.** A representation; a copy. **3.** The barest trace; a modicum. [ME < OFr. < *sembler*, to resemble. See SEMBLABLE.]

se•mé (sə-mā′) *adj. Her.* Having a design embellished with small delicate figures, such as a lacing of stars or flowers. [Fr. < OFr., p.part. of *semer*, to sow, scatter < Lat. *sēmināre* < *sēmen*, *sēmin-*, seed. See **sē-*.**]

se•mei•ol•o•gy (sē′mē-ŏl′ə-jē, sĕm′ē-, sē′mī-) *n.* Var. of **semiology.**

se•mei•ot•ic (sē′mē-ŏt′ĭk, sĕm′ē-, sē′mī-) also **se•mei•ot•i•cal** (-ĭ-kəl) *adj.* Var. of **semiotic.**

se•mei•ot•ics (sē′mē-ŏt′ĭks, sĕm′ē-, sē′mī-) *n.* Var. of **semiotics.**

se•meme (sē′mēm′) *n. Ling.* The meaning expressed by a morpheme. [Gk. *sēma*, sign + -EME.]

se•men (sē′mən) *n.* A viscous whitish secretion of the male reproductive organs, containing and transporting spermatozoa. [ME < Lat. *sēmen*, seed, semen. See **sē-*.**]

Se•me•nov (sə-myô′nəf), **Nikolai Nikolayevich.** 1896–1986. Soviet chemist who shared a 1956 Nobel Prize.

se•mes•ter (sə-mĕs′tər) *n.* One of two divisions of 15 to 18 weeks each of an academic year. [Ger. < Lat. *(cursus) sēmēstris*, (course) of six months < **sex-mēnstris* : *sē-*, six (< *sex*; see **s(w)eks***) + *mēnsis*, month; see **mē-²*.**]

sem•i (sĕm′ī, sĕm′ē) *n., pl.* **sem•is.** *Informal.* **1.a.** A semitrailer. **b.** A tractor-trailer. **2.** A semifinal.

semi– *pref.* **1.** Half: *semicircle.* **2.** Partial; partially: *semiconscious.* **3.** Resembling or having some of the characteristics of: *semiofficial.* **4.** Occurring twice during: *semimonthly.* See Usage Note at **bi–¹.** [ME < Lat. *sēmi-*, half. See **sēmi-*.**]

sem•i•ab•stract (sĕm′ē-ăb-străkt′, -ăb′străkt′, sĕm′ī-) *adj.* Of or relating to an art form characterized by stylized but recognizable subject matter. — **sem′i·ab·strac′tion** *n.*

sem·i·an·nu·al (sĕm′ē-ăn′yo͞o-əl, sĕm′ī-) *adj.* Occurring or issued twice a year. — **sem′i·an′nu·al·ly** *adv.*

sem·i·a·quat·ic (sĕm′ē-ə-kwŏt′ĭk, -kwăt′-, sĕm′ī-) *adj.* Adapted for living or growing in or near water; not entirely aquatic.

sem·i·ar·id (sĕm′ē-ăr′ĭd) *adj.* Characterized by relatively low annual rainfall of 25 to 50 centimeters (10 to 20 inches) and having scrubby vegetation with short coarse grasses; not completely arid. — **sem′i·a·rid′i·ty** (-ə-rĭd′ĭ-tē, -ă-rĭd′-) *n.*

sem·i·au·to·mat·ic (sĕm′ē-ô′tə-măt′ĭk, sĕm′ī-) *adj.* **1.** Partially automatic. **2.** Ejecting a shell and loading the next round of ammunition automatically but requiring a trigger squeeze for each shot. Used of a firearm. — *n.* A semiautomatic firearm.

sem·i·au·ton·o·mous (sĕm′ē-ô-tŏn′ə-məs, sĕm′ī-) *adj.* **1.** Partially self-governing. **2.** Having the powers of self-government within a larger organization or structure. — **sem′i·au·ton′o·my** *n.*

sem·i·breve (sĕm′ē-brĕv′, -brēv′, sĕm′ī-) *n. Chiefly British.* A whole note in music.

sem·i·cen·ten·ni·al (sĕm′ē-sĕn-tĕn′ē-əl, sĕm′ī-) *adj.* Marking the 50th anniversary of an event. — *n.* A 50th anniversary or its celebration.

sem·i·cir·cle (sĕm′ĭ-sûr′kəl) *n.* **1.** A half of a circle as divided by a diameter. **2.** An object or arrangement of objects or people in the shape of half a circle. — **sem′i·cir′cu·lar** (-kyə-lər) *adj.*

semicircular canal *n.* Any of three tubular and looped structures of the inner ear, together functioning in maintenance of the sense of balance in the body.

sem·i·clas·si·cal (sĕm′ē-klăs′ĭ-kəl, sĕm′ī-) *adj. Mus.* Of, relating to, or being a work that in style or form falls between the classical and popular genres.

sem·i·co·lon (sĕm′ĭ-kō′lən) *n.* A mark of punctuation (;) used to connect independent clauses and indicating a closer relationship between the clauses than a period.

sem·i·co·ma (sĕm′ē-kō′mə, sĕm′ī-) *n.* A partial or mild comatose state; a coma from which a person may be roused by stimuli. — **sem′i·co′ma·tose′** (-kō′mə-tōs′, -kŏm′ə-) *adj.*

sem·i·con·duc·tor (sĕm′ē-kən-dŭk′tər, sĕm′ī-) *n.* Any of various solid crystalline substances, such as germanium or silicon, having electrical conductivity greater than insulators but less than good conductors. — **sem′i·con·duct′ing** *adj.*

sem·i·con·scious (sĕm′ē-kŏn′shəs, sĕm′ī-) *adj.* Partially conscious; not completely aware of sensations. — **sem′i·con′scious·ly** *adv.* — **sem′i·con′scious·ness** *n.*

sem·i·des·ert (sĕm′ē-dĕz′ərt, sĕm′ī-) *n.* A semiarid area often located between a desert and a grassland or woodland.

sem·i·de·tached (sĕm′ē-dĭ-tăcht′, sĕm′ī-) *adj.* Attached to something on one side only: *a semidetached house.*

sem·i·di·am·e·ter (sĕm′ē-dī-ăm′ĭ-tər, sĕm′ī-) *n.* A celestial body's apparent radius when viewed as a disk from Earth.

sem·i·di·ur·nal (sĕm′ē-dī-ûr′nəl, sĕm′ī-) *adj.* **1.** Of, relating to, occurring, or performed during half a day. **2.** Occurring or coming approximately once every 12 hours, as the tides.

sem·i·dome (sĕm′ē-dōm′, sĕm′ī-) *n.* A roof covering a semicircular space; half a dome.

sem·i·el·lip·ti·cal (sĕm′ē-ĭ-lĭp′tĭ-kəl, sĕm′ī-) *adj.* Having the form or shape of half of an ellipse, esp. when divided along the major axis.

sem·i·fi·nal (sĕm′ē-fī′nəl, sĕm′ī-) *n.* **1.** A match, a competition, or an examination that precedes the final one. **2.** One of the two competitions of the next to the last round in an elimination tournament. — **sem′i·fi′nal** *adj.* — **sem′i·fi′nal·ist** *n.*

sem·i·fin·ished (sĕm′ē-fĭn′ĭsht, sĕm′ī-) *adj.* **1.** Made, treated, or sold to be used in a finished product. **2.** Partially finished.

sem·i·flex·ion (sĕm′ē-flĕk′shən, sĕm′ī-) *n.* The position of a limb or muscle halfway between flexion and extension.

sem·i·flu·id (sĕm′ē-flo͞o′ĭd, sĕm′ī-) *adj.* Intermediate in flow properties between solids and liquids; viscous. — **sem′i·flu′id** *n.* — **sem′i·flu·id′i·ty** *n.*

sem·i·gloss (sĕm′ē-glŏs′, -glôs′, sĕm′ī-) *n.* A paint that dries with a finish that is between gloss and flat. — **sem′i·gloss′**, **sem′i·gloss′y** *adj.*

sem·i·gov·ern·men·tal (sĕm′ē-gŭv′ərn-mĕn′tl, sĕm′ī-) *adj.* Partially owned or managed by a government or government agency.

sem·i·group (sĕm′ē-gro͞op′, sĕm′ī-) *n. Math.* A set for which there is a binary operation that is closed and associative.

sem·i·in·de·pend·ent (sĕm′ē-ĭn′dĭ-pĕn′dənt, sĕm′ī-) *adj.* **1.** Partially independent. **2.** Semiautonomous.

sem·i·in·fi·nite (sĕm′ē-ĭn′fə-nĭt, sĕm′ī-) *adj. Math.* Unbounded in one direction or dimension.

sem·i·liq·uid (sĕm′ē-lĭk′wĭd, sĕm′ī-) *adj.* Semifluid. — **sem′i·liq′uid** *n.* — **sem′i·liq·uid′i·ty** *n.*

sem·i·lit·er·ate (sĕm′ē-lĭt′ər-ĭt, sĕm′ī-) *adj.* **1.** Having achieved an elementary level of ability in reading and writing. **2.** Having limited knowledge or understanding, esp. of a technical subject. — **sem′i·lit′er·a·cy** (-ər-ə-sē) *n.*

Sé·mil·lon also **Se·mil·lon** (sā′mē-yôɴ) *n.* A variety of late-ripening grapes, often blended with sauvignon blanc grapes to produce a dry white wine with a crisp taste. [Fr. < obsolete *sémilion* < dial. *semilhoun* < OProv. *semilhar*, to sow < *seme*, seed < Lat. *sēmen*. See SEMEN.]

sem·i·log·a·rith·mic (sĕm′ē-lô′gə-rĭth′mĭk, -lŏg′ə-, sĕm′ī-) *adj. Math.* Having one logarithmic and one arithmetic scale: *semilogarithmic graph paper.*

sem·i·lu·nar (sĕm′ē-lo͞o′nər, sĕm′ī-) also **sem·i·lu·nate** (-lo͞o′nāt′) *adj.* Shaped like a half-moon; crescent-shaped.

semilunar cartilage *n.* Either of the crescent-shaped wedges of fibrocartilage found in the knee joint.

semilunar valve *n.* Either of two valves, one at the opening of the aorta and the other at the opening of the pulmonary artery, each made up of three crescent-shaped cusps and serving to keep blood from flowing back into the ventricles.

sem·i·month·ly (sĕm′ē-mŭnth′lē, sĕm′ī-) *adj.* Occurring or issued twice a month. — *n., pl.* **-lies.** A semimonthly publication. — *adv.* At intervals twice monthly. See Usage Note at **bi–¹**.

sem·i·nal (sĕm′ə-nəl) *adj.* **1.** Of, relating to, containing, or conveying semen or seed. **2.** Of, relating to, or having the power to originate; creative. **3.** Highly influential in an original way; constituting or providing a basis for further development. [ME < OFr. < Lat. *sēminālis* < *sēmen*, *sēmin-*, seed. See SEMEN.] — **sem′i·nal·ly** *adv.*

seminal duct *n.* The duct of the testis that carries semen outward, esp. the part of the duct that runs from the epididymis to the ejaculatory duct.

seminal fluid *n.* Semen, esp. the fluid part of semen without the spermatozoa.

seminal vesicle *n.* Either of a pair of pouchlike glands on each side of the male urinary bladder that secrete seminal fluid.

sem·i·nar (sĕm′ə-när′) *n.* **1.a.** A small group of students in a college or graduate school engaged in original research or intensive study under the guidance of a professor. **b.** A course of study so pursued. **c.** A scheduled meeting of such a group. **2.** A meeting for an exchange of ideas; a conference. [Ger. < Lat. *sēminārium*, seed plot. See SEMINARY.]

sem·i·nar·i·an (sĕm′ə-nâr′ē-ən) also **sem·i·nar·ist** (-ĭst) *n.* A student at a seminary.

sem·i·nar·y (sĕm′ə-nĕr′ē) *n., pl.* **-ies. 1.a.** A school, esp. a theological school for the training of priests, ministers, or rabbis. **b.** A school of higher education, esp. a private school for girls. **2.** A place or environment in which something is developed or nurtured. [ME, seed plot < Lat. *sēminārium* < *sēminārius*, of seed < *sēmen*, *sēmin-*, seed. See **sē-***.]

sem·i·nif·er·ous (sĕm′ə-nĭf′ər-əs) *adj. Biol.* **1.** Conveying, containing, or producing semen. **2.** Bearing seed. [Lat. *sēmen*, *sēmin-*, seed, semen; see SEMEN + –FEROUS.]

sem·i·niv·o·rous (sĕm′ə-nĭv′ər-əs) *adj.* Feeding on seeds. [Lat. *sēmen*, *sēmin-*, seed; see SEMEN + –VOROUS.]

Sem·i·nole (sĕm′ə-nōl′) *n., pl.* **Seminole** or **-noles. 1.** A member of a Native American people made up of various esp. Creek groups who moved into Florida during the 18th and 19th centuries, with present-day populations in Oklahoma and Florida. **2.** Either of their Muskogean languages. [Alteration of *Seminolie* < Creek *simalóoni*, *simanóoli*, runaway < Am.Sp. *cimarrón*. See MAROON¹.]

Seminole bread *n.* See **coontie**.

sem·i·no·ma (sĕm′ə-nō′mə) *n., pl.* **-mas** or **-ma·ta** (-mə-tə). A malignant tumor of the testis arising from sperm-forming tissue. [Lat. *sēmen*, *sēmin-*, semen; see SEMEN + –OMA.]

sem·i·no·mad (sĕm′ē-nō′măd′, sĕm′ī-) *n.* One of a people whose living habits are largely nomadic but who plant some crops at a base point. — **sem′i·no·mad′ic** *adj.*

se·mi·ol·o·gy also **se·mei·ol·o·gy** (sē′mē-ŏl′ə-jē, sĕm′ē-, sē′mī-) *n.* **1.a.** The scientific study of signs or sign language. **b.** The use of signs in signaling, as with a semaphore. **2.** *Medic.* Symptomatology. [Gk. *sēmeion*, sign; see SEMIOTIC + –LOGY.]

se·mi·ot·ic (sē′mē-ŏt′ĭk, sĕm′ē-, sē′mī-) also **se·mi·ot·i·**

semidome

sem′i·at·tached′ *adj.*
sem′i·au′to·bi′o·graph′i·cal *adj.*
sem′i·au′to·mat′ed *adj.*
sem′i·civ′i·lized′ *adj.*
sem′i·con′scious *adj.*
sem′i·con′scious·ly *adv.*
sem′i·con′scious·ness *n.*
sem′i·dark′ness *n.*
sem′i·di·vine′ *adj.*
sem′i·dry′ *adj.*
sem′i·feu′dal *adj.*
sem′i·flex′i·ble *adj.*
sem′i·for′mal *adj.*
sem′i·hard′ *adj.*
sem′i·liq′uid *adj. & n.*
sem′i·li·quid′i·ty *n.*
sem′i·mem′bra·nous *adj.*
sem′i·mys′ti·cal *adj.*
sem′i·nude′ *adv. & adj.*
sem′i·nu′di·ty *n.*
sem′i·of·fi′cial *adj.*
sem′i·of·fi′cial·ly *adv.*
sem′i·o·paque′ *adj.*
sem′i·po·lit′i·cal *adj.*
sem′i·re·tired′ *adj.*
sem′i·re·tire′ment *n.*
sem′i·rig′id *adj.*
sem′i·ru′ral *adj.*
sem′i·ster′ile *adj.*
sem′i·trans·par′ent *adj.*

ă pat	oi boy
ā pay	ou out
âr care	o͝o took
ä father	o͞o boot
ĕ pet	ŭ cut
ē be	ûr urge
ĭ pit	th thin
ī pie	*th* this
îr pier	hw which
ŏ pot	zh vision
ō toe	ə about, item
ô paw	

Stress marks:
′ (primary);
′ (secondary), as in dictionary (dĭk′shə-nĕr′ē)

cal (-ĭ-kəl) or **se•mei•ot•ic** (sē′mē-, sĕm′ē-, sē′mī-) also **se•mei•ot•i•cal** (-ĭ-kəl) *adj.* **1.** Of or relating to semantics. **2.** *Medic.* Relating to symptomatology. [Gk. *sēmeiōtikos*, significant < *sēmeiōsis*, indication < *sēmeioun*, to signal, to interpret as a sign < *sēmeion*, sign < *sēma*.]

se•mi•ot•ics also **se•mei•ot•ics** (sē′mē-ŏt′ĭks, sĕm′ē-, sē′mī-) *n. (used with a sing. v.)* Semantics. — **se′mi•o•ti′cian** (-ə-tĭsh′ən) *n.*

sem•i•o•vip•a•rous (sĕm′ē-ō-vĭp′ər-əs, sĕm′ī-) *adj.* Bearing living young that are incompletely developed, as a marsupial.

Sem•i•pa•la•tinsk (sĕm′ē-pə-lä′tĭnsk, syĭ-myĭ-). A city of NE Kazakhstan on the Irtysh R. NNE of Alma-Ata; founded 1718. Pop. 317,000.

sem•i•pal•mate (sĕm′ē-păl′māt′, -pä′-, -päl′māt′, sĕm′ī-) also **sem•i•pal•mat•ed** (-mā′tĭd) *adj.* Having partial or reduced webbing between the toes, as some wading birds.

sem•i•par•a•site (sĕm′ē-păr′ə-sīt′, sĕm′ī-) *n.* See **hemiparasite** 1. — **sem′i•par′a•sit′ic** (-sĭt′ĭk) *adj.* — **sem′i•par′a•sit•ism** (-sĭ-tĭz′əm) *n.*

sem•i•per•me•a•ble (sĕm′ē-pûr′mē-ə-bəl, sĕm′ī-) *adj.* **1.** Partially permeable. **2.** Allowing passage of certain, esp. small molecules or ions but barring others. Used of biological and synthetic membranes. — **sem′i•per′me•a•bil′i•ty** *n.*

sem•i•por•ce•lain (sĕm′ē-pôr′sə-lĭn, -pōr′-, sĕm′ī-) *n.* Any of several glazed ceramics resembling porcelain but opaque.

sem•i•pre•cious stone (sĕm′ē-prĕsh′əs, sĕm′ī-) *n.* A gem, such as an opal, that has commercial value but is not as rare or expensive as a precious stone.

sem•i•pri•vate (sĕm′ē-prī′vĭt, sĕm′ī-) *adj.* Shared with usu. one to three other hospital patients: *a semiprivate room.*

sem•i•pro (sĕm′ē-prō′, sĕm′ī-) *adj. Informal.* Semiprofessional: *a semipro baseball player.* — **sem′i•pro′** *n.*

sem•i•pro•fes•sion•al (sĕm′ē-prə-fĕsh′ə-nəl, sĕm′ī-) *adj. Sports.* **1.** Taking part in a sport for pay but not on a full-time basis. **2.** Composed of or engaged in by semiprofessional players. —*n.* **1.** *Sports.* A semiprofessional player. **2.** One whose occupation or work has some of the characteristics of a profession or of a professional.

sem•i•pub•lic (sĕm′ē-pŭb′lĭk, sĕm′ī-) *adj.* **1.** Partially but not entirely open to the use of the public. **2.** Partially but not totally owned by the public. **3.** Open to the knowledge and judgment of only a part of the public.

sem•i•qua•ver (sĕm′ē-kwā′vər) *n. Chiefly British & Mus.* A sixteenth note.

sem•i•round (sĕm′ē-round′, sĕm′ī-) *adj.* Having a round side and a flat side. —*n.* (sĕm′ē-round′, sĕm′ī-). Something that has a round side and a flat side.

sem•i•skilled (sĕm′ē-skĭld′, sĕm′ī-) *adj.* **1.** Possessing some skills but not enough to do specialized work. **2.** Requiring limited skills: *a semiskilled job.*

sem•i•soft (sĕm′ē-sôft′, -sŏft′, sĕm′ī-) *adj.* **1.** Of medium softness. **2.** Firm but easily sliced: *semisoft cheese.*

sem•i•sol•id (sĕm′ē-sŏl′ĭd, sĕm′ī-) *adj.* Intermediate in properties, esp. in rigidity, between solids and liquids. —*n.* (sĕm′ē-sŏl′ĭd, sĕm′ī-). A semisolid substance, as a stiff dough.

sem•i•staged (sĕm′ē-stājd′, sĕm′ī-) *adj.* Performed without all the usual stage effects, costumes, or participants.

sem•i•sub•mers•i•ble (sĕm′ē-səb-mûr′sə-bəl, sĕm′ī-) *n.* A seagoing self-propelled barge that rides at anchor, stands on partially submerged vertical legs, and serves as a base of operations in offshore drilling. — **sem′i•sub•mer′si•ble** *adj.*

sem•i•sweet (sĕm′ē-swēt′, sĕm′ī-) *adj.* Having a small amount of sweetening: *semisweet chocolate.*

sem•i•syn•thet•ic (sĕm′ē-sĭn-thĕt′ĭk, sĕm′ī-) *adj.* **1.** Prepared by chemical synthesis from natural materials. **2.** Consisting of a mixture of natural and synthetic substances.

Sem•ite (sĕm′īt′) *n.* **1.** A member of a group of Semitic-speaking peoples of the Near East and northern Africa, including the Arabs, Ethiopians, Hebrews, and Phoenicians. **2.** A Jew. **3.** *Bible.* A descendant of Shem.

sem•i•ter•res•tri•al (sĕm′ē-tə-rĕs′trē-əl, sĕm′ī-) *adj.* Not growing or living entirely on land; partly terrestrial.

Se•mit•ic (sə-mĭt′ĭk) *adj.* **1.** Of or relating to the Semites or their languages or cultures. **2.** Of, relating to, or being a subgroup of the Afro-Asiatic language group that includes Arabic, Hebrew, Amharic, and Aramaic. —*n.* **1.** The Semitic languages. **2.** Any one of the Semitic languages. [NLat. *Sēmiticus* < *Sēmita*, Semite < LLat. *Sēm*, Shem, eponymous ancestor of the Semites < Gk. < Heb. *Šēm*.]

Se•mit•ics (sə-mĭt′ĭks) *n. (used with a sing. v.)* The study of the history, languages, and cultures of the Semitic peoples. — **Se•mit′i•cist** (-ĭ-sĭst) *n.*

Sem•i•tism (sĕm′ĭ-tĭz′əm) *n.* **1.** A Semitic word or idiom. **2.** Semitic traits, attributes, or customs. **3.** A policy or predisposition in favor of Jews.

sem•i•tone (sĕm′ē-tōn′, sĕm′ī-) *n. Mus.* An interval equal to a half tone in the standard diatonic scale. — **sem′i•ton′ic** (-tŏn′ĭk) *adj.* — **sem′i•ton′i•cal•ly** *adv.*

sem•i•trail•er (sĕm′ē-trā′lər, sĕm′ī-) *n.* A trailer having one or more sets of wheels at the rear only, with the forward portion supported by the truck tractor or towing vehicle.

sem•i•trop•i•cal (sĕm′ē-trŏp′ĭ-kəl, sĕm′ī-) *adj.* Partly tropical; subtropical.

sem•i•vow•el (sĕm′ĭ-vou′əl) *n. Ling.* A sound with a high vowel quality, as (ē) or (o͞o), functioning as a consonant before vowels, as the initial sounds of *yell* and *well.*

sem•i•week•ly (sĕm′ē-wēk′lē, sĕm′ī-) *adj.* Issued or occurring twice a week. —*n., pl.* **-lies.** A semiweekly event or publication. —*adv.* Twice weekly. See Usage Note at **bi-**[1].

sem•i•year•ly (sĕm′ē-yîr′lē, sĕm′ī-) *adj.* Issued or occurring twice a year or once every half year. —*n., pl.* **-lies.** A semiyearly event or publication. —*adv.* Every half year.

sem•o•li•na (sĕm′ə-lē′nə) *n.* The coarse particles of wheat left after the finer flour has passed through a bolting machine, used for pasta. [Alteration of Ital. *semolino*, dim. of *semola*, bran < Lat. *simila*, fine flour, prob. of Semitic orig.]

sem•pi•ter•nal (sĕm′pĭ-tûr′nəl) *adj.* Enduring forever; eternal. See Syns at **infinite.** [Ult. < LLat. *sempiternālis* < Lat. *sempiternus* : *semper*, always; see **sem-**[1]* + *aeternus*, eternal; see **aiw-***.] — **sem′pi•ter′ni•ty** (-nĭ-tē) *n.*

sem•pli•ce (sĕm′plĭ-chā′) *adv. & adj. Mus.* In a simple or plain manner. [Ital. < Lat. *simplex*, *simplic-*, simple. See **sem-**[1]*.]

sem•pre (sĕm′prā) *adv. Mus.* In the same manner throughout. [Ital., always < Lat. *semper*. See **sem-**[1]*.]

sen[1] (sĕn) *n., pl.* **sen.** See table at **currency.** [J. < Chin. (Mandarin) *qián*, money, coin.]

sen[2] (sĕn) *n., pl.* **sen.** See table at **currency.** [Indonesian *senti*, *sen*, ult. < CENT.]

sen. or **Sen.** *abbr.* **1.** Senate; senator. **2.** Senior.

se•nar•i•us (sə-nâr′ē-əs) *n., pl.* **-i•i** (-ē-ī′, -ē-ē′). A Latin verse of six iambic feet. [Lat. *sēnārius*. See SENARY.]

sen•a•ry (sĕn′ə-rē) *adj.* **1.** Of or relating to the number six. **2.** Having six things or parts. [Lat. *sēnārius* < *sēnī*, six each < *sex*, six. See **s(w)eks***.]

sen•ate (sĕn′ĭt) *n.* **1.** An assembly or a council of citizens having the highest deliberative and legislative functions in a government, esp.: **a. Senate.** The upper house of the U.S. Congress, to which two members are elected from each state. **b.** Often **Senate.** The upper house in the bicameral legislature of many states in the United States. **c. Senate.** The upper legislative house in Canada, France, and some other countries. **d.** The supreme council of state of the ancient Roman Republic and later of the Roman Empire. **2.** The building or hall in which a senate meets. **3.** A governing, advisory, or disciplinary body of some colleges and universities. [ME *senat* < OFr. < Lat. *senātus* < *senex*, *sen-*, old, an elder. See **sen-***.]

sen•a•tor (sĕn′ə-tər) *n.* A member of a senate. — **sen′a•tor•ship′** *n.*

sen•a•to•ri•al (sĕn′ə-tôr′ē-əl, -tōr′-) *adj.* **1.** Of, concerning, or befitting a senator or senate. **2.** Composed of senators. — **sen′a•to′ri•al•ly** *adv.*

senatorial courtesy *n.* The custom in the U.S. Senate of refusing to confirm a presidential appointment to office opposed by both senators from the state of the appointee or by the senior senator of the President's party.

senatorial district *n.* A territorial district from which a senator is elected.

send[1] (sĕnd) *v.* **sent** (sĕnt), **send•ing, sends.** —*tr.* **1.** To cause to be conveyed by an intermediary to a destination. **2.** To dispatch, as by a communications medium. **3.a.** To direct to go on a mission. **b.** To require or enable to go: *sent her children to college.* **c.** To direct (a person) to a source of information; refer. **4.a.** To give off (heat, for example); emit or issue. **b.** To utter or otherwise emit (sound). **5.** To hit so as to direct or propel with force; drive. **6.** To cause to take place or occur: *whatever fate may send.* **7.a.** To put or drive into a given state or condition: *news that sent them into a panic.* **b.** *Slang.* To transport with delight; carry away. —*intr.* **1.** To dispatch someone to do an errand or convey a message: *sent out for pizza.* **2.** To dispatch a request or an order, esp. by mail. **3.** To transmit a message or messages. —***phrasal verbs.*** **send down.** *Chiefly British.* To suspend or dismiss from a university. **send for.** To request to come by means of a message or messenger; summon. **send in. 1.** To cause to arrive or to be delivered to the recipient. **2.** *Sports.* To put (a player) into or back into a game or contest. **3.** To cause (someone) to arrive in or become involved in a particular place or situation: *It's time to send in the lawyers.* **send up.** *Informal.* **1.** To send to jail. **2.** To make a parody of. —***idioms.*** **send flying.** *Informal.* To cause to be knocked or scattered about with force. **send packing.** To dismiss (someone) abruptly. [ME *senden* < OE *sendan*. See **sent-***.] — **send′er** *n.*

send[2] (sĕnd) *v. & n. Naut.* Var. of **scend.**

Sen•dai (sĕn-dī′). A city of NE Honshu, Japan, on an inlet of the Pacific N of Tokyo. Pop. 700,248.

sen•dal (sĕn′dl) *n.* A thin light silk used in the Middle Ages for fine garments, church vestments, and banners. [ME *cendal* < OFr., ult. < Gk. *sindōn*, fine linen.]

send•off (sĕnd′ôf′, -ŏf′) *n.* **1.** A demonstration of affection and good wishes for a new undertaking. **2.** A farewell.

send-up or **send•up** (sĕnd′ŭp′) *n. Informal.* An amusing imitation or parody; a takeoff.

se•ne (sä′nä) *n., pl.* **sene.** See table at **currency.** [Samoan < E. CENT.]

Sen•e•ca (sĕn′ĭ-kə) *n., pl.* **Seneca** or **-cas. 1.** A member of a Native American people formerly inhabiting western New York, with present-day populations in this same area and in southeast Ontario. **2.** The Iroquoian language of the Seneca. [< Du. *Sennecaas*, prob. of Mahican orig.]

Seneca, Lucius Annaeus. "the Younger." 4 B.C.?–A.D. 65. Roman Stoic philosopher and writer whose works include treatises on rhetoric and governance and numerous plays.

Seneca Falls. A village of W-central NY on the Seneca R. ESE of Rochester; site of the first women's rights convention (1848). Pop. 7,370.

Seneca Lake. A lake of W-central NY connected with Cayuga Lake by the **Seneca River,** c. 105 km (65 mi).

Seneca snakeroot *n.* An eastern North American plant *(Polygala senega)* with a terminal small white flower cluster.

se•nec•ti•tude (sĭ-nĕk′tĭ-to͞od′, -tyo͞od′) *n.* Old age; elderliness. [Med.Lat. *senectitūdō* < Lat. *senectūs* < *senex, sen-*, old, an elder. See **sen-*.**]

sen•e•ga (sĕn′ĭ-gə) *n.* The dried roots of the Seneca snakeroot, used as an expectorant. [Alteration of SENECA.]

Sen•e•gal (sĕn′ĭ-gôl′, -gäl′). A country of W Africa on the Atlantic Ocean; achieved independence from France in 1960. Cap. Dakar. Pop. 6,038,000. **—Sen′e•ga•lese′** (-gô-lēz′, -lēs′, -gə-) *adj. & n.*

Senegal River. A river of W Africa rising in W Mali and flowing c. 1,609 km (1,000 mi) to the Atlantic Ocean.

Sen•e•gam•bi•a (sĕn′ĭ-găm′bē-ə). A region of W Africa watered by the Senegal and Gambia rivers.

se•nes•cent (sĭ-nĕs′ənt) *adj.* Growing old; aging. [Lat. *senēscēns, senēscent-*, pr.part. of *senēscere*, to grow old, inchoative of *senēre*, to be old < *senex, sen-*, old. See **sen-*.**] **—se•nes′cence** *n.*

sen•e•schal (sĕn′ə-shəl) *n.* An official in a medieval noble household in charge of domestic arrangements and servants; a steward or major-domo. [ME < OFr., of Gmc. orig.]

se•nile (sē′nīl′, sĕn′īl′) *adj.* **1.** Relating to, characteristic of, or resulting from old age. **2.** Exhibiting the symptoms of senility. **3.** *Geol.* Eroded nearly to the base level. [Lat. *senīlis* < *senex, sen-*, old. See **sen-*.**] **—se′nile′ly** *adv.*

senile dementia *n.* A progressive, abnormally accelerated deterioration of mental faculties and emotional stability in old age, occurring esp. in Alzheimer's disease.

se•nil•i•ty (sĭ-nĭl′ĭ-tē) *n.* **1.** The state of being senile. **2.** The mental and physical deterioration characteristic of old age.

sen•ior (sēn′yər) *adj.* **1.** Of, relating to, or being the older of two, esp. the older of two persons having the same name, as father and son. **2.a.** Being in a position, rank, or grade above others of the same set or class: *a senior officer.* **b.** Having precedence in making certain decisions. **3.** Of or relating to the fourth and last year of high school or college. —*n.* **1.a.** A person who is older than another. **b.** A senior citizen. **2.a.** One that is senior, as in rank, to another. **b.** A student in the fourth year of high school or college. [ME < Lat., comp. of *senex*, old. See **sen-*.**]

senior chief petty officer *n.* A noncommissioned officer in the U.S. Navy ranking above chief petty officer and below master chief petty officer.

senior citizen *n.* A person of or over retirement age. **—sen′ior-cit′i•zen** (sēn′yər-sĭt′ĭ-zən) *adj.* **—senior citizenry** *n.*

senior high school *n.* A high school usu. constituting grades 10, 11, and 12.

sen•ior•i•ty (sēn-yôr′ĭ-tē, -yŏr′-) *n.* **1.** The state of being older or higher in rank than others. **2.** Precedence of position, esp. over others of the same rank because of longer service.

senior lecturer *n. Chiefly British.* A university teacher, esp. one ranking next below a reader.

senior master sergeant *n.* A noncommissioned officer in the U.S. Air Force ranking above master sergeant and below chief master sergeant.

sen•i•ti (sĕn′ĭ-tē) *n., pl.* **seniti.** See table at **currency.** [Tongan < E. CENT.]

Sen•lac (sĕn′lăk′). A hill in S England near Hastings; site of the Battle of Hastings (1066), in which William the Conqueror defeated Harold II.

sen•na (sĕn′ə) *n.* **1.** Any of various plants of the genus *Cassia*, having pinnately compound leaves and showy, usu. yellow flowers. **2.** The dried leaves of *C. angustifolia* or *C. acutifolia*, used medicinally as a cathartic. [NLat. < Ar. *sanā'*.]

Sen•nach•er•ib (sĭ-năk′ər-ĭb). d. 681 B.C. King of Assyria (704–681) who subjugated Babylon and rebuilt Nineveh.

sen•net[1] (sĕn′ĭt) *n.* A call on a trumpet or cornet signaling the ceremonial exits and entrances of actors in Elizabethan drama. [Perh. var. of SIGNET.]

sen•net[2] (sĕn′ĭt) *n.* Any of several barracudas, esp. *Sphyraena borealis*, of the western Atlantic. [?]

Sen•nett (sĕn′ĭt), **Mack.** 1880?–1960. Canadian-born Amer. filmmaker known for his slapstick motion pictures.

sen•night (sĕn′īt′) *n. Archaic.* A week. [ME *senight*, contraction of *seveniht* < OE *seofon nihta*, seven nights.]

sen•nit (sĕn′ĭt) *n.* **1.** *Naut.* Braided cordage formed by plaiting strands of rope fiber or similar material. **2.** Plaited straw, grass, or palm leaves for making hats. [?]

se•no•pi•a (sĭ-nō′pē-ə) *n.* Improvement of near vision sometimes in the aged because of swelling of the lens due to incipient cataract. [Lat. *senex, sen-*, old; see **sen-*** + -OPIA.]

se•ñor (sān-yôr′, sĕ-nyôr′) *n., pl.* **se•ño•res** (sān-yôr′ās, sĕ-nyô′rĕs). **1.a.** Used as a courtesy title before the surname, full name, or professional title of a man in a Spanish-speaking area. **b.** Used as a form of polite address for a man in a Spanish-speaking area. **2.** A Spanish or Spanish-speaking man. [Sp. < OSp. *sennor* < VLat. **senior*, lord < Lat., senior. See SENIOR.]

se•ño•ra (sān-yôr′ə, sĕ-nyô′rä) *n.* **1.a.** Used as a courtesy title before the surname or full name of a married woman in a Spanish-speaking area. **b.** Used as a form of polite address for a woman in a Spanish-speaking area. **2.** A Spanish or Spanish-speaking woman. [Sp., fem. of *señor*, señor. See SEÑOR.]

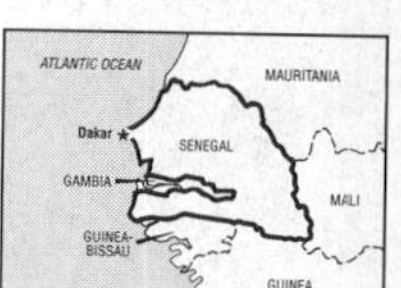

Senegal

se•ño•ri•ta (sān′yə-rē′tə, sĕ′nyô-rē′tä) *n.* **1.a.** Used as a courtesy title before the surname or full name of a girl or an unmarried woman in a Spanish-speaking area. **b.** Used as a form of address for a girl or young woman in a Spanish-speaking area. **2.** A Spanish or Spanish-speaking unmarried woman or girl. [Sp., dim. of *señora*, señora. See SEÑORA.]

sen•sate (sĕn′sāt′) also **sen•sat•ed** (-sā′tĭd) *adj.* **1.** Perceived by a sense or the senses. **2.** Having physical sensation. [ME *sensat* < LLat. *sēnsātus*, gifted with sense < Lat. *sēnsus*, sense. See SENSE.] **—sen′sate′ly** *adv.*

sen•sa•tion (sĕn-sā′shən) *n.* **1.a.** A perception associated with stimulation of a sense organ or with a specific body condition. **b.** The faculty to feel or perceive; physical sensibility. **c.** An indefinite, generalized body feeling. **2.** A state of heightened interest or emotion. **3.a.** A state of intense public interest and excitement. **b.** A cause of such interest and excitement. See Syns at **wonder.** [Fr. < OFr. < Med.Lat. *sēnsātiō, sēnsātiōn-* < LLat. *sēnsātus*, gifted with sense. See SENSATE.]

sen•sa•tion•al (sĕn-sā′shə-nəl) *adj.* **1.** Of or relating to sensation. **2.** Arousing or intended to arouse strong curiosity, interest, or reaction, esp. by exaggerated or lurid details. **3.** Outstanding; spectacular. **—sen•sa′tion•al•ly** *adv.*

sen•sa•tion•al•ism (sĕn-sā′shə-nə-lĭz′əm) *n.* **1.a.** The use of sensational matter or methods, esp. in writing, journalism, or politics. **b.** Sensational subject matter. **c.** Interest in or the effect of such subject matter. **2.** *Philos.* The theory that sensation is the only source of knowledge. **3.** The ethical doctrine that feeling is the only criterion of good. **—sen•sa′tion•al•ist** *n.* **—sen•sa′tion•al•is′tic** *adj.*

sennit

sen•sa•tion•al•ize (sĕn-sā′shə-nə-līz′) *tr.v.* **-ized, -iz•ing, -iz•es.** To cast and present in a sensational manner. **—sen•sa′tion•al•i•za′tion** (-shə-nə-lĭ-zā′shən) *n.*

sense (sĕns) *n.* **1.a.** Any of the faculties by which stimuli are received and felt, as the faculties of hearing, sight, and equilibrium. **b.** A perception or feeling produced by a stimulus; sensation. **2. senses.** The faculties of sensation as means of providing physical gratification and pleasure. **3.** Intuitive or acquired perception or ability to estimate: *a sense of timing.* **a.** A capacity to appreciate or understand: *a sense of humor.* **b.** A vague feeling or presentiment. **c.** Recognition or perception either through the senses or through the intellect; consciousness: *has no sense of shame.* **4.a.** Normal ability to think or reason soundly; correct judgment. Often used in the plural: *Come to your senses.* **b.** Something sound or reasonable. **5.a.** A meaning that is conveyed, as in speech or writing; signification. **b.** One of the meanings of a word or phrase. See Syns at **meaning. 6.a.** Judgment; consensus. **b.** Intellectual interpretation, as of the significance of an event or the conclusions reached by a group. —*tr.v.* **sensed, sens•ing, sens•es. 1.** To become aware of; perceive. **2.** To grasp; understand. **3.** To detect automatically: *sense radioactivity.* [ME, meaning < OFr. *sens* < Lat. *sēnsus*, the faculty of perceiving < p.part. of *sentīre*, to feel. See **sent-*.**]

sense datum *n.* A basic, unanalyzable sensation experienced upon stimulation of a sense organ or receptor.

sense•less (sĕns′lĭs) *adj.* **1.** Lacking sense or meaning; meaningless. **2.** Deficient in sense; foolish or stupid. **3.** Insensate; unconscious. **—sense′less•ly** *adv.* **—sense′less•ness** *n.*

sense organ *n.* A specialized organ or structure, such as the eye, ear, tongue, nose, or skin, that functions as a receptor.

sense perception *n.* Perception by or based on stimulation of the senses.

sen•si•bil•i•ty (sĕn′sə-bĭl′ĭ-tē) *n., pl.* **-ties. 1.** The ability to feel or perceive. **2.a.** Keen intellectual perception. **b.** Mental or emotional responsiveness toward something, such as the feelings of another. **3.** Receptiveness to impression, whether pleasant or unpleasant; acuteness of feeling. Often used in the plural. **4.** Refined awareness and appreciation in matters of feeling. **5.** The quality of being affected by changes in the environment.

sen•si•ble (sĕn′sə-bəl) *adj.* **1.** Perceptible by the senses or by the mind. **2.** Readily perceived; appreciable. **3.** Having the faculty of sensation; able to feel or perceive. **4.** Having a perception of something; cognizant. See Syns at **aware. 5.** Acting with or exhibiting good sense: *a sensible person.*

ă pat	oi boy
ā pay	ou out
âr care	o͝o took
ä father	o͞o boot
ĕ pet	ŭ cut
ē be	ûr urge
ĭ pit	th thin
ī pie	*th* this
îr pier	hw which
ŏ pot	zh vision
ō toe	ə about, item
ô paw	

Stress marks:
′ (primary);
′ (secondary), as in dictionary (dĭk′shə-nĕr′ē)

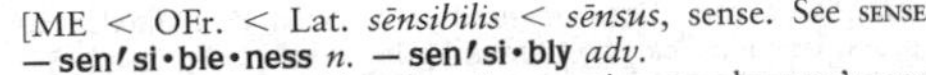
[ME < OFr. < Lat. *sēnsibilis* < *sēnsus*, sense. See SENSE.] —**sen′si·ble·ness** *n.* —**sen′si·bly** *adv.*

sensible horizon *n.* The plane intersecting an observer's position perpendicular to the line formed by the observer's nadir and zenith.

sen·sil·lum (sĕn-sĭl′əm) *n.*, *pl.* **-sil·la** (-sĭl′ə). A simple sensory receptor consisting of one cell or a few cells, esp. an epithelial cell projecting through the cuticle of arthropods. [NLat. *sēnsillum*, dim. of Lat. *sēnsus*, sense. See SENSE.]

sen·si·tive (sĕn′sĭ-tĭv) *adj.* **1.** Capable of perceiving with a sense or senses. **2.** Responsive to external conditions or stimulation. **3.** Susceptible to the attitudes, feelings, or circumstances of others. **4.** Quick to take offense; touchy. **5.** Easily irritated: *sensitive skin.* **6.** Readily altered by the action of an agent: *film that is sensitive to light.* **7.** Registering very slight differences or changes. Used of an instrument. **8.** Fluctuating or tending to fluctuate, as in price. **9.** Of or relating to classified information. —*n.* **1.** A sensitive person. **2.** One held to be endowed with psychic or occult powers. [ME < OFr. *sensitif* < Med.Lat. *sēnsitīvus* < Lat. *sēnsus*, sense. See SENSE.] —**sen′si·tive·ly** *adv.* —**sen′si·tive·ness** *n.*

sentry box
At Saint James's Palace, London

sensitive plant *n.* **1.** A shrubby tropical American plant *(Mimosa pudica)* having leaflets and leafstalks that fold and droop when touched. **2.** Any of various similar plants, such as *Cassia nictitans* of eastern and central North America.

sen·si·tiv·i·ty (sĕn′sĭ-tĭv′ĭ-tē) *n.*, *pl.* **-ties. 1.** The quality or condition of being sensitive. **2.** The capacity of an organ or organism to respond to stimulation. **3.** *Electron.* The degree of response of a receiver or an instrument to an incoming signal or a change in the incoming signal. **4.** The degree of response of a plate or film to light, esp. to light of a specified wavelength.

sen·si·tize (sĕn′sĭ-tīz′) *v.* **-tized, -tiz·ing, -tiz·es.** —*tr.* **1.** To make sensitive. **2.** To make (a film or plate) sensitive to light, esp. to light of a specific wavelength. **3.** To make hypersensitive or reactive to an antigen, such as pollen, esp. by repeated exposure. —*intr.* To become sensitive or hypersensitive. —**sen′si·ti·za′tion** (-tĭ-zā′shən) *n.* —**sen′si·tiz′er** *n.*

sen·si·tom·e·ter (sĕn′sĭ-tŏm′ĭ-tər) *n.* Any of various devices for measuring light sensitivity, as of photographic film. [SENSIT(IVITY) + -METER.] —**sen′si·to·met′ric** (-tə-mĕt′rĭk) *adj.* —**sen′si·tom′e·try** *n.*

sen·sor (sĕn′sər, -sôr′) *n.* **1.** A device that receives and responds to a signal or stimulus. **2.** See **sense organ.**

sen·so·ri·al (sĕn-sôr′ē-əl, -sōr′-) *adj.* Of or relating to sensations or sensory impressions. —**sen·so′ri·al·ly** *adv.*

sen·so·ri·mo·tor (sĕn′sə-rē-mō′tər) *adj.* Of, relating to, or combining the functions of the sensory and motor activities.

sen·so·ri·neu·ral (sĕn′sə-rē-nŏŏr′əl, -nyŏŏr′-) *adj.* Of, relating to, or involving the sensory nerves, esp. as they affect the hearing: *sensorineural deafness.*

sen·so·ri·um (sĕn-sôr′ē-əm, -sōr′-) *n.*, *pl.* **-so·ri·ums** or **-so·ri·a** (-sôr′ē-ə, -sōr′-). **1.** The part of the brain that receives and coordinates all the stimuli conveyed to various sensory centers. **2.** The entire sensory system of the body. [LLat. *sēnsōrium*, organ of sensation < Lat. *sēnsus*, sense. See SENSE.]

sen·so·ry (sĕn′sə-rē) *adj.* **1.** Of or relating to the senses or sensation. **2.** Transmitting impulses from sense organs to nerve centers; afferent.

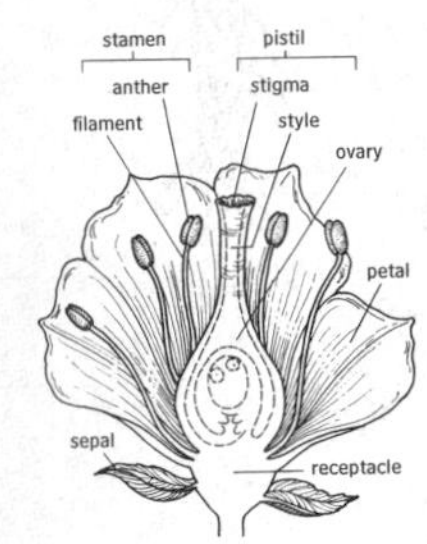

sepal

sensory deprivation *n.* Deprivation of sensory stimulation, as by prolonged isolation inside a sealed unlighted chamber, in order to observe physical and esp. psychological reactions.

sen·su·al (sĕn′shōō-əl) *adj.* **1.** Relating to or affecting any of the senses or a sense organ; sensory. **2.a.** Of, relating to, given to, or providing gratification of the physical and esp. the sexual appetites. **b.** Suggesting sexuality; voluptuous. **c.** Physical rather than spiritual or intellectual. **d.** Lacking in moral or spiritual interests; worldly. —**sen′su·al·ly** *adv.* —**sen′su·al·ness** *n.*

sen·su·al·ism (sĕn′shōō-ə-lĭz′əm) *n.* **1.** Sensuality. **2.** The ethical doctrine that the pleasures of the senses are the highest good. **3.** *Philos.* Sensationalism. —**sen′su·al·ist** *n.* —**sen′su·al·is′tic** *adj.*

sen·su·al·i·ty (sĕn′shōō-ăl′ĭ-tē) *n.* **1.** The quality or state of being sensual or lascivious. **2.** Excessive devotion to sensual pleasures.

sen·su·al·ize (sĕn′shōō-ə-līz′) *tr.v.* **-ized, -iz·ing, -iz·es.** To make sensual. —**sen′su·al·i·za′tion** (-ə-lĭ-zā′shən) *n.*

sen·su·ous (sĕn′shōō-əs) *adj.* **1.** Of, relating to, or derived from the senses. **2.** Appealing to or gratifying the senses. **3.a.** Readily affected through the senses. **b.** Highly appreciative of the pleasures of sensation. —**sen′su·os′i·ty** (-ŏs′ĭ-tē), **sen′su·ous·ness** (-əs-nĭs) *n.* —**sen′su·ous·ly** *adv.*

sent (sĕnt) *v.* P.t. and p.part. of **send**[1].

sen·te (sĕn′tä) *n.*, *pl.* **li·sen·te** (lē-sĕn′tä). See table at **currency.** [Sotho (Sesotho) < E. CENT.]

sen·tence (sĕn′təns) *n.* **1.** A grammatical unit that is syntactically independent and has a subject that is expressed or understood and a predicate that contains a finite verb. **2.** *Law.* **a.** A court judgment, esp. a judicial decision of the punishment to be inflicted on one adjudged guilty. **b.** The penalty meted out. **3.** *Archaic.* A maxim. **4.** *Obsolete.* An opinion, esp. one given formally after deliberation. —*tr.v.* **-tenced, -tenc·ing, -tenc·es.** *Law.* To pronounce sentence upon (one adjudged guilty). [ME, opinion < OFr. < Lat. *sententia* < *sentiēns, sentient-*, pr.part. of *sentīre*, to feel. See **sent-*.**] —**sen·ten′tial** (sĕn-tĕn′shəl) *adj.* —**sen·ten′tial·ly** *adv.*

sen·tenc·er (sĕn′tən-sər) *n.* *Law.* One, such as a court or judge, that pronounces sentence.

sentence stress *n.* *Ling.* The variation in emphasis or vocal stress on the syllables of words within a sentence.

sen·tenc·ing (sĕn′tən-sĭng) *Law.* —*adj.* **1.** Relating to a judicial sentence. **2.** Being or relating to the one who pronounces a judicial sentence. —*n.* **1.** The act of pronouncing a judicial sentence on a defendant. **2.** This sentence.

sen·ten·tia (sĕn-tĕn′shə, -shē-ə) *n.*, *pl.* **-ti·ae** (-shē-ē′). An adage or aphorism. [Lat. See SENTENCE.]

sen·ten·tious (sĕn-tĕn′shəs) *adj.* **1.** Terse and energetic in expression; pithy. **2.a.** Abounding in aphorisms. **b.** Given to aphoristic utterances. **3.a.** Abounding in pompous moralizing. **b.** Given to pompous moralizing. [ME < OFr. *sententieux* < Lat. *sententiōsus*, full of meaning < *sententia*, opinion. See SENTENCE.] —**sen·ten′tious·ly** *adv.* —**sen·ten′tious·ness** *n.*

sen·tience (sĕn′shəns, -shē-əns) *n.* **1.** The quality or state of being sentient; consciousness. **2.** Feeling as distinguished from perception or thought.

sen·tient (sĕn′shənt, -shē-ənt) *adj.* **1.** Having sense perception; conscious. **2.** Experiencing sensation or feeling. [Lat. *sentiēns, sentient-*, pr.part. of *sentīre*, to feel. See **sent-*.**] —**sen′tient·ly** *adv.*

sen·ti·ment (sĕn′tə-mənt) *n.* **1.a.** A cast of mind; general mental disposition: *anti-American sentiment.* **b.** An opinion about a specific matter; a view. **2.** A thought, a view, or an attitude based on feeling or emotion instead of reason. **3.** The emotional import of a passage. **4.a.** Susceptibility to tender, romantic, or nostalgic feeling. **b.** An expression of such susceptibility. **5.a.** Emotion that borders on mawkishness. **b.** Romantic nostalgic feeling verging on sentimentality. **6.** The expression of delicate and sensitive feeling, esp. in art and literature. See Syns at **feeling. 7.** A vague feeling or awareness; sensation. [ME *sentement* < OFr. < Med.Lat. *sentīmentum* < Lat. *sentīre*, to feel. See **sent-*.**]

sen·ti·men·tal (sĕn′tə-mĕn′tl) *adj.* **1.a.** Characterized or swayed by sentiment. **b.** Affectedly or extravagantly emotional. **2.** Resulting from or colored by emotion rather than reason or realism. **3.** Appealing to the sentiments, esp. to romantic feelings: *sentimental music.* —**sen′ti·men′tal·ly** *adv.*

sen·ti·men·tal·ism (sĕn′tə-mĕn′tl-ĭz′əm) *n.* **1.** A predilection for the sentimental. **2.** An idea or expression marked by excessive sentiment. —**sen′ti·men′tal·ist** *n.*

sen·ti·men·tal·i·ty (sĕn′tə-mĕn-tăl′ĭ-tē) *n.*, *pl.* **-ties. 1.** The quality or condition of being excessively or affectedly sentimental. **2.** A sentimental idea or an expression of it.

sen·ti·men·tal·ize (sĕn′tə-mĕn′tl-īz′) *v.* **-ized, -iz·ing, -iz·es.** —*tr.* To imbue or regard with sentiment; be sentimental about. —*intr.* To behave in a sentimental manner. —**sen′ti·men′tal·i·za′tion** (-mĕn′tl-ĭ-zā′shən) *n.*

sen·ti·nel (sĕn′tə-nəl) *n.* One that keeps guard; a sentry. —*tr.v.* **-neled, -nel·ing, -nels** or **-nelled, -nel·ling, -nels. 1.** To watch over as a guard. **2.** To provide with a guard. **3.** To post as a guard. [Fr. *sentinelle* < Ital. *sentinella*, prob. < OItal. *sentina*, vigilance < *sentire*, to watch < Lat. *sentīre*, to feel. See **sent-*.**]

sen·try (sĕn′trē) *n.*, *pl.* **-tries. 1.** A guard, esp. a soldier posted at a given spot to prevent the passage of unauthorized persons. **2.** The duty of a sentry; watch. [Perh. alteration of obsolete *sentrinel*, var. of SENTINEL.]

sentry box *n.* A small shelter for a posted sentry.

Seoul (sōl). The cap. of South Korea, in the NW part E of Inchon; founded in the 14th cent. Pop. 9,646,000.

sep. *abbr.* Separate; separation.

se·pal (sē′pəl) *n.* One of the separate, usu. green parts forming the calyx of a flower. [NLat. *sepalum*, perh. blend of Gk. *skepē*, covering, and Lat. *petalum*, petal; see PETAL.] —**se′paled, sep′a·lous** (sĕp′ə-ləs) *adj.*

se·pal·oid (sē′pə-loid′, sĕp′ə-) also **se·pal·ine** (-līn′, -lĭn) *adj.* Resembling or characteristic of a sepal.

-sepalous *suff.* Having a specified kind or number of sepals: *gamosepalous.*

sep·a·ra·ble (sĕp′ər-ə-bəl, sĕp′rə-) *adj.* Possible to separate. —**sep′a·ra·bil′i·ty** *n.* —**sep′a·ra·bly** *adv.*

sep·a·rate (sĕp′ə-rāt′) *v.* **-rat·ed, -rat·ing, -rates.** —*tr.* **1.a.** To set or keep apart; disunite. **b.** To space apart; scatter. **c.** To sort. **2.** To differentiate or discriminate between; distinguish. **3.** To remove from a mixture or combination; isolate. **4.** To part (a couple), often by decree. **5.** To terminate a contractual relationship with; discharge. —*intr.* **1.** To come apart. **2.** To withdraw. **3.** To part company; disperse. **4.** To stop living together as spouses. **5.** To become divided into components or parts. —*adj.* (sĕp′ər-ĭt, sĕp′rĭt). **1.** Set or kept apart; disunited. **2.a.** Existing as an independent entity. **b.** Often **Separate.** Having undergone schism or estrangement from a parent body. **3.** Dissimilar from all others; distinct.

4. Not shared; individual. **5.** *Archaic.* Withdrawn from others; solitary. —*n.* (sĕp′ər-ĭt, sĕp′rĭt). A garment, such as a skirt or jacket, that may be purchased separately and worn in various combinations with other garments. [ME *separaten* < Lat. *sēparātus*, p.part. of *sēparāre* : *sē-*, apart; see **s(w)e-*** + *parāre*, to prepare; see **perə-¹***.] —**sep′a·rate·ly** *adv.* —**sep′a·rate·ness** *n.*

Syns: *separate, divide, part, sever, sunder, divorce.* These verbs mean to become or cause to become parted, disconnected, or disunited. *Separate* applies both to putting apart and to keeping apart: *"In the darkness and confusion, the bands of these commanders became separated from each other"* (Washington Irving). *Divide* implies separation by or as if by cutting or splitting into parts or shares; the term often refers to separation into opposing or hostile groups: *" 'A house divided against itself cannot stand.' I believe this government cannot endure permanently half slave and half free"* (Abraham Lincoln). *Part* refers most often to the separation of closely associated persons or things: *"None shall part us from each other"* (W.S. Gilbert). *Sever* usually implies abruptness and force: *"His head was nearly severed from his body"* (H.G. Wells). *Sunder* stresses violent tearing or wrenching apart: *The country was sundered by civil war. Divorce* implies complete separation: *"a priest and a soldier, two classes of men circumstantially divorced from the kind and homely ties of life"* (Robert Louis Stevenson).

sep·a·ra·tion (sĕp′ə-rā′shən) *n.* **1.a.** The act or process of separating. **b.** The condition of being separated. **2.** The place at which a division or parting occurs. **3.** An interval or a space that separates; a gap. **4.a.** *Law.* An agreement or a court decree ending a spousal relationship. **b.** Discharge, as from employment.

sep·a·ra·tion·ist (sĕp′ə-rā′shə-nĭst) *n.* A separatist.

sep·a·ra·tist (sĕp′ər-ə-tĭst, sĕp′rə-, sĕp′ə-rā′-) *n.* **1.** One who secedes or advocates separation, esp. from an established church; a sectarian. **2.** One who advocates disjunction of a group from a larger group or political unit. **3.** One who advocates cultural, ethnic, or racial separation. —**sep′a·ra·tism** *n.* —**sep′a·ra·tist, sep′a·ra·tis′tic** *adj.*

sep·a·ra·tive (sĕp′ə-rā′tĭv, sĕp′ər-ə-, sĕp′rə-) *adj.* Tending to separate or to cause separation.

sep·a·ra·tor (sĕp′ə-rā′tər) *n.* One that separates, as a device for separating cream from milk.

sepd. *abbr.* Separated.

Se·phar·di (sə-fär′dē) *n., pl.* **-dim** (-dĭm). A descendant of the Jews who lived in Spain and Portugal during the Middle Ages until persecution forced them to leave. [Mod.Heb. *Sĕpāraddî*, Spaniard < *Sĕpārad*, Spain.] —**Se·phar′dic** (-dĭk) *adj.*

se·pi·a (sē′pē-ə) *n.* **1.a.** A dark brown ink or pigment originally prepared from the secretion of the cuttlefish. **b.** A drawing or picture done in sepia. **c.** A photograph in a brown tint. **2.** *Color.* A dark grayish yellow brown to dark or moderate olive brown. —*adj.* **1.** *Color.* Of the color sepia. **2.** Done or made in sepia. [ME, cuttlefish < Lat. *sēpia*, cuttlefish, ink < Gk., cuttlefish; perh. akin to *sēpein*, to make rotten.]

Se·pik (sā′pĭk). A river, c. 1,126 km (700 mi), of N Papua New Guinea.

se·pi·o·lite (sē′pē-ə-līt′) *n.* See **meerschaum** 1. [Gk. *sēpion*, cuttlebone (< *sēpia*, cuttlefish; see SEPIA) + -LITE.]

se·poy (sē′poi′) *n.* A regular soldier in some Middle Eastern countries, esp. an Indian soldier formerly serving under British command. [Prob. < Port. *sipae* < Urdu *sipāhī* < Pers., cavalryman < *sipāh*, army.]

sep·pu·ku (sĕp′o͞o-ko͞o, sĕ-po͞o′-) *n.* Hara-kiri. [J. : *seppu*, to cut + *ku*, abdomen.]

sep·sis (sĕp′sĭs) *n., pl.* **-ses** (-sēz). **1.** The presence of pathogenic organisms or their toxins in the blood or tissues. **2.** The poisoned condition resulting from sepsis, as in septicemia. [Gk. *sēpsis*, putrefaction < *sēpein*, to make rotten.]

sept (sĕpt) *n.* A division of a family, esp. a division of a clan. [Prob. alteration of SECT.]

Sept. or **Sept** *abbr.* September.

sep·ta (sĕp′tə) *n.* Pl. of **septum.**

sep·tage (sĕp′tĭj) *n.* The waste content found in a septic tank.

sep·tal (sĕp′təl) *adj.* Of or relating to a septum or septa.

sep·tar·i·um (sĕp-târ′ē-əm) *n., pl.* **-i·a** (-ē-ə). An irregular polygonal system of calcite-filled cracks occurring in certain rock concretions. [Lat. *saeptum*, partition; see SEPTUM + -ARIUM.] —**sep·tar′i·an** *adj.*

sep·tate (sĕp′tāt′) *adj.* Divided by a septum or septa.

Sep·tem·ber (sĕp-tĕm′bər) *n.* The ninth month of the year in the Gregorian calendar. [ME *Septembre* < OFr. < Lat. *September*, the seventh month < *septem*, seven. See **septm̥***.]

Sep·tem·brist (sĕp-tĕm′brĭst) *n.* **1.** A bloodthirsty revolutionist or terrorist. **2.** One of the mob that massacred the imprisoned royalists in Paris, France, in September 1792.

sep·te·nar·i·us (sĕp′tə-nâr′ē-əs) *n., pl.* **-i·i** (-ē-ī′). A Latin verse used only in comedy and consisting of seven iambic feet or a catalectic iambic tetrameter. [Lat. *septēnārius*, of seven < *septēnī*, seven each < *septem*, seven. See SEPTENNIAL.]

sep·ten·ni·al (sĕp-tĕn′ē-əl) *adj.* **1.** Occurring every seven years. **2.** Consisting of or continuing for seven years. —*n.* An event that occurs every seven years. [< LLat. *septennium*, period of seven years < Lat. *septennis*, of seven years : *septem*, seven; see **septm̥*** + *annus*, year; see **at-***.] —**sep·ten′ni·al·ly** *adv.*

sep·ten·tri·on (sĕp-tĕn′trē-ŏn′, -ən) *n. Obsolete.* Northern regions; the north. [ME < OFr. < Lat. *septentriōnēs*, seven plow oxen, the seven principal stars of Ursa Major : *septem*, seven; see **septm̥*** + *triōnēs* (pl. of *triō*, *triōn-*, plow ox; see **terə-¹***).] —**sep·ten′tri·o·nal** (-trē-ə-nəl) *adj.*

sep·tet also **sep·tette** (sĕp-tĕt′) *n.* **1.** A group of seven. **2.** *Mus.* **a.** A composition for seven voices or instruments. **b.** The performers playing such a composition. [Ger. *Septett* < Lat. *septem*, seven. See **septm̥***.]

sep·tic (sĕp′tĭk) *adj.* **1.** Of, relating to, having the nature of, or affected by sepsis. **2.** Causing sepsis; putrefactive. [Lat. *sēpticus*, putrefying < Gk. *sēptikos* < *sēptos*, rotten < *sēpein*, to make rotten.] —**sep·tic′i·ty** (-tĭs′ĭ-tē) *n.*

sep·ti·ce·mi·a (sĕp′tĭ-sē′mē-ə) *n.* A systemic disease caused by pathogenic organisms or their toxins in the bloodstream. [SEPTIC + -EMIA.] —**sep′ti·ce′mic** (-mĭk) *adj.*

sep·ti·ci·dal (sĕp′tĭ-sīd′l) *adj. Bot.* Dehiscing by splitting along or through the septa. Used of a seed capsule. [SEPT(UM) + Lat. *-cidere*, to cut (< *caedere*; see CAESURA) + -AL¹.]

septic sore throat *n.* An infection of the throat, often epidemic, caused by hemolytic streptococci and characterized by fever and inflammation of the tonsils.

septic tank *n.* A sewage-disposal tank in which a continuous flow of waste material is decomposed by anaerobic bacteria.

sep·tif·ra·gal (sĕp-tĭf′rə-gəl) *adj. Bot.* Dehiscing by the breaking away of the valves from its partitions. Used of a seed capsule. [SEPT(UM) + Lat. *frangere*, to break; see **bhreg-***.]

sep·ti·lat·er·al (sĕp′tə-lăt′ər-əl) *adj.* Seven-sided. [Lat. *septem*, seven; see SEPTET + LATERAL.]

Sept Îles or **Sept-Îles** (sĕt-ēl′). A city of E Quebec, Canada, on the St. Lawrence R. Pop. 29,262.

sep·til·lion (sĕp-tĭl′yən) *n.* **1.** The cardinal number equal to 10^{24}. **2.** *Chiefly British.* The cardinal number equal to 10^{42}. [Fr. : Lat. *septem*, seven; see SEPTET + Fr. *-illion* (as in *million*, million < OFr. *milion*; see MILLION).] —**sep·til′lion** *adj.*

sep·til·lionth (sĕp-tĭl′yənth) *n.* **1.** The ordinal number matching the number septillion in a series. **2.** One of a septillion equal parts. —**sep·til′lionth** *adv. & adj.*

sep·tu·a·ge·nar·i·an (sĕp′to͞o-ə-jə-nâr′ē-ən, -tyo͞o-, -cho͞o-) *n.* A person who is 70 years old or between the ages of 70 and 80. —*adj.* Of, relating to, or being a septuagenarian. [< Lat. *septuāgēnārius*, of the number seventy < *septuāgēnī*, seventy each < *septuāgintā*, seventy. See SEPTUAGINT.]

Sep·tu·a·gint (sĕp′to͞o-ə-jĭnt′, sĕp-to͞o′ə-jənt, -tyo͞o′-) *n.* A Greek translation of the Hebrew Bible made in the third century B.C. [Lat. *septuāgintā*, seventy (< the traditional number of its translators) : *septem*, seven; see **septm̥*** + *-gintā*, ten times; see **dekm̥***.]

sep·tum (sĕp′təm) *n., pl.* **-ta** (-tə). A thin partition or membrane that divides two cavities or soft masses of tissue in an organism: *the nasal septum.* [Lat. *saeptum*, partition < neut. p.part. of *saepīre*, to enclose < *saepēs*, fence.]

sep·tu·ple (sĕp-to͞o′pəl, -tyo͞o′-, -tŭp′əl) *adj.* **1.** Consisting of or containing seven. **2.** Multiplied by seven. —*tr.v.* **-pled, -pling, -ples.** To multiply by seven. [LLat. *septuplus*, sevenfold : Lat. *septem*, seven; see **septm̥*** + *-plus*, -fold; see **pel-²***.]

sep·tu·plet (sĕp-tŭp′lĭt, -to͞o′plĭt, -tyo͞o′-) *n.* **1.** One of seven offspring delivered at a single birth. **2. septuplets.** The seven offspring of one birth. **3.** A group of seven persons or things. [SEPTU(PLE) + (TRI)PLET.]

sep·ul·cher (sĕp′əl-kər) *n.* **1.** A burial vault. **2.** A receptacle for sacred relics, esp. in an altar. —*tr.v.* **-chered, -cher·ing, -chers.** To place into a sepulcher; inter. [ME *sepulcre* < OFr. < Lat. *sepulcrum* < *sepultus*, p.part. of *sepelīre*, to bury the dead.]

se·pul·chral (sə-pŭl′krəl, -po͝ol′-) *adj.* **1.** Of or relating to a sepulcher. **2.** Suggestive of the grave; funereal.

sep·ul·chre (sĕp′əl-kər) *n. & v. Chiefly British.* Var. of **sepulcher.**

sep·ul·ture (sĕp′əl-cho͝or′, -chər) *n.* **1.** The act of interment; burial. **2.** A sepulcher. [ME < OFr. < Lat. *sepultūra* < *sepultus*, p.part. of *sepelīre*, to bury the dead.]

seq. *abbr.* **1.** Sequel. **2.** *Lat.* Sequens (the following).

seqq. *abbr. Lat.* Sequentia (the following [things]).

se·qua·cious (sĭ-kwā′shəs) *adj.* **1.** Persisting in a continuous intellectual or stylistic direction. **2.a.** Disposed to follow another or others. **b.** Slavishly unthinking and uncritical. [< Lat. *sequāx*, *sequāc-*, pursuing < *sequī*, to follow. See **sekʷ-¹***.] —**se·qua′cious·ly** *adv.* —**se·quac′i·ty** (-kwăs′ĭ-tē) *n.*

se·quel (sē′kwəl) *n.* **1.** Something that follows; a continuation. **2.** A literary work complete in itself but continuing the narrative of an earlier work. **3.** A result or consequence. See Syns at **effect.** [ME *sequele* < OFr. *sequelle* < Lat. *sequēla* < *sequī*, to follow. See **sekʷ-¹***.]

se·quel·a (sĭ-kwĕl′ə) *n., pl.* **-quel·ae** (-kwĕl′ē). **1.** A pathological condition resulting from a disease. **2.** A secondary consequence or result. [Lat. *sequēla*, sequel. See SEQUEL.]

se·que·na·tor (sē′kwə-nā′tər) *n.* See **sequencer.**

ă pat	oi boy
ā pay	ou out
âr care	o͝o took
ä father	o͞o boot
ĕ pet	ŭ cut
ē be	ûr urge
ĭ pit	th thin
ī pie	*th* this
îr pier	hw which
ŏ pot	zh vision
ō toe	ə about, item
ô paw	

Stress marks:
′ (primary);
′ (secondary), as in
dictionary (dĭk′shə-nĕr′ē)

se•quence (sē′kwəns, -kwĕns′) *n.* **1.** A following of one thing after another; succession. **2.** An order of succession; an arrangement. **3.** A related or continuous series. **4.** *Games.* Three or more playing cards in consecutive order; a run. **5.** A series of single film shots so edited as to constitute an aesthetic or dramatic unit; an episode. **6.** *Mus.* A melodic or harmonic pattern successively repeated at different pitches with or without a key change. **7.** *Rom. Cath. Ch.* A hymn sung between the gradual and the Gospel. **8.** *Math.* An ordered set of quantities, as x, $2x^2$, $3x^3$, $4x^4$. **9.** *Biochem.* The order of constituents in a polymer, esp. the order of nucleotides in a nucleic acid or of amino acids in a protein. — *tr.v.* **-quenced, -quenc•ing, -quenc•es. 1.** To organize or arrange in a sequence. **2.** To determine the order of constituents in (a polymer). [ME, a type of hymn < OFr. < Med.Lat. *sequentia,* hymn, that which follows < LLat. < Lat. *sequēns, sequent-,* pr.part. of *sequī,* to follow. See **sek^{w}-1*.**]

Sequoya

se•quenc•er (sē′kwən-sər, -kwĕn′-) *n.* An apparatus for determining the order of constituents in a biological polymer.

se•quent (sē′kwənt) *adj.* **1.** Following in order or time; subsequent. **2.** Following as a result; consequent. — *n.* A result; a consequence. [Lat. *sequēns, sequent-,* pr.part. of *sequī,* to follow. See SEQUENCE.]

se•quen•tial (sĭ-kwĕn′shəl) *adj.* **1.** Forming or characterized by a sequence, as of units or musical notes. **2.** Sequent. — **se•quen′ti•al′i•ty** (-shē-ăl′ĭ-tē) *n.* — **se•quen′tial•ly** *adv.*

se•ques•ter (sĭ-kwĕs′tər) *v.* **-tered, -ter•ing, -ters.** — *tr.* **1.** To cause to withdraw into seclusion. **2.** To remove or set apart; segregate. **3.** *Law.* **a.** To take temporary possession of (property) as security against legal claims. **b.** To requisition and confiscate (enemy property). — *intr. Chem.* To undergo sequestration. [ME *sequestren* < OFr. < Lat. *sequestrāre,* to give up for safekeeping < Lat. *sequester,* depositary, trustee. See **sek^{w}-1*.**]

se•ques•trant (sĭ-kwĕs′trənt) *n.* A chemical that promotes sequestration.

serape

se•ques•trate (sē′kwĭ-strāt′, sĕk′wĭ-, sĭ-kwĕs′trāt′) *tr.v.* **-trat•ed, -trat•ing, -trates. 1.** *Chiefly British.* To seize; confiscate. **2.** To seclude; sequester. [Ult. < Lat. *sequestrāre, sequestrāt-,* to give up for safekeeping. See SEQUESTER.]

se•ques•tra•tion (sē′kwĭ-strā′shən, sĕk′wĭ-) *n.* **1.** The act of sequestering; segregation. **2.** *Law.* **a.** Seizure of property. **b.** A writ authorizing sequestration. **3.** The inhibition or prevention of normal ion behavior by combination with added materials, esp. by formation of a coordination compound.

se•ques•trum (sĭ-kwĕs′trəm) *n., pl.* **-tra** (-trə). A fragment of dead bone separated from healthy bone as a result of injury or disease. [Lat., deposit < neut. of *sequester,* depositary, trustee. See **sek^{w}-1*.**]

se•quin (sē′kwĭn) *n.* **1.** A small shiny ornamental disk, often sewn on cloth; a spangle. **2.** A gold coin of the Venetian Republic. — *tr.v.* **-quined, -quin•ing, -quins.** To affix sequins to (a garment, for example). [Fr. < OFr., Venetian coin < Ital. *zecchino* < *zecca,* mint < Ar. *sikkah,* coin die.]

se•quoi•a (sĭ-kwoi′ə) *n.* **1.** See **redwood 1. 2.** Giant sequoia. [NLat. *Sequoia,* genus name, after SEQUOYA.]

Se•quoy•a or **Se•quoy•ah** (sĭ-kwoi′ə). George Guess. 1770?–1843. Cherokee scholar who developed a system for transcribing the Cherokee language.

ser. *abbr.* **1.** Serial. **2.** Series. **3.** Sermon.

se•ra (sîr′ə) *n.* Pl. of **serum.**

sé•rac (sə-răk′, sā-) *n.* A large pointed mass of ice in a glacier isolated by intersecting crevasses. [Fr., cottage cheese, sérac, perh. < VLat. **serāceum,* whey < Lat. *serum.*]

seriema
Crested seriema
Cariama cristata

se•ra•glio (sə-răl′yō, -räl′-) *n., pl.* **-glios. 1.** A large harem. **2.** A sultan's palace. [Ital. *serraglio,* enclosure, seraglio, prob. partly < VLat. **serraculum,* enclosure (< **serrāre,* to lace up < Lat. *serāre* < *sera,* door bar) and partly < Turk. *saray,* palace (< Pers. *sarāī,* inn; see CARAVANSARY).]

ser•al (sîr′əl) *adj.* Of or relating to an ecological sere.

se•ra•pe also **sa•ra•pe** (sə-rä′pē, -răp′ē) *n.* A long blanket-like shawl worn esp. by Mexican men. [Am.Sp. *sarape.*]

ser•aph (sĕr′əf) *n., pl.* **-a•phim** (-ə-fĭm) or **-aphs. 1.** A celestial being having three pairs of wings. **2.** *Theol.* One of the first order of angels. [Back-formation < pl. *seraphim* < ME *seraphin* < OE < LLat. *seraphīn* < Gk. *seraphim* < Heb. *śərāpîm,* pl. of *śārāp.*] — **se•raph′ic** (sə-răf′ĭk), **se•raph′i•cal** (-ĭ-kəl) *adj.* — **se•raph′i•cal•ly** *adv.*

Se•ra•pis (sə-rā′pĭs) *n. Myth.* An ancient Egyptian god of the lower world, also worshiped in ancient Greece and Rome.

Serb (sûrb) *n.* A member of a southern Slavic people that is the principal ethnic group of Serbia. [Serbian *Srb.*]

Ser•bi•a (sûr′bē-ə). A region and former kingdom of the central Balkan Peninsula; a major component of the Kingdom of the Serbs, Croats, and Slovenes and a constituent republic of Yugoslavia after 1946. Serbia and Montenegro formed a new Yugoslavian country in 1992. Cap. Belgrade. Pop. 11,596,572.

E

serif

Ser•bi•an (sûr′bē-ən) *n.* **1.** A native or inhabitant of Serbia; a Serb. **2.** Serbo-Croatian as spoken in Serbia, written in a Cyrillic alphabet. — *adj.* Of or relating to Serbia or its people, language, or culture.

Ser•bo-Cro•a•tian (sûr′bō-krō-ā′shən) *n.* **1.** The Slavic language of the Serbs and the Croats. **2.** A native speaker of Serbo-Croatian. — *adj.* Of or relating to Serbo-Croatian or those who speak it.

sere[1] also **sear** (sîr) *adj.* Withered; dry. [ME < OE *sēar.*]

sere[2] (sîr) *n.* The sequence of successive ecological communities in an area from the initial stage to the climax. [< SERIES.]

ser•e•nade (sĕr′ə-nād′, sĕr′ə-nād′) *n.* **1.** *Mus.* A complimentary performance given to honor or express love for someone. **2.** *South Atlantic U.S.* See **shivaree.** See Regional Note at **shivaree. 3.** *Mus.* An instrumental composition written for a small ensemble and having characteristics of the suite and the sonata. — *v.* **-nad•ed, -nad•ing, -nades.** — *tr.* To perform a serenade for. — *intr.* To perform a serenade. [Fr. *sérénade* < Ital. *serenata* < *sereno,* calm, clear, the open air < Lat. *serēnus.* See SERENE.] — **ser′e•nad′er** *n.*

ser•en•dip•i•ty (sĕr′ən-dĭp′ĭ-tē) *n.* The faculty of making fortunate discoveries by accident. [From the characters in the Persian fairy tale *The Three Princes of Serendip,* who made such discoveries < Pers. *Sarandīp,* Sri Lanka < Ar. *Sarandīb.*] — **ser′en•dip′i•tous** *adj.* — **ser′en•dip′i•tous•ly** *adv.*

se•rene (sə-rēn′) *adj.* **1.** Unaffected by disturbance; calm and unruffled. See Syns at **calm. 2.** Unclouded; fair: *serene skies.* **3.** Often **Serene.** Used as a title and form of address for certain members of royalty: *Her Serene Highness.* [ME < Lat. *serēnus,* serene, clear.] — **se•rene′ly** *adv.* — **se•rene′ness** *n.*

Ser•en•get•i Plain (sĕr′ən-gĕt′ē). An area of N Tanzania bordering on Lake Victoria; noted for its wildlife preserve.

se•ren•i•ty (sə-rĕn′ĭ-tē) *n.* The state or quality of being serene; tranquillity.

serf (sûrf) *n.* **1.** A member of a servile feudal class of people in Europe, bound to the land and owned by a lord. **2.** One in servitude. [ME < OFr. < Lat. *servus,* slave.] — **serf′dom** *n.*

serge (sûrj) *n.* A twilled cloth of worsted or worsted and wool, often used for suits. [ME *sarge* < OFr. < VLat. **sārica* < Lat. *sērica (vestis),* silken (clothing), fem. of *sēricus,* silken < Gk. *sērikos,* of the Seres, silken < *Sēres,* a people of E Asia.]

ser•geant (sär′jənt) *n.* **1.** Any of several noncommissioned officers in the U.S. Army, Air Force, or Marine Corps. **2.** A police officer ranking next below a captain, lieutenant, or inspector. **3.** See **sergeant at arms.** [ME *sergeaunte,* a common soldier < OFr. *sergent* < Med.Lat. *serviēns, servient-,* servant, soldier < LLat., public official < Lat., pr.part. of *servīre,* to serve < *servus,* slave.] — **ser′gean•cy, ser′geant•ship′** *n.*

sergeant at arms *n., pl.* **sergeants at arms.** An officer appointed to keep order within an organization, such as a legislative, judicial, or social body.

sergeant first class *n., pl.* **sergeants first class.** A noncommissioned officer in the U.S. Army ranking above staff sergeant and below master sergeant.

sergeant fish *n.* **1.** See **cobia. 2.** See **snook**[1].

sergeant major *n., pl.* **sergeants major** or **sergeant majors. 1.** A noncommissioned officer serving as chief administrative assistant of a headquarters unit of the U.S. Army, Air Force, or Marine Corps. **2.** *Chiefly British.* A noncommissioned officer of the highest rank. **3.** A small damselfish *(Abudefduf saxatilis)* of warm seas, having dark vertical stripes.

se•ri•al (sîr′ē-əl) *adj.* **1.** Of, forming, or arranged in a series. **2.a.** Published or produced in installments. **b.** Relating to such publication or production. **3.** *Mus.* Relating to or based on a 12-tone row. **4.** *Comp. Sci.* **a.** Of or relating to the sequential transmission of the bits of a byte over one wire: *a serial port.* **b.** Of or relating to the sequential performance of multiple operations: *serial processing.* — *n.* A literary or dramatic work in installments. — **se′ri•al•ly** *adv.*

se•ri•al•ism (sîr′ē-ə-lĭz′əm) *n. Mus.* **1.** Serial compositions. **2.** The theory or composition of such music. — **se′ri•al•ist** *n.*

se•ri•al•ize (sîr′ē-ə-līz′) *tr.v.* **-ized, -iz•ing, -iz•es.** To write or publish in serial form. — **se′ri•al•i•za′tion** (-ə-lĭ-zā′shən) *n.*

serial killer *n.* A person who slays more than three victims one by one during a relatively short time. — **serial killing** *n.*

serial number *n.* A number that is one of a series and is used for identification, as of a machine, weapon, or motor vehicle.

se•ri•ate (sîr′ē-āt′, -ĭt) *adj.* Arranged or occurring in a series or in rows. — **se′ri•ate′ly** *adv.*

se•ri•a•tim (sîr′ē-ā′tĭm, -ăt′ĭm) *adv.* One after another; in a series. [Med.Lat. *seriātim* < Lat. *seriēs,* series. See SERIES.]

se•ri•ceous (sĭ-rĭsh′əs) *adj.* **1.** Silky. **2.** *Bot.* Covered with soft, silky hairs. [< Lat. *sēriceus,* silken, alteration of *sēricus.* See SERGE.]

ser•i•cin (sĕr′ĭ-sĭn) *n.* A viscous gelatinous protein that forms on the surface of raw-silk fibers. [Lat. *sēricus,* silken; see SERGE + -IN.]

ser•i•e•ma (sĕr′ē-ē′mə) *n.* Either of two cranelike birds *(Cariama cristata* or *Chunga burmeisteri)* of southern South America having a tuftlike crest at the base of the bill. [Sp. < Tupi *sariema.*]

se•ries (sîr′ēz) *n., pl.* **series. 1.** A number of objects or events arranged or coming one after the other in succession. **2.** *Phys. & Chem.* A group of objects related by linearly varying suc cessive differences in form or configuration: *a radioactive decay series.* **3.** *Math.* The sum of a sequentially ordered finite or infinite set of terms. **4.** *Geol.* A group of rock formations closely related in time of origin and distinct as a group from other formations. **5.** *Gram.* A succession of coordinate elements in a sentence. **6.a.** A succession of usu. continuously numbered issues or volumes of a publication, published with related authors or subjects and similar formats. **b.** A succession of regularly aired television programs, each one complete. **7.a.** *Sports.* A number of games played one after the other by the same opposing teams. **b.** *Baseball.* The World Series. **8.** *Ling.* A set of vowels or diphthongs related by ablaut. **—*idiom.* in series.** In an arrangement that forms a series. [Lat. *seriēs* < *serere*, to join. See **ser-**[2]*.]

Usage Note: *Series* is both a singular and a plural form. When it has the singular sense of "one set," it takes a singular verb, even when *series* is followed by *of* and a plural noun: *A series of lectures is scheduled.* When it has the plural sense of "one or more sets," it takes a plural verb: *Two series of lectures are scheduled: one for experts and one for laypeople.*

series circuit *n.* An electric circuit in which current passes through each circuit element in turn without branching.

se•ries-wound (sîr′ēz-wound′) *adj. Elect.* Of or being a motor or dynamo in which the armature circuit and the field circuit are connected in series with the external circuit.

ser•if (sĕr′ĭf) *n. Print.* A fine line finishing off the main strokes of a letter, as at the top and bottom of *M.* [Perh. < Du. *schreef*, line < MDu. *screve* < *scriven*, to write < Lat. *scrībere*. See **skrībh-***.]

ser•i•graph (sĕr′ĭ-grăf′) *n.* A silk-screen print. [Lat. *sēricum*, silk, neut. of *sēricus*, silken; see SERGE + -GRAPH.] **—se•rig′ra•pher** (sə-rĭg′rə-fər) *n.* **—se•rig′ra•phy** (-fē) *n.*

ser•in (sĕr′ĭn) *n.* Any of several Old World finches of the genus *Serinus*, esp. a European species *(S. serinus)* closely related to the canary. [Fr. < OFr., perh. < OProv. *serena*, a kind of bird < LLat. *sīrēna* < Lat. *sīrēn* < Gk. *seirēn*.]

ser•ine (sĕr′ēn′) *n.* An amino acid, $CH_2OHCH(NH_2)COOH$, occurring in many proteins. [SER(ICIN) + -INE[2].]

se•ri•o•com•ic (sîr′ē-ō-kŏm′ĭk) *adj.* Both serious and comic.

se•ri•ous (sîr′ē-əs) *adj.* **1.** Grave in quality or manner. **2.a.** Carried out in earnest. **b.** Deeply interested or involved. **c.** Designed for and addressing grave and earnest tastes. **d.** Not trifling or jesting. **e.** Of such character or quality as to appeal to the expert, the connoisseur, or the sophisticate. **3.** Concerned with important rather than trivial matters. **4.a.** Being of such import as to cause anxiety: *serious injuries.* **b.** Too complex to be easily answered or solved. [ME < OFr. *serieux* < LLat. *sēriōsus* < Lat. *sērius*.] **—se′ri•ous•ly** *adv.* **—se′ri•ous•ness** *n.*

Syns: *serious, sober, grave, solemn, earnest.* These adjectives refer to manner, appearance, disposition, or acts marked by absorption in thought, pressing concerns, or significant work. *Serious* implies a concern with responsibility and work as opposed to play: *serious students of music. Sober* emphasizes circumspection and self-restraint: *"My sober mind was no longer intoxicated by the fumes of politics"* (Edward Gibbon). *Grave* suggests the dignity and somberness associated with weighty matters: *"a quiet, grave man, busied in charts, exact in sums, master of the art of tactics"* (Walter Bagehot). *Solemn* often adds to *grave* the suggestion of impressiveness: *The judge's tone was solemn as he pronounced sentence. Earnest* implies sincerity and intensity of purpose: *Both disputants showed an earnest desire to reach an equitable solution.*

ser•jeant (sär′jənt) *n. Chiefly British.* Var. of **sergeant** 2.

Ser•kin (sûr′kĭn), **Rudolf.** 1903–91. Czech-born Amer. pianist known for his interpretations of the works of classical and romantic Austrian and German composers.

ser•mon (sûr′mən) *n.* **1.** A religious discourse, esp. as part of a church service. **2.** An often lengthy and tedious speech of reproof or exhortation. [ME < OFr. < Lat. *sermō, sermōn-*, discourse. See **ser-**[2]*.] **—ser•mon′ic** (-mŏn′ĭk), **ser•mon′i•cal** (-ĭ-kəl) *adj.*

ser•mon•ette (sûr′mə-nĕt′) *n.* A short sermon.

ser•mon•ize (sûr′mə-nīz′) *v.* **-ized, -iz•ing, -iz•es.** *—tr.* To deliver a sermon to (someone). *—intr.* To deliver or speak as though delivering a sermon. **—ser′mon•iz′er** *n.*

Ser•mon on the Mount (sûr′mən) *n.* In Matthew 5–7, a discourse of Jesus delivered on a Galilee mountainside, in which the Beatitudes are stated.

sero– *pref.* Serum: *serotherapy.* [< SERUM.]

se•ro•con•ver•sion (sîr′ō-kən-vûr′zhən, -shən) *n.* Development of antibodies in blood serum as a result of infection or immunization.

se•ro•di•ag•no•sis (sîr′ō-dī′əg-nō′sĭs) *n., pl.* **-ses** (-sēz). Diagnosis of disease based on reactions in the blood serum of the body. **—se′ro•di′ag•nos′tic** (-nŏs′tĭk) *adj.*

se•rol•o•gy (sĭ-rŏl′ə-jē) *n., pl.* **-gies. 1.** The science that deals with serums, esp. blood serum. **2.** The characteristics of a disease or an organism shown by study of blood serums. **—se′ro•log′ic** (sîr′ə-lŏj′ĭk), **se′ro•log′i•cal** (-ĭ-kəl) *adj.* **—se′ro•log′i•cal•ly** *adv.* **—se•rol′o•gist** *n.*

se•ro•neg•a•tive (sîr′ō-nĕg′ə-tĭv) *adj.* Showing a negative reaction to a blood serum test for a disease, esp. syphilis.

se•ro•pos•i•tive (sîr′ō-pŏz′ĭ-tĭv) *adj.* Showing a positive reaction to a blood serum test for a disease.

se•ro•pu•ru•lent (sîr′ō-pyo͝or′ə-lənt, -pyo͝or′yə-) *adj.* Consisting of serum and pus.

se•ro•sa (sĭ-rō′sə, -zə) *n., pl.* **-sas** or **-sae** (-sē, -zē). **1.** A serous membrane, esp. one that lines the pericardial, pleural, and peritoneal cavities. **2.** The chorion of a bird or reptile embryo. [NLat. *serōsa*, fem. of *serōsus*, serous < Lat. *serum*, serum.] **—se•ro′sal** (-zəl) *adj.*

se•ro•ther•a•py (sîr′ō-thĕr′ə-pē) *n., pl.* **-pies.** Treatment of disease by administration of a serum obtained from an immunized animal. **—se′ro•ther′a•pist** *n.*

se•rot•i•nal (sĭ-rŏt′n-əl, sĕr′ə-tī′nəl) *adj.* Serotinous.

ser•o•tine (sĕr′ə-tĭn, -tīn′) *n.* Any of a genus *(Eptesicus)* of usu. small brown bats of Europe and Asia, esp. *E. serotinus.* [< NLat. *sērōtinus*, species name < Lat., coming late (< its appearing late in the evening). See SEROTINOUS.]

se•rot•i•nous (sĭ-rŏt′n-əs, sĕr′ə-tī′nəs) *adj. Biol. & Bot.* Late in developing or blooming. [Lat. *sērōtinus*, coming late < *sērō*, at a late hour < *sērus*, late.]

se•ro•to•nin (sĕr′ə-tō′nĭn, sîr′-) *n.* An organic compound, $C_{10}H_{12}N_2O$, found esp. in the brain, blood serum, and gastric mucous membranes and active in vasoconstriction and transmission of nerve impulses. [SERO- + TON(E) + -IN.]

se•ro•type (sîr′ə-tīp′, sĕr′-) *n.* A group of closely related microorganisms distinguished by a characteristic set of antigens. *—tr.v.* **-typed, -typ•ing, -types.** To classify according to serotype; assign to a particular serotype.

se•rous (sîr′əs) *adj.* Secreting or resembling serum.

serous fluid *n.* Any of various body fluids resembling serum, esp. lymph.

serous membrane *n.* A thin membrane lining a closed body cavity and moistened with a serous fluid.

se•row (sə-rō′) *n.* Any of several goat antelopes of the genus *Capricornis* of mountainous regions of eastern Asia. [?]

Ser•pens (sûr′pənz, -pĕnz′) *n.* A constellation in the equatorial region of the northern sky near Hercules and Ophiuchus. [Lat. *Serpēns* < *serpēns*, serpent. See SERPENT.]

ser•pent (sûr′pənt) *n.* **1.** A reptile of the order Serpentes; a snake. **2.** Often **Serpent.** Satan. **3.** A subtle, sly, or treacherous person. **4.** A firework that writhes while burning. **5.** *Mus.* A wind instrument of serpentine shape, about 2.5 meters (8 feet) in length and made of brass or wood. **6. Serpent.** Serpens. [ME < OFr. < Lat. *serpēns, serpent-* < pr.part. of *serpere*, to creep.]

ser•pen•tar•i•um (sûr′pən-târ′ē-əm) *n., pl.* **-i•ums** or **-i•a** (-ē-ə). A place where snakes are kept for study or display.

ser•pen•tine (sûr′pən-tēn′, -tīn′) *adj.* **1.** Of or resembling a serpent, as in form or movement; sinuous. **2.** Subtly sly and tempting. *—n.* (-tēn′). Any of a group of minerals, $Mg_3Si_2O_5(OH)_4$, used as a source of magnesium and asbestos and as a decorative stone. [ME < OFr. *serpentin* < LLat. *serpentīnus* < Lat. *serpēns, serpent-*, serpent. See SERPENT.]

serpent star *n.* A brittle star.

ser•pi•go (sər-pī′gō) *n. Archaic.* A spreading skin eruption, such as ringworm. [ME < Med.Lat. *serpīgō* < Lat. *serpere*, to creep.] **—ser•pig′i•nous** (sər-pĭj′ə-nəs) *adj.*

Ser•ra (sĕr′ə), **Junípero.** "the Apostle of California." 1713–84. Spanish missionary who founded nine Franciscan missions in California (1769–82).

ser•rate (sĕr′āt′) *adj.* **1.** Having or forming a row of small sharp projections resembling the teeth of a saw: *serrate teeth.* **2.** Having a saw-toothed edge or margin notched with toothlike projections: *serrate leaves.* *—tr.v.* **-rat•ed, -rat•ing, -rates.** To make serrate or saw-toothed; jag the edge of. [Lat. *serrātus*, saw-shaped < *serra*, saw.]

ser•rat•ed (sĕr′ā′tĭd) *adj.* Saw-toothed; serrate.

ser•ra•tion (sə-rā′shən, sĕ-) *n.* **1.** The state of being serrate. **2.** A series or set of teeth or notches. **3.** A single tooth or notch in a serrate edge.

ser•ried (sĕr′ēd) *adj.* Pressed or crowded together, esp. in rows. [P.part. of obsolete *serry*, to close ranks < Fr. *serré*, p.part. of *serrer*, to crowd. See SEAR[2].] **—ser′ried•ly** *adv.*

ser•ru•late (sĕr′yə-lĭt, -lāt′, sĕr′ə-) also **ser•ru•lat•ed** (-lā′tĭd) *adj.* Having a minutely serrate margin, as in a rose leaflet. [NLat. *serrulātus* < Lat. *serrula*, dim. of *serra*, saw.]

ser•tu•lar•i•an (sûr′chə-lâr′ē-ən, sûr′tl-âr′-) *n.* Any of various colonial hydroids of the genus *Sertularia*, having stalkless polyps arranged in pairs along a long branching stem. [< NLat. *Sertularia*, genus name < Lat. *sertula*, dim. of *serta*, garland < fem. p.part. of *serere*, to join. See **ser-**[2]*.]

se•rum (sîr′əm) *n., pl.* **se•rums** or **se•ra** (sîr′ə). **1.** The clear yellowish fluid obtained upon separating whole blood into its solid and liquid components. **2.** Blood serum from immunized animals that contains antibodies, used to transfer immunity to another individual. **3.** Watery fluid from animal tissue. **4.** Whey. [Lat., whey, serum.]

serum albumin *n.* A protein fraction of serum, used as a substitute for plasma in the treatment of shock.

serum globulin *n.* A protein fraction of serum composed chiefly of antibodies.

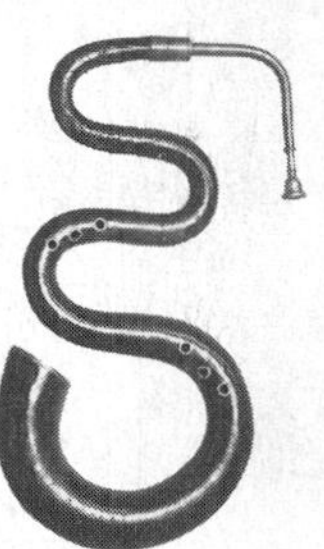

serpent
Top: Detail from a late 15th-century French manuscript, *De la Cité de Dieu*, translated from the Latin by Raoul de Presles
Bottom: 16th-century German or Italian

ă pat	oi boy
ā pay	ou out
âr care	o͝o took
ä father	o͞o boot
ĕ pet	ŭ cut
ē be	ûr urge
ĭ pit	th thin
ī pie	*th* this
îr pier	hw which
ŏ pot	zh vision
ō toe	ə about, item
ô paw	

Stress marks:
′ (primary);
′ (secondary), as in
dictionary (dĭk′shə-nĕr′ē)

serum hepatitis *n.* See **hepatitis B.**

serum sickness *n.* A hypersensitive reaction to the administration of a foreign serum, characterized by fever, swelling, skin rash, and enlargement of the lymph nodes.

serv. *abbr.* **1.** Servant. **2.** Service.

ser•val (sûr′vəl, sər-văl′) *n.* A long-legged wildcat *(Felis serval)* of Africa having a tawny coat with black spots and tuftless ears. [Fr. < Port. *(lobo) cerval*, deerlike (wolf), lynx < LLat. *cervālis* < Lat. *cervus*, deer. See **ker-^{1}*.**]

serval
Felis serval

ser•vant (sûr′vənt) *n.* **1.** One who is privately employed to perform domestic services. **2.** One who is publicly employed to perform services, as for a government. **3.** One who expresses submission, recognizance, or debt to another. [ME < OFr. < pr.part. of *servir*, to serve. See SERVE.]

serve (sûrv) *v.* **served, serv•ing, serves.** —*tr.* **1.a.** To work for. **b.** To be a servant to. **2.a.** To prepare and offer (food, for example). **b.** To place food before (someone); wait on. **3.a.** To provide goods and services for (customers). **b.** To supply (goods or services) to customers. **4.** To assist (the celebrant) during Mass. **5.** To be of assistance to or promote the interests of; aid. **6.** To spend or complete (time). **7.** To fight or undergo military service for. **8.** To give homage and obedience to: *served God.* **9.** To act toward (another) in a specified way; requite. **10.** To copulate with. Used of male animals. **11.** To meet the needs or requirements of; satisfy. **12.** *Law.* **a.** To deliver or present (a writ or summons). **b.** To present such a writ to. **13.** *Sports.* To put (a ball or shuttlecock) in play, as in tennis. **14.** To bind or whip (a rope) with fine cord or wire. —*intr.* **1.** To be employed as a servant. **2.** To do a term of duty. **3.** To act in a particular capacity. **4.** To be of service or use; function. **5.** To meet requirements or needs; satisfy. **6.** To wait on tables. **7.** *Sports.* To put a ball or shuttlecock into play, as in court games. **8.** To assist the celebrant during Mass. —*n. Sports.* The right, manner, or act of serving in many court games. —***idiom.* serve (someone) right.** To be deserved under the circumstances. [ME *serven* < OFr. *servir* < Lat. *servīre* < *servus*, slave.]

serv•er (sûr′vər) *n.* **1.a.** One who serves food and drink. **b.** Something that is used in serving food and drink. **2.** An acolyte at Mass. **3.** *Sports.* The player who serves.

Ser•ve•tus (sər-vē′təs), **Michael.** 1511–53. Spanish-born theologian and physician who described the circulation of blood and was executed for his denial of the Trinity.

sesame
Sesamum indicum

serv•ice (sûr′vĭs) *n.* **1.a.** Employment in duties or work for another, esp. for a government. **b.** A government branch or department and its employees. **2.a.** The armed forces of a nation. **b.** A branch of the armed forces of a nation. **3.a.** Work or duties performed for a superior. **b.** The occupation or duties of a servant. **4.a.** Work done for others as an occupation or a business: *a catering service.* **b.** A department or branch of a hospital staff that provides specified patient care. **5.** Installation, maintenance, or repairs provided or guaranteed by a dealer or manufacturer. **6.** A facility providing the public with the use of something, such as water. **7.a.** Acts of devotion to God; witness. **b.** A religious rite. **8.** An act of assistance or benefit to another or others; a favor. **9.a.** The serving of food or the manner in which it is served. **b.** A set of dishes or utensils. **10.** *Sports.* The act, manner, or right of serving in many court games; a serve. **11.** Copulation with a female. **12.** *Law.* The serving of a writ or summons. **13.** The material, such as cord, used in binding or wrapping rope. —*tr.v.* **-iced, -ic•ing, -ic•es. 1.** To make fit for use; adjust, repair, or maintain. **2.** To provide services to. **3.** To make interest payments on (a debt). **4.** To copulate with. —*adj.* **1.** Of or relating to the armed forces of a country. **2.** Intended for use in supplying or serving. **3.** Offering repairs or maintenance. **4.** Offering services to the public. [ME < OFr. < Lat. *servitium*, slavery < *servus*, slave.]

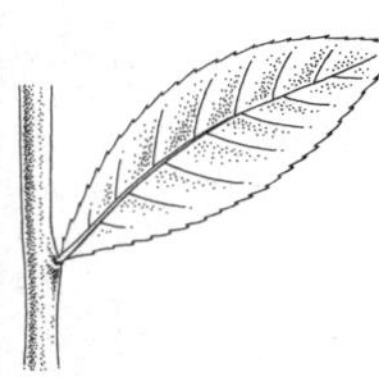

sessile

Ser•vice (sûr′vĭs), **Robert William.** 1874–1958. British-born Canadian writer of poetry and novels about life in the Yukon.

serv•ice•a•ble (sûr′vĭ-sə-bəl) *adj.* **1.** Ready for service; usable. **2.** Able to give long service; durable. —**serv′ice•a•bil′i•ty, serv′ice•a•ble•ness** *n.* —**serv′ice•a•bly** *adv.*

serv•ice•ber•ry (sûr′vĭs-bĕr′ē) *n.* The shadbush or one of its fruit. [SERVICE (TREE) + BERRY.]

service break *n. Sports.* A game won on an opponent's serve.

service cap *n.* A flat-topped military cap with a visor.

service charge *n.* An additional charge for a service for which there is already a basic fee.

service line *n. Sports.* A boundary line, as in tennis or handball, that must not be overstepped in serving.

serv•ice•man (sûr′vĭs-măn′, -mən) *n.* **1.** A man who is a member of the armed forces. **2.** Also **service man.** A man who maintains and repairs equipment.

service mark *n.* A mark used in the sale or advertising of services to distinguish them from the services of others.

serv•ice•per•son (sûr′vĭs-pûr′sən) *n.* **1.** A member of the armed forces. **2.** Also **service person.** A person who maintains and repairs equipment.

service road *n.* A local road that provides access to the property bordering an expressway or interstate highway.

service station *n.* **1.** A retail establishment at which motor vehicles are refueled, serviced, and sometimes repaired. **2.** A business or branch of a business where services, esp. repairs, can be obtained.

service stripe *n.* A stripe worn on the sleeve of a uniform, as of an enlisted person, to indicate years of service.

service tree *n.* Either of two Mediterranean trees *(Sorbus domestica* or *S. torminalis)* having white flowers, saw-toothed leaves, and edible fruit. [< ME *serves*, pl. of *serve*, the service tree < OE *syrfe* < VLat. **sorbea* < Lat. *sorbus.*]

serv•ice•wom•an (sûr′vĭs-wo͝om′ən) *n.* **1.** A woman who is a member of the armed forces. **2.** Also **service woman.** A woman who maintains and repairs equipment.

ser•vi•ette (sûr′vē-ĕt′) *n. Chiefly British.* A table napkin. [Fr. < OFr. *serviete*, perh. < *servir*, to serve. See SERVE.]

ser•vile (sûr′vəl, -vīl′) *adj.* **1.** Abjectly submissive; slavish. **2.a.** Of or suitable to a slave or servant. **b.** Of or relating to servitude or forced labor. [ME < Lat. *servīlis* < *servus*, slave.] —**ser′vile•ness, ser•vil′i•ty** (sər-vĭl′ĭ-tē) *n.*

serv•ing (sûr′vĭng) *n.* **1.** The act of one that serves. **2.** An individual portion or helping of food or drink.

ser•vi•tor (sûr′vĭ-tər, -tôr′) *n.* One that performs the duties of a servant to another; an attendant. [Ult. < Lat. *servītor* < *servīre*, to serve. See SERVE.] —**ser′vi•tor•ship′** *n.*

ser•vi•tude (sûr′vĭ-to͞od′, -tyo͞od′) *n.* **1.a.** A state of subjection to an owner or a master. **b.** Lack of personal freedom, as to act as one chooses. **2.** Forced labor imposed as a punishment for crime. **3.** *Law.* A right that grants use of another's property. [ME < OFr. < LLat. *servitūdō* < Lat. *servus*, slave.]

ser•vo (sûr′vō) *n., pl.* **-vos. 1.** A servomechanism. **2.** A servomotor.

ser•vo•mech•a•nism (sûr′vō-mĕk′ə-nĭz′əm) *n.* **1.** A feedback mechanism that consists of a sensing element, an amplifier, and a servomotor, used in the automatic control of a mechanical device. **2.** A self-regulating feedback system.

ser•vo•mo•tor (sûr′vō-mō′tər) *n.* A motor that controls the action of the mechanical device in a servomechanism. [Fr. *servomoteur* : Lat. *servus*, slave + Fr. *moteur*, motor (< OFr. < Lat. *mōtor*, that which sets in motion; see MOTOR).]

ses•a•me (sĕs′ə-mē) *n.* **1.** A tropical Asian plant *(Sesamum indicum)* bearing small flat seeds used as food and as a source of oil. **2.** The seed of this plant. [ME *sisamie* < Lat. *sēsamum* < Gk. *sēsamē, sēsamon*, of Semitic orig.]

ses•a•moid (sĕs′ə-moid′) *adj.* Of or being any of certain small modular bones or cartilages that develop in a tendon or in the capsule of a joint. —*n.* A sesamoid bone or cartilage. [Gk. *sēsamoeidēs*, shaped like a sesame seed : *sēsamon, sēsamē*, sesame; see SESAME + *-oeidēs*, -oid.] —**ses′a•moid′** *n.*

sesqui– *pref.* One and a half: *sesquicentennial.* [Lat. *sēsqui-* : *sēmis*, a half; see **sēmi-*** + *-que*, and; see **k^{w}e*.**]

ses•qui•cen•ten•ni•al (sĕs′kwĭ-sĕn-tĕn′ē-əl) *adj.* Of or relating to a period of 150 years. —*n.* A 150th anniversary or its celebration.

ses•quip•e•dal (sĕ-skwĭp′ĭ-dl) *adj.* Sesquipedalian. [Lat. *sēsquipedālis*, of a foot and a half in length : *sēsqui-*, sesqui- + *pēs, ped-*, foot; see **ped-*.**]

ses•qui•pe•da•lian (sĕs′kwĭ-pĭ-dāl′yən) *n.* A long word. —*adj.* **1.** Given to the use of long words. **2.** Long and ponderous; polysyllabic.

sess. *abbr.* Session.

ses•sile (sĕs′īl′, -əl) *adj.* **1.** *Bot.* Stalkless and attached directly at the base. **2.** *Zool.* Permanently attached or fixed; not free-moving. [Lat. *sessilis*, low, of sitting < *sessus*, p.part. of *sedēre*, to sit. See **sed-*.**] —**ses•sil′i•ty** (sĕ-sĭl′ĭ-tē) *n.*

ses•sion (sĕsh′ən) *n.* **1.a.** A meeting of a legislative or judicial body for the purpose of transacting business. **b.** A series of such meetings. **c.** The term or duration of such a series. **2.** The part of a year or of a day during which a school holds classes. **3.** An assembly of people for a common purpose or because of a common interest. **4.** *Law.* A court of criminal jurisdiction in the United States. **5.** A period of time devoted to a specific activity. [ME < OFr. < Lat. *sessiō, sessiōn-*, act of sitting < *sessus*, p.part. of *sedēre*, to sit. See **sed-*.**] —**ses′sion•al** *adj.*

Ses•sions (sĕsh′ənz), **Roger Huntington.** 1896–1985. Amer. composer whose works include *Montezuma* (1962).

ses•terce (sĕs′tûrs′) *n.* A silver or bronze coin of ancient Rome equivalent to one fourth of a denarius. [Lat. *sēstertius*, a coin worth two and a half asses : *sēmis*, half; see **sēmi-*** + *tertius*, third; see **trei-*.**]

ses•ter•tium (sĕ-stûr′shəm, -shē-əm) *n., pl.* **-tia** (-shə, -shē-ə). A monetary unit of ancient Rome equivalent to 1,000 sesterces. [Lat. *(mille) sēstertium*, (a thousand) sesterces, genitive pl. of *sēstertius*, sesterce. See SESTERCE.]

ses•tet (sĕ-stĕt′) *n.* **1.** A group of six lines of poetry, esp. the last six lines of a Petrarchan sonnet. **2.** A poem or stanza containing six lines. [Ital. *sestetto* < *sesto*, sixth < Lat. *sextus.* See **s(w)eks*.**]

ses•ti•na (sĕ-stē′nə) *n.* A verse form first used by the Provençal troubadours, consisting of six six-line stanzas and a three-line envoy, with the end words of the first stanza repeated in varied order as end words in the other stanzas and also recurring in the envoy. [Ital. < *sesto*, sixth < Lat. *sextus.* See **s(w)eks*.**]

Ses•tos (sĕs′təs, -tŏs). An ancient town of European Turkey at the narrowest point of the Dardanelles; site of a bridge of boats built by Xerxes in 481 B.C. to cross the Hellespont and invade Greece.

set[1] (sĕt) *v.* **set, set•ting, sets.** —*tr.* **1.** To put in a specified position; place. **2.** To put into a specified state: *set the prisoner at liberty.* **3.a.** To put into a stable position: *set the post into concrete.* **b.** To fix firmly or in an immobile manner. **4.** To restore to a normal state when dislocated or broken: *set a broken arm.* **5.a.** To adjust for proper functioning. **b.** To adjust (a saw) by deflecting the teeth. **c.** *Naut.* To spread open to the wind: *set the sails.* **6.** To adjust according to a standard. **7.** To adjust (an instrument) to a specific point or calibration. **8.** To arrange properly for use: *set a table.* **9.** To apply equipment, such as curlers, to (hair) in order to style. **10.** *Print.* **a.** To arrange (type) into words and sentences preparatory to printing; compose. **b.** To transpose into type. **11.** *Mus.* **a.** To compose (music) to fit a given text. **b.** To write (words) to fit a given melodic line. **12.** To arrange scenery on (a theater stage). **13.** To prescribe the unfolding of (a scene) in a specific place: *a play set in Venice.* **14.** To prescribe or establish: *set a precedent.* **15.** To prescribe as a time for: *set June 10 as the day.* **16.** To detail or assign (someone) to a particular duty, service, or station. **17.** To incite to hostile action. **18.a.** To establish as the highest level of performance: *set a record.* **b.** To establish as a model. **19.a.** To put in a mounting; mount. **b.** To apply jewels to; stud. **20.** To cause to sit. **21.a.** To put (a hen) on eggs to hatch them. **b.** To put (eggs) beneath a hen or in an incubator. **22.** *Sports.* To position (oneself) so as to be ready to start running a race. **23.a.** To value or regard something at the rate of: *She sets a great deal by good nutrition.* **b.** To fix at a given amount. **c.** To make as an estimate of worth: *We set a high value on human life.* **24.** To point to the location of (game) by holding a fixed attitude. Used of a hunting dog. **25.** *Bot.* To produce, as after pollination: *set seed.* **26.a.** To prepare (a trap) for catching prey. **b.** To fix (a hook) firmly into a fish's jaw. —*intr.* **1.** To disappear below the horizon. **2.** To diminish or decline; wane. **3.** To sit on eggs. Used of fowl. **4.a.** To become fixed; harden. **b.** To become permanent. Used of dye. **5.** To become whole; knit. Used of a broken bone. **6.** *Bot.* To mature or develop, as after pollination. **7.** *Non-Standard.* To sit. **8.** To position oneself preparatory to an action, such as running a race. —*adj.* **1.** Fixed or established by agreement. **2.** Established as by convention. **3.** Established deliberately; intentional. **4.** Fixed and rigid. **5.** Unwilling or very reluctant to change. **6.a.** Intent and determined: *dead set against it.* **b.** Ready: *We are set to leave.* —*n.* **1.a.** The act or process of setting. **b.** The condition resulting from setting. **2.** The manner in which something is positioned: *the set of her cap.* **3.** A permanent firming or hardening of a substance. **4.** The deflection of the teeth of a saw. **5.a.** The carriage or bearing of a part of the body. **b.** A particular psychological state, usu. that of anticipation or preparedness. **6.** A descent below the horizon. **7.a.** The direction or course of wind or water. **b.** The amount that a vessel is put off its course by current. **8.** A seedling, slip, or cutting that is ready for planting. **9.** The act of arranging hair by waving and curling it. —***phrasal verbs.*** **set about.** To begin or start. **set apart. 1.** To reserve for a specific use. **2.** To make noticeable. **set aside. 1.** To separate and reserve for a special purpose. **2.** To discard or reject. **3.** To declare invalid; annul or overrule. **set at.** To attack or assail. **set back. 1.** To slow down the progress of; hinder. **2.** *Informal.* To cost. **set by.** To reserve for future use. **set down. 1.** To cause to sit; seat. **2.** To put in writing; record. **3.a.** To regard; consider: *Just set him down as a sneak.* **b.** To assign to a cause; attribute. **4.** To land (an aircraft). **set forth. 1.** To present for consideration; propose. **2.** To express in words. **set forward.** To begin a journey. **set in. 1.** To insert. **2.** To begin to happen or be apparent. **3.** To move toward the shore. Used of wind or water. **set off. 1.a.** To give rise to; cause to occur. **b.** To cause to explode. **2.** To indicate as being different; distinguish. **3.** To direct attention to by contrast; accentuate. **4.** To start on a journey. **set out. 1.** To begin an earnest attempt; undertake. **2.** To lay out systematically or graphically: *set out a terrace.* **3.** To display for exhibition or sale. **4.** To plant. **5.** To start a journey. **set to. 1.** To begin working energetically; start in. **2.** To begin fighting. **set up. 1.** To place in an upright position. **2.a.** To elevate; raise. **b.** To raise in authority or power; invest with power. **c.** To put (oneself) forward as; claim to be. **d.** To assemble and erect. **3.** To establish; found. **4.** To cause. **5.** To establish in business by providing capital, equipment, or other backing. **6.** *Informal.* **a.** To treat (someone) to drinks. **b.** To pay for (drinks). **7.** *Informal.* To stimulate or exhilarate. **8.** To lay plans for. **9.** *Informal.* To put (someone else) into a compromising situation by deceit or trickery. **set upon.** To attack violently. —***idioms.*** **set fire to.** To cause to ignite and burn. **set foot in.** To enter. **set foot on.** To step on. **set in motion.** To give impetus to. **set (one's) heart on.** To be determined to do something. **set (one's) sights on.** To have as a goal. **set on fire. 1.** To cause to ignite and burn. **2.** To cause to become excited. **set sail.** *Naut.* To begin a voyage on water. **set (someone) straight.** To correct (someone) by providing full and accurate information. **set store by.** To regard as valuable or worthwhile. **set the pace. 1.** To go at a speed that other competitors attempt to match or surpass. **2.** To behave or perform in a way that others try to emulate. **set the stage for.** To provide the underlying basis for. **set up housekeeping.** To establish a household. **set up shop.** To establish one's business operations. [ME *setten* < OE *settan.* See **sed-***.]

Usage Note: Originally *set* meant "to cause (something) to sit," so that it is now in most cases a transitive verb: *She sets the book down. He sets the table. Sit* is generally an intransitive verb: *He sits down.* There are some exceptions: *The sun sets* (not *sits*). *A hen sets* (or *sits*) *on her eggs.*

set[2] (sĕt) *n.* **1.** A group of things of the same kind that belong together and are so used. **2.** A group of persons sharing a common interest. **3.** A group of books or periodicals published as a unit. **4.a.** A number of couples required for participation in a square dance. **b.** The movements constituting a square dance. **5.a.** The scenery constructed for a theatrical performance. **b.** The entire enclosure in which a movie is filmed; the sound stage. **6.** *Mus.* **a.** A session of music, typically dance music, played before an intermission. **b.** The music so played. **7.** The collective receiving apparatus assembled to operate a radio or television. **8.** *Math.* A collection of distinct elements having specific common properties. **9.** *Sports.* A group of tennis games constituting one division or unit of a match. [ME *sette* < OFr. < Med.Lat. *secta*, retinue < Lat., faction. See SECT.]

se•ta (sē′tə) *n., pl.* **-tae** (-tē). *Biol.* **1.** A stiff hair, bristle, or bristlelike process or part on an organism. **2.** *Bot.* The stalk of a moss capsule. [NLat. *sēta* < Lat. *saeta*, bristle.] —**se′tal** (sēt′l) *adj.*

se•ta•ceous (sĭ-tā′shəs) *adj.* **1.** Having or consisting of bristles; bristly. **2.** Resembling bristles or a bristle. [SET(A) + -ACEOUS.] —**se•ta′ceous•ly** *adv.*

set•back (sĕt′băk′) *n.* **1.** A check in progress; a change from better to worse. **2.** A steplike recession in a wall or a building.

set back *n. Football.* An offensive back who lines up behind the quarterback.

se-ten•ant or **se ten•ant** (sə-tĕn′ənt, sĕt′n-äɴ′, sə-tə-näɴ′) *n.* A block of commemorative stamps on one sheet but varying in design, color, value, or overprint. [Fr. : *se*, reflexive pron. + *tenant*, pr.part. of *tenir*, to hold.] —**se-ten′ant** *adj.*

Seth (sĕth). In the Bible, the third son of Adam and Eve.

se•ti•form (sē′tə-fôrm′) *adj.* Shaped like a seta or bristle.

set-in (sĕt′ĭn′) *adj.* **1.** Made or placed as a part of another unit or structure: *a set-in stereo cabinet.* **2.** Made separately and stitched into the main part: *a dress with set-in sleeves.* —*n.* Material, as for a book, that is inserted; an insert.

set•line (sĕt′līn′) *n.* A long fishing line towed by a boat and supporting many smaller lines bearing baited hooks.

set•off (sĕt′ôf′, -ŏf′) *n.* **1.** Something, such as a decoration, that sets off something else by contrast. **2.** Something that offsets or compensates for something else; a counterbalance. **3.a.** A counterclaim. **b.** Settlement of a debt by a debtor's establishing such a claim against a creditor. **4.** *Archit.* A flat projection, as from a wall; a ledge. **5.** *Print.* See **offset** 10a.

Se•ton (sēt′n), Saint **Elizabeth Ann Bayley.** "Mother Seton." 1774–1821. American religious leader who founded the Sisters of Charity (1809).

se•tose (sē′tōs′) *adj.* Bristly: setaceous.

set•out (sĕt′out′) *n.* **1.** A start or beginning; an outset. **2.a.** An arrangement or a display. **b.** An array of food; a spread. **3.** An entertaining event, such as a party.

set piece *n.* **1.** A realistic piece of stage scenery constructed to stand by itself. **2.** A formally patterned artistic or literary work. **3.a.** A carefully planned and executed military operation. **b.** A situation, an activity, or a speech planned beforehand and carried out according to a pattern or formula.

set point *n. Sports.* **1.** A situation in which the set will be won by the player who scores the next point in a net game such as tennis. **2.** The point so scored.

set•screw (sĕt′skrōō′) *n.* **1.** A screw, often without a head, used to hold two parts together. **2.** A screw used to regulate the tension of a spring.

Se•tswa•na (sĕt-swä′nə) also **Sech•ua•na** (sĕch-wä′-) *n.* See **Tswana** 2.

set•tee (sĕ-tē′) *n.* **1.** A long wood bench with a back. **2.** A small to medium-sized sofa. [Perh. alteration of SETTLE.]

set•ter (sĕt′ər) *n.* **1.** One that sets. **2.** Any of several breeds of longhaired hunting dogs originally trained to indicate the presence of game by crouching in a set position.

set theory *n. Math.* The study of the properties of sets.

set•ting (sĕt′ĭng) *n.* **1.** The position, direction, or way in which something, such as an automatic control, is set. **2.a.** The context in which a situation is set; the background. **b.** The time, place, and circumstances in which a narrative, drama, or film takes place. **3.** The scenery constructed for a theatrical performance or movie production. **4.** *Mus.* A composition written or arranged to fit a text, such as a poetical work. **5.** A mounting, as for a jewel. **6.** A place setting. **7.** A set of eggs in a hen's nest.

Elizabeth Seton

settee
c. 1805 American, attributed to John and Hugh Finlay (fl. 1799–1833)

ă **pat**	oi **boy**
ā **pay**	ou **out**
âr **care**	ŏŏ **took**
ä **father**	ōō **boot**
ĕ **pet**	ŭ **cut**
ē **be**	ûr **urge**
ĭ **pit**	th **thin**
ī **pie**	*th* **this**
îr **pier**	hw **which**
ŏ **pot**	zh **vision**
ō **toe**	ə **about,**
ô **paw**	**item**

Stress marks:
′ (primary);
′ (secondary), as in **dictionary** (dĭk′shə-nĕr′ē)

settle
Child's painted pine settle

Sèvres
c. 1780 vase

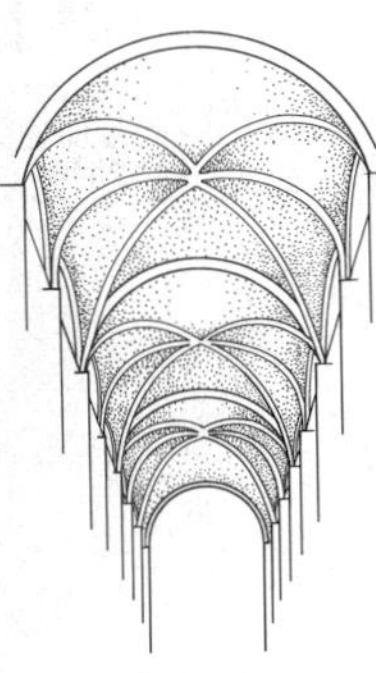

sexpartite
Series of sexpartite vaults

set•tle (sĕt′l) *v.* **-tled, -tling, -tles.** —*tr.* **1.** To put into order; arrange or fix definitely as desired. **2.** To put firmly into a desired position or place; establish. **3.a.** To establish as a resident or residents. **b.** To establish residence in; colonize. **c.** To establish in a residence, business, or profession. **4.** To restore calmness or comfort to. **5.a.** To cause to sink, become compact, or come to rest. **b.** To cause (a liquid) to become clear by forming a sediment. **6.** To subdue or make orderly. **7.** To establish on a permanent basis; stabilize. **8.a.** To make compensation for (a claim). **b.** To pay (a debt). **9.** To conclude (a dispute, for example) by a final decision. **10.** To decide (a lawsuit) by mutual agreement of the involved parties without court action. **11.** *Law.* To secure or assign (property or title) by legal action. —*intr.* **1.** To discontinue moving and come to rest in one place. **2.** To move downward; sink or descend, esp. gradually. **3.a.** To become clear by the sinking of suspended particles. Used of liquids. **b.** To be separated from a solution or mixture as a sediment. **c.** To become compact by sinking, as sediment when stirred up. **4.a.** To establish one's residence. **b.** To become established or localized: *The cold settled in my chest.* **5.** To reach a decision; determine. See Syns at **decide. 6.a.** To provide compensation for a claim. **b.** To pay a debt. —*n.* A long wooden bench with a high back, often including storage space beneath the seat. —***phrasal verbs.* settle down. 1.** To begin living a stable and orderly life. **2.** To become less nervous or restless. **settle for.** To accept in spite of incomplete satisfaction. [ME *setlen*, to seat < OE *setlan* < *setl*, seat. See **sed-***.] —**set′tle•a•ble** *adj.*

set•tle•ment (sĕt′l-mənt) *n.* **1.** The act or process of settling. **2.a.** Establishment, as of a person in a business or of people in a new region. **b.** A newly colonized region. **3.** A small community. **4.** An arrangement, adjustment, or other understanding reached, as in financial or business proceedings. **5.** *Law.* **a.** Transfer of property to provide for the future needs of a person. **b.** Property thus transferred. **6.** A center providing community services in an underprivileged area.

set•tler (sĕt′lər) *n.* One who settles in a new region.

set•tlings (sĕt′lĭngz) *pl.n.* Sediment; dregs.

set•tlor (sĕt′lər) *n. Law.* One that makes a business or financial settlement or a settlement of property.

set-to (sĕt′to͞o′) *n., pl.* **-tos.** A brief, usu. heated quarrel.

Se•tú•bal (sə-to͞o′bəl). A city of SW Portugal SE of Lisbon on the **Bay of Setúbal**, an inlet of the Atlantic. Pop. 77,885.

set•up (sĕt′ŭp′) *n.* **1.** The way in which something is constituted, arranged, or planned. **2.** The gathering and organization of the equipment for an operation, a procedure, or a task. **3.a.** Physical makeup; physique. **b.** Body posture or carriage, esp. militarily erect bearing. **4.a.** *Informal.* The collective ingredients, such as ice, mixers, and glasses, for serving various alcoholic drinks. Often used in the plural. **b.** A table setting, as in a restaurant. **5.** A camera position, as for a shot in a scene being filmed. **6.** *Slang.* **a.** A contest arranged to result in an easy or faked victory. **b.** An endeavor intentionally made easy. **c.** A deceptive scheme, such as a fraud or hoax. **7.** A plan or strategy for a projected course of action.

Seu•rat (sə-rä′, sœ-), **Georges Pierre.** 1859–91. French neo-impressionist painter who developed pointillism.

Seuss (so͞os), Doctor. See Theodor Seuss **Geisel.**

Se•vas•to•pol (sə-văs′tə-pōl′, sĕv′ə-stō′pəl, syĭ-və-). Formerly **Se•bas•to•pol** (sə-băs′tə-pōl′). A city of S Ukraine in the Crimea on the Black Sea W of Yalta; site of lengthy sieges during the Crimean War and World War II. Pop. 341,000.

sev•en (sĕv′ən) *n.* **1.** The cardinal number equal to 6 + 1. **2.** The seventh in a set or sequence. [ME < OE *seofon.* See **septm̥***.] —**sev′en** *adj. & pron.*

Sev•en Hills of Rome (sĕv′ən; rōm). The hills upon which the city of Rome was built, including the Aventine, Caelian, Capitoline, Esquiline, Palatine, Quirinal, and Viminal hills.

seven seas also **Seven Seas** *pl.n.* All the oceans of the world.

sev•en•teen (sĕv′ən-tēn′) *n.* **1.** The cardinal number equal to 16 + 1. **2.** The 17th in a set or sequence. [ME *seventene* < OE *seofontīne.* See **septm̥***.] —**sev′en•teen′** *adj. & pron.*

sev•en•teenth (sĕv′ən-tēnth′) *n.* **1.** The ordinal number matching the number 17 in a series. **2.** One of 17 equal parts. —**sev′en•teenth′** *adv. & adj.*

sev•en•teen-year locust (sĕv′ən-tēn′yîr′) *n.* See **periodical cicada.**

sev•enth (sĕv′ənth) *n.* **1.** The ordinal number matching the number seven in a series. **2.** One of seven equal parts. **3.** *Mus.* An interval encompassing seven diatonic degrees. [ME, alteration of *sefende* < OE *seofunda* < *seofon*, seven. See SEVEN.] —**sev′enth** *adv. & adj.*

Sev•enth-day Adventist (sĕv′ənth-dā′) *n.* A member of a sect of Adventism distinguished chiefly for its observance of the Sabbath on Saturday.

seventh heaven *n.* **1.** A state of great joy and satisfaction. **2.** The farthest of the concentric spheres containing the stars and constituting the dwelling place of God and the angels in the Muslim and cabalist systems.

sev•en•ti•eth (sĕv′ən-tē-ĭth) *n.* **1.** The ordinal number matching the number 70 in a series. **2.** One of 70 equal parts. —**sev′en•ti•eth** *adv. & adj.*

sev•en•ty (sĕv′ən-tē) *n.* **1.** The cardinal number equal to 7 × 10. **2. seventies. a.** Often **Seventies.** The decade from 70 to 79 in a century. **b.** A decade or the numbers from 70 to 79. [ME < OE *hundseofontig.* See **septm̥***.] —**sev′en•ty** *adj. & pron.*

sev•en-up (sĕv′ən-ŭp′) *n. Games.* A card game requiring seven points to win.

Seven Wonders of the World. In ancient times, the pyramids of Egypt; the Hanging Gardens of Babylon; Phidias's statue of Zeus at Olympia; the temple of Artemis at Ephesus; the tomb, or mausoleum, of King Mausolus at Halicarnassus; the Colossus of Rhodes; and either the Pharos, or lighthouse, at Alexandria or the walls of Babylon.

sev•er (sĕv′ər) *v.* **-ered, -er•ing, -ers.** —*tr.* **1.** To set or keep apart; divide or separate. **2.** To cut off (a part) from a whole. **3.** To break up (a relationship, for example); dissolve. See Syns at **separate.** —*intr.* **1.** To become cut or broken apart. **2.** To become separated or divided from each other. [ME *severen* < AN *severer* < VLat. **sēperāre* < Lat. *sēparāre.* See SEPARATE.]

sev•er•a•ble (sĕv′ər-ə-bəl, sĕv′rə-) *adj.* Capable of being severed or separated, as separable into legally distinct rights or obligations, as a contract. —**sev′er•a•bil′i•ty** *n.*

sev•er•al (sĕv′ər-əl, sĕv′rəl) *adj.* **1.** Being of a number more than two or three but not many. **2.** Single; distinct: *"Pshaw! said I . . . three several times"* (Laurence Sterne). **3.** Respectively different; various. **4.** *Law.* Relating separately to each party of a bond or note. —*pron.* (*used with a pl. v.*) An indefinite but small number; some or a few. [ME, separate < AN < Med.Lat. *sēparālis, sēperālis* < Lat. *sēpar* < *sēparāre*, to separate. See SEPARATE.] —**sev′er•al•ly** *adv.*

sev•er•al•fold (sĕv′ər-əl-fōld′, sĕv′rəl-) *adj.* **1.** Having several parts or members. **2.** Being several times as much or as many. —**sev′er•al•fold′** *adv.*

sev•er•al•ty (sĕv′ər-əl-tē, sĕv′rəl-) *n., pl.* **-ties. 1.** The quality or condition of being separate and distinct. **2.** *Law.* **a.** A separate and individual right to possession or ownership that is not shared with any other person. **b.** Land, property, or an estate owned in severalty. **c.** The quality or condition of being held or owned in severalty.

sev•er•ance (sĕv′ər-əns, sĕv′rəns) *n.* **1.a.** The act or process of severing. **b.** The condition of being severed. **2.** Separation; partition.

severance pay *n.* A sum of money, usu. based on length of employment, for which an employee is eligible upon termination.

severance tax *n.* A tax imposed by a state on the extraction of natural resources, such as oil, that will be used in other states.

se•vere (sə-vîr′) *adj.* **-ver•er, -ver•est. 1.** Unsparing or harsh, as in treatment of others; strict. **2.** Marked by or requiring strict adherence to rigorous standards or high principles. **3.** Austere or dour; forbidding. **4.** Extremely plain in substance or style. **5.** Causing sharp discomfort or distress; extremely violent or intense. **6.** Very serious; grave or grievous. **7.** Extremely difficult to perform or accomplish; trying. [Lat. *sevērus*, serious, strict. See **wēro-***.] —**se•vere′ly** *adv.* —**se•vere′ness** *n.*

Syns: *severe, stern, austere, ascetic, strict.* These adjectives mean unsparing and exacting with respect to discipline or control. *Severe* implies adherence to rigorous standards or high principles and often suggests harshness: *"Praise or blame has but a momentary effect on the man whose love of beauty in the abstract makes him a severe critic on his own works"* (John Keats). *Stern* suggests unyielding disposition, uncompromising resolution, or forbidding appearance or nature: *"a man fatally stern and implacable"* (George Meredith). *Austere* connotes aloofness or lack of feeling or sympathy and often rigid morality: *Austere officers demand meticulous conformity with military regulations. Ascetic* suggests self-discipline and often renunciation of worldly pleasures for spiritual improvement: *"Be systematically ascetic . . . do . . . something for no other reason than that you would rather not do it"* (William James). *Strict* means requiring or showing stringent observance of obligations, rules, or standards: *"He could not be severe nor even passably strict"* (W.H. Hudson).

se•ver•i•ty (sə-vĕr′ĭ-tē) *n., pl.* **-ties. 1.** The state or quality of being severe. **2.** The act or an instance of severe behavior, esp. punishment.

Sev•ern (sĕv′ərn). A community of N-central MD, a suburb of Baltimore. Pop. 24,499.

Se•ver•na•ya Zem•lya (sĕv′ər-nə-yä′ zĕm′lē-ä′, -lyä′, syĭ-vyĭr-). An archipelago of N-central Russia in the Arctic Ocean N of the Taimyr Peninsula.

Severn River. 1. A river of NW Ontario, Canada, flowing c. 676 km (420 mi) NE to Hudson Bay. **2.** A river of SW Great Britain rising in central Wales and flowing c. 338 km (210 mi) through W England to Bristol Channel.

Se•ve•rod•vinsk (sĕv′ər-əd-vĭnsk′, syĭ-vyĭ-rəd-). A city of NW Russia on an arm of the White Sea W of Arkhangelsk. Pop. 230,000.

Se•ve•rus (sə-vîr′əs), **Lucius Septimus.** A.D. 146–211. Emperor of Rome (193–211) who created a military monarchy.

se•vi•che (sə-vē′chā, sĕ-) *n.* Var. of **ceviche.**

Se•vier River (sə-vîr′). A river of W-central UT flowing c. 451 km (280 mi) through the **Sevier Desert** and emptying into **Sevier Lake,** a saline lake with no outlet.

Sé•vi•gné (sā-vēn-yā′), Marquise de. Marie de Rabutin-Chantal. 1626–96. French letter writer whose correspondence depicts aristocratic life in the age of Louis XIV.

Se•ville (sə-vĭl′). A city of SW Spain on the Guadalquivir R. NNE of Cádiz. Pop. 672,435.

Sè•vres (sĕv′rə) *n.* A fine French porcelain, often elaborately decorated. [After *Sèvres,* a city of N-central France.]

sew (sō) *v.* **sewed, sewn** (sōn) or **sewed, sew•ing, sews.** —*tr.* **1.** To make, repair, or fasten by stitching, as with a needle and thread. **2.** To furnish with stitches for the purpose of closing, fastening, or attaching. —*intr.* To work with a needle and thread or with a sewing machine. —***phrasal verb.* sew up.** *Informal.* **1.** To complete successfully. **2.** To gain complete control of; monopolize. **3.** To make sure of. [ME *sewen* < OE *seowian.* See **syū-*.**] —**sew′a•ble** *adj.*

sew•age (so͞o′ĭj) *n.* Liquid and solid waste carried off in sewers or drains. [Perh. *sew,* sewer (< ME, short for AN *sewere;* see SEWER[1]) + -AGE.]

Sew•all (so͞o′əl), **Samuel.** 1652–1730. English-born Amer. jurist who presided over the Salem witchcraft trials (1692).

Sew•ard (so͞o′ərd), **William Henry.** 1801–72. Amer. politician who as U.S. secretary of state (1861–69) arranged the purchase of Alaska from Russia (1867).

Seward Peninsula. A peninsula of W AK projecting into the Bering Sea just below the Arctic Circle.

Sew•ell (so͞o′əl), **Anna.** 1820–78. British writer of the children's classic *Black Beauty* (1877).

sew•er[1] (so͞o′ər) *n.* An artificial, usu. underground conduit for carrying off sewage or rainwater. [ME < AN *sewere* < VLat. **exaquāria* : Lat. *ex-,* ex- + Lat. *aquāria,* fem. of *aquārius,* pertaining to water (< *aqua,* water; see **akʷ-ā-*.**)]

sew•er[2] (so͞o′ər) *n.* A medieval servant in charge of meal service. [ME < AN *asseour* < *asseer,* to seat guests < Lat. *assidēre,* to sit down : *ad-,* ad- + *sedēre,* to sit; see **sed-*.**]

sew•er[3] (sō′ər) *n.* One that sews: *a sewer of fine clothing.*

sew•er•age (so͞o′ər-ĭj) *n.* **1.** A system of sewers. **2.** Removal of waste materials by means of a sewer system. **3.** Sewage.

sew•ing (sō′ĭng) *n.* **1.** The act, occupation, or hobby of one who sews. **2.** The article on which one is working with needle and thread; needlework.

sewing circle *n.* A group of people, esp. women, who meet regularly for the purpose of sewing, often for charity.

sewing machine *n.* A machine for sewing, often having additional attachments for special stitching.

sewn (sōn) *v.* A p.part. of **sew.**

sex (sĕks) *n.* **1.a.** The property or quality by which organisms are classified as female or male on the basis of their reproductive organs and functions. **b.** Either of the two divisions, designated female and male, of this classification. **2.** Females or males considered as a group. **3.** The condition or character of being female or male; the physiological, functional, and psychological differences that distinguish the female and the male. See Usage Note at **gender. 4.** The sexual urge or instinct as it manifests itself in behavior. **5.** Sexual intercourse. **6.** The genitalia. —*tr.v.* **sexed, sex•ing, sex•es. 1.** To determine the sex of (an organism, esp. a hatching chicken). **2.** *Slang.* **a.** To arouse sexually. Often used with *up.* **b.** To increase the appeal or attractiveness of. Often used with *up.* [ME < Lat. *sexus.*]

sex– *pref.* Six: *sexpartite.* [Lat. < *sex,* six. See **s(w)eks*.**]

sex•a•ge•nar•i•an (sĕk′sə-jə-nâr′ē-ən) *n.* A person who is 60 years old or between the ages of 60 and 70. —*adj.* **1.** Being 60 years old or between the ages of 60 and 70. **2.** Of or relating to a sexagenarian. [< Lat. *sexāgēnārius,* sexagenary. See SEXAGENARY.]

sex•ag•e•nar•y (sĕk-săj′ə-nĕr′ē) *adj.* **1.** Relating to or proceeding by sixties. **2.** Sexagenarian. —*n., pl.* **-ies.** A sexagenarian. [Lat. *sexāgēnārius* < *sexāgēnī,* sixty each < *sexāgintā,* sixty : *sex,* six; see SEX– + *-gintā,* ten times; see **dekm̥*.**]

sex•a•ges•i•mal (sĕk′sə-jĕs′ə-məl) *adj.* Of, relating to, or based on the number 60. [< Lat. *sexāgēsimus,* sixtieth < *sexāgintā,* sixty. See SEXAGENARY.]

sex cell *n.* A germ cell or gamete.

sex•cen•te•nar•y (sĕk-sĕn′tə-nĕr′ē, sĕk′sĕn-tĕn′ə-rē) *adj.* Relating to 600 or to a 600-year period. —*n., pl.* **-ies.** A 600th anniversary or its commemoration. [< Lat. *sexcentēnī,* six hundred each : *sex,* six; see SEX– + *centēnī,* a hundred each (< *centum,* hundred; see **dekm̥*).**]

sex change *n.* The modification of a person's biological sex characteristics, by surgery and hormone treatment, to approximate those of the opposite sex.

sex chromatin *n. Genet.* See **Barr body.**

sex chromosome *n.* Either of a pair of chromosomes, usu. designated X or Y, in the germ cells of most animals and some plants, that combine to determine the sex of an individual, XX resulting in a female and XY in a male.

sex•en•ni•al (sĕk-sĕn′ē-əl) *adj.* **1.** Occurring every six years. **2.** Relating to or lasting six years. —*n.* An event that occurs every six years. [< Lat. *sexennium,* of six years : *sex,* six; see SEX– + *annus,* year; see **at-*.**] —**sex•en′ni•al•ly** *adv.*

sex hormone *n.* Any of various hormones, such as estrogen and androgen, affecting the reproductive organs, behavior, and development of secondary sex characteristics.

sex•ism (sĕk′sĭz′əm) *n.* **1.** Discrimination based on gender, esp. against women. **2.** Attitudes, conditions, or behaviors that promote stereotyping of social roles based on gender. —**sex′ist** *adj. & n.*

sex kitten *n. Informal.* A young woman seen as sexually appealing.

sex•less (sĕks′lĭs) *adj.* **1.** Lacking sexual characteristics; neuter. **2.** Lacking in sexual interest or activity.

sex-lim•it•ed (sĕks′lĭm′ĭ-tĭd) *adj.* **1.** Occurring or appearing only in one sex. Used of a genetic character or phenotype. **2.** Having a sex-limited character or phenotype.

sex linkage *n.* The condition in which a gene responsible for a specific trait is located on a sex chromosome, resulting in sexually dependent inheritance of the trait.

sex-linked (sĕks′lĭngkt′) *adj.* **1.** Carried by a sex chromosome, esp. an X chromosome. Used of genes. **2.** Sexually determined. Used esp. of inherited traits.

sex object *n.* A person seen primarily as sexually attractive.

sex•ol•o•gy (sĕk-sŏl′ə-jē) *n.* The study of human sexual behavior. —**sex′o•log′ic** (sĕk′sə-lŏj′ĭk), **sex′o•log′i•cal** (-ĭ-kəl) *adj.* —**sex•ol′o•gist** *n.*

sex•par•tite (sĕks-pär′tīt′) *adj.* Composed of or divided into six parts, as a groined vault.

sex•pot (sĕks′pŏt′) *n. Informal.* A woman considered to be sexually attractive.

sex symbol *n.* A person, esp. a celebrity, who is widely acknowledged and appreciated for being sexually attractive.

sext also **Sext** (sĕkst) *n. Eccles.* The fourth of the seven canonical hours. [ME *sexte* < LLat. *sexta* < Lat. *sexta (hōra),* sixth (hour), fem. of *sextus,* sixth. See **s(w)eks*.**]

Sex•tans (sĕks′tənz) *n.* A constellation in the equatorial region of the sky near Leo and Hydra. [NLat. *sextāns,* sextant. See SEXTANT.]

sex•tant (sĕk′stənt) *n.* A navigational instrument containing a graduated 60-degree arc, used for measuring the altitudes of celestial bodies. [NLat. *sextāns, sextant-* < Lat., sixth part (the instrument's arc being a sixth of a circle) < *sextus,* sixth. See **s(w)eks*.**]

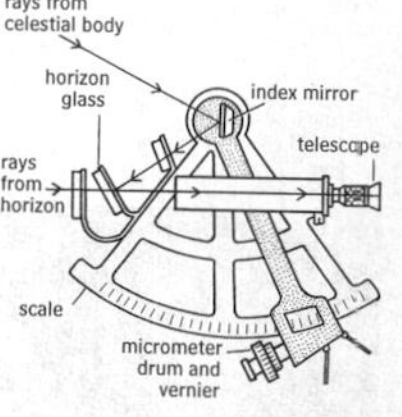

sextant

Sextant (sek′stənt) *n.* See **Sextans.**

sex•tet (sĕk-stĕt′) *n.* **1.** *Mus.* **a.** A group composed of six vocalists or musicians. **b.** A composition for six performers. **2.** A group of six. [Alteration of SESTET.]

sex therapy *n.* The treatment of sexual dysfunction, such as impotence or frigidity, by methods involving counseling, psychotherapy, or behavior modification. —**sex therapist** *n.*

sex•tile (sĕk′stĭl′, -stəl) *adj.* Of or relating to the position of two celestial bodies when they are 60° apart. [Lat. *sextīlis,* one sixth < *sextus,* sixth. See **s(w)eks*.**]

sex•til•lion (sĕk-stĭl′yən) *n.* **1.** The cardinal number equal to 10^{21}. **2.** *Chiefly British.* The cardinal number written 10^{36}. [Fr. : Lat. *sextus,* sixth; see SEXTILE + Fr. *-illion* (as in *million,* million < OFr. *milion;* see MILLION).] —**sex•til′lion** *adj. & pron.*

sex•til•lionth (sĕk-stĭl′yənth) *n.* **1.** The ordinal number matching the number sextillion in a series. **2.** One of sextillion equal parts. —**sex•til′lionth** *adv. & adj.*

sex•to•dec•i•mo (sĕk′stō-dĕs′ə-mō′) *n., pl.* **-mos.** *Print.* **1.** The page size of a book composed of printer's sheets folded into 16 leaves or 32 pages. **2.** A book composed of sextodecimo pages. [Lat. *sextōdecimō,* ablative of *sextusdecimus,* one sixteenth : *sextus,* sixth; see **s(w)eks*** + *decimus,* tenth (< *decem,* ten; see **dekm̥*).**]

sex•ton (sĕk′stən) *n.* An employee or officer of a church who is responsible for the care and upkeep of church property and sometimes for ringing bells and digging graves. [ME *sextein* < Anglo-Lat. *sextānus,* prob. alteration of Med.Lat. *secristānus,* sacristan, var. of *sacristānus.* See SACRISTAN.]

Anne Sexton

Sex•ton (sĕk′stən), **Anne.** 1928–74. Amer. poet whose works include the collection *Live or Die* (1966).

sex•tu•ple (sĕk-sto͞o′pəl, -styo͞o′-, -stŭp′əl, sĕk′stŭp′əl) *tr. & intr.v.* **-pled, -pling, -ples.** To multiply or be multiplied by six. —*adj.* **1.** Containing or consisting of six parts. **2.** Larger or greater by six parts; multiplied by six. **3.** *Mus.* Having six beats to the measure. —*n.* A number six times larger than another. [Prob. Lat. *sextus;* see SEXTILE + *-uple* (as in QUINTUPLE).] —**sex•tu′ply** *adv.*

sex•tup•let (sĕk-stŭp′lĭt, -sto͞o′plĭt, -styo͞o′-, sĕk′stŭp′lĭt) *n.* **1.** One of six offspring born in a single birth. **2.** A group of six similar persons or things; a sextet. [SEXTU(PLE) + (TRI)PLET.]

sex•u•al (sĕk′sho͞o-əl) *adj.* **1.** Of, relating to, involving, or characteristic of sex, sexuality, the sexes, or the sex organs and their functions. **2.** Implying or symbolizing erotic desires or activity. **3.** Of, relating to, or involving the union of male and female gametes: *sexual reproduction.* [LLat. *sexuālis* < Lat. *sexus,* sex.] —**sex′u•al•ly** *adv.*

sexual assault *n. Law.* Indecent conduct of a man toward another man, a woman, or a child or of a woman toward a child, accompanied by the threat or danger of physical suf-

ă pat	oi boy
ā pay	ou out
âr care	o͝o took
ä father	o͞o boot
ĕ pet	ŭ cut
ē be	ûr urge
ĭ pit	th thin
ī pie	*th* this
îr pier	hw which
ŏ pot	zh vision
ō toe	ə about,
ô paw	item

Stress marks:
′ (primary);
′ (secondary), as in
dictionary (dĭk′shə-nĕr′ē)

fering or injury or inducing fear, shame, humiliation, and mental anguish.

sexual harassment *n.* Unwanted and offensive sexual advances or sexually derogatory or discriminatory remarks.

sexual intercourse *n.* **1.** Coitus between human beings. **2.** Sexual union between human beings involving genital contact other than vaginal penetration by the penis.

sex•u•al•i•ty (sĕk′sho͞o-ăl′ĭ-tē) *n.* **1.** The condition of being characterized and distinguished by sex. **2.** Concern with or interest in sexual activity. **3.** Sexual character or potency.

sex•u•al•ize (sĕk′sho͞o-ə-līz′) *tr.v.* **-ized, -iz•ing, -iz•es.** To make sexual in character or quality. **— sex′u•al•i•za′tion** (-ə-lĭ-zā′shən) *n.*

sexually trans•mit•ted disease (trăns-mĭt′ĭd, trănz-) *n.* Any of various diseases, including chancroid, chlamydia, gonorrhea, and syphilis, that are usu. contracted through sexual intercourse or other intimate sexual contact.

sexual orientation *n.* The direction of one's sexual interest toward members of the same, opposite, or both sexes.

sexual relations *pl.n.* **1.** Sexual intercourse. **2.** Sexual activity between individuals.

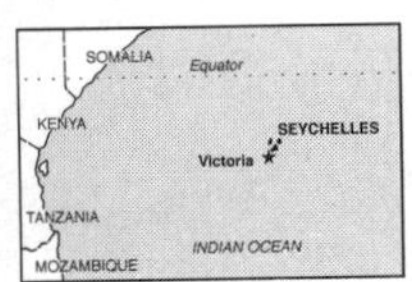

Seychelles

sex•y (sĕk′sē) *adj.* **-i•er, -i•est. 1.** Arousing or tending to arouse sexual desire or interest. **2.** *Slang.* Highly appealing or interesting; attractive. **— sex′i•ly** *adv.* **— sex′i•ness** *n.*

Sey•chelles (sā-shĕl′, -shĕlz′). An island country in the W Indian Ocean N of Madagascar; gained independence from Great Britain in 1976. Cap. Victoria. Pop. 64,718.

Sey•fert galaxy (sē′fərt, sī′-) *n.* A spiral galaxy with a small, compact, bright nucleus that exhibits variable light intensity and radio-wave emission. [After Carl K. *Seyfert* (1911–60), Amer. astronomer.]

Jane Seymour
1536 portrait by Hans Holbein the Younger

Sey•mour, Jane. 1509?–37. Queen of England (1536–37) as the third wife of Henry VIII.

sf or **SF** *abbr.* Science fiction.

sf. *abbr. Mus.* Sforzando.

SFC *abbr.* Sergeant first class.

sfer•ics also **spher•ics** (sfîr′ĭks, sfĕr′-) *n.* *(used with a sing. v.)* **1.** The study of atmospherics, esp. using electronic detectors. **2.** See **atmospherics** 1. [Alteration of ATMOSPHERICS.]

Sfor•za (sfôr′sə, sfôr′tsä). Family of Milanese political leaders, including **Ludovico** (1451?–1508), duke of Milan (1481–99) and a patron of Leonardo da Vinci.

sfor•zan•do (sfôrt-sän′dō) also **for•zan•do** (fôrt-sän′dō) *Mus.* — *adv. & adj.* Suddenly and strongly accented. — *n., pl.* **-dos** or **-di** (-dē). A sforzando tone or chord. [Ital., gerund of *sforzare*, to use force : *s-*, intensive pref. (< Lat. *ex-*; see EX–) + *forzare*, to force (< VLat. **fortiāre* < Lat. *fortis*, strong; see FORTIS).] **— sfor•zan′do** *adv.*

sfu•ma•to (sfo͞o-mä′tō) *n.* The blurring or softening of sharp outlines in painting by subtle and gradual blending of one tone into another. [Ital. < p.part. of *sfumare*, to evaporate, fade out : *s-*, from (< Lat. *ex-*; see EX–) + *fumare*, to smoke (< Lat. *fumāre*).]

sfz. *abbr. Mus.* Sforzando.

sg *abbr.* Specific gravity.

Sg *abbr. Bible.* Song of Songs.

SG *abbr.* **1.** Senior grade. **2.** Surgeon General.

S.G. or **SG** *abbr.* Solicitor general.

sgd. *abbr.* Signed.

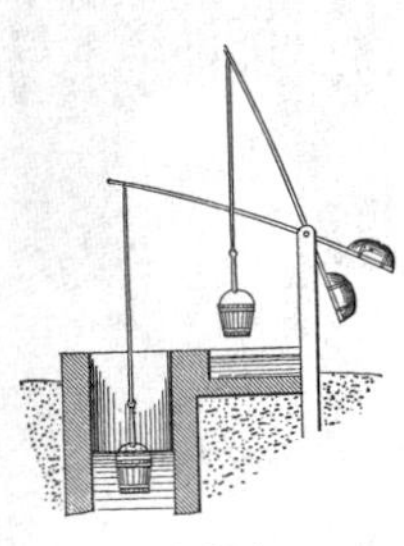
shadoof

sgraf•fi•to (skră-fē′tō, zgrä-) *n., pl.* **-ti** (-tē). **1.** Decoration produced on pottery or ceramic by scratching through a surface of plaster or glazing to reveal a different color underneath. **2.** Ware decorated in this manner. [Ital., p.part. of *sgraffire*, to scratch < *sgraffio*, a scratch < *sgraffiare*, to scratch < OItal. : *s-*, intensive pref.; see SFORZANDO + *graffiare*, to scratch; see GRAFFITO.]

's Gra•ven•ha•ge (skrä′vən-hä′gə, SKHrä′vən-hä′KHə). See The **Hague.**

Sgt. *abbr.* Sergeant.

Sgt. Maj. *abbr.* Sergeant major.

sh (sh) *interj.* Used to urge silence.

sh. *abbr.* **1.** Share. **2.** Sheet.

Shaan•xi (shän′shē′) also **Shen•si** (shĕn′sē′). A province of E-central China crossed by the Wei He. Cap. Xi'an. Pop. 30,020,000.

Sha•ba (shä′bə). Formerly **Ka•tan•ga** (kə-tăng′gə, -tăng′-). A region of SE Zaire bordering on Zambia; site of a secessionist state from 1960 to 1963.

Sha'•ban also **Shaa•ban** (shə-bän′, shä-, shô-) *n.* The eighth month of the year in the Muslim calendar. [Ar. *ša'bān.*]

Shab•bat (shə-bät′, shä′bəs) *n. Judaism.* The Sabbath. [Heb. *šabbāt*, sabbath.]

shab•by (shăb′ē) *adj.* **-bi•er, -bi•est. 1.** Wearing threadbare clothing. **2.a.** Showing signs of wear and tear; threadbare or worn-out. **b.** Dilapidated or deteriorated in condition, esp. through neglect; seedy. **3.a.** Despicable; mean. **b.** Not generous or just; unfair. **c.** Of mediocre or substandard quality. [< obsolete *shab*, scab < ME *shab* < OE *sceabb.*] **— shab′bi•ly** *adv.* **— shab′bi•ness** *n.*

Sha•bu•oth (shə-vo͞o′ōt′, -əs, shä′vo͞o-ôt′) *n.* Var. of **Shavuot.**

shack (shăk) *n.* A small, crudely built cabin; a shanty. — *intr.v.* **shack•ed, shack•ing, shacks.** To live or dwell. — *idiom.* **shack up.** *Slang.* **1.** To sleep together or live in sexual intimacy without being married. **2.** To live, room, or stay at a place. [Poss. < Am.Sp. *jacal* < Nahuat. *xacalli*, adobe hut : *xāmitl*, adobe + *calli*, house, hut.]

shack•le (shăk′əl) *n.* **1.** A metal fastening, usu. one of a pair, for encircling and confining the ankle or wrist of a prisoner or captive; a fetter or manacle. **2.** A hobble for an animal. **3.** Any of several devices, such as a clevis, used to fasten or couple. **4.** A restraint or check to action or progress. Often used in the plural. — *tr.v.* **-led, -ling, -les. 1.** To confine with shackles; fetter. **2.** To fasten or connect with a shackle. **3.** To restrict, confine, or hamper. [ME *schakel* < OE *sceacel*, fetter.] **— shack′ler** *n.*

shad (shăd) *n., pl.* **shad** or **shads.** Any of several food fishes of the genus *Alosa*, esp. the North American species *A. sapidissima*, related to the herrings. [ME **shad* < OE *sceadd.*]

shad•ber•ry (shăd′bĕr′ē) *n.* The fruit of the shadbush.

shad•bush (shăd′bo͝osh′) *n.* Any of various North American shrubs or trees of the genus *Amelanchier*, having edible blue-black or purplish fruit and smooth gray striped twigs.

shad•dock (shăd′ək) *n.* **1.** A tropical southeast Asian tree *(Citrus maxima)* having edible yellow pear-shaped fruit with thick rinds. **2.** The fruit of this tree. [After Captain *Shaddock*, 17th-cent. English ship commander.]

shade (shād) *n.* **1.** Light diminished in intensity as a result of the interception of the rays; partial darkness. **2.** An area or a space of partial darkness. **3.** Cover or shelter provided by interception by an object of the sun or its rays. **4.** Any of various devices used to reduce or screen light or heat. **5. shades.** *Slang.* Sunglasses. **6.** Relative obscurity. **7. shades.** Dark shadows gathering at dusk. **8.** The part of a picture or photograph depicting darkness or shadow. **9.** The degree to which a color is mixed with black or is decreasingly illuminated; gradation of darkness. **10.** A slight difference or variation; a nuance. **11.** A small amount; a trace. **12.** A disembodied spirit; a ghost. **13. shades.** A present reminder of a person or situation in the past. — *v.* **shad•ed, shad•ing, shades.** — *tr.* **1.** To screen from light or heat. **2.** To obscure or darken. **3.** To cause shade in or on. **4.a.** To represent degrees of shade or shadow in. **b.** To produce (gradations of light or color) in a drawing or picture. **5.** To change or vary by slight degrees. **6.** To make a slight reduction in. — *intr.* To pass from one quality, color, or thing to another by very slight changes or degrees. [ME < OE *sceadu.*] **— shad′er** *n.*

shade tree *n.* A tree planted chiefly to provide shade from sunlight.

shad•ing (shā′dĭng) *n.* **1.** A screening against light or heat. **2.** The lines or other marks used to fill in outlines of a sketch, an engraving, or a painting to represent gradations of color or darkness. **3.** A small variation, gradation, or difference.

sha•doof also **sha•duf** (shä-do͞of′) *n.* A device consisting of a long suspended pole weighted at one end and having a bucket at the other end, used in the Near East and esp. Egypt for raising water, as for the irrigation of land. [Ar. *šādūf.*]

shad•ow (shăd′ō) *n.* **1.** An area that is not or is only partially irradiated or illuminated because of the interception of radiation by an opaque object between the area and the source of radiation. **2.** The rough image cast by an object blocking rays of illumination. **3.** An imperfect imitation or copy. **4. shadows.** The darkness following sunset. **5.a.** A feeling of gloom or unhappiness. **b.** A cause of gloom or unhappiness. **6.** A shaded area in a picture or photograph. **7.** A mirrored image or reflection. **8.** A phantom; a ghost. **9.a.** One, such as a detective or spy, that follows or trails another. **b.** A constant companion. **10.** A faint indication; a premonition. **11.** A vestige or remnant. **12.** An insignificant portion or amount; a trace. **13.** Shelter; protection. — *v.* **-owed, -ow•ing, -ows.** — *tr.* **1.** To cast a shadow on; shade. **2.** To make gloomy or dark; cloud. **3.** To represent vaguely, mysteriously, or prophetically. **4.** To darken in a painting or drawing; shade in. **5.** To follow, esp. in secret; trail. — *intr.* **1.** To change by gradual degrees. **2.** To become clouded over as if with shadows. — *adj.* Not having official status. [ME < OE *sceaduwe*, oblique case of *sceadu.*] **— shad′ow•er** *n.*

shad•ow•box (shăd′ō-bŏks′) *intr.v.* **-boxed, -box•ing, -box•es.** To spar with an imaginary opponent, as for exercise or training purposes. **— shad′ow•box′ing** *n.*

shadow box *n.* A shallow rectangular box usu. with a glass front that is used for holding and protecting items on display.

shad•ow•graph (shăd′ō-grăf′) *n.* **1.** An image produced by casting a shadow on a screen. **2.** See **shadow play. 3.** See **radiograph.**

shadow play *n.* A play presented by casting shadows of puppets or actors on a screen.

shad•ow•y (shăd′ō-ē) *adj.* **-i•er, -i•est. 1.** Relating to or resembling a shadow. **2.** Full of or dark with shadow. **3.** Lacking distinctness; faint. **4.** Lacking substance; unsubstantial. **— shad′ow•i•ly** *adv.* **— shad′ow•i•ness** *n.*

Shad•rach (shăd′răk). In the Bible, a young man who with Abednego and Meshach emerged unharmed from the fiery furnace of Babylon.

shad•y (shā′dē) *adj.* **-i•er, -i•est. 1.** Full of shade; shaded. **2.** Casting shade: *a shady grove.* **3.** Quiet, dark, or concealed; hidden. **4.** Of dubious character or honesty; questionable. **— shad′i•ly** *adv.* **— shad′i•ness** *n.*

shaft (shăft) *n.* **1.a.** The long narrow stem or body of a spear or an arrow. **b.** A spear or an arrow. **2.a.** A projectile suggestive of a spear or an arrow in appearance or configuration. **b.** *Informal.* A scornfully satirical comment; a barb. **c.** *Slang.* Harsh, unfair treatment. **3.** A ray or beam of light. **4.** The handle of any of various tools or implements. **5.** The main axis of a feather, esp. its distal portion. **6.** *Anat.* **a.** The midsection of a long bone; diaphysis. **b.** The section of a hair projecting from the surface of the body. **7.** *Archit.* **a.** A column or an obelisk. **b.** The section of a column between the capital and the base. **8.** One of two parallel poles between which an animal is harnessed to a vehicle. **9.** A long, usu. cylindrical bar, esp. one that rotates and transmits power, as the drive shaft of an engine. **10.** A long, narrow, often vertical passage sunk into the earth; a tunnel. **11.** A vertical passage housing an elevator. **12.** A duct or conduit for the passage of air, as for ventilation or heating. *— tr.v.* **shaft•ed, shaft•ing, shafts. 1.** To equip with a shaft. **2.** *Slang.* To treat in a harsh, unfair way. [ME < OE *sceaft.*]

Shaftes•bur•y (shăfts′bĕr′ē, -bə-rē), First Earl of. Anthony Ashley Cooper. 1621–83. English politician considered the founder of the Whig Party.

shaft•ing (shăf′tĭng) *n.* **1.** A system of shafts, as in a machine, for transmitting motion or power. **2.** Material for making shafts. **3.** *Slang.* An instance of harsh or unfair treatment.

shag¹ (shăg) *n.* **1.** A tangle or mass, esp. of rough matted hair. **2.a.** A coarse long nap, as on a woolen cloth. **b.** Cloth having such a nap. **3.** A rug with a thick rough pile. **4.** Coarse shredded tobacco. *— tr.v.* **shagged, shag•ging, shags. 1.** To make shaggy; roughen. **2.a.** To chase and bring back; fetch. **b.** *Baseball.* To chase and catch (fly balls) in practice. [ME **shagge* < OE *sceacga,* matted hair.]

shag² (shăg) *n.* A dance step of the 1930's consisting of a hop on each foot in turn. *— intr.v.* **shagged, shag•ging, shags.** To perform or execute this dance. [?]

shag³ (shăg) *n.* Either of two marine birds *(Phalacrocorax aristotelis* or *P. punctatus)* of Europe and North Africa, related to the cormorant. [Perh. < its shaggy crest.]

shag•bark (shăg′bärk′) *n.* An eastern North American hickory tree *(Carya ovata)* having shaggy bark.

shag•gy (shăg′ē) *adj.* **-gi•er, -gi•est. 1.** Having, covered with, or resembling long rough hair or wool. **2.** Bushy and matted. **3.** Having a rough nap or surface, as a textile. **4.** Poorly groomed; unkempt. **5.** Lacking order or clarity, as in thinking. **— shag′gi•ly** *adv.* **— shag′gi•ness** *n.*

shaggy cap *n.* See **shaggymane.**

shag•gy-dog story (shăg′ē-dôg′, -dŏg′) *n. Informal.* A long anecdote with an absurd or anticlimactic punch line.

shag•gy•mane also **shag•gy mane** (shăg′ē-mān′) *n.* An edible mushroom *(Coprinus comatus)* having shaggy scales.

sha•green (shə-grēn′) *n.* **1.** The rough hide of a shark or ray, covered with numerous bony denticles and used as an abrasive and as leather. **2.** An untanned leather with a granular surface that is often dyed green. [Fr. *chagrin, sagrin* < Turk. *sağri,* crupper, leather.] **— sha•green′** *adj.*

shah (shä) *n.* Used formerly as a title for the hereditary monarch of Iran. [Pers. *shāh,* king < OPers. *khshāyathiya-.*] **— shah′dom** *n.*

Shah Ja•han (shä′ jə-hän′). 1592–1666. Mogul emperor of India (1628–58) whose reign ushered in the golden age of Mogul art and architecture.

Shahn (shän), **Ben(jamin).** 1898–1969. Lithuanian-born artist whose works reflect social and political themes.

shai•tan (shī-tän′, shā-) *n.* **1.** Often **Shaitan.** *Islam.* The Devil; Satan. **2.** An evil spirit; a fiend. [Ar. *šayṭān* < Heb. *śāṭān.* See SATAN.]

shake (shāk) *v.* **shook** (shŏŏk), **shak•en** (shā′kən), **shak•ing, shakes.** *— tr.* **1.** To cause to move to and fro with jerky movements. **2.** To cause to quiver, tremble, vibrate, or rock. **3.** To cause to lose stability or waver: *shook my beliefs.* **4.** To remove or dislodge by jerky movements. **5.a.** To bring to a specified condition by or as if by shaking: *shook me out of complacency.* **b.** *Slang.* To get rid of. **6.** To disturb or agitate; unnerve. See Syns at **dismay. 7.** To brandish or wave, esp. in anger. **8.** To clasp (hands) in greeting or leave-taking or as a sign of agreement. **9.** *Mus.* To trill (a note). **10.** *Games.* To rattle and mix (dice) before casting. *— intr.* **1.** To move to and fro in short, irregular, often jerky movements. **2.** To tremble, as from cold or in anger. **3.** To be unsteady; totter or waver. **4.** To move something vigorously up and down or from side to side, as in mixing. **5.** *Mus.* To trill. **6.** To shake hands. *— n.* **1.** The act of shaking. **2.** A trembling or quivering movement. **3.** *Informal.* An earthquake. **4.a.** A fissure in rock. **b.** A crack in timber caused by wind or frost. **5.** *Informal.* A moment or an instant; a trice. **6.** *Mus.* A trill. **7.a.** See **milk shake** 1. **b.** A beverage in which the ingredients are mixed by shaking. **8.** A rough shingle used to cover rustic buildings, such as barns. **9. shakes.** *Informal.* Uncontrollable trembling, as in a person who is cold, frightened, feverish, or ill. **10.** *Slang.* A bargain or deal. ***— phrasal verbs.*** **shake down. 1.** *Slang.* To extort money from. **2.** *Slang.* To make a thorough search of. **3.** To subject (a new ship or aircraft) to shakedown testing. **4.** To become acclimated or accustomed. **shake off.** To free oneself of; get rid of. **shake up. 1.** To upset by or as if by a physical jolt or shock. **2.** To subject to a drastic rearrangement or reorganization. ***— idioms.*** **give (someone) the shake.** *Slang.* To escape from or get rid of. **no great shakes.** *Slang.* Unexceptional; ordinary. **shake a leg.** *Informal.* **1.** To dance. **2.** To move quickly; hurry up. **shake (another's) tree.** *Slang.* To arouse to action or reaction; disturb. **shake a stick at.** *Slang.* To point out, designate, or name. [ME *shaken* < OE *sceacan.*] **— shak′a•ble, shake′a•ble** *adj.*

shake•down (shāk′doun′) *n.* **1.** *Slang.* Extortion of money, as by blackmail. **2.** *Slang.* A thorough search of a place or person. **3.** A period of appraisal followed by adjustments to improve efficiency or functioning. *— adj.* Serving to test a ship or an aircraft and familiarize the crew with its operation.

shake•out (shāk′out′) *n.* **1.** The elimination of competing businesses or products in a particular field. **2.** A decline in the values of certain securities that usu. results in a depressed stock market.

shak•er (shā′kər) *n.* **1.a.** One that shakes. **b.** One that impels, encourages, or supervises action. **2.a.** A container used for shaking. **b.** A container used to mix or blend by shaking. **3. Shaker.** A member of a Christian group originating in England in 1747, practicing communal living and observing celibacy. *— adj.* also **Shaker.** Relating to or constituting a style produced by Shakers that is distinctively simple, unornamented, functional, and finely crafted.

Shaker Heights. A city of NE OH, a suburb of Cleveland. Pop. 30,831.

Shake•speare (shāk′spîr), **William.** 1564–1616. English playwright and poet whose plays include historical works, such as *Richard II,* comedies, including *As You Like It,* and tragedies, such as *Hamlet* and *King Lear.* **— Shake•spear′e•an, Shake•spear′i•an** *adj. & n.*

Shakespearean sonnet *n.* The sonnet form perfected by Shakespeare, composed of three quatrains and a terminal couplet in iambic pentameter rhyming *abab cdcd efef gg.*

shake•up (shāk′ŭp′) *n.* A thorough, often drastic reorganization, as of the personnel in a business or government.

shak•ing palsy (shā′kĭng) *n.* See **Parkinson's disease.**

shak•o (shăk′ō, shā′kō, shä′-) *n., pl.* **-os** or **-oes.** A stiff, cylindrical military dress hat with a metal plate in front, a short visor, and a plume. [Fr. *schako* < Hung. *csákó* < *csákós (süveg),* pointed (cap) < *csák,* peak, perh. < MHGer. *zacke,* tack, nail.]

Shak•ta (shäk′tə, säk′-) *n. Hinduism.* One who worships Shakti. [Skt. *śāktaḥ* < *śaktiḥ,* Shakti. See SHAKTI.] **— Shak′tism** *n.* **— Shak′tist** *n.*

Shak•ti (shŭk′tē, shäk′-) *n. Hinduism.* **1.** The active manifest power that creates the universe. **2.** The consort of the male expression of the divine, esp. of the god Shiva. [Skt. *śaktiḥ* < *śaknoti,* he is strong.]

shak•y (shā′kē) *adj.* **-i•er, -i•est. 1.** Trembling or quivering; tremulous. **2.** Lacking soundness or sturdiness, as of construction. **3.a.** Not to be depended on; precarious. **b.** Wavering in firmness: *shaky confidence.* **c.** Open to question or doubt. **— shak′i•ly** *adv.* **— shak′i•ness** *n.*

shale (shāl) *n.* A fissile rock composed of layers of claylike fine-grained sediments. [Prob. < ME, shell < OE *scealu.* See **skel-¹*.**] **— shal′ey** *adj.*

shale oil *n.* A crude oil that is obtained from oil shale by heating and distillation.

shall (shăl) *aux.v.* p.t. **should** (shŏŏd). **1.** Used before a verb in the infinitive to show: **a.** Something that will take place or exist in the future: *We shall arrive tomorrow.* **b.** Something, such as an order, a promise, a requirement, or an obligation: *The penalty shall not exceed two years in prison.* **c.** The will to do something or have something take place: *I shall go out if I feel like it.* **d.** Something that is inevitable: *That day shall come.* **2.** *Archaic.* **a.** To be able to. **b.** To have to; must. [ME *shal* < OE *sceal.* See **skel-²*.**]

Usage Note: The traditional rules for using *shall* and *will* prescribe a highly complicated pattern of use in which the meanings of the forms change according to the person of the subject. In the first person *shall* is used to indicate simple futurity: *I shall have to buy another ticket.* In the second and third persons the same sense of futurity is expressed by *will: The comet will return in 87 years.* The use of *will* in the first person and of *shall* in the second and third may express determination, promise, obligation, or permission, depending on the context. Thus *I will leave tomorrow* indicates that the speaker is determined to leave; *You and she shall leave tomorrow* is likely to be interpreted as a command. In America, however, *will* is used to express most of the senses reserved for *shall* in British usage, and *shall* itself is restricted to first person interrogative proposals, as in *Shall we go?* and to certain fixed expressions, such as *We shall overcome. Shall* is also

shaggymane
Coprinus comatus

William Shakespeare
Portrait from title page of the First Folio, 1623, engraved by Martin Droeshout (1601–1650?)

ă pat	oi boy
ā pay	ou out
âr care	ŏŏ took
ä father	ōō boot
ĕ pet	ŭ cut
ē be	ûr urge
ĭ pit	th thin
ī pie	*th* this
îr pier	hw which
ŏ pot	zh vision
ō toe	ə about, item
ô paw	

Stress marks:
′ (primary);
′ (secondary), as in
dictionary (dĭk′shə-nĕr′ē)

used in formal style to express an explicit obligation, as in *Applicants shall provide a proof of residence.* In speech the distinction that the British signal by the choice of *shall* or *will* may be rendered by stressing the auxiliary, as in *I will leave tomorrow* ("I intend to leave"); by choosing another auxiliary, such as *must* or *have to*; or by using an adverb such as *certainly*. • Many earlier American writers observed the traditional distinction between *shall* and *will*, and some continue to do so. The practice cannot be called incorrect, though it may strike American ears as somewhat mannered. See Usage Note at **should.**

shal•loon (shə-lo͞on′, shă-) *n.* A lightweight wool or worsted twill fabric, used chiefly for coat linings. [Fr. *chalon*, after CHÂLONS-SUR-MARNE.]

shallop
Watercolor by John F. Leavitt

shal•lop (shăl′əp) *n. Naut.* A small open boat fitted with oars or sails, or both, and used primarily in shallow waters. [Fr. *chaloupe* < Du. *sloep*, sloop; see SLOOP, or perh. < obsolete Fr. *chaloppe*, nutshell (< OFr. *eschalope* < *escale, eschale*, shell, husk; see SCALE¹).]

shal•lot (shə-lŏt′, shăl′ət) *n.* **1.** A type of onion with long pear-shaped aggregated bulbs. **2.** The mild-flavored bulb of this plant, used in cookery. [Obsolete Fr. *eschalotte* < OFr. *eschaloigne* < VLat. **escalōnia*. See SCALLION.]

shal•low (shăl′ō) *adj.* **-er, -est. 1.** Measuring little from bottom to top or surface; lacking physical depth. **2.** Lacking depth of intellect, emotion, or knowledge. **3.** Marked by insufficient inhalation of air; weak. —*n.* A part of a body of water of little depth; a shoal. Often used in the plural. —*tr. & intr.v.* **-lowed, -low•ing, -lows.** To make or become shallow. [ME *shalowe*.] —**shal′low•ly** *adv.* —**shal′low•ness** *n.*

sha•lom (shä-lōm′, shə-) *interj.* Used as a traditional Jewish greeting or farewell. [Heb. *šālôm*, peace.]

shalt (shălt) *aux.v. Archaic.* A second pers. sing. pr.t. of **shall.**

sham (shăm) *n.* **1.** Something false or empty that is purported to be genuine; a spurious imitation. **2.** The quality of deceitfulness; empty pretense. **3.** One who assumes a false character; an impostor. **4.** A decorative cover made to simulate an article of household linen and used over or in place of it. —*adj.* Not genuine; fake. —*v.* **shammed, sham•ming, shams.** —*tr.* To put on the false appearance of; feign. —*intr.* To assume a false appearance or character; dissemble. [Perh. dialectal var. of SHAME.] —**sham′mer** *n.*

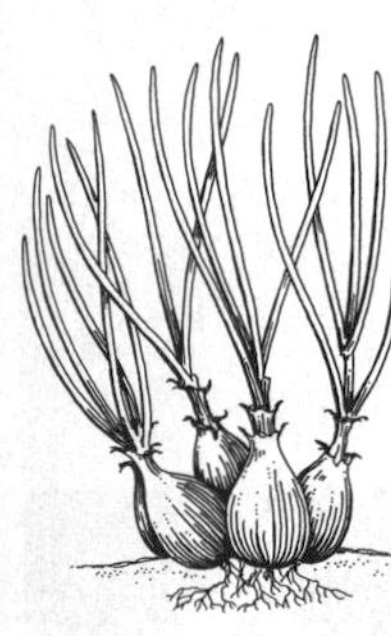

shallot
Allium ascalonicum

sha•man (shä′mən, shā′-) *n.* A member of certain tribal societies who acts as a medium between the visible world and an invisible spirit world and practices magic or sorcery for healing, divination, and control over natural events. [Russ. < Tungus *šaman*, Buddhist monk, shaman < Tocharian *samāne* < Prakrit *samaṇa* < Skt. *śramaṇaḥ* < *śrámaḥ*, religious exercise.] —**sha•man′ic** (shə-măn′ĭk) *adj.*

sha•man•ism (shä′mə-nĭz′əm, shā′-) *n.* **1.** The animistic religion of certain peoples of northern Asia in which shamans mediate between the visible and spirit worlds. **2.** A similar religion or set of beliefs, esp. among certain Native American peoples. —**sha′man•ist** *n.* —**sha′man•is′tic** *adj.*

sham•ble (shăm′bəl) *intr.v.* **-bled, -bling, -bles.** To walk in an awkward, lazy, or unsteady manner, shuffling the feet. [Prob. < obsolete *shamble*, awkward, ungainly < ME *schamil*, butcher's table. See SHAMBLES.] —**sham′ble** *n.*

sham•bles (shăm′bəlz) *pl.n. (used with a sing. v.)* **1.a.** A scene or condition of complete disorder or ruin. **b.** Great clutter or jumble; a total mess. **2.a.** A place or scene of bloodshed or carnage. **b.** A scene or condition of great devastation. **3.** A slaughterhouse. **4.** *Archaic.* A meat market or butcher shop. [< ME *shamel, shambil*, place where meat is butchered and sold < OE *sceamol*, table < Lat. *scabillum, scamillum*, dim. of *scamnum*, bench, stool.]

Word History: The history of the word *shambles* begins with the Latin word *scamnum*, "a stool or bench serving as a seat, step, or support for the feet, for example." The diminutive *scamillum*, "low stool," was borrowed by speakers of Old English as *sceamol*, "stool, bench, table." Old English *sceamol* became Middle English *shamel*, which developed the specific sense in the singular and plural of "a place where meat is butchered and sold." The Middle English compound *shamelhouse* meant "slaughterhouse," a sense that the plural *shambles* developed (first recorded in 1548) along with the figurative sense "a place or scene of bloodshed" (first recorded in 1593). Our current meanings, such as "a scene or condition of disorder," are first recorded as of 1926.

shame (shām) *n.* **1.a.** A painful emotion caused by a strong sense of guilt, embarrassment, unworthiness, or disgrace. **b.** Capacity for such a feeling. **2.** One that brings dishonor, disgrace, or condemnation. **3.** A condition of disgrace or dishonor; ignominy. **4.** A great disappointment. —*tr.v.* **shamed, sham•ing, shames. 1.** To cause to feel shame; put to shame. **2.** To bring dishonor or disgrace on. **3.** To disgrace by surpassing. **4.** To force by making ashamed. —***idiom.* put to shame. 1.** To fill with shame; disgrace. **2.** To outdo thoroughly; surpass. [ME < OE *sceamu*.]

shame•faced (shām′fāst′) *adj.* **1.** Indicative of shame; ashamed. **2.** Extremely modest or shy; bashful. [Alteration of obsolete *shamefast*, bashful, ashamed < ME < OE *sceamfæst* : *sceamu*, shame + *fæst*, fixed; see FAST¹.] —**shame′fac′ed•ly** (-fā′sĭd-lē) *adv.* —**shame′fac′ed•ness** *n.*

shame•ful (shām′fəl) *adj.* **1.a.** Causing shame; disgraceful. **b.** Giving offense; indecent. **2.** *Archaic.* Full of shame; ashamed. —**shame′ful•ly** *adv.* —**shame′ful•ness** *n.*

shame•less (shām′lĭs) *adj.* **1.** Feeling no shame; impervious to disgrace. **2.** Marked by a lack of shame: *a shameless lie.* —**shame′less•ly** *adv.* —**shame′less•ness** *n.*

sham•mes (shä′məs) *n., pl.* **sham•mo•sim** (shä-mô′sĭm). *Judaism.* **1.** A sexton in a synagogue. **2.** The candle used to light the other eight candles of a Hanukkah menorah. [Yiddish *shames* < Heb. *šammāš*.]

sham•my (shăm′ē) *n.* Var. of **chamois** 2.

sham•poo (shăm-po͞o′) *n., pl.* **-poos. 1.** Any of various liquid or cream preparations of soap or detergent used to wash the hair and scalp. **2.** Any of various cleaning agents for rugs, upholstery, or cars. **3.** The act or process of washing or cleaning with shampoo. —*tr. & intr.v.* **-pooed, -poo•ing, -poos.** To wash or undergo washing with shampoo. [< Hindi *cā̃pō*, imper. of *cā̃pnā*, to press.] —**sham•poo′er** *n.*

sham•rock (shăm′rŏk′) *n.* Any of several plants, such as the clover, having compound leaves with three leaflets. [Ir.Gael. *seamróg*, dim. of *seamar*, clover < MIr. *semar*.]

sha•mus (shä′məs, shā′-) *n. Slang.* **1.** A police officer. **2.** A private detective. [Perh. alteration of SHAMMES.]

Shan (shän, shăn) *n., pl.* **Shan** or **Shans. 1.** A member of any of a group of tribes inhabiting northeast Burma and adjacent parts of China, Laos, and Thailand. **2.** The Tai language of the Shan.

Shan•dong (shän′dông′) also **Shan•tung** (shăn′tŭng′, shän′to͝ong′). A province of E China bordered by the Gulf of Bo Hai and the Yellow Sea. The E part of the province forms the **Shandong Peninsula.** Cap. Jinan. Pop. 76,950,000.

shan•dy (shăn′dē) *n., pl.* **-dies. 1.** Shandygaff. **2.** A drink made of beer and lemonade.

shan•dy•gaff (shăn′dē-găf′) *n.* A drink made of beer or ale mixed with ginger beer, ginger ale, or lemonade. [?]

Shang (shäng). A Chinese dynasty traditionally dated 1766–1122 B.C., whose capital was present-day Anyang.

shang•hai (shăng-hī′, shăng′hī′) *tr.v.* **-haied, -hai•ing, -hais. 1.** To kidnap for compulsory service aboard a ship. **2.** To induce or compel (someone) to do something, esp. by fraud or force. [After SHANGHAI¹, < the former custom of kidnapping sailors to man ships going to China.] —**shang•hai′er** *n.*

Shang•hai¹ (shăng-hī′, shäng′-). A city of E China at the mouth of the Yangtze R. (Chang Jiang) SE of Nanjing; opened to foreign trade by the Treaty of Nanking (1842). Pop. 6,980,000. The municipality of **Shanghai** is administered as a separate governmental unit. Pop. 12,170,000.

Shang•hai² (shăng-hī′) *n.* See **Cochin China².**

Shan•gri-la (shăng′grĭ-lä′) *n.* **1.** An imaginary remote paradise on earth; utopia. **2.** A distant and secluded hideaway, usu. of great beauty and peacefulness. [After *Shangri-La*, the imaginary land in the novel *Lost Horizon* by James Hilton.]

shank (shăngk) *n.* **1.a.** The part of the human leg between the knee and ankle. **b.** A corresponding part in other vertebrates. **2.a.** The whole leg of a human being. **b.** A leg or leglike part. **3.** A cut of meat from the leg of a steer, calf, sheep, or lamb. **4.** The long narrow part of a nail or pin. **5.** A stem, stalk, or similar part. **6.** *Naut.* The stem of an anchor. **7.** The long shaft of a fishhook. **8.** The part of a tobacco pipe between the bowl and stem. **9.** The shaft of a key. **10.** The narrow section of the handle of a spoon. **11.a.** The narrow part of the sole of a shoe under the instep. **b.** A shankpiece. **12.** A projection, such as a ring, on the back of a button by which it is sewn to cloth. **13.a.** See **tang¹** 5. **b.** The part of a tool, such as a drill, that connects the functioning head to the handle. **14.a.** The latter or remaining part, esp. of a period of time. **b.** The early or primary part of a period of time. —*tr.v.* **shanked, shank•ing, shanks.** *Sports.* To hit (a golf ball) with the heel of the club, causing the ball to veer in the wrong direction. [ME *shanke* < OE *sceanca*.] —**shanked** *adj.*

Shan•kar (shän′kär, shăng′-), **Ravi.** b. 1920. Indian-born musician who popularized classical Indian music in the West.

shank•piece (shăngk′pēs′) *n.* An arch support inserted into the shank of a shoe.

Shan•non (shăn′ən). A river rising in N-central Ireland and flowing c. 386 km (240 mi) to the Atlantic Ocean.

shan't (shănt, shänt). Shall not.

shan•tey (shăn′tē) *n. Mus.* Var. of **chantey.**

Shan•tou (shän′tou′) also **Swa•tow** (swä′tou′). A city of SE China ENE of Hong Kong. Pop. 400,000.

shan•tung (shăn-tŭng′) *n.* **1.** A heavy fabric with a rough nubby surface, made of spun wild silk. **2.** A rayon or cotton fabric resembling shantung. [After *Shantung* (Shandong), China.]

Shan•tung (shăn′tŭng′, shän′to͝ong′). See **Shandong.**

shan•ty¹ (shăn′tē) *n., pl.* **-ties.** A roughly built, often ramshackle cabin; a shack. [Prob. < Canadian Fr. *chantier*, hut in a lumber camp < Fr., timberyard < OFr., gantry < Lat. *canthērius*, rafter, nag < Gk. *kanthēlios*, pack ass.]

shan•ty² (shăn′tē) *n. Mus.* Var. of **chantey.**

shan•ty•town (shăn′tē-toun′) *n.* A town or a section of a town consisting chiefly of shacks.

Shan•xi (shän′shē′) also **Shan•si** (-sē′). A province of NE China bordered on the N by a section of the Great Wall. Cap. Taiyuan. Pop. 26,270,000.

shape (shāp) *n.* **1.a.** The characteristic surface configuration of a thing; an outline or a contour. **b.** Something distinguished from its surroundings by its outline. **2.** The contour of a person's body; the figure. **3.a.** A definite, distinctive form: *a new shape to my life.* **b.** A desirable form: *a fabric that holds its shape.* **4.** A form or condition in which something may exist or appear; embodiment. **5.** Assumed or false appearance; guise. **6.** A ghostly form; a phantom. **7.** Something, such as a mold or pattern, used to give or determine form. **8.** The proper condition of something necessary for action, effectiveness, or use: *in good shape.* — *v.* **shaped, shap•ing, shapes.** — *tr.* **1.** To give a particular form to; create. **2.** To cause to conform to a particular form or pattern; adapt to fit. **3.a.** To plan to bring about the realization or accomplishment of; devise. **b.** To embody in a definite form. **4.a.** To adapt to a particular use or purpose; adjust. **b.** To direct the course of. — *intr.* **1.** To come to pass; happen. **2.** To take on a definite shape or form. Often used with *up* or *into.* — ***phrasal verb.* shape up. 1.** *Informal.* To turn out; develop. **2.** To improve so as to meet a standard. [ME < OE *gesceap*, a creation.] — **shap′a•ble, shape′a•ble** *adj.* — **shaped** *adj.* — **shap′er** *n.*

SHAPE *abbr.* Supreme Headquarters Allied Powers, Europe.

shape•less (shāp′lĭs) *adj.* **1.** Lacking a definite shape. **2.** Lacking symmetrical or attractive form; not shapely. — **shape′less•ly** *adv.* — **shape′less•ness** *n.*

shape•ly (shāp′lē) *adj.* **-li•er, -li•est. 1.** Having a distinct shape. **2.** Having a pleasing shape. — **shape′li•ness** *n.*

shape•up or **shape-up** (shāp′ŭp′) *n.* An assembled group of dock workers from which the day's work crew is chosen by a representative of the union.

Sha•pir•o (shə-pîr′ō), **Karl Jay.** b. 1913. Amer. poet known for his war poems and works in free verse.

Shap•ley (shăp′lē), **Harlow.** 1885–1972. Amer. astronomer noted for his work in spectroscopy and photometry.

shard (shärd) also **sherd** (shûrd) *n.* **1.** A piece of broken pottery, esp. one found in an archaeological dig; a potsherd. **2.a.** A fragment of a brittle substance, as of glass. **b.** A small piece or part. **3.** *Zool.* **a.** A tough sheath or covering, such as a shell. **b.** The elytron or outer wing covering of a beetle. [ME *sherd* < OE *sceard*, cut, notch. See **sker-**[1]*.]

share[1] (shâr) *n.* **1.** A part or portion belonging to, distributed to, contributed by, or owed by a person or group. **2.** An equitable portion. **3.** Any of the equal parts into which the capital stock of a corporation or company is divided. — *v.* **shared, shar•ing, shares.** — *tr.* **1.** To divide and parcel out in shares; apportion. **2.** To participate in, use, enjoy, or experience with another or others. **3.** To accord a share in (something) to another or others. — *intr.* To have a share or part. — ***idiom.* go shares.** To be concerned or partake equally or jointly, as in a business venture. [ME < OE *scearu*, division. See **sker-**[1]*.] — **share′a•ble, shar′a•ble** *adj.* — **shar′er** *n.*

share[2] (shâr) *n.* A plowshare. [ME < OE *scēar.* See **sker-**[1]*.]

share•crop (shâr′krŏp′) *v.* **-cropped, -crop•ping, -crops.** — *intr.* To work as a sharecropper. — *tr.* To work (land) or grow (crops) as a sharecropper.

share•crop•per (shâr′krŏp′ər) *n.* A tenant farmer who gives a share of the crops raised to the landlord in lieu of rent.

share•hold•er (shâr′hōl′dər) *n.* One that owns or holds a share or shares of stock; a stockholder. — **share′hold′ing** *n.*

share•own•er (shâr′ō′nər) *n.* See **shareholder.**

Sha•ri (shä′rē) also **Cha•ri** (shä′rē, shä-rē′). A river of N-central Africa rising in the Central African Republic and flowing c. 2,253 km (1,400 mi) to Lake Chad.

sha•ri•'a or **sha•ri•a** also **sha•ri•'ah** (shä-rē′ä) *n. Islam.* The code of law based on the Koran. [Ar. *šar'īya*, lawfulness < *šar'ī*, lawful < *aš-šar'*, Revelation, Islamic law.]

sha•rif (shə-rēf′) *n.* Var. of **sherif.**

shark (shärk) *n.* **1.** Any of numerous chiefly marine carnivorous fishes of the subclass Elasmobranchii, having a torpedolike body, five to seven gill openings on each side of the head, an oil-filled liver, a cartilaginous skeleton, and tough scaly skin. **2.a.** A person regarded as ruthless, greedy, or dishonest. **b.** A vicious usurer. **3.** *Slang.* A person unusually skilled in a particular activity. — *v.* **sharked, shark•ing, sharks.** — *tr. Archaic.* To obtain by deceitful means. — *intr.* To practice or live by fraud and trickery. [?]

shark•skin (shärk′skĭn′) *n.* **1.** The skin of a shark. **2.** Leather made from the skin of a shark. **3.** A rayon and acetate fabric having a smooth, somewhat shiny surface.

shark sucker *n.* See **remora.**

Shar•on (shăr′ən). A city of W PA on the OH border NNW of Pittsburgh. Pop. 17,493.

Sharon, Plain of. A fertile plain of W Israel extending along the Mediterranean coast S of Haifa.

sharp (shärp) *adj.* **sharp•er, sharp•est. 1.** Having a thin edge or a fine point suitable for or capable of cutting or piercing. **2.a.** Having clear form and detail. **b.** Terminating in an edge or a point. **c.** Clearly and distinctly set forth: *sharp contrasts.* **3.** Abrupt or acute: *a sharp drop.* **4.a.** Intellectually penetrating; astute. **b.** Marked by keenness and accuracy of perception. **5.** Crafty or deceitful. **6.** Vigilant; alert. **7.a.** Briskly or keenly cold and cutting. **b.** Harsh or biting in tone or character. **8.** Fierce or impetuous; violent: *a sharp temper.* **9.** Intense; severe: *a sharp pain.* **10.a.** Sudden and shrill. **b.** Sudden and brilliant or dazzling. **11.** Strongly affecting the senses of smell and taste. **12.** Composed of hard angular particles. **13.** *Mus.* **a.** Raised in pitch by a semitone. **b.** Being above the proper pitch. **c.** Having the key signature in sharps. **14.** *Ling.* Voiceless. Used of a consonant. **15.** *Informal.* Attractive or stylish. — *adv.* **1.** In a sharp manner. **2.** Punctually; exactly. **3.** *Mus.* Above the true or proper pitch. — *n.* **1.** *Mus.* **a.** A note or tone raised one semitone above its normal pitch. **b.** A sign (♯) indicating this. **2.** A slender sewing needle with a very fine point. **3.** *Informal.* **a.** An expert. **b.** A shrewd cheater; a sharper. — *v.* **sharped, sharp•ing, sharps.** — *tr.* To raise in pitch by a semitone. — *intr.* To play or sing above the proper pitch. [ME *sharp* < OE *scearp*, slope. See **sker-**[1]*.] — **sharp′ly** *adv.* — **sharp′ness** *n.*

Syns: sharp, keen, acute. These adjectives all apply literally to fine edges, points, or tips. Figuratively they indicate mental alertness and clarity of comprehension. *Sharp* suggests quickness and astuteness: *"a young man of sharp and active intellect"* (John Henry Newman). *Keen* implies clear-headedness and acuity: *a journalist with a keen mind. Acute* suggests penetrating perception or discernment: *an acute observer of politics.*

sharp•en (shär′pən) *tr. & intr.v.* **-ened, -en•ing, -ens.** To make or become sharp or sharper. — **sharp′en•er** *n.*

sharp•er (shär′pər) *n.* One that deals dishonestly with others, esp. a cheating gambler.

sharp-eyed (shärp′īd′) *adj.* **1.** Having keen eyesight. **2.** Keenly perceptive or observant; alert.

sharp•ie (shär′pē) *n., pl.* **-ies. 1.** *Naut.* A long narrow flat-bottom fishing boat having a centerboard and one or two masts, each rigged with a triangular sail. **2.a.** An alert quick-witted person. **b.** A sharper. [< SHARP.]

sharpie
Detail from an oil painting of a two-masted sharpie by Albert S. Bigelow

sharp-nosed (shärp′nōzd′) *adj.* **1.** Having a thin pointed nose or snout. **2.** Having a keen sense of smell.

Sharps•burg (shärps′bûrg′). A town of N MD W of Frederick; site of the Battle of Antietam (Sep. 16–17, 1862).

sharp-shinned hawk (shärp′shĭnd′) *n.* A small North American hawk *(Accipiter striatus)* that has short rounded wings and a long tail and preys on other birds.

sharp-shinned hawk
Accipiter striatus

sharp•shoot•er (shärp′sho͞o′tər) *n.* **1.** One who is highly proficient at shooting. **2.a.** The second military grade of proficiency in the use of rifles and other small arms. **b.** One who holds this grade of proficiency.

sharp•shoot•ing (shärp′sho͞o′tĭng) *n.* **1.** High proficiency in shooting firearms. **2.** Accurate, often unexpected verbal or written attack.

sharp-sight•ed (shärp′sī′tĭd) *adj.* **1.** Having keen eyesight. **2.** Keenly perceptive or alert. — **sharp′-sight′ed•ness** *n.*

sharp-tongued (shärp′tŭngd′) *adj.* Harsh, critical, or sarcastic in speech.

sharp-wit•ted (shärp′wĭt′ĭd) *adj.* Having or exhibiting keenly perceptive intellect. — **sharp′-wit′ted•ness** *n.*

shash•lik or **shash•lick** (shäsh-lĭk′, shäsh′lĭk) *n.* A dish consisting of marinated cubes of lamb or beef grilled or roasted on a spit, often with slices of eggplant, onion, and tomato; shish kebab. [Russ. *shashlyk*, of Turk. orig.]

Shas•ta (shăs′tə), **Mount.** A volcanic peak, 4,319.4 m (14,162 ft), of the Cascade Range in N CA.

Shasta daisy *n.* A hybrid daisy derived from *Chrysanthemum maximum* and *C. lacustre,* with large white flower heads.

shat (shăt) *v. Obscene.* A p.t. and p.part. of **shit.**

Shatt al Ar•ab or **Shatt-al-Ar•ab** (shăt′ ăl ăr′əb, shät′). A river channel, c. 193 km (120 mi), of SE Iraq formed by the confluence of the Tigris and Euphrates rivers and flowing to the Persian Gulf.

shat•ter (shăt′ər) *v.* **-tered, -ter•ing, -ters.** — *tr.* **1.** To cause to break or burst suddenly into pieces, as with a violent blow. **2.a.** To damage seriously; disable. **b.** To cause the destruction or ruin of; destroy: *shattered dreams.* — *intr.* To break into pieces; smash or burst. See Syns at **break.** — *n.* **1.a.** The act of shattering. **b.** The condition of being shattered. **2.** A splintered or fragmented condition. Often used in the plural. [ME *shateren* < OE **sceaterian*, to scatter.]

shatter cone *n.* A conical fragment of rock that is formed from the high pressure of volcanism or meteorite impact and has striations radiating from the apex.

shat•ter•proof (shăt′ər-pro͞of′) *adj.* Resistant to shattering.

Shav•a•no Peak (shăv′ə-nō). A mountain, 4,339.8 m (14,229 ft), in the Sawatch Range of the Rocky Mts. in central CO.

shave (shāv) *v.* **shaved, shaved** or **shav•en** (shā′vən), **shav•ing, shaves.** — *tr.* **1.a.** To remove the beard or other body hair from, with a razor or shaver. **b.** To cut (the beard, for example) at the surface of the skin with a razor or shaver. **2.** To crop, trim, or mow closely. **3.a.** To remove thin slices from. **b.** To cut or scrape into thin slices; shred. **4.** To come

ă pat	oi boy
ā pay	ou out
âr care	o͝o took
ä father	o͞o boot
ĕ pet	ŭ cut
ē be	ûr urge
ĭ pit	th thin
ī pie	*th* this
îr pier	hw which
ŏ pot	zh vision
ō toe	ə about, item
ô paw	

Stress marks:
′ (primary);
′ (secondary), as in dictionary (dĭk′shə-nĕr′ē)

George Bernard Shaw

shay

shears
Top: Straight-cut metal shears
Center: Pinking shears
Bottom: Pruning shears

ă pat oi boy
ā pay ou out
âr care o͝o took
ä father o͞o boot
ĕ pet ŭ cut
ē be ûr urge
ĭ pit th thin
ī pie *th* this
îr pier hw which
ŏ pot zh vision
ō toe ə about, item
ô paw

Stress marks:
ʹ (primary);
ʹ (secondary), as in dictionary (dĭkʹshə-nĕrʹē)

close to or graze in passing. **5.a.** To purchase (a note) at a reduction greater than the legal or customary rate. **b.** To cut (a price) by a slight margin. — *intr.* To remove beard or hair with a razor or shaver. — *n.* **1.** The act, process, or result of shaving. **2.** A thin slice or scraping; a shaving. **3.** A tool for shaving. [ME *shaven*, to scrape < OE *sceafan*.]

shav•er (shāʹvər) *n.* **1.a.** One who shaves. **b.** A shaving device, esp. an electric razor. **2.** *Informal.* A small, esp. male child.

Sha•vi•an (shāʹve-ən) *adj.* Of, relating to, or characteristic of George Bernard Shaw or his works: *Shavian wit.* — *n.* An admirer or a disciple of George Bernard Shaw. [< *Shavius*, pseudo-Latin form of the name *Shaw.*]

shav•ing (shāʹvĭng) *n.* **1.** A thin slice or sliver, as of wood or metal, that is shaved off. **2.** The act of one that shaves.

Sha•vu•ot also **Sha•bu•oth** (shə-vo͞oʹōt', -əs, shä'vo͞o-ôtʹ) *n. Judaism.* A feast held on the sixth and seventh days of Sivan in commemoration of the revelation of the Law on Mount Sinai and the celebration of the wheat festival in ancient times. [Heb. *šābūʿôt* < *šābûăʿ*, week.]

Shaw (shô), **Anna Howard.** 1847–1919. British-born Amer. physician who was president of the National American Woman Suffrage Association (1904–15).

Shaw, George Bernard. 1856–1950. Irish-born British playwright and critic who was a founder of the Fabian Society and won the 1925 Nobel Prize for literature.

Shaw, Henry Wheeler. Josh Billings. 1818–85. Amer. humorist noted for his essays in the *Farmers' Allminax* (1869–80).

Sha•win•i•gan (shə-wĭnʹĭ-gən). A city of S Quebec, Canada, on the St. Maurice R. NW of Trois Rivières. Pop. 23,011.

shawl (shôl) *n.* A square or oblong piece of cloth worn as a covering for the head, neck, and shoulders. — *tr.v.* **shawled, shawl•ing, shawls.** To cover with or as if with such a piece of cloth. [Ult. < Pers. *shāl.*]

shawm (shôm) *n. Mus.* Any of various early double-reed wind instruments, forerunners of the modern oboe. [ME *shalmie* < OFr. *chalemie*, alteration of *chalemel* < LLat. *calamellus*, dim. of Lat. *calamus*, reed < Gk. *kalamos.*]

Shawn (shôn), **Ted.** 1891–1972. Amer. dancer and choreographer noted for his partnership with Ruth Saint Denis.

Shaw•nee[1] (shô-nēʹ) *n., pl.* **Shawnee** or **-nees. 1.** A member of a Native American people formerly inhabiting parts of the Cumberland and central Ohio valleys, with present-day populations in Oklahoma. **2.** The Algonquian language of the Shawnee. [Back-formation < obsolete *Shawnese* < Shawnee *shaawanooki*, those of the south, Shawnee.]

Shaw•nee[2] (shô-nēʹ, shôʹnē). **1.** A city of NE KS, a suburb of Kansas City. Pop. 29,653. **2.** A city of central OK on the North Canadian R. ESE of Oklahoma City. Pop. 26,017.

Shawnee cake *n. New England.* See **johnnycake.** See Regional Note at **johnnycake.**

Shaw•wal (shə-wälʹ) *n.* The tenth month of the year in the Muslim calendar. [Ar. *šawwāl.*]

shay (shā) *n. Informal.* A chaise. [Back-formation < CHAISE (taken as pl.).]

Shays (shāz), **Daniel.** 1747?–1825. Amer. insurrectionist who led a raid on a government arsenal in Springfield MA to protest against the economic plight of farmers (1787).

she (shē) *pron.* **1.a.** Used to refer to the woman or girl previously mentioned or implied. See Usage Note at **I**[1]. **b.** Used to refer to a female animal. **2.** Used in place of *it* to refer to certain inanimate things, such as ships, traditionally perceived as female. — *n.* A female animal or person. [ME, prob. alteration of OE *sēo*, fem. demonstrative pron. See **so-*.**]

s/he (shēʹər-hēʹ, shēʹhēʹ) *pron.* Used as a gender-neutral alternative to *he* or *she.* See Usage Note at **he**[1].

shea butter (shē, shā) *n.* A fat obtained from the seeds of the shea tree, used as food and for making soap and candles.

sheaf (shēf) *n., pl.* **sheaves** (shēvz). **1.** A bundle of cut stalks of grain or similar plants bound with straw or twine. **2.** A collection of items held or bound together. **3.** An archer's quiver. — *tr.v.* **sheafed, sheaf•ing, sheafs.** To gather and bind into a bundle. [ME *sheef* < OE *scēaf.*]

shear (shîr) *v.* **sheared, sheared** or **shorn** (shôrn, shōrn), **shear•ing, shears.** — *tr.* **1.** To remove (fleece or hair) by cutting or clipping. **2.** To remove the hair or fleece from. **3.** To cut with or as if with shears. **4.** To divest or deprive as if by cutting: *shorn of all dignity.* — *intr.* **1.** To use a cutting tool such as shears. **2.** To move or proceed by or as if by cutting. **3.** *Phys.* To become deformed by forces tending to produce a shearing strain. — *n.* **1.a.** A pair of scissors. Often used in the plural. **b.** Any of various implements or machines that cut with a scissorlike action. Often used in the plural. **2.** The act, process, or result of shearing. **3.** Something cut off by shearing. **4.** The act, process, or fact of shearing. Used to indicate a sheep's age: *a two-shear ram.* **5.** An apparatus used to lift heavy weights, consisting of two or more spars joined at the top and spread at the base, the tackle being suspended from the top. Often used in the plural with a singular or plural verb. **6.** *Phys.* **a.** An applied force or system of forces that tends to produce a shearing strain. **b.** A shearing strain. [ME *sheren* < OE *sceran.* N. < ME *shere* < OE *scēar.* See **sker-**[1]***.**] — **shearʹer** *n.*

sheared (shîrd) *adj.* Shaped or finished by shearing, esp. cut or trimmed to a uniform length: *a sheared fur coat.*

shear•ing strain (shîrʹĭng) *n. Phys.* A deformation of an elastic body caused by forces that produce an opposite but parallel sliding motion of the body's planes.

shearing stress *n. Phys.* See **shear** 6a.

shear•ling (shîrʹlĭng) *n.* **1.** A year-old sheep that has been sheared once. **2.** The skin of a shearling or of a newly sheared sheep or lamb, tanned and with the wool on.

shear•wa•ter (shîrʹwôʹtər, -wŏtʹər) *n.* Any of various oceanic birds of the genus *Puffinus*, having slender wings that seem to shear the water as the bird flies along the surface.

sheath (shēth) *n., pl.* **sheaths** (shē*th*z, shēths). **1.a.** A case for a blade, as of a sword. **b.** Any of various similar coverings. **2.** *Biol.* An enveloping tubular structure, such as the tissue that encloses a muscle or nerve fiber. **3.** A close-fitting dress. — *tr.v.* **sheathed, sheath•ing, sheaths** (shē*th*z, shēths). To encase or cover with or as if with a sheath; sheathe. [ME *shethe* < OE *scēath.* See **skei-*.**]

sheath•bill (shēthʹbĭlʹ) *n.* Either of two pigeonlike shore birds *(Chionia alba* or *C. minor)* of Antarctic regions having white plumage and a horny covering on the base of the bill.

sheathe (shē*th*) *tr.v.* **sheathed, sheath•ing, sheathes. 1.** To insert into or provide with a sheath. **2.** To retract (a claw) into a sheath. **3.** To enclose with a protective covering; encase. [ME *shethen* < *shethe*, sheath. See SHEATH.] — **sheathʹer** *n.*

sheath•ing (shēʹ*th*ĭng) *n.* **1.** A layer of boards or of other wood or fiber materials applied to the outer studs, joists, and rafters of a building to strengthen the structure and serve as a base for a weatherproof cladding. **2.** *Naut.* An exterior covering on the underwater part of a ship's hull that protects it against marine growths. **3.** The act of providing sheathing.

sheath knife *n.* A knife that has a fixed blade and fits into a sheath.

shea tree (shē, shā) *n.* A tropical African tree *(Butyrospermum parkii)* having oily seeds that yield shea butter. [Mandingo (Bambara) *si.*]

sheave[1] (shēv) *tr.v.* **sheaved, sheav•ing, sheaves.** To collect and bind into a sheaf. [< SHEAF.]

sheave[2] (shēv, shĭv) *n.* A wheel or disk with a grooved rim, esp. one used as a pulley. [ME *sheve.* See **skei-*.**]

sheaves (shēvz) *n.* Pl. of **sheaf.**

She•ba (shēʹbə). An ancient country of S Arabia comprising present-day Yemen. Its people colonized Ethiopia in the 10th cent. B.C. and were known for their commercial prosperity.

she•bang (shə-băngʹ) *n. Slang.* A situation, an organization, a contrivance, or a set of facts or things. [?]

She•bat (shə-bätʹ, -vätʹ) *n.* Var. of **Shevat.**

she•been (shə-bēnʹ) *n.* An unlicensed drinking establishment, esp. in Ireland, Scotland, and South Africa. [Ir.Gael. *séibín*, grain measure or tax, bad ale, dim. of *séibe*, mug, bottle.]

She•bel•le or **She•be•li** (shə-bāʹlē). A river of NE Africa rising in central Ethiopia and flowing c. 1,609 km (1,000 mi) to S Somalia.

She•boy•gan (shə-boiʹgən). A city of E WI on Lake Michigan N of Milwaukee; founded c. 1835. Pop. 49,676.

shed[1] (shĕd) *v.* **shed, shed•ding, sheds.** — *tr.* **1.** To cause to pour forth. **2.** To diffuse or radiate; send forth or impart: *shed light.* **3.** To repel without allowing penetration. **4.a.** To lose by natural process: *a snake shedding its skin.* **b.** To rid oneself of (something not wanted or needed). — *intr.* **1.** To lose a natural growth or covering by natural process. **2.** To pour forth, fall off, or drop out. — *n.* **1.** Something that sheds, esp. an elevation in the earth's surface from which water flows in two directions; a watershed. **2.** Something shed. — *idiom.* **shed blood.** To take life, esp. with violence; kill. [ME *sheden*, to separate, shed < OE *scēadan*, to divide. See **skei-*.**]

shed[2] (shĕd) *n.* **1.** A small structure, either freestanding or attached to a larger structure, serving for storage or shelter. **2.** A large low structure often open on all sides. [Alteration of ME *shadde*, perh. var. of *shade*, shade. See SHADE.]

she'd (shēd). **1.** She had. **2.** She would.

shed•der (shĕdʹər) *n.* One that sheds, as a molting snake.

sheen (shēn) *n.* **1.** Glistening brightness; luster. **2.** Splendid attire. **3.** A glossy surface given to textiles. [< ME *shene*, beautiful < OE *scīene.* See **keu-*.**]

shee•ny[1] (shēʹnē) *adj.* Lustrous; glistening.

shee•ny[2] (shēʹnē) *n., pl.* **-nies.** *Offensive Slang.* Used as a disparaging term for a Jew. [?]

sheep (shēp) *n., pl.* **sheep. 1.** Any of various usu. horned ruminant mammals of the genus *Ovis* in the family Bovidae, esp. the domesticated species *O. aries* raised for wool, flesh, or skin. **2.** Leather made from the skin of one of these animals. **3.a.** A person regarded as timid, weak, or submissive. **b.** One easily swayed or led. [ME < OE *scēap.*]

sheep•ber•ry (shēpʹbĕrʹē) *n.* Either of two eastern North American shrubs or trees *(Viburnum lentago* or *V. prunifolium)* having white flowers and edible blue-black berries.

sheep•cote (shēpʹkōt', -kŏtʹ) *n. Chiefly British.* A sheepfold.

sheep dip also **sheep-dip** (shēpʹdĭpʹ) *n.* Any of various preparations of liquid disinfectant into which sheep are dipped to destroy parasites and clean their wool, esp. before shearing.

sheep•dog also **sheep dog** (shēp′dôg′, -dŏg′) *n.* A dog trained to guard and herd sheep.
sheep•fold (shēp′fōld′) *n.* A pen for sheep.
sheep•herd•er (shēp′hûr′dər) *n.* A person who herds sheep, esp. on an open range; a shepherd. **— sheep′herd′ing** *n.*
sheep•ish (shē′pĭsh) *adj.* **1.** Embarrassed, as by consciousness of a fault: *a sheepish grin.* **2.** Meek or stupid. **— sheep′ish•ly** *adv.* **— sheep′ish•ness** *n.*
sheep ked (kĕd) *n.* See **sheep tick.** [?]
sheep laurel *n.* An eastern North American evergreen shrub *(Kalmia angustifolia)* having flowers with rose-pink or crimson bell-shaped corollas and poisonous leaves.
sheep's eyes (shēps) *pl.n.* Shyly amorous glances.
sheep•shank (shēp′shăngk′) *n.* A knot used to shorten a line.
sheeps•head (shēps′hĕd′) *n.* **1.** A food fish *(Archosargus probatocephalus)* of the Atlantic and Gulf coasts of North America having dark markings. **2.** A freshwater drum *(Aplodinotus grunniens)* of central North America. **3.** A redfish *(Semicossyphus pulcher)* of the Gulf of California.
sheep•shear•ing (shēp′shîr′ĭng) *n.* **1.** The act of shearing sheep. **2.a.** The time or season when sheep are sheared. **b.** Festivities held at this time. **— sheep′shear′er** *n.*
sheep•skin (shēp′skĭn′) *n.* **1.** The skin of a sheep either tanned with the fleece left on or in the form of leather or parchment. **2.** *Informal.* A diploma.
sheep tick *n.* A wingless louselike fly *(Melophagus ovinus)* that is parasitic to sheep, causing loss of wool.
sheer[1] (shîr) *intr. & tr.v.* **sheered, sheer•ing, sheers.** To swerve or cause to swerve from a course. **—** *n.* **1.** A swerving or deviating course. **2.** *Naut.* The upward curve or amount of upward curve of the longitudinal lines of a ship's hull as viewed from the side. [Prob. partly < LGer. *scheren,* to move to and fro: said of boats, and partly < Du. *scheren,* to withdraw; see **sker-**[1]***.**]
sheer[2] (shîr) *adj.* **sheer•er, sheer•est. 1.** Thin, fine, and transparent. See Syns at **airy. 2.a.** Completely such, without qualification or exception. **b.** Free from admixture or adulterants; unmixed. See Syns at **pure. c.** Considered or operating apart from anything else. **3.** Almost perpendicular; steep. See Syns at **steep**[1]. **—** *adv.* **1.** Almost perpendicularly. **2.** Completely; altogether. [Obsolete *shere,* thin, clear, partly < ME *shir,* clear (< OE *scīr*) and partly < ME *skir,* clean (< ON *skærr*).] **— sheer′ly** *adv.* **— sheer′ness** *n.*
sheet[1] (shēt) *n.* **1.** A broad rectangular piece of fabric serving as a basic article of bedding. **2.a.** A broad, thin, usu. rectangular mass or piece of material, such as paper, metal, glass, or plywood. **b.** A flat or very shallow, usu. rectangular pan used for baking. **3.** A broad flat continuous surface or expanse. **4.** A moving expanse: *a sheet of flames.* **5.** A newspaper, esp. a tabloid. **6.** *Geol.* A broad, relatively thin deposit or layer of igneous or sedimentary rock. **7.** A large block of stamps printed by a single impression of a plate before the individual stamps have been separated. **—** *v.* **sheet•ed, sheet•ing, sheets. —** *tr.* **1.** To cover with, wrap in, or provide with a sheet. **2.** To make into sheets. **—** *intr.* To flow or fall in a sheet. **—** *adj.* Being in the form of a sheet. [ME *shete,* cloth < OE *scēte.* See **skeud-*.**]
sheet[2] (shēt) *Naut. n.* **1.** A line attached to a boom or a clew of a sail to control its position. **2. sheets.** The spaces at either end of an open boat in front of and behind the seats. **—** ***idiom.* three sheets to (or in) the wind.** *Informal.* Intoxicated; drunk. [ME *shete* < OE *scēat(line),* sheet (line) < *scēata,* corner of a sail. See **skeud-*.**]
sheet anchor *n.* **1.** *Naut.* A large extra anchor intended for use in an emergency. **2.** A source of aid in emergency or danger.
sheet bend *n.* *Naut.* A knot used to join together the ends of two ropes of different sizes.
sheet glass *n.* Glass drawn from a molten bath into a thin sheet of film, commonly used to make windows.
sheet•ing (shē′tĭng) *n.* **1.** Material, such as metal or cloth, used to make sheets or a sheet. **2.** The act or process of providing with or forming into sheets.
sheet lightning *n.* Lightning that appears as a broad sheetlike illumination of parts of a thundercloud, caused by the reflection of a lightning flash.
sheet metal *n.* Metal rolled into a sheet with a thickness between foil and plate. **— sheet′-met′al** (shēt′mĕt′l) *adj.*
sheet music *n.* *Mus.* Compositions printed on unbound sheets of paper.
Sheet•rock (shēt′rŏk′). A trademark used for plasterboard.
Shef•field (shĕf′ēld′). A borough of N-central England E of Manchester; long known for its cutlery. Pop. 547,600.
she•getz (shā′gĭts) *n., pl.* **shkotz•im** (shkôt′sĭm). *Offensive.* A non-Jewish boy or young man. [Yiddish *sheygets* < Heb. *šeqeṣ,* blemish.]
sheik also **sheikh** (shēk, shāk) *n.* **1.** *Islam.* **a.** A religious official, usu. male. **b.** A male leader of an Arab family or village. **c.** Used as a form of address for such an official or leader. **2. sheik.** *Slang.* A romantically alluring man. [Ar. *šayḫ,* old man, chief < *šāḫa,* to be old.]
sheik•dom also **sheikh•dom** (shēk′dəm, shāk′-) *n.* The area ruled by a sheik.
shei•la (shē′lə) *n.* *Australian.* A girl or young woman. [< the personal name *Sheila.*]
shek•el (shĕk′əl) *n.* **1.** See table at **currency. 2.a.** Any of several ancient units of weight, esp. a Hebrew unit equal to about a half ounce. **b.** A gold or silver coin equal in weight to one of these units, esp. the chief silver coin of the ancient Hebrews. **3.** *Slang.* **a.** A coin. **b. shekels.** Money. [Heb. *šeqel* < *šāqal,* to weigh < Canaanite *ṯql.*]
She•khi•nah (shĭ-KHē′nə, -hē′-) *n.* *Judaism.* The Divine Presence, considered female in Jewish mysticism. [Heb. *šĕkīnâ* < *šākan,* to dwell.]
shel•drake (shĕl′drāk′) *n.* **1.** Any of various large Old World ducks of the genus *Tadorna,* esp. *T. tadorna* having predominantly black and white plumage. **2.** See **merganser.** [ME *shelddrake* : *scheld,* variegated; see **skel-**[1]***** + *drake,* drake.]
shel•duck (shĕl′dŭk′) *n.* See **sheldrake** 1.
shelf (shĕlf) *n., pl.* **shelves** (shĕlvz). **1.a.** A flat, usu. rectangular structure composed of a rigid material, such as wood, glass, or metal, fixed at right angles to a wall or other vertical surface and used to hold or store objects. **b.** The contents or capacity of such a structure. **c.** Something, such as a projecting ledge of rock or a balcony, that resembles such a structure. **2.** A reef, sandbar, or shoal. **3.** Bedrock. **—** ***idioms.* off the shelf.** Available from merchandise in stock; not custom-made. **on the shelf. 1.** In a state of disuse. **2.a.** Unemployed. **b.** Out of circulation. **c.** Retired. [ME, prob. < MLGer. *schelf.* See **skel-**[1]***.**] **— shelf′ful′** (-fo͝ol′) *n.*
shelf ice *n.* An extension of glacial ice into coastal waters that is in contact with the bottom only near the shore.
shelf life *n.* Storage time of a product without deterioration.
shell (shĕl) *n.* **1.a.** The usu. hard outer covering that encases certain organisms, such as mollusks, insects, and turtles; the carapace. **b.** A similar outer covering on an egg, a fruit, or a nut. **c.** The material that constitutes such a covering. **2.** Something resembling or having the form of a shell, esp.: **a.** An external, usu. hard protective or enclosing case or cover. **b.** A framework or an exterior, as of a building. **c.** A thin layer of pastry. **d.** The external part of the ear. **3.** *Naut.* **a.** The hull of a ship. **b.** A long narrow racing boat propelled by rowers. **4.** A small glass for beer. **5.a.** A projectile or piece of ammunition, esp. the hollow tube containing the propulsive explosives. **b.** A metal or cardboard case containing the charge, primer, and shot fired from a shotgun. **6.** An attitude or a manner masking one's true feelings. **7.** *Phys.* **a.** A set of atomic energy levels occupied by electrons having the same principal quantum number. **b.** An analogous pattern of protons and neutrons within a nucleus. **8.a.** A usu. sleeveless and collarless blouse. **b.** The outermost layer of a lined garment such as a coat. **9.** *Comp. Sci.* A program that works with the operating system as a command processor, used to enter commands and initiate their execution. **—** *v.* **shelled, shell•ing, shells. —** *tr.* **1.a.** To remove the shell of; shuck. **b.** To remove from a shell. **2.** To separate the kernels of (corn) from the cob. **3.** To fire shells at; bombard. **4.** To defeat decisively. **—** *intr.* **1.** To shed or become free of a shell. **2.** To look for or collect shells, as on a seashore. **—** ***phrasal verb.* shell out.** *Informal.* To hand over; pay. [ME < OE *scell.* See **skel-**[1]***.**] **— shell** *adj.* **— shell′er** *n.*
she'll (shēl). **1.** She will. **2.** She shall.
shel•lac also **shel•lack** (shə-lăk′) **—** *n.* **1.** A purified lac in the form of thin yellow or orange flakes, often bleached white and widely used in varnishes, paints, and inks. **2.** A thin varnish made by dissolving this substance in denatured alcohol, used to finish wood. **—** *tr.v.* **-lacked, -lack•ing, -lacs. 1.** To coat or finish with shellac. **2.** *Slang.* **a.** To strike repeatedly and severely; batter. **b.** To defeat decisively. [SHEL(L) + LAC (transl. of Fr. *laque en écailles,* lac in thin plates).]
shell•back (shĕl′băk′) *n.* *Naut.* **1.** A sailor who has crossed the equator. **2.** A veteran sailor.
shell bean *n.* Any of various beans cultivated for their edible seeds rather than their pods.
Shel•ley (shĕl′ē), **Mary Godwin Wollstonecraft.** 1797–1851. British writer best known for the novel *Frankenstein* (1818).
Shelley, Percy Bysshe. 1792–1822. British romantic poet whose works include "To a Skylark" (1820) and the lyric drama *Prometheus Unbound* (1820).
shell•fire (shĕl′fīr′) *n.* The shooting or exploding of artillery shells.
shell•fish (shĕl′fĭsh′) *n., pl.* **shellfish** or **-fish•es.** An aquatic animal, such as a mollusk or crustacean, that has a shell or shell-like exoskeleton. **— shell′fish′ing** *n.*
shell•fish•er•y (shĕl′fĭsh′ə-rē) *n., pl.* **-ies. 1.** The industry or occupation of catching, processing, or selling shellfish. **2.** A fishing ground for shellfish.
shell game *n.* **1.** *Games.* A game in which a person hides a small object under one of three nutshells, thimbles, or cups, then shuffles them while spectators bet on the object's final location. **2.** A fraud or swindle.
shell jacket *n.* See **mess jacket.**
shell pink *n.* *Color.* A pinkish white to strong yellowish pink.
shell•proof (shĕl′pro͞of′) *adj.* Made to withstand shellfire.
shell shock *n.* **1.** Any of various acute, often hysterical neu-

sheath
Late 19th-century Ojibwa beaded knife sheath

sheet bend

sheldrake
Tadorna tadorna

Mary Wollstonecraft Shelley
Detail of a c. 1840 portrait by Richard Rothwell (1800–1868)

Percy Bysshe Shelley
1819 portrait by Amelia Curran (1775–1847)

roses originating in trauma suffered under fire in modern warfare. **2.** Combat fatigue.

shell-shocked or **shell•shocked** (shĕl′shŏkt′) *adj.* **1.** Suffering from shell shock. **2.** Stunned, distressed, or exhausted from a prolonged trauma or an unexpected difficulty.

Shel•ta (shĕl′tə) *n.* A secret jargon used by Gypsies in Great Britain and Ireland, based on systematic inversion or alteration of the initial consonants of Gaelic words. [< Shelta *Sheldrū*, perh. alteration of Ir.Gael. *béarla*, language, English < OIr. *bélrae*, language < *bél*, mouth.]

shel•ter (shĕl′tər) *n.* **1.a.** Something that provides cover or protection, as from the weather. **b.** A refuge; a haven. **c.** An establishment that provides temporary housing for homeless people. **2.** The state of being covered or protected. — *v.* **-tered, -ter•ing, -ters.** — *tr.* **1.** To provide cover or protection for. **2.** To invest (income) to protect it from taxation. — *intr.* To take cover; find refuge. [Perh. < ME *sheltron*, tight battle formation < OE *scildtruma* : *scield*, shield; see SHIELD + *truma*, troop; see **deru-***.] — **shel′ter•er** *n.*

Alan Shepard

shel•ter•belt (shĕl′tər-bĕlt′) *n.* A barrier of trees and shrubs that protects against the wind and reduces erosion.

shel•tered workshop (shĕl′tərd) *n.* A workplace that provides a supportive environment where physically or mentally disabled persons can acquire vocational skills and experience.

shelter tent *n.* A small tent usu. pitched by securing together two or more pieces of waterproof material.

shel•tie also **shel•ty** (shĕl′tē) *n., pl.* **-ties.** *Informal.* **1.** A Shetland pony. **2.** A Shetland sheepdog. [Prob. < ON *Hjalti*, Shetlander < *Hjaltland*, Shetland Is.]

Shel•ton (shĕl′tən). A city of SW CT on the Housatonic R. NNE of Bridgeport; settled in 1697. Pop. 35,418.

shelve (shĕlv) *v.* **shelved, shelv•ing, shelves.** — *tr.* **1.** To place or arrange on a shelf. **2.** To put away as though on a shelf; table. **3.** To cause to retire from service; dismiss. **4.** To furnish with shelves. — *intr.* To slope gradually; incline. [Back-formation < *shelves*, pl. of SHELF.] — **shelv′er** *n.*

William Tecumseh Sherman

shelves (shĕlvz) *n.* Pl. of **shelf.**

shelv•ing (shĕl′vĭng) *n.* **1.** Shelves considered as a group. **2.** Material for shelves. **3.** An incline; a slope.

Shem (shĕm). In the Bible, the eldest son of Noah and the brother of Japheth and Ham.

Shen•an•do•ah Valley (shĕn′ən-dō′ə). A valley of N VA between the Allegheny Mts. and the Blue Ridge; drained by the **Shenandoah River,** c. 241 km (150 mi).

she•nan•i•gan (shə-năn′ĭ-gən) *n. Informal.* **1.a.** A deceitful trick; an underhand act. **b.** Remarks intended to deceive; deceit. Often used in the plural. **2.a.** A playful or mischievous act; a prank. **b.** Mischief; prankishness. Often used in the plural. [?]

Shen•si (shĕn′sē′). See **Shaanxi.**

Shen•yang (shŭn′yăng′). Formerly **Muk•den** (mo͝ok′dən, -dĕn′, mo͝ok′-). A city of NE China ENE of Beijing; cap. of Liaoning province. Pop. 3,250,000.

She•ol (shē′ōl′, shē-ōl′) *n. Bible.* The underworld where the dead dwelt in darkness. [Heb. *šə'ôl.*]

Shep•ard (shĕp′ərd), **Alan Bartlett, Jr.** b. 1923. Amer. naval officer who on May 5, 1961, became the first U.S. astronaut in space.

Shetland pony

shep•herd (shĕp′ərd) *n.* **1.** One who herds, guards, and tends sheep. **2.** One who cares for and guides a group of people, as a minister. — *tr.v.* **-herd•ed, -herd•ing, -herds.** To herd, guard, tend, or guide as a shepherd. [ME *shepherde* < OE *scēaphierde* : *scēap*, sheep + *hierde*, herdsman.]

shepherd dog *n.* See **sheepdog.**

shep•herd•ess (shĕp′ər-dĭs) *n.* A girl or woman who herds, guards, and tends sheep.

shep•herd's pie (shĕp′ərdz) *n.* A meat pie baked in a crust of mashed potatoes.

shepherd's purse *n.* A common Eurasian weed *(Capsella bursa-pastoris)* having small white flowers and flat heart-shaped or triangular fruit. [< its pouchlike pods.]

Sher•a•ton (shĕr′ə-tn) *adj.* Of or relating to a style of English furniture that originated about 1800, characterized by simple designs and classical ornamentation.

Sheraton, Thomas. 1751–1806. British furniture designer known for his graceful neoclassical designs.

sher•bet (shûr′bĭt) *n.* **1.** Also **sher•bert** (-bûrt′). A frozen dessert made of fruit juice, sugar, and water mixed with milk, egg white, or gelatin. **2.** *Chiefly British.* A beverage made of sweetened diluted fruit juice. **3.** Also **sherbert.** *Australian.* An alcoholic beverage, esp. beer. [Ottoman Turk., sweet fruit drink < Pers. *sharbat* < Ar. *šarbah*, drink < *šariba*, to drink.]

Shetland sheepdog

Sher•brooke (shûr′bro͝ok′). A city of S Quebec, Canada, on the St. François R. E of Montreal. Pop. 74,075.

sherd (shûrd) *n.* Var. of **shard.**

Sher•i•dan (shĕr′ĭ-dn), **Philip Henry.** 1831–88. Amer. Union general who routed Confederate forces at the Battle of Five Forks (1865).

Sheridan, Richard Brinsley. 1751–1816. British playwright known for his comedies, including *The Rivals* (1775).

she•rif also **sha•rif** (shə-rēf′) *n.* **1.** A descendant of Muhammad through Fatima and her son Hussein (629?–680). **2.** The chief magistrate of Mecca in Ottoman times. **3.** A Moroccan prince or ruler. [Ar. *šarīf*, noble < *šarafa*, to be noble.]

sher•iff (shĕr′ĭf) *n.* **1.** The chief law enforcement officer for U.S. county courts. **2.** An officer of a county or an administrative region in England, Northern Ireland, and Scotland, charged mainly with judicial duties. [ME, the representative of royal authority in a shire < OE *scīrgerēfa* : *scīr*, shire + *gerēfa*, reeve.]

Sher•man (shûr′mən). A city of NE TX near the OK border N of Dallas. Pop. 31,601.

Sherman, James Schoolcraft. 1855–1912. Vice President of the U.S. (1909–12).

Sherman, John. 1823–1900. Amer. politician and U.S. senator who sponsored the Sherman Antitrust Act (1890).

Sherman, Mount. A peak, 4,281 m (14,036 ft), in the Park Range of the Rocky Mts. in central CO.

Sherman, Roger. 1721–93. Amer. Revolutionary patriot and a signer of the Declaration of Independence (1776), the Articles of Confederation (1781), and the U.S. Constitution (1787).

Sherman, William Tecumseh. 1820–91. Amer. Union general who captured Atlanta (1864) and led the destructive March to the Sea, which effectively cut the Confederacy in two.

she•root (shə-ro͞ot′) *n.* Var. of **cheroot**

Sher•pa (shûr′pə) *n., pl.* **Sherpa** or **-pas.** A member of a people of Tibetan descent living on the southern side of the Himalaya Mountains in Nepal and the region of Sikkim.

sher•ry (shĕr′ē) *n., pl.* **-ries.** **1.** A fortified Spanish wine ranging from very dry to sweet and from amber to brown. **2.** A similar wine made elsewhere. [Alteration of *sherris* (taken as pl.), after *Xeres* (Jerez), Spain.]

's Her•to•gen•bosch (sĕr′tō-gən-bôs′, -KHən-). A city of S-central Netherlands NNW of Eindhoven; chartered c. 1185. Pop. 89,059.

Sher•wood (shûr′wo͝od′), **Robert Emmet.** 1896–1955. Amer. writer whose works include *Idiot's Delight* (1936).

Sherwood Forest. A former royal forest of central England famed as the site of the legendary exploits of Robin Hood.

Sherwood Park. A city of central Alberta, Canada, a suburb of Edmonton. Pop. 29,285.

Shet•land (shĕt′lənd) *n.* **1.** A fine yarn made from the wool of sheep raised in the Shetland Islands. **2.** A garment, esp. a sweater, made of this yarn. [After the SHETLAND (ISLANDS).]

Shetland Islands. An archipelago of N Scotland in the Atlantic NE of the Orkney Is. — **Shet′land•er** *n.*

Shetland pony *n.* A small pony of a breed originating in the Shetland Islands and having a long thick mane and tail.

Shetland sheepdog *n.* A herding dog of a breed developed in the Shetland Islands resembling a small collie.

She•vat (shə-vät′, shvät) also **She•bat** (shə-bät′, -vät′) *n.* The year's fifth month in the Jewish calendar. [Heb. *šəbāṭ.*]

shew (shō) *v. Archaic.* Var. of **show.**

shew•bread (shō′brĕd′) *n. Archaic.* Var. of **showbread.**

Shey•enne (shī-ĕn′, -ăn′). A river rising in central ND and flowing c. 523 km (325 mi) to the Red R. of the North.

shf or **SHF** *abbr.* Superhigh frequency.

Shi•ah or **Shi•a** also **Shi•'ah** or **Shi•'a** (shē′ə) *Islam.* — *n.* **1.** *(used with a pl. v.)* The Shiites. **2.** *(used with a sing. v.)* A Shiite. — *adj.* Shiite. [Ar. *šī'ah*, following, sect < Syriac *sī'ā*, company, band.]

shi•at•su (shē-ät′so͞o) *n.* A form of therapeutic massage in which pressure is applied with the thumbs and palms to those areas of the body used in acupuncture. [Short for J. *shiatsuryōhō* : *shi*, finger + *atsu-*, pressure + *ryōhō*, treatment.]

shib•ah (shĭv′ə) *n. Judaism.* Var. of **shiva.**

shib•bo•leth (shĭb′ə-lĭth, -lĕth′) *n.* **1.** A word or pronunciation that distinguishes one group or class of people from another. **2.a.** A catchword serving to identify a particular group. **b.** A commonplace saying or idea. **3.** A custom or practice that betrays one as an outsider. [Ult. < Heb. *šibbōlet*, torrent of water, < the use of this word to distinguish one tribe from another, who pronounced it *sibbōleth* (Judges 12:4–6).]

shied[1] (shīd) *v.* P.t. and p.part. of **shy**[1].

shied[2] (shīd) *v.* P.t. and p.part. of **shy**[2].

shield (shēld) *n.* **1.** A broad piece of armor made of rigid material and strapped to the arm or carried for protection. **2.** A person or thing that provides protection. **3.** A protective device or structure, as: **a.** A steel sheet attached to an artillery piece to protect gunners. **b.** *Phys.* A wall or housing of concrete or lead built around a nuclear reactor to prevent the escape of radiation. **c.** *Electron.* A structure or arrangement of metal plates or mesh designed to protect a piece of electronic equipment from electrostatic or magnetic interference. **d.** A pad worn to protect a garment from perspiration. **4.** *Zool.* A protective plate or similar hard outer covering; a scute or scutellum. **5.** Something that resembles a shield, as: **a.** An escutcheon. **b.** A decorative emblem that often serves to identify an organization or a government. **c.** A police officer's badge. **6.** *Geol.* A large lowland area, the geologic nucleus of a continent, whose bedrock consists of usu. Precambrian igneous and metamorphic rocks. — *v.* **shield•ed, shield•ing, shields.** — *tr.* **1.** To protect or defend with or as if with a shield; guard. See Syns at **defend.** **2.** To cover up; conceal.

— *intr.* To act or serve as a shield or safeguard. [ME *sheld* < OE *scield.* See **skel-¹***.] — **shield′er** *n.*

shield law *n.* A law that protects journalists from being compelled to reveal confidential sources of information.

Shield of David (shēld) *n.* See **Magen David.**

shiel•ing (shē′lĭng, -lĭn) *n. Chiefly British.* **1.** A shepherd's hut. **2.** A mountain pasture used in the summer. [< Sc. *shiel*, hut < ME *shele*, poss. < OE **scēla*, prob. of Scand. orig. See **(s)keu-***.]

shi•er (shī′ər) *adj.* A comp. of **shy¹**.

shies¹ (shīz) *v.* Third pers. sing. pr.t. of **shy¹**. — *n.* Pl. of **shy¹**.

shies² (shīz) *v.* Third pers. sing. pr.t. of **shy²**. — *n.* Pl. of **shy²**.

shi•est (shī′ĭst) *adj.* A superl. of **shy¹**.

shift (shĭft) *v.* **shift•ed, shift•ing, shifts.** — *tr.* **1.** To exchange (one thing) for another of the same class: *shifted assignments.* **2.** To move or transfer from one place or position to another. **3.** To alter (position or place). **4.** To change (gears), as in an automobile. **5.** *Ling.* To alter phonetically as part of a systematic historical change. — *intr.* **1.** To change position, direction, place, or form. **2.a.** To provide for one's own needs; get along. **b.** To get along by tricky or evasive means. **3.** To change gears, as when driving. **4.** *Ling.* To be altered as part of a systematic historical change. Used of speech sounds. **5.** To select uppercase characters by depressing a shift key. — *n.* **1.** A change from one person or configuration to another; a substitution. **2.a.** A group of workers that relieve another on a regular schedule. **b.** The working period of such a group. **3.a.** A means to an end; an expedient. **b.** A stratagem; a trick. **4.** A change in direction. **5.** A change in attitude, judgment, or emphasis. **6.** A change in position, as: **a.** *Mus.* A change of the position of the hand in playing the violin or a similar instrument. **b.** *Football.* A rearrangement of players from one formation to another just prior to the snap of the ball. **c.** *Geol.* See **fault** 3. **7.** *Phys.* A change in wavelength, causing a movement of a spectral band or line. **8.** *Ling.* **a.** A systematic change of the phonetic or phonemic structure of a language. **b.** Functional shift. **9.a.** A loosely fitting dress that hangs straight from the shoulder; a chemise. **b.** A woman's undergarment; a slip or chemise. [ME *shiften* < OE *sciftan*, to arrange, divide.] — **shift′er** *n.*

shift key *n.* A key on a typewriter or computer keyboard that, when depressed, changes letters from lowercase to uppercase.

shift•less (shĭft′lĭs) *adj.* **1.a.** Lacking ambition or purpose; lazy. **b.** Marked by a lack of ambition or energy. **2.** Lacking resourcefulness or efficiency; incompetent. [SHIFT, expedient + -LESS.] — **shift′less•ly** *adv.* — **shift′less•ness** *n.*

shift•y (shĭf′tē) *adj.* **-i•er, -i•est. 1.** Having, displaying, or suggestive of deceitful character; untrustworthy. **2.** Marked by frequent changes in direction. **3.** Able to accomplish what is needed; resourceful. — **shift′i•ness** *n.*

shi•gel•la (shĭ-gĕl′ə) *n., pl.* **-gel•lae** (-gĕl′ē) also **-gel•las.** Any of various nonmotile rod-shaped bacteria of the genus *Shigella,* which includes some species that cause dysentery. [NLat. *Shigella*, genus name, after Kiyoshi *Shiga* (1870–1957), Japanese bacteriologist.]

shig•el•lo•sis (shĭg′ə-lō′sĭs) *n., pl.* **-ses** (-sēz). Dysentery caused by any of various species of shigellae.

Shih Tzu (shē′ dzo͞o′) *n.* A small dog of a breed first developed in Tibet, having a long thick coat and a square muzzle. [Chin. (Mandarin) *shī zi (gǒu)*, lion (dog), Shih Tzu.]

Shi•ism also **Shi•'ism** (shē′ĭz′əm) *n. Islam.* The religion or doctrines of the Shiites.

shi•i•ta•ke (shē-tä′kē, shē′ē-tä′kē) *n., pl.* **shiitake.** An edible eastern Asian mushroom *(Lentinus edodes)* having an aromatic fleshy golden or dark brown to blackish cap and an inedible tough stipe. [J. : *shi*, oak + *take*, mushroom.]

Shi•ite also **Shi•'ite** (shē′īt′) *Islam.* — *n.* A member of the branch of Islam that regards Ali and his descendants as the legitimate successors to Muhammad and rejects the first three caliphs. — *adj.* Of or relating to the Shiites or Shiism. — **Shi•it′ic** (-ĭt′ĭk) *adj.*

Shi•jia•zhuang (shœ′jyä′jwäng′) also **Shih•kia•chwang** (-kyä′chwäng′). A city of NE China SW of Beijing; cap. of Hebei province. Pop. 1,127,800.

shi•ka•ri (shĭ-kär′ē, -kăr′ē) *n., pl.* **-ris. 1.** A big-game hunter. **2.** A guide for big-game hunting. [Hindi *shikārī* < Pers. < *shikār*, hunting < MPers. *shkār*.]

Shi•ko•ku (shē-kô′ko͞o, shē′kô-ko͞o′). An island of S Japan between SW Honshu and E Kyushu.

shik•sa also **shik•se** (shĭk′sə) *n. Offensive.* Used as a disparaging term for a non-Jewish girl or woman. [Yiddish *shikse*.]

shill (shĭl) *Slang.* — *n.* One who poses as a satisfied customer or an enthusiastic gambler to dupe bystanders into participating in a swindle. — *v.* **shilled, shill•ing, shills.** — *intr.* To act as a shill. — *tr.* **1.** To act as a shill for (a deceitful enterprise). **2.** To lure (a person) into a swindle. [Perh. short for *shillaber*.]

shil•le•lagh also **shil•la•lah** (shə-lā′lē, -lə) *n.* A cudgel of oak, blackthorn, or other hardwood. [After *Shillelagh*, a village of E-central Ireland.]

shil•ling (shĭl′ĭng) *n.* **1.** A coin formerly used in the United Kingdom, worth 12 old pence prior to 1971. **2.** See table at **currency. 3.** *Print.* A virgule. [ME < OE *scilling*.]

Shil•luk (shĭ-lo͝ok′) *n., pl.* **Shilluk** or **-luks. 1.** A member of a people inhabiting the western bank of the Nile River in southern Sudan. **2.** The Nilotic language of the Shilluk.

shil•ly-shal•ly (shĭl′ē-shăl′ē) *intr.v.* **-lied** (-lēd), **-ly•ing, -lies** (-lēz). **1.** To procrastinate. **2.** To be unable to reach a decision; vacillate. **3.** To spend time on insignificant things; dawdle. — *adj.* Hesitant; vacillating. — *n., pl.* **-lies.** Procrastination; hesitation. — *adv.* Hesitantly; irresolutely. [Redup. of the question *shall I?*.] — **shil′ly-shal′li•er** *n.*

Shi•loh (shī′lō). **1.** An ancient village of central Palestine NW of the Dead Sea. In the Bible, it was a sanctuary for the Israelites and the site where the Ark of the Covenant was kept. **2.** A locality in SW TN E of Memphis; site of the Civil War Battle of Shiloh (Apr. 6–7, 1862), which ended in the withdrawal of Confederate troops.

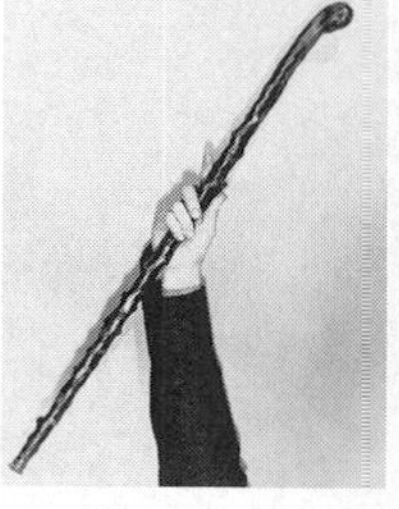
shillelagh

shim (shĭm) *n.* A thin, often tapered piece of material, such as wood, stone, or metal, used to fill gaps, make something level, or adjust something to fit properly. — *tr.v.* **shimmed, shim•ming, shims.** To fill in, level, or adjust with a shim. [?]

shim•mer (shĭm′ər) *intr.v.* **-mered, -mer•ing, -mers. 1.** To shine with a subdued flickering light. **2.** To appear as a wavering or flickering image, as in a reflection on water. — *n.* A flickering or tremulous light; a glimmer. [ME *shimeren* < OE *scimerian*.] — **shim′mer•ing•ly** *adv.* — **shim′mer•y** *adj.*

shim•my (shĭm′ē) *n., pl.* **-mies. 1.** Abnormal vibration or wobbling, as of car wheels. **2.** A dance popular in the 1920's, characterized by rapid shaking of the body. **3.** A chemise. — *intr.v.* **-mied, -my•ing, -mies. 1.** To vibrate or wobble abnormally. **2.** To shake the body in or as if in dancing the shimmy. [Perh. < alteration of CHEMISE.]

Shi•mo•no•se•ki (shĭm′ə-nō-sĕk′ē, shē′mô-nô-). A city of extreme SW Honshu, Japan; site of the signing (1895) of the treaty ending the Sino-Japanese War. Pop. 269,167.

shin¹ (shĭn) *n.* **1.a.** The front part of the leg below the knee and above the ankle. **b.** The shinbone. **2.** The lower foreleg in beef cattle. Used of cuts of meat. — *v.* **shinned, shin•ning, shins.** — *tr.* **1.** To climb (a rope or pole, for example) by gripping and pulling alternately with the hands and legs. **2.** To kick or hit in the shins. — *intr.* **1.** To climb by shinning. **2.** To move quickly on foot. [ME *shine* < OE *scinu*. See **skei-***.]

shin² (shēn, shĭn) *n.* The 22nd letter of the Hebrew alphabet. [Heb. *šîn*, var. of *šen*, tooth (< the shape of the letter).]

Shi•nar (shī′nər, -när′). An ancient country on the lower courses of the Tigris and Euphrates rivers.

shin•bone (shĭn′bōn′) *n.* See **tibia** 1.

shin•dig (shĭn′dĭg′) *n.* **1.** A festive party, often with dancing. **2.** See **shindy** 1. [Prob. alteration of SHINDY.]

shin•dy (shĭn′dē) *n., pl.* **-dies. 1.** A commotion; an uproar. **2.** See **shindig** 1. [Perh. alteration of SHINNY¹.]

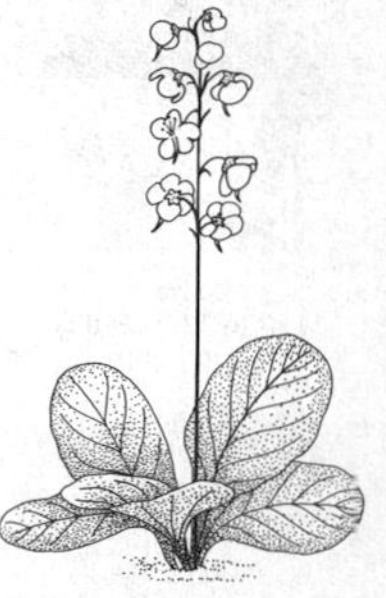
shinleaf
Pyrola elliptica

shine (shīn) *v.* **shone** (shōn) or **shined, shin•ing, shines.** — *intr.* **1.** To emit light. **2.** To reflect light; glisten. **3.** To distinguish oneself in an activity or a field; excel. **4.** To be immediately apparent: *Delight shone in her eyes.* — *tr.* **1.** To aim or cast the beam or glow of (a light). **2.** *p.t. and p.part.* **shined.** To make glossy or bright by polishing. — *n.* **1.** Brightness from a source of light; radiance. **2.** Brightness from reflected light; luster. **3.** A shoeshine. **4.** Excellence in quality or appearance; splendor. **5.** Fair weather. **6. shines.** *Informal.* Pranks or tricks. **7.** *Offensive Slang.* Used as a disparaging term for a Black person. — ***idiom.* take a shine to.** *Informal.* To like spontaneously. [ME *shinen* < OE *scīnan*.]

shin•er (shī′nər) *n.* **1.** One that shines, as a star or jewel. **2.** *Slang.* A black eye. **3.a.** Any of numerous small North American freshwater fishes of the family Cyprinidae, esp. one of the genus *Notropis.* **b.** Any of various similar fishes.

shin•gle¹ (shĭng′gəl) *n.* **1.** A thin oblong piece of material, such as wood, that is laid in overlapping rows to cover the roof or sides of a house or other building. **2.** *Informal.* A small signboard, as one indicating a professional office. **3.** A woman's close-cropped haircut. — *tr.v.* **-gled, -gling, -gles. 1.** To cover (a roof or building) with shingles. **2.** To cut (hair) short and close to the head. [ME < OE *scindel, scingal* < LLat. *scindula*, alteration of Lat. *scandula*.] — **shin′gler** *n.*

shin•gle² (shĭng′gəl) *n.* **1.** Beach gravel consisting of large smooth pebbles. **2.** A stretch of shore or beach covered with such gravel. [ME.] — **shin′gly** *adj.*

shin•gles (shĭng′gəlz) *pl.n. (used with a sing. or pl. v.)* An acute viral infection characterized by inflammation of the sensory ganglia of certain spinal or cranial nerves and the eruption of vesicles along the affected nerve path. [ME, alteration of Med.Lat. *cingulus*, var. of Lat. *cingulum*, girdle (the inflammation often girdling the body) < *cingere*, to gird. See **kenk-***.]

shin•leaf (shĭn′lēf′) *n.* Any of various Eurasian and North American woodland perennial herbs of the genera *Moneses* and *Pyrola,* esp. *P. elliptica,* having basal leaves.

shin•ny¹ also **shin•ney** (shĭn′ē) *n., pl.* **-nies** also **-neys.** *Sports.* **1.** Field hockey that is played informally with curved sticks and a ball, can, or similar object. **2.** The curved stick used in this game. [Prob. < *shin ye*, a cry used in the game.]

shin•ny² (shĭn′ē) *intr.v.* **-nied** (-nēd), **-ny•ing, -nies** (-nēz). To climb by shinning. [Alteration of SHIN¹.]

ă pat	oi boy
ā pay	ou out
âr care	o͝o took
ä father	o͞o boot
ĕ pet	ŭ cut
ē be	ûr urge
ĭ pit	th thin
ī pie	*th* this
îr pier	hw which
ŏ pot	zh vision
ō toe	ə about, item
ô paw	

Stress marks:
′ (primary);
′ (secondary), as in
dictionary (dĭk′shə-nĕr′ē)

shin•plas•ter (shĭn′plăs′tər) *n.* **1.** A piece of paper money issued privately and devalued by poor security or inflation. **2.** A piece of paper money of small value issued by the government, esp. by the U.S. government from 1862 to 1878.

shin splints also **shin•splints** (shĭn′splĭnts′) *pl.n.* *(used with a sing. or pl. v.)* Any of various painful conditions of the shins caused by inflammation of the surrounding muscles, frequently occurring among joggers and runners.

Shin•to (shĭn′tō) *n.* A religion native to Japan, characterized by veneration of nature spirits and ancestors and by a lack of formal dogma. [J. *shintō* : *shin*, gods (< Chin. *shén*) + *dō*, the Way of Taoism (< Chin. *dào*).] **—Shin′to** *adj.* **—Shin′to•ism** *n.* **—Shin′to•ist** *adj. & n.* **—Shin′to•is′tic** *adj.*

shin•y (shī′nē) *adj.* **-i•er, -i•est. 1.** Radiating light; bright. **2.** Bright from reflected light; glistening. **3.** Having a sheen from being rubbed or worn smooth. **—shin′i•ness** *n.*

ship (shĭp) *n.* **1.** *Naut.* **a.** A vessel of considerable size for deep-water navigation. **b.** A sailing vessel having three or more square-rigged masts. **2.** An aircraft or a spacecraft. **3.** The crew of one of these vessels. **4.** One's fortune. *—v.* **shipped, ship•ping, ships.** *—tr.* **1.** *Naut.* To place or receive on board a ship. **2.** To cause to be transported by or as if by ship; send. **3.** To hire (a person) for work on a ship. **4.** *Naut.* To take in (water) over the side of a ship. *—intr. Naut.* **1.** To go aboard a ship; embark. **2.** To travel by ship. **3.** To hire oneself out or enlist for service on a ship. ***—phrasal verb.* ship out. 1.** *Naut.* To accept a position as a crew member on a ship. **2.** To leave, as for a distant place. **3.** To send, as to a distant place. **4.** *Informal.* To quit, resign from, or otherwise vacate a position. [ME < OE *scip*.]

-ship *suff.* **1.a.** Quality, state, or condition: *scholarship*. **b.** Something that shows or possesses a quality, state, or condition: *courtship*. **2.** Rank, status, or office: *professorship*. **3.** Art, skill, or craft: *penmanship*. **4.** A collective body: *readership*. [ME < OE *-scipe*.]

ship biscuit *n.* See **hardtack.**

ship•board (shĭp′bôrd′, -bōrd′) *n.* **1.** *Naut.* The condition of being aboard a ship: *on shipboard*. **2.** *Archaic.* The side of a ship. *—adj. Naut.* Existing or occurring on board a ship.

ship•borne (shĭp′bôrn′, -bōrn′) *adj. Naut.* Transported by ship.

ship•build•ing (shĭp′bĭl′dĭng) *n.* The art or business of designing and constructing ships. **—ship′build′er** *n.*

ship canal *n.* A canal wide and deep enough to serve ships.

ship fitter *n.* **1.** One who positions the structural pieces of a ship for riveting and welding. **2.** A sailor in the U.S. Navy who does sheet-metal work and plumbing on board a ship.

ship•lap (shĭp′lăp′) *n.* Wooden siding rabbeted so that the edge of one board overlaps the one next to it in a flush joint. **—ship′lapped′** *adj.*

Shiva
11th- to 12th-century
Indian bronze

ship•load (shĭp′lōd′) *n.* The amount a ship can carry.

ship•man (shĭp′mən) *n. Naut.* **1.** A sailor. **2.** A shipmaster.

ship•mas•ter (shĭp′măs′tər) *n. Naut.* The officer in command of a merchant ship.

ship•mate (shĭp′māt′) *n. Naut.* A sailor serving on the same ship as another.

ship•ment (shĭp′mənt) *n.* **1.** The act or an instance of shipping goods. **2.** A quantity of cargo that is shipped together.

ship of the line *n., pl.* **ships of the line.** *Naut.* A warship large enough to take a position in the line of battle.

ship•per (shĭp′ər) *n.* One that consigns or receives goods for transportation.

ship•ping (shĭp′ĭng) *n.* **1.** The act or business of transporting goods. **2.** The body of ships belonging to one port, industry, or country, often referred to in aggregate tonnage. **3.** Passage or transport on a ship.

shipping clerk *n.* One who is employed to prepare, pack, receive, or record shipments of goods.

ship-rigged (shĭp′rĭgd′) *adj. Naut.* Rigged with three or more masts and square sails.

ship•shape (shĭp′shāp′) *adj.* Orderly and neat; tidy. See Syns at **neat¹.** [< obsolete *shipshapen*, arranged as a ship should be : SHIP + *shapen*, p.part. of SHAPE.] **—ship′shape′** *adv.*

ship•side (shĭp′sīd′) *n. Naut.* The area of a dock adjacent to a ship.

ship's papers (shĭps) *pl.n. Naut.* The documents, such as license, logbook, or bills of lading, that a ship must carry under international law and that must be shown on inspection.

ship•way (shĭp′wā′) *n.* **1.** The structure supporting a ship during construction or in dry dock. **2.** See **ship canal.**

ship•worm (shĭp′wûrm′) *n.* Any of various wormlike marine mollusks of the genera *Teredo* and *Bankia,* having rudimentary bivalve shells with which they bore into wood, esp. the submerged timbers of ships and wharves.

ship•wreck (shĭp′rĕk′) *n.* **1.** *Naut.* **a.** The destruction of a ship, as by storm. **b.** The remains of a wrecked ship. **2.** A complete failure or ruin. *—tr.v.* **-wrecked, -wreck•ing, -wrecks. 1.** *Naut.* **a.** To cause (a ship) to be destroyed. **b.** To cause (one on a ship) to suffer shipwreck. **2.** To ruin utterly.

ship•wright (shĭp′rīt′) *n.* One that builds or repairs ships.

ship•yard (shĭp′yärd′) *n.* A yard where ships are built or repaired.

Shi•ras (shī′rəs), **George.** 1832–1924. Amer. jurist; associate justice of the U.S. Supreme Court (1892–1903).

Shi•raz (shē-räz′). A city of SW-central Iran SSE of Tehran; long noted for its carpets and metalwork. Pop. 800,000.

shire (shīr) *n.* **1.** A former administrative division of Great Britain, equivalent to a county. **2.** Often **Shire.** A Shire horse. [ME < OE *scīr*, official charge, administrative district.]

Shire horse *n.* A large, powerful draft horse first bred in England, having long hair that grows from the knee and hock.

shire town *n. Chiefly British.* See **county town.**

shirk (shûrk) *v.* **shirked, shirk•ing, shirks.** *—tr.* To avoid or neglect (a duty or responsibility). *—intr.* To avoid work or duty. [Perh. < Ger. *Schurke*, scoundrel.] **—shirk′er** *n.*

Shir•ley (shûr′lē), **William.** 1694–1771. British governor of Massachusetts (1741–49 and 1753–56).

Shirley poppy *n.* A variety of the corn poppy with pink, salmon, or scarlet flowers. [After *Shirley*, district in SE England.]

shirr (shûr) *tr.v.* **shirred, shirr•ing, shirrs. 1.** To gather (cloth) into decorative rows by parallel stitching. **2.** To cook (unshelled eggs) by baking until set. [?]

shirt (shûrt) *n.* **1.** A garment for the upper part of the body, typically having a collar, sleeves, and a front opening. **2.** An undershirt. **3.** A nightshirt. ***—idioms.* keep (one's) shirt on.** *Slang.* To remain calm. **lose (one's) shirt.** *Slang.* To lose all one has. [ME *shirte* < OE *scyrte*, skirt. See **sker-¹*.**]

shirt•dress also **shirt-dress** (shûrt′drĕs′) *n.* A dress tailored like a shirt with a collar and buttons down the front.

shirt•ing (shûr′tĭng) *n.* Fabric suitable for making shirts.

shirt•sleeve (shûrt′slēv′) *n.* **1.** The sleeve of a shirt. **2. shirtsleeves.** The state of wearing no outer garment over one's shirt. *—adj.* **1.** Also **shirt•sleeved** (-slēvd′). Dressed without a coat. **2.** Also **shirtsleeves.** Calling for the removal of a coat or jacket. **3.** Also **shirtsleeves.** Marked by informality or straightforwardness.

shirt•tail (shûrt′tāl′) *n.* **1.** The part of a shirt that extends below the waist, esp. in the back. **2.** A brief addition at the end of a newspaper article. *—adj.* **1.** Very young: *shirttail kids*. **2.** Of little value; inadequate or small.

shirt•waist (shûrt′wāst′) *n.* **1.** A woman's blouse or bodice styled like a tailored shirt. **2.** See **shirtdress.**

shirt•y (shûr′tē) *adj.* **-i•er, -i•est.** *Chiefly British.* Ill-tempered; angry. [Prob. < *to get someone's shirt out*, to annoy, or *to keep one's shirt on*, to keep from being annoyed.]

shish ke•bab also **shish ke•bob** or **shish ka•bob** (shĭsh′ kə-bŏb′) *n.* A dish consisting of pieces of seasoned meat and sometimes vegetables roasted on skewers and served with condiments. [Armenian *shish kabab* < Turk. *şiş kebabiu* : *şiş*, skewer + *kebap*, roast meat.]

shit (shĭt) *Obscene.* *—v.* **shit** also **shat** (shăt), **shit•ting, shits.** *—intr.* To defecate. *—tr.* **1.** To defecate in. **2.** To tease or try to deceive. *—n.* **1.** Excrement. **2.** The act or an instance of defecating. **3. shits.** Diarrhea. Used with *the.* **4.a.** Something considered disgusting, shabby, foolish, or otherwise unacceptable. **b.** A person regarded as mean or contemptible. **5.** A narcotic or an intoxicant, such as heroin. **6.** Things; items. **7.** Foolishness; nonsense. **8.** Trouble or difficulty. *—interj.* Used to express surprise, anger, or extreme displeasure. [ME *shiten* < OE **scītan*. See **skei-*.**]

shit•list also **shit list** (shĭt′lĭst′) *n. Obscene.* A list of persons who are strongly disapproved of.

shit•tah (shĭt′ə) *n.* A tree, probably a species of acacia, that is mentioned frequently in the Bible. [Heb. *šiṭṭâ*.]

shit•ty (shĭt′ē) *adj.* **-ti•er, -ti•est.** *Obscene.* **1.** Of very poor quality; highly inferior. **2.** Contemptible; despicable. **3.** Unfortunate; unpleasant. **4.** Uncomfortable; unhappy; miserable. **5.** Incompetent; inept. **6.** Trivial; insignificant.

shiv (shĭv) *n. Slang.* A knife, razor, or other sharp implement, esp. one used as a weapon. [Prob. Romany *chiv*, blade.]

shiv•a also **shiv•ah** or **shib•ah** (shĭv′ə) *n. Judaism.* A seven-day period of formal mourning observed after the funeral of a close relative. [Yiddish *shive* < Heb. *šib'â*, seven.]

Shi•va (shē′və) also **Si•va** (shē′və, sē′-) *n. Hinduism.* One of the principal Hindu deities, worshiped as the destroyer and restorer of worlds and in numerous other complementary forms. [Skt. *śivaḥ* < *śiva-*, auspicious, dear. See **kei-¹*.**] **—Shi′va•ism** *n.* **—Shi′va•ist** *n.*

shiv•a•ree (shĭv′ə-rē′, shĭv′ə-rē′) *n. Midwestern & Western U.S.* A noisy mock serenade for newlyweds; a charivari. Also called regionally *belling, horning, serenade.* [Alteration of CHARIVARI.]

Regional Note: *Shivaree* is the most common American regional form of *charivari*, a French word meaning "a noisy mock serenade for newlyweds." The term, most likely borrowed from French traders and settlers along the Mississippi River, was well established in the United States by 1805. The word *shivaree* is especially common along and west of the Mississippi River, giving it an unusual north-south dialect boundary. Some regional equivalents are *belling,* used in Pennsylvania, West Virginia, and Ohio; *horning,* from upstate New York, Rhode Island, and western New England; and *serenade,* used chiefly in the South Atlantic states.

shiv•er¹ (shĭv′ər) *v.* **-ered, -er•ing, -ers.** *—intr.* **1.** To shake with or as if with cold; tremble. **2.** To quiver or vibrate, as by the force of the wind. — *tr. Naut.* To cause (a sail) to flutter by trimming it too close to the wind. — *n.* **1.** An instance of shivering or trembling. **2. shivers.** An attack of shivering. Used with *the.* [ME *chiveren, shiveren.*]

shiv•er[2] (shĭv′ər) *v.* **-ered, -er•ing, -ers.** — *intr.* To break into fragments or splinters; shatter. — *tr.* To cause to shiver. See Syns at **break.** — *n.* A fragment or splinter. [ME *shiveren* < *shivere,* splinter. See **skei-*.**]

shiv•er•y[1] (shĭv′ə-rē) *adj.* **1.** Trembling, as from cold or fear. **2.** Causing shivers; chilling.

shiv•er•y[2] (shĭv′ə-rē) *adj.* Easily broken; brittle.

Shi•zu•o•ka (shē′zo͞o-ô′kä). A city of E-central Honshu, Japan, on Suruga Bay SW of Yokohama. Pop. 468,362.

shkotz•im (shkôt′sĭm) *n. Offensive.* Pl. of **shegetz.**

shle•miel (shlə-mēl′) *n. Slang.* Var. of **schlemiel.**

shlep (shlĕp) *v. & n. Slang.* Var. of **schlep.**

shlock (shlŏk) *n. & adj.* Var. of **schlock.**

shmear (shmîr) *n. Slang.* Var. of **schmeer.**

shmuck (shmŭk) *n. Slang.* Var. of **schmuck.**

shoal[1] (shōl) *n.* A shallow place in a body of water. — *v.* **shoaled, shoal•ing, shoals.** — *intr.* To become shallow. — *adj.* Having little depth; shallow. [ME *shold,* shallow, shallows < OE *sceald,* shallow.]

shoal[2] (shōl) *n.* **1.** A large group; a crowd. **2.** A large school of fish or other marine animals. — *intr.v.* **shoaled, shoal•ing, shoals.** To come together in large numbers; throng. [Prob. MLGer. or MDu. *schōle;* see **skel-[1]*.**]

shoat also **shote** (shōt) *n.* A young pig just after weaning. [ME *shote,* perh. of MLGer. orig.]

shock[1] (shŏk) *n.* **1.a.** A violent collision or impact; a heavy blow. **b.** The effect of such a collision or blow. **2.a.** Something that jars the mind or emotions as if with a violent, unexpected blow. **b.** The disturbance of function, equilibrium, or mental faculties caused by such a blow; violent agitation. **3.** A severe offense to one's sense of propriety or decency; an outrage. **4.** A generally temporary state of massive physiological reaction to severe trauma, usu. characterized by marked loss of blood pressure and depression of vital processes. **5.** The sensation and muscular spasm caused by an electric current passing through the body. **6.** A sudden economic disturbance, such as a rise in the price of a commodity. **7.** A shock absorber. — *v.* **shocked, shock•ing, shocks.** — *tr.* **1.** To strike with great surprise and emotional disturbance. **2.** To strike with disgust; offend. **3.** To induce a state of physical shock in (a person). **4.** To subject (an animal or a person) to an electric shock. — *intr.* To come into contact violently, as in battle; collide. [Fr. *choc* < *choquer,* to collide with < OFr. *chuquier,* perh. of Gmc. orig.]

shock[2] (shŏk) *n.* **1.** A number of sheaves of grain stacked upright in a field for drying. **2.** A thick heavy mass: *a shock of hair.* — *tr.v.* **shocked, shock•ing, shocks.** To gather (grain) into shocks. [ME *shok.*]

shock absorber *n.* A device used to absorb mechanical shocks, as a hydraulic or pneumatic piston used to dampen the jarring sustained in a moving motor vehicle.

shock•er (shŏk′ər) *n.* One that startles, shocks, or horrifies.

shock•ing (shŏk′ĭng) *adj.* **1.** Highly disturbing emotionally. **2.** Highly offensive; indecent or distasteful. **3.** Very vivid or intense in tone: *shocking pink.* **—shock′ing•ly** *adv.*

Shock•ley (shŏk′lē), **William Bradford.** 1910–89. British-born Amer. physicist who shared a 1956 Nobel Prize.

shock•proof (shŏk′pro͞of′) *adj.* Constructed or designed to withstand blows or jarring.

shock therapy *n.* Any of various treatments for mental disorders, such as major depression, in which a convulsion or brief coma is induced by a drug or an electric current.

shock troops *pl.n.* Soldiers specially chosen, trained, and armed to lead an attack. [Transl. of Ger. *Stosstruppen.*]

shock wave *n.* **1.** A large-amplitude compression wave, as that produced by an explosion or by supersonic motion of a body in a medium. **2.** A violent disruption, disturbance, or reaction.

shod•dy (shŏd′ē) *adj.* **-di•er, -di•est. 1.** Made of or containing inferior material. **2.a.** Of poor quality or craft. **b.** Rundown; shabby. **3.** Dishonest or reprehensible: *shoddy business practices.* **4.** Conspicuously and cheaply imitative. — *n., pl.* **-dies. 1.a.** Woolen yarn made from scraps or used clothing, with some new wool added. **b.** Cloth made from or containing such yarn. **2.** Something of inferior quality; a cheap imitation. [?] **—shod′di•ly** *adv.* **—shod′di•ness** *n.*

shoe (sho͞o) *n.* **1.** A durable covering for the human foot, made of leather or similar material with a rigid sole and heel, usu. extending no higher than the ankle. **2.** A horseshoe. **3.** A part or device at the base of something or functioning as a protective covering, as: **a.** A strip of metal fitted onto the bottom of a sled runner. **b.** The base for the supports of the superstructure of a bridge. **c.** The ferrule on the end of a cane. **d.** The casing of a pneumatic tire. **4.** A device that retards or stops the motion of an object, as the part of a brake that presses against the wheel or drum. **5.** The sliding contact plate on an electric train or streetcar that conducts electricity from the third rail. **6.** A chute, as for conveying grain from a hopper. **7.** *Games.* A case from which playing cards are dealt one at a time. **8. shoes.** *Informal.* **a.** Position: *I'd love to be in your shoes.* **b.** Plight. — *tr.v.* **shod** (shŏd), **shod** or **shod•den** (shŏd′n), **shoe•ing, shoes. 1.** To furnish or fit with a shoe or shoes. **2.** To cover with a wooden or metal guard to protect against wear. [ME < OE *scōh.*]

shoe•bill (sho͞o′bĭl′) *n.* A tall wading bird *(Balaeniceps rex)* native to eastern tropical Africa and having dark plumage, long black legs, and a large shoelike bill.

shoe•box (sho͞o′bŏks′) *n.* **1.** An oblong box, usually made of cardboard, for holding a pair of shoes. **2.** Something resembling or suggestive of such a box.

shoe•horn (sho͞o′hôrn′) *n.* A smooth curved implement, often of plastic or metal, inserted at the heel to help put on a shoe. — *tr.v.* **-horned, -horn•ing, -horns.** To squeeze into or as if into an insufficient space.

shoe•lace (sho͞o′lās′) *n.* A string or cord used for lacing and fastening shoes.

shoe•mak•er (sho͞o′mā′kər) *n.* One that makes or repairs shoes. **—shoe′mak′ing** *n.*

shoe•pac also **shoe•pack** (sho͞o′păk′) *n.* A heavy warm waterproof boot. [Alteration of pidgin Delaware *seppock,* shoe, shoes < Unami (Delaware language) *chípahko,* shoes.]

shoe•shine (sho͞o′shīn′) *n.* **1.** A shiny finish put on a pair of shoes by brushing and buffing with polish. **2.** The act or an instance of putting a shiny finish on shoes.

shoe•string (sho͞o′strĭng′) *n.* **1.** See **shoelace. 2.** A small sum of money; capital that is barely adequate. — *adj.* **1.** Long and slender. **2.** Marked by or consisting of a small amount of money. **3.** *Sports.* At or near the feet.

shoe•tree (sho͞o′trē′) *n.* A form made of inflexible material inserted into a shoe to stretch it or preserve its shape.

sho•far (shō′fär′, -fər) *n., pl.* **sho•fars** or **sho•froth** (shō-frōt′, -frōs′). *Judaism.* A trumpet made of a ram's horn, blown by the ancient Hebrews on holidays and in battle, now sounded in the synagogue during Rosh Hashanah and at the end of Yom Kippur. [Heb. *šôpār,* ram's horn, shofar.]

sho•gi (shō′gē) *n. Games.* A Japanese game similar to chess that is played on a board with 81 squares, each side having 20 pieces. [J. < Chin. (Mandarin) *jiàng qí* : *jiàng,* commander in chief, chief chess piece + *qí,* board game, such as chess.]

sho•gun (shō′gən) *n.* The hereditary commander of the Japanese army who until 1867 exercised absolute rule under the nominal leadership of the emperor. [J. *shōgun,* general.]

sho•gun•ate (shō′gə-nĭt, -nāt′) *n.* The government, rule, or office of a shogun.

sho•ji (shō′jē) *n., pl.* **shoji** or **-jis.** A translucent screen consisting of a wooden frame covered in rice paper, used as a sliding door or partition in a Japanese house. [J. *shōji.*]

Sho•la•pur (shō′lə-po͝or′). A city of W-central India on the Deccan Peninsula ESE of Bombay. Pop. 511,103.

Sho•lo•khov (shô′lə-kôf′, -KHəf), **Mikhail Aleksandrovich.** 1905–84. Russian writer who won the 1965 Nobel Prize for literature.

shone (shōn) *v.* A p.t. and p.part. of **shine.**

shoo (sho͞o) *interj.* Used to frighten away animals or birds. — *tr.v.* **shooed, shoo•ing, shoos.** To drive or frighten away by or as if by crying "shoo."

shoo•fly (sho͞o′flī′) *n.* A child's rocker having the seat built between two flat sides cut in the shape of an animal.

shoofly pie *n.* A pie with a filling of molasses and brown sugar. [< shooing away the flies attracted to the sweet filling.]

shoo-in (sho͞o′ĭn′) *n. Informal.* **1.** A sure winner. **2.** One with a sure chance of being chosen, as for a job.

shook[1] (sho͝ok) *n.* A set of parts for assembling a barrel or packing box. [Prob. < *shook cask,* var. of *shaken cask,* cask broken down for shipment < *shaken,* dismantled and packed for transport, p.part. of SHAKE, to scatter, shed.]

shook[2] (sho͝ok) *v.* P.t. of **shake.**

shook-up (sho͝ok-ŭp′) *adj. Slang.* Emotionally upset or excited; shaken.

shoon (sho͞on) *n. Archaic.* Pl. of **shoe.**

shoot (sho͞ot) *v.* **shot** (shŏt), **shoot•ing, shoots.** — *tr.* **1.a.** To hit, wound, or kill with a missile fired from a weapon. **b.** To remove or destroy with a missile: *shot out the pane.* **c.** To make (a hole, for example) by firing a weapon. **2.** To fire or let fly (a missile) from a weapon. **3.a.** To discharge (a weapon). **b.** To detonate or cause to explode: *shot off a firecracker.* **4.** To inject (a drug, for example) with a hypodermic syringe. **5.** To throw out or release (a fishing line, for example). **6.a.** To send forth suddenly, intensely, or swiftly: *shot an angry look at me.* **b.** To emit (a form of energy). **c.** To utter (sounds or words) forcefully, rapidly, or suddenly. **7.** *Informal.* To spend, use up, or waste. **8.** To pass over or through swiftly: *shooting the rapids.* **9.** To cover (country) in hunting for game. **10.** To record on film. **11.** To cause to project or protrude; extend: *shot out her arm.* **12.** To begin to grow or produce; put forth. **13.** To pour, empty out, or discharge down or as if down a chute. **14.** *Sports & Games.* **a.** To throw or propel (a ball or other projectile in a game) in a specific direction. **b.** To accomplish (the objective) of a game involving projectiles; score (a point, basket, stroke, or goal).

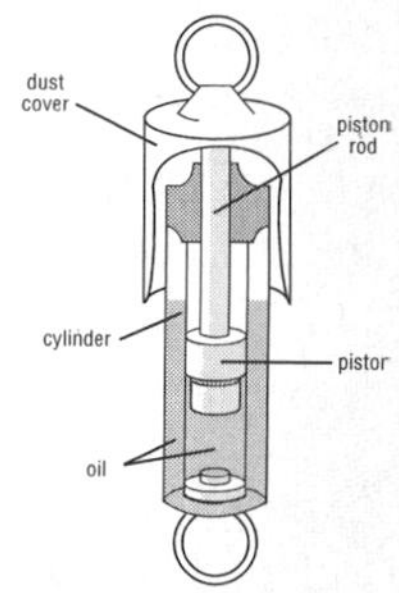

shock absorber
Hydraulic shock absorber

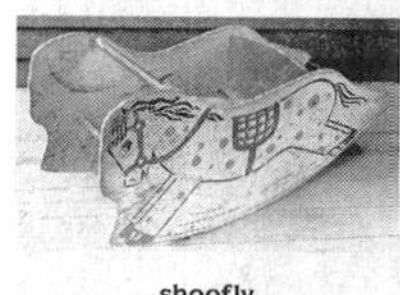

shoofly

ă pat	oi boy
ā pay	ou out
âr care	o͝o took
ä father	o͞o boot
ĕ pet	ŭ cut
ē be	ûr urge
ĭ pit	th thin
ī pie	*th* this
îr pier	hw which
ŏ pot	zh vision
ō toe	ə about,
ô paw	item

Stress marks:
′ (primary);
′ (secondary), as in
dictionary (dĭk′shə-nĕr′ē)

c. To play (a game involving projectiles or dice). d. To attain (a given score) in golf. e. To throw (the dice or a given score) in craps. 15. To slide (the bolt of a lock) into or out of its fastening. 16. To plane (the edge of a board) straight. 17. To variegate (colored cloth) by interweaving weft threads of a different color. 18. To measure the altitude of with an instrument: *shot the star.* — *intr.* 1. To discharge a missile from a weapon. 2. To discharge or fire; go off. 3.a. To gush or spurt: *Water shot out.* b. To appear suddenly: *The sun shot through the clouds.* 4. To move swiftly; dart. 5. To be felt moving or as if moving in the body. 6. To protrude; project. 7. To engage in hunting or the firing of weapons, esp. for sport. 8. To put forth new growth; germinate. 9.a. To take pictures. b. To begin filming a scene in a movie. 10. *Sports & Games.* To propel a ball or other object toward the goal or in a specific direction or manner. 11. *Games.* To throw dice. 12. *Slang.* To begin talking. Often used in the imperative: *I'm listening. Shoot!* 13. To slide into or out of a fastening. Used of the bolt of a lock. — *n.* 1. The motion or movement of something that is propelled, driven, or discharged. 2.a. The young growth arising from a germinating seed; a sprout. b. New growth on a plant. 3. A narrow, swift, or turbulent section of a stream. 4.a. The act of discharging a weapon or letting fly a missile. b. *Informal.* The launching of a rocket or similar missile. 5.a. An organized shooting activity, such as a hunt. b. A round of shots in a contest with firearms. 6.a. A photographic assignment or session. b. A cinematographic session. 7. The distance a shot travels; the range. 8. *Naut.* The interval between strokes in rowing. 9. A sharp twinge or spasm of pain. 10. An inclined channel for moving something; a chute. 11. A body of ore in a vein. — *interj.* Used to express surprise, annoyance, or disappointment. — ***phrasal verbs.*** **shoot down.** 1. To bring down (an aircraft, for example) with gunfire or a missile. 2. *Informal.* To ruin the aspirations of; disappoint. 3. *Informal.* a. To put an end to; defeat. b. To expose as false; discredit. **shoot for** (or **at**). *Informal.* To strive or aim for; have as a goal. **shoot up.** 1. *Informal.* To grow or get taller rapidly. 2. To increase dramatically in amount. 3. To riddle with bullets. 4. To damage or terrorize (a town, for example) by intense or random gunfire. 5. *Slang.* To inject a drug with a hypodermic syringe. — ***idioms.*** **shoot from the hip.** *Slang.* To act or speak without forethought. **shoot off (one's) mouth** (or **face**). *Slang.* 1. To speak indiscreetly. 2. To brag; boast. [ME *shoten* < OE *scēotan.* See **skeud-***.]

shoot•down (sho͞ot′doun′) *n.* Destruction or an instance of destruction of a flying aircraft with missiles or gunfire.

shoot-'em-up (sho͞ot′əm-ŭp′) *n. Informal.* An entertainment, such as a movie, featuring gunfire and violence.

shoot•ing gallery (sho͞o′tĭng) *n.* An enclosed target range for practice or competition with firearms.

shooting iron *n. Slang.* A firearm, esp. a handgun.

shooting script *n.* The version of a movie or television script with the scenes arranged in sequence for filming or taping.

shooting star *n.* 1. See **meteor.** 2. Any of several North American perennial herbs of the genus *Dodecatheon,* having nodding flowers with reflexed petals.

shooting stick *n.* A stick resembling a cane, pointed at one end with a folding seat at the other, typically used by spectators at outdoor sporting events.

shoot•out also **shoot-out** (sho͞ot′out′) *n.* 1.a. A gunfight. b. A battle between military forces. c. *Slang.* A dispute to settle a disagreement. 2. *Sports.* a. A high-scoring period or game. b. A means of resolving a tie after overtime in soccer, in which five players from each side alternately take individual shots on goal.

shoot-the-chute

shoot-the-chute also **chute-the-chute** (sho͞ot′*thə*-sho͞ot′) *n.* An amusement ride consisting of a steep slide often with a pool of water at the end.

shoot-up (sho͞ot′ŭp′) *n. Slang.* 1. The act or an instance of shooting up a drug. 2. A gunfight; a shootout.

shop (shŏp) *n.* 1. Also **shoppe.** A small retail store or a specialty department in a large store. 2. An atelier; a studio. 3. A place for manufacturing or repairing goods or machinery. 4. A commercial or industrial establishment: *a printing shop.* 5. A business establishment; an office or a center of activity. 6. A home workshop. 7.a. A schoolroom fitted with machinery and tools for instruction in industrial arts. b. The industrial arts as a technical science or course of study. — *v.* **shopped, shop•ping, shops.** — *intr.* 1. To visit stores in search of merchandise or bargains. 2. To look for something with the intention of acquiring it. — *tr.* To visit or buy from (a particular store). — ***phrasal verb.*** **shop around.** 1. To shop from store to store. 2. To look for something, such as a better job. 3. To offer (a large block of common stock, for example) for sale to various parties. — ***idiom.*** **talk shop.** To talk about one's work. [ME *shoppe* < OE *sceoppa,* treasure house.]

shop•keep•er (shŏp′kē′pər) *n.* One who owns or manages a shop.

shop•lift (shŏp′lĭft′) *v.* **-lift•ed, -lift•ing, -lifts.** — *intr.* To shoplift merchandise. — *tr.* To steal (articles or an article) from a store that is open for business. — **shop′lift′er** *n.* — **shop′lift′ing** *n.*

shop•per (shŏp′ər) *n.* 1. One who visits stores in search of merchandise or bargains. 2. A commercial agent who compares the merchandise and prices of competing merchants. 3. A commercial employee who fills mail or telephone orders. 4. A newspaper containing advertisements and local news.

shop•ping bag (shŏp′ĭng) *n.* A strong bag with handles for carrying a shopper's purchases.

shop•ping-bag lady (shŏp′ĭng-băg′) *n Slang.* A bag lady.

shopping center *n.* A group of stores and often restaurants and other businesses having a common parking lot.

shopping mall *n.* 1. An urban shopping area limited to pedestrians. 2. A shopping center with stores and businesses facing a system of enclosed walkways for pedestrians.

shop steward *n.* A union member elected to represent coworkers in dealings with management.

shop•talk (shŏp′tôk′) *n.* 1. Talk concerning one's work or business. 2. The jargon used in a specific business or field.

shop•worn (shŏp′wôrn′, -wōrn′) *adj.* 1. Tarnished, frayed, faded, or otherwise defective from being on display in a store. 2. Worn-out, as from overuse; trite: *shopworn anecdotes.*

sho•ran (shôr′ăn′, shōr′-) *n.* A short-range navigation system by which a ship or an aircraft can determine its position by measuring the times required for a radar signal to reach and return from each of two ground stations. [*sho(rt)-ra(nge) n(avigation).*]

shore[1] (shôr, shōr) *n.* 1. The land along the edge of an ocean, a sea, a lake, or a river; a coast. 2. Land; country. Often used in the plural: *native shores.* 3. Land as opposed to water. [ME *shore* < OE *scora.* See **sker-**[1]*.]

shore[2] (shôr, shōr) *tr.v.* **shored, shor•ing, shores.** To support by or as if by a prop: *shored up the sagging floors.* — *n.* A beam or timber propped against a structure to provide support. [ME *shoren* < *shore,* prop, prob. < MLGer. *schōre,* barrier, or MDu. *scōre,* prop.]

shore[3] (shôr, shōr) *v. Archaic.* A p.t. of **shear.**

shore bird also **shore•bird** (shôr′bûrd′, shōr′-) *n.* Any of various birds that frequent coastal or inland shores.

shore dinner *n.* A meal consisting of seafood.

shore leave *n.* A sailor's leave of absence to go ashore.

shore•line (shôr′līn′, shōr′-) *n.* The edge of a body of water.

shore patrol *n.* A detail of the U.S. Navy, Marine Corps, or Coast Guard serving as military police ashore.

Shore•view (shôr′vyo͞o′, shōr′-). A city of E MN, a suburb of St. Paul. Pop. 24,587.

shore•ward (shôr′wərd, shōr′-) *adv. & adj.* Toward, to, or on the shore. — **shore′wards** (-wərdz) *adv.*

shor•ing (shôr′ĭng, shōr′-) *n.* 1. The act or operation of propping with shores. 2. A system of supporting shores.

shorn (shôrn, shōrn) *v.* A p.part. of **shear.**

short (shôrt) *adj.* **short•er, short•est.** 1. Having little length; not long. 2. Having little height; not tall. 3. Extending not far or not far enough: *a short toss.* 4.a. Lasting a brief time. b. Appearing to pass quickly. 5. Not lengthy; succinct: *short and to the point.* 6.a. Rudely brief; abrupt. b. Easily provoked; irascible. 7. Inadequate; insufficient. 8. Lacking in length or amount: *a board short two inches.* 9. Lacking in breadth or scope. 10. Deficient in retentiveness: *a short memory.* 11.a. Not owning the stocks or commodities one is selling in anticipation of a fall in prices. b. Of or relating to a short sale. 12.a. Containing a large amount of shortening; flaky. b. Not ductile; brittle: *short iron.* 13.a. *Ling.* Of, relating to, or being a speech sound of brief duration, as the first vowel sound in the Latin word *mălus,* "evil," as compared with the same or a similar sound of long duration, as the first vowel sound in the Latin word *mālus,* "apple tree." b. *Gram.* Of, relating to, or being vowel sounds historically descended from vowels of brief duration, as (ă) in *pat* and (o͝o) in *put.* 14.a. Unstressed; unaccented. Used of a syllable in accentual prosody. b. Being of relatively brief duration. Used of a syllable in quantitative prosody. — *adv.* 1. Abruptly; quickly. 2. In a rude or curt manner. 3. At a point before a given limit or goal. 4. At a disadvantage: *caught short by the storm.* 5. Without owning what one is selling. — *n.* 1. Something short, as: a. A short sound or syllable. b. A brief film; a short subject. c. A size of clothing less long than the average for that size. d. **shorts.** Short trousers extending to the knee or above. e. **shorts.** Men's undershorts. 2.a. A short sale. b. One that sells short. 3. **shorts.** A byproduct of wheat processing that consists of germ, bran, and coarse meal or flour. 4. **shorts.** Clippings or trimmings that remain as byproducts in various manufacturing processes, often used to make an inferior variety of the product. 5.a. A short circuit. b. A malfunction caused by a short circuit. 6. *Baseball.* A shortstop. — *v.* **short•ed, short•ing, shorts.** — *tr.* 1. To cause a short circuit in. 2. *Informal.* To give (one) less than one is entitled to; shortchange. 3.a. To sell (a stock that one does not own) in anticipation of making a profit when its price falls. b. To sell unowned stock in (the stock market) in anticipation of making a profit when prices fall. — *intr.* To short-circuit. — ***idioms.*** **for short.** As an abbreviation. **in short.** In summary; briefly. **short for.** An abbreviation of. **short of.** 1. Having an inadequate supply of. 2. Less than.

3. Other than; without resorting to. **4.** Not quite willing to undertake or do; just this side of. **the short end of the stick.** The worst side of an unequal deal. [ME < OE *sceort, scort.* See **sker-**[1]*.] — **short′ness** *n.*

short account *n.* **1.** The account of one that sells short. **2.** The total number of open short shares in an account or in the market.

short•age (shôr′tĭj) *n.* A deficiency in amount.

short-billed marsh wren (shôrt′bĭld′) *n.* A small brownish wren *(Cistothorus platensis)* of eastern North America living in shallow sedge marshes and damp grassy meadows.

short•bread (shôrt′brĕd′) *n.* A cookie made of flour, sugar, and much butter or other shortening.

short•cake (shôrt′kāk′) *n.* A crisp light cake usu. served with fruit and topped with cream.

short•change (shôrt′chānj′) *tr.v.* **-changed, -chang•ing, -chang•es. 1.** To give (someone) less change than is due in a transaction. **2.** *Informal.* To treat unfairly or deceitfully; cheat. — **short′chang′er** *n.*

short circuit *n.* A low-resistance connection accidentally established between two points in an electric circuit.

short-cir•cuit (shôrt′sûr′kĭt) *v.* **-cuit•ed, -cuit•ing, -cuits.** — *tr.* **1.** To cause to have a short circuit. **2.** *Informal.* To hamper the progress of; impede. **3.** To bypass. — *intr.* To become affected with a short circuit.

short•com•ing (shôrt′kŭm′ĭng) *n.* A deficiency; a flaw.

short covering *n.* The buying of securities, stocks, or commodities in order to close out a short sale.

short•cut (shôrt′kŭt′) *n.* **1.** A more direct route than the customary one. **2.** A means of saving time or effort. [< CUT, direct route.] — **short′cut′** *v.*

short-day (shôrt′dā′) *adj.* Of, relating to, or being a plant that flowers only after exposure to light periods shorter than a certain critical length, as in early spring or fall.

short division *n. Math.* The process of dividing one number by another without writing down all the steps, esp. when the divisor is a single digit.

short•en (shôr′tn) *v.* **-ened, -en•ing, -ens.** — *tr.* **1.** To make short or shorter. **2.** *Naut.* To take in (a sail) so that less of its surface is exposed to the wind. **3.** To reduce in force, efficacy, or intensity. **4.** To add shortening to (dough) for flakiness. — *intr.* To become short or shorter. — **short′en•er** *n.*

short•en•ing (shôr′tn-ĭng, shôrt′nĭng) *n.* **1.** A fat used to make cake or pastry light or flaky. **2.** Something that has been shortened, as a word. **3.** The act or process of becoming or making shorter.

short•fall (shôrt′fôl′) *n.* **1.** A failure to attain a specified amount or level; a shortage. **2.** The amount by which a supply falls short of expectation, need, or demand.

short•hair (shôrt′hâr′) *n.* Either of two breeds of cats, characterized by short hair, a slender muscular body, large head, broad muzzle, and large round eyes.

short•haired (shôrt′hârd′) *adj.* Having a coat of short hair. Used of animals.

short•hand (shôrt′hănd′) *n.* **1.** A system of rapid handwriting using symbols for words, phrases, and letters. **2.** A system, a form, or an instance of abbreviated or formulaic reference.

short-hand•ed (shôrt′hăn′dĭd) *adj.* Lacking the usual or necessary number of workers, employees, players, or assistants.

short•horn (shôrt′hôrn′) *n.* Any of a breed of beef or dairy cattle that originated in northern England, having short curved horns or no horns and usu. red, white, or roan.

short-horned grasshopper (shôrt′hôrnd′) *n.* A grasshopper of the family Locustidae (or Acrididae), including the locusts that swarm over large areas destroying vegetation.

shor•ti•a (shôr′tē-ə) *n.* Any of various eastern North American and Asian evergreen stemless herbs of the genus *Shortia,* having glossy basal leaves and white, pink, or blue nodding flowers on long stalks. [NLat., genus name, after Charles Wilkins *Short* (1794–1863), Amer. physician and botanist.]

short•ie (shôr′tē) *n. & adj.* Var. of **shorty.**

short•leaf pine (shôrt′lēf′) *n.* A pine tree *(Pinus echinata)* common in the southeast United States and having dark bluish-green leaves grouped in fascicles of two.

short•list also **short-list** (shôrt′lĭst′) *n.* A list of preferable items or candidates that have been selected for final consideration, as in making an award. — **short′-list′** *v.*

short-lived (shôrt′lĭvd′, -līvd′) *adj.* Living or lasting only a short time; ephemeral.

Usage Note: The pronunciation (-līvd) is etymologically correct since the compound is derived from the noun *life,* rather than from the verb *live.* But the pronunciation (-lĭvd) is by now so common that it cannot be considered an error. In the most recent survey 43 percent of the Usage Panel preferred (-lĭvd), 39 percent preferred (-līvd), and 18 percent found both pronunciations equally acceptable.

short•ly (shôrt′lē) *adv.* **1.** In a short time; soon. **2.** In a few words; concisely. **3.** In an abrupt manner; curtly.

short order *n.* An order of food prepared and served quickly, as in a diner. — **short′-or′der** (shôrt′ôr′dər) *adj.*

short-range (shôrt′rānj′) *adj.* **1.** Designed for or limited to short distances. **2.** Of or relating to the near future.

short ribs *pl.n.* Beef rib ends between the rib roast and the plate.

short sale *n.* The sale of a security that one does not own but has borrowed in anticipation of making a profit by paying for it after its price has fallen.

short shrift *n.* **1.** Summary, careless treatment; scant attention. **2.** Quick work. **3.a.** A short respite, as from death. **b.** The brief time before execution granted a condemned prisoner for confession and absolution.

short sight *n.* See **myopia** 1.

short•sight•ed (shôrt′sī′tĭd) *adj.* **1.** Nearsighted; myopic. **2.** Lacking foresight. — **short′sight′ed•ly** *adv.* — **short′sight′ed•ness** *n.*

short-spo•ken (shôrt′spō′kən) *adj.* Given to shortness or abruptness in manner or speech; curt.

short•stop (shôrt′stŏp′) *n. Baseball.* **1.** The field position between second and third base. **2.** The infielder in this position.

short story *n.* A short piece of prose fiction, having few characters and aiming at unity of effect.

short subject *n.* A brief film often shown before a feature-length film.

short-tem•pered (shôrt′tĕm′pərd) *adj.* Easily or quickly moved to anger; irascible.

short-term (shôrt′tûrm′) *adj.* **1.** Involving or lasting a relatively brief time. **2.a.** Payable or reaching maturity within a relatively brief time, such as a year: *a short-term loan.* **b.** Acquired over a relatively brief time: *short-term capital gains.*

short ton *n.* See **ton** 1.

short•wave (shôrt′wāv′) *adj.* **1.** Having a wavelength of approx. 20 to 200 meters. **2.** Capable of receiving or transmitting at wavelengths of approx. 20 to 200 meters.

short wave *n.* An electromagnetic wave with a wavelength of approx. 200 meters or less, esp. a radio wave in the 20 to 200 meter range.

short-wind•ed (shôrt′wĭn′dĭd) *adj.* **1.** Breathing with quick labored breaths. **2.** Likely to have trouble breathing, esp. from exertion. **3.** Brief and succinct. **4.** Choppy; disconnected.

short•y also **short•ie** (shôr′tē) *Informal.* — *n., pl.* **-ies. 1.** A person short in stature. **2.** A thing of less than average size, length, extension, or duration. — *adj.* Of less than average size or length.

Sho•sho•ne also **Sho•sho•ni** (shō-shō′nē) *n., pl.* **Shoshone** or **-nes** also **Shoshoni** or **-nis. 1.** A member of a Native American people comprising three divisions, specifically: **a.** A group inhabiting parts of Idaho, northern Utah, eastern Oregon, and western Montana, now mostly in Idaho. **b.** A group inhabiting the Great Basin area of Idaho, Utah, and Nevada south to Death Valley, California, now mostly in Nevada. **c.** A group in western Wyoming. **2.** Any of the languages of the Shoshone people. [Prob. < an Eastern Shoshone band name.] — **Sho•sho′ne•an** *adj.*

Shoshone Falls. A waterfall, 64.7 m (212 ft), in the Snake R. of S ID.

Shoshone River. A river, c. 193 km (120 mi), of NW WY flowing NE to the Bighorn R.

Shos•ta•ko•vich (shŏs′tə-kō′vĭch, -kô′-, shə-stə-), **Dmitri.** 1906–75. Russian composer known esp. for his symphonies.

shot[1] (shŏt) *n.* **1.** The firing or discharge of a weapon. **2.** The distance over which something is shot; range. **3.a.** An attempt to hit a target with a projectile. **b.** An attempt to reach a target with a rocket. **4.a.** *Sports.* An attempt to score in a game, as in soccer. **b.** *Baseball.* A home run. **5.** *Sports & Games.* **a.** The flight or path of a projectile in a game. **b.** A stroke in a game, as in golf. **6.** A pointed or critical remark. **7.** *Informal.* **a.** An attempt; a try. **b.** A guess. **c.** An opportunity. **d.** A chance at odds; something to bet on: *a four-to-one shot.* **8.a.** *pl.* **shot.** A solid projectile designed to be discharged from a firearm or cannon. **b.** *pl.* **shot.** A tiny lead or steel pellet, esp. one used in a shotgun cartridge. **9.** *Sports.* The heavy metal ball that is put for distance in the shot put. **10.** One who shoots in a particular way: *a good shot.* **11.a.** A charge of explosives used in blasting mine shafts. **b.** A detonation of an explosive charge. **12.a.** A photographic view or exposure. **b.** A developed photographic image. **13.a.** A hypodermic injection. **b.** A small amount given or applied at one time. **14.** A drink, esp. a jigger of liquor. **15.** An amount to be paid, as for drinks; a bill. **16.** *Naut.* A length of chain equal to 15 fathoms (90 feet) in the United States and 12½ fathoms (75 feet) in Great Britain. — *tr.v.* **shot•ted, shot•ting, shots.** To load or weight with shot. — ***idioms.*** **like a shot.** Very quickly. **shot in the arm.** *Informal.* Something that boosts one's spirits. **shot in the dark.** *Informal.* **1.** A wild, unsubstantiated guess. **2.** An attempt that has little chance of succeeding. [ME < OE *sceot, scot.* See **skeud-***.]

shot[2] (shŏt) *v.* P.t. and p.part. of **shoot.** — *adj.* **1.a.** Of changeable or variegated color; iridescent. **b.** Streaked or flecked with or as if with yarn of a different color: *a blue suit shot with purple.* **c.** Interspersed or permeated with a distinctive quality: *shot with irony.* **2.** *Informal.* Worn-out; ruined.

shot clock *n. Basketball.* A device that shows how many seconds a team has to take a shot or else lose the ball.

ă pat	oi boy
ā pay	ou out
âr care	o͝o took
ä father	o͞o boot
ĕ pet	ŭ cut
ē be	ûr urge
ĭ pit	th thin
ī pie	*th* this
îr pier	hw which
ŏ pot	zh vision
ō toe	ə about, item
ô paw	

Stress marks:
′ (primary);
′ (secondary), as in
dictionary (dĭk′shə-nĕr′ē)

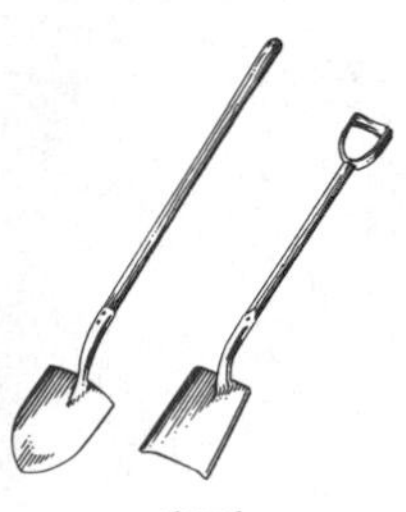

shovel
Left: Rounded mouth
Right: Tapered mouth

shrike
Loggerhead shrike
Lanius ludovicianus

shote (shōt) *n.* Var. of **shoat.**

shot•gun (shŏt′gŭn′) *n.* **1.** A smoothbore gun that fires shot over short ranges. **2.** *Football.* An offensive formation, used esp. for passing, in which the quarterback receives the snap several yards behind the line of scrimmage. **3.** *New Orleans.* A house in which several rooms join in a straight line from the front to the back. See Regional Note at **beignet.**

shotgun marriage *n.* A marriage necessitated by pregnancy.

shot hole *n.* **1.** A drilled hole in which an explosive charge is placed before detonation. **2.** An insect hole in wood.

shot put *n. Sports.* **1.** A competition in which contestants put a heavy metal ball as far as they can. **2.** This ball. **— shot′-put′ter** (shŏt′po͝ot′ər) *n.* **— shot′-put′ting** *n.*

shott (shŏt) *n.* Var. of **chott.**

shot•ten (shŏt′n) *adj.* Having recently spawned and thus being less desirable as food. Used of fish, esp. herring. [ME *shoten,* p.part. of *shoten,* to shoot. See SHOOT.]

should (sho͝od) *aux.v.* P.t. of **shall. 1.** Used to express obligation or duty: *You should call her.* **2.** Used to express probability or expectation: *They should arrive soon.* **3.** Used to express conditionality or contingency: *If she should fall, then so would I.* **4.** Used to moderate the directness or bluntness of a statement: *I should think he would like to go.*

Usage Note: Like the rules governing the use of *shall* and *will* on which they are based, the traditional rules governing the use of *should* and *would* are largely ignored in modern American practice. Either *should* or *would* can now be used in the first person to express conditional futurity: *If I had known that, I would* (or somewhat more formally, *should*) *have answered differently.* But in the second and third persons only *would* is used: *If he had known that, he would have answered differently. Would* cannot always be substituted for *should,* however. *Should* is used in all three persons in a conditional clause: *if I* (or *you* or *he*) *should decide to go. Should* is also used in all three persons to express duty or obligation (the equivalent of *ought to*): *I* (or *you* or *he*) *should go.* On the other hand, *would* is used to express volition or promise: *I agreed that I would do it.* Either *would* or *should* is possible as an auxiliary with *like, be inclined, be glad, prefer,* and related verbs: *I would* (or *should*) *like to call your attention to an oversight.* Here *would* was acceptable on all levels to a large majority of the Usage Panel in an earlier survey and is more common in American usage than *should.* • *Should have* is sometimes incorrectly written *should of* by writers who have mistaken the source of the spoken contraction *should've.* See Usage Notes at **if, rather, shall.**

shoul•der (shōl′dər) *n.* **1.a.** The joint connecting the arm with the torso. **b.** The part of the human body between the neck and upper arm. **2.a.** The joint of a vertebrate animal that connects the forelimb to the trunk. **b.** The part of an animal near this joint. **c.** The part of a bird's wing between the wrist and the trunk. **3.** The area of the back from one shoulder to the other. Often used in the plural. **4.** A cut of meat including the joint of the foreleg and adjacent parts. **5.** The portion of a garment that covers the shoulder. **6.** An angled or sloping part, as: **a.** The angle between the face and flank of a bastion in a fortification. **b.** The area between the body and neck of a bottle or vase. **7.** The area of an item or object that serves as an abutment or surrounds a projection, as: **a.** The end surface of a board from which a tenon projects. **b.** *Print.* The flat surface on the body of type that extends beyond the letter or character. **8.** The edge or border running on either side of a roadway. **—** *v.* **-dered, -der•ing, -ders.** **—** *tr.* **1.** To carry or place (a burden, for example) on the shoulders. **2.** To take on; assume: *shouldered the blame.* **3.** To push or apply force to, with or as if with the shoulder. **4.** To make (one's way) by or as if by shoving obstacles with one's shoulders. **—** *intr.* **1.** To push with the shoulders. **2.** To make one's way by or as if by shoving obstacles with one's shoulders. ***— idioms.*** **put (one's) shoulder to the wheel.** To apply oneself vigorously; make a concentrated effort. **shoulder to shoulder. 1.** In close proximity; side by side. **2.** In close cooperation. [ME *shulder* < OE *sculdor.*]

shoulder bag *n.* A handbag with a shoulder strap.

shoulder blade *n.* See **scapula.**

shoulder board *n.* One of a pair of oblong pieces of stiffened cloth worn on each shoulder of a military uniform and carrying insignia to show rank.

shoulder girdle *n.* The pectoral girdle, esp. of a human being.

shoulder harness *n.* A safety belt used with a seat belt in a vehicle and worn across the chest and over the shoulder.

shoulder knot *n.* **1.** Either of two detachable braided cords worn on each shoulder of a commissioned officer's full-dress uniform. **2.** An ornamental knot of ribbon or lace once worn on the shoulder.

shoulder patch *n.* A cloth patch bearing identifying markings, worn on the upper portion of the sleeve of a uniform.

shoulder strap *n.* **1.** A strap, usu. one of a pair, supporting a garment from the shoulder. **2.** A strap worn across the shoulder to support an item, such as a bag.

should•est (sho͝od′ĭst) or **shouldst** (sho͝odst) *aux.v. Archaic.* A second pers. sing. p.t. of **shall.**

should•n't (sho͝od′nt). Should not.

shout (shout) *n.* A loud cry. **—** *tr. & intr.v.* **shout•ed, shout•ing, shouts.** To say with or utter a shout. ***— phrasal verb.*** **shout down.** To overwhelm or silence by shouting loudly. [ME *shoute,* perh. < ON *skūta,* a taunt.] **— shout′er** *n.*

Syns: *shout, bawl, bellow, holler, howl, roar, whoop, yell.* The central meaning shared by these verbs is "to say with or make a loud, strong cry": *fans shouting their approval; bawling out orders; bellowing with rage; hollered a warning; howling with pain; a crowd roaring its disapproval; children whooping at play; troops yelling as they attacked.*

shout•ing distance (shou′tĭng) *n.* A short distance.

shove (shŭv) *v.* **shoved, shov•ing, shoves.** **—** *tr.* **1.** To push forward or along. **2.** To push rudely or roughly. See Syns at **push.** **—** *intr.* To push someone or something with force. **—** *n.* The act of shoving; a push. ***— phrasal verb.*** **shove off. 1.** To push (a boat) away from shore in leaving. **2.** *Informal.* To leave. [ME *shoven* < OE *scūfan.*] **— shov′er** *n.*

shov•el (shŭv′əl) *n.* **1.** A tool with a handle and a broad scoop or blade for digging and moving material, such as snow. **2.** A large mechanical device or vehicle for heavy digging or excavation. **3.** A shovelful. **—** *v.* **-eled, -el•ing, -els** also **-elled, -el•ling, -els.** **—** *tr.* **1.** To move or remove with a shovel. **2.** To make with a shovel. **3.** To convey or throw in a rough or hasty way, as if with a shovel. **4.** To clear or excavate with or as if with a shovel: *shoveling off the road.* **—** *intr.* To dig or work with a shovel. [ME < OE *scofl.*]

shov•el•er also **shov•el•ler** (shŭv′ə-lər, shŭv′lər) *n.* **1.** One that shovels: *a fast shoveler.* **2.** A duck *(Anas clypeata)* found esp. in marshes and having a long broad bill fringed with bristles, used to strain food from mud and water.

shov•el•ful (shŭv′əl-fo͝ol′) *n.* The amount a shovel can hold.

shovel hat *n.* A stiff broad-brimmed low-crowned hat, turned up at the sides and projecting in front, worn by some English clergymen.

shov•el•nose (shŭv′əl-nōz′) *n.* A sturgeon *(Scaphirhynchus platorhynchus)* of the Mississippi River having a broad flat snout.

shov•el-nosed (shŭv′əl-nōzd′) *adj.* Having a broad flattened snout, bill, or head.

show (shō) *v.* **showed, shown** (shōn) or **showed, show•ing, shows.** **—** *tr.* **1.a.** To cause or allow to be seen; display. **b.** To display for sale, in exhibition, or in competition. **2.** To conduct; guide. **3.** To direct one's attention to; point out. **4.** To manifest (an emotion, for example); reveal. **5.** To permit access to (a house, for example) when offering for sale or rent. **6.** To reveal (oneself) as in one's behavior or condition. **7.** To indicate; register. **8.a.** To demonstrate by reasoning or procedure: *showed that he was wrong.* **b.** To demonstrate to by reasoning or procedure; inform or prove to. **9.** To grant; bestow: *showed no mercy.* **10.** *Law.* To plead; allege: *show cause.* **—** *intr.* **1.** To be or become visible or evident. **2.** *Slang.* To make an appearance; show up. **3.a.** To be exhibited publicly. **b.** To give a performance or present an exhibition. **4.** *Sports.* To finish third or better in a horserace or dog race. **—** *n.* **1.** A display; a manifestation. **2.a.** A trace or an indication, as of oil in a well. **b.** The discharge of bloody mucus from the vagina indicating the start of labor. **c.** The first discharge of blood in menstruation. **3.** A false appearance; a pretense. **4.a.** A striking appearance or display; a spectacle. **b.** A pompous or ostentatious display. **5.** Display or outward appearance: *a smile for show.* **6.a.** A public exhibition or entertainment. **b.** A radio or television program. **c.** A movie. **d.** A theatrical troupe or company. **7.** *Informal.* An affair or undertaking: *ran the whole show.* **8.** *Sports.* Third place at the finish, as in a horserace. ***— phrasal verbs.*** **show off.** To display or behave ostentatiously or conspicuously. **show up. 1.** To be clearly visible. **2.** To put in an appearance; arrive. **3.** To expose or reveal the true character or nature of. **4.** *Informal.* To surpass, as in ability or intelligence. ***— idiom.*** **get the show on the road.** *Slang.* To get started. [ME *sheuen, shouen* < OE *scēawian,* to look at, display. See **keu-*.**]

show-and-tell or **show and tell** (shō′ən-tĕl′) *n.* **1.** An educational activity in which a child displays an object to the class and talks about it. **2.** A public presentation or display.

show bill *n.* An advertising poster.

show biz *n. Slang.* Show business.

show•boat (shō′bōt′) *n.* **1.** *Naut.* A river steamboat having performers and a theater aboard for performances on the river. **2.** One who seeks attention by ostentatious behavior; a showoff. **—** *intr.v.* **-boat•ed, -boat•ing, -boats.** To show off.

show•bread (shō′brĕd′) *n.* The 12 loaves of unleavened bread placed every Sabbath in the Jerusalem Temple sanctuary as an offering by the priests. [Transl. of Ger. *Schaubrot* (*Schau,* sight, show + *Brot,* bread), transl. of Gk. *artoi enōpioi* (*artoi,* pl. of *artos,* loaf of bread + *enōpioi,* pl. of *enōpios,* facing), transl. of Heb. *leḥem pānîm* (*leḥem,* bread + *pānîm,* divine presence).]

show business *n.* The entertainment industry.

show•case (shō′kās′) *n.* **1.** A display case or cabinet, as in a store. **2.** A setting in which someone or something may be displayed, esp. to advantage. **— show′case′** *v.*

show•down (shō′doun′) *n.* **1.** An event, esp. a confrontation, that forces an issue to a conclusion. **2.** *Games.* The showing of the players' cards to determine the winner of the pot in poker.
show•er¹ (shou′ər) *n.* **1.** A brief fall of precipitation, such as rain. **2.** A fall of a group of objects, esp. from the sky: *a meteor shower.* **3.** An abundant flow; an outpouring: *a shower of praise.* **4.** A party held to honor and present gifts to someone: *a bridal shower.* **5.a.** A bath in which the water is sprayed on the bather from a showerhead, usu. secured overhead; a showerbath. **b.** The stall or tub in which such a bath is taken. —*v.* **-ered, -er•ing, -ers.** —*tr.* **1.** To pour down in a shower: *showered confetti on them.* **2.** To cover with or as if with a shower. **3.** To bestow abundantly or liberally. —*intr.* **1.** To fall or pour down in or as if in a shower. **2.** To wash oneself in a shower. [ME *shour* < OE *scūr.*] —**show′er•y** *adj.*
show•er² (shō′ər) *n.* One that shows: *a shower of art.*
show•er bath (shou′ər) *n.* A shower.
show•er•head (shou′ər-hĕd′) *n.* A perforated nozzle for spraying water on a bather taking a shower.
show•girl (shō′gûrl′) *n.* A woman, usu. elaborately dressed, who performs in a musical or theatrical production.
show•ing (shō′ĭng) *n.* **1.** The act of presenting or displaying. **2.** Performance, as in a competition or test of skill: *a poor showing.* **3.** A presentation of evidence, facts, or figures.
show•man (shō′mən) *n.* **1.** A theatrical producer. **2.** A dramatic or ostentatious man. —**show′man•ship′** *n.*
shown (shōn) *v.* A p.part. of **show.**
show•off (shō′ôf′, -ŏf′) *n.* **1.** The act of showing off. **2.** One who shows off.
show•piece (shō′pēs′) *n.* Something exhibited, esp. as an outstanding example of its kind.
show place also **show•place** (shō′plās′) *n.* **1.** A place, such as an estate, that is viewed and frequented for its beauty or historical noteworthiness. **2.** A beautiful or ornate place.
show room *n.* A room for the display of merchandise.
show•stop•per (shō′stŏp′ər) *n. Informal.* **1.** A performance that evokes so much applause that the show is temporarily interrupted. **2.** A particularly arresting person or thing. —**show′stop′ping** *adj.*
show•time or **show time** (shō′tīm′) *n.* **1.** The time at which an entertainment, such as a movie, is scheduled to start. **2.** *Slang.* The time at which an activity is to begin.
show•y (shō′ē) *adj.* **-i•er, -i•est. 1.** Making an imposing or aesthetically pleasing display; striking: *showy flowers.* **2.** Displaying brilliance and virtuosity of ability or performance. **3.** Marked by or prone to ostentatious, often tasteless display; flashy. —**show′i•ly** *adv.* —**show′i•ness** *n.*

Syns: showy, flamboyant, ostentatious, pretentious, splashy. The central meaning shared by these adjectives is "marked by striking, often excessively conspicuous display": *a showy rhinestone bracelet; an entertainer's flamboyant personality; an ostentatious sable coat; a pretentious scholarly edition; a splashy advertising campaign.*

shp or **s.hp.** *abbr.* Shaft horsepower.
shpt. *n.* Shipment.
shr. *abbr.* Share.
shrank (shrăngk) *v.* A p.t. of **shrink.**
shrap•nel (shrăp′nəl) *n., pl.* **shrapnel. 1.a.** An artillery shell containing metal balls fused to explode in the air. **b.** The metal balls in such a weapon. **2.** Fragments from a high-explosive shell, mine, or bomb. [After Henry *Shrapnel* (1761–1842), British army officer.]
shred (shrĕd) *n.* **1.** A long irregular strip cut or torn off. **2.** A small amount; a particle: *a shred of evidence.* —*tr.v.* **shred•ded** or **shred, shred•ding, shreds.** To cut or tear into shreds. [ME *shrede* < OE *scrēade.*] —**shred′der** *n.*
Shreve•port (shrēv′pôrt′, -pōrt′). A city of NW LA on the Red R.; founded in the 1830's. Pop. 198,525.
shrew (shro͞o) *n.* **1.** Any of various small, chiefly insectivorous mammals of the family Soricidae, resembling a mouse but having a long pointed snout and small eyes and ears. **2.** A woman with a violent, scolding, or nagging temperament; a scold. [ME *shrewe,* villian < OE *scrēawa,* shrewmouse.]
shrewd (shro͞od) *adj.* **shrewd•er, shrewd•est. 1.** Marked by keen awareness, sharp intelligence, and often practicality. See Syns at **clever. 2.** Disposed to artful and cunning practices; tricky. **3.** Sharp; penetrating: *a shrewd wind.* [ME *shrewed,* wicked < *shrew,* rascal. See SHREW.] —**shrewd′ly** *adv.*
shrewd•ness (shro͞od′nĭs) *n.* **1.** The quality of being shrewd. **2.** An aggregation of apes.
shrew•ish (shro͞o′ĭsh) *adj.* Ill-tempered; nagging. —**shrew′ish•ly** *adv.* —**shrew′ish•ness** *n.*
shrew mole *n.* Any of several shrewlike moles of the family Talpidae, such as *Neurotrichus gibbsii* of western North America or *Uropsilus soricipes* of central Asia.
shrew•mouse (shro͞o′mous′) *n.* See **shrew 1.**
Shrews•bur•y (shro͞oz′bĕr′ē, -bə-rē). **1.** A municipal borough of W England WNW of Birmingham. Pop. 60,400. **2.** A town of central MA, a suburb of Worcester. Pop. 24,146.
shriek (shrēk) *n.* **1.** A shrill, often frantic cry. **2.** A sound suggestive of such a cry. —*v.* **shrieked, shriek•ing, shrieks.** —*intr.* **1.** To utter a shriek. **2.** To make a sound like a shriek. —*tr.* To utter with a shriek. [ME *shriken,* of Scand. orig.] —**shriek′er** *n.*
shrie•val (shrē′vəl) *adj.* Of or relating to a sheriff. [< obsolete *shrieve,* var. of SHERIFF.] —**shrie′val•ty** *n.*
shrift (shrĭft) *n. Archaic.* **1.** The act of shriving. **2.** Confession to a priest. **3.** Absolution given by a priest. [ME < OE *scrift* < Lat. *scrīptum,* something written < neut. p.part. of *scrībere,* to write. See SHRIVE.]
shrike (shrīk) *n.* Any of various carnivorous oscine birds of the family Laniidae, having a screeching call and a strong hooked bill. [Prob. < ME *shrik < OE *scrīc,* thrush.]
shrill (shrĭl) *adj.* **shrill•er, shrill•est. 1.** High-pitched and piercing in tone or sound: *a shrill wail.* **2.** Producing a sharp high-pitched tone or sound. **3.** Sharp or keen to the senses; harshly vivid. —*v.* **shrilled, shrill•ing, shrills.** —*tr.* To utter in a shrill manner; scream. —*intr.* To produce a shrill cry or sound. [ME *shrille.*] —**shrill′ness** *n.* —**shril′ly** *adv.*
shrimp (shrĭmp) *n., pl.* **shrimp** or **shrimps. 1.a.** Any of various small, chiefly marine decapod crustaceans of the suborder Natantia, many species of which are edible, having a compressed or elongated body with a well-developed abdomen and a long spinelike projection of the carapace. **b.** Any of various similar crustaceans. **2.** *Slang.* An unimportant or small person. —*intr.v.* **shrimped, shrimp•ing, shrimps.** To fish for shrimp. [ME *shrimpe,* poss. of LGer. orig.] —**shrimp′er** *n.*

shrimp

shrine (shrīn) *n.* **1.** A container or receptacle for sacred relics; a reliquary. **2.a.** The tomb of a venerated person, such as a saint. **b.** A place at which devotion is paid to a venerated person. **3.** A site hallowed by a venerated object or its associations. —*tr.v.* **shrined, shrin•ing, shrines.** To enshrine. [ME < OE *scrīn,* box < Lat. *scrīnium,* case for books or papers.]
Shrin•er (shrī′nər) *n.* A member of a U.S. secret fraternal order that admits only Knights Templars and 32nd-degree Masons as members. [After the Ancient Arabic Order of Nobles of the Mystic *Shrine,* their fraternal order.]

shrine
Offerings to Buddha

shrink (shrĭngk) *v.* **shrank** (shrăngk) or **shrunk** (shrŭngk), **shrunk** or **shrunk•en** (shrŭng′kən), **shrink•ing, shrinks.** —*intr.* **1.** To become constricted from heat, moisture, or cold. **2.** To become reduced in amount or value; dwindle. **3.** To draw back instinctively, as from something alarming; recoil. **4.** To show reluctance; hesitate. —*tr.* To cause to shrink. —*n.* **1.a.** The act of shrinking. **b.** The degree to which something shrinks; shrinkage. **2.** *Slang.* A psychiatrist. [ME *shrinken,* to wither, shrivel up < OE *scrincan.* See **sker-²*.**] —**shrink′a•ble** *adj.* —**shrink′er** *n.*
shrink•age (shrĭng′kĭj) *n.* **1.** The process of shrinking. **2.** The amount or proportion by which something shrinks. **3.** A reduction in value; depreciation. **4.** The total weight loss sustained by livestock in shipment to a market. **5.** Loss of merchandise, esp. by theft.
shrink•ing violet (shrĭng′kĭng) *n. Informal.* A shy or retiring person.
shrink-wrap (shrĭngk′răp′) *n.* A protective wrapping consisting of a clear plastic film that is wound about an article and then shrunk by heat to form a sealed tight-fitting package. —**shrink′-wrap′** *v.*

Shropshire²

shrive (shrīv) *v.* **shrove** (shrōv) or **shrived, shriv•en** (shrĭv′ən), **shriv•ing, shrives.** —*tr.* **1.** To hear the confession of and give absolution to (a penitent). **2.** To obtain absolution for (oneself) by confessing and doing penance. —*intr. Archaic.* **1.** To make or go to confession. **2.** To hear confessions. [ME *schriven* < OE *scrīfan* < Lat. *scrībere,* to write. See **skrībh-*.**] —**shriv′er** *n.*
shriv•el (shrĭv′əl) *intr. & tr.v.* **-eled, -el•ing, -els** or **-elled, -el•ling, -els. 1.** To become or make shrunken and wrinkled, often by drying: *Leaves fall and shrivel.* **2.** To lose or cause to lose vitality or intensity: *Inflation shriveled the dollar.* **3.** To become or make much less or smaller; dwindle. [?]
Shrop•shire¹ (shrŏp′shîr′, -shər). A historical region of W England on the Welsh border; part of the kingdom of Mercia during Anglo-Saxon times.
Shrop•shire² (shrŏp′shîr′, -shər, -shīr′) *n.* A large hornless black-faced sheep of a breed developed in Shropshire.
shroud (shroud) *n.* **1.** A cloth used to wrap a body for burial; a winding sheet. **2.** Something that conceals, protects, or screens: *a shroud of fog.* **3.a.** *Naut.* One of a set of ropes or wire cables stretched from a masthead to the sides of a vessel to support the mast. **b.** A similar supporting line for a smokestack or comparable structure. **c.** One of the ropes connecting the harness and the canopy of a parachute. —*v.* **shroud•ed, shroud•ing, shrouds.** —*tr.* **1.** To wrap (a corpse) in burial clothing. **2.** To shut off from sight; screen. See Syns at **block. 3.** *Archaic.* To shelter; protect. —*intr. Archaic.* To take cover; find shelter. [ME *shrud,* garment < OE *scrūd.*]
Shrove•tide (shrōv′tīd′) *n.* The three days preceding Ash Wednesday. [ME *shroftide* : *shrof-,* shriving (< *shriven,* to shrive; see SHRIVE) + *tid,* time; see TIDE¹.]
Shrove Tuesday *n.* The day before Ash Wednesday.
shrub¹ (shrŭb) *n.* A woody plant of relatively low height, hav-

ă pat	oi boy
ā pay	ou out
âr care	o͝o took
ä father	o͞o boot
ĕ pet	ŭ cut
ē be	ûr urge
ĭ pit	th thin
ī pie	*th* this
îr pier	hw which
ŏ pot	zh vision
ō toe	ə about, item
ô paw	

Stress marks:
′ (primary);
′ (secondary), as in **dictionary** (dĭk′shə-nĕr′ē)

ing several stems arising from the base and lacking a single trunk; a bush. [ME *shrubbe* < OE *scrybb*. See **sker-¹***.]

shrub² (shrŭb) *n.* A beverage made from fruit juice, sugar, and a liquor such as rum or brandy. [< Ar. *šurb*, a drink < *šariba*, to drink.]

shrub•ber•y (shrŭb′ə-rē) *n.*, *pl.* **-ies.** A group or planting of shrubs.

shrub•by (shrŭb′ē) *adj.* **-bi•er, -bi•est. 1.** Consisting of, planted with, or covered with shrubs. **2.** Of or resembling a shrub. **— shrub′bi•ness** *n.*

shrug (shrŭg) *v.* **shrugged, shrug•ging, shrugs.** *— tr.* To raise (the shoulders), esp. as a gesture of doubt, disdain, or indifference. *— intr.* To shrug the shoulders. *— n.* **1.** An expressive gesture of raising the shoulders. **2.** A woman's short jacket or sweater open down the front. ***— phrasal verb.*** **shrug off. 1.** To minimize the importance of. **2.** To get rid of. [ME *shruggen*.]

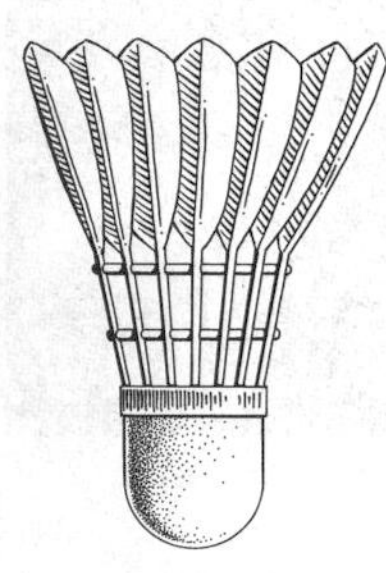

shuttlecock

shrunk (shrŭngk) *v.* A p.t. and p.part. of **shrink.**

shrunk•en (shrŭng′kən) *v.* A p.part. of **shrink.**

sht. *abbr.* Sheet.

shtetl (shtĕt′l, shtāt′l) *n.* A small Eastern European Jewish community of former times. [Yiddish < MHGer. *stetel*, dim. of *stat*, town < OHGer., place. See **stā-***.]

shtick also **schtick** or **shtik** (shtĭk) *n. Slang.* **1.** A characteristic attribute, talent, or trait that is helpful in securing recognition or attention. **2.** An entertainment routine or gimmick. [Yiddish *shtik*, piece, routine < MHGer. *stücke*, piece < OHGer. *stukki*, crust, fragment.]

shuck (shŭk) *n.* **1.a.** A husk, pod, or shell, as of an ear of corn, a pea, or a hickory nut. **b.** The shell of an oyster or a clam. **2.** *Informal.* Something worthless. Often used in the plural: *didn't amount to shucks.* *— tr.v.* **shucked, shuck•ing, shucks. 1.** To remove the husk or shell from. **2.** *Informal.* To cast off: *shucked their coats.* *— interj.* **shucks.** (shŭks). Used to express mild disappointment, disgust, or annoyance. [?] **— shuck′er** *n.*

shud•der (shŭd′ər) *intr.v.* **-dered, -der•ing, -ders. 1.** To shiver convulsively, as from fear or revulsion. **2.** To vibrate; quiver. *— n.* A convulsive shiver, as from fear or revulsion; a tremor. [ME *shodderen*, perh. of MDu. or MLGer. orig.]

Siamese cat

shuf•fle (shŭf′əl) *v.* **-fled, -fling, -fles.** *— tr.* **1.** To slide (the feet) along the floor or ground while walking. **2.** To move (something) from one place to another; transfer or shift. **3.** To put aside or under cover quickly; shunt. **4.** To mix together; jumble. **5.** *Games.* To mix together (playing cards, tiles, or dominoes) so as to make a random order of arrangement. *— intr.* **1.** To move with short sliding steps, without or barely lifting the feet. **2.** To dance with sliding and tapping steps. **3.** To move about from place to place; shift. **4.** To act in a shifty or deceitful manner; equivocate. **5.** *Games.* To shuffle playing cards, tiles, or dominoes. *— n.* **1.** A short sliding step or movement or a walk characterized by such steps. **2.** A dance in which the feet slide along or move close to the floor. **3.** An evasive or deceitful action; an equivocation. **4.** A confused mixture; a jumble. **5.** *Games.* **a.** An act of shuffling cards, dominoes, or tiles. **b.** A player's right or turn to do this. [ME *shovelen*, prob. of MDu. or MLGer. orig.] **— shuf′fler** *n.*

shuf•fle•board (shŭf′əl-bôrd′, -bōrd′) *n. Games.* **1.** A game in which disks are slid along a smooth surface toward one of two targets painted on the surface and divided into numbered scoring areas. **2.** A surface on which this game is played. [Alteration of obsolete *shove-board* : SHOVE + BOARD.]

shul (sho͝ol, sho͞ol) *n. Judaism.* A synagogue. [Yiddish < MHGer. *schuol*, school < OHGer. *scuola* < Lat. *scola*. See SCHOOL¹.]

Shu•men (sho͞o′mĕn′). A city of NE Bulgaria W of Varna; founded 927. Pop. 107,000.

shun (shŭn) *tr.v.* **shunned, shun•ning, shuns.** To avoid deliberately; keep away from. [ME *shunnen* < OE *scunian*, to abhor.] **— shun′ner** *n.*

shun•pike (shŭn′pīk′) *n.* A side road taken to avoid the tolls or traffic of a turnpike. *— intr.v.* **-piked, -pik•ing, -pikes.** To travel on side roads, avoiding turnpikes. **— shun′pik′er** *n.*

shunt (shŭnt) *n.* **1.** The act or process of turning aside or moving to an alternate course. **2.** A railroad switch. **3.** *Elect.* A low-resistance connection between two points in an electric circuit that forms an alternative path for a portion of the current. **4.** *Medic.* A passage between two natural body channels, such as blood vessels, esp. one created surgically to divert or permit flow from one pathway or region to another; a bypass. *— v.* **shunt•ed, shunt•ing, shunts.** *— tr.* **1.** To turn or move aside or onto another course. **2.** To evade by putting aside or ignoring. **3.** To switch (a train or car) from one track to another. **4.** *Elect.* To provide or divert (current) by means of a shunt. *— intr.* **1.** To move or turn aside. **2.** *Elect.* To become diverted by means of a shunt. Used of a circuit. [ME *shunten*, to flinch.] **— shunt′er** *n.*

shush (shŭsh) *interj.* Used to express a demand for silence. *— tr.v.* **shushed, shush•ing, shush•es.** To demand silence from by saying "shush."

shut (shŭt) *v.* **shut, shut•ting, shuts.** *— tr.* **1.** To move (a door or lid, for example) so as to block passage through an opening. **2.** To block entrance to or exit from; close. **3.** To fasten with a lock, catch, or latch. **4.** To confine in or as if in a closed space. **5.** To exclude from or as if from a closed space. **6.** To cause to stop operating: *shut down a restaurant.* *— intr.* **1.** To move or become moved so as to block passage; close. **2.** To stop operating, esp. automatically: *The electricity shuts off at midnight.* *— n.* **1.** The act or time of shutting. **2.** The line of connection between welded pieces of metal. ***— phrasal verbs.*** **shut off. 1.** To stop the flow or passage of; cut off. **2.** To close off; isolate. **shut out.** *Sports.* To prevent (an opponent) from scoring any runs or points. **shut up. 1.** To cause (someone) to stop speaking; silence. **2.** To stop speaking. ***— idiom.*** **shut (one's) eyes to.** To refuse to consider or acknowledge. [ME *shutten* < OE *scyttan*. See **skeud-***.]

shut•down (shŭt′doun′) *n.* A cessation of operations or activity, as at a factory.

Shute (sho͞ot), **Nevil.** Nevil Shute Norway. 1899–1960. British writer whose novels include *A Town Like Alice* (1950) and *On the Beach* (1957), both set in Australia.

shut•eye (shŭt′ī′) *n. Slang.* Sleep.

shut-in (shŭt′ĭn′) *n.* A person confined indoors by illness or disability. *— adj.* (shŭt-ĭn′). **1.** Confined to a home or hospital, as by illness. **2.** Disposed to avoid social contact.

shut•off (shŭt′ôf′, -ŏf′) *n.* **1.** A device that shuts something off. **2.** A stoppage; a cessation.

shut•out (shŭt′out′) *n.* **1.** See **lockout. 2.** *Sports.* A game in which one side does not score.

shut•ter (shŭt′ər) *n.* **1.** One that shuts, as: **a.** A hinged cover or screen for a window, usu. fitted with louvers. **b.** A mechanical device of a camera that opens and closes to control the duration of exposure of a plate or film to light. **2. shutters.** *Mus.* The movable louvers on a pipe organ, controlled by pedals, that open and close the swell box. *— tr.v.* **-tered, -ter•ing, -ters. 1.** To furnish or close with shutters. **2.** To cause to cease operations; close down.

shut•ter•bug (shŭt′ər-bŭg′) *n. Informal.* An enthusiastic amateur photographer.

shut•tle (shŭt′l) *n.* **1.** A device used in weaving to carry the woof thread back and forth between the warp threads. **2.** A device for holding the thread in tatting and netting and in a sewing machine. **3.a.** Regular travel back and forth over an established route by a vehicle. **b.** A vehicle used in such travel: *took the shuttle across town.* **c.** A route used in such travel. **4.** A space shuttle. *— v.* **-tled, -tling, -tles.** *— intr.* To go, move, or travel back and forth by or as if by a shuttle. *— tr.* **1.** To cause to move back and forth frequently. **2.** To transport by or as if by a shuttle. [ME *shutille* < OE *scytel*, dart. See **skeud-***.] **— shut′tler** *n.*

shut•tle•cock (shŭt′l-kŏk′) *n. Sports.* A small rounded piece of cork or rubber with a conical crown of feathers or plastic, used in badminton. *— tr.v.* **-cocked, -cock•ing, -cocks.** To throw or send back and forth like a shuttlecock.

shuttle diplomacy *n.* Diplomatic negotiations conducted by an official intermediary who travels frequently between the nations involved. **— shuttle diplomat** *n.*

shy¹ (shī) *adj.* **shi•er** (shī′ər) , **shi•est** (shī′ĭst) or **shy•er** or **shy•est. 1.** Easily startled; timid. **2.a.** Drawing back from contact or familiarity with others; retiring or reserved. **b.** Marked by reserve or diffidence. **3.** Distrustful; wary. **4.** Not having paid an amount due, as in poker. **5.** Short; lacking. *— intr.v.* **shied** (shīd), **shy•ing, shies** (shīz). **1.** To move suddenly, as if startled; start. **2.** To draw back, as from fear or caution; recoil. *— n.*, *pl.* **shies** (shīz). A sudden movement, as from fright; a start. [ME *shey* < OE *scēoh*.] **— shy′er** *n.* **— shy′ly** *adv.* **— shy′ness** *n.*

Syns: *shy, bashful, diffident, modest, coy, demure.* These adjectives mean not forward but marked by a retiring nature, reticence, or a reserve of manner. One who is *shy* draws back from others, either because of a withdrawn nature or out of timidity: *"The poor man was shy and hated society"* (George Bernard Shaw). *Bashful* suggests self-consciousness or awkwardness in the presence of others: *"I never laughed, being bashful/Lowering my head, I looked at the wall"* (Ezra Pound). *Diffident* implies lack of self-confidence: *He was too diffident to express his opinion. Modest* is associated with an unassertive nature and absence of vanity or pretension: *Despite her fame she remained a modest, unassuming person. Coy* usually implies feigned, often flirtatious shyness: *"yielded with coy submission"* (John Milton). *Demure* often denotes an affected shyness or modesty: *assented with a demure smile.*

shy² (shī) *v.* **shied** (shīd), **shy•ing, shies** (shīz). *— tr.* To throw (something) with a swift motion; fling. *— intr.* To throw something with a swift motion. *— n.*, *pl.* **shies** (shīz). **1.** A quick throw; a fling. **2.** *Informal.* A gibe; a sneer. **3.** *Informal.* An attempt; a try. [Perh. < SHY¹.]

shy•lock (shī′lŏk′) *n.* **1.** *Offensive.* A ruthless moneylender; a loan shark. **2. Shylock.** The ruthless usurer in Shakespeare's play *The Merchant of Venice.*

shy•ster (shī′stər) *n. Slang.* An unethical unscrupulous practitioner, esp. of law. [Prob. alteration of Ger. *Scheisser*, son of a bitch, bastard < *scheissen*, to defecate < MHGer. *schīzen* <

OHGer. *skīzzan.* See **skei-***.] —**shy′ster•ism** *n.*
si (sē) *n. Mus.* Ti. [Ital. < Med.Lat. See GAMUT.]
Si The symbol for the element **silicon.**
SI *abbr. Fr.* Système International [d'Unités] (International System [of Units]).
si•al (sī′ăl′) *n.* Rock rich in silicon and aluminum forming the upper layer of the earth's crust beneath all continental landmasses. [SI(LICON) + AL(UMINUM).]
si•al•a•gogue (sī-ăl′ə-gôg′, -gŏg′) *n.* A drug or other agent that increases the flow of saliva. [Gk. *sialon,* saliva + -AGOGUE.] —**si′al•a•gog′ic** (sī′ə-lə-gŏj′ĭk) *adj.*
si•al•ic acid (sī-ăl′ĭk) *n.* Any of a group of amino carbohydrates that are components of mucoproteins and glycoproteins, esp. in animal tissue and blood cells. [Gk. *sialon,* saliva + -IC.]
Si•al•kot (sē-äl′kōt′). A city of NE Pakistan N of Lahore. Pop. 252,000.
Si•am (sī-ăm′). See **Thailand.**
si•a•mang (sē′ə-măng′, sē-ăm′əng) *n.* A large black gibbon *(Symphalangus syndactylus* or *Hylobates syndactylus)* of Sumatra and the Malay Peninsula having an inflatable throat sac. [Malay.]
Si•a•mese (sī′ə-mēz′, -mēs′) *adj.* **1.** Of or relating to Siam; Thai. **2.** Closely connected or very similar; twin. **3. siamese.** Of or being a Y-shaped dual connection between two pipes or hoses and a larger pipe or hose. —*n., pl.* **Siamese. 1.** A native or inhabitant of Siam; a Thai. **2.** The Thai language. [After *Siam* (Thailand).]
Siamese cat *n.* A shorthaired cat of a breed developed in the Far East, having blue eyes and a pale fawn or gray coat with darker ears, face, tail, and feet.
Siamese fighting fish *n.* A small, often brightly colored aggressive freshwater fish *(Betta splendens)* native to Malaysia and Thailand and having large fins and tail.
Siamese twin *n.* Either of a pair of identical twins born with their bodies joined, a result of the incomplete division of the ovum from which they developed. [After Chang and Eng (1811–74), joined Chinese twins born in *Siam.*]
Si•an (sē′än′, shē′-). See **Xi'an.**
Siang Kiang (syäng′ kyäng′, shyäng′). See **Xiang Jiang.**
Siang•tan (syäng′tän′, shyäng′-). See **Xiangtan.**
Siau•liai (shyou′lyī′). A city of W Lithuania NW of Vilnius; under Polish rule from 1589 to 1772. Pop. 134,000.
sib (sĭb) *n.* **1.a.** A blood relation; a relative. **b.** A person's relatives considered as a group; kinfolk. **2.** A brother or sister; a sibling. **3.** *Anthro.* A kinship group consisting of two or more lineages considered as being related, as by common descent from a mythic ancestor. —*adj.* Related by blood; kindred. [ME *sibbe* < OE *sibb.* See **s(w)e-***.]
Sib. *abbr.* **1.** Siberia. **2.** Siberian.
Si•be•li•us (sĭ-bā′lē-əs, -bāl′yəs), **Jean.** 1865–1957. Finnish composer whose works include *Finlandia* (1899).
Si•be•ri•a¹ (sī-bîr′ē-ə). A region of central and E Russia stretching from the Ural Mts. to the Pacific; annexed by Russia during the 16th and 17th cent. and later used as a place of exile for political prisoners. —**Si•be′ri•an** *adj. & n.*
Si•be•ri•a² (sī-bîr′ē-ə) *n.* A remote undesirable locale.
Siberian husky *n.* See **husky³** 1.
sib•i•lant (sĭb′ə-lənt) *Ling.* —*adj.* Of, characterized by, or producing a hissing sound like that of (s) or (sh). —*n.* A sibilant speech sound, such as English (s), (sh), (z), or (zh). —**sib′i•lance, sib′i•lan•cy** *n.* —**sib′i•lant•ly** *adv.*
sib•i•late (sĭb′ə-lāt′) *intr. & tr.v.* **-lat•ed, -lat•ing, -lates.** To utter or pronounce with a hissing sound. [Lat. *sībilāre, sībilāt-,* to hiss.] —**sib′i•la′tion** *n.*
Si•biu (sē-byōō′). A city of central Romania NW of Bucharest; settled in the 12th cent. by German colonists. Pop. 172,117.
sib•ling (sĭb′lĭng) *n.* One of two or more individuals having one or both parents in common; a brother or sister. [ME < OE < *sibb,* kinsman. See SIB.]
Si•bu•yan Sea (sē′bōō-yän′). A sea in the central Philippines bordered by S Luzon, Mindoro, and the Visayan Is.
sib•yl (sĭb′əl) *n.* **1.** One of a number of women regarded as oracles or prophets by the ancient Greeks and Romans. **2.** A woman prophet. [ME *sibile* < OFr. < Lat. *Sibylla* < Gk. *Sibulla.*]
sib•yl•line (sĭb′ə-līn′, -lēn′) also **si•byl•ic** or **si•byl•lic** (sĭ-bĭl′ĭk) *adj.* **1.** Coming from, characteristic of, or relating to a sibyl. **2.** Prophetic; oracular.
sic¹ (sĭk) *adv.* Thus; so. Used in written texts to indicate that a surprising or paradoxical word, phrase, or fact is not a mistake and is to be read as it stands. [Lat. *sīc.* See **so-***.]
sic² also **sick** (sĭk) *tr.v.* **sicced, sic•cing, sics** also **sicked, sick•ing, sicks. 1.** To set upon; attack. **2.** To urge or incite to hostile action; set. [Dialectal var. of SEEK.]
Sic. *abbr.* **1.** Sicilian. **2.** Sicily.
sic•ca•tive (sĭk′ə-tĭv) *n.* A substance added to paints and some medicines to promote drying; a drier. [LLat. *siccātivus,* drying < Lat. *siccātus,* p.part. of *siccāre,* to dry < *siccus,* dry.]
Si•chuan also **Sze•chwan** or **Sze•chuan** (sĕch′wän′). A province of S-central China; incorporated into the empire c. 3rd cent. A.D. Cap. Chengdu. Pop. 101,800,000.
Si•ci•ly (sĭs′ə-lē). An island of S Italy in the Mediterranean Sea W of the S end of the Italian peninsula; came under the control of the Normans in the 11th cent. A.D. and formed the nucleus of the Kingdom of the Two Sicilies, consisting of Sicily and S Italy. A later Sicilian kingdom was conquered by Garibaldi in 1860. —**Si•cil′ian** (sĭ-sĭl′yən) *adj. & n.*
sick¹ (sĭk) *adj.* **sick•er, sick•est. 1.a.** Suffering from or affected with a physical illness; ailing. **b.** Of or for sick persons. **c.** Nauseated. **2.a.** Mentally ill or disturbed. **b.** Unwholesome; morbid. **3.** Defective; unsound: *a sick economy.* **4.a.** Deeply distressed; upset. **b.** Disgusted; revolted. **c.** Weary; tired. **d.** Pining; longing. **5.a.** In need of repairs: *a sick ship.* **b.** Constituting an unhealthy environment for those working or residing within: *a sick office building.* **6.** Unable to produce a profitable yield of crops. —***idiom.* sick and tired.** Thoroughly weary, discouraged, or bored. [ME < OE *sēoc.*]
sick² (sĭk) *v.* Var. of **sic².**
sick•bay (sĭk′bā′) *n.* **1.** The hospital and dispensary of a ship. **2.** A place where the sick or injured are treated.
sick•bed (sĭk′bĕd′) *n.* A sick person's bed.
sick call *n.* **1.** A lineup of military personnel requiring medical attention. **2.** A signal announcing the time for such a lineup.
sick•en (sĭk′ən) *tr. & intr.v.* **-ened, -en•ing, -ens.** To make or become sick. See Syns at **disgust.** —**sick′en•er** *n.*
sick•en•ing (sĭk′ə-nĭng) *adj.* **1.** Revolting or disgusting; loathsome. **2.** Causing sickness. —**sick′en•ing•ly** *adv.*
sick headache *n.* **1.** A headache accompanied by nausea. **2.** A migraine.
sick•ie (sĭk′ē) *n. Slang.* One who is deranged or perverted.
sick•ish (sĭk′ĭsh) *adj.* **1.** Somewhat sick. **2.** Somewhat nauseated. **3.** Somewhat revolting or nauseating. —**sick′ish•ly** *adv.* —**sick′ish•ness** *n.*
sick•le (sĭk′əl) *n.* **1.** An implement having a semicircular blade attached to a short handle, used for cutting grain or tall grass. **2.** The cutting mechanism of a reaper or mower. —*v.* **-led, -ling, -les.** —*tr.* **1.** To cut with a sickle. **2.** To deform (a red blood cell) into an abnormal crescent shape. —*intr.* To assume an abnormal crescent shape. Used of red blood cells. [ME *sikel* < OE *sicol* < VLat. **sicila* < Lat. *sēcula.* See **sek-***.]

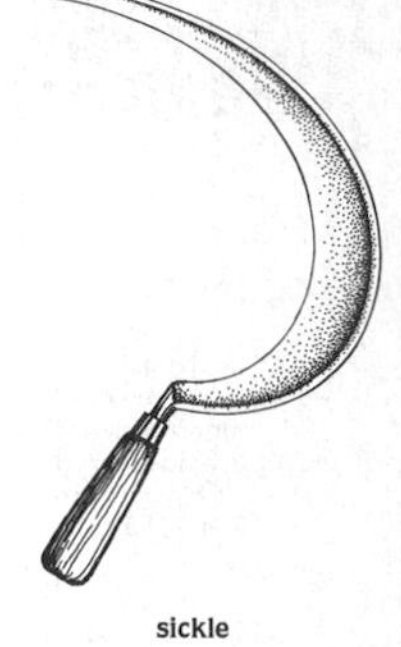
sickle

sick leave *n.* Paid absence from work allowed an employee because of sickness.
sick•le•bill (sĭk′əl-bĭl′) *n.* Any of several birds having long, sharply curved bills, such as *Hemignathus procerus,* a Hawaiian honeycreeper.
sickle cell *n.* An abnormal crescent-shaped red blood cell that results from a single change in the amino acid sequence of the cell's hemoglobin, which causes the cell to contort.
sickle cell anemia *n.* A chronic, usu. fatal anemia caused by a recessive gene and marked by crescent-shaped red blood cells, occurring almost exclusively in Black people of Africa or of African descent and characterized by episodic pain in the joints, fever, leg ulcers, and jaundice.
sickle cell trait *n.* A hereditary condition, usu. harmless and without symptoms, in which an individual carries only one gene for sickle cell anemia.
sickle feather *n.* Any of the long curving feathers in the tail of a rooster.
sick•le•mi•a (sĭk′ə-lē′mē-ə) *n.* Sickle cell anemia or sickle cell trait.

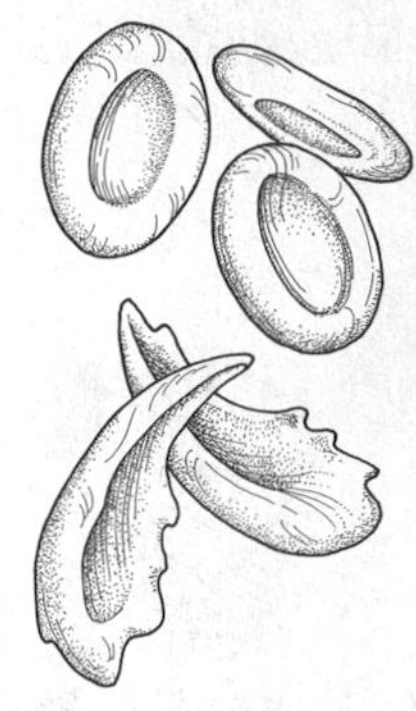
sickle cell
Top: Red blood cells
Bottom: Sickle cells

sick•ly (sĭk′lē) *adj.* **-li•er, -li•est. 1.** Prone to sickness. **2.** Of, caused by, or associated with sickness. **3.** Conducive to sickness. **4.** Causing nausea; nauseating. **5.** Lacking vigor or strength; feeble or weak. —*tr.v.* **-lied, -ly•ing, -lies.** To make sickly. —**sick′li•ness** *n.* —**sick′ly** *adv.*
sick•ness (sĭk′nĭs) *n.* **1.** The condition of being sick; illness. **2.** A disease; a malady. **3.** Nausea. **4.** A defective or unsound condition.
sick•o (sĭk′ō) *n., pl.* **-os.** *Slang.* One who is deranged or perverted. [< SICK¹.]
sick•out (sĭk′out′) *n.* An organized job action in which employees absent themselves from work on the pretext of illness.
sick pay *n.* Wages paid to an employee who is absent because of illness.
sick•room (sĭk′rōōm′, -rŏŏm′) *n.* A room occupied by a sick person.
sic pas•sim (sĭk păs′ĭm) *adv.* Thus everywhere. Used to indicate that a term or an idea is to be found throughout a text. [Lat. *sīc passim* : *sīc,* thus + *passim,* everywhere.]
Si•cy•on (sĭsh′ē-ŏn′, sĭs′-). An ancient city of S Greece in the NE Peloponnesus near the Gulf of Corinth; at the height of its power in the 6th cent. B.C.
Sid•dons (sĭd′nz), **Sarah.** 1755–1831. British actress known for her Shakespearean roles, esp. Lady Macbeth.
sid•dur (sĭd′ər, -ŏŏr′, sē-dŏŏr′) *n., pl.* **sid•du•rim** (sĭ-dŏŏr′-ĭm, sĭ′dŏŏ-rēm′). *Judaism.* A prayer book. [Heb. *siddûr,* arrangement, siddur < *siddēr,* to arrange.]
side (sīd) *n.* **1.** *Math.* **a.** A line bounding a plane figure. **b.** A surface bounding a solid figure. **2.** A surface of an object, esp. a surface joining a top and bottom: *the four sides of a box.* **3.** A surface of an object that extends more or less perpendicularly from an observer standing in front: *the side of the*

ă pat · oi boy
ā pay · ou out
âr care · ŏŏ took
ä father · ōō boot
ĕ pet · ŭ cut
ē be · ûr urge
ĭ pit · th thin
ī pie · *th* this
îr pier · hw which
ŏ pot · zh vision
ō toe · ə about, item
ô paw

Stress marks:
′ (primary);
′ (secondary), as in
dictionary (dĭk′shə-nĕr′ē)

ship. **4.** Either of the two surfaces of a flat object: *the two sides of a CD.* **5.a.** The part within an object or area to the left or right of the observer or of its vertical axis. **b.** The left or right half of the trunk of a human or animal body. **6.a.** The space immediately next to someone. **b.** The space immediately next to something. Often used in combination: *dockside.* **7.** One of two or more contrasted parts or places within an area, identified by its location with respect to a center: *the north side of the park.* **8.** An area separated from another area by an intervening feature, such as a line or barrier: *this side of the Atlantic.* **9.a.** One of two or more opposing individuals, groups, teams, or sets of opinions. **b.** One of the positions maintained in a dispute or debate. **10.** A distinct aspect: *his shy side.* **11.** Line of descent. **12.** *Chiefly British.* Affected superiority; arrogance. —*adj.* **1.** Located on a side. **2.** From or to one side; oblique: *a side view.* **3.** Minor; incidental. **4.** In addition to the main part; supplementary. —*v.* **sid•ed, sid•ing, sides.** —*tr.* **1.** To provide sides or siding for. **2.** To be positioned next to. **3.** To be in agreement with; support. —*intr.* To align oneself in a disagreement. —***idioms.* on the side. 1.** In addition to the main portion. **2.** In addition to the main occupation or activity. **side by side.** Next to each other; close together. **this side of.** *Informal.* Verging on; short of. [ME < OE *sīde.*]

sideboard
Late 18th- to early 19th-century American mahogany sideboard by Thomas Howard, Jr. (1774–1833)

side•arm (sīd′ärm′) *adj. Sports.* Thrown with or marked by a sideways motion of the arm between shoulder and hip height and relatively parallel to the ground. —**side′arm′** *adv.*

side arm *n.* A small weapon carried at the side or waist.

side•band also **side band** (sīd′bănd′) *n.* Either of the two bands of frequencies, one just above and one just below a carrier frequency, that result from modulation of a carrier wave.

side•bar (sīd′bär′) *n.* A short, often boxed auxiliary news story that is printed alongside a longer article and typically presents additional, contrasting, or late-breaking news.

side•board (sīd′bôrd′, -bōrd′) *n.* **1.** A piece of dining room furniture having drawers and shelves for linens and tableware. **2.** A board that forms a side or part of a side.

side•burns (sīd′bûrnz′) *pl.n.* Growths of hair down the sides of a man's face in front of the ears. [Alteration of BURNSIDES.]

sidecar

side•car (sīd′kär′) *n.* **1.** A one-wheeled car for a passenger, attached to the side of a motorcycle. **2.** A cocktail combining brandy, an orange-flavored liqueur, and lemon juice.

side chair *n.* A straight-backed chair without arms.

sid•ed (sī′dĭd) *adj.* Having sides usu. of a specified number or kind. Often used in combination: *many-sided; marble-sided.* —**sid′ed•ness** *n.*

side dish *n.* A dish served as an accompaniment to the main course.

side drum *n. Mus.* See **snare drum.**

side effect *n.* A peripheral or secondary effect, esp. an undesirable secondary effect of a drug or therapy.

side•kick (sīd′kĭk′) *n. Slang.* A close companion or comrade.

side•light (sīd′līt′) *n.* **1.** A light coming from the side. **2.** *Naut.* Either of two lights, red to port, green to starboard, shown by ships at night. **3.** A piece of incidental or contrasting information.

side•line (sīd′līn′) *n.* **1.** *Sports.* **a.** A line along either of the two sides of a playing court or field, marking its limits. **b. sidelines.** The space outside such limits. **2. sidelines.** The position or point of view of those who observe rather than participate in an activity: *the political sidelines.* **3.** A subsidiary line of merchandise. **4.** An activity pursued in addition to one's regular occupation. —*tr.v.* **-lined, -lin•ing, -lines.** *Informal.* To remove or keep from active participation.

side chair
1790–1800 American Classical Revival style

side•ling (sīd′lĭng) *adj.* **1.** Directed to one side; oblique. **2.** Sloping; inclined. —*adv.* Obliquely; sideways.

side•long (sīd′lông′, -lŏng′) *adj.* **1.** Directed to one side; sideways. **2.** So as to slant; sloping. —*adv.* **1.** On or toward the side; sideways. **2.** In an oblique manner. [Alteration of SIDELING.]

side•man (sīd′măn′) *n. Mus.* A member of a jazz band who is not the leader or a featured soloist.

side•piece (sīd′pēs′) *n.* A part forming the side of something.

si•de•re•al (sī-dîr′ē-əl) *adj.* **1.** Of, relating to, or concerned with the stars or constellations; stellar. **2.** Measured or determined by means of the apparent daily motion of the stars. [< Lat. *sīdereus* < *sīdus, sīder-*, constellation, star.]

sidereal day *n.* The time required for a complete rotation of the earth in reference to the vernal equinox at the meridian, equal to 23 hours, 56 minutes, 4.09 seconds of mean solar time.

sidereal hour *n.* A 24th part of a sidereal day.

sidereal month *n.* The average period of revolution of the moon around the earth in reference to a fixed star, equal to 27 days, 7 hours, 43 minutes of mean solar time.

sidereal time *n.* Time based on the rotation of the earth with reference to the background of stars.

sidereal year *n.* The time required for one complete revolution of the earth about the sun, relative to the fixed stars, or 365 days, 6 hours, 9 minutes, 9.54 seconds of mean solar time.

sid•er•ite (sĭd′ə-rīt′) *n.* **1.** An ore of iron, $FeCO_3$. **2.** A meteorite consisting mainly of iron and nickel.

sidero– or **sider–** *pref.* Iron: *siderolite.* [Gk. *sidēro-* < *sidēros*, iron.]

sid•er•o•lite (sĭd′ər-ə-līt′) *n.* A meteorite composed of a mixed mass of iron and stone.

sid•er•o•sis (sĭd′ə-rō′sĭs) *n.* Chronic inflammation of the lungs caused by excessive inhalation of dust containing iron.

side•sad•dle (sīd′săd′l) *n.* A saddle designed so that the rider sits with both legs on one side of the horse. —*adv.* On a sidesaddle.

side•show (sīd′shō′) *n.* **1.** A small show offered in addition to the main attraction. **2.** An incidental diversion or spectacle.

side•slip (sīd′slĭp′) *intr.v.* **-slipped, -slip•ping, -slips. 1.** To slip or skid to one side. **2.** *Sports.* To slide sideways and downward in skiing. **3.** To fly sideways and downward in an airplane along the lateral axis to reduce altitude without gaining speed or from banking too deeply. —**side′slip′** *n.*

side•spin (sīd′spĭn′) *n.* A rotary motion that spins a ball horizontally.

side•split•ting (sīd′splĭt′ĭng) *adj.* **1.** Convulsively hearty; uproarious. Used of laughter. **2.** Causing convulsive laughter; extremely funny. —**side′split′ting•ly** *adv.*

side•step (sīd′stĕp′) *v.* **-stepped, -step•ping, -steps.** —*intr.* **1.** To step aside: *sidestepped to make way.* **2.** To dodge an issue or a responsibility. —*tr.* **1.** To step out of the way of. **2.** To evade; skirt: *sidestep a question.* —**side′step′per** *n.*

side step *n.* A step to one side, as in boxing or dancing.

side•stroke (sīd′strōk′) *Sports. n.* A swimming stroke in which a person swims on one side and thrusts the arms forward and downward alternately while performing a scissors kick. —**side′stroke′** *v.* —**side′strok′er** *n.*

side•swipe (sīd′swīp′) *tr.v.* **-swiped, -swip•ing, -swipes.** To strike along the side in passing. —*n.* **1.** A glancing blow on the side. **2.** An incidental critical remark. —**side′swip′er** *n.*

side•track (sīd′trăk′) *v.* **-tracked, -track•ing, -tracks.** —*tr.* **1.** To divert from a main issue or course. **2.** To delay or block the progress of deliberately. **3.** To switch from a main railroad track to a siding. —*intr.* **1.** To deviate from a main issue or course. **2.** To run into a siding. —*n.* A railroad siding.

side•walk (sīd′wôk′) *n.* A paved walkway along a street.

sidewalk superintendent *n. Slang.* A pedestrian who stops to watch construction or demolition work.

side•wall (sīd′wôl′) *n.* **1.** A wall that forms the side of something. **2.** A side surface of an automobile tire, between the edge of the tread and the wheel rim.

side•ward (sīd′wərd) *adv. & adj.* Toward or at one side. —**side′wards** (-wərdz) *adv.*

side•ways (sīd′wāz′) also **side•way** (-wā′) *adv. & adj.* **1.** Toward one side: *took a step sideways.* **2.** From one side: *sideways pressure.* **3.** With the side forward: *turned sideways.*

side-wheel (sīd′hwēl′, -wēl′) *adj. Naut.* Of, relating to, or being a steamboat with a paddle wheel on each side.

side-wheel•er (sīd′hwē′lər, -wē′-) *n. Naut.* A side-wheel steamboat.

side-whis•kers (sīd′hwĭs′kərz, -wĭs′-) *pl.n.* Whiskers worn usu. long on the sides of a man's face.

side•wind•er (sīd′wīn′dər) *n.* **1.** A small rattlesnake *(Crotalus cerastes)* of the southwest United States and Mexico that moves by a distinctive lateral looping motion of its body. **2.** A powerful swinging punch delivered from the side.

side•wise (sīd′wīz′) *adv. & adj.* Sideways.

Si•di-bel-Ab•bès (sē′dē-bĕl-ə-bĕs′). A city of NW Algeria S of Oran; headquarters of the French Foreign Legion until 1962. Pop. 112,988.

sid•ing (sī′dĭng) *n.* **1.** Material, such as boards, used for surfacing the outside walls of a frame building. **2.** A short section of railroad track connected by switches with a main track.

si•dle (sīd′l) *v.* **-dled, -dling, -dles.** —*intr.* **1.** To move sideways. **2.** To advance in an unobtrusive, furtive, or coy way. —*tr.* To cause to move sideways. —*n.* **1.** An unobtrusive, furtive, or coy advance. **2.** A sideways movement. [Back-formation < SIDELING.] —**si′dling•ly** *adv.*

Sid•ney (sĭd′nē). A city of W-central OH WNW of Columbus. Pop. 18,710.

Sidney, Sir Philip. 1554–86. English poet, soldier, and politician whose works include the sonnet sequence *Astrophel and Stella* and the collection of pastoral idylls *Arcadia.*

Si•don (sīd′n). An ancient city of Phoenicia on the Mediterranean Sea in present-day SW Lebanon.

Sid•ra (sĭd′rə), **Gulf of.** An inlet of the Mediterranean Sea off N Libya W of Benghazi.

SIDS *abbr.* Sudden infant death syndrome.

siege (sēj) *n.* **1.** The surrounding and blockading of a city, town, or fortress by an army attempting to capture it. **2.** A prolonged period, as of illness: *a siege of asthma.* **3.** *Obsolete.* A seat, esp. a throne. —*tr.v.* **sieged, sieg•ing, sieg•es.** To subject to a siege; besiege. [ME *sege* < OFr., seat < VLat. **sedicum* < **sedicāre*, to sit < Lat. *sedēre.* See **sed-*.**]

Sie•gen (zē′gən). A city of W-central Germany E of Cologne; birthplace of the painter Rubens. Pop. 107,774.

Siege Perilous (sēj) *n.* In Arthurian legend, a seat at King Arthur's Round Table kept for the knight destined to find the Holy Grail and fatal for any other occupant.

Sieg•fried (sēg′frēd′, sĭg′-) *n.* The hero of the *Nibelungenlied* and other Germanic medieval epics. [Ger. < MHGer. *Sîfrit* < OHGer. *Sigifrith* : *sigu*, victory; see **segh-*** + *fridu*, peace; see **prī-***.]

sie•mens (sē′mənz) *n., pl.* **siemens.** A unit of electrical conductance in the International System, equal to one ampere per volt. [After Ernst Werner von SIEMENS.]

Siemens (sē′mənz, zē′-), Sir **Charles William.** 1823–83. German-born British engineer who invented a regenerative steam engine and designed a steamship for laying long-distance cables. His brother **Ernst Werner von Siemens** (1816–92) was a noted electrical engineer.

Si•en•a (sē-ĕn′ə, syĕ′nä). A city of W-central Italy S of Florence; founded by Etruscans. Pop. 61,888. **—Si′e•nese′** (-nēz′, -nēs′) *adj. & n.*

Sien•kie•wicz (shĕn-kyā′vĭch, -kyĕ′-), **Henryk.** 1846–1916. Polish writer who won the 1905 Nobel Prize for literature.

si•en•na (sē-ĕn′ə) *n.* **1.** A special clay containing iron and manganese oxides, used as a pigment for oil and watercolor painting. **2.** *Color.* **a.** Raw sienna. **b.** Burnt sienna. [Short for *terra-sienna* < Ital. *terra di Sienna*, earth of Siena, after SIENA.]

si•er•ra (sē-ĕr′ə) *n.* **1.** A rugged range of mountains having an irregular or jagged profile. **2.a.** A Spanish mackerel *(Scomberomorus sierra)* of the Pacific coast of tropical America. **b.** See **cero.** [Sp. < Lat. *serra*, saw.] **—si•er′ran** *adj.*

Si•er•ra Le•one (sē-ĕr′ə lē-ōn′, -ō′nē). A country of W Africa on the Atlantic coast; a British protectorate from 1896 until it achieved independence in 1961. Cap. Freetown. Pop. 3,381,000.

Si•er•ra Ma•dre del Sur (sē-ĕr′ə mä′drā dĕl so͝or′, syĕr′ä mä′*th*rĕ). A mountain range of S Mexico along the Pacific coast.

Sierra Madre Oc•ci•den•tal (ŏk′sĭ-dĕn′təl, ôk′sē-*th*ĕn-täl′). A mountain range of NW Mexico parallel to the Pacific coastline and extending c. 1,609 km (1,000 mi) S from AZ.

Sierra Madre Or•ien•tal (ôr′ē-ĕn-täl′, ô-ryĕn-). A mountain range of NE Mexico rising as barren hills S of the Rio Grande and roughly paralleling the coast of the Gulf of Mexico.

Si•er•ra Ne•va•da (sē-ĕr′ə nə-văd′ə, -vä′də). **1.** *(also* syĕr′ä nĕ-vä′*th*ä). A mountain range of S Spain along the Mediterranean coast E of Granada rising to 3,480.4 m (11,411 ft). **2.** A mountain range of E CA extending c. 644 km (400 mi) between the Sacramento and San Joaquin valleys and the NV border and rising to 4,420.7 m (14,494 ft).

Sierra Vis•ta (vĭs′tə). A city of SE AZ SE of Tucson near the Mexican border. Pop. 32,983.

si•es•ta (sē-ĕs′tə) *n.* A rest or nap after the midday meal. [Sp. < Lat. *sexta (hōra)*, sixth (hour), midday, fem. of *sextus*, sixth. See SEXT.]

sieve (sĭv) *n.* A utensil of wire mesh or closely perforated metal, used for straining, sifting, ricing, or puréeing. *—v.* **sieved, siev•ing, sieves.** *—tr.* To pass through a sieve. *—intr.* To use a sieve; sift. [ME *sive* < OE *sife.*]

sieve tube *n. Bot.* A series of cells joined end to end, forming a tube through which nutrients are conducted in flowering plants and brown algae.

sift (sĭft) *v.* **sift•ed, sift•ing, sifts.** *—tr.* **1.** To put (flour, for example) through a sieve or other straining device to separate out the coarse particles. **2.** To distinguish as if separating with a sieve. **3.** To apply by scattering with or as if with a sieve. **4.** To examine and sort carefully. *—intr.* **1.** To make use of a sieve. **2.** To pass through or as if through a sieve. **3.** To make a careful examination. [ME *siften* < OE *siftan.*] **—sift′er** *n.*

sig. *abbr.* **1.** Signal. **2.** Signature. **3.** Often **Sig.** Signor; signore.

Sig. *abbr.* **1.** *Lat.* Signa (mark or label it). **2.** *Medic.* Signature. **3.** *Lat.* Signetur (let it be marked or labeled).

sigh (sī) *v.* **sighed, sigh•ing, sighs.** *—intr.* **1.a.** To exhale audibly in a long deep breath, as in weariness or relief. **b.** To emit a similar sound: *willows sighing in the wind.* **2.** To feel longing or grief; yearn. *—tr.* **1.** To express with or as if with an audible exhalation. **2.** *Archaic.* To lament. *—n.* The act or sound of sighing. [ME *sighen*, prob. back-formation < *sighte*, p.t. of *siken*, to sigh < OE *sīcan.*] **—sigh′er** *n.*

sight (sīt) *n.* **1.** The ability to see. **2.** The act or fact of seeing. **3.** Field of vision. **4.** The foreseeable future; prospect: *no solution in sight.* **5.** Something seen; a view. **6.** Something worth seeing; a spectacle. **7.** *Informal.* Something unsightly. **8.a.** A device used to assist aim by guiding the eye, as on a firearm or surveying instrument. **b.** An aim or observation taken with such a device. **9.** An opportunity to observe or inspect. **10.** *Upper Southern U.S.* A large number or quantity. *—v.* **sight•ed, sight•ing, sights.** *—tr.* **1.** To perceive with the eyes; get sight of. **2.** To observe through a sight or an optical instrument. **3.** To adjust the sights of (a rifle, for example). **4.** To take aim with (a firearm). *—intr.* **1.** To direct one's gaze; look carefully. **2.** To take aim. ***—idioms.*** **on sight.** Immediately upon being seen. **out of sight.** *Slang.* Remarkable; incredible. **sight for sore eyes.** *Informal.* One whom it is a relief or joy to see. **sight unseen.** Without seeing the object in question. [ME < OE *sihth, gesiht*, something seen. See **sek^{w}-^{2}***.]

sight draft *n.* A draft or bill payable on demand or upon presentation.

sight•ed (sī′tĭd) *adj.* **1.** Having the ability to see. **2.** Having eyesight of a specified kind. Often used in combination: *keen-sighted.* **—sight′ed•ness** *n.*

sight gag *n.* A comic bit or effect that depends on sight.

sight•ing (sī′tĭng) *n.* The act of catching sight of something, esp. something unusual or searched for.

sight•less (sīt′lĭs) *adj.* **1.** Unable to see with the eyes; blind. **2.** Invisible. **—sight′less•ly** *adv.* **—sight′less•ness** *n.*

sight•line also **sight line** (sīt′līn′) *n.* A line of sight, esp. one between a spectator and a performance, as in a theater.

sight•ly (sīt′lē) *adj.* **-li•er, -li•est. 1.** Pleasing or appealing to see. **2.** Affording a fine view; scenic. **—sight′li•ness** *n.*

sight-read (sīt′rēd′) *v.* **-read** (-rĕd′), **-read•ing, -reads.** *—tr.* To read or perform (music, for example) without preparation or prior acquaintance. *—intr.* To sight-read something. **—sight′-read′er** *n.*

sight rhyme *n.* See **eye rhyme.**

sight•see (sīt′sē′) *intr.v.* **-saw** (-sô′), **-seen** (-sēn′), **-see•ing, -sees.** To tour sights of interest. **—sight′se′er** *n.*

sight•see•ing (sīt′sē′ĭng) *n.* The act or pastime of visiting sights of interest. *—adj.* Used or engaged in sightseeing.

sig•il (sĭj′əl, sĭg′ĭl) *n.* **1.** A seal; a signet. **2.** A sign or an image considered magical. [Lat. *sigillum*, dim. of *signum*, sign. See SIGN.]

Sig•is•mund (sĭg′ĭs-mənd). 1368–1437. Holy Roman emperor (1433–37) and king of Hungary (1387–1437) and Bohemia (1419–37) who helped end the Great Schism (1378–1417) by convening the Council of Constance (1414–18).

sig•ma (sĭg′mə) *n.* **1.** The 18th letter of the Greek alphabet. **2.** A sigma hyperon. [Gk., of Phoenician orig.; akin to Heb. *sāmek*, samekh.] **—sig′mate′** (-māt′) *adj.*

sigma hyperon *n.* Any of three unstable baryons having a mass of 2,328 to 2,343 times that of the electron and a positive, neutral, or negative elecric charge. See table at **subatomic particle.**

sig•moid (sĭg′moid′) also **sig•moi•dal** (sĭg-moid′l) *adj.* **1.** Having the shape of the letter S. **2.** Of or relating to the sigmoid flexure. [Gk. *sigmoeidēs* : *sigma*, sigma; see SIGMA + *-oeidēs*, -oid.]

sigmoid flexure *n.* An S-shaped section of the colon between the descending section and the rectum.

sig•moid•o•scope (sĭg-moi′də-skōp′) *n.* A tubular instrument for visual examination of the sigmoid flexure. **—sig•moid′o•scop′ic** (-skŏp′ĭk) *adj.* **—sig′moid•os′co•py** (sĭg′moi-dŏs′kə-pē) *n.*

sign (sīn) *n.* **1.** Something that suggests the presence or existence of a fact, condition, or quality. **2.a.** An act or a gesture used to convey an idea, a desire, information, or a command. **b.** Sign language. **3.a.** A displayed structure bearing lettering or symbols, used to identify or advertise a place of business. **b.** A posted notice bearing a designation, direction, or command. **4.** A conventional figure or device that stands for a word, a phrase, or an operation; a symbol, as in mathematics or in musical notation. **5.** *pl.* **sign.** An indicator, such as a footprint, of the trail of an animal. **6.** A trace or vestige: *no sign of life.* **7.** A portentous incident or event; a presage. **8.** A bodily manifestation that serves to indicate the presence of malfunction or disease. **9.** One of the 12 divisions of the zodiac, each represented by a symbol. *—v.* **signed, sign•ing, signs.** *—tr.* **1.** To affix one's signature to. **2.** To write (one's signature). **3.** To approve or ratify (a document) by affixing a signature, seal, or other mark: *sign a bill into law.* **4.** To hire or engage by obtaining a signature on a contract. **5.** To relinquish or transfer title to by signature: *signed away the estate.* **6.** To provide with a sign or signs. **7.** To communicate with a sign or by sign language. **8.** To consecrate with the sign of the cross. *—intr.* **1.** To make a sign or signs; signal. **2.** To use sign language. **3.** To write one's signature. ***—phrasal verbs.*** **sign in.** To record the arrival of (another or oneself) by signing a register. **sign off. 1.** To announce the end of a communication; conclude. **2.** To stop transmission after identifying the broadcasting station. **3.** *Informal.* To express approval formally or conclusively. **sign on. 1.** *Informal.* To enlist oneself, esp. as an employee. **2.** To start transmission with an identification of the broadcasting station. **sign out.** To record the departure of (another or oneself) by signing a register. **sign up.** To agree to be a participant or recipient by signing one's name; enlist. [ME *signe* < OFr. < Lat. *signum.* See **sek^{w}-^{1}***.] **—sign′er** *n.*

Si•gnac (sēn-yăk′), **Paul.** 1863–1935. French neoimpressionist painter whose works include *Port of St. Tropez* (1916).

sign•age (sī′nĭj) *n.* **1.** Signs considered as a group. **2.** The design or use of signs and symbols.

sig•nal (sĭg′nəl) *n.* **1.a.** An indicator, such as a gesture or colored light, that serves as a means of communication. **b.** A message communicated by such means. **2.** Something that incites action. **3.** *Electron.* An impulse or a fluctuating electric quantity, such as voltage, whose variations represent coded information. **4.** The sound, image, or message transmitted or received in telegraphy, telephony, radio, television, or radar.

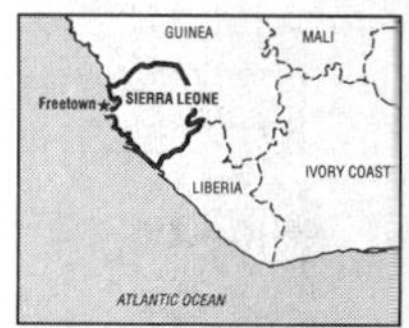

Sierra Leone

sieve
At an archaeological dig

ă **pat**	oi **boy**
ā **pay**	ou **out**
âr **care**	o͝o **took**
ä **father**	o͞o **boot**
ĕ **pet**	ŭ **cut**
ē **be**	ûr **urge**
ĭ **pit**	th **thin**
ī **pie**	*th* **this**
îr **pier**	hw **which**
ŏ **pot**	zh **vision**
ō **toe**	ə **about, item**
ô **paw**	

Stress marks:
′ (primary);
′ (secondary), as in
dictionary (dĭk′shə-nĕr′ē)

— *adj.* Notably out of the ordinary: *a signal feat.* — *v.* **-naled, -nal•ing, -nals** or **-nalled, -nal•ling, -nals.** — *tr.* **1.** To make a signal to. **2.** To relate or make known by signals. — *intr.* To make a signal or signals. [ME < OFr. < Med.Lat. *signāle* < neut. of LLat. *signālis*, of a sign < Lat. *signum*, sign. See SIGN.] — **sig′nal•er, sig′nal•ler** *n.*

sig•nal•ize (sĭg′nə-līz′) *tr.v.* **-ized, -iz•ing, -iz•es. 1.** To make remarkable or conspicuous. **2.** To point out particularly. — **sig′nal•i•za′tion** (-nə-lĭ-zā′shən) *n.*

sig•nal•ly (sĭg′nə-lē) *adv.* To a conspicuous degree; notably.

sig•nal•ment (sĭg′nəl-mənt) *n.* A detailed description of a person's appearance, as for police files. [Fr. *signalement* < *signaler*, to mark out < *signal*, signal. See SIGNAL.]

sig•na•to•ry (sĭg′nə-tôr′ē, -tōr′ē) *adj.* Bound by signed agreement. — *n.*, *pl.* **-ries.** One that has signed a treaty or other document. [Lat. *signātōrius* < *signātus*, p.part. of *signāre*, to mark < *signum*, sign. See SIGN.]

sig•na•ture (sĭg′nə-chər) *n.* **1.** One's name as written by oneself. **2.** The act of signing one's name. **3.** A distinctive mark, characteristic, or sound indicating identity. **4.** *Medic.* The part of a physician's prescription containing directions to the patient. **5.** *Mus.* **a.** A sign used to indicate key. **b.** A sign used to indicate tempo. **6.** *Print.* **a.** A letter, number, or symbol at the bottom of the first page on each sheet of printed pages as a guide to the sequence of the sheets in binding. **b.** A large sheet printed with a multiple of four pages that when folded becomes a section of the book. [Fr. < OFr. < Med.Lat. *signātūra* < Lat. *signātus*, p.part. of *signāre*, to mark < *signum*, sign. See SIGN.]

signpost

sign•board (sīn′bôrd′, -bōrd′) *n.* A board bearing a sign.

sig•net (sĭg′nĭt) *n.* **1.** A seal, esp. one used officially to mark documents. **2.** The impression made with such a seal. — *tr.v.* **-net•ed, -net•ing, -nets.** To mark or endorse with a signet. [ME < OFr., dim. of *signe*, sign. See SIGN.]

signet ring *n.* A finger ring bearing an engraved signet.

sig•nif•i•cance (sĭg-nĭf′ĭ-kəns) also **sig•nif•i•can•cy** (-kən-sē) *n.* **1.** The state or quality of being significant. See Syns at **importance. 2.** A meaning that is expressed. **3.** A covert or implied meaning. See Syns at **meaning.**

sig•nif•i•cant (sĭg-nĭf′ĭ-kənt) *adj.* **1.** Having or expressing a meaning; meaningful. **2.** Having or expressing a covert meaning; suggestive. See Syns at **expressive. 3.** Having or likely to have a major effect; important. **4.** Fairly large in amount or quantity. **5.** *Statistics.* Of or relating to observations or occurrences that are too closely correlated to be attributed only to chance. [Lat. *significāns*, *significant-*, pr.part. of *significāre*, to signify. See SIGNIFY.] — **sig•nif′i•cant•ly** *adv.*

silhouette
By an unidentified 18th-century artist

significant digits *pl.n. Math.* The digits of a decimal number beginning with the leftmost nonzero digit and extending to the right to include all digits warranted by the accuracy in measurement.

significant other *n.* **1.** A person with whom one shares a long-term sexual relationship. **2.** An important or influential person in one's life.

sig•ni•fi•ca•tion (sĭg′nə-fĭ-kā′shən) *n.* **1.** The established meaning of a word. See Syns at **meaning. 2.** The act of signifying; indication.

sig•nif•i•ca•tive (sĭg-nĭf′ĭ-kā′tĭv) *adj.* **1.** Tending to signify or indicate; indicative. **2.** Having meaning; significant. — **sig•nif′i•ca′tive•ness** *n.*

sig•ni•fy (sĭg′nə-fī′) *v.* **-fied, -fy•ing, -fies.** — *tr.* **1.** To denote; mean. **2.** To make known, as with a sign or word: *signify one's intent.* — *intr.* **1.** To have meaning or importance. See Syns at **count**[1]. **2.** *Slang.* To exchange humorous insults in a verbal game. [ME *signifien* < OFr. *signifier* < Lat. *significāre* : *signum*, sign; see SIGN + *-ficāre*, -fy.] — **sig′ni•fi′a•ble** *adj.* — **sig′ni•fi′er** *n.*

sign language *n.* **1.** A language that uses manual movements to convey grammatical structure and meaning. **2.** A method of communication, as between speakers of different languages, that uses hand movements and other gestures.

sign manual *n.*, *pl.* **signs manual.** A signature, esp. that of a monarch at the top of a royal decree.

sign of the cross *n.* A gesture describing the form of a cross, made in token of faith in Jesus or to invoke a blessing.

si•gnor also **si•gnior** (sēn-yôr′, -yōr′) *n.*, *pl.* **si•gno•ri** (sēn-yôr′ē, -yōr′ē) also **si•gniors** or **si•gnors.** Used as a courtesy title for a man in an Italian-speaking area. [Ital., var. of *signore.* See SIGNORE.]

si•gno•ra (sēn-yôr′ə, -yōr′ə, -yô′rä) *n.*, *pl.* **si•gno•re** (sēn-yôr′ā, -yōr′ā, -yô′rĕ) or **si•gno•ras.** Used as a courtesy title for a married woman in an Italian-speaking area. [Ital., fem. of *signore*, signore. See SIGNORE.]

si•gno•re (sēn-yôr′ā, -yōr′ā, -yô′rĕ) *n.*, *pl.* **si•gno•ri** (sēn-yô′rē, -yōr′ē). Used as a form of polite address for a man in an Italian-speaking area. [Ital. < Med.Lat. *senior*, lord < Lat., elder. See SENIOR.]

si•gno•ri•na (sēn′yə-rē′nə, -yô-rē′nä) *n.*, *pl.* **-ne** (-nā, -nĕ) or **-nas.** Used as a courtesy title for an unmarried woman or a girl in an Italian-speaking area. [Ital., dim. of *signora*, signora. See SIGNORA.]

si•gno•ry or **si•gnio•ry** (sēn′yə-rē) *n.*, *pl.* **-ries.** See **seigniory.** [ME *signorie* < OFr. *seigneurie* < *seigneur*, seignior. See SEIGNIOR.]

sign•post (sīn′pōst′) *n.* **1.** A post supporting a sign that has information or directions. **2.** An indication, a sign, or a guide.

Sig•urd (sĭg′ərd) *n. Myth.* A hero in Norse myth who wins an accursed hoard of gold and is slain.

Si•ha•nouk (sē′ə-no͝ok′), Prince **Norodom.** b. 1922. Cambodian politician who served as prime minister (1955–57) and head of state (1960–70 and 1975–76).

Si•ha•sa•pa (sə-hä′sə-pə) *n.*, *pl.* **Sihasapa** or **-pas.** A member of a Native American people constituting a subdivision of the Teton Sioux.

Sikes•ton (sīk′stən). A city of SE MO WSW of Cairo IL. Pop. 17,641.

Sikh (sēk) *n.* An adherent of Sikhism. — *adj.* Of or relating to the Sikhs or to Sikhism. [Hindi < Skt. *śiṣyaḥ*, disciple < *śikṣati*, he wishes to learn, desiderative of *śaknoti*, is able.]

Sikh•ism (sēk′ĭz′əm) *n.* The doctrines and practices of a monotheistic religion founded in northern India in the 16th century.

Si Kiang (sē′ kyäng′, shē′). See **Xi Jiang.**

Sik•kim (sĭk′ĭm). A region and former kingdom of NE India in the E Himalaya Mts. between Nepal and Bhutan; passed to India in 1949.

Si•kor•sky (sĭ-kôr′skē), **Igor Ivan.** 1889–1972. Russian-born Amer. aviation pioneer who designed (1939) an early helicopter.

si•lage (sī′lĭj) *n.* Fodder prepared by storing and fermenting green forage plants in a silo. [Short for ENSILAGE.]

sil•ane (sĭl′ān′) *n.* Any of a group of silicon hydrides having the general formula SiH that are analogous to the paraffin hydrocarbons. [SIL(ICON) + (METH)ANE.]

sild (sĭld) *n.*, *pl.* **sild** or **silds.** A young herring other than a sprat that is processed as a sardine in Norway. [Norw. and Dan. < ON *sīld*, herring.]

si•lence (sī′ləns) *n.* **1.** The condition or quality of being or keeping still and silent. **2.** The absence of sound; stillness. **3.** A period of time without speech or noise. **4.** Refusal or failure to speak out. — *tr.v.* **-lenced, -lenc•ing, -lenc•es. 1.** To make silent or bring to silence: *silenced the crowd.* **2.** To curtail the expression of; suppress. [ME < OFr. < Lat. *silentium* < *silēns*, *silent-*, pr.part. of *silēre*, to be silent.]

si•lenc•er (sī′lən-sər) *n.* One that silences, esp. a device on the muzzle of a firearm to muffle the sound of firing.

si•lent (sī′lənt) *adj.* **1.** Marked by absence of noise or sound; still. **2.** Not inclined to speak; not talkative. **3.** Unable to speak. **4.** Refraining from speech: *Do be silent.* **5.** Not voiced or expressed; unspoken: *a silent curse.* **6.** Inactive; quiescent: *a silent volcano.* **7.** *Ling.* Having no phonetic value; unpronounced, as the silent *b* in subtle. **8.** Having no spoken dialogue and usu. no soundtrack. Used of a film. — *n.* A silent movie. [Lat. *silēns*, *silent-*, pr.part. of *silēre*, to be silent.] — **si′lent•ly** *adv.* — **si′lent•ness** *n.*

Syns: *silent, reticent, reserved.* These adjectives describe people who are sparing with speech. *Silent* often implies a habitual disinclination to speak or to speak out: *"the great silent majority"* (Richard M. Nixon). The term may also mean refraining from speech, as out of fear or confusion: *"He must be warned . . . that he has the right to remain silent"* (Earl Warren). *Reticent* suggests a reluctance to share one's thoughts and feelings: *"She had been shy and reticent with me, and now . . . she was telling me aloud the secrets of her inmost heart"* (W.H. Hudson). *Reserved* suggests aloofness and reticence: *"a reserved man, whose inner life was intense and sufficient to him"* (Arnold Bennett).

silent butler *n.* A small receptacle with a handle and hinged cover, used for collecting ashes and crumbs.

silent partner *n.* One that makes financial investments in a business enterprise but does not share in management.

si•le•nus (sī-lē′nəs) *n.*, *pl.* **-ni** (-nī). *Gk. Myth.* Any of the minor woodland deities and companions of Dionysus, depicted as men with the tails, ears, and hoofs of horses. [Lat. *silēnus* < Gk. *silēnos* < *Silēnos*, Silenus.]

Si•le•nus (sī-lē′nəs) *n. Gk. Myth.* A satyr, usu. depicted as drunken and jolly, in the entourage of Dionysus. [Lat. < Gk. *Silēnos*.]

Si•le•sia (sī-lē′zhə, -shə, sī-). A region of central Europe primarily in SW Poland and N Czech Republic; settled by Slavic peoples c. A.D. 500. — **Si•le′sian** *adj. & n.*

si•lex (sī′lĕks′) *n.* **1.** Silica. **2.** Finely ground tripoli used as an inert paint filler. [Lat., hard stone, flint.]

sil•hou•ette (sĭl′o͞o-ĕt′) *n.* **1.** A drawing consisting of the outline of something, esp. a human profile, filled in with a solid color. **2.** An outline that appears dark against a light background. See Syns at **outline.** — *tr.v.* **-et•ted, -et•ting, -ettes.** To cause to be seen as a silhouette; outline. [Fr., after Étienne de *Silhouette* (1709–67), French finance minister.]

sil•i•ca (sĭl′ĭ-kə) *n.* An abundant crystalline compound, SiO_2, occurring as quartz, sand, flint, agate, and many other minerals and used to make a variety of materials, esp. glass and concrete. [NLat. < Lat. *silex*, *silic-*, hard stone, flint.]

silica gel *n.* Amorphous silica that is used as a drying and dehumidifying agent, as a catalyst and catalyst carrier, as an anticaking agent in cosmetics, and in chromatography.

sil•i•cate (sĭl′ĭ-kāt′, -kĭt) *n.* **1.** Any of numerous compounds containing silicon, oxygen, and one or more metals. **2.** Any of a large group of minerals, forming over 90 percent of the earth's crust, that combine SiO_2 or SiO_4 ions with one or more metals.

si•li•ceous (sĭ-lĭsh′əs) *adj.* Containing, resembling, relating to, or consisting of silica. [< Lat. *siliceus*, of flint < *silex*, *silic-*, flint.]

silici– or **silic–** *pref.* **1.** Silicon: *silicate.* **2.** Silica: *silicify.* [< SILICON and SILICA.]

si•lic•ic (sĭ-lĭs′ĭk) *adj.* Relating to, resembling, containing, or derived from silica or silicon.

silicic acid *n.* A jellylike substance, $SiO_2{\cdot}nH_2O$, produced when sodium silicate solution is acidified.

sil•i•cide (sĭl′ĭ-sīd′) *n.* A compound of silicon with another element or radical.

si•lic•i•fy (sĭ-lĭs′ə-fī′) *v.* **-fied, -fy•ing, -fies.** *—tr.* To convert into or impregnate with silica. *—intr.* To become converted into or impregnated with silica. **—si•lic′i•fi•ca′tion** (-fĭ-kā′shən) *n.*

sil•i•cle (sĭl′ĭ-kəl) *n. Bot.* A short silique usu. having a length less than three times its width. [Lat. *silicula*, dim. of *siliqua*, seed pod.]

sil•i•con (sĭl′ĭ-kən, -kŏn′) *n. Symbol* **Si** A nonmetallic element occurring extensively in the earth's crust in silica and silicates, having both an amorphous and a crystalline allotrope and used in glass, semiconducting devices, refractories, pottery, and silicones. Atomic number 14; atomic weight 28.086; melting point 1,410°C; boiling point 2,355°C; specific gravity 2.33; valence 4. See table at **element.** [< SILICA.]

silicon carbide *n.* A crystalline compound, SiC, one of the hardest known substances, used as an abrasive and heat-refractory material and in light-emitting diodes.

silicon dioxide *n.* Silica.

sil•i•cone (sĭl′ĭ-kōn′) *n.* Any of a group of semi-inorganic polymers of siloxane, characterized by high lubricity and thermal stability, extreme water repellence, and physiological inertness and used in adhesives, lubricants, paints, insulation, synthetic rubber, surgical implants, and prosthetics.

Sil•i•con Valley (sĭl′ĭ-kən, -kŏn′). A region of W CA SE of San Francisco known for its high-technology industries.

sil•i•co•sis (sĭl′ĭ-kō′sĭs) *n.* A disease of the lungs caused by continued inhalation of siliceous dust, marked by fibrosis and chronic shortness of breath. **—sil′i•cot′ic** (-kŏt′ĭk) *adj.*

si•lique (sĭ-lēk′) *n.* A dry dehiscent elongated fruit, characteristic of the mustard family, having two valves. [Fr. < OFr. < Lat. *siliqua*, seed pod.] **—sil′i•quous** (sĭl′ĭ-kwəs), **sil′i•quose′** (-kwōs′) *adj.*

silk (sĭlk) *n.* **1.a.** A fiber produced by certain insect larvae to form cocoons, esp. the strong elastic fibrous secretion of silkworms used to make thread and fabric. **b.** Thread or fabric made of silk. **c.** A garment made of silk. **2. silks.** *Sports.* The identifying garments of a jockey or harness driver. **3.** A silky filamentous material, such as the webbing spun by certain spiders or the styles forming a tuft on an ear of corn. *—adj.* Composed of or similar to silk. *—intr.v.* **silked, silk•ing, silks.** To develop silk. Used of corn. [ME < OE *sioloc*, prob. of Slav. orig., ult. from Chin.]

silk cotton *n.* A silky fiber on the seeds of certain trees.

silk-cot•ton tree (sĭlk′kŏt′n) *n.* **1.** A spiny deciduous North American tree *(Ceiba pentandra)* having palmately compound leaves and cultivated for its fruit that contain the silklike fiber kapok. **2.** Either of two trees *(Bombax ceiba* or *Cochlospermum religiosum)* having seeds surrounded by silky hairs.

silk•en (sĭl′kən) *adj.* **1.** Made of silk. **2.** Resembling silk in texture or appearance; smooth and lustrous. **3.** Delicately pleasing or caressing in effect. **4.** Luxurious.

silk hat *n.* A man's silk-covered top hat.

silk oak *n.* An Australian evergreen tree *(Grevillea robusta)* having divided fernlike leaves and showy orange flowers.

Silk Road (sĭlk). An ancient trade route between China and the Mediterranean Sea extending some 6,440 km (4,000 mi) and linking China with the Roman Empire.

silk-screen also **silk•screen** (sĭlk′skrēn′) *n.* **1.** A stencil method of printmaking in which a design is imposed on a screen of silk or other fine mesh, with blank areas coated with an impermeable substance, and ink is forced through the mesh onto the printing surface. **2.** A print made by this method. **—silk′-screen′** *v.*

silk stocking *n.* A wealthy, aristocratic, or elegantly dressed person.

silk-stock•ing (sĭlk′stŏk′ĭng) *adj.* Wealthy; aristocratic.

silk tree *n.* An Asian tree *(Albizzia julibrissin)* having pinnately compound leaves and pinkish flowers with many filaments.

silk•weed (sĭlk′wēd′) *n.* See **milkweed.**

silk•worm (sĭlk′wûrm′) *n.* Any of various caterpillars that produce silk cocoons, esp. the larva of a moth *(Bombyx mori)* native to Asia that spins a cocoon of fine, strong, lustrous fiber that is the source of commercial silk.

silk•y (sĭl′kē) *adj.* **-i•er, -i•est. 1.** Resembling silk; lustrous. **2.** Made of silk; silken. **3.** Covered with or characterized by fine soft hairs or feathers: *a silky chick.* **4.** Ingratiating; seductive. **—silk′i•ly** *adv.* **—silk′i•ness** *n.*

silky terrier *n.* A toy terrier characterized by long silky bluish-gray hair, tan markings, and erect ears.

sill (sĭl) *n.* **1.** The horizontal member that bears the upright portion of a frame, esp. that forming the base of a window. **2.** *Geol.* An approximately horizontal sheet of igneous rock intruded between older rock beds. [ME *sille* < OE *syll*, threshold.]

Sill (sĭl), **Mount.** A peak, 4,316.7 m (14,153 ft), in the Sierra Nevada of E-central CA.

sil•la•bub (sĭl′ə-bŭb′) *n.* Var. of **syllabub.**

Sil•lan•pää (sĭl′ən-pă′), **Frans Eemil.** 1888–1964. Finnish writer who won the 1939 Nobel Prize for literature.

Sills (sĭlz), **Beverly.** b. 1929. Amer. soprano who was the general director of the New York City Opera (1980–89).

sil•ly (sĭl′ē) *adj.* **-li•er, -li•est. 1.** Exhibiting a lack of wisdom or good sense; foolish. **2.** Lacking seriousness or responsibleness; frivolous. **3.** Semiconscious; dazed. [ME *seli, silli*, blessed, innocent, hapless < OE *gesælig*, blessed.] **—sil′li•ly** (sĭl′ə-lē) *adv.* **—sil′li•ness** *n.*

si•lo (sī′lō) *n.*, *pl.* **-los. 1.a.** A tall cylindrical structure, usu. beside a barn, in which fodder is stored. **b.** A pit dug for the same purpose. **2.** An underground shelter for a missile, usu. equipped to launch the missile or raise it into a launching position. *—tr.v.* **-loed, -lo•ing, -los.** To store in a silo. [Sp.]

Si•lo•ne (sĭ-lō′nē, sē-lô′nĕ), **Ignazio.** 1900–78. Italian novelist whose works include *Bread and Wine* (1937).

si•lox•ane (sĭ-lŏk′sān′, sī-) *n.* Any of a class of chemical compounds of silicon, oxygen, and usu. carbon and hydrogen, based on the structural unit R_2SiO, where R is an alkyl group, usu. methyl. [SIL(ICON) + OX(YGEN) + (METH)ANE.]

silt (sĭlt) *n.* A sedimentary material consisting of very fine particles intermediate in size between sand and clay. *—v.* **silt•ed, silt•ing, silts.** *—intr.* To become filled with silt: *The channel silted up.* *—tr.* To fill, cover, or obstruct with silt. [ME *cylte*, prob. of Scand. orig. See **sal-*.**] **—silt•a′tion** *n.* **—silt′y** *adj.*

silt•stone (sĭlt′stōn′) *n.* A fine-grained rock of consolidated silt.

Sil•u•res (sĭl′yə-rēz′) *pl.n.* A people described by Tacitus as occupying southeast Wales when the Romans invaded. [Lat.]

Si•lu•ri•an (sĭ-lo͝or′ē-ən, sī-) *adj.* **1.** Of or relating to the Silures or their culture. **2.** *Geol.* Of, belonging to, or being the geologic time of the third period of the Paleozoic Era, characterized by the appearance of invertebrate land animals and land plants. See table at **geologic time.** *—n. Geol.* The Silurian Period or its deposits. [< SILURES (because the Silures lived where the rocks were first identified).]

si•lu•rid (sĭ-lo͝or′ĭd, sī-) *adj.* Of or belonging to the family Siluridae, which includes various freshwater catfishes. [< NLat. *Silūridae*, family name < Lat. *silūrus*, a large freshwater fish < Gk. *silouros*, sheatfish. See **ors-*.**] **—si•lu′rid** *n.*

sil•va also **syl•va** (sĭl′və) *n.*, *pl.* **-vas** or **-vae** (-vē). **1.** The trees or forests of a region. **2.** A written work on the trees or forests of a region. [Lat., forest.]

sil•van (sĭl′vən) *adj. & n.* Var. of **sylvan.**

Sil•va•nus also **Syl•va•nus** (sĭl-vā′nəs) *n. Rom. Myth.* A god of forests, fields, and herding.

sil•ver (sĭl′vər) *n.* **1.** *Symbol* **Ag** A lustrous ductile malleable metallic element, occurring both uncombined and in ores such as argentite, having the highest thermal and electrical conductivity of the metals and used in jewelry, tableware, coinage, photography, dental and soldering alloys, electrical contacts, and printed circuits. Atomic number 47; atomic weight 107.868; melting point 960.8°C; boiling point 2,212°C; specific gravity 10.50; valence 1, 2. See table at **element. 2.** This metallic element as a commodity or medium of exchange. **3.** Coins made of this metallic element. **4.a.** Domestic articles, such as tableware, made of or plated with silver. **b.** Tableware, esp. eating and serving utensils, made of steel or another metal. **5.** *Color.* A lustrous medium gray. **6.** A silver salt, esp. silver nitrate, used to sensitize paper. *—adj.* **1.** Made of or containing silver. **2.** Resembling silver, esp. in having a lustrous shine; silvery. **3.** *Color.* Of a lustrous medium gray. **4.** Having a soft, clear, resonant sound. **5.** Eloquent; persuasive. **6.** Favoring the adoption of silver as a standard of currency. **7.** Of or constituting a 25th anniversary. *—v.* **-vered, -ver•ing, -vers.** *—tr.* **1.** To cover, plate, or adorn with silver or a similar lustrous substance. **2.** To give a silver color to. **3.** To coat (photographic paper) with a film of silver nitrate or other silver salt. *—intr.* To become silvery. [ME < OE *siolfor, seolfor*, prob. ult. < Akkadian *ṣarpu*, refined silver < *ṣarāpu*, to smelt, refine.]

silver age *n.* A period of history secondary in achievement to that of a golden age.

sil•ver•back (sĭl′vər-băk′) *n.* A mature male gorilla having silvery white hair across the back.

sil•ver•bell tree (sĭl′vər-bĕl′) *n.* Any of several trees or shrubs of the genus *Halesia*, esp. *H. carolina* of the southeast United States, having drooping, bell-shaped white flowers.

sil•ver•ber•ry (sĭl′vər-bĕr′ē) *n.* **1.** A northeast North Amer-

silk-cotton tree
Ceiba pentandra

Beverly Sills

silo

ă pat, ā pay, âr care, ä father, ĕ pet, ē be, ĭ pit, ī pie, îr pier, ŏ pot, ō toe, ô paw, oi boy, ou out, o͝o took, o͞o boot, ŭ cut, ûr urge, th thin, *th* this, hw which, zh vision, ə about, item

Stress marks: ′ (primary); ′ (secondary), as in dictionary (dĭk′shə-nĕr′ē)

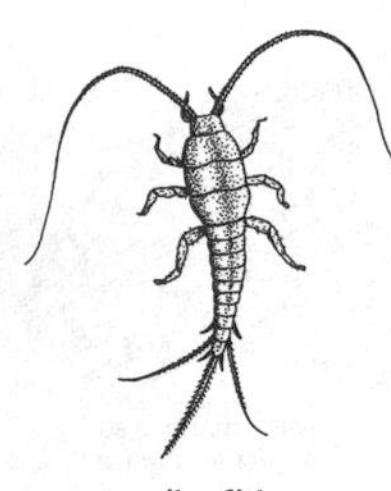
silverfish
Lepisma saccharina

Neil Simon

ican shrub *(Elaeagnus commutata)* having silvery flowers, leaves, and berries. **2.** See **oleaster.**

silver bromide *n.* A pale yellow crystalline compound, AgBr, that blackens on exposure to light and is used in photographic emulsions.

silver certificate *n.* A bill formerly issued as legal tender by the U.S. government in representation of deposited silver bullion.

silver chloride *n.* A white granular powder, AgCl, that turns dark on exposure to light and is used in photographic emulsions, photometry, and silver plating.

sil•ver•fish (sĭl′vər-fĭsh′) *n., pl.* **silverfish** or **-fish•es. 1.** Any of various fishes having silvery scales. **2.** A small silvery or gray bristletail *(Lepisma saccharina)* that feeds on the starchy material in bookbindings, wallpaper, clothing, and food.

silver fox *n.* **1.** A melanisitc red fox having black fur tipped with white. **2.** This fur, esp. as an article of clothing.

silver hake *n.* A marine food fish *(Merluccius bilinearis)* with silvery scales, common in American Atlantic coastal waters.

silver iodide *n.* A pale yellow odorless powder, AgI, that darkens on exposure to light and is used in photographic emulsions and medicine, esp. as an antiseptic.

silver lining *n.* A hopeful or cheerful prospect in the midst of trouble. [From the proverb "Every cloud has a silver lining."]

silver maple *n.* **1.** A North American deciduous tree *(Acer saccharinum)* having palmate leaves that are silvery below and light green above. **2.** The hard brittle wood of this tree.

sil•vern (sĭl′vərn) *adj.* **1.** Composed of silver. **2.** Resembling silver; silvery. [ME, alteration (influenced by *silver*, silver) of OE *silfren* < *siolfor*. See SILVER.]

silver nitrate *n.* A poisonous colorless crystalline compound, $AgNO_3$, that turns grayish black when exposed to light in the presence of organic matter and is used in manufacturing photographic film and in medicine as a cautery.

silver perch *n.* Any of various silvery fishes resembling perch.

silver plate *n.* **1.** A coating or plating of silver. **2.** Tableware, such as flatware, made of or coated with silver.

sil•ver-plate (sĭl′vər-plāt′) *tr.v.* **-plat•ed, -plat•ing, -plates.** To coat (an object) with a thin layer of silver, esp. by electroplating.

sil•ver•point (sĭl′vər-point′) *n.* **1.** A technique of drawing on specially prepared paper with a silver-tipped instrument. **2.** A drawing made by use of this technique.

silver protein *n.* A colloidal preparation of silver oxide and protein, usu. gelatin or albumin, used as an antibacterial agent.

silver screen *n.* See **screen** 6. [From a type of movie screen covered with silver-colored metallic paint.]

sil•ver•side (sĭl′vər-sīd′) also **sil•ver•sides** (-sīdz′) *n.* Any of various chiefly marine fishes of the family Atherinidae, characteristically having a broad silvery band along each side and including the grunion.

sil•ver•smith (sĭl′vər-smĭth′) *n.* One that makes, repairs, or replates articles of silver.

silver standard *n.* A monetary standard under which a specified quantity of silver constitutes the basic unit of currency.

Sil•ver Star (sĭl′vər) *n.* A U.S. military decoration awarded for gallantry.

sil•ver-tongued (sĭl′vər-tŭngd′) *adj.* Having or exhibiting the power of fluent and persuasive speech; eloquent.

sil•ver•ware (sĭl′vər-wâr′) *n.* **1.** Silver or silver-plated hollowware and flatware. **2.** Metal eating and serving utensils.

sil•ver•weed (sĭl′vər-wēd′) *n.* A stoloniferous plant *(Potentilla anserina)* having pinnate leaves that are silvery beneath.

sil•ver•y (sĭl′və-rē) *adj.* **1.** Containing or coated with silver. **2.** Resembling silver in color or luster. **3.** Having a clear, softly resonant sound: *a silvery laugh.* **—sil′ver•i•ness** *n.*

sil•vex (sĭl′vĕks′) *n.* A solid toxic selective herbicide, $C_9H_7O_3Cl_3$, used primarily against woody plants. [Prob. Lat. *silva*, forest + EX(TERMINATOR).]

sil•vi•cul•ture (sĭl′vĭ-kŭl′chər) *n.* The care and cultivation of forest trees; forestry. [Lat. *silva*, forest + CULTURE.] **—sil′vi•cul′tur•al** *adj.* **—sil′vi•cul′tur•ist** *n.*

si•ma (sī′mə) *n.* The lower layer of the earth's outer crust that underlies the sial and is rich in silica, iron, and magnesium. [SI(LICA) + MA(GNESIUM).]

Sim•chat To•rah (sēm-KHät′ tô-rä′) also **Sim•chas To•rah** (sĭm′KHəs tôr′ə, tōr′ə) *n. Judaism.* A festival celebrating the Torah and the completion of the year's reading cycle and its new beginning, observed on the 22nd or 23rd day of Tishri. [Heb. *śimḥat tôrâ*, rejoicing over the Law, Simchas Torah : *śimḥat*, inflectional form of *śimḥâ*, joy, merriment (< *śāmaḥ*, to rejoice) + *tôrâ*, torah.]

Sim•coe (sĭm′kō), **Lake.** A lake of SE Ontario, Canada, between Georgian Bay and Lake Ontario.

Si•me•non (sē-mə-nôN′), **Georges Joseph Christian.** 1903–89. Belgian-born French writer known esp. for his detective novels featuring Inspector Maigret.

Sim•e•on[1] (sĭm′ē-ən). In the Bible, a son of Jacob and Leah and the forebear of one of the tribes of Israel.

Sim•e•on[2]. In the Bible, the devout Jew who proclaimed the Nunc Dimittis while holding the infant Jesus.

Simeon Sty•li•tes (stī-lī′tēz), Saint. A.D. 390?–459. Syrian Christian ascetic who spent 30 years atop a column.

Sim•fer•o•pol (sĭm′fə-rō′pəl, syĭm-fyə-rô′-). A city of S Ukraine in the S Crimea NE of Sevastopol. Pop. 331,000.

sim•i•an (sĭm′ē-ən) *adj.* Relating to, characteristic of, or resembling an ape or a monkey. *—n.* An ape or a monkey. [< Lat. *sīmia*, ape, prob. < *sīmus*, snub-nosed < Gk. *simos*.]

sim•i•lar (sĭm′ə-lər) *adj.* **1.** Related in appearance or nature; alike though not identical. **2.** *Math.* Having corresponding angles equal and corresponding line segments proportional. Used of geometric figures: *similar triangles.* [Fr. *similaire* < Lat. *similis*, like. See **sem-**[1]*.] **—sim′i•lar•ly** *adv.*

sim•i•lar•i•ty (sĭm′ə-lăr′ĭ-tē) *n., pl.* **-ties. 1.** The quality or condition of being similar; resemblance. See Syns at **likeness. 2.** A corresponding aspect or feature; an equivalence.

sim•i•le (sĭm′ə-lē) *n.* A figure of speech in which two essentially unlike things are explicitly compared, usu. by means of *like* or *as*, as in "*So are you to my thoughts as food to life*" (Shakespeare). [ME < Lat. < neut. of *similis*, like. See SIMILAR.]

si•mil•i•tude (sĭ-mĭl′ĭ-to͞od′, -tyo͞od′) *n.* **1.** Similarity; resemblance. See Syns at **likeness. 2.a.** One closely resembling another; a counterpart. **b.** A perceptible likeness. **3.** *Archaic.* A simile, an allegory, or a parable. [ME < OFr. < Lat. *similitūdō* < *similis*, like. See SIMILAR.]

Si•mi Valley (sē′mē, sĭm′ē). A city of S CA, a suburb of Los Angeles. Pop. 100,217.

Sim•men•tal also **Sim•men•thal** (zĭm′ən-täl′) *n.* Any of a Swiss breed of large muscular cattle, having a reddish body and a white face and raised for meat and milk. [After *Simmental*, a valley of the Simme R. in SW-central Switzerland.]

sim•mer (sĭm′ər) *v.* **-mered, -mer•ing, -mers.** *—intr.* **1.** To be cooked gently or remain just at or below the boiling point. **2.a.** To be filled with pent-up emotion; seethe. **b.** To be in a state of gentle ferment. *—tr.* **1.** To cook (food) gently in a liquid just at or below the boiling point. **2.** To keep (a liquid) near or just below the boiling point. See Syns at **boil**[1]. *—n.* The state or process of simmering. ***—phrasal verb.* simmer down.** To become calm after excitement or anger. [Alteration of ME *simpire*, to simmer, prob. of imit. orig.]

sim•nel (sĭm′nəl) *n. Chiefly British.* **1.** A crisp bread made of fine wheat flour. **2.** A rich fruitcake eaten at mid-Lent, Easter, and Christmas. [ME < OFr. *siminel* < Med.Lat. *siminellus*, ult. < Lat. *simila*, fine flour, prob. of Semitic orig.]

si•mo•le•on (sĭ-mō′lē-ən) *n. Slang.* A dollar. [?]

Si•mon (sē-mōN′), **Claude Eugene Henri.** b. 1913. French writer who won the 1985 Nobel Prize for literature.

Si•mon (sī′mən), **Herbert Alexander.** b. 1916. Amer. economist who won a 1978 Nobel Prize.

Simon, Neil. b. 1927. Amer. playwright whose comedies include *The Odd Couple* (1965).

si•mo•ni•ac (sĭ-mō′nē-ăk′, sĭ-) *n.* One who practices simony. **—si•mo′ni•ac′, si′mo•ni′a•cal** (sī′mə-nī′ə-kəl, sĭm′ə-) *adj.* **—si′mo•ni′a•cal•ly** *adv.*

Si•mon•i•des of Ce•os (sĭ-mŏn′ĭ-dēz; sē′ŏs). 556?–468? B.C. Greek lyric poet known esp. for his elegies.

Simon Le•gree (lə-grē′) *n.* A brutal taskmaster. [After *Simon Legree*, a slave dealer in *Uncle Tom's Cabin.*]

si•mon-pure (sī′mən-pyo͝or′) *adj.* **1.** Genuinely and thoroughly pure. **2.** Superficially or hypocritically virtuous. [< *the real Simon Pure*, after *Simon Pure* in *A Bold Stroke for a Wife*, a play by Susannah Centlivre (1669–1723).]

si•mo•ny (sī′mə-nē, sĭm′ə-) *n.* The buying or selling of ecclesiastical pardons, offices, or emoluments. [ME *simonie* < OFr. < LLat. *simōnia*, after *Simon* Magus, a sorcerer who tried to buy spiritual powers from the Apostle Peter (Acts 8:9–24).] **—si′mo•nist** *n.*

Simon Ze•lo•tes (zē-lō′tēz) or **Simon the Ca•naan•ite** (kā′nə-nīt′). 1st cent. A.D. In the Bible, one of the 12 Apostles; thought to have been a member of the Zealots.

si•moom (sĭ-mo͞om′) also **si•moon** (-mo͞on′) *n.* A strong, hot, sand-laden wind of the Sahara and Arabian deserts. [Ar. *samūm*, poisonous, simoom < *samma*, to poison < Aram. *sammā*, drug, poison.]

simp (sĭmp) *n. Slang.* One who is regarded as simple or foolish. [Short for SIMPLETON.]

sim•pa•ti•co (sĭm-pä′tĭ-kō′, -păt′ĭ-) *adj.* **1.** Of like mind or temperament; compatible. **2.** Having attractive qualities; pleasing. [Ital. *simpatico* (< *simpatia*, sympathy) or Sp. *simpático* (< *simpatía*, sympathy), both < Lat. *sympathīa*. See SYMPATHY.]

sim•per (sĭm′pər) *v.* **-pered, -per•ing, -pers.** *—intr.* To smile in a silly, self-conscious, often coy manner. *—tr.* To utter or express with a simper. *—n.* A silly, self-conscious, often coy smile. [Perh. of Scand. orig.] **—sim′per•er** *n.*

sim•ple (sĭm′pəl) *adj.* **-pler, -plest. 1.** Having or composed of only one thing, element, or part. See Syns at **pure. 2.** Not involved or complicated; easy. See Syns at **easy. 3.** Being without additions or modifications; mere: *a simple "no."* **4.** Having little or no ornamentation; not embellished or adorned. **5.** Not elaborate, elegant, or luxurious. **6.** Unassuming or unpretentious; not affected. **7.a.** Having or manifesting little sense or intelligence. **b.** Uneducated; ignorant. **c.** Unworldly or unsophisticated. See Syns at **naive. 8.** Not guileful or deceitful; sincere. **9.** Humble or lowly in condition or rank. **10.** Ordinary or common. **11.a.** Being a fundamental or rudimentary element; basic. **b.** Not important or significant; trivial. **12.** *Biol.* Having no divisions or branches; not compound. **13.** *Mus.* Being without figuration or elaboration: *a simple tone.* — *n.* **1.** A single component of a complex, esp. one that is unanalyzable. **2.** A fool; a simpleton. **3.** A person of humble birth or condition. **4.** A medicinal plant or the medicine obtained from it. [ME < OFr. < Lat. *simplus*; see **sem-¹***, and < *simplex*; see SIMPLEX.] — **sim′ple·ness** *n.*

simple closed curve *n. Math.* A curve, such as a circle, that is closed and does not intersect itself.

simple equation *n. Math.* A linear equation.

simple fraction *n. Math.* A fraction in which both the numerator and the denominator are whole numbers.

simple fracture *n.* A bone fracture that causes little or no damage to the surrounding soft tissues.

simple interest *n.* Interest paid only on the original principal.

simple machine *n.* A simple device, such as a lever, a pulley, or an inclined plane; a machine.

sim·ple-mind·ed or **sim·ple·mind·ed** (sĭm′pəl-mīn′dĭd) *adj.* **1.** Lacking in subtlety or sophistication; naive. **2.** Stupid or silly; foolish. **3.** Mentally impaired. — **sim′ple-mind′ed·ly** *adv.* — **sim′ple-mind′ed·ness** *n.*

simple protein *n.* A protein, such as a globulin or histone, that yields only amino acids upon hydrolysis.

simple sentence *n.* A sentence having no coordinate or subordinate clauses, as *The cat purred.*

Sim·ple Si·mon (sĭm′pəl sī′mən) *n.* A foolish fellow; a simpleton. [After *Simple Simon*, a character in a nursery rhyme.]

simple sugar *n.* See **monosaccharide.**

sim·ple·ton (sĭm′pəl-tən) *n.* A person who is felt to be deficient in judgment, good sense, or intelligence; a fool. [SIMPLE + *-ton*, as in surnames such as *Chesterton*.]

sim·plex (sĭm′plĕks′) *adj.* **1.** Consisting of or marked by only one part or element. **2.** Of or relating to a telecommunications system in which only one message can be sent in either direction at one time. — *n., pl.* **-plex·es** or **-pli·ces** (-plĭ-sēz′). **1.** *Math.* A Euclidean geometric spatial element having the minimum number of boundary points, such as a line segment in one-dimensional space. **2.** *Ling.* A word that has no affixes and is not part of a compound; a simple word. [Lat., simple. See **sem-¹***.]

sim·plic·i·ty (sĭm-plĭs′ĭ-tē) *n., pl.* **-ties. 1.** The property, condition, or quality of being simple or uncombined. **2.** Absence of luxury or showiness; plainness. **3.** Absence of affectation or pretense. **4.a.** Lack of sophistication or subtlety; naiveté. **b.** Lack of good sense or intelligence; foolishness. **5.a.** Clarity of expression. **b.** Austerity in embellishment. [ME *simplicite* < OFr. < Lat. *simplicitās* < *simplex*, *simplic-*, simple. See **sem-¹***.]

sim·pli·fy (sĭm′plə-fī′) *tr.v.* **-fied, -fy·ing, -fies.** To make simple or simpler, as: **a.** To reduce in complexity or extent. **b.** To reduce to fundamental parts. **c.** To make easier to understand. [Fr. *simplifier* < OFr. < Med.Lat. *simplificāre* : Lat. *simplus*, simple; see SIMPLE + Lat. *-ficāre*, -fy.] — **sim′pli·fi·ca′tion** (-fĭ-kā′shən) *n.* — **sim′pli·fi′er** *n.*

sim·plism (sĭm′plĭz′əm) *n.* The tendency to oversimplify an issue or a problem by ignoring complexities or complications. — **sim·plis′tic** (sĭm-plĭs′tĭk) *adj.* — **sim·plis′ti·cal·ly** *adv.*

Sim·plon Pass (sĭm′plŏn′, săN-plôN′). A pass, 2,010 m (6,590 ft), between the Lepontine and Pennine Alps in S Switzerland.

sim·ply (sĭm′plē) *adv.* **1.a.** In a plain and unadorned way: *dresses simply.* **b.** In an unambiguous way; clearly. **2.** Not wisely or sensibly; foolishly. **3.** Merely; only: *simply a matter of time.* **4.** Absolutely; altogether: *simply delicious.* **5.** Frankly; candidly: *You are, quite simply, the best one for the job.*

Simp·son (sĭmp′sən), **O(renthal) J(ames).** b. 1947. Amer. football player; first to rush 2,000 yards in a season.

Simpson Desert. A barren uninhabited desert region of central Australia.

Sims·bur·y (sĭmz′bĕr′ē, -bə-rē). A town of N CT NW of Hartford; incorp. 1670. Pop. 22,023.

sim·u·la·cre (sĭm′yə-lā′kər, -lăk′ər) *n. Archaic.* A simulacrum. [ME < OFr. < Lat. *simulācrum.* See SIMULACRUM.]

sim·u·la·crum (sĭm′yə-lā′krəm, -lăk′rəm) *n., pl.* **-la·cra** (-lā′krə, -lăk′rə). **1.** An image or a representation. **2.** An unreal or vague semblance. [Lat. *simulācrum* (*simulāre*, to simulate; see SIMULATE) + *-crum*, n. suff.]

sim·u·lar (sĭm′yə-lər, -lär′) *Archaic.* — *n.* One that simulates; a pretender. — *adj.* Simulated; sham. [< Lat. *simulāre*, to simulate. See SIMULATE.]

sim·u·late (sĭm′yə-lāt′) *tr.v.* **-lat·ed, -lat·ing, -lates. 1.a.** To have or take on the appearance, form, or sound of; imitate. **b.** To make in imitation of or as a substitute for. See Syns at **imitate. 2.** To make a pretense of; feign: *simulate interest.* **3.** To create a representation or model of (a physical system, for example). [Lat. *simulāre*, *simulāt-* < *similis*, like. See SIMILAR.] — **sim′u·la′tive** *adj.*

sim·u·lat·ed (sĭm′yə-lā′tĭd) *adj.* Made in resemblance of or as a substitute for another. See Syns at **artificial.**

sim·u·la·tion (sĭm′yə-lā′shən) *n.* **1.** The act or process of simulating. **2.** An imitation; a sham. **3.** Assumption of a false appearance. **4.a.** Imitation or representation, as of a potential situation. **b.** Representation of the operation or features of one process or system through the use of another.

sim·u·la·tor (sĭm′yə-lā′tər) *n.* One that simulates, esp. an apparatus that generates test conditions approximating actual or operational conditions.

si·mul·cast (sī′məl-kăst′, sĭm′əl-) *v.* **-cast·ed, -cast·ing, -casts.** — *intr.* To broadcast simultaneously by FM and AM radio or by radio and television. — *tr.* To broadcast (a program) by simulcasting. — *n.* A broadcast so transmitted.

si·mul·ta·ne·ous (sī′məl-tā′nē-əs, sĭm′əl-) *adj.* **1.** Happening, existing, or done at the same time. **2.** *Math.* Containing variables for which there are values that can satisfy all the equations: *simultaneous equations.* [Lat. *simul*, at the same time; see **sem-¹*** + E. *-taneous*, as in INSTANTANEOUS.] — **si′mul·ta′ne·ous·ly** *adv.* — **si′mul·ta′ne·ous·ness, si′mul·ta·ne′i·ty** (-tə-nē′ĭ-tē, -nā′-) *n.*

sin¹ (sĭn) *n.* **1.** A transgression of a religious or moral law, esp. when deliberate. **2.** *Theol.* **a.** Deliberate disobedience to the known will of God. **b.** A condition of estrangement from God resulting from such disobedience. **3.** Something regarded as shameful, deplorable, or utterly wrong. — *intr.v.* **sinned, sin·ning, sins. 1.** To violate a religious or moral law. **2.** To commit an offense or a violation. [ME *sinne* < OE *synn.* See **es-***.]

sin² (sēn, sĭn) *n.* The 21st letter of the Hebrew alphabet. [Heb. *śîn.*]

sin³ *abbr. Math.* Sine.

Si·nai (sī′nī′), **Mount.** A mountain, c. 2,288 m (7,500 ft), of the S-central Sinai Peninsula; thought to be the biblical peak on which Moses received the Ten Commandments.

Sinai Peninsula. A peninsula linking SW Asia with NE Africa at the N end of the Red Sea between the Gulf of Suez and the Gulf of Aqaba; occupied by Israel in 1956 and from 1967 to 1982, when it was returned to Egyptian control.

sin·an·thro·pus (sī-năn′thrə-pəs, sĭ-, sī′năn-thrō′pəs, sĭn′-ăn-) *n.* See **Peking man.** [NLat. *Sinanthropus*, former genus name : SINO- + Gk. *anthrōpos*, human being.]

sin·a·pism (sĭn′ə-pĭz′əm) *n.* See **mustard plaster.** [Fr. *sinapisme* < LLat. *sinăpismus* < Gk. *sinapismos*, use of a mustard plaster < *sinapizein*, to apply a mustard plaster < *sinapi*, mustard.]

Si·na·tra (sə-nä′trə), **Francis Albert ("Frank").** b. 1915. Amer. singer and actor known for his mellifluous voice.

since (sĭns) *adv.* **1.** From then until now or between then and now: *They left and haven't been here since.* **2.** Before now; ago: *long since forgotten.* **3.** After some point in the past; at a subsequent time: *My friend has since moved.* — *prep.* **1.** Continuously from: *friends since childhood.* **2.** Intermittently from: *She's been skiing since childhood.* — *conj.* **1.** During the period subsequent to the time when: *He hasn't been home since he graduated.* **2.** Continuously from the time when: *They've been friends ever since they were in school.* **3.** Inasmuch as; because: *Since you're not interested, I won't tell you.* [ME *sinnes*, contraction of *sithenes* : *sithen*, since (< OE *siththan* : *sīth*, after + *than*, var. of *thām*, dative of *thæt*, that; see THAT) + *-es*, adv. suff.; see *-s*³.]

sin·cere (sĭn-sîr′) *adj.* **-cer·er, -cer·est. 1.** Not feigned or affected; genuine: *sincere rage.* **2.** Having no hypocrisy or pretense; true. **3.** *Archaic.* Pure; unadulterated. [Lat. *sincērus.* See **ker-²***.] — **sin·cere′ly** *adv.* — **sin·cere′ness** *n.*

sin·cer·i·ty (sĭn-sĕr′ĭ-tē) *n.* The quality or condition of being sincere; genuineness, honesty, and freedom from duplicity.

sin·ci·put (sĭn′sə-pət) *n., pl.* **sin·ci·puts** or **sin·cip·i·ta** (sĭn-sĭp′ĭ-tə). **1.** The upper half of the cranium, esp. the anterior portion above and including the forehead. **2.** The forehead. [Lat. : *sēmi-*, semi- + *caput*, head; see **kaput-***.] — **sin·cip′i·tal** (-sĭp′ĭ-tl) *adj.*

Sin·clair (sĭn-klâr′, sĭng-), **Harry Ford.** 1876–1956. Amer. oil executive involved in the Teapot Dome scandal (1923).

Sinclair, Upton Beall. 1878–1968. Amer. writer whose novels include *The Jungle* (1906).

Sind (sĭnd). A historical region of S Pakistan along the lower Indus R.; part of Pakistan since 1947.

Sin·dhi (sĭn′dē) *n., pl.* **Sindhi** or **-dhis. 1.** A member of the predominantly Muslim people of Sind. **2.** The Indic language of Sind. [Ar. *sindīy* < SIND.]

sine (sīn) *n. Math.* **1.** The ordinate of the endpoint of an arc of a unit circle centered at the origin of a Cartesian coordinate system, the arc being of length x and subtending a positive or negative angle. **2.** In a right triangle, the ratio of the length of the side opposite an acute angle to the length of the hypotenuse. [Med.Lat. *sinus* (mistransl. of Ar. *jayb*, sine, as if *jayb*, fold in a garment) < Lat., curve, fold.]

si·ne·cure (sī′nĭ-kyo͝or′, sĭn′ĭ-) *n.* **1.** A position or an office that requires little or no work but provides a salary. **2.** *Archaic.* An ecclesiastical benefice not attached to the spiritual duties of a parish. [< Med.Lat. *(beneficium) sine cūrā*, (benefice) without cure (of souls) : Lat. *sine*, without + Lat. *cūrā*, ablative of *cūra*, care; see CURE.] — **si′ne·cur·ism** *n.* — **si′ne·cur′ist** *n.*

O.J. Simpson

Sinai Peninsula
Aerial view from Gemini XI spacecraft, 1966

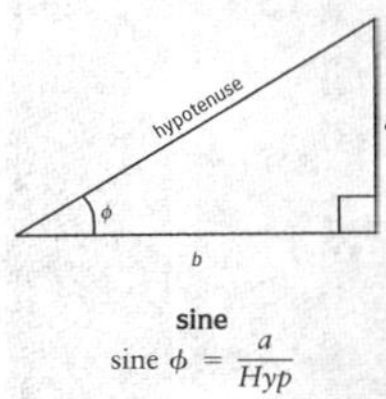

sine
sine $\phi = \dfrac{a}{Hyp}$

ă pat	oi boy
ā pay	ou out
âr care	o͝o took
ä father	o͞o boot
ĕ pet	ŭ cut
ē be	ûr urge
ĭ pit	th thin
ī pie	*th* this
îr pier	hw which
ŏ pot	zh vision
ō toe	ə about, item
ô paw	

Stress marks:
′ (primary);
′ (secondary), as in dictionary (dĭk′shə-nĕr′ē)

sine curve *n. Math.* The graph of the equation $y = \sin x$.

si•ne di•e (sī′nī dī′ē, sĭn′ā dē′ā′) *adv.* With no day fixed for a future meeting; indefinitely. [Med.Lat. : Lat. *sine*, without + Lat. *diē*, ablative of *diēs*, day.]

si•ne pro•le (sī′nī prō′lē, sĭn′ā) *adv. Law.* Without offspring. [NLat. *sine prōlē*.]

si•ne qua non (sĭn′ĭ kwä nŏn′, nōn′, sī′nĭ, kwā) *n.* An essential element or condition. [LLat. *sine quā (causā) nōn*, without which (cause) not.]

sin•ew (sĭn′yo͞o) *n.* **1.** A tendon. **2.** Vigorous strength; muscular power. **3.** The source or mainstay of vitality and strength. Often used in the plural. — *tr.v.* **-ewed, -ew•ing, -ews.** To strengthen with or as if with sinews. [ME *sinewe* < OE *sinewe*, oblique form of *seonu, sinu*.]

sine wave *n. Phys.* A waveform with deviation that can be graphically expressed as the sine curve.

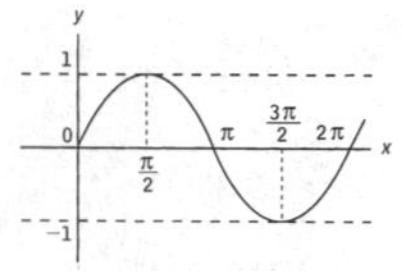

sine curve
$y = \sin x$

sin•ew•y (sĭn′yo͞o-ē) *adj.* **1.a.** Consisting of or resembling sinews. **b.** Having many sinews; stringy and tough: *a sinewy cut of beef.* **2.** Lean and muscular. See Syns at **muscular. 3.** Strong and vigorous: *sinewy prose.*

sin•fo•ni•a (sĭn-fō′nē-ə) *n. Mus.* **1.** An instrumental composition serving as an overture, as to an opera, esp. in the 18th century. **2.** A symphonic composition. [Ital. < Lat. *symphōnia*, group of musicians. See SYMPHONY.]

sin•fo•niet•ta (sĭn′fə-nyĕt′ə, -fō-) *n. Mus.* **1.** A symphony that is shorter than usual or calls for fewer than the usual number of instruments. **2.** A small symphony orchestra, esp. one consisting of stringed instruments only. [Ital., dim. of *sinfonia*, sinfonia. See SINFONIA.]

sin•ful (sĭn′fəl) *adj.* Marked by or full of sin; wicked. **— sin′ful•ly** *adv.* **— sin′ful•ness** *n.*

sing (sĭng) *v.* **sang** (săng) or **sung** (sŭng), **sung, sing•ing, sings.** — *intr.* **1.** *Mus.* **a.** To utter words or sounds in musical tones. **b.** To vocalize songs or selections. **c.** To perform songs or selections as a trained or professional singer. **d.** To produce sounds when played. **2.a.** To make melodious sounds: *birds singing.* **b.** To give or have the effect of melody; lilt. **3.** To make a high whining, humming, or whistling sound. **4.** To be filled with a buzzing or ringing sound. **5.a.** To proclaim or extol something in verse. **b.** To write poetry. **6.** *Slang.* To give information or evidence against someone. — *tr.* **1.** *Mus.* **a.** To produce the musical sound of: *sang a song.* **b.** To utter with musical inflections: *sang "hello."* **c.** To bring to a specified state by singing: *sang the baby to sleep.* **2.** To intone or chant. **3.** To proclaim or extol, esp. in verse: *sang praises.* — *n. Mus.* A gathering of people for group singing. **— *phrasal verb.* sing out.** To call out loudly. [ME *singen* < OE *singan*. See **seng^{w}h-***.] **— sing′a•ble** *adj.*

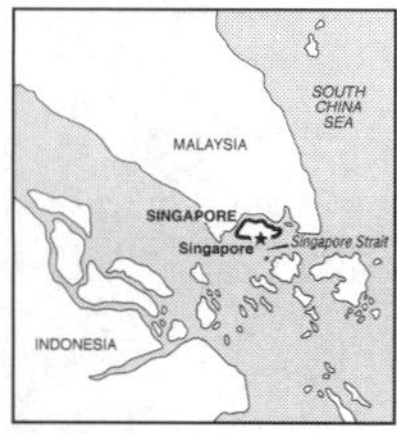

Singapore

sing. *abbr. Gram.* Singular.

sing-a•long (sĭng′ə-lông′, -lŏng′) *n. Mus.* **1.** A casual gathering for group singing; a songfest. **2.** A spontaneous group singing, as by an audience at a performance.

Sin•ga•pore (sĭng′gə-pôr′, -pōr′, sĭng′ə-). A country of SE Asia comprising **Singapore Island** and adjacent smaller islands; under British control from 1824 until 1965. The city of **Singapore** is the cap. Pop. 2,529,100. **— Sin′ga•por′e•an** *adj. & n.*

Singapore Strait. A strait off the S end of the Malay Peninsula between Singapore I. and the Riau Archipelago connecting the Strait of Malacca with the South China Sea.

singe (sĭnj) *tr.v.* **singed, singe•ing, sing•es. 1.** To burn superficially; scorch. **2.** To burn off the feathers or bristles of (a carcass of a bird or an animal) by subjecting briefly to flame. **3.** To burn the ends of (hair, for example). **4.** To burn the nap from (cloth) in manufacturing. — *n.* A slight or surface burn; a scorch. [ME *sengen* < OE *sengan*.]

sing•er¹ (sĭng′ər) *n.* **1.** *Mus.* One who sings, esp. a trained or professional vocalist. **2.** A poet. **3.** A songbird.

sing•er² (sĭn′jər) *n.* One that singes.

Isaac Bashevis Singer
Photographed in 1987

Sing•er (sĭng′ər), **Isaac Bashevis.** 1904–91. Polish-born writer who won the 1978 Nobel Prize for literature.

Singer, Isaac Merritt. 1811–75. Amer. inventor and manufacturer who patented (1851) a sewing machine.

Sin•gha•lese (sĭng′gə-lēz′, -lēs′) or **Sin•ha•lese** (sĭn′hə-) — *n., pl.* **Singhalese** or **Sinhalese. 1.** A member of a people constituting the majority of the population of Sri Lanka. **2.** The Indic language of the Singhalese that is the chief language of Sri Lanka. — *adj.* Of or relating to Sri Lanka, the Singhalese, or their language or culture. [Skt. *Siṁhalam*, Sri Lanka + -ESE.]

sin•gle (sĭng′gəl) *adj.* **1.** Not accompanied by another or others; solitary. **2.a.** Consisting of one part, aspect, or section. **b.** Having the same application for all; uniform. **c.** Consisting of one in number. **3.** Not divided; unbroken. **4.a.** Separate from others; individual and distinct. **b.** Having individual opponents; involving two individuals only. **5.a.** Honest; undisguised: *a single adoration.* **b.** Wholly attentive: *Watch with a single eye.* **6.** Designed to accommodate one person. **7.a.** Unmarried. **b.** Lacking a partner: *a single parent.* **c.** Relating to the unmarried state. **d.** Of or relating to celibacy. **8.** *Bot.* Having only one rank or row of petals. — *n.* **1.** One that is separate and individual. **2.** An accommodation for one person, as in a hotel. **3.a.** An unmarried person. **b. singles.** Unmarried persons considered as a group. **4.** A one-dollar bill. **5.** A phonograph record, esp. a forty-five, with one song on each side. **6.** *Baseball.* A hit by which a batter reaches first base safely; a one-base hit. **7.** *Sports.* **a.** A hit for one run in cricket. **b.** A golf match between two players. **c.** A tennis or badminton match between two players. Often used in the plural. — *v.* **-gled, -gling, -gles.** — *tr.* **1.** To choose or distinguish from others. Often used with *out*: *singled her out.* **2.** *Baseball.* **a.** To cause (a base runner) to score or advance by making a one-base hit. **b.** To cause the scoring of (a run) by a one-base hit. — *intr. Baseball.* To make a single. [ME *sengle* < OFr. < Lat. *singulus*. See **sem-¹***.] **— sin′gle•ness** *n.*

single blind *n.* A testing procedure in which the administrators do not tell the subjects if they are being given a test treatment or a control treatment in order to avoid accidental bias in the results. **— sin′gle-blind′** (sĭng′gəl-blīnd′) *adj.*

single bond *n.* A covalent bond in which one electron pair is shared by two atoms.

sin•gle-breast•ed (sĭng′gəl-brĕs′tĭd) *adj.* Closing with a narrow overlap and fastened down the front with a single row of buttons: *a single-breasted suit.*

single cross *n. Genet.* The hybrid of two inbred lines that can be represented as AB, the product of the cross A × B, where A and B represent inbred lines.

single entry *n. Accounting.* A system of bookkeeping in which a business keeps only a single account showing amounts due and amounts owed.

sin•gle-fam•i•ly (sĭng′gəl-făm′ə-lē, -făm′lē) *adj.* Relating to or being a dwelling designed for one family only.

single file *n.* A line of people, animals, or things standing or moving one behind the other. **— single file** *adv.*

sin•gle-foot (sĭng′gəl-fo͝ot′) *n.* A rapid gait of a horse in which each foot strikes the ground separately; the rack. No longer in technical use. — *intr.v.* **-foot•ed, -foot•ing, -foots.** To go at the single-foot. **— sin′gle-foot′er** *n.*

sin•gle-hand (sĭng′gəl-hănd′) *tr.v.* **-hand•ed, -hand•ing, -hands.** *Naut.* To sail (a boat) without the help of others. **— sin′gle-hand′er** *n.*

sin•gle-hand•ed (sĭng′gəl-hăn′dĭd) *adj.* **1.** Working or done without help; unassisted. **2.** Intended for use with one hand. **3.** Having or using only one hand. — *adv.* In a single-handed manner. **— sin′gle-hand′ed•ness** *n.*

sin•gle-heart•ed (sĭng′gəl-här′tĭd) *adj.* Sincerely dedicated. **— sin′gle-heart′ed•ness** *n.*

single knot *n.* See **overhand knot.**

sin•gle-mind•ed (sĭng′gəl-mīn′dĭd) *adj.* **1.** Having one overriding purpose. **2.** Steadfast; resolute. **— sin′gle-mind′ed•ness** *n.*

sin•gle-phase (sĭng′gəl-fāz′) *adj.* Producing, carrying, or powered by a single alternating voltage.

sin•gles bar (sĭng′gəlz) *n.* A bar for singles.

sin•gle-space (sĭng′gəl-spās′) *v.* **-spaced, -spac•ing, -spac•es.** — *tr.* To type or print (copy) with no blank line between lines. — *intr.* To type or print copy without line spaces.

single standard *n.* A set of principles with the same standard for all, esp. regarding the sexual behavior of men and women.

sin•gle•stick (sĭng′gəl-stĭk′) *n.* **1.** A one-handed fencing stick fitted with a hand guard. **2.** The art, sport, or exercise of fencing with such a stick.

sin•glet (sĭng′glĭt) *n.* **1.** *Chiefly British.* A man's jersey undershirt. **2.** *Phys.* A multiplet with a single member.

single tax *n.* A system by which all revenue is derived from a tax on one thing, esp. land.

sin•gle•ton (sĭng′gəl-tən) *n.* **1.** *Games.* A playing card that is the only one of its suit in a player's hand. **2.a.** An individual separate or distinct from two or more of its group. **b.** An offspring born alone. [< the name *Singleton*.]

sin•gle-track (sĭng′gəl-trăk′) *adj.* **1.** Having just one track. **2.** Lacking mental range or flexibility; one-track.

sin•gle•tree (sĭng′gəl-trē′) *n.* See **whiffletree.** [Alteration (influenced by DOUBLETREE) of SWINGLETREE.]

sin•gly (sĭng′glē) *adv.* **1.** Without the presence of others; alone. **2.** Without help; single-handed. **3.** One by one; individually.

sing•song (sĭng′sông′, -sŏng′) *n.* **1.** Verse characterized by mechanical regularity of rhythm and rhyme. **2.** A monotonously rising and falling inflection of the voice. — *adj.* Monotonous in vocal inflection or rhythm. **— sing′song′y** *adj.*

sing•spiel (sĭng′spēl′, zĭng′shpēl′) *n.* An 18th-century German musical comedy featuring folk songs interspersed with dialogue. [Ger. : *singen*, to sing (< MHGer. < OHGer. *singan*; see **seng^{w}h-***) + *Spiel*, play; see SPIEL.]

sin•gu•lar (sĭng′gyə-lər) *adj.* **1.** Being only one; individual. **2.** Being the only one of a kind; unique. **3.** Being beyond the ordinary or usual; remarkable. **4.** Deviating from the usual or expected; odd. See Syns at **strange. 5.** *Gram.* **a.** Of, relating to, or being a noun, pronoun, or adjective denoting a single person or thing or several entities considered as a single unit. **b.** Of, relating to, or being a verb expressing the action or state of a single subject. **6.** *Logic.* Of or relating to the specific as distinguished from the general; individual. — *n. Gram.* **1.** The singular number or a form designating it. **2.** A word in the singular. [ME *singuler* < OFr. < Lat. *singulāris* < *singulus*, single. See SINGLE.] — **sin′gu·lar·ly** *adv.* — **sin′gu·lar·ness** *n.*

sin·gu·lar·i·ty (sĭng′gyə-lăr′ĭ-tē) *n., pl.* **-ties. 1.** The quality or condition of being singular. **2.** A trait marking one as distinct from others; a peculiarity. **3.** Something uncommon or unusual. **4.** *Astrophys.* A point in space-time at which gravitational forces cause matter to have infinite density and infinitesimal volume. **5.** *Math.* A point at which the derivative does not exist for a given function of a real or complex variable but every neighborhood of which contains points for which the derivative exists.

sin·gu·lar·ize (sĭng′gyə-lə-rīz′) *tr.v.* **-ized, -iz·ing, -iz·es.** To make conspicuous; distinguish.

singular point *n. Math.* See **singularity** 5.

Sin·ha·lese (sĭn′hə-lēz′, -lēs′) *n. & adj.* Var. of **Singhalese.**

Si·ni·cism (sī′nĭ-sĭz′əm, sĭn′ĭ-) *n.* A custom or trait peculiar to the Chinese. [< *Sinic*, Chinese < Med.Lat. *Sīnicus* < LLat. *Sīnae*, the Chinese. See SINO–.]

Si·ni·cize (sī′nĭ-sīz′, sĭn′ĭ-) *tr.v.* **-cized, -ciz·ing, -ciz·es.** To make Chinese in character or to change or modify by Chinese influence. — **Si′ni·ci·za′tion** (-sĭ-zā′shən) *n.*

Si·ni·fy (sī′nə-fī′, sĭn′ə-) *tr.v.* **-fied, -fy·ing, -fies.** To Sinicize. [LLat. *Sīnae*, the Chinese; see SINO– + –FY.] — **Si′ni·fi·ca′tion** (-fĭ-kā′shən) *n.*

sin·is·ter (sĭn′ĭ-stər) *adj.* **1.** Suggesting or threatening evil. **2.** Presaging trouble; ominous: *sinister clouds.* **3.** Attended by or causing disaster or inauspicious circumstances. **4.** On the left side; left. **5.** *Her.* Located on or being the side of a shield on the wearer's left. [ME *sinistre*, unfavorable < OFr. < Lat. *sinister*, on the left, unlucky.] — **sin′is·ter·ly** *adv.* — **sin′is·ter·ness** *n.*

sin·is·tral (sĭn′ĭ-strəl, sĭ-nĭs′trəl) *adj.* **1.** Of or facing the left. **2.** Left-handed. **3.** *Zool.* Relating to or being a gastropod shell that has its aperture to the left when facing the observer with the apex upward. — **sin′is·tral·ly** *adv.*

sin·is·trorse (sĭn′ĭ-strôrs′) *adj.* Growing upward in a spiral that turns from right to left: *a sinistrorse vine.* [Lat. *sinistrōrsus*, turned toward the left < **sinistrōversus* : *sinistrō*, toward the left < ablative of *sinister*, left + *vorsus*, p.part. of *vortere*, var. of *vertere*, to turn. See **wer-**[2]***.**] — **sin′is·trorse′ly** *adv.*

sin·is·trous (sĭn′ĭ-strəs, sĭ-nĭs′trəs) *adj. Archaic.* Sinister; ill-omened. — **sin′is·trous·ly** *adv.*

Si·nit·ic (sī-nĭt′ĭk, sĭ-) *n.* The branch of Sino-Tibetan that comprises Chinese. — **Si·nit′ic** *adj.*

sink (sĭngk) *v.* **sank** (săngk) or **sunk** (sŭngk), **sunk, sink·ing, sinks.** — *intr.* **1.** To descend to the bottom; submerge. **2.a.** To fall or drop to a lower level, esp. slowly or in stages. **b.** To subside or settle gradually, as a massive structure. **3.** To appear to move downward, as the setting sun. **4.** To slope downward; incline. **5.** To pass into a specified condition: *sank into sleep.* **6.a.** To deteriorate in quality or condition. **b.** To diminish, as in value. **7.** To become weaker, quieter, or less forceful. **8.a.** To drop or fall slowly, as from weakness or fatigue. **b.** To feel great disappointment or discouragement. **9.** To seep or soak; penetrate. **10.** To make an impression; become felt or understood: *Her words sank in.* — *tr.* **1.** To cause to descend beneath a surface. **2.** To cause to drop or lower. **3.** To force into the ground. **4.** To dig or drill (a mine or well) in the earth. **5.** To occupy the full attention of; engross. **6.a.** To make weaker, quieter, or less forceful. **b.** To reduce in quantity or worth. **7.** To debase the nature of; degrade. **8.** To bring to a low or ruined state; defeat or destroy. **9.** To suppress or hide. **10.** *Informal.* To defeat, as in a game. **11.a.** To invest. **b.** To invest with no prospect of return. **12.** To pay off (a debt). **13.** *Sports.* To get (a ball) into a hole or basket. — *n.* **1.** A water basin with a drainpipe and generally a piped supply of water. **2.** A cesspool. **3.** A sinkhole. **4.** In thermodynamics, the part of a system that absorbs heat, or more generally, energy. **5.** A place regarded as wicked and corrupt. — ***idiom.* sink or swim.** *Informal.* To succeed or fail without alternative. [ME *sinken* < OE *sincan.*] — **sink′a·ble** *adj.*

sink·age (sĭng′kĭj) *n.* **1.** The process, amount, or degree of sinking. **2.** A sunken area; a depression.

sink·er (sĭng′kər) *n.* **1.** One that sinks, as a weight used for sinking fishing lines or nets. **2.** *Slang.* A doughnut.

sink·hole (sĭngk′hōl′) *n.* A surface depression communicating with a cave system, occurring in limestone regions and formed by collapse of a cavern roof or by solution.

Sin·kiang Ui·ghur or **Sin·kiang Ui·gur** (sĭn′kyăng′ wē′gər, shĭn′jyăng′). See **Xinjiang Uygur.**

sink·ing fund (sĭng′kĭng) *n. Accounting.* A fund accumulated to pay off a corporate or public debt.

sin·ner (sĭn′ər) *n.* **1.** One that sins. **2.** A scamp.

Sinn Fein (shĭn fān′, fĕ′ĭn) *n.* An Irish society founded about 1905 to promote political and economic independence from England, unification of Ireland, and Irish cultural renewal, now the political branch of the Irish Republican Army. [Ir. Gael. *sinn féin* : *sinn*, we (< MIr. < OIr.) + *féin*, self (< MIr. < OIr.; see **s(w)e-***).] — **Sinn Fein′er** *n.* — **Sinn′ Fein′ism** *n.*

Sino– *pref.* Chinese: *Sinology.* [< LLat. *Sīnae*, the Chinese < Gk. *Sinai* < Ar. *Ṣīn*, China, prob. < Chin. *Qin*, the first dynasty (221–206 B.C.) under which China was united.]

si·no·a·tri·al node (sī′nō-ā′trē-əl) *n.* A small mass of specialized cardiac muscle fibers in the right atrium of the heart that acts as a pacemaker by generating the regular electric impulses of the heartbeat.

Si·no·logue also **Sin·o·log** (sī′nə-lôg′, -lŏg′, sĭn′ə-) *n.* A student of or specialist in Sinology.

Si·nol·o·gy (sī-nŏl′ə-jē, sĭ-) *n.* The study of Chinese language, literature, or civilization. — **Si′no·log′i·cal** (sī′nə-lŏj′ĭ-kəl, sĭn′ə-) *adj.* — **Si·nol′o·gist** *n.*

Si·no·pe (sə-nō′pē) *n.* A satellite of Jupiter. [Lat. *Sinōpē*, woman unsuccessfully courted by Zeus < Gk.]

Si·no·phile (sī′nə-fīl′, sĭn′ə-) *n.* One who admires China, its people, or its culture. — **Si′no·phil′i·a** (-fĭl′ē-ə) *n.*

Si·no·phobe (sī′nə-fōb′, sĭn′-) *n.* One who fears or dislikes China, its people, or its culture. — **Si′no·pho′bi·a** (-fō′bē-ə) *n.* — **Si′no·pho′bic** (-fō′bĭk) *adj.*

Si·no-Ti·bet·an (sī′nō-tĭ-bĕt′n, sĭn′ō-) *n.* A language family that includes the Sinitic and Tibeto-Burman branches. — **Si′no-Ti·bet′an** *adj.*

sin·se·mil·la (sĭn′sə-mē′yə, -mĭl′ə) *n.* A highly potent form of marijuana obtained from unpollinated female plants. [Sp. : *sin*, without (< Lat. *sine*) + *semilla*, seed (< OSp. dial. *semilia*, alteration of LLat. *sēminia*, neut. pl. of *sēminium* < *sēmen*; see SEMEN).]

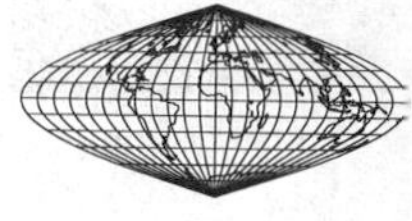

sinusoidal projection

sin tax *n. Informal.* A tax on certain items, such as cigarettes and alcohol, regarded as neither necessities nor luxuries.

sin·ter (sĭn′tər) *n.* **1.** *Geol.* A chemical sediment or crust deposited by a mineral spring. **2.** A mass formed by sintering. — *v.* **-tered, -ter·ing, -ters.** — *tr.* To cause (metallic powder, for example) to sinter. — *intr.* To form a coherent mass by heating without melting. [Ger. < MHGer., dross, metal slag < OHGer.] — **sin′ter·a·bil′i·ty** *n.*

sin·u·ate (sĭn′yo͞o-ĭt, -āt′) *intr.v.* **-at·ed, -at·ing, -ates.** To bend or curve; wind: *a sinuating road.* — *adj.* also **sin·u·at·ed** (-ā′tĭd). Having a wavy indented margin. [Lat. *sinuāre, sinuāt-*, to bend < *sinus*, curve.] — **sin′u·ate·ly** *adv.* — **sin′u·a′tion** *n.*

Sin·ui·ju (shĭn′wē-jo͞o′). A city of W North Korea on Korea Bay at the mouth of the Yalu R. Pop. 300,000.

sin·u·os·i·ty (sĭn′yo͞o-ŏs′ĭ-tē) *n., pl.* **-ties. 1.** The quality or condition of being sinuous. **2.** A bending or curving shape or movement.

sin·u·ous (sĭn′yo͞o-əs) *adj.* **1.** Characterized by many curves or turns; winding. **2.** Characterized by supple and lithe movements. **3.** Not direct; devious. **4.** Sinuate: *a sinuous leaf.* [< Lat. *sinuōsus* < *sinus*, curve.] — **sin′u·ous·ly** *adv.* — **sin′u·ous·ness** *n.*

si·nus (sī′nəs) *n.* **1.** A depression or cavity formed by a bending or curving. **2.** *Anat.* **a.** A dilated channel or receptacle containing chiefly venous blood. **b.** Any of various air-filled cavities in the bones of the skull, esp. one communicating with the nostrils. **3.** *Pathol.* A fistula leading from a pus-filled cavity. **4.** *Bot.* A recess or an indentation between lobes of a leaf or corolla. [ME, hollow in the body < Med.Lat. < Lat., curve, hollow.]

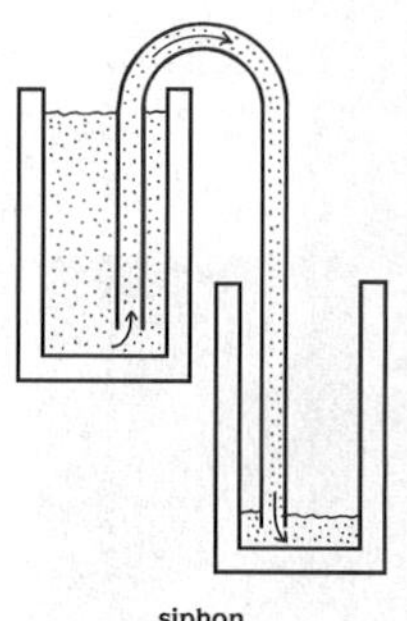

siphon

si·nus·i·tis (sī′nə-sī′tĭs) *n.* Inflammation of the sinuses or a sinus, esp. in the nasal region.

sinus node *n.* See **sinoatrial node.**

si·nu·soid (sī′nə-soid′, -nyə-) *n.* **1.** *Math.* See **sine curve. 2.** *Anat.* Any of the venous cavities through which blood passes in various glands and organs. [Med.Lat. *sinus*, sine; see SINE + –OID.] — **si′nu·soi′dal** (-soid′l) *adj.*

sinusoidal projection *n.* A map projection in which areas are equal to corresponding areas on a globe, the parallels and the prime meridian being straight lines and the other meridians being increasingly curved outward from the prime meridian.

Si·on (sī′ən) *n.* Var. of **Zion**[2].

Siou·an (so͞o′ən) *n.* **1.** A large North American Indian family of languages spoken from Lake Michigan to the Rocky Mountains and southward to Arkansas. **2.** A member of a Siouan-speaking people. — **Siou′an** *adj.*

Sioux (so͞o) *n., pl.* **Sioux** (so͞o, so͞oz). **1.** A member of a group of Native American peoples, also known as the Dakota, inhabiting the northern Great Plains from Minnesota to eastern Montana and from southern Saskatchewan to Nebraska, with present-day populations mainly in North and South Dakota. **2.** Any of the Siouan languages of the Sioux peoples. [N. Amer.Fr., short for *nadouéssioux* < Ottawa *naadowesiwag.*] — **Sioux** *adj.*

Sioux City. A city of NW IA on the Missouri R. near the SD–NE border. Pop. 80,505.

Sioux Falls. A city of SE SD near the MN border; first settled c. 1856. Pop. 100,814.

sip (sĭp) *v.* **sipped, sip·ping, sips.** — *tr.* **1.** To drink in small quantities. **2.** To sip from. — *intr.* To drink something in sips. — *n.* **1.** The act of sipping. **2.** A small quantity of liquid sipped. [ME *sippen.* See **seuə-**[2]***.**] — **sip′per** *n.*

si·phon also **sy·phon** (sī′fən) — *n.* **1.** A pipe or tube fashioned or deployed in an inverted U shape and filled until atmospheric pressure is sufficient to force a liquid from a reservoir

ă pat	oi boy
ā pay	ou out
âr care	o͝o took
ä father	o͞o boot
ĕ pet	ŭ cut
ē be	ûr urge
ĭ pit	th thin
ī pie	*th* this
îr pier	hw which
ŏ pot	zh vision
ō toe	ə about, item
ô paw	

Stress marks:
′ (primary);
′ (secondary), as in
dictionary (dĭk′shə-nĕr′ē)

at one end of the tube over a barrier higher than the reservoir and out the other end. **2.** *Zool.* A tubular organ, esp. of aquatic invertebrates such as squids, by which water is taken in or expelled. — *v.* **-phoned, -phon•ing, -phons.** — *tr.* To draw off or convey through or as if through a siphon. — *intr.* To pass through a siphon. [ME < Lat. *sīphō, sīphōn-* < Gk. *siphōn.*] — **si′phon•al, si•phon′ic** (sī-fŏn′ĭk) *adj.*

si•phon•o•phore (sī-fŏn′ə-fôr′, -fōr′, sī′fə-nə-) *n.* Any of various transparent marine hydrozoans of the order Siphonophora, including the Portuguese man-of-war. [< NLat. *Siphonophora*, order name : Gk. *siphō, siphōn-*, tube + Gk. *-phora*, neut. pl. of *-phoros*, -phore.]

si•phon•o•stele (sī-fŏn′ə-stēl′, sī′fə-nə-stē′lē) *n.* A type of stele in which the vascular cylinder surrounds a pith.

David Siqueiros

Sip•par (sĭ-pär′). An ancient city of N Babylonia on the Euphrates R. SSW of present-day Baghdad.

sip•pet (sĭp′ĭt) *n.* A small piece of toast or bread soaked in gravy or other liquid or used as a garnish. [< *sip*, alteration of SOP.]

Si•quei•ros (sĭ-kā′rōs), **David Alfaro.** 1896?–1974. Mexican painter known for his murals.

sir (sûr) *n.* **1. Sir.** Used as an honorific before the given name or the full name of baronets and knights. **2.** Used as a form of polite address for a man: *Don't forget your hat, sir.* **3.** Used as a salutation in a letter: *Dear Sir or Madam.* [ME, var. of *sire*, sire. See SIRE.]

sir•dar (sûr′där′, sər-där′) *n.* A person of high rank, esp. in India. [Hindi *sardār* < Pers. : *sar*, head; see **ker-¹*** + *-dār*, holder; see **dher-***.]

sire (sīr) *n.* **1.** A father. **2.** The father of an animal, esp. a domesticated mammal. **3.** *Archaic.* A male ancestor; a forefather. **4.** *Archaic.* A gentleman of rank. **5.** *Archaic.* Used as a form of address for a superior, esp. a king. — *tr.v.* **sired, sir•ing, sires.** To father; beget. [ME < OFr. < VLat. **seior* < Lat. *senior*, older, comp. of *senex*, old. See **sen-***.]

si•ren (sī′rən) *n.* **1.a.** A device in which compressed air or steam is driven against a rotating perforated disk to create a loud, often wailing sound as a signal or warning. **b.** An electronic device producing a similar sound as a signal or warning: *a fire siren.* **2.** Any of several salamanders of the family Sirenidae having an eellike body, external gills, and no hind limbs. [Fr. *sirène* < OFr. *sereine*, Siren < LLat. *Sīrēna* < Lat. *Sīrēn* < Gk. *Seirēn.*]

sisal
Agave sisalana

Si•ren (sī′rən) *n.* **1.** *Gk. Myth.* One of a group of sea nymphs whose sweet singing lured mariners to destruction on the rocks around their island. **2. siren.** A woman regarded as seductive and beautiful. [ME *serein* < OFr. *sereine.* See SIREN.]

si•re•ni•an (sī-rē′nē-ən) *n.* See **sea cow.** — *adj.* Of or belonging to the order of sea cows. [< NLat. *Sīrēnia*, order name < Lat. *Sīrēn*, Siren. See SIREN.]

Sir•i•us (sĭr′ē-əs) *n.* A star in the constellation Canis Major, the brightest star in the sky. [Lat. *Sīrius* < Gk. *Seirios* < *seirios*, burning.]

sir•loin (sûr′loin′) *n.* A cut of meat, esp. of beef, from the upper part of the loin just in front of the round. [ME *surloine* < OFr. *surlonge*, **surloigne* : *sur*, above (< Lat. *super*; see **uper***) + *longe, loigne*, loin; see LOIN.]

si•roc•co (sə-rŏk′ō) also **sci•roc•co** (shə-, sə-) *n.*, *pl.* **-cos.** **1.** A hot humid south or southeast wind blowing over the Mediterranean from North Africa to southern Europe. **2.** A hot or warm southerly wind, esp. one moving toward a low barometric pressure center. [Ital. *scirrocco* < Ar. *šarq*, east.]

sistrum
c. 2300–2000 B.C. bronze
Anatolian sistrum

Sí•ros (sē′rôs′). See **Syros.**

sir•rah (sĭr′ə) *n.* *Obsolete.* Mister; fellow. Used as a contemptuous form of address. [Alteration of SIR.]

sir•ree also **sir•ee** (sə-rē′) *n.* *Informal.* Sir. Used for emphasis after *yes* or *no.*

sir•up (sĭr′əp, sûr′-) *n.* Var. of **syrup.**

sir•up•y (sĭr′ə-pē, sûr′-) *adj.* Var. of **syrupy.**

sir•vente (sîr-vänt′, sər-vĕnt′) also **sir•ven•tes** (sər-vĕn′tĭs, -vĕnts′) *n.*, *pl.* **-ventes** (-vänt′, -vĕnts′) also **-vent•es** (-vĕn′təs). A satirical form of lyric verse of the Provençal troubadours. [Fr. < Prov. *sirventes* < OProv. < *sirvent*, servant (the position of a lover towards his mistress) < Lat. *serviēns, servient-*, pr.part. of *servīre*, to serve < *servus*, servant.]

sis (sĭs) *n.* *Informal.* Sister.

si•sal (sī′səl) *n.* **1.** A Mexican and Central American plant *(Agave sisalana)* widely cultivated for its large sword-shaped leaves that yield stiff fibers used for cordage and rope. **2.** The fiber of this plant or of other members of the genus *Agave.* [Am.Sp., after *Sisal*, a town of SE Mexico in the Yucatán.]

sis•kin (sĭs′kĭn) *n.* Any of several small finches, such as the pine siskin of North America. [Obsolete Du. *sisken* < MDu., dim. of *sīs* < MLGer. *csītze*, of Slav. orig.]

Sis•ley (sĭs′lē, sĭz′-, sēs-lā′), **Alfred.** 1839–99. British-born French impressionist painter noted for his outdoor scenes.

Sis•mon•di (sĭs-mŏn′dē, sēs-môN-dē′), **Jean Charles Léonard Simon de.** 1773–1842. Swiss historian and economist who attacked the classical economics of Adam Smith.

Sis•se•ton (sĭs′ĭ-tən) *n.*, *pl.* **Sisseton** or **-tons.** A member of a Native American people of the Santee branch of the Sioux.

sis•si•fied (sĭs′ə-fīd′) *adj.* Of, relating to, or having the characteristics of a sissy; timid, cowardly, or effeminate.

sis•sy (sĭs′ē) *n.*, *pl.* **-sies.** **1.** A boy or man regarded as effeminate. **2.** A person regarded as timid or cowardly. **3.** *Informal.* Sister. [Dim. of SIS.] — **sis′si•ness, sis′sy•ness** *n.* — **sis′sy** *adj.* — **sis′sy•ish** *adj.*

sis•ter (sĭs′tər) *n.* **1.a.** A girl or woman having the same parents as another. **b.** A girl or woman having one parent in common with another; a half sister. **c.** The daughter of a person's stepparent; a stepsister. **2.** A girl or woman who shares a common ancestry, allegiance, character, or purpose with another or others, specifically: **a.** A kinswoman. **b.** A woman fellow member of an organization: *my sorority sister.* **c.** A fellow woman, friend, or companion. **d.** A soul sister. **e.** A woman who is a feminist. **3.** *Informal.* Used as a form of address for a woman or girl. **4. Sister.** *Eccles.* **a.** A member of a women's religious order; a nun. **b.** Used as a form of address for such a woman, alone or followed by the woman's name. **5.** *Chiefly British.* A nurse, esp. the head nurse in a ward. — *adj.* **1.** Related by or as if by sisterhood; closely related. **2.** *Genet.* Of or being one of an identical pair. [ME, partly < OE *sweostor* and partly < ON *systir*; see **swesor-***.] — **sis′ter•ly** *adj.* & *adv.* — **sis′ter•li•ness** *n.*

sis•ter•hood (sĭs′tər-ho͝od′) *n.* **1.** The state or relationship of being a sister or sisters. **2.** The quality of being sisterly. **3.** A society, esp. a religious society, of women. **4.** Association or unification of women in a common cause.

sis•ter-in-law (sĭs′tər-ĭn-lô′) *n.*, *pl.* **sis•ters-in-law** (sĭs′tərz-). **1.** The sister of one's spouse. **2.** The wife of one's brother. **3.** The wife of the brother of one's spouse.

Sis•tine (sĭs′tēn′, sĭ-stēn′) also **Six•tine** (sĭk′stēn′, -stīn′) *adj.* **1.** Of or relating to one of the popes named Sixtus, esp. Sixtus IV (reigned 1471–1484). **2.** Of or relating to the Sistine Chapel in the Vatican. [Ital. *sistino* < NLat. *sixtīnus* < Med. Lat. *Sixtus*, the name of several popes < Lat. *Sextus*, Roman praenomen < *sextus*, sixth. See SEXT.]

sis•trum (sĭs′trəm) *n.*, *pl.* **-trums** or **-tra** (-trə). *Mus.* A percussion instrument of ancient Egypt consisting of metal rods or loops attached to a metal frame. [ME < Lat. *sīstrum* < Gk. *seistron* < *seiein*, to shake.]

Sis•y•phe•an (sĭs′ə-fē′ən) *adj.* **1.** *Gk. Myth.* Of or relating to Sisyphus. **2.** Endlessly laborious or futile. [< Lat. *Sisyphēius* < Gk. *Sisupheios* < *Sisuphos*, Sisyphus.]

Sis•y•phus (sĭs′ə-fəs) *n.* *Gk. Myth.* A cruel king of Corinth doomed forever to roll a huge stone to a hilltop in Hades only to have it roll back. [Lat. *Sisyphus* < Gk. *Sisuphos.*]

sit (sĭt) *v.* **sat** (săt), **sit•ting, sits.** — *intr.* **1.** To rest with the torso vertical and the body supported on the buttocks. **2.a.** To rest with the hindquarters lowered onto a supporting surface. Used of animals. **b.** To perch. Used of birds. **3.** To cover eggs for hatching; brood. **4.** To be situated or located. **5.** To lie or rest: *dishes sitting on a shelf.* See Usage Note at **set¹**. **6.** To pose for an artist or a photographer. **7.a.** To occupy a seat as a member of a body of officials. **b.** To be in session. **8.** To remain inactive or unused. **9.** To affect one with or as if with a burden; weigh. **10.** To fit, fall, or drape in a specified manner: *The jacket sits well on you.* **11.** To be agreeable to one; please: *The idea sat well with us.* **12.** *Chiefly British.* To take an examination, as for a degree. **13.** To blow from a particular direction. Used of the wind. **14.** To keep watch or take care of a child. — *tr.* **1.** To cause to sit; seat. **2.** To keep one's seat on (an animal). **3.** To sit on (eggs) for the purpose of hatching. **4.** To provide seating accommodation for. — *n.* **1.a.** The act of sitting. **b.** A period of time spent sitting. **2.** The way in which an article of clothing fits. — ***phrasal verbs.*** **sit down.** To take a seat. **sit in. 1.** To attend or participate in as a visitor. **2.** To take part in a sit-in. **sit on** (or **upon**). **1.** To confer about. **2.** *Informal.* To suppress or repress. **3.** *Informal.* To postpone action or resolution regarding. **sit out. 1.** To stay until the end of. **2.** To refrain from taking part in. **sit up. 1.** To rise from lying down to a sitting position. **2.** To sit with the spine erect. **3.** To stay up past the customary bedtime. **4.** To become suddenly alert. — ***idiom.*** **sit tight.** *Informal.* To be patient and await the next move. [ME *sitten* < OE *sittan.* See **sed-***.]

si•tar (sĭ-tär′) *n.* *Mus.* A stringed instrument of India made of seasoned gourds and teak and having a track of 20 metal frets with 6 or 7 main playing strings above and 13 sympathetic resonating strings below. [Hindi *sitār* < Pers. : *si*, three; see **trei-*** + *tār*, string; see **ten-***.] — **si•tar′ist** *n.*

sit•com also **sit-com** (sĭt′kŏm′) *n.* A situation comedy.

sit-down (sĭt′doun′) *n.* **1.** A work stoppage in which the workers refuse to leave their place of employment until their demands are considered or met. **2.** An obstruction of normal activity by the act of a large group sitting down in public to express a grievance or protest. **3.** *Informal.* An act, instance, or period of sitting. **4.** *Informal.* A meal for people seated at a table. — *adj.* **1.** Performed or accomplished while sitting down. **2.** Intended for people seated at a table.

site (sīt) *n.* **1.** The place where a structure or group of structures was, is, or is to be located. **2.** The place or setting of something. — *tr.v.* **sit•ed, sit•ing, sites.** To situate on a site. [ME < OFr. < Lat. *situs.* See SITUS.]

sith (sĭth) *conj. Archaic.* Since. [ME *sithe* < OE *siththa*, var. of *siththan.* See SINCE.] **— sith** *adv. & prep.*

sit-in (sĭt′ĭn′) *n.* **1.** See **sit-down** 1. **2.** An organized protest in which participants seat themselves and refuse to move. **3.** The act of occupying the seats or an area of a segregated establishment to protest racial discrimination.

Sit•ka (sĭt′kə). A town of SE AK on the W coast of Baranof I.; cap. of the territory from 1867 to 1906. Pop. 8,588.

si•tos•ter•ol (sī-tŏs′tə-rôl′, -rōl′, -rŏl′, sĭ-) *n.* Any of a group of sterols that occur in high concentrations in certain plants, such as yams, and are used in the synthesis of steroid hormones. [Gk. *sitos*, food, grain + STEROL.]

sit•ter (sĭt′ər) *n.* **1.** One that sits, esp.: **a.** A person who cares for young children when the parents are not home; a baby sitter. **b.** One who poses for artists. **2.** A brooding hen.

Sit•ter (sĭt′ər), **Willem de.** 1872–1934. Dutch astronomer noted for his work on cosmology and relativity.

sit•ting (sĭt′ĭng) *n.* **1.** The act or position of one that sits. **2.** A period during which one is seated and occupied with a single activity, such as reading a book. **3.** A session, as of a court. **4.a.** An act, a condition, or a period of brooding on eggs by a bird; incubation. **b.** The number of eggs under a brooding bird; a clutch. *— adj.* **1.** Incubating a nest of eggs. **2.** Occupying an official position; incumbent. **3.a.** Of or for sitting. **b.** Done or executed while sitting.

Sit•ting Bull (sĭt′ĭng bo͝ol′). 1834?–90. Hunkpapa Sioux leader who guided his people to victory against Gen. George A. Custer's cavalry at the Battle of the Little Bighorn (1876).

sitting duck *n. Informal.* An easy target or victim.

sitting room *n.* A living room.

sit•u•ate (sĭch′o͞o-āt′) *tr.v.* **-at•ed, -at•ing, -ates. 1.** To place in a certain spot or position; locate. **2.** To place under particular circumstances or in a given condition. *— adj.* (-ĭt, -āt′). *Archaic.* Situated. [ME < Med.Lat. *situāre, situāt-*, to place < Lat. *situs*, location. See **tkei-***.]

sit•u•at•ed (sĭch′o͞o-ā′tĭd) *adj.* **1.** Having a place or location; located. **2.** Supplied with money.

sit•u•a•tion (sĭch′o͞o-ā′shən) *n.* **1.a.** The way in which something is positioned vis-à-vis its surroundings. **b.** The place in which something is situated; a location. **2.** Position or status with regard to conditions and circumstances. **3.** The combination of circumstances at a given moment; a state of affairs. **4.** A critical, problematic, or striking set of circumstances. **5.** A position of employment; a post. **— sit′u•a′tion•al** *adj.* **— sit′u•a′tion•al•ly** *adv.*

situation comedy *n.* A humorous radio or television series featuring the reactions of a regular cast of characters to unusual situations, such as misunderstandings.

situation ethics *n. (used with a sing. or pl. v.)* A system of ethics that evaluates acts in light of their situational context rather than by the application of moral absolutes.

sit-up (sĭt′ŭp′) *n. Sports.* A physical exercise in which one raises the torso from a supine to a sitting position and then lies back down again without moving the legs.

si•tus (sī′təs) *n., pl.* **situs.** Position, esp. normal or original position, as of a body organ or part. [Lat. See **tkei-***.]

Sit•well (sĭt′wĕl′, -wəl). Family of British writers, including Dame **Edith Sitwell** (1887–1964) and her brothers Sir **Osbert** (1892–1969) and **Sacheverell** (1897–1988).

sitz bath (sĭts, zĭts) *n.* **1.** A bathtub shaped like a chair in which one bathes in a sitting position, immersing only the hips and buttocks. **2.** A bath taken in such a tub esp. for therapeutic reasons. [Partial transl. of Ger. *Sitzbad* : *Sitz*, act of sitting (< *sitzen*, to sit, ult. < OHGer. *sizzen*; see **sed-***) + *Bad*, bath.]

sitz•mark (sĭt′smärk′, zĭt′-) *n. Sports.* A hollow made in the snow by a skier who has fallen backward. [Partial transl. of Ger. *Sitzmarke* : *Sitz*, act of sitting (< *sitzen*, to sit < MHGer. < OHGer. *sizzen*; see **sed-***) – *Marke*, mark.]

Si•va (shē′və, sē′-) *n. Hinduism.* Var. of **Shiva.**

Si•van (sĭv′ən) *n.* The ninth month of the year in the Jewish calendar. [Heb. *sīwān* < Akkadian *Simānu*, the month Simanu.]

Si•vas (sĭ-väs′, sē-). A city of central Turkey E of Ankara; sacked by Tamerlane in 1400. Pop. 172,864.

Si•wa•lik Hills (sĭ-wä′lĭk). A range of the S Himalaya Mts. extending c. 1,689 km (1,050 mi) from SW Kashmir through N India into S Nepal.

six (sĭks) *n.* **1.** The cardinal number equal to 5 + 1. **2.** The sixth in a set or sequence. **3.** Something having six parts, units, or members, esp. a motor vehicle having six cylinders. **— *idiom.* at sixes and sevens.** In a state of confusion or disorder. [ME < OE. See **s(w)eks***.] **— six** *adj. & pron.*

six-gun (sĭks′gŭn′) *n.* A six-chambered revolver.

Six Nations (sĭks) *pl.n.* The Iroquois confederacy after it was joined by the Tuscarora in 1722.

six-pack (sĭks′păk′) *n.* **1.** Six units of a commodity, as six cans of beer, sold in a pack. **2.** The contents of a six-pack.

six•pence (sĭks′pəns) *n. Chiefly British.* **1.** A coin formerly used in Britain and worth six pennies. **2.** The sum of six pennies.

six•pen•ny (sĭks′pĕn′ē, -pə-nē) *adj.* **1.** Valued at, selling for, or worth sixpence. **2.** Of little worth; paltry.

sixpenny nail *n.* A nail 2 inches (5.1 centimeters) long.

six-shoot•er (sĭks′sho͞o′tər) *n. Informal.* A six-chambered revolver; a six-gun.

six•teen (sĭk-stēn′) *n.* **1.** The cardinal number equal to the sum of 15 + 1. **2.** The 16th in a set or sequence. [ME *sixtene* < OE *sixtȳne*. See **s(w)eks***.] **— six•teen′** *adj. & pron.*

six•teen•mo (sĭk-stēn′mō) *n., pl.* **-mos.** *Print.* See **sextodecimo.**

six•teenth (sĭk-stēnth′) *n.* **1.** The ordinal number matching the number 16 in a series. **2.** One of 16 equal parts. **— six•teenth′** *adv. & adj.*

sixteenth note *n. Mus.* A note having one sixteenth the time value of a whole note.

sixth (sĭksth) *n.* **1.** The ordinal number matching the number six in a series. **2.** One of six equal parts. **3.** *Mus.* **a.** An interval of six degrees in a diatonic scale. **b.** A tone separated by this interval from a given tone. **c.** The harmonic combination of two tones separated by this interval. **d.** The sixth tone of a scale; the submediant. **— sixth** *adv. & adj.*

sixth sense *n.* A power of perception seemingly independent of the five senses; keen intuition.

six•ti•eth (sĭk′stē-ĭth) *n.* **1.** The ordinal number matching the number 60 in a series. **2.** One of 60 equal parts. **— six′ti•eth** *adv. & adj.*

Six•tine (sĭk′stēn′, -stīn′) *adj.* Var. of **Sistine.**

six•ty (sĭks′tē) *n., pl.* **-ties. 1.** The cardinal number equal to 6 × 10. **2. sixties. a.** Often **Sixties.** The decade from 60 to 69 in a century. **b.** A decade or the numbers from 60 to 69. [ME < OE *sixtig*. See **s(w)eks***.] **— six′ty** *adj. & pron.*

six•ty-fourth note (sĭks′tē-fôrth′, -fōrth′) *n. Mus.* A note having one sixty-fourth the time value of a whole note.

six•ty-nine (sĭks′tē-nīn′) *n. Vulgar Slang.* Oral-genital sex between two people at the same time.

siz•a•ble also **size•a•ble** (sī′zə-bəl) *adj.* Of considerable size; fairly large. **— siz′a•ble•ness** *n.* **— siz′a•bly** *adv.*

size[1] (sīz) *n.* **1.** The physical dimensions, proportions, magnitude, or extent of an object. **2.** Any of a series of graduated categories of dimension whereby manufactured articles, such as shoes, are classified. **3.a.** Considerable extent, amount, or dimensions. **b.** Relative amount or number, as of population. **4.** Character, value, or status with reference to importance or the capacity to meet given requirements: *Try this on for size.* **5.** The actual state of affairs: *about the size of it.* *— tr.v.* **sized, siz•ing, siz•es. 1.** To arrange, classify, or distribute according to size. **2.** To make, cut, or shape to a required size. *— adj.* Sized. Often used in combination: *bite-size appetizers.* **— *phrasal verb.* size up.** To make an estimate, an opinion, or a judgment of. [ME *sise* < OFr., court session, law, short for *assise*. See ASSIZE.] **— siz′er** *n.*

size[2] (sīz) *n.* Any of several gelatinous or glutinous substances usu. made from glue, wax, or clay and used as a glaze or filler for porous materials such as paper, cloth, or wall surfaces. *— tr.v.* **sized, siz•ing, siz•es.** To treat or coat with size or a similar substance. [ME *sise*, prob. < OFr., a setting. See SIZE[1].]

sized (sīzd) *adj.* Having a particular or specified size. Often used in combination: *a medium-sized car.*

siz•ing (sī′zĭng) *n.* **1.** A glaze or filler; size. **2.** Treatment of a fabric or other surface with size.

siz•zle (sĭz′əl) *intr.v.* **-zled, -zling, -zles. 1.** To make the hissing sound characteristic of frying fat. **2.** To seethe with anger or indignation. **3.** To be very hot. *— n.* A hissing sound. [Perh. freq. of ME *sissen*, to hiss, of imit. orig.]

siz•zler (sĭz′lər) *n.* **1.** One that sizzles. **2.** *Informal.* A very hot day.

S.J. *abbr.* Society of Jesus.

Sjael•land (shĕl′än′) also **Zea•land** (zē′lənd). An island of E Denmark bounded by the Kattegat and the Baltic Sea and separated from Sweden by the Oresund.

S.J.D. *abbr. Lat.* Scientiae Juridicae Doctor (Doctor of Juridical Science).

SK *abbr.* Saskatchewan.

sk. *abbr.* Sack.

Skag•er•rak also **Skag•er•ak** (skăg′ə-răk′, skä′gə-räk′). A broad strait between Norway and Denmark linking the North Sea and the Kattegat.

Skag•way (skăg′wā′). A town of SE AK at the head of the Lynn Canal NNW of Juneau; a boom town during the Alaskan gold rush (1897–98). Pop. 692.

skald also **scald** (skôld, skäld) *n.* A medieval Scandinavian poet. [ON *skāld*. See **sekʷ-**[3]***.] **— skald′ic** *adj.*

skat (skăt) *n. Games.* **1.** A trick-taking card game for three active players using sevens through aces. **2.** A skat card combination. [Ger. < Ital. *scarto*, a discarded card < *scartare*, to reject : *s-*, out; see SFUMATO + *carta*, card (< Lat. *charta*, paper made of papyrus; see CARD[1]).]

skate[1] (skāt) *n. Sports.* **1.** An ice skate. **2.** A roller skate. **3.** The act or a period of skating. *— intr.v.* **skat•ed, skat•ing, skates. 1.** To glide or move along on or as if on skates. **2.** *Informal.* To act in an irresponsible or superficial manner. [< Du. *schaats*, stilt, skate (taken as pl.) < MDu. *schaetse* < ONFr. *escache*, stilt, perh. of Gmc. orig.]

skate[2] (skāt) *n.* Any of various rays of the genus *Raja*, having

sitar

Sitting Bull
Photographed in the 1880's

ă **pat**	oi **boy**
ā **pay**	ou **out**
âr **care**	o͝o **took**
ä **father**	o͞o **boot**
ĕ **pet**	ŭ **cut**
ē **be**	ûr **urge**
ĭ **pit**	th **thin**
ī **pie**	*th* **this**
îr **pier**	hw **which**
ŏ **pot**	zh **vision**
ō **toe**	ə **about,**
ô **paw**	**item**

Stress marks:
′ (primary);
′ (secondary), as in
dictionary (dĭk′shə-nĕr′ē)

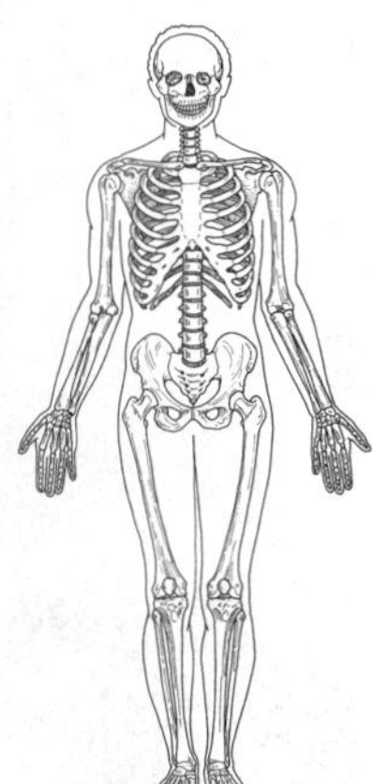
skeleton

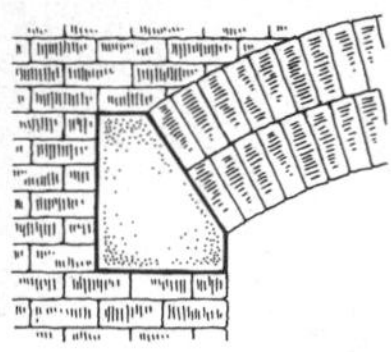
skewback

ski

a flattened body and greatly expanded pectoral fins that extend around the head. [ME *scate* < ON *skata.*]

skate³ (skāt) *n.* **1.** A person. **2.** A decrepit horse; a nag. [Perh. alteration of dial. *skite,* contemptible person, prob. < dial. *skite,* to defecate < ME *skiten* < ON *skīta.* See **skei-*.**]

skate•board (skāt′bôrd′, -bōrd′) *Sports. n.* A short narrow board with four wheels mounted under it. **— skate′board′** *v.* **— skate′board′er** *n.*

skat•er (skā′tər) *n.* **1.** One who skates, as on ice. **2.** See **water strider.**

skat•ole (skăt′ōl, -ôl) also **skat•ol** (-ôl, -ōl, -ŏl) *n.* A crystalline organic compound, C_9H_9N, having a strong fecal odor, found in feces, beets, and coal tar and used as a fixative in perfumery. [Gk. *skōr, skat-,* dung; see **sker-³*** + -OLE.]

Skaw (skô). A cape on the N extremity of Jutland, Denmark, extending into the Skagerrak.

skean (skēn) *n.* A double-edged dagger once used in Ireland and Scotland. [ME *skene* < Ir.Gael. *scian* < OIr. *scīan.* See **skei-*.**]

Skeat (skēt), **Walter William.** 1835–1912. English philologist who wrote *An Etymological Dictionary of the English Language* (1879–82).

ske•dad•dle (skĭ-dăd′l) *intr.v.* **-dled, -dling, -dles.** *Informal.* To leave hastily; flee. [?]

Skee•na (skē′nə). A river rising in W British Columbia, Canada, and flowing c. 579 km (360 mi) to the Pacific Ocean.

skeet (skēt) *n.* A form of trapshooting in which thrown clay targets are shot at from different stations. [Alteration of SHOOT.]

skee•ter (skē′tər) *n. Chiefly Southern U.S.* See **mosquito.** See Regional Note at **possum.**

skeeter hawk *n. South Atlantic U.S.* See **dragonfly.** See Regional Note at **dragonfly.**

skeg (skĕg) *n. Naut.* **1.** A structure that connects the keel and the sternpost of a ship. **2.** A vertical structure at the stern of a vessel that supports the rudder and protects the propeller. **3.** A small finlike structure at the stern of a small boat or surfboard, serving as a keel to keep the boat on course. [Du. *scheg,* perh. < ON *skegg,* beard, beak of a ship.]

skein (skān) *n.* **1.a.** A length of thread or yarn wound in a long, loose coil. **b.** Something suggesting the coil of a skein; a complex tangle: *a twisted skein of lies.* **2.** A flock of geese or similar birds in flight. [ME *skeine* < OFr. *escaigne.*]

skel•e•tal (skĕl′ĭ-tl) *adj.* **1.** Of, relating to, forming, or of the nature of a skeleton: *the skeletal system.* **2.** Attached to or formed by a skeleton: *skeletal muscles.* **— skel′e•tal•ly** *adv.*

skel•e•ton (skĕl′ĭ-tn) *n.* **1.a.** The internal structure composed of bone and cartilage that protects and supports a vertebrate organism; endoskeleton. **b.** The hard external supporting and protecting structure in many invertebrates, such as mollusks, and certain vertebrates, such as turtles; exoskeleton. **2.** A supporting structure or framework, as of a building. **3.** An outline or a sketch. **4.** Something reduced to its basic or minimal parts. **5.** One that is very thin or emaciated. *— adj.* **1.** Of, relating to, or resembling a skeleton. **2.** Reduced to the basic or minimal parts or members: *a skeleton crew.* **— *idiom.* skeleton in (one's) closet.** A source of shame that is kept secret. [Gk. *skeleton (sōma),* dried-up (body), neut. of *skeletos* < *skellesthai,* to dry up.]

skel•e•ton•ize (skĕl′ĭ-tn-īz′) *tr.v.* **-ized, -iz•ing, -iz•es. 1.** To reduce to skeleton form. **2.** To outline or sketch briefly. **3.** To reduce in size or number.

skeleton key *n.* A key with a large portion of the bit filed away so that it can open different locks.

skell (skĕl) *n. Slang.* A person without a home who lives as a derelict. [?]

skel•lum (skĕl′əm) *n. Scots.* A rascal; a rogue. [Du. *schelm* < LGer. < MLGer.]

Skel•ton (skĕl′tən), **John.** 1460?–1529. English poet and scholar whose satires include *Speke Parrot* (1521).

skep (skĕp) *n.* A beehive, esp. one of straw. [ME, basket < ON *skeppa,* a dry measure, and < OE *sceppe* (< ON *skeppa*).]

skep•tic also **scep•tic** (skĕp′tĭk) *n.* **1.** One who doubts, questions, or disagrees with assertions or generally accepted conclusions. **2.** One skeptical in religious matters. **3.** *Philos.* **a.** Often **Skeptic.** An adherent of a school of skepticism. **b. Skeptic.** A member of an ancient Greek school of skepticism, esp. that of Pyrrho of Elis (360?–272? B.C.). [Lat. *Scepticus,* disciple of Pyrrho of Elis < Gk. *Skeptikos* < *skeptesthai,* to examine. See **spek-*.**]

skep•ti•cal also **scep•ti•cal** (skĕp′tĭ-kəl) *adj.* **1.** Marked by or given to doubt; questioning. **2.** Relating to or characteristic of skeptics or skepticism. **— skep′ti•cal•ly** *adv.*

skep•ti•cism also **scep•ti•cism** (skĕp′tĭ-sĭz′əm) *n.* **1.** A doubting or questioning attitude or state of mind; dubiety. See Syns at **uncertainty. 2.** *Philos.* The doctrine that absolute knowledge is impossible and that inquiry must be a process of doubting in order to acquire approximate or relative certainty. **3.** Doubt or disbelief of religious tenets.

sker•ry (skĕr′ē) *n., pl.* **-ries.** A small rocky reef or island. [Sc., dim. of ON *sker.* See **sker-¹*.**]

sketch (skĕch) *n.* **1.** A hasty or undetailed drawing or painting often made as a preliminary study. **2.** A brief general account or presentation; an outline. **3.a.** A brief, light, or informal literary composition. **b.** *Mus.* A brief composition, esp. for the piano. **c.** A short, often satirical scene or play in a revue or variety show; a skit. **4.** *Informal.* An amusing person. *— v.* **sketched, sketch•ing, sketch•es.** *— tr.* To make a sketch of; outline. *— intr.* To make a sketch. [Du. *schets* < Ital. *schizzo* < *schizzare,* to splash, of imit. orig.] **— sketch′er** *n.*

sketch•book (skĕch′bo͝ok′) *n.* **1.** A pad of paper used for sketching. **2.** A book of literary sketches.

sketch•pad (skĕch′păd′) *n.* See **sketchbook** 1.

sketch•y (skĕch′ē) *adj.* **-i•er, -i•est. 1.** Resembling a sketch; giving only major points or parts. **2.a.** Lacking in substance or completeness; incomplete. **b.** Slight; superficial. **— sketch′i•ly** *adv.* **— sketch′i•ness** *n.*

skew (skyo͞o) *v.* **skewed, skew•ing, skews.** *— intr.* **1.** To take an oblique course or direction. **2.** To look obliquely or sideways. *— tr.* **1.** To turn or place at an angle. **2.** To give a bias to; distort. *— adj.* **1.** Placed or turned to one side; asymmetrical. **2.** Distorted or biased in meaning or effect. **3.** Having a part that diverges, as in gearing. **4.a.** *Math.* Neither parallel nor intersecting. Used of straight lines in space. **b.** *Statistics.* Not symmetrical about the mean. Used of distributions. *— n.* An oblique or slanting movement, position, or direction. [ME *skewen,* to escape, run sideways < ONFr. *eskiuer,* of Gmc. orig.] **— skew′ness** *n.*

skew arch *n. Archit.* An arch having sides not at right angles to the face of its abutments.

skew•back (skyo͞o′băk′) *n. Archit.* Either of two inset abutments sloped to support a segmental arch.

skew•bald (skyo͞o′bôld′) *adj.* Having spots or patches of white on a coat that is not black. *— n.* A skewbald animal, esp. a horse. [ME *skeued,* of mixed colors (prob. < *skeu,* sky, cloud, of Scand. orig.; see **(s)keu-***) + BALD.]

skew•er (skyo͞o′ər) *n.* **1.** A long metal or wooden pin used to secure or suspend food during cooking; a spit. **2.** Any of various picks or rods like a skewer in shape or function. *— tr.v.* **-ered, -er•ing, -ers.** To hold together or pierce with or as if with a skewer. [ME *skuer,* perh. of Scand. orig.]

skew lines *pl.n. Math.* Straight lines that are not in the same plane and do not intersect.

ski (skē) *n., pl.* **skis. 1.** *Sports.* **a.** One of a pair of long flat runners of plastic, metal, or wood that curve upward in front and may be attached to a boot for gliding or traveling over snow. **b.** A waterski. **2.** Something used as a runner on a vehicle. *— v.* **skied, ski•ing, skis.** *— intr.* To travel or glide on skis, esp. as a sport. *— tr.* To travel or glide over on skis. [Norw. < ON *skīdh,* stick, snowshoe. See **skei-*.**] **— ski′a•ble** *adj.* **— ski′er** *n.*

ski•a•gram (skī′ə-grăm′) *n.* **1.** A picture or photograph made up of shadows or outlines. **2.** See **radiograph.** [Gk. *skia,* shadow + -GRAM.]

ski boot *n. Sports.* A stiff padded boot that is fastened to the foot and locked into place in a ski binding.

skid (skĭd) *n.* **1.** The act of sliding or slipping over a surface, often sideways. **2.a.** A plank, log, or timber, usu. one of a pair, used as a support or track for sliding or rolling heavy objects. **b.** A pallet for loading or handling goods. **c.** One of several logs or timbers forming a skid road. **3. skids.** *Naut.* A wooden framework attached to the side of a ship to prevent damage, as when unloading. **4.** A shoe or drag applying pressure to a wheel to brake a vehicle. **5.** A runner in the landing gear of certain aircraft. **6. skids.** *Slang.* A path to ruin or failure. *— v.* **skid•ded, skid•ding, skids.** *— intr.* **1.** To slide sideways while moving because of loss of traction. See Syns at **slide. 2.** To slide without revolving. **3.** To move sideways in a turn because of insufficient banking. Used of an airplane. *— tr.* **1.** To brake (a wheel) with a skid. **2.** To haul on a skid or skids. [Perh. of Scand. orig.]

skid•der (skĭd′ər) *n.* **1.a.** One that skids. **b.** One that uses a skid. **2.** A heavy four-wheel tractor used to haul logs, esp. over rugged terrain.

skid•dy (skĭd′ē) *adj.* **-di•er, -di•est.** Liable to skid or cause skidding: *skiddy roads.*

skid road *n.* **1.** A track made of logs laid transversely about five feet apart and used to haul logs to a loading platform or a mill. **2.** *Slang.* Skid row.

skid row (rō) *n. Slang.* A squalid district inhabited chiefly by derelicts and vagrants. [Alteration of SKID ROAD (once a downtown area frequented by loggers).]

skied (skīd) *v.* P.t. and p.part. of **sky.**

skies (skīz) *n.* Pl. of **sky.** *— v.* Third pers. sing. pr.t. of **sky.**

skiff (skĭf) *n. Naut.* A flatbottom open boat of shallow draft, having a pointed bow and a square stern and propelled by oars, sail, or motor. [ME *skif* < OFr. *esquif* < OItal. *schifo,* of Gmc. orig.]

skif•fle (skĭf′əl) *n. Mus.* Jazz, folk, or country music played on instruments such as kazoos, washboards, or jugs. [?]

ski•jor•ing (skē′jôr′ĭng, -jōr′-) *n. Sports.* A sport in which a skier is drawn over ice or snow by a horse or vehicle. [Norw. *skikjøring* : *ski,* ski; see SKI + *kjøring,* driving (< *kjøre,* to drive < ON *keyra*).]

ski jump *Sports. n.* **1.** A jump or leap made by a skier. **2.** A course or chute prepared for a ski jump. — **ski jump** *v.* — **ski jumper** *n.*
ski jumping *n. Sports.* A competitive event in which a skier jumps from a ski jump and is judged on both form and the distance jumped.
ski lift *n. Sports.* A power-driven conveyer, usu. with attached tow bars, suspended chairs, or gondolas, used to carry skiers to the top of a trail or slope.
skill (skĭl) *n.* **1.** Proficiency, facility, or dexterity that is acquired or developed through training or experience. **2.a.** An art, a trade, or a technique, particularly one requiring use of the hands or body. **b.** A developed talent or ability: *writing skills.* **3.** *Obsolete.* A reason; a cause. [ME *skil* < ON, discernment. See **skel-¹***.]
skilled (skĭld) *adj.* **1.** Having or showing skill; expert. See Syns at **proficient. 2.** Requiring specialized ability or training.
skil•let (skĭl′ĭt) *n.* **1.** See Regional Note at **frying pan. 2.** *Chiefly British.* A long-handled stewing pan or saucepan sometimes having legs. [ME *skelet* < OFr. *escuelete,* dim. of *escuele,* plate < Lat. *scutella,* dim. of *scutra,* platter.]
skill•ful also **skil•ful** (skĭl′fəl) *adj.* **1.** Possessing or exercising skill; expert. See Syns at **proficient. 2.** Marked by, exhibiting, or requiring skill. — **skill′ful•ly** *adv.* — **skill′ful•ness** *n.*
skim (skĭm) *v.* **skimmed, skim•ming, skims.** —*tr.* **1.a.** To remove floating matter from (a liquid). **b.** To remove (floating matter) from a liquid. **c.** To take away the choicest or most readily attainable contents or parts from. **2.** To coat or cover with or as if with a thin layer, as of scum. **3.a.** To throw so as to bounce or slide. **b.** To glide or pass quickly and lightly over. **4.** To read or glance through (a book, for example) quickly or superficially. **5.** *Slang.* To fail to declare part of (certain income) to avoid tax payment. —*intr.* **1.** To move or pass swiftly and lightly over or near a surface; glide. **2.** To give a quick and superficial reading, scrutiny, or consideration; glance. **3.** To become coated with a thin layer. **4.** *Slang.* To fail to declare certain income to avoid tax payment. —*n.* **1.** The act of skimming. **2.** Something that has been skimmed. **3.** A thin layer or film. **4.** *Slang.* The profit gained by skimming. [ME *skimmen,* perh. < OFr. *escumer,* to remove scum < *escume,* scum, of Gmc. orig. See **(s)keu-***.]
ski mask *n.* A knitted covering for the head and face, worn especially by skiers for protection from the cold.
skim•mer (skĭm′ər) *n.* **1.** One that skims, such as a large perforated spoon used in skimming liquids. **2.** A light, usu. straw hat with a wide brim and a flat shallow crown. **3.a.** Any of several chiefly coastal birds of the genus *Rynchops,* having a long bill with a longer lower mandible for skimming the water's surface for food. **b.** A black skimmer.
skim milk *n.* Milk from which the cream has been removed.
ski•mo•bile (skē′mō-bēl′, -mə-) *n.* See **snowmobile.**
skimp (skĭmp) *v.* **skimped, skimp•ing, skimps.** —*tr.* **1.** To deal with hastily, carelessly, or with poor material. **2.** To give inadequate funds to; be stingy with. —*intr.* To be stingy or very thrifty. —*adj.* Scanty; skimpy. [Obsolete *skimp,* scanty, perh. < alteration of SCRIMP.]
skimp•y (skĭm′pē) *adj.* **-i•er, -i•est. 1.** Inadequate, as in size or fullness, esp. through economizing or stinting: *a skimpy meal.* **2.** Unduly thrifty; niggardly. — **skimp′i•ly** *adv.* — **skimp′i•ness** *n.*
skin (skĭn) *n.* **1.** The membranous tissue forming the external covering or integument of an animal and consisting in vertebrates of the epidermis and dermis. **2.** An animal pelt, esp. of a small or young animal. **3.** A usu. thin, closely adhering outer layer. **4.** A container for liquids that is made of animal skin. **5.** *Informal.* One's life or physical survival: *lied to save his skin.* —*v.* **skinned, skin•ning, skins.** —*tr.* **1.** To remove skin from. **2.** To bruise, cut, or injure the skin or surface of. **3.** To remove (an outer covering); peel off: *skin off the bark.* **4.** To cover with or as if with skin. **5.** *Slang.* To fleece; swindle. —*intr.* **1.** To become covered with or as if with skin: *The pond skins over with ice.* **2.** To pass with little room to spare: *barely skinned by.* —*adj. Slang.* Of, relating to, or depicting pornography. —***idioms.* by the skin of (one's) teeth.** By the smallest margin. **get under (one's) skin. 1.** To irritate or stimulate; provoke. **2.** To become an obsession. **under the skin.** Beneath the surface; fundamentally. [ME < ON *skinn.* See **sek-***.] — **skin′less** *adj.*
skin-deep (skĭn′dēp′) *adj.* Superficial; shallow: *skin-deep civility.* —*adv.* In a shallow manner; superficially.
skin-dive (skĭn′dīv′) *intr.v.* **-dived, -div•ing, -dives.** *Sports.* To engage in skin diving.
skin diving *n. Sports.* The sport of swimming under water with flippers and a face mask and usu. with a snorkel rather than a portable air supply. — **skin diver** *n.*
skin effect *n.* The tendency of alternating current to flow near the surface of a conductor.
skin flick *n. Slang.* A pornographic film.
skin•flint (skĭn′flĭnt′) *n.* One who is very reluctant to spend money; a miser.
skin game *n. Slang.* **1.** A fraudulent gambling game. **2.** A swindle.
skin graft *n.* A surgical graft of healthy skin from one part of the body to another or from one individual to another in order to replace damaged or lost skin. — **skin grafting** *n.*
skin•head (skĭn′hĕd′) *n. Slang.* **1.** A person with a shaven head. **2.** A member of any of various groups of white youths who shave their heads and sometimes participate in white-supremacist and anti-immigrant activities.
skink (skĭngk) *n.* Any of numerous smooth shiny lizards of the family Scincidae, having small or rudimentary legs. [Lat. *scincus* < Gk. *skinkos.*]
skinned (skĭnd) *adj.* Having skin of a specified kind. Often used in combination: *fair-skinned; dark-skinned.*
skin•ner (skĭn′ər) *n.* **1.** One that flays, dresses, or sells animal skins. **2.** *Western U.S.* A mule driver.
Skin•ner (skĭn′ər), **B(urrhus) F(rederick).** 1904–90. Amer. behavioristic psychologist noted for his theories of stimulus-response behavior. — **Skin•ner′i•an** (skĭ-nîr′ē-ən) *adj. & n.* — **Skin′ner•ism** *n.*
Skinner, Cornelia Otis. 1901–79. Amer. actress and writer known for her one-woman shows.
Skinner, Otis. 1858–1942. Amer. actor whose theater credits include *Kismet* (1911–14) and *Blood and Sand* (1921).
Skinner box *n.* A soundproof light-resistant box or cage used in laboratories to isolate an animal for experiments in operant conditioning. [After Burrhus Frederick SKINNER.]
skin•ny (skĭn′ē) *adj.* **-ni•er, -ni•est. 1.** Very thin. See Syns at **lean². 2.** Of, relating to, or resembling skin. —*n. Slang.* Inside information; the real facts. — **skin′ni•ness** *n.*
skin•ny-dip (skĭn′ē-dĭp′) *intr.v.* **-dipped, -dip•ping, -dips.** *Informal.* To swim nude. — **skin′ny-dip′per** *n.* — **skin′ny-dip′ping** *n.*
skin patch *n.* See **transdermal patch.**
skin test *n.* A test for detecting an allergy or infectious disease, performed by means of a patch test, a scratch test, or an intracutaneous injection of an allergen or extract of the disease-causing organism.
skin•tight (skĭn′tīt′) *adj.* Fitting closely to the skin.
skip (skĭp) *v.* **skipped, skip•ping, skips.** —*intr.* **1.a.** To move by hopping on one foot and then the other. **b.** To leap lightly about. **2.** To bounce over or be deflected from a surface; skim or ricochet. **3.** To pass from point to point, omitting or disregarding what intervenes. **4.** To be promoted in school beyond the next regular class or grade. **5.** *Informal.* To leave hastily; abscond: *skipped out of town.* **6.** To misfire. Used of an engine. —*tr.* **1.** To leap or jump lightly over: *skip rope.* **2.** To pass over without mentioning; omit. **3.** To cause to bounce lightly over a surface; skim. **4.** To be promoted beyond (the next grade or level). **5.** *Informal.* To leave hastily. **6.** *Informal.* To fail to attend. —*n.* **1.** A leaping or jumping movement, esp. a gait in which hops and steps alternate. **2.** An act of passing over something; an omission. [ME *skippen,* perh. of Scand. orig.] — **skip′pa•ble** *adj.*
skip•jack (skĭp′jăk′) *n., pl.* **skipjack** or **-jacks. 1.** Any of several marine food fishes of the genus *Euthynnus,* related to and resembling the tuna, esp. an economically important striped species *(E. pelamis)* occurring in all tropical areas. **2.** Any of various fishes, such as the bluefish, that habitually leap out of the water. **3.** *pl.* **-jacks.** *Naut.* A small sailboat having a bottom shaped like a flat V and vertical sides.
ski pole *n. Sports.* A lightweight pole with a handgrip, sometimes a wrist strap, and a sharp point encircled slightly above by a disk, used in pairs by snow skiers.
skip•per¹ (skĭp′ər) *n.* **1.** *Naut.* The master of a ship. **2.** A coach, director, or other leader. [ME < MDu. < *scip,* ship.] — **skip′per** *v.*
skip•per² (skĭp′ər) *n.* **1.** One that skips. **2.** Any of numerous butterflies of the families Hesperiidae and Megathymidae, having a hairy mothlike body, hooked tips on the antennae, and a darting flight pattern. **3.** Any of several marine fishes that often leap above water, esp. the saury *Cololabis saira* of Pacific waters.
skirl (skûrl) *v.* **skirled, skirl•ing, skirls.** —*intr.* To produce a high shrill wailing tone. Used of bagpipes. —*tr.* To play (a piece) on bagpipes. —*n.* **1.** *Mus.* The shrill sound made by the chanter pipe of bagpipes. **2.** A shrill wailing sound. [ME *skrillen, skirlen,* prob. of Scand. orig.]
skir•mish (skûr′mĭsh) *n.* **1.** A minor battle in war, as one between small forces or between large forces avoiding direct conflict. **2.** A minor or preliminary conflict or dispute. —*intr.v.* **-mished, -mish•ing, -mish•es.** To engage in a minor battle or dispute. [ME *skirmisshe,* alteration (influenced by ME *skirmisshen,* to brandish a weapon < OFr. *eskermir, eskirmiss-,* to fight with a sword, fence) of *skarmush* < OFr. *eskarmouch* < OItal. *scaramuccia,* of Gmc. orig. See **sker-¹***.] — **skir′mish•er** *n.*
Skí•ros also **Sky•ros** or **Scy•ros** (skī′rəs, skē′rôs). An island of E Greece in the Aegean Sea NE of Euboea; occupied by Athenians in the 5th cent. B.C.
skir•ret (skûr′ĭt) *n.* An eastern Asian plant *(Sium sisarum)* having sweet tuberous edible roots. [ME *skirwhit,* alteration of OFr. *eschervi,* prob. < Ar. *karawyā,* caraway.]
skirt (skûrt) *n.* **1.** The part of a garment, such as a dress, that

skiff
c. 1948 Seaford skiff by Paul A. Ketcham, after an 1880 boat by Samuel Gritman

skimmer
Black skimmer
Rynchops nigra

skink
Five-lined skink
Eumeces fasciatus

ă pat	oi boy
ā pay	ou out
âr care	ŏŏ took
ä father	ōō boot
ĕ pet	ŭ cut
ē be	ûr urge
ĭ pit	th thin
ī pie	*th* this
îr pier	hw which
ŏ pot	zh vision
ō toe	ə about,
ô paw	item

Stress marks:
′ (primary);
′ (secondary), as in
dictionary (dĭk′shə-nĕr′ē)

hangs freely from the waist down. **2.** A garment hanging from the waist and worn by women and girls. **3.** One of the leather flaps hanging from the side of a saddle. **4.** The lower outer section of a rocket vehicle. **5.** An outer edge; a border. **6. skirts.** The edge, as of a town; the outskirts. **7.** *Offensive Slang.* Used as a disparaging term for a woman. — *v.* **skirt•ed, skirt•ing, skirts.** — *tr.* **1.** To lie along or form the edge of; border. **2.** To pass around rather than across or through. **3.** To pass close to; miss narrowly. **4.** To evade, as by circumlocution: *skirted the issue.* — *intr.* To lie along, move along, or be an edge or a border. [ME < ON *skyrta*, shirt. See **sker-**[1]*.]

skirt steak *n.* A cut of beef from the lower part of the brisket.

skit (skĭt) *n.* **1.** A short, usu. comic dramatic performance or work; a sketch. **2.** A short humorous or satirical piece of writing. [?]

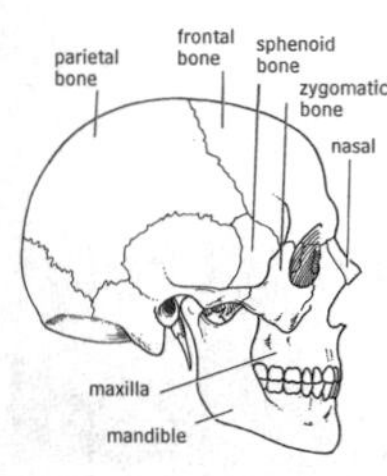

skull

ski tow *n. Sports.* **1.** A ski lift in which skiers cling to a continuous rope as they are pulled up a slope. **2.** See **ski lift.**

skit•ter (skĭt′ər) *v.* **-tered, -ter•ing, -ters.** — *intr.* **1.** To move rapidly along a surface, usu. with frequent light contacts or changes of direction; skip or glide quickly. **2.** To fish by drawing a lure or baited hook over the surface of the water with a skipping movement. — *tr.* To cause to skitter. [Prob. freq. of dial. *skite*, to run rapidly, perh. of Scand. orig.; akin to ON *skjōta*, to shoot. See SHOOT.]

skit•ter•y (skĭt′ə-rē) *adj.* Moving quickly, restlessly, or irregularly; skittish.

skit•tish (skĭt′ĭsh) *adj.* **1.** Moving quickly and lightly; lively. **2.** Restlessly active or nervous; restive. **3.** Undependably variable; mercurial or fickle. **4.** Shy; bashful. [ME, perh. of Scand. orig.; akin to ON *skjōta*, to shoot. See SHOOT.] — **skit′tish•ly** *adv.* — **skit′tish•ness** *n.*

skit•tle (skĭt′l) *n. Games.* **1. skittles.** *(used with a sing. v.)* A British form of ninepins, in which a wooden disk or ball is thrown to knock down the pins. **2.** One of the pins used in skittles. [Perh. of Scand. orig.]

skunk
Striped skunk
Mephitis mephitis

skive (skīv) *tr.v.* **skived, skiv•ing, skives.** To cut thin layers off (leather, for example); pare. [Of Scand. orig. See **skei-***.]

skiv•er (skī′vər) *n.* **1.** One, such as a cutting tool, that skives. **2.** A soft thin leather split off the outside of sheepskin and used for bookbinding.

Skiv•vies (skĭv′ēz). A trademark used for underwear.

skoal (skōl) *interj.* Used as a drinking toast. [Dan. and Norw. *skaal*, cup, skoal < ON *skāl*, bowl, drinking vessel. See **skel-**[1]*.]

Sko•kie (skō′kē). A village of NE IL, a suburb of Chicago. Pop. 54,432.

Skop•je (skôp′yā′, -yĕ) or **Skop•lje** (-lā′, -lyĕ). The cap. of Macedonia, in the N-central part on the Vardar R.; under Turkish control from 1392 to 1913. Pop. 406,400.

skosh (skōsh) *n. Slang.* A small amount; a bit. [J. *sukoshi.*]

Skr. *abbr.* Sanskrit.

Skt. *abbr.* Sanskrit.

skyscraper
John Hancock Center,
Chicago, Illinois

sku•a (skyo͞o′ə) *n.* **1.** Any of several large predatory sea birds of the genus *Catharacta* related to the jaeger, esp. the great skua. **2.** *Chiefly British.* See **jaeger** 1. [NLat., alteration of Faroese **skūvur* < ON *skūfr*, tassel, sea gull.]

skulk (skŭlk) *intr.v.* **skulked, skulk•ing, skulks.** **1.** To lie in hiding, as out of cowardice or bad conscience; lurk. **2.** To move about stealthily. **3.** To evade work or obligation; shirk. — *n.* **1.** One who hides, lurks, or practices evasion. **2.** A congregation of vermin, esp. foxes, or of thieves. [ME *skulken*, of Scand. orig.] — **skulk′er** *n.*

skull (skŭl) *n.* **1.** The bony or cartilaginous framework of the head of vertebrates, made up of the bones of the braincase and face; cranium. **2.** *Informal.* The head, regarded as the seat of thought or intelligence. **3.** A death's-head. [ME *skulle*, prob. of Scand. orig.]

skull•cap (skŭl′kăp′) *n.* **1.a.** A light close-fitting brimless cap. **b.** A yarmulke. **2.** Any of various plants of the genus *Scutellaria*, having clusters of two-lipped flowers.

skull•dug•ger•y or **skul•dug•ger•y** (skŭl-dŭg′ə-rē) *n., pl.* **-ger•ies.** Crafty deception or trickery or an instance of it. [Prob. alteration of Sc. *sculduddery*, obscenity, fornication.]

skulled (skŭld) *adj.* **1.** Having or provided with a skull: *skulled vertebrates.* **2.** Having a specified kind of skull. Often used in combination: *broad-skulled.*

skunk (skŭngk) *n.* **1.a.** Any of several small, mostly carnivorous New World mammals of the genus *Mephitis* and related genera, having a bushy tail and glossy black fur with white markings and ejecting a foul-smelling oily liquid from glands near the anus when frightened or in danger. **b.** The fur of this mammal. **2.** *Slang.* **a.** A person regarded as obnoxious or despicable. **b.** A person whose company is avoided. — *tr.v.* **skunked, skunk•ing, skunks.** *Slang.* **1.** To defeat overwhelmingly, esp. by keeping from scoring. **2.a.** To cheat (someone). **b.** To fail to pay (an amount due). [Of Massachusett orig.]

skunk bear *n.* See **wolverine** 1.

skunk cabbage *n.* **1.** An ill-smelling eastern North American swamp plant *(Symplocarpus foetidus)* having minute flowers enclosed in a mottled greenish or purplish spathe. **2.** A western North American plant *(Lysichitum americanum)* having a bright yellow spathe with an inflated upper part.

skunk grape *n.* See **fox grape.**

Skunk River (skŭngk). A river rising in central IA and flowing c. 425 km (264 mi) to the Mississippi R.

skunk•weed (skŭngk′wēd′) *n.* A dioecious, ill-smelling, dichotomously branched annual plant *(Croton texensis)* of the central and southwest United States.

sky (skī) *n., pl.* **skies** (skīz). **1.** The expanse of air over a given point on Earth; the upper atmosphere as seen from Earth's surface. **2.** The appearance of the upper atmosphere, esp. with reference to weather. Often used in the plural. **3.** The celestial regions; the heavens. **4.** The highest level or degree: *reaching for the sky.* — *tr.v.* **skied** (skīd), **sky•ing, skies** (skīz). **1.** To hit or throw (a ball, for example) high in the air. **2.** To hang (a painting, for example) on a wall above the line of vision. [ME < ON *sky̆*, cloud. See **(s)keu-***.]

sky blue *n. Color.* A light to pale blue.

sky•dive (skī′dīv′) *intr.v.* **-dived, -div•ing, -dives.** *Sports.* To jump and fall freely from an airplane, performing various maneuvers before pulling the ripcord of a parachute. — **sky′div′er** *n.* — **sky′div′ing** *n.*

Skye (skī), **Isle of.** An island of NW Scotland in the Inner Hebrides.

Skye terrier *n.* A small terrier of a breed native to the Isle of Skye, having a long low body, short legs, and shaggy hair.

sky•ey (skī′ē) *adj.* Of, from, or resembling the sky.

sky-high (skī′hī′) *adv.* **1.** To a very high level: *garbage piled sky-high.* **2.** In a lavish or enthusiastic manner. **3.** In pieces or to pieces; apart: *blew the bridge sky-high.* — *adj.* **1.** High up in the air. **2.** Exorbitantly high in cost or value.

sky-hook or **sky•hook** (skī′ho͝ok′) *n.* A helicopter whose fuselage is configured so as to be mounted with a steel line and hook used to lift and transport heavy objects.

sky•jack (skī′jăk′) *tr.v.* **-jacked, -jack•ing, -jacks.** To subject (an aircraft) to air piracy. [SKY + (HI)JACK.] — **sky′jack′er** *n.* — **sky′jack′ing** *n.*

sky•lark (skī′lärk′) *n.* An Old World lark *(Alauda arvensis)* with brown plumage, noted for singing while flying. — *intr.v.* **-larked, -lark•ing, -larks.** To play actively and boisterously.

sky•light (skī′līt′) *n.* An overhead window, as in a roof, admitting daylight.

sky•line (skī′līn′) *n.* **1.** The line along which the earth and the sky appear to meet; the horizon. **2.** The outline of a group of buildings or a mountain range seen against the sky.

sky•rock•et (skī′rŏk′ĭt) *n.* A firework that ascends high into the air where it explodes in a brilliant cascade of flares and starlike sparks. — *intr. & tr.v.* **-et•ed, -et•ing, -ets.** To rise or cause to rise rapidly and suddenly.

Sky•ros (skī′rəs, skē′rôs). See **Skíros.**

sky•sail (skī′səl, -sāl′) *n. Naut.* A small square sail above the royal in a square-rigged vessel.

sky•scrap•er (skī′skrā′pər) *n.* A very tall building.

sky•walk (skī′wôk′) *n.* An elevated, usu. enclosed walkway between two buildings.

sky•ward (skī′wərd) *adv. & adj.* At or toward the sky. — **sky′wards** *adv.*

sky wave *n.* A radio wave that travels upward.

sky•way (skī′wā′) *n.* **1.** A route regularly used by airplanes; an air lane. **2.** An elevated highway.

sky•writ•ing (skī′rī′tĭng) *n.* **1.** The process of writing in the sky by releasing a visible vapor from an airplane. **2.** The letters or words so formed. — **sky′writ′er** *n.*

SL *abbr.* **1.** Salvage loss. **2.** Sea level. **3.** Source language. **4.** South latitude.

sl. *abbr.* **1.** Slightly. **2.** Slow.

s.l. *abbr. Lat.* Sine loco (without place of publication).

slab[1] (slăb) *n.* **1.** A broad, flat, thick piece, as of cake, stone, or cheese. **2.** An outside piece cut from a log when squaring it for lumber. **3.** *Baseball.* The pitcher's rubber. — *tr.v.* **slabbed, slab•bing, slabs.** **1.** To make or shape into slabs or a slab. **2.** To cover or pave with slabs. **3.** To dress (a log) by cutting slabs. [ME.]

slab[2] (slăb) *adj. Archaic.* Viscid. [Prob. of Scand. orig.]

slab-sid•ed (slăb′sī′dĭd) *adj.* **1.** Having flat sides. **2.** *Informal.* Tall and slim; lanky.

slack[1] (slăk) *adj.* **slack•er, slack•est.** **1.** Moving slowly; sluggish. **2.** Lacking in activity; not busy: *a slack season for hotels.* **3.** Not tense or taut; loose: *a slack rope.* See Syns at **loose.** **4.** Lacking firmness; flaccid: *a slack grip.* **5.** Lacking in diligence or care; negligent: *a slack worker.* **6.** Flowing or blowing with little speed: *a slack current.* — *v.* **slacked, slack•ing, slacks.** — *tr.* **1.** To make slower or looser; slacken. **2.** To be careless or remiss in doing: *slack one's duty.* **3.** To slake (lime). — *intr.* **1.** To be or become slack. **2.** To evade work; shirk. — *n.* **1.** A loose part, as of a rope or sail. **2.** A lack of tension; looseness. **3.** A period of little activity; a lull. **4.a.** A cessation of movement in a current of air or water. **b.** An area of still water. **5.** Unused capacity. **6. slacks.** Casual trousers that are not part of a suit. — *adv.* In a slack manner: *a banner hanging slack.* — ***phrasal verb.*** **slack off.** To decrease in activity or intensity. [ME *slak* < CE *slæc.* See **slēg-***.] — **slack′ly** *adv.* — **slack′ness** *n.*

slack[2] (slăk) *n.* A mixture of coal fragments, coal dust, and dirt that remains after screening coal. [ME *sleck.*]

slack[3] (slăk) *n. Chiefly British.* **1.** A small dell or hollow. **2.** A bog; a morass. [ME *slak* < ON *slakki.*]

slack-baked (slăk′băkt′) *adj.* Not fully baked or done; half-baked: *slack-baked bread.*

slack•en (slăk′ən) *tr. & intr.v.* **-ened, -en•ing, -ens. 1.** To make or become slower; slow down: *Air speed slackened.* **2.** To make or become less tense, taut, or firm; loosen: *The tension in the room slackened.* **3.** To make or become less vigorous, intense, or severe; ease: *slacken discipline.*

slack•er (slăk′ər) *n.* One that shirks work or responsibility, esp. one that tries to evade military service in wartime.

slack water *n.* **1.** The period at high or low tide when there is no visible flow of water. **2.** An area in a sea or river unaffected by currents; still water.

slag (slăg) *n.* **1.** The vitreous mass left as a residue by the smelting of metallic ore. **2.** See **scoria** 1. *— tr. & intr.v.* **slagged, slag•ging, slags.** To change into slag or form slag. [LGer. *slagge* < MLGer.] **— slag′gy** *adj.*

slain (slān) *v.* P.part. of **slay.**

slake (slāk) *v.* **slaked, slak•ing, slakes.** *— tr.* **1.** To satisfy (a craving); quench: *slaked her thirst.* **2.** To lessen the force or activity of; moderate: *slaking his anger.* **3.** To cool or refresh by wetting or moistening. **4.** To combine (lime) chemically with water or moist air. *— intr.* To undergo a slaking process; crumble or disintegrate, as lime. [ME *slaken,* to abate < OE *slacian* < *slæc,* slack, sluggish. See SLACK[1].]

slaked lime (slākt) *n.* See **calcium hydroxide.**

sla•lom (slä′ləm) *Sports. — n.* **1.** The act or sport of skiing in a zigzag course. **2.** A race on skis or in vehicles along such a course laid out with flag-marked poles. *— intr.v.* **-lomed, -lom•ing, -loms.** To race in a slalom. [Norw. *slalåm* : *slad,* sloping + *låm,* path.] **— sla′lom•er, sla′lom•ist** *n.*

slam[1] (slăm) *v.* **slammed, slam•ming, slams.** *— tr.* **1.** To shut with force and loud noise. **2.** To put, throw, or otherwise forcefully move so as to produce a loud noise. **3.** To hit or strike with great force. **4.** *Slang.* To criticize harshly; censure forcefully. *— intr.* **1.** To close or swing into place with force so as to produce a loud noise. **2.** To hit something with force; crash. *— n.* **1.a.** A forceful impact that makes a loud noise. **b.** A noise so produced. **2.** An act of shutting forcefully and loudly. **3.** *Slang.* A harsh or devastating criticism. [Perh. of Scand. orig.]

slam[2] (slăm) *n. Games.* The winning of all the tricks or all but one during the play of one hand in bridge and other whist-derived card games. [?]

slam-bang (slăm′băng′) *adv. & adj. Slang.* **1.** With force and much noise. **2.** With heedless speed; slapdash. **3.** With vigorous, relentless action and pace.

slam-dunk or **slam dunk** (slăm′dŭngk′) *n. Basketball.* A dramatic, forceful dunk shot. **— slam′dunk′** *v.*

slam•mer (slăm′ər) *n. Slang.* A jail. [< SLAM[1].]

slan•der (slăn′dər) *n.* **1.** *Law.* Oral communication of false statements injurious to a person's reputation. **2.** A false and malicious statement or report about someone. *— v.* **-dered, -der•ing, -ders.** *— tr.* To communicate a slander about. *— intr.* To utter or spread slander. [ME *slaundre* < OFr. *esclandre,* alteration of *escandle* < Lat. *scandalum,* cause of offense, stumbling block. See SCANDAL.] **— slan′der•er** *n.* **— slan′der•ous** *adj.* **— slan′der•ous•ly** *adv.*

slang (slăng) *n.* **1.** A kind of language esp. occurring in casual and playful speech, usu. made up of short-lived coinages and figures of speech deliberately used in place of standard terms for effects such as raciness, humor, or irreverence. **2.** Language peculiar to a group; argot or jargon: *thieves' slang.* *— v.* **slanged, slang•ing, slangs.** *— intr.* **1.** To use slang. **2.** To use angry and abusive language. *— tr.* To attack with abusive language; vituperate. [?] **— slang′i•ly** *adv.* **— slang′i•ness** *n.* **— slang′y** *adj.*

slant (slănt) *v.* **slant•ed, slant•ing, slants.** *— tr.* **1.** To give a direction other than perpendicular or horizontal to; make diagonal; cause to slope. **2.** To present so as to conform to a particular bias or appeal to a certain audience. *— intr.* To have or go in a direction other than perpendicular or horizontal; slope. *— n.* **1.a.** A line, plane, course, or direction other than perpendicular or horizontal; a slope. **b.** A sloping thing or piece of ground. **2.** *Print.* A virgule. **3.a.** A personal point of view or opinion. **b.** A bias. [Alteration of obsolete *slent* < ME *slenten,* to fall aslant, perh. of Scand. orig.]

Syns: *slant, incline, lean, slope, tilt, tip.* The central meaning shared by these verbs is "to depart or cause to depart from true vertical or horizontal": *rays of light slanting through the window; inclined her head toward the speaker; leaned against the railing; a sloping driveway; tilted her hat at an angle; tipped his chair back.*

slant rhyme *n.* See **off rhyme.**

slant•ways (slănt′wāz′) *adv.* Slantwise.

slant•wise (slănt′wīz′) *adv.* At a slant or slope; obliquely. *— adj.* Slanting; oblique.

slap (slăp) *n.* **1.a.** A sharp blow made with the open hand or with a flat object; a smack. **b.** The sound of such a blow. **2.** A sharp insult. *— v.* **slapped, slap•ping, slaps.** *— tr.* **1.** To strike with a flat object, such as the palm of the hand. **2.** To cause to strike sharply and loudly. **3.** To put or place with a loud sharp sound. **4.** To criticize or insult sharply. *— intr.* To strike or beat with the force and sound of a slap. *— adv. Informal.* Directly and with force. ***— phrasal verb.*** **slap down. 1.** To restrain or correct by a sharp blow or emphatic censure. **2.** To put a sudden end to; suppress. ***— idiom.*** **slap on the wrist.** A nominal or token punishment. [ME *slappe.*] **— slap′per** *n.*

slap•dash (slăp′dăsh′) *adj.* Hasty and careless, as in execution. *— adv.* In a reckless, haphazard manner.

slap•hap•py (slăp′hăp′ē) *adj.* **-pi•er, -pi•est.** *Slang.* **1.** Dazed, silly, or incoherent from or as if from blows to the head; punch-drunk. **2.** Happy-go-lucky.

slap•jack (slăp′jăk′) *n.* A pancake; a flapjack.

slap shot *n. Sports.* A fast-moving shot made in hockey with a full swinging stroke.

slap•stick (slăp′stĭk′) *n.* **1.** A form of comedy marked by chases, collisions, and crude practical jokes. **2.** A paddle designed to make a loud whacking sound, once used in farces.

slash (slăsh) *v.* **slashed, slash•ing, slash•es.** *— tr.* **1.** To cut or form by cutting with forceful sweeping strokes. **2.** To lash with sweeping strokes. **3.** To make a gash or gashes in. **4.** To cut a slit or slits in, esp. to reveal an underlying color: *slash a sleeve.* **5.** To criticize sharply. **6.** To reduce or curtail greatly. *— intr.* **1.** To make forceful sweeping strokes with or as if with a sharp instrument. **2.** To cut one's way with such strokes. *— n.* **1.** A forceful sweeping stroke made with a sharp instrument. **2.** A long cut or other opening made by such a stroke; a gash or slit. **3.** A decorative slit in a fabric or garment. **4.** Branches and other residue left on a forest floor after the cutting of timber. **5.** Wet or swampy ground overgrown with bushes and trees. Often used in the plural. **6.** *Print.* A virgule. [Perh. < obsolete Fr. *esclachier,* to break, var. of *esclater* < OFr. < *esclat,* splinter. See SLAT.] **— slash′er** *n.*

slash•ing (slăsh′ĭng) *adj.* **1.** Bitingly critical or satiric: *slashing wit.* **2.** Dashing; pelting: *a slashing hailstorm.* **3.** Brilliant; intense: *slashing colors.* **— slash′ing•ly** *adv.*

slash pine *n.* A pine tree *(Pinus elliotti)* of swampy coastal areas of the southeast United States that yields pulp, rosin, timber, and turpentine.

slat (slăt) *n.* **1.** A narrow strip of metal or wood, as in a Venetian blind. **2.** A movable auxiliary airfoil running along the leading edge of the wing of an airplane. **3. slats.** *Slang.* The ribs. *— tr.v.* **slat•ted, slat•ting, slats.** To provide or make with slats: *slatting the back of a chair.* [ME *sclat* < OFr. *esclat,* splinter, prob. of Gmc. orig.]

slatch (slăch) *n. New England.* **1.** A momentary lull between breaking waves, favorable for launching a boat. **2.** A lull in a high windstorm. [Var. of SLACK[1].]

slate (slāt) *n.* **1.** A fine-grained metamorphic rock that splits into thin smooth-surfaced layers. **2.a.** A piece of this rock cut for use as roofing or surfacing material or as a writing surface. **b.** A writing tablet made of a similar material. **3.** A record of past performance or activity: *starting with a clean slate.* **4.** A list of the candidates of a political party running for various offices. **5.** *Color.* A dark or bluish gray to dark bluish or dark purplish gray. *— adj.* **1.** Made of slate. **2.** *Color.* Of the color slate. *— tr.v.* **slat•ed, slat•ing, slates. 1.** To cover (a roof, for example) with slate. **2.** To put on a list of candidates. **3.** To schedule or designate. [ME *sclate* < OFr. *esclate,* splinter, fem. of *esclat.* See SLAT.]

slate black *n. Color.* A purplish black.

slate blue *n. Color.* A grayish blue to dark bluish gray.

slate-col•ored junco (slāt′kŭl′ərd) *n.* A junco *(Junco hyemalis)* of eastern North America having dark gray upper parts and a white abdomen.

slat•er (slā′tər) *n.* **1.** One who lays slate surfaces, as on roofs. **2.** Any of several isopod crustaceans, such as the sow bug.

Sla•ter (slā′tər), **Samuel.** 1768–1835. British-born textile pioneer in America who oversaw construction of the nation's first successful water-powered cotton mill (1790–93).

slath•er (slăth′ər) *tr.v.* **-ered, -er•ing, -ers.** *Informal.* **1.** To use or give great amounts of; lavish. **2.a.** To spread thickly. **b.** To spread thickly with something. *— n. Slang.* A great amount. Often used in the plural: *slathers of jewels.* [?]

slat•ing (slā′tĭng) *n.* Slates for covering roofs, walls, or other surfaces.

slat•tern (slăt′ərn) *n.* An untidy dirty woman. [Perh. < dial. *slattering,* slovenly, pr.part. of dial. *slatter,* to slop.]

slat•tern•ly (slăt′ərn-lē) *adj.* **1.** Characteristic of or befitting a slattern. **2.** Slovenly; untidy. **— slat′tern•li•ness** *n.*

slat•y (slā′tē) *adj.* **-i•er, -i•est. 1.** Composed of or resembling slate. **2.** Having the color of slate.

slaugh•ter (slô′tər) *n.* **1.** The killing of animals esp. for food. **2.** The killing of a large number of people; a massacre. *— tr.v.* **-tered, -ter•ing, -ters. 1.** To kill (animals) esp. for food; butcher. **2.a.** To kill (people) in large numbers; massacre. **b.** To kill in a violent or brutal manner. [ME, of Scand. orig.] **— slaugh′ter•er** *n.* **— slaugh′ter•ous** *adj.*

slalom

slash
A Young Lady, 1567, by Steven van der Meulen

ă **pat**	oi **boy**
ā **pay**	ou **out**
âr **care**	o͝o **took**
ä **father**	o͞o **boot**
ĕ **pet**	ŭ **cut**
ē **be**	ûr **urge**
ĭ **pit**	th **thin**
ī **pie**	*th* **this**
îr **pier**	hw **which**
ŏ **pot**	zh **vision**
ō **toe**	ə **a**bout,
ô **paw**	it**e**m

Stress marks:
′ (primary);
′ (secondary), as in
dictionary (dĭk′shə-nĕr′ē)

slaugh•ter•house (slô′tər-hous′) *n.* **1.** A place where animals are butchered. **2.** A scene of massacre or carnage.

Slav (släv) *n.* A member of one of the Slavic-speaking peoples of eastern Europe. [ME *Sclave* < Med.Lat. *Sclāvus* < LGk. *Sklabos*, alteration of Old Slav. *Slověninŭ*.]

Slav. *abbr.* Slavic.

slave (slāv) *n.* **1.** One bound in servitude as the property of a person or household. **2.** One who is abjectly subservient to a specified person or influence. **3.** One who works extremely hard. **4.** A machine or component controlled by another machine or component. — *intr.v.* **slaved, slav•ing, slaves. 1.** To work very hard or doggedly; toil. **2.** To trade in or transport slaves. [ME *sclave* < OFr. *esclave* < Med.Lat. *sclāvus* < *Sclāvus*, Slav (< the widespread enslavement of captured Slavs in the early Middle Ages). See SLAV.]

slave ant *n.* An ant captured and raised as a worker by slave-making ants.

sled

Slave Coast (slāv). A region of W Africa bordering the Bight of Benin on the Gulf of Guinea; an exportation base for slaves from the 16th to the early 19th cent.

slave driver *n.* **1.** An overseer of slaves at work. **2.** A severely exacting employer or supervisor.

slave•hold•er (slāv′hōl′dər) *n.* One who owns or holds slaves. — **slave′hold′ing** *adj. & n.*

slave-mak•ing ant (slāv′mā′kĭng) *n.* Any of various species of ant, such as *Formica sanguinea* of Europe, that raid the nests of other ants and carry off the pupae in order to provide workers for their own colonies.

slav•er[1] (slăv′ər) *intr.v.* **-ered, -er•ing, -ers. 1.** To slobber; drool. **2.** To behave in an obsequious manner; fawn. — *n.* **1.** Saliva drooling from the mouth. **2.** Senseless and effusive talk; drivel. [ME *slaveren*, prob. < ON *slafra*.]

slav•er[2] (slā′vər) *n.* One, such as a person or ship, that is engaged in the trafficking of slaves.

Slave River. A river, c. 499 km (310 mi), of W-central Canada flowing between Lake Athabasca in NE Alberta and Great Slave Lake in the S Northwest Terrs.

sledge

slav•er•y (slā′və-rē, slāv′rē) *n.*, *pl.* **-ies. 1.** The state of one bound in servitude as the property of a slaveholder or household. **2.a.** The practice of owning slaves. **b.** A mode of production in which slaves constitute the principal work force. **3.** The condition of being subject or addicted to a specified influence. **4.** A condition of hard work and subjection.

slave state *n.* **1.** Any of the 15 states of the Union in which slavery was legal before the Civil War. **2.** A nation under totalitarian rule.

slave trade *n.* Traffic in slaves.

slav•ey (slā′vē) *n.*, *pl.* **-eys.** A household servant, esp. an overworked one.

Slav•ic (slä′vĭk) *adj.* Of or relating to the Slavs or their languages. — *n.* A branch of the Indo-European language family that includes Bulgarian, Belorussian, Czech, Macedonian, Polish, Russian, Serbo-Croatian, Slovak, Slovene, Ukrainian, and Wendish.

slav•ish (slā′vĭsh) *adj.* **1.** Of or characteristic of a slave or slavery; servile. **2.** Showing no originality; blindly imitative. — **slav′ish•ly** *adv.* — **slav′ish•ness** *n.*

slav•oc•ra•cy (slā-vŏk′rə-sē) *n.*, *pl.* **-cies.** A ruling group of slaveholders or advocates of slavery, as in the southern United States before 1865. — **slav′o•crat′** (slā′və-krăt′) *n.* — **slav′o•crat′ic** *adj.*

sledgehammer

Sla•vo•ni•a (slə-vō′nē-ə, -vōn′yə). A historical region of N Croatia between the Drava and Sava rivers; a Slavic state after the 7th cent. and part of Yugoslavia from 1918 to 1991. — **Sla•vo′ni•an** *adj. & n.*

Sla•von•ic (slə-vŏn′ĭk) *n.* Slavic. [< Med.Lat. *Sclāvōnia*, Slavic lands < *Sclāvus*, Slavic. See SLAVIC.] — **Sla•von′ic** *adj.*

Slav•o•phile (slä′və-fīl′) also **Slav•o•phil** (-fĭl) *n.* **1.** An admirer of Slavic peoples or their culture. **2.** A person advocating the supremacy of Slavic culture, esp. over western European influences, as in 19th-century Russia. — **Sla•voph′i•lism** (slə-vŏf′ə-lĭz′əm) *n.*

slaw (slô) *n.* Coleslaw.

slay (slā) *tr.v.* **slew** (slo͞o), **slain** (slān), **slay•ing, slays. 1.** To kill violently. **2.** *Slang.* To overwhelm, as with laughter or love. [ME *slen, slayen* < OE *slēan*.] — **slay′er** *n.*

sld. *abbr.* **1.** Sailed. **2.** Sealed. **3.** Sold.

SLE *abbr.* Systemic lupus erythematosus.

sleave (slēv) *n. Archaic.* A fine thread or skein of thread. [< ME **sleven*, to disentangle < OE **slǣfan*, to cut < *slāf*, p.t. of *slīfan*, to split.]

sleaze (slēz) *n.* A sleazy condition, quality, or appearance.

slea•zy (slē′zē) *adj.* **-zi•er, -zi•est. 1.a.** Shabby, dirty, and vulgar; tawdry. **b.** Dishonest or corrupt; disreputable. **2.** Made of low-quality materials; cheap or shoddy. **3.** Thin and loosely woven; flimsy. [?] — **slea′zi•ly** *adv.* — **slea′zi•ness** *n.*

sled (slĕd) *n.* **1.** A vehicle on runners, used for carrying people or loads over ice and snow; a sledge. **2.** A light wooden frame on runners, used for coasting over snow or ice. — *v.* **sled•ded, sled•ding, sleds.** — *tr.* To carry on a sled. — *intr.* To ride or use a sled. [ME *sledde* < MDu.] — **sled′der** *n.*

sled•ding (slĕd′ĭng) *n.* **1.** Use of a sled. **2.** Conditions conducive to the use of a sled. **3.** *Informal.* A specific kind of progress toward a goal; the going: *The plan faces tough sledding.*

sled dog *n.* A dog, such as a husky, used to pull a dogsled, esp. in Arctic regions.

sledge (slĕj) *n.* A vehicle on low runners drawn by work animals, such as horses, and used to transport loads across ice, snow, and rough ground. — *tr. & intr.v.* **sledged, sledg•ing, sledg•es.** To convey or travel on a sledge. [Du. dial. *sleedse*, perh. dim. of Du. *slede*, sled < MDu. *sledde*.]

sledge•ham•mer (slĕj′hăm′ər) *n.* A long heavy hammer, often wielded with both hands, used for driving wedges and for other heavy work. — *tr.v.* **-mered, -mer•ing, -mers.** To strike with or as if with a sledgehammer. — *adj.* Ruthlessly severe; crushing. [ME *slegge* (< OE *slecg*) + HAMMER.]

sleek (slēk) *adj.* **sleek•er, sleek•est. 1.** Smooth and lustrous as if polished; glossy. **2.** Well-groomed and neatly tailored. **3.** Healthy or well-fed; thriving. **4.** Polished or smooth in manner, esp. in an unctuous way; slick. — *tr.v.* **sleeked, sleek•ing, sleeks. 1.** To make sleek; slick. **2.** To gloss over; conceal. [Var. of SLICK.] — **sleek′ly** *adv.* — **sleek′ness** *n.*

sleep (slēp) *n.* **1.a.** A natural periodic state of rest for the mind and body, in which the eyes usu. close and consciousness is completely or partly lost, so that there is a decrease in bodily movement and responsiveness to external stimuli. **b.** A period of this form of rest. **c.** A state of inactivity resembling or suggesting sleep; unconsciousness, dormancy, hibernation, or death. **2.** *Bot.* The folding together of leaflets or petals at night or in the absence of light. — *v.* **slept** (slĕpt), **sleep•ing, sleeps.** — *intr.* **1.** To be in the state of sleep or fall asleep. **2.** To be in a condition resembling sleep. — *tr.* **1.** To pass or get rid of by sleeping: *slept away the day.* **2.** To provide sleeping accommodations for: *This tent sleeps three.* — ***phrasal verbs.*** **sleep around.** *Informal.* To be sexually active with more than one partner. **sleep in. 1.** To sleep at one's place of employment: *a cook who sleeps in.* **2.a.** To oversleep. **b.** To sleep late on purpose. **sleep out. 1.** To sleep at one's own home, not at one's place of employment. **2.** To sleep away from one's home. **sleep over.** To spend the night as a guest in another's home. **sleep with.** To have sexual relations with. — ***idiom.*** **sleep on it.** *Informal.* To consider something overnight before deciding. [ME *slepe* < OE *slǣp*. See **slēb-***.]

sleep apnea *n.* A temporary suspension of breathing occurring repeatedly during sleep that often affects overweight people or those having a neurological disorder.

sleep•er (slē′pər) *n.* **1.** One that sleeps. **2.** A sleeping car. **3.** Children's pajamas, usu. with legs that cover the feet. Often used in the plural. **4.** One that achieves unexpected recognition or success, as a racehorse or a movie. **5.** A horizontal structural member on or near the ground that supports weight. **6.** *Chiefly British.* A railroad crosstie. **7.** Any of various usu. small fishes of the family Eleotridae, noted for their habit of lying immobile.

sleep-in (slēp′ĭn′) *adj.* Living at one's place of employment.

sleep•ing bag (slē′pĭng) *n.* A large, warmly lined, usu. zippered bag for sleeping, esp. outdoors.

sleeping car *n.* A railroad car having accommodations for sleeping.

sleeping pill *n.* A sedative or hypnotic drug, esp. a barbiturate, in the form of a pill or capsule used to relieve insomnia.

sleeping sickness *n.* **1.** An often fatal, endemic infectious disease in tropical Africa, caused by either of two trypanosomes *(Trypanosoma rhodesiense* or *T. gambiense)* transmitted by the tsetse fly and characterized by fever, headache, and lymph node swelling, followed by weakness, sleepiness, and coma. **2.** See **encephalitis lethargica.**

sleep-learn•ing (slēp′lûr′nĭng) *n.* Instruction in a subject, such as a foreign language, during sleep, usu. by recordings.

sleep•less (slēp′lĭs) *adj.* **1.a.** Marked by a lack of sleep: *a sleepless night.* **b.** Unable to sleep. **2.** Always alert or active; never resting. — **sleep′less•ly** *adv.* — **sleep′less•ness** *n.*

sleep•o•ver (slēp′ō′vər) *n.* **1.** An instance of spending the night as a guest at another's home. **2.** An overnight guest.

sleep•walk•ing (slēp′wô′kĭng) *n.* The act or an instance of walking or performing another activity associated with wakefulness while asleep or in a sleeplike state. — **sleep′walk′** *v.* — **sleep′walk′er** *n.*

sleep•wear (slēp′wâr′) *n.* Nightclothes.

sleep•y (slē′pē) *adj.* **-i•er, -i•est. 1.a.** Ready for or needing sleep. **b.** Sluggish from sleep. **2.** Inducing sleep. **3.** Inactive; quiet: *a sleepy town.* — **sleep′i•ly** *adv.* — **sleep′i•ness** *n.*

sleep•y•head (slē′pē-hĕd′) *n. Informal.* A sleepy person.

sleepy sickness *n.* See **encephalitis lethargica.**

sleet (slēt) *n.* **1.** Precipitation consisting of usu. transparent frozen or partially frozen raindrops. **2.** A mixture of rain and snow or hail. **3.** A thin icy coating that forms when rain or sleet freezes, as on trees or streets. — *intr.v.* **sleet•ed, sleet•ing, sleets.** To shower sleet. [ME *slete* < OE **slēte*.] — **sleet′y** *adj.*

sleeve (slēv) *n.* **1.** A part of a garment that covers all or part of an arm. **2.** A case into which an object or a device fits: *a record sleeve.* — *tr.v.* **sleeved, sleev•ing, sleeves.** To furnish or fit with sleeves or a sleeve. — ***idiom.*** **up (one's) sleeve.**

Hidden but ready to be used. [ME *sleve* < OE *slēf.* See **sleubh-***.] — **sleeve′less** *adj.*

sleeve coupling *n.* A thin steel cylinder joining the ends of two lengths of shafting or pipe.

sleeve dog *n.* A very small Pekingese, usu. 15 centimeters (6 inches) or less in height.

sleigh (slā) *n.* A light vehicle mounted on runners and having one or more seats, usu. drawn by a horse over snow or ice. — *intr.v.* **sleighed, sleigh•ing, sleighs.** To ride in or drive a sleigh. [Du. *slee*, var. of *slede* < MDu. *slēde.*] — **sleigh′er** *n.*

sleight (slīt) *n.* **1.** Deftness; dexterity. **2.** A clever or skillful trick or deception; an artifice or a stratagem. [ME, alteration of *sleahthe* < ON *slœgdh* < *slœgr*, sly.]

sleight of hand *n., pl.* **sleights of hand. 1.** A trick or set of tricks performed by a juggler or magician so quickly that the manner of execution cannot be observed; legerdemain. **2.** Performance of conjuring tricks. **3.** Skill in such performance.

slen•der (slĕn′dər) *adj.* **-er, -est. 1.a.** Having little width in proportion to height or length; long and thin. **b.** Thin and delicate in build; gracefully slim. **2.** Small in amount or extent; meager: *slender wages.* [ME *sclendre, slendre.*] — **slen′der•ize′** *v.* — **slen′der•ly** *adv.* — **slen′der•ness** *n.*

slender loris *n.* A very small tailless loris *(Loris gracilis)* of southern India and Sri Lanka having large eyes with dark circles around them and very short fingers and toes.

slept (slĕpt) *v.* P.t. and p.part. of **sleep.**

sleuth (slo͞oth) *n.* **1.** A detective. **2.** See **sleuthhound** 1. — *v.* **sleuthed, sleuth•ing, sleuths.** — *tr.* To track or follow. — *intr.* To act as a detective. [Short for SLEUTHHOUND.]

sleuth•hound (slo͞oth′hound′) *n.* **1.** A dog used for tracking or pursuing, such as a bloodhound. **2.** A detective. [ME *sleuth*, animal track (< ON *slōdh*) + HOUND.]

slew¹ also **slue** (slo͞o) *n. Informal.* A large amount or number; a lot: *a slew of bills.* [Ir.Gael. *sluagh*, multitude < OIr. *slúag.*]

slew² (slo͞o) *v.* P.t. of **slay.**

slew³ (slo͞o) *n.* Var. of **slough¹.**

slew⁴ (slo͞o) *v. & n.* Var. of **slue¹.**

slice (slīs) *n.* **1.** A thin broad piece cut from a larger amount. **2.** A portion or share. **3.a.** A knife with a broad thin flexible blade, used for cutting and serving food. **b.** A similar implement for spreading printing ink. **4.** *Sports.* **a.** A stroke that causes a ball to curve off course to the right or, if the player is left-handed, to the left. **b.** The course followed by such a ball. — *v.* **sliced, slic•ing, slic•es.** — *tr.* **1.** To cut or divide into slices. **2.** To cut from a larger piece: *slice off a piece.* **3.** To cut through or across with or as if with a knife. **4.** To divide into portions or shares; parcel out. **5.** To spread, work at, or clear away with a bladed tool such as a slice bar. **6.** *Sports.* To hit (a ball) with a slice. — *intr.* **1.** To move like a knife. **2.** *Sports.* To hit a ball with a slice. [ME, splinter < OFr. *esclice* < *esclicier*, to splinter, of Gmc. orig.] — **slice′a•ble** *adj.* — **slic′er** *n.*

slice bar *n.* An iron tool with a broad flat end, used to loosen and clear out clinkers from furnace grates.

slice of life *n., pl.* **slices of life.** An episode of actual experience represented realistically in a dramatic, fictional, or reportorial work. — **slice′-of-life′** (slīs′əv-līf′) *adj.*

slick (slĭk) *adj.* **slick•er, slick•est. 1.** Smooth, glossy, and slippery. **2.** Deftly executed; adroit. **3.** Shrewd; wily. **4.** Superficially attractive or plausible but lacking depth or soundness; glib. — *n.* **1.** A smooth or slippery surface or area. **2.a.** A floating film of oil. **b.** A trail of floating material: *a garbage slick.* **3.** An implement that makes a surface slick, esp. a chisel for smoothing and polishing. **4.** *Informal.* A magazine, usu. of large popular readership, printed on high-quality glossy paper. **5.** A racing automobile tire with a smooth tread. — *tr.v.* **slicked, slick•ing, slicks. 1.** To make smooth, glossy, or oily. **2.** *Informal.* To make neat, trim, or tidy: *slicked themselves up.* [ME *slike* < OE **slice.* See **lei-***.] — **slick′ly** *adv.* — **slick′ness** *n.*

slick•en (slĭk′ən) *tr. & intr.v.* **-ened, -en•ing, -ens.** To make or become slick. — **slick′en•er** *n.*

slick•en•side (slĭk′ən-sīd′) *n.* A polished striated rock surface caused by one rock mass sliding over another in a fault plane. [Dial. *slicken*, glossy (alteration of SLICK) + SIDE.]

slick•er (slĭk′ər) *n.* **1.a.** A long water-repellant coat usu. made of oilskin. **b.** A raincoat made of a glossy or shiny material, such as plastic or rubber. **2.** A tool for dressing hides. **3.** *Informal.* A cheat; a swindler. **4.** *Informal.* A person with stylish clothing and manners.

slid•den (slĭd′n) *v. Archaic.* A p.part. of **slide.**

slide (slīd) *v.* **slid** (slĭd), **slid•ing, slides.** — *intr.* **1.** To move over a surface while maintaining smooth, continuous contact. **2.** To coast on a slippery surface, such as ice or snow. **3.** To pass smoothly and quietly; glide. **4.** To go unattended or unacted upon. **5.** To lose a secure footing or positioning; shift out of place; slip. **6.a.** To move downward. **b.** To return to a less favorable or less worthy condition. **7.** *Baseball.* To drop down and skid, usu. feet first, into a base to avoid being put out. — *tr.* To cause to slide or slip. — *n.* **1.** A sliding movement or action. **2.** A smooth surface or track for sliding, usu. inclined. **3.** A playground apparatus for children to slide on, typically consisting of a smooth chute mounted by a ladder. **4.** A part that operates by sliding, as the U-shaped section of tube on a trombone that is moved to produce various tones. **5.** An image on a transparent base for projection on a screen. **6.** A small glass plate for mounting specimens to be examined under a microscope. **7.** A fall of a mass of rock, earth, or snow down a slope; an avalanche or a landslide. **8.** *Mus.* **a.** A slight portamento used in violin playing, passing quickly from one note to another. **b.** An ornamentation consisting of two grace notes approaching the main note. [ME *sliden* < OE *slīdan.*]

Syns: *slide, slip, glide, coast, skid, slither.* These verbs mean to move smoothly and continuously over or as if over a slippery surface. *Slide* usually implies rapid, easy movement without loss of contact with the surface: *coal sliding down a chute. Slip* is often applied to accidental sliding resulting in loss of balance or foothold: *slipped on a patch of ice. Glide* refers to smooth, free-flowing, seemingly effortless movement: *"four snakes gliding up and down a hollow"* (Ralph Waldo Emerson). *Coast* applies especially to downward movement resulting from the effects of gravity or momentum: *The driver let the truck coast down the incline. Skid* implies an uncontrolled, often sideways sliding caused by a lack of traction: *The bus skidded on wet pavement. Slither* can mean to slip and slide, as on an uneven surface, often with friction and noise: *"The detached crystals slithered down the rock face"* (H.G. Wells). The word can also suggest the sinuous, gliding motion of a reptile: *An iguana slithered across the path.*

Sli•dell (slĭ-dĕl′). A city of SE LA NE of New Orleans. Pop. 24,124.

slid•er (slī′dər) *n.* **1.** One that slides. **2.** *Baseball.* A fast pitch that breaks in the same direction as a curve ball at the last moment.

slide rule *n.* A device consisting of logarithmically scaled rules mounted to slide along each other so that multiplication, division, and other more complex computations are reduced to the mechanical equivalent of addition or subtraction.

slide valve *n.* A valve that slides back and forth over ports, esp. one in the cylinder wall of a steam engine that permits the intake and outflow of steam to move the piston.

slid•ing scale (slī′dĭng) *n.* A scale in which indicated prices, taxes, or wages vary in accordance with another factor, as medical charges with a patient's income.

sli•er (slī′ər) *adj.* A comp. of **sly.**

sli•est (slī′ĭst) *adj.* A superl. of **sly.**

slight (slīt) *adj.* **slight•er, slight•est. 1.** Small in size, degree, or amount. **2.** Lacking strength, substance, or solidity; frail: *slight evidence.* **3.** Of small importance or consideration; trifling. **4.** Small and slender in build or construction; delicate. — *tr.v.* **slight•ed, slight•ing, slights. 1.** To treat as of small importance; make light of. **2.** To treat with discourteous reserve or inattention. **3.** To do negligently or thoughtlessly; scant. — *n.* **1.** The act or an instance of slighting. **2.** A deliberate discourtesy; a snub. [ME, slender, smooth, poss. of Scand. orig. See **lei-***.] — **slight′ness** *n.*

slight•ing (slī′tĭng) *adj.* Conveying or constituting a slight; belittling: *a slighting look.* — **slight′ing•ly** *adv.*

slight•ly (slīt′lē) *adv.* **1.** To a small degree or extent; somewhat. **2.** Slenderly; delicately: *slightly built.*

Sli•go (slī′gō). A municipal borough of N Ireland on **Sligo Bay,** an inlet of the Atlantic Ocean. Pop. 17,232.

slim (slĭm) *adj.* **slim•mer, slim•mest. 1.** Small in girth or thickness in proportion to height or length; slender. **2.** Small in quantity or amount; meager: *slim hopes.* — *intr. & tr.v.* **slimmed, slim•ming, slims. 1.** To become or make slim. **2.** To lose or cause to lose weight, as by dieting or exercise. [Du., bad, sly < MDu. *slimp, slim*, bad, crooked.] — **slim′ly** *adv.* — **slim′mer** *n.* — **slim′ness** *n.*

slime (slīm) *n.* **1.** A thick, sticky, slippery substance. **2.** A mucous substance secreted by certain animals, such as fish or slugs. **3.** Vile or disgusting matter. — *tr.v.* **slimed, slim•ing, slimes. 1.** To smear with slime. **2.** To remove slime from (fish to be canned, for example). [ME < OE *slīm.* See **lei-***.]

slime mold *n.* **1.** Any of various primitive organisms of the phylum Acrasiomycota, esp. of the genus *Dictyostelium*, that grow on dung and decaying vegetation and have a life cycle characterized by a slimelike amoeboid stage and a multicellular reproductive stage. **2.** Any of various organisms of the phylum Myxomycota that grow on decaying vegetation and in moist soil and have a similar but more advanced life cycle.

slim•sy (slĭm′zē) also **slimp•sy** (slĭmp′sē) *adj.* **-si•er, -si•est.** *Informal.* Frail; flimsy. [Blend of SLIM and FLIMSY.]

slim•y (slī′mē) *adj.* **-i•er, -i•est. 1.** Consisting of or resembling slime; viscous. **2.** Covered with or exuding slime. **3.** Vile; foul. — **slim′i•ly** *adv.* — **slim′i•ness** *n.*

sling¹ (slĭng) *n.* **1.a.** A weapon consisting of a looped strap in which a stone is whirled and then let fly. **b.** A slingshot. **2.** A loop for supporting, cradling, or hoisting something, esp.: **a.** A strap of a shoe that fits over the heel. **b.** A strap used to carry a rifle over the shoulder. **c.** *Naut.* A rope or chain for supporting a yard. **d.** A band suspended from the neck to support an injured arm or hand. **3.** The act of hurling a mis-

sleigh

ă pat	oi boy
ā pay	ou out
âr care	o͝o took
ä father	o͞o boot
ĕ pet	ŭ cut
ē be	ûr urge
ĭ pit	th thin
ī pie	*th* this
îr pier	hw which
ŏ pot	zh vision
ō toe	ə about, item
ô paw	

Stress marks:
′ (primary);
′ (secondary), as in
dictionary (dĭk′shə-nĕr′ē)

sile. — *tr.v.* **slung** (slŭng), **sling•ing, slings. 1.** To hurl with or as if with a sling. See Syns at **throw. 2.** To place or carry in a sling. **3.** To move with a sling: *sling cargo.* **4.** To hang loosely or freely; let swing. [ME *slinge.*] — **sling′er** *n.*

sling[2] (slĭng) *n.* A drink consisting of brandy, whiskey, or gin, sweetened and usu. lemon-flavored. [?]

sling•shot (slĭng′shŏt′) *n.* A Y-shaped stick having an elastic strap attached to the prongs, used for flinging small stones.

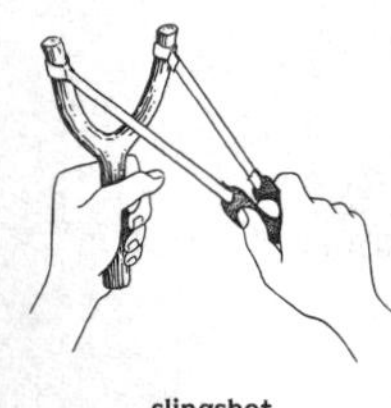
slingshot

slink (slĭngk) *v.* **slunk** (slŭngk) also **slinked, slink•ing, slinks.** — *intr.* To move in a quiet, furtive manner; sneak: *slunk away.* — *tr.* To give birth to prematurely. — *n.* An animal, esp. a calf, born prematurely. — *adj.* Born prematurely. [ME *slinken* < OE *slincan.*] — **slink′ing•ly** *adv.*

slink•y (sling′kē) *adj.* **-i•er, -i•est. 1.** Stealthy, furtive, and sneaking. **2.** *Informal.* Graceful, sinuous, and sleek: *wore a slinky outfit to the party.* — **slink′i•ly** *adv.* — **slink′i•ness** *n.*

slip[1] (slĭp) *v.* **slipped, slip•ping, slips.** — *intr.* **1.a.** To move smoothly, easily, and quietly. **b.** To move stealthily; steal. **2.** To pass gradually, easily, or imperceptibly: *The time slipped by.* **3.a.** To slide involuntarily and lose one's balance or foothold. See Syns at **slide. b.** To slide out of place; shift position: *The gear slipped.* **4.** To escape, as from a grasp, fastening, or restraint: *slipped away.* **5.** To decline from a former or standard level; fall off. **6.** To fall behind a scheduled production rate. **7.** To fall into fault or error. — *tr.* **1.** To cause to move in a smooth, easy, or sliding motion. **2.** To place or insert smoothly and quietly. **3.** To put on or remove (clothing) easily or quickly: *slip on a sweater.* **4.** To get loose or free from; elude. **5.** To bring forth (young) prematurely. Used of animals. **6.** To unleash or free (a dog or hawk) to pursue game. **7.** To release, loose, or unfasten: *slip a knot.* **8.** To dislocate (a bone). **9.** To pass (a knitting stitch) from one needle to another without knitting it. — *n.* **1.** The act or an instance of slipping or sliding. **2.** An accident or a mishap, esp. a falling down. **3.a.** An error in conduct or thinking; a mistake. **b.** A slight error or oversight, as in speech or writing: *a slip of the tongue.* **4.** *Naut.* **a.** A docking place for a ship between two piers. **b.** A slipway. **5.** *Naut.* The difference between a vessel's actual speed through water and the speed at which the vessel would move if the screw were propelling against a solid. **6.a.** A woman's undergarment of dress length. **b.** A half-slip. **7.** A pillowcase. **8.** *Geol.* The relative displacement of formerly adjacent points on opposite sides of a fault. **9.** The difference between optimal and actual output in a mechanical device. **10.** Movement between two parts where none should exist, as between a pulley and a belt. **11.** A sideways movement of an airplane when banked too far. — ***idioms.*** **give (someone) the slip.** *Slang.* To escape the pursuit of. **let slip.** To say inadvertently. **slip one over on.** *Informal.* To hoodwink; trick. [ME *slippen*, prob. of MLGer. or MDu. orig. See **lei-*.**]

slip[2] (slĭp) *n.* **1.** A part of a plant cut or broken off for grafting or planting; a scion or cutting. **2.** A long narrow piece; a strip. **3.** A slender youthful person. **4.** A small piece of paper, esp. a small form, document, or receipt: *a deposit slip; a sales slip.* **5.** A narrow pew in a church. — *tr.v.* **slipped, slip•ping, slips.** To make a slip from (a plant or plant part). [Prob. < MLGer. or MDu. *slippe.*]

slip[3] (slĭp) *n.* Thinned potter's clay used for decorating or coating ceramics. [ME, slime < OE *slypa.* See **sleubh-*.**]

slip•case (slĭp′kās′) *n.* A protective box with one open end or more, used for storing a book. — **slip′cased′** *adj.*

slip•cov•er (slĭp′kŭv′ər) *n.* A fitted removable cover, usu. of cloth, for a piece of upholstered furniture. — **slip′cov′er** *v.*

slip•knot (slĭp′nŏt′) *n.* **1.** A knot made with a loop so that it slips easily along the rope or cord around which it is tied. **2.** A knot that can readily be untied by pulling one free end.

slipknot

slip-on (slĭp′ŏn′, -ôn′) *n.* A garment easily donned or removed. — **slip′-on′** *adj.*

slip•o•ver (slĭp′ō′vər) *n.* A garment, such as a sweater, designed to be put on or taken off over the head.

slip•page (slĭp′ĭj) *n.* **1.** The act or an instance of slipping, esp. movement away from an original or secure place. **2.** The amount or extent of slipping. **3.** A decline in level, performance, or achievement. **4.** Loss of motion or power due to slipping.

slipped disk (slĭpt) *n.* Protrusion of a part of an intervertebral disk through the fibrocartilage, occurring usu. in the lower lumbar region and often causing back pain or sciatica.

slip•per (slĭp′ər) *n.* A low shoe that can be slipped on and off easily and usu. worn indoors. — **slip′pered** *adj.*

slipper flower *n.* See **calceolaria.**

slip•per•wort (slĭp′ər-wûrt′, -wôrt′) *n.* See **calceolaria.**

slip•per•y (slĭp′ə-rē) *adj.* **-i•er, -i•est. 1.** Causing or tending to cause sliding or slipping: *a slippery sidewalk.* **2.** Tending to slip, as from one's grasp: *a slippery bar of soap.* **3.** Not trustworthy; elusive or tricky. [Alteration of obsolete *slipper* < ME < OE *slipor.* See **lei-*.**] — **slip′per•i•ness** *n.*

slippery elm *n.* **1.** A deciduous eastern North American tree *(Ulmus rubra)* having hard wood and mucilaginous inner bark formerly used medicinally. **2.** Its wood.

slip ring *n.* A metal ring mounted on a rotating part of a machine to provide a continuous electrical connection through brushes on stationary contacts.

slip-sheet (slĭp′shēt′) *Print. n.* A blank sheet of paper slipped between newly printed sheets to prevent offsetting. — **slip′-sheet′** *v.*

slip•shod (slĭp′shŏd′) *adj.* **1.** Marked by carelessness; sloppy or slovenly. See Syns at **sloppy. 2.** Slovenly in appearance; shabby or seedy. — **slip′shod′di•ness** *n.*

slip•slop (slĭp′slŏp′) *n.* **1.** Trivial conversation or writing; twaddle. **2.** *Archaic.* Unappetizing liquid or watery food; slops. [Redup. of SLOP[1].]

slip•stitch (slĭp′stĭch′) *n.* A concealed stitch used for sewing together two layers of fabric, as with hems and facings.

slip•stream (slĭp′strēm′) *n.* **1.** The turbulent flow of air driven backward by the propeller or propellers of an aircraft. **2.** The region of reduced air pressure and forward suction produced by and immediately behind a fast-moving ground vehicle. — *intr.v.* **-streamed, -stream•ing, -streams.** To drive or cycle in the slipstream of a vehicle ahead.

slip-up (slĭp′ŭp′) *n.* An error; an oversight.

slip•ware (slĭp′wâr′) *n.* Pottery coated or decorated with slip.

slip•way (slĭp′wā′) *n. Naut.* A sloping surface leading down to the water, on which ships are built or repaired.

slit (slĭt) *n.* A long, straight, narrow cut or opening. — *tr.v.* **slit, slit•ting, slits. 1.** To make a slit or slits in. **2.** To cut lengthwise into strips; split. [ME *slitte* < *slitten*, to split < OE *slītan*, to cut up.] — **slit′ter** *n.* — **slit′ty** *adj.*

slith•er (slĭth′ər) *v.* **-ered, -er•ing, -ers.** — *intr.* **1.** To slip and slide, as on a loose or uneven surface, often with friction and noise. **2.** To glide or slide like a reptile. See Syns at **slide.** — *tr.* To cause to slither. — *n.* A slithering movement or gait. [ME *slethren*, var. of *sliddren* < OE *slidrian*, freq. of *slīdan*, to slide.] — **slith′er•y** *adj.*

Sli•ven (slĭv′ən). A city of E-central Bulgaria E of Sofia. Pop. 104,000.

sliv•er (slĭv′ər) *n.* **1.** A slender piece cut, split, or broken off; a splinter. **2.** A small narrow piece, portion, or plot: *a sliver of land.* **3.** (*also* slī′vər). A continuous strand of loose wool, flax, or cotton, ready for drawing and twisting. — *tr. & intr.v.* **-ered, -er•ing, -ers.** To split or become split into slivers. [ME *slivere* < *sliven*, to split < OE *slīfan.*]

sliv•o•vitz (slĭv′ə-vĭts) *n.* A dry colorless plum brandy. [Serbo-Croatian *šljivovica* < *šljiva*, plum. See **slī-*.**]

Sloan (slōn), **John French.** 1871–1951. Amer. painter whose works include *Sunday, Women Drying Their Hair* (1912).

slob (slŏb) *n. Informal.* A person regarded as slovenly, crude, or obnoxious. [Ir.Gael. *slab*, mud < OIr., prob. of Scand. orig.; akin to Swed. dial. *slabb*, mud.] — **slob′bish** *adj.*

slob•ber (slŏb′ər) *v.* **-bered, -ber•ing, -bers.** — *intr.* **1.** To let saliva or liquid spill out from the mouth; drool. **2.** To express sentiment or enthusiasm effusively or incoherently; gush. — *tr.* To wet or smear with or as if with slobber. — *n.* **1.** Saliva or liquid running from the mouth; drool. **2.** Effusive or incoherent expression; drivel. [ME *sloberen*, perh. of LGer. orig.] — **slob′ber•er** *n.* — **slob′ber•y** *adj.*

sloe (slō) *n.* **1.** See **blackthorn. 2.** Either of two eastern North American plum trees or shrubs, *Prunus alleghaniensis* having dark purple fruit or *P. americana* having yellow or red fruit. **3.** The tart plumlike fruit of either of these plants. [ME *slo* < OE *slā.* See **slī-*.**]

sloe-eyed (slō′īd′) *adj.* Having slanted dark eyes.

sloe gin *n.* A gin-based liqueur flavored with fresh sloes.

slog (slŏg) *v.* **slogged, slog•ging, slogs.** — *intr.* **1.** To walk or progress with a slow heavy pace; plod: *slog across the swamp.* **2.** To work diligently for long hours: *slogged away at Latin.* — *tr.* **1.** To make (one's way) with a slow heavy pace against resistance. **2.** To strike with heavy blows. — *n.* **1.** A long exhausting progress, march, or hike. **2.** Long hard work. [Perh. alteration of SLUG[3].] — **slog′ger** *n.*

slo•gan (slō′gən) *n.* **1.** A phrase expressing the aims or nature of an enterprise, an organization, or a candidate; a motto. **2.** A phrase used repeatedly, as in promotion. **3.** A battle cry of a Scottish clan. [Alteration of Sc. *slogorne*, battle cry < Gael. *sluagh-ghairm* : *sluagh*, host; see SLEW[1] + *gairm*, shout.]

slo•gan•eer (slō′gə-nîr′) *n.* One that invents or uses slogans. — **slo′gan•eer′** *v.*

slo•gan•ize (slō′gə-nīz′) *tr.v.* **-ized, -iz•ing, -iz•es.** To express as or in slogans or a slogan. — **slo′gan•iz•er** *n.*

sloop (slo͞op) *n. Naut.* A single-masted fore-and-aft-rigged sailing boat with a short standing bowsprit or none at all and a single headsail set from the forestay. [Du. *sloep* < MDu. *slūpen*, to glide. See **sleubh-*.**]

sloop of war *n., pl.* **sloops of war.** *Naut.* A small armed vessel larger than a gunboat, carrying guns on one deck only.

slop[1] (slŏp) *n.* **1.** Spilled or splashed liquid. **2.** Soft mud or slush. **3.** Unappetizing watery food or soup. **4.** Waste food used to feed pigs or other animals; swill. Often used in the plural. **5.** Mash remaining after alcohol distillation. Often used in the plural. **6.** Human excrement. Often used in the plural. **7.** Repulsively effusive writing or speech; drivel. — *v.* **slopped, slop•ping, slops.** — *intr.* **1.** To be spilled or splashed. **2.** To spill over; overflow. **3.** To walk heavily or messily in or as if in mud; plod. **4.** To express oneself effusively; gush. —*tr.* **1.** To spill (liquid). **2.** To spill liquid on. **3.** To serve unappetizingly or clumsily; dish out. **4.** To feed slops to (animals). [ME *sloppe*, a muddy place, perh. < OE **sloppe*, dung, slime. See **sleubh-***.]

slop² (slŏp) *n.* **1. slops.** Articles of clothing and bedding issued or sold to sailors. **2. slops.** Short full trousers worn in the 16th century. **3.** A loose outer garment, such as a smock or overalls. **4. slops.** *Chiefly British.* Cheap ready-made garments. [ME *sloppe*, a kind of garment < OE *-slop* (in *oferslop*, surplice; see **sleubh-***).]

slope (slōp) *v.* **sloped, slop•ing, slopes.** —*intr.* **1.** To diverge from the vertical or horizontal; incline. See Syns at **slant. 2.** To move on a slant; ascend or descend. —*tr.* To cause to slope. —*n.* **1.** An inclined line, surface, plane, position, or direction. **2.** A stretch of ground forming a natural or artificial incline: *ski slopes.* **3.a.** A deviation from the horizontal. **b.** The amount or degree of such deviation. **4.** *Math.* **a.** The rate at which an ordinate of a point of a line on a coordinate plane changes with respect to a change in the abscissa. **b.** The tangent of the angle of inclination of a line or the slope of the tangent line for a curve or surface. [Prob. < ME *aslope*, sloping.] —**slop′er** *n.* —**slop′ing•ly** *adv.*

slo-pitch (slō′pĭch′) *n. Sports.* Var. of **slow-pitch.**

slop•py (slŏp′ē) *adj.* **-pi•er, -pi•est. 1.** Lacking neatness or order; untidy: *a sloppy room.* **2.** Lacking care or precision; slipshod: *sloppy language.* **3.** *Informal.* Oversentimental; gushy. **4.** Of, resembling, or covered with slop; muddy or slushy. **5.** Watery and unappetizing. **6.** Spotted or splashed with liquid. —**slop′pi•ly** *adv.* —**slop′pi•ness** *n.*

Syns: *sloppy, slovenly, unkempt, slipshod.* These adjectives mean marked by an absence of due or proper care or attention. *Sloppy* evokes the idea of careless spilling, spotting, or splashing; it suggests slackness, untidiness, or diffuseness: *"I do not see how the sloppiest reasoner can evade that"* (H.G. Wells). *Slovenly* implies habitual negligence and a lack of system or thoroughness: *a slovenly appearance. Unkempt* stresses dishevelment resulting from a neglectful lack of proper maintenance: *"an unwashed brow, an unkempt head of hair"* (Sir Walter Scott). *Slipshod* suggests inattention to detail and a general absence of meticulousness: *"the new owners' camp . . . a slipshod and slovenly affair, tent half stretched, dishes unwashed"* (Jack London).

slosh (slŏsh) *v.* **sloshed, slosh•ing, slosh•es.** —*tr.* **1.** To spill or splash (a liquid) copiously or clumsily. **2.** To agitate in a liquid. —*intr.* To splash, wade, or flounder in water or another liquid. —*n.* **1.** Slush. **2.** The sound of splashing liquid. [Perh. blend of SLOP¹ and SLUSH.] —**slosh′y** *adj.*

sloshed (slŏsht) *adj. Slang.* Intoxicated; drunk.

slot¹ (slŏt) *n.* **1.** A narrow opening; a groove or slit: *a mail slot.* **2.** A gap between a main and an auxiliary airfoil to provide space for airflow and facilitate the passage of air over the wing. **3.a.** An assigned place in a sequence or schedule: *a new time slot for the show.* **b.** A position of employment in an organization or a hierarchy. **4.** *Comp. Sci.* A socket in a microcomputer that will accept a plug-in circuit board: *expansion slots.* —*tr.v.* **slot•ted, slot•ting, slots. 1.** To cut or make a slot or slots in. **2.** To put into or assign to a slot. [ME, hollow of the breastbone < OFr. *esclot.*]

slot² (slŏt) *n.* The track or trail of an animal, esp. a deer. [Obsolete Fr. *esclot*, horse's hoofprint < OFr., perh. < ON *slōdh*, track.]

sloth (slôth, slōth, slŏth) *n.* **1.** Aversion to work or exertion; laziness; indolence. **2.** Any of various slow-moving arboreal edentate mammals of the family Bradypodidae of South and Central America, having long hooklike claws by which they hang upside down from tree branches. **3.** A company of bears. [ME *slowth* < *slow*, slow. See **slow.**]

sloth bear *n.* A bear *(Melursus ursinus)* of India and Sri Lanka having a long snout, long sticky tongue, and dark shaggy hair.

sloth•ful (slôth′fəl, slōth′-, slŏth′-) *adj.* Disinclined to exertion or work. —**sloth′ful•ly** *adv.* —**sloth′ful•ness** *n.*

slot machine *n.* A vending or gambling machine operated by the insertion of coins into a slot.

slouch (slouch) *v.* **slouched, slouch•ing, slouch•es.** —*intr.* **1.** To sit, stand, or walk with an awkward, drooping, excessively relaxed posture. **2.** To droop or hang carelessly, as a hat. —*tr.* To cause to droop; stoop. —*n.* **1.** An awkward, drooping, excessively relaxed posture or gait. **2.** *Slang.* An awkward, lazy, or inept person: *no slouch at bridge.* [?] —**slouch′i•ly** *adv.* —**slouch′i•ness** *n.* —**slouch′y** *adj.*

slouch hat *n.* A soft hat with a broad flexible brim.

slough¹ (slo͞o, slou) also **slew** (slo͞o) *n.* **1.** A depression or hollow, usu. filled with deep mud or mire. **2.** Also **slue.** A stagnant swamp, marsh, bog, or pond, esp. as part of a bayou, an inlet, or a backwater. **3.** A state of deep despair or moral degradation. [ME < OE *slōh.*] —**slough′y** *adj.*

slough² (slŭf) *n.* **1.** The dead outer skin shed by a reptile or an amphibian. **2.** *Medic.* A layer or mass of dead tissue separated from surrounding living tissue, as in a wound. **3.** An outer layer or covering that is shed. —*v.* **sloughed, slough•ing, sloughs.** —*intr.* **1.** To be cast off or shed; come off. **2.** To shed a slough. **3.** *Medic.* To separate from surrounding living tissue. Used of dead tissue. —*tr.* To discard as undesirable or unfavorable; get rid of. [ME *slughe.*]

Slough (slou). A municipal borough of SE England, a suburb of London. Pop. 96,900.

Slo•vak (slō′väk′, -văk′) also **Slo•va•ki•an** (slō-vä′kē-ən, -văk′ē-ən) —*n.* **1.** A member of a Slavic people living in Slovakia. **2.** The Slavic language of the Slovaks. —*adj.* Of or relating to Slovakia or its people, language, or culture. [Slovak *Slovák.*]

Slo•vak•i•a (slō-vä′kē-ə, -văk′ē-ə). A country of central Europe; part of Czechoslovakia from 1918 to 1992. Cap. Bratislava. Pop. 4,991,168.

slov•en (slŭv′ən) *n.* One who is habitually careless in personal appearance or work. [ME *slovein*, perh. < MFlem. *sloovin*, a scold, gossip < MLGer. *slôven*, to dress carelessly; akin to Du. *sloof*, untidy woman. See **sleubh-***.]

Slo•vene (slō′vēn′) also **Slo•ve•ni•an** (slō-vē′nē-ən, -vēn′yən) —*n.* **1.** A member of a Slavic people living in Slovenia. **2.** The Slavic language of the Slovenes. —*adj.* Of or relating to Slovenia or its people, language, or culture. [Ger. *Slowene* < Slovene *Slovêenec*, ult. < Old Slav. *Slověninŭ*, Slav.]

Slo•ve•ni•a (slō-vē′nē-ə, -vēn′yə). A region of the NW Balkan Peninsula; came under Austrian control after 1335 and joined Yugoslavia in 1918. Slovenia declared its independence in 1991. Cap. Ljubljana. Pop. 1,697,068.

slov•en•ly (slŭv′ən-lē) *adj.* **1.** Untidy, as in dress or appearance. **2.** Marked by negligence; slipshod. See Syns at **sloppy.** —**slov′en•li•ness** *n.* —**slov′en•ly** *adv.*

slow (slō) *adj.* **slow•er, slow•est. 1.a.** Not moving or able to move quickly; proceeding at a low speed. **b.** Marked by a retarded tempo. **2.a.** Taking or requiring a long time. **b.** Taking more time than is usual. **3.** Registering a time or rate behind or below the correct one. **4.** Lacking in promptness or willingness; not precipitate. **5.** Characterized by a low volume of sales or transactions. **6.** Lacking liveliness or interest; boring: *a slow party.* **7.** Not having or exhibiting intellectual or mental quickness. **8.** Only moderately warm; low. —*adv.* **slower, slowest. 1.** So as to fall behind the correct time or rate. **2.** At a low speed. —*v.* **slowed, slow•ing, slows.** —*tr.* **1.** To make slow or slower. **2.** To delay; retard. —*intr.* To become slow or slower. [ME < OE *slāw.*] —**slow′ly** *adv.* —**slow′ness** *n.*

Usage Note: *Slow* may sometimes be used instead of *slowly* when it comes after the verb: *We drove the car slow.* In formal writing *slowly* is generally preferred. *Slow* is often used in speech and informal writing, especially when brevity and forcefulness are sought: *Drive slow! Slow* is also the established idiomatic form with certain senses of common verbs: *Take it slow.*

slow•down (slō′doun′) *n.* The act or process of slowing down; a slackening of pace: *a production slowdown.*

slow-foot•ed (slō′fo͝ot′ĭd) *adj.* Proceeding at a tediously slow pace: *a slow-footed story.* —**slow′-foot′ed•ness** *n.*

slow infection *n.* An infection having a long incubation period, as that caused by a slow virus or by a prion.

slow loris *n.* A large loris *(Nycticebus coucang)* of Indonesia, having a corpulent, almost tailless body and noted for its very slow cautious movements.

slow match *n.* A match or fuse that burns slowly at a known rate and is used to set off explosives.

slow motion *n.* A filmmaking technique in which the action as projected is slower than the original action. —**slow′-mo′tion** (slō′mō′shən) *adj.*

slow-pitch also **slo-pitch** (slō′pĭch′) *n. Sports.* Softball in which there are ten players to a team and legal pitches must travel in an arc from three to ten feet high.

slow•poke (slō′pōk′) *n. Informal.* One that moves, works, or acts slowly.

slow virus *n.* Any of a group of animal viruses that cause diseases having an unusually long incubation period, as Creutzfeldt-Jakob disease.

slow-wit•ted or **slow•wit•ted** (slō′wĭt′ĭd) *adj.* Slow to comprehend. —**slow′-wit′ted•ly** *adv.* —**slow′-wit′ted•ness** *n.*

slow•worm (slō′wûrm′) *n.* A limbless lizard *(Anguis fragilis)* of Europe, western Asia, and northern Africa having a smooth snakelike body and feeding chiefly on slugs. [Alteration (influenced by SLOW) of ME *slowurm* < OE *slāwyrm* : *slā-*, earthworm, slowworm + *wyrm*, worm; see WORM.]

SLR *abbr.* Single-lens reflex camera.

slub (slŭb) *tr.v.* **slubbed, slub•bing, slubs.** To draw out and twist (a strand of textile fiber) for spinning. —*n.* **1.** A soft thick nub in yarn that is an imperfection or purposely set for effect. **2.** A slightly twisted roll of fiber, as of silk. [?]

sludge (slŭj) *n.* **1.** Semisolid material such as the type precipitated by sewage treatment. **2.** Mud, mire, or ooze covering the ground or forming a deposit, as on a riverbed. **3.** Finely broken or half-formed ice on a body of water, esp. the sea. **4.** An agglutination of blood cells forming a semisolid mass that can impede circulation. —*intr.v.* **sludged, sludg•ing, sludg•es.** To agglutinate into a semisolid mass. Used of blood cells. [Perh. alteration of dial. *slutch*, mire.] —**sludg′y** *adj.*

sloop

sloth
Brown-throated three-toed sloth
Bradypus variegatus

ă pat	oi boy
ā pay	ou out
âr care	o͝o took
ä father	o͞o boot
ĕ pet	ŭ cut
ē be	ûr urge
ĭ pit	th thin
ī pie	*th* this
îr pier	hw which
ŏ pot	zh vision
ō toe	ə about, item
ô paw	

Stress marks:
′ (primary);
′ (secondary), as in **dictionary** (dĭk′shə-nĕr′ē)

slue[1] also **slew** (slo͞o) —*v.* **slued, slu•ing, slues** also **slewed, slew•ing, slews.** —*tr.* **1.** To turn (something) on an axis; rotate: *slued the chair around.* **2.** To turn sharply; veer: *slued the car around.* —*intr.* **1.** To turn about an axis; pivot. **2.** To turn or slide sideways or off course; skid. —*n.* **1.** The act of sluing. **2.** The position to which something has slued. [?]
slue[2] (slo͞o) *n.* Var. of **slew**[1].
slue[3] (slo͞o) *n.* Var. of **slough**[1] 2.
slug[1] (slŭg) *n.* **1.** A round bullet larger than buckshot. **2.** *Informal.* A shot of liquor. **3.** A small metal disk for use in a vending or gambling machine, esp. one used illegally. **4.** A lump of metal or glass prepared for further processing. **5.** *Print.* **a.** A strip of type metal, less than type-high and thicker than a lead, used for spacing. **b.** A line of cast type in a strip of metal. **c.** A compositor's type line of identifying marks or instructions, inserted temporarily in copy. **6.** *Phys.* The unit of mass accelerated at one foot per second per second when acted on by a force of one pound. —*tr.v.* **slugged, slug•ging, slugs.** *Print.* To add slugs to. [Perh. < SLUG[2] (from its shape).]

slug[2]
Limax maximus

slug[2] (slŭg) *n.* **1.** Any of various small, chiefly terrestrial gastropod mollusks of the genus *Limax* and related genera, having a slow-moving elongated body with no shell or only a flat rudimentary shell on or under the skin. **2.** The smooth soft larva of certain insects, such as the sawfly. **3.** A slimy mass of aggregated amoeboid cells from which the sporophore of a cellular slime mold develops. **4.** *Informal.* A sluggard. [ME *slugge*, sluggard, prob. of Scand. orig.]
slug[3] (slŭg) *tr.v.* **slugged, slug•ging, slugs.** To strike heavily, esp. with the fist or a bat. [Poss. < SLUG[1].] —**slug** *n.*
slug•a•bed (slŭg′ə-bĕd′) *n.* One inclined to stay in bed out of laziness.
slug•fest (slŭg′fĕst′) *n.* **1.** *Slang.* A fight marked by an extended exchange of heavy blows. **2.** *Baseball.* A game in which there are many hits and runs scored.
slug•gard (slŭg′ərd) *n.* A slothful person; an idler. —*adj.* Lazy. [ME *sluggart*, prob. < *sluggi*, lazy, prob. of Scand. orig.] —**slug′gard•ly** *adj.* —**slug′gard•ness** *n.*
slug•ger (slŭg′ər) *n.* **1.** One that slugs, as a fighter who delivers hard, swinging punches. **2.** *Baseball.* A batter who hits many extra-base hits.
slug•gish (slŭg′ĭsh) *adj.* **1.** Displaying little movement or activity; slow; inactive. **2.** Lacking alertness, vigor, or energy; indolent. **3.** Slow to perform or respond to stimulation. [ME, prob. < *slugge*, lazy person. See SLUG[2].] —**slug′gish•ly** *adv.*

sluice

sluice (slo͞os) *n.* **1.a.** An artificial channel for conducting water, with a valve or gate to regulate the flow. **b.** A valve or gate used in such a channel; a floodgate. **2.** A body of water impounded behind a floodgate. **3.** An artificial channel, esp. for carrying excess water. **4.** A long inclined trough, as for carrying logs or separating gold ore. —*v.* **sluiced, sluic•ing, sluic•es.** —*tr.* **1.** To flood or drench with or as if with a flow of released water. **2.** To wash with water flowing in a sluice. **3.** To draw off or let out by a sluice. **4.** To send (logs, for example) down a sluice. —*intr.* To flow out from or as if from a sluice. [ME *scluse* < OFr. *escluse* < LLat. *exclūsa* < Lat., fem. p.part. of *exclūdere*, to shut out. See EXCLUDE.]
slum (slŭm) *n.* A heavily populated urban area characterized by substandard housing and squalor. Often used in the plural. —*intr.v.* **slummed, slum•ming, slums.** To visit impoverished areas or squalid locales, esp. out of curiosity or for amusement. [?] —**slum′mer** *n.* —**slum′my** *adj.*
slum•ber (slŭm′bər) *v.* **-bered, -ber•ing, -bers.** —*intr.* **1.** To sleep. **2.** To be dormant or quiescent. —*tr.* To pass (time) in sleep. —*n.* **1.** Sleep. **2.** A state of inactivity or dormancy. [ME *slumeren, slumberen*, freq. of *slumen*, to doze, prob. < *slume*, light sleep < OE *slūma*.] —**slum′ber•er** *n.*
slum•ber•ous (slŭm′bər-əs) or **slum•brous** (-brəs) *adj.* **1.** Sleepy; drowsy. **2.a.** Suggestive of or resembling sleep. **b.** Quiet; tranquil. **3.** Causing or inducing sleep; soporific. —**slum′ber•ous•ly** *adv.* —**slum′ber•ous•ness** *n.*

smack[3]
Watercolor of the *Emma C. Berry* by John F. Leavitt

slum•ber•y (slŭm′bə-rē) *adj.* Slumberous.
slum•gul•lion (slŭm-gŭl′yən) *n.* A watery meat stew. [Perh. *slum*, muddy deposit in a mining sluice + dial. *gullion*, mud (perh. < Ir.Gael. *goilín*, pit).]
slum•lord (slŭm′lôrd′) *n.* An owner of slum property, esp. one that overcharges tenants and allows deterioration.
slump (slŭmp) *intr.v.* **slumped, slump•ing, slumps. 1.** To fall or sink heavily; collapse. **2.** To droop, as in sitting; slouch. **3.** To decline suddenly; fall off. **4.a.** To sink or settle, as into mud. **b.** To slide down or spread out thickly, as mud. —*n.* **1.** The act or an instance of slumping. **2.** A drooping or slouching posture. **3.** A sudden falling off or decline, as in activity or prices. **4.** An extended period of poor performance, as in a sport. [Prob. of Scand. orig.]
slung (slŭng) *v.* P.t. and p.part. of **sling**[1].
slunk (slŭngk) *v.* A p.t. and p.part. of **slink.**
slur (slûr) *tr.v.* **slurred, slur•ring, slurs. 1.** To pronounce indistinctly. **2.** To speak slightingly of; disparage. **3.** To pass over lightly or carelessly; treat without due consideration. **4.** *Mus.* **a.** To glide over (a series of notes) smoothly without a break. **b.** To mark with a slur. **5.** *Print.* To blur or smear. —*n.* **1.** A disparaging remark; an aspersion. **2.** A slurred utterance or sound. **3.** *Mus.* **a.** A curved line connecting notes on a score to indicate that they are to be played or sung legato. **b.** A passage played or sung in this manner. **4.** *Print.* A smeared or blurred impression. [Prob. < ME *sloor*, mud.]
slurp (slûrp) *v.* **slurped, slurp•ing, slurps.** —*tr.* To eat or drink noisily. —*intr.* To slurp something. —*n.* **1.** A loud sucking noise made in eating or drinking. **2.** *Slang.* A mouthful of a liquid. [Du. *slurpen*.]
slur•ry (slûr′ē) *n., pl.* **-ries.** A thin mixture of a liquid, esp. water, and any of several finely divided substances, such as cement or clay particles. [ME *slori*, perh. < *sloor*, mud.]
slush (slŭsh) *n.* **1.** Partially melted snow or ice. **2.** Soft mud; slop; mire. **3.** *Naut.* Grease or fat discarded from a ship's galley. **4.** A greasy compound used as a lubricant for machinery. **5.** Maudlin speech or writing; sentimental drivel. **6.** A drink made of flavored syrup poured over crushed ice. —*v.* **slushed, slush•ing, slush•es.** —*tr.* **1.** To daub (machinery) with slush. **2.** To fill (joints in masonry) with mortar. **3.** *Naut.* To wash down (a deck) by splashing with water. **4.** To splash or soak with slush or mud. —*intr.* **1.** To walk or proceed through slush. **2.** To make a splashing or slushy sound. [Perh. of Scand. orig.; akin to Norw. *slask*, sloppy weather.]
slush fund *n.* **1.** A fund raised for undesignated purposes, esp. one raised by a group for corrupt practices. **2.** Money formerly raised by the sale of garbage from a warship to buy small items of luxury for the crew.
slush•y (slŭsh′ē) *adj.* **-i•er, -i•est. 1.** Consisting of, covered with, or full of slush. **2.** Resembling slush, as in consistency. **3.** Revoltingly sentimental; maudlin. —**slush′i•ly** *adv.* —**slush′i•ness** *n.*
slut (slŭt) *n.* **1.a.** A woman considered sexually promiscuous. **b.** A prostitute. **2.** A slovenly woman; a slattern. [ME *slutte*.] —**slut′tish** *adj.* —**slut′tish•ly** *adv.* —**slut′tish•ness** *n.*
sly (slī) *adj.* **sli•er** (slī′ər) , **sli•est** (slī′ĭst) also **sly•er sly•est. 1.** Adept in craft or cunning. **2.** Lacking or marked by a lack of candor. **3.** Playfully mischievous; roguish. —***idiom.* on the sly.** In a way intended to escape notice: *took payments on the sly.* [ME *sleigh* < ON *slœgr*.] —**sly′ly** *adv.* —**sly′ness** *n.*
sly•boots (slī′bo͞ots′) *pl.n.* *(used with a sing. v.) Informal.* A sly person.
Sm The symbol for the element **samarium.**
SM *abbr.* **1.** Sergeant major. **2.** Service mark. **3.** Stage manager.
sm. *abbr.* Small.
S.M. *abbr. Lat.* Scientiae Magister (Master of Science).
S-M or **s-m** *abbr.* Sadomasochism.
smack[1] (smăk) *v.* **smacked, smack•ing, smacks.** —*tr.* **1.** To press together and open (the lips) quickly and noisily, as in eating. **2.** To kiss noisily. **3.** To strike sharply and with a loud noise. —*intr.* **1.** To make or give a smack. **2.** To collide sharply and noisily. —*n.* **1.** The loud sharp sound of smacking. **2.** A noisy kiss. **3.** A sharp blow or slap. —*adv.* **1.** With a smack: *fell smack on her head.* **2.** Directly. [Perh. of MFlem. orig., or perh. of imit. orig.]
smack[2] (smăk) *n.* **1.a.** A distinctive flavor or taste. **b.** A suggestion or trace. **2.** A small amount; a smattering. —*intr.v.* **smacked, smack•ing, smacks. 1.** To have a distinctive flavor or taste. Used with *of.* **2.** To give an indication; be suggestive. Often used with *of.* [ME < OE *smæc*.]
smack[3] (smăk) *n.* *Naut.* A sloop-rigged boat used chiefly in fishing, esp. to transport the catch to market. [Du. or LGer. *smak* < *smakken*, to fling, dash.]
smack[4] (smăk) *n.* *Slang.* Heroin. [Prob. var. of *smeck* < Yiddish *shmek*, a sniff, smell < *shmekn*, to sniff, smell < MHGer. *smecken, smacken*, to smell, taste < OHGer. *smac*, smell, taste.]
smack-dab (smăk′dăb′) *adv. Slang.* Squarely; directly. [SMACK[1] + DAB[1], with a sudden contact.]
smack•er (smăk′ər) *n.* **1.** One that smacks, as a loud kiss. **2.** *Slang.* A dollar.
smack•ing (smăk′ĭng) *adj.* Brisk; vigorous; spanking.
small (smôl) *adj.* **small•er, small•est. 1.** Being below the average in size or magnitude. **2.** Limited in importance or significance; trivial. **3.** Limited in degree or scope. **4.** Lacking position, influence, or status; minor. **5.** Unpretentious; modest. **6.** Not fully grown; very young. **7.** Narrow in outlook; petty. **8.** Having been belittled; humiliated: *felt small.* **9.** Diluted; weak. Used of alcoholic beverages. **10.** Lacking force or volume. —*adv.* **1.** In small pieces. **2.** Without loudness or forcefulness; softly. **3.** In a small manner. —*n.* **1.** Something smaller than the rest. **2. smalls. a.** Small things considered as a group. **b.** *Chiefly British.* Small items of clothing. [ME *smal* < OE *smæl*.] —**small′ish** *adj.* —**small′ness** *n.*
Syns: *small, diminutive, little, miniature, minuscule, minute, petite, tiny, wee.* The central meaning shared by these adjectives is "being notably below the average in size or magnitude": *a small house; diminutive in stature; little hands; a miniature camera; a minuscule amount of rain; minute errors; a petite figure; tiny feet; a wee bit better.* ***Ant:*** *large.*
small arm *n.* A firearm that can be carried in the hand.
small beer *n.* **1.** Weak or inferior beer. **2.** Unimportant things; trivia. —*adj.* Trivial; unimportant.

small-bore (smôl′bôr′, -bōr′) *adj.* **1.** Of, relating to, or being a firearm of .22 caliber. **2.** Trivial or parochial in character.
small calorie *n.* See **calorie** 1.
small capital *n.* A letter having the form of a capital letter but smaller; for example: SMALL CAPITALS.
small change *n.* **1.** Coins of low denomination. **2.** Something of little value or significance.
small-claims court (smôl′klāmz′) *n. Law.* A special court for simplified and efficient handling of small claims on debts.
small•clothes (smôl′klōthz′, -klōz′) *pl.n.* **1.** Men's close-fitting knee breeches worn in the 18th century. **2.** *Chiefly British.* Small items of clothing, such as underclothes.
small fry *n.* **1.** Small children. **2.** Young or small fish. **3.** Persons or things regarded as unimportant.
small hours *pl.n.* The early hours after midnight.
small intestine *n.* The upper part of the intestine, consisting of the duodenum, jejunum, and ileum, where digestion is completed and nutrients are absorbed by the blood.
small-mind•ed (smôl′mīn′dĭd) *adj.* **1.** Having a narrow or selfish attitude. **2.** Characterized by pettiness or selfishness. **—small′-mind′ed•ly** *adv.* **—small′-mind′ed•ness** *n.*
small•mouth bass (smôl′mouth′ băs) *n.* A North American freshwater food and game fish *(Micropterus dolomieui)* having a shorter upper jaw than the similar largemouth bass.
small potatoes *pl.n. Informal.* **1.** A person or thing regarded as unimportant. **2.** An insignificant amount or sum.
small•pox (smôl′pŏks′) *n.* An acute, highly infectious, often fatal disease caused by a poxvirus and marked by high fever, aches, and widespread skin eruptions that form pockmarks.
small print *n.* See **fine print.**
small-scale (smôl′skāl′) *adj.* **1.** Limited in scope or extent; modest. **2.** Created on a small scale: *a small-scale model.*
small talk *n.* Casual or trivial conversation.
small•time or **small-time** (smôl′tīm′) *adj. Informal.* Insignificant or unimportant; minor. **—small′tim′er** *n.*
small time *n. Informal.* A modest or minor level of attainment in a competitive field.
smalt (smôlt) *n.* A deep blue paint and ceramic pigment produced by pulverizing a glass made of silica, potash, and cobalt oxide. [Fr. < Ital. *smalto,* enamel, glaze, of Gmc. orig. See **mel-**[1]*.]
smalt•ite (smôl′tīt′) also **smalt•ine** (smôl′tĭn, -tēn′) *n.* A white to silver-gray mineral, $(Co,Ni)As_3$, that is an ore of cobalt.
smarm•y (smär′mē) *adj.* **-i•er, -i•est. 1.** Hypocritically, complacently, or effusively earnest; unctuous. **2.** Sleek. [< *smarm,* to smear.] **—smarm•i•ness** *n.*
smart (smärt) *adj.* **smart•er, smart•est. 1.a.** Characterized by sharp quick thought; bright. See Syns at **intelligent. b.** Amusingly clever; witty. **c.** Impertinent; insolent. **2.** Energetic or quick in movement: *a smart pace.* **3.** Canny and shrewd in dealings with others. **4.** Fashionable; elegant. **5.a.** Of, relating to, or being a highly automated device, esp. one that imitates human intelligence: *smart missiles.* **b.** *Comp. Sci.* Capable of performing operations independently of the computer. Used of a computer terminal. **6.** *New England & Southern U.S.* Accomplished; talented: *a right smart ball player.* —*intr.v.* **smart•ed, smart•ing, smarts. 1.a.** To cause a sharp, usu. superficial stinging pain. **b.** To be the location of such a pain: *My leg smarts.* **c.** To feel such a pain. **2.** To suffer acutely, as from mental distress or remorse. **3.** To suffer or pay a heavy penalty. —*n.* **1.** Sharp mental or physical pain. **2. smarts.** *Slang.* Intelligence; expertise. ***—phrasal verb.* smart off.** *Informal.* To speak or act impertinently. ***—idiom.* right smart.** *New England & Southern U.S.* A lot; a considerable amount. [ME, stinging, keen, alert < OE *smeart,* causing pain.] **—smart′ly** *adv.* **—smart′ness** *n.*
smart al•eck (ăl′ĭk) *n. Informal.* **1.** A person regarded as obnoxiously self-assertive. **2.** An impudent person. [Perh. after *Aleck* Hoag, 19th-cent. Amer. confidence man and thief.] **—smart′-al′eck** (smärt′ăl′ĭk), **smart′-al′eck•y** (-ĭ-kē) *adj.*
smart-ass (smärt′ăs′) *n. Slang.* A smart aleck. **—smart′-ass′** *adj.*
smart bomb *n.* A bomb that can be guided by radio waves, television, or a laser beam directly to its target.
smart•en (smär′tn) *v.* **-ened, -en•ing, -ens.** —*tr.* **1.** To improve in appearance or stylishness; spruce up. **2.** To make quicker: *smarten the pace.* —*intr.* To make oneself smart or smarter.
smart money *n.* **1.** *Games.* Bets or a bet placed by experienced gamblers or those having privileged information. **2.** *Informal.* **a.** Experienced, well-informed investors. **b.** Investments made by experienced and well-informed people.
smart•weed (smärt′wēd′) *n.* Any of various marsh plants of the genus *Polygonum,* having sheathlike stipules and small, densely clustered pink, white, or green flowers.
smart•y (smär′tē) *n., pl.* **-ies.** *Informal.* **1.** A smart aleck. **2.** A quick-witted person.
smar•ty-pants (smär′tē-pănts′) *pl.n. (used with a sing. v.) Informal.* A smart aleck.
smash (smăsh) *v.* **smashed, smash•ing, smash•es.** —*tr.* **1.** To break (something) into pieces suddenly, noisily, and violently; shatter. See Syns at **break. 2.a.** To throw or dash (something) violently so as to shatter or crush. **b.** To strike with a heavy blow; batter. **3.** *Sports.* To hit (a ball or shuttlecock) in a forceful overhand stroke. **4.** To crush or destroy completely. —*intr.* **1.** To strike or collide suddenly, noisily, and violently. **2.** To break suddenly into pieces, as from a violent blow or collision. **3.** *Sports.* To smash a ball or shuttlecock. **4.** To be crushed or destroyed. **5.** To go bankrupt. —*n.* **1.a.** The act or sound of smashing. **b.** The condition of having been smashed. **2.a.** Total defeat or destruction; ruin. **b.** Financial failure; bankruptcy. **3.** A collision or crash. **4.a.** A drink made of mint, sugar, soda water, and alcoholic liquor, usu. brandy. **b.** A soft drink made of crushed fruit. **5.** *Sports.* A violent overhand stroke, as in tennis. **6.** *Informal.* A resounding success. —*adj. Informal.* Of, relating to, or being a resounding success. —*adv.* With a sudden, violent crash. [Prob. of imit. orig.] **—smash′er** *n.*
smashed (smăsht) *adj. Slang.* Intoxicated; drunk.
smash•ing (smăsh′ĭng) *adj.* **1.** Serving to smash: *a smashing blow to the head.* **2.** *Informal.* Extraordinarily impressive or fine; wonderful: *a smashing success.* **—smash′ing•ly** *adv.*
smash•up (smăsh′ŭp′) *n.* **1.** A total collapse or defeat. **2.** A serious collision between vehicles; a wreck.
smat•ter (smăt′ər) *v.* **-tered, -ter•ing, -ters.** —*tr.* **1.** To speak (a language) without fluency: *smatters Russian.* **2.** To study or approach superficially; dabble in. —*intr.* To prattle. —*n.* A smattering. [ME *smateren,* to make dirty, speak foolishly, chatter.] **—smat′ter•er** *n.*
smat•ter•ing (smăt′ər-ĭng) *n.* **1.** Superficial or piecemeal knowledge. **2.** A small scattered amount or number.
smaze (smāz) *n.* A relatively dry atmospheric mixture of smoke and haze. [SM(OKE) + (H)AZE[1].]
smear (smîr) *v.* **smeared, smear•ing, smears.** —*tr.* **1.a.** To spread or daub with a sticky, greasy, or dirty substance. **b.** To apply by spreading or daubing: *smeared lotion on my face.* **2.** To stain by or as if by spreading or daubing with a sticky, greasy, or dirty substance. **3.** To stain or attempt to destroy the reputation of; vilify. **4.** *Slang.* To defeat utterly; smash. —*intr.* To be or become stained or dirtied. —*n.* **1.** A mark made by smearing; a spot or blot. **2.** A substance to be spread on a surface. **3.** *Biol.* A sample, as of blood, spread on a slide for microscopic examination or on the surface of a culture medium. **4.** An attempt to destroy a reputation; vilification or slander. [ME *smeren,* to anoint < OE *smerian.*]
smear•case (smîr′kās′) *n. Pennsylvania.* See **cottage cheese.** See Regional Note at **gum band.** [Penn.Du. *Schmierkees* < Ger. *Schmierkäse,* a kind of spreadable cheese : *schmieren,* to smear (< MHGer. *smirwen* < OHGer.) + *Käse,* cheese (< MHGer. *kaese* < OHGer. *kāsi* < Lat. *cāseus*).]
smear•y (smîr′ē) *adj.* **-i•er, -i•est. 1.** Having been smeared. **2.** Tending to smear or soil. **—smear′i•ness** *n.*
smeg•ma (smĕg′mə) *n.* A sebaceous secretion, esp. the cheesy one that collects under the prepuce or around the clitoris. [Lat., detergent < Gk. *smēgma* < *smēkhein,* to wash off.]
smell (smĕl) *v.* **smelled** or **smelt** (smĕlt), **smell•ing, smells.** —*tr.* **1.** To perceive the scent of (something) by means of the olfactory nerves. **2.** To sense the presence of by or as if by the olfactory nerves; detect or discover. —*intr.* **1.** To use the sense of smell; perceive the scent of something. **2.** To have or emit an odor. **3.** To be suggestive; have a touch of something. **4.** To have or emit an unpleasant odor; stink. **5.** To appear to be dishonest; suggest evil or corruption. —*n.* **1.** The sense by which odors are perceived; the olfactory sense. **2.** That quality of something that may be perceived by the olfactory sense. **3.** The act or an instance of smelling. **4.** A distinctive enveloping or characterizing quality; an aura or a trace: *the smell of success.* ***—idiom.* smell a rat.** *Slang.* To suspect that something is wrong. [ME *smellen.*]

Syns: *smell, aroma, odor, scent.* The central meaning shared by these nouns is "a quality that can be perceived by the olfactory sense": *the smell of gas; the aroma of frying onions; hospital odors; the scent of pine needles.*

smell•ing salts (smĕl′ĭng) *pl.n. (used with a sing. or pl. v.)* Any of various preparations of ammonium carbonate and perfume, sniffed as a restorative or stimulant.
smell•y (smĕl′ē) *adj.* **-i•er, -i•est.** *Informal.* Having a noticeable, usu. unpleasant or offensive odor.
smelt[1] (smĕlt) *v.* **smelt•ed, smelt•ing, smelts.** —*tr.* To melt or fuse (ores) in order to separate the metallic constituents. —*intr.* To melt or fuse. Used of ores. [Du. or LGer. *smelten* < MDu. or MLGer.; see **mel-**[1]*.]
smelt[2] (smĕlt) *n., pl.* **smelts** or **smelt.** Any of various small silvery marine and freshwater food fishes of the family Osmeridae found in cold waters of the Northern Hemisphere, esp. *Osmerus mordax* of North America and *O. eperlanus* of Europe. [ME < OE. See **mel-**[1]*.]
smelt[3] (smĕlt) *v.* A p.t. and p.part. of **smell.**
smelt•er (smĕl′tər) *n.* **1.a.** An apparatus for smelting. **b.** Also **smelt•er•y** (smĕl′tə-rē)., *pl.* **-ies.** An establishment for smelting. **2.** One who is engaged in the smelting industry.
Sme•ta•na (smĕt′n-ə, smĕ′tä-nä), **Bedřich.** 1824–84. Czech composer of *The Bartered Bride* (1866).

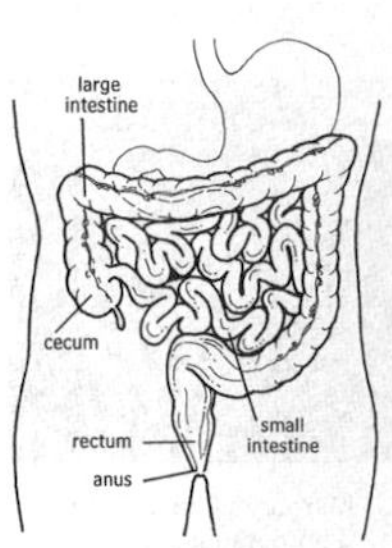

small intestine

ă pat	oi boy
ā pay	ou out
âr care	ŏŏ took
ä father	ōō boot
ĕ pet	ŭ cut
ē be	ûr urge
ĭ pit	th thin
ī pie	*th* this
îr pier	hw which
ŏ pot	zh vision
ō toe	ə about, item
ô paw	

Stress marks:
′ (primary);
′ (secondary), as in dictionary (dĭk′shə-nĕr′ē)

Smeth•wick (smĕth′ĭk). A borough of central England, a suburb of Birmingham. Pop. 309,900.

smew (smyo͞o) *n.* A small Old World merganser *(Mergus albellus),* the male of which has white and black plumage. [?]

smid•gen also **smid•geon** or **smid•gin** (smĭj′ən) *n.* A very small quantity or portion; a bit or mite. [Prob. alteration of dial. *smitch,* particle, perh. ult. < ME *smite,* perh. < p.part. of *smiten,* to smite. See SMITE.]

smi•lax (smī′lăks′) *n.* **1.** See **catbrier. 2.** A vine *(Asparagus asparagoides)* that has glossy foliage and is popular as a floral decoration. [Lat. *smīlax,* bindweed < Gk. *smilax.*]

smile (smīl) *n.* **1.** A facial expression characterized by an upward curving of the corners of the mouth and indicating pleasure, amusement, or derision. **2.** A pleasant or favorable disposition or aspect. *—v.* **smiled, smil•ing, smiles.** *—intr.* **1.** To have or form a smile. **2.a.** To look with favor or approval. **b.** To express cheerful acceptance or equanimity. *—tr.* **1.** To express with a smile. **2.** To effect or accomplish with or as if with a smile. [< ME *smilen,* to smile, prob. of Scand. orig. See **smei-***.] **—smil′er** *n.* **—smil′ey, smil′y** *adj.* **—smil′ing•ly** *adv.* **—smil′ing•ness** *n.*

Joseph Smith
A portrait executed in 1971 by Adrian Lamb (1901–1988)

smirch (smûrch) *tr.v.* **smirched, smirch•ing, smirch•es. 1.** To soil, stain, or dirty with or as if with a smearing agent. **2.** To dishonor; defame. *—n.* Something, such as a blot, smear, or stain, that smirches. [ME *smorchen.*]

smirk (smûrk) *intr.v.* **smirked, smirk•ing, smirks.** To smile in an affected, often offensively self-satisfied manner. *—n.* An affected, often offensively self-satisfied smile. [ME *smirken* < OE *smercian,* to smile. See **smei-***.] **—smirk′er** *n.* **—smirk′ing•ly, smirk′i•ly** *adv.* **—smirk′y** *adj.*

smite (smīt) *v.* **smote** (smōt), **smit•ten** (smĭt′n) or **smote, smit•ing, smites.** *—tr.* **1.a.** To inflict a heavy blow on, with or as if with the hand, a tool, or a weapon. **b.** To drive or strike (a weapon, for example) forcefully onto or into something else. **2.** To attack, damage, or destroy by or as if by blows. **3.a.** To afflict: *smitten by the plague.* **b.** To afflict retributively; chasten or chastise. **4.** To affect sharply with great feeling: *was smitten by remorse.* *—intr.* To deal a blow with or as if with the hand or a hand-held weapon. [ME *smiten* < OE *smītan,* to smear.] **—smit′er** *n.*

Margaret Chase Smith
Photographed in 1954

smith (smĭth) *n.* **1.** A metalworker. Often used in combination: *a silversmith.* **2.** A blacksmith. **3.** One who makes or works at something specified. Often used in combination: *a locksmith.* [ME < OE.]

Smith (smĭth), **Adam.** 1723–90. Scottish political economist and philosopher whose *Wealth of Nations* (1776) laid the foundations of classical free-market economic theory.

Smith, Alfred Emanuel. "the Happy Warrior." 1873–1944. Amer. politician who was defeated in the 1928 presidential election by Herbert Hoover.

Smith, Bessie. 1894?–1937. Amer. singer who became a leading jazz and blues singer in the 1920's.

Smith, Hannah Whitall. 1832–1911. Amer. evangelist who was a founder of the Woman's Christian Temperance Union (1874).

Smith, Ian. b. 1919. Zimbabwean politician who unilaterally declared the independence of Rhodesia in 1965.

Smith, Jedediah Strong. 1799–1831. Amer. trader and explorer who opened a number of frontier trade routes.

Smith, John. 1580?–1631. English colonist, explorer, and writer noted for his invaluable maps and accounts of explorations in Virginia and New England.

Smith, Joseph. 1805–44. Amer. religious leader who founded (1830) the Church of Jesus Christ of Latter-day Saints and led his congregation from NY to W IL, where he was murdered.

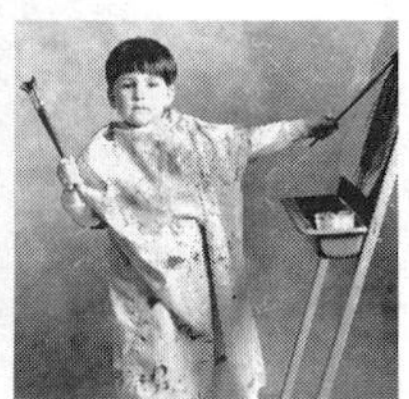

smock

Smith, Julia Evelina. 1792–1886. Amer. suffragist who with her sister **Abby Hadassah Smith** (1797–1878) refused to pay taxes until she could vote.

Smith, Kathryn ("Kate") Elizabeth. 1909–86. Amer. singer noted esp. for her rendition of "God Bless America."

Smith, Margaret Chase. b. 1897. Amer. politician who served as a U.S. representative (1940–49) and senator (1949–73) from ME.

Smith, Sydney. 1771–1845. British religious leader and advocate of the political emancipation of Catholics in England.

smith•er•eens (smĭth′ə-rēnz′) *pl.n. Informal.* Fragments or splintered pieces; bits. [< Ir.Gael. *smidirīn,* dim. of *smiodar,* small fragment.]

smith•er•y (smĭth′ə-rē) *n., pl.* **-ies. 1.** The occupation or craft of a smith. **2.** See **smithy.**

Smith•son (smĭth′sən), **James.** 1765–1829. British chemist, mineralogist, and philanthropist whose bequest to the U.S. helped establish (1846) the Smithsonian Institution.

smith•son•ite (smĭth′sə-nīt′) *n.* A mineral, $ZnCO_3$, sometimes used as a source of zinc. [After James SMITHSON.]

Smith•town (smĭth′toun′). A community of SE NY on N Long I. N of Islip. Pop. 25,638.

smith•y (smĭth′ē, smĭth′ē) *n., pl.* **-ies.** A blacksmith's shop; a forge. [ME < ON *smidhja.*]

smit•ten (smĭt′n) *v.* A p.part. of **smite.**

SMN *abbr.* Seaman.

smock (smŏk) *n.* A loose coatlike outer garment, often worn to protect the clothes. *—tr.v.* **smocked, smock•ing, smocks. 1.** To clothe in a smock. **2.** To decorate (fabric) with smocking. [ME, woman's undergarment < OE *smoc.*]

smock•ing (smŏk′ĭng) *n.* Needlework decoration of small, regularly spaced gathers stitched into a honeycomb pattern.

smog (smŏg, smôg) *n.* **1.** Fog that has become mixed and polluted with smoke. **2.** Air pollution produced when sunlight causes hydrocarbons and nitrogen oxides from automotive emissions to combine in a photochemical reaction. [SM(OKE) + (F)OG[1].] **—smog′gy** *adj.* **—smog′less** *adj.*

smoke (smōk) *n.* **1.** The vaporous system made up of small particles of carbonaceous matter in the air, resulting mainly from the burning of organic material. **2.** A suspension of fine solid or liquid particles in a gaseous medium. **3.** A cloud of fine particles. **4.** Something insubstantial, unreal, or transitory. **5.a.** The act of smoking tobacco. **b.** The duration of this act. **6.** *Informal.* Tobacco in a form that can be smoked, esp. a cigarette. **7.** A substance used in warfare to produce a smoke screen. **8.** Something used to conceal or obscure. **9.** *Color.* A pale to grayish blue to bluish or dark gray. *—v.* **smoked, smok•ing, smokes.** *—intr.* **1.a.** To draw in and exhale smoke from a cigarette, cigar, or pipe. **b.** To engage in smoking regularly or habitually. **2.** To emit smoke or a smokelike substance. **3.** To emit smoke excessively. **4.** *Slang.* **a.** To go or proceed at high speed. **b.** To play or perform energetically. *—tr.* **1.a.** To draw in and exhale the smoke of (tobacco, for example). **b.** To do so regularly or habitually. **2.** To preserve (meat or fish) by exposure to the aromatic smoke of burning hardwood, usu. after pickling. **3.a.** To fumigate (a house, for example). **b.** To expose (animals, esp. insects) to smoke in order to immobilize or drive away. **4.** To expose (glass) to smoke in order to darken or change its color. **5.** *Slang.* To kill; murder. ***—phrasal verb.*** **smoke out. 1.** To force out of a place of hiding or concealment by or as if by the use of smoke. **2.** To detect and bring to public view; expose or reveal. [ME < OE *smoca.*] **—smok′a•ble, smoke′a•ble** *adj.*

smoke bomb *n.* A bomb that gives out thick smoke upon exploding, used esp. to mark a target or create a smoke screen.

smoke detector *n.* An alarm device that automatically detects the presence of smoke.

smoke-filled room (smōk′fĭld′) *n.* A place, esp. a hotel room, where people gather to negotiate or make deals in private.

smoke•house (smōk′hous′) *n.* A structure in which meat or fish is cured with smoke.

smoke•jump•er (smōk′jŭm′pər) *n.* A firefighter who drops by parachute into a forest fire.

smoke•less (smōk′lĭs) *adj.* **1.** Emitting or containing little or no smoke. **2.** Free from the use of smoking tobacco or from the smoke generated by such use: *a smokeless office.*

smokeless powder *n.* A relatively smoke-free propellant charge composed mainly of nitrocellulose, used in ammunition.

smokeless tobacco *n.* **1.** Tobacco cut for chewing. **2.** See **snuff**[3] 1a.

smok•er (smō′kər) *n.* **1.** One who smokes tobacco. **2.** A device, such as a stove, that emits smoke. **3.** A smoking car. **4.** An informal social gathering for men.

smoke screen or **smoke•screen** (smōk′skrēn′) *n.* **1.** Artificial smoke used to conceal military areas or operations. **2.** An action or a statement used to conceal or deceive.

smoke•stack (smōk′stăk′) *n.* A large chimney or vertical pipe through which combustion vapors, gases, and smoke are discharged. *—adj.* Of, relating to, or involved in heavy manufacturing or the processing of materials.

smoke tree *n.* Either of two deciduous plants, *Cotinus obovatus,* a tree of the southern United States, or *C. coggygria,* a shrub of Eurasia, having plumelike clusters of small yellowish flowers.

smok•ing car (smō′kĭng) *n.* A railroad car in which smoking is allowed.

smoking gun *n. Informal.* Something that serves as indisputable evidence or proof, esp. of a crime.

smoking jacket *n.* A man's evening jacket, often made of a fine fabric, elaborately trimmed, and usu. worn at home.

smoking room *n.* A room set aside for smokers.

smok•y (smō′kē) *adj.* **-i•er, -i•est. 1.** Emitting smoke in profuse volume. **2.** Mixed or filled with smoke. **3.** Resembling smoke: *a smoky haze.* **4.** Discolored or soiled with or as if with smoke. **5.** Tasting of smoke: *smoky sausages.* **—smok′i•ly** *adv.* **—smok′i•ness** *n.*

Smok•y Hill River (smō′kē). A river rising in E CO and flowing c. 901 km (560 mi) E across central KS to join the Republican R. and form the Kansas R.

smoky quartz *n.* A transparent or semitransparent brown or gray to nearly black variety of quartz, used as a gemstone.

Smoky River. A river of W-central Alberta, Canada, flowing c. 402 km (250 mi) to the Peace R.

smol•der also **smoul•der** (smōl′dər) *—intr.v.* **-dered, -der•ing, -ders. 1.** To burn with little smoke and no flame. **2.** To exist in a suppressed state. **3.** To show signs of repressed anger or hatred. *—n.* Thick smoke resulting from a slow fire.

[ME *smolderen,* to suffocate < *smolder,* smoke, prob. alteration of *smorther* < OE *smorian,* to smoke.]

Smo•lensk (smō-lĕnsk′, smə-). A city of W Russia on the Dnieper R. WSW of Moscow. Pop. 331,000.

Smol•lett (smŏl′ĭt), **Tobias George.** 1721–71. British writer whose adventure novels include *Roderick Random* (1748).

smolt (smōlt) *n.* A young salmon at the stage when it becomes covered with silvery scales and first migrates from fresh water to the sea. [ME < Med.Lat. *smoltus,* prob. of OE orig.]

smooch (smo͞och) *Slang.* —*n.* A kiss. —*intr.v.* **smooched, smooch•ing, smooch•es.** To kiss. [Alteration of E. dial. *smouch,* perh. imit. of the sound of a kiss.]

smooth (smo͞o*th*) *adj.* **smooth•er, smooth•est. 1.** Having a surface free from irregularities, roughness, or projections; even. **2.** Having a fine texture. **3.** Having an even consistency. **4.** Having an even or gentle motion or movement. **5.** Having no obstructions or difficulties. See Syns at **easy. 6.** Serene: *a smooth temperament.* **7.** Bland: *a smooth wine.* **8.** Ingratiatingly polite and agreeable. **9.** Having no grossness or coarseness in dress or manner. —*v.* **smoothed, smooth•ing, smoothes.** —*tr.* **1.** To make (something) even, level, or unwrinkled. **2.** To rid of obstructions, hindrances, or difficulties. **3.** To soothe or tranquilize; make calm. **4.** To make less harsh or crude; refine. —*intr.* To become smooth. —*n.* **1.** The act of smoothing. **2.** A smooth surface or part. [ME *smothe* < OE *smōth.*] —**smooth′er** *n.* —**smooth′ly** *adv.* —**smooth′ness** *n.*

smooth•bore also **smooth bore** (smo͞o*th*′bôr′, -bōr′) —*adj.* Having no rifling within the barrel. Used of a firearm. —*n.* A firearm having no rifling.

smooth breathing *n.* **1.** The symbol (’) written over some initial vowels and diphthongs in ancient Greek to indicate that a word does not begin with the sound (h). **2.** In ancient Greek, an initial vowel or diphthong not preceded by the sound (h).

smooth dogfish *n.* Any of several dogfishes lacking a spine in front of the dorsal fin, esp. a species *(Mustelus canis)* found abundantly on the American Atlantic coast.

smooth•en (smo͞o′*th*ən) *tr. & intr.v.* **-ened, -en•ing, -ens.** To make or become smooth.

smooth hound *n.* Any dogfish of the genus *Mustelus,* esp. a smooth dogfish *(M. mustelus)* of southern Europe.

smooth•ie also **smooth•y** (smo͞o′*th*ē) *n., pl.* **-ies.** *Slang.* **1.** A person regarded as being assured and artfully ingratiating in manner. **2.** A smooth-tongued person.

smooth muscle *n.* Muscle tissue that contracts without conscious control, made up of spindle-shaped unstriated cells with single nuclei and found in the walls of the internal organs, excluding the heart.

smooth-tongued (smo͞o*th*′tŭngd′) *adj.* Speaking or spoken in an artfully suave manner; ingratiating.

smor•gas•bord (smôr′gəs-bôrd′, -bōrd′) *n.* **1.** A buffet meal featuring a varied number of dishes. **2.** A varied collection. [Swed. *smörgåsbord* : *smörgås,* bread and butter (*smör,* butter < ON + Swed. dial. *gå,* lump of butter < ON *gās,* goose; see GOSLING) + *bord,* table (< ON *bordh*).]

smote (smōt) *v.* P.t. and p.part. of **smite.**

smoth•er (smŭ*th*′ər) *v.* **-ered, -er•ing, -ers.** —*tr.* **1.a.** To suffocate (another). **b.** To deprive (a fire) of the oxygen necessary for combustion. **2.** To conceal, suppress, or hide. **3.** To cover (a foodstuff) thickly with another foodstuff. **4.** To lavish a surfeit of a given emotion on (someone). —*intr.* **1.a.** To suffocate. **b.** To be extinguished. **2.** To be concealed or suppressed. **3.** To be surfeited with an emotion. —*n.* Something, such as a dense cloud of smoke, that smothers or tends to smother. [ME *smotheren* < *smorther,* dense smoke. See SMOLDER.]

smoth•er•y (smŭ*th*′ə-rē) *adj. Upper Southern U.S.* Confined. Used of a place: *"Other places do seem so cramped up and smothery, but a raft don't"* (Mark Twain).

smoul•der (smōl′dər) *v. & n.* Var. of **smolder.**

smudge (smŭj) *v.* **smudged, smudg•ing, smudg•es.** —*tr.* **1.** To make dirty, esp. in one small area. **2.** To smear or blur (something). **3.** To fill (an orchard, for example) with smoke from a smudge pot to prevent damage from insects or frost. —*intr.* **1.** To smear something as with dirt, soot, or ink. **2.** To become smudged. —*n.* **1.** A blotch or smear. **2.** A smoky fire used as a protection against insects or frost. [ME *smogen.*] —**smudg′i•ly** *adv.* —**smudg′i•ness** *n.* —**smudg′y** *adj.*

smudge pot *n.* A receptacle in which oil or another smoky fuel is burned to protect an orchard from insects or frost.

smug (smŭg) *adj.* **smug•ger, smug•gest.** Exhibiting or feeling great or offensive satisfaction with oneself or with one's situation; self-righteously complacent. [Perh. akin to LGer. *smuck,* neat < MLGer. < *smucken,* to adorn.] —**smug′ly** *adv.* —**smug′ness** *n.*

smug•gle (smŭg′əl) *v.* **-gled, -gling, -gles.** —*tr.* **1.** To import or export without paying lawful customs charges or duties. **2.** To bring in or take out illicitly or by stealth. —*intr.* To engage in smuggling. [Prob. LGer. *smukkeln, smuggeln* or MDu. *smokkelen.*] —**smug′gler** *n.*

smut (smŭt) *n.* **1.a.** A particle of dirt. **b.** A smudge made by soot, smoke, or dirt. **2.a.** Obscenity in speech or writing. **b.** Pornography. **3.a.** Any of various plant diseases, esp. of cereal grasses, caused by parasitic fungi of the order Ustilaginales that form black powdery masses of spores on the affected parts. **b.** A fungus causing such a disease. —*v.* **smut•ted, smut•ting, smuts.** —*tr.* **1.** To blacken or smudge, as with smoke. **2.** To affect (a plant) with smut. **3.** To free (grain, for example) from smut. **4.** To make obscene. —*intr.* **1.** To emit smut. **2.** To be or become blackened or smudged. **3.** To become affected with smut, as a plant. [< ME *smotten, smutten,* to defile.] —**smut′ti•ly** *adv.* —**smut′ti•ness** *n.* —**smut′ty** *adj.*

smutch (smŭch) *tr.v.* **smutched, smutch•ing, smutch•es.** To soil or stain. —*n.* A stain or spot of dirt. [Perh. alteration of SMUDGE.] —**smutch′y** *adj.*

Smuts (smŭts, smœts), **Jan Christiaan.** 1870–1950. South African soldier and prime minister (1919–24 and 1939–48).

Smyr•na (smûr′nə). **1.** A city of NW GA, a residential suburb of Atlanta. Pop. 30,981. **2.** See **Izmir.**

Sn The symbol for the element **tin** 1. [< LLat. *stannum,* tin. See STANNIC.]

snack (snăk) *n.* **1.** A hurried or light meal. **2.** Food eaten between meals. —*intr.v.* **snacked, snack•ing, snacks.** To eat a hurried or light meal. [ME *snak,* var. of *snacche,* trap, bite < *snacchen,* to snap. See SNATCH.] —**snack′er** *n.*

snack bar *n.* A lunch counter or small restaurant where light meals are served.

snaf•fle (snăf′əl) *n.* A bit for a horse, consisting of two bars jointed at the center. —*tr.v.* **-fled, -fling, -fles.** To put on or control with a snaffle. [?]

snaffle

sna•fu (snă-fo͞o′) *Slang.* —*n., pl.* **-fus.** A chaotic or confused situation. —*adj.* In a state of confusion or chaos. —*tr.v.* **-fued, -fu•ing, -fus.** To make confused or chaotic. [*s(ituation) n(ormal), a(ll) f(ucked) u(p).*]

snag (snăg) *n.* **1.** A rough, sharp, or jagged protuberance, as: **a.** A tree or a part of a tree that protrudes above the surface in a body of water. **b.** A snaggletooth. **2.** A break, pull, or tear in fabric. **3.** An unforeseen or hidden obstacle. **4.** A short or imperfectly developed branch of a deer's antler. —*v.* **snagged, snag•ging, snags.** —*tr.* **1.** To tear, break, hinder, or destroy by or as if by a snag. **2.** *Informal.* To catch unexpectedly and quickly. **3.** To free of snags: *snagged the river.* **4.** *Missouri.* To catch (fish). —*intr.* To be damaged by a snag. [Of Scand. orig.] —**snag′gy** *adj.*

snag•gle•tooth (snăg′əl-to͞oth′) *n.* A tooth that is broken or not in alignment with the others. [< SNAG + TOOTH.]

snail (snāl) *n.* **1.** Any of numerous aquatic or terrestrial mollusks of the class Gastropoda, typically having a spirally coiled shell, a broad retractile foot, and a distinct head. **2.** A slow-moving, lazy, or sluggish person. [ME < OE *snægl.*]

snail

snail darter *n.* A small snail-eating darter *(Percina tanasi)* that formerly was found only in the Little Tennessee River of the southeast United States.

snail fever *n.* See **schistosomiasis.**

snail-paced (snāl′pāst′) *adj.* Moving with extreme slowness.

snake (snāk) *n.* **1.** Any of numerous scaly, legless, sometimes venomous reptiles of the suborder Serpentes or Ophidia (order Squamata), having a long tapering cylindrical body and found in most tropical and temperate regions. **2.** A treacherous person. **3.** A long, highly flexible metal wire or coil used for cleaning drains. —*v.* **snaked, snak•ing, snakes.** —*tr.* **1.** To drag or pull lengthwise, esp. to drag with a rope or chain. **2.** To pull with quick jerks. **3.** To move in a sinuous or gliding manner. —*intr.* To move with a sinuous motion. [ME < OE *snaca.*]

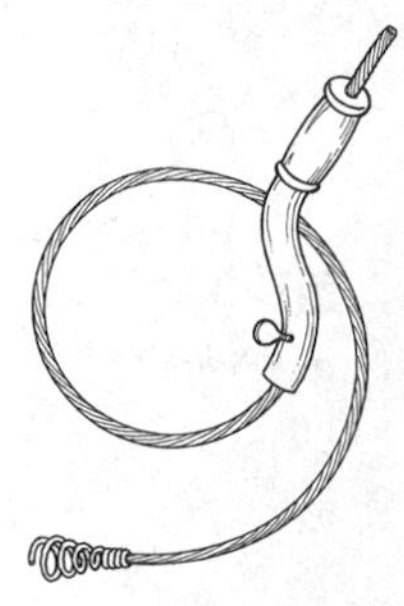
snake
Plumber's snake

Snake[1] (snāk) *n., pl.* **Snake** or **Snakes.** See **Shoshone** 1a.

Snake[2] (snāk) *n.* See **Hydra** 2.

snake•bird (snāk′bûrd′) *n.* See **anhinga.**

snake•bite (snāk′bīt′) *n.* **1.** The bite of a snake. **2.** Poisoning resulting from the bite of a venomous snake.

snake charmer *n.* One who uses rhythmic music and body movements to control snakes.

snake dance *n.* **1.** A ceremonial dance of the Hopi in which the dancers traditionally carry live snakes in their mouths. **2.** A procession of people who move forward in a zigzag line.

snake doctor *n.* **1.** *Chiefly Southern U.S.* See **dragonfly.** See Regional Note at **dragonfly. 2.** See **hellgrammite.**

snake eyes *pl.n. (used with a sing. v.) Games.* A throw of two dice that turns up one spot on each.

snake feeder *n. Midland U.S.* See **dragonfly.** See Regional Note at **dragonfly.**

snake fence *n.* See **worm fence.**

snake•fish (snāk′fĭsh′) *n., pl.* **snakefish** or **-fish•es.** Any of several fishes resembling a snake, esp. the lizardfish *Trachinocephalus myops* of the eastern Atlantic and western Pacific.

snake•head (snāk′hĕd′) *n. Bot.* See **turtlehead.**

snake in the grass *n., pl.* **snakes in the grass.** See **snake** 2.

snake•mouth (snāk′mouth′) *n.* A North American orchid *(Pogonia ophioglossoides)* having a solitary rose-purple flower with a fringed lip.

snake oil *n.* **1.** A preparation fraudulently peddled as a cure for many ills. **2.** Speech or writing intended to deceive; humbug.

ă pat	oi boy
ā pay	ou out
âr care	o͝o took
ä father	o͞o boot
ĕ pet	ŭ cut
ē be	ûr urge
ĭ pit	th thin
ī pie	*th* this
îr pier	hw which
ŏ pot	zh vision
ō toe	ə about, item
ô paw	

Stress marks:
′ (primary);
′ (secondary), as in **dictionary** (dĭk′shə-nĕr′ē)

snake pit *n. Slang.* **1.** A place of disorder and chaos. **2.** A mental health facility.

snake plant *n.* A stemless plant *(Sansevieria trifasciata)* having narrow, often mottled leaves and cultivated as a houseplant.

Snake River. A river of the NW U.S. rising in NW WY and flowing c. 1,670 km (1,038 mi) to the Columbia R. in SE WA.

snake•root (snāk′ro͞ot′, -ro͝ot′) *n.* Any of various plants, such as sanicle, having roots reputed to cure snakebite.

snake•skin (snāk′skĭn′) *n.* The skin of a snake, esp. when prepared as leather.

snake•weed (snāk′wēd′) *n.* Any of various plants, such as bistort, reputed to have the power to cure snakebite.

snak•y (snā′kē) *adj.* **-i•er, -i•est. 1.** Relating to or characteristic of snakes. **2.** Having the form or movement of a snake; serpentine. **3.** Overrun with snakes. **4.** Treacherous; sly. **—snak′i•ly** *adv.* **—snak′i•ness** *n.*

snap (snăp) *v.* **snapped, snap•ping, snaps.** *—intr.* **1.** To make a brisk sharp cracking sound. **2.** To break suddenly with a brisk sharp cracking sound. **3.a.** To give way abruptly under pressure or tension. **b.** To suffer a physical or mental breakdown, esp. while under stress. **4.** To bring the jaws briskly together, often with a clicking sound; bite. **5.** To snatch or grasp suddenly and with eagerness. **6.** To speak abruptly or sharply. **7.** To move swiftly and smartly. **8.** To flash or appear to flash light; sparkle. **9.** To open, close, or fit together with a click. *—tr.* **1.** To snatch at with or as if with the teeth; bite. **2.** To pull apart or break with a snapping sound. **3.** To utter abruptly or sharply: *snapped out a command.* **4.a.** To cause to emit a snapping sound. **b.** To close or latch with a snapping sound. **5.** To cause to move abruptly and smartly. **6.a.** To take (a photograph). **b.** To photograph. **7.** *Football.* To center (a football); hike. *—n.* **1.** A sudden sharp cracking sound or the action producing such a sound. **2.** A sudden breaking. **3.** A clasp, catch, or other fastening device that operates with a snapping sound. **4.** A sudden attempt to bite, snatch, or grasp. **5.a.** The sound produced by rapid movement of a finger from the thumb tip to the base of the thumb. **b.** The act of producing this sound. **6.** The sudden release of something held under pressure or tension. **7.** A thin, crisp, usu. circular cookie. **8.a.** Capacity to make a snapping sound; elasticity. **b.** *Informal.* Briskness, liveliness, or energy. **9.** A brief spell of brisk cold weather. **10.** Something accomplished without effort. **11.a.** A snapshot. **b.** The taking of a snapshot. **12.** A snap bean. **13.** *Football.* The passing of a football from the center to a back that initiates each play. *—adj.* **1.** Made or done suddenly, with little or no preparation. **2.** Fastening with a snap. **3.** *Informal.* Simple; easy. *—adv.* With a snap. ***—phrasal verbs.*** **snap back.** To recover quickly. **snap up.** To acquire quickly. ***—idiom.*** **snap out of it.** *Informal.* To move quickly back to one's normal condition from an undesirable condition, such as depression. [Prob. < ME *snappe,* a quick bite, prob. < MLGer. or MDu. *snappen,* to seize, snap.]

snapdragon

snap bean *n.* A string bean cultivated for its crisp edible pods.

snap-brim (snăp′brĭm′) *n.* A hat having a flexible brim, usu. turned down in front and up at the back.

snap•drag•on (snăp′drăg′ən) *n.* Any of several plants of the genus *Antirrhinum,* esp. the Mediterranean herb *A. majus,* having two-lipped, variously colored flowers. [< the imagined resemblance of the flowers to the mouth of a dragon.]

snap•per (snăp′ər) *n.* **1.** One that snaps. **2.** *pl.* **snapper** or **-pers.** Any of numerous widely distributed marine fishes of the family Lutjanidae (or Lutianidae), found chiefly in warm coastal waters of the Pacific and Atlantic. **3.** A snapping turtle. **4.** See **schnapper.**

snap•ping beetle (snăp′ĭng) *n.* See **click beetle.**

snapping turtle *n.* Any of several large freshwater turtles of the family Chelydridae of North, Central, and northern South America, having a rough shell and powerful hooked jaws that close with a snap.

snap•pish (snăp′ĭsh) *adj.* **1.** Likely to snap or bite. **2.** Irritable and curt. **—snap′pish•ly** *adv.* **—snap′pish•ness** *n.*

snap•py (snăp′ē) *adj.* **-pi•er, -pi•est. 1.** *Informal.* Lively or energetic; brisk. **2.** *Informal.* Smart or chic. **3.** Snappish: *a snappy retort.* **—snap′pi•ly** *adv.* **—snap′pi•ness** *n.*

snap roll *n.* An aerial maneuver in which an aircraft is put through a sharp roll of 360° about its longitudinal axis.

snap•shot (snăp′shŏt′) *n.* **1.** A photograph taken with a small hand-held camera. **2.** An isolated observation.

snare[1] (snâr) *n.* **1.** A trapping device, often consisting of a noose, used for capturing birds and small mammals. **2.** Something that serves to entangle the unwary. **3.** A surgical instrument with a wire loop controlled by a mechanism in the handle, used to remove growths. *—tr.v.* **snared, snar•ing, snares.** To trap with or as if with a snare. See Syns at **catch.** [ME < OE *snearu* and < ON *snara.*] **—snar′er** *n.*

snare[2] (snâr) *n. Mus.* **1.** Any of the wires or cords stretched across the lower skin of a snare drum to increase reverberation. **2.** A snare drum. [Prob. < Du. *snaar,* string < MDu. *snāre.*]

snare drum *n. Mus.* A small double-headed drum having one or more wires or cords stretched across the bottom head.

snarl[1] (snärl) *v.* **snarled, snarl•ing, snarls.** *—intr.* **1.** To growl viciously while baring the teeth. **2.** To speak angrily or threateningly. *—tr.* To utter with anger or hostility. *—n.* **1.** A vicious growl. **2.** A vicious, hostile utterance. [Freq. of obsolete *snar,* perh. < Du. or LGer. *snarren,* to rattle, prob. of imit. orig.] **—snarl′er** *n.* **—snarl′ing•ly** *adv.* **—snarl′y** *adj.*

snarl[2] (snärl) *n.* **1.** A tangled mass, as of hair or yarn. **2.** A confused, complicated, or tangled situation; a predicament. *—v.* **snarled, snarl•ing, snarls.** *—intr.* To become tangled or confused. *—tr.* **1.** To tangle or knot (hair, for example). **2.** To confuse; complicate. [ME *snarle,* trap, prob. dim. of *snare.* See SNARE[1].] **—snarl′er** *n.* **—snarl′y** *adj.*

snatch (snăch) *v.* **snatched, snatch•ing, snatch•es.** *—tr.* **1.a.** To grasp or seize hastily, eagerly, or suddenly. **b.** *Sports.* To raise (a weight) using a snatch. **2.** To grasp or seize illicitly. *—intr.* To make grasping or seizing motions. *—n.* **1.** The act of snatching; a quick grasp or grab. **2.** A brief period of time. **3.** A small amount; a bit or fragment. **4.** *Slang.* A kidnapping. **5.** *Sports.* A lift in weightlifting in which the weight is raised in one motion from the floor to an overhead position. [ME *snacchen.*] **—snatch′er** *n.*

snatch block *n. Naut.* A block that can be opened on one side to receive the looped part of a line without unreeving it.

snatch•y (snăch′ē) *adj.* **-i•er, -i•est.** Occurring in snatches; intermittent.

snaz•zy (snăz′ē) *adj.* **-zi•er, -zi•est.** *Slang.* Fashionable or flashy. [?] **—snaz′zi•ness** *n.*

SNCC *abbr.* Student Nonviolent Coordinating Committee.

sneak (snēk) *v.* **sneaked** also **snuck** (snŭk), **sneak•ing, sneaks.** *—intr.* **1.** To go or move in a quiet, stealthy way. **2.** To behave in a cowardly or servile manner. *—tr.* To move, give, take, or put in a quiet, stealthy manner. *—n.* **1.** A person regarded as stealthy, cowardly, or underhand. **2.** An instance of sneaking; a quiet, stealthy movement. **3.** *Informal.* A sneaker. *—adj.* **1.** Carried out in a clandestine manner. **2.** Perpetrated without warning. [Prob. akin to ME *sniken,* to creep < OE *snīcan.*]

Usage Note: *Snuck* is an Americanism first introduced in the 19th century as a nonstandard regional variant of *sneaked.* Many writers and editors have a lingering unease about the form, even though it is widely used, particularly if they recall its nonstandard origins. In fact, our evidence indicates that *sneaked* is preferred by a factor of 7 to 2. And 67 percent of the Usage Panel disapproves of *snuck.*

sneak•er (snē′kər) *n.* A sports shoe usu. made of canvas and having soft rubber soles.

sneak•ing (snē′kĭng) *adj.* **1.** Acting in a stealthy furtive way. **2.** Unavowed; secret. **3.** Gradually growing or persistent.

sneak preview *n.* A single public showing of a movie before its general release.

sneak thief *n.* One who steals without breaking into buildings or using violence.

sneak•y (snē′kē) *adj.* **-i•er, -i•est.** Furtive; surreptitious. **—sneak′i•ly** *adv.* **—sneak′i•ness** *n*

sneer (snîr) *n.* **1.** A scornful facial expression characterized by a slight raising of one corner of the upper lip. **2.** A contemptuous facial expression, sound, or statement. *—v.* **sneered, sneer•ing, sneers.** *—tr.* To utter with a sneer or in a sneering manner. *—intr.* **1.** To assume a scornful, contemptuous, or derisive facial expression. **2.** To speak in a scornful, contemptuous, or derisive manner. [< ME *sneren,* to mock, alteration of OE *fnǣran,* to breathe heavily. See **pneu-***.] **—sneer′er** *n.* **—sneer′ful, sneer′y** *adj.* **—sneer′ing•ly** *adv.*

sneeze (snēz) *intr.v.* **sneezed, sneez•ing, sneez•es.** To expel air forcibly from the mouth and nose in an explosive, spasmodic involuntary action resulting chiefly from irritation of the nasal mucous membrane. *—n.* An instance or the sound of sneezing. ***—phrasal verb.*** **sneeze at.** *Slang.* To treat as unimportant. [ME *snesen,* prob. alteration of *fnesen,* alteration of *fnesen* < OE *fnēosan.* See **pneu-***.] **—sneez′er** *n.* **—sneez′y** *adj.*

sneeze•weed (snēz′wēd′) *n.* Any of several New World herbs of the genus *Helenium* of the composite family, having yellow to red-purple rayed flower heads.

Snef•fels (snĕf′əlz), **Mount.** A peak, 4,315.8 m (14,150 ft), in the San Juan Mts. of SW CO.

snell (snĕl) *n.* A length of fine material, such as gut, that connects a fishhook to a heavier line; a length of leader. [?]

Snel•len chart (snĕl′ən) *n.* A chart for testing visual acuity, usu. with letters printed in lines of decreasing size, that a patient is asked to read or identify at a fixed distance. [After Herman *Snellen* (1834–1908), Dutch ophthalmologist.]

Snellen test *n.* A test for visual acuity using a Snellen chart.

SNG *abbr.* **1.** Substitute natural gas. **2.** Synthetic natural gas.

snick (snĭk) *v.* **snicked, snick•ing, snicks.** *—tr.* **1.** To cut with short strokes; snip. **2.** To make a small cut in; nick. **3.** To cause to click. *—intr.* **1.** To snip. **2.** To make a nick or nicks. **3.** To click. *—n.* **1.** A cut made by snicking. **2.** A clicking sound. [?]

snick•er (snĭk′ər) *intr.v.* **-ered, -er•ing, -ers.** To utter a snicker. *—n.* A slightly stifled laugh. [Perh imit.]

snick•er•snee (snĭk′ər-snē′) *n.* **1.** A knife resembling a sword. **2.** *Archaic.* The act of fighting with knives. [Alteration of obsolete *stick or snee*, to cut and thrust in knife fighting < Du. *steken of snijden* : *steken*, to stab (< MDu.; see **steig-***) + *of*, or (< MDu.) + *snijden*, to cut (< MDu. *sniden*).]

snide (snīd) *adj.* **snid•er, snid•est.** Derogatory in a malicious, superior way; sarcastic. [?] — **snide′ly** *adv.* — **snide′ness** *n.*

sniff (snĭf) *v.* **sniffed, sniff•ing, sniffs.** — *intr.* **1.a.** To inhale a short audible breath through the nose, as in smelling something. **b.** To sniffle. **2.** To use the sense of smell, as in savoring or investigating. **3.** To regard something in a contemptuous or dismissive manner. **4.** *Informal.* To pry; snoop. — *tr.* **1.** To inhale forcibly through the nose. **2.** To smell, as in savoring or investigating. **3.** To perceive or detect by or as if by sniffing. **4.** To utter in a contemptuous or haughty manner. — *n.* **1.** An instance or the sound of sniffing. **2.** Something sniffed or perceived by or as if by sniffing; a whiff. [ME *sniffen*, prob. of Scand. orig.] — **sniff′a•ble** *adj.* — **sniff′er** *n.*

snif•fle (snĭf′əl) *intr.v.* **-fled, -fling, -fles. 1.** To breathe audibly through a runny or congested nose. **2.** To weep or whimper lightly with spasmodic congestion of the nose. — *n.* **1.** The act or sound of sniffling. **2. sniffles.** A condition, such as a cold, accompanied by congestion of the nose. [Freq. of SNIFF.] — **snif′fler** *n.* — **snif′fly** (snĭf′ə-lē, snĭf′lē) *adj.*

sniff•y (snĭf′ē) *adj.* **-i•er, -i•est.** *Informal.* Disposed to show arrogance or contempt. — **sniff′i•ly** *adv.* — **sniff′i•ness** *n.*

snif•ter (snĭf′tər) *n.* **1.** A pear-shaped goblet with a narrow top, used esp. in serving brandy. **2.** *Slang.* A small portion of liquor. [< ME *snifteren*, to sniff, perh. of Scand. orig.]

snig•ger (snĭg′ər) *n.* A snicker. — *intr.v.* **-gered, -ger•ing, -gers.** To snicker. [Perh. alteration of SNICKER.]

snip (snĭp) *v.* **snipped, snip•ping, snips.** — *tr.* To cut, clip, or separate with short quick strokes. — *intr.* To cut or clip with short quick strokes. — *n.* **1.** An instance of snipping or the sound produced by snipping. **2.a.** A small cut made with scissors or shears. **b.** A small piece cut or clipped off. **c.** A bit or scrap. **3.** *Informal.* **a.** One that is small or slight in size or stature. **b.** A person regarded as impertinent or mischievous. **4. snips.** *(used with a sing. or pl. v.)* Hand shears used in cutting sheet metal. [Du. or LGer. *snippen.*]

snipe (snīp) *n.* **1.** *pl.* **snipe** or **snipes. a.** Any of various long-billed shore birds of the genus *Gallinago* or *Capella,* esp. the common, widely distributed species *G. gallinago* or *C. gallinago.* **b.** Any of various similar or related birds. **2.** A shot, esp. a gunshot, from a concealed place. — *intr.v.* **sniped, snip•ing, snipes. 1.** To shoot at individuals from a concealed place. **2.** To shoot snipe. **3.** To make malicious underhand remarks or attacks. [ME, prob. < ON *-snīpa*, as in *mȳrisnīpa*, marsh snipe.]

snip•er (snī′pər) *n.* **1.** A skilled military shooter detailed to spot and pick off enemy soldiers from a concealed place. **2.** One who shoots at other people from a concealed place.

snip•pet (snĭp′ĭt) *n.* **1.** A bit, scrap, or morsel. **2.** *Informal.* A small or mischievous person.

snip•pet•y (snĭp′ĭ-tē) *adj.* **-i•er, -i•est. 1.** Made up of snippets. **2.** *Informal.* Snippy; impertinent.

snip•py (snĭp′ē) *adj.* **-pi•er, -pi•est.** *Informal.* **1.** Sharp-tongued; impertinent. **2.** Occurring in pieces; fragmentary.

snit (snĭt) *n. Informal.* A state of agitation or irritation. [?]

snitch (snĭch) *Slang.* — *v.* **snitched, snitch•ing, snitch•es.** — *tr.* To steal (something, usu. something of little value); pilfer. — *intr.* To turn informer. — *n.* **1.** A thief. **2.** An informer. [?] — **snitch′er** *n.*

sniv•el (snĭv′əl) *intr.v.* **-eled, -el•ing, -els** or **-elled, -el•ling, -els. 1.** To sniffle. **2.** To complain or whine tearfully. **3.** To run at the nose. — *n.* **1.** The act of sniffling or sniveling. **2.** Nasal mucus. [ME *snivelen.*] — **sniv′el•er** *n.*

snob (snŏb) *n.* **1.** One who overtly imitates, obsequiously admires, and offensively seeks to associate only with those regarded as superiors, tending to rebuff or ignore altogether those regarded as inferiors. **2.** One who affects an offensive air of self-satisfied superiority in matters of taste or intellect. [Earlier *snob*, cobbler, lower-class person, person who aspires to social prominence.] — **snob′by** *adj.*

snob•ber•y (snŏb′ə-rē) *n., pl.* **-ies.** Snobbish behavior or an instance of it.

snob•bish (snŏb′ĭsh) *adj.* Of, befitting, or resembling a snob; pretentious. — **snob′bish•ly** *adv.* — **snob′bish•ness** *n.*

snob•bism (snŏb′ĭz′əm) *n.* Snobbery.

snood (sno͝od) *n.* **1.** A small netlike cap worn by women to keep the hair in place. **2.** A headband or fillet. — *tr.v.* **snood•ed, snood•ing, snoods.** To hold (the hair) in place with a snood. [ME *snod*, headband < OE *snōd.* See **(s)nē-***.]

snook[1] (sno͝ok, sno͞ok) *n., pl.* **snook** or **snooks.** Any of several chiefly marine percoid fishes of the family Centropomidae, esp. *Centropomus undecimalis*, a food and game fish of warm Atlantic waters. [Du. *snoek*, pike < MDu. *snoec.*]

snook[2] (sno͝ok, sno͞ok) *n.* A derisive or defiant gesture. — ***idiom.* cock a snook.** *Chiefly British.* To thumb one's nose; express scorn or ridicule. [?]

snook•er (sno͝ok′ər) *n. Games.* Pocket billiards played with 15 red balls and 6 balls of other colors. — *tr.v.* **-ered, -er•ing, -ers. 1.** *Slang.* **a.** To lead (another) into a situation in which all possible choices are undesirable; trap. **b.** To fool; dupe. **2.** *Games.* To leave one's opponent in the game of snooker unable to take a direct shot without striking a ball out of the required order. [?]

snoop (sno͞op) *intr.v.* **snooped, snoop•ing, snoops.** To pry into others' private affairs, esp. by prowling about. — *n.* One who snoops. [Du. *snoepen*, to eat on the sly.] — **snoop′er** *n.*

snoop•y (sno͞o′pē) *adj.* **-i•er, -i•est.** *Informal.* Likely to snoop. See Syns at **curious.** — **snoop′i•ly** *adv.* — **snoop′i•ness** *n.*

snoot (sno͞ot) *Informal.* — *n.* **1.** A snout or nose. **2.** A snob. — *tr.v.* **snoot•ed, snoot•ing, snoots.** To treat haughtily. [Dialectal var. of SNOUT.]

snoot•y (sno͞o′tē) *adj.* **-i•er, -i•est.** *Informal.* **1.** Snobbishly aloof; haughty. **2.** High-class; exclusive. — **snoot′i•ly** *adv.* — **snoot′i•ness** *n.*

snooze (sno͞oz) *intr.v.* **snoozed, snooz•ing, snooz•es.** To take a light nap; doze. — *n.* A brief light sleep. [?]

Sno•qual•mie Falls (snō-kwŏl′mē). A waterfall, 82.4 m (270 ft) high, in the **Snoqualmie River,** c. 113 km (70 mi), of W-central WA.

snore (snôr, snōr) *intr.v.* **snored, snor•ing, snores.** To breathe during sleep with harsh snorting noises caused by vibration of the soft palate. — *n.* **1.** The act or an instance of snoring. **2.** The noise so produced. [ME *snoren*, to snort < *fnoren* < OE *fnora*, sneezing. See **pneu-***.] — **snor′er** *n.*

snor•kel (snôr′kəl) *n.* **1.** A breathing apparatus used by skin divers, consisting of a long tube held in the mouth. **2.** A retractable vertical tube in a submarine that contains air-intake and exhaust pipes permitting extended periods of submergence at periscope depth. — *intr.v.* **-keled, -kel•ing, -kels.** To dive using a snorkel. [Ger. *Schnorchel* < dial., nose (< its resemblance in shape to a nose).] — **snor′kel•er** *n.*

snorkel

Snor•ri Stur•lu•son (snôr′ē stûr′lə-sən, snŏr′ē stœr′lə-sŏn). 1179–1241. Icelandic historian and chieftain whose works include *Heimskringla,* a series of sagas.

snort (snôrt) *n.* **1.a.** A rough noisy sound made by breathing forcefully through the nostrils, as a horse or pig does. **b.** A similar sound. **2.** *Slang.* **a.** A drink of liquor, esp. when swallowed in one gulp. **b.** A small amount of cocaine or heroin sniffed at one time. — *v.* **snort•ed, snort•ing, snorts.** — *intr.* **1.a.** To breathe noisily and forcefully through the nostrils. **b.** To make a sound resembling noisy inhalation. **2.** To make an abrupt noise expressive of scorn, ridicule, or contempt. **3.** *Slang.* To ingest a drug, such as cocaine, by sniffing. — *tr.* **1.** To express by snorting: *snorted his disapproval.* **2.** *Slang.* To ingest by sniffing. [< ME *snorten*, to snort < *fnorten*, var. of *fnoren.* See SNORE.] — **snort′er** *n.*

snot (snŏt) *n. Vulgar Slang.* **1.** Nasal mucus; phlegm. **2.** A person regarded as annoying, arrogant, or impertinent. [ME < OE *gesnot.*]

snot•ty (snŏt′ē) *adj.* **-ti•er, -ti•est.** *Vulgar Slang.* **1.** Dirtied with nasal mucus. **2.** Impertinent; arrogant. — **snot′ti•ly** *adv.* — **snot′ti•ness** *n.*

snout (snout) *n.* **1.a.** The projecting nose, jaws, or anterior facial part of an animal's head. **b.** A similar prolongation of the anterior portion of the head in certain insects, such as weevils; a rostrum. **c.** A spout or nozzle shaped like such a projection. **2.** *Slang.* The human nose. [ME, prob. of OE orig.]

snout beetle *n.* A weevil of the family Curculionidae, having the front of the head elongated to form a snout.

snow (snō) *n.* **1.** Frozen precipitation in the form of white or translucent hexagonal ice crystals that fall in soft white flakes. **2.** A falling of snow; a snowstorm. **3.** Something resembling snow, as: **a.** The white specks on a television screen resulting from weak reception. **b.** *Slang.* Cocaine. **c.** *Slang.* Heroin. — *v.* **snowed, snow•ing, snows.** — *intr.* To fall as or in snow. — *tr.* **1.** To cover, shut off, or close off with snow: *snowed in.* **2.** *Slang.* To overwhelm with insincere talk, esp. flattery. — ***phrasal verb.* snow under. 1.** To overwhelm. **2.** To defeat by a great margin. [ME < OE *snāw.*]

Snow (snō), **C(harles) P(ercy).** 1905–80. British writer known esp. for his series *Strangers and Brothers* (1940–70).

snow•ball (snō′bôl′) *n.* **1.a.** A mass of soft wet snow packed into a ball that can be thrown, as in play. **b.** *Chiefly Southern U.S.* A cup of crushed or shaved ice flavored with colored syrup. **2.** Any of several plants having rounded clusters of white flowers, as the guelder rose. — *v.* **-balled, -ball•ing, -balls.** — *intr.* **1.** To grow rapidly in significance, importance, or size. **2.** To throw snowballs. — *tr.* **1.** To cause to grow or increase rapidly. **2.** To throw snowballs at.

snow•bell (snō′bĕl′) *n.* Any of various shrubs or trees of the genus *Styrax*, esp. *S. japonicus* and *S. obassia* of eastern Asia, having bell-shaped white flowers.

Snow•belt also **Snow Belt** (snō′bĕlt′). The N and NE U.S.

snow•ber•ry (snō′bĕr′ē) *n.* **1.** Any of various shrubs of the genus *Symphoricarpos*, esp. *S. albus* of North America, having small pinkish flowers and white berries. **2.** Any of various tropical American shrubs or vines of the genus *Chiococca,* having white globular fruit and small yellow or white flowers.

snow•bird (snō′bûrd′) *n.* **1.** Any of several birds, such as the junco and the snow bunting, common in snowy regions. **2.** *Slang.* One who moves to a warm place in winter.

ă **pat**	oi **boy**
ā **pay**	ou **out**
âr **care**	o͝o **took**
ä **father**	o͞o **boot**
ĕ **pet**	ŭ **cut**
ē **be**	ûr **urge**
ĭ **pit**	th **thin**
ī **pie**	*th* **this**
îr **pier**	hw **which**
ŏ **pot**	zh **vision**
ō **toe**	ə **about, item**
ô **paw**	

Stress marks:
′ (primary);
′ (secondary), as in
dictionary (dĭk′shə-nĕr′ē)

snow blindness *n.* A usu. temporary loss of vision and inflammation of the eye, caused by exposure to bright sunlight and ultraviolet rays reflected from snow or ice. **— snow′-blind′** (snō′blīnd′), **snow′-blind′ed** (-blīn′dĭd) *adj.*

snow•blink (snō′blĭngk′) *n.* A white sky glow reflected from snow fields.

snow blower *n.* See **snow thrower.**

snow•board (snō′bôrd′, -bōrd′) *Sports. n.* A board resembling a small surfboard and equipped with bindings, used to descend snow-covered slopes on one's feet without ski poles. **—snow′board′** *v.*

snow•bound (snō′bound′) *adj.* Confined in one place by heavy snow.

snow bunting *n.* A finch *(Plectrophenax nivalis)* of northern regions having predominantly white winter plumage.

snow•bush (snō′bŏŏsh′) also **snow•brush** (-brŭsh′) *n.* A spiny shrub *(Ceanothus cordulatus)* of California and Oregon having large clusters of small white flowers.

snowboard

snow•cap (snō′kăp′) *n.* Snow covering a mountain peak, esp. such snow existing year-round. **— snow′capped′** *adj.*

snow cone *n.* A confection made of crushed ice and flavored syrup inserted into a paper cone and mounded on top.

Snow•don (snōd′n). A massif of NW Wales rising to 1,085.8 m (3,560 ft).

snow•drift (snō′drĭft′) *n.* A mass or bank of snow piled up by the wind.

snow•drop (snō′drŏp′) *n.* Any of several bulbous Eurasian plants of the genus *Galanthus,* having solitary nodding white flowers that bloom in early spring.

snow•fall (snō′fôl′) *n.* **1.** A fall of snow. **2.** The amount of snow that falls during a given period or in a specified area.

snow fence *n.* Temporary fencing made of slats wired together, used to prevent snow from drifting onto walks or roads.

snow•flake (snō′flāk′) *n.* **1.** A single flake or crystal of snow. **2.** Any of several bulbous European herbs of the genus *Leucojum,* having white flowers and fleshy fruit. **3.** See **snow bunting.**

snow goose *n.* A North American wild goose *(Chen caerulescens* or *Anser caerulescens)* that breeds in Arctic regions and has white plumage with black wingtips as an adult.

snow-in-sum•mer (snō′ĭn-sŭm′ər) *n.* A woolly mat-forming perennial herb *(Cerastium tomentosum)* native to Italy and cultivated in rock gardens for its white flowers.

snow job *n. Slang.* An effort to deceive, overwhelm, or persuade with insincere talk, esp. flattery.

snow leopard *n.* A large feline mammal *(Panthera uncia)* of the highlands of central Asia having long thick whitish-gray fur with dark markings like those of a leopard.

snow line *n.* **1.** The lower altitudinal boundary of a snow-covered area, esp. of one that is perennially covered, such as the snowcap of a mountain. **2.** The fluctuating latitudinal boundaries around the polar regions marking the extent of snow cover.

snow•mak•ing (snō′mā′kĭng) *n.* Production of artificial snow in the form of granular ice particles for ski slopes.

snow•man (snō′măn′) *n.* A human figure made from packed snow, usu. by piling large snowballs on top of each other.

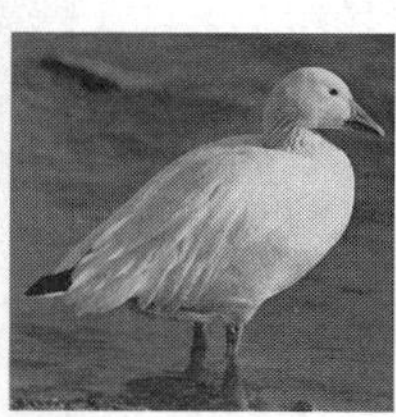

snow goose

Snow•mass Mountain (snō′măs). A peak, 4,298.1 m (14,092 ft), in the Elk Mts. of W-central CO.

snow•melt (snō′mĕlt′) *n.* **1.** The runoff from melting snow. **2.** A period or season when such runoff occurs.

snow•mo•bile (snō′mō-bēl′, -mə-) *n.* A small vehicle with skilike runners in front and tanklike treads, used for traveling on snow. [SNOW + (AUTO)MOBILE.] **— snow′mo•bil′er** *n.* **— snow′mo•bil′ing** *n.*

snow-on-the-moun•tain (snō′ŏn-*th*ə-moun′tən, -ôn-) *n.* A widely cultivated plant *(Euphorbia marginata)* of the central United States with white-margined leaves and white bracts.

snow pea *n.* **1.** A variety of the common pea having a soft thick pod. **2.** The edible young pod of this plant.

snow pellet *n.* A small white ice particle that falls as precipitation and typically breaks apart upon hitting a surface. Often used in the plural.

snow plant *n.* A fleshy saprophytic plant *(Sarcodes sanguinea)* of the mountains of western North America having a scaly reddish stalk and scarlet flowers.

snow•plow (snō′plou′) *n.* **1.** A plowlike device or vehicle used to remove snow, esp. from roads and railroad tracks. **2.** *Sports.* A maneuver in snow skiing in which the tips of the skis are brought together to slow or stop progress. *— intr.v.* **-plowed, -plow•ing, -plows.** *Sports.* To perform a snowplow maneuver.

snow•shoe (snō′shōō′) *n.* A racket-shaped frame containing interlaced strips that is attached to the foot for walking on deep snow. *— intr.v.* **-shoed, -shoe•ing, -shoes.** To travel on snowshoes. **— snow′sho′er** *n.*

snowshoe rabbit *n.* A medium-sized hare *(Lepus americanus)* of northern North America having large, heavily furred feet and fur that is white in winter and brown in summer.

snow•storm (snō′stôrm′) *n.* A storm with heavy snow.

snow•suit (snō′sōōt′) *n.* A child's zippered winter coverall.

snow thrower *n.* A machine that clears a surface of snow by scooping and projecting it forcefully through a chute.

snow tire *n.* A tire with a deep tread or studs to give added traction on snow-covered surfaces.

snow-white (snō′hwīt′, -wīt′) *adj.* White as snow.

snow•y (snō′ē) *adj.* **-i•er, -i•est. 1.a.** Abounding in or covered with snow. **b.** Subject to snow. **2.** Resembling snow, esp. in whiteness. **— snow′i•ly** *adv.* **— snow′i•ness** *n.*

snowy egret *n.* A medium-sized egret *(Egretta thula)* with white plumage, black legs, and yellow feet, found in warm parts of the Western Hemisphere.

snowy owl *n.* A large diurnal owl *(Nyctea scandiaca)* of Arctic and subarctic regions having snow-white plumage with dark markings.

snub (snŭb) *tr.v.* **snubbed, snub•bing, snubs. 1.** To ignore or behave coldly toward; slight. **2.** To dismiss, turn down, or frustrate the expectations of. **3.** *Naut.* **a.** To check the movement of (a rope or cable running out) by turning it quickly around a cleat or post. **b.** To secure (a vessel, for example) in this manner. **4.** To stub out (a cigarette, for example). *— n.* **1.** A deliberate slight or affront. **2.** *Naut.* A sudden checking, as of a rope or cable running out. *— adj.* Unusually short: *a snub nose.* [ME *snubben,* to rebuke.] **— snub′ber** *n.*

snub-nosed (snŭb′nōzd′) *adj.* **1.** Having a short turned-up nose. **2.** Having a very short barrel: *a snub-nosed pistol.*

snuck (snŭk) *v. Usage Problem.* A p.t. and p.part. of **sneak.** See Usage Note at **sneak.**

snuff[1] (snŭf) *v.* **snuffed, snuff•ing, snuffs.** *— tr.* **1.** To inhale audibly through the nose; sniff. **2.** To sense or examine by smelling; sniff at. *— intr.* To sniff; inhale. *— n.* The act of snuffing or the sound produced by it. [ME *snoffen,* to snuff a candle, sniffle, prob. < *snoffe,* snuff. See SNUFF[2].]

snuff[2] (snŭf) *n.* The charred portion of a candlewick. *— tr.v.* **snuffed, snuff•ing, snuffs. 1.** To extinguish: *snuffed out the candles.* **2.** To put a sudden end to; destroy: *lives snuffed out by war.* **3.** To cut off the charred portion of (a candlewick). [ME *snoffe,* poss. of LGer. orig.]

snuff[3] (snŭf) *n.* **1.a.** A preparation of finely pulverized tobacco that can be drawn up into the nostrils by inhaling. **b.** The quantity of this tobacco that is sniffed at a single time; a pinch. **2.** A powdery substance, such as a medicine, taken by sniffing. *— intr.v.* **snuffed, snuff•ing, snuffs.** To use or sniff snuff. **— *idiom.* up to snuff.** *Informal.* **1.** Normal in health. **2.** Up to standard; adequate. [Du. *snuf,* short for *snuftabak* : Du. *snuffen,* to sniff; see SNUFFLE + *tabak,* tobacco.]

snuff•box (snŭf′bŏks′) *n.* A small, often decorated box with a hinged lid, used for carrying snuff.

snuff•er[1] (snŭf′ər) *n.* One who uses snuff.

snuff•er[2] (snŭf′ər) *n.* **1.a.** A candlesnuffer. **b.** One who snuffs out candles. **2. snuffers.** An instrument resembling shears, used for cutting the snuff from or extinguishing candles.

snuff film *n. Slang.* A movie in which one or more actors is actually or ostensibly killed.

snuf•fle (snŭf′əl) *v.* **-fled, -fling, -fles.** *— intr.* **1.** To breathe noisily, as through a blocked nose. **2.** To sniff. **3.** To talk or sing nasally; whine. *— tr.* To utter in a snuffling tone. *— n.* **1.** The act of snuffling or the sound produced by it. **2. snuffles.** The sniffles. [Prob. < Du. *snuffelen,* to sniff about, prob. freq. of *snuffen,* to sniff < MDu. *snuiven.*] **— snuf′fler** *n.* **— snuf′fly** *adj.*

snug[1] (snŭg) *adj.* **snug•ger, snug•gest. 1.** Comfortably sheltered; cozy. **2.** Small but well arranged. **3.a.** Closely secured and well built; compact. **b.** Close-fitting. **c.** *Naut.* Seaworthy. **4.a.** Offering freedom from financial worry. **b.** Safe; secure. *— v.* **snugged, snug•ging, snugs.** *— tr.* To make snug or secure. *— intr.* To nestle; snuggle. **— *phrasal verb.* snug down.** *Naut.* To prepare (a vessel) to weather a storm, as by taking in sail. [Of Scand. orig.] **— snug, snug′ly** *adv.* **— snug′ness** *n.*

snug[2] (snŭg) *n. Chiefly British.* A very small private room in a pub. [Short for SNUGGERY.]

snug•ger•y (snŭg′ə-rē) *n., pl.* **-ies.** *Chiefly British.* A snug position or place.

snug•gle (snŭg′əl) *v.* **-gled, -gling, -gles.** *— intr.* **1.** To lie or press close together; cuddle. **2.** To curl up closely or comfortably; nestle. *— tr.* To draw close or hold closely, as for comfort or in affection; hug. [Freq. of SNUG[1].]

so[1] (sō) *adv.* **1.** In the condition or manner expressed or indicated; thus: *Hold the brush so.* **2.** To the amount or degree expressed or understood; to such an extent: *She was so weary that she fell.* **3.** To a great extent; to such an evident degree: *The idea is so obvious.* **4.** Because of the reason given; consequently: *She was weary and so fell.* **5.** Afterward; then: *to the gas station and so home.* **6.** In the same way; likewise: *You were on time and so was I.* **7.** Apparently; well, then. Used in expressing astonishment, disapproval, or sarcasm: *So you think you've got troubles?* **8.** In truth; indeed: *"You aren't right." "I am so!"* *— adj.* **1.** True; factual: *It isn't so.* **2.** In good order: *Everything must be exactly so.* *— conj. Usage Problem.* **1.** With the result or consequence that: *He failed to appear, so we went on without him.* **2.** In order that: *I stayed so I could see you.* *— pron.* Such as has already been suggested or specified; the same: *She became a loyal friend* *and remained so.* — *interj.* Used to express surprise or comprehension: *So! You've finished at last.* — **idioms. and so on (or forth).** And similarly; and continuing in a like manner. **so as to.** In order to. **so many. 1.** Forming an unspecified number: *so many memos each week.* **2.** Forming a group: *fought like so many tigers.* **so much. 1.** In that degree; to that extent: *so much the better.* **2.** In such a degree; to such an extent: *so much alike in ideas.* **3.** So great in quantity, degree, or extent: *so much rain.* **4.** Equivalent to in quantity, degree, or extent: *so much nonsense.* **5.** An unspecified amount or degree: *so much a yard.* **6.** Everything that can be said or done. Used to summarize or dismiss: *so much for that.* **so much as.** Used as an intensive to indicate something unexpected; even: *wouldn't so much as smile.* **so that. 1.** In order that. **2.** With the result or consequence that. [ME < OE *swā.* See **swo-*.**]

Usage Note: Many critics and grammarians have insisted that *so* must be followed by *that* in formal writing when used to introduce a clause giving the reason for or purpose of an action. But this rule is best regarded as a stylistic preference; in such clauses *that* is frequently omitted even by reputable writers in formal contexts, as in *They will have to double up so* (or *so that*) *room can be found for the new arrivals.* • Both *so* and *so that* are acceptably used to introduce clauses that state a result or consequence: *The bridge was closed, so* (or *so that*) *we went back.* • *So* is frequently used in informal speech to string together the elements of a narrative. This practice should not be carried over into formal writing, where the absence of contextual information generally requires that connections be made more explicit. See Usage Note at **as[1].**

so[2] (sō) *n. Mus.* Var. of **sol[1].**

so. or **So.** *abbr.* South; southern.

s.o. *abbr.* **1.** Seller's option. **2.** *Baseball.* Strikeout.

soak (sōk) *v.* **soaked, soak•ing, soaks.** — *tr.* **1.a.** To make thoroughly wet or saturated by or as if by placing in liquid. **b.** To immerse in liquid for a period of time. **2.** To absorb (liquid, for example) through or as if through pores or interstices: *soaked up the milk.* **3.** To remove (a stain, for example) by continued immersion: *soaked out the grease spots.* **4.** *Informal.* To take in or accept mentally, esp. eagerly and easily: *soaked up the gossip.* **5.** *Informal.* **a.** To drink (alcoholic liquor), esp. to excess. **b.** To make (a person) drunk. **6.** *Slang.* To overcharge (a person). — *intr.* **1.** To be immersed until thoroughly saturated. **2.** To penetrate or permeate; seep: *Let their words soak in.* **3.** *Slang.* To drink to excess. — *n.* **1.a.** The act or process of soaking. **b.** The condition of being soaked. **2.** Liquid for soaking something. **3.** *Slang.* A drunkard. [ME *soken* < OE *socian.* See **seuə-[2]*.**] — **soak′er** *n.*

soak•age (sō′kĭj) *n.* **1.a.** The process of soaking. **b.** The condition of being soaked. **2.** The amount of liquid that soaks into, through, or out of an object.

so-and-so (sō′ən-sō′) *n., pl.* **-sos. 1.** An unnamed or unspecified person or thing. **2.** *Informal.* A son of a gun.

soap (sōp) *n.* **1.** A cleansing agent made from a mixture of the sodium salts of various fatty acids of natural oils and fats. **2.** A metallic salt of a fatty acid. **3.** *Slang.* Money, esp. that which is used for bribery. **4.** *Slang.* A soap opera. — *tr.v.* **soaped, soap•ing, soaps. 1.** To treat or cover with or as if with soap. **2.a.** *Informal.* To soft-soap; cajole. **b.** *Slang.* To bribe. — **idiom. no soap.** *Slang.* **1.** Not possible or permissible. **2.** Unsuccessful; futile. [ME *sope* < OE *sāpe.*]

soap•bark (sōp′bärk′) *n.* **1.** A Chilean evergreen tree *(Quillaja saponaria)* of the rose family, having bark used as soap and as a source of saponin. **2.** The bark of this tree.

soap•ber•ry (sōp′bĕr′ē) *n.* **1.a.** Any of various chiefly tropical trees of the genus *Sapindus,* having pulpy fruit that lathers like soap. **b.** This fruit. **2.** The buffalo berry.

soap•box (sōp′bŏks′) *n.* **1.** A carton in which soap is packed. **2.** A temporary platform used while making an impromptu or nonofficial public speech. — *intr.v.* **-boxed, -box•ing, -box•es.** *Informal.* To engage in impromptu or nonofficial public speaking, often flamboyantly. — **idiom. on (one's) soapbox.** Speaking one's views passionately or self-importantly.

soap bubble *n.* **1.** A bubble formed from soapy water. **2.** Something beautiful but transient, insubstantial, or illusory.

soap opera *n.* A drama, typically performed as a serial on daytime television or radio, characterized by stock characters and situations, sentimentality, and melodrama. [< its originally having been sponsored by soap companies.]

soap plant *n.* **1.** Any of several bulbous plants of the genus *Chlorogalum,* esp. *C. pomeridianum,* of western North America, having small white flowers and bulbs formerly used as soap. **2.** Any of various plants having parts used as soap.

soap•stone (sōp′stōn′) *n.* A soft metamorphic rock composed mostly of the mineral talc. [< its smooth soapy feel.]

soap•suds (sōp′sŭdz′) *pl.n.* Suds from soapy water.

soap•wort (sōp′wûrt′, -wôrt′) *n.* See **bouncing Bet.** [< its yielding a soapy substance when the leaves are bruised.]

soap•y (sō′pē) *adj.* **-i•er, -i•est. 1.** Consisting of or containing soap. **2.** Covered with soap. **3.** Resembling soap. **4.** *Slang.* Unctuous; oily. — **soap′i•ly** *adv.* — **soap′i•ness** *n.*

soar (sôr, sōr) *intr.v.* **soared, soar•ing, soars. 1.** To rise, fly, or glide high and with little apparent effort. **2.** To climb swiftly or powerfully. **3.** To glide in an aircraft while maintaining altitude. **4.** To ascend suddenly above the normal or usual level: *Our spirits soared.* — *n.* **1.** The act of soaring. **2.** The altitude or scope attained in soaring. [ME *soren* < OFr. *essorer* < VLat. **exaurāre* : Lat. *ex-,* ex- + Lat. *aura,* air (< Gk., breeze; see AURA).] — **soar′er** *n.* — **soar′ing•ly** *adv.*

soar•ing (sôr′ĭng, sōr′-) *n.* The act of gliding while maintaining altitude, esp. the sport of flying a heavier-than-air craft by using ascending currents of air.

so•a•ve (sō-ä′vā) *n.* A dry white Italian table wine. [Ital. < Lat. *suāvis,* sweet, delightful. See **swād-*.**]

sob (sŏb) *v.* **sobbed, sob•bing, sobs.** — *intr.* **1.** To weep aloud with convulsive gasping; cry uncontrollably. See Syns at **cry. 2.** To make a sound resembling that of loud weeping. — *tr.* **1.** To utter with sobs. **2.** To put or bring (oneself) into a specified condition by sobbing: *sob oneself to sleep.* — *n.* The act or sound of sobbing. [ME *sobben,* perh. of LGer. orig.]

SOB *abbr. Vulgar.* Son of a bitch.

so•ber (sō′bər) *adj.* **-er, -est. 1.** Habitually abstemious in the use of alcoholic liquors or drugs; temperate. **2.** Not intoxicated or affected by the use of drugs. **3.** Plain or subdued: *sober attire.* **4.** Devoid of frivolity, excess, exaggeration, or speculative imagination; straightforward: *a sober assessment.* **5.** Marked by seriousness, gravity, or solemnity of conduct or character. See Syns at **serious. 6.** Marked by circumspection and self-restraint. — *tr. & intr.v.* **-bered, -ber•ing, -bers.** To make or become sober. [ME < OFr. *sobre* < Lat. *sōbrius.* See **s(w)e-*.**] — **so′ber•ly** *adv.* — **so′ber•ness** *n.*

so•ber-sid•ed (sō′bər-sī′dĭd) *adj.* Devoid of extreme qualities, such as exaggeration; sober. — **so′ber-sid′ed•ness** *n.*

so•ber•sides (sō′bər-sīdz′) *pl.n. (used with a sing. v.)* A sober-sided person.

so•bri•e•ty (sə-brī′ĭ-tē, sō-) *n.* **1.** Gravity in bearing, manner, or treatment. **2.** Moderation in or abstinence from consumption of alcoholic liquor or use of drugs. [ME *sobriete* < OFr. < Lat. *sōbrietās* < *sōbrius,* sober. See SOBER.]

so•bri•quet (sō′brĭ-kā′, -kĕt′, sō′brĭ-kā′, kĕt′) also **sou•bri•quet** (so͞o′brĭ-kā′, -kĕt′, so͞o′brĭ-kā′, -kĕt′) *n.* **1.** An affectionate or humorous nickname. **2.** An assumed name. [Fr. < OFr. *soubriquet,* chuck under the chin.]

sob sister *n.* **1.** A journalist, esp. a woman, employed as a writer or an editor of sob stories. **2.** A sentimental, ineffective person who seeks to do good.

sob story *n.* **1.** A tale of personal hardship or misfortune intended to arouse pity. **2.** A maudlin plea given as an explanation or a rationalization.

soc. *abbr.* **1.** Social. **2.** Socialist. **3.** Society.

so•ca (sō′kə) *n. Mus.* A style of music, originating in the West Indies, that is a blend of soul and calypso. [so(UL) + CA(LYPSO).]

soc•age (sŏk′ĭj, sō′kĭj) *n. Law.* Feudal tenure of land by a tenant, in return for agricultural or other nonmilitary services or for payment of rent in money. [ME *sokage* < *soke,* soke. See SOKE.] — **soc′ag•er** *n.*

so-called (sō′kôld′) *adj.* **1.** Commonly called. **2.** Incorrectly or falsely termed.

Usage Note: Quotation marks are not used to set off descriptions that follow expressions such as *so-called* and *self-styled*: *his so-called foolproof method* (not *"foolproof method"*).

soc•cer (sŏk′ər) *n. Sports.* A game played on a rectangular field with net goals at either end in which two teams of 11 players each maneuver a round ball mainly by kicking or butting or by using any part of the body except the arms and hands to score points. [Alteration of *assoc.,* abbreviation of *association football.*]

So•chi (sō′chē, sô′chĭ). A city of extreme SW Russia on the NE shore of the Black Sea. Pop. 310,000.

so•cia•bil•i•ty (sō′shə-bĭl′ĭ-tē) *n., pl.* **-ties. 1.** The disposition or quality of being sociable. **2.** An instance of being sociable.

so•cia•ble (sō′shə-bəl) *adj.* **1.** Fond of the company of others; gregarious. **2.** Marked by or affording occasion for agreeable conversation and conviviality. **3.** Pleasant, friendly, and affable. — *n.* A social. [Fr. < Lat. *sociābilis* < *sociāre,* to share, join < *socius,* companion. See **sekʷ-[1]*.**] — **so′cia•ble•ness** *n.* — **so′cia•bly** *adv.*

so•cial (sō′shəl) *adj.* **1.a.** Living together in communities. **b.** Of or relating to communal living. **c.** Of or relating to society. **2.** Living together in organized groups or similar close aggregates: *social insects.* **3.** Involving allies or members of a confederacy. **4.** Of or relating to the upper classes. **5.a.** Inclined to seek out or enjoy the company of others; sociable. **b.** Spent in or marked by friendly relations or companionship. **c.** Intended for convivial activities. **6.** Of, relating to, or occupied with matters affecting human welfare. — *n.* An informal social gathering, as of the members of a church congregation. [ME *sociale,* domestic < OFr. *social* < Lat. *sociālis,* of companionship < *socius,* companion. See **sekʷ-[1]*.**]

social contract *n.* An agreement among the members of an organized society or between the governed and the government defining and limiting the rights and duties of each.

social Darwinism *n.* The application of Darwinism to the study of human society, specifically a theory in sociology that

snowshoe
19th-century Eastern Plains Indians snowshoes

soccer
1982 World Cup soccer competition in Madrid, Spa n

ă pat	oi boy
ā pay	ou out
âr care	o͝o took
ä father	o͞o boot
ĕ pet	ŭ cut
ē be	ûr urge
ĭ pit	th thin
ī pie	*th* this
îr pier	hw which
ŏ pot	zh vision
ō toe	ə about, item
ô paw	

Stress marks:
′ (primary);
′ (secondary), as in
dictionary (dĭk′shə-nĕr′ē)

individuals or groups achieve advantage over others as the result of genetic or biological superiority.

social democracy *n.* A political theory advocating the use of democratic means to move gradually from capitalism to socialism. — **social democrat** *n.* — **social democratic** *adj.*

social disease *n.* **1.** A sexually transmitted disease; a venereal disease. **2.** A disease having its highest incidence among socioeconomic groups predisposed to it by a given set of adverse living or working conditions.

social engineering *n.* The practical application of sociological principles to social problems. — **social engineer** *n.*

social insurance *n.* An insurance program carried out or mandated by a government to provide economic assistance to the unemployed, the elderly, or the disabled.

socket wrench

so•cial•ism (sō′shə-lĭz′əm) *n.* **1.a.** A social system in which the means of producing and distributing goods are owned collectively and political power is exercised by the whole community. **b.** The theory or practice of those who support such a social system. **2.** The building of the material base for communism under the dictatorship of the proletariat in Marxist-Leninist theory.

so•cial•ist (sō′shə-lĭst) *n.* **1.** An advocate of socialism. **2.** Often **Socialist.** A member of a political party or group that advocates socialism. — *adj.* **1.** Of, promoting, or practicing socialism. **2.** Often **Socialist.** Of, belonging to, or constituting a socialist party or political group.

so•cial•is•tic (sō′shə-lĭs′tĭk) *adj.* Of, advocating, or tending toward socialism. — **so′cial•is′ti•cal•ly** *adv.*

socialist realism *n.* A Marxist aesthetic doctrine that seeks to promote the development of social consciousness through didactic use of literature, art, and music.

so•cial•ite (sō′shə-līt′) *n.* One prominent in society.

so•ci•al•i•ty (sō′shē-ăl′ĭ-tē) *n.*, *pl.* **-ties. 1.a.** The state or quality of being sociable; sociability. **b.** An instance of sociableness. **2.** The tendency to form communities and societies.

so•cial•ize (sō′shə-līz′) *v.* **-ized, -iz•ing, -iz•es.** — *tr.* **1.** To place under government or group ownership or control. **2.** To make fit for companionship with others; make sociable. **3.** To convert or adapt to the needs of society. — *intr.* To take part in social activities. — **so′cial•i•za′tion** (-shə-lĭ-zā′shən) *n.* — **so′cial•iz′er** *n.*

so•cial•ized medicine (sō′shə-līzd′) *n.* A system for providing medical and hospital care for all at a nominal cost by means of government regulation of health services and subsidies derived from taxation.

so•cial•ly (sō′shə-lē) *adv.* **1.** In a social way. **2.** With regard to society: *socially relevant.* **3.** By society: *socially accepted.*

soc•ial-mind•ed (sō′shəl-mīn′dĭd) *adj.* Interested in social service or the welfare of society in general.

social psychiatry *n.* The branch of psychiatry that deals with the relationship between social environment and mental illness. — **social psychiatrist** *n.*

Socrates
Copy of an early fourth-century B.C. herma

social psychology *n.* The branch of human psychology that deals with the behavior of groups and the influence of social factors on the individual. — **social psychologist** *n.*

social register *n.* A directory listing persons of social prominence in a community.

social science *n.* **1.** The study of human society and of individual relationships in and to society. **2.** Any of a group of disciplines that deal with such study, generally regarded as including sociology, psychology, anthropology, economics, political science, and history. — **social scientist** *n.*

social secretary *n.* A personal secretary who handles social correspondence and appointments.

social security *n.* **1.** A U.S. government program financed by employer and employee payments that provides retirement insurance, disability benefits, and unemployment compensation. **2.** The economic assistance provided by social security.

social service *n.* **1.** Organized efforts to advance human welfare; social work. **2.** A service, such as free school lunches, provided by a government for its disadvantaged citizens. Often used in the plural.

social studies *pl.n.* *(used with a sing. or pl. v.)* A course of study including geography, history, government, and sociology, taught in secondary and elementary schools.

social work *n.* Organized work intended to advance the social conditions of a community, esp. of the disadvantaged, by providing psychological counseling, guidance, and assistance, esp. in the form of social services. — **social worker** *n.*

so•ci•e•tal (sə-sī′ĭ-tl) *adj.* Of or relating to the structure, organization, or functioning of society. — **so•ci′e•tal•ly** *adv.*

so•ci•e•ty (sə-sī′ĭ-tē) *n.*, *pl.* **-ties. 1.a.** The totality of social relationships among human beings. **b.** A group of human beings broadly distinguished from other groups by mutual interests, participation in characteristic relationships, shared institutions, and a common culture. **c.** The institutions and culture of a distinct self-perpetuating group. **2.** An organization or association of persons engaged in a common profession, activity, or interest. **3.a.** The rich, privileged, and fashionable social class. **b.** The socially dominant members of a community. **4.** Companionship; company. **5.** *Biol.* A colony or community of organisms, usu. of the same species: *an insect society.* [Fr. *société* < OFr. < Lat. *societās*, fellowship < *socius*, companion. See **sekʷ-¹***.]

So•ci•e•ty Islands (sə-sī′ĭ-tē). An island group of W French Polynesia in the S Pacific E of Samoa; a French protectorate since 1843.

Society of Friends *n.* A Christian denomination, founded in the mid-17th century in England, that rejects formal sacraments and creed, a priesthood, and violence; the Quakers.

Society of Jesus *n.* The Jesuits.

So•cin•i•an (sō-sĭn′ē-ən) *n.* An adherent of a 16th-century Italian sect holding unitarian views, including denial of the divinity of Jesus. [NLat. *Sociniānus*, after Laelius *Socinus* and Faustus SOCINUS.] — **So•cin′i•an** *adj.* — **So•cin′i•an•ism** *n.*

So•ci•nus (sō-sī′nəs), **Faustus.** 1539–1604. Italian theologian who based his anti-Trinitarian teachings on the doctrine formulated by his uncle **Laelius Socinus** (1525–62).

socio– *pref.* **1.** Society: *sociometry.* **2.** Social: *socioeconomic.* [Fr. < Lat. *socius*, companion. See **sekʷ-¹***.]

so•ci•o•bi•ol•o•gy (sō′sē-ō-bī-ŏl′ə-jē, -shē-) *n.* The study of the biological determinants of social behavior, based on the theory that such behavior is often genetically transmitted and subject to evolutionary processes. — **so′ci•o•bi′o•log′i•cal** (-bī′ə-lŏj′ĭ-kəl) *adj.* — **so′ci•o•bi•ol′o•gist** *n.*

so•ci•o•cul•tur•al (sō′sē-ō-kŭl′chər-əl, -shē-) *adj.* Of or involving both social and cultural factors.

so•ci•o•ec•o•nom•ic (sō′sē-ō-ĕk′ə-nŏm′ĭk, -ē′kə-, -shē-) *adj.* Of or involving both social and economic factors.

so•ci•o•lin•guis•tics (sō′sē-ō-lĭng-gwĭs′tĭks, -shē-) *n.* *(used with a sing. v.)* The study of language and linguistic behavior as influenced by social and cultural factors. — **so′ci•o•lin′guist** *n.* — **so′ci•o•lin•guis′tic** *adj.*

so•ci•ol•o•gy (sō′sē-ŏl′ə-jē, -shē-) *n.* **1.** The study of human social behavior, esp. the study of the origins, organization, institutions, and development of human society. **2.** Analysis of a social institution or societal segment as a self-contained entity or in relation to society as a whole. — **so′ci•o•log′ic** (-ə-lŏj′ĭk), **so′ci•o•log′i•cal** (-ĭ-kəl) *adj.* — **so′ci•o•log′i•cal•ly** *adv.* — **so′ci•ol′o•gist** *n.*

so•ci•om•e•try (sō′sē-ŏm′ĭ-trē, -shē-) *n.* The quantitative study of interpersonal relationships in populations, esp. the study and measurement of preferences.

so•ci•o•path (sō′sē-ə-păth′, -shē-) *n.* One who is affected with a personality disorder marked by aggressive antisocial behavior. — **so′ci•o•path′ic** *adj.*

so•ci•o•po•li•ti•cal (sō′sē-ō-pə-lĭt′ĭ-kəl, -shē-) *adj.* Involving both social and political factors.

so•ci•o•psy•cho•log•i•cal (sō′sē-ō-sī′kə-lŏj′ĭ-kəl, -shē-) *adj.* **1.** Of or relating to social psychology. **2.** Of, relating to, or combining social and psychological factors.

so•ci•o•re•lig•ious (sō′sē-ō-rĭ-lĭj′əs, -shē-) *adj.* Involving social and religious factors.

sock¹ (sŏk) *n.* **1.** *pl.* **socks** or **sox** (sŏks). A short stocking reaching a point between the ankle and the knee. **2.** *Meteorol.* A windsock. **3.a.** A light shoe worn by comic actors in ancient Greek and Roman plays. **b.** Comic drama; comedy. — *tr.v.* **socked, sock•ing, socks.** To provide with socks. — ***phrasal verbs.*** **sock away.** *Informal.* To put (money) away in a safe place for future use. **sock in.** To close to air traffic. [ME *socke* < OE *socc*, a kind of light shoe < Lat. *soccus*, poss. < Gk. *sunkhis, sukkhos*, Phrygian shoe.]

sock² (sŏk) *v.* **socked, sock•ing, socks.** — *tr.* To hit or strike forcefully; punch. — *intr.* To deliver a blow. — ***idiom.*** **sock it to (someone).** *Slang.* To deliver a forceful comment or physical blow to someone else. [?] — **sock** *n.*

sock•dol•a•ger also **sock•dol•o•ger** (sŏk-dŏl′ə-jər) *n. Slang.* **1.** A final blow or remark. **2.** Something outstanding. [?]

sock•et (sŏk′ĭt) *n.* **1.** An opening or a cavity into which an inserted part is designed to fit: *a light bulb socket.* **2.** *Anat.* **a.** The concave part of a joint that receives the end of a bone. **b.** A hollow or concavity into which a part, such as the eye, fits. — *tr.v.* **-et•ed, -et•ing, -ets.** To furnish with or insert into a socket. [ME *soket* < AN, spearhead, dim. of *soc*, plowshare, prob. of Celt. orig. See **sū-***.]

socket wrench *n.* A wrench with a usu. interchangeable socket to fit over a nut or bolt.

sock•eye salmon (sŏk′ī′) *n.* A salmon *(Oncorhynchus nerka)* of northern Pacific coastal waters that is a commercially valuable food fish. [By folk ety. < Halkomelem (a Central Coast Salish language) *sthə́qə'y*.]

so•cle (sō′kəl) *n. Archit.* **1.** A plain square block higher than a plinth, serving as a pedestal for sculpture, a vase, or a column. **2.** A plain plinth supporting a wall. [Fr. < Ital. *zoccolo*, wooden shoe < Lat. *socculus*, dim. of *soccus*, a kind of light shoe. See SOCK¹.]

So•co•tra (sə-kō′trə). An island of Yemen in the Indian Ocean at the mouth of the Gulf of Aden; joined Southern Yemen (now Yemen) in 1967.

Soc•ra•tes (sŏk′rə-tēz′). 470?–399 B.C. Greek philosopher who initiated a question-and-answer method of teaching as a means of achieving self-knowledge.

So•crat•ic (sə-krăt′ĭk, sō-) *adj.* Of or relating to Socrates or his philosophizing.

Socratic irony *n.* Profession of ignorance while questioning another in order to arrive at the truth.

sod[1] (sŏd) *n.* **1.** A section of grass-covered surface soil held together by matted roots; turf. **2.** The ground, esp. when covered with grass. —*tr.v.* **sod•ded, sod•ding, sods.** To cover with sod. [ME < MLGer. or MDu. *sode.*]

sod[2] (sŏd) *Chiefly British.* —*n.* **a.** A sodomite. **b.** A person regarded as obnoxious or contemptible. **c.** A fellow; a guy. —*tr.v.* **sod•ded, sod•ding, sods.** To damn. Often used in the imperative with *off.* [Short for SODOMITE.]

so•da (sō′də) *n.* **1.a.** Any of various forms of sodium carbonate. **b.** Chemically combined sodium. **2.a.** Carbonated water. **b.** *Northeastern U.S.* See **soft drink.** See Regional Note at **tonic. 3.** A refreshment made from carbonated water, ice cream, and usu. a flavoring. **4.** *Games.* The card turned face up at the beginning of faro. [ME *sode, soda,* saltwort, soda < OItal. *soda,* perh. < Ar. *suwwād,* saltwort.]

soda ash *n.* Sodium carbonate in powdery white form, used esp. as an industrial chemical.

soda biscuit *n.* **1.** A breadlike biscuit leavened with baking soda. **2.** See **soda cracker.**

soda cracker *n.* A thin, usu. square cracker leavened slightly with baking soda.

soda fountain *n.* **1.** An apparatus with faucets for dispensing soda water. **2.** A counter equipped for preparing and serving soft drinks, ice-cream dishes, or sandwiches. Also called regionally *spa.*

soda lime *n.* A mixture of calcium oxide and sodium or potassium hydroxide, used as a drying agent and carbon dioxide absorbent.

so•da•lite (sōd′l-īt′) *n.* A blue-white vitreous mineral, $Na_4Al_3Si_3O_{12}Cl$, found in igneous rocks.

so•dal•i•ty (sō-dăl′ĭ-tē) *n., pl.* **-ties. 1.** A society or an association, esp. a devotional or charitable society for the laity in the Roman Catholic Church. **2.** Fellowship. [Fr. *sodalité* < OFr. < Lat. *sodālitās,* fellowship < *sodālis,* companion. See **s(w)e-*.**] —**so′da•list** (sōd′l-ĭst, sō-dăl′ĭst) *n.*

soda niter *n.* See **sodium nitrate.**

soda pop *n.* See **soft drink.**

soda water *n.* **1.a.** Effervescent water, usu. containing salts, charged under pressure with purified carbon dioxide gas and used as a beverage or mixer. **b.** See **soft drink. 2.** A solution of water, sodium bicarbonate, and acid.

sod•den (sŏd′n) *adj.* **1.** Thoroughly soaked; saturated. **2.** Soggy and heavy from improper cooking; doughy. **3.** Expressionless, stupid, or dull, esp. from drink. **4.** Unimaginative; torpid. [ME *soden,* boiled, p.part. of *sethen,* to boil. See SEETHE.] —**sod′den** *v.* —**sod′den•ly** *adv.* —**sod′den•ness** *n.*

Sod•dy (sŏd′ē), **Frederick.** 1877–1956. British chemist who won a 1921 Nobel Prize.

Sö•der•blom (sœ′dər-bloom′), **Nathan.** 1866–1931. Swedish prelate and historian who won the 1930 Nobel Peace Prize.

so•di•um (sō′dē-əm) *n. Symbol* **Na** A soft, light, highly reactive metallic element that is naturally abundant in combined forms, esp. in common salt, and is used in a wide variety of industrially important compounds. Atomic number 11; atomic weight 22.99; melting point 97.8°C; boiling point 892°C; specific gravity 0.971; valence 1. See table at **element.** [SOD(A) + -IUM.]

sodium alginate *n.* A powdery or crystalline compound, $C_6H_7O_6Na$, used as a food thickener and stabilizer.

sodium barbital *n.* A powder, $C_8H_{11}N_2NaO_3$, the soluble sodium salt of barbital, used as a hypnotic and sedative.

sodium benzoate *n.* The sodium salt of benzoic acid, $NaC_7H_5O_2$, used as a food preservative and an intermediate in dye manufacture and in the production of pharmaceuticals.

sodium bicarbonate *n.* See **baking soda.**

sodium borate *n.* A crystalline compound, $Na_2B_4O_7{\cdot}10H_2O$, used in making glass, detergents, and pharmaceuticals.

sodium carbonate *n.* A powdery compound, Na_2CO_3, used in making baking soda, glass, ceramics, detergents, and soap.

sodium chlorate *n.* A crystalline compound, $NaClO_3$, used as a bleaching and oxidizing agent and in explosives.

sodium chloride *n.* A colorless or white crystalline compound, NaCl, used in the manufacture of chemicals and as a food preservative and seasoning; common salt.

sodium citrate *n.* A crystalline or granular compound, $Na_3C_6H_5O_7{\cdot}2H_2O$, used in photography and in medicine esp. as an anticoagulant of blood stored for transfusion.

sodium cyanide *n.* A poisonous crystalline compound, NaCN, used in extracting gold and silver from ores.

sodium cyclamate *n.* An artificially prepared salt of cyclamic acid, $C_6H_{13}NO_3SNa$, once used as a low-calorie sweetener.

sodium dichromate *n.* A poisonous red-orange crystalline compound, $Na_2Cr_2O_7{\cdot}2H_2O$, used as an oxidizing agent.

sodium fluoride *n.* A crystalline salt, NaF, used in fluoridation of water, in treatment of tooth decay, and as a pesticide.

sodium glu•ta•mate (gloo′tə-māt′) *n.* Monosodium glutamate.

sodium hydroxide *n.* A strongly alkaline compound, NaOH, used in making chemicals and soaps.

sodium hypochlorite *n.* An unstable salt, NaOCl, usu. stored in solution and used as a fungicide and an oxidizing bleach.

sodium nitrate *n.* A crystalline compound, $NaNO_3$, used in the manufacture of explosives, in glass and pottery enamel, and as fertilizer.

sodium pentothal *n.* Thiopental sodium.

sodium perborate *n.* A crystalline compound, $NaBO_3{\cdot}4H_2O$, used as a mild alkaline oxidizing agent in dentifrices, a topical antiseptic and deodorant, and an industrial reagent.

sodium peroxide *n.* A powder, Na_2O_2, used industrially as an oxidizing and bleaching agent.

sodium phosphate *n.* Any of various sodium salts of phosphoric acid, esp. NaH_2PO_4, Na_2HPO_4, and Na_3PO_4, used in pharmaceutical manufacture, medicine, and chemistry.

so•di•um-po•tas•si•um pump (sō′dē-əm-pə-tăs′ē-əm) *n.* A mechanism of active transport that moves potassium ions into and sodium ions out of a cell.

sodium propionate *n.* A crystalline compound, CH_3CH_2COONa, used as a fungicide.

sodium silicate *n.* Any of various water-soluble silicate glass compounds used as a preservative for eggs, in plaster and cement, and in various purification and refining processes.

sodium sulfate *n.* A crystalline compound, Na_2SO_4, used to manufacture paper, glass, dyes, and pharmaceuticals.

sodium sulfide *n.* A hygroscopic compound, Na_2S, used as a metal ore reagent and in photography and printing.

sodium sulfite *n.* A crystalline or powdered compound, Na_2SO_3, used in preserving foods, developing photographs, and making paper.

sodium thiosulfate *n.* A translucent crystalline compound, $Na_2S_2O_3{\cdot}5H_2O$, used as a photographic fixing agent and a bleach.

so•di•um-va•por lamp (sō′dē-əm-vā′pər) *n.* An electric lamp containing a small amount of sodium and neon gas, used in generating yellow light for streetlights.

Sod•om[1] (sŏd′əm). A city of ancient Palestine possibly located S of the Dead Sea. In the Bible, it was destroyed along with Gomorrah because of its wickedness and depravity.

Sod•om[2] or **sod•om** (sŏd′əm) *n.* A place known for vice and corruption. [After SODOM[1].]

sod•om•y (sŏd′ə-mē) *n.* **1.** Anal copulation of one male with another. **2.** Anal or oral copulation with a member of the opposite sex. **3.** Copulation with an animal. [ME *sodomie* < OFr. < *Sodome,* Sodom < Lat. *Sodoma* < Gk. < Heb. *s'dōm.*] —**sod′om•ite′** *n.* —**sod′om•ize′** *v.*

so•ev•er (sō-ĕv′ər) *adv.* At all; in any way.

so•fa (sō′fə) *n.* A long upholstered seat usu. with a back and arms. [Turk. < Ar. *ṣuffah,* carpet, divan.]

sofa
Mid 19th-century American

so•far (sō′fär′) *n.* A system for determining the position of survivors lost at sea by which an explosion is set off underwater, the time needed for the waves to reach three different locations is calculated, and the position of the explosion is found by triangulation. [*so(und) f(ixing) a(nd) r(anging).*]

so far as *conj.* Insofar as: *So far as I am concerned, it is over.*

sof•fit (sŏf′ĭt) *n.* The underside of an architectural element, such as a cantilever, an arch, a staircase, or a cornice. [Fr. *soffite* < Ital. *soffitto* < VLat. **suffictus,* p.part. of *suffigere,* to fasten beneath. See SUFFIX.]

S. of Sol. *abbr. Bible.* Song of Solomon.

So•fi•a (sō′fē-ə, sō-fē′ə). The cap. of Bulgaria, in the W-central part; became the cap. in 1879. Pop. 1,102,100.

soft (sôft, sŏft) *adj.* **soft•er, soft•est. 1.a.** Easily molded, cut, or worked. **b.** Yielding readily to pressure or weight. **2.** Out of condition; flabby. **3.** Smooth or fine to the touch: *a soft fabric.* **4.a.** Not loud, harsh, or irritating: *a soft voice.* **b.** Not brilliant or glaring; subdued: *soft colors.* **5.** Not sharply drawn or delineated: *soft charcoal shading.* **6.** Mild; balmy: *a soft breeze.* **7.a.** Of a gentle disposition; tender. **b.** Affectionate: *a soft glance.* **c.** Attracted or emotionally involved: *soft on her.* **d.** Not stern; lenient. **e.** Lacking strength of character; weak. **f.** *Informal.* Simple; feeble. **g.** Gradually declining in trend; not firm: *a soft economy.* **8.a.** *Informal.* Easy: *a soft job.* **b.** Based on conciliation or negotiation rather than on threats or power plays. **9.** Informal and entertaining without confronting difficult issues or hard facts. **10.** Using or based on data not readily quantifiable or amenable to experimental verification or refutation: *soft sciences.* **11.** Of or relating to a paper currency as distinct from a hard currency backed by gold. **12.** Having low dissolved mineral content. **13.** *Ling.* **a.** Being the sound of *c* in *certain* or *g* in *gem.* **b.** Voiced and weakly articulated: *a soft consonant.* **c.** Palatalized, as certain consonants in Slavic languages. **14.** Unprotected against nuclear attack. —*n.* A soft object or part. —*adv.* In a soft manner; gently. [ME, pleasant, calm < OE *sōfte.*] —**soft′ly** *adv.* —**soft′ness** *n.*

soft•ball (sôft′bôl′, sŏft′-) *n. Sports.* **1.** A variation of baseball played on a smaller diamond with a larger, softer ball that is pitched underhand. **2.** The ball used in this game.

soft-boiled (sôft′boild′, sŏft′-) *adj.* **1.** Boiled in the shell to a soft consistency. Used of an egg. **2.** *Informal.* **a.** Softhearted; lenient. **b.** Sentimental.

soft•bound (sôft′bound′, sŏft′-) *adj.* Not bound between hard covers: *softbound books.*

ă **pat**	oi **boy**
ā **pay**	ou **out**
âr **care**	ŏŏ **took**
ä **father**	ōō **boot**
ĕ **pet**	ŭ **cut**
ē **be**	ûr **urge**
ĭ **pit**	th **thin**
ī **pie**	*th* **this**
îr **pier**	hw **which**
ŏ **pot**	zh **vision**
ō **toe**	ə **about, item**
ô **paw**	

Stress marks:
′ (primary);
′ (secondary), as in
dictionary (dĭk′shə-nĕr′ē)

soft chancre *n.* See **chancroid.**
soft clam *n.* See **soft-shell clam.**
soft coal *n.* See **bituminous coal.**
soft-core (sôft′kôr′, -kōr′, sŏft′-) *adj.* **1.** Being less explicit than hard-core material in depicting or describing sexual activity. **2.** Moderate: *a soft-core sports fan.*
soft•cov•er (sôft′kŭv′ər, sŏft′-) *adj.* Not bound between hard covers: *softcover books; a softcover edition.*
soft drink *n.* A nonalcoholic flavored carbonated beverage, usu. commercially prepared and sold in bottles or cans. Also called regionally *cold drink, pop, soda, tonic.* See Regional Note at **tonic.**
soft drug *n.* A drug that is believed to be nonaddictive and less damaging to the health than a hard drug.
soft•en (sô′fən, sŏf′ən) *v.* **-ened, -en•ing, -ens.** —*tr.* **1.** To make soft or softer. **2.** To undermine or reduce the strength, morale, or resistance of. **3.** To make less harsh, strident, or critical. —*intr.* To become soft or softer. —**soft′en•er** *n.*
soft-finned (sôft′fĭnd′, sŏft′-) *adj.* Having fins supported by flexible cartilaginous rays. Used of bony fishes.
soft goods *pl.n.* See **dry goods.**
soft hail *n.* See **snow pellet.**
soft•head (sôft′hĕd′, sŏft′-) *n.* A person regarded as foolish.
soft•head•ed (sôft′hĕd′ĭd, sŏft′-) *adj.* Lacking judgment, realism, or firmness. —**soft′head′-ed•ness** *n.*
soft•heart•ed (sôft′här′tĭd, sŏft′-) *adj.* Easily moved; tender. —**soft′heart′ed•ness** *n.*
soft•ie (sôf′tē, sŏf′-) *n.* Var. of **softy.**
soft landing *n.* The landing of a space vehicle on a celestial body or on Earth so as to prevent damage to the vehicle.
soft-lin•er (sôft′lī′nər, sŏft′-) *n.* One that takes a moderate or flexible approach, esp. on a political issue.
soft palate *n.* The movable fold that is suspended from the rear of the hard palate and closes off the nasal cavity from the oral cavity during swallowing or sucking.
soft paste also **soft-paste** (sôft′pāst′, sŏft′-) *n.* Any of various ceramics containing frit and refined clay.
soft pedal *n. Mus.* A pedal used to mute tone, as on a piano.
soft-ped•al (sôft′pĕd′l, sŏft′-) *tr.v.* **-aled, -al•ing, -als** or **-alled, -al•ling, -als. 1.** *Mus.* To soften or mute the tone of by depressing the soft pedal. **2.** *Informal.* To make less emphatic or obvious; play down.
soft rock *n. Mus.* A style of rock 'n' roll characterized by the predominance of melody and minimal electronic modulations.
soft roe *n.* The spermatozoa or testes of a fish; milt.
soft-shell (sôft′shĕl′, sŏft′-) also **soft-shelled** (-shĕld′) —*adj.* Having a soft, brittle, or unhardened shell. Used of an aquatic animal. —*n.* A soft-shelled aquatic animal.
soft-shell clam *n.* A common edible North American clam *(Mya arenaria)* having a thin elongated shell, found esp. along the Atlantic coast.
soft-shell crab *n.* A marine crab before its shell has hardened after molting, esp. the edible species *Callinectes sapidus* of eastern North America in this stage.
soft-shelled turtle *n.* Any of various freshwater turtles of the family Trionychidae, having a flat carapace covered with leathery skin and a fleshy elongated snout.

soft-shelled turtle
Eastern spiny soft-shelled turtle
Trionyx spiniferus spiniferus

soft-shoe (sôft′sho͞o′, sŏft′-) *n.* Tap dancing performed while wearing shoes without metal taps.
soft shoulder *n.* A border of soft earth running along the edge of a road.
soft soap *n.* **1.** A fluid or semifluid soap. **2.** *Informal.* Flattery; cajolery.
soft-soap (sôft′sōp′, sŏft′-) *tr.v.* **-soaped, -soap•ing, -soaps.** *Informal.* To flatter in order to gain something; cajole. —**soft′-soap′er** *n.*
soft-spo•ken (sôft′spō′kən, sŏft′-) *adj.* **1.** Speaking with a soft or gentle voice. **2.** Smooth; ingratiating.
soft spot *n.* **1.** A tender or sentimental feeling. **2.** A weak or vulnerable point: *a soft spot in his defenses.* **3.** See **fontanel.**
soft-top (sôft′tŏp′) *n.* A car having a top constructed of cloth or a combination of metal and cloth. —**soft′-top′** *adj.*
soft touch *n.* One easily persuaded or taken advantage of.
soft•ware (sôft′wâr′, sŏft′-) *n. Comp. Sci.* The programs, routines, and symbolic languages that control the functioning of hardware and direct its operation.
soft water *n.* Water containing little or no dissolved salts of calcium or magnesium, esp. water containing less than 85.5 parts per million of calcium carbonate.
soft•wood (sôft′wo͝od′, sŏft′-) *n.* **1.** The wood of a coniferous tree. **2.** A coniferous tree.
soft•y or **soft•ie** (sôf′tē, sŏf′-) *n., pl.* **-ies.** *Informal.* **1.** A person regarded as weak or sentimental. **2.** A person who finds it difficult to punish or be strict.
sog•gy (sŏg′ē, sô′gē) *adj.* **-gi•er, -gi•est. 1.** Saturated or sodden with moisture; soaked: *soggy clothes.* **2.** Lacking spirit; dull: *a soggy bit of dialogue.* **3.** Humid; sultry: *a soggy afternoon in August.* [< dial. *sog,* to be soaked (< ME *soggon,* soaked, prob. of Scand. orig.) or < dial. *sog,* swamp.] —**sog′gi•ly** *adv.* —**sog′gi•ness** *n.*
Sog•na•fjord or **Sog•ne Fjord** (sông′nə-fyôr′). A long narrow inlet of the Norwegian Sea in SW Norway.
So•ho (sō′hō′). **1.** A district of central London, England, known for its restaurants, theaters, and nightclubs. **2.** Also **So•Ho.** A district of New York City in SW Manhattan noted for its galleries, shops, restaurants, and artists' lofts.
soi-di•sant (swä′dē-zäN′) *adj.* Self-styled; so-called. [Fr. : *soi,* oneself + *disant,* saying.]
soi•gné also **soi•gnée** (swän-yā′) *adj.* **1.** Showing sophisticated elegance; fashionable. **2.** Well-groomed; polished. [Fr. < OFr., p.part. of *soigner,* to take care of, of Gmc. orig.]
soil[1] (soil) *n.* **1.** The top layer of the earth's surface, consisting of rock and mineral particles mixed with organic matter. **2.** A particular kind of earth or ground: *sandy soil.* **3.** Country; land: *native soil.* **4.** The agricultural life. **5.** A place or condition favorable to growth; a breeding ground. [ME < AN, a piece of ground < Lat. *solium,* seat. See **sed-*.**]
soil[2] (soil) *v.* **soiled, soil•ing, soils.** —*tr.* **1.** To make dirty, particularly on the surface. **2.** To disgrace; tarnish. **3.** To corrupt; defile. **4.** To dirty with excrement. —*intr.* To become dirty, stained, or tarnished. —*n.* **1.a.** The state of being soiled. **b.** A stain. **2.** Filth, sewage, or refuse matter. **3.** Manure, esp. human excrement, used as fertilizer. [ME *soilen* < OFr. *souiller* (< VLat. **suculāre* < LLat. *suculus,* dim. of Lat. *sūs,* pig; see **sū-***) or < *souil,* pigsty, wallow (< Lat. *solium,* seat; see SOIL[1]).]
soil[3] (soil) *tr.v.* **soiled, soil•ing, soils. 1.** To feed (livestock) soilage. **2.** To purge (livestock) by feeding with soilage. [?]
soil•age (soi′lĭj) *n.* Green crops cut to feed livestock.
soil pipe *n.* A drainpipe that carries off wastes from a plumbing fixture, esp. from a toilet.
soil•ure (soil′yər) *n.* **1.** Soiling or the condition of being soiled. **2.** A blot, stain, or smudge.
soi•ree also **soi•rée** (swä-rā′) *n.* An evening party or reception. [Fr. *soirée* < OFr. *seree* < *seir,* evening < Lat. *sērō,* at a late hour < *sērus,* late.]
so•journ (sō′jûrn′, sō-jûrn′) *intr.v.* **-journed, -journ•ing, -journs.** To reside temporarily. See Syns at **stay**[1]. —*n.* A temporary stay; a brief period of residence. [ME *sojournen* < OFr. *sojorner* < VLat. **subdiurnāre* : Lat. *sub-,* sub- + LLat. *diurnum,* day (< Lat., daily ration < neut. of *diurnus,* daily < *diēs,* day; see **deiw-***).] —**so′journ′er** *n.*
soke (sōk) *n.* **1.** In early English law, the right of local jurisdiction, generally one of the feudal rights of lordship. **2.** The district over which soke jurisdiction was exercised. [ME < Med.Lat. *sōca* < OE *sōcn,* act of seeking. See **sāg-*.**]
sol[1] (sōl) also **so** (sō) *n. Mus.* The fifth tone of the diatonic scale in solfeggio. [ME < Med.Lat. See GAMUT.]
sol[2] (sŏl) *n.* An old French coin worth 12 deniers. [Fr. < OFr. < LLat. *solidus,* solidus. See SOLIDUS.]
sol[3] (sōl) *n., pl.* **so•les** (sō′lās). A monetary unit fomerly used in Peru, worth 1/1000 of an inti. [Sp., sun (< the drawing on the coin) < Lat. *sōl,* sun. See **sāwel-*.**]
sol[4] (sôl, sōl) *n.* A colloidal solution. [< SOLUTION.]
Sol (sŏl, sōl) *n.* The sun. [ME < Lat. *sōl.* See **sāwel-*.**]
sol. *abbr.* **1.** Solicitor. **2.** Soluble. **3.** Solution.
so•la[1] (sō′lə) *n.* Pl. of **solum.**
so•la[2] (sō′lə) *adv.* By oneself; alone. Used as a stage direction to a female character. [Ital., fem. of *solo,* solo. See SOLO.]
sol•ace (sŏl′ĭs) *n.* **1.** Comfort in sorrow, misfortune, or distress; consolation. **2.** A source of comfort or consolation. —*tr.v.* **-aced, -ac•ing, -ac•es. 1.** To comfort, cheer, or console, as in trouble or sorrow. **2.** To allay or assuage. [ME *solas* < OFr. < Lat. *sōlācium* < *sōlārī,* to console.] —**sol′ac•er** *n.*
so•lan (sō′lən) *n.* See **gannet.** [ME *soland* : ON *sūla,* pillar, gannet + ON *önd,* duck.]
so•la•nine (sō′lə-nēn′, -nĭn) also **so•a•nin** (-nĭn) *n.* A poisonous alkaloid, $C_{45}H_{73}NO_{15}$, found in potato sprouts, tomatoes, and nightshade. [Fr. < Lat. *sōlānum,* nightshade < *sōl,* sun. See **sāwel-*.**]
so•lar (sō′lər) *adj.* **1.** Of, relating to, or proceeding from the sun. **2.** Using or operated by energy derived from the sun. **3.** Determined or measured in reference to the sun: *the solar year.* [ME < Lat. *sōlāris* < *sōl,* sun. See **sāwel-*.**]
solar battery *n.* A system consisting of a large number of connected solar cells.
solar cell *n.* A semiconductor device that converts the energy of sunlight into electric energy.
solar constant *n.* The average density of solar radiation measured outside Earth's atmosphere and at Earth's mean distance from the sun, equal to 1.4 kilowatts per square meter.
solar day *n.* A mean solar day.
solar flare *n.* A sudden eruption of hydrogen gas on the surface of the sun, usu. associated with sunspots and often followed by disturbances in Earth's magnetic field.
solar furnace *n.* A parabolic reflector that focuses solar radiation to obtain temperatures as high as 4,000°C (7,200°F).
so•lar•im•e•ter (sō′lə-rĭm′ĭ-tər) *n.* An instrument used to measure the flux of solar radiation through a surface.
so•lar•i•um (sō-lâr′ē-əm, sə-) *n., pl.* **-i•a** (-ē-ə) or **-i•ums.** A room, gallery, or glassed-in porch exposed to the sun. [Lat. *sōlārium,* terrace, flat housetop < *sōl,* sun. See **sāwel-*.**]
so•lar•ize (sō′lə-rīz′) *v.* **-ized, -iz•ing, -iz•es.** —*tr.* To affect by exposing to sunlight. —*intr.* To be overexposed. Used of

photographic film. — **so′lar·i·za′tion** (-lər-ĭ-zā′shən) *n.*

solar month *n.* One twelfth of a solar year, totaling 30 days, 10 hours, 29 minutes, 3.8 seconds.

solar panel *n.* A group of connected solar cells.

solar plexus *n.* **1.** The large network of sympathetic nerves and ganglia located in the peritoneal cavity behind the stomach and having branching tracts that supply nerves to the abdominal viscera. **2.** The pit of the stomach. [< its radially branching ganglia.]

solar system *n.* The sun together with the nine planets and all other celestial bodies that orbit the sun.

solar wind (wĭnd) *n.* A stream of ionized particles ejected at high speeds from the surface of the sun.

solar year *n.* The period of time required for the earth to make one complete revolution around the sun, measured from one vernal equinox to the next and equal to 365 days, 5 hours, 48 minutes, 45.51 seconds.

sold (sōld) *v.* P.t. and p.part. of **sell.**

sol·dan (sŏl′dən, sŏl′-) also **sou·dan** (so͞od′n) *n.* A sultan in Egypt. [ME < OFr. < Ar. *sulṭān.*]

sol·der (sŏd′ər) *n.* **1.** Any of various fusible alloys, usu. tin and lead, used to join metallic parts. **2.** Something that joins or cements. — *v.* **-dered, -der·ing, -ders.** — *tr.* To serve as a bond between; join. — *intr.* **1.** To unite or repair things with solder. **2.** To be joined by or as if by solder. [ME *soudur* < OFr. *soldure* < *soulder*, to solder < Lat. *solidāre*, to make solid < *solidus*, solid. See SOLID.] — **sol′der·er** *n.*

sol·dier (sōl′jər) *n.* **1.** One who serves in an army. **2.** An enlisted person or a noncommissioned officer. **3.a.** An active, loyal, and militant follower. **b.** A trusted follower of an organized crime leader. **4.** A sexually undeveloped form of certain ants and termites, having large heads and powerful jaws specialized to serve as fighting weapons. — *intr.v.* **-diered, -dier·ing, -diers. 1.** To be or serve as a soldier. **2.** To make a show of working. [ME *soudier*, mercenary < AN *soldeier* and OFr. *soudier*, both < OFr. *sol, soud*, sou < LLat. *solidum, soldum*, pay < *solidus*, solidus. See SOLIDUS.]

Word History: Why do soldiers fight? The Old French word *soudoior* or *soudier,* from which our word comes, is derived from *sol* or *soud,* Old French forms of Modern French *sou.* There is no longer a French coin named *sou,* but the meaning of the word *sou* alerts us to the fact that money is involved. Indeed, Old French *sol* referred to a coin and also meant "pay," and a *soudoior* was one who fought for pay. This was a concept worth expressing in an era when others were not paid for fighting but did it in service to a feudal superior.

sol·dier·ly (sōl′jər-lē) *adj.* Of or befitting a soldier.

soldier of fortune *n., pl.* **soldiers of fortune.** One who will serve in any army for personal gain or love of adventure.

sol·dier·y (sōl′jə-rē) *n.* **1.** Soldiers considered as a group. **2.** The profession of soldiering.

sold-out (sōld′out′) *adj.* Having all tickets or accommodations completely sold, esp. ahead of time.

sole[1] (sōl) *n.* **1.** The underside of the foot. **2.** The underside of a shoe or boot, often excluding the heel. **3.** The part on which something else rests while in a vertical position, esp.: **a.** The bottom surface of a plow. **b.** *Sports.* The bottom surface of the head of a golf club. — *tr.v.* **soled, sol·ing, soles. 1.** To furnish (a shoe or boot) with a sole. **2.** *Sports.* To put the sole of (a golf club) on the ground, as in preparing to make a stroke. [ME < OFr. < Lat. *solea*, sandal < *solum*, bottom, sole of the foot.]

sole[2] (sōl) *adj.* **1.** Being the only one: *the sole survivor of the crash.* **2.** Of or relating to only one individual or group; exclusive: *The court has the sole right to decide.* **3.** *Law.* Single; unmarried. [ME, alone < OFr. *sol* < Lat. *sōlus.* See **s(w)e-*.**]

sole[3] (sōl) *n., pl.* **sole** or **soles. 1.** Any of various chiefly marine flatfish of the family Soleidae, related to and resembling the flounders, esp. any of several European species, such as *Solea solea,* valued as food fishes. **2.** Any of various other flatfish, esp. certain coastal flounders. [ME < OFr. < Lat. *solea*, sandal, flatfish (< its shape). See SOLE[1].]

sol·e·cism (sŏl′ĭ-sĭz′əm, sō′lĭ-) *n.* **1.** A nonstandard usage or grammatical construction. **2.** A violation of etiquette. **3.** An impropriety, a mistake, or an incongruity. [Lat. *soloecismus* < Gk. *soloikismos* < *soloikizein*, to speak incorrectly < *soloikos*, speaking incorrectly, after *Soloi* (Soli), an Athenian colony in Cilicia where a dialect regarded as substandard was spoken.] — **sol′e·cist** *n.* — **sol′e·cis′tic** *adj.*

sole·ly (sōl′lē, sō′lē) *adv.* **1.** Alone; singly: *solely responsible.* **2.** Entirely; exclusively: *did it solely for love.*

sol·emn (sŏl′əm) *adj.* **1.** Deeply earnest, serious, and sober. **2.** Somberly or gravely impressive. See Syns at **serious. 3.** Performed with full ceremony. **4.** Invoking the force of religion; sacred: *a solemn vow.* **5.** Gloomy; somber. [ME *solemne* < OFr. < Lat. *sollemnis*, established, customary. See **sol-*.**] — **sol′emn·ly** *adv.* — **sol′emn·ness** *n.*

so·lem·ni·ty (sə-lĕm′nĭ-tē) *n., pl.* **-ties. 1.** The quality or condition of being solemn. **2.** A solemn observance or proceeding.

sol·em·nize (sŏl′əm-nīz′) *tr.v.* **-nized, -niz·ing, -niz·es. 1.** To celebrate or observe with dignity and gravity. **2.** To perform with formal ceremony. **3.** To make serious or grave. — **sol′em·ni·za′tion** (-nĭ-zā′shən) *n.*

so·le·noid (sō′lə-noid′) *n.* **1.** A coil of wire that acts like a magnet when a current passes through it. **2.** An assembly used as a switch, consisting of a coil and a metal core free to slide along the coil axis under the influence of the magnetic field. [Fr. *solénoïde* < Gk. *sōlēnoeidēs*, pipe-shaped : *sōlēn*, pipe + *-oeidēs*, -oid.] — **so′le·noi′dal** (-noid′l) *adj.* — **so′le·noi′dal·ly** *adv.*

So·lent (sō′lənt). A narrow channel between the Isle of Wight and the S mainland of England.

sole·plate (sōl′plāt′) *n.* The underside of a clothes iron.

sole·print (sōl′prĭnt′) *n.* **1.** A print of the sole of the foot. **2.** A print of the sole of the foot made for identification.

so·les (sō′lās) *n.* Pl. of **sol**[3].

so·le·us (sō′lē-əs) *n., pl.* **-le·i** (-lē-ī′). A broad flat muscle of the calf of the leg, situated under the gastrocnemius. [NLat. < Lat. *solea*, sandal. See SOLE[1].]

sol-fa (sōl-fä′) *Mus.* — *n.* **1.** The set of syllables *do, re, mi, fa, sol, la,* and *ti,* used to represent the tones of the scale. **2.** Use of these syllables. — *intr. & tr.v.* **-faed, -fa·ing, -fas.** To use the sol-fa syllables or sing using these syllables. [Ital. *solfa* < Med.Lat. : *sol*, note of the scale; see GAMUT + *fa*, note of the scale; see GAMUT.]

sol·fa·ta·ra (sōl′fə-tär′ə) *n.* A volcanic area that gives off sulfurous gases and steam. [Ital. < *solfo*, sulfur < Lat. *sulfur.*]

sol·fège (sŏl-fĕzh′, sōl-) *n. Mus.* Solfeggio. [Fr. < Ital. *solfeggio.* See SOLFEGGIO.]

sol·feg·gio (sōl-fĕj′ē-ō′, -fĕj′ō) *n., pl.* **-feg·gi** (-fĕj′ē) or **-gios.** *Mus.* **1.** Use of the sol-fa syllables to note the tones of the scale; solmization. **2.** A singing exercise in which the sol-fa syllables are used. [Ital. < *solfa*, sol-fa. See SOL-FA.]

sol·fe·ri·no (sŏl′fə-rē′nō) *n. Color.* A moderate purplish red. [After *Solferino*, a village of N Italy.]

so·lic·it (sə-lĭs′ĭt) *v.* **-it·ed, -it·ing, -its.** — *tr.* **1.** To seek to obtain by persuasion, entreaty, or formal application. **2.** To petition persistently; importune. **3.** To entice or incite to evil or illegal action. **4.** To approach or accost (a person) with an offer of sexual services. — *intr.* **1.** To make solicitation or petition for something desired. **2.** To solicit someone sexually. [ME *soliciten*, to disturb < OFr. *solliciter* < Lat. *sollicitāre* < *sollicitus*, troubled. See SOLICITOUS.] — **so·lic′i·ta′tion** *n.*

so·lic·i·tor (sə-lĭs′ĭ-tər) *n.* **1.** One that solicits, esp. one that seeks trade or contributions. **2.** The chief law officer of a city, town, or government department. **3.** *Chiefly British.* An attorney who is not a member of the bar and may be heard only in the lower courts.

solicitor general *n., pl.* **solicitors general. 1.** A law officer assisting an attorney general. **2.** The chief law officer in a state not having an attorney general.

so·lic·i·tous (sə-lĭs′ĭ-təs) *adj.* **1.a.** Anxious or concerned. **b.** Expressing care or concern. See Syns at **thoughtful. 2.** Full of desire; eager. **3.** Marked by anxious care and often hovering attentiveness. **4.** Extremely careful; meticulous. [Lat. *sollicitus* : *sollus*, entire; see **sol-*** + *citus*, p.part. of *ciēre*, to set in motion; see **kei-**[2]***.**] — **so·lic′i·tous·ly** *adv.* — **so·lic′i·tous·ness** *n.*

so·lic·i·tude (sə-lĭs′ĭ-to͞od′, -tyo͞od′) *n.* **1.** The state of being solicitous; care or concern, as for the well-being of another. See Syns at **anxiety. 2.** A cause of anxiety or concern. Often used in the plural.

sol·id (sŏl′ĭd) *adj.* **-er, -est. 1.a.** Of definite shape and volume; not liquid or gaseous. **b.** Firm or compact in substance. See Syns at **firm**[1]. **2.** Not hollowed out: *a solid block of wood.* **3.** Being the same substance or color throughout: *solid gold.* **4.** *Math.* Of, relating to, or being a three-dimensional geometric figure or body. **5.** Having no gaps or breaks; continuous: *a solid line of people.* **6.** Of good quality and substance: *a solid foundation.* **7.** Substantial; hearty: *a solid meal.* **8.** Sound; reliable: *solid facts.* **9.** Financially sound. **10.** Upstanding and dependable: *a solid citizen.* **11.** Written without a hyphen or space. For example, the word *software* is a solid compound. **12.** *Print.* Having no leads between the lines. **13.** Acting together; unanimous: *a solid voting bloc.* — *n.* **1.** A substance having a definite shape and volume; one that is neither liquid nor gaseous. **2.** *Math.* A geometric figure having three dimensions. [ME *solide* < OFr. < Lat. *solidus.* See **sol-*.**] — **sol′id·ly** *adv.* — **sol′id·ness** *n.*

solid angle *n. Math.* An angle formed by all rays from a common point that pass through a closed curve.

sol·i·dar·i·ty (sŏl′ĭ-dăr′ĭ-tē) *n.* A union of interests, purposes, or sympathies among members of a group; fellowship of responsibilities and interests. [Fr. *solidarité* < *solidaire*, interdependent < OFr., in common < Lat. *solidus*, solid, whole. See SOLID.]

solid geometry *n. Math.* The branch of mathematics that deals with three-dimensional figures and surfaces.

so·lid·i·fy (sə-lĭd′ə-fī′) *v.* **-fied, -fy·ing, -fies.** — *tr.* **1.** To make solid, compact, or hard. **2.** To make strong or united. — *intr.* To become solid or united. — **so·lid′i·fi·ca′tion** (-fĭ-kā′shən) *n.*

solar panel
On the Skylab satellite

ă pat	oi boy
ā pay	ou out
âr care	o͝o took
ä father	o͞o boot
ĕ pet	ŭ cut
ē be	ûr urge
ĭ pit	th thin
ī pie	*th* this
îr pier	hw which
ŏ pot	zh vision
ō toe	ə about, item
ô paw	

Stress marks:
′ (primary);
′ (secondary), as in
dictionary (dĭk′shə-nĕr′ē)

so•lid•i•ty (sə-lĭd′ĭ-tē) *n.* **1.** The condition or property of being solid. **2.** Soundness of mind, moral character, or finances.

solid of revolution *n. Math.* A volume generated by the rotation of a plane figure about an axis in its plane.

solid propellant *n.* A rocket propellant in solid form, combining fuel and oxidizer to form a compact cohesive grain.

solid solution *n.* A homogeneous crystalline structure in which two or more types of atoms or molecules share a common lattice, as in certain alloys.

sol•id-state (sŏl′ĭd-stāt′) *adj.* **1.** Characteristic of or relating to the physical properties of solid materials, esp. to the electromagnetic properties of crystalline solids. **2.** Based on or consisting of semiconducting materials, components, and related devices.

solleret
Pair of 1460 Italian sollerets

sol•i•dus (sŏl′ĭ-dəs) *n., pl.* **-di** (-dī′). **1.** A gold coin of the Roman Empire used in Europe until the 15th century. **2.** *Print.* A virgule; a slash. [ME < LLat. *(nummus) solidus,* a solid (sesterce) < Lat. *solidus,* solid. See SOLID.]

so•lil•o•quy (sə-lĭl′ə-kwē) *n., pl.* **-quies. 1.a.** A dramatic or literary form of discourse in which a character reveals his or her thoughts when alone or unaware of the presence of other characters. **b.** A specific speech or piece of writing in this form of discourse. **2.** The act of speaking to oneself. [LLat. *sōliloquium* : Lat. *sōlus,* alone; see **s(w)e-*** + Lat. *loquī,* to speak; see **tolkʷ-*.**] **—so•lil′o•quist** (-kwĭst) **—so•lil′o•quiz′er** (-kwī′zər) *n.* **—so•lil′o•quize′** (-kwīz′) *v.*

So•ling•en (zō′lĭng-ən). A city of W-central Germany ESE of Düsseldorf; chartered 1374. Pop. 158,418.

sol•ip•sism (sŏl′ĭp-sĭz′əm, sō′lĭp-) *n. Philos.* The theory that the self is the only thing that has reality or can be known and verified. [Lat. *sōlus,* alone; see **s(w)e-*** + Lat. *ipse,* self + -ISM.] **—sol′ip•sist** *n.* **—sol′ip•sis′tic** *adj.*

sol•i•taire (sŏl′ĭ-târ′) *n.* **1.** A gem, such as a diamond, that is set alone. **2.** *Games.* Any of a number of card games played by one person. **3.** Any of several thrushes of the genus *Myadestes,* found in North and Central America and noted for their beautiful song. [Fr., solitary < OFr. See SOLITARY.]

sol•i•tar•y (sŏl′ĭ-tĕr′ē) *adj.* **1.** Existing, living, or going without others; alone. See Syns at **alone. 2.** Happening, done, or made alone. **3.** Remote from civilization; secluded. **4.** Having no companions; lonesome or lonely. **5.** *Zool.* Living alone or in pairs only. **6.** Single and set apart from others. *—n., pl.* **-ies. 1.** A person who lives alone; a recluse. **2.** Solitary confinement. [ME < OFr. *solitaire* < Lat. *sōlitārius* < *sōlitās,* solitude < *sōlus,* alone. See **s(w)e-*.**] **—sol′i•tar′i•ly** (-târ′ə-lē) *adv.* **—sol′i•tar′i•ness** *n.*

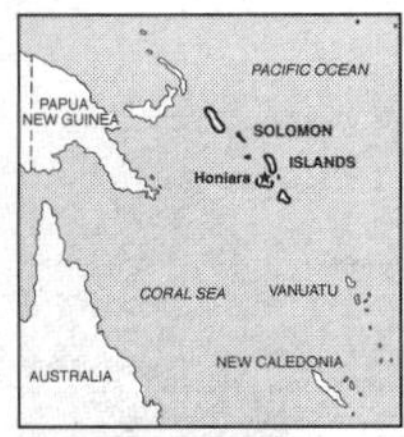

Solomon Islands[2]

sol•i•tude (sŏl′ĭ-to͞od′, -tyo͞od′) *n.* **1.** The state or quality of being alone or remote from others. **2.** A lonely or secluded place. [ME < OFr. < Lat. *sōlitūdō* < *sōlus,* alone. See **s(w)e-*.**]

sol•i•tud•i•nar•i•an (sŏl′ĭ-to͞od′n-âr′ē-ən, -tyo͞od′-) *n.* One leading a solitary or secluded life. [Lat. *sōlitūdō, sōlitūdin-,* solitude; see SOLITUDE + -ARIAN.]

sol•ler•et (sŏl′ə-rĕt′) *n.* A steel shoe made of overlapping plates, forming a part of a medieval suit of armor. [Fr. < OFr., dim. of *soller,* shoe < LLat. *subtēlāris (calceus),* (shoe gear) for the sole of the foot < *subtēl,* the hollow of the foot : Lat. *sub-,* sub- + Lat. *talus,* ankle; see TALUS[1].]

sol•mi•za•tion (sŏl′mĭ-zā′shən) *n. Mus.* The act or a system of using syllables, such as *do, re,* and *mi,* to represent the tones of the scale. [Fr. *solmisation* < *solmiser,* to sol-fa : *sol,* note of the scale (< Med.Lat.; see GAMUT) + *mi,* note of the scale (< Med.Lat.; see GAMUT).]

soln. *abbr.* Solution.

so•lo (sō′lō) *n., pl.* **-los. 1.** *Mus.* A composition or passage for an individual voice or instrument, with or without accompaniment. **2.** A performance by or intended for a single individual. **3.** *Games.* Any of various card games in which one player singly opposes others. *—adj.* **1.** *Mus.* Composed, arranged for, or performed by a single voice or instrument. **2.** Made or done by a single individual. *—adv.* Unaccompanied; alone. *—intr.v.* **-loed, -lo•ing, -los. 1.** To perform a solo. **2.** To fly an airplane without a companion or an instructor, esp. for the first time. [Ital. < Lat. *sōlus,* alone. See **s(w)e-*.**]

Solomon's seal

so•lo•ist (sō′lō-ĭst) *n.* One who performs a solo.

so•lo•is•tic (sō′lō-ĭs′tĭk) *adj. Mus.* **1.** Of, relating to, or containing a solo or soloist. **2.** Having elements or qualities of or appropriate to a solo or a soloist.

So•lo man (sō′lō) *n.* An extinct hominid primate *(Homo soloensis)* known from fossil remains of the late Pleistocene Epoch. [After the *Solo* R. of central Java.]

Sol•o•mon (sŏl′ə-mən). fl. 10th cent. B.C. King of Israel famous for his wisdom.

Sol•o•mon•ic (sŏl′ə-mŏn′ĭk) *adj.* Exhibiting or requiring the exercise of great wisdom, esp. in making difficult decisions.

Solomon Islands[1]. An island group of the W Pacific E of New Guinea. The N Solomons are part of Papua New Guinea; the S islands are an independent country.

Solomon Islands[2]. A country comprising the Solomon Is. SE of Bougainville; a British protectorate after 1893 and independent since 1978. Cap. Honiara. Pop. 212,868.

Sol•o•mon's feather (sŏl′ə-mənz) *n* See **false Solomon's seal.**

Solomon's plume *n.* See **false Solomon's seal.**

Solomon's seal *n.* **1.** A six-pointed star or hexagram supposed to possess mystical powers. **2.** Any of several plants of the genus *Polygonatum,* having paired drooping flowers.

so•lon (sō′lən, -lŏn′) *n.* **1.** A wise lawgiver. **2.** A legislator. [After SOLON.]

So•lon (sō′lən, -lŏn′). 638?–559? B.C. Athenian lawgiver and poet whose reforms ended class privilege by birth.

so long *interj. Informal.* Used to express good-bye.

so long as *conj.* **1.** During the time that; while. **2.** Provided that.

sol•stice (sŏl′stĭs, sōl′-, sôl′-) *n.* **1.** *Astron.* Either of two times of the year, the summer solstice or the winter solstice, when the sun is at its greatest distance from the celestial equator. **2.** A highest point or culmination. [ME < OFr. < Lat. *sōlstitium* : *sōl,* sun; see **sāwel-*** + *-stitium,* a stoppage; see **stā-*.**] **—sol•sti′tial** (-stĭsh′əl) *adj.*

sol•u•bil•i•ty (sŏl′yə-bĭl′ĭ-tē) *n., pl.* **-ties. 1.** The quality or condition of being soluble. **2.** The amount of a substance that can be dissolved in a given amount of solvent.

sol•u•bi•lize (sŏl′yə-bə-līz′) *tr.v.* **-lized, -liz•ing, -liz•es.** To make (substances such as fats and lipids) soluble in water by the action of a detergent or similar agent.

sol•u•ble (sŏl′yə-bəl) *adj.* **1.** That can be dissolved, esp. easily dissolved: *soluble fats.* **2.** Possible to solve or explain: *soluble mysteries.* [ME < OFr. < LLat. *solūbilis* < Lat. *solvere,* to loosen. See **leu-*.**] **—sol′u•ble•ness** *n.* **—sol′u•bly** *adv.*

soluble glass *n.* See **sodium silicate.**

soluble RNA *n.* Transfer RNA.

so•lum (sō′ləm) *n., pl.* **-la** (-lə) or **-lums.** The upper layers of a soil profile in which topsoil formation occurs. [Lat., base, ground.]

so•lus (sō′ləs) *adv. & adj.* By oneself; alone. Used as a stage direction to a male character. [Lat. *sōlus,* alone. See SOLO.]

sol•ute (sŏl′yo͞ot, sō′lo͞ot) *n.* A substance dissolved in another substance. *—adj.* Being in solution; dissolved. [< ME, loose, porous < Lat. *solūtus,* p.part. of *solvere,* to loosen. See **leu-*.**]

so•lu•tion (sə-lo͞o′shən) *n.* **1.a.** A homogeneous mixture of two or more substances, which may be solids, liquids, gases, or a combination of these. **b.** The process of forming such a mixture. **2.** The state of being dissolved. **3.a.** The method or process of solving a problem. **b.** The answer to or disposition of a problem. **4.** *Law.* Payment or satisfaction of a claim or debt. **5.** The act of separating or breaking up; dissolution. [ME < OFr. < Lat. *solūtiō, solūtiōn-* < *solūtus,* p.part. of *solvere,* to loosen. See SOLUTE.]

So•lu•tre•an also **So•lu•tri•an** (sə-lo͞o′trē-ən) *adj.* Of or relating to the Old World Upper Paleolithic culture that succeeded the Aurignacian and was characterized by improved flint implements and stylized symbolic forms of art. [Fr. *solutréen,* after *Solutré-Pouilly,* a village of E-central France.]

solv•a•ble (sŏl′və-bəl, sôl′-) *adj.* Possible to solve: *solvable problems.* **—solv′a•bil′i•ty, solv′a•ble•ness** *n.*

sol•va•tion (sŏl-vā′shən, sôl-) *n.* Any of a class of chemical reactions in which solute and solvent molecules combine with relatively weak covalent bonds. [SOLV(ENT) + -ATION.]

Sol•vay process (sŏl′vā, sôl-vā′) *n.* A process used to produce large quantities of sodium carbonate from sodium chloride, ammonia, and carbon dioxide. [After Ernest *Solvay* (1838–1922), Belgian chemist.]

solve (sŏlv, sôlv) *tr.v.* **solved, solv•ing, solves. 1.** To find a solution to. **2.** To work out a correct solution to (a problem). [ME *solven,* to loosen < Lat. *solvere.* See **leu-*.**] **—solv′er** *n.*

Syns: solve, decipher, resolve, unravel. The central meaning shared by these verbs is "to clear up or explain something puzzling or unintelligible": *solve a riddle; can't decipher his handwriting; resolve a problem; unravel a mystery.*

sol•vent (sŏl′vənt, sôl′-) *adj.* **1.** Capable of meeting financial obligations. **2.** *Chem.* Capable of dissolving another substance. *—n.* **1.** *Chem.* **a.** A substance in which another substance is dissolved, forming a solution. **b.** A substance, usu. a liquid, capable of dissolving another substance. **2.** Something that solves or explains. [Fr. < Lat. *solvēns, solvent-,* pr.part. of *solvere,* to loosen. See SOLVE.] **—sol′ven•cy** *n.*

sol•vol•y•sis (sŏl-vŏl′ĭ-sĭs, sôl-) *n.* A chemical reaction in which the solute and solvent react to form a new compound. [SOLV(ENT) + -LYSIS.] **—sol′vo•lyt′ic** (-və-lĭt′ĭk) *adj.*

Sol•way Firth (sŏl′wā′). An arm of the Irish Sea separating NW England from SW Scotland.

Sol•zhe•ni•tsyn (sōl′zhə-nēt′sĭn, səl-zhə-nyē′tsĭn), **Aleksandr Isayevich.** b. 1918. Soviet writer and dissident who won the 1970 Nobel Prize for literature.

so•ma (sō′mə) *n., pl.* **-ma•ta** (-mə-tə) or **-mas. 1.** The entire body of an organism, exclusive of the germ cells. **2.** See **cell body. 3.** The body of an individual as contrasted with the mind or psyche. [NLat. *sōma* < Gk., body. See **teuə-*.**]

So•ma•li (sō-mä′lē) *n., pl.* **Somali** or **-lis. 1.** A member of a Muslim people of Somalia and adjacent parts of Ethiopia, Kenya, and Djibouti. **2.** The Cushitic language of the Somali and an official language of Somalia.

So•ma•li•a (sō-mä′lē-ə, -mäl′yə). A country of extreme E Africa on the Gulf of Aden and the Indian Ocean; formed in 1960 from colonies previously held by Italy and Great Britain. Cap. Mogadishu. Pop. 3,645,000. **— So•ma′li•an** *adj. & n.*

So•ma•li•land (sō-mä′lē-lănd′, sə-). A region of E Africa comprising Somalia, Djibouti, and SE Ethiopia.

so•mat•ic (sō-măt′ĭk) *adj.* **1.** Of, relating to, or affecting the body, esp. as distinguished from a body part, the mind, or the environment; corporeal or physical. See Syns at **bodily. 2.** Of or relating to the wall of the body cavity, esp. as distinguished from the head, limbs, or viscera. **3.** Of or relating to a somatic cell or the somatoplasm. [Fr. *somatique* < Gk. *sōmatikos* < *sōma, sōmat-*, body. See SOMA.] **— so•mat′i•cal•ly** *adv.*

somatic cell *n.* Any cell of a plant or an animal other than a germ cell.

somato– *pref.* **1.** Body: *somatology.* **2.** Soma: *somatoplasm.* [Gk. *sōmato-* < *sōma, sōmat-*, body. See **teuə-***.]

so•ma•tol•o•gy (sō′mə-tŏl′ə-jē) *n.* **1.** The physiological and anatomical study of the body. **2.** See **physical anthropology. — so′ma•to•log′ic** (sō′mə-tl-ŏj′ĭk, sō-măt′l-), **so′ma•to•log′i•cal** (-ĭ-kəl) *adj.* **— so′ma•tol′o•gist** *n.*

so•mat•o•me•din (sō-măt′ə-mēd′n, sō′mə-tə-) *n.* Any of a group of peptides produced by the liver upon stimulation by somatotropin that act directly on cartilage cells to stimulate skeletal growth. [Perh. SOMATO(TROPIN) + (INTER)MED(IARY) + -IN.]

so•mat•o•plasm (sō-măt′ə-plăz′əm, sō′mə-tə-) *n.* **1.** The entirety of specialized protoplasm, other than germ plasm, constituting the body. **2.** The protoplasm of a somatic cell. **— so′ma•to•plas′tic** (sō′mə-tə-plăs′tĭk) *adj.*

so•mat•o•pleure (sō-măt′ə-plo͝or′, sō′mə-tə-) *n.* A complex sheet of embryonic cells in craniate vertebrates, formed by association of part of the mesoderm with the ectoderm and developing as the internal body wall. [NLat. *somatopleura* : SOMATO- + Gk. *pleura*, side.]

so•mat•o•stat•in (sō-măt′ə-stăt′n, sō′mə-tə-) *n.* A polypeptide hormone produced chiefly by the hypothalamus that inhibits the secretion of various other hormones, such as somatotropin and insulin. [SOMATO(TROPIN) + -STAT + -IN.]

so•mat•o•tro•pin (sə-măt′ə-trō′pĭn, sō′mə-tə-) also **so•mat•o•tro•phin** (-trō′fĭn) *n.* A polypeptide hormone secreted by the anterior lobe of the pituitary gland that promotes growth of the body, esp. by stimulating the release of somatomedin. [SOMATO- + -TROP(IC) + -IN.]

so•mat•o•type (sō-măt′ə-tīp′, sō′mə-tə-) *n.* Body type; physique. **— so•mat′o•typ′ic** (-tĭp′ĭk) *adj.*

som•ber (sŏm′bər) *adj.* **1.a.** Dark; gloomy. **b.** Dull or dark in color. **2.a.** Melancholy; dismal. **b.** Serious; grave. [Fr. *sombre* < OFr. < **sombrer*, to cast a shadow < LLat. *subumbrāre* < Lat. *sub umbrā*, in shadow : *sub*, sub- + *umbrā*, ablative of *umbra*, shadow.] **— som′ber•ly** *adv.* **— som′ber•ness** *n.*

som•bre (sŏm′bər) *adj. Chiefly British.* Var. of **somber.**

som•bre•ro (sŏm-brâr′ō, səm-) *n., pl.* **-ros.** A large straw or felt hat with a broad brim and tall crown, worn esp. in Mexico and the American southwest. [Sp., perh. < *sombra*, shade, prob. < *sombrar*, to shade < LLat. *subumbrāre*, to cast a shadow. See SOMBER.]

Som•bre•ro (sŏm-brâr′ō, səm-). An island of St. Christopher-Nevis in the Leeward Is. of the West Indies.

som•brous (sŏm′brəs) *adj. Archaic.* Somber in aspect or in character.

some (sŭm) *adj.* **1.** Being an unspecified number or quantity: *some people.* **2.** Unknown or unspecified by name: *Some man called.* **3.** *Logic.* Being part and perhaps all of a class. **4.** *Informal.* Remarkable: *She is some skier.* *—pron.* **1.** An indefinite or unspecified number or portion: *We took some of the books.* See Usage Note at **every. 2.** An indefinite additional quantity: *did the work and then some.* *—adv.* **1.** Approximately; about: *Some 40 people attended the rally.* **2.** *Informal.* Somewhat. [ME < OE *sum*, a certain one. See **sem-¹***.]

–some¹ *suff.* Characterized by a specified quality, condition, or action: *bothersome.* [ME *-som* < OE *-sum*, -like. See **sem-¹***.]

–some² *suff.* A group of a specified number of members: *threesome.* [ME *-sum* < OE *sum*, some. See SOME.]

–some³ *suff.* **1.** Body: *centrosome.* **2.** Chromosome: *monosome.* [< Gk. *sōma*, body. See **teuə-***.]

some•bod•y (sŭm′bŏd′ē, -bŭd′ē, -bə-dē) *pron.* An unspecified or unknown person; someone. See Usage Note at **he¹.** *—n., pl.* **-ies.** *Informal.* A person of importance.

some•day (sŭm′dā′) *adv.* At an indefinite time in the future.

Usage Note: *Someday* (adverb) and *sometime* express future time indefinitely. For example, *We'll succeed someday. I'll come sometime.* This sense can also be conveyed by *some day* and *some time.* The two word forms are always used when *some* is an adjective modifying and specifying a more particular *day* or *time* (used as nouns): *Come some day soon.*

some•how (sŭm′hou′) *adv.* In a way not specified, understood, or known.

some•one (sŭm′wŭn′, -wən) *pron.* An unspecified or unknown person; somebody. *—n. Informal.* A somebody.

some•place (sŭm′plās′) *adv. & n.* Somewhere. See Usage Note at **everyplace.**

som•er•sault also **sum•mer•sault** (sŭm′ər-sôlt′) *—n.* **1.** An acrobatic stunt in which the body rolls in a complete circle, heels over head. Also called regionally *tumbleset.* **2.** A complete reversal, as of sympathies or opinions. *—intr.v.* **-sault•ed, -sault•ing, -saults.** To perform a somersault. [Obsolete Fr. *sombresault*, var. of *sobresault* < OProv. *sobresaut* : *sobre-*, above (< Lat. *suprā*; see **uper***) + *saut*, leap (< Lat. *saltus* < p.part. of *salīre*, to leap; see **sel-***).]

som•er•set also **sum•mer•set** (sŭm′ər-sĕt′) *—n.* See **somersault** 1. *—intr.v.* **-set•ted, -set•ting, -sets.** To perform a somersault. [Alteration of SOMERSAULT.]

Som•er•set (sŭm′ər-sĕt′, -sĭt). A town of SE MA, a suburb of Fall River. Pop. 17,655.

Som•er•ville (sŭm′ər-vĭl′). A city of E MA, a suburb of Boston. Pop. 76,210.

Somerville, Mary Fairfax Greig. 1780–1872. British mathematician and astronomer.

so•mes•thet•ic (sō′mĕs-thĕt′ĭk) *adj.* Somatosensory. [*som(a)* + Gk. *aisthētikos*, of sense perception; see AESTHETIC.]

some•thing (sŭm′thĭng) *pron.* **1.** An undetermined or unspecified thing. **2.** One having essentially the same attributes, character, or essence as another: *something of an optimist.* *—n. Informal.* A remarkable or important thing or person: *He thinks he is something in that uniform.* *—adv.* **1.** A little; somewhat: *looks something like her.* **2.** *Informal.* To an extreme degree: *drinks something fierce.* **—*idioms.* something else.** *Informal.* One that is very special or quite remarkable. **something of.** To some extent: *something of an eccentric.*

some•time (sŭm′tīm′) *adv.* **1.** At an indefinite or unstated time: *Let's meet sometime today.* **2.** At an indefinite time in the future: *Let's get together sometime.* **3.** *Obsolete.* Sometimes. **4.** *Archaic.* Formerly. *—adj.* **1.** Having been at some prior time; former. **2.** *Usage Problem.* Occasional.

Usage Note: *Sometime* as an adjective has been employed to mean "former" since the 15th century. It has come to be used in the 20th century with the meaning "occasional": *the team's sometime star and sometime problem child.* This latter use, however, is unacceptable to a majority of the Usage Panel. See Usage Note at **someday.**

some•times (sŭm′tīmz′) *adv.* **1.** At times; now and then. **2.** *Obsolete.* At some previous time; formerly.

some•way (sŭm′wā′) also **some•ways** (-wāz′) *adv.* In some way or another; somehow.

some•what (sŭm′hwŏt′, -wŏt′, -hwŭt′, -wŭt′, -hwət, -wət) *adv.* To some extent or degree; rather. *—pron.* Something.

some•where (sŭm′hwâr′, -wâr′) *adv.* **1.** At, in, or to a place not specified or known: *found it somewhere in the woods.* **2.** To a place or state of further development or progress: *finally getting somewhere.* **3.** Approximately; roughly. *—n.* An unknown or unspecified place.

some•wheres (sŭm′hwârz′, -wârz′) *adv. Informal.* Somewhere.

so•mite (sō′mīt′) *n.* **1.** *Zool.* See **metamere. 2.** A segmental mass of mesoderm in the vertebrate embryo that develops into muscles and vertebrae. [Gk. *sōma*, body; see SOMA + -ITE¹.] **— so•mit′ic** (sō-mĭt′ĭk) *adj.*

Somme (sŏm, sôm). A river of N France flowing c. 241 km (150 mi) W and NW to the English Channel.

som•me•lier (sŭm′əl-yā′, sô′mə-lyā′) *n.* A wine steward in a restaurant. [Fr. < OFr., officer in charge of provisions, pack-animal driver, alteration of **sommerier* < *sommier*, beast of burden < VLat. **saumārius.* See SUMMER².]

som•nam•bu•late (sŏm-năm′byə-lāt′) *intr.v.* **-lat•ed, -lat•ing, -lates.** To walk or perform another act while asleep or in a sleeplike condition. **— som•nam′bu•lar** (-lər) *adj.* **— som′nam•bu•la′tion** *n.*

som•nam•bu•lism (sŏm-năm′byə-lĭz′əm) *n.* See **sleepwalking. — som•nam′bu•list** *n.* **— som•nam′bu•lis′tic** *adj.*

somni– or **somn–** *pref.* Sleep: *somnambulate.* [< Lat. *somnus*, sleep. See **swep-***.]

som•ni•fa•cient (sŏm′nə-fā′shənt) *adj.* Tending to produce sleep; hypnotic. **— som′ni•fa′cient** *n.*

som•nif•er•ous (sŏm-nĭf′ər-əs) also **som•nif•ic** (-nĭf′ĭk) *adj.* Inducing sleep; soporific. **— som•nif′er•ous•ly** *adv.*

som•nil•o•quy (sŏm-nĭl′ə-kwē) *n., pl.* **-quies.** The act or habit of talking in one's sleep. [SOMNI- + Lat. *loquī*, to speak; see SOLILOQUY.] **— som•nil′o•quist** *n.*

som•no•lent (sŏm′nə-lənt) *adj.* **1.** Drowsy; sleepy. **2.** Inducing or tending to induce sleep; soporific. [ME *sompnolent* < OFr. < Lat. *somnolentus* : *somnus*, sleep; see **swep-*** + *-olentus*, abounding in.] **— som′no•lence** *n.* **— som′no•lent•ly** *adv.*

So•mo•za De•bay•le (sə-mō′zə də-bī′lā, sô-mô′sä thĕ-vī′lĕ), **Anastasio.** 1925–80. Nicaraguan president (1963–79) who was overthrown by the Sandinista National Liberation Front and later assassinated.

son (sŭn) *n.* **1.** One's male child. **2.** A male descendant. **3.** A man considered as if in a relationship of child to parent: *a son of the soil.* **4.** One personified or regarded as a male descendant. **5.** Used as a familiar form of address for a young man. **6. Son.** The second person of the Trinity. [ME < OE *sunu.* See **seuə-¹***.] **— son′ly** *adj.*

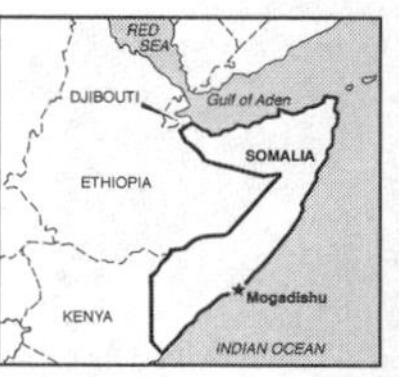

Somalia

sombrero

ă pat	oi boy
ā pay	ou out
âr care	o͝o took
ä father	o͞o boot
ĕ pet	ŭ cut
ē be	ûr urge
ĭ pit	th thin
ī pie	*th* this
îr pier	hw which
ŏ pot	zh vision
ō toe	ə about, item
ô paw	

Stress marks:
′ (primary);
′ (secondary), as in
dictionary (dĭk′shə-nĕr′ē)

so•nance (sō′nəns) *n.* Sound.
so•nant (sō′nənt) *adj. Ling.* Voiced, as a speech sound. —*n.* **1.** A voiced speech sound. **2.** A syllabic consonant in Indo-European. [Lat. *sonāns, sonant-,* pr.part. of *sonāre,* to sound. See **swen-*.**]
so•nar (sō′när′) *n.* **1.** A system using transmitted and reflected underwater sound waves to detect and locate submerged objects or measure the distance to the floor of a body of water. **2.** An apparatus, as one in a submarine, using sonar. **3.** Echolocation. [*so(und) na(vigation and) r(anging).*]
so•na•ta (sə-nä′tə) *n. Mus.* A composition for one to four instruments, one of which is usu. a keyboard instrument, typically consisting of three or four independent movements varying in key, mood, and tempo. [Ital. < fem. p.part. of *sonare,* to sound < Lat. *sonāre.* See **swen-*.**]
sonata form *n. Mus.* A form having three sections, the exposition, development, and recapitulation, often with a coda.
son•a•ti•na (sŏn′ə-tē′nə) *n. Mus.* A sonata having shorter movements than the typical sonata. [Ital., dim. of *sonata,* sonata. See SONATA.]
Sond•heim (sŏnd′hīm′), **Stephen.** b. 1930. Amer. composer and lyricist whose musicals include *Gypsy* (1959).
sone (sōn) *n.* A subjective unit of loudness, equal to the loudness of a pure tone having a frequency of 1,000 hertz at 40 decibels as perceived by a person with normal hearing. [Lat. *sonus,* a sound. See **swen-*.**]
son et lu•mière (sôn′ ā lüm-yâr′) *n.* A historical theatrical entertainment using recorded sound, lighting, and other effects and presented at night in a historic, usu. outdoor setting. [Fr. : *son,* sound + *et,* and + *lumière,* light.]
song (sông, sŏng) *n.* **1.** *Mus.* **a.** A brief composition written or adapted for singing. **b.** The act or art of singing. **2.** A distinctive or characteristic sound made by an animal, such as a bird or an insect. **3.a.** Poetry; verse. **b.** A lyric poem or ballad. —***idiom.*** **for a song.** *Informal.* At a low price. [ME < OE *sang.* See **seng^{wh}-*.**]
Song also **Sung** (sŏŏng). A Chinese dynasty (960–1279) marked by cultural advance and prosperity.
song and dance *n., pl.* **song and dances** or **songs and dances. 1.** A theatrical performance that combines singing and dancing. **2.** *Slang.* An excessively elaborate story or explanation, sometimes intended to deceive or mislead.
song•bird (sông′bûrd′, sŏng′-) *n.* A bird, esp. of the suborder Oscines of passerines, with a melodious song or call.
Song Da (sông′ dä′). See **Black River** 1.
song•fest (sông′fĕst′, sŏng′-) *n.* A casual group sing.
song•ful (sông′fəl, sŏng′-) *adj.* Melodious; tuneful. —**song′ful•ly** *adv.* —**song′ful•ness** *n.*
Song•hai also **Song•hay** (sông′hī′, sŏng-gī′). An ancient empire of W Africa in present-day Mali; founded c. 700 by Berbers and at the height of its power around 1500.
Song Hong (sông′ hông′). See **Red River** 1.
Song•hua (sŏŏng′hwä′) also **Sun•ga•ri** (sŏŏng′gə-rē′). A river of NE China rising near the North Korean border and flowing c. 1,850 km (1,150 mi) to the Amur R.
Song of Solomon (sông, sŏng) *n.* See table at **Bible.**
Song of Songs (sôngz, sŏngz) *n.* See table at **Bible.**
song•smith (sông′smĭth′, sŏng′-) *n. Mus.* See **songwriter.**
song sparrow *n.* A common North American sparrow *(Melospiza melodia)* having streaked brownish plumage and noted for its melodious song.
song•ster (sông′stər, sŏng′-) *n.* **1.** *Mus.* **a.** One who sings. **b.** See **songwriter. 2.** A songbird.
song•stress (sông′strĭs, sŏng′-) *n. Mus.* **1.** A woman who performs songs. **2.** A woman who writes songs.
song thrush *n.* An Old World songbird *(Turdus philomelos)* having brown upper plumage and a spotted breast.
song•writ•er (sông′rī′tər, sŏng′-) *n. Mus.* One who writes lyrics or tunes, or both, for songs.
son•ic (sŏn′ĭk) *adj.* **1.** Of or relating to audible sound. **2.** Having a speed approaching or being that of sound in air, about 1,220 kilometers (760 miles) per hour at sea level. **3.** *Slang.* Extremely exciting and fast-paced. [< Lat. *sonus,* a sound. See **swen-*.**] —**son′ic•al•ly** *adv.*
sonic barrier *n.* The sudden sharp increase in aerodynamic drag experienced by aircraft approaching the speed of sound.
sonic boom *n.* An explosive sound due to the shock wave radiating from aircraft traveling at or above the speed of sound.
son-in-law (sŭn′ĭn-lô′) *n., pl.* **sons-in-law** (sŭnz′-). The husband of one's daughter.
son•net (sŏn′ĭt) *n.* **1.** A 14-line verse form usu. having one of several conventional rhyme schemes. **2.** A poem in this form. [Fr. or Ital. *sonetto* (Fr. < Ital.) < OProv. *sonet,* dim. of *son,* song < Lat. *sonus,* a sound. See **swen-*.**]
son•net•eer (sŏn′ĭ-tîr′) *n.* **1.** A composer of sonnets. **2.** An inferior poet.
son•ny (sŭn′ē) *n., pl.* **-nies.** Used as a familiar form of address for a boy or young man. [Dim. of SON.]
sono– *pref.* Sound: *sonobuoy.* [< Lat. *sonus,* sound. See SONIC.]
so•no•buoy (sŏn′ə-bōō′ē, -boi′) *n.* A buoy equipped with an acoustic receiver and a radio transmitter that emits radio signals when it detects underwater sounds.
son of a bitch *Vulgar.* —*n., pl.* **sons of bitches.** A person regarded as thoroughly mean or disagreeable. —*interj.* Used in annoyance, disgust, disappointment, or amazement.
son of a gun *Informal.* —*n., pl.* **sons of guns.** A person; a fellow. —*interj.* Used to express annoyance, disappointment, or surprise.
Son of God *n.* Jesus.
Son of Man *n.* Jesus.
son•o•gram (sŏn′ə-grăm′, sō′nə-) *n.* An image, as of an unborn fetus, produced by ultrasonography.
So•no•ma (sə-nō′mə). A district of W CA N of San Francisco; famous for its numerous vineyards.
so•no•rant (sə-nôr′ənt, -nōr′-, sŏn′ər-) *n. Ling.* A voiced consonant regarded as a syllabic sound, as the last sound in the word *sudden.* [SONOR(OUS) + –ANT.]
so•nor•i•ty (sə-nôr′ĭ-tē, -nŏr′-) *n., pl.* **-ties. 1.** The quality or state of being sonorous; resonance. **2.** A sound.
so•no•rous (sə-nôr′əs, -nōr′-, sŏn′ər-) *adj.* **1.** Having or producing sound. **2.** Having or producing a full, deep, or rich sound. **3.** Impressive in style of speech: *a sonorous oration.* [< Lat. *sonōrus* < *sonor,* sound < *sonāre,* to sound. See **swen-*.**] —**so•no′rous•ly** *adv.* —**so•no′rous•ness** *n.*
sons-in-law (sŭnz′ĭn-lô′) *n.* Pl. of **son-in-law.**
Son•tag (sŏn′tăg′), **Susan.** b. 1933. Amer. writer noted esp. for her essays in *Against Interpretation* (1966).
Soo Canals (sōō). See **Sault Sainte Marie Canals.**
Soo•chow (sōō′chou′, -jō′). See **Suzhou.**
soon (sōōn) *adv.* **soon•er, soon•est. 1.** In the near future; shortly. **2.** Without hesitation; promptly: *as soon as possible.* **3.** Before the usual or appointed time; early. **4.** With willingness; readily: *I'd as soon leave right now.* **5.** *Obsolete.* Immediately. —***idioms.*** **no sooner than.** As soon as. **sooner or later.** At some time; eventually. [ME *sone* < OE *sōna,* immediately.]

Usage Note: *No sooner* as a comparative adverb should be followed by *than* not *when,* as in this example: *No sooner had she come than the maid knocked.*

soon•er (sōō′nər) *n. Slang.* **1.** A person who settled homestead land in the western United States before it was officially made available, in order to have first choice of location. **2. Sooner.** A native or resident of Oklahoma. [< SOON.]
soot (sŏŏt, sōōt) *n.* The fine black particles, chiefly composed of carbon, produced by incomplete combustion of coal, oil, wood, or other fuels. [ME < OE *sōt.* See **sed-*.**] —**soot** *v.*
sooth (sōōth) *Archaic.* —*adj.* **1.** Real; true. **2.** Soft; smooth. —*n.* Truth; reality. [ME < OE *sōth.* See **es-*.**]
soothe (sōōth) *v.* **soothed, sooth•ing, soothes.** —*tr.* **1.** To calm or placate. **2.** To ease or relieve (pain, for example). —*intr.* To bring comfort, composure, or relief. [ME *sothen,* to verify < OE *sōthian* < *sōth,* true. See **es-*.**] —**sooth′er** *n.*
sooth•fast (sōōth′făst′) *adj. Archaic.* **1.** Truthful; honest. **2.** True; real. [ME *sothfast* < OE *sōthfæst* : *sōth,* truth; see SOOTH + *fæst,* fixed, fast; see FAST[1].]
sooth•ing (sōō′thĭng) *adj.* Tending to soothe. —**sooth′ing•ly** *adv.* —**sooth′ing•ness** *n.*
sooth•say (sōōth′sā′) *intr.v.* **-said** (-sĕd′), **-say•ing, -says** (-sĕz′). To foretell future events; predict.
sooth•say•er (sōōth′sā′ər) *n.* One who claims to be able to foretell events or predict the future; a seer.
sooth•say•ing (sōōth′sā′ĭng) *n.* **1.** The art or practice of foretelling events. **2.** A prediction; a prophecy.
soot•y (sŏŏt′ē, sōō′tē) *adj.* **-i•er, -i•est. 1.** Covered with or as if with soot. **2.** Of or producing soot. —**soot′i•ness** *n.*
sooty mold *n.* **1.** A blackish growth produced by fungi of the genus *Capnodium,* which grows in the droppings of aphids on plants. **2.** Any of the fungi that produce such growth.
sooty tern *n.* A tern *(Sterna fuscata)* found along most tropical coasts, having black plumage above and white below.
sop (sŏp) *v.* **sopped, sop•ping, sops.** —*tr.* **1.** To dip, soak, or drench in a liquid; saturate. **2.** To take up by absorption: *sop up water.* —*intr.* To be or become thoroughly soaked or saturated. —*n.* **1.** A piece of food soaked or dipped in a liquid. **2.a.** Something yielded to placate or soothe. **b.** A bribe. [< ME *soppe,* bread dipped in liquid < OE *sopp-,* in *soppcuppe,* cup for dipping bread in. See **seuə-[2]*.**]
SOP *abbr.* Standard operating procedure.
sop. *abbr. Mus.* Soprano.
soph. *abbr.* Sophomore.
soph•ism (sŏf′ĭz′əm) *n.* **1.** A plausible but fallacious argument. **2.** Deceptive or fallacious argumentation. [ME *sophime, sophisme* < OFr. *sophime* < Lat. *sophisma* < Gk. < *sophizesthai,* to be subtle < *sophos,* clever, wise.]
soph•ist (sŏf′ĭst) *n.* **1.a.** One skilled in elaborate and devious argumentation. **b.** A scholar or thinker. **2. Sophist.** A professional philosopher and teacher, esp. one belonging to a group of fifth-century B.C. Greek philosophers who specialized in dialectic, argumentation, and rhetoric. [ME *sophiste* < Lat. *sophista* < Gk. *sophistēs* < *sophizesthai,* to become wise < *sophos,* clever.]
so•phis•tic (sə-fĭs′tĭk) or **so•phis•ti•cal** (-tĭ-kəl) *adj.* **1.** Of, relating to, or characteristic of sophists. **2.** Apparently sound but really fallacious; specious. —**so•phis′ti•cal•ly** *adv.*

so•phis•ti•cate (sə-fĭs′tĭ-kāt′) *v.* **-cat•ed, -cat•ing, -cates.** —*tr.* **1.** To cause to become less natural, esp. to make less naive and more worldly. **2.** To make impure; adulterate. **3.** To make more complex or inclusive; refine. —*intr.* To use sophistry. —*n.* (-kĭt). A sophisticated person. [ME *sophisticaten*, to adulterate < Med.Lat. *sophisticāre, sophisticāt-* < Lat. *sophisticus*, sophistic < Gk. *sophistikos* < *sophistēs*, sophist. See SOPHIST.] —**so•phis′ti•ca′tion** *n.* —**so•phis′ti•ca′tor** *n.*

so•phis•ti•cat•ed (sə-fĭs′tĭ-kā′tĭd) *adj.* **1.** Having acquired worldly knowledge or refinement; lacking natural simplicity or naiveté. **2.** Very complex or complicated. **3.** Suitable for or appealing to the tastes of sophisticates.

soph•is•try (sŏf′ĭ-strē) *n., pl.* **-tries. 1.** Plausible but fallacious argumentation. **2.** A plausible but misleading or fallacious argument.

Soph•o•cles (sŏf′ə-klēz′). 496?–406 B.C. Greek dramatist whose plays include *Oedipus Rex.* —**Soph′o•cle′an** *adj.*

soph•o•more (sŏf′ə-môr′, -mōr′, sŏf′môr′, -mōr′) *n.* **1.a.** A second-year student in a U.S. college. **b.** A tenth-grade student in a U.S. high school. **2.** A person in the second year of carrying out an endeavor. [Alteration (prob. influenced by Gk. *sophos*, wise and *mōros*, dull) of *sophumer* < obsolete *sophom*, sophism, dialectic exercise, var. of SOPHISM.]

soph•o•mor•ic (sŏf′ə-môr′ĭk, -mōr′-, -mŏr′-) *adj.* **1.** Of or characteristic of a sophomore. **2.** Exhibiting great immaturity and lack of judgment. —**soph′o•mor′i•cal•ly** *adv.*

so•por (sō′pər, -pôr′) *n.* A deep, lethargic, or unnatural sleep. [Lat. See **swep-***.]

sop•o•rif•er•ous (sŏp′ə-rĭf′ər-əs, sō′pə-) *adj.* Inducing or tending to induce sleep; soporific. —**sop′o•rif′er•ous•ly** *adv.* —**sop′o•rif′er•ous•ness** *n.*

sop•o•rif•ic (sŏp′ə-rĭf′ĭk, sō′pə-) *adj.* **1.** Inducing or tending to induce sleep. **2.** Drowsy. —*n.* A drug or other substance that induces sleep; a hypnotic.

sop•ping (sŏp′ĭng) *adj.* Thoroughly soaked; drenched. —*adv.* Extremely; very: *sopping wet.*

sop•py (sŏp′ē) *adj.* **-pi•er, -pi•est. 1.** Soaked; sopping. **2.** Rainy. **3.** Sentimental; maudlin.

so•pra•ni•no (sō′prə-nē′nō, sŏp′rə-) *n., pl.* **-nos.** *Mus.* An instrument, such as a recorder, that is higher in pitch than the soprano of its family. [Ital., dim. of *soprano*, soprano. See SOPRANO.]

so•pran•o (sə-prăn′ō, -prä′nō) *n., pl.* **-os.** *Mus.* **1.** The highest singing voice of a woman or young boy. **2.** A singer having such a voice. **3.** A part written in the range of such a voice. **4.** The tonal range characteristic of a soprano. **5.** An instrument with this range. [Ital. < *sopra*, above < Lat. *suprā*. See **uper***.]

soprano clef *n. Mus.* The C clef positioned to indicate that the bottom line of a staff represents the pitch of middle C.

so•ra (sôr′ə, sōr′ə) *n.* A North American rail *(Porzana carolina)* having grayish-brown plumage and a short stout bill, commonly found in freshwater bogs or swamps. [?]

sorb[1] (sôrb) *tr.v.* **sorbed, sorb•ing, sorbs.** To take up and hold, as by absorption or adsorption. —**sorb′a•bil′i•ty** *n.* —**sorb′a•ble** *adj.* —**sorb′ent** *adj. & n.*

sorb[2] (sôrb) *n.* **1.** Any of several Old World trees of the genus *Sorbus* in the rose family, as the service tree or the rowan. **2.** The fruit of any of these plants. [Fr. *sorbe*, sorb fruit < OFr. *sourbe* < VLat. **sorba* < Lat. *sorbum.*]

Sorb (sôrb) *n.* See **Wend.** [Ger. *Sorbe*, perh. var. of *Serbe*, Serb < Serbian *Serb.*]

sor•bet (sôr′bĭt, sôr-bā′) *n.* A frozen dessert similar to a frappé, usu. made from fruit juice and mushy in consistency. [Fr. < Ottoman Turk. *sherbet*, sweet fruit drink. See SHERBET.]

Sor•bi•an (sôr′bē-ən) *n.* **1.** See **Wend. 2.** See **Wendish.**

sor•bic acid (sôr′bĭk) *n.* A white crystalline solid, $C_6H_8O_2$, found in the berries of the mountain ash and also synthesized, used as a food preservative and fungicide. [< SORB[2].]

sor•bi•tol (sôr′bĭ-tôl′, -tōl′, -tŏl′) *n.* A white sweetish crystalline alcohol, $C_6H_8(OH)_6$, found in various berries and fruits or prepared synthetically and used as a flavoring agent, a sugar substitute for people with diabetes, and a moisturizer in cosmetics and other products. [SORB[2] + -IT(E)[2] + -OL[1].]

sor•cer•er (sôr′sər-ər) *n.* One who practices sorcery; a wizard. [ME *sorser, sorcerer* < OFr. *sorcier* < VLat. **sortiārius* < Lat. *sors, sort-*, lot, fortune. See **ser-**[2]*.]

sor•cer•ess (sôr′sər-ĭs) *n.* A woman who practices sorcery.

sor•cer•y (sôr′sə-rē) *n.* Use of supernatural power over others through the assistance of spirits; witchcraft. [ME *sorcerie* < OFr. < *sorcier*, sorcerer. See SORCERER.] —**sor′cer•ous** *adj.* —**sor′cer•ous•ly** *adv.*

sor•did (sôr′dĭd) *adj.* **1.** Filthy or dirty; foul. **2.** Depressingly squalid; wretched. **3.** Morally degraded. **4.** Exceedingly mercenary; grasping. [ME *sordide*, festering, purulent < Lat. *sordidus*, dirty < *sordēre*, to be dirty.] —**sor′did•ly** *adv.* —**sor′did•ness** *n.*

sor•di•no (sôr-dē′nō) *n., pl.* **-ni** (-nē). *Mus.* A mute for an instrument. [Ital. < *sordo*, deaf, mute < Lat. *surdus.*]

sore (sôr, sōr) *adj.* **sor•er, sor•est. 1.** Painful to the touch; tender. **2.** Feeling physical pain; hurting. **3.** Causing misery, sorrow, or distress; grievous: *in sore need.* **4.** Causing embarrassment or irritation: *a sore subject.* **5.** Full of distress; sorrowful. **6.** *Informal.* Angry; offended. —*n.* **1.** An open skin lesion, wound, or ulcer. **2.** A source of pain, distress, or irritation. —*tr.v.* **sored, sor•ing, sores.** To mutilate the legs or feet of (a horse) to induce a particular gait in the animal. —*adv. Archaic.* Sorely. [ME < OE *sār.*] —**sore′ness** *n.*

sore•head (sôr′hĕd′, sōr′-) *n. Slang.* One who is easily offended, annoyed, or angered.

So•rel (sə-rĕl′, sô-). A city of S Quebec, Canada, at the confluence of the St. Lawrence and Richelieu rivers; founded 1672. Pop. 20,347.

So•rel (sô-rĕl′), **Georges.** 1847–1922. French political philosopher whose works include *Reflections on Violence* (1906).

sore•ly (sôr′lē, sōr′-) *adv.* **1.** Painfully; grievously. **2.** Extremely; greatly: *Their skills were sorely needed.*

sore throat *n.* Any of various inflammations of the tonsils, pharynx, or larynx characterized by pain in swallowing.

sor•ghum (sôr′gəm) *n.* **1.** An Old World grass *(Sorghum bicolor),* several varieties of which are widely cultivated as grain and forage or as a source of syrup. **2.** Syrup made from the juice of this plant. [NLat. *Sorghum*, genus name < Ital. *sorgo*, a tall cereal grass, prob. < Med.Lat. *surgum*, perh. var. of VLat. **syricum* < neut. of Lat. *Syricus*, Syrian < SYRIA.]

sor•go also **sor•gho** (sôr′gō) *n., pl.* **-gos** also **-ghos.** Any of various sorghums that are cultivated as a source of syrup. [Ital. See SORGHUM.]

so•ri (sôr′ī, sōr′ī) *n.* Pl. of **sorus.**

so•ri•tes (sə-rī′tēz, sô-) *n., pl.* **sorites.** *Logic.* A form of argument in which a series of incomplete syllogisms is so arranged that the predicate of each premise forms the subject of the next until the subject of the first is joined with the predicate of the last in the conclusion. [Lat. *sōrītēs* < Gk. *sōreitēs* < *sōros*, heap. See **teuə-***.]

Sophocles

So•ro•ca•ba (sôr′o͝o-kä′bä). A city of S Brazil W of São Paulo. Pop. 254,672.

so•ro•ral (sə-rôr′əl, -rōr′-) *adj.* Of, relating to, or resembling a sister; sisterly. [< Lat. *soror*, sister. See **swesor-***.]

so•ror•ate (sə-rôr′ĭt, -rōr′-) *n.* The custom of marriage of a man to his wife's sister or sisters, usu. after the wife has died or proved sterile. [< Lat. *soror*, sister. See SORORAL.]

so•ror•i•cide (sə-rôr′ĭ-sīd′, -rŏr′-) *n.* **1.** The killing of one's sister. **2.** One who kills one's own sister. [Lat. *soror*, sister; see SORORITY + -CIDE.] —**so•ror′i•cid′al** (-sīd′l) *adj.*

so•ror•i•ty (sə-rôr′ĭ-tē, -rŏr′-) *n., pl.* **-ties. 1.** A chiefly social organization of women students at a college or university. **2.** An association or a society of women. [Med.Lat. *sorōritās* < Lat. *soror, sorōr-*, sister. See **swesor-***.]

sorp•tion (sôrp′shən) *n.* **1.** The process of sorbing. **2.** The state of being sorbed. —**sorp′tive** *adj.*

sor•rel[1] (sôr′əl, sŏr′-) *n.* **1.** Any of several plants of the genus *Rumex*, having acid-flavored leaves sometimes used as salad greens, esp. *R. acetosella*, a widely naturalized Eurasian species. **2.** Any of various plants of the genus *Oxalis*, having usu. compound leaves with three leaflets. [ME *sorel* < OFr. *surele* < *sur*, sour, of Gmc. orig.]

sor•rel[2] (sôr′əl, sŏr′-) *n.* **1.** *Color.* A brownish orange to light brown. **2.** A sorrel-colored horse or other animal. [< ME *sorel*, sorrel-colored < OFr. < *sor*, red-brown, of Gmc. orig.]

sorrel tree *n.* See **sourwood.**

Sor•ren•to (sə-rĕn′tō, sôr-rĕn′tô). A resort town of S Italy on the **Sorrento Peninsula,** separating the Bay of Naples from the Gulf of Salerno. Pop. 17,301.

sorrel[1]
Yellow oxalis
Oxalis europaea

sor•row (sŏr′ō, sôr′ō) *n.* **1.** Mental suffering or pain caused by injury, loss, or despair. See Syns at **regret. 2.** A source or cause of sorrow; a misfortune. **3.** Expression of sorrow; grieving. —*intr.v.* **-rowed, -row•ing, -rows.** To feel or express sorrow; grieve. See Syns at **grieve.** [ME *sorwe* < OE *sorg.*] —**sor′row•er** *n.*

sor•row•ful (sŏr′ō-fəl, -ə-fəl, sôr′-) *adj.* Affected with, marked by, causing, or expressing sorrow. See Syns at **sad.** —**sor′row•ful•ly** *adv.* —**sor′row•ful•ness** *n.*

sor•ry (sŏr′ē, sôr′ē) *adj.* **-ri•er, -ri•est. 1.** Feeling or expressing sympathy, pity, or regret. **2.** Worthless or inferior; paltry: *a sorry excuse.* **3.** Causing sorrow, grief, or misfortune; grievous: *a sorry development.* [ME *sori* < OE *sārig*, sad < *sār*, sore.] —**sor′ri•ly** *adv.* —**sor′ri•ness** *n.*

sort (sôrt) *n.* **1.** A group of persons or things of the same general character; a kind. See Usage Note at **kind**[2]. **2.** Character or nature: *books of all sorts.* **3.** One that typifies a group or exemplifies a characteristic: *The clerk is a decent sort.* **4.** A way of acting or behaving. **5.** *Print.* One of the characters in a font of type. Often used in the plural. —*tr.v.* **sort•ed, sort•ing, sorts. 1.** To arrange according to class, kind, or size; classify. See Syns at **arrange. 2.** To separate from others: *sort out the wheat from the chaff.* **3.** To clarify by going over mentally: *sorting out her problems.* —*idioms.* **after a sort.** In a haphazard or imperfect way. **of sorts (or of a sort). 1.** Of a mediocre or inferior kind. **2.** Of one kind or another. **out of sorts. 1.** Slightly ill. **2.** Irritable; cross. **sort of.** *Informal.* Somewhat; rather. [ME < OFr. < Lat. *sors, sort-*, lot. See **ser-**[2]*.] —**sort′a•ble** *adj.* —**sort′er** *n.*

sor•tie (sôr′tē, sôr-tē′) *n.* **1.a.** An armed attack made from a

ă pat	oi boy
ā pay	ou out
âr care	o͝o took
ä father	o͞o boot
ĕ pet	ŭ cut
ē be	ûr urge
ĭ pit	th thin
ī pie	*th* this
îr pier	hw which
ŏ pot	zh vision
ō toe	ə about,
ô paw	item

Stress marks:
′ (primary);
′ (secondary), as in
dictionary (dĭk′shə-nĕr′ē)

place surrounded by enemy forces. **b.** The troops making such an attack. **2.** A flight of a combat aircraft on a mission. — *intr.v.* **-tied, -tie•ing, -ties.** To go on a sortie. [Fr. < fem. p.part. of *sortir*, to go out < OFr.]

sor•ti•lege (sôr′tl-ĭj) *n.* **1.** The act or practice of foretelling the future by drawing lots. **2.** Sorcery; witchcraft. [ME < OFr. < Med.Lat. *sortilegium* < *sortilegus*, diviner : Lat. *sors, sort-*, lot; see **ser-²*** + Lat. *legere*, to read; see **leg-***.]

so•rus (sôr′əs, sōr′-) *n., pl.* **so•ri** (sôr′ī, sōr′ī). **1.** A cluster of sporangia borne on the underside of a fern frond. **2.** A reproductive structure in certain fungi and lichens. [NLat. *sōrus* < Gk. *sōros*, heap. See **teuə-***.]

S O S (ĕs′ō-ĕs′) *n.* **1.** The letters represented by the Morse signal · · · — — — · · ·, used as an international distress signal, esp. by ships and aircraft. **2.** A call or signal for help.

So•sno•wiec (sŏs-nô′vyĕts). A city of S Poland, a suburb of Katowice. Pop. 255,000.

so-so (sō′sō′) *adj.* Neither very good nor very bad; passable. — *adv.* Neither very well nor very poorly; passably.

so•ste•nu•to (sō′stə-no͞o′tō, sô′-) *Mus.* — *adv. & adj.* Beyond or being sustained beyond a note's full value. — *n., pl.* **-tos** or **-ti** (-tē). A sostenuto passage or movement. [Ital., p.part. of *sostenere*, to sustain < Lat. *sustinēre*. See SUSTAIN.]

sot (sŏt) *n.* A drunkard. [ME, fool < OE *sott* < OFr. *sot.*]

so•te•ri•ol•o•gy (sō-tîr′ē-ŏl′ə-jē) *n.* The theological doctrine of salvation as effected by Jesus. [Gk. *sōtērion*, deliverance (< *sōtēr*, savior < *saos, sōs*, safe; see **teuə-***) + -LOGY.] — **so•te′ri•o•log′ic** (-ə-lŏj′ĭk), **so•te′ri•o•log′i•cal** (-ĭ-kəl) *adj.*

So•thic (sō′thĭk, sŏth′ĭk) *adj.* **1.** Of, relating to, or deriving from the name of Sothis. **2.** Being the ancient Egyptian calendar year, consisting of 365¼ days. **3.** Being a cycle consisting of 1,460 years of 365 days in the ancient Egyptian calendar. [< Gk. *Sōthis*, the star Sirius. See SOTHIS.]

So•this (sō′thĭs) *n.* See **Sirius.** [Gk. *Sōthis* < Egypt. *spdt.*]

So•tho (sō′tō) *n.* **1.** A group of Bantu languages that are closely related, including Tswana, spoken in southern Africa. **2.** Any of these languages.

so•tol (sō′tōl′) *n.* **1.** Any of several tall woody plants of the genus *Dasylirion* of southwest North America having prickly leaves and whitish flowers. **2.** An alcoholic beverage produced from the trunks of these plants. [Perh. < Sp. *soto*, thicket, woods < Lat. *saltus*, narrow pass, woodland.]

sot•ted (sŏt′ĭd) *adj.* Muddled or stupefied, esp. with liquor; besotted. — **sot′ted•ly** *adv.* — **sot′ted•ness** *n.*

sot•tish (sŏt′ĭsh) *adj.* **1.** Stupefied from or as if from drink. **2.** Tending to drink excessively; drunken. — **sot′tish•ly** *adv.* — **sot′tish•ness** *n.*

sot•to vo•ce (sŏt′ō vō′chē, sôt′tô vô′chĕ) *adv. & adj.* **1.** In soft tones, so as not to be overheard; in an undertone. **2.** *Mus.* In very soft tones. [Ital. : *sotto*, under + *voce*, voice.]

sou (so͞o) *n.* One of several coins formerly used in France, worth a small amount. [Fr. < OFr. *sol* < LLat. *solidus*, solidus. See SOLIDUS.]

sou. or **Sou.** *abbr.* South; southern.

sou•a•ri nut (so͞o-är′ē) *n.* **1.** A South American evergreen tree *(Caryocar nuciferum)* having drupes with nutlike stones containing seeds used as food and a source of cooking oil. **2.** The nut of this tree. [Fr. *saouari* < Galibi *sawarra.*]

sou•bise (so͞o-bēz′) *n.* A sauce of onions or onion purée. [Fr., after Charles de Rohan, Prince de *Soubise* (1715–87).]

sou•brette (so͞o-brĕt′) *n.* **1.a.** A saucy coquettish maidservant in comedies or comic opera. **b.** An actress or a singer taking such a part. **2.** A young woman regarded as flirtatious or frivolous. [Fr. < Prov. *soubreto*, fem. of *soubret*, conceited < *soubra*, to leave aside < OProv. *sobrar*, to be excessive < Lat. *superāre* < *super*, above. See **uper***.]

sou•bri•quet (so͞o′brĭ-kā′, -kĕt′, so͞o′brĭ-kā′, -kĕt′) *n.* Var. of **sobriquet.**

sou•chong (so͞o′chŏng′, -shŏng′) *n.* Any of several varieties of black tea native to China and adjacent regions. [Chin. (Mandarin) *xiăo zhŏng* : *xiăo*, small + *zhŏng*, kind.]

sou•dan (so͞od′n) *n.* Var. of **soldan.**

souf•flé (so͞o-flā′) *n.* A light fluffy baked dish made with egg yolks and beaten egg whites combined with various other ingredients. [Fr. < p.part. of *souffler*, to puff up < OFr. *soffler* < Lat. *sufflāre* : *sub–*, sub- + *flāre*, to blow; see **bhlē-***.] — **souf•flé′** *adj.* — **souf•fléd′** *adj.*

sough (sŭf, sou) *intr.v.* **soughed, sough•ing, soughs.** To make a soft murmuring or rustling sound. — *n.* A soft murmuring or rustling sound. [ME *swowen, soughen* < OE *swōgan.*]

sought (sôt) *v.* P.t. and p.part. of **seek.**

souk (so͞ok, sho͝ok) *n.* An open-air market or a part of such a market in an Arab city. [Ar. *sūq.*]

soul (sōl) *n.* **1.** The animating and vital principle in human beings, credited with the faculties of thought, action, and emotion and often conceived as an immaterial entity. **2.** The spiritual nature of human beings, regarded as immortal, separable from the body at death, and susceptible to happiness or misery in a future state. **3.** The disembodied spirit of a dead human being; a shade. **4.** A human being. **5.** The central or integral part; the vital core. **6.** A person considered as the perfect embodiment of an intangible quality; a personification: *I am the very soul of discretion.* **7.** A person's emotional or moral nature. **8.** A sense of ethnic pride among Black people, esp. African-Americans, as expressed in culture, esp. music. **9.** A strong, deeply felt emotion conveyed by a speaker, a performer, or an artist. **10.** Soul music. [ME < OE *sāwol.*]

soul brother *n. Slang.* A fellow Black man.

soul food *n.* Food, such as ham hocks and collard greens, traditionally eaten by southern American Black people.

soul•ful (sōl′fəl) *adj.* Full of or expressing deep feeling; profoundly emotional. — **soul′ful•ly** *adv.* — **soul′ful•ness** *n.*

soul kiss *n.* A kiss in which the tongue enters the partner's mouth; a French kiss.

soul•less (sōl′lĭs) *adj.* Lacking sensitivity or the capacity for deep feeling. — **soul′less•ly** *adv.* — **soul′less•ness** *n.*

soul mate *n.* One of two persons compatible with each other in disposition, point of view, or sensitivity.

soul music *n. Mus.* Popular music developed by American Black people, based on gospel music and rhythm and blues.

soul-search•ing (sōl′sûr′chĭng) *n.* A penetrating examination of one's motives, convictions, and attitudes.

soul sister *n. Slang.* A fellow Black woman.

sound¹ (sound) *n.* **1.a.** Vibrations transmitted through an elastic material, either solid, liquid, or gas, with frequencies from approx. 20 to 20,000 hertz, capable of being detected by the human ear. **b.** Transmitted vibrations of any frequency including those outside the range of human hearing. **c.** The sensation stimulated in the organs of hearing by such vibrations in the air or other medium. **d.** Such sensations considered as a group. **2.** A distinctive noise **3.** The distance over which something can be heard. **4.** *Ling.* **a.** An articulation made by the vocal apparatus. **b.** The distinctive character of such an articulation: *The words* bear *and* bare *have the same sound.* **5.** A mental impression; an implication: *didn't like the sound of it.* **6.** Auditory material that is recorded, as for a movie. **7.** Meaningless noise. **8.** *Mus.* A distinctive style, as of an orchestra or a singer. **9.** *Archaic.* Rumor; report. — *v.* **sound•ed, sound•ing, sounds.** — *intr.* **1.a.** To make or give forth a sound. **b.** To be given forth as a sound. **2.** To present a particular impression: *That sounds reasonable.* — *tr.* **1.** To cause to give forth or produce a sound. **2.** To summon, announce, or signal by a sound. **3.** *Ling.* To articulate; pronounce. **4.** To make known; celebrate. **5.** To examine (a body organ or part) by causing to emit sound; auscultate. — ***phrasal verb.* sound off. 1.** To express one's views vigorously. **2.** To count cadence when marching in military formation. [ME *soun* < OFr. *son* < Lat. *sonus.* See **swen-***.]

sound² (sound) *adj.* **sound•er, sound•est. 1.** Free from defect, decay, or damage; in good condition. **2.** Free from disease or injury. See Syns at **healthy. 3.** Having a firm basis; unshakable. **4.** Financially secure or safe. **5.a.** Based on valid reasoning. See Syns at **valid. b.** Free from logical flaws. **6.** Thorough; complete: *a sound flogging.* **7.** Deep and unbroken; undisturbed. **8.** Free from moral defect; upright. **9.** Worthy of confidence; trustworthy. **10.** Marked by or showing common sense and good judgment; levelheaded. **11.** Compatible with an accepted point of view; conservative. **12.** *Law.* Legally valid. — *adv.* Thoroughly; deeply. [ME < OE *gesund.*] — **sound′ly** *adv.* — **sound′ness** *n.*

sound³ (sound) *n.* **1.** A long, relatively wide body of water, larger than a strait or a channel, connecting larger bodies of water. **2.** A long wide ocean inlet. **3.** The air bladder of a fish. [ME < OE *sund*, swimming, sea.]

sound⁴ (sound) *v.* **sound•ed, sound•ing, sounds.** — *tr.* **1.** To measure the depth of (water), esp. by means of a weighted line; fathom. **2.** To try to learn the attitudes or opinions of. **3.** To probe (a body cavity) with a sound. — *intr.* **1.** To measure depth. **2.** To dive swiftly downward. Used of a whale or fish. **3.** To look into a possibility; investigate. — *n.* An instrument used to examine or explore body cavities or dilate strictures in them. [ME *sounden* < OFr. *sonder* < *sonde*, sounding line, prob. of Gmc. orig.] — **sound′a•ble** *adj.*

sound-a•like (sound′ə-līk′) *n.* One that closely resembles another in sound, esp. by imitation.

sound barrier *n.* **1.** See **sonic barrier. 2.** A set of tall wooden, plastic, or concrete barriers placed along a road or highway to muffle the sound of traffic.

sound bite *n. Slang.* A very brief broadcast statement, as by a politician during a news report.

sound•board (sound′bôrd′, -bōrd′) *n. Mus.* See **sounding board** 1.

sound box *n. Mus.* A chamber in the body of an instrument, such as a cello, that intensifies the resonance of the tone.

sound effects *pl.n.* Imitative sounds, as of thunder or an explosion, produced artificially, as for a film.

sound•er¹ (soun′dər) *n.* One that makes a sound.

sound•er² (soun′dər) *n.* One that sounds, esp. a device for making soundings of the sea.

sound•er³ (soun′dər) *n.* A herd of wild boar. [ME < OFr. *sondre*, of Gmc. orig.]

sound•ing¹ (soun′dĭng) *n.* **1.** The act of one that sounds. **2.** A probe of the environment for scientific observation. **3.a.** A measured depth of water. **b.** Water shallow enough for depth measurements to be taken by a hand line. Often used in the plural.

sound•ing[2] (soun′dĭng) *adj.* **1.** Emitting a full sound; resonant. **2.** Noisy but with little significance.

sounding board *n.* **1.** *Mus.* **a.** A thin board forming the upper portion of the resonant chamber in an instrument, such as a piano, and serving to increase resonance. **b.** A structure placed behind or over a podium or platform to reflect music or a speaker's voice to an audience. **2.** A person or group whose reactions to an idea or a point of view serve as a measure of its effectiveness or acceptability. **3.** A device or means serving to spread or popularize an idea or a point of view.

sounding lead (lĕd) *n. Naut.* The metal weight at the end of a sounding line.

sounding line *n. Naut.* A line marked at intervals of fathoms and weighted at one end, used to determine water depth.

sounding rocket *n.* A rocket used to make observations anywhere within Earth's atmosphere.

sound•man (sound′măn′) *n.* One in charge of recording, transmitting, or amplifying sound or producing sound effects.

sound•proof (sound′pro͞of′) *adj.* Not penetrable by audible sound. **— sound′proof′** *v.*

sound stage also **sound•stage** (sound′stāj′) *n.* A usu. soundproof room or studio used in producing sound movies.

sound•track also **sound track** (sound′trăk′) *n.* **1.** The narrow strip at one side of a movie film that carries the sound recording. **2.a.** The music that accompanies a movie. **b.** A commercial recording of such music.

sound truck *n.* A truck or other vehicle having one or more loudspeakers used for broadcasting messages.

sound wave *n.* A longitudinal pressure wave of audible or inaudible sound.

soup (so͞op) *n.* **1.** A liquid food prepared from meat, fish, or vegetable stock and often containing solid ingredients. **2.** *Slang.* Something having the appearance or a consistency suggestive of soup, esp.: **a.** Dense fog. **b.** Nitroglycerine. **3.** A chaotic or unfortunate situation. ***— phrasal verb.* soup up.** *Slang.* To modify (something) so as to increase its capacity to perform or satisfy, esp. to add horsepower to (a vehicle). ***— idiom.* in the soup.** *Slang.* Having difficulties; in trouble. [ME *soupe* < OFr., of Gmc. orig. See **seuə-[2]*.**]

soup•çon (so͞op-sôN′, so͞op′sŏn′) *n.* A very small amount; a trace. [Fr. < OFr. *sospeçon*, suspicion < Lat. *suspectiō, suspectiōn-*, fear < *suspectus*, p.part. of *suspicere*, to suspect. See SUSPECT.]

soup du jour (so͞op′ də zho͝or′) *n., pl.* **soups du jour.** A soup featured by a restaurant on a given day. [Fr. *soupe du jour* : *soupe*, soup + *du*, of the + *jour*, day.]

soup kitchen *n.* A place where food is offered free or at very low cost to the needy.

soup•spoon (so͞op′spo͞on′) *n.* A spoon somewhat larger than a teaspoon, used for eating soup.

soup•y (so͞o′pē) *adj.* **-i•er, -i•est. 1.** Having the appearance or consistency of soup. **2.** *Slang.* Foggy: *soupy weather.* **3.** *Informal.* Sentimental.

sour (sour) *adj.* **sour•er, sour•est. 1.** Having a taste characteristic of that produced by acids; sharp, tart, or tangy. **2.** Made acid or rancid by fermentation. **3.** Having the characteristics of fermentation or rancidity; tasting or smelling of decay. **4.a.** Bad-tempered and morose; peevish: *a sour temper.* **b.** Displeased with something one formerly admired or liked; disenchanted. **5.** Not measuring up to the expected or usual ability or quality; bad. **6.** Of, relating to, or being excessively acid soil that is damaging to crops. **7.** Containing excessive sulfur compounds. Used of gasoline. *— n.* **1.** The sensation of sour taste, one of the four primary tastes. **2.** Something sour. **3.** A mixed drink made esp. with whiskey, lemon or lime juice, and sugar. *— tr. & intr.v.* **soured, sour•ing, sours. 1.** To make or become sour. **2.** To make or become disagreeable, disillusioned, or disenchanted. [ME < OE *sūr.*] **— sour′ish** *adj.* **— sour′ly** *adv.* **— sour′ness** *n.*

sour•ball (sour′bôl′) *n.* A round piece of hard tart candy.

source (sôrs, sōrs) *n.* **1.** The point at which something springs into being or from which it derives or is obtained. **2.** The point of origin, such as a spring, of a stream or river. See Syns at **origin. 3.** One that causes, creates, or initiates; a maker. **4.** One, such as a person or document, that supplies information. **5.** *Phys.* The point or part of a system where energy or mass is added to the system. *— v.* **sourced, sourc•ing, sourc•es.** *— tr.* **1.** To specify the origin of (a communication); document. **2.** To obtain (parts or materials) from another business, country, or locale for manufacture. *— intr.* To source parts or materials. [ME < OFr. *sourse* < fem. p.part. of *sourdre*, to rise < Lat. *surgere.* See SURGE.]

source book *n.* **1.** A primary document, as of history, literature, or religion, on which secondary writings are based. **2.** A collection of such documents.

source language *n.* The language from which a translation is to be made.

sour cherry *n.* **1.** A deciduous shrub or small tree *(Prunus cerasus)* having white flowers and tart red fruit. **2.** This fruit.

sour cream *n.* Cream that has been soured artificially or naturally by the action of lactic-acid bacteria, widely used in cooking and as a garnish.

sour•dine (so͝or-dēn′) *n. Mus.* **1.** An obsolete double-reed instrument with a soft tone. **2.** A mute, esp. one for a violin. [Fr. < Ital. *sordina*, fem. of *sordino*, a mute, dim. of *sordo*, deaf, mute < Lat. *surdus.*]

sour•dough (sour′dō′) *n.* **1.** Sour fermented dough used as leaven in making bread. **2.** An early settler or prospector, esp. in Alaska and northwest Canada.

sour grapes *pl.n.* Denial of the desirability of something after finding that it cannot be reached or acquired.

sour gum *n.* A deciduous tree *(Nyssa sylvatica)* of eastern North America having glossy, somewhat leathery leaves and soft wood.

Sou•ris (so͝or′ĭs). A river, c. 724 km (450 mi), rising in S Saskatchewan, Canada, and flowing SE in a great loop into N ND then NE to the Assiniboine R. in SW Manitoba.

sour mash *n.* **1.** A mixture of new mash and mash from a preceding run used to distill certain malt whiskeys. **2.** Whiskey so distilled.

sour orange *n.* A spiny evergreen tree *(Citrus aurantium)* native to southern Vietnam and widely cultivated in warmer regions, having globose, reddish-orange, highly acidic fruit.

sour•puss (sour′po͝os′) *n. Slang.* A habitually gloomy or sullen person. [SOUR + PUSS[2].]

sour salt *n.* Crystals of citric acid used in cooking.

sour•sop (sour′sŏp′) *n.* **1.** A tropical American evergreen tree *(Annona muricata)* bearing spiny fruit with tart edible pulp. **2.** The fruit of this tree.

sour•wood (sour′wo͝od′) *n.* A deciduous tree *(Oxydendrum arboreum)* of eastern North America having small white urn-shaped flowers. [So called < its sour-tasting leaves.]

sousaphone

Sou•sa (so͞o′zə, -sə), **John Philip.** "the March King." 1854–1932. Amer. composer of *Stars and Stripes Forever* (1897).

sou•sa•phone (so͞o′zə-fōn′, -sə-) *n. Mus.* A large brass wind instrument, similar in range to the tuba, having a flaring bell and a shape adapted to being carried in marching bands.

souse[1] (sous) *v.* **soused, sous•ing, sous•es.** *— tr.* **1.** To plunge into a liquid. **2.** To make soaking wet; drench. **3.** To steep in a mixture, as in pickling. **4.** *Slang.* To make intoxicated. *— intr.* To become immersed or soaking wet. *— n.* **1.** The act or process of sousing. **2.a.** Food steeped in pickle, esp. pork trimmings. **b.** The liquid used in pickling; brine. **3.** *Slang.* **a.** A drunkard. **b.** A period of heavy drinking; a binge. [ME *sousen*, prob. < OFr. **souser*, to pickle < *souz, sous*, pickled meat, of Gmc. orig. See **sal-*.**]

souse[2] (sous) *v.* **soused, sous•ing, sous•es.** *— tr.* To pounce on; attack. *— intr.* To swoop down, as an attacking hawk does. *— n. Obsolete.* A swooping motion of attack. [< ME *souse*, swooping motion, alteration of *sours*, source, a rising. See SOURCE.]

sous•lik (sŭs′lĭk) *n.* Var. of **suslik.**

Sousse (so͞os) also **Su•sah** or **Su•sa** (so͞o′sə, -zə). A city of NE Tunisia on an inlet of the Mediterranean; founded in ancient times by the Phoenicians. Pop. 69,530.

sous vide (so͞o vēd′) *n.* The cooking of various ingredients in a plastic pouch. [Fr., in a vacuum, vacuum-packed : *sous*, under + *vide*, vacuum.] **— sous-vide′** (so͞o-vēd′) *adj.*

sou•tache (so͞o-tăsh′) *n.* A narrow flat braid in a herringbone pattern. [Fr. < Hung. *sujtás.*]

sou•tane (so͞o-tän′ -tăn′) *n.* A cassock, esp. one that buttons up and down the front. [Fr., alteration (influenced by Fr. *sous*, under) of obsolete *sottane* < Ital. *sottana* < *sotto*, under < Lat. *subtus* < *sub.* See **upo*.**]

Sou•ter (so͞o′tər), **David Hackett.** b. 1939. Amer. jurist; appointed associate justice of the Supreme Court in 1990.

south (south) *n.* **1.a.** The direction along a meridian 90° clockwise from east; the direction to the right of sunrise. **b.** The cardinal point on the compass 180° clockwise from due north and directly opposite north. **2.** An area or a region lying in the south. **3.** Often **South. a.** The southern part of the earth. **b.** The southern part of a region or country. **4. South.** The southern part of the United States, esp. the states that fought for the Confederacy in the Civil War. *— adj.* **1.** To, toward, of, facing, or in the south. **2.** Originating in or coming from the south. *— adv.* In, from, or toward the south. [ME < OE *sūth.* See **sāwel-*.**]

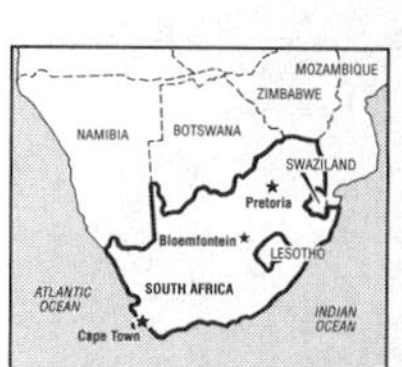

South Africa

South Af•ri•ca (ăf′rĭ-kə). A country of S Africa on the Atlantic and Indian oceans. Orig. inhabited by Khoikhoin, San, and Bantu-speaking peoples, it was administered by a union of British and Boer colonies after 1910 and became a republic in 1961. Caps. Pretoria, Cape Town, and Bloemfontein. Pop. 24,208,140. **— South Af′ri•can** *adj. & n.*

South A•mer•i•ca (ə-mĕr′ĭ-kə). A continent of the S Western Hemisphere SE of North America between the Atlantic and Pacific oceans extending from the Caribbean Sea S to Cape Horn. **— South A•mer′i•can** *adj. & n.*

South•amp•ton (south-hămp′tən, sou-thămp′-). A borough of S-central England on an inlet of the English Channel opposite the Isle of Wight. Pop. 208,800.

Southampton Island. An island of E Northwest Terrs., Canada, at the entrance to Hudson Bay.

ă pat	oi boy
ā pay	ou out
âr care	o͝o took
ä father	o͞o boot
ĕ pet	ŭ cut
ē be	ûr urge
ĭ pit	th thin
ī pie	*th* this
îr pier	hw which
ŏ pot	zh vision
ō toe	ə about, item
ô paw	

Stress marks:
′ (primary);
′ (secondary), as in
dictionary (dĭk′shə-nĕr′ē)

South At•lan•tic Ocean (ăt-lăn′tĭk). The S part of the Atlantic, extending S from the equator to Antarctica.

South•a•ven (south′ā′vən). A community of extreme NW MS, a suburb of Memphis TN. Pop. 17,949.

South Bend. A city of N IN NW of Fort Wayne; built on the site of a fur-trading post estab. 1820. Pop. 105,511.

south•bound (south′bound′) *adj.* Going toward the south.

South•bridge (south′brĭj′). A town of S-central MA SW of Worcester; incorp. 1816. Pop. 17,816.

south by east *n.* The direction or compass point halfway between due south and south-southeast, or 168°45′ east of due north. *—adv. & adj.* Toward or from south by east.

south by west *n.* The direction or compass point halfway between due south and south-southwest, or 168°45′ west of due north. *—adv. & adj.* Toward or from south by west.

South Car•o•li•na (kăr′ə-lī′nə). A state of the SE U.S. bordering on the Atlantic; admitted as one of the original Thirteen Colonies in 1788. It seceded from the Union in 1860, precipitating the Civil War. Cap. Columbia. Pop. 3,505,707. **—South Car′o•lin′i•an** (-lĭn′ē-ən) *adj. & n.*

South Central Niger-Congo *n.* A branch of the Niger-Congo language family.

South Chi•na Sea (chī′nə). An arm of the W Pacific Ocean bounded by SE China, Taiwan, the Philippines, Borneo, and Vietnam.

South Da•ko•ta (də-kō′tə). A state of the N-central U.S.; admitted as the 40th state in 1889. The region was split off from ND at the time it achieved statehood. Cap. Pierre. Pop. 699,999. **—South Da•ko′tan** *adj. & n.*

South Korea

South•down (south′doun′) *n.* Any of a breed of small hornless sheep of English origin, having short dense fine-textured wool. [After the SOUTH DOWNS.]

South Downs (dounz). See **Downs.**

south•east (south-ēst′, sou-ēst′) *n.* **1.** The direction or compass point halfway between due south and due east, or 135° east of due north. **2.** An area or a region lying in the southeast. **3. Southeast.** A region of the southeast United States generally including Alabama, Georgia, South Carolina, and Florida. *—adj.* **1.** To, toward, of, facing, or in the southeast. **2.** Originating in or coming from the southeast. *—adv.* In, from, or toward the southeast. **—south•east′ern** *adj.*

Southeast A•sia (ā′zhə, ā′shə). A region of Asia bounded by the Indian subcontinent, China, and the Pacific Ocean and including Indochina, the Malay Peninsula, and the Malay Archipelago. **—Southeast A′sian** *adj. & n.*

southeast by east *n.* The direction or compass point halfway between southeast and east-southeast, or 123°45′ east of due north. *—adv. & adj.* Toward or from southeast by east.

southeast by south *n.* The direction or compass point halfway between southeast and south-southeast, or 146°15′ east of due north. *—adv. & adj.* Toward or from southeast by south.

south•east•er (south-ē′stər, sou-ē′-) *n.* A storm or gale blowing from the southeast.

south•east•er•ly (south-ē′stər-lē, sou-ē′-) *adj.* **1.** Situated toward the southeast. **2.** Coming or being from the southeast. **—south•east′er•ly** *adv.*

south•east•ward (south-ēst′wərd, sou-ēst′-) *adv. & adj.* Toward, to, or in the southeast. *—n.* A southeastward direction, point, or region. **—south•east′ward•ly** *adv. & adj.* **—south•east′wards** *adv.*

South El Mon•te (ĕl môn′tē). A city of S CA, a suburb of Los Angeles. Pop. 20,850.

South•end-on-Sea (sou′thĕnd-ŏn-sē′, -ôn-). A borough of SE England at the mouth of the Thames R. Pop. 157,100.

south•er (sou′*th*ər) *n.* A strong wind coming from the south.

south•er•ly (sŭ*th*′ər-lē) *adj.* **1.** Situated toward the south. **2.** Coming or being from the south. *—n., pl.* **-lies.** A storm or wind coming from the south. **—south′er•ly** *adv.*

south•ern (sŭ*th*′ərn) *adj.* **1.** Situated in, toward, or facing the south. **2.** Coming from the south. **3.** Native to or growing in the south. **4.** Often **Southern.** Of, relating to, or characteristic of southern regions or the South. **5.** Being south of the equator. [ME *southerne* < OE *sūtherne.* See **sāwel-*.**] **—south′ern•ness′** *n.*

Southern Alps (ălps). A mountain range of South I., New Zealand, rising to 3,766.4 m (12,349 ft).

Southern Bug (bo͞og, bo͝ok). See **Bug** 2.

Southern Cross *n.* A constellation in the Southern Hemisphere near Centaurus and Musca.

Southern Crown *n.* See **Corona Australis.**

Southern Educated Standard *n.* See **Received Pronunciation.**

south•ern•er also **South•ern•er** (sŭ*th*′ər-nər) *n.* A native or inhabitant of the south, esp. the southern United States.

Southern Hemisphere *n.* **1.** The half of the earth south of the equator. **2.** *Astron.* The half of the celestial sphere south of the celestial equator.

South•ern•ism (sŭ*th*′ər-nĭz′əm) *n.* **1.** An expression or a pronunciation characteristic of the southern United States or southern England. **2.** A trait, attitude, or practice typical of the South or southerners, esp. in the United States.

southern lights *pl.n.* See **aurora australis.**

south•ern•most (sŭ*th*′ərn-mōst′) *adj.* Farthest south.

Southern Paiute *n.* **1.** See **Paiute** 1. **2.** The Uto-Aztecan language of the Southern Paiute.

south•ern•wood (sŭ*th*′ərn-wo͝od′) *n.* An aromatic southern European shrubby plant *(Artemisia abrotanum)* having finely divided grayish foliage and globose white flower heads.

Southern Yem•en (yĕm′ən, yā′mən). A former country of SW Asia on the Arabian Peninsula; became independent in 1967 and united with North Yemen in 1990.

South Eu•clid (yo͞o′klĭd). A city of NE OH, a suburb of Cleveland. Pop. 23,866.

Sou•they (sou′*th*ē, sŭ*th*′ē), **Robert.** 1774–1843. British writer noted for his poetry, criticism, and biographical works.

South•field (south′fēld′). A city of SE MI, a suburb of Detroit on the Rouge R. Pop. 75,728.

South Frig•id Zone (frĭj′ĭd). See **Frigid Zone.**

South•gate (south′gāt′). A city of SE MI, a residential suburb of Detroit. Pop. 30,771.

South Gate. A city of S CA, a suburb of Los Angeles. Pop. 86,284.

South Geor•gia (jôr′jə). A British-administered island in the S Atlantic E of Cape Horn, a dependency of the Falkland Is.

South Had•ley (hăd′lē). A town of W MA N of Springfield; site of Mount Holyoke College (estab. 1837). Pop. 16,685.

South Hol•land (hŏl′ənd). A village of NE IL, a suburb of Chicago. Pop. 22,105.

south•ing (sou′*th*ĭng) *n.* **1.** The difference in latitude between two positions as a result of a movement to the south. **2.** Progress toward the south.

South•ing•ton (sŭ*th*′ĭng-tən). A town of central CT NE of Waterbury. Pop. 38,518.

South Island. An island of New Zealand SW of North I., from which it is separated by Cook Strait.

South Ko•re•a (kə-rē′ə, kô-, kō-). A country of E Asia at the S end of the Korean peninsula. Part of the ancient country of Korea, its present border with North Korea was set at the end of the Korean War (1950–53). Cap. Seoul. Pop. 39,951,000. **—South Ko•re′an** *adj. & n.*

South Lake Ta•hoe (tä′hō). A resort city of E CA on Lake Tahoe near the NV border. Pop. 21,586.

south•land or **South•land** (south′lănd′, -lənd) *n.* A region in the south of a country or an area. **—south′land•er** *n.*

South Mi•am•i Heights (mī-ăm′ē, -ăm′ə). A city of SE FL, a suburb of Miami. Pop. 30,030.

South Mil•wau•kee (mĭl-wô′kē). A city of SE WI, a suburb of Milwaukee. Pop. 20,958.

South Na•han•ni (nə-hăn′ē). A river of SW Northwest Terrs., Canada, flowing c. 563 km (350 mi) to the Liard R.

South Or•ange (ôr′ĭnj, ŏr′-). A village of NE NJ west of Newark. Pop. 16,390.

South Ork•ney Islands (ôrk′nē). A group of British-administered islands in the S Atlantic SE of Cape Horn.

South Pa•cif•ic Ocean (pə-sĭf′ĭk). The S part of the Pacific, extending S from the equator to Antarctica.

South Pas•a•de•na (păs′ə-dē′nə). A city of S CA, a suburb of Los Angeles. Pop. 23,936.

south•paw (south′pô′) *n. Slang.* A left-handed person, esp. a left-handed baseball pitcher. [< the batter facing east.]

South Plain•field (plān′fēld′). A borough of NE-central NJ SW of Elizabeth. Pop. 20,489.

South Platte River (plăt). A river of central and NE CO and W-central NE flowing c. 724 km (450 mi) E to the North Platte R. to form the Platte R.

South Po•lar Region (pō′lər). See **Polar Regions.**

South Pole *n.* **1.a.** The southern end of Earth's axis of rotation, a point in Antarctica. **b.** The celestial zenith of this terrestrial point. **c. south pole.** The southern end of the axis of rotation of a planet or other celestial body. **2. south pole.** The south-seeking magnetic pole of a straight magnet.

South•port (south′pôrt′, -pōrt′). A borough of NW England on Liverpool Bay N of Liverpool. Pop. 90,000.

South Port•land (pôrt′lənd, pōrt′-). A city of SW ME, a suburb of Portland. Pop. 23,163.

south•ron (sŭ*th*′rən) *n.* **1.** Often **Southron.** A person who lives in the south, esp. an Englishman as called by a Scot. **2.** A native or inhabitant of the American South. Used by the Confederates in the Civil War. *—adj. Scots.* Southern. [ME, var. of *southerne,* southern. See SOUTHERN.]

South Saint Paul (sānt pôl′). A city of SE MN, a suburb of St. Paul on the Mississippi R. Pop. 20,197.

South Sand•wich Islands (sănd′wĭch′, săn′-). A group of British-administered volcanic islands in the S Atlantic ESE of Cape Horn; now included in the British Antarctic Terr.

South San Fran•cis•co (săn′ frən-sĭs′kō). A city of W CA, a suburb of San Francisco on San Francisco Bay. Pop. 54,312.

South Sas•katch•e•wan River (să-skăch′ə-wän′, -wən). A river of Canada flowing c. 885 km (550 mi) from S Alberta to central Saskatchewan to form the Saskatchewan R.

South Sea Islands. The islands of the S Pacific, roughly coextensive with Oceania. **—South Sea Is′land•er** *n.*

South Seas. The oceans S of the equator, esp. the S Pacific. The name **South Sea,** or *El Mar del Sur,* was first used by Balboa for the entire Pacific Ocean.

South Shet•land Islands (shĕt′lənd). An archipelago in the S Atlantic off Antarctica, part of the British Antarctic Terr.

South Shields (shēldz). A borough of NE England E of Newcastle upon Tyne; founded in the 13th cent. Pop. 162,500.

south-south•east (south′south-ēst′, sou′sou-ēst′) *n.* The direction or compass point halfway between south and southeast, or 157°30′ east of due north. —*adj.* To, toward, of, facing, or in the south-southeast. —*adv.* In, from, or toward the south-southeast.

south-south•west (south′south-wĕst′, sou′sou-wĕst′) *n.* The direction or compass point halfway between due south and southwest, or 157°30′ west of due north. —*adj.* To, toward, of, facing, or in the south-southwest. —*adv.* In, from, or toward the south-southwest.

South Tem•per•ate Zone (tĕm′pər-ĭt, tĕm′prĭt). See **Temperate Zone.**

South Vi•et•nam (vē-ĕt′näm′, -năm′, vē′ĭt-, vyĕt′-). A former country of SE Asia (1954–75) that became part of Vietnam after the Vietnam War. —**South Vi•et′nam•ese′** (-nə-mēz′, -mēs′) *adj. & n.*

south•ward (south′wərd, sŭth′ərd) *adv. & adj.* Toward, to, or in the south. —*n.* A southward direction, point, or region. —**south′ward•ly** *adv. & adj.* —**south′wards** *adv.*

South Wa•zir•i•stan (wə-zîr′ĭ-stăn′, -stän′). See **Waziristan.**

south•west (south-wĕst′, sou-wĕst′) *n.* **1.** The direction or compass point halfway between due south and due west, or 135° west of due north. **2.** An area or a region lying in the southwest. **3. Southwest.** A region of the southwest United States generally including New Mexico, Arizona, Texas, California, and Nevada and sometimes Utah and Colorado. —*adj.* **1.** To, toward, of, facing, or in the southwest. **2.** Originating in or coming from the southwest. —*adv.* In, from, or toward the southwest. —**south•west′ern** *adj.*

South-West Af•ri•ca (south′wĕst ăf′rĭ-kə). See **Namibia.**

southwest by south *n.* The direction or compass point halfway between southwest and south-southwest, or 146°15′ west of due north. —*adv. & adj.* Toward or from southwest by south.

southwest by west *n.* The direction or compass point halfway between southwest and west-southwest, or 123°45′ west of due north. —*adv. & adj.* Toward or from southwest by west.

south•west•er (south-wĕs′tər, sou-wĕs′-) also **sou′•west•er** (sou-wĕs′-) *n.* **1.** A storm or gale from the southwest. **2.** A waterproof hat with a broad brim for the neck.

south•west•er•ly (south-wĕs′tər-lē, sou-wĕs′-) *adj.* **1.** Situated toward the southwest. **2.** Coming or being from the southwest. —**south•west′er•ly** *adv.*

south•west•ward (south-wĕst′wərd, sou-wĕst′-) *adv. & adj.* Toward, to, or in the southwest. —*n.* A southwestward direction, point, or region. —**south•west′ward•ly** *adv. & adj.* —**south•west′wards** *adv.*

South Wind•sor (wĭn′zər). A town of N-central CT NNE of Hartford. Pop. 22,090.

Sou•tine (so͞o-tēn′), **Chaim.** 1893–1943. Lithuanian-born expressionist painter known for his distorted figures.

sou•ve•nir (so͞o′və-nîr′, so͞o′və-nîr′) *n.* A token of remembrance. [Fr. < OFr., memory < Lat. *subvenīre*, to come to mind : *sub-*, sub- + *venīre*, to come; see **gʷā-*.**]

sov•er•eign (sŏv′ər-ĭn, sŏv′rĭn) *n.* **1.** One that exercises supreme, permanent authority, esp. in a nation or other governmental unit, as: **a.** A king, queen, or other noble person who serves as chief of state; a ruler or monarch. **b.** A national governing council or committee. **2.** A nation that governs territory outside its borders. **3.** A gold coin formerly used in Great Britain. —*adj.* **1.** Self-governing; independent. **2.** Having supreme rank or power. **3.** Paramount; supreme. **4.a.** Of superlative strength or efficacy. **b.** Unmitigated: *sovereign contempt.* [ME *soverain* < OFr. < VLat. **superānus* < Lat. *super*, above. See **uper*.**] —**sov′er•eign•ly** *adv.*

sov•er•eign•ty (sŏv′ər-ĭn-tē, sŏv′rĭn-) *n., pl.* **-ties. 1.** Supremacy of authority or rule as exercised by a sovereign or sovereign state. **2.** Royal rank, authority, or power. **3.** Complete independence and self-government. **4.** A territory existing as an independent state.

so•vi•et (sō′vē-ĕt′, -ĭt, sŏv′ē-, sō′vē-ĕt′) *n.* **1.** One of the popularly elected legislative assemblies that existed at local, regional, and national levels in the Soviet Union. **2.a. Soviet.** A native or inhabitant of the former Soviet Union. **b. Soviets.** The government of the former Soviet Union. Used with *the.* —*adj.* **1.** Often **Soviet.** Of or relating to the Union of Soviet Socialist Republics. **2.** Of or relating to a soviet. [Russ. *sovét*, council, soviet < ORuss. *sŭvětŭ.* See **ksun-*.**]

so•vi•et•ize also **So•vi•et•ize** (sō′vē-ĭ-tīz′, sŏv′ē-) *tr.v.* **-ized, -iz•ing, -iz•es. 1.** To cause to come under Soviet control. **2.** To cause to conform to Soviet political, social, and cultural policy. —**so′vi•et•i•za′tion** (-ĭ-tĭ-zā′shən) *n.*

So•vi•et•ol•o•gy (sō′vē-ĭ-tŏl′ə-jē, sŏv′ē-) *n.* Study of the former Soviet Union. —**So′vi•et•ol′o•gist** *n.*

Soviet Union. See **Union of Soviet Socialist Republics.**

sow[1] (sō) *v.* **sowed, sown** (sōn) or **sowed, sow•ing, sows.** —*tr.* **1.** To scatter (seed) over the ground for growing. **2.** To impregnate (a growing medium) with seed. **3.** To propagate; disseminate: *sow rumors.* **4.** To strew or cover with something; spread thickly. —*intr.* To scatter seed for growing. [ME *sowen* < OE *sāwan.* See **sē-*.**] —**sow′er** *n.*

sow[2] (sou) *n.* **1.a.** An adult female hog. **b.** The adult female of several other animals, such as the bear. **2.a.** A channel that conducts molten iron to the molds in a pig bed. **b.** The mass of metal solidified in such a mold. [ME < OE *sugu* and OE *sū*; see **sū-*.**]

sow•bel•ly (sou′bĕl′ē) *n. Informal.* Salt pork.

sow bug (sou) *n.* Any of various small terrestrial isopod crustaceans, chiefly of the genera *Oniscus* and *Porcellio*, having an oval segmented body. [< its piglike shape.]

So•we•to (sə-wē′tō, -wā′-). A city of NE South Africa SW of Johannesburg; a center of racial strife since the late 1970's. Pop. 868,580.

sow thistle (sou) *n.* Any of various plants of the genus *Sonchus*, esp. *S. oberaceus* of Eurasia, having prickly leaves and rayed yellow flower heads.

sox (sŏks) *n.* Pl. of **sock**[1] 1.

soy (soi) *n.* **1.** The soybean. **2.** A salty brown liquid condiment made by fermenting soybeans in brine. [Du. *soja, soya* < J. *shō-yu* < Chin. (Mandarin) *jiàng yóu*, soy sauce : *jiàng*, soy paste + *yóu*, sauce.]

soy•a (soi′ə) *n.* The soybean. [Du. See SOY.]

soybean
Glycine max

soy•bean (soi′bēn′) *n.* **1.** A southeast Asian leguminous plant *(Glycine max)*, widely cultivated for forage and soil improvement and for its nutritious seeds. **2.** The seed of this plant.

So•yin•ka (shô-yĭng′kə), **Wole.** b. 1934. Nigerian writer who won the 1986 Nobel Prize for literature.

Wole Soyinka

soy•milk (soi′mĭlk′) *n.* A milk substitute made from soybeans.

SP *abbr.* **1.** Self-propelled. **2.** Shore patrol. **3.** Single pole. **4.** Specialist. **5.** Submarine patrol.

sp. *abbr.* **1.** Special. **2.** Species. **3.** Specific. **4.** Specimen. **5.** Spelling.

Sp. *abbr.* Spanish.

s.p. *abbr. Law.* Sine prole.

spa (spä) *n.* **1.** A resort providing therapeutic baths. **2.** A resort area having mineral springs. **3.** A fashionable hotel or resort. **4.** A health spa. **5.** A tub for relaxation or invigoration, usu. including a device for raising whirlpools. **6.** *Eastern New England.* See **soda fountain** 2. [After *Spa* in E Belgium.]

space (spās) *n.* **1.a.** *Math.* A set of elements or points satisfying specified geometric postulates: *non-Euclidean space.* **b.** The infinite extension of the three-dimensional field in which all matter exists. **2.a.** The expanse in which the solar system, stars, and galaxies exist; the universe. **b.** The region of this expanse beyond Earth's atmosphere. **3.** A blank or empty area. **4.** An area provided for a particular purpose. **5.** Reserved or available accommodation on a public transportation vehicle. **6.a.** A period or interval of time. **b.** A little while. **7.** Sufficient freedom from external pressure for oneself and one's needs. **8.** *Mus.* One of the intervals between the lines of a staff. **9.** *Print.* One of the blank pieces of type or other means used for separating words or characters. **10.** One of the intervals during the telegraphic transmission of a message when the key is open or not in contact. **11.** Blank sections in printed material or broadcast time available for use by advertisers. —*v.* **spaced, spac•ing, spac•es.** —*tr.* **1.** To organize or arrange with spaces between. **2.** To separate or keep apart. **3.** *Slang.* To stupefy or disorient from or as if from a drug. Often used with *out.* —*intr. Slang.* To be or become stupefied or disoriented. Often used with *out.* [ME, area < OFr. *espace* < Lat. *spatium.*] —**spac′er** *n.*

space age also **Space Age** (spās) *n.* The period from 1957 through the present, in which spacecraft have orbited Earth and explored celestial bodies. —**space′-age′** (spās′āj′) *adj.*

space bar *n.* **1.** A bar at the bottom of the keyboard of a typewriter that when pressed down introduces a blank horizontal space into the typewritten matter, as between words. **2.** *Comp. Sci.* A similar bar on the keyboard of a terminal.

space cadet *n. Slang.* One who shows difficulty in grasping reality or in responding appropriately to it; a spacy person.

space capsule *n.* A vehicle or compartment for transporting, protecting, and supporting human beings or animals in outer space or at very high atmospheric altitudes.

space charge *n.* The excess of electrons or ions in a given volume.

space•craft (spās′krăft′) *n., pl.* **spacecraft.** A vehicle intended to be launched into space.

spaced (spāst) *adj. Slang.* Spaced-out.

spaced-out (spāst′out′) *adj. Slang.* Stupefied or disoriented from or as if from a drug.

space flight *n.* Flight beyond the atmosphere of Earth.

space heater *n.* An appliance that warms a small area, such as one room, typically by radiant electric heat.

space lattice *n.* See **crystal lattice.**

space•less (spās′lĭs) *adj.* Having no limits or boundaries.

space medicine *n.* The medical science concerned with the biological, physiological, and psychological effects of space flight on human beings.

space•port (spās′pôrt′, -pōrt′) *n.* An installation for sheltering, testing, maintaining, and launching spacecraft.

ă pat	oi boy
ā pay	ou out
âr care	o͝o took
ä father	o͞o boot
ĕ pet	ŭ cut
ē be	ûr urge
ĭ pit	th thin
ī pie	*th* this
îr pier	hw which
ŏ pot	zh vision
ō toe	ə about, item
ô paw	

Stress marks:
′ (primary);
′ (secondary), as in
dictionary (dĭk′shə-nĕr′ē)

space shuttle
Atlantis landing at Edwards Air Force Base, California, March 1990

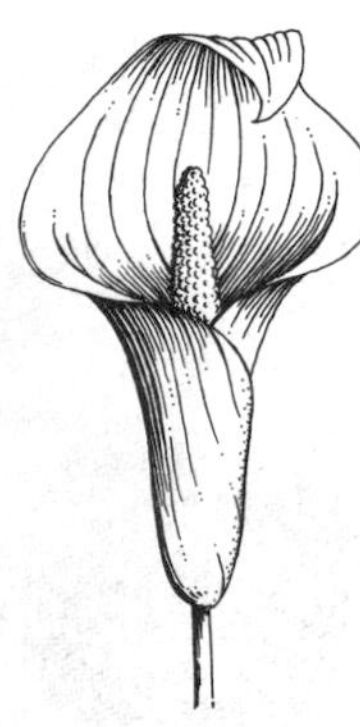

spadix
Calla lily
Zantedeschia aethiopica

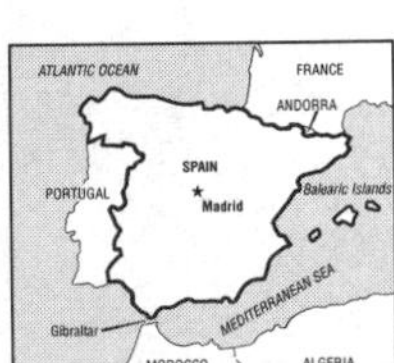

Spain

spanker

space probe *n.* A spacecraft carrying instruments intended for use in exploration of the physical properties of outer space or celestial bodies other than Earth.

space•ship or **space ship** (spās′shĭp′) *n.* See **spacecraft.**

space shuttle *n.* A reusable spacecraft with wings for controlled descent in the atmosphere, designed to transport astronauts between Earth and an orbiting space station.

space station *n.* A large satellite that can support a human crew and remain in orbit around Earth for an extended period and serve as a base for activities, such as scientific research.

space suit *n.* A protective pressure suit designed to permit the wearer relatively free movement in space.

space-time (spās′tīm′) *n. Phys.* The four-dimensional continuum of one temporal and three spatial coordinates in which any event or physical object is located.

space walk *n.* An excursion by an astronaut outside a spacecraft in space. **— space walk** *v.* **— space walker** *n.*

space writer *n.* A writer who is paid according to the amount of space his or her material occupies in print.

spa•cial (spā′shəl) *adj.* Var. of **spatial.**

spac•ing (spā′sĭng) *n.* **1.a.** The act of arranging with intervening spaces. **b.** The result of so arranging. **c.** A system of or allowance for intervals. **2.** Spaces or a space, as in print.

spa•cious (spā′shəs) *adj.* **1.** Generous or large in area or extent; roomy. **2.** Vast in range or scope: *a spacious view.* **— spa′cious•ly** *adv.* **— spa′cious•ness** *n.*

Spack•le (spăk′əl). A trademark used for a powder to be mixed with water or a ready-to-use plastic paste designed to fill cracks and holes in plaster before painting or papering.

spac•y or **spac•ey** (spā′sē) *adj.* **-i•er, -i•est.** *Slang.* **1.** Stupefied or disoriented from or as if from drug use. **2.** Eccentric.

spade¹ (spād) *n.* **1.** A sturdy digging tool having a thick handle and a heavy flat blade that can be pressed into the ground with the foot. **2.** Any of various similar digging or cutting tools. *— tr.v.* **spad•ed, spad•ing, spades.** To dig or cut with a spade. [ME < OE *spadu.*] **— spad′er** *n.*

spade² (spād) *n.* **1.** *Games.* **a.** A black leaf-shaped figure on certain playing cards. **b.** A playing card with this figure. **c. spades.** *(used with a sing. or pl. v.)* The suit of cards represented by this figure. **2.** *Offensive Slang.* Used as a disparaging term for a Black person. **—*idiom.* in spades.** To a considerable degree; in the extreme. [Ital. *spade,* pl. of *spada,* card suit < Lat. *spatha,* sword, broad-bladed stirrer < Gk. *spathē,* broad blade.]

spade•fish (spād′fĭsh′) *n., pl.* **spadefish** or **-fish•es.** Any of several food fishes of the family Ephippidae, esp. *Chaetodipterus faber,* of Atlantic coastal waters. [< its shape.]

spade•work (spād′wûrk′) *n.* **1.** Work requiring a spade. **2.** Preparatory work necessary for a project or an activity.

spa•dix (spā′dĭks) *n., pl.* **-di•ces** (-dĭ-sēz′). *Bot.* A fleshy club-like spike bearing minute flowers, usu. enclosed within a sheathlike spathe, as in the jack-in-the-pulpit. [Lat. *spādīx,* broken-off palm branch < Gk. < *span,* to stretch.]

spa•ghet•ti (spə-gĕt′ē) *n.* **1.** A pasta made into long solid strings and cooked by boiling. **2.** *Elect.* A slender tube of insulating material that covers bare wire. [Ital., pl. dim. of *spago,* cord.]

spa•ghet•ti•ni (spăg′ĭ-tē′nē) *n.* A form of pasta that is thinner than spaghetti but not as thin as vermicelli. [Ital., dim. of *spaghetti,* spaghetti. See SPAGHETTI.]

spaghetti Western *n.* A low-budget Western film made by a European, esp. an Italian, film company.

Spain (spān). A country of SW Europe comprising most of the Iberian Peninsula and the Balearic and Canary Is.; first colonized by Phoenicians and Greeks and unified as a kingdom in 1479. Cap. Madrid. Pop. 38,872,389.

spake (spāk) *v. Archaic.* A p.t. of **speak.**

spall (spôl) *n.* A chip, fragment, or flake from a piece of stone or ore. *— v.* **spalled, spall•ing, spalls.** *— tr.* To break up into chips or fragments. *— intr.* To chip or crumble. [ME *spalle.*]

spal•la•tion (spô-lā′shən) *n.* A nuclear reaction in which many particles are ejected from an atomic nucleus by incident particles of sufficiently high energy.

Spam (spăm). A trademark used for a canned meat product consisting primarily of chopped pork pressed into a loaf.

span¹ (spăn) *n.* **1.** The extent or measure of space between two points or extremities, as of a bridge; the breadth. **2.** The distance between the tips of the wings of an airplane. **3.** The section between two intermediate supports of a bridge. **4.** Something, such as a bridge, that extends from one point to another. **5.** The distance from the tip of the thumb to the tip of the little finger when the hand is fully extended, formerly used as a unit of measure equal to about nine inches (23 centimeters). **6.** A period of time. *— tr.v.* **spanned, span•ning, spans. 1.** To measure by or as if by the fully extended hand. **2.** To encircle with the hand or hands in or as if in measuring. **3.** To extend across in space or time. [ME, unit of measurement < OE *spann.* See **(s)pen-*.**]

span² (spăn) *tr.v.* **spanned, span•ning, spans.** To bind or fetter. *— n.* A pair of animals, such as oxen, matched in size, strength, or color and driven as a team. [Du. *spannen,* to harness < MDu. See **(s)pen-*.**]

span³ (spăn) *v. Archaic.* A p.t. of **spin.**

Span. *abbr.* Spanish.

Span•dau (spăn′dou′, shpän′-). A district of Berlin, Germany; site of a fortress used for Nazi war criminals after the Nuremburg trials of 1945 to 1946.

span•dex (spăn′dĕks) *n.* A synthetic fiber or fabric made from a polymer containing polyurethane, used in the manufacture of elastic clothing. *— adj.* Of or relating to spandex or its elastic qualities. [By alteration of *expands.*]

span•drel also **span•dril** (spăn′drəl) *n. Archit.* **1.** The triangular space between the left or right exterior curve of an arch and the rectangular framework surrounding it. **2.** The space between two arches and a horizontal molding or cornice above them. [ME *spaundrell,* prob. < *spandre,* space between supporting timbers < AN *spaundre* < *spandre,* to spread out < Lat. *expandere.* See EXPAND.]

spang (spăng) *adv. Informal.* Precisely; squarely. [Prob. < dial. *spang,* to leap, jerk, bang, prob. of imit. orig.]

span•gle (spăng′gəl) *n.* **1.** A small, often circular piece of sparkling metal or plastic sewn esp. on garments for decoration. **2.** A small sparkling object, drop, or spot: *spangles of sunlight.* *— v.* **-gled, -gling, -gles.** *— tr.* To adorn or cause to sparkle by covering with or as if with spangles. *— intr.* To sparkle in the manner of spangles. [ME *spangel,* dim. of *spange* < MDu., clasp. See **(s)pen-*.**] **— span′gly** *adj.*

Spang•lish (spăng′glĭsh) *n.* Spanish characterized by numerous borrowings from English.

Span•iard (spăn′yərd) *n.* A native or inhabitant of Spain. [ME < OFr. *Espaniard* < *Espaigne,* Spain < Lat. *Hispānia.*]

span•iel (spăn′yəl) *n.* **1.** Any of several breeds of small-sized to medium-sized dogs, usu. having drooping ears and a wavy silky coat. **2.** A docile or servile person. [ME *spainol* < OFr. *espaignol,* Spaniard, Spanish dog < VLat. **Hispāniōlus,* Spanish < *Hispānia,* Spain.]

Span•ish (spăn′ĭsh) *adj.* **1.** Of or relating to Spain or its people or culture. **2.** Of or relating to the Spanish language. *— n.* **1.** The Romance language of the largest part of Spain and most of Central and South America. **2.** The people of Spain. [Alteration (influenced by Lat. *Hispānia,* Spain) of ME *Spainish* < *Spaine,* Spain < OFr. *Espaigne.* See SPANIARD.]

Spanish A•mer•i•ca (ə-mĕr′ĭ-kə). The former Spanish possessions in the New World, including most of South and Central America, Mexico, Cuba, Puerto Rico, the Dominican Republic, and other small islands in the Caribbean.

Spanish American *n.* **1.** A native or inhabitant of Spanish America. **2.** A U.S. citizen or resident of Hispanic descent. *— adj.* **Span•ish-A•mer•i•can.** (spăn′ĭsh-ə-mĕr′ĭ-kən). **1.** Of or relating to Spanish America or its peoples or cultures. **2.** Of or relating to Spain and America, esp. the United States.

Spanish bayonet *n.* Any of several New World plants of the genus *Yucca,* esp. *Y. aloifolia* or *Y. baccata,* having a tall woody stem, stiff swordlike pointed leaves, and white flowers.

Spanish cedar *n.* **1.** Any of several tropical American trees of the genus *Cedrela,* esp. *C. odorata,* having reddish aromatic wood used for cabinetwork and cigar boxes. **2.** This wood.

Spanish chestnut *n.* **1.** A deciduous Mediterranean tree *(Castanea sativa)* with edible nuts in a spiny bur. **2.** This nut.

Spanish fly *n.* See **cantharis.**

Spanish Lake. A community of E-central MO, a suburb of St. Louis. Pop. 20,322.

Spanish lime *n.* See **genip** 2.

Spanish mackerel *n.* Any of various marine food fishes of the genus *Scomberomorus,* esp. a commercially important species, *S. maculatus,* of American Atlantic coastal waters.

Spanish Main (mān). **1.** The coastal region of mainland Spanish America in the 16th and 17th cent., from the Isthmus of Panama to the mouth of the Orinoco R. **2.** The section of the Caribbean crossed by Spanish ships in colonial times.

Spanish moss *n.* An epiphytic bromeliad plant *(Tillandsia usneoides)* of the southeast United States and tropical America having gray threadlike stems drooping in long matted clusters.

Spanish needles *pl.n.* *(used with a sing. or pl. v.)* See **beggar ticks** 1a.

Spanish omelet *n.* An omelet served with an often spicy sauce of tomatoes, onions, and peppers.

Spanish onion *n.* A mild-flavored yellow-skinned onion *(Allium fistulosum)* having yellowish-white flowers.

Spanish paprika *n.* A mild seasoning made from pimientos.

Spanish rice *n.* A dish consisting of rice cooked with tomatoes, spices, chopped onions, and green peppers.

Spanish Sa•ha•ra (sə-hâr′ə, -hăr′ə, -hä′rə). See **Western Sahara.**

spank (spăngk) *v.* **spanked, spank•ing, spanks.** *— tr.* To slap on the buttocks with a flat object or with the open hand, as for punishment. *— intr.* To move briskly or spiritedly. *— n.* A slap on the buttocks. [Perh. of imit. orig.]

spank•er (spăng′kər) *n. Naut.* A usu. gaff-headed sail set from the aftermost lower mast of a sailing ship.

spank•ing (spăng′kĭng) *adj.* **1.** *Informal.* Exceptional of its kind; remarkable. **2.** Swift and vigorous. **3.** Brisk and fresh: *a spanking breeze.* *— adv.* Used as an intensive: *a spanking clean shirt.* *— n.* A number of spanks delivered in rapid succession, as for punishment. [Perh. of Scand. orig.]

span•ner (spăn′ər) *n.* **1.** A wrench having a hook, hole, or pin at the end for meshing with a related device on another object. **2.** *Chiefly British.* A wrench. [Ger., winding tool < *spannen*, to stretch < MHGer. < OHGer. *spannan.* See **(s)pen-*.**]

span-new (spăn′no͞o′, -nyo͞o′) *adj.* Entirely new. [ME *spanneue*, partial transl. of ON *spánnýr* : *spánn*, shingle, chip + *nýr*, new; see **newo-*.**]

span•worm (spăn′wûrm′) *n.* See **measuring worm.** [< SPAN[1].]

spar[1] (spär) *n.* **1.** *Naut.* A wooden or metal pole, such as a mast, boom, yard, or bowsprit, used to support sails and rigging. **2.** A usu. metal pole used as part of a crane or derrick. **3.** A principal structural member in an airplane wing or a tail assembly that runs from tip to tip or from root to tip. *— tr.v.* **sparred, spar•ring, spars. 1.** To supply with spars. **2.** *Archaic.* To fasten with a bolt. [ME *sparre*, rafter.]

spar[2] (spär) *intr.v.* **sparred, spar•ring, spars. 1.a.** To box, esp. to make boxing motions without hitting one's opponent. **b.** To participate in a practice or exhibition boxing match. **2.** To bandy words about in argument; dispute. **3.** To fight by striking with the feet and spurs. Used of gamecocks. *— n.* **1.** A motion of attack or defense in boxing. **2.** A sparring match. [ME *sparren*, to thrust or strike rapidly, perh. < OFr. *esparer*, to kick < OItal. *sparare*, to fling : *s-*, intensive pref. (< Lat. *ex-*, ex-) + *parare*, to ward off; see PARRY.]

spar[3] (spär) *n.* A nonmetallic, readily cleavable translucent or transparent light-colored mineral with a shiny luster, such as feldspar. [LGer. < MLGer.]

spare (spâr) *v.* **spared, spar•ing, spares.** *— tr.* **1.** To refrain from treating harshly; treat mercifully or leniently. **2.** To refrain from harming or destroying. **3.** To save or relieve from experiencing or doing (something): *spared herself the trouble.* **4.** To hold back from; withhold or avoid. **5.** To use with restraint. **6.** To give or grant out of one's resources; afford. *— intr.* **1.** To be frugal. **2.** To refrain from inflicting harm; be merciful or lenient. *— adj.* **spar•er, spar•est. 1.a.** Kept in reserve. **b.** Being in excess of what is needed; extra. See Syns at **superfluous. c.** Free for other use; unoccupied. **2.a.** Not lavish, abundant, or excessive. **b.** Lean and trim. See Syns at **lean[2]. 3.** Not profuse or copious. *— n.* **1.** A replacement, esp. a tire, reserved for future need. **2.** *Sports.* **a.** The act of knocking down all ten pins with two successive rolls of a bowling ball. **b.** The score so made. *— **idiom.*** **to spare.** In addition to what is needed. [ME *sparen* < OE *sparian.*] **— spare′ly** *adv.* **— spare′ness** *n.* **— spar′er** *n.*

spare•ribs (spâr′rĭbz′) *pl.n.* Pork ribs with most of the meat trimmed off. [Alteration of obsolete *ribspare* < LGer. *ribbesper*, pickled pork ribs roasted on a spit < MLGer. *ribbespēr* : *ribbe*, rib + *spēr*, spear, spit.]

sparge (spärj) *tr.v.* **sparged, sparg•ing, sparg•es. 1.** To spray or sprinkle. **2.** To introduce air or gas into (a liquid). *— n.* A sprinkle. [Obsolete Fr. *espargier* < OFr. < Lat. *spargere.*]

spar•ing (spâr′ĭng) *adj.* **1.** Given to or marked by prudence and restraint in the use of material resources. **2.** Deficient or limited in quantity, fullness, or extent. **3.** Forbearing; lenient. **— spar′ing•ly** *adv.* **— spar′ing•ness** *n.*

Syns: sparing, frugal, thrifty, economical. These adjectives mean exercising or reflecting care in the use of resources, such as money. *Sparing* stresses restraint, as in expenditure: *sparing of words. Frugal* implies self-denial and abstention from luxury: *a frugal diet. Thrifty* suggests industry, care, and diligence in conserving means: *grew up during the Depression and learned to be thrifty. Economical* emphasizes prudence, skillful management, and the avoidance of waste: *an economical shopper; an economical use of energy.*

spark[1] (spärk) *n.* **1.** An incandescent particle, esp.: **a.** One thrown off from a burning substance. **b.** One resulting from friction. **c.** One remaining in an otherwise extinguished fire; an ember. **2.** A glistening particle, as of metal. **3.** A flash of light. **4.** A trace or suggestion, as: **a.** A quality or feeling with latent potential; a seed or germ. **b.** A vital, animating, or activating factor. **5. sparks.** *(used with a sing. v.) Informal.* A radio operator aboard a ship. **6.** *Elect.* **a.** The flash of light resulting from a disruptive discharge through an insulating material. **b.** The discharge itself. *— v.* **sparked, spark•ing, sparks.** *— intr.* **1.** To give off sparks. **2.** To give an enthusiastic response. **3.** To operate correctly. Used of the ignition system of an internal-combustion engine. *— tr.* **1.** To set in motion; activate. **2.** To rouse to action; spur. [ME *sparke* < OE *spearca.*] **— spark′er** *n.*

spark[2] (spärk) *n.* **1.** An elegantly dressed, self-conscious young man. **2.** A male suitor; a beau. *— v.* **sparked, spark•ing, sparks.** *— tr.* To court or woo. *— intr.* To play the suitor. [Perh. of Scand. orig., or < SPARK[1].] **— spark′er** *n.*

Spark (spärk), **Muriel Sarah.** b. 1918. Scottish writer known for her satirical novels, including *Memento Mori* (1958).

spark arrester *n.* A device designed to keep sparks from escaping, as at a chimney opening.

spark chamber *n.* A device consisting of electrically charged parallel metal plates in a chamber filled with inert gas, used to detect a charged subatomic particle as it passes through the chamber, leaving a trail of sparks.

spark coil *n.* An induction coil used to produce a spark, as in an internal-combustion engine.

spark gap *n.* A gap in an otherwise complete electric circuit across which a discharge occurs at a prescribed voltage.

spark•ing plug (spär′kĭng) *n. Chiefly British.* A spark plug.

spar•kle (spär′kəl) *v.* **-kled, -kling, -kles.** *— intr.* **1.** To give off sparks. **2.** To give off or reflect flashes of light; glitter. **3.** To be brilliant in performance. **4.a.** To shine with animation. **b.** To flash with wit. **5.** To release gas bubbles; effervesce. *— tr.* To cause to flash and glitter. *— n.* **1.** A small spark or gleaming particle. **2.** A glittering quality. **3.** Brilliant animation; vivacity. **4.** Emission of gas bubbles; effervescence. [ME *sparklen*, freq. of *sparken*, to spark. See SPARK[1].]

spar•kler (spär′klər) *n.* **1.** One, such as a highly polished metallic surface, that sparkles. **2.** *Informal.* A diamond. **3.** A firework that burns slowly and gives off a shower of sparks.

spar•kling water (spär′klĭng) *n.* Water charged with carbon dioxide.

sparkling wine *n.* Any of various effervescent wines produced by a process involving fermentation in the bottle.

spark•ly (spär′klē) *adj.* **-li•er, -li•est. 1.a.** Giving off tiny flashes of light; glittery. **b.** Lively; vivacious. **2.** Effervescent.

spark plug *n.* **1.** A device inserted in the head of an internal-combustion engine cylinder that ignites the fuel mixture by means of an electric spark. **2.** *Informal.* One who gives life or energy to an endeavor.

Sparks (spärks). A resort city of W NV E of Reno. Pop. 53,367.

spark transmitter *n.* A now obsolete radio transmitter that derives its output from the oscillating discharge of a capacitor to an inductor and across a spark gap.

spark•y (spär′kē) *adj.* **-i•er, -i•est.** Animated; lively.

spar•ling (spär′lĭng) *n.* **1.** The common European smelt *(Osperus eperlanus).* **2.** A young or immature herring. [ME *sperlinge* < OFr. *esperlinge*, of Gmc. orig.]

spar•row (spăr′ō) *n.* **1.** Any of various small New World finches of the family Emberizidae, having brownish or grayish plumage and including the song sparrow and other closely related species. **2.** Any of several similar or related birds, such as the house sparrow. [ME *sparowe* < OE *spearwa.*]

spar•row•grass (spăr′ə-grăs′, spăr′ō-) *n. Eastern U.S.* Asparagus. [By folk ety. < ASPARAGUS.]

sparrow hawk *n.* **1.** A small hawk *(Accipter nisus)* of Europe, Africa, and central Asia that has short broad wings and preys on small birds. **2.** A small North American falcon *(Falco sparverius)* that feeds chiefly on insects and mice.

sparse (spärs) *adj.* **spars•er, spars•est.** Occurring, growing, or settled at widely spaced intervals; not thick or dense. [Lat. *sparsus*, p.part. of *spargere*, to scatter.] **— sparse′ly** *adv.* **— sparse′ness, spar′si•ty** (spär′sĭ-tē) *n.*

Spar•ta (spär′tə) also **Lac•e•dae•mon** (lăs′ĭ-dē′mən). A city-state of ancient Greece in the SE Peloponnesus; noted for its militarism. The Peloponnesian Wars (460–404) with Athens led to Sparta's hegemony over all of Greece.

Spar•ta•cus (spär′tə-kəs). Died 71 B.C. Thracian gladiator who led a slave revolt in Italy (73–71) that was ultimately crushed at Lucania (71), where he was killed.

Spar•tan (spär′tn) *adj.* **1.** Of or relating to Sparta or its people. **2.a.** Rigorously self-disciplined or self-restrained. **b.** Simple, frugal, or austere: *a Spartan diet.* **c.** Marked by brevity of speech; laconic. **d.** Courageous in the face of pain, danger, or adversity. *— n.* **1.** A citizen of Sparta. **2.** One of Spartan character. **— Spar′tan•ism** *n.* **— Spar′tan•ly** *adv.*

Spar•tan•burg (spär′tn-bûrg′). A city of NW SC NW of Columbia at the foot of the Blue Ridge. Pop. 43,467.

spar•te•ine (spär′tē-ēn′, -ĭn) *n.* A bitter poisonous liquid alkaloid, $C_{15}H_{26}N_2$, obtained from the broom *Cytisus scoparius* or the lupin *Lupinus luteus.* [NLat. *Spartium*, broom genus (< Lat. *spartum*, a kind of broom < Gk. *sparton*) + -INE[2].]

spar varnish *n.* A waterproof varnish.

spasm (spăz′əm) *n.* **1.** A sudden involuntary contraction of a muscle or group of muscles. **2.** A sudden burst of energy, activity, or emotion. [ME *spasme* < OFr. < Lat. *spasmus* < Gk. *spasmos* < *span*, to pull.]

spas•mod•ic (spăz-mŏd′ĭk) *adj.* **1.** Relating to, affected by, or having the character of a spasm; convulsive. **2.** Happening intermittently; fitful. **3.** Given to sudden outbursts of energy or feeling; excitable. [NLat. *spasmōdicus* < Gk. *spasmōdēs* < *spasmos*, spasm. See SPASM.] **— spas•mod′i•cal•ly** *adv.*

spas•tic (spăs′tĭk) *adj.* **1.** Of, relating to, or characterized by spasms: *a spastic colon.* **2.** Affected by spastic paralysis. *— n.* A person affected with spastic paralysis. [Lat. *spasticus* < Gk. *spastikos* < *span*, to pull.] **— spas′ti•cal•ly** *adv.* **— spas•tic′i•ty** (spă-stĭs′ĭ-tē) *n.*

spastic paralysis *n.* A chronic pathological condition marked by persistent muscle spasms and exaggerated tendon reflexes due to damage to motor nerves of the central nervous system.

spat[1] (spăt) *v.* A p.t. and p.part. of **spit[1].**

spat[2] (spăt) *n., pl.* **spat** or **spats. 1.** An oyster or similar bivalve mollusk in the larval stage, esp. when it settles to the bottom and begins to develop a shell. **2.** The spawn of an oyster or a similar mollusk. *— intr.v.* **spat•ted, spat•ting, spats.** To

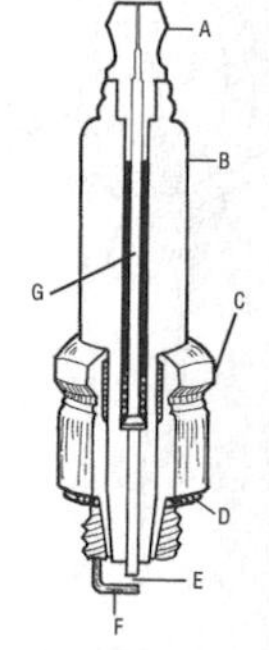

spark plug
Cross section of a spark plug
A. Terminal
B. Insulator
C. Body
D. Gasket
E. Gap
F. Ground electrode
G. Center electrode

sparrow hawk
Falco sparverius

ă pat	oi boy
ā pay	ou out
âr care	o͝o took
ä father	o͞o boot
ĕ pet	ŭ cut
ē be	ûr urge
ĭ pit	th thin
ī pie	*th* this
îr pier	hw which
ŏ pot	zh vision
ō toe	ə about,
ô paw	item

Stress marks:
′ (primary);
′ (secondary), as in
dictionary (dĭk′shə-nĕr′ē)

spawn. Used of oysters and similar mollusks. [ME.]

spat³ (spăt) *n.* A cloth or leather gaiter covering the shoe upper and the ankle and fastening under the shoe with a strap. Often used in the plural. [Short for *spatterdash* : SPATTER + DASH¹.]

spat⁴ (spăt) *n.* **1.** A brief quarrel. **2.** *Informal.* A slap or smack. **3.** A spattering sound, as of raindrops. — *v.* **spat•ted, spat•ting, spats.** — *intr.* **1.** To engage in a brief quarrel. **2.** To strike with a light spattering sound; slap. — *tr. Informal.* To slap. [?]

spatch•cock (spăch′kŏk) *n.* A dressed and split chicken for roasting or broiling on a spit. — *tr.v.* **-cocked, -cock•ing, -cocks. 1.** To prepare (a dressed chicken) for grilling by splitting open. **2.** To introduce or interpose, esp. in a labored or unsuitable manner. [Perh. alteration of *spitchcock*, a way of cooking an eel.]

spathe
Calla lily
Zantedeschia aethiopica

spate (spāt) *n.* **1.** A sudden flood, rush, or outpouring. **2.** *Chiefly British.* **a.** A flash flood. **b.** A freshet resulting from rain or melting snow. **c.** A sudden heavy fall of rain. [ME.]

spathe (spāth) *n. Bot.* A leaflike bract that encloses or subtends a flower cluster or spadix, as in the jack-in-the-pulpit. [Lat. *spatha*, broadsword < Gk. *spathē*, broad blade.]

spath•ic (spăth′ĭk) *adj.* Having good cleavage. Used of minerals. [Ger. *Spath, Spat*, spar (< MHGer. *spāt*) + -IC.]

spa•tial also **spa•cial** (spā′shəl) *adj.* Of, relating to, involving, or having the nature of space. [< Lat. *spatium*, space.] — **spa′ti•al′i•ty** (spā′shē-ăl′ĭ-tē) *n.* — **spa′tial•ly** *adv.*

spa•ti•o•tem•po•ral (spā′shē-ō-tĕm′pər-əl) *adj.* **1.** Of, relating to, or existing in both space and time. **2.** Of or relating to space-time. [Lat. *spatium*, space + TEMPORAL¹.]

spat•ter (spăt′ər) *v.* **-tered, -ter•ing, -ters.** — *tr.* **1.** To scatter (a liquid) in drops or small splashes. **2.** To spot, splash, or soil. **3.** To sully the reputation of; defame. — *intr.* **1.** To come forth in drops or small splashes: *Grease spattered everywhere.* **2.** To fall in or as if in a shower, as rain. — *n.* **1.a.** The act of spattering. **b.** The condition of being spattered. **2.** A spattering sound. **3.a.** A drop or splash of something spattered. **b.** A small amount; a smattering. [Perh. of LGer. orig.]

spat•ter•dock (spăt′ər-dŏk′) *n.* An aquatic plant *(Nuphar advena)* of eastern Mexico and the eastern and central United States, having emergent broad leaves and globe-shaped yellow flowers. [SPATTER + DOCK⁴.]

spat•u•la (spăch′ə-lə) *n.* **1.** A small implement having a broad flat flexible blade used esp. to mix, spread, or lift material. **2.** A device used to press down the tongue while examining the mouth or throat. [Lat., flat piece of wood, splint, dim. of *spatha*, broadsword. See SPATHE.] — **spat′u•lar** *adj.*

spat•u•late (spăch′ə-lĭt) *adj.* Shaped like a spatula.

spav•in (spăv′ĭn) *n.* A disease affecting horses in which the accumulation of new bone or lymph enlarges the hock joint. [ME *spaven* < OFr. *espavain*, swelling, perh. of Gmc. orig.]

spav•ined (spăv′ĭnd) *adj.* **1.** Afflicted with spavin: *a spavined horse.* **2.** Marked by damage, deterioration, or ruin.

spearmint
Mentha spicata

spawn (spôn) *n.* **1.** The eggs of aquatic animals such as bivalve mollusks, fishes, and amphibians. **2.** Offspring occurring in numbers; brood. **3.** A person who is the issue of a parent or family. **4.** The source of something; a germ or seed. **5.** A product or an outcome. **6.** Mycelia of mushrooms or other fungi grown in specially prepared organic matter for planting in beds. — *v.* **spawned, spawn•ing, spawns.** — *intr.* **1.** To deposit eggs; produce spawn. **2.** To produce offspring in large numbers. — *tr.* **1.** To produce or deposit (spawn). **2.** To produce in large numbers. **3.** To give rise to; engender: *tyranny that spawned revolt.* **4.** To cause to spawn; bring forth; produce. **5.** To plant with mycelia grown in specially prepared organic matter. [ME *spawne* < *spawnen*, to spawn < AN *espaundre* < Lat. *expandere*. See EXPAND.] — **spawn′er** *n.*

spay (spā) *tr.v.* **spayed, spay•ing, spays.** To remove surgically the ovaries of (an animal). [ME *spaien* < AN *espeier*, to cut with a sword < *espee*, sword < Lat. *spatha*. See SPATHE.]

SPCA *abbr.* Society for the Prevention of Cruelty to Animals.

SPCC *abbr.* Society for the Prevention of Cruelty to Children.

speak (spēk) *v.* **spoke** (spōk), **spo•ken** (spō′kən), **speak•ing, speaks.** — *intr.* **1.** To utter words or articulate sounds with ordinary speech modulation; talk. **2.a.** To convey thoughts, opinions, or emotions orally. **b.** To express oneself. **c.** To be on speaking terms. **3.** To deliver an address or a lecture. **4.a.** To make a statement in writing: *The biography speaks of loneliness.* **b.** To act as spokesperson. **5.a.** To convey a message by nonverbal means. **b.** To be expressive. **c.** To be appealing. **6.** To make a reservation or request. Often used with *for: Is this dance spoken for?* **7.a.** To produce a characteristic sound: *The drums spoke.* **b.** To give off a sound on firing. Used of guns or cannon. **8.** To make communicative sounds. **9.** To give an indication or a suggestion. — *tr.* **1.** To articulate in a speaking voice. **2.** To converse in or be able to converse in (a language). **3.a.** To express aloud; tell: *speak the truth.* **b.** To express in writing. **4.** *Naut.* To hail and communicate with (another vessel) at sea. **5.** To convey by nonverbal means. — ***phrasal verbs.*** **speak out.** To talk freely and fearlessly, as about a public issue. **speak up. 1.** To speak loud enough to be audible. **2.** To speak without fear or hesitation. — ***idioms.*** **so to speak.** In a manner of speaking. **speak down to.** To speak condescendingly to. **to speak of.** Worthy of mention. [ME *speken* < OE *sprecan, specan.*] — **speak′a•ble** *adj.*

Syns: *speak, talk, converse, discourse.* These verbs mean to express one's thoughts by uttering words. *Speak* and *talk* are the most general: *"On an occasion of this kind it becomes more than a moral duty to speak one's mind. It becomes a pleasure"* (Oscar Wilde). *"Let's talk sense to the American people"* (Adlai E. Stevenson). *Converse* stresses interchange of thoughts and ideas: *"With thee conversing I forget all time"* (John Milton). *Discourse* usually refers to formal, extended speech: *"striding through the city, stick in hand, discoursing spontaneously on the writings of Hazlitt"* (Manchester Guardian Weekly).

speak•eas•y (spēk′ē′zē) *n., pl.* **-ies.** A place for the illegal sale and consumption of alcoholic drinks, as during Prohibition.

speak•er (spē′kər) *n.* **1.a.** One who speaks. **b.** A spokesperson. **2.** One who delivers a public speech. **3.** Often **Speaker.** The presiding officer of a legislative assembly. **4.** A loudspeaker. — **speak′er•ship′** *n.*

speak•er•phone (spē′kər-fōn′) *n.* A telephone or telephone attachment that contains both a loudspeaker and a microphone, allowing several persons to participate in a call at the same time.

speak•ing (spē′kĭng) *adj.* **1.a.** Capable of speech. **b.** Involving speaking or talking: *a speaking part in the play.* **2.** Expressive or telling; eloquent. **3.** True to life; lifelike: *a speaking likeness.* — ***idiom.*** **on speaking terms. 1.** Friendly enough to exchange superficial remarks. **2.** Ready and willing to communicate; not alienated or estranged.

speaking in tongues *n.* See **gift of tongues.**

speaking tube *n.* A tube used for speaking from one room of a building or ship to another.

spear¹ (spîr) *n.* **1.** A weapon consisting of a long shaft with a sharply pointed end. **2.** A shaft with a sharp point and barbs for spearing fish. **3.** A soldier armed with a spear. — *v.* **speared, spear•ing, spears.** — *tr.* **1.** To pierce with or as if with a spear. **2.** To catch with a thrust of the arm. — *intr.* To stab at something with or as if with a spear. [ME *spere* < OE.] — **spear′er** *n.* — **spear′like′** *adj.*

spear² (spîr) *n.* A slender stalk, as of asparagus. — *intr.v.* **speared, spear•ing, spears.** To sprout like a spear. [Alteration of SPIRE².]

spear-car•ri•er (spîr′kăr′ē-ər) *n.* **1.** A minor member of an operatic or dramatic cast, usu. having no speaking part. **2.** One whose presence or performance has little effect.

spear•fish (spîr′fĭsh′) *n., pl.* **spearfish** or **-fish•es.** Either of two large marine game fishes *(Tetrapturus angustirostris* or *T. belone)* related to the sailfish and marlin, having the upper jaw elongated into a spearlike projection. — *intr.v.* **-fished, -fish•ing, -fish•es.** To fish with a spear, spearlike implement, or spear gun. — **spear′fish′er** *n.* — **spear′fish′ing** *n.*

spear gun *n.* A device for mechanically shooting a spearlike missile under water, as in spearfishing.

spear•head (spîr′hĕd′) *n.* **1.** The sharp head of a spear. **2.a.** The leading forces in a military thrust. **b.** The driving force in a given action, endeavor, or movement. — *tr.v.* **-head•ed, -head•ing, -heads.** To be the leader of (a movement, for example).

spear•man (spîr′mən) *n.* A man armed with a spear.

spear•mint (spîr′mĭnt′) *n.* An aromatic Eurasian plant *(Mentha spicata)* having clusters of small purplish flowers and yielding an oil used widely as a flavoring.

spear•wort (spîr′wûrt′, -wôrt′) *n.* Any of several plants related to the buttercups, esp. *Ranunculus flammula* of Eurasia, having lance-shaped leaves and yellow flowers.

spec (spĕk) *Informal.* — *n.* **1. specs.** The specifications, as for a building to be constructed. **2.** Speculation. — *tr.v.* **spec'd, spec'ing, specs** or **specced** (spĕkt), **spec•cing** (spĕk′ĭng), **specs.** To write or supply specifications for. — *adj.* **1.** Of or relating to specifications. **2.** Done, constructed, produced, or purchased as a speculation. — ***idiom.*** **on spec.** On a speculation basis; with no assurance of profit: *writes TV scripts on spec.* — **spec′′er** *n.*

spec. *abbr.* **1.** Special. **2.** Specifically. **3.** Specification. **4.** Speculation.

spe•cial (spĕsh′əl) *adj.* **1.** Surpassing what is common or usual; exceptional. **2.a.** Distinct among others of a kind: *a special medication.* **b.** Primary; chief. **3.** Peculiar to a specific person or thing; particular. **4.a.** Having a limited or specific function, application, or scope: *a special role.* **b.** Arranged for a particular occasion or purpose. **5.** Regarded with particular affection and admiration. **6.** Additional; extra. — *n.* **1.** Something arranged, issued, or appropriated to a particular service or occasion: *the commuter special.* **2.** A featured attraction, such as a reduced price. **3.** A television production that features a specific work, a given topic, or a particular performer. [ME < OFr. *especial* < Lat. *speciālis* < *speciēs*, kind. See SPECIES.] — **spe′cial•ly** *adv.* — **spe′cial•ness** *n.*

special delivery *n.* The delivery of a piece of mail, for an additional charge, by a special messenger.

special education *n.* Instruction for students whose learning needs cannot be met by a standard school curriculum.

special effect *n.* A visual or sound effect added to a film, for example, to create an illusion. Often used in the plural.

Spe•cial Forces (spĕsh′əl) *pl.n.* A division of the U.S. Army composed of soldiers specially trained in guerrilla fighting.

special handling *n.* The handling of fourth-class or parcel-post mail as first-class mail for an extra charge.

special interest *n.* A person, a group, or an organization attempting to influence legislators in favor of one particular interest or issue. **—spe′cial-in′ter•est** (spĕsh′əl-ĭn′trĭst, -tər-ĭst, -trĕst′) *adj.*

spe•cial•ism (spĕsh′ə-lĭz′əm) *n.* **1.** Concentration of one's efforts in a given occupation or field of study. **2.** A field of specialization.

spe•cial•ist (spĕsh′ə-lĭst) *n.* **1.** One who is devoted to a particular occupation or branch of study or research. **2.** A physician whose practice is limited to a particular branch of medicine or surgery, esp. one certified by a board of physicians. **3.** Any of several noncommissioned ranks in the U.S. Army that correspond to that of corporal through sergeant first class. **—spe′cial•ist, spe′cial•is′tic** *adj.*

spe•ci•al•i•ty (spĕsh′ē-ăl′ĭ-tē) *n., pl.* **-ties. 1.** A distinguishing mark or feature. **2. specialities.** Special points of consideration; particulars. **3.** *Chiefly British.* A specialty.

spe•cial•i•za•tion (spĕsh′ə-lĭ-zā′shən) *n.* **1.** The act of specializing or the process of becoming specialized. **2.** *Biol.* **a.** Adaptation, as of an organ, to a specific function or environment. **b.** A character, a feature, or an organism resulting from such adaptation.

spe•cial•ize (spĕsh′ə-līz′) *v.* **-ized, -iz•ing, -iz•es.** —*intr.* **1.** To pursue a special activity, occupation, or field of study. **2.** *Biol.* To develop so as to become adapted to a specific function or environment. **3.** To concentrate on a particular activity or product. —*tr.* **1.** To make specific mention of; particularize. **2.** To give a particular character or function to. **3.** *Biol.* To adapt to a particular function or environment. **4.** To specify the payee in endorsing (a check).

special jury *n. Law.* See **blue-ribbon jury.**

Special Olympics *pl.n.* A program of competitive sports for physically or mentally disabled athletes.

special pleading *n.* **1.** *Law.* Assertion of new or special matter to offset the opposing party's allegations, as an alternative to direct denial. **2.** A presentation of an argument that emphasizes only a favorable or single aspect of the question at issue.

special relativity *n.* The physical theory of space and time developed by Albert Einstein, based on the postulates that the laws of physics are identical in all frames of reference moving at a uniform velocity and that the speed of light from a uniformly moving source is always the same, regardless of how fast or slow the source or its observer is moving.

spe•cial•ty (spĕsh′əl-tē) *n., pl.* **-ties. 1.** A special pursuit, occupation, aptitude, or skill. **2.** A branch of medicine or surgery, such as cardiology, in which a physician specializes. **3.** A special feature or characteristic; a peculiarity. **4.** The state or quality of being special or distinctive. **5.** An item or a product of a distinctive kind or of particular superiority: *Pastry is the chef's specialty.* **6.** *Law.* A special contract or agreement, esp. a deed kept under seal.

spe•ci•a•tion (spē′shē-ā′shən, -sē-) *n.* The evolutionary formation of new biological species, usu. by the division of a single species into two or more genetically distinct ones. [SPECI(ES) + -ATION.] **—spe′ci•a′tion•al** *adj.*

spe•cie (spē′shē, -sē) *n.* Coined money; coin. **—*idiom.* in specie. 1.** In coin. **2.** In a similar manner; in kind: *repaid the offense in specie.* **3.** *Law.* In the same kind or shape; as specified. [< *(in) specie,* (in) the actual form < Lat. *(in) speciē,* (in) kind, ablative of *speciēs.* See SPECIES.]

spe•cies (spē′shēz, -sēz) *n., pl.* **species. 1.** *Biol.* **a.** A fundamental category of taxonomic classification, ranking below a genus and consisting of related organisms capable of interbreeding. See table at **taxonomy. b.** An organism belonging to such a category, represented in binomial nomenclature by an uncapitalized Latin adjective or noun following a capitalized genus name, as in *Equus caballus,* the horse. **2.** *Logic.* A class of individuals or objects grouped by virtue of their common attributes; a division subordinate to a genus. **3.a.** A kind, variety, or type. **b.** The human race; humankind. **4.** *Rom. Cath. Ch.* **a.** The outward appearance or form of the Eucharistic elements that is retained after their consecration. **b.** Either of the consecrated elements of the Eucharist. **5.** *Obsolete.* **a.** An outward form or appearance. **b.** Specie. **6.** *Chem.* A chemical entity, such as an atom or ion. [ME, logical classification < Lat. *speciēs,* a seeing, kind, form. See **spek-*.**]

spe•cies•ism (spē′shē-zĭz′əm, -sē-) *n.* Human intolerance or discrimination on the basis of species.

specif. *abbr.* **1.** Specific. **2.** Specifically.

spec•i•fi•a•ble (spĕs′ə-fī′ə-bəl) *adj.* Possible to specify.

spe•cif•ic (spĭ-sĭf′ĭk) *adj.* **1.** Explicitly set forth; definite. **2.** Relating to, characterizing, or distinguishing a species. **3.** Special, distinctive, or unique. **4.a.** Intended for, applying to, or acting on a particular thing. **b.** Concerned particularly with the subject specified. Often used in combination: *"age-specific voting patterns"* (A. Dianne Schmidley). **5.a.** Being a disease produced by a particular microorganism or condition. **b.** Having a remedial influence or effect on a particular disease. **6.** *Immunol.* Having an affinity limited to a particular antibody or antigen. **7.a.** Being a customs charge levied on merchandise by unit or weight rather than according to value. **b.** Being a commodity rate applicable to the transportation of a single commodity between named points. —*n.* **1.a.** Something particularly fitted to a use or purpose. **b.** A remedy intended for a particular ailment or disorder. **2.a.** A distinguishing quality or attribute. **b. specifics.** Distinct items or details; particulars. [LLat. *specificus* : Lat. *speciēs,* kind, species; see SPECIES + Lat. *-ficus,* -fic.] **—spe•cif′i•cal•ly** *adv.* **—spec′i•fic′i•ty** (spĕs′ə-fĭs′ĭ-tē) *n.*

spec•i•fi•ca•tion (spĕs′ə-fĭ-kā′shən) *n.* **1.** The act of specifying. **2.a. specifications.** A detailed exact statement of particulars, esp. a statement prescribing materials, dimensions, and quality of work for something to be built, installed, or manufactured. **b.** A single item specified. **3.** An exact written description of an invention by a patent applicant.

specific epithet *n.* The uncapitalized Latin adjective or noun that follows a capitalized genus name in binomial nomenclature and serves to distinguish a species from others in the same genus, as *saccharum* in *Acer saccharum* (sugar maple).

specific gravity *n.* The ratio of the mass of a solid or liquid to the mass of an equal volume of distilled water at 4°C (39°F) or of a gas to an equal volume of air or hydrogen under prescribed conditions of temperature and pressure.

specific heat *n.* **1.** The ratio of the amount of heat required to raise the temperature of a unit mass of a substance by one unit of temperature to that required to raise the temperature of a unit mass of a reference material, usu. water, by the same amount. **2.** The amount of heat, in calories, required to raise the temperature of one gram of a substance by one Celsius degree.

specific impulse *n.* A performance measure for rocket propellants that is equal to units of thrust per unit weight of propellant consumed per unit time.

specific performance *n. Law.* The performance of a contract as specified in its terms.

specific resistance *n. Elect.* Electrical resistivity.

spec•i•fy (spĕs′ə-fī′) *tr.v.* **-fied, -fy•ing, -fies. 1.** To state explicitly or in detail: *specified the amount needed.* **2.** To include in a specification. **3.** To state as a condition. [ME *specifien* < OFr. *specifier* < LLat. *specificāre* < *specificus,* specific. See SPECIFIC.] **—spec′i•fi′er** *n.*

spec•i•men (spĕs′ə-mən) *n.* **1.** An individual, an item, or a part representative of a class, genus, or whole. **2.** A sample, as of tissue, blood, or urine, used for analysis and diagnosis. **3.** *Informal.* An individual; a person: *a disagreeable specimen.* [Lat., example < *specere,* to look at. See **spek-*.**]

spe•cious (spē′shəs) *adj.* **1.** Having the ring of truth or plausibility but actually fallacious. **2.** Deceptively attractive. [ME, attractive < Lat. *speciōsus* < *speciēs,* appearance. See **spek-*.**] **—spe′cious•ly** *adv.* **—spe′ci•os′i•ty** (-shē-ŏs′ĭ-tē), **spe′cious•ness** (-shəs-nĭs) *n.*

Usage Note: A *specious* argument is not simply a false one but one that has the ring of truth. Those aware of the specialized use of the word may therefore sense a certain contradiction in hearing an argument described as *obviously specious* or *specious on the face of things.*

speck (spĕk) *n.* **1.** A small spot, mark, or discoloration. **2.** A tiny amount; a bit. —*tr.v.* **specked, speck•ing, specks.** To mark with specks. [ME *specke* < OE *specca.*]

speck•le (spĕk′əl) *n.* A speck or small spot, esp. a natural dot of color on skin, plumage, or foliage. [ME *spakle.*] **—speck′le** *v.*

speck•led (spĕk′əld) *adj.* **1.** Dotted or covered with speckles, esp. flecked with small spots of contrasting color. **2.** Of a mixed character; motley.

speckled trout *n.* See **brook trout.**

specs also **specks** (spĕks) *pl.n. Informal.* Eyeglasses; spectacles.

spec•ta•cle (spĕk′tə-kəl) *n.* **1.a.** Something that can be seen or viewed, esp. something of a remarkable or impressive nature. **b.** A public performance or display, esp. one on a large or lavish scale. **c.** A regrettable public display, as of bad behavior: *made a spectacle of himself.* **2. spectacles. a.** A pair of eyeglasses. **b.** Something resembling eyeglasses in shape or suggesting them in function. [ME < OFr. < Lat. *spectāculum* < *spectāre,* to watch, freq. of *specere,* to look at. See **spek-*.**]

spec•ta•cled (spĕk′tə-kəld) *adj.* **1.** Wearing spectacles. **2.** Having markings suggesting spectacles. Used of animals.

spec•tac•u•lar (spĕk-tăk′yə-lər) *adj.* Of the nature of a spectacle; impressive or sensational. —*n.* Something that is spectacular, as: **a.** A single dramatic production of unusual length or lavishness. **b.** An elaborate display. **—spec•tac′u•lar′i•ty** (-lăr′ĭ-tē) *n.* **—spec•tac′u•lar•ly** *adv.*

spec•tate (spĕk′tāt) *intr.v.* **-tat•ed, -tat•ing, -tates.** *Sports.* To attend (a horserace or other sporting event, for example) as a spectator. [Back-formation < SPECTATOR.]

spec•ta•tor (spĕk′tā′tər) *n.* An observer of an event. [Lat. *spectātor* < *spectāre,* to watch. See SPECTACLE.] **—spec′ta•**

spectacled
Spectacled bear
Tremarctos ornatus

ă pat	oi boy
ā pay	ou out
âr care	o͝o took
ä father	o͞o boot
ĕ pet	ŭ cut
ē be	ûr urge
ĭ pit	th thin
ī pie	*th* this
îr pier	hw which
ŏ pot	zh vision
ō toe	ə about, item
ô paw	

Stress marks:
′ (primary);
′ (secondary), as in
dictionary (dĭk′shə-nĕr′ē)

to′ri•al (-tə-tôr′ē-əl, -tôr′-) *adj.* — **spec′ta•tor•ship′** *n.*

spec•ter (spĕk′tər) *n.* **1.** A ghostly apparition; a phantom. **2.** A haunting or disturbing image or prospect. [Fr. *spectre* < Lat. *spectrum*, appearance, apparition. See SPECTRUM.]

spec•ti•no•my•cin (spĕk′tə-nō-mī′sĭn) *n.* A broad-spectrum antibiotic, $C_{14}H_{24}N_2O_7$, obtained from a species of gram-negative bacteria *(Streptomyces spectabilis)* or produced synthetically, used esp. in the treatment of penicillin-resistant gonorrhea. [NLat. : *spect(abilis)*, species name (< Lat., visible < *spectāre*, to watch; see SPECTACLE) + (ACT)INOMYCIN.]

spec•tra (spĕk′trə) *n.* Pl. of **spectrum.**

spec•tral (spĕk′trəl) *adj.* **1.** Of or resembling a specter. **2.** Of, relating to, or produced by a spectrum. — **spec•tral′i•ty** (-trăl′ĭ-tē), **spec′tral•ness** (-trəl-nĭs) *n.* — **spec′tral•ly** *adv.*

spectral line *n.* A bright or dark line in a spectrum produced by emission or absorption of light of a single wavelength.

spec•tre (spĕk′tər) *n. Chiefly British.* Var. of **specter.**

spectro– *pref.* Spectrum: *spectrograph.* [< SPECTRUM.]

spec•tro•gram (spĕk′trə-grăm′) *n.* A graphic or photographic representation of a spectrum.

spec•tro•graph (spĕk′trə-grăf′) *n.* **1.** A spectroscope equipped to photograph or otherwise record spectra. **2.** A spectrogram. — **spec′tro•graph′ic** *adj.* — **spec′tro•graph′i•cal•ly** *adv.* — **spec•trog′ra•phy** (-trŏg′rə-fē) *n.*

spec•tro•he•li•o•gram (spĕk′trō-hē′lē-ə-grăm′) *n.* A photograph of the sun taken in a narrow wavelength band centered on a selected wavelength.

spec•tro•he•li•o•graph (spĕk′trō-hē′lē-ə-grăf′) *n.* An instrument used to make spectroheliograms. — **spec′tro•he′li•og′ra•phy** (-ŏg′rə-fē) *n.*

spec•tro•he•li•o•scope (spĕk′trō-hē′lē-ə-skōp′) *n.* An instrument used to observe solar radiation directly.

spec•trom•e•ter (spĕk-trŏm′ĭ-tər) *n.* A spectroscope equipped with scales for measuring wavelengths or indexes of refraction. — **spec′tro•met′ric** (-trə-mĕt′rĭk) *adj.* — **spec•trom′e•try** *n.*

spec•tro•pho•tom•e•ter (spĕk′trō-fō-tŏm′ĭ-tər) *n. Phys.* An instrument used to determine the intensity of various wavelengths in a spectrum of light. — **spec′tro•pho′to•met′ric** (-fō′tə-mĕt′rĭk) *adj.* — **spec′tro•pho•tom′e•try** *n.*

spec•tro•scope (spĕk′trə-skōp′) *n.* An instrument for producing and observing spectra. — **spec′tro•scop′ic** (-skŏp′ĭk), **spec′tro•scop′i•cal** (-ĭ-kəl) *adj.*

spec•tros•co•py (spĕk-trŏs′kə-pē) *n., pl.* **-pies.** Study of spectra, esp. experimental observation of optical spectra. — **spec•tros′co•pist** *n.*

spectroscope

spec•trum (spĕk′trəm) *n., pl.* **-tra** (-trə) or **-trums. 1.** *Phys.* The distribution of a characteristic of a physical system, esp.: **a.** A distribution of electromagnetic energies arranged in order of wavelengths. **b.** A distribution of charged atomic or subatomic particles arranged in order of masses. **2.** A graphic or photographic representation of such a distribution. **3.a.** A range of values of a quantity or set of related quantities. **b.** A broad sequence or range of related qualities, ideas, or activities. [Lat., appearance < *specere*, to look at. See **spek-***.]

spec•u•lar (spĕk′yə-lər) *adj.* Of, resembling, or produced by a mirror or speculum. — **spec′u•lar•ly** *adv.*

spec•u•late (spĕk′yə-lāt′) *v.* **-lat•ed, -lat•ing, -lates.** — *intr.* **1.** To meditate on a subject; reflect. **2.** To engage in a course of reasoning often based on inconclusive evidence. **3.** To engage in the buying or selling of a commodity with an element of risk on the chance of profit. — *tr.* To assume to be true without conclusive evidence. [Lat. *speculārī*, *speculāt-*, to observe < *specula*, watchtower < *specere*, to look at. See **spek-***.]

spec•u•la•tion (spĕk′yə-lā′shən) *n.* **1.a.** Contemplation or consideration of a subject; meditation. **b.** A conclusion, an opinion, or a theory reached by conjecture. **c.** Reasoning based on inconclusive evidence; conjecture; supposition. **2.a.** Engagement in risky business transactions on the chance of quick or considerable profit. **b.** A commercial or financial transaction involving speculation.

spec•u•la•tive (spĕk′yə-lə-tĭv, -lā′-) *adj.* **1.** Of, marked by, or based upon contemplative speculation. **2.a.** Given to conjecture or speculation. **b.** Marked by inquisitive interest. **3.a.** Engaging in, given to, or involving financial speculation. **b.** Spent in speculation. **c.** Involving chance; risky. — **spec′u•la•tive•ly** *adv.* — **spec′u•la•tive•ness** *n.*

spec•u•la•tor (spĕk′yə-lā′tər) *n.* One that speculates.

spec•u•lum (spĕk′yə-ləm) *n., pl.* **-la** (-lə) or **-lums. 1.** A mirror or polished metal plate used as a reflector in optical instruments. **2.** An instrument for dilating the opening of a body cavity for medical examination. **3.** *Zool.* **a.** A bright, often iridescent patch of color on the wings of certain birds, esp. ducks. **b.** A transparent spot in the wings of some butterflies or moths. [ME, surgical speculum < Lat., mirror < *specere*, to look at. See **spek-***.]

speech (spēch) *n.* **1.a.** The faculty or act of speaking. **b.** The faculty or act of expressing or describing thoughts, feelings, or perceptions by the articulation of words. **2.** Something spoken; an utterance. **3.** Vocal communication; conversation. **4.** A talk or public address. **5.** One's habitual manner or style of speaking. **6.** The language or dialect of a nation or region: *American speech.* **7.** The study of oral communication, speech sounds, and vocal physiology. **8.** *Archaic.* Rumor. [ME *speche* < OE *sprǣc, spǣc.*]

speech community *n.* A group of speakers who recognize the same language or dialect of a language as a standard.

speech•i•fy (spē′chə-fī′) *intr.v.* **-fied, -fy•ing, -fies.** To give a speech. — **speech′i•fi′er** *n.*

speech•less (spēch′lĭs) *adj.* **1.** Lacking the faculty of speech. **2.** Temporarily unable to speak, as through wonder. See Syns at **dumb. 3.** Refraining from speech; silent. **4.** Unexpressed or inexpressible in words. — **speech′less•ness** *n.*

speech•mak•er (spēch′mā′kər) *n.* One who makes a speech. — **speech′mak′ing** *n.*

speech pathology *n.* The study of speech defects and disorders such as stuttering and dysphasia. — **speech pathologist** *n.*

speech therapy *n.* Treatment of speech defects and disorders, esp. through use of exercises and audio-visual aids that develop new speech habits. — **speech therapist** *n.*

speech•writ•er (spēch′rī′tər) *n.* One who writes speeches for others, esp. as a profession. — **speech′writ′ing** *n.*

speed (spēd) *n.* **1.** *Phys.* The rate or a measure of the rate of motion, esp.: **a.** Distance traveled divided by the time of travel. **b.** The first derivative of distance with respect to time. **c.** The magnitude of a velocity. **2.** Swiftness of action. **3.a.** The act of moving rapidly. **b.** The state of being in rapid motion; rapidity. See Syns at **haste. 4.** A transmission gear or set of gears in a vehicle. **5.a.** A numerical expression of the sensitivity of a photographic film, plate, or paper to light. **b.** The capacity of a lens to accumulate light at an appropriate aperture. **c.** The length of time required or permitted for a camera shutter to open and admit light. **6.** *Slang.* Amphetamine. **7.** *Slang.* One that suits or appeals to a person's inclinations, skills, or character. **8.** *Archaic.* Prosperity; luck. — *v.* **sped** (spĕd) or **speed•ed, speed•ing, speeds.** — *tr.* **1.** To cause to go, move, or proceed quickly; hasten. **2.** To increase the speed or rate of; accelerate: *speed up a car.* **3.** To wish Godspeed to. **4.** To further, promote, or expedite (a legal action, for example). **5.** *Archaic.* To help to succeed or prosper; aid. — *intr.* **1.a.** To go, move, or proceed quickly. **b.** To drive at a speed exceeding a legal limit. **2.** To pass quickly: *The days sped by.* **3.** To move, work, or happen at a faster rate; accelerate: *His pulse sped up.* **4.** *Archaic.* **a.** To prove successful; prosper. **b.** To get along in a specified manner; fare. — ***idiom.* up to speed. 1.a.** Operating at maximum speed. **b.** Producing something or performing at an acceptable rate or level. **2.** *Informal.* Fully informed or conversant. [ME *spede* < OE *spēd*, success, swiftness. See **spē-***.]

speed•ball (spēd′bôl′) *n. Slang.* An intravenous dose of cocaine mixed with heroin or an amphetamine.

speed•boat (spēd′bōt′) *n. Naut.* A fast motorboat.

speed brake *n.* A flap on an aircraft for decreasing speed while in flight in preparation for landing.

speed bump *n.* A ridge set crosswise into a paved surface or a dirt road to make the operators of vehicles slow down.

speed•er (spē′dər) *n.* One that speeds, esp. a driver who exceeds a legal or safe speed.

speed•ing (spē′dĭng) *adj.* Moving with speed. — *n.* The act or an instance of driving faster than is allowed by law.

speed limit *n.* The maximum speed legally permitted on a given stretch of road.

speed•om•e•ter (spĭ-dŏm′ĭ-tər, spē-) *n.* **1.** An instrument for indicating speed. **2.a.** An instrument for indicating distance traveled as well as rate of speed. **b.** An odometer.

speed-read•ing (spēd′rē′dĭng) *n.* A method of reading rapidly by assimilating several words or phrases at a glance or by skimming. — **speed′-read′** *v.*

speed skate *n. Sports.* An ice skate for racing, having a long blade that extends beyond the heel and toe of the sole of the boot. — **speed skater** *n.* — **speed skat′ing** *n.*

speed•ster (spēd′stər) *n.* **1.** A fast driver. **2.** A fast car.

speed trap *n.* A deployment of concealed police officers or electronic devices on a stretch of road to catch speeders.

speed•up (spēd′ŭp′) *n.* **1.** An increase in speed; acceleration. **2.** A required increase of production with no pay increase.

speed•way (spēd′wā′) *n.* **1.** *Sports.* A course for automobile or motorcycle racing. **2.** A road for fast-moving traffic.

speed•well (spēd′wĕl′) *n.* Any of various plants of the genus *Veronica*, having opposite leaves and small, usu. blue flowers.

speed•writ•ing (spēd′rī′tĭng) *n.* A form of shorthand that uses letters of the alphabet. — **speed′writ′er** *n.*

speed•y (spē′dē) *adj.* **-i•er, -i•est. 1.** Characterized by rapid motion. **2.** Accomplished or arrived at without delay; prompt. See Syns at **fast**[1]. — **speed′i•ly** *adv.* — **speed′i•ness** *n.*

Speer (spîr, shpâr), **Albert.** 1905–81. German Nazi politician who was Hitler's official architect (1934–45).

speiss (spīs) *n.* An arsenic compound or a mixture of arsenic compounds resulting from the smelting of iron, cobalt, nickel, and copper ores. [Ger. *Speise*, food, speiss < MHGer. *spīse*, food < OHGer. *spīsa*, prob. < Med.Lat. *spēnsa*, storehouse, or *spēsa*, provisions, both < Lat. *expēnsa (pecūnia)*, (money) paid out. See EXPENSE.]

Speke (spēk), **John Hanning.** 1827–64. British explorer in Africa who was one of the first Europeans to explore Lake Tanganyika (1858).

spe•le•ol•o•gy (spē′lē-ŏl′ə-jē) *n.* **1.** The scientific study of caves. **2.** Exploration of caves. [Fr. *spéléologie* : Lat. *spēlēum*, cave (< Gk. *spēlaion*) + *-logie*, -logy.] — **spe′le•o•log′i•cal** (-ə-lŏj′ĭ-kəl) *adj.* — **spe′le•ol′o•gist** *n.*

spell[1] (spĕl) *v.* **spelled** or **spelt** (spĕlt), **spell•ing, spells.** — *tr.* **1.** To name or write in order the letters constituting (a word or part of a word). **2.** To constitute the letters of (a word). **3.** To add up to; signify. — *intr.* To form words by means of letters. — ***phrasal verbs.* spell down.** To defeat in a spelling bee. **spell out. 1.** To make perfectly clear and understandable. **2.** To read slowly and laboriously. **3.** To puzzle out; comprehend by study. [ME *spellen*, to read letter by letter < OFr. *espeller* (of Gmc. orig.) and < OE *spellian*, to tell (< *spell*, discourse).]

spell[2] (spĕl) *n.* **1.a.** A word or formula believed to have magic power. **b.** A bewitched state; a trance. **2.** A compelling attraction; charm or fascination. — *tr.v.* **spelled, spell•ing, spells.** To put (someone) under a spell. [ME, discourse < OE.]

spell[3] (spĕl) *n.* **1.** A short indefinite period of time. **2.** *Informal.* A period of weather of a particular kind: *a dry spell.* **3.a.** One's turn at work. **b.** A period of work; a shift. **4.** *Australian.* A period of rest. **5.** *Informal.* A period of physical or mental disorder or distress: *a dizzy spell.* **6.** *Informal.* A short distance. — *v.* **spelled, spell•ing, spells.** — *tr.* **1.** To relieve (someone) from work temporarily by taking a turn. **2.** To allow to rest a while. — *intr.* **1.** To take turns working. **2.** *Australian.* To rest for a time from an activity. [< ME *spelen*, to spare < OE *spelian*, substitute for.]

spell•bind (spĕl′bīnd′) *tr.v.* **-bound** (-bound′), **-bind•ing, -binds.** To hold under or as if under a spell; enchant or fascinate. [Back-formation < SPELLBOUND.]

spell•bind•er (spĕl′bīn′dər) *n.* One that holds others spellbound, esp. an enthralling speaker or an interesting book.

spell•bound (spĕl′bound′) *adj.* Entranced by or as if by a spell; fascinated.

spell•down (spĕl′doun′) *n.* See **spelling bee.**

spell•er (spĕl′ər) *n.* **1.** One who spells words. **2.** An elementary textbook containing exercises that teach spelling.

spell•ing (spĕl′ĭng) *n.* **1.a.** The forming of words with letters in an accepted order; orthography. **b.** The art or study of orthography. **2.** The way in which a word is spelled.

spelling bee *n.* A contest in which competitors are eliminated as they fail to spell a given word correctly.

spelt[1] (spĕlt) *n.* A hardy wheat grown mostly in Europe. [ME < OE < LLat. *spelta*, prob. of Gmc. orig.]

spelt[2] (spĕlt) *v.* A p.t. and p.part. of **spell**[1].

spel•ter (spĕl′tər) *n.* Zinc, esp. in the form of ingots, slabs, or plates. [Prob. of Du. or LGer. orig.]

spe•lunk•er (spĭ-lŭng′kər, spē′lŭng′-) *n.* One who explores and studies caves chiefly as a hobby. [< obsolete *spelunk*, cave < ME < OFr. *spelunque* < Lat. *spēlunca* < Gk. *spēlunx.*] — **spe′lunk′ing** *n.*

spen•cer[1] (spĕn′sər) *n. Naut.* A gaff-headed sail on any mast of a ship except the mizzenmast, serving as a trysail. [Perh. < the name *Spencer.*]

spen•cer[2] (spĕn′sər) *n.* **1.** A short double-breasted overcoat worn by men in the early 19th century. **2.** A close-fitting waist-length jacket worn by women. [After George John *Spencer*, 2nd Earl Spencer (1758–1834).]

Spen•cer (spĕn′sər), **Herbert.** 1820–1903. British philosopher who applied the theory of evolution to philosophy and ethics.

Spencer Gulf. An inlet of the Indian Ocean off S-central Australia.

Spen•ce•ri•an[1] (spĕn-sîr′ē-ən) *adj.* Of or relating to Herbert Spencer or his philosophy. — *n.* A follower of Spencer.

Spen•ce•ri•an[2] (spĕn-sîr′ē-ən) *adj.* Of or relating to an ornate style of writing using rounded letters slanted to the right. [After P.R. *Spencer* (1800–64), Amer. handwriting expert.]

spend (spĕnd) *v.* **spent** (spĕnt), **spend•ing, spends.** — *tr.* **1.** To use up or put out; expend. **2.** To pay out (money). **3.** To wear out; exhaust. **4.** To pass (time) in a specified manner or place. **5.a.** To throw away; squander. **b.** To give up (one's time or efforts, for example) to a cause; sacrifice. — *intr.* **1.** To pay out or expend money. **2.** To be exhausted or consumed. [ME *spenden*, partly < OE *-spendan* (< Lat. *expendere*, to expend; see EXPEND) and partly < OFr. *despendre*, to weigh out; see DISPENSE.] — **spend′a•ble** *adj.* — **spend′er** *n.*

Syns: *spend, disburse, expend.* The central meaning shared by these verbs is "to pay or give out money or an equivalent in return for something": *spent five dollars for a ticket; disbursing funds from the account; expending energy on a project.* ***Ant:*** *save.*

Spen•der (spĕn′dər), Sir **Stephen Harold.** b. 1909. British writer whose works include *Poems of Dedication* (1947).

spend•ing money (spĕn′dĭng) *n.* Cash for small personal needs.

spend•thrift (spĕnd′thrĭft′) *n.* One who spends money recklessly or wastefully. — *adj.* Wasteful or extravagant. [SPEND + THRIFT, accumulated wealth (obsolete).]

Speng•ler (spĕng′lər, -glər, shpĕng′-), **Oswald.** 1880–1936. German philosopher who argued that civilizations are subject to the same cycle of growth and decay as human beings.

Spen•ser (spĕn′sər), **Edmund.** 1552?–99. English poet known chiefly for his allegorical epic romance *The Faerie Queene* (1590–96). — **Spen•se′ri•an** (spĕn-sîr′ē-ən) *adj.*

Spenserian sonnet *n.* A sonnet form composed of three quatrains and a couplet in iambic pentameter with the rhyme scheme *abab bcbc cdcd ee.*

Spenserian stanza *n.* A stanza consisting of eight lines of iambic pentameter and a final alexandrine, rhymed *ababbcbcc.*

spent (spĕnt) *adj.* **1.** Used up; consumed: *a spent youth.* **2.** Having come to an end; passed. **3.** Depleted of energy, force, or strength; exhausted: *spent workers.* **4.** *Naut.* Of or relating to a vessel at the end of a voyage, with fuel, stores, and water consumed and cargo discharged.

sperm[1] (spûrm) *n., pl.* **sperm** or **sperms. 1.** A male gamete or reproductive cell; a spermatozoon. **2.** Semen. [ME *sperme*, semen < OFr. *esperme* < LLat. *sperma* < Gk. See **sper-***.] — **sperm′ous** *adj.*

sperm[2] (spûrm) *n.* A substance, such as spermaceti, associated with the sperm whale. [Short for SPERMACETI.]

sperm– *pref.* Var. of **spermi–.**

–sperm *suff.* Seed: *endosperm.* [Gk. *-spermos* < *sperma*, seed. See SPERM[1].]

sperma– *pref.* Var. of **spermi–.**

sper•ma•ce•ti (spûr′mə-sē′tē, -sĕt′ē) *n., pl.* **-tis.** A waxy white substance from the head of the sperm whale or another cetacean and used for making candles, ointments, and cosmetics. [ME < Med.Lat. *spermacētī* : LLat. *sperma*, semen; see SPERM[1] + Lat. *cētī*, genitive of *cētus*, whale; see CETUS.]

sper•ma•go•ni•um also **sper•mo•go•ni•um** (spûr′mə-gō′nē-əm) *n., pl.* **-ni•a** (-nē-ə). *Bot.* A cup-shaped cavity or receptacle in which the spermatia of certain lichens and fungi are produced. [NLat. : *sperma*, sperm; see SPERM[1] + *-gonium*, seed, cell (< Gk. *gonos*, seed; see GONO–).]

sper•ma•ry (spûr′mə-rē) *n., pl.* **-ries.** An organ or a gland in which male gametes are formed, esp. in invertebrate animals. [NLat. *spermārium* < LLat. *sperma*, semen. See SPERM[1].]

sper•ma•the•ca (spûr′mə-thē′kə) *n.* A receptacle in the reproductive tracts of certain female invertebrates, esp. insects, in which spermatozoa are stored.

sper•mat•ic (spər-măt′ĭk) *adj.* **1.** Of, relating to, or resembling sperm. **2.** Containing, conveying, or producing sperm. **3.** Of or relating to a spermary.

spermatic cord *n.* A cordlike structure that includes the vas deferens and passes from the abdominal cavity via the inguinal canal into the scrotum to the back of the testicle.

sper•ma•tid (spûr′mə-tĭd) *n.* Any of the four haploid cells formed by meiosis in a male organism that develop into spermatozoa without further division.

sper•ma•ti•um (spər-mā′shē-əm, -shəm) *n., pl.* **-ti•a** (-shē-ə, -shə). A nonmotile cell in red algae and certain lichens and fungi that functions as a male gamete. [NLat. < Gk. *spermation*, dim. of *sperma, spermat-*, semen. See SPERM[1].] — **sper•ma′tial** (-shəl) *adj.*

spermato– or **spermat–** *pref.* **1.** Seed: *spermatophyte.* **2.a.** Sperm: *spermatic.* **b.** Spermatozoon: *spermatophore.* [Gk. < *sperma, spermat-*, seed. See SPERM[1].]

sper•mat•o•cyte (spər-măt′ə-sīt′, spûr′mə-tə-) *n.* A diploid cell that undergoes meiosis to form four spermatids.

sper•mat•o•gen•e•sis (spər-măt′ə-jĕn′ĭ-sĭs, spûr′mə-tə-) *n.* Formation and development of spermatozoa by meiosis and spermiogenesis.

sper•mat•o•go•ni•um (spər-măt′ə-gō′nē-əm, spûr′mə-tə-) *n., pl.* **-ni•a** (-nē-ə). Any of the cells of the gonads in male organisms that are the progenitors of spermatocytes. [NLat. : SPERMATO– + *-gonium*, seed; see SPERMAGONIUM.] — **sper•mat′o•go′ni•al** (-nē-əl) *adj.*

sper•mat•o•phore (spər-măt′ə-fôr′, -fōr′, spûr′mə-tə-) *n.* A capsule or compact mass of spermatozoa extruded by the males of certain invertebrates and primitive vertebrates and directly transferred to the reproductive parts of the female. — **sper′ma•toph′o•ral** (spûr′mə-tŏf′ər-əl) *adj.*

sper•mat•o•phyte (spər-măt′ə-fīt′, spûr′mə-tə-) *n.* A seed-bearing plant, such as a conifer or a flowering plant. — **sper•mat′o•phyt′ic** (-fĭt′ĭk) *adj.*

sper•mat•or•rhe•a also **sper•mat•or•rhoe•a** (spər-măt′ə-rē′ə, spûr′mə-tə-) *n.* Involuntary discharge of semen without orgasm.

sper•mat•o•zo•id (spər-măt′ə-zō′ĭd, spûr′mə-tə-) *n.* A ciliated male gamete produced in an antheridium.

sper•mat•o•zo•on (spər-măt′ə-zō′ŏn′, -ən, spûr′mə-tə-) *n., pl.* **-zo•a** (-zō′ə). The mature fertilizing gamete of a male organism, usu. consisting of a round or cylindrical nucleated cell, a short neck, and a thin, motile tail. — **sper•mat′o•zo′al** (-zō′əl), **sper•mat′o•zo′an** (-zō′ən), **sper•mat′o•zo′ic** (-zō′ĭk) *adj.*

spermi– or **sperma–** or **spermo–** or **sperm–** *pref.* **1.** Seed: *spermophile.* **2.** Sperm: *spermicide.* [Gk. *spermo-, sperm-* < *sperma*, seed. See SPERM[1].]

sper•mi•cide (spûr′mĭ-sīd′) *n.* An agent that kills spermato-

ă pat	oi boy
ā pay	ou out
âr care	ŏŏ took
ä father	ōō boot
ĕ pet	ŭ cut
ē be	ûr urge
ĭ pit	th thin
ī pie	*th* this
îr pier	hw which
ŏ pot	zh vision
ō toe	ə about, item
ô paw	

Stress marks:
′ (primary);
′ (secondary), as in
dictionary (dĭk′shə-nĕr′ē)

zoa, esp. a contraceptive. —**sper′mi•cid′al** (-sīd′l) *adj.*

sper•mi•o•gen•e•sis (spûr′mē-ō-jĕn′ĭ-sĭs) *n.* Transformation of a spermatid into a spermatozoon. [NLat. *spermium,* spermatozoon (prob. < LLat. *sperma,* semen; see SPERM[1]) + -GENESIS.] —**sper′mi•o•ge•net′ic** (-jə-nĕt′ĭk) *adj.*

sper•mo•go•ni•um (spûr′mə-gō′nē-əm) *n. Bot.* Var. of **spermagonium.**

sperm oil *n.* A waxy yellow oil obtained from the head of the sperm whale and used as an industrial lubricant.

sperm•o•phile (spûr′mə-fīl′) *n.* The ground squirrel.

sperm whale *n.* Any of several large, toothed whales of the family *Physeteridae,* esp. *Physeter catadon* or *P. macrocephalus,* of tropical and temperate oceans, whose massive head has a cavity containing sperm oil and spermaceti and whose long intestines often contain ambergris.

sphinx
c. 530 B.C. Greek grave monument

Sper•ry (spĕr′ē), **Elmer Ambrose.** 1860–1930. Amer. engineer and inventor of the gyrocompass (1910).

sper•ry•lite (spĕr′ĭ-līt′) *n.* A white crystalline platinum mineral, essentially $PtAs_2$. [After Francis L. *Sperry,* 19th-cent. Canadian chemist.]

spes•sar•tite (spĕs′ər-tīt′) also **spes•sar•tine** (-tēn′) *n.* A red to brownish-red mineral of the garnet group, $Mn_3Al_2(SiO_4)_3$. [Fr., after *Spessart,* a hilly area of central Germany.]

spew (spyo͞o) *v.* **spewed, spew•ing, spews.** —*tr.* **1.** To send or force out in or as if in a stream; eject forcefully or in large amounts. **2.** To vomit or otherwise cast out through the mouth. —*intr.* **1.** To flow or gush forth. **2.** To vomit. —*n.* Something spewed. [ME *spewen* < OE *spīwan.*]

Spey•er (spīr, spī′ər, shpī′ər) also **Spires** (spīrz). A city of SW Germany on the Rhine R.; became a free imperial city in 1111. Pop. 43,748.

SPF also **spf** *abbr.* Sun protection factor.

sp gr *abbr.* Specific gravity.

sphag•num (sfăg′nəm) *n.* Any of various pale or ashy mosses of the genus *Sphagnum,* the decomposed remains of which form peat. [NLat. < Lat. *sphagnos,* a kind of moss < Gk., a kind of shrub.] —**sphag′nous** *adj.*

sphal•er•ite (sfăl′ə-rīt′) *n.* The primary ore of zinc, ZnS, occurring in usu. yellow-brown or brownish-black crystals or cleavage masses. [Gk. *sphaleros,* deceitful (< *sphallein,* to trip, it being easily mistaken for galena) + -ITE[1].]

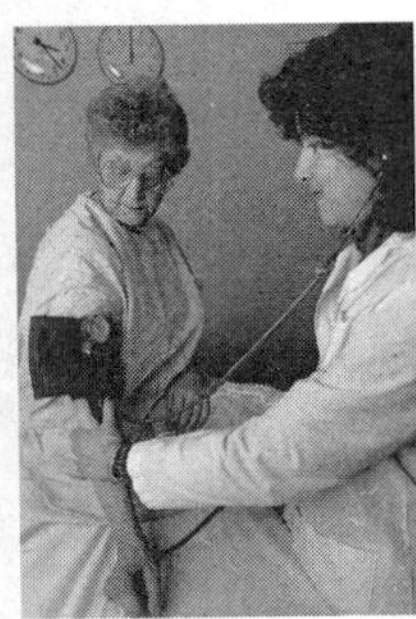
sphygmomanometer

sphene (sfēn) *n.* A titanium mineral in some granite and metamorphic rocks, $CaTiSiO_5$, occurring in usu. small brown or yellow crystals. [Fr. *sphène* < Gk. *sphēn,* wedge.]

sphe•nic (sfē′nĭk) *adj.* Shaped like a wedge.

spheno– or **sphen–** *pref.* Wedge; wedge-shaped: *sphenodon.* [Gk. *sphēno-* < *sphēn,* wedge.]

sphe•no•don (sfē′nə-dŏn′, sfĕn′ə-) *n.* See **tuatara.**

sphe•no•gram (sfē′nə-gram′, sfĕn′ə-) *n.* A cuneiform character.

sphe•noid (sfē′noid′) *n.* The sphenoid bone. —*adj.* **1.** Wedge-shaped. **2.** Of or relating to the sphenoid bone. —**sphe•noi′dal** (-noid′l) *adj.*

sphenoid bone *n.* A compound bone with winglike processes, situated at the base of the skull.

spher– *pref.* Var. of **sphero–.**

spher•al (sfîr′əl) *adj.* **1.** Of, relating to, or having the shape of a sphere; spherical. **2.** Symmetrical.

sphere (sfîr) *n.* **1.** *Math.* A three-dimensional surface, all points of which are equidistant from a fixed point. **2.** A spherical object or figure. **3.** A celestial body, such as a planet or star. **4.** The sky, appearing as a hemisphere to an observer. **5.** Any of a series of postulated concentric, transparent revolving globes that together contained the moon, sun, planets, and stars. **6.** The extent of a person's knowledge, interests, or social position. **7.** An area of power, control, or influence; domain. —*tr.v.* **sphered, spher•ing, spheres. 1.** To form into a sphere. **2.** To put in or within a sphere. **3.** To surround or encompass. [ME *spere* < OFr. *espere* < Lat. *sphaera* < Gk. *sphaira.*] —**sphe•ric′i•ty** (sfĭ-rĭs′ĭ-tē) *n.*

sphere of influence *n., pl.* **spheres of influence.** A territorial area over which influence is wielded by one nation.

spher•i•cal (sfîr′ĭ-kəl, sfĕr′-) also **spher•ic** (-ĭk) *adj.* **1.a.** Having the shape of a sphere; globular. **b.** Having a shape approximating that of a sphere. **2.** Of or relating to a sphere. **3.** Of or relating to celestial bodies. —**spher′i•cal•ly** *adv.* —**spher′i•cal•ness** *n.*

spherical aberration *n.* A blurred image that occurs when light from the margin of a lens or mirror with a spherical surface comes to a shorter focus than light from the central portion.

spherical angle *n. Math.* The angle formed at the intersection of the arcs of two great circles.

spher•i•cal-co•or•di•nate system (sfîr′ĭ-kəl-kō-ôr′dn-ĭt, -āt′, sfĕr′-) *n. Math.* A system for locating points in space by means of a radius vector and two angles measured from the center of a sphere with respect to two perpendicular axes.

spherical geometry *n. Math.* The geometry of circles, angles, and figures on the surface of a sphere.

spherical polygon *n.* A part of a spherical surface that is bounded by arcs of three or more great circles.

spherical triangle *n.* A triangle the three sides of which are arcs of great circles.

spherical trigonometry *n. Math.* The modified form of trigonometry applied to spherical triangles.

spher•ics[1] (sfîr′ĭks, sfĕr′-) *n.* (*used with a sing. v.*) *Math.* **1.** Spherical geometry. **2.** Spherical trigonometry.

spher•ics[2] (sfîr′ĭks, sfĕr′-) *n.* Var. of **sferics.**

sphero– or **spher–** *pref.* Sphere: *spherometer.* [Lat. *sphaero-* < Gk. *sphairo-* < *sphaira,* sphere.]

sphe•roid (sfîr′oid′, sfĕr′-) *n.* A body that is shaped like a sphere but is not perfectly round, esp. an ellipsoid that is generated by revolving an ellipse around one of its axes. —**sphe•roi′dal** (-oid′l), **sphe•roi′dic** (-oi′dĭk) *adj.* —**sphe•roi′dal•ly** *adv.* —**sphe′roi•dic′i•ty** (-dĭs′ĭ-tē) *n.*

sphe•rom•e•ter (sfĭ-rŏm′ĭ-tər) *n.* An instrument for measuring the curvature of a surface, as of a sphere or cylinder.

spher•o•plast (sfîr′ə-plăst′, sfĕr′-) *n.* A bacterial cell whose cell wall is absent or deficient, giving it a spherical form.

spher•ule (sfîr′o͞ol, -yo͞ol, sfĕr′-) *n.* A miniature sphere; a globule. [LLat. *sphaerula,* dim. of Lat. *sphaera,* ball. See SPHERE.] —**spher′u•lar** (sfîr′yə-lər, sfĕr′-) *adj.*

spher•u•lite (sfîr′yə-līt′, -ə-līt′, sfĕr′-) *n.* A small, usu. spheroid body consisting of radiating crystals, found in obsidian and other glassy lava rocks. —**spher′u•lit′ic** (-lĭt′ĭk) *adj.*

spher•y (sfîr′ē) *adj.* **-i•er, -i•est. 1.** Of or relating to the celestial spheres. **2.** Resembling a celestial body.

sphinc•ter (sfĭngk′tər) *n.* A ringlike muscle that constricts a body passage or orifice and relaxes as required by normal physiological functioning. [LLat. *sphincter* < Gk. *sphinktēr* < *sphingein,* to bind tight.] —**sphinc′ter•al** *adj.*

sphin•gid (sfĭn′jĭd) *n.* A moth of the family Sphingidae; a hawk moth. [< NLat. *Sphingidae,* family name < *Sphinx,* type genus < Lat., sphinx. See SPHINX.] —**sphin′gid** *adj.*

sphinx (sfĭngks) *n., pl.* **sphinx•es** or **sphin•ges** (sfĭn′jēz′). **1.** *Myth.* A figure in Egyptian myth having the body of a lion and the head of a man, ram, or hawk. **2.** *Gk. Myth.* A winged creature having the head of a woman and the body of a lion, who killed those unable to answer its riddle. **3.** A puzzling or mysterious person. [ME *Spynx* < Lat. *Sphinx* < Gk.]

sphinx moth *n.* See **hawk moth.**

sp ht *abbr.* Specific heat.

sphyg•mic (sfĭg′mĭk) *adj. Physiol.* Of or relating to the pulse.

sphygmo– or **sphygm–** *pref.* Pulse: *sphygmograph.* [Gk. *sphugmo-* < *sphugmos,* pulsation < *sphuzein, sphug-,* to throb.]

sphyg•mo•gram (sfĭg′mə-grăm′) *n.* The record or tracing produced by a sphygmograph.

sphyg•mo•graph (sfĭg′mə-grăf′) *n.* An instrument for graphically recording the form, strength, and variations of the arterial pulse. —**sphyg′mo•graph′ic** *adj.* —**sphyg•mog′ra•phy** (-mŏg′rə-fē) *n.*

sphyg•mo•ma•nom•e•ter (sfĭg′mō-mə-nŏm′ĭ-tər) also **sphyg•mom•e•ter** (sfĭg-mŏm′ĭ-tər) *n.* An instrument for measuring blood pressure in the arteries, esp. one consisting of a pressure gauge and a rubber cuff that wraps around the upper arm. —**sphyg′mo•ma•nom′e•try** *n.*

spic also **spick** (spĭk) *n. Offensive Slang.* Used as a disparaging term for a Hispanic person. [Alteration of obsolete *spig,* a Mexican, short for *spiggoty,* perh. < an accented pronunciation of *(No) speak the (English).*]

spi•ca (spī′kə) *n., pl.* **-cae** (-kē, -sē) or **-cas.** A bandage applied in overlapping opposite spirals to immobilize a digit or limb. [Lat. *spīca,* ear of grain (< its shape).]

Spi•ca (spī′kə) *n.* A binary star in the constellation Virgo. [Lat. *Spīca* < *spīca,* ear of grain.]

spi•cate (spī′kāt′) *adj.* Borne in or forming a spike. [Lat. *spīcātus* < *spīca,* ear of grain.]

spic•ca•to (spĭ-kä′tō) *Mus.* —*n., pl.* **-tos.** A technique of bowing in which the bow is made to bounce slightly from the string. —*adj.* Of or employing spiccato. [Ital., p.part. of *spiccare,* to separate : *s-,* from (< Lat. *ex-;* see EX–) + *piccare,* to pierce, impale (< VLat. **piccāre;* see PICK[1]).]

spice (spīs) *n.* **1.a.** Any of various pungent aromatic plant substances, such as nutmeg, used to flavor foods or beverages. **b.** These substances considered as a group. **2.** Something adding zest or flavor. **3.** A pungent aroma; a perfume. —*tr.v.* **spiced, spic•ing, spic•es. 1.** To season with spices. **2.** To add zest or flavor to: *spiced up their lives.* [ME < OFr. *espice* < LLat. *speciēs,* wares, spices < Lat., kind. See SPECIES.]

spice•bush (spīs′bo͝osh′) *n.* An aromatic deciduous shrub *(Lindera benzoin)* of eastern North America having clusters of early-blooming small yellow flowers.

spicebush swallowtail *n.* A large swallowtail *(Papilio troilus)* of eastern North America that feeds on spicebushes, having dark forewings and bluish-green hindwings.

Spice Islands (spīs). See **Moluccas.**

spic•er•y (spī′sə-rē) *n., pl.* **-ies. 1.** Spices considered as a group. **2.** The aromatic or pungent quality of spices. **3.** *Archaic.* A place where spices are stored.

spick-and-span also **spic-and-span** (spĭk′ən-spăn′) *adj.* **1.** Immaculately clean; spotless. **2.** Brand-new; fresh. [Short for obsolete *spick and span-new* : *spick,* spike (var. of SPIKE[1]) + SPAN-NEW.]

spic•ule (spĭk′yo͞ol) also **spic•u•la** (-yə-lə) *n., pl.* **-ules** also

-u•lae (-yə-lē). A small needlelike structure or part, such as one of the silicate or calcium carbonate processes supporting the soft tissue of certain invertebrates. [Lat. *spīculum.* See SPICULUM.] — **spic′u•lar** (-yə-lər), **spic′u•late** (-yə-lĭt, -lāt′) *adj.*

spic•u•lum (spĭk′yə-ləm) *n., pl.* **-la** (-lə). A spicule or similar needlelike structure, such as a spine of an echinoderm. [Lat. *spīculum,* dim. of *spīca,* point, ear of grain.]

spic•y (spī′sē) *adj.* **-i•er, -i•est. 1.** Having the flavor, aroma, or quality of spice. **2.** Piquant; zesty: *a spicy tomato sauce.* **3.** High-spirited; lively. **4.** Slightly scandalous; risqué. — **spic′i•ly** *adv.* — **spic′i•ness** *n.*

spi•der (spī′dər) *n.* **1.** Any of numerous arachnids of the order Araneae, having a body divided into a cephalothorax bearing eight legs and an unsegmented abdomen bearing spinnerets that produce silk used esp. to make webs for trapping insects. **2.** One that resembles a spider, as in appearance, character, or movement. **3.** *New England, Upper Northern, & South Atlantic U.S.* See **frying pan.** See Regional Note at **frying pan. 4.** A trivet. [ME *spither* < OE *spīthra.* See **(s)pen-*.**]

spider crab *n.* Any of various crabs, such as those of the genera *Libinia* and *Macrocheira,* having long legs and a relatively small triangular body.

spider flower *n.* See **cleome.**

spider mite *n.* See **red spider.**

spider monkey *n.* Any of several tropical American monkeys of the genus *Ateles,* having long legs and a long prehensile tail and lacking a thumb.

spi•der•wort (spī′dər-wûrt′, -wôrt′) *n.* Any of various New World herbs of the genus *Tradescantia,* having blue or purple flowers with six hairy stamens. [Prob. from its thin, hairy stamens.]

spi•der•y (spī′də-rē) *adj.* **1.a.** Resembling a spider in form, characteristics, or behavior. **b.** Resembling a spider's web; very fine: *spidery handwriting.* **2.** Infested with spiders.

spied (spīd) *v.* P.t. and p.part. of **spy.**

spie•gel (spē′gəl) *n.* Spiegeleisen. [Short for SPIEGELEISEN.]

spie•gel•ei•sen (spē′gə-lī′zən) *n.* An alloy of iron containing approx. 15 percent manganese and small quantities of carbon and silicon, used in the Bessemer process. [Ger. : *Spiegel,* mirror (ult. < Lat. *speculum;* see SPECULUM) + *Eisen,* iron (< MHGer. *īsen* < OHGer. *īsan;* see **eis-***).]

spiel (spēl, shpēl) *Informal.* — *n.* A lengthy, usu. extravagant speech or argument, esp. one intended to persuade. — *intr. & tr.v.* **spieled, spiel•ing, spiels.** To talk or say (something) at length or extravagantly. [Ger., play, or Yiddish *shpil,* both < MHGer. *spil* < OHGer.] — **spiel′er** *n.*

spies (spīz) *n.* Pl. of **spy.** — *v.* Third pers. sing. pr.t. of **spy.**

spiff (spĭf) *Informal.* — *tr.v.* **spiffed, spiff•ing, spiffs.** To make attractive, stylish, or up-to-date: *spiffed up the the old storefront.* — *n.* Attractiveness or charm in appearance, dress, or manners. [Poss. < dial. *spiff,* well-dressed.]

spiff•y (spĭf′ē) *Informal.* — *adj.* **-i•er, -i•est.** Smart in appearance or dress; stylish. — *tr.v.* **-ied, -y•ing, -ies.** To make attractive, stylish, or up-to-date: *spiffying up my wardrobe.* [Poss. < dial. *spiff,* dandified.] — **spiff′i•ly** *adv.* — **spiff′i•ness** *n.*

spig•ot (spĭg′ət) *n.* **1.** A faucet. **2.** A wooden faucet placed in the bunghole of a cask. **3.** The vent plug of a cask. [ME, perh. < OFr. **espigot,* dim. of OProv. *espiga,* ear of grain < Lat. *spīca.*]

spike¹ (spīk) *n.* **1.a.** A long thick sharp-pointed piece of wood or metal. **b.** A heavy nail. **2.** A sharp-pointed projection on the top of a fence or wall. **3.a.** One of several sharp metal projections set in the sole and often the heel of an athletic shoe for grip. **b. spikes.** A pair of athletic shoes with such spikes. **4. spikes.** A pair of spike heels. **5.** An unbranched antler of a young deer. **6.** A young mackerel usu. 15 centimeters (6 inches) or less in length. **7.** A sharp rise followed by a sharp decline in a graph or in the tracing of a scientific instrument. **8.** *Sports.* The act of driving a volleyball at a sharp angle into the opponent's court. — *tr.v.* **spiked, spik•ing, spikes. 1.** To secure or provide with a spike. **2.a.** To pierce or injure with a spike. **b.** *Sports.* To injure with spiked shoes. **3.** *Informal.* To put an end to; block. **4.** *Informal.* To add alcoholic liquor to: *spiked punch.* **5.** *Sports.* To drive (a ball) in a spike. **6.** To render (a muzzleloading gun) useless by driving a spike into the vent. [ME < ON *spīk.*] — **spiked** *adj.*

spike² (spīk) *n.* **1.** An ear of grain, as of wheat. **2.** *Bot.* A usu. elongated unbranched inflorescence with stalkless flowers arranged along an axis. [ME < Lat. *spīca.*]

spike heel *n.* **1.** A very thin high heel used on a woman's shoe. **2.** A woman's shoe with a very thin high heel.

spike lavender *n.* An aromatic Mediterranean plant *(Lavandula latifolia)* of the mint family, yielding an oil similar to that of true lavender.

spike•let (spīk′lĭt) *n.* A small or secondary spike, characteristic of grasses and sedges.

spike•nard (spīk′närd′) *n.* **1.** An aromatic perennial herb *(Nardostachys jatamansi)* of the Himalaya Mountains having rose-purple flowers. **2.** An ointment of antiquity, probably prepared from this herb. **3.** A North American plant *(Aralia racemosa)* having aromatic roots and bipinnately compound leaves. [ME < AN < Med.Lat. *spīca nardī* : Lat. *spīca,* spike, ear + Lat. *nardī,* genitive of *nardus,* nard.]

spik•y (spī′kē) *adj.* **-i•er, -i•est. 1.** Having one or more projecting sharp points. **2.** Grouchy or cross in temperament. — **spik′i•ly** *adv.* — **spik′i•ness** *n.*

spile (spīl) *n.* **1.** A post used as a foundation; a pile. **2.** A wooden plug; a bung. **3.** A spigot used in taking sap from a tree. — *tr.v.* **spiled, spil•ing, spiles.** To support, plug, or tap with a spile. [Du. *spijl,* wooden pin < MDu. *spīle.*]

spill¹ (spĭl) *v.* **spilled** or **spilt** (spĭlt), **spill•ing, spills.** — *tr.* **1.** To cause or allow (a substance) to run or fall out of a container. **2.** To scatter (objects) from containment. **3.** To shed (blood). **4.** *Naut.* **a.** To relieve the pressure of wind on (a sail). **b.** To cause or allow (wind) to be lost from a sail. **5.** To cause to fall. **6.** *Informal.* To disclose (something previously unknown); divulge. — *intr.* **1.** To run or fall out of a container or containment. **2.** To come to the ground suddenly and involuntarily. **3.** To pour out or spread beyond limits. — *n.* **1.** The act of spilling. **2.** An amount spilled. **3.** A fall, as from a horse. **4.** A spillway. [ME *spillen,* to shed blood, to spill < OE *spillan,* to kill.] — **spill′er** *n.*

spill² (spĭl) *n.* **1.** A piece of wood or rolled paper used to light a fire. **2.** A small peg or rod, esp. one used as a plug. [ME *spille.*]

spill•age (spĭl′ĭj) *n.* **1.** The act of spilling. **2.** An amount spilled.

spil•li•kin (spĭl′ĭ-kĭn) *n. Games.* **1. spillikins.** *(used with a sing. v.)* The game of jackstraws. **2.** A jackstraw. [Prob. alteration of Flem. *spelleken,* dim. of *spelle,* pin < MFlem., ult. < Med.Lat. *spīnula,* dim. of Lat. *spīna,* thorn.]

spill•o•ver (spĭl′ō′vər) *n.* **1.** The act or an instance of spilling over. **2.** An amount or a quantity spilled over.

spill•way (spĭl′wā′) *n.* A channel for an overflow of water, as from a reservoir.

spilth (spĭlth) *n.* **1.** The act of spilling. **2.** An amount spilled.

spin (spĭn) *v.* **spun** (spŭn), **spin•ning, spins.** — *tr.* **1.a.** To draw out and twist (fibers) into thread. **b.** To form (thread or yarn) in this manner. **2.** To form (a web or cocoon, for example) by extruding viscous filaments. **3.** To make or produce by or as if by drawing out and twisting. **4.a.** To tell, esp. imaginatively. **b.** To prolong or extend: *spin out a visit.* **5.** To cause to rotate swiftly; twirl. **6.** To shape or make by a twirling or rotating process. **7.** *Slang.* To play (a recording), esp. as a disc jockey. — *intr.* **1.** To spin thread or yarn. **2.** To spin a web or cocoon, for example. **3.** To rotate rapidly; whirl. **4.** To seem to be whirling, as from dizziness; reel. **5.** To ride or drive rapidly. **6.** To fish with a light rod, lure, and line and a reel with a stationary spool. — *n.* **1.** The act of spinning. **2.** A swift whirling motion. **3.** A state of mental confusion. **4.** *Informal.* A short drive in a vehicle. **5.** The flight condition of an aircraft in a nose-down, spiraling, stalled descent. **6.a.** A distinctive point of view or interpretation. **b.** *Slang.* Interpretation, esp. of a politician's words, designed to sway public opinion. **7.** *Phys.* **a.** The intrinsic angular momentum of a subatomic particle. **b.** The total intrinsic angular momentum of an atomic nucleus. **c.** A quantum number expressing spin. — ***phrasal verb.* spin off.** To derive (a product, for example) from something larger. — ***idiom.* spin (one's) wheels.** *Informal.* To expend effort in vain. [ME *spinnen* < OE *spinnan.* See **(s)pen-*.**]

spi•na bif•i•da (spī′nə bĭf′ĭ-də) *n.* A congenital defect in which the spinal column is imperfectly closed so that part of the meninges or spinal cord protrudes, often resulting in hydrocephalus and other neurological disorders. [NLat. *spīna bifida* : Lat. *spīna,* spine + Lat. *bifida,* split in two.]

spin•ach (spĭn′ĭch) *n.* **1.** A widely cultivated southwest Asian plant *(Spinacia oleracea)* having succulent edible leaves. **2.** The leaves of this plant, eaten as a vegetable. [ME < OFr. *espinache* < Med.Lat. *spinăchium* < Ar. *'isfānāḫ* < Pers. *aspanākh.*]

spi•nal (spī′nəl) *adj.* **1.** Of, relating to, or situated near the spine or spinal cord; vertebral: *spinal injury.* **2.** Resembling a spine or spinous part. — *n.* An anesthetic injected into the spinal cord to induce anesthesia. — **spi′nal•ly** *adv.*

spinal anesthesia *n.* Partial or complete anesthesia produced by injecting an anesthetic into the spinal canal.

spinal canal *n.* The passage formed by successive openings in the articulated vertebrae in the spinal column.

spinal column *n.* The series of articulated vertebrae that extends from the cranium to the coccyx or the end of the tail, encasing the spinal cord and forming the supporting axis of the body.

spinal cord *n.* The cord of nerve tissue that extends from the medulla oblongata down through the spinal column and from which the spinal nerves branch off to various body parts.

spinal nerve *n.* Any of the nerves that arise in pairs from the spinal cord, of which there are 31 pairs in the human body.

spin control *n. Slang.* Efforts made esp. by politicians to ensure a favorable interpretation of their words and actions.

spin•dle (spĭn′dl) *n.* **1.a.** A rod or pin, tapered at one end, on which fibers are spun into thread. **b.** A pin or rod holding a bobbin or spool on which thread is wound on an automated

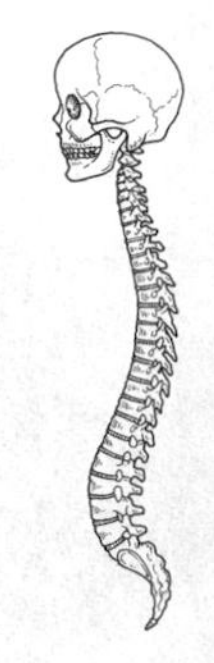

spinal column

ă pat	oi boy
ā pay	ou out
âr care	o͝o took
ä father	o͞o boot
ĕ pet	ŭ cut
ē be	ûr urge
ĭ pit	th thin
ī pie	*th* this
îr pier	hw which
ŏ pot	zh vision
ō toe	ə about, item
ô paw	

Stress marks:
′ (primary);
′ (secondary), as in
dictionary (dĭk′shə-nĕr′ē)

spinning machine. **2.** Any of various mechanical parts that revolve or serve as axes for larger revolving parts, as in a lock or a lathe. **3.** Any of various long thin stationary rods, as: **a.** A spike on which papers may be impaled. **b.** A baluster. **4.** *Biol.* The spindle-shaped achromatic structure, composed of microtubules, along which the chromosomes are distributed in mitosis and meiosis. **5.** *Coastal New Jersey.* See **dragonfly.** See Regional Note at **dragonfly.** —*v.* **-dled, -dling, -dles.** —*tr.* To impale or perforate on a spindle. —*intr.* To grow into a thin, elongated, or weak form. [ME *spindel*, alteration of OE *spinel.* See **(s)pen-***.]

spindle fiber *n.* One of a network of achromatic filaments that extend inward from the poles of a dividing cell, forming a spindle-shaped figure.

spindle tree *n.* Any of various shrubs or trees of the genus *Euonymus*, having brightly colored arillate seeds.

spin•dling (spĭnd′lĭng) *adj.* Spindly.

spin•dly (spĭnd′lē) *adj.* **-dli•er, -dli•est.** Slender and elongated, esp. in a way that suggests weakness.

spin-doc•tor (spĭn′dŏk′tər) *n. Slang.* A representative, esp. for a politician, who favorably interprets words or actions.

spin•drift (spĭn′drĭft′) *n.* Windblown sea spray. [Var. of Sc. *spenedrift* : *spene* (var. of obsolete *spoon*, to run before the wind) + DRIFT.]

spinnaker
Parachute spinnaker on a catamaran

spine (spīn) *n.* **1.** The spinal column of a vertebrate. **2.** *Zool.* Any of various pointed projections, processes, or appendages of animals. **3.** *Bot.* A strong, sharp-pointed, usu. woody outgrowth from a stem or leaf; a thorn. **4.** Something that resembles or suggests a backbone, as: **a.** The hinged back of a book. **b.** The crest of a ridge. **5.** Strength of character; courage or willpower. [ME < OFr. *espine* < Lat. *spīna.*]

spi•nel also **spi•nelle** (spĭ-nĕl′) *n.* A hard, variously colored mineral, $MgAl_2O_4$, of which the red variety is valued as a gem and is sometimes confused with ruby. [Ital. *spinella*, dim. of *spina*, thorn (from its sharply pointed crystals) < Lat. *spīna.*]

spine•less (spīn′lĭs) *adj.* **1.** Lacking courage or willpower. **2.** *Biol.* **a.** Having no spiny processes. **b.** Lacking a spinal column; invertebrate. —**spine′less•ness** *n.*

spi•nes•cent (spī-nĕs′ənt) *adj. Biol.* **1.** Having a spine or spines. **2.** Terminating in a spine. [LLat. *spīnēscēns*, *spīnēscent-*, pr.part. of *spīnēscere*, to become thorny < Lat. *spīna*, thorn.] —**spi•nes′cence** *n.*

spin•et (spĭn′ĭt) *n. Mus.* **1.a.** A small compact upright piano. **b.** A small compact upright electronic organ. **2.** A small harpsichord with a single keyboard. [< obsolete Fr. *espinette*, small harpsichord < Ital. *spinetta*, perh. dim. of *spina*, thorn (presumably so called because the strings of the original instrument were plucked with quills). See SPINEL.]

spinning wheel
Foot-operated spinning wheel

Spin•garn (spĭn′gärn′), **Joel Elias.** 1875–1939. Amer. poet and critic who was a founder (1909) and president (1930–39) of the NAACP.

spi•ni•fex (spī′nə-fĕks′) *n.* Any of various clump-forming perennial Australian grasses, chiefly of the genus *Triodia*, growing in arid regions and having awl-shaped pointed leaves. [NLat. *Spīnifex*, former genus name : Lat. *spīna*, thorn + Lat. *-fex*; see **dhē-***.]

spin•na•ker (spĭn′ə-kər) *n. Naut.* A large triangular sail set forward of all other sails, used by racing and cruising yachts when sailing downwind. [Prob. alteration of *Sphinx's acre* or *sphinxer* < *Sphinx*, name of the first yacht to use it.]

spin•ner (spĭn′ər) *n.* **1.** One that spins. **2.** A fishing lure that rotates rapidly. **3.** A fairing fitted over the hub of the propeller in some aircraft. **4.** *Games.* An arrow that is spun on a dial to indicate the next move in some board games.

spin•ner•et (spĭn′ə-rĕt′) *n.* **1.** Any of various tubular structures from which spiders and certain insect larvae, such as silkworms, secrete the silk threads from which they form webs or cocoons. **2.** A device for making nylon and other synthetic fibers, consisting of a plate pierced with holes through which plastic material is extruded in filaments.

spiral
Staircase

spin•ney (spĭn′ē) *n., pl.* **-neys.** *Chiefly British.* A small grove; a copse. [Obsolete Fr. *espinoi* < OFr. *espinei*, thorny place < VLat. **spīnēta*, pl. of Lat. *spīnētum*, thorn hedge < *spīna*, thorn.]

spin•ning (spĭn′ĭng) *n.* **1.** The process of making fibrous material into yarn or thread. **2.** The act of fishing with a light rod, lure, and line and a reel with a stationary spool.

spinning frame *n.* A machine that draws and twists fibers into yarn and winds it on spindles.

spinning jenny *n.* An early form of spinning machine having several spindles.

spinning wheel *n.* A device for making yarn or thread, having a foot-driven or hand-driven wheel and a single spindle.

spin•off or **spin-off** (spĭn′ôf′, -ŏf′) *n.* **1.a.** A divestiture by a corporation of a division or subsidiary by issuing to stockholders shares in a new company set up to continue operating the division or subsidiary. **b.** This new company. **2.** Something, such as a product, derived from something larger and more or less unrelated; a byproduct. **3.** Something derived from an earlier work, such as a television show starring a character with a minor role in another show.

spi•nose (spī′nōs′) *adj.* Bearing spines; spiny: *a spinose plant.* [Lat. *spīnōsus* < *spīna*, thorn.] —**spi′nose′ly** *adv.* —**spi•nos′i•ty** (-nŏs′ĭ-tē) *n.*

spi•nous (spī′nəs) *adj.* **1.** Resembling a spine or thorn. **2.** Having spines or similar projections; spiny.

Spi•no•za (spĭ-nō′zə), **Baruch** or **Benedict.** 1632–77. Dutch philosopher and theologian whose pantheistic doctrine advocated an intellectual love of God.

Spi•no•zism (spĭ-nō′zĭz′əm) *n. Philos.* A monistic approach to philosophy in which all reality is held to consist of one substance, usu. termed God or Nature, of which minds and bodies are both attributes. [After Baruch SPINOZA.] —**Spi•no′zist** *adj. & n.* —**Spi•no•zis′tic** *adj.*

spin•ster (spĭn′stər) *n.* **1.** A woman who has remained single beyond the conventional age for marrying. **2.** A single woman. **3.** A person whose occupation is spinning. [ME *spinnestere*, female spinner : *spinnen*, to spin; see SPIN + *-estere*, *-ster*, -ster.] —**spin′ster•hood′** *n.* —**spin′ster•ish** *adj.*

spin-the-bot•tle (spĭn′*thə*-bŏt′l) *n. Games.* A game in which players take turns spinning a bottle and kissing the person it points toward when it comes to rest.

spin•to (spĭn′tō) *adj. Mus.* Of, relating to, or being a lyric operatic voice with some attributes of the dramatic voice: *a spinto soprano.* [Ital., p.part. of *spingere*, to push < VLat. **expingere* : Lat. *ex-*, ex- + Lat. *pangere*, to fasten; see IMPINGE.] —**spin′to** *n.*

spi•nule (spīn′yo͞ol) *n.* A small spine or thorn. [Lat. *spīnula*, dim. of *spīna*, thorn.]

spin•y (spī′nē) *adj.* **-i•er, -i•est.** **1.** Bearing or covered with spines, thorns, or similar stiff projections. **2.** Shaped like a spine. **3.** Difficult; troublesome. —**spin′i•ness** *n.*

spiny anteater *n.* See **echidna.**

spin•y-finned (spī′nē-fĭnd′) *adj.* Having fins supported by sharp spiny inflexible rays. Used of a fish.

spin•y-head•ed worm (spī′nē-hĕd′ĭd) *n.* Any of various worms of the phylum Acanthocephala that live parasitically in the intestines of vertebrates and have a cylindrical retractile proboscis with many rows of hooked spines.

spiny lobster *n.* Any of various edible marine decapod crustaceans of the family Palinuridae, having a spiny carapace and lacking the large pincers characteristic of true lobsters.

spin•y-rayed (spī′nē-rād′) *adj.* Spiny-finned.

spir•a•cle (spĭr′ə-kəl, spī′rə-) *n.* **1.** *Zool.* A respiratory aperture, esp.: **a.** Any of several tracheal openings in the exoskeleton of an insect or a spider. **b.** A small respiratory opening behind the eye of certain fishes, such as sharks, rays, and skates. **c.** The blowhole of a cetacean. **2.** An aperture or opening through which air is admitted and expelled. [ME < Lat. *spīrāculum* < *spīrāre*, to breathe.] —**spi•rac′u•lar** (spī-răk′yə-lər, spĭ-) *adj.*

spi•ral (spī′rəl) *n.* **1.a.** A curve on a plane that winds around a fixed center point at a continuously increasing or decreasing distance from the point. **b.** A three-dimensional curve that turns around an axis at a constant or continuously varying distance while moving parallel to the axis; a helix. **c.** Something with the form of such a curve: *a spiral of smoke.* **2.** *Print.* A spiral binding. **3.** The course of an object rotating on its longitudinal axis. **4.** A continuously accelerating increase or decrease: *the wage-price spiral.* —*adj.* **1.** Of or resembling a spiral. **2.** Circling around a center at a continuously increasing or decreasing distance. **3.** Coiling around an axis in a constantly changing series of planes; helical. **4.** *Print.* Relating to or having a spiral binding. —*v.* **-raled, -ral•ing, -rals** also **-ralled, -ral•ling, -rals.** —*intr.* **1.** To take a spiral form or course. **2.** To rise or fall with steady acceleration. —*tr.* To cause to take a spiral form or course. [Med.Lat. *spīrālis*, of a spiral < Lat. *spīra*, coil. See SPIRE².] —**spi•ral′i•ty** (spī-răl′ĭ-tē) *n.* —**spi′ral•ly** *adv.*

spiral binding *n. Print.* A binding for notebooks and booklets in which a cylindrical spiral of wire or plastic is passed through a row of punched holes at the edge of a tablet. —**spi′ral-bound′** (spī′rəl-bound′) *adj.*

spiral galaxy *n.* A galaxy having a spiral structure.

spi•rant (spī′rənt) *Ling.* —*n.* See **fricative.** —*adj.* Fricative. [Lat. *spīrāns*, *spīrant-*, pr.part. of *spīrāre*, to breathe.]

spire¹ (spīr) *n.* **1.** A top part or point that tapers upward; a pinnacle. **2.** A structure or formation that tapers to a point at the top. **3.** A slender tapering part, such as a newly sprouting blade of grass. —*v.* **spired, spir•ing, spires.** —*tr.* To furnish with a spire. —*intr.* To rise and taper steeply. [ME < OE *spīr.*]

spire² (spīr) *n.* **1.a.** A spiral. **b.** A single turn of a spiral. **2.** The area farthest from the aperture and nearest the apex on a coiled gastropod shell. [Lat. *spīra*, coil < Gk. *speira.*]

spi•re•a also **spi•rae•a** (spī-rē′ə) *n.* Any of various shrubs of the genus *Spiraea* of the rose family, having clusters of small white or pink flowers and including the meadowsweet. [Lat. *spiraea*, meadowsweet < Gk. *speiraia*, privet < *speira*, coil.]

spi•reme (spī′rēm′) also **spi•rem** (-rĕm′) *n. Biol.* The tangle of filaments that appears at the beginning of the prophase portion of meiosis or mitosis. [Ger. *Spirem* < Gk. *speirēma*, coil < *speirasthai*, to be coiled around < *speira*, coil.]

Spires (spīrz). See **Speyer.**

spi•rif•er•ous (spī-rĭf′ər-əs) *adj.* Having a spiral structure or spiral parts. [Prob. < NLat. *spirifer* : Lat. *spīra*, coil; see SPIRE[2] + Lat. *-fer*, -fer.]

spi•ril•lum (spī-rĭl′əm) *n., pl.* **-ril•la** (-rĭl′ə). **1.** Any of various aerobic bacteria of the genus *Spirillum*, having an elongated spiral form and bearing a tuft of flagella. **2.** Any of various other spiral-shaped microorganisms. [NLat. *Spīrillum*, genus name, dim. of Lat. *spīra*, coil. See SPIRE[2].]

spir•it (spĭr′ĭt) *n.* **1.a.** The vital principle or animating force within living beings. **b.** Incorporeal consciousness. **2.** The soul, considered as departing from a person's body at death. **3. Spirit.** The Holy Spirit. **4.** A supernatural being, as: **a.** An angel or a demon. **b.** A being inhabiting or embodying a particular place, object, or natural phenomenon. **c.** A fairy or sprite. **5.a.** The part of a human being associated with the mind, will, and feelings: *with us in spirit.* **b.** The essential nature of a person or group. **6.** A person as characterized by a stated quality: *a proud spirit.* **7.a.** An inclination or a tendency of a specified kind: *a generous spirit.* **b.** A causative, activating, or essential principle: *The party was announced in a joyous spirit.* **8. spirits.** A mood or an emotional state. **9.** A particular mood or an emotional state characterized by vigor and animation: *sang with spirit.* **10.** Strong loyalty or dedication. **11.** The predominant mood of an occasion or a period. **12.** The actual though unstated sense or significance of something: *the spirit of the law.* **13.** An alcohol solution of an essential or volatile substance. Often used in the plural with a singular verb. **14. spirits.** An alcoholic beverage, esp. distilled liquor. —*tr.v.* **-it•ed, -it•ing, -its. 1.** To carry off mysteriously or secretly: *spirited away the papers.* **2.** To impart courage, animation, or determination to; inspirit. [ME < OFr. *espirit* < Lat. *spīritus*, breath < *spīrāre*, to breathe.]

spir•it•ed (spĭr′ĭ-tĭd) *adj.* **1.** Animated, vigorous, or courageous. **2.** Having a given mood or nature. Used in combination: *high-spirited.* —**spir′it•ed•ness** *n.*

spir•it•ism (spĭr′ĭ-tĭz′əm) *n.* Spiritualism. —**spir′it•ist** *n.* —**spir′it•is′tic** *adj.*

spir•it•less (spĭr′ĭt-lĭs) *adj.* Lacking energy or enthusiasm; listless. —**spir′it•less•ly** *adv.* —**spir′it•less•ness** *n.*

spirit level *n.* See **level** 7a.

spirit of turpentine *n.* See **turpentine** 1.

spirit of wine *n.* Rectified ethyl alcohol.

spir•it•ous (spĭr′ĭ-təs) *adj.* **1.** Spirituous. **2.** *Archaic.* Highly refined; pure.

spir•i•tu•al (spĭr′ĭ-cho͞o-əl) *adj.* **1.** Of, relating to, consisting of, or having the nature of spirit; not tangible or material. **2.** Of, concerned with, or affecting the soul. **3.** Of, from, or relating to God; deific. **4.** Of or belonging to a church or religion; sacred. **5.** Relating to or having the nature of spirits or a spirit; supernatural. —*n.* **1.** *Mus.* **a.** A religious folk song of American Black origin. **b.** A work composed in imitation of such a song. **2.** Religious, spiritual, or ecclesiastical matters. Often used in the plural. [ME < OFr. *spirituel* < Lat. *spīrituālis*, of breathing, spiritual < *spīritus*, breath. See SPIRIT.] —**spir′i•tu•al•ly** *adv.* —**spir′i•tu•al•ness** *n.*

spir•i•tu•al•ism (spĭr′ĭ-cho͞o-ə-lĭz′əm) *n.* **1.a.** The belief that the dead communicate with the living, as through a medium; spiritism. **b.** The practices or doctrines of those holding such a belief; spiritism. **2.** A philosophy, doctrine, or religion emphasizing the spiritual aspect of being. —**spir′i•tu•al•ist** *n.* —**spir′i•tu•al•is′tic** *adj.*

spir•i•tu•al•i•ty (spĭr′ĭ-cho͞o-ăl′ĭ-tē) *n., pl.* **-ties. 1.** The state, quality, manner, or fact of being spiritual. **2.** The clergy. **3.** Something, such as property or revenue, that belongs to the church or to a cleric. Often used in the plural.

spir•i•tu•al•ize (spĭr′ĭ-cho͞o-ə-līz′) *tr.v.* **-ized, -iz•ing, -iz•es. 1.** To impart a spiritual nature to. **2.** To invest with or treat as having a spiritual sense or meaning. —**spir′i•tu•al•i•za′tion** (-ə-lĭ-zā′shən) *n.* —**spir′i•tu•al•iz′er** *n.*

spir•i•tu•al•ty (spĭr′ĭ-cho͞o-əl-tē) *n., pl.* **-ties.** Property or revenue belonging to the church or to a cleric; spirituality. Often used in the plural.

spir•i•tu•el also **spir•i•tu•elle** (spĭr′ĭ-cho͞o-ĕl′, spē′rē-to͞o-ĕl′, -tü-) *adj.* Having or evidencing a refined mind and wit. [Fr. < OFr., spiritual. See SPIRITUAL.]

spir•i•tu•ous (spĭr′ĭ-cho͞o-əs) *adj.* **1.** Having the nature of or containing alcohol; alcoholic. **2.** Distilled. Used of an alcoholic beverage. —**spir′i•tu•os′i•ty** (-ŏs′ĭ-tē), **spir′i•tu•ous•ness** (-əs-nĭs) *n.*

spiro– *pref.* Respiration: *spirometer.* [< Lat. *spīrāre*, to breathe.]

spi•ro•chete (spī′rə-kēt′) *n.* Any of various slender spiral motile bacteria of the order Spirochaetales, many of which are pathogenic, causing syphilis and other diseases. [NLat. *Spīrochaeta*, genus name : Lat. *spīra*, coil; see SPIRE[2] + NLat. *chaeta*, bristle, hair; see CHAETA.] —**spi′ro•chet′al** (-kēt′l) *adj.*

spi•ro•che•to•sis (spī′rə-kē-tō′sĭs) *n., pl.* **-ses** (-sēz). Any of various diseases, such as syphilis, caused by spirochetes.

spi•ro•graph (spī′rə-grăf′) *n.* An instrument for registering the depth and rapidity of respiratory movements. —**spi′ro•graph′ic** *adj.* —**spi•rog′ra•phy** (spī-rŏg′rə-fē) *n.*

spi•ro•gy•ra (spī′rə-jī′rə) *n.* Any of various filamentous freshwater green algae of the genus *Spirogyra*, having chloroplasts in spirally twisted bands. [NLat. *Spīrogyra*, genus name : Lat. *spīra*, coil; see SPIRE[2] + Gk. *guros*, ring.]

spi•roid (spī′roid′) *adj.* Resembling a spiral.

spi•rom•e•ter (spī-rŏm′ĭ-tər) *n.* An instrument for measuring the volume of air entering and leaving the lungs. —**spi′ro•met′ric** (-rə-mĕt′rĭk) *adj.* —**spi•rom′e•try** *n.*

spirt (spûrt) *n. & v. Chiefly British.* Var. of **spurt.**

spir•u•la (spĭr′yə-lə, spĭr′ə-) *n., pl.* **-lae** (-lē′). A small cephalopod mollusk of the genus *Spirula*, having a spirally coiled, partitioned internal shell. [LLat. *spīrula*, twisted cake, dim. of Lat. *spīra*, coil. See SPIRE[2].]

spit[1] (spĭt) *n.* **1.** Saliva, esp. when expectorated; spittle. **2.** The act of expectorating. **3.** Something, such as the frothy secretion of spittle bugs, that resembles expectorated saliva. **4.** A brief scattered fall of rain or snow. **5.** *Informal.* The perfect likeness: *He's the spit and image of his father.* —*v.* **spat** (spăt) or **spit, spit•ting, spits.** —*tr.* **1.** To eject from the mouth: *spat out the date pits.* **2.** To eject as if from the mouth: *a fire spitting sparks.* **3.** To emit suddenly and forcefully: *spat out an insult.* —*intr.* **1.** To eject matter from the mouth; expectorate. **2.** To express contempt or animosity by or as if by ejecting matter from the mouth. **3.** To make a hissing or sputtering noise. **4.** To rain or snow in light scattered drops or flakes. —***phrasal verb.* spit up.** To vomit. [ME < *spitten*, to spit < OE *spittan*, ult. of imit. orig.]

spit[2] (spĭt) *n.* **1.** A slender pointed rod on which meat is impaled for broiling. **2.** A narrow point of land extending into a body of water. —*tr.v.* **spit•ted, spit•ting, spits.** To impale on or as if on a spit. [ME < OE *spitu.*]

spit•al (spĭt′l) *n. Archaic.* A hospital, esp. one for contagious patients. [ME *spitel*, short for *hospital.* See HOSPITAL.]

spit and polish *n.* Attention to appearance and order, as in a military unit. —**spit′-and-pol′ish** (spĭt′n-pŏl′ĭsh) *adj.*

spit•ball (spĭt′bôl′) *n.* **1.** A piece of paper chewed, crumpled, and used as a projectile. **2.** *Baseball.* An illegal pitch in which a foreign substance, such as saliva, is applied to the ball.

spit curl *n.* A spiral curl of hair pressed flat against the cheek, temple, or forehead. [< the use of saliva to fix the curl.]

spite (spīt) *n.* **1.** Malicious ill will prompting an urge to hurt or humiliate. **2.** An instance of malicious feeling. —*tr.v.* **spit•ed, spit•ing, spites. 1.a.** To show spite toward. **b.** To vent spite on. **2.a.** To fill with spite. **b.** To annoy. —***idiom.* in spite of.** Not stopped by; regardless of: *They kept going in spite of their fears.* [ME, short for *despit.* See DESPITE.]

spite•ful (spīt′fəl) *adj.* Filled with, prompted by, or showing spite; malicious. —**spite′ful•ly** *adv.* —**spite′ful•ness** *n.*

spit•fire (spĭt′fīr′) *n.* A quick-tempered or highly excitable person.

Spits•ber•gen (spĭts′bûr′gən). An island of Norway in Svalbard in the Arctic Ocean E of N Greenland.

Spit•te•ler (shpĭt′l-ər, shpĭt′lər, spĭt′-), **Carl.** 1845–1924. Swiss writer who won the 1919 Nobel Prize for literature.

spit•ter (spĭt′ər) *n.* **1.** One that spits: *a spitter of invective.* **2.** *Baseball.* See **spitball** 2.

spit•ting cobra (spĭt′ĭng) *n.* See **ringhals.**

spitting image *n.* A perfect likeness or counterpart. [Alteration of *spit and image* < *spit*, an exact likeness. See SPIT 1.]

spit•tle (spĭt′l) *n.* **1.** Spit; saliva. **2.** The frothy liquid secreted by spittlebugs. [ME *spitel*, alteration of *spatel* < OE *spātl.*]

spit•tle•bug (spĭt′l-bŭg′) *n.* Any of various leaping homopterous insects of the family Cercopidae, the nymphs of which form frothy masses of liquid on plant stems.

spit•toon (spĭ-to͞on′) *n.* A bowl-shaped, usu. metal vessel, often with a funnel-shaped cover, into which tobacco chewers periodically spit. [SPIT[1] + *-oon*, as in BALLOON.]

spitz (spĭts) *n.* A dog of any of several northern breeds, such as the Samoyed, having a long, thick, usu. white coat, pointed muzzle and ears, and a tail curled over the back. [Ger. *Spitz* < *spitz*, pointed < MHGer. *spiz* < OHGer. *spizzi.*]

spiv (spĭv) *n. Chiefly British.* **1.** One, usu. unemployed, who lives by one's wits. **2.** One who shirks work or responsibility; a slacker. [Dial. *spif*, dandified, dandy.]

splanch•nic (splăngk′nĭk) *adj.* Of or relating to the viscera; visceral: *a splanchnic nerve.* [NLat. *splanchnicus* < Gk. *splankhnikos* < *splankhna*, inward parts.]

splash (splăsh) *v.* **splashed, splash•ing, splash•es.** —*tr.* **1.** To propel or scatter (a fluid) about in flying masses. **2.** To scatter fluid onto in flying masses; wet, stain, or soil with flying fluid. **3.** To cause (something) to scatter fluid in flying masses: *splashed their hands in the water.* **4.** To make (one's way) with or by scattering of fluid. **5.** To apply patches or spots of a contrasting, usu. bright color to. **6.** To display or publicize very noticeably. —*intr.* **1.a.** To cause a fluid to scatter in flying masses: *splashed about in the pool.* **b.** To fall into or move through fluid with this effect: *We splashed through the waves.* **2.a.** To move, spill, or fly about in scattered masses. **b.** To produce a sound or sight associated with this effect. —*n.* **1.** The act or sound of splashing. **2.a.** A flying mass of fluid. **b.** A small amount, esp. of a fluid. **3.** A marking produced by or as if by scattered fluid. **4.** A great though often short-lived impression; a stir. [Prob. alteration of PLASH.]

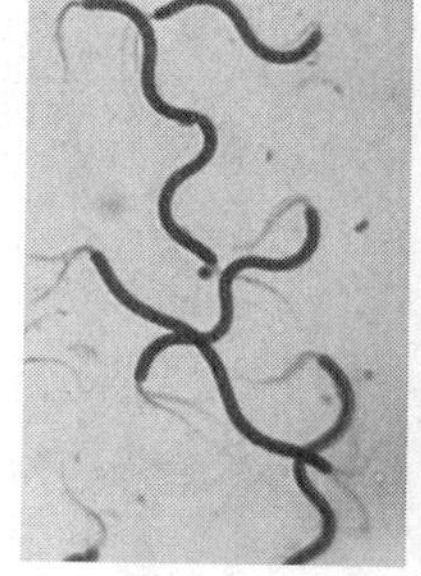
spirillum
Magnified image of spirilla

spittlebug
Top: Adult European spittlebug *Aphrophora alvi*
Bottom: Nymph enclosed in mass of spittle

ă pat	oi boy
ā pay	ou out
âr care	o͝o took
ä father	o͞o boot
ĕ pet	ŭ cut
ē be	ûr urge
ĭ pit	th thin
ī pie	*th* this
îr pier	hw which
ŏ pot	zh vision
ō toe	ə about, item
ô paw	

Stress marks:
′ (primary);
′ (secondary), as in
dictionary (dĭk′shə-nĕr′ē)

splash•board (splăsh′bôrd′, -bōrd′) *n.* **1.** A structure that protects the upper part of a vehicle from splashes of mud. **2.** *Naut.* A screen on a boat to keep water from splashing onto the deck. **3.** A board for closing a spillway or sluice.

splash•down (splăsh′doun′) *n.* The landing of a spacecraft or missile in water.

splash•guard (splăsh′gärd′) *n.* See **mudguard.**

splash•y (splăsh′ē) *adj.* **-i•er, -i•est. 1.** Making or likely to make splashes. **2.** Covered with splashes of color. **3.** Showy; ostentatious. See Syns at **showy.** **—splash′i•ly** *adv.* **—splash′i•ness** *n.*

splat[1] (splăt) *n.* A slat of wood, as one in the middle of a chair back. [Perh. < ME *splatten,* to split open, perh. < Med.Lat. *splattāre,* of LGer. orig.]

splat[1]

splat[2] (splăt) *n.* A smacking or splashing noise. —*adv.* With a smacking or splashing noise: *fell splat on the floor.* [Imit.]

splat•ter (splăt′ər) *v.* **-tered, -ter•ing, -ters.** —*tr.* To spatter (something), esp. to soil with splashes of liquid. —*intr.* To spatter, esp. to move or fall so as to cause splashes. —*n.* A splash of liquid. [Perh. blend of SPLASH and SPATTER.]

splay (splā) *adj.* **1.** Spread or turned out. **2.** Clumsy or clumsily formed; awkward. —*n. Archit.* An oblique angle or bevel given to the sides of an opening in a wall so that the opening is wider on one side of the wall than on the other. —*v.* **splayed, splay•ing, splays.** —*tr.* **1.** To spread (the limbs, for example) out or apart, esp. clumsily. **2.** To make slanting or sloping; bevel. **3.** To dislocate (a bone). Used of an animal. —*intr.* **1.** To be spread out or apart. **2.** To slant or slope. [< ME *splayen,* to spread out, short for *displayen.* See DISPLAY.]

splay•foot (splā′fo͝ot′) *n.* **1.** A physical deformity characterized by abnormally flat and turned-out feet. **2.** A foot so affected. **—splay′foot′ed** *adj.*

spleen (splēn) *n.* **1.a.** A large, highly vascular lymphoid organ, lying in the human body to the left of the stomach below the diaphragm, serving to filter and store blood and produce lymphocytes. **b.** A homologous organ or tissue in other vertebrates. **2.** *Obsolete.* This organ conceived as the seat of emotions or passions. **3.** Ill temper: *vent one's spleen.* **4.** *Archaic.* Melancholy. **5.** *Obsolete.* A whim; a caprice. [ME *splen* < OFr. *esplen* < Lat. *splēn* < Gk.] **—spleen′y** *adj.*

spleen•ful (splēn′fəl) *adj.* Affected by or filled with spleen.

spleen•wort (splēn′wûrt′, -wôrt′) *n.* Any of numerous widely distributed evergreen ferns of the genus *Asplenium,* having undivided to featherlike fronds and oblong to linear sori.

splen•dent (splĕn′dənt) *adj.* **1.** Shining or lustrous; brilliant. **2.** Admired by many; illustrious. [ME < OFr. *esplendent* < Lat. *splendēns, splendent-,* pr.part. of *splendēre,* to shine.]

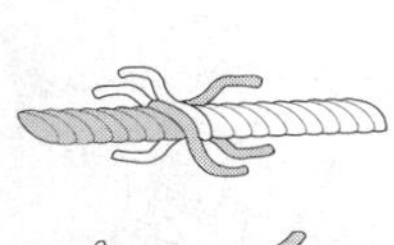

splice

splen•did (splĕn′dĭd) *adj.* **1.** Brilliant with light or color; radiant: *a splendid field of poppies.* **2.** Magnificent; grand; sumptuous: *splendid costumes.* **3.** Outstanding; surpassing: *a splendid day.* **4.** Very good or satisfying: *a splendid character.* [Lat. *splendidus* < *splendēre,* to shine.] **—splen′did•ly** *adv.* **—splen′did•ness** *n.*

splen•dif•er•ous (splĕn-dĭf′ər-əs) *adj.* Splendid. [ME < Med. Lat. *splendiferus* < LLat. *splendōrifer* : Lat. *splendor,* splendor; see SPLENDOR + Lat. *-fer,* -fer.]

splen•dor (splĕn′dər) *n.* **1.** Great light or luster; brilliance. **2.a.** Magnificent appearance or display; grandeur. **b.** Something grand or magnificent. **3.** Great fame; glory. [ME *splendoure* < OFr. *splendour* < Lat. *splendor* < *splendēre,* to shine.] **—splen′dor•ous, splen′drous** (splĕn′drəs) *adj.*

splen•dour (splĕn′dər) *n. Chiefly British.* Var. of **splendor.**

sple•nec•to•my (splĭ-nĕk′tə-mē) *n., pl.* **-mies.** Surgical removal of the spleen. **—sple•nec′to•mize′** (-mīz′) *v.*

sple•net•ic (splĭ-nĕt′ĭk) also **sple•net•i•cal** (-ĭ-kəl) —*adj.* **1.** Of or relating to the spleen. **2.** Ill-humored or irritable. —*n.* A person regarded as irritable. [LLat. *splēnēticus* < Lat. *splēn,* spleen. See SPLEEN.] **—sple•net′i•cal•ly** *adv.*

splen•ic (splĕn′ĭk) *adj.* Of, in, near, or relating to the spleen.

sple•ni•us (splē′nē-əs) *n., pl.* **-ni•i** (-nē-ī′). Either of two muscles of the back of the neck that rotate and extend the head and neck. [NLat. *splēnius* < Lat. *splēnium,* patch, plaster (< its shape) < Gk. *splēnion* < *splēn,* spleen.]

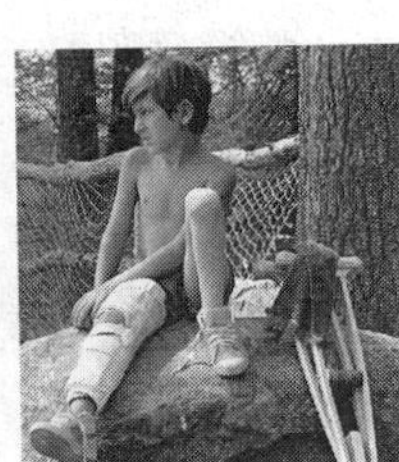

splint

spleno– or **splen–** *pref.* Spleen: *splenomegaly.* [Gk. *splēno-* < *splēn,* spleen.]

sple•no•meg•a•ly (splē′nō-mĕg′ə-lē, splĕn′ō-) *n., pl.* **-lies.** Enlargement of the spleen.

splice (splīs) *tr.v.* **spliced, splic•ing, splic•es. 1.a.** To join (film, for example) at the ends. **b.** To join (ropes, for example) by interweaving strands. **2.** To join (pieces of wood) by overlapping and binding at the ends. **3.** To join together or insert (segments of DNA or RNA) so as to form new genetic combinations or alter a genetic structure. **4.** *Slang.* To marry. —*n.* **1.** A joining by splicing. **2.** A place where parts have been spliced. [Obsolete Du. *splissen* < MDu.] **—splic′er** *n.*

spline (splīn) *n.* **1.a.** Any of a series of projections on a shaft that fit into slots on a corresponding shaft, enabling both to rotate together. **b.** The groove or slot for such a projection. **2.** A flexible piece of wood, hard rubber, or metal used in drawing curves. **3.** A wooden or metal strip; a slat. [?]

splint (splĭnt) *n.* **1.** A thin piece split off from a larger one; a splinter. **2.a.** A rigid device used to prevent motion of a joint or of the ends of a fractured bone. **b.** A dental appliance to protect teeth from grinding or moving out of place. **3.** A thin flexible wooden strip, such as one used in basketry. **4.** A plate or strip of metal. **5.** A bony enlargement of a horse's cannon bone or splint bone. —*tr.v.* **splint•ed, splint•ing, splints.** To support or restrict with or as if with a splint. [ME < MDu. or MLGer. *splinte.*]

splint bone *n.* Either of two small metacarpal or metatarsal bones in horses or related animals.

splin•ter (splĭn′tər) *n.* **1.** A sharp slender piece, as of wood or metal, split or broken off from a main body. **2.** A splinter group. —*v.* **-tered, -ter•ing, -ters.** —*intr.* To split or break into sharp slender pieces. See Syns at **break.** —*tr.* To cause to splinter. [ME < MDu.] **—splin′ter•y** *adj.*

splinter group *n.* A group, such as a religious sect or political faction, that has broken away from a parent group.

split (splĭt) *v.* **split, split•ting, splits.** —*tr.* **1.** To divide from end to end or along the grain by or as if by a sharp blow. See Syns at **tear**[1]. **2.a.** To break, burst, or rip apart with force; rend. See Syns at **break. b.** To affect with force in a way that suggests tearing apart: *A lightning bolt split the night sky.* **3.** To separate (people or groups, for example); disunite. **4.** To divide and share. **5.** To divide, as for convenience or proper ordering: *split the project up.* **6.** To separate (leather, for example) into layers. **7.** To mark (a vote or ballot) in favor of candidates from different parties. **8.** To divide (stock) by issuing multiples of the existing stock with a corresponding reduction in the price of each share, so that the total value of the stock is unchanged. **9.** *Sports.* To win half the games of (a series or double-header). **10.** *Slang.* To depart from; leave. —*intr.* **1.** To become separated into parts, esp. to undergo lengthwise division. **2.** To become broken or ripped apart, esp. from internal pressure. **3.** To become or admit of being divided: *split up into teams.* **4.** *Informal.* To become divided or part company as a result of discord or disagreement. **5.** To divide or share something with others. **6.** *Slang.* To depart; leave. —*n.* **1.** The act of splitting or the result of it. **2.** A breach or rupture in a group. **3.** A splinter. **4.** Something divided and portioned out; a share. **5.** A strip of flexible wood used for making baskets. **6.a.** A bottle of an alcoholic or carbonated beverage half the usual size. **b.** A drink of half the usual quantity. **c.** A half pint. **7.** A dessert of sliced fruit, ice cream, and toppings. **8.** *Sports.* An acrobatic feat in which the legs are stretched out straight in opposite directions at right angles to the trunk. Often used in the plural. **9.** *Sports.* An arrangement of bowling pins left standing, in which two or more pins remain standing with one or more pins between them knocked down. **10.** A single thickness of a split hide. —*adj.* **1.** Having been divided or separated. **2.** Fissured longitudinally; cleft. **3.a.** Quoted in 16ths rather than in 8ths. Used of stocks. **b.** Having been split. Used of stocks. —***idiom.*** **split hairs.** To see or make trivial distinctions; quibble. [Du. *splitten* < MDu.] **—split′ter** *n.*

Split (splĭt). A city of SW Croatia on the Dalmatian coast of the Adriatic Sea; founded as a Roman colony. Pop. 193,600.

split-brain (splĭt′brān′) *adj.* Of, relating to, or subjected to surgical separation of the hemispheres of the brain by severing the corpus callosum: *split-brain operations.*

split infinitive *n. Gram.* An infinitive verb form with an element, usu. an adverb, interposed between *to* and the verb form, as in *to boldly go.*

Usage Note: The split infinitive was first labeled and condemned in the 19th century. No plausible rationale has ever been advanced for the rule, though it may arise from a hazy notion that because the Latin infinitive is a single word, the equivalent English construction must be treated as if it were indivisible. In some cases avoidance of the split infinitive may result in a stylistic improvement. The sentence *We are seeking a plan to gradually, systematically, and economically relieve the burden on our employees* becomes clearer if the adverbs are placed at the end: *We are seeking a plan to relieve the burden on our employees gradually, systematically, and economically.* (In an earlier survey the example having the split infinitive was accepted by only 23 percent of the Usage Panel.) But in other cases the effort to avoid a split infinitive may have unfortunate consequences. In *We expect our output to more than double in a year,* the phrase *more than* is intrinsic to the sense of the infinitive phrase, though the split infinitive could be avoided by use of another phrase, such as *to increase by more than 100 percent.* In this example the split infinitive is accepted by 87 percent of the Usage Panel.

split-lev•el (splĭt′lĕv′əl) *adj.* Having the floors of adjoining rooms separated by about half a story. **—split′-lev′el** *n.*

split personality *n.* See **multiple personality.**

split rail *n.* A fence rail split lengthwise from a log. **—split′-rail′** (splĭt′rāl′) *adj.*

split second *n.* An instant; a flash. [Short for *split second hands,* a stopwatch with two independent second hands.]

split ticket *n.* A ballot cast for candidates of two or more political parties.

split•ting (splĭt′ĭng) *adj.* Very severe: *a splitting headache.*

splotch (splŏch) *n.* An irregularly shaped spot, stain, or colored or discolored area. — *tr.v.* **splotched, splotch•ing, splotch•es.** To mark with splotches or a splotch. [Perh. blend of SPOT, BLOT[1], and BOTCH.] **— splotch′i•ness** *n.* **— splotch′y** *adj.*

splurge (splûrj) *v.* **splurged, splurg•ing, splurg•es.** — *intr.* **1.** To indulge in an extravagant expense or luxury. **2.** To be showy or ostentatious. — *tr.* To spend extravagantly or wastefully. — *n.* **1.** An extravagant display. **2.** An expensive indulgence; a spree. [Perh. blend of SPLASH and SURGE.] **— splurg′y** *adj.*

splut•ter (splŭt′ər) *v.* **-tered, -ter•ing, -ters.** — *intr.* **1.** To make a spitting sound. **2.** To speak incoherently, as when confused or angry. — *tr.* To utter or express hastily and incoherently. — *n.* A spluttering noise. [Perh. alteration of SPUTTER.] **— splut′ter•er** *n.* **— splut′ter•y** *adj.*

Spock (spŏk), **Benjamin McLane.** b. 1903. Amer. pediatrician who wrote *Baby and Child Care* (orig. published 1946).

Spode (spōd). A trademark used for a brand of fine china and earthenware.

spod•u•mene (spŏj′ə-mēn′) *n.* A greenish to pinkish mineral, $LiAlSi_2O_6$, used as a lithium ore and in transparent varieties as a gemstone. [Fr. *spodumène* < Ger. *Spodumen* < Gk. *spodoumenos*, pr.part. of *spodousthai*, to be burned to ashes < *spodos*, wood ashes (the mineral becoming gray in air).]

spoil (spoil) *v.* **spoiled** or **spoilt** (spoilt), **spoil•ing, spoils.** — *tr.* **1.a.** To impair the value or quality of. **b.** To damage irreparably; ruin. **2.** To impair the completeness, perfection, or unity of; flaw grievously. **3.** To harm the character, nature, or attitude of by oversolicitude, overindulgence, or excessive praise. **4.** *Archaic.* **a.** To plunder; despoil. **b.** To take by force. — *intr.* **1.** To become unfit for use or consumption, as from decay. Used esp. of perishables, such as food. **2.** To pillage. — *n.* **1. spoils. a.** Goods or property seized from a victim after a conflict. **b.** Incidental benefits reaped by a winner, esp. political patronage enjoyed by a party or candidate. **2.** An object of plunder; prey. **3.** Refuse material removed from an excavation. **4.** *Archaic.* The act of plundering; spoliation. **—*phrasal verb.* spoil for.** To be eager for. [ME *spoilen*, to plunder < OFr. *espoillier* < Lat. *spoliāre* < *spolium*, booty.]

Syns: *spoil, injure, harm, hurt, damage, impair, mar.* The central meaning shared by these verbs is "to affect detrimentally or adversely": *spoiled our party; was badly injured; insects that harmed the foliage; situation that hurt their profits; scandal damaging a reputation; vision impaired by poor lighting; a performance marred by error.*

spoil•age (spoi′lĭj) *n.* **1.a.** The process of becoming spoiled. **b.** The condition of being spoiled. **2.a.** Something spoiled. **b.** The degree to which something has been spoiled.

spoil•er (spoi′lər) *n.* **1.** One who seizes spoils or booty. **2.** Something that causes spoilage. **3.a.** A long narrow hinged plate on the upper surface of an airplane wing that reduces lift and increases drag when raised. **b.** An air deflector mounted usu. at the rear of an automobile to reduce lift at high speeds. **4.** A candidate for office who has little chance of winning but may prevent another candidate from winning.

spoil•sport (spoil′spôrt′, -spōrt′) *n.* One who mars the pleasure of others.

spoils system (spoilz) *n.* The postelection practice of rewarding the winner's loyal supporters with public offices.

Spo•kane (spō-kăn′). A city of E WA near the ID border on the falls of the **Spokane River,** c. 193 km (120 mi); settled on the site of a trading fort estab. 1810. Pop. 177,196.

spoke[1] (spōk) *n.* **1.** One of the rods or braces connecting the hub and rim of a wheel. **2.** *Naut.* One of the handles projecting from the rim of a ship's wheel. **3.** A rod or stick that may be inserted into a wheel to prevent it from turning. **4.** A rung of a ladder. — *tr.v.* **spoked, spok•ing, spokes. 1.** To equip with spokes. **2.** To impede (a wheel) by inserting a rod. [ME < OE *spāca.*]

spoke[2] (spōk) *v.* **1.** P.t. of **speak. 2.** *Archaic.* A p.part. of **speak.**

spo•ken (spō′kən) *v.* P.part. of **speak.** — *adj.* **1.** Expressed orally; uttered. **2.** Speaking or using speech in a certain way or voice. Often used in combination: *plainspoken.*

spoke•shave (spōk′shāv′) *n.* A drawknife originally used for shaping spokes, now used for making rounded edges.

spokes•man (spōks′mən) *n.* A man who speaks on behalf of another or others. See Usage Note at **man.** [Prob. *spoke*, p.part. of SPEAK + MAN.]

spokes•per•son (spōks′pûr′sən) *n.* A spokesman or a spokeswoman. See Usage Note at **man.**

spokes•wom•an (spōks′wo͝om′ən) *n.* A woman who speaks on behalf of another or others. See Usage Note at **man.**

spo•li•a•tion (spō′lē-ā′shən) *n.* **1.** The act of despoiling or plundering. **2.** Seizure of neutral vessels at sea by a belligerent power in time of war. **3.** *Law.* Intentional alteration or destruction of a document. [ME < AN *spoliacioun* < Lat. *spoliātiō, spoliātiōn-* < *spoliātus*, p.part. of *spoliāre*, to despoil. See SPOIL.] **— spo′li•a′tor** *n.*

spon•da•ic (spŏn-dā′ĭk) *adj.* Of or written in spondees. [Fr. *spondaïque* < LLat. *spondaicus*, alteration of *spondīacus* < Gk. *spondeiakos* < *spondeios*, spondee. See SPONDEE.]

spon•dee (spŏn′dē′) *n.* A metrical foot consisting of two long or stressed syllables. [ME *sponde* < OFr. *spondee* < Lat. *spondēum* < neut. of *spondēus*, of libations, spondaic < Gk. *spondeios* < *spondē*, libation. See **spend-*.**]

spon•dy•li•tis (spŏn′dl-ī′tĭs) *n.* Inflammation of the vertebrae. [Gk. *spondulos*, vertebra + -ITIS.]

sponge (spŭnj) *n.* **1.a.** Any of numerous sessile, chiefly marine invertebrate animals of the phylum Porifera, having a porous fibrous skeleton and often forming irregularly shaped colonies attached to an underwater surface. **b.** The light fibrous flexible absorbent skeleton of certain of these organisms, used for bathing and cleaning. **2.** Porous plastic, rubber, or other material, similar in absorbency to this skeleton and used for the same purposes. **3.** A gauze pad used to absorb blood and other fluids, as in surgery. **4.** A small contraceptive pad that contains a spermicide and is placed against the cervix. **5.** Dough that has been or is being leavened. **6.** A light cake, such as sponge cake. **7.** A sponge bath. **8.** One who habitually depends on others for one's own maintenance. **9.a.** *Informal.* A glutton. **b.** *Slang.* A drunkard. — *v.* **sponged, spong•ing, spong•es.** — *tr.* **1.** To moisten, wipe, or clean with or as if with a sponge: *sponge off the table.* **2.** To wipe out; erase. **3.** To absorb with or as if with a sponge: *sponge up the mess.* **4.** *Informal.* To obtain free: *sponge a meal.* — *intr.* **1.** To fish for sponges. **2.** *Informal.* To live by relying on the generosity of others: *sponged off her parents.* [ME < OE < Lat. *spongia* < Gk. < *spongos.*]

sponge bath *n.* A bath in which the bather washes with a wet sponge or washcloth without immersing.

sponge cake *n.* A very light porous cake made of flour, sugar, beaten eggs, and flavoring and containing no shortening.

spong•er (spŭn′jər) *n.* **1.** One that gathers sponges. **2.** *Informal.* A person who sponges on others; a parasite.

sponge rubber *n.* A soft porous rubber used in toys, cushions, gaskets, and weather stripping and as a vibration dampener.

spon•gin (spŭn′jĭn) *n.* A horny sulfur-containing protein related to keratin that forms the skeletal structure of certain classes of sponges.

spong•y (spŭn′jē) *adj.* **-i•er, -i•est.** Resembling a sponge in elasticity, absorbency, or porousness. **— spong′i•ness** *n.*

spongy mesophyll *n.* A leaf tissue consisting of loosely arranged, chloroplast-bearing, usu. lobed cells.

spon•son (spŏn′sən) *n.* **1.** *Naut.* Any of several structures that project from the side of a boat or ship, esp. a gun platform. **2.** A short curved air-filled projection on the hull of a seaplane, imparting stability in the water. [Perh. alteration of EXPANSION.]

spon•sor (spŏn′sər) *n.* **1.** One who assumes responsibility for another person or a group during a period of instruction, apprenticeship, or probation. **2.** One who vouches for the suitability of a candidate for admission. **3.** A legislator who proposes and urges adoption of a bill. **4.** One who presents a candidate for baptism or confirmation; a godparent. **5.** One that finances a project or an event carried out by another, esp. a business enterprise that pays for radio or television programming in return for advertising time. — *tr.v.* **-sored, -sor•ing, -sors.** To act as a sponsor for. [LLat. *spōnsor*, sponsor in baptism < Lat., surety < *spōnsus*, p.part. of *spondēre*, to pledge. See **spend-*.**] **— spon•so′ri•al** (-sôr′ē-əl, -sōr′-) *adj.* **— spon′sor•ship′** *n.*

spon•ta•ne•i•ty (spŏn′tə-nē′ĭ-tē, -nā′-) *n., pl.* **-ties. 1.** The quality or condition of being spontaneous. **2.** Spontaneous behavior, impulse, or movement.

spon•ta•ne•ous (spŏn-tā′nē-əs) *adj.* **1.** Happening or arising without apparent external cause; self-generated. **2.** Arising from a natural inclination or impulse and not from external incitement or constraint. **3.** Unconstrained and unstudied in manner or behavior. **4.** Growing without cultivation or human labor; indigenous. [< LLat. *spontāneus*, of one's own accord < Lat. *sponte.* See **(s)pen-*.**] **— spon•ta′ne•ous•ly** *adv.* **— spon•ta′ne•ous•ness** *n.*

spontaneous abortion *n.* See **miscarriage** 1.

spontaneous combustion *n.* Ignition of a substance caused by a localized heat-increasing reaction between the oxidant and the fuel and not involving an outside source of heat.

spontaneous generation *n.* See **abiogenesis.**

spon•toon (spŏn-to͞on′) *n.* A short pike carried by infantry officers in the 18th century. [Fr. *sponton* < Ital. *spuntone* : *s-*, intensive pref.; see SFORZANDO + *puntone*, kind of weapon, aug. of *punto*, point (< Lat. *pūnctum* < neut. p.part. of *pungere*, to pierce, prick; see **peuk-***).]

spoof (spo͞of) *n.* **1.** Nonsense; tomfoolery. **2.** A hoax. **3.** A gentle satirical imitation; a light parody. — *tr.v.* **spoofed, spoof•ing, spoofs. 1.** To deceive. **2.** To satirize gently. [?]

spook (spo͝ok) *n.* **1.** *Informal.* A ghost; a specter. **2.** *Slang.* A secret agent. — *v.* **spooked, spook•ing, spooks.** — *tr.* **1.** To haunt. **2.** To frighten, esp. to startle and cause nervous activity in (an animal or animals). — *intr.* To become frightened and nervous. Used esp. of animals. [Du. < MDu. *spooc.*]

spook•y (spo͞o′kē) *adj.* **-i•er, -i•est.** *Informal.* **1.** Suggestive of ghosts or a ghost; eerie. **2.** Easily startled; skittish. **— spook′i•ly** *adv.* **— spook′i•ness** *n.*

spool (spo͞ol) *n.* **1.a.** A cylinder on which wire, thread, or string

split rail
Split-rail fence

Benjamin Spock
Photographed in 1982

ă **pat**	oi **boy**
ā **pay**	ou **out**
âr **care**	o͝o **took**
ä **father**	o͞o **boot**
ĕ **pet**	ŭ **cut**
ē **be**	ûr **urge**
ĭ **pit**	th **thin**
ī **pie**	*th* **this**
îr **pier**	hw **which**
ŏ **pot**	zh **vision**
ō **toe**	ə **about,**
ô **paw**	**item**

Stress marks:
′ (primary);
′ (secondary), as in dictionary (dĭk′shə-nĕr′ē)

is wound. **b.** The amount of wire, thread, or string wound on a spool. **c.** Something like a spool in shape or function. **2.** A reel for magnetic tape. — *tr. & intr.v.* **spooled, spool•ing, spools.** To wind or be wound on or off a spool. [ME *spole* < ONFr. *espole* and < MDu. and MLGer. *spoele* (ONFr. < MDu.).]

spool•ing (spo͞o′lĭng) *n. Comp. Sci.* The temporary storage of information that occurs while further processing is awaited. [< *s(imultaneous) p(eripheral) o(perations) o(n) l(ine)*.]

spoon (spo͞on) *n.* **1.** A utensil consisting of a small, shallow bowl on a handle, used in preparing, serving, or eating food. **2.** Something similar to this utensil or its bowl, as: **a.** A shiny curved metallic fishing lure. **b.** A paddle or an oar with a curved blade. **3.** *Sports.* The three wood golf club. — *v.* **spooned, spoon•ing, spoons.** — *tr.* **1.** To lift, scoop up, or carry with or as if with a spoon. **2.** *Sports & Games.* To shove or scoop (a ball) into the air. — *intr.* **1.** To fish with a spoon lure. **2.** *Sports & Games.* To give a ball an upward scoop. **3.** *Informal.* To engage in amorous behavior, such as caressing. [ME < OE *spōn*, chip of wood.] — **spoon′a•ble** *adj.*

spoonbill
Roseate spoonbill
Ajaia ajaja

spoon•bill (spo͞on′bĭl′) *n.* **1.a.** Any of several long-legged wading birds similar to the ibis but having a long flat bill with a broadly spatulate tip. **b.** Any of various broad-billed ducks, such as the shoveler. **2.** See **paddlefish.**

spoon bread *n. Chiefly Southern U.S.* A soft light bread made with cornmeal, eggs, butter, and milk, baked in a bowl.

spoon•drift (spo͞on′drĭft′) *n.* See **spindrift.** [Obsolete *spoon*, to run before the wind + DRIFT.]

spoon•er•ism (spo͞o′nə-rĭz′əm) *n.* A transposition of sounds of two or more words, esp. a ludicrous one, such as *Let me sew you to your sheet* for *Let me show you to your seat.* [After William A. *Spooner* (1844–1930), British cleric.]

spoon-feed (spo͞on′fēd′) *tr.v.* **-fed** (-fĕd′), **-feed•ing, -feeds. 1.** To feed (another) with a spoon. **2.** To treat (another) so as to discourage independence, as by overindulgence. **3.a.** To inform or teach (another) in an oversimplified way. **b.** To provide (knowledge or information) in an oversimplified way.

spoon•ful (spo͞on′fo͝ol′) *n., pl.* **-fuls.** The amount that a spoon holds.

spoon•y also **spoon•ey** (spo͞o′nē) *adj.* **-i•er, -i•est. 1.** Enamored in a silly or sentimental way. **2.** Feebly sentimental.

spoor (spo͝or) *n.* The track or trail of an animal, esp. a wild animal. — *tr. & intr.v.* **spoored, spoor•ing, spoors.** To track (an animal) by following its spoor or engage in such tracking. [Afr. < MDu. See **sperə-*.**]

Spor•a•des (spôr′ə-dēz′, spô-rä′*th*ēs). Two island groups of Greece in the Aegean Sea, the **Northern Sporades** off the central mainland and the **Southern Sporades** off Turkey.

spo•rad•ic (spə-răd′ĭk, spô-) also **spo•rad•i•cal** (-ĭ-kəl) *adj.* **1.** Occurring irregularly; having no pattern or order in time. See Syns at **periodic. 2.** Appearing singly or at widely scattered localities. **3.** Isolated; unique. [Med.Lat. *sporadicus*, scattered < Gk. *sporadikos* < *sporas*, *sporad-*. See **sper-*.**] — **spo•rad′i•cal•ly** *adv.* — **spo•rad′i•cal•ness** *n.*

spo•ran•gi•o•phore (spə-răn′jē-ə-fôr′, -fōr′) *n.* **1.** A specialized branch bearing one or more sporangia. **2.** A stalk of a sporangium. [SPORANGI(UM) + -PHORE.]

spo•ran•gi•um (spə-răn′jē-əm) *n., pl.* **-gi•a** (-jē-ə). A single-celled or many-celled structure in which spores are produced, as in fungi and ferns. [NLat. : SPOR(O)- + Gk. *angeion*, vessel; see ANGIO-.] — **spo•ran′gi•al** (-jē-əl) *adj.*

spore (spôr, spōr) *n.* **1.** A small, usu. single-celled reproductive body that is capable of growing into a new organism, produced esp. by certain bacteria, fungi, algae, and nonflowering plants. **2.** A dormant nonreproductive body formed by certain bacteria in response to adverse environmental conditions. — *intr.v.* **spored, spor•ing, spores.** To produce spores. [Gk. *spora*, seed. See **sper-*.**]

spore case *n.* See **sporangium.**

spo•ri•cide (spôr′ĭ-sīd′, spōr′-) *n.* An agent used to kill spores. — **spo′ri•cid′al** (-sīd′l) *adj.*

spo•rif•er•ous (spə-rĭf′ər-əs, spô-, spō-) *adj.* Producing spores.

sporo– or **spor–** *pref.* Spore: *sporocyst.* [Gk. < *spora*, seed. See **sper-*.**]

spo•ro•carp (spôr′ə-kärp′, spōr′-) *n.* **1.** A multicellular structure in which spores are formed, esp. in red algae and certain fungi and slime molds. **2.** A receptacle containing sporangia.

spo•ro•cyst (spôr′ə-sĭst′, spōr′-) *n.* **1.** A resting cell that produces asexual plant spores. **2.a.** A protective case or cyst in which sporozoites develop and from which they are transferred to different hosts. **b.** A sporozoite enclosed in such a case. **3.** A saclike larval stage in many trematode worms.

spo•ro•gen•e•sis (spôr′ə-jĕn′ĭ-sĭs, spōr′-) *n.* **1.** Production or formation of spores. **2.** Reproduction by means of spores. — **spo′ro•gen′ic** (-jĕn′ĭk), **spo•rog′e•nous** (spə-rŏj′ə-nəs, spô-, spō-) *adj.*

spo•rog•o•ny (spə-rŏg′ə-nē, spô-, spō-) *n.* Reproduction by multiple fission of a spore or zygote, characteristic of many sporozoans.

spo•ro•phore (spôr′ə-fôr′, spōr′ə-fōr′) *n.* A spore-bearing structure, esp. in fungi.

spo•ro•phyll (spôr′ə-fĭl′, spōr′-) *n.* A leaf or leaflike organ that bears spores.

spo•ro•phyte (spôr′ə-fīt′, spōr′-) *n.* The spore-producing phase in the life cycle of a plant that exhibits alternation of generations. — **spo′ro•phyt′ic** (-fĭt′ĭk) *adj.*

–sporous *suff.* Having a specified number or kind of spores: *heterosporous.*

spo•ro•zo•an (spôr′ə-zō′ən, spōr′-) *n.* Any of numerous parasitic protozoans of the class Sporozoa, most of which reproduce sexually and asexually in alternate generations by means of spores. [< NLat. *Sporozoa*, class name : SPORO- + *-zoa*, pl. of *-zoon*, -zoon.] — **spo′ro•zo′an** *adj.*

spo•ro•zo•ite (spôr′ə-zō′īt′, spōr′-) *n.* Any of the minute undeveloped sporozoans produced by sporogony.

spor•ran (spôr′ən, spŏr′-) *n.* A leather or fur pouch traditionally worn at the front of the kilt. [Sc.Gael. *sporan* < MIr. *sparán*, poss. < LLat. *bursa*, bag. See BURSA.]

sport (spôrt, spōrt) *n.* **1.** An activity involving physical exertion and skill, governed by rules or customs and often undertaken competitively. **2.** An active pastime; recreation. **3.a.** Mockery; jest. **b.** An object of mockery, jest, or play. **c.** A joking mood or attitude. **4.a.** One known for the manner of one's acceptance of rules, esp. of a game, or of a difficult situation. **b.** *Informal.* One who accepts rules or difficult situations well. **c.** *Informal.* A pleasant companion. **5.** *Informal.* **a.** A person who lives a jolly, extravagant life. **b.** A gambler at sporting events. **6.** *Biol.* An organism that shows a marked change from the normal type or parent stock, typically as a result of mutation. **7.** *Maine.* See **summercater. 8.** *Obsolete.* Amorous dalliance; lovemaking. — *v.* **sport•ed, sport•ing, sports.** — *intr.* **1.** To play or frolic. **2.** To joke or trifle. **3.** *Biol.* To mutate. — *tr.* To display or show off. — *adj.* or **sports. 1.** Of, relating to, or appropriate for sports. **2.** Designed or appropriate for outdoor or informal wear. [ME *sporte*, short for *disporte* < OFr. *desport*, pleasure < *desporter*, to divert. See DISPORT.] — **sport′ful** *adj.* — **sport′ful•ly** *adv.* — **sport′ful•ness** *n.*

sport•ing (spôr′tĭng, spōr′-) *adj.* **1.** Used in or appropriate for sports: *sporting goods.* **2.** Characterized by sportsmanship. **3.** Of or associated with gambling. — **sport′ing•ly** *adv.*

sporting chance *n. Informal.* A fair chance for success.

spor•tive (spôr′tĭv, spōr′-) *adj.* **1.** Playful; frolicsome. **2.** Relating to or interested in sports. **3.** *Archaic.* Amorous or wanton. — **spor′tive•ly** *adv.* — **spor′tive•ness** *n.*

sports car (spôrts, spōrts) *n.* An automobile equipped for racing, esp. an aerodynamically shaped one-passenger or two-passenger vehicle having a low center of gravity and steering and suspension designed for precise control at high speeds.

sports•cast (spôrts′kăst′, spōrts′-) *n.* A broadcast of a sports event or of sports news. — **sports′cast′er** *n.*

sports•man (spôrts′mən, spōrts′-) *n.* **1.** A man who is active in sports. **2.** A person whose conduct and attitude exhibit sportsmanship. — **sports′man•like′, sports′man•ly** *adj.*

sports•man•ship (spôrts′mən-shĭp′, spōrts′-) *n.* **1.** The fact or practice of participating in sports or a sport. **2.** Conduct and attitude viewed as befitting athletes, as fair play.

sports medicine *n.* The branch of medicine that deals with injuries or illnesses resulting from sports and athletics.

sports•wear (spôrts′wâr′, spōrts′-) *n.* Clothes designed for comfort and casual wear.

sports•wom•an (spôrts′wo͝om′ən, spōrts′-) *n.* **1.** A woman who is active in sports. **2.** A woman whose conduct and attitude exhibit sportsmanship.

sports•writ•er (spôrts′rī′tər, spōrts′-) *n.* A person who writes about sports, esp. for a newspaper or magazine.

sport•y (spôr′tē, spōr′-) *adj.* **-i•er, -i•est. 1.** Appropriate for sport or participation in sports. **2.** Exhibiting sportsmanship. **3.** Flashy; jazzy. — **sport′i•ly** *adv.* — **sport′i•ness** *n.*

spor•u•late (spôr′yə-lāt′, spōr′-) *intr.v.* **-lat•ed, -lat•ing, -lates.** To produce or release spores. [< NLat. *sporula*, small spore, dim. of *spora*, spore < Gk., seed. See SPORE.] — **spor′u•la′tion** *n.*

spot (spŏt) *n.* **1.** A place of relatively small and definite limits. **2.a.** A mark on a surface contrasting in color to its surroundings. **b.** A stain or blot. **3.** *Games.* **a.** A mark or pip on a playing card; a spade, club, diamond, or heart. **b.** A playing card with a specified number of such spots indicating its value. **4.** *Informal.* A piece of paper money worth a specified number of dollars. **5.a.** A location; a locale. **b.** A point of interest. **c.** A position or an item in an ordered arrangement. **6.** *Informal.* A situation, esp. a troublesome one. **7.** A flaw in one's reputation or character. **8.** A short presentation or commercial on television or radio. **9.** *Informal.* A spotlight. **10.** *pl.* **spot** or **spots.** A small edible croaker *(Leiostomus xanthurus)* of North American Atlantic waters having a dark mark above each pectoral fin. **11.** *Chiefly British.* A small amount; a bit. — *v.* **spot•ted, spot•ting, spots.** — *tr.* **1.** To cause a spot or spots to appear on, esp.: **a.** To soil with spots. **b.** To decorate with spots; dot. **2.** To harm; besmirch. **3.** To place in a particular location; situate precisely. **4.** To detect or discern, esp. visually; spy. **5.** To remove spots from, as in a laundry. **6.** *Sports.* To yield a favorable scoring margin to.

—*intr.* **1.** To become marked with spots. **2.** To cause a discoloration or make a stain. **3.** To locate targets from the air during combat or training missions. —*adj.* **1.** Made, paid, or delivered immediately: *a spot sale.* **2.** Of, relating to, or being a market in which payment or delivery is immediate. **3.** Involving random or selective instances or actions. **4.** Presented between major radio or television programs. —***idiom.* on the spot. 1.** Without delay; at once. **2.** At the scene of action. **3.** Under pressure or attention; in a pressed position. [ME < OE.] —**spot′ta•ble** *adj.*

spot check *n.* A random or selective inspection or investigation. —**spot′-check′** (spŏt′chĕk′) *v.*

spot•less (spŏt′lĭs) *adj.* **1.** Perfectly clean. See Syns at **clean. 2.** Unblemished; impeccable. —**spot′less•ness** *n.*

spot•light (spŏt′līt′) *n.* **1.** A strong beam of light that illuminates a small area, used esp. to center attention on a stage performer. **2.** Public notoriety or prominence. **3.** An artificial source of light with a strongly focused beam, esp. a lamp that produces a spotlight. —*tr.v.* **-light•ed** or **-lit** (-lĭt), **-light•ing, -lights. 1.** To light with a spotlight. **2.** To focus attention on.

spot price *n.* The market price of a commodity.

Spot•syl•va•nia (spŏt′səl-vān′yə). A village of NE VA SW of Fredericksburg; site of a major but inconclusive Civil War battle (May 8–21, 1864).

spot•ted (spŏt′ĭd) *adj.* Marked or stained with or as if with spots: *a spotted fabric.*

spotted fever *n.* **1.** Any of various often fatal infectious diseases, such as typhus, characterized by skin eruptions and caused by rickettsia that are transmitted by ticks and mites. **2.** An epidemic form of cerebrospinal meningitis.

spot•ter (spŏt′ər) *n.* **1.** One that applies spots. **2.** One that looks for, locates, and reports something, as: **a.** A military lookout. **b.** *Informal.* A person hired to detect dishonest acts by employees. **3.** *Sports.* **a.** One who identifies players on the field, as for an announcer. **b.** One who watches and guards a performer during practice to prevent injury, as in gymnastics. **4.** One employed by a dry cleaner to remove spots.

spot•ty (spŏt′ē) *adj.* **-ti•er, -ti•est. 1.** Lacking consistency; uneven. **2.** Having or marked with spots; spotted. —**spot′ti•ly** *adv.* —**spot′ti•ness** *n.*

spot weld•ing (wĕl′dĭng) *n.* Welding of overlapping pieces of metal at circular areas by application of great pressure and electric current. —**spot′-weld′** (spŏt′wĕld′) *v.* —**spot′-weld′er** *n.*

spou•sal (spou′zəl, -səl) *adj.* **1.** Of or concerning marriage; nuptial. **2.** Of or concerning a spouse. —*n.* Marriage; nuptials. Often used in the plural. [< ME *spousaille*, marriage < OFr. *espousaille* < Lat. *spōnsālia*, betrothal < neut. pl. of *spōnsālis*, of marriage < *spōnsus*, p.part. of *spondēre*, to pledge. See SPOUSE.]

spousal equivalent or **spouse equivalent** *n.* One who cohabits and shares responsibility for common welfare with a nonrelative of the same sex in an exclusive relationship that one intends to maintain indefinitely: *health insurance for spousal equivalents.* —**spousal equivalence, spousal equivalency** *n.* —**spousal equivalent** *adj.*

spouse (spous, spouz) *n.* A marriage partner; a husband or wife. —*tr.v.* (spouz, spous). **spoused, spous•ing, spous•es.** *Archaic.* To marry; wed. [ME < OFr. *spous* < Lat. *spōnsus* < p.part. of *spondēre*, to pledge. See **spend-***.]

spout (spout) *v.* **spout•ed, spout•ing, spouts.** —*intr.* **1.** To gush forth in a rapid stream or in spurts. **2.** To discharge a liquid or other substance continuously or in spurts. **3.** *Informal.* To speak volubly and tediously. —*tr.* **1.** To cause to flow or spurt out. **2.** To utter volubly and tediously. **3.** *Chiefly British.* To pawn. —*n.* **1.** A tube, mouth, or pipe through which liquid is released or discharged. **2.** A continuous stream of liquid. **3.** The burst of spray from the blowhole of a whale. **4.** *Chiefly British.* A pawnshop. [ME *spouten*, ult. of imit. orig.] —**spout′er** *n.*

spout•ing (spou′tĭng) *n. Chiefly Pennsylvania & New Jersey.* See **gutter** 2. See Regional Note at **gutter.**

spp. *abbr.* Species (plural).

S.P.Q.R. or **SPQR** *abbr. Lat.* Senatus Populusque Romanus (the Senate and the people of Rome).

spr. *abbr.* Spring.

sprach•ge•fühl (shpräкн′gə-fül′) *n.* An ear for idiomatically correct or appropriate language. [Ger. : *Sprache*, language (ult. < OHGer. *sprāhha*) + *Gefühl*, feeling (< *fühlen*, to feel < MHGer. *vuelen* < OHGer. *vuolen*; see **pōl-***).]

sprag (sprăg) *n.* **1.a.** A piece of wood or metal wedged under a wheel or between spokes to prevent rolling. **b.** A pointed stake angled into the ground from a vehicle to prevent motion. **2.** A prop for a mine roof. [Perh. of Scand. orig.]

sprain (sprān) *n.* **1.** A painful wrenching or laceration of the ligaments of a joint. **2.** The condition resulting from a sprain. —*tr.v.* **sprained, sprain•ing, sprains.** To cause a sprain to (a joint or ligament). [?]

sprang (sprăng) *v.* A p.t. of **spring.**

sprat (sprăt) *n.* **1.** A small marine food fish *(Clupea sprattus)* of northeast Atlantic waters. **2.** Any of various other similar fishes, such as a young herring. [ME *sprot, spratte* < OE *sprot.*]

sprawl (sprôl) *v.* **sprawled, sprawl•ing, sprawls.** —*intr.* **1.** To sit or lie with the body and limbs spread out awkwardly. **2.** To spread out in a straggling or disordered fashion. —*tr.* To cause to spread out in a straggling or disordered fashion. —*n.* **1.** A sprawling position or posture. **2.** Haphazard growth or extension outward, esp. that due to real estate development on the outskirts of a city. [ME *sprawlen* < OE *sprēawlian*, to writhe. See **sper-***.] —**sprawl′er** *n.*

spray¹ (sprā) *n.* **1.** Water or other liquid moving in a mass of dispersed droplets. **2.a.** A fine jet of liquid discharged from a pressurized container. **b.** Such a pressurized container or an atomizer. **c.** Any of numerous commercial products, including paints, that are dispensed from containers in this manner. —*v.* **sprayed, spray•ing, sprays.** —*tr.* **1.** To disperse (a liquid) in a mass or jet of droplets. **2.** To apply a spray to (a surface). —*intr.* **1.** To discharge sprays of liquid. **2.** To move in the form of a spray. [< obsolete *spray*, to sprinkle < MDu. *sprayen.*] —**spray′er** *n.*

spray² (sprā) *n.* **1.** A small branch bearing buds, flowers, or berries. **2.** Something, such as a decorative motif, that resembles a floral spray. [ME < OE **spræg.*]

spread (sprĕd) *v.* **spread, spread•ing, spreads.** —*tr.* **1.** To open to a fuller extent or width; stretch. **2.** To widen the gap between; move farther apart. **3.a.** To distribute over a surface in a layer. **b.** To cover with a layer: *spread bread with butter.* **4.a.** To distribute widely. **b.** To make a wide or extensive arrangement of: *spread the parts out on the floor.* **c.** To exhibit or display the full extent of. **5.** To cause to become widely seen or known; scatter or disseminate. **6.a.** To prepare (a table) for eating; set. **b.** To arrange (food or a meal) on a table. **7.** To flatten (a rivet end, for example) by pounding. —*intr.* **1.** To be extended or enlarged. **2.** To become distributed or widely dispersed. **3.** To increase in range of occurrence; become known or prevalent over a wide area. **4.** To be exhibited, displayed, or visible in broad or full extent. **5.** To become or admit of being distributed in a layer. **6.** To become separated; be forced farther apart. —*n.* **1.a.** The act of spreading. **b.** Dissemination, as of news; diffusion. **2.a.** An open area of land; an expanse. **b.** A ranch, a farm, or an estate. **3.** The extent or limit to which something is or can be spread; range. **4.** A cloth covering for a bed, table, or other piece of furniture. **5.** *Informal.* An abundant meal laid out on a table. **6.** A food to be spread on bread or crackers. **7.a.** Two facing pages of a magazine or newspaper, often with related matter extending across the fold. **b.** A story or advertisement running across two or more columns of a magazine or newspaper. **8.** A difference, as between two figures. **9.a.** A position taken in two or more options or futures contracts in order to profit from a change in their relative prices. **b.** The difference between the price asked and bid for a particular security. [ME *spreden* < OE *-sprǣdan*, as in *tōsprǣdan*, to spread out. See **sper-***.] —**spread′a•bil′i•ty** *n.* —**spread′a•ble** *adj.* —**spread′a•bly** *adv.*

spread eagle *n.* **1.a.** The figure of an eagle with wings and legs spread. **b.** The emblem on the obverse of the Great Seal of the United States. **2.** A posture or design resembling such an emblem or figure.

spread-ea•gle (sprĕd′ē′gəl) *adj.* **1.** Having the arms and legs stretched out. **2.** *Informal.* Full of patriotic or jingoistic rhetoric. —*v.* **-gled, -gling, -gles.** —*tr.* To place in a spread-eagle position, esp. as a punishment. —*intr.* **1.** To assume a spread-eagle position. **2.** To make a grandiloquent patriotic speech.

spread•er (sprĕd′ər) *n.* One that spreads, as: **a.** A butter knife. **b.** An implement for distributing fertilizer or seed. **c.** A device, such as a bar, for keeping wires or stays apart.

spread•ing factor (sprĕd′ĭng) *n.* See **hyaluronidase.**

spread•sheet (sprĕd′shēt′) *n. Comp. Sci.* **1.** An accounting or bookkeeping program for a computer. **2.** The display, with multiple columns and rows, that such a program allows to be printed.

sprech•stim•me (shprĕкн′shtĭm′ə) *n.* A form of dramatic declamation, in which the speaker uses lilt and rhythm but not precise pitches. [Ger. : *sprechen*, to speak (< MHGer. *sprĕchen* < OHGer. *sprehhan*) + *Stimme*, voice (< MHGer. *stimme* < OHGer. *stimma*).]

spree (sprē) *n.* **1.** A carefree, lively outing. **2.** A drinking bout. **3.** Overindulgence in an activity. See Syns at **binge.** [Perh. alteration of Sc. *spreath*, cattle raid < Ir. and Sc.Gael. *spréidh, spré*, cattle, wealth < MIr. *preit, preid*, booty, ult. < Lat. *praeda*. See **ghend-***.]

Spree (sprā, shprā). A river of E Germany flowing c. 402 km (250 mi) N to the Havel R. at Berlin.

spri•er (sprī′ər) *adj.* A comp. of **spry.**

spri•est (sprī′ĭst) *adj.* A superl. of **spry.**

sprig (sprĭg) *n.* **1.a.** A small shoot or twig of a plant. **b.** An ornament in this shape. **2.** A small brad without a head. **3.** A young, immature person. —*tr.v.* **sprigged, sprig•ging, sprigs. 1.** To decorate with a design of sprigs. **2.** To remove a sprig or sprigs from (a bush or tree). **3.** To fasten with a small headless brad. [ME *sprigge*, alteration of *spring* < OE, source of water.] —**sprig′ger** *n.*

spright (sprīt) *n.* Var. of **sprite.**

spotter
Spotter at a weightlifting workout

spread eagle
Detail from a mid 19th-century American quilt

ă **pat**	oi **boy**
ā **pay**	ou **out**
âr **care**	o͝o **took**
ä **father**	o͞o **boot**
ĕ **pet**	ŭ **cut**
ē **be**	ûr **urge**
ĭ **pit**	th **thin**
ī **pie**	*th* **this**
îr **pier**	hw **which**
ŏ **pot**	zh **vision**
ō **toe**	ə **about, item**
ô **paw**	

Stress marks:
′ (primary);
′ (secondary), as in
dictionary (dĭk′shə-nĕr′ē)

spright•ly (sprīt′lē) *adj.* **-li•er, -li•est.** Full of spirit and vitality; lively; brisk. —*adv.* In a lively, animated manner. —**spright′li•ness** *n.*
sprig•tail (sprĭg′tāl′) *n.* **1.** See **pintail. 2.** See **ruddy duck.**
spring (sprĭng) *v.* **sprang** (sprăng) or **sprung** (sprŭng), **sprung, spring•ing, springs.** —*intr.* **1.** To move upward or forward in a single quick motion or a series of such motions; leap. **2.** To move suddenly on or as if on a spring: *The door sprang shut.* **3.** To appear or come into being quickly: *New businesses were springing up.* See Syns at **stem**[1]. **4.** To issue or emerge suddenly: *A cry sprang from her lips.* **5.** To extend or curve upward, as an arch. **6.** To arise from a source; develop. See Syns at **stem**[1]. **7.** To become warped, split, or cracked. Used of wood. **8.** To move out of place; come loose, as parts of a mechanism. **9.** *Slang.* To pay another's expenses: *He sprang for the dinner.* —*tr.* **1.** To cause to leap, dart, or come forth suddenly. **2.** To jump over; vault. **3.** To release from a checked or inoperative position; actuate: *spring a trap.* **4.a.** To cause to warp, split, or crack, as a mast. **b.** To bend by force. **5.** To present or disclose unexpectedly or suddenly. **6.** *Slang.* To release from prison or other confinement. —*n.* **1.** An elastic device, such as a coil of wire, that regains its original shape after compression or extension. **2.** An actuating force or factor; a motive. **3.a.** Elasticity; resilience. **b.** Energetic bounce. **4.** The act or an instance of jumping or leaping. **5.** A usu. rapid return to normal shape after removal of stress; recoil. **6.** A small stream of water flowing naturally from the earth. **7.** A source, an origin, or a beginning. **8.a.** The season of the year between winter and summer, comprising March, April, and May in the Northern Hemisphere or, as calculated astronomically, extending from the vernal equinox to the summer solstice. **b.** A time of growth and renewal. **9.** A warping, bending, or cracking, as that caused by excessive force. **10.** *Archit.* The point at which an arch or a vault rises from its support. —*adj.* **1.** Of or acting like a spring; resilient. **2.** Having or supported by springs. **3.a.** Of, having to do with, occurring in, or appropriate to the season of spring. **b.** Grown during the season of spring. [ME *springen* < OE *springan.* N., ME *springe* < OE *spring,* wellspring.]

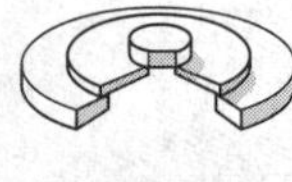

spring
Top: Spiral
Center: Disk
Bottom: Helical

spring beauty *n.* Any of various spring-flowering plants of the genus *Claytonia,* esp. *C. virginica* of eastern North America, having narrow leaves and white or pinkish flowers.
spring•board (sprĭng′bôrd′, -bōrd′) *n.* **1.** *Sports.* **a.** A flexible board mounted on a fulcrum with one end secured, used by gymnasts in vaulting. **b.** See **diving board. 2.** Something that helps to launch a career or an activity.
spring•bok (sprĭng′bŏk′) also **spring•buck** (-bŭk′) *n., pl.* **springbok** or **-boks** also **springbuck** or **-bucks.** A small brown and white gazelle *(Antidorcas marsupialis)* of southern Africa noted for its habit of repeatedly leaping high into the air when startled. [Afr. : *spring,* to leap up (< MDu. *springhen*) + *bok,* male deer (< MDu. *boc*).]
spring chicken *n.* **1.** A young chicken, esp. one from two to ten months old. **2.** *Slang.* A young person.
spring-clean•ing (sprĭng′klē′nĭng) *n.* A thorough cleaning, esp. of a residence when winter is over.
Spring•dale (sprĭng′dāl′). A city of NW AR N of Fayetteville. Pop. 29,941.
springe (sprĭnj) *n.* **1.** A device for snaring small game, made by attaching a noose to a branch under tension. **2.** A trap or snare. [ME, branch, spring. See SPRING.]
spring•er (sprĭng′ər) *n.* **1.** A springer spaniel. **2.** *Western U.S.* A cow about to give birth. **3.** *Archit.* The bottom stone of an arch resting on the impost.

springer spaniel
English springer spaniel

springer spaniel *n.* A dog of either of two breeds of spaniels, the English springer spaniel or the Welsh springer spaniel.
spring fever *n.* A feeling of languor or yearning brought on by the coming of spring.
Spring•field (sprĭng′fēld′). **1.** The cap. of IL, in the central part; became state cap. in 1837. Pop. 105,227. **2.** A city of SW MA on the Connecticut R. near the CT border; settled 1636. Pop. 156,983. **3.** A city of SW MO SSW of Kansas City. Pop. 140,494. **4.** A city of W-central OH W of Columbus. Pop. 70,487. **5.** A city of W-central OR E of Eugene. Pop. 44,683. **6.** A community of SE PA, a suburb of Philadelphia. Pop. 24,160.
Springfield rifle *n.* A magazine-fed breechloading bolt-action .30-caliber rifle used by the U.S. Army esp. in World War I. [After SPRINGFIELD MA.]

spruce[1]
Norway spruce
Picea abies

spring•form pan (sprĭng′fôrm′) *n.* A cake pan having an upright rim that can be detached from the bottom.
spring•halt (sprĭng′hôlt′) *n.* See **stringhalt.** [Alteration of STRINGHALT.]
spring•head (sprĭng′hĕd′) *n.* A fountainhead; a source.
spring•house (sprĭng′hous′) *n.* A small storehouse constructed over a spring and used to keep food cool.
spring•let (sprĭng′lĭt) *n.* A small spring of water; a rill.
spring-load•ed (sprĭng′lō′dĭd) *adj.* Secured or loaded by means of a spring.
spring lock *n.* A lock in which the bolt shoots automatically by means of a spring.
spring peeper *n.* A small brown tree frog *(Hyla crucifer)* of eastern North America having a shrill high-pitched call.
spring roll *n.* See **egg roll.** [Transl. of Chin. (Mandarin) *chūn juǎn.*]
spring•tail (sprĭng′tāl′) *n.* Any of various small wingless insects of the order Collembola, having abdominal appendages that act as springs to catapult them through the air.
spring•tide (sprĭng′tīd′) *n.* Springtime.
spring tide *n.* **1.** The exceptionally high and low tides that occur when the moon is new or full and the sun, moon, and earth are aligned. **2.** A great flood or rush, as of emotion.
spring•time (sprĭng′tīm′) *n.* The season of spring.
Spring Valley (sprĭng). A village of SE NY near the NJ border WNW of White Plains. Pop. 21,802.
spring•wood (sprĭng′wo͝od′) *n.* Young, usu. soft wood that lies directly beneath the bark and develops in early spring.
spring•y (sprĭng′ē) *adj.* **-i•er, -i•est. 1.** Marked by resilience; elastic. **2.** Abounding in freshwater springs. —**spring′i•ly** *adv.* —**spring′i•ness** *n.*
sprin•kle (sprĭng′kəl) *v.* **-kled, -kling, -kles.** —*tr.* **1.** To scatter in drops or particles. **2.** To scatter drops or particles on. **3.** To intersperse with something as if by scattering. **4.** To distribute or intersperse at random. —*intr.* **1.** To scatter something in drops or particles. **2.** To fall or rain in small or infrequent drops. —*n.* **1.** The act of sprinkling. **2.** A light rainfall. **3.** A small amount; a sprinkling. **4.** A small particle of candy sprinkled on ice cream as a topping. Often used in the plural. [ME *sprenklen,* perh. of MDu. or MLGer. orig.]
sprin•kler (sprĭng′klər) *n.* **1.** One that sprinkles, esp.: **a.** An outlet on a sprinkler system. **b.** A device with perforations through which water issues from a hose to sprinkle a lawn. **2.** A sprinkler system. —*tr.v.* **-klered, -kler•ing, -klers.** To equip with a sprinkler system.
sprinkler system *n.* A fire-extinguishing system consisting of a network of overhead pipes that release water automatically when a predetermined temperature has been reached.
sprin•kling (sprĭng′klĭng) *n.* **1.** A small amount or quantity; a modicum. **2.** A small quantity sparsely distributed.
sprint (sprĭnt) *n.* **1.** *Sports.* A short race at top speed. **2.** A burst of speed or activity. —*intr.v.* **sprint•ed, sprint•ing, sprints.** To run or move at top speed for a brief period. [Poss. alteration of ME *sprenten,* to spring up, of Scand. orig.; akin to Swed. dial. *sprinta* and ON *spretta,* to jump.] —**sprint′er** *n.*
sprit (sprĭt) *n. Naut.* **1.** A spar extending diagonally across a fore-and-aft sail from the lower part of the mast to the peak of the sail. **2.** A bowsprit. [ME < OE *sprēot,* pole. See **sper-*.**]
sprite also **spright** (sprīt) *n.* **1.** A small or elusive supernatural being; an elf or a pixy. **2.** An elflike person. **3.** A specter or ghost. **4.** *Archaic.* A soul. [ME *spreit* < OFr. *espirit* < Lat. *spīritus.* See SPIRIT.]
sprit•sail (sprĭt′səl, -sāl′) *n. Naut.* A sail extended by a sprit.
spritz (sprĭts, shprĭts) *tr.v.* **spritzed, spritz•ing, spritz•es.** To squirt or spray (something) quickly. —*n.* A quick squirt or spray, as of carbonated water. [Penn.Du. *schpritze* < MHGer. *sprützen,* to spray. See **sper-*.**]
spritz•er (sprĭt′sər, shprĭt′-) *n.* A drink made of wine and carbonated water. [Ger. < *spritzen,* to spray < MHGer. *sprützen.* See **sper-*.**]
sprock•et (sprŏk′ĭt) *n.* **1.** Any of various toothlike projections arranged on a wheel rim to engage the links of a chain. **2.** A cylinder with a toothed rim that engages in the perforations of photographic or movie film to pull it through a camera or projector. [?]
sprocket wheel *n.* A wheel rimmed with toothlike projections, used to engage the links of a chain in a pulley or drive system.
sprout (sprout) *v.* **sprout•ed, sprout•ing, sprouts.** —*intr.* **1.** To begin to grow; give off shoots or buds. **2.** To emerge and develop rapidly. —*tr.* To cause to emerge and grow. —*n.* **1.** A young plant growth, such as a bud or shoot. **2.** Something resembling a sprout, as in rapid growth. **3. sprouts.** Brussels sprouts. [ME *spruten* < OE *sprūtan.* See **sper-*.**]
spruce[1] (spro͞os) *n.* **1.a.** Any of various coniferous evergreen trees of the genus *Picea,* having needlelike foliage, drooping cones, and soft wood often used for paper pulp. **b.** Any of various similar or related trees. **c.** The wood of any of these trees. **2.** *Color.* A grayish green to dark greenish black. [Short for obsolete *Spruce fir,* Prussian fir < ME *spruce,* Prussia, alteration of *Pruce* < AN *Pruz* < Med.Lat. *Prussia.*]
spruce[2] (spro͞os) *adj.* **spruc•er, spruc•est.** Neat, trim, and smart in appearance. —*v.* **spruced, spruc•ing, spruc•es.** —*tr.* To make neat and trim: *spruce up the house.* —*intr.* To make oneself neat and smart in appearance. [Perh. < obsolete *spruce leather,* Prussian leather < ME *spruce,* Prussia. See SPRUCE[1].] —**spruce′ly** *adv.* —**spruce′ness** *n.*
spruce budworm *n.* The highly destructive larva of a tortricid moth *(Choristoneura fumiferana)* of the northern United States and southern Canada that feeds on the needles, buds, and branch tips of spruce, fir, and other forest conifers.
spruce grouse *n.* A grouse *(Canachites canadensis)* that is dark gray barred with black, found in swampy forests of northern North America and popular as a game bird.
spruce pine *n.* See **scrub pine** 1.

sprue (sproo) *n.* A chronic, chiefly tropical disease marked by diarrhea, emaciation, and anemia, caused by malabsorption of nutrients from the intestinal tract. [Du. *spruw* < MDu. *sprouwe.*]

sprung (sprŭng) *v.* A p.t. and the p.part. of **spring.**

sprung rhythm *n.* A poetic rhythm designed to imitate the rhythm of speech, in which each foot has one stressed syllable, either standing alone or followed by a varying number of unstressed syllables. [Coined by Gerard Manley HOPKINS.]

spry (sprī) *adj.* **spri•er** (sprī′ər), **spri•est** (sprī′ĭst) or **spry•er** or **spry•est.** Lively, active, and brisk; vigorous. [Perh. of Scand. orig.] — **spry′ly** *adv.* — **spry′ness** *n.*

spt. *abbr.* Seaport.

spud (spŭd) *n.* **1.** *Slang.* A potato. **2.** A sharp spadelike tool for rooting or digging out weeds. — *v.* **spud•ded, spud•ding, spuds.** — *tr.* **1.** To remove with a sharp spadelike tool. **2.** To begin drilling operations on. [ME *spudde,* short knife.]

spue (spyoo) *v. & n. Obsolete.* Var. of **spew.**

spume (spyoom) *n.* Foam or froth on a liquid, as on the sea. — *intr.v.* **spumed, spum•ing, spumes.** To froth or foam. [ME < OFr. *espume* < Lat. *spūma.*] — **spu′mous, spum′y** *adj.*

spu•mo•ni or **spu•mo•ne** (spoo-mō′nē) *n.* An Italian ice cream with layers of different colors or flavors and often fruits and nuts. [Ital., aug. of *spuma,* foam < Lat. *spūma.*]

spun (spŭn) *v.* P.t. and p.part. of **spin.**

spun glass *n.* **1.** See **fiberglass. 2.** Fine blown glass having delicate threading or filigree.

spunk (spŭngk) *n.* **1.** *Informal.* Spirit; pluck. **2.** Punk, touchwood, or other tinder. [Sc.Gael. *spong,* tinder < Lat. *spongia,* sponge. See SPONGE.]

spunk•y (spŭng′kē) *adj.* **-i•er, -i•est.** *Informal.* Spirited; plucky. — **spunk′i•ly** *adv.* — **spunk′i•ness** *n.*

spun silk *n.* A yarn made from short-fibered silk and silk waste.

spun sugar *n.* See **cotton candy.**

spur (spûr) *n.* **1.** A short spike or spiked wheel that attaches to the heel of a rider's boot and is used to urge a horse forward. **2.** Something that serves as a goad or an incentive. **3.** A spurlike attachment or projection, as: **a.** A spinelike process on the leg of some birds. **b.** A climbing iron; a crampon. **c.** A gaff attached to the leg of a gamecock. **d.** A short or stunted branch of a tree. **e.** A bony outgrowth or protuberance. **4.** A lateral ridge projecting from a mountain or mountain range. **5.** An oblique reinforcing prop or stay of timber or masonry. **6.** *Bot.* A tubular or saclike extension of the corolla or calyx of a flower, as in a columbine or larkspur. **7.** An ergot growing on rye. **8.** A spur track. — *v.* **spurred, spur•ring, spurs.** — *tr.* **1.** To urge (a horse) on by the use of spurs. **2.** To incite or stimulate. — *intr.* **1.** To ride quickly by spurring a horse. **2.** To proceed in haste. [ME *spure* < OE *spura.* See **sperə-*.**]

spurge (spûrj) *n.* Any of various plants of the genus *Euphorbia,* having milky juice and small unisexual flowers surrounded by a cuplike structure of fused bracts. [ME < OFr. *espurge* < *espurgier,* to purge (< its use as a purgative) < Lat. *expūrgāre.* See EXPURGATE.]

spur gear *n.* A gear with teeth radially arrayed on the rim parallel to its axis.

spu•ri•ous (spyoor′ē-əs) *adj.* **1.** Lacking authenticity or validity in essence or origin; not genuine; false. **2.** Born to parents not married to each other. **3.** *Bot.* Similar in appearance but unlike in structure or function. Used of plant parts. [< LLat. *spurius* < Lat., illegitimate, prob. of Etruscan orig.] — **spu′ri•ous•ly** *adv.* — **spu′ri•ous•ness** *n.*

spurious wing *n.* See **alula.**

spurn (spûrn) *v.* **spurned, spurn•ing, spurns.** — *tr.* **1.** To reject disdainfully or contemptuously; scorn. See Syns at **refuse[1]. 2.** To kick at or tread on disdainfully. — *intr.* To reject something contemptuously. — *n.* **1.** A contemptuous rejection. **2.** *Archaic.* A kick. [ME *spurnen* < OE *spurnan.* See **sperə-*.**] — **spurn′er** *n.*

spur-of-the-mo•ment (spûr′əv-*th*ə-mō′mənt) *adj.* Occurring or made hastily on impulse: *a spur-of-the moment choice.*

spurred (spûrd) *adj.* **1.** Wearing spurs. **2.** Having spurs or a spur: *spurred flowers; spurred boots.*

spur•ry also **spur•rey** (spûr′ē, spŭr′ē) *n., pl.* **-ries** also **-reys.** Any of several weedy low-growing herbs of the genera *Spergula* or *Spergularia,* esp. *Spergula arvensis* of Europe, having linear whorled leaves and small white flowers. [Du. *spurrie* < MDu. *speurie,* prob. < Med.Lat. *spergula,* prob. < Lat. *spargere,* to scatter.]

spurt (spûrt) *n.* **1.** A sudden forcible gush or jet. **2.** A sudden short burst, as of activity. — *v.* **spurt•ed, spurt•ing, spurts.** — *intr.* **1.** To gush forth suddenly in a jet. **2.** To make a brief intense effort. — *tr.* To force out in a spurt. [?]

spur track *n.* A short side track that connects with the main track of a railroad system.

sput•nik (spoot′nĭk, spŭt′-, spoot′nyĭk) *n.* Any of a series of Soviet satellites sent into Earth orbit, esp. the first, launched October 4, 1957. [Russ. *sputnik (zemlyi),* fellow traveler (of Earth) : *so-, s-,* together; see **ksun*** + *put′,* path, way; see **pent-*** + *-nik,* n. suff.]

sput•ter (spŭt′ər) *v.* **-tered, -ter•ing, -ters.** — *intr.* **1.** To spit out or spray particles of saliva or food from the mouth in noisy bursts. **2.** To spit out words or sounds in an excited or confused manner. **3.** To make sporadic spitting or popping sounds. **4.** *Phys.* To cause the atoms of a solid to be removed from the surface by bombardment with atoms in a discharge tube. — *tr.* **1.** To eject in short bursts with spitting or popping sounds. **2.** To utter in an excited or confused manner. **3.** *Phys.* To coat (a solid surface) with metal atoms by sputtering. — *n.* **1.** The act or sound of sputtering. **2.** Matter emitted in sputtering. **3.** Excited or confused utterance. [Prob. of LGer. orig.; akin to Du. *sputteren.*] — **sput′ter•er** *n.* — **sput′ter•y** *adj.*

spu•tum (spyoo′təm) *n., pl.* **-ta** (-tə). Matter coughed up and usu. ejected from the mouth, including saliva, foreign material, and substances such as mucus or phlegm, from the respiratory tract. [Lat. *spūtum* < neut. p.part. of *spuere,* to spit.]

Spuy•ten Duy•vil Creek (spīt′n dī′vəl). A narrow channel in SE NY separating N Manhattan I. from the mainland and linking the Harlem and Hudson rivers.

spy (spī) *n., pl.* **spies** (spīz). **1.** An agent employed by a state to obtain secret information concerning its potential or actual enemies. **2.** One employed by a company to obtain confidential information about its competitors. **3.** One who secretly keeps watch on another or others. **4.** An act of spying. — *v.* **spied** (spīd), **spy•ing, spies** (spīz). — *tr.* **1.** To observe secretly with hostile intent. **2.** To discover by close observation. **3.** To catch sight of. **4.** To investigate intensively. — *intr.* **1.** To engage in espionage. **2.** To seek or observe something secretly and closely. **3.** To make a careful investigation. [ME *spie* < OFr. *espie* < *espier,* to watch, of Gmc. orig. See **spek-*.**]

spy•glass (spī′glăs′) *n.* **1.** A small telescope. **2.** A pair of binoculars. Often used in the plural.

spy•mas•ter (spī′măs′tər) *n.* One who directs clandestine intelligence activities.

sq. *abbr.* **1.** Squadron. **2.** Square.

squab (skwŏb) *n.* **1.** A newly hatched or unfledged pigeon. **2.a.** A soft thick cushion, as for a couch. **b.** A couch. — *adj.* Young and undeveloped; newly hatched or unfledged. [Prob. of Scand. orig.]

squab•ble (skwŏb′əl) *intr.v.* **-bled, -bling, -bles.** To engage in a disagreeable argument, usu. over a trivial matter; wrangle. — *n.* A noisy quarrel, usu. about a trivial matter. [Prob. of Scand. orig.] — **squab′bler** *n.*

squad (skwŏd) *n.* **1.** A small group of people organized in an endeavor or activity. **2.** The smallest tactical unit of military personnel. **3.** A small unit of police officers. **4.** *Sports.* An athletic team. [Obsolete Fr. *esquade* < OFr. *escadre* < OSp. *escuadra* and OItal. *squadra,* both < VLat. **exquadra,* square. See SQUARE.]

spur
c. 1730 American silver spur

squad car *n.* A police automobile connected by radio with headquarters.

squad•ron (skwŏd′rən) *n.* **1.** A naval unit consisting of two or more divisions of a fleet. **2.** An armored cavalry unit subordinate to a regiment and consisting of two or more troops. **3.** A basic tactical air force unit, subordinate to a group and consisting of two or more flights. **4.** An organized multitude. [Ital. *squadrone,* aug. of *squadra,* squad. See SQUAD.]

squa•lene (skwā′lēn′) *n.* An unsaturated aliphatic hydrocarbon, $C_{30}H_{50}$, found esp. in human sebum and in the liver oil of sharks, that is an intermediate in the biosynthesis of cholesterol. [NLat. *Squalus,* shark genus (< Lat. *squalus,* a sea fish) + -ENE.]

squal•id (skwŏl′ĭd) *adj.* **1.** Dirty and wretched, as from poverty or lack of care. **2.** Morally repulsive; sordid. [Lat. *squālidus* < *squālēre,* to be filthy < *squālus,* filthy.] — **squal′id•ly** *adv.* — **squal′id•ness, squa•lid′i•ty** (skwŏ-lĭd′ĭ-tē) *n.*

squall[1] (skwôl) *n.* A loud, harsh cry. — *intr.v.* **squalled, squall•ing, squalls.** To scream or cry loudly and harshly. [Prob. of Scand. orig.; akin to ON *skvala,* to squeal.] — **squall′er** *n.*

squall[2] (skwôl) *n.* **1.** A brief sudden violent windstorm, often accompanied by rain or snow. **2.** *Informal.* A brief commotion. — *intr.v.* **squalled, squall•ing, squalls.** To blow strongly for a brief period. [Prob. of Scand. orig.]

squall line *n.* A line of thunderstorms preceding a cold front.

squall•y (skwô′lē) *adj.* **-i•er, -i•est. 1.** Characterized by gusts of wind. **2.** *Informal.* Marked by commotion or disturbance.

squal•or (skwŏl′ər) *n.* A filthy and wretched condition or quality. [Lat. *squālor* < *squālēre,* to be filthy. See SQUALID.]

squa•ma (skwā′mə, skwä′-) *n., pl.* **-mae** (-mē′). **1.** A scale or scalelike structure. **2.** A thin platelike mass, as of bone. [Lat. *squāma.*] — **squa′mate′** (-māt′) *adj.*

squa•ma•tion (skwə-mā′shən) *n.* **1.** The condition of being scaly. **2.** An arrangement of scales, as on a fish.

squa•mo•sal (skwə-mō′səl) *adj.* Of or relating to the thin platelike part of the human temporal bone or to a corresponding part in other vertebrates. — *n.* A squamosal bone. [< Lat. *squāmōsus,* squamous. See SQUAMOUS.]

squa•mous (skwā′məs, skwä′-) also **squa•mose** (-mōs′) *adj.* **1.** Covered with or formed of scales; scaly. **2.** Resembling a scale or scales; thin and flat like a scale. **3.** Of or relating to the thin platelike part of the temporal bone. [Lat. *squāmōsus* < *squāma,* scale.] — **squa′mous•ness** *n.*

squamous epithelium *n.* Epithelium consisting of one or more

ă **pat**	oi **boy**
ā **pay**	ou **out**
âr **care**	ŏŏ **took**
ä **father**	ōō **boot**
ĕ **pet**	ŭ **cut**
ē **be**	ûr **urge**
ĭ **pit**	th **thin**
ī **pie**	*th* **this**
îr **pier**	hw **which**
ŏ **pot**	zh **vision**
ō **toe**	ə **a**bout,
ô **paw**	it**e**m

Stress marks:
′ (primary);
′ (secondary), as in
dictionary (dĭk′shə-nĕr′ē)

cell layers, the most superficial of which is composed of flat scalelike or platelike cells.

squa•mu•lose (skwā′myə-lōs′, skwä′-) *adj.* Having or consisting of minute scales. [Lat. *squāmula*, dim. of *squāma*, scale + -OSE[1].]

squan•der (skwŏn′dər) *tr.v.* **-dered, -der•ing, -ders. 1.** To spend wastefully or extravagantly; dissipate. **2.** *Obsolete.* To scatter. —*n.* Extravagant expenditure; prodigality. [?] —**squan′der•er** *n.* —**squan′der•ing•ly** *adv.*

Squan•to (skwŏn′tō). d. 1622. Native American who helped the colonists in Massachusetts develop agricultural techniques and served as an interpreter with the Wampanoag.

square (skwâr) *n.* **1.** A plane figure having four equal sides. **2.** Something having an equal-sided rectangular form. **3.** A T-shaped or L-shaped instrument for drawing or testing right angles. **4.** *Math.* The product obtained when a number or quantity is multiplied by itself. **5.** *Games.* Any of the quadrilateral spaces on a board, as in chess. **6.a.** An open, usu. four-sided area at the intersection of two or more streets, often planted with grass and trees for use as a park. **b.** A rectangular space enclosed by streets and occupied by buildings; a block. **7.** *Slang.* A person who is regarded as dull, rigidly conventional, and out of touch with current trends. —*adj.* **squar•er, squar•est. 1.** Having four equal sides and four right angles. **2.** Forming a right angle. **3.a.** Expressed in units measuring area: *square feet.* **b.** Having a specified length in each of two equal dimensions. **4.** *Naut.* Set at right angles to the mast and keel. Used of the yards of a square-rigged ship. **5.** Approximately rectangular and equilateral in cross section. **6.** Characterized by blocklike solidity or sturdiness. **7.** Honest; direct. **8.** Just; equitable. **9.** Having been paid up; settled. **10.** *Sports.* Even; tied. **11.** *Slang.* Rigidly conventional; dull. —*v.* **squared, squar•ing, squares.** —*tr.* **1.** To cut to a square or rectangular shape. **2.** To test for conformity to a desired plane, straight line, or right angle. **3.** To mark into squares. Often used with *off.* **4.a.** To bring into conformity or agreement. **b.** To bring (oneself) into a better position or relation. **5.** To set straight or at approximate right angles: *square one's cap.* **6.** To bring into balance; settle. **7.** *Sports.* To even the score of. **8.** *Math.* **a.** To raise (a number or quantity) to the second power. **b.** To find a square equal in area to (the area of a given figure). **9.** *Informal.* To bribe or fix. —*intr.* **1.** *Math.* To be at right angles. **2.** To agree or conform. —*adv.* **1.** *Math.* At right angles. **2.** In a square shape. **3.** In a solid manner; firmly. **4.** Directly; straight: *ran square into it.* **5.** In an honest, straightforward manner. —***phrasal verbs.*** **square away. 1.** *Naut.* To square the yards of a sailing vessel. **2.** To put away or in order. **square off.** To assume a fighting stance; prepare to fight. **square up.** To settle a bill or debt. —***idioms.*** **on the square. 1.** *Math.* At right angles. **2.** Honestly and openly. **out of square. 1.** *Math.* Not at exact right angles. **2.** Not in agreement. **square peg in a round hole.** *Informal.* A misfit. [ME < OFr. *esquarre* < VLat. **exquadra* < **exquadrāre*, to square : Lat. *ex-*, ex- + *quadrāre*, to square (< *quadrum*, a square; see **kʷetwer-***).] —**square′ly** *adv.* —**square′ness** *n.* —**squar′er** *n.*

square bracket *n.* See **bracket** 4a.

square dance *n.* **1.** A dance in which sets of four couples form squares. **2.** Any of various similar group dances of rural origin. —**square′-dance′** (skwâr′dăns′) *v.* —**square dancer** *n.* —**square danc′ing** *n.*

square knot *n.* A common double knot in which the loose ends are parallel to the standing parts, most often used to join the ends of two cords or lines.

square knot

square matrix *n.* *Math.* A matrix with equal numbers of rows and columns.

square meal *n.* A substantial nourishing meal.

square measure *n.* A system of units used in measuring area.

square one *n.* *Informal.* The starting point. [Alluding to board games with numbered squares.]

square-rigged (skwâr′rĭgd′) *adj.* *Naut.* Fitted with square sails as the principal sails.

square-rig•ger (skwâr′rĭg′ər) *n.* *Naut.* A square-rigged vessel.

square root *n.* *Math.* A divisor of a quantity that when squared gives the quantity.

square sail *n.* *Naut.* A four-sided sail extended by a yard suspended horizontally across the mast.

square•tail (skwâr′tāl′) *n.* See **brook trout.**

squar•ish (skwâr′ĭsh) *adj.* Somewhat or almost square. —**squar′ish•ly** *adv.* —**squar′ish•ness** *n.*

squar•rose (skwăr′ōs′, skwär′-) *adj.* **1.** *Biol.* Having rough or spreading scalelike processes. **2.** *Bot.* Spreading or recurved at the tip: *squarrose bracts.* [Lat. *squarrōsus*, scabby.]

squash[1] (skwŏsh, skwôsh) *n.* **1.** Any of various tendril-bearing plants of the genus *Cucurbita*, having fleshy edible fruit with a leathery rind. **2.** The fruit of any of these plants. [< alteration of Narragansett *askútasquash*.]

squash[1]

squash[2] (skwŏsh, skwôsh) *v.* **squashed, squash•ing, squash•es.** —*tr.* **1.** To beat, squeeze, or press into a pulp or a flattened mass; crush. **2.** To put down or suppress; quash. **3.** To silence or fluster, as with crushing words. —*intr.* **1.** To become crushed, flattened, or pulpy, as by pressure or impact. **2.** To move with a splashing or sucking sound. —*n.* **1.a.** The act or sound of squashing. **b.** The fact or condition of being squashed. **2.** A crushed or crowded mass. **3.** *Sports.* A racket game played in a closed walled court with a rubber ball. **4.** *Chiefly British.* A citrus-based soft drink. —*adv.* With a squashing sound. [ME *squachen* < OFr. *esquasser* < VLat. **exquassāre* : Lat. *ex-*, intensive pref.; see EX- + Lat. *quassāre*, to shatter, freq. of *quatere*, to shake; see **kwēt-***.]

squash•y (skwŏsh′ē, skwô′shē) *adj.* **-i•er, -i•est. 1.** Easily squashed. **2.** Overripe and soft; pulpy. **3.** Boggy; marshy: *squashy ground.* —**squash′i•ly** *adv.* —**squash′i•ness** *n.*

squat (skwŏt) *v.* **squat•ted, squat•ting, squats.** —*intr.* **1.** To crouch with knees bent and the hams resting on or near the heels. **2.** To crouch down, as an animal does. **3.** To settle on unoccupied land without legal claim. **4.** To occupy a given piece of public land in order to acquire title to it. —*tr.* **1.** To put (oneself) into a squat. **2.** To occupy as a squatter. —*adj.* **squat•ter, squat•test. 1.** Short and thick; low and broad. **2.** Crouched in a squat. —*n.* **1.** The act of squatting. **2.** A squatting or crouching posture. **3.** *Sports.* A lift or a weight-lifting exercise in which one squats and stands while holding a weighted barbell supported by the back of the shoulders. **4.** The place occupied by a squatter. **5.** The lair of an animal such as a hare. [ME *squatten* < OFr. *esquatir*, to crush : *es-*, intensive pref. (< Lat. *ex-*; see EX-) + *quatir*, to press flat (< VLat. **coāctire* < Lat. *coāctus*, p.part. of *cōgere*, to compress : *co-*, co- + *agere*, to drive; see **ag-***).] —**squat′ter** *n.*

squaw (skwô) *n.* *Offensive.* **1.** A Native American woman, esp. a wife. **2.** A woman or wife. [Massachusett *squa*, younger woman.]

squaw•fish (skwô′fĭsh′) *n., pl.* **squawfish** or **-fish•es.** Any of several large cyprinid freshwater fishes of the genus *Ptychocheilus* of western North America.

squawk (skwôk) *v.* **squawked, squawk•ing, squawks.** —*intr.* **1.** To utter a harsh scream; screech. **2.** *Informal.* To complain or protest noisily or peevishly. —*tr.* To utter with or as if with a squawk. [Imit.] —**squawk** *n.* —**squawk′er** *n.*

squaw•root (skwô′rōōt′, -rŏŏt′) *n.* **1.** A parasitic eastern North American plant *(Conopholis americana)* having yellowish flowers and a brown scaly stem. **2.** An eastern North American plant *(Trillium erectum)* having ill-smelling purple to yellow flowers and dark red fruit.

Squaw Valley (skwô). A resort area of NE CA in the Sierra Nevada W of Lake Tahoe.

squeak (skwēk) *v.* **squeaked, squeak•ing, squeaks.** —*intr.* **1.** To give forth a squeak. **2.** *Slang.* To turn informer. —*tr.* To utter in a thin shrill voice. —*n.* **1.** A short shrill cry or sound. **2.** An escape. —***phrasal verb.*** **squeak through** (or **by**). To manage barely to pass, win, or survive. [ME *squeken*, perh. of Scand. orig.]

squeak•er (skwē′kər) *n.* **1.** One that squeaks. **2.** *Informal.* Something, such as an election, that is won, passed, or achieved by the narrowest of margins or time periods.

squeak•y (skwē′kē) *adj.* **-i•er, -i•est. 1.** Characterized by squeaking tones: *a squeaky voice.* **2.** Tending to squeak: *squeaky shoes.* —**squeak′i•ly** *adv.* —**squeak′i•ness** *n.*

squeal (skwēl) *v.* **squealed, squeal•ing, squeals.** —*intr.* **1.** To give forth a squeal. **2.** *Slang.* To turn informer; betray an accomplice or a secret. —*tr.* To utter or produce with a squeal. —*n.* A loud shrill cry or sound: *a squeal of surprise.* [ME *squelen*, prob. of imit. orig.] —**squeal′er** *n.*

squea•mish (skwē′mĭsh) *adj.* **1.a.** Easily nauseated or sickened. **b.** Nauseated. **2.** Easily shocked or disgusted. **3.** Excessively fastidious or scrupulous. [ME *squeimous*, alteration of AN *escoymous*.] —**squea′mish•ly** *adv.* —**squea′mish•ness** *n.*

squee•gee (skwē′jē) *n.* **1.** A T-shaped implement having a crosspiece edged with rubber or leather that is drawn across a surface to remove water, as in washing windows. **2.** *Print.* A similar implement or a rubber roller used in printing and photography. [Perh. < obsolete *squeege*, to press, alteration of SQUEEZE.] —**squee′gee** *v.*

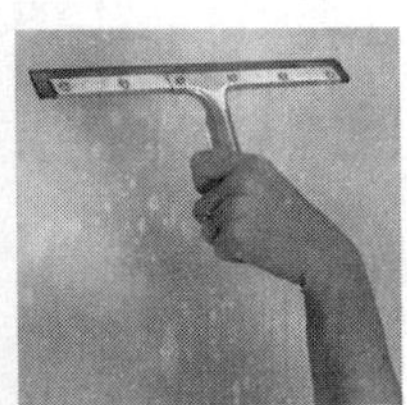

squeegee

squeeze (skwēz) *v.* **squeezed, squeez•ing, squeez•es.** —*tr.* **1.** To press hard on or together; compress. **2.** To press gently, as in affection. **3.** To exert pressure on, as by way of extracting liquid. **4.** To extract by or as if by applying pressure. **5.** To extract by dishonest means; extort. **6.** To oppress with burdensome demands. **7.** To obtain room for by pressure; cram. **8.** To manage to find time or space for. **9.** *Games.* To force (an opponent) to discard a potentially winning card in bridge. —*intr.* **1.** To give way under pressure. **2.** To exert pressure. **3.** To force one's way. —*n.* **1.** The act or an instance of squeezing. **2.** An amount squeezed out. **3.** A handclasp or brief embrace. **4.** A group crowded together; a crush. **5.** *Informal.* A squeeze play. **6.** Financial pressure caused by shortages or narrowing economic margins. **7.** *Games.* A forced discard of a potentially winning card in bridge. —***phrasal verbs.*** **squeeze off.** To fire (a round of bullets) by squeezing the trigger. **squeeze through** (or **by**). To manage narrowly to pass, win, or survive. [Prob. alteration of obsolete *quease*, to press < ME *queisen* < OE *cwȳsan*.] —**squeez′a•ble** *adj.* —**squeez′er** *n.*

squeeze play *n.* **1.** *Baseball.* A play in which the batter attempts to bunt so that a runner on third base may score. **2.** *Informal.* Pressure exerted, as to achieve a goal.

squelch (skwĕlch) *v.* **squelched, squelch•ing, squelch•es.** *— tr.* **1.** To crush by or as if by trampling; squash. **2.** To put down or silence, as with a crushing retort. *— intr.* To produce a splashing, squishing, or sucking sound, as when walking through ooze. *— n.* **1.** A squishing sound. **2.** A crushing reply. **3.** An electric circuit that cuts off a radio receiver when the signal is too weak for reception of anything but noise. [Prob. imit.] **— squelch′er** *n.*

sque•teague (skwĭ-tēg′) *n., pl.* **squeteague. 1.** See **weakfish. 2.** Any of several related fishes. [Of Algonquian orig.]

squib (skwĭb) *n.* **1.a.** A small firecracker. **b.** A broken firecracker that burns but does not explode. **2.a.** A brief satirical or witty writing or speech, such as a lampoon. **b.** A short, sometimes humorous piece in a newspaper or magazine, usu. used as a filler. *— v.* **squibbed, squib•bing, squibs.** *— intr.* To write or utter squibs. *— tr.* **1.** To write or utter squibs against; lampoon. **2.** *Football.* To kick (the ball) low on a kickoff so that it bounces along the ground. [Prob. imit.]

squid (skwĭd) *n., pl.* **squids** or **squid.** Any of various marine cephalopod mollusks of the genus *Loligo* and related genera, having an elongated body, ten arms surrounding the mouth, and a vestigial internal shell. [?]

squig•gle (skwĭg′əl) *n.* A small wiggly mark or scrawl. *— intr.v.* **-gled, -gling, -gles. 1.** To squirm and wriggle. **2.** To make squiggles. [Perh. blend of SQUIRM and WIGGLE.] **— squig′gly** *adj.*

squill (skwĭl) *n.* **1.** Any of several bulbous Eurasian and African plants of the genus *Scilla,* having narrow leaves and bell-shaped blue, white, or pink flowers. **2.** See **sea onion** 1. **3.** The dried inner scales of the bulbs of any of these plants, used as rat poison and formerly as a cardiac stimulant, expectorant, and diuretic. [ME < Lat. *scilla, squilla,* shrimp, squill < Gk. *skilla.*]

squil•la (skwĭl′ə) *n., pl.* **squil•las** or **squil•lae** (skwĭl′ē′). Any of various burrowing predatory marine crustaceans of the order Stomatopoda, having movable stalked eyes and a pair of jointed grasping appendages. [NLat. *Squilla,* genus name < Lat. *squilla,* shrimp. See SQUILL.]

squinch¹ (skwĭnch) *n.* A quarter-spherical segment of masonry vaulting or corbeling carried across an interior angle of a square tower to support a circular or octagonal superstructure. [Alteration of *scuncheon* < ME *sconchon* < OFr. *escoinson* : *es-,* out of (< Lat. *ex-*; see EX–) + *coin,* angle, wedge; see COIN.]

squinch² (skwĭnch) *tr.v.* **squinched, squinch•ing, squinch•es.** To squeeze, twist, or draw together. [Alteration of SQUINT.]

squint (skwĭnt) *v.* **squint•ed, squint•ing, squints.** *— intr.* **1.** To look with the eyes partly closed, as in bright sunlight. **2.a.** To look or glance sideways. **b.** To look askance, as in disapproval. **3.** To have an indirect reference or inclination. **4.** To be affected with strabismus. *— tr.* **1.** To cause to squint. **2.** To close (the eyes) partly while looking. *— n.* **1.** The act or an instance of squinting. **2.a.** A sideways glance. **b.** A quick look or glance. **3.** An oblique reference or inclination. **4.** See **strabismus. 5.** A hagioscope. *— adj.* **1.** Looking obliquely or askance. **2.** Squint-eyed. [Short for ASQUINT.] **— squint′er** *n.* **— squint′y** *adj.*

squint-eyed (skwĭnt′īd′) *adj.* **1.** Affected with strabismus. **2.** Looking with narrowed or squinting eyes. **3.** Looking askance, as in envy.

squire (skwīr) *n.* **1.** A man who attends or escorts a woman; a gallant. **2.** An English country gentleman, esp. the chief landowner in a district. **3.** A judge or another local dignitary. **4.** A young nobleman attendant upon a knight and ranked next below a knight in feudal hierarchy. *— tr.v.* **squired, squir•ing, squires.** To attend as a squire; escort. [ME *squier* < OFr. *esquier.* See ESQUIRE.]

squire•ar•chy or **squir•ar•chy** (skwīr′är′kē) *n., pl.* **-chies.** The landed gentry considered as a group or class.

squirm (skwûrm) *intr.v.* **squirmed, squirm•ing, squirms. 1.** To twist about in a wriggling snakelike motion; writhe. **2.** To feel or exhibit signs of humiliation or embarrassment. *— n.* **1.** The act of squirming. **2.** A squirming movement. [?] **— squirm′er** *n.* **— squirm′y** *adj.*

squir•rel (skwûr′əl, skwŭr′-) *n.* **1.** Any of various arboreal rodents of the genus *Sciurus* and related genera of the family Sciuridae, having a long flexible bushy tail and including the gray squirrel. **2.** Any of various other rodents of the family Sciuridae, as the flying squirrel. **3.** The fur of one of these rodents. *— tr.v.* **-reled, -rel•ing, -rels** or **-relled, -rel•ling, -rels.** To hide or store: *squirreled it away.* [ME *squirel* < AN *esquirel* < VLat. **scūriolus,* dim. of **scūrius,* alteration of Lat. *sciūrus* < Gk. *skiouros* : *skia,* shadow + *oura,* tail; see **ors-*.**]

squir•rel•ly (skwûr′ə-lē, skwŭr′-) *adj. Slang.* **1.** Eccentric. **2.** Cunningly unforthcoming or reticent.

squirrel monkey *n.* Any of several small, brightly colored arboreal monkeys of the genus *Saimiri,* widely distributed in South and Central American jungles and having a white face, a black nose and mouth, and a long nonprehensile tail.

squirt (skwûrt) *v.* **squirt•ed, squirt•ing, squirts.** *— intr.* **1.** To issue forth in a thin forceful stream or jet; spurt. **2.** To eject liquid in a jet. *— tr.* **1.** To eject (liquid) forcibly in a thin stream from a narrow opening. **2.** To wet with a spurt of liquid. *— n.* **1.** The act of squirting. **2.** An instrument used for squirting. **3.** A squirted jet of liquid. [ME *squirten,* poss. of MDu. or MLGer. orig.] **— squirt′er** *n.*

squirt gun *n.* A toy gun designed to squirt a stream of water.

squirt•ing cucumber (skwûr′tĭng) *n.* A hairy Mediterranean vine *(Ecballium elaterium)* having fruit that when ripe discharges its seeds and juice explosively.

squish (skwĭsh) *v.* **squished, squish•ing, squish•es.** *— tr.* To squeeze or crush together or into a flat mass; squash. *— intr.* To emit the gurgling or sucking sound of soft mud being walked on. *— n.* **1.** A squishing sound. **2.** *Slang.* A weak and ineffective person. [Prob. alteration of SQUASH².]

squish•y (skwĭsh′ē) *adj.* **squish•i•er, squish•i•est. 1.** Soft and wet; spongy. **2.** Sloppily sentimental.

sr *abbr.* Steradian.

Sr The symbol for the element **strontium.**

Sr. *abbr.* **1.** Or **sr.** Senior. **2.** Señor. **3.** *Eccles.* Sister (religious).

Sra. *abbr.* Señora.

Sra•nan•ton•go (srä′nən-tŏng′gō) *n.* A creole based on English, spoken in coastal Suriname and widely used as a lingua franca. [Sranantongo : *Sranan,* Suriname + *tongo,* tongue (< E. TONGUE).]

Sri Lan•ka (srē läng′kə). Formerly **Cey•lon** (sĭ-lŏn′, sā-). An island country in the Indian Ocean off SE India; became a British colony in 1798 and achieved independence in 1948. Cap. Colombo. Pop. 14,848,364. **— Sri Lan′kan** *adj. & n.*

Sri•na•gar (srē-nŭg′ər). A city of N India on the Jhelum R. N of Amritsar; founded in the 6th cent. A.D. Pop. 594,775.

sRNA *n.* Soluble RNA.

SRO *abbr.* **1.** Single room occupancy. **2.** Standing room only.

Srta. *abbr.* Señorita.

SS¹ (ĕs′ĕs′) *n.* An elite quasi-military unit of the Nazi party that served as Hitler's personal guard and as a special security force in Germany and the occupied countries. [Ger., abbr. for *Schutzstaffel* : *Schutz,* defense + *Staffel,* echelon.]

SS² *abbr.* Saints.

ss. *abbr.* **1.** Or **ss** Scilicet. **2.** *Lat.* Semis (one half).

S.S. *abbr.* **1.** Social Security. **2.** Or **SS** Steamship. **3.** Sunday school. **4.** Sworn statement.

s/s *abbr.* Same size.

SSA *abbr.* Social Security Administration.

SSE *abbr.* South-southeast.

S.Sgt. or **SSGT** *abbr.* Staff sergeant.

SSI *abbr.* Supplemental Security Income.

ssp. *abbr.* Subspecies.

S.S.R. or **SSR** *abbr.* Soviet Socialist Republic.

SST *abbr.* Supersonic transport.

SSW *abbr.* South-southwest.

ST *abbr.* Standard time.

st. *abbr.* **1.** Stanza. **2.** Start. **3.** State. **4.** Or **St.** Statute. **5.** *Print.* Stet. **6.** Stitch. **7.** Stone (weight). **8.** Or **St.** Strait. **9.** Or **St.** Street. **10.** Strophe.

St. *abbr.* Saint.

s.t. *abbr.* Short ton.

–st *suff.* Var. of **–est².**

sta. *abbr.* Station.

stab (stăb) *v.* **stabbed, stab•bing, stabs.** *— tr.* **1.** To pierce or wound with or as if with a pointed weapon. **2.** To plunge (a pointed weapon or instrument) into something. **3.** To make a thrusting or poking motion at or into. *— intr.* **1.** To thrust with or as if with a pointed weapon. **2.** To inflict a wound with or as if with a pointed weapon. *— n.* **1.** A thrust with a pointed weapon or instrument. **2.** A wound inflicted with or as if with a pointed weapon. **3.** A sudden piercing pain. **4.** An attempt; a try: *made a stab at the answer.* ***— idiom.*** **stab (someone) in the back.** To harm (someone) by treachery or betrayal of trust. [ME *stabben.*] **— stab′ber** *n.*

sta•bile (stā′bĭl, -bəl, -bīl′, -bēl′) *adj.* Immobile; unchangeable; stable. *— n.* An abstract sculpture, usu. of sheet metal, resembling a mobile but having no moving parts. [Lat. *stabilis,* stable. See STABLE¹.]

sta•bil•i•ty (stə-bĭl′ĭ-tē) *n., pl.* **-ties. 1.** The state or quality of being stable, esp.: **a.** Resistance to change, deterioration, or displacement. **b.** Constancy of character or purpose; steadfastness. **c.** Reliability; dependability. **2.** The ability of an object, such as a ship, to maintain equilibrium or resume its original position after displacement, as by the sea.

sta•bi•lize (stā′bə-līz′) *v.* **-lized, -liz•ing, -liz•es.** *— tr.* **1.** To make stable or steadfast. **2.** To maintain the stability of (an airplane, for example) by means of a stabilizer. **3.** To keep from fluctuating; fix the level of. *— intr.* To become stable, steadfast, or fixed. **— sta′bi•li•za′tion** (-lĭ-zā′shən) *n.*

sta•bi•liz•er (stā′bə-lī′zər) *n.* **1.** One that makes or keeps something stable. **2.** *Naut.* A device, such as a gyroscopically controlled fin, that prevents excessive rolling of a ship in heavy seas. **3.** An airfoil that stabilizes an aircraft or a missile in flight. **4.** *Chem.* A substance that renders a solution, mix-

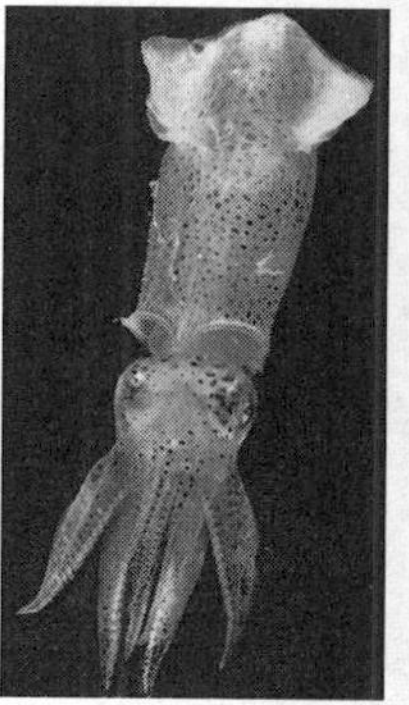
squid

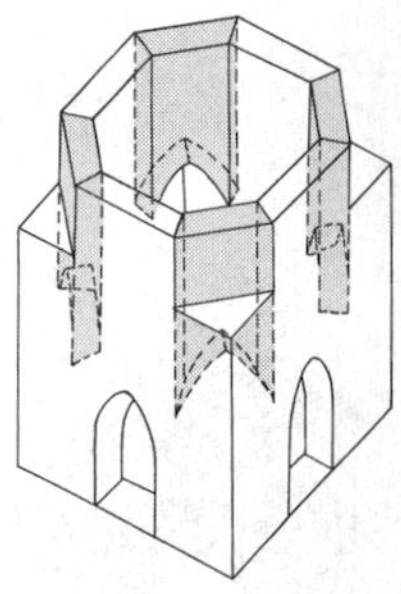
squinch¹

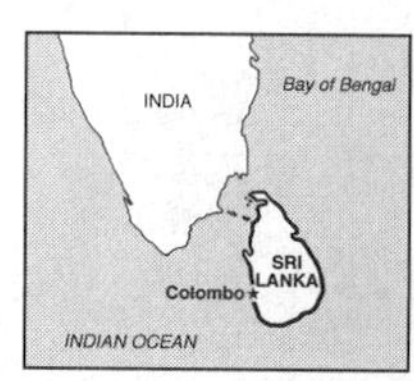

Sri Lanka

ă pat	oi boy
ā pay	ou out
âr care	ŏŏ took
ä father	ōō boot
ĕ pet	ŭ cut
ē be	ûr urge
ĭ pit	th thin
ī pie	*th* this
îr pier	hw which
ŏ pot	zh vision
ō toe	ə about, item
ô paw	

Stress marks:
′ (primary);
′ (secondary), as in dictionary (dĭk′shə-nĕr′ē)

ture, suspension, or state resistant to chemical change.

stabilizer bar *n.* See **anti-sway bar.**

sta•ble[1] (stā′bəl) *adj.* **-bler, -blest. 1.a.** Resistant to change of position or condition; steadfast. **b.** Maintaining equilibrium; self-restoring. **2.** Immutable; permanent; enduring. **3.a.** Consistently dependable. **b.** Not subject to mental illness or irrationality. **4.** *Phys.* Having no known mode of decay; indefinitely long-lived. Used of atomic particles. **5.** *Chem.* Not easily decomposed or otherwise modified chemically. [ME < OFr. *estable* < Lat. *stabilis.* See **stā-*.**] **— sta′ble•ness** *n.* **— sta′bly** *adv.*

sta•ble[2] (stā′bəl) *n.* **1.a.** A building for the shelter and feeding of domestic animals, esp. horses and cattle. **b.** A group of animals lodged in such a building. **2.a.** All the racehorses of an owner or racing establishment. **b.** The personnel employed to keep and train a stable. **3.** A group, as of athletes, under common management, authority, or ownership. *— v.* **-bled, -bling, -bles.** *— tr.* To put or keep in or as if in a stable. *— intr.* To live in or as if in a stable. [ME < OFr. *estable* < Lat. *stabulum,* stable, standing place. See **stā-*.**]

Madame de Staël
1810 portrait by
Jean Baptiste Isabey
(1767 – 1855)

stab•lish (stăb′lĭsh) *tr.v.* **-lish, -lished, -lish•ing.** *Archaic.* To establish.

stac•ca•to (stə-kä′tō) *adj.* **1.** *Mus.* Cut short crisply; disconnected: *staccato octaves.* **2.** Marked by or composed of abrupt disconnected parts or sounds: *staccato applause.* *— n., pl.* **-tos** or **-ti** (-tē). A staccato manner or sound. [Ital., p.part. of *staccare,* to detach, short for *distaccare* < obsolete Fr. *destacher* < OFr. *destachier.* See DETACH.] **— stac•ca′to** *adv.*

stack (stăk) *n.* **1.** A large, usu. conical pile of straw or fodder arranged for outdoor storage. **2.** An orderly pile, esp. one arranged in layers. **3.** *Comp. Sci.* A section of memory and its associated registers used for temporary storage of information in which the item most recently stored is the first to be retrieved. **4.** A group of three rifles supporting each other, butt downward and forming a cone. **5.a.** A chimney or flue. **b.** A group of chimneys arranged together. **6.** A vertical exhaust pipe, as on a ship. **7.a.** An extensive arrangement of bookshelves. **b.** The area of a library in which most of the books are shelved. In both senses, often used in the plural. **8.** A stackup. **9.** An English measure of coal or cut wood, equal to 108 cubic feet (3.06 cubic meters). **10.** *Informal.* A large quantity. *— v.* **stacked, stack•ing, stacks.** *— tr.* **1.** To arrange in a stack; pile. **2.** To load or cover with stacks or piles. **3.a.** *Games.* To prearrange the order of (a deck of cards) so as to increase the chance of winning. **b.** To prearrange or fix unfairly so as to favor a particular outcome. **4.** To direct (aircraft) to circle at different altitudes while waiting to land. *— intr.* To form a stack. ***— phrasal verb.* stack up.** *Informal.* **1.** To measure up or equal. **2.** To make sense; add up. [ME *stac* < ON *stakkr.*] **— stack′a•ble** *adj.* **— stack′er** *n.*

stagecoach
c. 1890 Concord stagecoach

stacked (stăkt) *adj. Slang.* Attractively formed and buxom.

stack•up (stăk′ŭp′) *n.* A deployment of aircraft circling an airport at designated altitudes while waiting to land.

stad•dle (stăd′l) *n.* A base or support, esp. a platform on which hay or straw is stacked. [ME *stathel* < OE *stathol.* See **stā-*.**]

stad•hold•er (stăd′hōl′dər) also **stadt•hold•er** (stăt′-) *n.* **1.** A governor or viceroy formerly stationed in a province of the Netherlands. **2.** The chief magistrate of the former Netherlands republic. [Partial transl. of Du. *stadhouder* : *stad,* place; see **stā-*** + *houder,* holder.]

sta•di•a[1] (stā′dē-ə) *n.* **1.a.** A telescopic instrument having two parallel lines through which intervals on a calibrated rod are observed, used to measure distances. **b.** The parallel lines in this instrument. **c.** The calibrated rod so used. **2.** The technique of measuring distances with this instrument. [Ital., prob. < Lat., pl. of *stadium,* a unit of length. See STADIUM.]

sta•di•a[2] (stā′dē-ə) *n.* Pl. of **stadium.**

sta•di•um (stā′dē-əm) *n., pl.* **-di•ums** or **-di•a** (-dē-ə). **1.** A large, usu. open structure for sports events with tiered seating for spectators. **2.** A course on which foot races were held in ancient Greece, having tiers of seats for spectators. **3.** An ancient Greek measure of distance, based on the length of such a course and equal to about 185 meters (607 feet). **4.** *Medic.* A stage or period in the course of a disease. **5.** *Biol.* A stage in the development or life history of an organism. [ME, unit of length < Lat. < Gk. *stadion,* perh. alteration (influenced by *stadios,* firm) of *spadion,* racetrack < *span,* to pull.]

stained glass
Tiffany stained glass window

Staël (stäl), Madame de. Baronne Anne Louise Germaine Necker de Staël-Holstein. 1766 – 1817. French writer and literary patron who introduced romanticism to French literature.

staff[1] (stăf) *n., pl.* **staffs** or **staves** (stāvz). **1.a.** A stick or cane carried as an aid in walking or climbing. **b.** A stout stick used as a weapon; a cudgel. **c.** A pole on which a flag is displayed; a flagstaff. **d.** A rod or baton carried as a symbol of authority. **2.** *pl.* **staffs.** A rule or similar graduated stick used for testing or measuring, as in surveying. **3.** *pl.* **staffs. a.** A group of assistants to a manager, an executive, or another person in authority. **b.** A group of military officers assigned to assist a commanding officer in an executive or advisory capacity. **c.** The personnel who carry out a specific enterprise. **4.** Something that serves as a staple or support. **5.** *Mus.* A set of five horizontal lines and four intermediate spaces used in notation to represent a sequence of pitches. *— tr.v.* **staffed, staff•ing, staffs. 1.** To provide with a staff of workers or assistants. **2.** To serve on the staff of. [ME *staf* < OE *stæf.*]

staff[2] (stăf) *n.* A building material of plaster and fiber used as an exterior wall covering of temporary buildings, as at expositions. [Perh. < Ger. *stoff,* stuff.]

Staf•fa (stăf′ə). An island of W Scotland in the Inner Hebrides W of Mull.

staff•er (stăf′ər) *n. Informal.* A member of a staff.

Staf•ford (stăf′ərd). A municipal borough of W-central England NNW of Birmingham. Pop. 55,100.

Staf•ford•shire terrier (stăf′ərd-shîr′, -shər) *n.* See **American Staffordshire terrier.** [After *Staffordshire,* a county of W-central England.]

staff sergeant *n.* **1.** A noncommissioned officer in the U.S. Army ranking above sergeant and below sergeant first class. **2.** A noncommissioned officer in the U.S. Air Force ranking above sergeant and below technical sergeant. **3.** A noncommissioned officer in the U.S. Marine Corps ranking above sergeant and below gunnery sergeant.

staff tree *n.* See **bittersweet** 1.

stag (stăg) *n.* **1.** The adult male of various deer, esp. the red deer. **2.** A male animal, esp. a pig, castrated after reaching sexual maturity. **3.** A member of one sex who attends a social gathering unaccompanied by a member of the other sex. **4.** A social gathering for men only. *— adj.* **1.** Of or for men only. **2.** Pornographic. *— adv.* Unaccompanied. *— intr.v.* **stagged, stag•ging, stags.** To attend a social gathering as a stag. [ME *stagge* < OE *stagga.* See **stegh-*.**]

stag beetle *n.* Any of numerous large beetles of the family Lucanidae, having large branched mandibles in the male.

stage (stāj) *n.* **1.** A raised and level floor or platform. **2.a.** A raised platform on which theatrical performances are presented. **b.** An area in which actors perform. **c.** The acting profession, or the world of theater. Used with *the.* **3.** The scene of an event or a series of events. **4.** A platform on a microscope that supports a slide for viewing. **5.** A scaffold for workers. **6.** A resting place on a journey, esp. one providing overnight accommodations. **7.** The distance between stopping places on a journey; a leg. **8.** A stagecoach. **9.** A level or story of a building. **10.** The height of the surface of a river or other fluctuating body of water above a set point. **11.a.** A level, degree, or period of time in the course of a process, esp. a step in development. **b.** A point in the course of an action or series of events. **12.** One of two or more successive propulsion units of a rocket vehicle, each of which fires after the preceding one has been jettisoned. **13.** *Geol.* A subdivision in the classification of stratified rocks, ranking just below a series and representing rock formed during a chronological age. **14.** *Electron.* An element or a group of elements in a complex arrangement of parts, esp. a single tube or transistor and its accessory components in an amplifier. *— v.* **staged, stag•ing, stag•es.** *— tr.* **1.** To exhibit or present on or as if on a stage. **2.** To produce or direct (a theatrical performance). **3.** To arrange and carry out. *— intr.* **1.** To be adaptable to or suitable for theatrical presentation. **2.** To stop at a designated place in the course of a journey. [ME < OFr. *estage* < VLat. **staticum* < Lat. *status,* p.part. of *stāre,* to stand. See **stā-*.**] **— stage′ful′** *n.*

stage•coach (stāj′kōch′) *n.* A four-wheeled horse-drawn vehicle formerly used to transport mail, parcels, and passengers over a regular route.

stage•craft (stāj′krăft′) *n.* Skill in the techniques and devices of the theater.

stage fright *n.* Acute nervousness associated with performing or speaking before an audience.

stage•hand (stāj′hănd′) *n.* A worker who shifts scenery, adjusts lighting, and performs other tasks required in a theatrical production.

stage left *n.* The area of the stage to one's left when facing the audience.

stage-man•age (stāj′măn′ĭj) *tr.v.* **-aged, -ag•ing, -ag•es. 1.** To serve as overall supervisor of the stage and actors for (a theatrical production). **2.** To direct or manipulate from behind the scenes, as to achieve a desired effect; orchestrate. **— stage management** *n.* **— stage manager** *n.*

stag•er (stā′jər) *n.* One who possesses the wisdom of long experience.

stage right *n.* The area of the stage to one's right when facing the audience.

stage-struck (stāj′strŭk′) *adj.* Enthralled by the theater or intensely eager for a career in acting.

stage whisper *n.* **1.** The conventional whisper of an actor, intended to be heard by the audience but supposedly inaudible to others on stage. **2.** A whisper intended to be overheard.

stag•ey (stā′jē) *adj.* Var. of **stagy.**

stag•gard (stăg′ərd) *n.* A male red deer in its fourth year. [ME < *stagge,* stag. See STAG.]

stag•ger (stăg′ər) *v.* **-gered, -ger•ing, -gers.** *— intr.* **1.** To move or stand unsteadily, as if under a great weight; totter. **2.** To begin to lose confidence or strength of purpose; waver.

—*tr.* **1.** To cause to totter, sway, or reel. **2.a.** To overwhelm with emotion or astonishment. **b.** To cause to waver or lose confidence. **3.** To place on or as if on alternating sides of a center line; set in a zigzag row or rows. **4.** To arrange in alternating or overlapping time periods. **5.** To arrange (the wings of a biplane) so that the leading edge of one wing is either ahead of or behind the leading edge of the other wing. —*n.* **1.** A tottering, swaying, or reeling motion. **2.** A staggered pattern, arrangement, or order. **3. staggers.** *(used with a sing. v.)* Any of various diseases of the nervous system in animals, esp. horses, cattle, or other domestic animals, marked by a staggering gait and frequent falling. [Alteration of ME *stakeren* < ON *stakra*, freq. of *staka*, to push.] —**stag′ger·er** *n.* —**stag′ger·y** *adj.*

stag·ger·bush (stăg′ər-bo͝osh′) *n.* A deciduous shrub *(Lyonia mariana)* of the eastern United States having poisonous foliage and white or pink flowers clustered in racemes.

stag·ger·ing (stăg′ər-ĭng) *adj.* Causing great astonishment, amazement, or dismay; overwhelming: *a staggering defeat.*

stag·horn fern (stăg′hôrn′) *n.* Any of several tropical epiphytic ferns of the genus *Platycerium,* having large, dichotomously divided fertile fronds that resemble antlers.

staghorn sumac *n.* An eastern North American deciduous shrub or tree *(Rhus typhina)* having pinnately compound leaves, small greenish flowers, and hairy crimson fruit.

stag·hound (stăg′hound′) *n.* Any of several dogs formerly used in hunting stags and other large game.

stag·ing (stā′jĭng) *n.* **1.** A temporary platform or system of platforms used for support; scaffolding. **2.** The process or manner of staging a play. **3.** The act of jettisoning a stage of a multistage rocket. **4.a.** The operation of stagecoaches as an enterprise. **b.** Travel by stagecoach.

staging area *n.* A place where troops or equipment in transit are assembled and processed, as before a military operation.

Sta·gi·ra (stə-jī′rə) or **Sta·gi·rus** (-rəs). An ancient city of Macedonia in NE Greece; birthplace of Aristotle.

stag·nant (stăg′nənt) *adj.* **1.** Not moving or flowing; motionless. **2.** Foul or stale from standing. **3.a.** Showing little or no sign of activity or advancement; not developing or progressing; inactive. **b.** Lacking vitality or briskness; sluggish or dull. —**stag′nan·cy** *n.* —**stag′nant·ly** *adv.*

stag·nate (stăg′nāt′) *intr.v.* **-nat·ed, -nat·ing, -nates.** To be or become stagnant. [Lat. *stagnāre, stagnāt-* < *stagnum,* swamp.] —**stag·na′tion** *n.*

stag·y also **stag·ey** (stā′jē) *adj.* **-i·er, -i·est.** Having a theatrical character or quality; artificial and affected. —**stag′i·ly** *adv.* —**stag′i·ness** *n.*

staid (stād) *adj.* **1.** Characterized by sedate dignity and often a strait-laced sense of propriety; sober. **2.** Fixed; permanent. [< obsolete *staid,* p.part. of STAY[1].] —**staid′ly** *adv.* —**staid′ness** *n.*

stain (stān) *v.* **stained, stain·ing, stains.** —*tr.* **1.** To discolor, soil, or spot. **2.** To bring into disrepute; taint. **3.** To color (glass, for example) with a coat of penetrating liquid dye or tint. **4.** To treat (specimens for the microscope) with a reagent or dye that makes visible certain structures without affecting others. —*intr.* To produce or receive discolorations. —*n.* **1.** A discolored or soiled spot or smudge. **2.** A blemish on one's character or reputation. **3.** A liquid applied esp. to wood that penetrates the surface and imparts a rich color. **4.** A reagent or dye used for staining microscopic specimens. [ME *steinen,* partly < OFr. *desteindre, desteign-,* to deprive of color (*des-,* dis- + Lat. *tingere, tīnct-,* to dye) and partly < ON *steina,* to paint.] —**stain′a·ble** *adj.* —**stain′er** *n.*

stained glass (stānd) *n.* Glass colored by mixing pigments into the glass, fusing colored metallic oxides onto the glass, or painting and baking transparent colors on the glass surface.

Staines (stānz). An urban district of SE England on the Thames R. WSW of London. Pop. 92,800.

stain·less (stān′lĭs) *adj.* **1.** Without stain or blemish. **2.** Resistant to stain or corrosion. —**stain′less·ly** *adv.*

stainless steel *n.* Any of various steels that are alloyed with at least 10 percent chromium and sometimes contain other elements and are resistant to corrosion or rusting.

stair (stâr) *n.* **1.** A series or flight of steps; a staircase. Often used in the plural. **2.** One of a flight of steps. [ME < OE *stǣger.* See **steigh-***.]

stair·case (stâr′kās′) *n.* A flight or series of flights of steps and a supporting structure connecting separate levels.

stair·way (stâr′wā′) *n.* See **staircase.**

stair·well (stâr′wĕl′) *n.* A vertical shaft around which a staircase has been built.

stake (stāk) *n.* **1.** A piece of wood or metal pointed at one end for driving into the ground as a marker, fence pole, or tent peg. **2.a.** A vertical post to which an offender is bound for execution by burning. **b.** Execution by burning. Used with *the.* **3.** A vertical post secured in a socket at the edge of a platform, as on a truck bed, to help retain the load. **4.** *Mormon Ch.* A territorial division consisting of a group of wards under the jurisdiction of a president. **5.** *Sports & Games.* **a.** Money or property risked in a wager or gambling game. See Syns at **bet. b.** The prize awarded the winner of a contest or race. **c.** A race offering a prize to the winner, esp. a horserace in which the prize consists of money contributed equally by the horse owners. In all three senses, often used in the plural. **6.a.** A share or an interest in an enterprise, esp. a financial share. **b.** Personal interest or involvement. **7.** A grubstake. —*tr.v.* **staked, stak·ing, stakes. 1.a.** To mark the location or limits of with or as if with stakes: *staked out a claim.* **b.** To claim as one's own. **2.** To fasten, secure, or support with a stake or stakes. **3.** To tether or tie to a stake. **4.** To gamble or risk; hazard. **5.** To provide working capital for; finance. —***phrasal verb.* stake out. 1.** To assign (a police officer, for example) to an area to conduct surveillance. **2.** To keep under surveillance. —***idiom.* at stake.** At risk; in question. [ME < OE *staca.*]

stake·hold·er (stāk′hōl′dər) *n.* **1.** *Games.* One who holds the bets in a game or contest. **2.** One who has a share or an interest, as in an enterprise.

stake·out (stāk′out′) *n.* Surveillance of an area, a building, or a person, esp. by the police.

sta·lac·tite (stə-lăk′tīt′, stăl′ək-) *n.* An icicle-shaped mineral deposit, usu. calcite or aragonite, hanging from the roof of a cavern, formed from the dripping of mineral-rich water. [NLat. *stalactītēs* < Gk. *stalaktos,* dripping < *stalassein, stalak-,* to drip.] —**sta·lac′ti·form′** *adj.* —**stal′ac·tit′ic** (stăl′ăk-tĭt′ĭk, stə-lăk′-) *adj.*

stalactite and stalagmite

sta·lag (stä′läg′, stăl′ăg′) *n.* A German prisoner of war camp. [Ger., short for *Stammlager,* base camp : *Stamm,* base, stem (< MHGer. *stam* < OHGer.) + *Lager,* camp, bed (< MHGer. *leger* < OHGer. *legar,* bed, lair; see LAGER).]

sta·lag·mite (stə-lăg′mīt′, stăl′əg-) *n.* A conical mineral deposit, usu. calcite or aragonite, built up on the floor of a cavern, formed from the dripping of mineral-rich water. [NLat. *stalagmītēs,* a drop < Gk. *stalagma,* a drop, or *stalagmos,* dropping, both < *stalassein, stalak-,* to drip.] —**stal′ag·mit′ic** (stăl′əg-mĭt′ĭk, stə-lăg′-) *adj.*

stale[1] (stāl) *adj.* **stal·er, stal·est. 1.** Having lost freshness, effervescence, or palatability. **2.** Lacking originality or spontaneity. **3.** Impaired in efficacy, vigor, or spirit, as from inactivity. [ME, settled, clear: used of beer or wine, prob. < OFr. *estale,* slack, settled, clear < *estaler,* to halt < *estal,* standing place, stand, of Gmc. orig. See **stel-***.] —**stale** *v.* —**stale′ly** *adv.* —**stale′ness** *n.*

stale[2] (stāl) *intr.v.* **staled, stal·ing, stales.** To urinate. Used esp. of horses and camels. —*n.* The urine of these animals. [ME *stalen,* poss. of LGer. orig.; akin to MLGer. *stallen.*]

stale·mate (stāl′māt′) *n.* **1.** A situation in which further action is blocked; a deadlock. **2.** *Games.* A drawing position in chess in which the king, although not in check, can move only into check and no other piece can move. [Obsolete *stale* (< ME, prob. < AN *estale,* fixed position < OFr. *estal;* see STALE[1]) + MATE[2].] —**stale′mate′** *v.*

Sta·lin (stä′lĭn, stăl′ĭn), **Joseph.** 1879–1953. Soviet politician who was general secretary of the Communist Party (1922–53) and premier (1941–53) of the U.S.S.R.

Joseph Stalin

Sta·lin·grad (stä′lĭn-grăd′, stə-lyĭn-grät′). See **Volgograd.**

Sta·lin·ism (stä′lə-nĭz′əm) *n.* The bureaucratic, authoritarian exercise of state power and mechanistic application of Marxist-Leninist principles associated with Stalin. —**Sta′lin·ist** *adj. & n.* —**Sta′lin·ize′** *v.*

stalk[1] (stôk) *n.* **1.a.** A stem or main axis of a herbaceous plant. **b.** A stem or similar structure that supports a plant part such as a flower, flower cluster, or leaf. **2.** A slender or elongated support or structure, as one that holds up an organ or another body part. [ME, prob. dim. of *stale,* upright of a ladder, post, handle < OE *stalu.* See **stel-***.] —**stalk′y** *adj.*

stalk[2] (stôk) *v.* **stalked, stalk·ing, stalks.** —*intr.* **1.** To walk with a stiff, haughty, or angry gait. **2.** To move threateningly or menacingly. **3.** To track prey or quarry. —*tr.* **1.** To pursue by tracking stealthily. **2.** To go through (an area) in pursuit of prey or quarry. [ME *stalken* < OE *-stealcian,* to move stealthily (in *bestealcian*).] —**stalk′er** *n.*

stalked (stôkt) *adj.* Having a stalk or stem. Often used in combination: *long-stalked.*

stalk·ing-horse (stô′kĭng-hôrs′) *n.* **1.** Something used to cover one's true purpose; a decoy. **2.** A sham candidate put forward, as to divide the opposition. **3.a.** A horse trained to conceal the hunter while stalking. **b.** A canvas screen made in the figure of a horse, used for similar concealment.

stall[1] (stôl) *n.* **1.** A compartment for one domestic animal in a barn or shed. **2.a.** A booth, cubicle, or stand used by a vendor, as at a market. **b.** A small compartment. **3.a.** An enclosed seat in the chancel of a church. **b.** A pew in a church. **4.** *Chiefly British.* A seat in the front part of a theater. **5.** A space marked off, as in a garage, for parking a motor vehicle. **6.** A protective sheath for a finger or toe. **7.** The sudden unintended loss of power or effectiveness in an engine. **8.** A condition in which an aircraft or airfoil experiences an interruption of airflow resulting in loss of lift and a tendency to drop. —*v.* **stalled, stall·ing, stalls.** —*tr.* **1.** To put or lodge in a stall. **2.** To maintain in a stall for fattening: *to stall cattle.* **3.** To check the motion or progress of; bring to a standstill. **4.** To cause (an engine) to stop running. **5.** To cause (an air-

ă pat	oi boy
ā pay	ou out
âr care	o͝o took
ä father	o͞o boot
ĕ pet	ŭ cut
ē be	ûr urge
ĭ pit	th thin
ī pie	*th* this
îr pier	hw which
ŏ pot	zh vision
ō toe	ə about, item
ô paw	

Stress marks:
′ (primary);
′ (secondary), as in
dictionary (dĭk′shə-nĕr′ē)

craft) to go into a stall. —*intr.* **1.** To live or be lodged in a stall. Used of an animal. **2.** To stick fast in mud or snow. **3.** To come to a standstill: *Negotiations stalled.* **4.** To stop running as a result of mechanical failure. **5.** To lose forward flying speed, causing a stall. Used of an aircraft. [ME *stalle* < OE *steall*, standing place, stable. See **stel-***.]

stall[2] (stôl) *n.* A ruse or tactic used to mislead or delay. —*v.* **stalled, stall•ing, stalls.** —*tr.* To employ delaying tactics against: *stall off creditors.* —*intr.* To employ delaying tactics. [Alteration (influenced by STALL[1]) of obsolete *stale*, pickpocket's accomplice < ME, decoy < AN *estale*, of Gmc. orig.; poss. akin to OE *stǣl, stathol*, place, position. See STADDLE.]

stall-feed (stôl′fēd′) *tr.v.* **-fed** (-fĕd′), **-feed•ing, -feeds.** To lodge and feed (an animal) in a stall for fattening.

stal•lion (stăl′yən) *n.* An adult male horse that has not been castrated, esp. one kept for breeding. [ME *stalione*, alteration of *staloun* < AN *estaloun*, of Gmc. orig. See **stel-***.]

stal•wart (stôl′wərt) *adj.* **1.** Having or marked by imposing physical strength. **2.** Firm and resolute; stout. —*n.* **1.** One who is physically and morally strong. **2.** One who steadfastly supports an organization or a cause. [ME, alteration of *stalworth* < OE *stǣlwierthe*, serviceable, prob. alteration of **statholwierthe*, steadfast : *stathol*, foundation; see STADDLE + *weorth*, valuable; see **wer-[2]***.] —**stal′wart•ly** *adv.* —**stal′wart•ness** *n.*

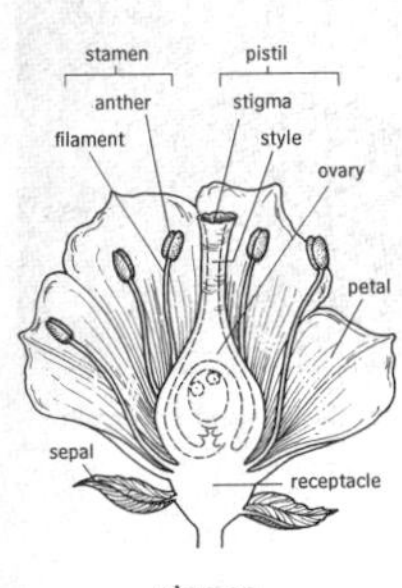

stamen

sta•men (stā′mən) *n., pl.* **sta•mens** or **sta•mi•na** (stā′mə-nə, stăm′ə-). The pollen-producing reproductive organ of a flower, usu. consisting of a filament and an anther. [Lat. *stāmen*, thread. See **stā-***.]

Stam•ford (stăm′fərd). A city of SW CT on Long Island Sound and the NY border; settled in 1641. Pop. 108,056.

stamin– *pref.* Stamen: *staminate.* [Lat. *stāmen, stāmin-*, thread, warp. See STAMEN.]

stam•i•na[1] (stăm′ə-nə) *n.* Physical or moral strength to resist or withstand illness, fatigue, or hardship; endurance. [Lat. *stāmina*, pl. of *stāmen*, thread. See STAMEN.]

sta•mi•na[2] (stā′mə-nə, stăm′ə-) *n.* Pl. of **stamen.**

stam•i•nal[1] (stăm′ə-nəl) *adj.* Of or relating to stamina or endurance.

sta•mi•nal[2] (stā′mə-nəl, stăm′ə-) *adj.* Of or relating to stamens or a stamen.

sta•mi•nate (stā′mə-nĭt, -nāt′, stăm′ə-) *adj.* Having stamens but lacking pistils: *staminate flowers.*

stam•i•node (stā′mə-nōd′, stăm′ə-) also **stam•i•no•di•um** (stā′mə-nō′dē-əm, stăm′ə-) *n., pl.* **-nodes** also **-no•di•a** (-nō′dē-ə). A sterile stamen, sometimes resembling a petal, as in the canna. [NLat. *stamīnōdium* < Lat. *stāmen, stāmin-*, thread. See STAMEN.]

stam•mel (stăm′əl) *n.* **1.** *Archaic.* The red color of a coarse woolen cloth sometimes used for undergarments. **2.** *Obsolete.* A coarse woolen cloth for undergarments. [Prob. alteration of *stamin* < ME *stamyn* < OFr. *estamine* < VLat. **stāminea* < Lat., fem. of *stāmineus*, consisting of threads < *stāmen, stāmin-*, thread. See **stā-***.]

stam•mer (stăm′ər) *v.* **-mered, -mer•ing, -mers.** —*intr.* To speak with a stammer. —*tr.* To utter with a stammer. —*n.* A way of speaking marked by involuntary pauses or repetitions. [ME *stameren* < OE *stamerian*.] —**stam′mer•er** *n.*

stamp (stămp) *v.* **stamped, stamp•ing, stamps.** —*tr.* **1.** To bring down (the foot) forcibly. **2.** To bring the foot down onto (an object or a surface) forcibly. **3.** To extinguish or destroy by or as if by trampling underfoot: *stamp out a fire.* **4.** To crush or grind with a heavy instrument: *stamp ore.* **5.** To form or cut out by application of a mold, form, or die. **6.** To imprint or impress with a mark, design, or seal. **7.** To impress forcibly or permanently. **8.** To affix an adhesive stamp to. **9.** To identify, characterize, or reveal. —*intr.* **1.** To thrust the foot forcibly downward. **2.** To walk with forcible heavy steps. See Usage Note at **stomp.** —*n.* **1.** The act of stamping. **2.a.** An implement or a device used to impress, cut out, or shape something to which it is applied. **b.** An impression or a shape formed by such an implement or device. **3.** An official mark, design, or seal that indicates ownership, approval, completion, or the payment of a tax. **4.a.** A small piece of gummed paper sold by a government for attachment to an article that is to be mailed; a postage stamp. **b.** A similar piece of gummed paper issued for a specific purpose. **5.** An identifying or characterizing mark or impression. **6.** Characteristic nature or quality: *a person of her stamp.* [ME *stampen*, poss. alteration of OE *stempan*, to pound in a mortar.]

standard
1812 American standard of the New England Guards by Jesse Churchill (1773–1819)

stam•pede (stăm-pēd′) *n.* **1.** A sudden frenzied rush of panic-stricken animals. **2.** A sudden headlong rush or flight of a crowd of people. **3.** A mass impulsive action. —*v.* **-ped•ed, -ped•ing, -pedes.** —*tr.* **1.** To cause (a herd of animals) to flee in panic. **2.** To cause (a crowd of people) to act on mass impulse. —*intr.* **1.** To flee in a headlong rush. **2.** To act on mass impulse. [Sp. *estampida*, uproar, stampede < Prov. < *estampir*, to stamp, of Gmc. orig.] —**stam•ped′er** *n.*

stamp•er (stăm′pər) *n.* One that stamps: *a metal stamper.*

stamp mill *n.* **1.** A machine that crushes ore. **2.** A building in which ore is crushed.

stance (stăns) *n.* **1.** The attitude or position of a standing person or animal, esp. the position assumed by an athlete preparatory to action. **2.** Mental posture; point of view. [Fr., position < Ital. *stanza* < VLat. **stantia* < Lat. *stāns, stant-*, pr.part. of *stāre*, to stand. See **stā-***.]

stanch[1] (stônch, stänch, stănch) also **staunch** (stônch, stänch) *tr.v.* **stanched, stanch•ing, stanch•es** also **staunched, staunch•ing, staunch•es. 1.** To stop or check the flow of (blood or tears, for example). **2.** To stop the flow of blood from (a wound). **3.** To check or allay. See Usage Note at **staunch[1].** [ME *stanchen* < OFr. *estanchier* < VLat. **stanticāre*, to stop, prob. < Lat. *stāns, stant-*, pr.part. of *stāre*, to stand. See **stā-***.] —**stanch′er** *n.*

stanch[2] (stônch, stänch, stănch) *adj.* Var. of **staunch[1].** See Usage Note at **staunch[1].**

stan•chion (stăn′chən, -shən) *n.* **1.** An upright pole, post, or support. **2.** A framework consisting usu. of two vertical bars, used to secure cattle in a stall. —*tr.v.* **-chioned, -chion•ing, -chions. 1.** To equip with stanchions. **2.** To confine (cattle) by means of stanchions. [ME *stanchon* < OFr. *estanchon*, prob. < *estance*, act of standing upright, prop < *estans*, pr.part. of *ester*, to stand < Lat. *stāre.* See **stā-***.]

stand (stănd) *v.* **stood** (sto͝od), **stand•ing, stands.** —*intr.* **1.a.** To rise to an upright position on the feet. **b.** To assume or maintain an upright position as specified: *stand to one side.* **2.a.** To maintain an upright position on the feet. **b.** To maintain an upright or vertical position on a base or support. **c.** To be placed or situated. **3.a.** To remain stable, upright, or intact. **b.** To remain valid, effective, or unaltered. **4.** To be or show a specified figure or amount. **5.** To measure a specified height when in an upright position: *stands six feet tall.* **6.** To take up or maintain a specified position, altitude, or course. **7.** To be in a position of possible gain or loss. **8.a.** To be in a specified state or condition. **b.** To exist in a particular form. **9.** To be at a specified level on or as if on a scale: *stands third in her class.* **10.a.** To come to a stop; remain motionless. **b.** To remain stationary or inactive. **11.** To remain without flowing or being disturbed; be or become stagnant. **12.** *Naut.* To take or hold a particular course or direction: *a ship standing in toward shore.* **13.** To be available as a sire. Used of horses. **14.** *Chiefly British.* To be a candidate for public office. —*tr.* **1.** To cause to stand; place upright. **2.** To engage in or encounter. **3.a.** To resist successfully; withstand. **b.** To put up with patiently or resolutely; bear. See Syns at **bear[1]. 4.** To submit to or undergo: *stand trial.* **5.** To tolerate and benefit from: *I could stand some sleep.* **6.** To perform the duty of: *stand guard.* **7.** *Informal.* To treat (someone) or pay the cost of (food or drink): *We'll stand dinner.* —*n.* **1.** The act of standing. **2.** A ceasing of work or activity; a standstill or halt. **3.** A stop on a performance tour. **4.** The place or station where a person stands. **5.** A booth, stall, or counter for the display of goods for sale. **6.** A parking space reserved for taxis. **7.** A desperate or decisive effort at defense or resistance, as in a battle. **8.** A position or an opinion one is prepared to uphold. **9. stands.** The bleachers at a playing field or stadium. **10.** *Law.* A witness stand. **11.** A small rack, prop, or table for holding any of various articles. **12.** A group or growth of tall plants or trees. —***phrasal verbs.* stand by. 1.** To be ready or available to act. **2.** To wait for something, such as a broadcast, to resume. **3.** To remain uninvolved; refrain from acting. **4.** To remain loyal to; aid or support. **5.** To keep or maintain. **stand down. 1.** *Law.* To leave a witness stand. **2.** To withdraw, as from a political contest. **3.** To go off duty. **stand for. 1.** To represent; symbolize. **2.** To advocate or support. **3.** To put up with; tolerate. **stand in.** To act as a stand-in. **stand off. 1.** To stay at a distance; remain apart or aloof. **2.** To put off; evade. **3.** *Naut.* To maintain a course away from shore. **stand on. 1.** To be based on; depend on. **2.** To insist on observance of. **stand out. 1.** To protrude; project. **2.** To be conspicuous, distinctive, or prominent. **3.** To refuse compliance or maintain opposition; hold out. **4.** *Naut.* To maintain a course away from shore. **stand over. 1.** To watch or supervise closely. **2.** To hold over; postpone. **stand to.** To take up positions for action. **stand up. 1.** To remain valid, sound, or durable. **2.** *Informal.* To fail to keep a date with. —***idioms.* stand a chance.** To have a chance, as of gaining or accomplishing something. **stand on (one's) own (or two) feet.** To be independent and responsible for oneself. **stand pat. 1.** To refuse to change one's position or opinion. **2.** *Games.* To play one's poker hand without drawing. **stand to reason.** To be consistent with reason. **stand up for.** To side with; defend. **stand up to.** To confront fearlessly; face up to. [ME *standen* < OE *standan.* See **stā-***.] —**stand′er** *n.*

stand-a•lone (stănd′ə-lōn′) *adj. Comp. Sci.* Of, relating to, or being a self-contained, usu. independently operating computer system or device: *a stand-alone terminal.*

stan•dard (stăn′dərd) *n.* **1.** A flag, banner, or ensign, esp.: **a.** The ensign of a chief of state, nation, or city. **b.** A long tapering flag bearing heraldic devices distinctive of a person or corporation. **c.** An emblem or flag of an army, raised on a pole to indicate the rallying point in battle. **d.** The colors of a mounted or motorized military unit. **2.a.** An acknowledged measure of comparison for quantitative or qualitative value; a criterion. **b.** An object that under specified conditions defines, represents, or records the magnitude of a unit. **3.** The set proportion by weight of gold or silver to alloy metal for use in coinage. **4.** The commodity or commodities backing a monetary system. **5.a.** A degree or level of requirement, excellence, or attainment. **b.** A requirement of moral conduct. Often used in the plural. **6.** *Chiefly British.* A grade level in elementary schools. **7.** A pedestal, stand, or base. **8.** *Bot.* **a.** The large upper petal of the flower of a pea or related plant. **b.** One of the narrow upright petals of an iris. **9.** A shrub or small tree that through grafting or training has a single stem of limited height with a crown of leaves and flowers at its apex. **10.** *Mus.* A composition continually used in repertoires. — *adj.* **1.** Serving as or conforming to a standard of measurement or value. **2.** Widely recognized as a model of authority or excellence. **3.** Acceptable but of less than top quality. **4.** Normal, familiar, or usual. **5.** Commonly used or supplied. **6.** *Ling.* Conforming to established educated usage in speech or writing. [ME < OFr. *estandard,* rallying place, prob. < Frankish **standhard* : **standan,* to stand; see **stā-*** + **hard,* fast, hard; see **kar-*.**] — **stan′dard·ly** *adv.*

stan·dard-bear·er (stăn′dərd-bâr′ər) *n.* **1.** One who carries a standard or banner, esp. of a military unit. **2.** An outstanding leader or representative, as of a political party.

stan·dard·bred (stăn′dərd-brĕd′) *n.* Any of an American breed of trotting and pacing horses developed esp. for harness racing by crossing esp. Thoroughbreds with Morgans.

standard candle *n.* A candela.

standard deviation *n. Statistics.* A statistic used as a measure of the dispersion or variation in a distribution, equal to the square root of the mean of the squares of the deviations from the mean of the distribution.

Stan·dard English (stăn′dərd) *n.* The variety of English that is most widely accepted as the spoken and written language of educated speakers in formal and informal contexts and is characterized by generally accepted conventions of spelling, grammar, and vocabulary while admitting some regional differences, esp. in pronunciation and vocabulary.

standard gauge *n.* **1.** A railroad track having a width of 56½ inches (143.5 centimeters). **2.** A railroad or railroad car built to standard gauge specification.

stan·dard·ize (stăn′dər-dīz′) *tr.v.* **-ized, -iz·ing, -iz·es. 1.** To cause to conform to a standard. **2.** To evaluate by comparing with a standard. — **stan′dard·i·za′tion** (-dər-dĭ-zā′shən) *n.*

standard time *n.* The time in any of 24 time zones, usu. the mean solar time at the central meridian of each zone.

stand·by (stănd′bī′) *n., pl.* **-bys. 1.** One that can always be relied on, as in an emergency. **2.** A favorite or frequent choice. **3.** One kept in readiness to serve as a substitute. — *adj.* **1.** Kept in reserve for use when needed. **2.** Of, relating to, or waiting for unreserved travel space that is made available by an airline only shortly before departure. — *adv.* On a standby basis. — ***idiom.* on standby.** Ready and waiting.

stand-down or **stand·down** (stănd′doun′) *n.* A withdrawal, as of a military presence.

stand·ee (stăn-dē′) *n.* One using standing room. See Usage Note at **-ee¹.**

stand-in (stănd′ĭn′) *n.* **1.** One who substitutes for an actor while lights and camera are adjusted or during hazardous action. **2.** A substitute.

stand·ing (stăn′dĭng) *n.* **1.a.** Status with respect to rank, reputation, or position in society or a profession. **b.** High reputation; esteem. **2.** Continuance in time; duration. **3.** *Law.* The right or capacity to initiate a suit. **4.** The act of one that stands. **5.** A place where a person or thing stands. — *adj.* **1.a.** Remaining upright; erect. **b.** Not cut down: *standing timber.* **2.** Performed or done from a standing position. **3.** Permanent and unchanging; fixed. **4.** Remaining in force or use indefinitely: *a standing invitation.* **5.** Not movable; stationary. **6.** Not flowing or circulating; stagnant.

standing crop *n.* The total amount of living organisms, as of plankton, in a specific area at a given time.

standing order *n.* An order or rule held to be in force until specifically changed or withdrawn, esp. a regulation relating to military or parliamentary procedure.

standing room *n.* Space in which to stand, as in a public place where all seats are filled. — **stand′ing-room′** (stăn′dĭng-ro͞om′, -ro͝om′) *adj.*

standing wave *n.* A wave having points of periodic maximum vibration in between fixed points of zero vibration, produced whenever a wave is confined within boundaries.

Stan·dish (stăn′dĭsh′), **Miles** or **Myles.** 1584?–1656. English colonial leader in America hired by the Pilgrims to accompany them to the New World (1620).

stand·off (stănd′ôf′, -ŏf′) *n.* **1.** A tie or draw, as in a contest. **2.** A situation in which one force neutralizes or counterbalances the other. — *adj.* Standoffish.

stand·off·ish (stănd-ô′fĭsh, -ŏf′ĭsh) *adj.* Aloof or reserved. — **stand·off′ish·ness** *n.*

stand·out (stănd′out′) *n. Informal.* One that is conspicuous by virtue of excellence or superiority.

stand·pat·ter (stănd′păt′ər) *n.* One who maintains opposition to change, as in politics. — **stand′pat′tism** *n.*

stand·pipe (stănd′pīp′) *n.* A large vertical pipe into which water is pumped in order to produce a desired pressure.

stand·point (stănd′point′) *n.* A position from which things are considered or judged; a point of view.

stand·still (stănd′stĭl′) *n.* Total cessation, as of activity.

stand·up or **stand-up** (stănd′ŭp′) *adj.* **1.** Standing erect; upright. **2.** Taken, done, or used while standing. **3.** Of or being a performer who stands alone on a stage and delivers a comic monologue. **4.** *Slang.* Courageous and steadfast.

Stan·ford-Bi·net test (stăn′fərd-bĭ-nā′) *n.* A standard intelligence test adapted from the Binet-Simon scale for use in the United States, esp. in the assessment of children. [After *Stanford* University in W CA near Palo Alto.]

stang (stăng) *v. Obsolete.* A p.t. of **sting.**

stan·hope (stăn′hōp′, stăn′əp) *n.* A light open horse-drawn carriage with one seat and two or four wheels. [After the Reverend Fitzroy *Stanhope* (1787–1864), British cleric.]

Stan·is·las I Lesz·czyń·ski (stăn′ĭ-slôs lĕsh-chĭn′skē). 1677–1766. King of Poland (1704–09 and 1733–36) who ruled during the War of the Polish Succession (1733–35).

Stan·i·slav·sky (stăn′ĭ-släv′skē, -släf′-, stə-nyĭ-), **Konstantin.** 1863–1938. Russian director who developed a method of acting emphasizing psychological motivation.

stank (stăngk) *v.* A p.t. of **stink.**

Stan·ley or **Port Stan·ley** (stăn′lē). A town of the E Falkland Is., administrative cap. of the British dependency. Pop. 1,050.

Stanley, Edward George Geoffrey Smith. 14th Earl of Derby. 1799–1869. British politician who served as prime minister (1852, 1858–59, and 1866–68).

Stanley, Sir **Henry Morton.** 1841–1904. British journalist known esp. for his expedition into Africa in search of David Livingstone.

Stanley, Wendell Meredith. 1904–71. Amer. biochemist who shared a 1946 Nobel Prize.

Stanley Pool. An expansion of the Congo R. in W-central Africa on the Congo-Zaire border.

Stan·ley·ville (stăn′lē-vĭl′). See **Kisangani.**

stan·nic (stăn′ĭk) *adj.* Of, relating to, or containing tin, esp. with valence 4. [LLat. *stannum,* tin (< Lat., an alloy of silver and lead, alteration of *stagnum,* prob. of Celt. orig.) + -IC.]

stannic chloride *n.* A caustic liquid, $SnCl_4$, used as a conductive coating and in ceramics.

stan·nite (stăn′īt′) *n.* A gray to black mineral, Cu_2FeSnS_4, with a metallic luster. [< LLat. *stannum,* tin. See STANNIC.]

stan·nous (stăn′əs) *adj.* Of, relating to, or containing tin, esp. with valence 2. [LLat. *stannum,* tin; see STANNIC + -OUS.]

stannous fluoride *n.* A powder, SnF_2, used to fluoridate toothpaste.

Stan·o·voy Range or **Stan·o·voi Range** (stăn′ə-voi′, stə-nə-voi′). A mountain range of SE Russia N of the Amur R.

Stan·ton (stăn′tən). A city of S CA, a suburb of Los Angeles. Pop. 30,491.

Stanton, Edwin McMasters. 1814–69. Amer. public official who served as U.S. secretary of war (1862–68). His dismissal by President Andrew Johnson and his subsequent refusal to leave office precipitated the impeachment of Johnson.

Stanton, Elizabeth Cady. 1815–1902. Amer. feminist and social reformer who helped organize the first women's rights convention, held in Seneca Falls NY (1848).

Elizabeth Cady Stanton
Photographed in the 1890's

stan·za (stăn′zə) *n.* One of the divisions of a poem, composed of two or more lines and usu. characterized by a common pattern of meter, rhyme, and number of lines. [Ital. See STANCE.] — **stan·za′ic** (-zā′ĭk) *adj.*

sta·pe·dec·to·my (stā′pĭ-dĕk′tə-mē, -pē-) *n., pl.* **-mies.** Surgical removal of the stapes. [NLat. *stapēs, stapēd-,* stapes; see STAPES + -ECTOMY.]

sta·pe·li·a (stə-pē′lē-ə) *n.* Any of various plants of the genus *Stapelia,* including the starfish flower. [NLat. *Stapelia,* genus name, after Jan Bode van *Stapel* (d. 1636), Dutch botanist.]

sta·pes (stā′pēz) *n., pl.* **stapes** or **sta·pe·des** (stā′pĭ-dēz′). The innermost of the three small bones of the middle ear, shaped somewhat like a stirrup. [NLat. *stapēs, stapēd-* < Med. Lat., stirrup.] — **sta·pe′di·al** (stā-pē′dē-əl) *adj.*

staph (stăf) *n. Informal.* Staphylococcus. — **staph** *adj.*

staphylo– *pref.* Cluster; resembling a cluster: *staphylococcus.* [NLat. < Gk. *staphulē,* bunch of grapes.]

staph·y·lo·coc·cus (stăf′ə-lō-kŏk′əs) *n., pl.* **-coc·ci** (-kŏk′sī, -kŏk′ī). A spherical gram-positive bacterium of the genus *Staphylococcus,* usu. occurring in clusters and causing boils, septicemia, and other infections. — **staph′y·lo·coc′cal** (-kŏk′əl), **staph′y·lo·coc·′cic** (-kŏk′sĭk, -kŏk′ĭk) *adj.*

sta·ple¹ (stā′pəl) *n.* **1.** A principal raw material or commodity grown or produced in a region. **2.** A major item of trade in steady demand. **3.** A basic dietary item, such as flour. **4.** A principal element or feature. **5.** The fiber of cotton, wool, or flax, graded as to length and fineness. — *adj.* **1.** Produced or stocked in large quantities to meet steady demand. **2.** Principal; main. — *tr.v.* **-pled, -pling, -ples.** To grade (fibers) according to length and fineness. [ME, official export market < AN *estaple,* perh. < MDu. *stāpel,* heap, emporium.]

sta·ple² (stā′pəl) *n.* **1.** A U-shaped metal loop with pointed

ă pat	oi boy
ā pay	ou out
âr care	o͝o took
ä father	o͞o boot
ĕ pet	ŭ cut
ē be	ûr urge
ĭ pit	th thin
ī pie	*th* this
îr pier	hw which
ŏ pot	zh vision
ō toe	ə about, item
ô paw	

Stress marks:
′ (primary);
′ (secondary), as in
dictionary (dĭk′shə-nĕr′ē)

ends, driven into a surface to hold a bolt, hook, or hasp or hold wiring in place. **2.** A thin piece of wire in the shape of a square bracket that is driven by a device through sheets of paper or similar material and flattened to serve as a fastening. — *tr.v.* **-pled, -pling, -ples.** To secure or fasten by means of a staple or staples. [ME < OE *stapol*, post, pillar.]

sta•pler¹ (stā′plər) *n.* A dealer in staple goods or fibers.

sta•pler² (stā′plər) *n.* A device used to bind material together by means of staples.

star (stär) *n.* **1.** *Astron.* **a.** A self-luminous celestial body that consists of a mass of gas held together by its own gravity and generates energy by nuclear reactions in its interior. **b.** Any of the celestial bodies visible at night from Earth as relatively stationary, usu. twinkling points of light. **c.** Something regarded as resembling a star. **2.** A graphic design having five or more radiating points, often used as a symbol of rank or merit. **3.** An artistic performer or athlete whose leading role or superior performance is acknowledged. **4.** An asterisk (*). **5.** A white spot on the forehead of a horse. **6.** A planet or constellation of the zodiac believed in astrology to influence personal destiny. **7. stars.** The future; destiny. — *adj.* Of, relating to, or being an outstanding, famous performer. — *v.* **starred, star•ring, stars.** — *tr.* **1.a.** To ornament with stars. **b.** To award or mark with a star for excellence. **2.** To mark with an asterisk. **3.** To present or feature (a performer) in a leading role. — *intr.* **1.** To play the leading role in a theatrical or film production. **2.** To do an outstanding job; perform excellently. — ***idioms.*** **have stars in (one's) eyes.** To be dazzled or enraptured. **see stars.** To experience bright flashing sensations, as from a blow to the head. [ME *sterre* < OE *steorra.* See **ster-³***.]

star-nosed mole
Condylura cristata

star anise *n.* **1.** An aromatic eastern Asian evergreen tree *(Illicium verum)* having purple-red flowers and starlike clusters of anise-scented fruit. **2.** The fruit of this plant.

star apple *n.* **1.** A tropical American evergreen tree *(Chrysophyllum cainito)* having smooth-skinned green or purple fruit and purplish flowers. **2.** The edible fruit of this tree.

Sta•ra Za•go•ra (stä′rə zə-gôr′ə, stä′rä zä-gô′rä). A city of central Bulgaria ENE of Plovdiv. Pop. 152,000.

star•board (stär′bərd) *n.* The right-hand side of a ship or an aircraft as one faces forward. — *adj.* On the right-hand side as one faces forward. — *adv.* To or toward the right-hand side as one faces forward. [ME *sterbord* < OE *stēorbord* : *stēor-*, a steering; see **stā-*** + *bord*, side of a ship.]

star•burst (stär′bûrst′) *n.* A shape or design with emanating rays that resembles the flash produced by an exploding star.

starch (stärch) *n.* **1.** A naturally abundant nutrient carbohydrate, $(C_6H_{10}O_5)_n$, found chiefly in the seeds, fruits, tubers, roots, and stem pith of plants, notably in corn, potatoes, wheat, and rice, and commonly prepared as a white amorphous tasteless powder. **2.** Any of various substances, such as natural starch, used to stiffen cloth, as in laundering. **3. starches.** Foods having a high content of starch, as breads and potatoes. **4.a.** Stiff behavior. **b.** Vigor; mettle. — *tr.v.* **starched, starch•ing, starch•es.** To stiffen with starch. [ME *starche*, substance used to stiffen cloth (sense uncertain) < *sterchen*, to stiffen < OE **stercan.* See **ster-¹***.]

Ringo Starr

Star Chamber (stär) *n.* **1.** A 15th- to 17th-century English court consisting of judges who were appointed by the Crown and sat in closed session on cases involving state security. **2. star chamber.** A court or group that engages in secret, harsh, or arbitrary procedures. [So called because the ceiling of the original courtroom was decorated with stars.]

starch syrup *n.* See **glucose** 2.

starch wheat *n.* See **emmer.**

starch•y (stär′chē) *adj.* **-i•er, -i•est. 1.a.** Containing starch. **b.** Stiffened with starch. **2.** Of or resembling starch. **3.** Stiff; formal. — **starch′i•ly** *adv.* — **starch′i•ness** *n.*

star-crossed (stär′krôst′, -krŏst′) *adj.* Ill-fated.

star•dom (stär′dəm) *n.* **1.** The status of a performer acknowledged as a star. **2.** Star performers considered as a group.

star•dust (stär′dŭst′) *n.* **1.** A dreamlike, romantic, or uncritical sense of well-being. **2.** A cluster of stars too distant to be seen individually, resembling a dimly luminous cloud of dust. Not in scientific use. **3.** Minute particles of matter that are supposed to fall to Earth from the stars. Not in scientific use.

stare (stâr) *v.* **stared, star•ing, stares.** — *intr.* **1.** To look directly and fixedly, often with a wide-eyed gaze. **2.** To be conspicuous; stand out. **3.** To stand on end; bristle, as hair or feathers. — *tr.* To look at directly and fixedly. — *n.* An intent gaze. — ***phrasal verb.*** **stare down.** To cause to waver or give in by or as if by staring. — ***idiom.*** **stare (one) in the face. 1.** To be plainly visible or obvious; force itself on (one's) attention. **2.** To be imminent or unavoidable. [ME *staren* < OE *starian.* See **ster-¹***.] — **star′er** *n.*

sta•rets (stär′yĭts) *n., pl.* **star•tsy** (stärt′sē). A male spiritual adviser, often a monk or hermit, in the Russian Orthodox Church. [Russ., elder, starets < Old Church Slavonic *starĭtsĭ*, elder < *starŭ*, old. See **stā-***.]

star facet *n.* One of the eight small triangular facets in the crown of a brilliant-cut gem.

star•fish (stär′fĭsh′) *n., pl.* **starfish** or **-fish•es.** Any of various marine echinoderms of the class Asteroidea, having a thick, often spiny body with five arms extending from a central disk.

star•flow•er (stär′flou′ər) *n.* **1.** Any of several small plants of the genus *Trientalis,* esp. *T. borealis* of northeast North America, having white starlike flowers. **2.** Any of several plants having starlike flowers.

star fruit *n.* See **carambola** 2. [< its cross section.]

star•gaze (stär′gāz′) *intr.v.* **-gazed, -gaz•ing, -gaz•es. 1.** To gaze at the stars. **2.** To daydream.

star•gaz•er (stär′gā′zər) *n.* **1.a.** *Informal.* An astronomer. **b.** An astrologer. **2.** A daydreamer. **3.** Any of various bottom-dwelling marine percoid fishes of the families Uranoscopidae and Dactyloscopidae, having eyes on the top of the head.

star grass *n.* **1.** Any of various plants of the genus *Hypoxis,* having grasslike leaves and star-shaped white or yellow flowers. **2.** See **colicroot.**

stark (stärk) *adj.* **stark•er, stark•est. 1.** Bare; blunt: *stark language.* **2.** Complete or utter; extreme: *a stark contrast.* **3.** Harsh; grim: *the stark reality of an epidemic.* — *adv.* Utterly; entirely: *stark raving mad.* [ME, stiff, severe, strong < OE *stearc.* See **ster-¹***.] — **stark′ly** *adv.* — **stark′ness** *n.*

stark•ers (stär′kərz) *adj. Chiefly British.* Stark naked. [Alteration of *stark naked.*]

star•let (stär′lĭt) *n.* **1.** A small star. **2.** A young film actress publicized as a future star.

star•light (stär′līt′) *n.* The light from the stars.

star•ling¹ (stär′lĭng) *n.* Any of various Old World passerine birds of the family Sturnidae, having a short tail, pointed wings, and dark, often iridescent plumage, esp. *Sturnus vulgaris,* widely naturalized in North America. [ME < OE *stærlinc* : *stær*, starling + *-linc*, noun suff.; see -LING¹.]

star•ling² (stär′lĭng) *n.* A protective structure of pilings surrounding a pier of a bridge. [Perh. alteration of ME *stadelinge* < *stathel*, foundation < OE *stathol.* See **stā-***.]

star•lit (stär′lĭt′) *adj.* Illuminated by starlight.

star-nosed mole (stär′nōzd′) *n.* A mole *(Condylura cristata)* of North America having 22 small fleshy tentacles encircling the end of its nose in a starlike pattern.

star-of-Beth•le•hem (stär′əv-bĕth′lĭ-hĕm′) *n., pl.* **star-of-Bethlehem** or **stars-of-Bethlehem** (stärz′-). **1.** Any of numerous bulbous perennial herbs of the genus *Ornithogalum* in the lily family, esp. *O. arabicum* or *O. umbellatum* of the Mediterranean region, having narrow leaves and a cluster of star-shaped white flowers. **2.** Any of several similar or related plants. [After the star that guided the Magi to Bethlehem.]

Star of David *n., pl.* **Stars of David** or **Star of Davids.** See **Magen David.**

Starr (stär), **Ringo.** b. 1940. British musician who was the drummer of The Beatles (1962–70).

star•ry (stär′ē) *adj.* **-ri•er, -ri•est. 1.** Marked or set with stars or starlike objects. **2.** Shining or glittering like stars. **3.** Shaped like a star. **4.** Illuminated by stars; starlit. **5.** Of or coming from the stars; stellar. — **star′ri•ness** *n.*

star•ry-eyed (stär′ē-īd′) *adj.* Having a naively enthusiastic, overoptimistic, or romantic view; unrealistic.

Stars and Bars (stärz) *n. (used with a sing. or pl. v.)* The first Confederate flag.

Stars and Stripes *n. (used with a sing. or pl. v.)* The flag of the United States.

star sapphire *n.* A sapphire with a polished convex surface exhibiting asterism.

star shell *n.* An artillery shell that explodes in midair with a shower of lights, used for illumination and signaling.

star•ship (stär′shĭp′) *n.* A spacecraft designed for human interstellar travel.

Star-Span•gled Banner (stär′spăng′gəld) *n.* The flag of the United States.

star•struck or **star-struck** (stär′strŭk′) *adj.* Fascinated by or exhibiting a fascination with fame or famous people.

start (stärt) *v.* **start•ed, start•ing, starts.** — *intr.* **1.** To begin an activity or a movement; set out. **2.** To have a beginning; commence. **3.** To move suddenly or involuntarily. **4.** To come quickly into view, life, or activity; spring forth. **5.** *Sports.* To be in the initial lineup of a game or race. **6.** To protrude or bulge. **7.** To become loosened or disengaged. — *tr.* **1.** To commence; begin. **2.** To set into motion, operation, or activity. **3.** To introduce; originate. **4.** *Sports.* **a.** To play in the initial lineup of (a game). **b.** To put (a player) into the initial lineup of a game. **c.** To enter (a participant) into a race or game. **5.** To found; establish. **6.** To tend in an early stage of development. **7.** To rouse (game) from its hiding place or lair; flush. **8.** To cause to become displaced or loosened. — *n.* **1.a.** A beginning; a commencement. **b.** The beginning of a new construction project. **2.** A place or time of beginning. **3.** *Sports.* **a.** A starting line for a race. **b.** A signal to begin a race. **c.** An instance of beginning a game or race. **4.** A startled reaction or movement. **5.** A part that has become dislocated or loosened. **6.** A position of advantage over others, as in a race; a lead. **7.** An opportunity granted to pursue a career or course of action. — ***idioms.*** **start something.** *Informal.* To cause trouble. **to start with. 1.** At the beginning; initially.

2. In any case. [ME *sterten*, to move or leap suddenly < OE **styrtan*. See **ster-**[1]*.]

start•er (stär′tər) *n.* **1.** One that starts. **2.** An attachment for starting an internal-combustion engine without hand cranking. **3.** A device that initiates a flow of high voltage across the electrodes of a fluorescent lamp. **4.** *Sports.* **a.** One who signals the start of a race. **b.** A participant that starts in a game or race. **5.** *Baseball.* **a.** The first pitcher for a team in a game. **b.** A pitcher who regularly begins games for a team. **6.** The first in a series, esp. the first course of a meal; an appetizer. —***idiom.* for starters.** *Informal.* To begin with; initially.

star thistle *n.* Any of several Eurasian plants of the genus *Centaurea*, esp. *C. calcitrapa*, having spiny purplish flower heads.

start•ing block (stär′tĭng) *n. Sports.* An apparatus that braces a runner's feet at the start of a race, consisting of two angled supports adjustably mounted on a rigid frame that is usu. anchored to the track.

starting gate *n. Sports.* **1.** A series of stalls with interconnected doors that open simultaneously at the beginning of a race. **2.** A movable barrier that starts an automatic timer when pushed aside by a competitor, such as a skier.

star•tle (stär′tl) *v.* **-tled, -tling, -tles.** —*tr.* **1.** To cause to make a quick involuntary movement or start. **2.** To alarm, frighten, or surprise suddenly. —*intr.* To become alarmed, frightened, or surprised. —*n.* A sudden mild shock; a start. [ME *stertlen*, to run about < OE *steartlian*, to kick. See **ster-**[1]*.] —**star′tling•ness** *n.*

star•tsy (stärt′sē) *n.* Pl. of **starets.**

start-up or **start•up** (stärt′ŭp′) *n.* The act or process of setting into operation or motion.

star•va•tion (stär-vā′shən) *n.* **1.** The act or process of starving. **2.** The condition of being starved.

starve (stärv) *v.* **starved, starv•ing, starves.** —*intr.* **1.** To suffer or die from extreme or prolonged lack of food. **2.** *Informal.* To be hungry. **3.** To suffer from deprivation. **4.** *Archaic.* To suffer or die from cold. —*tr.* **1.** To cause to starve. **2.** To force to a specified state by starving. [ME *sterven*, to die < OE *steorfan*. See **ster-**[1]*.]

starve•ling (stärv′lĭng) *n.* One that is starving or being starved. —*adj.* **1.** Starving. **2.** Poor in quality; inadequate.

star•wort (stär′wûrt′, -wôrt′) *n.* Any of various plants having star-shaped flowers or flower heads, as the aster.

stash (stăsh) *Slang.* —*tr.v.* **stashed, stash•ing, stash•es.** To hide or store away in a secret place. —*n.* **1.** A store or cache of money or valuables. **2.** Something hidden away. [?]

sta•sis (stā′sĭs, stăs′ĭs) *n., pl.* **sta•ses** (stā′sēz, stăs′ēz). **1.** A condition of balance among various forces; motionlessness. **2.** *Pathol.* Stoppage of the normal flow of a body substance, as of blood through an artery. [Gk., stationariness. See **stā-***.]

–stasis *suff.* **1.** Slowing; stoppage: *bacteriostasis.* **2.** Stable state: *homeostasis.* [< Gk. *stasis*, standstill. See STASIS.]

Stas•sen (stăs′ən), **Harold Edward.** b. 1907. Amer. politician who has made numerous unsuccessful bids for the Republican presidential nomination.

stat[1] (stăt) *n.* A statistic.

stat[2] (stăt) *adv.* With no delay; at once. —*adj.* Immediate. [Short for Lat. *statim.* See **stā-***.]

stat. *abbr.* **1.** Statistic; statistics. **2.** Statuary. **3.** Statute.

–stat *suff.* **1.** Something that stabilizes: *rheostat.* **2.** A device for reflecting something specified in a constant direction: *heliostat.* **3.** Something that inhibits: *fungistat.* [NLat. *-stata* < Gk. *-statēs*, one that causes to stand, or < *statos*, standing; see **stā-***.]

state (stāt) *n.* **1.** A condition or mode of being, as with regard to circumstances: *a state of confusion.* **2.** A condition of being in a stage or form, as of structure, growth, or development: *the larval state.* **3.** A mental or emotional condition: *in a manic state.* **4.** *Informal.* A condition of excitement or distress. **5.** *Phys.* The condition of a physical system with regard to phase, form, composition, or structure. **6.** Social position or rank. **7.** Ceremony; pomp. **8.a.** The supreme public power within a sovereign political entity. **b.** The sphere of supreme civil power within a given polity: *matters of state.* **9.** A specific mode of government. **10.** A body politic, esp. one constituting a nation. **11.** One of the more or less internally autonomous territorial and political units composing a federation under a sovereign government. —*adj.* **1.** Of or relating to a body politic or to an internally autonomous territorial or political unit constituting a federation under one government. **2.** Owned and operated by a state. —*tr.v.* **stat•ed, stat•ing, states.** To set forth in words; declare. [ME < OFr. *estat* < Lat. *status.* See **stā-***.]

state attorney *n. Law.* A prosecuting attorney for a state.

State Col•lege (stāt kŏl′ĭj). A borough of central PA NW of Harrisburg. Pop. 38,923.

state•craft (stāt′krăft′) *n.* The art of leading a country.

state•hood (stāt′ho͝od′) *n.* The status of being a state, esp. of the United States.

state•house also **state house** (stāt′hous′) *n.* A building in which a state legislature holds sessions; a state capitol.

state•less (stāt′lĭs) *adj.* **1.** Having no state. **2.** Having no recognized citizenship in a state or nation. —**state′less•ness** *n.*

state•ly (stāt′lē) *adj.* **-li•er, -li•est. 1.** Dignified and impressive, as in size or proportions. See Syns at **grand. 2.** Majestic; lofty. —*adv.* In a ceremonious or imposing manner. [ME *statly* < *state*, state, rank. See STATE.] —**state′li•ness** *n.*

state•ment (stāt′mənt) *n.* **1.** The act of stating or declaring. **2.** Something stated; a declaration. **3.** *Law.* A formal pleading. **4.** An abstract of a commercial or financial account showing an amount due; a bill. **5.** A monthly report sent to a debtor or bank depositor. **6.** *Comp. Sci.* An elementary instruction in a source language. —***idiom.* make a statement.** To create a certain impression.

Stat•en Island (stăt′n). Formerly **Rich•mond** (rĭch′mənd). A borough of New York City coextensive with **Staten Island** in New York Bay SW of Manhattan I. The island was permanently settled in the mid-1600's and became part of New York City in 1898. Pop. 378,977.

state of the art *n.* The highest level of development, as of a device, technique, or scientific field, achieved at a particular time. —**state′-of-the-art′** (stāt′əv-*thē*-ärt′) *adj.*

stat•er[1] (stā′tər) *n.* A resident of a particular state or type of state. Often used in combination: *Lone Star staters.*

sta•ter[2] (stā′tər) *n.* Any of various gold, silver, or electrum coins of ancient Greece. [ME < LLat. *statēr* < Gk. < *histanai, sta-*, to set on a scale, weigh. See SYSTEM.]

state•room (stāt′ro͞om′, -ro͝om′) *n.* A private cabin or compartment with sleeping accommodations on a ship or train.

state's evidence (stāts) *n. Law.* **1.** Evidence for the prosecution in U.S. state or federal trials. **2.** One that gives evidence for the state in criminal proceedings.

States-Gen•er•al (stāts′jĕn′ər-əl) *pl.n.* **1.** A legislative assembly of representatives from the estates of a nation, as opposed to a provincial assembly. **2.** The legislative assembly in France before the Revolution.

state•side (stāt′sīd′) *adj.* **1.** Of or in the continental United States. **2.** *Alaska.* Of or in the 48 contiguous states of the United States. —*adv. Informal.* **1.** To, toward, or in the continental United States. **2.** *Alaska.* To, toward, or in the 48 contiguous states of the United States.

Regional Note: After World War II the term *stateside* gained currency among Alaskans, as in *"Most of the owners live in Anchorage; some 14% live stateside"* (Alaska Magazine). It may or may not be capitalized. *Stateside, the lower states, the South,* and (*the*) *Outside* are all used in Alaska to denote "the 48 contiguous states." All these terms, however, are losing out to *the Lower 48.*

states•man (stāts′mən) *n.* **1.** A man who is a leader in national or international affairs. **2.** A male political leader seen as disinterestedly promoting the public good. —**states′man•like′, states′man•ly** *adj.* —**states′man•ship′** *n.*

states' rights also **States' rights** (stāts) *pl.n.* **1.** All rights not delegated to the federal government by the Constitution nor denied by it to the states. **2.** The political position advocating strict interpretation of the Constitution with regard to the limitation of federal powers and the extension of the autonomy of the individual state to the greatest possible degree. —**states' righter** *n.*

States' Rights Party *n.* A former political party founded in 1948 by Southern Democrats to consolidate opposition to civil rights policies of the regular Democratic Party.

States•ville (stāts′vĭl′, -vəl). A city of W-central NC N of Charlotte; founded 1789. Pop. 17,567.

states•wom•an (stāts′wo͝om′ən) *n.* **1.** A woman who is a leader in national or international affairs. **2.** A woman political leader seen as disinterestedly promoting the public good.

state•wide (stāt′wīd′) *adj.* Occurring or extending throughout a state. —*adv.* Throughout a state.

stat•ic (stăt′ĭk) *adj.* **1.a.** Having no motion; being at rest; quiescent. **b.** Fixed; stationary. **2.** *Phys.* Of or relating to bodies at rest or forces that balance each other. **3.** *Elect.* Of, relating to, or producing stationary charges; electrostatic. **4.** Of, relating to, or produced by random radio noise. —*n.* **1.** Random noise, such as crackling in a receiver, produced by atmospheric disturbance of the signal. **2.** *Informal.* **a.** Back talk. **b.** Interference; obstruction. **c.** Angry or heated criticism. [NLat. *staticus*, relating to weight < Gk. *statikos*, causing to stand < *statos*, standing. See **stā-***.] —**stat′i•cal** *adj.* —**stat′i•cal•ly** *adv.*

stat•i•ce (stăt′ĭ-sē′, stăt′ĭs) *n.* See **sea lavender.** [Lat. *staticē*, an astringent plant < Gk. *statikē* < fem. of *statikos*, causing to stand, astringent < *statos*, standing. See **stā-***.]

static electricity *n.* **1.** An accumulation of electric charge on an insulated body. **2.** Electric discharge resulting from the accumulation of electric charge on an insulated body.

static pressure *n.* The pressure exerted by a still liquid or gas.

stat•ics (stăt′ĭks) *n.* (*used with a sing. or pl. v.*) The equilibrium mechanics of stationary bodies.

static tube *n.* A specialized tube used to measure the static pressure in a stream of fluid.

sta•tion (stā′shən) *n.* **1.** The place or position where a person or thing stands or is assigned to stand; a post. **2.** The place, building, or establishment from which a service is provided or

ă pat	oi boy
ā pay	ou out
âr care	o͝o took
ä father	o͞o boot
ĕ pet	ŭ cut
ē be	ûr urge
ĭ pit	th thin
ī pie	*th* this
îr pier	hw which
ŏ pot	zh vision
ō toe	ə about, item
ô paw	

Stress marks:
′ (primary);
′ (secondary), as in
dictionary (dĭk′shə-nĕr′ē)

operations are directed. **3.** A stopping place along a route, esp. a stop for refueling or for taking on passengers; a depot. **4.** Social position; rank. **5.** An establishment equipped for observation and study. **6.** An establishment equipped for radio or television transmission. **7.** An input or output point along a communications system. **8.** *Ecol.* **a.** The normal habitat of a particular plant or animal community. **b.** The exact place of occurrence of a species or individual within a given habitat. — *tr.v.* **-tioned, -tion•ing, -tions.** To assign to a position; post. [ME *stacioun* < OFr. *station* < Lat. *statiō, statiōn-*. See **stā-***.]

sta•tion•ar•y (stā′shə-nĕr′ē) *adj.* **1.a.** Not moving. **b.** Not capable of being moved. **2.** Unchanging: *a stationary sound.* — *n., pl.* **-ar•ies.** One that is stationary. [ME *stacionarie* < OFr. *stationnaire* < Med.Lat. *statiōnārius* < Lat., of a military station < *statiō, statiōn-*, station. See STATION.]

steamboat

stationary front *n.* A transition zone between two nearly stationary air masses of different density.

stationary orbit *n.* A geostationary orbit.

stationary wave *n.* See **standing wave.**

station break *n.* An intermission in a radio or television program for identification of the network or station.

sta•tion•er (stā′shə-nər) *n.* **1.** One that sells stationery. **2.** *Archaic.* **a.** A publisher. **b.** A bookseller. [ME *staciouner*, a bookseller < Med.Lat. *statiōnārius*, shopkeeper (as against a peddler), prob. < Lat. *statiō, statiōn-*, place of business. See STATION.]

sta•tion•er•y (stā′shə-nĕr′ē) *n.* **1.** Writing paper and envelopes. **2.** Writing materials and office supplies.

station house also **sta•tion•house** (stā′shən-hous′) *n.* **1.** A police station. **2.** A fire station.

sta•tion•mas•ter (stā′shən-măs′tər) *n.* An official in charge of a railroad or bus station.

Sta•tions of the Cross (stā′shənz) *pl.n.* **1.** A devotion in some Christian churches consisting of prayers before representations of the Passion of Jesus. **2.** The 14 crucifixes or images representing the sufferings of Jesus.

sta•tion-to-sta•tion (stā′shən-tə-stā′shən) *adj.* Of, relating to, or designating a long-distance telephone call in which the caller is charged upon reaching anyone at the receiving number. — *adv.* By station-to-station long-distance telephone.

station wagon *n.* An automobile having an extended interior with a third seat or luggage platform and a tailgate. [Originally a covered wagon traveling from a train station to a hotel.]

stat•ism (stā′tĭz′əm) *n.* The practice or doctrine of giving a centralized government control over economic planning and policy. — **stat′ist** *adj. & n.*

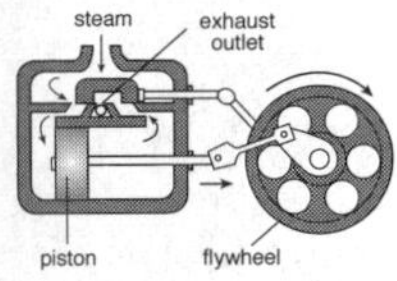

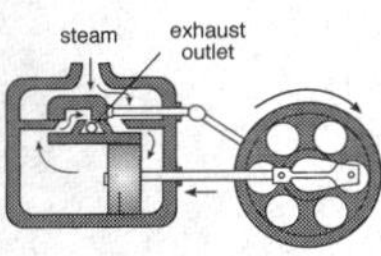

steam engine
Rightward (*top*) and leftward (*bottom*) movements of a slide valve steam engine

sta•tis•tic (stə-tĭs′tĭk) *n.* **1.** A numerical datum. **2.** A numerical value, such as standard deviation or mean, that characterizes the sample or population from which it was derived. [Ult. < NLat. *statisticus*, of statecraft. See STATISTICS.]

stat•is•ti•cian (stăt′ĭ-stĭsh′ən) *n.* **1.** A mathematician specializing in statistics. **2.** A compiler of statistical data.

sta•tis•tics (stə-tĭs′tĭks) *n.* **1.** *(used with a sing. v.)* The mathematics of the collection, organization, and interpretation of numerical data, esp. the analysis of population characteristics by inference from sampling. **2.** *(used with a pl. v.)* Numerical data. [< Ger. *Statistik*, political science < NLat. *statisticus*, of state affairs < Ital. *statista*, person skilled in statecraft < *stato*, state < OItal. < Lat. *status*, position, form of government. See **stā-***.] — **sta•tis′ti•cal** (-tĭ-kəl) *adj.* — **sta•tis′ti•cal•ly** *adv.*

Sta•tius (stā′shəs, -shē-əs), **Publius Papinus.** A.D. 45?–96? Roman poet known for his epics *Thebaid* and *Achilleid.*

sta•tive (stā′tĭv) *Gram.* — *adj.* Belonging to or designating a class of verbs that express a state or condition. — *n.* A verb of the stative class.

stato– *pref.* **1.** Resting; remaining: *statoblast.* **2.** Equilibrium; balance: *statocyst.* [< Gk. *statos*, standing, placed. See **stā-***.]

stat•o•blast (stăt′ə-blăst′) *n.* An asexually produced encapsulated bud of a freshwater bryozoan that remains inactive through winter and develops into a new organism in spring.

stat•o•cyst (stăt′ə-sĭst′) *n.* A small organ of balance in many invertebrates, consisting of a fluid-filled sac containing statoliths that stimulate sensory cells when the animal moves.

stat•o•lith (stăt′l-ĭth′) *n.* A small movable concretion of calcium carbonate found in statocysts; an otolith.

sta•tor (stā′tər) *n.* The stationary part of a motor, dynamo, turbine, or other working machine about which a rotor turns. [Lat., one that stands < *stāre*, to stand. See **stā-***.]

stat•u•ar•y (stăch′o͞o-ĕr′ē) *n., pl.* **-ies. 1.** Statues considered as a group. **2.** The art of making statues. **3.** A sculptor. — *adj.* Of, relating to, or suitable for a statue. [< Lat. *statuārius*, of a statue < *statua*, statue. See STATUE.]

stat•ue (stăch′o͞o) *n.* A three-dimensional form sculpted, modeled, carved, or cast in material such as clay or bronze. [ME < OFr. < Lat. *statua* < *statuere*, to set up. See STATUTE.]

stat•u•esque (stăch′o͞o-ĕsk′) *adj.* Suggestive of a statue, as in proportion, grace, or dignity; stately. — **stat′u•esque′ly** *adv.*

stat•u•ette (stăch′o͞o-ĕt′) *n.* A small statue.

stat•ure (stăch′ər) *n.* **1.** The natural height of a human being or an animal in an upright position. **2.** An achieved level; status. [ME < OFr. < Lat. *statūra.* See **stā-***.]

sta•tus (stā′təs, stăt′əs) *n.* **1.** Position relative to that of others; standing. **2.** High standing; prestige. **3.** *Law.* The legal character or condition of a person or thing. **4.** A state of affairs; situation. [Lat. See **stā-***.]

status quo (kwō) *n.* The existing condition or state of affairs. [Lat. *status quō*, state in which.]

status symbol *n.* Something, such as a possession or an activity, by which one's social or economic prestige is measured.

stat•u•ta•ble (stăch′ə-tə-bəl) *adj.* **1.** Enacted, regulated, or authorized by statute; statutory. **2.** *Law.* Legally punishable; recognized by statute: *a statutable offense.*

stat•ute (stăch′o͞ot) *n.* **1.** *Law.* A law enacted by a legislature. **2.** A decree or an edict, as of a ruler. **3.** An established law or rule, as of a corporation. [ME < OFr. *estatut* < LLat. *statūtum* < neut. of Lat. *statūtus*, p.part. of *statuere*, to set up < *status*, position. See **stā-***.]

statute law *n.* A law established by legislative enactment.

statute mile *n.* See **mile** 1.

statute of limitations *n., pl.* **statutes of limitations.** *Law.* A statute setting a time limit on legal action in certain cases.

stat•u•to•ry (stăch′ə-tôr′ē, -tōr′ē) *adj.* **1.** Of or relating to a statute. **2.** Enacted, regulated, or authorized by statute. — **stat′u•to′ri•ly** *adv.*

statutory offense *n.* *Law.* A legal offense declared by statute.

statutory rape *n.* Sexual relations with a person under the statutory age of consent.

staunch^1 (stônch, stänch) also **stanch** (stônch, stänch, stănch) *adj.* **staunch•er, staunch•est** also **stanch•er, stanch•est. 1.** Firm and steadfast; true. See Syns at **faithful. 2.** Strong or substantial in construction or constitution. [ME *staunche* < AN *estaunche* < *estaunchier*, to stanch, var. of OFr. *estanchier.* See STANCH^1.] — **staunch′ly** *adv* — **staunch′ness** *n.*

Usage Note: *Staunch* is more common than *stanch* as the spelling of the adjective. *Stanch* is more common than *staunch* as the spelling of the verb.

staunch^2 (stônch, stänch) *v.* Var. of **stanch^1**. See Usage Note at **staunch^1**.

Staun•ton (stăn′tən). An independent city of N-central VA WNW of Charlottesville. Pop. 24,461.

stau•ro•lite (stôr′ə-līt′) *n.* A brownish to black mineral, chiefly $(FeMg)_2Al_9Si_4O_{23}(OH)$, often having crossed intergrown crystals and sometimes used as a gem. [Gk. *stauros*, cross; see **stā-*** + -LITE.] — **stau′ro•lit′ic** (-lĭt′ĭk) *adj.*

Sta•vang•er (stə-văng′ər). A city of SW Norway S of Bergen on an inlet of the North Sea; probably founded in the 8th cent. Pop. 92,012.

stave (stāv) *n.* **1.** A narrow strip of wood forming part of the sides of a barrel, tub, or similar structure. **2.** A rung of a ladder or chair. **3.** A staff or cudgel. **4.** *Mus.* See **staff^1** 5. **5.** A set of verses; a stanza. — *v.* **staved** or **stove** (stōv), **stav•ing, staves.** — *tr.* **1.** To break in or puncture the staves of. **2.** To break or smash a hole in. **3.** To crush or smash inward. **4.** To furnish with staves. — *intr.* To be or become crushed in. — ***phrasal verb.* stave off.** To keep or hold off; repel. [Back-formation < *staves*, pl. of STAFF^1.]

staves (stāvz) *n.* Pl. of **staff^1**.

staves•a•cre (stāvz′ā′kər) *n.* **1.** A larkspur, *Delphinium staphisagria,* of southern Europe with greenish-white flowers. **2.** The seeds of this plant, formerly used medicinally. [By folk ety. < ME *staphisagre* < Lat. *staphis agria* < Gk. : *staphis*, stavesacre + *agria*, fem. of *agrios*, wild; see **agro-***.]

Stav•ro•pol (stăv-rō′pəl, stäv′rə-pəl). A city of SW Russia SE of Rostov; founded 1777. Pop. 293,000.

stay^1 (stā) *v.* **stayed, stay•ing, stays.** — *intr.* **1.** To continue to be in a place or condition. **2.** To remain or sojourn as a guest or lodger. **3.** To stop moving; halt. **4.** To wait; pause. **5.** To endure or persist. **6.** To keep up in a race or contest. **7.** *Games.* To meet a bet in poker without raising it. **8.** To stand one's ground; remain firm. **9.** *Archaic.* To cease from a specified activity. — *tr.* **1.** To stop or halt; check. **2.** To postpone; delay. **3.** To delay or stop the effect of (an order, for example) by legal action or mandate. **4.** To satisfy or appease temporarily. **5.** To remain during. **6.** To wait for; await. — *n.* **1.** The act of halting; check. **2.** The act of coming to a halt. **3.** A brief period of residence or visiting. **4.** A suspension or postponement of a legal action or an execution. — ***idioms.* stay put.** To remain in a fixed or established position. **stay the course.** To hold out or persevere to the end of a race or challenge. [ME *steien* < OFr. *ester, esteir* < Lat. *stāre.* See **stā-***.]

Syns: *stay, remain, wait, abide, tarry, linger, sojourn.* These verbs mean to continue to be in a given place. *Stay* is the least specific, though it can also suggest that the person involved is a guest or visitor: *"Must you go? Can't you stay?"* (Charles J. Vaughan). *Remain* often implies continuing or being left after others have gone: *remained at the end of the meeting. Wait* suggests remaining in readiness, anticipation, or expectation: *"Your father is waiting for me to take a walk with him"* (Booth Tarkington). *Abide* implies continuing for a lengthy period: *"Abide with me"* (Henry Francis Lyte). *Tarry* and *linger* both imply a delayed departure, but *linger* more strongly suggests reluctance to leave: *"She was not anxious but puzzled that her husband tarried"* (Eden Phillpotts). *"I alone sit lingering here"* (Henry Vaughan). To *sojourn* is to reside temporarily in a place: *"He was sojourning at* [a] *hotel in Bond Street"* (Anthony Trollope).

stay² (stā) *tr.v.* **stayed, stay•ing, stays. 1.** To brace, support, or prop up. **2.** To strengthen or sustain mentally or spiritually. **3.** To rest or fix on for support. — *n.* **1.** A support or brace. **2.** A strip of bone, plastic, or metal, used to stiffen a garment or part, such as a corset or shirt collar. **3. stays.** A corset. [ME *staien* < OFr. *estaiier* < *estaie*, a support, of Gmc. orig.]

stay³ (stā) *n.* **1.** *Naut.* A heavy rope or cable, usu. of wire, that provides fore-and-aft support for a mast or spar. **2.** A rope used to steady, guide, or brace. [ME < OE *stæg.*]

stay•ing power (stā′ĭng) *n.* The ability to endure or last.

stay•sail (stā′səl, -sāl′) *n.* *Naut.* A triangular sail hoisted on a stay.

stbd. *abbr.* Starboard.

STD *abbr.* Sexually transmitted disease.

std. *abbr.* Standard.

Ste. *abbr.* *Fr.* Sainte (feminine form of saint).

stead (stĕd) *n.* **1.** The place, position, or function properly or customarily occupied by another. **2.** Advantage; service; purpose. — *tr.v.* **stead•ed, stead•ing, steads.** To be of advantage or service to; benefit. [ME *stede* < OE. See **stā-*.**]

stead•fast also **sted•fast** (stĕd′făst′, -fəst) *adj.* **1.** Fixed or unchanging; steady. **2.** Firmly loyal or constant; unswerving. See Syns at **faithful.** [ME *stedefast* < OE *stedefæst* : *stede*, place; see STEAD + *fæst*, fixed, fast; see **past-*.**] — **stead′fast′ly** *adv.* — **stead′fast′ness** *n.*

stead•y (stĕd′ē) *adj.* **-i•er, -i•est. 1.** Firm in position or place; fixed. **2.** Direct and unfaltering; sure. **3.** Free or almost free from change, variation, or fluctuation; uniform. **4.** Not easily excited or upset. **5.** Unwavering, as in purpose; steadfast. **6.** Reliable; dependable. **7.** Temperate; sober. — *tr. & intr.v.* **stead•ied, stead•y•ing, stead•ies.** To make or become steady. — *interj.* *Naut.* Used to direct a helmsman to keep a ship's head in the same direction. — *n., pl.* **-ies.** The person whom one dates regularly, usu. exclusively. — **stead′i•er** *n.* — **stead′i•ly** *adv.* — **stead′i•ness** *n.*

steady state *n.* *Phys.* A stable condition that does not change over time or in which change in one direction is continually balanced by change in another.

stead•y-state theory (stĕd′ē-stāt′) *n.* A cosmological theory that assumes the average density of matter in the universe is constant in space and time and the expansion of the universe is compensated for by the continuous creation of matter.

steak (stāk) *n.* **1.** A slice of meat, typically beef, usu. cut across the muscle grain and served broiled or fried. **2.** A thick slice of a large fish cut across the body. **3.** A patty of ground meat broiled or fried. [ME *steike* < ON *steik.* See **steig-*.**]

steak house or **steak•house** (stāk′hous′) *n.* A restaurant that specializes in beefsteak dishes.

steak knife *n.* A table knife with a sharp, usu. serrated blade.

steak tartare *n.* An appetizer of raw ground beef mixed with onion, seasoning, and raw egg. [STEAK + Fr. *tartare*, Tartar.]

steal (stēl) *v.* **stole** (stōl), **sto•len** (stō′lən), **steal•ing, steals.** — *tr.* **1.** To take (the property of another) without right or permission. **2.** To get or effect surreptitiously or artfully: *stole the ball.* **3.** To move, carry, or place surreptitiously. **4.** To draw attention unexpectedly in (an entertainment), esp. by being the outstanding performer. **5.** *Baseball.* To advance safely to (another base) during the delivery of a pitch, without the aid of a base hit, walk, passed ball, or wild pitch. — *intr.* **1.** To commit theft. **2.** To move, happen, or elapse stealthily or unobtrusively. **3.** *Baseball.* To steal a base. — *n.* **1.** The act of stealing. **2.** *Slang.* A bargain. — ***idiom.* steal (someone's) thunder.** To use, appropriate, or preempt the use of another's idea. [ME *stelen* < OE *stelan.*] — **steal′er** *n.*

stealth (stĕlth) *n.* **1.** The act of moving, proceeding, or acting in a covert way. **2.** The quality or characteristic of being furtive or covert. **3.** *Archaic.* The act of stealing. [ME *stelth*, prob. < OE **stǣlth.*]

stealth•y (stĕl′thē) *adj.* **-i•er, -i•est.** Marked by or acting with quiet, caution, and secrecy intended to avoid notice. — **stealth′i•ly** *adv.* — **stealth′i•ness** *n.*

steam (stēm) *n.* **1.a.** The vapor phase of water. **b.** A mist of cooling water vapor. **2.a.** Pressurized water vapor used for heating, cooking, or to provide mechanical power. **b.** The power produced by using steam. **c.** Steam heating. **3.** Power; energy. — *v.* **steamed, steam•ing, steams.** — *intr.* **1.** To produce or emit steam. **2.** To become or rise up as steam. **3.** To become misted or covered with steam. **4.** To move by means of steam power. **5.** *Informal.* To become very angry; fume. — *tr.* To expose to steam. [ME *steme* < OE *stēam.*]

steam bath *n.* **1.** Bathing by exposure to steam. **2.** A room or building that provides bathing with steam.

steam•boat (stēm′bōt′) *n.* *Naut.* A steamship, esp. one used on rivers and other inland waterways.

steam boiler *n.* A closed tank in which water is converted into steam under pressure.

steam chest *n.* A compartment in a steam engine through which steam is delivered from the boiler to a cylinder.

steam engine *n.* An engine that converts the heat energy of pressurized steam into mechanical energy, esp. one in which steam drives a piston in a closed cylinder.

steam•er (stē′mər) *n.* **1.** *Naut.* A steamship. **2.** A vehicle, a machine, or an engine driven by steam. **3.** A container in which something is steamed. **4.** See **soft-shell clam.**

steamer rug *n.* A warm blanket used esp. by shipboard passengers while sitting in deck chairs.

steamer trunk *n.* A small trunk originally designed to fit under the bunk of a steamship cabin.

steam•fit•ter (stēm′fĭt′ər) *n.* One who installs and repairs heating, ventilating, refrigerating, and air-conditioning systems. — **steam′fit′ting** *n.*

steam heat•ing (hē′tĭng) *n.* A heating system in which steam is generated in a boiler and piped to radiators.

steam iron *n.* A pressing iron that holds and heats water to be emitted as steam on the cloth being pressed.

steamroller

steam•rol•ler (stēm′rō′lər) *n.* **1.a.** A steam-driven machine equipped with a heavy roller for smoothing road surfaces. **b.** A similar machine with an internal-combustion engine. **2.** A ruthless or irresistible force or power. — *v.* also **steam•roll** (-rōl′). **-rol•lered, -rol•ler•ing, -rol•lers** also **-rolled, -roll•ing, -rolls.** — *tr.* **1.** To smooth or level (a road) with a steamroller. **2.** To overwhelm or suppress ruthlessly; crush. — *intr.* To move or proceed with overwhelming force.

steam•ship (stēm′shĭp′) *n.* *Naut.* A large vessel propelled by one or more steam-driven screws, propellers, or paddles.

steam shovel *n.* **1.** A large steam-driven machine for digging. **2.** See **power shovel.**

steam table *n.* A table in which containers of cooked food are kept warm by hot water or steam circulating below.

steam turbine *n.* A turbine operated by highly pressurized steam directed against vanes on a rotor.

steam•y (stē′mē) *adj.* **-i•er, -i•est. 1.** Filled with or emitting steam. **2.** Erotic. — **steam′i•ly** *adv.* — **steam′i•ness** *n.*

ste•ap•sin (stē-ăp′sĭn) *n.* A digestive enzyme of pancreatic juice that catalyzes the hydrolysis of fats to fatty acids and glycerol. [Gk. *stear*, tallow; see **stei-*** + (PE)PSIN.]

ste•a•rate (stē′ə-rāt′, stîr′āt′) *n.* A salt or an ester of stearic acid. [STEAR(IC) + -ATE².]

ste•ar•ic (stē-ăr′ĭk, stîr′ĭk) *adj.* **1.** Of, relating to, or similar to stearin or fat. **2.** Of or relating to stearic acid. [Fr. *stéarique* < Gk. *stear*, tallow. See **stei-*.**]

stearic acid *n.* A colorless waxlike fatty acid, $CH_3(CH_2)_{16}COOH$, occurring in natural animal and vegetable fats and used in making soaps, candles, and lubricants.

steel band

ste•a•rin (stē′ər-ĭn, stîr′ĭn) also **ste•a•rine** (stē′ər-ĭn, -ə-rēn′, stîr′ĭn) *n.* **1.** A colorless ester of glycerol and stearic acid, $C_3H_5(C_{18}H_{35}O_2)_3$, found in most animal and vegetable fats and used in the manufacture of soaps, candles, and adhesives and for textile sizing. **2.** The solid form of fat. [Fr. *stéarine* : Gk. *stear*, tallow; see **stei-*** + Fr. *-ine*, -in.]

ste•a•tite (stē′ə-tīt′) *n.* See **soapstone.** [Lat. *steatītis*, a precious stone < Gk. < *stear, steat-*, tallow. See **stei-*.**]

steato– or **steat–** *pref.* Fat: *steatopygia.* [Gk. < *stear, steat-*, tallow. See **stei-*.**]

ste•at•o•pyg•i•a (stē-ăt′ə-pĭj′ē-ə, -pī′jē-ə) *n.* An extreme accumulation of fat on the buttocks. [STEATO– + Gk. *pugē*, rump + -IA¹.] — **ste′at•o•pyg′ic** (-pĭj′ĭk, -pī′jĭk), **ste′a•to•py′gous** (-pī′gəs) *adj.*

ste•at•or•rhe•a also **ste•at•or•rhoe•a** (stē′ə-tə-rē′ə, stē-ăt′ə-) *n.* **1.** Overaction of the sebaceous glands. **2.** Excessive discharge of fat in the feces.

sted•fast (stĕd′făst′, -fəst) *adj.* Var. of **steadfast.**

steed (stēd) *n.* A horse, esp. a spirited one. [ME *stede* < OE *stēda*, stallion. See **stā-*.**]

steel (stēl) *n.* **1.** A generally hard, strong durable malleable alloy of iron and carbon, usu. containing between 0.2 and 1.5 percent carbon, often with other constituents such as manganese, chromium, nickel, or silicon, depending on the desired alloy properties, and widely used as a structural material. **2.** Something made of steel. **3.** A quality suggestive of this alloy, esp. a hard, unflinching character. **4.** *Color.* Steel gray. — *adj.* **1.a.** Made with, relating to, or consisting of steel: *steel beams.* **b.** Very firm or strong: *a steel grip.* **2.** *Color.* Of a steel gray. — *tr.v.* **steeled, steel•ing, steels. 1.** To cover, plate, edge, or point with steel. **2.** To make hard, strong, or obdurate; strengthen. [ME *stel* < OE *stȳle, stēl.*]

steel band *n.* *Mus.* A steel drum band.

steel blue *n.* **1.** *Color.* A medium grayish blue. **2.** One of several blue colors taken on by steel while being tempered.

steel drum *n.* *Mus.* A metal percussion instrument of Trinidadian origin, fashioned from an oil barrel and having a concave array of flattened areas that produce different tones when struck. — **steel drummer** *n.*

Steele (stēl), **Mount.** A mountain, 5,076.4 m (16,644 ft), in the St. Elias Mts. of SW Yukon Terr., Canada.

Steele, Sir **Richard.** 1672–1729. English writer of plays and essays who founded and edited *The Tatler* (1709–11) and with Joseph Addison *The Spectator* (1711–12).

ă pat	oi boy
ā pay	ou out
âr care	o͝o took
ä father	o͞o boot
ĕ pet	ŭ cut
ē be	ûr urge
ĭ pit	th thin
ī pie	*th* this
îr pier	hw which
ŏ pot	zh vision
ō toe	ə about, item
ô paw	

Stress marks:
′ (primary);
′ (secondary), as in
dictionary (dĭk′shə-nĕr′ē)

steel engraving *n.* **1.** The art or process of engraving on a steel plate. **2.** An impression produced with such a plate.

steel gray *n. Color.* A dark to purplish gray.

steel guitar *n. Mus.* **1.** An acoustic guitar with a metal resonator built into the body, often played with a slide and producing a twangy variable tone. **2.** See **Hawaiian guitar.**

steel•head (stēl′hĕd′) *n.* The anadromous variety of rainbow trout, larger and darker than the freshwater variety.

steel-trap (stēl′trăp′) *adj.* Very quick and keen; trenchant.

steel wool *n.* Fine fibers of steel, matted or woven together to form an abrasive for cleaning, smoothing, or polishing.

steel•work (stēl′wûrk′) *n.* **1.** Something made of steel. **2. steelworks.** *(used with a sing. v.)* A plant where steel is made; a foundry. **— steel′work′er** *n.*

steel•y (stē′lē) *adj.* **-i•er, -i•est. 1.** Made of steel. **2.** Resembling steel, as in color or hardness. **— steel′i•ness** *n.*

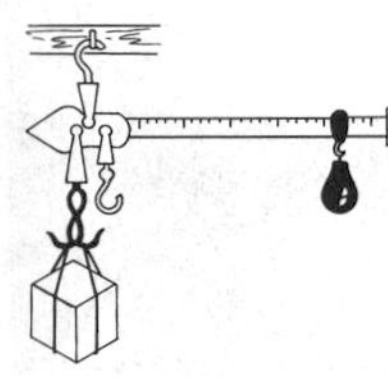

steelyard

steel•yard (stēl′yärd′) *n.* A balance consisting of a scaled arm suspended off center, a hook at the shorter end on which to hang the object being weighed, and a counterbalance at the longer end that can be moved to find the weight. [STEEL + YARD¹, rod.]

Steen (stān), **Jan.** 1626?–79. Dutch genre painter whose depictions of domestic life include *Village Wedding.*

steen•bok (stēn′bŏk′, stān′-) also **stein•bok** (stīn′-) *n.* A small antelope *(Raphicerus campestris)* of southern and eastern Africa having a brownish coat and short pointed horns in the male. [Afr. < MDu. *steenboc,* ibex : *steen,* stone; see **stei-*** + *boc,* buck.]

steep¹ (stēp) *adj.* **steep•er, steep•est. 1.** Having a sharp inclination; precipitous. **2.** At a rapid or precipitous rate: *a steep rise in salaries.* **3.a.** Excessive; stiff: *a steep price.* **b.** Ambitious; difficult. *— n.* A precipitous slope. [ME *stepe* < OE *stēap.*] **— steep′ly** *adv.* **— steep′ness** *n.*

Syns: *steep, abrupt, precipitous, sheer.* The central meaning shared by these adjectives is "so sharply inclined as to be almost perpendicular": *steep cliffs; an abrupt drop-off; precipitous hills; a sheer descent.*

steep² (stēp) *v.* **steeped, steep•ing, steeps.** *— tr.* **1.** To soak in liquid in order to cleanse, soften, or extract a given property from. **2.** To infuse or subject thoroughly to. **3.** To make thoroughly wet; saturate. *— intr.* To undergo a soaking in liquid. *— n.* **1.a.** The act or process of steeping. **b.** The state of being steeped. **2.** A liquid, bath, or solution in which something is steeped. [ME *stepen,* perh. of OE orig.] **— steep′er** *n.*

steep•en (stē′pən) *tr. & intr.v.* **-ened, -en•ing, -ens.** To make or become steep or steeper.

steeple
Place of Meditation, Eisenhower Center, Abilene, Kansas

stee•ple (stē′pəl) *n.* **1.** A tall tower forming the superstructure of a building, such as a church or temple, and usu. surmounted by a spire. **2.** A spire. [ME *stepel* < OE *stēpel.*]

stee•ple•bush (stē′pəl-bo͝osh′) *n.* See **hardhack.**

stee•ple•chase (stē′pəl-chās′) *n. Sports.* **1.** A horserace across open country or over an obstacle course. **2.** A footrace over a closed track with four hurdles and a water obstacle. [Church steeples being landmarks.] **— stee′ple•chas′er** *n.*

stee•pled (stē′pəld) *adj.* **1.** Having steeples or a steeple: *a tiny, steepled church.* **2.** Steeply inclined: *steepled roofs.*

stee•ple•jack (stē′pəl-jăk′) *n.* One who builds or maintains very high structures, such as steeples.

steer¹ (stîr) *v.* **steered, steer•ing, steers.** *— tr.* **1.** To guide by means of a device such as a rudder, paddle, or wheel. **2.a.** To direct the course of. **b.** To maneuver (a person) into a place or course of action. *— intr.* **1.** To guide a vessel or vehicle. **2.** To follow or move in a set course. **3.** To admit of being steered or guided. *— n.* A piece of advice. [ME *steren* < OE *stēran.* See **stā-***.] **— steer′a•ble** *adj.* **— steer′er** *n.*

steer² (stîr) *n.* A male bovine animal castrated before reaching sexual maturity. [ME < OE *stēor.* See **stā-***.]

steer•age (stîr′ĭj) *n.* **1.** The act or practice of steering. **2.** *Naut.* **a.** The effect of the helm on a ship. **b.** The section of a passenger ship, originally near the rudder, providing the cheapest passenger accommodations.

John Steinbeck

steer•age•way (stîr′ĭj-wā′) *n. Naut.* The minimum forward speed through the water required for a vessel's rudder to be effective.

steer•ing committee (stîr′ĭng) *n.* A committee that sets agendas and schedules of business, as for a legislative body.

steering gear *n.* The mechanism by which dispositions of the steering controls of a vehicle are transferred to a rudder, wheel, or other part that directs the vehicle's course.

steering wheel *n.* A wheel that controls steering, as on a boat.

steers•man (stîrz′mən) *n. Naut.* One who steers a ship.

steeve¹ (stēv) *Naut. — n.* A spar or derrick with a block at one end, used for stowing cargo. *— tr.v.* **steeved, steev•ing, steeves.** To stow or pack (cargo) in the hold of a ship. [< ME *steven,* to stow, prob. < OSp. *estibar,* to steeve, or < Old Catalan *stivar,* both < Lat. *stīpāre.*]

steeve² (stēv) *Naut. — n.* The angle formed by the bowsprit and the horizon or the keel. *— v.* **steeved, steev•ing, steeves.** *— tr.* To incline (a bowsprit) upward at an angle with the horizon or the keel. *— intr.* To have an upward inclination. Used of a bowsprit. [?]

Ste•fáns•son (stĕf′ən-sən), **Vilhjálmur.** 1879–1962. Canadian-born explorer and ethnologist who studied the language and culture of the Eskimo.

Stef•fens (stĕf′ənz), **(Joseph) Lincoln.** 1866–1936. Amer. journalist considered a pioneer of muckraking journalism.

steg•o•don (stĕg′ə-dŏn′) *n.* Any of various extinct elephantlike mammals of the genus *Stegodon* and related genera of the Pliocene to the Pleistocene. [NLat. *Stegodon,* genus name : Gk. *stegos,* roof (< *stegein,* to cover; see **(s)teg-***) + -ODON (so called because of the distinctive ridges on its molars).]

steg•o•saur (stĕg′ə-sôr′) also **steg•o•sau•rus** (stĕg′ə-sôr′-əs) *n.* Any of several herbivorous dinosaurs of the suborder *Stegosauria* of the Jurassic to the Cretaceous, having a double row of upright bony plates along the back and a relatively small head. [NLat. *Stegosaurus,* genus name : Gk. *stegos,* roof; see STEGODON + NLat. *saurus,* lizard; see SAURY.]

Stei•chen (stī′kən), **Edward Jean.** 1879–1973. Amer. photographer who was a pioneer of photography as a fine art.

stein (stīn) *n.* A mug, esp. one for beer, usu. holding about a pint. [Ger., prob. short for *Steinkrug,* stone jug : *Stein,* stone (< MHGer. < OHGer.; see **stei-***) + *Krug,* jug.]

Stein (stīn), **Gertrude.** 1874–1946. Amer. writer whose works include *The Autobiography of Alice B. Toklas* (1933).

Stein•beck (stīn′bĕk′), **John Ernst.** 1902–68. Amer. writer of short stories and novels, most notably *The Grapes of Wrath* (1939). He won the 1962 Nobel Prize for literature.

stein•bok (stīn′bok′) *n.* Var. of **steenbok.**

Stein•em (stī′nəm), **Gloria.** b. 1934. Amer. feminist who was a founding editor (1972) of *Ms.* magazine.

Stein•er (stī′nər, shtī′-), **Rudolf.** 1861–1925. Austrian social philosopher who founded a Christianized school of theosophy, called anthroposophy.

Stein•heim man (stīn′hīm′, shtīn′-) *n.* An extinct hominid *(Homo steinheimensis)* known from skull fragments of the middle Pleistocene and thought to be an ancestor of Neanderthal man. [After *Steinheim,* in S-central Germany.]

Stein•metz (stīn′mĕts′, shtīn′-), **Charles Proteus.** 1865–1923. German-born Amer. electrical engineer and inventor known for his theoretical studies of alternating current.

Stein•way (stīn′wā′), **Henry Engelhard.** 1797–1871. German-born Amer. piano maker who founded the Steinway & Sons piano company in New York City (1853).

ste•le (stē′lē) *n., pl.* **-les** or **-lae** (-lē). **1.a.** An upright stone or slab with an inscribed or sculptured surface, used for commemorative purposes. **b.** A similar tablet in the surface of a building. **2.** *Bot.* The central core of vascular tissue in a plant stem or root. [Gk. *stēlē,* pillar. See **stel-***.] **— ste′lar** (-lər) *adj.*

Stel•la (stĕl′ə), **Frank Philip.** b. 1936. Amer. painter known for his geometric abstract works.

stel•lar (stĕl′ər) *adj.* **1.** Of, relating to, or consisting of stars. **2.a.** Of or relating to a star performer. **b.** Outstanding; principal. [LLat. *stēllāris* < Lat. *stēlla,* star. See **ster-³***.]

stellar wind (wĭnd) *n.* The varying flow of plasma ejected from the surface of a star into interstellar space.

stel•late (stĕl′āt′) also **stel•lat•ed** (-ā′tĭd) *adj.* Arranged or shaped like a star; radiating from a center. [Lat. *stēllātus* < *stēlla,* star. See **ster-³***.] **— stel′late•ly** *adv.*

stel•li•form (stĕl′ə-fôrm′) *adj.* Shaped like a star. [NLat. *stēllifōrmis* : Lat. *stēlla,* star; see STELLAR + Lat. *-formis,* form (< *fōrma*).]

stel•lu•lar (stĕl′yə-lər) *adj.* **1.** Having the form of a small star. **2.** Bespangled with small stars. [< LLat. *stēllula,* dim. of Lat. *stēlla,* star. See STELLAR.]

stem¹ (stĕm) *n.* **1.a.** The main ascending axis of a plant; a stalk or trunk. **b.** A slender stalk supporting or connecting another plant part, such as a leaf or flower. **2.** A banana stalk bearing several bunches of bananas. **3.** A connecting or supporting part, esp.: **a.** The tube of a tobacco pipe. **b.** The slender upright support of a wineglass or goblet. **c.** The small projecting shaft with an expanded crown by which a watch is wound. **d.** The rounded rod in the center of certain locks about which the key fits and is turned. **e.** The shaft of a feather or hair. **f.** The upright stroke of a typeface or letter. **g.** *Mus.* The vertical line extending from the head of a note. **4.** The main line of descent of a family. **5.** *Ling.* The main part of a word to which affixes are added. **6.** *Naut.* The curved upright beam at the fore of a vessel into which the hull timbers are scarfed to form the prow. **7.** The tubular glass structure mounting the filament or electrodes in an incandescent bulb or vacuum tube. *— v.* **stemmed, stem•ming, stems.** *— intr.* To have or take origin or descent. *— tr.* **1.** To remove the stem of. **2.** To provide with a stem. **3.** To make headway against: *stemmed the rebellion.* **— *idiom.* from stem to stern.** From one end to another. [ME < OE *stefn, stemn.* See **stā-***.]

Syns: *stem, arise, derive, emanate, flow, issue, originate, proceed, rise, spring.* The central meaning shared by these verbs is "to come forth or come into being": *customs stemming from the past; misery arising from war; rights deriving from citizenship; approval emanating from them; joy that flows from friendship; hate that issues from fear; a bill originating in Congress; a mistake proceeding from haste; rebellion rising in the towns; new industries springing up.*

stem² (stĕm) *v.* **stemmed, stem•ming, stems.** —*tr.* **1.** To stop or hold back by or as if by damming; stanch. **2.** To plug or tamp (a blast hole, for example). **3.** *Sports.* To point (skis) inward. —*intr. Sports.* To point skis inward in order to slow down or turn. [ME *stemmen* < ON *stemma.*]

stem cell *n.* An unspecialized cell that gives rise to a specific specialized cell, such as a blood cell.

stem•ma (stĕm′ə) *n., pl.* **stem•ma•ta** (stĕm′ə-tə) or **stem•mas. 1.** A scroll recording the genealogy of an ancient Roman family; a family tree. **2.** The genealogy of the manuscripts of a literary work. **3.** A small circular simple eye present in various insect larvae. [Lat. *stemma, stemmat-* < Gk., garland < *stephein,* to encircle.]

stemmed (stĕmd) *adj.* **1.** Having the stems removed. **2.** Provided with a stem or a specific type of stem. Often used in combination: *long-stemmed roses.*

stem rust *n.* A rust disease affecting the stem of a plant.

stem•son (stĕm′sən) *n. Naut.* A piece of supporting timber bolted to the stem and keelson at their junction near the bow of a wooden vessel. [STEM¹ + (KEEL)SON.]

stem turn *n. Sports.* A turn in skiing made by stemming the uphill ski, transferring weight to its inside edge, and bringing the other ski into a parallel position after making the turn.

stem•ware (stĕm′wâr′) *n.* Glassware mounted on a stem with a broad base.

stem-wind•er (stĕm′wīn′dər) *n.* **1.** A stem-winding watch. **2.** A rousing oration, esp. a political one.

stem-wind•ing (stĕm′wīn′dĭng) *adj.* Wound by turning an expanded crown on the stem.

sten. *abbr.* Stenographer; stenography.

stench (stĕnch) *n.* A strong foul odor; a stink. [ME < OE *stenc,* odor.]

sten•cil (stĕn′səl) *n.* **1.** A sheet, as of plastic, in which lettering or a design has been cut so that ink or paint applied to the sheet will reproduce the pattern on the surface beneath. **2.** The lettering or design so produced. **3.** The process of printing with such a sheet. —*tr.v.* **-ciled, -cil•ing, -cils** or **-cilled, -cil•ling, -cils. 1.** To mark with a stencil. **2.** To produce by stencil. [< ME *stencellen,* adorned brightly < OFr. *estenceler,* to adorn brightly < *estencele,* spark < VLat. **stincilla,* alteration of Lat. *scintilla,* spark.] —**sten′cil•er** *n.*

Sten•dhal (stĕn-däl′, stăn-, stăɴ-). Pen name of Marie Henri Beyle. 1783–1842. French writer who influenced the development of the modern novel with his psychological romances.

Sten•gel (stĕng′gəl), **Charles ("Casey") Dillon.** 1890?–1975. Amer. baseball player and manager, most notably of the New York Yankees (1948–60).

sten•o (stĕn′ō) *n., pl.* **-os. 1.** A stenographer. **2.** Stenography.

steno– *pref.* Narrow; small: *stenotopic.* [Gk. < *stenos.*]

sten•o•bath•ic (stĕn′ə-băth′ĭk) *adj.* Limited to or able to live only within a narrow range of water depths. [STENO– + Gk. *bathos,* depth + –IC.] —**sten′o•bath′** *n.*

stenog. *abbr.* Stenographer; stenography.

sten•o•graph (stĕn′ə-grăf′) *n.* **1.** A keyboard machine for reproducing letters in a shorthand system. **2.** A character in shorthand.

ste•nog•ra•pher (stə-nŏg′rə-fər) *n.* One who is skilled in stenography, esp. one employed to take and transcribe dictation or testimony.

ste•nog•ra•phy (stə-nŏg′rə-fē) *n.* **1.** The art or process of writing in shorthand. **2.** The art or practice of transcribing speech with a stenograph. **3.** Material transcribed in shorthand. —**sten′o•graph′ic** (stĕn′ə-grăf′ĭk), **sten′o•graph′i•cal** (-ĭ-kəl) *adj.* —**sten′o•graph′i•cal•ly** *adv.*

sten•o•ha•line (stĕn′ə-hā′līn, -hăl′īn) *adj.* Limited to or able to live only within a narrow range of saltwater concentrations. [STENO– + Gk. *halinos,* of salt (< *hals, hal-,* salt; see HALO–).]

ste•nosed (stə-nōzd′, -nōst′) *adj.* Characterized by stenosis.

ste•no•sis (stə-nō′sĭs) *n., pl.* **-ses** (-sēz). A constriction or narrowing of a duct or passage; a stricture. [NLat. < Gk. *stenōsis,* a narrowing < *stenoun,* to narrow < *stenos,* narrow.] —**ste•not′ic** (-nŏt′ĭk) *adj.*

sten•o•ther•mal (stĕn′ə-thûr′məl) also **sten•o•ther•mic** (-mĭk) or **sten•o•ther•mous** (-məs) *adj.* Capable of living or growing only within a limited range of temperature. —**sten′o•therm′** *n.*

sten•o•top•ic (stĕn′ə-tŏp′ĭk) *adj.* Able to adapt only to a narrow range of environmental conditions. Used of a plant or an animal. [STENO– + Gk. *topos,* place + –IC.]

sten•o•type (stĕn′ə-tīp′) *n.* **1.** A keyboard machine used to record dictation in shorthand by a series of phonetic symbols. **2.** A phonetic symbol or combination of symbols produced by such a machine. —*tr.v.* **-typed, -typ•ing, -types.** To record or transcribe (matter) with a stenotype machine. [STENO(GRAPHY) + TYPE.] —**sten′o•typ′ist** *n.*

sten•o•typ•y (stĕn′ə-tī′pē) *n., pl.* **-ies.** The art or process of transcribing with a stenotype machine.

sten•tor (stĕn′tôr′) *n.* Any of several trumpet-shaped ciliate protozoans of the genus *Stentor,* living in dark freshwater pools and feeding chiefly on smaller microorganisms. [After *Stentor,* a Greek herald,. See STENTORIAN.]

sten•to•ri•an (stĕn-tôr′ē-ən, -tōr′-) *adj.* Extremely loud. [After *Stentor,* a loud-voiced Greek herald in the *Iliad.*]

step (stĕp) *n.* **1.a.** The single complete movement of raising one foot and putting it down in another spot, as in walking. **b.** A manner of walking; a particular gait. **c.** A fixed rhythm or pace, as in marching: *keep step.* **d.** The sound of a footstep. **e.** A footprint. **2.a.** The distance traversed by moving one foot ahead of the other. **b.** A very short distance. **c. steps.** Course; path. **3.a.** A rest for the foot in ascending or descending. **b. steps.** Stairs. **c.** Something, such as a ledge, that resembles a step of a stairway. **4.a.** One of a series of actions, processes, or measures taken to achieve a goal. **b.** A stage in a process. **5.** A degree in progress or a grade or rank in a scale. **6.** *Mus.* The interval that separates two successive tones of a scale. **7.** *Naut.* The frame or support in which the heel of a mast is fixed. —*v.* **stepped, step•ping, steps.** —*intr.* **1.** To put or press the foot. **2.** To shift or move slightly by taking a step or two. **3.** To walk a short distance to a given place or in a given direction. **4.** To move with the feet in a given manner: *step lively.* **5.** To move into a new situation by or as if by taking a single step. **6.** To treat with arrogant indifference: *stepped on them.* —*tr.* **1.** To put or set (the foot) down. **2.** To measure by pacing: *step off ten yards.* **3.** To furnish with steps; make steps in. **4.** *Comp. Sci.* To cause (a computer) to execute a single instruction. **5.** *Naut.* To place (a mast) in its step. —***phrasal verbs.*** **step down. 1.** To resign from a high post. **2.** To reduce, esp. in stages. **step in. 1.** To enter into an activity or a situation. **2.** To intervene. **step out. 1.** To walk briskly. **2.** To go outside for a short time. **3.** *Informal.* To go out for a special evening of entertainment. **4.** To withdraw; quit. **step up. 1.** To increase, esp. in stages. **2.** To come forward. —***idioms.*** **in step. 1.** Moving in rhythm. **2.** In conformity with one's environment. **out of step. 1.** Not moving in rhythm. **2.** Not in conformity with one's environment. **step by step.** By degrees. **step on it.** *Informal.* To go faster; hurry. [ME < OE *stæpe, stepe.*]

step– *pref.* Related by means of a remarriage rather than by blood: *stepparent.* [ME < OE *stēop-.*]

step•broth•er (stĕp′brŭ*th*′ər) *n.* A son of one's stepparent.

step•child (stĕp′chīld′) *n.* **1.** A spouse's child by a previous marriage. **2.** Something that does not receive appropriate care, respect, or attention.

step dance *n.* A dance focusing mainly on steps.

step•daugh•ter (stĕp′dô′tər) *n.* A spouse's daughter by a previous marriage.

step-down (stĕp′doun′) *adj.* **1.** Decreasing in stages: *a step-down gear.* **2.** *Elect.* Serving to reduce voltage: *a step-down transformer.* —*n.* A reduction in amount or size.

step•fam•i•ly (stĕp′făm′ə-lē, -făm′lē) *n., pl.* **-lies.** A family with one or more stepchildren.

step•fa•ther (stĕp′fä′*th*ər) *n.* The husband of one's mother and not one's natural father.

steph•a•no•tis (stĕf′ə-nō′tĭs) *n., pl.* **-tis•es.** Any of various woody climbing plants of the genus *Stephanotis,* esp. *S. floribunda* of Madagascar cultivated for its showy fragrant white flowers. [Gk. *stephanōtis,* deserving a crown < *stephanos,* crown, wreath < *stephein,* to crown.]

Ste•phen (stē′vən), Saint. d. c. A.D. 36. Christian protomartyr who according to tradition was stoned to death.

Stephen I. Saint Stephen. 975?–1038. King of Hungary (997?–1038) considered the founder of the Hungarian state.

Stephen, Sir **Leslie.** 1832–1904. British writer and editor whose works include *The History of English Thought in the Eighteenth Century* (1876).

Stephen of Blois (blwä). 1097?–1154. King of England (1135–54) who was the last Norman king of the realm.

Ste•phens (stē′vənz), **Alexander Hamilton.** 1812–83. Amer. politician and vice president of the Confederacy (1861–65).

Stephens, James. 1882–1950. Irish writer of poems and novels, such as *The Crock of Gold* (1912).

Ste•phen•son (stē′vən-sən), **George.** 1781–1848. British railway pioneer who built the first passenger railway (1825). His son **Robert** (1803–59) built railroads and bridges.

step-in (stĕp′ĭn′) *adj.* Put on by stepping into. —*n.* **1. step-ins.** Panties with wide legs. **2.** A step-in garment.

step•lad•der (stĕp′lăd′ər) *n.* A portable ladder with a hinged supporting frame and usu. topped with a small platform.

step•moth•er (stĕp′mŭ*th*′ər) *n.* The wife of one's father and not one's natural mother.

step•par•ent (stĕp′pâr′ənt, -păr′-) *n.* A stepfather or stepmother.

steppe (stĕp) *n.* A vast semiarid grass-covered plain, as found in southeast Europe, Siberia, and central North America. [Ger. < Russ. *step′.*]

stepped-up (stĕpt′ŭp′) *adj.* Increased in pace or intensity; heightened: *a stepped-up political campaign.*

step•per (stĕp′ər) *n.* **1.** One that steps, esp. in a fast or spirited manner. **2.** *Informal.* A dancer.

step•ping•stone (stĕp′ĭng-stōn′) *n.* **1.** A stone that provides a place to step, as in crossing a stream. **2.** An advantageous position for advancement toward a goal.

step•sis•ter (stĕp′sĭs′tər) *n.* A daughter of one's stepparent.

Gloria Steinem

stencil

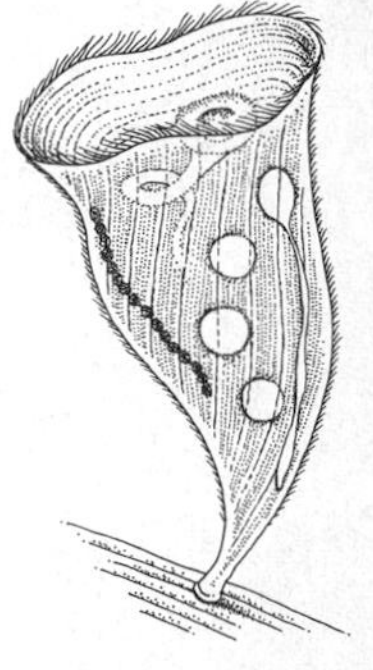

stentor

ă pat	oi boy
ā pay	ou out
âr care	ŏŏ took
ä father	ōō boot
ĕ pet	ŭ cut
ē be	ûr urge
ĭ pit	th thin
ī pie	*th* this
îr pier	hw which
ŏ pot	zh vision
ō toe	ə about, item
ô paw	

Stress marks:
′ (primary);
′ (secondary), as in **dictionary** (dĭk′shə-nĕr′ē)

step•son (stĕp′sŭn′) *n.* A spouse's son by a previous marriage.

step stool *n.* A stool, often with folding steps attached, on which one stands to reach high objects.

step-up (stĕp′ŭp′) *adj.* **1.** Increasing in steps or by stages. **2.** *Elect.* Serving to increase voltage: *a step-up transformer.* —*n.* An increase in size, amount, or activity.

step•wise (stĕp′wīz′) *adj.* **1.** Marked by a gradual progression as if step by step. **2.** *Mus.* Moving from one tone to an adjacent one. —**step′wise′** *adv.*

ster. *abbr.* Sterling.

-ster *suff.* **1.** One that is associated with, participates in, makes, or does: *songster.* **2.** One that is: *youngster.* [ME < OE *-estre*, female agent suff.]

ste•ra•di•an (stĭ-rā′dē-ən) *n.* A unit of measure equal to the solid angle subtended at the center of a sphere by an area on the surface of the sphere that is equal to the radius squared. See table at **measurement.** [STE(REO)- + RADIAN.]

ster•co•ra•ceous (stûr′kə-rā′shəs) also **ster•co•rous** (stûr′kər-əs) *adj.* Consisting of or relating to excrement. [Lat. *stercus, stercor-*, dung; see **sker-³*** + -ACEOUS.]

stere (stîr) *n.* A unit of volume equal to one cubic meter. [Fr. *stère* < Gk. *stereos*, solid, hard. See **ster-¹*.**]

ster•e•o (stĕr′ē-ō′, stîr′-) *n., pl.* **-os. 1.a.** A stereophonic sound-reproduction system. **b.** Stereophonic sound. **2.** A stereotype. **3.** A stereoscopic system or photograph. —*adj.* **1.** Stereophonic. **2.** Stereoscopic.

stereo- *pref.* **1.** Solid; solid body: *stereotropism.* **2.** Three-dimensional: *stereoscope.* [Gk. < *stereos*, solid. See **ster-¹*.**]

Isaac Stern
Photographed in 1990

ster•e•o•bate (stĕr′ē-ō-bāt′, stîr′-) *n. Archit.* **1.** See **stylobate. 2.** The foundation of a stone building, its top course sometimes being a stylobate. [Lat. *stereobatēs* < Gk. **stereobatēs* : *stereos*, solid; see STEREO- + *-batēs*, walker (< *bainein*, to go; see **gʷā-***).]

ster•e•o•chem•is•try (stĕr′ē-ō-kĕm′ĭ-strē, stîr′-) *n.* The branch of chemistry that deals with spatial arrangements of atoms in molecules and the chemical and physical effects of these arrangements. —**ster′e•o•chem′i•cal** (-ĭ-kəl) *adj.*

ster•e•o•chro•my (stĕr′ē-ə-krō′mē, stîr′-) *n., pl.* **-mies.** The art or process of mural painting with pigments mixed with water glass. —**ster′e•o•chrome′** *n.* —**ster′e•o•chro′mic** *adj.* —**ster′e•o•chro′mi•cal•ly** *adv.*

ster•e•o•gram (stĕr′ē-ə-grăm′, stîr′-) *n.* **1.** A picture or diagram that gives the impression of solidity. **2.** A stereograph.

ster•e•o•graph (stĕr′ē-ə-grăf′, stîr′-) *n.* Two stereoscopic pictures or one picture with two superposed stereoscopic images, designed to give a three-dimensional effect when viewed through a stereoscope or special glasses. —*tr.v.* **-graphed, -graph•ing, -graphs.** To make a stereographic picture of.

ster•e•og•ra•phy (stĕr′ē-ŏg′rə-fē, stîr′-) *n.* **1.** The art or technique of depicting solid bodies on a plane surface. **2.** Photography that involves the use of stereoscopic equipment. —**ster′e•o•graph′ic** (-ə-grăf′ĭk), **ster′e•o•graph′i•cal** (-ĭ-kəl) *adj.* —**ster′e•o•graph′i•cal•ly** *adv.*

ster•e•o•i•so•mer (stĕr′ē-ō-ī′sə-mər, stîr′-) *n.* One of a set of isomers whose molecules have the same atoms bonded to each other but differ in the way these atoms are arranged in space.

ster•e•o•i•som•er•ism (stĕr′ē-ō-ī-sŏm′ə-rĭz′əm, stîr′-) *n.* Isomerism due to differences in the spatial arrangement of atoms in a molecule. —**ster′e•o•i′so•mer′ic** (-ī′-sə-mĕr′ĭk) *adj.*

ster•e•ol•o•gy (stĕr′ē-ŏl′ə-jē, stîr′-) *n.* The study of three-dimensional properties of objects or matter usu. observed two-dimensionally. —**ster′e•o•log′ic** (-ə-lŏj′ĭk), **ster′e•o•log′i•cal** (-ĭ-kəl) *adj.* —**ster′e•ol′o•gist** *n.*

ster•e•o•phon•ic (stĕr′ē-ə-fŏn′ĭk, stîr′-) *adj.* Of or used in a sound-reproduction system that uses two or more separate channels to give a more natural distribution of sound. —**ster′e•o•phon′i•cal•ly** *adv.* —**ster′e•oph′on•y** (-ē-ŏf′ə-nē) *n.*

ster•e•op•sis (stĕr′ē-ŏp′sĭs, stîr′-) *n.* Stereoscopic vision.

ster•e•op•ti•con (stĕr′ē-ŏp′tĭ-kŏn′, stîr′-) *n.* A magic lantern, esp. one with two projectors arranged so as to produce dissolving views. [New Latin : STEREO- + Gk. *optikon*, neut. of *optikos*, optic; see OPTIC.]

ster•e•o•scope (stĕr′ē-ə-skōp′, stîr′-) *n.* An instrument with two eyepieces used to impart a three-dimensional effect to two photographs of the same scene from slightly different angles.

ster•e•o•scop•ic (stĕr′ē-ə-skŏp′ĭk, stîr′-) *adj.* **1.** Of or relating to stereoscopy. **2.** Of or relating to a stereoscope. —**ster′e•o•scop′i•cal•ly** *adv.*

ster•e•os•co•py (stĕr′ē-ŏs′kə-pē, stîr′-) *n.* **1.** The viewing of objects as three-dimensional. **2.** The technique of making or using stereoscopes and stereoscopic slides.

ster•e•o•tax•is (stĕr′ē-ə-tăk′sĭs, stîr′-) *n.* **1.** A method in neurosurgery and neurological research for locating points within the brain using an external three-dimensional frame of reference usu. based on the Cartesian coordinate system. **2.** Movement of an organism in response to contact with a solid body. —**ster′e•o•tac′tic** (-tăk′tĭk) *adj.*

ster•e•ot•ro•pism (stĕr′ē-ŏt′rə-pĭz′əm, stîr′-) *n.* See **thigmotropism.** —**ster′e•o•trop′ic** (-ē-ə-trŏp′ĭk) *adj.*

ster•e•o•type (stĕr′ē-ə-tīp′, stîr′-) *n.* **1.** A conventional, formulaic, and oversimplified conception or image. **2.** One seen as embodying or conforming to a stereotype. **3.** *Print.* A metal printing plate cast from a matrix molded from a raised printing surface. —*tr.v.* **-typed, -typ•ing, -types. 1.** To make a stereotype of. **2.** To characterize by a stereotype. **3.** To give a fixed, unvarying form to. **4.** To print from a stereotype. [Fr. *stéréotype*, stereotype printing : *stéréo-*, solid (< Gk. *stereo-*; see STEREO-) + *type*, printing type (< OFr., symbol < LLat. *typus*; see TYPE).] —**ster′e•o•typ′er** *n.* —**ster′e•o•typ′ic** (-tĭp′ĭk), **ster′e•o•typ′i•cal** (-ĭ-kəl) *adj.* —**ster′e•o•typ′i•cal•ly** *adv.*

ster•e•o•typed (stĕr′ē-ə-tīpt′, stîr′-) *adj.* **1.** Lacking originality or creativity. **2.** *Print.* Made from stereotype plates.

ster•e•o•ty•py (stĕr′ē-ə-tī′pē, stîr′-) *n., pl.* **-pies. 1.** Excessive repetition or lack of variation in movements, ideas, or patterns of speech. **2.** *Print.* The process or art of making stereotype plates.

ster•ic (stĕr′ĭk, stîr′-) also **ster•i•cal** (-ĭ-kəl) *adj. Phys. & Chem.* Of or relating to the spatial arrangement of atoms in a molecule. [STER(EO)- + -IC.] —**ster′i•cal•ly** *adv.*

ste•rig•ma (stə-rĭg′mə) *n., pl.* **-ma•ta** (-mə-tə). A slender projection of the basidium of some fungi that bears a basidiospore. [NLat. < Gk. *stērigma*, support < *stērizein, stērig-*, to support. See **ster-¹*.**]

ster•il•ant (stĕr′ə-lənt) *n.* A sterilizing agent.

ster•ile (stĕr′əl, -īl′) *adj.* **1.** Not producing or incapable of producing offspring. **2.a.** Not producing or incapable of producing seed, fruit spores, or other reproductive structures. Used of plants or their parts. **b.** Producing little or no vegetation; unfruitful. **3.** Free from live bacteria or other microorganisms. **4.** Lacking imagination, creativity, or vitality. **5.** Lacking the power to function; not productive or effective; fruitless. [ME < OFr. < Lat. *sterilis*.] —**ster′ile•ly** *adv.* —**ster′ile•ness, ste•ril′i•ty** (stə-rĭl′ĭ-tē) *n.*

ster•il•i•za•tion (stĕr′ə-lĭ-zā′shən) *n.* **1.** The act or procedure of sterilizing. **2.** The condition of being sterile or sterilized.

ster•il•ize (stĕr′ə-līz′) *tr.v.* **-ized, -iz•ing, -iz•es. 1.** To remove live bacteria or other microorganisms from. **2.** To make (a person or an animal) unable to produce offspring. **3.a.** To make incapable of bearing fruit or germinating. **b.** To render (land) unfruitful. **4.** *Econ.* To place (gold) in safekeeping so as not to affect the supply of money or credit. **5.** To make inoffensive or innocuous. —**ster′il•iz′er** *n.*

ster•let (stûr′lĭt) *n.* A sturgeon (*Acipenser ruthenus*) of the Black and Caspian seas, used as a source of caviar. [Russ. *sterlyad'* < ORuss. *sterlyagi*, of Gmc. orig.]

ster•ling (stûr′lĭng) *n.* **1.** British money, esp. the pound as the basic monetary unit of the United Kingdom. **2.** British coinage of silver or gold, having as a standard of fineness 0.500 for silver and 0.91666 for gold. **3.a.** Sterling silver. **b.** Articles made of sterling silver. —*adj.* **1.** Consisting of or relating to sterling or British money. **2.** Made of sterling silver: *a sterling teaspoon.* **3.** Of the highest quality: *a sterling character.* [ME, silver penny : poss. *sterre*, star; see STAR + *-ling*, dim. suff. (< the small star stamped on the coin); see -LING¹.]

Ster•ling Heights (stûr′lĭng). A city of SE MI, a suburb of Detroit. Pop. 117,810.

sterling silver *n.* **1.** An alloy of 92.5 percent silver with copper or another metal. **2.** Objects made of this alloy.

stern¹ (stûrn) *adj.* **stern•er, stern•est. 1.** Hard, harsh, or severe in manner or character: *a stern disciplinarian.* See Syns at **severe. 2.** Grim, gloomy, or forbidding in appearance or outlook. **3.** Firm or unyielding; uncompromising. **4.** Inexorable; relentless: *stern necessity.* [ME *sterne* < OE *styrne.* See **ster-¹*.**] —**stern′ly** *adv.* —**stern′ness** *n.*

stern² (stûrn) *n.* **1.** *Naut.* The rear part of a ship or boat. **2.** A rear part or section. [ME *sterne*, perh. of Scand. orig.; akin to ON *stjórn*, rudder. See **stā-*.**]

Stern (stûrn), **Isaac.** b. 1920. Russian-born Amer. violinist considered among the great virtuosos of the 20th cent.

ster•na (stûr′nə) *n.* Pl. of **sternum.**

ster•nal (stûr′nəl) *adj.* Of, relating to, or near the sternum.

stern chaser *n.* A gun or cannon mounted on the stern of a ship for firing at a pursuing vessel.

Sterne (stûrn), **Laurence.** 1713–68. British writer whose works include *Tristram Shandy* (1761-67).

stern•fore•most (stûrn′fôr′mōst′, -fōr′-) *adv. Naut.* With the stern foremost; backward.

stern•most (stûrn′mōst′) *adj. Naut.* Closest to the stern.

stern•post (stûrn′pōst′) *n. Naut.* The principal upright post at the stern of a vessel, usu. serving to support the rudder.

stern sheets *pl.n. Naut.* The stern area of an open boat.

stern•son (stûrn′sən) *n. Naut.* A bar of metal or wood set between the keelson and the sternpost to fortify the joint. [STERN² + (KEEL)SON.]

ster•num (stûr′nəm) *n., pl.* **-nums** or **-na** (-nə). A long flat bone in most vertebrates that is situated along the ventral midline of the thorax and articulates with the ribs. [NLat. < Gk. *sternon*, breast, breastbone. See **ster-²*.**]

ster•nu•ta•tion (stûr′nyə-tā′shən) *n.* **1.** The act of sneezing.

2. A sneeze. [ME *sternutacioun* < Lat. *sternūtātiō, sternūtātiōn-* < *sternūtātus*, p.part. of *sternūtāre*, freq. of *sternuere*, to sneeze.]

ster•nu•ta•tor (stûr′nyə-tā′tər) *n.* A substance that irritates the nasal and respiratory passages and causes coughing, sneezing, lacrimation, and sometimes vomiting.

ster•nu•ta•to•ry (stûr-nyōō′tə-tôr′ē, -tōr′ē, -nōō′-) *adj.* Causing or tending to cause sneezing. **—ster•nu′ta•to′ry** *n.*

stern•ward (stûrn′wərd) *adv. & adj. Naut.* Toward, to, or in the stern. **—stern′wards** *adv.*

stern•way (stûrn′wā′) *n. Naut.* The backward movement of a vessel.

stern-wheel•er (stûrn′hwē′lər, -wē′lər) *n. Naut.* A steamboat propelled by a paddle wheel at the stern.

ster•oid (stîr′oid′, stĕr′-) *n.* Any of numerous fat-soluble organic compounds having as a basis 17 carbon atoms arranged in four rings and including sterols, adrenal and sex hormones, and the precursors of certain vitamins. [STER(OL) + -OID.] **—ster′oid′, ste•roi′dal** (stĭ-roid′l, stĕ-) *adj.*

ste•roid•o•gen•e•sis (stĭ-roi′də-jĕn′ĭ-sĭs, stîr′oi-, stĕr′-) *n.* Production of steroids by living organisms. **—ste•roid′o•gen′ic** (-jĕn′ĭk) *adj.*

ster•ol (stîr′ôl′, -ōl′, -ŏl′, stĕr′-) *n.* Any of a group of predominantly unsaturated solid alcohols of the steroid group, such as cholesterol and ergosterol, present in the fatty tissues of plants and animals. [Short for CHOLESTEROL.]

ster•tor (stûr′tər) *n.* A heavy snoring sound in respiration. [NLat. < Lat. *stertere*, to snore.] **—ster′to•rous** *adj.*

stet (stĕt) *v.* **stet•ted, stet•ting, stets.** *—intr.* To direct that a letter, word, or other matter marked for omission or correction be retained. Used in the imperative. *—tr.* To nullify (a correction or deletion) in printed matter. [Lat., third pers. sing. pr. subjunctive of *stāre*, to stand. See **stā-***.]

steth•o•scope (stĕth′ə-skōp′) *n.* Any of various instruments used for listening to sounds produced within the body. [Fr. *stéthoscope* : Gk. *stēthos*, chest + Fr. *-scope*, an instrument for viewing (< Lat. *-scopium*; see -SCOPE).] **—steth′o•scop′ic** (-skŏp′ĭk), **steth′o•scop′i•cal** (-ĭ-kəl) *adj.* **—ste•thos′co•py** (stĕ-thŏs′kə-pē) *n.*

Stet•son (stĕt′sən). A trademark used for a hat having a high crown and wide brim.

Stet•tin (stə-tēn′, shtĕ-). See **Szczecin.**

Steu•ben (stōō′bən, styōō′-, stōō-bĕn′, styōō-, shtoi′bən), Baron **Friedrich Wilhelm Ludolf Gerhard Augustin von.** 1730–94. Prussian-born Amer. Revolutionary military leader who trained the troops under Gen. George Washington.

Steu•ben•ville (stōō′bĭn-vĭl′, styōō′-). A city of E OH on the Ohio R. S of Youngstown; settled in 1797. Pop. 22,125.

ste•ve•dore (stē′vĭ-dôr′, -dōr′) *n.* One who is employed in the loading or unloading of ships. *—tr. & intr.v.* **-dored, -dor•ing, -dores.** To load or unload the cargo of (a ship) or engage in the process of loading or unloading such a vessel. [Sp. *estibador* < *estibar*, to stow < Lat. *stīpāre*, to pack.]

ste•ve•dore's knot (stē′vĭ-dôrz′, -dōrz′) also **stevedore knot** *n. Naut.* A knot tied in the end of a line to prevent it from unreeving.

Ste•vens (stē′vənz), **John Paul.** b. 1920. Amer. jurist; associate justice of the U.S. Supreme Court (since 1975).

Stevens, Nettie Marie. 1861–1912. Amer. cytogeneticist whose studies led to the discovery of the chromosomal determination of sex.

Stevens, Thaddeus. 1792–1868. Amer. politician who led the impeachment proceedings against Andrew Johnson (1868).

Stevens, Wallace. 1879–1955. Amer. poet whose works include "Sunday Morning" (1923).

Ste•ven•son (stē′vən-sən), **Adlai Ewing.** 1835–1914. Vice President of the U.S. (1893–97). His grandson **Adlai Ewing Stevenson** (1900–65) ran unsuccessfully for President in 1952 and 1956.

Stevenson, Robert Louis Balfour. 1850–94. British writer of essays, poetry, and novels, including *Treasure Island* (1883) and *The Strange Case of Dr. Jekyll and Mr. Hyde* (1886).

Stevens Point. A city of central WI S of Wausau. Pop. 23,006.

stew[1] (stōō, styōō) *v.* **stewed, stew•ing, stews.** *—tr.* To cook (food) by boiling slowly. *—intr.* **1.** To undergo cooking by boiling slowly. See Syns at **boil**[1]. **2.** *Informal.* To suffer with oppressive heat or stuffy confinement; swelter. **3.** *Informal.* To be anxious or agitated. See Syns at **brood.** *—n.* **1.a.** A dish cooked by stewing, esp. a mixture of meat or fish and vegetables with stock. **b.** A mixture like this. **2.** *Informal.* Mental agitation. **3.** *Archaic.* A brothel. Often used in the plural. [ME *stewen*, to bathe in a steam bath, stew < OFr. *estuver*, poss. < VLat. **extūpāre*, to bathe, evaporate : Lat. *ex-*, ex- + VLat. **tūfus*, hot vapor (< Gk. *tuphos*, fever; see TYPHUS).] **—stew′y** *adj.*

stew[2] (stōō, styōō) *n. Informal.* A flight attendant.

stew•ard (stōō′ərd, styōō′-) *n.* **1.** One who manages another's property, finances, or other affairs. **2.** One who is in charge of the household affairs of a large estate, club, hotel, or resort. **3.** A ship's officer in charge of provisions and dining arrangements. **4.** An attendant on a ship or an airplane. **5.** An official who supervises or helps to manage an event. **6.** A shop steward. *—intr. & tr.v.* **-ard•ed, -ard•ing, -ards.** To serve as a steward or as the steward of. [ME < OE *stīward* : *stig, stī*, hall + *weard*, keeper; see **wer-**[3]*.] **—stew′ard•ship′** *n.*

stew•ard•ess (stōō′ər-dĭs, styōō′-) *n.* A woman flight attendant. See Usage Note at **-ess.**

Stew•art (stōō′ərt, styōō′-), **Henry.** See Lord **Darnley.**

Stewart, James. b. 1908. Amer. actor whose motion pictures include *It's a Wonderful Life* (1946).

Stewart, Potter. 1915–85. Amer. jurist; associate justice of the U.S. Supreme Court (1958–81).

Stewart, Robert. See Viscount **Castlereagh.**

Stewart Island. A volcanic island of S New Zealand off the S coast of South I.

Stewart River. A river of central Yukon Terr., Canada, flowing c. 533 km (331 mi) to the Yukon R.

stewed (stōōd, styōōd) *adj.* **1.** Cooked by stewing: *stewed prunes.* **2.** *Informal.* Intoxicated; drunk.

St. Ex. *abbr.* Stock Exchange.

stg. *abbr.* Sterling.

stge. *abbr.* Storage.

sthe•ni•a (sthə-nī′ə, sthē′nē-ə) *n.* A condition of bodily strength, vigor, or vitality. [NLat. < Gk. *sthenos*, strength.] **—sthen′ic** (sthĕn′ĭk) *adj.*

stib•ine (stĭb′ēn) *n.* A colorless flammable poisonous gas, SbH_3, often used as a fumigant. [< ME *stibium*, antimony < Lat., var. of *stimi* < Gk. *stibi, stimmi*, of Coptic orig.; akin to Egypt. *stm*.]

stib•nite (stĭb′nīt′) *n.* A lead-gray mineral, Sb_2S_3, that is the chief source of antimony. [Fr. *stibine*, stibnite (< Lat. *stibium*, antimony; see STIBINE) + -ITE[1].]

stich (stĭk) *n.* A line of verse. [Gk. *stikhos*. See **steigh-***.]

stich•ic (stĭk′ĭk) *adj.* Composed of verses in the same meter.

sti•chom•e•try (stĭ-kŏm′ĭ-trē) *n.* The division of prose into lines of fixed length or into lines whose lengths correspond to the natural divisions of sense, as in manuscripts preceding the adoption of punctuation. [Gk. *stikhos*, stich; see **steigh-*** + -METRY.] **—stich′o•met′ric** (stĭk′ə-mĕt′rĭk) *adj.*

stich•o•myth•i•a (stĭk′ə-mĭth′ē-ə) also **sti•chom•y•thy** (stĭ-kŏm′ə-thē) *n.* Alteration between speakers of lines or parts of lines of verse in Greek drama. [Gk. *stikhomuthia* < *stikhomuthein*, to speak in alternating lines : *stikhos*, stich; see **steigh-*** + *muthos*, speech.] **—stich′o•myth′ic** *adj.*

stick (stĭk) *n.* **1.** A long slender piece of wood, esp.: **a.** A branch or stem cut from a tree or shrub. **b.** A piece of wood, such as a tree branch, that is used for fuel, lumber, or another specific purpose. **c.** A wand, staff, baton, or rod. **d.** *Sports & Games.* Any of various implements shaped like a rod and used in play. **2.** A walking stick; a cane. **3.** Something slender and often cylindrical in form. **4.** *Slang.* A marijuana cigarette. **5.a.** The control device of an aircraft that operates the elevators and ailerons. **b.** *Informal.* A stick shift. **6.** *Naut.* A mast or a part of a mast. **7.** *Print.* **a.** A composing stick. **b.** A stickful. **8.** A timber tree. **9.** *Informal.* A piece of furniture. **10.** A poke, thrust, or stab with a stick or similar object. **11.** A threatened penalty. **12.** The condition or power of adhering. **13. sticks.** *Informal.* **a.** A remote area; backwoods. **b.** A city or town regarded as dull or unsophisticated. **14.** *Informal.* A person regarded as stiff, boring, or spiritless. **15.** *Archaic.* A difficulty or an obstacle; a delay. *—v.* **stuck** (stŭk), **stick•ing, sticks.** *—tr.* **1.** To pierce, puncture, or penetrate with a pointed instrument. **2.** To kill by piercing. **3.** To thrust or push (a pointed instrument) into or through another object. **4.** To fasten into place by forcing an end or point into something. **5.** To fasten or attach with or as if with pins, nails, or similar devices. **6.** To fasten or attach with an adhesive material, such as glue. **7.** To cover or decorate with objects piercing the surface. **8.** To fix, impale, or transfix on a pointed object. **9.** To put, thrust, or push: *stuck a flower in his buttonhole.* **10.** To detain or delay. **11.** *p.t. and p.part.* **sticked** (stĭkt). To prop (a plant) with sticks or brush on which to grow. **12.** *p.t. and p.part.* **sticked.** *Print.* To set (type) in a composing stick. **13.** *Informal.* To confuse, baffle, or puzzle. **14.** To cover or smear with something sticky. **15.** *Informal.* To put blame or responsibility on; burden. **16.** *Slang.* To defraud or cheat. *—intr.* **1.** To be or become fixed or embedded in place by having the point thrust in. **2.** To become or remain attached or in close association by or as if by adhesion; cling: *stick together in a crowd.* **3.a.** To remain firm, determined, or resolute. **b.** To remain loyal or faithful. **c.** To persist or endure. **4.** To scruple or hesitate. **5.** To be at or come to a standstill; become fixed, blocked, checked, or obstructed. **6.** To project or protrude: *hair sticking out.* ***—phrasal verbs.*** **stick around.** *Informal.* To remain; linger. **stick out. 1.** To be prominent. **2.** *Informal.* To put up with. **stick up.** To rob, esp. at gunpoint. ***—idioms.*** **be stuck on.** *Informal.* To be very fond of. **stick (one's) neck out.** *Informal.* To make oneself vulnerable; take a risk. **stick to (or by) one's guns.** To hold fast to an opinion or a set course of action. **stick up for.** To defend or support. [ME *stikke* < OE *sticca*. See **steig-***.]

stick•ball (stĭk′bôl′) *n. Sports.* A form of baseball played with a rubber ball and a stick, such as one made from the handle of a broom, for a bat. **—stick′ball′er** *n.*

ă pat	oi boy
ā pay	ou out
âr care	ŏŏ took
ä father	ōō boot
ĕ pet	ŭ cut
ē be	ûr urge
ĭ pit	th thin
ī pie	*th* this
îr pier	hw which
ŏ pot	zh vision
ō toe	ə about, item
ô paw	

Stress marks:
′ (primary);
′ (secondary), as in **dictionary** (dĭk′shə-nĕr′ē)

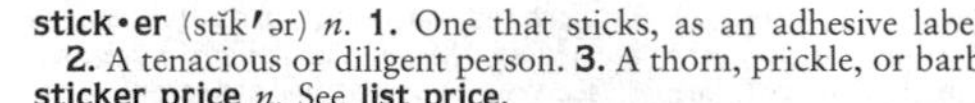

stick•er (stĭk′ər) *n.* **1.** One that sticks, as an adhesive label. **2.** A tenacious or diligent person. **3.** A thorn, prickle, or barb.

sticker price *n.* See **list price.**

stick figure *n.* A picture of a human or animal figure showing the head as a circle and the other body parts as straight lines.

stick•ful (stĭk′fo͝ol′) *n. Print.* The amount of type a composing stick will hold.

stick•han•dle (stĭk′hăn′dl) *intr.v.* **-dled, -dling, -dles.** *Sports.* To move, maneuver, and have control over the puck in ice hockey or the ball in lacrosse and field hockey. **— stick′han′dler** *n.*

stick•ing plaster (stĭk′ĭng) *n.* See **plaster** 3.

sticking point *n.* A point, an issue, or a situation that causes or is likely to cause an impasse.

stick insect *n.* Any of several insects of the family Phasmidae, such as the walking stick, that resemble sticks or twigs.

stick-in-the-mud (stĭk′ĭn-*th*ə-mŭd′) *n., pl.* **stick-in-the-muds.** *Informal.* One without initiative, imagination, or enthusiasm.

stickleback
Three-spine stickleback
Gasterosteus aculeatus

stick•le (stĭk′əl) *intr.v.* **-led, -ling, -les. 1.** To argue or contend stubbornly, esp. about trivial points. **2.** To have or raise objections; scruple. [Var. of ME *stightlen,* to contend, freq. of *stighten,* to arrange < OE *stihtian, stihtan.* See **steigh-*.**]

stick•le•back (stĭk′əl-băk′) *n.* Any of various small freshwater and marine fishes of the family Gasterosteidae, having erectile spines along the back. [ME *stikelbak* : OE *sticel,* prick; see **steig-*** + ME *bak,* back; see BACK[1].]

stick•ler (stĭk′lər) *n.* **1.** One who insists on something unyieldingly. **2.** Something puzzling or difficult.

stick•pin (stĭk′pĭn′) *n.* A decorative pin worn on a necktie.

stick•seed (stĭk′sēd′) *n.* Any of various plants of the genera *Hackelia* or *Lappula,* with clinging barbed fruits.

stick shift *n.* An automotive transmission with a shift lever operated by hand.

stick•tight (stĭk′tīt′) *n.* See **beggar ticks** 1a.

stick-to-it•ive•ness (stĭk-to͞o′ĭ-tĭv-nĭs) *n. Informal.* Unwavering pertinacity; perseverance.

stick•um (stĭk′əm) *n.* An adhesive substance. [STICK + *-um* (var. of 'EM).]

stick•up (stĭk′ŭp′) *n. Slang.* A robbery, esp. at gunpoint. [< the expression *"Stick up your hands!"*]

stick•weed (stĭk′wēd′) *n.* Any of various plants having clinging seeds or fruit, esp. ragweed.

stick•y (stĭk′ē) *adj.* **-i•er, -i•est. 1.** Having the property of adhering or sticking to a surface; adhesive. **2.** Covered with an adhesive agent. **3.** Warm and humid; muggy. **4.** *Informal.* Painful or difficult. **5.** *Econ.* Tending to remain the same despite changes in the economy. Used of prices or wages. **— stick′i•ly** *adv.* **— stick′i•ness** *n.*

sticky wicket *n. Informal.* A difficult or embarrassing problem or situation.

stied (stīd) *v.* P.t. and p.part. of **sty[1].**

Stieg•litz (stēg′lĭts), **Alfred.** 1864–1946. Amer. photographer known for his stark black-and-white images.

sties[1] (stīz) *n.* Pl. of **sty[1].** — *v.* Third pers. sing. pr.t. of **sty[1].**

sties[2] (stīz) *n.* Pl. of **sty[2].**

stiff (stĭf) *adj.* **stiff•er, stiff•est. 1.** Difficult to bend; rigid. **2.a.** Not moving or operating easily or freely; resistant. **b.** Lacking ease or comfort of movement; not limber: *a stiff neck.* **3.** Drawn tightly; taut. **4.a.** Rigidly formal. **b.** Lacking ease or grace. **5.** Not liquid, loose, or fluid; thick. **6.** Firm, as in purpose; resolute. **7.** Having a strong, swift, steady force or movement. **8.** Potent or strong. **9.** Difficult, laborious, or arduous. **10.** Difficult to comprehend or accept; harsh or severe. **11.** Excessively high: *a stiff price.* **12.** *Naut.* Not likely to heel excessively under sail. — *adv.* **1.** In a stiff manner: *frozen stiff.* **2.** To a complete extent; totally. — *n. Slang.* **1.** A corpse. **2.** A person seen as constrained, priggish, or overformal. **3.** A drunk. **4.** A person: *a lucky stiff.* **5.** A hobo; a tramp. **6.** A person who tips poorly. — *tr.v.* **stiffed, stiff•ing, stiffs.** *Slang.* **1.** To tip (someone) inadequately or not at all, as for a service rendered. **2.a.** To cheat (someone) of something owed. **b.** To fail to give or supply (something that is expected or promised). [ME < OE *stīf.*] **— stiff′ish** *adj.* **— stiff′ly** *adv.* **— stiff′ness** *n.*

Syns: *stiff, rigid, inflexible, inelastic, tense.* These adjectives describe what is very firm and does not easily bend or give way. *Stiff,* the least specific, refers to what can be flexed only with difficulty (*a brush with stiff bristles*); with reference to persons it often suggests a lack of ease, cold formality, or fixity, as of purpose: *"stiff in opinions"* (John Dryden). *Rigid* and *inflexible* apply to what cannot be bent without damage or deformation (*an inflexible knife blade*); figuratively they describe what does not relent or yield: *"under the dictates of a rigid disciplinarian"* (Thomas B. Aldrich). *"In religion the law is written, and inflexible, never to do evil"* (Oliver Goldsmith). *Inelastic* refers largely to what will not stretch and spring back without marked physical change: *an inelastic substance. Tense* means stretched tight and figuratively applies to what is marked by tautness or strain: *"that tense moment of expectation"* (Arnold Bennett).

still life
Fruit, 1868, by Paul Lacroix
(active in America
1858–1869)

stiff-arm (stĭf′ärm′) *Football.* — *tr.v.* **-armed, -arm•ing, -arms.** To straight-arm. — *n.* A straight-arm.

stiff•en (stĭf′ən) *tr. & intr.v.* **-ened, -en•ing, -ens.** To make or become stiff or stiffer. **— stiff′en•er** *n.*

stiff-necked (stĭf′nĕkt′) *adj.* Stubborn and arrogant or aloof. See Syns at **obstinate.**

sti•fle[1] (stī′fəl) *v.* **-fled, -fling, -fles.** — *tr.* **1.** To interrupt or cut off (the voice, for example). **2.** To keep in or hold back; repress. **3.** To kill by preventing respiration; smother or suffocate. — *intr.* **1.** To feel smothered or suffocated by or as if by close confinement in a stuffy room. **2.** To die of suffocation. [ME *stifilen,* alteration (influenced by ON *stīfla,* to stop up) of *stuffen, stuflen,* to stifle, choke, drown < OFr. *estoufer,* of Gmc. orig.] **— sti′fler** *n.*

sti•fle[2] (stī′fəl) *n.* The joint of the hind leg analogous to the human knee in certain quadrupeds, such as the horse. [ME, poss. < OFr. *estivel,* pipe, leg, tibia < Lat. *stīpes,* stick.]

sti•fling (stī′flĭng) *adj.* **1.** Very hot or stuffy almost to the point of being suffocating. **2.** Engendering a feeling of stultification, repression, or suffocation. **— sti′fling•ly** *adv.*

stig•ma (stĭg′mə) *n., pl.* **stig•ma•ta** (stĭg-mä′tə, -măt′ə, stĭg′mə-) or **stig•mas. 1.** A mark or token of infamy, disgrace, or reproach. **2.** A small mark; a scar or birthmark. **3.** *Medic.* **a.** A mark or spot on the skin that bleeds as a symptom of hysteria. **b.** A mark or characteristic indicative of a history of a disease or abnormality. **4. stigmata.** Marks or sores corresponding to the wounds of Jesus. **5.** *Biol.* A small mark, spot, or pore, such as an eyespot in certain algae. **6.** *Bot.* The receptive apex of the pistil of a flower, on which pollen is deposited. **7.** *Archaic.* A mark burned into the skin of a criminal or slave; a brand. [ME *stigme,* brand < Lat. *stigma, stigmat-* < Gk., tattoo mark < *stizein, stig-,* to prick. See **steig-*.**] **— stig′mal** *adj.*

stig•mas•ter•ol (stĭg-măs′tə-rôl′, -rōl′) *n.* A sterol, $C_{29}H_{48}O$, obtained from soybeans or Calabar beans. [< NLat. *(Physo)stigma,* Calabar bean genus. See PHYSOSTIGMINE.]

stig•mat•ic (stĭg-măt′ĭk) *adj.* **1.** Relating to, resembling, or having stigmata or a stigma. **2.** Anastigmatic. — *n.* A person marked with religious stigmata. **— stig•mat′i•cal•ly** *adv.*

stig•ma•tism (stĭg′mə-tĭz′əm) *n.* **1.** The condition of being affected by stigmata. **2.** The state of a refracting or reflecting system in which light rays from a single point are accurately focused at another point. **3.** Normal eyesight.

stig•ma•tist (stĭg′mə-tĭst) *n.* A stigmatic.

stig•ma•tize (stĭg′mə-tīz′) *tr.v.* **-tized, -tiz•ing, -tiz•es. 1.** To characterize or brand as disgraceful or ignominious. **2.** To mark with stigmata or a stigma. **3.** To cause stigmata to appear on. [Med.Lat. *stigmatizāre,* to brand < Gk. *stigmatizein,* to mark < *stigma, stigmat-,* tattoo mark. See STIGMA.] **— stig′ma•ti•za′tion** (-tĭ-zā′shən) *n.* **— stig′ma•tiz′er** *n.*

Sti•kine (stĭ-kēn′). A river rising in the **Stikine Mountains** of NW British Columbia, Canada, and flowing c. 539 km (335 mi) through SE AK to the Pacific Ocean.

stil•bene (stĭl′bēn′) *n.* A crystalline compound, $C_{14}H_{12}$, used in dyes and optical bleaches and as a phosphor. [Gk. *stilbos,* shining (< *stilbein,* to shimmer) + -ENE.]

stil•bes•trol (stĭl-bĕs′trôl′, -trōl′, -trŏl′) *n.* DES. [STILB(ENE) + ESTR(US) + -OL[1].]

stil•bite (stĭl′bīt′) *n.* A white or yellow zeolite mineral, $(Ca,Na)_2Al_2Si_7O_{18}\cdot 7H_2O$. [Fr. < Gk. *stilbos,* shining. See STILBENE.]

stile[1] (stīl) *n.* **1.** A set or series of steps for crossing a fence or wall. **2.** A turnstile. [ME < OE *stigel.* See **steigh-*.**]

stile[2] (stīl) *n.* A vertical part of a panel or frame, as in a door. [Prob. < Du. *stijl,* doorpost < MDu., poss. < Lat. *stilus,* pole, post.]

sti•let•to (stĭ-lĕt′ō) *n., pl.* **-tos** or **-toes. 1.a.** A small dagger with a slender tapering blade. **b.** Something shaped like such a dagger. **2.** A small sharp-pointed instrument that makes eyelet holes in needlework. [Ital., dim. of *stilo,* dagger < Lat. *stilus,* stylus, spike.]

stiletto heel *n.* A high heel on women's shoes that is thinner than a spike heel.

still[1] (stĭl) *adj.* **still•er, still•est. 1.** Free of sound. **2.** Low in sound; hushed or subdued. **3.** Not moving or in motion. **4.** Free from disturbance, agitation, or commotion. **5.** Free from a noticeable current: *still waters.* **6.** Not carbonated; lacking effervescence. **7.** Of or relating to a single or static photograph as opposed to a movie. — *n.* **1.** Silence; quiet. **2.** A still photograph, esp. one taken from and used to promote a movie. **3.** A still-life picture. — *adv.* **1.** Without movement; motionlessly. **2.** Up to or at the time indicated; yet. **3.** In increasing amount or degree: *and still further complaints.* **4.** All the same; nevertheless. — *v.* **stilled, still•ing, stills.** — *tr.* **1.** To make still or tranquil. **2.** To make quiet; silence. **3.** To make motionless. **4.** To allay; calm. — *intr.* To become still. [ME < OE *stille.* See **stel-*.**]

still[2] (stĭl) *n.* **1.** An apparatus for distilling liquids consisting of a vessel in which the substance is vaporized by heat and a cooling device in which the vapor is condensed. **2.** A distillery. [< ME *stillen,* to distill < *distillen.* See DISTILL.]

still alarm *n.* A fire alarm transmitted silently, as by telephone, rather than by sounding the conventional signal apparatus.

still and all *adv. Informal.* After taking everything into consideration; nevertheless; however: *Still and all, we may win.*

still•birth (stĭl′bûrth′) *n.* **1.** The birth of a dead child or fetus. **2.** A child or fetus dead at birth.

still•born (stĭl′bôrn′) *adj.* **1.** Dead at birth. **2.** Failing before or at the very beginning or inception; abortive.

still hunt *n.* The hunting of game by stalking or ambushing. **— still′-hunt′** (stĭl′hŭnt′) *v.* **— still′-hunt′er** *n.*

still life *n., pl.* **still lifes. 1.** Representation of inanimate objects, such as fruit, in painting or photography. **2.** Such a representation. **— still′-life′** (stĭl′līf′) *adj.*

still•ness (stĭl′nĭs) *n.* The state or an instance of being quiet.

Still•son (stĭl′sən). A trademark used for a monkey wrench having serrated jaws that tighten as pressure is applied to the handle.

still water *n.* A flat or level section of a stream without discernible water motion or current. **— still′-wa′ter** (stĭl′wô′tər, -wŏt′ər) *adj.*

Still•wa•ter (stĭl′wô′tər, -wŏt′ər). A city of N-central OK NNE of Oklahoma City. Pop. 36,676.

still•y (stĭl′ē) *adj.* **-i•er, -i•est.** Quiet; calm. **— stil′ly** *adv.*

stilt (stĭlt) *n.* **1.** Either of a pair of long slender poles each equipped with a raised footrest to enable the user to walk above the ground. **2.** Any of various tall posts or pillars used as support, as for a dock or building. **3.** *pl.* **stilt** or **stilts. a.** A wide-ranging American wading bird *(Himantopus mexicanus)* with long pink legs, black and white plumage, and a long slender bill. **b.** A related bird *(Cladorhyncus leucocephala)* of Australia. *— tr.v.* **stilt•ed, stilt•ing, stilts.** To place or raise on stilts. [ME *stilte.* See **stel-*.**]

stilt•ed (stĭl′tĭd) *adj.* **1.** Stiffly or artificially formal; stiff. **2.** *Archit.* Having some vertical length between the impost and the beginning of the curve. Used of an arch. **— stilt′ed•ly** *adv.* **— stilt′ed•ness** *n.*

Stil•ton (stĭl′tən) *n.* A rich waxy cheese with a blue-green mold. [After *Stilton,* a village of E-central England.]

Stil•well (stĭl′wĕl′, -wəl), **Joseph Warren.** "Vinegar Joe." 1883–1946. Amer. army officer who commanded Allied forces in China, Burma, and India during World War II.

Stim•son (stĭm′sən), **Henry Lewis.** 1867–1950. Amer. public official who served as U.S. secretary of state (1929–33) and secretary of war (1940–45).

stim•u•lant (stĭm′yə-lənt) *n.* **1.** An agent, esp. a chemical agent such as caffeine, that temporarily arouses or accelerates physiological or organic activity. **2.** A stimulus or an incentive. **3.** A food or drink believed to have a stimulating effect. *— adj.* Serving as a stimulus; stimulating.

stim•u•late (stĭm′yə-lāt′) *v.* **-lat•ed, -lat•ing, -lates.** *— tr.* **1.** To rouse to activity or heightened action, as by spurring; excite. **2.** To increase temporarily the activity of (a body part). **3.** To excite or invigorate (a person, for example) with a stimulant. *— intr.* To act as a stimulant or stimulus. [Lat. *stimulāre, stimulāt-,* to goad on < *stimulus,* goad.] **— stim′u•lat′er, stim′u•la′tor** *n.* **— stim′u•la′tion** *n.* **— stim′u•la′tive, stim′u•la•to′ry** (-lə-tôr′ē, -tōr′ē) *adj.*

stim•u•lus (stĭm′yə-ləs) *n., pl.* **-li** (-lī′). **1.** Something causing or regarded as causing a response. **2.** An agent, an action, or a condition that elicits or accelerates a physiological or psychological activity or response. **3.** Something that incites or rouses to action; an incentive. [Latin, goad.]

sting (stĭng) *v.* **stung** (stŭng), **sting•ing, stings.** *— tr.* **1.** To pierce or wound painfully with or as if with a sharp-pointed structure or organ, as that of certain insects. **2.** To cause to feel a sharp smarting pain by or as if by pricking with a sharp point. **3.** To cause to suffer keenly in the mind or feelings. **4.** To spur on by or as if by sharp irritation. **5.** *Slang.* To cheat or overcharge. *— intr.* **1.** To have, use, or wound with or as if with a sharp-pointed structure or organ, as that of certain insects. **2.** To cause or feel a sharp smarting pain. *— n.* **1.** The act of stinging. **2.** The wound or pain caused by or as if by stinging. **3.** A sharp piercing organ or part, often ejecting a venomous secretion, as the modified ovipositor of a bee. **4.** A stinging power, quality, or capacity. **5.** A keen stimulus or incitement; a goad or spur. **6.** *Slang.* A complicated confidence game planned and executed with great care, esp. an operation organized and implemented by undercover agents to apprehend criminals. [ME *stingen* < OE *stingan.* See **stegh-*.**]

sting•er (stĭng′ər) *n.* **1.** One that stings, esp. mentally. **2.** A stinging organ or part. **3.** A sharp blow. **4.** *Slang.* One who participates in or organizes the operation of a sting. **5.** A cocktail of crème de menthe and brandy.

sting•ing hair (stĭng′ĭng) *n.* A glandular plant hair that expels an irritating fluid.

sting•ray (stĭng′rā′) *n.* Any of various rays of the family Dasyatidae, having a whiplike tail armed with one or more venomous spines capable of inflicting severe injury.

stin•gy (stĭn′jē) *adj.* **-gi•er, -gi•est. 1.** Giving or spending reluctantly. **2.** Scanty or meager: *a stingy meal.* [Perh. alteration of dial. *stingy,* stinging < STING.] **— stin′gi•ly** *adv.* **— stin′gi•ness** *n.*

stink (stĭngk) *v.* **stank** (stăngk) or **stunk** (stŭngk), **stunk, stink•ing, stinks.** *— intr.* **1.** To emit a strong foul odor. **2.a.** To be highly offensive or abhorrent. **b.** To be in extremely bad repute. **3.** *Slang.* To have something to an extreme or offensive degree. **4.** *Slang.* To be of an extremely low or bad quality. *— tr.* To cause to stink: *garbage that stinks up the yard.* *— n.* A strong offensive odor; a stench. ***— idiom.* make (or raise) a stink.** *Slang.* To make a great fuss. [ME *stinken* < OE *stincan,* to emit a smell.] **— stink′y** *adj.*

stink bomb *n.* A small bomb, often in the form of a capsule, that emits a foul odor on detonation.

stink•bug (stĭngk′bŭg′) *n.* Any of numerous hemipterous insects of the family Pentatomidae, having a broad flattened body and emitting a foul odor.

stink•er (stĭng′kər) *n. Slang.* **1.** One seen as irritating, disgusting, or contemptible. **2.** *Slang.* Something very difficult.

stink•er•oo also **stink•a•roo** (stĭng′kə-ro͞o′, stĭng′kə-ro͞o′) *n., pl.* **-er•oos** also **-a•roos.** *Slang.* One that is contemptible, disgusting, irritating, or very bad. [< STINKER.]

stink•horn (stĭngk′hôrn′) *n.* Any of several foul-smelling fungi of the order Phallales, such as *Phallus impudicus* or *P. ravenelii,* having a thick cylindrical stalk and a narrow cap.

stink•ing (stĭng′kĭng) *adj.* **1.** Having a foul smell; fetid. **2.** *Slang.* Very drunk. *— adv. Slang.* Used as an intensive: *stinking rich.* **— stink′ing•ly** *adv.* **— stink′ing•ness** *n.*

stink•o (stĭng′kō) *adj. Slang.* **1.** Very drunk. **2.** Of poor or inferior quality. [< STINK.]

stink•pot (stĭngk′pŏt′) *n.* **1.** *Slang.* One who is despised. **2.** A small musk turtle *(Sternotherus odoratus)* of the eastern and southern United States. **3.** *Slang.* A motorboat. **4.** An earthenware jar with combustibles emitting a suffocating smoke, once used in naval warfare.

stink stone also **stink•stone** (stĭngk′stōn′) *n.* A variety of limestone that emits a disagreeable odor when struck or rubbed.

stink•weed (stĭngk′wēd′) *n.* Any of various plants that have flowers or foliage with an unpleasant odor.

stink•wood (stĭngk′wo͝od′) *n.* **1.a.** A southern African deciduous tree *(Ocotea bullata)* having wood with an unpleasant odor. **b.** The hard heavy wood of this tree. **2.** Any of several trees having wood with an unpleasant odor.

stint[1] (stĭnt) *v.* **stint•ed, stint•ing, stints.** *— tr.* **1.** To restrict or limit, as in amount; be sparing with. **2.** *Archaic.* To stop. *— intr.* **1.** To subsist on a meager allowance; be frugal. **2.** *Archaic.* To stop or desist. *— n.* **1.** A fixed amount of work allotted. See Syns at **task. 2.** A limit or restriction. [ME *stinten,* to cease < OE *styntan,* to blunt.] **— stint′er** *n.*

stint[2] (stĭnt) *n.* Any of several small sandpipers of the genera *Erolia* or *Calidris* of northern regions. [ME *stint* < OE.]

stipe (stīp) *n. Bot.* A supporting stalk or stemlike structure, esp. the stalk of a pistil, the petiole of a fern frond, or the stalk that supports the cap of a mushroom. [Fr. < Lat. *stīpes,* post.]

sti•pel (stī′pəl, stī-pĕl′) *n. Bot.* A minute stipule at the base of a leaflet. [NLat. *stipella,* dim. of *stipula,* stipule. See STIPULE.] **— sti•pel′late** (stī-pĕl′ĭt, stī′pə-lāt′) *adj.*

sti•pend (stī′pĕnd′, -pənd) *n.* A fixed and regular payment, such as a salary for services rendered. [ME *stipendie* < OFr. < Lat. *stīpendium,* soldier's pay < **stipipendium* : *stips, stip-,* a small payment + *pendere,* to weigh, pay; see SUSPEND.]

sti•pen•di•ar•y (stī-pĕn′dē-ĕr′ē) *adj.* **1.** Receiving a stipend. **2.** Compensated by stipend: *stipendiary services.* *— n., pl.* **-ies.** A recipient of a stipend.

sti•pes (stī′pēz) *n., pl.* **stip•i•tes** (stĭp′ĭ-tēz′). **1.** The basal segment of the maxilla of an insect or a crustacean. **2.** *Bot.* A stalklike support or structure; a stipe. [NLat. *stīpes, stīpit-* < Lat., post.] **— sti′pi•form′** (stī′pə-fôrm′), **stip′i•ti•form′** (stĭp′ĭ-tə-) *adj.*

stip•ple (stĭp′əl) *tr.v.* **-pled, -pling, -ples. 1.** To draw, engrave, or paint in dots or short strokes. **2.** To apply (paint, for example) in dots or short strokes. **3.** To dot, fleck, or speckle. *— n.* **1.** A method of drawing, engraving, or painting using dots or short strokes. **2.** The effect thus produced or a similar appearance. [Du. *stippelen,* freq. of *stippen,* to speckle < *stip,* dot < MDu.] **— stip′pler** *n.*

stip•u•lar (stĭp′yə-lər) *adj.* Of, relating to, or resembling a stipule.

stip•u•late[1] (stĭp′yə-lāt′) *v.* **-lat•ed, -lat•ing, -lates.** *— tr.* **1.a.** To lay down as a condition of an agreement; require by contract. **b.** To specify or arrange in an agreement: *stipulate a price.* **2.** To guarantee or promise (something) in an agreement. *— intr.* **1.** To make an express demand or provision in an agreement. **2.** To form an agreement. [Lat. *stipulārī, stipulāt-,* to bargain.] **— stip′u•la′tor** *n.*

stip•u•late[2] (stĭp′yə-lĭt) *adj. Bot.* Having stipules.

stip•u•la•tion (stĭp′yə-lā′shən) *n.* **1.** The act of stipulating. **2.** Something stipulated, esp. a term or condition in an agreement. **— stip′u•la•to′ry** (-lə-tôr′ē, -tōr′ē) *adj.*

stip•ule (stĭp′yo͞ol) *n. Bot.* One of the usu. small paired appendages at the base of a leafstalk in certain plants, such as roses. [NLat. *stipula* < Lat., stalk. See STUBBLE.]

stir[1] (stûr) *v.* **stirred, stir•ring, stirs.** *— tr.* **1.a.** To pass an implement through (a liquid, for example) in circular motions so as to mix or cool the contents. **b.** To introduce (an ingredient, for example) into a liquid or mixture. **c.** To mix to-

stilt
A pair of stilts

stinkbug
Harlequin stinkbug
Murgantia histrionica

ă pat	oi boy
ā pay	ou out
âr care	o͝o took
ä father	o͞o boot
ĕ pet	ŭ cut
ē be	ûr urge
ĭ pit	th thin
ī pie	*th* this
îr pier	hw which
ŏ pot	zh vision
ō toe	ə about, item
ô paw	

Stress marks:
′ (primary);
′ (secondary), as in
dictionary (dĭk′shə-nĕr′ē)

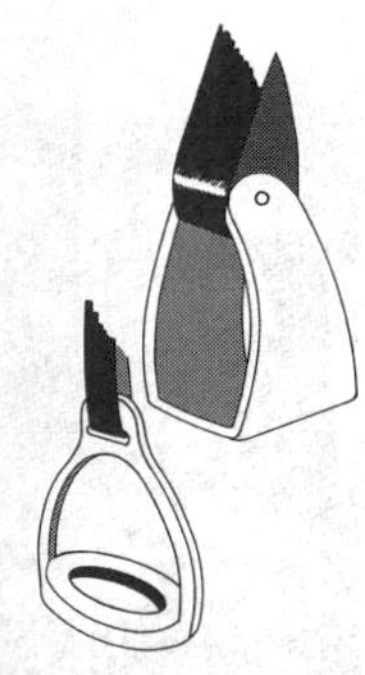

stirrup
Top: Western
Bottom: English

stocks

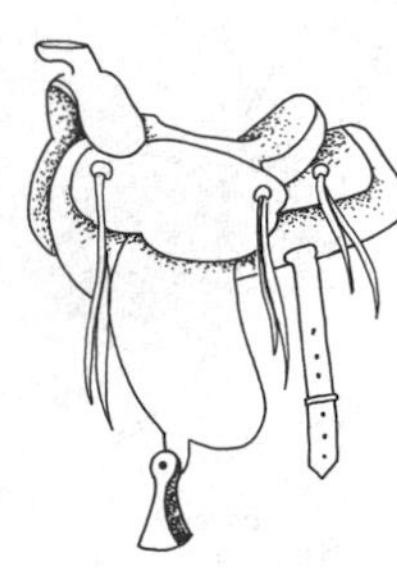

stock saddle

stole¹
Ecclesiastical stole

gether the ingredients of before cooking or use. **2.** To alter the placement of slightly; disarrange. **3.** To cause to move briskly or vigorously; bestir. **4.a.** To rouse, as from indifference, and prompt to action. **b.** To provoke deliberately. **5.** To excite strong feelings in. —*intr.* **1.** To change position slightly. **2.a.** To move about actively; bestir oneself. **b.** To move away from a customary or usual place or position. **3.** To take place; happen. **4.** To be capable of being stirred. **5.** To be roused or affected by strong feelings. —*n.* **1.** A stirring, mixing, or poking movement. **2.** A slight movement. **3.** A disturbance or commotion. **4.** An excited reaction. [ME *stiren* < OE *styrian,* to excite, agitate.] —**stir′rer** *n.*

stir² (stûr) *n. Slang.* Prison. [?]

stir-cra•zy (stûr′krā′zē) *adj. Informal.* Distraught or restless from long confinement in or as if in prison.

stir-fry (stûr′frī′) *tr.v.* **-fried** (-frīd′), **-fry•ing, -fries** (-frīz′). To fry quickly in a small amount of oil over high heat while stirring continuously. —*n.* Stir-fried food.

stirk (stûrk) *n. Chiefly British.* A heifer or bullock, esp. between one and two years old. [ME < OE *stirc.* See **stā-***.]

Stir•ling (stûr′lĭng). A borough of central Scotland on the Forth R.; birthplace of James II. Pop. 38,400.

stirps (stûrps) *n., pl.* **stir•pes** (stûr′pēz). **1.** A line of descendants of common ancestry; stock. **2.** *Law.* A person from whom a family is descended. [Lat., stem, lineage.]

stir•ring (stûr′ĭng) *adj.* **1.** Exciting strong feelings, as of inspiration; rousing. **2.** Active; lively. —*n.* A slight motion or moving about. —**stir′ring•ly** *adv.*

stir•rup (stûr′əp, stĭr′-) *n.* **1.** A flat-based loop or ring hung from either side of a horse's saddle to support the rider's foot. **2.** A part or device shaped like an inverted U in which something is supported, held, or fixed. **3.** *Naut.* A rope on a ship that hangs from a yard and has an eye at the end through which a footrope is passed for support. [ME *stirope* < OE *stigrāp* : *stīgan,* to mount; see **steigh-*** + *rāp,* rope.]

stirrup bone *n.* See **stapes.**

stir•rup-cup (stûr′əp-kŭp′, stĭr′-) *n.* A farewell drink, esp. for a rider who is mounted to depart.

stirrup leather *n.* The strap fastening a stirrup to a saddle.

stitch (stĭch) *n.* **1.** A single complete movement of a threaded needle in sewing or surgical suturing. **2.a.** A single loop of yarn around an implement such as a knitting needle. **b.** The link, loop, or knot made in this way. **3.** A mode of arranging the threads in sewing, knitting, or crocheting: *a purl stitch.* **4.** A sudden sharp pain, esp. in the side. **5.** *Informal.* An article of clothing. **6.** *Informal.* The least part; a bit. **7.** A ridge between two furrows. —*v.* **stitched, stitch•ing, stitch•es.** —*tr.* **1.a.** To fasten or join with or as if with stitches. **b.** To mend or repair with stitches: *stitched up the tear.* **2.** To decorate or ornament with or as if with stitches. **3.** To fasten together with staples or thread. —*intr.* To make stitches; sew. —***idiom.*** **in stitches.** *Informal.* Laughing uncontrollably. [ME *stiche* < OE *stice,* sting. See **steig-***.] —**stitch′er** *n.*

stitch•er•y (stĭch′ə-rē) *n.* Needlework; sewing.

stitch•wort (stĭch′wûrt′, -wôrt′) *n.* Any of several low-growing plants of the genus *Stellaria,* having opposite leaves and star-shaped flowers. [ME < OE *sticwyrt,* agrimony : *stice,* side pain; see STITCH + *wyrt,* plant; see WORT¹.]

stith•y (stĭth′ē, stĭth′ē) *n., pl.* **-ies. 1.** An anvil. **2.** A forge or smithy. [ME *stethi* < ON *stedhi.* See **stā-***.]

sti•ver (stī′vər) *n.* **1.** A nickel coin used in the Netherlands and worth 1/20 of a guilder. **2.** Something of small value. [Du. *stuiver* < MDu. *stuyver.*]

stk. *abbr.* Stock.

S.T.M. *abbr. Lat.* Sacrae Theologiae Magister (Master of Sacred Theology).

sto•a (stō′ə) *n., pl.* **sto•as** or **sto•ae** (stō′ē′). An ancient Greek covered walk or colonnade, usu. having columns on one side and a wall on the other. [Gk., porch. See **stā-***.]

stoat (stōt) *n., pl.* **stoat** or **stoats.** *Chiefly British.* The ermine, esp. when in its brown color phase. [ME *stote.*]

stob (stŏb) *n. Chiefly Southern U.S.* A short straight piece of wood. [ME, stump, var. of *stubbe, stub.* See STUB.]

sto•chas•tic (stō-kăs′tĭk) *adj.* **1.** Of, relating to, or marked by conjecture; conjectural. **2.** *Statistics.* **a.** Involving or containing a random variable or variables: *stochastic calculus.* **b.** Involving chance or probability. [Gk. *stokhastikos* < *stokhastēs,* diviner < *stokhazesthai,* to guess at < *stokhos,* aim, goal. See **stegh-***.] —**sto•chas′ti•cal•ly** *adv.*

stock (stŏk) *n.* **1.** A supply accumulated for future use; a store. **2.** The total merchandise kept on hand, as by a commercial establishment or warehouse. **3.** All the animals kept or raised on a farm; livestock. **4.a.** The capital or fund that a corporation raises by selling shares entitling the stockholder to dividends and other rights of ownership. **b.** The number of shares that each stockholder possesses. **c.** The part of a tally or record of account formerly given to a creditor. **d.** A debt symbolized by a tally. **5.** The trunk or main stem of a tree or another plant. **6.a.** A plant or stem onto which a graft is made. **b.** A plant or tree from which cuttings and slips are taken. **7.a.** The original progenitor of a family line. **b.** The descendants of a common ancestor; a family line, esp. of a specified character: *comes from farming stock.* **c.** Ancestry or lineage; antecedents. **d.** The type from which a group of animals or plants has descended. **e.** A race, family, or other related group of animals or plants. **f.** An ethnic group or other major division of the human race. **g.** A group of related languages or families of languages. **8.** The raw material out of which something is made. **9.** The broth in which meat, fish, bones, or vegetables are simmered, used as a base for soup, gravy, or sauces. **10.a.** A main upright part, esp. a supporting structure or block. **b. stocks.** *Naut.* The timber frame that supports a ship during construction. **c.** A frame in which an animal is held for shoeing or for veterinary treatment. Often used in the plural. **11. stocks.** A former punitive device consisting of a heavy timber frame with holes for confining the ankles and sometimes the wrists. **12.** *Naut.* A crosspiece at the end of the shank of an anchor. **13.** The wooden block from which a bell is suspended. **14.a.** The rear handle or support of a rifle, a pistol, or an automatic weapon, to which the barrel and mechanism are attached. **b.** The long supporting structure and mooring beam of field-gun carriages that trails along the ground to provide stability and support. **15.** A handle, such as that of various carpentry tools. **16.** The frame of a plow, to which the share, coulter, and other parts are fastened. **17.a.** A theatrical stock company. **b.** The repertoire of such a company. **c.** A theater or theatrical activity, esp. outside of a main theatrical center. **18.** *Bot.* Any of several Eurasian and Mediterranean plants of the genus *Matthiola* in the mustard family, esp. *M. incana,* having variously colored flower clusters. **19.** *Games.* The portion of a card deck or of a domino set that is not dealt out but is drawn from during a game. **20.** *Geol.* A body of intrusive igneous rock of which less than 100 square kilometers (40 square miles) is exposed. **21.** *Zool.* A compound organism. **22.a.** Personal reputation or status. **b.** Confidence or credence. **23.a.** A long white neckcloth worn as part of a formal riding habit. **b.** A broad scarf worn around the neck, esp. by certain clerics. **24.** Rolling stock. —*v.* **stocked, stock•ing, stocks.** —*tr.* **1.** To provide or furnish with a stock of something, esp.: **a.** To supply (a shop) with merchandise. **b.** To supply (a farm) with livestock. **c.** To fill (a stream, for example) with fish. **2.** To keep for future sale or use. **3.** *Obsolete.* To put (someone) in the stocks as a punishment. —*intr.* **1.** To gather and lay in a supply of something: *stock up on canned goods.* **2.** To put forth new shoots. Used of a plant. —*adj.* **1.** Kept regularly in stock. **2.** Repeated often without any thought or originality; routine. **3.** Employed in dealing with stock or merchandise. **4.a.** Of or relating to the raising of livestock. **b.** Used for breeding. **5.a.** Of or relating to a stock company or its repertoire. **b.** Of or being a conventional character or situation in literary or cinematic works. —***idioms.*** **in stock.** Available for sale or use. **out of stock.** Not available for sale or use. [ME *stok* < OE *stocc,* tree trunk.] —**stock′age** *n.* —**stock′er** *n.*

stock•ade (stŏ-kād′) *n.* **1.** A defensive barrier made of strong posts or timbers driven upright side by side into the ground. **2.a.** A similar fenced or enclosed area, esp. one for protection. **b.** A jail on a military base. —*tr.v.* **-ad•ed, -ad•ing, -ades.** To fortify, protect, or surround with a stockade. [Obsolete Fr. *estocade* < Sp. *estacada* < *estaca,* stake, of Gmc. orig.]

stock•breed•ing (stŏk′brē′dĭng) *n.* The breeding and raising of livestock. —**stock′breed′er** *n.*

Stock•bridge (stŏk′brĭj′) *n.* A subtribe of the Mahican confederacy formerly inhabiting southwest Massachusetts, with a present-day population in central Wisconsin.

stock•bro•ker (stŏk′brō′kər) *n.* One that acts as an agent in the buying and selling of stocks or other securities; a broker. —**stock′bro′ker•age** *n.* —**stock′brok′ing** *n.*

stock car *n.* **1.** *Sports.* An automobile of a standard make modified for racing. **2.** A railroad car for carrying livestock.

stock certificate *n.* A certificate establishing ownership of a stated number of shares in a corporation's stock.

stock company *n.* **1.** A company or corporation whose capital is divided into shares. **2.** A permanent company that performs a repertoire of plays, usu. at a single theater.

stock dove (dŭv) *n.* An Old World bird *(Columba oenas)* having grayish plumage. [Prob. < living in tree trunks.]

stock exchange *n.* **1.** A place where stocks, bonds, or other securities are bought and sold. **2.** An association of stockbrokers who meet to trade stocks and bonds according to fixed regulations.

stock•fish (stŏk′fĭsh′) *n., pl.* **stockfish** or **-fish•es.** A fish, such as a cod, cured by being split and air-dried without salt. [ME *stokfish,* transl. of MDu. *stocvisch* : *stoc,* tree limb (perh. < its being dried on wooden racks) + *vische,* fish.]

stock•hold•er (stŏk′hōl′dər) *n.* One who owns a share or shares of stock in a company. —**stock′hold′ing** *n.*

Stock•holm (stŏk′hōlm′, -hōm′). The cap. of Sweden, in the E part on the Baltic Sea; founded in the mid-13th cent. Pop. 653,455.

stock•i•nette also **stock•i•net** (stŏk′ə-nĕt′) *n.* An elastic knitted fabric used esp. in making undergarments, bandages, and babies' clothes. [Alteration of *stocking net.*]

stockinette stitch *n.* A knitting pattern made by alternating rows of plain stitches and purl stitches.
stock•ing (stŏk′ĭng) *n.* **1.** A close-fitting, usu. knitted covering for the foot and leg. **2.** An item resembling this covering. [< dial. *stock* < ME *stokke*, leg covering, prob. < *stok*, stock. See STOCK.] **—stock′inged** *adj.*
stocking cap *n.* A close-fitting knitted cap that resembles a stocking and often has a long tapering tail with a tassel.
stock-in-trade also **stock in trade** (stŏk′ĭn-trād′, stŏk′ĭn-trād′) *n.* **1.** All the merchandise and equipment kept on hand and used in carrying on a business. **2.** The resources available to and habitually used by a person in a given situation.
stock•job•ber (stŏk′jŏb′ər) *n. Chiefly British.* A stock-exchange operator who deals only with brokers. **—stock′-job′ber•y** *n.*
stock•man (stŏk′mən) *n.* **1.** A man who owns or raises livestock. **2.** A man who is in charge of livestock or works on a stock farm. **3.** A man who is employed in a stockroom or warehouse.
stock market *n.* **1.** See **stock exchange. 2.** The business transacted at a stock exchange. **3.** The prices offered for stocks and bonds in general. **—stock′-mar′ket** (stŏk′mär′kĭt) *adj.*
stock•own•er (stŏk′ō′nər) *n.* See **stockholder.**
stock•pile (stŏk′pīl′) *n.* A supply stored for future use, usu. carefully accrued and maintained. **—***tr.v.* **-piled, -pil•ing, -piles.** To stock a supply of for future use. **—stock′pil′er** *n.*
Stock•port (stŏk′pôrt′, -pōrt′). A borough of NW England S of Manchester; chartered 1220. Pop. 291,000.
stock•pot (stŏk′pŏt′) *n.* **1.** A pot used for preparing soup stock. **2.** A rich supply or resource.
stock•room also **stock room** (stŏk′ro͞om′, -ro͝om′) *n.* A room in which a store of goods or materials is kept.
stock saddle *n.* A large, heavy, often ornamented saddle with a raised curved pommel originally used on cattle ranches in the West and Southwest.
stock-still (stŏk′stĭl′) *adj.* Completely still; motionless.
stock•tak•ing (stŏk′tā′kĭng) *n.* **1.** A reappraisal of a situation, a person, or one's own position or prospects. **2.** The act or process of inventorying stock.
Stock•ton (stŏk′tən). A city of central CA on the San Joaquin R. S of Sacramento; settled in 1848. Pop. 210,943.
Stock•ton-on-Tees (stŏk′tən-ŏn-tēz′, -ôn-). A borough of NE England WNW of Middlesbrough. Pop. 172,600.
stock•y (stŏk′ē) *adj.* **-i•er, -i•est. 1.** Solidly built; sturdy. **2.** Chubby; plump. **—stock′i•ly** *adv.* **—stock′i•ness** *n.*
stock•yard (stŏk′yärd′) *n.* A large enclosed yard, usu. with pens or stables, in which livestock, such as cattle or pigs, are temporarily kept until slaughtered, sold, or shipped elsewhere.
stodg•y (stŏj′ē) *adj.* **-i•er, -i•est. 1.a.** Dull, unimaginative, and commonplace. **b.** Prim or pompous; stuffy. **2.** Indigestible and starchy; heavy: *stodgy food.* **3.** Solidly built; stocky. [< *stodge*, thick filling food < *stodge*, to cram.] **—stodg′i•ly** *adv.* **—stodg′i•ness** *n.*
sto•gy or **sto•gie** (stō′gē) *n., pl.* **-gies. 1.** A cheap cigar. **2.** A rough heavy shoe or boot. [After *Conestoga* in SE PA.]
sto•ic (stō′ĭk) *n.* **1.** One who is seemingly indifferent to or unaffected by joy, grief, pleasure, or pain. **2. Stoic.** *Philos.* A member of a Greek school of philosophy, founded by Zeno about 308 B.C., believing that human beings should be free from passion and should calmly accept all occurrences as the unavoidable result of divine will or the natural order. **—***adj.* also **sto•i•cal** (-ĭ-kəl). Seemingly indifferent to or unaffected by pleasure or pain; impassive. [ME *Stoic*, a Stoic < Lat. *Stōicus* < Gk. *Stōikos* < *stoa (poikilē)*, (Painted) Porch, where Zeno taught. See **stā-*.**] **—sto′i•cal•ly** *adv.* **—sto′-i•cal•ness** *n.*
stoi•chi•om•e•try (stoi′kē-ŏm′ĭ-trē) *n.* **1.** Calculation of the quantities of reactants and products in a chemical reaction. **2.** The quantitative relationship between reactants and products in a chemical reaction. [Gk. *stoikheion*, element; see **steigh-*** + -METRY.] **—stoi′chi•o•met′ric** (-ə-mĕt′rĭk) *adj.* **—stoi′chi•o•met′ri•cal•ly** *adv.*
sto•i•cism (stō′ĭ-sĭz′əm) *n.* **1.** Indifference to pleasure or pain; impassiveness. **2. Stoicism.** *Philos.* The doctrines or philosophy of the Stoics.
stoke (stōk) *v.* **stoked, stok•ing, stokes. —***tr.* **1.** To stir up and feed (a fire or furnace). **2.** To feed fuel to and tend the fire of (a furnace). **—***intr.* **1.** To stoke a furnace or fire. **2.** *Informal.* To eat steadily and in large quantities.
stoke•hold (stōk′hōld′) *n. Naut.* The area or compartment into which a ship's furnaces or boilers open.
stoke•hole (stōk′hōl′) *n.* **1.** The space about the opening in a furnace or boiler. **2.** *Naut.* A stokehold.
Stoke-on-Trent (stōk′ŏn-trĕnt′, -ôn-). A borough of W-central England S of Manchester. Pop. 250,700.
Stoke Po•ges (stōk pō′jĭs). A village of SE-central England W of London; thought to be the setting for Thomas Gray's *Elegy Written in a Country Churchyard* (published 1751).
stok•er (stō′kər) *n.* **1.** One who is employed to feed fuel to and tend a furnace, as on a steam locomotive or a steamship. **2.** A mechanical device for feeding coal to a furnace. [Du. < *stoken*, to stoke < MDu. *stōken*, to poke.]
Sto•ker (stō′kər), **Abraham ("Bram").** 1847–1912. British writer of the gothic horror novel *Dracula* (1897).
Sto•kow•ski (stə-kôv′skē, -kôf′-, -kou′-), **Leopold Antoni Stanislaw.** 1882–1977. British-born Amer. conductor of the Philadelphia Orchestra (1914–36).
STOL *abbr.* Short takeoff and landing.
stole[1] (stōl) *n.* **1.** *Eccles.* A long scarf, usu. of embroidered silk or linen, worn over the left shoulder by deacons and over both shoulders by priests and bishops while officiating. **2.** A woman's long scarf worn about the shoulders. **3.** A long robe or outer garment worn by matrons in ancient Rome. [ME < OE < Lat. *stola*, garment, robe < Gk. *stolē*. See **stel-*.**]
stole[2] (stōl) *v.* P.t. of **steal.**
sto•len (stō′lən) *v.* P.part. of **steal.**
stol•id (stŏl′ĭd) *adj.* **-er, -est.** Having or revealing little emotion or sensibility; impassive. [Lat. *stolidus*, unmoving, stupid. See **stel-*.**] **—sto•lid′i•ty** (stə-lĭd′ĭ-tē, stə-), **stol′id•ness** (stŏl′ĭd-nĭs) *n.* **—stol′id•ly** *adv.*
stol•len (stō′lən) *n., pl.* **stollen** or **-lens.** A rich yeast bread containing raisins, citron, and chopped nutmeats. [Ger., prop, support, stollen. See STULL.]
sto•lon (stō′lŏn′, -lən) *n.* **1.** *Bot.* A shoot that bends to the ground or grows horizontally above the ground and produces roots and shoots at the nodes. **2.** *Zool.* A stemlike structure of certain colonial organisms from which new individuals arise by budding. [Lat. *stolō, stolōn-*, shoot. See **stel-*.**] **—sto′lon•ate′** (-lə-nāt′) *adj.*
sto•lon•if•er•ous (stō′lə-nĭf′ər-əs) *adj.* Bearing or forming stolons. **—sto′lon•if′er•ous•ly** *adv.*
sto•ma (stō′mə) *n., pl.* **-ma•ta** (-mə-tə) or **-mas. 1.** *Bot.* One of the minute pores in the epidermis of a leaf or stem through which gases and water vapor pass. **2.** *Anat.* A small aperture in the surface of a membrane. **3.** A surgically constructed opening, esp. one in the abdominal wall that permits the passage of waste after a colostomy or an ileostomy. **4.** *Zool.* A mouthlike opening, such as the oral cavity of a nematode. [NLat. < Gk., mouth.]
stom•ach (stŭm′ək) *n.* **1.a.** The enlarged saclike portion of the alimentary canal, one of the principal organs of digestion, located in vertebrates between the esophagus and the small intestine. **b.** A similar digestive structure of many invertebrates. **c.** Any of the four compartments into which the stomach of a ruminant is divided. **2.** The abdomen or belly. **3.** An appetite for food. **4.** A desire or inclination, esp. for something difficult or unpleasant. **5.** Courage; spirit. **6.** *Obsolete.* Pride. **—***tr.v.* **-ached, -ach•ing, -achs. 1.** To bear; tolerate. **2.** *Obsolete.* To resent. [ME < OFr. *stomaque, estomac* < Lat. *stomachus* < Gk. *stomakhos* < *stoma*, mouth.]
stom•ach•ache (stŭm′ək-āk′) *n.* Pain in the stomach or abdomen.
stom•ach•er (stŭm′ə-kər) *n.* A heavily embroidered or jeweled garment formerly worn over the chest and stomach.
sto•mach•ic (stə-măk′ĭk) *adj.* **1.** Of or relating to the stomach; gastric. **2.** Beneficial to or stimulating digestion in the stomach. **—***n.* An agent, such as a medicine, that strengthens or stimulates the stomach. **—sto•mach′i•cal•ly** *adv.*
stomach pump *n.* A suction pump with a flexible tube inserted into the stomach through the mouth and esophagus to empty the stomach in an emergency, as in a case of poisoning.
sto•ma•tal (stō′mə-təl) *adj.* Of, relating to, resembling, or having a stoma.
sto•mate (stō′māt′) *n. Bot.* See **stoma** 1. [Perh. back-formation < STOMATA.]
sto•mat•ic (stō-măt′ĭk) *adj.* **1.** Of or relating to the mouth. **2.** Of, having, or resembling a stoma.
sto•ma•ti•tis (stō′mə-tī′tĭs) *n.* Inflammation of the mucous tissue of the mouth.
stomato– or **stomat–** *pref.* Mouth; stoma: *stomatitis.* [< Gk. *stoma, stomat-*, mouth.]
sto•mat•o•pod (stō-măt′ə-pŏd′) *n.* Any of various marine crustaceans of the order Stomatopoda, which includes the squilla. [< NLat. *Stomatopoda*, order name : STOMATO– + –POD.]
sto•ma•tous (stō′mə-təs) *adj.* Of, having, or like a stoma.
–stome *suff.* Mouth; stoma: *peristome.* [< Gk. *stoma*, mouth.]
sto•mo•de•um also **sto•mo•dae•um** (stō′mə-dē′əm) *n., pl.* **-de•a** also **-dae•a** (-dē′ə). The anterior or oral portion of the alimentary canal of an embryo. [NLat. : Gk. *stoma*, mouth + Gk. *hodaios*, on the way (< *hodos*, road).]
stomp (stŏmp, stômp) *v.* **stomped, stomp•ing, stomps. —***tr.* To tread or trample heavily or violently on. **—***intr.* To tread or trample heavily or violently. **—***n.* **1.** A dance involving a rhythmic heavy step. **2.** The jazz music for this dance. [Var. of STAMP.] **—stomp′er** *n.* **—stomp′ing•ly** *adv.*

Usage Note: *Stomp* and *stamp* are interchangeable in the sense "to trample" or "to tread on violently": *stomped* (or *stamped) to death; stomping* (or *stamping) horses.* Only *stamp* is used in the sense "to eliminate": *stamp out a fire. Stamp* is also standard in the sense "to strike the ground with the foot, as in anger or frustration," as in *He stamped his foot and began to cry.*

–stomy *suff.* A surgical operation in which an artificial open-

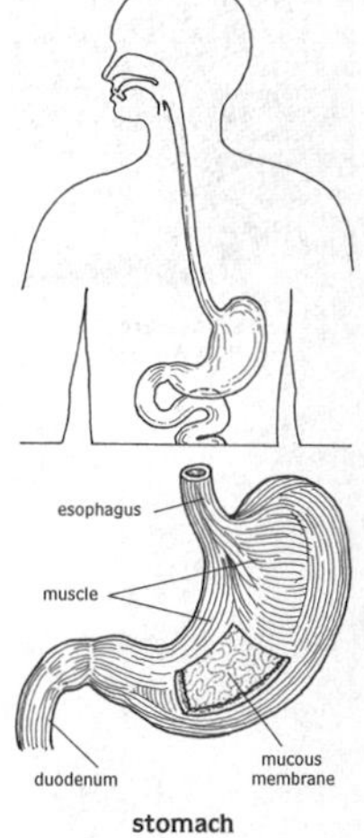

stomach

stomacher
Portrait of a Woman,
c. 1625–1630, attributed to
Pieter Claesz Soutman
(1580?–1657)

ă pat	oi boy
ā pay	ou out
âr care	o͝o took
ä father	o͞o boot
ĕ pet	ŭ cut
ē be	ûr urge
ĭ pit	th thin
ī pie	*th* this
îr pier	hw which
ŏ pot	zh vision
ō toe	ə about, item
ô paw	

Stress marks:
′ (primary);
′ (secondary), as in
dictionary (dĭk′shə-nĕr′ē)

ing is made into a specified organ or part: *colostomy.* [Gk. *stoma,* opening, mouth + -Y².]

stone (stōn) *n.* **1.a.** Concreted earthy or mineral matter; rock. **b.** Such concreted matter of a particular type. Often used in combination: *sandstone.* **2.** A small piece of rock. **3.** Rock or a piece of rock shaped or finished for a particular purpose, esp.: **a.** A piece of rock that is used in construction: *a coping stone.* **b.** A gravestone or tombstone. **c.** A grindstone, millstone, or whetstone. **d.** A milestone or boundary. **4.** A gem or precious stone. **5.** Something resembling a stone in shape or hardness. **6.** *Bot.* The hard covering enclosing the seed in certain fruits, such as the plum. **7.** *Pathol.* A mineral concretion in a body part or organ, such as the kidney; a calculus. **8.** *pl.* **stone.** A unit of weight in Great Britain, 14 pounds (6.4 kilograms). **9.** *Print.* A table with a smooth surface on which page forms are composed. —*adj.* **1.** Relating to or made of stone: *a stone wall.* **2.** Made of stoneware or earthenware. —*adv.* Used as an intensive. Often used in combination: *stone cold.* —*tr.v.* **stoned, ston•ing, stones. 1.** To hurl or throw stones at, esp. to kill with stones. **2.** To remove the stones or pits from. **3.** To furnish, fit, pave, or line with stones. **4.** To rub on or with a stone in order to polish or sharpen. **5.** *Obsolete.* To make hard or indifferent. [ME < OE *stān.* See **stei-***.] —**ston′er** *n.*

stoneware
c. 1830 American

Stone (stōn), **Edward Durell.** 1902–78. Amer. architect who was an exponent of the International Style.

Stone, Harlan Fiske. 1872–1946. Amer. jurist; associate justice (1925–41) and chief justice (1941–46) of the U.S. Supreme Court.

Stone, Lucy. 1818–93. Amer. feminist who organized the first national women's rights convention (1850).

Stone Age *n.* The earliest known period of human culture, characterized by the use of stone tools.

stone-blind (stōn′blīnd′) *adj.* Completely blind. —**stone′-blind′ness** *n.*

stone-broke (stōn′brōk′) *adj. Informal.* Completely broke; having no money.

stone•chat (stōn′chăt′) *n.* A small Old World thrush *(Saxicola torquata)* of open grassy regions, the male of which has dark plumage and chestnut underparts. [< the resemblance of its call to the sound of falling pebbles.]

stone crab *n.* A large edible crab *(Menippe mercenaria)* found along the Atlantic coast of the southern United States.

stone•crop (stōn′krŏp′) *n.* **1.** Any of various plants of the genus *Sedum,* having fleshy leaves and variously colored flowers. **2.** Any of various related plants. [ME < OE *stāncropp* : *stān,* stone; see STONE + *cropp,* cluster, sprout.]

stone•cut•ter (stōn′kŭt′ər) *n.* **1.** One that cuts or carves stone. **2.** A machine for dressing stone. —**stone′cut′ting** *n.*

stoned (stōnd) *adj. Slang.* **1.** Intoxicated; drunk. **2.** Under the influence of a mind-altering drug.

stone-deaf (stōn′dĕf′) *adj.* Completely deaf.

stone•fish (stōn′fĭsh′) *n., pl.* **stonefish** or **-fish•es.** Any of several tropical scorpion fishes of the genus *Synanceja,* esp. *S. verrucosa,* resembling a rock and ejecting a deadly venom.

stone•fly (stōn′flī′) *n.* Any of numerous weak-flying insects of the order Plecoptera, whose flat elongated nymphs live under stones along the banks of streams.

stone fruit *n.* See **drupe.**

stone-ground (stōn′ground′) *adj.* Ground between millstones, esp. buhrstones: *stone-ground flour.*

Stone•ham (stō′nəm). A town of NE MA, a suburb of Boston. Pop. 22,203.

stone•heart•ed (stōn′här′tĭd) *adj.* Var. of **stonyhearted.**

Stone•henge (stōn′hĕnj′). A group of standing stones on Salisbury Plain in S England. Dating to c. 2000–1800 B.C., Stonehenge was probably a religious center and astronomical observatory.

stonework
Whitefield House Museum, the oldest stone house in the United States, in Guilford, Connecticut

stone marten *n.* **1.** A Eurasian marten *(Martes foina)* having brown fur with lighter underfur and often inhabiting rocky inlets and crevices. **2.** The fur of this animal.

stone•ma•son (stōn′mā′sən) *n.* One that prepares and lays stones in building. —**stone′ma′son•ry** *n.*

Stone Mountain. A massive granite monadnock, 514.2 m (1,686 ft), in NW-central GA E of Atlanta; site of a huge Confederate memorial (carved 1917–67).

stone•roll•er (stōn′rō′lər) *n.* **1.** A minnow *(Campostoma anomalum)* of the central and southern United States, having a horny ridge near the edge of the lower lip used for scraping food from the bottom of a body of water. **2.** A sucker *(Hypentelium nigricans)* of the central and southern United States, common in swift or rocky streams.

stone's throw (stōnz) *n.* A short distance.

stone•wall (stōn′wôl′) *v.* **-walled, -wall•ing, -walls.** —*intr.* **1.** *Informal.* **a.** To engage in delaying tactics; stall. **b.** To refuse to answer or cooperate. **2.** *Sports.* To play defensively rather than trying to score in cricket. —*tr. Informal.* To refuse to answer or cooperate with; resist or rebuff.

stone•ware (stōn′wâr′) *n.* A heavy nonporous nontranslucent pottery, such as jasper ware, that is fired at a high temperature.

stone•work (stōn′wûrk′) *n.* **1.** The technique or process of working in stone. **2.** Work made of stone; stone masonry. —**stone′work′er** *n.*

stone•wort (stōn′wûrt′, -wôrt′) *n.* Any of various submerged aquatic algae of the genus *Chara* that are frequently encrusted with calcium carbonate deposits.

Ston•ey Creek (stō′nē). A town of SE Ontario, Canada, at the W end of Lake Ontario S of Hamilton. Pop. 36,762.

Ston•ing•ton (stō′nĭng-tən). A town of SE CT on Long Island Sound E of New London; settled in 1649. Pop. 16,919.

ston•y also **ston•ey** (stō′nē) *adj.* **-i•er, -i•est. 1.** Covered with or full of stones. **2.** Resembling stone, as in hardness. **3.a.** Hardhearted and unfeeling; unemotional. **b.** Exhibiting no feeling or warmth; impassive. **4.** Emotionally numbing or paralyzing. —**ston′i•ly** *adv.* —**ston′i•ness** *n.*

ston•y•heart•ed (stō′nē-här′tĭd) also **stone•heart•ed** (stōn′-) *adj.* Devoid of kindness or sympathy; hardhearted.

Ston•y Tun•gus•ka (stō′nē tŏŏng-gŏŏ′skə, tŏŏn-). See **Tunguska.**

stood (stŏŏd) *v.* P.t. and p.part. of **stand.**

stooge (stōōj) *n.* **1.** One who feeds straight lines to a comedian. **2.** One who allows oneself to be used for another's advantage; a puppet. **3.** *Slang.* A stool pigeon. —*intr.v.* **stooged, stoog•ing, stoog•es.** To be a stooge or behave like one. [?]

stool (stōōl) *n.* **1.** A backless and armless single seat supported on legs or a pedestal. **2.** A low bench or support for the feet or knees in sitting or kneeling, as a footrest. **3.** A toilet seat; a commode. **4.a.** A bowel movement. **b.** Evacuated fecal matter. **5.** *Bot.* **a.** A stump or rootstock that produces shoots or suckers. **b.** A shoot or growth from a stool. —*intr.v.* **stooled, stool•ing, stools. 1.** *Bot.* To send up shoots or suckers. **2.** To evacuate the bowels; defecate. **3.** *Slang.* To act as a stool pigeon. [ME < OE *stōl.* See **stā-***.]

stool•ie (stōō′lē) *n. Slang.* A stool pigeon.

stool pigeon *n.* **1.** *Slang.* A person acting as a decoy or as an informer, esp. one who is a spy for the police. **2.** A pigeon used as a decoy. [< the practice of tying decoy pigeons to a stool to attract other pigeons.]

stoop[1] (stōōp) *v.* **stooped, stoop•ing, stoops.** —*intr.* **1.** To bend forward and down from the waist or the middle of the back. **2.** To walk or stand, esp. habitually, with the head and upper back bent forward. **3.** To bend or sag downward. **4.a.** To lower or debase oneself. **b.** To descend from a superior position; condescend. **5.** To yield; submit. **6.** To swoop down, as a bird in pursuing its prey. —*tr.* **1.** To bend (the head or body) forward and down. **2.** To debase; humble. —*n.* **1.** The act of stooping. **2.** A forward bending of the head and upper back, esp. when habitual. **3.** An act of self-abasement or condescension. **4.** A descent, as of a bird of prey. [ME *stoupen* < OE *stūpian.*] —**stoop′er** *n.*

stoop[2] (stōōp) *n. Northeastern U.S.* A small porch, platform, or staircase leading to the entrance of a house or building. [Du. *stoep,* front verandah < MDu.]

stoop[3] (stōōp) *n.* Var. of **stoup.**

stoop•ball (stōōp′bôl′) *n. Sports.* A game patterned on baseball in which a player throws a ball against a stoop or wall and the number of bounces indicates the bases reached.

stop (stŏp) *v.* **stopped, stop•ping, stops.** —*tr.* **1.** To close (an opening) by covering, filling in, or plugging up. **2.** To constrict (an opening). **3.** To obstruct or block passage on (a road, for example). **4.** To prevent the flow or passage of. **5.** To cause to halt, cease, or desist. **6.** To desist from; cease. **7.** To order a bank to withhold payment of. **8.** To cause (a motor, for example) to cease operation or function; halt. **9.** *Mus.* **a.** To press down (a string on a stringed instrument) on the fingerboard to produce a desired pitch. **b.** To close (a hole on a wind instrument) with the finger in sounding a desired pitch. —*intr.* **1.** To cease moving, progressing, acting, or operating; come to a halt. **2.** To put an end to what one is doing; cease. **3.** To interrupt one's course or journey for a brief visit or stay. —*n.* **1.** The act of stopping or the condition of being stopped; cessation. **2.** A finish; an end. **3.** A stay or visit, as one taken during a trip. **4.** A place at which someone or something stops. **5.** A device or means that obstructs, blocks, or plugs up. **6.** An order given to a bank to withhold payment on a check. **7.** A part in a machine that stops or regulates movement. **8.** The effective aperture of a lens, controlled by a diaphragm. **9.** A mark of punctuation, esp. a period. **10.** *Mus.* **a.** The act of stopping a string or hole on an instrument. **b.** A fret on a stringed instrument. **c.** A hole on a wind instrument. **d.** A device such as a key for closing the hole on a wind instrument. **e.** A tuned set of pipes. **f.** A knob, key, or pull that regulates such a set of pipes. **11.** *Naut.* A line used for securing something temporarily: *a sail stop.* **12.** *Ling.* See **plosive. 13.** The depression between the muzzle and top of the skull of an animal, esp. a dog. **14.** *Games.* A stopper. **15.** *Archit.* A projecting stone, often carved, at the end of a molding. —*adj.* Of, relating to, or being of use at the end of an operation or activity: *a stop code.* [ME *stoppen* < OE *-stoppian,* prob. < VLat. **stuppāre,* to caulk < Lat. *stuppa,* tow, broken flax < Gk. *stuppē.*] —**stop′pa•ble** *adj.*

Syns: *stop, cease, desist, discontinue, halt, quit.* The central meaning shared by these verbs is "to bring or come to a cessation": *stop arguing; ceased crying; desist from lying; discontinued treatment; halted him; quit going.* **Ant:** *start.*

stop•cock (stŏp′kŏk′) *n.* A valve that regulates the flow of fluid through a pipe; a faucet.

stope (stōp) *n.* An excavation in the form of steps made by the mining of ore from steeply inclined or vertical veins. —*tr.v.* **stoped, stop•ing, stopes.** To remove (ore) from or mine by means of a stope. [Perh. < LGer., step < MLGer. *stōpe.*] —**stop′er** *n.*

stop•gap (stŏp′găp′) *n.* An improvised substitute for something lacking; a temporary expedient.

stop•light (stŏp′līt′) *n.* **1.** A light on the rear of a vehicle that is activated when the brakes are applied. **2.** See **traffic light.**

stop order *n.* An order to a broker to buy or sell a stock when it reaches a specified level of decline or gain in price.

stop•o•ver (stŏp′ō′vər) *n.* **1.** An interruption of a trip for stopping somewhere. **2.** A place visited briefly during a trip.

stop•page (stŏp′ĭj) *n.* The act of stopping or the condition of being stopped; a halt: *called for a work stoppage.*

stop payment *n.* An order to one's bank not to honor a check one has drawn.

stop•per (stŏp′ər) *n.* **1.** A device, such as a plug, that is inserted to close an opening. **2.** One that stops something: *a conversation stopper.* —*tr.v.* **-pered, -per•ing, -pers.** To close with or as if with a stopper.

stop•ple (stŏp′əl) *n.* A stopper; a plug. —*tr.v.* **-pled, -pling, -ples.** To close with a stopper or plug. [ME *stoppell* < ME *stoppen,* to stop. See STOP.]

stop sign *n.* A traffic sign that indicates that traffic is required to come to a complete stop before proceeding.

stop street *n.* A street intersection at which a vehicle must come to a complete stop before entering a through street.

stop•watch (stŏp′wŏch′) *n.* A watch that can be instantly started and stopped by pushing a button, used to measure an exact duration of time.

stor•age (stôr′ĭj, stōr′-) *n.* **1.a.** The act of storing goods or the state of being stored. **b.** A space for storing goods. **c.** The price charged for storing goods. **2.** The charging or regenerating of a storage battery. **3.** *Comp. Sci.* The part of a computer that stores information for subsequent use or retrieval.

storage battery *n. Elect.* A group of reversible or rechargeable secondary cells acting as a unit.

storage cell *n.* **1.** See **secondary cell. 2.** *Comp. Sci.* An elementary unit of storage.

sto•rax (stôr′ăks′, stōr′-) *n.* **1.** See **snowbell. 2.** *Bot.* An aromatic resin obtained from the snowbell. **3.** *Bot.* A brownish aromatic resin used in perfume and medicine and obtained from any of several trees of the genus *Liquidambar,* esp. *L. orientalis* of Turkey. [ME < Lat., alteration of *styrax* < Gk. *sturax,* perh. of Semitic orig.]

store (stôr, stōr) *n.* **1.** A place where merchandise is sold; a shop. **2.** A stock or supply reserved for future use. **3. stores.** Supplies, esp. of food, clothing, or arms. **4.** A place where commodities are kept; a warehouse or storehouse. **5.** A great quantity or number; an abundance. —*tr.v.* **stored, stor•ing, stores. 1.** To reserve for future use. **2.** To fill, supply, or stock. **3.** To deposit or receive in a storehouse or warehouse for safekeeping. —***idiom.* in store.** Forthcoming. [ME *stor,* supply < OFr. *estor* < *estorer,* to build < Lat. *īnstaurāre,* to restore. See **stā-*.**] —**stor′a•ble** *adj.* —**stor′er** *n.*

store-bought (stôr′bôt′, stōr′-) *adj. Informal.* Manufactured and bought at retail; not homemade: *store-bought pie.*

store•front (stôr′frŭnt′, stōr′-) *n.* **1.** The side of a store or shop facing a street. **2.** A room or suite of rooms in a commercial building at street level. —**store′front′** *adj.*

store•house (stôr′hous′, stōr′-) *n.* **1.** A place or building in which goods are stored; a warehouse. **2.** An abundant source or supply: *a storehouse of knowledge.*

store•keep•er (stôr′kē′pər, stōr′-) *n.* **1.** One who keeps a retail store or shop. **2.** One in charge of receiving or distributing stores or supplies. —**store′keep′ing** *n.*

store•own•er (stôr′ō′nər) *n.* One who owns or operates a store or shop.

store•room (stôr′ro͞om′, -ro͝om′, stōr′-) *n.* A room in which things are stored.

store•wide (stôr′wīd′, stōr′-) *adj.* Involving, applying to, or occurring throughout a whole store: *a storewide sale.*

sto•rey (stôr′ē, stōr′ē) *n. Chiefly British.* Var. of **story[2].**

sto•reyed (stôr′ēd, stōr′-) *adj. Chiefly British.* Var. of **storied[2].**

sto•ried[1] (stôr′ēd, stōr′-) *adj.* **1.** Celebrated or famous in history or story. **2.** Ornamented with designs representing scenes from history, legend, or story: *storied tapestry.*

sto•ried[2] (stôr′ēd, stōr′-) *adj.* Having or consisting of a given number of stories: *a two-storied house.*

stork (stôrk) *n.* Any of various large wading birds of the family Ciconiidae, chiefly of the Eastern Hemisphere, having long legs and a long straight bill. [ME < OE *storc.* See **ster-[1]*.**]

storks•bill (stôrks′bĭl′) *n.* **1.** Any of various plants of the genus *Erodium,* having fruit with a narrow beaklike tip. **2.** See **geranium** 2.

storm (stôrm) *n.* **1.** An atmospheric disturbance manifested in strong winds accompanied by rain, snow, hail, or sleet and often by thunder and lightning. **2.** *Meteorol.* A wind with a speed from 64 to 73 miles (from 103 to 117 kilometers) per hour, according to the Beaufort scale. **3.** A heavy shower of objects, such as missiles. **4.** A strong or violent outburst, as of emotion or excitement. **5.** A violent disturbance or upheaval, as in political, social, or domestic affairs. **6.** A sudden violent attack on a fortified place. —*v.* **stormed, storm•ing, storms.** —*intr.* **1.a.** To blow forcefully. **b.** To precipitate rain, snow, hail, or sleet. **2.** To be extremely angry; rant and rage. **3.** To move or rush tumultuously, violently, or angrily. —*tr.* To assault, capture, or captivate by storm. [ME < OE.]

storm•bound (stôrm′bound′) *adj.* Delayed, confined, or cut off from communication by a storm.

storm cellar *n.* See **cyclone cellar.**

storm center *n.* **1.** The central area of a storm, esp. the point of lowest barometric pressure within a storm. **2.** A center of trouble, disturbance, or argument.

storm door *n.* An outer or additional door added for protection against inclement weather.

storm petrel *n.* Any of various small sea birds of the family Hydrobatidae, esp. *Hydrobates pelagicus* of the North Atlantic and the Mediterranean, having sooty plumage.

storm trooper *n.* **1.a.** A member of the Nazi militia noted for brutality and violence. **b.** One who resembles a member of the Nazi militia. **2.** A member of a force of shock troops.

storm window *n.* A secondary window attached over the usual window to protect against the wind and cold.

storm•y (stôr′mē) *adj.* **-i•er, -i•est. 1.** Subject to, marked by, or affected by storms; tempestuous. **2.** Marked by violent emotions, speech, or actions. —**storm′i•ly** *adv.* —**storm′i•ness** *n.*

stormy petrel *n.* **1.** See **storm petrel. 2.** One who brings discord or appears at the onset of trouble; a rebel.

sto•ry[1] (stôr′ē, stōr′ē) *n., pl.* **-ries. 1.** An account or a recital of an event or series of events. **2.** A usu. fictional narrative intended to interest or amuse the hearer or reader; a tale. **3.** A short story. **4.** An incident, experience, or subject that furnishes or would be interesting material for a narrative. **5.** The plot of a narrative or dramatic work. **6.** A report, a statement, or an allegation of facts. **7.a.** A news article or broadcast. **b.** The event, situation, or other material for such an article or broadcast. **8.** An anecdote. **9.** A lie. **10.** Romantic legend or tradition. —*tr.v.* **-ried, -ry•ing, -ries. 1.** To decorate with scenes representing historical or legendary events. **2.** *Archaic.* To tell as a story. [ME *storie* < OFr. *estorie, estoire* < Lat. *historia.* See HISTORY.]

sto•ry[2] (stôr′ē, stōr′ē) *n., pl.* **-ries. 1.** A complete horizontal division of a building, constituting the area between two adjacent levels. **2.** The set of rooms on the same level of a building. [ME *storie, story* < Med.Lat. *historia,* picture, story (prob. < painted windows or sculpture on the front of buildings) < Lat., history. See HISTORY.]

Sto•ry (stôr′ē, stōr′ē), **Joseph.** 1779–1845. Amer. jurist; associate justice of the U.S. Supreme Court (1811–45).

sto•ry•board (stôr′ē-bôrd′, stōr′ē-bōrd′) *n.* A hanging panel of sketches depicting sequential scenes, as of a film being proposed or made. —**sto′ry•board′** *v.*

sto•ry•book (stôr′ē-bo͝ok′, stōr′-) *n.* A book containing a collection of stories, usu. for children. —**sto′ry•book′** *adj.*

story line *n.* The plot of a story or dramatic work.

sto•ry•tell•er (stôr′ē-tĕl′ər, stōr′-) *n.* **1.a.** One who tells or writes stories. **b.** One who relates anecdotes. **2.** *Informal.* One who tells lies. —**sto′ry•tell′ing** *n.*

sto•ry•writ•er (stôr′ē-rī′tər, stōr′-) *n.* **1.** One who writes stories. **2.** One who writes news stories, as for the media.

stoss (stŏs, stôs, shtōs) *adj.* Facing the direction from which a glacier moves. Used of a rock or slope in its path. [< Ger. *Stoss,* push, blow < *stossen,* to push < MHGer. *stōzen* < OHGer. *stōzan.*]

sto•tin•ka (stō-tĭng′kə) *n., pl.* **-ki** (-kē). See table at **currency.** [Bulgarian < *sto,* hundred < Old Church Slavonic *sŭto.* See **dekm̥*.**]

Stough•ton (stōt′n). A town of E MA NW of Brockton. Pop. 26,777.

stound (stound) *n. Archaic.* A short time; a while. [ME < OE *stund.* See **stā-*.**]

stoup also **stoop** (sto͞op) *n.* **1.** *Eccles.* A basin or font for holy water at the entrance of a church. **2.** A drinking vessel, such as a cup or tankard. **3.** *Scots.* A bucket or pail. [ME *stoup,* bucket, jar < ON *staup,* cup.]

Stour (stour, sto͝or, stōr). A river, c. 64 km (40 mi), of SE England emptying into the North Sea in two channels.

stout (stout) *adj.* **stout•er, stout•est. 1.** Bold, brave, or determined; firm and resolute. **2.** Strong in body; sturdy. **3.** Strong in structure or substance; solid or substantial. **4.** Bulky in figure; thickset or corpulent. See Syns at **fat. 5.** Powerful; forceful. **6.** Stubborn or uncompromising. —*n.* **1.a.** A thickset or corpulent person. **b.** A garment size for a large or heavy figure. **2.** A strong, very dark beer or ale. [ME < OFr. *estout,* of Gmc. orig. See **stel-*.**] —**stout′ish** *adj.* —**stout′ly** *adv.* —**stout′ness** *n.*

stopwatch

stork
Yellow-billed stork
Ibis ibis

ă pat	oi **boy**
ā **pay**	ou **out**
âr **care**	o͝o **took**
ä **father**	o͞o **boot**
ĕ **pet**	ŭ **cut**
ē **be**	ûr **urge**
ĭ **pit**	th **thin**
ī **pie**	*th* **this**
îr **pier**	hw **which**
ŏ **pot**	zh **vision**
ō **toe**	ə **about, item**
ô **paw**	

Stress marks:
′ (primary);
′ (secondary), as in
dictionary (dĭk′shə-nĕr′ē)

stout•en (stout′n) *tr. & intr.v.* **-ened, -en•ing, -ens.** To make or become stout or stouter.

stout•heart•ed (stout′här′tĭd) *adj.* Brave; courageous. **—stout′heart′ed•ly** *adv.* **—stout′heart′ed•ness** *n.*

stove¹ (stōv) *n.* **1.** An apparatus in which electricity or a fuel is used to furnish heat, as for cooking or warmth. **2.** A device that produces heat for specialized, esp. industrial purposes. **3.** A kiln. **4.** *Chiefly British.* A hothouse. [ME, heated room, prob. < MLGer. or MDu., both prob. < VLat. **extūfa* < **extūfāre*, to heat with steam. See STEW¹.]

stove² (stōv) *v.* A p.t. and p.part. of **stave.**

stove•pipe (stōv′pīp′) *n.* **1.** A pipe, usu. of thin sheet iron, used to conduct smoke or fumes from a stove into a chimney flue. **2.** A man's tall silk hat.

stovepipe

sto•ver (stō′vər) *n.* The dried stalks and leaves of a cereal crop, used as fodder after the grain has been harvested. [ME, provisions < Norman Fr. *estovers* < OFr. *estovier*, to be necessary < Lat. *est opus*, it is necessary : *est*, third pers. sing. pr.t. of *esse*, to be; see ESSENCE + *opus*, need, work; see OPUS.]

stow (stō) *tr.v.* **stowed, stow•ing, stows. 1.a.** To place or arrange, esp. in a neat, compact way. **b.** To fill (a place or container) by packing tightly. **2.** To store for future use. **3.** *Slang.* To refrain from; stop. **4.** To provide lodging for; quarter. **—*phrasal verb.* stow away. 1.** To hide oneself aboard a conveyance to obtain free transportation. **2.** *Informal.* To consume (food or drink) greedily. [ME *stowen* < *stowe*, place < OE *stōw*. See **stā-*.**]

Stow (stō). A city of NE OH, a suburb of Akron. Pop. 27,702.

stow•age (stō′ĭj) *n.* **1.a.** The act, manner, or process of stowing. **b.** The state of being stored. **2.a.** Space or room for storage. **b.** A place or container for storage. **3.** Goods in storage or to be stowed. **4.** A charge for storing goods.

stow•a•way (stō′ə-wā′) *n.* A person who hides aboard a ship or other conveyance in order to obtain free passage.

Stowe (stō), **Harriet (Elizabeth) Beecher.** 1811–96. Amer. writer noted esp. for her novel *Uncle Tom's Cabin* (1852).

Harriet Beecher Stowe
Photographed c. 1880

STP *abbr.* Standard temperature and pressure.

str. *abbr.* **1.** Steamer. **2.** Or **Str.** Strait. **3.** *Mus.* Stringed. **4.** Strophe.

stra•bis•mus (strə-bĭz′məs) *n.* A visual defect in which one eye cannot focus with the other because of imbalance of the eye muscles. [NLat. < Gk. *strabismos*, condition of squinting < *strabizein*, to squint < *strabos*, squinting. See **streb(h)-*.**] **—stra•bis′mal** (-məl), **stra•bis′mic** (-mĭk) *adj.*

Stra•bo (strā′bō′). 63? B.C.–A.D. 24? Greek geographer and historian whose work describes the people and countries known during the reign of Augustus.

Stra•chey (strā′kē), **(Giles) Lytton.** 1880–1932. British historian best known for *Eminent Victorians* (1918).

strad•dle (străd′l) *v.* **-dled, -dling, -dles.** —*tr.* **1.a.** To stand or sit with a leg on each side of; bestride. **b.** To be on both sides of; extend over or across. **2.** To appear to favor both sides of (an issue). **3.** To fire shots behind and in front of (a target) to determine the range. —*intr.* **1.** To walk, stand, or sit with the legs wide apart, esp. to sit astride. **2.** To spread out in a disorderly way; sprawl. **3.** To appear to favor both sides of an issue. —*n.* **1.** The act or posture of sitting astride. **2.** An equivocal or a noncommittal position. **3.** The option to buy or sell a specific asset, such as a block of stock, at a set price before a certain date. **—*idiom.* straddle the fence.** *Informal.* To be undecided or uncommitted. [Akin to STRIDE.] **—strad′dler** *n.*

Stra•di•va•ri (străd′ə-vâr′ē, -vär′ē), **Antonio.** Often **Antonius Stradivarius.** 1644?–1737. Italian violinmaker who developed the proportions of the modern violin.

strafe (strāf) *tr.v.* **strafed, straf•ing, strafes.** To attack (ground troops, for example) with a machine gun or cannon from a low-flying aircraft. [< Ger. *(Gott) strafe (England)*, (God) punish (England), World War I slogan < *strafen*, to punish < MHGer. *strāfen*, to admonish.] **—strafe** *n.* **—straf′er** *n.*

Straf•ford (străf′ərd), 1st Earl of. Thomas Wentworth. 1593–1641. English politician and principal minister to Charles I who was convicted of treason by Parliament and executed.

strag•gle (străg′əl) *intr.v.* **-gled, -gling, -gles. 1.** To stray or fall behind. **2.** To proceed or spread out in a scattered or irregular group. —*n.* A scattered or disorderly group, as of people or things. [ME *straglen*, to wander.] **—strag′gler** *n.*

strag•gly (străg′lē) *adj.* **-gli•er, -gli•est.** Growing or spread out in a disorderly or aimless way: *straggly ivy.*

straight (strāt) *adj.* **straight•er, straight•est. 1.** Extending continuously in the same direction without curving. **2.** Having no waves or bends: *straight hair.* **3.** Erect; upright. **4.** Perfectly horizontal or vertical; level or even. **5.a.** Direct and candid. **b.** Following a direct or correct method or approach; systematic: *straight reasoning.* **c.** Coming from a reliable source; factual. **6.a.** Showing or marked by honesty or fair-mindedness. **b.** Right; correct. **7.** Neatly arranged; orderly. **8.a.** Uninterrupted; consecutive. **b.** Having the parts or details in correct sequence. **c.** *Games.* Made up of five cards constituting a straight. **9.** Undeviatingly supportive, as of a principle or a political party. **10.a.** Not deviating from the socially normal, usual, or acceptable; conventional. **b.** Conventional to an extreme degree. **c.** Heterosexual. **11.** *Slang.* Not being under the influence of alcohol or drugs. **12.a.** Not deviating from the normal or strict form. **b.** Not altered, embellished, or modified. **13.a.** Concerned with serious or important matters: *a straight drama.* **b.** Of or relating to a straight man. **14.** Not mixed with anything else; undiluted. **15.** Sold without discount regardless of the amount purchased. —*adv.* **1.** In a straight line; directly. **2.** In an erect posture; upright. **3.** Without detour or delay. **4.** Without circumlocution; candidly. **5.** In a neat and orderly condition. **6.** In an honest, law-abiding, or virtuous manner. **7.** Without stopping; continuously. **8.** Without embellishment or modification. **9.** Without ice, water, or a mixer. —*n.* **1.a.** The straight part, as of a road. **b.** *Sports & Games.* The straight part of a racecourse between the winning post and the last turn. **2.** A straight line. **3.** A straight form or position. **4.** *Games.* A poker hand containing five cards of various suits in numerical sequence, ranked above three of a kind and below a flush. **5.a.** A conventional person, esp. a member of established society. **b.** A heterosexual person. **6.** *Slang.* A person who does not use illegal drugs. **—*idiom.* straight up.** Served without ice. [ME < p.part. of *strecchen*, to stretch. See STRETCH.] **—straight′ly** *adv.* **—straight′ness** *n.*

straight-a•head (strāt′ə-hĕd′) *adj.* Conforming to a conventional style or mode; standard.

straight and narrow *n.* The way of proper conduct and moral integrity. [Prob. alteration of *"Strait is the gate, and narrow is the way, which leadeth unto life"* (Matthew 7:14).]

straight angle *n. Math.* An angle of 180°.

straight-arm (strāt′ärm′) *tr.v.* **-armed, -arm•ing, -arms. 1.** *Football.* To ward off (a tackler) by holding the arm out straight with the elbow locked and the palm of the hand placed against the opponent's body; stiff-arm. **2.** To force or ward off by or as if by holding the arm out straight. **—straight′-arm′** *n.*

straight•a•way (strāt′ə-wā′) *adj.* **1.** Extending in a straight line or course without a curve or turn. **2.** Unhesitating; immediate: *a straightaway denial.* —*n.* A straight course, stretch, or track. —*adv.* (strāt′ə-wā′). At once; immediately.

straight-backed (strāt′băkt′) *adj.* Having a straight back.

straight chain *n.* An organic molecular structure in the form of an unbranched open chain.

straight•edge (strāt′ĕj′) *n.* A rigid flat rectangular bar, as of wood or metal, with a straight edge for testing or drawing straight lines. **—straight′edged′** *adj.*

straight•en (strāt′n) *tr. & intr.v.* **-ened, -en•ing, -ens.** To make or become straight or straighter. **—straight′en•er** *n.*

straight face *n.* A face that betrays no sign of emotion. **—straight′-faced′** (strāt′fāst′) *adj.*

straight flush *n. Games.* A hand in which all five cards are of the same suit and in numerical sequence, ranked above four of a kind in poker.

straight•for•ward (strāt-fôr′wərd) *adj.* **1.** Proceeding in a straight course; direct. **2.a.** Not circuitous or evasive; honest and frank. See Syns at **frank¹. b.** Free from ambiguity or pretense; plain and open. —*adv.* In a direct course or an honest manner. **—straight•for′ward•ly** *adv.* **—straight•for′ward•ness** *n.* **—straight•for′wards** *adv.*

straight•jack•et (strāt′jăk′ĭt) *n. & v.* Var. of **straitjacket.**

straight-laced (strāt′lāst′) *adj.* Var. of **strait-laced.**

straight-line (strāt′līn′) *adj.* **1.** Lying in a straight line. **2.** Relating to or being a device whose linkage produces or copies motion in straight lines. **3.** *Accounting.* Of or being a mode of amortization by equal payments at stated intervals over a given period of time.

straight man *n.* The partner in a comedy team who feeds lines to the other comedian, who then makes witty replies.

straight off *adv.* At once; immediately.

straight-out (strāt′out′) *adj.* **1.** Straightforward; blunt. **2.** Complete; unmitigated.

straight poker *n. Games.* Poker in which each player is dealt five cards face down, bets are made, and the showdown takes place without any new cards being drawn.

straight razor *n.* A razor consisting of a blade hinged to a handle into which it slips when not in use.

straight ticket *n.* A ballot cast for one party's candidates.

straight•way (strāt′wā′, -wā′) *adv.* **1.** In a direct course. **2.** Without delay; at once.

strain¹ (strān) *v.* **strained, strain•ing, strains.** —*tr.* **1.** To pull, draw, or stretch tight. **2.** To exert or tax to the utmost. **3.** To injure or impair by overuse or overexertion; wrench. **4.** To stretch or force beyond the proper or legitimate limit. **5.** To alter (the relations between the parts of a structure or shape) by applying an external force; deform. **6.a.** To pass (gravy, for example) through a filter such as a strainer. **b.** To draw off or remove by filtration. **7.** To embrace or clasp tightly; hug. —*intr.* **1.** To make violent or steady efforts; strive hard. **2.** To be or become wrenched or twisted. **3.** To be subjected to great stress. **4.** To pull forcibly or violently. **5.** To stretch or exert one's muscles or nerves to the utmost. **6.** To filter, trickle, or ooze. **7.** To be extremely hesitant; balk. —*n.* **1.a.** The act of straining. **b.** The state of being strained.

2.a. Extreme or laborious effort, exertion, or work. **b.** A great or excessive pressure, demand, or stress on one's body, mind, or resources. **3.** A wrench, twist, or other physical injury due to excessive tension, effort, or use. **4.** *Phys.* A deformation caused by stress. **5.** An exceptional degree or pitch. [ME *streinen* < OFr. *estreindre, estrein-*, to bind tightly < Lat. *stringere.* See **streig-*.**]

strain[2] (strān) *n.* **1.** The collective descendants of a common ancestor; a race, stock, line, or breed. **2.** Any of the various lines of ancestry united in an individual or a family; ancestry or lineage. **3.** *Biol.* A group of organisms of the same species, having distinctive characteristics but not usu. considered a separate breed or variety. **4.** An artificial variety of a domestic animal or cultivated plant. **5.** A kind or sort. **6.a.** An inborn or inherited tendency or character. **b.** A streak; a trace. **7.a.** The tone, tenor, or substance of an utterance or of an action. **b.** A prevailing quality, as of attitude or behavior. **8.** *Mus.* A passage of musical expression; a tune or an air. Often used in the plural. **9.a.** A passage of poetic and esp. lyrical expression. **b.** An outburst or a flow of eloquent or impassioned language. [ME *strene* < OE *strēon*, something gained, offspring. See **ster-[2]*.**]

strained (strānd) *adj.* **1.** Having been passed through a strainer. **2.** Done with or marked by excessive effort; forced. **3.** Extended beyond proper limits: *a strained meaning.* **4.** Antagonized to the verge of open conflict.

strain•er (strā′nər) *n.* **1.** One that strains, as a device used to separate liquids from solids. **2.** An apparatus for tightening, stretching, or strengthening.

strain gauge *n.* An extensometer.

strain•ing beam (strā′nĭng) *n. Archit.* A horizontal tie beam connecting two queen posts in a roof truss.

strain•om•e•ter (strā-nŏm′ĭ-tər) *n.* An extensometer.

strait (strāt) *n.* **1.** A narrow channel joining two larger bodies of water. Often used in the plural with a singular verb. **2.** A position of difficulty, perplexity, distress, or need. Often used in the plural: *in desperate straits.* —*adj.* **1.a.** Difficult; stressful. **b.** Having or marked by limited funds or resources. **2.** *Archaic.* **a.** Narrow. **b.** Affording little space or room; confined. **c.** Fitting tightly; constricted. **3.** *Archaic.* Strict, rigid, or righteous. [ME *streit*, narrow, a strait < OFr. *estreit*, tight, narrow < Lat. *strictus*, p.part. of *stringere*, to draw tight. See **streig-*.**] —**strait′ly** *adv.* —**strait′ness** *n.*

strait•en (strāt′n) *tr.v.* **-ened, -en•ing, -ens. 1.a.** To make narrow. **b.** To enclose in a limited area; confine. **2.** To put or bring into difficulties or distress, esp. financial hardship. **3.** *Archaic.* To restrict in latitude or scope.

strait•jack•et also **straight•jack•et** (strāt′jăk′ĭt) *n.* **1.** A long-sleeved jacketlike garment used to bind the arms tightly against the body as a means of restraining a violent patient or prisoner. **2.** Something that restricts, hinders, or confines. —**strait′jack′et** *v.*

strait-laced also **straight-laced** (strāt′lāst′) *adj.* **1.** Excessively strict in behavior, morality, or opinions. **2.** Having or wearing a tightly laced garment. —**strait′-lac′ed•ly** (-lā′sĭd-lē, -lāst′lē) *adv.* —**strait′-lac′ed•ness** *n.*

Straits Settlements (strāts). A former British crown colony comprising parts of the S and W Malay Peninsula and adjacent islands, including Singapore.

strake (strāk) *n. Naut.* A single continuous line of planking or metal plating extending on a vessel's hull from stem to stern. [ME, prob. < OE **straca.*]

Stral•sund (străl′so͝ont′, shträl′zo͝ont′). A city of NE Germany on an inlet of the Baltic Sea opposite Rügen I.; chartered 1234. Pop. 75,335.

stra•mo•ni•um (strə-mō′nē-əm) *n.* **1.** See **jimsonweed. 2.** The dried poisonous leaves of the jimsonweed, used in the treatment of asthma. [NLat.]

strand[1] (strănd) *n.* The land bordering a body of water; a beach. —*v.* **strand•ed, strand•ing, strands.** —*tr.* **1.** To drive or run ashore or aground. **2.** To bring into or leave in a difficult or helpless position. **3.** *Baseball.* To leave (a base runner) on base at the end of an inning. —*intr.* **1.** To be driven or run ashore or aground. **2.** To be brought into or left in a difficult or helpless position. [ME < OE.]

strand[2] (strănd) *n.* **1.** A complex of fibers or filaments twisted together into a cable, rope, thread, or yarn. **2.a.** A single filament, such as a fiber or thread, of a woven or braided material. **b.** A wisp or a tress of hair. **3.** Something, such as a string of pearls, plaited or twisted into a ropelike length. **4.** One of the elements woven into an intricate whole. —*tr.v.* **strand•ed, strand•ing, strands. 1.** To make or form (a rope, for example) by twisting strands together. **2.** To break a strand of (a rope, for example). [ME *strond.*]

strand line also **strand•line** (strănd′līn′) *n.* A shoreline, esp. one marking an earlier and higher water level.

strange (strānj) *adj.* **strang•er, strang•est. 1.** Not previously known; unfamiliar. **2.a.** Out of the ordinary; unusual or striking. **b.** Differing from the normal. **3.** Not of one's own or a particular locality, environment, or kind; exotic. **4.a.** Reserved in manner; distant. **b.** Not comfortable or at ease; constrained. **5.** Not accustomed or conditioned. **6.** *Archaic.* Of, relating to, or characteristic of another place or part of the world; foreign. —*adv.* In a strange manner. [ME < OFr. *estrange*, extraordinary, foreign < Lat. *extrāneus*, adventitious, foreign < *extrā*, outside < fem. ablative of *exter*, outward. See **eghs*.**] —**strange′ly** *adv.*

Syns: *strange, peculiar, odd, queer, quaint, outlandish, singular, eccentric, curious.* These adjectives describe what deviates from the usual or customary. *Strange* refers especially to what is unfamiliar, unknown, or inexplicable: *traveling through strange lands. Peculiar* particularly describes what is distinct from all others: *the peculiar odor of cloves.* Something that is *odd* or *queer* fails to accord with what is ordinary, usual, or expected; both terms can suggest strangeness or peculiarity: *odd that his name is never mentioned. "Now, my suspicion is that the universe is not only queerer than we suppose, but queerer than we can suppose"* (J.B.S. Haldane). *Quaint* refers to pleasing or old-fashioned peculiarity: *"the quaint streets of New Orleans, that most foreign of American cities"* (Winston Churchill). *Outlandish* suggests alien or bizarre strangeness: *outlandish clothes. Singular* describes what is unique or unparalleled; the term often suggests a quality that arouses curiosity or wonder: *singular poise in one so young. Eccentric* refers particularly to what is strange and departs strikingly from the conventional: *innovative but eccentric. Curious* suggests strangeness that excites interest: *Americans abroad often acquire a curious accent.*

strange•ness (strānj′nĭs) *n.* **1.** The quality or condition of being strange. **2.** *Phys.* A quantum property of the strange quark whose conservation accounts for the absence of certain strong-interaction decay modes among hadrons.

strange particle *n. Phys.* An unstable elementary particle with nonzero total strangeness.

strange quark *n. Phys.* A quark with a charge of −⅓, a mass about 988 times that of the electron, and a strangeness of −1. See table at **subatomic particle.**

strang•er (strān′jər) *n.* **1.** One who is neither a friend nor an acquaintance. **2.** A foreigner, a newcomer, or an outsider. **3.** One who is unaccustomed to or unacquainted with something specified; a novice. **4.** A visitor or guest. **5.** *Law.* One that is neither privy nor party to a title, an act, or a contract. [ME < OFr. *estrangier* < *estrange*, strange. See STRANGE.]

stran•gle (străng′gəl) *v.* **-gled, -gling, -gles.** —*tr.* **1.a.** To kill by squeezing the throat so as to choke or suffocate; throttle. **b.** To cut off the oxygen supply of; smother. **2.** To suppress, repress, or stifle. **3.** To inhibit the growth or action of; restrict. —*intr.* **1.** To become strangled. **2.** To die from suffocation or strangulation; choke. [ME *stranglen* < OFr. *estrangler* < Lat. *strangulāre* < Gk. *strangalan* < *strangalē*, halter.] —**stran′gler** *n.*

stran•gle•hold (străng′gəl-hōld′) *n.* **1.** *Sports.* An illegal wrestling hold used to choke an opponent. **2.** A force or action that restricts or suppresses freedom or progress.

stran•gles (străng′gəlz) *pl.n.* *(used with a sing. v.)* An infectious disease of horses, caused by the bacterium *Streptococcus equi* and marked by inflammation of the mucous membranes that causes a strangling or choking sensation. [< ME *strangle*, strangulation < *stranglen*, to strangle. See STRANGLE.]

stran•gu•late (străng′gyə-lāt′) *v.* **-lat•ed, -lat•ing, -lates.** —*tr.* **1.** To strangle. **2.** *Pathol.* To compress, constrict, or obstruct (an organ, a duct, or other body part) so as to cut off the flow of blood or other fluid. —*intr.* To be or become strangled, compressed, constricted, or obstructed. [Lat. *strangulāre, strangulāt-*. See STRANGLE.] —**stran′gu•la′tion** *n.*

stran•gu•ry (străng′gyə-rē) *n.* Slow painful urination drop by drop. [ME < Lat. *strangūria* < Gk. *strangouria* : *stranx, strang-*, drop, trickle + *-ouria*, -uria.]

strap (străp) *n.* **1.a.** A long narrow strip of pliant material such as leather. **b.** Such a strip equipped with a buckle or similar fastener to bind or secure objects. **2.** A thin flat metal or plastic band used to fasten or clamp objects together or into position. **3.** A narrow band formed into a loop for grasping with the hand. **4.** A razor strop. **5.** A strip of leather used in flogging. —*tr.v.* **strapped, strap•ping, straps. 1.** To fasten or secure with a strap. **2.** To beat with a strap. **3.** To sharpen (a razor, for example). [Alteration of STROP.]

strap•hang•er (străp′hăng′ər) *n.* **1.** One who grips a hanging strap or similar device for support while riding as a passenger on a bus or subway. **2.** One who uses public transportation.

strap•less (străp′lĭs) *adj.* Having no strap or straps, as a dress or an undergarment. —**strap′less** *n.*

strap•pa•do (stră-pā′dō, -pä′-) *n., pl.* **-does. 1.** A form of torture in which the victim is first lifted off the ground by a rope attached to the wrists and tied behind the back and then dropped partway to the ground with a jerk. **2.** The apparatus used in this torture. [Alteration of Fr. *strapade* < OFr. < OItal. *strappata* < *strappare*, to stretch tight, of Gmc. orig.]

strapped (străpt) *adj. Informal.* In financial need.

strap•per (străp′ər) *n.* A powerfully built, robust person.

strap•ping (străp′ĭng) *adj.* Having a sturdy muscular physique; robust. —*n.* **1.** Straps considered as a group. **2.** Material for making straps.

Stras•bourg (sträs′bo͝org′, sträz′-, sträz-bo͝or′). A city of NE

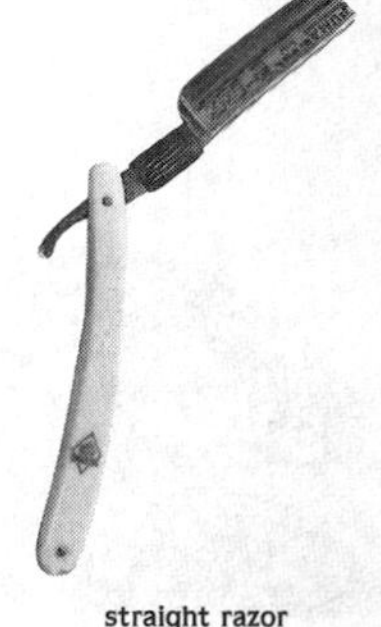

straight razor

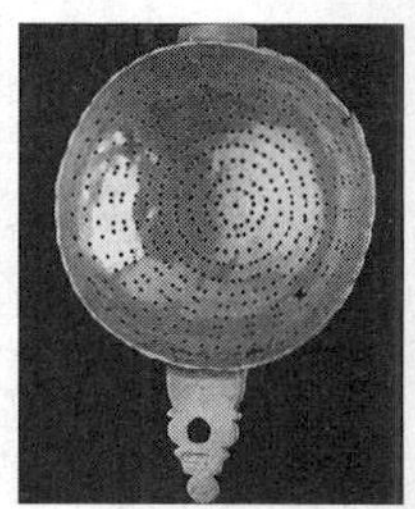

strainer
c. 1740 silver punch strainer, 3⅛″ diameter, by Peter David (1707–1755)

ă pat	oi boy
ā pay	ou out
âr care	o͝o took
ä father	o͞o boot
ĕ pet	ŭ cut
ē be	ûr urge
ĭ pit	th thin
ī pie	*th* this
îr pier	hw which
ŏ pot	zh vision
ō toe	ə about, item
ô paw	

Stress marks:
′ (primary);
′ (secondary), as in dictionary (dĭk′shə-nĕr′ē)

Johann Strauss the Younger
Photographed in the 1890's

strawberry

France near the German border E of Nancy; under German control from 1871 to 1919. Pop. 248,712.

strass (străs) *n.* See **paste**[1] 4. [Ger. *Strass* or Fr. *stras*, both perh. after Josef *Strasser*, 18th-cent. German jeweler.]

stra•ta (strā′tə, străt′ə) *n.* Pl. of **stratum.**

strat•a•gem (străt′ə-jəm) *n.* **1.** A military maneuver to deceive or surprise an enemy. **2.** A clever, often underhand scheme to achieve an objective. [ME < OFr. *stratageme* < OItal. *stratagemma* < Lat. *stratēgēma* < Gk. < *stratēgein*, to be a general < *stratēgos*, general : *stratos*, army; see **ster-**[2]* + *agein*, to lead; see **ag-***.]

stra•te•gic (strə-tē′jĭk) also **stra•te•gi•cal** (-jĭ-kəl) *adj.* **1.** Of or relating to strategy. **2.a.** Important or essential to a plan of action. **b.** Essential to the conduct of war. **c.** Highly important to an objective. **3.** Intended to destroy the military potential of an enemy. **—stra•te′gi•cal•ly** *adv.*

stra•te•gics (strə-tē′jĭks) *n. (used with a sing. v.)* The art of strategy.

strat•e•gist (străt′ə-jĭst) *n.* One who is skilled in strategy.

strat•e•gize (străt′ə-jīz′) *v.* **-gized, -giz•ing, -giz•es.** *—tr.* To plan a strategy for (a business or financial venture, for example). *—intr.* To determine strategies; plan.

strat•e•gy (străt′ə-jē) *n., pl.* **-gies. 1.a.** The science and art of using a nation's forces to execute approved plans as effectively as possible. **b.** The science and art of military command in the planning and conduct of war. **2.** A plan of action resulting from strategy or intended to accomplish a specific goal. See Syns at **plan. 3.** The art or skill of using stratagems in endeavors such as politics. [Fr. *stratégie* < Gk. *stratēgia*, office of a general < *stratēgos*, general. See STRATAGEM.]

Strat•ford (străt′fərd). **1.** A city of SE Ontario, Canada, WSW of Toronto. Pop. 26,262. **2.** A town of SW CT on Long Island Sound NE of Bridgeport; settled in 1639. Pop. 49,389.

Strat•ford-up•on-Av•on (străt′fərd-ə-pŏn-ā′vən, -pôn-) also **Strat•ford-on-Av•on** (-ŏn-, -ôn-). A municipal borough of central England SSE of Birmingham; birthplace and home of William Shakespeare. Pop. 20,800.

strath (străth) *n. Scots.* A wide flat river valley. [Sc.Gael. *srath* < OIr. See **ster-**[2]*.]

stra•ti (strā′tī, străt′ī) *n.* Pl. of **stratus.**

strati– *pref.* Stratum: *stratiform.* [< STRATUM.]

stra•tic•u•late (stră-tĭk′yə-lĭt) *adj. Geol.* Having thin layers. [< STRATUM.] **—stra•tic′u•la′tion** (-lā′shən) *n.*

strat•i•fi•ca•tion (străt′ə-fĭ-kā′shən) *n.* **1.a.** Formation or deposition of layers, as of rock or sediments. **b.** The condition of being stratified. **2.** A layered configuration.

strat•i•fi•ca•tion•al grammar (străt′ə-fĭ-kā′shə-nəl) *n.* A grammar based on the theory that language is made up of a hierarchical series of layers linked by rules.

strat•i•fied charge engine (străt′ə-fīd′) *n.* An internal-combustion engine with a divided ignition cylinder that burns rich fuel in a chamber near the spark plug to improve the combustion of a very lean mixture throughout the rest of the cylinder.

strat•i•form (străt′ə-fôrm′) *adj.* Forming a layer or arranged in layers.

strat•i•fy (străt′ə-fī′) *v.* **-fied, -fy•ing, -fies.** *—tr.* **1.** To form, arrange, or deposit in layers. **2.** To preserve (seeds) by placing them between layers of moist sand or similar material. **3.a.** To arrange or separate into castes, classes, or social levels. **b.** To separate into a sequence of graded status levels. *—intr.* **1.** To become layered; form strata. **2.** To develop different levels of caste, class, privilege, or status.

stra•tig•ra•phy (strə-tĭg′rə-fē) *n.* The study of rock strata, esp. the distribution, deposition, and age of sedimentary rocks. **—strat′i•graph′ic** (străt′ĭ-grăf′ĭk), **strat′i•graph′i•cal** (-ĭ-kəl) *adj.* **—strat′i•graph′i•cal•ly** *adv.*

stra•toc•ra•cy (strə-tŏk′rə-sē) *n., pl.* **-cies.** Government by the armed forces. [Gk. *stratos*, army; see **ster-**[2]* + -CRACY.] **—strat′o•crat′ic** (străt′ə-krăt′ĭk) *adj.*

stra•to•cu•mu•lus (strā′tō-kyo͞om′yə-ləs, străt′ō-) *n., pl.* **-li** (-lī′). A low-lying cloud formation occurring in extensive horizontal layers with rounded summits. [STRAT(US) + CUMULUS.]

strat•o•pause (străt′ə-pôz′) *n.* The boundary between the stratosphere and the mesosphere located about 55 kilometers (35 miles) above the earth's surface. [STRATO(SPHERE) + PAUSE.]

strat•o•sphere (străt′ə-sfîr′) *n.* **1.** The region of the atmosphere above the troposphere and below the mesosphere. **2.** An extremely high or the highest point or degree on a ranked scale. [Fr. *stratosphère* : Lat. *strātus*, a spreading out; see STRATUS + *-sphère*, sphere (< OFr. *espere*; see SPHERE).]

strat•o•spher•ic (străt′ə-sfîr′ĭk, -sfĕr′-) *adj.* **1.** Of, relating to, or characteristic of the stratosphere. **2.** Extremely or unreasonably high. **—strat′o•spher′i•cal•ly** *adv.*

strat•o•vol•ca•no (străt′ō-vŏl-kā′nō, strā′tō-) *n., pl.* **-nos.** A volcano composed of alternating layers of lava and ash.

stra•tum (strā′təm, străt′əm) *n., pl.* **-ta** (-tə) or **-tums. 1.** A horizontal layer of material, esp. one of several stacked parallel layers. **2.** *Geol.* A bed or layer of sedimentary rock of approximately uniform composition. **3.** A level of society of people with similar social, cultural, or economic status. **4.** One of a number of layers, levels, or divisions in an organized system. [Lat. *strātum*, a covering < neut. p.part. of *sternere*, to spread. See STRATUS.] **—stra′tal** (-təl) *adj.*

Usage Note: The standard singular form is *stratum*; the standard plural is *strata* (sometimes *stratums*), not *stratas*.

stra•tus (strā′təs, străt′əs) *n., pl.* **stra•ti** (-tī). A low-altitude cloud formation consisting of a horizontal layer of gray clouds. [< Lat. *strātus*, p.part. of *sternere*, to stretch, extend. See **ster-**[2]*.]

Straus (strous, shtrous), **Oscar.** 1870–1954. Austrian-born composer whose operettas include *The Chocolate Soldier* (1908).

Strauss (strous, shtrous), **Johann.** 1804–49. Austrian violinist and composer of waltzes and other works, notably *Redetzky March* (1848). His son **Johann** (1825–99) is remembered for his waltzes, such as "The Blue Danube" (1867).

Strauss, Richard. 1864–1949. German composer known chiefly for his symphonic poems, such as *Don Quixote* (1897), and his operas, including *Salome* (1905).

Stra•vin•sky (strə-vĭn′skē), **Igor Fyodorovich.** 1882–1971. Russian-born composer whose ballets include *The Rite of Spring* (1913).

straw (strô) *n.* **1.a.** Stalks of threshed grain, used as bedding and fodder, for thatching, and for weaving or braiding. **b.** A single stalk of threshed grain. **2.** Something, such as a basket, made of straw. **3.** A slender tube used for sucking up a liquid. **4.a.** Something of minimal value or importance. **b.** Something with too little substance to provide support in a crisis. *—adj.* **1.** Of, relating to, or made of straw. **2.** Containing or used for straw, as a barn. **3.** *Color.* Of the color of straw; yellowish. **4.** Having little or no value or substance; unimportant. **5.** Of or constituting a straw man. ***—idiom.* straw in the wind.** A slight hint of something to come. [ME < OE *strēaw*. See **ster-**[2]*.] **—straw′y** *adj.*

straw•ber•ry (strô′bĕr′ē) *n.* **1.** Any of various low-growing plants of the genus *Fragaria*, having white flowers and an aggregate fruit consisting of a red fleshy edible receptacle and numerous seedlike fruitlets. **2.** The fruit of this plant. [ME < OE *strēawberige* : *strēaw*, straw; see STRAW + *berige, berie*, berry; see BERRY.]

strawberry bush *n.* A shrub *(Euonymus americanus)* of the eastern United States having showy pinkish fruit.

strawberry mark *n.* A red nevus or birthmark, occurring usu. on the face or scalp and resembling a strawberry.

strawberry roan *n.* A horse having reddish and white hair.

strawberry shrub *n.* See **Carolina allspice.**

strawberry tomato *n.* **1.** Any of several plants of the genus *Physalis*, such as *P. pubescens* and *P. pruinosa* of eastern North America, having yellow flowers and edible yellowish fruit. **2.** The fruit of this plant.

strawberry tree *n.* Any of several evergreen shrubs of the genus *Arbutus*, esp. *A. unedo*, native to southern Europe and having scarlet strawberrylike fruit.

straw•board (strô′bôrd′, -bōrd′) *n.* A coarse yellow cardboard made of straw pulp.

straw boss *n. Informal.* A worker who acts as a boss or crew leader in addition to performing regular duties.

straw•flow•er (strô′flou′ər) *n.* A stout Australian plant *(Helichrysum bracteatum)* having flower heads with showy, variously colored bracts that retain their color when dried.

straw-hat (strô′hăt′) *adj.* Of or relating to summer theater that operates in suburban or resort areas.

straw man *n.* **1.** A person who is set up as cover or a front for a questionable enterprise. **2.** An argument or opponent set up so as to be easily defeated. **3.** A bundle of straw made into the likeness of a man and often used as a scarecrow.

straw mushroom *n.* A tropical and subtropical edible mushroom *(Volvariella volvacea)* having a white cap and a long stipe with a swollen base.

straw vote *n.* An unofficial vote or poll indicating the trend of opinion on a candidate or an issue.

straw wine *n.* A sweet dessert wine made from grapes that have been dried on straw.

straw•worm (strô′wûrm′) *n.* The larva of the wasp *Harmolita grandis* of western North America that damages grain.

straw yellow *n. Color.* A pale yellow.

stray (strā) *intr.v.* **strayed, stray•ing, strays. 1.a.** To move away from a group, deviate from the correct course, or go beyond established limits. **b.** To become lost. **2.** To wander about without a goal; roam. See Syns at **wander. 3.** To follow a winding course; meander. **4.** To deviate from a moral, proper, or right course; err. **5.** To become diverted from a subject or train of thought; digress. See Syns at **swerve.** *—n.* One that has strayed, esp. a domestic animal wandering about. *—adj.* **1.** Straying or having strayed; wandering or lost. **2.** Scattered or separate. [ME *straien* < OFr. *estraier* < *estree*, highway < Lat. *strāta*. See STREET.] **—stray′er** *n.*

streak (strēk) *n.* **1.** A line, mark, smear, or band differentiated by color or texture from its surroundings. **2.** A slight contrasting element; a trace. **3.** *Informal.* **a.** A brief run or stretch, as of luck. **b.** An unbroken series, as of wins or losses. **4.** *Mineral.* The color of the fine powder produced when a mineral is rubbed against a hard surface. Used as a distinguishing characteristic. **5.** *Microbiol.* A bacterial culture inoculated by drawing a bacteria-laden needle across the surface of a solid culture medium. —*v.* **streaked, streak•ing, streaks.** —*tr.* **1.** To mark with streaks: *rain streaking the pavement.* **2.** To lighten (strands of hair) with a chemical preparation. **3.** *Microbiol.* To inoculate in order to produce a streak. —*intr.* **1.** To form streaks. **2.** To be or become streaked. **3.** To move at high speed; rush. [ME *streke,* line < OE *strica.* See **streig-***.] —**streak′er** *n.*

streak•y (strē′kē) *adj.* **-i•er, -i•est. 1.** Marked with, characterized by, or occurring in streaks. **2.** Variable or uneven in character or quality. —**streak′i•ly** *adv.* —**streak′i•ness** *n.*

stream (strēm) *n.* **1.a.** A flow of water in a channel or bed, as a brook or small river. **b.** A steady current in such a flow of water. **2.** A steady current of a fluid. **3.** A steady flow or succession. **4.** A trend, course, or drift, as of opinion. **5.** A beam or ray of light. —*v.* **streamed, stream•ing, streams.** —*intr.* **1.** To flow in or as if in a stream. **2.** To pour forth or give off a stream; flow. **3.** To come or go in large numbers; pour. **4.** To extend, wave, or float outward. **5.a.** To leave a continuous trail of light. **b.** To give forth a continuous stream of light rays or beams; shine. —*tr.* To emit, discharge, or exude (a body fluid, for example). —***idiom.* on stream.** In or into operation or production. [ME *streme* < OE *strēam.* See **sreu-***.] —**stream′y** *adj.*

stream•bed (strēm′bĕd′) *n.* The channel through which a natural stream of water runs or used to run.

stream•er (strē′mər) *n.* **1.a.** A long narrow flag, banner, or pennant. **b.** A long narrow strip of material used for ornament or decoration. **2.** A column of light shooting across the sky in the aurora borealis. **3.** An extension of rays from the sun's corona. **4.** A newspaper headline across a full page.

stream•let (strēm′lĭt) *n.* A small stream.

stream•line (strēm′līn′) *tr.v.* **-lined, -lin•ing, -lines. 1.** To construct or design in a form that offers the least resistance to fluid flow. **2.** To improve the appearance or efficiency of; modernize. **3.a.** To organize. **b.** To simplify. —*n.* **1.** A line parallel to the direction of flow of a fluid at a given instant. **2.** The path of one particle in a flowing fluid. **3.** A contour that offers minimum resistance to fluid flow.

stream•lined (strēm′līnd′) *adj.* **1.a.** Designed or arranged to offer the least resistance to fluid flow. **b.** Reduced to essentials; lacking anything extra. **c.** Effectively organized or simplified. **2.** Having flowing, graceful lines; sleek. **3.** Improved in appearance or efficiency; modernized.

stream of consciousness *n., pl.* **streams of consciousness. 1.** A literary technique that presents the thoughts and feelings of a character as they develop. **2.** *Psychol.* The conscious experience of an individual regarded as a continuous flowing series of images and ideas running through the mind. —**stream′-of-con′scious•ness** (strēm′əv-kŏn′shəs-nĭs) *adj.*

stream•side (strēm′sīd′) *n.* The land adjacent to a stream.

Stream•wood (strēm′wo͝od′). A village of NE IL, a suburb of Chicago. Pop. 30,987.

street (strēt) *n.* **1.a.** A public way or thoroughfare in a city or town, usu. with a sidewalk or sidewalks. **b.** Such a public way considered apart from the sidewalks. **c.** A public way or road along with the houses or buildings abutting it. **2.** The people living, working, or habitually gathering in or along a street. **3. Street.** A district identified with a specific profession. **4.** The streets of a city viewed as the scene of crime, poverty, or dereliction. —*adj.* **1.** Near or giving passage to a street. **2.a.** Taking place in the street. **b.** Living or making a living on the streets. **c.** Performing on the street. **d.** Crude; vulgar. **3.** Appropriate for wear or use in public. —***idiom.* on (or in) the street. 1.** Without a job; idle. **2.** Without a home; homeless. **3.** Out of prison; at liberty. [ME *strete* < OE *strǣt, strēt* < LLat. *strāta,* paved road < Lat., fem. p.part. of *sternere,* to stretch, extend, pave. See **ster-²***.]

street•car (strēt′kär′) *n.* A public vehicle operated on rails along a regular route, usu. through the streets of a city.

street fighter *n.* One who has learned fighting skills in the streets as opposed to being formally trained in boxing.

street•light (strēt′līt′) *n.* One of a series of lights that are usu. attached to tall poles, spaced at intervals along a public street or roadway, and illuminated from dusk to dawn.

street-smart (strēt′smärt′) *adj. Informal.* Having or displaying street smarts.

street smarts *pl.n. Informal.* Shrewd awareness of how to survive in an often hostile urban environment.

street theater *n.* Dramatization of social and political issues, usu. enacted outside, as on the street or in a park.

street•walk•er (strēt′wô′kər) *n.* A prostitute, esp. one who solicits in the streets. —**street′walk′ing** *n.*

street•wise (strēt′wīz′) *adj. Informal.* Having the shrewd awareness, experience, and resourcefulness needed for survival in a difficult, often dangerous urban environment.

strength (strĕngkth, strĕngth, strĕnth) *n.* **1.** The state, property, or quality of being strong. **2.** The power to resist attack; impregnability. **3.** The power to resist strain or stress; durability. **4.** The ability to maintain a moral or intellectual position firmly. **5.** Capacity or potential for effective action. **6.a.** The number of people constituting a normal or ideal organization. **b.** Military capability in terms of personnel and materiel. **7.a.** A source of power or force. **b.** One regarded as the embodiment of protective or supportive power; a support or mainstay. **c.** An attribute or a quality of particular worth or utility; an asset. **8.** Degree of intensity, force, effectiveness, or potency in terms of a particular property, as: **a.** Degree of concentration, distillation, or saturation; potency. **b.** Operative effectiveness or power. **c.** Intensity, as of sound or light. **d.** Intensity or vehemence, as of emotion or language. **9.** Effective or binding force; efficacy: *the strength of an argument.* **10.** Firmness of or a continuous rising tendency in prices, as on the stock market. **11.** *Games.* Power to take tricks derived from the value of cards held. —***idiom.* on the strength of.** On the basis of. [ME < OE *strengthu.*]

Syns: *strength, power, might, energy, force.* These nouns denote the capacity to act or work effectively. *Strength* refers especially to physical, mental, or moral robustness or vigor: *"enough work to do, and strength enough to do the work"* (Rudyard Kipling). *Power* is the ability to do something and especially to produce an effect: *"I do not think the United States would come to an end if we lost our power to declare an Act of Congress void"* (Oliver Wendell Holmes, Jr.). *Might* often implies abundant or extraordinary power: *"He could defend the island against the whole might of the German Air Force"* (Winston S. Churchill). *Energy* refers especially to a latent source of power: *"The same energy of character which renders a man a daring villain would have rendered him useful to society"* (Mary Wollstonecraft). *Force* is the application of power or strength: *"the overthrow of our institutions by force and violence"* (Charles Evans Hughes).

strength•en (strĕngk′thən, strĕng′-, strĕn′-) *v.* **-ened, -en•ing, -ens.** —*tr.* To make strong or increase the strength of. —*intr.* To become strong or stronger. —**strength′en•er** *n.*

stren•u•ous (strĕn′yo͞o-əs) *adj.* **1.** Requiring great effort, energy, or exertion. **2.** Vigorously active; energetic or zealous. [< Lat. *strēnuus.*] —**stren′u•os′i•ty** (-ŏs′ĭ-tē), **stren′u•ous•ness** (-əs-nĭs) *n.* —**stren′u•ous•ly** *adv.*

strep (strĕp) *adj.* Streptococcal. —*n.* Streptococcus.

strep throat *n.* See **septic sore throat.**

strepto– *pref.* **1.** Twisted; twisted chain: *streptococcus.* **2.** Streptococcus: *streptokinase.* [< Gk. *streptos* < *strephein,* to turn. See **streb(h)-***.]

strep•to•ba•cil•lus (strĕp′tō-bə-sĭl′əs) *n., pl.* **-cil•li** (-sĭl′ī). Any of various gram-negative, rod-shaped, often pathogenic bacteria of the genus *Streptobacillus,* occurring in chains, esp. *S. moniliformis,* which causes a type of rat-bite fever.

strep•to•coc•cus (strĕp′tə-kŏk′əs) *n., pl.* **-coc•ci** (-kŏk′sī, -kŏk′ī). A round to ovoid, gram-positive, often pathogenic bacterium of the genus *Streptococcus* that occurs in pairs or chains and causes various diseases in human beings, including scarlet fever and septic sore throat. —**strep′to•coc′cal, strep′to•coc′cic** (-kŏk′sĭk, -kŏk′ĭk) *adj.*

strep•to•kin•ase (strĕp′tō-kĭn′ās, -āz, -kī′nās, -nāz) *n.* A streptococcal enzyme used medically to dissolve blood clots.

strep•to•my•ces (strĕp′tə-mī′sēz) *n., pl.* **streptomyces.** Any of various actinomycetes of the genus *Streptomyces,* including several strains that produce antibiotics. [NLat. *Streptomyces,* genus name : STREPTO– + Gk. *mukēs,* fungus.]

strep•to•my•cin (strĕp′tə-mī′sĭn) *n.* An antibiotic, $C_{21}H_{39}O_{12}N_7$, produced by the actinomycete *Streptomyces griseus,* used on bacterial infections such as tuberculosis. [STREPTOMYC(ES) + –IN.]

strep•to•thri•cin (strĕp′tə-thrī′sĭn, -thrĭs′ĭn) *n.* Any of a group of antibiotics produced by an actinomycete *(Streptomyces lavendulae)* and active against bacteria and some fungi. [NLat. *Streptothrix, Streptothric-,* genus of bacteria (STREPTO– + Gk. *thrix, trikh-,* hair) + –IN.]

Stre•se•mann (strā′zə-män′, shtrā′-), **Gustav.** 1878–1929. German politician who shared the 1929 Nobel Peace Prize.

stress (strĕs) *n.* **1.** Importance, significance, or emphasis placed on something. See Syns at **emphasis. 2.** *Ling.* **a.** The relative force with which a sound or syllable is spoken. **b.** The emphasis placed on the sound or syllable spoken most forcefully in a word or phrase. **3.a.** The relative force of sound or emphasis given a syllable or word in accordance with a metrical pattern. **b.** A syllable having strong relative emphasis in a metrical pattern. **4.** *Mus.* Accent or a mark representing it. **5.** *Phys.* **a.** An applied force or system of forces that tends to strain or deform a body. **b.** The internal resistance of a body to such an applied force or system of forces. **6.a.** A mentally or emotionally disruptive or upsetting condition occurring in response to adverse external influences and usu. characterized by increased heart rate, a rise in blood pressure, muscular tension, irritability, and depression. **b.** A stimulus or circumstance causing such a condition. **7.** A state of extreme difficulty, pressure, or strain. —*tr.v.* **stressed, stress•ing, stress•es. 1.** To place emphasis on: *stressed safety.* **2.** To give prominence to (a syllable or word) in pronouncing or in accordance with a metrical pattern. **3.** To subject to physical or mental pressure, tension, or strain. **4.** To subject to mechanical pressure or force. **5.** To construct so as to withstand a

streetcar

ă pat · ā pay · âr care · ä father · ĕ pet · ē be · ĭ pit · ī pie · îr pier · ŏ pot · ō toe · ô paw · oi boy · ou out · o͝o took · o͞o boot · ŭ cut · ûr urge · th thin · *th* this · hw which · zh vision · ə about, item

Stress marks: ′ (primary); ′ (secondary), as in dictionary (dĭk′shə-nĕr′ē)

specified stress. — *phrasal verb.* **stress out.** *Slang.* To subject to or undergo extreme stress, as from working. [ME *stresse,* hardship, partly < *destresse* (< OFr.; see DISTRESS) and partly < OFr. *estrece,* narrowness, oppression (< VLat. **strictia* < Lat. *strictus,* p.part. of *stringere,* to draw tight; see STRAIT).]

STRESS (strĕs) *n. Comp. Sci.* A programming language designed for use in solving structural analysis problems in civil engineering. [*str(uctural) e(ngineering) s(ystems) s(olver).*]

stressed-out (strĕsd′out′) *adj. Slang.* Undergoing or suffering the effects of extreme stress.

stress fracture *n.* A fracture of bone caused by repeated application of a heavy load, such as the constant pounding on a surface by runners, gymnasts, and dancers.

stress•ful (strĕs′fəl) *adj.* Full of or tending to cause stress. — **stress′ful•ly** *adv.* — **stress′ful•ness** *n.*

stres•sor (strĕs′ər) *n.* An agent, a condition, or another stimulus that causes stress to an organism.

stress test *n.* A graded test to measure an individual's heart rate and oxygen intake during strenuous physical exercise.

stretch (strĕch) *v.* **stretched, stretch•ing, stretch•es.** — *tr.* **1.** To lengthen, widen, or distend. **2.** To cause to extend from one place to another or across a given space. **3.** To make taut; tighten. **4.** To reach or put forth; extend: *stretched out his hand.* **5.a.** To extend (oneself or one's limbs, for example) to full length. **b.** To extend (oneself) when lying down. **c.** To put to torture on the rack. **6.** To wrench or strain (a muscle, for example). **7.a.** To extend or enlarge beyond the usual or proper limits. **b.** To subject to undue strain. **8.a.** To expand in order to fulfill a larger function: *stretch a paycheck.* **b.** To increase the quantity of by admixture or dilution. **9.** To prolong: *stretch out an argument.* **10.** *Informal.* To fell by a blow. — *intr.* **1.** To become lengthened, widened, or distended. **2.** To extend or reach over a distance or an area or in a given direction. **3.** To lie down at full length: *stretched out for a nap.* **4.** To extend one's muscles or limbs, as on awakening. **5.** To extend over a given period of time. — *n.* **1.** The act of stretching or the state of being stretched. **2.** The extent or scope to which something can be stretched; elasticity. **3.** A continuous or unbroken length, area, or expanse. **4.** A straight section of a racecourse or track, esp. the section leading to the finish line. **5.a.** A continuous period of time. **b.** *Slang.* A term of imprisonment. **c.** *Informal.* The last stage of an event, a period, or a process. **6.** *Baseball.* The movement in which a pitcher raises both hands to the height of the head and then lowers them to the waist briefly before pitching the ball. — *adj.* **1.** Made of an elastic material that stretches easily. **2.** Of, relating to, or being a vehicle, such as a limousine, having an extended seating area. — ***idiom.*** **stretch (one's) legs.** To go for a walk, esp. after a lengthy period of sitting. [ME *strecchen* < OE *streccan.*] — **stretch′a•bil′i•ty** *n.* — **stretch′a•ble** *adj.*

stretch•er (strĕch′ər) *n.* **1.** A litter, usu. of canvas stretched over a frame, for the sick, wounded, or dead. **2.** One that stretches, such as the wooden framework on which canvas is stretched for an oil painting. **3.** A usu. horizontal tie beam or brace serving to support or extend a framework. **4.** A brick or stone laid parallel to the face of a wall.

stretch mark *n.* A white, shiny line on the skin of the abdomen, breasts, thighs, or buttocks caused by the stretching and weakening of elastic tissues, as during pregnancy.

stretch-out (strĕch′out′) *n.* **1.a.** The act of stretching out. **b.** The condition of being stretched out. **c.** An extension or a prolongation. **2.** An increase in the work required of industrial workers without a commensurate pay increase.

stretch receptor *n.* A sensory receptor in a muscle that responds to the stretching of tissue.

stretch runner *n. Sports.* A runner or racehorse that makes a strong effort in the last stretch of a race.

stretch•y (strĕch′ē) *adj.* **-i•er, -i•est.** **1.** Capable of being stretched: *a stretchy fabric.* **2.** Tending to stretch excessively.

stret•ta (strĕt′ə) *n., pl.* **stret•te** (strĕt′ā) or **stret•tas.** *Mus.* See **stretto** 2. [Ital., fem. of *stretto,* stretto. See STRETTO.]

stret•to (strĕt′ō) *n., pl.* **stret•ti** (strĕt′ē) or **stret•tos.** *Mus.* **1.** A close succession or overlapping of voices in a fugue, esp. in the final section. **2.** A final section, as of an oratorio, performed with an acceleration in tempo to produce a climax. [Ital., narrow, stretto < Lat. *strictus,* strict. See STRICT.]

streu•sel (strōō′zəl, stroi′-) *n.* A crumblike topping for coffee cakes and rich breads, consisting of flour, sugar, butter, cinnamon, and sometimes chopped nutmeats. [Ger., streusel < MHGer. *ströusel,* something strewn < *ströuwen,* to sprinkle < OHGer. *strouwen.* See **ster-**[2]***.**]

strew (strōō) *tr.v.* **strewed, strewn** (strōōn) or **strewed, strew•ing, strews.** **1.** To spread about; scatter. **2.** To cover (an area) with things scattered or sprinkled. **3.** To be or become dispersed over (a surface). **4.** To spread (something) over a wide area; disseminate. [ME *strewen* < OE *strēowian.* See **ster-**[2]***.**]

stri•a (strī′ə) *n., pl.* **stri•ae** (strī′ē). **1.** A thin narrow groove or channel. **2.** A thin line or band, esp. one of several that are parallel or close together. [Lat. See **streig-*.**]

stri•ate (strī′āt′) *tr.v.* **-at•ed, -at•ing, -ates.** To mark with striae or striations. — *adj.* also **stri•at•ed** (-ā′tĭd). **1.** Marked with striae; striped, grooved, or ridged. **2.** Consisting of a stria or striae. [< Lat. *striātus,* furrowed < *stria,* furrow. See STRIA.]

stri•a•tion (strī-ā′shən) *n.* **1.** The state of being striated or having striae. **2.** One of a number of parallel lines or scratches on the surface of a rock that were inscribed by rock fragments embedded in the base of a glacier as it moved across the rock. **3.** The form taken by striae. **4.** A stria.

strick•en (strĭk′ən) *v.* A p.part. of **strike.** — *adj.* **1.** Struck or wounded, as by a projectile. **2.a.** Overwhelmingly afflicted, as by disease, trouble, or painful emotion. **b.** Incapacitated; disabled. **3.** Having the contents made even with the top of a measuring device or container; level.

strick•le (strĭk′əl) *n.* **1.** An instrument used to level off grain or other material in a measure. **2.** A foundry tool used to shape a mold in sand or loam. **3.** A tool for sharpening scythes. [ME *strikelle,* perh. < OE *stricel,* teat, strickle. See **streig-*.**] — **strick′le** *v.*

strict (strĭkt) *adj.* **strict•er, strict•est.** **1.** Precise; exact: *a strict definition.* **2.** Complete; absolute. **3.** Kept within narrowly specific limits. **4.** Rigorous in discipline. **5.** Exacting in enforcement, observance, or requirement. See Syns at **severe. 6.** Conforming completely to rule, principle, or condition. **7.** *Bot.* Stiff, narrow, and upright. [ME *stricte,* narrow, small < Lat. *strictus,* tight, strict, p.part. of *stringere,* to draw tight. See **streig-*.**] — **strict′ly** *adv.* — **strict′ness** *n.*

stric•ture (strĭk′chər) *n.* **1.** A restraint, limit, or restriction. **2.** An adverse remark or criticism; censure. **3.** *Pathol.* An abnormal narrowing of a duct or passage. [ME, an abnormal narrowing of a bodily part < LLat. *strictūra,* contraction < Lat. *strictus,* p.part. of *stringere,* to draw tight. See STRICT.]

stride (strīd) *v.* **strode** (strōd), **strid•den** (strĭd′n), **strid•ing, strides.** — *intr.* **1.** To walk with long steps, esp. in a hasty or vigorous way. **2.** To take a single long step, as in passing over an obstruction. **3.** To stand or sit astride; straddle. — *tr.* **1.** To walk with long steps on, along, or over. **2.** To step over or across. **3.** To be astride of; straddle. — *n.* **1.** The act of striding. **2.a.** A single long step. **b.** The distance traveled in such a step. **3.a.** A single coordinated movement of the four legs of a horse or other animal, completed when the legs return to their initial relative position. **b.** The distance traveled in such a movement. **4.** A step of progress; an advance. Often used in the plural. — ***idioms.*** **hit (one's) stride. 1.** To achieve a steady effective pace. **2.** To attain a maximum level of competence. **take in (one's) stride.** To cope with calmly, without a break in routine. [ME *striden* < OE *strīdan.*] — **strid′er** *n.*

stri•dent (strīd′nt) *adj.* Loud, harsh, grating, or shrill; discordant. [Lat. *strīdēns, strīdent-,* pr.part. of *strīdēre,* to make harsh sounds, ult. of imit. orig.] — **stri′dence, stri′den•cy** *n.* — **stri′dent•ly** *adv.*

stride piano *n. Mus.* A style of jazz piano playing in which the melody is played by the right hand while a single note is played by the left hand in alternation with a chord that is an octave or more higher. [< *stride bass.*] — **stride pianist** *n.*

stri•dor (strī′dər, -dôr′) *n.* **1.** A harsh, shrill, grating, or creaking sound. **2.** *Pathol.* A harsh high-pitched sound in inhalation or exhalation. [Lat. *strīdor* < *strīdēre,* to make harsh sounds, ult. of imit. orig.]

strid•u•late (strĭj′ə-lāt′) *v.* **-lat•ed, -lat•ing, -lates.** — *intr.* To produce a shrill grating, chirping, or hissing sound by rubbing body parts together, as certain insects do. — *tr.* To produce by rubbing body parts together. — **strid′u•la′tion** *n.* — **strid′u•la•to′ry** (-lə-tôr′ē, -tōr′ē) *adj.*

strid•u•lous (strĭj′ə-ləs) *adj.* **1.** Characterized by or making a shrill grating sound or noise. **2.** Relating to or characterized by stridor. [< Lat. *strīdulus* < *strīdēre,* to make harsh sounds, ult. of imit. orig.] — **strid′u•lous•ly** *adv.*

strife (strīf) *n.* **1.** Heated, often violent dissension; bitter conflict. **2.** A struggle, fight, or quarrel. **3.** Contention or competition between rivals. **4.** *Archaic.* Earnest endeavor or striving. [ME *strif* < OFr. *estrit, estrif* < Frankish **strīd.*]

strig•il (strĭj′əl) *n.* An instrument used in ancient Greece and Rome for scraping the skin after a bath. [Lat. *strigilis.* See **streig-*.**]

stri•gose (strī′gōs′) *adj.* **1.** *Zool.* Marked with fine close-set grooves, ridges, or streaks. **2.** *Bot.* Having stiff, straight, closely appressed hair: *strigose leaves.* [NLat. *strigōsus* < *striga,* bristle < Lat., windrow, furrow. See **streig-*.**]

strike (strīk) *v.* **struck** (strŭk), **struck** or **strick•en** (strĭk′ən), **strik•ing, strikes.** — *tr.* **1.a.** To hit sharply, as with the hand, the fist, or a weapon. **b.** To inflict (a blow). **2.** To penetrate or pierce. **3.a.** To collide with or crash into. **b.** To cause to come into violent or forceful contact: *She struck her knee against the desk.* **c.** To thrust (a weapon, for example) in or into someone or something. **d.** To damage or destroy, as by forceful contact. **4.** To make a military attack on; assault. **5.** To afflict suddenly, as with a disease or an impairment. **6.** To cause to become by or as if by a blow: *struck him dead.* **7.a.** To snap at or seize (a bait). **b.** To hook (a fish that has taken the bait) by a pull on the line. **8.** To wound by biting. Used esp. of a snake. **9.** To form by stamping, printing, or *punching.* **10.** To produce or play by manipulating strings or keys. **11.** To indicate by a percussive or chiming sound: *The clock struck nine.* **12.** To produce as if by playing a musical instrument: *The report struck a positive note.* **13.a.** To produce by friction or a blow: *struck fire from the flints.* **b.** To produce flame, light, or a spark from by friction: *strike a match.* **14.** To remove or separate with or as if with a blow. **15.** To eliminate or expunge. **16.a.** To come upon; discover: *struck gold.* **b.** To come to; attain: *finally struck the main trail.* **17.a.** To fall upon; shine on. **b.** To become audible to. **18.** To affect keenly or forcibly; impress. **19.** To enter one's mind; occur to. **20.a.** To cause (a strong emotion) to penetrate deeply. **b.** To affect or overcome with strong emotion. **21.a.** To make and confirm the terms of (a bargain). **b.** To achieve (a balance, for example) by careful weighing or reckoning. **22.** To take on or assume (a pose, for example). **23.** *Naut.* **a.** To haul down (a mast or sail). **b.** To lower (a flag or sail) in salute or surrender. **c.** To lower (cargo) into a hold. **24.** To remove (a theatrical set or properties) from the stage. **25.** To dismantle and pack up for departure. **26.** To undertake a strike against (an employer). **27.a.** To level or even (a measure, as of grain). **b.** To smooth or shape with a strickle. **28.a.** To send (plant roots) out or down. **b.** To cause (a plant cutting) to take root. — *intr.* **1.** To deal a blow or blows with or as if with the fist or a weapon; hit. **2.** To aim a stroke or blow. **3.** To make contact suddenly or violently; collide. **4.** To begin a military attack. **5.** To penetrate or pierce. **6.** To take bait. **7.** To dart or shoot suddenly forward in an attempt to inflict a bite or wound. Used of snakes and wild animals. **8.** To set out or proceed, esp. in a new direction: *struck off into the woods.* **9.** To begin to move: *The horse struck into a gallop.* **10.a.** To send out roots. **b.** To sprout. **11.a.** To indicate the time by making a percussive or chiming sound. **b.** To become indicated by percussive or chiming sounds. **12.** To become ignited. **13.** To discover something suddenly or unexpectedly. **14.** To fall, as light or sound. **15.** To have an effect; make an impression. **16.** To engage in a strike against an employer. **17.** To interrupt by pushing oneself forward. **18.** To strive diligently for a specific technical rating in the U.S. Navy. — *n.* **1.** An act or a gesture of striking. **2.** An attack, esp. a military air attack on a cluster of targets. **3.a.** A cessation of work by employees in support of demands made on their employer, as for higher pay or improved conditions. **b.** A temporary stoppage of normal activity undertaken as a protest. **4.** A sudden achievement or valuable discovery, as of a precious mineral. **5.a.** The taking of bait by a fish. **b.** A pull on a fishing line indicating this. **6.** A quantity of coins or medals struck at the same time. **7.** *Baseball.* **a.** A pitched ball that is counted against the batter, typically one that is swung at and missed, fouled off, or judged to have passed through the strike zone. **b.** A perfectly thrown ball. **8.** An unfavorable condition, circumstance, or characteristic; a disadvantage. **9.** *Sports.* The knocking down of all the pins in bowling with the first bowl of a frame. **10.** The taking root and growing of a plant cutting. **11.** *Geol.* The course or bearing of the outcrop of an inclined bed or structure on a level surface. **12.** A strickle. — ***phrasal verbs.* strike down. 1.** To cause to fall by a blow. **2.** To incapacitate or kill. **3.** To render ineffective; cancel. **strike out. 1.** To begin a course of action. **2.** To set out energetically. **3.** *Baseball.* **a.** To pitch three strikes to (a batter), putting the batter out. **b.** To be struck out. **4.** To fail in an endeavor. **strike up. 1.a.** To start to play music or sing. **b.** To start to play or sing (something). **c.** To cause to start to play or sing. **2.** To initiate or begin. — ***idioms.* on strike.** Engaged in a work stoppage. **strike hands.** To conclude a bargain or reach an agreement. **strike it rich.** *Informal.* To have sudden financial success. [ME *striken* < OE *strīcan,* to stroke. See **streig-***.]

strike•bound (strīk′bound′) *adj.* Closed, immobilized, or slowed down by a strike: *a strikebound airline.*

strike•break•er (strīk′brā′kər) *n.* One who works or provides an employer with workers during a strike. — **strike′-break′ing** *n.*

strike•out (strīk′out′) *n. Baseball.* An out made by a batter charged with three strikes and credited to the pitcher.

strike•o•ver (strīk′ō′vər) *n.* The act or an instance of typing a character over one already typed.

strik•er (strī′kər) *n.* **1.** One who strikes, as an employee on strike. **2.** One that strikes, as the clapper in a bell. **3.a.** A harpoon. **b.** One who uses a harpoon; a harpooner. **4.** An enlisted person in usu. intensive training for a naval technical rating. **5.** *Sports.* A forward on a soccer team.

strike zone *n. Baseball.* The area over home plate through which a pitch must pass to be called a strike, roughly between the batter's armpits and knees.

strik•ing (strī′kĭng) *adj.* Producing a vivid impression on the sight or the mind. — **strik′ing•ly** *adv.* — **strik′ing•ness** *n.*

striking price *n.* The price at which a put or call option may be exercised.

Strind•berg (strĭnd′bûrg, strĭn′-, strĭn′bĕr′ē), **(Johan) August.** 1849–1912. Swedish writer whose plays include *Miss Julie* (1888). — **Strind•berg′i•an** *adj.*

string (strĭng) *n.* **1.** A cord usu. made of fiber, used for fastening, tying, or lacing. **2.** Something configured as a long, thin line. **3.** A plant fiber. **4.** A set of objects threaded together. **5.** A series of similar or related acts, events, or items arranged or falling in or as if in a line. **6.** *Comp. Sci.* A set of consecutive characters treated by a computer as a single item. **7.** *Informal.* **a.** A set of animals, esp. racehorses, belonging to one owner; a stable. **b.** A scattered group of businesses under one ownership or management. **8.** *Sports.* A group of players ranked according to ability on a team. **9.** *Mus.* **a.** A cord stretched on an instrument and struck, plucked, or bowed to produce tones. **b. strings.** The section of a band or an orchestra composed of stringed instruments. **c. strings.** Stringed instruments or their players considered as a group. **10.** *Archit.* **a.** A stringboard. **b.** A stringcourse. **11.** *Games.* The balk line in billiards. **12.** *Sports.* A complete game consisting of ten frames in bowling. **13.** *Informal.* A limiting or hidden condition. Often used in the plural. — *v.* **strung** (strŭng), **string•ing, strings.** — *tr.* **1.** To fit or furnish with strings or a string. **2.** To thread on a string. **3.** To arrange in a string or series. **4.** To fasten, tie, or hang with a string or strings. **5.** To stretch out or extend. **6.** To strip (vegetables) of fibers. — *intr.* **1.** To form strings or become stringlike. **2.** To extend or progress in a string, line, or succession. — ***phrasal verbs.* string along.** *Informal.* **1.** To go along with something; agree. **2.** To keep (someone) waiting or in uncertainty. **3.** To fool, cheat, or deceive. **string up.** *Informal.* To kill (someone) by hanging. — ***idiom.* on the string.** Under one's control or influence. [ME < OE *streng.*]

string bass (bās) *n. Mus.* See **double bass.**

string bean *n.* **1.a.** A bushy or climbing tropical American plant *(Phaseolus vulgaris)* having narrow green edible pods. **b.** The pod of this plant. **2.** *Slang.* A tall thin person.

string•board (strĭng′bôrd′, -bōrd′) *n.* A board along the side of a staircase supporting or covering the ends of the steps.

string•course (strĭng′kôrs′, -kōrs′) *n. Archit.* A decorative horizontal band or molding set in the face of a building.

stringed (strĭngd) *adj. Mus.* **1.** Having strings. Often used in combination: *a six-stringed lute.* **2.** Produced by stringed instruments: *stringed chamber music.*

stringed instrument *n. Mus.* An instrument, such as a violin, viola, cello, or double bass, in which sound is produced by plucking, striking, or bowing taut strings.

strin•gen•do (strĭn-jĕn′dō) *adj. Mus.* Played with an accelerating tempo. [Ital., gerund of *stringere,* to draw tight < Lat. See **streig-***.] — **strin•gen′do** *adv.*

strin•gent (strĭn′jənt) *adj.* **1.** Imposing rigorous standards of performance; severe. **2.** Constricted; tight: *a stringent time limit.* **3.** Characterized by scarcity of money, credit restrictions, or other financial strain. [Lat. *stringēns, stringent-,* pr.part. of *stringere,* to draw tight. See **streig-***.] — **strin′gen•cy** *n.* — **strin′gent•ly** *adv.*

string•er (strĭng′ər) *n.* **1.** One that strings: *a stringer of beads.* **2.** *Archit.* **a.** A long heavy horizontal timber used as a support or connector. **b.** A stringboard. **3.** A horizontal timber supporting upright posts. **4.** *Sports.* A member of a string or squad on a team. Often used in combination: *a first-stringer.* **5.** A part-time or freelance correspondent for the news media.

string•halt (strĭng′hôlt′) *n.* A nervous disorder in horses marked by spasmodic movements in the hind legs that cause the feet to rise abnormally high. [STRING, tendon + HALT[2].]

string quartet *n. Mus.* **1.** Four people playing stringed instruments, traditionally including a first and second violinist, a violist, and a cellist. **2.** A composition for such a group.

string•y (strĭng′ē) *adj.* **-i•er, -i•est. 1.** Consisting of, resembling, or containing strings or a string. **2.** Slender and sinewy; wiry. **3.** Forming strings, as a viscous liquid; ropy. — **string′i•ly** *adv.* — **string′i•ness** *n.*

strip[1] (strĭp) *v.* **stripped, strip•ping, strips.** — *tr.* **1.a.** To remove clothing or covering from. **b.** To deprive of (clothing or covering). **2.** To deprive of honors, rank, office, privileges, or possessions; divest. **3.a.** To remove all excess detail from; reduce to essentials. **b.** To remove equipment, furnishings, or supplementary parts or attachments from. **4.** To clear of a natural covering or growth; make bare. **5.** To remove an exterior coating, as of paint, from. **6.** To remove the leaves from the stalks of. **7.** To dismantle (a firearm, for example) piece by piece. **8.** To damage or break the threads of (a screw, for example) or the teeth of (a gear). **9.** To press the last drops of milk from (a cow, for example). **10.** To rob of wealth or property; despoil. **11.** To mount (a photographic positive or negative) on paper to be used in making a printing plate. — *intr.* **1.a.** To undress completely. **b.** To perform a striptease. **2.** To fall away or be removed; peel. — *n.* A striptease. [ME *stripen* < OE *-strȳpan,* to plunder.]

strip[2] (strĭp) *n.* **1.a.** A long narrow piece, usu. of uniform width: *a strip of paper.* **b.** A long narrow region of land or body of water. **2.** A comic strip. **3.** An airstrip. **4.** An area, as along a busy street or highway, lined with a great number and variety of commercial establishments. — *tr.v.* **stripped, strip•ping, strips.** To cut or tear into strips. [ME, perh. < MLGer. *strippe,* strap, thong.]

ă pat	oi boy
ā pay	ou out
âr care	o͝o to͝ok
ä father	o͞o bo͞ot
ĕ pet	ŭ cut
ē be	ûr urge
ĭ pit	th thin
ī pie	*th* this
îr pier	hw which
ŏ pot	zh vision
ō toe	ə about, item
ô paw	

Stress marks:
′ (primary);
′ (secondary), as in dictionary (dĭk′shə-nĕr′ē)

strip-crop•ping (strĭp′krŏp′ĭng) *n.* The growing of a cultivated crop, such as cotton, and a sod-forming crop, such as alfalfa, in alternating strips following the contour of the land, in order to minimize erosion.

stripe¹ (strīp) *n.* **1.a.** A long narrow band distinguished, as by color or texture, from the surrounding material or surface. **b.** A textile pattern of parallel bands or lines on a contrasting background. **c.** A fabric having such a pattern. **2.** A strip of cloth or braid worn on a uniform to indicate rank, awards received, or length of service; a chevron. **3.** Sort; kind. —*tr.v.* **striped, strip•ing, stripes.** To mark with stripes or a stripe. [ME, poss. < MDu. or MLGer. *strīpe.*]

stripe² (strīp) *n.* A stroke or blow, as with a whip. [ME.]

striped (strīpt, strī′pĭd) *adj.* Having lines or bands of different color or texture.

striped bass (băs) *n.* A North American food and game fish *(Morone saxatilis)* chiefly of coastal waters, having dark longitudinal stripes along its sides.

striped gopher *n.* A ground squirrel *(Citellus decemlineatus)* of western North America with streaks of white fur.

strip•er (strī′pər) *n.* **1.** *Slang.* A member of the armed forces, a cadet corps, or a commercial flight crew who wears stripes designating rank or length of service. Often used in combination: *a four-striper.* **2.** See **striped bass.**

strip•film (strĭp′fĭlm′) *n.* See **filmstrip.**

strip•ing (strī′pĭng) *n.* **1.** The act or process of marking or decorating with stripes. **2.a.** The stripes placed on something. **b.** A pattern of stripes.

strip•ling (strĭp′lĭng) *n.* An adolescent youth. [ME, poss. < *strip*, strip. See STRIP².]

strip mine *n.* An open mine, esp. a coal mine, whose seams or outcrops run close to ground level and are exposed by the removal of topsoil and overburden.

stroller
Baby stroller

strip-mine (strĭp′mīn′) *v.* **strip-mined, strip-min•ing, strip-mines.** —*tr.* **1.** To mine (ore) from a strip mine. **2.** To subject to strip mining: *strip-mined the land.* —*intr.* To engage in strip mining. —**strip miner** *n.*

stripped-down (strĭpt′doun′) *adj.* Having only essential or minimal features; lacking anything extra.

strip•per (strĭp′ər) *n.* **1.** One that strips, as one that strips photographic negatives or positives. **2.** A chemical product for removing a surface covering, such as paint or varnish, from furniture or floors. **3.** *Slang.* One who performs a striptease. **4.** An oil well that produces ten barrels or fewer per day.

strip-search (strĭp′sûrch′) *tr.v.* **-searched, -search•ing, -search•es.** To search (a person) for illegal articles by first requiring the removal of all clothing. —**strip search** *n.*

strip•tease also **strip tease** (strĭp′tēz′) *n.* A performance, as in a burlesque act, in which a person slowly removes clothing, usu. to musical accompaniment. —**strip′teas′er** *n.*

strip•y (strī′pē) *adj.* **-i•er, -i•est.** Marked with or suggestive of stripes; striped.

strive (strīv) *intr.v.* **strove** (strōv), **striv•en** (strĭv′ən) or **strived, striv•ing, strives. 1.** To exert much effort or energy; endeavor. **2.** To struggle or fight forcefully; contend: *strive for justice.* [ME *striven* < OFr. *estriver* < *estrit, estrif,* quarrel. See STRIFE.] —**striv′er** *n.* —**striv′ing•ly** *adv.*

strobe (strōb) *n.* **1.** A strobe light. **2.** A stroboscope. **3.** A spot of higher than normal intensity in the sweep of an indicator, as on a radar screen, used as a reference mark.

strobe light *n.* A flash lamp that produces high-intensity short-duration light pulses by electric discharge in a gas.

stro•bi•la (strō-bī′lə) *n., pl.* **-lae** (-lē). A part or structure that buds to form a series of segments, as the main body part of a tapeworm. [NLat. < Gk. *strobilē*, twisted plug of lint < *strobilos*, pine cone. See STROBILUS.] —**stro•bi′lar** *adj.*

stro•bi•lus (strō-bī′ləs) also **stro•bile** (strō′bīl′, -bəl) *n., pl.* **-bi•li** (-bī′lī) or **-biles.** A conelike structure, such as a pine cone, that consists of overlapping sporophylls spirally arranged along a central axis. [LLat., pine cone < Gk. *strobilos* < *strobos*, a whirling. See **streb(h)-*.**]

strob•o•scope (strō′bə-skōp′) *n.* Any of various instruments used to observe moving objects by making them appear stationary, esp. with pulsed illumination or mechanical devices that intermittently interrupt observation. [Gk. *strobos*, a whirling; see **streb(h)-*** + -SCOPE.] —**stro′bo•scop′ic** (-skŏp′ĭk) *adj.* —**stro′bo•scop′i•cal•ly** *adv.*

stro•bo•tron (strō′bə-trŏn′) *n.* A gas-filled cathode tube that produces bright flashes of light for a stroboscope.

strode (strōd) *v.* P.t. of **stride.**

Stro•heim (strō′hīm′), **Erich von.** 1885–1957. Austrian-born Amer. actor and director who is best known for his roles in *La Grande Illusion* (1937) and *Sunset Boulevard* (1950).

stroke¹ (strōk) *n.* **1.** The act or an instance of striking, as with the hand; a blow or an impact. **2.a.** The striking of a bell or gong. **b.** The sound so produced. **c.** The time so indicated. **3.** A sudden action or process having a strong impact or effect. **4.** A sudden occurrence or result. **5.** A sudden severe attack, as of paralysis or sunstroke. **6.** A sudden loss of brain function caused by a blockage or rupture of a blood vessel to the brain, characterized by loss of muscular control, diminution or loss of sensation or consciousness, dizziness, or slurred speech. **7.** An inspired or effective idea or act. **8.a.** A single uninterrupted movement, esp. when repeated or in a back-and-forth motion. **b.** Any of a series of movements of a piston from one end of the limit of its motion to another. **9.a.** A single completed movement of the limbs and body, as in swimming. **b.** The manner or rate of executing such a movement. **10.** *Naut.* **a.** The rower who sits nearest the coxswain or the stern and sets the tempo for the other rowers. **b.** The position occupied by this person. **11.** *Sports.* **a.** A movement of the upper torso and arms for the purpose of striking a ball, as in golf. **b.** The manner of executing such a movement. **12.a.** A mark made by a writing or marking implement. **b.** The act of making such a mark. **c.** A printed line in a graphic character that resembles such a mark. **13.** A distinctive effect or deft touch. —*v.* **stroked, strok•ing, strokes.** —*tr.* **1.a.** To mark with a single short line. **b.** To draw a line through; cancel: *stroked out the words.* **2.** *Naut.* To set the pace for (a rowing crew). **3.** To hit or propel (a ball, for example) with a smooth swing. —*intr.* **1.** To make or perform a stroke. **2.** *Naut.* To row at a particular rate per minute. [ME, prob. < OE **strāc.* See **streig-*.**]

stroke² (strōk) *tr.v.* **stroked, strok•ing, strokes. 1.** To rub lightly, with or as if with the hand or something in it; caress. **2.** *Informal.* To behave attentively or flatteringly toward, as to win over. —*n.* A light caressing movement. [ME *stroken* < OE *strācian* < **strāc*, stroke. See STROKE¹.] —**strok′er** *n.*

stroll (strōl) *v.* **strolled, stroll•ing, strolls.** —*intr.* **1.** To go for a leisurely walk. **2.** To travel from place to place seeking work or gain. —*tr.* To walk along or through at a leisurely pace. —*n.* A leisurely walk. [Prob. Ger. dial. *strollen*, var. of *strolchen* < *Strolch*, fortuneteller, vagabond, perh. < Ital. dial. *strolegh* < Ital. *astròlogo*, astrologer, fortuneteller, ult. < Gk. *astrologos*, astronomer, astrologer. See ASTROLOGY.]

stroll•er (strō′lər) *n.* **1.** One who strolls. **2.** A light four-wheeled chairlike carriage for transporting small children. **3.** An itinerant actor or performer. **4.** A vagabond.

stro•ma (strō′mə) *n., pl.* **-ma•ta** (-mə-tə). **1.** The connective tissue framework of an organ, a gland, or other structure. **2.** The spongy colorless framework of a red blood cell or other cell. [LLat. *strōma*, mattress, covering < Gk., bed. See **ster-²*.**] —**stro′mal** *adj.* —**stro•mat′ic** (-măt′ĭk) *adj.*

stro•mat•o•lite (strō-măt′l-īt′) *n.* A sedimentary structure of laminated carbonate or silicate rocks, produced over geologic time by the trapping of sediment by groups of microorganisms, esp. cyanobacteria. [LLat. *strōma, strōmat-*, covering; see STROMA + -LITE.] —**stro•mat′o•lit′ic** (-măt′l-ĭt′ĭk) *adj.*

Strom•bo•li (strŏm′bə-lē, strôm′bô-). An island of S Italy in the Lipari Is. off NE Sicily in the Tyrrhenian Sea. Its volcano, 926.6 m (3,038 ft), erupted violently in 1930 and 1966.

strong (strông) *adj.* **strong•er, strong•est. 1.a.** Physically powerful; capable of exerting great physical force. **b.** Marked by great physical power. **2.** In good or sound health; robust. **3.** Economically or financially sound or thriving. **4.** Having force of character, will, morality, or intelligence. **5.** Having or showing ability or achievement in a specified field. **6.** Capable of the effective exercise of authority. **7.a.** Capable of withstanding force or wear; solid, tough, or firm. **b.** Having great binding strength. **8.** Not easily captured or defeated. **9.** Not easily upset; resistant to harmful or unpleasant influences. **10.** Having force or rapidity of motion. **11.a.** Persuasive, effective, and cogent. **b.** Forceful and pointed; emphatic. **c.** Forthright and explicit, often offensively so. **12.** Extreme; drastic. **13.** Having force of conviction or feeling; uncompromising. **14.** Intense in degree or quality. **15.a.** Having an intense or offensive effect on the senses: *strong light.* **b.** Clear and loud. **c.** Readily noticeable; remarkable. **d.** Readily detected or received: *a strong signal.* **16.a.** Having a high concentration of an essential or active ingredient. **b.** Containing a considerable percentage of alcohol. **c.** Powerfully effective. **17.** *Color.* Marked by a high degree of saturation. **18.** Having a specified number of units or members: *100,000 strong.* **19.** Marked by steady or rising prices. **20.** *Ling.* **a.** Of or relating to verbs in Germanic languages that form their past tense and their past participle by a change in stem vowel, sometimes adding the suffix *-(e)n,* to the participle, as *take, took, taken.* **b.** Of or relating to the inflection of nouns or adjectives in Germanic languages with endings that historically did not contain a suffix with an *-n-*. **21.** Stressed or accented in pronunciation or poetic meter. Used of a word or syllable. —*adv.* In a strong, powerful, or vigorous manner; forcefully. [ME < OE *strang.*] —**strong′ish** *adj.* —**strong′ly** *adv.*

Strong (strông), **William.** 1808–95. Amer. jurist; associate justice of the U.S. Supreme Court (1870–80).

strong-arm (strông′ärm′) *Informal.* —*adj.* Using physical force or coercion. —*tr.v.* **-armed, -arm•ing, -arms. 1.** To use physical force or coercion against. **2.** To rob by force.

strong•box (strông′bŏks′) *n.* A stoutly made box or safe in which valuables are deposited.

strong force *n. Phys.* See **strong interaction.**

strong•hold (strông′hōld′) *n.* **1.** A fortified place or a fortress. **2.a.** A place of survival or refuge. **b.** An area specially

dominated or occupied by a group or marked by a quality.
strong interaction *n.* A fundamental interaction between elementary particles that causes protons and neutrons to bind together in the atomic nucleus.
strong•man (strông′măn′) *n.* **1.** A powerful influential political figure who exercises leadership and control by force. **2.** One who performs feats of strength, as at a circus.
strong-mind•ed (strông′mīn′dĭd) *adj.* **1.** Having a determined will. **2.** Having a vigorous, independent mind. **—strong′-mind′ed•ly** *adv.* **—strong′-mind′ed•ness** *n.*
strong•point (strông′point′) *n.* A military stronghold.
strong room *n.* A strongly built fireproof room designed for the safekeeping of money or valuables.
strong side *n. Football.* The side of a formation having more players; the side on which the tight end is positioned.
strong suit *n.* **1.** A quality, an activity, or a skill in which a person excels. **2.** *Games.* A long suit in a card game such as bridge that contains high cards.
Strongs•ville (strôngz′vĭl′). A city of NE OH, a suburb of Cleveland. Pop. 35,308.
stron•gyle also **stron•gyl** (strŏn′jīl′, -jəl) *n.* Any of various nematode worms of the family Strongylidae, often parasitic in the gastrointestinal tract of mammals, esp. horses. [NLat. *Strongylus*, type genus < Gk. *strongulos*, compact.]
stron•gy•lo•sis (strŏn′jə-lō′sĭs) *n.* Infestation with strongyles.
stron•ti•an•ite (strŏn′chē-ə-nīt′, -shə-nīt′) *n.* A gray to yellowish-green ore of strontium, $SrCO_3$. [< *strontian*, strontianite, ultimately after *Strontian* in W-central Scotland.]
stron•ti•um (strŏn′chē-əm, -tē-əm, -shəm) *n. Symbol* **Sr** A soft, easily oxidized metallic element that ignites spontaneously in air when finely divided and is used in pyrotechnic compounds and various alloys. Atomic number 38; atomic weight 87.62; melting point 769°C; boiling point 1,384°C; specific gravity 2.54; valence 2. See table at **element.** [< NLat. *strontia*, strontium oxide < *strontian.* See STRONTIANITE.] **—stron′tic** (-tĭk) *adj.*
strontium 90 *n.* The strontium isotope with mass 90, having a half-life of 28 years, that is a high-energy beta emitter and constitutes a radiation hazard in fallout.
strop (strŏp) *n.* **1.** A strap, esp. a short rope whose ends are spliced together to make a ring. **2.** A flexible strip of leather or canvas used for sharpening a razor. —*tr.v.* **stropped, strop•ping, strops.** To sharpen (a razor) on a strop. [ME *strope*, band of leather, prob. < OE, thong for an oar < Lat. *stroppus*, twisted cord < Gk. *strophos* < *strephein*, to turn. See **streb(h)-*.**]
stro•phan•thin (strō-făn′thĭn) *n.* A toxic glycoside or mixture of glycosides obtained from the seeds of certain plants of the genus *Strophanthus*, esp. *S. kombé*, used medicinally as a cardiac stimulant. [NLat. *Strophanthus*, genus name (Gk. *strophos*, twisted cord; see STROP + Gk. *anthos*, flower) + -IN.]
stro•phe (strō′fē) *n.* **1.a.** The first of a pair of stanzas of alternating form on which the structure of a given poem is based. **b.** A stanza containing irregular lines. **2.** The first division of the triad constituting a section of a Pindaric ode. **3.a.** The first movement of the chorus in classical Greek drama while turning from one side of the orchestra to the other. **b.** The part of a choral ode sung while this movement is executed. [Gk. *strophē*, a turning, stanza < *strephein*, to turn. See **streb(h)-*.**] **—stro′phic** (strō′fĭk, strŏf′ĭk) *adj.*
stro•phoid (strō′foid′) *n.* A plane curve generated by a point that maintains a distance from the y-axis along a straight line equal to the y-intercept. [Gk. *strophos*, twisted cord (< *strephein*, to turn; see **streb(h)-***) + -OID.]
stroph•u•lus (strŏf′yə-ləs) *n., pl.* **-li** (-lē). A disease, common esp. among children, sometimes associated with intestinal disturbances and characterized by a papular eruption of the skin. [NLat. < Gk. *strophos*, twisted cord < *strephein*, to turn. See **streb(h)-*.**]
strop•py (strŏp′ē) *adj.* **-pi•er, -pi•est.** *Chiefly British.* Easily offended or annoyed; ill-tempered or belligerent. [Perh. alteration of OBSTREPEROUS.]
stroud (stroud) *n.* A coarse woolen cloth or blanket. [After *Stroud*, an urban district of SW-central England.]
strove (strōv) *v.* P.t. of **strive.**
struck (strŭk) *v.* P.t. and p.part. of **strike.** —*adj.* Affected or shut down by a labor strike.
struc•tur•al (strŭk′chər-əl) *adj.* **1.a.** Of, relating to, having, or characterized by structure. **b.** Affecting structure. **2.** Used in or necessary to building. **3.** Concerned with or resulting from political or esp. economic structure. **4.** *Geol.* Of or relating to the structure of rocks and other aspects of the earth's crust. **5.** *Biol.* Of or relating to organic structure; morphological. **6.** Relating to or concerned with systematic structure in a field of study, such as linguistics or the behavioral sciences. —*n.* A part of a structure that bears a weight or the structural piece used for such a part. **—struc′tur•al•ly** *adv.*
structural formula *n.* A chemical formula that shows how the atoms and bonds in a molecule are arranged.
structural gene *n.* A gene that determines the amino acid sequence of a protein.
struc•tur•al•ism (strŭk′chər-ə-lĭz′əm) *n.* **1.** A method of analyzing phenomena, as in linguistics or psychology, marked by contrasting the elemental structures of the phenomena in a system of binary opposition. **2.** A school that advocates and employs such a method. **—struc′tur•al•ist** *adj. & n.*
struc•tur•al•ize (strŭk′chər-ə-līz′) *tr.v.* **-ized, -iz•ing, -iz•es.** To form, organize, or incorporate into a structure. **—struc′tur•al•i•za′tion** (-ə-lĭ-zā′shən) *n.*
structural linguistics *n.* (*used with a sing. v.*) **1.** A method of synchronic linguistic analysis employing structuralism, esp. in contrasting those formal structures, such as phonemes or sentences, that make up systems, such as phonology or syntax. **2.** A school of such a method of linguistics, developed in the United States from the 1930's to the 1950's.
structural steel *n.* Steel shaped for use in construction.
struc•ture (strŭk′chər) *n.* **1.** Something made up of a number of parts that are held or put together in a particular way. **2.** The way in which parts are arranged or put together to form a whole; makeup. **3.** The interrelation or arrangement of parts in a complex entity. **4.** Something constructed. **5.** *Biol.* **a.** The arrangement or formation of the tissues, organs, or other parts of an organism. **b.** An organ or other part of an organism. —*tr.v.* **-tured, -tur•ing, -tures.** To give form or arrangement to. [ME, the process of building < Lat. *strūctūra* < *strūctus*, p.part. of *struere*, to construct. See **ster-²*.**]
struc•tured (strŭk′chərd) *adj.* **1.** Highly organized. **2.** *Psychol.* Having a limited number of correct or nearly correct answers. Used of a test.
structured programming *n. Comp. Sci.* A method of designing and writing programs in which the statements are organized to minimalize error or misinterpretation.
stru•del (strōōd′l, shtrōōd′l) *n.* A pastry made with fruit or cheese rolled up in a thin sheet of dough and then baked. [Ger. < MHGer., whirlpool.]
strug•gle (strŭg′əl) *v.* **-gled, -gling, -gles.** —*intr.* **1.** To exert muscular energy, as against a material force or mass. **2.** To be strenuously engaged with a problem, a task, or an undertaking. **3.** To make a strenuous effort; strive. **4.** To contend or compete. **5.** To progress with difficulty. —*tr.* To move or place (something) with an effort. —*n.* **1.** The act of struggling. **2.** Strenuous effort; striving. **3.** Combat; strife. [ME *struglen.*] **—strug′gler** *n.* **—strug′gling•ly** *adv.*
strum (strŭm) *v.* **strummed, strum•ming, strums.** —*tr.* **1.** To play (a stringed musical instrument) by stroking or brushing the strings. **2.** To play (music) in this way. —*intr.* To strum a stringed instrument. —*n.* The act or sound of strumming. [Perh. imit.] **—strum′mer** *n.*
stru•ma (strōō′mə) *n., pl.* **-mae** (-mē) or **-mas. 1.a.** See **scrofula. b.** See **goiter. 2.** *Bot.* A cushionlike swelling at a moss capsule base. [Lat. *strūma*, scrofulous tumor.] **—stru•mat′ic** (-măt′ĭk), **stru′mose′** (-mōs′), **stru′mous** (-məs) *adj.*
Stru•ma (strōō′mə). A river of W Bulgaria and NE Greece flowing c. 348 km (216 mi) to the Aegean Sea.
strum•pet (strŭm′pĭt) *n.* A prostitute. [ME.]
strung (strŭng) *v.* P.t. and p.part. of **string.** —*adj.* Tense or exhausted.
strung-out (strŭng′out′) *adj. Slang.* **1.a.** Stupefied from ingestion of a drug. **b.** Addicted to a drug. **2.a.** Debilitated from long drug use. **b.** Physically or emotionally exhausted.
strut (strŭt) *v.* **strut•ted, strut•ting, struts.** —*intr.* To walk with pompous bearing; swagger. —*tr.* **1.** To display in order to impress others. **2.** To brace with a supporting bar or rod. —*n.* **1.** A pompous self-important gait. **2.** A bar or rod used to brace a structure against forces applied from the side. —***idiom.* strut (one's) stuff.** *Slang.* To behave or perform ostentatiously; show off. [ME *strouten*, to stand out < OE *strūtian*, to stand out stiffly. See **ster-¹*.**] **—strut′ter** *n.*
stru•thi•ous (strōō′thē-əs, -thē-) *adj.* Of, relating to, or resembling an ostrich or a related bird; ratite. [< LLat. *strūthiō*, ostrich < LGk. *strouthiōn* < Gk. *strouthos.*]
strych•nine (strĭk′nīn′, -nĭn, -nēn′) *n.* An extremely poisonous crystalline alkaloid, $C_{21}H_{22}O_2N_2$, derived from nux vomica and related plants and used as a poison for rodents and other pests and topically in medicine as a stimulant for the central nervous system. [Fr. < NLat. *Strychnos*, genus name < Lat. *strychnon*, a kind of nightshade < Gk. *strukhnon.*]
strych•nin•ism (strĭk′nĭ-nĭz′əm, -nī-, -nē-) *n.* A pathological condition induced by strychnine poisoning.
Stu•art (stōō′ərt, styōō′-). Ruling house of Scotland (1371–1603) and of England and Scotland (1603–49 and 1660–1714).
Stuart, Charles Edward. "the Young Pretender." 1720–88. Pretender to the British throne who led the last Jacobite rising (1745–46) but was defeated in battle and fled to France.
Stuart, Gilbert Charles. 1755–1828. Amer. painter particularly known for his portraits of George Washington.
Stuart, Henry. See Lord **Darnley.**
Stuart, James Ewell Brown ("Jeb"). 1833–64. Amer. Confederate general who was mortally wounded during the Wilderness Campaign (1864).
Stuart, James (Francis) Edward. "the Old Pretender." 1688–1766. Pretender to the British throne who made two unsuc-

Gilbert Stuart
Self-portrait

J.E.B. Stuart
Photographed in the early 1860's

ă pat	oi boy
ā pay	ou out
âr care	ŏŏ took
ä father	ōō boot
ĕ pet	ŭ cut
ē be	ûr urge
ĭ pit	th thin
ī pie	*th* this
îr pier	hw which
ŏ pot	zh vision
ō toe	ə about, item
ô paw	

Stress marks:
′ (primary);
′ (secondary), as in dictionary (dĭk′shə-nĕr′ē)

cessful attempts to take the throne (1708–15).

stub (stŭb) *n.* **1.** The usu. short end remaining after something bigger has been used up. **2.** Something cut short or arrested in development. **3.a.** The part of a check or receipt retained as a record. **b.** The part of a ticket returned as a voucher of payment. —*tr.v.* **stubbed, stub•bing, stubs. 1.a.** To pull up (weeds) by the roots. **b.** To clear (a field) of weeds. **2.** To strike (one's toe or foot) against something accidentally. **3.** To snuff out (a cigarette butt) by crushing. [ME *stubbe*, tree stump < OE *stybb*.]

stub•ble (stŭbʹəl) *n.* **1.** The short stiff stalks of grain or hay left after harvest. **2.** Something similar, esp. the short bristly hairs on a man's unshaven face. [ME *stuble* < OFr. *estuble* < Lat. *stupula, stupla*, var. of *stipula*, straw, dim. of *stīpes*, stalk.] —**stubʹbled** *adj.* —**stubʹbly** *adj.*

stub•born (stŭbʹərn) *adj.* **-er, -est. 1.a.** Unreasonably, often perversely unyielding; bullheaded. **b.** Firmly resolved or determined; resolute. See Syns at **obstinate. 2.** Characterized by perseverance; persistent. **3.** Difficult to treat or deal with. [ME *stuborn*.] —**stubʹborn•ly** *adv.* —**stubʹborn•ness** *n.*

Stubbs (stŭbz), **William.** 1825–1901. British historian and prelate known for his study of the constitutional history of medieval England.

stub•by (stŭbʹē) *adj.* **-bi•er, -bi•est. 1.a.** Having the nature of or suggesting a stub, as in shortness or thickness. **b.** Having a short, stocky build; thickset. **2.** Short and blunt, as from much use. **3.** Covered with or made of stubs. **4.** Short and bristly. —**stubʹbi•ly** *adv.* —**stubʹbi•ness** *n.*

stub nail *n.* A short thick nail.

sturgeon

stuc•co (stŭkʹō) *n., pl.* **-coes** or **-cos. 1.** A durable finish for exterior walls, usu. composed of cement, sand, and lime, and applied while wet. **2.** A fine plaster for interior wall ornamentation, such as moldings. **3.** A plaster or cement finish for interior walls. **4.** Stuccowork. —*tr.v.* **-coed, -co•ing, -coes** or **-cos.** To finish or decorate with stucco. [Ital., of Gmc. orig.]

stuc•co•work (stŭkʹō-wûrkʹ) *n.* Ornamental work or moldings or a finish done in stucco. —**stucʹco•workʹer** *n.*

stuck (stŭk) *v.* P.t. and p.part. of **stick.**

stuck-up (stŭkʹŭpʹ) *adj. Informal.* Snobbish; conceited.

stud¹ (stŭd) *n.* **1.** An upright post in the framework of a wall for supporting sheets of lath, wallboard, or similar material. **2.** A small knob, nail head, or rivet fixed in and slightly projecting from a surface. **3.a.** A small ornamental button mounted on a short post for insertion through an eyelet, as on a dress shirt. **b.** A buttonlike earring mounted on a slender post, as of gold or steel, for wearing in a pierced earlobe. **4.a.** Any of various protruding pins or pegs in machinery, used mainly as a support or pivot. **b.** One of a number of small metal cleats embedded in a snow tire to increase traction on slippery or snowy roads. **5.** A metal crosspiece used as a brace in a link, as in a chain cable. —*tr.v.* **stud•ded, stud•ding, studs. 1.** To provide with or construct with studs or a stud. **2.** To set with studs or a stud. **3.** To be scattered over. [ME *stode* < OE *studu*. See **stā-*.**]

stud² (stŭd) *n.* **1.a.** A group of animals, esp. horses, kept for breeding. **b.** A male animal, such as a stallion, kept for breeding. **c.** A stable or farm where these animals are kept. **2.** *Slang.* A man regarded as virile and sexually active. **3.** *Games.* Stud poker. —***idiom.* at stud.** Available or offered for breeding. Used of animals. [ME *stod*, establishment for breeding horses < OE *stōd*. See **stā-*.**]

stud. *abbr.* Student.

stud•book (stŭdʹbo͝okʹ) *n.* A book registering the pedigrees of thoroughbred animals, esp. horses.

stud•ding (stŭdʹĭng) *n.* **1.a.** The wood framework of a wall or partition. **b.** Lumber cut for studs. **2.** Something with which a surface is studded.

stud•ding•sail (stŭnʹsəl, stŭdʹing-sālʹ) *n. Naut.* A narrow rectangular sail set from an extension of a yard of a square-rigged ship. [?]

stu•dent (sto͞odʹnt, styo͞odʹ-) *n.* **1.** One who attends a school, college, or university. **2.a.** One who makes a study of something. **b.** An attentive observer. [ME, alteration (influenced by Lat. *studēre*, to study) of *studient, studiant* < OFr. *estudiant*, one who studies < pr.part. of *estudier*, to study < Med.Lat. *studiāre* < Lat. *studium*, study. See STUDY.]

student lamp *n.* A reading lamp having a flexible adjustable neck and intended for use on a desk.

student teacher *n.* A college student pursuing a degree in education who as an intern teaches in a classroom under an experienced, certified teacher. —**student teaching** *n.*

student union *n.* A building on a college campus with facilities for social and organizational activities.

stud•fish (stŭdʹfĭshʹ) *n., pl.* **studfish** or **-fish•es.** Either of two small, brightly colored topminnows *(Fundulus catenatus* or *F. stellifer)* of the southeast United States.

stud•horse also **stud horse** (stŭdʹhôrsʹ) *n.* A stallion kept for breeding.

stud•ied (stŭdʹēd) *adj.* **1.** Resulting from deliberation and careful thought. **2.** Lacking spontaneity; contrived. **3.** Learned; knowledgeable. —**studʹied•ly** *adv.* —**studʹied•ness** *n.*

stu•di•o (sto͞oʹdē-ō, styo͞oʹ-) *n., pl.* **-os. 1.** An artist's workroom. **2.** A photographer's establishment. **3.** An establishment where an art is taught or studied. **4.a.** A room or building for movie, television, or radio productions. **b.** A room or building where tapes and records are produced. [Ital. < Lat. *studium*, eagerness, application. See STUDY.]

studio apartment *n.* A small apartment usu. consisting of one main living space, a small kitchen, and a bathroom.

studio couch *n.* A couch that can be made to serve as a double bed by sliding the frame of a cot from beneath it.

stu•di•ous (sto͞oʹdē-əs, styo͞oʹ-) *adj.* **1.a.** Given to diligent study. **b.** Conducive to study. **2.** Marked by steady attention and effort; assiduous. **3.** Giving or evincing careful regard; heedful. **4.** Deliberate; contrived. [ME < Lat. *studiōsus* < *studium*, eagerness. See STUDY.] —**stuʹdi•ous•ly** *adv.* —**stuʹdi•ous•ness** *n.*

stud poker *n. Games.* Poker in which the first round of cards, and often the last, is dealt face down and the others face up. [Prob. short for *studhorse poker*.]

stud•work (stŭdʹwûrkʹ) *n.* **1.** Work ornamented or covered with studs. **2.** The supportive framework, as of a wall.

stud•y (stŭdʹē) *n., pl.* **-ies. 1.a.** The act or process of studying. **b.** The pursuit of knowledge, as by observation or research. **2.** Attentive scrutiny. **3.** A branch of knowledge. **4. studies.** A branch or department of learning: *African studies.* **5.a.** A work, such as a thesis, that results from studious endeavor. **b.** A literary work on a given subject. **c.** A preliminary sketch, as for a work of art. **6.** *Mus.* A composition intended as a technical exercise. **7.** A state of mental absorption. **8.** A room intended or equipped for studying or writing. **9.a.** One who memorizes something, esp. a performer with reference to the ability to memorize a part: *a quick study.* **b.** Memorization of a part in a play. —*v.* **-ied, -y•ing, -ies.** —*tr.* **1.** To apply one's mind purposefully to the acquisition of knowledge or understanding of (a subject). **2.** To read carefully. **3.** To memorize. **4.** To take (a course) at a school. **5.** To inquire into; investigate. **6.** To examine closely; scrutinize. **7.** To give careful thought to; contemplate: *study the next move.* —*intr.* **1.** To apply oneself to learning, esp. by reading. **2.** To pursue a course of study. **3.** To ponder; reflect. [ME *studie* < OFr. *estudie* < Lat. *studium* < *studēre*, to study.]

study hall *n.* **1.** A schoolroom reserved for study. **2.** A period set aside for study.

stuff (stŭf) *n.* **1.** The material out of which something is made or formed; substance. **2.** The essential substance or elements; essence. **3.** *Informal.* **a.** Unspecified material. **b.** Household or personal articles considered as a group. **c.** Worthless objects. **4.** *Slang.* Specific talk or actions. **5.** *Sports.* **a.** The control a player has over a ball, esp. to give it spin, english, curve, or speed. **b.** The result of such control. **6.** Special capability. **7.** *Chiefly British.* Woven material, esp. woolens. **8.** *Slang.* Money; cash. **9.** *Slang.* A habit-forming drug, esp. heroin. —*v.* **stuffed, stuff•ing, stuffs.** —*tr.* **1.a.** To pack tightly; cram. **b.** To block (a passage); plug. **2.a.** To fill with an appropriate stuffing. **b.** To fill (an animal skin) for mounting or display. **3.** To cram with food. **4.** To fill (the mind). **5.** To put fraudulent votes into (a ballot box). **6.** To apply a preservative and softening agent to (leather). —*intr.* To overeat; gorge. —***idiom.* stuff (one's) face.** *Slang.* To eat greedily. [ME < OFr. *estoffe* < *estoffer*, to equip, of Gmc. orig.] —**stuffʹer** *n.*

stuffed shirt (stŭft) *n. Informal.* A person regarded as pompous or stiff.

stuff•ing (stŭfʹĭng) *n.* **1.** Padding put in cushions and upholstered furniture. **2.** Food put into the cavity of a piece of meat or a hollowed-out vegetable.

stuffing box *n.* An enclosure containing packing to prevent leakage around a moving machine part.

stuff•y (stŭfʹē) *adj.* **-i•er, -i•est. 1.** Insufficiently ventilated; close. **2.** Having the respiratory passages blocked. **3.a.** Dull; boring. **b.** Rigidly adhering to standards of conduct; straitlaced. —**stuffʹi•ly** *adv.* —**stuffʹi•ness** *n.*

stull (stŭl) *n.* **1.** A supporting prop in a mine. **2.** A platform braced against the sides of a work area in a mine. [Prob. < Ger. *Stollen* < MHGer. *stolle*, prop, support < OHGer. *stollo*. See **stel-*.**]

stul•ti•fy (stŭlʹtə-fīʹ) *tr.v.* **-fied, -fy•ing, -fies. 1.** To render useless or ineffectual; cripple. **2.** To cause to appear stupid, inconsistent, or ridiculous. [LLat. *stultificāre*, to make foolish : Lat. *stultus*, foolish; see **stel-*** + Lat. *-ficāre*, -fy.] —**stulʹti•fi•caʹtion** (-fĭ-kāʹshən) *n.* —**stulʹti•fiʹer** *n.*

stum (stŭm) *n.* **1.** Unfermented or partly fermented grape juice; must. **2.** Vapid wine renewed by an admixture of stum. —*tr.v.* **stummed, stum•ming, stums.** To ferment (vapid wine) by adding stum. [Du. *stom*, dumb, stum < MDu.]

stum•ble (stŭmʹbəl) *v.* **-bled, -bling, -bles.** —*intr.* **1.a.** To miss one's step; trip and almost fall. **b.** To proceed unsteadily or falteringly; flounder. See Syns at **blunder. c.** To act or speak falteringly or clumsily. **2.** To make a mistake; blunder. **3.** To fall into evil ways. **4.** To come upon accidentally or unexpectedly. —*tr.* To cause to stumble. —*n.* **1.** The act of stumbling. **2.** A mistake or blunder. [ME *stumblen*, prob. of Scand. orig.] —**stumʹbler** *n.* —**stumʹbling•ly** *adv.*

stum•ble•bum (stŭmʹbəl-bŭmʹ) *n. Slang.* **1.** A person regarded as blundering or inept. **2.** *Sports.* A punch-drunk or second-rate prizefighter.

stum•bling block (stŭm′blĭng) *n.* An obstacle or impediment.

stump (stŭmp) *n.* **1.** The part of a tree trunk left protruding from the ground after the tree has come down. **2.** A part, as of a tooth, remaining after the main part has been cut away, broken off, or worn down. **3.a. stumps.** *Informal.* The legs. **b.** An artificial leg. **4.** A short thickset person. **5.** A heavy footfall. **6.** A place or an occasion used for political oratory. **7.** A roll or piece of soft leather, paper, or similar material that is rubbed on the surface of a charcoal or pencil drawing to shade or soften it. **8.** *Sports.* Any one of the three upright sticks in a cricket wicket. —*tr.v.* **stumped, stump•ing, stumps. 1.** To reduce to a stump. **2.** To clear stumps from. **3.** To stub (a toe or foot). **4.** To traverse (a district) making political speeches. **5.** To shade (a drawing) with a stump. **6.** *Informal.* To challenge (someone); defy. **7.** *Informal.* To bring to a halt; baffle. [ME *stumpe,* poss. < MLGer. *stump.*] —**stump′er** *n.* —**stump′i•ness** *n.* —**stump′y** *adj.*

stump•age (stŭm′pĭj) *n.* **1.** Standing timber regarded as a commodity. **2.** The value of standing timber. **3.** The right to cut standing timber.

stun (stŭn) *tr.v.* **stunned, stun•ning, stuns. 1.** To daze or render senseless, by or as if by a blow. **2.** To overwhelm or daze with a loud noise. **3.** To stupefy, as with the emotional impact of an experience; astound. —*n.* A blow or shock that stupefies. [ME *stonen* < OFr. *estoner* < VLat. **extonāre* : Lat. *ex-,* ex- + Lat. *tonāre,* to thunder; see **(s)tenə-*.**]

stung (stŭng) *v.* P.t. and p.part. of **sting.**

stun gun *n.* A weapon designed to stun or temporarily immobilize a victim by firing pellets or bags of shot or sand or by delivering a high-voltage electric shock.

stunk (stŭngk) *v.* A p.t. and the p.part. of **stink.**

stun•ner (stŭn′ər) *n.* One that stuns, as: **a.** An astounding, unexpected event. **b.** An exceptionally good-looking person.

stun•ning (stŭn′ĭng) *adj.* **1.** Causing or capable of causing emotional shock or loss of consciousness. **2.** Of a strikingly attractive appearance. **3.a.** Impressive. **b.** Surprising.

stunt[1] (stŭnt) *tr.v.* **stunt•ed, stunt•ing, stunts.** To check the growth or development of. —*n.* **1.** One that stunts. **2.** One that is stunted. **3.** A plant disease that causes dwarfing. [< ME *stunnt,* foolish, short-witted, short (influenced by ON *stuttr,* short, dwarfish) < OE *stunt.*] —**stunt′ed•ness** *n.*

stunt[2] (stŭnt) *n.* **1.** A feat displaying unusual strength, skill, or daring. **2.** Something unusual done for publicity. —*intr.v.* **stunt•ed, stunt•ing, stunts.** To perform stunts or a stunt. [?]

stunt•man (stŭnt′măn′) *n.* A man who substitutes for a performer in scenes involving physical risk.

stunt•wom•an (stŭnt′wo͝om′ən) *n.* A woman who substitutes for a performer in scenes involving physical risk.

stu•pa (sto͞o′pə) *n.* See **tope**[3]. [Skt. *stūpaḥ,* summit, stupa.]

stupe (sto͞op, styo͞op) *n.* A hot, wet, often medicated cloth used as a compress. [ME < Lat. *stuppa, stūpa,* tow < Gk. *stuppē.*]

stu•pe•fa•cient (sto͞o′pə-fā′shənt, styo͞o′-) *adj.* Inducing stupor. —*n.* A drug that induces stupor. [Lat. *stupefaciēns, stupefacient-,* pr.part. of *stupefacere,* to stupefy. See STUPEFY.]

stu•pe•fac•tion (sto͞o′pə-făk′shən, styo͞o′-) *n.* **1.a.** The act or an instance of stupefying. **b.** The state of being stupefied. **2.** Great astonishment or consternation. —**stu′pe•fac′tive** (-făk′tĭv) *adj. & n.*

stu•pe•fy (sto͞o′pə-fī′, styo͞o′-) *tr.v.* **-fied, -fy•ing, -fies. 1.** To dull the senses or faculties of. **2.** To amaze. [ME *stupefien* < OFr. *stupefier* < Lat. *stupefacere* : *stupēre,* to be stunned + *facere,* to make; see FACT.] —**stu′pe•fi′er** *n.*

stu•pen•dous (sto͞o-pĕn′dəs, styo͞o-) *adj.* **1.** Of astounding force, volume, degree, or excellence; marvelous. **2.** Amazingly large or great; huge. [< LLat. *stupendus,* stunning, gerundive of Lat. *stupēre,* to be stunned.] —**stu•pen′dous•ly** *adv.* —**stu•pen′dous•ness** *n.*

stu•pid (sto͞o′pĭd, styo͞o′-) *adj.* **-er, -est. 1.** Slow to learn or understand; obtuse. **2.** Lacking or marked by a lack of intelligence. **3.** In a stupor; stupefied. **4.** In a dazed or stunned state. **5.** Pointless; worthless: *a stupid job.* —*n.* A person regarded as stupid. [Lat. *stupidus* < *stupēre,* to be stunned.] —**stu′pid•ly** *adv.* —**stu′pid•ness** *n.*

stu•pid•i•ty (sto͞o-pĭd′ĭ-tē, styo͞o-) *n., pl.* **-ties. 1.** The quality or condition of being stupid. **2.** A stupid act, remark, or idea.

stu•por (sto͞o′pər, styo͞o′-) *n.* **1.** A state of reduced or suspended sensibility. **2.** A state of mental numbness, as from shock; a daze. [ME < Lat. < *stupēre,* to be stunned.] —**stu′por•ous** *adj.*

stur•dy (stûr′dē) *adj.* **-di•er, -di•est. 1.** Having or showing rugged physical strength. **2.** Substantially made or built; stout: *sturdy canvas.* **3.** Marked by resoluteness or determination; firm. **4.** Vigorous or robust. —*n.* See **gid.** [ME, stubborn, reckless, sturdy < OFr. *estourdi,* p.part. of *estourdir,* to stun, perh. < VLat. **exturdīre,* to be giddy as a thrush : Lat. *ex-,* intensive pref.; see EX- + Lat. *turdus,* thrush.] —**stur′di•ly** *adv.* —**stur′di•ness** *n.*

stur•geon (stûr′jən) *n.* Any of various large freshwater and marine fishes of the family Acipenseridae of the Northern Hemisphere, having edible flesh and valued as a source of caviar. [ME < AN < OFr. *estourgeon,* of Gmc. orig.]

Sturm und Drang (shto͝orm′ o͝ont drăng′) *n.* **1.** Turmoil; ferment. **2.** A late-18th-century German romantic literary movement whose works typically depicted the struggles of a highly emotional individual against conventional society. [Ger., storm and stress, after *Sturm und Drang,* a drama by Friedrich Maximilian von Klinger (1752–1831).]

stut•ter (stŭt′ər) *v.* **-tered, -ter•ing, -ters.** —*intr.* To speak with a spasmodic repetition or prolongation of sounds. —*tr.* To utter with spasmodic repetition or prolongation of sounds. —*n.* The act or habit of stuttering. [Freq. of dial. *stut* < ME *stutten.*] —**stut′ter•er** *n.* —**stut′ter•ing•ly** *adv.*

Stutt•gart (stŭt′gärt′, sto͝ot′-, shto͝ot′-). A city of SW Germany on the Neckar R. SSE of Heidelberg; chartered in the 13th cent. Pop. 561,567.

Stuy•ve•sant (stī′vĭ-sənt), **Peter** or **Petrus.** 1592?–1672. Dutch colonial governor of New Netherland (1646–64), who was forced to surrender the colony to England.

sty[1] (stī) *n., pl.* **sties** (stīz). **1.** An enclosure for swine. **2.** A filthy place. —*tr. & intr.v.* **stied** (stīd), **sty•ing, sties** (stīz). To shut up in or live in a sty. [ME < OE *stī-, stig.*]

sty[2] also **stye** (stī) *n., pl.* **sties** also **styes** (stīz). An inflammation of one or more sebaceous glands of an eyelid. [Alteration of ME *styanye* : *styan,* sty (< OE *stīgend* < pr.part. of *stīgan,* to rise; see **steigh-***) + *eye, ye,* eye; see EYE.]

styg•i•an also **Styg•i•an** (stĭj′ē-ən) *adj.* **1.a.** Gloomy and dark. **b.** Infernal; hellish. **2.** Of or relating to the river Styx. [< Lat. *Stygius* < Gk. *Stugios* < *Stux, Stug-,* Styx.]

styl– *pref.* Var. of **stylo–.**

sty•lar (stī′lər, -lär′) *adj.* **1.** Of, relating to, or resembling a stylus. **2.** *Bot. & Zool.* Of or relating to a style.

sty•late (stī′lāt′) *adj.* Having a style or styles.

style (stīl) *n.* **1.** The way in which something is said, done, expressed, or performed. **2.** The combination of distinctive features of literary or artistic expression, execution, or performance characterizing a particular person, group, school, or era. **3.** Sort; type. **4.** A quality of imagination and individuality expressed in one's actions and tastes. **5.a.** A comfortable and elegant mode of existence. **b.** A mode of living. **6.a.** The fashion of the moment, esp. of dress; vogue. **b.** A particular fashion. **7.** A customary manner of presenting printed material, including punctuation, spelling, and typography. **8.** A form of address; a title. **9.a.** An implement used for etching or engraving. **b.** A slender pointed writing instrument used by the ancients on wax tablets. **10.** The needle of a phonograph. **11.** The gnomon of a sundial. **12.** *Bot.* The usu. slender part of a pistil, situated between the ovary and the stigma. **13.** *Zool.* A slender, tubular, or bristlelike process. **14.** *Medic.* A surgical probing instrument; a stylet. **15.** *Obsolete.* A pen. —*tr.v.* **styled, styl•ing, styles. 1.** To call or name; designate. **2.** To make consistent with rules of style. **3.** To give style to: *style hair.* [ME < OFr. < Lat. *stylus, stilus,* spike, pointed instrument used for writing, style. See STYLUS.] —**styl′er** *n.* —**styl′ing** *n.*

style•book (stīl′bo͝ok′) *n.* A book giving rules and examples, as of usage, punctuation, and typography, used esp. in preparation of copy for publication.

sty•let (stī-lĕt′, stī′lĭt) *n.* **1.** A slender pointed instrument or weapon. **2.a.** A surgical probe. **b.** A fine wire that is run through a catheter, cannula, or hollow needle to keep it stiff or clear of debris. **3.** *Zool.* A small stiff needlelike organ or appendage. [Fr. < Ital. *stiletto,* stiletto. See STILETTO.]

sty•li (stī′lī) *n.* Pl. of **stylus.**

sty•li•form (stī′lə-fôrm′) *adj.* Having the shape of a style; slender and pointed: *a styliform bone or appendage.*

styl•ish (stī′lĭsh) *adj.* Conforming to the current fashion. —**styl′ish•ly** *adv.* —**styl′ish•ness** *n.*

styl•ist (stī′lĭst) *n.* **1.** One with an artful literary style. **2.** One who designs or consults on decorating, dress, or beauty styles.

sty•lis•tic (stī-lĭs′tĭk) *adj.* Of or relating to style, esp. literary style. —**sty•lis′ti•cal•ly** *adv.*

sty•lis•tics (stī-lĭs′tĭks) *n.* *(used with a sing. v.)* The study of the use of elements of language style in particular contexts.

sty•lite (stī′līt′) *n.* One of a number of early Christian ascetics who lived unsheltered on the tops of high pillars. [LGk. *stulitēs* < Gk. *stulos,* pillar. See **stā-*.**] —**sty•lit′ic** (-lĭt′ĭk) *adj.* —**sty′lit•ism** (stī′lī-tĭz-əm) *n.*

styl•ize (stī′līz′) *tr.v.* **-ized, -iz•ing, -iz•es. 1.** To restrict or make conform to a particular style. **2.** To represent conventionally. —**styl′i•za′tion** (stī′lĭ-zā′shən) *n.* —**styl′iz′er** *n.*

stylo– or **styli–** or **styl–** *pref.* Style: *stylopodium.* [< Lat. *stilus, stylus,* stake, stem, style. See STYLUS.]

sty•lo•bate (stī′lə-bāt′) *n.* *Archit.* The immediate foundation of a row of classical columns. [Lat. *stylobata* < Gk. *stulobatēs* : *stulos,* pillar; see **stā-*** + *bainein,* to walk; see **gʷā-*.**]

sty•loid (stī′loid′) *adj.* **1.** Resembling a style in shape; slender and pointed: *styloid muscles.* **2.** *Anat.* Of, relating to, or being any of several slender pointed bone processes.

sty•lo•lite (stī′lə-līt′) *n.* A contact zone found along adjacent calcareous rock layers, appearing in cross section as a series of jagged interlocking up-and-down projections that resemble a suture. [Gk. *stulos,* pillar; see STYLITE + -LITE.]

Peter Stuyvesant
c. 1660 portrait attributed to Henri Couturrier

ă pat	oi boy
ā pay	ou out
âr care	o͝o took
ä father	o͞o boot
ĕ pet	ŭ cut
ē be	ûr urge
ĭ pit	th thin
ī pie	*th* this
îr pier	hw which
ŏ pot	zh vision
ō toe	ə about, item
ô paw	

Stress marks:
′ (primary);
′ (secondary), as in
dictionary (dĭk′shə-nĕr′ē)

sty•lo•po•di•um (stī′lə-pō′dē-əm) *n.*, *pl.* **-di•a** (-dē-ə). An enlargement at the base of the style of flowers in certain plants of the parsley family.

sty•lus (stī′ləs) *n.*, *pl.* **-lus•es** or **-li** (-lī). **1.** A sharp pointed instrument used for writing, marking, or engraving. **2.** A phonograph needle. **3.** A sharp pointed tool used for cutting record grooves. [Lat., alteration of *stilus.*]

sty•mie also **sty•my** (stī′mē) —*tr.v.* **-mied** (-mēd), **-mie•ing** also **-my•ing** (-mē-ĭng), **-mies** (-mēz). To thwart; stump. —*n.* **1.** An obstacle or obstruction. **2.** *Sports.* A situation in golf in which an opponent's ball obstructs the line of play of one's own ball on the putting green. [?]

styp•sis (stĭp′sĭs) *n.* The action or application of a styptic. [LLat. *stypsis* < Gk. *stupsis* < *stuphein*, to contract.]

styp•tic (stĭp′tĭk) *adj.* **1.** Contracting the tissues or blood vessels; astringent. **2.** Tending to check bleeding by contracting the tissues or blood vessels; hemostatic. —*n.* A styptic drug or substance. [ME *stiptik* < OFr. *stiptique* < Lat. *stypticus* < Gk. *stuptikos* < *stuphein*, to contract.]

styptic pencil *n.* A short medicated stick, often of alum, applied to a cut to check bleeding.

Styr (stîr). A river of NW Ukraine flowing c. 436 km (271 mi) N to the Pripet R.

sty•rene (stī′rēn′) *n.* A colorless oily liquid, $C_6H_5CH:CH_2$, the monomer for polystyrene. [Lat. *styrax*, storax; see STORAX + -ENE.]

Sty•ro•foam (stī′rə-fōm′). A trademark used for a light resilient polystyrene plastic.

Sty•ron (stī′rən), **William.** b. 1925. Amer. writer whose novels include *Lie Down in Darkness* (1951).

William Styron
Photographed in 1990

Styx (stĭks) *n. Gk. Myth.* The river in Hades across which the souls of the dead are ferried. [Lat. < Gk. *Stux.*]

su•a•ble (so͞o′ə-bəl) *adj. Law.* Subject to suit in a court of law. —**su′a•bil′i•ty** *n.*

sua•sion (swā′zhən) *n.* Persuasion. [Ult. < Lat. *suāsiō, suāsiōn-* < *suāsus*, p.part. of *suādēre*, to advise. See **swād-***.]

sua•sive (swā′sĭv) *adj.* Having the power to persuade or convince; persuasive. [Lat. *suāsus*, p.part. of *suādēre*, to advise; see SUASION + -IVE.] —**sua′sive•ly** *adv.* —**sua′sive•ness** *n.*

suave (swäv) *adj.* **suav•er, suav•est.** Smoothly agreeable and courteous. [Fr., agreeable < OFr. < Lat. *suāvis*, delightful, sweet. See **swād-***.] —**suave′ly** *adv.* —**suave′ness, suav′i•ty** (swä′vĭ-tē) *n.*

sub[1] (sŭb) *n. Informal.* **1.** See **submarine** 1. **2.** See **submarine** 2. See Regional Note at **submarine.**

sub[2] (sŭb) *Informal.* —*n.* A substitute. —*intr.v.* **subbed, sub•bing, subs.** To act as a substitute.

sub. *abbr.* **1.** Subaltern. **2.** Suburb; suburban.

sub– *pref.* **1.** Below; under; beneath: *subsoil.* **2.a.** Subordinate; secondary: *subplot.* **b.** Subdivision: *subregion.* **3.** Less than completely or normally; nearly; almost: *subhuman.* [ME < Lat. < *sub*, under. See **upo***.]

sub•ac•id (sŭb-ăs′ĭd) *adj.* Somewhat sharp or acid in character: *subacid remarks.*

sub•a•cute (sŭb′ə-kyo͞ot′) *adj.* **1.** Somewhat or moderately acute: *subacute petals.* **2.** Between acute and chronic.

subacute scle•ros•ing panencephalitis (sklə-rō′sĭng) *n.* An often fatal viral disease of the central nervous system occurring chiefly in young people.

sub•aer•i•al (sŭb-âr′ē-əl) *adj.* Located or occurring on or near the surface of the earth.

sub•al•pine (sŭb-ăl′pīn′) *adj.* **1.** Of or relating to regions at or near the foot of the Alps. **2.** Of, relating to, inhabiting, or growing in mountainous regions just below the timberline.

sub•al•tern (sŭb-ôl′tərn, sŭb′əl-tûrn′) *adj.* **1.** Lower in position or rank; secondary. **2.** *Chiefly British.* Holding a military rank just below that of captain. **3.** *Logic.* In the relation of a particular proposition to a universal with the same subject, predicate, and quality. [Fr. *subalterne* < OFr. < LLat. *subalternus* : Lat. *sub-*, sub- + Lat. *alternus*, alternate (< *alter*, other; see **al-**[1]*).] —**sub•al′tern** *n.*

sub•al•ter•nate (sŭb-ôl′tər-nĭt) *adj.* **1.** Subordinate. **2.** *Bot.* Arranged in an alternating pattern but tending to become opposite. Used of leaves. —**sub•al′ter•na′tion** (-nā′shən) *n.*

sub•ant•arc•tic (sŭb′ănt-ärk′tĭk, -är′tĭk) *adj.* Of or resembling regions just north of the Antarctic Circle.

sub•a•que•ous (sŭb-ā′kwē-əs, -ăk′wē-) *adj.* **1.** Formed or adapted for underwater use or operation; submarine. **2.** Found or occurring underwater: *subaqueous organisms.*

sub•a•rach•noid (sŭb′ə-răk′noid) *adj.* Situated or occurring beneath the arachnoid membrane or between the arachnoid and the pia mater: *subarachnoid space.*

sub•arc•tic (sŭb-ärk′tĭk, -är′tĭk) *adj.* Of or resembling regions just south of the Arctic Circle.

sub•as•sem•bly (sŭb′ə-sĕm′blē) *n.*, *pl.* **-blies.** An assembled unit designed to be incorporated into a larger unit.

sub•a•tom•ic (sŭb′ə-tŏm′ĭk) *adj.* **1.** Of or relating to the constituents of the atom. **2.** Having dimensions or participating in reactions characteristic of the constituents of the atom.

subatomic particle *n.* Any of various units of matter smaller than an atom, as an elementary particle or a hadron.

sub•au•di•tion (sŭb′ô-dĭsh′ən) *n.* **1.** The act of understanding and mentally supplying a word or thought that has been implied but not expressed. **2.** A word or thought supplied by subaudition. [LLat. *subaudītiō, subaudītiōn-* < *subaudītus*, p.part. of *subaudīre*, to supply an omitted word : Lat. *sub-*, sub- + Lat. *audīre*, to hear; see **au-***.]

sub•base (sŭb′bās′) *n.* The lowermost strip or molding of a baseboard.

sub•cab•i•net (sŭb′kăb′ə-nĭt) *adj.* Of, relating to, or being an administrative position below cabinet level.

sub•ce•les•tial (sŭb′sĭ-lĕs′chəl) *adj.* **1.** Lower than celestial; terrestrial. **2.** Mundane.

sub•cel•lu•lar (sŭb-sĕl′yə-lər) *adj.* **1.** Situated or occurring within a cell. **2.** Smaller in size than ordinary cells: *subcellular organisms.* **3.** Below the cellular level: *subcellular research.*

sub•cen•ter (sŭb′sĕn′tər) *n.* A secondary center, esp. a commercial or shopping area located away from the main business sector of a city. —**sub•cen′tral** (-trəl) *adj.*

sub•chas•er (sŭb′chā′sər) *n. Informal.* A submarine chaser.

sub•class (sŭb′klăs′) *n.* **1.** A subdivision of a set or class. **2.** *Biol.* A taxonomic category of related organisms ranking between a class and an order.

sub•cla•vi•an (sŭb-klā′vē-ən) *adj. Anat.* **1.** Situated beneath the clavicle. **2.** Of or relating to a subclavian part. **3.** Of or relating to the subclavian artery or vein. [< NLat. *subclāvius* : SUB– + Lat. *clāvis*, key; see CLAVICLE.] —**sub•cla′vi•an** *n.*

subclavian artery *n.* A part of a major artery of the upper extremities or forelimbs that passes beneath the clavicle and is continuous with the axillary artery.

subclavian vein *n.* A part of a major vein of the upper extremities or forelimbs that passes beneath the clavicle and is continuous with the axillary vein.

sub•cli•max (sŭb-klī′măks′) *n. Ecol.* A stage in the ecological succession of a plant or animal community immediately preceding a climax and often persisting because of the effects of fire, flood, or other conditions.

sub•clin•i•cal (sŭb-klĭn′ĭ-kəl) *adj.* Not manifesting characteristic clinical symptoms. Used of a disease or condition.

sub•com•pact (sŭb-kŏm′păkt′) *n.* An automobile smaller than a compact.

sub•com•po•nent (sŭb′kəm-pō′nənt) *n.* A portion of a component, esp. an electronic component; a subassembly.

sub•con•scious (sŭb-kŏn′shəs) *adj.* Not wholly conscious; partially or imperfectly conscious. —*n. Psychol.* The part of the mind below the level of conscious perception. —**sub•con′scious•ly** *adv.* —**sub•con′scious•ness** *n.*

sub•con•ti•nent (sŭb′kŏn′tə-nənt, sŭb-kŏn′-) *n.* **1.** A large landmass, such as India, that is part of a continent but is considered either geographically or politically as an independent entity. **2.** A large landmass, such as Greenland, smaller than a continent. —**sub′con•ti•nen′tal** (-nĕn′tl) *adj.*

sub•con•tract (sŭb-kŏn′trăkt′, sŭb′kŏn′trăkt) *n.* A contract that assigns some obligations of a prior contract to another party. —*intr.* & *tr.v.* (sŭb-kŏn′trăkt′, sŭb′kən-trăkt′) **-tract•ed, -tract•ing, -tracts.** To make a subcontract or a subcontract for.

sub•con•trac•tor (sŭb-kŏn′trăk′tər, sŭb′kən-trăk′tər) *n.* One that enters into a subcontract and assumes some of the obligations of the primary contractor.

sub•con•trar•y (sŭb-kŏn′trĕr′ē) *n.*, *pl.* **-ries.** *Logic.* A proposition related to another in such a way that both may be true, but both cannot be false.

sub•cor•tex (sŭb-kôr′tĕks) *n.*, *pl.* **-ti•ces** (-tĭ-sēz′). The portion of the brain immediately below the cerebral cortex. —**sub•cor′ti•cal** (-tĭ-kəl) *adj.* —**sub•cor′ti•cal•ly** *adv.*

sub•cul•ture (sŭb′kŭl′chər) *n.* **1.** A subdivision of a cultural group differentiated by status, ethnicity, residence, religion, or other factors that unify the group and act on each member. **2.** One culture of microorganisms derived from another. —**sub•cul′tur•al** *adj.*

sub•dea•con (sŭb-dē′kən) *n.* **1.** A cleric ranking just below a deacon. **2.** A cleric who assists the deacon at High Mass.

sub•deb (sŭb′dĕb′) *n. Informal.* A subdebutante.

---

sub′ab•dom′i•nal *adj.*
sub•ap′i•cal *adj.*
sub•ap′i•cal•ly *adv.*
sub•arc′tic *adj.*
sub•ar′id *adj.*
sub•ax′il•lar′y *adj.*
sub′base′ment *n.*
sub•cat′e•go′ry *n.*
sub′com•mit′tee *n.*
sub′cu•ta′ne•ous *adj.*
sub′cu•ta′ne•ous•ly *adv.*
sub•dur′al *adj.*
sub•freez′ing *adj.*
sub′gen′re *n.*
sub•le′thal *adj.*
sub•le′thal•ly *adv.*
sub′o•ce•an′ic *adj.*
sub′per•i•os′te•al *adj.*
sub′pop•u•la′tion *n.*
sub′re′gion *n.*
sub′re′gion•al *adj.*
sub′-Sa•har′an *adj.*
sub′sam′ple *n.* & *tr.v.*
sub•spe′cial•ist *n.*
sub•spe′cial•i•za′tion *n.*
sub′spe′cial•ize′ *intr.v.*
sub′spe′cial•ty *n.*
sub•strat′o•sphere′ *n.*
sub′strat•o•spher′ic *adj.*
sub′top′ic *n.*
sub′tribe′ *n.*

SUBATOMIC PARTICLES

Subatomic particles fall into two major groups: the elementary particles and the hadrons. An **elementary particle** is not composed of any smaller particles and therefore represents the most fundamental form of matter. A **hadron** is composed of elementary particles called **quarks**. This table contains the most common subatomic particles, including the major constituents of the **atom**—the **electron** (an elementary particle), and the **proton** and the **neutron** (hadrons).

Explanation of Column Headings:

PARTICLE SYMBOL A superscript indicates charge.

ANTIPARTICLE SYMBOL Typically the same as the particle symbol but with a bar above or parentheses around it.

COMPOSITION The combination of quarks that make up the hadron. Some hadrons are members of **multiplets** that differ in **isospin** and their compositions are best described by using mathematical expressions.

MASS Expressed as a multiple of an electron's mass, 9.1066 x 10^{-28}g or 0.511 MeV.

ELECTRIC CHARGE Expressed as a multiple of an electron's charge, 1.602 x 10^{-19} coulomb. The antiparticle has a charge opposite that of its corresponding particle, except when both are neutral.

LIFETIME The average time in seconds that the particle exists. "Stable" means that the particle has no known mode of decay.

ELEMENTARY PARTICLES

FAMILY NAME	PARTICLE NAME	PARTICLE SYMBOL	ANTI-PARTICLE SYMBOL	MASS	ELECTRIC CHARGE	LIFETIME IN SECONDS
classon	photon	γ	(γ)	0	0	stable
	graviton	g	(g)	0	0	stable
weakon	W particle	W^-	W^+	160,000	−1	?
	Z particle	Z	Z	180,000	0	?
lepton	electron	e or e^-	e^+	1	−1	stable
	electron neutrino	ν_e	$\bar{\nu}_e$	about 0	0	stable
	muon	μ or μ^-	μ^+	209	−1	2.2 x 10^{-6}
	muon neutrino	ν_μ	$\bar{\nu}_\mu$	<0.49	0	stable
	tau	τ or τ^-	τ^+	3,490	−1	3.0 x 10^{-13}
	tau neutrino	ν_τ	$\bar{\nu}_\tau$	<69	0	stable (?)
quark	up	u	$\bar{u}$	607	+⅔	stable
	down	d	$\bar{d}$	607	−⅓	stable
	charm	c	$\bar{c}$	2,900	+⅔	?
	strange	s	$\bar{s}$	988	−⅓	?
	top	t	$\bar{t}$	> 100,000	+⅔	?
	bottom	b	$\bar{b}$	10,000	−⅓	?

HADRONS

FAMILY NAME	PARTICLE NAME	PARTICLE SYMBOL	ANTI-PARTICLE SYMBOL	COMPOSITION	MASS	ELECTRIC CHARGE	LIFETIME IN SECONDS
baryon							
nucleon	proton	p	$\bar{p}$	uud	1,836	+1	stable
	neutron	n	$\bar{n}$	udd	1,839	0	8.98 x 10^{2}*
hyperon	lambda	Λ^0	$\overline{\Lambda}^0$	uds	2,183	0	2.6 x 10^{-10}
	sigma	Σ^+	$\overline{\Sigma}^+$	uus	2,328	+1	0.8 x 10^{-10}
		Σ^0	$\overline{\Sigma}^0$	$\frac{(ud \pm du)s}{\sqrt{2}}$	2,334	0	6.0 x 10^{-20}
		Σ^-	$\overline{\Sigma}^-$	dds	2,343	−1	1.5 x 10^{-10}
	xi	Ξ^0	$\overline{\Xi}^0$	uss	2,573	0	2.9 x 10^{-10}
		Ξ^-	$\overline{\Xi}^-$	dss	2,585	−1	1.6 x 10^{-10}
	omega	Ω^-	$\overline{\Omega}^-$	sss	3,272	−1	0.8 x 10^{-10}
meson	pion	π^+	π^-	$u\bar{d}$	273	+1	2.6 x 10^{-8}
		π^0	π^0	$\frac{(u\bar{u} - d\bar{d})}{\sqrt{2}}$	264	0	8.4 x 10^{-17}
	kaon**	K^+	K^-	$u\bar{s}$	966	+1	1.2 x 10^{-8}
		K^0	$\overline{K}^0$	$d\bar{s}$	974	0	8.9 x 10^{-11} or 5.2 x 10^{-8}
	J particle	J or Ψ	J or Ψ	$c\bar{c}$	6,060	0	1.0 x 10^{-20}
	omega	ω	ω	$\frac{(u\bar{u} + d\bar{d})}{\sqrt{2}}$	1,532	0	6.6 x 10^{-23}

* Neutrons are stable when bound within the nucleus.

** The neutral kaon is composed of two particles; the average lifetime of each particle is given.

sub•deb•u•tante (sŭb-dĕb′yə-tänt′) *n.* A teenage girl approaching her debut.

sub•di•ac•o•nate (sŭb′dī-ăk′ə-nĭt) *n.* The office, order, or rank of subdeacon. [LLat. *subdiāconātus* < *subdiāconus*, subdeacon (partial transl. of LGk. *hupodiakonos*) : Lat. *sub-*, sub- + Gk. *diakonos*, attendant.] —**sub′di•ac′o•nal** *adj.*

sub•di•vide (sŭb′dĭ-vīd′, sŭb′dĭ-vīd′) *v.* **-vid•ed, -vid•ing, -vides.** —*tr.* **1.** To divide a part or parts of into smaller parts. **2.** To divide into a number of parts, esp. to divide (land) into lots. —*intr.* To form into subdivisions. —**sub′di•vid′er** *n.*

sub•di•vi•sion (sŭb′dĭ-vĭzh′ən, sŭb′dĭ-vĭzh′ən) *n.* **1.a.** The act or process of subdividing. **b.** A subdivided part. **2.** An area composed of subdivided lots: *There are several new subdivisions in our area.* —**sub′di•vi′sion•al** *adj.*

sub•dom•i•nant (sŭb-dŏm′ə-nənt) *n. Mus.* The fourth tone of a diatonic scale, next below the dominant. —*adj.* **1.** *Zool.* Less than dominant; ranking below one that is dominant. **2.** *Ecol.* Prevalent in a community but below the dominant in importance. Used of a species.

sub•duc•tion (səb-dŭk′shən) *n.* A geologic process in which one edge of one lithospheric plate is forced below the edge of another. [Fr. < Lat. *subductus*, p.part. of *subdūcere*, to draw away from below : *sub-*, sub- + *dūcere*, to lead; see **deuk-***.]

sub•due (səb-do͞o′, -dyo͞o′) *tr.v.* **-dued, -du•ing, -dues. 1.** To conquer and subjugate; vanquish. See Syns at **defeat. 2.** To quiet or bring under control by physical force or persuasion; make tractable. **3.** To make less intense or prominent; tone down: *I tried to subdue my excitement about the upcoming holiday.* **4.** To bring (land) under cultivation. [ME *subduen*, alteration (influenced by Lat. *subdere*, to subject) of OFr. *suduire*, to seduce < Lat. *subdūcere*, to withdraw : *sub-*, away; see SUB– + *dūcere*, to lead; see **deuk-***.] —**sub•du′a•ble** *adj.* —**sub•du′er** *n.*

sub•em•ployed (sŭb′em-ploid′) *adj.* Of or relating to work-

ă pat | oi boy
ā pay | ou out
âr care | o͝o took
ä father | o͞o boot
ĕ pet | ŭ cut
ē be | ûr urge
ĭ pit | th thin
ī pie | *th* this
îr pier | hw which
ŏ pot | zh vision
ō toe | ə about, item
ô paw |

Stress marks:
′ (primary);
′ (secondary), as in dictionary (dĭk′shə-nĕr′ē)

ers or segments of the paid labor force that are unemployed, underemployed, or underpaid. **—sub′em•ploy′ment** *n.*

sub•en•try (sŭb′ĕn′trē) *n., pl.* **-tries.** An entry, such as one in a reference work, that is included within a main entry.

sub•e•qua•to•ri•al (sŭb′ē-kwə-tôr′ē-əl, -tōr′-, -ĕk-wə-) *adj.* Belonging to a region adjacent to an equatorial area.

su•ber•ic acid (so͞o-bĕr′ĭk) *n.* A crystalline dibasic acid, $HOOC(CH_2)_6COOH$, used in the manufacture of plastics. [Fr. *subérique* < Lat. *sūber*, cork.]

su•ber•in (so͞o′bər-ĭn) *n.* A waxy waterproof substance present in the cell walls of cork tissue in plants. [Fr. *subérine* : Lat. *sūber*, cork + Fr. *-ine*, adj. suff.; see -INE[2].]

su•ber•i•za•tion (so͞o′bər-ĭ-zā′shən) *n.* Deposition of suberin on plant cell walls, converting them into cork tissue.

su•ber•ize (so͞o′bə-rīz′) *tr.v.* **-ized, -iz•ing, -iz•es.** To cause to undergo suberization. [< Lat. *sūber*, cork.]

sub•fam•i•ly (sŭb′făm′ə-lē) *n., pl.* **-lies. 1.** *Biol.* A taxonomic category of related organisms ranking between a family and a genus. **2.** *Ling.* A division of languages below a family and above a branch.

sub•floor•ing (sŭb′flôr′ĭng, -flōr′-) or **sub•floor** (-flôr′, -flōr′) *n.* A rough floor over which a finished floor, flooring material, or carpet is laid.

sub•fusc (sŭb-fŭsk′) *adj.* Of a dark, dull, or somber color. *—n.* Dark, dull clothing. [Lat. *subfuscus*, brownish : *sub-*, sub- + *fuscus*, dark.]

sub•ge•nus (sŭb′jē′nəs) *n., pl.* **-gen•e•ra** (-jĕn′ər-ə). *Biol.* An occasionally used taxonomic category ranking between a genus and a species. **—sub′ge•ner′ic** (-jə-nĕr′ĭk) *adj.*

sub•gla•cial (sŭb-glā′shəl) *adj.* Formed or deposited beneath a glacier. **—sub′gla′cial•ly** *adv.*

sub•grade (sŭb′grād′) *n.* The level layer of rock or earth upon which the foundation of a road or railway is laid.

sub•group (sŭb′gro͞op′) *n.* **1.** A distinct group within a group; a subdivision of a group. **2.** A subordinate group. **3.** *Math.* A nonempty subset of a group.

sub•gum (sŭb′gŭm′) *n.* A dish of Chinese origin made with mixed vegetables. [Chin. (Cantonese) *shap kam.*]

sub•head (sŭb′hĕd′) *n.* **1.** The heading or title of a subdivision of a printed subject. **2.** A subordinate heading or title.

sub•hu•man (sŭb-hyo͞o′mən) *adj.* **1.** Below the human race in evolutionary development. **2.** Regarded as not being fully human. **—sub•hu′man** *n.*

Su•bic Bay (so͞o′bĭk). An inlet of the South China Sea off W-central Luzon, Philippines, W of Manila Bay.

sub•in•dex (sŭb-ĭn′dĕks) *n., pl.* **-di•ces** (-dĭ-sēz′). **1.** *Math.* A subscript. **2.** *pl.* **-dic•es** or **-dex•es.** An index of measurement based on relatively few variables, esp. a trade index based on the performance of a particular group or type of stocks.

sub•in•feu•date (sŭb′ĭn-fyo͞o′dāt′) also **sub•in•feud** (-fyo͞od′) *tr.v.* **-dat•ed, -dat•ing, -dates** also **-feud•ed, -feud•ing, -feuds.** To lease (lands) by subinfeudation.

sub•in•feu•da•tion (sŭb′ĭn-fyo͞o-dā′shən) *n.* **1.** The sublease of a portion of a feudal estate by a vassal to a subtenant who pays fealty to the vassal. **2.** The lands so leased. **—sub′in•feu′da•to′ry** (-fyo͞o′də-tôr′ē, -tōr′ē) *adj.*

sub•ir•ri•gate (sŭb-ĭr′ĭ-gāt′) *tr.v.* **-gat•ed, -gat•ing, -gates.** To irrigate from beneath, as by underground pipes. **—sub′ir•ri•ga′tion** *n.*

su•bi•to (so͞o′bē-tō′) *adv. Mus.* Quickly; suddenly. [Ital. < Lat. *subitō* < neut. ablative sing. of *subitus*, sudden < p.part. of *subīre*, to come secretly. See SUDDEN.]

subj. *abbr.* **1.** Subject. **2.** Subjective. **3.** Subjunctive.

sub•ja•cent (sŭb-jā′sənt) *adj.* **1.** Located beneath or below; underlying. **2.** Lying lower but not directly beneath. [Lat. *subiacēns*, *subiacent-*, pr.part. of *subiacēre*, to lie below : *sub-*, sub- + *iacēre*, to lie; see **yē-***.] **—sub•ja′cen•cy** *n.*

sub•ject (sŭb′jĭkt) *adj.* **1.** Being under the power or authority of another or others. **2.** Prone; disposed. **3.** Likely to incur or receive; exposed: *subject to misinterpretation.* **4.** Contingent or dependent. *—n.* **1.** One who is under the rule of another or others, esp. one who owes allegiance to a government or ruler. **2.a.** One concerning which something is said or done. **b.** Something treated or indicated in a work of art. **c.** *Mus.* A theme of a composition, esp. of a fugue. **3.** A course or area of study. **4.** A basis for action; a cause. **5.a.** One that experiences or is subjected to something. **b.** One that is the object of clinical study. **c.** One who is under surveillance. **6.** *Gram.* The noun, noun phrase, or pronoun in a sentence or clause that denotes the doer of the action or what is described by the predicate and that in some languages can be identified by its position in simple sentences and in other languages by inflectional endings. **7.** *Logic.* The term of a proposition about which something is affirmed or denied. **8.** *Philos.* **a.** The essential nature or substance of something as distinguished from its attributes. **b.** The mind or thinking part as distinguished from the object of thought. *—tr.v.* (səb-jĕkt′) **-ject•ed, -ject•ing, -jects. 1.** To submit for consideration. **2.** To submit to the authority of someone or something. **3.** To expose to something: *subjected to infection.* **4.** To cause to experience something: *subjected to cold.* **5.** To subjugate; subdue. [ME < OFr. < Lat. *sūbiectus* < p.part. of *sūbicere*, to subject : *sub-*, sub- + *iacere*, to throw; see **yē-***.] **—sub•jec′tion** (səb-jĕk′shən) *n.*

Syns: *subject, matter, topic, theme.* These nouns denote the principal idea or point of a speech, a piece of writing, or an artistic work. *Subject* is the most general: *"Well, honor is the subject of my story"* (Shakespeare). *Matter* refers to the material that is the object of thought or discourse: *"This distinction seems to me to go to the root of the matter"* (William James). A *topic* is a subject of discussion or argument: *"They would talk of . . . other fashionable topics, such as pictures, taste, Shakespeare"* (Oliver Goldsmith). *Theme* refers especially to an idea, a point of view, or a perception that is developed in a work of art: *"To produce a mighty book, you must choose a mighty theme"* (Herman Melville).

sub•jec•tive (səb-jĕk′tĭv) *adj.* **1.a.** Proceeding from or taking place within a person's mind such as to be unaffected by the external world. **b.** Particular to a given person; personal. **2.** Moodily introspective. **3.** Existing only in the mind; illusory. **4.** *Psychol.* Existing only within the experiencer's mind. **5.** *Medic.* Of, relating to, or being a symptom or condition perceived by the patient and not by the examiner. **6.** Expressing or bringing into prominence the individuality of the artist or author. **7.** *Gram.* Relating to or being the nominative case. **8.** Relating to the real nature of something; essential. **—sub•jec′tive•ly** *adv.* **—sub•jec′tive•ness, sub′jec•tiv′i•ty** (sŭb′jĕk-tĭv′ĭ-tē) *n.*

subjective idealism *n. Philos.* The theory that nature has no objective existence independent of the minds that perceive it.

sub•jec•tiv•ism (səb-jĕk′tə-vĭz′əm) *n.* **1.** The quality of being subjective. **2.a.** The doctrine that all knowledge is restricted to the conscious self and its sensory states. **b.** A theory or doctrine that emphasizes the subjective elements in experience. **3.** The theory that individual conscience is the only valid standard of moral judgment. **—sub•jec′tiv•ist** *n.* **—sub•jec′tiv•is′tic** *adj.*

subject matter *n.* Matter under consideration in a written work or speech; a theme.

sub•join (səb-join′) *tr.v.* **-joined, -join•ing, -joins.** To add at the end; append. [Obsolete Fr. *subjoindre* < Lat. *subiungere* : *sub-*, sub- + *iungere*, to join; see **yeug-***.]

sub•join•der (səb-join′dər) *n.* Something subjoined. [< SUBJOIN (on the model of REJOINDER).]

sub ju•di•ce (sŭb jo͞o′dĭ-sē′, so͝ob yo͞o′dĭ-kā′) *adv. Law.* Under judicial deliberation; before a judge or court of law. [Lat. *sub iūdice.*]

sub•ju•gate (sŭb′jə-gāt′) *tr.v.* **-gat•ed, -gat•ing, -gates. 1.** To bring under control; conquer. See Syns at **defeat. 2.** To make subservient; enslave. [ME *subjugaten* < Lat. *subiugāre*, *subiugāt-* : *sub-*, sub- + *iugum*, yoke; see **yeug-***.] **—sub′ju•ga′tion** *n.* **—sub′ju•ga′tor** *n.*

sub•junc•tion (səb-jŭngk′shən) *n.* **1.** The act of subjoining or the condition of being subjoined. **2.** Something subjoined. [LLat. *subiūnctiō*, *subiūnctiōn-* < Lat. *subiūnctus*, p.part. of *subiungere*, to subjoin. See SUBJOIN.]

sub•junc•tive (səb-jŭngk′tĭv) *Gram. —adj.* Of, relating to, or being a mood of a verb used in some languages for contingent or hypothetical action, action viewed subjectively, or grammatically subordinate statements. *—n.* **1.** The subjunctive mood. **2.** A subjunctive construction. See Usage Note at **if.** [LLat. *subiūnctīvus* < Lat. *subiūnctus*, p.part. of *subiungere*, to subjoin, subordinate. See SUBJOIN.]

sub•king•dom (sŭb′kĭng′dəm) *n. Biol.* A taxonomic category of related organisms that is a major division of a kingdom.

sub•late (sŭb′lāt′) *tr.v.* **-lat•ed, -lat•ing, -lates.** *Logic.* To negate, deny, or contradict. [< Lat. *sublātus*, p.part. of *tollere*, to take away : *sub-*, sub- + *lātus*, taken; see **telə-***.]

sub•lease (sŭb′lēs′) *tr.v.* **-leased, -leas•ing, -leas•es. 1.** To sublet (property). **2.** To rent (property) under a sublease. *—n.* (sŭb′lēs′). A lease of property granted by a lessee.

sub•let (sŭb′lĕt′) *tr.v.* **-let, -let•ting, -lets. 1.** To rent (property one holds by lease) to another. **2.** To subcontract (work). *—n.* (sŭb′lĕt′). Sublet property, esp. an apartment.

sub•li•mate (sŭb′lə-māt′) *v.* **-mat•ed, -mat•ing, -mates.** *—tr.* **1.** *Chem.* To cause (a solid or gas) to change state without becoming a liquid. **2.** *Psychol.* To modify the natural expression of (an instinctual impulse, esp. a sexual one) in a socially acceptable manner. *—intr. Chem.* To be sublimated. Used of a solid or gas. [Lat. *sublīmāre*, *sublīmāt-*, to elevate < *sublīmis*, uplifted.]

sub•li•ma•tion (sŭb′lə-mā′shən) *n.* **1.** The act or process of sublimating. **2.** Something that has been sublimated.

sub•lime (sə-blīm′) *adj.* **1.** Characterized by nobility; majestic. **2.a.** Of high spiritual, moral, or intellectual worth. **b.** Not to be excelled; supreme. **3.** Inspiring awe; impressive. **4.** *Archaic.* Raised aloft; set high. **5.** *Obsolete.* Of lofty appearance or bearing; haughty. *—n.* **1.** Something sublime. **2.** An ultimate example. *—v.* **-limed, -lim•ing, -limes.** *—tr.* **1.** To render sublime. **2.** *Chem.* To cause to sublimate. *—intr. Chem.* To sublimate. [Fr. < OFr., sublimated < Lat. *sublīmis*, uplifted.] **—sub•lime′ly** *adv.* **—sub•lime′ness, sub•lim′i•ty** (sə-blĭm′ĭ-tē) *n.*

sub•lim•i•nal (sŭb-lĭm′ə-nəl) *adj. Psychol.* **1.** Below the threshold of conscious perception. Used of stimuli. **2.** Inadequate to produce conscious awareness but able to evoke a response: *subliminal propaganda.* [SUB– + Lat. *līmen, līmin-,* threshold.] — **sub·lim′i·nal·ly** *adv.*

sub·lin·gual (sŭb-lĭng′gwəl) *adj.* Situated beneath or on the underside of the tongue. — *n.* A sublingual part, such as a gland, an artery, or a duct. — **sub·lin′gual·ly** *adv.*

sub·lit·to·ral (sŭb-lĭt′ər-əl) *adj.* **1.** Of or situated near the seashore. **2.** Lying between the low tide line and the edge of the continental shelf or ranging in depth to about 100 fathoms or 200 meters (660 feet).

sub·lu·na·ry (sŭb-lo͞o′nə-rē, sŭb′lo͞o-nĕr′ē) also **sub·lu·nar** (-lo͞o′nər) *adj.* **1.** Situated beneath the moon. **2.** Of this world; earthly. [LLat. *sublūnāris* : Lat. *sub-*, sub- + Lat. *lūna*, moon; see **leuk-***.]

sub·lux·a·tion (sŭb′lŭk-sā′shən) *n.* Incomplete or partial dislocation of a bone in a joint.

sub·ma·chine gun (sŭb′mə-shēn′) *n.* A lightweight automatic or semiautomatic gun that fires pistol cartridges.

sub·man·dib·u·lar (sŭb′măn-dĭb′yə-lər) *adj.* Submaxillary.

sub·mar·gin·al (sŭb-mär′jə-nəl) *adj.* **1.** Near the margin of a body, an organ, or a part. **2.** Of low productivity; infertile.

sub·ma·rine (sŭb′mə-rēn′, sŭb′mə-rēn′) *n.* **1.** A ship capable of operating submerged. **2.** A large sandwich on a long split roll filled with layers of meat, cheese, tomatoes, lettuce, and condiments. Also called regionally *bomber, Cuban sandwich, grinder, hoagie, Italian, Italian sandwich, poor boy, torpedo, wedge, zep.* — *adj.* Beneath the surface of the water; undersea. — *v.* **-rined, -rin·ing, -rines.** — *tr.* **1.** To attack by submarine, esp. with torpedoes. **2.** *Sports.* To knock down with a blow to the legs. **3.** *Baseball.* To pitch (a ball) with an underhand motion. — *intr.* **1.** To operate a submarine. **2.** To slide, drive, or throw under something.

Regional Note: The long sandwich featuring layers of meat and cheese on a crusty Italian roll goes by a variety of names. *Submarine, sub,* and *hero* are widespread. Jane Stern, an expert on regional cooking, finds that upstate New Yorkers call it a *bomber,* while speakers downstate refer to a *wedge.* In the Delaware Valley, including Philadelphia and southern New Jersey, the term is *hoagie;* in Italian restaurants in New England one asks for a *grinder;* in Miami, a *Cuban sandwich;* and in Maine, an *Italian sandwich.* In the southern Midwest, according to Stern, the name *Italian* is common. In New Orleans the same sandwich is called a *poor boy* and is likely to be offered in a most un-Italian version featuring fried oysters.

submarine chaser *n.* A small fast ship equipped to pursue and attack submarines.

sub·ma·rin·er (sŭb-mə-rē′nər, sŭb′măr′ə-nər) *n.* A member of the crew of a submarine.

sub·max·il·la (sŭb′măk-sĭl′ə) *n., pl.* **-max·il·lae** (-măk-sĭl′ē). The lower jaw or mandible, esp. in human beings.

sub·max·il·lar·y (sŭb-măk′sə-lĕr′ē) *adj.* **1.** Of or relating to the lower jaw: *a submaxillary fracture.* **2.** Situated beneath the maxilla. — *n., pl.* **-ies.** An anatomical part, such as a gland, situated beneath the maxilla.

sub·me·di·ant (sŭb-mē′dē-ənt) *n. Mus.* The sixth tone of a diatonic scale.

sub·merge (səb-mûrj′) *v.* **-merged, -merg·ing, -merg·es.** — *tr.* **1.** To place under water. **2.** To cover with water; inundate. **3.** To hide from view; obscure. — *intr.* To go under or as if under water. [Lat. *submergere* : *sub-*, sub- + *mergere*, to plunge.] — **sub·mer′gence** *n.*

sub·merged (səb-mûrjd′) *adj.* **1.** *Bot.* Growing or remaining under water: *submerged leaves.* **2.** Living in poverty or misery. **3.** Having been hidden.

sub·mer·gi·ble (səb-mûr′jə-bəl) *adj.* That can be immersed in or can remain under water. — **sub·mer′gi·bil′i·ty** *n.*

sub·merse (səb-mûrs′) *tr.v.* **-mersed, -mers·ing, -mers·es.** To submerge. [Prob. back-formation < SUBMERSION < LLat. *submersiō, submersiōn-* < Lat. *submersus*, p.part. of *submergere*, to submerge. See SUBMERGE.] — **sub·mer′sion** (-mûr′zhən, -shən) *n.*

sub·mersed (səb-mûrst′) *adj. Bot.* Growing or remaining under water.

sub·mers·i·ble (səb-mûr′sə-bəl) *adj.* Submergible. — *n.* A vessel capable of operating or remaining under water.

sub·mi·cro·scop·ic (sŭb′mī-krə-skŏp′ĭk) *adj.* Too small to be resolved by an optical microscope.

sub·min·i·a·ture (sŭb-mĭn′ē-ə-cho͝or′, -chər) *adj.* Smaller than miniature; exceedingly small.

sub·min·i·a·tur·ize (sŭb′mĭn′ē-ə-chə-rīz′) *tr.v.* **-ized, -iz·ing, -iz·es.** To make subminiature, esp. to manufacture or design (electronic equipment) in subminiature size. — **sub·min′i·a·tur·i·za′tion** (-chər-ĭ-zā′shən) *n.*

sub·miss (səb-mĭs′) *adj. Archaic.* Submissive. [Lat. *submissus*, p.part. of *submittere*, to set under. See SUBMIT.]

sub·mis·sion (səb-mĭsh′ən) *n.* **1.a.** The act of submitting to the power of another. **b.** The state of having submitted. **2.** The state of being submissive or compliant; meekness. **3.a.** The act of submitting something, such as a manuscript, for consideration. **b.** Something so submitted. [Ult. < Lat. *submissiō, submissiōn-*, a lowering < *submissus*, p.part. of *submittere*, to set under. See SUBMIT.]

sub·mis·sive (səb-mĭs′ĭv) *adj.* Inclined or willing to submit. — **sub·mis′sive·ly** *adv.* — **sub·mis′sive·ness** *n.*

sub·mit (səb-mĭt′) *v.* **-mit·ted, -mit·ting, -mits.** — *tr.* **1.** To yield or surrender (oneself) to the will or authority of another. **2.** To subject to a condition or process. **3.** To commit (something) to the consideration or judgment of another. **4.** To offer as a proposition or contention. — *intr.* **1.** To give in to the authority, power, or desires of another. See Syns at **yield. 2.** To allow oneself to be subjected to something. [ME *submitten* < Lat. *submittere*, to set under : *sub-*, sub- + *mittere*, to cause to go.] — **sub·mit′tal** (-mĭt′l) *n.* — **sub·mit′ter** *n.*

sub·mon·tane (sŭb′mŏn′tān′, -mŏn-tān′) *adj.* Located under or at the base of a mountain or mountain range.

sub·nor·mal (sŭb-nôr′məl) *adj.* Less than normal; below the average. — *n.* One viewed as subnormal in some respect, such as in coordination. — **sub′nor·mal′i·ty** (-nôr-măl′ĭ-tē) *n.*

sub·or·bi·tal (sŭb-ôr′bĭ-tl) *adj.* **1.** Having or following a trajectory of less than one orbit. Used of a rocket or spacecraft. **2.** *Anat.* Situated on or below the floor of the orbit of the eye. — *n.* A suborbital part, such as a bone, nerve, or cartilage.

sub·or·der (sŭb′ôr′dər) *n.* **1.** *Biol.* A taxonomic category of related organisms ranking between an order and a family. **2.** A subdivision of a category termed an order.

sub·or·di·nate (sə-bôr′dn-ĭt) *adj.* **1.** Belonging to a lower or inferior class or rank; secondary. **2.** Subject to the authority or control of another. — *n.* One that is subordinate. — *tr.v.* (sə-bôr′dn-āt′) **-nat·ed, -nat·ing, -nates. 1.** To put in a lower or inferior rank or class. **2.** To make subservient; subdue. [ME *subordinat* < Med.Lat. *subōrdinātus*, p.part. of *subōrdināre*, to subordinate : Lat. *sub-*, sub- + Lat. *ōrdināre*, to set in order (< *ōrdō, ōrdin-*, order; see **ar-***).] — **sub·or′di·nate·ly** *adv.* — **sub·or′di·nate·ness, sub·or′di·na′tion** (-nā′shən) *n.* — **sub·or′di·na′tive** (-nə′tĭv) *adj.*

subordinate clause *n. Gram.* See **dependent clause.**

subordinate conjunction *n. Gram.* A conjunction, such as *that, who,* and *where,* that introduces a dependent clause.

sub·orn (sə-bôrn′) *tr.v.* **-orned, -orn·ing, -orns. 1.** To induce (a person) to commit an unlawful or evil act. **2.** *Law.* **a.** To induce (a person) to commit perjury. **b.** To procure (perjured testimony). [Lat. *subōrnāre* : *sub-*, secretly; see SUB– + *ōrnāre*, to equip; see **ar-***.] — **sub′or·na′tion** (sŭb′ôr-nā′shən) *n.* — **sub·orn′er** *n.*

Su·bo·ti·ca also **Su·bo·ti·tsa** (so͞o′bə-tē′tsə, -bô-). A city of N Serbia near the Hungarian border. Pop. 93,500.

sub·ox·ide (sŭb-ŏk′sīd′) *n.* An oxide containing a relatively small amount of oxygen.

sub·phy·lum (sŭb′fī′ləm) *n., pl.* **-la** (-lə). *Biol.* A taxonomic category of related organisms ranking between a phylum and a class.

sub·plot (sŭb′plŏt′) *n.* **1.** A plot subordinate to the main plot of a literary work or film. **2.** A subdivision of a plot of land, esp. a plot used for experimental purposes.

sub·poe·na (sə-pē′nə) *Law.* — *n.* A writ summoning a person to court to give testimony. — *tr.v.* **-naed, -na·ing, -nas.** To serve with such a writ. [ME *suppena* < Med.Lat. *sub poenā*, under a penalty : Lat. *sub*, under; see SUB– + Lat. *poenā*, ablative of *poena*, penalty (< Gk. *poinē*); see **kʷei-¹***.]

sub·prin·ci·pal (sŭb-prĭn′sə-pəl) *n.* **1.** An assistant school principal. **2.** An auxiliary or bracing rafter in a frame.

sub·pro·fes·sion·al (sŭb′prə-fĕsh′ə-nəl) *n.* A paraprofessional. — **sub′pro·fes′sion·al** *adj.*

sub·pro·gram (sŭb′prō′grăm, -grəm) *n. Comp. Sci.* A program contained within another program that operates semi-independently of the encasing program.

sub·rep·tion (sŭb-rĕp′shən) *n.* **1.** A calculated misrepresentation through concealment of the facts. **2.** An inference drawn from a subreption. [LLat. *subreptiō, subreptiōn-* < Lat., theft < *subreptus*, p.part. of *surripere*, to take away secretly. See SURREPTITIOUS.] — **sub′rep·ti′tious** (-tĭsh′əs) *adj.*

sub·ro·gate (sŭb′rō-gāt′) *tr.v.* **-gat·ed, -gat·ing, -gates.** To substitute (one person) for another. [ME *subrogaten* < Lat. *subrogāre, subrogāt-* : *sub-*, instead of; see SUB– + *rogāre*, to ask; see **reg-***.]

sub·ro·ga·tion (sŭb′rō-gā′shən) *n.* The substitution of one person for another, esp. the legal doctrine of substituting one creditor for another.

sub ro·sa (sŭb rō′zə) *adv.* In secret; privately or confidentially. [Lat. *sub rosā*, under the rose (< hanging a rose over a meeting as a symbol of confidentiality).]

sub·rou·tine (sŭb′ro͞o-tēn′) *n. Comp. Sci.* A set of instructions that performs a specific task for a main routine, requiring direction back to the main routine when finished.

subs. *abbr.* Subscription.

sub-Sa·har·an (sŭb′sə-hâr′ən, -hăr′-, -här′-) *adj.* Of, relating to, or situated in the region of Africa south of the Sahara.

sub·scribe (səb-skrīb′) *v.* **-scribed, -scrib·ing, -scribes.** — *tr.* **1.** To pledge or contribute (a sum of money). **2.** To sign (one's name) at the end of a document. **3.** To sign one's name to in attestation, testimony, or consent: *subscribe a will.* — *intr.* **1.** To contract to purchase a certain number of issues of a

submersible
Underwater submersible *Alvin*, Woods Hole Oceanographic Institution

ă **pat**	oi **boy**
ā **pay**	ou **out**
âr **care**	o͝o **took**
ä **father**	o͞o **boot**
ĕ **pet**	ŭ **cut**
ē **be**	ûr **urge**
ĭ **pit**	th **thin**
ī **pie**	*th* **this**
îr **pier**	hw **which**
ŏ **pot**	zh **vision**
ō **toe**	ə **about, item**
ô **paw**	

Stress marks:
′ (primary);
′ (secondary), as in
dictionary (dĭk′shə-nĕr′ē)

publication, tickets to a series of events or performances, or a utility service, for example. **2.** To promise to pay or contribute money. **3.** To feel or express hearty approval. See Syns at **assent. 4.** To sign one's name. **5.** To affix one's signature to a document as a witness or to show consent. [ME *subscriben* < Lat. *subscrībere* : *sub-*, sub- + *scrībere*, to write; see **skrībh-*.**] — **sub•scrib′er** *n.*

sub•script (sŭb′skrĭpt′) *n.* A character set, printed, or written below and immediately to one side of another. [< Lat. *subscrīptus*, p.part. of *subscrībere*, to subscribe. See SUBSCRIBE.] — **sub′script′** *adj.*

sub•scrip•tion (səb-skrĭp′shən) *n.* **1.** A purchase made by signed order, as for a periodical for a given time period or for a series of performances. **2.** Acceptance, as of a doctrine, demonstrated by signing one's name. **3.a.** The raising of money from subscribers. **b.** A sum of money so raised. **4.** The signing of one's name. **5.** Something subscribed. [Ult. < Lat. *subscrīptiō, subscrīptiōn-*, something written underneath < *subscrīptus*, p.part. of *subscrībere*, to subscribe. See SUBSCRIBE.] — **sub•scrip′tive** *adj.* — **sub•scrip′tive•ly** *adv.*

sub•se•quence (sŭb′sĭ-kwĕns′, -kwəns) *n.* **1.** Something subsequent; a sequel. **2.** The fact or quality of being subsequent. **3.** (-sē′kwəns). *Math.* A sequence contained in another sequence.

sub•se•quent (sŭb′sĭ-kwĕnt′, -kwənt) *adj.* Following in time or order; succeeding. [ME < OFr. < Lat. *subsequēns, subsequent-*, pr.part. of *subsequī*, to follow close after : *sub-*, close after; see SUB- + *sequī*, to follow; see **sek^{w}-^{1}*.**] — **sub′se•quent′ly** *adv.* — **sub′se•quent′ness** *n.*

sub•serve (səb-sûrv′) *tr.v.* **-served, -serv•ing, -serves.** To serve to promote (an end); be useful to. [Lat. *subservīre* : *sub-*, sub- + *servīre*, to serve; see SERVE.]

sub•ser•vi•ent (səb-sûr′vē-ənt) *adj.* **1.** Subordinate in capacity or function. **2.** Obsequious; servile. **3.** Useful as a means or a tool; promoting an end. [Lat. *subserviēns, subservient-*, pr.part. of *subservīre*, to subserve. See SUBSERVE.] — **sub•ser′vi•ence, sub•ser′vi•en•cy** *n.* — **sub•ser′vi•ent•ly** *adv.*

sub•set (sŭb′sĕt′) *n.* A set contained within a set.

sub•shell (sŭb′shĕl′) *n.* One of the energy levels in the electron shell of an atom.

sub•shrub (sŭb′shrŭb′) *n.* **1.** An herb having a woody lower stem. **2.** A low shrub; an undershrub.

subway
Prague subway system

sub•side (səb-sīd′) *intr.v.* **-sid•ed, -sid•ing, -sides. 1.** To sink to a lower or normal level. **2.** To sink or settle down, as into a sofa. **3.** To sink to the bottom, as a sediment. **4.** To become less agitated or active; abate. See Syns at **decrease.** [Lat. *subsīdere* : *sub-*, sub- + *sīdere*, to settle; see **sed-*.**] — **sub•si′dence** (səb-sīd′ns, sŭb′sĭ-dns) *n.*

sub•sid•i•ar•y (səb-sĭd′ē-ĕr′ē) *adj.* **1.** Serving to assist or supplement; auxiliary. **2.** Secondary in importance; subordinate. **3.** Of, relating to, or of the nature of a subsidy. — *n., pl.* **-ar•ies. 1.** One that is subsidiary to another. **2.** A subsidiary company. **3.** *Mus.* A theme subordinate to a main theme or subject. [Lat. *subsidiārius* < *subsidium*, support. See SUBSIDY.] — **sub•sid′i•ar′i•ly** (-âr′ə-lē) *adv.*

subsidiary cell *n.* A plant epidermal cell associated with guard cells and morphologically different from other epidermal cells.

subsidiary company *n.* A company having more than half of its stock owned by another company.

sub•si•dize (sŭb′sĭ-dīz′) *tr.v.* **-dized, -diz•ing, -diz•es. 1.** To assist or support with a subsidy. **2.** To secure the assistance of by granting a subsidy. — **sub′si•di•za′tion** (-dĭ-zā′shən) *n.* — **sub′si•diz′er** *n.*

sub•si•dy (sŭb′sĭ-dē) *n., pl.* **-dies. 1.** Monetary assistance granted by a government in support of an enterprise regarded as being in the public interest. See Syns at **bonus. 2.** Financial assistance given by one person or government to another. **3.** Money formerly granted to the British Crown by Parliament. [ME *subsidie* < AN < Lat. *subsidium*, support : *sub-*, behind, beneath; see SUB- + *sedēre*, to sit; see **sed-*.**]

sub•sist (səb-sĭst′) *v.* **-sist•ed, -sist•ing, -sists.** — *intr.* **1.a.** To exist; be. **b.** To stay in existence. **2.** To maintain life; live: *subsisted on oats.* **3.** To be logically conceivable. — *tr.* To maintain with provisions. [Lat. *subsistere*, to support : *sub-*, sub- + *sistere*, to stand; see **stā-*.**] — **sub•sist′er** *n.*

sub•sis•tence (səb-sĭs′təns) *n.* **1.** The act or state of subsisting. **2.** A means of subsisting, esp. one barely sufficient to maintain life. **3.** Something with real or substantial existence. **4.** *Theol.* Hypostasis. — **sub•sis′tent** *adj.*

sub•soil (sŭb′soil′) *n.* The layer or bed of earth beneath the topsoil. — *tr.v.* **-soiled, -soil•ing, -soils.** To plow or turn up the subsoil of. — **sub′soil′er** *n.*

sub•so•lar (sŭb-sō′lər) *adj.* **1.** Situated directly beneath the sun. **2.** Located between the tropics; equatorial.

sub•son•ic (sŭb-sŏn′ĭk) *adj.* **1.** Of less than audible frequency. **2.** Having a speed less than that of sound in a designated medium.

subsp. *abbr.* Subspecies.

sub•spe•cies (sŭb′spē′shēz, -sēz) *n., pl.* **subspecies.** *Biol.* A subdivision of a taxonomic species, usu. based on geographic distribution. — **sub′spe•cif′ic** (-spĭ-sĭf′ĭk) *adj.*

subst. *abbr.* **1.** Substantive. **2.** Substitute.

sub•stage (sŭb′stāj′) *n.* The part of a microscope located below the stage, on which accessories are held in place.

sub•stance (sŭb′stəns) *n.* **1.a.** That which has mass and occupies space; matter. **b.** A material of a particular kind or constitution. **2.a.** Essential nature; essence. **b.** Gist; heart. **3.** That which is solid and practical in character, quality, or importance. **4.** Density; body: *Air has little substance.* **5.** Material possessions; goods; wealth. [ME < OFr. < Lat. *substantia* < *substāns, substant-*, pr.part. of *substāre*, to be present : *sub-*, sub- + *stāre*, to stand; see **stā-*.**]

substance abuse *n.* Excessive use of addictive substances, esp. alcohol and narcotic drugs. — **substance abuser** *n.*

substance P *n.* A short-chain polypeptide that functions as a neurotransmitter esp. in the transmission of pain impulses.

sub•stan•dard (sŭb-stăn′dərd) *adj.* **1.** Failing to meet a standard; below standard. **2.** *Ling.* **a.** Of, relating to, or indicating a speech pattern that does not conform to that of the prestige group in a speech community or to that of the standard language. **b.** Not in accord with notions of good English; nonstandard.

sub•stan•tial (səb-stăn′shəl) *adj.* **1.** Of, relating to, or having substance; material. **2.** True or real; not imaginary. **3.** Solidly built; strong. **4.** Ample; sustaining: *a substantial breakfast.* **5.** Considerable in importance, value, degree, amount, or extent. **6.** Possessing wealth or property; well-to-do. — *n.* **1.** An essential. Often used in the plural. **2.** A solid thing. Often used in the plural. [ME *substancial* < OFr. *substantiel* < Lat. *substantiālis* < *substantia*, substance. See SUBSTANCE.] — **sub•stan′ti•al′i•ty** (-shē-ăl′ĭ-tē), **sub•stan′tial•ness** (-shəl-nĭs) *n.* — **sub•stan′tial•ly** *adv.*

sub•stan•ti•a ni•gra (səb-stăn′shē-ə nī′grə, nĭg′rə) *n.* A layer of large pigmented nerve cells in the mesencephalon that produce dopamine and whose destruction is associated with Parkinson's disease. [NLat. : Lat. *substantia*, substance + Lat. *nigra*, fem. of *niger*, black.]

sub•stan•ti•ate (səb-stăn′shē-āt′) *tr.v.* **-at•ed, -at•ing, -ates. 1.** To support with proof or evidence; verify. **2.a.** To give material form to; embody. **b.** To make firm or solid. **3.** To give substance to; make real or actual. [NLat. *substantiāre, substantiāt-* < Lat. *substantia*, substance. See SUBSTANCE.] — **sub•stan′ti•a′tion** *n.*

sub•stan•ti•val (sŭb′stən-tī′vəl) *adj. Gram.* Of or relating to a substantive. — **sub′stan•ti′val•ly** *adv.*

sub•stan•tive (sŭb′stən-tĭv) *adj.* **1.** Substantial; considerable. **2.** Independent in existence or function; not subordinate. **3.** Not imaginary; real. **4.** Of or relating to the essence or substance; essential. **5.** Having a solid basis; firm. **6.** *Gram.* Expressing or designating existence; for example, the verb *to be.* **7.** *Gram.* Being a noun or noun equivalent. — *n. Gram.* A word or group of words functioning as a noun. [ME *substantif*, self-sufficient, independent < OFr., substantive < LLat. *substantīvus* < Lat. *substantia*, substance. See SUBSTANCE.] — **sub′stan•tive•ly** *adv.* — **sub′stan•tive•ness** *n.*

substantive right *n.* A basic right seen as part of the order of society and independent of, not subordinate to, human law.

sub•sta•tion (sŭb′stā′shən) *n.* A subsidiary or branch station, as of a post office or an electric utility.

sub•stit•u•ent (səb-stĭch′o͞o-ənt) *n.* An atom, a radical, or a group substituted for another in a molecule. [Lat. *substituēns, substituent-*, pr.part. of *substituere*, to substitute. See SUBSTITUTE.] — **sub•stit′u•ent** *adj.*

sub•sti•tute (sŭb′stĭ-to͞ot′, -tyo͞ot′) *n.* **1.** One that takes the place of another; a replacement. **2.** *Gram.* A word or construction used in place of another. — *v.* **-tut•ed, -tut•ing, -tutes.** — *tr.* To put or use (a person or thing) in place of another. — *intr.* To take the place of another. [ME < OFr. *substitut* < Lat. *substitūtus*, p.part. of *substituere*, to substitute : *sub-*, in place of; see SUB- + *statuere*, to cause to stand; see **stā-*.**] — **sub′sti•tut′a•bil′it•y** *n.* — **sub′sti•tut′a•ble** *adj.*

sub•sti•tu•tion (sŭb′stĭ-to͞o′shən, -tyo͞o′-) *n.* **1.a.** The act or an instance of substituting. **b.** The state of being substituted. **2.** One substituted; a replacement. — **sub′sti•tu′tion•al, sub′sti•tu′tion•ar′y** *adj.* — **sub′sti•tu′tion•al•ly** *adv.*

sub•sti•tu•tive (sŭb′stĭ-to͞o′tĭv, -tyo͞o′-) *adj.* Serving or capable of serving as a substitute.

sub•strate (sŭb′strāt′) *n.* **1.** The material or substance on which an enzyme acts. **2.** *Biol.* A surface on which an organism grows or is attached. **3.** An underlying layer; a substratum. [< SUBSTRATUM.]

sub•stra•tum (sŭb′strā′təm, -străt′əm) *n., pl.* **-stra•ta** (-strā′tə, -străt′ə) or **-stra•tums. 1.a.** An underlying layer. **b.** Subsoil. **2.** A foundation or groundwork. **3.** The material on which another material is coated or fabricated. **4.** *Philos.* The characterless substance that supports attributes of reality. **5.** *Biol.* A substrate. [NLat. < neut. of Lat. *substrātus*, p.part. of *substernere*, to lay under : *sub-*, sub- + *sternere*, to stretch, spread; see **ster-^{2}*.**] — **sub•stra′tive** *adj.*

sub•struc•tion (sŭb-strŭk′shən) *n.* A foundation; a substructure. [Lat. *substrūctiō, substrūctiōn-* < *substrūctus*, p.part. of *substruere*, to build beneath : *sub-*, sub- + *struere*, to build, pile up; see **ster-^{2}*.**] — **sub•struc′tion•al** *adj.*

sub•struc•ture (sŭb′strŭk′chər) *n.* **1.** The supporting part of a structure; the foundation. **2.** The earth bank or bed supporting railroad tracks. —**sub•struc′tur•al** *adj.*

sub•sume (səb-so͞om′) *tr.v.* **-sumed, -sum•ing, -sumes.** To classify, include, or incorporate in a more comprehensive category or under a general principle. [Med.Lat. *subsūmere* : Lat. *sub-*, sub- + Lat. *sūmere*, to take; see **em-***.] —**sub•sum′a•ble** *adj.*

sub•sump•tion (səb-sŭmp′shən) *n.* **1.a.** The act of subsuming. **b.** Something subsumed. **2.** *Logic.* The minor premise of a syllogism. [Lat. *subsūmptiō*, *subsūmptiōn-*, a subsuming < *subsūmptus*, p.part. of *subsūmere*, to subsume. See SUBSUME.] —**sub•sump′tive** *adj.*

sub•sur•face (sŭb′sûr′fəs, sŭb-sûr′-) *adj.* Of, relating to, or situated in an area beneath a surface, esp. the surface of the earth or a body of water.

sub•teen (sŭb′tēn′) *adj.* Relating to, intended for, or being a preadolescent child or children; preteen: *a subteen dance.* —*n.* **1.** See **preteen. 2. subteens.** The preadolescent years.

sub•tem•per•ate (sŭb-tĕm′pər-ĭt, -tĕm′prĭt) *adj.* Of or occurring within the colder regions of the Temperate Zones.

sub•ten•ant (sŭb-tĕn′ənt) *n.* One that rents property, such as land or a house, from a tenant. —**sub•ten′an•cy** *n.*

sub•tend (səb-tĕnd′) *tr.v.* **-tend•ed, -tend•ing, -tends. 1.** *Math.* To be opposite to and delimit: *The side of a triangle subtends the opposite angle.* **2.** To underlie so as to enclose or surround. [Lat. *subtendere*, to extend underneath : *sub-*, sub- + *tendere*, to extend; see **ten-***.]

sub•ter•fuge (sŭb′tər-fyo͞oj′) *n.* A deceptive stratagem or device. [Fr. < OFr. *suterfuge* < LLat. *subterfugium* < Lat. *subterfugere*, to escape : *subter*, secretly, beneath; see **upo*** + *fugere*, to flee.]

sub•ter•mi•nal (sŭb-tûr′mə-nəl) *adj.* Located or occurring near an end.

sub•ter•ra•ne•an (sŭb′tə-rā′nē-ən) *adj.* **1.** Situated or operating beneath the earth's surface; underground. **2.** Hidden; secret. [Lat. *subterrāneus* : *sub-*, sub- + *terra*, earth; see **ters-***.] —**sub′ter•ra′ne•an•ly** *adv.*

sub•ter•res•tri•al (sŭb′tə-rĕs′trē-əl) *adj.* Subterranean; underground.

sub•text (sŭb′tĕkst′) *n.* **1.** The implicit meaning or theme of a literary text. **2.** The underlying personality of a dramatic character as implied by a script or text and interpreted by an actor in performance. —**sub•tex•tu•al** (-tĕks′cho͞o-əl) *adj.*

sub•tile (sŭt′l, sŭb′təl) *adj.* Subtle. [ME < OFr. *subtil* < Lat. *subtīlis*, fine, delicate. See SUBTLE.] —**sub′tile•ly** *adv.* —**sub•til′i•ty** (səb-tĭl′ĭ-tē), **sub′tile•ness** (sŭt′l-nĭs, sŭb′təl-), **sub′til•ty** (sŭt′l-tē, sŭb′təl-) *n.*

sub•til•ize (sŭt′l-īz′, sŭb′tə-līz′) *v.* **-ized, -iz•ing, -iz•es.** —*tr.* To render subtle. —*intr.* To argue or discuss with fine subtlety. —**sub′til•i•za′tion** (-ĭ-zā′shən) *n.*

sub•ti•tle (sŭb′tīt′l) *n.* **1.** A secondary, usu. explanatory title, as of a book. **2.a.** A printed translation of the dialogue of a foreign-language film shown at the bottom of the screen. **b.** A printed portion of narration or dialogue flashed on the screen between the scenes of a silent film. —*tr.v.* **-tled, -tling, -tles. 1.** To give a subtitle to. **2.** To provide with subtitles.

sub•tle (sŭt′l) *adj.* **sub•tler, sub•tlest. 1.a.** So slight as to be difficult to detect or analyze; elusive. **b.** Not immediately obvious; abstruse. **2.** Able to make fine distinctions: *a subtle mind.* **3.a.** Characterized by skill or ingenuity; clever. **b.** Crafty or sly; devious. **c.** Operating in a hidden, usu. injurious way; insidious. [ME *sotil* < OFr. < Lat. *subtīlis*. See **teks-***.] —**sub′tle•ness** *n.* —**sub′tly** *adv.*

sub•tle•ty (sŭt′l-tē) *n., pl.* **-ties. 1.** The quality or state of being subtle. **2.** Something subtle, as a nicety of thought.

sub•ton•ic (sŭb-tŏn′ĭk) *n. Mus.* The seventh tone of a diatonic scale, immediately below the tonic.

sub•tor•rid (sŭb-tôr′ĭd, -tŏr′-) *adj.* Subtropical.

sub•to•tal (sŭb-tōt′l) *adj.* Less than total; incomplete. —*n.* (sŭb′tōt′l). The total of part of a series of numbers. —*v.* (sŭb′tōt′l) **-taled, -tal•ing, -tals** also **-talled, -tal•ling, -tals.** —*tr.* To total part of (a series of numbers). —*intr.* To arrive at a subtotal.

sub•tract (səb-trăkt′) *v.* **-tract•ed, -tract•ing, -tracts.** —*tr.* To take away; deduct. —*intr. Math.* To perform the arithmetic operation of subtraction. [Lat. *subtrahere*, *subtract-* : *sub-*, sub- + *trahere*, to draw.] —**sub•tract′er** *n.*

sub•trac•tion (səb-trăk′shən) *n.* **1.** The act or process of subtracting; deduction. **2.** *Math.* The arithmetic operation of finding the difference between two quantities or numbers.

sub•trac•tive (səb-trăk′tĭv) *adj.* **1.** Producing or involving subtraction. **2.** *Color.* Of or being a color produced by light passing through more than one colorant, each of which inhibits certain wavelengths. **3.** Of or being a photographic process that produces a positive image by superposing or mixing substances that selectively absorb colored light.

sub•tra•hend (sŭb′trə-hĕnd′) *n. Math.* A quantity or number to be subtracted from another. [< Lat. *subtrahendum*, neut. gerundive of *subtrahere*, to subtract. See SUBTRACT.]

sub•trop•i•cal (sŭb-trŏp′ĭ-kəl) *adj.* Of, relating to, or being the geographic areas adjacent to the Tropics.

sub•trop•ics (sŭb-trŏp′ĭks) *pl.n.* Subtropical regions.

su•bu•late (so͞o′byə-lĭt, -lāt′, sŭb′yə-) *adj. Biol.* Tapering to a point; awl-shaped: *a subulate leaf.* [NLat. *sūbulātus* < Lat. *sūbula*, awl. See **syū-***.]

sub•um•brel•la (sŭb′ŭm-brĕl′ə) *n.* The concave underside of the body of a jellyfish.

sub•u•nit (sŭb′yo͞o′nĭt) *n.* A subdivision of a larger unit.

sub•urb (sŭb′ûrb′) *n.* **1.** A usu. residential area or community outlying a city. **2. suburbs.** The usu. residential region around a major city; the environs. [ME *suburbe* < OFr. < Lat. *suburbium* : *sub-*, sub- + *urbs*, *urb-*, city.]

sub•ur•ban (sə-bûr′bən) *adj.* **1.** Of, relating to, or characteristic of a suburb. **2.** Located or residing in a suburb. **3.** Of, relating to, or characteristic of the culture, customs, and manners typical of life in the suburbs. —*n.* A suburbanite.

sub•ur•ban•ite (sə-bûr′bə-nīt′) *n.* One living in a suburb.

sub•ur•ban•ize (sə-bûr′bə-nīz′) *tr.v.* **-ized, -iz•ing, -izes.** To render suburban; impart a suburban character to. —**sub•ur′ban•i•za′tion** (-bə-nĭ-zā′shən) *n.*

sub•ur•bi•a (sə-bûr′bē-ə) *n.* **1.** The suburbs. **2.** Suburbanites considered as a group.

sub•ven•tion (səb-vĕn′shən) *n.* **1.** Provision of help or support. **2.** An endowment or a subsidy, as one from a government to a research institution; a financial aid grant. [Ult. < LLat. *subventiō*, *subventiōn-*, assistance < Lat. *subventus*, p.part. of *subvenīre*, to come to help : *sub-*, beneath, behind; see SUB- + *venīre*, to come; see **gʷā-***.] —**sub•ven′tion•ar′y** *adj.*

sub•ver•sion (səb-vûr′zhən, -shən) *n.* **1.a.** The act or an instance of subverting. **b.** The condition of being subverted. **2.** *Obsolete.* A cause of overthrow or ruin. [Ult. < LLat. *subversiō*, *subversiōn-* < Lat. *subversus*, p.part. of *subvertere*, to subvert. See SUBVERT.] —**sub•ver′sion•ar′y** *adj.*

sub•ver•sive (səb-vûr′sĭv, -zĭv) *adj.* Intended or serving to subvert, esp. intended to overthrow or undermine an established government. —**sub•ver′sive** *n.* —**sub•ver′sive•ly** *adv.* —**sub•ver′sive•ness** *n.*

sub•vert (səb-vûrt′) *tr.v.* **-vert•ed, -vert•ing, -verts. 1.** To destroy completely; ruin. **2.** To undermine the character, morals, or allegiance of; corrupt. **3.** To overthrow completely. See Syns at **overthrow.** [ME *subverten* < OFr. *subvertir* < Lat. *subvertere* : *sub-*, sub- + *vertere*, to turn; see **wer-**[2]***.] —**sub•vert′er** *n.*

sub•vi•rus (sŭb-vī′rəs) *n., pl.* **-rus•es.** A viral protein or other substance smaller than a virus and having some of the properties of a virus. —**sub•vi′ral** (-rəl) *adj.*

sub•vo•cal (sŭb-vō′kəl) *adj.* Characterized by movement of the lips or other speech organs without audible sounds. —**sub•vo′cal•ly** *adv.*

sub•vo•cal•ize (sŭb-vō′kə-līz′) *tr. & intr.v.* **-ized, -iz•ing, -iz•es.** To articulate subvocally or engage in subvocal articulation. —**sub•vo′cal•i•za′tion** *n.* —**sub•vo′cal•iz′er** *n.*

sub•way (sŭb′wā′) *n.* **1.a.** An underground urban railroad, usu. operated by electricity. **b.** A passage for such a railroad. **2.** An underground tunnel or passage, as for pedestrians.

suc•ce•da•ne•um (sŭk′sĭ-dā′nē-əm) *n., pl.* **-ne•a** (-nē-ə). A substitute. [NLat. *succēdāneum* < Lat., neut. sing. of *succēdāneus*, substituted < *succēdere*, to succeed. See SUCCEED.]

suc•ceed (sək-sēd′) *v.* **-ceed•ed, -ceed•ing, -ceeds.** —*intr.* **1.** To come next in time or succession; follow after another; replace another in an office or a position. **2.** To accomplish something desired or intended. **3.** *Obsolete.* To devolve upon a person by way of inheritance. —*tr.* **1.** To follow in time or order. **2.** To come after and take the place of. See Syns at **follow.** [ME *succeden* < OFr. *succeder* < Lat. *succēdere* : *sub-*, near; see SUB- + *cēdere*, to go; see **ked-***.] —**suc•ce′dent** (sək-sēd′nt) *adj.* —**suc•ceed′er** *n.*

suc•cès d'es•time (sük-sĕ′ dĕs-tēm′) *n.* An important but unpopular success or achievement. [Fr. : *succès*, success + *de*, of + *estime*, esteem.]

suc•cès fou (sük-sĕ′ fo͞o′) *n.* A wild success. [Fr. : *succès*, success + *fou*, mad.]

suc•cess (sək-sĕs′) *n.* **1.** The achievement of something desired, planned, or attempted. **2.a.** The gaining of fame or prosperity. **b.** The extent of such gain. **3.** One that is successful. **4.** *Obsolete.* A result or an outcome. [Lat. *successus* < p.part. of *succēdere*, to succeed. See SUCCEED.]

suc•cess•ful (sək-sĕs′fəl) *adj.* **1.** Having a favorable outcome. **2.** Having obtained something desired or intended: *was successful in stopping the leak.* **3.** Having achieved wealth or eminence. —**suc•cess′ful•ly** *adv.* —**suc•cess′ful•ness** *n.*

suc•ces•sion (sək-sĕsh′ən) *n.* **1.** The act or process of following in order or sequence. **2.** A group of people or things arranged or following in order; a sequence. **3.a.** The sequence in which one person after another succeeds to a title, throne, dignity, or estate. **b.** The right of a person or line of persons to so succeed. **c.** The person or line having such a right. **4.a.** The act or process of succeeding to the rights or duties of another. **b.** The act or process of becoming entitled as a legal beneficiary to the property of a deceased person. **5.** *Ecol.* The gradual and orderly evolution of an ecosystem until a climax is reached. [ME < OFr. < Lat. *successiō*, *successiōn-* < *suc-*

ă pat	oi boy
ā pay	ou out
âr care	o͝o took
ä father	o͞o boot
ĕ pet	ŭ cut
ē be	ûr urge
ĭ pit	th thin
ī pie	*th* this
îr pier	hw which
ŏ pot	zh vision
ō toe	ə about, item
ô paw	

Stress marks:
′ (primary);
′ (secondary), as in
dictionary (dĭk′shə-nĕr′ē)

cessus, p.part. of *succēdere*, to succeed. See SUCCEED.] — **suc•ces′sion•al** *adj.* — **suc•ces′sion•al•ly** *adv.*

suc•ces•sive (sək-sĕs′ĭv) *adj.* **1.** Following in uninterrupted order; consecutive. **2.** Of, characterized by, or involving succession. — **suc•ces′sive•ly** *adv.* — **suc•ces′sive•ness** *n.*

successive approximation *n. Math.* A method for estimating the value of an unknown quantity by repeated comparison to a sequence of known quantities.

suc•ces•sor (sək-sĕs′ər) *n.* One that succeeds another.

suc•ci•nate (sŭk′sə-nāt′) *n.* A salt or an ester of succinic acid.

suc•cinct (sək-sĭngkt′) *adj.* **-er, -est. 1.** Concise and terse: *a succinct reply.* **2.** *Archaic.* Encircled as if by a girdle; girded. [ME *succincte*, girt < OFr. < Lat. *succīnctus*, p.part. of *succingere*, to gird from below : *sub-*, sub- + *cingere*, to gird; see **kenk-***.] — **suc•cinct′ly** *adv.* — **suc•cinct′ness** *n.*

suc•cin•ic acid (sək-sĭn′ĭk) *n.* A crystalline dicarboxylic acid, $C_4H_6O_4$, occurring naturally as an intermediate in the Krebs cycle and synthesized for use in pharmaceuticals and perfumes. [Fr. *succinique* < Lat. *succinum*, amber.]

suc•cin•yl•cho•line (sŭk′sə-nĭl-kō′lēn) *n.* A crystalline compound, $C_{14}H_{30}N_2O_4$, formed by esterification of succinic acid with choline and used medically to produce brief but complete muscular relaxation. [SUCCIN(IC ACID) + -YL + CHOLINE.]

Sudan

suc•cor (sŭk′ər) *n.* **1.** Assistance in time of want, difficulty, or distress; relief. **2.** One that affords succor. — *tr.v.* **-cored, -cor•ing, -cors.** To give succor to. See Syns at **help.** [ME *sucur*, back-formation < *sucurs* (taken as pl.) < OFr. *secors* < Med.Lat. *succursus* < p.part. of Lat. *succurrere*, to run to the aid of, succor : *sub-*, sub- + *currere*, to run; see **kers-***.] — **suc′cor•a•ble** *adj.* — **suc′cor•er** *n.*

suc•co•ry (sŭk′ə-rē) *n.*, *pl.* **-ries.** See **chicory** 1. [Perh. alteration of ME *cicoree*. See CHICORY.]

suc•co•tash (sŭk′ə-tăsh′) *n.* A dish consisting of kernels of corn and beans, esp. lima beans. [Narragansett *msíckquatash*, boiled whole-kernel corn.]

Suc•coth also **Suk•koth** (so͝ok′əs, so͞o-kōs′, so͞o-kôt′) *n. Judaism.* A harvest festival lasting for 7 days beginning on the 15th of Tishri that commemorates the open huts in which the Israelites resided during their 40 years in the wilderness. [Heb. *sukkôt*, open huts, Succoth, pl. of *sukkâ*, open hut.]

suc•cour (sŭk′ər) *n.* & *v. Chiefly British.* Var. of **succor.**

suc•cu•bus (sŭk′yə-bəs) also **suc•cu•ba** (-bə) *n.*, *pl.* **-bus•es** or **-bi** (-bī′, -bē′) also **-bae** (-bē′, -bī′). **1.** A female demon supposed to descend upon and have sexual intercourse with a man while he sleeps. **2.** An evil spirit; a demon. [ME < Med. Lat., alteration of Lat. *succuba*, paramour < *succubāre*, to lie under : *sub-*, sub- + *cubāre*, to lie down.]

suc•cu•lent (sŭk′yə-lənt) *adj.* **1.** Full of juice or sap. **2.** *Bot.* Having thick fleshy water-storing leaves or stems. **3.** Highly interesting or enjoyable; delectable. — *n. Bot.* A succulent plant. [Lat. *succulentus* < *succus*, juice. See **seuə-**[2]*.] — **suc′cu•lence, suc′cu•len•cy** *n.* — **suc′cu•lent•ly** *adv.*

suc•cumb (sə-kŭm′) *intr.v.* **-cumbed, -cumb•ing, -cumbs. 1.** To submit to an overpowering force or yield to an overwhelming desire; give up or give in. See Syns at **yield. 2.** To die. [ME *succomben*, to bring down < OFr. *succomber* < Lat. *succumbere*, to lie under, yield : *sub-*, sub- + *-cumbere*, to lie down, as in *accumbere*, to lie down.]

suc•cus•sion (sə-kŭsh′ən) *n.* **1.** The act or process of shaking violently, esp. as a method of diagnosis to detect the presence of fluid and air in a body cavity. **2.** The condition of being shaken violently. [Lat. *succussiō*, *succussiōn-* < *succussus*, p.part. of *succutere*, to toss up : *sub-*, up from below; see SUB- + *quatere*, to shake; see **kwēt-***.] — **suc•cus′sa•to′ry** (sə-kŭs′ə-tôr′ē, -tōr′ē) *adj.*

such (sŭch) *adj.* **1.a.** Of this kind: *a single parent, one of many such people in town.* **b.** Of a kind specified or implied: *a boy such as yourself.* **2.a.** Of a degree or quality indicated: *His anxiety was such that he twitched.* **b.** Of so extreme a degree or quality: *never dreamed of such wealth.* — *adv.* **1.** To so extreme a degree; so: *such beautiful flowers.* **2.** Very; especially: *has been in such poor health.* — *pron.* **1.a.** Such a person or persons or thing or things: *was the mayor and as such presided.* **b.** Itself alone or within itself: *Money as such is seldom enough.* **2.** Someone or something implied or indicated: *Such are the fortunes of war.* **3.** Similar things or people; the like: *pins, needles, and such.* — ***idiom.* such as.** For example. [ME < OE *swylc*. See **swo-***.]

such and such *adj.* Not specified; unnamed or undetermined: *They agreed to meet at such and such a place.*

such•like (sŭch′līk′) *adj.* Of the same kind; similar. — *pron.* Persons or things of such a kind.

Sü•chow (so͞o′chou′, sü′jō′). See **Xuzhou.**

suck (sŭk) *v.* **sucked, suck•ing, sucks.** — *tr.* **1.** To draw (liquid) into the mouth by movements of the tongue and lips that create suction. **2.a.** To draw in by establishing a partial vacuum: *This device sucks up dirt.* **b.** To draw in by or as if by a current in a fluid. **c.** To draw or pull as if by suction. **3.** To draw nourishment through or from. **4.** To hold, moisten, or maneuver (a sweet, for example) in the mouth. **5.** *Vulgar Slang.* To perform fellatio on. — *intr.* **1.** To draw something in by or as if by suction. **2.** To draw nourishment; suckle. **3.** To make a sound caused by suction. **4.** *Slang.* To behave obsequiously; fawn. Often used with *up.* **5.** *Vulgar Slang.* To be disgustingly disagreeable or offensive. — *n.* **1.** The act or sound of sucking. **2.** Suction. **3.** Something drawn in by sucking. — ***phrasal verb.* suck in.** To take advantage of; cheat. [ME *suken* < OE *sūcan*. See **seuə-**[2]*.]

suck•er (sŭk′ər) *n.* **1.** One that sucks, esp. an unweaned domestic animal. **2.** *Informal.* **a.** One who is easily deceived; a dupe. **b.** One that is indiscriminately attracted to something specified: *a sucker for pizza.* **3.** *Slang.* **a.** An unspecified thing. Used as a generalized term of reference, often as an intensive. **b.** A person. Used as a generalized term of reference, often as an intensive: *He's a mean sucker.* **4.** A lollipop. **5.a.** A piston or piston valve, as in a syringe. **b.** A tube or pipe, such as a siphon, through which something is sucked. **6.** Any of numerous chiefly North American freshwater fishes of the family Catostomidae, having a thick-lipped mouth adapted for feeding by suction. **7.** *Zool.* An organ or other structure adapted for sucking nourishment or for clinging to objects by suction. **8.** *Bot.* A secondary shoot produced from the base or roots of a woody plant that gives rise to a new plant. — *v.* **-ered, -er•ing, -ers.** — *tr.* **1.** To strip suckers or shoots from (plants). **2.** *Informal.* To trick; dupe. — *intr. Bot.* To send out suckers or shoots.

suck•er•fish (sŭk′ər-fĭsh′) *n.*, *pl.* **suckerfish** or **-fish•es.** See **remora.**

sucker punch *n. Slang.* An unexpected punch or blow.

suck•ing (sŭk′ĭng) *adj.* Not yet weaned.

sucking louse *n.* Any of various small insects of the order Anoplura with mouthparts for piercing and sucking.

suck•le (sŭk′əl) *v.* **-led, -ling, -les.** — *tr.* **1.a.** To cause or allow to take milk at the breast or udder; nurse. **b.** To take milk at the breast or udder of. **2.** To take in as sustenance; have as nourishment. **3.** To nourish as if with the milk of the breast; nurture. — *intr.* To suck at the breast or udder. [ME *suclen*, perh. < *suklinge*, suckling. See SUCKLING.]

suck•ler (sŭk′lər) *n.* **1.** An unweaned mammal, esp. a suckling calf. **2.** An animal that suckles its young; a mammal.

suck•ling (sŭk′lĭng) *n.* A young mammal that has not been weaned. — *adj.* Unweaned. [ME *suklinge* : *souken*, *suken*, to suck; see SUCK + *-ling*, one that is young; see -LING[1].]

Suck•ling (sŭk′lĭng), Sir **John.** 1609–42. English poet and courtier whose works include *Aglaura* (1637).

su•crase (so͞o′krās′, -krāz′) *n.* See **invertase.** [Fr. *sucre*, sugar (< OFr. *sukere*; see SUGAR) + -ASE.]

su•cre (so͞o′krā) *n.* See table at **currency.** [Am.Sp., after Antonio José de SUCRE.]

Su•cre (so͞o′krā, -krĕ). The constitutional cap. of Bolivia, in the S-central part SE of La Paz; founded in 1538 as Chuquisaca and renamed in 1840. Pop. 86,609.

Su•cre (so͞o′krā), **Antonio José de.** 1795–1830. South American military leader who helped secure independence from Spain and served as the first president of Bolivia (1826–28).

su•crose (so͞o′krōs′) *n.* A crystalline disaccharide carbohydrate, $C_{12}H_{22}O_{11}$, found in many plants but extracted as ordinary sugar mainly from sugar cane and sugar beets, widely used as a sweetener or preservative and in the manufacture of plastics and cellulose. [Fr. *sucre*, sugar; see SUCRASE + -OSE[2].]

suc•tion (sŭk′shən) *n.* **1.** The act or process of sucking. **2.** A force that causes a fluid or solid to be drawn into an interior space or to adhere to a surface because of the difference between the external and internal pressures. — *tr.v.* **-tioned, -tion•ing, -tions. 1.** To draw away or remove by the force of suction. **2.** To clean or evacuate (a body cavity, for example) by the force of suction. — *adj.* **1.** Creating suction. **2.** Operating or operated by suction. [LLat. *sūctiō*, *sūctiōn-* < Lat. *sūctus*, p.part. of *sūgere*, to suck. See **seuə-**[2]*.]

suction pump *n.* A pump for drawing up a liquid by means of suction produced by a piston drawn through a cylinder.

suction stop *n. Ling.* See **click** 3.

suc•to•ri•al (sŭk-tôr′ē-əl, -tōr′-) *adj.* **1.** Adapted for sucking or clinging by suction: *a suctorial organ.* **2.** Having organs or parts adapted for sucking or clinging. [< NLat. *sūctōrius* < Lat. *sūctus*, p.part. of *sūgere*, to suck. See **seuə-**[2]*.]

suc•to•ri•an (sŭk-tôr′ē-ən, -tōr′-) *n.* A protozoan of the class Suctoria, in its adult form being sessile and feeding by means of suctorial tentacles. [< NLat. *Suctoria*, class name < neut. pl. of *suctorius*, suctorial. See SUCTORIAL.]

Su•dan (so͞o-dăn′). **1.** A region of N Africa S of the Sahara and N of the equator extending from the Atlantic coast to the mountains of Ethiopia. **2.** A country of NE Africa S of Egypt; jointly administered by Great Britain and Egypt from 1899 to 1956. Cap. Khartoum. Pop. 20,564,364. — **Su′da•nese′** (so͞od′n-ēz′, -ēs′) *adj.* & *n.*

su•da•to•ri•um (so͞o′də-tôr′ē-əm, -tōr′-) *n.*, *pl.* **-to•ri•a** (-tôr′ē-ə, -tōr′ē-ə). A hot-air room used for sweat baths. [Lat. *sūdātōrium* < neut. of *sūdātōrius*, for sweating < *sūdātus*, p.part. of *sūdāre*, to sweat. See **sweid-***.]

su•da•to•ry (so͞o′də-tôr′ē, -tōr′ē) *adj.* Sudorific. — *n.*, *pl.* **-ries. 1.** See **sudatorium. 2.** See **sudorific.**

Sud•bur•y (sŭd′bĕr′ē, -bə-rē). A city of SE Ontario, Canada, N of Georgian Bay. Pop. 91,829.

sudd (sŭd) *n.* A floating mass of vegetation that often obstructs navigation in tropical rivers. [Ar., obstruction, sudd < *sadda*, to obstruct.]

sud•den (sŭd′n) *adj.* **1.** Happening without warning; unforeseen. **2.** Characterized by hastiness; abrupt or rash. **3.** Characterized by rapidity; quick and swift. **—*idiom.* all of a sudden.** Very quickly and unexpectedly; suddenly. [ME *sodain* < OFr. < VLat. **subitānus* < Lat. *subitāneus* < *subitus* < p.part. of *subīre*, to approach stealthily : *sub-*, secretly; see SUB- + *īre*, to go; see **ei-***.] **—sud′den•ly** *adv.* **—sud′den•ness** *n.*

sudden death *n. Sports.* Extra play added to a tied game, the winner of which being the first to score. **—sud′den-death′** (sŭd′n-dĕth′) *adj.*

sudden infant death syndrome *n.* A fatal syndrome that affects sleeping infants under a year old, characterized by a sudden cessation of breathing.

Su•de•ten (so͞o-dā′tn, zo͞o-) also **Su•de•tes** (so͞o-dē′tēz). A series of mountain ranges along the Czech-Polish border between the Elbe and Oder rivers extending for c. 298 km (185 mi) and rising to 1,603 m (5,256 ft).

Su•de•ten•land (so͞o-dāt′n-lănd′, -länt′, zo͞o-). A historical region of N Czech Republic along the Polish border; occupied by Germany from 1938 to 1945.

su•dor•if•er•ous (so͞o′də-rĭf′ər-əs) *adj.* Producing or secreting sweat: *sudoriferous glands.* [< LLat. *sūdōrifer* : Lat. *sūdor*, sweat; see **sweid-*** + Lat. *-fer*, -fer.]

su•dor•if•ic (so͞o′də-rĭf′ĭk) *adj.* Causing or increasing sweat. —*n.* A sudorific medicine. [NLat. *sūdōrificus* : Lat. *sūdor*, sweat; see **sweid-*** + Lat. *-ficus*, -fic.]

Su•dra (so͞o′drə) *n.* A member of the fourth of the four Hindu classes, comprising artisans, laborers, and menials. [Skt. *śūdraḥ*.]

suds (sŭdz) *pl.n.* **1.** Soapy water. **2.** Foam; lather. **3.** *Slang.* Beer. [Perh. < obsolete Du. *zudse*, marsh < MDu. *sudse*.]

suds•y (sŭd′zē) *adj.* **-i•er, -i•est.** Full of or resembling suds.

sue (so͞o) *v.* **sued, su•ing, sues.** —*tr.* **1.** *Law.* **a.** To petition (a court) for redress of grievances or recovery of a right. **b.** To institute proceedings against (a person) for redress of grievances. **c.** To carry (an action) through to a final decision. **2.** To court; woo. **3.** *Obsolete.* To make a petition to; appeal to; beseech. —*intr.* **1.** *Law.* To institute legal proceedings; bring suit. **2.** To make an appeal or entreaty. **3.** To pay court; woo. [ME *sewen* < AN *suer* < VLat. **sequere*, to follow < Lat. *sequī*. See **sekʷ-¹***.] **—su′er** *n.*

Sue (so͞o, sü), **Eugène.** 1804–57. French writer whose novels include *The Mysteries of Paris* (1842–43).

suede also **suède** (swād) *n.* **1.** Leather with a soft napped surface. **2.** Fabric made to resemble suede. [Short for *Suède gloves* < Fr. *gants de Suède*, gloves of Sweden < *Suède*, Sweden.]

su•et (so͞o′ĭt) *n.* The hard fat around the kidneys of cattle and sheep, used in cooking and for making tallow. [ME < AN **suet*, accusative of *sue*, tallow, var. of OFr. *sieu* < Lat. *sēbum*.]

Sue•to•ni•us (swē-tō′nē-əs). fl. 2nd cent. A.D. Roman historian whose major work, *Lives of the Caesars*, is an account of the first 12 Roman emperors.

Su•ez (so͞o-ĕz′, so͞o′ĕz′). A city of NE Egypt on the Gulf of Suez at the S terminus of the Suez Canal. Pop. 254,000.

Suez, Gulf of. An arm of the Red Sea off NE Egypt W of the Sinai Peninsula.

Suez, Isthmus of. An isthmus of NE Egypt connecting Africa and Asia and bordered by the Mediterranean Sea on the N and the Gulf of Suez on the S.

Suez Canal. A ship canal, c. 166 km (103 mi), traversing the Isthmus of Suez and linking the Red Sea and the Gulf of Suez with the Mediterranean Sea; built under the supervision of Ferdinand de Lesseps and opened in 1869.

suf. *abbr.* **1.** Sufficient. **2.** *Gram.* Suffix.

suff. *abbr.* **1.** Sufficient. **2.** *Gram.* Suffix.

Suff. *abbr.* Suffragan.

suf•fer (sŭf′ər) *v.* **-fered, -fer•ing, -fers.** —*intr.* **1.** To feel pain or distress; sustain loss, injury, harm, or punishment. **2.** To tolerate or endure evil, injury, pain, or death. See Syns at **bear¹**. **3.** To appear at a disadvantage. —*tr.* **1.** To undergo or sustain (something painful, injurious, or unpleasant). **2.** To experience; undergo. **3.** To endure or bear; stand. **4.** To permit; allow. [ME *suffren* < OFr. *sufrir* < VLat. **sufferīre* < Lat. *sufferre* : *sub-*, sub- + *ferre*, to carry; see **bher-¹***.] **—suf′fer•er** *n.* **—suf′fer•ing•ly** *adv.*

Usage Note: In general usage *suffer* is preferably used with *from*, rather than *with*, in constructions such as *He suffered from hypertension.* According to 94 percent of the Usage Panel, *suffered with* would be unacceptable in the preceding example. In medical usage *suffer with* sometimes refers to the actual pain or discomfort caused by a condition, while *suffer from* is used more broadly in reference to a detrimental condition that is not necessarily painful.

suf•fer•a•ble (sŭf′ər-ə-bəl, sŭf′rə-) *adj.* Possible to suffer, endure, or permit; tolerable. **—suf′fer•a•ble•ness** *n.* **—suf′fer•a•bly** *adv.*

suf•fer•ance (sŭf′ər-əns, sŭf′rəns) *n.* **1.** Patient endurance, esp. of pain or distress. **2.** Suffering; misery. **3.** Sanction or permission implied or given by failure to prohibit; tacit consent. [ME *suffrance* < OFr. *sufrance* < Lat. *sufferentia* < *sufferēns*, *sufferent-*, pr.part. of *sufferre*, to suffer. See SUFFER.]

suf•fer•ing (sŭf′ər-ĭng, sŭf′rĭng) *n.* **1.** The condition of one who suffers; pain or distress. **2.** A source of pain or distress.

suf•fice (sə-fīs′) *v.* **-ficed, -fic•ing, -fic•es.** —*intr.* **1.** To meet present needs or requirements; be sufficient. **2.** To be equal to a specified task; be capable. —*tr.* To satisfy the needs or requirements of; be enough for. [ME *suffisen* < OFr. *suffire*, *suffis-* < Lat. *sufficere* : *sub-*, sub- + *facere*, to make; see **dhē-***.] **—suf•fic′er** *n.*

suf•fi•cien•cy (sə-fĭsh′ən-sē) *n.*, *pl.* **-cies.** **1.** The condition or quality of being sufficient. **2.** An adequate amount or quantity. **3.** Adequate means to live in modest comfort.

suf•fi•cient (sə-fĭsh′ənt) *adj.* **1.** Being as much as is needed. **2.** *Archaic.* Competent; qualified. [ME < OFr. < Lat. *sufficiēns*, *sufficient-*, pr.part. of *sufficere*, to suffice. See SUFFICE.] **—suf•fi′cient•ly** *adv.*

suf•fix (sŭf′ĭks) *Gram.* —*n.* An affix added to the end of a word or stem, serving to form a new word or functioning as an inflectional ending, such as *-ness* in *gentleness* or *-s* in *sits.* —*tr.v.* **-fixed, -fix•ing, -fix•es.** To add as a suffix. [NLat. *suffixum* < Lat., neut. of *suffixus*, p.part. of *suffīgere*, to fasten underneath, affix : *sub-*, sub- + *fīgere*, to fix, fasten; see **dhīgʷ-***.] **—suf′fix•al** *adj.* **—suf′fix•a′tion, suf•fix′ion** (sə-fĭk′shən) *n.*

suf•fo•cate (sŭf′ə-kāt′) *v.* **-cat•ed, -cat•ing, -cates.** —*tr.* **1.** To kill or destroy by preventing access to air or oxygen. **2.** To impair the respiration of; asphyxiate. **3.** To cause discomfort to by or as if by cutting off the supply of fresh air. **4.** To suppress the development, imagination, or creativity of; stifle. —*intr.* **1.** To die from lack of air or oxygen; be asphyxiated. **2.** To feel discomfort from lack of fresh air. **3.** To become or feel suppressed; be stifled. [Lat. *suffōcāre*, *suffōcāt-* : *sub-*, sub- + *faucēs*, throat.] **—suf′fo•ca′ting•ly** *adv.* **—suf′fo•ca′tion** *n.* **—suf′fo•ca′tive** *adj.*

Suf•folk¹ (sŭf′ək). **1.** A historical region of E England bordering on the North Sea; formerly part of the Anglo-Saxon kingdom of East Anglia. **2.** (*also* -ôk′). An independent city of SE VA SE of Portsmouth. Pop. 52,141.

Suf•folk² (sŭf′ək) *n.* **1.** Any of an English breed of hornless sheep with black face and black legs, raised for high-quality mutton. **2.** Any of a breed of English draft horses of a chestnut color, having short legs and a thickset heavy body. [After *Suffolk*, a county of E England.]

suf•fra•gan (sŭf′rə-gən) *n.* **1.** A bishop elected or appointed as an assistant to the bishop or ordinary of a diocese. **2.** A bishop regarded in position as subordinate to an archbishop or a metropolitan. [ME < OFr. < Med.Lat. *suffrāgāneus*, voting, supporting < Lat. *suffrāgium*, support, right to vote < *suffrāgārī*, to express support. See **bhreg-***.] **—suf′fra•gan** *adj.* **—suf′fra•gan•ship′** *n.*

suf•frage (sŭf′rĭj) *n.* **1.a.** The right or privilege of voting; franchise. **b.** The exercise of such a right. **2.** A vote cast in deciding a disputed question or in electing a person to office. **3.** A short intercessory prayer. [ME, intercessory prayer < OFr. < Med.Lat. *suffrāgium* < Lat., the right to vote < *suffrāgārī*, to express support. See **bhreg-***.]

suf•fra•gette (sŭf′rə-jĕt′) *n.* An advocate of woman suffrage, esp. in the United Kingdom. See Usage Note at **-ette.** **—suf′fra•get′tism** *n.*

suf•fra•gist (sŭf′rə-jĭst) *n.* An advocate of the extension of political voting rights, esp. to women. **—suf′fra•gism** *n.*

suf•fru•tes•cent (sŭf′ro͞o-tĕs′ənt) also **suf•fru•ti•cose** (sŭf-ro͞o′tĭ-kōs′) *adj. Bot.* Having a stem that is woody only at the base. [NLat. *suffrutēscēns*, *suffrutēscent-* : Lat. *sub-*, sub- + NLat. *frutēscēns*, frutescent (< Lat. *frutex*, shrub).]

suf•fuse (sə-fyo͞oz′) *tr.v.* **-fused, -fus•ing, -fus•es.** To spread through or over, as with liquid or light. [Lat. *suffundere*, *suffūs-* : *sub-*, sub- + *fundere*, to pour; see **gheu-***.] **—suf•fu′sion** *n.* **—suf•fu′sive** (-fyo͞o′sĭv, -zĭv) *adj.*

Su•fi (so͞o′fē) *Islam.* —*n.* A Muslim mystic. —*adj.* Of or relating to the Sufis. [Ar. *Ṣūfīy*, (man) of wool, Sufi < *ṣūf*, wool (prob. from their woolen garments).] **—Su′fic** (-fĭk), **Su•fis′tic** (-fĭs′tĭk) *adj.* **—Su′fism** (-fĭz′əm) *n.*

sug•ar (sho͝og′ər) *n.* **1.** A sweet crystalline or powdered substance, consisting of sucrose obtained mainly from sugar cane and sugar beets and used esp. in foods to improve taste. **2.** Any of a class of water-soluble crystalline carbohydrates, including sucrose and lactose, having a sweet taste and classified as monosaccharides, disaccharides, and trisaccharides. **3.** A unit, such as a lump or cube, in which sugar is dispensed or taken. **4.** *Slang.* Sweetheart. Used as a term of endearment. —*v.* **-ared, -ar•ing, -ars.** —*tr.* **1.** To coat, cover, or sweeten with sugar. **2.** To make less distasteful or more appealing. —*intr.* **1.** To form sugar. **2.** To form granules; granulate. **3.** To make sugar or syrup from sugar maple sap. Often used with *off.* [ME *sugre* < OFr. *sukere* < Med.Lat. *succārum* < OItal. *zucchero* < Ar. *sukkar* < Pers. *shakar* < Skt. *śarkarā*, grit, ground sugar.] **—sug′ar•er** *n.*

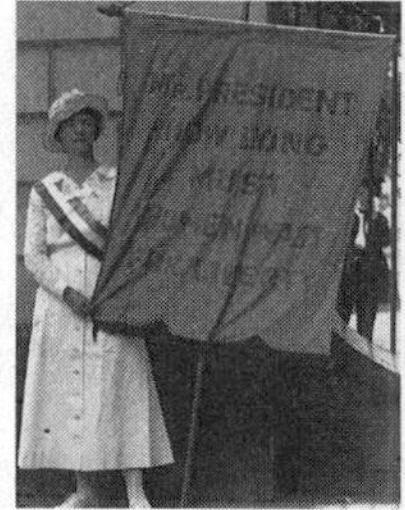

suffragist
Demonstrating outside the White House, 1917

ă pat	oi boy
ā pay	ou out
âr care	o͝o took
ä father	o͞o boot
ĕ pet	ŭ cut
ē be	ûr urge
ĭ pit	th thin
ī pie	*th* this
îr pier	hw which
ŏ pot	zh vision
ō toe	ə about, item
ô paw	

Stress marks:
′ (primary);
′ (secondary), as in **dictionary** (dĭk′shə-nĕr′ē)

sugar apple *n.* See **sweetsop.**
sugar beet *n.* A form of the common beet *(Beta vulgaris)* having fleshy white roots from which sugar is obtained.
sug•ar•ber•ry (sho͝og′ər-bĕr′ē) *n.* See **hackberry.**
sugar bush *n.* A grove of sugar maples.
sugar cane *n.* A tall tropical southeast Asian grass *(Saccharum officinarum)* having thick tough stems that are a chief source of sugar.
sug•ar•coat (sho͝og′ər-kōt′) *tr.v.* **-coat•ed, -coat•ing, -coats. 1.** To cause to seem more appealing or pleasant. **2.** To coat with sugar: *sugarcoat a pill.*
sug•ar-cured (sho͝og′ər-kyo͝ord′) *adj.* Cured with a preparation of sugar, salt, and nitrate: *a sugar-cured ham.*
sugar daddy *n. Slang.* A wealthy, usu. older man who gives expensive gifts to a young person in return for sexual favors or companionship.
sug•ared (sho͝og′ərd) *adj.* **1.** Sweetened with sugar. **2.** Made more appealing or pleasant.
sug•ar•house (sho͝og′ər-hous′) *n.* A sugar refinery or processing plant, esp. a building in which maple sap is boiled down to yield maple syrup and maple sugar.
sug•ar•less (sho͝og′ər-lĭs) *adj.* **1.** Containing no sugar. **2.** Sweetened with a substance other than sucrose.
sugar loaf *n.* **1.** A large conical loaf of pure concentrated sugar. **2.** Something, such as a mountain, that resembles a loaf of sugar in shape. **—sug′ar-loaf′** (sho͝og′ər-lōf′) *adj.*

Sugarloaf Mountain

Sug•ar•loaf Mountain (sho͝og′ər-lōf′). A peak, 395.3 m (1,296 ft), in Rio de Janeiro, Brazil, at the entrance to Guanabara Bay.
sugar maple *n.* **1.** An eastern North American maple tree *(Acer saccharum)* having sap that is the source of maple syrup and maple sugar and hard wood used in cabinetmaking. **2.** The wood of this tree

sugar maple
Acer saccharum

sugar of lead (lĕd) *n.* See **lead acetate.**
sugar of milk *n.* Lactose.
sugar orchard *n.* See **sugar bush.**
sugar pea *n.* See **snow pea.**
sugar pine *n.* A tall evergreen timber tree *(Pinus lambertiana)* of the Pacific coast of North America having needles with white lines on the back that are grouped in fascicles of five.
sug•ar•plum (sho͝og′ər-plŭm′) *n.* A small round piece of sugary candy.
sug•ar•y (sho͝og′ə-rē) *adj.* **-i•er, -i•est. 1.** Characterized by or containing sugar. **2.** Tasting or looking like sugar. **3.** Excessively or cloyingly sweet: *a sugary smile.* **—sug′ar•i•ness** *n.*
sug•gest (səg-jĕst′, sə-jĕst′) *tr.v.* **-gest•ed, -gest•ing, -gests. 1.** To offer for consideration or action; propose. **2.** To bring or call to mind by logic or association; evoke. **3.** To make evident indirectly; intimate or imply. **4.** To serve as or provide a motive for; prompt or demand. [Lat. *suggerere, suggest-* : *sub-*, up; see SUB- + *gerere*, to carry.] **—sug•gest′er** *n.*
Syns: *suggest, imply, hint, intimate, insinuate.* These verbs mean to convey thoughts or ideas by indirection. *Suggest* refers to the calling of something to mind as the result of an association of ideas: *"his erect and careless attitude suggesting assurance and power"* (Joseph Conrad). To *imply* is to suggest a thought or an idea by letting it be inferred from something else, such as a statement, that is more explicit: *The effusive praise the professor heaped on one of the students seemed to imply disapproval of the rest. Hint* refers to an oblique or covert suggestion that often contains clues: *My imagination supplied the explanation you only hinted at. Intimate* applies to indirect, subtle expression that often reflects discretion, tact, or reserve: *She intimated that the couple had had marital problems.* To *insinuate* is to suggest something, usually something unpleasant, in a sly manner: *The columnist insinuated that the candidate had underworld ties.*
sug•gest•i•bil•i•ty (səg-jĕs′tə-bĭl′ĭ-tē, sə-jĕs′-) *n.* Responsiveness or susceptibility to suggestion.
sug•gest•i•ble (səg-jĕs′tə-bəl, sə-jĕs′-) *adj.* Readily influenced by suggestion: *suggestible young minds.*
sug•ges•tion (səg-jĕs′chən, sə-jĕs′-) *n.* **1.** The act of suggesting. **2.** Something suggested. **3.** The process by which one thought or mental image leads to another. **4.a.** A psychological process by which an idea is induced in or adopted by another without argument, command, or coercion. **b.** An idea or response so induced. **5.** A hint or trace.
sug•ges•tive (səg-jĕs′tĭv, sə-jĕs′-) *adj.* **1.a.** Tending to suggest; evocative. **b.** Stimulating further thought. **c.** Conveying a hint or suggestion. **2.** Tending to suggest something improper or indecent. **—sug•ges′tive•ly** *adv.* **—sug•ges′tive•ness** *n.*

Suleiman I

Su•har•to (sə-här′tō, so͞o-). b. 1921. Indonesian military and political leader who seized power from Sukarno (1967) and became president in 1969.
Sui (swā). A Chinese dynasty (581–618) that reunified China after a period of declining centralized government.
su•i•cid•al (so͞o′ĭ-sīd′l) *adj.* **1.** Causing, intending, or relating to suicide. **2.** Dangerous to oneself or to one's interests; self-destructive or ruinous. **—su′i•cid′al•ly** *adv.*
su•i•cide (so͞o′ĭ-sīd′) *n.* **1.** The act or an instance of intentionally killing oneself. **2.** The destruction or ruin of one's own interests. **3.** One who commits suicide. [Lat. *suī*, of oneself; see **s(w)e-*** + -CIDE.]
su•i ge•ne•ris (so͞o′ī′ jĕn′ər-ĭs, so͞o′ē) *adj.* Being the only example of its kind; unique. [Lat. *suī generis* : *suī*, of its own + *generis*, genitive of *genus*, kind.]
su•int (so͞o′ĭnt, swĭnt) *n.* A grease formed from dried perspiration found in the fleece of sheep, used as a source of potash. [Fr. < OFr. < *suer*, to sweat < Lat. *sūdāre*. See **sweid-***.]
suit (so͞ot) *n.* **1.a.** A set of matching outer garments, esp. one consisting of a coat with trousers or a skirt. **b.** A costume for a special activity: *a diving suit.* **2.** A group of things used together; a set or collection. **3.** *Games.* Any of the four sets of 13 playing cards (clubs, diamonds, hearts, and spades) in a standard deck. **4.** Attendance required of a vassal at his feudal lord's court or manor. **5.** *Law.* A court proceeding to recover a right or claim. **6.** The act or an instance of courting a woman; courtship. **—*v.* suit•ed, suit•ing, suits. —*tr.* 1.** To meet the requirements of; fit. **2.** To make appropriate or suitable; adapt. **3.** To be appropriate for; befit. **4.** To please; satisfy. **5.** To provide with clothing; dress. **—*intr.* 1.** To be suitable or acceptable. **2.** To be in accord; agree or match. **—*phrasal verb.* suit up.** To put on clothing designed for a special activity. [ME *sute* < AN < VLat. **sequita*, act of following, fem. of **sequitus*, p.part. of **sequere*, to follow < Lat. *sequī*. See SUITOR.]
suit•a•ble (so͞o′tə-bəl) *adj.* Appropriate to a purpose or an occasion. **—suit′a•bil′i•ty, suit′a•ble•ness** *n.* **—suit′a•bly** *adv.*
suit•case (so͞ot′kās′) *n.* A usu. rectangular piece of luggage for carrying clothing.
suite (swēt) *n.* **1.** A staff of attendants or followers; a retinue. **2.a.** A group of related things intended to be used together; a set. **b.** (*also* so͞ot). A set of matching furniture. **3.** A series of connected rooms used as a living unit. **4.** *Mus.* An instrumental composition consisting of a succession of dances in the same or related keys. [Fr. < OFr. See SUIT.]
suit•ing (so͞o′tĭng) *n.* Fabric from which suits are made.
suit•or (so͞o′tər) *n.* **1.** A man who is courting a woman. **2.** A person who makes a petition or request. **3.** *Law.* A person who sues in court; a plaintiff; a petitioner. **4.** A person or group seeking to purchase controlling interest in a company. [ME, plaintiff < AN < Lat. *secūtor*, follower < *secūtus*, p.part. of *sequī*, to follow. See **sekʷ-¹***.]
Su•kar•no (so͞o-kär′nō). 1901–70. Indonesian politician who served as Indonesia's first president (1949–67) and was ousted from office by a coup d'état.
su•ki•ya•ki (so͞o′kē-yä′kē, skē-yä′kē) *n.* A Japanese dish of thinly sliced meat, bean curd, and vegetables. [J.]
Suk•koth (so͝ok′əs, so͞o-kōs′, so͞o-kôt′) *n. Judaism.* Var. of **Succoth.**
Su•la•we•si (so͞o′lä-wā′sē). See **Celebes.**
sul•cate (sŭl′kāt′) *adj. Biol.* Having narrow, deep furrows or grooves, as a stem or tissue. [Lat. *sulcātus*, p.part. of *sulcāre*, to furrow < *sulcus*, furrow.]
sul•cus (sŭl′kəs) *n., pl.* **-ci** (-kī, -sī). **1.** A deep narrow furrow or groove, as in an organ or a tissue. **2.** *Anat.* Any of the narrow fissures separating adjacent convolutions of the brain. [Lat.] **—sul′cal** *adj.*
Su•lei•man I (so͞o′lā-män′, -lə-). "Suleiman the Magnificent." 1494?–1566. Sultan of Turkey (1520–66) under whose governance the Ottoman Empire reached the height of its power.
sul•fa (sŭl′fə) *adj.* Of, relating to, or containing sulfanilamide or any sulfa drug. [Short for SULFA(NILAMIDE).]
sul•fa•di•a•zine (sŭl′fə-dī′ə-zēn′) *n.* A sulfa drug, $C_{10}H_{10}N_4O_2S$, used esp. in the treatment of meningitis.
sulfa drug *n.* Any of a group of synthetic organic compounds, derived chiefly from sulfanilamide and capable of inhibiting bacterial growth and activity.
sul•fa•nil•a•mide (sŭl′fə-nĭl′ə-mīd′, -mĭd) *n.* A white crystalline sulfonamide, $C_6H_8N_2SO_2$, used in the treatment of various bacterial infections. [SULF(O)- + ANIL(INE) + AMIDE.]
sul•fate (sŭl′fāt′) *n.* A chemical compound containing the bivalent group SO_4. **—*v.* -fat•ed, -fat•ing, -fates. —*tr.* 1.** To treat or react with sulfuric acid or a sulfate. **2.** *Elect.* To cause lead sulfate to accumulate on (the plates of a lead-acid battery). **—*intr.*** To become sulfated. [Fr. < Lat. *sulfur*, sulfur.]
sul•fide (sŭl′fīd′) *n.* A compound of bivalent sulfur with an electropositive element or group, esp. a binary compound of sulfur with a metal.
sul•fi•nyl (sŭl′fə-nĭl′) *n.* The bivalent group SO. [SULF(O)- + -IN + -YL.]
sul•fite (sŭl′fīt′) *n.* A salt or an ester of sulfurous acid. **—sul•fit′ic** (-fĭt′ĭk) *adj.*
sulfo– or **sulf–** *pref.* Sulfur: *sulfate.* [< SULFUR.]
sulfon– *pref.* Sulfonic: *sulfonamide.* [< SULFONE.]
sul•fon•a•mide (sŭl-fŏn′ə-mīd′, -mĭd) *n.* **1.** Any of a group of organic sulfur compounds containing the radical O_2NH_2 and including the sulfa drugs. **2.** See **sulfa drug.**
sul•fo•nate (sŭl′fə-nāt′) *n.* A salt or an ester of sulfonic acid. **—*tr.v.* -nat•ed, -nat•ing, -nates. 1.** To introduce into (an organic compound) one or more sulfonic acid groups. **2.** To treat with sulfonic acid. **—sul′fo•na′tion** *n.*

sul•fone (sŭl′fōn′) *n.* Any of various organic sulfur compounds having a sulfonyl group that is attached to two carbon atoms.
sul•fon•ic (sŭl-fŏn′ĭk) *adj.* Of or relating to the chemical group SO_2OH.
sulfonic acid *n.* Any of several organic acids containing one or more sulfonic groups.
sul•fo•ni•um (sŭl-fō′nē-əm) *n.* A positive ion or univalent radical containing trivalent sulfur, such as H_3S. [SULF(O)- + (AMM)ONIUM.]
sul•fo•nyl (sŭl′fə-nĭl′) *n.* The bivalent radical SO_2.
sulf•ox•ide (sŭl-fŏk′sīd′) *n.* Any of various organic compounds that contain a sulfinyl group.
sul•fur also **sul•phur** (sŭl′fər) —*n. Symbol* **S** A yellow nonmetallic element occurring widely in nature in several free and combined allotropic forms and used in rubber vulcanization and in the manufacture of insecticides, pharmaceuticals, and many sulfur compounds, esp. sulfuric acid. Atomic number 16; atomic weight 32.064; melting point (rhombic) 112.8°C; (monoclinic) 119.0°C; boiling point 444.6°C; specific gravity (rhombic) 2.07; (monoclinic) 1.957; valence 2, 4, 6. See table at **element.** —*tr.v.* **-fured, -fur•ing, -furs** also **-phured, -phur•ing, -phurs.** To treat with sulfur or a compound of sulfur. [ME < AN *sulfre* < Lat. *sulfur.*]
sul•fu•rate (sŭl′fə-rāt′, -fyə-) *tr.v.* **-rat•ed, -rat•ing, -rates.** To treat or combine with sulfur. —**sul′fu•ra′tion** *n.*
sulfur bacterium *n.* Any of several bacteria that oxidize inorganic sulfur compounds, esp. a rod-shaped gram-negative bacterium of the genus *Thiobacillus.*
sulfur dioxide *n.* A colorless, extremely irritating gas or liquid, SO_2, used in many industrial processes.
sul•fu•re•ous (sŭl-fyŏŏr′ē-əs) *adj.* Of or relating to sulfur; sulfurous.
sul•fu•ret (sŭl′fə-rĕt′, -fyə-) *tr.v.* **-ret•ed, -ret•ing, -rets** or **-ret•ted, -ret•ting, -rets.** To sulfurize. —*n.* A sulfide. [< NLat. *sulfurētum,* sulfide : *sulf-,* sulfur (< Lat. *sulfur*) + *-urētum,* obsolete chemical suff.]
sul•fu•ric (sŭl-fyŏŏr′ĭk) *adj.* Of, relating to, or containing sulfur, esp. with valence 6.
sulfuric acid *n.* A highly corrosive dense oily liquid, H_2SO_4, used to manufacture a wide variety of chemicals and materials including fertilizers, paints, detergents, and explosives.
sul•fur•ize (sŭl′fə-rīz′, -fyə-) *tr.v.* **-ized, -iz•ing, -iz•es. 1.** To treat or impregnate with sulfur; sulfuret. **2.** To bleach or fumigate with sulfur or sulfur dioxide. —**sul′fur•i•za′tion** (-fər-ĭ-zā′shən, -fyər-) *n.*
sul•fur•ous (sŭl′fər-əs, -fyər-, sŭl-fyŏŏr′əs) *adj.* **1.** Of, relating to, derived from, or containing sulfur, esp. with valence 4. **2.** Characteristic of or emanating from burning sulfur. **3.** Also **sul•phur•ous.** Fiery; hellish.
sulfurous acid *n.* A colorless solution of sulfur dioxide in water, H_2SO_3, characterized by a suffocating sulfurous odor, used as a bleaching agent, preservative, and disinfectant.
sul•fur•yl (sŭl′fə-rĭl′, -fyə-) *n.* See **sulfonyl.**
sulk (sŭlk) *intr.v.* **sulked, sulk•ing, sulks.** To be sullenly aloof or withdrawn, as in silent resentment or protest. —*n.* A mood or display of sullen aloofness or withdrawal.
sulk•y[1] (sŭl′kē) *adj.* **-i•er, -i•est. 1.** Sullenly aloof or withdrawn. **2.** Gloomy; dismal. [Perh. alteration of obsolete *sulke,* sluggish, perh. ult. < OE *āsolcen* < p.part. of *āseolcan,* to become sluggish.] —**sulk′i•ly** *adv.* —**sulk′i•ness** *n.*
sulk•y[2] (sŭl′kē) *n., pl.* **-ies.** An open two-wheeled vehicle accommodating only the driver and drawn by one horse, used esp. in harness racing. [< SULKY[1] (, from its having only one seat).]
Sul•la (sŭl′ə), **Lucius Cornelius.** 138–78 B.C. Roman general and dictator (82–79) who marched on Rome and seized power from his political rival Marius (88).
sul•lage (sŭl′ĭj) *n.* **1.** Silt deposited by a current of water. **2.** Waste materials or sewage; refuse. [Perh. < Fr. *souiller,* to soil. See SULLY.]
sul•len (sŭl′ən) *adj.* **-er, -est. 1.** Showing a brooding ill humor or silent resentment; morose or sulky. **2.** Gloomy or somber in tone, color, or portent. **3.** Sluggish; slow. [ME *solein* < AN *solein,* alone < *sol,* single < Lat. *sōlus,* by oneself alone. See **s(w)e-*.**] —**sul′len•ly** *adv.* —**sul′len•ness** *n.*
Sul•li•van (sŭl′ə-vən), **Anne Mansfield.** 1866–1936. Amer. educator who was the teacher of Helen Keller.
Sullivan, Sir **Arthur Seymour.** 1842–1900. British composer known for a series of comic operas, including *H.M.S. Pinafore* (1878), written with the lyricist W.S. Gilbert.
Sullivan, John Lawrence. 1858–1918. Amer. prizefighter who was the heavyweight champion from 1882 to 1892.
Sullivan, Louis Henry or **Henri.** 1856–1924. Amer. architect known for his early steel-frame designs for skyscrapers.
sul•ly (sŭl′ē) *tr.v.* **-lied, -ly•ing, -lies. 1.** To mar the cleanness or luster of; soil or stain. **2.** To defile; taint. —*n., pl.* **-lies.** *Archaic.* Something that stains or spots. [Prob. < Fr. *souiller* < OFr. See SOIL[2].]
Sul•ly (sŭl′ē, sōō-lē′, sü-), Duc de. Maximilien de Béthune. 1560–1641. French politician and chief minister to Henry IV who replenished the treasury and encouraged industry.
Sul•ly (sŭl′ē), **Thomas.** 1783–1872. British-born Amer. painter of *Washington's Passage of the Delaware* (c. 1818).
Sul•ly-Prud•homme (sŭl′ē-prōō′dəm, sü-lē′prü-dôm′), **René François Armand.** 1839–1907. French poet who won the 1901 Nobel Prize for literature.
sul•phur[1] (sŭl′fər) *n.* Any of various butterflies of the genus *Colias* and related genera of the family Pieridae, having yellow or orange wings marked with black. [< *sulphur,* var. of SULFUR (< its color).]
sul•phur[2] (sŭl′fər) *n. & v.* Var. of **sulfur.**
Sul•phur (sŭl′fər). A city of SW LA W of Lake Charles. Pop. 20,125.
sul•phur-bot•tom (sŭl′fər-bŏt′əm) *n.* See **blue whale.**
sul•phur•ous (sŭl′fər-əs, -fyər-, sŭl-fyŏŏr′əs) *adj.* Var. of **sulfurous** 3.
sul•tan (sŭl′tən) *n.* **1.** A ruler of a Muslim country, esp. of the former Ottoman Empire. **2.** A powerful person. [Fr. < OFr., ruler of Turkey < Turk. < Ar. *sulṭān* < Aram. *šulṭānā* < *šĕlēṭ,* to rule.]
sul•tan•a (sŭl-tăn′ə, -tä′nə) *n.* **1.a.** The wife, mother, sister, or daughter of a sultan. **b.** The mistress of a sultan, king, or prince. **2.** A yellow seedless raisin of a kind originally produced in Asia Minor. [Ital., fem. of *sultano,* sultan < Ar. *sulṭān.* See SULTAN.]
sul•tan•ate (sŭl′tə-nāt′) *n.* **1.** The office, power, or reign of a sultan. **2.** A country ruled by a sultan.
sul•try (sŭl′trē) *adj.* **-tri•er, -tri•est. 1.a.** Very humid and hot. **b.** Extremely hot; torrid. **2.** Arousing passion or desire. [< obsolete *sulter,* to swelter, poss. alteration of SWELTER.] —**sul′tri•ly** *adv.* —**sul′tri•ness** *n.*
Su•lu (sōō′lōō) *n., pl.* **Su•lu** or **-lus.** A member of a Muslim people inhabiting the Sulu Archipelago. [Sama *sulu,* current.]
Sulu Sea. An arm of the W Pacific between the Philippines and N Borneo. The **Sulu Archipelago,** a chain of small islands belonging to the Philippines, separates the Sulu Sea from the Celebes Sea SW of Mindanao.
sum (sŭm) *n. Math.* **1.a.** An amount obtained as a result of adding numbers. **b.** An arithmetic problem. **2.** The whole amount, quantity, or number; an aggregate. **3.** An amount of money. **4.** A summary. **5.** The central idea or point; the gist. —*tr.v.* **summed, sum•ming, sums. 1.** *Math.* To add. **2.** To give a summary of; summarize. —***phrasal verb.*** **sum up. 1.** To present the substance of (material) in a condensed form; summarize. **2.** To describe or assess concisely. [ME *summe* < OFr. < Lat. *summa* < fem. of *summus,* highest. See **uper*.**]
su•mac also **su•mach** (sōō′măk, shōō′-) *n.* Any of various shrubs or small trees of the genus *Rhus,* having compound leaves and usu. red hairy fruit and including poison ivy and poison oak. [ME, preparation made from sumac < OFr. (poss. via Med.Lat. *sumach*) < Ar. *summāq,* sumac tree, prob. < Aram. *sĕmēq,* to be red.]
Su•ma•tra (sōō-mä′trə). An island of W Indonesia in the Indian Ocean S of the Malay Peninsula; under Dutch control from the 17th cent. until it joined newly independent Indonesia in 1949. —**Su•ma′tran** *adj. & n.*
Sum•ba (sōōm′bə, -bä). An island of S-central Indonesia in the Lesser Sunda Is. S of Flores.
Sum•ba•wa (sōōm-bä′wə, -wä). A volcanic island of S-central Indonesia in the Lesser Sunda Is. W of Flores.
Su•mer (sōō′mər). An ancient country of S Mesopotamia in present-day S Iraq; reached the height of its power under the Akkadian dynasty founded (c. 2340) by Sargon I.
Su•me•ri•an (sōō-mîr′ē-ən, -mĕr′-) *adj.* Of or relating to ancient Sumer or its people, language, or culture. —*n.* **1.** A member of an ancient people, probably of non-Semitic origin, who established a nation of city-states in Sumer in the fourth millennium B.C. **2.** The language of the Sumerians.
sum•ma cum lau•de (sōōm′ə kōōm lou′də, -dā, -dē) *adv. & adj.* With the greatest honor. Used to express the highest academic distinction. [Lat. *summā cum laude,* with highest praise : *summā,* fem. ablative of *summus,* highest + *cum,* with + *laude,* ablative of *laus,* praise.]
sum•ma•rize (sŭm′ə-rīz′) *intr. & tr.v.* **-rized, -riz•ing, -riz•es.** To make a summary or make a summary of. —**sum′ma•ri•za′tion** (sŭm′ər-ĭ-zā′shən) *n.* —**sum′ma•ri′zer** *n.*
sum•ma•ry (sŭm′ə-rē) *adj.* **1.** Presenting the substance in a condensed form; concise. **2.** Performed speedily and without ceremony: *a summary rejection.* —*n., pl.* **-ries.** A presentation of a body of material in condensed form or by reducing it to its main points; an abstract. [ME < Med.Lat. *summārius,* of or concerning the sum < Lat. *summa,* sum. See SUM.] —**sum•mar′i•ly** (sə-mĕr′ə-lē) *adv.* —**sum′ma•ri•ness** *n.*
sum•mate (sə-māt′) *v.* **-ma•ted, -ma•ting, -mates.** —*tr.* To sum up. —*intr.* To form or constitute a cumulative effect.
sum•ma•tion (sə-mā′shən) *n.* **1.** The act or process of adding; addition. **2.** A sum or an aggregate. **3.** A concluding part of a speech or an argument containing a summary of principal points, esp. of a case before a court of law. [NLat. *summātiō, summātiōn-* < LLat. *summātus,* p.part. of *summāre,* to sum up < Lat. *summa,* sum. See SUM.]
sum•mer[1] (sŭm′ər) *n.* **1.** The usu. warmest season of the year, occurring between spring and autumn and constituting June,

sulky[2]
Harness racing

sumac
Staghorn sumac
Rhus typhina

ă pat	oi boy
ā pay	ou out
âr care	ŏŏ took
ä father	ōō boot
ĕ pet	ŭ cut
ē be	ûr urge
ĭ pit	th thin
ī pie	*th* this
îr pier	hw which
ŏ pot	zh vision
ō toe	ə about, item
ô paw	

Stress marks:
′ (primary);
′ (secondary), as in **dictionary** (dĭk′shə-nĕr′ē)

July, and August in the Northern Hemisphere or, as calculated astronomically, extending from the summer solstice to the autumnal equinox. **2.** A period of fruition, fulfillment, happiness, or beauty. **3.** A year. — *v.* **-mered, -mer•ing, -mers.** — *tr.* To lodge or keep during the summer. — *intr.* To pass the summer. — *adj.* **1.** Of, having to do with, occurring in, or appropriate to the season of summer. **2.** Grown during the season of summer. [ME *sumer* < OE *sumor.* See **sem-²*.**] — **sum′mer•ly** *adv. & adj.*

sum•mer² (sŭm′ər) *n. Archit.* **1.** A heavy horizontal timber that serves as a supporting beam, esp. for a floor. **2.** A lintel. **3.** A large stone usu. set on top of a column or pilaster to support an arch or a lintel. [ME, beam, pack animal < AN *sumer* < VLat. **saumārius* < LLat. *sagmārius,* pertaining to a packsaddle, packhorse < *sagma,* packsaddle. See SUMPTER.]

sum•mer•ca•ter (sŭm′ər-kā′tər) *n. Maine.* A summer resident of Maine. Also called regionally *sport.* [Prob. SUMMER¹ + (VA)CAT(ION) + -ER¹.]

summer cypress *n.* A Eurasian annual plant *(Kochia scoparia)* having narrow dense foliage that turns bright red.

summer flounder *n.* A fluke *(Paralichthys dentatus)* of the Atlantic coast of the United States.

sum•mer•house (sŭm′ər-hous′) *n.* A small roofed structure in a park or garden affording shade and rest; a gazebo.

sum•mer•sault (sŭm′ər-sôlt′) *n. & v.* Var. of **somersault.**

summer savory *n.* See **savory²** 1.

summer school *n.* An academic session held during the summer, chiefly for supplementary and remedial study.

sum•mer•set (sŭm′ər-sĕt′) *n. & v.* Var. of **somerset.**

summer solstice *n.* In the Northern Hemisphere, the solstice that occurs on about June 21.

summer squash *n.* Any of several varieties of squash, such as the crookneck or the cymling, that are eaten shortly after being picked rather than kept in storage.

summer stock *n.* Theatrical productions of stock companies presented during the summer.

sum•mer•time (sŭm′ər-tīm′) *n.* The summer season.

sum•mer•wood (sŭm′ər-wo͝od′) *n.* Wood that is produced during the latter part of the growing season and is harder and less porous than springwood.

sum•mer•y (sŭm′ə-rē) *adj.* Of, for, or suggesting summer.

sum•ming-up (sŭm′ĭng-ŭp′) *n., pl.* **sum•mings-up** (sŭm′ĭngz-). A summary, often including an assessment.

sum•mit (sŭm′ĭt) *n.* **1.** The highest point or part; the top. **2.** The highest level or degree that can be attained. **3.a.** The highest level, as of government officials. **b.** A summit conference. [ME *somet* < OFr. *sommette,* dim. of *som,* top < Lat. *summum* < neut. of *summus,* highest. See **uper*.**]

Sum•mit (sŭm′ĭt). A city of NE NJ W of Newark. Pop. 19,757.

summit conference *n.* A conference of leaders, esp. of the highest-ranking officials of two or more governments.

sum•mit•eer (sŭm′ĭ-tîr′) *n.* An official who takes part in a summit conference.

sum•mit•ry (sŭm′ĭ-trē) *n.* **1.** The holding of a summit conference. **2.** Participation in summit conferences.

sum•mon (sŭm′ən) *tr.v.* **-moned, -mon•ing, -mons. 1.** To call together; convene. **2.** To request to appear; send for. **3.** *Law.* To order to appear in court by the issuance of a summons. **4.** To order to take a specified action; bid. **5.** To call forth; evoke: *Summon up your courage.* [ME *somonen* < OFr. *somondre* < VLat. **summonere* < Lat. *summonēre,* to remind privately, hint to : *sub-,* secretly; see SUB- + *monēre,* to warn; see **men-¹*.**] — **sum′mon•er** *n.*

sum•mons (sŭm′ənz) *n., pl.* **-mons•es. 1.** A call by an authority to appear, come, or do something. **2.** *Law.* **a.** A notice summoning a defendant to appear in court. **b.** A notice summoning a person to report to court as a juror or witness. — *tr.v.* **-monsed, -mons•ing, -mons•es.** *Law.* To serve a court summons to. [ME *somons* < OFr. *somonse* < fem. p.part. of *somondre,* to summon. See SUMMON.]

sum•mum bo•num (so͞om′əm bō′nəm) *n.* The greatest or supreme good. [Lat. : *summum,* neut. of *summus,* highest + *bonum,* good.]

Sum•ner (sŭm′nər), **Charles.** 1811–74. Amer. politician who was an outspoken opponent of slavery.

Sumner, William Graham. 1840–1910. Amer. sociologist who developed the concepts of folkways and mores.

su•mo (so͞o′mō) *n. Sports.* A Japanese form of men's wrestling in which a fighter loses if forced from the ring or if he touches the ground other than with the soles of his feet. [J. *sumō.*]

sump (sŭmp) *n.* **1.a.** A low-lying place, such as a pit, that receives drainage. **b.** A cesspool. **2.** A hole at the lowest point of a mine shaft into which water is drained in order to be pumped out. **3.** The crankcase or oil reservoir of an internal-combustion engine. [ME *sompe,* marsh < MLGer. *sump* or < MDu. *somp.* Sense 2 < Ger. *Sumpf,* swamp, sump < MHGer., swamp.]

sump•ter (sŭmp′tər) *n.* A pack animal, such as a horse or mule. [ME, driver of a packhorse < OFr. *sometier* < VLat. **saumatārius* < LLat. *sagma, sagmat-,* packsaddle < Gk. < *sattein,* to pack.]

sump•tu•ar•y (sŭmp′cho͞o-ĕr′ē) *adj.* **1.** Regulating or limiting personal expenditures. **2.a.** Regulating commercial or real-estate activities. **b.** Regulating personal behavior on moral or religious grounds. [Lat. *sūmptuārius* < *sūmptus,* expense < p.part. of *sūmere,* to take, buy. See **em-*.**]

sump•tu•ous (sŭmp′cho͞o-əs) *adj.* Of a size or splendor suggesting great expense; lavish. [ME < OFr. *sumptueux* < Lat. *sūmptuōsus* < *sūmptus,* expense. See SUMPTUARY.] — **sump′tu•ous•ly** *adv.* — **sump′tu•ous•ness** *n.*

Sum•ter (sŭm′tər). A city of central SC E of Columbia; founded 1799. Pop. 41,943.

Su•my (so͞o′mē). A city of N Ukraine NW of Kharkov. Pop. 256,000.

sun (sŭn) *n.* **1.** A star that is the basis of the solar system and sustains life on Earth as the source of heat and light, having a mean distance from Earth of about 150 million kilometers (93 million miles) and a diameter of approx. 1,390,000 kilometers (864,000 miles). **2.** A star that is the center of a planetary system. **3.** The radiant energy, esp. heat and visible light, emitted by the sun; sunshine. — *v.* **sunned, sun•ning, suns.** — *tr.* To expose to the sun's rays, as for warming, drying, or tanning. — *intr.* To expose oneself or itself to the sun. — ***idiom.* under the sun.** On earth; in the world. [ME < OE *sunne.* See **sāwel-*.**]

Sun. *abbr.* Sunday.

sun•baked (sŭn′bākt′) *adj.* Baked, dried, or hardened by exposure to sunlight: *sunbaked bricks.*

sun•bath (sŭn′băth′, -bäth′) *n.* An exposure of the body to sun.

sun•bathe (sŭn′bāth′) *intr.v.* **-bathed, -bath•ing, -bathes.** To expose the body to the sun. — **sun′bath′er** (-bā′*th*ər) *n.*

sun•beam (sŭn′bēm′) *n.* A ray of sunlight. [ME *sunnebem* < OE *sunnebēam* (transl. of LLat. *columna lūcis,* pillar of light) : *sunne,* sun; see SUN + *bēam,* tree, building post; see BEAM.]

Word History: The word *sunbeam* is believed to have entered English in the ninth century through the work of the English king Alfred the Great, who undertook a number of translations of great Latin writings. In one of these works appears several times the Latin phrase *columna lucis,* which we would today translate as "a column of light." Since the Old English translator did not have the word *column* in his vocabulary, he substituted *beam,* which meant "a tree" or "a wood building post." *Columna lucis* thus became *sunnebēam,* or "sun post," which survives as our *sunbeam.*

Sun•belt also **Sun Belt** (sŭn′bĕlt′). The S and SW U.S.

sun•bird (sŭn′bûrd′) *n.* Any of various tropical Old World passerine birds of the family Nectariniidae, having a curved bill and often brightly colored plumage in the male.

sun bittern *n.* A cranelike tropical American bird *(Eurypyga helias)* having mottled brownish plumage and often spreading its wings and tail in a showy display.

sun block also **sun blocker** *n.* A preparation, as of PABA, that prevents sunburn by filtering out the sun's ultraviolet rays.

sun•bon•net (sŭn′bŏn′ĭt) *n.* A woman's wide-brimmed bonnet with a flap at the back to protect the neck from the sun.

sun•bow (sŭn′bō′) *n.* A rainbow resulting from refraction of sunlight through a spray of water.

sun•burn (sŭn′bûrn′) *n.* Inflammation or blistering of the skin caused by overexposure to direct sunlight. — *tr. & intr.v.* **-burned** or **-burnt** (-bûrnt′), **-burn•ing, -burns.** To affect or be affected with sunburn.

sun•burst (sŭn′bûrst′) *n.* **1.** A sudden burst of sunlight, as through clouds. **2.a.** A pattern or design consisting of a central disk with radiating spires. **b.** A brooch with such a design.

sunburst

Sun City. A community of S-central AZ, a suburb of Phoenix. Pop. 40,505.

sun•dae (sŭn′dē, -dā′) *n.* A dish of ice cream with a topping such as syrup, fruits, nuts, or whipped cream. [?]

Sun•da Islands (sŭn′də, so͞on′-). A group of islands of the W Malay Archipelago between the South China Sea and the Indian Ocean. The **Greater Sunda Islands** include Sumatra, Borneo, Java, and Celebes; the **Lesser Sunda Islands** lie E of Java and extend from Bali to Timor.

sun dance *n.* A religious ceremony practiced among Native American peoples of the Great Plains, marked by several days of fasting and group dancing.

Sun•day (sŭn′dē, -dā′) *n.* **1.** The first day of the week. **2.** The Sabbath for many Christians. [ME < OE *sunnandæg.* See **sāwel-*.**]

Sunday, William ("Billy") Ashley. 1862–1935. Amer. evangelist who was a professional baseball player (1883–91) before he became a Presbyterian minister in 1903.

Sunday punch *n. Slang.* **1.** A knockout blow. **2.** Something capable of destroying an opponent or opposing force.

Sunday school *n.* **1.** A school, generally affiliated with a church or synagogue, that offers religious instruction for children on Sundays. **2.** The teachers and pupils of such a school.

sun deck *n.* A roof, balcony, or terrace used for sunbathing.

sun•der (sŭn′dər) *v.* **-dered, -der•ing, -ders.** — *tr.* To break or wrench apart; sever. See Syns at **separate.** — *intr.* To break into parts. — *n.* A division or separation. [ME *sundren* < OE *sundrian.*] — **sun′der•ance** *n.*

Sun·der·land (sŭn′dər-lənd). A borough of NE England on the North Sea ESE of Newcastle. Pop. 299,100.

sun·dew (sŭn′do͞o′, -dyo͞o′) *n.* Any of several insectivorous plants of the genus *Drosera,* growing in wet ground and having leaves covered with sticky hairs. [Obsolete Du. *sondauw* : *son,* sun (< MDu. *sonne;* see **sāwel-***) + *dauw,* dew (< MDu. *dau;* see **dheu-¹***).]

sun·di·al (sŭn′dī′əl) *n.* An instrument that indicates local apparent solar time by the shadow cast by a central projecting pointer on a surrounding calibrated dial.

sun disk *n.* An ancient Middle Eastern symbol consisting of a disk set between outspread wings, representing the sun god.

sun·dog (sŭn′dôg′, -dŏg′) *n.* **1.** A parhelion. **2.** A small halo or rainbow near the horizon just off the parhelic circle.

sun·down (sŭn′doun′) *n.* The time of sunset.

sun·down·er (sŭn′dou′nər) *n.* **1.** *Australian.* A vagrant; a tramp. **2.** *Chiefly British.* A drink taken at sundown.

sun·dress (sŭn′drĕs′) *n.* A light summer dress with a bodice that exposes the arms and shoulders.

sun·dries (sŭn′drēz) *pl.n.* Articles too small or numerous to be specified; miscellaneous items. [< SUNDRY.]

sun·drops (sŭn′drŏps′) *pl.n. (used with a sing. or pl. v.)* See **evening primrose.**

sun·dry (sŭn′drē) *adj.* Various; miscellaneous. [ME *sundri* < OE *syndrig,* separate.]

sun·fish (sŭn′fĭsh′) *n., pl.* **sunfish** or **-fish·es. 1.** Any of various small North American percoid freshwater fishes of the family Centrarchidae, having laterally compressed, often brightly colored bodies. **2.** Any of several large marine fishes of the family Molidae, esp. the ocean sunfish.

sun·flow·er (sŭn′flou′ər) *n.* **1.** Any of several plants of the genus *Helianthus,* esp. *H. annuus,* having tall coarse stems and large yellow-rayed flower heads that produce edible seeds rich in oil. **2.** The seeds of this plant.

sung (sŭng) *v.* A p.t. and the p.part. of **sing.**

Sung (so͝ong). See **Song.**

Sun·ga·ri (so͝ong′gə-rē). See **Songhua.**

sun·glass (sŭn′glăs′) *n.* **1.** A convex lens used to focus the sun's rays and produce heat. **2. sunglasses.** Eyeglasses with tinted or polarizing lenses to protect the eyes from the sun.

sun·glow (sŭn′glō′) *n.* A rose or yellow glow in the sky preceding sunrise or following sunset.

sun god *n. Myth.* A god that personifies the sun.

sunk (sŭngk) *v.* A p.t. and the p.part. of **sink.**

sunk·en (sŭng′kən) *v. Obsolete.* A p.part. of **sink.** —*adj.* **1.** Depressed, fallen in, or hollowed: *sunken cheeks.* **2.** Situated beneath the surface of the water or ground; submerged. **3.** Below a surrounding level: *a sunken meadow.*

sunk fence *n.* A ditch with a retaining wall set into it to divide lands without marring the landscape.

sun lamp *n.* **1.** A lamp that radiates ultraviolet rays used in therapeutic and cosmetic treatments. **2.** A high-intensity lamp with parabolic mirrors, used in photography.

sun·less (sŭn′lĭs) *adj.* **1.** Being without sunlight; dark or overcast. **2.** Gloomy; cheerless. —**sun′less·ness** *n.*

sun·light (sŭn′līt′) *n.* The light of the sun; sunshine.

Sun·light Peak (sŭn′līt′). A mountain, 4,288 m (14,059 ft), in the San Juan Mts. of SW CO.

sun·lit (sŭn′lĭt′) *adj.* Illuminated by the sun.

sunn (sŭn) *n.* **1.** A tropical Asian plant *(Crotalaria juncea)* having yellow flowers. **2.** A tough fiber obtained from the stems of this plant. [Hindi *san* < Skt. *śāṇa-,* hempen.]

Sun·na also **Sun·nah** (so͝on′ə) *n. Islam.* **1.** The way of life prescribed as normative in Islam, based on the teachings and practices of Muhammad and on exegesis of the Koran. **2.** Muhammad's way of life viewed as a model for Muslims. [Ar. *sunnah,* custom, rule, Sunna.]

Sun·ni (so͝on′ē) *n. Islam.* **1.** The branch of Islam that accepts the first four caliphs as rightful successors of Muhammad. **2.** *pl.* **Sunni** or **-nis.** A Muslim belonging to this branch; a Sunnite. [Ar. *sunnīy,* adherent of the Sunna < *sunnah,* Sunna.] —**Sun′ni** *adj.*

Sun·nite (so͝on′īt′) *n. Islam.* A Sunni Muslim. [< SUNNI.]

sun·ny (sŭn′ē) *adj.* **-ni·er, -ni·est. 1.** Exposed to or abounding in sunshine: *a sunny room.* **2.** Cheerful; genial: *a sunny smile.* —**sun′ni·ly** *adv.* —**sun′ni·ness** *n.*

sun·ny-side up (sŭn′ē-sīd′) *adj.* Fried only on one side. Used of eggs.

Sun·ny·vale (sŭn′ē-vāl′). A city of W CA WNW of San Jose. Pop. 117,229.

sun protection factor *n.* The degree to which a sun block, a sunscreen, suntan lotion, or a similar preparation protects the skin from ultraviolet rays.

sun·rise (sŭn′rīz′) *n.* **1.** The event or time of the daily first appearance of the sun above the eastern horizon. **2.** A beginning or an emergence: *the sunrise of classical art.*

Sun·rise (sŭn′rīz′). A city of SE FL E of Fort Lauderdale. Pop. 64,407.

Sunrise Manor. A community of SE NV, a suburb of Las Vegas. Pop. 95,362.

sun·roof (sŭn′ro͞of′, -ro͝of′) *n.* A roof on a motor vehicle having a panel that can be slid back or raised.

sun·room (sŭn′ro͞om′, -ro͝om′) *n.* A room or an enclosed porch with large windows designed to admit much sunlight.

sun·scald (sŭn′skôld′) *n.* Localized injury or death of the tissues of a woody plant caused by excessive sun in summer and by the combined effects of sun and cold in winter.

sun·screen (sŭn′skrēn′) *n.* A preparation, often in the form of a cream or lotion, used to protect the skin from the ultraviolet rays of the sun. —**sun′screen′ing** *adj.*

sun·set (sŭn′sĕt′) *n.* **1.** The event or time of the daily disappearance of the sun below the western horizon. **2.** A decline or final phase: *the sunset of an empire.* —*adj.* Providing for the automatic termination of a government program or agency unless deliberately reauthorized by law.

sun·shade (sŭn′shād′) *n.* Something, such as an awning or a billed cap, used or worn as a protection from the sun's rays.

sun·shine (sŭn′shīn′) *n.* **1.** The light or the direct rays from the sun. **2.a.** Radiant cheerfulness; geniality. **b.** A source of cheerfulness. —*adj.* Requiring governmental bodies to hold open meetings and sometimes to permit public access to records. —**sun′shin′y** *adj.*

sun·spot (sŭn′spŏt′) *n.* Any of the relatively cool dark spots that appear periodically in groups on the surface of the sun and are associated with strong magnetic fields.

sun·stroke (sŭn′strōk′) *n.* Heat stroke caused by exposure to the sun and characterized by a rise in temperature, convulsions, and coma.

sun·tan (sŭn′tăn′) *n.* A tan color on the skin resulting from exposure to the sun. —**sun′tanned′** *adj.*

sun·up (sŭn′ŭp′) *n.* The time of sunrise.

Sun Valley. A resort area of S-central ID E of Boise; first promoted by the Union Pacific Railroad in the 1930's.

sun·ward (sŭn′wərd) *adv. & adj.* Toward or at the sun: *bathers facing sunward.* —**sun′wards** *adv.*

Sun Yat-sen (so͝on′ yät′sĕn′). 1866–1925. Chinese politician who served as provisional president of the republic after the fall of the Manchu (1911–12).

sup¹ (sŭp) *tr. & intr.v.* **supped, sup·ping, sups.** To eat or drink (something) or engage in eating or drinking by taking small swallows or mouthfuls. —*n.* A sip. [ME *soupen* < OE *sūpan.* See **seuə-²*.**]

sup² (sŭp) *intr.v.* **supped, sup·ping, sups.** To eat an evening meal; have supper. [ME *soupen* < OFr. *souper* < *soupe,* soup. See SOUP.]

sup. *abbr.* **1.** Superior. **2.** *Gram.* **a.** Superlative. **b.** Supine. **3.a.** Supplement. **b.** Supplementary. **4.** Supply. **5.** *Lat.* Supra (above).

Sup.Ct. *abbr. Law.* **1.** Superior court. **2.** Supreme court.

su·per (so͞o′pər) *n.* **1.** *Informal.* An article or a product of superior size, quality, or grade. **2.** *Informal.* **a.** A superintendent in an apartment or office building. **b.** A supernumerary. **3.** *Print.* A thin starched cotton mesh used to super spines and covers of books. —*adj. Informal.* **1.** Very large, great, or extreme. **2.** Excellent; first-rate. —*adv. Informal.* Especially; extremely. —*tr.v.* **-pered, -per·ing, -pers.** *Print.* To reinforce (a book spine or cover) with super. [< SUPER–.]

super. *abbr.* Superior.

super– *pref.* **1.** Above; over; upon: *superimpose.* **2.** Superior in size, quality, number, or degree: *superfine.* **3.a.** Exceeding a norm: *supersaturate.* **b.** Excessive in degree or intensity: *supersubtle.* **c.** Containing a specified ingredient in an unusually high proportion: *superphosphate.* **4.** More inclusive than a specified category: *superorder.* [Lat. < *super,* over, above. See **uper*.**]

su·per·a·ble (so͞o′pər-ə-bəl) *adj.* Possible to overcome; surmountable: *superable problems.* [Lat. *superābilis* < *superāre,* to overcome < *super,* over. See **uper*.**] —**su′per·a·ble·ness** *n.* —**su′per·a·bly** *adv.*

su·per·a·bound (so͞o′pər-ə-bound′) *intr.v.* **-bound·ed, -bound·ing, -bounds.** To be unusually or excessively abundant.

su·per·a·bun·dant (so͞o′pər-ə-bŭn′dənt) *adj.* Abundant to excess. —**su′per·a·bun′dance** *n.* —**su′per·a·bun′dant·ly** *adv.*

su·per·al·loy (so͞o′pər-ăl′oi) *n.* Any of several complex temperature-resistant alloys.

su·per·an·nu·ate (so͞o′pər-ăn′yo͞o-āt′) *tr.v.* **-at·ed, -at·ing, -ates. 1.** To allow to retire on a pension because of age or infirmity. **2.** To set aside or discard as old-fashioned or obsolete. [Back-formation < SUPERANNUATED.]

su·per·an·nu·at·ed (so͞o′pər-ăn′yo͞o-ā′tĭd) *adj.* **1.** Retired or ineffective because of advanced age. **2.** Outmoded; obsolete. [< Med.Lat. *superannuātus,* over one year old : Lat. *super-,* super- + Lat. *annus,* year; see **at-*.**]

su·perb (so͞o-pûrb′) *adj.* **1.** Of unusually high quality; excellent. **2.** Majestic; imposing: *The cheetah is a superb animal.* **3.** Rich; luxurious. [Lat. *superbus,* arrogant, superior. See **uper*.**] —**su·perb′ly** *adv.* —**su·perb′ness** *n.*

su·per·cal·en·der (so͞o′pər-kăl′ən-dər) *n.* A calender with a number of rollers for giving a high finish or gloss to paper. —*tr.v.* **-dered, -der·ing, -ders.** To process (paper) in a supercalender.

su·per·car·go (so͞o′pər-kär′gō) *n., pl.* **-goes** or **-gos.** An of-

sundial

sunflower
Helianthus annuus

Sun Yat-sen
Photographed in the 1920's

ă pat	oi boy
ā pay	ou out
âr care	o͝o took
ä father	o͞o boot
ĕ pet	ŭ cut
ē be	ûr urge
ĭ pit	th thin
ī pie	*th* this
îr pier	hw which
ŏ pot	zh vision
ō toe	ə about, item
ô paw	

Stress marks:
′ (primary);
′ (secondary), as in
dictionary (dĭk′shə-nĕr′ē)

ficer on a merchant ship who has charge of the cargo and its sale and purchase. [Alteration of *supracargo*, alteration of Sp. *sobrecargo* : *sobre-*, over (< Lat. *super-*; see SUPER-) + *cargo*, cargo; see CARGO.]

su·per·charge (so͞o′pər-chärj′) *tr.v.* **-charged, -charg·ing, -charg·es. 1.** To increase the power of (an engine, for example), as by fitting with a supercharger. **2.** To charge heavily or excessively: *an atmosphere supercharged with tension.*

su·per·charg·er (so͞o′pər-chär′jər) *n.* A blower or compressor, usu. driven by the engine, for supplying air under high pressure to the cylinders of an internal-combustion engine.

su·per·cil·i·ar·y (so͞o′pər-sĭl′ē-ĕr′ē) *adj.* **1.** Of, relating to, or being in the area of the eyebrow. **2.** Located over the eyebrow or the eye. [NLat. *superciliāris* < Lat. *supercilium*, eyebrow. See SUPERCILIOUS.]

su·per·cil·i·ous (so͞o′pər-sĭl′ē-əs) *adj.* Feeling or showing haughty disdain. See Syns at **proud.** [Lat. *superciliōsus* < *supercilium*, eyebrow, pride : *super-*, super- + *cilium*, lower eyelid; see **kel-**[1]*.] **—su′per·cil′i·ous·ly** *adv.* **—su′per·cil′i·ous·ness** *n.*

su·per·class (so͞o′pər-klăs′) *n. Biol.* A taxonomic category ranking below a phylum and above a class.

su·per·clus·ter (so͞o′pər-klŭs′tər) *n.* A group of neighboring clusters of galaxies.

su·per·col·lid·er (so͞o′pər-kə-lĭd′ər) *n. Phys.* A high-energy particle accelerator.

su·per·com·put·er (so͞o′pər-kəm-pyo͞o′tər) *n. Comp. Sci.* A mainframe computer that is among the largest, fastest, or most powerful of those available at a given time.

su·per·con·duc·tiv·i·ty (so͞o′pər-kŏn′dŭk-tĭv′ĭtē) *n.* The vanishing of electrical resistance in certain metals, alloys, and ceramics at temperatures near absolute zero and in some compounds at much higher temperatures. **—su′per·con·duc′tive** (-kən-dŭk′tĭv) *adj.* **—su′per·con·duc′tor** (-dŭk′tər) *n.*

su·per·con·ti·nent (so͞o′pər-kŏn′tə-nənt) *n.* A large hypothetical continent, esp. Pangaea, that is thought to have split into smaller ones in the geologic past.

su·per·cool (so͞o′pər-ko͞ol′) *v.* **-cooled, -cool·ing, -cools.** —*tr.* To cool (a liquid) below a transition temperature without the transition occurring, esp. to cool below the freezing point without solidification. —*intr.* To become supercooled.

su·per·dom·i·nant (so͞o′pər-dŏm′ə-nənt) *n. Mus.* See **submediant.**

su·per·du·per (so͞o′pər-do͞o′pər) *adj. Slang.* Great; marvelous. [Redup. of SUPER.]

su·per·e·go (so͞o′pər-ē′gō, -ĕg′ō) *n., pl.* **-gos.** In Freudian theory, the division of the psyche formed through the internalization of moral standards of parents and society, which censors and restrains the ego.

su·per·em·i·nent (so͞o′pər-ĕm′ə-nənt) *adj.* Preeminent. **—su′per·em′i·nence** *n.* **—su′per·em′i·nent·ly** *adv.*

su·per·er·o·gate (so͞o′pər-ĕr′ə-gāt′) *intr.v.* **-gat·ed, -gat·ing, -gates.** To do more than is required, ordered, or expected. [LLat. *supererōgāre, supererōgāt-*, to spend over and above : Lat. *super-*, super- + Lat. *ērogāre*, to spend (*ē-*, *ex-*, ex- + *rogāre*, to ask; see **reg-***).] **—su′per·er′o·ga′tion** (-gā′shən) *n.*

su·per·e·rog·a·to·ry (so͞o′pər-ĭ-rŏg′ə-tôr′ē, -tōr′ē) also **su·per·e·rog·a·tive** (-tĭv) *adj.* **1.** Performed or observed beyond the required or expected degree. **2.** Superfluous; unnecessary.

su·per·fam·i·ly (so͞o′pər-făm′ə-lē) *n., pl.* **-lies.** *Biol.* A taxonomic category ranking below an order or its subdivisions and above a family.

su·per·fec·ta (so͞o′pər-fĕk′tə) *n. Sports & Games.* A method of betting in which the bettor, in order to win, must pick the first four finishers of a race in the correct sequence. [SUPER- + (PER)FECTA.]

su·per·fe·cun·da·tion (so͞o′pər-fē′kən-dā′shən, -fĕk′ən-) *n.* Fertilization of more than one ovum within a single menstrual cycle by separate acts of coitus, esp. by different males.

su·per·fe·tate (so͞o′pər-fē′tāt′) *intr.v.* **-tat·ed, -tat·ing, -tates.** To conceive when a fetus is already present in the uterus. [Lat. *superfētāre, superfētāt-* : *super-*, super- + *fētāre*, to breed (< *fētus*, offspring; see **dhē(i)-***).] **—su′per·fe·ta′tion** *n.*

su·per·fi·cial (so͞o′pər-fĭsh′əl) *adj.* **1.** Of, affecting, or being on or near the surface: *a superficial wound.* **2.** Concerned with or comprehending only what is apparent or obvious; shallow. **3.** Apparent rather than actual or substantial: *a superficial resemblance.* **4.** Trivial; insignificant. [ME < OFr. *superficiel* < Lat. *superficiālis* < *superficiēs*, surface. See SUPERFICIES.] **—su′per·fi′ci·al′i·ty** (-fĭsh′ē-ăl′ĭ-tē), **su′per·fi′cial·ness** (-fĭsh′əl-nĭs) *n.* **—su′per·fi′cial·ly** *adv.*

su·per·fi·cies (so͞o′pər-fĭsh′ēz, -fĭsh′ē-ēz′) *n., pl.* **superficies. 1.** The outer surface of an area or a body. **2.** External appearance or aspect. [Lat. *superficiēs* : *super-*, super- + *faciēs*, face; see FACE.]

su·per·fine (so͞o′pər-fīn′) *adj.* **1.** Of exceptional quality or refinement. **2.** Excessively delicate or refined. **3.** Of extra fine texture: *superfine sandpaper.* **—su′per·fine′ness** *n.*

su·per·flu·id (so͞o′pər-flo͞o′ĭd) *n.* A fluid, such as a liquid form of helium, exhibiting a frictionless flow at temperatures close to absolute zero. **—su′per·flu·id′i·ty** (-flo͞o-ĭd′ĭ-tē) *n.*

su·per·flu·i·ty (so͞o′pər-flo͞o′ĭ-tē) *n., pl.* **-ties. 1.** The quality or condition of being superfluous. **2.** Something superfluous. **3.** Overabundance; excess.

su·per·flu·ous (so͞o-pûr′flo͞o-əs) *adj.* Being beyond what is required or sufficient. [ME < OFr. *superflueux* < Lat. *superfluus* < *superfluere*, to overflow : *super-*, super- + *fluere*, to flow; see **bhleu-***.] **—su·per′flu·ous·ly** *adv.* **—su·per′flu·ous·ness** *n.*

Syns: *superfluous, excess, extra, spare, supernumerary, surplus.* The central meaning shared by these adjectives is "being more than is needed, desired, required, or appropriate": *delete superfluous words; trying to lose excess weight; found some extra change on the dresser; sleeping in the spare room; supernumerary ornamentation; distributed surplus food.*

su·per·gene (so͞o′pər-jēn′) *n.* A group of closely linked genes occupying a large chromosomal segment and frequently functioning as a genetic unit.

su·per·gi·ant (so͞o′pər-jī′ənt) *n.* Any of various very large bright stars, such as Betelgeuse or Rigel, having a luminosity that is thousands of times greater than that of the sun.

su·per·graph·ics (so͞o′pər-grăf′ĭks) *n.* (*used with a sing. or pl. v.*) Brightly colored and simply designed graphic shapes of billboard proportions.

su·per·heat (so͞o′pər-hēt′) *tr.v.* **-heat·ed, -heat·ing, -heats. 1.** To heat excessively; overheat. **2.** To heat (steam or other vapor not in contact with its own liquid) beyond its saturation point at a given pressure. **3.** To heat (a liquid) above its boiling point without causing vaporization. —*n.* (so͞o′pər-hēt′). **1.** The amount by which a vapor is superheated. **2.** The heat imparted during the process of superheating. **—su′per·heat′er** *n.*

su·per·he·lix (so͞o′pər-hē′lĭks) *n., pl.* **-he·lix·es** or **-hel·i·ces** (hĕl′ĭ-sēz′, hē′lĭ-). A molecular structure, as of a protein or DNA, in which a helix is itself coiled into a helix. **—su′per·hel′i·cal** (-hĕl′ĭ-kəl, -hē′lĭ-) *adj.*

su·per·he·ro (so͞o′pər-hîr′ō) *n., pl.* **-roes.** A figure, esp. in a comic strip or cartoon, endowed with superhuman powers and usu. portrayed as fighting evil or crime.

su·per·het·er·o·dyne (so͞o′pər-hĕt′ər-ə-dīn′) *adj.* Of, relating to, or being a form of radio reception in which the frequency of an incoming radio signal is mixed with a locally generated signal and converted to an intermediate frequency in order to facilitate amplification. —*n.* A superheterodyne radio receiver. [SUPER(SONIC) + HETERODYNE.]

su·per·high frequency (so͞o′pər-hī′) *n.* A radio frequency between 3,000 and 30,000 megahertz.

su·per·high·way (so͞o′pər-hī′wā′) *n.* **1.** A broad highway, often with six or more lanes, used for high-speed traffic. **2.** See **expressway.**

su·per·hu·man (so͞o′pər-hyo͞o′mən) *adj.* **1.** Above or beyond the human; preternatural or supernatural. **2.** Beyond ordinary or normal human ability, power, or experience. **—su′per·hu·man′i·ty** (-măn′ĭ-tē) *n.* **—su′per·hu′man·ly** *adv.*

su·per·im·pose (so͞o′pər-ĭm-pōz′) *tr.v.* **-posed, -pos·ing, -pos·es. 1.** To lay or place (something) on or over something else. **2.** To add as a distinct feature, element, or quality. **—su′per·im·pos′a·ble** *adj.* **—su′per·im′po·si′tion** (-ĭm′pə-zĭsh′ən) *n.*

su·per·in·cum·bent (so͞o′pər-ĭn-kŭm′bənt) *adj.* Lying or resting on or above something. **—su′per·in·cum′bence, su′per·in·cum′ben·cy** *n.*

su·per·in·duce (so͞o′pər-ĭn-do͞os′, -dyo͞os′) *tr.v.* **-duced, -duc·ing, -duc·es.** To introduce as an addition. [Lat. *superindūcere* : *super-*, super- + *indūcere*, to lead in; see INDUCE.] **—su′per·in·duc′tion** (-dŭk′shən) *n.*

su·per·in·fect (so͞o′pər-ĭn-fĕkt′) *tr.v.* **-fect·ed, -fect·ing, -fects.** To cause (a cell, for example) to be further infected with a microorganism; infect a second time or more.

su·per·in·fec·tion (so͞o′pər-ĭn-fĕk′shən) *n.* **1.** The act or process of superinfecting a cell or an organism. **2.** An infection following a previous one, esp. when caused by microorganisms that have become resistant to antibiotics used earlier.

su·per·in·tend (so͞o′pər-ĭn-tĕnd′, so͞o′prĭn-) *tr.v.* **-tend·ed, -tend·ing, -tends.** To oversee and direct; supervise. [LLat. *superintendere* : Lat. *super-*, super- + Lat. *intendere*, to direct one's attention to; see INTEND.] **—su′per·in·ten′dence** *n.*

su·per·in·ten·dent (so͞o′pər-ĭn-tĕn′dənt, so͞o′prĭn-) *n.* **1.** A person who has the authority to supervise or direct. **2.** A janitor or custodian in a building, esp. in an apartment house. **—su′per·in·ten′dent** *adj.*

su·pe·ri·or (so͝o-pîr′ē-ər) *adj.* **1.** Higher than another in rank, station, or authority. **2.** Of a higher nature or kind. **3.** Of great value or excellence; extraordinary. **4.** Greater in number or amount than another. **5.** Affecting an attitude of disdain or conceit; haughty and supercilious. **6.** Above being affected or influenced; indifferent or immune. **7.** Located higher than another; upper. **8.** *Bot.* Inserted or situated above the perianth. Used of an ovary. **9.** *Print.* Set above the main line of type. **10.** *Logic.* Of wider or more comprehensive application; generic. Used of a term or proposition. —*n.* **1.** One that surpasses another in rank or quality. **2.** *Eccles.* The head of a religious community, such as a monastery or a convent. **3.** *Print.* A superior character, as the number 2 in x^2. [ME < OFr. < Lat., comp. of *superus*, upper < *super*, over. See **uper*.**] **— su·pe′ri·or′i·ty** (-ôr′ĭ-tē, -ŏr′-) *n.*

Su·pe·ri·or (so͝o-pîr′ē-ər). A city of NW WI on Lake Superior opposite Duluth MN. Pop. 27,134.

Superior, Lake. The largest and westernmost of the Great Lakes, between the N-central U.S. and S Ontario, Canada.

superior conjunction *n.* The position of a celestial body when it is on the opposite side of the sun from Earth.

superior court *n. Law.* A court of general jurisdiction, above the inferior courts and below the higher courts of appeal.

superiority complex *n.* **1.** An exaggerated feeling of being superior to others. **2.** A psychological defense mechanism in which feelings of superiority counter or conceal feelings of inferiority.

superior planet *n.* A planet whose mean distance from the sun is greater than that of Earth.

su·per·ja·cent (so͞o′pər-jā′sənt) *adj.* Resting or lying immediately above or on something else. [Lat. *superiacēns, superiacent-*, pr.part. of *superiacēre*, to lie over : *super-*, super- + *iacēre*, to lie down; see **yē-*.**]

su·per·la·tive (so͝o-pûr′lə-tĭv) *adj.* **1.** Of the highest order, quality, or degree; surpassing or superior to all others. **2.** Excessive or exaggerated. **3.** *Gram.* Of, relating to, or being the extreme degree of comparison of an adjective or adverb, as in *best* or *most brightly.* — *n.* **1.** Something of the highest possible excellence. **2.** The highest degree; the acme. **3.** *Gram.* **a.** The superlative degree. **b.** An adjective or adverb expressing the superlative degree. [ME *superlatif* < OFr. < LLat. *superlātīvus* < Lat. *superlātus*, p.part. of *superferre*, to carry over a person or thing, exaggerate : *super-*, super- + *lātus*, p.part. of *ferre*, to carry; see **telə-*.**] **— su·per′la·tive·ly** *adv.*

su·per·li·ner (so͞o′pər-lī′nər) *n.* **1.** *Naut.* A very large luxurious oceangoing passenger ship. **2.a.** A railway car fitted with more capacious, comfortable, or luxurious accommodations than usual. **b.** A railway train with such cars.

su·per·lu·na·ry (so͞o′pər-lo͞o′nə-rē) also **su·per·lu·nar** (-nər) *adj.* Situated beyond the moon. [SUPER- + (SUB)LUNARY.]

su·per·man (so͞o′pər-măn′) *n.* **1.** A man with more than human powers. **2.** An ideal superior man who, according to Nietzsche, forgoes transient pleasure, exercises creative power, and is the goal of human evolution. [Transl. of Ger. *Übermensch* : *über-*, super- + *Mensch*, man.]

su·per·mar·ket (so͞o′pər-mär′kĭt) *n.* A large self-service retail market that sells food and household goods.

su·per·mol·e·cule (so͞o′pər-mŏl′ĭ-kyo͞ol′) *n.* See **macromolecule.**

su·per·nal (so͝o-pûr′nəl) *adj.* **1.** Celestial; heavenly. **2.** Of, coming from, or being in the sky or high above. [ME < OFr. < Lat. *supernus*. See **uper*.**] **— su·per′nal·ly** *adv.*

su·per·na·tant (so͞o′pər-nāt′nt) *adj.* Floating on the surface. — *n.* also **su·per·nate** (so͞o′pər-nāt′). The clear fluid above a sediment or precipitate. [Lat. *supernatāns, supernatant-*, pr.part. of *supernatāre*, to float : *super-*, super- + *natāre*, to swim; see **snā-*.**]

su·per·nat·u·ral (so͞o′pər-năch′ər-əl) *adj.* **1.** Of or relating to existence outside the natural world. **2.** Attributed to a power that seems to violate or go beyond natural forces. **3.** Of or relating to a deity. **4.** Of or relating to the immediate exercise of divine power; miraculous. **5.** Of or relating to the miraculous. — *n.* That which is supernatural. **— su′per·nat′u·ral·ly** *adv.* **— su′per·nat′u·ral·ness** *n.*

su·per·nat·u·ral·ism (so͞o′pər-năch′ər-ə-lĭz′əm) *n.* **1.** The quality of being supernatural. **2.** Belief in a supernatural agency that intervenes in the course of natural laws. **— su′per·nat′u·ral·ist** *n.* **— su′per·nat′u·ral·is′tic** *adj.*

su·per·nor·mal (so͞o′pər-nôr′məl) *adj.* **1.** Greatly exceeding the normal but still obeying natural laws. **2.** Paranormal.

su·per·no·va (so͞o′pər-nō′və) *n., pl.* **-vae** (-vē) or **-vas.** A rare celestial phenomenon involving the explosion of most of the material in a star, resulting in an extremely bright short-lived object that emits vast amounts of energy.

su·per·nu·mer·ar·y (so͞o′pər-no͞o′mə-rĕr′ē, -nyo͞o′-) *adj.* **1.** Exceeding a fixed, prescribed, or standard number; extra. **2.** Exceeding the required or desired number or amount; superfluous. See Syns at **superfluous.** — *n., pl.* **-ies. 1.** One that is in excess of the regular, necessary, or usual number. **2.** An actor without a speaking part, as one who appears in a crowd scene. [Lat. *supernumerārius* : *super*, above; see SUPER- + *numerum*, accusative of *numerus*, number; see **nem-*.**]

su·per·or·der (so͞o′pər-ôr′dər) *n. Biol.* A taxonomic category ranking below a class or subclass and above an order.

su·per·or·di·nate (so͞o′pər-ôr′dn-ĭt) *adj.* **1.** Of higher rank, status, or value. **2.** *Logic.* Of or being the relation of a universal proposition to a particular proposition in which the terms are the same and occur in the same order. [SUPER- + (SUB)ORDINATE.] **— su′per·or′di·nate** *n.* **— su′per·or′di·nate′** (-ôr′dn-āt′) *v.* **— su′per·or′di·na′tion** *n.*

su·per·or·gan·ism (so͞o′pər-ôr′gə-nĭz′əm) *n.* A group of organisms, such as an insect colony, that functions as a unit.

su·per·o·vu·late (so͞o′pər-ō′vyə-lāt′, -ŏv′yə-) *v.* **-lat·ed, -lat·ing, -lates.** — *intr.* To produce mature ova at an accelerated rate or in a large number at one time. — *tr.* To cause (an animal) to superovulate. **— su′per·o·vu·la′tion** *n.*

su·per·par·a·sit·ism (so͞o′pər-păr′ə-sĭ-tĭz′əm, -sī-) *n.* Infestation of parasites by other parasites.

su·per·phos·phate (so͞o′pər-fŏs′fāt′) *n.* **1.** An acid phosphate. **2.** A mixture of gypsum and monobasic calcium phosphate resulting from the action of sulfuric acid on phosphate rock, used as a fertilizer.

su·per·phys·i·cal (so͞o′pər-fĭz′ĭ-kəl) *adj.* **1.** Exceeding or going beyond the purely physical. **2.** Not explained by known physical laws; preternatural or supernatural.

su·per·pose (so͞o′pər-pōz′) *tr.v.* **-posed, -pos·ing, -pos·es. 1.** To set or place (one thing) over or above something else. **2.** *Math.* To place (one geometric figure) over another so that all like parts coincide. [Prob. Fr. *superposer*, back-formation < *superposition*, superposition < LLat. *superpositiō, superpositiōn-* < Lat. *superpositus*, p.part. of *superpōnere*, to place over : *super-*, super- + *pōnere*, to place; see POSITION.]

su·per·po·si·tion (so͞o′pər-pə-zĭsh′ən) *n.* **1.** The act of superposing or the state of being superposed. **2.** *Geol.* The principle that in a group of stratified sedimentary rocks the lowest were the earliest to be deposited.

su·per·pow·er (so͞o′pər-pou′ər) *n.* A powerful and influential nation, esp. a nuclear power that dominates its allies or client states in an international power bloc.

su·per·re·al·ism (so͞o′pər-rē′ə-lĭz′əm) *n.* An artistic and literary movement characterized by extreme realism. **— su′per·re′al, su′per·re′al·is′tic** *adj.* **— su′per·re′al·ist** *n.*

su·per·sat·u·rate (so͞o′pər-săch′ə-rāt′) *tr.v.* **-rat·ed, -rat·ing, -rates. 1.** To cause (a chemical solution) to be more highly concentrated than is normally possible under given conditions of temperature and pressure. **2.** To cause (a vapor) to exceed the normal saturation vapor pressure at a given temperature. **— su′per·sat′u·ra′tion** *n.*

su·per·sav·er (so͞o′pər-sā′vər) *n.* An airline ticket, purchased typically well ahead of the departure date, that affords the purchaser considerable savings over regular fare.

su·per·scribe (so͞o′pər-skrīb′) *tr.v.* **-scribed, -scrib·ing, -scribes. 1.** To write on the outside or upper part of (a letter, for example). **2.** To write (a name or an address, for example) on the top or outside. [Lat. *superscrībere*, to write over : *super-*, super- + *scrībere*, to write; see **skrībh-*.**]

su·per·script (so͞o′pər-skrĭpt′) *n.* A character set, printed, or written above and immediately to one side of another. [Lat. *superscrīptus*, p.part. of *superscrībere*, to write over. See SUPERSCRIBE.] **— su′per·script** *adj.*

su·per·scrip·tion (so͞o′pər-skrĭp′shən) *n.* **1.** Something written above or outside something else. **2.** The act of superscribing. **3.** The part of a prescription that bears the Latin word *recipe* represented by the symbol ℞.

su·per·sede (so͞o′pər-sēd′) *tr.v.* **-sed·ed, -sed·ing, -sedes. 1.** To take the place of; replace. **2.** To cause to be set aside, esp. to displace as inferior or antiquated. See Syns at **replace.** [ME *superceden*, to postpone < OFr. *superceder* < Lat. *supersedēre*, to refrain from : *super-*, super- + *sedēre*, to sit; see **sed-*.**] **— su′per·sed′er** *n.* **— su′per·ses′sion** (-sĕsh′ən) *n.*

su·per·se·de·as (so͞o′pər-sē′dē-əs) *n. Law.* A writ containing a command to stay legal proceedings, as in the halting or delaying of the execution of a sentence. [ME < Med.Lat. *supersedeās* < Lat., you must desist, second pers. sing. pr. subjunctive of *supersedēre*, to desist from. See SUPERSEDE.]

su·per·se·dure (so͞o′pər-sē′jər) *n.* **1.** The act or process of superseding. **2.** Replacement of a queen bee that has grown old or weak by one that is younger or more vigorous.

su·per·sen·si·ble (so͞o′pər-sĕn′sə-bəl) *adj.* Beyond or above perception by the senses. **— su′per·sen′si·bly** *adv.*

su·per·son·ic (so͞o′pər-sŏn′ĭk) *adj.* **1.** Having, caused by, or relating to a speed greater than the speed of sound in a given medium, esp. air. **2.** Of or relating to sound waves beyond human audibility. **— su′per·son′i·cal·ly** *adv.*

su·per·son·ics (so͞o′pər-sŏn′ĭks) *n.* *(used with a sing. v.)* The study of phenomena produced by the motion of a body through a medium at velocities greater than that of sound.

supersonic transport *n.* A large transport airplane engineered to operate at supersonic speeds.

su·per·star (so͞o′pər-stär′) *n.* **1.** A widely acclaimed star, as in movies or sports, who has great popular appeal. **2.** One that is extremely popular or prominent or is a major attraction. **— su′per·star′dom** (so͞o′pər-stär′dəm) *n.*

su·per·sta·tion (so͞o′pər-stā′shən) *n.* A television or radio station that broadcasts to a nationwide audience by satellite, cable, or both.

su·per·sti·tion (so͞o′pər-stĭsh′ən) *n.* **1.** An irrational belief that something unrelated to an event influences its outcome. **2.a.** A belief, practice, or rite maintained by ignorance of the laws of nature or by faith in magic or chance. **b.** A fearful or abject state of mind due to such ignorance or irrationality. **c.** Idolatry. [Ult. < Lat. *superstitiō, superstitiōn-* < *superstes, superstit-*, standing over. See **stā-*.**]

ă pat	oi **boy**
ā pay	ou **out**
âr care	o͝o to͝ok
ä father	o͞o bo͞ot
ĕ pet	ŭ cut
ē be	ûr **urge**
ĭ pit	th **thin**
ī pie	*th* **this**
îr pier	hw **which**
ŏ pot	zh vision
ō toe	ə about, item
ô paw	

Stress marks:
′ (primary);
′ (secondary), as in
dictionary (dĭk′shə-nĕr′ē)

su•per•sti•tious (so͞o′pər-stĭsh′əs) *adj.* **1.** Inclined to believe in superstition. **2.** Of, characterized by, or due to superstition. —**su′per•sti′tious•ly** *adv.* —**su′per•sti′tious•ness** *n.*

su•per•store (so͞o′pər-stôr′, -stōr′) *n.* A very large supermarket that stocks diversified merchandise.

su•per•stra•tum (so͞o′pər-strā′təm, -străt′əm) *n., pl.* **-stra•ta** (-strā′tə, -străt′ə). **1.** One layer or stratum superimposed on another. **2.** *Ling.* The language of a later invading people imposed on and leaving features in an indigenous language.

su•per•string (so͞o′pər-strĭng′) *n. Phys.* The elementary particle in a theory of space-time incorporating supersymmetry. [SUPER(SYMMETRY) + STRING.]

su•per•struc•ture (so͞o′pər-strŭk′chər) *n.* **1.** A physical or conceptual structure extended or developed from a basic form. **2.** The part of a building or other structure above the foundation. **3.** *Naut.* The parts of a ship's structure above the main deck. **4.** The rails, sleepers, and other parts of a railway. **5.** In Marxism, the ideologies or institutions of a society as distinct from the basic processes and direct social relations of material production and economics.

su•per•sym•me•try (so͞o′pər-sĭm′ĭ-trē) *n. Phys.* A hypothetical symmetry that relates fermions to bosons and gravitational force to forces that operate on the subatomic level.

su•per•tank•er (so͞o′pər-tăng′kər) *n. Naut.* A very large ship, usu. between 100,000 and 400,000 displacement tons, used for transporting oil and other liquids in large quantities.

su•per•ti•tle (so͞o′pər-tīt′l) *n.* A written translation of the dialogue or lyrics of a foreign-language performance of an opera, for example, shown on a screen above the performers.

su•per•ton•ic (so͞o′pər-tŏn′ĭk) *n. Mus.* The second tone of a diatonic scale.

su•per•vene (so͞o′pər-vēn′) *intr.v.* **-vened, -ven•ing, -venes.** **1.** To come or occur as something extraneous, additional, or unexpected. See Syns at **follow.** **2.** To follow immediately after; ensue. [Lat. *supervenīre* : *super-*, super- + *venīre*, to come; see **gʷā-*.**] —**su′per•ven′ient** (-vēn′yənt) *adj.* —**su′per•ven′tion** (-vĕn′shən) *n.*

su•per•vise (so͞o′pər-vīz′) *tr.v.* **-vised, -vis•ing, -vis•es.** To have the charge and direction of; superintend. [ME **supervisen* < Med.Lat. *supervidēre, supervīs-* : Lat. *super-*, super- + Lat. *vidēre*, to see; see **weid-*.**]

su•per•vi•sion (so͞o′pər-vĭzh′ən) *n.* The act, process, or function of supervising. See Syns at **care.**

su•per•vi•sor (so͞o′pər-vī′zər) *n.* **1.** One who supervises. **2.** One who is in charge of a particular department or unit, as in a governmental agency or school system. **3.** One who is an elected administrative officer in certain U.S. counties and townships. —**su′per•vi′so•ry** (-vī′zə-rē) *adj.*

su•per•wom•an (so͞o′pər-wo͝om′ən) *n.* **1.** A woman who performs all the duties typically associated with several different full-time roles, such as wage earner, mother, and wife. **2.** A woman with more than human powers.

su•pi•nate (so͞o′pə-nāt′) *v.* **-nat•ed, -nat•ing, -nates.** —*tr.* **1.** To turn (the hand and forearm) so that the palm is upward or forward. **2.** To turn (the foot or leg) so that the sole is outward. —*intr.* To be supinated; undergo supination. [Lat. *supīnāre, supīnāt-* < *supīnus*, backward. See SUPINE.] —**su′pi•na′tion** *n.*

su•pi•na•tor (so͞o′pə-nā′tər) *n.* A muscle, esp. in the forearm, that effects or assists supination.

su•pine (so͞o-pīn′, so͞o′pīn′) *adj.* **1.** Lying on the back or having the face upward. **2.** Having the palm upward. **3.** Marked by or showing lethargy, passivity, or blameworthy indifference. **4.** Inclined; sloping. —*n. Gram.* A defective Latin verbal noun of the fourth declension, having very limited syntax and only two cases. [ME *supin*, Lat. verbal noun < LLat. *supīnum* < neut. of Lat. *supīnus*, lying on the back. See **upo*.**] —**su•pine′ly** *adv.* —**su•pine′ness** *n.*

supp. *abbr.* **1.** Supplement. **2.** Supplementary.

sup•per (sŭp′ər) *n.* **1.a.** A light evening meal when dinner is taken at midday. **b.** A light meal eaten before going to bed. **2.** A dance or social affair where supper is served. [ME < OFr. *souper*, to sup, supper. See SUP[2].]

suppl. *abbr.* **1.** Supplement. **2.** Supplementary.

sup•plant (sə-plănt′) *tr.v.* **-plant•ed, -plant•ing, -plants.** **1.** To usurp the place of, esp. through intrigue or underhanded tactics. **2.** To displace and substitute for (another). See Syns at **replace.** [ME *supplanten* < OFr. *supplanter* < Lat. *supplantāre*, to trip up : *sub-*, sub- + *planta*, sole; see **plat-*.**]

sup•ple (sŭp′əl) *adj.* **-pler, -plest.** **1.** Readily bent; pliant. **2.** Moving and bending with agility; limber. **3.** Yielding or changing readily; compliant or adaptable. [ME *souple* < OFr. < Lat. *supplex*, suppliant. See **plāk-[1]*.**] —**sup′ple** *v.* —**sup′ple•ness** *n.* —**sup′ply, sup′ple•ly** *adv.*

sup•ple•ment (sŭp′lə-mənt) *n.* **1.** Something added to complete a thing, make up for a deficiency, or extend or strengthen the whole. **2.** A section added to a book or document to give further information or correct errors. **3.** A separate section devoted to a special subject inserted into a newspaper, for example. **4.** *Math.* The angle or arc that when added to a given angle or arc makes 180° or a semicircle. —*tr.v.* (-mĕnt′) **-ment•ed, -ment•ing, -ments.** To provide or form a supplement to. [ME < OFr. < Lat. *supplēmentum* < *supplēre*, to complete. See SUPPLY.] —**sup′ple•men•tar′i•ty** (-târ′ĭ-tē) *n.* —**sup′ple•men′ta•ry** (-mĕn′tə-rē, -trē), **sup′ple•men′tal** (-mĕn′tl) *adj.* —**sup′ple•men•ta′tion** (-mĕn-tā′shən) *n.*

supplementary angle *n. Math.* See **supplement** 4.

sup•ple•tion (sə-plē′shən) *n. Ling.* The use of an unrelated form to complete a paradigm, as the past tense *went* of the verb *go, goes, going, gone.* [< Lat. *supplētus*, p.part. of *supplēre*, to supply. See SUPPLY.]

sup•pli•ant (sŭp′lē-ənt) *adj.* Asking humbly and earnestly; beseeching. —*n.* A supplicant. [< ME, one who supplicates < OFr., pr.part. of *supplier*, to entreat < Lat. *supplicāre*. See SUPPLICATE.] —**sup′pli•ance** *n.* —**sup′pli•ant•ly** *adv.*

sup•pli•cant (sŭp′lĭ-kənt) *n.* One who supplicates; a suppliant. [< Lat. *supplicāns, supplicant-*, pr.part. of *supplicāre*, to kneel down. See SUPPLICATE.] —**sup′pli•cant** *adj.*

sup•pli•cate (sŭp′lĭ-kāt′) *v.* **-cat•ed, -cat•ing, -cates.** —*tr.* **1.** To ask for humbly or earnestly, as by praying. **2.** To make a humble entreaty to; beseech. —*intr.* To make a humble, earnest petition; beg. [ME *supplicaten* < Lat. *supplicāre, supplicāt-* < *supplex, supplic-*, suppliant. See SUPPLE.] —**sup′pli•ca′tion** *n.* —**sup′pli•ca•to′ry** (-kə-tôr′ē, -tōr′ē) *adj.*

sup•ply (sə-plī′) *v.* **-plied, -ply•ing, -plies.** —*tr.* **1.** To make available for use; provide. **2.** To furnish or equip with. **3.** To fill sufficiently; satisfy. **4.** To make up for (a deficiency, for example); compensate for. **5.** To serve temporarily as a substitute in (a church, for example). —*intr.* To fill a position as a substitute. —*n., pl.* **-plies.** **1.** The act of supplying. **2.** Something that is or can be supplied. **3.** An amount available or sufficient for a given use; stock. **4.** Materials or provisions stored and used as needed. Often used in the plural. **5.** *Econ.* The amount of a commodity available for meeting a demand or for purchase at a given price. **6.** A cleric serving as a substitute or temporary pastor. [ME *supplien*, to help, complete < OFr. *soupleer*, to fill up < Lat. *supplēre* : *sub-*, from below; see SUB- + *plēre*, to fill; see **pelə-[1]*.**] —**sup•pli′er** *n.*

sup•ply-side (sə-plī′sīd′) *adj.* Of, relating to, or being an economic theory stating that reduction of taxes, esp. in the higher tax brackets, will increase investment, productivity, and income throughout an economic system. —**supply side** *n.*

sup•port (sə-pôrt′, -pōrt′) *tr.v.* **-port•ed, -port•ing, -ports.** **1.** To bear the weight of, esp. from below. **2.** To hold in position so as to keep from falling, sinking, or slipping. **3.** To be capable of bearing; withstand. **4.** To keep from weakening or failing; strengthen. **5.** To provide for or maintain by supplying with money or necessities. **6.** To furnish corroborating evidence for. **7.** To aid the cause, policy, or interests of. **8.** To endure; tolerate. **9.a.** To act (a part or role). **b.** To act in a secondary or subordinate role to (a leading performer). —*n.* **1.a.** The act of supporting. **b.** The state of being supported. **2.** One that supports. **3.** Maintenance, as of a family, with the necessities of life. [ME *supporten* < OFr. *supporter* < Lat. *supportāre*, to carry : *sub-*, from below; see SUB- + *portāre*, to carry; see **per-[2]*.**]

Syns: *support, uphold, back, advocate, champion.* These verbs mean to give aid or encouragement to a person or cause. *Support* is the most general: *"the policy of Cromwell, who supported the growing power of France against the declining power of Spain"* (William E.H. Lecky). To *uphold* is to maintain or affirm in the face of a challenge or strong opposition: *"The Declaration of Right upheld the principle of hereditary monarchy"* (Edmund Burke). *Back* suggests material or moral support intended to contribute to or assure success: *research backed by the government. Advocate* implies verbal support, often in the form of pleading or arguing: *Scientists advocate reducing saturated fats in the diet.* To *champion* is to fight for one that is under attack or lacks the strength or ability to act in its own behalf: *"championed the government and defended the system of taxation"* (Samuel Chew).

sup•port•a•ble (sə-pôr′tə-bəl, -pōr′-) *adj.* Bearable; endurable. —**sup•port′a•bil′i•ty** *n.* —**sup•port′a•bly** *adv.*

sup•port•er (sə-pôr′tər, -pōr′-) *n.* **1.** One that supports, as a structural member of a building. **2.** One who promotes or advocates; an adherent. **3.** An athletic supporter. **4.** *Her.* An animal or a figure that supports a shield in a coat of arms.

support group *n.* A group of people, sometimes led by a therapist, who provide each other moral support, information, and advice on problems relating to some shared characteristic or experience: *a support group for incest survivors.*

support hose *pl.n.* Elasticized stockings designed to reduce stress on the blood vessels in the legs.

sup•por•tive (sə-pôr′tĭv, -pōr′-) *adj.* Furnishing support or assistance. —**sup•por′tive•ly** *adv.* —**sup•por′tive•ness** *n.*

support level *n.* A price at which a security or the market becomes attractive to investors.

support system *n.* A network of personal or professional contacts available to a person or an organization for practical or moral support when needed.

sup•pos•a•ble (sə-pō′zə-bəl) *adj.* That can be supposed or conjectured. —**sup•pos′a•bly** *adv.*

sup•pose (sə-pōz′) *v.* **-posed, -pos•ing, -pos•es.** —*tr.* **1.** To assume to be true or real for the sake of argument or explanation. **2.a.** To believe, esp. on uncertain or tentative grounds. **b.** To consider to be probable or likely. **3.** To imply as an antecedent condition; presuppose. **4.** To consider as a suggestion. — *intr.* To imagine; conjecture. [ME *supposen* < OFr. *supposer*, alteration (influenced by *poser*, to place; see POSE[1]) of Med.Lat. *suppōnere* < Lat., to put under : *sub-*, sub- + *pōnere*, to place; see **apo-***.]

sup•posed (sə-pōzd′, -pō′zĭd) *adj.* **1.** Presumed to be true or real without conclusive evidence. **2.** Intended. **3.a.** Required. **b.** Permitted. **c.** Firmly believed; expected. — **sup•pos′ed•ly** (-pō′zĭd-lē) *adv.*

sup•pos•ing (sə-pō′zĭng) *conj.* Assuming that.

sup•po•si•tion (sŭp′ə-zĭsh′ən) *n.* **1.** The act of supposing. **2.** Something supposed; an assumption. — **sup′po•si′tion•al** *adj.* — **sup′po•si′tion•al•ly** *adv.*

sup•po•si•tious (sŭp′ə-zĭsh′əs) *adj.* Supposititious.

sup•pos•i•ti•tious (sə-pŏz′ĭ-tĭsh′əs) *adj.* **1.** Substituted with fraudulent intent; spurious. **2.** Hypothetical; supposed. [< Lat. *supposītīcius* < *suppositus*, p.part. of *suppōnere*, to substitute. See SUPPOSE.] — **sup•pos′i•ti′tious•ly** *adv.* — **sup•pos′i•ti′tious•ness** *n.*

sup•pos•i•tive (sə-pŏz′ĭ-tĭv) *adj.* Of the nature of, including, or involving supposition. — *n. Gram.* A conjunction, such as *if*, that introduces a supposition. — **sup•pos′i•tive•ly** *adv.*

sup•pos•i•to•ry (sə-pŏz′ĭ-tôr′ē, -tōr′ē) *n., pl.* **-ries.** *Medic.* A plug of medication designed to melt at body temperature within a body cavity other than the mouth, esp. the rectum. [ME < OFr. *suppositorie* < Med.Lat. *suppositōrium* < LLat., neut. of *suppositōrius*, placed under < Lat. *suppositus*, p.part. of *suppōnere*, to put under. See SUPPOSE.]

sup•press (sə-prĕs′) *tr.v.* **-pressed, -press•ing, -press•es. 1.** To put an end to forcibly; subdue. **2.** To curtail or prohibit the activities of. **3.** To keep from being revealed, published, or circulated. **4.** To deliberately exclude (unacceptable desires or thoughts) from the mind. **5.** To inhibit the expression of (an impulse, for example); check. **6.** To reduce the incidence or severity of (a cough, for example); arrest. [ME *suppressen* < Lat. *supprimere*, *suppress-* : *sub-*, sub- + *premere*, to press; see **per-**[4]*.] — **sup•press′ant** *n.* — **sup•press′i•ble** *adj.*

sup•pres•sion (sə-prĕsh′ən) *n.* **1.** The act of suppressing. **2.** The state of being suppressed. **3.** *Psychiat.* Conscious exclusion of unacceptable desires, thoughts, or memories from the mind.

sup•pres•sive (sə-prĕs′ĭv) *adj.* Tending or serving to suppress.

sup•pres•sor (sə-prĕs′ər) *n.* **1.** Or **sup•press•er.** One that suppresses. **2.** A gene that suppresses the phenotypic expression of another gene, esp. of a mutant gene. **3.** A device, such as a resistor or grid, that is used in an electrical or electronic system to reduce unwanted currents.

sup•pu•rate (sŭp′yə-rāt′) *intr.v.* **-rat•ed, -rat•ing, -rates.** To form or discharge pus. [ME *suppuraten* < Lat. *suppūrāre*, *suppūrāt-* : *sub-*, sub- + *pūs*, *pūr-*, pus; see **pū-***.]

sup•pu•ra•tion (sŭp′yə-rā′shən) *n.* **1.** The formation or discharge of pus. **2.** Pus. — **sup′pu•ra′tive** *adj.*

supr. *abbr.* Supreme.

supra– *pref.* **1.** Above; over; on top of: *suprarenal.* **2.** Greater than; transcending: *supramolecular.* [Lat. < *suprā*, above, beyond. See **uper***.]

su•pra•lim•i•nal (so͞o′prə-lĭm′ə-nəl) *adj.* Being above the threshold of consciousness or of sensation. Used of stimuli.

su•pra•mo•lec•u•lar (so͞o′prə-mə-lĕk′yə-lər) *adj.* **1.** Consisting of more than one molecule. **2.** Of greater complexity than a molecule.

su•pra•or•bi•tal (so͞o′prə-ôr′bĭ-tl) *adj.* Located above the orbit of the eye: *the supraorbital ridge.*

su•pra•re•nal (so͞o′prə-rē′nəl) *adj.* Located on or above the kidney. — *n.* A suprarenal part, esp. an adrenal gland.

suprarenal gland *n.* See **adrenal gland.**

su•pra•vi•tal (so͞o′prə-vīt′l) *adj.* Relating to or capable of staining living cells after their removal from a living or recently dead organism: *a supravital stain.*

su•prem•a•cist (so͝o-prĕm′ə-sĭst) *n.* One who believes that a certain group is or should be supreme.

su•prem•a•cy (so͝o-prĕm′ə-sē) *n., pl.* **-cies. 1.** The quality or condition of being supreme. **2.** Supreme power or authority.

su•prem•a•tism (so͝o-prĕm′ə-tĭz′ən) *n.* A school and theory of geometric abstract art that originated in Russia in the early 20th century and influenced constructivism. [Russ. *suprematizm* < Fr. *suprématie*, supremacy < SUPREMACY.] — **su•prem′a•tist** *adj. & n.*

su•preme (so͝o-prēm′) *adj.* **-er, -est. 1.** Greatest in power, authority, or rank; paramount or dominant. **2.** Greatest in importance, degree, character, or achievement. **3.** Ultimate; final. [Lat. *suprēmus*, superl. of *superus*, upper < *super*, over. See **uper***.] — **su•preme′ly** *adv.* — **su•preme′ness** *n.*

su•prême (so͝o-prēm′, -prĕm′) *n.* **1.** A velouté made with chicken stock, cream, and egg yolks. **2.** A dish made or served with this sauce, esp. chicken. [Fr., supreme, suprême < Lat. *suprēmus*, supreme. See SUPREME.]

Su•preme Being (so͝o-prēm′) *n.* God.

Supreme Court *n. Law.* **1.** The highest federal court in the United States, consisting of nine justices and having jurisdiction over all other courts in the nation. **2. supreme court.** The highest court in most states within the United States.

Supreme Soviet *n.* The legislature of the former Soviet Union.

su•pre•mo (so͞o-prē′mō′, sə-) *n., pl.* **-mos.** *Chiefly British.* One who is highest in authority or command. [Sp. and Ital., supreme, supremo < Lat. *suprēmus*. See SUPREME.]

supt. or **Supt.** *abbr.* Superintendent.

supvr. *abbr.* Supervisor.

Su•qua•mish (sə-kwä′mĭsh) *n., pl.* **Suquamish** or **-mish•es. 1.** A member of an extinct Native American people formerly inhabiting an area of the eastern shore of Puget Sound. **2.** The Salish language of the Suquamish.

sur. *abbr.* Surface.

Sur. *abbr.* Suriname.

sur– *pref.* **1.** Over; above; upon: *surprint.* **2.** Additional: *surtax.* [ME < OFr. < Lat. *super-*. See **uper***.]

su•ra (so͝or′ə) *n. Islam.* Any of the 114 chapters of the Koran. [Ar. *sūrah* < Heb. *šûrâ*, row, line.]

Su•ra•ba•ya also **Su•ra•ba•ja** (so͝or′ə-bä′yə). A city of NE Java, Indonesia, on the Java Sea. Pop. 2,027,913.

su•rah (so͝or′ə) *n.* A soft twilled fabric of silk or of a blend of silk and rayon. [Fr. *surat*, after SURAT.]

Su•ra•kar•ta (so͝or′ə-kär′tə). A city of S-central Java, Indonesia, E of Bandung. Pop. 469,888.

su•ral (so͝or′əl) *adj.* Of or relating to the calf of the leg. [NLat. *sūrālis* < Lat. *sūra*, calf of the leg.]

Su•rat (so͝or′ət, sə-răt′). A city of W-central India on the Gulf of Cambay N of Bombay. Pop. 776,583.

sur•base (sûr′bās′) *n. Archit.* A molding or border above the base of a structure such as a baseboard.

sur•cease (sûr′sēs′, sər-sēs′) *tr. & intr.v.* **-ceased, -ceas•ing, -ceas•es.** To bring or come to an end; stop. — *n.* Cessation. [ME *surcesen*, var. (influenced by *cesen*, to cease; see CEASE) of *sursesen* < AN *surseser* < OFr. *surseoir*, *sursis-*, to refrain < Lat. *supersedēre*. See SUPERSEDE.]

sur•charge (sûr′chärj′) *n.* **1.** A sum added to the usual amount or cost. **2.** An overcharge, esp. when unlawful. **3.** An additional or excessive burden; an overload. **4.a.** A new value or denomination overprinted on a postage or revenue stamp. **b.** The stamp to which a new value has been applied. **5.** *Law.* The act of surcharging. — *tr.v.* **-charged, -charg•ing, -charg•es. 1.** To charge (a person) an additional sum. **2.** To overcharge (a person). **3.** To place an excessive burden on; overload. **4.** To fill beyond capacity; overfill. **5.** To print a surcharge on (a postage or revenue stamp). **6.** *Law.* To show an omission of a credit in (an account). **7.** To require (a person) to reimburse funds spent without authorization. [ME < *surchargen*, to overtax < OFr. *surcharger* : *sur-*, sur- + *chargier*, to charge; see CHARGE.]

sur•cin•gle (sûr′sĭng′gəl) *n.* **1.** A girth that binds a saddle, pack, or blanket to the body of a horse. **2.** *Archaic.* The fastening belt on a clerical cassock; a cincture. [ME *sursengle* < OFr. *surcengle* : *sur-*, sur- + *cengle*, belt (< Lat. *cingula* < *cingere*, to gird; see CINGULUM).] — **sur′cin′gle** *v.*

sur•coat (sûr′kōt′) *n.* **1.** A loose outer coat or gown. **2.** A tunic worn in the Middle Ages by a knight over his armor. [ME *surcote* < OFr. : *sur-*, sur- + *cote*, coat; see COAT.]

surcoat
Detail from an early 16th-century breviary of Queen Eleanor of Portugal, showing Saint Barbara wearing a sleeveless surcoat

surd (sûrd) *n.* **1.** *Math.* An irrational number, such as $\sqrt{2}$. **2.** *Ling.* A voiceless sound in speech. — *adj. Ling.* Voiceless, as a sound. [Med.Lat. *surdus* (< Lat., speechless), transl. of Ar. *(jadr) ʾaṣamm*, deaf (root), surd, transl. of Gk. *alogos*, speechless, surd.]

sure (sho͝or) *adj.* **sur•er, sur•est. 1.** Impossible to doubt or dispute; certain. **2.** Not hesitating or wavering; firm. **3.** Confident, as of something awaited or expected. **4.a.** Bound to come about or happen; inevitable. **b.** Having one's course directed; destined or bound. **5.** Certain not to miss or err; steady. **6.a.** Worthy of being trusted or depended on; reliable. **b.** Free from or marked by freedom from doubt. **7.** Careful to do something. **8.** *Obsolete.* Free from harm or danger; safe. — *adv. Informal.* Surely; certainly. — ***idioms.* for sure.** *Informal.* Certainly; unquestionably. **make sure.** To establish something without doubt; make certain. **to be sure.** Indeed; certainly. [ME < OFr., safe < Lat. *sēcūrus*. See SECURE.]

sure-fire (sho͝or′fīr′) *adj. Informal.* Bound to be successful or perform as expected: *a sure-fire solution to the problem.*

sure-foot•ed or **sure•foot•ed** (sho͝or′fo͝ot′ĭd) *adj.* **1.** Not liable to stumble or fall. **2.** Confident and capable. — **sure′-foot′ed•ly** *adv.* — **sure′-foot′ed•ness** *n.*

sure•ly (sho͝or′lē) *adv.* **1.** With confidence; unhesitatingly. **2.** Undoubtedly; certainly. **3.** Without fail.

sur•e•ty (sho͝or′ĭ-tē) *n., pl.* **-ties. 1.** The condition of being sure, esp. of oneself; self-assurance. **2.** Something beyond doubt; a certainty. **3.** A pledge or promise made to secure against loss, damage, or default; a guarantee. **4.** One contracted to be responsible for another, esp. one who assumes responsibilities or debts in the event of default. [ME *surte* < OFr. < Lat. *sēcūritās* < *sēcūrus*, sure. See SECURE.] — **sur′e•ty•ship′** *n.*

surf (sûrf) *n.* The waves of the sea as they break upon a shore or reef. — *intr.v.* **surfed, surf•ing, surfs.** *Sports.* To engage in surfing. [?] — **surf′y** *adj.*

ă pat	oi boy
ā pay	ou out
âr care	o͝o took
ä father	o͞o boot
ĕ pet	ŭ cut
ē be	ûr urge
ĭ pit	th thin
ī pie	*th* this
îr pier	hw which
ŏ pot	zh vision
ō toe	ə about, item
ô paw	

Stress marks:
′ (primary);
′ (secondary), as in dictionary (dĭk′shə-nĕr′ē)

sur•face (sûr′fəs) *n.* **1.a.** The outer or the topmost boundary of an object. **b.** A material layer constituting such a boundary. **2.** *Math.* **a.** The boundary of a three-dimensional figure. **b.** The two-dimensional locus of points located in three-dimensional space. **c.** A portion of space having length and breadth but no thickness. **3.** The superficial or external aspect. **4.** An airfoil. — *adj.* **1.** Relating to, on, or at a surface. **2.a.** Superficial. **b.** Apparent as opposed to real. — *v.* **-faced, -fac•ing, -fac•es.** — *tr.* **1.** To form the surface of. **2.** To apply a surface to. **3.** To provide with a surface. — *intr.* **1.** To rise to the surface. **2.** To emerge after concealment. **3.** To work or dig a mine at or near the surface of the ground. — ***idiom.* on the surface.** To all intents and purposes; to all outward appearances. [Fr. : *sur-*, above (< OFr.; see SUR–) + *face*, face (< OFr.; see FACE).]

sur•face-ac•tive (sûr′fəs-ăk′tĭv) *adj.* Of, relating to, or being a substance capable of reducing the surface tension of a liquid in which it is dissolved. Used esp. of detergents.

surface of revolution *n.*, *pl.* **surfaces of revolution.** *Math.* A surface generated by revolving a plane curve about an axis in its plane.

surface plate *n.* See **planometer.**

surface tension *n.* **1.** A property of liquids arising from unbalanced molecular cohesive forces at or near the surface, as a result of which the surface tends to contract. **2.** A measure of this property.

sur•face-to-air missile (sûr′fəs-to͞o-âr′) *n.* A guided missile launched from the ground against an airborne target.

sur•fac•tant (sər-făk′tənt, sûr′făk′-) *n.* **1.** A surface-active substance. **2.** A substance that is secreted by the alveolar cells of the lung and serves to maintain the stability of pulmonary tissue by reducing the surface tension of fluids that coat the lung. [SURF(ACE)-ACT(IVE) + A(GE)NT.]

surf•bird (sûrf′bûrd′) *n.* A shore bird *(Aphriza virgata)* of the Pacific coast of North and South America having dark spotted plumage and a black tail with a broad white base.

surf•board (sûrf′bôrd′, -bōrd′) *n. Sports.* A long, narrow, somewhat rounded board, used for surfing.

surfboard

surf•board•er (sûrf′bôr′dər, -bōr′-) *n. Sports.* See **surfer.**

surf•board•ing (sûrf′bôr′dĭng, -bōr′-) *n. Sports.* See **surfing.**

surf•boat (sûrf′bōt′) *n. Naut.* A strong seaworthy boat that can be launched or landed in heavy surf.

surf•cast•ing (sûrf′kăs′tĭng) *n.* The activity of fishing from shore, esp. by casting a line into the surf. — **surf′cast′er** *n.*

surf clam *n.* Any of various usu. large edible clams of the family Mactridae, commonly living in the surf of coastal waters.

surf duck *n.* A scoter, esp. the surf scoter.

sur•feit (sûr′fĭt) *v.* **-feit•ed, -feit•ing, -feits.** — *tr.* To feed or supply to excess, satiety, or disgust. — *intr. Archaic.* To overindulge. — *n.* **1.a.** Overindulgence in food or drink. **b.** The result of such overindulgence; satiety or disgust. **2.** An excessive amount. [ME *surfeten* < *surfait*, excess < OFr. < p.part. of *surfaire*, to overdo : *sur-*, sur- + *faire*, to do (< Lat. *facere*; see **dhē-***).] — **sur′feit•er** *n.*

surf•er (sûr′fər) *n. Sports.* One who engages in surfing.

surf fish *n.* See **surfperch.**

sur•fi•cial (sər-fĭsh′əl) *adj.* Of, relating to, or occurring on or near the surface of the earth. [SURF(ACE) + (SUPERF)ICIAL.]

surf•ing (sûr′fĭng) *n. Sports.* The sport of riding on the crest or along the tunnel of a wave, esp. on a surfboard.

surf•perch (sûrf′pûrch′) *n.*, *pl.* **surfperch** or **-perch•es.** Any of various viviparous marine fishes of the family Embiotocidae, found along the North American Pacific coast.

surf scoter *n.* A North American sea duck *(Melanitta perspicillata)*, the male of which is black with a white forehead.

surf•side (sûrf′sīd′) *adj.* Situated at or near the seashore.

surg. *abbr.* Surgeon; surgery; surgical.

surge (sûrj) *v.* **surged, surg•ing, surg•es.** — *intr.* **1.** To move in a billowing or swelling manner in or as if in waves. **2.** To roll or be tossed about on waves, as a boat. **3.** To move like advancing waves. **4.** To increase suddenly. Used of electric current or voltage. **5.** *Naut.* To slip around a windlass, capstan, or winch. Used of a cable or hawser. — *tr. Naut.* To loosen or slacken (a cable) by letting it slip around a windlass or winch. — *n.* **1.** A heavy billowing or swelling motion like that of great waves. **2.a.** Wave motion with low height and a shorter period than a swell. **b.** A coastal rise in water level caused by wind. **3.** A sudden onrush: *a surge of joy.* **4.** A sudden transient increase or oscillation in electric current or voltage. **5.** An instability in the power output of an engine. **6.** *Astron.* A brief violent disturbance occurring during the eruption of a solar flare. **7.** *Naut.* **a.** The part of a windlass into which the cable surges. **b.** A temporary release or slackening of a cable. [Prob. Fr. *sourdre, sourge-* (< OFr.) and Fr. *surgir*, to rise (< OFr., to cast anchor < Old Catalan), both < Lat. *surgere*, to rise : *sub-*, from below; see SUB– + *regere*, to lead straight; see **reg-***.]

sur•geon (sûr′jən) *n.* A physician specializing in surgery. [ME *surgien* < AN, short for OFr. *cirurgien* < *cirurgie*, surgery. See SURGERY.]

sur•geon•fish (sûr′jən-fĭsh′) *n.*, *pl.* **surgeonfish** or **-fish•es.** Any of various bright-colored tropical marine fishes of the family Acanthuridae, having one or more sharp erectile spines near the base of the tail.

Sur•geon General (sûr′jən) *n.*, *pl.* **Surgeons General. 1.** The chief general officer in the medical departments of the U.S. Army, Navy, or Air Force. **2.** The chief medical officer in the U.S. Public Health Service or in a state public health service.

sur•geon's knot (sûr′jənz) *n.*, *pl.* **surgeons' knots.** Any of several knots, esp. one similar to a square knot, used in surgery for tying ligatures or stitching incisions.

sur•ger•y (sûr′jə-rē) *n.*, *pl.* **-ies. 1.** The branch of medicine that deals with the diagnosis and treatment of injury, deformity, and disease by manual and instrumental means. **2.** A surgical operation or procedure, esp. one involving the removal or replacement of a diseased organ or tissue. **3.** An operating room or a laboratory of a surgeon or of a hospital's surgical staff. **4.** The skill or work of a surgeon. **5.** *Chiefly British.* **a.** A physician's, dentist's, or veterinarian's office. **b.** The period during which a physician, dentist, or veterinarian consults with or treats patients in the office. [ME *surgerie* < OFr., short for *cirurgerie* < *cirurgie* < Lat. *chīrūrgia* < Gk. *kheirourgia* < *kheirourgos*, working by hand : *kheir*, hand; see **ghesor-*** + *ergon*, work; see **werg-***.]

sur•gi•cal (sûr′jĭ-kəl) *adj.* **1.** Of, relating to, or characteristic of surgeons or surgery. **2.** Used in surgery. **3.** Resulting from or occurring after surgery. [< SURGEON.] — **sur′gi•cal•ly** *adv.*

Su•ri•ba•chi (so͝or′ə-bä′chē), **Mount.** A volcanic hill on Iwo Jima in the W Pacific; captured by U.S. Marines in 1945 during World War II.

su•ri•cate (so͝or′ĭ-kāt′) *n.* A small burrowing carnivorous mammal *(Suricata suricatta)* of southern Africa, related to the mongoose. [Fr. < obsolete Du. *surikat*, macaque, prob. of South African orig.]

su•ri•mi (sə-rē′mē, so͞o-) *n.* Minced processed fish used in the preparation of imitation seafood, esp. imitation crabmeat, lobster, and scallops. [J. < *suru*, to process, mash.]

Su•ri•na•me (sü′rē-nä′mə) also **Su•ri•nam** (so͝or′ə-năm′, -näm′). Formerly **Dutch Gui•a•na** (dŭch gē-ăn′ə, -ä′nə, gī-). A country of NE South America on the Atlantic Ocean; ceded to the Dutch in 1667 and gained full independence in 1975. Cap. Paramaribo. Pop. 354,860. — **Su′ri•na•mese′** (-nä-mēz′, -mēs′) *adj.* & *n.*

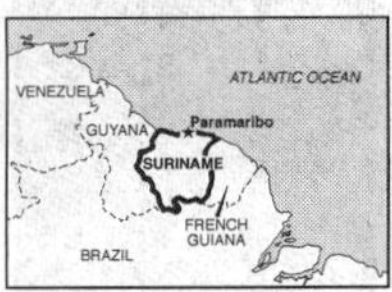

Suriname

Suriname River also **Surinam River.** A river of Suriname flowing c. 644 km (400 mi) to the Atlantic Ocean.

sur•ly (sûr′lē) *adj.* **-li•er, -li•est. 1.** Sullenly ill-humored; gruff. **2.** *Obsolete.* Arrogant; domineering. [ME *sirly*, masterful, lordly < *sir*, lord. See SIR.] — **sur′li•ly** *adv.* — **sur′li•ness** *n.*

sur•mise (sər-mīz′) *v.* **-mised, -mis•ing, -mis•es.** — *tr.* To infer (something) without sufficient evidence. — *intr.* To make a conjecture; guess. — *n.* A guess; a conjecture. [ME *surmisen*, to accuse < OFr. *surmise*, fem. p.part. of *surmettre* : *sur-*, sur- + *mettre*, to put (< Lat. *mittere*).]

sur•mount (sər-mount′) *tr.v.* **-mount•ed, -mount•ing, -mounts. 1.** To overcome (an obstacle, for example); conquer. **2.** To ascend to the top of; climb. **3.a.** To place something above; top. **b.** To be above or on top of. **4.** *Obsolete.* To surpass or exceed in amount. [ME *surmonten* < OFr. *surmonter* : *sur-*, sur- + *monter*, to mount; see MOUNT[1].] — **sur•mount′a•ble** *adj.* — **sur•mount′er** *n.*

sur•mul•let (sər-mŭl′ĭt, sûr′mŭl′-) *n.*, *pl.* **surmullet** or **-lets.** See **goatfish.** [Fr. *surmulet* < OFr. *sormulet* : prob. *sor*, reddish brown (of Gmc. orig.) + *mulet*, mullet; see MULLET.]

sur•name (sûr′nām′) *n.* **1.** A name shared in common to identify the members of a family, as distinguished from each member's given name. **2.** A nickname or an epithet added to a person's name. — *tr.v.* **-named, -nam•ing, -names.** To give a surname to. [ME, partial transl. of OFr. *surnom* : *sur-*, sur- + *nom*, name.]

sur•pass (sər-păs′) *tr.v.* **-passed, -pass•ing, -pass•es. 1.** To be beyond the limit, powers, or capacity of; transcend. **2.** To be or go beyond, as in degree; exceed. [Fr. *surpasser* < OFr., to transgress : *sur-*, sur- + *passer*, pass; see PASS.]

sur•pass•ing (sər-păs′ĭng) *adj.* Exceptional; exceeding.

sur•plice (sûr′plĭs) *n.* A loose-fitting white ecclesiastical gown with wide sleeves, worn over a cassock. [ME *surplis* < AN *surpliz*, var. of OFr. *sourpeliz* < Med.Lat. *superpellīcium* : Lat. *super-*, super- + Med.Lat. *pellīcium*, fur coat (< Lat., neut. of *pellīcius*, made of skin < *pellis*, skin; see **pel-³***).]

surplice

sur•plus (sûr′pləs, -plŭs′) *adj.* Being more than or in excess of what is needed or required. See Syns at **superfluous.** — *n.* **1.** An amount or a quantity in excess of what is needed. **2.** *Accounting.* **a.** Total assets minus the sum of all liabilities. **b.** Excess of a corporation's net assets over the face value of its capital stock. **c.** Excess of receipts over expenditures. [ME, an excess, surplus < OFr., an excess < Med.Lat. *superplūs* : Lat. *super-*, super- + Lat. *plūs*, more; see **pelə-¹***.]

sur•plus•age (sûr′plə-sĭj) *n.* **1.** Surplus, excess. **2.** An excess of words; verbiage. **3.** *Law.* Irrelevant matter in a pleading.

surplus value *n.* The difference between the value of the product produced by labor and the actual price of labor as paid out in wages in Marxian analysis of capitalism.

sur•print (sûr′prĭnt′) *tr.v.* **-print•ed, -print•ing, -prints. 1.** To overprint. **2.** To superimpose (a second negative) on a previously printed image of the first negative. — **sur′print′** *n.*

sur•pris•al (sər-prī′zəl) *n.* The act of surprising or the state of being surprised.

sur•prise also **sur•prize** (sər-prīz′) — *tr.v.* **-prised, -pris•ing, -pris•es** also **-prized, -priz•ing, -priz•es. 1.** To encounter suddenly or unexpectedly; take or catch unawares. **2.** To attack or capture suddenly and without warning. **3.** To cause to feel wonder, astonishment, or amazement, as at something unanticipated. **4.a.** To cause (someone) to do or say something unintended. **b.** To elicit or detect through surprise. — *n.* **1.** The act of surprising or the condition of being surprised. **2.** Something, such as an unexpected gift, that surprises. [ME *surprisen,* to overcome < OFr. *surprise,* fem. p.part. of *surprendre,* to surprise : *sur-,* sur- + *prendre,* to take (< Lat. *prehendere, prendere,* to seize; see **ghend-***).] — **sur•pris′er** *n.* — **sur•pris′ing** *adj.* — **sur•pris′ing•ly** *adv.*

Syns: *surprise, astonish, amaze, astound.* These verbs mean to affect a person strongly as being unexpected or unusual. To *surprise* is to fill with often sudden wonder or disbelief as being unanticipated or out of the ordinary: *"Poetry should surprise by a fine excess"* (John Keats). *Astonish* suggests overwhelming surprise: *The sight of such an enormous crowd astonished us. Amaze* implies astonishment and often bewilderment: *The violinist's virtuosity amazed the audience. Astound* connotes shock, as from something unprecedented in one's experience: *They were astounded at her beauty.*

surr. *abbr.* Surrender.

Sur•ratt (sə-răt′), **Mary Eugenia Jenkins.** 1820?–65. Amer. alleged conspirator in Abraham Lincoln's assassination who was convicted and executed although she probably knew nothing about the plot to kill the President.

sur•re•al (sə-rē′əl) *adj.* **1.** Having qualities attributed to or associated with surrealism. **2.** Having an oddly dreamlike quality. [Back-formation < SURREALISM.] — **sur•re′al•ly** *adv.*

sur•re•al•ism (sə-rē′ə-lĭz′əm) *n.* **1.** A 20th-century literary and artistic movement that attempts to express the workings of the subconscious and is characterized by fantastic imagery and incongruous juxtaposition of subject matter. **2.** Literature or art produced in this style. [Fr. *surréalisme* : *sur-,* beyond (< OFr.; see SUR–) + *réalisme,* realism (< *réalité,* reality < Med. Lat. *reālitās* < *reālis,* real; see REAL[1]).] — **sur•re′al•ist** *n.*

sur•re•al•is•tic (sə-rē′ə-lĭs′tĭk) *adj.* **1.** Of or relating to surrealism. **2.** Having an oddly dreamlike or unreal quality.

sur•re•but•ter (sûr′rĭ-bŭt′ər) also **sur•re•but•tal** (-bŭt′l) *n. Law.* A plaintiff's reply to a defendant's rebuttal.

sur•re•join•der (sûr′rĭ-join′dər) *n. Law.* A plaintiff's reply to a defendant's rejoinder.

sur•ren•der (sə-rĕn′dər) *v.* **-dered, -der•ing, -ders.** — *tr.* **1.** To relinquish possession or control of to another because of demand or compulsion. See Syns at **relinquish. 2.** To give up in favor of another. **3.** To give up or give back (something granted). **4.** To give up or abandon: *surrender all hope.* **5.** To give over or resign (oneself) to something, as to an emotion. **6.** *Law.* To restore (an estate, for example), esp. to give up (a lease) before expiration of the term. — *intr.* To give oneself up, as to an enemy. — *n.* **1.** The act or an instance of surrendering. **2.** *Law.* **a.** The delivery of a prisoner, fugitive from justice, or other principal in a suit into legal custody. **b.** The act of surrendering or of being surrendered to bail. **c.** Restoration of an estate. [ME *surrenderen* < OFr. *surrendre* : *sur-,* sur- + *rendre,* to deliver; see RENDER.]

sur•rep•ti•tious (sûr′əp-tĭsh′əs) *adj.* **1.** Obtained, done, or made by clandestine or stealthy means. **2.** Acting with or marked by stealth. [ME < Lat. *surreptīcius* < *surreptus,* p.part. of *surripere,* to take away secretly : *sub-,* secretly; see SUB– + *rapere,* to seize; see **rep-***.] — **sur′rep•ti′tious•ly** *adv.* — **sur′rep•ti′tious•ness** *n.*

sur•rey (sûr′ē, sŭr′ē) *n., pl.* **-reys.** A four-wheeled horse-drawn pleasure carriage having two or four seats. [Short for *Surrey cart,* after *Surrey,* a county of SE England.]

Sur•rey (sûr′ē, sŭr′ē). A historical region of SE England; dominated by Mercia and Wessex in Anglo-Saxon times and overrun by the Danes in the 9th cent.

Surrey, Earl of. See Henry **Howard.**

sur•ro•ga•cy (sûr′ə-gə-sē, sŭr′-) *n., pl.* **-cies. 1.** The condition of being a surrogate, esp. a surrogate mother. **2.** *Law.* The office of a surrogate.

sur•ro•gate (sûr′ə-gĭt, -gāt′, sŭr′-) *n.* **1.** One that takes the place of another; a substitute. **2.a.** A person or an animal that functions as a substitute for another, as in a social or family role. **b.** A surrogate mother. **3.** *Psychol.* A figure of authority who takes the place of the father or mother in a person's unconscious or emotional life. **4.** *Law.* A judge in New York and some other states having jurisdiction over the probate of wills and the settlement of estates. — *adj.* Substitute. — *tr.v.* (-gāt′) **-gat•ed, -gat•ing, -gates. 1.** To put in the place of another, esp. as a successor; replace. **2.** To appoint (another) as a replacement for oneself. [ME < Lat. *surrogātus,* p.part. of *surrogāre,* to substitute, var. of *subrogāre.* See SUBROGATE.]

surrogate mother *n.* **1.** A woman who is paid to bear a child for another woman. **2.** One that acts as, serves as, or is a mother substitute. — **surrogate motherhood** *n.*

sur•round (sə-round′) *tr.v.* **-round•ed, -round•ing, -rounds. 1.** To extend on all sides of simultaneously; encircle. **2.** To enclose or confine on all sides so as to bar escape or outside communication. — *n.* **1.** Something, such as fencing or a border, that surrounds. **2.a.** The area around a thing or place. **b.** Surroundings; environment. **3.** A method of hunting wild animals by surrounding them and driving them to a place from which they cannot escape. [ME *surrounden,* to inundate < OFr. *suronder* < LLat. *superundāre* : Lat. *super-,* super- + Lat. *undāre,* to rise in waves (< *unda,* wave; see **wed-[1]***).]

sur•round•ings (sə-roun′dĭngz) *pl.n.* The external circumstances, conditions, and objects that affect existence and development; the environment.

sur•tax (sûr′tăks′) *n.* **1.** An additional tax. **2.** A tax levied on corporations or individuals after net income has exceeded a certain level. — *tr.v.* **-taxed, -tax•ing, -tax•es.** To levy a surtax on.

sur•ti•tle (sûr′tīt′l) *n.* See **supertitle.**

sur•veil•lance (sər-vā′ləns) *n.* **1.** Close observation of a person or group, esp. one under suspicion. **2.** The act of observing or the condition of being observed.

sur•veil•lant (sər-vā′lənt) *adj.* Exercising surveillance. — *n.* One that exercises surveillance. [Fr., pr.part. of *surveiller,* to watch over : *sur-,* over (< OFr.; see SUR–) + *veiller,* to watch (< OFr. *veillier* < Lat. *vigilāre* < *vigil,* watchful; see **weg-***).]

sur•vey (sər-vā′, sûr′vā′) *v.* **-veyed, -vey•ing, -veys.** — *tr.* **1.** To examine or look at comprehensively. **2.** To inspect carefully; scrutinize. See Syns at **see[1]. 3.** To determine the boundaries, area, or elevations of (land or structures on the earth's surface) by surveying. **4.** *Chiefly British.* To inspect and determine the structural condition of (a building). **5.** To conduct a statistical survey on. **6.** To range one's gaze leisurely over. — *intr.* To make a survey. — *n.* (sûr′vā′), *pl.* **-veys. 1.** A detailed inspection or investigation. **2.** A general or comprehensive view. **3.a.** The process of surveying. **b.** A report on or map of what has been surveyed. [ME *surveien* < OFr. *surveeir* < Med.Lat. *supervidēre* : Lat. *super-,* super- + Lat. *vidēre,* to look; see **weid-***.] — **sur•vey′or** *n.*

survey course *n.* An academic course consisting of an overview of a broad topic or field of knowledge.

sur•vey•ing (sər-vā′ĭng) *n.* The measurement of dimensional relationships, as of horizontal distances, elevations, directions, and angles, on the earth's surface esp. for locating property boundaries, construction layout, and mapmaking.

sur•vey•or's level (sər-vā′ərz) *n., pl.* **surveyors' levels.** An instrument having a telescope and attached spirit level mounted on a tripod and rotating around a vertical axis.

sur•viv•a•ble (sər-vī′və-bəl) *adj.* **1.** Capable of surviving. **2.** That can be survived. — **sur•viv′a•bil′i•ty** *n.*

sur•viv•al (sər-vī′vəl) *n.* **1.a.** The act or process of surviving. **b.** The fact of having survived. **2.** Something, such as an ancient custom or belief, that has survived.

sur•viv•al•ist (sər-vī′və-lĭst) *n.* One whose primary goal is personal or group survival, as after nuclear war.

survival of the fittest *n.* Natural selection conceived of as a struggle for life in which only those organisms best adapted to existing conditions are able to survive and reproduce.

sur•vive (sər-vīv′) *v.* **-vived, -viv•ing, -vives.** — *intr.* To remain alive or in existence. — *tr.* **1.** To live longer than; outlive. **2.** To live or persist through. [ME *surviven* < OFr. *sourvivre* < Lat. *supervīvere* : *super-,* super- + *vīvere,* to live; see **g[w]ei-***.] — **sur•vi′vor** *n.*

sur•vi•vor•ship (sər-vī′vər-shĭp′) *n.* **1.** *Law.* The right of a person who survives a partner or joint owner to the entire ownership of something that was previously owned jointly. **2.** The condition of being a survivor.

Su•sa (so͞o′sə, -zə). A ruined city of SW Iran S of Hamaden; cap. of the kingdom of Elam.

Su•sah or **Su•sa** (so͞o′sə, -zə). See **Sousse.**

Su•san B. An•tho•ny Day (so͞o′zən bē′ ăn′thə-nē) *n.* February 15, observed in the United States in commemoration of the birth in 1820 of Susan B. Anthony.

Su•san•na (so͞o-zăn′ə). In the Apocrypha, a captive in Babylon who was falsely accused of adultery.

sus•cep•tance (sə-sĕp′təns) *n. Electron.* The imaginary part of the complex admittance. [(*electric*) *suscept*(*ibility*), a measure of the ease of polarization of a dielectric + -ANCE.]

sus•cep•ti•bil•i•ty (sə-sĕp′tə-bĭl′ĭ-tē) *n., pl.* **-ties. 1.** The quality or condition of being susceptible. **2.** The capacity to be affected by deep emotions or strong feelings; sensitivity. **3. susceptibilities.** Sensibilities; feelings.

sus•cep•ti•ble (sə-sĕp′tə-bəl) *adj.* **1.** Easily influenced or affected. **2.** Likely to be affected, as with an infection. **3.** Especially sensitive; highly impressionable. **4.** Capable of accepting or permitting: *susceptible of proof.* [LLat. *susceptibilis* < Lat. *susceptus,* p.part. of *suscipere,* to receive : *sub-,* from below; see SUB– + *capere,* to take; see **kap-***.] — **sus•cep′ti•ble•ness** *n.* — **sus•cep′ti•bly** *adv.*

sus•cep•tive (sə-sĕp′tĭv) *adj.* **1.** Receptive. **2.** Susceptible. — **sus•cep′tive•ness, sus•cep′tiv′i•ty** *n.*

su•shi (so͞o′shē) *n.* Small cakes of cold cooked rice wrapped in seaweed, dressed with vinegar, and topped or wrapped with

Mary Surratt
19th-century mezzotint

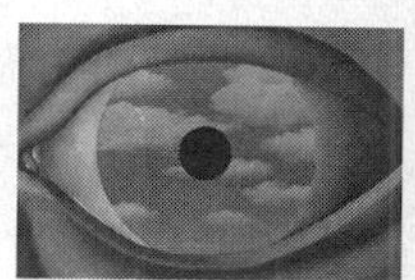

surrealism
The False Mirror,
1928, by René Magritte
The Museum of Modern Art, New York. Purchase. Oil on canvas, 21¼" × 31⅞".

ă pat	oi boy
ā pay	ou out
âr care	o͝o took
ä father	o͞o boot
ĕ pet	ŭ cut
ē be	ûr urge
ĭ pit	th thin
ī pie	*th* this
îr pier	hw which
ŏ pot	zh vision
ō toe	ə about, item
ô paw	

Stress marks:
′ (primary);
′ (secondary), as in
dictionary (dĭk′shə-nĕr′ē)

slices of raw or cooked fish, egg, or vegetables. [J.]

Su·si·a·na (so͞o′zē-ä′nə, -ăn′ə). See **Elam.**

sus·lik (sŭs′lĭk) also **sous·lik** (so͞os′-) *n.* **1.** Any of several ground squirrels of Europe and Asia, esp. the small grayish European species *Citellus citellus.* **2.** The pelt or fur of this animal. [Russ. < ORuss. *susolŭ.*]

sus·pect (sə-spĕkt′) *v.* **-pect·ed, -pect·ing, -pects.** *—tr.* **1.** To surmise to be true or probable; imagine. **2.** To have doubts about; distrust. **3.** To think (a person) guilty without proof. *—intr.* To have suspicion. *—n.* (sŭs′pĕkt′). One who is suspected, esp. of having committed a crime. *—adj.* (sŭs′-pĕkt′, sə-spĕkt′). Open to or viewed with suspicion. [ME *suspecten* < OFr. *suspecter* < Lat. *suspectāre,* freq. of *suspicere,* to look up at, suspect : *su-, sub-,* from below; see SUB- + *specere,* to look at; see **spek-*.**]

suspender
A pair of suspenders

sus·pend (sə-spĕnd′) *v.* **-pend·ed, -pend·ing, -pends.** *—tr.* **1.** To bar for a period from a privilege, office, or position, usu. as a punishment. **2.** To cause to stop for a period; interrupt. **3.a.** To hold in abeyance; defer. **b.** To render temporarily ineffective. **4.** To hang so as to allow free movement. **5.** To support or keep from falling without apparent attachment, as by buoyancy. *—intr.* **1.** To cease for a period; delay. **2.** To fail to make payments or meet obligations. [ME *suspenden* < OFr. *suspendre* < Lat. *suspendere* : *sub-,* from below; see SUB- + *pendere,* to hang; see **(s)pen-*.**]

sus·pend·ed animation (sə-spĕn′dĭd) *n.* A temporary interruption of the vital functions resembling death.

sus·pend·er (sə-spĕn′dər) *n.* **1.** One, such as a hook, that suspends something else. **2.** An often elastic strap worn over the shoulders to support trousers. Often used in the plural. **3.** *Chiefly British.* A garter.

sus·pense (sə-spĕns′) *n.* **1.** The condition of being physically suspended. **2.a.** The state or quality of being undecided, uncertain, or doubtful. **b.** Pleasurable excitement and anticipation regarding an outcome. **3.** Anxiety or apprehension due to an uncertain, undecided, or mysterious situation. [ME < OFr. *suspens* < Lat. *suspēnsus,* p.part. of *suspendere,* to suspend. See SUSPEND.] **—sus·pense′ful** *adj.*

suspense account *n.* A temporary account in which entries of credits or charges are made until their proper disposition can be determined.

sus·pen·sion (sə-spĕn′shən) *n.* **1.** The act of suspending or the condition of being suspended, esp.: **a.** A temporary abrogation or deferment. **b.** A debarment, as from office. **c.** A postponement, as of judgment or decision. See Syns at **pause. 2.** *Mus.* **a.** The prolongation of one or more tones of a chord into a following chord to create a temporary dissonance. **b.** The tone so prolonged. **3.** A device from which a mechanical part is suspended. **4.** The system of springs and other devices that insulates the chassis of a vehicle from shocks transmitted through the wheels. **5.** *Chem.* A relatively coarse noncolloidal dispersion of solid particles in a liquid.

suspension
From Bach's Fourth Fugue

suspension bridge *n.* A bridge having the roadway suspended from cables that are anchored at either end and usu. supported at intervals by towers.

suspension point *n.* One of a series of dots, usu. three, used to indicate an incomplete statement or the omission of a word or words from a written text. Often used in the plural.

sus·pen·sive (sə-spĕn′sĭv) *adj.* **1.** Serving or tending to suspend or temporarily stop something. **2.** Marked by or causing suspense. **—sus·pen′sive·ly** *adv.* **—sus·pen′sive·ness** *n.*

sus·pen·sor (sə-spĕn′sər) *n.* **1.** *Bot.* A multicellular filamentous structure in seed-bearing plants that connects the embryo to the endosperm. **2.** An athletic supporter. [NLat. *suspēnsor,* one that suspends < Lat. *suspēnsus,* p.part. of *suspendere,* to suspend. See SUSPEND.]

sus·pen·so·ry (sə-spĕn′sə-rē) *adj.* **1.** Supporting or suspending. **2.** Delaying completion. *—n., pl.* **-ries. 1.** A support or truss. **2.** An athletic supporter.

suspension bridge
San Francisco–Oakland Bay Bridge

suspensory ligament *n.* A ligament that supports an organ or a body part, esp. a fibrous membrane that holds the lens of the eye in place.

sus·pi·cion (sə-spĭsh′ən) *n.* **1.** The act of suspecting something, esp. something wrong, on little evidence or without proof. **2.** The condition of being suspected, esp. of wrongdoing. **3.** A state of uncertainty; doubt. See Syns at **uncertainty. 4.** A minute amount; trace. *—tr.v.* **-cioned, -cion·ing, -cions.** *Non-Standard.* To suspect. [ME, alteration of *suspecioun* < AN, var. of OFr. *sospeçon* < Lat. *suspectiō, suspectiōn-* < *suspectus,* p.part. of *suspicere,* to watch. See SUSPECT.]

sus·pi·cious (sə-spĭsh′əs) *adj.* **1.** Arousing or apt to arouse suspicion; questionable: *suspicious behavior.* **2.** Tending to suspect; distrustful. **3.** Expressing suspicion. **—sus·pi′cious·ly** *adv.* **—sus·pi′cious·ness** *n.*

sus·pire (sə-spīr′) *intr.v.* **-pired, -pir·ing, -pires. 1.** To breathe. **2.** To sigh. [ME *suspiren,* to sigh < OFr. < Lat. *suspīrāre* : *sub-,* from below; see SUB- + *spīrāre,* to breathe.] **—sus′pi·ra′tion** (sŭs′pə-rā′shən) *n.*

Sus·que·han·na (sŭs′kwə-hăn′ə) *n., pl.* **Susquehanna** or **-nas.** See **Susquehannock** 1.

Susquehanna River. A river of the NE U.S. rising in central NY and flowing c. 714 km (444 mi) to Chesapeake Bay.

Sus·que·han·nock (sŭs′kwə-hăn′ək) *n., pl.* **Susquehannock** or **-nocks. 1.** A member of an extinct Native American people formerly located along the Susquehanna River in New York, Pennsylvania, and Maryland. **2.** The Iroquoian language of the Susquehannock.

Sus·sex (sŭs′ĭks). An Anglo-Saxon kingdom of S England bordering on the English Channel; founded in the 5th cent. A.D. and captured by the kingdom of Wessex in 825.

Sussex spaniel *n.* A strong stocky dog of a breed developed in Sussex, a county of southeast England, having long ears, short legs, and a silky golden-brown coat.

sus·tain (sə-stān′) *tr.v.* **-tained, -tain·ing, -tains. 1.** To keep in existence; maintain. **2.** To supply with necessities or nourishment; provide for. **3.** To support from below; keep from falling or sinking; prop. **4.** To support the spirits, vitality, or resolution of; encourage. **5.** To bear up under; withstand. **6.** To experience or suffer. **7.** To affirm the validity of. **8.** To prove or corroborate; confirm. **9.** To keep up (a joke or an assumed role, for example) competently. [ME *sustenen* < OFr. *sustenir* < Lat. *sustinēre* : *sub-,* from below; see SUB- + *tenēre,* to hold; see **ten-*.**] **—sus·tain′a·ble** *adj.* **—sus·tain′er** *n.* **—sus·tain′ment** *n.*

sus·tained yield (sə-stānd′) *n.* **1.** The continuing yield of a biological resource, such as timber, by controlled periodic harvesting. **2.** The quantity of a resource so harvested.

sus·tain·ing pedal (sə-stā′nĭng) *n. Mus.* The right pedal of a piano, which stops the action of the dampers and allows the strings to vibrate freely.

sus·te·nance (sŭs′tə-nəns) *n.* **1.a.** The act of sustaining. **b.** The condition of being sustained. **2.** The supporting of life or health; maintenance. **3.** Something, esp. food, that sustains life or health. **4.** Means of livelihood. [ME < OFr. < *sustenir,* to sustain. See SUSTAIN.]

sus·ten·tac·u·lar (sŭs′tən-tăk′yə-lər, -tĕn-) *adj. Anat.* Serving to support. [< LLat. *sustentāculum,* support < Lat. *sustentāre,* to support, freq. of *sustinēre,* to sustain. See SUSTAIN.]

sus·ten·ta·tion (sŭs′tən-tā′shən, -tĕn-) *n.* **1.** Something that sustains; a support. **2.** Sustenance. [ME < OFr. < Lat. *sustentātiō, sustentātiōn-* < *sustentātus,* p.part. of *sustentāre,* to support. See SUSTENTACULAR.] **—sus′ten·ta′tive** (-tā′tĭv) *adj.*

Su·su (so͞o′so͞o) *n., pl.* **Susu** or **Su·sus. 1.** A member of a West African people inhabiting parts of Guinea and Sierra Leone. **2.** The Mande language of the Susu.

su·sur·ra·tion (so͞o′sə-rā′shən) also **su·sur·rus** (so͞o-sûr′əs, -sŭr′-) *n.* A soft whispering or rustling sound; a murmur. [ME *susurracioun* < LLat. *susurrātiō, susurrātiōn-* < Lat. *susurrātus,* p.part. of *susurrāre,* to whisper < *susurrus,* whisper, ult. of imit. orig.] **—su·sur′rant** (so͞o-sûr′ənt, -sŭr′-), **su·sur′rous** (-sûr′əs, -sŭr′-) *adj.*

Suth·er·land (sŭth′ər-lənd), **George.** 1862–1942. Amer. jurist; associate justice of the U.S. Supreme Court (1922–38).

Sutherland, Joan. b. 1926. Australian soprano noted for her interpretations of the works of Bellini and Donizetti.

Sutherland Falls. A waterfall, 581 m (1,904 ft), of SW South I., New Zealand.

Sut·lej (sŭt′lĕj′). A river, c. 1,448 km (900 mi), flowing from SW Xizang (Tibet) through N India and E Pakistan to join the Chenab R.; one of the five rivers of the Punjab.

sut·ler (sŭt′lər) *n.* An army camp follower who peddles provisions to the soldiers. [Obsolete Du. *soeteler* < LGer. *sudeler, suteler* < Ger. *sudeln,* to dirty < MHGer. *sudelen.*]

su·tra (so͞o′trə) *n.* **1.** *Hinduism.* Any of various aphoristic doctrinal summaries produced generally between 500 and 200 B.C. and later incorporated into Hindu literature. **2.** Also **sut·ta** (so͝ot′ə). *Buddhism.* A scriptural narrative, esp. one regarded as by the Buddha. [Skt. *sūtram.* See **syū-*.**]

sut·tee also **sa·ti** (sŭ-tē′, sŭt′ē′) *n.* **1.** The now illegal act or practice by a Hindu widow of cremating herself on her husband's funeral pyre to fulfill her true role as wife. **2.** *pl.* **-tees** *also* **-tis.** A widow who commits such an act. [Skt. *satī,* suttee, fem. of *sant-, sat-,* true, virtuous. See **es-*.**]

Sut·ter (sŭt′ər), **John Augustus.** 1803–80. Amer. pioneer who emigrated from Switzerland. The discovery of gold on his land led to the California gold rush (1848–49).

Sutt·ner (zo͝ot′nər, so͝ot′-), **Bertha von.** 1843–1914. Austrian pacifist who won the 1905 Nobel Peace Prize.

su·ture (so͞o′chər) *n.* **1.a.** The joining of two surfaces or edges together along a line by or as if by sewing. **b.** The material, such as thread, gut, or wire, used in this procedure. **c.** The line or stitch so formed. **2.** *Medic.* **a.** The fine thread or other material used surgically to close a wound or join tissues. **b.** The stitch so formed. **3.** *Anat.* The line of junction or an immovable joint between two bones, esp. of the skull. **4.** *Biol.* A seamlike joint or line of articulation, such as the line of dehiscence in a dry fruit. *—tr.v.* **-tured, -tur·ing, -tures.** To join by sutures or a suture. [ME < Lat *sūtūra* < *sūtus,* p.part. of *suere,* to sew. See **syū-*.**] **—su′tur·al** *adj.*

Su·va (so͞o′və, -vä). The cap. of Fiji, on the SE coast of Viti Levu. Pop. 74,000.

Su·vo·rov (so͞o-vôr′əf), Count **Aleksandr Vasilevich.** 1729–1800. Russian field marshal famous for his campaigns in the Russo-Turkish War (1787–92).

Su•wan•nee (sə-wä′nē). A river, c. 386 km (240 mi), flowing from SE GA across N FL to the Gulf of Mexico.

Su•won (so͞o′wŭn′). A city of NW South Korea S of Seoul. Pop. 374,000.

su•ze•rain (so͞o′zər-ən, -zə-rān′) *n.* **1.** A nation that controls another nation in international affairs but allows it domestic sovereignty. **2.** A feudal lord to whom fealty was due. [Fr. < OFr. *suserain* : prob. *sus*, up (< Lat. *sūrsum, sūsum*, upward < **subsvorsum*, turned upward : *subs-, sub-*, from under; see SUB- + *vorsum*, neut. of *vorsus*, var. of *versus*, p.part. of *vertere*, to turn; see VERSUS) + *souverein*, sovereign; see SOVEREIGN.] — **su′ze•rain** *adj.*

su•ze•rain•ty (so͞o′zər-ən-tē, -zə-rān′tē) *n., pl.* **su•ze•rain•ties.** The power or domain of a suzerain.

Su•zhou (so͞o′jō′) also **Soo•chow** (-chou′, -jō′). A city of E China WNW of Shanghai. Pop. 695,500.

Sval•bard (säl′bär′). A Norwegian archipelago comprising Spitsbergen and other islands in the Arctic Ocean.

svc *abbr.* Service.

svelte (svĕlt) *adj.* **svelt•er, svelt•est.** Slender or graceful in figure or outline; slim. [Fr. < Ital. *svelto* < p.part. of *svellere*, to stretch out < VLat. **exvellere* < Lat. *ēvellere* : *ē, ex-*, ex- + *vellere*, to pull.] — **svelte′ly** *adv.* — **svelte′ness** *n.*

Sven•ga•li (svĕn-gä′lē, sfĕn-) *n. pl.* **-lis.** A person who evilly tempts another to do what is desired. [After *Svengali*, the hypnotist villain in the novel *Trilby* by George du Maurier.]

Sverd•lovsk (sfĕrd-lôfsk′, svyĭrd-). Officially (since 1991) **Ye•ka•te•rin•burg** (yĭ-kăt′ər-ĭn-bûrg′). A city of W-central Russia in the E foothills of the Ural Mts. Pop. 1,300,000.

Sver•drup Islands (sfĕr′drəp, svĕr′-). A group of islands of the N Northwest Terrs., Canada, in the Arctic Ocean W of Ellesmere I.

svgs. *abbr.* Savings.

sw *abbr.* Short wave.

SW *abbr.* **1.** Southwest. **2.** Southwestern.

sw. *abbr.* Switch.

Sw. *abbr.* Swedish.

swab also **swob** (swŏb) — *n.* **1.a.** A small piece of absorbent material on the end of a stick or wire, used for cleansing or applying medicine. **b.** A specimen of mucus or other material removed with a swab. **2.** A sponge or patch of absorbent material used to clean the bore of a firearm or cannon. **3.** A mop used for cleaning floors or decks. **4.a.** One who uses such a mop, esp. on a ship. **b.** *Slang.* A sailor. **5.** A lout. — *tr.v.* **swabbed, swab•bing, swabs** also **swobbed, swob•bing, swobs. 1.** To use a swab on. **2.** To clean with a swab. [Back-formation < *swabber*, mop for a ship's deck (< obsolete Du. **zwabber* < *zwabben*, to mop) or < obsolete Du. *swabbe*, mop (< MDu.).]

swab•bie also **swab•by** (swŏb′ē) *n., pl.* **-bies.** *Slang.* See **swab** 4.

Swa•bi•a (swā′bē-ə). A historical region of SW Germany with parts of present-day France and Switzerland; center of the **Swabian League** from 1488 to 1534. — **Swa′bi•an** *adj. & n.*

swad•dle (swŏd′l) *tr.v.* **-dled, -dling, -dles. 1.** To wrap or bind in bandages; swathe. **2.** To wrap (a baby) in swaddling clothes. **3.** To restrain or restrict. — *n.* A band or cloth used for swaddling. [ME *swadlen*, prob. back-formation < *swadling (band)*, swaddling (cloth), or *swathelbonde*, both < *swathel-*, prob. freq. of OE *swathian*, to swathe.]

swad•dling clothes (swŏd′lĭng) *pl.n.* **1.** Strips of cloth wrapped around a newborn infant to hold its legs and arms still. **2.** Restrictions imposed on the immature.

swag (swăg) *n.* **1.a.** An ornamental drapery or curtain draped in a curve between two points. **b.** An ornamental festoon of flowers or fruit. **c.** A carving or plaster molding of such an ornament. **2.** *Slang.* Stolen property; loot. **3.** *Australian.* The pack or bundle containing the personal belongings of a swagman. — *intr.v.* **swagged, swag•ging, swags. 1.** *Chiefly British.* To lurch or sway. **2.** *Australian.* To travel about with a pack or swag. [Prob. of Scand. orig.]

swage (swāj) *n.* **1.** A tool used to bend or shape cold metal. **2.** A stamp or die for marking or shaping metal. **3.** A swage block. — *tr.v.* **swaged, swag•ing, swag•es.** To bend or shape by or as if by using a swage. [ME, ornamental border < OFr. *souage*.]

swage block *n.* A metal block with holes or grooves for shaping metal objects.

swag•ger (swăg′ər) *v.* **-gered, -ger•ing, -gers.** — *intr.* **1.** To walk or conduct oneself insolently or arrogantly; strut. **2.** To brag; boast. — *tr.* To browbeat or bully (someone). — *n.* **1.** A swaggering movement or gait. **2.** Boastful or conceited expression. [Prob. freq. of SWAG.] — **swag′ger•er** *n.*

swagger stick *n.* A short metal-tipped cane carried esp. by officers in the armed forces.

swag•man (swăg′măn′) *n.* *Australian.* A man who seeks casual work while traveling about carrying his swag.

Swa•hi•li (swä-hē′lē) *n., pl.* **Swahili** or **-lis. 1.** A member of a predominantly Muslim people inhabiting much of the coast and islands of eastern Africa. **2.** The Bantu language of the Swahili that is the official language of Tanzania and is widely used as a lingua franca in eastern and east-central Africa. [Swahili < Ar. *sawāḥilīy*, belonging to the coasts : *sawāḥil*, pl. of *sāḥil*, coast + *-īy*, belonging to.] — **Swa•hi′li•an** *adj.*

swain (swān) *n.* **1.** A country lad, esp. a young shepherd. **2.** A beau. [ME, young man, servant < ON *sveinn*. See **s(w)e-*.**]

swale (swāl) *n.* A low tract of land, esp. when moist or marshy. [Perh. < ME, shade, perh. of Scand. orig.]

swal•low¹ (swŏl′ō) *v.* **-lowed, -low•ing, -lows.** — *tr.* **1.** To cause (food or drink, for example) to pass through the mouth and throat into the stomach. **2.** To put up with (something unpleasant). **3.** To refrain from expressing; suppress. **4.** To consume or destroy as if by ingestion; devour. **5.** *Slang.* To believe without question. **6.** To take back; retract. — *intr.* To perform the act of swallowing. — *n.* **1.** The act of swallowing. **2.** An amount swallowed. [ME *swalowen* < OE *swelgan*. See **swel-*.**] — **swal′low•er** *n.*

swal•low² (swŏl′ō) *n.* **1.** Any of various small graceful swift-flying passerine birds of the family Hirundinidae, having long pointed wings, a usu. notched or forked tail, and a large mouth for catching flying insects. **2.** Any of various similar birds, such as a swift. [ME *swalowe* < OE *swealwe*.]

swal•low•tail (swŏl′ō-tāl′) *n.* **1.a.** The deeply forked tail of a swallow. **b.** Something similar to the tail of a swallow. **2.** *Informal.* A swallow-tailed coat. **3.** Any of various colorful, widely distributed butterflies of the family Papilionidae, usu. having an extension at the end of each hind wing that resembles the tails of certain swallows. — **swal′low-tailed′** *adj.*

swallow-tailed coat *n.* A man's black coat worn for formal daytime occasions and having a long rounded and split tail.

swal•low•wort (swŏl′ō-wûrt′, -wôrt′) *n.* **1.** See **celandine** 1. **2.** Any of several vines of the genus *Cynanchum*, esp. *C. nigrum* of Europe having small brownish-purple flowers. [From the shape of its pod.]

swam (swăm) *v.* P.t. of **swim.**

swa•mi (swä′mē) *n., pl.* **swa•mis. 1.a.** *Hinduism.* A religious teacher. **b.** A mystic; a yogi. **2.** Used as a form of address for such a person. [Hindi *svāmī*, master, swami < Skt., nominative sing. of *svāmin-*, being one's own master, possessing proprietary rights. See **s(w)e-*.**]

Swam•mer•dam (svä′mər-däm′), **Jan.** 1637–80. Dutch naturalist known for his pioneering microscopic research.

swamp (swŏmp, swômp) *n.* **1.a.** A seasonally flooded bottomland with more woody plants than a marsh and better drainage than a bog. **b.** A lowland region saturated with water. **2.** A situation or place fraught with difficulties and imponderables. — *v.* **swamped, swamp•ing, swamps.** — *tr.* **1.** To drench in or cover with or as if in or with water. **2.** To inundate or burden; overwhelm. **3.** *Naut.* To fill (a ship or boat) with water to the point of sinking it. — *intr.* To become full of water or sink. [Perh. of Low German origin.] — **swamp′i•ness** *n.* — **swamp′y** *adj.*

swamp boat *n.* *Naut.* A flat-bottomed boat propelled by an airplane propeller projecting above the stern and used in swamps or shallow waters.

swamp•er (swŏm′pər, swôm′-) *n.* **1.** One who lives in or close to a swamp. **2.** One who clears a swamp or forest. **3.a.** A helper, as in a restaurant. **b.** A truck driver's assistant.

swamp fever *n.* **1.** See **malaria** 1. **2.** A viral disease in horses marked by progressive anemia, a staggering gait, and fever. **3.** See **leptospirosis.**

swamp pink *n.* An orchid *(Arethusa bulbosa)* of northeast North America having a usu. rose-colored flower.

swamp potato *n.* *Bot.* Arrowhead.

swan (swŏn) *n.* Any of various large aquatic birds of the family Anatidae chiefly of the genera *Cygnus* and *Olor*, having webbed feet, a long slender neck, and usu. white plumage. — *intr.v.* **swanned, swan•ning, swans.** *Chiefly British.* To travel around from place to place. [ME < OE. See **swen-*.**]

Swan (swŏn) *n.* See **Cygnus.**

swan dive *n.* *Sports.* A dive made with the legs straight together, the back arched, and the arms out from the sides.

swank (swăngk) *adj.* **swank•er, swank•est. 1.** Imposingly fashionable or elegant; grand. **2.** Ostentatious; pretentious. — *n.* **1.** Smartness in style or bearing; elegance. **2.** Swagger. — *intr.v.* **swanked, swank•ing, swanks.** To act in an ostentatious or pretentious way; swagger. [Perh. akin to MHGer. *swanken*, to swing.]

swank•y (swăng′kē) *adj.* **-i•er, -i•est.** Swank. — **swank′i•ly** *adv.* — **swank′i•ness** *n.*

swan•ny (swŏn′ē) *interj.* *Chiefly Southern U.S.* Used to express surprise: *Well, I swanny!* [Prob. alteration of dial. *I s'wan ye*, I shall warrant ye.]

swan's-down also **swans•down** (swŏnz′doun′) *n.* **1.** The soft down of a swan. **2.** A soft woolen fabric used esp. for baby clothes. **3.** Flannelette.

Swan•sea (swän′zē, -sē). A borough of S Wales on **Swansea Bay**, an inlet of the Bristol Channel. Pop. 188,500.

swan•skin (swŏn′skĭn′) *n.* **1.** The skin of a swan with the feathers attached. **2.** Any of several flannel or cotton fabrics with a soft nap.

swan song *n.* **1.** A farewell or final appearance, action, or work. **2.** The beautiful legendary song sung only once by a swan in its lifetime, as it is dying.

Joan Sutherland

swallowtail
Black swallowtail butterfly
Papilio polyxenes asterius

swan
Mute swan
Cygnus olor

ă pat	oi boy
ā pay	ou out
âr care	o͝o took
ä father	o͞o boot
ĕ pet	ŭ cut
ē be	ûr urge
ĭ pit	th thin
ī pie	*th* this
îr pier	hw which
ŏ pot	zh vision
ō toe	ə about, item
ô paw	

Stress marks:
′ (primary);
′ (secondary), as in
dictionary (dĭk′shə-nĕr′ē)

swap also **swop** (swŏp) *Informal.* —*v.* **swapped, swap•ping, swaps** also **swopped, swop•ping, swops.** —*intr.* To trade one thing for another. —*tr.* To exchange (one thing) for another. —*n.* An exchange of one thing for another. [ME *swappen,* to strike, strike hands in a bargain.] —**swap′per** *n.*

sward (swôrd) also **swarth** (swôrth) *n.* **1.** Land covered with grassy turf. **2.** A lawn or meadow. [ME < OE *sweard,* skin.]

sware (swâr) *v. Archaic.* A p.t. of **swear.**

swarf (swôrf) *n.* Fine metallic filings or shavings removed by a cutting tool. [Of Scand. orig.; akin to ON *svarf.*]

swarm[1] (swôrm) *n.* **1.** A large number of insects or other small organisms, esp. when in motion. **2.** A group of bees with a queen bee in migration to establish a new colony. **3.** An aggregation of persons or animals, esp. when in turmoil or moving in mass. —*v.* **swarmed, swarm•ing, swarms.** —*intr.* **1.a.** To move or emerge in a swarm. **b.** To leave a hive as a swarm. Used of bees. **2.** To move or gather in large numbers. **3.** To be overrun; teem. —*tr.* To fill with a crowd. [ME, group of bees < OE *swearm.*] —**swarm′er** *n.*

swarm[2] (swôrm) *v.* **swarmed, swarm•ing, swarms.** —*intr.* To climb by gripping with the arms and legs. —*tr.* To climb (something) in this manner. [?]

swarm spore *n.* See **zoospore.**

swart (swôrt) *adj. Archaic.* Swarthy. [ME *swarte* < OE *sweart.*]

swarth•y (swôr′thē) *adj.* **-i•er, -i•est.** Having a dark complexion or color. [Alteration of *swarty* < SWART.] —**swarth′i•ly** *adv.* —**swarth′i•ness** *n.*

swash (swŏsh, swôsh) *n.* **1.a.** A splash of water or other liquid hitting a solid surface. **b.** The sound of such a splash. **2.a.** A narrow channel through which tides flow. **b.** A bar over which waves wash freely. **3.a.** Swagger or bluster. **b.** A swaggering or blustering person. —*v.* **swashed, swash•ing, swash•es.** —*intr.* **1.** To strike, move, or wash with a splashing sound. **2.** To swagger. —*tr.* **1.** To splash (a liquid). **2.** To splash a liquid against. [Prob. imit.]

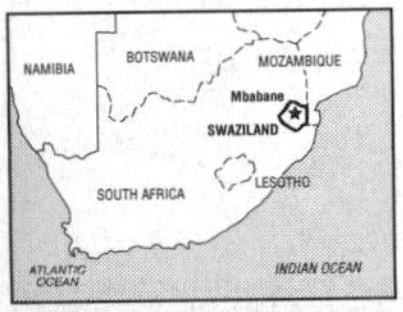

swash•buck•ler (swŏsh′bŭk′lər, swôsh′-) *n.* **1.** A flamboyant swordsman or adventurer. **2.** A sword-wielding ruffian or bully. **3.** A dramatic or literary work dealing with a swashbuckler. [Prob. from the striking of bucklers in fighting.] —**swash′buck′ling** *adj.*

Swaziland

swash letter *n. Print.* An ornamental italic letter with elaborate flowing flourishes and tails. [?]

swas•ti•ka (swŏs′tĭ-kə) *n.* **1.** The emblem of Nazi Germany, officially adopted in 1935. **2.** An ancient cosmic or religious symbol formed by a cross with the ends of the arms bent at right angles in either a clockwise or a counterclockwise direction. [Skt. *svastikaḥ,* sign of good luck, swastika < *svasti,* well-being. See **su-*.**]

swat (swŏt) *tr.v.* **swat•ted, swat•ting, swats.** To deal a sharp blow to; slap. —*n.* A sharp blow; a slap. [Alteration of SQUAT, to squash (obsolete and dialectal).]

swatch (swŏch) *n.* A sample strip or piece of material. [?]

swath (swŏth, swôth) also **swathe** (swŏth, swôth, swāth) *n.* **1.a.** The width of a scythe stroke or a mowing-machine blade. **b.** A path of this width made in mowing. **c.** The mown grass or grain lying on such a path. **2.** Something likened to a swath; a strip. —***idiom.* cut a swath. 1.** To create a great stir, impression, or display. **2.** To extend in distinctive physical length and width. [ME *swathe* < OE *swæth,* track.]

swathe[1] (swŏth, swôth, swāth) *tr.v.* **swathed, swath•ing, swathes. 1.** To wrap or bind with or as if with bandages. **2.** To enfold or constrict. —*n.* A wrapping, binding, or bandage. [ME *swathen* < OE *swathian.*] —**swath′er** *n.*

swathe[2] (swŏth, swôth, swāth) *n.* Var. of **swath.**

Swa•tow (swä′tou′). See **Shantou.**

swat•ter (swŏt′ər) *n.* **1.** A fly swatter. **2.** *Baseball.* A hard-hitting batter.

sway (swā) *v.* **swayed, sway•ing, sways.** —*intr.* **1.** To swing back and forth or to and fro. **2.** To incline or bend to one side; veer. **3.a.** To incline toward change, as in opinion. **b.** To fluctuate, as in outlook. —*tr.* **1.** To cause to swing back and forth or to and fro. **2.** To cause to incline or bend to one side. **3.** *Naut.* To hoist (a mast or yard) into position. **4.a.** To divert; deflect. **b.** To exert influence on or control over. **5.** *Archaic.* **a.** To rule or govern. **b.** To wield, as a scepter. —*n.* **1.** The act of moving from side to side with a swinging motion. **2.** Power; influence. **3.** Dominion or control. [ME *sweien,* prob. of Scand. orig.] —**sway′er** *n.*

sway•back (swā′băk′) *n.* Excessive inward or downward curvature of the spine, esp. in a horse. —**sway′backed′** *adj.*

Swayne (swān), **Noah Haynes.** 1804–84. Amer. jurist; associate justice of the U.S. Supreme Court (1862–81).

Swaz. *abbr.* Swaziland.

Swa•zi (swä′zē) *n., pl.* **Swazi** or **-zis. 1.** A member of a southeast African people of Swaziland and adjacent parts of South Africa. **2.** The Nguni language of this people.

Swa•zi•land (swä′zē-lănd′). A country of SE Africa between South Africa and Mozambique; gained independence from Great Britain in 1968. Cap. Mbabane. Pop. 585,000.

SWbS *abbr.* Southwest by south.

SWbW *abbr.* Southwest by west.

Swe. *abbr.* Sweden; Swedish.

swear (swâr) *v.* **swore** (swôr, swōr), **sworn** (swôrn, swōrn), **swear•ing, swears.** —*intr.* **1.** To make a solemn declaration, invoking a deity or a sacred person or thing. **2.** To make a solemn promise; vow. **3.** To use profane oaths; curse. **4.** *Law.* To give evidence or testimony under oath. —*tr.* **1.** To declare or affirm solemnly by invoking a deity or a sacred person or thing. **2.** To promise or pledge with a solemn oath; vow. **3.** To utter or bind oneself to (an oath). **4.** *Law.* To administer a legal oath to. **5.** To say or affirm earnestly and with great conviction. —***phrasal verbs.* swear at.** To use abusive, violent, or blasphemous language against; curse. **swear by. 1.** To have great reliance on or confidence in. **2.** To have reliable knowledge of; be sure of. **3.** To take an oath by. **swear in.** To administer a legal or official oath to. **swear off.** *Informal.* To pledge to renounce or give up. **swear out.** *Law.* To obtain (an arrest warrant) by making a charge under oath. [ME *sweren* < OE *swerian.* See **swer-*.**] —**swear′er** *n.*

swear•word (swâr′wûrd′) *n.* An obscene or blasphemous word.

sweat (swĕt) *v.* **sweat•ed** or **sweat, sweat•ing, sweats.** —*intr.* **1.** To excrete perspiration through the pores in the skin; perspire. **2.** To exude in droplets. **3.** To condense atmospheric moisture. **4.a.** To release moisture, as hay in the swath. **b.** To ferment, as tobacco during curing. **5.** *Informal.* **a.** To work long and hard. **b.** To suffer much, as for a misdeed. **6.** *Informal.* To fret or worry. —*tr.* **1.** To excrete (moisture) through a porous surface. **2.** To gather and condense (moisture) on a surface. **3.** To cause to perspire, as by exercise. **4.** To make damp or wet with perspiration. **5.** To cause to work excessively; overwork. **6.** To overwork and underpay (employees). **7.** *Slang.* **a.** To interrogate (someone) under duress. **b.** To extract (information) from someone under duress. **8.** *Metall.* To join (metal parts) by interposing cold solder and then heating. **9.** To steam (vegetables or other food). —*n.* **1.** The colorless saline moisture excreted by the sweat glands; perspiration. **2.** Condensation of moisture in the form of droplets on a surface. **3.a.** The process of sweating. **b.** *Slang.* The condition of being sweated. **4.** Strenuous, exhaustive labor; drudgery. **5.** A run given to a horse as exercise before a race. **6.** *Informal.* An anxious, fretful condition. **7. sweats.** *Informal.* A sweat suit. —***phrasal verb.* sweat out.** *Slang.* **1.** To endure anxiously. **2.** To await (something) anxiously. —***idioms.* no sweat.** *Slang.* Easily done or handled. **sweat blood.** *Informal.* **1.** To work diligently or strenuously. **2.** To worry intensely. **sweat bullets.** *Slang.* To sweat profusely. **sweat of (one's) brow.** Hard work. [ME *sweten* < OE *swǣtan.* See **sweid-*.**]

sweat•band (swĕt′bănd′) *n.* **1.** A band of fabric or leather sewn inside the crown of a hat as protection against sweat. **2.** A band of material worn around the forehead or wrist to absorb sweat.

sweat•box (swĕt′bŏks′) *n.* **1.** A box in which something, such as hides or fruit, is fermented by sweating. **2.** *Slang.* A confined place where a person sweats, esp.: **a.** An interrogation room. **b.** A prison cell used for special punishment.

sweat•er (swĕt′ər) *n.* **1.** One that sweats, esp. profusely. **2.** A jacket or pullover made esp. of knit, crocheted, or woven wool, cotton, or synthetic yarn. **3.** Something, esp. a sudorific, that induces sweating.

sweat gland *n.* Any of the numerous small, tubular glands found in human skin that secrete perspiration externally through pores to help regulate body temperature.

sweat•house (swĕt′hous′) *n.* Any of various structures often heated by fire or by pouring water over hot stones and used by some Native American peoples to induce sweating, as for medicinal or spiritual purposes.

sweat•pants (swĕt′pănts′) *pl.n.* Pants made traditionally of cotton jersey usu. having a drawstring or elasticized waist and elasticized cuffs and worn esp. for exercising.

sweat•shirt (swĕt′shûrt′) *n.* A usu. long-sleeved collarless oversize pullover made traditionally of heavy cotton jersey that has a fleeced backing.

sweat•shop (swĕt′shŏp′) *n.* A shop or factory in which employees work long hours at low wages under poor conditions.

sweat suit *n.* A two-piece outfit consisting of a sweatshirt and sweat pants, usu. worn for exercise.

sweat•y (swĕt′ē) *adj.* **-i•er, -i•est. 1.** Covered with or smelling of sweat. **2.** Causing sweat: *a sweaty job.* —**sweat′i•ly** *adv.* —**sweat′i•ness** *n.*

Swed. *abbr.* Sweden.

swede (swēd) *n.* See **rutabaga.** [Introduced from Sweden.]

Swede (swēd) *n.* A native or inhabitant of Sweden. [LGer. (< MLGer. *Swēde*) or Du. *Zweed* (< MDu. *Swēde*).]

Swe•den (swēd′n). A country of N Europe on the E Scandinavian Peninsula. Cap. Stockholm. Pop. 8,342,621.

Swe•den•borg (swēd′n-bôrg′, svād′n-bôr′ē), **Emanuel.** 1688–1772. Swedish scientist and theologian whose visions and writings inspired his followers to establish the Church of the New Jerusalem. —**Swe′den•bor′gi•an** *adj. & n.*

Swed•ish (swē′dĭsh) *adj.* Of or relating to Sweden, the Swedes, or their culture or language. —*n.* The North Germanic language of Sweden and Finland.

Swedish massage *n.* A system of massage for the muscles and joints, developed in Sweden in the 19th century.

Swedish turnip *n.* See **rutabaga.**

sweep (swēp) *v.* **swept** (swĕpt), **sweep•ing, sweeps.** —*tr.* **1.** To clean or clear, as of dirt, with or as if with a broom or brush. **2.** To clear away with or as if with a broom or brush. **3.** To clear (a path or space) with or as if with a broom. **4.a.** To search thoroughly. **b.** *Electron.* To search for and remove (eavesdropping devices) from a place. **5.** To touch or brush lightly, as with a trailing garment. **6.** To pass over or through a surface or medium with a continuous movement. **7.** To clear, drive, or convey with relentless force: *The floods swept away everything.* **8.** To wipe out at a single stroke. Often used with *away.* **9.** To remove or carry off with a swift brushing motion. **10.** To move across or through swiftly or with great intensity. **11.** To pass quickly across, as when searching. **12.** To drag the bottom of (a body of water). **13.a.** To win all the stages of (a game or contest). **b.** To win overwhelmingly in. —*intr.* **1.** To clean or clear a surface with or as if with a broom or brush. **2.** *Electron.* To search for and remove eavesdropping devices. **3.** To move swiftly with strong, steady force. **4.** To move swiftly in a lofty manner, as if in a trailing robe: *She swept by in silence.* **5.** To trail, as a long garment. **6.** To extend gracefully, esp. in a long curve: *The hills sweep down to the sea.* **7.** To extend in a wide range. —*n.* **1.** A clearing out or removal with or as if with a broom or brush. **2.** *Electron.* The act or an instance of sweeping. **3.a.** A wide curving motion. **b.** The range or scope encompassed by sweeping. **4.** A broad reach or extent. **5.** A curve or contour. **6.** One who sweeps, esp. a chimney sweep. **7.** Sweepings. Often used in the plural. **8.a.** The winning of all stages of a game or contest. **b.** An overwhelming victory or success. **9.** *Naut.* A long oar used to propel a boat. **10.** A long pole attached to a pivot and used to raise or lower a bucket in a well. **11. sweeps.** *(used with a sing. or pl. v.) Informal.* Sweepstakes. **12.a. sweeps.** The period every fall, winter, and spring when television ratings are accrued and studied and advertising rates are reset. **b.** The survey conducted to determine these ratings. **13.** *Electron.* The steady motion of an electron beam across a cathode-ray tube. —***idiom.* sweep (one) off (one's) feet.** To cause an immediate and strongly positive response in (a person); impress deeply. [ME *swepen,* perh. < *swepe,* p.t. of *swopen,* to sweep along. See SWOOP.] —**sweep′er** *n.*

sweep•back (swēp′băk′) *n.* The backward slant of the leading edge of an airfoil.

sweep•ing (swē′pĭng) *adj.* **1.** Having wide-ranging influence or effect. **2.** Moving in or as if in a wide curve. **3.** Indiscriminate; wholesale. **4.** Overwhelming; complete. —*n.* **1.** The action of one that sweeps. **2. sweepings.** Things swept up; refuse. —**sweep′ing•ly** *adv.*

sweep•stakes (swēp′stāks′) *pl.n. (used with a sing. or pl. v.)* **1.** A lottery in which the participants' stakes form a fund awarded as a prize to one or several winners. **2.** An event or a contest, esp. a horserace, the result of which determines the winner of such a lottery. **3.** The prize won in such a lottery.

sweet (swēt) *adj.* **sweet•er, sweet•est. 1.** Having the taste of sugar or a substance containing or resembling sugar, as honey. **2.a.** Containing or derived from sugar. **b.** Retaining some natural sugar; not dry: *a sweet wine.* **3.a.** Pleasing to the senses; agreeable. **b.** Pleasing to the mind or feelings; gratifying. **4.** Having a pleasing disposition; lovable. **5.** Kind; gracious. **6.** Fragrant; perfumed. **7.** Not saline or salted. **8.** Not spoiled, sour, or decaying; fresh. **9.** Free of acid or acidity: *sweet soil.* **10.** Low in sulfur content: *sweet fuel oil.* **11.** *Mus.* Of, relating to, or being a form of jazz characterized by adherence to a melodic line and a time signature. —*adv.* In a sweet manner; sweetly. —*n.* **1.** Sweet taste or quality; sweetness. **2.** Something sweet to the taste. **3. sweets. a.** Foods, such as candy or pastries, that are high in sugar content. **b.** *Informal.* Sweet potatoes. **4.** *Chiefly British.* **a.** A sweet dish, such as pudding, served as dessert. **b.** A sweetmeat or confection. **5.** A dear or beloved person. **6.** Something pleasing to the mind or feelings. —***idiom.* sweet on.** *Informal.* Enamored of; in love with. [ME *swete* < OE *swēte.* See **swād-*.**] —**sweet′ly** *adv.* —**sweet′ness** *n.*

Sweet (swēt), **Henry.** 1845–1912. British phonetician known esp. for his *History of English Sounds* (1874).

sweet alyssum *n.* An annual or perennial Mediterranean herb *(Lobularia maritima)* of the mustard family, having long-lasting flowers varying in size and color.

sweet-and-sour (swēt′n-sour′) *adj.* Flavored with a sauce containing sugar and vinegar: *sweet-and-sour pork.*

sweet basil *n.* See **basil** 1.

sweet bay *n.* **1.** A shrub or small tree *(Magnolia virginiana)* of the southeast United States and eastern coastal areas, having large fragrant white flowers and red fruit. **2.** See **laurel** 1.

sweet birch *n.* **1.** An eastern North American birch *(Betula lenta)* having aromatic stems with brownish bark that does not peel into papery flakes. **2.** The wood of this tree.

sweet•bread (swēt′brĕd′) *n.* The thymus gland or pancreas of a young animal, esp. a calf or lamb, used for food.

sweet•bri•er also **sweet•bri•ar** (swēt′brī′ər) *n.* A Eurasian rose *(Rosa eglanteria)* having prickly stems, fragrant leaves, bright pink flowers, and scarlet hips.

sweet cherry *n.* **1.** A large deciduous Eurasian tree *(Prunus avium)* of the rose family, having red-brown birchlike bark and sweet edible fruit. **2.** The fruit of the sweet cherry.

sweet cicely *n.* **1.** Any of various perennial New World herbs of the genus *Osmorhiza,* having fleshy aromatic roots, compound leaves, and white flowers. **2.** An aromatic European perennial herb *(Myrrhis odorata)* having compound leaves and white flowers. [ME *seseli* < Lat. *seselis* < Gk.]

sweet cider *n.* Unfermented cider.

sweet clover *n.* See **melilot.**

sweet corn *n.* The common table and canning variety of corn *(Zea mays* var. *rugosa),* having sweet kernels when young.

sweet•en (swēt′n) *v.* **-ened, -en•ing, -ens.** —*tr.* **1.** To make sweet or sweeter by adding sugar, honey, or another sweet substance. **2.** To make more pleasant or agreeable. **3.** To soften or soothe. **4.** To make bearable; alleviate. **5.** *Informal.* **a.** To increase the value of (collateral for a loan) by adding more securities. **b.** To enhance the attractiveness or financial desirability of (an offer, for example). **6.** *Games.* To increase the value of (an unwon poker pot) by adding stakes before reopening. **7.** To make less acidic. **8.** To remove sulfur compounds from (fuel oil or gas). —*intr.* To become sweet.

sweet•en•er (swēt′n-ər) *n.* **1.** Something that sweetens. **2.** *Informal.* An added inducement or incentive.

sweet•en•ing (swēt′n-ĭng) *n.* **1.** The act or process of making sweet. **2.** Something that sweetens; a sweetener.

sweet fern *n.* An aromatic deciduous shrub *(Comptonia peregrina)* of eastern North America having narrow, deeply lobed fernlike leaves and clusters of minute flowers.

sweet flag *n.* A hardy perennial herb *(Acorus calamus)* of the Northern Hemisphere growing in marshy places and having grasslike leaves and aromatic rhizomes.

sweet gale *n.* A deciduous swamp shrub *(Myrica gale)* of northern Eurasia and North America having aromatic resinous leaves used in medicine and tiny yellowish fruits.

sweet gum *n.* **1.** Any of several trees of the genus *Liquidambar,* esp. *L. styraciflua* of North America and Central America, having prickly fruit clusters and wood used to make furniture. **2.** The aromatic resin obtained from this tree.

sweet•heart (swēt′härt′) *n.* **1.** One who is loved. **2.** Used as a familiar term of endearment. **3.** *Informal.* **a.** A person regarded as generous or lovable. **b.** Something cherished for its excellent qualities. —*adj.* Involving privileged treatment of a favored party; illegally or unethically favorable.

sweet•ie (swē′tē) *n. Informal.* Sweetheart; dear.

sweet•ing (swē′tĭng) *n.* **1.** A sweet apple. **2.** *Archaic.* Sweetheart.

sweet marjoram *n.* See **marjoram.**

sweet•meat (swēt′mēt′) *n.* A sweet delicacy.

sweet pea *n.* An annual climbing herb *(Lathyrus odoratus)* of the pea family, native to Italy and having variously colored fragrant flowers.

sweet pepper *n.* The bell pepper.

sweet potato *n.* **1.a.** A tropical American vine *(Ipomoea batatas),* cultivated for its fleshy tuberous orange-colored root. **b.** The root of this vine, eaten cooked as a vegetable. Also called regionally *yam* **2.** *Informal.* An ocarina.

sweet•shop (swēt′shŏp′) *n. Chiefly British.* A candy store.

sweet•sop (swēt′sŏp′) *n.* **1.** A tropical American evergreen tree *(Annona squamosa)* cultivated for its yellowish-green fruit with sweet edible pulp. **2.** The fruit of this tree.

sweet sorghum *n.* See **sorgo.**

sweet spot *n. Sports.* The place on a racket, club, bat, paddle, or ball where hits are most effective.

sweet talk *n. Informal.* Flattery; cajolery. —**sweet-talk** (swēt′tôk′) *v.*

sweet tooth *n. Informal.* A fondness or craving for sweets.

sweet William *n.* An annual, biennial, or perennial herb *(Dianthus barbatus)* native to Eurasia and having flat-topped dense clusters of varicolored flowers.

swell (swĕl) *v.* **swelled, swelled** or **swol•len** (swō′lən), **swell•ing, swells.** —*intr.* **1.** To increase in size or volume as a result of internal pressure; expand. **2.a.** To increase in force, size, number, or degree. **b.** To grow in loudness or intensity. **3.** To bulge out, as a sail. **4.a.** To rise or extend above the surrounding level, as clouds. **b.** To rise in swells, as the sea. **5.a.** To be or become filled or puffed up, as with pride. **b.** To rise from within. —*tr.* **1.** To cause to increase in volume, size, number, degree, or intensity. **2.** To fill with emotion. —*n.* **1.a.** The act or process of swelling. **b.** The condition of being swollen. **2.** A swollen part; a bulge or protuberance. **3.** A long deep wave on water that travels a long distance at sea. **4.** A rise in the land; a rounded elevation. **5.** *Informal.* One who is fashionably dressed or socially prominent. **6.** *Mus.* **a.** A crescendo followed by a gradual diminuendo. **b.** The sign indicating this. **c.** A device on an instrument, such as an organ, for regulating volume. —*adj.* **swell•er, swell•est.** *Informal.* **1.** Fashionably elegant; stylish. **2.** Excellent; wonderful. [ME *swellen* < OE *swellan.*]

Sweden

ă pat	oi boy
ā pay	ou out
âr care	o͝o took
ä father	o͞o boot
ĕ pet	ŭ cut
ē be	ûr urge
ĭ pit	th thin
ī pie	*th* this
îr pier	hw which
ŏ pot	zh vision
ō toe	ə about,
ô paw	item

Stress marks:
′ (primary);
′ (secondary), as in
dictionary (dĭk′shə-nĕr′ē)

swell box *n. Mus.* A chamber containing organ pipes, with shutters that can be opened or shut to regulate the volume.

swelled head (swĕld) *n. Informal.* An unduly high opinion of oneself.

swell•fish (swĕl′fĭsh′) *n., pl.* **swellfish** or **-fish•es.** See **puffer.**

swell•head (swĕl′hĕd′) *n. Informal.* An arrogant or conceited person. — **swell′head′ed** *adj.* — **swell′head′ed•ness** *n.*

swell•ing (swĕl′ĭng) *n.* **1.** The state of being swollen. **2.** Something swollen, esp. an abnormally swollen body part or area.

swel•ter (swĕl′tər) *v.* **-tered, -ter•ing, -ters.** — *intr.* To suffer from oppressive heat. — *tr.* **1.** To affect with oppressive heat. **2.** *Archaic.* To exude (venom, for example). — *n.* A condition of oppressive heat. [ME *swelteren,* freq. of *swelten,* to faint from heat < OE *sweltan,* to perish.]

swel•ter•ing (swĕl′tər-ĭng) *adj.* **1.** Oppressively hot and humid; sultry. **2.** Suffering from heat. — **swel′ter•ing•ly** *adv.*

swel•try (swĕl′trē) *adj.* **-tri•er, -tri•est.** Sweltering.

swept (swĕpt) *v.* P.t. and p.part. of **sweep.**

swept•back (swĕpt′băk′) *adj.* **1.** Angled rearward from the points of attachment. Used esp. of aircraft wings. **2.** Having wings of this type. Used of an aircraft.

swept•wing (swĕpt′wĭng′) *adj.* Having sweptback wings. Used of an aircraft. — *n.* A sweptback wing.

swerve (swûrv) *tr. & intr.v.* **swerved, swerv•ing, swerves.** To turn aside or be turned aside from a straight course. — *n.* The act of swerving. [ME *swerven* < OE *sweorfan,* to rub, scour.]

Syns: swerve, depart, deviate, digress, diverge, stray, veer. The central meaning shared by these verbs is "to turn away from a straight or prescribed course": *a gaze that never swerved; won't depart from traditions; deviated from their original plan; digressing from the topic; opinions that diverged; straying from the truth; veered the conversation.*

SWG *abbr.* Standard wire gauge.

swift (swĭft) *adj.* **swift•er, swift•est. 1.** Moving or capable of moving with great speed; fast. See Syns at **fast**[1]. **2.** Coming, occurring, or done quickly; instant. **3.** Quick to act or react; prompt: *swift to act.* — *adv.* Swiftly. Often used in combination: *swift-running.* — *n.* **1.a.** A cylinder on a carding machine. **b.** A reel that holds yarn as it is being wound. **2.** Any of various small dark insect-eating birds of the family Apodidae, related to the hummingbirds and noted for their swift flight. **3.** Any of various small fast-moving North American lizards of the genera *Sceloporus* and *Uta.* [ME < OE.] — **swift′ly** *adv.* — **swift′ness** *n.*

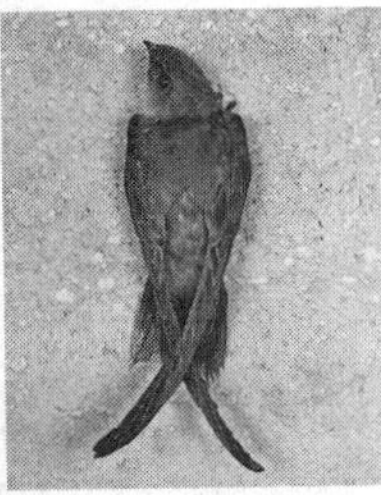

swift
Top: Collapsible boxwood swift for yarn
Bottom: Chimney swift *Chaetura pelagica*

Swift (swĭft), **Jonathan.** 1667–1745. Irish-born English writer whose satirical works include *Gulliver's Travels* (1726).

Jonathan Swift
Detail of a c. 1718 portrait by Charles Jervas (1675–1739)

swig (swĭg) *Informal. n.* A deep draft, esp. of liquor; a gulp. [?] — **swig** *v.* — **swig′ger** *n.*

swill (swĭl) *v.* **swilled, swill•ing, swills.** — *tr.* **1.** To drink greedily or grossly. **2.** To flood with water, as for washing. **3.** To feed (animals) with swill. — *intr.* To drink or eat greedily or to excess. — *n.* **1.** A mixture of liquid and solid food fed to animals, esp. pigs; slop. **2.** Kitchen waste; garbage. **3.** A deep draft of liquor. **4.** Nonsense; rubbish. [ME *swilen,* to wash out < OE *swilian.* See **swel-***.] — **swill′er** *n.*

swim (swĭm) *v.* **swam** (swăm), **swum** (swŭm), **swim•ming, swims.** — *intr.* **1.** To move through water by means of the limbs, fins, or tail. **2.** To move as though gliding through water. **3.** To float on water or another liquid. **4.a.** To be covered or flooded with or as if with a liquid. **b.** To possess a superfluity; abound. **5.** To experience a floating or giddy sensation; be dizzy. **6.** To appear to spin or reel lazily. — *tr.* **1.** To move through or across (a body of water) by swimming. **2.** To execute (a given stroke) in swimming. **3.** To cause to swim or float. — *n.* **1.a.** The act of swimming. **b.** A period of time spent swimming. **2.** A gliding motion. **3.** A state of dizziness. **4.** An area, as of a river, abounding in fish. — *adj.* Of, relating to, or used for swimming. — ***idioms.* in the swim.** Active in the general current of affairs. **swim against the stream.** To move counter to a prevailing trend. [ME *swimmen* < OE *swimman.*] — **swim′ma•ble** *adj.* — **swim′mer** *n.*

swim bladder *n.* See **air bladder** 1.

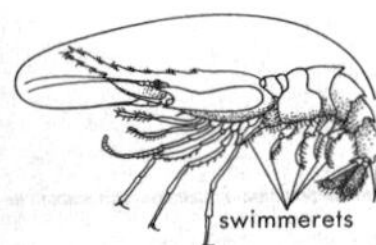

swimmeret
Of a shrimp

swim•mer•et (swĭm′ə-rĕt′, swĭm′ə-rĕt′) *n.* One of the paired abdominal appendages of certain aquatic crustaceans, such as shrimp, lobsters, and isopods, that function primarily for carrying the eggs in females and are usu. adapted for swimming.

swim•ming (swĭm′ĭng) *n.* The act, sport, or technique of one that swims. — *adj.* **1.** Relating to or used in swimming. **2.** That swims: *swimming insects.*

swim•ming•ly (swĭm′ĭng-lē) *adv.* Very easily and successfully.

swimming pool *n.* A structure, often a rectangular concrete-lined excavation, filled with water and used for swimming.

swim•suit (swĭm′so͞ot′) *n.* A garment worn while swimming.

swim•wear (swĭm′wâr′) *n.* Clothing designed to be worn for swimming or with swimsuits.

Swin•burne (swĭn′bûrn′), **Algernon Charles.** 1837–1909. British writer best known for his unconventional verse.

swin•dle (swĭn′dl) *v.* **-dled, -dling, -dles.** — *tr.* **1.** To cheat or defraud, as of money. **2.** To obtain by fraud. — *intr.* To use fraud to obtain money or property. — *n.* The act or an instance of swindling. [Back-formation < *swindler,* one who swindles < Ger. *Schwindler,* giddy person, cheat < *schwindeln,* to be dizzy, swindle < MHGer. < OHGer. *swintilōn,* freq. of *swintan,* to languish.] — **swin′dler** *n.*

Swin•don (swĭn′dən). A municipal borough of S-central England ENE of Bristol. Pop. 151,600.

swine (swīn) *n., pl.* **swine. 1.** Any of various omnivorous ungulates of the family Suidae, including pigs, having a stout body, a thick skin, and a short neck. **2.** A person regarded as brutish or contemptible. [ME < OE *swīn.* See **sū-***.]

swine•herd (swīn′hûrd′) *n.* One who tends swine.

swine•pox (swīn′pŏks′) *n.* An infectious viral disease of domesticated swine marked by skin lesions.

swing (swĭng) *v.* **swung** (swŭng), **swing•ing, swings.** — *intr.* **1.** To move back and forth suspended or as if suspended from above. **2.** To hit at something with a sweeping motion of the arm: *swung at the ball.* **3.** To move laterally or in a curve. **4.** To turn in place on or as if on a hinge or pivot. **5.** To move along with an easy swaying gait. **6.** To propel oneself from one place or position to another by grasping a fixed support. **7.** To ride on a swing. **8.** To shift from one attitude, opinion, or condition to another; vacillate. **9.** *Slang.* To be put to death by hanging. **10.** *Mus.* **a.** To have a subtle, intuitively felt rhythm or sense of rhythm. **b.** To play with such a sense of rhythm. **11.** *Slang.* **a.** To be lively, trendy, and exciting. **b.** To engage in promiscuous sex. **c.** To exchange sex partners. Used esp. of married couples. — *tr.* **1.** To cause to move back and forth, as on a swing. **2.** To cause to move in a broad arc or curve. **3.a.** To cause to move with a sweeping motion. **4.** To lift and convey with a sweeping motion. **4.** To suspend so as to sway or turn freely. **5.a.** To suspend on hinges. **b.** To cause to turn on hinges. **6.** To cause to shift from one attitude, opinion, or condition to another. **7.** *Informal.* **a.** To manage or arrange successfully. **b.** To bring around to the desired result. **8.** *Mus.* To play (music) with a subtle, intuitively felt sense of rhythm. — *n.* **1.** The act or an instance of swinging; movement back and forth or in one particular direction. **2.** The sweep or scope of something that swings. **3.** A blow or stroke executed with a sweeping motion of the arm. **4.** The manner in which one swings something, such as a bat. **5.** A shift from one attitude, opinion, or condition to another. **6.** Freedom of action. **7.a.** A swaying graceful motion. **b.** A sweep back and forth. **8.** A course or tour that returns to the starting point. **9.** A seat suspended from above, as by ropes, on which one can ride back and forth for recreation. **10.** The normal rhythm of life or pace of activities. **11.** A steady vigorous rhythm or movement, as in verse. **12.** A regular movement up or down, as in stock prices. **13.** *Mus.* **a.** A type of popular dance music developed about 1935 and based on jazz but employing simpler harmonic and rhythmic patterns. **b.** A ballroom dance performed to this music. **c.** A subtle, intuitively felt rhythmic quality or sense of rhythm. — *adj.* **1.** *Mus.* Relating to or performing swing. **2.** Determining an outcome; decisive. — ***idiom.* in full swing.** At the highest level of activity or operation. [ME *swingen,* to beat, brandish < OE *swingan,* to flog, strike, swing.] — **swing′y** *adj.*

swing-by (swĭng′bī′) *n., pl.* **-bys.** An interplanetary mission in which a space vehicle uses planetary gravitation for changes in course.

swinge (swĭnj) *tr.v.* **swinged, swinge•ing** also **swing•ing, swing•es.** *Archaic.* To punish with blows; thrash. [ME *swengen* < OE *swengan,* to shake.] — **swing′er** (swĭn′jər) *n.*

swing•er (swĭng′ər) *n.* **1.** One that swings. **2.** *Slang.* **a.** One who actively seeks excitement and follows the latest trends. **b.** One who engages in promiscuous sex. **c.** A member of a couple, esp. a married couple, who exchanges sexual partners.

swing•ing (swĭng′ĭng) *Slang. adj.* **1.** Spirited; up-to-date. **2.** Attracting a lively, trendy crowd. **3.** *Slang.* **a.** Sexually promiscuous. **b.** Exchanging sexual partners, esp. spouses.

swin•gle•tree (swĭng′gəl-trē) *n.* See **whiffletree.** [< E. *swingle,* wooden instrument used for beating flax < ME < MDu. *swinghel.*]

swing•man (swĭng′mən) *n. Basketball.* A player who plays well in two different positions, esp. forward and guard.

swing shift *n.* The work shift between the day and the night shifts, usu. 4 P.M. to midnight.

swing-wing (swĭng′wĭng′) *adj.* Of or being an airplane with wings constructed to allow the outer portion to fold back along the fuselage to produce streamlining at high speeds.

swin•ish (swī′nĭsh) *adj.* **1.** Resembling or befitting swine. **2.** Bestial or brutish.

swipe (swīp) *n.* **1.** A sweeping blow or stroke. **2.** *Informal.* A critical remark. **3.** A lever, esp. one that raises the bucket in a well. — *v.* **swiped, swip•ing, swipes.** — *tr.* **1.** To hit with a sweeping motion. **2.** *Informal.* To steal; filch. — *intr.* To make a sweeping stroke. [Perh. var. of SWEEP.]

swirl (swûrl) *v.* **swirled, swirl•ing, swirls.** — *intr.* **1.** To move with a twisting or whirling motion; eddy. **2.** To be dizzy; swim. **3.** To be arranged in a spiral, whorl, or twist. — *tr.* **1.** To cause to move in a swirl. **2.** To form into or arrange in a spiral, whorl, or twist. — *n.* **1.** A whirling or eddying motion or mass. **2.** Something that coils, twists, or whirls. **3.** Whirling confusion or disorder. [ME *swyrl,* eddy, prob. of LGer. or Scand. orig.] — **swirl′y** *adj*

swish (swĭsh) *v.* **swished, swish•ing, swish•es.** — *intr.* **1.** To move with a hissing or whistling sound. **2.** To rustle, as silk. — *tr.* **1.** To cause to make a swishing sound. **2.** To strike or cut with a swishing sound. **3.** To whip with a rod. — *n.* **1.a.** A sharp whistling or rustling sound. **b.** A movement making such a sound. **2.a.** A rod used for flogging. **b.** A stroke made with such a rod. **3.** *Offensive Slang.* Used as a disparaging term for a gay or homosexual man. — *adj.* **1.** *Informal.* Fashionable; posh. **2.** *Slang.* Effeminate. [Imit.]

swish•y (swĭsh′ē) *adj.* **-i•er, -i•est. 1.** Producing a swishing sound. **2.** *Slang.* Effeminate.

Swiss (swĭs) *adj.* Of or relating to Switzerland or its people or culture. — *n.* **1.** *pl.* **Swiss.** A native or inhabitant of Switzerland. **2.** Also **swiss.** A crisp sheer cotton fabric used for curtains or light garments. **3.** A firm white or pale yellow cheese with holes, originally produced in Switzerland. [Fr. *Suisse* < MHGer. *Swīzer* < *Swīz*, Switzerland.]

Swiss chard *n.* A variety of beet *(Beta vulgaris* var. *cicla)* having large succulent leaves used as a vegetable.

Swiss Guard *n.* A member of a corps of soldiers of Swiss birth employed at the Vatican as bodyguards to the pope.

Swiss steak *n.* A round steak pounded with flour and braised in stock with vegetables.

switch (swĭch) *n.* **1.** A thin flexible rod, stick, or twig, esp. one used for whipping. **2.** The bushy tip of the tail of certain animals. **3.** A thick strand of real or synthetic hair used as part of a coiffure. **4.** A flailing or lashing, as with a switch. **5.** A device used to break or open an electric circuit or divert current from one conductor to another. **6.** A device consisting of two sections of railroad track and accompanying apparatus used to transfer rolling stock from one track to another. **7.a.** The operating of a switching device. **b.** The result of such an act. **8.** An exchange or a swap, esp. a secret one. **9.** A transference or shift, as of opinion. — *v.* **switched, switch•ing, switch•es.** — *tr.* **1.** *Chiefly Southern U.S.* To whip with or as if with a switch, esp. in punishing a child. **2.** To jerk or swish abruptly or sharply. **3.** To shift, transfer, or divert. **4.** To exchange. **5.** To connect, disconnect, or divert (an electric current) by operating a switch. **6.** To cause (an electric current or appliance) to begin or cease operation: *switched the lights on.* **7.** *Informal.* To produce as if by operating a control. Often used with *on.* **8.** To move (rolling stock) from one track to another; shunt. — *intr.* **1.** To make or undergo a shift or an exchange. **2.** To swish sharply from side to side. [Prob. of LGer. or Flem. orig.] — **switch′a•ble** *adj.*

switch•back (swĭch′băk′) *n.* **1.** A road, trail, or railroad track that ascends a steep incline in a zigzag course. **2.** A sharp bend in a road or trail ascending a steep incline. **3.** *Chiefly British.* A roller coaster.

switch•blade (swĭch′blād′) *n.* A pocketknife with a spring-operated blade that opens when a release on the handle is pressed.

switch•board (swĭch′bôrd′, -bōrd′) *n.* **1.** One or more panels accommodating control switches and other apparatus for operating electric circuits. **2.** See **telephone exchange.**

switch•er•oo (swĭch′ə-ro͞o′) *n., pl.* **-oos.** *Slang.* An unexpected variation or reversal. [Alteration of SWITCH.]

switch hitter *n. Baseball.* A player who can bat either right-handed or left-handed. — **switch′-hit′** (swĭch′hĭt′) *v.*

switch knife *n.* See **switchblade.**

switch•man (swĭch′mən) *n.* A man who operates railroad switches.

switch•o•ver (swĭch′ō′vər) *n.* A complete shift, as from one system to another.

switch•yard (swĭch′yärd′) *n.* An area where railroad cars are switched and trains assembled.

Switz. *abbr.* Switzerland.

Swit•zer (swĭt′sər) *n.* A Swiss. [Ult. < MHGer. *Swīzer.* See SWISS.]

Swit•zer•land (swĭt′sər-lənd). A country of W-central Europe; became part of the Holy Roman Empire in the 10th cent. by 1499 achieved independence as a confederation of cantons. Cap. Bern. Pop. 6,455,900.

swiv•el (swĭv′əl) *n.* **1.** A link, pivot, or other fastening that permits the free turning of attached parts. **2.** A pivoted support that allows an attached object, such as a chair, to turn in a horizontal plane. **3.** A gun that turns on a pivot. — *v.* **-eled, -el•ing, -els** or **-elled, -el•ling, -els.** — *tr.* **1.** To turn or rotate on or as if on a swivel. **2.** To secure, fit, or support with a swivel. — *intr.* To turn on or as if on a swivel. [ME *swyvel.*]

swivel chair *n.* A chair that swivels on its base.

swiv•el-hipped (swĭv′əl-hĭpt′) *adj.* Characterized by an exaggerated swinging movement of the hips.

swiv•et (swĭv′ĭt) *n. Informal.* Extreme distress or discomposure. [?]

swiz•zle (swĭz′əl) *n.* Any of various tall mixed drinks usu. made with rum. [?]

swizzle stick *n.* A small thin rod for stirring mixed drinks.

swob (swŏb) *n. & v.* Var. of **swab.**

swol•len (swō′lən) *v.* A p.part. of **swell.** — *adj.* **1.** Expanded by or as if by internal pressure; distended: *a swollen toe.* **2.** Overblown; bombastic: *swollen rhetoric.*

swoon (swo͞on) *intr.v.* **swooned, swoon•ing, swoons. 1.** To faint. **2.** To be overwhelmed by ecstatic joy. — *n.* **1.** A fainting spell; syncope. **2.** A state of ecstasy or rapture. [ME *swounen,* prob. < *iswowen,* in a swoon < OE *geswōgen,* p.part. of **swōgan,* to suffocate.]

swoop (swo͞op) *v.* **swooped, swoop•ing, swoops.** — *intr.* **1.** To move in a sudden sweep. **2.** To make a rush or an attack with or as if with a sudden sweeping movement. Often used with *down.* — *tr.* To seize or snatch in or as if in a sudden sweeping movement. — *n.* The act or an instance of swooping. [ME *swopen,* to sweep along < OE *swāpan,* to sweep, swing.]

swoosh (swo͞osh, swo͝osh) *v.* **swooshed, swoosh•ing, swoosh•es.** — *intr.* **1.** To move with or make a rushing sound. **2.** To flow or swirl copiously. — *tr.* To cause to move with or make a rushing or swirling sound. [Imit.]

swop (swŏp) *v. & n.* Var. of **swap.**

sword (sôrd) *n.* **1.** A weapon consisting typically of a long straight or slightly curved pointed blade having one or two cutting edges and set into a hilt. **2.** An instrument of death or destruction. **3.a.** The use of force, as in war. **b.** Military power or jurisdiction. — ***idioms.* at swords' points.** Ready for a fight. **put to the sword.** To kill; slay. [ME < OE *sweord.*]

sword cane *n.* A cane with a hollow shaft in which a sword can be concealed.

sword dance *n.* A dance performed with swords, esp. one performed around swords laid on the ground.

sword fern *n.* Any of various ferns of the genus *Nephrolepis,* including the Boston fern, having bipinnately compound fronds and sori at the vein tips.

sword•fish (sôrd′fĭsh′) *n., pl.* **swordfish** or **-fish•es.** A large marine fish *(Xiphias gladius)* with a long swordlike extension of the upper jaw that serves as a weapon.

sword grass *n.* Any of various grasses or grasslike plants having pointed swordlike leaves.

sword knot *n.* A decorative loop or tassel on a sword hilt.

sword lily *n. Bot.* See **gladiolus** 1.

sword of Damocles *n.* Constant threat; imminent peril.

sword•play (sôrd′plā′) *n.* The act or art of using a sword.

swords•man (sôrdz′mən) *n.* **1.** A man who is skilled in the use of swords. **2.** A fencer. — **swords′man•ship′** *n.*

sword•tail (sôrd′tāl′) *n.* A small, brightly colored live-bearing freshwater fish *(Xiphophorus helleri)* of Central America having a long tapering extension of the caudal fin in the male.

swore (swôr, swōr) *v.* P.t. of **swear.**

sworn (swôrn, swōrn) *v.* P.part. of **swear.** — *adj.* **1.** Having been asserted as true under oath: *sworn statements.* **2.** Bound or empowered by an oath. **3.** Avowed: *a sworn friend.*

swum (swŭm) *v.* P.part. of **swim.**

swung (swŭng) *v.* P.t. and p.part. of **swing.**

swung dash *n. Print.* A character (~) used to stand for all or part of a word that has previously been spelled out.

Syb•a•ris (sĭb′ər-ĭs). An ancient Greek city of S Italy on the Gulf of Taranto; noted for its wealth and luxury.

Syb•a•rite (sĭb′ə-rīt′) *n.* **1.** Often **sybarite.** A person devoted to pleasure and luxury; a voluptuary. **2.** A native or inhabitant of Sybaris. [Lat. *Sybarīta,* native of Sybaris < Gk. *Subaritēs* < *Subaris,* Sybaris.] — **syb′a•rit•ism** (-rĭ-tĭz′əm) *n.*

syb•a•rit•ic (sĭb′ə-rĭt′ĭk) *adj.* **1.** Devoted to or marked by often excessive or effete luxury. **2. Sybaritic.** Of or relating to Sybaris or its people. — **syb′a•rit′i•cal•ly** *adv.*

syc•a•mine (sĭk′ə-mīn′, -mĭn) *n.* A tree mentioned in the Bible, thought to be a species of mulberry. [Lat. *sȳcamīnus* < Gk. *sukaminos,* of Semitic orig.]

syc•a•more (sĭk′ə-môr′, -mōr′) *n.* **1.** Any of various deciduous trees of the genus *Platanus,* esp. *P. occidentalis* of eastern North America, having palmately lobed leaves, ball-like, hairy fruit clusters, and bark that flakes off in large colorful patches. **2.** A Eurasian deciduous maple tree *(Acer pseudoplatanus)* having palmately lobed leaves, winged fruits, and greenish flowers. **3.** A fig tree *(Ficus sycomorus)* of Africa and adjacent southwest Asia, having clusters of figs borne on short leafless twigs. [ME *sicamour,* a kind of fig tree < OFr. *sicamor* < Lat. *sȳcomorus* < Gk. *sukomoros* : *sukon,* fruit of the fig + *moron,* black mulberry.]

syce (sīs) *n.* A stableman or groom, esp. in India. [Hindi *sā'is* < Ar. < *sāsa,* to administer.]

sy•cee (sī-sē′) *n.* Lumps of pure silver stamped by a banker or an assayer and formerly used in China as money. [Chin. (Cantonese) *sai sz,* fine silk.]

sy•co•ni•um (sī-kō′nē-əm) *n., pl.* **-ni•a** (-nē-ə). The fleshy multiple fruit of the fig, having an enlarged, hollow globose floral receptacle open at the apex. [NLat. < Gk. *sukon,* fig.]

syc•o•phan•cy (sĭk′ə-fən-sē, sī′kə-) *n., pl.* **-cies.** The fawning behavior of a sycophant; servile flattery.

syc•o•phant (sĭk′ə-fənt, sī′kə-) *n.* A servile self-seeker who seeks favor by flattering influential people. [Lat. *sȳcophanta,* informer, slanderer < Gk. *sukophantēs,* informer : *sukon,* fig + *-phantēs,* one who shows (< *phainein,* to show; see **bhā-**[1]*).] — **syc′o•phan′tic** (-făn′tĭk), **syc′o•phan′ti•cal** (-tĭ-kəl) *adj.* — **syc′o•phan•tism** *n.*

sy•co•sis (sī-kō′sĭs) *n.* A chronic inflammation of the hair fol-

FRANCE GERMANY LIECHTENSTEIN AUSTRIA Bern SWITZERLAND ITALY

Switzerland

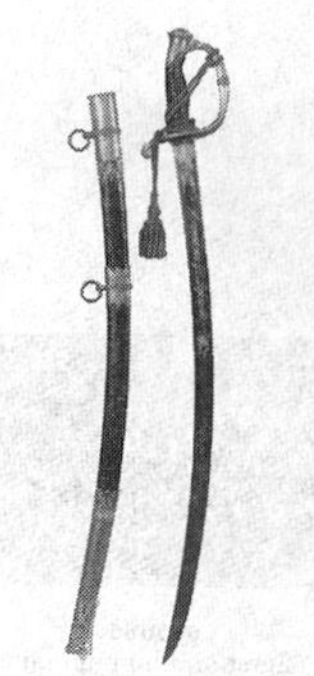

sword
Dress sword used by Lafayette

sycamore
American sycamore
Platanus occidentalis

ă pat	oi boy
ā pay	ou out
âr care	o͝o took
ä father	o͞o boot
ĕ pet	ŭ cut
ē be	ûr urge
ĭ pit	th thin
ī pie	*th* this
îr pier	hw which
ŏ pot	zh vision
ō toe	ə about, item
ô paw	

Stress marks:
′ (primary);
′ (secondary), as in dictionary (dĭk′shə-nĕr′ē)

licles, esp. of the beard, marked by eruption of pimples and nodules. [Gk. *sukōsis*, ulcer resembling a fig < *sukon*, fig.]

Syd•en•ham's chorea (sĭd′n-əmz) *n.* A nervous disorder occurring chiefly in childhood or during pregnancy, closely associated with rheumatic fever and characterized by rapid jerky involuntary movements of the body. [After Thomas *Sydenham* (1624–89), English physician.]

Syd•ney (sĭd′nē). **1.** A city of SE Australia on an inlet of the Tasman Sea. Met. area pop. 3,358,550. **2.** A city of Nova Scotia, Canada, on E Cape Breton I. Pop. 29,444.

sy•e•nite (sī′ə-nīt′) *n.* An igneous rock composed primarily of alkali feldspar. [Lat. *Syēnītēs (lapis)*, (stone) of Syene < *Syēnē*, Syene, an ancient city of S Egypt < Gk. *Suēnē*.] **— sy′e•nit′ic** (-nĭt′ĭk) *adj.*

syl. *abbr.* Syllable.

syll. *abbr.* Syllable.

syl•la•bar•y (sĭl′ə-bĕr′ē) *n., pl.* **-ies. 1.** A list of syllables. **2.** A list or set of written characters for a language, each character representing a syllable. [NLat. *syllabārium* < Lat. *syllaba*, syllable. See SYLLABLE.]

syl•lab•ic (sĭ-lăb′ĭk) *adj.* **1.** *Ling.* **a.** Of or consisting of a syllable or syllables. **b.** Being a consonant that forms a syllable without a vowel, such as the (l) in *riddle* (rĭd′l). **c.** Pronounced with every syllable distinct. **2.** Of or being a form of verse based on the number of syllables in a line rather than the arrangement of accents or quantities. *—n. Ling.* A syllabic sound. [Med.Lat. *syllabicus* < Gk. *sullabikos* < *sullabē*, syllable. See SYLLABLE.] **— syl•lab′i•cal•ly** *adv.*

syl•lab•i•fy (sĭ-lăb′ĭ-fī′) or **syl•lab•i•cate** (-kāt′) *tr.v.* **-fied** (-fīd′), **-fy•ing, -fies** (-fīz′) or **-cat•ed, -cat•ing** or **-cates.** To form or divide into syllables. **— syl•lab′i•fi•ca′tion** (-fĭ-kā′shən), **syl•lab′i•ca′tion** (-kā′shən) *n.*

symbiosis
Egret and hippopotamus

syl•la•bism (sĭl′ə-bĭz′əm) *n.* **1.** Division of a word or phrase into syllables. **2.** Use of syllabic characters in writing. [Lat. *syllaba*, syllable; see SYLLABLE + -ISM.]

syl•la•bize (sĭl′ə-bīz′) *tr.v.* **-bized, -biz•ing, -biz•es.** To syllabify. [Med.Lat. *syllabizāre*, to quibble < Gk. *sullabizein*, to syllabify < *sullabē*, syllable. See SYLLABLE.]

syl•la•ble (sĭl′ə-bəl) *n.* **1.** *Ling.* **a.** A unit of spoken language consisting of an uninterrupted sound formed by a vowel, diphthong, or syllabic consonant alone or by any of these sounds with one or more consonants. **b.** One or more written letters or phonetic symbols that approximate a spoken syllable. **2.** The slightest bit of spoken or written expression. *—tr.v.* **-bled, -bling, -bles.** *Ling.* To pronounce in syllables. [ME *sillable* < AN, alteration of OFr. *sillabe* < Lat. *syllaba* < Gk. *sullabē* < *sullabein*, second aorist of *sullambanein*, to combine in pronunciation : *sun-*, syn- + *lambanein*, to take.]

syl•la•bub also **sil•la•bub** (sĭl′ə-bŭb′) *n.* **1.** A drink made of sweetened milk or cream curdled with wine or spirits. **2.** A cold dessert made with sweetened cream thickened with gelatin and beaten with wine, spirits, or fruit juice. [?]

syl•la•bus (sĭl′ə-bəs) *n., pl.* **-bus•es** or **-bi** (-bī′). **1.** An outline or a summary of the main points of a text, lecture, or course of study. **2.** *Law.* A short statement preceding a report on an adjudged case and summarizing the court's rulings. [Med. Lat., prob. alteration (influenced by Gk. *sullambanein*, to put together; see SYLLABLE) of Lat. *sillybus*, parchment label < Gk. *sillubos*.]

syl•lep•sis (sĭ-lĕp′sĭs) *n., pl.* **-ses** (-sēz). A construction in which a word governs two or more other words but agrees in number, gender, or case with only one or has a different meaning when applied to each, as in *He lost his coat and his temper.* [LLat. *syllēpsis* < Gk. *sullēpsis* : *sun-*, syn- + *lēpsis*, a taking (< *lambanein*, to take).] **— syl•lep′tic** (-lĕp′tĭk) *adj.*

syl•lo•gism (sĭl′ə-jĭz′əm) *n.* **1.** *Logic.* A form of deductive reasoning consisting of a major premise, a minor premise, and a conclusion; for example, *All human beings are mortal,* the major premise, *I am a human being,* the minor premise, *therefore, I am mortal,* the conclusion. **2.** Reasoning from the general to the specific; deduction. **3.** A subtle or specious piece of reasoning. [ME *silogisme* < OFr. < Lat. *syllogismus* < Gk. *sullogismos* < *sullogizesthai*, to infer : *sun-*, syn- + *logizesthai*, to count, reckon (< *logos*, reason; see **leg-***).] **— syl′lo•gist** *n.* **— syl′lo•gis′tic, syl′lo•gis′ti•cal** *adj.*

syl•lo•gize (sĭl′ə-jīz′) *v.* **-gized, -giz•ing, -giz•es.** *—intr.* To reason or argue by syllogisms. *—tr.* To deduce by syllogism. **— syl′lo•gi•za′tion** (-jĭ-zā′shən) *n.* **— syl′lo•giz′er** *n.*

sylph (sĭlf) *n.* **1.** A slim graceful woman or girl. **2.** According to Paracelsus, any of a class of elemental soulless beings thought to inhabit the air. [NLat. *sylpha*, perh. blend of Lat. *sylvestris*, of the forest (< *silva, sylva*, forest) and Lat. *nympha*, nymph; see NYMPH.]

sylph•id (sĭl′fĭd) *n.* A young or diminutive sylph. *—adj.* Relating to or resembling a sylph. [Fr. *sylphide* < *sylphe*, sylph < NLat. *sylpha*. See SYLPH.]

syl•va (sĭl′və) *n.* Var. of **silva.**

syl•van also **sil•van** (sĭl′vən) *—adj.* **1.** Relating to or characteristic of woods or forest regions. **2.** Located in or inhabiting a wood or forest. **3.** Abounding in trees; wooded. *—n.* One that lives in or frequents the woods. [Med.Lat. *sylvānus* < Lat. *Silvānus*, god of the woods < *silva*, forest.]

Syl•va•nia (sĭl-vān′yə). A city of N OH on the MI border NW of Toledo. Pop. 17,301.

syl•van•ite (sĭl′və-nīt′) *n.* A pale yellow to silver-white ore of gold and silver, (Au,Ag)Te_2. [Fr., after TRANSYLVANIA.]

Syl•va•nus (sĭl-vā′nəs) *n. Rom. Myth.* Var. of **Silvanus.**

syl•vat•ic (sĭl-văt′ĭk) *adj.* **1.** Affecting only wild animals. **2.** Sylvan. [Lat. *sylvāticus*, wild < *silva, sylva*, forest.]

syl•vite (sĭl′vīt′) also **syl•vine** (-vēn′) or **syl•vin•ite** (-vĭ-nīt′) *n.* A colorless vitreous mineral, KCl, the major ore of potassium. [Alteration of *sylvine* < Fr. < NLat. *(sal digestivus) Sylvii*, (digestive salt) of Sylvius, prob. after Franciscus *Sylvius* (1614–72), Dutch physician.]

sym. *abbr.* **1.** Symbol. **2.** Symmetrical. **3.** *Mus.* Symphony.

sym– *pref.* Var. of **syn–.**

sym•bi•ont (sĭm′bē-ŏnt′, -bī-) *n.* An organism in a symbiotic relationship. [Gk. *sumbiōn, sumbiount-*, pr.part. of *sumbioun*, to live together. See SYMBIOSIS.] **— sym′bi•on′tic** *adj.*

sym•bi•o•sis (sĭm′bē-ō′sĭs, -bī-) *n., pl.* **-ses** (-sēz). **1.** *Biol.* A close prolonged association between two or more different organisms of different species. **2.** A relationship of mutual benefit or dependence. [Gk. *sumbiōsis*, companionship < *sumbioun*, to live together < *sumbios*, living together : *sun-*, syn- + *bios*, life; see **g^{w}ei-*.**] **— sym′bi•ot′ic** (-ŏt′ĭk), **sym′bi•ot′i•cal** (-ĭ-kəl) *adj.* **— sym′bi•ot′i•cal•ly** *adv.*

sym•bol (sĭm′bəl) *n.* **1.** One that represents something else by association, resemblance, or convention, esp. a material object representing something invisible. **2.** A printed or written sign used to represent an operation, an element, a quantity, a quality, or a relation, as in music. *—tr.v.* **-boled, -bol•ing, -bols.** To symbolize. [ME *symbole*, creed < OFr. < Lat. *symbolum*, token, mark < Gk. *sumbolon*, token for identification (by comparison with a counterpart) : *sun-*, syn- + *ballein*, to throw; see **g^{w}elə-*.**]

sym•bol•ic (sĭm-bŏl′ĭk) also **sym•bol•i•cal** (-ĭ-kəl) *adj.* **1.** Of, relating to, or expressed by means of symbols or a symbol. **2.** Serving as a symbol. **3.** Using symbolism: *symbolic art.* **— sym•bol′i•cal•ly** *adv.* **— sym•bol′i•cal•ness** *n.*

symbolic address *n. Comp. Sci.* An address expressed in symbolic form as a convenience to the programmer.

symbolic language *n. Comp. Sci.* A high-level programming language.

symbolic logic *n.* A treatment of formal logic in which a system of symbols is used to represent quantities and relationships.

sym•bol•ism (sĭm′bə-lĭz′əm) *n.* **1.** The practice of representing things by means of symbols or of attributing symbolic meanings or significance to objects, events, or relationships. **2.** A system of symbols or representations. **3.** A symbolic meaning or representation. **4.** Revelation or suggestion of intangible conditions or truths by artistic invention. **5. Symbolism.** The movement, theory, or practice of the late 19th-century Symbolists.

sym•bol•ist (sĭm′bə-lĭst) *n.* **1.** One who uses symbols or symbolism. **2.a.** One who interprets or represents conditions or truths with symbols or symbolism. **b.** Often **Symbolist.** Any of a group of chiefly French writers and artists of the late 19th century who expressed their ideas and emotions indirectly through symbols. *—adj.* **1.** Of or relating to symbolism. **2.** Often **Symbolist.** Of or relating to the Symbolists. **— sym′bol•is′tic** *adj.* **— sym′bol•is′ti•cal•ly** *adv.*

sym•bol•ize (sĭm′bə-līz′) *v.* **-ized, -iz•ing, -iz•es.** *—tr.* **1.** To serve as a symbol of. **2.** To represent or identify by a symbol. *—intr.* To use symbols. **— sym′bol•i•za′tion** (-bə-lĭ-zā′shən) *n.* **— sym′bol•iz′er** *n.*

sym•bol•o•gy (sĭm-bŏl′ə-jē) *n.* **1.** The study or interpretation of symbols or symbolism. **2.** The use of symbols.

sym•met•al•lism (sĭm-mĕt′l-ĭz′əm) *n.* A system of coinage in which a unit of currency is pegged to a combination of two or more metals in fixed proportions.

sym•met•ri•cal (sĭ-mĕt′rĭ-kəl) also **sym•met•ric** (-rĭk) *adj.* Of or exhibiting symmetry. **— sym•met′ri•cal•ly** *adv.*

symmetric matrix *n. Math.* A matrix that is its own transpose.

sym•me•trize (sĭm′ĭ-trīz′) *tr.v.* **-trized, -triz•ing, -triz•es.** To give symmetry to; make symmetrical or proportional. **— sym′me•tri•za′tion** (-trĭ-zā′shən) *n.*

sym•me•try (sĭm′ĭ-trē) *n., pl.* **-tries. 1.** Exact correspondence of form and constituent configuration on opposite sides of a dividing line or plane or about a center or an axis. See Syns at **proportion. 2.** A relationship of characteristic correspondence, equivalence, or identity among constituents of an entity or between different entities. **3.** Beauty as a result of balance or harmonious arrangement. [Lat. *symmetria* < Gk. *summetria* < *summetros*, of like measure : *sun-*, syn- + *metron*, measure; see **mē-[2]*.**]

Sym•onds (sĭm′əndz, sī′məndz), **John Addington.** 1840–93. British writer of *The Renaissance in Italy* (1875–86).

Sy•mons (sī′mənz), **Arthur.** 1865–1945. British writer whose works include *The Symbolist Movement in Literature* (1899).

sym•pa•thec•to•my (sĭm′pə-thĕk′tə-mē) *n., pl.* **-mies.** Surgical removal of a part of the sympathetic nervous system.

sym•pa•thet•ic (sĭm′pə-thĕt′ĭk) *adj.* **1.** Of, expressing, feeling, or resulting from sympathy. **2.** Favorably inclined.

3. Agreeably suited to one's disposition or mood; congenial. **4.** Of, relating to, or acting on the sympathetic nervous system. **5.a.** Relating to or being vibrations, esp. musical tones, produced in one body by and at the same frequency as vibrations from a nearby body. **b.** Emitting such vibrations. [Gk. *sumpathētikos* < *sumpatheia*, sympathy. See SYMPATHY.] —**sym'pa·thet'i·cal·ly** *adv.*

sympathetic ink *n.* See **invisible ink.**

sympathetic nervous system *n. Anat.* The part of the autonomic nervous system originating in the thoracic and lumbar regions of the spinal cord that inhibits or opposes the physiological effects of the parasympathetic nervous system, as in speeding up the heart and contracting blood vessels.

sym·pa·thize (sĭm'pə-thīz') *intr.v.* **-thized, -thiz·ing, -thiz·es. 1.** To feel or express compassion, as for another's suffering; commiserate. **2.** To share or understand the feelings or ideas of another. **3.** To be in accord; correspond. —**sym'pa·thiz'er** *n.* —**sym'pa·thiz'ing·ly** *adv.*

sym·pa·tho·lyt·ic (sĭm'pə-thō-lĭt'ĭk) *adj.* Opposing the physiological effects caused by stimulation of the sympathetic nervous system. [SYMPATH(ETIC) + -LYTIC.]

sym·pa·tho·mi·met·ic (sĭm'pə-thō-mĭ-mĕt'ĭk, -mī-) *adj.* Producing physiological effects resembling those caused by the sympathetic nervous system. —*n.* A sympathomimetic drug or agent. [SYMPATH(ETIC) + MIMETIC.]

sym·pa·thy (sĭm'pə-thē) *n., pl.* **-thies. 1.a.** A relationship or an affinity between people or things in which whatever affects one correspondingly affects the other. **b.** Mutual understanding or affection arising from this relationship or affinity. **2.a.** The act or power of sharing the feelings of another. **b.** A feeling or an expression of pity or sorrow for the distress of another; compassion or commiseration. Often used in the plural. **3.** Harmonious agreement; accord. **4.** A feeling of loyalty; allegiance. Often used in the plural. **5.** *Physiol.* A relation between parts or organs by which a disease or disorder in one induces an effect in the other. [Lat. *sympathīa* < Gk. *sumpatheia* < *sumpathēs*, affected by like feelings : *sun-*, syn- + *pathos*, emotion; see **kʷent(h)-*.**]

sympathy strike *n.* A strike by a body of workers for the purpose of supporting a cause or another group of strikers.

sym·pat·ric (sĭm-păt'rĭk) *adj. Ecol.* Occupying the same or overlapping geographic areas without interbreeding. Used of populations of closely related species. [SYN- + Gk. *patra*, fatherland (< *patēr*, father; see **pəter-***) + -IC.] —**sym·pat'ri·cal·ly** *adv.* —**sym'pat'ry** (sĭm'păt'rē, -pə-trē) *n.*

sym·pet·al·ous (sĭm-pĕt'l-əs) *adj.* Having united petals; gamopetalous.

sym·phon·ic (sĭm-fŏn'ĭk) *adj.* **1.** *Mus.* Relating to, being, or similar to a symphony. **2.** Harmonious in sound.

symphonic poem *n. Mus.* A piece of music, popular in the late 19th century, based on an extramusical theme and consisting of a single extended movement for a symphony orchestra.

sym·pho·ni·ous (sĭm-fō'nē-əs) *adj.* Being in a state of accord; harmonious. —**sym·pho'ni·ous·ly** *adv.*

sym·pho·nist (sĭm'fə-nĭst) *n. Mus.* One who composes symphonies.

sym·pho·ny (sĭm'fə-nē) *n., pl.* **-nies. 1.** *Mus.* **a.** An extended piece for symphony orchestra in three or more independent movements varying in key, mood, and tempo. **b.** An instrumental passage in a vocal or choral composition. **c.** An instrumental overture or interlude, as in early opera. **2.** *Mus.* **a.** A symphony orchestra. **b.** An orchestral concert. **3.** Harmony, esp. of sound or color. **4.** Something marked by a harmonious combination of elements. [ME *symphonye*, harmony < OFr. *symphonie* < Lat. *symphōnia* < Gk. *sumphōnia* < *sumphōnos*, harmonious : *sun-*, syn- + *phōnē*, sound; see **bhā-²*.**]

symphony orchestra *n. Mus.* A large orchestra composed of string, wind, and percussion sections.

sym·phy·sis (sĭm'fĭ-sĭs) *n., pl.* **-ses** (-sēz'). **1.a.** A growing together of bones originally separate, as of the two pubic bones. **b.** A line or junction thus formed. **c.** An articulation in which bones are united by cartilage without a synovial membrane. **2.** The coalescence of similar parts or organs. [Gk. *sumphusis* < *sumphuein*, to cause to grow together : *sun-*, syn- + *phuein*, to cause to grow; see **bheuə-*.**] —**sym'phy·se'al** (sĭm'-fĭ-sē'əl), **sym·phys'i·al** (sĭm-fĭz'ē-əl) *adj.*

sym·po·di·um (sĭm-pō'dē-əm) *n., pl.* **-di·a** (-dē-ə). *Bot.* A primary axis that develops from a series of short lateral branches, as in the grapevine. [NLat. : SYN- + Gk. *podion*, base (< *pous*, *pod-*, foot; see **ped-***).]

sym·po·si·ac (sĭm-pō'zē-ăk') *adj.* Of, relating to, or appropriate to a symposium. —*n. Archaic.* A symposium.

sym·po·si·arch (sĭm-pō'zē-ärk') *n.* **1.** The master or director of a symposium, esp. one in ancient Greece. **2.** A toastmaster. [Gk. *sumposiarkhos* : *sumposion*, symposium; see SYMPOSIUM + *arkhos*, ruler; see -ARCH.]

sym·po·si·ast (sĭm-pō'zē-ăst', -əst) *n.* A participant in a symposium.

sym·po·si·um (sĭm-pō'zē-əm) *n., pl.* **-si·ums** or **-si·a** (-zē-ə). **1.** A meeting or conference for discussion of a topic, esp. one in which the participants form an audience and make presentations. **2.** A collection of writings on a particular topic, as in a magazine. **3.** A convivial meeting for drinking, music, and intellectual discussion among the ancient Greeks. [Lat., drinking party < Gk. *sumposion* : *sun-*, syn- + *posis*, drinking; see **pō(i)-*.**]

symp·tom (sĭm'təm, sĭmp'-) *n.* **1.** A characteristic sign or indication of the existence of something else. **2.** A sign or an indication of disorder or disease, esp. when experienced by an individual as a change from normal function, sensation, or appearance. [Alteration (influenced by LLat. *symptōma*) of ME *sinthoma*, symptom of a disease < Med.Lat. *sinthōma* < LLat. *symptōma* < Gk. *sumptōma*, *sumptōmat-*, a happening, symptom of a disease < *sumpiptein*, to coincide : *sun-*, syn- + *piptein*, to fall; see **pet-*.**]

symp·to·mat·ic (sĭm'tə-măt'ĭk, sĭmp'-) *adj.* **1.** Of, relating to, or based on symptoms. **2.** Being a symptom, as of a disease. —**symp'to·mat'i·cal·ly** *adv.*

symp·to·ma·tol·o·gy (sĭm'tə-mə-tŏl'ə-jē, sĭmp'-) *n.* **1.** The medical science of symptoms. **2.** The combined symptoms of a disease. [NLat. *symptōmatologia* : Gk. *sumptōma*, *sumptōmat-*, symptom; see SYMPTOM + Lat. *-logia*, -logy.] —**symp'to·mat'o·log'i·cal** (-măt'l-ŏj'ĭ-kəl) *adj.*

symp·tom·ize (sĭm'tə-mīz', sĭmp'-) or **symp·tom·a·tize** (-tə-mə-tīz') *tr.v.* **-ized, -iz·ing, -iz·es** or **-tized, -tiz·ing, -tiz·es.** To be a symptom of (a disease, for example).

syn. *abbr.* Synonym; synonymous; synonymy.

syn– or **sym–** *pref.* **1.a.** Together; with: *synecology.* **b.** United: *syncarp.* **2.a.** Same; similar: *sympatric.* **b.** At the same time: *synesthesia.* [Gk. *sun-* < *sun.* See **ksun*.**]

syn·aer·e·sis (sĭ-nĕr'ĭ-sĭs) *n.* Var. of **syneresis.**

syn·aes·the·sia (sĭn'ĭs-thē'zhə) *n.* Var. of **synesthesia.**

synagogue
Temple Ohabei Shalom, Brookline, Massachusetts

syn·a·gogue also **syn·a·gog** (sĭn'ə-gŏg', -gôg') *n.* **1.** A place of meeting for worship and religious instruction in the Jewish faith. **2.** A congregation of Jews for the purpose of worship or religious study. **3.** Judaism as organized or typified in local congregations. [ME < OFr. *sinagoge* < LLat. *synagōga* < Gk. *sunagōgē*, assembly, synagogue < *sunagein*, to bring together : *sun-*, syn- + *agein*, to lead; see **ag-*.**] —**syn'a·gog'i·cal** (-gŏj'ĭ-kəl), **syn'a·gog'al** (-gŏg'əl, -gôg'-) *adj.*

syn·a·le·pha also **syn·a·loe·pha** (sĭn'ə-lē'fə) *n.* The blending into one syllable of two successive vowels of adjacent syllables, esp. to fit a poetic meter; for example, *th' elite* for *the elite.* [NLat. < Gk. *sunaloiphē* < *sunaleiphein*, to unite two syllables : *sun-*, syn- + *aleiphein*, to smear; see **leip-*.**]

syn·apse (sĭn'ăps', sĭ-năps') *n.* The junction across which a nerve impulse passes from an axon terminal to a neuron, a muscle cell, or a gland cell. —*intr.v.* **-apsed, -aps·ing, -aps·es. 1.** To form a synapse. **2.** To undergo synapsis. [Gk. *sunapsis*, point of contact < *sunaptein*, to join together : *sun-*, syn- + *haptein*, to fasten.]

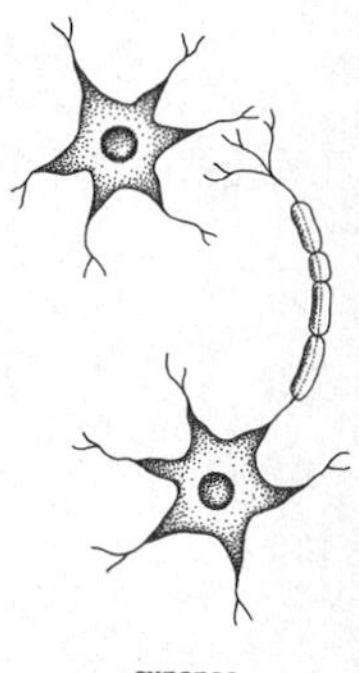
synapse

syn·ap·sis (sĭ-năp'sĭs) *n., pl.* **-ses** (-sēz). The side-by-side association of homologous paternal and maternal chromosomes during the early prophase of meiosis. [NLat. < Gk. *sunapsis*, point of contact. See SYNAPSE.]

syn·ap·tic (sĭ-năp'tĭk) *adj.* Of or relating to synapsis or a synapse. [< Gk. *sunaptos*, joined together < *sunaptein*, to join together. See SYNAPSE.] —**syn·ap'ti·cal·ly** *adv.*

syn·ap·to·some (sĭ-năp'tə-sōm') *n.* A saclike structure formed by nerve endings at a synapse that remains intact after homogenization of nerve tissue. —**syn·ap'to·so'mal** *adj.*

syn·ar·thro·sis (sĭn'är-thrō'sĭs) *n., pl.* **-ses** (-sēz). *Anat.* A form of articulation in which the bones are rigidly joined by fibrous tissue. [Gk. < *sunarthrousthai*, to be joined by articulation : *sun-*, syn- + *arthron*, a joint; see **ar-*.**]

sync or **synch** (sĭngk) *Informal.* —*n.* **1.** Synchronization. **2.** Harmony; accord. —*intr. & tr.v.* **synced, sync·ing, syncs** or **synched, synch·ing, synchs.** To synchronize.

syn·car·pous (sĭn-kär'pəs) *adj.* Having or consisting of united carpels. Used of a pistil. —**syn'car·py** *n.*

syn·chro (sĭng'krō, sĭn'-) *n., pl.* **-chros.** A selsyn.

synchro– *pref.* Synchronized; synchronous: *synchrotron.*

syn·chro·cy·clo·tron (sĭng'krō-sī'klə-trŏn', sĭn'-) *n.* A cyclotron that accelerates protons and positive ions by synchronizing the frequency of the accelerating potential with the frequency of the accelerated particles to compensate for increases in particle mass at relativistic speeds.

syn·chro·flash (sĭng'krō-flăsh', sĭn'-) *n.* A device used in photography to synchronize the peak of a flash with the opening of the camera shutter. —**syn'chro·flash'** *adj.*

syn·chro·mesh (sĭng'krə-mĕsh', sĭn'-) *n.* **1.** An automotive gear-shifting system in which the gears are synchronized at the same speeds before engaging to effect a smooth shift. **2.** A gear in such a system. —**syn'chro·mesh'** *adj.*

syn·chro·nal (sĭng'krə-nəl, sĭn'-) *adj.* Synchronous.

syn·chron·ic (sĭn-krŏn'ĭk, sĭng-) *adj.* **1.** Synchronous. **2.a.** Of or relating to the study of language at a given point in time without regard to its historical development. **b.** Relating to or being the study of events of a particular time or era without reference to historical context. —**syn·chron'i·cal·ly** *adv.*

syn·chro·nic·i·ty (sĭng'krə-nĭs'ĭ-tē, sĭn'-) *n., pl.* **-ties. 1.** The state or fact of being synchronous or simultaneous; synchronism. **2.** Coincidence of events that seem to be meaningfully

ă pat	oi boy
ā pay	ou out
âr care	o͝o took
ä father	o͞o boot
ĕ pet	ŭ cut
ē be	ûr urge
ĭ pit	th thin
ī pie	*th* this
îr pier	hw which
ŏ pot	zh vision
ō toe	ə about, item
ô paw	

Stress marks:
' (primary);
' (secondary), as in
dictionary (dĭk'shə-nĕr'ē)

related, conceived in the theory of Carl Jung as an explanatory principle on the same order as causality.

synchronic linguistics *n. (used with a sing. v.)* Descriptive linguistics.

syn•chro•nism (sĭng′krə-nĭz′əm, sĭn′-) *n.* **1.** Coincidence in time; simultaneousness. **2.** A chronological listing of historical personages or events so as to indicate parallel existence or occurrence. **3.** Representation in the same artwork of events that occurred at different times. —**syn′chro•nis′tic, syn′chro•nis′ti•cal** (-tĭ-kəl) *adj.* —**syn′chro•nis′ti•cal•ly** *adv.*

syn•chro•nize (sĭng′krə-nīz′, sĭn′-) *v.* **-nized, -niz•ing, -niz•es.** —*intr.* **1.** To be simultaneous. **2.** To operate in unison. —*tr.* **1.a.** To cause to occur or operate with exact coincidence in time or rate. **b.** To cause to occur or operate at the same time as something else. **2.** To arrange (historical events) in a synchronism so as to indicate parallel occurrence. **3.** To cause (soundtrack and action) to match exactly in a film. [Gk. *sunkhronizein*, to be contemporary < *sunkhronos*, contemporaneous. See SYNCHRONOUS.] —**syn′chro•ni•za′tion** (-nĭ-zā′shən) *n.*

syn•chro•nized swimming (sĭng′krə-nīzd′, sĭn′-) *n. Sports.* A sport or an exhibition in which swimmers, singly or in groups, perform dancelike movements often to music.

syn•chro•niz•er (sĭng′krə-nī′zər, sĭn′-) *n.* **1.** One that synchronizes. **2.** *Comp. Sci.* A storage device that compensates for a difference between the rates at which information is processed in two or more devices.

syn•chro•nous (sĭng′krə-nəs, sĭn′-) *adj.* **1.** Occurring or existing at the same time. **2.** Moving or operating at the same rate. **3.a.** Having identical periods. **b.** Having identical period and phase. [< LLat. *synchronus* < Gk. *sunkhronos* : *sun-*, syn- + *khronos*, time.] —**syn′chro•nous•ly** *adv.* —**syn′chro•nous•ness** *n.*

synchronous motor *n.* A motor with a speed directly proportional to the frequency of its alternating current power.

synchronous orbit *n.* A geostationary orbit.

syn•chro•ny (sĭng′krə-nē, sĭn′-) *n., pl.* **-nies.** Simultaneous occurrence; synchronism. [< SYNCHRONOUS.]

syn•chro•tron (sĭng′krə-trŏn′, sĭn′-) *n.* An accelerator in which charged particles are accelerated around a fixed circular path by an electric field and held to the path by an increasing magnetic field.

synchrotron radiation *n.* Electromagnetic radiation emitted by high-energy particles when accelerated to relativistic speeds in a magnetic field.

syn•cli•nal (sĭn-klī′nəl) *adj.* **1.** Sloping downward from opposite directions to meet in a common point or line. **2.** *Geol.* Relating to, formed by, or forming a syncline.

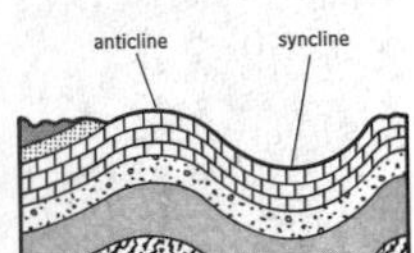

syncline

syn•cline (sĭn′klīn′) *n. Geol.* A fold in rocks in which the rock layers dip inward from both sides toward the axis.

syn•co•pate (sĭng′kə-pāt′, sĭn′-) *tr.v.* **-pat•ed, -pat•ing, -pates. 1.** *Gram.* To shorten (a word) by syncope. **2.** *Mus.* To modify (rhythm) by syncopation. [LLat. *syncopāre*, *syncopāt-* < *syncopē*, syncope. See SYNCOPE.] —**syn′co•pa′tor** *n.*

syn•co•pa•tion (sĭng′kə-pā′shən, sĭn′-) *n.* **1.** *Mus.* A shift of accent in a passage or composition that occurs when a normally weak beat is stressed. **2.** Something, such as rhythm, that is syncopated. **3.** *Gram.* Syncope.

syn•co•pe (sĭng′kə-pē, sĭn′-) *n.* **1.** *Gram.* The shortening of a word by omission of a sound, letter, or syllable from the middle of the word; for example, *bos'n* for *boatswain*. **2.** *Pathol.* A brief loss of consciousness due to a temporary deficiency of oxygen in the brain. [Ult. < LLat. *syncopē* < Gk. *sunkopē* < *sunkoptein*, to cut short : *sun-*, syn- + *koptein*, to strike.] —**syn′co•pal** (sĭng′kə-pəl, sĭn′-), **syn•cop′ic** (sĭn-kŏp′ĭk) *adj.*

syncopation
From Mozart's
Symphony no. 25

syn•cre•tism (sĭng′krĭ-tĭz′əm, sĭn′-) *n.* **1.** Reconciliation or fusion of differing systems of belief, esp. with partial success or a heterogeneous result. **2.** *Ling.* The merging of two or more originally different inflectional forms. [Gk. *sunkrētismos*, union < *sunkrētizein*, to unite (in the manner of the Cretan cities) : *sun-*, syn- + *Krēs*, *Krēt-*, Cretan.] —**syn•cret′ic** (-krĕt′ĭk), **syn′cre•tis′tic** (-krĭ-tĭs′tĭk) *adj.* —**syn′cre•tist** *n.*

syn•cre•tize (sĭng′krĭ-tīz′, sĭn′-) *v.* **-tized, -tiz•ing, -tiz•es.** —*tr.* To reconcile and unite (differing religious beliefs, for example), esp. with partial success or a heterogeneous result. —*intr.* To syncretize differing elements or beliefs. [Gk. *sunkrētizein*, to unite against a common enemy. See SYNCRETISM.]

syn•cy•ti•um (sĭn-sĭsh′ē-əm) *n., pl.* **-cy•ti•a** (-sĭsh′ē-ə). A mass of cytoplasm with many nuclei but no internal cell boundaries. [NLat. : SYN– + CYT(O)– + –IUM.]

synd. *abbr.* Syndicate.

syn•dac•tyl (sĭn-dăk′təl) *Biol. n.* An animal, esp. a bird or mammal, that has two or more fused digits. [Fr. *syndactyle* : Gk. *sun-*, syn- + Gk. *daktulos*, finger.] —**syn•dac′tyl, syn•dac′ty•lous** (-tə-ləs) *adj.*

syn•dac•ty•ly (sĭn-dăk′tə-lē) or **syn•dac•tyl•ism** (-tə-lĭz′əm) *n. Biol.* **1.** The condition of having two or more fused digits, as occurs normally in certain mammals and birds. **2.** A congenital anomaly in human beings characterized by two or more fused fingers or toes.

syn•des•mo•sis (sĭn′dĕz-mō′sĭs, -dĕs-) *n., pl.* **-ses** (-sēz). An articulation in which the bones are joined by a ligament. [NLat. < Gk. *sundesmos*, bond, ligament < *sundein*, to bind together. See SYNDETIC.] —**syn′des•mot′ic** (-mŏt′ĭk) *adj.*

syn•det•ic (sĭn-dĕt′ĭk) *adj.* **1.** Serving to connect, as a conjunction; copulative or conjunctive. **2.** Connected by a conjunction. [Gk. *sundetikos* < *sundetos*, bound together < *sundein*, to bind together : *sun-*, syn- + *dein*, to bind.]

syn•dic (sĭn′dĭk) *n.* **1.** One appointed to represent an organization in business transactions; a business agent. **2.** A civil magistrate or similar government official in some European countries. [Fr. < OFr. *sindiz* < LLat. *syndicus* < Gk. *sundikos*, public advocate : *sun-*, syn- + *dikē*, justice; see **deik-***.] —**syn′di•cal** *adj.*

syn•di•cal•ism (sĭn′dĭ-kə-lĭz′əm) *n.* A radical political movement that advocates bringing industry and government under the control of federations of labor unions by the use of direct action, such as general strikes and sabotage. [Fr. *syndicalisme* < *(chambre) syndicale*, trade union, fem. of *syndical*, of a labor union < *syndic*, delegate. See SYNDIC.] —**syn′di•cal•ist** *adj. & n.* —**syn′di•cal•is′tic** *adj.*

syn•di•cate (sĭn′dĭ-kĭt) *n.* **1.** An association of people or firms authorized to undertake a duty or transact specific business. **2.** An association of people or firms formed to engage in an enterprise or promote a common interest. **3.** A loose affiliation of gangsters in control of organized criminal activities. **4.** An agency that sells articles, features, or photographs for publication in a number of newspapers or periodicals simultaneously. **5.** A company consisting of a number of separate newspapers; a newspaper chain. **6.** The office, position, or jurisdiction of a syndic or body of syndics. —*v.* (-kāt′) **-cat•ed, -cat•ing, -cates.** —*tr.* **1.a.** To organize into or manage as a syndicate. **b.** To sell shares in. **2.** To sell (an article, feature, or photograph) through a syndicate. **3.** To sell (a television series, for example) directly to independent stations. —*intr.* To join together in a syndicate. [Fr. *syndicat* < OFr., office of syndic < Med.Lat. *syndicātus* < LLat. *syndicus*, syndic. See SYNDIC.] —**syn′di•ca′tion** *n.* —**syn′di•ca′tor** *n.*

syn•drome (sĭn′drōm′) *n.* **1.** A group of symptoms that collectively indicate or characterize a disease or another abnormal condition. **2.a.** A complex of symptoms indicating the existence of an undesirable condition or quality. **b.** A distinctive or characteristic pattern of behavior. [Gk. *sundromē*, concurrence of symptoms < *sundromos*, running together : *sun-*, syn- + *dromos*, a running.] —**syn•drom′ic** (-drō′mĭk, -drŏm′ĭk) *adj.*

syne (sīn) *Scots.* —*adv.* **1.** Before now; ago. **2.** Afterward; since then; since. **3.** Thereupon; next. —*conj.* Since. —*prep.* Since. [Sc. < ME *sitthen* < OE *siththan*.]

syn•ec•do•che (sĭ-nĕk′də-kē) *n.* A figure of speech in which a part is used for the whole (as *hand* for *sailor*), the whole for a part (as *the law* for *police officer*), the specific for the general (as *cutthroat* for *assassin*), the general for the specific (as *thief* for *pickpocket*), or the material for the thing made from it (as *steel* for *sword*). [Ult. < Lat. *synecdochē* < Gk. *sunekdokhē* < *sunekdekhesthai*, to take on a share of : *sun-*, syn- + *ekdekhesthai*, to understand (*ek-*, out of; see **eghs*** + *dekhesthai*, to take; see **dek-***).] —**syn′ec•doch′ic** (sĭn′ĕk-dŏk′ĭk), **syn′ec•doch′i•cal** (-ĭ-kəl) *adj.*

syn•e•col•o•gy (sĭn′ĭ-kŏl′ə-jē) *n.* The study of the ecological interrelationships among communities of organisms. —**syn′e•co•log′ic** (-kə-lŏj′ĭk), **syn′e•co•log′i•cal** (-ĭ-kəl) *adj.*

syn•er•e•sis also **syn•aer•e•sis** (sĭ-nĕr′ĭ-sĭs) *n., pl.* **-ses** (-sēz′). **1.** *Ling.* The combining into one syllable of two consecutive vowels or syllables, as in a diphthong. **2.** *Chem.* Exudation of the liquid component of a gel. [LLat. *synaeresis* < Gk. *sunairesis* < *sunairein*, to contract : *sun-*, syn- + *hairein*, to take, grasp.]

syn•er•get•ic (sĭn′ər-jĕt′ĭk) also **syn•er•gic** (sĭ-nûr′jĭk) *adj.* Synergistic.

syn•er•gid (sĭ-nûr′jĭd, sĭn′ər-) *n.* One of two small cells lying near the egg in the embryo sac of a flowering plant. [NLat. *synergida* < Gk. *sunergos*, working together. See SYNERGISM.]

syn•er•gism (sĭn′ər-jĭz′əm) *n.* **1.** Synergy. **2.** *Theol.* The doctrine that individual salvation is achieved through a combination of human will and divine grace. [NLat. *synergismus* < Gk. *sunergos*, working together : *sun-*, syn- + *ergon*, work; see **werg-***.]

syn•er•gist (sĭn′ər-jĭst) *n.* **1.** A synergistic organ, drug, or agent. **2.** *Theol.* An adherent of synergism.

syn•er•gis•tic (sĭn′ər-jĭs′tĭk) *adj.* **1.** Of or relating to synergy. **2.** Producing or capable of producing synergy. **3.** *Theol.* Of or relating to synergism. —**syn′er•gis′ti•cal•ly** *adv.*

syn•er•gy (sĭn′ər-jē) *n., pl.* **-gies. 1.** The interaction of two or more agents or forces so that their combined effect is greater than the sum of their individual effects. **2.** Cooperative interaction among groups, such as corporate subsidiaries, that creates an enhanced combined effect. [< Gk. *sunergia*, cooperation < *sunergos*, working together. See SYNERGISM.]

syn•e•sis (sĭn′ĭ-sĭs) *n.* A construction in which a form, such as a pronoun, differs in number but agrees in meaning with the word governing it, as in *If the group is too large, split them* *in two.* [Gk. *sunesis*, union, understanding < *sunienai*, to bring together : *sun-*, syn- + *hienai*, to send, hurl; see **yē-***.]

syn•es•the•sia also **syn•aes•the•sia** (sĭn′ĭs-thē′zhə) *n.* **1.** A condition in which one type of stimulation evokes the sensation of another, as when the hearing of a sound produces the visualization of a color. **2.** A sensation felt in one part of the body as a result of a stimulus applied to another, as in referred pain. **3.** The description of one kind of sense impression by using words that normally describe another. **— syn′es•thet′ic** (-thĕt′ĭk) *adj.*

syn•es•thete (sĭn′ĭs-thēt′) *n.* A person who experiences synesthesia, as by having a secondary sensation of sound as color.

syn•fu•el (sĭn′fyo͞o′əl) *n.* A liquid or gaseous fuel derived from coal, shale, or tar sand or obtained by fermentation of certain substances, such as grain. [SYN(THETIC) + FUEL.]

syn•ga•my (sĭng′gə-mē) *n.* The fusion of two gametes in fertilization. **— syn•gam′ic** (sĭn-găm′ĭk), **syn′ga•mous** (sĭng′gə-məs) *adj.*

Synge (sĭng), **John Millington.** 1871–1909. Irish playwright whose works, based on rural Irish life, include *The Playboy of the Western World* (1907).

Synge, Richard Laurence Millington. b. 1914. British biochemist who shared a 1952 Nobel Prize.

syn•i•ze•sis (sĭn′ĭ-zē′sĭs) *n., pl.* **-ses** (-sēz). *Ling.* The union in pronunciation of two adjacent vowels into one syllable without forming a diphthong. [LLat. *synizēsis* < Gk. *sunizēsis* < *sunizein*, to collapse : *sun-*, syn- + *hizein*, to settle down; see **sed-***.]

syn•kar•y•on (sĭn-kăr′ē-ŏn′, -ē-ən) *n.* The nucleus of a fertilized egg immediately after the male and female nuclei have fused. [SYN- + Gk. *karuon*, nut, seed; see **kar-***.]

syn•od (sĭn′əd) *n.* **1.** An ecclesiastical council or assembly. **2.** A council or an assembly. [ME < Lat. *synodus* < Gk. *sunodos*, meeting, assembly : *sun-*, syn- + *hodos*, way, course.] **— syn′od•al** (sĭn′ə-dl) *adj.*

syn•od•ic (sĭ-nŏd′ĭk) or **syn•od•i•cal** (-nŏd′ĭ-kəl) *adj.* **1.** Of or relating to a synod; synodal. **2.** Relating to the conjunction of celestial bodies, esp. the interval between two successive conjunctions of a planet or the moon with the sun.

synodic month *n.* See **lunar month.**

syn•o•nym (sĭn′ə-nĭm′) *n.* **1.** A word having the same or nearly the same meaning as another word or other words in a language. **2.** A word or an expression that serves as a figurative or symbolic substitute for another. **3.** *Biol.* An obsolete taxonomic name. [ME *sinonyme* < OFr. *synonyme* < Lat. *synōnymum* < Gk. *sunōnumon* < neut. of *sunōnumos*, synonymous. See SYNONYMOUS.] **— syn′o•nym′ic, syn′o•nym′i•cal** *adj.* **— syn′o•nym′i•ty** *n.*

syn•on•y•mize (sĭ-nŏn′ə-mīz′) *tr.v.* **-mized, -miz•ing, -miz•es.** To analyze or provide the synonyms of (words or a word).

syn•on•y•mous (sĭ-nŏn′ə-məs) *adj.* **1.** Having the same or a similar meaning. **2.** Equivalent in connotation. [Med.Lat. *synōnymus* < Gk. *sunōnumos* : *sun-*, syn- + *onoma, onuma*, name; see **nō-men-***.] **— syn•on′y•mous•ly** *adv.*

syn•on•y•my (sĭ-nŏn′ə-mē) *n., pl.* **-mies.** **1.** The quality of being synonymous; equivalence of meaning. **2.** Study and classification of synonyms. **3.** A list, book, or system of synonyms. **4.** *Biol.* A list or record of the scientific names that have been applied to a taxonomic group.

syn•op•sis (sĭ-nŏp′sĭs) *n., pl.* **-ses** (-sēz). A brief outline or general view; an abstract; a summary. [LLat. < Gk. *sunopsis*, general view : *sun-*, syn- + *opsis*, view; see **ok^{w}-***.]

syn•op•size (sĭ-nŏp′sīz′) *tr.v.* **-sized, -siz•ing, -siz•es.** To make a synopsis of; summarize. [Gk. *sunopsizein*, to sum up < *sunopsis*, general view. See SYNOPSIS.]

syn•op•tic (sĭ-nŏp′tĭk) also **syn•op•ti•cal** (-tĭ-kəl) *adj.* **1.** Of or constituting a synopsis; presenting a summary of the principal parts or a general view of the whole. **2.a.** Taking the same point of view. **b.** Often **Synoptic.** Relating to or being the first three gospels of the New Testament, which correspond closely. [Gk. *sunoptikos* < *sunopsis*, general view. See SYNOPSIS.] **— syn•op′ti•cal•ly** *adv.*

syn•os•to•sis (sĭn′ŏs-tō′sĭs) *n., pl.* **-ses** (-sēz). The fusion of normally separate skeletal bones. [SYN- + Gk. *osteon*, bone; see **ost-*** + -OSIS.] **— syn′os•tot′ic** (-tŏt′ĭk) *adj.*

syn•o•vi•a (sĭ-nō′vē-ə) *n.* A clear viscid lubricating fluid secreted by membranes in joint cavities, sheaths of tendons, and bursae. [NLat.] **— syn•o′vi•al** *adj.*

sy•no•vi•tis (sī′nə-vī′tĭs) *n.* Inflammation of a synovial membrane. [NLat. *synovium*, synovia-secreting membrane (< SYNOVIA) + -ITIS.]

syn•sep•al•ous (sĭn-sĕp′ə-ləs) *adj. Bot.* Having united sepals; gamosepalous.

syn•tac•tic (sĭn-tăk′tĭk) or **syn•tac•ti•cal** (-tĭ-kəl) *adj.* **1.** Of or relating to the rules of syntax. **2.** Conforming to accepted patterns of syntax. [Gk. *suntaktikos*, putting together < *suntaktos*, constructed < *suntassein*, to construct. See SYNTAX.] **— syn•tac′ti•cal•ly** *adv.*

syn•tac•tics (sĭn-tăk′tĭks) *n. (used with a sing. v.)* The branch of semiotics that deals with the formal properties of signs and symbols. [< SYNTACTIC.]

syn•tax (sĭn′tăks′) *n.* **1.a.** The study of the rules for forming grammatical sentences. **b.** A publication, such as a book, that presents such rules. **c.** The pattern of formation of sentences or phrases in a language. **d.** Such a pattern in a particular sentence or discourse. **2.** *Comp. Sci.* The rules governing construction of a machine language. **3.** A systematic orderly arrangement. [Fr. *syntaxe* < LLat. *syntaxis* < Gk. *suntaxis* < *suntassein*, put in order : *sun-*, syn- + *tassein*, *tag-*, to arrange.]

syn•the•sis (sĭn′thĭ-sĭs) *n., pl.* **-ses** (-sēz′). **1.a.** The combining of separate elements or substances to form a coherent whole. **b.** The complex whole so formed. **2.** *Chem.* Formation of a compound from simpler compounds or elements. **3.** *Philos.* **a.** Reasoning from the general to the particular; logical deduction. **b.** The combination of thesis and antithesis in the Hegelian dialectical process whereby a new and higher level of truth is produced. [Lat., collection < Gk. *sunthesis* < *suntithenai*, to put together : *sun-*, syn- + *tithenai*, to put; see **dhē-***.] **— syn′the•sist** *n.*

synthesis gas *n.* A mixture of gases made as feedstock, esp. a fuel produced by controlled combustion of coal in the presence of water vapor.

syn•the•size (sĭn′thĭ-sīz′) *v.* **-sized, -siz•ing, -siz•es.** *—tr.* **1.** To combine so as to form a new, complex product. **2.** To form or produce by chemical synthesis. *—intr.* To form a synthesis.

syn•the•sized (sĭn′thĭ-sīzd′) *adj. Mus.* **1.** Relating to or being an instrument whose sound is modified or augmented by a synthesizer. **2.** Relating to or being compositions performed on synthesizers or synthesized instruments.

syn•the•siz•er (sĭn′thĭ-sī′zər) *n.* **1.** One that synthesizes. **2.** *Mus.* An electronic instrument, often played with a keyboard, that combines simple waveforms to produce more complex sounds, such as those of various other instruments.

syn•the•tase (sĭn′thĭ-tās′, -tāz′) *n.* See **ligase.**

syn•thet•ic (sĭn-thĕt′ĭk) *adj.* **1.** Relating to, involving, or of the nature of synthesis. **2.** *Chem.* Produced by synthesis, esp. not of natural origin. **3.a.** Not natural or genuine; artificial or contrived. **b.** Prepared or made artificially: *synthetic leather.* See Syns at **artificial. 4.** *Ling.* Relating to or being a language, such as Russian, that uses inflectional affixes to express syntactic relationships. **5.** *Logic & Philos.* Relating to or being a proposition that attributes to a subject a predicate not inherent in the subject and that does not result in a contradiction if negated. *—n.* A synthetic chemical compound or material. [Gk. *sunthetikos*, skilled in putting together, component < *sunthetos*, combined < *suntithenai*, to put together. See SYNTHESIS.] **— syn•thet′i•cal•ly** *adv.*

synthetic division *n. Math.* A method of dividing polynomials when the divisor is a polynomial of the first degree, by using only the coefficients of the terms.

syph•i•lis (sĭf′ə-lĭs) *n.* A chronic infectious disease caused by a spirochete *(Treponema pallidum)*, either transmitted by direct contact, usu. in sexual intercourse, or passed from mother to child in utero and characterized by local formation of chancres and systemic infection leading to general paresis. [NLat. < *Syphilis, sive Morbus Gallicus*, "Syphilis, or the French Disease," title of a poem by Girolamo Fracastoro (1478?–1553) < *Syphilus*, the poem's protagonist.]

syph•i•lit•ic (sĭf′ə-lĭt′ĭk) *adj.* Of, relating to, or affected with syphilis. *—n.* A person affected with syphilis. [NLat. *syphiliticus* < *syphilis*, syphilis. See SYPHILIS.]

syph•i•loid (sĭf′ə-loid′) *adj.* Characteristic of or resembling syphilis.

sy•phon (sī′fən) *n. & v.* Var. of **siphon.**

Syr. *abbr.* Syria.

Syr•a•cuse (sîr′ə-kyo͞os′, -kyo͞oz′). **1.** A city of SE Sicily, Italy, on the Ionian Sea SSE of Catania; founded by colonists from Corinth in the 8th cent. B.C. Pop. 117,689. **2.** A city of central NY ESE of Rochester. Pop. 163,860.

Syr Dar•ya (sîr där′yə, dər-yä′). A river of S Kirghiz, W Uzbekistan, N Tadzhikistan, and S Kazakhstan, flowing c. 2,220 km (1,380 mi) to the Aral Sea.

Sy•ri•a (sîr′ē-ə). A country of SW Asia on the E Mediterranean coast; a province of the Ottoman Empire (1516–1918) and a French territory from 1920 to 1944. Cap. Damascus. Pop. 9,052,628. **— Syr′i•an** *adj. & n.*

Syr•i•ac (sîr′ē-ăk′) *n.* An ancient Aramaic language spoken in Syria from the 3rd to the 13th century that survives as the liturgical language of several Eastern Christian churches.

Syrian Desert. A desert region of N Arabia in N Saudi Arabia, W Iraq, SE Syria, and E Jordan.

sy•rin•ga (sə-rĭng′gə) *n.* The mock orange. [NLat. < Gk. *surinx, suring-*, shepherd's pipe (its hollow stems making pipes).]

sy•ringe (sə-rĭnj′, sîr′ĭnj) *n.* **1.** A medical instrument used to inject fluids into the body or draw them from it. **2.** A hypodermic syringe. [ME, alteration of *syryng* < Med.Lat. *syringa* < LLat., injection < Gk. *surinx, suring-*, shepherd's pipe.]

sy•rin•go•my•e•li•a (sə-rĭng′gō-mī-ē′lē-ə) *n.* A chronic disease of the spinal cord characterized by the presence of fluid-filled cavities. [NLat. : Gk. *surinx, suring-*, spinal cavity + Gk. *muelos*, marrow (< *mus*, mouse, muscle; see **mūs-***).]

John Millington Synge
1905 portrait by
John Butler Yeats
(1839–1922)

synthesizer

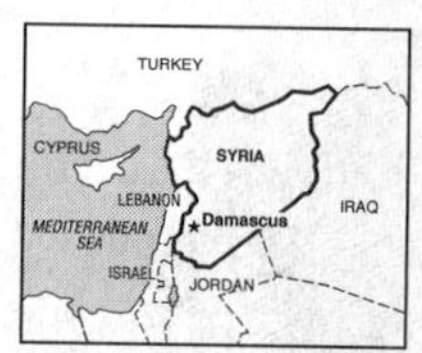

Syria

ă pat	oi boy
ā pay	ou out
âr care	o͝o to͝ok
ä father	o͞o bo͞ot
ĕ pet	ŭ cut
ē be	ûr urge
ĭ pit	th thin
ī pie	*th* this
îr pier	hw which
ŏ pot	zh vision
ō toe	ə about,
ô paw	item

Stress marks:
′ (primary);
′ (secondary), as in
dictionary (dĭk′shə-nĕr′ē)

syr•inx (sîr′ĭngks) *n., pl.* **sy•rin•ges** (sə-rĭn′jēz, -rĭng′gēz) or **syr•inx•es. 1.** *Mus.* See **panpipe. 2.** *Zool.* The vocal organ of a bird, located at or close to the division of the trachea into the bronchi. [Lat. *sȳrinx* < Gk. *surinx*.]

Sy•ros (sī′rŏs′) also **Sí•ros** (sē′rôs′). An island of Greece in the N-central Cyclades.

syr•phid (sûr′fĭd) *n.* Any of numerous flies of the family Syrphidae, many of which have a form or coloration mimicking that of bees or wasps. [< NLat. *Syrphidae*, family name < *Syrphus*, type genus < Gk. *surphos*, gnat.] **— syr′phid** *adj.*

syr•phus fly (sûr′fəs) *n.* See **syrphid.** [NLat. *Syrphus*, fly genus. See SYRPHID.]

syr•up also **sir•up** (sĭr′əp, sûr′-) *n.* **1.** A thick sweet sticky liquid, consisting of a sugar base, natural or artificial flavorings, and water. **2.** The juice of a fruit or plant boiled with sugar until thick and sticky. **3.** A concentrated solution of sugar in water, often used as a vehicle for medicine. [ME *sirup* < OFr. *sirop* < Med.Lat. *siropus* < Ar. *šarāb* < *šariba*, to drink.]

syr•up•y also **sir•up•y** (sĭr′ə-pē, sûr′-) *adj.* **1.** Resembling syrup in taste or consistency. **2.** Cloyingly sweet or sentimental.

syst. *abbr.* System.

Henrietta Szold

sys•tal•tic (sĭ-stôl′tĭk, -stăl′-) *adj.* Alternately contracting and dilating, as the heart; pulsating. [LLat. *systalticus* < Gk. *sustaltikos* < *sustellein*, to contract : *sun-*, syn- + *stellein*, to send; see **stel-***.]

sys•tem (sĭs′təm) *n.* **1.** A group of interacting, interrelated, or interdependent elements forming a complex whole. **2.** A functionally related group of elements, esp.: **a.** The human body regarded as a functional physiological unit. **b.** An organism as a whole, esp. with regard to its vital processes or functions. **c.** A group of physiologically or anatomically complementary organs or parts: *the nervous system.* **d.** A group of interacting mechanical or electrical components. **e.** A network of structures and channels, as for communication, travel, or distribution. **3.** An organized set of interrelated ideas or principles. **4.** A social, economic, or political organizational form. **5.** A naturally occurring group of objects or phenomena: *the solar system.* **6.** A set of objects or phenomena grouped together for classification or analysis. **7.** A condition of harmonious, orderly interaction. **8.** An organized and coordinated method; a procedure. See Syns at **method. 9.** The prevailing social order; the establishment. Used with *the.* [LLat. *systēma*, *systēmat-* < Gk. *sustēma* < *sunistanai*, to combine : *sun-*, syn- + *histanai*, set up, establish; see **stā-***.]

sys•tem•at•ic (sĭs′tə-măt′ĭk) also **sys•tem•at•i•cal** (-ĭ-kəl) *adj.* **1.** Of, characterized by, based on, or constituting a system. **2.** Carried on using step-by-step procedures. **3.** Purposefully regular; methodical. See Syns at **orderly. 4.** Of classification or taxonomy. **— sys′tem•at′i•cal•ly** *adv.*

sys•tem•at•ics (sĭs′tə-măt′ĭks) *n. (used with a sing. v.)* **1.** The science of systematic classification. **2.** A system of classification. **3.** *Biol.* The systematic classification of organisms and their evolutionary relationships; taxonomy.

sys•tem•a•tism (sĭs′tə-mə-tĭz′əm, sĭ-stĕm′ə-) *n.* **1.** The practice of classifying or systematizing. **2.** Adherence to a system or systems.

sys•tem•a•tist (sĭs′tə-mə-tĭst, sĭ-stĕm′ə-) *n.* **1.** One who adheres to or formulates a system or systems. **2.** A taxonomist.

sys•tem•a•tize (sĭs′tə-mə-tīz′) *tr.v.* **-tized, -tiz•ing, -tiz•es.** To form into a system. See Syns at **arrange. — sys′tem•a•ti•za′tion** (-tĭ-zā′shən) *n.* **— sys′tem•a•tiz′er** *n.*

sys•tem•ic (sĭ-stĕm′ĭk) *adj.* **1.** Of or relating to systems or a system. **2.a.** Of, relating to, or affecting the entire body or an entire organism. **b.** Relating to or affecting a given body system. **— sys•tem′i•cal•ly** *adv.*

systemic lupus er•y•the•ma•to•sus (ĕr′ə-thē′mə-tō′sĭs) *n.* A chronic disease of the connective tissue, characterized by fever, skin eruptions, pain in the muscles and joints, and anemia and often affecting the kidneys and other organs.

sys•tem•ize (sĭs′tə-mīz′) *tr.v.* **-ized, -iz•ing, -iz•es.** To systematize. **— sys′tem•i•za′tion** (-tə-mĭ-zā′shən) *n.* **— sys′tem•iz′er** *n.*

sys•tems analysis (sĭs′təmz) *n.* **1.** The study of an activity or a procedure to determine the desired end and the most efficient method of obtaining this end. **2.** The act, process, or profession of systems analysis. **— systems analyst** *n.*

sys•to•le (sĭs′tə-lē) *n.* The rhythmic contraction of the heart, esp. of the ventricles, by which blood is pumped. [Gk. *sustolē*, contraction < *sustellein*, to contract. See SYSTALTIC.] **— sys•tol′ic** (sĭ-stŏl′ĭk) *adj.*

Syz•ran (sĭz′rən). A city of W Russia on the Volga R. W of Kuibyshev. Pop. 173,000.

syz•y•gy (sĭz′ə-jē) *n., pl.* **-gies. 1.** *Astron.* **a.** Either of two points in the orbit of a celestial body, esp. the moon, where the body is in opposition to or in conjunction with the sun. **b.** The configuration of the sun, the moon, and Earth lying in a straight line. **2.** The combining of two feet into a single metrical unit in classical prosody. [LLat. *sȳzygia* < Gk. *suzugia*, union < *suzugos*, paired : *sun-*, syn- + *zugon*, yoke; see **yeug-***.] **— sy•zyg′i•al** (sĭ-zĭj′ē-əl) *adj.*

Szcze•cin (shchĕ′chēn′) also **Stet•tin** (stə-tēn′, shtĕ-). A city of NW Poland near the mouth of the Oder R.; ruled by Sweden from 1648 to 1720. Pop. 390,800.

Sze•chuan (sĕch′wän′) or **Sze•chwan.** See **Sichuan.**

Sze•ged (sĕg′ĕd′). A city of S Hungary on the Tisza R. near the Serbian border. Pop. 178,591.

Szé•kes•fe•hér•vár (sā′kĕsh-fĕ′hâr-vär′). A city of central Hungary on the Danube R. SSW of Budapest; coronation place of Hungary's kings from 1027 to 1527. Pop. 110,203.

Szell (sĕl, zĕl), **George.** 1897–1970. Hungarian-born Amer. conductor of the Cleveland Orchestra (1946–70).

Szent-Györ•gyi (sānt-jôr′jē, sĕnt-dyœr′dyĭ), **Albert.** 1893–1986. Hungarian-born Amer. biochemist who isolated vitamin C and won a 1937 Nobel Prize.

Szi•lard (zĭl′ərd, zə-lärd′), **Leo.** 1898–1964. Hungarian-born Amer. physicist who helped develop the first atomic bomb but later opposed the construction of nuclear weapons.

Szold (zōld), **Henrietta.** 1860–1945. Amer. Zionist leader who was a founder of Hadassah (1912).

Szol•nok (sōl′nōk′). A city of central Hungary ESE of Budapest. Pop. 79,619.

Szom•bat•hely (sōm′bôt-hā′). A city of W Hungary near the Austrian border; founded in Roman times. Pop. 85,830.

T t

tabard
Worn by armored knight

t¹ or **T** (tē) *n., pl.* **t's** or **T's. 1.** The 20th letter of the modern English alphabet. **2.** Any of the speech sounds represented by the letter *t.* **3.** The 20th in a series. **4.** Something shaped like the letter T. **— *idiom.* to a T.** Perfectly; precisely.

t² *abbr.* **1.** Troy (system of weights). **2.** *Phys.* Top quark.

T¹ The symbol for the isotope tritium.

T² *abbr.* **1.** Temperature. **2.** Tesla. **3.** *Math.* Time reversal.

t. *abbr.* **1.** Tare. **2.** Teaspoon; teaspoonful. **3.** *Mus.* Tempo. **4.** *Lat.* Tempore (in the time of). **5.** Or **T.** *Mus.* Tenor. **6.** *Gram.* Tense. **7.** Terminal. **8.** Or **T.** Territory. **9.** Or **T.** Time. **10.** Ton. **11.** Or **T.** Town; township. **12.** Transit. **13.** *Gram.* Transitive.

T. *abbr.* **1.** Tablespoon; tablespoonful. **2.** *Bible.* Testament. **3.** Tuesday.

ta (tä) *interj. Chiefly British.* Used to express thanks.

Ta The symbol for the element **tantalum.**

TA *abbr.* Teaching assistant.

Taal¹ (tä-äl′). A lake of SW Luzon, Philippines, S of Manila. It contains Volcano I., site of the active volcano **Mount Taal.**

Taal² (täl) *n.* See **Afrikaans.** [Afr. < MDu. *tāle*, speech. See **del-²***.]

tab¹ (tăb) *n.* **1.** A projection, flap, or short strip attached to an object to facilitate opening, handling, or identification. **2.** A small, usu. decorative flap or tongue on a garment. **3.** A small auxiliary airfoil that is attached to a larger one and helps stabilize an aircraft. **— *tr.v.*** **tabbed, tab•bing, tabs.** To supply with a tab or tabs. [?]

tab² (tăb) *n.* **1.** *Informal.* A bill or check, such as one for a meal in a restaurant. **2.** A tabulator on a typewriter. **— *idiom.* keep tabs on.** *Informal.* To observe carefully. [Short for TABLET or TABULATION. Sense 2, short for TABULATOR.]

tab. *abbr.* Table.

ta•ba•nid (tə-bā′nĭd, -băn′ĭd) *n.* Any of various bloodsucking dipterous flies of the family Tabanidae, which includes the horseflies. [NLat. *Tabānidae*, family name < Lat. *tabānus*, horsefly.] **— ta•ba′nid** *adj.*

tab•ard (tăb′ərd) *n.* **1.** A short heavy cape of coarse cloth, formerly worn outdoors. **2.a.** A tunic or capelike garment worn by a knight over his armor and emblazoned with his coat of arms. **b.** A similar garment worn by a herald and bearing his lord's coat of arms. **3.** An embroidered pennant attached to a trumpet. [ME < OFr. *tabart* or OSp. *tabardo.*]

Ta•bas•co (tə-băs′kō). A trademark used for a spicy sauce made from a strong-flavored red pepper.

ta•bas•co pepper (tə-băs′kō) *n.* A very pungent pepper *(Capsicum frutescens)* grown principally in the Gulf Coast states for commercial production of hot sauces.

tab•bou•leh (tə-bo͞o′lē) *n.* A Lebanese salad of bulgur wheat,

scallions, tomatoes, mint, and parsley. [Ar. *tabbūlah*.]
tab•by (tăb′ē) *n., pl.* **-bies. 1.** A rich watered silk. **2.** A fabric of plain weave. **3.a.** A domestic cat with a striped or brindled coat of a gray or tawny color. **b.** A domestic cat, esp. a female. **4.** *South Atlantic U.S.* A mixture of oyster shells, lime, sand, and water used as a building material. —*adj.* **1.** Having light and dark striped markings. **2.** Made of or resembling watered silk. [Fr. *tabis* < OFr. *atabis* < Med.Lat. *attabī* < Ar. *'attābī*, after *al-'Attābīya*, a suburb of Baghdad, Iraq.]
tab•er•na•cle (tăb′ər-năk′əl) *n.* **1.** Often **Tabernacle.** The portable sanctuary in which the Jews carried the Ark of the Covenant through the desert. **2.** Often **Tabernacle.** A case or box on a church altar containing the consecrated host and wine of the Eucharist. **3.** A place of worship. **4.** A niche for a statue or relic. **5.** *Naut.* A hinged support by means of which a mast can be stepped on deck and raised and lowered at will. [ME < OFr. < LLat. *tabernāculum* < Lat., tent, dim. of *taberna*, hut. See TAVERN.] —**tab′er•nac′u•lar** *adj.*
ta•bes (tā′bēz) *n., pl.* **tabes. 1.** Progressive bodily wasting or emaciation. **2.** Tabes dorsalis. [Lat. *tābēs*.]
ta•bes•cent (tə-bĕs′ənt) *adj.* Progressively wasting away. [Lat. *tābēscēns, tābēscent-*, pr.part. of *tābēscere*, to waste away, inchoative of *tābēre* < *tābēs*, a wasting away.] —**ta•bes′cence** *n.*
tabes dor•sa•lis (dôr-sā′lĭs, -săl′ĭs) *n.* A late form of syphilis marked by a hardening of the dorsal columns of the spinal cord, shooting pains, emaciation, loss of muscular coordination, and disturbances of sensation and digestion. [NLat. *tābēs dorsālis*.]
tab•la (tä′blə, tŭb′lə) *n. Mus.* A small hand drum of India. [Hindi *tablā* < Ar. *ṭabla* < *ṭabl*, drum.]
tab•la•ture (tăb′lə-cho͝or′, -chər) *n.* **1.** An engraved tablet or surface. **2.** *Mus.* A system of notation that uses letters and symbols to indicate playing directions rather than tones. [Fr., alteration of Ital. *intavolatura* < *intavolare*, to put on a board : Lat. *in-*, in- + *tavola*, table, board (< Lat. *tabula*).]
ta•ble (tā′bəl) *n.* **1.a.** An article of furniture supported by one or more vertical legs and having a flat horizontal surface. **b.** The objects laid out for a meal on a table. **2.** The food and drink served at meals; fare. **3.** The company of people assembled around a table, as for a meal. **4.** *Games.* A piece of furniture serving as a playing surface, as for faro, roulette, or dice. Often used in the plural. **5.** *Games.* **a.** Either of the leaves of a backgammon board. **b. tables.** *Obsolete.* The game of backgammon. **6.** A plateau or tableland. **7.a.** A flat facet cut across the top of a precious stone. **b.** A stone or gem cut in this fashion. **8.** *Archit.* **a.** A raised or sunken rectangular panel on a wall. **b.** A raised horizontal surface or continuous band on an exterior wall; a stringcourse. **9.** An orderly arrangement of data, esp. one in columns and rows. **10.** An abbreviated list, as of contents; a synopsis. **11.** An engraved slab or tablet bearing an inscription or a device. **12. tables.** A system of laws or decrees; a code. —*tr.v.* **-bled, -bling, -bles. 1.** To put or place on a table. **2.** To postpone consideration of; shelve. **3.** To enter in a list or table; tabulate. —***idioms.* on the table. 1.** Up for discussion. **2.** Postponed or put aside for consideration at a later date. **under the table. 1.** In secret. **2.** Into a completely intoxicated state. [ME < OFr. < Lat. *tabula*, board.]
tab•leau (tăb′lō′, tă-blō′) *n., pl.* **tab•leaux** or **tab•leaus** (tăb′lōz′, tă-blōz′). **1.** A vivid or graphic description. **2.** A striking incidental scene. **3.** An interlude during a scene when all the performers on stage freeze in position and then resume action. **4.** A tableau vivant. [Fr. < OFr. *tablel*, dim. of *table*, surface prepared for painting. See TABLE.]
tableau vi•vant (vē-văN′) *n., pl.* **tab•leaux vi•vants** (tă-blō′ vē-văN′). A scene presented on stage by costumed actors who remain silent and motionless as if in a picture. [Fr. : *tableau*, picture + *vivant*, living.]
ta•ble•cloth (tā′bəl-klôth′, -klŏth′) *n.* A cloth to cover a table, esp. during a meal.
ta•ble d'hôte (tä′bəl dōt′, tä′blə) *n., pl.* **ta•bles d'hôte** (tä′bəl dōt′, tä′blə). A full-course meal offering a limited number of choices and served at a fixed price in a restaurant or hotel. [Fr. : *table*, table + *de*, of + *hôte*, host.]
ta•ble-hop (tā′bəl-hŏp′) *intr.v.* **-hopped, -hop•ping, -hops.** *Informal.* To move around from table to table greeting friends, as in a restaurant or nightclub. —**ta′ble-hop′per** *n.*
ta•ble•land (tā′bəl-lănd′) *n.* A flat elevated region; a plateau or mesa.
ta•ble linen (tā′bəl) *n.* Tablecloths and napkins.
table salt *n.* See **salt** 1.
ta•ble•spoon (tā′bəl-spo͞on′) *n.* **1.** A large spoon used for serving food. **2.** A cooking measure equal to 3 teaspoons, or ½ fluid ounce (15 milliliters). See table at **measurement.**
ta•ble•spoon•ful (tā′bəl-spo͞on-fo͝ol′) *n., pl.* **-fuls.** The amount that a tablespoon can hold.
tab•let (tăb′lĭt) *n.* **1.** A slab or plaque, as of stone or ivory, with a surface that is intended for or bears an inscription. **2.a.** A thin sheet or leaf, used as a writing surface. **b.** A set of such leaves fastened together, as in a book. **c.** A pad of writing paper glued together along one edge. **3.** A small flat pellet of medication to be taken orally. **4.** A small flat cake of a prepared substance, such as soap. —*tr.v.* **-let•ed, -let•ing, -lets. 1.** To inscribe on a tablet. **2.** To form into a tablet. [ME *tablette* < OFr. *tablete*, dim. of *table*, table. See TABLE.]
table talk *n.* Casual mealtime conversation.
table tennis *n.* A game similar to lawn tennis, played on a table with wooden bats and a small hollow plastic ball.
ta•ble•top (tā′bəl-tŏp′) *n.* The flat surface of a table. —*adj.* Made or designed for use on the top of a table.
ta•ble•ware (tā′bəl-wâr′) *n.* The dishes, glassware, and silverware used in setting a table for a meal.
table wine *n.* A wine suitable for serving with a meal.
tab•loid (tăb′loid′) *n.* A newspaper of small format giving the news in condensed form, usu. with illustrated, often sensational material. [< *tabloid journalism* < *Tabloid*, trademark for a drug or chemical in condensed form.]
ta•boo also **ta•bu** (tə-bo͞o′, tă-) —*n., pl.* **-boos** also **-bus. 1.** A ban or an inhibition resulting from social custom or emotional aversion. **2.a.** A prohibition, esp. in Polynesia and other South Pacific islands, excluding something from use, approach, or mention because of its sacred and inviolable nature. **b.** An object, a word, or an act protected by such a prohibition. —*adj.* Excluded or forbidden from use, approach, or mention. —*tr.v.* **-booed, -boo•ing, -boos** also **-bued, -bu•ing, -bus.** To exclude from use, approach, or mention. [Tongan *tabu*, under prohibition.]

Word History: Among the many discoveries of Capt. James Cook was a linguistic one, the term *taboo*. Cook used this word in his journal of 1777 while he was in the Friendly Islands (now Tonga). Hence, even though similar words occur in other Polynesian languages, the form *taboo* from Tongan *tabu* is the form we have borrowed. The Tongans used *tabu* as an adjective; they spoke of persons or things that were *tabu*, that is, "under prohibition, forbidden, or set apart." From its origins in Polynesian society the word *taboo* has spread throughout the English-speaking world.

ta•bor also **ta•bour** (tā′bər) *n. Mus.* A small drum played by a fifer to accompany the fife. [ME *tabur* < OFr., alteration of *tambur*. See TAMBOUR.]
tab•o•ret also **tab•ou•ret** (tăb′ə-rĕt′, -rā′) *n.* **1.** A low stool without a back or arms. **2.** A low stand or cabinet. **3.** An embroidery frame. [Fr. *tabouret* < OFr. *taburet*, dim. of *tabur*, tabor. See TABOR.]
Ta•briz[1] (tə-brēz′, tä-). A city of NW Iran E of Lake Urmia. Pop. 852,000.
Ta•briz[2] (tä-brēz′) *n.* A cotton and wool Persian rug with designs of stylized animals, hunting scenes, and floral motifs.
tab•u•lar (tăb′yə-lər) *adj.* **1.** Having a plane surface; flat. **2.** *Geol.* Tending to split into thin flat pieces. **3.** Organized as a table or list. **4.** Calculated by means of a table. [Lat. *tabulāris*, of boards < *tabula*, board.] —**tab′u•lar•ly** *adv.*
tab•u•la ra•sa (tăb′yə-lə rä′sə, -zə) *n., pl.* **tab•u•lae ra•sae** (tăb′yə-lē′ rä′sē, -zē). **1.a.** The mind before it receives the impressions gained from experience. **b.** The unformed featureless mind in the philosophy of John Locke. **2.** A need or an opportunity to start from the beginning. [Med.Lat. *tabula rāsa* : Lat. *tabula*, tablet + Lat. *rāsa*, fem. of *rāsus*, erased.]
tab•u•lar•ize (tăb′yə-lə-rīz′) *tr.v.* **-ized, -iz•ing, -iz•es.** To put into tabular form; tabulate. —**tab′u•lar•i•za′tion** (-lər-ĭ-zā′shən) *n.*
tab•u•late (tăb′yə-lāt′) *tr.v.* **-lat•ed, -lat•ing, -lates. 1.** To arrange in tabular form; condense and list. **2.** To cut or form with a plane surface. —*adj.* (tăb′yə-lĭt, -lāt′). Having a plane surface. [Lat. *tabula*, writing + -ATE[1].] —**tab′u•la′tion** *n.*
tab•u•la•tor (tăb′yə-lā′tər) *n.* **1.** One who tabulates: *a tabulator of racing scores.* **2.** A machine that reads, sorts, and prints out information from punched cards. **3.** A mechanism on a typewriter for setting automatic stops or margins.
tac•a•ma•hac (tăk′ə-mə-hăk′) *n.* **1.** Any of several aromatic resinous substances used in ointments and incense. **2.** See **balsam poplar.** [Sp. *tacamahaca* < Nahuatl *tecamaca*.]
ta•cet (tā′sĭt, tăs′ĭt, tä′kĕt′) *v. Mus.* Be silent. [Lat., third pers. sing. pr.t. of *tacēre*, to be silent.]
tach (tăk) *n. Informal.* A tachometer.
tach•i•na fly (tăk′ə-nə) *n.* Any of several bristly, usu. grayish dipterous flies of the family Tachinidae, the larvae of which are parasitic on other insects. [NLat. *Tachina*, type genus < Gk. *takhinē*, fem. of *takhinos*, swift < *takhos*, speed.]
tach•i•nid (tăk′ə-nĭd′) *n.* See **tachina fly.** —*adj.* Of or belonging to the family Tachinidae. [NLat. *Tachinidae*, family name < *Tachina*, type genus. See TACHINA FLY.]
tach•isme or **tach•ism** (tăsh′ĭz′əm) *n.* A French school of art originating in the 1950's and characterized by irregular splotches of color applied haphazardly to the canvas. [Fr. *tachisme* < *tache*, stain < OFr. *teche*, mark, of Gmc. orig. See **deik-*.**] —**tach′iste, tach′ist** *n.*
ta•chis•to•scope (tă-kĭs′tə-skōp′, tə-) *n.* An apparatus that projects a series of images onto a screen at rapid speed to test visual perception, memory, and learning. [Gk. *takhistos*, superl. of *takhus*, swift + -SCOPE.]
ta•chom•e•ter (tă-kŏm′ĭ-tər, tə-) *n.* An instrument used to measure the rotations per minute of a rotating shaft. [Gk.

table tennis

taboret

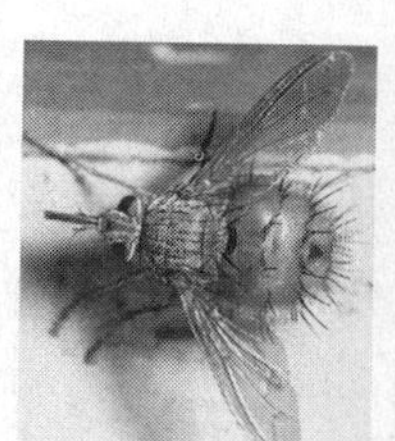
tachina fly

ă pat	oi boy
ā pay	ou out
âr care	o͝o took
ä father	o͞o boot
ĕ pet	ŭ cut
ē be	ûr urge
ĭ pit	th thin
ī pie	*th* this
îr pier	hw which
ŏ pot	zh vision
ō toe	ə about, item
ô paw	

Stress marks:
′ (primary);
′ (secondary), as in
dictionary (dĭk′shə-nĕr′ē)

takhos, speed + -METER.] —**tach′o·met′ric** (tăk′ə-mĕt′rĭk) *adj.* —**ta·chom′e·try** *n.*

tachy– *pref.* Rapid; accelerated: *tachymeter.* [Gk. *takhu-* < *takhus*, swift.]

tach·y·car·di·a (tăk′ĭ-kär′dē-ə) *n.* A rapid heart rate, esp. one above 100 beats per minute in an adult. [TACHY- + Gk. *kardia*, heart; see CARDIA.]

ta·chyg·ra·phy (tă-kĭg′rə-fē, tə-) *n.* The art or practice of rapid writing or shorthand, esp. the stenography of the ancient Greeks and Romans.

tach·y·lyte also **tach·y·lite** (tăk′ə-līt′) *n.* A glassy black basalt of volcanic origin. [Ger. *Tachylyt* : Gk. *takhu-*, tachy- + Gk. *lutos*, soluble (< *luein*, to loosen; see **leu-***).]

taco

ta·chym·e·ter (tă-kĭm′ĭ-tər, tə-) *n.* A surveying instrument used for the rapid determination of distances, elevations, and bearings. —**ta·chym′e·try** *n.*

tach·y·on (tăk′ē-ŏn′) *n.* A hypothetical subatomic particle that travels faster than the speed of light. —**tach′y·on′ic** *adj.*

tac·it (tăs′ĭt) *adj.* **1.** Not spoken. **2.** Implied by or inferred from actions or statements. **3.** *Archaic.* Not speaking; silent. [Lat. *tacitus*, silent, p.part. of *tacēre*, to be silent.] —**tac′it·ly** *adv.* —**tac′it·ness** *n.*

tac·i·turn (tăs′ĭ-tûrn′) *adj.* Habitually untalkative. [Fr. *taciturne* < OFr. < Lat. *taciturnus* < *tacitus*, silent. See TACIT.] —**tac′i·tur′ni·ty** (-tûr′nĭ-tē) *n.* —**tac′i·turn·ly** *adv.*

Tac·i·tus (tăs′ĭ-təs), **Publius Cornelius.** A.D. 55?–120? Roman historian whose works concern Rome in the 1st cent. A.D.

tack¹ (tăk) *n.* **1.** A short light nail with a sharp point and a flat head. **2.** *Naut.* **a.** A line for holding down the weather clew of a course. **b.** A line for hauling the outer lower corner of a studdingsail to the boom. **c.** The part of a sail, such as the weather clew of a course, to which this line is fastened. **d.** The lower forward corner of a fore-and-aft sail. **3.** *Naut.* **a.** The position of a vessel relative to the side from which the wind is blowing. **b.** The act of changing a sailing vessel's course by bringing the bow across the wind. **c.** The distance or leg sailed between changes of position or direction. **4.a.** A course of action meant to minimize opposition to the attainment of a goal. **b.** An approach, esp. one of a series of changing approaches. **5.** A large loose stitch made as a temporary binding or as a marker. **6.** Stickiness, as that of a newly painted surface. —*v.* **tacked, tack·ing, tacks.** —*tr.* **1.** To fasten or attach with or as if with a tack. **2.** To fasten or mark (cloth or a seam, for example) with a loose basting stitch. **3.** To put together loosely and arbitrarily. **4.** To add as an extra item; append. **5.** *Naut.* To bring (a vessel) into the wind in order to change course or direction. —*intr.* **1.** *Naut.* **a.** To change the direction or course of a vessel by bringing the bow across the wind. **b.** To change tack: *The ship tacked to starboard.* **2.** To change one's course of action. [ME *tak*, fastener < ONFr. *taque*, prob. of Gmc. orig.] —**tack′er** *n.*

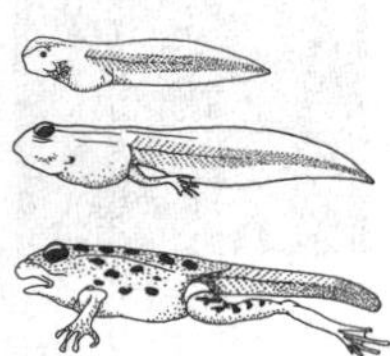
tadpole
Development of a northern leopard frog
Rana pipiens

tack² (tăk) *n.* Food, esp. coarse or inferior foodstuffs. [?]

tack³ (tăk) *n.* The harness for a horse, including the bridle and saddle. [Short for TACKLE.]

tack·le (tăk′əl) *n.* **1.** The equipment used in a sport or an occupation, esp. in fishing; gear. **2.** (*also* tā′kəl). *Naut.* **a.** A system of ropes and blocks that provides a mechanical advantage, used for lifting weights and controlling spars and rigging. **b.** A rope and its pulley. **3.** *Football.* **a.** Either of the two line players on a team positioned between the guard and the end. **b.** This position. **c.** The act of stopping an opponent carrying the ball, esp. by forcing the opponent to the ground. —*v.* **-led, -ling, -les.** —*tr.* **1.** To take on and wrestle with (an opponent or a problem, for example). **2.** *Football.* To make a tackle on (an opponent carrying the ball). **3.** To harness (a horse). —*intr. Football.* To tackle an opponent. [ME *takel* < MDu. or MLGer.] —**tack′ler** *n.*

Tadzhikistan

tack·ling (tăk′lĭng) *n.* Gear; tackle.

tack·y¹ (tăk′ē) *adj.* **-i·er, -i·est.** Slightly adhesive or gummy to the touch; sticky. [< TACK¹.] —**tack′i·ness** *n.*

tack·y² (tăk′ē) *adj.* **-i·er, -i·est.** *Informal.* **1.** Neglected and in a state of disrepair. **2.a.** Lacking style or good taste; tawdry. **b.** Distasteful or offensive; tasteless. [< *tackey*, an inferior horse.] —**tack′i·ly** *adv.* —**tack′i·ness** *n.*

Tac·na (tăk′nə, täk′nä). A town of S Peru N of Arica, Chile; became part of Peru in 1929. Pop. 97,173.

ta·co (tä′kō) *n., pl.* **-cos.** A corn tortilla folded around a filling such as ground meat or cheese. [Am.Sp. < Sp., plug, wad of bank notes.]

Ta·co·ma (tə-kō′mə). A city of W-central WA on an arm of Puget Sound S of Seattle. Pop. 176,664.

Ta·con·ic Mountains (tə-kŏn′ĭk). A range of the Appalachian Mts. rising to 1,163.9 m (3,816 ft).

tac·o·nite (tăk′ə-nīt′) *n.* A variety of chert containing magnetite and hematite, mined as an iron ore. [After the TACONIC (MOUNTAINS).]

tact (tăkt) *n.* **1.** Acute sensitivity to what is proper and appropriate in dealing with others, including the ability to speak or act without offending. **2.** *Archaic.* The sense of touch. [Fr. < OFr., sense of touch < Lat. *tāctus* < p.part. of *tangere*, to touch. See **tag-***.]

tact·ful (tăkt′fəl) *adj.* Possessing or exhibiting tact; considerate and discreet. —**tact′ful·ly** *adv.* —**tact′ful·ness** *n.*

tac·tic (tăk′tĭk) *n.* An expedient for achieving a goal; a maneuver. [Fr. *tactique*, tactics < Gk. *taktika*. See TACTICS.]

tac·ti·cal (tăk′tĭ-kəl) *adj.* **1.** Of, relating to, or using tactics. **2.a.** Of, relating to, used in, or involving military or naval operations that are smaller, closer to base, and less significant than strategic operations. **b.** Carried out in support of military or naval operations. **3.** Marked by adroitness, ingenuity, or skill. —**tac′ti·cal·ly** *adv.*

tac·ti·cian (tăk-tĭsh′ən) *n.* **1.** One who is skilled in the planning and execution of military tactics. **2.** A clever maneuverer.

tac·tics (tăk′tĭks) *n.* **1.a.** (*used with a sing. v.*) The military art that deals with securing objectives set by strategy, esp. the technique of deploying and directing troops, ships, and aircraft in efficient maneuvers against an enemy. **b.** (*used with a pl. v.*) Maneuvers used against an enemy. **2.** (*used with a sing. or pl. v.*) A procedure or set of maneuvers engaged in to achieve an end, an aim, or a goal. [NLat. *tactica* < Gk. *taktika* < neut. pl. of *taktikos*, of order < *taktos*, arranged < *tassein*, *tag-*, to arrange.]

tac·tile (tăk′təl, -tīl′) *adj.* **1.a.** Perceptible to the sense of touch; tangible. **b.** Characterized by or conveying an illusion of tangibility. **2.** Used for feeling: *a tactile organ.* **3.** Of, relating to, or proceeding from the sense of touch; tactual. [< Lat. *tāctilis* < *tāctus*, p.part. of *tangere*, to touch. See TACT.] —**tac′tile·ly** *adv.* —**tac·til′i·ty** (-tĭl′ĭ-tē) *n.*

tactile corpuscle *n.* Any of numerous minute oval end organs of touch in sensitive skin, as in the fingertips.

tac·tion (tăk′shən) *n.* The act of touching; contact. [Lat. *tāctiō*, *tāctiōn-* < *tāctus*, p.part. of *tangere*, to touch. See TACT.]

tact·less (tăkt′lĭs) *adj.* Lacking or exhibiting a lack of tact; bluntly inconsiderate or indiscreet. —**tact′less·ly** *adv.* —**tact′less·ness** *n.*

tac·tu·al (tăk′cho͞o-əl) *adj.* Tactile. [Lat. *tāctus*, touch; see TACT + -AL¹.] —**tac′tu·al·ly** *adv.*

tad (tăd) *n. Informal.* **1.** A small boy. **2.** A small amount or degree; a bit. [Perh. short for TADPOLE.]

tad·pole (tăd′pōl′) *n.* The limbless aquatic larva of a frog or toad, having gills and a long flat tail. [ME *taddepol* : *tadde*, *tode*, toad; see TOAD + *pol*, head; see POLL.]

Ta·dzhik (tä-jĭk′, tə-) *n. & adj.* Var. of **Tajik.**

Ta·dzhik·i (tä-jĭk′ē, tə-) *n. & adj.* Var. of **Tajiki.**

Ta·dzhik·i·stan also **Ta·jik·i·stan** (tä-jĭk′ĭ-stăn′, -stän′, tə-jĭ-kyĭ-stän′). A region and republic of W-central Asia bordering on Afghanistan and China; settled by the Tajik by the 10th cent. and a constituent republic of the U.S.S.R. from 1929 to 1991. Cap. Dushanbe. Pop. 4,499,000.

Tae·gu (tī-go͞o′). A city of SE South Korea NNW of Pusan. Pop. 2,031,000.

Tae·jon (tī-jôn′, -jŏn′). A city of central South Korea SSE of Seoul. Pop. 800,000.

tae kwon do (tī′ kwŏn′ dō′) *n.* A Korean art of self-defense; a style of karate. [Korean *t'aekwŏndo* : *tae-*, to trample + *kwŏn*, fist + *-do*, way.]

tael (tāl) *n.* **1.** Any of various units of weight used in eastern Asia, roughly equivalent to 38 grams (1⅓ ounces). **2.** A monetary unit formerly used in China, equivalent in value to this weight of standard silver. [Port. < Malay *tahil, tael.*]

tae·ni·a also **te·ni·a** (tē′nē-ə) *n., pl.* **-ni·ae** (-nē-ē′) or **-ni·as.** **1.** A narrow band or ribbon for the hair that was worn in ancient Greece. **2.** *Archit.* A band in the Doric order that separates the frieze from the architrave. **3.** *Anat.* A ribbonlike band of tissue or muscle. **4.** A flatworm of the genus *Taenia*, which includes many tapeworms. [Lat., ribbon, tapeworm < Gk. *tainia*. See **ten-***.]

tae·ni·a·sis also **te·ni·a·sis** (tē-nī′ə-sĭs) *n.* Infestation with tapeworms.

taf·fe·ta (tăf′ĭ-tə) *n.* A crisp smooth plain-woven fabric with a slight sheen, made of various fibers, such as silk, rayon, or nylon, and used esp. for women's garments. [ME < OFr. *taffetas* < OItal. *taffetà* < Turk. *tafta* < Pers. *tāftah*, silk or linen cloth < p.part. of *tāftan*, to twist, spin.] —**taf′fe·ta** *adj.*

taff·rail (tăf′rāl′, -rəl) *n. Naut.* **1.** The rail around the stern of a vessel. **2.** The flat upper part of the stern of a vessel, made of wood and often richly carved. [Alteration of *tafferel*, carved panel < Du. *tafereel*, panel for carving or painting < MDu. *tafeleel*, *tafereel* < OFr. *tablel*. See TABLEAU.]

taffrail log *n. Naut.* See **patent log.**

taf·fy (tăf′ē) *n., pl.* **-fies.** A sweet chewy candy of molasses or brown sugar boiled until very thick and then pulled until the candy is glossy and holds its shape. [?]

taf·i·a also **taf·fi·a** (tăf′ē-ə) *n.* A cheap rum distilled from molasses and refuse sugar in the West Indies. [Fr., perh. of West Indian Creole orig.]

Taft (tăft), **Helen.** 1861–1943. First Lady of the U.S. (1909–13).

Taft, Lorado. 1860–1936. Amer. sculptor whose works include *The Fountain of Time* in Chicago (1922).

Taft, William Howard. 1857–1930. The 27th President of the U.S. (1909–13), who later served as chief justice of the U.S. Supreme Court (1921–30).

tag¹ (tăg) *n.* **1.** A strip of leather, paper, metal, or plastic attached to something or hung from a wearer's neck to identify, classify, or label. **2.** The plastic or metal tip at the end of a shoelace. **3.** The contrastingly colored tip of an animal's tail. **4.** *Sports.* A bright piece of feather, floss, or tinsel surrounding the shank of the hook on a fishing fly. **5.a.** A dirty matted lock of wool. **b.** A loose lock of hair. **6.** A rag; a tatter. **7.** A fragment. **8.** An ornamental flourish, esp. at the end of a signature. **9.** A designation or an epithet, esp. an unwelcome one. **10.a.** A brief quotation used in a discourse to give it an air of erudition or authority. **b.** A cliché, saw, or similar short conventional idea used to embellish a discourse. **c.** The refrain or last lines of a song or poem. **d.** The closing lines of a speech in a play; a cue. **11.** *Comp. Sci.* A label assigned to identify data in memory. —*v.* **tagged, tag•ging, tags.** —*tr.* **1.** To label, identify, or recognize with or as if with a tag. See Syns at **mark¹**. **2.** To put a ticket on (a motor vehicle) for a traffic or parking violation. **3.** To charge with a crime. **4.** To add as an appendage. **5.** To follow closely. **6.** To cut the tags from (sheep). —*intr.* To follow after; accompany: *insisted on tagging along.* [ME *tagge,* dangling piece of cloth on a garment, poss. of Scand. orig.]

tag² (tăg) *n.* **1.** *Games.* A children's game in which one player pursues the others in order to tag one of them, who then pursues in turn. **2.** *Baseball.* The act of tagging a player who is not on base. **3.** *Sports.* The act of tagging a player. —*tr.v.* **tagged, tag•ging, tags. 1.** To touch (another player) in the game of tag. **2.** *Baseball.* To touch (a runner) with the ball in order to put that player out. **3.** *Sports.* To touch (the runner) instead of tackling in touch football. —***phrasal verb.* tag up.** *Baseball.* To return to and touch a base with one foot before running to the next base after a fielder catches a fly. [Perh. var. of Sc. *tig,* touch, tap, prob. alteration of ME *tek.*]

Ta•ga•log (tə-gä′lôg, -ləg) *n., pl.* **Tagalog** or **-logs. 1.** A member of a people native to the Philippines and inhabiting Manila and its adjacent provinces. **2.** The Austronesian language of the Tagalog. [Tagalog : *taga,* native of + *ílog,* river.]

tag•a•long also **tag-a-long** (tăg′ə-lông′, -lŏng′) *n.* One that persistently follows another.

Tag•an•rog (tăg′ən-rŏg′, tə-gən-rôk′). A city of SW Russia on the **Gulf of Taganrog,** an arm of the Sea of Azov; annexed by Russia in 1769. Pop. 289,000.

tag day *n.* A day on which collectors for a charitable fund solicit contributions, giving each contributor a tag.

tag end *n.* **1.** The very end. **2.** Something left over; a remnant.

tag•ger (tăg′ər) *n.* **1.** One that tags, esp. in the game of tag. **2. taggers.** Very thin sheet iron, usu. plated with tin.

tag line also **tag•line** (tăg′līn′) *n.* **1.** An ending line, as in a play or joke, that makes a point. **2.** An often repeated phrase associated with an individual, organization, or product.

Ta•gore (tə-gôr′, -gōr′, tä-), Sir **Rabindranath.** 1861–1941. Bengali writer who won the 1913 Nobel Prize for literature.

tag sale *n.* See **garage sale.**

Ta•gus (tā′gəs) also **Ta•jo** (tä′hō). A river of the Iberian Peninsula flowing c. 941 km (585 mi) to the Atlantic Ocean.

ta•hi•ni (tə-hē′nē) *n.* A thick paste made from ground sesame seeds. [Turk. *tāhin,* sesame flour or oil < Ar. dial. *ṭaḥīne* < *ṭaḥan,* to grind.]

Ta•hi•ti (tə-hē′tē). An island of the S Pacific in the Windward group of the Society Is. in French Polynesia; first settled by Polynesians in the 14th cent.

Ta•hi•tian (tə-hē′shən) *adj.* Of or relating to Tahiti or its people, language, or culture. —*n.* **1.** A native or inhabitant of Tahiti. **2.** The Polynesian language of Tahiti.

Ta•hoe (tä′hō), **Lake.** A lake on the CA-NV border W of Carson City, NV.

tah•sil•dar also **tah•seel•dar** (tə-sēl′där′) *n.* A district official in India in charge of revenues and taxation. [Urdu *taḥsīldār* < Pers. : *taḥṣīl,* collection, revenue (< Ar. < *ḥaṣṣala,* to collect < *ḥaṣala,* to acquire) + *-dār,* having; see **dher-*.**]

Tai (tī) *n., pl.* **Tai** or **Tais. 1.** A family of languages spoken in southeast Asia and southern China that includes Thai, Lao, and Shan. **2.** A member of any of the Tai-speaking peoples of Thailand, Burma, Laos, China, and Vietnam. **3.** Thai. —*adj.* **1.** Of or relating to Tai, its speakers, or their culture. **2.** Thai.

tai chi or **Tai Chi** (tī′ chē′, jē′) also **tai chi chuan** or **Tai Chi Chuan** (chwän′) *n.* A Chinese system of physical exercises esp. for self-defense and meditation. [Chin. (Mandarin) *taì jí quán* : *taì,* highest + *jí,* reach + *quán,* boxing.]

Tai•chung (tī′cho͝ong′, -jo͝ong′) also **Tai•zhong** (-jông′). A city of W-central Taiwan SW of Taipei. Pop. 621,566.

tai•ga (tī′gə) *n.* A subarctic evergreen coniferous forest of northern Eurasia located just south of the tundra and dominated by firs and spruces. [Russ. *taĭga,* of Altaic orig.]

tail¹ (tāl) *n.* **1.** The posterior part of an animal, esp. when elongated and extending beyond the trunk or main part of the body. **2.** The bottom, rear, or hindmost part. **3.** The rear end of a wagon or other vehicle. **4.a.** The rear portion of the fuselage of an aircraft. **b.** An assembly of stabilizing planes and control surfaces in this rear portion. **5.** The vaned rear portion of a bomb or missile. **6.** An appendage to the rear or bottom of a thing. **7.** The long luminous stream of gas and dust forced from the head of a comet when it is close to the sun. **8.** A braid of hair; a pigtail. **9.** Something that follows or takes the last place: *the tail of a journey.* **10.** A train of followers; a retinue. **11.** The end of a line of persons or things. **12.** The short closing line of certain stanzas of verse. **13.** The refuse or dross remaining from processes such as distilling or milling. **14.** *Print.* The bottom of a page; the bottom margin. **15.** The side of a coin not having the principal design and the date. Often used in the plural with a singular verb. **16.** *Informal.* The trail of a person or an animal in flight. **17.** *Informal.* A person assigned or employed to follow and report on someone else's movements and actions. **18. tails. a.** A formal evening costume typically worn by men. **b.** A swallow-tailed coat. **19.a.** *Slang.* The buttocks. **b.** *Vulgar Slang.* A sexual partner, esp. a woman. —*adj.* **1.** Of or relating to a tail or tails. **2.** Situated in the tail, as of an airplane. —*v.* **tailed, tail•ing, tails.** —*tr.* **1.** To provide with a tail. **2.** To deprive of a tail; dock. **3.** To serve as the tail of. **4.** To connect (often dissimilar or incongruous objects) by or as if by the tail or end. **5.** *Archit.* To set one end of (a beam, board, or brick) into a wall. **6.** *Informal.* To follow and keep under surveillance. —*intr.* **1.** To become lengthened or spaced when moving in a line: *The patrol tailed out in pairs.* **2.** *Archit.* To be inserted at one end into a wall, as a floor timber or beam. **3.** *Informal.* To follow. **4.** *Naut.* **a.** To go aground with the stern foremost. **b.** To lie or swing with the stern in a named direction, as when riding at anchor or on a mooring. —***phrasal verbs.* tail down.** To ease a heavy load down a steep slope. **tail off (**or **away).** To diminish gradually; dwindle or subside. [ME < OE *tægel.*]

tail² (tāl) *Law. n.* Limitation of the inheritance of an estate to a particular party. [ME *taille* < OFr., division < *taillier,* to cut. See TAILOR.]

tail•back (tāl′băk′) *n. Football.* The back on an offensive team who lines up farthest from the line of scrimmage.

tail beam *n. Archit.* See **tailpiece** 3.

tail•board (tāl′bôrd′, -bōrd′) *n.* See **tailgate** 1.

tail•bone (tāl′bōn′) *n.* See **coccyx.**

tail•coat (tāl′kōt′) *n.* See **swallow-tailed coat.**

tail end *n.* **1.** The rear or hindmost part. **2.** The very end.

tail fan *n.* The fanlike posterior structure of a lobster, shrimp, or other crustacean, formed from the telson and the last pair of uropods and used for backward locomotion.

tail fin also **tail•fin** (tāl′fĭn′) *n.* **1.** A fin at the posterior part of the body of a fish, crustacean, whale, or other aquatic animal. **2.** An ornamental projection shaped like a fin on the rear fender of an automobile.

tail•gate (tāl′gāt′) *n.* **1.** A hinged board or closure at the rear of a vehicle, such as a truck, that can be lowered during loading and unloading. **2.** One of the pair of gates downstream in a canal lock. —*v.* **-gat•ed, -gat•ing, -gates.** —*tr.* To drive so closely behind (another vehicle) that one risks collision in an emergency. —*intr.* **1.** To follow another vehicle too closely. **2.** To participate in a picnic that is served from the tailgate of a vehicle. —**tail′gat′er** *n.*

tail•ing (tā′lĭng) *n.* **1. tailings.** Refuse or dross remaining after ore has been processed. **2.** *Archit.* The portion of a tailed beam, brick, or board inside a wall.

tail lamp *n.* See **taillight.**

taille (tāl, tä′yə) *n.* A form of direct royal taxation that was levied in France before 1789 on nonprivileged subjects and lands. [Fr. < OFr., division. See TAIL².]

tail•light (tāl′līt′) *n.* A red light or one of a pair mounted on the rear end of a vehicle.

tai•lor (tā′lər) *n.* One that makes, repairs, and alters garments such as suits, coats, and dresses. —*v.* **-lored, -lor•ing, -lors.** —*tr.* **1.** To make (a garment), esp. to specific requirements or measurements. **2.** To fit or provide (a person) with clothes made to that person's measurements. **3.** To make, alter, or adapt for a particular end or purpose. —*intr.* To pursue the trade of a tailor. [ME < AN *taillour* < OFr. *tailleor* < *taillier,* to cut < LLat. *tāliāre* < Lat. *tālea,* a cutting.]

tai•lor•bird (tā′lər-bûrd′) *n.* Any of several Old World tropical passerine birds of the genus *Orthotomus* that characteristically stitch leaves together with plant fibers to make nests.

tai•lored (tā′lərd) *adj.* **1.** Made by a tailor; custom-made. **2.** Simple, trim, or severe in line or design.

tai•lor-made (tā′lər-mād′) *adj.* **1.** Made by a tailor. **2.** Perfectly fitted to a condition, preference, or purpose; made or as if made to order. —*n.* A garment made by a tailor.

tai•lor's chalk (tā′lərz) *n.* A thin piece of hard chalk used in tailoring for making temporary alteration marks on clothing.

tail•piece (tāl′pēs′) *n.* **1.** A piece forming an end; an appendage. **2.** *Print.* An ornamental engraving or a design at the end of a chapter or the bottom of a page. **3.** *Archit.* A beam tailed into a wall. **4.** *Mus.* A triangular piece of ebony to which the lower ends of violin or cello strings are attached.

tail•pipe also **tail pipe** (tāl′pīp′) *n.* The pipe through which exhaust gases from an engine are discharged.

tail•race (tāl′rās′) *n.* **1.** The part of a millrace below the water wheel through which the spent water flows. **2.** A channel for floating away mine tailings and refuse.

Helen Taft

William Howard Taft

ă pat	oi boy
ā pay	ou out
âr care	o͝o took
ä father	o͞o boot
ĕ pet	ŭ cut
ē be	ûr urge
ĭ pit	th thin
ī pie	*th* this
îr pier	hw which
ŏ pot	zh vision
ō toe	ə about, item
ô paw	

Stress marks:
′ (primary);
′ (secondary), as in
dictionary (dĭk′shə-nĕr′ē)

tail•spin (tāl′spĭn′) *n.* **1.** The rapid descent of an aircraft in a steep, spiral spin. **2.** *Informal.* A loss of emotional control sometimes resulting in emotional collapse.
tail•stock (tāl′stŏk′) *n.* The movable part of a lathe that supports the dead center.
tail wind or **tail•wind** (tāl′wĭnd′) *n.* A wind blowing in the same direction as that of a ship or another vehicle.
Tai•myr Peninsula also **Tai•mir Peninsula** or **Tay•myr Peninsula** (tī-mîr′). A peninsula of N-central Russia extending N between the Laptev and Kara seas.
Tai•nan (tī′nän′). A city of SW Taiwan on the South China Sea; settled in 1590. Pop. 609,934.
Taí•na•ron (tā′nə-rôn′, tĕ′nä-), **Cape.** Formerly **Cape Mat•a•pan** (măt′ə-păn′). A cape of S mainland Greece.
Taine (tān, tĕn), **Hippolyte Adolphe.** 1828–93. French philosopher and historian who was an exponent of positivism.
Tai•no (tī′nō) *n., pl.* **Taino** or **-nos. 1.** A member of an Arawak people of the Greater Antilles and the Bahamas who became extinct under Spanish colonization during the 16th century. **2.** The language of this people. [Sp., of American Indian orig.]
taint (tānt) *v.* **taint•ed, taint•ing, taints.** *—tr.* **1.** To affect with or as if with a disease. **2.** To affect with decay or putrefaction; spoil. **3.** To corrupt morally. **4.** To affect with a tinge of something reprehensible. *—intr.* To become affected with decay or putrefaction; spoil. *—n.* **1.** A moral defect considered as a stain or spot. **2.** An infecting touch, influence, or tinge. [Partly < obsolete *taynt,* to color, dye (< AN *teint* < p.part. of *teindre* < Lat. *tingere*) and partly < ME *tainten,* to convict (< OFr. *ataint,* p.part. of *ataindre,* to attain, touch upon; see ATTAIN).]
tai•pan¹ (tī′păn′) *n.* **1.** A foreign businessman or a trader in China. **2.** A foreigner who is a chief executive of a business or company operating in China or Hong Kong; a tycoon. [Chin. *tài pān* : *tài,* big + *pān,* company.]
tai•pan² (tī′păn) *n.* A large, extremely venomous elapid snake *(Oxyuranus scutellatus)* of Australia and New Guinea having long fangs and large venom glands. [Wik Munkan (Aboriginal language of NE Australia) *dhayban.*]

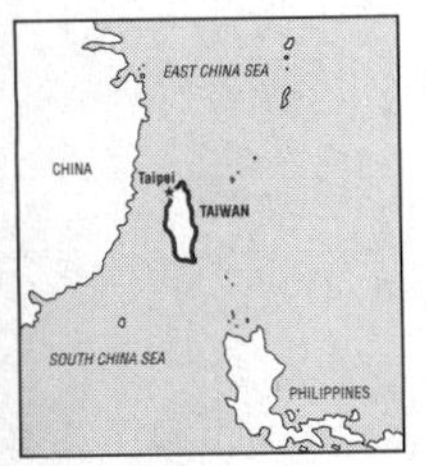

Taiwan

Tai•pei also **Tai•peh** (tī′pā′, -bā′). The cap. of Taiwan, in the N part; headquarters of Chiang Kai-shek and the Chinese Nationalists after 1949. Pop. 2,327,641.
Tai•wan (tī′wän′). Officially **Republic of Chi•na** (chī′nə). Formerly **For•mo•sa** (fôr-mō′sə). A country off the SE coast of China comprising the island of **Taiwan,** the Pescadores, and other smaller islands. Cap. Taipei. Pop. 18,457,923.
Tai•wan•ese (tī′wä-nēz′, -nēs′) *adj.* Of or relating to Taiwan or its peoples, languages, or cultures. *—n., pl.* **Taiwanese. 1.** A native or inhabitant of Taiwan. **2.** The Minnan dialect of Chinese spoken on Taiwan.
Taiwan Strait. See **Formosa Strait.**
Tai•yu•an also **Tai•yü•an** (tī′yo͞o-än′, -yüän′). A city of NE China SW of Beijing. Pop. 1,390,000.
Tai•zhong (tī′jông′). See **Taichung.**
Ta•jik also **Ta•dzhik** (tä-jĭk′, tə-) *—n., pl.* **Tajik** or **-jiks** also **Tadzhik** or **-dzhiks. 1.** A member of a people inhabiting Tadzhikistan and neighboring areas in Afghanistan and China. **2.** Tajiki. *—adj.* Tajiki.
Ta•jik•i also **Ta•dzhik•i** (tä-jĭk′ē, tə-) *—n.* The Iranian language of the Tajik people, closely related to Persian. *—adj.* Of or relating to the Tajik people or their language or culture.
Ta•jik•i•stan (tä-jĭk′ĭ-stăn′, -stän′, tə-jĭ-kyĭ-stän′). See **Tadzhikistan.**
Ta•jo (tä′hō). See **Tagus.**
ta•ka (tä′kə) *n.* See table at **currency.** [Bengali *ṭākā* < Skt. *ṭaṅkaḥ,* stamped coin.]
Ta•ka•mat•su (tä′kä-mät′so͞o). A city of NE Shikoku, Japan, on the Inland Sea. Pop. 327,001.
Ta•ka•tsu•ki (tə-kät′so͞o-kē, tä′kä-tso͞o′kē). A city of SW Honshu, Japan, between Osaka and Kyoto. Pop. 348,743.
take (tāk) *v.* **took** (to͝ok), **tak•en** (tā′kən), **tak•ing, takes.** *—tr.* **1.** To get into one's possession by force, skill, or artifice, esp.: **a.** To capture physically; seize. **b.** To seize with authority; confiscate. **c.** To kill, snare, or trap (fish or game, for example). **d.** *Sports & Games.* To acquire in a game or competition; win. **e.** *Sports & Games.* To defeat. **f.** *Sports.* To catch (a ball in play), esp. in baseball. **2.** To grasp with the hands; grip. **3.** To be affected with; come down with; contract. **4.** To encounter or catch in a particular situation; come upon; discover. **5.** To deal a blow to; strike or hit. **6.** To affect favorably or winsomely; charm or captivate. **7.a.** To put (food or drink, for example) into the body; eat or drink. **b.** To draw in; inhale. **8.** To expose one's body to (healthful or pleasurable treatment, for example). **9.** To bring or receive into a particular relation, association, or other connection. **10.** To engage in sex with. **11.** To accept and place under one's care or keeping. **12.** To appropriate for one's own or another's use or benefit; obtain by purchase; secure or buy. **13.** To assume for oneself. **14.a.** To charge or oblige oneself with the fulfillment of (a task or duty, for example); commit oneself to. **b.** To pledge one's obedience to; impose (a vow or promise) upon oneself. **c.** To subject oneself to. **d.** To accept or adopt for one's own. **e.** To put forth or adopt as a point of argument, defense, or discussion. **f.** To require or have as a fitting or proper accompaniment: *Intransitive verbs take no direct object.* **15.** To pick out; select or choose. **16.a.** To choose for one's own use; avail oneself of the use of. **b.** To use (something) as when in operation. **c.** To use (something) as a means of conveyance or transportation. **d.** To use (something) as a means of safety or refuge. **e.** To choose and then adopt (a particular route or direction) while on foot or while operating a vehicle. **17.** To assume occupancy of: *take a seat.* **18.** To require (something) as a basic necessity. **19.** To obtain from a source; derive or draw. **20.** To obtain, as through measurement or a specified procedure. **21.** To put down in shorthand or cursive writing. **22.** To put down an image, a likeness, or a representation of by or as by drawing, painting, or photography. **23.a.** To accept (something owed, offered, or given) either reluctantly or willingly: *take criticism.* **b.** *Baseball.* To refrain from swinging at (a pitched ball). **c.** To submit to (something inflicted); endure. **d.** To withstand. **24.a.** To accept or believe (something put forth) as true. **b.** To follow (advice or a lead, for example). **c.** To accept, handle, or deal with in a particular way: *took it in stride.* **d.** To consider in a particular relation or from a particular viewpoint: *take the bitter with the sweet.* **25.** To make or perform. **26.a.** To allow to come in; give access or admission to; admit. **b.** To provide room for; accommodate. **c.** To become saturated or impregnated with (dye, for example). **27.a.** To understand or interpret. **b.** To consider; assume: *Take the matter as settled.* **c.** To consider to be equal to; reckon: *We take their number at 1,000.* **d.** To perceive or feel; experience. **28.** To carry, convey, lead, or cause to go along to another place. **29.** To remove from a place. **30.** To cause to die; kill or destroy. **31.** To subtract. **32.a.** To commit and apply oneself to the study of. **b.** To study for with success. **33.** *Informal.* To swindle, defraud, or cheat. *—intr.* **1.** To acquire possession. **2.** To engage or mesh; catch, as gears or other mechanical parts. **3.** To start growing; root or germinate. **4.** To have the intended effect; operate or work. **5.** To gain popularity or favor. **6.** To become: *He took sick.* *—n.* **1.a.** The act or process of taking. **b.** That which is taken. **2.a.** A quantity collected at one time, esp. the amount of profit or receipts taken on a business arrangement or venture. **b.** The number of fish, game birds, or other animals killed or captured at one time. **3.** *Sports.* The amount of money collected as admission to a sporting event; the gate. **4.** The uninterrupted running of a movie or television camera or a set of recording equipment in filming a movie or television program or cutting a record. **5.a.** A scene filmed or televised without interrupting the run of the camera. **b.** A recording made in a single session. **6.a.** A physical reaction, such as a rash, indicating a successful vaccination. **b.** A successful graft. **7.** *Slang.* An attempt or a try. ***—phrasal verbs.*** **take after. 1.** To follow as an example. **2.** To resemble in appearance, temperament, or character. **take apart. 1.** To divide into parts after disassembling. **2.** To dissect or analyze (a theory, for example), usu. in an effort to discover flaws. **3.** *Slang.* To beat up; thrash. **take back.** To retract (something stated or written). **take down. 1.** To bring to a lower position from a higher one. **2.** To take apart; dismantle. **3.** To lower the arrogance or the self-esteem of (a person). **4.** To put down in writing. **take for. 1.** To regard as. **2.** To consider mistakenly. **take in. 1.** To grant admittance to; receive as a guest or an employee. **2.** To reduce in size; make smaller or shorter. **3.** To include or constitute. **4.** To understand. **5.** To deceive or swindle. **6.** To look at thoroughly; view. **7.** To accept (work) to be done in one's house for pay. **8.** To convey (a prisoner) to a police station. **take off. 1.** To remove, as clothing. **2.** To release: *took the brake off.* **3.** To deduct as a discount. **4.** To carry off or away. **5.** *Slang.* **a.** To go off; leave. **b.** To achieve wide use or popularity. **6.** To rise in flight. **7.** To discontinue. **8.** To withhold service due, as from one's work. **take on. 1.** To undertake or begin to handle. **2.** To hire; engage. **3.** To oppose in competition. **4.** *Informal.* To display violent or passionate emotion. **5.** To acquire (an appearance, for example) as or as if one's own. **take out. 1.** To extract; remove. **2.** To secure (a license, for example) by application to an authority. **3.** *Informal.* To escort, as a date. **4.** To give vent to. **5.** To obtain as an equivalent in a different form. **6.** *Informal.* To begin a course; set out. **7.** *Slang.* **a.** To kill; murder. **b.** To search for and destroy in an armed attack or other such encounter. **take over.** To assume the control or management of. **take to. 1.** To have recourse to; go to, as for safety. **2.** To develop as a habit or a steady practice. **3.** To become fond of or attached to. **take up. 1.** To raise; lift. **2.** To reduce in size; shorten or tighten. **3.** To pay off (an outstanding debt, mortgage, or note). **4.** To accept (an option, a bet, or a challenge) as offered. **5.** To begin again; resume. **6.** To use up, consume, or occupy. **7.** To develop an interest in or devotion to. **8.** To deal with. **9.** To assume: *took up a friendly attitude.* **10.** To absorb or adsorb. **11.** To enter into (a profession or business). ***—idioms.*** **on the take.** *Informal.* Taking or seeking to take bribes or illegal income. **take a bath.** *Informal.* To experience financial loss. **take account of.** To take into consideration. **take away from.** To detract from. **take care.** To be careful.

take care of. To assume responsibility for the maintenance, support, or treatment of. **take charge.** To assume control or command. **take effect. 1.** To become operative, as under law or regulation. **2.** To produce the desired reaction. **take exception.** To express opposition by argument; object to. **take five** (or **ten**). *Slang.* To take a short rest or break, as of five or ten minutes. **take for granted. 1.** To consider as true, real, or forthcoming; anticipate correctly. **2.** To underestimate the value of. **take heart.** To be confident or courageous. **take hold. 1.** To seize, as by grasping. **2.** To become established. **take it. 1.** To understand; assume. **2.** *Informal.* To endure abuse, criticism, or other harsh treatment. **take it on the chin.** *Slang.* To endure punishment, suffering, or defeat. **take it or leave it.** To accept or reject unconditionally. **take it out on.** *Informal.* To abuse (someone) in venting one's own anger. **take notice of.** To pay attention to. **take (one's) breath away.** To put into a state of awe or shock. **take (one's) time.** To act slowly or at one's leisure. **take place.** To happen; occur. **take root. 1.** To become established or fixed. **2.** To become rooted. **take shape.** To take on a distinctive form. **take sick.** *Chiefly Southern U.S.* To become ill. **take sides.** To associate with and support a particular faction, group, cause, or person. **take stock. 1.** To take an inventory. **2.** To make an estimate or appraisal, as of resources or of oneself. **take stock in.** To trust, believe in, or attach importance to. **take the cake. 1.** To be the most outrageous or disappointing. **2.** To win the prize; be outstanding. **take the fall** (or **hit**). *Slang.* To incur blame or censure, either willingly or unwillingly. **take the heat.** *Slang.* To incur and endure heavy censure or criticism. **take to the cleaners.** *Slang.* **1.** To rob or swindle. **2.** To take all the money or possessions of. **3.** To subject to withering criticism. **take up with.** *Informal.* To begin to associate with; consort with. [ME *taken* < OE *tacan* < ON *taka.*]

take-a•way (tāk′ə-wā′) *adj. Chiefly British.* Take-out.

take•down (tāk′doun′) *adj.* Having the capability of being taken down or apart. —*n.* **1.a.** A takedown article or apparatus. **b.** The mechanism that makes this procedure easy. **2.** *Sports.* A move in wrestling or the martial arts in which a standing opponent is forced to the floor. **3.** *Informal.* **a.** The act of humiliating a person. **b.** An instance of such humiliation.

take-home pay (tāk′hōm′) *n.* The amount of one's salary remaining after federal, state, and often city income taxes and various other deductions have been withheld.

take-in (tāk′ĭn′) *n. Informal.* The act or an instance of swindling or cheating; a deception.

take•off (tāk′ôf′, -ŏf′) *n.* **1.** The act of rising in flight. Used of an aircraft or a rocket. **2.** The point or place of takeoff. **3.** *Informal.* An amusing imitative caricature or burlesque.

take•out also **take-out** (tāk′out′) *adj.* **1.** Intended to be eaten off the premises. **2.** Selling or intended for the sale of takeout food products. —**take′-out′** *n.*

take•o•ver also **take-o•ver** (tāk′ō′vər) *n.* The act or an instance of assuming control or management of or responsibility for something, such as a nation. —**take′o′ver** *adj.*

tak•er (tā′kər) *n.* One that takes or takes up something, such as a wager or purchase: *There were no takers on the bets.*

take-up (tāk′ŭp′) *n.* **1.** The act of taking or tightening up. **2.** A device for reducing slack or taking up lost motion.

ta•kin (tä′kēn′) *n.* A large ruminant mammal *(Budorcas taxicolor)* of the mountains of China, Burma, and the Himalayas, having backward-pointing horns and a shaggy coat. [Poss. of Tibeto-Burman orig.]

tak•ing (tā′kĭng) *adj.* **1.** Capturing interest; fetching. **2.** Contagious; catching. Used of an infectious disease. —*n.* **1.** The act of one that takes. **2.** Something taken, as a catch of fish. **3. takings.** *Informal.* Receipts, esp. of money.

ta•ki-ta•ki (tä′kē-tä′kē) *n.* See **Sranantongo.** [Prob. alteration and redup. of TALK.]

Tak•ka•kaw (tăk′ə-kô′). A waterfall, 503.3 m (1,650 ft), in SE British Columbia, Canada.

Ta•kli•ma•kan also **Ta•kla•ma•kan** (tä′klə-mə-kän′). A desert of W China between the Tien Shan and the Kunlun Mts.

Ta•ko•ma Park (tə-kō′mə). A city of central MD, a suburb of Washington DC. Pop. 16,700.

ta•la (tä′lə) *n.* See table at **currency.** [Samoan < E. DOLLAR.]

Ta•la•ud Islands (tə-lout′, tä-lä′o͞od) or **Ta•laur Islands** (-lour′, -lä′o͝or). An island group of NE Indonesia.

Tal•bot (tôl′bət, tăl′-) *n.* A large white or light-colored English hound, having long ears and heavy jaws, formerly used for tracking and hunting. [ME, personal name < OFr.]

talc (tălk) *n.* A fine-grained white, greenish, or gray mineral, $Mg_3Si_4O_{10}(OH)_2$, having a soft soapy feel and used in talcum and face powder and as a filler in paper and plastics. —*tr.v.* **talcked, talck•ing, talcs** or **talced, talc•ing, talcs.** To apply this substance to (a photographic plate, for example). [Fr. < Med.Lat. *talcum* and OSp. *talco,* both < Ar. *ṭalq* < Pers. *talk.*] —**talc′ose′** (tăl′kōs′), **talc′ous, talck′y** *adj.*

Tal•ca (täl′kä). A city of central Chile between Santiago and Concepción. Pop. 128,544.

Tal•ca•hua•no (täl′kə-wä′nō, -hwä′-, täl′kä-). A city of central Chile on the Pacific near Concepción. Pop. 202,368.

tal•cum (tăl′kəm) *n.* **1.** Talc. **2.** Talcum powder. [See TALC.]

talcum powder *n.* A fine, often perfumed powder made from purified talc for use on the skin.

tale (tāl) *n.* **1.** A recital of events or happenings; a report or revelation. **2.** A malicious story, piece of gossip, or petty complaint. **3.** A deliberate lie; a falsehood. **4.** A narrative of real or imaginary events; a story. **5.** *Archaic.* A tally or reckoning; a total. [ME < OE *talu.* See **del-[2]*.**]

tale•bear•er (tāl′bâr′ər) *n.* One who spreads malicious stories or gossip. —**tale′bear′ing** *adj. & n.*

tal•ent (tăl′ənt) *n.* **1.** A marked innate ability, as for artistic accomplishment. **2.a.** Natural endowment or ability of a superior quality. **b.** A person or group of people having such ability. **3.** A variable unit of weight and money used in ancient Greece, Rome, and the Middle East. [ME, inclination, disposition < OFr. < Med.Lat. < Lat., balance, sum of money < Gk. *talanton.* See **telə-*.**] —**tal′ent•ed** *adj.*

talent scout *n.* An agent who goes in search of talented people for acting, sports, or business.

talent show *n.* A show that features amateur performers whose talents may win them recognition or awards.

ta•ler also **tha•ler** (tä′lər) *n., pl.* **taler** or **-lers** also **thaler** or **-lers.** Any of numerous silver coins that once served as a currency unit in certain Germanic countries. [Ger. See DOLLAR.]

tales (tālz, tā′lēz) *n., pl.* **tales.** *Law.* A writ allowing for a summons of jurors. [ME < Med.Lat. *tālēs dē circumstantibus,* such (persons) from those standing about (a phrase used in the writ) < Lat., pl. of *tālis,* such. See **to-*.**]

tale•tell•er (tāl′tĕl′ər) *n.* **1.** One who tells stories; a storyteller. **2.** A talebearer; a tattletale. —**tale′tell′ing** *adj. & n.*

ta•li (tā′lī′) *n.* Pl. of **talus[1].**

Ta•lien (tä′lyĕn′). See **Dalian.**

tal•i•on (tăl′ē-ən) *n.* A punishment identical to the offense. [ME *talioun* < AN < Lat. *tāliō, tāliōn-.* See **telə-*.**]

tal•i•ped (tăl′ə-pĕd′) *adj.* Having a clubfoot; clubfooted. —*n.* A person with a clubfoot. [< NLat. *tālipēs, tāliped-,* clubfoot. See TALIPES.]

tal•i•pes (tăl′ə-pēz′) *n.* See **clubfoot** 1. [NLat. *tālipēs, tāliped-* : Lat. *tālus,* ankle + Lat. *pēs, ped-,* foot; see -PED.]

tal•i•pot (tăl′ə-pŏt′) *n.* A tall palm tree *(Corypha umbraculifera)* of India and Sri Lanka having a spreading crown of very large fanlike leaves and a giant inflorescence. [Ult. < Skt. *tālapattram,* palm leaf used for writing : *tālaḥ,* fan palm; see TODDY + *pattram,* leaf; see **pet-*.**]

tal•is•man (tăl′ĭs-mən, -ĭz-) *n., pl.* **-mans. 1.** An object marked with magic signs, believed to confer on its bearer supernatural powers or protection. **2.** Something that seems magical in power. [Ult. < Ar. *ṭilasm* < LGk. *telesma* < Gk., consecration ceremony < *telein,* to consecrate, fulfill < *telos,* result. See **k^{w}el-[1]*.**] —**tal′is•man′ic** (-ĭs-măn′ĭk, -ĭz-), **tal′is•man′i•cal** (-ĭ-kəl) *adj.*

talk (tôk) *v.* **talked, talk•ing, talks.** —*tr.* **1.** To articulate (words). **2.** To give expression to in words. **3.** To speak of or discuss (something). **4.** To speak or know how to speak in (an idiom or a language). **5.** To gain, influence, or bring into a specified state by talking. **6.** To spend (a period of time) by or as if by talking. —*intr.* **1.** To converse by means of spoken language. See Syns at **speak. 2.** To articulate words. **3.** To imitate the sounds of human speech. **4.** To express one's thoughts or emotions by means of spoken language. **5.** To convey one's thoughts in a way other than by spoken words. **6.** To express one's thoughts in writing. **7.** To parley or negotiate with someone. **8.** To spread rumors; gossip. **9.** To allude to something. **10.** To consult or confer with someone. **11.** To reveal information concerning oneself or others, esp. under pressure. **12.** *Informal.* To be efficacious: *Money talks.* —*n.* **1.** An exchange of ideas or opinions; a conversation. **2.** A speech or lecture. **3.** Hearsay, rumor, or speculation. **4.** A subject of conversation. **5.** A conference or negotiation. Often used in the plural. **6.** Jargon; slang. **7.** Empty speech or unnecessary discussion. **8.** A particular manner of speech. **9.** Something, such as the sounds of animals, felt to resemble human talk. —***phrasal verbs.*** **talk around. 1.** To persuade. **2.** To speak indirectly about. **talk at.** To address orally with no regard for or interest in reaction or response. **talk back. 1.** To make an impertinent reply. **2.** To make a belligerent response. **talk down. 1.** To depreciate. **2.** To speak with insulting condescension. **3.** To silence (a person), esp. by speaking in a loud and domineering manner. **4.** To direct and control (an aircraft during an approach for landing) by radioed instructions. **talk out. 1.** To discuss (a matter) exhaustively. **2.** To resolve or settle by discussion. **3.** *Chiefly British.* To block (proposed legislation) by filibustering. **talk over. 1.** To consider thoroughly in conversation; discuss. **2.** To win (someone) over by persuasion. **talk up. 1.** To speak in favor of; promote. **2.** To speak up in a frank, often insolent manner. —***idioms.*** **talk big.** *Informal.* To brag. **talk sense.** To speak rationally. [ME *talken.* See **del-[2]*.**] —**talk′er** *n.*

talk•a•thon (tôk′ə-thŏn′) *n.* A lengthy session of discussions, speeches, or debate. [TALK + (MAR)ATHON.]

talk•a•tive (tô′kə-tĭv) *adj.* Marked by or having a disposition to talk. —**talk′a•tive•ly** *adv.* —**talk′a•tive•ness** *n.*

talisman
Late 19th-century reliquary figure from central Africa

ă pat	oi boy
ā pay	ou out
âr care	o͝o took
ä father	o͞o boot
ĕ pet	ŭ cut
ē be	ûr urge
ĭ pit	th thin
ī pie	*th* this
îr pier	hw which
ŏ pot	zh vision
ō toe	ə about, item
ô paw	

Stress marks:
′ (primary);
′ (secondary), as in
dictionary (dĭk′shə-nĕr′ē)

talk•back (tôk′băk′) *n.* A one-way communications link from a control booth to a recording or broadcasting studio.
talk•ie (tô′kē) *n. Informal.* A movie with a sound track.
talk•ing book (tô′kĭng) *n.* A recording of a reading of a book, designed for use by the visually impaired.
talking head *n. Slang.* The image of a person, as on a television news show, who talks at length directly to the camera.
talking point *n.* Something, such as a persuasive point, that helps support an argument or a discussion.
talk•ing-to (tô′kĭng-to͞o′) *n., pl.* **-tos.** *Informal.* A scolding.
talk show *n.* A television or radio show featuring talk, as among hosts, guests, and listeners.
talk•y (tô′kē) *adj.* **-i•er, -i•est. 1.** Talkative; loquacious. **2.** Containing or given to too much talk. **—talk′i•ness** *n.*
tall (tôl) *adj.* **tall•er, tall•est. 1.a.** Having greater than ordinary height. **b.** Having considerable height, esp. in relation to width; lofty. **2.** Having a specified height. **3.** *Informal.* Fanciful or exaggerated; boastful. **4.** Impressively great or difficult: *a tall order.* **5.** *Archaic.* Excellent; fine. *—adv.* With proud bearing; straight. [ME, brave, quick < OE *getæl*, swift. See **del-**[2]*.] **—tall′ness** *n.*
Tal•la•de•ga (tăl′ə-dē′gə). A city of E-central AL E of Birmingham; incorp. 1835. Pop. 18,175.
tal•lage (tăl′ĭj) *n.* An occasional tax levied by the Anglo-Norman kings on crown lands and royal towns. *—tr.v.* **-laged, -lag•ing, -lag•es.** To levy a tax on. [ME *taillage* < OFr. < *taillier*, to cut, tax. See TAILOR.]
Tal•la•has•see (tăl′ə-hăs′ē). The cap. of FL, in the NW part; founded as cap. of the Florida Terr. in 1824. Pop. 124,773.
Tal•la•hatch•ie (tăl′ə-hăch′ē). A river rising in N MS and flowing c. 371 km (230 mi) generally SW to the Yazoo R.
Tal•la•poo•sa (tăl′ə-po͞o′sə). A river rising in NW GA and flowing c. 431 km (268 mi) to the Coosa R.
tall•boy (tôl′boi′) *n. Chiefly British.* A highboy.
Tal•ley•rand-Pé•ri•gord (tăl′ē-rănd′pĕr′ĭ-gôr′, tä-lĕ-räN-pā-rē-gôr′), **Charles Maurice de.** 1754–1838. French public official during the French Revolution, Napoleon's reign, the Bourbon restoration, and the reign of Louis Philippe.
Tal•linn also **Tal•lin** (tăl′ĭn, tä′lĭn). The cap. of Estonia, in the NW part on the Gulf of Finland. Pop. 464,000.
tal•lith also **tal•lis** (tä′lĭs, tä-lēt′) *n., pl.* **tal•lith•im** (tä-lē′-sĭm, -lä′-, tä′lē-tēm′) or **tal•liths** also **tal•li•sim** (tä-lē′sĭm, -lä′-). *Judaism.* A shawl with zizith worn by many observant Jews during morning prayer. [Mishnaic Heb. *ṭallît*, cover < Heb. *ṭillēl*, to cover.]
tall oil (täl, tôl) *n.* A resinous liquid mixture of rosin acids and fatty acids obtained as a byproduct in the treatment of pine pulp and used in soaps, emulsions, and lubricants. [Partial transl. of Ger. *Tallöl* < partial transl. of Swed. *tallolja* : *tall*, pine (< ON *thöll*, young pine tree) + *olja*, oil.]
tal•low (tăl′ō) *n.* **1.** Hard fat obtained from cattle, sheep, or horses and used in foodstuffs or to make candles, leather dressing, soap, and lubricants. **2.** Any of various similar fats, such as those obtained from plants. *—tr.v.* **-lowed, -low•ing, -lows. 1.** To smear or cover with tallow. **2.** To fatten (animals) to obtain tallow. [ME *talow*.] **—tal′low•y** *adj.*
tal•ly (tăl′ē) *n., pl.* **-lies. 1.** A reckoning or score. **2.a.** A stick on which notches keep a count or score. **b.** A tally once used to keep a record of amounts paid or owed. **3.** A mark used in recording a number of acts or objects, most often in series of five, consisting of four vertical lines canceled diagonally or horizontally by a fifth line. **4.** An identifying or classifying label, ticket, or piece of metal or wood, esp. in gardens and greenhouses. **5.** Something that is very similar or corresponds to something else; a double or counterpart. *—v.* **-lied, -ly•ing, -lies.** *—tr.* **1.** To reckon or count. **2.** To record by making a mark. **3.** To label, as with a tally, for identification or classification. **4.** To cause to tally. *—intr.* **1.** To be alike; correspond or agree. **2.** To keep score. [ME *taly* < AN *tallie* < Med.Lat. *tallia* < Lat. *tālea*, stick.]
tal•ly•ho (tăl′ē-hō′) *interj.* Used to urge hounds on during a fox hunt. *—v.* **-hoed, -ho•ing, -hos.** *—tr.* To urge (hounds) on during a fox hunt by shouting "tallyho" when the fox is sighted. *—intr.* To shout "tallyho" as a hunting cry. *—n., pl.* **-hos. 1.** The cry of "tallyho." **2.** A fast coach drawn by four horses. [Prob. alteration of Fr. *taïaut* < OFr. *thialau, taho.*]
Tal•mud (täl′mo͝od, tăl′məd) *n. Judaism.* The collection of ancient Rabbinic writings consisting of the Mishnah and the Gemara, constituting the basis for much of Jewish law. [Mishnaic Heb. *talmûd*, learning, instruction < *lāmad*, to learn.] **—Tal•mu′dic** (tăl-mo͞o′dĭk, -myo͞o′-, tăl-), **Tal•mu′di•cal** (-dĭ-kəl) *adj.* **—Tal′mud•ist** (täl′mo͝o-dĭst, tăl′mə-) *n.*
tal•on (tăl′ən) *n.* **1.a.** The claw of a bird of prey. **b.** The similar claw of a predatory animal. **2.** Something similar to or suggestive of an animal's claw. **3.** The part of a lock that the key presses in order to shoot the bolt. **4.** *Games.* The part of the deck of cards in certain card games left on the table after the deal. **5.** *Archit.* An ogee molding. [ME *taloun* < OFr. *talon*, heel < VLat. **tālō, tālōn-* < Lat. *tālus*, ankle.]
ta•lus[1] (tā′ləs) *n., pl.* **-li** (-lī′). **1.** The bone of the ankle that articulates with the tibia and fibula to form the ankle joint. **2.** The ankle. [Lat. *tālus*, ankle.]

talon
Of a bald eagle

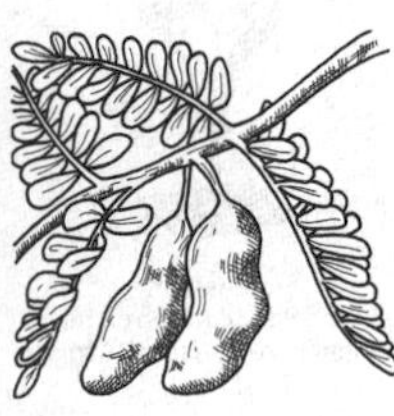
tamarind
Tamarindus indica

tambourine

ta•lus[2] (tā′ləs) *n., pl.* **-lus•es.** A sloping mass of rock debris at a cliff base. [Fr. *talus* < OFr. *talu*, earthwork slope < Lat. *talūtium*, gold-bearing outcrop, perh. of Celt. orig.]
tam (tăm) *n.* A tam-o'-shanter.
ta•ma•le (tə-mä′lē) *n.* A Mexican dish made of fried chopped meat and crushed peppers, rolled in cornmeal dough, wrapped in cornhusks, and steamed. [< Am.Sp. *tamales*, pl. of *tamal*, tamale < Nahuatl *tamalli.*]
ta•man•du•a (tə-măn′do͞o-ə) *n.* Either of two small nocturnal anteaters *(Tamandua tetradactyla* or *T. mexicana)* of Central and South America having thick bristly fur. [Port. *tamanduá* < Tupi *ta-monduá* < *monduar*, to catch.]
Tam•a•rac (tăm′ə-răk′). A city of SE FL NW of Fort Lauderdale. Pop. 44,822.
tam•a•rack (tăm′ə-răk′) *n.* A deciduous North American larch tree *(Larix laricina)* having short needles borne on spur shoots. [Canadian Fr. *tamarac*, prob. of Algonquian orig.]
tam•a•rau also **tam•a•rao** (tăm′ə-rou′) *n., pl.* **-raus** also **-raos.** A small grayish-black short-horned buffalo *(Bubalus mindorensis)* of the island of Mindoro. [Tagalog *tamaráw.*]
tam•a•rin (tăm′ə-rĭn, -răn′) *n.* Any of various small long-tailed arboreal monkeys of the genera *Leontideus* and *Saguinus* of Central and South America. [Fr. < Galibi.]
tam•a•rind (tăm′ə-rĭnd′) *n.* **1.** A tropical Asian evergreen tree *(Tamarindus indica)* having pinnately compound leaves, pale yellow flowers, and thick pods containing an edible acid pulp. **2.** The fruit of this tree, eaten fresh or used in the preparation of chutney, curry, or soft drinks. [ME < OFr. *tamarinde* < Ar. *tamr hindī* : *tamr*, date + *hindī*, of India.]
tam•a•risk (tăm′ə-rĭsk′) *n.* Any of numerous African and Eurasian shrubs or small trees of the genus *Tamarix*, having small scalelike leaves. [ME *tamarisc* < LLat. *tamariscus*, var. of Lat. *tamarīx, tamarīc-.*]
Ta•ma•yo (tä-mä′yō), **Rufino.** 1899–1991. Mexican artist whose works were influenced by pre-Columbian symbols.
tam•ba•la (täm-bä′lə) *n.* See table at **currency.** [Perh. < Chewa or Nyanja, cockerels.]
tam•bour (tăm′bo͝or′, tăm-bo͝or′) *n.* **1.** *Mus.* A drum or drummer. **2.a.** A small wooden embroidery frame consisting of two concentric hoops between which fabric is stretched. **b.** Embroidery made on such a frame. **3.** A rolling front or top for a desk or table, consisting of narrow strips of wood glued to canvas. **4.** *Archit.* **a.** The wall of a circular building surrounded with columns. **b.** The vertical part of a cupola. *—v.* **-boured, -bour•ing, -bours.** *—tr.* To do (embroidery) on a tambour. *—intr.* To embroider at or on a tambour. [ME < OFr., ult. < Ar. *ṭanbūr*, lute.]
tam•bou•ra or **tam•bu•ra** (tŭm-bo͝or′ə) *n. Mus.* An unfretted lute of India and Turkey, used as a harmonic drone. [Urdu *ṭambūra* < Pers. *ṭanbūra* < Ar. *ṭanbūr.*]
tam•bou•rin (tăm′bo͝o-rĭn, tăN-bo͝o-răN′) *n.* **1.** *Mus.* **a.** A long narrow drum used in Provence. **b.** One who plays this drum. **2.** A style of dance in lively two-beat rhythm, accompanied by this drum. [Prov. *tambourin* < OFr., dim. of *tambour*, tambour. See TAMBOUR.]
tam•bou•rine (tăm′bə-rēn′) *n. Mus.* A percussion instrument made up of a small drumhead with jingling disks fitted into the rim. [Fr. *tambourin*, small drum < OFr. See TAMBOURIN.]
Tam•bov (täm-bôf′, -bôv′). A city of W Russia SE of Moscow; founded as a fortress in 1636. Pop. 296,000.
tam•bu•rit•za (tăm-bo͝or′ĭt-sə, tăm′bə-rĭt′sə) *n. Mus.* A Serbo-Croatian mandolinlike stringed instrument. [Serbo-Croatian *tàmburica*, dim. of *tàmbura*, stringed instrument < Ottoman Turk. *ṭambūra* < Pers. *ṭanbūra*. See TAMBOURA.]
tame (tām) *adj.* **tam•er, tam•est. 1.** Brought from wildness into a domesticated or tractable state. **2.** Naturally unafraid; not timid. **3.** Submissive; docile; fawning. **4.** Insipid; flat: *a tame party.* **5.** Sluggish; languid; inactive. *—tr.v.* **tamed, tam•ing, tames. 1.** To make tractable; domesticate. **2.** To subdue or curb. **3.** To tone down; soften. [ME < OE *tam*. See **demə-***.] **—tam′a•ble, tame′a•ble** *adj.* **—tame′ly** *adv.* **—tame′ness** *n.* **—tam′er** *n.*
Tam•er•lane (tăm′ər-lān′) or **Tam•bur•laine** (-bər-). 1336–1405. Mongolian conqueror of Persia, Turkey, and India.
Tam•il (tăm′əl, tŭm′-, tä′məl) *n., pl.* **Tamil** or **-ils. 1.** A member of a Dravidian people of southern India and northern Sri Lanka. **2.** The Dravidian language of the Tamil. *—adj.* Of or relating to the Tamil or their language or culture. [Tamil.]
Tamm (tăm), **Igor Yevgeneevich.** 1895–1971. Russian physicist who shared a 1958 Nobel Prize.
Tam•muz also **Tham•muz** (tä′mo͞oz) *n.* The tenth month of the year in the Jewish calendar. [Heb. *Tammûz* < Babylonian *Du'uzu*, the name of a god.]
tam-o'-shan•ter (tăm′ə-shăn′tər) *n.* A Scottish cap or braided bonnet, sometimes having a pompon, tassel, or feather in the center. [After "*Tam o' Shanter*" by Robert Burns.]
tamp (tămp) *tr.v.* **tamped, tamp•ing, tamps. 1.** To pack down tightly by a succession of blows or taps. **2.** To pack clay, sand, or dirt into (a drill hole) above an explosive. [Perh. back-formation < *tampin*, var. of TAMPION.]
Tam•pa (tăm′pə). A city of W-central FL on **Tampa Bay,** an inlet of the Gulf of Mexico. Pop. 280,015.

tam•per[1] (tăm′pər) *v.* **-pered, -per•ing, -pers.** —*intr.* **1.** To interfere in a harmful manner. **2.** To tinker with rashly or foolishly. **3.** To engage in improper or secret dealings, as in an effort to influence. See Syns at **interfere.** —*tr.* To alter improperly. [Prob. alteration of TEMPER.] —**tam′per•er** *n.*

tamp•er[2] (tăm′pər) *n.* A neutron reflector in an atomic bomb that delays the expansion of the exploding material, making possible a longer-lasting and more energetic explosion.

Tam•pe•re (tăm′pə-rā′, täm′-). A city of SW Finland NNW of Helsinki. Pop. 168,150.

Tam•pi•co (tăm-pē′kō, täm-). A city of E-central Mexico near the Gulf of Mexico NNE of Mexico City. Pop. 267,957.

tam•pi•on (tăm′pē-ən) also **tom•pi•on** (tŏm′-) *n.* A plug or cover for the muzzle of a cannon or gun to keep out dust and moisture. [ME < OFr. *tampon*, var. of *tapon*, rag for stopping a hole, of Gmc. orig.]

tam•pon (tăm′pŏn′) *n.* A plug of absorbent material inserted into a body cavity or wound to check a flow of blood or to absorb secretions, esp. one for the vagina during menstruation. [Fr. < OFr. See TAMPION.] —**tam′pon′** *v.*

tam-tam[1] (tŭm′tŭm′, tăm′tăm′) *n. Mus.* A gong having a metal disk struck with a felt-covered hammer or stick, used in a gamelan orchestra. [Ult. of imit. orig.]

tam-tam[2] (tŭm′tŭm′, tăm′tăm′) *n.* Var. of **tom-tom.**

tan[1] (tăn) *v.* **tanned, tan•ning, tans.** —*tr.* **1.** To convert (hide) into leather, as by treating with tannin. **2.** To make brown by exposure to the sun. **3.** *Informal.* To thrash; beat. —*intr.* To become suntanned. —*n.* **1.** *Color.* A light or moderate yellowish brown to brownish orange. **2.** The brown color that sun rays impart to light skin. **3.** Tanbark. **4.a.** Tannin. **b.** A solution derived from tannin. —*adj.* **tan•ner, tan•nest. 1.** *Color.* Of the color tan. **2.** Having a suntan. **3.** Used in or relating to tanning. [ME *tannen* < OE **tannian* < Med.Lat. *tannāre* < *tannum*, tanbark, prob. of Celt. orig.]

tan[2] *abbr. Math.* Tangent.

Ta•na (tä′nə, -nä), **Lake.** Also **Lake Tsa•na** (tsä′-). A lake of NW Ethiopia; source of the Blue Nile.

tan•a•ger (tăn′ĭ-jər) *n.* Any of various small New World passerine birds of the family Thraupidae, often having brightly colored plumage in the males and usu. living in forests. [NLat. *tanagra*, alteration of Port. *tangará* < Tupi *tanagorá*.]

Tan•a•gra (tăn′ə-grə, tə-năg′rə). An ancient city of E-central Greece in E Boeotia; site of a Spartan defeat of Athenian forces in 457 B.C.

Ta•nakh (tä-näKH) *n.* The sacred book of Judaism, consisting of the Torah, the Prophets, and the Writings.

Tan•a•na (tăn′ə-nô′). A river of E and S AK flowing c. 764 km (475 mi) from the Wrangell Mts. to the Yukon R.

Ta•nan•a•rive (tə-năn′ə-rēv′, tä-nä-nä-rēv′). See **Antananarivo.**

Tana River. 1. A river of central Kenya flowing c. 805 km (500 mi) to the Indian Ocean. **2.** A river, c. 322 km (200 mi), of NE Norway emptying into an inlet of the Arctic Ocean.

tan•bark (tăn′bärk′) *n.* **1.** The bark of various trees used as a source of tannin. **2.** Shredded bark from which the tannin has been extracted, used to cover circus arenas and other surfaces.

Tan•cred (tăng′krĭd). 1078?–1112. Norman soldier who was a leader of the First Crusade (1096–99).

tan•dem (tăn′dəm) *n.* **1.** A two-wheeled carriage drawn by horses harnessed one before the other. **2.** A team of carriage horses harnessed in single file. **3.** A tandem bicycle. **4.** An arrangement of two or more persons or objects placed one behind the other. —*adv.* One behind the other. [Lat., at last, at length. See **to-*.**] —**tan′dem** *adj.*

tandem bicycle *n.* A bicycle built for two or more people sitting one behind the other.

tan•door (tän-do͝or′) *n., pl.* **-doors** or **-door•i** (-do͝or′ē). A cylindrical oven made of clay, heated to a high heat over charcoal or wood and used in India. [Hindi and Urdu *tandūr* < Pers., var. of *tannūr* < MPers. < Ar. < *nūr*, light, fire.]

tan•door•i (tän-do͝or′ē) *adj.* Cooked in a tandoor. [Hindi *tandūri* < *tandūr*, tandoor. See TANDOOR.]

Ta•ney (tô′nē), **Roger Brooke.** 1777–1864. Amer. jurist; chief justice of the U.S. Supreme Court (1836–64).

tang[1] (tăng) *n.* **1.** A distinctively sharp taste, flavor, or odor. **2.** A distinctive quality that adds piquancy. **3.** A trace, hint, or smattering. **4.** A sharp point, tongue, or prong. **5.** A projection by which a tool, such as a knife, is attached to its handle or stock. **6.** A surgeonfish. —*tr.v.* **tanged, tang•ing, tangs. 1.** To furnish with a tang. **2.** To give a tang to. [ME *tange*, of Scand. orig.] —**tang′i•ness** *n.* —**tang′y** *adj.*

tang[2] (tăng) *n.* A loud ringing sound; a twang. [Imit.] —**tang** *v.*

Tang (täng). A Chinese dynasty (618–907) known for its wealth and its encouragement of the arts and literature.

Tan•gan•yi•ka (tăn′gən-yē′kə, tăng′-). A former country of E-central Africa; gained independence from Great Britain in 1961 and joined with Zanzibar to form Tanzania in 1964. —**Tan′gan•yi′kan** *adj. & n.*

Tanganyika, Lake. A lake of E-central Africa between Zaire and Tanzania.

tan•ge•lo (tăn′jə-lō′) *n., pl.* **-los. 1.** A hybrid citrus tree derived from grapefruit and tangerine. **2.** The aromatic fruit of this tree. [Blend of TANGERINE and POMELO.]

tan•gen•cy (tăn′jən-sē) also **tan•gence** (-jəns) *n.* The condition of being tangent.

tan•gent (tăn′jənt) *adj.* **1.** Making contact at a single point or along a line; touching but not intersecting. **2.** Irrelevant. —*n.* **1.** A line, curve, or surface touching but not intersecting another line, curve, or surface. **2.** *Math.* The trigonometric function of an acute angle in a right triangle that is the ratio of the length of the side opposite the angle to the length of the side adjacent to the angle. **3.** A sudden digression or change of course. **4.** *Mus.* An upright pin in a keyboard instrument, esp. in a clavichord, that rises to sound a string when a key is depressed and stops the string at a preset length to set the pitch. [Lat. *(linea) tangēns*, *tangent-*, touching (line), pr.part. of *tangere*, to touch. See **tag-*.**]

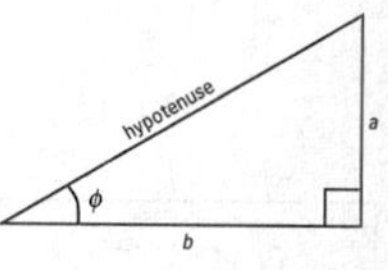

tangent
tangent $\phi = \frac{a}{b}$

tan•gen•tial (tăn-jĕn′shəl) also **tan•gen•tal** (-jĕn′tl) *adj.* **1.** Of, relating to, or moving along or in the direction of a tangent. **2.** Merely touching or slightly connected. **3.** Only superficially relevant; divergent: *a tangential remark.* —**tan•gen′ti•al′i•ty** (-shē-ăl′ĭ-tē) *n.* —**tan•gen′tial•ly** *adv.*

tan•ger•ine (tăn′jə-rēn′, tăn′jə-rēn′) *n.* **1.** A small southeast Asian spiny evergreen tree *(Citrus reticulata)* having sweet edible fruit. **2.** The loose-skinned fruit of this tree. **3.** *Color.* A strong reddish orange to strong or vivid orange. [Short for *tangerine orange*, after *Tanger* (Tangier), Morocco.]

tan•gi•ble (tăn′jə-bəl) *adj.* **1.a.** Discernible by the touch; palpable. **b.** Possible to touch. **c.** Possible to be treated as fact; real or concrete. **2.** Possible to understand or realize. **3.** *Law.* That can be valued monetarily. —*n.* **1.** Something palpable or concrete. **2. tangibles.** Material assets. [LLat. *tangibilis* < Lat. *tangere*, to touch. See **tag-*.**] —**tan′gi•bil′i•ty, tan′gi•ble•ness** *n.* —**tan′gi•bly** *adv.*

Tan•gier (tăn-jîr′) also **Tan•giers** (-jîrz′). A city of N Morocco at the W end of the Strait of Gibraltar. Pop. 266,346.

tan•gle[1] (tăng′gəl) *v.* **-gled, -gling, -gles.** —*tr.* **1.** To mix together or intertwine in a confused mass; snarl. **2.** To involve in hampering or awkward complications; entangle. **3.** To catch and hold in or as if in a net; entrap. See Syns at **catch.** —*intr.* **1.** To be or become entangled. **2.** *Informal.* To enter into argument, dispute, or conflict. —*n.* **1.** A confused, intertwined mass. **2.** A jumbled or confused state. **3.** A state of bewilderment. **4.** *Informal.* An argument or altercation. [ME *tangilen*, to involve in an embarrassing situation, var. of *tagilen*, prob. of Scand. orig.] —**tan′gly** *adj.*

tan•gle[2] (tăng′gəl) *n.* A large seaweed of the genus *Laminaria.* [Of Scand. orig.; akin to ON *thöngull*, seaweed.]

tan•gled (tăng′gəld) *adj.* Complicated and difficult to unravel. See Syns at **complex.**

tan•go (tăng′gō) *n., pl.* **-gos. 1.** A Latin American ballroom dance in 2/4 or 4/4 time. **2.** The music for this dance. —*intr.v.* **-goed, -go•ing, -gos.** To perform this dance. [Am. Sp., poss. of Niger-Congo orig.; akin to Ibibio *tamgu*, to dance.] —**tan′go•like′** *adj.*

tan•gram (tăng′grəm) *n. Games.* A Chinese puzzle consisting of a square cut into five triangles, a square, and a rhomboid, to be reassembled into different figures. [Perh. partial transl. of Chin. *táng tú* : *táng*, Tang + *tú*, picture, diagram.]

Tang•shan (tăng′shăn′, däng′-). A city of NE China ESE of Beijing. Pop. 921,100.

Tan•guy (täN-gē′), **Yves.** 1900–55. French-born Amer. painter whose works include *Indefinite Divisibility* (1942).

Ta•nis (tā′nĭs). An ancient city of Egypt in the E delta of the Nile R.; important during the XIX and XXI Dynasties.

tan•ist (tăn′ĭst, thô′nĭst) *n.* In ancient Ireland, the heir apparent to a Celtic chief, elected during the chief's lifetime. [Ir. Gael. *tánaiste*, second, tanist < OIr. *tānaise.* See **sed-*.**] —**tan′ist•ry** *n.*

tank (tăngk) *n.* **1.a.** A large, often metallic container for holding or storing liquids or gases. **b.** The amount that a tank can hold. **2.** A usu. artificial pond or cistern, used to hold water for drinking or irrigation. **3.** An enclosed, heavily armored combat vehicle mounted with cannon and guns and moving on caterpillar treads. **4.** *Slang.* A jail or jail cell. —*tr.v.* **tanked, tank•ing, tanks.** To place, store, or process in a tank. —***phrasal verb.* tank up. 1.** *Slang.* To drink to the point of intoxication. **2.** To fill the tank of a motor vehicle with gasoline. [Partly < Gujarati *tānkh*, cistern (< Skt. *taḍāgaḥ*, pond, perh. of Dravidian orig.) and partly < Port. *tanque*, reservoir (var. of *estanque* < *estancar*, to dam up < VLat. **stanticāre*; see STANCH[1]).] —**tank′ful′** (-fo͝ol′) *n.*

tank
Top: Fuel storage tanks
Bottom: M-1 army tank

tan•ka[1] (täng′kə) *n.* A Japanese verse form in five lines, the first and third of five syllables and the rest of seven. [J.]

tan•ka[2] *n.* A Tibetan religious painting on fabric, usu. portraying the Buddha or lamas in stereotyped aspects. [Tibetan *thaṅka*, something rolled up.]

tank•age (tăng′kĭj) *n.* **1.a.** The act or process of putting or storing in a tank. **b.** The amount that a tank can hold. **c.** A fee for tank storage. **2.** Animal residues that remain after rendering fat in a slaughterhouse, used for fertilizer or feed.

tank•ard (tăng′kərd) *n.* A large drinking cup having a single handle and often a hinged cover. [ME.]

tankard
Late 18th-century American pewter tankard by Frederick Bassett (1740–1800)

ă pat	oi boy
ā pay	ou out
âr care	o͝o took
ä father	o͞o boot
ĕ pet	ŭ cut
ē be	ûr urge
ĭ pit	th thin
ī pie	*th* this
îr pier	hw which
ŏ pot	zh vision
ō toe	ə about,
ô paw	item

Stress marks:
′ (primary);
′ (secondary), as in
dictionary (dĭk′shə-nĕr′ē)

tank destroyer *n.* A high-speed armored vehicle equipped with antitank guns.

tanked (tăngkt) *adj. Slang.* Intoxicated; drunk.

tank•er (tăng′kər) *n.* **1.** A ship, plane, or truck for transporting liquids in bulk. **2.** A member of a military tank crew.

tank farm *n.* A group of tanks, as for the commercial storage of oil.

tank suit *n.* A simply designed one-piece swimsuit with shoulder straps.

tank top *n.* A sleeveless, tight-fitting, usu. knit shirt with no front opening. [< its resemblance to a TANK SUIT.]

tank town *n.* A small town. [So called because trains would stop there only to replenish water.]

tan•nate (tăn′āt′) *n.* A salt or an ester of tannic acid. [TANN(IN) + -ATE[2].]

Tanzania

tan•ner[1] (tăn′ər) *n.* One that tans hides.

tan•ner[2] (tăn′ər) *n. Chiefly British.* A sixpenny coin formerly used in Britain; a sixpence. [?]

tan•ner•y (tăn′ə-rē) *n., pl.* **-ies.** An establishment where hides are tanned.

tan•nic (tăn′ĭk) *adj.* Of, relating to, or obtained from tannin.

tannic acid *n.* Any of various yellowish complex organic compounds, esp. $C_{14}H_{10}O_9$, derived from nutgalls and certain plants and used in tanning and in dyeing as a mordant.

tan•nif•er•ous (tă-nĭf′ər-əs) *adj.* Having or yielding tannin.

tan•nin (tăn′ĭn) *n.* **1.** Tannic acid. **2.** Any of various chemically different substances capable of promoting tanning. [Fr. < *tan,* crushed oak bark < OFr. < Med.Lat. *tannum.* See TAN[1].]

tan•ning (tăn′ĭng) *n.* **1.** The art or process of making leather from rawhides. **2.** Browning of the skin by exposure to sun and weather. **3.** *Informal.* A beating; a whipping.

Ta•no•an (tä′nō-ən) *n.* An American Indian language family of New Mexico and Arizona. [< Sp. *Tano,* name for the Southern Tewas of NM < Tewa.] **—Ta′no•an** *adj.*

tapa[1]

tan•sy (tăn′zē) *n., pl.* **-sies.** Any of several Eurasian plants of the genus *Tanacetum,* esp. *T. vulgare,* having buttonlike yellow flower heads and aromatic leaves. [ME < OFr. *tanesie* < VLat. **tanacēta* < LLat. *tanacētum,* wormwood.]

Tan•ta (tän′tä). A city of N Egypt in the Nile R. delta N of Cairo. Pop. 364,700.

tan•tal•ic (tăn-tăl′ĭk) *adj.* Of or containing tantalum.

tan•ta•lite (tăn′tə-līt′) *n.* A black to red-brown mineral, $(Fe,Mn)(Ta,Nb)_2O_6$, distinguished from columbite by the predominance of tantalum over niobium and used as an ore of both elements. [TANTAL(UM) + -ITE[1].]

tan•ta•lize (tăn′tə-līz′) *tr.v.* **-lized, -liz•ing, -liz•es.** To excite (another) by exposing something desirable while keeping it out of reach. [< Lat. *Tantalus,* Tantalus. See TANTALUS.] **—tan′ta•li•za′tion** (-lĭ-zā′shən) *n.* **—tan′ta•liz′er** *n.*

tan•ta•lum (tăn′tə-ləm) *n. Symbol* **Ta** A hard heavy metallic element that is exceptionally resistant to chemical attack below 150°C and is used to make electronic components, nuclear reactor parts, and surgical instruments. Atomic number 73; atomic weight 180.948; melting point 2,996°C; boiling point 5,425°C; specific gravity 16.6; valence 2, 3, 4, 5. See table at **element.** [NLat. < Lat. *Tantalus,* Tantalus (< its high resistance to acids). See TANTALUS.]

Tan•ta•lus (tăn′tə-ləs) *n. Gk. Myth.* A king who was condemned in Hades to stand in water that receded when he tried to drink and under fruit that receded when he reached for it. [Lat. < Gk. *Tantalos.* See **telə-*.**]

tan•ta•mount (tăn′tə-mount′) *adj.* Equivalent in effect or value: *a request tantamount to a demand.* [< obsolete *tantamount,* an equivalent < AN *tant amunter,* to amount to as much : *tant,* so much, so great (< Lat. *tantum,* neut. of *tantus* < *tam,* so; see **to-***) + *amunter,* to amount to, var. of OFr. *amonter.* See AMOUNT.]

tan•ta•ra (tăn-tăr′ə, -tär′ə) *n.* **1.a.** *Mus.* A trumpet or horn fanfare. **b.** A sound like a tantara. **2.** A hunting cry. [Imit.]

tan•tiv•y (tăn-tĭv′ē) *adv.* At full gallop; at top speed. *—n., pl.* **-ies. 1.** A hunting cry. **2.** A fast furious gallop; top speed. [?]

tan•tra (tŭn′trə, tăn′-) *n.* The esoteric books or teachings of Hinduism, Buddhism, or Jainism, using symbolic, often sexual language and relying on secret rites to attain transcendent states. [Skt. *tantram,* doctrine, loom. See **ten-*.**] **—tan′tric** (-trĭk) *adj.* **—tan′trism** (-trĭz′əm) *n.*

tapir
Baird's tapir
Tapirus bairdii

tan•trum (tăn′trəm) *n.* A fit of bad temper. Also called regionally *hissy fit.* [?]

Tan•tung (tän′to͝ong′). See **Dandong.**

Tan•za•ni•a (tăn′zə-nē′ə). A country of E-central Africa on the Indian Ocean; formed by Tanganyika and Zanzibar in 1964. Official cap. Dodoma. De facto cap. Dar es Salaam. Pop. 17,557,000. **—Tan•za′ni•an** *adj. & n.*

tan•zan•ite (tăn′zə-nīt′) *n.* A transparent variety of zoisite, used as a gem. [After TANZANIA.]

Tao•ism (tou′ĭz′əm, dou′-) *n.* A principal philosophy and system of religion of China based on the teachings of Lao-tzu in the sixth century B.C. [< Chin. (Mandarin) *dào,* way.] **—Tao′ist** *n.* **—Tao•is′tic** *adj.*

Taos[1] (tous, tä′ōs) *n., pl.* **Taos. 1.** A member of a Pueblo people located north-northeast of Santa Fe, New Mexico. **2.** The Tanoan language of the Taos people.

Taos[2] (tous, tä′ōs). A resort town of N NM NNE of Santa Fe. Pop. 4,065.

tap[1] (tăp) *v.* **tapped, tap•ping, taps.** *—tr.* **1.** To strike gently with a light blow or blows. **2.** To give a light rap with. **3.** To produce with a succession of light blows: *tap out a rhythm.* **4.** To select, as for membership in an organization; designate. **5.a.** To repair (shoe heels or toes) by applying a thin layer of leather or a substitute material. **b.** To attach metal plates to (shoe toes or heels). *—intr.* **1.** To deliver a gentle light blow or blows. **2.** To walk making light clicks. *—n.* **1.a.** A gentle blow. **b.** The sound of such a blow. **2.a.** A thin layer of leather or a substitute applied to a worn-down shoe heel or toe. **b.** A metal plate attached to the toe or heel of a shoe. [ME *tappen,* poss. < OFr. *taper.*]

tap[2] (tăp) *n.* **1.** A valve and spout used to regulate delivery of a fluid at the end of a pipe. **2.** A plug for a bunghole; a spigot. **3.a.** Liquor drawn from a spigot. **b.** Liquor of a particular brew, cask, or quality. **4.** *Medic.* The removal of fluid from a body cavity. **5.** A tool for cutting an internal screw thread. **6.** A makeshift terminal in an electric circuit. *—tr.v.* **tapped, tap•ping, taps. 1.** To furnish with a spigot or tap. **2.** To pierce in order to draw off liquid. **3.** To draw (liquid) from a vessel or container. **4.** *Medic.* To withdraw fluid from (a body cavity). **5.** To make a connection with or open outlets from. **6.a.** To wiretap (a telephone). **b.** To establish an electric connection in (a power line), as to divert current secretly. **7.** To cut screw threads in (a collar, socket, or other fitting). **8.** *Informal.* To ask (a person) for money. **—*idiom.* on tap. 1.** Ready to be drawn; in a tapped cask. **2.** Available for immediate use; ready. [ME *tappe* < OE *tæppa.*]

ta•pa[1] (tä′pə, tăp′ə) *n.* **1.** The inner bark of the paper mulberry. **2.** A paperlike cloth made in the South Pacific islands from this bark or similar bark. [Marquesan and Tahitian.]

ta•pa[2] (tä′pä) *n.* Any of various small, often spicy dishes served as appetizers, typically in sherry bars in Spain. [Sp., cap, appetizer, of Gmc. orig.]

Ta•pa•jós also **Ta•pa•joz** (tăp′ə-zhôs′, tä′pä-). A river of N Brazil flowing c. 965 km (600 mi) NE to the Amazon R.

tap dance *n.* A dance in which the rhythm is sounded out by the clicking taps on the heels and toes of a dancer's shoes. **—tap dancer** *n.*

tap-dance (tăp′dăns′) *intr.v.* **-danced, -danc•ing, -danc•es.** To perform a tap dance.

tape (tāp) *n.* **1.** A narrow strip of strong woven fabric, as that used in sewing or bookbinding. **2.** A continuous narrow, flexible strip of cloth, metal, paper, or plastic, such as adhesive tape or magnetic tape. **3.** A string stretched across the finish line of a racetrack to be broken by the winner. **4.** A tape recording. *—v.* **taped, tap•ing, tapes.** *—tr.* **1.a.** To fasten, secure, strengthen, or wrap with a tape. **b.** To bind together (book sections) by applying strips of tape to. **2.** To measure with a tape measure. **3.** To record sounds or pictures on magnetic tape. *—intr.* To make a recording on magnetic tape. [ME < OE *tæppe.*] **—tape′a•ble** *adj*

tape deck *n.* A tape recorder and player having no built-in amplifiers or speakers, used as an audio system component.

tape grass *n.* See **eelgrass.**

tape•line (tāp′līn′) *n.* See **tape measure.**

tape measure *n.* A tape of cloth, paper, or steel marked off in a linear scale, as of inches, for taking measurements.

tape player *n.* A self-contained machine for playing back recorded magnetic tapes.

ta•per (tā′pər) *n.* **1.** A small or very slender candle. **2.** A long wax-coated wick used to light candles or gas lamps. **3.** A source of feeble light. **4.a.** A gradual decrease in thickness or width of an elongated object. **b.** A gradual decrease, as in action or force. *—v.* **-pered, -per•ing, -pers.** *—intr.* **1.** To become gradually narrower or thinner toward one end. **2.** To diminish or lessen gradually. Often used with *off.* *—tr.* **1.** To make thinner or narrower at one end. **2.** To make smaller gradually. *—adj.* Gradually decreasing in size toward a point. [ME < OE *tapor,* poss. ult. < Lat. *papyrus,* papyrus (sometimes used for candlewicks). See PAPER.] **—ta′per•ing•ly** *adv.*

tape-re•cord (tāp′rĭ-kôrd′) *tr.v.* **-cord•ed, -cord•ing, -cords.** To record on magnetic tape.

tape recorder *n.* A mechanical device for recording on magnetic tape and usu. for playing back the recorded material.

tape recording *n.* **1.a.** A magnetic tape on which sound or visual images have been recorded. **b.** The material recorded on a magnetic tape. **2.** The act of recording on magnetic tape.

tap•es•try (tăp′ĭ-strē) *n., pl.* **-tries. 1.** A heavy cloth woven with rich, often varicolored designs or scenes, usu. hung on walls for decoration and sometimes used to cover furniture. **2.** Something felt to resemble a tapestry. *—tr.v.* **-es•tried** (-ĭ-strēd), **-es•try•ing, -es•tries** (-ĭ-strēz). **1.** To hang or decorate with tapestry. **2.** To make, weave, or depict in a tapestry. [ME *tapiceri, tapstri* < OFr. *tapisserie* < *tapisser,* to cover with carpet < *tapis,* carpet < Gk. *tapētion,* dim. of *tapēs,* perh. of Iran. orig.]

ta•pe•tum (tə-pē′təm) *n., pl.* **-ta** (-tə). **1.** *Bot.* A nutritive tissue within the sporangium, particularly within an anther. **2.** *Anat.* **a.** A membranous layer or region, esp. the iridescent membrane of the choroid of certain mammals. **b.** A layer of fibers of the corpus callosum. [Med.Lat. *tapētum*, coverlet < Lat. *tapēte*, *tapētum < Gk. *tapēs*, *tapēt-*. See TAPESTRY.]

tape•worm (tāp′wûrm′) *n.* Any of various ribbonlike, often very long flatworms of the class Cestoda, parasitic in the intestines of vertebrates, including human beings.

ta•phon•o•my (tə-fŏn′ə-mē) *n.* **1.** The study of the conditions and processes of fossilization. **2.** The conditions and processes of fossilization. [Gk. *taphē*, grave + -NOMY.]

tap house *n.* A tavern or bar.

tap•i•o•ca (tăp′ē-ō′kə) *n.* A beady starch obtained from the root of the cassava, used for puddings and as a thickening agent in cooking. [Port. < Tupi *typióca* : *ty*, juice + *pyá*, heart + *oca*, to remove.]

ta•pir (tā′pər, tə-pîr′) *n.* Any of several large, chiefly nocturnal ungulates of the genus *Tapirus* of tropical areas, having a heavy body, short legs, and a long fleshy flexible upper lip. [Perh. Fr., ult. < Tupi *tapiira*, tapir.]

tap•is (tăp′ē, tăp′ĭs, tă-pē′) *n.* *Obsolete.* Tapestry or comparable material used for draperies, carpeting, and furniture covering. — ***idiom.* on the tapis.** Under consideration. [ME < OFr. See TAPESTRY.]

Tap•pan Zee (tăp′an zē). A section of the Hudson R. in SE NY.

tap•per (tăp′ər) *n.* One that taps.

tap•pet (tăp′ĭt) *n.* A lever or projecting arm that moves or is moved by contact with another part, usu. to communicate a certain motion. [Prob. < TAP¹.]

tap•ping (tăp′ĭng) *n.* **1.a.** The act of one that taps. **b.** The process or means by which something is tapped. **2.** Something that is taken or drawn by tapping.

tap•pit-hen (tăp′ĭt-hĕn′) *n.* *Scots.* **1.** A crested hen. **2.** A large mug with a knobbed lid. [Sc. *tappit*, crested (var. of *topped*, p.part. of TOP¹) + HEN.]

tap•room (tăp′ro͞om′, -ro͝om′) *n.* A bar or barroom.

tap•root (tăp′ro͞ot′, -ro͝ot′) *n.* The main root of a plant, usu. growing straight downward from the stem.

taps (tăps) *pl.n.* *(used with a sing. or pl. v.)* A bugle call or drum signal sounded at night as an order to put out lights, as at a military camp, and also sounded at military funerals. [Perh. alteration of *taptoo*, tattoo, var. of TATTOO¹.]

tap•ster (tăp′stər) *n.* One who draws and serves liquor for customers; a bartender.

tar¹ (tär) *n.* **1.** A dark oily viscous material, consisting mainly of hydrocarbons, produced by the destructive distillation of organic substances such as wood, coal, or peat. **2.** Coal tar. **3.** A solid residue of tobacco smoke containing byproducts of combustion. — *tr.v.* **tarred, tar•ring, tars.** To coat with or as if with tar. — ***idiom.* tar and feather. 1.** To punish (a person) by covering with tar and feathers. **2.** To criticize severely and devastatingly; excoriate. [ME < OE *teru*. See **deru-*.**]

tar² (tär) *n.* *Informal.* A sailor. [Poss. short for TARPAULIN.]

tar•a•did•dle (tăr′ə-dĭd′l) *n.* Var. of **tarradiddle.**

Ta•ra•hu•ma•ra (tär′ə-ho͞o-mär′ə, tär′-) *n.*, *pl.* **Tarahumara** or **-ras. 1.** A member of a Native American people of north-central Mexico. **2.** Their Uto-Aztecan language.

tar•an•tel•la (tăr′ən-tĕl′ə) *n.* **1.** A lively whirling Italian dance. **2.** Its music, in 6/8 time. [Ital., after TARANTO.]

tar•an•tism (tăr′ən-tĭz′əm) *n.* A disorder marked by an uncontrollable urge to dance, esp. prevalent in Italy from the 15th to the 17th century. [NLat. *tarantismus*, after TARANTO.]

Ta•ran•to (tär′ən-tō′, tə-răn′tō, tä′rän-tô′). A city of SE Italy ESE of Naples on the **Gulf of Taranto,** an arm of the Ionian Sea; founded in the 8th cent. B.C. Pop. 242,774.

ta•ran•tu•la (tə-răn′chə-lə) *n.*, *pl.* **-las** or **-lae** (-lē′). **1.** Any of various large, hairy, chiefly tropical spiders of the family Theraphosidae, capable of inflicting a painful but not seriously poisonous bite. **2.** A large wolf spider *(Lycosa tarentula)* of southern Europe, once thought to cause tarantism. [Med. Lat. < OItal. *tarantola*, after TARANTO.]

Ta•ra•wa (tə-rä′wə, tăr′ə-wä′, tä′rä-). An atoll of Kiribati in the N Gilbert Is. of the W Pacific.

tar baby *n.* A situation or problem from which it is virtually impossible to disentangle oneself. [After "Bre'r Rabbit and the *Tar Baby*," an Uncle Remus story by Joel Chandler Harris.]

Tar•bell (tär′bəl), **Ida Minerva.** 1857–1944. Amer. writer and editor noted for her muckraking investigations of industry.

tar•boosh also **tar•bush** (tär-bo͞osh′) *n.* A brimless, usu. red felt cap with a silk tassel, worn by some Muslim men either by itself or as the base of a turban. [Ar. (Egypt.) *ṭarbūš* < Turk. *terposh*, prob. < Pers. *sarposh*, headdress : *sar*, head + *pūsh*, covering.]

tar camphor *n.* See **naphthalene.**

tar•di•grade (tär′dĭ-grād′) *n.* Any of various slow-moving microscopic invertebrates of the phylum Tardigrada related to the arthropods and living in water or damp moss. — *adj.* **1.** Of or belonging to the Tardigrada. **2.** Slow in action; slow-moving. [Lat. *tardigradus*, slow-moving : *tardus*, slow + *-gradus*, walking, moving (< *gradī*, to go; see TRANSGRESS).]

tar•dive (tär′dĭv) *adj.* Having symptoms that develop slowly or appear long after inception. Used of a disease. [Fr., fem. of *tardif* < OFr., slow. See TARDY.]

tardive dyskinesia *n.* A chronic disorder of the nervous system characterized by involuntary jerky movements, usu. caused by prolonged treatment with antipsychotic drugs.

tar•dy (tär′dē) *adj.* **-di•er, -di•est. 1.** Occurring, arriving, acting, or done after the scheduled, expected, or usual time; late. **2.** Moving slowly; sluggish. [Alteration of ME *tardive*, slow, ult. < Lat. *tardus*.] — **tar′di•ly** *adv.* — **tar′di•ness** *n.*

tare¹ (târ) *n.* **1.** Any of various weedy plants of the genus *Vicia*, esp. the common vetch. **2.** Any of several weedy plants that grow in grain fields. **3. tares.** An unwelcome or objectionable element. [ME.]

tare² (târ) *n.* **1.** The weight of a container or wrapper deducted from the gross weight to obtain net weight. **2.** A deduction from gross weight to allow for the weight of a container. **3.** *Chem.* A counterbalance, esp. an empty vessel counterbalancing the weight of a similar container. — *tr.v.* **tared, tar•ing, tares.** To determine or indicate the tare of. [ME < OFr., ult. < Ar. *ṭarḥah*, that thrown away < *ṭaraḥa*, to reject.]

targe (tärj) *n.* *Archaic.* A light shield or buckler. [ME < OFr. See TARGET.]

tar•get (tär′gĭt) *n.* **1.a.** An object that is shot at to test accuracy in rifle or archery practice. **b.** Something aimed or fired at. **2.** An object of criticism or attack. **3.** One to be influenced or changed by an action or event. **4.** A desired goal. **5.** A railroad signal that indicates the position of a switch by its color, position, and shape. **6.** The sliding sight on a surveyor's leveling rod. **7.** A small round shield. **8.a.** A structure in a television camera tube with a storage surface that is scanned by an electron beam to generate a signal output current similar to the charge-density pattern stored on the surface. **b.** A usu. metal part in an x-ray tube on which a beam of electrons is focused and from which x-rays are emitted. — *tr.v.* **-get•ed, -get•ing, -gets. 1.** To make a target of. **2.** To aim at or for. **3.** To establish as a target or goal. — ***idiom.* on target.** Completely accurate, precise, or valid. [ME, small targe < OFr. *targuete*, var. of *targete*, dim. of *targe*, light shield, of Gmc. orig.] — **tar′get•a•ble** *adj.*

target date *n.* A date established as a target or goal.

target language *n.* **1.** The language into which a text written in another language is to be translated. **2.** A language that a nonnative speaker is in the process of learning.

Tar•gum (tär′go͝om′, -go͞om′) *n.* Any of several Aramaic translations or paraphrasings of the Old Testament. [Mishnaic Heb. *targûm* < Heb. *tirgēm*, to interpret.]

Tar Heel or **Tar•heel** (tär′hēl′) *n.* A native or resident of North Carolina. [Perh. < tar once being a major product.]

tar•iff (tăr′ĭf) *n.* **1.a.** A list or system of duties imposed by a government on imported or exported goods. **b.** Duties or a duty imposed by a government on imported or exported goods. **2.** A schedule of prices or fees. — *tr.v.* **-iffed, -iff•ing, -iffs.** To fix a duty or price on. [Ital. *tariffa* < OItal. < Ar. *ta'rīf*, notification < *'arafa*, to know.]

Ta•rim He (tä′rēm′ hə′). A river of W China flowing c. 2,092 km (1,300 mi) E to Lop Nur.

Tarim Pen•di (pŭn′dē′). An arid basin of W China S of the Tien Shan and traversed by the Tarim He.

Tar•king•ton (tär′kĭng′tən), **(Newton) Booth.** 1869–1946. Amer. writer whose novels include *Alice Adams* (1921).

tar•la•tan also **tar•le•tan** (tär′lə-tən, -lə-tn) *n.* A thin, stiffly starched muslin in open plain weave. [Fr. *tarlatane*, alteration of earlier *tarnatane*.]

tar•mac (tär′măk′) *n.* A tarmacadam road or surface, esp. an airport runway. — *v.* **-macked, -mack•ing, -macs.** — *tr.* To cause (an aircraft) to sit on a taxiway. — *intr.* To sit on a taxiway. Used of an aircraft. [Originally a trademark.]

tar•mac•ad•am (tär′mə-kăd′əm) *n.* A pavement of layers of crushed stone with a tar binder pressed to a smooth surface.

tarn (tärn) *n.* A small mountain lake, esp. one formed by glaciers. [ME *tarne*, of Scand. orig.]

Tarn (tärn). A river of S France flowing c. 378 km (235 mi) generally W and SW to the Garonne R.

tar•nal (tär′nəl) *adj.* & *adv.* *Chiefly New England & Upper Southern U.S.* Damned. See Regional Note at **tarnation.** [Alteration of ETERNAL.] — **tar′nal•ly** *adv.*

tar•na•tion (tär-nā′shən) *New England & Southern U.S.* — *n.* The act of damning or the condition of being damned. — *interj.* Used to express anger or annoyance. [TARN(AL) + (DAMN)ATION.]

Regional Note: The noun and interjection *tarnation* illustrate the addition of a suffix to a word. *Tarnation* and *darnation* are both euphemistic forms of *damnation*. *Tarnation* seems to have been influenced by *tarnal*, another mild oath derived from *(e)ternal!*

tar•nish (tär′nĭsh) *v.* **-nished, -nish•ing, -nish•es.** — *tr.* **1.** To dull the luster of; discolor, esp. by exposure to air or dirt. **2.a.** To detract from or spoil; taint. **b.** To cast aspersions on; sully. — *intr.* **1.** To lose luster; become discolored. **2.** To diminish or become tainted. — *n.* **1.** The condition of being tarnished. **2.** Discoloration of a metal surface caused by corrosion or oxidation. **3.** The condition of being sullied or tainted. [ME *ternisshen* < OFr. *ternir*, *terniss-*, to dull < *terne*, dull, of Gmc. orig.] — **tar′nish•a•ble** *adj.*

tarantula

targe
16th-century Italian

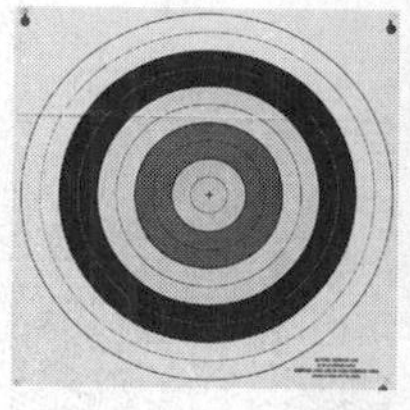

target

ă **pat**	oi **boy**
ā **pay**	ou **out**
âr **care**	o͝o **took**
ä **father**	o͞o **boot**
ĕ **pet**	ŭ **cut**
ē **be**	ûr **urge**
ĭ **pit**	th **thin**
ī **pie**	*th* **this**
îr **pier**	hw **which**
ŏ **pot**	zh **vision**
ō **toe**	ə **about, item**
ô **paw**	

Stress marks:
′ (primary);
′ (secondary), as in **dictionary** (dĭk′shə-nĕr′ē)

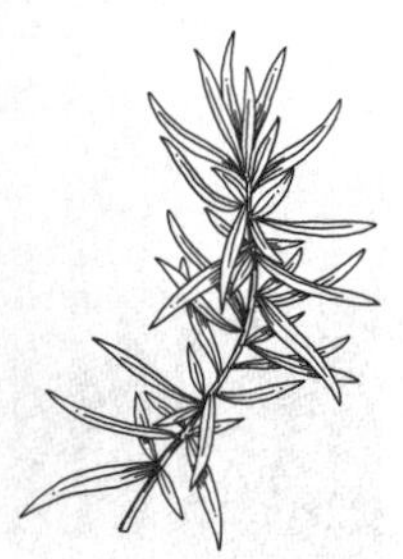

tarragon
Artemisia dracunculus

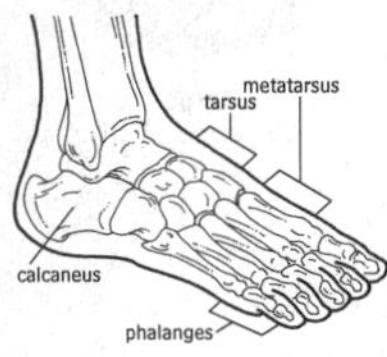

tarsus

tartan[1]

Tar•nów (tär′no͞of′). A city of SE Poland E of Cracow; a cultural center in the 15th and 16th cent. Pop. 113,200.

ta•ro (tär′ō, tăr′ō) *n., pl.* **-ros. 1.** A widely cultivated tropical Asian plant *(Colocasia esculenta)* having broad peltate leaves and a large, starchy edible tuber. **2.** The tuber of this plant. [Of Polynesian orig.]

tar•ok also **tar•oc** (tăr′ək) *n. Games.* A card game developed in Italy in the 14th century, played with a 78-card pack consisting of four suits plus the 22 tarot cards as trumps. [Ital. *tarocchi*, pl. of *tarocco*, tarot.]

tar•ot (tăr′ō, tə-rō′) *n. Games.* **1.** Any of a set of 22 playing cards consisting of a joker plus 21 cards depicting vices, virtues, and elemental forces, used in fortunetelling and as trump in tarok. **2. tarots.** Tarok. [Fr. < Ital. *tarocco.*]

tarp (tärp) *n. Informal.* A tarpaulin.

tar•pa•per (tär′pā′pər) *n.* Heavy paper impregnated or coated with tar, used as a waterproof material in building.

tar•pau•lin (tär-pô′lĭn, tär′pə-) *n.* **1.** Material, such as waterproofed canvas, used to cover and protect things from moisture. **2.** A sheet of this material. [Prob. alteration of TAR[1] + PALL[1] + -ING[2].]

tar pit *n.* An exposed accumulation of natural tar or asphalt, esp. one that traps animals and preserves their bones.

tar•pon (tär′pən) *n., pl.* **tarpon** or **-pons.** Any of several fishes of the family Elopidae or Megalopidae, esp. a large silvery game fish *(Megalops atlanticus)* of Atlantic coastal waters. [?]

tar•ra•did•dle also **tar•a•did•dle** (tăr′ə-dĭd′l) *n.* **1.** A petty falsehood; a fib. **2.** Silly pretentious language; twaddle. [?]

tar•ra•gon (tăr′ə-gŏn′, -gən) *n.* **1.** An aromatic Eurasian herb *(Artemisia dracunculus)* having linear to lance-shaped leaves and small whitish-green flower heads arranged in loose, spreading panicles. **2.** The leaves of this plant used as seasoning. [NLat. *tarchon* < Med.Gk. *tarkhōn* < Ar. *ṭarḫūn*, perh. < Gk. *drakōn*, dragon, tarragon.]

Tar•ra•go•na (tăr′ə-gō′nə, tä′rä-gô′nä). A city of NE Spain on the Mediterranean WSW of Barcelona. Pop. 113,075.

Tar•ra•sa (tə-rä′sə, tä-rä′sä). A city of NE Spain NNW of Barcelona; founded in Roman times. Pop. 165,233.

tar•ri•ance (tăr′ē-əns) *n. Archaic.* **1.** The act of tarrying. **2.** A temporary stay; a sojourn.

Tar River. A river of NE NC flowing c. 346 km (215 mi) to an estuary of Pamlico Sound.

tar•ry[1] (tăr′ē) *v.* **-ried, -ry•ing, -ries.** —*intr.* **1.** To delay or be late in going, coming, or doing. See Syns at **stay[1]**. **2.** To wait. **3.** To remain or stay temporarily, as in a place; sojourn. —*tr. Archaic.* To wait for; await. —*n.* A temporary stay; a sojourn. [ME *tarien.*] —**tar′ri•er** *n.*

tar•ry[2] (tär′ē) *adj.* **-ri•er, -ri•est.** Of, resembling, or covered with tar.

tar•sal (tär′səl) *adj.* **1.** Of, relating to, or situated near the tarsus of the foot or eyelid. **2.** Of or relating to the tarsus of the eyelid. [NLat. *tarsālis* < *tarsus*, tarsus. See TARSUS.]

tarsal plate *n.* See **tarsus** 2.

tar•si•er (tär′sē-ər, -sē-ā′) *n.* Any of several small nocturnal arboreal primates of the genus *Tarsius* of the East Indies and the Philippines, having large round eyes, a long tail, and long digits tipped with soft disklike pads. [Fr. < *tarse*, tarsus (< its elongated ankles) < NLat. *tarsus.* See TARSUS.]

tar•so•met•a•tar•sus (tär′sō-mĕt′ə-tär′səs) *n., pl.* **-si** (-sī, -sē). A compound bone between the tibia and the toes of a bird's leg. —**tar′so•met′a•tar′sal** (-tär′səl) *adj.*

tar•sus (tär′səs) *n., pl.* **-si** (-sī, -sē). **1.a.** The section of the vertebrate foot between the leg and the metatarsus. **b.** The bones making up this section, esp. the seven small bones of the human ankle. **2.** A fibrous plate that supports and shapes the edge of the eyelid. **3.** *Zool.* **a.** The tarsometatarsus. **b.** The distal part of the leg of an arthropod. [NLat. < Gk. *tarsos*, ankle. See **ters-***.]

Tar•sus (tär′səs). A city of S Turkey near the Mediterranean Sea W of Adana. Pop. 121,074.

tart[1] (tärt) *adj.* **tart•er, tart•est. 1.** Having a sharp pungent taste; sour. **2.** Sharp or bitter in tone or meaning; cutting. [ME < OE *teart*, severe. See **der-***.] —**tart′ly** *adv.* —**tart′ness** *n.*

tart[2] (tärt) *n.* **1.a.** A small open pie with a sweet filling. **b.** *Chiefly British.* A pie. **2.a.** A prostitute. **b.** A woman considered sexually promiscuous. —*tr.v.* **tart•ed, tart•ing, tarts.** *Chiefly British.* To dress up or make fancy in a tawdry garish way. [ME *tarte* < OFr., perh. alteration of *tartane* < LLat. *torta*, a bread.]

tar•tan[1] (tär′tn) *n.* **1.a.** Any of numerous textile patterns consisting of stripes of varying widths and colors crossed at right angles against a solid background, each forming a distinctive design worn by the members of a Scottish clan. **b.** A twilled wool fabric or garment having such a pattern. **2.** A plaid fabric. [ME *tartane*, poss. < OFr. *tiretaine*, linsey-woolsey, prob. < *tiret*, a kind of cloth < *tire*, silk cloth < Lat. *Tyrius*, Tyrian (cloth) < *Tyrus*, Tyre.] —**tar′tan** *adj.*

tar•tan[2] (tär′tn, tär-tăn′) *n. Naut.* A small single-masted Mediterranean ship with a large lateen sail. [Fr. *tartane* < Prov. *tartano* < OProv. *tartana*, buzzard, of imit. orig.]

tar•tar (tär′tər) *n.* **1.** *Dentistry.* A hard yellowish deposit on the teeth, consisting of organic secretions and food particles deposited in various salts. **2.** A reddish acid compound, chiefly potassium bitartrate, in the juice of grapes, deposited on casks during winemaking. [ME *tartre*, potassium bitartrate < OFr. < Med.Lat. *tartarum* < Med.Gk. *tartaron.*]

Tar•tar (tär′tər) *n.* **1.** Also **Ta•tar** (tä′tər). A member of any of the Turkic and Mongolian peoples of central Asia who invaded western Asia and eastern Europe in the Middle Ages. **2.** Var. of **Tatar** 1, 2. **3.** Often **tartar.** A person regarded as ferocious or violent. [ME *Tartre* < OFr. *Tartare* < Med.Lat. *Tartarus*, alteration of Pers. *Tātār*, of Turkic orig.]

tartar emetic *n.* A poisonous crystalline compound, $K(SbO)C_4H_4O_6 \cdot \frac{1}{2}H_2O$, used in medicine as an expectorant and in the treatment of parasitic infections, such as schistosomiasis.

tar•tare steak (tär-tär′, tär′tər) *n.* See **steak tartare.**

tar•tar•ic (tär-tăr′ĭk) *adj.* Of, relating to, or derived from tartar or tartaric acid.

tartaric acid *n.* Any of four isomeric crystalline organic compounds, $C_4H_6O_6$, used to make cream of tartar and baking powder, as a sequestrant, in tanning, and in effervescent beverages and photographic chemicals.

tar•tar•ous (tär′tər-əs) *adj.* Consisting of, derived from, or containing tartar.

tartar sauce *n.* Mayonnaise mixed with chopped onion, olives, pickles, and capers and served as a sauce with fish. [Transl. of Fr. *sauce tartare* : *sauce*, sauce + *tartare*, Tartar.]

Tar•ta•rus (tär′tər-əs) *n.* **1.** *Gk. Myth.* The regions below Hades where the Titans were confined. **2.** An infernal region. [Lat. < Gk. *Tartaros.*] —**Tar•tar′e•an** (-târ′ē-ən) *adj.*

Tar•ta•ry (tär′tə-rē) or **Ta•ta•ry** (tä′-). A vast region of E Europe and W Asia controlled by the Mongols in the 13th and 14th cent.

tart•let (tärt′lĭt) *n.* A small pastry tart.

tar•trate (tär′trāt′) *n.* A salt or an ester of tartaric acid.

tar•trat•ed (tär′trā′tĭd) *adj.* Containing, combined with, or derived from tartaric acid.

Tar•tu (tär′to͞o). A city of SE Estonia SE of Tallinn; became part of Russia after 1704. Pop. 111,000.

tar•tuffe also **tar•tufe** (tär-to͝of′, -to͞of′) *n.* A hypocrite, esp. one who affects religious piety. [After the protagonist of *Tartuffe*, a play by Molière.] —**tar•tuf′fe•ry** *n.*

tart•y (tär′tē) *adj.* **-i•er, -i•est.** Of, relating to, or suggestive of a prostitute. —**tart′i•ly** *adv.* —**tart′i•ness** *n.*

tar•weed (tär′wēd′) *n.* **1.** Any of several resinous western American and Chilean plants of the genus *Madia*, having rayed yellow flower heads. **2.** Any of several similar plants.

Tar•zan (tär′zən, -zăn) *n.* A powerfully built man of great agility and valor. [After *Tarzan*, the hero of a series of jungle tales by Edgar Rice Burroughs.]

Tas. *abbr.* Tasmania.

Tash•kent (tăsh-kĕnt′, täsh-). The cap. of Uzbekistan, in the NE part near the Kazakhstan border. Pop. 2,030,000.

task (tăsk) *n.* **1.** A piece of work assigned or done as part of one's duties. **2.** A difficult or tedious undertaking. **3.** A function to be performed; an objective. —*tr.v.* **tasked, task•ing, tasks. 1.** To assign a task to or impose a task on. **2.** To overburden with labor; tax. —*idiom.* **take** (or **call** or **bring**) **to task.** To reprimand or censure. [ME *taske*, imposed work, tax < ONFr. *tasque* < VLat. **tasca*, alteration of **taxa* < Lat. *taxāre*, to feel, reproach, reckon. See TAX.]

Syns: task, job, chore, stint, assignment. These nouns denote a piece of work that one must do. A *task* is a well-defined, sometimes burdensome responsibility usu. imposed by another: *the task at hand. Job* often suggests a short-term undertaking: *"did little jobs about the house with skill"* (W.H. Auden). *Chore* generally denotes a minor, routine, or odd job: *morning chores. Stint* refers to a prescribed share of work: *her daily three-hour stint as a lifeguard. Assignment* generally denotes a task allotted by one in authority: *the homework assignment.*

task force *n.* **1.** A temporary grouping of military units or forces under one commander for a specific operation or assignment. **2.** A temporary grouping of individuals and resources for a specific objective.

task•mas•ter (tăsk′măs′tər) *n.* **1.** One, often a man, who imposes tasks, esp. burdensome or laborious ones. **2.** A source of burden or responsibility.

task•mis•tress (tăsk′mĭs′trĭs) *n.* A woman who imposes tasks, esp. burdensome or laborious ones.

Tas•man (tăz′mən, täs′män), **Abel Janszoon.** 1603?–59. Dutch navigator who was the first European to sight Tasmania and New Zealand (1642).

Tas•ma•ni•a (tăz-mā′nē-ə, -mān′yə). Formerly **Van Die•men's Land** (văn dē′mənz, vän) An island of SE Australia separated from the mainland by Bass Strait. —**Tas•ma′ni•an** *adj. & n.*

Tasmanian devil *n.* A burrowing nocturnal carnivorous marsupial *(Sarcophilus harrisii)* of Tasmania having a predominantly blackish coat and a long, almost hairless tail.

Tasmanian tiger *n.* See **Tasmanian wolf.**

Tasmanian wolf *n.* A large wolflike carnivorous marsupial

(*Thylacinus cynocephalus*) of Tasmania, believed to be extinct, having a pointed head and dark stripes across its back.

Tas•man Sea (tăz′mən). An arm of the S Pacific between SW Australia and W New Zealand.

tasse (tăs) also **tas•set** (tăs′ĭt) *n.* One of a series of jointed overlapping metal splints hanging from a corselet, used as armor for the lower trunk and thighs. [Poss. Fr., pouch < OFr., perh. ult. < VLat. **tasca*, task, money pouch. See TASK.]

tas•sel (tăs′əl) *n.* **1.** A bunch of loose threads or cords bound at one end and hanging free at the other, used as an ornament. **2.** Something that resembles such an ornament, esp. the pollen-bearing inflorescence of a corn plant. — *v.* **-seled, -sel•ing, -sels** or **-selled, -sel•ling, -sels.** — *tr.* To fringe or decorate with tassels. — *intr.* To put forth a tassellike inflorescence. Used esp. of corn. [ME < OFr., fastening, clasp < VLat. **tassellus*, blend of Lat. *tessella*, small die; see TESSELLATE, and *taxillus*, dim. of *tālus*, knucklebone, ankle.]

Tas•so (tăs′ō, tä′sō), **Torquato.** 1544–95. Italian poet known for the epic *Jerusalem Delivered* (1581).

taste (tāst) *v.* **tast•ed, tast•ing, tastes.** — *tr.* **1.** To distinguish the flavor of by taking into the mouth. **2.** To eat or drink a small quantity of. **3.** To partake of, esp. for the first time; experience. **4.** To perceive as if by the sense of taste. **5.** *Archaic.* To appreciate or enjoy. — *intr.* **1.** To distinguish flavors in the mouth. **2.** To have a distinct flavor. **3.** To eat or drink a small amount. **4.** To have experience or enjoyment; partake. — *n.* **1.a.** The sense that distinguishes the sweet, sour, salty, and bitter qualities of dissolved substances in contact with the taste buds on the tongue. **b.** This sense in combination with the senses of smell and touch, which together receive a sensation of a substance in the mouth. **2.a.** The sensation of sweet, sour, salty, or bitter qualities produced by or as if by a substance placed in the mouth. **b.** The unified sensation produced by any of these qualities plus a distinct smell and texture; flavor. **c.** A distinctive perception as if by the sense of taste. **3.** The act of tasting. **4.** A small quantity eaten or tasted. **5.** A limited or first experience; a sample. **6.** A personal preference or liking. **7.a.** The faculty of discerning what is aesthetically excellent or appropriate. **b.** A manner indicative of the quality of such discernment. **8.a.** The sense of what is proper, seemly, or least likely to give offense in a given social situation. **b.** A manner indicative of the quality of this sense. **9.** *Obsolete.* The act of testing; trial. [ME *tasten*, to touch, taste < OFr. *taster* < VLat. **tastāre*, prob. alteration of Lat. **taxāre*, prob. freq. of *tangere*, to touch. See **tag-***.] — **tast′a•ble** *adj.*

taste bud *n.* Any of numerous spherical or ovoid clusters of receptor cells found mainly in the epithelium of the tongue and constituting the end organs of the sense of taste.

taste•ful (tāst′fəl) *adj.* **1.** Having, showing, or being in keeping with good taste. **2.** Pleasing in flavor; tasty. — **taste′ful•ly** *adv.* — **taste′ful•ness** *n.*

taste•less (tāst′lĭs) *adj.* **1.** Lacking flavor; insipid. **2.** Not having or showing good taste. — **taste′less•ly** *adv.* — **taste′less•ness** *n.*

taste•mak•er (tāst′mā′kər) *n.* One that determines or strongly influences current trends or styles, as in fashion.

tast•er (tā′stər) *n.* **1.** One that tastes, esp. one who samples a food or beverage for quality. **2.** Any of several devices or implements used in tasting.

tast•y (tā′stē) *adj.* **-i•er, -i•est. 1.** Having a pleasing flavor; savory. **2.** Having or showing good taste; tasteful. — **tast′i•ly** *adv.* — **tast′i•ness** *n.*

tat[1] (tăt) *intr. & tr.v.* **tat•ted, tat•ting, tats.** To do tatting or make (lace) by tatting. [Prob. back-formation < TATTING.]

tat[2] also **TAT** (tăt) *n.* A gene in the AIDS virus that stimulates the host cell to replicate genetic components of the virus. [*t(rans)a(c)t(ivator) (gene)*.]

TAT *abbr.* Thematic Apperception Test.

ta•ta•mi (tä-tä′mē, tə-) *n., pl.* **tatami** or **-mis.** Straw matting used as a floor covering esp. in a Japanese house. [J.]

Ta•tar (tä′tər) *n.* **1.** Also **Tar•tar** (tär′tər). A member of a group of Turkic peoples inhabiting southeast Europe and west-central Asia. **2. Tartar.** Any of the Turkic languages of the Tatars. **3.** Var. of **Tartar** 1. **4. tatar.** A ferocious or violent person; a tartar.

Ta•ta•ry (tä′tə-rē). See **Tartary.**

Tate (tāt), **Allen.** 1899–1979. Amer. writer and leading exponent of New Criticism known esp. for his poetry.

Tate, Nahum. 1652–1715. English poet and playwright who was appointed poet laureate in 1692.

ta•ter (tā′tər) *n. Upper Southern U.S.* Var. of **potato.** See Regional Notes at **holler[2], possum.**

Ta•tra Mountains (tä′trə). A range of the Carpathian Mts. in E-central Europe along the Slovakian-Polish border.

tat•ter[1] (tăt′ər) *n.* **1.** A torn and hanging piece of cloth; a shred. **2. tatters.** Torn and ragged clothing; rags. — *tr. & intr.v.* **-tered, -ter•ing, -ters.** To make or become ragged. [ME *tater*, of Scand. orig.]

tat•ter[2] (tăt′ər) *n.* One that makes tatting.

tat•ter•de•mal•ion (tăt′ər-dĭ-māl′yən, -mā′lē-ən) *n.* A person wearing ragged or tattered clothing; a ragamuffin. — *adj.* Ragged; tattered. [Prob. TATTERED + *-demalion*, of unknown meaning.]

tat•tered (tăt′ərd) *adj.* **1.** Torn into shreds; ragged. **2.** Having ragged clothes; dressed in tatters. **3.a.** Shabby or dilapidated. **b.** Disordered or disrupted.

tat•ter•sall also **Tat•ter•sall** (tăt′ər-sôl′, -səl) — *n.* **1.** A pattern of dark lines forming squares on a light background. **2.** Cloth having this pattern. — *adj.* Having such a pattern. [After *Tattersall's* horse market in London, England, after Richard *Tattersall* (1724–95), British auctioneer.]

tat•ting (tăt′ĭng) *n.* **1.** Handmade lace fashioned by looping and knotting a single strand of heavy-duty thread on a small hand shuttle. **2.** The act or art of making such lace. [?]

tat•tle (tăt′l) *v.* **-tled, -tling, -tles.** — *intr.* **1.** To reveal the plans or activities of another; gossip. **2.** To chatter aimlessly; prate. — *tr.* To reveal through gossiping. — *n.* **1.** Aimless chatter; prattle. **2.** Gossip; talebearing. **3.** A tattletale. [ME *tatelen*, to stammer, prob. < MDu., of imit. orig.]

tat•tler (tăt′lər) *n.* **1.** One who tattles. **2.** Any of several shore birds related to and resembling the sandpipers, esp. one of the genus *Heteroscelus* that is noted for its loud cry.

tat•tle•tale (tăt′l-tāl′) *n.* One who tattles on others; an informer or a talebearer. — *adj.* Revealing; telltale.

tattletale gray *n. Color.* Grayish white.

tat•too[1] (tă-to͞o′) *n., pl.* **-toos. 1.** A signal sounded on a drum or bugle to summon soldiers or sailors to their quarters at night. **2.** A display of military exercises offered as evening entertainment. **3.** A continuous even drumming or rapping. — *v.* **-tooed, -too•ing, -toos.** — *intr.* To beat out an even rhythm, as with the fingers. — *tr.* To beat or tap rhythmically on; rap or drum on. [Alteration of Du. *taptoe*, tap-shut (closing time for taverns), tattoo : *tap*, spigot, tap (< MDu. *tappe*) + *toe*, shut (< MDu.; see **de-***).]

tat•too[2] (tă-to͞o′) *n., pl.* **-toos.** A permanent mark made on the skin by pricking and ingraining an indelible pigment or by raising scars. — *tr.v.* **-tooed, -too•ing, -toos. 1.** To mark (the skin) thus. **2.** To form (a tattoo) on the skin. [Of Polynesian orig.] — **tat•too′er** *n.* — **tat•too′ist** *n.*

tat•ty (tăt′ē) *adj.* **-ti•er, -ti•est.** Somewhat worn, shabby, or dilapidated. [Prob. < *tat*, a rag, shabby person.]

Ta•tum (tā′təm), **Arthur ("Art").** 1910–56. Amer. jazz pianist noted for his harmonic and rhythmic innovations.

Tatum, Edward Lawrie. 1909–75. Amer. biochemist who shared a 1958 Nobel Prize.

Ta•tung (tä′to͝ong′). See **Datong.**

tau (tou, tô) *n.* **1.** The 19th letter of the Greek alphabet. **2.** A negatively charged elementary particle of the lepton family, having a mass about 3,490 times that of the electron and a mean lifetime of 3×10^{-13} seconds. See table at **subatomic particle.** [Gk., of Phoenician orig.; akin to Heb. *tāw*, tav.]

Tau•ba•té (tou′bä-tē′). A city of SE Brazil NE of São Paulo; founded 1645. Pop. 155,376.

tau cross *n.* A cross in the form of a T.

taught (tôt) *v.* P.t. and p.part. of **teach.**

tau neutrino *n.* A probably stable elementary particle in the lepton family having a mass less than 69 times that of the electron and no charge. See table at **subatomic particle.**

taunt[1] (tônt) *tr.v.* **taunt•ed, taunt•ing, taunts. 1.** To reproach in a mocking, insulting, or contemptuous manner. See Syns at **ridicule. 2.** To drive or incite (a person) by taunting. — *n.* A scornful remark or tirade; a jeer. [?] — **taunt′er** *n.*

taunt[2] (tônt) *adj. Naut.* Unusually tall. Used of masts. [?]

Taun•ton (tôn′tən, tŏn′-). A city of SE MA on the **Taunton River** N of Fall River; settled in the 1630's. Pop. 49,832.

Tau•nus Mountains (tou′nəs, -no͝os′). A range of W Germany extending NE from the Rhine R.

taupe (tōp) *n. Color.* A brownish gray. [Fr. < OFr., mole < Lat. *talpa*.] — **taupe** *adj.*

tau•rine[1] (tôr′īn′) *adj.* Of, relating to, or resembling a bull. [Lat. *taurīnus* < *taurus*, bull. See **tauro-***.]

tau•rine[2] (tôr′ēn′) *n.* A colorless crystalline substance, $C_2H_7NO_3S$, formed by the hydrolysis of taurocholic acid and found in the fluids of the muscles and lungs of many animals. [Gk. *tauros*, bull; see **tauro-*** + -INE[2].]

tau•ro•cho•lic acid (tôr′ō-kō′lĭk, -kŏl′ĭk) *n.* A crystalline acid, $C_{26}H_{45}NO_7S$, involved in the emulsification of fats and occurring as a sodium salt in the bile of human beings, oxen, and other mammals. [< Gk. *tauros*, bull. See **tauro-*.**]

Tau•rus (tôr′əs) *n.* **1.** A constellation in the Northern Hemisphere near Orion and Aries. **2.a.** The second sign of the zodiac. **b.** One who is born under this sign. [ME < Lat., bull, the constellation Taurus. See **tauro-*.**]

Taurus Mountains. A range of S Turkey parallel to the Mediterranean coast that rises to 3,736.6 m (12,251 ft).

Tau•sug (tô′so͞og′) *n.* An Austronesian language spoken in the Sulu Archipelago. [Tausug : *ta'u*, people + *su:g*, current.]

taut (tôt) *adj.* **taut•er, taut•est. 1.** Pulled or drawn tight; not slack. See Syns at **tight. 2.** Strained; tense. **3.a.** Kept in trim shape; neat and tidy. **b.** Marked by the efficient, sparing, or concise use of something, such as language. [ME *tohte*, distended, perh. ult. < OE *togian*, to drag. See TOW[1].] — **taut′ly** *adv.* — **taut′ness** *n.*

tassel
On a mortarboard

tau cross

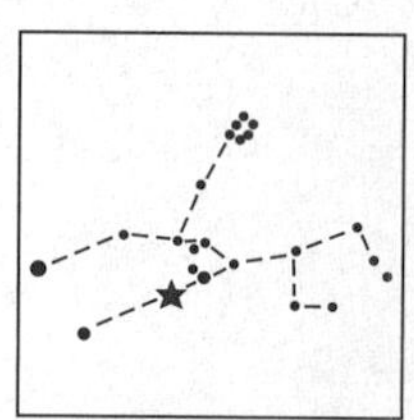
Taurus

ă pat	oi boy
ā pay	ou out
âr care	o͝o took
ä father	o͞o boot
ĕ pet	ŭ cut
ē be	ûr urge
ĭ pit	th thin
ī pie	*th* this
îr pier	hw which
ŏ pot	zh vision
ō toe	ə about, item
ô paw	

Stress marks:
′ (primary);
′ (secondary), as in **dictionary** (dĭk′shə-nĕr′ē)

taut•en (tôt′n) *tr. & intr.v.* **-ened, -en•ing, -ens.** To make or become taut.

tauto– or **taut–** *pref.* Same; identical: *tautomerism.* [Gk. < *tauto*, the same, contraction of *to auto* : *to*, the; see **to-*** + *auto*, neut. of *autos*, same, self.]

tau•tog also **tau•taug** (tô′tôg′, -tŏg′, tô-tôg′, -tŏg′) *n.* A dark-colored edible marine fish *(Tautoga onitis)* found along the North American Atlantic coast. [Narragansett *tautaûg.*]

tau•tol•o•gize (tô-tŏl′ə-jīz′) *intr.v.* **-gized, -giz•ing, -giz•es.** To use tautology. **—tau•tol′o•gist** (-jĭst) *n.*

tau•tol•o•gy (tô-tŏl′ə-jē) *n., pl.* **-gies. 1.a.** Needless repetition of the same sense in different words; redundancy. **b.** An instance of such repetition. **2.** *Logic.* An empty statement composed of simpler statements in a fashion that makes it logically true whether the simpler statements are factually true or false; for example, *Either we'll go or we'll stay.* [LLat. *tautologia* < Gk. < *tautologos*, redundant : *tauto-*, tauto- + *logos*, saying; see -LOGY.] **—tau′to•log′i•cal** (tôt′l-ŏj′ĭ-kəl), **tau′to•log′ic** (-ĭk) *adj.* **—tau′to•log′i•cal•ly** *adv.*

Zachary Taylor

tau•tom•er•ism (tô-tŏm′ə-rĭz′əm) *n.* Chemical isomerism characterized by relatively easy interconversion of isomeric forms in equilibrium. [TAUTO– + (ISO)MERISM.] **—tau′to•mer** (tô′tə-mər) *n.* **—tau′to•mer′ic** (tô′tə-mĕr′ĭk) *adj.*

tau•to•nym (tô′tə-nĭm′) *n.* A taxonomic designation, such as *Gorilla gorilla,* in which the genus and species names are the same, commonly used in zoology. **—tau′to•nym′ic, tau•ton′y•mous** (tô-tŏn′ə-məs) *adj.* **—tau•ton′y•my** *n.*

tav also **taw** (täf, tôf) *n.* The 23rd letter of the Hebrew alphabet. [Heb. *tāw*, mark, cross (sense uncertain).]

tav•ern (tăv′ərn) *n.* **1.** An establishment licensed to sell alcoholic beverages to be consumed on the premises. **2.** An inn for travelers. [ME *taverne* < OFr. < Lat. *taberna*, hut, tavern, prob. < **traberna* < *trabs, trab-*, beam. See TRAVE.]

ta•ver•na (tə-vûr′nə, tä-vĕr′nä) *n.* A café or small restaurant in Greece. [Mod.Gk. *taberna*, ult. < Lat. See TAVERN.]

taw[1] (tô) *tr.v.* **tawed, taw•ing, taws.** To convert (skin) into white leather by mineral tanning, as with alum and salt. [ME *tawen* < OE *tawian*, to prepare.] **—taw′er** *n.*

taw[2] (tô) *n.* **1.** *Chiefly Southern U.S.* A large fancy marble used for shooting. **2.** The line from which a player shoots in marbles. **3.** A game of marbles. *—intr.v.* **tawed, taw•ing, taws.** To shoot a marble. [?]

Peter Ilich Tchaikovsky
Photographed in 1888

taw[3] (täf, tôf) *n.* Var. of **tav.**

taw•dry (tô′drē) *adj.* **-dri•er, -dri•est.** Gaudy and cheap in nature or appearance. *—n.* Cheap and gaudy finery. [< *tawdry lace*, lace necktie, alteration of *Saint Audrey's lace*, after *St. Audrey* (St. Etheldreda), queen of Northumbria, who died in 679 of a throat tumor, supposedly because when young she liked fancy necklaces.] **—taw′dri•ly** *adv.* **—taw′dri•ness** *n.*

Taw•ney (tô′nē), **Richard Henry.** 1880–1962. British historian noted for his studies of the development of capitalism.

taw•ny (tô′nē) *n. Color.* A light brown to brownish orange. [ME < AN *taune*, var. of OFr. *tane* < p.part. of *taner*, to tan. See TAN[1].] **—taw′ni•ness** *n.* **—taw′ny** *adj.*

tax (tăks) *n.* **1.** A contribution for the support of a government required of persons, groups, or businesses within the domain of that government. **2.** A fee or dues levied on the members of an organization to meet its expenses. **3.** A burdensome or excessive demand; a strain. *—tr.v.* **taxed, tax•ing, tax•es. 1.** To place a tax on (income, property, or goods). **2.** To exact a tax from. **3.** *Law.* To assess (court costs, for example). **4.** To make difficult or excessive demands upon: *taxed my patience.* **5.** To make a charge against; accuse. [ME < *taxen*, to tax < OFr. *taxer* < Med.Lat. *taxāre* < Lat., to touch, reproach, reckon, freq. of *tangere*, to touch. See **tag-***.] **—tax′er** *n.*

tax– *pref.* Var. of **taxo–.**

ta•xa (tăk′sə) *n.* Pl. of **taxon.**

tax•a•ble (tăk′sə-bəl) *adj.* Subject to taxation. *—n.* One that is subject to taxation. **—tax′a•bil′i•ty, tax′a•ble•ness** *n.* **—tax′a•bly** *adv.*

tax•a•tion (tăk-sā′shən) *n.* **1.a.** The act or practice of imposing taxes. **b.** The fact of being taxed. **2.** An assessed amount of tax. **3.** Revenue gained from taxes.

tax-de•duct•i•ble (tăks′dĭ-dŭk′tə-bəl) *adj.* Exempt from inclusion in one's taxable income.

tax•eme (tăk′sēm′) *n. Ling.* A grammatical feature that cannot be analyzed or has no meaning by itself, as the order of phonemes or the stress of syllables in a word. [Gk. *taxis*, order, arrangement + -EME.] **—tax•e′mic** *adj.*

tax-ex•empt (tăks′ĭg-zĕmpt′) *adj.* **1.** Not subject to taxation. **2.** Producing interest that is exempt from income tax. *—n.* A tax-exempt security.

tax-free (tăks′frē′) *adj.* Not subject to taxation; tax-exempt.

tax•i (tăk′sē) *n., pl.* **tax•is** or **tax•ies.** A taxicab. *—v.* **tax•ied** (tăk′sēd), **tax•i•ing** or **tax•y•ing, tax•ies** or **tax•is** (tăk′sēz). *—intr.* **1.** To be transported by taxi. **2.** To move slowly on the ground or on the surface of the water before takeoff or after landing. Used of an aircraft. *—tr.* **1.** To transport (someone or something) by or as if by taxi. **2.** To cause (an aircraft) to taxi. [Short for TAXIMETER or TAXICAB.]

taxi– *pref.* Var. of **taxo–.**

tax•i•cab (tăk′sē-kăb′) *n.* An automobile that carries passengers for a fare, usu. calculated by a taximeter.

taxi dancer *n.* A woman employed, as by a dance hall or nightclub, to dance with the patrons for a fee.

tax•i•der•my (tăk′sĭ-dûr′mē) *n.* The art or operation of preparing, stuffing, and mounting the skins of dead animals for exhibition in a lifelike state. **—tax′i•der′mal, tax′i•der′mic** *adj.* **—tax′i•der′mist** *n.*

tax•i•me•ter (tăk′sē-mē′tər) *n.* An instrument installed in a taxicab to compute and indicate the fare. [Fr. *taximètre*, alteration of *taxamètre* < Ger. *Taxameter* : Med.Lat. *taxa*, tax (< *taxāre*, to tax; see TAX) + *-meter*, meter (< Gk. *metron*, measure; see -METER).]

tax•ing (tăk′sĭng) *adj.* Burdensome; wearing.

tax•is (tăk′sĭs) *n., pl.* **tax•es** (tăk′sēz). **1.** *Biol.* The movement of a free-moving organism or cell toward or away from an external stimulus, such as light. **2.** *Medic.* The moving of a body part by manipulation into normal position, as after a dislocation. [Gk., arrangement < *tassein, tag-*, to arrange.]

–taxis *suff.* **1.** Order; arrangement: *homotaxis.* **2.** Responsive movement; taxis: *chemotaxis.* [Gk. < *taxis.* See TAXIS.]

taxi squad *n. Football.* **1.** A group of professional players who are under contract to and practice with a team but are ineligible to play in official games. **2.** The four extra players of a professional team who are prepared to play on short notice.

taxi stand *n.* An area reserved for waiting taxicabs.

tax•i•way (tăk′sē-wā′) *n.* A usu. paved strip at an airport for use by aircraft in taxiing to and from a runway.

tax•man (tăks′măn′) *n.* One that is responsible for the collection of federal, state, or local taxes.

taxo– or **taxi–** or **tax–** *pref.* Order; arrangement: *taxidermy.* [< Gk. *taxis.* See TAXIS.]

Tax•ol (tăk′sôl, -sŏl). A trademark used for a colorless crystalline compound, $C_{47}H_5NO_{14}$, found in the bark of a species of yew *(Taxus brevifolia* var. *Nuttallii,* and used in the treatment of ovarian and other types of cancer.

tax•on (tăk′sŏn′) *n., pl.* **ta•xa** (tăk′sə). *Biol.* A taxonomic category or group, such as a phylum, order, family, genus, or species. [NLat., back-formation < TAXONOMY.]

tax•o•nom•ic (tăk′sə-nŏm′ĭk) also **tax•o•nom•i•cal** (-ĭ-kəl) *adj.* Of or relating to taxonomy. **—tax′o•nom′i•cal•ly** *adv.*

tax•on•o•my (tăk-sŏn′ə-mē) *n., pl.* **-mies. 1.** The classification of organisms in an ordered system that indicates natural relationships. **2.** The science, laws, or principles of classification; systematics. **3.** Division into ordered groups or categories. [Fr. *taxonomie* : Gk. *taxis*, arrangement; see TAXIS + *-nomie*, method (< Gk. *-nomia*; see -NOMY).] **—tax•on′o•mist** *n.*

tax•pay•er (tăks′pā′ər) *n.* One that pays taxes or is subject to taxation. **—tax′pay′ing** *adj.*

tax return *n.* See **return** 16.

tax shelter *n.* A financial arrangement, such as the use of special depletion allowances, that reduces taxes on current earnings. **—tax′-shel′tered** (tăks′shĕl′tərd) *adj.*

–taxy *suff.* Order; arrangement: *phyllotaxy.* [Gk. *-taxia* < *taktos*, arranged. See TAXIS.]

Tay (tā). A river of central Scotland rising in the Grampian Mts. and flowing c. 190 km (118 mi) through **Loch Tay** to the **Firth of Tay,** an inlet of the North Sea.

Tay•lor (tā′lər). A city of SE MI, a suburb of Detroit. Pop. 70,811.

Taylor, Elizabeth. b. 1932. British-born Amer. actress whose film credits include *National Velvet* (1944).

Taylor, (James) Bayard. 1825–78. Amer. writer known esp. for his translation (1870–71) of Goethe's *Faust.*

Taylor, Jeremy. 1613–67. English bishop and writer whose works include *The Rule and Exercises of Holy Living* (1650).

Taylor, Paul. b. 1930. Amer. choreographer whose avant-garde works include *Three Epitaphs* (1956) and *Orbs* (1966).

Taylor, Zachary. "Old Rough and Ready." 1784–1850. The 12th President of the U.S. (1849–50), who became a national hero during the Mexican War (1846–48).

Tay•lors•ville (tā′lərz-vĭl′). A community of N-central UT, a suburb of Salt Lake City. Pop. 52,351.

Tay•myr Peninsula (tī-mîr′). See **Taimyr Peninsula.**

Tay-Sachs disease (tā′săks′) *n.* A fatal hereditary disease that affects young children almost exclusively of eastern European Jewish descent, in which an enzyme deficiency leads to the accumulation of gangliosides in nervous tissue. [After Warren *Tay* (1843–1927), British physician, and Bernard *Sachs* (1858–1944), Amer. neurologist.]

taz•za (tät′sə, -tsä) *n.* A shallow ornamental vessel usu. on a pedestal. [Ital., cup, tazza < Ar. *ṭašt*, basin.]

Tb[1] The symbol for the element **terbium.**

Tb[2] *abbr. Bible.* Tobit.

TB also **T.B.** *abbr.* Tuberculosis.

t.b. *abbr.* **1.** Trial balance. **2.** Also **T.B.** Tubercle bacillus.

TBA or **tba** *abbr.* To be announced.

T-bar (tē′bär′) *n. Sports.* A ski lift consisting of a bar suspended like an inverted T against which skiers lean.

Tbi•li•si (tə-bə-lē′sē, -byĭ-lē′syĭ) also **Tif•lis** (tĭf′lĭs, tyə-flēs′). The cap. of Georgia, in the SE part on the Kura R.; came

TAXONOMY OF LIFE

The taxonomic organization of species is hierarchical. Each species belongs to a genus, each genus belongs to a family, and so on through order, class, phylum, and kingdom. Associations within the hierarchy reflect evolutionary relationships, which are deduced typically from morphological and physiological similarities between species. So, for example, species in the same genus are more closely related and more alike than species in the same family.

Carolus Linnaeus, an eighteenth-century Swedish botanist, devised the system of **binomial nomenclature** used for naming species. In this system, each species is given a two-part Latin name, formed by appending a **specific epithet** to the genus name. By convention, the genus name is capitalized, and both the genus name and specific epithet are italicized, for example, *Canis familiaris* or simply *C. familiaris*.

Modern taxonomy recognizes five kingdoms, into which the estimated five million species of the world are divided. This table presents a familiar organism from each kingdom and the names of the taxonomic groups to which it belongs.

	DOG	SUGAR MAPLE	BREAD MOLD	INTESTINAL BACTERIUM	POND ALGA
KINGDOM	Animalia (animals)	Plantae (plants)	Fungi (fungi)	Prokaryotae (bacteria)	Protoctista (algae, protozoans, slime molds)
PHYLUM*	Chordata	Magnoliophyta	Zygomycota	Omnibacteria	Chlorophyta
CLASS	Mammalia	Rosidae	Zygomycetes	Enterobacteria	Euconjugatae
ORDER	Carnivora	Sapindales	Mucorales	Eubacteriales	Zygnematales
FAMILY	Canidae	Aceraceae	Mucoraceae	**	Zygnemataceae
GENUS	*Canis*	*Acer*	*Rhizopus*	*Escherichia*	*Spirogyra*
SPECIES	*C. familiaris*	*A. saccharum*	*R. stolonifer*	*E. coli*	*S. crassa*

* In botanical nomenclature, "division" is used instead of "phylum."
** *Escherichia coli* does not have a family classification.

under Russian control in 1801. Pop. 1,158,000.

T-bill (tē′bĭl′) *n.* A U.S. Treasury note.

T-bone (tē′bōn′) *n.* A thick porterhouse steak taken from the small end of the loin and containing a T-shaped bone.

tbs. *abbr.* **1.** Tablespoon. **2.** Tablespoonful.

tbsp. *abbr.* **1.** Tablespoon. **2.** Tablespoonful.

Tc The symbol for the element **technetium.**

T cell *n.* A type of white blood cell that matures in the thymus and has various roles in the immune system, including the identification of specific foreign antigens and the regulation of other immune cells. [*t(hymus-derived) cell.*]

Tchai•kov•sky (chī-kôf′skē), **Peter Ilich.** 1840–93. Russian composer whose works include the ballet *Swan Lake* (1877). **—Tchai•kov′sky•an, Tchai•kov′ski•an** *adj.*

tchotch•ke (chŏch′kə) *n.* Var. of **chachka.**

tchr. *abbr.* Teacher.

TD *abbr.* **1.** Tank destroyer. **2.** Also **td.** *Football.* Touchdown. **3.** Also **T.D.** Treasury Department.

TDD *abbr.* Telecommunications device for the deaf.

TDN also **T.D.N.** *abbr.* Total digestible nutrients.

Te *n.* The symbol for the element **tellurium.**

tea (tē) *n.* **1.a.** An eastern Asian evergreen shrub or small tree *(Camellia sinensis)* having fragrant nodding cup-shaped white flowers and glossy leaves. **b.** The young dried leaves of this plant, used to make a hot beverage. **2.** An aromatic, slightly bitter beverage made by steeping tea leaves in boiling water. **3.** Any of various beverages, made as by steeping the leaves of certain plants or by extracting an infusion esp. from beef. **4.** Any of various plants having leaves used to make a tealike beverage. **5.** *Chiefly British.* **a.** An afternoon refreshment consisting usu. of sandwiches and cakes served with tea. **b.** High tea. **6.** An afternoon reception or social gathering at which tea is served. **7.** *Slang.* Marijuana. [Prob. Du. *thee* < Malay *teh* < Chin. (Amoy) *te.*]

tea bag *n.* A small porous sack holding enough tea leaves to make an individual serving of tea.

tea ball *n.* A small perforated metal ball for holding tea leaves that are to be steeped in hot water.

tea•ber•ry (tē′bĕr′ē) *n.* **1.** See **wintergreen** 1a. **2.** See **withe rod.** [< the use of its leaves as a tea substitute.]

tea biscuit *n.* Any of various plain cookies or biscuits often served with tea.

tea caddy *n.* A small box or container for holding loose tea.

tea•cake (tē′kāk′) *n.* See **tea biscuit.**

tea•cart (tē′kärt′) *n.* See **tea wagon.**

teach (tēch) *v.* **taught** (tôt), **teach•ing, teach•es.** —*tr.* **1.** To impart knowledge or skill to. **2.** To provide knowledge of; instruct in. **3.** To condition to a certain action or frame of mind. **4.** To cause to learn by example or experience. **5.** To advocate or preach. **6.** To carry on instruction on a regular basis in. —*intr.* To give instruction, esp. as an occupation. [ME *techen* < OE *tǣcan.* See **deik-*.**]

Syns: *teach, instruct, educate, train, school.* These verbs mean to impart knowledge or skill. *Teach* is the most widely applicable: *"We shouldn't teach great books; we should teach a love of reading"* (B.F. Skinner). *Instruct* usually suggests methodical teaching: *instructed them in music theory. Educate* often implies formal instruction but especially stresses the development of innate capacities: *"All educated Americans, first or last, go to Europe"* (Ralph Waldo Emerson). *Train* suggests concentration on particular skills intended to fit a person for a desired role: *trained as a computer technician. School* often implies an arduous learning process: *schooled to play accurate intonation.*

Usage Note: Some grammarians have objected to the use of *teach* as a transitive verb when its object denotes an institution of learning, as in *Kim teaches grade school.* This usage has wide currency at all levels, however, and is supported by the analogy to phrases such as *grade-school teacher.*

Teach (tēch) also **Thatch** (thăch), **Edward.** "Blackbeard." d. 1718. English pirate in the Caribbean.

teach•a•ble (tē′chə-bəl) *adj.* **1.** That can be taught: *teachable skills.* **2.** Able and willing to learn. **—teach′a•bil′i•ty, teach′a•ble•ness** *n.* **—teach′a•bly** *adv.*

teach•er (tē′chər) *n.* One who teaches, esp. one hired to teach.

teacher bird *n.* See **ovenbird** 1. [Imit. of the bird's song.]

teach•ers college also **teach•ers' college** (tē′chərz) *n.* A college with a special curriculum for training teachers.

teach•er's pet (tē′chərz) *n., pl.* **teacher's pets** or **teachers' pets. 1.** A student in special favor with a teacher. **2.** One who has gained favor with an authority.

teach-in (tēch′ĭn′) *n.* An extended session, as at a college, for lectures and discussions on a usu. controversial issue.

teach•ing (tē′chĭng) *n.* **1.** The act, practice, occupation, or profession of a teacher. **2.a.** Something taught. **b.** A precept or doctrine. Often used in the plural. —*adj.* **1.** Of, involving, or used for teaching. **2.** Working as a teacher.

teaching fellow *n.* A graduate student in a university or college who is awarded a fellowship that provides financial aid in exchange for teaching duties. **—teaching fellowship** *n.*

teaching hospital *n.* A hospital associated with a medical school and serving as a practical educational site for medical students, interns, residents, and other health workers.

tea•cup (tē′kŭp′) *n.* A small cup used with a saucer for serving tea. **—tea′cup•ful′** *n.*

tea dance *n.* A late-afternoon dance.

tea garden *n.* **1.** A garden open to the public where tea and light refreshments are served. **2.** A tea plantation.

tea•house (tē′hous′) *n.* A public establishment serving tea and light refreshments.

teak (tēk) *n.* **1.a.** A tall evergreen tree *(Tectona grandis)* of southeast Asia having hard heavy durable yellowish-brown wood. **b.** The wood of this tree, used esp. for furniture and in shipbuilding. **2.** *Color.* A grayish yellowish brown or grayish to moderate brown. [Port. *teca* < Malayalam *tēkka.*]

tea•ket•tle (tē′kĕt′l) *n.* A covered kettle with a spout and handle, used for boiling water, as for tea.

teak•wood (tēk′wo͝od′) *n.* Teak.

teal (tēl) *n., pl.* **teal** or **teals. 1.** Any of several small short-necked freshwater ducks, esp. of the genus *Anas,* that feed on the surface of the water and often have brightly marked plumage. **2.** *Color.* A moderate or dark bluish green to greenish blue. [ME *tele.*] **—teal** *adj.*

team (tēm) *n.* **1.** *Sports & Games.* A group on the same side. **2.** A group organized to work together. **3.a.** Two or more draft animals used to pull a vehicle or farm implement. **b.** A

tea caddy
1737 English silver tea caddy by John Swift

ă pat	oi boy
ā pay	ou out
âr care	o͝o took
ä father	o͞o boot
ĕ pet	ŭ cut
ē be	ûr urge
ĭ pit	th thin
ī pie	*th* this
îr pier	hw which
ŏ pot	zh vision
ō toe	ə about, item
ô paw	

Stress marks:
′ (primary);
′ (secondary), as in **dictionary** (dĭk′shə-nĕr′ē)

vehicle along with the animal or animals harnessed to it. **4.** A group of animals exhibited or performing together. **5.** A brood or flock. **6.** *Obsolete.* Offspring; lineage. See Usage Note at **collective noun.** —*v.* **teamed, team•ing, teams.** —*tr.* **1.** To harness or join together to form a team. **2.** To transport or haul with a draft team. —*intr.* **1.** To form a team or an association. Often used with *up.* **2.** To drive a team or truck. [ME, draft team < OE *tēam.* See **deuk-*.**]

team•mate (tēm′māt′) *n.* A fellow member of a team.

team play *n.* **1.** Collective play participated in by team members. **2.** Collective effort and cooperation. —**team player** *n.*

team•ster (tēm′stər) *n.* **1.** One who drives a truck for hauling loads, esp. as an occupation. **2.** One who drives a team.

team-teach (tēm′tēch′) *v.* **-taught** (-tôt′), **-teach•ing, -teach•es.** *tr. & intr.v.* To teach cooperatively with other teachers or engage in such teaching.

team teaching *n.* A method of classroom instruction in which several teachers combine their individual subjects into one course that they teach as a team to a group of students.

team•work (tēm′wûrk′) *n.* Cooperative effort by the members of a group or team to achieve a common goal.

Tea•neck (tē′něk′). A township of NE NJ ESE of Paterson. Pop. 37,825.

tea party *n.* An afternoon social gathering at which tea and light refreshments are served.

tea•pot (tē′pŏt′) *n.* A covered pot with a spout in which tea is steeped and from which it is served.

tea•poy (tē′poi′) *n.* **1.** A small table for holding a tea service. **2.** A small decorative three-legged table. [Hindi *tipāī,* alteration (influenced by Hindi *tir,* three) of Pers. *si-pāya,* three : *si,* three + MPers. *pāī,* foot; see **ped-*.**]

tear¹ (târ) *v.* **tore** (tôr, tōr), **torn** (tôrn, tōrn), **tear•ing, tears.** —*tr.* **1.** To pull apart or into pieces by force; rend. **2.** To make (an opening) by ripping. **3.** To lacerate (the skin, for example). **4.** To separate forcefully; wrench. **5.** To divide or disrupt. —*intr.* **1.** To become torn. **2.** To move with heedless speed; rush headlong. —*n.* **1.** The act of tearing. **2.** The result of tearing; a rip or rent. **3.** A great rush; a hurry. **4.** *Slang.* A carousal; a spree. —***phrasal verbs.*** **tear around.** *Informal.* **1.** To move about in excited, often angry haste. **2.** To lead a wild life. **tear at. 1.** To pull at or attack violently. **2.** To distress greatly. **tear away.** To remove (oneself, for example) unwillingly or reluctantly. **tear down. 1.** To demolish. **2.** To take apart; disassemble. **3.** To vilify or denigrate. **tear into.** To attack with great vigor or violence. **tear up. 1.** To tear to pieces. **2.** To make an opening in. [ME *teren* < OE *teran.* See **der-*.**] —**tear′er** *n.*

Syns: *tear, rip, rend, split, cleave.* These verbs mean to separate or pull apart by force. *Tear* involves pulling something apart or into pieces: *"She tore the letter in shreds"* (Edith Wharton). *Rip* implies rough or forcible tearing, often along a dividing line: *ripped up the old floorboards. Rend* usually refers to violent tearing or wrenching apart: *"Come as the winds come, when/Forests are rended"* (Sir Walter Scott). To *split* is to cut or break something into parts or layers, especially along its entire length or along a natural line of division: *"They* [wood stumps] *warmed me twice—once while I was splitting them, and again when they were on the fire"* (Henry David Thoreau). *Cleave* most often refers to splitting with or as if with a sharp instrument: *"The apple's cleft right through the core"* (J.C.F. von Schiller).

teasel
Dipsacus sylvestris

tear² (tîr) *n.* **1.a.** A drop of the clear salty liquid that is secreted by the lachrymal gland of the eye to lubricate the surface between the eyeball and eyelid and to wash away irritants. **b. tears.** A profusion of this liquid spilling from the eyes and wetting the cheeks, esp. as an expression of emotion. **c. tears.** The act of weeping: *criticism that left me in tears.* **2.** A drop of a liquid or hardened fluid. —*intr.v.* **teared, tear•ing, tears.** To fill with tears. [ME < OE *tēar.* See **dakru-*.**]

tear•drop (tîr′drŏp′) *n.* **1.** A single tear. **2.** An object shaped like a tear.

tear•ful (tîr′fəl) *adj.* **1.** Filled with or accompanied by tears. **2.** So piteous as to excite tears. —**tear′ful•ness** *n.*

tear gas (tîr) *n.* Any of various agents that on dispersal, usu. from grenades or projectiles, irritate the eyes and cause blinding tears. —**tear′-gas′** (tîrgăs′) *v.*

tear•ing (târ′ĭng) *adj.* Marked by great or violent haste.

tear•jerk•er (tîr′jûr′kər) *n. Slang.* A grossly sentimental story, drama, or performance. —**tear′-jerk′ing** *adj.*

tea•room (tē′ro͞om′, -ro͝om′) *n.* A restaurant or shop serving tea and other refreshments.

tea rose *n.* **1.** Any of several cultivated roses derived from *Rosa odorata,* native to China and having fragrant yellowish or pink flowers. **2.** *Color.* A pale to strong yellowish pink.

tear sheet or **tear•sheet** (târ′shēt′) *n. Print.* A page taken from a book or periodical.

tear•stain (tîr′stān′) *n.* A track or mark left by tears.

tear•y (tîr′ē) *adj.* **-i•er, -i•est. 1.a.** Filled or wet with tears. **b.** Of or resembling tears. **2.** Causing weeping: *a teary goodbye.* **3.** Inclined to weep. —**tear′i•ly** *adv.* —**tear′i•ness** *n.*

tear•y-eyed (tîr′ē-īd′) *adj.* **1.** Having tears in the eyes, as from emotion. **2.** Marked by tears or weeping.

Teas•dale (tēz′dāl′), **Sara.** 1884–1933. Amer. poet whose collections include *Love Songs* (1917).

tease (tēz) *v.* **teased, teas•ing, teas•es.** —*tr.* **1.** To annoy or pester; vex. **2.** To make fun of; mock playfully. **3.** To arouse hope, desire, or curiosity in without affording satisfaction. **4.a.** To urge persistently; coax. **b.** To gain by persistent coaxing. **c.** To deal with or have an effect on as if by teasing. **5.** To cut (tissue, for example) into pieces for examination. **6.** To disentangle and dress the fibers of (wool, for example). **7.** To raise the nap of (cloth) by dressing, as with a fuller's teasel. **8.** To ruffle (the hair) by combing from the ends toward the scalp for an airy effect. —*intr.* To annoy or make fun of someone persistently. —*n.* **1.a.** The act of teasing. **b.** The state of being teased. **2.** One that teases, as: **a.** One given to playful mocking. **b.** A flirt. **c.** A preliminary remark or act intended to whet the curiosity. —***phrasal verb.*** **tease out.** To get by or as if by untangling or releasing with a pointed tool or device. [ME *tesen,* to comb apart < OE *tǣsan.*]

tea•sel (tē′zəl) *n.* **1.** Any of several plants of the genus *Dipsacus,* native to the Old World and having flower heads surrounded by spiny bracts. **2.a.** The bristly flower head of *D. sativus,* used to make a napped surface, as on wool. **b.** A wire device used to make a napped surface. —*tr.v.* **-seled, -sel•ing, -sels** or **-selled, -sel•ling, -sels.** To make a napped surface on (a fabric). [ME *tesel* < OE *tǣsel.*]

teas•er (tē′zər) *n.* **1.a.** One that teases, as a device for teasing wool. **b.** One who engages in teasing; a tease. **2.** A puzzling problem. **3.** An advertisement that attracts customers by offering something extra or free. **4.** *Slang.* An attention-getting vignette or highlight presented before a television show.

tea service *n.* A set of articles, such as matching cups and a teapot, used in serving tea.

tea•shop (tē′shŏp′) *n.* **1.** See **tearoom. 2.** *Chiefly British.* A luncheonette or small restaurant.

tea•spoon (tē′spo͞on′) *n.* **1.** The common small spoon used esp. in serving and consuming tea, coffee, and desserts. **2.** A household cooking measure equal to ⅓ tablespoon (about 5 milliliters). See table at **measurement.**

tea•spoon•ful (tē′spo͞on-fo͝ol′) *n., pl.* **-fuls.** The amount that a teaspoon can hold.

teat (tēt, tĭt) *n.* A nipple of the mammary gland; a mamilla. [ME *tete* < OFr., of Gmc. orig.] —**teat′ed** *adj.*

tea table *n.* A small table used for serving tea.

tea•time (tē′tīm′) *n.* The usual or traditional time for serving tea, as late afternoon.

tea towel *n.* A cloth for drying dishes; a dishtowel.

tea tray *n.* A tray for holding a tea service.

tea wagon *n.* A small table on wheels for serving tea or holding dishes.

Te•bal•di (tə-băl′dē, tĕ-), **Renata.** b. 1922. Italian-born operatic soprano known for her portrayal of dramatic heroines.

Te•bet or **Te•beth** (tā′vās, tĕ-vĕt′) *n.* Var. of **Tevet.**

tec. *abbr.* **1.** Technical. **2.** Technician.

tech. *abbr.* **1.** Technical. **2.** Technician.

teched (tĕcht) *adj.* Var. of **tetched.**

tech•ie also **tek•kie** (tĕk′ē) *n. Informal.* One who studies or is interested or proficient in a technical field, esp. electronics.

tech•ne•ti•um (tĕk-nē′shē-əm, -shəm) *n. Symbol* **Tc** A radioactive metal, the first synthetically produced element, used as a tracer and to inhibit corrosion in steel; its longest-lived isotope is Tc 97 with a half-life of 2.6 × 10^6 years. Atomic number 43; melting point 2,200°C; specific gravity 11.50; valence 0, 2, 4, 5, 6, 7. See table at **element.** [< Gk. *tekhnētos,* artificial < *teknasthai,* to make by art < *tekhnē,* art. See TECHNICAL.]

tech•ne•tron•ic (tĕk′nĭ-trŏn′ĭk) *adj.* Of or marked by the changes effected by modern technology and electronics.

tech•nic (tĕk′nĭk) *n.* **1. technics.** *(used with a sing. or pl. v.)* The theory, principles, or study of an art or a process. **2. technics.** *(used with a pl. v.)* Technical details, rules, or methods. —*adj.* Technical. [< Gk. *tekhnikos,* of art < *tekhnē,* art. See TECHNICAL.]

tech•ni•cal (tĕk′nĭ-kəl) *adj.* **1.** Of or derived from technique. **2.a.** Having special skill or practical knowledge esp. in a mechanical or scientific field. **b.** Used in or peculiar to a given field or profession; specialized. **3.a.** Belonging or relating to a given subject. **b.** Of, relating to, or involving the practical, mechanical, or industrial arts or the applied sciences. **4.a.** Abstract or theoretical. **b.** Of or employing the methodology of science; scientific. **5.** According to principle; formal rather than practical: *a technical advantage.* **6.** Industrial and mechanical; technological. **7.** Indicating or relating to a stock market in which prices are determined or affected by internal manipulation and speculation. —*n. Sports.* A technical foul. [< Gk. *tekhnikos,* of art < *tekhnē,* art. See **teks-*.**] —**tech′ni•cal•ly** *adv.* —**tech′ni•cal•ness** *n.*

technical foul *n. Sports.* A foul, esp. in basketball, that is called, as for unsportsmanlike conduct, and does not usu. involve physical contact with an opponent during play.

tech•ni•cal•i•ty (tĕk′nĭ-kăl′ĭ-tē) *n., pl.* **-ties. 1.** The quality or condition of being technical. **2.** Something meaningful or relevant only to a specialist: *a legal technicality.*

technical knockout *n. Sports.* A victory in boxing awarded by the referee when it appears that one fighter is too badly injured to continue.

technical sergeant *n.* A noncommissioned officer in the U.S. Air Force ranking above staff sergeant and below master sergeant.

tech•ni•cian (tĕk-nĭsh′ən) *n.* An expert in a technique, as: **a.** One whose occupation requires training in a specific technical process: *an electronics technician.* **b.** One who is known for skill in an intellectual or artistic technique.

Tech•ni•col•or (tĕk′nĭ-kŭl′ər). A trademark used for a method of making color motion pictures in which films sensitive to different primary colors are exposed simultaneously and are later superimposed to produce the full-color print.

tech•nique (tĕk-nēk′) *n.* **1.** The systematic procedure by which a complex or scientific task is accomplished. **2.** Also **tech•nic** (tĕk′nĭk). **a.** The way in which the fundamentals, as of an artistic work, are handled. **b.** Skill or command in handling such fundamentals. [Fr., technical, technique < Gk. *tekhnikos*, technical. See TECHNICAL.]

tech•noc•ra•cy (tĕk-nŏk′rə-sē) *n., pl.* **-cies.** A government or social system controlled by technicians, esp. technical experts. [Gk. *tekhnē*, skill; see TECHNICAL + -CRACY.] **—tech′no•crat′** *n.* **—tech′no•crat′ic** *adj.*

technol. *abbr.* Technology.

tech•no•log•i•cal (tĕk′nə-lŏj′ĭ-kəl) also **tech•no•log•ic** (-lŏj′ĭk) *adj.* **1.** Relating to or involving technology, esp. scientific technology. **2.** Affected by or resulting from scientific and industrial progress. **—tech′no•log′i•cal•ly** *adv.*

tech•nol•o•gist (tĕk-nŏl′ə-jĭst) *n.* A specialist in technology.

tech•nol•o•gize (tĕk-nŏl′ə-jīz′) *tr.v.* **-gized, -giz•ing, -giz•es.** To modify or affect by technology; make technological.

tech•nol•o•gy (tĕk-nŏl′ə-jē) *n., pl.* **-gies. 1.a.** The application of science, esp. to industrial or commercial objectives. **b.** The scientific method and material used to achieve a commercial or industrial objective. **2.** *Anthro.* The body of knowledge available to a civilization that is of use in fashioning implements, practicing manual arts and skills, and extracting or collecting materials. [Gk. *tekhnologia*, systematic treatment of an art or craft : *tekhnē*, skill; see **teks-*** + *-logia*, -logy.]

tech•no•struc•ture (tĕk′nō-strŭk′chər) *n.* **1.** A large-scale corporate system. **2.** A network of skilled professionals who control such a corporate system. [TECHNO(LOGY) + STRUCTURE.]

tech•y (tĕch′ē) *adj.* Var. of **tetchy.**

tec•ton•ic (tĕk-tŏn′ĭk) *adj.* **1.** *Geol.* Relating to, causing, or resulting from structural deformation of the earth's crust. **2.a.** Relating to construction or building. **b.** Architectural. [LLat. *tectonicus* < Gk. *tektonikos* < *tektōn*, builder. See **teks-*.**] **—tec•ton′i•cal•ly** *adv.*

tec•ton•ics (tĕk-tŏn′ĭks) *n. (used with a sing. v.)* **1.** The study of the earth's structural features. **2.** The art or science of construction, esp. of large buildings.

tec•ton•ism (tĕk′tə-nĭz′əm) *n. Geol.* **1.** The structural behavior of an element of the earth's crust. **2.** Crustal instability.

tec•trix (tĕk′trĭks) *n., pl.* **-tri•ces** (-trĭ-sēz′). One of the coverts of a bird's wing. Often used in the plural. [Lat. *tēctrix*, fem. of *tēctor*, plasterer < *tēctus*, p.part. of *tegere*, to cover. See **(s)teg-*.**]

tec•tum (tĕk′təm) *n., pl.* **-ta** (-tə). A rooflike structure of the body, esp. the dorsal part of the mesencephalon. [Lat. *tēctum*, roof < neut. p.part. of *tegere*, to cover. See **(s)teg-*.**]

Te•cum•seh (tĭ-kŭm′sə) or **Te•cum•tha** (-thə). 1768–1813. Shawnee leader who attempted to establish a confederacy to unify Native Americans against white encroachment.

ted (tĕd) *tr.v.* **ted•ded, ted•ding, teds.** *Chiefly New England.* To strew or spread (newly mown grass, for example) for drying. [ME *tedden.*]

ted•der (tĕd′ər) *n. Chiefly New England.* A machine that spreads newly mown hay for drying. **—ted′der** *v.*

ted•dy (tĕd′ē) *n., pl.* **-dies. 1.** A woman's undergarment combining a camisole top and panties. **2.** A teddy bear.

teddy bear also **Teddy bear** *n.* A child's toy bear, usu. stuffed with soft material and covered with furlike plush. [After *Teddy*, nickname of Theodore Roosevelt.]

Teddy boy *n.* A tough British youth wearing a modified style of Edwardian clothes. [< the name *Teddy*, nickname for *Edward*, after EDWARD VII.]

Te De•um (tā′ dā′əm, -ōōm, tē′ dē′əm) *n.* A hymn of praise to God sung as part of a liturgy. [< LLat. *Tē Deum (laudāmus)*, You, God, (we praise).]

te•di•ous (tē′dē-əs) *adj.* **1.** Tiresome by reason of length, slowness, or dullness; boring. See Syns at **boring. 2.** *Obsolete.* Moving or progressing very slowly. [ME < LLat. *taediōsus* < Lat. *taedium*, tedium. See TEDIUM.] **—te′di•ous•ly** *adv.* **—te′di•ous•ness** *n.*

te•di•um (tē′dē-əm) *n.* The quality or condition of being tedious; boredom. [Lat. *taedium* < *taedēre*, to weary.]

tee[1] (tē) *n.* **1.** The letter *t.* **2.** Something shaped like a T. **3.** *Sports & Games.* A mark aimed at in certain games, such as curling or quoits. **—*idiom.* to a tee.** Perfectly; exactly.

tee[2] (tē) *n. Sports.* **1.** A small peg with a concave top for holding a golf ball for an initial drive. **2.** The designated area of each golf hole from which a player makes the first stroke. **—*tr.v.*** **teed, tee•ing, tees.** *Sports.* To place (a golf ball) on a tee. Often used with *up.* **—*phrasal verb.* tee off. 1.** *Sports.* To drive a golf ball from the tee. **2.** *Slang.* To start or begin. **3.** *Slang.* To make or become angry or disgusted. [Back-formation < obsolete Sc. *teaz* (taken as a pl.).]

tee•dle board (tēd′l) *n. Northeastern Massachusetts.* See **seesaw** 1. See Regional Note at **teeter-totter.** [Prob. alteration of TEETERBOARD.]

teem[1] (tēm) *v.* **teemed, teem•ing, teems.** **—*intr.*** **1.** To be full of things; abound or swarm. **2.** *Obsolete.* To be or become pregnant; bear or produce young. **—*tr. Archaic.*** To give birth to. [ME *temen*, to beget, bear < OE *tīeman, tēman.* See **deuk-*.**] **—teem′er** *n.* **—teem′ing•ly** *adv.*

Syns: *teem, abound, bristle, crawl, overflow, swarm.* The central meaning shared by these verbs is "to be abundantly filled or richly supplied": *a street teeming with pedestrians; a garden abounding with flowers; roofs bristling with television antennas; a highway crawling with cars; a house overflowing with guests; a parade route swarming with spectators.*

teem[2] (tēm) *tr.v.* **teemed, teem•ing, teems.** To pour out or empty. [ME *temen* < ON *tōma.*]

teen[1] (tēn) *n.* **1. teens. a.** The numbers 13 through 19. **b.** The 13th through 19th items in a series or scale, as years of a century. **2.** A teenager. **—*adj.*** Teenage.

teen[2] (tēn) *n. Archaic.* Misery; grief. [ME *tene* < OE *tēona.*]

teen•age or **teen-age** (tēn′āj′) also **teen•aged** or **teen-aged** (-ājd′) *adj.* Of, relating to, or applicable to teenagers.

teen•ag•er also **teen-ag•er** (tēn′ā′jər) *n.* A person between the ages of 13 and 19; an adolescent.

teen•er (tē′nər) *n. Informal.* A teenager.

teen•sy-ween•sy (tēn′sē-wēn′sē) or **teen•y-ween•y** (tē′nē-wē′nē) *adj. Informal.* Tiny. [Alteration of *teeny-weeny*, redup. and alteration of TEENY.]

tee•ny (tē′nē) also **teen•sy** (tēn′sē) *adj.* **-ni•er, -ni•est** also **-si•er, -si•est.** *Informal.* Tiny. [Alteration of TINY.]

teen•y•bop•per (tē′nē-bŏp′ər) *n. Slang.* **1.** A young teenage girl. **2.** A teenager who follows the latest fad or craze.

tee•pee (tē′pē) *n.* Var. of **tepee.**

Tees (tēz). A river of NE England flowing c. 113 km (70 mi) to the North Sea.

tee shirt *n.* Var. of **T-shirt.**

tee•ter (tē′tər) *v.* **-tered, -ter•ing, -ters.** **—*intr.*** **1.** To walk or move unsteadily or unsurely; totter. **2.** To alternate, as between opposing positions; vacillate. **3.** To seesaw. **—*tr.*** To cause to teeter or seesaw. **—*n. Northeastern U.S.*** **1.** See **seesaw** 1. See Regional Note at **teeter-totter. 2.** A teetering motion. [ME *titeren*, prob. < ON *titra*, to shake.]

tee•ter•board (tē′tər-bôrd′, -bōrd′) *n. Northeastern U.S.* **1.** See **seesaw** 1. See Regional Note at **teeter-totter. 2.** *Sports.* A board with one end raised so that when an acrobat or a tumbler jumps onto it, another performer standing on the opposite end is tossed into the air.

tee•ter-tot•ter (tē′tər-tŏt′ər) *n. Inland Northern & Western U.S.* See **seesaw** 1.

Regional Note: The outdoor toy usually called a *seesaw* has a number of regional names. In southeast New England it is called a *tilt* or a *tilting board.* Speakers in northeast Massachusetts call it a *teedle board*; in the Narragansett Bay area the term changes to *dandle* or *dandle board. Teeter* or *teeterboard* is used more generally in the northeast United States, while *teeter-totter*, probably the most common term after *seesaw*, is used across the inland northern states and westward to the West Coast.

teeth (tēth) *n.* Pl. of **tooth.**

teethe (tē*th*) *intr.v.* **teethed, teeth•ing, teethes.** To grow teeth; cut one's teeth. [ME *tethen* < *teth*, pl. of *tooth*, tooth. See TOOTH.]

teeth•er (tē′*th*ər) *n.* An object or a device, such as a teething ring, for a baby to bite on during teething.

teeth•ing (tē′*th*ĭng) *n.* The eruption and cutting of teeth, esp. the milk teeth; dentition.

teething ring *n.* A ring of hard plastic or rubber upon which a teething baby can bite.

teeth•ridge (tēth′rĭj′) *n.* The ridge of gum behind the upper front teeth.

tee•to•tal (tē′tōt′l) *adj.* **1.** Of, relating to, or practicing complete abstinence from alcoholic beverages. **2.** Total; absolute. [Prob. partly TEE[1] (pronunciation of the first letter in *total*) + *total (abstinence)*, and partly redup. of TOTAL.]

tee•to•tal•er or **tee•to•tal•ler** (tē′tōt′l-ər) also **tee•to•tal•ist** (-ĭst) *n.* One who abstains completely from alcoholic beverages. **—tee•to′tal•ism** *n.*

tee•to•tum (tē-tō′təm) *n. Games.* A top, usu. having four lettered sides, used to play various games of chance. [< earlier *T totum* (< the letter tee) < *totum*, teetotum < Lat. *tōtum*, neut. sing. of *tōtus*, all. See **teutā-*.**]

te•fil•lin (tə-fĭl′ĭn, -fē-lēn′) *pl.n.* Two small leather boxes, each containing parchment with quotations from the Hebrew Bible, worn by some observant Jews during morning worship, except on holidays. [Heb. *tĕpillîn* < Aram., attachments.]

TEFL *abbr.* Teaching English as a foreign language.

teem[2]

ă pat	oi boy
ā pay	ou out
âr care	ŏŏ took
ä father	ōō boot
ĕ pet	ŭ cut
ē be	ûr urge
ĭ pit	th thin
ī pie	*th* this
îr pier	hw which
ŏ pot	zh vision
ō toe	ə about, item
ô paw	

Stress marks:
′ (primary);
′ (secondary), as in
dictionary (dĭk′shə-nĕr′ē)

Tef•lon (tĕf′lŏn′). A trademark for a waxy opaque material, polytetrafluoroethylene, as a coating on cooking utensils and in industry to prevent sticking.
teg also **tegg** (tĕg) *n.* A sheep in its second year or before its first shearing. [?]
teg•men (tĕg′mən) *n., pl.* **-mi•na** (-mə-nə). A covering or an integument, such as the inner coat of a seed. [Lat., covering < *tegere*, to cover. See **(s)teg-***.]
teg•men•tum (tĕg-mĕn′təm) *n.* **1.** See **tegmen. 2.** A part of the mesencephalon consisting of white fibers running lengthwise through gray matter. [Lat., covering < *tegere*, to cover. See **(s)teg-***.] **—teg•men′tal** (-təl) *adj.*
Te•gu•ci•gal•pa (tə-go͞o′sə-găl′pə, tĕ-go͞o′sē-gäl′pä). The cap. of Honduras, in the S-central part. Pop. 532,500.
teg•u•lar (tĕg′yə-lər) also **teg•u•lat•ed** (-lā′tĭd) *adj.* Of or resembling a tile. [< Lat. *tēgula*, tile < *tegere*, to cover. See **(s)teg-***.] **—teg′u•lar•ly** *adv.*
teg•u•ment (tĕg′yə-mənt) *n.* A natural outer covering; an integument. [ME < Lat. *tegumentum* < *tegere*, to cover. See **(s)teg-***.] **—teg′u•men′ta•ry** (-mĕn′tə-rē, -mĕn′trē), **teg′u•men′tal** (-mĕn′tl) *adj.*
Teh•ran or **Te•he•ran** (tĕ′ə-răn′, -rän′, tĕ-răn′, -rän′). The cap. of Iran, in the N-central part. Pop. 5,734,199.
Te•huan•te•pec (tə-wän′tə-pĕk′, tĕ-wän′tĕ-), **Isthmus of.** An isthmus of S Mexico between the Bay of Campeche and the **Gulf of Tehuantepec**, a wide inlet of the Pacific.
Te•huel•che (tə-wĕl′chē, tā-wĕl′chā) *n., pl.* **Tehuelche** or **-ches. 1.** A member of a South American Indian people of Patagonia, who were virtually exterminated. **2.** The language of the Tehuelche. **—Te•huel′che•an** (-chē-ən) *adj.*
Teil•hard de Char•din (tā-yär′ də shär-dăN′), **Pierre.** 1881–1955. French philosopher who maintained that the universe and humankind are evolving toward a perfect state.
Te Ka•na•wa (tĭ kä′nə-wə), Dame **Kiri.** b. 1944. New Zealand operatic soprano noted for her rich lyric voice.
tek•kie (tĕk′ē) *n. Informal.* Var. of **techie.**
tek•tite (tĕk′tīt′) *n.* Any of numerous generally small rounded dark brown to green glassy objects composed of silicate glass, thought to have been formed by the impact of a meteorite with the earth's surface. [Gk. *tēktos*, molten (< *tēkein*, to melt) + -ITE[1].] **—tek•tit′ic** (-tĭt′ĭk) *adj.*
tel. *abbr.* **1.** Telegram. **2.** Telegraph. **3.** Telegraphic. **4.** Telephone.
tel–[1] *pref.* Var. of **tele–.**
tel–[2] *pref.* Var. of **telo–.**
tel•aes•the•sia (tĕl′ĭs-thē′zhə) *n.* Var. of **telesthesia.**
tel•a•mon (tĕl′ə-mŏn′) *n., pl.* **-mon•es** (-mō′nēz). *Archit.* A figure of a man used as a supporting pillar. [Lat. *telamōn* < Gk., bearer. See **telə-***.]
Tel•a•mon (tĕl′ə-mən, -mŏn′) *n. Gk. Myth.* One of the Argonauts and the father of Ajax.
tel•an•gi•ec•ta•sia (tĕl-ăn′jē-ĕk-tā′zhə) also **tel•an•gi•ec•ta•sis** (-ĕk′tə-sĭs) *n.* Chronic dilation of groups of capillaries causing elevated dark red blotches on the skin. [NLat. : TEL(O)– + Gk. *angeion*, vessel; see ANGIO– + Gk. *ektasis*, expansion (< *ekteinein*, to stretch out : *ek-*, *ex*, ex- + *teinein*, to stretch; see **ten-***).] **—tel•an′gi•ec•tat′ic** (-tăt′ĭk) *adj.*
Tel A•viv–Jaf•fa (tĕl′ ə-vēv′-jăf′ə, -yäf′ə, ä-vēv′-). A city of W-central Israel WNW of Jerusalem. Tel Aviv was founded in 1909 by settlers from the ancient city of Jaffa; the communities merged in 1950. Pop. 323,400.
tele– or **tel–** *pref.* **1.** Distance; distant: *telesthesia.* **2.a.** Telegraph; telephone: *telegram.* **b.** Television: *telecast.* [Gk. *tēle-* < *tēle*, far off. See **kʷel-²***.]
tel•e•cast (tĕl′ĭ-kăst′) *v.* **-cast** or **-cast•ed, -cast•ing, -casts.** *—intr.* To broadcast a television program. *—tr.* To broadcast (a program) by television. *—n.* A television broadcast. **—tel′e•cast′er** *n.*
tel•e•com (tĕl′ĭ-kŏm′) *n. Informal.* Telecommunication.
tel•e•com•mu•ni•cate (tĕl′ĭ-kə-myo͞o′nĭ-kāt′) *v.* **-cat•ed, -cat•ing, -cates.** *—tr.* To transmit (data, for example) by telecommunication. *—intr.* To communicate by means of telecommunication. **—tel′e•com•mu′ni•ca′tor** *n.*
tel•e•com•mu•ni•ca•tion (tĕl′ĭ-kə-myo͞o′nĭ-kā′shən) *n.* **1.** The science and technology of communication at a distance by electronic transmission of impulses, as by telegraph, telephone, radio, or television. Often used in the plural with a singular verb. **2.** The electronic systems used in such transmission. Often used in the plural. **3.** A message so transmitted.
tel•e•com•mut•ing (tĕl′ĭ-kə-myo͞o′tĭng) *n. Comp. Sci.* The practice of working at home by using a modem and a computer terminal connected with one's business office. **—tel′e•com•mute′** *v.* **—tel′e•com•mut′er** *n.*
tel•e•con•fer•ence (tĕl′ĭ-kŏn′fər-əns, -frəns) *n.* A conference held among people in different locations by means of telecommunications equipment, such as closed-circuit television. **—tel′e•con′fer•ence** *v.* **—tel′e•con′fer•enc•ing** *n.*
tel•e•course (tĕl′ĭ-kôrs′, -kōrs′) *n.* A course of televised lectures, as one offered by a university.
tel•e•fac•sim•i•le (tĕl′ə-făk-sĭm′ə-lē) *n.* A method for the electronic transmission and reproduction of graphic images or printed matter via signals sent over telephone lines.
tel•e•film (tĕl′ə-fĭlm′) *n.* A film made for television.
teleg. *abbr.* **1.** Telegram. **2.** Telegraph. **3.** Telegraphic. **4.** Telegraphy.
tel•e•gen•ic (tĕl′ə-jĕn′ĭk) *adj.* Having physical and personal qualities deemed appealing on television.
tel•e•gram (tĕl′ĭ-grăm′) *n.* A message transmitted by telegraph. *—tr. & intr.v.* **-grammed, -gram•ming, -grams.** To telegraph (something) or be telegraphed.
tel•e•graph (tĕl′ĭ-grăf′) *n.* **1.** A communications system that transmits and receives simple unmodulated electric impulses, esp. one in which the transmission and reception stations are directly connected by wires. **2.** A message transmitted by telegraph; a telegram. *—v.* **-graphed, -graph•ing, -graphs.** *—tr.* **1.** To transmit (a message) by telegraph. **2.** To send or convey a message to (a recipient) by telegraph. **3.a.** To make known (a feeling, for example) by nonverbal means. **b.** To make known (an intended action, for example) in advance or unintentionally. *—intr.* To send or transmit a telegram. **—te•leg′ra•pher** (tə-lĕg′rə-fər), **te•leg′ra•phist** (-fĭst) *n.*
tel•e•graph•ic (tĕl′ĭ-grăf′ĭk) also **tel•e•graph•i•cal** (-ĭ-kəl) *adj.* **1.** Of or transmitted by telegraph. **2.** Brief or concise.
telegraph plant *n.* A tropical Asian plant *(Desmodium motorium)* having trifoliolate compound leaves, whose very small lateral leaflets move by jerks under the sun's influence.
te•leg•ra•phy (tə-lĕg′rə-fē) *n.* Communication by means of the telegraph.
Tel•e•gu (tĕl′ə-go͞o′) *n. & adj.* Var. of **Telugu.**
tel•e•ki•ne•sis (tĕl′ĭ-kĭ-nē′sĭs, -kī-) *n.* The movement of objects by scientifically inexplicable means, as by the exercise of an occult power. **—tel′e•ki•net′ic** (-nĕt′ĭk) *adj.*
Te•lem•a•chus (tə-lĕm′ə-kəs) *n. Gk. Myth.* The son of Odysseus and Penelope, who helped kill Penelope's suitors.
Te•le•mann (tā′lə-män′), **Georg Philipp.** 1681–1767. German composer of the late baroque period.
tel•e•mark (tĕl′ə-märk′) *Sports. n.* A downhill turn performed on cross-country skis in which the outside ski is advanced ahead of the other and angled inward until the turn is complete. [Norw., after *Telemark*, a region of S Norway.]
tel•e•mar•ket•ing (tĕl′ə-mär′kĭ-tĭng) *n.* Use of the telephone in marketing. **—tel′e•mar′ket•er** *n.*
tel•e•me•ter (tĕl′ə-mē′tər, tə-lĕm′ĭ-tər) *n.* Any of various measuring, transmitting, and receiving systems used in telemetry. *—tr.v.* (tĕl′ə-mē′tər) **-tered, -ter•ing, -ters.** To measure and transmit (data) using telemetry.
te•lem•e•try (tə-lĕm′ĭ-trē) *n.* The science or process of transmitting, as by wire or radio, data measured at a remote location to a distant receiving station for recording and analysis. **—tel′e•met′ric** (tĕl′ə-mĕt′rĭk), **tel′e•met′ri•cal** (-rĭ-kəl) *adj.*
tel•en•ceph•a•lon (tĕl′ĕn-sĕf′ə-lŏn′, -lən) *n.* The anterior portion of the forebrain, constituting the cerebral hemispheres and related parts. **—tel′en•ce•phal′ic** (-sə-făl′ĭk) *adj.*
tel•e•ol•o•gy (tĕl′ē-ŏl′ə-jē, tē′lē-) *n., pl.* **-gies. 1.** *Philos.* The study of design or purpose in natural phenomena. **2.** The use of ultimate purpose or design as a means of explaining natural phenomena. **3.** Purposeful development, as in nature or history, toward a final end. [Gk. *teleios*, *teleos*, perfect, complete (< *telos*, end, result; see **kʷel-¹***) + -LOGY.] **—tel′e•o•log′i•cal** (-ə-lŏj′ĭ-kəl), **tel′e•o•log′ic** (-ĭk) *adj.* **—tel′e•o•log′i•cal•ly** *adv.* **—tel′e•ol′o•gist** *n.*
tel•e•ost (tĕl′ē-ŏst′, tē′lē-) also **tel•e•os•te•an** (-ŏs′tē-ən) *adj.* Of or belonging to the Teleostei or Teleostomi, a group of fishes with bony skeletons, including most common fishes. [< NLat. *Teleostei*, group name (Gk. *teleos*, complete; see TELEOLOGY + *osteon*, bone; see **ost-***) and < NLat. *Teleostomi*, group name (Gk. *teleos*, complete + Gk. *stoma*, mouth).] **—tel′e•ost′** *n.*
te•lep•a•thy (tə-lĕp′ə-thē) *n.* Communication through means other than the senses, as by the exercise of an occult power. **—tel′e•path′ic** (tĕl′ə-păth′ĭk) *adj.* **—tel′e•path′i•cal•ly** *adv.* **—te•lep′a•thist** *n.*
tel•e•phone (tĕl′ə-fōn′) *n.* An instrument that converts voice and other sound signals into a form that can be transmitted to remote locations and receives and reconverts waves into sound signals. *—v.* **-phoned, -phon•ing, -phones.** *—tr.* **1.** To speak with (a person) by telephone. **2.** To initiate or make a telephone connection with; place a call to. **3.** To transmit (a message, for example) by telephone. *—intr.* To engage in communication by telephone. **—tel′e•phon′er** *n.*
telephone book *n.* A directory of telephone subscribers with their telephone numbers and often their addresses.
telephone booth *n.* A small enclosure for a public telephone.
telephone exchange *n.* A central system of equipment that establishes connections between individual telephones.
telephone receiver *n.* The part of a telephone in which incoming electrical impulses are converted into sound.
tel•e•phon•ic (tĕl′ə-fŏn′ĭk) *adj.* **1.** Of or relating to telephones. **2.** Transmitted or conveyed by telephone. **—tel′e•phon′i•cal•ly** *adv.*
te•leph•o•ny (tə-lĕf′ə-nē) *n.* **1.** The transmission of sound between distant stations, esp. by radio or telephone. **2.** The

telephone booth

technology and manufacture of telephone equipment. —**te•leph′o•nist** *n.*

tel•e•pho•to (tĕl′ə-fō′tō) *adj.* **1.** Of, relating to, or being a photographic lens or lens system used to produce a large image of a distant object. **2.** Of or relating to an instrument that electrically transmits photographs. —*n., pl.* **-tos. 1.** A telephoto lens. **2.** A photograph made with a telephoto lens.

tel•e•pho•to•graph (tĕl′ə-fō′tə-grăf′) *n.* **1.** A telephoto. **2.** A photograph transmitted and reproduced by telephotography. —**tel′e•pho′to•graph′** *v.*

tel•e•pho•tog•ra•phy (tĕl′ə-fə-tŏg′rə-fē) *n.* **1.** The process or technique of photographing distant objects, using a telephoto lens on a camera. **2.** The technique or process of transmitting photographs over a distance. —**tel′e•pho′to•graph′ic** (-fō′tə-grăf′ĭk) *adj.*

tel•e•play (tĕl′ə-plā′) *n.* A play written or adapted for television.

tel•e•print•er (tĕl′ə-prĭn′tər) *n.* A teletypewriter.

tel•e•proc•ess•ing (tĕl′ə-prŏs′ĕs′ĭng, -prō′sĕs′-) *n. Comp. Sci.* Data processing by means of remote terminals.

Tel•e•Promp•Ter (tĕl′ə-prŏmp′tər). A trademark for a device used in television to show an actor or a speaker an enlarged line-by-line reproduction of a script, unseen by the audience.

tel•e•ran (tĕl′ə-răn′) *n.* An air-traffic control system in which the image of a ground-based radar unit is televised to aircraft in the vicinity as a navigational aid. [Originally a trademark, short for *tele(vision) r(adar) a(ir) n(avigation).*]

tel•e•scope (tĕl′ĭ-skōp′) *n.* **1.** An arrangement of lenses or mirrors or both that gathers visible light, permitting observation or photographic recording of distant objects. **2.** Any of various devices, such as a radio telescope, used to observe distant objects by detecting and collecting invisible radiation. —*v.* **-scoped, -scop•ing, -scopes.** —*tr.* **1.** To cause to slide inward or outward in overlapping sections, as the cylindrical sections of a small hand telescope do. **2.** To make more compact or concise; condense. —*intr.* To slide inward or outward in or as if in overlapping cylindrical sections. [NLat. *telescopium* or Ital. *telescopio*, both < Gk. *tēleskopos*, far-seeing : *tēle-*, tele- + *skopos*, watcher; see **spek-***.]

tel•e•scop•ic (tĕl′ĭ-skŏp′ĭk) *adj.* **1.** Of or relating to a telescope. **2.** Seen or obtained by means of a telescope. **3.** Visible only by means of a telescope. **4.** Capable of discerning distant objects. **5.** Extensible or compressible by or as if by the sliding of overlapping sections. —**tel′e•scop′i•cal•ly** *adv.*

Tel•e•sco•pi•um (tĕl′ĭ-skō′pē-əm) *n.* A constellation in the Southern Hemisphere between Pavo and Sagittarius. [NLat. < *telescopium*, telescope. See TELESCOPE.]

te•les•co•py (tə-lĕs′kə-pē) *n.* The art or study of making and operating telescopes. —**te•les′co•pist** *n.*

tel•e•shop•ping (tĕl′ə-shŏp′ĭng) *n.* The buying and selling of consumer products by way of television and telephone.

Te•les Pi•res (tĕl′ĭs pîr′ĭs). A river of central Brazil flowing c. 965 km (600 mi) NW as a tributary of the Tapajós R.

tel•es•the•sia also **tel•aes•the•sia** (tĕl′ĭs-thē′zhə) *n.* Response to or perception of distant stimuli by extrasensory means. —**tel′es•thet′ic** (-thĕt′ĭk) *adj.*

tel•e•text (tĕl′ĭ-tĕkst′) *n.* An electronic communications system in which printed information is broadcast by television signal to sets equipped with decoders.

tel•e•thon (tĕl′ə-thŏn′) *n.* A lengthy television program to raise funds for a charity. [TELE- + (MARA)THON.]

Tel•e•type (tĕl′ĭ-tīp′). A trademark used for a teletypewriter.

tel•e•type•writ•er (tĕl′ĭ-tīp′rī′tər) *n.* An electromechanical typewriter that either transmits or receives messages coded in electrical signals carried by telegraph or telephone wires.

te•leu•to•spore (tə-lo͞o′tə-spôr′, -spōr′) *n.* See **teliospore.** [Gk. *teleutē*, termination (< *telos*, end; see **kʷel-¹***) + SPORE.]

tel•e•van•gel•ist (tĕl′ĭ-văn′jə-lĭst) *n.* An evangelist who conducts religious telecasts. —**tel′e•van′gel•ism** *n.*

tel•e•vise (tĕl′ə-vīz′) *tr. & intr v.* **-vised, -vis•ing, -vis•es.** To broadcast or be broadcast by television. —**tel′e•vi′sor** *n.*

tel•e•vi•sion (tĕl′ə-vĭzh′ən) *n.* **1.** The transmission of successive visual images, generally with accompanying sound, as electromagnetic waves and the reconversion of received waves into visual images. **2.a.** An electronic apparatus that receives electromagnetic waves and displays the reconverted images on a screen. **b.** The integrated audible and visible content of the electromagnetic waves received and converted by such an apparatus. **3.** The industry of producing and broadcasting television programs. [Fr. *télévision* : *télé-*, far (< Gk. *tēle-*, tele–) + *vision*, vision; see VISION.]

tel•ex (tĕl′ĕks′) *n.* **1.** A communications system consisting of teletypewriters connected to a telephonic network to send and receive signals. **2.** A message sent or received by such a system. [TEL(ETYPEWRITER) + EX(CHANGE).] —**tel′ex′** *v.*

Tel•ford (tĕl′fərd). A borough of W-central England WNW of Birmingham. Pop. 123,525.

tel•ic (tĕl′ĭk, tē′lĭk) *adj.* Directed or tending toward a goal or purpose; purposeful. [Gk. *telikos* < *telos*, end. See **kʷel-¹***.]

te•li•o•spore (tē′lē-ə-spôr′, -spōr′) *n.* A thick-walled, usu. blackish resting spore of some rusts and smuts, from which the basidium arises. [TELI(UM) + SPORE.]

te•li•um (tē′lē-əm) *n., pl.* **-li•a** (-lē-ə). A pustulelike sorus formed on the tissue of a plant infected by a rust fungus and producing teliospores. [NLat. < Gk. *teleios*, complete. See TELEOLOGY.] —**te′li•al** (-lē-əl) *adj.*

tell (tĕl) *v.* **told** (tōld), **tell•ing, tells.** —*tr.* **1.** To give a detailed account of; narrate. **2.** To communicate by speech or writing; express with words. **3.** To make known; reveal. **4.** To notify; inform. **5.** To inform positively; assure. **6.** To give instructions to; direct. **7.** To discover by observation; discern. **8.** To name or number one by one; count. —*intr.* **1.** To give an account or a revelation. **2.** To give evidence; inform. **3.** To have an effect or impact. —***phrasal verb.* tell off.** *Informal.* To rebuke severely; reprimand. [ME *tellen* < OE *tellan*. See **del-²***.] —**tell′a•ble** *adj.*

tell•er (tĕl′ər) *n.* **1.** One who tells. **2.a.** A bank employee who receives and pays out money. **b.** A machine, as in a bank, that automatically conducts transactions in response to a client's use of a coded card. **3.** A person who counts votes in a legislative assembly. —**tell′er•ship′** *n.*

Tel•ler (tĕl′ər), **Edward.** b. 1908. Hungarian-born Amer. physicist who helped develop the atomic bomb.

tell•ing (tĕl′ĭng) *adj.* Having force and producing a striking effect. See Syns at **valid.** —**tell′ing•ly** *adv.*

tell•tale (tĕl′tāl′) *n.* **1.** One who informs on another; a talebearer. **2.** Something that indicates or reveals information; a sign. **3.** Any of various devices that indicate or register information, esp.: **a.** A time clock. **b.** *Naut.* One of the brightly colored lengths of yarn or string attached to the shrouds and stays of a sailboat, indicating wind direction relative to the boat's motion. **c.** A row of strips hung above a railroad track to warn a passing train of low clearance ahead. **4.** *Sports.* A resonant metal strip across the bottom of the front wall of a racquets or squash court above which the ball must be hit.

tel•lu•ri•an (tĕ-lo͝or′ē-ən) *adj.* Of, relating to, or inhabiting Earth. —*n.* An inhabitant of Earth; a terrestrial.

tel•lu•ric (tĕ-lo͝or′ĭk) *adj.* **1.** Of or relating to Earth. **2.** Derived from or containing tellurium, esp. with valence 6.

telluric acid *n.* A white crystalline inorganic acid, H_6TeO_6, used as a chemical reagent.

tel•lu•ride (tĕl′yə-rīd′) *n.* A binary compound of tellurium.

tel•lu•ri•on (tĕ-lo͝or′ē-ŏn′) also **tel•lu•ri•an** (-ən) *n.* An apparatus that shows how the movement of Earth on its axis and around the sun causes day and night and the seasons. [NLat. : TELLURO- + Gk. *-ion*, dim. suff.]

tel•lu•ri•um (tĕ-lo͝or′ē-əm) *n. Symbol* **Te** A brittle metallic element usu. found in combination with gold and other metals, produced commercially as a byproduct of copper refining and used to alloy stainless steel and lead, in ceramics, and, as bismuth telluride, in thermoelectric devices. Atomic number 52; atomic weight 127.60; melting point 449.5°C; boiling point 989.8°C; specific gravity 6.24; valence 2, 4, 6. See table at **element.**

telluro– or **tellur–** *pref.* **1.** Earth: *tellurian.* **2.** Tellurium: *tellurous.* [< Lat. *tellūs, tellūr-*, earth.]

tel•lu•rom•e•ter (tĕl′yə-rŏm′ĭ-tər) *n.* A surveying instrument that measures distance by timing reflected microwaves.

tel•lu•rous (tĕl′yər-əs, tĕ-lo͝or′əs) *adj.* Of, relating to, or derived from tellurium, esp. with valence 4.

tel•ly (tĕl′ē) *n., pl.* **-lies.** *Chiefly British.* A television set.

telo– or **tel–** *pref.* End: *telophase.* [< Gk. *telos*, end. See **kʷel-¹***.]

tel•o•cen•tric (tĕl′ə-sĕn′trĭk, tē′lə-) *adj.* Having the centromere in a terminal position. Used of a chromosome.

tel•o•mere (tĕl′ə-mîr′, tē′lə-) *n.* Either end of a chromosome.

tel•o•phase (tĕl′ə-fāz′, tē′lə-) *n.* The final stage of mitosis or meiosis during which the chromosomes of daughter cells are grouped in new nuclei. —**tel′o•phas′ic** *adj.*

tel•o•tax•is (tĕl′ə-tăk′sĭs) *n.* Movement or orientation of an organism toward or away from a particular stimulus.

tel•pher (tĕl′fər) *n.* **1.** A small traveling car, usu. driven by electricity, suspended from or moving on an overhead rail or cable. **2.** A transportation system using telphers. —*tr.v.* **-phered, -pher•ing, -phers.** To transport by telpher. [Alteration of *telepher* : TELE- + Gk. *pherein*, to carry; see **bher-¹***.]

tel•son (tĕl′sən) *n.* **1.** The rearmost segment of the body of certain arthropods. **2.** An extension of this segment, such as the middle lobe of the tail fan of a lobster. [Gk., limit.]

Tel•u•gu also **Tel•e•gu** (tĕl′ə-go͞o′) —*n., pl.* **Telugu** or **-gus** also **Telegu** or **-gus. 1.** A Dravidian language spoken in central India. **2.** A member of the Dravidian people who speak Telugu. —*adj.* Of Telugu, its speakers, or their culture.

tem•blor (tĕm′blər, -blôr′) *n.* See **earthquake.** [Sp., a trembling, earthquake < *temblar*, to shake < VLat. **tremulāre* < Lat. *tremulus*, shaking. See TREMULOUS.]

tem•er•ar•i•ous (tĕm′ə-râr′ē-əs) *adj.* Presumptuously or recklessly daring. [< Lat. *temerārius* < *temere*, rashly.] —**tem′er•ar′i•ous•ly** *adv.* —**tem′er•ar′i•ous•ness** *n.*

te•mer•i•ty (tə-mĕr′ĭ-tē) *n.* Foolhardy disregard of danger. [ME *temerite* < OFr. < Lat. *temeritās* < *temere*, rashly.]

Tem•ne (tĕm′nē) *n., pl.* **Temne** or **-nes. 1.** A member of a people living in Sierra Leone. **2.** The West Atlantic language of this people.

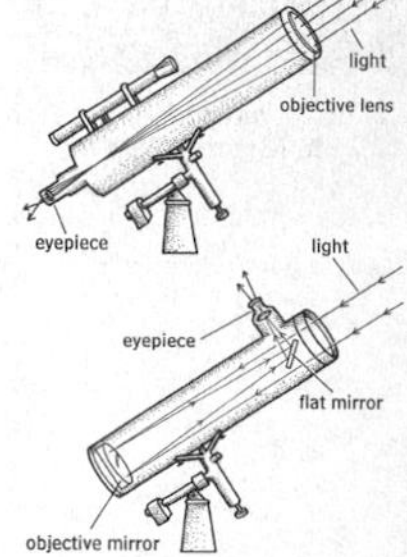

telescope
Top: Refracting telescope
Bottom: Reflecting telescope

ă pat	oi boy
ā pay	ou out
âr care	o͝o took
ä father	o͞o boot
ĕ pet	ŭ cut
ē be	ûr urge
ĭ pit	th thin
ī pie	*th* this
îr pier	hw which
ŏ pot	zh vision
ō toe	ə about,
ô paw	item

Stress marks:
′ (primary);
′ (secondary), as in
dictionary (dĭk′shə-nĕr′ē)

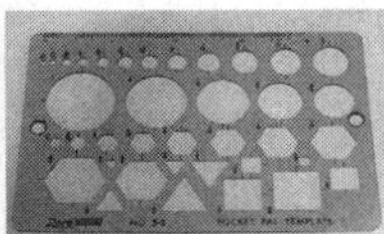

template

temple[1]
In Mysore, India

Ten Commandments
Moses holding the Ten Commandments

temp (tĕmp) *n. Informal.* A temporary worker, as in an office.

temp. *abbr.* **1.** Temperance. **2.** Temperature. **3.** Template. **4.** Temporal. **5.** Temporary. **6.** *Lat.* Tempore (in the time of).

Tem•pe (tĕm′pē′). A city of S-central AZ E of Phoenix; seat of Arizona State University (estab. 1885). Pop. 141,865.

Tempe, Vale of. A valley of NE Greece between Mt. Olympus and Mt. Ossa.

tem•per (tĕm′pər) *v.* **-pered, -per•ing, -pers.** —*tr.* **1.** To modify by the addition of a moderating element; moderate. **2.** To bring to a desired consistency, texture, hardness, or other physical condition by or as if by blending, admixing, or kneading: *temper clay.* **3.** To harden or strengthen (metal or glass) by application of heat or by heating and cooling. **4.** To strengthen through experience or hardship; toughen. **5.a.** To attune. **b.** *Mus.* To adjust (the pitch of an instrument) to a temperament. —*intr.* To be or become tempered. —*n.* **1.** A state of mind or emotions; disposition. See Syns at **mood**[1]. **2.** Calmness of mind or emotions; composure. **3.a.** A tendency to become easily angry or irritable. **b.** An outburst of rage. **4.** A characteristic general quality; tone. **5.a.** The condition of being tempered. **b.** The degree of hardness and elasticity of a metal, chiefly steel, achieved by tempering. **6.** A modifying substance or agent added to something else. **7.** *Archaic.* A middle course between extremes; a mean. [ME *temperen* < OE *temprian* < Lat. *temperāre*, prob. < *temper-*, var. of *tempor-*, stem of *tempus*, time, season.] —**tem′per•a•bil′i•ty** *n.* —**tem′per•a•ble** *adj.* —**tem′per•er** *n.*

tem•per•a (tĕm′pər-ə) *n.* **1.** A painting medium in which pigment is mixed with water-soluble glutinous materials such as size or egg yolk. **2.** Painting done in this medium. [Ital. < *temperare*, to mingle < Lat. *temperāre*. See TEMPER.]

tem•per•a•ment (tĕm′prə-mənt, tĕm′pər-ə-) *n.* **1.a.** The manner of thinking, behaving, or reacting typical of a specific person. **b.** One's distinguishing mental and physical characteristics according to medieval physiology, resulting from dominance of one of the four humors. **2.** Excessive irritability or sensitiveness. **3.** *Mus.* Equal temperament. [ME < Lat. *temperāmentum* < *temperāre*, to temper. See TEMPER.]

tem•per•a•men•tal (tĕm′prə-mĕn′tl, tĕm′pər-ə-) *adj.* **1.** Relating to or caused by temperament. **2.** Excessively sensitive or irritable; moody. **3.** Likely to perform unpredictably; undependable. —**tem′per•a•men′tal•ly** *adv.*

tem•per•ance (tĕm′pər-əns, tĕm′prəns) *n.* **1.** Moderation and self-restraint, as in behavior. **2.** Restraint in the use of or abstinence from alcoholic liquors.

tem•per•ate (tĕm′pər-ĭt, tĕm′prĭt) *adj.* **1.** Exercising moderation and self-restraint. **2.** Moderate in degree or quality; restrained. **3.** Marked by moderate temperatures, weather, or climate; neither hot nor cold. [ME *temperat* < Lat. *temperātus* < p.part. of *temperāre*, to temper. See TEMPER.] —**tem′per•ate•ly** *adv.* —**tem′per•ate•ness** *n.*

Tem•per•ate Zone (tĕm′pər-ĭt, tĕm′prĭt). Either of two intermediate latitude zones of the earth, the **North Temperate Zone,** between the Arctic Circle and the Tropic of Cancer, or the **South Temperate Zone,** between the Antarctic Circle and the Tropic of Capricorn.

tem•per•a•ture (tĕm′pər-ə-cho͝or′, -chər, tĕm′prə-) *n.* **1.a.** The degree of hotness or coldness of a body or an environment. **b.** A specific degree of hotness or coldness as indicated on or referred to a standard scale. **2.a.** The degree of heat in the body of a living organism, usu. about 37.0°C (98.6°F) in humans. **b.** An abnormally high condition of body heat caused by illness; a fever. [ME, temperate weather < Lat. *temperātūra*, due measure < *temperātus*, p.part. of *temperāre*, to mix. See TEMPER.]

temperature gradient *n.* The rate of change of temperature with displacement in a given direction from a given point.

tem•pered (tĕm′pərd) *adj.* **1.** Having a specified temper or disposition. Often used in combination: *sweet-tempered.* **2.** Adjusted or attuned by the addition of a counterbalancing element; moderated or measured. **3.** Made appropriately hard or flexible by tempering: *tempered steel.* **4.** Having the requisite degree of hardness or elasticity. Used of glass or a metal. **5.** *Mus.* Tuned to temperament. Used of a scale, an interval, a semitone, or intonation.

tem•pest (tĕm′pĭst) *n.* **1.** A violent windstorm, frequently accompanied by rain, snow, or hail. **2.** Furious agitation, commotion, or tumult; an uproar. —*tr.v.* **-pest•ed, -pest•ing, -pests.** To cause a tempest around or in. —***idiom.* tempest in a teacup** (or **teapot**). A great disturbance or uproar over a matter of little or no importance. [ME < OFr. *tempeste* < VLat. **tempesta*, var. of Lat. *tempestās* < *tempus*, time.]

tem•pes•tu•ous (tĕm-pĕs′cho͞o-əs) *adj.* **1.** Of, relating to, or resembling a tempest. **2.** Tumultuous; stormy: *a tempestuous relationship.* [ME < LLat. *tempestuōsus* < *tempestūs*, tempest, var. of *tempestās*. See TEMPEST.] —**tem•pes′tu•ous•ly** *adv.* —**tem•pes′tu•ous•ness** *n.*

tem•pi (tĕm′pē) *n.* Pl. of **tempo.**

Tem•plar (tĕm′plər) *n.* **1.** A Knight Templar. **2. templar.** A lawyer or student of law having chambers in the Temple in London. [ME *templer* < AN < Med.Lat. *templārius* < Lat. *templum*, temple. See TEMPLE[1].]

tem•plate also **tem•plet** (tĕm′plĭt) *n.* **1.** A pattern or gauge, such as a thin metal plate with a cut pattern, used as a guide in making something accurately, as in woodworking. **2.** A horizontal piece of stone or timber used to distribute weight or pressure, as over a door frame. **3.** *Biochem.* A molecule of a nucleic acid, such as DNA, that serves as a pattern for the synthesis of a macromolecule, as of RNA. [Prob. < Fr. *templet*, dim. of *temple*, temple of a loom. See TEMPLE[3].]

tem•ple[1] (tĕm′pəl) *n.* **1.a.** A building dedicated to religious ceremonies or worship. **b. Temple.** Either of two successive buildings in ancient Jerusalem serving as the primary center for Jewish worship. **c.** *Judaism.* A synagogue, esp. of a Reform or Conservative congregation. **2.** Something regarded as having within it a divine presence. **3.** A building used for meetings by a fraternal order. **4.** A building reserved for a highly valued function. **5. Temple.** Either of two groups of buildings in London, the Inner Temple and the Middle Temple, that house two of the four Inns of Court and occupy the site of the medieval Knights Templars establishment. [ME < OE *tempel* < Lat. *templum*. See **tem-***.]

tem•ple[2] (tĕm′pəl) *n.* **1.** The flat region on either side of the forehead. **2.** Either of the sidepieces of an eyeglasses frame that extends along the temple and over the ear. [ME < OFr. < VLat. **tempula* < Lat. *tempora*, pl. of *tempus*, temple of the head.]

tem•ple[3] (tĕm′pəl) *n.* A device in a loom that keeps the cloth stretched to the correct width. [ME *tempille* < OFr. *temple*, poss. < Lat. *templum*, small piece of timber. See **tem-***.]

Temple. A city of central TX S of Fort Worth. Pop. 46,109.

Temple, Shirley. See Shirley Temple **Black.**

Temple, Sir **William.** 1628–99. English politician and writer whose prose style influenced Jonathan Swift and others.

Temple City. A city of S CA, a suburb of Los Angeles. Pop. 31,100.

temple tree *n.* See **frangipani** 1.

tem•po (tĕm′pō) *n., pl.* **-pos** or **-pi** (-pē). **1.** *Mus.* The relative speed at which music is or ought to be played. **2.** A characteristic rate or rhythm of activity. [Ital. < Lat. *tempus*, time.]

tem•po•ral[1] (tĕm′pər-əl, tĕm′prəl) *adj.* **1.** Of, relating to, or limited by time. **2.** Of or relating to the material world; worldly. **3.** Lasting only for a time; not eternal; passing. **4.** Secular or lay; civil. **5.** *Gram.* Expressing time: *a temporal adverb.* [ME < OFr. < Lat. *temporālis* < *tempus*, *tempor-*, time.] —**tem′po•ral•ly** *adv.*

tem•po•ral[2] (tĕm′pər-əl, tĕm′prəl) *adj.* Of, relating to, or near the temples of the skull. [LLat. *temporālis* < Lat. *tempora*, pl. of *tempus*, temple.]

temporal bone *n.* Either of a pair of compound bones forming the sides and base of the skull.

temporal lobe *n.* The lower lateral lobe of either cerebral hemisphere, located in front of the occipital lobe and containing the sensory center of hearing in the brain.

tem•po•ral•i•ty (tĕm′pə-răl′ĭ-tē) *n., pl.* **-ties. 1.** The condition of being temporal or bounded in time. **2. temporalities.** Temporal possessions, esp. of the Church or clergy.

tem•po•rar•y (tĕm′pə-rĕr′ē) *adj.* Lasting, used, serving, or enjoyed for a limited time. —*n., pl.* **-ies.** *Informal.* One that serves for a limited time: *an office staffed by temporaries.* [Lat. *temporārius* < *tempus*, *tempor-*, time.] —**tem′po•rar′i•ly** *adv.* —**tem′po•rar′i•ness** *n*

tem•po•rize (tĕm′pə-rīz′) *intr.v.* **-rized, -riz•ing, -riz•es. 1.** To act evasively to gain time, avoid argument, or postpone a decision. **2.** To engage in discussions or negotiations, esp. to achieve a compromise or gain time. **3.** To yield to current circumstances or necessities; act to suit the time. [Fr. *temporiser* < OFr. < Med.Lat. *temporizāre*, to pass one's time < Lat. *tempus*, *tempor-*, time.] —**tem′po•ri•za′tion** (-pər-ĭ-zā′shən) *n.* —**tem′po•riz′er** *n.*

tem•po•ro•man•dib•u•lar (tĕm′pə-rō-măn-dĭb′yə-lər) *adj.* Of or formed by the temporal bone and the mandible.

temporomandibular joint syndrome *n.* A disorder caused by faulty articulation of the temporomandibular joint and marked by pain in the head and neck, tinnitus, and dizziness.

tempt (tĕmpt) *v.* **tempt•ed, tempt•ing, tempts.** —*tr.* **1.** To try to get (someone) to do wrong, esp. by a promise of reward. **2.** To be inviting or attractive to. **3.** To provoke or to risk provoking. **4.** To cause to be strongly disposed. —*intr.* To be attractive or inviting. [ME *tempten* < OFr. *tempter* < Lat. *temptāre*, to feel, try.] —**tempt′a•ble** *adj.* —**tempt′er** *n.*

temp•ta•tion (tĕmp-tā′shən) *n.* **1.** The act of tempting or the state of being tempted. **2.** Something tempting or enticing.

tempt•ing (tĕmp′tĭng) *adj.* Having strong appeal; enticing: *a tempting repast.* —**tempt′ing•ly** *adv.* —**tempt′ing•ness** *n.*

tempt•ress (tĕmp′trĭs) *n.* A woman who tempts or allures. See Usage Note at **-ess.**

tem•pu•ra (tĕm′po͝o-rə, tĕm-po͝or′ə) *n* A dish of vegetables and seafood dipped in batter and deep-fried. [J.]

Te•mu•co (tĕ-mo͞o′kō). A city of central Chile SSW of Concepción; founded 1881. Pop. 157,297.

ten (tĕn) *n.* **1.** The cardinal number equal to 9 + 1. **2.** The tenth in a set or sequence. **3.** Something having ten parts, units, or members. **4.** *Games.* A playing card marked with ten spots. **5.** A ten-dollar bill. [ME < OE *tīen.* See **dekm̥*.**] **—ten** *adj. & pron.*

ten. *abbr.* **1.** Tenor. **2.** *Mus.* Tenuto.

ten•a•ble (tĕn′ə-bəl) *adj.* **1.** Capable of being maintained in argument; rationally defensible: *a tenable theory.* **2.** Capable of being held against assault; defensible: *a tenable outpost.* [Fr. < OFr. < *tenir,* to hold < Lat. *tenēre.* See **ten-*.**] **—ten′a•bil′i•ty, ten′a•ble•ness** *n.* **—ten′a•bly** *adv.*

ten•ace (tĕn′ās′, tĕ-nās′, tĕn′ĭs) *n. Games.* A combination of two nonsequential high cards of the same suit, esp. in a bridge or whist hand. [Fr. < Sp. *tenaza,* tongs, tenace < *tenaces,* pl. of *tenaz,* tenacious < Lat. *tenāx, tenāc-.* See TENACIOUS.]

te•na•cious (tə-nā′shəs) *adj.* **1.** Holding or tending to hold persistently to something, such as a point of view. **2.** Holding together firmly; cohesive. **3.** Clinging to another object or surface; adhesive. **4.** Tending to retain; retentive. [< Lat. *tenāx, tenāc-,* holding fast < *tenēre,* to hold. See **ten-*.**] **—te•na′cious•ly** *adv.* **—te•na′cious•ness** *n.*

te•nac•i•ty (tə-năs′ĭ-tē) *n.* The state or quality of being tenacious.

te•nac•u•lum (tə-năk′yə-ləm) *n., pl.* **-la** (-lə). A slender hooked surgical instrument for lifting parts. [LLat. *tenāculum,* holder < Lat. *tenēre,* to hold. See **ten-*.**]

ten•an•cy (tĕn′ən-sē) *n., pl.* **-cies. 1.** Possession or occupancy of a property by title, under a lease, or on payment of rent. **2.** The period of a tenant's occupancy or possession. **3.** A habitation held or occupied by a tenant.

ten•ant (tĕn′ənt) *n.* **1.** One that pays rent to use or occupy property owned by another. **2.** A dweller in a place; an occupant. **3.** *Law.* One who holds or possesses lands, tenements, or sometimes personal property by any kind of title. **—** *tr. & intr.v.* **-ant•ed, -ant•ing, -ants.** To hold as a tenant or be a tenant. [ME < OFr. < pr.part. of *tenir,* to hold < Lat. *tenēre.* See **ten-*.**]

tenant farmer *n.* One who farms land owned by another and pays rent in cash or in kind.

ten•ant•ry (tĕn′ən-trē) *n.* **1.** Tenants considered as a group. **2.** The condition of being a tenant; tenancy.

ten-cent store (tĕn′sĕnt′) *n.* See **five-and-ten.**

tench (tĕnch) *n., pl.* **tench** or **tench•es.** An edible Eurasian freshwater fish *(Tinca tinca)* having small scales and two barbels near the mouth. [ME *tenche* < OFr. < LLat. *tinca,* prob. of Celt. orig.]

Ten Commandments (tĕn) *pl.n. Bible.* The ten injunctions given by God to Moses on Mount Sinai.

tend[1] (tĕnd) *intr.v.* **tend•ed, tend•ing, tends. 1.** To have a tendency. **2.** To be disposed or inclined. **3.** To move or extend in a certain direction. [ME *tenden* < OFr. *tendre* < Lat. *tendere.* See **ten-*.**]

tend[2] (tĕnd) *v.* **tend•ed, tend•ing, tends. —** *tr.* **1.** To have the care of; watch over; look after: *tend a child.* **2.** To manage the activities and transactions of; run: *tend bar.* **—** *intr.* **1.** To be an attendant or a servant. **2.** To apply one's attention; attend. [ME *tenden,* short for *attenden,* to wait on. See ATTEND.]

Syns: *tend, attend, mind, minister, watch.* The central meaning shared by these verbs is "to have the care or supervision of": *tended her plants; attending the sick; minded the furnace; ministering to flood victims; watched the house for the owners.*

ten•den•cy (tĕn′dən-sē) *n., pl.* **-cies. 1.** Movement or prevailing movement in a given direction. **2.** A characteristic likelihood. **3.** A predisposition to think, act, behave, or proceed in a particular way. **4.a.** An implicit direction or purpose. **b.** An implicit point of view in written or spoken matter; a bias. [Med.Lat. *tendentia* < Lat. *tendēns, tendent-,* pr.part. of *tendere,* to tend. See TEND[1].]

ten•den•tious also **ten•den•cious** (tĕn-dĕn′shəs) *adj.* Marked by a strong implicit point of view; partisan: *a tendentious account.* [< Med.Lat. *tendentia,* a cause. See TENDENCY.] **—ten•den′tious•ly** *adv.* **—ten•den′tious•ness** *n.*

ten•der[1] (tĕn′dər) *adj.* **-er, -est. 1.a.** Easily crushed or bruised; fragile. **b.** Easily chewed or cut. **2.** Young and vulnerable. **3.** Frail; delicate. **4.** Sensitive to frost or severe cold; not hardy. **5.a.** Easily hurt; sensitive. **b.** Painful; sore. **6.a.** Considerate and protective; solicitous. **b.** Marked by or expressing gentle emotions; loving. **c.** Given to sympathy or sentimentality; soft. **7.** *Naut.* Likely to heel easily under sail; crank. **—** *tr.v.* **-dered, -der•ing, -ders. 1.** To make tender. **2.** *Archaic.* To treat with tender regard. [ME < OFr. *tendre* < Lat. *tener.* See **ten-*.**] **—ten′der•ly** *adv.* **—ten′der•ness** *n.*

ten•der[2] (tĕn′dər) *n.* **1.** A formal offer, as: **a.** *Law.* An offer of money or service in payment of an obligation. **b.** A written offer to contract goods or services at a specified cost or rate; a bid. **2.** Something, esp. money, offered in payment. **—** *tr.v.* **-dered, -der•ing, -ders.** To offer formally. See Syns at **offer.** [< Fr. *tendre,* to offer < OFr. < Lat. *tendere,* to hold forth, extend. See **ten-*.**] **—ten′der•er** *n.*

tend•er[3] (tĕn′dər) *n.* **1.** One who tends something. **2.** *Naut.* A vessel attendant on other vessels, esp. one that ferries supplies between ship and shore. **3.** A railroad car attached to the rear of a locomotive and designed to carry fuel and water.

ten•der•foot (tĕn′dər-fo͝ot′) *n., pl.* **-foots** or **-feet** (-fēt′). **1.** A newcomer not yet hardened to rough outdoor life; a greenhorn. **2.** An inexperienced person; a novice. **3.** Often **Tenderfoot.** A Boy Scout of the lowest rank.

ten•der•heart•ed (tĕn′dər-här′tĭd) *adj.* Easily moved by another's distress; compassionate. **—ten′der•heart′ed•ly** *adv.* **—ten′der•heart′ed•ness** *n.*

ten•der•ize (tĕn′də-rīz′) *tr.v.* **-ized, -iz•ing, -iz•es.** To make (meat) tender, as by marinating, pounding, or applying a tenderizer. **—ten′der•i•za′tion** (-dər-ĭ-zā′shən) *n.*

ten•der•iz•er (tĕn′də-rī′zər) *n.* A substance, such as a plant enzyme, applied to meat to make it tender.

ten•der•loin (tĕn′dər-loin′) *n.* **1.** The tenderest part of a loin of beef or pork or a similar cut of meat. **2.** A city district known for vice and graft. [Sense 2, after the *Tenderloin,* an area of New York City.]

ten•di•ni•tis also **ten•do•ni•tis** (tĕn′də-nī′tĭs) *n.* Inflammation of a tendon. [NLat. *tendō, tendin-,* tendon; see TENDINOUS + -ITIS.]

ten•di•nous (tĕn′də-nəs) *adj.* **1.** Of, having, or resembling a tendon. **2.** Sinewy. [NLat. *tendō, tendin-,* tendon (< Med.Lat. *tendō;* see TENDON) + -OUS.]

ten•don (tĕn′dən) *n.* A band of tough inelastic fibrous tissue that connects a muscle with its bony attachment. [Med.Lat. *tendō, tendōn-,* alteration of Gk. *tenōn.* See **ten-*.**]

ten•dril (tĕn′drəl) *n.* **1.** A twisting threadlike structure by which a twining plant, such as a grape, grasps an object or a plant for support. **2.** Something, such as a ringlet of hair, that is long, slender, and curling. [Fr. *tendrillon* < OFr., dim. of *tendron,* young shoot < *tendre,* tender. See TENDER[1].]

Ten•e•brae (tĕn′ə-brā′, -brē′) *pl.n. (used with a sing. or pl. v.) Rom. Cath. Ch.* The office of matins and lauds sung on the last three days of Holy Week, with a ceremony of candles. [Med.Lat. < Lat. *tenebrae,* darkness.]

ten•e•brif•ic (tĕn′ə-brĭf′ĭk) *adj.* **1.** Serving to obscure or darken. **2.** Gloomy; dark. [Lat. *tenebrae,* darkness + -FIC.]

te•neb•ri•o•nid (tə-nĕb′rē-ə-nĭd′, tĕn′ə-brī′-) *n.* See **darkling beetle.** [< NLat. *Tenebriōnidae,* family name < *Tenebriō,* type genus < Lat. *tenebriō,* one who avoids light < *tenebrae,* darkness.] **—te•neb′ri•o•nid′** *adj.*

ten•e•brous (tĕn′ə-brəs) also **te•neb•ri•ous** (tə-nĕb′rē-əs) *adj.* Dark and gloomy. [Ult. < Lat. *tenebrōsus* < *tenebrae,* darkness.] **—ten′e•bros′i•ty** (-brŏs′ĭ-tē) *n.*

ten•e•ment (tĕn′ə-mənt) *n.* **1.** A building for human habitation, esp. one rented to tenants. **2.** A rundown low-rental apartment building that just meets minimum standards. **3.** *Chiefly British.* An apartment or a room leased to a tenant. **4.** *Law.* Property, such as land or franchises, held by one person leasing it from another. [ME, house < OFr. < Med. Lat. *tenēmentum* < Lat. *tenēre,* to hold. See **ten-*.**] **—ten′e•men′tal** (-mĕn′tl), **ten′e•men′ta•ry** (-mĕn′tə-rē) *adj.*

Ten•er•ife (tĕn′ə-rĭf′, -rēf′, tĕ′nĕ-rē′fĕ). A Spanish island of the Canary Is. in the Atlantic Ocean.

te•nes•mus (tə-nĕz′məs) *n.* A painfully urgent but ineffectual attempt to urinate or defecate. [Med.Lat. *tēnesmus,* var. of Lat. *tēnesmos* < Gk. *teinesmos* < *teinein,* to strain, stretch. See **ten-*.**]

ten•et (tĕn′ĭt) *n.* An opinion, doctrine, or principle held as truth by a person or esp. by an organization. [Prob. < Med. Lat. < Lat., third pers. sing. pr. indic. of *tenēre,* to hold. See **ten-*.**]

ten-gal•lon hat (tĕn′găl′ən) *n.* See **cowboy hat.** [Perh. < Sp. *galón,* braid, galloon (wrapped in rows above the brim) < Fr. *galon.* See GALLOON.]

Teng Hsiao-ping (tŭng′ shyou′pĭng′). See **Deng Xiaoping.**

te•ni•a (tē′nē-ə) *n.* Var. of **taenia.**

te•ni•a•sis (tē-nī′ə-sĭs) *n.* Var. of **taeniasis.**

Te•niers (tə-nîrz′, -nîrs′, tĕ-nyā′), **David.** "the Elder." 1582–1649. Flemish painter of religious subjects. His son **David** (1610–90), "the Younger," painted landscapes, religious subjects, and genre scenes.

Tenn. *abbr.* Tennessee.

Ten•nes•see (tĕn′ĭ-sē′, tĕn′ĭ-sē′). A state of the SE U.S. S of KY; admitted as the 16th state in 1796. Cap. Nashville. Pop. 4,896,641. **—Ten′nes•se′an** *adj. & n.*

Tennessee River. A river of the SE U.S. rising in E TN and flowing c. 1,049 km (652 mi) to the Ohio R.

Tennessee walking horse *n.* Any of a breed of lightly built saddle horses developed in Tennessee from Morgan and standardbred stock and having an easy gait.

Tennessee warbler *n.* A small wood warbler *(Vermivora peregrina)* of North America with green and white plumage.

Ten•niel (tĕn′yəl), Sir **John.** 1820–1914. British cartoonist and illustrator of *Alice's Adventures in Wonderland* (1865).

ten•nis (tĕn′ĭs) *n. Sports.* **1.** A game played with rackets and a light ball by two players or two pairs of players on a rectangular court, as of grass or clay, divided by a net. **2.** Court tennis. [ME *tenetz, tenyes,* court tennis < AN *tenetz* and OFr. *tenez,* pl. imper. of *tenir,* to hold < Lat. *tenēre.* See DETAIN.]

tennis bracelet *n.* A bracelet containing many small gemstones set and linked one after the other into a narrow chain.

tennis elbow *n.* A painful inflammation of the tissue surround-

Tennessee walking horse

tennis
Serving at a pro tennis competition

ă pat	oi boy
ā pay	ou out
âr care	o͝o took
ä father	o͞o boot
ĕ pet	ŭ cut
ē be	ûr urge
ĭ pit	th thin
ī pie	*th* this
îr pier	hw which
ŏ pot	zh vision
ō toe	ə about, item
ô paw	

Stress marks:
′ (primary);
′ (secondary), as in
dictionary (dĭk′shə-nĕr′ē)

ing the elbow, caused by strain from sports such as tennis.

tennis shoe *n.* See **sneaker.**

Ten•ny•son (tĕn′ĭ-sən), **Alfred.** 1st Baron Tennyson. 1809–92. British poet whose works include *In Memoriam* (1850). —**Ten′ny•so′ni•an** (-sō′nē-ən) *adj.*

teno– *pref.* Tendon: *tenotomy.* [< Gk. *tenōn,* tendon. See **ten-***.]

Te•noch•ti•tlán (tĕ-nôch′tē-tlän′). An ancient Aztec cap. on the site of present-day Mexico City; founded c. 1325 and destroyed by the Spanish in 1521.

ten•on (tĕn′ən) *n.* A projection on the end of a piece of wood shaped for insertion into a mortise to make a joint. —*tr.v.* **-oned, -on•ing, -ons.** To provide with or join with a tenon. [ME < OFr. < *tenir,* to hold < Lat. *tenēre.* See **ten-***.]

ten•or (tĕn′ər) *n.* **1.** A continuous unwavering course. **2.** The word, phrase, or subject with which the vehicle of a metaphor is identified, as *life* in *"Life's but a walking shadow"* (Shakespeare). **3.a.** The course of thought or argument running through something written or spoken. **b.** General sense; purport. **4.** *Law.* **a.** The exact meaning or actual wording of a document as distinct from its effect. **b.** An exact copy of a document. **5.** *Mus.* **a.** The highest natural adult male voice. **b.** A part for this voice. **c.** One who sings this part. [ME < AN < Lat., uninterrupted course < *tenēre,* to hold, continue. See **ten-***.]

tenor clef *n. Mus.* The C clef positioned to indicate that the fourth line from the bottom of a staff represents the pitch of middle C.

te•nor•rha•phy (tĕ-nôr′ə-fē) *n., pl.* **-phies.** The surgical uniting of divided tendons with sutures. [TENO– + Gk. *rhaphē,* suture (< *rhaptein,* to sew; see **wer-[2]***) + -Y[2].]

ten•o•syn•o•vi•tis (tĕn′ō-sĭn′ə-vī′tĭs) *n.* Inflammation of a tendon sheath.

te•not•o•my (tĕ-nŏt′ə-mē) *n., pl.* **-mies.** Surgical cutting or division of a tendon.

ten•pen•ny nail (tĕn′pĕn′ē, -pə-nē) *n.* A nail 3.0 inches (7.6 centimeters) long. [< its original price per hundred.]

ten•pin (tĕn′pĭn′) *n. Sports & Games.* **1.** One of the bottle-shaped pins used in bowling. **2. tenpins.** *(used with a sing. v.)* See **bowling** 1a.

ten•pound•er (tĕn′poun′dər) *n.* See **ladyfish.**

ten•rec (tĕn′rĕk′) also **tan•rec** (tän′-) *n.* Any of various insectivorous mammals of the family Tenrecidae of Madagascar and adjacent islands, similar to the hedgehog but having a long snout and often no tail. [Fr. < Malagasy *tandraka.*]

TENS (tĕnz) *n.* A technique used to relieve pain in a body part in which electrodes on the skin intermittently stimulate surface nerves, blocking the transmission of pain signals. [*t(ranscutaneous) e(lectrical) n(erve) s(timulation).*]

Ten•sas (tĕn′sô′). A river of NE LA flowing c. 402 km (250 mi) S to the Ouachita R.

tense[1] (tĕns) *adj.* **tens•er, tens•est. 1.** Tightly stretched; taut. See Syns at **stiff, tight. 2.** In a state of mental or nervous tension. **3.** Characterized by nervous tension or suspense. **4.** *Ling.* Enunciated with taut muscles, as the sound (t). —*tr. & intr.v.* **tensed, tens•ing, tens•es.** To make or become tense. [Lat. *tēnsus,* p.part. of *tendere,* to stretch. See **ten-***.] —**tense′ly** *adv.* —**tense′ness** *n.*

tense[2] (tĕns) *n. Gram.* **1.** Any one of the inflected forms in the conjugation of a verb that indicates the time, such as past, present, or future, as well as the continuance or completion of the action or state. **2.** A set of tense forms indicating a particular time. [ME *tens* < OFr., time < Lat. *tempus.*]

ten•sile (tĕn′səl, -sīl′) *adj.* **1.** Of or relating to tension. **2.** Capable of being stretched or extended; ductile. [NLat. *tēnsilis* < Lat. *tēnsus,* stretched out. See TENSE[1].] —**ten•sil′i•ty** (tĕn-sĭl′ĭ-tē) *n.*

tensile strength *n.* The maximum tension a material can withstand without tearing.

ten•sim•e•ter (tĕn-sĭm′ĭ-tər) *n.* An apparatus for measuring differences in vapor pressure. [TENSI(ON) + -METER.]

ten•si•om•e•ter (tĕn′sē-ŏm′ĭ-tər) *n.* **1.** An instrument for measuring tensile strength. **2.** An instrument used to measure the surface tension of a liquid. [TENSIO(N) + -METER.] —**ten′si•o•met′ric** (-ə-mĕt′rĭk) *adj.* —**ten′si•om′e•try** *n.*

ten•sion (tĕn′shən) *n.* **1.a.** The act or process of stretching something tight. **b.** The condition of so being stretched; tautness. **2.a.** A force tending to stretch or elongate something. **b.** A measure of such a force. **3.a.** Mental, emotional, or nervous strain. **b.** Barely controlled hostility or a strained relationship between people or groups. **4.** The interplay of conflicting elements in a piece of literature, esp. a poem. **5.** A balanced relation between strongly opposing elements. **6.** A device for regulating tautness, esp. that of thread on a sewing machine or loom. **7.** *Elect.* Voltage or potential; electromotive force. —*tr.v.* **-sioned, -sion•ing, -sions.** To subject to tension; tighten. [Lat. *tēnsiō, tēnsiōn-,* a stretching out < *tēnsus,* p.part. of *tendere,* to stretch. See TENSE[1].] —**ten′sion•al** *adj.*

ten•si•ty (tĕn′sĭ-tē) *n., pl.* **-ties.** The state of being tense.

ten•sive (tĕn′sĭv) *adj.* **1.** Of or causing tension. **2.** *Physiol.* Giving or causing the sensation of stretching or tension.

ten•sor (tĕn′sər, -sôr′) *n.* **1.** *Anat.* A muscle that stretches or tightens a body part. **2.** *Math.* A set of quantities that obey certain transformation laws relating the bases in one generalized coordinate system to those of another and involving partial derivative sums. [NLat. *tēnsor* < Lat. *tēnsus,* p.part. of *tendere,* to stretch. See TENSE[1].] —**ten•so′ri•al** (-sôr′ē-əl, -sōr′-) *adj.*

ten-speed (tĕn′spēd′) *n.* A bicycle having ten different gears.

ten-strike (tĕn′strīk′) *n.* **1.** *Sports & Games.* A strike in bowling. **2.** *Informal.* A remarkably successful stroke or act.

tent[1] (tĕnt) *n.* **1.** A portable shelter, as of canvas, stretched over a supporting framework of poles with ropes and pegs. **2.** Something resembling such a portable shelter. —*v.* **tent•ed, tent•ing, tents.** —*intr.* To camp in a tent. —*tr.* **1.** To form a tent over. **2.** To supply with or put up in tents. [ME < OFr. *tente* < VLat. **tendita* < fem. p.part. of Lat. *tendere,* to stretch out. See **ten-***.]

tent[1]
Top: Baker tent
Bottom: Pop tent

tent[2] (tĕnt) *n.* A small cylindrical plug of lint or gauze used to keep open or probe a wound or an orifice. —*tr.v.* **tent•ed, tent•ing, tents.** To keep (a wound or an orifice) open with such a plug. [ME *tente* < OFr. < *tenter,* to probe < Lat. *tentāre,* to feel, try. See TENTATIVE.]

tent[3] (tĕnt) *tr.v.* **tent•ed, tent•ing, tents.** *Scots.* **1.** To pay heed to. **2.** To attend; wait on. [ME *tenten* < *tent,* attention, short for *attent* < OFr. *attente* < VLat. **attendita* < fem. p.part. of Lat. *attendere,* to wait on. See ATTEND.]

ten•ta•cle (tĕn′tə-kəl) *n.* **1.** *Zool.* An elongated flexible unsegmented extension, used for feeling, grasping, or locomotion. **2.** *Bot.* One of the sensitive hairs on the leaves of insectivorous plants, such as the sundew. **3.** A similar part or extension. [NLat. *tentaculum* < Lat. *tentāre,* to feel, try. See TENTATIVE.] —**ten•tac′u•lar** (-tăk′yə-lər) *adj.*

ten•ta•cled (tĕn′tə-kəld) *adj.* Having tentacles.

tent•age (tĕn′tĭj) *n.* A group or supply of tents.

ten•ta•tive (tĕn′tə-tĭv) *adj.* **1.** Not fully worked out, concluded, or agreed on; provisional. **2.** Uncertain; hesitant. [Med. Lat. *tentātīvus* < Lat. *tentātus,* p.part. of *tentāre,* to try, var. of *temptāre.*] —**ten′ta•tive•ly** *adv.* —**ten′ta•tive•ness** *n.*

tent caterpillar *n.* Any of several destructive caterpillars of the family Lasiocampidae, esp. of the genus *Malacosoma,* whose colonies construct silken tentlike webs in tree branches.

tent•ed (tĕn′tĭd) *adj.* **1.** Covered with tents. **2.** Sheltered in tents. **3.** Resembling a tent.

ten•ter (tĕn′tər) *n.* **1.** A framework on which milled cloth is stretched for drying without shrinkage. **2.** *Archaic.* A tenterhook. —*tr.v.* **-tered, -ter•ing, -ters.** To stretch (cloth) on a tenter. [ME *teyntur, tentour,* prob. ult. < Lat. *tentōrium,* shelter made of stretched skins < *tendere,* to stretch. See TENT[1].]

ten•ter•hook (tĕn′tər-ho͝ok′) *n.* A hooked nail for securing cloth on a tenter. —*idiom.* **on tenterhooks.** In a state of uneasiness, suspense, or anxiety.

tenth (tĕnth) *n.* **1.** The ordinal number matching the number ten in a series. **2.** One of ten equal parts. [ME *tenthe,* alteration of *tethe* < OE *tēotha.* See **dekm̥***.] —**tenth** *adv. & adj.*

tent stitch *n.* A short diagonal embroidery stitch that forms close, even, parallel rows to fill in a pattern or background.

ten•u•is (tĕn′yo͞o-ĭs) *n., pl.* **-u•es** (-yo͞o-ēz′). *Ling.* **1.** A voiceless stop. **2.** A voiceless unaspirated stop in ancient Greek. [NLat. (transl. of Gk. *psilos*) < Lat., thin. See TENUOUS.]

te•nu•i•ty (tĕ-no͞o′ĭ-tē, -nyo͞o′-) *n.* The quality or condition of being tenuous. [ME *tenuite* < OFr. < Lat. *tenuitās,* thinness < *tenuis,* thin. See TENUOUS.]

ten•u•ous (tĕn′yo͞o-əs) *adj.* **1.** Long and thin; slender: *tenuous strands.* **2.** Having a thin consistency; dilute. **3.** Having little substance; flimsy: *a tenuous argument.* [Lat. *tenuis.* See **ten-***.] —**ten′u•ous•ly** *adv.* —**ten′u•ous•ness** *n.*

ten•ure (tĕn′yər, -yo͝or′) *n.* **1.a.** The act, fact, or condition of holding something in one's possession, as real estate or an office; occupation. **b.** A period during which something is held. **2.** The status of holding one's position on a permanent basis without periodic contract renewals. [ME < OFr. *teneure* < *tenir,* to hold < Lat. *tenēre,* to hold. See **ten-***.] —**ten•u′ri•al** (-yo͝or′ē-əl) *adj.* —**ten•u′ri•al•ly** *adv.*

ten•ured (tĕn′yərd, -yo͝ord′) *adj.* Having tenure.

te•nu•to (tā-no͞o′tō) *adv. & adj. Mus.* So as to be held for the full time value; sustained. [Ital. < p.part. of *tenere,* to hold < Lat. *tenēre.* See **ten-***.]

te•o•cal•li (tē′ə-kăl′ē, tē′ô-kä′lē) *n., pl.* **-lis.** A temple of ancient Mexico and Central America, usu. built on a pyramidal mound. [Nahuatl : *teōtl,* god + *calli,* house.]

te•o•sin•te (tē′ə-sĭn′tē, tā′ō-) *n.* A tall Mexican and Central American annual plant *(Zea mexicana)* related to corn and cultivated for fodder. [Am.Sp. < Nahuatl *teocintli* : *teōtl,* sacred + *cintli,* dried ear of corn.]

Te•o•ti•hua•cán (tā′ə-tē′wä-kän′, tĕ′ô-). An ancient city of central Mexico NE of present-day Mexico City.

te•pal (tē′pəl, tĕp′əl) *n. Bot.* A division of the perianth of a flower having a virtually indistinguishable calyx and corolla, as in tulips and lilies. [Fr. *tépale,* alteration of *pétale,* petal < NLat. *petalum.* See PETAL.]

tep•a•ry bean (tĕp′ə-rē) *n.* **1.** An annual twining plant *(Phaseolus acutifolius* var. *latifolius),* of southwest North America. **2.** The edible bean of this plant. [?]

te•pee also **tee•pee** or **ti•pi** (tē′pē) *n.* A portable dwelling of certain Native American peoples, esp. on the Great Plains, consisting of a conical framework of poles covered with skins or bark. [Sioux *tʰípi*, dwelling.]

Te•pic (tě-pēk′). A city of W Mexico NW of Guadalajara. Pop. 145,741.

tep•id (těp′ĭd) *adj.* **1.** Moderately warm; lukewarm. **2.** Lacking in emotional warmth or enthusiasm; halfhearted. [ME < Lat. *tepidus* < *tepēre*, to be lukewarm.] **—te•pid′i•ty, tep′id•ness** *n.* **—tep′id•ly** *adv.*

TEPP (těp) *n.* A crystalline organophosphorus compound, $C_8H_{20}O_7P_2$, that inhibits the action of acetylcholinesterase and is used as an insecticide and in medicine as a stimulant. [*t(etra)e(thyl)p(yro)p(hosphate).*]

te•qui•la (tə-kē′lə) *n.* An alcoholic liquor distilled from the fermented juice of the Central American century plant *Agave tequilana.* [Am.Sp., after *Tequila* in W-central Mexico.]

ter. *abbr.* **1.** Terrace. **2.** Territorial; territory.

tera– *pref.* One trillion (10^{12}): *terahertz.* [< Gk. *teras*, monster. See **kʷer-***.]

ter•a•hertz (tĕr′ə-hûrts′) *n.* One trillion (10^{12}) hertz.

ter•aph (tĕr′əf) *n., pl.* **ter•a•phim** (-ə-fĭm). A small image or idol of an ancient Semitic household god. [Back-formation < *teraphim*, teraphim < Heb. *tĕrāpîm*, household gods.]

te•rat•o•gen (tə-răt′ə-jən, tĕr′ə-tə-) *n.* An agent, such as a virus or drug, that causes malformation of an embryo or a fetus. [Gk. *teras, terat-*, monster; see **kʷer-*** + -GEN.]

ter•a•to•gen•e•sis (tĕr′ə-tə-jĕn′ĭ-sĭs) *n.* Development of malformed organisms or growths. [Gk. *teras, terat-*, monster; see TERATOID + GENESIS.]

ter•a•to•gen•ic (tĕr′ə-tə-jĕn′ĭk) *adj.* Of, relating to, or causing malformations of an embryo or a fetus. **—ter′a•to•ge•nic′i•ty** (-jə-nĭs′ĭ-tē) *n.*

ter•a•toid (tĕr′ə-toid′) *adj. Biol.* Grotesquely deformed. [Gk. *teras, terat-*, monster; see **kʷer-*** + -OID.]

ter•a•tol•o•gy (tĕr′ə-tŏl′ə-jē) *n.* The biological study of malformations and monstrosities. [Gk. *teras, terat-*, monster; see TERATOID + -LOGY.] **—ter′a•to•log′i•cal** (-ə-tl-ŏj′ĭ-kəl) *adj.*

ter•a•to•ma (tĕr′ə-tō′mə) *n., pl.* **-mas** or **-ma•ta** (-mə-tə). A tumor consisting of different types of tissue, as of skin, hair, and muscle, caused by the development of independent germ cells. [Gk. *teras, terat-*, monster; see **kʷer-*** + -OMA.]

ter•bi•um (tûr′bē-əm) *n. Symbol* **Tb** A soft metallic rare-earth element used in x-ray and color television tubes. Atomic number 65; atomic weight 158.924; melting point 1,356°C; boiling point 3,123°C; specific gravity 8.229; valence 3, 4. See table at **element.** [After *Ytterby*, a town in Sweden.]

terbium metal *n.* Any of several rare-earth metals separable from other metals as a group and including europium, terbium, and gadolinium.

Ter•borch or **Ter Borch** (tər-bôrk′, -bôrkh′), **Gerard.** 1617–81. Dutch painter of portraits and genre scenes.

terce (tûrs) *n.* Var. of **tierce** 1.

Ter•cei•ra (tər-sîr′ə, tĕr-sā′rə). A Portuguese island of the central Azores in the N Atlantic.

ter•cel (tûr′səl) also **tier•cel** (tîr′səl) *n.* A male hawk used in falconry. [ME < OFr. *terçuel* < VLat. **tertiōlus*, dim. of Lat. *tertius*, third. See **trei-***.]

ter•cen•ten•a•ry (tûr′sĕn-tĕn′ə-rē, tər-sĕn′tə-nĕr′ē) *n., pl.* **-ries.** A 300th anniversary or its celebration. *—adj.* Of or relating to a span of 300 years or to a 300th anniversary. [Lat. *ter*, thrice; see TERN[2] + CENTENARY.]

ter•cen•ten•ni•al (tûr′sĕn-tĕn′ē-əl) *n.* A tercentenary. **—ter′cen•ten′ni•al** *adj.*

ter•cet (tûr′sĭt) *n.* **1.** A group of three lines of verse, often rhyming together or with another triplet. **2.** *Mus.* See **triplet** 4. [Fr. < Ital. *terzetto* < dim. of *terzo*, third < Lat. *tertius.* See **trei-***.]

ter•e•bene (tĕr′ə-bēn′) *n.* A mixture of terpenes prepared from oil of turpentine, used as an expectorant and antiseptic. [Fr. *térébène* < *térébinthe*, terebinth < OFr. *terebinte.* See TEREBINTH.]

ter•e•binth (tĕr′ə-bĭnth′) *n.* A small Mediterranean tree *(Pistacia terebinthus)* that is a source of tanning material and turpentine. [ME *terebinthe* < OFr. *terebinte* < Lat. *terebinthus* < Gk. *terebinthos.*]

ter•e•bin•thine (tĕr′ə-bĭn′thĭn, -thīn′) also **ter•e•bin•thic** (-thĭk) *adj.* **1.** Of or relating to the terebinth. **2.** Relating to, consisting of, or resembling turpentine.

te•re•do (tə-rē′dō, -rā′dō) *n., pl.* **-dos.** A shipworm of the genus *Teredo.* [NLat. *Terēdō*, mollusk genus < Lat. *terēdō*, a kind of worm < Gk. *terēdōn.* See **terə-[1]***.]

Ter•ence (tĕr′əns). 185?–159? B.C. Greek-born Roman playwright whose comedies include *Phormio* and *Adelphi.*

Te•re•sa (tə-rē′sə, -zə, -rā′-), Mother. b. 1910. Albanian-born Indian nun who won the 1979 Nobel Peace Prize.

Te•resh•ko•va (tə-rĕsh-kō′və, tyĭ-ryĭ-shkô′və), **Valentina Vladmirovna.** b. 1937. Soviet cosmonaut who was the first woman in space (Jun. 1963).

Te•re•si•na (tĕr′ĭ-zē′nə). A city of NE Brazil on the Parnaíba R. ESE of Belém; founded 1852. Pop. 339,042.

te•rete (tĕ-rēt′) *adj.* Cylindrical but usu. slightly tapering at both ends, circular in cross section, and smooth-surfaced. [< Lat. *teres, teret-*, rounded. See **terə-[1]***.]

Te•reus (tîr′ē-əs, tîr′yo͞os′) *n. Gk. Myth.* A king of Thrace who raped Philomela and who was changed into a hoopoe.

ter•giv•er•sate (tər-jĭv′ər-sāt′, tûr′jĭ-vər-) *intr.v.* **-sat•ed, -sat•ing, -sates. 1.** To use evasions or ambiguities; equivocate. **2.** To change sides; apostatize. [Lat. *tergiversārī, tergiversāt-* : *tergum*, the back + *versāre*, to turn; see **wer-[2]***.] **—ter′gi•ver•sa′tion** *n.* **—ter′gi•ver•sa′tor** (-sā′tər) *n.*

ter•gum (tûr′gəm) *n., pl.* **-ga** (-gə). The upper or dorsal surface, esp. of a body segment of an insect or other arthropod. [Lat., back.] **—ter′gal** (-gəl) *adj.*

ter•i•ya•ki (tĕr′ē-yä′kē) *n.* A Japanese dish consisting of grilled or broiled slices of marinated meat or shellfish. [J. : *teri*, glaze + *yaki*, to broil.]

term (tûrm) *n.* **1.a.** A limited period of time. **b.** A period of time assigned to a person to serve. **c.** A period when a school or court is in session. **2.a.** A point in time at which something ends; termination. **b.** The end of a normal gestation period. **c.** A deadline, as for making a payment. **3.** *Law.* **a.** A fixed period of time for which an estate is granted. **b.** An estate granted for a fixed period. **4.a.** A word or group of words having a particular meaning: *explained the term* gridlock. **b. terms.** Language of a certain kind; chosen words. **5.** One of the elements of a proposed or concluded agreement; a condition. Often used in the plural. **6. terms.** The relationship between two people or groups; personal footing. **7.** *Math.* **a.** One of the quantities composing a ratio or fraction or forming a series. **b.** One of the quantities connected by addition or subtraction signs in an equation; a member. **8.** *Logic.* Each of the two concepts being compared or related in a proposition. **9.** A stone or post marking a boundary, esp. a pillar adorned with a head and upper torso. *—tr.v.* **termed, term•ing, terms.** To designate; call. **—*idiom.* in terms of. 1.** As measured or indicated by; in units of. **2.** In relation to; with reference to. [ME *terme* < OFr. < Lat. *terminus*, boundary. N., senses 4-8 < ME < Med.Lat. *terminus* < LLat., mathematical or logical term < Lat., boundary, limit.]

term. *abbr.* **1.** Terminal. **2.** Termination.

ter•ma•gant (tûr′mə-gənt) *n.* A quarrelsome scolding woman. *—adj.* Shrewish; scolding. [< ME *Termagaunt*, imaginary Muslim deity, alteration of *Tervagant* < OFr.]

term•er (tûr′mər) *n.* One serving a specified term.

ter•mi•na•ble (tûr′mə-nə-bəl) *adj.* **1.** Possible to terminate. **2.** Terminating after a designated date. **—ter′mi•na•bil′i•ty, ter′mi•na•ble•ness** *n.* **—ter′mi•na•bly** *adv.*

ter•mi•nal (tûr′mə-nəl) *adj.* **1.** Of, relating to, situated at, or forming a limit, a boundary, an extremity, or an end. **2.** *Bot.* Growing or appearing at the end of a stem, branch, stalk, or similar part. **3.** Of, relating to, occurring at, or being the end of a section or series; final. See Syns at **last[1]**. **4.** Relating to or occurring in a term or each term: *terminal inventories.* **5.** Causing, ending in, or approaching death; fatal. *—n.* **1.** A point or part that forms the end. **2.** An ornamental figure or object placed at the end of a larger structure; a finial. **3.** *Elect.* **a.** A position in a circuit or device at which a connection is normally established or broken. **b.** A passive conductor at such a position used to facilitate the connection. **4.a.** Either end of a railroad or other transportation line; a terminus. **b.** A station at the end of a transportation line or at a major junction on a transportation line. **c.** A town at the end of a transportation line. **5.** *Comp. Sci.* A device, often equipped with a keyboard and a video display, through which data or information can enter or leave a computer system. [ME < Lat. *terminālis* < *terminus*, boundary.] **—ter′mi•nal•ly** *adv.*

ter•mi•nate (tûr′mə-nāt′) *v.* **-nat•ed, -nat•ing, -nates.** *—tr.* **1.** To bring to an end or a halt. **2.** To occur at or form the end of; conclude. **3.** To discontinue the employment of; dismiss. *—intr.* **1.** To come to an end. **2.** To have as an end or a result. [Lat. *termināre, termināt-* < *terminus*, end.]

ter•mi•na•tion (tûr′mə-nā′shən) *n.* **1.** The act of terminating or the condition of being terminated. **2.a.** The end of something in time; the conclusion. **b.** An end of something in space; a limit or an edge. **3.** A result; an outcome. **4.** *Ling.* The end of a word, as an inflectional ending, a suffix, or a final morpheme. **—ter′mi•na′tion•al** *adj.*

ter•mi•na•tive (tûr′mə-nā′tĭv) *adj.* Serving, designed, or tending to terminate; conclusive. **—ter′mi•na′tive•ly** *adv.*

ter•mi•na•tor (tûr′mə-nā′tər) *n.* **1.** One that terminates. **2.** The dividing line between the bright and shaded regions of the disk of the moon or an inner planet.

ter•mi•nol•o•gy (tûr′mə-nŏl′ə-jē) *n., pl.* **-gies. 1.** The technical terms used in a particular field, subject, science, or art; nomenclature. **2.** The study of nomenclature. [Ger. *Terminologie* < Med.Lat. *terminus*, expression. See TERM.] **—ter′mi•no•log′i•cal** (-nə-lŏj′ĭ-kəl) *adj.* **—ter′mi•nol′o•gist** *n.*

term insurance *n.* Insurance providing coverage for losses during a stated period but becoming void upon its expiration.

ter•mi•nus (tûr′mə-nəs) *n., pl.* **-nus•es** or **-ni** (-nī′). **1.** The final point; the end. **2.** An end point on a transportation line or the town in which it is located. **3.a.** A boundary or border. **b.** A stone or post marking a border. [Lat.]

tepee
Modern Cheyenne tepee

Mother Teresa

Valentina Tereshkova

ă pat	oi boy
ā pay	ou out
âr care	o͝o took
ä father	o͞o boot
ĕ pet	ŭ cut
ē be	ûr urge
ĭ pit	th thin
ī pie	*th* this
îr pier	hw which
ŏ pot	zh vision
ō toe	ə about, item
ô paw	

Stress marks:
′ (primary);
′ (secondary), as in
dictionary (dĭk′shə-nĕr′ē)

ter•mi•tar•i•um (tûr′mĭ-târ′ē-əm) *n., pl.* **-i•a** (-ē-ə). A nest built by a colony of termites.

ter•mi•tar•y (tûr′mĭ-tĕr′ē) *n., pl.* **-ies.** See **termitarium.**

ter•mite (tûr′mīt′) *n.* Any of numerous pale-colored, usu. soft-bodied social insects of the order Isoptera, many species of which feed on wood, often destroying trees and wooden structures. [NLat. *Termes*, genus name < LLat. *termes, termit-*, woodworm, alteration of Lat. *tarmes.*]

ter•mit•ic (tər-mĭt′ĭk) *adj.* Of or formed by termites.

term•less (tûrm′lĭs) *adj.* **1.** Having no bounds or limits; unending. **2.** Unconditional: *termless surrender.*

term paper *n.* A lengthy written work required of a student on a topic drawn from the subject matter of a course of study.

tern[1] (tûrn) *n.* Any of various sea birds of the genus *Sterna* and related genera, related to and resembling the gulls but smaller and having a forked tail. [Of Scand. orig.]

tern[2] (tûrn) *n.* **1.** *Games.* A set of three, esp. a combination of three numbers that wins a lottery prize. **2.** *Naut.* A three-masted schooner. [ME *terne* < OFr. < *ternes* < Lat. *ternās*, accusative pl. of *ternī*, three each < *ter*, thrice. See **trei-*.**]

termitarium

ter•na•ry (tûr′nə-rē) *adj.* **1.** Composed of three or arranged in threes. **2.** *Math.* **a.** Having the base three. **b.** Involving three variables. —*n., pl.* **-ries.** A group of three. [ME < Lat. *ternārius* < *ternī*, three each. See TERN[2].]

ter•nate (tûr′nāt′, -nĭt) *adj.* Arranged in or consisting of sets or groups of three, as a compound leaf with three leaflets. [NLat. *ternātus* < Med.Lat., p.part. of *ternāre*, treble < Lat. *ternī*, three each. See TERN[2].] —**ter′nate′ly** *adv.*

Ter•na•te (tər-nä′tā, tĕr-nä′tĕ). An island of E Indonesia in the N Moluccas W of NE Celebes.

terne•plate (tûrn′plāt′) *n.* Sheet iron or steel plated with an alloy of three or four parts of lead to one part of tin, used as roofing. [Prob. Fr. *terne*, dull (< OFr.; see TARNISH) + PLATE.]

Ter•ni (tĕr′nē). A city of central Italy N of Rome; part of the Papal States in the 14th cent. Pop. 111,401.

ter•pene (tûr′pēn′) *n.* Any of various unsaturated hydrocarbons, $C_{10}H_{16}$, found in essential oils and oleoresins of plants such as conifers and used in organic syntheses. [Obsolete *terp(entine)*, var. of TURPENTINE + -ENE.] —**ter•pe′nic** *adj.* —**ter′pe•noid′** *adj. & n.*

ter•pin•e•ol (tər-pĭn′ē-ôl′, -ōl′, -ŏl′) *n.* Any of three isomeric alcohols, $C_{10}H_{17}OH$, occurring naturally in the essential oils of certain plants and used as solvents in perfumes, soaps, and medicine. [TERP(ENE) + -INE[2] + -OL[1].]

ter•pol•y•mer (tər-pŏl′ə-mər) *n.* A polymer that consists of three distinct monomers. [< Lat. *ter*, thrice. See **trei-*.**]

Terp•sich•o•re (tûrp-sĭk′ə-rē) *n.* **1.** *Gk. Myth.* The Muse of dancing and choral singing. **2. terpsichore.** The art of dancing. [Lat. *Terpsichorē* < Gk. *Terpsikhorē* < fem. of *terpsikhoros*, dance-loving : *terpein*, to delight + *khoros*, dance; see **gher-**[1]**.*]

terp•si•cho•re•an (tûrp′sĭ-kə-rē′ən, tûrp′sĭ-kôr′ē-ən, -kōr′-) *adj.* Of or relating to dancing. —*n.* A dancer.

terr. *abbr.* **1.** Terrace. **2.** Territorial; territory.

ter•ra (tĕr′ə) *n., pl.* **ter•rae** (tĕr′ē). A rough upland or mountainous region of the moon with a relatively high albedo. [Lat., earth, land. See TERRACE.]

terra al•ba (ăl′bə, ôl′bə) *n.* **1.** Finely pulverized gypsum used in making paper, paints, and as a nutrient for growing yeast. **2.** Kaolin. [NLat. : Lat. *terra*, earth + Lat. *alba*, fem. of *albus*, white.]

terrace
Terraced rice fields in China

ter•race (tĕr′ĭs) *n.* **1.a.** A porch or walkway bordered by colonnades. **b.** A platform extending outdoors from a floor of a house or an apartment building. **2.** An open, often paved area adjacent to a house serving as an outdoor living space; a patio. **3.** A raised bank of earth having vertical or sloping sides and a flat top. **4.** A flat narrow stretch of ground, often having a steep slope facing a river, lake, or sea. **5.a.** A row of buildings erected on raised ground or on a sloping site. **b.** A section of row houses. **c.** A residential street on top of or climbing a slope. **6.** A narrow strip of landscaped earth in the middle of a street. —*tr.v.* **-raced, -rac•ing, -rac•es. 1.** To provide (a house, for example) with a terrace or terraces. **2.** To form (a hillside or sloping lawn, for example) into terraces. [Fr. < OFr. < OProv. *terrassa* < VLat. **terrācea*, fem. of **terrāceus*, earthen < Lat. *terra*, earth. See **ters-*.**]

terra cot•ta (kŏt′ə) *n.* **1.a.** A hard semifired waterproof ceramic clay used in pottery and building construction. **b.** Ceramic wares made of this material. **2.** *Color.* A brownish orange. [Ital. : *terra*, earth (< Lat.; see TERRACE) + *cotta*, baked, cooked (< Lat. *cōcta*, fem. p.part. of *coquere*, to cook; see **pekʷ-*.**)] —**ter′ra-cot′ta** (tĕr′ə-kŏt′ə) *adj.*

terra fir•ma (fûr′mə) *n.* Solid ground; dry land. [NLat.]

ter•rain (tə-rān′) *n.* **1.a.** An area of land; ground. **b.** A particular geographic area; a region: *knows this terrain well.* **2.** The surface features of an area of land; topography. [Fr. < OFr. < VLat. **terrānum*, alteration of Lat. *terrēnum* < neut. of *terrēnus*, of the earth. See TERRENE.]

terra in•cog•ni•ta (ĭn′kŏg-nē′tə, -kŏg′nĭ-tə) *n., pl.* **terrae in•cog•ni•tae** (ĭn′kŏg-nē′tē, -kŏg′nĭ-tē′). **1.** An unknown land; an unexplored region. **2.** A new or unexplored field of knowledge. [NLat.]

Ter•ra•my•cin (tĕr′ə-mī′sĭn). A trademark used for oxytetracycline.

ter•rane also **ter•rain** (tə-rān′, tĕr′ān′) *n.* **1.** A series of related rock formations. **2.** An area having a preponderance of a particular rock or rock groups. [Alteration of TERRAIN.]

ter•ra•pin (tĕr′ə-pĭn) *n.* Any of various North American aquatic turtles of the family Emydidae, esp. of the genus *Malaclemys.* [Alteration of *torope* < Virginia Algonquian.]

ter•ra•que•ous (tĕr-ā′kwē-əs, -ăk′wē-) *adj.* Composed of land and water. [Lat. *terra*, earth; see **ters-*** + AQUEOUS.]

ter•rar•i•um (tə-râr′ē-əm) *n., pl.* **-i•ums** or **-i•a** (-ē-ə). A small enclosure or closed container in which selected living plants and sometimes small land animals, such as turtles, are kept. [NLat. : Lat. *terra*, earth; see TERRENE + -ARIUM.]

ter•raz•zo (tə-răz′ō, tĕ-rät′sō) *n.* A flooring material of marble or stone chips set in mortar and polished when dry. [Ital., perh. < OProv. *terrassa*, terrace. See TERRACE.]

Ter•re Haute (tĕr′ə hōt′, hŭt′, hôt′). A city of W IN on the Wabash R. WSW of Indianapolis. Pop. 57,483.

ter•rene (tĕ-rēn′, tĕr′ēn′) *adj.* Of or relating to Earth; earthly. [ME < Lat. *terrēnus* < *terra*, earth. See **ters-*.**]

ter•re•plein (tĕr′ə-plān′) *n.* A platform or level ground surface on which heavy guns are mounted. [Fr. *terreplein* < Ital. *terrapieno* < *terrapienare*, to fill with earth : *terra*, earth (< Lat.; see **ters-***) + *pieno*, full (< Lat. *plēnus*; see **pelə-**[1]**.*)]

ter•res•tri•al (tə-rĕs′trē-əl) *adj.* **1.** Of or relating to Earth or its inhabitants. **2.** Having a worldly, mundane character or quality. **3.** Of, relating to, or composed of land. **4.** *Biol.* Living on land; not aquatic: *a terrestrial animal.* —*n.* An inhabitant of Earth. [ME < Lat. *terrestris* < *terra*, earth. See **ters-*.**] —**ter•res′tri•al•ly** *adv.* —**ter•res′tri•al•ness** *n.*

terrestrial planet *n.* Any of the four planets, Mercury, Venus, Earth, or Mars, nearest the sun and similar in size and density.

ter•ret (tĕr′ĭt) *n.* **1.** One of the metal rings on a harness through which the reins pass. **2.** A ring on an animal's collar, used for attaching a leash. [ME *teret*, var. of *toret* < OFr., dim. of *tour, tor*, a round. See TOUR.]

terre-verte (tĕr′vĕrt′) *n.* An olive-green pigment commonly made from glauconite, used by artists. [Fr. : *terre*, earth (< Lat. *terra*; see **ters-***) + *verte*, fem. of *vert*, green (< OFr. *verd*; see VERDANT).]

ter•ri•ble (tĕr′ə-bəl) *adj.* **1.** Causing great fear or alarm; dreadful. **2.** Extremely formidable. **3.** Extreme in extent or degree. **4.a.** Unpleasant; disagreeable. **b.** Markedly objectionable. [ME < OFr. < Lat. *terribilis* < *terrēre*, to frighten.] —**ter′ri•ble•ness** *n.* —**ter′ri•bly** *adv.*

ter•ric•o•lous (tĕ-rĭk′ə-ləs) *adj. Biol.* Living on or in the ground: *terricolous worms.* [< Lat. *terricola*, earth-dweller : *terra*, earth; see **ters-*** + *-cola*, -colous.]

ter•ri•er (tĕr′ē-ər) *n.* Any of several breeds of hunting dog originally developed for driving game from burrows. [ME < OFr. *(chien) terrier*, ground (dog), terrier < Med.Lat. *terrārius*, of the earth < Lat. *terra.* See **ters-*.**]

ter•ri•fic (tə-rĭf′ĭk) *adj.* **1.** Causing terror or great fear; terrifying. **2.** Very bad or unpleasant; frightful: *a terrific headache.* **3.** Very good or fine; splendid: *a terrific fiddler.* **4.** Awesome; astounding: *terrific speed.* [Lat. *terrificus* : *terrēre*, to frighten + *-ficus*, -fic.] —**ter•rif′i•cal•ly** *adv.*

ter•ri•fy (tĕr′ə-fī′) *tr.v.* **-fied, -fy•ing, -fies. 1.** To fill with terror; make deeply afraid; alarm. **2.** To menace or threaten; intimidate. [Lat. *terrificāre* < *terrificus*, terrific. See TERRIFIC.]

ter•rig•e•nous (tĕ-rĭj′ə-nəs) *adj. Geol.* Derived from the land, esp. by erosive action. Used primarily of sediments. [< Lat. *terrigena*, earth-born : *terra*, earth; see **ters-*** + -GENOUS.]

ter•rine (tə-rēn′) *n.* **1.** An earthenware dish for cooking and serving food. **2.** A food, such as pâté, cooked or served in such a dish. [Fr. See TUREEN.]

ter•ri•to•ri•al (tĕr′ĭ-tôr′ē-əl, -tōr′-) *adj.* **1.** Of or relating to the geographic area under a given jurisdiction. **2.** Relating or restricted to a particular territory; regional. **3.** Often **Territorial.** Of or relating to an administrative territory. **4.** Often **Territorial.** Organized for national or home defense. **5.** *Biol.* Displaying territoriality; defending a territory from intruders. —*n.* also **Territorial.** A member of a territorial army. —**ter′ri•to′ri•al•ly** *adv.*

ter•ri•to•ri•al•ism (tĕr′ĭ-tôr′ē-ə-lĭz′əm, -tōr′-) *n.* **1.** A social system that gives authority and influence in a state to the landowners. **2.** A system of church government based on primacy of civil power. —**ter′ri•to′ri•al•ist** *n.*

ter•ri•to•ri•al•i•ty (tĕr′ĭ-tôr′ē-ăl′ĭ-tē, -tōr′-) *n., pl.* **-ties. 1.** The status of a territory. **2.** A behavior pattern in animals consisting of the occupation and defense of a territory.

ter•ri•to•ri•al•ize (tĕr′ĭ-tôr′ē-ə-līz′, -tōr′-) *tr.v.* **-ized, -iz•ing, -iz•es. 1.** To make a territory of; organize as a territory. **2.** To extend by adding territory. —**ter′ri•to′ri•al•i•za′tion** (-ə-lĭ-zā′shən) *n.*

territorial waters *pl.n.* Inland and coastal waters under the jurisdiction of a nation or state, esp. the ocean waters within 3 or 12 miles (4.8 or 19.3 kilometers) of the shoreline.

ter•ri•to•ry (tĕr′ĭ-tôr′ē, -tōr′ē) *n., pl.* **-ries. 1.** An area of land; a region. **2.** The land and waters under the jurisdiction of a government. **3.a.** A political subdivision of a country.

b. A geographic region, such as a colonial possession, dependent on an external government. **4.** Often **Territory. a.** A subdivision of the United States that is administered by an appointed or elected governor and elected legislature. **b.** A similarly organized political subdivision of Canada or Australia. **5.** An area for which a person is responsible as a representative or an agent. **6.** *Sports.* The area of a field defended by a specified team. **7.** *Biol.* An area occupied by a single animal, mating pair, or group and often vigorously defended against intruders. **8.** A sphere of action or interest; a province. [ME < Lat. *territōrium* < *terra*, earth. See **ters-*.**]

ter•ror (tĕr′ər) *n.* **1.** Intense, overpowering fear. See Syns at **fear. 2.** One that instills intense fear. **3.** The ability to instill intense fear. **4.** Violence committed or threatened to intimidate or coerce, as for military or political purposes. **5.** *Informal.* An annoying or intolerable pest. [ME *terrour* < OFr. *terreur* < Lat. *terror* < *terrēre*, to frighten.]

ter•ror•ism (tĕr′ə-rĭz′əm) *n.* The unlawful use or threatened use of force or violence to intimidate or coerce societies or governments, often for ideological or political reasons.

ter•ror•ist (tĕr′ər-ĭst) *n.* One that engages in acts or an act of terrorism. **—ter′ror•ist, ter′ror•is′tic** *adj.*

ter•ror•ize (tĕr′ə-rīz′) *tr.v.* **-ized, -iz•ing, -iz•es. 1.** To fill or overpower with terror; terrify. **2.** To coerce by intimidation or fear. **—ter′ror•i•za′tion** (-ər-ĭ-zā′shən) *n.* **—ter′ror•iz′er** *n.*

ter•ry (tĕr′ē) *n., pl.* **-ries. 1.** One of the uncut loops that form the pile of a fabric. **2.** A pile fabric, usu. of cotton, with uncut loops on both sides, used for bath towels and robes. [?]

Ter•ry (tĕr′ē), Dame **Ellen Alice** or **Alicia.** 1847–1928. British actress known for her Shakespearean roles.

terse (tûrs) *adj.* **ters•er, ters•est.** Brief and to the point; effectively concise: *a terse one-word answer.* [Lat. *tersus*, p.part. of *tergēre*, to cleanse.] **—terse′ly** *adv.* **—terse′ness** *n.*

ter•tial (tûr′shəl) *adj.* Of, relating to, or being the third row of flight feathers on the basal section of a bird's wing. —*n.* A tertial feather. [Lat. *tertius*, third; see TERTIARY + -AL[1].]

ter•tian (tûr′shən) *adj.* Recurring every other day or, when considered inclusively, every third day: *tertian malaria.* —*n.* *Pathol.* A tertian fever, such as vivax malaria. [ME *terciane*, tertian fever < Lat. *(febris) tertiāna*, (fever) of the third (day) < *tertius*, third. See **trei-*.**]

ter•ti•ar•y (tûr′shē-ĕr′ē) *adj.* **1.** Third in place, order, degree, or rank. **2.** Of, relating to, or being the short flight feathers nearest the body on the rear edge of a bird's wing. **3.** *Chem.* **a.** Of or relating to salts of acids containing three replaceable hydrogen atoms. **b.** Of or being an organic compound in which a group, such as an amine, is bound to three nonelementary radicals. **4. Tertiary.** *Geol.* Of, belonging to, or being the geologic time of the first period of the Cenozoic Era, extending from the end of the Mesozoic Era to the Quaternary Period of the Cenozoic Era and characterized by the appearance of modern flora and of apes and other large mammals. See table at **geologic time.** —*n., pl.* **-ies. 1.** A tertiary feather. **2. Tertiary.** *Geol.* The Tertiary Period or its system of deposits. **3.** *Rom. Cath. Ch.* A member of a religious Third Order. [Lat. *tertiārius* < *tertius*, third. See **trei-*.**]

tertiary color *n.* A color resulting from the mixture of two secondary colors.

ter•ti•um quid (tûr′shē-əm kwĭd′, tĕr′tē-o͝om′) *n.* Something that cannot be classified into either of two groups considered exhaustive; an intermediate thing or factor. [LLat. : Lat. *tertium*, neut. of *tertius*, third + *quid*, something.]

Ter•tul•lian (tər-tŭl′yən, -tŭl′ē-ən). A.D. 160?–230? Carthaginian theologian who formed his own schismatic sect.

ter•va•lent (tər-vā′lənt, tûr′vā′-) *adj.* Trivalent.

ter•za ri•ma (tĕr′tsə rē′mə) *n., pl.* **ter•ze ri•me** (tĕr′tsĕ rē′mĕ). A verse form of Italian origin consisting of tercets of 10 or 11 syllables with the middle line rhyming with the first and third lines of the following tercet. [Ital. : *terza*, third + *rima*, rhyme.]

TESL *abbr.* Teaching English as a second language.

tes•la (tĕs′lə) *n.* The unit of magnetic flux density in the International System, equal to one weber per square meter. See table at **measurement.** [After Nikola TESLA.]

Tes•la (tĕs′lə), **Nikola.** 1856–1943. Serbian-born physicist who discovered the principles of alternating current (1881).

tesla coil *n.* An air-core transformer used as a source of high-frequency power, as for x-ray tubes. [After Nikola TESLA.]

TESOL *abbr.* Teachers of English to speakers of other languages.

tes•sel•late (tĕs′ə-lāt′) *tr.v.* **-lat•ed, -lat•ing, -lates.** To form into a mosaic pattern, as with tesserae. [< Lat. *tessellātus*, of small square stones < *tessella*, small cube, dim. of *tessera*, a square. See TESSERA.] **—tes′sel•la′tion** *n.*

tes•ser•a (tĕs′ər-ə) *n., pl.* **tes•ser•ae** (tĕs′ə-rē′). One of the small glass or stone squares used to make mosaic patterns. [Lat. < Gk., neut. of *tesseres*, var. of *tessares*, four. See **kʷetwer-*.**]

tes•ser•act (tĕs′ə-răkt′) *n.* The four-dimensional equivalent of a cube. [Gk. *tessera*, neut. pl. of *tesseres*, four; see TESSERA + *aktis*, ray of light; see ACTINO-.]

tes•si•tu•ra (tĕs′ĭ-to͝or′ə) *n.* *Mus.* The prevailing range of a vocal or instrumental part, within which most of the tones lie. [Ital. < Lat. *textūra*, web, structure. See TEXTURE.]

test[1] (tĕst) *n.* **1.** A procedure for critical evaluation; a means of determining the presence, quality, or truth of something; a trial. **2.** A series of questions, problems, or physical responses designed to determine knowledge, intelligence, or ability. **3.** A basis for evaluation or judgment. **4.** *Chem.* **a.** A physical or chemical change by which a substance may be detected or its properties ascertained. **b.** A reagent used to cause or promote such a change. **c.** A positive result obtained. **5.** A cupel. —*v.* **test•ed, test•ing, tests.** —*tr.* **1.** To subject to a test; try. **2.a.** To determine the presence or properties of (a substance). **b.** To assay (metal) in a cupel. —*intr.* **1.** To undergo a test. **2.** To administer a test. **3.** To achieve a score or rating on tests. **4.** To exhibit a given characteristic when subjected to a test. [ME, cupel < OFr., pot < Lat. *testū, testum.*] **—test′a•bil′i•ty** *n.* **—test′a•ble** *adj.*

test[2] (tĕst) *n.* A hard external covering, as that of certain amoebas, dinoflagellates, and sea urchins. [Lat. *testa*, shell.]

Test. *abbr.* *Bible.* Testament.

tes•ta (tĕs′tə) *n., pl.* **-tae** (-tē′). The often thick or hard outer coat of a seed. [Lat., shell.]

tes•ta•cean (tĕ-stā′shən) *n.* Any of various rhizopods of the order Testacea, characterized by the presence of a shell. [< NLat. *Testācea*, order name < Lat., neut. pl. of *testāceus*, covered with a shell < *testa*, shell.] **—tes•ta′cean** *adj.*

tes•ta•ceous (tĕ-stā′shəs) *adj.* **1.** *Biol.* **a.** Having a hard shell or shell-like outer covering. **b.** Composed of a shell or shell-like material. **2.** *Color.* Having the reddish-brown or brownish-yellow hue of bricks. [< Lat. *testāceus* < *testa*, shell.]

tes•ta•cy (tĕs′tə-sē) *n.* *Law.* The condition of being testate.

tes•ta•ment (tĕs′tə-mənt) *n.* **1.** Something that serves as tangible proof. **2.** A statement of belief; a credo. **3.** *Law.* A written document providing for the disposition of a person's property after death; a will. **4. Testament.** *Bible.* Either of the two main divisions of the Christian Bible. **5.** *Archaic.* A covenant between human beings and God. [ME, a will < Lat. *testāmentum* < *testārī*, to make a will < *testis*, witness. See **trei-*.**] **—tes′ta•men′tar•y** (-mĕn′tə-rē, -mĕn′trē) *adj.*

tes•tate (tĕs′tāt′) *adj.* *Law.* Having made a legally valid will before death. [ME < Lat. *testātus*, p.part. of *testārī*, to make one's will. See TESTAMENT.]

tes•ta•tor (tĕs′tā′tər, tĕ-stā′tər) *n.* *Law.* One who has made a legally valid will before death. [ME *testatour* < AN < Lat. *testātor* < *testārī*, to make one's will. See TESTAMENT.]

tes•ta•trix (tĕ-stā′trĭks) *n., pl.* **-tri•ces** (-trĭ-sēz′). *Law.* A woman who has made a legally valid will before death. [Lat., fem. of *testātor*, testator. See TESTATOR.]

test case *n.* *Law.* A legal action whose outcome is likely to set a precedent or test the constitutionality of a statute.

test•cross (tĕst′krôs′, -krŏs′) *Genet.* *n.* A cross between an individual exhibiting the dominant phenotype of a trait and an individual that is homozygous recessive for that trait in order to determine the genotype of the dominant individual. **—test′cross′** *v.*

test-drive (tĕst′drīv′) *tr.v.* **-drove** (-drōv′), **-driv•en** (-drĭv′ən), **-driv•ing, -drives.** To drive (a motor vehicle) to evaluate it.

test•er[1] (tĕs′tər) *n.* One that tests: *a battery tester.*

tes•ter[2] (tĕs′tər, tē′stər) *n.* A canopy, as over a bed or pulpit. [ME < Med.Lat. *testrum* < LLat. *testa*, skull < Lat., shell.]

tes•ter[3] (tĕs′tər) *n.* See **teston** 2. [Alteration of TESTON.]

tes•ti•cle (tĕs′tĭ-kəl) *n.* A testis, esp. within a scrotum. [ME *testicule* < Lat. *testiculus*, dim. of *testis*, testis. See TESTIS.]

tes•tic•u•lar (tĕ-stĭk′yə-lər) *adj.* Of or relating to a testis.

tes•tic•u•late (tĕ-stĭk′yə-lĭt) *adj.* **1.** Having the shape of a testicle; ovoid. **2.** *Bot.* Having two oblong tubes, as some orchids. **3.** Testicular.

tes•ti•fy (tĕs′tə-fī′) *v.* **-fied, -fy•ing, -fies.** —*intr.* **1.** To make a declaration of truth or fact under oath; submit testimony. **2.** To express or declare a strong belief, esp. to make a declaration of faith. **3.** To make a statement based on personal knowledge in support of an asserted fact; bear witness. **4.** To serve as evidence. —*tr.* **1.** To declare publicly; make known. **2.** To state or affirm under oath. **3.** To bear witness to; provide evidence for. [ME *testifien* < Lat. *testificārī* : *testis*, witness; see **trei-*** + *-ficārī*, -fy.] **—tes′ti•fi•ca′tion** (-fĭ-kā′shən) *n.* **—tes′ti•fi′er** *n.*

tes•ti•mo•ni•al (tĕs′tə-mō′nē-əl) *n.* **1.** A statement in support of a particular truth, fact, or claim. **2.** A written affirmation of another's character or worth; a personal recommendation. **3.** Something given in appreciation of a person's service or achievement; a tribute. —*adj.* Relating to or constituting a testimony or testimonial: *testimonial statements.* [ME < OFr., of evidence < LLat. *testimōniālis* < Lat. *testimōnium*, testimony. See TESTIMONY.]

tes•ti•mo•ny (tĕs′tə-mō′nē) *n., pl.* **-nies. 1.a.** A declaration by a witness under oath, as that given before a court. **b.** All such declarations, spoken or written, offered in a legal case or deliberative hearing. **2.** Evidence in support of a fact or an assertion; proof. **3.** A public declaration regarding a religious experience. **4.a.** The stone tablets inscribed with the Law of

terrapin
Diamondback terrapin

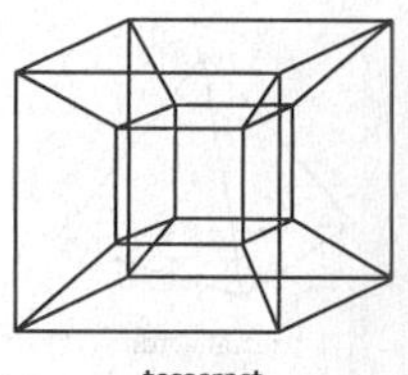
tesseract

ă **pat**	oi **boy**
ā **pay**	ou **out**
âr **care**	o͝o **took**
ä **father**	o͞o **boot**
ĕ **pet**	ŭ **cut**
ē **be**	ûr **urge**
ĭ **pit**	th **thin**
ī **pie**	*th* **this**
îr **pier**	hw **which**
ŏ **pot**	zh **vision**
ō **toe**	ə **about,**
ô **paw**	**item**

Stress marks:
′ (primary);
′ (secondary), as in
dictionary (dĭk′shə-nĕr′ē)

Moses. **b.** The ark containing these tablets. [ME < OFr. *testimonie* < Lat. *testimōnium* < *testis*, witness. See TESTIFY.]

tes•tis (tĕs′tĭs) *n.*, *pl.* **-tes** (-tēz). **1.** The reproductive gland in a male vertebrate, the source of spermatozoa and the androgens. **2.** An analogous gland in an invertebrate animal, such as a hydra. [Lat., witness, testis. See TESTIFY.]

test match *n. Sports.* A match in cricket or Rugby played by all-star teams from different countries.

tes•ton (tĕs′tŏn′) also **tes•toon** (tĕ-sto͞on′) *n.* **1.** A 16th-century French silver coin. **2.** An English coin stamped with the image of Henry VIII's head. [Fr. < Ital. *testone*, aug. of *testa*, head < LLat., skull < Lat., shell.]

tes•tos•ter•one (tĕs-tŏs′tə-rōn′) *n.* A crystalline steroid hormone, $C_{19}H_{28}O_2$, produced in the testes or synthetically and responsible for male secondary sex characteristics. [TEST(IS) + STER(OL) + -ONE.]

test paper *n.* **1.** A paper bearing a student's work for an examination. **2.** Paper saturated with a reagent, such as litmus, used in making chemical tests.

testudo

test pattern *n.* A geometric chart transmitted by a television station to assist viewers in adjusting reception.

test pilot *n.* A pilot who tests new or experimental aircraft.

test tube *n.* A clear cylindrical glass tube usu. open at one end and rounded at the other, used in laboratory experimentation.

test-tube (tĕst′to͞ob′, -tyo͞ob′) *adj.* Produced or cultivated in a test tube.

test-tube baby *n.* A baby developed from an egg fertilized outside the body and implanted in the uterus.

tes•tu•di•nal (tĕs-to͞od′n-əl, -tyo͞od′-) *adj.* Testudinate.

tes•tu•di•nate (tĕs-to͞od′n-ĭt, -āt′, -tyo͞od′-) *adj.* Of, relating to, or resembling a turtle or tortoise. —*n.* A turtle or tortoise. [< NLat. *Testūdināta*, order name < *Testūdō*, *Testūdin-*, type genus < Lat., tortoise. See TESTUDO.]

tes•tu•do (tĕ-sto͞o′dō, -styo͞o′-) *n.*, *pl.* **-dos. 1.** A Roman siege device consisting of a movable screen protecting the besiegers' approach to a wall. **2.** An overhead cover formed by the overlapping shields of besiegers. [Lat. *testūdō* < *testa*, shell.]

tes•ty (tĕs′tē) *adj.* **-ti•er, -ti•est.** Irritated, impatient, or exasperated; peevish: *a testy refusal to help.* [Alteration of ME *testif*, headstrong < OFr. *testu* < *teste*, head < LLat. *testa*, skull. See TESTON.] —**tes′ti•ly** *adv.* —**tes′ti•ness** *n.*

Tet (tĕt) *n.* The lunar New Year as celebrated in Vietnam. [Vietnamese *têt.*]

te•tan•ic (tĕ-tăn′ĭk) *adj.* **1.** Of, relating to, or causing tetanus. **2.** Of, relating to, or causing tetany. —**te•tan′i•cal•ly** *adv.*

tet•a•nize (tĕt′-n-īz′) *tr.v.* **-nized, -niz•ing, -niz•es.** To affect with tetanic convulsions; produce or induce tetanus in. —**tet′a•ni•za′tion** (-nĭ-zā′shən) *n.*

tet•a•nus (tĕt′n-əs) *n.* **1.** An acute, often fatal disease marked by spasmodic contraction of voluntary muscles, esp. those of the neck and jaw, and caused by the toxin of the bacillus *Clostridium tetani*, which typically infects the body through a deep wound. **2.** *Physiol.* A state of continuous muscular contraction, esp. when induced artificially by rapidly repeated stimuli. [ME < Lat. < Gk. *tetanos*, rigid, tetanus. See **ten-***.] —**tet′a•nal** (tĕt′n-əl) *adj.*

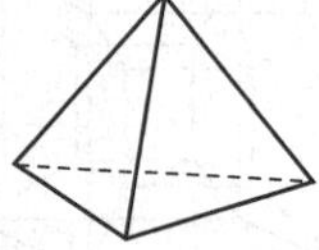

tetrahedron

tet•a•ny (tĕt′n-ē) *n.*, *pl.* **-nies.** An abnormal condition characterized by periodic painful muscular spasms and tremors, caused by faulty calcium metabolism and associated with diminished function of the parathyroid glands. [< TETANUS.]

tetched also **teched** (tĕcht) *adj. Informal.* Somewhat unbalanced mentally; touched. [Alteration of TOUCHED.]

tetch•y also **tech•y** (tĕch′ē) *adj.* **-i•er, -i•est.** Peevish; testy. [Prob. < ME *tache, teche*, blemish < OFr. *tache, teche* < VLat. **tacca* < Goth. *taikns*, sign. See **deik-***.] —**tetch′i•ly** *adv.* —**tetch′i•ness** *n.*

tête-à-tête (tāt′ə-tāt′, tĕt′ə-tĕt′) *adv. & adj.* Without the intrusion of a third person; in intimate privacy: *talk tête-à-tête.* —*n.* **1.** A private conversation between two persons. **2.** A sofa for two, esp. an S-shaped one allowing the occupants to face each other. [Fr. : *tête*, head + *à*, to + *tête*, head.]

tête-bêche (tĕt′bĕsh′) *adj.* Of, relating to, or being a pair of postage stamps printed with one upside-down in relation to the other. [Fr. : *tête*, head + *bêche* (short for obsolete *béchevet*, double head of a bed).]

teth (tĕt, tĕs) *n.* The ninth letter of the Hebrew alphabet. [Heb. *ṭêt.*]

teth•er (tĕth′ər) *n.* **1.** A rope or chain for holding an animal in place, allowing it a short radius in which to move about. **2.** The extent or limit of one's resources, abilities, or endurance. —*tr.v.* **-ered, -er•ing, -ers.** To fasten or restrict with or as if with a tether. [ME *tedir, tethir* < ON *tjōdhr.*]

teth•er•ball (tĕth′ər-bôl′) *n. Games.* A game in which two people hit a ball hung by a cord from an upright post until one has wound the cord around the post.

Te•thys (tē′thĭs) *n.* **1.** *Gk. Myth.* A Titan and sea goddess who was sister and wife of Oceanus. **2.** *Astron.* A satellite of Saturn. [Gk. *Tēthus.*]

Te•ton (tē′tŏn′) *n.*, *pl.* **Teton** or **-tons.** A member of the largest and westernmost of the Sioux peoples, including the Oglala, Hunkpapa, Brulé, and Miniconjou.

Teton Dakota *n.* See **Teton.**

Teton Range. A range of the Rocky Mts. in NW WY and SE ID rising to 4,198.6 m (13,766 ft).

Teton Sioux *n.* See **Teton.**

tet•ra (tĕt′rə) *n.* Any of numerous small, colorful tropical freshwater fish of the family Characidae, such as the neon tetra, often kept in home aquariums. [Short for NLat. *Tetragonopterini*, group name : LLat. *tetragōnum*, tetragon; see TETRAGON + Gk. *pteron*, wing.]

tetra– or **tetr–** *pref.* **1.** Four: *tetrode.* **2.** Containing four of a specified kind of atom, radical, or group: *tetrachloride.* [Gk. See **kʷetwer-***.]

tet•ra•ba•sic (tĕt′rə-bā′sĭk) *adj.* **1.** Containing four replaceable hydrogen atoms in a molecule. Used of acids. **2.** Containing four univalent basic atoms or radicals. Used of bases or salts. —**tet′ra•ba•sic′i•ty** (-sĭs′ĭ-tē) *n.*

tet•ra•caine (tĕt′rə-kān′) *n.* A crystalline compound, $C_{15}H_{24}N_2O_2$, related to procaine and used as a local anesthetic.

tet•ra•chlo•ride (tĕt′rə-klôr′īd′, -klōr′-) *n.* A chemical compound containing four chlorine atoms per molecule.

tet•ra•chord (tĕt′rə-kôrd′) *n. Mus.* A series of four diatonic tones encompassing the interval of a perfect fourth. [Gk. *tetrakhordon* < neut. of *tetrakhordos*, four-stringed : *tetra-*, tetra- + *khordē*, string; see **gherə-***.] —**tet′ra•chor′dal** (-kôr′dl) *adj.*

tet•ra•cy•cline (tĕt′rə-sī′klēn′, -klĭn) *n.* **1.** A crystalline compound, $C_{22}H_{24}N_2O_8$, derived from certain microorganisms of the genus *Streptomyces* or synthesized and used as a broad-spectrum antibiotic. **2.** An antibiotic having the same basic structure. [TETRA– + CYCL(IC) + –INE[2].]

tet•rad (tĕt′răd′) *n.* **1.** A group or set of four. **2.** A tetravalent atom, radical, or element. **3.** *Biol.* **a.** A group of four chromatids formed from each of a pair of homologous chromosomes that split longitudinally during the prophase of meiosis. **b.** *Bot.* A group of four cells, as of spores, formed by division of one mother cell. [Gk. *tetras, tetrad-*. See **kʷetwer-***.]

tet•ra•dy•na•mous (tĕt′rə-dī′nə-məs) *adj. Bot.* Having six stamens, two of which are shorter than the others. [TETRA– + Gk. *dynamis*, strength; see DYNAMIC + –OUS.]

tet•ra•eth•yl lead also **tet•ra•eth•yl•lead** (tĕt′rə-ĕth′əl-lĕd′) *n.* A poisonous oily liquid, $Pb(C_2H_5)_4$, used in gasoline for internal-combustion engines as an antiknock agent.

tetraethyl pyrophosphate *n.* TEPP.

tet•ra•gon (tĕt′rə-gŏn′) *n.* A four-sided polygon; a quadrilateral. [LLat. *tetragōnum* < Gk. *tetragōnon* : *tetra-*, tetra- + *-gonon*, -gon.] —**te•trag′o•nal** (tĕ-trăg′ə-nəl) *adj.* —**te•trag′o•nal•ly** *adv.*

Tet•ra•gram•ma•ton (tĕt′rə-grăm′ə-tŏn′) *n.* The four Hebrew letters usu. transliterated as YHWH or JHVH, used as a biblical proper name for God. [ME *Tetragramaton* < Gk. *tetragrammaton*, four-letter word < neut. of *tetragrammatos*, four-lettered : *tetra-*, tetra- + *gramma, grammat-*, letter; see **gerbh-***.]

tet•ra•he•dral (tĕt′rə-hē′drəl) *adj.* **1.** Of or relating to a tetrahedron. **2.** Having four faces. —**tet′ra•he′dral•ly** *adv.*

tet•ra•he•drite (tĕt′rə-hē′drīt′) *n.* A grayish-black mineral, $(CuFe)_{12}Sb_4S_{13}$, often containing other elements and used as an ore of copper. [Ger. *Tetraëdrit* < Gk. *tetraedros*, four-faced (< its four-faced crystals). See TETRAHEDRON.]

tet•ra•he•dron (tĕt′rə-hē′drən) *n.*, *pl.* **-drons** or **-dra** (-drə). A polyhedron with four faces. [LGk. *tetraedron* < Gk., neut. of *tetraedros*, four-faced : *tetra-*, tetra- + *hedra*, face of a geometric solid; see **sed-***.]

tet•ra•hy•dro•can•nab•i•nol (tĕt′rə-hī′drə-kə-năb′ə-nôl′, -nōl′, -nŏl′) *n.* THC.

te•tral•o•gy (tĕ-trăl′ə-jē, -trŏl′-) *n.*, *pl.* **-gies. 1.** A series of four related dramatic, operatic, or literary works. **2.** *Medic.* A complex of four symptoms. [Gk. *tetralogia* : *tetra-*, tetra- + *-logia*, -logy.]

tet•ra•mer (tĕt′rə-mər) *n.* A polymer consisting of four identical monomers. —**tet′ra•mer′ic** (-mĕr′ĭk) *adj.*

te•tram•er•ous (tĕ-trăm′ər-əs) *adj.* **1.** Having or consisting of four similar parts. **2.** *Bot.* Having flower parts, such as petals, in sets of four. —**te•tram′er•ism** *n.*

te•tram•e•ter (tĕ-trăm′ĭ-tər) *n.* **1.** A line of verse consisting of four metrical feet. **2.** A unit consisting of two pairs of feet in classical prosody. [LLat. *tetrametrus* < Gk. *tetrametron* < neut. of *tetrametros*, having four measures : *tetra-*, tetra- + *-metron*, measure; see –METER.] —**te•tram′e•ter** *adj.*

tet•ra•ploid (tĕt′rə-ploid′) *Genet.* —*adj.* Having four times the haploid number of chromosomes in the cell nucleus. —*n.* A tetraploid individual. —**tet′ra•ploi′dy** *n.*

tet•ra•pod (tĕt′rə-pŏd′) *adj.* Having four feet, legs, or leglike appendages. —*n.* A tetrapod vertebrate. —**tet′ra•pod′** *n.*

te•trap•ter•ous (tĕ-trăp′tər-əs) *adj.* Having four wings.

tet•rarch (tĕt′rärk′, tē′trärk′) *n.* **1.a.** A subordinate ruler. **b.** One of four joint rulers. **2.** A governor of one of four divisions of a country or province, esp. in the ancient Roman Empire. **3.** The commander of a subdivision of a phalanx in ancient Greece. [ME *tetrarche*, a Roman tetrarch < OFr. < LLat. *tetrarcha* < Lat. *tetrarchēs* < Gk. *tetrarkhēs* : *tetra-*, tetra- + *-arkhēs*, -arch.] —**te•trar′chic** (tĕ-trär′kĭk, tē-) *adj.*

tet•rar•chy (tĕt′rär′kē, tē′trär′-) also **tet•rar•chate** (-kāt′, -kĭt) *n., pl.* **-chies** also **-chates. 1.** The area ruled by a tetrarch. **2.a.** Joint rule by four governors. **b.** The four governors so ruling.
tet•ra•spore (tĕt′rə-spôr′, -spōr′) *n.* One of four spores produced by meiosis in certain red algae.
tet•ra•va•lent (tĕt′rə-vā′lənt) *adj. Chem.* Having valence 4.
tet•raz•zi•ni also **Tet•raz•zin•i** (tĕt′rə-zē′nē) *adj.* Made with noodles, mushrooms, and almonds in a cream sauce topped with cheese: *turkey tetrazzini.* [After Luisa *Tetrazzini* (1871–1940), Italian operatic soprano.]
tet•rode (tĕt′rōd′) *n.* A four-element electron tube with an anode, a cathode, a control grid, and an additional electrode.
te•tro•do•tox•in (tĕ-trō′də-tŏk′sĭn) *n.* A potent neurotoxin, $C_{11}H_{17}N_3O_3$, found in many puffers and certain newts. [NLat. *Tetrodon*, genus name (Gk. *tetra-*, tetra- + NLat. *-odon*, -odon) + TOXIN.]
te•trox•ide (tĕ-trŏk′sīd′) *n.* A chemical compound containing four oxygen atoms per molecule.
tet•ryl (tĕt′rəl) *n.* A yellow crystalline compound, $C_7H_5N_5O_8$, used as a detonator.
tet•ter (tĕt′ər) *n. Chiefly Southern U.S.* Any of various skin diseases, such as eczema, psoriasis, or herpes, characterized by eruptions and itching. [ME *teter* < OE. See **der-*.**]
Tet•zel (tĕt′səl), **Johann.** 1465?–1519. German monk whose sale of indulgences and simplistic sermons provoked Martin Luther's *95 theses* (1517).
Teut. *abbr.* Teuton; Teutonic.
Teu•to•bur•ger Wald (to͞o′tə-bûr′gər wôld′, toi′tō-bo͝or′-gər vält′). A range of hills in NW Germany between the upper Ems and the Weser rivers.
Teu•ton (to͞ot′n, tyo͞ot′n) *n.* **1.** A member of an ancient people, probably of Germanic or Celtic origin, who lived in Jutland until about 100 B.C. **2.** A member of any of the peoples speaking a Germanic language, esp. a German. [Lat. *Teutonī*, Teutons. See **teutā-*.**]
Teu•ton•ic (to͞o-tŏn′ĭk, tyo͞o-) *adj.* **1.** Of or relating to the ancient Teutons. **2.** Of or relating to the Germanic languages or their speakers. — *n.* Germanic. [Lat. *Teutonicus* < *Teutonī*, Teutons. See TEUTON.]
Teu•ton•ism (to͞ot′n-ĭz′əm, tyo͞ot′-) also **Teu•ton•i•cism** (to͞o-tŏn′ĭ-sĭz′əm, tyo͞o-) *n.* **1.** A Germanism. **2.** German character or civilization. — **Teu′ton•ist** *n.*
Teu•ton•ize (to͞ot′n-īz′, tyo͞ot′-) *tr.v.* **-ized, -iz•ing, -iz•es.** To Germanize. — **Teu′ton•i•za′tion** (-ĭ-zā′shən) *n.*
Te•vet also **Te•bet** or **Te•beth** (tā′vās, tĕ-vĕt′) *n.* The fourth month of the year in the Jewish calendar. [Heb. *ṭēbēt* < Akkadian *ṭebētu*, the month Tebetu (December/January).]
Te•wa (tā′wə, tē′wə) *n., pl.* **Tewa** or **-was. 1.** A member of a group of Pueblo peoples of northern New Mexico. **2.** The group of Tanoan languages spoken by the Tewa.
Tewkes•bur•y (to͞oks′bĕr′ē, -bə-rē, -brē, tyo͞oks′-). A municipal borough of W-central England on the Severn R.; site of the last battle of the Wars of the Roses (1471). Pop. 9,554.
Tewks•bur•y (to͞oks′bĕr′ē, -bə-rē, tyo͞oks′-). A town of NE MA S of Lowell. Pop. 27,266.
Tex. *abbr.* Texas.
Tex•ar•kan•a (tĕk′sär-kăn′ə). A city of SW AR on the TX border SW of Little Rock. Pop. 22,631. It is adjacent to **Texarkana** TX, in the NE part of that state. Pop. 31,656.
tex•as (tĕk′səs) *n. Naut.* A structure on a river steamboat containing the pilothouse and the officers' quarters. [After TEXAS.]
Tex•as (tĕk′səs). A state of the S-central U.S.; admitted as the 28th state in 1845. The region won its independence from Mexico in 1836 and was a self-governing republic until 1845. Cap. Austin. Pop. 17,059,805. — **Tex′an** *adj. & n.*
Texas City. A city of SE TX, a suburb of Galveston on Galveston Bay. Pop. 40,822.
Texas fever *n.* An infectious disease of cattle first identified in Texas, characterized by high fever, anemia, and emaciation and caused by a parasitic protozoan *(Babesia bigemina).*
Texas leagu•er (lē′gər) *n. Baseball.* A fly ball that drops between an infielder and an outfielder for a hit. [After the *Texas League*, a baseball minor league.]
Texas Ranger *n.* **1.** A member of a division of the Texas state highway patrol. **2.** A member of a mounted force of Texans organized in 1835 to maintain order on the frontier.
Tex-Mex (tĕks′mĕks′) *adj. Informal.* Of or marked by a blend of Mexican and southwest U.S. cultural elements.
text (tĕkst) *n.* **1.a.** The original words of something written or printed, as opposed to a paraphrase, translation, revision, or condensation. **b.** The printed version of a speech. **2.** The body of a printed work as distinct from headings, illustrative matter, or front and back matter in a book. **3.** One of the editions or forms of a written work. **4.** A passage from the Scriptures or another authoritative source used as the basis for a discourse or an argument. **5.** A passage from a written work used as the starting point of a discussion. **6.** A subject; a topic. **7.** A textbook. [ME *texte* < OFr. < LLat., written account < Lat., structure, context, body of a passage < p.part. of *texere*, to weave, fabricate. See **teks-*.**]
text•book (tĕkst′bo͝ok′) *n.* A book used for the formal study of a subject. — *adj.* Being a typical example of its kind; classic: *a textbook case of schizophrenia.* — **text′book′ish** *adj.*
text edition *n.* An edition of a book designed esp. for use in schools or colleges.
tex•tile (tĕks′tīl′, -təl) *n.* **1.** A cloth, esp. one manufactured by weaving or knitting; a fabric. **2.** Fiber or yarn for weaving or knitting into cloth. [Lat. < neut. of *textilis*, woven < *textus*, p.part. of *texere*, to weave. See TEXT.]
tex•tu•al (tĕks′cho͞o-əl) *adj.* Of, relating to, or conforming to a text. — **tex′tu•al•ly** *adv.*
textual criticism *n.* **1.** The study of manuscripts or printings to determine the original or most authoritative form of a text, esp. of a piece of literature. **2.** Literary criticism stressing close reading and detailed analysis of a particular text.
tex•tu•al•ism (tĕks′cho͞o-ə-lĭz′əm) *n.* **1.** Strict adherence to a text, esp. of the Scriptures. **2.** Textual criticism, esp. of the Scriptures. — **tex′tu•al•ist** *n.*
tex•tu•ar•y (tĕks′cho͞o-ĕr′ē) *adj.* Of or contained in a text; textual. — *n., pl.* **-ies.** A specialist in the Scriptures.
tex•ture (tĕks′chər) *n.* **1.** A structure of interwoven fibers or other elements. **2.** The basic structure or composition, esp. of something complex or fine. **3.a.** The appearance and feel of a surface: *the smooth texture of soap.* **b.** A rough or grainy surface quality. **4.** Distinctive or identifying character or characteristics. — *tr.v.* **-tured, -tur•ing, -tures.** To give texture to, esp. to impart desirable surface characteristics to. [ME < OFr. < Lat. *textūra* < *textus*, p.part. of *texere*, to weave. See TEXT.] — **tex′tur•al** *adj.* — **tex′tur•al•ly** *adv.* — **tex′tured** *adj.*
tex•tur•ize (tĕks′chə-rīz′) *tr.v.* **-ized, -iz•ing, -iz•es.** To give a desired texture to by a special process. — **tex′tur•iz′er** *n.*
tfr. *abbr.* Transfer.
TG *abbr.* Transformational grammar.
t.g. *abbr.* Type genus.
TGIF *abbr.* Thank God it's Friday.
Th[1] The symbol for the element **thorium.**
Th[2] *abbr. Bible.* Thessalonians.
Th. *abbr.* Thursday.
-th[1] *suff.* Var. of **-eth**[1].
-th[2] *suff.* **1.** Act; process: *spilth.* **2.** State; quality: *dearth.* [ME < OE *-thu*, n. suff.]
-th[3] also **-eth** *suff.* Used to form ordinal numbers: *millionth.* [ME *-the* < OE *-tha, -the.*]
Thack•er•ay (thăk′ə-rē, thăk′rē), **William Makepeace.** 1811–63. British writer whose novels include *Vanity Fair* (1847–48). — **Thack′er•ay•an** *adj.*
Thai (tī) *n., pl.* **Thai** or **Thais. 1.a.** A native or inhabitant of Thailand. **b.** A member of a Tai-speaking people who constitute the predominant ethnic group of Thailand. **2.** The language of the Tai family that is the official language of Thailand. **3.** Tai. — *adj.* **1.** Of or relating to Thailand or its peoples, languages, or cultures. **2.** Tai.
Thai•land (tī′lănd′, -lənd). Formerly **Si•am** (sī-ăm′). A country of SE Asia on the **Gulf of Thailand** (formerly the Gulf of Siam), an arm of the South China Sea; became a constitutional monarchy in 1932. Cap. Bangkok. Pop. 49,515,074.
thal•a•men•ceph•a•lon (thăl′ə-mĕn-sĕf′ə-lŏn′) *n. Anat.* See **diencephalon.** [THALAM(US) + ENCEPHALON.]
thal•a•mus (thăl′ə-məs) *n., pl.* **-mi** (-mī′). **1.** *Anat.* A large ovoid mass of gray matter situated in the posterior part of the forebrain that relays sensory impulses to the cerebral cortex. **2.** *Bot.* The receptacle of a flower. [Lat., inner chamber < Gk. *thalamos.*] — **tha•lam′ic** (thə-lăm′ĭk) *adj.*
thal•as•se•mi•a (thăl′ə-sē′mē-ə) *n.* An inherited form of anemia occurring chiefly among people of Mediterranean descent, caused by faulty synthesis of part of the hemoglobin molecule. [Gk. *thalassa*, sea + -EMIA.] — **thal′as•se′mic** *adj.*
tha•las•sic (thə-lăs′ĭk) *adj.* Of or relating to seas or oceans, esp. smaller seas. [Fr. *thalassique* < Gk. *thalassa*, sea.]
thal•as•soc•ra•cy (thăl′ə-sŏk′rə-sē) *n., pl.* **-cies.** Naval or commercial supremacy on the seas. [Gk. *thalassokratia* : *thalassa*, sea + *-kratia*, -cracy.]
tha•ler (tä′lər) *n.* Var. of **taler.**
Tha•les (thā′lēz). 624?–546? B.C. Greek philosopher who was a founder of geometry and abstract astronomy. — **Tha•le′sian** (thā-lē′zhən) *adj.*
Tha•li•a (thə-lī′ə, thā′lē-ə, thāl′yə) *n. Gk. Myth.* **1.** The Muse of comedy and pastoral poetry. **2.** One of the three Graces.
tha•lid•o•mide (thə-lĭd′ə-mīd′) *n.* A sedative and hypnotic drug, $C_{13}H_{10}N_2O_4$, withdrawn from sale after it was found to cause severe birth defects, esp. of the limbs, when taken during pregnancy. [(PH)THAL(IC ACID) + (IM)ID(E) + (I)MIDE.]
thal•lic (thăl′ĭk) *adj.* Of, relating to, or containing thallium, esp. with valence 3.
thal•li•um (thăl′ē-əm) *n. Symbol* **Tl** A soft, malleable, highly toxic metallic element, used in photocells, infrared detectors, and low-melting glass. Atomic number 81; atomic weight 204.37; melting point 303.5°C; boiling point 1,457°C; specific gravity 11.85; valence 1, 3. See table at **element.** [THALL(O)- (< its green spectral line) + -IUM.]
thallo- or **thall-** *pref.* **1.a.** Young, green shoot: *thallium.* **b.** Thallus: *thalloid.* **2.** Thallium: *thallous.* [Gk. < *thallos.* See THALLUS.]

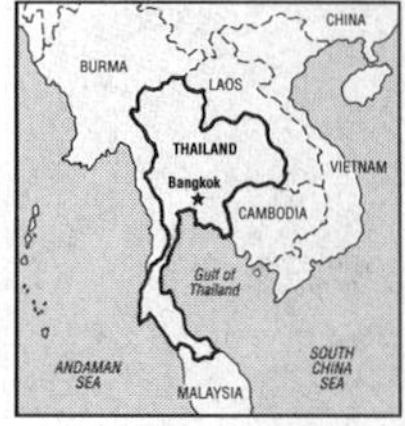

Thailand

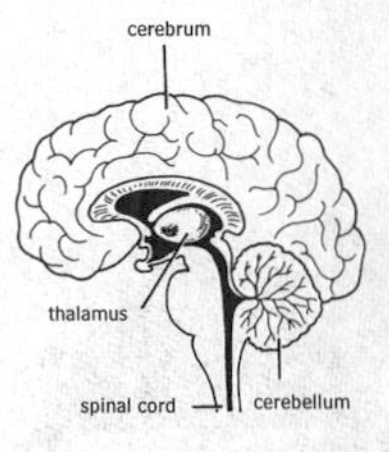

thalamus

ă pat	oi boy
ā pay	ou out
âr care	o͝o took
ä father	o͞o boot
ĕ pet	ŭ cut
ē be	ûr urge
ĭ pit	th thin
ī pie	*th* this
îr pier	hw which
ŏ pot	zh vision
ō toe	ə about, item
ô paw	

Stress marks:
′ (primary);
′ (secondary), as in **dictionary** (dĭk′shə-nĕr′ē)

U Thant
Photographed in the early 1960's

thatch
Thatched roof on a cottage in Hungary

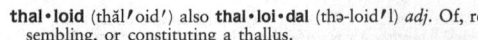

thal•loid (thăl′oid′) also **thal•loi•dal** (thə-loid′l) *adj.* Of, resembling, or constituting a thallus.

thal•lo•phyte (thăl′ə-fīt′) *n.* Any of a group of plantlike organisms showing no differentiation into stem, root, or leaf, such as algae. **—thal′lo•phyt′ic** (-fĭt′ĭk) *adj.*

thal•lous (thăl′əs) *adj.* Of, relating to, or containing thallium, esp. with valence 1.

thal•lus (thăl′əs) *n., pl.* **thal•li** (thăl′ī) or **-lus•es.** A plant body undifferentiated into stem, root, or leaf. [Lat., green stalk < Gk. *thallos* < *thallein*, to sprout.]

Thames (tĕmz). **1.** A river of SE Ontario, Canada, flowing c. 257 km (160 mi) SW to Lake St. Clair. **2.** A river of S England flowing c. 338 km (210 mi) E to a wide estuary on the North Sea. **3.** (thāmz, tāmz). A tidal estuary of SE CT flowing c. 24 km (15 mi) to Long Island Sound.

Tham•muz (tä′mo͝oz′) *n.* Var. of **Tammuz.**

than (*th*ăn, *th*ən) *conj.* Used to introduce the second element or clause of an unequal comparison: *She is a better athlete than I.* *—prep. Usage Problem.* In comparison with: *disliked no one more than her.* [ME < OE *thanne, than.* See **to-*.**]

Usage Note: According to the traditional view, the case of a pronoun following *than* is determined by whether the pronoun serves as the subject or object of the verb that is "understood." Thus, the standard rule requires *Pat is taller than I* on the assumption that this sentence is elliptical for *Pat is taller than I am* but allows *The news surprised Pat more than me,* since this sentence is taken as elliptical for *The news surprised Pat more than it surprised me.* However, *than* is quite commonly treated as a preposition when followed by an isolated noun phrase, and as such occurs with a pronoun in the objective case: *John is taller than me.* Though this usage is predominant in speech and has reputable literary precedent, it is still widely regarded as incorrect. • Comparatives using *as ... as* can be analyzed in a parallel way to those using *than.* Traditional grammarians insist that *I am not as tall as he* is the only correct form, and though both literary precedent and syntactic arguments can support the analysis of the second *as* as a preposition, one should treat this use of *as* as a conjunction in formal writing. See Usage Note at **as[1].**

than•age (thā′nĭj) *n.* **1.** The rank, jurisdiction, or office of a thane. **2.** The land held by a thane.

than•a•tol•o•gy (thăn′ə-tŏl′ə-jē) *n.* The study of death and dying, esp. in their psychological and social aspects. [Gk. *thanatos*, death + -LOGY.] **—than′a•to•log′i•cal** (-tl-ŏj′ĭ-kəl) *adj.* **—than′a•tol′o•gist** *n.*

than•a•top•sis (thăn′ə-tŏp′sĭs) *n.* A meditation upon death. [Gk. *thanatos*, death + -OPSIS.]

Than•a•tos (thăn′ə-tŏs′) *n.* **1.** Death as a personification or as a philosophical notion. **2.** *Psychiat.* See **death instinct** 1. [Gk.] **—than′a•tot′ic** (-tŏt′ĭk) *adj.*

thane (thān) *n.* **1.** A freeman granted land by the king in return for military service in Anglo-Saxon England and ranking above an ordinary freeman and below a nobleman. **2.** A feudal lord or baron in Scotland. [ME < OE *thegn.* See **tek-*.**] **—thane′ship′** *n.*

thank (thăngk) *tr.v.* **thanked, thank•ing, thanks. 1.** To express gratitude to; give thanks to. **2.** To hold responsible; credit. [ME *thanken* < OE *thancian.* See **tong-*.**]

thank•ful (thăngk′fəl) *adj.* **1.** Aware and appreciative of a benefit; grateful. **2.** Expressive of gratitude: *a thankful smile.* **—thank′ful•ly** *adv.* **—thank′ful•ness** *n.*

thank•less (thăngk′lĭs) *adj.* **1.** Not feeling or showing gratitude; ungrateful. **2.** Not likely to be appreciated: *a thankless job.* **—thank′less•ly** *adv.* **—thank′less•ness** *n.*

thanks (thăngks) *pl.n.* **1.** Grateful feelings or thoughts; gratitude. **2.** An expression of gratitude. *—interj.* Used to express thanks. **—*idioms.* no thanks to.** Without the benefit of help from. **thanks to.** On account of; because of.

thanks•giv•ing (thăngks-gĭv′ĭng) *n.* **1.** An act of giving thanks; an expression of gratitude, esp. to God: *a hymn of thanksgiving.* **2. Thanksgiving.** Thanksgiving Day.

Thanksgiving Day *n.* **1.** The fourth Thursday of November, observed as a legal holiday in the United States to commemorate the feast held at Plymouth in 1621 by the colonists and the Wampanoag people and marked by the giving of thanks to God for harvest and health. **2.** The second Monday of October, celebrated in Canada by the giving of thanks to God for harvest and health.

thank•wor•thy (thăngk′wûr′*th*ē) *adj.* **-thi•er, -thi•est.** Worthy of or deserving thanks.

thank-you (thăngk′yo͞o′) *n.* An expression of gratitude.

Thant (thänt, thănt), **U.** 1909–74. Burmese diplomat who served as secretary-general of the United Nations (1961–71).

Thap•sus (thăp′səs). An ancient city of N Africa on the Mediterranean Sea in present-day Tunisia.

Thar Desert (tär) also **Great In•di•an Desert** (ĭn′dē-ən). A sandy region of NW India and SE Pakistan between the Indus and Sutlej river valleys.

Tharp (thärp), **Twyla.** b. 1941. Amer. dancer and choreographer whose works include *Deuce Coupe* (1973).

Thá•sos (thā′sŏs′, thä′sôs). An island of NE Greece in the N Aegean Sea; ceded to Greece in 1913.

that (*th*ăt, *th*ət) *pron., pl.* **those** (*th*ōz). **1.a.** Used to refer to the one designated, implied, mentioned, or understood: *Whose soup is that?* **b.** Used to refer to the one, thing, or type specified as follows: *The relics found were those of an earlier time.* **c.** Used to refer to the event, action, or time just mentioned: *After that, he fled.* **2.** Used to indicate the farther or less immediate one: *That is for sale; this is not.* **3.** Used to emphasize the idea of a previously expressed word or phrase: *He was fed up, and that to a great degree.* **4.** The one, kind, or thing; something: *She followed the calling of that she loved.* **5. those.** Used to indicate an unspecified number of people. **6.** Used as a relative pronoun to introduce a clause, esp. a restrictive clause: *the car that has the flat tire.* **7.a.** In, on, by, or with which: *each summer that the concerts are performed.* **b.** According to what; insofar as: *not that I know of.* *—adj., pl.* **those. 1.** Being the one singled out, implied, or understood: *that place.* **2.** Being the one farther removed or less obvious: *That route is shorter than this one.* *—adv.* **1.** To such an extent or degree: *Is your problem that complicated?* **2.** To a high degree; very: *didn't take him that seriously.* *—conj.* **1.** Used to introduce a noun clause that is usu. the subject or object of a verb or a predicate nominative: *That your dogs bark is inevitable.* **2.** Used to introduce a subordinate clause stating a result, wish, purpose, reason, or cause: *hoped that he would stop.* **3.a.** Used to introduce an anticipated subordinate clause following the expletive *it* occurring as subject of the verb: *It is true that I want to stop.* **b.** Used to introduce a subordinate clause modifying an adverb or adverbial expression: *will go anywhere that they can.* **c.** Used to introduce a subordinate clause that is joined to an adjective or noun as a complement: *was sure that she was right.* **4.** Used to introduce an elliptical exclamation of desire: *Oh, that I were rich!* **—*idioms.* at that. 1.** In addition; besides. **2.** Regardless of what has been said or implied. **that is.** To explain more clearly; in other words: *the first floor, that is, the floor at street level.* [ME < OE *thæt.* See **to-*.**]

Usage Note: The standard rule is that *that* should be used only to introduce a restrictive (or "defining") relative clause, which serves to identify the entity being talked about; in this use it should never be preceded by a comma. Thus, we say *The house that Jack built has been torn down,* where the clause *that Jack built* tells which house was torn down. Only *which* is to be used with nonrestrictive (or "nondefining") clauses, which give additional information about an entity that has already been identified in the context; in this use, *which* is always preceded by a comma. Thus, we say *The students in Chemistry 10 complain about the textbook, which is hard to follow.* The clause *which is hard to follow* does not indicate which text is being complained about. The use of *that* in nonrestrictive clauses like this, though once common in writing and still frequent in speech, is best avoided in formal style. • Some grammarians have argued that symmetry requires that *which* should be used only in nonrestrictive clauses, as *that* is to be used only in restrictive clauses. Thus, they suggest that we should avoid sentences such as *I need a book which will help me.* Such use of *which* is useful where two or more relative clauses are joined by *and* or *or,* as in *It is a philosophy in which the common man may find solace and which many have found reason to praise.* *Which* is also preferred to introduce a restrictive relative clause when the preceding phrase itself contains a *that,* as in *I can only give you that which I don't need.* • *That* may be omitted in a relative clause when the subject of the clause is different from the referent of the phrase preceding the clause. Thus, we may say either *the book that I was reading* or *the book I was reading,* where the subject of the clause (*I*) is not the referent of the phrase *the book.* • There have also been occasional objections to the omission of *that* in its use to introduce a subordinate clause, as in *I think we should try again.* But this usage is entirely idiomatic. *That* should not be omitted, however, when the subordinate clause begins with an adverbial phrase or any element other than the subject: *The book argues that eventually the housing supply will increase.* This last sentence would be ambiguous if *that* were omitted, since the adverb *eventually* could then be construed as modifying either *argues* or *will increase.* See Usage Notes at **this, whatever, which, who.**

that•a•way (*th*ăt′ə-wā′) *adv. Southern & Midland U.S.* That way. [Alteration of *that way.*]

thatch (thăch) *n.* **1.** Plant stalks or foliage, such as reeds, used for roofing. **2.** Something that resembles thatch. **3.** Dead turf. *—tr.v.* **thatched, thatch•ing, thatch•es.** To cover with or as if with thatch. [ME *thacche,* alteration of *thak* < OE *thæc.* See **(s)teg-*.**] **—thatch′er** *n.* **—thatch′y** *adj.*

Thatch (thăch), **Edward.** See Edward **Teach.**

Thatch•er (thăch′ər), **Margaret Hilda.** b. 1925. British politician who served as prime minister (1979–90).

thau•ma•tol•o•gy (thô′mə-tŏl′ə-jē) *n., pl.* **-gies. 1.** The study of miracles. **2.** A discourse on miracles. [Gk. *thauma, thaumat-,* wonder + -LOGY.]

thau•ma•turge (thô′mə-tûrj′) also **thau•ma•tur•gist** (-tûr′jĭst) *n.* A performer of miracles or magic feats. [Gk.

thaumatourgos : *thauma, thaumat-*, wonder + *ergon*, work; see **werg-***.]

thau•ma•tur•gy (thô′mə-tûr′jē) *n.* The working of miracles or magic. **—thau′ma•tur′gic, thau′ma•tur′gi•cal** *adj.*

thaw (thô) *v.* **thawed, thaw•ing, thaws.** *—intr.* **1.** To change from a frozen solid to a liquid by gradual warming. **2.** To lose stiffness, numbness, or impermeability by being warmed: *thawed out by the stove.* **3.** To become warm enough for snow and ice to melt. **4.** To become less formal, aloof, or reserved. *—tr.* To cause to thaw. *—n.* **1.** The process of thawing. **2.** A warm period in the cold season when ice and snow melt. **3.** A relaxation of reserve, restraints, or tensions. [ME *thawen* < OE *thawian.*]

Thay•er (thā′ər, thâr), **Sylvanus.** 1785–1872. Amer. soldier and superintendent (1817–33) of the U.S. Military Academy.

Th.B. *abbr. Lat.* Theologiae Baccalaureus (Bachelor of Theology).

THC (tē′āch-sē′) *n.* A compound, $C_{21}H_{30}O_2$, obtained from cannabis or made synthetically, that is the primary intoxicant in marijuana and hashish. [T(ETRA)H(YDRO)C(ANNABINOL).]

Th.D. *abbr. Lat.* Theologiae Doctor (Doctor of Theology).

the[1] (*thē before a vowel and for emphasis; thə before a consonant*) *def.art.* **1.a.** Used before singular or plural nouns and noun phrases that denote particular, specified persons or things: *the dress I wore.* **b.** Used before a noun, and generally stressed, to emphasize one of a group or type as the most outstanding or prominent: *considered it* the *neighborhood.* **c.** Used to indicate uniqueness: *the moon.* **d.** Used before nouns that designate natural phenomena or points of the compass: *the weather.* **e.** Used as the equivalent of a possessive adjective before names of some parts of the body: *a wave of the hand.* **f.** Used before a noun specifying a field of endeavor: *the law.* **g.** Used before a proper name, as of a monument or ship: *the Alamo.* **h.** Used before the plural form of a numeral denoting a specific decade of a century or of a life span: *the Thirties.* **2.** Used before a singular noun indicating that the noun is generic: *The wolf is endangered.* **3.a.** Used before an adjective extending it to signify a class and giving it the function of a noun: *the rich.* **b.** Used before an absolute adjective: *the best we have.* **4.** Used before a present participle, signifying the action in the abstract: *the weaving of rugs.* **5.** Used before a noun with the force of *per*: *$1.50 the box.* [ME < OE *the*, alteration (influenced by *thæt*, neut. demonstrative pron., *thæs*, genitive demonstrative pron., etc.) of *se*, masc. demonstrative pron. See **so-***.]

the[2] (*thē before a vowel; thə before a consonant*) *adv.* **1.** Because of that. Used before a comparative: *thinks the worse of you.* **2.** To that extent; by that much: *the sooner the better.* **3.** Beyond any other: *enjoyed reading the most.* [ME < OE *thȳ, thē.* See **to-***.]

the– *pref.* Var. of **theo–.**

the•an•throp•ic (thē′ăn-thrŏp′ĭk) also **the•an•throp•i•cal** (-ĭ-kəl) *adj.* Having both divine and human natures. [< LGk. *theanthrōpos*, god-man : Gk. *theo-*, theo- + Gk. *anthrōpos*, man.]

the•an•thro•pism (thē-ăn′thrə-pĭz′əm) *n.* **1.** Attribution of human traits to God; anthropomorphism. **2.** *Theol.* The doctrine of the theanthropic nature of Jesus.

the•ar•chy (thē′är′kē) *n., pl.* **-chies. 1.** Government or rule by a god or by priests; theocracy. **2.** A hierarchy of gods.

the•a•ter or **the•a•tre** (thē′ə-tər) *n.* **1.** A building, room, or outdoor structure for plays, films, or other dramatic performances. **2.** A room with tiers of seats used for lectures or demonstrations. **3.a.** Dramatic literature or its performance; drama. **b.** The milieu of actors and playwrights. **4.a.** The quality or effectiveness of a theatrical production. **b.** Dramatic material or the use of such material. **5.** The audience assembled for a dramatic performance. **6.** A place that is the setting for dramatic events. **7.** A large geographic area in which military operations are coordinated. [ME *theatre* < OFr. < Lat. *theātrum* < Gk. *theatron* < *theasthai*, to watch < *thea*, a viewing.]

the•a•ter•go•er (thē′ə-tər-gō′ər) *n.* One who often attends the theater. **—the′a•ter•go′ing** *adj. & n.*

the•a•ter-in-the-round (thē′ə-tər-ĭn-*thə*-round′) *n., pl.* **the•a•ters-in-the-round** (thē′ə-tərz-). See **arena theater.**

theater of the absurd *n.* A form of drama that emphasizes the absurdity of human existence, as by illogical plots.

the•at•ri•cal (thē-ăt′rĭ-kəl) also **the•at•ric** (-rĭk) *—adj.* **1.** Of, relating to, or suitable for dramatic performance or the theater. **2.** Marked by exaggerated self-display and unnatural behavior; affectedly dramatic. *—n.* **1.** Stage performances or a stage performance, esp. by amateurs. Often used in the plural. **2. theatricals.** Affectedly dramatic gestures or behavior; histrionics. **—the•at′ri•cal′i•ty** (-kăl′ĭ-tē), **the•at′ri•cal•ness** (-kəl-nĭs) *n.* **—the•at′ri•cal•ly** *adv.*

the•at•ri•cal•ism (thē-ăt′rĭ-kə-lĭz′əm) *n.* Theatrical manner or style; showiness.

the•at•ri•cal•ize (thē-ăt′rĭ-kə-līz′) *tr.v.* **-ized, -iz•ing, -iz•es. 1.** To adapt to performance on the stage; dramatize. **2.** To make a spectacle of; display showily. **—the•at′ri•cal•i•za′tion** (-kə-lĭ-zā′shən) *n.* **—the•at′ri•cal•iz′er** *n.*

the•at•rics (thē-ăt′rĭks) *n.* **1.** *(used with a sing. v.)* The art of the theater. **2.** *(used with a pl. v.)* Theatrical effects or mannerisms; histrionics.

the•ba•ine (thē′bə-ēn′, thĭ-bā′ĭn) *n.* A poisonous alkaloid, $C_{19}H_{21}NO_3$, obtained from opium. [< NLat. *(herba) thēbaia*, (herb of) Thebes, Egyptian opium < Lat. *Thēbaea*, fem. of *Thēbaeus*, Theban < *Thēbae*, Thebes < Gk. *Thēbai.*]

the•be (tĕ′bĕ) *n.* See table at **currency.**

The•be (thē′bē) *n.* A satellite of Jupiter. [Lat. *Thēbē*, a nymph, daughter of the river god Asopus < Gk.]

Thebes (thēbz). **1.** An ancient city of Upper Egypt on the Nile R.; flourished from the mid-22nd to the 18th cent. B.C. **2.** An ancient city of Boeotia in E-central Greece NW of Athens. **—The′ban** (thē′bən) *adj. & n.*

the•ca (thē′kə) *n., pl.* **-cae** (-sē′, -kē′). A case, covering, or sheath, such as the pollen sac of an anther. [Lat., case, receptacle < Gk. *thēkē.* See **dhē-***.] **—the′cal** (-kəl) *adj.*

the•cate (thē′kāt′) *adj.* Having a theca; encased or sheathed.

thee (*thē*) *pron.* The objective case of **thou**[1]. **1.a.** Used as the direct object of a verb. **b.** Used as the indirect object of a verb. **2.** Used as the object of a preposition. **3.** Used in the nominative as well as the objective case, esp. by members of the Society of Friends.

thee•lin (thē′lĭn) *n.* See **estrone.** [Gk. *thēlus*, female; see **dhē(i)-*** + -IN.]

thee•lol (thē′lôl′, -lōl′, -lŏl′) *n.* See **estriol.** [THEEL(IN) + -OL[2].]

theft (thĕft) *n.* **1.** The act or an instance of stealing; larceny. **2.** *Obsolete.* Something stolen. [ME < OE *thīefth.*]

their (*thâr*) *adj.* The possessive form of **they. 1.** Used as a modifier before a noun: *their home.* **2.** *Usage Problem.* His, her, or its: *"It is fatal for anyone who writes to think of their sex"* (Virginia Woolf). See Usage Note at **he**[1]. [ME < ON *theira*, theirs. See **to-***.]

theirs (*thârz*) *pron. (used with a sing. or pl. v.)* **1.** Used to indicate the one or ones belonging to them: *The red house is theirs.* **2.** *Usage Problem.* His or hers. See Usage Note at **he**[1]. [ME < *their*, their. See THEIR.]

the•ism (thē′ĭz′əm) *n.* Belief in a god or gods, esp. belief in a personal God as creator and ruler of the world. **—the′ist** *n.* **—the•is′tic, the•is′ti•cal** *adj.* **—the•is′ti•cal•ly** *adv.*

The•lon (thē′lŏn′). A river, c. 885 km (550 mi), of S-central Northwest Terrs., Canada, E of Great Slave Lake.

them (*thĕm, thəm*) *pron.* The objective case of **they. 1.a.** Used as the direct object of a verb: *We saw them at camp.* **b.** Used as the indirect object of a verb: *We gave them cake.* **2.** Used as the object of a preposition: *This is for them.* **3.** *Informal.* Used as a predicate nominative: *It's them.* See Usage Notes at **be, I**[1]. [ME < ON *theim* and OE *thǣm*; see **to-***.]

the•mat•ic (thĭ-măt′ĭk) *adj.* **1.** Of, relating to, or being a theme. **2.** *Ling.* Of, constituting, or relating to the theme of a word: *a thematic vowel.* [Gk. *thematikos* < *thema, themat-*, theme. See THEME.] **—the•mat′i•cal•ly** *adv.*

The•mat•ic Apperception Test (thĭ-măt′ĭk) *n.* A projective test in which the subject tells a story suggested by each of a standard set of pictures showing everyday situations.

theme (thēm) *n.* **1.** A topic of discourse or discussion. See Syns at **subject. 2.** A subject of artistic representation. **3.** An implicit or recurrent idea; a motif. **4.** A short composition assigned to a student as a writing exercise. **5.** *Mus.* A principal melodic phrase in a composition, esp. a melody forming the basis of a set of variations. **6.** *Ling.* A root accompanied by derivational affixes. [ME *teme, theme* < OFr. *tesme* < Lat. *thema* < Gk. See **dhē-***.]

theme park *n.* An amusement park in which all the settings and attractions have a central theme, such as the future.

theme song *n. Mus.* **1.** An often repeated song in a musical play that is identified with the work or a character. **2.** A song identified with a performer or radio or television program.

The•mis•to•cles (thə-mĭs′tə-klēz′). 527?–460? B.C. Athenian official who directed the naval victory over Persia (480).

them•selves (*thĕm-sĕlvz′, thəm-*) *pron.* **1.** Those ones identical with them: **a.** Used reflexively as the direct or indirect object of a verb or as the object of a preposition: *They prepared themselves.* **b.** Used for emphasis: *The cooks themselves eat later.* **c.** Used in an absolute construction: *Newcomers themselves, they knew few people.* **2.** Their normal or healthy condition: *They're fully recovered and quite themselves again.*

then (*thĕn*) *adv.* **1.** At that time: *I was still in school then.* **2.** Next in time, space, or order; immediately afterward: *watched the movie and then went to bed.* **3.** In addition; moreover; besides: *It costs $20, and then there's the sales tax.* **4.** Used after *but* to qualify or balance a preceding statement: *The star was nervous, but then who isn't on the first night.* **5.** In that case; accordingly: *If traffic is heavy, then allow extra time.* **6.** As a consequence; therefore: *The case, then, is closed.* *—n.* That time or moment: *The plane leaves at four; until then let's shop.* *—adj.* Being so at that time: *the then president.* **—idiom. and then some.** *Informal.* With considerably more in addition. [ME < OE *thenne.* See **to-***.]

then and there *adv.* At that precise time and place; on the spot: *resigned then and there.*

Margaret Thatcher

ă pat	oi boy
ā pay	ou out
âr care	o͝o took
ä father	o͞o boot
ĕ pet	ŭ cut
ē be	ûr urge
ĭ pit	th thin
ī pie	*th* this
îr pier	hw which
ŏ pot	zh vision
ō toe	ə about, item
ô paw	

Stress marks:
′ (primary);
′ (secondary), as in dictionary (dĭk′shə-nĕr′ē)

the•nar (thē′när′) *n.* The fleshy mass on the palm of the hand at the base of the thumb. —*adj.* Of or relating to the thenar. [Gk., palm of the hand.]

thence (*th*ĕns, thĕns) *adv.* **1.** From that place; from there: *flew to Helsinki and thence to Moscow.* **2.** From that circumstance or source; therefrom. **3.** *Archaic.* From that time; thenceforth. See Usage Note at **whence.** [ME *thennes* : *thenne,* from there (< OE *thanon*; see **to-***) + *-es,* genitive sing. suff.; see **-s**[3].]

thence•forth (*th*ĕns-fôrth′, -fōrth′, thĕns-) *adv.* From that time forward; thereafter.

thence•for•ward (*th*ĕns-fôr′wərd, thĕns-) also **thence•for•wards** (-wərdz) *adv.* **1.** Thenceforth. **2.** From that time or place onward.

theo– or **the–** *pref.* God: *theomorphism.* [Gk. < *theos.* See **dhēs-***.]

the•o•bro•mine (thē′ō-brō′mēn′) *n.* A bitter alkaloid, $C_7H_8N_4O_2$, derived from the cacao bean and used as a diuretic, vasodilator, and myocardial stimulant. [NLat. *Theobroma,* genus of trees (Gk. *theo-,* theo- + *brōma,* food) + -INE[2].]

the•o•cen•tric (thē′ō-sĕn′trĭk) *adj.* Centering on God as the prime concern: *a theocentric cosmology.*

the•oc•ra•cy (thē-ŏk′rə-sē) *n., pl.* **-cies. 1.** A government ruled by or subject to religious authority. **2.** A state so governed.

the•o•crat (thē′ə-krăt′) *n.* **1.** A ruler of a theocracy. **2.** A believer in theocracy. —**the′o•crat′ic, the′o•crat′i•cal** *adj.*

The•oc•ri•tus (thē-ŏk′rĭ-təs). 3rd cent. B.C. Greek poet who composed the earliest known pastoral poems.

the•od•i•cy (thē-ŏd′ĭ-sē) *n., pl.* **-cies.** A vindication of God's goodness and justice in the face of the existence of evil. [After *Théodicée,* a work by Baron Gottfried Wilhelm von Leibnitz, : Gk. *theo-,* theo- + Gk. *dikē,* order, right; see **deik-***.]

the•od•o•lite (thē-ŏd′l-īt′) *n.* An optical instrument consisting of a small mounted telescope rotatable in horizontal and vertical planes, used in surveying and meteorology. [NLat. *theodolitus, theodelitus.*] —**the•od′o•lit′ic** (-lĭt′ĭk) *adj.*

The•o•do•ra (thē′ə-dôr′ə, -dōr′-). 508?–548. Byzantine empress (525–548) as the wife and adviser of Justinian I.

The•od•o•ric (thē-ŏd′ər-ĭk). A.D. 454?–526. King of the Ostrogoths (474–526) who founded a kingdom in Italy (493).

The•o•do•sius I (thē′ə-dō′shəs, -shē-əs). A.D. 346?–395. Emperor of Rome who ruled jointly (379–392) with Gratian and Valentinian II and independently (392–395).

the•og•o•ny (thē-ŏg′ə-nē) *n., pl.* **-nies.** An account of the gods' origin and genealogy. —**the′o•gon′ic** (-ə-gŏn′ĭk) *adj.*

theol. *abbr.* Theologian; theological; theology.

the•o•lo•gi•an (thē′ə-lō′jən) *n.* One learned in theology.

the•o•log•i•cal (thē′ə-lŏj′ĭ-kəl) also **the•o•log•ic** (-lŏj′ĭk) *adj.* Of or relating to theology or to specialized religious study. —**the′o•log′i•cal•ly** *adv.*

the•ol•o•gize (thē-ŏl′ə-jīz′) *v.* **-gized, -giz•ing, -giz•es.** —*tr.* To make theological in form or significance. —*intr.* To speculate about theology. —**the•ol′o•giz′er** *n.*

the•ol•o•gy (thē-ŏl′ə-jē) *n., pl.* **-gies. 1.** The study of the nature of God and religious truth. **2.** A system or school of opinions concerning God and religious questions. **3.** A course of specialized religious study usu. at a college or seminary.

the•om•a•chy (thē-ŏm′ə-kē) *n., pl.* **-chies.** Strife or battle among gods, as in the Homeric poems. [Gk. *theomakhia* : *theo-,* theo- + *makhia,* fighting (< *makhē,* battle).]

the•o•mor•phism (thē′ō-môr′fĭz′əm) *n.* Depiction or conception of human beings as having the form of a god. —**the′o•mor′phic** *adj.*

the•oph•a•ny (thē-ŏf′ə-nē) *n., pl.* **-nies.** An appearance of a god to a human being; a divine manifestation. [Med.Lat. *theophania* < LGk. *theophaneia* : Gk. *theo-,* theo- + Gk. *phainein, phan-,* to show; see **bhā-**[1]*.]

The•o•phras•tus (thē′ə-frăs′təs). 371?–287? B.C. Greek philosopher who succeeded Aristotle as leader of the Peripatetics.

the•oph•yl•line (thē-ŏf′ə-lĭn, thē′ō-fĭl′ēn′) *n.* A crystalline alkaloid, $C_7H_8N_4O_2H_2O$, derived from tea leaves or made synthetically and used as a cardiac stimulant and diuretic. [THEO(BROMINE) + PHYLL(O)- + -INE[2].]

the•o•rem (thē′ər-əm, thîr′əm) *n.* **1.** An idea that is demonstrably true or is assumed to be so. **2.** *Math.* A proposition that has been or is to be proved on the basis of explicit assumptions. [LLat. *theōrēma* < Gk. < *theōrein,* to look at < *theōros,* spectator. See THEORY.]

the•o•ret•i•cal (thē′ə-rĕt′ĭ-kəl) also **the•o•ret•ic** (-rĕt′ĭk) *adj.* **1.** Of, relating to, or based on theory. **2.** Restricted to theory; not practical: *theoretical physics.* **3.** Given to theorizing; speculative. [LLat. *theōrēticus* < Gk. *theōrētikos* < *theōrētos,* observable < *theōrein,* to look at. See THEOREM.] —**the′o•ret′i•cal•ly** *adv.*

the•o•re•ti•cian (thē′ər-ĭ-tĭsh′ən, thîr′ĭ-) *n.* One who formulates, studies, or is expert in the theory of a science or an art.

the•o•ret•ics (thē′ə-rĕt′ĭks) *n.* (*used with a sing. v.*) The theoretical part of a science or an art.

the•o•rist (thē′ər-ĭst, thîr′ĭst) *n.* One who theorizes; a theoretician.

the•o•rize (thē′ə-rīz′, thîr′īz) *v.* **-rized, -riz•ing, -riz•es.** —*intr.* To formulate theories or a theory; speculate. —*tr.* To propose a theory about. —**the′o•ri•za′tion** (-ər-ĭ-zā′shən) *n.* —**the′o•riz′er** *n.*

the•o•ry (thē′ə-rē, thîr′ē) *n., pl.* **-ries. 1.a.** Systematically organized knowledge applicable in a wide variety of circumstances, esp. a system of assumptions, principles, and rules of procedure devised to analyze, predict, or otherwise explain the nature or behavior of specified phenomena. **b.** Such knowledge or such a system. **2.** Abstract reasoning; speculation. **3.** A belief that guides action or assists comprehension or judgment: *the theory that less is more.* **4.** An assumption based on limited information or knowledge; a conjecture. [LLat. *theōria* < Gk. < *theōros,* spectator : prob. *thea,* a viewing + *-oros,* seeing.]

theory of games *n.* See **game theory.**

the•os•o•phy (thē-ŏs′ə-fē) *n., pl.* **-phies. 1.** Religious philosophy or speculation about the soul based on mystical insight into the nature of God. **2.** Often **Theosophy.** The beliefs of a religious sect, the Theosophical Society, founded in New York City in 1875, incorporating aspects of Buddhism and Brahmanism. [Med.Lat. *theosophia* < LGk. : Gk. *theo-,* theo- + Gk. *sophia,* wisdom.] —**the′o•soph′ic** (-ə-sŏf′ĭk), **the′o•soph′i•cal** (-ĭ-kəl) *adj.* —**the•os′o•phist** *n.*

ther•a•peu•tic (thĕr′ə-pyōō′tĭk) also **ther•a•peu•ti•cal** (-tĭ-kəl) *adj.* **1.** Having or exhibiting healing powers: *a therapeutic agent.* **2.** Of or relating to therapeutics. [NLat. *therapeuticus* < Gk. *therapeutikos* < *therapeutēs,* one who administers < *therapeuein* < *theraps, therap-,* attendant. See THERAPY.] —**ther′a•peu′ti•cal•ly** *adv.*

therapeutic abortion *n.* An abortion induced for medical reasons, as when a woman's health is in danger.

therapeutic index *n.* The ratio between the toxic dose and the therapeutic dose of a drug, used as a measure of the relative safety of the drug for a particular treatment.

ther•a•peu•tics (thĕr′ə-pyōō′tĭks) *n* (*used with a sing. v.*) Medical treatment of disease; the art or science of healing. —**ther′a•peu′tist** *n.*

ther•a•pist (thĕr′ə-pĭst) *n.* One who specializes in the provision of a particular therapy.

the•rap•sid (thə-răp′sĭd) *n.* Any of various reptiles of the order Therapsida of the Permian and Triassic periods, many of which are considered direct ancestors of mammals. [< NLat. *Thērapsida,* order name : Gk. *thēr,* wild animal; see THEROPOD + Gk. *hapsis, hapsid-,* arch, vault (< their enlarged lower temporal opening); see APSIS.] —**the•rap′sid** *adj.*

ther•a•py (thĕr′ə-pē) *n., pl.* **-pies. 1.** Treatment of illness or disability. **2.** Psychotherapy. **3.** Healing power or quality: *the therapy of fresh air and sun.* [NLat. *therapia* < Gk. *therapeia* < *therapeuein,* to treat medically. See THERAPEUTIC.]

Ther•a•va•da (thĕr′ə-vä′də) *n. Buddhism.* A form of Hinayana prevalent in Sri Lanka and Indochina. [Pali *theravāda* : *thera,* an elder (< Skt. *sthavira-,* old, venerable; see **stā-***) + *vāda,* doctrine (< Skt. *vādaḥ,* statement, doctrine; see **wed-**[2]*).]

there (*th*âr) *adv.* **1.** At or in that place: *sit over there.* **2.** To, into, or toward that place: *wouldn't go there.* **3.** At that stage, moment, or point: *Stop there!* **4.** In that matter: *I can't agree with him there.* —*pron.* **1.** Used to introduce a clause or sentence: *There must be another exit.* **2.** Used to indicate an unspecified person in direct address: *Hello there.* —*adj.* Used as an intensive: *Ask that person there.* —*n.* That place or point: *went on from there.* —*interj.* Used to express feelings such as relief, satisfaction, sympathy, or anger: *There, now I can have some peace!* [ME < OE *thǣr, thēr.* See **to-***.]

Usage Note: The standard rule states that when the pronoun *there* precedes a verb such as *be, seem,* or *appear,* the verb agrees in number with the following grammatical subject: *There is a great Italian deli across the street. There are fabulous wildflowers in the hills.* • The demonstrative forms *that there* and *this here* are nonstandard.

there•a•bouts (*th*âr′ə-bouts′) also **there•a•bout** (-bout′) *adv.* **1.** Near that place; about there: *somewhere in New York or thereabouts.* **2.** About that number, amount, or time.

there•af•ter (*th*âr-ăf′tər) *adv.* From a specified time onward; from then on.

there•a•gainst (*th*âr′ə-gĕnst′) *adv.* Against or in opposition to that.

there•at (*th*âr-ăt′) *adv.* **1.** At that place; there. **2.** At that event; on account of that.

there•by (*th*âr-bī′) *adv.* **1.** By that means; because of that. **2.** In connection with that.

there•for (*th*âr-fôr′) *adv.* For that.

there•fore (*th*âr′fôr′, -fōr′) *adv.* For that reason or cause; consequently or hence. [ME : *there,* there; see THERE + *for, fore,* for; see FOR.]

there•from (*th*âr-frŭm′, -frŏm′) *adv.* From that place, time, or thing.

there•in (*th*âr-ĭn′) *adv.* **1.** In that place, time, or thing. **2.** In that circumstance or respect.

there•in•af•ter (*th*âr′ĭn-ăf′tər) *adv.* In a later part, as of a speech or book.

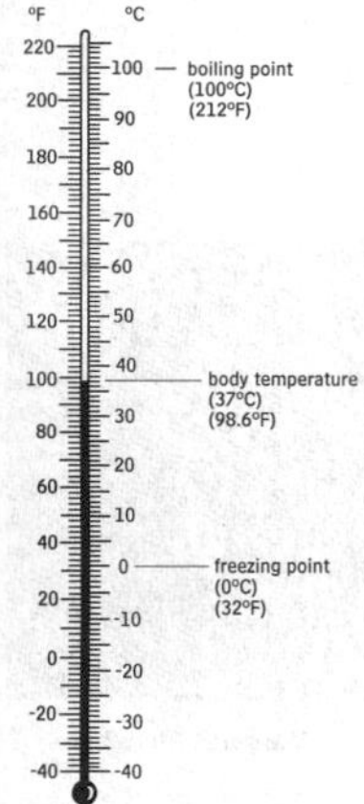

thermometer

ther•e•min (thĕr′ə-mĭn) *n. Mus.* An electronic instrument played by moving the hands near its two antennas, often used for high tremolo effects. [After Leo *Theremin* (b. 1896), Russian engineer and inventor.]

there•of (*th*âr-ŭv′, -ŏv′) *adv.* **1.** Of or concerning this, that, or it. **2.** From that cause or origin; therefrom.

there•on (*th*âr-ŏn′, -ôn′) *adv.* **1.** On or upon this, that, or it. **2.** *Archaic.* Following that immediately; thereupon.

The•re•sa (tə-rē′sə, -zə, -rā′-), Saint. "Theresa of Ávila." 1515–82. Spanish nun who founded the reformed order of Carmelites (1562).

there•to (*th*âr-to͞o′) *adv.* **1.** To that, this, or it. **2.** *Archaic.* In addition to that; furthermore.

there•to•fore (*th*âr′tə-fôr′, -fōr′) *adv.* Until that time; before that.

there•un•der (*th*âr-ŭn′dər) *adv.* Under this, that, or it.

there•un•to (*th*âr′ŭn-to͞o′) *adv. Archaic.* To that, this, or it; thereto.

there•up•on (*th*âr′ə-pŏn′, -pôn′) *adv.* **1.** Concerning that matter; upon that. **2.** Directly following that; forthwith. **3.** In consequence of that; therefore.

there•with (*th*âr-wĭ*th*′, -wĭth′) *adv.* **1.** With that, this, or it. **2.** In addition to that. **3.** *Archaic.* Immediately thereafter.

there•with•al (*th*âr′wĭ*th*-ôl′, -wĭth-) *adv.* With all that, this, or it; besides.

the•ri•o•mor•phic (thîr′ē-ə-môr′fĭk) also **the•ri•o•mor•phous** (-fəs) *adj.* Thought of as having the form of a beast. Used of a deity. [Gk. *thērion*, dim. of *thēr*, wild beast; see THEROPOD + -MORPHIC.]

therm (thûrm) *n.* A unit of heat equal to 100,000 British thermal units. [Gk. *thermē*, heat < *thermos*, warm, hot. See **g**ʷ**her-***.]

therm. *abbr.* Thermometer.

therm– *pref.* Var. of **thermo–**.

–therm *suff.* An animal having a specified kind of body temperature: *poikilotherm.* [< Gk. *thermē*, heat < *thermos*, warm, hot. See **g**ʷ**her-***.]

ther•mal (thûr′məl) *adj.* **1.** Of, relating to, using, producing, or caused by heat. **2.** Intended or designed to help retain body heat. —*n.* A rising current of warm air. —**ther′mal•ly** *adv.*

thermal noise *n.* Unwanted currents or voltages in an electronic component resulting from the agitation of electrons by heat.

thermal pollution *n.* Industrial discharge of heated water into a river, lake, or other body of water, causing a rise in temperature that endangers aquatic life.

ther•mic (thûr′mĭk) *adj.* Thermal.

therm•i•on (thûr′mī′ən) *n.* An electrically charged particle, esp. an electron, emitted by a conducting material at high temperatures. —**therm′i•on′ic** (-mī-ŏn′ĭk) *adj.*

thermionic current *n.* A flow of thermions.

thermionic emission *n.* Emission of thermions, esp. electrons, from a conducting material at high temperatures.

therm•i•on•ics (thûr′mī-ŏn′ĭks) *n.* *(used with a sing. or pl. v.)* The physics of thermionic phenomena.

thermionic tube *n.* An electron tube in which the source of electrons is a heated electrode.

therm•is•tor (thûr′mĭs′tər) *n.* A resistor made of semiconductors having resistance that varies rapidly and predictably with temperature. [THERM(AL) + (RES)ISTOR.]

Ther•mit (thûr′mĭt, -mīt′). A trademark used for a welding and incendiary mixture of fine aluminum powder with a metallic oxide that when ignited yields an intense heat.

thermo– or **therm–** *pref.* **1.** Heat: *thermochemistry.* **2.** Thermoelectric: *thermojunction.* [< Gk. *thermē*, heat < *thermos*, warm, hot. See **g**ʷ**her-***.]

ther•mo•chem•is•try (thûr′mō-kĕm′ĭ-strē) *n.* The chemistry of heat and heat-associated chemical phenomena. —**ther′mo•chem′i•cal** (-ĭ-kəl) *adj.* —**ther′mo•chem′ist** *n.*

ther•mo•cline (thûr′mə-klīn′) *n.* A layer in a large body of water that sharply separates regions differing in temperature, so that the temperature gradient across the layer is abrupt.

ther•mo•cou•ple (thûr′mə-kŭp′əl) *n.* A thermoelectric device used to measure temperatures accurately, esp. one consisting of two dissimilar metals joined so that a potential difference generated between the points of contact is a measure of the temperature difference between the points.

ther•mo•dur•ic (thûr′mō-do͝or′ĭk, -dyo͝or′-) *adj.* Capable of surviving high temperatures, esp. those of pasteurization. Used of a microorganism. [THERMO– + Lat. *dūrāre*, to last; see **deuə-*** + -IC.]

ther•mo•dy•nam•ic (thûr′mō-dī-năm′ĭk) *adj.* **1.** Characteristic of or resulting from the conversion of heat into other forms of energy. **2.** Of or relating to thermodynamics. —**ther′mo•dy•nam′i•cal•ly** *adv.*

ther•mo•dy•nam•ics (thûr′mō-dī-năm′ĭks) *n.* **1.** *(used with a sing. v.)* The branch of physics that deals with the relationships between heat and other forms of energy. **2.** *(used with a pl. v.)* Thermodynamic phenomena and processes.

ther•mo•e•lec•tric (thûr′mō-ĭ-lĕk′trĭk) also **ther•mo•e•lec•tri•cal** (-trĭ-kəl) *adj.* Characteristic of, resulting from, or using electrical phenomena occurring in conjunction with a flow of heat. —**ther′mo•e•lec′tri•cal•ly** *adv.*

ther•mo•e•lec•tric•i•ty (thûr′mō-ĭ-lĕk-trĭs′ĭ-tē, -ē′lĕk-) *n.* Electricity generated by a flow of heat, as in a thermocouple.

ther•mo•e•lec•tron (thûr′mō-ĭ-lĕk′trŏn′) *n.* An electron emitted by a material at high temperatures.

ther•mo•gram (thûr′mə-grăm′) *n.* A record made by a thermograph.

ther•mo•graph (thûr′mə-grăf′) *n.* **1.** A thermometer that records the temperature it indicates. **2.** The apparatus used in diagnostic thermography.

ther•mog•ra•phy (thər-mŏg′rə-fē) *n.*, *pl.* **-phies.** **1.** A process for producing raised lettering, as on stationery, by application of a powder fused by heat to the fresh ink. **2.** A diagnostic technique in which an infrared camera produces images that reveal sites of abnormal tissue growth by measuring temperature variations on the surface of the body. —**ther′mo•graph′ic** (-mə-grăf′ĭk) *adj.* —**ther′mo•graph′i•cal•ly** *adv.*

ther•mo•junc•tion (thûr′mō-jŭngk′shən) *n.* The point of contact between two dissimilar metals in a thermocouple.

ther•mo•la•bile (thûr′mō-lā′bĭl, -bīl′) *adj.* Subject to destruction, decomposition, or great change by heating. Used esp. of biochemical substances.

ther•mo•lu•mi•nes•cence (thûr′mō-lo͞o′mə-nĕs′əns) *n.* A phenomenon in which certain minerals release previously absorbed radiation upon being moderately heated.

ther•mol•y•sis (thər-mŏl′ĭ-sĭs) *n.*, *pl.* **-ses** (-sēz′). **1.** *Physiol.* Dissipation of heat from the body, as by evaporation. **2.** *Chem.* Dissociation or decomposition of compounds by heat. —**ther′mo•lyt′ic** (thûr′mə-lĭt′ĭk) *adj.*

ther•mom•e•ter (thər-mŏm′ĭ-tər) *n.* An instrument for measuring temperature, esp. one having a graduated glass tube with a bulb containing a liquid, such as mercury, that expands and rises in the tube as the temperature increases.

ther•mom•e•try (thər-mŏm′ĭ-trē) *n.* **1.** Measurement of temperature. **2.** The technology of temperature measurement. —**ther′mo•met′ric** (thûr′mō-mĕt′rĭk) *adj.*

ther•mo•nu•cle•ar (thûr′mō-no͞o′klē-ər, -nyo͞o′-) *adj.* **1.** Of, relating to, or derived from the fusion of atomic nuclei at high temperatures: *thermonuclear reactions.* **2.** Of, relating to, or characterized by the use of atomic weapons based on fusion, esp. as distinguished from those based on fission.

ther•mo•pe•ri•od•ism (thûr′mō-pîr′ē-ə-dĭz′əm) also **ther•mo•pe•ri•o•dic•i•ty** (-dĭs′ĭ-tē) *n.* The effect on an organism of the rhythmic fluctuation of temperature, as that accompanying the alternation of day and night.

ther•mo•phil•ic (thûr′mə-fĭl′ĭk) *adj.* Requiring high temperatures for normal development, as certain bacteria. —**ther′mo•phile′** (-fīl′) *n.*

ther•mo•pile (thûr′mə-pīl′) *n.* A device consisting of a number of connected thermocouples, used for measuring temperature or generating current. [THERMO– + PILE[1].]

ther•mo•plas•tic (thûr′mə-plăs′tĭk) *adj.* Becoming soft when heated and hard when cooled. —*n.* A thermoplastic resin. —**ther′mo•plas•tic′i•ty** (-plă-stĭs′ĭ-tē) *n.*

Ther•mop•y•lae (thər-mŏp′ə-lē). A narrow pass of E-central Greece; site of an unsuccessful Spartan stand against the Persians in 480 B.C.

ther•mo•re•cep•tor (thûr′mō-rĭ-sĕp′tər) *n. Biol.* A sensory receptor that responds to heat and cold.

ther•mo•reg•u•late (thûr′mō-rĕg′yə-lāt′) *intr.v.* **-lat•ed, -lat•ing, -lates.** **1.** To regulate body temperature. **2.** To undergo thermoregulation.

ther•mo•reg•u•la•tion (thûr′mō-rĕg′yə-lā′shən) *n.* Maintenance of a constant internal body temperature independent from the environmental temperature. —**ther′mo•reg′u•la•to′ry** (-rĕg′yə-lə-tôr′ē, -tōr′ē) *adj.*

Ther•mos (thûr′məs). A trademark used for a brand of vacuum bottles and other insulated containers.

ther•mo•set•ting (thûr′mō-sĕt′ĭng) *adj.* Permanently solidifying on being heated. Used of certain synthetic resins.

ther•mo•sphere (thûr′mə-sfîr′) *n.* The outermost shell of the atmosphere, between the mesosphere and outer space, where temperatures increase steadily with altitude. —**ther′mo•spher′ic** (-sfîr′ĭk, -sfĕr′ĭk) *adj.*

ther•mo•sta•ble (thûr′mō-stā′bəl) also **ther•mo•sta•bile** (-bəl, -bīl′) *adj.* Unaffected by relatively high temperatures, as certain ferments. —**ther′mo•sta•bil′i•ty** (-stə-bĭl′ĭ-tē) *n.*

ther•mo•stat (thûr′mə-stăt′) *n.* A device, as in a home heating system, that automatically responds to temperature changes and activates switches controlling the equipment. —**ther′mo•stat′ic** *adj.* —**ther′mo•stat′i•cal•ly** *adv.*

ther•mo•tax•is (thûr′mə-tăk′sĭs) *n.*, *pl.* **-tax•es** (-tăk′sēz). **1.** Movement of a living organism in response to temperature changes. **2.** Normal regulation or adjustment of body temperature. —**ther′mo•tac′tic** (-tăk′tĭk), **ther′mo•tax′ic** (-tăk′sĭk) *adj.*

ther•mot•ro•pism (thər-mŏt′rə-pĭz′əm) *n. Biol.* The tendency of plants or other organisms to bend toward or away from heat. —**ther′mo•trop′ic** (thûr′mə-trŏp′ĭk) *adj.*

–thermy *suff.* Heat: *diathermy.* [NLat. *-thermia* < Gk. *thermē*, heat < *thermos*, warm, hot. See **g**ʷ**her-***.]

the•ro•pod (thîr′ə-pŏd′) *n.* Any of various carnivorous dino-

ă pat	oi boy
ā pay	ou out
âr care	o͝o took
ä father	o͞o boot
ĕ pet	ŭ cut
ē be	ûr urge
ĭ pit	th thin
ī pie	*th* this
îr pier	hw which
ŏ pot	zh vision
ō toe	ə about, item
ô paw	

Stress marks:
′ (primary);
′ (secondary), as in
dictionary (dĭk′shə-nĕr′ē)

saurs of the suborder Theropoda of the Jurassic and Cretaceous periods, characterized by short forelimbs. [< NLat. *Theropoda*, suborder name : Gk. *thēr*, wild beast; see **ghwer-*** + NLat. *-poda*, -pod.] —**the·rop′o·dan** (thĭ-rŏp′ə-dən) *adj.* & *n.*

the·sau·rus (thĭ-sôr′əs) *n., pl.* **-sau·ri** (-sôr′ī′) or **-sau·rus·es. 1.** A book of synonyms, often including related and contrasting words and antonyms. **2.** A book of selected words or concepts, such as a specialized vocabulary of a particular field. [Lat. *thēsaurus*, treasury < Gk. *thēsauros*.]

these (*th*ēz) *pron.* & *adj.* Pl. of **this.** [ME < OE *thæs*, var. of *thās*, pl. of *thes, this*, this. See **to-*.**]

The·se·us (thē′sē-əs, -syo͞os′) *n. Gk. Myth.* A hero and king of Athens who slew the Minotaur and united Attica.

the·sis (thē′sĭs) *n., pl.* **-ses** (-sēz). **1.** A proposition maintained by argument. **2.** A dissertation advancing an original point of view based on research, esp. as required for an academic degree. **3.** A hypothetical proposition, esp. one not proved. **4.** The first stage of the Hegelian dialectic process. **5.a.** The long or accented part of a metrical foot, esp. in quantitative verse. **b.** The unaccented or short part of a metrical foot, esp. in accentual verse. **6.** *Mus.* The accented section of a measure. [Lat. < Gk. < *tithenai*, to put. See **dhē-*.**]

thes·pi·an (thĕs′pē-ən) *adj.* **1.** Of or relating to drama; dramatic. **2. Thespian.** Of Thespis. —*n.* An actor or actress.

Thes·pis (thĕs′pĭs). 6th cent. B.C. Greek poet who reputedly originated Greek tragedy.

Thes·sa·lo·ni·ans (thĕs′ə-lō′nē-ənz) *pl.n. (used with a sing. v.)* See table at **Bible.**

Thes·sa·lo·ní·ki (thĕ′sä-lô-nē′kē) also **Thes·sa·lo·ni·ca** (-lô-nī′kə, -lŏn′ĭ-kə) or **Sa·lo·ni·ka** (sə-lŏn′ĭ-kə, săl′ə-nē′kə). A city of NE Greece on an inlet of the Aegean Sea; flourished after c. 146 as the cap. of Macedon. Pop. 406,413.

Theseus
Theseus and the Minotaur
by Antoine Louis Barye
(1796–1875)

Thes·sa·ly (thĕs′ə-lē). A region of E-central Greece between the Pindus Mts. and the Aegean Sea. —**Thes·sa′lian** (thĕ-sā′lē-ən, -săl′yən), **Thes′sa·lo′ni·an** (-lō′nē-ən) *adj.* & *n.*

the·ta (thā′tə, thē′-) *n.* The eighth letter of the Greek alphabet. [Gk. *thēta*, of Phoenician orig.; akin to Heb. *ṭēt*, teth.]

theta rhythm *n.* A waveform on an electroencephalogram with a frequency of 4 to 8 hertz, recorded chiefly in the hippocampus of carnivorous mammals when alert or aroused.

Thet·ford Mines (thĕt′fərd). A city of S Quebec, Canada, S of Quebec City. Pop. 19,965.

thet·ic (thĕt′ĭk, thē′tĭk) also **thet·i·cal** (thĕt′ĭ-kəl, thē′tĭ-) *adj.* **1.** Beginning with, constituting, or relating to the thesis in prosody. **2.** Presented dogmatically; arbitrarily prescribed. [Gk. *thetikos* < *thetos*, placed < *tithenai*, to put. See **dhē-*.**]

The·tis (thē′tĭs) *n. Gk. Myth.* One of the Nereids, the wife of Peleus and mother of Achilles.

the·ur·gy (thē′ûr-jē) *n., pl.* **-gies. 1.** Divine or supernatural intervention in human affairs. **2.** The performance of miracles with supernatural assistance. **3.** Magic performed with the aid of beneficent spirits, as formerly practiced by the Neo-Platonists. [LLat. *theurgia* < Gk. *theourgia*, sacramental rite, mystery : *theo-*, theo- + *-ourgia*, -urgy.] —**the·ur′gic, the·ur′gi·cal** *adj.* —**the·ur′gi·cal·ly** *adv.* —**the′ur·gist** *n.*

thew (thyo͞o) *n.* **1.** A well-developed sinew or muscle. **2.** Muscular power or strength. Often used in the plural. [ME, a virtue < OE *thēaw*, a custom, habit.] —**thew′y** *adj.*

they (*th*ā) *pron.* **1.** Used to refer to the ones previously mentioned or implied. **2.** *Usage Problem.* Used to refer to the one previously mentioned or implied, esp. as a substitute for generic *he*. See Usage Note at **he¹**. **3.a.** Used to refer to people in general. **b.** Used to refer to people in general as seen in a position of authority. [ME < ON *their*, masc. pl. demonstrative and personal pron. See **to-*.**]

they'd (*th*ād). **1.** They had. **2.** They would.

they'll (*th*āl). **1.** They will. **2.** They shall.

they're (*th*âr). They are.

they've (*th*āv). They have.

thi– *pref.* Var. of **thio–.**

thi·a·mine (thī′ə-mĭn, -mēn′) also **thi·a·min** (-mĭn) *n.* A vitamin, $C_{12}H_{17}ClN_4OS$, of the vitamin B complex, found in meat, yeast, and the bran coat of grains and necessary for carbohydrate metabolism. [Alteration of *thiamin* : THI(O)– + (VIT)AMIN.]

thi·a·zide (thī′ə-zīd′, -zĭd) *n.* Any of a group of drugs that block reabsorption of sodium in the distal tubules of the kidneys, used to treat hypertension. [THI(O)– + AZ(O)– + –IDE.]

thi·a·zine (thī′ə-zēn′) *n.* Any of a class of organic chemical compounds with a ring composed of one sulfur atom, one nitrogen atom, and four carbon atoms, used in making dyes.

thi·a·zole (thī′ə-zōl′) *n.* **1.** A colorless or pale yellow liquid, C_3H_3NS, with a five-member ring composed of a nitrogen atom, a sulfur atom, and three carbon atoms, used in making dyes and fungicides. **2.** Any of its various derivatives.

thick (thĭk) *adj.* **thick·er, thick·est. 1.a.** Relatively great in extent from one surface to the opposite, usu. in the smallest solid dimension; not thin. **b.** Measuring a specified number of units in this dimension: *two inches thick.* **2.** Heavy in form, build, or stature; thickset. **3.** Having component parts in a close, crowded state or arrangement; dense: *a thick forest.* **4.** Having or suggesting a heavy or viscous consistency. **5.** Having a great number; abounding. **6.** Impenetrable by the eyes. **7.a.** Not easy to hear or understand; indistinctly articulated. **b.** Producing indistinctly articulated sounds. **8.** Noticeably affecting sound; conspicuous: *a thick brogue.* **9.** *Informal.* Lacking mental agility; stupid. **10.** *Informal.* Very friendly; intimate. **11.** *Informal.* Going beyond what is tolerable; excessive. —*adv.* **1.** In a thick manner; deeply or heavily. **2.** In a close, compact state or arrangement; densely. **3.** So as to be thick; thickly: *Slice the bread thick.* —*n.* **1.** The thickest part. **2.** The most active or intense part. —***idiom.* thick and thin.** Good and bad times. [ME *thicke* < OE *thicce.* See **tegu-*.**] —**thick′ish** *adj.* —**thick′ly** *adv.*

thick·en (thĭk′ən) *tr.* & *intr.v.* **-ened, -en·ing, -ens. 1.** To make or become thick or thicker. **2.** To make or become more intense, intricate, or complex. —**thick′en·er** *n.*

thick·en·ing (thĭk′ə-nĭng) *n.* **1.** The act or process of making or becoming thick. **2.** Material used to thicken. **3.** A thickened part.

thick·et (thĭk′ĭt) *n.* **1.** A dense growth of shrubs or underbrush; a copse. **2.** Something suggestive of a dense growth of plants, as in thickness. [OE *thiccet* < *thicce*, thick. See THICK.]

thick·head (thĭk′hĕd′) *n.* A person regarded as stupid; a blockhead. —**thick′head′ed** *adj.*

thick milk *n. Pennsylvania.* See **clabber.**

thick·ness (thĭk′nĭs) *n.* **1.** The quality or condition of being thick. **2.** The dimension between two surfaces of an object, usu. the dimension of smallest measure. **3.** A layer, sheet, stratum, or ply: *Each floor is a single thickness of concrete.*

thick·set (thĭk′sĕt′) *adj.* **1.** Having a solid stocky form or body; stout. **2.** Positioned or placed closely together.

thick-skinned (thĭk′skĭnd′) *adj.* **1.** Having a thick skin or rind. **2.** Not easily offended. **3.** Largely unaffected by the needs and feelings of other people; insensitive.

thick-wit·ted (thĭk′wĭt′ĭd) *adj.* Stupid; dull.

thief (thēf) *n., pl.* **thieves** (thēvz). One who steals, esp. one who steals movable property by stealth. [ME < OE *thēof.*]

thieve (thēv) *tr.* & *intr.v.* **thieved, thiev·ing, thieves.** To take (something) by theft or commit theft. [Perh. < OE *thēofian* < *thēof*, thief.]

thiev·er·y (thē′və-rē) *n., pl.* **-ies.** Thieving.

thiev·ish (thē′vĭsh) *adj.* **1.** Given to thieving. **2.** Of, similar to, or characteristic of a thief; furtive.

thigh (thī) *n.* **1.a.** The portion of the human leg between the hip and the knee. **b.** The corresponding part of the hind leg of a quadruped or other vertebrate animal. **2.** The second segment of a bird's leg, containing the tibia and fibula. **3.** The femur of an insect's leg. [ME < OE *thēoh.* See **teuə-*.**]

thigh·bone (thī′bōn′) *n.* See **femur** 1.

thig·mo·tax·is (thĭg′mə-tăk′sĭs) *n.* See **stereotaxis** 2. [Gk. *thigma*, touch (< *thinganein*, to touch; see **dheigh-***) + -TAXIS.] —**thig′mo·tac′tic** (-tăk′tĭk) *adj.*

thig·mot·ro·pism (thĭg-mŏt′rə-pĭz′əm) *n.* The turning or bending response of an organism upon direct contact with a solid surface or object. [Gk. *thigma*, touch; see THIGMOTAXIS + -TROPISM.] —**thig′mo·trop′ic** (thĭg′mə-trŏp′ĭk, -trō′pĭk)

thill (thĭl) *n.* Either of the two long shafts between which an animal is fastened when pulling a wagon. [ME *thille*, perh. < OE, plank.]

thim·ble (thĭm′bəl) *n.* **1.** A small cup made of metal, plastic, leather, or other hard material, worn to protect the finger that pushes the needle in sewing. **2.** Any of various tubular sockets or sleeves in machinery. **3.** *Naut.* **a.** A metal ring fitted in an eye of a sail to prevent chafing. **b.** A metal ring around which a rope splice is passed. [ME *thimbil*, alteration of OE *thȳmel*, leather finger covering < *thūma*, thumb. See **teuə-*.**]

thim·ble·ber·ry (thĭm′bəl-bĕr′ē) *n.* **1.** Any of several North American raspberries, esp. *Rubus parviflorus, R. occidentalis*, or *R. odoratus* of the rose family, having thimble-shaped aggregate fruit. **2.** The fruit of any of these plants.

thim·ble·ful (thĭm′bəl-fo͝ol′) *n.* **1.** A very small quantity. **2.** The amount that a thimble can hold.

thim·ble·rig (thĭm′bəl-rĭg′) *Games.* —*n.* **1.** See **shell game** 1. **2.** One who operates a thimblerig. —*tr.v.* **-rigged, -rig·ging, -rigs.** To swindle with or as if with a thimblerig.

thim·ble·weed (thĭm′bəl-wēd′) *n.* Any of several North American plants of the genus *Anemone*, having cylindrical thimblelike fruit clusters.

Thim·bu (thĭm′bo͞o′, tĭm′-) also **Thim·phu** (-po͞o′). The cap. of Bhutan, in the W part in the E Himalaya Mts. Pop. 8,982.

thi·mer·o·sal (thī-mĕr′ə-săl′) *n.* A cream-colored crystalline powder, $C_9H_9HgNaO_2S$, used as a local antiseptic. [THI(O)– + MER(CURY) + –O– + SAL(ICYLATE).]

thin (thĭn) *adj.* **thin·ner, thin·nest. 1.a.** Relatively small in extent from one surface to the opposite, usu. in the smallest solid dimension. **b.** Not great in diameter or cross section; fine: *thin wire.* **2.** Lean or slender in form, build, or stature. **3.a.** Not dense or concentrated; sparse. **b.** More rarefied than normal: *thin air.* **4.a.** Flowing with relative ease; not viscous. **b.** Watery. **5.** Sparsely supplied or provided; scanty: *a thin menu.* **6.** Lacking force or substance; flimsy. **7.** Lacking resonance or fullness; tinny. **8.** Lacking radiance or intensity.

9. Not having enough photographic density or contrast to make satisfactory prints. Used of a negative. *—adv.* **1.** In a thin manner. **2.** So as to be thin: *Cut the cheese thin.* *—tr. & intr.v.* **thinned, thin•ning, thins.** To make or become thin or thinner. [ME < OE *thynne.* See **ten-***.] **—thin′ly** *adv.* **—thin′ness** *n.* **—thin′nish** *adj.*

thine (thīn) *pron. (used with a sing. or pl. v.)* Used to indicate the one or ones belonging to thee. *—adj.* A possessive form of **thou**[1]. Used instead of *thy* before an initial vowel or *h*: *thine orchard.* [ME < OE *thīn.* See **tu-***.]

thing (thĭng) *n.* **1.** An entity, an idea, or a quality perceived, known, or thought to have its own existence. **2.a.** The real or concrete substance of an entity. **b.** An entity existing in space and time. **c.** An inanimate object. **3.** Something referred to by a word, a symbol, a sign, or an idea; a referent. **4.** A creature: *poor thing.* **5.** An individual object: *There wasn't a thing in sight.* **6.a.** *Law.* That which can be possessed or owned. Often used in the plural: *things personal.* **b. things.** Possessions; belongings: *packed her things.* **c.** An article of clothing: *Put on your things.* **7. things.** The equipment needed for an activity or a special purpose: *cleaning things.* **8.** An object or entity that is not or cannot be named specifically. **9.a.** An act, deed, or work. **b.** The result of work or activity: *always building things.* **10.** A thought, a notion, or an utterance. **11.** A piece of information. **12.** A means to an end: *just the thing to increase sales.* **13.** An end or objective. **14.** A matter of concern. **15.** A turn of events; a circumstance. **16.a. things.** The general state of affairs; conditions. **b.** A particular state of affairs; a situation. **17.** *Informal.* A persistent illogical feeling, as a desire or an aversion; an obsession: *has a thing about seafood.* **18.** *Informal.* The latest fad or fashion; the rage. **19.** *Slang.* An activity uniquely suitable and satisfying to one: *do your own thing.* **—*idioms.* first thing.** *Informal.* Right away; before anything else. **see (or hear) things.** To have hallucinations. **sure thing.** *Informal.* **1.** A certainty. **2.** Of course; certainly. [ME < OE.]

thing•a•ma•bob or **thing•u•ma•bob** (thĭng′ə-mə-bŏb′) also **thing•um•bob** (thĭng′əm-bŏb′) *n. Informal.* A thingamajig. [Alteration of *thingumbob* : *thingum* (< THING) + BOB[2].]

thing•a•ma•jig also **thing•um•a•jig** (thĭng′ə-mə-jĭg′) *n. Informal.* Something difficult to classify or whose name has been forgotten or is not known. [Alteration of obsolete *thingum* (< THING) + JIG.]

thing-in-it•self (thĭng′ĭn-ĭt-sĕlf′) *n., pl.* **things-in-them•selves** (thĭngz′ĭn-*th*ĕm-sĕlvz′). *Philos.* See **noumenon** 2.

think (thĭngk) *v.* **thought** (thôt), **think•ing, thinks.** *—tr.* **1.** To have or formulate in the mind. **2.a.** To reason about or reflect on; ponder: *Think it through.* **b.** To decide by reasoning, reflection, or pondering. **3.** To judge or regard; look upon: *I think it fair.* **4.** To believe; suppose. **5.a.** To expect; hope. **b.** To intend. **6.** To call to mind; remember. **7.** To visualize; imagine. **8.** To devise or evolve; invent: *thought up a plan.* **9.** To bring into a given condition by mental preoccupation. **10.** To concentrate one's thoughts on. *—intr.* **1.** To exercise the power of reason, as by conceiving ideas, drawing inferences, and using judgment. **2.** To weigh or consider an idea: *thinking about moving.* **3.a.** To bring a thought to mind by imagination or invention. **b.** To recall a thought or an image to mind. **4.** To believe; suppose. **5.** To have care or consideration. **6.** To dispose the mind in a given way: *Do you think so?* *—adj. Informal.* Requiring much thought to create or assimilate. *—n.* The act or an instance of deliberate or extended thinking; a meditation. **—*idioms.* come to think of it.** *Informal.* When one considers the matter; on reflection. **think aloud (or out loud).** To speak one's thoughts audibly. **think nothing of.** To give little consideration to; regard as routine or usual. **think twice.** To weigh something carefully. [ME *thenken* < OE *thencan.* See **tong-***.]

think•a•ble (thĭng′kə-bəl) *adj.* Possible to consider or be considered; conceivable. **—think′a•bly** *adv.*

think•er (thĭng′kər) *n.* **1.** One who devotes much time to thought or meditation. **2.** One who thinks or reasons in a certain way: *a careful thinker.*

think•ing (thĭng′kĭng) *n.* **1.** The act or practice of one that thinks; thought. **2.** A way of reasoning; judgment. *—adj.* Marked by thought or thoughtfulness; rational.

thinking cap *n.* A state in which one thinks, esp. carefully.

think piece *n.* A newspaper article consisting of news analysis, background material, and personal opinions.

think tank also **think-tank** (thĭngk′tăngk′) *n.* A group or an institution for intensive research and problem solving, esp. in technology, social or political strategy, or armament.

thin•ner (thĭn′ər) *n.* A liquid, such as turpentine, mixed with paint or varnish to reduce its viscosity.

thin-skinned (thĭn′skĭnd′) *adj.* **1.** Having a thin rind or skin. **2.** Oversensitive, esp. to criticism or insult.

thio– or **thi–** *pref.* Containing sulfur, used esp. of a compound in which a divalent sulfur has replaced oxygen: *thiourea.* [Gk. *theio-* < *theion,* sulfur.]

thi•o•car•ba•mide (thī′ō-kär′bə-mīd′) *n.* See **thiourea.**

thi•o•cy•a•nate (thī′ō-sī′ə-nāt′) *n.* A salt or an ester of thiocyanic acid.

thi•o•cy•an•ic acid (thī′ō-sī-ăn′ĭk) *n.* An unstable colorless liquid, HSCN, used in the form of esters as an insecticide.

Thi•o•kol (thī′ə-kôl′, -kōl′, -kŏl′). A trademark used for any of various polysulfide polymers in the form of liquids, water dispersions, and rubbers used in seals and sealants.

thi•ol (thī′ôl′, -ōl′, -ŏl′) *n.* See **mercaptan.**

thion– *pref.* Sulfur: *thionic.* [< Gk. *theion,* sulfur.]

thi•on•ic (thī-ŏn′ĭk) *adj.* Of, relating to, containing, or derived from sulfur.

thi•o•nyl (thī′ə-nĭl′) *n.* See **sulfinyl.**

thi•o•pen•tal sodium (thī′ō-pĕn′tăl′, -tôl′) *n.* A yellowish-white hygroscopic powder, $C_{11}H_{17}N_2O_2SNa$, injected intravenously as a general anesthetic and used in psychotherapy to induce a relaxed state. [THIO– + PENT(OBARBIT)AL SODIUM.]

thi•o•phene (thī′ə-fēn′) *n.* A colorless liquid, C_4H_4S, used as a solvent. [THIO– + *-phene* (var. of PHENO–).]

thi•o•sul•fate (thī′ō-sŭl′fāt′) *n.* A salt or an ester of thiosulfuric acid.

thi•o•sul•fu•ric acid (thī′ō-sŭl-fyo͝or′ĭk) *n.* An unstable acid, $H_2S_2O_3$, formed by replacement of an oxygen atom by a sulfur atom in sulfuric acid.

thi•o•ur•a•cil (thī′ō-yo͝or′ə-sĭl′) *n.* A crystalline compound, $C_4H_4N_2OS$, that interferes with the synthesis of thyroxine, used to reduce the action of the thyroid gland.

thi•o•u•re•a (thī′ō-yo͞o-rē′ə) *n.* A lustrous crystalline compound, $(NH_2)_2CS$, used as a developer in photography and photocopying and in various organic syntheses.

Thí•ra (thîr′ə, thē′rä). Formerly **San•to•rin** (săn′tə-rēn′). A volcanic island of SE Greece in the S Cyclades Is. N of Crete.

third (thûrd) *n.* **1.** The ordinal number matching the number three in a series. **2.** One of three equal parts. **3.** *Mus.* **a.** An interval of three degrees in a diatonic scale. **b.** A tone separated by three degrees from a given tone, esp. the third tone of a scale. **4.** The transmission gear or gear ratio for forward speeds next higher to those of second in a motor vehicle. **5.** *Baseball.* Third base. **6. thirds.** Merchandise whose quality is below the standard set for seconds. [ME *thridde, therdde,* third < OE *thridda.* See **trei-***.] **—third** *adv. & adj.*

third base *n. Baseball.* **1.** The third of the bases on the diamond counterclockwise from home plate. **2.** The position played by the third baseman.

third baseman *n. Baseball.* The infielder near third base.

third class *n.* **1.** A class of mail in the U.S. postal system including all printed matter, except newspapers and magazines, that weighs less than 16 ounces and is unsealed. **2.** Accommodations, as on a ship or train, of the third and usu. lowest order of luxury and price. **—third′-class′** *adv. & adj.*

third degree *n.* Mental or physical torture used to obtain information or a confession from a prisoner.

third-de•gree burn (thûrd′dĭ-grē′) *n.* A severe burn in which the skin and underlying tissues are destroyed.

third dimension *n.* **1.** The quality of depth or thickness in an object or a space. **2.** The quality of seeming real or lifelike. **—third′-di•men′sion•al** (thûrd′dĭ-mĕn′shə-nəl) *adj.*

third eyelid *n.* See **nictitating membrane.**

third force *n.* A group of people or nations that mediates between two opposed groups, such as hostile nations.

third•hand (thûrd′hănd′) *adj.* **1.** Acquired from or through two intermediate sources: *a thirdhand report.* **2.a.** Previously used by two other owners. **b.** Dealing in merchandise previously used by two other owners. **—third′hand′** *adv.*

third•ly (thûrd′lē) *adv.* In the third place, rank, or order.

Third Order (thûrd) *n. Rom. Cath. Ch.* A confraternity of laypersons associated with a religious order.

third party *n.* **1.** A political party organized as opposition to the existing parties in a two-party system. **2.** One other than the principals involved in a transaction.

third person *n. Gram.* **1.** A set of grammatical forms used in referring to a person or thing other than the speaker or the one spoken to. **2.** A grammatical form belonging to such a set. **3.** Reference of a grammatical form to a person or thing other than the speaker or the one spoken to.

third rail *n.* The rail that supplies the high voltage to power a train on an electric railway.

third-rate (thûrd′rāt′) *adj.* Of third quality or value, esp. of less quality or value than second-rate.

third-stream (thûrd′strēm′) *adj. Mus.* Of, relating to, or being music that blends classical music with jazz improvisation.

Third World also **third world** *n.* The developing nations of Africa, Asia, and Latin America. **—Third World′er** *n.*

thirst (thûrst) *n.* **1.a.** A sensation of dryness in the mouth and throat related to a need or desire to drink. **b.** The desire to drink. **2.** An insistent desire; a craving: *a thirst for knowledge.* *—intr.v.* **thirst•ed, thirst•ing, thirsts. 1.** To feel a need to drink. **2.** To have a strong craving; yearn. [ME < OE *thurst.* See **ters-***.] **—thirst′er** *n.*

thirst•y (thûr′stē) *adj.* **-i•er, -i•est. 1.** Desiring to drink. **2.** Arid; parched. **3.** Craving something. **4.** Very absorbent: *a thirsty sponge.* **—thirst′i•ly** *adv.* **—thirst′i•ness** *n.*

thir•teen (thûr-tēn′) *n.* **1.** The cardinal number that is equal to the sum of 12 + 1. **2.** The 13th in a set or sequence. **3.** Something having 13 parts, units, or members. [ME *thyrtene,* al-

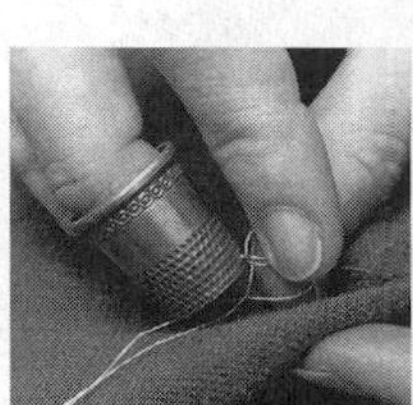

thimble

ă pat	oi boy
ā pay	ou out
âr care	o͝o took
ä father	o͞o boot
ĕ pet	ŭ cut
ē be	ûr urge
ĭ pit	th thin
ī pie	*th* this
îr pier	hw which
ŏ pot	zh vision
ō toe	ə about, item
ô paw	

Stress marks:
′ (primary);
′ (secondary), as in
dictionary (dĭk′shə-nĕr′ē)

teration of *thrittene* < OE *thrēotīne.* See **trei-***.] **—thir•teen′** *adj.* & *pron.*

thir•teenth (thûr-tēnth′) *n.* **1.** The ordinal number matching the number 13 in a series. **2.** One of 13 equal parts. **—thir•teenth′** *adv.* & *adj.*

thir•ti•eth (thûr′tē-ĭth) *n.* **1.** The ordinal number matching the number 30 in a series. **2.** One of 30 equal parts. **—thir′ti•eth** *adv.* & *adj.*

thir•ty (thûr′tē) *n., pl.* **-ties. 1.** The cardinal number equal to 3 × 10. **2. thirties. a.** Often **Thirties.** The decade from 30 to 39 in a century. **b.** A decade or the numbers from 30 to 39: *They settled down in their thirties.* **3.** An indication of the end of a news story, usu. written 30. [ME *thritty, thirty* < OE *thrītig.* See **trei-***.] **—thir′ty** *adj.* & *pron.*

thir•ty-sec•ond note (thûr′tē-sĕk′ənd) *n. Mus.* A musical note with a time value equivalent to 1/32 of a whole note.

thir•ty-two•mo (thûr′tē-to͞o′mō) *n., pl.* **-mos.** *Print.* **1.** The page size (3½ by 5½ inches) that results when a printer's sheet is folded into 32 equal sections. **2.** A book composed of pages of this size.

thistle
Scotch thistle
Onopordum ancanthium

this (*th*ĭs) *pron., pl.* **these** (*th*ēz). **1.a.** Used to refer to the person or thing present, nearby, or just mentioned: *This is my cat.* **b.** Used to refer to what is about to be said: *Listen to this.* **c.** Used to refer to the present event, action, or time: *said he'd be back before this.* **2.** Used to indicate the nearer or the more immediate one: *This is mine and that is yours.* —*adj., pl.* **these. 1.** Being just mentioned or present in space, time, or thought: *early this morning.* **2.** Being nearer or more immediate: *this side and that side.* **3.** Being about to be stated or described: *Wait for this story.* **4.** *Informal.* Used as an emphatic substitute for the indefinite article: *lost this book.* —*adv.* To this extent; so: *this late.* [ME < OE. See **to-***.]

Usage Note: *This* and *that* are both used as demonstrative pronouns to refer to a thought expressed earlier: *The letter was unopened; that* (or *this*) *in itself casts doubt on the inspector's theory. That* is sometimes prescribed as the better choice in referring to what has gone before (as in the preceding example). When the referent is yet to be mentioned, only *this* is used: *This is what bothers me. We have no time to consider late applications.* • *This* is often used in speech and informal writing as an emphatic substitute for the use of the indefinite article to refer to a specific thing or person: *I have this feeling that I forgot it.* This informal usage is best avoided in formal writing except where conversational tone is deliberately being sought. See Usage Note at **that.**

this•a•way (*th*ĭs′ə-wā′) *adv. Southern & Midland U.S.* This way.

This•be (thĭz′bē) *n. Gk. & Rom. Myth.* A young woman who killed herself after the suicide of her lover, Pyramus.

this•tle (thĭs′əl) *n.* **1.** Any of numerous weedy plants, chiefly of the genera *Cirsium, Carduus,* or *Onopordum* of the composite family, having prickly leaves and variously colored flower heads surrounded by prickly bracts. **2.** Any of various similar or related plants. [ME < OE *thistel.*]

this•tle•down (thĭs′əl-doun′) *n.* The silky down attached to the seedlike fruit of a thistle; pappus.

thith•er (thĭ*th*′ər, *th*ĭ*th*′-) *adv.* To or toward that place; in that direction; there. —*adj.* Located or being on the more distant side; farther. [ME < OE *thider.* See **to-***.]

thith•er•to (thĭ*th*′ər-to͞o′, *th*ĭ*th*′-) *adv.* Up to that time.

thith•er•ward (thĭ*th*′ər-wərd, *th*ĭ*th*′-) *adv.* Thither.

thoroughbred
Secretariat, winner of the Triple Crown in 1973

thix•ot•ro•py (thĭk-sŏt′rə-pē) *n.* The property exhibited by certain gels of becoming fluid when stirred or shaken and returning to the semisolid state upon standing. [< Gk. *thixis,* touch < *thinganein, thig-,* to touch. See **dheigh-***.]

Th.M. *abbr. Lat.* Theologiae Magister (Master of Theology).

tho also **tho'** (*th*ō) *conj.* & *adv. Informal.* Though.

thole (thōl) *n. Naut.* A thole pin.

thole pin *n. Naut.* A wooden peg set in pairs in the gunwales of a boat as an oarlock. [ME *tholle* < OE *thol.* See **teuə-***.]

Thom•as (tŏm′əs), Saint. One of the 12 Apostles, who doubted that Jesus had risen from the dead until he saw the wounds.

Thomas, Clarence. b. 1948. Amer. jurist; associate justice of the U.S. Supreme Court (since 1991).

Thomas, Dylan Marlais. 1914–53. Welsh poet known for his bardic voice experiments with syllabic verse.

Thomas, George Henry. 1816–70. Amer. Union general who fought at Shiloh (1862) and Chickamauga (1863).

Thomas, Norman Mattoon. 1884–1968. Amer. socialist who was a founder of the American Civil Liberties Union (1920).

Thomas, Seth. 1785–1859. Amer. clockmaker and a pioneer in the mass production of clocks.

Thomas à Kem•pis (ə kĕm′pĭs, ä). 1380?–1471. German ecclesiastic and writer of devotional literature, most probably including *The Imitation of Christ* (1426).

Thomas of Er•cel•doune (ûr′səl-do͞on′). "Thomas the Rhymer." fl. 1220–97. Scottish poet and seer associated with Merlin and other legendary soothsayers.

Thom•as•ville (tŏm′əs-vĭl′). A city of S GA W of Valdosta. Pop. 17,457.

Tho•mism (tō′mĭz′əm) *n.* The theological and philosophical system of Saint Thomas Aquinas, a system that dominated scholasticism. **—Tho′mist** *n.* **—Tho•mis′tic** *adj.*

Thomp•son (tŏmp′sən, tŏm′-), **Benjamin.** Count Rumford. 1753–1814. Amer.-born British public official and physicist who concluded that heat is produced by moving particles.

Thompson, Dorothy. 1894–1961. Amer. journalist noted for her radio broadcasts and syndicated column "On the Record" (1936–41).

Thompson, Francis. 1859–1907. British poet whose works include "The Hound of Heaven" (1893).

Thompson, Sir **John Sparrow David.** 1844–94. Canadian politician who served as prime minister (1892–94).

Thompson, Smith. 1768–1843. Amer. jurist; associate justice of the U.S. Supreme Court (1823–43).

Thompson River. A river, c. 489 km (304 mi), of S British Columbia, Canada, flowing W and SW to the Fraser R.

Thompson submachine gun *n.* A .45-caliber submachine gun. [After John *Thompson* (1860–1940), Amer. army officer.]

Thom•son (tŏm′sən), Sir **George Paget.** 1892–1975. British physicist who shared a 1937 Nobel Prize.

Thomson, James[1]. 1700–48. Scottish-born British poet whose works presaged romanticism.

Thomson, James[2]. "Bysshe Vanolis" or "B.V." 1834–82. Scottish-born British poet whose pessimistic works include *The City of Dreadful Night* (1874).

Thomson, Sir **Joseph John.** 1856–1940. British physicist who won a 1906 Nobel Prize.

Thomson, Virgil Garnett. 1896–1989. Amer. composer best known for the opera *Four Saints in Three Acts* (1927).

thong (thông, thŏng) *n.* **1.** A narrow strip, as of leather, used for binding or lashing. **2.** A whip of plaited leather or cord. **3.** A sandal held on the foot by a strip that fits between the first and second toes and a strap. [ME < OE *thwong.*]

Thor (thôr) *n. Myth.* The Norse god of thunder. [ON *Thōrr.* See **(s)tenə-***.]

tho•rac•ic (thə-răs′ĭk) *adj.* Of, relating to, or located in or near the thorax: *the thoracic cavity.* **—tho•rac′i•cal•ly** *adv.*

thoracic duct *n.* The main duct of the lymphatic system, ascending through the thoracic cavity along the spinal column and discharging lymph and chyle into the left subclavian vein.

tho•ra•cot•o•my (thôr′ə-kŏt′ə-mē, thōr′-) *n., pl.* **-mies.** Surgical incision of the chest wall. [Lat. *thōrāx, thōrāc-,* thorax + -TOMY.]

tho•rax (thôr′ăks′, thōr′-) *n., pl.* **tho•rax•es** or **tho•ra•ces** (thôr′ə-sēz′, thōr′-). **1.** The part of the human body between the neck and the diaphragm, partially encased by the ribs and containing the heart and lungs; the chest. **2.** A part in other vertebrates that corresponds to the human thorax. **3.** The second or middle region of the body of an arthropod, between the head and the abdomen. [ME < Lat. *thōrāx,* breastplate, chest < Gk. *thōrax.*]

Tho•ra•zine (thôr′ə-zēn′, thōr′-). A trademark used for chlorpromazine.

Tho•reau (thə-rō′, thôr′ō), **Henry David.** 1817–62. Amer. writer whose works include "Civil Disobedience" (1849) and *Walden* (1854). **—Tho•reau′vi•an** (-vē-ən) *adj.*

tho•ri•a (thôr′ē-ə, thōr′-) *n.* See **thorium dioxide.**

tho•rite (thôr′īt′, thōr′-) *n.* A vitreous brownish-yellow to black radioactive mineral, $ThSiO_4$, an ore of thorium.

tho•ri•um (thôr′ē-əm, thōr′-) *n. Symbol* **Th** A radioactive metallic element that is recovered commercially from monazite and used in magnesium alloys; its longest-lived isotope, Th 232, has a half-life of 1.41×10^{10} years and is used as a source of nuclear energy. Atomic number 90; atomic weight 232.038; approx. melting point 1,750°C; approx. boiling point 4,500°C; approx. specific gravity 11.7; valence 4. See table at **element.** [After THOR.] **—tho′ric** (thôr′ĭk, thŏr′-, thōr′-) *adj.*

thorium dioxide *n.* A heavy powder, ThO_2, obtained from monazite and used in gas mantles and as a catalyst.

thorn (thôrn) *n.* **1.** *Bot.* **a.** A modified branch in the form of a sharp, woody spine. **b.** Any of various plants bearing thorns. **2.** Any of various sharp spiny protuberances; a prickle. **3.** One that causes sharp pain, irritation, or discomfort. **4.** The runic letter þ originally representing either sound of the Modern English *th,* as in *the* and *thin,* used in Old English and Middle English manuscripts. [ME < OE.]

thorn apple *n.* See **datura.**

thorn•back (thôrn′băk′) *n.* **1.** A European ray *(Raja clavata)* having spines along the back. **2.** A fish *(Platyrhinoidis triseriata)* of Pacific waters, related to the guitarfish.

Thorn•dike (thôrn′dīk′), **Edward Lee.** 1874–1949. Amer. psychologist noted for his study of animal intelligence.

Thorndike, Dame **Sybil.** 1882–1976. British actress known for her role in George Bernard Shaw's *Saint Joan* (1924).

Thorn•ton (thôrn′tən). A city of N-central CO, a suburb of Denver. Pop. 55,031.

thorn•y (thôr′nē) *adj.* **-i•er, -i•est. 1.** Full of or covered with thorns. **2.** Spiny. **3.** Painfully controversial; vexatious: *thorny issues.* **—thorn′i•ly** *adv.* **—thorn′i•ness** *n.*

tho•ron (thôr′ŏn′, thōr′-) *n.* A radioactive isotope of radon, Rn 220, having a half-life of 54.5 seconds and produced by the disintegration of thorium. [THOR(IUM) + -ON[2].]

thor•ough (thûr′ō, thŭr′ō) *adj.* **1.** Exhaustively complete. **2.** Painstakingly accurate or careful. **3.** Absolute; utter. —*prep. & adv. Archaic.* Var. of **through.** [ME *thorow,* through, thorough < OE *thuruh,* from end to end, through. See **terə-**[2]*.] —**thor′ough•ly** *adv.* —**thor′ough•ness** *n.*

thor•ough•bass or **thor•ough bass** (thûr′ō-bās′, thûr′ə-, thŭr′-) *n. Mus.* See **continuo.**

thorough brace *n.* One of several leather bands passed from front to back of a carriage, supporting it and serving as a spring. —**thor′ough-braced′** (thûr′ō-brāst′, thŭr′-) *adj.*

thor•ough•bred (thûr′ō-brĕd′, thûr′ə-, thŭr′-) *n.* **1.** A purebred or pedigreed animal, esp. a horse. **2. Thoroughbred.** Any of a breed of horses, bred chiefly for racing, originating from a cross between Arabian stallions and English mares. **3.** A well-bred person. —**thor′ough•bred′** *adj.*

thor•ough•fare (thûr′ō-fâr′, thûr′ə-, thŭr′-) *n.* **1.** A main road or public highway. **2.a.** A place of passage from one location to another. **b.** Right to such passage. **3.** A heavily traveled passage, such as a strait. [ME *thurghfare* : *thurgh, thorow,* through; see THOROUGH + *fare,* road (< OE *faru, fær* < *faran,* to go; see FARE).]

thor•ough•go•ing (thûr′ō-gō′ĭng, thûr′ə-, thŭr′-) *adj.* **1.** Very thorough; complete. **2.** Unmitigated; unqualified.

thor•ough•paced (thûr′ō-pāst′, thûr′ə-, thŭr′-) *adj.* **1.** Trained in all paces or gaits, as a horse. **2.** Thoroughgoing.

thor•ough•pin (thûr′ō-pĭn′, thûr′ə-, thŭr′-) *n.* An abnormal swelling of the hock joint in horses and related animals.

thor•ough•wort (thûr′ō-wûrt′, -wôrt′, thûr′ə-, thŭr′-) *n.* See **boneset.** [THOROUGH, through + WORT[1].]

thorp (thôrp) *n. Archaic.* A hamlet. [ME < OE. See **treb-***.]

Thorpe (thôrp), **James ("Jim") Francis.** 1888–1953. Amer. athlete who won the decathlon and pentathlon in the 1912 Olympics.

Thor•vald•sen or **Thor•wald•sen** (tôr′wôl′sən, thôr′-, to͝or′väl′-), **(Albert) Bertel.** 1768?–1844. Danish sculptor whose neoclassical works include *Lion of Lucerne* (1819).

those (*th*ōz) *pron. & adj.* Pl. of **that.** [ME *thos* < OE *thās,* these. See THESE.]

Thoth (thōth, tōt) *n. Myth.* The Egyptian god of the moon and of wisdom and learning.

thou[1] (*th*ou) *pron.* Used to address a single person, esp. as a familiar form in a literary or devotional context. [ME < OE *thū,* second pers. nominative sing. personal pron. See **tu-***.]

thou[2] (thou) *n. Slang.* A thousand, esp. of dollars.

though (*th*ō) *conj.* **1.** Despite the fact that; although: *He still argues, though he's wrong.* **2.** Conceding or supposing that; even if: *Though I may fail, I will still try.* See Usage Note at **although.** —*adv.* **1.** However; nevertheless. **2.** *Informal.* Used as an intensive: *Wouldn't that beat all, though?* [ME, of Scand. orig. See **to-***.]

thought (thôt) *v.* P.t. and p.part. of **think.** —*n.* **1.** The act or process of thinking; cogitation. **2.** A product of thinking. See Syns at **idea. 3.** The faculty of thinking or reasoning. **4.** The intellectual activity or production of a particular time or group: *feminist thought.* **5.** Consideration; attention. **6.a.** Intention; purpose. **b.** Expectation or conception: *no thought of being wrong.* **7.** A trifle; a bit: *a thought more considerate.* [ME < OE *gethōht, thōht.* See **tong-***.]

thought•ful (thôt′fəl) *adj.* **1.** Engrossed in thought; contemplative. **2.** Exhibiting or marked by careful thought. **3.** Having or showing heed for the happiness of others and a propensity for anticipating their needs or wishes. —**thought′ful•ly** *adv.* —**thought′ful•ness** *n.*

Syns: *thoughtful, considerate, attentive, solicitous.* These adjectives mean having or showing concern for the well-being of others. Although *thoughtful* and *considerate* are often used interchangeably, *thoughtful* implies a tendency to anticipate needs or wishes, whereas *considerate* stresses sensitivity to another's feelings: *It was thoughtful of you to bring flowers. I wish I had more considerate neighbors. Attentive* suggests devoted, assiduous attention: *attentive to his clients. Solicitous* implies deep concern that often verges on anxiety or expresses itself in exaggerated and sometimes cloying attentiveness: *a solicitous friend.* See also Syns at **pensive.**

thought•less (thôt′lĭs) *adj.* **1.** Marked by or showing lack of due thought or care; careless. **2.** Inconsiderate; inattentive. **3.** Lacking thought: *thoughtless bickering.* —**thought′less•ly** *adv.* —**thought′less•ness** *n.*

thou•sand (thou′zənd) *n.* The cardinal number equal to 10 × 100 or 10^3. [ME < OE *thūsend.* See **teuə-***.] —**thou′sand** *adj. & pron.*

Thou•sand Island dressing (thou′zənd) *n.* A salad dressing made with mayonnaise, chili sauce, and seasonings. [Perh. after the THOUSAND ISLANDS.]

Thousand Islands. A group of more than 1,800 islands of N NY and SE Ontario, Canada, in the St. Lawrence R.

Thousand Oaks. A city of S CA W of Los Angeles. Pop. 104,352.

thou•sandth (thou′zəndth, -zənth) *n.* **1.** The ordinal number matching the number 1,000 in a series. **2.** One of 1,000 equal parts. —**thou′sandth** *adv. & adj.*

thp also **t.hp.** *abbr.* Thrust horsepower.

Thrace (thrās). A region and ancient country of the SE Balkan Peninsula N of the Aegean Sea; colonized by Greeks in the 7th cent. B.C.

Thra•cian (thrā′shən) *adj.* Of or relating to Thrace or its people. —*n.* **1.** A native or inhabitant of Thrace. **2.** The Indo-European language of the ancient Thracians.

Thrale (thrāl), Mrs. See Hester Lynch **Piozzi.**

thrall (thrôl) *n.* **1.** One, such as a slave, held in bondage. **2.** One intellectually or morally enslaved. **3.** Servitude; bondage. —*tr.v.* **thralled, thrall•ing, thralls.** *Archaic.* To enslave. [ME < OE *thrǣl* < ON *thrǣll.*] —**thrall′dom, thral′dom** *n.*

thrash (thrăsh) *v.* **thrashed, thrash•ing, thrash•es.** —*tr.* **1.** To beat with or as if with a flail, esp. as a punishment. **2.** To flail. **3.** To defeat utterly. **4.** To thresh. **5.** *Naut.* To sail (a boat) against opposing winds or tides. —*intr.* **1.** To move wildly or violently. **2.** To strike or flail. **3.** To thresh. **4.** *Naut.* To sail against opposing tides or winds. —*n.* The act or an instance of thrashing. —***phrasal verb.*** **thrash out.** To discuss fully. [Var. of THRESH.] —**thrash′er** *n.*

thrash•er (thrăsh′ər) *n.* Any of various New World songbirds of the genus *Toxostoma,* having a long curved beak and usu. a brown head and back. [Perh. alteration of THRUSH[1].]

thrash•ing (thrăsh′ĭng) *n.* A severe beating.

thra•son•i•cal (thrā-sŏn′ĭ-kəl, thrə-) *adj.* Boastful. [After *Thrasō,* a character in *Eunuchus,* a play by Terence.]

thread (thrĕd) *n.* **1.a.** Fine cord of a fibrous material, such as flax, made of two or more filaments twisted together and used in needlework and weaving. **b.** A piece of such cord. **2.a.** A thin strand, cord, or filament of natural or manufactured material. **b.** Something that suggests the fineness or thinness of such a strand, cord, or filament: *a thread of smoke.* **c.** Something that suggests the continuousness of such a thread: *the thread of his argument.* **3.** A helical or spiral ridge on a screw, nut, or bolt. **4. threads.** *Slang.* Clothes. —*v.* **thread•ed, thread•ing, threads.** —*tr.* **1.a.** To pass one end of a thread through the eye of (a needle, for example). **b.** To pass (something) through in the manner of a thread. **c.** To pass a tape or film into or through (a device). **d.** To pass (a tape or film) into or through a device. **2.** To connect by running a thread through; string: *thread beads.* **3.a.** To make one's way cautiously through: *threading dark alleys.* **b.** To make (one's way) cautiously through something. **4.** To occur here and there throughout; pervade. **5.** To machine a thread on (a screw, nut, or bolt). —*intr.* **1.** To make one's way cautiously. **2.** To proceed by a winding course. **3.** To form a thread when dropped from a spoon, as boiling sugar syrup. [ME < OE *thrǣd.* See **terə-**[1]*.] —**thread′er** *n.*

thread•bare (thrĕd′bâr′) *adj.* **1.** Having the nap worn down so that the filling or warp shows through; frayed or shabby: *threadbare rugs.* **2.** Wearing old, shabby clothing. **3.** Overused and worn out; hackneyed: *threadbare excuses.*

thread•fin (thrĕd′fĭn′) *n., pl.* **threadfin** or **-fins.** Any of various chiefly tropical marine fishes of the family Polynemidae, having threadlike rays extending from the pectoral fin.

thread•worm (thrĕd′wûrm′) *n.* See **pinworm.**

thread•y (thrĕd′ē) *adj.* **-i•er, -i•est. 1.** Consisting of or resembling thread; filamentous. **2.** Capable of forming or tending to form threads; viscid. **3.** *Medic.* Weak and shallow. Used of a pulse. **4.** Lacking fullness of tone; thin: *a thready voice.* —**thread′i•ness** *n.*

threat (thrĕt) *n.* **1.** An expression of an intention to inflict pain, injury, evil, or punishment. **2.** An indication of impending danger or harm. **3.** One that is regarded as a possible danger; a menace. —*tr.v.* **threat•ed, threat•ing, threats.** *Archaic.* To threaten. [ME < OE *thrēat,* oppression. See **treud-***.]

threat•en (thrĕt′n) *v.* **-ened, -en•ing, -ens.** —*tr.* **1.** To express a threat against. **2.** To be a source of danger to; menace. **3.** To give signs or warning of; portend. **4.** To announce the possibility of in a threat. —*intr.* **1.** To express or use threats. **2.** To indicate danger or harm. —**threat′en•er** *n.*

threat•ened (thrĕt′nd) *adj. Ecol.* At risk of becoming endangered. Used of a plant or an animal.

three (thrē) *n.* **1.** The cardinal number equal to the sum of 2 + 1. **2.** The third in a set or sequence. **3.** Something having three parts, units, or members. [ME < OE *thrī.* See **trei-***.] —**three** *adj. & pron.*

three-bag•ger (thrē′băg′ər) *n. Baseball.* See **three-base hit.**

three-base hit (thrē′bās′) *n. Baseball.* A base hit that allows the batter to reach third base without being put out.

three-card monte (thrē′kärd) *n. Games.* A gambling game in which the dealer shows a player three cards, then turns them face down and moves them around, and the player must guess the position of a particular card.

three-col•or (thrē′kŭl′ər) *adj.* Of, relating to, or being a color printing or photographic process in which three primary colors are transferred by three different plates or filters to a surface, reproducing all the colors of the subject matter.

3-D or **3D** also **three-D** (thrē′dē′) —*adj.* Three-dimensional. —*n.* A three-dimensional medium, display, or performance, esp. a cinematic or graphic medium in three dimensions.

three-deck•er (thrē′dĕk′ər) *n.* **1.** *Naut.* A ship having three

Jim Thorpe

Thoth
Detail of a XIX Dynasty relief of Pharaoh Seti I presenting an offering to Thoth

three-decker
H.M.S. *Victory,* commanded by Admiral Nelson

ă pat	oi boy
ā pay	ou out
âr care	o͝o to͝ok
ä father	o͞o bo͞ot
ĕ pet	ŭ cut
ē be	ûr urge
ĭ pit	th thin
ī pie	*th* this
îr pier	hw which
ŏ pot	zh vision
ō toe	ə about, item
ô paw	

Stress marks:
′ (primary);
′ (secondary), as in
dictionary (dĭk′shə-nĕr′ē)

throne
Coronation throne of Edward the Confessor

decks, esp. one of a class of sail-powered warships with guns on three decks. **2.** Something with three levels or layers, as: **a.** A three-story apartment building. **b.** A sandwich having three slices of bread.

three-di•men•sion•al (thrē′dĭ-mĕn′shə-nəl, -dī-) *adj.* **1.** Of, relating to, having, or existing in three dimensions. **2.** Having or appearing to have extension in depth. **3.** Treating many aspects of a subject; lifelike.

three-gait•ed (thrē′gā′tĭd) *adj.* Trained in the walk, trot, and canter. Used of a horse.

three-leg•ged race (thrē′lĕg′ĭd, -lĕgd′) *n. Games.* A race in which runners are in pairs with their near legs tied together.

Three Mile Island (thrē). An island in the Susquehanna R. in SE PA; site of a major nuclear accident in Mar. 1979.

three•pence (thrĕp′əns, thrĭp′-, thrŭp′-) *n., pl.* **threepence** or **-penc•es. 1.** A coin worth three pennies, formerly used in Great Britain. **2.** The sum of three pennies.

three•pen•ny (thrĕp′ə-nē, thrĭp′-, thrŭp′-) *adj.* **1.** Worth or priced at threepence. **2.** Very small; trifling.

three-piece (thrē′pēs′) *adj.* Made in or consisting of three parts or pieces, as a suit with a jacket, trousers, and a vest.

three-ply (thrē′plī′) *adj.* Consisting of three layers or strands.

three-point landing (thrē′point′) *n.* An airplane landing in which the two main wheels and the nose wheel, tail wheel, or rear skid all touch the ground simultaneously.

three-quar•ter (thrē′kwôr′tər) *adj.* **1.** Of or extending to three fourths of the usual full length. **2.** Depicting the subject turned slightly from a full frontal view.

three-quarter binding *n. Print.* A bookbinding in which the leather or fabric covering the spine extends onto the covers for one third of their width.

three-ring circus (thrē′rĭng′) *n.* **1.** A circus having simultaneous performances in three separate rings. **2.** *Informal.* A confusing, engrossing, or amusing situation.

three R's *pl.n.* Reading, writing, and arithmetic, considered as the fundamentals of elementary education. [< the phrase *reading, 'riting, and 'rithmetic.*]

three•score (thrē′skôr′, -skōr′) *adj.* Being three times twenty; sixty. **—three′score′** *n. & pron.*

three•some (thrē′səm) *n.* **1.** A group of three persons or things. **2.** An activity involving three people, esp. a golf match in which one player competes against two others who alternate their play. *—adj.* Consisting of or performed by three.

three-square (thrē′skwâr′) *adj.* Having an equilateral triangular cross section: *a three-square file.*

three-wheel•er (thrē′hwē′lər, -wē′-) *n.* A vehicle having three wheels, as a small all-terrain motor vehicle.

thren•o•dy (thrĕn′ə-dē) *n., pl.* **-dies.** A poem or song of mourning or lamentation. [Gk. *thrēnōidia* : *thrēnos*, lament + *ōidē*, song; see ODE.] **—thre•no′di•al** (thrə-nō′dē-əl), **thre•nod′ic** (-nŏd′ĭk) *adj.* **—thren′o•dist** *n.*

thre•o•nine (thrē′ə-nēn′, -nĭn) *n.* A crystalline essential amino acid, $C_4H_9NO_3$, that is derived from the hydrolysis of protein. [Prob. < *threose*, a kind of sugar (alteration of *erythrose* : ERYTHRO- + -OSE[2]) + -INE[2].]

thresh (thrĕsh) *v.* **threshed, thresh•ing, thresh•es.** *—tr.* **1.a.** To beat the stems and husks of (grain or cereal plants) with a machine or flail to separate the grains or seeds from the straw. **b.** To separate (grains or seeds) in this manner. **2.** To discuss or examine (an issue, for example) repeatedly. **3.** To beat severely; thrash. *—intr.* **1.** To thresh grain or seeds. **2.** To thrash about; toss. [ME *thresshen* < OE *therscan.* See **terə-**[1]*.]

thresh•er (thrĕsh′ər) *n.* **1.** One that threshes: *a thresher of grain.* **2.** A threshing machine. **3.** Any of various large sharks of the genus *Alopias,* having a tail with a long whiplike upper lobe with which it strikes the surface of the water.

thresh•ing machine (thrĕsh′ĭng) *n.* A farm machine used in threshing grain or seed plants.

thresh•old (thrĕsh′ōld′, -hōld′) *n.* **1.** A piece of wood or stone beneath a door; a doorsill. **2.** An entrance or a doorway. **3.** The place or point of beginning; the outset. **4.** A point separating conditions that will produce a given effect from those of a higher or lower degree that will not produce the effect. [ME *thresshold* < OE *therscold.* See **terə-**[1]*.]

threw (thrōō) *v.* P.t. of **throw.**

thrice (thrīs) *adv.* **1.** Three times. **2.** In a threefold quantity or degree. **3.** *Archaic.* Extremely; greatly. [ME *thries,* adverbial genitive of *thrie* < OE *thrīga.* See **trei-***.]

thrift (thrĭft) *n.* **1.** Wise economy in the management of money and other resources; frugality. **2.** Vigorous growth of living things, such as plants. **3.** Any of several densely tufted plants of the genus *Armeria,* esp. *A. maritima,* having white to pink flower heads with a funnel-shaped scarious calyx. **4.** A savings and loan association, credit union, or savings bank. [ME, prosperity, perh. < ON < *thrīfask,* to thrive. See THRIVE.]

thrift•less (thrĭft′lĭs) *adj.* **1.** Careless in handling money; wasteful. **2.** *Archaic.* Lacking usefulness or value. **—thrift′less•ly** *adv.* **—thrift′less•ness** *n.*

thrift shop *n.* A shop that sells used articles, esp. clothing, as to benefit a charitable organization.

thrift•y (thrĭf′tē) *adj.* **-i•er, -i•est. 1.** Practicing or marked by the practice of thrift; wisely economical. See Syns at **sparing. 2.** Industrious and thriving; prosperous. **3.** Growing vigorously, as a plant. **—thrift′i•ly** *adv.* **—thrift′i•ness** *n.*

thrill (thrĭl) *v.* **thrilled, thrill•ing, thrills.** *—tr.* **1.** To cause a sudden intense sensation; excite greatly. **2.** To give great pleasure to; delight. **3.** To cause to quiver, tremble, or vibrate. *—intr.* **1.** To feel a sudden quiver of excitement or emotion. **2.** To quiver, tremble, or vibrate. *—n.* **1.** A quivering or trembling caused by sudden excitement or emotion. **2.** A source or cause of excitement or emotion. **3.** *Pathol.* A slight palpable vibration accompanying certain cardiac and circulatory abnormalities. [ME *thrillen,* alteration of *thirlen,* to pierce < OE *thȳrlian* < *thȳrel,* hole. See **terə-**[2]*.]

thrill•er (thrĭl′ər) *n.* One that thrills, esp. a sensational or suspenseful book, story, play, or movie.

thrips (thrĭps) *n., pl.* **thrips.** Any of various minute insects of the order Thysanoptera, many of which are major pests of cereals and fruit trees. [Lat., woodworm < Gk.]

thrive (thrīv) *intr.v.* **thrived** or **throve** (thrōv), **thrived** or **thriv•en** (thrĭv′ən), **thriv•ing, thrives. 1.** To make steady progress; prosper. **2.** To grow vigorously; flourish. [ME *thriven* < ON *thrīfask,* reflexive of *thrīfa,* to seize.] **—thriv′er** *n.*

throat (thrōt) *n.* **1.** The anterior portion of the neck. **2.** *Anat.* The portion of the digestive tract that lies between the rear of the mouth and the esophagus and includes the fauces and the pharynx. **3.** A narrow passage or part suggestive of the human throat. *—tr.v.* **throat•ed, throat•ing, throats.** To pronounce with a harsh or guttural voice. **—*idiom.* ram (or shove) down (someone's) throat.** *Informal.* To compel to accept or consider. [ME *throte* < OE.]

throat•latch (thrōt′lăch′) *n.* A strap passing under the neck of a horse for holding a bridle or halter in place.

throat•y (thrō′tē) *adj.* **-i•er, -i•est.** Uttered or sounding as if uttered deep in the throat; guttural, hoarse, or husky. **—throat′i•ly** *adv.* **—throat′i•ness** *n.*

throb (thrŏb) *intr.v.* **throbbed, throb•bing, throbs. 1.** To beat rapidly or violently, as the heart; pound. **2.** To vibrate, pulsate, or sound with a steady pronounced rhythm: *boat engines throbbing.* *—n.* The act of throbbing; a beating, palpitation, or vibration. [ME *throbben,* of imit. orig.]

throe (thrō) *n.* **1.** A severe pang or spasm of pain, as in childbirth. **2. throes.** A condition of agonizing struggle or trouble: *the throes of poverty.* [ME *throwe,* perh. alteration of *thrawe* < OE *thrawu,* genitive of *thrēah,* pain, affliction.]

throm•bi (thrŏm′bī) *n.* Pl. of **thrombus.**

throm•bin (thrŏm′bĭn) *n.* An enzyme in blood that facilitates blood clotting by reacting with fibrinogen to form fibrin.

thrombo– or **thromb–** *pref.* Blood clot; blood clotting: *thromboplastic.* [Gk. < *thrombos,* clot.]

throm•bo•cyte (thrŏm′bə-sīt′) *n.* See **platelet. —throm′bo•cyt′ic** (-sĭt′ĭk) *adj.*

throm•bo•cy•to•pe•ni•a (thrŏm′bə-sī′tə-pē′nē-ə) *n.* An abnormal decrease in the number of platelets in circulatory blood. **—throm′bo•cy′to•pe′nic** *adj.*

throm•bo•em•bo•lism (thrŏm′bō-ĕm′bə-lĭz′əm) *n.* The blocking of a blood vessel by a blood clot dislodged from its site of origin. **—throm′bo•em•bol′ic** (-ĕm-bŏl′ĭk) *adj.*

throm•bo•ki•nase (thrŏm′bō-kī′nās, -nāz) *n.* See **thromboplastin.**

throm•bo•phle•bi•tis (thrŏm′bō-flĭ-bī′tĭs) *n.* Inflammation of a vein associated with the formation of a blood clot.

throm•bo•plas•tic (thrŏm′bō-plăs′tĭk) *adj.* **1.** Causing or promoting blood clotting: *a thromboplastic protein.* **2.** Of or relating to thromboplastin. **—throm′bo•plas′ti•cal•ly** *adv.*

throm•bo•plas•tin (thrŏm′bō-plăs′tĭn) *n.* An enzyme that converts prothrombin to thrombin in blood clotting.

throm•bo•sis (thrŏm-bō′sĭs) *n., pl.* **-ses** (-sēz). The formation, presence, or development of a thrombus. [NLat. *thrombōsis* < Gk., a clotting < *thromboustha*i, to clot < *thrombos,* clot.]

throm•box•ane (thrŏm-bŏk′sān) *n.* Any of several compounds, derived from platelets or synthesized, that stimulate clotting and constriction of blood vessels.

throm•bus (thrŏm′bəs) *n., pl.* **-bi** (-bī). A fibrinous clot formed in a blood vessel or in a chamber of the heart. [NLat. < Gk. *thrombos,* clot.]

throne (thrōn) *n.* **1.** A chair occupied by an exalted personage on state or ceremonial occasions, often situated on a dais and sometimes having ornate decoration. **2.a.** A personage who occupies a throne. **b.** The power, dignity, or rank of such a personage; sovereignty. **3. thrones.** *Theol.* The third of the nine orders of angels. *—tr. & intr.v.* **throned, thron•ing, thrones.** To install in or occupy a throne. [ME, alteration of *trone* < OFr. < Lat. *thronus* < Gk. *thronos.* See **dher-***.]

throng (thrông, thrŏng) *n.* **1.** A large group of people close together; a multitude. **2.** A large group of things; a host. *—v.* **thronged, throng•ing, throngs.** *—tr.* **1.** To crowd into; fill. **2.** To press in on. *—intr.* To gather, press, or move in a throng. [ME < OE *gethrang.*]

thros•tle (thrŏs′əl) *n.* **1.** Any of various Old World thrushes, esp. a song thrush. **2.** A machine formerly used for spinning fibers such as cotton or wool. [ME < OE.]

throt•tle (thrŏt′l) *n.* **1.** A valve that regulates the flow of a fluid, as in an internal-combustion engine. **2.** A lever or pedal controlling such a valve. — *tr.v.* **-tled, -tling, -tles. 1.a.** To regulate the flow of (fuel) in an engine. **b.** To regulate the speed of (an engine) with a throttle. **2.** To suppress: *throttled the press.* **3.** To strangle; choke. [Short for *throttle valve* < *throttle*, to strangle, choke < ME *throtelen*, prob. < *throte*, throat. See THROAT.] — **throt′tler** *n.*

throt•tle•hold (thrŏt′l-hōld′) *n.* See **stranglehold** 2.

through (thro͞o) *prep.* **1.** In one side and out the opposite or another side of: *through the tunnel.* **2.** Among or between; in the midst of: *a walk through the flowers.* **3.** By way of: *climbed in through the window.* **4.a.** By the means or agency of: *bought through a dealer.* **b.** Into and out of the handling, care, processing, modification, or consideration of: *The report went through our office.* **5.** Here and there in; around: *a tour through France.* **6.** From the beginning to the end of: *through the night.* **7.** At or to the end of; done or finished with, esp. successfully: *through the initial period.* **8.** Up to and including: *The play runs through May.* **9.** Past and without stopping for: *drove through a red light.* **10.** Because of; on account of: *succeeded through hard work.* — *adv.* **1.** From one end or side to another or an opposite end or side: *opened it and went through.* **2.** From beginning to end; completely: *read it through.* **3.** Throughout the whole extent or thickness; thoroughly: *got soaked through.* **4.** Over the total distance; all the way: *drove through.* **5.** To a conclusion or an accomplishment: *see it through.* — *adj.* **1.** Allowing continuous passage; unobstructed. **2.a.** Affording transportation to a destination with few or no stops and no transfers. **b.** Continuing on a highway without exiting. **3.** Passing or extending from one end, side, or surface to another. **4.** Having finished; at completion: *through with the job.* **5.** Having no further concern, dealings, or connection: *I'm through with him.* **6.** Having no more use, value, or potential; washed up: *He's through as an athlete.* — ***idiom.*** **through and through. 1.** In every part; throughout. **2.** In every aspect; completely. [ME *thurh, through* < OE *thurh.* See **terə-²***.]

through•ly (thro͞o′lē) *adv. Archaic.* Thoroughly.

through•out (thro͞o-out′) *prep.* In, to, through, or during every part of; all through. — *adv.* **1.** In or through all parts; everywhere. **2.** During the entire time or extent.

through•put (thro͞o′po͝ot′) *n.* Output or production, as of a computer program, over a period of time.

through•way (thro͞o′wā′) *n.* Var. of **thruway.**

throve (thrōv) *v.* A p.t. of **thrive.**

throw (thrō) *v.* **threw** (thro͞o), **thrown** (thrōn), **throw•ing, throws.** — *tr.* **1.** To propel through the air with a motion of the hand or arm. **2.** To discharge into the air by any means: *a machine that throws tennis balls.* **3.** To hurl or fling with great force or speed: *threw themselves on the food.* **4.a.** To hurl to the ground or floor, as in a wrestling contest. **b.** To cause to fall off. **5.** *Informal.* To cause confusion or perplexity in; disconcert or nonplus. **6.** To put on or off hastily or carelessly. **7.a.** To put (suddenly or forcefully) into a given condition, position, or activity: *threw some supper together.* **b.** To devote, apply, or direct. **8.** To form on a potter's wheel. **9.** To twist (fibers) into thread. **10.** *Games.* **a.** To roll (dice). **b.** To roll (a particular combination) with dice. **c.** To discard or play (a card). **11.** To send forth; project: *threw me a look of pity.* **12.** To cause to fall on or over something; cast. **13.** To bear (young). Used of cows or horses, for example. **14.** To arrange or give (a party, for example). **15.** To move (a lever or switch) in order to activate, deactivate, or control a device. **16.** *Informal.* To lose or give up (a contest, for example) purposely. **17.** To abandon oneself to; have: *threw a fit.* **18.** To commit (oneself), esp. for leniency or support. **19.** To deliver (a punch), as in boxing. — *intr.* To cast, fling, or hurl something. — *n.* **1.** The act or an instance of throwing. **2.** The distance to which something is or can be thrown: *a stone's throw away.* **3.** *Games.* **a.** A roll or cast of dice. **b.** The combination of numbers so obtained. **4.** *Informal.* A single chance, venture, or instance. **5.** *Sports.* The act of throwing or a technique used to throw an opponent, as in wrestling. **6.a.** A light coverlet, such as an afghan. **b.** A scarf or shawl. **7.a.** The radius of a circle described by a crank, cam, or similar machine part. **b.** The maximum displacement of a machine part moved by another part, such as a cam. **8.** *Geol.* The amount of vertical displacement of a fault. — ***phrasal verbs.*** **throw away. 1.a.** To get rid of as useless. **b.** *Games.* To discard. **2.a.** To fail to take advantage of. **b.** To waste or use foolishly. **3.** To utter or perform in an offhand, seemingly careless way: *threw the best line away.* **throw back. 1.** To hinder the progress of; check. **2.** To revert to an earlier type or stage in one's past. **3.** To cause to depend; make reliant. **throw in. 1.** To insert or introduce into the course of something. **2.** To add (an extra thing or amount) with no additional charge. **3.** To engage (a clutch, for example). **throw off. 1.** To cast out; rid oneself of. **2.** To give off; emit. **3.** To distract, divert, or mislead. **4.** To do, finish, or accomplish in a casual or offhand way; toss off. **throw open.** To make more accessible, esp. suddenly or dramatically. **throw out. 1.** To give off; emit. **2.** To reject or discard. **3.** To get rid of as useless. **4.** *Informal.* To offer, as a suggestion or plan. **5.** To force to leave a place or position, esp. in an abrupt or unexpected manner. **6.a.** To disengage (a clutch, for example). **b.** To put out of alignment. **7.** *Baseball.* To put out (a base runner) by throwing the ball to the player guarding the base to which the base runner is moving. **throw over. 1.** To overturn. **2.** To abandon. **3.** To reject. **throw up. 1.** To vomit. **2.** To abandon; relinquish. **3.** To construct hurriedly. **4.** To refer to something repeatedly. **5.** To project, play, or otherwise display (a slide, videotape, or other recorded image). — ***idioms.*** **throw (one's) weight around.** *Slang.* To use power or authority, esp. in an excessive or heavy-handed way. **throw the baby out with the bath water.** *Slang.* To discard something valuable along with something not desired, usu. unintentionally. **throw up (one's) hands.** To indicate or express utter hopelessness. [ME *throwen*, to turn, twist, hurl < OE *thrāwan.* See **terə-¹***.] — **throw′er** *n.*

Syns: *throw, cast, hurl, fling, pitch, toss, sling.* These verbs mean to propel something through the air with a motion of the hand or arm. *Throw* is the least specific: *throw a ball. Cast* usually refers to throwing something light: *cast her line into the stream. Hurl* and *fling* mean to throw with great force: *"Him the Almighty Power/Hurl'd headlong flaming from th' Ethereal Sky"* (John Milton). *The guests flung confetti. Pitch* often means to throw with careful aim: *"a special basket in my study . . . into which I pitch letters, circulars, pamphlets and so forth"* (H.G. Wells). *Toss* usually means to throw lightly or casually: *"Campton tossed the card away"* (Edith Wharton). *Sling* stresses force of propulsion: *slung the heavy bag over her shoulder.* See also Syns at **confuse.**

throw•a•way (thrō′ə-wā′) *adj.* **1.a.** Designed or intended to be discarded after use. **b.** Readily discarding things. **c.** Having been rejected by parents or guardians. **2.** Written or delivered in a low-key or offhand manner. — **throw′a•way′** *n.*

throw•back (thrō′băk′) *n.* **1.** A reversion to a former type or ancestral characteristic. **2.** See **atavism** 2.

throw pillow *n.* A pillow used esp. for decoration, as on a sofa.

throw rug *n.* See **scatter rug.**

throw•ster (thrō′stər) *n.* One that twists fibers into thread.

throw-weight or **throw weight** (thrō′wāt′) *n.* The total weight of a missile's explosive and nonexplosive payload.

thru (thro͞o) *prep., adv., & adj. Informal.* Through.

thrum¹ (thrŭm) *v.* **thrummed, thrum•ming, thrums.** — *tr.* **1.** *Mus.* To play (a stringed instrument) idly or monotonously. **2.** To speak, repeat, or recite in a monotonous tone of voice; drone. — *intr.* **1.** *Mus.* To thrum a stringed instrument. **2.** To drone. — *n.* A thrumming sound. [Imit.]

thrum² (thrŭm) *n.* **1.a.** The fringe of warp threads left on a loom after the cloth has been cut off. **b.** One of these threads. **2.** A loose end, fringe, or tuft of thread. **3. thrums.** *Naut.* Short bits of rope yarn inserted into canvas to roughen the surface. — *tr.v.* **thrummed, thrum•ming, thrums. 1.** To cover or trim with thrums; fringe. **2.** *Naut.* To sew thrums in (canvas). [ME < OE *(tunge)thrum*, ligament (of the tongue).]

thrush¹ (thrŭsh) *n.* **1.** Any of numerous migratory songbirds of the family Turdidae, usu. having brownish upper plumage and a spotted breast. **2.** Any of various similar or related birds, as a water thrush. [ME *thrushe* < OE *thrysce.*]

thrush² (thrŭsh) *n.* **1.** A contagious disease caused by the fungus *Candida albicans,* marked by small whitish eruptions on the mouth, throat, and tongue. **2.** An infection of the frog of a horse's foot, often resulting from unhygienic stall conditions. [Prob. of Scand. orig.]

thrust (thrŭst) *v.* **thrust, thrust•ing, thrusts.** — *tr.* **1.** To push or drive quickly and forcibly. See Syns at **push. 2.** To issue or extend. **3.** To force into a given condition or situation. **4.** To include or interpolate improperly. **5.** To force on an unwilling or improper recipient. **6.** *Archaic.* To stab; pierce. — *intr.* **1.** To shove something into or at something else; push. **2.** To pierce or stab with or as if with a pointed weapon. **3.** To force one's way. — *n.* **1.** A forceful shove or push. **2.a.** A driving force or pressure. **b.** The forward-directed force developed in a jet or rocket engine as a reaction to the rearward ejection of exhaust gases. **3.** A piercing movement made with or as if with a pointed weapon; a stab. **4.** The essence; the point. **5.** *Archit.* Outward or lateral stress in a structure. **6.** An attack or assault, esp. by an armed force. [ME *thrusten* < ON *thrȳsta.* See **treud-***.] — **thrust′er** *n.* — **thrust′ful** *adj.*

thrust stage *n.* A stage that extends into the audience's portion of a theater beyond the usual location of the proscenium and often has seats facing it on three sides.

thru•way also **through•way** (thro͞o′wā′) *n.* See **expressway.**

Thu or **Thu.** *abbr.* Thursday.

Thu•cyd•i•des (tho͞o-sĭd′ĭ-dēz′). 460?–400? B.C. Greek historian noted for his account of the Peloponnesian War.

thud (thŭd) *n.* **1.** A dull sound, as of a heavy object falling. **2.** A blow or fall causing a thud. — *intr.v.* **thud•ded, thud•ding, thuds.** To make a heavy dull sound. [Perh. < ME *thudden*, to strike with a weapon < OE *thyddan*, of imit. orig.]

thug (thŭg) *n.* **1.** A cutthroat or ruffian; a hoodlum. **2.** One of a band of professional assassins formerly active in northern India. [Hindi *ṭhag*, perh. < Skt. *sthagaḥ*, a cheat < *sthagati*,

ă pat	oi boy
ā pay	ou out
âr care	o͝o took
ä father	o͞o boot
ĕ pet	ŭ cut
ē be	ûr urge
ĭ pit	th thin
ī pie	*th* this
îr pier	hw which
ŏ pot	zh vision
ō toe	ə about,
ô paw	item

Stress marks:
′ (primary);
′ (secondary), as in
dictionary (dĭk′shə-nĕr′ē)

thunderbird
Pueblo sand painting

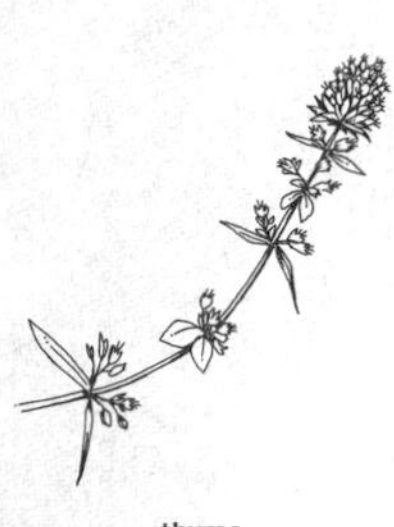
thyme

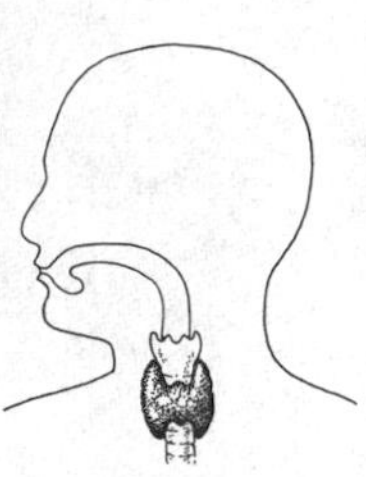
thyroid gland

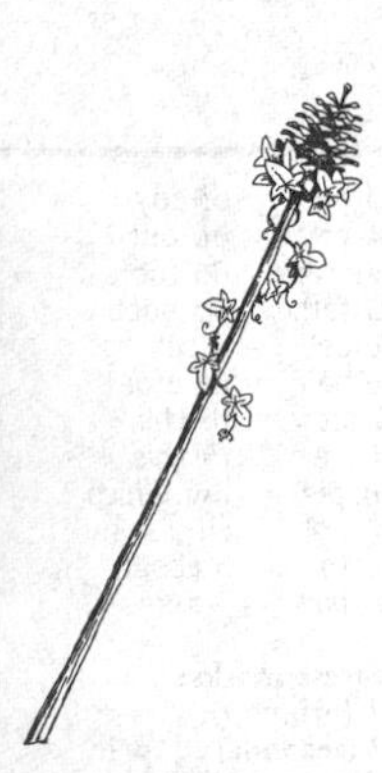
thyrsus

sthagayati, he conceals. See **(s)teg-*.**] **—thug′ger·y** *n.* **—thug′gish** *adj.*

thu·ja (thōō′jə, thyōō′-) *n.* See **arborvitae** 1. [NLat. *Thuja,* arborvitae genus < Med.Lat. *thuia,* cedar < Gk.]

Thu·le¹ (thōō′lē). The most northerly region of the habitable world to ancient Greek geographers, variously identified as Iceland, Norway, and the Shetland Is.

Thu·le² (tōō′lē). A town of NW Greenland NW of Cape York; site of a U.S. naval base during World War II. Pop. 449.

thu·li·um (thōō′lē-əm, thyōō′-) *n. Symbol* **Tm** A rare-earth element obtained commercially from monazite, having an x-ray emitting isotope that is used in small portable medical x-ray units. Atomic number 69; atomic weight 168.934; melting point 1,545°C; boiling point 1,727°C; specific gravity 9.3; valence 2, 3. See table at **element.** [After THULE¹.]

thumb (thŭm) *n.* **1.a.** The short thick digit of the human hand, next to the index finger and opposable to each of the other four digits. **b.** A corresponding digit in other animals, esp. primates. **2.** The part of a glove or mitten that covers the thumb. *—v.* **thumbed, thumb·ing, thumbs.** *—tr.* **1.** To scan (written matter) by turning over pages with or as if with the thumb. **2.** To disarrange, soil, or wear by careless or frequent handling. **3.** *Informal.* To solicit (a ride) from a vehicle by signaling with the thumb. *—intr.* **1.** To thumb written matter. **2.** *Informal.* To hitchhike. **—*idioms.* all thumbs.** Lacking physical coordination, skill, or grace; clumsy. **thumb (one's) nose.** To express scorn or ridicule by or as if by placing the thumb on the nose and wiggling the fingers. **thumbs down.** An expression of rejection, refusal, or disapproval. **thumbs up.** An expression of approval, success, or hope. **under (one's) thumb.** Under the control of or subordinate to someone. [ME < OE *thūma.* See **teuə-*.**]

thumb·hole (thŭm′hōl′) *n.* **1.** An opening made to fit a thumb, as in a bowling ball. **2.** *Mus.* The hole on a wind instrument that is opened or closed with the thumb.

thumb index *n. Print.* A series of rounded indentations in the front edge of a book, each labeled, as with a letter, to indicate a section of the book. **—thumb′-in′dex** (thŭm′ĭn′dĕks) *v.*

thumb·nail (thŭm′nāl′) *n.* The nail of the thumb. *—adj.* **1.** Of or of the size of a thumbnail. **2.** Brief; cursory.

thumb piano *n. Mus.* An African musical instrument, such as the kalimba or mbira, that has a small sound box fitted with a row of tuned tabs that are plucked with the thumbs.

thumb·print (thŭm′prĭnt′) *n.* A print made by the thumb, esp. by the pad of the thumb.

thumb·screw (thŭm′skrōō′) *n.* **1.** A screw designed so that it can be turned with the thumb and fingers. **2.** An instrument of torture formerly used to compress the thumb.

thumb·tack (thŭm′tăk′) *n.* A tack with a smooth rounded head that can be pressed into place with the thumb. *—tr.v.* **-tacked, -tack·ing, -tacks.** To affix with a thumbtack.

thump (thŭmp) *n.* **1.** A blow with a blunt object. **2.** The muffled sound produced by or as if by a thump; a thud. *—v.* **thumped, thump·ing, thumps.** *—tr.* **1.** To beat with or as if with a blunt object so as to produce a thud. **2.** *Informal.* To beat soundly or thoroughly; drub. *—intr.* **1.** To hit or fall in such a way as to produce a thump; pound. **2.** To walk with heavy steps; stump. **3.** To throb audibly. [Prob. of imit. orig.] **—thump′er** *n.*

thump·ing (thŭm′pĭng) *adj. Informal.* Outstanding.

Thun (tōōn), **Lake of.** A lake of central Switzerland SE of Bern at the foot of the Bernese Alps.

thun·der (thŭn′dər) *n.* **1.** The crashing or booming sound produced by rapidly expanding air along the path of the electrical discharge of lightning. **2.** A sound that resembles or suggests thunder. *—v.* **-dered, -der·ing, -ders.** *—intr.* **1.** To produce thunder. **2.** To produce sounds like thunder. **3.** To utter loud vociferous remarks or threats. *—tr.* To express violently, commandingly, or angrily; roar. [ME < OE *thunor.* See **(s)tenə-*.**] **—thun′der·er** *n.*

Thun·der Bay (thŭn′dər). A city of SW Ontario, Canada, on **Thunder Bay,** an inlet of Lake Superior. Pop. 112,486.

thun·der·bird (thŭn′dər-bûrd′) *n.* A spirit of thunder, lightning, and rain in the form of a huge bird in the mythology of certain Native American peoples.

thun·der·bolt (thŭn′dər-bōlt′) *n.* **1.** A discharge of lightning accompanied by thunder. **2.** A flash of lightning conceived as a bolt or dart from the heavens. **3.a.** One that acts with sudden destructive fury. **b.** A startling, forceful action.

thun·der·clap (thŭn′dər-klăp′) *n.* **1.** A single sharp crash of thunder. **2.** Something, such as a startling piece of news, that is similar to a crash of thunder in suddenness or violence.

thun·der·cloud (thŭn′dər-kloud′) *n.* **1.** A large dark cloud charged with electricity and producing thunder and lightning; a cumulonimbus cloud. **2.** Something menacing or dreadful.

thun·der·head (thŭn′dər-hĕd′) *n.* The swollen upper portion of a thundercloud, usu. associated with a thunderstorm.

thun·der·ous (thŭn′dər-əs) *adj.* **1.** Producing thunder or a similar sound. **2.** Loud and unrestrained like thunder.

thun·der·show·er (thŭn′dər-shou′ər) *n.* A brief rainstorm accompanied by thunder and lightning.

thun·der·stone (thŭn′dər-stōn′) *n.* **1.** Any of various mineral concretions, such as a belemnite, formerly supposed to be thunderbolts. **2.** *Archaic.* A flash of lightning conceived as a stone; a thunderbolt.

thun·der·storm (thŭn′dər-stôrm′) *n.* A transient, sometimes violent storm of thunder and lightning, often accompanied by rain and sometimes hail.

thun·der·struck (thŭn′dər-strŭk′) *adj.* Affected with sudden astonishment or amazement.

thunk¹ (thŭngk) *n.* A dull, hollow sound. *—intr.v.* **thunked, thunk·ing, thunks.** To make a dull, hollow sound. [Imit.]

thunk² (thŭngk) *v. Non-Standard.* A p.t. and p.part. of **think.**

Thur. *abbr.* Thursday.

Thur·ber (thûr′bər), **James Grover.** 1894–1961. Amer. writer and cartoonist known for his humorous essays and drawings.

thu·ri·ble (thŏŏr′ə-bəl) *n.* A censer used in certain ecclesiastical ceremonies or liturgies. [ME *thoríble* < OFr. *thurible* < Lat. *thūribulum* < *thūs, thūr-,* incense < Gk. *thuos* < *thuein,* to sacrifice.]

thu·ri·fer (thŏŏr′ə-fər) *n.* An acolyte who carries a thurible. [Lat. *thūrifer,* incense-bearing : *thūs, thūr-,* incense; see THURIBLE + *-fer,* -fer.]

Thu·rin·gi·a (thōō-rĭn′jē-ə, -jə). A historical region of central Germany crossed by the **Thuringian Forest.**

Thu·rin·gi·an (thōō-rĭn′jē-ən, -jən) *adj.* Of or relating to Thuringia or its people or culture. *—n.* **1.** A member of an ancient tribe inhabiting central Germany until the sixth century A.D. **2.** A native or inhabitant of Thuringia.

Thurs·day (thûrz′dē, -dā′) *n.* The fifth day of the week. [ME < OE *thūres dæg,* alteration of *thunres dæg,* Thor's day (transl. of LLat. *Iovis diēs,* Jupiter's day) : *thunres,* genitive of *thunor,* thunder; see **(s)tenə-*** + *dæg,* day; see DAY.]

Thursday Island. An island of NE Australia in Torres Strait NW of Cape York; noted for its pearl fishing beds.

Thurs·ton Island (thûr′stən). An island off Antarctica between the Bellinghausen and Amundsen seas.

thus (*th*ŭs) *adv.* **1.** In this manner: *Lay the pieces out thus.* See Usage Note at **thusly. 2.** To a stated degree or extent; so. **3.** Therefore; consequently: *Thus I had to resign.* **4.** For example: *Few large U.S. cities are state capitals; thus New York is not the seat of its state's government.* [ME < OE. See **to-*.**]

thus·ly (*th*ŭs′lē) *adv. Usage Problem.* Thus.

Usage Note: Although the word *thusly* has since gained some currency in educated usage, it is widely regarded as incorrect. In an earlier survey the use of the word was judged unacceptable by a large majority of the Usage Panel. In formal writing *thus* can still be used as in *Hold it thus;* in other styles, expressions such as *this way* and *like this* are more natural.

Thut·mo·se III (thōōt-mō′sə). d. 1450 B.C. King of Egypt (1504?–1450) who conquered Syria.

thwack (thwăk) *tr.v.* **thwacked, thwack·ing, thwacks.** To strike or hit with a flat object; whack. *—n.* A hard blow with a flat object; a whack. [Imit.]

thwart (thwôrt) *tr.v.* **thwart·ed, thwart·ing, thwarts. 1.** To prevent the occurrence, realization, or attainment of. **2.** To oppose and defeat the efforts, plans, or ambitions of. *—n. Naut.* A seat across a boat on which a rower may sit. *—adj.* **1.** Extending, lying, or passing across; transverse. **2.** Eager to oppose, esp. wrongly; perverse. *—adv. & prep. Archaic.* Athwart; across. [ME *thwerten* < *thwert,* across < ON *thvert,* neut. of *thverr,* transverse. See **terkʷ-*.**]

thy (*th*ī) *adj.* The possessive form of **thou.** Used as a modifier before a noun. [ME, var. of *thin,* thine < OE *thīn.* See **tu-*.**]

Thy·es·te·an (thī-ĕs′tē-ən, thī′ĭ-stē′ən) *adj.* Cannibalistic.

Thy·es·tes (thī-ĕs′tēz) *n. Gk. Myth.* A king of Mycenae who unknowingly ate the flesh of his own sons, served to him by his brother Atreus as revenge for seducing his wife and usurping the throne. [Gk. *Thuestēs.*]

thy·la·cine (thī′lə-sīn′) *n.* See **Tasmanian wolf.** [< NLat. *Thylacinus,* genus name < Gk. *thulakos,* sack.]

thyme (tīm) *n.* **1.** Any of several aromatic Eurasian herbs or low shrubs of the genus *Thymus,* esp. *T. vulgaris* of southern Europe. **2.** The leaves of this plant, used as a seasoning. [ME < OFr. *thym* < Lat. *thymum* < Gk. *thumon.*]

thy·mec·to·my (thī-mĕk′tə-mē) *n., pl.* **-mies.** Surgical removal of the thymus.

–thymia *suff.* State or condition of mind: *schizothymia.* [NLat. < Gk. < *thumos,* mind, soul.]

thy·mic¹ (tī′mĭk, thī′-) *adj.* Of or relating to thyme.

thy·mic² (thī′mĭk) *adj.* Of or relating to the thymus.

thy·mi·dine (thī′mĭ-dēn′) *n.* A nucleoside, $C_{10}H_{14}N_2O_5$, composed of thymine and deoxyribose, that is a constituent of DNA. [THYM(INE) + –ID(E) + –INE².]

thy·mine (thī′mēn′) *n.* A pyrimidine base, $C_5H_6N_2O_2$, that is an essential constituent of DNA. [THYM(US) + –INE².]

thy·mo·cyte (thī′mə-sīt′) *n.* A lymphocyte that derives from the thymus and is the precursor of a T cell.

thy·mol (thī′mōl′, -mōl′) *n.* A white crystalline aromatic compound, $C_{10}H_{14}O$, derived from thyme oil and other oils or synthesized and used as an antiseptic and a preservative.

thy·mo·sin (thī′mə-sĭn) *n.* A hormone secreted by the thymus that stimulates development of T cells.

thy·mus (thī′məs) *n., pl.* **-mus·es.** A small gland situated behind the breastbone, consisting mainly of lymphatic tissue and serving as the site of T cell differentiation. [NLat. < Gk. *thumos*, warty excrescerce, thymus.]

thyro– or **thyr–** *pref.* Thyroid: *thyroxine.* [< THYROID.]

thy•ro•cal•ci•to•nin (thī′rō-kăl′sĭ-tō′nĭn) *n.* See **calcitonin.**

thy•roid (thī′roid′) *n.* **1.** The thyroid gland. **2.** The thyroid cartilage. **3.** A preparation of the thyroid gland of certain animals, used to treat hypothyroid conditions. **4.** An artery, a vein, a nerve, or another part in the thyroid region. [Gk. *thureoeidēs* : *thureos*, oblong shield (< *thura*, door; see **dhwer-***) + *-oeidēs*, -oid.] **—thy•roi′dal** *adj.*

thyroid cartilage *n.* The largest cartilage of the larynx, forming the Adam's apple.

thy•roid•ec•to•my (thī′roi-dĕk′tə-mē) *n., pl.* **-mies.** Surgical removal of the thyroid gland. **—thy′roid•ec′to•mize′** *v.*

thyroid gland *n.* A two-lobed endocrine gland found in all vertebrates, located at the base of the neck and producing various hormones, such as triiodothyronine and calcitonin.

thy•roid•i•tis (thī′roi-dī′tĭs) *n.* Inflammation of the thyroid gland.

thy•roid-stim•u•lat•ing hormone (thī′roid-stĭm′yə-lā′tĭng) *n.* See **thyrotropin.**

thy•ro•tox•i•co•sis (thī′rō-tŏk′sĭ-kō′sĭs) *n.* A toxic condition resulting from excessive amounts of thyroid hormones in the body.

thy•ro•tro•pin (thī′rə-trō′pĭn, thī-rŏt′rə-) also **thy•ro•tro•phin** (-fĭn) *n.* A hormone secreted by the anterior lobe of the pituitary gland that stimulates and regulates the activity of the thyroid gland. [THYRO– + –TROP(HIC) + –IN.]

thy•ro•tro•pin-re•leas•ing hormone (thī′rə-trō′pĭn-rĭ-lē′sĭng, thī-rŏt′rə-) *n.* A hormone secreted by the hypothalamus that stimulates release of thyrotropin.

thy•rox•ine (thī-rŏk′sēn′, -sĭn) also **thy•rox•in** (-rŏk′sĭn) *n.* An iodine-containing hormone, $C_{15}H_{11}I_4NO_4$, produced by the thyroid gland, that increases the rate of cell metabolism and regulates growth and is made synthetically for treatment of thyroid disorders. [THYR(O)– + OX(Y)– + IN(DOLE).]

thyrse (thûrs) *n.* A dense paniclelike flower cluster, as of the lilac, in which the lateral branches terminate in cymes. [Lat., thyrsus. See THYRSUS.]

thyr•sus (thûr′səs) *n., pl.* **-si** (-sī). **1.** *Myth.* A staff tipped with a pine cone and twined with ivy, carried by Dionysus and Dionysian revelers. **2.** *Bot.* A thyrse. [Lat. < Gk. *thursos.*]

thy•sa•nu•ran (thī′sə-no͝or′ən, -nyo͝or′-) *n.* A wingless insect of the order Thysanura, constituting the bristletails. [< NLat. *Thysanura*, order name : Gk. *thusanos*, tassel + Gk. *-oura*, neut. pl. of *-ouros*, tailed (< *oura*, tail; see –UROUS).] **—thy′sa•nu′ran** *adj.*

thy•self (*th*ī-sĕlf′) *pron. Archaic.* Yourself. Used as the reflexive or emphatic form of *thee* or *thou.*

THz *abbr.* Terahertz.

ti[1] (tē) *n. Mus.* The seventh tone in the diatonic scale in solfeggio. [Alteration of SI.]

ti[2] (tē) *n., pl.* **tis.** An eastern Asian tropical shrub *(Cordyline terminalis)* having a terminal tuft of long narrow leaves and edible roots. [Tahitian and Maori.]

Ti The symbol for the element **titanium.**

Ti•a•hua•na•co (tē′ə-wə-nä′kō). A site of pre-Incan ruins in W Bolivia near the S end of Lake Titicaca.

Tian•an•men Square (tyän′än′mĕn′). An extensive open area in central Beijing, China, adjacent to the Forbidden City.

Tian•jin (tyän′jĭn′) also **Tien•tsin** (tyĕn′tsĭn′). A city of NE China near the Gulf of Bo Hai SE of Beijing. Pop. 5,380,000.

Tian Shan (tyän′ shän′). See **Tien Shan.**

ti•ar•a (tē-ăr′ə, -âr′ə, -är′ə) *n.* **1.** An ornamental, often jeweled crownlike semicircle worn on the head by women on formal occasions. **2.** The triple crown worn by the pope. [Lat. *tiāra*, turban, headband < Gk. *tiara.*]

Ti•ber (tī′bər). A river of central Italy flowing c. 406 km (252 mi) through Rome to the Tyrrhenian Sea.

Ti•be•ri•as (tī-bîr′ē-əs), **Lake.** See Sea of **Galilee.**

Ti•be•ri•us (tī-bîr′ē-əs). 42 B.C.–A.D. 37. Emperor of Rome (A.D. 14–37) who was chosen by Augustus as his heir. **—Ti•be′ri•an** (-ən) *adj.*

Ti•bet (tə-bĕt′). **1.** A historical region of central Asia between the Himalaya and Kunlun mountains; under Chinese control after 1720. **2.** See **Xizang.**

Ti•bet•an (tĭ-bĕt′n) *adj.* Of or relating to Tibet, the Tibetans, or their language or culture. **—** *n.* **1.a.** A native or inhabitant of Tibet. **b.** A member of a Buddhist people constituting the main ethnic population of Tibet and neighboring regions. **2.** The Tibeto-Burman language of the Tibetans.

Tibetan Buddhism *n.* A form of Buddhism with an admixture of indigenous animism that is practiced in Tibet, Mongolia, Bhutan, and neighboring areas.

Tibetan spaniel *n.* Any of a breed of small dog that originated in Tibet, having a thick silky coat and a plumed tail that curls over the back.

Tibetan terrier *n.* Any of a breed of medium-sized dog that originated in Tibet, having thick long hair over the eyes and a fluffy tail that curls over the back.

Ti•bet•o-Bur•man (tĭ-bĕt′ō-bûr′mən) *n.* A branch of the Sino-Tibetan family that includes Tibetan and Burmese.

tib•i•a (tĭb′ē-ə) *n., pl.* **-i•ae** (-ē-ē′) or **-i•as. 1.a.** The inner and larger of the two bones of the lower human leg, extending from the knee to the ankle. **b.** A corresponding bone in other vertebrates. **2.** The fourth division of an insect's leg, between the femur and the tarsi. **3.** *Mus.* An ancient flute originally made from an animal's leg bone. [Lat. *tībia*, pipe, shinbone.] **—tib′i•al** *adj.*

Ti•bur (tī′bər). See **Tivoli.**

tic (tĭk) *n.* A habitual spasmodic muscular movement or contraction, usu. of the face or extremities. **—** *intr.v.* **ticced, tic•cing, tics.** To have a tic; produce tics. [Fr.]

tic dou•lou•reux (do͞o′lə-ro͞o′) *n.* See **trigeminal neuralgia.** [Fr. : *tic*, tic + *douloureux*, painful.]

Ti•ci•no (tĭ-chē′nō). A river of S Switzerland and N Italy flowing c. 248 km (154 mi) generally S to the Po R.

tick[1] (tĭk) *n.* **1.** A light sharp clicking sound made repeatedly by a machine, such as a clock. **2.** *Chiefly British.* A moment. **3.** A light mark used to check off or call attention to an item. **4.** *Informal.* A unit on a scale; a degree. **—** *v.* **ticked, tick•ing, ticks. —** *intr.* **1.** To emit recurring clicking sounds. **2.** To function characteristically or well: *what makes people tick.* **—** *tr.* **1.** To count or record with or as if with the sound of ticks. **2.** To mark or check off (a listed item) with a tick: *ticked off each name.* **—*phrasal verb.* tick off.** *Informal.* To make angry or annoyed. [ME *tek*, light tap.]

tiara
Jeweled tiara
worn by Nancy Astor

tick[2] (tĭk) *n.* **1.** Any of numerous small bloodsucking parasitic arachnids of the family Ixodidae, many of which transmit febrile diseases, such as Lyme disease. **2.** Any of various usu. wingless louselike insects of the family Hippoboscidae that are parasitic, as on sheep. [ME *tik*, perh. < OE **ticca.*]

tick[3] (tĭk) *n.* **1.a.** A cloth case for a mattress or pillow. **b.** A light mattress without inner springs. **2.** Ticking. [ME *tikke*, prob. < MDu. *tike*, ult. < Lat. *thēca*, receptacle < Gk. *thēkē.* See **dhē-*.**]

tick[4] (tĭk) *n. Chiefly British.* Credit or an amount of credit. [Short for TICKET.]

tick-borne (tĭk′bôrn′, -bōrn′) *adj.* Carried or transmitted by ticks: *a tick-borne disease.*

tick•er (tĭk′ər) *n.* **1.a.** A telegraphic instrument that receives news reports and prints them on paper tape. **b.** Any of various devices that receive and display similar information electronically. **2.** *Slang.* A watch. **3.** *Slang.* The heart.

ticker tape *n.* The paper strip used by a telegraphic ticker.

tick•et (tĭk′ĭt) *n.* **1.** A paper slip or card indicating that its holder has paid for or is entitled to a specified service, right, or consideration. **2.** A certifying document, esp. a captain's or pilot's license. **3.** An identifying or descriptive tag attached to merchandise; a label. **4.** A list of candidates proposed or endorsed by a political party; a slate. **5.** A legal summons, esp. for a traffic violation. **6.** The proper or desirable thing. **7.** *Informal.* A means to an end. **—** *tr.v.* **-et•ed, -et•ing, -ets. 1.** To provide with a ticket for passage or admission. **2.** To attach a ticket to; tag. See Syns at **mark[1]. 3.** To designate for a specified use or end; destine. **4.** To serve (an offender) with a legal summons. [Obsolete Fr. *etiquet*, label, note < OFr. *estiquet*, notice, label < OSp. *etiqueta* < OFr. *estiquet*, post serving as a target in certain sports < *estiquier*, to stick, of Gmc. orig. See **steig-*.**]

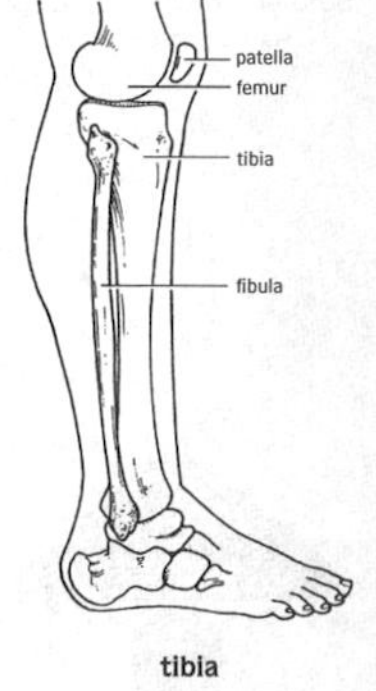

tibia

tick fever *n.* Any of various febrile diseases transmitted by ticks, such as Rocky Mountain spotted fever and Texas fever.

tick•ing (tĭk′ĭng) *n.* A strong, tightly woven fabric of cotton or linen used to make pillow and mattress coverings.

tick•le (tĭk′əl) *v.* **-led, -ling, -les. —** *tr.* **1.** To touch (the body) lightly so as to cause laughter or twitching movements. **2.a.** To tease or excite pleasurably; titillate: *suspense that tickles one's curiosity.* **b.** To fill with mirth or pleasure; delight. See Syns at **please. —** *intr.* To feel or cause a tingling sensation. **—** *n.* **1.** The act of tickling. **2.** A tickling sensation. **—*idiom.* tickle (one) pink.** *Informal.* To please; delight. [ME *tikelen*, perh. freq. of *ticken*, to touch lightly.]

tick•lish (tĭk′lĭsh) *adj.* **1.** Sensitive to tickling. **2.** Easily offended or upset; touchy. **3.** Requiring skillful or tactful handling; delicate. **—tick′lish•ly** *adv.* **—tick′lish•ness** *n.*

tick•seed (tĭk′sēd′) *n.* **1.** See **coreopsis. 2.** See **beggar ticks** 1a. [< TICK[2] (< its seed's shape).]

tick•tack also **tic-tac** (tĭk′tăk′) *n.* **1.** A steady ticking sound, as of a clock. **2.** A prankster's device for tapping on a door or window from a distance. [Imit.]

tick•tack•toe also **tick-tack-toe** (tĭk′tăk′tō′) *n. Games.* A game played by two people, each trying to make a line of three X's or three O's in a boxlike figure with nine spaces. [Prob. imit. of the sounds of the original children's game, played with a pencil and a slate.]

tick•tock (tĭk′tŏk′) *n.* A clock's ticking sound. [Imit.]

tick trefoil *n.* Any of various plants of the genus *Desmodium*, usu. having trifoliolate compound leaves and jointed seedpods. [< TICK[2] (< the way its pods adhere to animals).]

tick•y-tack•y (tĭk′ē-tăk′ē) *n.* Shoddy material, as for building standardized housing. **—** *adj.* **1.** Made of shoddy material; cheaply built. **2.a.** Marked by mediocre uniformity of look or style. **b.** Tawdry; tacky. [Redup. of TACKY[2].]

ă pat	oi boy
ā pay	ou out
âr care	o͝o took
ä father	o͞o boot
ĕ pet	ŭ cut
ē be	ûr urge
ĭ pit	th thin
ī pie	*th* this
îr pier	hw which
ŏ pot	zh vision
ō toe	ə about, item
ô paw	

Stress marks:
′ (primary);
′ (secondary), as in
dictionary (dĭk′shə-nĕr′ē)

Ti•con•der•o•ga (tī′kŏn-də-rō′gə). A village of NE NY between Lake George and Lake Champlain; orig. a French fortress.

t.i.d. *abbr. Lat.* Ter in die (three times a day).

tid•al (tīd′l) *adj.* **1.** Relating to or affected by tides. **2.** Dependent on or scheduled by the time of high tide. **—tid′al•ly** *adv.*

tidal wave *n.* **1.** An unusual rise or incursion of water along the seashore, as from a storm. **2.** A tsunami. **3.** An overwhelming manifestation; a flood.

tid•bit (tĭd′bĭt′) also **tit•bit** (tĭt′-) *n.* A choice morsel, as of gossip or food. [Perh. obsolete and dial. *tid*, tender + BIT[1].]

tid•dly•winks (tĭd′lē-wĭngks′) also **tid•dle•dy•winks** (tĭd′l-dē-) *pl.n. (used with a sing. v.) Games.* A game in which players try to snap small disks into a cup by pressing them on the edge with a larger disk. [Poss. dial. *tiddly*, little + WINK.]

tide[1] (tīd) *n.* **1.a.** The periodic variation in the surface level of the oceans and of bays, gulfs, inlets, and estuaries, caused by gravitational attraction of the moon and sun. **b.** A specific occurrence of such a variation. **c.** Flood tide. **2.** Stress exerted on a body or part of a body by gravitational attraction of another. **3.** Something that fluctuates like the waters of the tide. **4.** A time or season. Often used in combination: *eventide.* **5.** A favorable occasion; an opportunity. **—*v.* tid•ed, tid•ing, tides.** —*intr.* **1.** To rise and fall like the tide. **2.** *Naut.* To drift or ride with the tide: *tided off the reef.* —*tr.* To carry along with or as if with the tide. ***—phrasal verb.* tide over.** To support through a difficult period. [ME < OE *tīd*, division of time. See **dā-***.]

tide[2] (tīd) *intr.v.* **tid•ed, tid•ing, tides.** *Archaic.* To betide; befall. [ME *tiden* < OE *tīdan*. See **dā-***.]

tide•land (tīd′lănd′) *n.* Coastal land submerged during high tide.

tide•mark (tīd′märk′) *n.* **1.** A line or an artificial indicator marking the high-water or low-water limit of the tides. **2.** A trace or an indication of past activity.

tide•rip (tīd′rĭp′) *n.* See **rip current.**

tide•wa•ter (tīd′wô′tər, -wŏt′ər) *n.* **1.** Water that inundates land at flood tide. **2.** Water affected by the tides, esp. tidal streams. **3.** Low coastal land drained by tidal streams.

tide•way (tīd′wā′) *n.* A channel in which a tidal current runs.

tid•ing (tī′dĭng) *n.* A piece of information or news. Often used in the plural: *sad tidings.* [ME *tiding*, perh. < ON *tīdhendi*, events < *tīdhr*, occurring. See **dā-***.]

ti•dy (tī′dē) *adj.* **-di•er, -di•est. 1.** Orderly and neat in appearance or procedure. See Syns at **neat[1]**. **2.** *Informal.* Adequate; satisfactory. **3.** *Informal.* Substantial; considerable. **—*v.* -died, -dy•ing, -dies.** —*tr.* To put in order: *tidied up the house.* —*intr.* To make things tidy: *tidied up after dinner.* **—*n., pl.* -dies.** A decorative protective covering for the arms or headrest of a chair. [ME *tidi*, in season, healthy < *tide*, time. See TIDE[1].] **—ti′di•ly** *adv.* **—ti′di•ness** *n.*

ti•dy•tips (tī′dē-tĭps′) *pl.n. (used with a sing. or pl. v.)* A Californian herb *(Layia platyglossa)* with daisylike flowers.

tie (tī) *v.* **tied, ty•ing** (tī′ĭng), **ties.** —*tr.* **1.** To fasten or secure with or as if with a cord, rope, or strap. **2.** To fasten by drawing together the parts or sides and knotting with strings or laces: *tied her shoes.* **3.a.** To make by fastening ends or parts: *tie a knot.* **b.** To put a knot or bow in: *tie a scarf.* **4.** To confine or restrict as if with cord. **5.** To bring together in relationship; connect or unite. **6.a.** To equal (an opponent or an opponent's score) in a contest. **b.** To equal an opponent's score in (a contest). **7.** *Mus.* To join (notes) by a tie. —*intr.* **1.** To be fastened or attached. **2.** To achieve equal scores in a contest. —*n.* **1.** A cord, string, or other means by which something is tied. **2.** Something that connects or unites; a link: *marital ties.* **3.** A necktie. **4.** A beam or rod that joins parts and gives support. **5.** One of the beams, usu. made of wood, laid across a railroad bed to secure the rails. **6.a.** An equality of scores, votes, or performance in a contest. **b.** A contest so resulting; a draw. **7.** *Mus.* A curved line above or below two notes of the same pitch, indicating that the tone is to be sustained for their combined duration. ***—phrasal verbs.* tie in.** To bring into or have a close or effective relation; connect or coordinate. **tie into.** To attack energetically. **tie up. 1.** *Naut.* To secure or be secured to a shore or pier; dock. **2.** To impede the progress of; block. **3.** To keep occupied; engage. **4.** To place (funds) so as to make inaccessible for other uses. ***—idioms.* tie one on.** *Slang.* To become intoxicated; go on a drinking spree. **tie the knot.** *Slang.* **1.** To get married. **2.** To perform a marriage ceremony. [ME *tien* < OE *tīgan*. See **deuk-***.]

tie•back (tī′băk′) *n.* **1.** A decorative loop of fabric, cord, or metal for parting and draping a curtain to the side. **2. tiebacks.** A pair of curtains intended to be tied back.

tie beam *n.* A horizontal beam that connects roof rafters.

tie•break•er (tī′brā′kər) *n. Sports & Games.* An additional contest or period of play designed to establish a winner among tied contestants. **—tie′break′ing** *adj.*

tie-dye (tī′dī′) *tr.v.* **-dyed, -dye•ing, -dyes.** To dye (fabric) after tying parts of the fabric so that they will not absorb dye, giving the fabric a streaked or mottled look. —*n.* **1.** The process of tie-dyeing. **2.** A tie-dyed fabric or garment.

tie-in (tī′ĭn′) *n.* A thing related to or connected with another.

tie line *n.* **1.** A communications link between extensions of a private telephone system. **2.** A connection between systems, such as electrical power or communications systems.

Tien Shan (tyĕn′ shän′) also **Tian Shan** (tyän′). A mountain range of W Kirghiz, SW Kazakhstan, and NW China rising to 7,443.8 m (24,406 ft).

Tien•tsin (tyĕn′tsĭn′). See **Tianjin.**

Tie•po•lo (tē-ĕp′ə-lō′, tyĕ′pô-lô′), **Giovanni Battista.** 1696–1770. Italian painter noted for his command of perspective.

tier[1] (tîr) *n.* **1.** One of a series of rows placed one above another. **2.** A rank or class. **—*tr. & intr.v.* tiered, tier•ing, tiers.** To arrange (something) into or rise in tiers. [ME *tire*, row, rank < OFr. < *tirer*, to draw out. See TIRADE.]

ti•er[2] (tī′ər) *n.* One that ties: *a tier of knots.*

tierce (tîrs) *n.* **1.** Also **terce** (tûrs). The third of the seven canonical hours. No longer in liturgical use. **2.** A measure of liquid capacity, equal to a third of a pipe, or 42 gallons (159 liters). **3.** *Games.* A sequence of three cards of the same suit. **4.** *Sports.* The third position from which a parry or thrust can be made in fencing. **5.** *Mus.* An interval of a third. [ME < OFr. < fem. of *tiers*, third < Lat. *tertius*. See **trei-***.]

tier•cel (tîr′səl) *n.* Var. of **tercel.**

Ti•er•ra del Fue•go (tē-ĕr′ə dĕl fwā′gō, tyĕr′rä *th*ĕl fwĕ′gô). An archipelago off S South America separated from the mainland by the Strait of Magellan. The main island, also called **Tierra del Fuego,** is divided between Chile and Argentina.

tier table (tîr) *n.* A table having several shelflike tops, one above the other.

tie tack *n.* A short pin with a decorative head, used to attach a tie to a shirt front by means of a snap or chain.

Tie•tê (tyə-tā′, tyĭ-tĕ′). A river of SE Brazil flowing c. 805 km (500 mi) to the Paraná R.

tie-up (tī′ŭp′) *n.* A temporary immobilization, as of traffic.

tie vine *n. Lower Southern U.S.* The bindweed.

tiff (tĭf) *n.* **1.** A fit of irritation. **2.** A petty quarrel. **—*intr.v.* tiffed, tiff•ing, tiffs.** To quarrel. [?]

tif•fa•ny (tĭf′ə-nē) *n., pl.* **-nies.** A thin transparent gauze of silk or cotton muslin. [Prob. < obsolete Fr. *tiphanie*, Epiphany < OFr. < LLat. *theophania*. See THEOPHANY.]

Tif•fa•ny (tĭf′ə-nē), **Louis Comfort.** 1848–1933. Amer. artist who developed an opalescent colored glass.

Tiffany glass *n.* Stained or iridescent glass of a kind popular in the early 1900's for vases and lampshades.

tif•fin (tĭf′ĭn) *n. Chiefly British.* A meal at midday; a luncheon. [Short for *tiffing*, gerund of *tiff*, to sip.]

Tif•fin (tĭf′ĭn). A city of N-central OH SSW of Toledo. Pop. 18,604.

Tif•lis (tĭf′lĭs, tyə-flēs′). See **Tbilisi.**

ti•ger (tī′gər) *n.* **1.a.** A large carnivorous feline mammal *(Panthera tigris)* of Asia having a tawny coat with transverse black stripes. **b.** Any of various similar wild felines, such as the jaguar, mountain lion, or lynx. **2.** A person regarded as aggressive, audacious, or fierce. [ME *tigre* < OE *tigras*, tigers, and < OFr. *tigre*, both < Lat. *tigris* < Gk., of Iran. orig. See **steig-***.] **—ti′ger•ish** *adj.*

tiger beetle *n.* Any of numerous brightly colored predatory beetles of the family Cicindelidae, chiefly of warm sandy regions, having larvae that live in vertical burrows.

tiger cat *n.* **1.** Any of various small wild felines, such as the ocelot, margay, or jaguarundi, that resemble the tiger in appearance or behavior. **2.** A domestic cat, esp. a tabby, having markings like those of a tiger.

ti•ger-eye (tī′gər-ī′) also **ti•ger's-eye** (tī′gərz-) *n.* A yellow-brown semiprecious chatoyant gemstone consisting of quartz with parallel veins of silicified altered crocidolite.

tiger lily *n.* An eastern Asian perennial *(Lilium lancifolium)* having large black-spotted reddish-orange flowers.

tiger moth *n.* Any of numerous often brightly colored moths of the family Arctiidae, having spotted or striped wings.

tiger salamander *n.* A large terrestrial salamander *(Ambystoma tigrinum)* found in most parts of North America and having distinctive light olive bars or spots.

tiger shark *n.* A large voracious shark *(Galeocerdo cuvieri)* of tropical waters, grayish brown in color with vertical bars.

tiger swallowtail *n.* A large swallowtail butterfly *(Papilio glaucus)* of eastern North America, mostly yellow with narrow black bands across the wings.

tight (tīt) *adj.* **tight•er, tight•est. 1.** Fixed or fastened firmly in place. **2.** Stretched or drawn out fully. **3.** Of such close construction as to be impermeable. **4.a.** Leaving little empty space through compression; compact: *a tight weave.* **b.** Affording little spare time; full. **5.** Closely reasoned or concise: *a tight argument.* **6.** Fitting close or too close to the skin; snug. **7.** *Slang.* Personally close; intimate. **8.** Constricted. **9.** Reluctant to spend or give; stingy. **10.a.** Obtainable with difficulty or only at a high price. **b.** Affected by scarcity: *a tight market.* **11.** Difficult to deal with or get out of: *a tight spot.* **12.** Barely profitable: *a tight bargain.* **13.** Closely contested; close. **14.** *Chiefly British.* Neat and trim in appearance or arrangement. **15.** Marked by full control over elements or

tide[1]
Top: High tide in the Bay of Fundy
Bottom: Low tide from the same perspective

Tiffany glass

subordinates; firm: *tight management.* **16.** *Slang.* Intoxicated; drunk. **17.** *Baseball.* Inside. — *adv.* **tighter, tightest. 1.** Firmly; securely. **2.** Soundly: *sleep tight.* **3.** Snugly or with constriction: *shoes laced too tight.* [ME, dense, of Scand. orig.] — **tight′ly** *adv.* — **tight′ness** *n.*

Syns: *tight, taut, tense.* The central meaning shared by these adjectives is "not slack or loose but pulled or drawn out fully": *a tight skirt; taut sails; tense piano strings.*

tight•en (tīt′n) *tr. & intr.v.* **-ened, -en•ing, -ens.** To make or become tight or tighter. — **tight′en•er** *n.*

tight end *n. Football.* An offensive end who lines up close to a tackle.

tight•fist•ed (tīt′fĭs′tĭd) *adj.* Close-fisted; stingy. — **tight′fist′ed•ness** *n.*

tight•lipped also **tight-lipped** (tīt′lĭpt′) *adj.* **1.** Having the lips pressed together. **2.** Loath to speak; close-mouthed. — **tight′lipped′ness** *n.*

tight•rope (tīt′rōp′) *n.* **1.** A tightly stretched rope or wire on which acrobats perform high above the ground. **2.** An extremely precarious course or situation.

tights (tīts) *pl.n.* **1.** A snug stretchable garment for the lower body and the legs, generally worn by women and girls. **2.** A similar, often full-length garment designed for athletic use, worn esp. by acrobats and dancers.

tight•wad (tīt′wŏd′) *n. Slang.* A miser.

Tig•lath•pi•le•ser III (tĭg′lăth-pə-lē′zər, -pī-). d. 727 B.C. King of Assyria (745–727).

tig•lic acid (tĭg′lĭk) *n.* A syrupy poisonous liquid, $C_5H_8O_2$, derived from croton oil and used in making perfumes and flavoring agents. [< NLat. *tiglium*, specific epithet of *Croton tiglium*, perh. < Gk. *tilos*, liquid feces (< the use of croton oil as a purgative).]

ti•glon (tī′glən) also **ti•gon** (gən) *n.* The hybrid offspring of a male tiger and a female lion. [TIG(ER) + L(I)ON.]

Ti•gré (tē-grā′) *n.* A Semitic language of northern Ethiopia.

ti•gress (tī′grĭs) *n.* **1.** A female tiger. **2.** A woman regarded as daring or fierce.

Ti•gri•nya (tə-grēn′yə) *n.* A Semitic language of Ethiopia.

Ti•gris (tī′grĭs). A river rising in E Turkey and flowing c. 1,850 km (1,150 mi) through Iraq to the Euphrates R.

Ti•jua•na (tē′ə-wä′nə, tē-hwä′nä). A city of extreme NW Mexico on the U.S. border S of San Diego. Pop. 429,500.

Ti•kal (tē-käl′). A ruined Mayan city of N Guatemala; the largest and possibly the oldest of the Mayan cities.

tike (tīk) *n.* Var. of **tyke.**

ti•ki (tē′kē) *n., pl.* **-kis. 1. Tiki.** *Myth.* A male figure in Polynesian myth, sometimes identified as the first man. **2.** A wooden or stone image of a Polynesian god. **3.** A Maori figurine representing an ancestor. [Maori.]

til¹ (tĭl) *n.* See **sesame.** [Hindi < Skt. *tilaḥ.*]

til² (tĭl) *prep.* Until. — *conj.* Until. See Usage Note at **till².**

ti•la•pi•a (tə-lä′pē-ə, -lā′-) *n.* Any of various African cichlid food fishes of the genus *Tilapia.* [NLat. *Tilapia*, genus name.]

Til•burg (tĭl′bûrg′, -bœrкн′). A city of S Netherlands near the Belgian border SE of Rotterdam. Pop. 154,094.

til•bur•y (tĭl′bĕr′ē, -bə-rē) *n., pl.* **-ies.** A light two-wheeled open carriage with two seats, used in the 19th century. [After *Tilbury*, a 19th-cent. London coach builder.]

til•de (tĭl′də) *n.* A diacritical mark (˜) placed over the letter *n* in Spanish to indicate the palatal nasal sound (ny), as in *cañon*, or over a vowel in Portuguese to indicate nasalization, as in *lã, pão.* [Sp., alteration of obsolete Catalan *title* < Lat. *titulus*, superscription.]

Til•den (tĭl′dən), **Samuel Jones.** 1814–86. Amer. politician who ran unsuccessfully for President in 1876.

tile (tīl) *n.* **1.** A thin flat or convex slab of hard material, such as baked clay or plastic, laid in rows to cover walls, floors, and roofs. **2.** A short length of pipe made of clay or concrete, used in sewers and drains. **3.** A hollow fired clay or concrete block used for building walls. **4.** Tiles considered as a group. **5.** *Games.* A marked playing piece, as in mahjong. — *tr.v.* **tiled, til•ing, tiles.** To cover or provide with tiles. [ME < OE *tigele* < Lat. *tēgula* < *tegere*, to cover. See **(s)teg-*.**]

tile•fish (tīl′fĭsh′) *n., pl.* **tilefish** or **-fish•es.** A reddish-blue percoid marine food fish *(Lopholatilus chamaeleonticeps)* of deep Atlantic waters having a fleshy flap on the nape and small yellow spots on the upper sides and fins. [*Tile-* (short for NLat. *Lopholatilus*, genus name : Gk. *lophos*, crest, fin + *-latilus*, Latinized dim. of Gk. *latos*, a kind of perch) + FISH.]

til•er (tī′lər) *n.* **1.** One who lays tiles. **2.** The doorkeeper of a Masonic or other fraternal society's lodge.

til•ing (tī′lĭng) *n.* **1.** Tile laying. **2.** Tiles. **3.** A tiled surface.

till¹ (tĭl) *tr.v.* **tilled, till•ing, tills.** To prepare (land) for the raising of crops, as by plowing and harrowing; cultivate. [ME *tilen* < OE *tilian.*] — **till′a•ble** *adj.*

till² (tĭl) *prep.* Until. — *conj.* Until. [ME < OE *til* < ON.]

Usage Note: *Till* and *until* are generally interchangeable in both writing and speech, though as the first word in a sentence *until* is usually preferred. In the 18th century the spelling *'till* became fashionable, as if *till* were a shortened form of *until.* Although *'till* is now nonstandard, *'til* is sometimes used in this way and is considered acceptable.

till³ (tĭl) *n.* **1.** A drawer, small chest, or compartment for money, as in a store. **2.** A supply of money; a purse. [ME *tille.*]

till⁴ (tĭl) *n.* Glacial drift made up of an unconsolidated mixture of clay, sand, pebbles, cobbles, and boulders. [?]

till•age (tĭl′ĭj) *n.* **1.** Cultivation of land. **2.** Tilled land.

til•land•si•a (tĭ-lănd′zē-ə) *n.* Any of various usu. epiphytic bromeliad plants of the genus *Tillandsia*, such as Spanish moss, of tropical and subtropical America. [NLat. *Tillandsia*, after Elias *Tillands* (1640–93), Finno-Swedish botanist.]

till•er¹ (tĭl′ər) *n.* One that tills land: *a tiller of soil.*

til•ler² (tĭl′ər) *n. Naut.* A lever used to turn a rudder and steer a boat. [ME *tiler*, stock of a crossbow < OFr. *telier* < Med. Lat. *tēlārium*, weaver's beam < Lat. *tēla.* See **teks-*.**]

til•ler³ (tĭl′ər) *n.* A shoot, esp. from the base of a grass. — *intr.v.* **-lered, -ler•ing, -lers.** To send forth shoots from the base. Used of a grass. [ME **tiller* < OE *telgor.*]

Til•lich (tĭl′ĭk, -ĭкн), **Paul Johannes.** 1886–1965. German-born Amer. theologian and philosopher.

Til•ly (tĭl′ē), Count of. Johann Tserclaas. 1559–1632. Flemish field marshal during the Thirty Years' War.

tilt¹ (tĭlt) *v.* **tilt•ed, tilt•ing, tilts.** — *tr.* **1.** To cause to slope, as by raising one end; incline. **2.a.** To aim or thrust (a lance) in a joust. **b.** To charge (an opponent); attack. **3.** To forge with a tilt hammer. — *intr.* **1.** To slope; incline. See Syns at **slant. 2.** To favor one side over another in a dispute; lean. **3.a.** To fight with lances; joust. **b.** To engage in a combat or struggle; fight. — *n.* **1.** The act of tilting or the condition of being tilted. **2.a.** An inclination from the horizontal or vertical; a slant. **b.** A sloping surface, as of the ground. **3.a.** A tendency to favor one side in a dispute. **b.** An implicit preference; a bias. **4.a.** A medieval sport in which two mounted knights with lances charged together and attempted to unhorse one another. **b.** A thrust or blow with a lance. **5.** A combat, esp. a verbal one; a debate. **6.** A tilt hammer. **7.** *New England.* See **seesaw** 1. See Regional Note at **teeter-totter.** — ***idiom.* at full tilt.** *Informal.* At full speed. [ME *tilten*, to cause to fall, perh. of Scand. orig.] — **tilt′er** *n.*

tilt² (tĭlt) *n.* A canopy or an awning for a boat, wagon, or cart. — *tr.v.* **tilt•ed, tilt•ing, tilts.** To cover (a vehicle) with a tilt. [ME *telte*, tent < OE *teld.*]

tilth (tĭlth) *n.* **1.** Cultivation of land; tillage. **2.** Tilled earth. [ME < OE < *tilian*, to labor.]

tilt hammer *n.* A heavy forge hammer having a pivoted lever by which it is tilted up and then allowed to drop.

tilt•ing board (tĭl′tĭng) *n. New England.* See **seesaw** 1. See Regional Note at **teeter-totter.**

tilt•yard (tĭlt′yärd′) *n.* An enclosed yard for tilting contests.

Tim. *abbr. Bible.* Timothy.

tim•bal also **tym•bal** (tĭm′bəl) *n.* A kettledrum. [Fr. *timbale* < OFr., alteration of *tamballe*, alteration of OSp. *atabal*, small drum < Ar. *aṭ-ṭabl*, the drum.]

tim•bale (tĭm′bəl, tĭm-bäl′, tăm-) *n.* **1.** A custardlike dish of cheese, chicken, fish, or vegetables baked in a drum-shaped pastry mold. **2.** The pastry mold in which this food is baked. [Fr., timbal, mold. See TIMBAL.]

tim•ber (tĭm′bər) *n.* **1.a.** Trees or wooded land considered as a source of wood. **b.** Wood used as a building material; lumber. **2.a.** A dressed piece of wood, esp. a beam in a structure. **b.** *Naut.* A rib in a ship's frame. **3.** A person considered to have qualities suited for a particular activity. — *tr.v.* **-bered, -ber•ing, -bers.** To support or frame with timbers. [ME < OE, building, trees for building. See **dem-*.**]

tim•bered (tĭm′bərd) *adj.* **1.** Covered with trees; wooded. **2.** Made of or framed by timbers, esp. exposed timbers.

tim•ber•head (tĭm′bər-hĕd′) *n. Naut.* An upper end of a timber that projects above a deck and is used as a bollard.

timber hitch *n.* A knot used for fastening a rope around a spar or log to be hoisted or towed.

tim•ber•ing (tĭm′bər-ĭng) *n.* Timber or objects made of it.

tim•ber•land (tĭm′bər-lănd′) *n.* Forested land, esp. land containing timber of commercial value.

tim•ber•line (tĭm′bər-līn′) *n.* **1.** The elevation in a mountainous region above which trees do not grow. **2.** The northern or southern latitude beyond which trees do not grow.

timber rattlesnake *n.* A venomous snake *(Crotalus horridus* subsp. *horridus)* of the United States having a yellowish-brown color and wide transverse bands on the back.

timber right *n.* A claim to the trees on property belonging to another. Often used in the plural.

timber wolf *n.* See **gray wolf.**

tim•ber•work (tĭm′bər-wûrk′) *n.* A structure made with timbers, as the framework of a boat or house.

tim•bre (tăm′bər, tĭm′-) *n.* **1.** The quality of a sound that distinguishes it from other sounds of the same pitch and volume. **2.** *Mus.* The distinctive tone of an instrument or a singing voice. [Fr. < OFr., drum, clapperless bell, prob. < Med. Gk. **timbanon*, drum < Gk. *tumpanon*, kettledrum.]

tim•brel (tĭm′brəl) *n. Mus.* An ancient tambourinelike instrument. [Dim. of ME *timbre*, drum < OFr. See TIMBRE.]

Tim•buk•tu (tĭm′bŭk-to͞o′, tĭm-bŭk′to͞o). A city of central Mali near the Niger R. NE of Bamako; founded in the 11th cent. Pop. 19,166.

tightrope
Philippe Petit at the Jerusalem Festival in 1987

tile
Top: Roofing tiles arranged in the mission pattern
Bottom: 18th-century Spanish tile representing Asia

ă pat	oi boy
ā pay	ou out
âr care	o͝o took
ä father	o͞o boot
ĕ pet	ŭ cut
ē be	ûr urge
ĭ pit	th thin
ī pie	*th* this
îr pier	hw which
ŏ pot	zh vision
ō toe	ə about, item
ô paw	

Stress marks:
′ (primary);
′ (secondary), as in **dictionary** (dĭk′shə-nĕr′ē)

time (tīm) *n.* **1.a.** A nonspatial continuum in which events occur in apparently irreversible succession from the past through the present to the future. **b.** An interval separating two points on this continuum; a duration: *passed the time reading.* **c.** A number, as of years, days, or minutes, representing such an interval. **d.** A similar number representing a specific point on this continuum, reckoned in hours and minutes: *The time is 6:17* A.M. **e.** A system by which such intervals are measured or such numbers are reckoned: *solar time.* **2.a.** An interval, esp. a span of years, marked by similar events, conditions, or phenomena; an era. Often used in the plural: *hard times.* **b. times.** The present with respect to prevailing conditions and trends: *change with the times.* **3.** A suitable or opportune moment or season. **4.a.** Periods or a period designated for a given activity: *time for bed.* **b.** Periods or a period necessary or available for a given activity. **c.** A period at one's disposal. **5.** An appointed or fated moment, esp. of death or giving birth. **6.a.** One of several instances. **b. times.** Used to indicate the number of instances by which something is multiplied or divided: *many times smaller.* **7.a.** One's lifetime. **b.** One's period of greatest activity or engagement. **c.** A person's experience during a specific period or on a certain occasion: *had a good time.* **8.a.** A period of military service. **b.** A period of apprenticeship. **c.** *Informal.* A prison sentence. **9.a.** The customary period of work: *full time.* **b.** The period spent working. **c.** The hourly pay rate. **10.** The period during which a radio or television program or commercial is broadcast. **11.** The rate of speed of a measured activity: *double time.* **12.** *Mus.* **a.** The characteristic beat of musical rhythm: *three-quarter time.* **b.** The rate of speed at which a piece of music is played; the tempo. **13.** *Chiefly British.* The hour at which a pub closes. **14.** *Sports.* A time-out. —*adj.* **1.** Of, relating to, or measuring time. **2.** Constructed so as to operate at a particular moment: *a time release.* **3.** Payable on a future date or dates. **4.** Of or relating to installment buying: *time payments.* —*tr.v.* **timed, tim•ing, times. 1.** To set the time for (an event or occasion). **2.** To adjust to keep accurate time. **3.** To adjust so that a force is applied or an action occurs at the desired time. **4.** To record the speed or duration of. **5.** To set or maintain the tempo, speed, or duration of. —***idioms.*** **against time.** With a quickly approaching time limit. **at one time. 1.** Simultaneously. **2.** At a period or moment in the past. **at the same time.** However; nonetheless. **at times.** On occasion; sometimes. **behind the times.** Out-of-date; old-fashioned. **for the time being.** Temporarily. **from time to time.** Once in a while; at intervals. **high time.** Long overdue. **in good time. 1.** In a reasonable length of time. **2.** When or before due. **3.** Quickly. **in no time.** Almost instantly; immediately. **in time. 1.** Before a time limit expires. **2.** Within an indefinite time; eventually. **3.** *Mus.* In the proper tempo. **on time. 1.** According to schedule; punctual or punctually. **2.** By paying in installments. **time after time.** Again and again; repeatedly. **time and again.** Again and again; repeatedly. **time of (one's) life.** A highly pleasurable experience. **time on (one's) hands.** An interval with nothing to do. **time was.** There was once a time. [ME < OE *tīma.* See **dā-*.**]

time and a half *n.* A rate of pay that is one and a half times the regular rate, as for overtime work.

time and motion study *n.* An analysis of the efficiency with which an industrial operation is performed.

time bill *n.* A bill of exchange payable at an indicated future time.

time bomb *n.* **1.** A bomb with a detonating mechanism that can be set for a particular time. **2.** Something that threatens to have an abruptly disastrous outcome in the future.

time capsule *n.* A sealed container preserving contemporary articles and records for future scientists and scholars.

time•card (tīm′kärd′) *n.* A card, either filled out by an employee or stamped by a time clock, recording the employee's starting and quitting times or work hours each workday.

time clock *n.* A clock that records the starting and quitting times of employees, usu. by punching timecards.

time deposit *n.* A bank deposit that cannot be withdrawn before a date specified at the time of deposit.

time dilatation *n.* The relativistic slowing of a clock that moves with respect to a stationary observer.

time dilation *n.* See **time dilatation.**

timed-re•lease (tīmd′rĭ-lēs′) or **time-re•lease** (tīm′-) *adj.* Releasing ingredients gradually to produce a sustained effect.

time exposure *n.* **1.** A photographic exposure made by leaving the shutter open a relatively long time, generally a second or more. **2.** An image so made.

time frame *n.* A period in which something occurs or is to occur.

time-hon•ored (tīm′ŏn′ərd) *adj.* Respected or adhered to because of age or age-old observance.

time immemorial *n., pl.* **times immemorial. 1.** Time long past, beyond memory or record. **2.** *Law.* Time antedating legal records.

time•keep•er (tīm′kē′pər) *n.* **1.** One who records time, as: **a.** *Sports.* One who keeps track of elapsed time in a sporting event. **b.** One who keeps records of the hours worked by employees. **2.** A device for keeping time; a timepiece. —**time′keep′ing** *adj.*

time-lapse (tīm′lăps′) *adj.* Of, using, or being a technique that photographs a naturally slow process, such as plant growth, on movie film at intervals, so that continuous projection of the frames gives an accelerated view of the process.

time•less (tīm′lĭs) *adj.* **1.** Independent of time; eternal. **2.** Unaffected by time; ageless. **3.** *Archaic.* Untimely or premature. —**time′less•ly** *adv.* —**time′less•ness** *n.*

time loan *n.* A loan to be paid within or by a specified time.

time lock *n.* A lock, as for a bank vault, containing a mechanism that prevents its being opened before a fixed time.

time•ly (tīm′lē) *adj.* **-li•er, -li•est. 1.** Occurring at a suitable or opportune time; well-timed. **2.** *Archaic.* Coming too early; premature. —*adv.* **1.** In time; opportunely. **2.** *Archaic.* Early; soon. —**time′li•ness** *n.*

time machine *n.* A fictional or hypothetical device by means of which one may travel into the future and the past.

time note *n.* An instrument, such as a promissory note, that specifies dates or a date of payment.

time•ous (tī′məs) *adj.* Timely. —**time′ous•ly** *adv.*

time-out also **time out** (tīm′out′) *n.* **1.** *Sports.* A brief cessation of play at the request of a team or an official for rest, consultation, or substitution. **2.** A short break.

time out of mind *n., pl.* **times out of mind.** See **time immemorial** 1.

time•piece (tīm′pēs′) *n.* An instrument, such as a clock or watch, that measures, registers, or records time.

tim•er (tī′mər) *n.* **1.** One who keeps track of time; a timekeeper. **2.** A timepiece, esp. one used for measuring and signaling the end of time intervals, as on a stove. **3.** A switch or regulator that controls or activates and deactivates another mechanism at set times. **4.** A device that times the sparks igniting the fuel in an internal-combustion engine.

time-re•lease (tīm′rĭ-lēs′) *adj.* Var. of **timed-release.**

time reversal *n. Math.* An operation representing a transformation from a given physical system undergoing a given sequence of events to a system in which the exact reverse sequence of events takes place.

times (tīmz) *prep. Math.* Multiplied by: *Five times two is ten.*

time•sav•ing (tīm′sā′vĭng) *adj.* Serving to save time through an efficient method or a shorter route. —**time′sav′er** *n.*

time•serv•er also **time-serv•er** (tīm′sûr′vər) *n.* One who conforms to the prevailing ways and opinions of one's time or condition for personal advantage; an opportunist. —**time′-serv′ing** *adj. & n.*

time-share (tīm′shâr′) *v.* **-shared, -shar•ing, -shares.** —*tr.* **1.** *Comp. Sci.* To use (a computer) by time-sharing. **2.** To occupy (a vacation property) by time-sharing. —*intr.* To engage in time-sharing. —*n.* A property jointly owned or leased by time-sharing. —**time′-shar′er** *n.*

time-shar•ing (tīm′shâr′ĭng) *n.* **1.** *Comp. Sci.* A technique permitting many users simultaneous access to a central computer through remote terminals. **2.** Also **time-share** (-shâr′). Joint ownership or lease of vacation property by several people who take turns occupying the premises for fixed periods.

time sheet *n.* A sheet that records the number of hours worked by employees during a pay period.

time signature *n. Mus.* A sign placed on a staff to indicate the meter, commonly a numerical fraction of which the numerator is the number of beats per measure and the denominator represents the kind of note getting one beat.

times sign *n. Math.* The symbol × for multiplication.

Times Square (tīmz). An intersection in New York City at the juncture of Broadway, Seventh Avenue, and 42nd Street.

time study *n.* See **time and motion study.**

time•ta•ble (tīm′tā′bəl) *n.* A schedule listing the times at which certain events are expected to take place.

time-test•ed (tīm′tĕs′tĭd) *adj.* Proved effective over time.

time warp *n.* A hypothetical discontinuity or distortion occurring in the flow of time that would move events from one time period to another or suspend the passage of time.

time•work (tīm′wûrk′) *n.* Work paid for at a rate per unit of time, as by the hour. —**time′work′er** *n.*

time•worn (tīm′wôrn′, -wōrn′) *adj.* **1.** Showing the effects of long use or wear: *timeworn lanes.* **2.** Used too often; trite.

time zone *n.* Any of the 24 longitudinal divisions of Earth's surface in which a standard time is kept, each being about 15° of longitude in width and observing a clock time one hour earlier than the zone immediately to the east.

tim•id (tĭm′ĭd) *adj.* **-er, -est. 1.** Lacking self-confidence; shy. **2.** Fearful and hesitant. [Lat. *timidus* < *timēre,* to fear.] —**ti•mid′i•ty, tim′id•ness** *n.* —**tim′id•ly** *adv.*

tim•ing (tī′mĭng) *n.* The art or operation of regulating occurrence, pace, or coordination to achieve the most desirable effects, as in music, the theater, athletics, or mechanics.

timing chain *n.* The chain that drives the camshaft in an internal combustion engine.

Ti•mi•şoa•ra (tē′mē-shwär′ə). A city of W Romania near the Yugoslavian border WNW of Bucharest. Pop. 303,499.

Tim•mins (tĭm′ĭnz). A city of central Ontario, Canada, NE of Sault Sainte Marie. Pop. 46,114.

ti•moc•ra•cy (tī-mŏk′rə-sē) *n.*, *pl.* **-cies. 1.** A state described by Plato as being governed on principles of honor and military glory. **2.** An Aristotelian state in which civic honor or political power is proportional to the property one owns. [Ult. < Gk. *timokratia* : *timē*, honor, value + *-kratia*, -cracy.] **—ti′mo•crat′ic** (tī′mə-krăt′ĭk) *adj.*

Ti•mor (tē′môr, tē-môr′). An island of SE Indonesia in the E Lesser Sundas. The W half of the island, formerly Netherlands Timor, became part of Indonesia in 1949; the E half was an overseas province of Portugal from 1914 until 1975.

tim•or•ous (tĭm′ər-əs) *adj.* Full of apprehensiveness; timid. [ME < OFr. *timoureus* < Med.Lat. *timōrōsus* < Lat. *timor*, *timōr-*, fear < *timēre*, to fear.] **—tim′or•ous•ly** *adv.* **—tim′or•ous•ness** *n.*

Timor Sea. An arm of the Indian Ocean between Timor and Australia.

tim•o•thy (tĭm′ə-thē) *n.*, *pl.* **-thies.** Any of several grasses of the genus *Phleum*, esp. *P. pratense* of Eurasia and *P. alpinum* of North America, widely cultivated for hay. [Prob. after *Timothy* Hanson, an 18th-cent. Amer. farmer.]

Tim•o•thy (tĭm′ə-thē) *n.* See table at **Bible.**

Timothy, Saint. 1st cent. A.D. Christian leader and companion of St. Paul. Two epistles of the Bible are addressed to him.

tim•pa•ni also **tym•pa•ni** (tĭm′pə-nē) *pl.n. Mus.* A set of kettledrums. [Ital., pl. of *timpano*, kettledrum < Lat. *tympanum*, drum. See TYMPANUM.]

tim•pa•nist also **tym•pa•nist** (tim′pə-nĭst) *n. Mus.* One who plays the kettledrums and other percussion instruments in an orchestra.

tim•pa•num (tĭm′pə-nəm) *n.* Var. of **tympanum.**

Tim•u•cu•a (tĭm′ə-ko͞o′ə) *n.*, *pl.* **Timucua** or **-cu•as. 1.** A member of an extinct Native American people formerly inhabiting Florida. **2.** The extinct language of the Timucua.

tin (tĭn) *n.* **1.** *Symbol* **Sn** A malleable metallic element obtained chiefly from cassiterite and used to coat other metals to prevent corrosion and in numerous alloys, such as soft solder, pewter, type metal, and bronze. Atomic number 50; atomic weight 118.69; melting point 231.89°C; boiling point 2,270°C; specific gravity 7.31; valence 2, 4. See table at **element. 2.** Tin plate. **3.** A container or box made of tin plate. **4.** *Chiefly British.* **a.** A container for preserved foodstuffs; a can. **b.** Its contents. *—tr.v.* **tinned, tin•ning, tins. 1.** To plate or coat with tin. **2.** *Chiefly British.* To preserve or pack in tins; can. *—adj.* **1.** Of or made of tin. **2.a.** Constructed of inferior material. **b.** Spurious. [ME < OE.]

tin•a•mou (tĭn′ə-mo͞o′) *n.* Any of various chickenlike or quaillike birds of the family Tinamidae of Central and South America. [Fr., perh. of Galibi orig.]

Tin•ber•gen (tĭn′bər-gən, -bĕr′KHən), **Jan.** b. 1903. Dutch economist who shared a 1969 Nobel Prize. His brother **Nikolaas** (b. 1907), a Dutch-born British ethologist, shared a 1973 Nobel Prize.

tin•cal (tĭng′kəl) *n.* Crude borax. [Malay *tingkal.*]

tin can *n.* **1.** A container of tin-coated sheet metal used esp. for preserving food. **2.** *Informal.* A naval destroyer.

tinct (tĭngkt) *n.* A color or tint. *—adj.* Colored lightly or faintly; tinged. [ME, a transforming elixir < Lat. *tīnctus*, a dyeing < p.part. of *tingere*, to dye.]

tinct. *abbr.* Tincture.

tinc•to•ri•al (tĭngk-tôr′ē-əl, -tōr′-) *adj.* Relating to the processes of dyeing or coloring. [< Lat. *tīnctōrius* < *tīnctus*, p.part. of *tingere*, to dye.] **—tinc•to′ri•al•ly** *adv.*

tinc•ture (tĭngk′chər) *n.* **1.** A coloring or dyeing substance; a pigment. **2.** An imparted color; a tint. **3.** A quality that colors, pervades, or distinguishes. **4.** A trace or vestige. **5.** An alcohol solution of a nonvolatile medicine: *tincture of iodine.* **6.** *Her.* A metal, color, or fur. *—tr.v.* **-tured, -tur•ing, -tures. 1.** To stain or tint with a color. **2.** To infuse, as with a quality; impregnate. [ME < Lat. *tīnctūra*, a dyeing < *tīnctus*, p.part. of *tingere*, to dye.]

Tin•dal or **Tin•dale** (tĭn′dl), **William.** See William **Tyndale.**

tin•der (tĭn′dər) *n.* Readily combustible material, such as dry twigs, used to kindle fires. [ME < OE *tynder.*]

tin•der•box (tĭn′dər-bŏks′) *n.* **1.** A metal box for holding tinder. **2.** A potentially explosive place or situation.

tine (tīn) *n.* **1.** A branch of a deer's antlers. **2.** A prong on an implement such as a fork or pitchfork. [ME < OE *tind.*] **—tined** (tīnd) *adj.*

tin•e•a (tĭn′ē-ə) *n.* Any of several infections of the skin, such as ringworm, caused by fungi. [ME < Med.Lat. < Lat., a gnawing worm.] **—tin′e•al** *adj.*

tinea cru•ris (kro͝or′ĭs) *n.* A fungal infection of the skin of the groin, occurring esp. in males. [NLat. : Med.Lat. *tinea*, tinea + Lat. *crūris*, genitive of *crūs*, leg.]

tin ear *n. Informal.* An insensitivity to music or to sounds of a given kind: *a writer with a tin ear for dialogue.*

tin•foil also **tin foil** (tĭn′foil′) *n.* A thin pliable sheet of aluminum or tin-lead alloy, used as a protective wrapping.

ting (tĭng) *n.* A single light metallic sound, as of a small bell. *—intr.v.* **tinged** (tĭngd), **ting•ing, tings.** To give forth a light metallic sound. [< ME *tingen*, to cause to ring, of imit. orig.]

tinge (tĭnj) *tr.v.* **tinged** (tĭnjd), **tinge•ing** or **ting•ing** (tĭn′jĭng), **ting•es. 1.** To apply a trace of color to; tint. **2.** To affect slightly, as with a contrasting quality. *—n.* **1.** A small amount of a color incorporated or added. **2.** A slight added element, property, or influence. [ME *tingen* < Lat. *tingere.*]

tin•gle (tĭng′gəl) *v.* **-gled, -gling, -gles.** *—intr.* **1.** To have a prickly stinging sensation, as from cold. **2.** To cause a prickly stinging sensation or feeling. *—tr.* To cause to tingle. *—n.* A prickly stinging sensation. [ME *tinglen*, alteration of *tinklen.* See TINKLE.] **—tin′gler** *n.* **—tin′gly** *adj.*

tin•horn (tĭn′hôrn′) *n. Slang.* A petty braggart pretending to be rich and important. [< the horn-shaped metal can used in chuck-a-luck for shaking the dice.] **—tin′horn′** *adj.*

Ti•ni•an (tĭn′ē-ăn′, tē′nē-än′). An island of the W Pacific in the S Mariana Is.; departure point for the planes that dropped atomic bombs on Hiroshima and Nagasaki (1945).

tin•ker (tĭng′kər) *n.* **1.** A traveling mender of metal household utensils. **2.** One who enjoys experimenting with and repairing machine parts. **3.** A clumsy repairer or worker; a meddler. *—v.* **-kered, -ker•ing, -kers.** *—intr.* **1.** To work as a tinker. **2.** To make unskilled or experimental efforts at repair; fiddle: *tinkering with the economy.* *—tr.* **1.** To mend as a tinker. **2.** To manipulate unskillfully or experimentally. [ME *tinkere.*]

tin•ker's damn also **tin•ker's dam** (tĭng′kərz) *n. Slang.* The smallest degree or amount.

Tin•ker•toy (tĭng′kər-toi′). A trademark used for a construction toy consisting of pieces that fit together.

tin•kle (tĭng′kəl) *v.* **-kled, -kling, -kles.** *—intr.* To make light metallic sounds, as those of a small bell. *—tr.* **1.** To cause to tinkle. **2.** To signal or call by tinkling. *—n.* **1.** A light clear metallic sound or a sound suggestive of it. **2.** The act of tinkling. [ME *tinklen*, freq. of *tinken*, to emit a brief metallic sound, perh. of imit. orig.] **—tin′kly** *adj.*

Tin•ley Park (tĭn′lē). A city of NE IL, a suburb of Chicago. Pop. 37,121.

tin liz•zie (lĭz′ē) *n. Slang.* A dilapidated or cheap car. [< the name *Lizzie*, a nickname for Elizabeth.]

tin•ner (tĭn′ər) *n.* **1.** A tin miner. **2.** One that makes or deals in tinware; a tinsmith.

tin•ni•tus (tĭ-nī′təs, tĭn′ĭ-) *n.*, *pl.* **-tus•es.** A chronic ringing or buzzing sound in one or both ears usu. caused by a specific condition, such as an ear infection. [Lat. *tinnītus* < p.part. of *tinnīre*, to ring, of imit. orig.]

tin•ny (tĭn′ē) *adj.* **-ni•er, -ni•est. 1.** Of, containing, or yielding tin. **2.** Tasting or smelling of tin: *tinny canned food.* **3.** Having a thin metallic sound: *a high tinny voice.* **4.** Weak or thin; flimsy. **—tin′ni•ly** *adv.* **—tin′ni•ness** *n.*

Tin Pan Alley (tĭn) *n. Mus.* **1.** A district associated with musicians, composers, and publishers of popular music. **2.** The publishers and composers of popular music considered as a group. [Prob. < *tin pan*, tinny piano + ALLEY[1].]

tin plate *n.* Thin sheet iron or steel coated with tin to prevent rusting, used esp. to make cans and pots.

tin-plate (tĭn′plāt′) *tr.v.* **-plat•ed, -plat•ing, -plates.** To coat with tin by dipping or electroplating. **—tin′-plat′er** *n.*

tin pyrites *n.* See **stannite.**

tin•sel (tĭn′səl) *n.* **1.** Very thin sheets, strips, or threads of a glittering material used as a decoration. **2.** Something sparkling or showy but basically valueless. *—adj.* **1.** Made of or decorated with tinsel. **2.** Gaudy, showy, and valueless. *—tr.v.* **-seled, -sel•ing, -sels** or **-selled, -sel•ling, -sels. 1.** To decorate with or as if with tinsel. **2.** To give a false sparkle to. [ME *tineseile* < OFr. *estincelle*, spangle. See STENCIL.]

tin•smith (tĭn′smĭth′) *n.* One that makes and repairs things made of light metal.

tin•stone (tĭn′stōn′) *n.* See **cassiterite.**

tint (tĭnt) *n.* **1.** A shade of a color, esp. a pale or delicate variation. **2.** A gradation of a color made by adding white to it to lessen its saturation. **3.** A slight coloration; a tinge. **4.** A barely detectable amount or degree; a trace. **5.** A shaded effect in engraving produced by fine, close, parallel lines. **6.** *Print.* A panel of light color on which matter in another color is to be printed, as in an illustration. **7.** A dye for the hair. *—tr. & intr.v.* **tint•ed, tint•ing, tints.** To give a tint to or take on a tint. [Alteration of TINCT.] **—tint′er** *n.*

Tin•tag•el Head (tĭn-tăj′əl). A promontory in SW England NE of Plymouth; reputed birthplace of King Arthur.

tin•tin•nab•u•lar (tĭn′tĭ-năb′yə-lər) also **tin•tin•nab•u•lar•y** (-lĕr′ē) or **tin•tin•nab•u•lous** (-ləs) *adj.* Of or relating to bells or the ringing of bells. [< TINTINNABULUM.]

tin•tin•nab•u•la•tion (tĭn′tĭ-năb′yə-lā′shən) *n.* The ringing or sounding of bells. [< TINTINNABULUM.]

tin•tin•nab•u•lum (tĭn′tĭ-năb′yə-ləm) *n.*, *pl.* **-la** (-lə). A small tinkling bell. [ME < Lat. *tintinnābulum* < *tintinnāre*, to jingle, redup. of *tinnīre*, to ring, of imit. orig.]

Tin•to•ret•to (tĭn′tə-rĕt′ō, tĕn′tô-rĕt′tô). 1518–94. Italian painter of *St. George and the Dragon* (c. 1550).

tin•type (tĭn′tīp′) *n.* See **ferrotype** 1.

tin•work (tĭn′wûrk′) *n.* **1.** Articles made of tin or tin plate. **2. tinworks.** *(used with a sing. v.)* A place where tin is worked.

ti•ny (tī′nē) *adj.* **-ni•er, -ni•est.** Extremely small; minute. See Syns at **small.** [Alteration of ME *tine.*] **—ti′ni•ness** *n.*

tinamou

ă pat	oi boy
ā pay	ou out
âr care	o͝o took
ä father	o͞o boot
ĕ pet	ŭ cut
ē be	ûr urge
ĭ pit	th thin
ī pie	*th* this
îr pier	hw which
ŏ pot	zh vision
ō toe	ə about, item
ô paw	

Stress marks:
′ (primary);
′ (secondary), as in
dictionary (dĭk′shə-nĕr′ē)

tip[1] (tĭp) *n.* **1.** The end of a pointed or projecting object. **2.** A piece or an attachment, such as a cap or ferrule, to be fitted to the end of something else. —*tr.v.* **tipped, tip•ping, tips. 1.** To furnish with a tip. **2.** To cover or decorate the tip of. **3.** To remove the tip of. **4.** To dye the ends of (hair or fur) in order to blend or improve appearance. —***phrasal verb.* tip in.** *Print.* To attach (an insert) in a book by gluing along the binding edge. [ME.]

tip[2] (tĭp) *v.* **tipped, tip•ping, tips.** —*tr.* **1.** To push or knock over; overturn or topple. **2.** To move to a slanting position; tilt. **3.** To touch or raise (one's hat) in greeting. **4.** *Chiefly British.* **a.** To empty (something) by overturning; dump. **b.** To dump (rubbish, for example). —*intr.* **1.** To topple over; overturn. **2.** To become tilted; slant. See Syns at **slant.** —*n.* **1.** The act of tipping. **2.** A tilt or slant; an incline. **3.** *Chiefly British.* A place for dumping something, such as rubbish, from a mine. —***idiom.* tip the scales. 1.** To register weight at a certain amount. **2.** To offset the balance of a situation. [ME *tipen.*]

tippet

tip[3] (tĭp) *v.* **tipped, tip•ping, tips.** —*tr.* **1.** To strike gently; tap. **2.a.** *Baseball.* To hit (a pitched ball) with the side of the bat so that it glances off. **b.** *Sports.* To tap or deflect (a ball, for example), esp. in scoring. —*intr.* **1.** *Sports.* To deflect or glance off. Used of a ball or puck. **2.** *Lower Southern U.S.* To tiptoe. —*n.* **1.** A light blow; a tap. **2.** *Baseball.* A tipped pitched ball. [< ME *tippe*, a tap, perh. of LGer. orig.]

tip[4] (tĭp) *n.* **1.** A small sum of money given to someone for performing a service; a gratuity. **2.a.** A piece of confidential, advance, or inside information. **b.** A helpful hint. —*v.* **tipped, tip•ping, tips.** —*tr.* **1.a.** To give a tip to. **b.** To give as a tip. **2.** To provide with an informational tip. —*intr.* To give tips or a tip: *tips lavishly.* —***idiom.* tip (one's) hand.** To reveal one's resources or intentions. [?] —**tip′per** *n.*

tip•cart (tĭp′kärt′) *n.* A cart having a body that can be tilted to dump the contents.

ti•pi (tē′pē) *n.* Var. of **tepee.**

tip-in (tĭp′ĭn′) *n.* **1.** *Basketball.* A field goal scored by tapping the ball into the basket with the fingertips. **2.** *Sports.* A goal in hockey scored at close range by a short stroke of a stick.

tip-off[1] (tĭp′ôf′, -ŏf′) *n. Informal.* **1.** An informational tip. **2.** An indication of an otherwise unknown fact or probability.

tip-off[2] (tĭp′ôf′, -ŏf′) *n. Basketball.* An act of starting play at the beginning of a period with a jump ball. [TIP[3] + (KICK)OFF.]

tip of the iceberg *n., pl.* **tips of the iceberg.** A small evident part or aspect of something largely hidden.

Tip•pe•ca•noe (tĭp′ē-kə-no͞o′). A river, c. 274 km (170 mi), rising in NE IN and flowing to the Wabash R.; site of Gen. William Henry Harrison's defeat of the Shawnee (1811).

Tip•per•ar•y (tĭp′ə-râr′ē). A town of S-central Ireland SW of Dublin. The song "It's a Long Way to Tipperary" was used as a march by the British in World War I. Pop. 4,984.

tip•pet (tĭp′ĭt) *n.* **1.** A covering for the shoulders, as of fur, with long ends that hang in front. **2.** A long stole worn by members of the Anglican clergy. **3.** A long hanging part, as of a sleeve. [ME *tipet*, perh. < *tip*, tip of an object.]

tip•ple[1] (tĭp′əl) *tr. & intr.v.* **-pled, -pling, -ples.** To drink (alcoholic liquor) or engage in such drinking, esp. habitually or to excess. —*n.* Alcoholic liquor. [Perh. back-formation < ME *tipeler*, bartender.] —**tip′pler** *n.*

tip•ple[2] (tĭp′əl) *n.* **1.a.** An apparatus for unloading freight cars by tipping them. **b.** The place where this is done. **2.** A place for screening coal and loading it into trucks or railroad cars. [< dial. *tipple*, to overturn, freq. of TIP[2].]

tit[1]
Blue tit
Parus caeruleus

tip•py (tĭp′ē) *adj.* **-pi•er, -pi•est.** Likely to tip or tilt.

tip•staff (tĭp′stăf′) *n., pl.* **-staves** (-stāvz′, -stăvz′) or **-staffs. 1.** A staff with a metal tip, carried as a sign of office. **2.** An officer, such as a bailiff or constable, who carries a tipstaff.

tip•ster (tĭp′stər) *n. Informal.* One who sells tips or information, as to bettors or speculators.

tip•sy (tĭp′sē) *adj.* **-si•er, -si•est. 1.** Slightly intoxicated. **2.** Unsteady or crooked. [< TIP[2].] —**tip′si•ly** *adv.* —**tip′si•ness** *n.*

tip•toe (tĭp′tō′) *intr.v.* **-toed, -toe•ing, -toes.** To walk or move quietly on one's toes. —*n.* The tip of a toe. —*adj.* **1.** Standing or walking on one's toes. **2.** Stealthy; wary. —*adv.* **1.** On one's toes. **2.** Stealthily; warily. —***idiom.* on tiptoe.** Full of anticipation; eager.

tip•top (tĭp′tŏp′) *n.* **1.** The highest point; the summit. **2.** The highest degree of quality or excellence. —*adj.* Excellent; first-rate: *in tiptop condition.* —*adv.* Very well; excellently.

ti•rade (tī′rād′, tī-rād′) *n.* A long angry or violent speech, usu. censorious or denunciatory; a diatribe. [Fr. < OFr., act of firing < *tirer*, to draw out, endure, prob. back-formation < *martirant*, pr.part. of *martirer*, to torture (influenced by *mar*, to one's misfortune, and *tiranz*, executioner, tyrant) < *martir*, martyr < LLat. *martyr.* See MARTYR.]

Ti•ran (tə-rän′). A strait off the S tip of the Sinai Peninsula in NE Egypt connecting the Red Sea with the Gulf of Aqaba.

Ti•ra•në also **Ti•ra•na** (tə-rä′nə, tē-). The cap. of Albania, in the W-central part; became cap. in 1920. Pop. 206,100.

tire[1] (tīr) *v.* **tired, tir•ing, tires.** —*intr.* **1.** To grow weary. **2.** To grow bored or impatient. —*tr.* **1.** To diminish the strength or energy of; fatigue. **2.** To exhaust the interest or patience of; bore. [ME *tiren* < OE *tēorian, tyrian.* See **deu-**[1]*.]

tire[2] (tīr) *n.* **1.** A covering for a wheel, usu. made of rubber reinforced with cords of nylon, fiberglass, or other material and filled with compressed air. **2.** A hoop of metal or rubber fitted around a wheel. [ME, iron rim of a wheel, prob. < *tir*, attire, short for *atire* < *attiren*, to attire. See ATTIRE.]

tire[3] (tīr) *Archaic.* —*tr.v.* **tired, tir•ing, tires.** To adorn or attire. —*n.* **1.** Attire. **2.** A headband or headdress. [ME *tiren*, short for *attiren*, to attire. See ATTIRE.]

tired (tīrd) *adj.* **1.a.** Exhausted; fatigued. **b.** Impatient; bored. **2.** Overused; hackneyed. —**tired′ly** *adv.* —**tired′ness** *n.*

tire•less (tīr′lĭs) *adj.* Not yielding to fatigue; untiring or indefatigable. —**tire′less•ly** *adv.* —**tire′less•ness** *n.*

tire•some (tīr′səm) *adj.* Causing fatigue or boredom; wearisome. See Syns at **boring.** —**tire′some•ness** *n.*

Tîr•gu-Mu•reş (tîr′go͞o-mo͝or′ĕsh). A city of N-central Romania ESE of Cluj; ceded by Hungary in 1918. Pop. 154,506.

Ti•rich Mir (tîr′ĭch mîr′). A mountain, 7,695.2 m (25,230 ft), of the Hindu Kush in N Pakistan.

ti•ro (tī′rō) *n.* Var. of **tyro.**

Ti•rol (tə-rōl′, tī-, tī′rōl′). See **Tyrol.**

Tir•so de Mo•li•na (tîr′sō dā mə-lē′nə, *thĕ* mô-lē′nä). 1584?–1648. Spanish playwright who introduced the character Don Juan in *The Seducer of Seville* (1630).

Ti•ruch•chi•rap•pal•li (tîr′ə-chə-rä′pə-lē). A city of SE India SSW of the Madras R. Pop. 362,045.

Tir•yns (tîr′ĭnz, tī′rĭnz). An ancient city of S Greece in the E Peloponnesus; site of ruined Mycenaean palaces.

'tis (tĭz). It is.

ti•sane (tĭ-zăn′, -zän′) *n.* A herbal infusion or similar preparation drunk as a beverage or for its mildly medicinal effect. [*tisan*, barley water < OFr. *tisane* < Lat. *ptisana.* See PTISAN.]

Tish•ri (tĭsh′rē, -rā) *n.* The first month of the year in the Jewish calendar. [Heb. *tišrî* < Akkadian *tašrītu*, the month Tashritu (September/October).]

Ti•siph•o•ne (tĭ-sĭf′ə-nē) *n. Gk. & Rom. Myth.* One of the three Furies.

tis•sue (tĭsh′o͞o) *n.* **1.** A fine, very thin fabric, such as gauze. **2.** Tissue paper. **3.** A soft absorbent piece of paper used as toilet paper, a handkerchief, or a towel. **4.** An interwoven or interrelated number of things; a web; a network. **5.** *Biol.* An aggregation of morphologically similar cells and intercellular matter performing one or more functions in the body. [ME *tissu*, a rich kind of cloth < OFr. < p.part. of *tistre*, to weave < Lat. *texere.* See **teks-*.**] —**tis′su•ey** *adj.* —**tis′su•lar** *adj.*

tissue culture *n.* **1.** The technique or process of keeping tissue alive and growing in a culture medium. **2.** A culture of tissue grown by this technique or process.

tissue paper *n.* Thin translucent paper used for packing, wrapping, or protecting delicate articles.

tissue plasminogen activator *n.* An enzyme that converts plasminogen to plasmin, used to dissolve blood clots rapidly and selectively, esp. in the treatment of heart attacks.

Ti•sza (tĭs′ô) also **Ti•sa** (tē′sə). A river of central Europe rising in the Carpathian Mts. in W Ukraine and flowing c. 965 km (600 mi) to the Danube R.

tit[1] (tĭt) *n.* **1.** A titmouse. **2.** Any of various small similar or related birds. —*adj. New England & Upstate New York.* Small; undersized. [Short for TITMOUSE. Adj., ME *tit-*, as in *titmose*, titmouse. See TITMOUSE.]

tit[2] (tĭt) *n.* **1.** *Vulgar Slang.* A woman's breast. **2.** A teat. [ME < OE *titt.*]

tit. *abbr.* Title.

Tit. *abbr. Bible.* Titus.

Ti•tan (tīt′n) *n.* **1.** *Gk. Myth.* One of a family of giants, the children of Uranus and Gaea, who sought to rule heaven and were overthrown in turn by the family of Zeus. **2. titan.** A person of colossal size, strength, or achievement. **3.** The largest satellite of Saturn. [Ult. < Lat. *Tītān* < Gk. *Titan.*]

ti•tan•ate (tīt′n-āt′) *n.* A salt or an ester of titanic acid.

Ti•tan•ess (tīt′n-ĭs) *n. Gk. Myth.* One of the daughters of Gaea and Uranus.

Ti•ta•ni•a (tĭ-tā′nē-ə, -tān′yə, tī-) *n.* **1.** The queen of the fairies and wife of Oberon in medieval folklore. **2.** A satellite of Uranus. [< Lat. *Tītānia*, the goddess Diana, sister to the sun < fem. of *Tītānius*, of the Titans < *Tītān*, Titan. See TITAN.]

ti•tan•ic[1] (tī-tăn′ĭk) *adj.* **1. Titanic.** Of or relating to the Titans. **2.a.** Having great stature or enormous strength; huge or colossal: *titanic creatures of the deep.* **b.** Of enormous scope, power, or influence. —**ti•tan′i•cal•ly** *adv.*

ti•tan•ic[2] (tī-tăn′ĭk, -tā′nĭk, tĭ-) *adj.* Relating to or containing titanium, esp. with valence 4.

titanic acid (tī-tăn′ĭk, -tā′nĭk, tĭ-) *n.* A powdered inorganic acid, H_2TiO_3, used as a mordant.

ti•tan•if•er•ous (tīt′n-ĭf′ər-əs) *adj.* Containing or yielding titanium.

Ti•tan•ism (tīt′n-ĭz′əm) *n.* The spirit of revolt against an established order; rebelliousness.

ti•tan•ite (tīt′n-īt′) *n.* See **sphene.**

ti•ta•ni•um (tī-tā′nē-əm, tĭ-) *n. Symbol* **Ti** A strong, low-density, highly corrosion-resistant metallic element that occurs widely in igneous rocks and is used to alloy aircraft metals for low weight, strength, and high-temperature stability. Atomic number 22; atomic weight 47.90; melting point 1,660°C; boiling point 3,287°C; specific gravity 4.54; valence 2, 3, 4. See table at **element.** [< Lat. *Tītān*, Titan. See TITAN.]

titanium dioxide *n.* A white powder, TiO_2, used as an exceptionally opaque white pigment.

titanium white *n.* Titanium dioxide.

ti•tan•ous (tī-tăn′əs, -tā′nəs, tĭ-) *adj.* Relating to or containing titanium, esp. with valence 3.

tit•bit (tĭt′bĭt′) *n.* Var. of **tidbit.**

ti•ter also **ti•tre** (tī′tər) *n.* **1.** Concentration of a substance in solution determined by titration. **2.** The minimum volume needed to cause a particular result in titration. [Fr. *titre* < OFr. *title*, title. See TITLE.]

tit for tat *n.* Repayment in kind, as for an injury; retaliation. [Prob. alteration of *tip for tap*.]

tithe (tīth) *n.* **1.a.** A tenth part of one's annual income contributed voluntarily or due as a tax, esp. for the support of the clergy or church. **b.** The institution or obligation of paying tithes. **2.** A tax or an assessment of one tenth. **3.a.** A tenth part. **b.** A very small part. —*v.* **tithed, tith•ing, tithes.** —*tr.* **1.** To contribute or pay a tenth part of (one's annual income). **2.** To levy a tithe on. —*intr.* To pay a tithe. [ME < OE *tēotha*. See TENTH.] —**tith′a•ble** (tī′thə-bəl) *adj.* —**tith′er** *n.*

tith•ing (tī′thĭng) *n.* An administrative division consisting of ten householders in the old English system of frankpledge.

ti•ti¹ (tī′tī′, tē′tē′) *n., pl.* **-tis. 1.** A New World shrub or small tree *(Cyrilla racemiflora)* of warm swampy areas having leathery leaves and yellow fruit. **2.** An evergreen shrub or small tree *(Cliftonia monophylla)* of the southeast United States having glossy leathery leaves and winged fruit. [?]

ti•ti² (tē-tē′) *n., pl.* **-tis.** Any of various small long-tailed arboreal monkeys of the genus *Callicebus*, living in tropical regions of South America. [Sp. *tití* < Aymara *titi*.]

ti•tian (tĭsh′ən) *n.* A brownish orange. [After TITIAN.]

Ti•tian (tĭsh′ən). 1488?–1576. Italian painter of the Venetian school. —**Ti′tian•esque′** *adj.*

Ti•ti•ca•ca (tĭt′ĭ-kä′kə, tē′tē-kä′kä), **Lake.** A freshwater lake of South America in the Andes on the Bolivia-Peru border.

tit•il•late (tĭt′l-āt′) *v.* **-lat•ed, -lat•ing, -lates.** —*tr.* **1.** To stimulate by touching lightly; tickle. **2.** To excite (another) pleasurably, superficially, or erotically. —*intr.* To excite another, esp. in a superficial pleasurable manner. [Lat. *tītillāre*, *tītillāt-*, to tickle.] —**tit′il•lat′er** *n.* —**tit′il•lat′ing•ly** *adv.* —**tit′il•la′tion** *n.* —**tit′il•la′tive** *adj.*

tit•i•vate (tĭt′ə-vāt′) *tr.v.* **-vat•ed, -vat•ing, -vates.** To make decorative additions to; spruce up. [Alteration of earlier *tidivate* : perh. TIDY + (ELE)VATE.] —**tit′i•va′tion** *n.*

tit•lark (tĭt′lärk′) *n.* See **pipit.** [*tit-*, as in TIT(MOUSE) + LARK¹.]

ti•tle (tīt′l) *n.* **1.** An identifying name given to a book, play, film, musical composition, or other work. **2.** A general or descriptive heading, as of a book chapter. **3.a.** Written material in a film or television show, typically presenting credits, narration, or dialogue. **b.** A written piece of translated dialogue superimposed at the bottom of the frame during a film; a subtitle. In both senses often used in the plural. **4.** *Law.* A heading that names a document, statute, or proceeding. **5.** A division of a law book, declaration, or bill, generally larger than a section or an article. **6.** A written work that is published or about to be published. **7.** *Law.* **a.** The coincidence of all the elements that constitute the fullest legal right to control and dispose of property or a claim. **b.** The aggregate evidence that gives rise to a legal right of possession or control. **c.** The instrument, such as a deed, that constitutes this evidence. **8.a.** Something that provides a basis for or justifies a claim. **b.** A legitimate or alleged right. **9.** A formal appellation attached to the name of a person or family by virtue of office, rank, hereditary privilege, noble birth, or attainment or used as a mark of respect. **10.** A descriptive name; an epithet. **11.** *Sports.* A championship. **12.** *Eccles.* **a.** A source of income or area of work required of a candidate for ordination in the Church of England. **b.** A Roman Catholic church in or near Rome having a cardinal for its nominal head. —*tr.v.* **-tled, -tling, -tles. 1.** To give a title to; entitle. **2.** To call by a name; style. [ME < OE *titul*, superscription, and < OFr. *title*, title, both < Lat. *titulus*.]

ti•tled (tīt′ld) *adj.* Having a title, esp. a noble title.

ti•tle•hold•er (tīt′l-hōl′dər) *n.* **1.** One, esp. a champion, who holds a title. **2.** One that holds legal title to something.

title page *n. Print.* A front page of a book with its title, author and publisher names, and place of publication.

ti•tlist (tīt′lĭst, -l-ĭst) *n.* The holder of a competitive title; a champion: *a chess titlist.*

tit•man (tĭt′mən) *n. New England & Upstate New York.* **1.** A runt, esp. a piglet. **2.** A small person. [TIT¹ + MAN.]

tit•mouse (tĭt′mous′) *n., pl.* **-mice** (-mīs′). Any of numerous small insect-eating passerine birds of the family Paridae, including esp. members of the genus *Parus*, such as the chickadee. [Alteration of ME *titmose* : *tit- (prob. < ON *tittr*, titmouse) + *mose*, titmouse (< OE *māse*, titmouse).]

Ti•to (tē′tō), Marshal. Orig. Josip Broz. 1892–1980. Yugoslavian politician who served as president (1953–80). —**Ti′to•ism** *n.*

Ti•to•grad (tē′tō-grăd′, -gräd′). The cap. of Montenegro, in the SE part near the Albanian border. Pop. 73,000.

ti•trant (tī′trənt) *n.* A substance, such as a solution, of known concentration used in titration.

ti•trate (tī′trāt′) *tr. & intr.v.* **-trat•ed, -trat•ing, -trates.** To determine the concentration of (a solution) by titration or perform the act of titration. [< Fr. *titrer* < *titre*, titer. See TITER.] —**ti′trat′a•ble** *adj.* —**ti′tra′tor** *n.*

ti•tra•tion (tī-trā′shən) *n.* The process, act, or method of determining the concentration of a substance in solution by adding to it a standard reagent of known concentration in measured amounts until a reaction of definite and known proportion is completed and then calculating the unknown concentration.

ti•tre (tī′tər) *n.* Var. of **titer.**

ti•tri•met•ric (tī′trə-mĕt′rĭk) *adj.* Of or relating to measurement by titration. —**ti′tri•met′ri•cal•ly** *adv.*

tit•ter (tĭt′ər) *intr.v.* **-tered, -ter•ing, -ters.** To laugh in a restrained nervous way; giggle. —*n.* A nervous giggle. [Prob. imit.] —**tit′ter•er** *n.* —**tit′ter•ing•ly** *adv.*

tit•tle (tĭt′l) *n.* **1.** *Ling.* A small diacritic mark, such as an accent, a vowel mark, or a dot over an *i*. **2.** The tiniest bit; an iota. [ME *titil* < Med.Lat. *titulus*, diacritical mark < Lat., title, superscription.]

tit•tle-tat•tle (tĭt′l-tăt′l) *n.* Petty gossip; trivial talk. [Redup. of TATTLE.] —**tit′tle-tat′tle** *v.*

tit•tup (tĭt′əp) *intr.v.* **-tuped, -tup•ing, -tups** or **-tupped, -tup•ping, -tups.** To move in a lively capering manner; prance. —*n.* A lively capering manner of moving or walking; a prance. [Perh. imit. of the sound of a horse's hoofs.]

tit•u•ba•tion (tĭch′ə-bā′shən) *n.* The staggering or stumbling gait characteristic of certain nervous disorders. [Lat. *titubātiō*, *titubātiōn-*, a staggering < *titubātus*, p.part. of *titubāre*, to stagger.]

tit•u•lar (tĭch′ə-lər) *adj.* **1.** Relating to, having the nature of, or constituting a title. **2.a.** Existing in name only; nominal. **b.** Bearing the title of a church or monastery no longer active. **3.** Bearing a title. **4.** Derived from a title: *the titular role in a play.* —*n.* One holding a title. [< Lat. *titulus*, title.]

tit•u•lar•y (tĭch′ə-lĕr′ē) *n., pl.* **-ies.** A titleholder; a titular.

Ti•tus¹ (tī′təs). A.D. 39–81. Emperor of Rome (79–81) whose reign was marked by the capture of Jerusalem (70).

Ti•tus² (tī′təs) *n.* See table at **Bible.**

Titus, Saint. 1st cent. A.D. Christian leader and companion of St. Paul. An epistle of the Bible is addressed to him.

Ti•tus•ville (tī′təs-vĭl′). A city of E FL E of Orlando; incorp. 1886. Pop. 39,394.

Ti•u (tē′o͞o) *n. Myth.* The Germanic god of war and the sky. [OE *Tīw*. See **deiw-*.**]

Ti•vo•li (tĭv′ə-lē, tē′vô-lē) also **Ti•bur** (tī′bər). A city of central Italy ENE of Rome. Pop. 50,969.

Ti•wa (tē′wə) *n., pl.* **Tiwa** or **-was. 1.** A member of a group of Pueblo peoples of northern New Mexico. **2.** The group of Tanoan languages spoken by the Tiwa.

tiz•zy (tĭz′ē) *n., pl.* **-zies.** *Slang.* A state of nervous excitement or confusion; a dither. [?]

tk. *abbr.* Truck.

TKO (tē′kā-ō′) *abbr. Sports.* A technical knockout.

tkt. *abbr.* Ticket.

Tl The symbol for the element **thallium.**

Tlal•ne•pan•tla (tläl′nə-pänt′lä, -nĕ-). A city of S-central Mexico N of Mexico City. Pop. 778,173.

TLC *abbr.* Tender loving care.

Tlin•git (tlĭng′gĭt, tlĭng′ĭt) *n., pl.* **Tlingit** or **-gits. 1.** A member of a Native American people inhabiting the coastal and island areas of southeast Alaska. **2.** The language of the Tlingit.

T lymphocyte *n.* See **T cell.**

Tm¹ The symbol for the element **thulium.**

Tm² *abbr.* Timothy.

TM *abbr.* Trademark.

T.M. *abbr.* Transcendental meditation.

tme•sis (tmē′sĭs, mē′-) *n., pl.* **-ses** (-sēz). Separation of the parts of a compound word by one or more intervening words; for example, *where I go ever* instead of *wherever I go*. [LLat. *tmēsis* < Gk., a cutting < *temnein*, to cut. See **tem-*.**]

TN *abbr.* Tennessee.

tn. *abbr.* **1.** Ton. **2.** Town. **3.** Train.

tng. *abbr.* Training.

tnpk. *abbr.* Turnpike.

TNT (tē′ĕn-tē′) *n.* A crystalline compound, $CH_3C_6H_2(NO_2)_3$, used as a high explosive. [*t(ri)n(itro)t(oluene)*.]

to (to͞o; tə *when unstressed*) *prep.* **1.a.** In a direction toward so as to reach: *went to the city.* **b.** Toward: *turned to me.* **2.a.** Reaching as far as: *The water was clear to the bottom.* **b.** To the extent or degree of: *loved him to distraction.* **c.** With the resultant condition of: *nursed her back to health.* **3.** Toward a given state: *helping women to equality.* **4.** In contact with; against: *faces pressed to the windows.* **5.** In front of: *face to face.* **6.** Used to indicate appropriation or

Titian
c. 1550 self-portrait

Tito
Photographed in 1962

ă pat	oi boy
ā pay	ou out
âr care	o͝o took
ä father	o͞o boot
ĕ pet	ŭ cut
ē be	ûr urge
ĭ pit	th thin
ī pie	*th* this
îr pier	hw which
ŏ pot	zh vision
ō toe	ə about, item
ô paw	

Stress marks:
′ (primary);
′ (secondary), as in **dictionary** (dĭk′shə-nĕr′ē)

possession: *the top to the jar.* **7.** Concerning; regarding: *an answer to my letter.* **8.** In a particular relationship with: *parallel to the road.* **9.** As an accompaniment or a complement of: *danced to the tune.* **10.** Composing; constituting: *two cups to a pint.* **11.** In accord with: *suited to her abilities.* **12.** As compared with: *superior to the others.* **13.a.** Before: *The time is ten to five.* **b.** Up till; until: *worked from nine to five.* **14.a.** For the purpose of: *out to lunch.* **b.** In honor of: *a toast to the queen.* **15.a.** Used before a verb to indicate the infinitive: *I'd like to go.* **b.** Used alone when the infinitive is understood: *Go if you want to.* **16.a.** Used to indicate the relationship of a verb with its complement: *refer to a dictionary; refer me to a dictionary.* **b.** Used with a reflexive pronoun to indicate exclusivity or separateness: *had it to ourselves.* — *adv.* **1.** In one direction; toward a person or thing. **2.** Into a shut or closed position: *pushed the door to.* **3.** Into a state of consciousness: *The patient came to.* **4.** Into a state of action or attentiveness: *sat down for lunch and fell to.* **5.** *Naut.* Into the wind. [ME < OE *tō.* See **de-***.]

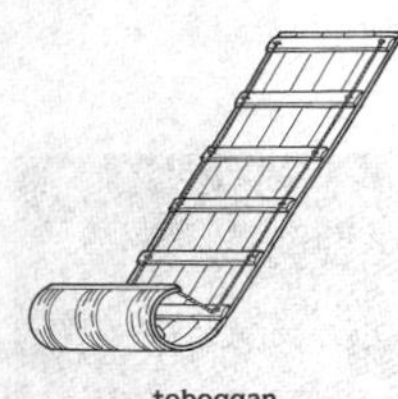
toboggan

t.o. *abbr.* Turnover.

toad (tōd) *n.* **1.** Any of numerous tailless amphibians chiefly of the family Bufonidae, related to the frogs but more terrestrial and with a broader body and rougher drier skin. **2.** The horned toad. **3.** A repulsive person. [ME *tode* < OE *tādige.*]

toad•eat•er (tōd′ē′tər) *n.* A toady. [Originally an eater or pretend eater of poisonous toads who was part of a scam.]

toad•fish (tōd′fĭsh′) *n., pl.* **toadfish** or **-fish•es.** Any of various scaleless fishes of the family Batrachoididae of warm waters, having a broad flattened head and a wide mouth.

toad•flax (tōd′flăks′) *n.* **1.** Any of various plants of the genus *Linaria*, having narrow leaves and spurred two-lipped flowers. **2.** See **butter-and-eggs.**

toad•stone (tōd′stōn′) *n.* A stone once worn as a charm and believed to have been formed in the body of a toad.

toad•stool (tōd′sto͞ol′) *n.* An inedible or poisonous fungus with an umbrella-shaped fruiting body.

toad•y (tō′dē) *n., pl.* **-ies.** A person who flatters or defers to others for self-serving reasons; a sycophant. — *tr. & intr.v.* **-ied** (tō′dēd), **-y•ing, -ies** (tō′dēz). To be a toady to or behave like a toady. [< TOAD.]

to and fro *adv.* Back and forth.

to-and-fro (to͞o′ən-frō′) *n.* **1.** Movement back and forth; reciprocating movement. **2.** Debate over an issue; vacillation. — **to′-and-fro′** *adj.*

toast¹ (tōst) *v.* **toast•ed, toast•ing, toasts.** — *tr.* **1.** To heat and brown (bread, for example) by placing in a toaster or an oven or close to a fire. **2.** To warm thoroughly, as before a fire. — *intr.* To become toasted. — *n.* Sliced bread heated and browned. [ME *tosten* < OFr. *toster* < VLat. **tostāre*, freq. of Lat. *torrēre*, to parch, burn. See **ters-***.]

toast² (tōst) *n.* **1.a.** The act of raising a glass and drinking in honor of a person or thing. **b.** A proposal to drink to someone or something or a speech given before such a drink. **c.** The one honored by a toast. **2.** A person receiving much attention or acclaim. — *v.* **toast•ed, toast•ing, toasts.** — *tr.* To drink to the honor of. — *intr.* To propose or drink a toast. [Perh. < TOAST¹, < using spiced toast to flavor drinks.]

toby
c. 1780 Leeds creamware toby

toast•er (tō′stər) *n.* A mechanical device used to toast bread, esp. by exposure to electrically heated wire coils.

toast•mas•ter (tōst′măs′tər) *n.* A man who proposes the toasts and introduces the speakers at a banquet.

toast•mis•tress (tōst′mĭs′trĭs) *n.* A woman who proposes the toasts and introduces the speakers at a banquet.

toast•y (tō′stē) *adj.* **-i•er, -i•est.** Pleasantly warm.

to•bac•co (tə-băk′ō) *n., pl.* **-cos** or **-coes. 1.** Any of various plants of the genus *Nicotiana*, esp. *N. tabacum*, native to tropical America and widely cultivated for their leaves, which are dried and processed chiefly for use in snuff or for smoking. **2.** The leaves of these plants. **3.** Products made from these plants. **4.** The habit of smoking tobacco. **5.** A crop of tobacco. [Sp. *tabaco*, poss. < Ar. *ṭabbâq*, name of various medicinal herbs.]

tobacco budworm *n.* The destructive larva of a noctuid moth *(Heliothis virescens)* that feeds on tobacco plants.

tobacco hornworm *n.* The destructive larva of a hawk moth *(Manduca sexta)* of the southern United States and the West Indies that feeds on the leaves of tobacco plants.

tobacco mosaic virus *n.* A retrovirus that causes mosaic in tobacco and some other plants.

to•bac•co•nist (tə-băk′ə-nĭst) *n.* A dealer in tobacco and smoking supplies.

tobacco worm *n.* See **tobacco hornworm.**

To•ba•go (tə-bā′gō). An island of Trinidad and Tobago in the SE West Indies NE of Trinidad; became a British colony in 1899 and gained independence with Trinidad in 1962.

to-be (to͞o-bē′) *adj.* That is to be; future. Often used postpositively and in combination: *a graduate-to-be.*

To•bey (tō′bē), **Mark.** 1890–1976. Amer. painter whose distinctive abstract style was inspired by Oriental calligraphy.

To•bit (tō′bĭt) *n.* **1.** In the Bible, a Hebrew captive in Nineveh. **2.** See table at **Bible.** [Gk. *Tōbit* < Heb. *Ṭôbîyāh* : *ṭôb*, good + *yāh*, God.]

to•bog•gan (tə-bŏg′ən) *n.* A long narrow runnerless sled made of thin boards curled upward in front. — *intr.v.* **-ganed, -gan•ing, -gans. 1.** To coast or ride on a toboggan. **2.** *Slang.* To decline or fall rapidly. [Canadian Fr. *tobagan* < Micmac *topaghan.*] — **to•bog′gan•er, to•bog′gan•ist** *n.*

To•bol (tə-bôl′). A river rising in the SE Ural Mts. and flowing c. 1,690 km (1,050 mi) to the Irtysh R.

to•by also **To•by** (tō′bē) *n., pl.* **-bies.** A drinking mug, usu. in the shape of a stout man wearing a large three-cornered hat. [After *Toby*, a nickname for *Tobias.*]

To•can•tins (tō′kän-tēns′). A river, c. 2,639 km (1,640 mi), flowing from central Brazil near Brasília N to the Pará R.

toc•ca•ta (tə-kä′tə) *n. Mus.* A composition, usu. for the organ or another keyboard instrument, in free style with full chords and elaborate runs. [Ital. < fem. p.part. of *toccare*, to touch < VLat. **toccāre.*]

To•char•i•an also **To•khar•i•an** (tō-kâr′ē-ən, -kär′-, -kăr′-) *n.* **1.** A member of a people of possible European origin, living in Chinese Turkistan until about the tenth century. **2.** The language of this people, recorded in two dialects dating from the seventh century and forming its own branch within Indo-European. [< Lat. *Tocharī*, the Tocharians < Gk. *Tokharoi.*]

to•col•o•gy also **to•kol•o•gy** (tō-kŏl′ə-jē) *n.* The science of childbirth; midwifery or obstetrics. [Gk. *tokos*, childbirth; see **tek-*** + -LOGY.]

to•coph•er•ol (tō-kŏf′ə-rôl′, -rōl′, -rŏl′) *n.* Any of a group of fat-soluble alcohols that constitute vitamin E and are present in milk, lettuce, and wheat germ oil. [< Gk. *tokos*, offspring; see TOCOLOGY + Gk. *pherein*, to carry; see **bher-¹***.]

Tocque•ville (tōk′vĭl, tŏk′-, tôk-vēl′), **Alexis Charles Henri Clérel de.** 1805–59. French politician and historian who wrote *Democracy in America* (1835).

toc•sin (tŏk′sĭn) *n.* **1.a.** An alarm sounded on a bell. See Syns at **alarm. b.** A bell used to sound an alarm. **2.** A warning; an omen. [Fr., alteration of *toquassen* < OFr. *touque-sain* < OProv. *tocasenh* : *tocar*, to strike (< VLat. **toccāre*) + *senh*, bell (< LLat. *signum* < Lat., signal; see SIGN).]

tod (tŏd) *n. Chiefly British.* **1.** A unit of weight for wool, esp. one equivalent to about 28 pounds (12.7 kilograms). **2.** A bushy clump, as of ivy. [ME *todde.*]

to•day (tə-dā′) *n.* The present day, time, or age. — *adv.* **1.** During or on the present day. **2.** During or at the present time. — *adj.* Of the present time. [ME *to dai* < OE *tō dæge* : *tō*, to; see TO + *dæge*, dative of *dæg*, day; see **agh-***.]

Todd (tŏd), Sir **Alexander Robertus.** b. 1907. British chemist who won a 1957 Nobel Prize.

Todd, Thomas. 1765–1826. Amer. jurist; associate justice of the U.S. Supreme Court (1807–26).

tod•dle (tŏd′l) *intr.v.* **-dled, -dling, -dles. 1.** To walk with short, unsteady steps. **2.** To walk leisurely; stroll. — *n.* An unsteady gait. [?]

tod•dler (tŏd′lər) *n.* **1.** One who toddles, esp. a young child learning to walk. **2.** A size of clothing for children between the ages of about one and three.

tod•dy (tŏd′ē) *n., pl.* **-dies. 1.** A hot toddy. **2.a.** The sweet sap of several tropical Asian palm trees, esp. palmyra and *Caryota urens*, used as a beverage. **b.** A liquor fermented from this sap. [Hindi *tāṛī*, sap of palm < *tāṛ*, palm < Skt. *tālaḥ*, perh. of Dravidian orig.]

to-do (tə-do͞o′) *n., pl.* **-dos** (-do͞oz′). A commotion or stir.

to•dy (tō′dē) *n., pl.* **-dies.** Any of various small birds of the family Todidae of the West Indies, having colorful, predominantly green plumage and a red throat. [Prob. < Fr. *todier* < NLat. *Todus*, genus name < Lat. *todus*, a small bird.]

toe (tō) *n.* **1.a.** One of the digits of a vertebrate. **b.** The forepart of a foot or hoof. **c.** The terminal segment of an invertebrate's limb. **2.** The part of a sock, shoe, or boot that covers the digits of the foot. **3.** *Sports.* The end of the head on a golf club. **4.** The part of a vertical shaft that turns in a bearing. **5.** The lowest part, as of an embankment or a dam. — *v.* **toed, toe•ing, toes.** — *tr.* **1.** To touch, kick, or reach with the toe. **2.** *Sports.* To drive (a golf ball) with the toe of the club. **3.a.** To drive (a nail or spike) at an oblique angle. **b.** To fasten or secure with obliquely driven nails or spikes. — *intr.* To stand, walk, move, or be formed with the toes pointed in a specified direction: *He toes out.* — ***idioms.* on (one's) toes.** Ready to act; alert. **step (or tread) on (someone's) toes.** To hurt, offend, or encroach on the feelings, actions, or province of. **toe the line (or mark). 1.** To adhere to doctrines or rules conscientiously; conform. **2.** *Sports & Games.* To touch a mark or line with the toe or hands in readiness for the start of a race or competition. [ME < OE *tā.* See **deik-***.]

toe•a (toi′ə) *n., pl.* **toea.** See table at **currency.** [Perh. Pidgin E. < E. DOLLAR.]

toe•cap (tō′kăp′) *n.* A reinforced covering of leather or metal for the toe of a shoe or boot.

toe crack *n.* A sand crack in the front part of a horse's hoof.

toed (tōd) *adj.* **1.** Having a toe, esp. of a specified number or kind. Often used in combination: *even-toed.* **2.a.** Driven obliquely: *a toed nail.* **b.** Secured by toed nails.

toe dance *n.* A dance that is performed on the toes, esp. in ballet. — **toe dancer** *n.*

toe•hold (tō′hōld′) *n.* **1.** A small indentation or ledge on which the foot can find support in climbing. **2.** A slight or initial advantage useful for future progress. **3.** *Sports.* A wrestling hold in which one competitor wrenches the other's foot.

toe loop *n. Sports.* A jump in figure skating in which the skater, moving backward, takes off from the back outer edge of one skate, makes a full spin in the air, and lands on the back outer edge of the same skate.

toe•nail (tō′nāl′) *n.* **1.** The nail on a toe. **2.** A nail driven obliquely, as to join vertical and horizontal beams. **—toe′nail′** *v.*

toff (tŏf) *n. Chiefly British.* An elegantly dressed young man, often having affected manners. [Prob. var. of TUFT, a gold tassel worn by titled students at Oxford and Cambridge.]

tof•fee (tô′fē, tŏf′ē) *n.* A hard chewy candy made of brown sugar or molasses and butter. [Alteration of TAFFY.]

toft (tôft, tŏft) *n. Chiefly British.* **1.** A homestead. **2.** A hillock. [ME < OE < ON *topt.* See **dem-***.]

to•fu (tō′fo͞o) *n.* A protein-rich food made from soybean extract. [J. *tōfu* < Chin. *dòufu* : *dòu*, bean + *fŭ*, curdled.]

tog (tŏg, tôg) *Informal.* **—***n.* **1. togs.** Clothes: *gardening togs.* **2.** A coat or cloak. **—***tr.v.* **togged, tog•ging, togs.** To dress or clothe. [Short for obsolete *togeman* < obsolete Fr. *togue*, cloak < Lat. *toga*, garment. See TOGA.]

to•ga (tō′gə) *n.* **1.** A loose one-piece outer garment worn in public by male citizens in ancient Rome. **2.** A robe of office; a professional or ceremonial gown. [Lat. See **(s)teg-***.] **—to′gaed** (tō′gəd) *adj.*

to•geth•er (tə-gĕth′ər) *adv.* **1.** In or into a single group, mass, or place: *gather together.* **2.** In or into contact: *mixed together.* **3.a.** In association with or in relationship to one another; mutually or reciprocally: *getting along together.* **b.** By joint or cooperative effort: *ironed together.* **4.** Regarded collectively; in total: *worth more than all of us together.* **5.** In or into a unified structure or arrangement: *put it together.* **6.** Simultaneously: *rang out together.* **7.** In harmony or accord: *stand together.* **8.** *Informal.* Into an effective, coherent condition: *Get yourself together.* **—***adj. Slang.* **1.** Emotionally stable and effective in performance: *She's really together.* **2.** In tune with what is going on; hip. [ME < OE *tōgædere.* See **ghedh-***.] **—to•geth′er•ness** *n.*

Usage Note: *Together with,* like *in addition to,* is often employed following the subject of a sentence or clause to introduce an addition. The addition, however, does not alter the number of the verb, which is governed by the subject: *The king* (singular), *together with two aides, is expected in an hour.* The same is true of *along with, besides,* and *in addition to.* See Usage Notes at **besides, like²**.

tog•gle (tŏg′əl) *n.* **1.** A pin, rod, or crosspiece fitted or inserted into a loop in a rope, chain, or strap to tighten, prevent slipping, or hold an attached object. **2.** A device or an apparatus with a toggle joint. **—***v.* **-gled, -gling, -gles.** **—***tr.* To furnish or fasten with a toggle. **—***intr.* To alternate between circuit configurations, usu. by a single switch. [?]

toggle bolt *n.* A fastener consisting of a threaded bolt and a spring-loaded toggle, used to secure objects to thin or hollow walls.

toggle joint *n.* A joint made of two arms attached by a pivot shaped like an elbow, allowing force to be exerted at the ends of the arms as the joint is expanded.

toggle switch *n.* A switch that uses a toggle joint with a spring to open or close an electric circuit as an attached lever is pushed through a small arc.

To•gliat•ti also **Tol•yat•ti** (tōl-yä′tē, tô-lyät′tē). A city of W Russia on the Volga R. NW of Kuibyshev. Pop. 594,000.

To•go (tō′gō′). A country of W Africa on the Gulf of Guinea; gained independence in 1960. Cap. Lomé. Pop. 2,742,945.

togue (tōg) *n.* See **lake trout.** [Canadian Fr. < Micmac *atoghwaasu.*]

To•ho•no O'o•dham (tō-hō′nō ō′ə-däm) *n., pl.* **Tohono O'odham** or **Tohono O'o•dhams.** See **Papago.**

toil¹ (toil) *intr.v.* **toiled, toil•ing, toils.** **1.** To labor continuously; work strenuously. **2.** To proceed with difficulty: *toiling over the mountains.* **—***n.* **1.** Exhausting labor or effort. **2.** *Archaic.* Strife; contention. [ME *toilen* < AN *toiler*, to stir about < Lat. *tudiculāre* < *tudicula*, a machine for bruising olives, dim. of *tudēs*, hammer.] **—toil′er** *n.*

toil² (toil) *n.* **1.** Something that binds, snares, or entangles; an entrapment. Often used in the plural: *caught in the toils of despair.* **2.** *Archaic.* A net for trapping game. [Fr. *toile*, cloth < OFr. *teile* < Lat. *tēla*, web. See **teks-***.]

toile (twäl) *n.* A sheer fabric, such as linen. [Fr. See TOIL².]

toi•let (toi′lĭt) *n.* **1.a.** A fixture for defecation and urination, consisting of a bowl fitted with a hinged seat and connected to a waste pipe and a flushing apparatus; a privy. **b.** A room or booth containing such a fixture. **2.** The act or process of dressing or grooming oneself. **3.** Dress; attire; costume. **4.** The cleansing of a body area as part of a surgical or medical procedure. **5.** *Archaic.* A dressing table. [Fr. *toilette*, clothes bag < OFr. *tellette*, dim. of *teile*, cloth. See TOIL².]

toilet paper *n.* Thin absorbent paper, usu. in rolls, used to clean oneself after defecation or urination.

toi•let•ry (toi′lĭ-trē) *n., pl.* **-ries.** An article, such as toothpaste or a hairbrush, used in personal grooming or dressing.

toi•lette (twä-lĕt′) *n.* **1.** The act or process of dressing or grooming oneself; toilet. **2.** A person's dress or style of dress. **3.** A gown or costume. [Fr. See TOILET.]

toilet tissue *n.* See **toilet paper.**

toilet training *n.* The training of a child to use a toilet.

toilet water *n.* A scented liquid with a high alcohol content used in bathing or applied as a skin freshener.

toil•some (toil′səm) *adj.* Characterized by or requiring toil. **—toil′some•ly** *adv.* **—toil′some•ness** *n.*

To•jo Hi•de•ki (tō′jō′ hē′dĕ-kē). 1884–1948. Japanese army officer who ruled as dictator (1941–44).

to•ka•mak (tô′kə-măk′, tŏk′ə-) *n.* A doughnut-shaped chamber used in fusion research in which a plasma is heated and confined by magnetic fields. [Russ. < *to(roidal'naya) kam(era s) ak(sial'nym magnitnym polem)*, toroidal chamber with axial magnetic field.]

To•ka•ra Islands (tō-kär′ə, -kä′rä). A group of islands of Japan in the N Ryukyu group S of Kyushu.

To•kay (tō-kā′) *n.* **1.** A variety of grape originally grown near Tokaj (formerly Tokay), a town of eastern Hungary. **2.** A wine made from these grapes.

toke (tōk) *Slang. n.* A puff on a cigarette, esp. a marijuana one, or a pipe of marijuana or hashish. [Perh. < Sp. *toque*, a hit, a turn < *tocar*, to touch < VLat. **toccāre.*] **—toke** *v.*

To•ke•lau Islands (tō′kə-lou′). An island group of New Zealand in the central Pacific in the N Ryukyu Is. N of Samoa.

to•ken (tō′kən) *n.* **1.** Something serving as an indication, a proof, or an expression of something else; a sign. **2.** Something that signifies or evidences authority, validity, or identity: *The scepter is a token of regal status.* **3.** A distinguishing feature or characteristic. **4.** One that represents a group, as an employee whose presence is used to prevent the employer from being accused of discrimination. **5.** A keepsake or souvenir. **6.** A piece of stamped metal used as a substitute for currency. **—***tr.v.* **-kened, -ken•ing, -kens.** To betoken or symbolize; portend. **—***adj.* **1.** Done as an indication or a pledge. **2.a.** Perfunctory; minimal. **b.** Merely symbolic. **—*idioms.* by the same token.** In like manner; similarly. **in token of.** As an indication of. [ME < OE *tācen.* See **deik-***.]

to•ken•ism (tō′kə-nĭz′əm) *n.* **1.** The policy of making only a symbolic gesture, as toward racial integration. **2.** The practice of hiring or appointing a token number of people from underrepresented groups, as to deflect criticism.

To•khar•i•an (tō-kâr′ē-ən, -kär′-, -kăr′-) *n.* Var. of **Tocharian.**

To•klas (tō′kləs), **Alice B.** 1877–1967. Amer. writer who was the secretary and longtime companion of Gertrude Stein.

to•kol•o•gy (tō-kŏl′ə-jē) *n.* Var. of **tocology.**

to•ko•no•ma (tō′kə-nō′mə) *n.* A niche or an alcove in a Japanese home for displaying a piece of art. [J. : *toko*, alcove + *no*, of + *ma*, room.]

Tok Pis•in (tŏk′ pĭs′ĭn) *n.* A pidgin based on English and spoken in Papua New Guinea. [Pidgin E. : TALK + PIDGIN.]

To•ku•shi•ma (tō′kə-shē′mä). A city of E Shikoku, Japan, on the Inland Sea. Pop. 257,886.

To•ky•o (tō′kē-ō′, -kyō). Formerly **E•do** (ĕd′ō). The cap. of Japan, in E-central Honshu on **Tokyo Bay,** an inlet of the Pacific; founded in the 12th cent. Pop. 8,353,674.

to•la (tō′lə, tō-lä′) *n.* A unit of weight used in India, equal to the weight of one silver rupee (11.7 grams or 180 troy grains). [Hindi *tolā* < Skt. *tulā*, weight. See **telə-***.]

tol•booth also **toll•booth** (tōl′bo͞oth′) *n. Scots.* A prison; a jail. [ME *tolbothe*, town hall containing customs offices and prison cells : *tol*, toll; see TOLL¹ + *bothe*, booth; see BOOTH.]

Tol•bu•khin (tôl-bo͞o′kĭn, -KHĭn). A city of NE Bulgaria N of Varna. Pop. 105,000.

tol•bu•ta•mide (tŏl-byo͞o′tə-mīd′) *n.* A white powder, $C_{12}H_{18}N_2O_3S$, that lowers the level of sugar in the blood and is used in the treatment of diabetes. [TOL(U) + BUT- + AMIDE.]

told (tōld) *v.* P.t. and p.part. of **tell.**

tole also **tôle** (tōl) *n.* A lacquered or enameled metalware, usu. gilded and elaborately painted. [Fr. *tôle*, sheet metal, var. of *table*, table, slab < OFr. < Lat. *tabula*, board.]

To•le•do¹ (tə-lē′dō). **1.** (*also* tô-lĕ′thô). A city of central Spain near the Tagus R. SSW of Madrid; a provincial cap. (712–1031) of Moorish Spain. Pop. 57,778. **2.** A city of NW OH on Lake Erie; incorp. 1837. Pop. 332,943.

To•le•do² also **to•le•do** (tə-lē′dō) *n., pl.* **-dos.** A fine-tempered sword or steel sword blade made in Toledo, Spain.

tol•er•a•ble (tŏl′ər-ə-bəl) *adj.* **1.** Capable of being tolerated; endurable. **2.** Fairly good. See Syns at **average.** **—tol′er•a•bil′i•ty, tol′er•a•ble•ness** *n.* **—tol′er•a•bly** *adv.*

tol•er•ance (tŏl′ər-əns) *n.* **1.** The capacity for or the practice of recognizing and respecting the beliefs or practices of others. **2.a.** Leeway for variation from a standard. **b.** The permissible deviation from a specified value of a structural dimension, often expressed as a percent. **3.** The capacity to endure hardship or pain. **4.** *Medic.* **a.** Physiological resistance to a poison. **b.** The capacity to absorb a drug continuously or in large doses without adverse effect. **5.a.** Acceptance of a tissue graft

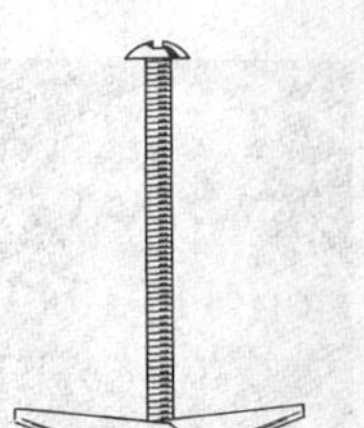
toggle bolt

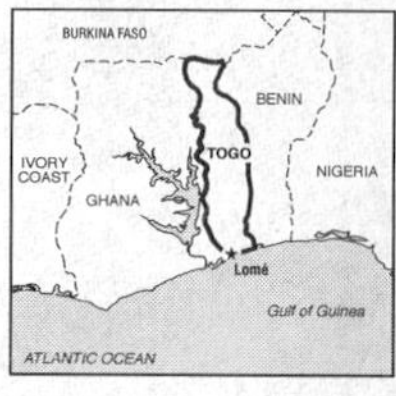

Togo

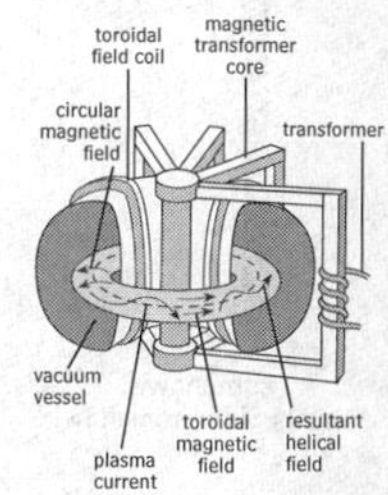

tokamak

ă pat	oi boy
ā pay	ou out
âr care	o͝o took
ä father	o͞o boot
ĕ pet	ŭ cut
ē be	ûr urge
ĭ pit	th thin
ī pie	*th* this
îr pier	hw which
ŏ pot	zh vision
ō toe	ə about, item
ô paw	

Stress marks:
′ (primary);
′ (secondary), as in
dictionary (dĭk′shə-nĕr′ē)

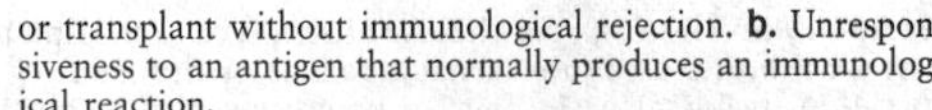

or transplant without immunological rejection. **b.** Unresponsiveness to an antigen that normally produces an immunological reaction.

tol•er•ant (tŏl′ər-ənt) *adj.* **1.** Inclined to tolerate the beliefs, practices, or traits of others; forbearing. See Syns at **broad-minded. 2.** Able to withstand or endure an adverse environmental condition. **—tol′er•ant•ly** *adv.*

tol•er•ate (tŏl′ə-rāt′) *tr.v.* **-at•ed, -at•ing, -ates. 1.** To allow without prohibiting or opposing; permit. **2.** To recognize and respect (the rights, beliefs, or practices of others). **3.** To put up with; endure. See Syns at **bear**[1]. **4.** *Medic.* To have tolerance for (a substance or pathogen). [Lat. *tolerāre, tolerāt-,* to bear. See **telə-***.] **—tol′er•a′tive** *adj.* **—tol′er•a′tor** *n.*

tol•er•a•tion (tŏl′ə-rā′shən) *n.* **1.** Tolerance with respect to the actions and beliefs of others. **2.** Official recognition of the right to hold dissenting opinions, esp. on religion.

Leo Tolstoy

tol•i•dine (tŏl′ĭ-dēn′) *n.* Any of several isomeric bases, $C_{14}H_{16}N_2$, derived from toluene, one of which is used as an analytical reagent. [TOL(UENE) + -ID(E) + -INE[2].]

Tol•kien (tōl′kēn′, tŏl′-), **J(ohn) R(onald) R(euel).** 1892–1973. British philologist and writer of the fantasies *The Hobbit* (1937) and *The Lord of the Rings* (1954–55).

toll[1] (tōl) *n.* **1.** A fixed charge or tax for a privilege, esp. for passage across a bridge or along a road. **2.** A charge for a service, such as a long-distance telephone call. **3.** The amount or extent of loss or destruction caused by a disaster. *—tr.v.* **tolled, toll•ing, tolls. 1.** To exact as a toll. **2.** To charge a fee for using (a structure, such as a bridge). [ME < OE, var. of *toln* < Med.Lat. *tolōnīum* < Lat. *telōnēum,* tollbooth < Gk. *telōneion* < *telōnēs,* tax collector < *telos,* tax. See **telə-***.]

toll[2] (tōl) *v.* **tolled, toll•ing, tolls.** *—tr.* **1.** To sound (a large bell) slowly at regular intervals. **2.** To announce or summon by tolling. *—intr.* To sound in slowly repeated single tones. *—n.* **1.** The act of tolling. **2.** The sound of a bell being struck. [ME *tollen,* to ring an alarm, perh. < *tollen,* to entice, pull, var. of *tillen* < OE *-tyllan.*]

toll•booth[1] (tōl′bo͞oth′) *n.* A booth where a toll is collected.

toll•booth[2] (tōl′bo͞oth′) *n.* Var. of **tolbooth.**

toll bridge *n.* A bridge at which a toll is charged for crossing.

toll call *n.* A telephone call for which a higher rate is charged than that standard for a local call.

toll•gate (tōl′gāt′) *n.* **1.** A gate barring passage, as to a road, until a toll is collected. **2.** A tollbooth equipped with a gate.

toll•house (tōl′hous′) *n.* **1.** A house adjoining a tollgate and occupied by a toll collector. **2.** See **tollbooth**[1].

tollhouse cookie *n.* A cookie made with flour, brown sugar, semisweet chocolate chips, and often chopped nuts.

Tol•stoy or **Tol•stoi** (tōl′stoi, tŏl′-, təl-stoi′), Count **Leo** or **Lev Nikolayevich.** 1828–1910. Russian writer whose works include *War and Peace* (1864–69) and *Anna Karenina* (1873–76). **—Tol•stoy′an, Tol•stoi′an** *adj.*

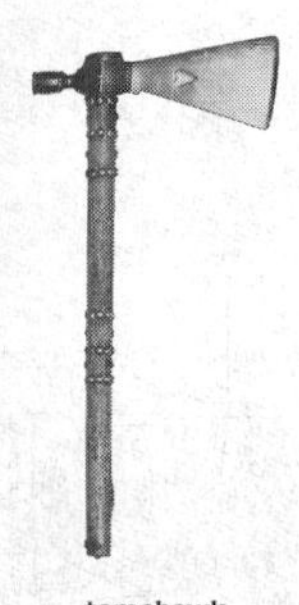

tomahawk
Oglala Sioux tomahawk

Tol•tec (tōl′tĕk′, tŏl′-) *n., pl.* **Toltec** or **-tecs.** A member of a Nahuatl-speaking people of central and southern Mexico whose empire flourished from the 10th to the 12th century. [Sp. *tolteca* < Nahuatl *toltecatl,* artisan, mechanic.] **—Tol′tec′, Tol•tec′an** *adj.*

to•lu (tə-lo͞o′) *n.* Balsam of Peru. [Sp. *tolú,* after *Tolú,* a seaport of NW Colombia.]

tol•u•ate (tŏl′yo͞o-āt′) *n.* A salt or an ester of toluic acid.

tol•u•ene (tŏl′yo͞o-ēn′) also **tol•u•ol** (-ôl′, -ōl′, -ŏl′) *n.* A flammable liquid, $CH_3C_6H_5$, obtained from coal tar or petroleum and used in aviation fuel and other high-octane fuels, in dyestuffs and explosives, and as a solvent. [TOLU (< which it was originally obtained) + -ENE.]

to•lu•ic acid (tə-lo͞o′ĭk) *n.* Any of three isomeric acids, $C_8H_8O_2$, derived from toluene. [TOLU(ENE) + -IC.]

to•lu•i•dine (tə-lo͞o′ĭ-dēn′) *n.* Any of three isomers, C_7H_9N, used to make dyes. [TOLU(ENE) + -ID(E) + -INE[2].]

Tol•yat•ti (tōl-yä′tē, tô-lyät′tē). See **Togliatti.**

tol•yl (tŏl′əl) *n.* The group C_7H_7, derived from toluene.

tom (tŏm) *n.* The male of various animals, esp. a male cat or turkey. [*Tom,* nickname for *Thomas.*]

Tom (tŏm) *n. Slang.* An Uncle Tom.

tom•a•hawk (tŏm′ə-hôk′) *n.* **1.** A light ax formerly used as a tool or weapon by certain Native American peoples. See Regional Note at **pone. 2.** A similar implement or weapon. [Virginia Algonquian *tamahaac.*] **—tom′a•hawk′** *v.*

to•mal•ley (tə-măl′ē, tŏm′ăl′ē) *n., pl.* **-leys.** The soft green liver of cooked lobster, considered a delicacy. [Galibi *tamali.*]

Tom and Jer•ry (jĕr′ē) *n., pl.* **Tom and Jer•ries.** A hot drink consisting usu. of rum, a beaten egg, milk or water, sugar, and spices. [After Corinthian *Tom* and *Jerry* Hawthorn, characters in *Life in London,* a novel by Pierce Egan (1772–1849).]

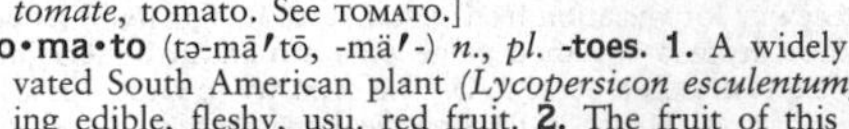

to•ma•til•lo (tō′mə-tē′yō, -tēl′yō) *n., pl.* **-los.** A species of ground cherry *(Physalis ixocarpa)* native to Mexico and having an edible yellow to purple viscid fruit. [Am.Sp., dim. of *tomate,* tomato. See TOMATO.]

to•ma•to (tə-mā′tō, -mä′-) *n., pl.* **-toes. 1.** A widely cultivated South American plant *(Lycopersicon esculentum)* having edible, fleshy, usu. red fruit. **2.** The fruit of this plant. [Alteration of Sp. *tomate* < Nahuatl *tomatl.*]

tomato fruit•worm (fro͞ot′wûrm′) *n.* The destructive larva of a noctuid moth *(Heliothis zea)* of the United States that burrows into the fruit of tomato plants.

tomato hornworm *n.* The destructive larva of a North American hawk moth *(Manduca quinquemaculata)* that feeds on the leaves of tomato plants.

tomb (to͞om) *n.* **1.** A grave or other place of burial. **2.** A vault or chamber for burial of the dead. **3.** A monument commemorating the dead. [ME < OFr. *tombe* < LLat. *tumba* < Gk. *tumbos.* See **teuə-***.]

tom•bac (tŏm′băk) *n.* An alloy of copper with zinc and sometimes other metals, used in making inexpensive jewelry. [Fr. < Du. *tombak* < Malay *tĕmbaga.*]

Tom•baugh (tŏm′bô′), **Clyde William.** b. 1906. Amer. astronomer who discovered the planet Pluto (1930).

Tom•big•bee (tŏm-bĭg′bē). A river, c. 544 km (400 mi), rising in NE MS and flowing through W AL to join the Alabama R.

tom•bo•lo (tŏm′bə-lō′) *n., pl.* **-los.** A sandbar that connects an island to the mainland or to another island. [Ital. < Lat. *tumulus,* mound. See TUMULUS.]

tom•boy (tŏm′boi′) *n.* A girl considered boyish or masculine.

tomb•stone (to͞om′stōn′) *n.* A stone placed over a grave as a marker; a gravestone.

Tomb•stone (to͞om′stōn′). A city of SE AZ NNW of Bisbee; site of a rich silver strike in 1877. Pop. 1,220.

tom•cat (tŏm′kăt′) *n.* A male cat. *—intr.v.* **-cat•ted, -cat•ting, -cats.** *Slang.* To pursue women sexually. Used of men.

tom•cod (tŏm′kŏd′) *n., pl.* **tomcod** or **-cods.** Either of two edible marine fishes, *Microgadus tomcod* of northern Atlantic waters or *M. proximus* of northern Pacific waters.

Tom Col•lins (kŏl′ĭnz) *n.* A drink consisting of gin, lemon or lime juice, carbonated water, and sugar. [< the name *Tom Collins.*]

Tom, Dick, and Har•ry (tŏm′ dĭk′ ən hăr′ē) *n. Informal.* Anybody at all; a member of the public at large.

tome (tōm) *n.* **1.** One of the books in a work of several volumes. **2.** A book, esp. a large or scholarly one. [Fr. < Lat. *tomus* < Gk. *tomos,* section < *temnein,* to cut. See **tem-***.]

-tome *suff.* **1.** Part; area; segment: *dermatome.* **2.** Cutting instrument: *microtome.* [NLat. *-tomus* < Gk. *-tomos,* a cutting < *tomos.* See TOME.]

to•men•tose (tō-mĕn′tōs′, tō′mən-) *adj. Biol.* Covered with short dense matted hairs. [NLat. *tōmentōsus* < Lat. *tōmentum,* cushion stuffing.]

to•men•tum (tō-mĕn′təm) *n., pl.* **-ta** (-tə). **1.** *Anat.* A network of extremely small blood vessels passing between the pia mater and the cerebral cortex. **2.** *Biol.* A covering of closely matted woolly hairs. [Lat. *tōmentum,* cushion stuffing.]

tom•fool (tŏm′fo͞ol′) *n.* A person considered stupid or foolish. *—adj.* Extremely foolish or stupid.

tom•fool•er•y (tŏm-fo͞o′lə-rē) *n., pl.* **-ies. 1.** Foolish behavior. **2.** Something trivial or foolish; nonsense.

tom•my also **Tom•my** (tŏm′ē) *n., pl.* **-mies.** *Chiefly British.* A British soldier. [Short for *Tommy Atkins* < *Thomas Atkins,* a name often used on sample forms.]

Tommy gun *n. Informal.* A Thompson submachine gun.

tom•my•rot (tŏm′ē-rŏt′) *n. Informal.* Utter foolishness; nonsense. [Dial. *tommy,* fool (< *Tom,* Tom) + ROT.]

to•mog•ra•phy (tō-mŏg′rə-fē) *n.* Any of several techniques for making detailed x-rays of a plane section of a solid object while blurring out the images of other planes. [Gk. *tomos,* section; see TOME + -GRAPHY.] **—to′mo•gram′** (tō′mə-grăm′) *n.* **—to′mo•graph′** (-grăf′) *n.*

to•mor•row (tə-môr′ō, -mŏr′ō) *n.* **1.** The day following today. **2.** The near future. *—adv.* On or for the day following today. [ME *to morow* < OE *tō morgenne,* in the morning : *tō,* at, on; see TO + *morgenne,* dative of *morgen,* morning.]

tom•pi•on (tŏm′pē-ən) *n.* Var. of **tampion.**

Tomp•kins (tŏmp′kĭnz, tŏm′-), **Daniel D.** 1774–1825. Vice President of the U.S. (1817–25).

Tomsk (tŏmsk, tômsk). A city of central Russia NE of Novosibirsk. Pop. 475,000.

Tom Thumb *n.* **1.** A hero of English folklore, who was no bigger than his father's thumb. **2.** A very small person.

tom•tit (tŏm′tĭt′) *n.* A small bird, such as a titmouse.

tom-tom (tŏm′tŏm′) also **tam-tam** (tŭm′tŭm′, tăm′tăm′) *n.* **1.** Any of various small-headed drums, usu. long and narrow, beaten with the hands. **2.** A monotonous rhythmic drumbeat or similar sound. [Hindi *ṭamṭam,* prob. of imit. orig.]

-tomy *suff.* Act of cutting; incision: *gastrotomy.* [NLat. *-tomia* < Gk. < *tomos,* a cutting < *temnein,* to cut. See **tem-***.]

ton (tŭn) *n.* **1.** A unit of weight equal to 2,000 pounds (0.907 metric ton or 907.18 kilograms). **2.** A unit of weight equal to 2,240 pounds (1.016 metric tons or 1,016.05 kilograms). **3.** A metric ton. See table at **measurement. 4.** A unit of capacity for cargo in maritime shipping, normally estimated at 40 cubic feet. **5.** A unit of internal capacity of a ship equal to 100 cubic feet. **6.** A unit for measuring the displacement of ships, equal to 35 cubic feet, and supposed to equal the volume taken by a long ton of seawater. **7.** *Informal.* A very large quantity. [ME *tonne,* a measure of weight. See TUN.]

ton•al (tō′nəl) *adj.* Of or relating to tones, a tone, or tonality. **—ton′al•ly** *adv.*

to•nal•i•ty (tō-năl′ĭ-tē) *n.*, *pl.* **-ties. 1.** *Mus.* **a.** A system or an arrangement of seven tones built on a tonic key. **b.** The arrangement of all the tones and chords of a composition in relation to a tonic. **2.** The scheme of the tones in a painting.

Ton•a•wan•da (tŏn′ə-wŏn′də). A city of W NY, a suburb of Buffalo. Pop. 17,284.

ton•do (tŏn′dō, tôn′-) *n.*, *pl.* **-dos** also **-di** (-dē). A round painting, relief, or similar work of art. [Ital., short for *rotondo*, round < Lat. *rotundus*. See ROTUND.]

tone (tōn) *n.* **1.** *Mus.* **a.** A sound of distinct pitch, quality, and duration; a note. **b.** The interval of a major second in the diatonic scale; a whole step. **c.** A recitational melody in a Gregorian chant. **2.a.** The quality or character of sound. **b.** The characteristic quality or timbre of a particular instrument or voice. **3.a.** The pitch of a word used to determine its meaning or to distinguish differences in meaning. **b.** The particular or relative pitch of a word, phrase, or sentence. **4.** Manner of expression in speech or writing. **5.** A general quality, effect, or atmosphere. **6.** *Color.* **a.** A color or shade of color. **b.** Quality of color. **7.** The general effect in painting of light, color, and shade. **8.** *Physiol.* **a.** The normal state of elastic tension or partial contraction in resting muscles. **b.** Normal firmness of a tissue or an organ. —*v.* **toned, ton•ing, tones.** —*tr.* **1.** To give a particular tone or inflection to. **2.** To soften or change the color of (a photographic negative, for example). **3.** To sound monotonously; intone. —*intr.* **1.** To assume a particular color quality. **2.** To harmonize in color. —***phrasal verbs.*** **tone down.** To make less vivid, harsh, or violent; moderate. **tone up.** To make or become brighter or more vigorous. [ME *ton* < OFr. < Lat. *tonus* < Gk. *tonos*, a stretching, string. See **ten-***.]

tone arm *n.* The arm of a phonograph turntable that holds the cartridge.

tone cluster *n.* *Mus.* A dissonant group of close notes played at the same time.

tone color *n.* *Mus.* The timbre of a voice or an instrument.

tone-deaf (tōn′dĕf′) *adj.* Unable to distinguish differences in musical pitch.

tone language *n.* A language that distinguishes meanings among words of similar form by variations in pitch and tone.

tone•less (tōn′lĭs) *adj.* **1.** Lacking tone. **2.** Lacking vitality; listless. —**tone′less•ly** *adv.* —**tone′less•ness** *n.*

ton•eme (tō′nēm) *n.* A type of phoneme that occurs in languages that use tone to convey differences in lexical meaning.

tone poem *n.* *Mus.* See **symphonic poem.**

ton•er (tō′nər) *n.* One that tones, as: **a.** A chemical bath used to change the color of a photographic print or preserve black-and-white prints or movie film. **b.** A powdery ink used dry or suspended in a liquid to produce a photocopy. **c.** A mildly astringent cream or lotion used to refresh the skin.

tone row (rō) *n.* *Mus.* A unique arbitrary series of notes used in the 12-tone system of composition.

ton•ey (tō′nē) *adj.* Var. of **tony.**

tong[1] (tông, tŏng) *tr.v.* **tonged, tong•ing, tongs.** To seize, hold, or manipulate with tongs. [Back-formation < TONGS.]

tong[2] (tông, tŏng) *n.* **1.** A Chinese association or political party. **2.** An association of Chinese in the United States, believed to be involved in organized crime. [Chin. (Cantonese), assembly hall, familial relationship between cousins.]

Ton•ga (tŏng′gə) also **Friend•ly Islands** (frĕnd′lē). A country in the SW Pacific E of Fiji comprising c. 150 islands; gained independence in 1970. Cap. Nukualofa. Pop. 96,592.

Ton•gan (tŏng′gən, tŏng′ən) *adj.* Of or relating to Tonga or its people, language, or culture. —*n.* **1.** A native or inhabitant of Tonga. **2.** The Polynesian language of Tonga.

tongs (tôngz, tŏngz) *pl.n.* *(used with a sing. or pl. v.)* A grasping device made up of two arms joined at one end by a pivot or hingelike scissors. [ME *tonges*, pl. of *tonge* < OE *tong.*]

tongue (tŭng) *n.* **1.a.** The fleshy movable muscular organ, attached in most vertebrates to the floor of the mouth, that is the principal organ of taste, an aid in chewing and swallowing, and an important organ of speech in human beings. **b.** An analogous organ or part in invertebrate animals, as in certain insects or mollusks. **2.** The tongue of an animal, such as a cow, used as food. **3.** A spoken language or dialect. **4.a.** Speech; talk. **b.** The act or power of speaking: *had no tongue to answer.* **c. tongues.** Speech or vocal sounds produced in a state of religious ecstasy. **d.** Style or quality of utterance: *a sharp tongue.* **5.** The bark or baying of a hunting dog that sees game. **6.** Something resembling a tongue in shape or function, as: **a.** The vibrating end of a reed in a wind instrument. **b.** A flame. **c.** The flap of material under the laces or buckles of a shoe. **d.** A spit of land; a promontory. **e.** A bell clapper. **f.** The harnessing pole attached to the front axle of a horse-drawn vehicle. **7.** A protruding strip along the edge of a board that fits into a groove on the edge of another board. —*v.* **tongued, tongu•ing, tongues.** —*tr.* **1.** *Mus.* To separate or articulate (notes played on a brass or wind instrument) by shutting off the stream of air with the tongue. **2.** To touch or lick with the tongue. **3.a.** To provide (a board) with a tongue. **b.** To join by means of a tongue and groove. **4.** *Archaic.* To scold. —*intr.* **1.** *Mus.* To articulate notes on a brass or wind instrument. **2.** To project. —***idioms.*** **hold (one's) tongue.** To be or keep silent. **lose (one's) tongue.** To lose the capacity to speak, as from shock. **on the tip of (one's) tongue.** On the verge of being recalled or expressed. [ME < OE *tunge.* See **dn̥ghū-***.]

tongue and groove *n.* A joint made by fitting a tongue on the edge of a board into a matching groove on another board.

tongue depressor *n.* A thin blade for pressing down the tongue during a medical examination of the mouth and throat; a spatula.

tongue•fish (tŭng′fĭsh′) *n.*, *pl.* **tonguefish** or **-fish•es.** Any of various marine flatfishes of the family Cynoglossidae, having the posterior part of the body tapering to a point.

tongue-in-cheek (tŭng′ĭn-chēk′) *adj.* Meant or expressed ironically or facetiously.

tongue-lash•ing (tŭng′lăsh′ĭng) *n.* *Informal.* A scolding.

tongue•less (tŭng′lĭs) *adj.* **1.** Having no tongue. **2.** Lacking the faculty of speech; mute. **3.** Speechless; silent.

tongue-tie (tŭng′tī′) *n.* Restricted mobility of the tongue resulting from abnormal shortness of the frenum. —*tr.v.* **-tied, -ty•ing, -ties.** To make tongue-tied.

tongue-tied (tŭng′tīd′) *adj.* **1.** Speechless or confused in expression, as from shyness. **2.** Affected with tongue-tie.

tongue twister *n.* **1.** A word or group of words difficult to articulate rapidly, as *Shall she sell seashells?* **2.** Something difficult to pronounce.

tongu•ing (tŭng′ĭng) *n.* *Mus.* Movement of the tongue in order to articulate notes on an instrument.

-tonia *suff.* Degree or state of tonicity: *myotonia.* [NLat. < Lat. *tonus.* See TONE.]

ton•ic (tŏn′ĭk) *n.* **1.** An agent, such as a medication, that restores or increases bodily tone. **2.** An invigorating, refreshing, or restorative agent or influence. **3.a.** Quinine water. **b.** *Boston.* See **soft drink. 4.** *Mus.* The first note of a diatonic scale; the keynote. **5.** A tonic accent. —*adj.* **1.** Producing or stimulating physical, mental, or emotional vigor. **2.a.** *Physiol.* Of, relating to, or producing tone or tonicity in muscles or tissue. **b.** *Medic.* Marked by continuous tension or contraction of muscles: *a tonic spasm.* **3.** *Mus.* Of or based on the keynote. **4.** Stressed, as a syllable; accented. [NLat. *tonicus*, of tension or tone < Gk. *tonikos*, capable of extension < *tonos*, a stretching, tone. See TONE.] —**ton′i•cal•ly** *adv.*

Regional Note: Generic terms for carbonated soft drinks vary widely in the United States. Probably the two most common words competing for precedence are *soda*, used in the northeast United States, and *pop*, used from the Midwest westward. Speakers in Western Maryland and Boston and its environs have a term of their own: *tonic.*

tonic accent *n.* *Ling.* A stress produced by a change, esp. a rise, in pitch as distinguished from increased volume.

to•nic•i•ty (tō-nĭs′ĭ-tē) *n.*, *pl.* **-ties. 1.** Normal firmness or functional readiness in body tissues or organs. **2.** The sustained partial contraction of resting or relaxed muscles.

tonic sol-fa *n.* *Mus.* A system of notation based on relationships between tones in a key and replacing the usual staff notation with solmization syllables or their abbreviations.

to•night (tə-nīt′) *adv.* On or during the present or coming night. —*n.* This night or this day's night. [ME *to night* < OE *tō niht*, at night : *tō*, at, on; see TO + *niht*, night; see NIGHT.]

ton•ka bean (tŏng′kə) *n.* **1.** A tropical South American tree *(Dipteryx odorata)* having pulpy egg-shaped one-seeded pods and fragrant seeds used as a flavoring. **2.** The seed of this tree. [Perh. < Galibi *tonka.*]

Ton•kin (tŏn′kĭn′, tŏng′-). A historical region of SE Asia in present-day N Vietnam on the **Gulf of Tonkin**, an arm of the South China Sea. —**Ton′kin•ese′** (-ēz′, -ēs′) *adj. & n.*

Ton•le Sap (tŏn′lā săp′, säp′). A lake of central Cambodia; an outlet for the floodwaters of the Mekong R.

ton-mile (tŭn′mīl′) *n.* A unit of freight transportation equivalent to a ton of freight moved one mile.

ton•nage (tŭn′ĭj) *n.* **1.** The number of tons of water that a ship displaces when afloat. **2.** The capacity of a merchant ship in units of 100 cubic feet. **3.** A duty or charge per ton on cargo, as at a port or canal. **4.** The total shipping of a country or port, figured in tons, with reference to carrying capacity. **5.** Weight measured in tons. [TON + -AGE. Sense 3, ME < OFr. < *tonne*, tun. See TONNE.]

tonne (tŭn) *n.* A metric ton. [Fr. < OFr., tun < LLat. *tunna*, prob. of Celt. orig.]

ton•neau (tə-nō′, tŏn′ō′) *n.*, *pl.* **-neaus.** The rear seating compartment of an early type of automobile. [Fr. < OFr. *tonnel*, cask. See TUNNEL.]

to•nom•e•ter (tō-nŏm′ĭ-tər) *n.* **1.** Any of various instruments for measuring pressure or tension. **2.** An instrument for measuring hydrostatic pressure within the eyeball, used in the detection of glaucoma. **3.** *Mus.* An instrument used to determine the pitch or vibration rate of tones. [Gk. *tonos*, tension; see TONE + -METER.] —**to′no•met′ric** (tō′nə-mĕt′rĭk) *adj.* —**to•nom′e•try** *n.*

to•no•plast (tō′nə-plăst′) *n.* The cytoplasmic membrane that surrounds a vacuole of a plant cell. [Gk. *tonos*, string, tension; see **ten-*** + -PLAST.]

tom-tom

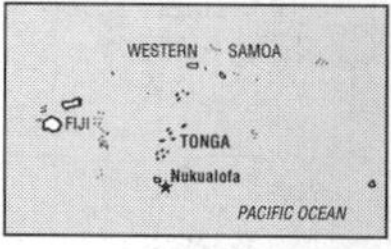

Tonga

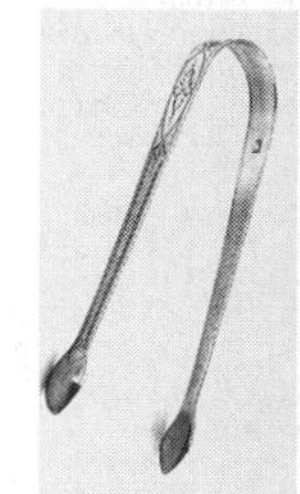

tongs
1802 English silver sugar tongs

ă pat	oi boy
ā pay	ou out
âr care	ŏŏ took
ä father	ōō boot
ĕ pet	ŭ cut
ē be	ûr urge
ĭ pit	th thin
ī pie	*th* this
îr pier	hw which
ŏ pot	zh vision
ō toe	ə about, item
ô paw	

Stress marks:
′ (primary);
′ (secondary), as in
dictionary (dĭk′shə-nĕr′ē)

ton•sil (tŏn′səl) *n.* A small oral mass of lymphoid tissue, esp. either of two such masses embedded in the lateral walls of the opening between the mouth and the pharynx, of uncertain function but believed to help protect the body from respiratory infections. [< Lat. *tōnsillae*, tonsils.] **—ton′sil•lar** *adj.*
ton•sil•lec•to•my (tŏn′sə-lĕk′tə-mē) *n., pl.* **-mies.** Surgical removal of tonsils or a tonsil.
ton•sil•li•tis (tŏn′sə-lī′tĭs) *n.* Inflammation of the tonsils.
tonsillo– or **tonsill–** *pref.* Tonsil: *tonsillectomy.* [< Lat. *tōnsillae*, tonsils.]
ton•sil•lot•o•my (tŏn′sə-lŏt′ə-mē) *n., pl.* **-mies.** Surgical incision of a tonsil.
ton•so•ri•al (tŏn-sôr′ē-əl, -sōr-) *adj.* Of or relating to barbering or a barber. [< Lat. *tōnsōrius* < *tōnsor*, barber < *tōnsus*, p.part. of *tondēre*, to shear. See **tem-*.**]
ton•sure (tŏn′shər) *n.* **1.** The act of shaving the head or part of the head, esp. as a preliminary to becoming a priest or a member of a monastic order. **2.** The shaved part of a monk's or priest's head. *—tr.v.* **-sured, -sur•ing, -sures.** To shave the head of. [ME < OFr. < Med.Lat. *tōnsūra* < Lat., a shearing < *tōnsus*, p.part. of *tondēre*, to shear. See **tem-*.**]
ton•tine (tŏn′tēn′, tŏn-tēn′) *n.* An investment plan in which participants buy shares in a common fund and receive an annuity, with the entire fund going to the final survivor or to those who survive after a specified time. [Fr., after Lorenzo *Tonti* (1635–90?), Italian-born French banker.]
to•nus (tō′nəs) *n., pl.* **-nus•es.** Bodily or muscular tone; tonicity. [Lat., tone. See TONE.]
ton•y also **ton•ey** (tō′nē) *adj.* **-i•er, -i•est.** *Informal.* Viewed as expensive, luxurious, or exclusive. [< TONE.]
To•ny (tō′nē) *n., pl.* **-nys.** An annual award for outstanding achievement in the theater. [After *Tony*, nickname of Antoinette Perry (1888–1946), Amer. actress and director.]
too (to͞o) *adv.* **1.** In addition; also: *He's coming too.* **2.** More than enough; excessively: *worries too much.* **3.** To a regrettable degree: *an error all too apparent.* **4.** Very; extremely; immensely: *only too willing.* **5.** *Informal.* Indeed; so: *You will too!* [ME *to* < OE *tō*, to, furthermore. See **de-*.**]
took (to͝ok) *v.* P.t. of **take.**
tool (to͞ol) *n.* **1.** A device, such as a saw, used to perform or facilitate manual or mechanical work. **2.a.** A machine, such as a lathe, used to cut and shape machine parts or other objects. **b.** The cutting part of such a machine. **3.** Something regarded as needed for carrying out an occupation or profession. **4.** Something used in the performance of an operation; an instrument. **5.** *Vulgar Slang.* A penis. **6.** A person used to carry out the designs of another; a dupe. **7.a.** A bookbinder's hand stamp. **b.** A design impressed on a book cover by such a stamp. *—v.* **tooled, tool•ing, tools.** *—tr.* **1.** To form, work, or decorate with a tool. **2.** To ornament (a book cover) with a bookbinder's tool. **3.** *Slang.* To drive (a vehicle). *—intr.* **1.** To work with a tool. **2.** *Slang.* To drive or ride in a vehicle. ***—phrasal verb.*** **tool up.** To provide an industry or a factory with machinery and tools suitable for a job. [ME < OE *tōl*, poss. < ON.]

Syns: *tool, instrument, implement, utensil, appliance.* These nouns refer to devices used in the performance of work. *Tool* applies broadly to a device that facilitates work; specifically it denotes a small manually operated device: *a box full of tools for repair jobs. Instrument* refers especially to one of the relatively small precision tools used by trained professionals: *sterilized the scalpel along with the other instruments. Implement* is the preferred term for tools used in agriculture and certain building trades: *rakes, hoes, and other implements. Utensil* often refers to an implement used in doing household work: *cooking utensils laid out on the table. Appliance* most frequently denotes a power-driven device that performs a specific function: *toasters and other appliances.*

tool•box (to͞ol′bŏks′) *n.* A case for carrying or storing tools.
tool•ing (to͞o′lĭng) *n.* **1.** Work or ornamentation done with tools, esp. on leather. **2.** The process of providing a factory with machinery in preparation for production.
tool•mak•er (to͞ol′mā′kər) *n.* A skilled machinist trained in making and repairing tools and parts.
Toombs (to͞omz), **Robert Augustus.** 1810–85. Amer. politician who served as Confederate secretary of state (1861).
toon (to͞on) *n.* **1.** A tall tree *(Cedrela toona)* of tropical Asia and Australia having dark red aromatic wood. **2.** The wood of this tree. [Hindi *tūn* < Skt. *tunnaḥ.*]
toot (to͞ot) *v.* **toot•ed, toot•ing, toots.** *—intr.* **1.** To sound a horn or whistle in short blasts. **2.** To make this or a similar sound. **3.** *Slang.* To snort cocaine. *—tr.* **1.** To blow or sound (a horn or whistle). **2.** To sound (a blast, for example) on a horn or whistle. **3.** *Slang.* To snort (cocaine). *—n.* **1.** A blast, as of a horn. **2.** *Slang.* A drinking binge. **3.** *Slang.* Cocaine, esp. a small amount snorted at one time. [Ult. of imit. orig.] **—toot′er** *n.*
tooth (to͞oth) *n., pl.* **teeth** (tēth). **1.a.** One of a set of hard bonelike structures rooted in sockets in the jaws of vertebrates, typically composed of a core of soft pulp surrounded by a layer of hard dentin coated with cement or enamel at the crown and used for biting or chewing food or as a means of attack or defense. **b.** A similar structure in invertebrates, such as one of the pointed ridges on the shell of a mollusk. **2.** A projecting part resembling a tooth in shape or function, as on a comb, gear, or saw. **3.** A small notched projection along a margin, esp. of a leaf. **4.** A rough surface, as of metal. **5.a.** Something that injures or destroys with force. Often used in the plural. **b. teeth.** Effective means of enforcement; muscle. **6.** Taste or appetite. *—v.* (to͞oth, to͞oth) **toothed, tooth•ing, tooths.** *—tr.* **1.** To furnish (a tool, for example) with teeth. **2.** To make a jagged edge on. *—intr.* To become interlocked; mesh. ***—idioms.*** **get** (or **sink**) **(one's) teeth into.** *Slang.* To be actively involved in; get a firm grasp of. **show** (or **bare**) **(one's) teeth.** To express a readiness to fight; threaten defiantly. **to the teeth.** Lacking nothing; completely. [ME < OE *tōth.* See **dent-*.**]

Word History: The words *eat, tooth,* and *dentist* are all related etymologically. The Proto-Indo-European root **ed–*, meaning "to eat" and the source of our word *eat,* originally meant "to bite." A participial form of **ed–* in this sense was **dent–*, "biting," which came to mean "tooth." Our word *tooth* comes from **dont–*, a form of **dent–*, with sound changes that resulted in the Germanic word **tanthuz.* This word became Old English *tōth* and Modern English *tooth.* Meanwhile the Proto-Indo-European form **dent–* itself became in Latin *dēns* (stem *dent–*), "tooth," from which is derived our word *dentist.*

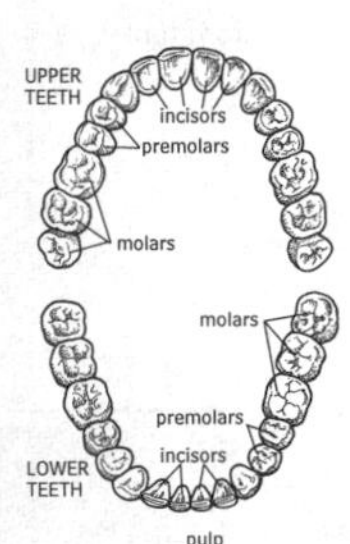

tooth
Top: Permanent teeth of an adult human
Bottom: Cross section of an incisor

tooth•ache (to͞oth′āk′) *n.* An aching pain in or near a tooth.
tooth and nail *adv.* With every available resource; with unrelenting effort.
tooth•brush (to͞oth′brŭsh′) *n.* A brush for cleaning teeth.
toothed (to͞otht, to͞othd) *adj.* Having teeth, esp. of a certain number or type. Often used in combination: *saw-toothed.*
toothed whale *n.* Any of various whales of the suborder Odontoceti, having numerous conical teeth.
tooth fairy *n.* A fairy supposed to leave money under a child's pillow in place of a baby tooth that has just fallen out.
tooth•less (to͞oth′lĭs) *adj.* **1.** Lacking teeth. **2.** Lacking force; ineffectual. **—tooth′less•ly** *adv.* **—tooth′less•ness** *n.*
tooth•paste (to͞oth′pāst′) *n.* A paste for cleaning teeth.
tooth•pick (to͞oth′pĭk′) *n.* A small piece of wood or other material for removing food particles from between the teeth.
tooth•pow•der (to͞oth′pou′dər) *n.* Powder for cleaning teeth.
tooth shell *n.* Any of various burrowing marine mollusks of the class Scaphopoda, having a long tapering curved shell.
tooth•some (to͞oth′səm) *adj.* **1.** Delicious; luscious. **2.** Pleasant; attractive. **3.** Sexually attractive or exciting. **—tooth′some•ly** *adv.* **—tooth′some•ness** *n.*
tooth•wort (to͞oth′wûrt′, -wôrt′) *n.* **1.** Any of several eastern North American plants of the genus *Cardamine,* such as the crinkleroot, having fleshy rhizomes and palmately divided leaves. **2.** A parasitic European plant *(Lathraea squamaria)* having scaly stems and pinkish flowers.
tooth•y (to͞o′thē) *adj.* **-i•er, -i•est.** Having or showing prominent teeth. **—tooth′i•ly** *adv.*
too•tle (to͞ot′l) *intr.v.* **-tled, -tling, -tles. 1.** To toot softly and repeatedly, as on a flute. **2.** *Informal.* To walk or drive in a leisurely manner; amble. *—n.* The act or sound of tootling, as on a flute. [Freq. of TOOT.]
toots (to͝ots) *n. Slang.* Babe; sweetie. [Perh. short for TOOTSIE.]
toot•sie (to͝ot′sē) *n. Slang.* **1.** Toots. **2.** A girl or young woman. [?]
toot•sy (to͝ot′sē) *n., pl.* **-sies.** *Slang.* A person's foot. [Alteration of *footsy* < FOOT.]
top¹ (tŏp) *n.* **1.** The uppermost part, point, surface, or end. **2.** The crown of the head. **3.** The part of a plant, such as a rutabaga, above the ground. **4.** Something, such as a lid, that covers or forms an uppermost part. **5.** The upper half of a two-piece garment. **6.** *Naut.* A platform enclosing the head of each mast of a sailing ship, to which the topmast rigging is attached. **7.** The highest degree, pitch, or point; the peak, acme, or zenith. **8.a.** The highest position or rank. **b.** A person in this position. **9.** *Games.* The highest card or cards in a suit or hand. **10.** The best part. **11.** The earliest part or beginning. **12.** *Baseball.* The first half of an inning. **13.** *Sports.* **a.** A stroke that lands above the center of a ball, as in golf or tennis, giving it a forward spin. **b.** This forward spin. *—adj.* **1.** Situated at the top. **2.** Of the highest degree, quality, or amount. **3.** In a position of preeminence. *—v.* **topped, top•ping, tops.** *—tr.* **1.** To form, furnish with, or serve as a top. **2.** To reach the top of. **3.** To go over the top of. **4.** To exceed or surpass. **5.** To be at the head of. **6.** To remove the top or uppermost part from; crop: *topped the trees.* **7.** *Sports.* **a.** To strike the upper part of (a ball), giving it forward spin. **b.** To make (a stroke) in this way. *—intr.* To make a finish, an end, or a conclusion. ***—phrasal verbs.*** **top off. 1.** To fill up (a container), esp. when it is almost full to begin with. **2.** To finish up. **top out. 1.** To put the framework for the top story on (a building). **2.** To fill up (a ship, for example). **3.** To cease rising. ***—idioms.*** **off the top of (one's) head.** *Informal.* In an impromptu way. **on top. 1.** At the highest point or peak. **2.** In a dominant, controlling, or successful position. **on top of.** *Informal.* **1.** In control of. **2.** Fully

informed about. **3.** In addition to; besides. **4.** Following closely on; coming immediately after. **on top of the world.** *Informal.* In a position of great happiness or success. **over the top.** **1.** Surpassing a goal or quota. **2.** Over the breastwork, as an attack in trench warfare. [ME < OE.]

top² (tŏp) *n.* A toy having one end tapered to a point, allowing it to be spun, as by suddenly pulling a string wound around it. [ME < OE.]

top– *pref.* Var. of **topo–**.

to•paz (tō′păz′) *n.* **1.a.** A colorless, blue, yellow, brown, or pink aluminum silicate mineral, often found in association with granitic rocks and valued as a gemstone, esp. in the brown and pink varieties. **b.** Any of various yellow gemstones, esp. a yellow variety of sapphire or corundum. **2.** A light yellow variety of quartz. **3.** Either of two colorful South American hummingbirds *(Topaza pyra* or *T. pella).* [ME *topace* < OFr. < Lat. *topazus* < Gk. *topazos.*]

top banana *n. Slang.* **1.** The main comic in a burlesque show. **2.** The head person, as of a group or project. [So called from the presentation of a banana to the comedian who has the punch line in a three-man burlesque routine.]

top boot *n.* A high boot usu. having its upper part made of a different material or with leather of a contrasting color or texture.

top•coat (tŏp′kōt′) *n.* A lightweight overcoat.

top dog *n. Slang.* One seen to have the dominant position or highest authority. **—top′-dog′** (tŏp′dôg′, -dŏg′) *adj.*

top-drawer (tŏp′drôr′) *adj.* Of the highest importance, rank, privilege, or merit.

top-dress (tŏp′drĕs′) *tr.v.* **-dressed, -dress•ing, -dress•es. 1.** To cover (a road surface) with loose material that is not worked in. **2.** To cover (farmland) with fertilizer.

top dressing *n.* **1.** A covering of loose gravel on a road. **2.** A fertilizer covering put on soil without being plowed under.

tope¹ (tōp) *tr. & intr.v.* **toped, top•ing, topes.** To drink (liquor) habitually and excessively or engage in such drinking. [Poss. < obsolete *tope,* interjection used in proposing a toast.]

tope² (tōp) *n.* A small, rough-skinned, widely distributed shark *(Galeorhinus galeus)* having an elongated conical snout. [?]

tope³ (tōp) *n.* A dome-shaped monument used to house Buddhist relics or commemorate significant facts of Buddhism or Jainism. [Hindi *top,* prob. < Prakrit *thūpo* < Skt. *stūpaḥ.*]

to•pee (tō-pē′, tō′pē) *n.* Var. of **topi¹**.

To•pe•ka (tə-pē′kə). The cap. of KS, in the NE part W of Kansas City; founded 1854. Pop. 119,883.

top•er (tō′pər) *n.* A chronic drinker.

top•flight (tŏp′flīt′) *adj. Informal.* First-rate; excellent.

top•gal•lant (tə-găl′ənt, tŏp-) *adj.* **1.** *Naut.* Of, relating to, or being the mast above the topmast, its sails, or its rigging. **2.** Raised above adjacent parts or structures.

top-ham•per also **top ham•per** (tŏp′hăm′pər) *n.* **1.** *Naut.* Weight or materials, such as spars, stored either aloft or on the upper decks. **2.** Cumbersome unnecessary matter.

top hat *n.* A man's hat having a narrow brim and a tall cylindrical crown, usu. made of silk.

top-heav•y (tŏp′hĕv′ē) *adj.* **-i•er, -i•est. 1.** Likely to topple because of too much weight at the top. **2.** *Accounting.* Overcapitalized. **3.** Having an excessive number of managers. **—top′-heav′i•ness** *n.*

To•phet (tō′fĕt′, -fĭt) *n.* **1.** An extremely unpleasant or painful condition or place. **2.** Hell. [ME < Heb. *tōpet,* a place where children were burned.]

top-hole (tŏp′hōl′) *adj. Chiefly British.* First-rate; excellent.

to•phus (tō′fəs) *n., pl.* **-phi** (-fī). **1.** *Pathol.* A deposit of urates in the skin and tissue around a joint or in the external ear, occurring in gout. **2.** A concretion of mineral salts and organic matter on the teeth. [Lat. *tōphus,* tufa.]

to•pi¹ also **to•pee** (tō-pē′, tō′pē) *n., pl.* **-pis** also **-pees.** A pith helmet worn to protect against sun and heat. [Hindi *ṭopī,* hat.]

to•pi² (tō′pē) *n., pl.* **topi** or **-pis.** A sassaby *(Damaliscus lunatus* subsp. *topi)* of eastern Africa having a glossy dark brown coat. [Prob. of Swahili orig.]

to•pi•ar•y (tō′pē-ĕr′ē) *adj.* Of or characterized by the clipping or trimming of live shrubs or trees into decorative shapes, as of animals. *—n., pl.* **-ies. 1.** Topiary work or art. **2.** A topiary garden. [Lat. *topiārius* < *topia,* ornamental gardening < Gk. *topia,* pl. of *topion,* field, dim. of *topos,* place.]

top•ic (tŏp′ĭk) *n.* **1.** The subject of a speech, an essay, a thesis, or a discourse. **2.** A subject of discussion or conversation. **3.** A subdivision of a theme, a thesis, or an outline. See Syns at **subject.** [Obsolete *topic,* rhetorical argument, sing. of *Topics,* work by Aristotle < Lat. *Topica* < Gk. *Topika,* commonplaces < neut. pl. of *topikos,* of a place < *topos,* place.]

top•i•cal (tŏp′ĭ-kəl) *adj.* **1.** Of or belonging to a particular location or place; local. **2.** Currently of interest; contemporary. **3.** *Medic.* Of or applied to an isolated or localized area of the body. **4.** Of, arranged by, or relating to a particular topic or topics. [< Gk. *topikos* < *topos,* place.] **—top′i•cal′i•ty** (-kăl′ĭ-tē) *n.* **—top′i•cal•ly** *adv.*

topic sentence *n.* The sentence within a paragraph or discourse that states the main thought, usu. at the beginning.

top•knot (tŏp′nŏt′) *n.* **1.** A crest or knot of hair or feathers on the crown of the head. **2.** A ribbon or bow worn as a headdress.

top•less (tŏp′lĭs) *adj.* **1.** Having no top: *topless jars.* **2.** So high as to appear to extend out of sight. **3.** Of, relating to, or wearing a garment that does not cover the breasts.

top-lev•el (tŏp′lĕv′əl) *adj.* **1.** Of or relating to the highest office or rank. **2.** Of or relating to top-level people.

top•loft•y (tŏp′lôf′tē, -lŏf′-) *adj.* **-i•er, -i•est.** Haughty; pretentious. **—top′loft′i•ness** *n.*

top•mast (tŏp′məst, -măst′) *n. Naut.* A mast extending upward from the top of a lower mast of a sailing ship.

top•min•now (tŏp′mĭn′ō) *n.* **1.** Any of several small New World freshwater fishes of the genus *Fundulus,* related to the killifishes. **2.** Any of various small viviparous New World fishes of the family Poeciliidae of fresh or brackish waters.

top•most (tŏp′mōst′) *adj.* Highest; uppermost.

top•notch (tŏp′nŏch′) *adj. Informal.* First-rate; excellent.

topo– or **top–** *pref.* Place; region: *toponymy.* [Gk. < *topos,* place.]

topog. *abbr.* Topography

to•pog•ra•pher (tə-pŏg′rə-fər) *n.* **1.** One who is skilled in topography. **2.** One who describes and maps the surface features of geographic regions.

to•pog•ra•phy (tə-pŏg′rə-fē) *n., pl.* **-phies. 1.** Detailed precise description of a place or region. **2.** Graphic representation of the surface features of a place or region on a map, indicating their relative positions and elevations. **3.** A description or an analysis of a structured entity. **4.a.** The surface features of a place or region. **b.** The surface features of an object: *The topography of a crystal.* **5.** The surveying of the features of a place or region. **6.** The study or description of an anatomical region or part. **—top′o•graph′** (tŏp′ə-grăf′) *n.* **—top′o•graph′ic** (-grăf′ĭk), **top′o•graph′i•cal** (-ĭ-kəl) *adj.* **—top′o•graph′i•cal•ly** *adv.*

to•pol•o•gy (tə-pŏl′ə-jē) *n., pl.* **-gies. 1.** Topographic study of a given place, esp. the history of a region as indicated by topography. **2.** *Medic.* The anatomical structure of a specific area or part of the body. **3.** *Math.* The study of the properties of geometric figures or solids not normally affected by changes in size or shape. **—top′o•log′ic** (tŏp′ə-lŏj′ĭk), **top′o•log′i•cal** (-ĭ-kəl) *adj.* **—top′o•log′i•cal•ly** *adv.* **—to•pol′o•gist** *n.*

top•o•nym (tŏp′ə-nĭm′) *n.* **1.** A place name. **2.** A name derived from a place or region. [Back-formation < TOPONYMY.] **—top′o•nym′ic, top′o•nym′i•cal** *adj.*

to•pon•y•my (tə-pŏn′ə-mē) *n., pl.* **-mies. 1.a.** The place names of a region or language. **b.** The study of such place names. **2.** *Anat.* Nomenclature with respect to a region of the body rather than to organs or structures.

to•pos (tō′pōs, -pŏs) *n., pl.* **-poi** (-poi). A traditional theme or motif. [Gk., short for *(koinos) topos,* (common)place.]

top•per (tŏp′ər) *n.* **1.** One that removes tops or puts tops on. **2.a.** One that is exceedingly good of its kind. **b.** *Slang.* Something, such as a witticism, that surpasses all before it. **3.** A woman's short lightweight coat. **4.** *Slang.* A top hat.

top•ping (tŏp′ĭng) *n.* **1.** A sauce, frosting, or garnish for food. **2.** A part or layer that forms the top. **3. toppings.** The cropped parts of plants or trees after pruning. *—adj.* **1.** Highest in rank or eminence. **2.** *Chiefly British.* First-rate.

top•ple (tŏp′əl) *v.* **-pled, -pling, -ples.** *—tr.* To push or throw over; overturn. See Syns at **overthrow.** *—intr.* **1.** To totter and fall. **2.** To lean over as if about to fall. [Freq. of TOP¹.]

top quark *n.* A hypothetical quark with a charge of +⅔ and a mass more than 100,000 times that of the electron. See table at **subatomic particle.**

top round *n.* A cut of meat, such as a steak or roast, taken from the inner section of a round of beef.

tops (tŏps) *adj. Slang.* First-rate; excellent.

top•sail (tŏp′səl, -sāl′) *n. Naut.* **1.** A square sail set above the lowest sail on the mast of a square-rigged ship. **2.** A triangular or square sail set above the gaff of a lower sail on a fore-and-aft-rigged ship.

topsail schooner *n. Naut.* A schooner carrying two or more square topsails on its foremast.

top-se•cret (tŏp′sē′krĭt) *adj.* Containing information, the disclosure of which poses the gravest threat to national security.

top•side (tŏp′sīd′) *n.* **1.** *Naut.* The surface of a ship's hull above the water line. Often used in the plural. **2.** The highest position of authority. *—adv. & adj.* **1.** *Naut.* On or to the upper parts of a ship; on deck. **2.** In a position of authority.

top•soil (tŏp′soil′) *n.* The upper part of the soil. *—tr.v.* **-soiled, -soil•ing, -soils.** To remove topsoil from (land).

top•spin (tŏp′spĭn′) *n. Sports.* Forward rotation imparted to a ball by a stroke, as in tennis.

top•stitch (tŏp′stĭch′) *tr.v.* **-stitched, -stitch•ing, -stitch•es.** To sew a row of stitching close to the seam or edge of (a garment) on the outer side of the fabric.

top•sy-tur•vy (tŏp′sē-tûr′vē) *adv.* **1.** With the top downward and the bottom up; upside-down. **2.** In a state of utter disorder or confusion. *—adj.* **-vi•er, -vi•est.** Being in a confused or disordered condition. *—n., pl.* **-vies.** The quality, the con-

top hat

topiary

ă pat	oi boy
ā pay	ou out
âr care	o͝o took
ä father	o͞o boot
ĕ pet	ŭ cut
ē be	ûr urge
ĭ pit	th thin
ī pie	*th* this
îr pier	hw which
ŏ pot	zh vision
ō toe	ə about, item
ô paw	

Stress marks:
′ (primary);
′ (secondary), as in
dictionary (dĭk′shə-nĕr′ē)

dition, or an instance of confusion or chaos. [Prob. < TOP¹ + obsolete *terve*, to overturn (< ME *terven*).] **—top′sy-tur′vi•ly** *adv.* **—top′sy-tur′vi•ness** *n.*

toque (tōk) *n.* **1.** A woman's small, brimless, close-fitting hat. **2.** A plumed velvet cap with a full crown and small rolled brim, worn in 16th-century France. [Fr. < Sp. *toca*, perh. < Ar. **ṭâqa* < OPers. *tāq*, veil, shawl.]

tor (tôr) *n.* **1.** A high rock or pile of rocks on the top of a hill. **2.** A rocky peak or hill. [ME < OE *torr*, prob. of Celt. orig.]

To•rah also **to•rah** (tôr′ə, tōr′ə, toir′ə, tô-rä′) *n. Judaism.* **1.** The first five books of the Hebrew Bible. See table at **Bible. 2.** The entire body of Jewish religious law and learning including both sacred literature and oral tradition. **3.** A scroll of parchment containing the first five books of the Hebrew Bible, read during certain Jewish services. [Heb. *tôrâ*.]

Torah
18th-century Torah scroll

Tor•bay (tôr-bā′, tôr′bā′). A borough of SW England ENE of Plymouth. Pop. 112,400.

torch (tôrch) *n.* **1.a.** A portable light produced by a burning stick of resinous wood or burning material wound about the end of a stick of wood; a flambeau. **b.** *Chiefly British.* A flashlight. **2.** Something that serves to illuminate, enlighten, or guide. **3.** *Slang.* An arsonist. **4.** A portable apparatus that produces a very hot flame by the combustion of gases, used in welding and construction. *—tr.v.* **torched, torch•ing, torch•es.** *Slang.* To cause to burn or undergo combustion. [ME *torche* < OFr. < VLat. **torca*, alteration of Lat. *torqua*, var. of *torquēs*, torque < Lat. *torquēre*, to twist. See **terkʷ-***.]

torch•bear•er (tôrch′bâr′ər) *n.* **1.** One that carries a torch. **2.** One who imparts knowledge or inspiration to others.

tor•chère (tôr-shâr′) also **tor•chier** or **tor•chiere** (-chîr′) *n.* A usu. tall floor lamp with a bowl-shaped part that diffuses the light or directs it upward. [Fr. < *torche*, torch. See TORCH.]

tor•chon lace (tôr′shŏn′) *n.* Lace made of coarse linen or cotton thread twisted in geometric patterns. [Fr. *torchon*, duster < OFr. < *torche*, twisted straw, torch. See TORCH.]

torch song *n. Mus.* A sentimental love song, typically one in which the singer laments a lost love. **—torch singer** *n.*

torch•wood (tôrch′wo͝od′) *n.* **1.** Any of several tropical American trees of the genus *Amyris*, esp. *A. balsamifera*, having resinous wood that burns with a torchlike flame. **2.** The wood of any of these trees.

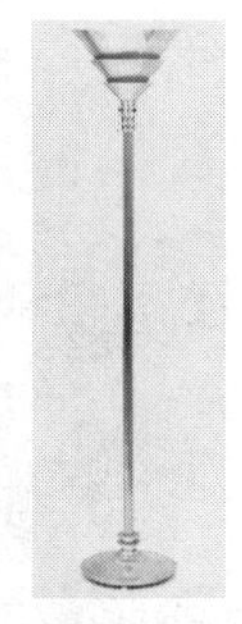
torchère
c. 1932 aluminum torchère, designed by Walter von Nessen (1889–1943) with modifications by Eliel Saarinen (1873–1950)

tore¹ (tôr, tōr) *v.* P.t. of **tear¹**.

tore² (tôr, tōr) *n. Math.* See **torus** 4. [Fr. < Lat. *torus*.]

tor•e•a•dor (tôr′ē-ə-dôr′) *n.* A matador; a bullfighter. [Sp. < *torear*, to fight bulls < *toro*, bull < Lat. *taurus*. See **tauro-***.]

to•re•ro (tə-râr′ō, tō-rĕ′rō) *n., pl.* **-ros.** A matador or one of the supporting team. [Sp. < LLat. *taurārius* < Lat. *taurus*, bull. See **tauro-***.]

to•reu•tics (tə-ro͞o′tĭks) *n. (used with a sing. v.)* The art of working metal or other materials by the use of embossing and chasing to form minute detailed reliefs. [< Gk. *toreutikos*, of metal work < *toreutos*, worked in relief < *toreuein*, to work thus < *toreus*, a boring tool. See **terə-¹***.] **—to•reu′tic** *adj.*

to•ri (tôr′ī, tōr′ī) *n.* Pl. of **torus.**

to•ri•i (tôr′ē-ē′, tōr′-) *n., pl.* **torii.** The gateway of a Shinto temple, consisting of two uprights supporting a concave crosspiece with projecting ends and a straight crosspiece beneath it. [J. : *tori*, bird + *i-* (< *iru*, to dwell).]

To•ri•no (tô-rē′nô). See **Turin.**

tor•ment (tôr′mĕnt′) *n.* **1.** Great physical pain or mental anguish. **2.** A source of harassment, annoyance, or pain. **3.** The torture inflicted on prisoners under interrogation. *—tr.v.* (tôr-mĕnt′, tôr′mĕnt′) **-ment•ed, -ment•ing, -ments. 1.** To cause to undergo physical or mental torture. **2.** To agitate or upset greatly. **3.** To annoy, pester, or harass. [ME < OFr. < Lat. *tormentum* (< *torquēre*, to twist; see **terkʷ-***).]

torii
The Grand Torii of Itsukushima, Japan

tor•men•til (tôr′mən-tĭl′) *n.* A perennial Eurasian plant *(Potentilla erecta)* having yellow flowers and astringent roots. [ME *tormentille* < Med.Lat. *tormentilla*, fem. dim. of Lat. *tormentum*, torment (used as an analgesic). See TORMENT.]

tor•men•tor also **tor•ment•er** (tôr-mĕn′tər, tôr′mĕn′-) *n.* **1.** One that torments. **2.** A hanging at each side of a stage directly behind the proscenium that blocks the wing area and sidelights from the audience. **3.** A sound-absorbent screen used on a movie set to prevent echo.

torn (tôrn, tōrn) *v.* P.part. of **tear¹**.

tor•na•do (tôr-nā′dō) *n., pl.* **-does** or **-dos. 1.** A rotating column of air usu. accompanied by a funnel-shaped downward extension of a cumulonimbus cloud and having a vortex several hundred yards in diameter whirling destructively at high speeds. **2.** A violent thunderstorm in western Africa or nearby Atlantic waters. **3.** A whirlwind or hurricane. [Alteration of Sp. *tronada*, thunderstorm < *tronar*, to thunder < Lat. *tonāre*. See **(s)tenə-***.] **—tor•na′dic** (-nā′dĭk, -năd′ĭk) *adj.*

Tor•ne (tôr′nə) also **Tor•ni•o** (tôr′nē-ō′). A river of N Sweden rising near the Norwegian border in **Lake Torne** and flowing c. 402 km (250 mi) to the Gulf of Bothnia.

tor•nil•lo (tôr-nĭl′ō, -nē′ō) *n., pl.* **-los.** See **screw bean.** [Am. Sp. < Sp., small lathe, screw, dim. of *torno*, lathe < Lat. *tornus*. See TURN.]

to•roid (tôr′oid′, tōr′-) *n.* **1.** *Math.* **a.** A surface generated by a closed curve rotating about but not intersecting or containing an axis in its own plane. **b.** A solid having such a surface. **2.** A body having the shape of a toroid. [TOR(US) + -OID.] **—to•roi′dal** (tô-roid′l) *adj.*

To•ron•to (tə-rŏn′tō). The cap. of Ontario, Canada, in the S part of the province on Lake Ontario. Pop. 599,217.

to•rose (tôr′ōs′, tōr′-) *adj.* Cylindrical and having ridges or swellings. [Lat. *torōsus* < *torus*, knot, bulge.]

tor•pe•do (tôr-pē′dō) *n., pl.* **-does. 1.** A cigar-shaped self-propelled underwater projectile launched from a submarine, an aircraft, or a ship and designed to detonate on contact with or in the vicinity of a target. **2.** Any of various submarine explosive devices, esp. a submarine mine. **3.** A small explosive warning device placed on a railroad track and fired by the weight of the train. **4.** An explosive fired in an oil or gas well to begin or increase the flow. **5.** A small firework consisting of some gravel wrapped in tissue paper with a percussion cap. **6.** See **electric ray. 7.** *Slang.* A professional assassin or thug. **8.** *Chiefly New Jersey.* See **submarine** 2. See Regional Note at **submarine.** *—tr.v.* **-doed, -do•ing, -does. 1.** To attack, strike, or sink with a torpedo. **2.** To destroy decisively; wreck. [Lat. *torpēdō*, numbness; electric ray < *torpēre*, to be stiff. See **ster-¹***.]

torpedo boat *n.* A small, fast, thinly plated warship equipped for firing torpedoes.

tor•pid (tôr′pĭd) *adj.* **1.** Deprived of the power of motion or feeling; benumbed. **2.** Dormant; hibernating. **3.** Lethargic; apathetic. [Lat. *torpidus* < *torpēre*, to be stiff. See **ster-¹***.] **—tor′pid•ly** *adv.*

tor•pid•i•ty (tôr-pĭd′ĭ-tē) *n.* Torpor.

tor•por (tôr′pər) *n.* **1.** A state of mental or physical inactivity or insensibility. **2.** Lethargy; apathy. **3.** The dormant state of a hibernating or estivating animal. [Lat. < *torpēre*, to be stiff. See **ster-¹***.] **—tor′po•rif′ic** (-pə-rĭf′ĭk) *adj.*

torque¹ (tôrk) *n.* **1.** The moment of a force, equal to the vector product of the force and the radius vector from the axis about which the force produces torsion or rotation. **2.** A turning or twisting force. *—tr.v.* **torqued, torqu•ing, torques.** To impart torque to. [< Lat. *torquēre*, to twist. See **terkʷ-***.]

torque² (tôrk) *n.* A collar, a necklace, or an armband made of a strip of twisted metal, worn by the ancient Gauls, Germans, and Britons. [Fr. < OFr. < Lat. *torquēs* < *torquēre*, to twist. See **terkʷ-***.]

torque converter *n.* A mechanical or hydraulic device for changing the ratio of torque to speed between the input and output shafts of a mechanism.

Tor•que•ma•da (tôr′kə-mä′də, tôr′kĕ-mä′*th*ä), **Tomás de.** 1420–98. Spanish Dominican monk who was appointed grand inquisitor in 1487.

torr (tôr) *n., pl.* **torr.** A unit of pressure that is equal to approx. 1.316×10^{-3} atmosphere or 1,333 pascals. [After Evangelista TORRICELLI.]

Tor•rance (tôr′əns, tŏr′-). A city of S CA S of Los Angeles; founded c. 1912. Pop. 133,107.

Tor•re del Gre•co (tŏr′ā dĕl grĕk′ō, tŏr′ĕ). A city of S Italy on the Bay of Naples near Mt. Vesuvius. Pop. 102,890.

Tor•rens (tôr′ənz, tŏr′-). A salt lake of S-central Australia NNW of Adelaide.

tor•rent (tôr′ənt, tŏr′-) *n.* **1.** A turbulent swift-flowing stream. **2.** A heavy downpour; a deluge. **3.** A heavy uncontrolled outpouring: *a torrent of insults.* [Lat. *torrēns*, *torrent-* < pr.part. of *torrēre*, to burn. See **ters-***.]

tor•ren•tial (tô-rĕn′shəl, tə-) *adj.* **1.** Resembling, flowing in, or forming torrents. **2.** Resulting from the action of fast-flowing streams: *torrential erosion.* **3.** Flowing or surging abundantly; wild: *torrential applause.* **—tor•ren′tial•ly** *adv.*

Tor•re•ón (tôr′ē-ōn′, -rĕ-ôn′). A city of N Mexico W of Monterrey; founded 1893. Pop. 328,086.

Tor•res Strait (tôr′ĭs). A strait between New Guinea and NE Australia connecting the Arafura Sea with the Coral Sea.

Tor•reys Peak (tôr′ēz, tŏr′-). A mountain, 4,351.4 m (14,267 ft) in the Front Range of the Rocky Mts. in central CO.

Tor•ri•cel•li (tôr′ə-chĕl′ē, tôr′ē-), **Evangelista.** 1608–47. Italian physicist who invented the mercury barometer.

tor•rid (tôr′ĭd, tŏr′-) *adj.* **-er, -est. 1.** Parched with the heat of the sun; intensely hot. **2.** Scorching; burning: *the torrid noonday sun.* **3.** Passionate; ardent: *a torrid love scene.* **4.** Hurried; rapid: *a torrid pace.* [Lat. *torridus* < *torrēre*, to parch. See **ters-***.] **—tor•rid′i•ty, tor′rid•ness** *n.* **—tor′rid•ly** *adv.*

Tor•rid Zone (tôr′ĭd, tŏr′-). The central latitude zone of the earth, between the Tropics of Cancer and Capricorn.

Tor•ri•jos Her•re•ra (tôr-rē′hôs ĕr-rĕ′rä), **Omar.** 1929–81. Panamanian military and political leader who seized power in a coup d'état and ruled as a virtual dictator (1968–81).

Tor•ring•ton (tôr′ĭng-tən, tŏr′-). A city of NW CT W of Hartford. Pop. 33,687.

tor•sade (tôr-säd′, -sād′) *n.* A trimming of twisted ribbon or cord, used esp. on hats. [Fr. < *tors* < VLat. **torsus*, alteration of Lat. *tortus*, p.part. of *torquēre*, to twist. See **terkʷ-***.]

Tór•shavn (tôr′shouN′). The cap. of the Faeroe Is., on SE Straymoy I. Pop. 14,443.

tor•sion (tôr′shən) *n.* **1.a.** The act of twisting or turning. **b.** The condition of being twisted or turned. **2.** The stress or deformation caused when one end of an object is twisted in one direction and the other is held motionless or twisted oppositely. [Ult. < LLat. *torsiō, torsiōn-*, a wringing pain, var. of Lat. *tortiō* < *tortus*, p.part. of *torquēre*, to twist. See TORSADE.] **—tor′sion•al** *adj.* **—tor′sion•al•ly** *adv.*

torsion balance *n.* An instrument with which small forces, as of electricity or magnetism, are measured by means of the torsion they produce in a wire or slender rod.

torsion bar *n.* A part of an automotive suspension consisting of a bar that twists to maintain stability.

tor•so (tôr′sō) *n., pl.* **-sos** or **-si** (-sē). **1.** The human body excluding the head and limbs; trunk. **2.** A statue of the human body with the head and limbs omitted or removed. **3.** A truncated or unfinished thing. [Ital., trunk of a statue < OItal., stalk, stem < VLat. **tursus* < Lat. *thyrsus*, stalk. See THYRSUS.]

tort (tôrt) *n. Law.* Damage, injury, or a wrongful act done willfully, negligently, or in circumstances involving strict liability but not involving breach of contract, for which a civil suit can be brought. [ME, injury < OFr. < Med.Lat. *tortum* < Lat., neut. p.part. of *torquēre*, to twist. See **terkʷ-***.]

torte (tôrt, tôr′tə) *n.* A rich cake made with many eggs and little flour and usu. containing chopped nuts. [Prob. Ger., perh. < Ital. *torta*, cake, tart < LLat. *tōrta*, a kind of bread.]

tor•tel•li•ni (tôr′tl-ē′nē) *n.* Small ring-shaped pasta stuffed usu. with meat or cheese and served in soup or with a sauce. [Ital., dim. of *tortelli*, a kind of pasta, pl. dim. of *torta*, cake < LLat. *torta*, a kind of bread.]

tor•ti•col•lis (tôr′tĭ-kŏl′ĭs) *n.* A contracted state of the neck muscles producing an unnatural position of the head. [NLat. : Lat. *tortus*, twisted, p.part. of *torquēre*, to twist; see **terkʷ-*** + *collum*, neck; see **kʷel-**[1]*.]

tor•til•la (tôr-tē′yə) *n.* A thin disk of unleavened bread made from cornmeal or wheat flour, baked on a hot surface and often served with a topping. [Am.Sp., dim. of Sp. *torta*, cake < LLat., a kind of bread.]

tor•toise (tôr′tĭs) *n.* **1.a.** Any of various terrestrial turtles, esp. one of the family Testudinidae, having thick clublike hind limbs and a high rounded carapace. **b.** *Chiefly British.* A terrestrial or freshwater chelonian. **2.** One that moves slowly; a laggard. [Alteration (influenced by PORPOISE) of ME *tortuce* < Med.Lat. *tortūca*, alteration of LLat. *tartarūcha*, fem. of *tartarūchus*, of the underworld. See TURTLE[1].]

tortoise beetle *n.* Any of several small, brightly colored beetles of the subfamily Cassidinae, shaped like a tortoise.

tor•toise•shell also **tor•toise-shell** or **tor•toise shell** (tôr′tĭs-shĕl′) *n.* **1.a.** The mottled, horny, translucent brownish covering of the carapace of certain tortoises or turtles, esp. the hawksbill, used to make combs, jewelry, and other articles. **b.** A synthetic imitation of natural tortoiseshell. **2.** See **hawksbill. 3.** A domestic cat having fur with brown, black, and yellowish markings. **4.** Any of several butterflies, chiefly of the genus *Nymphalis,* having wings with orange, black, and brown markings. **—tor′toise•shell′** *adj.*

Tor•to•la (tôr-tō′lə). An island of the British Virgin Is. in the West Indies E of Puerto Rico.

tor•tri•cid (tôr′trĭ-sĭd) *n.* Any of various small thick-bodied moths of the family Tortricidae, having larvae that feed on the leaves of trees. [< NLat. *Tortricidae*, family name < *Tortrix*, *Tortric-*, type genus. See TORTRIX.] **—tor′tri•cid** *adj.*

tor•trix (tôr′trĭks) *n.* A moth of the family Tortricidae; a tortricid. [New Latin *Tortrix*, genus name < Lat. *tortus*, p.part. of *torquēre*, to twist. See TORTUOUS.]

Tor•tu•ga (tôr-tōō′gə). An island in the West Indies off N Haiti; a pirate refuge in the 17th cent.

tor•tu•os•i•ty (tôr′chōō-ŏs′ĭ-tē) *n., pl.* **-ties. 1.** The quality or condition of being tortuous; twistedness or crookedness. **2.** A bent or twisted part, passage, or thing.

tor•tu•ous (tôr′chōō-əs) *adj.* **1.** Having or marked by repeated turns or bends; winding or twisting. **2.** Not straightforward; circuitous; devious. **3.** Highly involved; complex. [ME < AN < Lat. *tortuōsus* < *tortus*, a twisting < p.part. of *torquēre*, to twist. See **terkʷ-***.] **—tor′tu•ous•ly** *adv.*

Usage Note: Although *tortuous* and *torturous* both come from the Latin word *torquēre,* "to twist," their primary meanings are distinct. *Tortuous* means "twisting" (*a tortuous road*) or by extension "complex" or "devious." *Torturous* refers primarily to torture and its pain. However, *torturous* also can be used in the sense of "twisted" or "strained," and *tortured* is an even stronger synonym: *tortured reasoning.*

tor•ture (tôr′chər) *n.* **1.a.** Infliction of severe physical pain as a means of punishment or coercion. **b.** An instrument or a method for inflicting such pain. **2.** Excruciating physical or mental pain; agony. **3.** Something causing severe pain or anguish. *—tr.v.* **-tured, -tur•ing, -tures. 1.** To subject (a person or an animal) to torture. **2.** To bring great physical or mental pain upon (another). **3.** To twist or turn abnormally; distort. [ME < OFr. < LLat. *tortūra* < Lat. *tortus*, p.part. of *torquēre*, to twist. See **terkʷ-***.] **—tor′tur•er** *n.*

tor•tur•ous (tôr′chər-əs) *adj.* **1.** Of, relating to, or causing torture. **2.** Twisted; strained. See Usage Note at **tortuous. —tor′tur•ous•ly** *adv.*

tor•u•la (tôr′yə-lə, -ə-lə, tŏr′-) *n., pl.* **-lae** (-lē′, -lī′) or **-las.** Any of a group of fungi similar to the yeasts but lacking asci, many of which ferment sugars. [NLat. *Torula*, fungus genus, fem. dim. of *torus*, bulge.]

To•ruń (tôr′ōōn′, -ōōn′yə). A city of N-central Poland on the Vistula R. NW of Warsaw; founded 1231. Pop. 186,200.

to•rus (tôr′əs, tōr′-) *n., pl.* **to•ri** (tôr′ī, tōr′ī). **1.** *Archit.* A large convex molding, semicircular in cross section, at the base of a classical column. **2.** *Anat.* A bulging or rounded projection or swelling. **3.** *Bot.* The receptacle of a flower. **4.** *Math.* A toroid generated by a circle; a surface having the shape of a doughnut. [Lat., bulge, knot, torus.] **—tor′ic** *adj.*

To•ry (tôr′ē, tōr′ē) *n., pl.* **-ries. 1.a.** A member of a British political party, founded in 1689, that was the opposition party to the Whigs and has been known as the Conservative Party since about 1832. **b.** A member of a Conservative Party, as in Canada. **2.** An American who favored the British side during the period of the American Revolution. **3.** Often **tory.** A supporter of traditional political and social institutions; a political conservative. [Ir.Gael. *tóraidhe*, robber < OIr. *tōir*, pursuit. See **ret-***.] **—To′ry** *adj.* **—To′ry•ism** *n.*

Tos•ca•ni•ni (tŏs′kə-nē′nē, tôs′kä-), **Arturo.** 1867–1957. Italian conductor of the Metropolitan Opera (1908–21) and the New York Philharmonic (1928–36).

toss (tôs, tŏs) *v.* **tossed, toss•ing, toss•es.** *—tr.* **1.** To throw lightly or casually or with a sudden slight jerk. See Syns at **throw. 2.** To throw, fling, or heave continuously about; pitch to and fro: *boats tossed about.* **3.** To mix (a salad) lightly so as to cover with dressing. **4.** To discuss informally; bandy. **5.** To move or lift (the head) with a sudden motion. **6.** To disturb or agitate; upset. **7.** To throw to the ground. **8.a.** To flip (coins) in order to decide an issue. **b.** To flip coins with. *—intr.* **1.** To be thrown here and there; be flung to and fro. **2.** To move about restlessly; twist and turn. **3.** To flip a coin to decide an issue. *—n.* **1.** The act of tossing or the condition of being tossed. **2.** The distance that something is or can be tossed. **3.** An abrupt upward movement, as of the head. **4.** A flipping of a coin to decide an issue. ***—phrasal verbs.* toss down.** *Informal.* To drink in one draft by suddenly tilting. **toss off.** *Informal.* **1.** To drink up in one draft. **2.** To do or finish effortlessly or casually. [ME *tossen*, poss. of Scand. orig.] **—toss′er** *n.*

toss•pot (tôs′pŏt′, tŏs′-) *n.* A drunkard.

toss•up (tôs′ŭp′, tŏs′-) *n. Informal.* **1.** An even chance or choice. **2.** The flipping of a coin to decide an issue.

tos•ta•da (tō-stä′də) or **tos•ta•do** (-dō) *n., pl.* **-das** or **-dos.** A tortilla or tortilla chip deep-fried until crisp. [Am.Sp. < Sp., fem. p.part. of *tostar*, to toast < VLat. **tostāre*. See TOAST[1].]

tot[1] (tŏt) *n.* **1.** A small child. **2.** A small amount. [?]

tot[2] (tŏt) *tr.v.* **tot•ted, tot•ting, tots.** To total: *totted it up.*

to•tal (tōt′l) *n.* **1.** An amount obtained by addition; a sum. **2.** A whole quantity; an entirety. *—adj.* **1.** Of, relating to, or constituting the whole; entire. See Syns at **whole. 2.** Complete; utter; absolute. *—v.* **-taled, -tal•ing, -tals** or **-talled, -tal•ling, -tals.** *—tr.* **1.** To determine the total of; add up. **2.** To equal a total of; amount to. **3.** *Slang.* To wreck completely; demolish. *—intr.* To add up; amount. [ME, whole < OFr. < Med.Lat. *tōtālis* < Lat. *tōtus*. See **teutā-***.]

total eclipse *n.* An eclipse in which the entire surface of a celestial body is obscured.

to•tal•i•tar•i•an (tō-tăl′ĭ-târ′ē-ən) *adj.* Of, being, or imposing a form of government in which the political authority exercises absolute and centralized control over all aspects of life. *—n.* A practitioner or supporter of such a government. [TOTAL + (AUTHOR)ITARIAN.] **—to•tal′i•tar′i•an•ism** *n.*

to•tal•i•ty (tō-tăl′ĭ-tē) *n., pl.* **-ties. 1.** The quality or state of being total. **2.** An aggregate amount; a sum. **3.** The phase of an eclipse when it is total.

to•tal•i•za•tor (tōt′l-ĭ-zā′tər) *n.* A machine for computing and showing totals, esp. a pari-mutuel machine showing the total number and amounts of bets at a racetrack.

to•tal•ize (tōt′l-īz′) *tr.v.* **-ized, -iz•ing, -iz•es.** To make or combine into a total. **—to′tal•i•za′tion** (-ĭ-zā′shən) *n.*

to•tal•iz•er (tōt′l-ī′zər) *n.* A pari-mutuel machine.

to•tal•ly (tōt′l-ē) *adv.* Entirely; wholly; completely.

tote[1] (tōt) *tr.v.* **tot•ed, tot•ing, totes.** *Informal.* **1.** To haul; lug. **2.** To have on one's person; pack: *toting guns.* *—n.* **1.** *Informal.* A load; a burden. **2.** A tote bag. [Perh. (via Black West African E.) of Bantu orig.; akin to Kongo *-tota*, to pick up, Swahili *-tuta*, to pile up, carry.] **—tot′er** *n.*

tote[2] (tōt) *tr.v.* **tot•ed, tot•ing, totes.** *Informal.* **1.** To determine the total of; add up. **2.** To sum up; summarize.

tote[3] (tōt) *n. Informal.* A pari-mutuel machine.

tote bag *n.* A large handbag or shopping bag.

tote board *n.* A large, usu. electrically operated board that displays changing numerical information.

to•tem (tō′təm) *n.* **1.a.** An animal, a plant, or a natural object serving among certain tribal or traditional peoples as the emblem of a clan or family and sometimes revered as its founder, ancestor, or guardian. **b.** A representation of such an object. **c.** A social group having a common affiliation to such an object. **2.** A venerated emblem or symbol. [Ojibwa *nindoodem*, my totem.] **—to•tem′ic** (-tĕm′ĭk) *adj.*

tornado

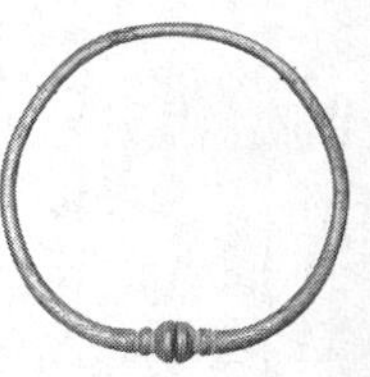
torque[2]
Fourth- to second-century B.C. Celtic bronze torque

tortoise
Galápagos giant tortoise
Geochelone elephantopus

ă pat	oi boy
ā pay	ou out
âr care	ŏŏ took
ä father	ōō boot
ĕ pet	ŭ cut
ē be	ûr urge
ĭ pit	th thin
ī pie	*th* this
îr pier	hw which
ŏ pot	zh vision
ō toe	ə about, item
ô paw	

Stress marks:
′ (primary);
′ (secondary), as in
dictionary (dĭk′shə-nĕr′ē)

totem pole
Tlingit totem pole

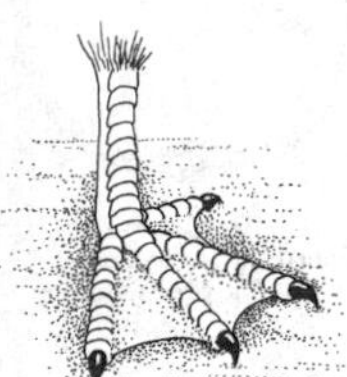

totipalmate
Totipalmate foot

toucan

to•tem•ism (tō′tə-mĭz′əm) *n.* **1.** A belief in totems or in kinship through common affiliation to a totem. **2.** A social system based on affiliations to totems. —**to′tem•ist** *n.* —**to′tem•is′tic** *adj.*

totem pole *n.* **1.** A post carved and painted with a series of totemic symbols and erected before a dwelling, as among certain Native American peoples of the northwest coast of North America. **2.** *Slang.* A hierarchy: *low on the totem pole.*

toth•er or **t'oth•er** (tŭth′ər) *pron. & adj. Informal.* The other. [< ME *the tother*, alteration of *thet other*, that other : *thet*, the (< OE *thæt*; see THAT) + *other*, other; see OTHER.]

to•ti•pal•mate (tō′tĭ-păl′māt′) *adj.* Having webbing that connects each of the four anterior toes, as in water birds. [Lat. *tōtus*, whole; see TOTAL + PALMATE.] —**to′ti•pal•ma′tion** *n.*

to•tip•o•ten•cy (tō-tĭp′ə-tən-sē, tō′tĭ-pōt′n-sē) also **to•tip•o•tence** (tō-tĭp′ə-təns, tō′tĭ-pōt′ns) *n., pl.* **-cies** also **-ten•ces.** The ability of a cell, such as an egg, to give rise to unlike cells and thus develop into a new organism or part. [Lat. *tōtus*, whole; see TOTAL + POTENCY.] —**to•tip′o•tent** *adj.*

tot•ter (tŏt′ər) *intr.v.* **-tered, -ter•ing, -ters. 1.a.** To sway as if about to fall. **b.** To appear about to collapse. **2.** To walk unsteadily or feebly; stagger. [ME *toteren*, perh. of Scand. orig.] —**tot′ter** *n.* —**tot′ter•er** *n.* —**tot′ter•y** *adj.*

tou•can (to͞o′kăn′, -kän′, to͞o-kăn′, -kän′) *n.* Any of various tropical American birds of the family Ramphastidae, having brightly colored plumage and a very large bill. [Fr. < Port. *tucano* or Sp. *tucán*, both < Tupi *tucano*, bird.]

touch (tŭch) *v.* **touched, touch•ing, touch•es.** —*tr.* **1.** To cause or permit a part of the body, esp. the hand or fingers, to come in contact with so as to feel. **2.a.** To bring something into light contact with. **b.** To bring (one thing) into light contact with something else. **3.** To press or push lightly; tap. **4.** To lay hands on in violence. **5.** To eat or drink; taste. **6.** To disturb or move by handling. **7.a.** To meet without going beyond; adjoin. **b.** *Math.* To be tangent to. **c.** To come up to; reach. **d.** To match in quality; equal. **8.** To deal with, esp. in passing; treat briefly or allusively. **9.** To be pertinent to; concern. **10.** To affect the emotions of; move to tender response. **11.** To injure slightly: *plants touched by frost.* **12.** To color slightly; tinge. **13.a.** To draw with light strokes. **b.** To change or improve by adding fine lines or strokes. **14.** To stamp (tested metal). **15.** *Slang.* To wheedle a loan or handout from. **16.a.** *Archaic.* To strike or pluck the keys or strings of (a musical instrument). **b.** To play (a musical piece). —*intr.* **1.** To touch someone or something. **2.** To be or come into contact. —*n.* **1.** The act or an instance of touching. **2.** The physiological sense by which external objects or forces are perceived through contact with the body. **3.** A sensation experienced in touching something with a characteristic texture. **4.** A light push; a tap. **5.** A discernible mark or effect left by contact with something. **6.** A small change or addition, or the effect achieved by it. **7.** A suggestion, hint, or tinge. **8.** A mild attack: *a touch of the flu.* **9.** A small amount; a dash. **10.a.** A manner or technique of striking the keys of a keyboard instrument. **b.** The resistance to pressure characteristic of the keys of a keyboard. **11.** A characteristic way of doing things. **12.** A facility; a knack: *lose one's touch.* **13.** The state of being in contact or communication: *out of touch.* **14.** An official stamp indicating the quality of a metal product. **15.** *Slang.* **a.** The act of approaching someone for a loan or handout. **b.** A prospect for a loan or handout. **16.** *Sports.* The area just outside the sidelines in Rugby and soccer. —***phrasal verbs.*** **touch down.** To make contact with the ground; land. **touch off. 1.** To cause to explode; fire. **2.** To initiate; trigger. **3.** To describe or portray with deft precision. **touch on** (or **upon**). **1.** To deal with (a topic) in passing. **2.** To pertain to; concern. **3.** To approach being; verge on. **touch up.** To improve by making minor corrections, changes, or additions. —***idiom.*** **touch base** (or **bases**). *Informal.* To renew a line of communication. [ME *touchen* < OFr. *touchier*, perh. of imit. orig.] —**touch′a•ble** *adj.* —**touch′er** *n.*

touch-and-go (tŭch′ən-gō′) *adj.* Dangerous and uncertain in nature or outcome; precarious; delicate.

touch•back (tŭch′băk′) *n. Football.* A play in which the defensive team recovers and downs the ball behind its own goal line after the offense has kicked or passed it there.

touch•down (tŭch′doun′) *n.* **1.** *Football.* An act of carrying, receiving, or gaining possession of the ball across the opponent's goal line for a score of six points. **2.** The contact, or moment of contact, of a landing aircraft or spacecraft with the landing surface. [< the earlier practice of touching the ball to the ground behind the goal line.]

tou•ché (to͞o-shā′) *interj.* Used to acknowledge a hit in fencing or a successful criticism or an effective point in argument. [Fr. < p.part. of *toucher*, to hit or wound in fencing < OFr. *touchier*, to touch. See TOUCH.]

touched (tŭcht) *adj.* **1.** Emotionally affected; moved. **2.** Somewhat demented or mentally unbalanced.

touch football *n. Sports.* A variety of football in which ball carriers are downed by touching instead of tackling.

touch•hole (tŭch′hōl′) *n.* The opening in early firearms and cannons through which the powder was ignited.

touch•ing (tŭch′ĭng) *adj.* Eliciting or capable of eliciting sympathy or tenderness. —*prep.* Concerning; about. —**touch′ing•ly** *adv.* —**touch′ing•ness** *n.*

touch•line (tŭch′līn′) *n. Sports.* Either of the sidelines bordering the playing field in soccer and Rugby.

touch-me-not (tŭch′mē-nŏt′) *n.* **1.** See **jewelweed. 2.** See **sensitive plant** 1. [< ripe seedpods bursting when touched.]

touch•stone (tŭch′stōn′) *n.* **1.** A hard black stone, such as jasper or basalt, formerly used to test the quality of gold and silver by comparing the streak left on the stone by one of these metals with that of a standard alloy. **2.** A quality or example used to test the excellence or genuineness of others.

touch-tone also **touch•tone** (tŭch′tōn′) —*adj.* Of or being a telephone with a dialing system that has push buttons that generate tones of differing pitch corresponding to the digits of the number being called. —*n.* A touch-tone telephone.

touch-type (tŭch′tīp′) *tr. & intr.v.* **-typed, -typ•ing, -types.** To type (a document, for example) or engage in typing without having to look at the keyboard, the fingers having been trained to locate the keys by position. —**touch′-typ′ist** *n.*

touch•up (tŭch′ŭp′) *n.* The act or an instance of finishing or improving by small changes, corrections, or additions.

touch•wood (tŭch′wo͝od′) *n.* Material, such as decayed wood, that is used as tinder; punk. [< its being easy to ignite.]

touch•y (tŭch′ē) *adj.* **-i•er, -i•est. 1.** Tending to take offense with slight cause; oversensitive. **2.** Requiring special tact or skill in handling; delicate: *a touchy situation.* **3.** Highly sensitive to touch. Used of a body part. **4.** Easily ignited; flammable. —**touch′i•ly** *adv.* —**touch′i•ness** *n.*

tough (tŭf) *adj.* **tough•er, tough•est. 1.** Able to withstand great strain without tearing or breaking; strong and resilient. **2.** Hard to cut or chew. **3.** Physically hardy; rugged. **4.** Severe; harsh: *a tough winter.* **5.a.** Aggressive; pugnacious. **b.** Inclined to violent or disruptive behavior; rowdy or rough. **6.** Demanding or troubling; difficult: *tough questions.* **7.** Strong-minded; resolute. **8.** *Slang.* Unfortunate; too bad: *a tough break.* **9.** *Slang.* Fine; great. —*n.* A violent or rowdy person; a hoodlum or thug. —***idiom.*** **tough it out.** *Slang.* To get through despite hardship; endure. [ME < OE *tōh.*] —**tough′ly** *adv.* —**tough′ness** *n.*

tough•en (tŭf′ən) *tr. & intr.v.* **-ened, -en•ing, -ens.** To make or become tough. —**tough′en•er** *n.*

tough•ie (tŭf′ē) *n. Informal.* **1.** A thug. **2.** A difficult problem.

tough-mind•ed (tŭf′mīn′dĭd) *adj.* Facing facts and difficulties with strength and determination; realistic and resolute. —**tough′-mind′ed•ly** *adv.* —**tough′-mind′ed•ness** *n.*

Tou•lon (to͞o-lôɴ′). A city of SE France on the Mediterranean Sea ESE of Marseille. Pop. 179,423.

Tou•louse (to͞o-lo͞oz′). A city of S France on the Garonne R. SE of Bordeaux; cap. of the Visigoths (419–507) and the Carolingian kingdom of Aquitaine (781–843). Pop. 347,995.

Tou•louse-Lau•trec (to͞o-lo͞os′lō-trĕk′, to͞o-lo͞oz′-), **Henri de.** 1864–1901. French artist known for his images of the music halls and cafés of Montmartre.

tou•pee (to͞o-pā′) *n.* **1.** A partial wig or hairpiece worn to cover a bald spot. **2.** A curl or lock of hair worn during the 18th century as a topknot on a periwig. [Fr. *toupet*, dim. of OFr. *toupe*, tuft of hair < Frankish **top.*]

tour (to͝or) *n.* **1.** A trip with visits to various places of interest for business, pleasure, or instruction. **2.** A group organized for such a trip or for a shorter sightseeing excursion. **3.** A brief trip to or through a place for the purpose of seeing it. **4.** A journey to fulfill a round of engagements in several places: *a concert tour.* **5.** A shift, as in a factory. **6.** A period of duty at a single place or job. —*v.* **toured, tour•ing, tours.** —*intr.* **1.** To travel from place to place, esp. for pleasure. **2.** To travel among various places while fulfilling engagements. —*tr.* **1.** To make a tour of. **2.** To present (a play, for example) on a tour. [ME, a turn < OFr. < Lat. *tornus*, lathe. See TURN.] —**tour′er** *n.*

tou•ra•co also **tu•ra•co** (to͝or′ə-kō′) *n., pl.* **-cos.** Any of various weak-flying cuckoolike African birds of the family Musophagidae, many of which have brightly colored plumage and long tails. [Fr., perh. of West African orig.]

Tou•raine (to͞o-rān′, -rĕn′). A historical region and former province of W-central France; taken by the English in 1152 and recaptured by the French in 1204.

Tou•rane (to͞o-rän′). See **Da Nang.**

tour•bil•lion (to͝or-bĭl′yən) *n.* **1.a.** A whirlwind. **b.** A vortex, as of a whirlwind or whirlpool. **2.** A skyrocket that has a spiral flight. [ME *turbilloun* < OFr. *torbeillon*, ult. < Lat. *turbō* < Gk. *turbē*, noise, confusion. See TURBID.]

Tour•coing (to͝or-kwăɴ′). A city of N France NE of Lille near the Belgian border. Pop. 96,908.

tour de force (to͝or′ də fôrs′, fōrs′) *n., pl.* **tours de force** (to͝or′). A feat requiring great virtuosity or strength. [Fr. : *tour*, turn, feat + *de*, of + *force*, strength.]

Tou•rette's syndrome (to͞o-rĕts′) or **Tou•rette syndrome** (-rĕt′) *n.* A severe neurological disorder characterized by facial and body tics, often accompanied by grunts and compulsive utterances, as of obscenities. [After Georges Gilles de la *Tourette* (1857–1904), French physician.]

tour•ism (to͝or′ĭz′əm) *n.* **1.** The practice of traveling for pleasure. **2.** The business of providing tours and tourist services.
tour•ist (to͝or′ĭst) *n.* One who travels for pleasure. **—tour•is′tic** *adj.* **—tour′ist•y** *adj.*
tourist class *n.* The lowest class of accommodations on some passenger ships and airplanes.
tourist trap *n.* A place, such as a shop or resort area, that offers overpriced goods and services to tourists.
tour•ma•line also **tur•ma•line** (to͝or′mə-lĭn, -lēn′) *n.* A complex crystalline silicate containing aluminum, boron, and other elements, used esp. in its green, clear, and blue varieties as a gemstone. [Fr. < Singhalese *toramalli,* carnelian.]
tour•na•ment (to͝or′nə-mənt, tûr′-) *n.* **1.** A series of contests in which a number of contestants compete and the one that prevails through the final round or that finishes with the best record is declared the winner. **2.** A medieval martial sport in which two groups of mounted and armored combatants fought against each other with blunted lances or swords. [ME *tournement,* a medieval sport < OFr. *torneiement* < *torneier,* to tourney. See TOURNEY.]
tour•ne•dos (to͝or′nə-dō′) *n., pl.* **tour•ne•dos** (-dō′, -dōz′). A fillet of beef cut from the tenderloin, often bound in bacon or suet for cooking. [Fr. : *tourner,* to turn (< OFr.; see TURN) + *dos,* the back (< Lat. *dorsum*).]
tour•ney (to͝or′nē, tûr′-) *intr.v.* **-neyed, -ney•ing, -neys.** To compete in a tournament. **—** *n., pl.* **-neys.** A tournament. [ME *torneien* < OFr. *torneier* < VLat. **tornizāre,* to turn around < Lat. *tornāre,* to turn in a lathe. See TURN.]
tour•ni•quet (to͝or′nĭ-kĭt, tûr′-) *n.* A device, typically a tightly encircling bandage, used to check bleeding by temporarily stopping the flow of blood through a limb. [Fr. : *tourner,* to turn (< OFr.; see TURN) + *-iquet,* dim. suff. (< OFr.).]
Tours (to͝or). A city of W-central France on the Loire R.; a Huguenot stronghold before 1685. Pop. 132,209.
tou•sle (tou′zəl) *tr.v.* **-sled, -sling, -sles.** To disarrange or rumple; dishevel. **—** *n.* A disheveled mass, as of hair. [ME *touselen,* freq. of *tousen,* to pull roughly.]
Tous•saint L'Ou•ver•ture (to͞o-săN′ lo͞o-vĕr-tür′), **François Dominique.** 1743?–1803. Haitian revolutionary who led a force that expelled the British and Spanish from Haiti (1798).
tout (tout) *v.* **tout•ed, tout•ing, touts.** **—** *intr.* **1.** To solicit customers, votes, or patronage, esp. in a brazen way. **2.** To tout information on racehorses. **—** *tr.* **1.** To solicit or importune. **2.** To obtain or sell information on (a racehorse or stable) for the guidance of bettors. **3.** To promote or praise energetically; publicize. **—** *n.* **1.** One who touts information on racehorses. **2.** One who solicits customers brazenly or persistently. [ME *tuten,* to peer.] **—tout′er** *n.*
to•va•rich or **to•va•rish** (tə-vär′ĭch, -ĭsh, -ĭshch) *n.* A comrade. [Russ. *tovarishch* < ORuss. *tovarishchĭ,* sing. of *tovarishchi,* business associates < Old Turkic *tavar ishchi,* businessman, merchant : *tavar,* wealth, trade + *ishchi,* one who works (< *ish,* work, business).]
tow¹ (tō) *tr.v.* **towed, tow•ing, tows.** To draw or pull behind by a chain or line. See Syns at **pull.** **—** *n.* **1.a.** The act or an instance of towing. **b.** The condition of being towed. **2.** Something that tows. **3.** Something, such as a barge, that is towed. **4.** A rope or cable used in towing. **—*idiom.* in tow.** **1.** Under close guidance; in one's charge. **2.** As a companion or follower. [ME *towen* < OE *togian.* See **deuk-*.**] **—tow′a•ble** *adj.* **—tow′er** *n.*
tow² (tō) *n.* Coarse broken flax or hemp fiber prepared for spinning. See Regional Note at **gunnysack.** [ME, poss. < OE *tōw-,* spinning.]
tow•age (tō′ĭj) *n.* **1.** The act or service of towing. **2.** A charge for towing.
to•ward (tôrd, tōrd, tə-wôrd′) *prep.* also **to•wards** (tôrdz, tōrdz, tə-wôrdz′). **1.** In the direction of: *toward home.* **2.** In a position facing: *his back toward me.* **3.** Somewhat before in time: *toward morning.* **4.** With regard to; in relation to: *turned toward the future.* **5.** In furtherance or partial fulfillment of: *five dollars toward the bill.* **6.** By way of achieving; with a view to: *efforts toward peace.* **—** *adj.* (tôrd, tōrd). **1.** Favoring success or a good outcome; propitious. **2.** Often **towards.** Happening soon; imminent. **3.** *Obsolete.* Being quick to understand or learn. [ME < OE *tōweard* : *tō,* to; see TO + *-weard,* -ward.]

Usage Note: Some critics have tried to discern a semantic distinction between *toward* and *towards,* but the difference is entirely dialectal. *Toward* is more common in American English; *towards* is the predominant form in British English.

to•ward•ly (tôrd′lē, tōrd′-) *adj. Archaic.* **1.** Appearing likely to succeed; promising. **2.** Advantageous; favorable.
tow-a•way zone (tō′ə-wā′) *n.* A no-parking zone from which motor vehicles may be towed away.
tow bag *n. Eastern North Carolina.* See **gunnysack.** See Regional Note at **gunnysack.**
tow•boat (tō′bōt′) *n. Naut.* **1.** See **tugboat.** **2.** A powerful shallow-draft boat with a broad bow, intended to push barges on rivers and canals.
tow•el (tou′əl) *n.* A piece of absorbent cloth or paper for wiping or drying. **—** *v.* **-eled, -el•ing, -els** or **-elled, -el•ling, -els.** **—** *tr.* To wipe or rub dry with a towel. **—** *intr.* To towel oneself. [ME *towaille* < OFr. *toaille,* of Gmc. orig.]
tow•el•ette (tou′ə-lĕt′) *n.* A small, usu. moistened piece of paper or cloth used for cleansing.
tow•el•ing also **tow•el•ling** (tou′ə-lĭng) *n.* Any of various fabrics of cotton or linen used for making towels.
tow•er (tou′ər) *n.* **1.** A building or part of a building that is exceptionally high in proportion to its width and length. **2.** A tall slender structure used for observation, signaling, or pumping. **3.** One that conspicuously embodies strength, firmness, or another virtue. **—** *intr.v.* **-ered, -er•ing, -ers.** **1.** To appear at or rise to a conspicuous height; loom. **2.** To fly directly upward before swooping or falling. Used of certain birds. **3.** To demonstrate great superiority; be preeminent. [ME *tur, tour, towr* < OE *torr* and < OFr. *tur,* both < Lat. *turris,* prob. < Gk. *tursis, turris.*]
tow•er•ing (tou′ər-ĭng) *adj.* **1.** Of imposing height. **2.** Outstanding; preeminent. **3.** Very great or intense.
tow•head (tō′hĕd′) *n.* **1.** A head of white-blond hair resembling tow. **2.** A person having such hair. **—tow′head′ed** *adj.*
tow•hee (tō′hē, tō-hē′) *n.* **1.** A North American bird *(Pipilo erythrophthalmus)* that has black, white, and rust-colored plumage in the male. **2.** Any of several finches of the genera *Pipilo* or *Chlorura,* found in the western United States. [Imit. of the song of some of these birds.]
tow•line (tō′līn′) *n.* A line used in towing a vessel or vehicle.
town (toun) *n.* **1.a.** A population center, often incorporated, larger than a village and usu. smaller than a city. **b.** The residents of such a population center. **2.** A township. **3.** *Informal.* A city. **4.** *Chiefly British.* A rural village that has a market or fair periodically. **5.** The commercial district or center of an area. **—*idiom.* on the town.** *Informal.* In spirited pursuit of the entertainment offered by a city or town. [ME < OE *tūn,* enclosed place, village. See **dhū-no-*.**]
town clerk *n.* A public official who keeps the records of a town.
town crier *n.* **1.** A person formerly employed by a town to proclaim announcements in the streets. **2.** *Informal.* A gossip.
town hall *n.* A building containing the offices of the public officials of a town and housing the town council and courts.
town•house or **town house** (toun′hous′) *n.* **1.** A city residence. **2.** One of a row of houses joined by common side walls.
town•ie also **town•y** (tou′nē) *n., pl.* **-ies.** *Informal.* A permanent resident of a town, esp. one in a college town who is academically unaffiliated with the local college or university.
town manager *n.* An administrator appointed to manage the government of a town.
town meeting *n.* A legislative assembly of townspeople.
towns•folk (tounz′fōk′) *pl.n.* The people of a town.
Town•shend (toun′zənd), **Charles.** 1725–67. British politician who sponsored the Townshend Acts (1767), which levied duties on imports to the American colonies.
town•ship (toun′shĭp′) *n.* **1.** A subdivision of a county in most northeast and Midwest U.S. states, having the status of a unit of local government with varying governmental powers; a town. **2.** A public land surveying unit of 36 sections or 36 square miles. **3.** An ancient administrative division of a large parish in England. **4.** A racially segregated area in South Africa established by the government as a residence for people of color.
towns•man (tounz′mən) *n.* **1.** A man who resides in a town. **2.** A male fellow resident of one's town.
towns•peo•ple (tounz′pē′pəl) *pl.n.* The inhabitants or citizens of a town or city.
towns•wom•an (tounz′wo͝om′ən) *n.* **1.** A woman who resides in a town. **2.** A female fellow resident of one's town.
tow•path (tō′păth′, -päth′) *n.* A path along a canal or river used by animals towing boats.
tow sack *n. Upper Southern U.S.* See **gunnysack.** See Regional Note at **gunnysack.**
Tow•son (tou′sən). A city of N MD, a suburb of Baltimore. Pop. 49,445.
tox•a•phene (tŏk′sə-fēn′) *n.* A toxic solid compound, $C_{10}H_{10}Cl_8$, used as an insecticide. [TOX(I)– + (C)A(M)PHENE.]
tox•e•mi•a (tŏk-sē′mē-ə) *n.* A condition in which the blood contains toxins, as from the growth of microorganisms. **—tox•e′mic** *adj.*
toxi– or **toxo–** or **tox–** *pref.* Poison; poisonous: *toxaphene.* [< Lat. *toxicum.* See TOXIC.]
tox•ic (tŏk′sĭk) *adj.* **1.** Of or caused by a toxin or other poison. **2.** Capable of causing injury or death, esp. by chemical means; poisonous. **—** *n.* A toxic chemical or other substance. [LLat. *toxicus* < Lat. *toxicum,* poison < Gk. *toxikon,* poison for arrows, poison < neut. of *toxikos,* of a bow < *toxon,* bow < OPers. **taxša-,* an arrow.] **—tox′i•cal•ly** *adv.*
tox•i•cant (tŏk′sĭ-kənt) *n.* A poison or poisonous agent. **—** *adj.* Poisonous; toxic.
tox•ic•i•ty (tŏk-sĭs′ĭ-tē) *n., pl.* **-ties.** **1.** The quality or condition of being toxic. **2.** The degree of toxicity.
toxico– or **toxic–** *pref.* Poison: *toxicosis.* [< Lat. *toxicum.* See TOXIC.]

François Dominique Toussaint L'Ouverture

tower
Eiffel Tower, Paris, France

towhee
Pipilo erythrophthalmus

ă pat	oi boy
ā pay	ou out
âr care	o͝o took
ä father	o͞o boot
ĕ pet	ŭ cut
ē be	ûr urge
ĭ pit	th thin
ī pie	*th* this
îr pier	hw which
ŏ pot	zh vision
ō toe	ə about, item
ô paw	

Stress marks:
′ (primary);
′ (secondary), as in
dictionary (dĭk′shə-nĕr′ē)

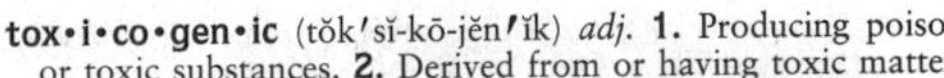

tox•i•co•gen•ic (tŏk′sĭ-kō-jĕn′ĭk) *adj.* **1.** Producing poison or toxic substances. **2.** Derived from or having toxic matter.
tox•i•col•o•gy (tŏk′sĭ-kŏl′ə-jē) *n.* The study of the nature, effects, and detection of poisons and the treatment of poisoning. **—tox′i•co•log′i•cal** (-kə-lŏj′ĭ-kəl), **tox′i•co•log′ic** (-ĭk) *adj.* **—tox′i•co•log′i•cal•ly** *adv.* **—tox′i•col′o•gist** *n.*
tox•i•co•sis (tŏk′sĭ-kō′sĭs) *n., pl.* **-ses** (-sēz). A diseased condition resulting from poisoning.
toxic shock syndrome *n.* An acute infection marked by high fever, a sunburnlike rash, vomiting, and diarrhea, followed in severe cases by shock, caused by a toxin-producing strain of the bacterium *Staphylococcus aureus* and occurring chiefly among menstruating women who use tampons.
tox•i•gen•ic (tŏk′sə-jĕn′ĭk) *adj.* Producing poison; toxicogenic. **—tox′i•ge•nic′i•ty** (-jə-nĭs′ĭ-tē) *n.*
tox•in (tŏk′sĭn) *n.* A poisonous substance, esp. a protein, that is produced by living cells or organisms and is capable of causing disease but is often also capable of inducing neutralizing antibodies or antitoxins.
tox•in-an•ti•tox•in (tŏk′sĭn-ăn′tĭ-tŏk′sĭn) *n.* A mixture of a toxin and its antitoxin with a slight excess of toxin, formerly used as a vaccine.
toxo– *pref.* Var. of **toxi–.**
tox•oid (tŏk′soid′) *n.* A substance that has been treated to destroy its toxic properties but retains the capacity to stimulate production of antitoxins, used in immunization.
tox•o•plas•ma (tŏk′sə-plăz′mə) *n.* Any of various parasitic sporozoans of the genus *Toxoplasma.*
tox•o•plas•mo•sis (tŏk′sō-plăz-mō′sĭs) *n., pl.* **-mo•ses** (-mō′sēz). A disease caused by the sporozoan *Toxoplasma gondii,* esp.: **a.** A congenital disease marked by lesions of the central nervous system that can cause blindness and brain damage. **b.** An acquired disease marked by fever, swollen lymph nodes, and lesions in the liver, heart, lungs, and brain.
toy (toi) *n.* **1.** An object for children to play with. **2.** Something of little importance; a trifle. **3.** An amusement; a pastime. **4.** A small ornament; a bauble. **5.** A diminutive thing or person. **6.** A dog of a very small breed or of a variety smaller than the standard variety of its breed. **7.** *Scots.* A loose covering for the head, formerly worn by women. **8.** *Chiefly Southern U.S.* A shooter marble. *—intr.v.* **toyed, toy•ing, toys. 1.** To amuse oneself idly; trifle. **2.** To treat something casually or without seriousness. [ME *toye,* amorous play, some fun.]
To•ya•ma (tō-yä′mä). A city of W-central Honshu, Japan, on **Toyama Bay,** an inlet of the Sea of Japan. Pop. 314,111.
toy line *n. Chiefly Southern U.S.* The line used in a game of marbles.
Toyn•bee (toin′bē), **Arnold Joseph.** 1889–1975. British historian who studied cyclical patterns in civilizations.
To•yo•ha•shi (tô′yô-hä′shē). A city of S-central Honshu, Japan, on the Pacific Ocean SE of Nagoya. Pop. 287,700.
toy•on (toi′ŏn′) *n.* An evergreen Californian shrub *(Heteromeles arbutifolia)* having leathery leaves, white flowers, and red fleshy berrylike fruit. [Sp. *tollon* < Gk. *tolon.*]
To•yo•na•ka (tô′yô-nä′kä). A city of S Honshu, Japan, a suburb of Osaka. Pop. 413,219.
To•yo•ta (toi-ō′tə, tô-yô′tä). A city of S-central Honshu, Japan, ESE of Nagoya. Pop. 308,106.
tp. *abbr.* Township.
t.p. *abbr. Print.* Title page.
TPA or **tPA** *abbr.* Tissue plasminogen activator.
tpk. *abbr.* Turnpike.
TR or **T-R** *abbr.* Transmit-receive.
tr. *abbr.* **1.** *Gram.* Transitive. **2.a.** Translated. **b.** Translation; translator. **3.** Transpose; transposition. **4.** Treasurer. **5.** Troop. **6.** *Law.* Trust; trustee.
tra•be•at•ed (trā′bē-ā′tĭd) also **tra•be•ate** (-bē-ĭt, -āt′) *adj. Archit.* Having horizontal beams or lintels. [< Lat. *trabs,* beam. See **treb-*.**] **—tra′be•a′tion** *n.*
tra•bec•u•la (trə-bĕk′yə-lə) *n., pl.* **-lae** (-lē′). **1.** A small supporting beam or bar. **2.** *Anat.* Any of the supporting strands of connective tissue projecting into an organ and constituting part of the framework of that organ. [Lat., dim. of *trabs,* beam. See **treb-*.**] **—tra•bec′u•lar** *adj.*
Trab•zon (trăb-zŏn′, träb-zôn′) or **Treb•i•zond** (trĕb′ĭ-zŏnd′). A city of NE Turkey on the Black Sea; founded in the 8th cent. B.C. Pop. 108,403.
trace¹ (trās) *n.* **1.a.** A visible mark, such as a footprint, made or left by the passage of a person, an animal, or a thing. **b.** Evidence or an indication of the former presence or existence of something; a vestige. **2.** A barely perceivable indication; a touch: *a trace of sarcasm.* **3.a.** An extremely small amount. **b.** A constituent, such as a chemical element, present in quantities less than a standard limit. **4.** A path or trail beaten out by the passage of animals or people. **5.** A way or route followed. **6.** A line drawn by a recording instrument, such as a cardiograph. **7.** *Math.* **a.** The point at which a line or the curve in which a surface intersects a coordinate plane. **b.** The sum of the elements of the principal diagonal of a matrix. **8.** An engram. *—v.* **traced, trac•ing, trac•es.** *—tr.* **1.** To follow the course or trail of. **2.** To ascertain the successive stages in the development or progress of. **3.** To locate or discover by searching or researching evidence. **4.** To draw (a line or figure); sketch; delineate. **5.** To form (letters) with special concentration or care. **6.** To copy by following lines seen through a sheet of transparent paper. **7.a.** To imprint (a design) by pressure with an instrument on a superimposed pattern. **b.** To make a design or series of markings on (a surface) by such pressure on a pattern. **8.** To record (a variable), as on a graph. *—intr.* **1.** To make one's way along a trail or course. **2.** To have origins; be traceable. [ME, track < OFr. < *tracier,* to make one's way < VLat. **tractiāre* < Lat. *tractus,* a dragging, course < p.part. of *trahere,* to draw.] **—trace′a•bil′i•ty, trace′a•ble•ness** *n.* **—trace′a•ble** *adj.* **—trace′a•bly** *adv.*

tracery
South transept of the Cathedral of Notre Dame, Paris

trace² (trās) *n.* **1.** One of two side straps or chains connecting a harnessed draft animal to a vehicle or whiffletree. **2.** A bar or rod, hinged at either end to another part, that transfers movement from one part of a machine to another. [ME *trais* < OFr., pl. of *trait,* a hauling, harness strap < Lat. *trāctus,* a hauling < p.part. of *trahere,* to haul.]
trace element *n.* **1.** A chemical element required in minute quantities by an organism to maintain proper physical functioning. **2.** A minute quantity or amount.
trac•er (trā′sər) *n.* **1.a.** One who is employed to locate missing goods or persons. **b.** An investigation or inquiry organized to trace missing goods or persons. **2.** Any of several instruments used in making tracings or in imprinting designs by tracing. **3.** A tracer bullet. **4.** *Chem.* An identifiable substance, such as a radioactive isotope, that is introduced into a biological or mechanical system and can be followed through the course of a process.
tracer bullet *n.* A bullet that leaves a luminous or smoky trail.
trac•er•y (trā′sə-rē) *n., pl.* **-ies.** Ornamental work of interlaced and branching lines, esp. the lacy openwork in a Gothic window. [< TRACE¹.] **—trac′er•ied** *adj.*
tra•che•a (trā′kē-ə) *n., pl.* **-che•ae** (-kē-ē′) or **-che•as. 1.** *Anat.* A thin-walled tube of cartilaginous and membranous tissue descending from the larynx to the bronchi and carrying air to the lungs. **2.** *Zool.* One of the internal respiratory tubes of insects and some other terrestrial arthropods. **3.** *Bot.* One of the tubular conductive vessels in the xylem of vascular plants. [ME *trache* < Med.Lat. *trāchēa* < LLat. *trāchīa* < Gk. *(artēria) trakheia,* rough (artery), trachea < fem. of *trakhus,* rough.] **—tra′che•al** *adj.*
tra•che•ate (trā′kē-āt′, -ĭt) *adj.* Having tracheae. Used of arthropods. *—n.* A tracheate arthropod.
tra•che•id (trā′kē-ĭd, -kēd′) *n. Bot.* A xylem cell in vascular plants. **—tra•che′i•dal** (trā-kē′ĭ-dl, -kēd′l) *adj.*

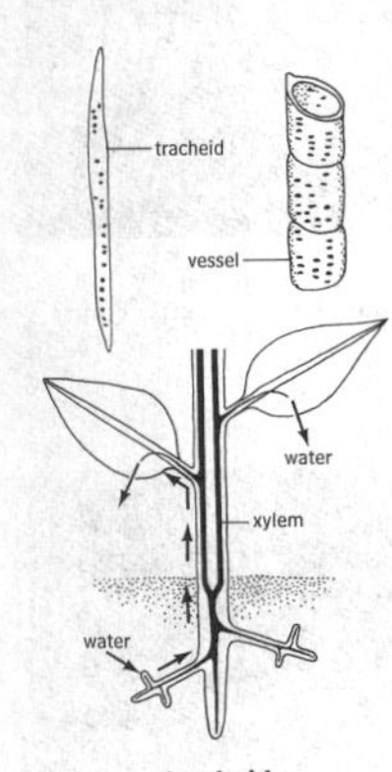

tracheid

tra•che•i•tis (trā′kē-ī′tĭs) *n.* Inflammation of the trachea.
tracheo– or **trache–** *pref.* Trachea: *tracheid.* [NLat. *trāchēo-* < Med.Lat. *trāchēa.* See TRACHEA.]
tra•che•o•bron•chi•al (trā′kē-ō-brŏng′kē-əl) *adj.* Of or relating to the trachea and the bronchi.
tra•che•ole (trā′kē-ōl′) *n.* One of the fine branching tubes of the trachea of an insect. [TRACHE(A) + *-ole,* dim. suff. (< Fr. < Lat. *-olus*).]
tra•che•o•phyte (trā′kē-ə-fīt′) *n.* Any of various vascular plants having a conducting system of xylem and phloem. [< NLat. *Tracheophyta,* division name : TRACHEO– + Gk. *phuta,* pl. of *phuton,* plant; see **bheuə-*.**]
tra•che•os•to•my (trā′kē-ŏs′tə-mē) *n., pl.* **-mies. 1.** Surgical construction of a respiratory opening in the trachea. **2.** The opening so made.
tra•che•ot•o•my (trā′kē-ŏt′ə-mē) *n., pl.* **-mies.** The act or procedure of cutting into the trachea through the neck, as to make an artificial opening for breathing.
tra•cho•ma (trə-kō′mə) *n.* A contagious disease of the conjunctiva and cornea, caused by the gram-negative bacterium *Chlamydia trachomatis* and characterized by inflammation, hypertrophy, and formation of granules of adenoid tissue. [NLat. *trachōma* < Gk. *trakhōma* < *trakhus,* rough.]
tra•chyte (trā′kīt′, trăk′īt′) *n.* A light-colored igneous rock consisting essentially of alkali feldspar. [Fr. < Gk. *trakhus,* rough.] **—tra•chyt′ic** (trə-kĭt′ĭk) *adj.*
trac•ing (trā′sĭng) *n.* **1.** A reproduction made by superimposing a transparent sheet and copying the lines of the original on it. **2.** A graphic record made by a recording instrument, such as a cardiograph or seismograph.
track (trăk) *n.* **1.a.** A mark or succession of marks left by something that has passed. **b.** A path, route, or course indicated by such marks. **2.** A path along which something moves; a course. **3.a.** A course of action; a method of proceeding. **b.** An intended or proper course. **4.** A succession of ideas; a train of thought. **5.** Awareness of something occurring or passing: *lost track of time.* **6.** *Sports.* **a.** A course laid out for running or racing. **b.** Athletic competition on such a course; track events. **c.** Track and field. **7.** A rail or set of parallel rails upon which railroad cars or other vehicles run. **8.** A metal groove or ridge that holds, guides, and reduces friction for a moving device or apparatus. **9.** Any of several courses of study to which students are assigned according to ability,

achievement, or needs. **10.a.** A distinct path, as along a length of film or magnetic tape, on which sound or other information is recorded. **b.** A distinct selection from a sound recording, usu. containing an individual work or part of a larger work. **c.** One of the separate sound recordings that are combined so as to be heard simultaneously, as in stereophonic sound reproduction. — *v.* **tracked, track•ing, tracks.** — *tr.* **1.** To follow the tracks of; trail. **2.** To pursue successfully. **3.** To move over or along; traverse. **4.** To carry on the shoes and deposit. **5.** To observe or monitor the course of (aircraft, for example), as by radar. **6.** To observe the progress of; follow. **7.** To equip with a track. **8.** To assign (a student) to a curricular track. — *intr.* **1.** To move along a track. **2.** To follow a course; travel. **3.** To keep a constant distance apart. Used of a pair of wheels. **4.** To be in alignment. — ***idiom.*** **in (one's) tracks.** Exactly where one is standing. [ME *trak* < OFr. *trac*, perh. of Gmc. orig.] — **track′a•ble** *adj.* — **track′er** *n.*

track•age (trăk′ĭj) *n.* **1.** Railway tracks. **2.a.** The right of one railroad company to use the track system of another. **b.** The charge for this right.

track and field *n. Sports.* Athletic events performed on a running track and the field associated with it. — **track′-and-field′** (trăk′ən-fēld′) *adj.*

track•ing (trăk′ĭng) *n.* The placing of students in any of several tracks.

tracking shot *n.* A movie sequence made by a camera moving steadily on a track or dolly.

tracking station *n.* A station for observing the path of and maintaining contact with an object in the atmosphere or in space esp. by means of radar or radio.

track•less (trăk′lĭs) *adj.* **1.** Not running on tracks or rails. **2.** Unmarked by trails or paths.

trackless trolley *n.* A trolley bus.

track light *n.* A light mounted on and movable along an electrified metal track. — **track lighting** *n.*

track•man (trăk′mən) *n.* A worker employed to maintain or inspect railroad tracks.

track record *n. Informal.* A record of actual performance or accomplishment.

track•suit (trăk′so͞ot′) *n.* A loose-fitting jacket and pants worn by athletes and exercisers usu. preceding and following workouts.

track•walk•er (trăk′wô′kər) *n.* A worker employed to inspect a section of railroad track.

tract[1] (trăkt) *n.* **1.a.** An expanse of land or water. **b.** A specified or limited area of land. **2.** *Anat.* **a.** A system of organs and tissues that together perform a specialized function: *the alimentary tract.* **b.** A bundle of nerve fibers having a common origin, termination, and function. **3.** *Archaic.* A stretch or lapse of time. [ME, period of time < Lat. *trāctus*, course, space, period of time < p.part. of *trahere*, to draw.]

tract[2] (trăkt) *n.* A leaflet or pamphlet containing a declaration or an appeal, esp. one put out by a religious or political group. [ME *tracte*, treatise, prob. short for Lat. *trāctātus* < p.part. of *trāctāre*, to discuss, freq. of *trahere*, to draw.]

tract[3] (trăkt) *n.* The verses from Scripture sung during Lent or on Ember Days after the gradual in the Roman Catholic Mass. [ME *tracte* < Med.Lat. *tractus* < Lat., a drawing out (< its being an uninterrupted solo). See TRACT[1].]

trac•ta•ble (trăk′tə-bəl) *adj.* **1.** Easily managed or controlled; governable. **2.** Easily handled or worked; malleable. [Lat. *trāctābilis* < *trāctāre*, to manage, freq. of *trahere*, to draw.] — **trac′ta•bil′i•ty, trac′ta•ble•ness** *n.* — **trac′ta•bly** *adv.*

Trac•tar•i•an•ism (trăk-târ′ē-ə-nĭz′əm) *n.* The religious opinions and principles of the founders of the Oxford movement, put forth in a series of pamphlets entitled *Tracts for the Times.* — **Trac•tar′i•an** *adj. & n.*

trac•tate (trăk′tāt′) *n.* A treatise; an essay. [Lat. *trāctātus*. See TRACT[2].]

tract house *n.* One of numerous houses of similar or complementary design built on a tract of land. — **tract housing** *n.*

trac•tile (trăk′təl, -tīl′) *adj.* Capable of being drawn out in length; ductile: *a tractile metal.* [< Lat. *trāctus*, p.part. of *trahere*, to draw.] — **trac•til′i•ty** (-tĭl′ĭ-tē) *n.*

trac•tion (trăk′shən) *n.* **1.a.** The act of drawing or pulling, esp. the drawing of a vehicle or load over a surface by motor power. **b.** The condition of being drawn or pulled. **2.** Pulling power, as of a draft animal or an engine. **3.** Adhesive friction, as of a tire on a road. **4.** *Medic.* A sustained pull applied mechanically, as to the neck, so as to correct fractured or dislocated bones, overcome muscle spasms, or relieve pressure. [Med.Lat. *trāctiō*, *trāctiōn-* < Lat. *trāctus*, p.part. of *trahere*, to pull, draw.] — **trac′tion•al** *adj.*

trac•tive (trăk′tĭv) *adj.* Serving to pull or draw; exerting traction. [< Lat. *trāctus*, p.part. of *trahere*, to draw.]

trac•tor (trăk′tər) *n.* **1.** A vehicle, powered by a gasoline or diesel motor, having large heavily treaded tires and used in mowing, farming, or other applications. **2.** A truck having a cab and no body, used for pulling large vehicles such as vans or trailers. **3.** Something that pulls or draws. **4.a.** An airplane propeller mounted in front of the supporting surfaces. **b.** An airplane having such a propeller. **5.** A toothed mechanism that automatically advances perforated continuous-form paper through a computer printer.

trac•tor-trail•er (trăk′tər-trā′lər) *n.* A truck consisting of a tractor attached to a semitrailer or trailer.

Tra•cy (trā′sē). A city of W-central CA SSW of Stockton. Pop. 33,558.

Tracy, Spencer. 1900–67. Amer. actor whose motion pictures include *Captains Courageous* (1937) and *Boys Town* (1938).

trade (trād) *n.* **1.** The business of buying and selling commodities; commerce. See Syns at **business. 2.** The people working in or associated with a business or an industry. **3.** The customers of a specified business or industry; clientele. **4.** The act or an instance of buying or selling; transaction. **5.** An exchange of one thing for another. **6.** An occupation, esp. one requiring skilled labor; craft. **7.** The trade winds. Often used in the plural. — *v.* **trad•ed, trad•ing, trades.** — *intr.* **1.** To engage in buying and selling for profit. **2.** To make an exchange of one thing for another. **3.** To shop or buy regularly. — *tr.* **1.** To give in exchange for something else. **2.** To buy and sell (stock, for example). **3.** To pass back and forth. — ***phrasal verbs.*** **trade down.** To trade something in for something else of lower value or price. **trade in.** To surrender or sell (an old or used item), using the proceeds as partial payment on a new purchase. **trade on.** To put to calculated and often unscrupulous advantage; exploit. **trade up.** To trade something in for something else of greater value or price. [ME, course < MLGer.] — **trad′a•ble** *adj.*

trade acceptance *n.* A bill of exchange for the amount of a purchase drawn by the seller on the purchaser, with the purchaser's signature and time and place of payment.

trade book *n.* A book published for distribution to the general public through booksellers.

trade discount *n.* A discount on the list price granted by a manufacturer or wholesaler to buyers in the same trade.

trade edition *n.* An book edition published as a trade book.

trade-in (trād′ĭn′) *n.* **1.** Merchandise accepted as partial payment for a new purchase. **2.** A transaction involving such merchandise.

trade language *n.* A language, esp. a pidgin, used by speakers of different native languages for communication in commercial trade.

trade-last (trād′lăst′) *n. Informal.* A compliment overheard about someone else that one offers to repeat to that person in return for a similar remark overheard about oneself.

trade•mark (trād′märk′) *n.* **1.** A name, symbol, or other device identifying a product, officially registered and legally restricted to the use of the owner or manufacturer. **2.** A distinctive characteristic by which a person or thing comes to be known. — *tr.v.* **-marked, -mark•ing, -marks. 1.** To label (a product) with proprietary identification. **2.** To register (something) as a trademark.

trade name *n.* **1.** A name identifying a commercial product or service, which may or may not be a registered trademark. **2.** The name by which the trade knows a commodity, service, or process. **3.** The name under which a business firm operates.

trade•off or **trade-off** (trād′ôf′, -ŏf′) *n.* An exchange of one thing in return for another, esp. relinquishment of one benefit or advantage for another regarded as more desirable.

trad•er (trā′dər) *n.* **1.** One that trades; a dealer: *a gold trader; a trader in bonds.* **2.** *Naut.* A ship employed in foreign trade.

trade route *n.* A route used by traveling traders or merchant ships.

trade school *n.* A secondary school that offers instruction in skilled trades; a vocational school.

trade secret *n.* A secret formula, method, or device that gives one an advantage over competitors.

trades•man (trādz′mən) *n.* **1.** A man engaged in retail trade. **2.** A craftsman.

trades•peo•ple (trādz′pē′pəl) *pl.n.* **1.** People engaged in retail trade. **2.** Skilled workers.

trade union *n.* A labor union, esp. one limited to people in the same trade. — **trade unionism** *n.* — **trade unionist** *n.*

trade wind (wĭnd) *n.* Any of a consistent system of prevailing winds occupying most of the Tropics and blowing northeasterly in the Northern Hemisphere and southeasterly in the Southern Hemisphere. Often used in the plural. [< obsolete *to blow trade*, to blow in a regular course < TRADE, regular course (obsolete).]

trad•ing card (trā′dĭng) *n.* A card with a picture or design printed on it, often one of a set collected and traded.

trading post *n.* A station or store in a sparsely settled area established by traders to barter supplies for local products.

trading stamp *n.* A stamp given by a retailer to a buyer for a purchase of a specified amount and intended to be redeemed in quantity for merchandise.

tra•di•tion (trə-dĭsh′ən) *n.* **1.** The passing down of elements of a culture from generation to generation, esp. by oral communication. **2.a.** A mode of thought or behavior followed by a people continuously from generation to generation; a custom or usage. **b.** A set of such customs and usages viewed as a coherent body of precedents influencing the present. **3.** A

track and field
Top: Foot race
Bottom: Long jump by Carl Lewis in 1987

tractor

ă pat	oi boy
ā pay	ou out
âr care	o͝o took
ä father	o͞o boot
ĕ pet	ŭ cut
ē be	ûr urge
ĭ pit	th thin
ī pie	*th* this
îr pier	hw which
ŏ pot	zh vision
ō toe	ə about, item
ô paw	

Stress marks:
′ (primary);
′ (secondary), as in
dictionary (dĭk′shə-nĕr′ē)

body of unwritten religious precepts. **4.** A time-honored practice or set of such practices. [Ult. < Lat. *trāditiō, trāditiōn-* < *trāditus,* p.part. of *trādere,* to hand over, deliver, entrust : *trā-, trāns-,* trans- + *dare,* to give; see **dō-*.**]

tra•di•tion•al (trə-dĭsh′ə-nəl) *adj.* Of, relating to, or in accord with tradition. —**tra•di′tion•al•ly** *adv.*

tra•di•tion•al•ism (trə-dĭsh′ə-nə-lĭz′əm) *n.* **1.** Adherence to tradition, esp. in cultural or religious practice. **2.** *Philos.* A system holding that all knowledge is derived from original divine revelation and is transmitted by tradition. —**tra•di′tion•al•ist** *adj. & n.* —**tra•di′tion•al•is′tic** *adj.*

tra•di•tion•al•ize (trə-dĭsh′ə-nə-līz′) *tr.v.* **-ized, -iz•ing, -iz•es.** To make traditional.

tra•duce (trə-do͞os′, -dyo͞os′) *tr.v.* **-duced, -duc•ing, -duc•es.** To cause humiliation or disgrace to by making malicious and false statements. [Lat. *trādūcere,* to lead as a spectacle, dishonor : *trā-, trāns-,* trans- + *dūcere,* to lead; see **deuk-*.**] —**tra•duce′ment** *n.* —**tra•duc′er** *n.*

tra•du•cian•ism (trə-do͞o′shə-nĭz′əm, -dyo͞o′-) *n. Theol.* The belief that the soul is inherited from the parents along with the body. [< LLat. *trādūciānus,* believer in traducianism < *trādux, trāduc-,* inheritance < Lat., vine-branch trained for propagation < *trādūcere,* to lead across. See TRADUCE.]

Tra•fal•gar (trə-făl′gər), **Cape.** A cape on the SW coast of Spain NW of the Strait of Gibraltar. The British navy defeated the French and Spanish fleets off Cape Trafalgar in 1805.

traf•fic (trăf′ĭk) *n.* **1.a.** The commercial exchange of goods; trade. **b.** Illegal or improper commercial activity. **2.a.** The business of moving passengers and cargo through a transportation system. See Syns at **business. b.** The amount of cargo or number of passengers conveyed. **3.a.** The passage of people, vehicles, or messages along routes of transportation or communication. **b.** Vehicles or pedestrians in transit. **4.** Social or verbal exchange; communication. —*intr.v.* **-ficked, -fick•ing, -fics.** To carry on trade or other dealings. [Fr. *trafic* < OFr. *trafique* < OItal. *traffico* < *trafficare,* to trade, perh. < Catalan *trafegar,* to decant < VLat. **trānsfaecāre* : *trāns-,* trans- + *faex, faec-,* dregs; see FECES.] —**traf′fick•er** *n.*

traffic circle *n.* A circular one-way road at a junction of thoroughfares, facilitating an uninterrupted flow of traffic.

traffic island *n.* A raised area over which cars may not pass at a junction of thoroughfares or between opposing traffic lanes.

traffic light *n.* A road signal for directing vehicular traffic by means of colored lights, typically red for stop, green for go, and yellow for proceed with caution.

trag•a•canth (trăg′ə-kănth′, trăj′-) *n.* **1.** Any of various thorny Middle Eastern shrubs of the genus *Astragalus,* esp. *A. gummifer,* yielding a gum used in pharmaceuticals, adhesives, and textile printing. **2.** The gum of this plant. [Lat. *tragacantha* < Gk. *tragakantha* : *tragos,* goat + *akantha,* thorn.]

tra•ge•di•an (trə-jē′dē-ən) *n.* **1.** A writer of tragedies. **2.** One who performs tragic roles in the theater.

tra•ge•di•enne (trə-jē′dē-ĕn′) *n.* A woman who performs tragic roles in the theater. [Fr., fem. of *tragédien,* tragedian < OFr. *tragedian* < *tragedie,* tragedy. See TRAGEDY.]

trag•e•dy (trăj′ĭ-dē) *n., pl.* **-dies. 1.a.** A drama or literary work in which the main character is brought to ruin or suffers extreme sorrow, esp. as a consequence of a tragic flaw, a moral weakness, or an inability to cope with unfavorable circumstances. **b.** The genre made up of such works. **c.** The art or theory of writing or producing these works. **2.** A play, film, television program, or other narrative work that portrays or depicts calamitous events and has an unhappy ending. **3.** A disastrous event, esp. one involving distressing loss or injury to life. **4.** A tragic aspect or element. [ME *tragedie* < OFr. < Lat. *tragoedia* < Gk. *tragōidia* : *tragos,* goat + *ōidē,* song; see **wed-**[2]***.**]

trag•ic (trăj′ĭk) *adj.* **1.** Relating to or characteristic of dramatic tragedy or tragedies. **2.** Writing or performing in tragedy. **3.** Having the elements of tragedy; involving death, grief, or destruction. [Lat. *tragicus* < Gk. *tragikos* < *tragos,* goat.]

trag•i•cal (trăj′ĭ-kəl) *adj.* Tragic. —**trag′i•cal•ly** *adv.* —**trag′i•cal•ness** *n.*

tragic flaw *n.* A flaw in the character of the protagonist of a tragedy that brings the protagonist to ruin or sorrow.

tragic irony *n.* Dramatic irony in a tragedy.

trag•i•com•e•dy (trăj′ĭ-kŏm′ĭ-dē) *n., pl.* **-dies. 1.** A drama combining elements of tragedy and comedy. **2.** The genre made up of such works. **3.** An incident or a situation having both comic and tragic elements. [Fr. *tragicomédie* < Ital. *tragicommedia* < LLat. *tragicōmoedia,* short for Lat. *tragicocōmoedia* : *tragicus,* tragic; see TRAGIC + *cōmoedia,* comedy; see COMEDY.] —**trag′i•com′ic** (-kŏm′ĭk), **trag′i•com′i•cal** (-ĭ-kəl) *adj.* —**trag′i•com′i•cal•ly** *adv.*

tragopan
Satyr tragopan
Tragopan satyra

trag•o•pan (trăg′ə-păn′) *n.* Any of several Asian pheasants of the genus *Tragopan,* the male of which has two blue hornlike appendages on the head. [Lat. *tragopān,* fabulous bird < Gk. : *tragos,* goat + *Pan,* Pan; see PAN.]

tra•gus (trā′gəs) *n., pl.* **-gi** (-gī, -jī). **1.** The projection of skin-covered cartilage in front of the meatus of the external ear. **2.** Any of the hairs growing in the meatus of the external ear. [NLat. < Gk. *tragos,* goat, hairy part of the ear.]

trail (trāl) *v.* **trailed, trail•ing, trails.** —*tr.* **1.** To allow to drag or stream behind, as along the ground. **2.** To drag (the body, for example) wearily or heavily. **3.a.** To follow the traces or scent of, as in hunting; track. **b.** To follow the course taken by; pursue. **4.** To follow behind. **5.** To lag behind (an opponent). —*intr.* **1.** To drag or be dragged along, brushing the ground. **2.** To extend, grow, or droop loosely over a surface. **3.** To drift in a thin stream, as smoke. **4.** To become gradually fainter; dwindle: *His voice trailed off.* **5.** To walk or proceed with dragging steps; trudge. **6.** To be behind in competition; lag. —*n.* **1.** Something that hangs loose and long. **2.** Something that is drawn along or follows behind; a train. **3.** A succession of things that come afterward or are left behind. **4.a.** A mark or trace left by something that has moved or been dragged by. **b.** A succession of such marks indicating a course taken; a track. **5.a.** A marked or beaten path, as through woods or wilderness. **b.** An overland route. **6.** The part of a gun carriage that rests or slides on the ground. **7.** The act of trailing. [ME *trailen,* prob. < OFr. *trailler,* to hunt without a foreknown course < VLat. **trāgulāre,* to make a deer double back and forth, perh. alteration of Lat. *trahere,* to pull, draw.]

trail bike *n.* A small motorcycle with rugged tires and suspension, designed for cross-country off-road riding.

trail•blaz•er (trāl′blā′zər) *n.* **1.** One that blazes a trail. **2.** An innovative leader in a field; a pioneer. —**trail′blaz′ing** *adj.*

trail•er (trā′lər) *n.* **1.** A large transport vehicle designed to be hauled by a truck or tractor. **2.** A furnished van drawn by a truck or an automobile and used when parked as a dwelling or an office. **3.a.** A short filmed advertisement for a movie. **b.** A short blank strip of film at the end of a reel. —*v.* **-ered, -er•ing, -ers.** —*tr.* To transport by a trailer. —*intr.* To travel or live in a trailer.

trailer camp *n.* See **trailer park.**

trailer park *n.* An area in which parking space for house trailers is rented, usu. providing utilities and services.

trail•ing arbutus (trā′lĭng) *n.* A low-growing evergreen shrub *(Epigaea repens)* of eastern North America having leathery leaves and clusters of fragrant pink or white flowers.

trailing edge *n.* The rearmost edge of a structure that moves, as an airfoil.

train (trān) *n.* **1.** A series of connected railroad cars pulled or pushed by one or more locomotives. **2.** A long line of moving people, animals, or vehicles. **3.** The personnel, vehicles, and equipment following and providing supplies and services to a combat unit. **4.** A part of a gown that trails behind the wearer. **5.** A staff of people following in attendance; a retinue. **6.a.** An orderly succession of related events or thoughts; a sequence. **b.** A series of consequences wrought by an event; aftermath. **7.** A set of linked mechanical parts: *a train of gears.* **8.** A string of gunpowder that acts as a fuse for exploding a charge. —*v.* **trained, train•ing, trains.** —*tr.* **1.** To coach in or accustom to a mode of behavior or performance. **2.** To make proficient with specialized instruction and practice. See Syns at **teach. 3.** To prepare physically, as with a regimen. **4.** To cause (a plant or one's hair) to take a desired course or shape, as by manipulating. **5.** To focus on or aim at (a goal, mark, or target); direct. **6.** To let drag behind; trail. —*intr.* **1.** To give or undergo a course of training. **2.** To travel by railroad train. [ME, trailing part of a gown < OFr. < *trainer,* to drag < VLat. **tragināre* < **tragere,* to pull, back-formation < *tractus,* p.part. of Lat. *trahere.*] —**train′a•bil′i•ty** *n.* —**train′a•ble** *adj.*

train•band (trān′bănd′) *n.* A company of trained militia in England or America from the 16th to the 18th century. [Contraction of *trained band.*]

train•ee (trā-nē′) *n.* One who is being trained. —**train•ee′ship′** *n.*

train•er (trā′nər) *n.* **1.** One who trains, esp. one who coaches athletes, racehorses, or show animals. **2.** A contrivance or an apparatus used in training.

train•ing (trā′nĭng) *n.* **1.** The process or routine of one who trains. **2.** The state of being trained.

training school *n.* **1.** A school that gives practical vocational and technical instruction. **2.** A detention home that offers vocational training to juvenile offenders.

train•load (trān′lōd′) *n.* The number of occupants or the amount of material that a passenger or freight train can hold.

train•man (trān′mən) *n.* A member of the operating crew on a railroad train, esp. the brakeman.

train oil *n.* Oil obtained from the blubber of a whale or other marine animal. [ME *trane* < MDu. See **dakru-*.**]

traipse (trāps) *intr.v.* **traipsed, traips•ing, traips•es.** To walk or tramp about; gad. [?]

trait (trāt) *n.* **1.** A distinguishing feature, as of a person's character. **2.** A genetically determined characteristic or condition. **3.a.** A stroke with or as if with a pencil. **b.** A slight degree or amount, as of a quality; a touch or trace. [ME, shot < OFr. < Lat. *tractus,* a drawing out, line. See TRACT[1].]

trai•tor (trā′tər) *n.* One who betrays one's country, a cause, or a trust, esp. one who commits treason. [ME < OFr. < Lat. *trāditor, trāditōr-* < *trāditus,* p.part. of *trādere,* to betray. See TRADITION.]

trai•tor•ous (trā′tər-əs) *adj.* **1.** Having the character of a traitor; disloyal. **2.** Constituting treason. —**trai′tor•ous•ly** *adv.* —**trai′tor•ous•ness** *n.*

Tra•jan (trā′jən). A.D. 53–117. Roman emperor (98–117) whose reign was marked by an extensive building program.

tra•ject (trə-jĕkt′) *tr.v.* **-ject•ed, -ject•ing, -jects.** To transmit. [Lat. *trāicere, trāiect-*, to throw across : *trā-, trāns-*, trans- + *iacere*, to throw; see **yē-***.] —**tra•jec′tion** *n.*

tra•jec•to•ry (trə-jĕk′tə-rē) *n., pl.* **-ries. 1.a.** The path of a projectile or other moving body through space. **b.** A chosen course or a course taken. **2.** *Math.* A curve that cuts all of a given family of curves or surfaces at the same angle.

Tra•lee (trə-lē′). An urban district of SW Ireland at the head of **Tralee Bay,** an inlet of the Atlantic Ocean. Pop. 16,495.

tram[1] (trăm) *n.* **1.** *Chiefly British.* **a.** A streetcar. **b.** A streetcar line. **2.** A cable car, esp. one suspended from an overhead cable. **3.** A four-wheeled open box-shaped wagon or iron car run on tracks in a coal mine. —*tr.v.* **trammed, tram•ming, trams.** To move or convey in a tram. [Sc., shaft of a barrow, prob. < MFlem.]

tram[2] (trăm) *n.* **1.** An instrument for gauging and adjusting machine parts; a trammel. **2.** Accurate mechanical adjustment. —*tr.v.* **trammed, tram•ming, trams.** To adjust or align (mechanical parts) with a trammel. [Short for TRAMMEL.]

tram[3] (trăm) *n.* A heavy silk thread used for the weft in fine velvet or silk. [ME, contrivance < OFr. *traime*, contrivance, weft < Lat. *trāma*, weft, woof.]

tram•line (trăm′līn′) *n. Chiefly British.* A streetcar line.

tram•mel (trăm′əl) *n.* **1.** A shackle used to teach a horse to amble. **2.** Something that restricts activity, expression, or progress; a restraint. **3.** A vertically set fishing net of three layers, consisting of a finely meshed net between two nets of coarse mesh. **4.** An instrument for describing ellipses. **5.** An instrument for gauging and adjusting parts of a machine; a tram. **6.** An arrangement of links and a hook in a fireplace for raising and lowering a kettle. —*tr.v.* **-meled, -mel•ing, -mels** or **-melled, -mel•ling, -mels. 1.** To enmesh in or as if in a fishing net. **2.** To hinder the activity or free movement of. [ME *tramale*, a kind of net < OFr. *tramail* < LLat. *trēmaculum* : Lat. *trēs*, three; see **trei-*** + Lat. *macula*, mesh.] —**tram′mel•er** *n.*

tra•mon•tane (trə-mŏn′tān′, trăm′ən-tān′) *adj.* **1.** Dwelling beyond or coming from the far side of the mountains, esp. the Alps as viewed from Italy. **2.** From another country; foreign. —*n.* **1.** A person who lives beyond the mountains. **2.** A foreigner; a stranger. **3.** A cold north wind in Italy. [Ital. *tramontano* < Lat. *trānsmontānus* : *trāns-*, trans- + *montānus*, of a mountain; see MOUNTAIN.]

tramp (trămp) *v.* **tramped, tramp•ing, tramps.** —*intr.* **1.** To walk with a firm heavy step; trudge. **2.a.** To travel on foot; hike. **b.** To wander about aimlessly. —*tr.* **1.** To traverse on foot: *tramp the fields.* **2.** To tread down; trample. —*n.* **1.a.** A heavy footfall. **b.** The sound produced by heavy walking or marching. **2.** A walking trip; a hike. **3.** One who travels aimlessly about on foot, doing odd jobs or begging for a living; a vagrant. **4.a.** A prostitute. **b.** A person regarded as promiscuous. **5.** *Naut.* A tramp steamer. **6.** A metal plate attached to the sole of a shoe for protection, as when spading ground. [ME *trampen*, to walk heavily < MLGer.] —**tramp′er** *n.* —**tramp′ish** *adj.* —**tramp′y** *adj.*

tram•ple (trăm′pəl) *v.* **-pled, -pling, -ples.** —*tr.* **1.** To beat down with the feet so as to crush, bruise, or destroy; tramp on. **2.** To treat harshly or ruthlessly. —*intr.* **1.** To tread heavily or destructively. **2.** To inflict injury as if by treading heavily. —*n.* The action or sound of trampling. [ME *tramplen*, freq. of *trampen*, to tramp. See TRAMP.] —**tram′pler** *n.*

tram•po•line (trăm′pə-lēn′, -lĭn) *n. Sports.* A strong taut sheet, usu. of canvas, attached with springs to a metal frame and used for gymnastic springing and tumbling. [Sp. *trampolín* and Ital. *trampolino* (Ital. < Sp.) < *tràmpoli*, stilts, of Gmc. orig.] —**tram′po•lin′er, tram′po•lin′ist** *n.*

tramp steamer *n. Naut.* A commercial vessel with no regular schedule that takes on and discharges cargo as hired.

tram•way (trăm′wā′) *n.* **1.** A track or way for trams, as in a mine. **2.** *Chiefly British.* A streetcar line. **3.** A cable or system of cables for a cable car.

trance (trăns) *n.* **1.** A hypnotic, cataleptic, or ecstatic state. **2.** Detachment from one's physical surroundings, as in contemplation or daydreaming. **3.** A semiconscious state, as between sleeping and waking; a daze. —*tr.v.* **tranced, tranc•ing, tranc•es.** To put into a trance; entrance. [ME *traunce* < OFr. *transe*, passage, fear, vision < *transir*, to die, be numb with fear < Lat. *trānsīre*, to go over or across. See TRANSIENT.]

tran•quil (trăng′kwəl, trăn′-) *adj.* **1.** Free from commotion or disturbance. See Syns at **calm. 2.** Free from anxiety, tension, or restlessness; composed. **3.** Steady; even: *a tranquil flame.* [ME *tranquill* < Lat. *tranquillus*. See **kʷeiə-***.] —**tran′quil•ly** *adv.* —**tran′quil•ness** *n.*

tran•quil•ize also **tran•quil•lize** (trăng′kwə-līz′, trăn′-) —*v.* **-ized, -iz•ing, -iz•es** also **-lized, -liz•ing, -liz•es.** —*tr.* **1.** To make tranquil; pacify. **2.** To sedate or relieve of anxiety or tension by the administration of a drug. —*intr.* **1.** To become tranquil; relax. **2.** To have a calming or soothing effect. —**tran′quil•i•za′tion** (-kwə-lĭ-zā′shən) *n.*

tran•quil•iz•er (trăng′kwə-lī′zər, trăn′-) *n.* **1.** One that serves to tranquilize. **2.** Any of various depressant drugs used to reduce tension or anxiety and treat psychotic states.

tran•quil•li•ty or **tran•quil•i•ty** (trăng-kwĭl′ĭ-tē, trăn-) *n.* The quality or state of being tranquil; serenity.

trans. *abbr.* **1.** Transaction. **2.** Transfer. **3.** *Gram.* Transitive. **4.a.** Translated. **b.** Translation; translator. **5.** Transportation. **6.** Transpose; transposition. **7.** Transverse.

trans– *pref.* **1.** Across; on the other side; beyond: *transpolar.* **2.** Through: *transcontinental.* **3.** Change; transfer: *transliterate.* **4.** Having a pair of identical atoms on opposite sides of two atoms linked by a double bond. Used of a geometric isomer: trans-*butene.* [< Lat. *trāns-* < *trāns*, across, beyond, through. See **terə-**[2]*.]

trans•act (trăn-săkt′, -zăkt′) *v.* **-act•ed, -act•ing, -acts.** —*tr.* To do, carry on, or conduct: *transact business.* —*intr.* To conduct business. [Lat. *trānsigere, trānsāct-* : *trāns-*, trans- + *agere*, to drive, do; see **ag-***.] —**trans•ac′tor** *n.*

trans•ac•ti•nide (trăn-săk′tə-nīd′, -zăk′-) *adj.* Of or belonging to the series of elements whose atomic numbers are greater than 103.

trans•ac•tion (trăn-săk′shən, -zăk′-) *n.* **1.** The act of transacting or the fact of being transacted. **2.** Something transacted, esp. a business agreement or exchange. **3.** Communication involving two or more people that affects all those involved; personal interaction. **4. transactions.** A record of business at a meeting; proceedings. —**trans•ac′tion•al** *adj.*

transactional analysis *n.* A system of psychotherapy that analyzes personal relationships and interactions in terms of conflicting or complementary ego states that correspond to the roles of parent, child, and adult.

Trans A•lai (trăns′ ə-lī′, trănz′). A range of the Pamir Mts. in E Tadzhikistan and S Kirghiz rising to 7,138.5 m (23,405 ft).

trans•al•pine (trăns-ăl′pīn′, trănz-) *adj.* Of, living on, or coming from the other side of the Alps, esp. as seen from Italy.

Trans•al•pine Gaul (trăns-ăl′pīn′ gôl′, trănz-). The part of ancient Gaul NW of the Alps, including France and Belgium.

trans•am•i•nase (trăns-ăm′ə-nās′, -nāz′, trănz-) *n.* Any of a group of enzymes that catalyze transamination.

trans•am•i•na•tion (trăns-ăm′ə-nā′shən, trănz-) *n.* **1.** Transfer of an amino group from one chemical compound to another. **2.** Transposition of an amino group within a chemical compound.

trans•at•lan•tic (trăns′ət-lăn′tĭk, trănz′-) *adj.* **1.** Situated on or coming from the other side of the Atlantic Ocean. **2.** Spanning or crossing the Atlantic Ocean.

trans•ax•le (trăns-ăk′səl, trănz-) *n.* An automotive part that combines the transmission and the differential and is used on vehicles with front-wheel drive. [TRANS(MISSION) + AXLE.]

Trans•cau•ca•sia (trăns′kô-kā′zhə, -zhē-ə, trănz′-). A region of Georgia, Armenia, and Azerbaijan between the Caucasus Mts. and Turkey and Iran. —**Trans′cau•ca′sian** *adj.* & *n.*

trans•ceiv•er (trăn-sē′vər) *n.* A transmitter and receiver in a single unit sharing some circuits.

tran•scend (trăn-sĕnd′) *v.* **-scend•ed, -scend•ing, -scends.** —*tr.* **1.** To pass beyond the limits of. **2.** To be greater than, as in intensity or power; surpass. **3.** To exist above and independent of (material experience or the universe). —*intr.* To be transcendent; excel. [Ult. < Lat. *trānscendere* : *trāns-*, trans- + *scandere*, to climb; see **skand-***.]

tran•scen•dent (trăn-sĕn′dənt) *adj.* **1.** Surpassing others; preeminent or supreme. **2.** Lying beyond ordinary perception. **3.** *Philos.* **a.** Transcending the Aristotelian categories. **b.** In Kant's theory of knowledge, being beyond the limits of experience and hence unknowable. **4.** Being above and independent of the material universe. Used of the Deity. —**tran•scen′dence, tran•scen′den•cy** *n.* —**tran•scen′dent•ly** *adv.*

tran•scen•den•tal (trăn′sĕn-dĕn′tl) *adj.* **1.** *Philos.* **a.** Concerned with the a priori or intuitive basis of knowledge as independent of experience. **b.** Asserting a fundamental irrationality or supernatural element in experience. **2.** Surpassing all others; superior. **3.** Beyond common thought or experience; mystical or supernatural. **4.** *Math.* **a.** Not capable of being determined by any combination of a finite number of equations with rational integral coefficients. **b.** Not expressible as an integer or as the root or quotient of integers. Used of numbers, esp. nonrepeating infinite decimals. —**tran′scen•den′tal•ly** *adv.*

tran•scen•den•tal•ism (trăn′sĕn-dĕn′tl-ĭz′əm) *n.* **1.** A philosophy associated with Kant, holding that one must transcend empiricism or experience in order to find the a priori principles of all knowledge. **2.** A literary and philosophical movement asserting the existence of an ideal spiritual reality transcending the empirical and knowable through intuition. **3.** The quality or state of being transcendental. —**tran′scen•den′tal•ist** *n.*

transcendental meditation *n.* A technique of meditation derived from Hindu traditions that promotes deep relaxation through the use of a mantra.

ă pat	oi boy
ā pay	ou out
âr care	o͝o took
ä father	o͞o boot
ĕ pet	ŭ cut
ē be	ûr urge
ĭ pit	th thin
ī pie	*th* this
îr pier	hw which
ŏ pot	zh vision
ō toe	ə about, item
ô paw	

Stress marks:
′ (primary);
′ (secondary), as in **dictionary** (dĭk′shə-nĕr′ē)

trans•con•ti•nen•tal (trăns′kŏn-tə-nĕn′tl) *adj.* Spanning or crossing a continent.

tran•scribe (trăn-skrīb′) *tr.v.* **-scribed, -scrib•ing, -scribes. 1.** To make a full written or typewritten copy of (dictated material, for example). **2.** *Comp. Sci.* To transfer (information) from one recording and storing system to another. **3.** *Mus.* To adapt or arrange (a composition) for a voice or an instrument other than the original. **4.** To record, usu. on tape, for later broadcast. **5.** *Ling.* To represent (speech sounds) by phonetic symbols. **6.** To translate or transliterate. **7.** *Biol.* To cause (DNA or RNA) to undergo transcription. [Lat. *trānscrībere* : *trāns-*, trans- + *scrībere*, to write; see **skrībh-*.**] **—tran•scrib′a•ble** *adj.* **—tran•scrib′er** *n.*

tran•script (trăn′skrĭpt′) *n.* **1.** Something transcribed, esp. a written or typewritten copy. **2.** *Biol.* A sequence of RNA produced by transcription. [ME < Med.Lat. *trānscrīptum* < Lat., neut. p.part. of *trānscrībere*, to transcribe. See TRANSCRIBE.]

tran•scrip•tase (trăn-skrĭp′tās, -tāz) *n.* **1.** A polymerase that catalyzes the formation of RNA from a DNA template in the process of transcription. **2.** Reverse transcriptase.

tran•scrip•tion (trăn-skrĭp′shən) *n.* **1.** The act or process of transcribing. **2.** Something that has been transcribed, esp.: **a.** *Mus.* An adaptation of a composition. **b.** A recorded radio or television program. **c.** *Ling.* A representation of speech sounds in phonetic symbols. **3.** *Biol.* The process by which messenger RNA is synthesized from a DNA template. **—tran•scrip′tion•al** *adj.* **—tran•scrip′tion•ist** *n.*

trans•cur•rent (trăns-kûr′ənt, -kŭr′-) *adj.* Extending or running transversely.

trans•cu•ta•ne•ous (trăns′kyo͞o-tā′nē-əs) *adj.* Transdermal.

trans•der•mal (trăns-dûr′məl, trănz-) *n.* Through or by way of the skin.

transdermal patch *n.* An adhesive pad that delivers a time-release dose of medication through the skin into the bloodstream.

trans•duce (trăns-do͞os′, -dyo͞os′, trănz-) *tr.v.* **-duced, -duc•ing, -duc•es. 1.** To convert (energy) from one form to another. **2.** To transfer (genetic material or characteristics) from one bacterial cell to another. Used of a bacteriophage or plasmid. [Back-formation < TRANSDUCER.]

trans•duc•er (trăns-do͞o′sər, -dyo͞o′-, trănz-) *n.* A substance or device that converts input energy of one form into output energy of another. [< Lat. *trānsdūcere*, to transfer : *trāns-*, trans- + *dūcere*, to lead; see **deuk-*.**]

trans•duc•tion (trăns-dŭk′shən, trănz-) *n.* *Genet.* The act or process of transducing. [< Lat. *transductus*, p.part. of *trānsdūcere*, to transfer. See TRANSDUCER.] **—trans•duc′tion•al** *adj.*

tran•sect (trăn-sĕkt′) *tr.v.* **-sect•ed, -sect•ing, -sects.** To divide by cutting transversely. **—tran•sec′tion** *n.*

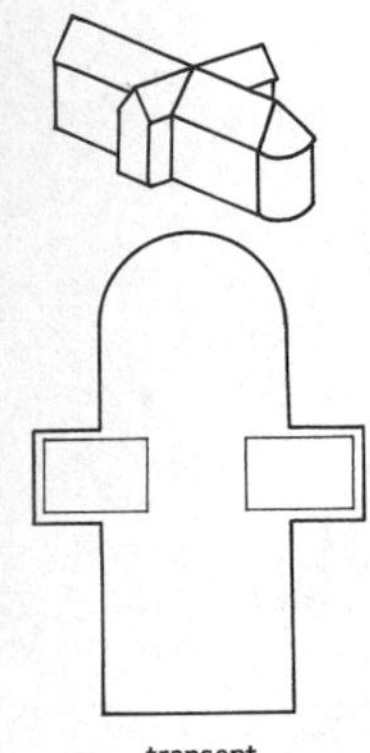

transept

tran•sept (trăn′sĕpt′) *n.* *Archit.* **1.** The transverse part of a cruciform church, crossing the nave at right angles. **2.** Either of the two lateral arms of such a part. [NLat. *trānseptum* : Lat. *trāns-*, trans- + Lat. *saeptum*, partition; see SEPTUM.]

tran•se•unt (trăn′sē-ənt) *adj.* *Philos.* Productive of effects outside the mind. [Lat. *trānsiēns*, *trānseunt-*, pr.part. of *trānsīre*, to go over. See TRANSIENT.]

transf. *abbr.* **1.** Transfer. **2.** Transferred.

trans•fec•tion (trăns-fĕk′shən) *n.* Infection of a cell with purified viral nucleic acid, resulting in subsequent replication of the virus in the cell. [TRANS- + (IN)FECTION.] **—trans•fect′** *v.*

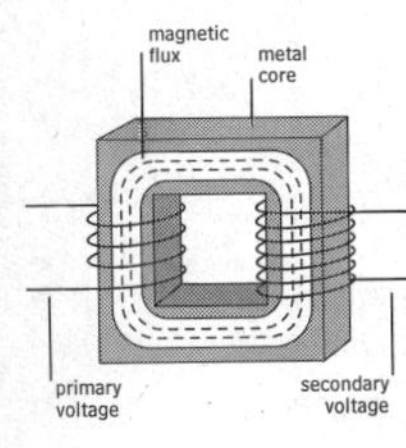

transformer
Iron core transformer

trans•fer (trăns-fûr′, trăns′fər) *v.* **-ferred, -fer•ring, -fers.** —*tr.* **1.** To convey or cause to pass from one place, person, or thing to another. **2.** *Law.* To make over the possession or legal title of; convey. **3.** To convey (a design, for example) from one surface to another, as by impression. —*intr.* **1.** To move oneself from one location or job to another. **2.** To withdraw from one educational institution or course of study and enroll in another. **3.** To change from one public conveyance to another: *transferred to another bus.* —*n.* (trăns′fər). **1.** Also **trans•fer•al** (trăns-fûr′əl). The conveyance or removal of something from one place, person, or thing to another. **2.** One who transfers or is transferred. **3.** A design conveyed by contact from one surface to another. **4.a.** A ticket entitling a passenger to transfer as part of one trip. **b.** A place where such a change is made. **5.** Also **transferal.** *Law.* A conveyance of title or property from one person to another. [ME *transferren* < OFr. *transferer* < Lat. *trānsferre* : *trāns-*, trans- + *ferre*, to carry; see **bher-[1]*.**] **—trans•fer′a•bil′i•ty** *n.* **—trans•fer′a•ble, trans•fer′ra•ble** *adj.* **—trans•fer′rer** *n.*

trans•fer•ase (trăns′fə-rās′, -rāz′) *n.* Any of various enzymes that catalyze the transfer of a chemical group, such as a phosphate or an amine, from one molecule to another.

trans•fer•ee (trăns′fə-rē′) *n.* **1.** *Law.* One to whom a conveyance of title or property is made. **2.** One who is transferred.

trans•fer•ence (trăns-fûr′əns, trăns′fər-əns) *n.* **1.a.** The act or process of transferring. **b.** The fact of being transferred. **2.** In psychoanalysis, the process by which emotions associated with one person, such as a parent, unconsciously shift to another, esp. to the analyst. **—trans′fer•en′tial** (trăns′fə-rĕn′shəl) *adj.*

transfer factor *n.* A polypeptide secreted by lymphocytes that can transfer immunity from one cell or individual to another.

trans•fer•or (trăns′fə-rôr′) *n.* *Law.* One who conveys a title or property.

trans•fer•rin (trăns-fĕr′ĭn) *n.* A beta globulin in blood serum that transports iron. [TRANS- + FERR(C)- + -IN.]

transfer RNA *n.* One of a class of RNA molecules that transport amino acids to ribosomes for incorporation into a polypeptide undergoing synthesis.

trans•fig•u•ra•tion (trăns-fĭg′yə-rā′shən) *n.* **1.a.** A marked change in form or appearance; a metamorphosis. **b.** A change that glorifies or exalts. **2. Transfiguration. a.** The emanation of radiance from Jesus on the mountain. **b.** The Christian feast marking this event, observed on August 6 or 19.

trans•fig•ure (trăns-fĭg′yər) *tr.v.* **-ured, -ur•ing, -ures. 1.** To alter the outward appearance of; transform. **2.** To exalt or glorify. [Ult. < Lat. *trānsfigūrāre* : *trāns-*, trans- + *figūra*, form; see **dheigh-*.**] **—trans•fig′ure•ment** *n.*

trans•fi•nite (trăns-fī′nīt′) *adj.* Going beyond the finite.

transfinite number *n.* *Math.* A number that is greater than any finite number.

trans•fix (trăns-fĭks′) *tr.v.* **-fixed, -fix•ing, -fix•es. 1.** To pierce with or as if with a pointed weapon. **2.** To fix fast; impale. **3.** To render motionless, as with terror, amazement, or awe. [Lat. *trānsfigere*, *trānsfīx-* : *trāns-*, trans- + *fīgere*, to pierce, fasten; see **dhīgʷ-*.**] **—trans•fix′ion** (-fĭk′shən) *n.*

trans•form (trăns-fôrm′) *v.* **-formed, -form•ing, -forms.** —*tr.* **1.** To change markedly the appearance or form of. **2.** To change the nature, function, or condition of; convert. **3.** *Math.* To subject to a transformation. **4.** *Ling.* To subject (a construction) to a transformation. **5.** *Elect.* To subject to the action of a transformer. **6.** *Genet.* To subject (a bacterial cell) to transformation. —*intr.* To undergo a transformation. —*n.* (trăns′fôrm′). The result, as a mathematical quantity, of a transformation. [Ult. < Lat. *trānsfōrmāre* : *trāns-*, trans- + *fōrma*, form.] **—trans•form′a•ble** *adj.*

trans•for•ma•tion (trăns′fər-mā′shən, -fôr-) *n.* **1.a.** The act or an instance of transforming. **b.** The state of being transformed. **2.** A marked change, as in appearance, usu. for the better. **3.** *Math.* **a.** Replacement of the variables in an algebraic expression by their values in terms of another set of variables. **b.** A mapping of one space onto another or onto itself. **4.** *Ling.* **a.** The conversion of a sentence, clause, or phrase into a semantically equivalent one by the particular syntactic rules of a language. **b.** A construction derived by such transformation. **5.** *Genet.* Alteration of a bacterial cell by introduction of DNA from another cell or from a virus. **—trans•form′a•tive** (-fôr′mə-tĭv) *adj.*

trans•for•ma•tion•al grammar (trăns′fər-mā′shə-nəl, -fôr-) *n.* *Ling.* A grammar that accounts for the constructions of a language by transformations and phrase structures.

trans•form•er (trăns-fôr′mər) *n.* A device used to transfer electric energy from one circuit to another, esp. a pair of inductively coupled wire coils that effect such a transfer with a change in voltage, current, phase, or impedance.

trans•fuse (trăns-fyo͞oz′) *tr.v.* **-fused, -fus•ing, -fus•es. 1.** To pour (something) out of one vessel into another. **2.** To instill or impart. **3.** To diffuse through; permeate. **4.** *Medic.* To administer a transfusion of or to. [ME *transfusen*, to transmit < Lat. *trānsfundere*, *trānsfūs-*, to transfuse : *trāns-*, trans- + *fundere*, to pour; see **gheu-*.**] **—trans•fus′i•ble, trans•fus′a•ble** *adj.* **—trans•fu′sive** (-fyo͞o′sĭv, -zĭv) *adj.*

trans•fu•sion (trăns-fyo͞o′zhən) *n.* **1.** The act or process of transfusing. **2.** *Medic.* The transfer of blood or blood products from one person to another. **—trans•fu′sion•al** *adj.*

trans•gen•ic (trăns-jĕn′ĭk, trănz-) *adj.* Carrying genes transferred from another species or breed.

trans•gress (trăns-grĕs′, trănz-) *v.* **-gressed, -gress•ing, -gress•es.** —*tr.* **1.** To go beyond or over (a limit or boundary); exceed or overstep. **2.** To act in violation of (the law, for example). —*intr.* **1.** To commit an offense by violating a law or command; sin. **2.** To spread over land. Used of the sea. [Ult. < Lat. *trānsgredī*, *trānsgress-*, to step across : *trāns-*, trans- + *gradī*, to go; see **ghredh-*.**] **—trans•gress′i•ble** *adj.* **—trans•gres′sive** *adj.* **—trans•gres′sor** *n.*

trans•gres•sion (trăns-grĕsh′ən, trănz-) *n.* **1.** A violation of a law, command, or duty. See Syns at **breach. 2.** The exceeding of due bounds. **3.** The spread of the sea over land.

tran•ship (trăn-shĭp′) *v.* Var. of **transship.**

trans•hu•mance (trăns-hyo͞o′məns, trănz-) *n.* Transfer of livestock from one grazing ground to another with the changing of seasons. [Fr. < *transhumer*, to move livestock seasonally < Sp. *trashumar* : Lat. *trāns-*, trans- + Lat. *humus*, ground; see **dhghem-*.**] **—trans•hu′mant** *adj. & n.*

tran•sient (trăn′shənt, -zhənt, -zē-ənt) *adj.* **1.** Passing with time; transitory. **2.** Remaining in a place only a brief time. **3.** *Phys.* Decaying with time, esp. as a simple exponential function of time. —*n.* **1.** One that is transient, esp. a hotel guest or boarder of brief duration. **2.** *Phys.* A transient disturbance or oscillation, esp. in an electric current. [Alteration of Lat. *trānsiēns*, *trānseunt-*, pr.part. of *trānsīre*, to go over : *trāns*, over; see **tera-[2]*** + *īre*, to go; see **ei-*.**] **—tran′sient•ly** *adv.* **—tran′sience, tran′sien•cy** *n.*

trans•il•lu•mi•na•tion (trăns′ĭ-lo͞o′mə-nā′shən, trănz′-) *n.* *Medic.* The passing of a light through the walls of a body part or organ to facilitate medical inspection. —**trans′il•lu′mi•nate′** (-lo͞o′mə-nāt′) *v.* —**trans′il•lu′mi•na′tor** *n.*

tran•sis•tor (trăn-zĭs′tər, -sĭs′-) *n.* **1.** A small electronic device containing a semiconductor and having at least three electrical contacts, used in a circuit as an amplifier, a detector, or a switch. **2.** A transistor radio. [TRANS(FER) + (RES)ISTOR.]

tran•sis•tor•ize (trăn-zĭs′tə-rīz′, -sĭs′-) *tr.v.* **-ized, -iz•ing, -iz•es.** To equip (an electronic device) with transistors.

transistor radio *n.* A small portable radio using transistors.

tran•sit (trăn′sĭt, -zĭt) *n.* **1.** The act of passing over, across, or through; passage. **2.** Conveyance of people or goods from one place to another, esp. on a local public transportation system. **3.** A transition or change, as to a spiritual existence at death. **4.** *Astron.* **a.** The passage of a celestial body across the observer's meridian. **b.** The passage of a smaller celestial body or its shadow across the disk of a larger celestial body. **5.** A surveying instrument similar to a theodolite that measures horizontal and vertical angles. —*v.* **-sit•ed, -sit•ing, -sits.** —*tr.* **1.** To pass over, across, or through. **2.** To revolve (the telescope of a surveying transit) about its horizontal transverse axis in order to reverse its direction. —*intr. Astron.* To make a transit. [ME *transite* < Lat. *trānsitus* < p.part. of *trānsīre*, to go across. See TRANSIENT.]

tran•si•tion (trăn-zĭsh′ən, -sĭsh′-) *n.* **1.** Passage from one form, state, style, or place to another. **2.a.** Passage from one subject to another in discourse. **b.** A word, phrase, sentence, or series of sentences connecting one part of a discourse to another. **3.** *Mus.* **a.** A modulation, esp. a brief one. **b.** A passage connecting two themes. —**tran•si′tion•al, tran•si′tion•ar′y** (-zĭsh′-ə-nĕr′ē) *adj.* —**tran•si′tion•al•ly** *adv.*

transition element *n.* Any of the metallic elements having an incomplete inner electron shell, marked by multiple valences, colored compounds, and the formation of stable complex ions.

transition metal *n.* A transition element.

tran•si•tive (trăn′sĭ-tĭv, -zĭ-) *adj.* **1.** *Gram.* Expressing an action that is carried from the subject to the object; requiring a direct object to complete meaning. Used of a verb or verb construction. **2.** Marked by or involving transition. —*n.* *Gram.* A transitive verb. —**tran′si•tive•ly** *adv.* —**tran′si•tive•ness, tran′si•tiv′i•ty** *n.*

tran•si•to•ry (trăn′sĭ-tôr′ē, -tōr′ē, trăn′zĭ-) *adj.* Existing or lasting only a short time; short-lived or temporary. —**tran′si•to′ri•ly** *adv.* —**tran′si•to′ri•ness** *n.*

Trans•jor•dan (trăns′jôr′dn, trănz′-). See **Jordan.** —**Trans′jor•da′ni•an** (-jôr-dā′nē-ən) *adj. & n.*

Trans•kei (trăns-kā′, -kī′). An internally self-governing Black African homeland in SE South Africa on the Indian Ocean coast; granted nominal independence in 1976. Cap. Umtata. Pop. 2,400,000. —**Trans•kei′an** *adj. & n.*

transl. *abbr.* **1.** Translated. **2.** Translation.

trans•late (trăns-lāt′, trănz-, trăns′lāt′, trănz′-) *v.* **-lat•ed, -lat•ing, -lates.** —*tr.* **1.** To render in another language. **2.a.** To put into simpler terms; explain. **b.** To express in different words; paraphrase. **3.a.** To change from one form, function, or state to another; transform: *translate ideas into reality.* **b.** To express in another medium. **4.** To transfer from one place or condition to another. **5.** To forward or retransmit (a telegraphic message). **6.a.** *Eccles.* To transfer (a bishop) to another see. **b.** *Theol.* To convey to heaven without death. **7.** *Phys.* To subject (a body) to translation. **8.** *Biol.* To subject (messenger RNA) to translation. **9.** *Archaic.* To enrapture. —*intr.* **1.a.** To make a translation. **b.** To work as a translator. **2.** To admit of translation. **3.** To be changed or transformed in effect. Often used with *into* or *to.* [ME *translaten* < OFr. *translater* < Lat. *trānslātus*, p.part. of *trānsferre*, to transfer : *trāns-*, trans- + *lātus*, brought; see **telə-*.**] —**trans•lat′a•bil′i•ty, trans•lat′a•ble•ness** *n.* —**trans•lat′a•ble** *adj.*

trans•la•tion (trăns-lā′shən, trănz-) *n.* **1.a.** The act or process of translating, esp. from one language into another. **b.** The state of being translated. **2.** A translated version of a text. **3.** *Phys.* Motion of a body in which every point of the body moves parallel to and the same distance as every other point of the body; nonrotational displacement. **4.** *Biol.* The process by which messenger RNA directs the amino acid sequence of a growing polypeptide during protein synthesis. —**trans•la′tion•al** *adj.*

trans•la•tor (trăns-lā′tər, trănz-, trăns′lā′tər, trănz′-) *n.* **1.** One that translates, esp. one employed to render written works into another language. **2.** An interpreter. —**trans′la•to′ri•al** (-lə-tôr′ē-əl, -tōr′-) *adj.*

trans•lit•er•ate (trăns-lĭt′ə-rāt′, trănz-) *tr.v.* **-at•ed, -at•ing, -ates.** To represent (letters or words) in the corresponding characters of another alphabet. [TRANS- + Lat. *littera, lītera*, letter + -ATE[1].] —**trans•lit′er•a′tion** *n.*

trans•lo•cate (trăns-lō′kāt′, trănz-) *tr.v.* **-cat•ed, -cat•ing, -cates.** **1.** To cause to change from one place or position to another; displace. **2.** *Genet.* To cause (a chromosomal segment) to undergo translocation.

trans•lo•ca•tion (trăns′lō-kā′shən, trănz′-) *n.* **1.** A change of location. **2.** *Genet.* **a.** A transfer of a chromosomal segment to a new position. **b.** A translocated chromosomal segment.

trans•lu•cent (trăns-lo͞o′sənt, trănz-) *adj.* **1.** Transmitting light but causing sufficient diffusion to prevent perception of distinct images. **2.** Clear; lucid. [Lat. *trānslūcēns, trānslūcent-*, pr.part. of *trānslūcēre*, to shine through : *trāns-*, trans- + *lūcēre*, to shine; see **leuk-*.**] —**trans•lu′cence, trans•lu′cen•cy** *n.* —**trans•lu′cent•ly** *adv.*

trans•lu•nar (trăns′lo͞o′nər, trănz′-, trăns-lo͞o′-, trănz-) *adj.* Extending beyond the moon or its orbit around Earth.

trans•ma•rine (trăns′mə-rēn′, trănz′-) *adj.* **1.** Crossing the sea. **2.** Beyond or coming from across the sea.

trans•mem•brane (trăns-mĕm′brān, trănz-) *adj.* Passing or occurring across a membrane.

trans•mi•grant (trăns-mī′grənt, trănz-) *n.* **1.** One that transmigrates. **2.** One in transit through a country on the way to the country in which one intends to settle.

trans•mi•grate (trăns-mī′grāt′, trănz-) *intr.v.* **-grat•ed, -grat•ing, -grates.** **1.** To migrate. **2.** To pass into another body after death. Used of the soul. —**trans′mi•gra′tion** *n.* —**trans′mi•gra′tion•ism** *n.* —**trans•mi′gra′tor** *n.* —**trans•mi′gra•to′ry** (-mī′grə-tôr′ē, -tōr′ē) *adj.*

trans•mis•si•ble (trăns-mĭs′ə-bəl, trănz-) *adj.* That can be transmitted. —**trans•mis′si•bil′i•ty** *n.*

trans•mis•sion (trăns-mĭsh′ən, trănz-) *n.* **1.a.** The act or process of transmitting. **b.** The fact of being transmitted. **2.** Something, such as a message, that is transmitted. **3.** An automotive assembly including gears that transmit power from the engine to a driving axle. **4.** The sending of information from a transmitter. [Lat. *trānsmissiō, trānsmissiōn-*, a sending across < *trānsmissus*, p.part. of *trānsmittere*, to transmit. See TRANSMIT.] —**trans•mis′sive** (-mĭs′ĭv) *adj.*

trans•mis•som•e•ter (trăns′mĭ-sŏm′ĭ-tər, trănz′-) *n.* A device used to measure transmission of light through a medium. [TRANSMISS(ION) + -METER.] —**trans′mis•som′e•try** *n.*

trans•mit (trăns-mĭt′, trănz-) *v.* **-mit•ted, -mit•ting, -mits.** —*tr.* **1.** To send from one person, thing, or place to another; convey. **2.** To cause to spread; pass on. **3.** To impart or convey to others by heredity or inheritance; hand down. **4.** To pass along (information); communicate. **5.a.** *Electron.* To send (a signal), as by wire or radio. **b.** *Phys.* To cause (a disturbance) to propagate through a medium. **6.** To convey (force or energy) from one part of a mechanism to another. —*intr.* To send out a signal. [Ult. < Lat. *trānsmittere* : *trāns-*, trans- + *mittere*, to send.] —**trans•mit′ta•ble** *adj.* —**trans•mit′tal** (-mĭt′l) *n.*

trans•mit•tance (trăns-mĭt′ns, trănz-) *n.* **1.** A transmission. **2.** *Phys.* The ratio of the radiant energy transmitted to the total radiant energy incident on a given body.

trans•mit•ter (trăns-mĭt′ər, trănz-) *n.* **1.** One that transmits. **2.a.** An electronic device that generates a carrier wave, modulates it with a signal to be broadcast, and radiates the resulting wave from an antenna. **b.** The portion of a telephone that converts the incident sounds into electrical impulses that are conveyed to a remote receiver. **c.** A telegraphic sending instrument.

trans•mog•ri•fy (trăns-mŏg′rə-fī′, trănz-) *tr.v.* **-fied** (-fīd′), **-fy•ing, -fies** (-fīz′). To change into a different shape or form, esp. one that is fantastic or bizarre. [?] —**trans•mog′ri•fi•ca′tion** (-fĭ-kā′shən) *n.*

trans•mon•tane (trăns-mŏn′tān′, trănz-, trăns′mŏn-tān′, trănz′-) *adj.* Tramontane. [Lat. *trānsmontānus*. See TRAMONTANE.]

trans•mun•dane (trăns′mŭn-dān′, trănz′-, trăns-mŭn′dā′, trănz-) *adj.* Existing or extending beyond the physical world.

trans•mu•ta•tion (trăns′myo͞o-tā′shən, trănz′-) *n.* **1.a.** The act or an instance of transmuting; transformation. **b.** The state of being transmuted. **2.** *Phys.* Transformation of one element into another by one or a series of nuclear reactions. **3.** The supposed conversion of base metals into gold or silver in alchemy. —**trans′mu•ta′tion•al, trans•mut′a•tive** (-myo͞o′tə-tĭv) *adj.*

trans•mute (trăns-myo͞ot′, trănz-) *v.* **-mut•ed, -mut•ing, -mutes.** —*tr.* To change from one form, nature, substance, or state into another; transform. —*intr.* To undergo transmutation. [ME *transmuten* < Lat. *trānsmūtāre* : *trāns-*, trans- + *mūtāre*, to change; see **mei-[1]*.**] —**trans•mut′a•bil′i•ty, trans•mut′a•ble•ness** *n.* —**trans•mut′a•ble** *adj.* —**trans•mut′a•bly** *adv.* —**trans•mut′er** *n.*

trans•na•tion•al (trăns-năsh′ə-nəl, trănz-) *adj.* **1.** Reaching beyond or transcending national boundaries. **2.** Relating to or involving several nations or nationalities.

trans•o•ce•an•ic (trăns′ō-shē-ăn′ĭk, trănz′-) *adj.* **1.** Situated beyond or on the other side of the ocean. **2.** Spanning or crossing the ocean.

tran•som (trăn′səm) *n.* **1.a.** A crosspiece over a door or between a door and a window above it. **b.** A small hinged window above a door or window. **2.** A horizontal dividing bar of wood or stone in a window. **3.** A lintel. **4.** *Naut.* A flat or nearly flat surface at the stern of a vessel. **5.** The horizontal beam on a cross or gallows. [ME *traunsom*, prob. alteration of Lat. *trānstrum*, crossbeam < *trāns*, across. See TRANS-.]

transit

transom

ă pat	oi boy
ā pay	ou out
âr care	o͝o took
ä father	o͞o boot
ĕ pet	ŭ cut
ē be	ûr urge
ĭ pit	th thin
ī pie	*th* this
îr pier	hw which
ŏ pot	zh vision
ō toe	ə about, item
ô paw	

Stress marks:
′ (primary);
′ (secondary), as in
dictionary (dĭk′shə-nĕr′ē)

tran•son•ic (trăn-sŏn′ĭk) *adj.* Of or relating to aerodynamic flow or flight conditions at speeds close to the speed of sound. [TRAN(S)- + SONIC.]

transp. *abbr.* Transportation.

trans•pa•cif•ic (trăns′pə-sĭf′ĭk, trănz′-) *adj.* **1.** Situated on or coming from the other side of the Pacific Ocean. **2.** Spanning or crossing the Pacific Ocean.

trans•par•en•cy (trăns-pâr′ən-sē, -păr′-) *n., pl.* **-cies. 1.** A transparent object, esp. a photographic slide that is viewed by light shining through it from behind or by projection. **2.** Also **trans•par•ence** (-pâr′əns, -păr′-). The quality or state of being transparent.

trans•par•ent (trăns-pâr′ənt, -păr′-) *adj.* **1.** Capable of transmitting light so that objects or images can be seen as if there were no intervening material. **2.** Permeable to electromagnetic radiation of specified frequencies, as to visible light waves. **3.** So fine in texture that it can be seen through; sheer. See Syns at **airy. 4.a.** Easily seen through or detected; obvious. **b.** Free from guile; candid or open. **5.** *Obsolete.* Shining through; luminous. [ME < OFr. < Med.Lat. *trānspārēns, trānspārent-*, pr.part. of *trānspārēre*, to show through : Lat. *trāns-*, trans- + Lat. *pārēre*, to show.] **—trans•par′ent•ly** *adv.* **—trans•par′ent•ness** *n.*

trans•per•son•al (trăns-pûr′sə-nəl, trănz-) *adj.* Transcending or reaching beyond the personal or individual.

tran•spic•u•ous (trăn-spĭk′yo͞o-əs) *adj.* Easily understood or seen through. [< NLat. *trānspicuus* < Lat. *trānspicere*, to see through : *trāns-*, trans- + *specere*, to look at; see **spek-***.]

tran•spi•ra•tion (trăn′spə-rā′shən) *n.* The act or process of transpiring, esp. through the stomata of plant tissue or the pores of the skin. **—tran′spi•ra′tion•al** *adj.*

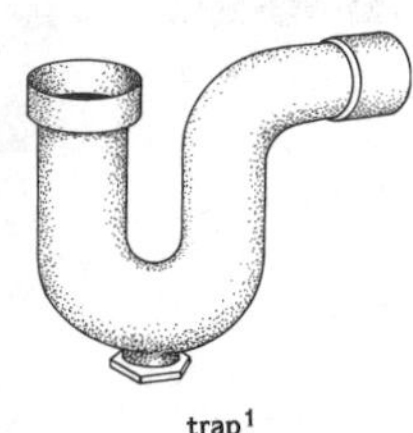

trap[1]
Drainpipe trap

tran•spire (trăn-spīr′) *v.* **-spired, -spir•ing, -spires.** *—tr.* To give off (vapor containing waste products) through the pores of the skin or the stomata of plant tissue. *—intr.* **1.** To become known; come to light. **2.** *Usage Problem.* To come about; happen or occur. **3.** To give off vapor containing waste products, as through pores. [Fr. *transpirer* < Med.Lat. *trānspīrāre* : Lat. *trāns-*, trans- + Lat. *spīrāre*, to breathe.]

Usage Note: In a 1969 survey the usage of *transpire* to mean "to happen" was acceptable only to 38 percent of the Usage Panel; in the most recent survey it was acceptable to 58 percent in the sentence *All of these events transpired after last week's announcement* (though many of the Panelists who accepted the usage also remarked that it was pretentious or pompous).

trans•pla•cen•tal (trăns′plə-sĕn′tl) *adj.* Passing through or occurring across the placenta. **—trans′pla•cen′tal•ly** *adv.*

trans•plant (trăns-plănt′) *v.* **-plant•ed, -plant•ing, -plants.** *—tr.* **1.** To uproot and replant (a growing plant). **2.** To transfer from one place or residence to another; relocate. **3.** *Medic.* To transfer (tissue or an organ) from one body or body part to another. *—intr.* To be capable of undergoing transplantation. *—n.* (trăns′plănt′). **1.** The act or process of transplanting. **2.** Something transplanted. **3.** *Medic.* An operation for transplanting. [Ult. < LLat. *trānsplantāre* : Lat. *trāns*, trans- + Lat. *plantāre*, to plant; see **plat-***.] **—trans•plant′a•ble** *adj.* **—trans′plan•ta′tion** *n.* **—trans•plant′er** *n.*

trans•po•lar (trăns-pō′lər) *adj.* Extending across or crossing either of the Polar Regions.

tran•spond•er (trăn-spŏn′dər) *n.* A radio or radar transceiver activated for transmission by reception of a predetermined signal. [TRAN(SMITTER) + (RE)SPONDER.]

trans•pon•tine (trăns-pŏn′tīn′) *adj.* **1.** Situated on the other side of a bridge. **2.** Similar to or characteristic of melodramas once performed in London theaters south of the Thames.

trans•port (trăns-pôrt′, -pōrt′) *tr.v.* **-port•ed, -port•ing, -ports. 1.** To carry from one place to another; convey. **2.** To move to strong emotion; carry away; enrapture. **3.** To send abroad to a penal colony; deport. See Syns at **banish.** *—n.* (trăns′pôrt′, -pōrt′). **1.** The act of transporting; conveyance. **2.** The condition of being transported by emotion; rapture. **3.** A vehicle used to transport passengers, mail, freight, or military equipment. **4.** A system for transporting passengers. **5.** A deported convict. [Ult. < Lat. *trānsportāre* : *trāns-*, trans- + *portāre*, to carry; see **per-[2]***.] **—trans•port′a•bil′i•ty** *n.* **—trans•port′a•ble** *adj.* **—trans•port′er** *n.* **—trans•por′tive** *adj.*

trans•por•ta•tion (trăns′pər-tā′shən) *n.* **1.a.** The act or an instance of transporting. **b.** The state of being transported. **2.** A means of conveyance. **3.** The business of conveying passengers or goods. **4.** A charge for public conveyance; a fare. **5.** Deportation to a penal colony.

trans•pose (trăns-pōz′) *v.* **-posed, -pos•ing, -pos•es.** *—tr.* **1.** To reverse or transfer the order or place of; interchange. **2.** To put into a different place or order. **3.** *Math.* To move (a term) from one side of an algebraic equation to the other side, reversing its sign to maintain equality. **4.** *Mus.* To write or perform (a composition) in a key other than the original or given key. **5.** To render into another language. **6.** To alter in form or nature; transform. *—intr.* **1.** *Mus.* To write or perform music in a different key. **2.** To admit of being transposed. *—n. Math.* A matrix formed by interchanging the rows and columns of a given matrix. [ME *transposen*, to transform < OFr. *transposer*, alteration (influenced by *poser*, to put, place; see POSE[1]) of Lat. *trānspōnere*, to transfer : *trāns-*, trans- + *pōnere*, to place; see **apo-***.] **—trans•pos′a•ble** *adj.*

trans•po•si•tion (trăns′pə-zĭsh′ən) *n.* **1.a.** The act or an instance of transposing. **b.** The state of being transposed. **2.** Something transposed. **3.** *Genet.* Transfer of a segment of DNA to a new position on the same or another chromosome, plasmid, or cell. **—trans′po•si′tion•al** *adj.*

trans•po•son (trăns-pō′zŏn) *n.* A segment of DNA that is capable of moving to a new position within the same or another chromosome, plasmid, or cell. [TRANSPOS(ITION) + -ON[1].]

trans•sex•u•al (trăns-sĕk′sho͞o-əl) *n.* **1.** One whose primary sexual identification is with the opposite sex. **2.** One who has undergone a sex change. **—trans•sex′u•al** *adj.* **—trans•sex′u•al•ism, trans•sex′u•al′i•ty** (-ăl′ĭ-tē) *n.*

trans•ship (trăns-shĭp′) also **tran•ship** (trăn-shĭp′) *tr. & intr.v.* **-shipped, -ship•ping, -ships.** To transfer or be transferred from one conveyance to another for reshipment. **—trans•ship′ment** *n.*

tran•sub•stan•ti•ate (trăn′səb-stăn′shē-āt′) *tr.v.* **-at•ed, -at•ing, -ates. 1.** To change (one substance) into another; transmute. **2.** *Theol.* To change the substance of (the Eucharistic bread and wine) into the body and blood of Jesus. [Med. Lat. *trānsubstantiāre, trānsubstantiāt-* : Lat. *trāns-*, trans- + Lat. *substantia*, substance; see SUBSTANCE.]

tran•sub•stan•ti•a•tion (trăn′səb-stăn′shē-ā′shən) *n.* **1.** Conversion of one substance into another. **2.** *Theol.* The doctrine that the Eucharistic bread and wine become the body and blood of Jesus. **—tran′sub•stan′ti•a′tion•al•ist** *n.*

tran•su•date (trăn-so͞o′dāt′, -syo͞o′-, trăn′so͞o-dāt′, -syo͞o-) also **tran•su•da•tion** (trăn′so͞o-dā′shən, -syo͞o-) *n.* **1.** A product of transuding. **2.** A substance that transudes.

tran•sude (trăn-so͞od′, -syo͞od′, -zo͞od′, -zyo͞od′) *intr.v.* **-sud•ed, -sud•ing, -sudes.** To pass through pores or interstices in the manner of perspiration. [NLat. *trānsūdāre* : Lat. *trāns-*, trans- + Lat. *sūdāre*, to sweat; see **sweid-***.] **—tran•su′da•to′ry** (trăn-so͞o′də-tôr′ē, -tōr′ē, -syo͞o′-) *adj.*

trans•u•ran•ic (trăns′yo͞o-răn′ĭk, -rā′nĭk, trănz′-) also **trans•u•ra•ni•um** (-rā′nē-əm) *adj.* Having an atomic number greater than 92. [TRANS- + URAN(IUM) + -IC.]

Trans•vaal (trăns-väl′, trănz-). A region of NE South Africa (since 1910); an independent Boer state after the 1850's and a British territory (1877) and crown colony (after 1900).

trans•val•ue (trăns-văl′yo͞o, trănz-) *tr.v.* **-ued, -u•ing, -ues.** To evaluate by a new standard or principle, esp. by one that varies from conventional standards. **—trans•val′u•a′tion** *n.*

trans•ver•sal (trăns-vûr′səl, trănz-) *adj.* Transverse. *—n. Math.* A line that intersects a system of other lines.

trans•verse (trăns-vûrs′, trănz-, trăns′vûrs′, trănz′-) *adj.* Situated or lying across; crosswise. *—n.* Something that is transverse. [Lat. *trānsversus* < p.part. of *trānsvertere*, to turn across : *trāns-*, trans- + *vertere*, to turn; see **wer-[2]***.] **—trans•verse′ly** *adv.* **—trans•verse′ness** *n.*

transverse colon *n.* The part of the colon that lies across the upper part of the abdominal cavity.

transverse flute *n. Mus.* See **flute** 1a.

transverse process *n.* A process projecting outward from the side of a vertebra.

trans•ves•tite (trăns-vĕs′tīt′, trănz-) *n.* A person who dresses and acts in a style or manner traditionally associated with the opposite sex. [Ger. *Transvestit* : Lat. *trāns-*, trans- + Lat. *vestīre*, to dress; see TRAVESTY.] **—trans•ves′tism** (-tĭz′əm), **trans•ves′ti•tism** (-tĭ-tĭz′əm) *n.*

Tran•syl•va•nia (trăn′sĭl-vān′yə, -vā′nē-ə). A historical region of W Romania bounded by the Transylvanian Alps and the Carpathian Mts. **—Tran′syl•va′ni•an** *adj. & n.*

Transylvanian Alps. A range of the S Carpathian Mts. extending across central Romania and rising to 2,544.6 m (8,343 ft).

trap[1] (trăp) *n.* **1.** A contrivance for catching and holding animals, as a concealed pit or a clamplike device that springs shut suddenly. **2.** A stratagem for catching or tricking an unwary person. **3.** A device for sealing a passage against the escape of gases, esp. a bend in a drainpipe that prevents the return flow of sewer gas by means of a water barrier. **4.** *Sports.* **a.** A device that hurls clay pigeons into the air in trapshooting. **b.** A land hazard or bunker on a golf course; a sand trap. **c. traps.** A measured length of roadway over which electronic timers register the speed of a racing vehicle. **5.** A light two-wheeled carriage with springs. **6.** A trap door. **7. traps.** *Mus.* Percussion instruments, esp. in a jazz band. **8.** *Slang.* The human mouth. *—v.* **trapped, trap•ping, traps.** *—tr.* **1.** To catch in or as if in a trap; ensnare. See Syns at **catch. 2.** To place in a confining or embarrassing position. **3.** To seal off (gases) by a trap. **4.** To furnish with traps or a trap. *—intr.* **1.** To set traps for game. **2.** To engage in trapping furbearing animals. [ME < OE *træppe*.]

trap[2] (trăp) *Informal.* *—n.* Personal belongings or household goods. Often used in the plural. *—tr.v.* **trapped, trap•ping, traps.** To furnish with trappings. [ME *trap*, trapping, perh. alteration of OFr. *drap*, cloth < LLat. *drappus*.]

trap³ (trăp) *n.* Any of several dark fine-grained igneous rocks often used in making roads. [Swed. *trapp* < *trappa*, step < MLGer. *trappe*.]

tra•pan (trə-păn′) *v.* Var. of **trepan²**.

trap door *n.* A hinged or sliding door in a floor, roof, or ceiling.

trap-door spider (trăp′dôr′, -dōr′) *n.* Any of various spiders of the family Ctenizidae, found in warm climates, that construct a silk-lined burrow with a hinged lid.

tra•peze (tră-pēz′, trə-) *n. Sports.* **1.** A short horizontal bar suspended from two parallel ropes, used for exercises or acrobatic stunts. **2.** An article of women's clothing that hangs down from the shoulders and swings out around the hips and legs. [Fr. *trapèze* < LLat. *trapezium*, trapezoid. See TRAPEZIUM.]

tra•pe•zi•um (trə-pē′zē-əm) *n., pl.* **-zi•ums** or **-zi•a** (-zē-ə). **1.** A quadrilateral having no parallel sides. **2.** *Chiefly British.* A trapezoid. **3.** A bone in the wrist at the base of the thumb. [LLat. *trapezium*, trapezoid < Gk. *trapezion*, dim. of *trapeza*, table : *tra-*, four; see **kʷetwer-*** + *peza*, foot; see **ped-***.]

tra•pe•zi•us (trə-pē′zē-əs) *n., pl.* **-us•es.** Either of two large flat triangular muscles running from the base of the occiput to the middle of the back. [NLat. < LLat. *trapēzium*, trapezium (< the shape of the muscles paired). See TRAPEZIUM.]

tra•pe•zo•he•dron (trə-pē′zō-hē′drən, trăp′ĭ-zō-) *n., pl.* **-drons** or **-dra** (-drə). Any of several forms of crystal with trapeziums as faces. [TRAPEZ(IUM) + -HEDRON.]

trap•e•zoid (trăp′ĭ-zoid′) *n.* **1.** A quadrilateral having two parallel sides. **2.** A small bone in the wrist, situated near the base of the index finger. [NLat. *trapezoidēs* < Gk. *trapezoeidēs*, trapezium-shaped : *trapeza*, table; see TRAPEZIUM + *-oeidēs*, -oid.] **—trap′e•zoid′, trap′e•zoi′dal** *adj.*

trap•per (trăp′ər) *n.* One who traps animals for their fur.

trap•ping (trăp′ĭng) *n.* **1.** An ornamental covering or harness for a horse; a caparison. Often used in the plural. **2. trappings. a.** Articles of dress or adornment, esp. accessories. **b.** Characteristic or symbolic signs: *all the trappings of power.*

Trap•pist (trăp′ĭst) *n.* A member of the main, reformed branch of Cistercian monks, established in 1664 at La Trappe Monastery in northwest France. **—Trap′pist** *adj.*

trap•shoot•ing (trăp′shoo͞′tĭng) *n. Sports.* Shooting at clay pigeons hurled up from spring traps. **—trap′shoot′er** *n.*

tra•pun•to (trə-po͞on′tō) *n., pl.* **-tos.** Quilting in which the design is outlined with running stitches and then padded from underneath. [Ital. < p.part. of *trapungere*, to embroider : Lat. *trāns-*, trans- + Lat. *pungere*, to prick; see **peuk-***.]

trash (trăsh) *n.* **1.a.** Worthless or discarded material or objects; refuse or rubbish. **b.** Something broken off or removed to be discarded, esp. plant trimmings. **c.** The refuse of sugar cane after extraction of the juice. **2.a.** Empty words or ideas. **b.** Worthless or offensive literary or artistic material. **3.** A person or group regarded as worthless or contemptible. *—tr.v.* **trashed, trash•ing, trash•es. 1.** *Slang.* **a.** To throw away; discard. **b.** To wreck or destroy by or as if by vandalism; reduce to trash or ruins. **c.** To beat up; assault. **d.** To subject to scathing criticism or abuse. **2.a.** To remove twigs or branches from. **b.** To cut off the outer leaves of (growing sugar cane). [Prob. of Scand. orig.]

trash•y (trăsh′ē) *adj.* **-i•er, -i•est. 1.** Resembling or containing trash; cheap or worthless. **2.** In very poor taste or of very poor quality. **—trash′i•ly** *adv.* **—trash′i•ness** *n.*

Tra•si•me•no (trä′zə-mā′nō, -zē-mĕ′-), **Lake.** A lake in central Italy W of Perugia; site of Hannibal's defeat of a Roman force in 217 B.C.

trass (trăs) *n.* A light-colored tuff used in hydraulic cement. [Du. *tras*, short for obsolete *terras, tiras*, poss. < Ital. *terrazzo*, stone chips. See TERRAZZO.]

trat•to•ri•a (trä′tə-rē′ə, trät′tô-rē′ä) *n., pl.* **-ri•as** or **-ri•e** (-rē′ĕ). An informal restaurant or tavern serving simple Italian dishes. [Ital. < *trattore*, host < *trattare*, to treat < Lat. *tractāre*. See TREAT.]

trau•ma (trou′mə, trô′-) *n., pl.* **-mas** or **-ma•ta** (-mə-tə). **1.** *Medic.* A serious injury or shock to the body, as from violence or an accident. **2.** *Psychiat.* An emotional wound or shock that creates substantial lasting damage to the psychological development of a person. [Gk. See **terə-¹***.] **—trau•mat′ic** (-măt′ĭk) *adj.* **—trau•mat′i•cal•ly** *adv.*

trau•ma•tism (trou′mə-tĭz′əm, trô′-) *n.* **1.** The condition produced by a trauma. **2.** A wound or an injury.

trau•ma•tize (trou′mə-tīz′, trô′-) *tr.v.* **-tized, -tiz•ing, -tiz•es. 1.** To wound or injure (a tissue), as in a surgical operation. **2.** To subject to psychological trauma.

trau•ma•tol•o•gy (trou′mə-tŏl′ə-jē, trō′-) *n.* The branch of medicine that deals with serious wounds and injuries. **—trau′ma•to•log′i•cal** *adj.* **—trau′ma•tol′o•gist** *n.*

tra•vail (trə-vāl′, trăv′āl′) *n.* **1.** Work, esp. when arduous; toil. **2.** Tribulation or agony; anguish. **3.** The labor of childbirth. *—intr.v.* **-vailed, -vail•ing, -vails. 1.** To work strenuously; toil. **2.** To be in the labor of childbirth. [ME < OFr. < *travailler*, to work hard < VLat. **tripāliāre*, to torture with a tripalium < LLat. *tripālium*, instrument of torture, prob. < Lat. *tripālis*, having three stakes : *tri-*, tri- + *pālus*, stake; see **pag-***.]

trave (trāv) *n.* **1.** *Archit.* **a.** A crossbeam. **b.** A section, as of a ceiling, formed by crossbeams. **2.** A wooden frame that confines a horse being shod. [ME < OFr. < Lat. *trabs, trab-*. See **treb-***.]

trav•el (trăv′əl) *v.* **-eled, -el•ing, -els** or **-elled, -el•ling, -els.** *—intr.* **1.** To go from one place to another, as on a trip; journey. **2.** To go from place to place as a salesperson or an agent. **3.** To be transmitted, as light; move or pass. **4.** To advance or proceed. **5.** To go about in the company of a particular group; associate: *travels in wealthy circles.* **6.** To move along a course, as in a groove. **7.** To admit of being transported without loss of quality. **8.** *Informal.* To move swiftly. **9.** *Basketball.* To walk or run illegally while holding the ball. *—tr.* To pass or journey over or through; traverse. *—n.* **1.** The act or process of traveling; movement or passage from one place to another. **2. travels. a.** A series of journeys. **b.** An account of one's journeys. **3.** Activity or traffic along a route or through a given point. [ME *travelen*, alteration of *travailen*, to toil < OFr. *travailler*. See TRAVAIL.]

travel agency *n.* A business attending to travelers' transportation, itinerary, and accommodations. **—travel agent** *n.*

travel bureau *n.* See **travel agency.**

trav•eled or **trav•elled** (trăv′əld) *adj.* **1.** Having made journeys; experienced in travel. **2.** Frequented by travelers.

trav•el•er or **trav•el•ler** (trăv′əl-ər, trăv′lər) *n.* **1.** One who travels or has traveled. **2.** *Chiefly British.* A traveling salesperson. **3.** *Naut.* **a.** A metal ring that moves freely back and forth on a rope, rod, or spar. **b.** This rope, rod, or spar.

trav•el•er's check (trăv′əl-ərz, trăv′lərz) *n., pl.* **traveler's checks** or **travelers' checks.** An internationally redeemable draft valid only with the purchaser's endorsement against his or her original signature on the draft.

trav•el•ing salesman (trăv′ə-lĭng, trăv′lĭng) *n.* A salesman who travels throughout a given territory.

trav•e•logue also **trav•e•log** (trăv′ə-lôg′, -lŏg′) *n.* **1.** A lecture with travel slides or films. **2.** A narrated travel film.

Tra•ven (trā′vən), **B.** Orig. Berick Traven Torsvan? 1890–1969. Amer.-born writer best known for his novel *The Treasure of the Sierra Madre* (1935).

Trav•ers (trăv′ərz), **P(amela) L.** b. 1906. Australian-born British writer whose works include *Mary Poppins* (1934).

tra•verse (trə-vûrs′, trăv′ərs) *v.* **-versed, -vers•ing, -vers•es.** *—tr.* **1.** To travel or pass across, over, or through. **2.** To move to and fro over; cross and recross. **3.** *Sports.* To go up, down, or across (a slope) diagonally or in a zigzag manner, as in skiing. **4.** To cause to move laterally on a pivot; swivel. **5.** To extend across; cross. **6.** To look over carefully; examine. **7.** To go counter to; thwart. **8.** *Law.* **a.** To deny formally (an allegation of fact by the opposing party) in a suit. **b.** To join issue upon (an indictment). **9.** To survey by traverse. *—intr.* **1.** To move to the side or back and forth. **2.** To turn laterally; swivel. **3.** *Sports.* **a.** To traverse a slope. **b.** To slide one's blade with pressure toward the hilt of the opponent's foil in fencing. *—n.* **trav•erse.** (trăv′ərs, trə-vûrs′). **1.** A passing across, over, or through. **2.** A route or path across or over. **3.** Something that lies across, esp.: **a.** An intersecting line; a transversal. **b.** *Archit.* A structural crosspiece; a transom. **c.** A gallery, deck, or loft crossing from one side of a building to the other. **d.** A railing, curtain, screen, or similar barrier. **e.** A defensive barrier across a rampart or trench. **4.** Something that obstructs and thwarts; an obstacle. **5.** *Naut.* The zigzag route of a vessel forced by contrary winds to sail on different courses. **6.** *Sports.* A zigzag or diagonal course on a steep slope, as in skiing. **7.a.** A lateral movement, as of a lathe tool across a piece of wood. **b.** A part of a mechanism that moves in this manner. **c.** The lateral swivel of a mounted gun. **8.** A line established by sighting in surveying a tract of land. **9.** *Law.* A formal denial of the opposing party's allegation of fact in a suit. *—adj.* **trav•erse.** (trăv′ərs, trə-vûrs′). Lying or extending across; transverse. [ME *traversen* < OFr. *traverser* < VLat. **trāversāre* < LLat. *trānsversāre* < Lat. *trānsversus*, transverse. See TRANSVERSE.] **—tra•vers′a•ble** *adj.* **—tra•vers′al** *n.* **—tra•vers′er** *n.*

trav•erse rod (trăv′ərs) *n.* A horizontal rod having a mechanism for drawing attached draperies with a pull cord.

trav•er•tine (trăv′ər-tēn′, -tĭn) *n.* **1.** A light-colored porous calcite, $CaCO_3$, deposited from solution in ground or surface waters. **2.** A compact calcium carbonate used as a facing material in construction. [Fr. < Ital. *travertino*, alteration of *tivertino* < Lat. *(lapis) tīburtīnus*, (stone) of Tibur (Tivoli), an ancient city of central Italy.]

trav•es•ty (trăv′ĭ-stē) *n., pl.* **-ties. 1.** An exaggerated or grotesque imitation. **2.** A debased or grotesque likeness: *a travesty of justice.* *—tr.v.* **-es•tied** (-ĭ-stēd), **-es•ty•ing, -es•ties** (-ĭ-stēz). To make a travesty of; parody or ridicule. [< obsolete, disguised, burlesqued < Fr. *travesti*, p.part. of *travestir*, to disguise, parody < Ital. *travestire* : Lat. *trāns-*, trans- + Lat. *vestīre*, to dress (< *vestis*, garment; see **wes-²***).]

Trav•is (trăv′ĭs), **William Barret.** 1809–36. Amer. military leader who commanded the defense of the Alamo (1836).

tra•vois (trə-voi′, trăv′oi′) also **tra•voise** (trə-voiz′, trăv′oiz′) *n., pl.* **tra•vois** (trə-voiz′, trăv′oiz′) also **tra•vois•es** (trə-voi′zĭz, trăv′oi′zĭz). A conveyance formerly used by

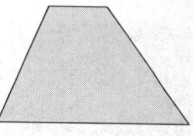

trapezoid

ă pat	oi boy
ā pay	ou out
âr care	o͝o took
ä father	o͞o boot
ĕ pet	ŭ cut
ē be	ûr urge
ĭ pit	th thin
ī pie	*th* this
îr pier	hw which
ŏ pot	zh vision
ō toe	ə about, item
ô paw	

Stress marks:
′ (primary);
′ (secondary), as in dictionary (dĭk′shə-nĕr′ē)

trawler
Oil painting by
Ellery F. Thompson
(1899–1986)

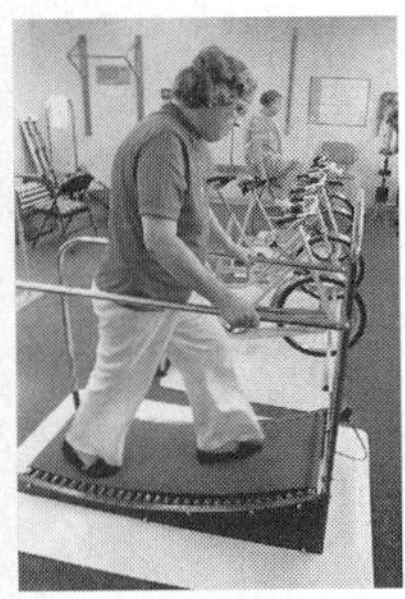

treadmill
Exercise treadmill

treble clef

Plains Indians consisting of a frame slung between poles and pulled by a dog or horse. [Canadian Fr., alteration of obsolete *travoy* < *travail*, cart-shaft < Fr., horse restraining frame, alteration of LLat. *tripālium*, device with three stakes, prob. < Lat. *tripālis*, having three stakes. See TRAVAIL.]

trawl (trôl) *n.* **1.** A trawl net. **2.** See **setline.** —*v.* **trawled, trawl•ing, trawls.** —*tr.* To catch (fish) with a trawl. —*intr.* **1.** To fish with a trawl. **2.** To troll. [Poss. ME *trawelle*, perh. < MDu. *tragel*, dragnet, poss. < Lat. *trāgula* < *trahere*, to drag.]

trawl•er (trô′lər) *n.* **1.** *Naut.* A vessel used for trawling. **2.** One who trawls.

trawl line *n.* See **setline.**

trawl net *n.* A large tapered fishing net that is towed along the sea bottom.

tray (trā) *n.* **1.** A shallow flat receptacle with a raised edge or rim, used for carrying, holding, or displaying articles. **2.** A tray with its contents. [ME < OE *trēg.* See **deru-*.**]

treach•er•ous (trĕch′ər-əs) *adj.* **1.** Marked by betrayal of fidelity, confidence, or trust; perfidious. **2.** Not to be relied on; not dependable or trustworthy. **3.** Marked by unforeseen hazards; dangerous or deceptive. —**treach′er•ous•ly** *adv.* —**treach′er•ous•ness** *n.*

treach•er•y (trĕch′ə-rē) *n., pl.* **-ies. 1.** Willful betrayal of fidelity, confidence, or trust; perfidy. **2.** The act or an instance of such betrayal. [ME *trecherie* < OFr. < *trichier*, to trick, prob. < VLat. **triccāre.* See TRICK.]

trea•cle (trē′kəl) *n.* **1.** Cloying speech or sentiment. **2.** *Chiefly British.* Molasses. **3.** A medicinal compound formerly used as an antidote for poison. [ME *triacle*, antidote for poison < OFr. < Lat. *thēriaca* < Gk. *thēriakē (antidotos)*, (antidote against) wild animals, fem. of *thēriakos*, of wild animals < *thērion*, dim. of *thēr*, beast. See **ghwer-*.**]

trea•cly (trē′klē) *adj.* Cloyingly sweet or sentimental.

tread (trĕd) *v.* **trod** (trŏd), **trod•den** (trŏd′n) or **trod, tread•ing, treads.** —*tr.* **1.** To walk on, over, or along. **2.** To press beneath the feet; trample. **3.** To subdue harshly or cruelly; crush. **4.** To form by walking or trampling: *tread a path.* **5.** To execute by walking or dancing: *tread a measure.* **6.** To copulate with. Used of a male bird. —*intr.* **1.a.** To go on foot; walk. **b.** To set down the foot; step. **2.** To press, crush, or injure something by or as if by trampling. Often used with *on* or *upon.* **3.** To copulate. Used of birds. —*n.* **1.a.** The act, manner, or sound of treading. **b.** An instance of treading; a step. **2.** The upper horizontal part of a step in a staircase. **3.a.** The part of a wheel or tire that makes contact with the road or rails. **b.** The grooved face of a tire. **4.** The part of a shoe sole that touches the ground. —***idiom.* tread water. 1.** To keep the head above water while in an upright position by pumping the legs. **2.** To expend effort but make little or no progress. [ME *treden* < OE *tredan.*] —**tread′less** *adj.*

tread•le (trĕd′l) *n.* A pedal or lever operated by the foot for circular drive, as in a sewing machine. —*intr.v.* **-led, -ling, -les.** To work a treadle. [ME *tredel* < OE, step of a stair < *tredan*, to tread.] —**tread′ler** *n.*

tread•mill (trĕd′mĭl′) *n.* **1.a.** A mechanism rotated by people treading on the moving steps of a wheel. **b.** A similar device operated by an animal treading an endless sloping belt. **2.** An exercise device consisting of an endless moving belt on which a person can walk or jog while remaining in one place. **3.** A monotonous task or set of tasks seeming to have no end.

treas. *abbr.* Treasurer; treasury.

trea•son (trē′zən) *n.* **1.** Violation of allegiance toward one's country or sovereign, esp. the betrayal of one's country by waging war against it or by purposely aiding its enemies. **2.** A betrayal of trust or confidence. [ME < AN *treson* < Lat. *trāditiō, trāditiōn-*, a handing over. See TRADITION.]

trea•son•a•ble (trē′zə-nə-bəl) *adj.* Relating to, constituting, or involving treason. —**trea′son•a•ble•ness** *n.* —**trea′son•a•bly** *adv.*

trea•son•ous (trē′zə-nəs) *adj.* Treasonable. —**trea′son•ous•ly** *adv.*

treas•ure (trĕzh′ər) *n.* **1.** Accumulated or stored wealth such as jewels or other valuables. **2.** Valuable or precious possessions of any kind. **3.** One considered esp. precious or valuable. —*tr.v.* **-ured, -ur•ing, -ures. 1.** To keep or regard as precious; value highly. See Syns at **appreciate. 2.** To accumulate and store away. [ME *tresure* < OFr. *tresor* < Lat. *thēsaurus* < Gk. *thēsauros.*] —**treas′ur•a•ble** *adj.*

treasure hunt *n.* *Games.* A game in which the players attempt to find hidden articles by means of a series of clues.

treas•ur•er (trĕzh′ər-ər) *n.* One who has charge of funds or revenues, esp. the chief financial officer of a government, a corporation, or an association. [ME *tresurer* < AN *tresorer* < LLat. *thēsaurārius* < Lat., of treasure < *thēsaurus*, treasure. See TREASURE.]

treas•ure-trove (trĕzh′ər-trōv′) *n.* **1.** Treasure found hidden. **2.** *Law.* Silver or gold in the form of bullion, plate, or money that is found hidden and has no known owner. **3.** A discovery of great value. [AN *tresor trove* : OFr. *tresor*, treasure; see TREASURE + OFr. *trove*, p.part. of *trover*, to find; see TROVER.]

treas•ur•y (trĕzh′ə-rē) *n., pl.* **-ies. 1.** A place in which treasure is kept. **2.** A place in which private or public funds are received, kept, and managed. **3.** Such funds or revenues. **4.** A collection of literary or artistic treasures. **5. Treasury. a.** The department of a government in charge of the collection, management, and expenditure of the public revenue. **b.** A security, such as a note, issued by the U.S. Treasury.

Treasury bill *n.* A short-term obligation of the U.S. Treasury having a maturity period of one year or less and sold at a discount from face value.

Treasury bond *n.* A long-term obligation of the U.S. Treasury having a maturity period of more than ten years and paying interest semiannually.

Treasury note *n.* An intermediate-term obligation of the U.S. Treasury having a maturity period of one to ten years and paying interest semiannually.

treat (trēt) *v.* **treat•ed, treat•ing, treats.** —*tr.* **1.** To act or behave in a specified manner toward. **2.** To regard and handle in a certain way. Often used with *as.* **3.** To deal with in writing or speech; discuss. **4.** To deal with or represent artistically in a specified manner or style. **5.a.** To provide with food, entertainment, or gifts at one's own expense. **b.** To give (someone or oneself) something pleasurable. **6.** To subject to a process, an action, or a change, esp. to a chemical or physical process or application. **7.a.** To give medical aid to (someone). **b.** To give medical aid to counteract (a disease or condition). —*intr.* **1.** To deal with a subject or topic in writing or speech. Often used with *of.* **2.** To pay for another's entertainment, food, or drink. **3.** To engage in negotiations, as to reach a settlement or agree on terms. —*n.* **1.** Something, such as one's food or entertainment, that is paid for by someone else. **2.** A source of special delight or pleasure. [ME *tretien* < OFr. *traitier* < Lat. *tractāre*, freq. of *trahere*, to draw.] —**treat′er** *n.*

Syns: *treat, deal, handle.* The central meaning shared by these verbs is "to act in a specified way with regard to someone or something": *treats his guests with courtesy; dealt rationally with the problem; handling a case with discretion.*

treat•a•ble (trē′tə-bəl) *adj.* Possible to treat; responsive to treatment.

trea•tise (trē′tĭs) *n.* **1.** A systematic, usu. extensive written discourse on a topic. **2.** *Obsolete.* A tale or narrative. [ME *treatis* < AN *tretiz*, alteration of *treteiz* < VLat. **tractāticius* < Lat. *tractātus*, p.part. of *tractāre*, to drag about, deal with. See TREAT.]

treat•ment (trēt′mənt) *n.* **1.a.** The act, manner, or method of handling or dealing with someone or something. **b.** *Informal.* The usual methods of dealing with a given situation: *gave the opposing team the treatment.* **2.a.** Administration or application of remedies to a patient or for a disease or an injury; therapy. **b.** The substance or remedy so applied.

trea•ty (trē′tē) *n., pl.* **-ties. 1.a.** A formal agreement between two or more states, as to terms of peace or trade. **b.** The document in which such an agreement is set down. **2.** A contract or an agreement. **3.** *Obsolete.* **a.** Negotiation for the purpose of reaching an agreement. **b.** An entreaty. [ME *tretee* < OFr. *traite* < Lat. *tractātus*, discussion < p.part. of *tractāre*, to drag about, deal with. See TREAT.]

treaty port *n.* A port kept open for foreign trade according to a treaty, esp. formerly in China, Korea, and Japan.

Treb•bia (trĕb′yä). A river of NW Italy flowing c. 113 km (70 mi) N to the Po R.

Treb•i•zond (trĕb′ĭ-zŏnd′). **1.** A former Greek empire bordering the Black Sea; founded in 1204 and conquered by Ottoman Turks in 1461. **2.** See **Trabzon.**

treb•le (trĕb′əl) *adj.* **1.** Triple. **2.** *Mus.* Relating to or having the highest part, voice, or range. **3.** High-pitched; shrill. —*n.* **1.** *Mus.* **a.** The highest part, voice, instrument, or range. **b.** A singer or player of this part. **2.** A high shrill sound or voice. —*tr. & intr.v.* **-led, -ling, -les.** To make or become triple. [ME < OFr. < Med.Lat. *triplum* < Lat., neut. of *triplus*, triple. See TRIPLE.] —**treb′le•ness** *n.* —**treb′ly** *adv.*

treble clef *n.* *Mus.* A symbol indicating the second line from the bottom of a staff as the pitch of G above middle C.

treb•u•chet (trĕb′yə-shĕt′) also **treb•uc•ket** (-ə-kĕt′) *n.* A medieval catapult for hurling heavy stones. [ME < OFr. < *trebucher*, to overthrow : *tre-*, over (< Lat. *trāns-*; see TRANS–) + *but*, trunk of the body (of Gmc. orig.).]

tre•cen•to (trā-chĕn′tō) *n.* The 14th century, esp. with reference to Italian art and literature. [Ital. < *(mil) trecento*, (one thousand) three hundred : *tre*, three (< Lat. *trēs*; see **trei-***) + *cento*, hundred (< Lat. *centum*; see **dekm̥***).]

tree (trē) *n.* **1.a.** A perennial woody plant having a main trunk and usu. a distinct crown. **b.** A plant or shrub resembling a tree in form or size. **2.** Something, such as a clothes tree, that resembles a tree in form. **3.** A wooden beam, post, stake, or bar used as part of a framework or structure. **4.** A saddletree. **5.** A diagram showing a family lineage; a family tree. **6.** *Archaic.* **a.** A gallows. **b.** The cross on which Jesus was crucified. —*tr.v.* **treed, tree•ing, trees. 1.** To force up a tree. **2.** *Informal.* To force into a difficult position; corner. **3.** To supply with trees. **4.** To stretch (a shoe or boot) onto a shoetree. —***idiom.* up a tree.** *Informal.* In a situation of great difficulty

or perplexity; helpless. [ME < OE *trēow*. See **deru-***.]
Tree (trē), Sir **Herbert Beerbohm.** 1853–1917. British actor who founded the Royal Academy of Dramatic Art (1904).
tree farm *n.* An area of forest land for commercial use.
tree fern *n.* Any of various tropical treelike ferns with a terminal crown of large, pinnately divided fronds.
tree frog *n.* Any of various small arboreal frogs of the family Hylidae, having long toes terminating in adhesive disks.
tree•hop•per (trē′hŏp′ər) *n.* Any of numerous, generally small tropical homopterous insects of the family Membracidae, having mouthparts for sucking the sap from trees.
tree house *n.* A structure built among the limbs of a tree.
tree line *n.* **1.** The limit of northern or southern latitude beyond which trees will not grow except as stunted forms. **2.** See **timberline.**
tre•en (trē′ən) *n.* Wooden cookware, tableware, or eating utensils. [< ME, made of wood < OE *trēowen* < *trēow*, tree. See TREE.]
tree•nail or **tre•nail** (trē′nāl′, trĕn′əl, trŭn′əl) also **trun•nel** (trŭn′əl) *n.* A wooden peg that swells when wet and is used to fasten timbers, esp. in shipbuilding.
tree-of-heav•en (trē′əv-hĕv′ən) *n.* A deciduous, rapidly growing tree *(Ailanthus altissima)* native to China and having sweetish fetid male flowers.
tree of knowledge *n.* The tree in the Garden of Eden whose forbidden fruit Adam and Eve tasted.
tree of life *n., pl.* **trees of life. 1.** A tall palm *(Mauritia flexuosa)* of South America having fan-shaped leaves. **2.** A tree in the Garden of Eden whose fruit, if eaten, gave eternal life.
tree shrew *n.* Any of various small squirrellike arboreal mammals of the family Tupaiidae, found in southern Asia and thought to be related to both insectivores and primates.
tree squirrel *n.* See **squirrel** 1.
tree surgery *n.* Treatment of diseased or damaged trees by filling cavities and pruning and bracing branches. **—tree surgeon** *n.*
tree toad *n.* See **tree frog.**
tree•top (trē′tŏp′) *n.* The uppermost part of a tree.
tref (trāf) *adj. Judaism.* Not kosher according to dietary law. [Yiddish *treyf* < Heb. *ṭĕrēpâ*, carrion < *ṭārap*, to tear.]
tre•foil (trē′foil′, trĕf′oil′) *n.* **1.** Any of various plants of the genera *Trifolium, Lotus,* and related genera of the pea family, having compound trifoliate leaves. **2.** An ornament or symbol having the appearance of a trifoliate leaf. [ME < AN *trifoil* < Lat. *trifolium* : *tri-*, tri- + *folium*, leaf; see **bhel-³***.]
tre•ha•la (trĭ-hä′lə) *n.* A sugarlike edible substance obtained from the pupal case of an Old World beetle of the genus *Larinus.* [NLat. *trehāla* < Turk. *tiqāla* < Pers. *tighāl*.]
tre•ha•lose (trĭ-hä′lōs′, -lōz′) *n.* A sweet-tasting crystalline disaccharide, $C_{12}H_{22}O_{11}$, found in trehala and in many fungi.
treil•lage (trĕ-yäzh′, trā′lĭj) *n.* Latticework, esp. a trellis for a vine. [Fr. < OFr. *treille*, bower supported by trelliswork < Lat. *trichila*, bower, arbor.]
trek (trĕk) *intr.v.* **trekked, trek•king, treks. 1.** To make a slow or arduous journey. **2.** To journey on foot, esp. through mountainous areas. **3.** *South African.* To travel by ox wagon. —*n.* **1.** A journey or leg of a journey, esp. when slow or difficult. **2.** *South African.* A journey by ox wagon, esp. a migration such as that of the Boers from 1835 to 1837. [Afr., to travel by ox wagon < Du. *trekken*, to travel < MDu. *trecken*, to pull.] **—trek′ker** *n.*
trel•lis (trĕl′ĭs) *n.* **1.** A structure of open latticework, esp. one used as a support for creeping plants. **2.** An arbor or arch made of latticework. —*tr.v.* **-lised, -lis•ing, -lis•es. 1.** To provide with a trellis, esp. to train (a vine) on a trellis. **2.** To make (something) in the form of a trellis. [ME *trelis* < OFr. < VLat. **trilīcius* < Lat. *trilīx, trilīc-*, woven with three threads : *tri-*, tri- + *līcium*, thread.]
trel•lis•work (trĕl′ĭs-wûrk′) *n.* Latticework.
trem•a•tode (trĕm′ə-tōd′) *n.* Any of numerous parasitic flatworms of the class Trematoda, having a thick outer cuticle and one or more suckers or hooks for attaching to host tissue. [< NLat. *Trematoda*, class name < Gk. *trēmatōdēs*, having holes < *trēma, trēmat-*, perforation. See **terə-¹***.] **—trem′a•tode′** *adj.*
trem•ble (trĕm′bəl) *intr.v.* **-bled, -bling, -bles. 1.** To shake involuntarily, as from excitement, weakness, or anger; quake. **2.** To feel fear or anxiety. **3.** To vibrate or quiver. —*n.* **1.** The act or state of trembling. **2.** A convulsive fit of shaking. Often used in the plural. **3. trembles.** *(used with a sing. v.)* **a.** An infectious viral disease of sheep that affects the nervous system, often causing prolonged trembling. **b.** Poisoning of domestic animals, esp. cattle and sheep, caused by eating white snakeroot or rayless goldenrod and marked by muscular tremors and weakening. [ME *tremblen* < OFr. *trembler* < VLat. **tremulāre* < Lat. *tremulus*, trembling. See TREMULOUS.] **—trem′bler** *n.* **—trem′bly** *adj.*
tre•men•dous (trĭ-mĕn′dəs) *adj.* **1.a.** Extremely large in amount, extent, or degree; enormous. **b.** *Informal.* Marvelous; wonderful. **2.** Capable of making one tremble; terrible. [< Lat. *tremendus*, gerundive of *tremere*, to tremble.] **—tre•men′dous•ly** *adv.* **—tre•men′dous•ness** *n.*
trem•o•lite (trĕm′ə-līt′) *n.* A white to gray amphibole mineral, $Ca_2Mg_5Si_8O_{22}(OH)_2$, typically occurring in aggregates. [Fr. *trémolite*, after *Tremola*, a valley in the Swiss Alps.]
trem•o•lo (trĕm′ə-lō′) *n., pl.* **-los.** *Mus.* **1.a.** A tremulous effect produced by rapid repetition of a single tone. **b.** A similar effect produced by rapid alternation of two tones. **2.** A device on an organ for producing a tremulous effect. **3.** A vibrato in singing, often excessive or poorly controlled. [Ital. < Lat. *tremulus*, tremulous. See TREMULOUS.]
trem•or (trĕm′ər) *n.* **1.** A shaking or vibrating movement, as of the earth. **2.** A trembling or quivering effect. **3.** An involuntary trembling or quivering, as from nervous agitation. **4.** A nervous quiver or thrill. **5.** A state or feeling of nervous agitation or tension. **6.** A tremulous sound; a quaver. [ME, terror < OFr. < Lat., a trembling < *tremere*, to tremble.]
trem•u•lant (trĕm′yə-lənt) *adj.* Tremulous; trembling.
trem•u•lous (trĕm′yə-ləs) *adj.* **1.** Marked by trembling, quivering, or shaking. **2.** Timid or fearful; timorous. [< Lat. *tremulus* < *tremere*, to tremble.] **—trem′u•lous•ly** *adv.* **—trem′u•lous•ness** *n.*
tre•nail (trē′nāl′, trĕn′əl, trŭn′əl) *n.* Var. of **treenail.**
trench (trĕnch) *n.* **1.** A deep furrow or ditch. **2.** A long narrow ditch embanked with its own soil and used for concealment and protection in warfare. **3.** A long steep-sided valley on the ocean floor. —*v.* **trenched, trench•ing, trench•es.** —*tr.* **1.** To cut a trench in. **2.** To fortify with trenches. **3.** To place in a trench. **4.** To make a cut in; carve. —*intr.* **1.** To dig trenches or a trench. **2.** To verge or encroach. Often used with *on* or *upon.* [ME *trenche* < OFr. < *trenchier*, to cut, perh. < VLat. **trincāre*, var. of Lat. *truncāre* < *truncus*, trunk. See **terə-²***.]
trench•ant (trĕn′chənt) *adj.* **1.** Keen; incisive. **2.** Forceful, effective, and vigorous. **3.** Caustic; cutting. **4.** Distinct; clear-cut. [ME < OFr., cutting < pr.part. of *trenchier*, to cut. See TRENCH.] **—trench′an•cy** *n.* **—trench′ant•ly** *adv.*
trench coat *n.* A belted raincoat in a military style, having straps on the shoulders and deep pockets.
trench•er¹ (trĕn′chər) *n.* **1.** A wooden board or platter on which food is carved or served. **2.** *Archaic.* The pleasure of the table; food. [ME *trenchur* < AN *trenchour* < *trencher*, to cut, perh. < VLat. **trincāre.* See TRENCH.]
trench•er² (trĕn′chər) *n.* One that digs trenches.
trench•er•man (trĕn′chər-mən) *n.* **1.** A hearty eater. **2.** *Archaic.* One who frequents another's table; a parasite.
trench fever *n.* An acute infectious disease characterized by chills and fever, caused by the microorganism *Rickettsia quintana* and transmitted by the louse *Pediculus humanus.*
trench foot *n.* A condition of the foot resembling frostbite, caused by prolonged exposure to cold and dampness.
trench mortar *n.* See **mortar** 3a.
trench mouth *n.* A painful infection of the mouth and throat caused by the bacterium *Fusobacterium fusiforme* in combination with the spirochete *Treponema vincentii* and marked by ulcerations of the mucous membranes, bleeding, and foul breath.
trend (trĕnd) *n.* **1.** The general direction in which something tends to move. **2.** A general tendency or inclination. **3.** Current style; vogue. —*intr.v.* **trend•ed, trend•ing, trends. 1.** To extend, incline, or veer in a specified direction. **2.** To show a general tendency; tend. [< ME *trenden*, to revolve < OE *trendan.*]
trend•set•ter (trĕnd′sĕt′ər) *n.* One that initiates or popularizes a trend. **—trend′set′ting** *adj.*
trend•y (trĕn′dē) *Informal. adj.* **-i•er, -i•est.** Of or in accord with the latest fad or fashion: *trendy clothes.* **—trend′i•ly** *adv.* **—trend′i•ness** *n.* **—trend′y** *n.*
Trent (trĕnt) also **Tren•to** (trĕn′tō). A city of N Italy NW of Venice; site of the Council of Trent (1545–63). Pop. 98,833.
Tren•ti•no-Al•to-A•di•ge (trĕn-tē′nō-äl′tō-ä′dē-jĕ′). A region of NE Italy bordering on Switzerland and Austria.
Tren•ton (trĕn′tən). **1.** A city of SE MI, a suburb of Detroit. Pop. 20,586. **2.** The cap. of NJ, in the W-central part on the Delaware R.; settled c. 1679 by Quakers. Pop. 88,675.
Trent River. A river of central England flowing c. 274 km (170 mi) NE to join the Ouse R. and form the Humber estuary.
tre•pan¹ (trĭ-păn′) *n.* **1.** A rock-boring tool used in mining for sinking shafts. **2.** *Medic.* A trephine. —*tr.v.* **-panned, -pan•ning, -pans. 1.** To bore (a shaft) with a trepan. **2.** *Medic.* To trephine. [ME *trepane*, surgical crown saw < Med.Lat. *trepanum* < Gk. *trupanon*, borer < *trupan*, to pierce < *trupē*, hole. See **terə-¹***.] **—trep′a•na′tion** (trĕp′ə-nā′shən) *n.*
tre•pan² (trĭ-păn′) also **tra•pan** (trə-) *Archaic.* —*tr.v.* **-panned, -pan•ning, -pans.** To trap; ensnare. —*n.* **1.** A trickster. **2.** A trick or snare. [?]
tre•pang (trĭ-păng′) *n.* A sea cucumber of the genus *Holothuria* of the southern Pacific and Indian oceans, used in soup, esp. in China and Indonesia. [Malay *tĕripang.*]
tre•phine (trĭ-fīn′) *Medic.* —*n.* A surgical instrument having circular sawlike edges, used to cut out disks of bone, usu. from the skull. —*tr.v.* **-phined, -phin•ing, -phines.** To operate on with a trephine. [Fr. *tréphine* < obsolete E. *trefine* < Lat. *trēs fīnēs*, three ends : *trēs*, three; see **trei-*** + *fīnēs*, pl.

tree frog
Anderson tree frog
Hyla andersonii

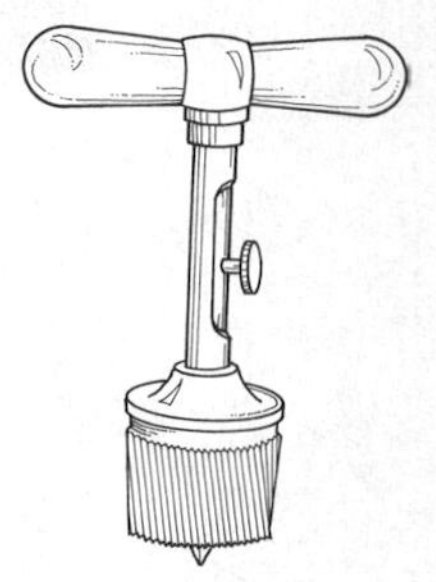

trellis

trephine

ă pat	oi boy
ā pay	ou out
âr care	o͝o took
ä father	o͞o boot
ĕ pet	ŭ cut
ē be	ûr urge
ĭ pit	th thin
ī pie	*th* this
îr pier	hw which
ŏ pot	zh vision
ō toe	ə about, item
ô paw	

Stress marks:
′ (primary);
′ (secondary), as in dictionary (dĭk′shə-nĕr′ē)

of *finis,* end.] —**treph′i•na′tion** (trĕf′ə-nā′shən) *n.*

trep•id (trĕp′ĭd) *adj.* Timid; timorous. [Lat. *trepidus,* anxious.]

trep•i•da•tion (trĕp′ĭ-dā′shən) *n.* **1.** A state of alarm or dread; apprehension. See Syns at **fear. 2.** An involuntary trembling. [Lat. *trepidātiō, trepidātiōn-* < *trepidātus,* p.part. of *trepidāre,* to be in a state of confusion < *trepidus,* anxious.]

trep•o•ne•ma (trĕp′ə-nē′mə) *n., pl.* **-ma•ta** (-mə-tə) or **-mas.** Any of a group of spirochetes of the genus *Treponema,* including those that cause syphilis. [NLat. *Treponema,* genus name : Gk. *trepein,* to turn; see **trep-*** + Gk. *nēma,* thread; see **(s)nē-*.**] —**trep′o•ne′mal, trep′o•nem′a•tous** (-nĕm′ə-təs) *adj.*

trep•o•ne•ma•to•sis (trĕp′ə-nē′mə-tō′sĭs) *n., pl.* **-ses** (-sēz). An infection or a disease caused by a treponema.

trep•o•neme (trĕp′ə-nēm′) *n.* A treponema.

tres•pass (trĕs′pəs, -păs′) *intr.v.* **-passed, -pass•ing, -pass•es. 1.** To commit an offense or a sin; transgress or err. **2.** *Law.* To commit an unlawful injury to the person, property, or rights of another, with actual or implied force or violence, esp. to enter onto another's land wrongfully. **3.** To infringe on the privacy, time, or attention of another. —*n.* (trĕs′păs′, -pəs). **1.** Transgression of a moral or social law, code, or duty. **2.** *Law.* **a.** The act of trespassing. **b.** A suit brought for trespassing. **3.** An intrusion or infringement on another. See Syns at **breach.** [ME *trespassen* < OFr. *trespasser* : *tres-,* over (< Lat. *trāns-*; see TRANS–) + *passer,* to pass; see PASS.] —**tres′pass•er** *n.*

tress (trĕs) *n.* **1.** A long lock or ringlet of hair. **2.** *Archaic.* A plait of hair. [ME *tresse* < OFr., perh. < VLat. **trichia, tricia,* rope, braid < Gk. *trikhia,* rope < *thrix, trikh-,* hair.]

tres•tle (trĕs′əl) *n.* **1.** A horizontal beam or bar held up by two pairs of divergent legs and used as a support. **2.** A framework consisting of vertical slanted supports and horizontal crosspieces supporting a bridge. [ME *trestel* < OFr., alteration of VLat. **trāstellum, trānstellum,* dim. of Lat. *trānstrum,* beam. See TRANSOM.]

tres•tle•tree (trĕs′əl-trē′) *n. Naut.* One of a pair of horizontal beams set into a masthead to support the crosstrees.

tres•tle•work (trĕs′əl-wûrk′) *n.* A trestle or system of trestles, as that supporting a bridge.

tret•i•noin (trĕt′ĭ-noin′) *n.* An isomer of retinoic acid, used in the treatment of acne. [T(RANS–), type of chemical bond + *retinoic acid* (RETINO– + –IC) + –IN.]

tre•val•ly (trə-văl′ē) *n., pl.* **-lies.** An Australian food fish of the genus *Caranx.* [Perh. alteration of CAVALLA.]

Tre•vel•yan (trə-vĕl′yən, -vĭl′-), Sir **George Otto.** 1838–1928. British historian whose works include *The American Revolution* (1899–1907). His son **George Macaulay Trevelyan** (1876–1962) wrote three biographical works (1907–11) about Garibaldi.

Trèves (trĕv). See **Trier.**

Tre•vi•so (trə-vē′zō, trĕ-). A city of NE Italy NNW of Venice; formerly the seat of a Lombard duchy. Pop. 87,089.

trews (tro͞oz) *pl.n.* Close-fitting trousers, usu. of tartan. [Var. of obsolete *trouse.* See TROUSER.]

trey (trā) *n., pl.* **treys.** *Games.* A card, die, or domino with three pips. [ME *treye* < OFr. *treie* < Lat. *tria,* neut. of *trēs,* three. See **trei-*.**]

tri– *pref.* **1.** Three: *trilobate.* **2.a.** Occurring at intervals of three: *trimonthly.* **b.** Occurring three times during: *triweekly.* [ME < Lat. and Gk.; see **trei-*.**]

tri•a•ble (trī′ə-bəl) *adj.* **1.** That can be tried or tested. **2.** *Law.* Subject to judicial examination. —**tri′a•ble•ness** *n.*

tri•ad (trī′ăd′, -əd) *n.* **1.** A group of three. **2.** *Mus.* A chord of three tones, esp. one built on a given root tone plus a major or minor third and a perfect fifth. **3.** A section of a Pindaric ode consisting of the strophe, antistrophe, and epode. [LLat. *trias, triad-* < Gk., three. See **trei-*.**] —**tri•ad′ic** *adj.*

tri•age (trē-äzh′, trē′äzh′) *n.* **1.** A process for sorting injured people into groups based on their need for immediate medical treatment. **2.** A system used to allocate a scarce commodity, such as food, only to those capable of deriving the greatest benefit from it. [Fr. < *trier,* to sort < OFr.]

tri•al (trī′əl, trīl) *n.* **1.** *Law.* Examination of evidence and applicable law by a competent tribunal to determine the issue of specified charges or claims. **2.a.** The act or process of testing, trying, or putting to the proof. **b.** An instance of such testing, esp. as part of a series of tests or experiments. **3.** An effort or attempt. **4.** A state of pain or anguish that tests patience, endurance, or belief. **5.** A trying, troublesome, or annoying person or thing. See Syns at **burden[1]. 6.** A preliminary competition or test to determine qualifications, as in a sport. —*adj.* **1.** Of, relating to, or used in a trial. **2.** Attempted or advanced on a provisional or experimental basis: *a trial separation.* **3.** Made or done in the course of a trial or test. —***idioms.* on trial.** In the process of being tried, as in a court of law. **trial by fire.** A test of one's abilities, esp. the ability to perform well under pressure. [ME *triall,* a testing < AN *trial* < *trier,* to sort, try.]

trial and error *n.* A method of reaching a correct solution or satisfactory result by trying out various means or theories until error is sufficiently reduced or eliminated. —**tri′al-and-er′ror** (trī′əl-ən-ĕr′ər, trīl′-) *adj.*

trial balance *n.* A statement of all the open debit and credit items in a double-entry ledger, made to test their equality.

trial balloon *n.* An idea or a plan advanced tentatively to test reaction. [< testing weather conditions with balloons.]

trial jury *n. Law.* See **petit jury.**

tri•a•logue (trī′ə-lôg′, -lŏg′) *n.* A conversation or discussion involving three people or groups.

trial run *n.* A test, as of performance.

tri•am•cin•o•lone (trī′ăm-sĭn′ə-lōn′) *n.* A synthetic glucocorticoid, $C_{21}H_{27}FO_6$, used in the treatment of allergic and respiratory disorders. [Perh. < TRI– + AM(YL) + *cin(ene),* a turpene + *(prednis)olone,* a corticoid.]

tri•an•gle (trī′ăng′gəl) *n.* **1.a.** The plane figure formed by connecting three points not in a straight line by straight line segments; a three-sided polygon. **b.** Something shaped like such a figure. **2.** Any of various flat three-sided drawing and drafting guides, used esp. to draw straight lines at specific angles. **3.** *Mus.* A percussion instrument consisting of a piece of metal in the shape of a triangle open at one angle. **4.** A relationship involving three people, esp. a ménage à trois. [ME < OFr. < Lat. *triangulum* < neut. of *triangulus,* three-angled : *tri-,* tri- + *angulus,* angle.]

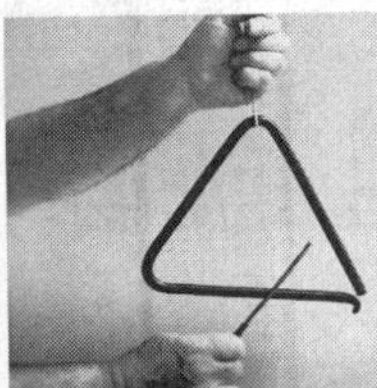

triangle
Top: Right triangle (*left*) and equilateral triangle (*right*)
Bottom: Musical instrument

tri•an•gu•lar (trī-ăng′gyə-lər) *adj.* **1.** Of, relating to, or shaped like a triangle. **2.** Having a triangle for a base: *a triangular pyramid.* **3.** Relating to or involving three entities, such as three people, objects, or ideas. —**tri•an′gu•lar′i•ty** (-lăr′ĭ-tē) *n.* —**tri•an′gu•lar•ly** *adv.*

tri•an•gu•late (trī-ăng′gyə-lāt′) *tr.v.* **-lat•ed, -lat•ing, -lates. 1.** To divide into triangles. **2.** To survey by triangulation. **3.** To make triangular. **4.** To measure by using trigonometry. —*adj.* (trī-ăng′gyə-lĭt). **1.** Of or relating to triangles; triangular. **2.** Made up of or marked with triangles.

tri•an•gu•la•tion (trī-ăng′gyə-lā′shən) *n.* **1.a.** A surveying technique in which a region is divided into triangular elements based on a line of known length so that measurements may be made by the application of trigonometry. **b.** The network of triangles so laid out. **2.** The location of an unknown point by the formation of a triangle with the unknown point and two known points as the vertices.

Tri•an•gu•lum (trī-ăng′gyə-ləm) *n.* A northern constellation near Aries. [Lat. *triangulum,* triangle. See TRIANGLE.]

Triangulum Aus•tra•le (ô-strā′lē) *n.* A southern constellation near Apus. [NLat. : Lat. *triangulum,* triangle + Lat. *austrālis,* southern.]

tri•ar•chy (trī′är′kē) *n., pl.* **-chies. 1.** Government by three people; a triumvirate. **2.** A country governed by three rulers.

Tri•as•sic (trī-ăs′ĭk) *adj.* Of, belonging to, or being the geologic time of the first period of the Mesozoic Era, after the end of the Paleozoic Era and before the Jurassic Period of the Mesozoic Era. See table at **geologic time.** —*n.* The Triassic Period or its deposits. [LLat. *trias,* triad (< the subdivision of this period into three parts); see TRIAD + –IC.]

tri•ath•lete (trī-ăth′lēt) *n. Sports.* One in a triathlon.

tri•ath•lon (trī-ăth′lən, -lŏn′) *n. Sports.* An athletic contest consisting of three successive events, usu. long-distance swimming, bicycling, and running. [TRI– + (DEC)ATHLON.]

tri•a•tom•ic (trī′ə-tŏm′ĭk) *adj.* **1.** Containing three atoms per molecule. **2.** Containing three replaceable atoms or radicals.

tri•ax•i•al (trī-ăk′sē-əl) *adj.* Having three axes. —**tri•ax′i•al′i•ty** (-ăl′ĭ-tē) *n.*

tri•a•zine (trī′ə-zēn′, trī-ăz′ēn′) *n.* A compound having three carbon and three nitrogen atoms in a six-membered ring, esp. any of three isomers of $C_3H_3N_3$.

tri•a•zole (trī′ə-zōl′, trī-ăz′ōl′) *n.* Any of several compounds with composition $C_2H_3N_3$, having a five-membered ring of two carbon atoms and three nitrogen atoms.

trib. *abbr.* Tributary.

trib•ade (trĭb′əd) *n.* A lesbian. [Fr. < Lat. *tribas, tribad-* < Gk. < *tribein,* to rub. See TRIBOLOGY.] —**trib′a•dism** *n.*

trib•al (trī′bəl) *adj.* Of, relating to, or characteristic of a tribe. —**trib′al•ly** *adv.*

trib•al•ism (trī′bə-lĭz′əm) *n.* **1.** The organization, culture, or beliefs of a tribe. **2.** A strong feeling of identity with and loyalty to one's tribe or group. —**trib′al•ist** *n.* —**trib′al•is′tic** *adj.*

tri•ba•sic (trī-bā′sĭk) *adj.* **1.** Containing three replaceable hydrogen atoms. Used of an acid. **2.** Containing three univalent basic atoms or radicals. Used of a base or salt.

tribe (trīb) *n.* **1.** A unit of social organization consisting of a number of groups who share a common ancestry, culture, and leadership. **2.** An ancient political, ethnic, or ancestral division, esp.: **a.** Any of the three divisions of the ancient Romans, namely, the Latin, Sabine, and Etruscan. **b.** Any of the 12 divisions of ancient Israel. **c.** A phyle of ancient Greece. **3.** A group of people sharing an occupation, an interest, or a habit. **4.** *Informal.* A large family. **5.** *Biol.* A taxonomic category placed between a subfamily and a genus or between a suborder and a family. [ME < OFr. *tribu* < Lat. *tribus,* division of the Roman people, perh. of Etruscan orig., or poss. < *tri-,* three; see **trei-*.**]

tribes•man (trībz′mən) *n.* **1.** A man who is a member of one's own tribe. **2.** A member of a tribal aboriginal people.

tribes•peo•ple (trībz′pē′pəl) *pl.n.* **1.** The people of one's own tribe. **2.** An aboriginal people living in tribes.

tribes•wom•an (trībz′wo͝om′ən) *n.* **1.** A woman who is a member of one's own tribe. **2.** A woman who is a member of a tribal aboriginal people.

tri•bo•e•lec•tric•i•ty (trī′bō-ĭ-lĕk-trĭs′ĭ-tē, -ē′lĕk-, trĭb′ō-) *n., pl.* **-ties.** An electrical charge produced by friction between two objects. [Gk. *tribos,* a rubbing < *tribein,* to rub; see **terə-**[1]* + ELECTRICITY.] **—tri′bo•e•lec′tric** *adj.*

tri•bol•o•gy (trī-bŏl′ə-jē, trĭb-) *n.* The science of the mechanisms of friction, lubrication, and wear of interacting surfaces that are in relative motion. [Gk. *tribos,* a rubbing (< Gk. *tribein,* to rub; see **terə-**[1]*) + -LOGY.] **—tri′bo•log′i•cal** (trī′bə-lŏj′ĭ-kəl, trĭb′ə-) *adj.* **—tri•bol′o•gist** *n.*

tri•brach (trī′brăk′) *n.* A metrical foot having three short or unstressed syllables. [Lat. *tribrachys* < Gk. *tribrakhus* : *tri-,* tri- + *brakhus,* short; see **mregh-u-***.]

trib•u•la•tion (trĭb′yə-lā′shən) *n.* **1.** Great affliction, trial, or distress; suffering. **2.** An experience that tests one's endurance, patience, or faith. See Syns at **burden**[1]. [Ult. < Lat. *trībulātiō, trībulātiōn-* < *trībulātus,* p.part. of *trībulāre,* to oppress < Lat. *trībulum,* threshing-sledge. See **terə-**[1]*.]

tri•bu•nal (trī-byo͞o′nəl, trĭ-) *n.* **1.** *Law.* **a.** A seat or court of justice. **b.** The bench on which a judge or other presiding officer sits in court. **2.** A committee or board appointed to adjudicate in a particular matter. **3.** Something that has the power to determine or judge. [ME < OFr. < Lat. *tribūnal,* judge's platform < *tribūnus,* tribune. See TRIBUNE[1].]

trib•u•nate (trĭb′yə-nāt′, trĭ-byo͞o′nĭt) *n.* The rank, office, dignity, or authority of a tribune.

trib•une[1] (trĭb′yo͞on′, trĭ-byo͞on′) *n.* **1.** An officer of ancient Rome elected by the plebeians to protect their rights from arbitrary acts of the patrician magistrates. **2.** A protector or champion of the people. [ME < OFr. *tribun* < Lat. *tribūnus* < *tribus,* tribe. See TRIBE.] **—trib′u•nar′y** (trĭb′yə-nĕr′ē) *adj.*

trib•une[2] (trĭb′yo͞on′, trĭ-byo͞on′) *n.* A raised platform or dais from which a speaker addresses an assembly. [Fr. < OFr., part of a church, speaking platform < OItal. *tribuna* < Med. Lat. *tribūna,* alteration of Lat. *tribūnal.* See TRIBUNAL.]

trib•u•tar•y (trĭb′yə-tĕr′ē) *adj.* **1.** Making additions or yielding supplies; contributory. **2.** Paid in tribute. **3.** Paying tribute: *a tributary colony.* **—***n., pl.* **-ies. 1.** A stream that flows into a larger stream or other body of water. **2.** A ruler or nation that pays tribute. [ME *tributarie,* paying tribute < Lat. *tribūtārius* < *tribūtum,* tribute. See TRIBUTE.]

trib•ute (trĭb′yo͞ot) *n.* **1.** A gift, payment, declaration, or other acknowledgment of gratitude, respect, or admiration. **2.** Evidence attesting to some praiseworthy quality or characteristic. **3.a.** A payment made by one ruler or nation to another in acknowledgment of submission or as the price of security. **b.** A tax imposed for such payment. **4.** Any payment exacted for protection. **5.a.** A payment or tax given by a feudal vassal to an overlord. **b.** The obligation to make such a payment. [ME *tribut* < OFr. < Lat. *tribūtum* < neut. p.part. of *tribuere,* to pay, distribute < *tribus,* tribe. See TRIBE.]

tri•cam•er•al (trī-kăm′ər-əl) *adj.* Of or being a legislature composed of three chambers. [TRI- + Lat. *camera,* chamber; see CAMERA + -AL[1].]

tri•car•box•yl•ic (trī′kär-bŏk-sĭl′ĭk) *adj.* Having three carboxyl groups.

tricarboxylic acid cycle *n.* See **Krebs cycle.**

trice (trīs) *n.* A very short period of time; an instant. **—***tr.v.* **triced, tric•ing, tric•es.** *Naut.* To hoist and secure with a rope: *trice up a sail.* [< ME *(at a) trise,* at one pull < *trisen,* to hoist < MDu. *trīsen* < *trīse,* pulley. V. < ME *trisen.*]

tri•cen•ten•ni•al (trī′sĕn-tĕn′ē-əl) *adj.* Tercentenary. **—***n.* A tercentenary event or celebration.

tri•ceps (trī′sĕps′) *n., pl.* **-ceps•es** (-sĕp′sĭz) also **triceps.** A large three-headed extensor muscle of the upper arm. [< Lat., three-headed : *tri-,* tri- + *caput,* head; see **kaput-***.]

tri•cer•a•tops (trī-sĕr′ə-tŏps′) *n.* A herbivorous Cretaceous dinosaur of the genus *Triceratops,* having a large horn above either eye and a smaller horn on the nose. [NLat. *Triceratops,* genus name : Gk. *tri-,* tri- + Gk. *keras, kerat-,* horn; see **ker-**[1]* + Gk. *ōps,* eye, face; see **ok^{w}-***.]

tri•chi•a•sis (trĭ-kī′ə-sĭs) *n.* A condition of ingrowing hairs about an orifice, esp. ingrowing eyelashes.

tri•chi•na (trĭ-kī′nə) *n., pl.* **-nae** (-nē) or **-nas.** A small slender parasitic nematode worm *(Trichinella spiralis)* that infests the intestines of various mammals and whose larvae become encysted in muscles. [NLat. < Gk. *trikhinē,* fem. of *trikhinos,* hairy < *thrix, trikh-,* hair.]

trich•i•nize (trĭk′ə-nīz′) *tr.v.* **-nized, -niz•ing, -niz•es.** To infect with trichinae. **—trich′i•ni•za′tion** (-nĭ-zā′shən) *n.*

trich•i•no•sis (trĭk′ə-nō′sĭs) *n.* A disease caused by eating undercooked trichinous meat, usu. pork, and characterized by fever, nausea, muscular pain, and edema of the face.

tri•chi•nous (trĭ-kī′nəs, trĭk′ə-nəs) *adj.* **1.** Containing trichinae. **2.** Of or relating to trichinae or trichinosis.

trich•ite (trĭk′īt′) *n.* A small dark needle-shaped crystal.

tri•chlo•ride (trī-klôr′īd′, -klōr′-) also **tri•chlo•rid** (-klôr′-ĭd, -klōr′-) *n.* A compound containing three chlorine atoms per molecule.

tri•chlo•ro•a•ce•tic acid (trī-klôr′ō-ə-sē′tĭk, -klōr′-) *n.* A deliquescent corrosive crystalline compound, CCl_3COOH, used as a herbicide, an astringent, and an antiseptic.

tri•chlo•ro•eth•yl•ene (trī-klôr′ō-ĕth′ə-lēn′, -klōr′-) also **tri•chlor•eth•yl•ene** (trī′klôr-, -klōr-) *n.* A heavy toxic liquid, $CHCl{:}CCl_2$, used as a solvent for oils and waxes.

tricho– or **trich–** *pref.* Hair; thread; filament: *trichocyst.* [Gk. *trikho-* < *thrix, trikh-,* hair.]

trich•o•cyst (trĭk′ə-sĭst′) *n.* A hairlike stinging or grasping organ in the outer cytoplasm of certain protozoans. **—trich′o•cys′tic** *adj.*

trich•o•gyne (trĭk′ə-jīn′, -gīn′) *n.* A hairlike terminal process forming the receptive part of the female reproductive structure in certain fungi or algae.

trich•oid (trĭk′oid′, trī′koid′) *adj.* Resembling hair.

trich•ome (trĭk′ōm′, trī′kōm′) *n.* A hairlike or bristlelike outgrowth, as from the epidermis of a plant. [Gk. *trikhōma,* growth of hair < *trikhoun,* to cover with hair < *thrix, trikh-,* hair.] **—tri•chom′ic** (trĭ-kŏm′ĭk, -kō′mĭk, trī-) *adj.*

trich•o•mo•nad (trĭk′ə-mō′năd′) *n.* Any of various flagellate protozoans of the genus *Trichomonas,* occurring as parasites in the digestive and urogenital tracts of vertebrates. [NLat. *Trichomonas, Trichomonad-,* genus name : TRICHO- + LLat. *monas, monad-,* unit; see MONAD.] **—trich′o•mo•nad′al** (-năd′l), **trich′o•mon′al** (-mō′nəl) *adj.*

trich•o•mo•ni•a•sis (trĭk′ə-mə-nī′ə-sĭs) *n., pl.* **-ses** (-sēz′). **1.** A vaginal inflammation caused by a trichomonad *(Trichomonas vaginalis)* that results in a persistent discharge and itching. **2.** An infection caused by trichomonads, as a disease of cattle that commonly results in infertility or abortion.

tri•chop•ter•an (trĭ-kŏp′tər-ən) *n.* An insect of the order Trichoptera, constituting the caddis flies. [< NLat. *Trichoptera,* order name : Gk. *trikho-,* tricho- + Gk. *-ptera,* pl. of *-pteros,* winged (< *pteron,* wing; see -PTER).]

tri•cho•sis (trĭ-kō′sĭs) *n., pl.* **-ses** (-sēz). Any hair disease.

tri•chot•o•my (trī-kŏt′ə-mē) *n., pl.* **-mies. 1.** Division into three parts or elements. **2.** A system based on three parts or elements. [NLat. *trichotomia* : Gk. *trikha,* in three parts; see **trei-*** + NLat. *-tomia,* -tomy.] **—tri•chot′o•mous** *adj.*

–trichous *suff.* Having a specified kind of hair or hairlike part: *peritrichous.* [< Gk. *-trikhos* < *thrix, trikh-,* hair.]

tri•chro•ism (trī′krō-ĭz′əm) *n.* The property possessed by certain minerals of exhibiting three different colors when viewed from three different directions under white lights. [< Gk. *trikhroos,* three-colored : *tri-,* tri- + *khrōs,* color.] **—tri•chro′ic** *adj.*

tri•chro•mat (trī′krō-măt′) *n.* A trichromatic person.

tri•chro•mat•ic (trī′krō-măt′ĭk) also **tri•chrome** (trī′-krōm′) or **tri•chro•mic** (trī-krō′mĭk) *adj.* **1.** Of, relating to, or having three colors, as in photography. **2.** Having perception of the three primary colors, as in normal vision. **—tri•chro′ma•tism** (trī-krō′mə-tĭz′əm) *n.*

trick (trĭk) *n.* **1.** An act or a procedure intended to achieve an end by deceptive or fraudulent means. **2.** A mischievous action; a prank. **3.** A stupid, disgraceful, or childish act or performance. **4.a.** A peculiar trait or characteristic; a mannerism. **b.** A peculiar event with unexpected, often deceptive results. **c.** A deceptive or illusive appearance; an illusion. **5.a.** A special skill; a knack. **b.** A convention or specialized skill peculiar to a particular field. **6.** A feat of magic or legerdemain. **7.** A difficult, dexterous, or clever act designed to amuse. **8.** *Games.* **a.** All the cards played in a single round, one from each player. **b.** One such round. **9.a.** A period or turn of duty, as at the helm of a ship. **b.** *Slang.* A prison term. **10.** *Slang.* **a.** An act of prostitution. **b.** A prostitute's customer. **11.** *Slang.* A robbery or theft. **—***tr. & intr.v.* **tricked, trick•ing, tricks.** To cheat or deceive or to practice trickery or deception. **—***adj.* **1.** Of, relating to, or involving tricks. **2.** Capable of performing tricks: *a trick dog.* **3.** Designed or made for doing a trick or tricks: *trick dice.* **4.** Weak, defective, or liable to fail: *a trick knee.* **—*phrasal verb.* trick out (**or **up).** *Informal.* To ornament or adorn, often garishly. **—*idioms.* how's tricks.** *Informal.* Used to make a friendly inquiry about a person or that person's affairs. **not miss a trick.** To be extremely alert. [ME *trik* < ONFr. *trique* < *trikier,* to deceive, prob. < VLat. **triccāre* < Lat. *trīcārī,* to play tricks < *trīcae,* tricks.] **—trick′er** *n.*

trick•er•y (trĭk′ə-rē) *n., pl.* **-ies.** The practice or use of tricks; deception by stratagem.

trick•ish (trĭk′ĭsh) *adj.* Characterized by or tending to use tricks or trickery. **—trick′ish•ly** *adv.* **—trick′ish•ness** *n.*

trick•le (trĭk′əl) *v.* **-led, -ling, -les.** **—***intr.* **1.** To flow or fall in drops or in a thin stream. **2.** To move or proceed slowly or bit by bit: *People trickled in.* **—***tr.* To cause to trickle. **—***n.* **1.** The act or condition of trickling. **2.** A slow, small, or irregular quantity that moves, proceeds, or occurs intermittently. [ME *triklen,* perh. var. of *striklen,* freq. of *striken,* to flow. See STRIKE.]

trickle charge *n.* An electric charge supplied to a storage bat-

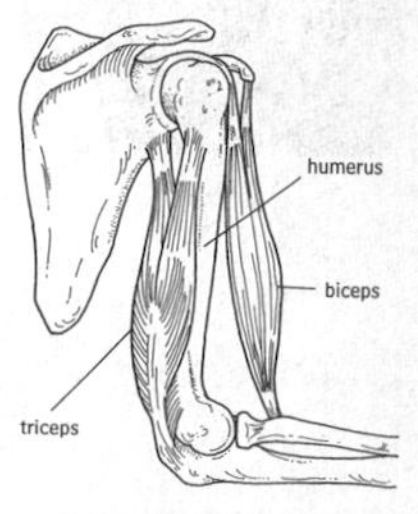

triceps

triceratops

ă pat	oi boy
ā pay	ou out
âr care	o͝o took
ä father	o͞o boot
ĕ pet	ŭ cut
ē be	ûr urge
ĭ pit	th thin
ī pie	*th* this
îr pier	hw which
ŏ pot	zh vision
ō toe	ə about, item
ô paw	

Stress marks:
′ (primary);
′ (secondary), as in
dictionary (dĭk′shə-nĕr′ē)

tricorn

trident
Detail of a bell krater showing Poseidon holding a trident

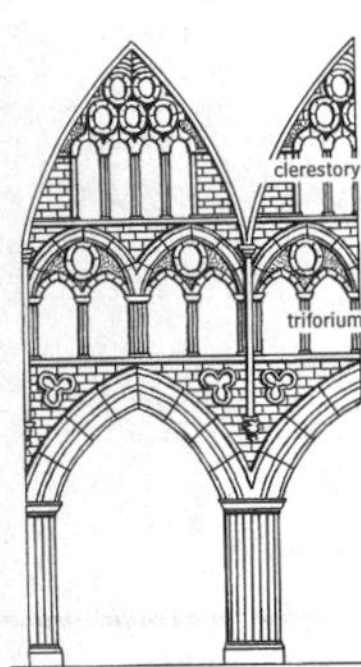

triforium

tery at a continuous low rate to keep it fully charged.

trick•le-down also **trick•le•down** (trĭk′əl-doun′) *adj.* Of or relating to the trickle-down theory: *the trickle-down effect.*

trickle-down theory *n.* An economic theory that financial benefits to big business will in turn pass down to smaller businesses and consumers.

trick or treat *interj.* Used as a greeting by children when trick-or-treating.

trick-or-treat (trĭk′ər-trēt′) *intr.v.* **-treat•ed, -treat•ing, -treats.** To engage in the practice of asking for treats on Halloween and threatening to play tricks on those who refuse.

trick•ster (trĭk′stər) *n.* One that swindles or plays tricks.

trick•sy (trĭk′sē) *adj.* **-si•er, -si•est. 1.** Smartly attired; dapper. **2.** Sportive; mischievous. **3.** Crafty; cunning; devious. **4.** Likely to cause trouble and therefore requiring special care.

trick•y (trĭk′ē) *adj.* **-i•er, -i•est. 1.** Given to or characterized by trickery. **2.** Requiring caution or skill: *a tricky recipe.* —**trick′i•ly** *adv.* —**trick′i•ness** *n.*

tri•clin•ic (trī-klĭn′ĭk) *adj.* Having three unequal axes intersecting at oblique angles. Used of certain crystals.

tri•clin•i•um (trī-klĭn′ē-əm) *n., pl.* **-i•a** (-ē-ə). **1.** A couch facing three sides of a rectangular table, used by the ancient Greeks and Romans for reclining at meals. **2.** A room with such a couch or couches; a dining room. [Lat. *trīclīnium* < Gk. *triklinion*, dim. of *triklinos*, room with three couches : *tri-*, three; see **trei-*** + *klinē*, couch; see **klei-***.]

tri•col•or (trī′kŭl′ər) *n.* **1.** A flag having three colors. **2.** Also **Tricolor.** The French flag. —*adj.* also **tri•col•ored** (-ərd). Having three colors.

tri•corn also **tri•corne** (trī′kôrn′) —*n.* A hat having the brim turned up on three sides. —*adj.* Having three corners, horns, or projections. [Fr. *tricorne* < Lat. *tricornis*, three-horned : *tri-*, tri- + *cornū*, horn; see **ker-¹***.]

tri•cor•nered (trī′kôr′nərd) *adj.* Having three corners.

tri•cos•tate (trī-kŏs′tāt′) *adj.* Having three costae.

tri•cot (trē′kō) *n.* **1.** A plain knitted cloth of any of various yarns. **2.** A soft ribbed cloth of wool or a wool blend, usu. used for dresses. [Fr. < *tricoter*, to knit < OFr., to beat, run < *tricote*, short thick stick, dim. of *estrique, trique*, stick for leveling measures of grain < *estriquier*, to strike off, of Gmc. orig. See **streig-***.]

tric•o•tine (trĭk′ə-tēn′, trē′kə-) *n.* A sturdy worsted fabric with a double twill. [Fr. < *tricot*, tricot. See TRICOT.]

tri•crot•ic (trī-krŏt′ĭk) *adj. Medic.* Having three waves or elevations to one beat of the pulse. [< Gk. *trikrotos*, having a triple beat : *tri-*, three; see **trei-*** + *krotein*, to beat.]

tri•cus•pid (trī-kŭs′pĭd) *n.* An organ or a part, esp. a tooth, having three cusps. —*adj.* also **tri•cus•pi•dal** (-pĭ-dəl) or **tri•cus•pi•date** (-pĭ-dāt′). **1.** Having three cusps. **2.** Of or relating to the tricuspid valve. [< Lat. *tricuspis, tricuspid-*, having three points : *tri-*, tri- + *cuspis*, point.]

tricuspid valve *n.* The three-segmented valve of the heart that keeps blood in the right ventricle from flowing back into the right atrium.

tri•cy•cle (trī′sĭk′əl, -sĭ-kəl) *n.* A three-wheeled vehicle, used esp. by small children and usu. propelled by pedals. [Fr. : *tri-*, three (< Gk. *tri-*; see TRI-) + Gk. *kuklos*, wheel; see CYCLE.]

tri•cy•clic (trī-sī′klĭk, -sĭk′lĭk) *adj. Chem.* Having or being a molecular structure that contains three closed rings: *a tricyclic molecule.* —*n.* A tricyclic antidepressant drug.

tri•dac•tyl (trī-dăk′təl) also **tri•dac•ty•lous** (-tə-ləs) *adj.* Having three digits or claws on each limb. [Gk. *tridaktulos*, three-fingered : *tri-*, tri-; see **trei-*** + *daktulos*, finger.]

tri•dent (trīd′nt) *n.* **1.** A long three-pronged fork or weapon, esp. a three-pronged spear used for fishing. **2.** *Gk. & Rom. Myth.* The three-pronged spear carried by Neptune or Poseidon. —*adj.* also **tri•den•tate** (trī-dĕn′tāt). Having three protrusions, such as teeth or prongs. [ME < OFr. < Lat. *tridēns, trident-* : *tri-*, tri- + *dēns*, tooth; see **dent-***.]

Tri•den•tine (trī-dĕn′tīn′, -tēn′) *adj.* Of or relating to a council held by the Roman Catholic Church in Trent, Italy, from 1545 to 1563 or to the results of that council. —*n.* A Roman Catholic who conforms to the Tridentine Creed. [Med.Lat. *Tridentīnus* < Lat., area around Tridentum, from *Tridentum* (Trent).]

tri•di•men•sion•al (trī′dĭ-mĕn′shə-nəl, -dī-) *adj.* Of, relating to, or having three dimensions.

tried (trīd) *v.* P.t. and p.part. of **try.** —*adj.* **1.** Thoroughly tested and proved to be good or trustworthy. **2.** Made to undergo trials or distress. Often used in combination: *a much-tried teacher.*

tried and true *adj.* Tested and proved to be worthy or good.

tri•en•ni•al (trī-ĕn′ē-əl) *adj.* **1.** Occurring every third year. **2.** Lasting three years. —*n.* **1.** A third anniversary. **2.** An event occurring every three years. [< Lat. *triennis* < *triennium*, triennium. See TRIENNIUM.] —**tri•en′ni•al•ly** *adv.*

tri•en•ni•um (trī-ĕn′ē-əm) *n., pl.* **-en•ni•ums** or **-en•ni•a** (-ĕn′ē-ə). A period of three years. [Lat. : *tri-*, tri- + *annus*, year; see **at-***.]

tri•er (trī′ər) *n.* **1.a.** One that tries; a test or tester. **b.** One who keeps attempting something despite failure. **2.** *Law.* One who examines and settles a case; a judge or juror. **3.a.** An instrument or a device that sifts, filters, or separates grain, for example, from impurities. **b.** An instrument or a device, such as a tube, for taking samples, as of wine.

Trier (trîr) also **Trèves** (trĕv). A city of SW Germany on the Moselle R. near the Luxembourg border; under French control from 1797 until 1815. Pop. 94,190.

tri•er•arch (trī′ə-rärk′) *n.* **1.** The captain of a Greek trireme. **2.** An Athenian who outfitted and maintained a trireme as a part of his civic duties. [Lat. *triērarchus* < Gk. *triērarkhos* : *triērēs*, trireme; see **trei-*** + *arkhos*, ruler; see -ARCH.]

tri•er•ar•chy (trī′ə-rär′kē) *n., pl.* **-chies. 1.** The authority or office of a trierarch. **2.** The system whereby an Athenian furnished and maintained a trireme for the polis.

tries (trīz) *v.* Third pers. sing. pr.t. of **try.** —*n.* Pl. of **try.**

Tri•este (trē-ĕst′, -ĕs′tĕ). A city of extreme NE Italy on the **Gulf of Trieste,** an inlet of the Gulf of Venice at the head of the Adriatic Sea. From 1947 to 1954 it was the center of the **Free Territory of Trieste** administered by the United Nations. Pop. 251,380.

tri•fa•cial (trī-fā′shəl) *adj.* Trigeminal.

tri•fec•ta (trī-fĕk′tə) *n. Sports & Games.* A system of betting in which the bettor must pick the first three winners in the correct sequence. [TRI- + (PER)FECTA.]

tri•fid (trī′fĭd′) *adj.* Divided or cleft into three narrow parts or lobes. [Lat. *trifidus* : *tri-*, tri- + *findere, fid-*, to split.]

tri•fle (trī′fəl) *n.* **1.** Something of little importance or value. **2.** A small amount; a jot. **3.** A dessert typically consisting of plain or sponge cake soaked in sherry, rum, or brandy and topped with jam or jelly, custard, and whipped cream. **4.a.** A moderately hard variety of pewter. **b. trifles.** Utensils made from this variety of pewter. —*v.* **-fled, -fling, -fles.** —*intr.* **1.** To deal with something as if it were of little significance or value. **2.** To act, perform, or speak with little seriousness or purpose; jest. **3.** To play or toy with something. —*tr.* To waste (time, for example). —***idiom.* a trifle.** Very little; somewhat. [ME *trufle, trifle* < OFr. *trufle*, mockery, dim. of *truffe*, deception.] —**tri′fler** (trī′flər) *n.*

tri•fling (trī′flĭng) *adj.* **1.** Of slight worth or importance. **2.** Frivolous or idle. —**tri′fling•ly** *adv.*

tri•fo•cal (trī-fō′kəl, trī′fō′-) *adj.* **1.** Having three focal lengths. **2.** Having one section that corrects for distant vision, a second section that corrects for medium vision, and a third that corrects for near vision, as an eyeglass lens. —*n.* **1.** A trifocal lens. **2. trifocals.** Eyeglasses having trifocal lenses.

tri•fo•li•ate (trī-fō′lē-ĭt) also **tri•fo•li•at•ed** (-ā′tĭd) *adj.* Having three leaves or leaflike parts, as in the trillium.

tri•fo•li•o•late (trī-fō′lē-ə-lāt′) *adj.* Having three leaflets.

tri•fo•ri•um (trī-fôr′ē-əm, -fōr′-) *n., pl.* **-fo•ri•a** (-fôr′ē-ə, -fōr′-). *Archit.* A gallery of arches above the side-aisle vaulting in the nave of a church. [Med.Lat., a gallery in Canterbury Cathedral (later taken to mean "with three openings").]

tri•formed (trī′fôrmd′) also **tri•form** (-fôrm′) *adj.* Having three different forms or parts.

tri•fur•cate (trī-fûr′kĭt, -kāt′, trī′fər-kāt′) also **tri•fur•cat•ed** (trī′fər-kā′tĭd) *adj.* Having three forks or branches: *trifurcate antennae.* —**tri′fur•ca′tion** *n.*

trig¹ (trĭg) *adj.* **1.** Smart and trim, as in looks. **2.** Being in good condition. —*tr.v.* **trigged, trig•ging, trigs.** To make trim or neat, esp. in dress. [ME, true < ON *tryggr*, loyal, true. See **deru-***.] —**trig′ly** *adv.* —**trig′ness** *n.*

trig² (trĭg) *tr.v.* **trigged, trig•ging, trigs. 1.** To stop (a wheel) from rolling, as with a wedge. **2.** To prop up; support. —*n.* A wedge or other braking device. [Perh. of Scand. orig.; akin to ON *tryggr*, firm. See TRIG¹.]

trig. *abbr. Math.* **1.** Trigonometric. **2.** Trigonometry.

tri•gem•i•nal (trī-jĕm′ə-nəl) *adj.* Of or relating to the trigeminal nerves; trifacial.

trigeminal nerve *n.* Either of the fifth pair of cranial nerves, having sensory and motor functions in the face, teeth, mouth, and nasal cavity.

trigeminal neuralgia *n.* Paroxysmal shooting pains of the facial area around one or more branches of the trigeminal nerve, often precipitated by irritation of the affected area.

trig•ger (trĭg′ər) *n.* **1.a.** The lever pressed by the finger to discharge a firearm. **b.** A similar device used to release or activate a mechanism. **2.** An event that precipitates other events. **3.** *Electron.* A pulse or circuit that initiates the action of another component. —*tr.v.* **-gered, -ger•ing, -gers. 1.** To set off; initiate. **2.** To fire or explode (a weapon or an explosive charge). [Du. *trekker* < MDu. *trecker* < *trecken*, to pull.]

trig•ger•fish (trĭg′ər-fĭsh′) *n., pl.* **triggerfish** or **-fish•es.** Any of various brightly colored fishes of the family Balistidae of warm coastal waters, having an erectile spine.

trig•ger-hap•py (trĭg′ər-hăp′ē) *adj. Slang.* **1.** Tending or desiring to shoot a firearm before adequately identifying the target. **2.** Inclined to react violently at slight provocation.

trig•ger•man (trĭg′ər-mən) *n.* **1.** An underworld gunman who in premeditation shoots a victim. **2.** A gunman; a shooter.

tri•glyc•er•ide (trī-glĭs′ə-rīd′) *n.* An ester of three fatty acids and glycerol that is the chief constituent of fats and oils.

tri•glyph (trī′glĭf′) *adj. Archit.* An ornament in a Doric frieze, consisting of a projecting block having on its face two parallel vertical glyphs or grooves and two half grooves or chamfers on either vertical end, that separates the metopes. [Lat. *triglyphus* < Gk. *trigluphos* : *tri-*, three; see **trei-*** + *gluphē*, carving; see GLYPH.] —**tri•glyph′ic** *adj.*

tri•gon (trī′gŏn′) *n.* **1.** *Mus.* A triangular lyre or harp of Roman and Greek antiquity. **2.** See **triplicity** 3. **3.** *Archaic.* A triangle. [Lat. *trigōnum* < Gk. *trigōnon* < neut. of *trigōnos*, triangular : *tri-*, tri- + *gōnia*, angle; see -GON.]

trigonometric function *n. Math.* A function of an angle expressed as the ratio of two of the sides of a right triangle that contains that angle; the sine, cosine, tangent, cotangent, secant, and cosecant.

trig•o•nom•e•try (trĭg′ə-nŏm′ĭ-trē) *n. Math.* The branch of mathematics that deals with the relationships between the sides and the angles of triangles and the calculations based on them, particularly the trigonometric functions. [NLat. *trigōnometria* : Gk. *trigōnon*, triangle; see TRIGON + Gk. *-metria*, -metry.] —**trig′o•no•met′ric** (-nə-mĕt′rĭk), **trig′o•no•met′ri•cal** (-rĭ-kəl) *adj.* —**trig′o•no•met′ri•cal•ly** *adv.*

tri•gram (trī′grăm′) *n.* **1.** A figure composed of three solid or interrupted parallel lines, esp. as used in Chinese philosophy or divination according to the I Ching. **2.** See **trigraph** 3. —**tri′gram•mat′ic** (-grə-măt′ĭk) *adj.*

tri•graph (trī′grăf′) *n.* **1.** Three letters spelling one consonant, vowel, or diphthong, such as *igh* in *high*. **2.** A group of three letters, esp. of frequent occurrence in a given language, as *ing* in English. **3.** Any combination of three letters of an alphabet. —**tri•graph′ic** *adj.* —**tri•graph′i•cal•ly** *adv.*

tri•he•dral (trī-hē′drəl) *adj.* Having or formed by three planes meeting at a point. —*n.* See **trihedron.**

tri•he•dron (trī-hē′drən) *n., pl.* **-drons** or **-dra** (-drə). A figure formed by three planes meeting at a point.

tri•hy•brid (trī-hī′brĭd) *n. Genet.* The hybrid of parents that differ at only three gene loci, for which each parent is homozygous.

tri•i•o•do•thy•ro•nine (trī′ī-ō′dō-thī′rə-nēn′, -ī-ŏd′ō-) *n.* A thyroid hormone, $C_{15}H_{12}I_3NO_4$, similar to thyroxine but more potent, used in the treatment of hypothyroidism. [TRI- + IODO- + *thyronine* (THYR(O)- + -ON(E) + -INE[2]).]

trike (trīk) *n. Informal.* A tricycle.

tri•lat•er•al (trī-lăt′ər-əl) *adj.* Having or involving three sides, countries, or parties. [< Lat. *trilaterus* : *tri-*, tri- + *latus*, *later-*, side.] —**tri•lat′er•al•ly** *adv.*

tril•by (trĭl′bē) *n., pl.* **tril•bies.** A soft felt hat with a deeply creased crown. [After *Trilby* by George du Maurier.]

tri•lin•e•ar (trī-lĭn′ē-ər) *adj.* Relating to, having, or bounded by three lines.

tri•lin•gual (trī-lĭng′gwəl) *adj.* **1.** Using or able to use three languages, esp. with equal fluency. **2.** Of, relating to, or expressed in three languages. —*n.* One who can use three languages, esp. with equal fluency. —**tri•lin′gual•ism** *n.*

tri•lit•er•al (trī-lĭt′ər-əl) *adj.* Consisting of three letters, esp. of three consonants. Used chiefly of roots in Semitic languages. —*n.* **1.** A three-letter word or word element. **2.** A triliteral root or word.

tri•lith•on (trī-lĭth′ŏn, trī′lĭ-thŏn′) also **tri•lith** (trī′lĭth) *n.* A prehistoric structure consisting of two large stones set upright to support a third on their tops. [Gk., neut. of *trilithos*, having three stones : *tri-*, tri- + *lithos*, stone.]

trill (trĭl) *n.* **1.** A fluttering or tremulous sound, as that made by certain birds; a warble. **2.** *Mus.* **a.** The rapid alternation of two tones either a whole or a half tone apart. **b.** A vibrato. **3.** *Ling.* **a.** A rapid vibration of one speech organ against another, as of the tongue against the alveolar ridge in Spanish *rr*. **b.** A speech sound pronounced with such a vibration. —*v.* **trilled, trill•ing, trills.** —*tr.* **1.** To sound, sing, or play with a trill. **2.** To articulate (a sound) with a trill. —*intr.* To produce or give forth a trill. [Ital. *trillo* < *trillare*, to trill, prob. ult. of imit. orig.]

Tril•ling (trĭl′ĭng), **Lionel.** 1905–75. Amer. literary critic whose works include *Beyond Culture* (1965).

tril•lion (trĭl′yən) *n.* **1.** The cardinal number equal to 10^{12}. **2.** *Chiefly British.* The cardinal number equal to 10^{18}. [Fr. : *tri-*, third power (< Lat. *tri-*, tri-) + *(m)illion*, million (< OFr. *milion*; see MILLION).] —**tril′lion** *adj.*

tril•lionth (trĭl′yənth) *n.* **1.** The ordinal number matching the number one trillion in a series. **2.** One of a trillion equal parts. —**tril′lionth** *adv. & adj.*

tril•li•um (trĭl′ē-əm) *n.* Any of various plants of the genus *Trillium*, usu. having a single cluster of three leaves and a three-petaled flower. [NLat. *Trillium*, genus name, prob. < Swed. *trilling*, triplet (< its three leaves) < obsolete Swed. *tri*, three < OSwed. *thrīr*. See **trei-***.]

tri•lo•bate (trī-lō′bāt′) or **tri•lo•bat•ed** (-bā′tĭd) also **tri•lobed** (trī′lōbd′) *adj.* Having three lobes, as certain leaves.

tri•lo•bite (trī′lə-bīt′) *n.* Any of numerous extinct marine arthropods of the class Trilobita of the Paleozoic Era, having a segmented body divided into three vertical lobes. [NLat. *Trilobītēs*, former class name < Gk. *trilobos*, three-lobed : *tri-*, tri- + *lobos*, lobe.] —**tri′lo•bit′ic** (-bĭt′ĭk) *adj.*

tri•loc•u•lar (trī-lŏk′yə-lər) *adj.* Having three chamberlike divisions or cavities, as the capsule of a plant.

tril•o•gy (trĭl′ə-jē) *n., pl.* **-gies.** A group of three dramatic or literary works related in subject or theme. [Gk. *trilogia*, series of three related tragedies : *tri-*, tri- + *-logia*, -logy.]

trim (trĭm) *v.* **trimmed, trim•ming, trims.** —*tr.* **1.** To make neat or tidy by clipping, pruning, or smoothing. **2.a.** To remove (excess) by cutting. **b.** To remove the excess from by or as if by cutting. **3.** To ornament; decorate. **4.** *Informal.* **a.** To thrash; beat. **b.** To defeat soundly. **c.** To cheat. **d.** To rebuke; scold. **5.** *Naut.* **a.** To adjust (the sails and yards) so that they receive the wind properly. **b.** To balance (a ship) by shifting its cargo or ballast. **6.** To balance (an aircraft) in flight by regulating the control surfaces and tabs. **7.** To furnish or equip. —*intr.* **1.** *Naut.* **a.** To be in or retain equilibrium. **b.** To make sails and yards ready for sailing. **2.a.** To affect or maintain cautious neutrality. **b.** To fashion one's views for momentary popularity or advantage. —*n.* **1.a.** State of order, arrangement, or appearance; condition: *in good trim.* **b.** A condition of good health or fitness. **2.a.** Exterior ornamentation on a building or vehicle. **b.** Decoration or ornament, as for clothing. **3.** Material used in commercial window displays. **4.** Dress or equipment. **5.** Excised or rejected material, such as film cut in editing. **6.** Personal quality; character. **7.** A cutting or clipping to make neat. **8.** *Naut.* **a.** The readiness of a vessel for sailing with regard to ballast, sails, and yards. **b.** The balance of a ship. **c.** The difference between the draft at the bow and at the stern. **9.** The position of an aircraft relative to its horizontal axis. —*adj.* **trim•mer, trim•mest. 1.a.** In good or neat order. **b.** In good physical condition; fit; slim. **2.** Having lines, edges, or forms of neat and pleasing simplicity. See Syns at **neat**[1]. —*adv.* In a trim manner. [ME *trimmen*, to make firm < OE *trymman* < *trum*, strong. See **deru-***.] —**trim′ly** *adv.* —**trim′ness** *n.*

tri•ma•ran (trī′mə-răn′) *n. Naut.* A fast sailboat with three parallel hulls. [TRI- + (CATA)MARAN.]

Trim•ble (trĭm′bəl), **Robert.** 1777–1828. Amer. jurist; associate justice of the U.S. Supreme Court (1826–28).

tri•mer (trī′mər) *n.* A molecule formed by combining three identical smaller molecules. [TRI- + (POLY)MER.] —**tri•mer′ic** (-mĕr′ĭk) *adj.*

trim•er•ous (trĭm′ər-əs) *adj.* **1.** Having three similar segments or parts. **2.** *Bot.* Having flower parts, such as petals, sepals, and stamens, in sets of three. —**trim′er•ism** *n.*

tri•mes•ter (trī-mĕs′tər, trī′mĕs′-) *n.* **1.** A period or term of three months. **2.** One of three terms into which an academic year is divided in some universities and colleges. [Fr. *trimestre* < Lat. *trimēstris*, of three months : *tri-*, tri- + *mēnsis*, month; see **mē-**[2]*.] —**tri•mes′tral** (-trəl), **tri•mes′tri•al** *adj.*

trim•e•ter (trĭm′ĭ-tər) *n.* A line of verse consisting of three metrical feet. [LLat. < Lat. *trimetrus* < Gk. *trimetros* : *tri-*, tri- + *metron*, measure; see METER[1].] —**tri•met′ric** (trī-mĕt′rĭk), **tri•met′ri•cal** (-rĭ-kəl) *adj.*

tri•met•ro•gon (trī-mĕt′rə-gŏn′) *n.* A system of aerial photography in which one vertical and two oblique photographs are simultaneously taken for use in topographic mapping. [TRI- + *Metrogon*, a kind of camera lens.]

trim•mer (trĭm′ər) *n.* **1.** One that trims: *a hedge trimmer.* **2.** One who changes one's opinions, esp. political opinions, to suit the needs of the moment. **3.** *Electron.* A variable component used to make fine adjustments to capacitance or resistance. **4.** *Archit.* A beam across an opening, such as a hearth, into which the ends of joists can be fitted.

trim•ming (trĭm′ĭng) *n.* **1.** The act of one that trims. **2.** Something added as ornament, esp. a band of lace or embroidery on clothing. **3. trimmings.** Accessories; extras. **4. trimmings.** Scraps or material removed when something is trimmed. **5.** *Informal.* A sound defeat, beating, or punishment.

tri•month•ly (trī-mŭnth′lē) *adj.* Done, occurring, or appearing every three months. —**tri•month′ly** *adv.*

tri•morph (trī′môrf′) *n.* **1.** A substance that occurs in three distinct crystalline forms. **2.** One of the crystalline forms in which a trimorphic substance occurs.

tri•mor•phic (trī-môr′fĭk) also **tri•mor•phous** (-fəs) *adj.* **1.** *Biol.* Having or occurring in three differing forms. **2.** *Chem.* Crystallizing in three distinct forms. —**tri•mor′phi•cal•ly** *adv.* —**tri•mor′phism** *n.*

Tri•mur•ti (trĭ-mo͝or′tē) *n. Hinduism.* The triad of Brahma the creator, Vishnu the preserver, and Shiva the destroyer. [Skt. *trimūrtiḥ* : *tri-*, three; see **trei-*** + *mūrtiḥ*, form.]

tri•nal (trī′nəl) *adj.* Having three parts; threefold.

tri•na•ry (trī′nə-rē) *adj.* Consisting of three parts or proceeding by threes; ternary.

trine (trīn) *adj.* **1.** Threefold; triple. **2.a.** Of or relating to an astrologically favorable positioning of two celestial bodies 120° apart. **b.** In astrology, situated 120° apart. —*n.* **1.** A group of three. **2.** In astrology, the aspect of two planets when 120° apart. **3. Trine.** *Theol.* See **Trinity** 2. [ME < OFr. < Lat. *trīnus*, sing. of *trīnī*, three each. See **trei-***.]

Trin•i•dad (trĭn′ĭ-dăd′). An island of Trinidad and Tobago in the Atlantic off NE Venezuela; ceded to Great Britain in 1802 and joined with Tobago in 1888 to form the colony of Trinidad and Tobago (1898). —**Trin′i•dad′i•an** *adj. & n.*

Trinidad and To•ba•go (tə-bā′gō). An island country of the

trilithon
Stonehenge, Salisbury Plain, England

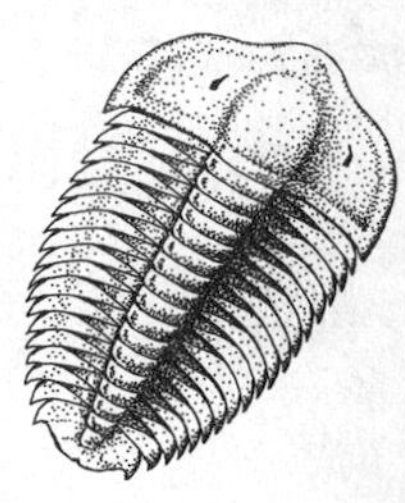

trilobite

Trinidad and Tobago

ă pat	oi boy
ā pay	ou out
âr care	o͝o took
ä father	o͞o boot
ĕ pet	ŭ cut
ē be	ûr urge
ĭ pit	th thin
ī pie	*th* this
îr pier	hw which
ŏ pot	zh vision
ō toe	ə about, item
ô paw	

Stress marks:
′ (primary);
′ (secondary), as in **dictionary** (dĭk′shə-nĕr′ē)

Trinity
Detail from *The Book of Hours of Catherine of Cleves*

triplane
Fokker Dr-I
World War I fighter

tripod
12th- to 11th-century B.C.
Chinese bronze wine vessel

SE West Indies off NE Venezuela; gained independence from Great Britain in 1962. Cap. Port of Spain. Pop. 1,059,825.

Trin•i•tar•i•an (trĭn′ĭ-târ′ē-ən) *adj.* **1.** Of, relating to, or believing in the Christian Trinity or the doctrine of the Trinity. **2. trinitarian.** Having three members, parts, or facets. —*n.* One who believes in the Christian doctrine of the Trinity. —**Trin′i•tar′i•an•ism** *n.*

tri•ni•tro•ben•zene (trī-nī′trō-bĕn′zēn′, -bĕn-zēn′) *n.* A crystalline compound, $C_6H_3(NO_2)_3$, derived from trinitrotoluene and used as an explosive.

tri•ni•tro•phe•nol (trī-nī′trō-fē′nōl′, -nôl′, -nŏl′) *n.* Picric acid.

tri•ni•tro•tol•u•ene (trī-nī′trō-tŏl′yo͞o-ēn′) also **tri•ni•tro•tol•u•ol** (-ôl′, -ōl′, -ŏl′) *n.* TNT.

trin•i•ty (trĭn′ĭ-tē) *n., pl.* **-ties. 1.** A group consisting of three closely related members. **2. Trinity.** *Theol.* The union of three divine persons, the Father, Son, and Holy Spirit, in one God. **3. Trinity.** Trinity Sunday. [ME *trinite* < OFr. < Lat. *trīnitās* < *trīnus*, trine. See TRINE.]

Trinity River. A river, c. 821 km (510 mi), of E TX formed near Dallas and flowing to **Trinity Bay**, an arm of Galveston Bay.

Trinity Sunday *n.* The first Sunday after Pentecost, celebrated by a feast in honor of the Trinity.

trin•ket (trĭng′kĭt) *n.* **1.** A small ornament, such as a piece of jewelry. **2.** A trivial thing; a trifle. [?]

tri•no•mi•al (trī-nō′mē-əl) *adj.* Consisting of three names or terms, as a taxonomic designation. —*n.* **1.** A three-part taxonomic designation indicating genus, species, and subspecies or variety, such as *Brassica oleracea botrytis*, the cauliflower. **2.** *Math.* A polynomial with three terms. [TRI– + (BI)NOMIAL.] —**tri•no′mi•al•ism** *n.*

tri•nu•cle•o•tide (trī-no͞o′klē-ə-tīd′, -nyo͞o′-) *n.* A triplet of nucleotides; a codon.

tri•o (trē′ō) *n., pl.* **-os. 1.** A group of three people or things joined or associated. **2.** *Mus.* **a.** A composition for three performers. **b.** The group performing such a composition. **c.** The middle section of a minuet or scherzo, a march, or of various dance forms. [Fr., composition for three voices < Ital. : *tri-*, three (< Lat.; see **trei-***) + *(du)o*, duet; see DUO.]

tri•ode (trī′ōd′) *n.* A highly evacuated electron tube containing an anode, a cathode, and a control grid.

tri•ol (trī′ôl′, -ōl′, -ŏl′) *n.* A chemical compound containing three hydroxyl groups.

tri•o•let (trē′ə-lĭt, trī′-, trē′ə-lā′) *n.* A poem or stanza of eight lines with a rhyme scheme *abaaabab*, in which the fourth and seventh lines duplicate the first and the eighth line the second. [Fr., dim. of *trio*, trio. See TRIO.]

tri•ose (trī′ōs′) *n.* One of a group of monosaccharides that contain three carbon atoms.

tri•ox•ide (trī-ŏk′sīd′) also **tri•ox•id** (-ŏk′sĭd) *n.* An oxide containing three oxygen atoms per molecule.

trip (trĭp) *n.* **1.** A going from one place to another; a journey. **2.** A stumble or fall. **3.** A maneuver causing someone to stumble or fall. **4.** A mistake. **5.** *Slang.* **a.** A hallucinatory experience induced by a psychedelic drug. **b.** An intense, stimulating, or exciting experience: *a power trip.* **6.** *Slang.* **a.** A usu. temporary but absorbing interest. **b.** A certain way of life or situation. **7.** A light or nimble tread. **8.a.** A device, such as a pawl, for triggering a mechanism. **b.** The action of such a device. —*v.* **tripped, trip•ping, trips.** —*intr.* **1.** To stumble. **2.** To make a mistake: *I tripped up on the question.* **3.** To move nimbly with light rapid steps; skip. **4.** To be released, as a tooth on an escapement wheel in a watch. **5.** To make a trip. **6.** *Slang.* To have a drug-induced hallucination. —*tr.* **1.** To cause to stumble or fall. **2.** To trap or catch in an error or inconsistency. **3.** To release (a catch, trigger, or switch), thereby setting something in operation. **4.** *Naut.* **a.** To raise (an anchor) from the bottom. **b.** To tip or turn (a yardarm) into a position for lowering. **c.** To lift (an upper mast) in order to remove the fid before lowering. —*idiom.* **trip the light fantastic.** To dance. [ME, act of tripping < *trippen*, to trip < OFr. *tripper*, to stamp the foot, of Gmc. orig.]

tri•pal•mi•tin (trī-păl′mĭ-tĭn) *n.* See **palmitin.**

tri•par•tite (trī-pär′tīt) *adj.* **1.** Composed of or divided into three parts. **2.** Relating to or executed by three parties.

tri•par•ti•tion (trī′pär-tĭsh′ən) *n.* Division into three parts or among three parties.

tripe (trīp) *n.* **1.** The light-colored rubbery lining of the stomach of cattle or other ruminants, used as food. **2.** *Informal.* Something of no value. [ME < OFr. *tripes*, intestines, tripe.]

tri•ped•al (trī-pĕd′l) *adj.* Having three feet or legs; tripodal.

tri•pet•al•ous (trī-pĕt′l-əs) *adj. Bot.* Having three petals.

trip ham•mer also **trip•ham•mer** or **trip-ham•mer** (trĭp′-hăm′ər) *n.* A heavy power-operated hammer that is lifted by a cam or lever and then dropped.

tri•phen•yl•meth•ane (trī-fĕn′əl-mĕth′ān′, -fē′nəl-) *n.* A colorless crystalline hydrocarbon, $(C_6H_5)_3CH$, from which a large number of synthetic dyes are derived by substitution.

tri•phib•i•an (trī-fĭb′ē-ən) *adj.* Operating on land, on water, or in air. —*n.* A triphibian aircraft. [TRI– + (AM)PHIBIAN.]

tri•phos•phate (trī-fŏs′fāt′) *n.* A salt or an ester containing three phosphate groups.

tri•phos•pho•py•ri•dine nucleotide (trī-fŏs′fō-pĭr′ĭ-dēn′) *n.* NADP.

triph•thong (trĭf′thông′, -thŏng′, trĭp′-) *n. Ling.* A compound vowel sound resulting from the succession of three simple ones and functioning as a unit. [TRI– + (DI)PHTHONG.] —**triph•thon′gal** (-thông′əl, -thŏng′əl) *adj.*

tri•pin•nate (trī-pĭn′āt′) *adj. Bot.* Divided into pinnae that are subdivided into smaller, further subdivided leaflets or lobes, as in many ferns. —**tri•pin′nate′ly** *adv.*

tripl. *abbr.* Triplicate.

tri•plane (trī′plān′) *n.* An airplane with wings placed above each other in three levels.

tri•ple (trĭp′əl) *adj.* **1.** Consisting of three parts. **2.** Three times as many or as much. **3.** Repeated three times. **4.** *Mus.* Marked by three beats in a measure. —*n.* **1.** A number or quantity three times as great as another. **2.** A group of three. **3.** *Baseball.* See **three-base hit. 4.** *Sports & Games.* See **trifecta.** —*v.* **-pled, -pling, -ples.** —*tr.* To make three times as great in number or amount. —*intr.* **1.** To be or become tripled. **2.** *Baseball.* To make a three-base hit. [ME < OFr. < Lat. *triplus* (on the model of Gk. *triploos*) : Lat. *tri-*, three; see **trei-*** + *-plus*, -fold; see **pel-**[2]*.]

triple bond *n.* A covalent bond in which three electron pairs are shared between two atoms.

Tri•ple Crown (trĭp′əl) *n.* **1.** *Sports & Games.* An unofficial championship title attained by a horse that wins the three traditional races for a specified category. **2.** *Baseball.* An unofficial championship title achieved by a player who leads the league in batting average, home runs, and runs batted in.

tri•ple-deck•er (trĭp′əl-dĕk′ər) *n. Informal.* Something, such as a structure, that has three decks, floors, or layers.

tri•ple-head•er also **tri•ple•head•er** (trĭp′əl-hĕd′ər) *n. Sports.* A contest consisting of three games or events in a row.

triple measure *n. Mus.* See **triple time.**

triple play *n. Baseball.* A defensive play that suddenly ends the inning by executing three consecutive putouts.

triple point *n.* The temperature and pressure at which the gaseous, liquid, and solid phases of a substance coexist in equilibrium.

trip•let (trĭp′lĭt) *n.* **1.** A group or set of three of one kind. **2.** One of three children born at one birth. **3.** A group of three lines of verse. **4.** *Mus.* A group of three notes having the time value of two notes of the same kind. **5.** *Phys.* A multiplet with three components. **6.** *Genet.* A unit of three successive nucleotides in a molecule of DNA or RNA that codes for a specific amino acid; a codon or anticodon. [TRIPL(E) + (DOUBL)ET.]

tri•ple•tail (trĭp′əl-tāl′) *n.* Any of several chiefly marine percoid fishes of the family Lobotidae of warm waters, having dorsal and anal fins that resemble extra tails.

triple time *n. Mus.* A time or rhythm having three beats to the measure, with the accent on the first beat. —**tri′ple-time′** (trĭp′əl-tīm′) *adj.*

tri•plex (trĭp′lĕks′, trī′plĕks′) *adj.* **1.** Composed of three parts; threefold; triple. **2.** Having three apartments, divisions, or floors. —*n.* Something that is triplex. [Lat. See **trei-*.**]

trip•li•cate (trĭp′lĭ-kĭt) *n.* One of three identical objects or copies. —*tr.v.* (-kāt′) **-cat•ed, -cat•ing, -cates. 1.** To triple. **2.** To make three identical copies of. [< ME, triple < Lat. *triplicātus*, p.part. of *triplicāre*, to triple < *triplex, triplic-*, threefold. See TRIPLEX.] —**trip′li•ca′tion** *n.*

tri•plic•i•ty (trĭ-plĭs′ĭ-tē, trī-) *n., pl.* **-ties. 1.** The quality or condition of being triple. **2.** A group of three. **3.** In astrology, one of four zodiac groups consisting of three signs separated from each other by 120°. [ME, three signs < LLat. *triplicitās*, triplicity < Lat. *triplex, triplic-*, triplex. See TRIPLEX.]

trip•lo•blas•tic (trĭp′lō-blăs′tĭk) *adj.* Having three germ layers. Used of the vertebrate embryo. [Gk. *triploos*, triple; see **pel-**[2]* + –BLASTIC.]

trip•loid (trĭp′loid′) *Genet.* —*adj.* Having three times the haploid number of chromosomes in the cell nucleus. —*n.* A triploid organism or cell. —**trip′loi•dy** *n.*

trip•ly (trĭp′lē) *adv.* **1.** In three ways. **2.** To a triple degree. **3.** Three times.

tri•pod (trī′pŏd′) *n.* **1.** A three-legged object, such as a stool. **2.** An adjustable three-legged stand, as for a camera. [Lat. *tripūs, tripod-* < Gk. *tripous*, three-footed : *tri-*, tri- + *pous*, foot; see –POD.] —**trip′o•dal** (trĭp′ə-dl, trī′pŏd′l) *adj.*

trip•o•li (trĭp′ə-lē) *n., pl.* **-lis.** A porous lightweight siliceous sedimentary rock composed of the shells of diatoms or radiolarians or of finely weathered chert, used as an abrasive and a polish. [Fr., prob. after TRIPOLI, Lebanon.]

Trip•o•li (trĭp′ə-lē). **1.** A historical region of N Africa roughly coextensive with Tripolitania; became part of the Barbary States in the 16th cent. **2.** A city of NW Lebanon on the Mediterranean NNE of Beirut; probably founded after the 7th cent. B.C. Pop. 198,000. **3.** The cap. of Libya, in the NW part on the Mediterranean; settled by Phoenicians from Tyre. Pop. 858,500. —**Tri•pol′i•tan** (trĭ-pŏl′ĭ-tn) *adj. & n.*

Tri•pol•i•ta•ni•a (trĭ-pŏl′ĭ-tā′nē-ə, -tān′yə, trĭp′ə-lĭ-). A historical region of N Africa bordering on the Mediterranean Sea; orig. a Phoenician colony and later held by Carthage and Rome (after 46 B.C.). —**Tri•pol′i•ta′ni•an** *adj. & n.*

tri·pos (trīʹpŏsʹ) *n., pl.* **-pos·es.** Any of the examinations for the B.A. degree with honors at Cambridge University in England. [Alteration of Lat. *tripūs*, *tripod-*, tripod (< the stool upon which a degree holder was appointed to sit and dispute humorously with candidates for that degree). See TRIPOD.]

trip·per (trĭpʹər) *n.* **1.** *Slang.* One who is hallucinating from a psychedelic drug. **2.** A tripping or triggering device on a mechanism. **3.** *Chiefly British.* One on a short pleasure trip.

trip·pet (trĭpʹĭt) *n.* A cam or projection in a mechanism designed to strike another part at regular intervals. [ME *tripet*, piece of wood used in a game < *trippen*, to trip. See TRIP.]

trip·ping·ly (trĭpʹĭng-lē) *adv.* Lightly and easily; fluently.

trip·tane (trĭpʹtānʹ) *n.* A colorless liquid antiknock additive, C_7H_{16}, used in aviation fuels. [Shortening and alteration of *trimethylbutane* : TRI- + METHYL + BUTANE.]

trip·tych (trĭpʹtĭk) *n.* **1.** A hinged writing tablet consisting of three leaves, used in ancient Rome. **2.** A work consisting of three painted or carved panels that are hinged together. [< Gk. *triptukhos*, threefold : *tri-*, tri- + *ptux*, *ptukh-*, fold.]

trip·wire (trĭpʹwīrʹ) *n.* **1.** A wire set near ground level to trip or trap an enemy. **2.** A wire or line that activates a trap, for example, when pulled. **3.** A small frontline military force whose involvement in hostilities will engage a larger force.

tri·que·trous (trī-kwēʹtrəs, -kwĕtʹrəs) *adj.* Three-edged; having three salient angles. [< Lat. *triquetrus*, three-cornered : *tri-*, tri- + *-quetrus*, -cornered.]

tri·reme (trīʹrēmʹ) *n. Naut.* An ancient Greek or Roman galley or warship, having three tiers of oars on each side. [Lat. *trirēmis* : *tri-*, tri- + *rēmus*, oar; see **erə-***.]

tri·sac·cha·ride (trī-săkʹə-rīdʹ, -rĭd) *n.* A carbohydrate that yields three monosaccharides upon hydrolysis.

tri·sect (trīʹsĕktʹ, trī-sĕktʹ) *tr.v.* **-sect·ed, -sect·ing, -sects.** To divide into three equal parts. —**triʹsecʹtion** (trīʹsĕkʹshən, trī-sĕkʹ-) *n.* —**triʹsecʹtor** (trīʹsĕkʹtər, trī-sĕkʹ-) *n.*

tri·sep·al·ous (trī-sĕpʹə-ləs) *adj. Bot.* Having three sepals. Used of the calyx of a flower.

tris·kai·dek·a·pho·bi·a (trĭsʹkī-dĕkʹə-fōʹbē-ə, trĭsʹkĭ-) *n.* An abnormal fear of the number 13. [Gk. *triskaideka*, thirteen (*treis*, *tris*, three; see **trei-*** + *kai*, and + *deka*, ten; see DECA-) + PHOBIA.]

tri·skel·i·on (trī-skĕlʹē-ən, trĭ-) also **tri·skele** (trīʹskēlʹ, trĭsʹkēlʹ) *n., pl.* **-skel·i·a** (-skĕlʹē-ə) also **-skeles.** A figure consisting of three curved lines or branches or three stylized human arms or legs radiating from a common center. [NLat. < Gk. *triskelēs*, three-legged : *tri-*, tri- + *skelos*, leg.]

tris·mus (trĭzʹməs) *n.* See **lockjaw** 2. [NLat. < Gk. *trismos*, a grinding.] —**trisʹmic** (-mĭk) *adj.*

tris·oc·ta·he·dron (trĭs-ŏkʹtə-hēʹdrən) *n., pl.* **-drons** or **-dra** (-drə). *Math.* A solid figure having 24 equal faces, every three of which correspond to one face of an octahedron. [Gk. *tris*, thrice; see **trei-*** + OCTAHEDRON.] —**tris·ocʹta·heʹdral** *adj.*

tri·so·di·um (trī-sōʹdē-əm) *adj.* Having three sodium atoms.

tri·so·my (trī-sōʹmē, trīʹsōʹ-) *n., pl.* **-mies.** The condition of having three copies of a given chromosome in each somatic cell rather than the normal number of two. [TRI- + -SOM(E)[3] + -Y[2].] —**triʹsomeʹ** *n.* —**tri·soʹmic** *adj.*

trisomy 21 *n.* See **Down syndrome.**

Tris·tan (trĭsʹtən, -tänʹ, -tănʹ) or **Tris·tram** (-trəm) *n.* In Arthurian legend, a knight who loved the Irish princess Iseult, the betrothed of his uncle King Mark of Cornwall.

Tris·tan da Cun·ha (trĭsʹtən də ko͞oʹnə). An island and volcanic island group of the S Atlantic between S Africa and S South America; administered as a dependency of St. Helena.

triste (trēst) *adj.* Sad; wistful. [ME < OFr. < Lat. *tristis*.]

trist·ful (trĭstʹfəl) *adj.* Sorrowful; gloomy. [ME : *triste*, sad; see TRISTE + *-ful*, -ful.] —**tristʹful·ness** *n.*

tris·tich (trĭsʹtĭk) *n.* A strophe, stanza, or poem consisting of three lines. [TRI- + (DI)STICH.]

tri·sul·fide (trī-sŭlʹfīdʹ) *n.* A sulfide containing three sulfur atoms per molecule.

tri·syl·la·ble (trīʹsĭlʹə-bəl) *n. Ling.* A three-syllable word. —**triʹsyl·labʹic** (-sĭ-lăbʹĭk), **triʹsyl·labʹi·cal** (-ĭ-kəl) *adj.*

trite (trīt) *adj.* **trit·er, trit·est. 1.** Lacking power to evoke interest from overuse or repetition; hackneyed. **2.** *Archaic.* Frayed or worn out by use. [Lat. *trītus* < p.part. of *terere*, to wear out. See **terə-**[1]*.] —**triteʹly** *adv.* —**triteʹness** *n.*

tri·the·ism (trīʹthē-ĭzʹəm) *n. Theol.* The belief that God the Father, God the Son, and God the Holy Spirit are three gods. —**triʹthe·ist** *n.* —**triʹthe·isʹtic, triʹthe·isʹti·cal** *adj.*

trit·i·ca·le (trĭtʹĭ-kāʹlē) *n.* **1.** A hardy hybrid of wheat and rye having a high yield. **2.** The grain of this hybrid. [Lat. *trīticum*, wheat (< *trītus*, p.part. of *terere*, to rub, thresh; see TRITE) + *sēcale*, rye.]

trit·i·um (trĭtʹē-əm, trĭshʹē-) *n.* A rare radioactive hydrogen isotope with atomic mass 3 and half-life 12.5 years, prepared artificially for use as a tracer and a constituent of hydrogen bombs. [< Gk. *tritos*, third. See **trei-***.]

tri·ton[1] (trītʹn) *n.* Any of various chiefly tropical marine gastropod mollusks of the family Cymatiidae, having a pointed spiral shell. [Lat. *Trītōn*, Triton. See TRITON.]

tri·ton[2] (trīʹtŏnʹ) *n.* The nucleus of tritium, consisting of two neutrons and one proton. [TRIT(IUM) + -ON[1].]

Tri·ton (trītʹn) *n.* **1.** *Gk. Myth.* A god of the sea, son of Poseidon and Amphitrite, portrayed as having the head and trunk of a man and the tail of a fish. **2.** *Astron.* A satellite of Neptune. [Lat. *Trītōn* < Gk.]

tri·tone (trīʹtōnʹ) *n. Mus.* An interval composed of three whole tones. [Med.Lat. *tritonus* < Gk. *tritonos*, having three tones : *tri-*, three; see **trei-*** + *tonos*, tone; see TONE.]

trit·u·rate (trĭchʹə-rātʹ) *tr.v.* **-rat·ed, -rat·ing, -rates.** To pulverize. —*n.* (-ər-ĭt). A triturated substance, esp. a powdered drug. [LLat. *trītūrāre*, *trītūrāt-*, to thresh < Lat. *trītūra*, a threshing < *trītus*, p.part. of *terere*, to thresh. See **terə-**[1]*.] —**tritʹu·ra·ble** *adj.* —**tritʹu·raʹtor** *n.*

trit·u·ra·tion (trĭchʹə-rāʹshən) *n.* **1.** The act or process of triturating. **2.** The composing of a dental amalgam by mortar and pestle.

tri·umph (trīʹəmf) *intr.v.* **-umphed, -umph·ing, -umphs. 1.** To be victorious or successful; win. **2.** To rejoice over a success or victory; exult. **3.** To receive honors upon return from a victory in ancient Rome. Used of a general. —*n.* **1.** The fact of being victorious; victory or conquest. **2.** A noteworthy or spectacular success. **3.** Exultation or rejoicing over victory or success. **4.** A public celebration in ancient Rome for a victorious commander and his army. **5.** *Obsolete.* A public celebration or spectacular pageant. [Ult. < Lat. *triumphāre* < *triumphus*, triumph (prob. via Etruscan) < Gk. *thriambos*, hymn to Dionysus.]

tri·um·phal (trī-ŭmʹfəl) *adj.* **1.** Relating or similar to a triumph. **2.** Celebrating a triumph: *a triumphal ode.*

tri·umph·al·ism (trī-ŭmʹfə-lĭzʹəm) *n.* The attitude or belief that a particular doctrine, esp. a religion or political theory, is superior to all others. —**tri·umphʹal·ist** *n.*

tri·um·phant (trī-ŭmʹfənt) *adj.* **1.** Exulting in success or victory. **2.** Victorious; conquering. **3.** *Archaic.* Triumphal. **4.** *Obsolete.* Magnificent; splendid. —**tri·umʹphant·ly** *adv.*

tri·um·vir (trī-ŭmʹvər) *n., pl.* **-virs** or **-vi·ri** (-və-rīʹ). **1.** One of three men sharing public administration or civil authority in ancient Rome. **2.** One of three people sharing public administration or civil authority. [ME < Lat., back-formation < *triumvirī*, board of three < *trium virum*, of three men : *trium*, genitive pl. of *trēs*, three; see **trei-*** + *virum*, var. of *virōrum*, genitive pl. of *vir*, man. See **wī-ro-***.] —**tri·umʹvi·ral** *adj.*

tri·um·vi·rate (trī-ŭmʹvər-ĭt) *n.* **1.** Government by triumvirs. **2.** The office or term of a triumvir. **3.** A body or group of triumvirs. **4.** An association or a group of three. [Lat. *triumvirātus* < *triumvirī*, board of three. See TRIUMVIR.]

tri·une (trīʹyo͞onʹ) *adj.* Being three in one. Used esp. of the Christian Trinity. —*n.* A trinity. [TRI- + Lat. *ūnus*, one; see **oi-no-***.] —**tri·uʹni·ty** (trī-yo͞oʹnĭ-tē) *n.*

tri·va·lent (trī-vāʹlənt) *adj.* Having valence 3. —**tri·vaʹlence, tri·vaʹlen·cy** *n.*

tri·valve (trīʹvălvʹ) *adj.* Having three valves.

Tri·van·drum (trə-vănʹdrəm). A city of SW India on the Arabian Sea SSW of Bangalore. Pop. 483,086.

triv·et (trĭvʹĭt) *n.* **1.** A metal stand with short feet, used under a hot dish on a table. **2.** A three-legged metal stand for cooking vessels in a hearth. [ME *trevet*, stand for cooking vessels < OE *trefet*, prob. alteration of Lat. *tripēs*, *triped-* : *tri-*, tri- + *pēs*, foot; see **ped-***.]

triv·i·a[1] (trĭvʹē-ə) *pl.n. (used with a sing. or pl. v.)* Insignificant or inessential matters; trifles. [Lat. *trivia*, neut. pl. of *trivium*, crossroads, gutter (influenced by TRIVIAL). See TRIVIUM.]

triv·i·a[2] (trĭvʹē-ə) *n.* Pl. of **trivium.**

triv·i·al (trĭvʹē-əl) *adj.* **1.** Of little significance or value. **2.** Ordinary; commonplace. **3.** Concerned with or involving trivia. **4.** *Biol.* Relating to or designating a species; specific. **5.** *Math.* **a.** Of, relating to, or being the solution of an equation in which every variable is equal to zero. **b.** Of, relating to, or being the simplest possible case; self-evident. [ME *trivialle*, of the trivium (< Med.Lat. *triviālis* < *trivium*, trivium; see TRIVIUM) and Lat. *triviālis*, ordinary (< *trivium*, crossroads).] —**trivʹi·al·ly** *adv.*

triv·i·al·i·ty (trĭvʹē-ălʹĭ-tē) *n., pl.* **-ties. 1.** The quality or condition of being trivial. **2.** Something trivial.

triv·i·al·ize (trĭvʹē-ə-līzʹ) *tr.v.* **-ized, -iz·ing, -iz·es.** To reduce to triviality. —**trivʹi·al·i·za·ʹtion** (-ə-lĭ-zāʹshən) *n.*

trivial name *n.* **1.** A common or vernacular name as distinguished from a specific name, as *chimpanzee* for *Pan troglodytes.* **2.** See **specific epithet. 3.** *Chem.* A common or historic name for a substance, not used in official nomenclature, as *sucrose* for *α-D-Glucopyranosyl β-D-fructo-furanoside.*

triv·i·um (trĭvʹē-əm) *n., pl.* **-i·a** (-ē-ə). The lower division of the seven liberal arts in medieval schools, consisting of grammar, logic, and rhetoric. [Med.Lat. < Lat., crossroads : *tri-*, tri- + *via*, road; see **wegh-***.]

tri·week·ly (trī-wēkʹlē) *adj.* **1.** Happening, done, or appearing three times a week. **2.** Happening, done, or appearing every three weeks. —*adv.* **1.** Three times a week. **2.** Every three weeks. —*n., pl.* **-lies.** A periodical published triweekly.

-trix *suff.* **1.** A female that is connected with a specified thing: *testatrix.* **2.** A geometric point, line, or surface: *directrix.* [ME < Lat. *-trīx*, fem. of *-tor*, noun suff.]

tRNA (tēʹär-ĕn-āʹ) *n.* See **transfer RNA.**

triptych
14th-century French ivory

triskelion
Detail of an amphora showing triskelion pattern on a warrior's shield

Triton

ă pat	oi boy
ā pay	ou out
âr care	o͝o took
ä father	o͞o boot
ĕ pet	ŭ cut
ē be	ûr urge
ĭ pit	th thin
ī pie	*th* this
îr pier	hw which
ŏ pot	zh vision
ō toe	ə about, item
ô paw	

Stress marks:
ʹ (primary);
ʹ (secondary), as in
dictionary (dĭkʹshə-nĕrʹē)

Tro•as (trō′ăs′) also **Tro•ad** (-ăd′). An ancient region of NW Asia Minor surrounding the city of Troy.

Tro•bri•and Islands (trō′brē-ănd′, -änd′). An island group of Papua New Guinea in the Solomon Sea off E New Guinea.

tro•car (trō′kär′) *n.* A sharp-pointed surgical instrument, used with a cannula to puncture a body cavity for fluid aspiration. [Fr. *trocart* : *trois*, three (< OFr. < Lat. *trēs*; see **trei-***) + *carre*, side of an instrument (< OFr. < *carrer*, to square < Lat. *quadrāre* < *quadrum*, square; see **kʷetwer-***).]

tro•cha•ic (trō-kā′ĭk) *adj.* Of, relating to, or consisting of trochees. [Lat. *trochāicus* < Gk. *trokhaikos* < *trokhaios*, trochee. See TROCHEE.] —**tro•cha′ic** *n.*

Trojan horse
Engraving after a painting by Henri Paul Motte (1846–1922)

tro•chan•ter (trō-kăn′tər) *n.* **1.** Any of several bony processes on the upper part of the femur of many vertebrates. **2.** The second proximal segment of the leg of an insect. [NLat. < Gk. *trokhantēr*, ball of the hip joint < *trekhein*, to run.] —**tro•chan′ter•al, tro′chan•ter′ic** (trō′kən-tĕr′ĭk, -kăn-) *adj.*

tro•che (trō′kē) *n.* A small circular medicinal lozenge; a pastille. [Back-formation < ME *trocis, troches* (taken as pl.) < OFr. *trocisse* < LLat. *trochiscus* < Gk. *trokhiskos*, dim. of *trokhos*, wheel < *trekhein*, to run.]

tro•chee (trō′kē) *n.* A metrical foot consisting of a stressed syllable followed by an unstressed one, as in *season*, or of a long syllable followed by a short. [Fr. *trochée* < Lat. *trochaeus* < Gk. *trokhaios* < *trokhos*, a running < *trekhein*, to run.]

troch•le•a (trŏk′lē-ə) *n.*, *pl.* **-le•ae** (-lē-ē′). An anatomical structure that resembles a pulley, esp. the part of the distal end of the humerus that articulates with the ulna. [Lat., system of pulleys < Gk. *trokhileia*; akin to *trekhein*, to run.]

troch•le•ar (trŏk′lē-ər) *adj.* **1.** Of, resembling, or situated near a trochlea. **2.** Of or relating to the trochlear nerve. **3.** *Bot.* Shaped like a pulley.

trochlear nerve *n.* Either of the fourth pair of cranial nerves that innervate the superior oblique muscles of the eyeballs.

tro•choid (trō′koid′, trŏk′oid′) *n.* A curve traced by a point on or connected with a circle as the circle rolls along a fixed straight line. —*adj.* also **tro•choi•dal** (trō-koid′l, trŏk-oid′l). **1.** Capable of or exhibiting rotation about a central axis. **2.** Permitting rotation, as a pivot. [Gk. *trokhoeidēs*, wheellike : *trokhos*, wheel; see TROCHEE + *-oeidēs*, -oid.]

trombone

troch•o•phore (trŏk′ə-fôr′, -fōr′) *n.* The small free-swimming ciliated aquatic larva of various invertebrates, including certain mollusks and annelids. [Gk. *trokhos*, wheel (< *trekhein*, to run) + -PHORE.]

trod (trŏd) *v.* P.t. and p.part. of **tread.**

trod•den (trŏd′n) *v.* A p.part. of **tread.**

trof•fer (trŏf′ər, trô′fər) *n.* An inverted, usu. metal trough suspended from a ceiling as a fixture for fluorescent lighting tubes. [Alteration of TROUGH.]

trog•lo•dyte (trŏg′lə-dīt′) *n.* **1.a.** A member of a fabulous or prehistoric race of people that lived in caves, dens, or holes. **b.** A person considered to be reclusive, reactionary, out of date, or brutish. **2.** An anthropoid ape, such as a gorilla. **3.** An animal that lives underground. [< Lat. *Trōglodytae* < Gk. *Trōglodutai*, alteration (influenced by *trōglē*, hole and *-dutai*, those who enter) of *Trōgodutai*.] —**trog′lo•dyt′ic** (-dĭt′ĭk), **trog′lo•dyt′i•cal** (-ĭ-kəl) *adj.*

tro•gon (trō′gŏn′) *n.* Any of various colorful tropical or subtropical birds of the family Trogonidae. [Gk. *trōgōn*, pr.part. of *trōgein*, to gnaw. See **terə-¹***.]

troi•ka (troi′kə) *n.* **1.** A Russian carriage drawn by a team of three horses abreast. **2.** See **triumvirate** 4. [Russ. *troĭka* < *troe*, group of three. See **trei-***.]

Troi•lus (troi′ləs, trō′ə-ləs) *n.* A son of King Priam of Troy, depicted as Cressida's lover in medieval romance.

Trois Ri•vières or **Trois-Rivières** (trwä rē-vyĕr′). A city of S Quebec, Canada, at the confluence of the St. Lawrence and St. Maurice rivers; founded 1634. Pop. 50,466.

trophy
José Luis Clerc after winning the U.S. Pro Tennis Championship, 1983

Tro•jan (trō′jən) *n.* **1.** A native or inhabitant of ancient Troy. **2.** A person of courageous determination or energy. [ME < Lat. *Trōiānus* < *Trōia*, Troy < Gk. < *Trōs*, the mythical founder of Troy.] —**Tro′jan** *adj.*

Trojan horse *n.* **1.** A subversive group or device placed within enemy ranks. **2.** The wooden horse in which, according to legend, Greeks hid and gained access to Troy. **3.** *Comp. Sci.* A set of instructions hidden inside a legitimate program, causing a computer to perform illegitimate functions.

Trojan War *n. Gk. Myth.* The ten-year war waged against Troy by the Greeks, caused by the abduction of Helen by Paris and resulting in the burning and destruction of Troy.

troll¹ (trōl) *v.* **trolled, troll•ing, trolls.** —*tr.* **1.a.** To fish for by trailing a baited line from behind a slowly moving boat. **b.** To fish in by trailing a baited line. **c.** To trail (a baited line) in fishing. **2.** *Slang.* To patrol (an area) in search for someone or something. **3.** *Mus.* **a.** To sing in succession the parts of (a round, for example). **b.** To sing heartily: *troll a carol.* **4.** To roll or revolve. —*intr.* **1.** To fish by trailing a line, as from a moving boat. **2.a.** To wander about; ramble. **b.** *Slang.* To troll an area. **3.** *Mus.* To sing heartily or gaily. **4.** To roll or spin around. —*n.* **1.a.** The act of trolling for fish. **b.** A lure, such as a spoon, that is used for trolling. **2.** *Mus.* A vocal composition in successive parts; a round. [ME *trollen*, to wander about < OFr. *troller*, of Gmc. orig.] —**troll′er** *n.*

troll² (trōl) *n.* A supernatural creature of Scandinavian folklore, variously portrayed as a friendly or mischievous dwarf or as a giant, that lives in caves or under bridges. [Ult. < ON.]

trol•ley also **trol•ly** (trŏl′ē) —*n.*, *pl.* **-leys** also **-lies. 1.** A streetcar. **2.** A device that conducts current, as from a third rail, to the motor of an electric vehicle. **3.** A small truck or car on a track used, as in a mine, for conveying materials. **4.** A wheeled carriage, cage, or basket that travels on an overhead track. **5.** *Chiefly British.* A cart. —*tr.* & *intr.v.* **-leyed, -ley•ing, -leys** also **-lied** (-lēd), **-ly•ing, -lies** (-lēz). To convey (passengers) or travel by trolley. [Prob. < TROLL¹.]

trolley bus *n.* An electric bus that does not run on tracks and is powered by electricity from an overhead wire.

trolley car *n.* A streetcar.

trol•lop (trŏl′əp) *n.* **1.** A slovenly or untidy woman; a slattern. **2.** A prostitute. [Perh. < TROLL¹, to roll about, wallow.]

Trol•lope (trŏl′əp), **Anthony.** 1815–82. British writer whose works include *Barchester Towers* (1857). —**Trol•lo•pi•an** (trə-lŏp′ē-ən, -lō′pē-, trŏl′ə-pē′-) *adj.*

trom•bone (trŏm-bōn′, trəm-, trŏm′bōn′) *n. Mus.* **1.** A brass instrument consisting of a long cylindrical tube bent upon itself twice, ending in a bell-shaped mouth, and having a movable U-shaped slide for producing different pitches. **2.** A member of an orchestra who plays the trombone. [Fr. < Ital., aug. of *tromba*, trumpet, of Gmc. orig.] —**trom•bon′ist** *n.*

trom•mel (trŏm′əl) *n.* A revolving cylindrical sieve used for screening or sizing rock and ore. [Ger. < MHGer. *trummel*, dim. of *trumme*, drum, prob. of imit. orig.]

tromp (trŏmp) *v.* **tromped, tromp•ing, tromps.** —*intr.* **1.** To walk heavily and noisily; tramp. **2.** To apply heavy foot pressure on something. —*tr.* **1.** To trample underfoot. **2.** To defeat soundly; trounce. [Var. of TRAMP.]

trompe (trŏmp) *n.* A device in which water falling through a perforated pipe entrains air through the pipe to produce an air blast for a furnace or forge. [Fr. < OFr., trumpet. See TRUMP².]

trompe l'oeil (trômp′ loi′) *n.*, *pl.* **trompe l'oeils** (loi′). **1.** A style of painting that gives an illusion of photographic reality. **2.** A painting or effect created in this style. [Fr. : *trompe*, third pers. sing. pr.t. of *tromper*, to deceive + *le*, the + *oeil*, eye.]

-tron *suff.* **1.** Vacuum tube: *dynatron.* **2.** Device for manipulating subatomic particles: *betatron.* [Gk., instrumental noun suff.]

tro•na (trō′nə) *n.* A vitreous gray or white mineral, $Na_2CO_3{\cdot}NaHCO_3{\cdot}2H_2O$, used as a source of sodium carbonate. [Swed., prob. < Ar. dial. *ṭrōn*, var. of Ar. *naṭrūn*, natron. See NATRON.]

Trond•heim (trŏn′hām′, trôn′-). A city of central Norway on **Trondheim Fjord,** an inlet of the Norwegian Sea; founded in 997 and the cap. of Norway until 1380. Pop. 134,652.

troop (tro͞op) *n.* **1.** A group or company. **2.a.** A group of soldiers. **b. troops.** Military units; soldiers. **3.** A unit of Boy Scouts or Girl Scouts with an adult leader. **4.** A great many; a lot. —*intr.v.* **trooped, troop•ing, troops. 1.** To move or go as a throng. **2.** To assemble or move in crowds. **3.** To consort; associate. [Fr. *troupe* < OFr. *trope*, prob. < VLat. **troppu-*.]

troop•er (tro͞o′pər) *n.* **1.a.** A member of a cavalry unit. **b.** A cavalry horse. **2.a.** A mounted police officer. **b.** A state police officer.

troop•ship (tro͞op′shĭp′) *n.* A ship for transporting troops.

trop. *abbr.* Tropic; tropical.

trop- *pref.* Var. of **tropo-.**

trope (trōp) *n.* **1.** A figure of speech using words in nonliteral ways, such as a metaphor. **2.** *Mus.* A word or phrase interpolated as an embellishment in the sung parts of certain medieval liturgies. [Lat. *tropus* < Gk. *tropos*, turn, figure of speech. See **trep-***.] —**trop′i•cal** (trŏp′ĭ-kəl) *adj.*

troph- *pref.* Var. of **tropho-.**

troph•al•lax•is (trŏf′ə-lăk′sĭs, trō′fə-) *n.*, *pl.* **-lax•es** (-lăk′sēz). Mutual exchange of food between adults and larvae of certain social insects such as bees. [TROPH(O)- + Gk. *allaxis*, exchange (< *allassein*, to exchange < *allos*, other; see **al-¹***).]

troph•ic (trŏf′ĭk, trō′fĭk) *adj.* **1.** Of or relating to nutrition. **2.** *Ecol.* Of or involving the feeding habits or food relationship of different organisms in a food chain.

-trophic *suff.* **1.** Of, relating to, or characterized by a specified kind of nutrition: *polytrophic.* **2.** Acting on something specified: *gonadotrophic.* [< TROPHIC.]

trophic level *n. Ecol.* A group of organisms that occupy the same position in a food chain.

tropho- or **troph-** *pref.* Nutrition; nutritive: *trophoblast.* [Gk. < *trophē* < *trephein*, to nourish.]

tro•pho•blast (trō′fə-blăst′) *n.* The outermost layer of cells of the blastocyst that functions in the implantation and nutrition of the embryo. —**tro′pho•blas′tic** *adj.*

tro•pho•zo•ite (trō′fə-zō′īt′) *n.* A protozoan, esp. of the class Sporozoa, in the active stage of its life cycle.

tro•phy (trō′fē) *n.*, *pl.* **-phies. 1.a.** A prize or memento received as a symbol of victory, esp. in sports. **b.** A specimen or part, such as a lion's head, preserved as a token of a successful hunt. **c.** A memento, as of one's personal achievements. **d.** The spoils of war, dedicated in classical antiquity with an inscription to a deity. **2.** *Archit.* A painted or sculpted representation of a group of weapons or armor. [Fr. *trophée* < OFr. *trophee* < Lat. *trophaeum*, monument to victory, var. of *tropaeum* < Gk. *tropaion* < neut. of *tropaios*, of defeat < *tropē*, a turning, rout. See **trep-***.]

–trophy *suff.* Nutrition; growth: *hypertrophy.* [Gk. *-trophia* < *trophē* < *trephein*, to nourish.]

trop•ic (trŏp′ĭk) *n.* **1.a.** Either of two parallels of latitude, the tropic of Cancer or the tropic of Capricorn, representing the points farthest north and south at which the sun can shine directly overhead. **b. Tropics or tropics.** The region of the earth's surface lying between these latitudes. **2.** *Astron.* Either of two corresponding parallels of celestial latitude that are the limits of the apparent northern and southern passages of the sun. *—adj.* Of or relating to the Tropics; tropical. [ME *tropik* < OFr. *tropique* < LLat. *tropicus* < Lat., of a turn < Gk. *tropikos* < *tropē*, a turning. See **trep-***.]

–tropic *suff.* **1.** Turning or changing in a specified way or in response to a specified stimulus: *heliotropic.* **2.** Affecting or attracted to something specified: *gonadotropic.* [< Gk. *tropē*, a turning. See TROPIC.]

trop•i•cal (trŏp′ĭ-kəl) *adj.* **1.** Of, occurring in, or characteristic of the Tropics. **2.** Hot and humid; torrid. *—n.* A tropical plant. **—trop′i•cal•ly** *adv.*

tropical cyclone *n.* A cyclone originating over tropical oceans, characterized by violent rainstorms and winds with velocities of up to 320 kilometers (200 miles) per hour.

tropical fish *n.* Any of various small brightly colored fishes native to tropical waters and often kept in home aquariums.

tropical storm *n.* A cyclonic storm having winds ranging from approx. 48 to 121 kilometers (30 to 75 miles) per hour.

tropical year *n.* See **solar year.**

trop•ic•bird (trŏp′ĭk-bûrd′) *n.* Any of several predominantly white, swift-flying sea birds of the genus *Phaethon* of warm regions, having small weak legs and a pair of long central tail feathers.

tropic of Cancer *n.* The parallel of latitude 23°27′ north of the equator, the northern limit of the Torrid Zone.

tropic of Capricorn *n.* The parallel of latitude 23°27′ south of the equator, the southern limit of the Torrid Zone.

tro•pine (trō′pēn′, -pĭn) also **tro•pin** (-pĭn) *n.* A white crystalline poisonous alkaloid, $C_8H_{15}NO$, obtained chiefly by hydrolysis of atropine. [< ATROPINE.]

tro•pism (trō′pĭz′əm) *n.* The movement of an organism or a part toward or away from an external stimulus, such as light, heat, or gravity. [< –TROPISM.] **—tro•pis′tic** *adj.*

–tropism *suff.* Tropism: *phototropism.* [< Gk. *tropē*, a turning. See –TROPIC.]

tropo– or **trop–** *pref.* **1.** Turning; change: *troposphere.* **2.** Tropism: *tropotaxis.* [Gk. < *tropē*, turn. See **trep-***.]

tro•po•col•la•gen (trō′pə-kŏl′ə-jən, trŏp′ə-) *n.* The molecular component of a collagen fiber, consisting of three polypeptide chains coiled around each other.

tro•pol•o•gy (trō-pŏl′ə-jē) *n., pl.* **-gies. 1.** The use of tropes in speech or writing. **2.** A mode of biblical interpretation that finds moral meanings in the tropes of the Bible. [LLat. *tropologia* < LGk. : Gk. *tropos*, trope; see TROPE + Gk. *-logia*, -logy.] **—tro′po•log′ic** (trō′pə-lŏj′ĭk, trŏp′ə-), **tro′po•log′i•cal** (-ĭ-kəl) *adj.* **—tro′po•log′i•cal•ly** *adv.*

tro•po•pause (trō′pə-pôz′, trŏp′ə-) *n.* The boundary between the troposphere and the stratosphere varying in altitude from approx. 8 kilometers (5 miles) at the poles to approx. 18 kilometers (11 miles) at the equator.

tro•po•phyte (trō′pə-fīt′, trŏp′ə-) *n.* A plant adapted to climatic conditions in which periods of heavy rainfall alternate with periods of drought. **—tro′po•phyt′ic** (-fĭt′ĭk) *adj.*

tro•po•sphere (trō′pə-sfîr′, trŏp′ə-) *n.* The lowest region of the atmosphere between the earth's surface and the tropopause, characterized by decreasing temperature with increasing altitude. **—tro′po•spher′ic** (-sfîr′ĭk, -sfĕr′-) *adj.*

tro•po•tax•is (trō′pə-tăk′sĭs, trŏp′ə-) *n.* The movement or orientation of an organism in response to two stimuli, esp. lights, by means of different sense organs.

–tropous *suff.* Turning in a specified way or from a specified stimulus: *amphitropous.* [< Gk. *-tropos*, of turning < *tropos*, changeable < *trepein*, to turn. See **trep-***.]

–tropy *suff.* The state of turning in a specified way or from a specified stimulus: *thixotropy.* [Gk. *-tropia* < *-tropos*, -tropous.]

trot (trŏt) *n.* **1.a.** The gait of a horse or other four-footed animal, between a walk and a canter in speed, in which diagonal pairs of legs move forward together. **b.** A ride on a horse at this pace. **2.** A gait of a person, faster than a walk; a jog. **3.** *Sports.* A race for trotters. **4.** See **pony** 4. **5. trots.** *Informal.* Diarrhea. Used with *the.* **6.** A toddler. **7.** *Archaic.* An old woman; a crone. *—v.* **trot•ted, trot•ting, trots.** *—intr.* **1.** To go or move at a trot. **2.** To proceed rapidly; hurry. *—tr.* To cause to move at a trot. **—*phrasal verb.* trot out.** *Informal.* To present for inspection or admiration. [ME < OFr. < *troter*, to trot, of Gmc. orig.]

troth (trôth, trŏth, trōth) *n.* **1.a.** Betrothal. **b.** One's pledged fidelity. **2.** Good faith; fidelity. *—tr.v.* **trothed, troth•ing, troths.** To pledge or betroth. [ME *trouthe, trothe*, var. of *treuthe* < OE *trēowth*, truth. See **deru-***.]

troth•plight (trôth′plīt′, trŏth′-, trōth′-) *Archaic. —n.* A betrothal. *—tr.v.* **-plight•ed, -plight•ing, -plights.** To betroth.

trot•line (trŏt′līn′) *n.* See **setline.** [Perh. < TROT.]

Trot•sky or **Trot•ski** (trŏt′skē, trôt′-), **Leon.** 1879–1940. Russian revolutionary theoretician who was a leader of the Bolshevik Revolution (1917) but was banished (1929) for his opposition to Stalin. **—Trots′ky•ism** *n.* **—Trots′ky•ist, Trots′ky•ite′** (-īt′) *n.*

trot•ter (trŏt′ər) *n.* **1.** A horse that trots, esp. one trained for harness racing. **2.** *Informal.* A foot, esp. the foot of a pig or sheep prepared as food.

trou•ba•dour (tro͞o′bə-dôr′, -dōr′, -do͝or′) *n.* **1.** One of a class of 12th- and 13th-century lyric poets in Provence, northern Italy, and northern Spain, who wrote songs in langue d'oc often about courtly love. **2.** A strolling minstrel. [Fr. < Prov. *trobador* < OProv. < *trobar*, to compose, perh. < VLat. **tropāre* < LLat. *tropus*, trope, song < Lat., trope. See TROPE.]

trou•ble (trŭb′əl) *n.* **1.** A state of distress, affliction, danger, or need. **2.** A cause or source of distress, disturbance, or difficulty. **3.** An effort, esp. one that causes inconvenience or bother. **4.** A condition of pain, disease, or malfunction. *—v.* **-led, -ling, -les.** *—tr.* **1.** To agitate; stir up. **2.** To afflict with pain or discomfort. **3.** To cause mental agitation or distress to; worry. **4.** To inconvenience; bother. *—intr.* To take pains. [ME < OFr. < *troubler*, to trouble < VLat. **turbulāre*, alteration of LLat. *turbidāre* < Lat. *turbidus*, confused. See TURBID.] **—trou′bler** *n.*

Syns: *trouble, ail, distress, worry.* The central meaning shared by these verbs is "to cause anxious uneasiness in": *questions that trouble all parents; asked what's ailing him; events that distress us; a fever that worries the doctor.*

trou•ble•mak•er (trŭb′əl-mā′kər) *n.* One that stirs up trouble or strife.

trou•ble•shoot also **trou•ble-shoot** (trŭb′əl-sho͞ot′) *—v.* **-shot** (-shŏt′), **-shoot•ing, -shoots.** *—intr.* To work or serve as a troubleshooter. *—tr.* To investigate as a troubleshooter and eliminate or settle problems with.

trou•ble•shoot•er also **trou•ble-shoot•er** (trŭb′əl-sho͞o′tər) *n.* **1.** A worker whose job is to locate and eliminate sources of trouble, as in mechanical operations. **2.** A mediator skilled in settling disputes esp. of a diplomatic or industrial nature.

trou•ble•some (trŭb′əl-səm) *adj.* **1.** Causing trouble or anxiety; worrisome. **2.** Difficult; trying. **—trou′ble•some•ly** *adv.* **—trou′ble•some•ness** *n.*

trouble spot *n.* A location or site of possible difficulty.

trou•blous (trŭb′ləs) *adj.* **1.a.** Full of trouble. **b.** Uneasy; troubled. **2.** Causing trouble; troublesome.

trough (trôf, trŏf) *n.* **1.a.** A long, narrow, generally shallow receptacle for holding water or feed for animals. **b.** Any of various similar containers for domestic or industrial use, such as washing. **2.** A gutter under the eaves of a roof. **3.** A long narrow depression, as between waves. **4.** A low point in a business cycle or on a statistical graph. **5.** *Meteorol.* An elongated region of relatively low atmospheric pressure, often associated with a front. **6.** *Phys.* A minimum point in a wave or an alternating signal. [ME < OE *trog.* See **deru-***.]

trounce (trouns) *v.* **trounced, trounc•ing, trounc•es.** *—tr.* **1.** To thrash; beat. **2.** To defeat decisively. *—intr.* To censure something or someone forcefully. [?]

troupe (tro͞op) *n.* A company or group, esp. of touring actors, singers, or dancers. *—intr.v.* **trouped, troup•ing, troupes.** To tour with a theatrical company. [Fr., troop. See TROOP.]

troup•er (tro͞o′pər) *n.* **1.** A member of a theatrical company. **2.** A veteran actor or performer. **3.** A reliable, uncomplaining, often hard-working person.

trou•pi•al (tro͞o′pē-əl) *n.* Any of several tropical American birds of the genus *Icterus*, related to the orioles and New World blackbirds, esp. *I. icterus*, having orange and black plumage. [Fr. *troupiale* < *troupe*, flock. See TROOP.]

trou•ser also **trow•ser** (trou′zər) *—n.* An outer garment for covering the body from the waist to the ankles, divided into sections to fit each leg separately and worn esp. by men and boys. Often used in the plural. *—adj.* Of, designed for, or to be found on trousers: *trouser legs.* [Back-formation < *trousers*, alteration of obsolete *trouse* < Sc.Gael. *triubhas.*]

trous•seau (tro͞o′sō, tro͞o-sō′) *n., pl.* **-seaux** (-sōz, -sōz′) or **-seaus.** The possessions, such as clothing and linens, that a bride assembles for her marriage. [Fr. < OFr., dim. of *trousse*, bundle. See TRUSS.]

trout (trout) *n., pl.* **trout** or **trouts. 1.** Any of various freshwater or anadromous food and game fishes of the family Salmonidae, esp. of the genera *Salmo* and *Salvelinus*, usu. having a speckled body with small scales. **2.** Any of various similar but unrelated fishes, such as the troutperch. [ME *troute* < OE *trūht* < LLat. *tructa*, perh. < Gk. *trōktēs*, a sea fish with sharp teeth < *trōgein*, to gnaw. See **terə-¹***.]

trout lily *n.* See **dogtooth violet.**

troutperch (trout′pûrch′) *n., pl.* **troutperch** or **-perch•es.** A small North American freshwater fish *(Percopsis omiscomaycus)* having a translucent body and an adipose fin.

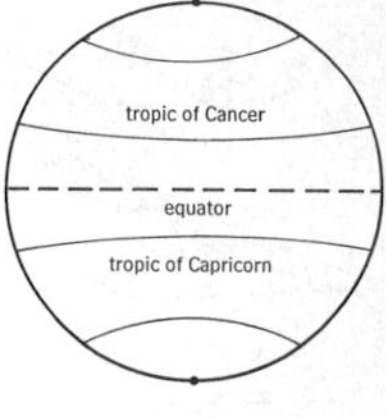

tropic

Leon Trotsky
Photographed c. 1917

ă pat	oi boy
ā pay	ou out
âr care	o͝o took
ä father	o͞o boot
ĕ pet	ŭ cut
ē be	ûr urge
ĭ pit	th thin
ī pie	*th* this
îr pier	hw which
ŏ pot	zh vision
ō toe	ə about, item
ô paw	

Stress marks:
′ (primary);
′ (secondary), as in
dictionary (dĭk′shə-nĕr′ē)

trou•vère (trōō-vâr′) also **trou•veur** (-vûr′, -vœr′) *n.* One of a class of poet-musicians flourishing in northern France in the 12th and 13th centuries, who composed chiefly narrative works, such as the chansons de geste, in langue d'oïl. [Fr. < OFr. *trovere* < *trover*, to compose < VLat. **tropāre*. See TROUBADOUR.]

Trou•ville (trōō-vēl′) or **Trou•ville-sur-Mer** (-sŏŏr-mĕr′, -sür-). A resort town of NW France on the English Channel S of Le Havre. Pop. 6,008.

trove (trōv) *n.* A collection of valuable items discovered or found; a treasure-trove. [Short for (TREASURE-)TROVE.]

tro•ver (trō′vər) *n. Law.* A common-law action to recover damages for property illegally withheld or wrongfully converted to use by another. [< AN, to compose, invent, find, prob. < VLat. **tropāre*. See TROUBADOUR.]

trow (trō) *intr.v.* **trowed, trow•ing, trows. 1.** *Archaic.* To think. **2.** *Obsolete.* To suppose. [ME *trowen* < OE *trēowian*, to trust. See **deru-*.**]

trow•el (trou′əl) *n.* **1.** A flat-bladed hand tool for leveling, spreading, or shaping substances such as cement or mortar. **2.** A small implement with a pointed scoop-shaped blade used for digging, as in setting plants. —*tr.v.* **-eled, -el•ing, -els** or **-elled, -el•ling, -els.** To spread, smooth, form, or scoop with a trowel. [ME *trowell* < OFr. *truele* < LLat. *truella*, dim. of Lat. *trua*, ladle.] —**trow′el•er, trow′el•ler** *n.*

trowel
Top: Corner trowel
Center: Pointing trowel
Bottom: Finishing trowel

troy (troi) *adj.* Of or expressed in troy weight. [ME *troye*, after TROYES.]

Troy (troi). **1.** Also **Il•i•on** (ĭl′ē-ən, -ŏn′) or **Il•i•um** (-ē-əm). An ancient city of NW Asia Minor; legendary site of the Trojan War. **2.** A city of SE MI, a suburb of Detroit. Pop. 72,884. **3.** A city of E NY on the Hudson R. NE of Albany; settled in the 1780's. Pop. 54,269. **4.** A city of W-central OH N of Dayton. Pop. 19,478.

Troyes (trwä). A city of NE France on the Seine ESE of Paris; noted in medieval times for its annual fairs, which set standards of weights and measures for Europe. Pop. 63,581.

troy weight *n.* A system of units of weight in which the grain is the same as in the avoirdupois system and the pound contains 12 ounces, 240 pennyweights, or 5,760 grains.

trp. *abbr.* Troop.

tru•an•cy (trōō′ən-sē) also **tru•ant•ry** (-ən-trē) *n., pl.* **-cies** also **-ries.** The act or condition of being absent without permission.

tru•ant (trōō′ənt) *n.* **1.** One who is absent without permission, esp. from school. **2.** One who shirks work or duty. —*adj.* **1.** Absent without permission, esp. from school. **2.** Idle, lazy, or neglectful. —*intr.v.* **-ant•ed, -ant•ing, -ants.** To be truant. [ME, beggar < OFr. See **terə-¹*.**]

truant officer *n.* An official who investigates school truancy.

truce (trōōs) *n.* **1.** A temporary cessation or suspension of hostilities by agreement of the opposing sides; an armistice. **2.** A respite from a disagreeable state of affairs. —*tr. & intr.v.* **truced, truc•ing, truc•es.** To end or be ended with a truce. [ME *trewes*, pl. of *trewe*, treaty, pledge < OE *trēow*. See **deru-*.**]

Tru•cial O•man (trōō′shəl ō-män′). See **United Arab Emirates.**

Bess Truman
Photographed in 1948

truck¹ (trŭk) *n.* **1.** Any of various heavy motor vehicles designed for carrying or pulling loads. **2.** A two-wheeled barrow for moving heavy objects by hand. **3.** A wheeled platform, sometimes equipped with a motor, for conveying loads in a warehouse or freight yard. **4.** One of the swiveling frames of wheels under each end of a railroad car or trolley car. **5.** A set of bookshelves mounted on four wheels or casters, used in libraries. **6.** *Naut.* A small piece of wood placed at the top of a mast or flagpole, usu. having holes or sheaves through which halyards can be passed. **7.** *Chiefly British.* A railroad freight car without a top. —*v.* **trucked, truck•ing, trucks.** —*tr.* To transport by truck. —*intr.* **1.** To carry goods by truck. **2.** To drive a truck. **3.** *Slang.* To move or travel in a steady but easy manner. [Short for TRUCKLE, or < Lat. *trochus*, iron hoop (< Gk. *trokhos*, wheel).]

truck² (trŭk) *v.* **trucked, truck•ing, trucks.** —*tr.* **1.** To exchange; barter. **2.** To peddle. —*intr.* To have dealings or commerce; traffic. —*n.* **1.** Articles of commerce; trade goods. **2.** Garden produce raised for the market. **3.** *Informal.* Worthless goods; stuff or rubbish. **4.** Barter; exchange. **5.** *Informal.* Dealings; business. [ME *trukien* < ONFr. *troquer*.]

Harry S. Truman
Photographed c. 1945

truck•age (trŭk′ĭj) *n.* **1.** Transportation of goods by truck. **2.** A charge for transportation by truck.

Truck•ee (trŭk′ē). A river, c. 193 km (120 mi), rising in E CA and flowing E and NE into NW NV.

truck•er (trŭk′ər) *n.* **1.** One who drives a truck. **2.** One engaged in trucking goods.

truck farm *n.* A farm producing vegetables for the market. [< TRUCK².] —**truck farmer** *n.* —**truck farming** *n.*

truck•le (trŭk′əl) *n.* A small wheel or roller; a caster. —*intr.v.* **-led, -ling, -les.** To be servile or submissive. [ME *trocle*, pulley < AN < Lat. *trochlea*, system of pulleys. See TROCHLEA.] —**truck′ler** *n.*

truckle bed *n.* A trundle bed.

truck•load (trŭk′lōd′) *n.* The quantity that a truck can hold.

truck stop *n.* An establishment that sells fuel for trucks and usu. maintains a restaurant for truck drivers.

truc•u•lence (trŭk′yə-ləns) also **truc•u•len•cy** (-lən-sē) *n.* **1.** A disposition or apparent disposition to fight, esp. fiercely. **2.** Ferociously cruel actions or behavior.

truc•u•lent (trŭk′yə-lənt) *adj.* **1.** Disposed to fight; pugnacious. **2.** Expressing bitter opposition; scathing. **3.** Disposed to or exhibiting violence or destructiveness; fierce. [Lat. *truculentus* < *trux*, *truc-*, fierce. See **terə-²*.**]

Tru•deau (trōō-dō′, trōō′dō′), **Pierre Elliott.** b. 1919. Canadian prime minister (1968–79 and 1980–84).

trudge (trŭj) *intr.v.* **trudged, trudg•ing, trudg•es.** To walk in a laborious heavy-footed way; plod. —*n.* A long tedious walk. [?] —**trudg′er** *n.*

trudg•en also **trudg•eon** (trŭj′ən) *n. Sports.* A swimming stroke in which an alternating overarm movement is combined with a scissors kick. [After John *Trudgen* (1852–1902), British swimmer.]

true (trōō) *adj.* **tru•er, tru•est. 1.a.** Consistent with fact or reality; not false or erroneous. See Usage Note at **fact. b.** Truthful. **2.** Real; genuine. See Syns at **authentic. 3.** Reliable; accurate: *a true prophecy.* **4.** Faithful, as to a friend, vow, or cause; loyal. See Syns at **faithful. 5.** Sincerely felt or expressed; unfeigned. **6.** Fundamental; essential: *his true motive.* **7.** Rightful; legitimate. **8.** Exactly conforming to a rule, standard, or pattern. **9.** Accurately shaped or fitted. **10.** Accurately placed, delivered, or thrown. **11.** Quick and exact in sensing and responding. **12.** Determined with reference to the earth's axis, not the magnetic poles: *true north.* **13.** Conforming to the definitive criteria of a natural group; typical: *a true crab.* **14.** Narrowly particularized; highly specific: *the truest sense of the word.* —*adv.* **1.** In accord with reality, fact, or truthfulness. **2.** Unswervingly; exactly. **3.** So as to conform to a type, standard, or pattern. —*tr.v.* **trued, tru•ing** or **true•ing, trues.** To position (something) so as to make it balanced, level, or square: *trued up the planks.* —*n.* **1.** Truth or reality. Used with *the.* **2.** Proper alignment or adjustment: *out of true.* [ME *trewe* < OE *trēowe*, firm, trustworthy. See **deru-*.**] —**true′ness** *n.*

true bill *n. Law.* A bill of indictment endorsed by a grand jury.

true-blue (trōō′blōō′) *adj.* Loyal or faithful; staunch. [< the adoption of the color blue by 17th-century Scottish Presbyterians in opposition to the Royalists' red.]

true•born (trōō′bôrn′) *adj.* Being authentically or genuinely such by birth.

true bug *n.* A wingless or four-winged insect of the order Hemiptera, esp. of the suborder Heteroptera, including the bedbug and louse, having mouthparts adapted for sucking.

true-false test (trōō′fôls′) *n.* A test in which statements are to be marked either true or false.

true-life (trōō′līf′) *adj.* Presenting conditions and esp. human relationships accurately; true to life: *a true-life romance.*

true•love (trōō′lŭv′) *n.* One's beloved; a sweetheart.

true lovers' knot *n.* See **love knot.**

true•pen•ny (trōō′pĕn′ē) *n., pl.* **-nies.** An honest, trustworthy person.

true rib *n.* Any of the ribs attached to the sternum by a costal cartilage, esp. any of the seven upper ribs on either side of the thorax in human beings.

true seal *n.* See **earless seal.**

Truf•faut (trōō-fō′), **François.** 1932–84. French New Wave filmmaker whose works include *The 400 Blows* (1959).

truf•fle (trŭf′əl) *n.* **1.** Any of various fleshy ascomycetous edible fungi, chiefly of the genus *Tuber*, that grow underground on or near the roots of trees and are valued as a delicacy. **2.** Any of various chocolate confections, esp. one made of a mixture including chopped nuts, rolled into balls and covered with cocoa powder. [Alteration of Fr. *truffe* < OFr. < OProv. *trufa* < VLat. **tūfera*, truffles < dialectal var. of Lat. *tūber*, lump. See **teuə-*.**]

tru•ism (trōō′ĭz′əm) *n.* A self-evident truth. —**tru•is′tic** (trōō-ĭs′tĭk) *adj.*

Tru•ji•llo (trōō-hē′ō, -yō). A city of NW Peru NW of Lima; founded 1534. Pop. 202,469.

Trujillo Mo•li•na (mō-lē′nə, -nä), **Rafael Leónidas.** 1891–1961. Dominican soldier and dictator (1930–61).

Truk Islands (trŭk, trŏŏk). An island group in the central Caroline Is.; part of the U.S. Trust Territory of the Pacific Is.

trull (trŭl) *n.* A prostitute. [Perh. < Ger. *Trulle* < MHGer. *trulle*; akin to ON *troll*, creature, troll.]

tru•ly (trōō′lē) *adv.* **1.** Sincerely; genuinely. **2.** Truthfully; accurately. **3.** Indeed: *truly ugly.* **4.** Properly: *not truly civilized.*

Tru•man (trōō′mən), **Elizabeth ("Bess").** 1885–1982. First Lady of the U.S. (1945–53).

Truman, Harry S. 1884–1972. The 33rd President of the U.S. (1945–53), who authorized the use of the atomic bomb against Japan (1945).

Trum•bo (trŭm′bō), **Dalton.** 1905–76. Amer. screenwriter who was blacklisted and imprisoned for his refusal to testify before the House Un-American Activities Committee.

Trum•bull (trŭm′bəl). A town of SW CT N of Bridgeport. Pop. 32,016.

Trumbull, John. 1756–1843. Amer. painter of historical scenes, such as *The Battle of Bunker's Hill* (1786).

Trumbull, Jonathan. 1710–85. Amer. politician who as governor of Connecticut (1769–84) provided support for the Continental Army during the American Revolution.

trump[1] (trŭmp) *n.* **1.** *Games.* **a.** A suit in card games that outranks all others for the duration of a hand. Often used in the plural. **b.** A card of such a suit. **c.** A trump card. **2.** A key resource to be used at an opportune moment. **3.** *Informal.* A reliable or admirable person. —*v.* **trumped, trump•ing, trumps.** —*tr.* **1.** *Games.* To take (a card or trick) with a trump. **2.** To get the better of (an adversary or a competitor, for example) by using a key, often hidden resource. —*intr. Games.* To play a trump. —***phrasal verb.*** **trump up.** To devise fraudulently. [Alteration of TRIUMPH.]

trump[2] (trŭmp) *n. Mus.* A trumpet. [ME *trompe* < OFr. See TRUMPET.]

trump card *n.* **1.** *Games.* A card in the trump suit, held in reserve for winning a trick. **2.** A trump.

trump•er•y (trŭm′pə-rē) *n., pl.* **-ies. 1.** Showy but worthless finery; bric-a-brac. **2.** Nonsense; rubbish. **3.** Deception; trickery; fraud. [ME *trompery*, deceit < OFr. *tromperie* < *tromper*, to deceive.]

trum•pet (trŭm′pĭt) *n.* **1.a.** *Mus.* A soprano brass wind instrument consisting of a long metal tube looped once and ending in a flared bell, the modern type having three valves for producing variations in pitch. **b.** Something like this instrument in shape or sound. **2.** A resounding call, as that of the elephant. —*v.* **-pet•ed, -pet•ing, -pets.** —*intr.* **1.** *Mus.* To play a trumpet. **2.** To give forth a resounding call. —*tr.* To sound or proclaim loudly. [ME *trumpette* < OFr. *trompette*, dim. of *trompe*, horn < OHGer. *trumpa*.]

trumpet creeper *n.* A deciduous woody vine *(Campsis radicans)* of the eastern United States having opposite compound leaves and trumpet-shaped reddish-orange flowers.

trum•pet•er (trŭm′pĭ-tər) *n.* **1.** *Mus.* One who plays the trumpet. **2.** One who announces something, as a herald. **3.** Any of several large cranelike birds of the genus *Psophia* of tropical South America, having a loud resonant call. **4.a.** The trumpeter swan. **b.** A variety of domestic pigeon having a shell-shaped crest and heavily feathered feet.

trumpeter swan *n.* A large white swan *(Olor buccinator)* of western North America having a loud buglelike call.

trumpet honeysuckle *n.* A vine *(Lonicera sempervirens)* of the eastern United States having tubular reddish flowers.

trumpet vine *n.* See **trumpet creeper.**

trun•cate (trŭng′kāt′) *tr.v.* **-cat•ed, -cat•ing, -cates. 1.** To shorten by or as if by cutting off. **2.** To shorten (a number) by dropping one or more digits after the decimal point. **3.** To replace (the edge of a crystal) with a plane face. —*adj.* **1.** Appearing to terminate abruptly, as a leaf of a tulip tree. **2.** Truncated. [Lat. *truncāre*, *truncāt-* < *truncus*, trunk. See **terə-[2]*.**] —**trun′cate′ly** *adv.* —**trun•ca′tion** *n.*

trun•ca•ted (trŭng′kā′tĭd) *adj.* **1.** Having the apex cut off and replaced by a plane, esp. one parallel to the base. Used of a cone or pyramid. **2.a.** Lacking one or more syllables, esp. in the final foot; catalectic. **b.** Lacking an initial or final syllable. Used of a line of verse. **3.** Truncate.

trun•cheon (trŭn′chən) *n.* **1.** A short stick carried by police; a billy club. **2.** A staff carried as a symbol of office or authority; a baton. **3.** *Obsolete.* **a.** A heavy club; a cudgel. **b.** A thick cutting from a plant, as for grafting. [ME *tronchon*, piece broken off, club < ONFr. < VLat. **trunciō, trunciōn-* < Lat. *truncus*, trunk. See TRUNK.] —**trun′cheon** *v.*

trun•dle (trŭn′dl) *n.* **1.** A small wheel or roller. **2.** The motion or noise of rolling. **3.** A trundle bed. **4.** A low-wheeled cart; a dolly. —*v.* **-dled, -dling, -dles.** —*tr.* **1.** To push or propel on wheels or rollers. **2.** To spin; twirl. —*intr.* To move along by or as if by rolling or spinning. [Var. of dial. *trendle*, wheel < ME < OE *trendel*, circle.] —**trun′dler** *n.*

trundle bed *n.* A low bed on casters that can be rolled under another bed for storage.

trunk (trŭngk) *n.* **1.a.** The main woody axis of a tree. **b.** *Archit.* The shaft of a column. **2.a.** The body of a human being or an animal excluding the head and limbs. **b.** The thorax of an insect. **3.** A proboscis, esp. that of an elephant. **4.a.** A main body, apart from tributaries or appendages. **b.** The main stem of a blood vessel or nerve apart from the branches. **5.** A trunk line. **6.** A chute or conduit. **7.** *Naut.* **a.** A shaft connecting two or more decks. **b.** The housing for the centerboard of a vessel. **8.** *Naut.* Any of certain structures projecting above part of a main deck, as: **a.** A covering over the hatches of a ship. **b.** An expansion chamber on a tanker. **c.** A cabin on a small boat. **9.a.** A covered compartment for storage, generally at the rear of an automobile. **b.** A large packing case or box that clasps shut, used as luggage or for storage. **10. trunks.** Shorts worn for swimming or other athletics. [ME *trunke* < OFr. *tronc* < Lat. *truncus.* See **terə-[2]*.**]

trunk•fish (trŭngk′fĭsh′) *n., pl.* **trunkfish** or **-fish•es.** Any of various colorful tropical marine fishes of the family Ostraciidae, having a body enclosed in bony armorlike plates.

trunk hose *pl.n.* Short ballooning breeches worn by men in Europe in the 16th and 17th centuries. [Perh. < obsolete *trunk*, to cut off < Lat. *truncāre.* See TRUNCATE.]

trunk line *n.* **1.** A direct line between two telephone switchboards. **2.** The main line of a communications or transportation system.

trun•nel (trŭn′əl) *n.* Var. of **treenail.**

trun•nion (trŭn′yən) *n.* A pin or gudgeon, esp. either of two small cylindrical projections on a cannon forming an axis on which it pivots. [Fr. *trognon*, stump.]

truss (trŭs) *n.* **1.** *Medic.* A supportive device, usu. consisting of a pad with a belt, worn to prevent enlargement of a hernia or the return of a reduced hernia. **2.a.** A rigid framework, as of wooden beams or metal bars, designed to support a structure, such as a roof. **b.** *Archit.* A bracket. **3.** Something gathered into a bundle; a pack. **4.** *Naut.* An iron fitting by which a lower yard is secured to a mast. **5.** *Bot.* A compact cluster of flowers at the end of a stalk. —*tr.v.* **trussed, truss•ing, truss•es. 1.** To tie up or bind tightly. **2.** To bind or skewer the wings or legs of (a fowl) before cooking. **3.** To support or brace with a truss. [ME *trusse*, bundle < OFr. *trousse* < *torser, trousser*, to truss, poss. < VLat. **torsāre* < **torsus*, var. of Lat. *tortus*, p.part. of *torquēre*, to twist. See **terk^{w}-*.**]

trumpet

truss bridge *n.* A bridge supported by trusses.

trust (trŭst) *n.* **1.** Firm reliance on the integrity, ability, or character of a person or thing. **2.** Custody; care. See Syns at **care. 3.** Something committed into the care of another; a charge. **4.a.** The condition and resulting obligation of having confidence placed in one: *a public trust.* **b.** One in which confidence is placed. **5.** Reliance on something in the future; hope. **6.** Reliance on the intention and ability of a purchaser to pay in the future; credit. **7.** *Law.* **a.** A legal title to property held by one party for the benefit of another. **b.** The confidence reposed in a trustee when giving the trustee legal title to property to administer for another, together with the trustee's obligation regarding that property and the beneficiary. **c.** The property so held. **8.** A combination of firms or corporations for the purpose of reducing competition and controlling prices throughout a business or an industry. —*v.* **trust•ed, trust•ing, trusts.** —*intr.* **1.** To have or place reliance; depend: *Trust to destiny.* **2.** To be confident; hope. **3.** To sell on credit. —*tr.* **1.** To have or place confidence in; depend on. **2.** To expect with assurance; assume. **3.** To believe. **4.** To place in the care of another; entrust. **5.** To grant discretion to confidently. **6.** To extend credit to. —***idiom.*** **in trust.** In the possession or care of a trustee. [ME *truste*, perh. < ON *traust*, confidence. See **deru-*.**] —**trust′er** *n.*

truss bridge

trust•bust•er (trŭst′bŭs′tər) *n.* One that seeks to prosecute or dissolve business trusts. —**trust′bust′ing** *adj. & n.*

trust company *n.* A commercial bank or other corporation that manages trusts.

trus•tee (trŭ-stē′) *n.* **1.** *Law.* One, such as a bank, that holds legal title to property to administer it for a beneficiary. **2.** A member of a board elected or appointed to direct the funds and policy of an institution. **3.** A country responsible for supervising a trust territory. See Usage Note at **-ee[1].** —*tr. & intr.v.* **-teed, -tee•ing, -tees.** To place (property) in the care of a trustee or to function or serve as a trustee.

trus•tee•ship (trŭ-stē′shĭp′) *n.* **1.** The position or function of a trustee. **2.a.** Administration of a territory by a country or countries so commissioned by the United Nations. **b.** See **trust territory.**

trust•ful (trŭst′fəl) *adj.* Inclined to believe or confide readily; full of trust. —**trust′ful•ly** *adv.* —**trust′ful•ness** *n.*

trust fund *n.* Property, esp. money and securities, held or settled in trust.

trust territory *n.* A colony or territory placed under the administration of a country or countries by the United Nations.

trust•wor•thy (trŭst′wûr′thē) *adj.* **-thi•er, -thi•est.** Warranting trust; reliable. —**trust′wor′thi•ness** *n.*

Sojourner Truth
Photographed c. 1870

trust•y (trŭs′tē) *adj.* **-i•er, -i•est.** Meriting trust; trustworthy. —*n., pl.* **-ies. 1.** A convict regarded as worthy of trust and therefore granted special privileges. **2.** A trusted person. —**trust′i•ly** *adv.* —**trust′i•ness** *n.*

truth (tro͞oth) *n., pl.* **truths** (tro͞o*th*z, tro͞oths). **1.** Conformity to fact or actuality. **2.** A statement proven to be or accepted as true. **3.** Sincerity; integrity. **4.** Fidelity to an original or a standard. **5.** Reality; actuality. [ME *trewthe*, loyalty < OE *trēowth.* See **deru-*.**]

Truth (tro͞oth), **Sojourner.** 1797?–1883. Amer. abolitionist and feminist who was freed from slavery in 1827.

truth•ful (tro͞oth′fəl) *adj.* **1.** Consistently telling the truth; honest. **2.** Corresponding to reality; true. —**truth′ful•ly** *adv.* —**truth′ful•ness** *n.*

truth quark *n.* See **top quark.**

truth serum *n.* Any of various hypnotic or anesthetic drugs, such as scopolamine or thiopental sodium, used to induce a subject under questioning to talk without inhibition.

truth table *n. Logic.* A table that displays the truth-value of a compound sentence as a function of the varying truth-values of its components.

truth-val•ue (tro͞oth′văl′yo͞o) *n. Logic.* The truth or falsity of a statement or sentence.

ă **pat**	oi **boy**
ā **pay**	ou **out**
âr **care**	o͝o **took**
ä **father**	o͞o **boot**
ĕ **pet**	ŭ **cut**
ē **be**	ûr **urge**
ĭ **pit**	th **thin**
ī **pie**	*th* **this**
îr **pier**	hw **which**
ŏ **pot**	zh **vision**
ō **toe**	ə **about,**
ô **paw**	**item**

Stress marks:
′ (primary);
′ (secondary), as in
dictionary (dĭk′shə-nĕr′ē)

try (trī) *v.* **tried** (trīd), **try•ing, tries** (trīz). —*tr.* **1.** To make an effort to do or accomplish (something); attempt. **2.** To taste, sample, or otherwise test in order to determine strength, effect, worth, or desirability. **3.** *Law.* **a.** To examine or hear (evidence or a case) by judicial process. **b.** To put (an accused person) on trial. **4.** To subject to great strain or hardship; tax. **5.** To melt (lard, for example) to separate out impurities; render. **6.** To smooth, fit, or align accurately. —*intr.* To make an effort; strive. —*n., pl.* **tries** (trīz). An attempt; an effort. —***phrasal verbs.*** **try on. 1.** To don (a garment) to test its fit. **2.** To test or use experimentally. **try out. 1.** To undergo a competitive qualifying test, as for a job or an athletic team. **2.** To test or use experimentally. —***idiom.*** **try (one's) hand.** To attempt to do something for the first time. [ME *trien* < OFr. *trier,* to pick out < VLat. **triāre.*]

Usage Note: The phrase *try and* is commonly used as a substitute for *try to,* as in *Could you try and make less noise?* The usage strikes an inappropriately conversational note in formal writing. In the most recent survey 65 percent of the Usage Panel rejected the use in writing of the sentence *Why don't you try and see if you can work the problem out between yourselves?* See Usage Note at **and.**

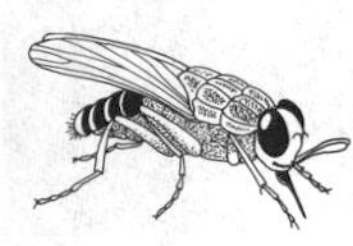
tsetse fly

try•ing (trī′ĭng) *adj.* Causing strain, hardship, or distress.

try•out (trī′out′) *n.* **1.** A test to ascertain the qualifications of applicants, as for an athletic team. **2.** An experimental performance of a play before its official opening.

try•pan•o•some (trĭ-păn′ə-sōm′) *n.* Any of various parasitic flagellate protozoans of the genus *Trypanosoma,* transmitted to vertebrates by certain insects and often causing diseases such as sleeping sickness and nagana. [< NLat. *Trypanosoma,* genus name : Gk. *trupanon,* auger (< *trupan,* to bore < *trupē,* hole; see **terə-¹***) + Gk. *sōma,* body; see -SOME³.]

try•pan•o•so•mi•a•sis (trĭ-păn′ə-sō-mī′ə-sĭs) *n., pl.* **-ses** (-sēz′). A disease or an infection caused by a trypanosome.

tryp•sin (trĭp′sĭn) *n.* An enzyme of pancreatic juice that hydrolyzes proteins to form smaller polypeptide units. [Perh. Gk. *tripsis,* a rubbing (< its having been first obtained by rubbing a pancreas with glycerin) < *tribein,* to rub; see **terə-¹*** + -IN.] —**tryp′tic** (-tĭk) *adj.*

tryp•sin•o•gen (trĭp-sĭn′ə-jən) *n.* The inactive precursor of trypsin, produced by the pancreas and converted to trypsin in the small intestine by enterokinase.

tryp•ta•mine (trĭp′tə-mēn′) *n.* A crystalline substance, $C_{10}H_{12}N_2$, that is formed from tryptophan and is an intermediate in various metabolic processes. [TRYPT(OPHAN) + AMINE.]

tryp•to•phan (trĭp′tə-făn′) also **tryp•to•phane** (-fān′) *n.* An essential amino acid, $C_{11}H_{12}N_2O_2$, formed from proteins during the digestive process by the action of proteolytic enzymes. [*tryptic,* of trypsin; see TRYPSIN + -PHAN(E).]

try•sail (trī′səl, -sāl′) *n. Naut.* A small fore-and-aft sail hoisted abaft the foremast and mainmast in a storm to keep a ship's bow to the wind. [< TRY, a lying to (obsolete).]

try square *n.* A carpenter's measuring tool consisting of a ruled metal straightedge at right angles to a straight piece.

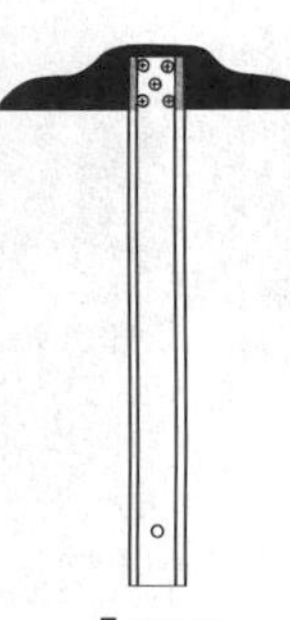
T-square

tryst (trĭst) *n.* **1.** An agreement, as between lovers, to meet at a certain time and place. **2.** A meeting or meeting place that has been agreed on. See Syns at **engagement.** —*intr.v.* **tryst•ed, tryst•ing, trysts.** To keep a tryst. [ME *trist* < OFr. *triste,* a waiting place (in hunting). See **deru-*.**] —**tryst′er** *n.*

T.S. or **t.s.** *abbr.* Tensile strength.

tsa•de (tsä′də, -dē) *n.* Var. of **sadhe.**

Tsa•na (tsä′nə, -nä), **Lake.** See Lake **Tana.**

tsar (zär, tsär) *n.* Var. of **czar** 1. See Usage Note at **czar.**

tsats•ke (tsäts′kə) *n.* Var. of **chachka.**

Tse•lin•o•grad (tsə-lĭn′ə-grăd′, tsĭ-lyĭ-nə-grät′). A city of N-central Kazakhstan NNW of Karaganda. Pop. 262,000.

tset•se disease (tsĕt′sē, tsē′tsē) *n.* See **nagana.**

tsetse fly also **tzet•ze fly** (tsĕt′sē, tsē′tsē) *n.* Any of several two-winged bloodsucking African flies of the genus *Glossina,* often carrying and transmitting pathogenic trypanosomes to human beings and livestock. [Afr. < Sotho (Setswana) *tsêtsê.*]

T.Sgt. *abbr.* Technical sergeant.

TSH *abbr.* Thyroid-stimulating hormone.

Tshi•lu•ba (chĭ-lo͞o′bə) *n.* See **Luba** 2.

T-shirt also **tee shirt** (tē′shûrt′) *n.* **1.** A short-sleeved collarless undershirt. **2.** An outer shirt of a design similar to the T-shirt.

tsim•mes or **tzim•mes** (tsĭm′ĭs) *n.* **1.** A stew of vegetables or fruits cooked slowly over very low heat. **2.** *Informal.* A state of confusion. [Yiddish *tsimes* : MHGer. *ze, zuo,* to, for (< OHGer.; see **de-***) + MHGer. *imbiz,* light meal (< OHGer. < *enbizzan,* to eat : *in,* in; see **en*** + *bīzan, bizzan,* to bite; see **bheid-***).]

Tsi•mshi•an (chĭm′shē-ən, tsĭm′-) *n., pl.* **Tsimshian** or **-ans. 1.** A member of a Native American people inhabiting a coastal area of western British Columbia and extreme southeast Alaska. **2.** The family of languages spoken by the Tsimshian and related peoples.

Tsi•nan (jē′nän′). See **Jinan.**

Tsing•hai (tsĭng′hī′). See **Qinghai.**

Tsing•tao (tsĭng′dou′). See **Qingdao.**

Tsi•tsi•har (tsē′tsē′här′). See **Qiqihar.**

tsk (*a t-like sound produced by suction rather than plosion; conventional spelling pronunciation,* tĭsk) *interj.* Used to express disappointment or sympathy. —*n.* A sucking noise made by suddenly releasing the tongue from the hard palate, used to express disappointment or sympathy. —**tsk** *v.*

tsp. or **tsp** *abbr.* Teaspoon; teaspoonful.

T-square (tē′skwâr′) *n.* A rule having a short, sometimes sliding perpendicular crosspiece at one end, used by drafters for establishing and drawing parallel lines.

TSS *abbr.* Toxic shock syndrome.

Tsu•ga•ru Strait (tso͞o-gä′ro͞o). A channel between Honshu and Hokkaido in N Japan.

tsu•na•mi (tso͞o-nä′mē) *n., pl.* **-mis.** A very large ocean wave caused by an underwater earthquake or volcanic eruption. [J. : *tsu,* port + *nami,* wave.] —**tsu•na′mic** *adj.*

tsu•ris also **tzu•ris** (tso͝or′ĭs, tsûr′-) *n. Informal.* Trouble; aggravation. [Yiddish *tsores,* pl. of *tsure* < Heb. *ṣarā.*]

Tsu•shi•ma (tso͞o-shē′mə, tso͞o′shē-mä′). Two islands of SW Japan separated from Kyushu by **Tsushima Strait.**

tsu•tsu•ga•mu•shi disease (tso͞o′tso͞o-gə-mo͞o′shē) *n.* See **scrub typhus.** [J. *tsutsugamushi,* typhus mite : *tsutsuga,* illness + *mushi,* tick.]

Tswa•na (tswä′nə, swä′-) *n., pl.* **Tswana** or **-nas. 1.** A member of a Bantu people inhabiting Botswana and western South Africa. **2.** The Sotho language of the Tswana.

Tt *abbr. Bible.* Titus.

TT *abbr.* **1.** Teletypewriter. **2.** Trust territory.

Tu. *abbr.* Tuesday.

T.U. *abbr.* **1.** Trade union. **2.** Transmission unit.

Tu•a•mo•tu Archipelago (to͞o′ə-mō′to͞o). An island group of French Polynesia in the S Pacific E of Tahiti.

Tuan (twän) *n.* Used in Malay as a form of respectful address for a man. [Malay.]

Tua•reg (twä′rĕg′) *n., pl.* **Tuareg** or **-regs.** A member of a Muslim Berber-speaking people inhabiting the western and central Sahara and western Sahel. [Ar. *Tawāriq.*]

tu•a•ta•ra (to͞o′ə-tär′ə) *n.* A lizardlike reptile *(Sphenodon punctatus)* of New Zealand, the sole extant member of the Rhynchocephalia, an order that flourished during the Mesozoic Era. [Maori *tuatàra* : *tua,* back + *tàra,* spine.]

tub (tŭb) *n.* **1.a.** An open flatbottom vessel, usu. round and typically wider than it is deep, used for washing, packing, or storing. **b.** The amount that such a vessel can hold. **c.** The contents of such a vessel. **2.a.** A bathtub. **b.** *Informal.* A bath taken in a bathtub. **3.** *Informal.* A wide, clumsy, slow-moving boat. **4.a.** A bucket used for conveying ore or coal up a mine shaft. **b.** A coal car used in a mine. —*v.* **tubbed, tub•bing, tubs.** —*tr.* **1.** To pack or store in a tub. **2.** To wash or bathe in a tub. —*intr.* To take a bath. [ME < MDu. or MLGer.] —**tub′ba•ble** *adj.* —**tub′ber** *n.*

tu•ba (to͞o′bə, tyo͞o′-) *n. Mus.* A large valved brass wind instrument with a bass pitch. [Ital. < Lat., trumpet; akin to *tubus,* tube.] —**tu′ba•ist, tu′bist** *n.*

tu•bal (to͞o′bəl, tyo͞o′-) *adj.* Of, relating to, or occurring in a tube, such as the fallopian tube or the eustachian tube.

tubal ligation *n.* A method of sterilization in which the fallopian tubes are surgically tied.

tu•bate (to͞o′bāt′, tyo͞o′-) *adj.* Forming or having a tube.

tub•by (tŭb′ē) *adj.* **-bi•er, -bi•est. 1.** Short and fat. **2.** Having a dull sound; lacking resonance. —**tub′bi•ness** *n.*

tube (to͞ob, tyo͞ob) *n.* **1.a.** A hollow cylinder, esp. one that conveys a fluid or functions as a passage. **b.** An organic structure having the shape or function of a tube; a duct: *a bronchial tube.* **2.** A small flexible cylindrical container sealed at one end and having a screw cap at the other, for pigments, toothpaste, or other pastelike substances. **3.** *Mus.* The cylindrical part of a wind instrument. **4.** *Electron.* **a.** An electron tube. **b.** A vacuum tube. **5.** *Bot.* The lower cylindrical part of a gamopetalous corolla or a gamosepalous calyx. **6.** *Chiefly British.* A subway; an underground. **7.** A tunnel. **8.** An inner tube. **9.** *Slang.* **a.** Television. **b.** A television set. —*v.* **tubed, tub•ing, tubes.** —*tr.* **1.** To provide with a tube; insert a tube in. **2.** To place in or enclose in a tube. —***idiom.*** **down the tubes (or tube).** *Slang.* Into a state of failure or ruin. [Fr. < OFr. < Lat. *tubus.*]

tube foot *n.* One of the numerous external fluid-filled muscular tubes of echinoderms, such as the starfish or sea urchin, serving as organs of locomotion, food handling, and respiration.

tube•less tire (to͞ob′lĭs, tyo͞ob′-) *n.* A pneumatic vehicular tire in which the air is held in the assembly of casing and rim without an inner tube.

tube pan *n.* A round pan with a hollow cylinder or cone in the middle, used for baking or molding foods in ring shape.

tu•ber (to͞o′bər, tyo͞o′-) *n.* **1.** *Bot.* A swollen, fleshy, usu. underground stem, such as the potato, bearing buds from which new plant shoots arise. **2.** *Biol.* A rounded projection or swelling; a tubercle. [Lat. *tūber,* lump. See **teuə-*.**]

tu•ber•cle (to͞o′bər-kəl, tyo͞o′-) *n.* **1.** *Pathol.* A nodule or swelling, esp. a mass of lymphocytes and epithelioid cells forming the characteristic lesion of tuberculosis. **2.** A small rounded prominence or process, such as a wartlike excrescence on the roots of some leguminous plants. [Lat. *tūberculum,* dim. of *tūber,* lump. See TUBER.]

tubercle bacillus *n.* A rod-shaped aerobic bacterium *(Mycobacterium tuberculosis)* that causes tuberculosis.

tu•ber•cu•lar (to͞o-bûr′kyə-lər, tyo͞o-) *adj.* **1.** Of, relating to, or covered with tubercles; tuberculate. **2.** Of, relating to, or affected with tuberculosis. —*n.* A person having tuberculosis.

tu•ber•cu•late (to͞o-bûr′kyə-lĭt, tyo͞o-) also **tu•ber•cu•la•ted** (-lā′tĭd) *adj.* **1.** Having or affected with tubercles. **2.** Tubercular. —**tu•ber′cu•late•ly** *adv.* —**tu•ber′cu•la′tion** *n.*

tu•ber•cu•lin (to͞o-bûr′kyə-lĭn, tyo͞o-) *n.* A sterile liquid containing proteins extracted from cultures of tubercle bacilli and used in tests for tuberculosis. [Lat. *tūberculum*, tubercle; see TUBERCLE + -IN.]

tu•ber•cu•loid (to͞o-bûr′kyə-loid′, tyo͞o-) *adj.* **1.** Resembling tuberculosis. **2.** Resembling a tubercle.

tu•ber•cu•lo•sis (to͞o-bûr′kyə-lō′sĭs, tyo͞o-) *n.* **1.** An infectious disease of humans and animals caused by the tubercle bacillus and characterized by the formation of tubercles on the lungs and other tissues of the body, often developing long after the initial infection. **2.** Tuberculosis of the lungs, marked by fever and the coughing up of mucus and sputum. [Lat. *tūberculum*, tubercle; see TUBERCLE + -OSIS.]

tu•ber•cu•lous (to͞o-bûr′kyə-ləs, tyo͞o-) *adj.* **1.** Of, relating to, or having tuberculosis. **2.** Of, affected with, or caused by tubercles. —**tu•ber′cu•lous•ly** *adv.*

tube•rose[1] (to͞ob′rōz′, tyo͞ob′-, to͞o′bə-) *n.* A tuberous perennial Mexican herb *(Polianthes tuberosa)* having grasslike leaves and cultivated for its highly fragrant white flowers. [< NLat. *tūberōsa*, species name < fem. of Lat. *tūberōsus*, full of lumps < *tūber*, lump. See TUBER.]

tu•ber•ose[2] (to͞o′bə-rōs′, tyo͞o′-) *adj.* Var. of **tuberous.**

tu•ber•os•i•ty (to͞o′bə-rŏs′ĭ-tē, tyo͞o′-) *n., pl.* **-ties. 1.** The quality or condition of being tuberous. **2.** A projection or protuberance, esp. one at the end of a bone for the attachment of a muscle or tendon.

tu•ber•ous (to͞o′bər-əs, tyo͞o′-) also **tu•ber•ose** (-bə-rōs′) *adj.* **1.** Producing or bearing tubers. **2.** Being or resembling a tuber: *a tuberous root.*

tu•bi•fex (to͞o′bə-fĕks′, tyo͞o′-) *n., pl.* **tubifex** or **-fex•es.** Any of various small slender reddish freshwater worms of the genus *Tubifex*. [NLat. *Tubifex*, genus name : Lat. *tubus*, tube + Lat. *-fex*, maker; see **dhē-*.**]

tub•ing (to͞o′bĭng, tyo͞o′-) *n.* **1.a.** Tubes considered as a group. **b.** A system of tubes. **c.** A piece or length of tube. **2.** Tubular fabric, such as that used for making pillowcases.

Tü•bing•en (to͞o′bĭng-ən, tü′-). A city of SW Germany on the Neckar R. S of Stuttgart. Pop. 75,333.

Tub•man (tŭb′mən), **Harriet.** 1820?–1913. Amer. abolitionist who helped organize the Underground Railroad.

Tubman, William Vacanarat Shadrach. 1895–1971. Liberian politician who served as president (1944–71).

tu•bo•cu•ra•rine (to͞o′bō-ko͞o-rä′rĭn, -rēn′, -kyo͞o, tyo͞o′-) *n.* **1.** An alkaloid that is the active component of curare. **2.** The chloride of this alkaloid, $C_{38}H_{44}Cl_2N_2O_6$, used as a muscle relaxant. [Lat. *tubus*, tube (< the practice of shipping it in bamboo tubes) + *curarine* (CURARE + -INE[2]).]

tu•bo•plas•ty (to͞o′bō-plăs′tē, tyo͞o′-) *n., pl.* **-ties.** Surgical repair of one or both fallopian tubes.

tub-thump (tŭb′thŭmp′) *intr.v.* **-thumped, -thump•ing, -thumps.** *Slang.* To argue for or promote something vigorously. —**tub′-thump′er** *n.*

tu•bu•lar (to͞o′byə-lər, tyo͞o′-) *adj.* **1.** Of or relating to a tube. **2.** Constituting or consisting of tubes or a tube. **3.** Shaped like a tube. —**tu′bu•lar′i•ty** (-lăr′ĭ-tē) *n.* —**tu′bu•lar•ly** *adv.*

tu•bu•late (to͞o′byə-lĭt, -lāt′, tyo͞o′-) also **tu•bu•lat•ed** (-lā′tĭd) *adj.* **1.** Formed into or resembling a tube; tubular. **2.** Having a tube. [Lat. *tubulātus* < *tubulus*, dim. of *tubus*, tube.] —**tu′bu•la′tion** *n.* —**tu′bu•la′tor** *n.*

tu•bule (to͞o′byo͞ol, tyo͞o′-) *n.* A very small tube or tubular structure. [Lat. *tubulus*, dim. of *tubus*, tube.]

tu•bu•li•flo•rous (to͞o′byə-lə-flôr′əs, -flōr′-, tyo͞o′-) *adj.* Having flowers or florets with tubular corollas.

tu•bu•lin (to͞o′byə-lĭn, tyo͞o′-) *n.* A globular protein that is the basic structural constituent of microtubules.

tu•bu•lous (to͞o′byə-ləs, tyo͞o′-) *adj.* **1.** Shaped like a tube; tubular. **2.a.** Composed of tubes. **b.** Having tubular parts.

Tu•ca•na (to͞o-kā′nə, -kä′-, tyo͞o-) *n.* A polar constellation in the Southern Hemisphere. [Tupi *tucana*, toucan.]

Tuch•man (tŭck′mən), **Barbara Wertheim.** 1912–89. Amer. historian whose works include *The Guns of August* (1962).

tu•chun (to͞o′cho͞on′, do͞o′jün′) *n., pl.* **-chuns** or **tuchun.** A Chinese provincial military governor. [Chin. (Mandarin) *dū jūn* : *dū*, to supervise + *jūn*, army.]

tuck[1] (tŭk) *v.* **tucked, tuck•ing, tucks.** —*tr.* **1.** To make one fold or several folds in. **2.** To gather up and fold, thrust, or turn in so as to secure or confine. **3.a.** To put in a snug spot. **b.** To put in an out-of-the-way, snug place. **c.** To store in a safe spot; save. **4.a.** To draw in; contract. **b.** *Sports.* To bring (a body part) into a tuck position. —*intr.* To make tucks. —*n.* **1.** The act of tucking. **2.** A flattened pleat or fold, esp. a very narrow one stitched in place. **3.** *Naut.* The part of a ship's hull under the stern where the ends of the bottom planks come together. **4.** *Sports.* **a.** A mid-air position in sports such as diving in which the contestant bends the knees, draws the thighs close to the chest, and clasps the hands around the shins. **b.** A position in skiing in which the skier squats while holding the poles parallel to the ground and under the arms. **5.** *Chiefly British.* Food, esp. sweets and pastry. —***phrasal verbs.* tuck away.** *Informal.* To consume (food) heartily. **tuck in.** To make secure in bed for sleep, esp. by tucking bedclothes into the bed. [ME *tukken*, poss. < MLGer. or MDu. *tocken, tucken.*]

tuck[2] (tŭk) *n.* A beat or tap, esp. on a drum. [< ME *tukken*, to beat a drum < ONFr. *toquer*, to strike < VLat. **toccāre.*]

tuck[3] (tŭk) *n. Archaic.* A slender sword; a rapier. [Perh. < Fr. dial. *étoc* < OFr. *estoc*, of Gmc. orig.]

tuck[4] (tŭk) *n.* Energy; vigor. [?]

tuck•a•hoe (tŭk′ə-hō′) *n.* Any of various plants or plant parts used by certain Native American peoples as food, esp. the edible root of certain arums or the sclerotium of certain fungi. [Of Virginia Algonquian orig.]

tuck•er[1] (tŭk′ər) *n.* **1.** One that tucks, esp. an attachment on a sewing machine for making tucks. **2.** A piece of linen or lace formerly worn by women around the neck and shoulders.

tuck•er[2] (tŭk′ər) *tr.v.* **-ered, -er•ing, -ers.** *Informal.* To make weary; exhaust. [Perh. < TUCK[1].]

tuck•et (tŭk′ĭt) *n. Mus.* A trumpet fanfare. [Prob. < obsolete *tuk* < ME < *tukken*, to beat a drum. See TUCK[2].]

tuck-point (tŭk′point′) *tr.v.* **-point•ed, -point•ing, -points.** To point (grooved mortar joints) with a thin ridge of fine lime mortar or putty.

tuck-shop (tŭk′shŏp′) *n. Chiefly British.* A shop where candy and other sweets are sold; a confectionery.

Tuc•son (to͞o′sŏn′). A city of SE AZ SSE of Phoenix; first settled permanently in 1775. Pop. 405,390.

-tude *suff.* Condition, state, or quality: *exactitude.* [Fr. < OFr. < Lat. *-tūdō, -tūdin-.*]

Tu•dor[1] (to͞o′dər, tyo͞o′-). English ruling dynasty (1485–1603).

Tu•dor[2] (to͞o′dər, tyo͞o′-) *adj.* **1.** Of or relating to the royal house of Tudor. **2.** Of, relating to, or characteristic of the Tudor period or of an architectural style derived from it, having exposed beams as a typical feature.

Tudor, Antony. 1909–87. British-born Amer. dancer and choreographer whose ballets include *Undertow* (1945).

Tues•day (to͞oz′dē, -dā′, tyo͞oz′-) *n.* The third day of the week. [ME *Tuesdai* < OE *Tīwesdæg*, Tiu's day : *Tīwes*, genitive of *Tīw*, Tiu; see TIU + *dæg*, day; see DAY (transl. of Lat. *diēs Mārtis*, Mars' day).]

tu•fa (to͞o′fə, tyo͞o′-) *n.* **1.** The calcareous and siliceous rock deposits of springs, lakes, or ground water. **2.** See **tuff.** [Obsolete Ital. *tufo, tufa* < Lat. *tōfus*.] —**tu•fa′ceous** *adj.*

tuff (tŭf) *n.* A rock of compacted volcanic ash varying in size from fine sand to coarse gravel. [Fr. *tuf* < OFr. < OItal. *tufo*, tufa. See TUFA.] —**tuff•a′ceous** (tŭ-fā′shəs) *adj.*

tuf•fet (tŭf′ĭt) *n.* **1.** A clump or tuft of grass. **2.** A low seat, such as a stool. [Alteration of TUFT.]

tuft (tŭft) *n.* **1.** A short cluster of elongated strands, as of yarn, hair, or grass, attached at the base or growing close together. **2.** A dense clump, esp. of trees or bushes. **3.** A goatee. —*v.* **tuft•ed, tuft•ing, tufts.** —*tr.* **1.** To furnish or ornament with tufts or a tuft. **2.** To pass threads through the layers of (a quilt, a mattress, or upholstery), securing the thread ends with a knot or button. —*intr.* **1.** To separate or form into tufts. **2.** To grow in a tuft. [ME, prob. alteration of OFr. *tofe* < LLat. *tufa*, helmet crest, or of Gmc. orig.] —**tuft′er** *n.* —**tuft′y** *adj.*

tuft•ed duck (tŭf′tĭd) *n.* An Old World duck *(Aythya fuligula)* having a short plump body and a crest on its head.

tufted titmouse *n.* A bluish-gray titmouse *(Parus bicolor)* of the eastern and southern United States, having brown flanks and a crest on its head.

tug (tŭg) *v.* **tugged, tug•ging, tugs.** —*tr.* **1.** To pull at vigorously; strain at. **2.** To move by pulling with great effort or exertion; drag. **3.** *Naut.* To tow by tugboat. —*intr.* **1.** To pull hard. See Syns at **pull. 2.** To toil or struggle; strain. **3.** To vie; contend. —*n.* **1.** A strong pull or pulling force. **2.** A contest; a struggle. **3.a.** *Naut.* A tugboat. **b.** A land, air, or space vehicle that moves or tows other vehicles. **4.** A rope, chain, or strap used in hauling, esp. a harness trace. [ME *tuggen* < OE *tēon*. See **deuk-*.**] —**tug′ger** *n.*

tug•boat (tŭg′bōt′) *n. Naut.* A small powerful boat designed for towing or pushing larger vessels.

tug of war *n., pl.* **tugs of war. 1.** *Games.* A contest in which two teams tug on opposite ends of a rope, each trying to pull the other across a dividing line. **2.** A struggle for supremacy.

tu•grik (to͞o′grĭk) *n.* See table at **currency.** [Mongolian *dughurik*, wheel, tugrik.]

tu•i (to͞o′ē) *n., pl.* **-is.** A honeyeater *(Prosthemadera novaeseelandiae)* of New Zealand having dark plumage with white feathers on the throat. [Maori *tūī.*]

tuille (twēl) *n.* A steel plate used in medieval armor for protecting the thigh. [ME *toile* < OFr. *teuille, tuille* < Lat. *tēgula*, tile. See **(s)teg-*.**]

tu•i•tion (to͞o-ĭsh′ən, tyo͞o-) *n.* **1.** A fee for instruction, esp. at

tuberose[1]
Polianthes tuberosa

Harriet Tubman

ă pat	oi boy
ā pay	ou out
âr care	o͝o took
ä father	o͞o boot
ĕ pet	ŭ cut
ē be	ûr urge
ĭ pit	th thin
ī pie	*th* this
îr pier	hw which
ŏ pot	zh vision
ō toe	ə about,
ô paw	item

Stress marks:
′ (primary);
′ (secondary), as in
dictionary (dĭk′shə-nĕr′ē)

a formal institution of learning. **2.** Instruction; teaching. **3.** *Archaic.* Guardianship. [ME *tuicion*, protection < OFr. *tuition* < Lat. *tuitiō, tuitiōn-* < *tuitus*, p.part. of *tuērī*, to protect.] **—tu·i′tion·al, tu·i′tion·ar′y** (-ĭsh′ə-nĕr′ē) *adj.*

Tu·la (to͞o′lə). A city of W Russia S of Moscow; first mentioned in 1146. Pop. 532,000.

Tu·lare (to͞o-lâr′ē, -lâr′). A city of S-central CA SE of Fresno in the San Joaquin Valley. Pop. 33,249.

tu·la·re·mi·a (to͞o′lə-rē′mē-ə, tyo͞o′-) *n.* An infectious disease of rodents and humans caused by the bacterium *Francisella tularensis* that in humans is characterized by intermittent fever and swelling of the lymph nodes. [NLat., after *Tulare*, a county of S-central CA.] **—tu′la·re′mic** *adj.*

tu·le (to͞o′lē) *n.* **1.** Any of several bulrushes of the genus *Scirpus,* growing in marshy lowlands of the southwest United States. **2. tu·les** (to͞o′lēz). *Northern California.* Marshy or swampy land. Also called regionally *tule land.* [Am.Sp. < Nahuatl *tollin*, reed.]

Regional Note: Low swampy land is *tules* in the parlance of northern California. The Spanish word *tule,* from Nahuatl *tollin,* "bulrush," was borrowed by the English-speaking settlers of the West to refer to certain varieties of bulrushes native to California. Eventually the meaning of the word was extended to the marshy land where they grew.

tulip

tu·lip (to͞o′lĭp, tyo͞o′-) *n.* **1.** Any of several bulbous plants of the genus *Tulipa,* native chiefly to Asia and having showy, variously colored flowers. **2.** The flower of any of these plants. [Fr. *tulipe*, alteration of *tulipan* < Ottoman Turk. *tülbend*, muslin, gauze, turban.]

tulip tree *n.* A tall deciduous eastern North American tree *(Liriodendron tulipifera)* having large tuliplike green and orange flowers, aromatic twigs, and yellowish, easily worked wood.

tu·lip·wood (to͞o′lĭp-wo͝od′, tyo͞o′-) *n.* **1.** The wood of the tulip tree. **2.** The irregularly striped ornamental wood of any of several related or similar trees.

tulle (to͞ol) *n.* A fine, often starched net used esp. for veils, tutus, or gowns. [Fr., after *Tulle*, a city of S-central France.]

tul·li·bee (tŭl′ə-bē′) *n.* A large thick-backed cisco *(Coregonus artedi* or *Leucichthys artedi)* of the Great Lakes. [Canadian Fr. *toulibi* < Ojibwa dial. **oto·lipi·*.]

Tul·sa (tŭl′sə). A city of NE OK on the Arkansas R. NE of Oklahoma City. Pop. 367,302.

tum·ble (tŭm′bəl) *v.* **-bled, -bling, -bles.** *—intr.* **1.** To perform acrobatic feats such as somersaults, rolls, or twists. **2.a.** To fall or roll end over end. **b.** To spill or roll out in confusion or disorder. **c.** To pitch headlong; fall. **d.** To proceed haphazardly. **3.a.** To topple, as from power or a high position; fall. **b.** To collapse. **c.** To drop. **4.** To come upon accidentally; happen on. **5.** *Slang.* To come to a sudden understanding; catch on. *—tr.* **1.** To cause to fall; bring down. **2.** To put, spill, or toss haphazardly. **3.** To toss or whirl in a drum, tumbler, or tumbling box. *—n.* **1.** An act of tumbling; a fall. **2.** Confusion; disorder. [ME *tumblen*, freq. of *tumben*, to dance about < OE *tumbian*.]

tum·ble·bug (tŭm′bəl-bŭg′) *n.* Any of various dung beetles, esp. of the genera *Canthon* and *Phanaeus,* that roll up balls of fresh dung, inside which the female deposits her eggs.

tum·ble·down (tŭm′bəl-doun′) *adj.* Being in such bad repair as to seem in danger of collapsing; very dilapidated.

tum·ble·home (tŭm′bəl-hōm′) *n. Naut.* The inward curve of a ship's topsides. [< TUMBLE, to slope inward (obsolete).]

tum·bler (tŭm′blər) *n.* **1.** One that tumbles, esp. an acrobat or a gymnast. **2.a.** A drinking glass, originally with a rounded bottom. **b.** A flatbottom glass having no handle, foot, or stem. **c.** The contents of such a drinking glass. **3.** A toy made with a weighted rounded base so that it can rock over and then right itself. **4.** One of a breed of domestic pigeons characteristically tumbling or somersaulting in flight. **5.** A piece in a gunlock that forces the hammer forward by action of the mainspring. **6.** The part in a lock that releases the bolt when moved by a key. **7.a.** The drum of a clothes dryer. **b.** A tumbling box. **8.a.** A projecting piece on a revolving or rocking part in a mechanism that transmits motion to the part it engages. **b.** The rocking frame that moves a gear into place in a selective transmission.

tulip tree
Liriodendron tulipifera

tumbleset (tŭm′bəl-sĕt′) *n. Lower Southern U.S.* See **somersault** 1. [Blend of TUMBLE and *somerset* (alteration of *somersaut*, var. of SOMERSAULT).]

Regional Note: In the Lower Southern word *tumbleset* for *somersault –set* at first glance seems not to have any relationship to *–sault* in *somersault*. However, *–set* is an old *l*-less variant of *–sault* (from Latin *saltus,* "a leap") that has been an alternative pronunciation throughout the word's history; hence, the variant *somerset. Somer–* is an alteration of Old French *sobre–*, from Latin *supra,* "over." In the word *tumbleset,* as in a folk etymology, *somer–*, part of a compound word that no longer bears any meaning for the speakers, has been replaced by *tumble.*

tum·ble·weed (tŭm′bəl-wēd′) *n.* Any of various densely branched annual plants, such as amaranth and Russian thistle, that break off from the roots at the end of the growing season and are rolled about by the wind.

tum·bling (tŭm′blĭng) *n. Sports.* Gymnastics, such as somersaults and rolls, performed without specialized apparatus.

tumbling box *n.* A revolving drum in which objects are dried, reduced in size, polished, or cleaned.

tum·brel or **tum·bril** (tŭm′brəl) *n.* **1.** A two-wheeled cart, esp. a farmer's cart that can be tilted to dump a load. **2.** A crude cart used to carry condemned prisoners to their place of execution, as during the French Revolution. [ME *tumberell* < OFr. *tomberel* < *tomber*, to let fall, perh. of Gmc. orig.]

tu·me·fa·cient (to͞o′mə-fā′shənt, tyo͞o′-) *adj.* Producing or tending to produce swelling or tumefaction. [Lat. *tumefaciēns, tumefacient-*, pr.part. of *tumefacere*, to tumefy : *tumēre*, to swell; see **teuə-*** + *facere*, to make; see **dhē-***.]

tu·me·fac·tion (to͞o′mə-făk′shən, tyo͞o′-) *n.* **1.a.** The act or process of puffing or swelling. **b.** A swollen condition. **2.** A puffy or swollen part. **—tu′me·fac′tive** (-tĭv) *adj.*

tu·me·fy (to͞o′mə-fī′, tyo͞o′-) *intr. & tr.v.* **-fied** (-fīd′), **-fy·ing, -fies** (-fīz′). To swell or cause to swell. [Fr. *tuméfier* < Lat. *tumefacere.* See TUMEFACIENT.]

tu·mes·cence (to͞o-mĕs′əns, tyo͞o-) *n.* **1.a.** A swelling or an enlarging. **b.** A swollen condition. **2.** A swollen part or organ.

tu·mes·cent (to͞o-mĕs′ənt, tyo͞o-) *adj.* **1.** Somewhat tumid. **2.** Becoming swollen; swelling. [Lat. *tumēscēns, tumēscent-*, pr.part. of *tumēscere*, to begin to swell, inchoative of *tumēre*, to swell. See **teuə-***.]

tu·mid (to͞o′mĭd, tyo͞o′-) *adj.* **1.** Swollen; distended. Used of a body part or organ. **2.** Of a bulging shape; protuberant. **3.** Overblown; bombastic. [Lat. *tumidus* < *tumēre*, to swell. See **teuə-***.] **—tu·mid′i·ty, tu′mid·ness** *n.*

tumm·ler (to͝om′lər) *n.* **1.** One, such as a social director or an entertainer, who encourages guest or audience participation. **2.** One who incites others to action. [Yiddish *tumler* < *tumlen*, to make a racket.]

tum·my (tŭm′ē) *n., pl.* **-mies.** *Informal.* The human stomach or belly. [Baby-talk alteration of STOMACH.]

tu·mor (to͞o′mər, tyo͞o′-) *n.* **1.** An abnormal growth of tissue resulting from uncontrolled progressive multiplication of cells and serving no physiological function; a neoplasm. **2.** A swollen part; a swelling. [ME *tumour* < Lat. *tumor* < *tumēre*, to swell. See **teuə-***.] **—tu′mor·al, tu′mor·ous** *adj.*

tu·mor·i·gen·e·sis (to͞o′mər-ə-jĕn′ĭ-sĭs, tyo͞o′-) *n., pl.* **-ses** (-sēz′). Formation or production of tumors.

tu·mor·i·gen·ic (to͞o′mər-ə-jĕn′ĭk, tyo͞o′-) *adj.* Capable of causing tumors. **—tu′mor·i·ge·nic′i·ty** (-jə-nĭs′ĭ-tē) *n.*

tumor necrosis factor *n.* A protein produced by macrophages in the presence of an endotoxin and shown experimentally to be capable of attacking and destroying cancerous tumors.

tump[1] (tŭmp) *v.* **tumped, tump·ing, tumps.** *—tr.* To overturn. Often used with *over.* *—intr.* To fall over. Often used with *over.* [Prob. akin to TUMBLE.]

tump[2] (tŭmp) *n.* **1.** A mound. **2.** A clump of trees, shrubs, or grass. [?]

tump·line (tŭmp′līn′) *n.* A strap slung across the forehead or the chest to support a load carried on the back. [*tump* (alteration of *mattump*, of Southern New England Algonquian orig.) + LINE[1].]

tu·mu·lar (to͞o′myə-lər, tyo͞o′-) *adj.* Relating to or having the shape of a tumulus.

tu·mu·lose (to͞o′myə-lōs′, tyo͞o′-) also **tu·mu·lous** (-ləs) *adj.* Having many mounds or small hills. [Lat. *tumulōsus* < *tumulus*. See TUMULUS.] **—tu′mu·los′i·ty** (-lŏs′ĭ-tē) *n.*

tu·mult (to͞o′mŭlt′, tyo͞o′-) *n.* **1.** The din and commotion of a great crowd. **2.a.** A disorderly commotion or disturbance. **b.** A tempestuous uprising; a riot. **3.** Agitation of the mind or emotions. [ME *tumulte* < Lat. *tumultus*.]

tu·mul·tu·ar·y (to͞o-mŭl′cho͞o-ĕr′ē, tyo͞o-) *adj.* Marked by haste, confusion, disorder, and irregularity. [Lat. *tumultuārius* < *tumultus*, commotion. See TUMULT.]

tu·mul·tu·ous (to͞o-mŭl′cho͞o-əs, tyo͞o-) *adj.* **1.** Characterized by tumult; noisy and disorderly: *tumultuous applause.* **2.** Tending to cause tumult. **3.** Confusedly or violently agitated. **—tu·mul′tu·ous·ly** *adv.* **—tu·mul′tu·ous·ness** *n.*

tu·mu·lus (to͞o′myə-ləs, tyo͞o′-) *n., pl.* **-li** (-lī′). An ancient grave mound; a barrow. [Lat. See **teuə-***.]

tun (tŭn) *n.* **1.** A large cask for liquids, esp. wine. **2.** A measure of liquid capacity, esp. one equivalent to approx. 252 gallons (954 liters). [ME < OE *tunne*, poss. of Celt. orig.]

Tun. *abbr.* Tunisia; Tunisian.

tu·na[1] (to͞o′nə, tyo͞o′-) *n., pl.* **tuna** or **-nas. 1.a.** Any of various often large scombroid marine food and game fishes of the genus *Thunnus* and related genera, many of which, including *T. thynnus* and the albacore, are commercially important sources of canned fish. **b.** Any of several related fishes, such as the bonito. **2.** The edible flesh of tuna. [Am.Sp. < Sp. *atún* < Ar. *at-tūn*, the tuna < Lat. *thunnus*. See TUNNY.]

tu·na[2] (to͞o′nə, tyo͞o′-) *n.* **1.** Any of several flat-jointed tropical American cacti of the genus *Opuntia,* esp. *O. tuna,* having yellow flowers and edible red fruit. **2.** The edible fruit of any of these cacti. [Am.Sp. < Taino.]

tun·a·ble also **tune·a·ble** (to͞o′nə-bəl, tyo͞o′-) *adj.* **1.** That can be tuned: *a tunable wind instrument; a tunable radio.* **2.** *Archaic.* Tuneful. **—tun′a·ble·ness** *n.* **—tun′a·bly** *adv.*

tuna fish *n.* See **tuna**[1] 2.
tun•dra (tŭnʹdrə) *n.* A treeless area between the icecap and the tree line of Arctic regions, having a permanently frozen subsoil and supporting low-growing vegetation. [Russ. < Sami *tūndar*, flat-topped hill.]
tune (to͞on, tyo͞on) *n.* **1.** *Mus.* **a.** A melody, esp. a simple and easily remembered one. **b.** A song. **c.** Correct pitch. **d.** The state of being properly adjusted for pitch. **e.** Agreement in pitch. **f.** *Obsolete.* A musical tone. **2.a.** Concord or agreement; harmony. **b.** *Archaic.* Frame of mind; disposition. **3.** *Electron.* Adjustment of a receiver or circuit for maximum response to a given signal or frequency. —*v.* **tuned, tun•ing, tunes.** —*tr.* **1.a.** *Mus.* To put into proper pitch. **b.** *Archaic.* To utter musically; sing. **2.** To adopt or adjust, esp. to bring into harmony. **3.** *Electron.* **a.** To adjust (a receiver) to a desired frequency. **b.** To adjust (a circuit) so as to make it resonant with a given input signal. **4.** To adjust (an engine, for example) for maximum usability or performance. —*intr.* To become attuned. —***phrasal verbs.*** **tune in. 1.** *Electron.* To adjust a receiver to receive signals at a particular frequency or a particular program. **2.** *Slang.* To make or become aware or responsive. **tune out. 1.** *Electron.* To adjust a receiver so as not to receive a particular signal. **2.** *Slang.* **a.** To disassociate oneself from one's environment. **b.** To become unresponsive to; ignore. **tune up. 1.** *Mus.* To adjust an instrument to a desired pitch or key. **2.** To adjust a machine so as to put it into proper condition. **3.** To prepare (oneself) for a specified activity. —***idiom.*** **to the tune of.** To the sum or extent of. [ME, var. of *tone*, tone. See TONE.]
tune•ful (to͞onʹfəl, tyo͞onʹ-) *adj.* **1.** Full of tune; melodious. **2.** Producing musical sounds. —**tuneʹful•ly** *adv.* —**tuneʹful•ness** *n.*
tune•less (to͞onʹlĭs, tyo͞onʹ-) *adj.* **1.** Deficient in melody; not tuneful. **2.** Producing no music; silent. —**tuneʹless•ness** *n.*
tun•er (to͞oʹnər, tyo͞oʹ-) *n.* **1.** One that tunes: *a piano tuner.* **2.** A device for tuning, esp. an electronic circuit or device used to select signals at a specific radio frequency for amplification and conversion to sound.
tune•smith (to͞onʹsmĭthʹ, tyo͞onʹ-) *n. Mus.* One who composes melodies, esp. for popular songs.
tune-up (to͞onʹŭpʹ, tyo͞onʹ-) *n.* An adjustment, as of a motor or an engine, made to improve working order or efficiency.
tung oil (tŭng) *n.* A yellow or brownish oil extracted from the seeds of the tung tree and used as a drying agent in varnishes and paints and for waterproofing.
tung•state (tŭngʹstātʹ) *n.* A salt of tungstic acid.
tung•sten (tŭngʹstən) *n. Symbol* **W** A hard brittle corrosion-resistant metallic element extracted from wolframite, scheelite, and other minerals, having the highest melting point of any metal and used, along with its alloys, in high-temperature structural materials and in electrical elements, notably lamp filaments. Atomic number 74; atomic weight 183.85; melting point 3,410°C; boiling point 5,900°C; specific gravity 19.3 (20°C); valence 2, 3, 4, 5, 6. See table at **element.** [Swed. : *tung*, heavy (< ON *thungr*) + *sten*, stone (< ON *steinn*; see **stei-***).] —**tung•stenʹic** (-stĕnʹĭk) *adj.*
tungsten carbide *n.* A very hard fine powder, WC, used in tools, dies, wear-resistant machine parts, and abrasives.
tungsten lamp *n.* An incandescent electric lamp with a tungsten filament.
tungsten steel *n.* A very hard heat-resistant steel containing tungsten.
tung•stic (tŭngʹstĭk) *adj.* Of, relating to, or containing tungsten, esp. with valence 6.
tungstic acid *n.* A yellow powder, H_2WO_4, used in textiles and plastics.
tung tree *n.* Any of several eastern Asian trees of the genus *Aleurites*, esp. *A. montana* and *A. fordii*, whose seeds yield a commercially valuable drying oil. [Chin. (Mandarin) *tóng*.]
Tun•gus (to͝ong-go͞ozʹ, tŭn-) *n., pl.* **Tungus** or **-gus•es.** See **Evenki.** [Russ. < East Turkic *tunguz*, wild pig, boar < Old Turkic *tonguz*.]
Tun•gus•ic (to͝ong-go͞oʹzĭk, tŭn-) *n.* A subfamily of the Altaic language family spoken in eastern Siberia and northern Manchuria including Tungus and Manchu. —**Tun•gusʹic** *adj.*
Tun•gus•ka (to͝ong-go͞oʹskə, to͞on-). The name of three rivers of central Russia. The **Upper Tunguska** is the lower course of the Angara R. The **Lower Tunguska** flows c. 3,218 km (2,000 mi) N and W to the Yenisei R. The **Stony Tunguska**, c. 1,609 km (1,000 mi), flows WNW to the Yenisei.
tu•nic (to͞oʹnĭk, tyo͞oʹ-) *n.* **1.a.** A loose-fitting garment extending to the knees and worn esp. in ancient Greece and Rome. **b.** A medieval surcoat. **2.a.** A long plain close-fitting military jacket, usu. with a stiff high collar. **b.** A long plain sleeved or sleeveless blouse. **c.** A short pleated and belted dress worn by women for some sports. **3.** *Anat.* A coat or layer enveloping an organ or a part. **4.** *Bot.* A loose membranous outer covering of a bulb or corm. **5.** See **tunicle.** [ME *tunik* < OFr. *tunique* < Lat. *tunica*, prob. of Semitic orig.]
tu•ni•ca (to͞oʹnĭ-kə, tyo͞oʹ-) *n., pl.* **-cae** (-kēʹ, -sēʹ). An enclosing membrane or layer of tissue. [Lat., tunic. See TUNIC.]
tu•ni•cate (to͞oʹnĭ-kĭt, -kātʹ, tyo͞oʹ-) *n.* Any of various chordate marine animals of the subphylum Tunicata or Urochordata, having a cylindrical or globular body enclosed in a tough outer covering and including the sea squirts and salps. —*adj.* **1.** Of or relating to the tunicates. **2.** *Anat.* Having a tunic. **3.** *Bot.* Having a tunic. [Lat. *tunicātus*, p.part. of *tunicāre*, to clothe with a tunic < *tunica*, tunic. See TUNIC.]
tu•ni•cle (to͞oʹnĭ-kəl, tyo͞oʹ-) *n.* A sleeved outer vestment reaching to the knees, worn over the alb by a subdeacon or sometimes under the dalmatic by a bishop or cardinal. [ME < Lat. *tunicula*, dim. of *tunica*, tunic. See TUNIC.]
tun•ing fork (to͞oʹnĭng, tyo͞oʹ-) *n.* A small two-pronged metal device that when struck produces a sound of fixed pitch that is used as a reference, as in tuning musical instruments.

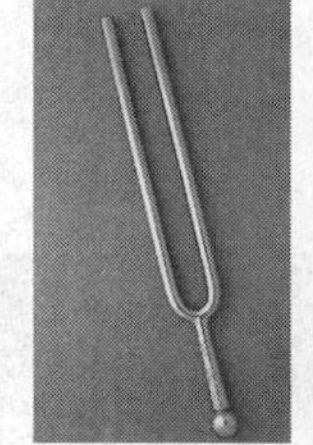
tuning fork

Tu•nis (to͞oʹnĭs, tyo͞oʹ-). **1.** A former Barbary state on the N coast of Africa SW of Carthage; conquered by the Turks in 1575. **2.** The cap. of Tunisia, in the N part on the **Gulf of Tunis**, an inlet of the Mediterranean Sea. Pop. 550,404.
Tu•ni•sia (to͞o-nēʹzhə, -shə, -nĭzhʹə, -nĭshʹə, tyo͞o-). A country of N Africa bordering on the Mediterranean; a French protectorate from 1881 to 1956. Cap. Tunis. Pop. 5,588,209.
Tu•ni•sian (to͞o-nēʹzhən, -shən, -nĭzhʹən, -nĭshʹ-, tyo͞o-) *adj.* Of or relating to Tunisia or Tunis or their inhabitants. —*n.* A native or inhabitant of Tunisia or Tunis.
tun•nel (tŭnʹəl) *n.* **1.** An underground or underwater passage. **2.** A passage through or under a barrier. **3.** *Obsolete.* The main flue on a chimney. —*v.* **-neled, -nel•ing, -nels** or **-nelled, -nel•ling, -nels.** —*tr.* **1.** To make a tunnel through or under. **2.** To produce, shape, or dig in the form of a tunnel. —*intr.* To make a tunnel. [ME *tonel*, tubular net < OFr. *tonnelle*, dim. of *tonne*, tun, poss. of Celt. orig.] —**tunʹnel•er, tunʹnel•ler** *n.*
tunnel disease *n.* See **ancylostomiasis.**
tunnel vision *n.* **1.** Vision in which the visual field is severely constricted, as from within a tunnel looking out. **2.** An extremely narrow point of view; narrow-mindedness.
Tun•ney (tŭnʹē), **James Joseph ("Gene").** 1898–1978. Amer. prizefighter who won the world heavyweight championship in 1926 by defeating Jack Dempsey.

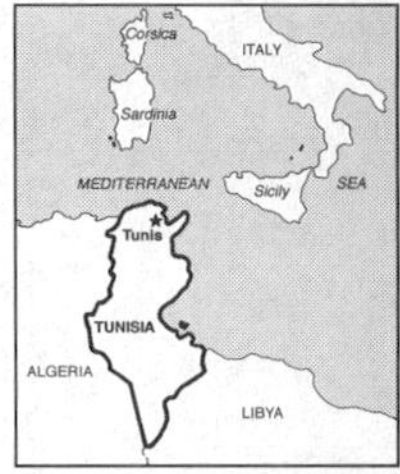

Tunisia

tun•ny (tŭnʹē) *n., pl.* **tunny** or **-nies.** See **tuna**[1] 1a. [Ult. < OProv. *ton* < Lat. *thynnus* < Gk. *thunnos*.]
tup (tŭp) *n.* **1.** *Chiefly British.* A male sheep; a ram. **2.** A heavy metal body, esp. the head of a power hammer. —*v.* **tupped, tup•ping, tups.** —*tr.* To copulate with (a ewe). Used of a ram. —*intr.* To copulate with a ewe. [ME *tupe*.]
tu•pe•lo (to͞oʹpə-lōʹ, tyo͞oʹ-) *n., pl.* **-los. 1.** Any of several trees of the genus *Nyssa*, esp. *N. aquatica* of the southeast United States, having soft light wood. **2.** The wood of this tree. [Prob. Creek *'topilwa* : *íto*, tree + *opílwa*, swamp.]
Tu•pe•lo (to͞oʹpə-lōʹ, tyo͞oʹ-). A city of NE MS NNW of Columbus; site of a Union victory (Jul. 1864). Pop. 30,685.
Tu•pi (to͞oʹpē, to͞o-pēʹ) *n., pl.* **Tupi** or **-pis. 1.** A member of any of a group of South American Indian peoples living along the coast of Brazil, in the Amazon River valley, and in Paraguay. **2.** The Tupian language of the Tupi.
Tu•pi•an (to͞oʹpē-ən, to͞o-pēʹ-) *n.* **1.** A subdivision of Tupi-Guarani that includes Tupi. **2.** A member of a Tupian-speaking people. —**Tuʹpi•an** *adj.*
Tu•pi-Gua•ra•ni (to͞o-pēʹgwär-ə-nēʹ, to͞oʹpē-) *n.* A language family widely spread throughout the Amazon River valley, coastal Brazil, and northeast South America. —**Tu•piʹ-Gua•ra•niʹ, Tu•piʹ-Gua•ra•niʹan** *adj.*
tup•pence (tŭpʹəns) *n.* Var. of **twopence.**
tup•pen•ny (tŭpʹnē) *adj. Chiefly British.* Var. of **twopenny.**
Tup•per (tŭpʹər), Sir **Charles.** 1821–1915. Canadian politician who served as prime minister (1896).
Tu•pun•ga•to (to͞oʹpo͝ong-gäʹtō). A mountain, 6,804.6 m (22,310 ft), in the Andes on the Chile-Argentina border.
tuque (to͞ok, tyo͞ok) *n.* A knitted cap in the form of a cylindrical bag often with tapered ends, worn with one end tucked into the other. [Canadian Fr. < Fr. *toque*, toque. See TOQUE.]

turban

tu quo•que (to͞o kwōʹkwē, -kwā, tyo͞o) *n.* A retort accusing an accuser of a similar offense or similar behavior. [Lat. *tū quoque*, you also : *tū*, you + *quoque*, also.]
Tur. *abbr.* Turkey; Turkish.
tu•ra•co (to͝orʹə-kōʹ) *n.* Var. of **touraco.**
Tu•ra•ni•an (to͝o-rāʹnē-ən, -räʹ-, tyo͝o-) *n.* **1.** See **Ural-Altaic. 2.** A member of any of the peoples who speak languages of the Ural-Altaic group. [< Pers. *Tūrān*, Turkistan.] —**Tu•raʹni•an** *adj.*
tur•ban (tûrʹbən) *n.* **1.** A traditionally Muslim headdress consisting of a long scarf wound around a small cap or directly around the head. **2.** A woman's close-fitting hat that consists of material wound around a small inner cap. [Fr. *turbant* < Ital. *turbante* < Ottoman Turk. *tülbend*, muslin, gauze.]
tur•bel•lar•i•an (tûrʹbə-lârʹē-ən) *n.* Any of various free-living, chiefly aquatic ciliate flatworms of the class Turbellaria, which includes the common planarians of the genus *Dugesia*. [< NLat. *Turbellāria*, class name < Lat. *turbella*, bustle, dim. of *turba*, turmoil (from the motion of their cilia in the water). See TURBID.] —**turʹbel•larʹi•an** *adj.*
tur•bid (tûrʹbĭd) *adj.* **1.** Having sediment or foreign particles stirred up or suspended; muddy. **2.** Heavy, dark, or dense, as

ă pat	oi boy
ā pay	ou out
âr care	o͝o took
ä father	o͞o boot
ĕ pet	ŭ cut
ē be	ûr urge
ĭ pit	th thin
ī pie	*th* this
îr pier	hw which
ŏ pot	zh vision
ō toe	ə about,
ô paw	item

Stress marks:
ʹ (primary);
ʹ (secondary), as in
dictionary (dĭkʹshə-nĕrʹē)

smoke or fog. **3.** In a state of turmoil; muddled. [Lat. *turbidus*, disordered < *turba*, turmoil, prob. < Gk. *turbē*.] —**tur′bid·ly** *adv.* —**tur′bid·ness, tur·bid′i·ty** *n.*

tur·bi·dim·e·ter (tûr′bĭ-dĭm′ĭ-tər) *n.* An instrument for measuring the loss in intensity of a light beam through a solution that contains suspended particulate matter. —**tur′bi·di·met′ric** (-də-mĕt′rĭk) *adj.* —**tur′bi·dim′e·try** *n.*

tur·bi·nate (tûr′bə-nĭt, -nāt′) also **tur·bi·nat·ed** (-nā′tĭd) *adj.* **1.** Shaped like a top. **2.** Spinning like a top. **3.** *Zool.* Spiral and decreasing sharply in diameter from base to apex. Used esp. of shells. **4.** *Anat.* Of, relating to, or being a small curved bone that extends horizontally along the lateral wall of the nasal passage in higher vertebrates. [Lat. *turbinātus* < *turbō, turbin-*, spinning top. See TURBINE.]

tur·bi·na·tion (tûr′bə-nā′shən) *n.* A turbinate formation.

tur·bine (tûr′bĭn, -bīn′) *n.* Any of various machines in which the kinetic energy of a moving fluid is converted to rotary mechanical power. [Fr. < Lat. *turbō, turbin-*, spinning top, perh. < Gk. *turbē*, turmoil.]

tureen
Mid 18th-century porcelain tureen with cover

tur·bit (tûr′bĭt) *n.* Any of a breed of domestic pigeons having a small crested head and a ruffled breast. [?]

turbo– *pref.* **1.** Turbine: *turbocharger.* **2.** Driven by a turbine: *turbojet.* [< TURBINE.]

tur·bo·charg·er (tûr′bō-chär′jər) *n.* See **turbosupercharger.** —**tur′bo·charged′** *adj.*

tur·bo·fan (tûr′bō-făn′) *n.* **1.** A turbojet engine in which a fan supplements the total thrust by forcing air directly into the hot turbine exhaust. **2.** An aircraft using a turbofan.

tur·bo·jet (tûr′bō-jĕt′) *n.* **1.** A jet engine having a turbine-driven compressor and developing thrust from the exhaust of hot gases. **2.** An aircraft in which a turbojet is used.

tur·bo·prop (tûr′bō-prŏp′) *n.* **1.** A turbojet engine used to drive an external propeller. **2.** An aircraft using a turboprop.

tur·bo·su·per·charg·er (tûr′bō-sōō′pər-chär′jər) *n.* A supercharger that uses an exhaust-driven turbine to maintain air-intake pressure esp. in high-altitude aircraft. —**tur′bo·su′per-charged′** *adj.*

tur·bot (tûr′bət) *n., pl.* **turbot** or **-bots. 1.** A European flatfish, *Scophthalmus maximus,* that has a brown, knobby upper side and is prized as food. **2.** Any of various flatfishes similar or related to this fish. [ME *turbut* < OFr. *tourbout*, prob. of Scand. orig.; akin to OSwed. *törnbut* : *törn*, thorn + *but*, flatfish; see **bhau-*.**]

tur·bu·lence (tûr′byə-ləns) *n.* **1.** The state or quality of being turbulent. **2.** *Phys.* Turbulent flow. **3.** An eddying motion of the atmosphere that interrupts the flow of wind.

tur·bu·lent (tûr′byə-lənt) *adj.* **1.** Violently agitated or disturbed; tumultuous: *turbulent rapids.* **2.** Having a chaotic or restless character or tendency: *a turbulent period.* **3.** Causing unrest or disturbance; unruly. [ME < OFr. < Lat. *turbulentus* < *turba*, turmoil. See TURBID.] —**tur′bu·lent·ly** *adv.*

turbulent flow *n. Phys.* The motion of a fluid having local velocities and pressures that fluctuate randomly.

Tur·co·man (tûr′kə-mən) *n. & adj.* Var. of **Turkmen.**

turd (tûrd) *n. Vulgar Slang.* **1.** A piece of excrement. **2.** A person regarded as contemptible. [ME < OE *tord.* See **der-*.**]

tu·reen (tŏŏ-rēn′, tyŏŏ-) *n.* A broad, deep, usu. covered dish used for serving foods such as soups or stews. [Fr. *terrine* < OFr. < fem. of *terrin*, earthen < VLat. **terrīnus* < Lat. *terra*, earth. See **ters-*.**]

Tu·renne (tŏŏ-rĕn′, tü-), Vicomte de. Henri de La Tour d'Auvergne. 1611–75. French military leader noted for his campaigns (1635–42) during the Thirty Years' War.

turf (tûrf) *n., pl.* **turfs** also **turves** (tûrvz). **1.a.** A surface layer of earth containing a dense growth of grass and its matted roots; sod. **b.** An artificial substitute for such a grassy layer, as on a playing field. **2.** A piece cut from a layer of earth or sod. **3.** A piece of peat that is burned for use as fuel. **4.** *Slang.* **a.** A range of authority or influence; a bailiwick. **b.** A geographical area; a territory. **c.** The area claimed by a gang as its personal territory. **5.** *Sports.* **a.** A racetrack. **b.** The sport or business of racing horses. —*tr.v.* **turfed, turf·ing, turfs. 1.** To spread with turf: *turfed the front yard.* **2.** *Chiefly British.* To discard or eject. [ME < OE.] —**turf′y** *adj.*

Turkey

Tur·ge·nev (tŏŏr-găn′yəf, -gĕn′-, tŏŏr-gyĕ′nyĭf), **Ivan Sergeevich.** 1818–83. Russian writer whose works include stories, plays, and novels, most notably *Fathers and Sons* (1862).

tur·ges·cence (tûr-jĕs′əns) *n.* **1.a.** The condition of being swollen. **b.** The process of swelling. **2.** Pomposity; self-importance. [< Lat. *turgēscere*, to begin to swell, inchoative of *turgēre*, to be swollen.] —**tur·ges′cent** *adj.*

tur·gid (tûr′jĭd) *adj.* **1.** Excessively ornate or complex in style or language; grandiloquent. **2.** Swollen or distended, as from a fluid; bloated. [Lat. *turgidus* < *turgēre*, to be swollen.] —**tur·gid′i·ty, tur′gid·ness** *n.* —**tur′gid·ly** *adv.*

tur·gor (tûr′gər, -gôr′) *n.* **1.** The state of being turgid. **2.** *Biol.* The normal fullness or tension produced by the fluid content of blood vessels, capillaries, and plant or animal cells. [LLat. < Lat. *turgēre*, to be swollen.]

Tur·got (tŏŏr-gō′, tür-), **Anne Robert Jacques.** 1727–81. French economist and controller general (1774–76).

Tu·rin (tŏŏr′ĭn, tyŏŏr′-) also **To·ri·no** (tô-rē′nô). A city of NW Italy on the Po R. WSW of Milan; former cap. of the kingdom of Sardinia (1720–1861). Pop. 1,103,520.

tu·ri·on (tŏŏr′ē-ŏn′, tyŏŏr′-) *n. Bot.* A thick fleshy young shoot or sucker. [Lat. *turiō, turiōn-*.]

Turk (tûrk) *n.* **1.a.** A native or inhabitant of Turkey. **b.** A native or inhabitant of the Ottoman Empire. **2.** A member of the principal ethnic group of modern-day Turkey. **3.** A member of any of the Turkic-speaking peoples. **4.** *Archaic.* A Muslim. [ME < OFr. *Turc* < Turk. *Türk* < Old Turkic *türk*, strong.]

Turk. *abbr.* Turkey; Turkish.

Tur·ka·na (tər-kăn′ə, tŏŏr-kä′nə), **Lake.** Also **Lake Ru·dolf** (rōō′dŏlf′). A lake of NW Kenya in the Great Rift Valley.

Tur·ke·stan (tûr′kĭ-stăn′, -stän′). See **Turkistan.**

tur·key (tûr′kē) *n., pl.* **-keys. 1.a.** A large North American bird *(Meleagris gallopavo)* that has brownish plumage and a bare wattled head and neck and is widely domesticated for food. **b.** A related bird *(Agriocharis ocellata)* of Mexico and Central America, brilliantly colored and having eyelike spots on its tail. **2.** *Slang.* **a.** A person considered inept or undesirable. **b.** A failure, esp. a failed theatrical production or movie. **3.** *Sports.* Three consecutive strikes in bowling. —***idiom.* talk turkey.** *Informal.* To speak frankly and get down to the basic facts of a matter. [After TURKEY, from a confusion with the guinea fowl, once believed to have a Turkish orig.]

Tur·key (tûr′kē). A country of SW Asia and SE Europe between the Mediterranean and the Black seas; center of the Ottoman Empire for more than 600 years (until 1918) and a republic since 1923. Cap. Ankara. Pop. 44,736,957.

turkey buzzard *n.* See **turkey vulture.**

turkey cock *n.* **1.** A male turkey. **2.** A strutting and conceited person.

Turkey red *n. Color.* A moderate red.

turkey trot *n.* A ragtime dance characterized by a springy walk and a swinging up-and-down movement of the shoulders.

turkey vulture *n.* A New World vulture *(Cathartes aura)* having dark plumage and a bare red head and neck.

Tur·ki (tûr′kē) *adj.* Of or relating to the Turkic language subfamily, esp. the eastern Turkic languages. —*n., pl.* **Turki** or **-kis. 1.** The Turkic language subfamily, esp. the eastern Turkic languages. **2.** A member of a Turki-speaking people. [Pers. *turkī* < *Turk*, Turk < Turk. *Türk.* See TURK.]

Turk·ic (tûr′kĭk) *n.* A subfamily of the Altaic language family that includes Turkish. —*adj.* **1.** Of or relating to Turkic or the peoples who speak Turkic. **2.** Turkish.

Turk·ish (tûr′kĭsh) *adj.* Of or relating to Turkey or its peoples, languages, or cultures. —*n.* Ottoman Turkish.

Turkish bath *n.* A steam bath that induces heavy perspiration and is followed by a shower and massage.

Turkish coffee *n.* A sweetened brew of pulverized coffee.

Turkish delight *n.* A candy usu. consisting of jellylike cubes covered with powdered sugar.

Turkish Empire. See **Ottoman Empire.**

Turkish towel *n.* A thick towel with a nap of uncut pile.

Turk·ism (tûr′kĭz′əm) *n.* The culture, religion, or social system of the Turks.

Tur·ki·stan also **Tur·ke·stan** (tûr′kĭ-stăn′, -stän′). A historical region of W-central Asia extending E from the Caspian Sea to the border of China.

Turk·men (tûrk′mĕn, -mən) also **Tur·ko·man** or **Tur·co·man** (tûr′kə-mən) —*n., pl.* **Turkmen** or **-mens** also **-ko·mans** or **-co·mans. 1.** A member of a traditionally nomadic Turkic people inhabiting Turkmenistan and neighboring areas in Iran and Afghanistan. **2.** The Turkic language of the Turkmen. —*adj.* Of or relating to the Turkmen or their language or culture. [Med.Lat. *Turcomannus* < Pers. *Turkmān* < *turkmān*, like a Turk < *Turk*, Turk. See TURKI.]

Turk·men·i·stan (tûrk′mĕn-ĭ-stăn′, -stän′). A region and republic of W-central Asia E of the Caspian Sea; annexed by Russia in 1881 and a constituent republic from 1925 to 1991. Cap. Ashkhabad. Pop. 3,189,000.

Turks and Cai·cos Islands (tûrks; kā′kəs, kī′kōs). Two island groups of the British West Indies in the SE Bahama Is.

Turk's-cap lily (tûrks′kăp′) *n.* **1.** Either of two North American lilies, *Lilium michauxii* or *L. superbum,* having spotted orange-red flowers with a reflexed perianth. **2.** See **martagon.**

Turk's-head (tûrks′hĕd′) *n.* A turban-shaped knot made by winding a smaller rope around a larger one.

Tur·ku (tŏŏr′kōō′). A city of SW Finland on the Baltic Sea W of Helsinki; settled in the early 13th cent. Pop. 162,282.

Tur·lock (tûr′lŏk′). A city of central CA SE of Modesto. Pop. 42,198.

tur·ma·line (tŏŏr′mə-lĭn, -lēn′) *n.* Var. of **tourmaline.**

tur·mer·ic (tûr′mər-ĭk) *n.* **1.** A widely cultivated tropical plant *(Curcuma domestica)* of India having yellow flowers and an aromatic, somewhat fleshy rhizome. **2.** The powdered rhizome of this plant, used as a condiment and a yellow dye. **3.** Any of several other plants having similar rhizomes. [Alteration of ME *termeryte* < OFr. *terre-merite*, saffron < Med. Lat. *terra merita* : Lat. *terra*, earth; see **ters-*** + Lat. *merita*, fem. p.part. of *merēre*, to deserve; see **(s)mer-²*.**]

tur·moil (tûr′moil′) *n.* A state of extreme confusion or agitation; commotion or tumult. [?]

turn (tûrn) *v.* **turned, turn•ing, turns.** —*tr.* **1.** To cause to move around an axis or a center; cause to rotate or revolve. **2.** To cause to move around in order to achieve a result, such as opening, closing, or tightening. **3.** To alter or control the functioning of (a mechanical device, for example) by the use of a rotating or similar movement: *turn the iron to a hotter setting.* **4.** To perform or accomplish by rotating or revolving: *turn a somersault.* **5.a.** To change the position of so that the underside becomes the upper side. **b.** To spade or plow (soil) to bring the undersoil to the surface. **c.** To reverse and resew the material of (a collar, for example). **6.** To revolve in the mind; meditate on; ponder. **7.a.** To give a rounded form to (wood, for example) by rotating against a cutting tool. **b.** To give a rounded shape to (clay, for example) by rotating and shaping with the hands or tools. **c.** To give a rounded form to: *turn a heel in knitting a sock.* **d.** To give distinctive, artistic, or graceful form to: *knows how to turn a line.* **8.a.** To change the position of by traversing an arc of a circle; pivot. **b.** To cause (a scale) to move up or down so as to register weight. **9.a.** To fold, bend, or twist (something). **b.** To change the position or disposition of by folding, bending, or twisting: *Turn the hat inside out.* **c.** To make a bend or curve in: *turn steel.* **d.** To blunt or dull (the edge of a cutting instrument). **e.** To injure by twisting. **f.** To upset or make nauseated. **10.** To change the direction or course of. **11.a.** To divert or deflect: *turn a stampede.* **b.** To reverse the course of; cause to retreat. **12.** To make a course around or about: *turn a corner.* **13.** To change the purpose, intention, or content of by persuasion or influence. **14.** To change the order or disposition of; unsettle: *turned my head.* **15.a.** To set in a specified way or direction by or as if by rotating or pivoting; point. **b.** To present in a specified direction by or as if by rotating or pivoting: *turn one's face to the wall.* **16.a.** To aim or focus; train. **b.** To devote or apply (oneself, for example) to something. **17.** To cause to act or go against; make antagonistic. **18.** To cause to go in a specific direction; direct: *They turned their way back.* **19.** To send, drive, or let go. **20.** To pour, let fall, or otherwise release (contents) from or into a receptacle. **21.** To cause to take on a specified character, nature, identity, or appearance; change or transform. Used with *to* or *into.* **22.** To make sour; ferment. **23.** To affect or change the color of. **24.** To exchange; convert. Used with *to* or *into.* **25.** To keep in circulation; sell and restock. **26.** To get by buying and selling: *turn a fair profit.* **27.** *Slang.* To perform (an act of prostitution). —*intr.* **1.** To move around an axis or a center; rotate or revolve. **2.** To have a sensation of revolving or whirling, esp. as a result of dizziness or giddiness. **3.** To change position from side to side or back and forth. **4.** To progress through pages so as to arrive at a given place. **5.a.** To operate a lathe. **b.** To be formed on a lathe. **6.** To direct one's way or course. **7.** To change or reverse one's way, course, or direction. **8.** To have a specific reaction or effect, esp. when adverse. **9.** To change one's actions or attitudes adversely; become hostile or antagonistic. **10.** To attack suddenly and violently with no apparent motive: *The tiger turned on the trainer.* **11.** To channel one's attention, interest, or thought toward or away from something. **12.** To devote or apply oneself to something, as to a field of study. **13.** To convert to a religion. **14.** To switch one's loyalty from one side or party to another. **15.** To have recourse to a person or thing for help, support, or information. **16.** To depend on something for success or failure; hinge. **17.a.** To change so as to be; become. **b.** To change; become transformed. Used with *to* or *into*: *The sky turned to pink at dawn.* **c.** To reach and pass (a certain age, for example). **18.** To become sour. **19.** To change color. **20.** To be stocked and sold. **21.** To become dull or blunt by bending back. Used of the edge of a cutting instrument. —*n.* **1.** The act of turning or the condition of being turned; rotation or revolution. **2.** A change of direction, motion, or position. **3.** A place, as in a road or path, where a change in direction occurs; a curve. **4.** A departure or deviation, as in a trend. **5.** A point marking the end of one period of time and the beginning of the next. **6.a.** A chance or an opportunity. **b.** One of a series of such opportunities accorded people in succession or in scheduled order. **7.** A period of participation. **8.a.** An attack of illness or severe nervousness. **b.** *Informal.* A momentary shock or scare. **9.** A characteristic mood, style, or habit; a natural inclination. **10.** A propensity or an adeptness. **11.** A distinctive, graceful, or artistic expression or arrangement of words: *the poetic turn of a phrase.* **12.a.** A movement or development in a particular direction: *a turn for the worse.* **b.** A variation of a given kind or type. **13.** A deed or an action having a good or bad effect on another: *a good turn.* **14.** Advantage or purpose. **15.** A short walk or excursion out and back. **16.** A distortion in shape. **17.** The condition of being twisted or wound. **18.a.** A winding of one thing about another. **b.** A single wind or convolution, as of wire on a spool. **19.** Something that winds or turns around a center axis. **20.** *Mus.* A figure or an ornament consisting of four or more notes in rapid succession and including in addition to the principal note the one that is a degree above and the one that is a degree below it. **21.** A brief theatrical act or stage appearance. **22.** A transaction on the stock market involving both a sale and a purchase. **23.** *South Atlantic U.S.* The amount that can be carried in the arms in one load. —***phrasal verbs.*** **turn away. 1.** To send away; dismiss. **2.** To repel. **3.** To avert; deflect. **turn back. 1.** To reverse one's direction of motion. **2.** To drive back and away. **3.** To halt the advance of. **4.** To fold down. **turn down. 1.** To diminish the speed, volume, intensity, or flow of. **2.** To reject or refuse, as a person, advice, or a suggestion. **3.** To fold or be capable of folding down. **turn in. 1.** To hand in; give over. **2.** To inform on or deliver. **3.** To produce: *turned in a good performance.* **4.** *Informal.* To go to bed. **turn off. 1.** To stop the operation, activity, or flow of; shut off. **2.** *Slang.* **a.** To affect with dislike, displeasure, or revulsion. **b.** To affect with boredom. **c.** To lose or cause to lose interest; withdraw. **d.** To cease paying attention to. **3.** To divert; deflect. **4.** *Chiefly British.* To dismiss (an employee). **turn on. 1.** To cause to begin the operation, activity, or flow of. **2.** To begin to display, employ, or exude. **3.** *Slang.* **a.** To take or cause to take a mind-altering drug, esp. for the first time. **b.** To be or cause to become interested, pleasurably excited, or stimulated. Often used with *to.* **c.** To excite or become excited sexually. **turn out. 1.** To shut off. **2.** To arrive or assemble, as for a public event or entertainment. **3.** To produce, as by a manufacturing process; make. **4.** To be found to be, as after experience or trial. **5.** To end up; result. **6.** To equip; outfit. **7.** *Informal.* To get out of bed. **8.** To evict; expel. **turn over. 1.** To bring the bottom to the top or vice versa; invert. **2.a.** To shift the position of, as by rolling from one side to the other. **b.** To shift one's position by rolling from one side to the other. **3.** To rotate; cycle: *The engine turned over.* **4.** To think about; consider. **5.** To transfer to another; surrender. **6.** To do business to the extent or amount of. **7.** To seem to lurch or heave convulsively: *My stomach turned over.* **turn to.** To begin work. **turn up. 1.** To increase the speed, volume, intensity, or flow of. **2.a.** To find. **b.** To be found. **3.** To make an appearance; arrive. **4.** To fold or be capable of folding up. **5.** To happen unexpectedly. **6.** To be evident. —***idioms.*** **at every turn.** In every place; at every moment. **by turns.** One after another; alternately. **in turn.** In the proper order or sequence. **out of turn. 1.** Not in the proper order or sequence. **2.** At an inappropriate time or in an inappropriate manner. **to a turn.** To a precise degree; perfectly. **turn a blind eye.** To refuse to see or recognize something. **turn a deaf ear.** To refuse to listen to or hear something. **turn a hair.** To become afraid or upset. **turn (one's) back on. 1.** To deny; reject. **2.** To abandon; forsake. **turn (one's) hand.** To apply oneself, as to a task. **turn (one's) head. 1.** To cause to become infatuated. **2.** To cause to become egotistical and conceited. **turn over a new leaf.** To change, as one's attitude or conduct, for the better. **turn tail.** To run away. **turn the (**or **a) corner.** To reach and surpass a midpoint or milestone. **turn the other cheek.** To respond to insult or injury by patiently eschewing retaliation. **turn the scales.** To offset the balance of a situation. **turn the tables.** To reverse a situation and gain the upper hand. **turn turtle.** To capsize or turn upside-down. **turn up (one's) nose.** To regard something with disdain or scorn. [ME *turnen* < OE *turnian, tyrnan* and OFr. *torner,* both < Lat. *tornāre,* to turn in a lathe < *tornus,* lathe < Gk. *tornos.* See **terə-**[1]***.**]

turn•a•bout (tûrn′ə-bout′) *n.* **1.** The act of turning about and facing or moving in the opposite direction. **2.** A shift or change in opinion, loyalty, or allegiance. **3.** A dance or party to which girls invite boys.

turn•a•round (tûrn′ə-round′) *n.* **1.** A space, as in a driveway, permitting the turning around of a vehicle. **2.** The act or an instance of turning about and facing or moving in the opposite direction; a reversal. **3.** A shift or change in opinion, loyalty, or allegiance. **4.a.** The process of or time needed for loading, unloading, and servicing a vehicle. **b.** The process of or time needed for performing a task.

turn•buck•le (tûrn′bŭk′əl) *n.* A metal coupling device consisting of an oblong piece internally threaded at both ends into which the two sections of a threaded rod are screwed in order to adjust the tension of the rod.

turn•coat (tûrn′kōt′) *n.* One who traitorously switches allegiance.

turn•down (tûrn′doun′) *n.* **1.** A rejection. **2.** One who has been turned down or rejected. **3.** Something that is folded down, as on a garment. **4.** A downturn. —*adj.* Being or capable of being turned or folded down: *a turndown collar.*

turned-on (tûrnd′ŏn′, -ôn′) *adj. Slang.* **1.** Highly aware of and responsive to what is fashionable and up-to-date. **2.a.** Pleasantly excited or stimulated. **b.** Sexually aroused. **c.** Under the influence of a mind-altering drug.

turn•er[1] (tûr′nər) *n.* One that turns, esp. a person who operates a lathe or similar device.

turn•er[2] (tûr′nər) *n. Sports.* A tumbler or gymnast, esp. a member of a turnverein. [Ger. < *turnen,* to do gymnastics < OHGer. *turnēn,* to turn < Lat. *tornāre,* to turn in a lathe. See TURN.]

Tur•ner (tûr′nər), **Frederick Jackson.** 1861–1932. Amer. historian who emphasized the importance of the frontier.

Turkmenistan

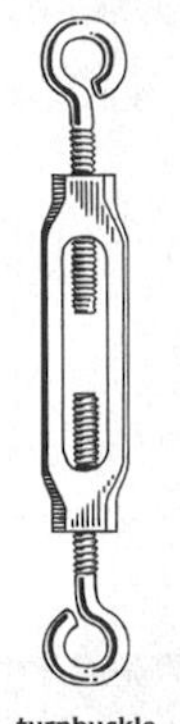

turnbuckle

ă pat oi boy
ā pay ou out
âr care ŏŏ took
ä father ōō boot
ĕ pet ŭ cut
ē be ûr urge
ĭ pit th thin
ī pie *th* this
îr pier hw which
ŏ pot zh vision
ō toe ə about, item
ô paw

Stress marks:
′ (primary);
′ (secondary), as in
dictionary (dĭk′shə-nĕr′ē)

turtle[1]
Florida box turtle
Terrapene carolina bauri

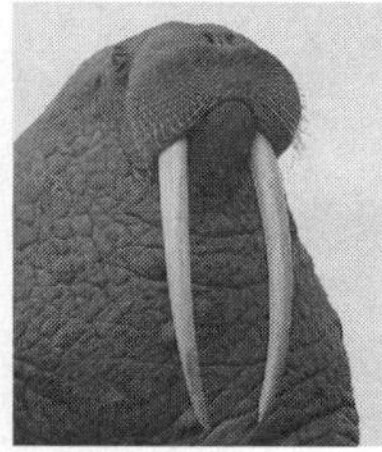
tusk
Bull walrus

Tutankhamen
Gold funerary portrait

Turner, Joseph Mallord William. 1775–1851. British painter who influenced the French impressionists.
Turner, Nat. 1800–31. Amer. slave who led a rebellion against whites in VA (1831).
Tur•ner's syndrome (tûr′nərz) *n.* A congenital condition of females associated with a defect or an absence of an X-chromosome, characterized by short stature and sexual underdevelopment. [After Henry Hubert *Turner* (1892–1970), Amer. endocrinologist.]
turn•er•y (tûr′nə-rē) *n., pl.* **-ies.** The work or workshop of a lathe operator.
turn•ing (tûr′nĭng) *n.* **1.** A deviation from a straight course; a turn. **2.a.** The shaping of metal or wood on a lathe. **b. turnings.** Shavings produced in shaping metal on a lathe.
turning point *n.* **1.** The point at which a significant change occurs; a decisive moment. **2.** *Math.* A maximum or minimum point on a curve.
tur•nip (tûr′nĭp) *n.* **1.** A widely cultivated Eurasian plant *(Brassica rapa)* of the mustard family, having a large fleshy edible yellow or white root. **2.** The root of this plant, eaten as a vegetable. [*tur-*, of unknown orig. + dial. *nepe*, turnip (< ME < OE *nǣp* < Lat. *nāpus*).]
turn•key (tûrn′kē′) *n., pl.* **-keys.** The keeper of the keys in a prison; a jailer. —*adj.* **1.** Supplied, installed, or purchased in a condition ready for immediate use, occupation, or operation. **2.** Of or relating to something in this condition.
turn•off (tûrn′ôf′, -ŏf′) *n.* **1.** A branch of a road or path leading away from a main thoroughfare. **2.** The act or an instance of turning off. **3.** *Slang.* **a.** One that is distasteful. **b.** Something that causes loss of interest.
turn-on (tûrn′ŏn′, -ôn′) *n. Slang.* Something that causes pleasure or excitement.
turn•out (tûrn′out′) *n.* **1.** The number of people gathered for a particular event or purpose; attendance. **2.** A number of things produced; output. **3.** The act or an instance of turning out. **4.** *Chiefly British.* **a.** A labor strike. **b.** A laborer on strike. **5.** An array of equipment; an outfit. **6.** An outfit of a carriage with its horse or horses; equipage. **7.** A railroad siding. **8.** A widening in a highway to allow vehicles to pass or park. **9.** The rotation of a dancer's legs from the hip sockets in classical ballet.
turn•o•ver (tûrn′ō′vər) *n.* **1.** The act of turning over; an upset or overthrow. **2.** An abrupt change; a reversal. **3.** A small pastry made by covering one half of a piece of dough with fruit or other filling and folding the other half over on top. **4.a.** The number of times a particular stock of goods is sold and restocked during a given period of time. **b.** The amount of business transacted during a given period of time. **c.** The number of shares of stock sold on the market during a given period of time. **5.a.** The number of workers hired by an establishment to replace those who have left in a given period of time. **b.** The ratio of this number to the number of employed workers. **6.** *Sports.* A loss of possession of the ball to the opposing team, as by a misplay. —*adj.* Capable of being turned or folded down or over: *a turnover collar.*
turn•pike (tûrn′pīk′) *n.* **1.** A toll road, esp. an expressway. **2.** A tollgate. [ME *turnepike*, spiked barrier : *turnen*, to turn; see TURN + *pike*, sharp point; see PIKE[5].]
turn signal *n.* See **directional signal.**
turn•sole (tûrn′sōl′) *n.* **1.** Any of various plants that move or are believed to move in response to the sun. **2.** See **heliotrope** 1a. [ME *turnesole*, purple dye obtained from the plant < OFr. *tournesol* < OItal. *tornasole*, heliotrope : *tornare*, to turn (< Lat. *tornāre*; see TURN) + *sole*, sun (< Lat. *sōl*; see **sāwel-***).]
turn•spit (tûrn′spĭt′) *n.* **1.a.** One that turns a roasting spit. **b.** A roasting spit that can be turned. **2.** A dog formerly used in a treadmill to turn a roasting spit.
turn•stile (tûrn′stīl′) *n.* **1.** A mechanical device typically consisting of several horizontal arms supported by and radially projecting from a central post and allowing only the passage of individuals on foot. **2.** A similar structure that permits the passage of an individual once a charge has been paid or counts the number of individuals passing through.
turn•stone (tûrn′stōn′) *n.* Any of several wading birds of the genus *Arenaria*, esp. *A. interpres*, which is dark brown above with large areas of chestnut and black.
turn•ta•ble (tûrn′tā′bəl) *n.* **1.a.** The rotating platform of a record player. **b.** The unit housing this platform. **2.** A rotating platform equipped with a railway track, used for turning locomotives. **3.** A rotating platform or disk.
turn•up (tûrn′ŭp′) *n.* Something, such as the cuff on a trouser leg, that is turned up or can be turned up. —*adj.* Turned up or capable of being turned up.
turn•ver•ein (tûrn′və-rīn′, to͝orn′-) *n. Sports.* A club of tumblers or gymnasts. [Ger. : *turnen*, to do gymnastics; see TURNER[2] + *Verein*, club (< obsolete *vereine*, back-formation < MHGer. *vereinen*, to unite : *ver-*, intensive pref. < OHGer. *far-*; see **per**[1]* + *einen*, to make one < *ein*, one < OHGer.; see **oi-no-***).]
tur•pen•tine (tûr′pən-tīn′) *n.* **1.** A thin volatile essential oil, $C_{10}H_{16}$, distilled or extracted from the wood or exudate of certain pine trees and used as a paint thinner, solvent, and liniment. **2.** The sticky mixture of resin and volatile oil from which turpentine is distilled. **3.** A brownish-yellow resinous liquid obtained from the terebinth. —*tr.v.* **-tined, -tin•ing, -tines. 1.** To apply turpentine to or mix turpentine with. **2.** To extract turpentine from (a tree). [ME, resin of the terebinth < OFr. *terebentine* < Lat. *terebinthina (rēsīna)*, terebinth (resin) < Gk. *terebinthinē*, fem. of *terebenthinos* < *terebinthos*, terebinth tree.] —**tur′pen•tin′ic** (-tĭn′ĭk), **tur′pen•tin′ous** (-tĭn′əs) *adj.*
tur•pi•tude (tûr′pĭ-to͞od′, -tyo͞od′) *n.* **1.** Depravity; baseness. **2.** A base act. [Ult. < Lat. *turpitūdō* < *turpis*, shameful.]
turps (tûrps) *pl.n. (used with a sing. v.) Informal.* Turpentine.
tur•quoise (tûr′kwoiz′, -koiz′) *n.* **1.** A blue to blue-green mineral of aluminum and copper, essentially $CuAl_6(PO_4)_4(OH)_8{\cdot}4H_2O$, prized as a gemstone in its polished blue form. **2.** *Color.* A light to brilliant bluish green. [ME *turkeis* and Fr. *turquoise*, both < OFr. *(pierre) turqueise*, Turkish (stone), turquoise, fem. of *turqueis*, Turkish < *Turc*, Turk. See TURK.] —**tur′quoise′** *adj*
tur•ret (tûr′ĭt, tŭr′-) *n.* **1.** A small tower or tower-shaped projection on a building. **2.a.** A low, heavily armored structure, usu. rotating horizontally, containing mounted guns and their gunners, as on a warship or tank. **b.** A domelike gunner's enclosure of a combat aircraft. **3.** A tall wooden structure mounted on wheels and used in ancient warfare to scale an enemy fortress. **4.** An attachment for a lathe consisting of a rotating cylindrical block holding cutting tools. **5.** A rotating device holding various lenses, as for a microscope. [ME *turet* < OFr. *torete*, dim. of *tor*, tower. See TOWER.]
tur•ret•ed (tûr′ĭ-tĭd, tŭr′-) *adj.* **1.** Furnished with turrets or a turret. **2.** Having the shape or form of a turret.
tur•tle[1] (tûr′tl) *n.* **1.** Any of various aquatic or terrestrial reptiles of the order Testudines (or Chelonia), having horny toothless jaws and a bony or leathery shell into which the head, limbs, and tail can be withdrawn in most species. **2.** *Chiefly British.* A sea turtle. —*intr.v.* **-tled, -tling, -tles. 1.** To hunt for turtles, esp. as an occupation. **2.** *Naut.* To capsize. [Perh. < Fr. *tortue* < OFr. < Med.Lat. **tortūca*, perh. alteration of VLat. **tartarūca*, fem. of **tartarūcus*, of Tartarus < LLat. *tartarūchus* < LGk. *tartaroukhos*, occupying Tartarus : *Tartaros*, Tartarus + *ekhein*, to hold; see EUNUCH.] —**tur′tler** *n.*
tur•tle[2] (tûr′tl) *n. Archaic.* A turtledove. [ME < OE < Lat. *turtur*, prob. of imit. orig.]
tur•tle[3] (tûr′tl) *n.* A turtleneck.
tur•tle•back (tûr′tl-băk′) *n.* Something shaped like the back of a turtle, esp.: **a.** *Naut.* An arched structure erected over the deck of a ship as protection from heavy seas. **b.** *Archaeol.* A stone tool with a convex side. —**tur′tle•back′, tur′tle•backed′** *adj.*
tur•tle•dove (tûr′tl-dŭv′) *n.* **1.** A small slender European dove *(Streptopelia turtur)* having a white-edged tail and a soft purring voice. **2.** See **mourning dove.**
tur•tle•head (tûr′tl-hĕd′) *n.* Any of several perennial North American herbs of the genus *Chelone*, esp. *C. glabra*, having white or pink flowers. [< the shape of its flowers.]
tur•tle•neck (tûr′tl-nĕk′) *n.* **1.** A high, tubular, turned-down collar that fits closely about the neck. **2.** A garment, such as a sweater, that has this type of collar
turves (tûrvz) *n.* Pl. of **turf.**
Tus•ca•loo•sa (tŭs′kə-lo͞o′sə). A city of W-central AL SW of Birmingham; estab. 1819. Pop. 77,759.
Tus•can (tŭs′kən) *adj.* **1.** Of or relating to Tuscany, its people, or their language. **2.** *Archit.* Of or relating to the Tuscan order. —*n.* **1.** A native or inhabitant of Tuscany. **2.a.** Any of the dialects of Italian spoken in Tuscany. **b.** The standard literary form of Italian. [ME < Lat. *Tuscānus*, Etruscan < *Tuscus*, an Etruscan.]
Tuscan order *n. Archit.* A classical order similar to Roman Doric but having columns with an unfluted shaft and a simplified base, capital, and entablature.
Tus•ca•ny (tŭs′kə-nē′). A region of NW Italy between the N Apennines and the Ligurian and Tyrrhenian seas.
Tus•ca•ro•ra (tŭs′kə-rôr′ə, -rōr′ə) *n., pl.* **Tuscarora** or **-ras. 1.** A member of a Native American people formerly inhabiting parts of North Carolina, with present-day populations in western New York and southeast Ontario, Canada. **2.** The Iroquoian language of the Tuscarora.
tu•sche (to͝osh′ə) *n.* A black liquid used for drawing in lithography and as a resist in etching and silk-screen work. [Ger., back-formation < *tuschen*, to lay on colors < Fr. *toucher* < OFr. *tochier, touchier*, to touch. See TOUCH.]
tush[1] (tŭsh) *interj.* Used to express mild reproof, disapproval, or admonition.
tush[2] (tŭsh) *n.* **1.** A canine tooth, esp. of a horse. **2.** *Chiefly Southern U.S.* See **tusk** 1. [ME *tusche* < OE *tūsc*. See TUSK.]
tush[3] (to͝osh) *n. Slang.* The buttocks. [Alteration of Yiddish *tokhes* < Heb. *taḥat*, under, buttocks.]
tush•y also **tush•ie** (to͝osh′ē) *n., pl.* **-ies.** *Slang.* The buttocks.
tusk (tŭsk) *n.* **1.** An elongated pointed tooth extending outside the mouth in certain animals such as the walrus or elephant. Also called regionally *tush.* **2.** A long projecting tooth or

toothlike part. —*tr. & intr.v.* **tusked, tusk•ing, tusks.** To gore or dig with the tusks or a tusk. [ME *tux, tusce* < OE *tūx, tūsc,* canine tooth. See **dent-*.**] —**tusked** *adj.*

Tus•ke•gee (tŭs-kē′gē). A city of E AL E of Montgomery; seat of the Tuskegee Institute (founded 1881). Pop. 12,257.

tusk•er (tŭs′kər) *n.* An animal that has tusks.

tusk shell *n.* See **tooth shell.**

tus•sah (tŭs′ə, tŭs′ô′) also **tus•sore** (tŭs′ôr′, -ōr′) *n.* **1.** An Asian silkworm, the larva of a large saturniid moth *(Antheraea paphia),* that produces a coarse brownish silk. **2.** This silk or a fabric woven from it. [Hindi *tasar* < Skt. *tasaram,* shuttle (prob. < the shape of its cocoon).]

tus•sie-mus•sie (tŭs′ē-mŭs′ē) or **tuz•zy-muz•zy** (tŭz′ē-mŭz′ē) *n., pl.* **-sies** or **-zies. 1.** A small bouquet of flowers; a nosegay. **2.** A cone-shaped holder for such a bouquet. [ME *tussemose,* perh. redup. of **tusse.*]

tus•sis (tŭs′ĭs) *n., pl.* **-ses** (-sēz). A cough. [Lat.] —**tus′sal** (tŭs′əl) *adj.*

tus•sle (tŭs′əl) *intr.v.* **-sled, -sling, -sles.** To struggle roughly; scuffle. —*n.* A rough or vigorous struggle; a scuffle. [ME *tussillen,* freq. of *-tousen,* to pull roughly.]

tus•sock (tŭs′ək) *n.* **1.** A clump or tuft, as of growing grass. **2.** A tuft of hair or feathers. [?] —**tus′sock•y** *adj.*

tussock moth *n.* Any of various dull-colored moths of the family Lymantriidae, the caterpillars of which have tufts of hair along the back and are often destructive to trees.

Tus•tin (tŭs′tĭn). A city of S CA, a suburb of the Greater Los Angeles area. Pop. 50,689.

tut (*a* t*-like sound produced by suction rather than plosion; conventional spelling pronunciation,* tŭt) *interj.* Used to express annoyance, impatience, or mild reproof. —**tut** *n. & v.*

Tut•ankh•a•men (to͞ot′äng-kä′mən). fl. c. 1358 B.C. King of Egypt during the XVIII Dynasty whose tomb was found almost intact by Howard Carter in 1922.

tu•tee (to͞o-tē′, tyo͞o-) *n.* One that is being tutored. [TUT(OR) + -EE[1].]

tu•te•lage (to͞ot′l-ĭj, tyo͞ot′-) *n.* **1.** The capacity or activity of a guardian; guardianship. **2.** The capacity or activity of a tutor; instruction or teaching. **3.** The state of being under the direction of a guardian or tutor. [Lat. *tūtēla* (< *tūtus,* var. p.part. of *tuērī,* to guard) + -AGE.]

tu•te•lar•y (to͞ot′l-ĕr′ē, tyo͞ot′-) also **tu•te•lar** (to͞ot′l-ər, -är′, tyo͞ot′-) —*adj.* **1.** Being or serving as a guardian or protector: *tutelary gods.* **2.** Of or relating to a guardian or guardianship. —*n., pl.* **-lar•ies** also **-lars.** One that serves as a guardian or protector.

tu•tor (to͞o′tər, tyo͞o′-) *n.* **1.a.** A private instructor. **b.** One that gives additional, special, or remedial instruction. **2.** A teacher or teaching assistant in some universities and colleges having a rank lower than that of an instructor. **3.** A graduate responsible for the supervision of an undergraduate at some British universities. —*v.* **-tored, -tor•ing, -tors.** —*tr.* **1.** To act as a tutor to; instruct or teach privately. **2.** To have the guardianship, tutelage, or care of. —*intr.* **1.** To function as a tutor. **2.** To be instructed by a tutor; study under a tutor. [Ult. < Lat. *tūtor* < *tūtus,* var. p.part. of *tuērī,* to guard.]

tu•to•ri•al (to͞o-tôr′ē-əl, -tōr′-, tyo͞o-) *adj.* Of or relating to tutors or a tutor. —*n.* Something that provides special, often individual instruction, esp.: **a.** A book or class that provides instruction in a particular area. **b.** *Comp. Sci.* A program that instructs the user of a system or software package.

tut•ti (to͞o′tē) *Mus.* —*adv. & adj.* All. Used chiefly as a direction to indicate that all performers are to take part. —*n., pl.* **-tis.** A passage of ensemble music executed by all the performers simultaneously. [Ital., pl. of *tutto,* all < VLat. **tōttus,* var. of Lat. *tōtus.* See **teutā-*.**]

tut•ti-frut•ti (to͞o′tē-fro͞o′tē) *n., pl.* **-tis. 1.** A confection, esp. ice cream, containing a variety of chopped and usu. candied fruits. **2.** A flavoring simulating the flavor of many fruits. [Ital. : *tutti,* pl. of *tutto,* all + *frutti,* pl. of *frutto,* fruit.]

tut-tut (*two* t*-like sounds produced by suction rather than plosion; conventional spelling pronunciation,* tŭt′tŭt′) *intr.v.* **-tut•ted, -tut•ting, -tuts.** To express annoyance, impatience, or mild reproof. [Imit.]

tut•ty (tŭt′ē) *n., pl.* **-ties.** An impure zinc oxide obtained as a sublimate from the flues of zinc-smelting furnaces and used as a polishing powder. [ME *tutie* < OFr. < Ar. *tūtiyā* < Pers. < Skt. *tuttham,* blue vitriol.]

tu•tu (to͞o′to͞o) *n.* A short skirt, usu. made of layers of sheer fabric, worn by ballerinas. [Fr., perh. alteration of *cucu,* baby-talk redup. of *cul,* buttocks. See CULOTTE.]

Tu•tu (to͞o′to͞o), **Desmond.** b. 1931. South African prelate who won the 1984 Nobel Peace Prize.

Tu•tu•i•la (to͞o′to͞o-ē′lə). An island of American Samoa in the SW-central Pacific Ocean.

Tu•va•lu (to͞o-vä′lo͞o, to͞o′və-lo͞o′). Formerly **El•lice Islands** (ĕl′ĭs). An island country of the W Pacific N of Fiji; organized as a British protectorate in 1892 and independent after 1978. Cap. Fongafale. Pop. 7,349.

tux (tŭks) *n. Informal.* A tuxedo.

tux•e•do (tŭk-sē′dō) *n., pl.* **-dos** or **-does. 1.** A man's dress jacket, usu. black with satin or grosgrain lapels, worn for formal or semiformal occasions. **2.** A complete outfit including this jacket, trousers usu. with a silken stripe down the side, a bow tie, and often a cummerbund. [Short for *Tuxedo coat,* after a country club at *Tuxedo* Park, a village of SE NY.]

Tux•tla Gu•tiér•rez (to͞os′tlə go͞o-tyĕr′ĕs). A city of SE Mexico near the Isthmus of Tehuantepec. Pop. 131,096.

tu•yère (twē-yâr′) *n.* The pipe, nozzle, or other opening through which air is forced into a blast furnace or forge to facilitate combustion. [Fr. < OFr. < *tuyau,* pipe, prob. of Gmc. orig.]

tuz•zy-muz•zy (tŭz′ē-mŭz′ē) *n.* Var. of **tussie-mussie.**

TV (tē′vē′) *n., pl.* **TVs** or **TV's.** Television.

TVA *abbr.* Tennessee Valley Authority.

TV dinner *n.* A frozen prepared meal, usu. packaged in a disposable serving tray, that needs to be heated before serving.

twa (twä, twô) *n., adj., & pron. Scots.* Two. [ME, var. of *two.* See TWO.]

twad•dle (twŏd′l) *intr.v.* **-dled, -dling, -dles.** To talk foolishly; prate. —*n.* Foolish, trivial, or idle talk or chatter. [Prob. var. of dial. *twattle,* perh. alteration of TATTLE.] —**twad′dler** *n.*

twain (twān) *n., adj., & pron.* Two. [ME *tweien, twaine* < OE *twēgen.* See **dwo-*.**]

Twain (twān), **Mark.** See Samuel Langhorne **Clemens.**

twang (twăng) *v.* **twanged, twang•ing, twangs.** —*intr.* **1.** To emit a twang. **2.** To resound with a twang. **3.** To speak in a twang. —*tr.* **1.** To cause to make a twang. **2.** To utter with a twang. —*n.* **1.** A sharp vibrating sound, as that of a plucked string. **2.** A strongly nasal tone of voice, esp. as a peculiarity of certain regional dialects. [Imit.] —**twang′y** *adj.*

'twas (twŭz, twŏz, twəz *when unstressed*). It was.

twat (twŏt) *n. Obscene.* **1.** The vulva. **2.** Used as a disparaging term for a woman. [?]

tway•blade (twā′blād′) *n.* Any of numerous small terrestrial orchids of the genera *Liparis* and *Listera,* having usu. two basal leaves. [Obsolete *tway,* two (short for ME *twaine;* see TWAIN) + BLADE (transl. of Med.Lat. *bifolium,* two-leaf).]

tweak (twēk) *tr.v.* **tweaked, tweak•ing, tweaks. 1.** To pinch, pluck, or twist sharply. **2.** To adjust; fine-tune. —*n.* A sharp twisting pinch. [Prob. var. of dial. *twick* < ME *twikken* < OE *twiccian.*] —**tweak′y** *adj.*

twee (twē) *adj. Chiefly British.* Overly precious or nice. [Alteration of *tweet,* baby-talk alteration of SWEET.]

tweed (twēd) *n.* **1.** A coarse, rugged, often nubby woolen fabric made in any of various twill weaves and used chiefly for casual suits and coats. **2. tweeds.** Clothing made of this fabric. [Alteration (poss. influenced by the river TWEED) of Sc. *tweel,* twill < ME *twile.* See TWILL.]

Tweed (twēd). A river of SE Scotland flowing 156 km (97 mi) E to the North Sea.

Tweed, William Marcy. "Boss Tweed." 1823–78. Amer. politician who as the Democratic boss of New York City in the 1860's defrauded the city of millions of dollars.

twee•dle•dum and twee•dle•dee (twēd′l-dŭm′ ən twēd′l-dē′) *n.* Two people or two groups that are practically indistinguishable. [After *Tweedledum and Tweedledee,* names of two proverbial rival fiddlers, of imitative origin.]

tweed•y (twē′dē) *adj.* **-i•er, -i•est. 1.** Made of tweed. **2.** Wearing tweeds. **3.** *Informal.* Suggestive of casual, informal taste, habits, and lifestyle.

'tween (twēn) *prep.* Between.

tweet (twēt) *n.* A weak chirping sound. —*intr.v.* **tweet•ed, tweet•ing, tweets.** To utter a tweet. [Imit.]

tweet•er (twē′tər) *n.* A small loudspeaker designed to reproduce high-pitched sounds in a high-fidelity audio system.

tweeze (twēz) *tr.v.* **tweezed, tweez•ing, tweez•es.** To handle or extract with tweezers. [Back-formation < TWEEZERS.]

tweez•er (twē′zər) *n.* Tweezers.

tweez•ers (twē′zərz) *pl.n. (used with a sing. or pl. v.)* Small pincers, usu. of metal, used for plucking or handling small objects. [< obsolete *tweezes,* pl. of *tweeze,* a case for tweezers or other small instruments, alteration of *etweese* < Fr. *étuis,* pl. of *étui.* See ÉTUI.]

twelfth (twĕlfth) *n.* **1.** The ordinal number matching the number 12 in a series. **2.** One of 12 equal parts. **3.** *Mus.* **a.** A 12-degree interval in a diatonic scale. **b.** A tone 12 degrees below or above a given tone. [ME *twelfthe,* alteration of OE *twelfta.* See **dwo-*.**] —**twelfth** *adv. & adj.*

Twelfth Day (twĕlfth) *n. Eccles.* Epiphany.

Twelfth Night *n.* January 5, the eve of Epiphany and the beginning of Carnival, celebrated as a holiday in parts of Europe and the United States.

twelve (twĕlv) *n.* **1.** The cardinal number equal to the sum of 11 + 1. **2.** The twelfth in a set or sequence. **3. Twelve.** See **Minor Prophets.** [ME < OE *twelf.* See **dwo-*.**] —**twelve** *adj. & pron.*

twelve•mo (twĕlv′mō′) *n., pl.* **-mos.** *Print.* See **duodecimo** 1.

twelve•month (twĕlv′mŭnth′) *n.* A year.

twelve•pen•ny nail (twĕlv′pĕn′ē) *n.* A nail 3¼ inches (8.25 centimeters) long. [< the original price per hundred.]

twelve-tone (twĕlv′tōn′) *adj. Mus.* Relating to, consisting of, or based on an atonal arrangement of the traditional 12 chromatic tones.

tutu

Desmond Tutu

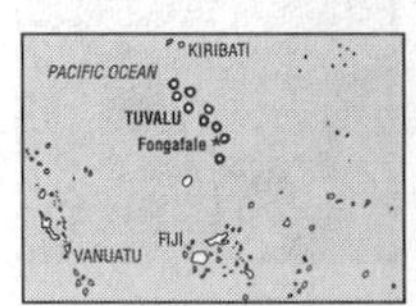

Tuvalu

ă pat	oi boy
ā pay	ou out
âr care	o͝o to͝ok
ä father	o͞o bo͞ot
ĕ pet	ŭ cut
ē be	ûr urge
ĭ pit	th thin
ī pie	*th* this
îr pier	hw which
ŏ pot	zh vision
ō toe	ə about,
ô paw	item

Stress marks:
′ (primary);
′ (secondary), as in
dictionary (dĭk′shə-nĕr′ē)

twinflower
Linnaea borealis

John Tyler
Detail of an 1842 portrait by George Peter Alexander Healy (1813?–1894)

twen•ti•eth (twĕn′tē-ĭth, twŭn′-) *n.* **1.** The ordinal number matching the number 20 in a series. **2.** One of 20 equal parts. —**twen′ti•eth** *adv. & adj.*

twen•ty (twĕn′tē, twŭn′-) *n.* **1.** The cardinal number equal to 2 × 10. **2. twenties. a.** Often **Twenties.** The decade from 20 to 29 in a century. **b.** A decade or the numbers from 20 to 29. [ME < OE *twēntig*. See **dwo-***.] —**twen′ty** *adj. & pron.*

twen•ty-one (twĕn′tē-wŭn′, twŭn′-) *n.* See **blackjack** 3.

twen•ty-twen•ty or **20/20** (twĕn′tē-twĕn′tē, twŭn′tē-twŭn′tē) *adj.* Having normal visual acuity. [< a method of testing vision by reading charts at a distance of 20 feet.]

'twere (twûr). It were.

twerp also **twirp** (twûrp) *n. Slang.* A person regarded as insignificant and contemptible. [?]

Twi (chwē, chē) *n.* A variety of the Akan language spoken in Ghana.

twi•bill (twī′bĭl′) *n. Archaic.* **1.** A battle-ax with two cutting edges. **2.** A mattock with one blade like an ax and the other like an adz. [ME < OE : *twi-*, two; see **dwo-*** + *bil*, billhook.]

twice (twīs) *adv.* **1.** In two cases or on two occasions; two times: *I rewrote the essay twice.* **2.** In doubled degree or amount: *twice as many.* [ME < OE *twiga*. See **dwo-***.]

twice-laid (twīs′lād′) *adj.* Made from strands of old or used rope. Used of rope.

twice-told (twīs′tōld′) *adj.* Very familiar because of repeated telling: *a twice-told tale.*

twid•dle (twĭd′l) *v.* **-dled, -dling, -dles.** —*tr.* To turn over or around idly or lightly; fiddle with. —*intr.* **1.** To trifle with something. **2.** To be busy about trifles. **3.** To twirl or rotate without purpose. —*n.* The act or an instance of twiddling. —***idiom.* twiddle (one's) thumbs.** To do little or nothing; be idle. [Poss. blend of TWIST and FIDDLE.] —**twid′dler** *n.*

twig¹ (twĭg) *n.* **1.** A young shoot representing the current season's growth of a woody plant. **2.** Any small leafless branch of a woody plant. [ME < OE *twigge*. See **dwo-***.]

twig² (twĭg) *v.* **twigged, twig•ging, twigs.** —*tr.* **1.** To observe or notice. **2.** To understand or figure out. —*intr.* To be or become aware of the situation; understand. [Ir.Gael. *tuigim*, I understand < OIr. *tuicse*, var. of *to-ucc-*, to understand.]

twig³ (twĭg) *n. Chiefly British.* The current style. [?]

twig•gy (twĭg′ē) *adj.* **-gi•er, -gi•est. 1.** Resembling a twig or twigs, as in slenderness or fragility. **2.** Abounding in twigs.

twi•light (twī′līt′) *n.* **1.a.** The diffused light from the sky during the early evening or early morning when the sun is just below the horizon. **b.** The time of the day when the sun is just below the horizon, esp. the period between sunset and dark. **2.** Dim or diffused illumination. **3.** A period or condition of decline following growth, glory, or success: *in the twilight of his life.* **4.** A state of ambiguity or obscurity. [ME *twilighte* : OE *twi-*, two, half; see **dwo-*** + OE *līht*, light; see LIGHT¹.]

twilight zone *n.* An area of ambiguity between two distinct states or conditions.

twill (twĭl) *n.* **1.** A fabric with diagonal parallel ribs. **2.** The weave used to produce such a fabric. —*tr.v.* **twilled, twill•ing, twills.** To weave (cloth) so as to produce a pattern of diagonal parallel ribs. [ME *twile* < OE *twilīc*, woven of double thread. See **dwo-***.]

twin (twĭn) *n.* **1.** One of two offspring born at the same birth. **2.** One of two identical or similar people, animals, or things; a counterpart. **3. twins.** *Mineral.* Two interwoven crystals that are mirror images of each other. **4.** A twin-size bed. —*adj.* **1.** Being two or one of two offspring born at the same birth: *twin sisters.* **2.** Being two or one of two identical or similar people, animals, or things. **3.** Consisting of two identical or similar parts: *a twin lamp fixture.* —*v.* **twinned, twin•ning, twins.** —*intr.* **1.a.** To give birth to twins. **b.** *Archaic.* To be one of twin offspring. **2.** To be paired or coupled. —*tr.* **1.** To pair or couple. **2.** To provide a match or counterpart to. [ME < OE *twinn*, twofold. See **dwo-***.]

twin•ber•ry (twĭn′bĕr′ē) *n.* **1.** See **partridgeberry. 2.** A deciduous North American shrub *(Lonicera involucrata)* having shiny purple-black berries.

twin bill *n.* **1.** A double feature. **2.** *Sports.* A double-header.

twin•born (twĭn′bôrn′) *adj.* Born a twin or twins.

twine (twīn) *v.* **twined, twin•ing, twines.** —*tr.* **1.** To twist together (threads, for example); intertwine. **2.** To form by twisting, intertwining, or interlacing. **3.** To encircle or coil about. **4.** To wind, coil, or wrap around something. —*intr.* **1.** To become twisted, interlaced, or interwoven. **2.** To go in a winding course; twist about. —*n.* **1.** A strong string or cord made of two or more threads twisted together. **2.** Something formed by twining. **3.** A tangle; a knot. [ME *twinen* < *twin*, twine < OE *twīn*, double thread. See **dwo-***.] —**twin′er** *n.*

twin-en•gine (twĭn′ĕn′jĭn) *adj.* Powered by two engines.

Twin Falls (twĭn). A city of S-central ID W of Pocatello near the **Twin Falls** of the Snake R. Pop. 27,591.

twin•flow•er (twĭn′flou′ər) *n.* A shrubby creeping evergreen plant *(Linnaea borealis)* of northern regions, having roundish opposite leaves and paired, bell-shaped pinkish flowers.

twinge (twĭnj) *n.* **1.** A sudden sharp physical pain. **2.** A mental or emotional pain: *a twinge of guilt.* —*v.* **twinged, twing•ing, twing•es.** —*tr.* **1.** To cause to feel a sharp pain. **2.** *Obsolete.* To tweak; pinch. —*intr.* To feel a twinge or twinges. [< ME *twengen*, to pinch < OE *twengan*.]

twi•night (twī′nīt′) *adj. Baseball.* Of or being a double-header in which the first game begins in late afternoon.

twin•kle (twĭng′kəl) *v.* **-kled, -kling, -kles.** —*intr.* **1.** To shine with slight intermittent gleams, as stars; flicker; glimmer. **2.** To be bright or sparkling, as with merriment. **3.** To blink or wink the eyes. **4.** To move about or to and fro rapidly and gracefully; flit. —*tr.* To emit (light) in slight intermittent gleams. —*n.* **1.** A slight intermittent gleam of light; a sparkling flash; a glimmer. **2.** A sparkle of merriment or delight in the eye. **3.** A brief interval; a twinkling. **4.** A rapid to-and-fro movement. [ME *twinklen* < OE *twinclian*, freq. of *twincan*, to blink.] —**twin′kler** *n.* —**twink′ly** *adj.*

twin•kling (twĭng′klĭng) *n.* **1.** The act of blinking. **2.** A blink or twinkle. **3.** The time it takes to blink once; an instant.

twin•ning (twĭn′ĭng) *n. Mineral.* The formation of twin crystals. —**twinned** *adj.*

Twins (twĭnz) *pl.n. (used with a sing. v.)* See **Gemini** 1, 2a.

twin-screw (twĭn′skrōō′) *adj. Naut.* Having two propellers, one on either side of the keel, that usu. revolve in opposite directions.

twin-size (twĭn′sīz′) *adj.* **1.** Measuring about 39 by 75 inches (99 by 190 centimeters). Used of a bed. **2.** Being of a size that will fit such a bed. [< *twin bed*, one of a matching pair of single beds.]

twirl (twûrl) *v.* **twirled, twirl•ing, twirls.** —*tr.* **1.** To rotate or revolve briskly; swing in a circle; spin: *twirl a baton.* **2.** To twist or wind around. —*intr.* **1.** To move or spin around rapidly, suddenly, or repeatedly. **2.** To whirl or turn suddenly; make an about-face. **3.** *Baseball.* To pitch. —*n.* **1.** The act of twirling or the condition of being twirled. **2.** Something twirled; a twist. [?] —**twirl′er** *n.*

twirp (twûrp) *n. Slang.* Var. of **twerp.**

twist (twĭst) *v.* **twist•ed, twist•ing, twists.** —*tr.* **1.a.** To wind together (threads, for example) so as to produce a single strand. **b.** To form in this manner. **2.** To wind or coil (rope, for example) about something. **3.** To interlock or interlace: *twist flowers in one's hair.* **4.** To make (one's way) in a tortuous manner. **5.** To turn so as to face another direction. **6.** To impart a spiral or coiling shape to. **7.a.** To turn or open by turning. **b.** To pull, break, or snap by turning: *twist off a dead branch.* **8.** To wrench or sprain. **9.** To alter the normal aspect of; contort. **10.** To alter or distort the intended meaning of. **11.** To alter or distort the mental, moral, or emotional character of. —*intr.* **1.** To be or become twisted. **2.** To move or progress in a winding course; meander. **3.** To squirm; writhe. **4.** To rotate or revolve. **5.** To dance the twist. **6.** To move so as to face in another direction. —*n.* **1.** Something twisted or formed by twisting, esp.: **a.** A length of yarn, cord, or thread, esp. a strong silk thread. **b.** Tobacco leaves processed into the form of a rope or roll. **c.** A loaf of bread or other bakery product made from pieces of dough twisted together. **d.** A sliver of citrus peel twisted over or dropped into a beverage for flavoring. **2.** The act of twisting or the condition of being twisted; a spin, twirl, or rotation. **3.** *Sports.* **a.** A complete rotation of the body around its vertical axis, as in diving. **b.** A spinning motion given to a ball. **4.a.** The state of being twisted spirally; torsional stress or strain. **b.** The degree or angle of torsional stress. **5.a.** A contortion or distortion of the body, esp. the face. **b.** A distortion of meaning. **6.** A sprain or wrench, as of an ankle. **7.** A change in direction; a turn. **8.** An unexpected change in a process or a departure from a pattern, often producing a distortion or perversion. **9.** A personal inclination or eccentricity; a penchant or flaw. **10.** A dance characterized by vigorous gyrations of the hips and arms. —***idiom.* twist (someone's) arm.** *Slang.* To coerce by or as if by physical force. [ME *twisten* < *twist*, a divided object, fork, rope < OE *-twist*. See **dwo-***.] —**twist′a•bil′i•ty** *n.* —**twist′a•ble** *adj.* —**twist′y** *adj.*

twist drill *n.* A drill having deep helical grooves along the shank from the point.

twist•er (twĭs′tər) *n.* **1.** One that twists, as in the manufacture of rope or yarn. **2.** *Informal.* **a.** A cyclone. **b.** A tornado.

twit (twĭt) *tr.v.* **twit•ted, twit•ting, twits.** To taunt, ridicule, or tease, esp. for embarrassing mistakes or faults. See Syns at **ridicule.** —*n.* **1.** The act or an instance of twitting. **2.** A reproach, gibe, or taunt. **3.** *Slang.* A person regarded as foolishly annoying. [Short for obsolete *atwite* < ME *atwiten* < OE *ætwītan* : *æt*, at; see AT¹ + *wītan*, to reproach; see **weid-***.] —**twit′ter** *n.*

twitch (twĭch) *v.* **twitched, twitch•ing, twitch•es.** —*tr.* To draw, pull, or move suddenly and sharply; jerk. —*intr.* **1.** To move jerkily or spasmodically. **2.** To ache sharply from time to time; twinge. —*n.* **1.** A sudden involuntary or spasmodic muscular movement. **2.** A sudden pulling; a tug. **3.** A looped cord used to restrain a horse by tightening it around the animal's upper lip. [ME *twicchen*.] —**twitch′y** *adj.*

twitch•y (twĭch′ē) *adj.* **-i•er, -i•est. 1.** Characterized by jerky or spasmodic motion: *the twitchy whiskers of a cat.* **2.** Nervous; jittery. **—twitch′i·ly** *adv.* **—twitch′i·ness** *n.*

twit·ter (twĭt′ər) *v.* **-tered, -ter·ing, -ters.** *—intr.* **1.** To utter a succession of light chirping or tremulous sounds; chirrup. **2.a.** To speak rapidly and in a tremulous manner. **b.** To giggle nervously; titter. **3.** To tremble with nervous agitation or excitement. *—tr.* To utter or say with a twitter. *—n.* **1.a.** The light chirping sound made by certain birds. **b.** A similar sound, esp. light tremulous speech or laughter. **2.** Agitation or excitement; flutter. [ME *twiteren*, ult. of imit. orig.] **—twit′ter·er** *n.* **—twit′ter·y** *adj.*

twixt also **'twixt** (twĭkst) *prep.* Betwixt.

two (to͞o) *n.* **1.** The cardinal number equal to the sum of 1 + 1. **2.** The second in a set or sequence. **3.** Something having two parts, units, or members, such as a playing card. **—*idiom.* in two.** Into two separate parts; in half. [ME < OE *twā*. See **dwo-***.] **—two** *adj. & pron.*

two-bag·ger (to͞o′băg′ər) *n. Baseball.* See **two-base hit.**

two-base hit (to͞o′bās′) *n. Baseball.* A hit enabling the batter to reach second base.

two-bit (to͞o′bĭt′) *adj.* **1.** *Informal.* Costing or worth 25 cents. **2.** *Slang.* Worth very little; petty or insignificant.

two bits *pl.n.* **1.** *Informal.* Twenty-five cents. **2.** *Slang.* A petty sum.

two-by-four (to͞o′bī-fôr′, -fōr′, to͞o′bə-) *adj.* **1.** Measuring two units by four units, esp. inches. **2.** *Slang.* Small in size; boxed in or cramped. *—n.* A length of lumber that is 2 inches thick and 4 inches wide, or that is trimmed to slightly smaller dimensions.

two-di·men·sion·al (to͞o′dĭ-mĕn′shə-nəl, -dī-) *adj.* **1.** Having only two dimensions. **2.** Lacking range or depth.

two-edged (to͞o′ĕjd′) *adj.* **1.** Having two keen edges. **2.** Being such that two contrasting meanings, effects, or interpretations are possible: *a two-edged compliment.*

two-faced (to͞o′fāst′) *adj.* **1.** Having two faces or surfaces. **2.** Hypocritical or double-dealing; deceitful. **—two′-fac′ed·ly** (-fā′sĭd-lē, -fāst′lē) *adv.* **—two′-fac′ed·ness** *n.*

two·fer (to͞o′fər) *n. Informal.* **1.** A coupon offering two items for the price of one. **2.** An offer, a deal, or an arrangement in which a single expense yields a dual return.

two-fist·ed (to͞o′fĭs′tĭd) *adj.* **1.** Using or able to use two fists. **2.** *Informal.* Marked by great vigor, energy, or enthusiasm.

two-grained spelt (to͞o′grānd′) *n.* See **emmer.**

two-hand·ed (to͞o′hăn′dĭd) *adj.* **1.** Requiring the use of two hands at once. **2.** Made to be operated by two people: *a two-handed crosscut saw.* **3.** Able to use both hands with equal facility; ambidextrous. **4.** Having two hands.

two-mast·er (to͞o′măs′tər) *n. Naut.* A sailing vessel having two masts.

two·pence or **tup·pence** (tŭp′əns) *n.* **1.a.** *Chiefly British.* Two pennies regarded as a monetary unit. **b.** A very small amount; a whit: *didn't care twopence about politics.* **2.** *pl.* **twopence** or **-penc·es.** A British coin worth two pennies.

two·pen·ny (tŭp′ə-nē, to͞o′pĕn′ē) *adj.* **1.** Worth or costing two pennies: *twopenny candy.* **2.** Cheap; worthless.

two-phase (to͞o′fāz′) *adj. Elect.* Relating to two alternating currents with phases at 90°.

two-piece (to͞o′pēs′) *adj.* Made in or consisting of two parts or pieces. *—n.* A garment consisting of two parts.

two-ply (to͞o′plī′) *adj.* **1.** Made of two interwoven layers. **2.** Consisting of two thicknesses or strands: *two-ply yarn.*

two-seat·er (to͞o′sē′tər) *n.* A vehicle for two people.

Two Sic·i·lies (to͞o sĭs′ə-lēz). A former kingdom comprising Sicily and Naples; annexed to Italy by Garibaldi in 1860.

two·some (to͞o′səm) *n.* **1.** Two people or things together; a pair or couple. **2.** *Sports.* A round of golf played by two people.

two-spot (to͞o′spŏt′) *n.* **1.** *Games.* A playing card bearing two spots or pips; a deuce. **2.** *Slang.* **a.** A two-dollar bill. **b.** Two dollars.

two-step (to͞o′stĕp′) *n.* **1.** A ballroom dance in 2/4 time, marked by long sliding steps. **2.** The music for this dance.

two-time (to͞o′tīm′) *tr.v.* **-timed, -tim·ing, -times.** *Slang.* **1.** To be unfaithful to (a spouse or lover). **2.** To deceive; double-cross. **—two′-tim′er** *n.*

two-tone (to͞o′tōn′) or **two-toned** (-tōnd′) *adj.* Having two colors or two shades of a single color.

two-way (to͞o′wā′) *adj.* **1.a.** Affording passage in two directions: *a two-way street.* **b.** Moving in two directions: *two-way traffic.* **2.a.** Permitting communication in two directions: *a two-way radio.* **b.** Permitting flow in two directions: *a two-way valve.* **3.a.** Expressive of or involving mutual action, relationship, or responsibility. **b.** Involving two participants.

two-wheel·er (to͞o′hwē′lər, -wē′-) *n.* A vehicle with two wheels, esp. a bicycle.

twp. *abbr.* Township.

TX *abbr.* Texas.

-ty *suff.* Condition; quality: *realty.* [ME *-te* < OFr. < Lat. *-tās.*]

Ty·chy (tĭk′ē, tĭ′KHĭ). A town of S-central Poland S of Katowice. Pop. 181,800.

ty·coon (tī-ko͞on′) *n.* **1.** A wealthy and powerful businessperson or industrialist; a magnate. **2.** Used formerly as a title for a Japanese shogun. [J. *taikun*, title of a shogun, of Chin. orig.]

ty·ing (tī′ĭng) *v.* Pr.part. of **tie.**

tyke also **tike** (tīk) *n.* **1.** A small child. **2.** A mongrel or cur. **3.** *Chiefly British.* A man considered uncouth or mean; a boor. [ME, mongrel < ON *tīk*, bitch.]

Ty·le·nol (tī′lə-nôl′, -nŏl′). A trademark used for a brand of acetaminophen.

Ty·ler (tī′lər). A city of NE TX ESE of Dallas. Pop. 75,450.

Tyler, John. 1790–1862. The 10th President of the U.S. (1841–45), whose administration was marked by the annexation of Texas (1845).

Tyler, Royall. 1757–1826. Amer. jurist and writer whose plays include *The Contrast* (first produced 1787).

Tyler, Wat. d. 1381. English revolutionary who led the Peasants' Revolt against Richard II's poll tax in June 1381.

tym·bal (tĭm′bəl) *n.* Var. of **timbal.**

tym·pan (tĭm′pən) *n.* **1.** *Print.* A padding, as of paper or cloth, placed over the platen of a press to regulate pressure. **2.** *Archit.* A tympanum. **3.** A tightly stretched sheet or membrane, as on a drum. [ME *timpan*, drum < OE *timpana* < Lat. *tympanum* < Gk. *tumpanon.*]

tym·pa·ni (tĭm′pə-nē) *pl.n. Mus.* Var. of **timpani.**

tym·pan·ic (tĭm-păn′ĭk) *adj.* **1.** Relating to or resembling a drum. **2.** *Anat.* Of or relating to the middle ear or eardrum. [< Lat. *tympanum*, drum. See TYMPANUM.]

tympanic bone *n.* The part of the temporal bone that partially encloses the middle ear and supports the eardrum.

tympanic membrane *n. Anat.* See **eardrum.**

tym·pa·nist (tĭm′pə-nĭst) *n. Mus.* Var. of **timpanist.**

tym·pa·ni·tes (tĭm′pə-nī′tēz) *n.* A distention of the abdomen resulting from the accumulation of gas or air in the intestine or peritoneal cavity. [ME < LLat. *tympanītēs* < Gk. *tumpanītēs* < *tumpanon*, drum.] **—tym′pa·nit′ic** (-nĭt′ĭk) *adj.*

tym·pa·num also **tim·pa·num** (tĭm′pə-nəm) *n., pl.* **-na** (-nə) or **-nums. 1.a.** *Anat.* See **middle ear. b.** See **eardrum. 2.** *Zool.* A membranous external auditory structure, as in certain insects. **3.** *Archit.* **a.** The ornamental recessed space or panel enclosed by the cornices of a triangular pediment. **b.** A similar space between an arch and the lintel of a portal or window. **4.** The diaphragm of a telephone. [Med.Lat. < Lat., drum < Gk. *tumpanon.*]

tym·pa·ny (tĭm′pə-nē) *n., pl.* **-nies. 1.** *Archaic.* Inflated manner or style; bombast. **2.** See **tympanites.** [Med.Lat. *tympanias*, tympanites < Gk. *tumpanias* < *tumpanon*, drum.]

Tyn·dale also **Tin·dal** or **Tin·dale** (tĭn′dl), **William.** 1494?–1536. English religious reformer whose translation of the New Testament was the basis of the King James Bible.

Tyn·dall, Mount. A mountain, 4,275.8 m (14,019 ft), in the Sierra Nevada of S-central CA.

Tyn·dar·e·us (tĭn-dâr′ē-əs) *n. Gk. Myth.* A king of Sparta and the husband of Leda.

Tyne (tīn). A river of N England flowing c. 129 km (80 mi) E to the North Sea.

Tyne·mouth (tīn′mouth′, -məth). A borough of NE England on the North Sea at the mouth of the Tyne R. Pop. 200,100.

typ. *abbr.* Typographer; typography.

typ·al (tī′pəl) *adj.* Of, relating to, or serving as a type; typical.

type (tīp) *n.* **1.** A number of people or things having in common traits or characteristics that distinguish them as a group or class. **2.** The general character or structure held in common by a number of people or things considered as a group or class. **3.** A person or thing having the features of a group or class. **4.** An example or a model having the ideal features of a group or class; an embodiment. **5.** A person regarded as exemplifying a particular profession, rank, or social group: *a group of executive types.* **6.** A figure, representation, or symbol of something to come, such as an event in the Old Testament that foreshadows another in the New Testament. **7.a.** A taxonomic group, esp. a genus or species, chosen as the representative example of a larger taxonomic group. **b.** The specimen on which the original description and naming of a taxon is based. **8.** *Print.* **a.** A small block of metal or wood bearing a raised letter or character on the upper end that leaves a printed impression when inked. **b.** Such pieces considered as a group. **c.** Printed or typewritten characters; print. **d.** A size or style of printed or typewritten characters; a typeface: *a sans-serif type.* **9.** A pattern, a design, or an image impressed or stamped onto the face of a coin. *—v.* **typed, typ·ing, types.** *—tr.* **1.** To write (something) with a typewriter; typewrite. **2.** To determine the antigenic characteristics of (a blood or tissue sample). **3.** To typecast. **4.** To represent or typify. **5.** To prefigure. *—intr.* To write with a typewriter; typewrite. [ME, symbol < LLat. *typus*, type < Lat., image < Gk. *tupos*, impression.]

type A or **Type A** *—adj.* Of or relating to a behavior pattern characterized by tenseness, impatience, and aggressiveness that possibly increases one's risk of heart disease. *—n., pl.* **type A's** or **Type A's.** One who exhibits this behavior pattern.

type B or **Type B** *—adj.* Of or relating to a behavior pattern characterized by a relaxed manner, patience, and friendliness that possibly decreases one's risk of heart disease. *—n., pl.* **type B's** or **Type B's.** One who exhibits this behavior pattern.

tympanum

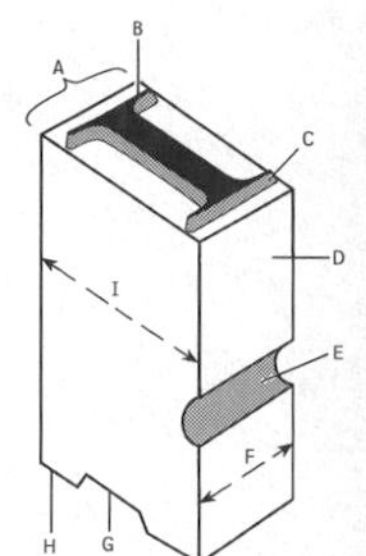

type
A. Face
B. Serif
C. Beard
D. Body
E. Nick
F. Set width
G. Groove
H. Foot
I. Point size

ă pat	oi boy
ā pay	ou out
âr care	o͝o took
ä father	o͞o boot
ĕ pet	ŭ cut
ē be	ûr urge
ĭ pit	th thin
ī pie	*th* this
îr pier	hw which
ŏ pot	zh vision
ō toe	ə about,
ô paw	item

Stress marks:
′ (primary);
′ (secondary), as in
dictionary (dĭk′shə-nĕr′ē)

Tyr

Tzu Hsi

type•cast (tīp′kăst′) *tr.v.* **-cast, -cast•ing, -casts. 1.** To cast in an acting role akin or natural to one's own personality or fitted to one's physical appearance. **2.** To assign (a performer) repeatedly to the same kind of part.

type•face (tīp′fās′) *n. Print.* **1.a.** The surface of a block of type that makes the impression. **b.** The impression made by this surface. **2.** The size or style of the letter or character on a block of type. **3.** The full range of type of the same design.

type genus *n.* The taxonomic genus that is designated as representative of the family to which it belongs.

type-high (tīp′hī′) *adj. Print.* As high as the standard height of type, measured from the face to the foot, 23.3 millimeters (0.9186 inch).

type metal *n. Print.* An alloy used for making metal type, consisting mainly of lead, antimony, and tin.

type•script (tīp′skrĭpt′) *n.* **1.** A typewritten copy, as of a manuscript. **2.** Typewritten matter. [TYPE + (MANU)SCRIPT.]

type•set (tīp′sĕt′) *tr.v.* **-set, -set•ting, -sets.** *Print.* To set (written material) into type; compose. —**type′set′ter** *n.*

type-site (tīp′sīt′) *n.* An archaeological site regarded as definitively characteristic of a particular culture and whose name is often applied to the culture.

type species *n.* The taxonomic species that is designated as representative of the genus to which it belongs.

type specimen *n.* The individual specimen used as a basis for determining the characteristics of a species.

type•style or **type style** (tīp′stīl′) *n. Print.* A specific style of type, as Roman.

type•write (tīp′rīt′) *tr. & intr.v.* **-wrote** (-rōt′), **-writ•ten** (-rĭt′n), **-writ•ing, -writes.** To engage in writing or to write (matter) with a typewriter. [Back-formation < TYPEWRITER.]

type•writ•er (tīp′rī′tər) *n.* **1.** A writing machine that produces characters by a manually operated keyboard that actuates a set of raised types, which strike the paper through an inked ribbon. **2.** *Print.* A typestyle like that of typewritten copy.

type•writ•ing (tīp′rī′tĭng) *n.* **1.** The act, process, or skill of using a typewriter. **2.** Copy produced on a typewriter; typescript.

ty•phoid (tī′foid′) *n.* Typhoid fever. —*adj.* also **ty•phoi•dal** (tī-foid′l). Of, relating to, or resembling typhoid fever. [TYPH(US) + -OID.]

typhoid fever *n.* An acute, highly infectious disease that is caused by a bacillus *(Salmonella typhi)* transmitted chiefly by contaminated food or water and is marked by high fever, coughing, intestinal hemorrhaging, and reddish spots on the skin.

Ty•phoid Mar•y (tī′foid′ mâr′ē) *n.* A person from whom something undesirable or deadly spreads to those nearby. [After *Mary* Mallon, a carrier of typhoid.]

Ty•phon (tī′fŏn′) *n. Gk. Myth.* A monster with one hundred heads, thrown by Zeus into Tartarus.

ty•phoon (tī-fo͞on′) *n.* A tropical cyclone occurring in the western Pacific or Indian oceans. [Prob. alteration of Chin. (Cantonese) *toi fung* : Mandarin *tái*, great + Mandarin *fēng*, wind.]

Word History: Few words better illustrate the polyglot background of English than *typhoon,* with its Chinese, Arabic, East Indian, and Greek background. The Greek word *typhon,* both the name of the father of the winds and a common noun meaning "whirlwind, typhoon," was borrowed into Arabic. *Ṭūfān,* the Arabic version of the Greek word, passed into languages spoken in India, where Arabic-speaking Muslim invaders had settled in the 11th century. Thus the descendant of the Arabic word, passing into English (first recorded in 1588) through an Indian language and appearing in English in forms such as *touffon* and *tufan,* originally referred specifically to a severe storm in India. China, another great empire, gave us yet another word for a storm, in this case the hurricane that occurred in the waters around China. This Chinese word in its Cantonese form, *toi fung,* was similar to our Arabic borrowing and is first recorded in English guise as *tuffoon* in 1699. The various forms coalesced and finally became *typhoon.*

ty•phus (tī′fəs) *n.* Any of several forms of infectious disease caused by rickettsia, esp. those transmitted by fleas, lice, or mites, and marked by headache, high fever, and red rashes on the skin. [NLat. < Gk. *tuphos*, stupor arising from a fever, vapor < *tuphein*, to smoke.] —**ty′phous** (-fəs) *adj.*

typ•i•cal (tĭp′ĭ-kəl) *adj.* **1.** Exhibiting the qualities, traits, or characteristics that identify a kind, class, group, or category. **2.** Of or relating to a representative specimen; characteristic or distinctive. **3.** Conforming to a type: *typical of the baroque period.* **4.** Also **typ•ic** (-ĭk). Of the nature of, constituting, or serving as a type; emblematic. [LLat. *typicālis* < *typicus* < Gk. *tupikos* < *tupos*, impression.] —**typ′i•cal•ly** *adv.* —**typ′i•cal•ness, typ′i•cal′i•ty** (-kăl′ĭ-tē) *n.*

typ•i•fy (tĭp′ə-fī′) *tr.v.* **-fied** (-fīd′), **-fy•ing, -fies** (-fīz′). **1.** To serve as a typical example of; embody the essential characteristics of. **2.** To represent by an image, a form, or a model; symbolize or prefigure. —**typ′i•fi•ca′tion** (-fĭ-kā′shən) *n.* —**typ′i•fi′er** *n.*

typ•ist (tī′pĭst) *n.* One who operates a typewriter.

ty•po (tī′pō) *n., pl.* **-pos.** *Informal.* A typographical error.

typo. *abbr. Print.* Typographer; typography.

ty•pog•ra•pher (tī-pŏg′rə-fər) *n. Print.* One that sets written material into type; a compositor or printer.

typographical error *n. Print.* A mistake in printing, typesetting, or typing, esp. one caused by striking an incorrect key on a keyboard.

ty•pog•ra•phy (tī-pŏg′rə-fē) *n., pl.* **-phies.** *Print.* **1.a.** The art and technique of printing with movable type. **b.** The composition of printed material from movable type. **2.** The arrangement and appearance of printed matter. [Fr. *typographie* < Med.Lat. *typographia* : Gk. *tupos*, impression + Lat. *-graphia*, -graphy.] —**ty′po•graph′i•cal** (tī′pə-grăf′ĭ-kəl), **ty′po•graph′ic** (-grăf′ĭk) *adj.* —**ty′po•graph′i•cal•ly** *adv.*

ty•pol•o•gy (tī-pŏl′ə-jē) *n., pl.* **-gies. 1.** The study or systematic classification of types. **2.** A theory or doctrine of types, as in scriptural studies. —**ty′po•log′i•cal** (tī′pə-lŏj′ĭ-kəl), **ty′po•log′ic** (-lŏj′ĭk) *adj.* —**ty′po•log′i•cal•ly** *adv.* —**ty•pol′o•gist** *n.*

Tyr (tîr) *n. Myth.* A Norse god of war, son of Odin. [ON *Týr*. See **deiw-***.]

ty•ra•mine (tī′rə-mēn′) *n.* A colorless crystalline amine, $C_8H_{11}NO$, used in medicine as a sympathomimetic agent. [TYR(OSINE) + AMINE.]

ty•ran•ni•cal (tĭ-răn′ĭ-kəl, tī-) also **ty•ran•nic** (-răn′ĭk) *adj.* **1.** Of or relating to a tyrant or tyranny. **2.** Characteristic of a tyrant or tyranny; despotic and oppressive. —**ty•ran′ni•cal•ly** *adv.* —**ty•ran′ni•cal•ness** *n.*

tyr•an•nize (tĭr′ə-nīz′) *v.* **-nized, -niz•ing, -niz•es.** —*tr.* To treat tyrannically; oppress. —*intr.* **1.** To exercise absolute power. **2.** To rule as a tyrant. [ME < OFr. *tyranniser* < *tyran*, tyrant. See TYRANT.] —**tyr′an•niz′er** *n.*

ty•ran•no•saur (tĭ-răn′ə-sôr′, tī-) also **ty•ran•no•saur•us** (tĭ-răn′ə-sôr′əs, tī-) *n.* A large bipedal carnivorous dinosaur of the Upper Cretaceous Period of North America, having small forelimbs and a large head. [NLat. *Tyrannosaurus*, genus name : Gk. *turannos*, tyrant + Gk. *sauros*, lizard.]

tyr•an•nous (tĭr′ə-nəs) *adj.* Characterized by tyranny; despotic. —**tyr′an•nous•ly** *adv.*

tyr•an•ny (tĭr′ə-nē) *n., pl.* **-nies. 1.** A government in which a single ruler is vested with absolute power. **2.** The office, authority, or jurisdiction of an absolute ruler. **3.** Absolute power, esp. when exercised unjustly or cruelly. **4.a.** Use of absolute power. **b.** A tyrannical act. **5.** Extreme harshness or severity; rigor. [ME *tyrannie* < OFr. < LLat. *tyrannia* < Gk. *turannia* < *turannos*, tyrant.]

ty•rant (tī′rənt) *n.* **1.** An absolute ruler who governs without restrictions. **2.** A ruler who exercises power in a harsh cruel manner. **3.** An oppressive, harsh, arbitrary person. [ME < OFr., alteration of *tyran* < Lat. *tyrannus* < Gk. *turannos.*]

tyrant flycatcher *n.* See **flycatcher** 2.

tyre (tīr) *n. Chiefly British.* Var. of **tire**².

Tyre (tīr). An ancient Phoenician city on the E Mediterranean Sea in S Lebanon; cap. of Phoenicia after the 11th cent. B.C. and a flourishing commercial center noted for its purple dyestuffs and rich, silken clothing.

Tyr•i•an purple (tĭr′ē-ən) *n.* A reddish dyestuff obtained from the bodies of certain mollusks of the genus *Murex* and highly prized in ancient times. [After TYRE.]

ty•ro also **ti•ro** (tī′rō) *n., pl.* **-ros.** A beginner in learning something. [Med.Lat. *tȳrō*, squire, var. of Lat. *tīrō*, recruit.]

ty•ro•ci•dine also **ty•ro•ci•din** (tī′rə-sīd′n) *n.* A polypeptide antibiotic produced by the soil microorganism *Bacillus brevis.* [*tyrothricin*, an antibiotic (NLat. *Tyrothrix*, former bacteria genus name < Gk. *turos*, cheese; see TYROSINE + Gk. *thrix*, hair) + (GRAMI)CID(IN) + -INE².]

Ty•rol or **Ti•rol** (tə-rōl′, tī-, tī′rōl′). A region of the E Alps in W Austria and N Italy. —**Ty•rol′le•an, Tyr′o•lese′** (tĭr′ə-lēz′, -lēs′, tī′rə-) *adj. & n.*

ty•ros•i•nase (tī-rŏs′ə-nās′, -nāz′) *n.* A copper-containing enzyme of plant and animal tissues that catalyzes the production of melanin and other pigments from tyrosine.

ty•ro•sine (tī′rə-sēn′) *n.* A white crystalline amino acid, $C_9H_{11}NO_3$, that is derived from the hydrolysis of proteins such as casein and is a precursor of epinephrine, thyroxine, and melanin. [Gk. *turos*, cheese; see **teuə-*** + -INE².]

Tyr•rhe•ni•an Sea (tə-rē′nē-ən). An arm of the Mediterranean Sea between the Italian peninsula and the islands of Corsica, Sardinia, and Sicily; connected with the Ionian Sea by the Strait of Messina.

Tyu•men (tyo͞o-mĕn′). A city of W-central Russia E of Sverdlovsk; founded 1585 and the oldest Russian settlement E of the Ural Mts. Pop. 425,000.

tzar (zär, tsär) *n.* Var. of **czar** 1. See Usage Note at **czar.**

Tze•kung (tsŭ′ko͝ong′, dzŭ′go͝ong′). See **Zigong.**

Tze•po (tsŭ′pō′, dzŭ′bō′). See **Zibo.**

tzet•ze fly (tsĕt′sē, tsē′tsē) *n.* Var. of **tsetse fly.**

tzim•mes (tsĭm′ĭs) *n.* Var. of **tsimmes.**

Tzu Hsi (tso͞o′ shē′). 1835–1908. The dowager empress of China (1861–1908), who was hostile to foreign influences and supported the Boxer Rebellion (1898–1900).

tzu•ris (tso͝or′ĭs, tsûr′-) *n.* Var. of **tsuris.**

U u

u¹ or **U** (yo͞o) *n., pl.* **u's** or **U's. 1.** The 21st letter of the modern English alphabet. **2.** Any of the speech sounds represented by the letter *u.* **3.** The 21st in a series. **4.** Something shaped like the letter U.

u² *abbr. Phys.* Up quark.

U¹ (yo͞o) *adj. Chiefly British.* Of or appropriate to the upper class, esp. in language usage. [U(PPER CLASS).]

U² (o͞o) *n.* Used as a courtesy title before the name of a man in a Burmese-speaking area. [Burmese.]

U³ 1. The symbol for the element **uranium. 2.** The symbol for **internal energy.**

u. *abbr.* **1.** Or **U.** Uncle. **2.** Unit. **3.** Or **U.** Upper.

U. or **U** *abbr.* University.

U.A.E. *abbr.* United Arab Emirates.

U.A.R. *abbr.* United Arab Republic.

Uau•pés (wou-pĕs′). In its upper course **Vau•pés** (vou-pās′, -pĕs′). A river of NW South America rising in S-central Colombia and flowing c. 805 km (500 mi) to the Río Negro.

UAW or **U.A.W.** *abbr.* **1.** United Automobile, Aerospace, and Agricultural Implement Workers. **2.** United Automobile Workers.

U•ban•gi (yo͞o-băng′gē, o͞o-bäng′-). A river of central Africa flowing c. 1,126 km (700 mi) along the NW border of Zaire to the Congo R.

U•be•ra•ba (o͞o′bĭ-rä′bə, -bä). A city of E Brazil W of Belo Horizonte. Pop. 180,228.

U•ber•lân•di•a (o͞o′bĭr-lăn′dē-ə, -dyä). A city of E Brazil WNW of Belo Horizonte. Pop. 230,185.

u•bi•e•ty (yo͞o-bī′ĭ-tē) *n.* The condition of being located in a particular place. [Lat. *ubī,* where; see UBIQUITY + -TY.]

u•biq•ui•tous (yo͞o-bĭk′wĭ-təs) *adj.* Being or seeming to be everywhere at the same time; omnipresent. **— u•biq′ui•tous•ly** *adv.* **— u•biq′ui•tous•ness** *n.*

u•biq•ui•ty (yo͞o-bĭk′wĭ-tē) *n.* Existence or apparent existence everywhere at the same time; omnipresence. [NLat. *ubīquitās* < Lat. *ubīque,* everywhere : *ubī,* where; see **kʷo-*** + *-que,* and, generalizing particle; see **kʷe*.**]

U-boat (yo͞o′bōt′) *n.* A submarine of the German navy. [Transl. of Ger. *U-Boot,* short for *Unterseeboot* : *unter,* under (< MHGer. *under* < OHGer. *untar;* see **n̥dher-***) + *See,* sea (< MHGer. *sē* < OHGer.) + *Boot,* boat.]

U-bolt (yo͞o′bōlt′) *n.* A bolt shaped like the letter U, fitted with threads and a nut at each end.

u.c. also **UC** *abbr. Print.* Uppercase.

U•ca•ya•li (o͞o′kä-yä′lē). A river of E Peru flowing c. 1,609 km (1,000 mi) to join the Marañón and form the Amazon R.

Uc•cel•lo (o͞o-chĕl′lō), **Paolo.** 1397–1475. Italian painter whose works include *The Battle of San Romano* (c. 1456).

UCMJ *abbr.* Uniform Code of Military Justice.

UCS *abbr.* Universal character set.

UDC *abbr.* Universal decimal system.

ud•der (ŭd′ər) *n.* A baglike organ containing the mammary glands, characteristic of certain female mammals, such as cows, sheep, and goats. [ME < OE *ūder.* See **euə-dh-r̥*.**]

U•di•ne (o͞o′dē-nā′). A city of NE Italy NE of Venice. Pop. 101,264.

u•do (o͞o′dō) *n., pl.* **u•dos.** A perennial Japanese plant *(Aralia cordata)* having bipinnately compound leaves and young shoots that are cooked and eaten as a vegetable. [J.]

Ue•le (wĕl′ē, wĕl′ā). A river of N Zaire flowing c. 1,126 km (700 mi) W as a tributary of the Ubangi R.

U•fa (o͞o-fä′). A city of SW Russia in the S Ural Mts. at the confluence of the **Ufa River** with the Belaya. The Ufa flows about 965 km (600 mi) NW and SW. Pop. 1,064,000.

UFO (yo͞o′ĕf-ō′) *n., pl.* **UFOs** or **UFO's.** An unidentified flying object.

u•fol•o•gy (yo͞o-fŏl′ə-jē) *n.* The study of unidentified flying objects. [UFO + -LOGY.] **— u′fo•log′i•cal** (yo͞o′fə-lŏj′ĭ-kəl) *adj.* **— u•fol′o•gist** *n.*

U•gan•da (yo͞o-găn′də, o͞o-gän′-dä). A country of E-central Africa; gained independence from Great Britain in 1962. Cap. Kampala. Pop. 12,636,179. **— U•gan′dan** *adj. & n.*

U•ga•rit (o͞o′gə-rēt′). An ancient city of W Syria on the Mediterranean Sea; flourished from c. 1450 to 1195 B.C.

U•ga•rit•ic (o͞o′gə-rĭt′ĭk, yo͞o′-) *n.* The Semitic language of Ugarit. **— U′ga•rit′ic** *adj.*

ugh (ŭg, ŭk) *interj.* Used to express horror, disgust, or repugnance.

Ug•li (ŭg′lē). A trademark used for a citrus fruit produced by a cross of a grapefruit, an orange, and a tangerine.

ug•li•fy (ŭg′lə-fī′) *tr.v.* **-fied** (-fīd′), **-fy•ing, -fies** (-fīz′). To make ugly; disfigure. **— ug′li•fi•ca′tion** (-fĭ-kā′shən) *n.* **— ug′li•fi′er** *n.*

ug•ly (ŭg′lē) *adj.* **-li•er, -li•est. 1.** Displeasing to the eye; unsightly. **2.a.** Repulsive or offensive; objectionable: *an ugly remark.* **b.** *Chiefly Southern U.S.* Rude: *Don't be ugly to your grandparents.* **c.** *New England.* Unmanageable. Used of animals, esp. cows or horses. **3.** Morally reprehensible; bad. **4.** Threatening or ominous: *ugly black clouds.* **5.a.** Likely to cause embarrassment or trouble: *ugly rumors.* **b.** Marked by or inclined to anger or bad feelings; cross or disagreeable: *an ugly scene.* —*n., pl.* **-lies.** *Informal.* One that is ugly. [ME, frightful, repulsive < ON *uggligr* < *uggr,* fear.] **— ug′li•ly** *adv.* **— ug′li•ness** *n.*

ugly duckling *n.* One considered ugly or unpromising at first but having the potential of becoming beautiful or admirable in maturity. [After *The Ugly Duckling,* a story by Hans Christian Andersen.]

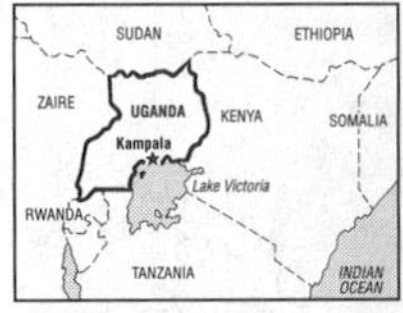

Uganda

U•gri•an (o͞o′grē-ən, yo͞o′-) *n.* **1.** A member of a group of Finno-Ugric peoples of western Siberia and Hungary, including the Magyars. **2.** Ugric. [< ORuss. *Ugre,* Hungarians, of Turkic orig.] **— U′gri•an** *adj.*

U•gric (o͞o′grĭk, yo͞o′-) *n.* The branch of the Finno-Ugric subfamily of languages that includes Hungarian. **— U′gric** *adj.*

ug•some (ŭg′səm) *adj.* Disgusting; loathsome. [ME : *uggen,* to fear (< ON *ugga* < *uggr,* fear) + *-some,* characterized by; see -SOME¹.] **— ug′some•ness** *n.*

UGT *abbr.* Urgent (telegram).

uh (ŭ) *interj.* Used to express hesitation or uncertainty.

uhf or **UHF** *abbr.* Ultrahigh frequency.

uh-huh (ə-hŭ′) *interj. Informal.* Used to express agreement or an answer in the affirmative.

uh•lan also **u•lan** (o͞o′län′, yo͞o′lən) *n.* A member of a body of horse cavalry that was part of the former Polish army and the former German army. [Ger. < Pol. *ulan* < Turk. *oğlan,* youth < *oğul,* son.]

Uh•land (o͞o′länt′), **Johann Ludwig.** 1787–1862. German romantic poet known for his lyrical ballads and plays.

uh-uh (ŭɴ′ŭɴ′) *interj. Informal.* Used to express disagreement or an answer in the negative.

Ui•gur also **Ui•ghur** (wē′go͝or) *n., pl.* **Uigur** or **-gurs** also **Uighur** or **-ghurs. 1.** A member of a mainly agricultural Turkic people inhabiting the Xinjiang region in China. **2.** The Turkic language of the Uigurs. [Uigur.] **— Ui•gu′ri•an** (-go͝or′ē-ən), **Ui•gu′ric** (-go͝or′ĭk) *adj.*

U•in•ta Mountains (yo͞o-ĭn′tə). A range of the Rocky Mts. in NE UT and SW WY rising to 4,116.9 m (13,498 ft).

uit•land•er (oit′lăn′dər, īt′-) *n. South African.* **1.** An outlander; a foreigner. **2. Uitlander.** A native of Great Britain who resided in either of the former republics of the Orange Free State and Transvaal. [Afr. < MDu. *utelander* < *utelant,* foreign land : *ute,* out; see **ud-*** + *land,* land; see **lendh-*.**]

Uj•jain (o͞o′jīn′). A city of W-central India E of Ahmadabad; a Hindu pilgrimage site. Pop. 278,454.

U•jung Pan•dang (o͞o-jo͝ong′ pän-däng′). Formerly **Ma•kas•sar** or **Ma•ka•sar** (mə-kăs′ər). A city of central Indonesia on SW Celebes I.; settled by the Dutch in 1607. Pop. 709,038.

U.K. or **UK** *abbr.* United Kingdom.

Galina Ulanova

u•kase (yo͞o-kās′, -kāz′, yo͞o′kās′, -kāz′) *n.* **1.** An authoritative order or decree; an edict. **2.** A proclamation of a czar having the force of law in imperial Russia. [Fr. < Russ. *ukaz,* decree < Old Church Slavonic *ukazŭ,* a showing, proof : *u-,* at, to + *kazati,* to point out, show.]

uke (yo͞ok) *n. Mus.* A ukulele.

U•kraine (yo͞o-krān′). A region and republic of E Europe; came under the control of Lithuania in the mid-14th cent. and was a constituent republic of the U.S.S.R. from 1922 to 1991. Cap. Kiev. Pop. 50,840,000.

U•krain•i•an (yo͞o-krā′nē-ən) *n.* **1.** A native or inhabitant of the Ukraine. **2.** The Slavic language of the Ukrainians, which is closely related to Russian. **— U•krain′i•an** *adj.*

u•ku•le•le (yo͞o′kə-lā′lē, o͞o′kə-) *n. Mus.* A small four-stringed guitar popularized in Hawaii. [Hawaiian *'ukulele* : *'uku,* flea + *lele,* jumping.]

Regional Note: The word *ukulele* is one of a small stock of Polynesian borrowings into American English. Other Hawaiian words now common in American English are *aloha* (a greeting or farewell) and *luau* (an outdoor picnic usually featuring a whole barbecued pig). *Haole,* a word common in Hawaii itself but not well known on the American mainland, is the Hawaiian word for a white resident of Hawaii.

u•lan (o͞o′län′, yo͞o′lən) *n.* Var. of **uhlan.**

U•lan Ba•tor (o͞o′län bä′tôr′). The cap. of Mongolia, in the N-central part; founded 1649. Pop. 488,200.

U•la•no•va (o͞o-lä′nə-və), **Galina.** b. 1910. Russian-born dancer with the Bolshoi Ballet (1944–62).

U•lan-U•de (o͞o′län-o͞o-dā′, o͞o-län′o͞o-dĕ′). A city of S-central Russia near Lake Baikal and the Mongolian border;

ă pat	oi boy
ā pay	ou out
âr care	o͝o took
ä father	o͞o boot
ĕ pet	ŭ cut
ē be	ûr urge
ĭ pit	th thin
ī pie	*th* this
îr pier	hw which
ŏ pot	zh vision
ō toe	ə about, item
ô paw	

Stress marks:
′ (primary);
′ (secondary), as in
dictionary (dĭk′shə-nĕr′ē)

founded as a Cossack fortress in 1649. Pop. 335,000.

–ular *suff.* Of, relating to, or resembling: *tubular.* [Lat. *-ulāris* < *-ulus*, dim. suff.]

Ul•bricht (o͝ol′brĭkt, -brĭKHt), **Walter.** 1893–1973. German politician who ordered the building of the Berlin Wall (1961).

ul•cer (ŭl′sər) *n.* **1.** A lesion of the skin or a mucous membrane such as the one lining the stomach that is accompanied by formation of pus and necrosis of surrounding tissue, usu. resulting from inflammation or ischemia. **2.** A corrupting condition or influence. [ME < OFr. *ulcere* < Lat. *ulcus, ulcer-*.]

ul•cer•ate (ŭl′sə-rāt′) *v.* **-at•ed, -at•ing, -ates.** *—intr.* To develop an ulcer; become ulcerous. *—tr.* To cause ulceration of. **—ul′cer•a′tive** (-sə-rā′tĭv, -sər-ə-tĭv) *adj.*

ul•cer•a•tion (ŭl′sə-rā′shən) *n.* **1.** Development of an ulcer. **2.** An ulcer or an ulcerous condition.

ul•cer•o•gen•ic (ŭl′sə-rō-jĕn′ĭk) *adj.* Tending to be the cause of an ulcer.

ul•cer•ous (ŭl′sər-əs) *adj.* **1.** Of the nature of ulcers or an ulcer. **2.** Having ulcers or an ulcer. **—ul′cer•ous•ly** *adv.* **—ul′cer•ous•ness** *n.*

–ule *suff.* Small one: *valvule.* [Fr. < Lat. *-ulus, -ula, -ulum*, dim. suff.]

u•le•ma or **u•la•ma** (o͞o′lə-mä′) *pl.n.* Muslim scholars trained in Islam and Islamic law. [Turk. *'ulemā* < Ar. *'ulamā'*, wise men < pl. of *'alim*, wise, learned < *'alima*, to know.]

u•lex•ite (yo͞o′lĭk-sīt′, yo͞o-lĕk′-) *n.* A white mineral, $NaCaB_5O_9 \cdot 8H_2O$, that forms rounded masses of very fine needle-shaped crystals. [After G.L. *Ulex*, 19th-cent. German chemist.]

ul•lage (ŭl′ĭj) *n.* **1.** The amount of liquid within a container that is lost during shipment or storage. **2.** The amount by which a container, such as a bottle, falls short of being full. [ME *ulage* < OFr. *ouillage* < *ouiller*, to fill up a cask < *ouil*, eye, bunghole < Lat. *oculus*, eye. See **okʷ-***.] **—ul′laged** *adj.*

Ulm (o͝olm). A city of S Germany on the Danube R. SE of Stuttgart; site of Napoleon's defeat of Austrian troops in Oct. 1805. Pop. 98,604.

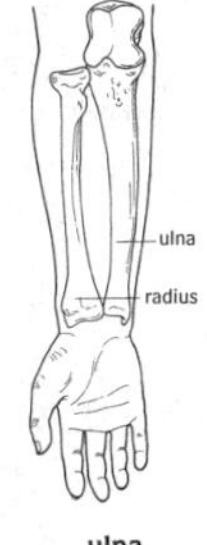

ulna

ul•na (ŭl′nə) *n., pl.* **-nas** or **-nae** (-nē). *Anat.* **1.** The bone extending from the elbow to the wrist on the side opposite to the thumb in human beings. **2.** A corresponding bone in the forelimb of other vertebrates. [Lat., elbow, forearm. See **el-***.] **—ul′nar** *adj.*

Ul•san (o͞ol′sän′). A city of SW South Korea on Korea Strait NNE of Pusan. Pop. 345,700.

ul•ster (ŭl′stər) *n.* A long loose overcoat made of heavy rugged fabric and often belted. [After ULSTER.]

Ul•ster (ŭl′stər). A historical region and ancient kingdom of N Ireland; now divided between Ireland and Northern Ireland, which is often called Ulster.

ult. *abbr.* **1.** Ultimate. **2.** Ultimately. **3.** Ultimo.

ul•te•ri•or (ŭl-tîr′ē-ər) *adj.* **1.** Lying beyond what is evident, revealed, or avowed, esp. being concealed intentionally so as to deceive: *an ulterior motive.* **2.** Lying beyond or outside the area of immediate interest. **3.** Occurring later; subsequent. [Lat., farther, comp. of **ulter*, on the other side. See **al-¹***.] **—ul•te′ri•or•ly** *adv.*

ul•ti•ma (ŭl′tə-mə) *n. Ling.* The last syllable of a word. [Lat., fem. of *ultimus*, last. See ULTIMATE.]

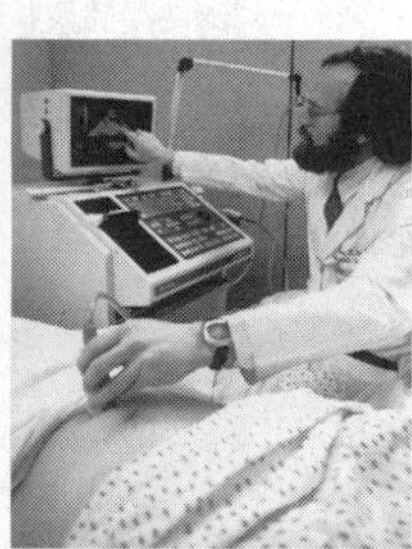
ultrasonograph

ul•ti•mate (ŭl′tə-mĭt) *adj.* **1.** Being last in a series, process, or progression. **2.** Fundamental; elemental: *an ultimate truth.* **3.a.** Of the greatest possible size or significance; maximum. **b.** Representing or exhibiting the greatest possible development or sophistication: *the ultimate bicycle.* **c.** Utmost; extreme: *the ultimate insult.* **4.** Being most distant or remote; farthest. See Syns at **last¹**. **5.** Eventual. *—n.* **1.** The basic or fundamental fact, element, or principle. **2.** The final point; the conclusion. **3.** The greatest extreme; the maximum. [Lat. *ultimātus*, p.part. of *ultimāre*, to come to an end < *ultimus*, last, superl. of **ulter*, on the other side. See **al-¹***.]

ul•ti•mate•ly (ŭl′tə-mĭt-lē) *adv.* At last; in the end.

ultima Thu•le (tho͞o′lē) *n.* **1.** The northernmost region of the habitable world to ancient geographers. **2.** A distant territory or destination. **3.** A remote goal or ideal. [Lat. *ultima Thūlē* : *ultima*, fem. of *ultimus*, farthest + *Thūlē*, Thule.]

ul•ti•ma•tum (ŭl′tə-mā′təm, -mä′-) *n., pl.* **-tums** or **-ta** (-tə). **1.** A final statement of terms made by one party to another. **2.** A statement, esp. in diplomatic negotiations, that expresses or implies the threat of serious penalties if the terms are not accepted. [NLat. < neut. of Lat. *ultimātus*, last. See ULTIMATE.]

ul•ti•mo (ŭl′tə-mō′) *adv.* In or of the month before the present one. [Lat. *ultimō (mēnse)*, in the last (month), ablative of *ultimus*, last. See ULTIMATE.]

ul•tra (ŭl′trə) *adj.* Immoderately adhering to a belief, fashion, or course of action; extreme. *—n.* An extremist. [Fr. < Lat. *ultrā-*, ultra-.]

ultra– *pref.* **1.** Beyond; on the other side of: *ultraviolet.* **2.** Beyond the range, scope, or limit of: *ultrasonic.* **3.** Beyond the normal or proper degree; excessively: *ultraconservative.* [Lat. *ultrā-* < *ultrā*, beyond. See **al-¹***.]

ul•tra•ba•sic (ŭl′trə-bā′sĭk) *adj. Geol.* Containing magnesium and iron but poor in silica. Used of igneous rock.

ul•tra•cen•tri•fuge (ŭl′trə-sĕn′trə-fyo͞oj′) *n.* A high-velocity centrifuge used in the separation of colloidal or submicroscopic particles.

ul•tra•con•ser•va•tive (ŭl′trə-kən-sûr′və-tĭv) *adj.* Conservative to an extreme, esp. in political beliefs; reactionary. *—n.* One who is ultraconservative. **—ul′tra•con•ser′va•tism** *n.*

ul•tra•fiche (ŭl′trə-fēsh′) *n.* A microfiche on which material is reduced by a factor of 100 or more.

ul•tra•fil•tra•tion (ŭl′trə-fĭl-trā′shən) *n.* The filtration of a colloidal substance through a semipermeable medium that allows only the passage of small molecules.

ul•tra•high (ŭl′trə-hī′) *adj.* Exceedingly high.

ultrahigh frequency *n.* A band of radio frequencies from 300 to 3,000 megahertz.

ul•tra•ism (ŭl′trə-ĭz′əm) *n.* Extremism, esp. in politics or government; radicalism. **—ul′tra•ist** *n.*

ul•tra•lib•er•al (ŭl′trə-lĭb′ər-əl, -lĭb′rəl) *adj.* Liberal to an extreme, esp. in political beliefs; radical. *—n.* One who is extremely liberal.

ul•tra•light (ŭl′trə-līt′, ŭl′trə-līt′) *n.* A recreational aircraft constructed of lightweight materials such as aluminum, graphite compositions, or high-strength plastics, having an engine of 15 to 40 horsepower and resembling a motorized hang glider with wings. **—ul′tra•light′** *adj.*

ul•tra•maf•ic (ŭl′trə-măf′ĭk) *adj. Geol.* Ultrabasic.

ul•tra•mar•a•thon (ŭl′trə-măr′ə-thŏn′) *n. Sports.* A cross-country footrace with distances of 30 miles (48 kilometers) or more. **—ul′tra•mar′a•thon′er** *n.*

ul•tra•ma•rine (ŭl′trə-mə-rēn′) *n.* **1.a.** A blue pigment made from powdered lapis lazuli. **b.** A similar pigment made synthetically by heating clay, sodium carbonate, and sulfur together. **2.** *Color.* A vivid or strong blue to purplish blue. *—adj.* **1.** *Color.* Of the color ultramarine. **2.** Of or from a place beyond the sea. [< Med.Lat. *ultrāmarīnus*, from beyond the sea : Lat. *ultrā*, ultra- + Lat. *marīnus*, of the sea (< *mare*, sea; see **mori-***).]

ul•tra•mi•cro•fiche (ŭl′trə-mī′krō-fēsh′, -krə-) *n.* See **ultrafiche.**

ul•tra•mi•cro•scope (ŭl′trə-mī′krə-skōp′) *n.* A microscope with high-intensity illumination used to study very minute objects, such as colloidal particles that scatter the light and appear as bright spots against a dark background. **—ul′tra•mi•cros′co•py** (-krŏs′kə-pē) *n.*

ul•tra•mi•cro•scop•ic (ŭl′trə-mī′krə-skŏp′ĭk) *adj.* **1.** Too minute to be seen with an ordinary microscope. **2.** Of or relating to an ultramicroscope.

ul•tra•mi•cro•tome (ŭl′trə-mī′krə-tōm′) *n.* A microtome for cutting very thin sections of material for use in electron microscopy. **—ul′tra•mi•crot′o•my** (-mī-krŏt′ə-mē) *n.*

ul•tra•mil•i•tant (ŭl′trə-mĭl′ĭ-tənt) *adj.* Militant to an extreme. *—n.* One who is extremely militant.

ul•tra•min•i•a•ture (ŭl′trə-mĭn′ē-ə-cho͝or′, -chər, -mĭn′ə-) *adj.* Subminiature. **—ul′tra•min′i•a•tur•ize′** (-īz′) *v.* **—ul′tra•min′i•a•tur•i•za′tion** (-chə-rĭ-zā′shən) *n.*

ul•tra•mod•ern (ŭl′trə-mŏd′ərn) *adj.* Extremely modern in ideas or style; completely up-to-date. **—ul′tra•mod′ern•ism** *n.* **—ul′tra•mod′ern•ist** *n.* **—ul′tra•mod′ern•is′tic** *adj.*

ul•tra•mon•tane (ŭl′trə-mŏn′tān′, -mŏn-tān′) *adj.* **1.** Of or relating to peoples or regions lying beyond the mountains, esp. the Alps. **2.** *Rom. Cath. Ch.* **a.** Supporting the authority of the papal court over national or diocesan authority. **b.** Relating to or supporting the doctrine of papal supremacy. *—n.* **1.** One who lives beyond the mountains, esp. south of the Alps. **2.** Often **Ultramontane.** *Rom. Cath. Ch.* One who advocates support of papal policy in ecclesiastical and political matters. [Med.Lat. *ultrāmontānus* : Lat. *ultrā-*, ultra- + Lat. *montānus*, of mountains (< *mōns, mont-*, mountain; see **men-²***).]

ul•tra•mon•ta•nism or **Ul•tra•mon•ta•nism** (ŭl′trə-mŏn′tə-nĭz′əm) *n. Rom. Cath. Ch.* The policy that absolute authority in the Church should be vested in the pope. **—ul′tra•mon′ta•nist** *n.*

ul•tra•mun•dane (ŭl′trə-mŭn′dān′, -mŭn-dān′) *adj.* Extending or being beyond the world or the limits of the universe. [Lat. *ultrāmundānus* : *ultrā-*, ultra- + *mundānus*, of the world; see MUNDANE.]

ul•tra•na•tion•al•ism (ŭl′trə-năsh′ə-nə-lĭz′əm) *n.* Extreme nationalism, esp. when opposed to international cooperation. **—ul′tra•na′tion•al** *adj.* **—ul′tra•na′tion•al•ist** *n.* **—ul′tra•na′tion•al•is′tic** *adj.*

ul•tra•pure (ŭl′trə-pyo͝or′) *adj.* Exceedingly pure.

ul•tra•short (ŭl′trə-shôrt′) *adj.* **1.** Of or relating to radio waves with a wavelength less than 10 meters (33 feet). **2.** Of extremely short duration. **3.** Extremely short.

ul•tra•son•ic (ŭl′trə-sŏn′ĭk) *adj.* **1.** Of or relating to acoustic frequencies above the range audible to the human ear, or above approx. 20,000 hertz. **2.** Of, relating to, or involving ultrasound. **—ul′tra•son′i•cal•ly** *adv.*

ul•tra•son•ics (ŭl′trə-sŏn′ĭks) *n.* (*used with a sing. v.*) **1.** The acoustics of ultrasonic sound. **2.** The science and technology that deals with the study and application of ultrasound.

ul•tra•son•o•gram (ŭl′trə-sŏn′ə-grăm′, -sō′nə-) *n.* See **sonogram.**

ul•tra•son•o•graph (ŭl′trə-sŏn′ə-grăf′, -sō′nə-) *n.* An apparatus for producing images obtained by ultrasonography.

ul•tra•so•nog•ra•phy (ŭl′trə-sə-nŏg′rə-fē) *n.* Diagnostic imaging in which ultrasound is used to visualize an internal body structure or a developing fetus. [ULTRASON(IC) + -GRAPHY.] **—ul′tra•so•nog′ra•pher** *n.* **—ul′tra•son′o•graph′ic** (-sŏn′ə-grăf′ĭk, -sō′nə-) *adj.*

ul•tra•so•phis•ti•cat•ed (ŭl′trə-sə-fĭs′tĭ-kā′tĭd) *adj.* Very sophisticated.

ul•tra•sound (ŭl′trə-sound′) *n.* **1.** Ultrasonic sound. **2.** *Medic.* The use of ultrasonic waves for diagnostic or therapeutic purposes, esp. to visualize an internal body structure, monitor a fetus, or generate deep heat to the tissues.

ul•tra•struc•ture (ŭl′trə-strŭk′chər) *n. Biol.* The detailed structure of a biological specimen, such as a cell, a tissue, or an organ, that can be observed only by electron microscopy.

ul•tra•thin (ŭl′trə-thĭn′) *adj.* Very thin.

ul•tra•vi•o•let (ŭl′trə-vī′ə-lĭt) *adj.* Of or relating to the range of invisible radiation wavelengths from about 4 nanometers, on the border of the x-ray region, to about 380 nanometers, just beyond the violet in the visible spectrum. *—n.* Ultraviolet light or the ultraviolet part of the spectrum.

ul•tra•vi•rus (ŭl′trə-vī′rəs) *n., pl.* **-rus•es.** See **filterable virus.**

U•lugh Muz•tagh (o͞o′lə məz-tä′, -täg′). A mountain, 7,729 m (25,341 ft), of the Kunlun Mts. in W China.

ul•u•late (ŭl′yə-lāt′, yo͞ol′-) *intr.v.* **-lat•ed, -lat•ing, -lates.** To howl, wail, or lament loudly. [Lat. *ululāre, ululāt-*, ult. of imit. orig.] **—ul′u•lant** (-lənt) *adj.* **—ul′u•la′tion** *n.*

Ul•ya•novsk (o͞ol-yä′nəfsk). A city of W Russia on the Volga R. ESE of Moscow; founded 1648. Pop. 544,000.

U•lys•ses (yo͞o-lĭs′ēz′) *n. Myth.* Odysseus.

um also **umm** (ŭm, əm) *interj.* Used to express doubt or uncertainty or to fill a pause when hesitating in speaking.

U•ma•til•la (yo͞o′mə-tĭl′ə) *n., pl.* **Umatilla** or **-las. 1.** A member of a Native American people of northeast Oregon. **2.** The dialect of Sahaptin spoken by the Umatilla.

U•may•yad (o͞o-mī′ăd) or **Om•mi•ad** also **O•may•yad** (ō-mī′ăd). The first dynasty of Arab caliphs (661–750).

um•bel (ŭm′bəl) *n.* A flower cluster in which the individual stalks arise from about the same point, as in the geranium. [NLat. *umbella* < Lat., parasol, dim. of *umbra*, shadow.]

um•bel•late (ŭm′bə-lāt′, ŭm-bĕl′ĭt) also **um•bel•lat•ed** (-bə-lā′tĭd) *adj.* Having, forming, or of the nature of an umbel. **—um′bel•late′ly** *adv.*

um•bel•lif•er•ous (ŭm′bə-lĭf′ər-əs) *adj. Bot.* Bearing umbels.

um•bel•lule (ŭm′bəl-yo͞ol′, ŭm-bĕl′-) *n. Bot.* A secondary umbel in a compound umbel, as in the carrot. [NLat. *umbellula*, dim. of *umbella*, umbel. See UMBEL.]

um•ber (ŭm′bər) *n.* **1.** A natural brown earth containing ferric oxide and manganese oxides, used as pigment. **2.** *Color.* Any of the shades of brown produced by umber in its various states. *—adj.* **1.** Of or related to umber. **2.** *Color.* Having a brownish color. *—tr.v.* **-bered, -ber•ing, -bers.** To darken with or as if with umber. [Fr. *(terre d')ombre* or Ital. *(terra di) ombra*, shadow (earth), both poss. < alteration (influenced by Fr. *ombre* and Ital. *ombra*, shadow < Lat. *umbra*) of Lat. *Umbria*, a region of ancient Italy.]

um•bil•i•cal (ŭm-bĭl′ĭ-kəl) *adj.* **1.** Of, relating to, or resembling a navel or an umbilical cord. **2.** Located near the central area of the abdomen. *—n. Aerospace.* An umbilical cord. **—um•bil′i•cal•ly** *adv.*

umbilical cord *n.* **1.a.** *Anat.* The flexible cordlike structure connecting a fetus at the navel with the placenta that transports nourishment to the fetus and removes its wastes. **b.** Something likened to this structure; a source or means of support or sustenance. **2.** *Aerospace.* **a.** Any of the external electrical lines or fluid tubes that supply a rocket before launch. **b.** The line that supplies an astronaut with oxygen while outside the spacecraft.

um•bil•i•cate (ŭm-bĭl′ĭ-kĭt) also **um•bil•i•cat•ed** (-kā′tĭd) *adj.* **1.** Having a central mark or depression resembling a navel. **2.** Having a navel. **—um•bil′i•ca′tion** *n.*

um•bil•i•cus (ŭm-bĭl′ĭ-kəs, ŭm′bə-lī′kəs) *n., pl.* **-ci** (-sī′). **1.** See **navel** 1. **2.** *Biol.* A small opening or depression similar to a navel. [Lat. *umbilīcus.* See **nobh-*.**]

um•bo (ŭm′bō) *n., pl.* **um•bo•nes** (ŭm-bō′nēz) or **um•bos. 1.** The boss or knob at the center of a shield. **2.a.** *Biol.* A knoblike protuberance, as the prominence near the hinge of a bivalve shell. **b.** *Anat.* A small projection at the center of the outer surface of the eardrum. [Lat. *umbō, umbōn-.* See **nobh-*.**] **—um′bo•nal** (ŭm′bə-nəl, ŭm-bō′nəl) *adj.*

um•bo•nate (ŭm′bə-nāt′, ŭm-bō′nĭt) *adj.* Having or resembling a knob or knoblike protuberance.

um•bra (ŭm′brə) *n., pl.* **-bras** or **-brae** (-brē). **1.** A dark area, esp. the blackest part of a shadow from which all light is cut off. **2.** *Astron.* **a.** The completely dark portion of the shadow cast by the earth, moon, or other body during an eclipse. **b.** The darkest region of a sunspot. [Lat., shadow.] **—um′bral** *adj.*

um•brage (ŭm′brĭj) *n.* **1.** Offense; resentment: *took umbrage at their rudeness.* **2.a.** Something that affords shade. **b.** Shadow or shade. **3.** A vague or indistinct indication; a hint. [ME, shade < OFr. < Lat. *umbrāticum*, neut. of *umbrāticus*, of shade < *umbra*, shadow.]

um•bra•geous (ŭm-brā′jəs) *adj.* **1.** Affording or forming shade; shady. **2.** Easily offended; irritable. **—um•bra′geous•ly** *adv.* **—um•bra′geous•ness** *n.*

um•brel•la (ŭm-brĕl′ə) *n.* **1.** A device for protection from the weather consisting of a collapsible, usu. circular canopy mounted on a central rod. **2.a.** Something that covers or protects. **b.** Air cover, esp. during a military operation. **3.** Something that encompasses or covers many different elements or groups. **4.** *Zool.* The gelatinous rounded mass that is the major part of the body of most jellyfish. [Ital. *ombrella* < LLat. *umbrella*, alteration (influenced by *umbra*, shade) of Lat. *umbella*, parasol. See UMBEL.]

umbrella

umbrella bird *n.* Any of several tropical American birds of the genus *Cephalopterus*, esp. *C. ornatus*, having a retractile umbrellalike black crest and a long feathered wattle.

umbrella plant *n.* **1.** A widely cultivated ornamental robust sedge *(Cyperus alternifolius)* native to Madagascar and Mauritius and having a terminal umbrellalike cluster of grasslike leaves. **2.** *Midland U.S.* The May apple.

umbrella tree *n.* **1.** Either of two trees *(Magnolia fraseri* or *M. tripetala)* of the southeast United States having large leaves clustered in an umbrellalike form at the ends of the branches. **2.** An Australian evergreen tree *(Brassasia actinophylla)* having palmately compound leaves. **3.** See **schefflera.**

um•brette (ŭm-brĕt′) *n.* See **hammerhead** 3. [NLat. *umbretta*, species name < Fr. *ombrette*, shadow, dim. of *ombre*, shade < OFr. < Lat. *umbra.*]

Um•bri•a (ŭm′brē-ə, o͞om′brē-ä). A region of central Italy in the Apennines; came under the control of the papacy in the 16th cent. and joined the kingdom of Sardinia in 1860.

Um•bri•an (ŭm′brē-ən) *adj.* Of or relating to Umbria. *—n.* **1.** The Italic language of ancient Umbria. **2.** A native or inhabitant of Umbria.

Um•bri•el (ŭm′brē-əl′) *n.* A satellite of Uranus. [After *Umbriel*, a character in Pope's *Rape of the Lock.*]

Um•bun•du (o͞om-bo͞on′do͞o, əm-) *n.* See **Mbundu** 2.

U•me (o͞o′mə, ü′mə). A river of northern Sweden flowing c. 459 km (285 mi) SE into the Gulf of Bothnia.

u•mi•ak also **oo•mi•ak** (o͞o′mē-ăk′) *n. Naut.* A large open Eskimo boat made of skins stretched on a wooden frame and usu. paddled. [Canadian and Greenlandic Eskimo *umiaq.*]

um•laut (o͞om′lout′) *Ling. —n.* **1.a.** A change in a vowel sound caused by partial assimilation esp. to a vowel or semivowel in the following syllable. **b.** A vowel sound changed in this manner. **2.** The diacritic mark (¨) over a vowel, indicating an umlaut, esp. in German. *—tr.v.* **-laut•ed, -laut•ing, -lauts. 1.** To modify by umlaut. **2.** To write or print (a vowel) with an umlaut. [Ger. : *um-*, around, alteration (< MHGer. *umb-* < *umbe* < OHGer. *umbi*; see **ambhi***) + *Laut*, sound (< MHGer. *lūt* < OHGer. *hlūt*; see **kleu-***).]

Um•nak Island (o͞om′năk′). An island of SW AK in the Aleutian Is. separated from Unalaska I. by **Umnak Pass.**

ump (ŭmp) *Sports. —n.* An umpire. *—intr.v.* **umped, ump•ing, umps.** To serve as an umpire.

umbrella bird

um•pire (ŭm′pīr′) *n.* **1.** *Sports.* A person appointed to rule on plays, esp. in baseball. **2.** A person appointed to settle a dispute that arbitrators have been unable to resolve. *—v.* **-pired, -pir•ing, -pires.** *—tr.* To act as referee for; rule or judge. *—intr.* To be or act as a referee or an arbitrator. [ME *(an) oumpere*, (an) umpire, alteration of *(a) noumpere*, a mediator < OFr. *nonper* : *non-*, non- + *per*, equal, even, paired (< Lat. *pār*; see PAIR).]

ump•teen (ŭmp′tēn′, ŭm′-) *adj. Informal.* Relatively large but unspecified in number: *umpteen guests.* [Slang *ump(ty)*, dash in Morse code (of imit. orig.) + *-teen* (as in THIRTEEN).] **—ump′teenth′** *adj.*

Um•ta•ta (o͞om-tä′tə). The cap. of Transkei, in the W-central part; founded 1860. Pop. 30,000.

UMW *abbr.* United Mine Workers.

UN or **U.N.** *abbr.* United Nations.

un–¹ *pref.* **1.** Not: *unhappy.* **2.** Opposite of; contrary to: *unrest.* [ME < OE. See **ne*.**]

un–² *pref.* **1.** To reverse or undo the result of a specified action: *unbind.* **2.a.** To deprive of or remove a specified thing: *unfrock.* **b.** To release, free, or remove from: *unyoke.* **3.** Used as an intensive: *unloose.* [ME < OE *on-*, alteration (influenced by *un-*, not; see UN-¹) of *ond-, and-, an-*, against, opposing. See **ant-*.**]

un•a•bashed (ŭn′ə-băsht′) *adj.* **1.** Not disconcerted or embarrassed; poised. **2.** Not concealed or disguised; obvious.

un•a•bat•ed (ŭn′ə-bā′tĭd) *adj.* Sustaining an original intensity or maintaining full force with no decrease.

un•a•bridged (ŭn′ə-brĭjd′) *adj.* Containing the original content; not condensed. Used of books, articles, and documents.

un•ac•cent•ed (ŭn-ăk′sĕn-tĭd) *adj. Ling.* **1.** Having no diacritical mark. Used of a word, syllable, or letter. **2.** Having weak stress or no stress, as in pronunciation or metrical rhythm.

un•ac•com•mo•dat•ed (ŭn′ə-kŏm′ə-dā′tĭd) *adj.* **1.** Not

ă pat	oi boy
ā pay	ou out
âr care	o͝o took
ä father	o͞o boot
ĕ pet	ŭ cut
ē be	ûr urge
ĭ pit	th thin
ī pie	*th* this
îr pier	hw which
ŏ pot	zh vision
ō toe	ə about,
ô paw	item

Stress marks:
′ (primary);
′ (secondary), as in
dictionary (dĭk′shə-nĕr′ē)

adapted or accommodated. **2.** Lacking accommodations.

un•ac•com•pa•nied (ŭn′ə-kŭm′pə-nēd) *adj.* **1.** Going or acting without companions or a companion. **2.** *Mus.* Performed or scored without accompaniment.

un•ac•count•ed-for (ŭn′ə-koun′tĭd-fôr′) *adj.* **1.** Not explained, understood, or taken into account. **2.** Missing or absent without explanation, as from a roll call.

un•ac•cred•it•ed (ŭn′ə-krĕd′ĭ-tĭd) *adj.* **1.** Not having the proper credentials; unauthorized: *an unaccredited school.* **2.** Not ascribed or attributed to a source.

u•na cor•da (o͞o′nə kôr′də) *adv. & adj. Mus.* With the soft pedal of the piano depressed. Used chiefly as a direction. [Ital. : *una*, one + *corda*, string (so called because depressing the soft pedal causes only one string to be struck of the two or three provided for each note).]

un•ad•dressed (ŭn-ə-drĕst′) *adj.* **1.** Not brought up for discussion or solution: *questions that remain unaddressed.* **2.** Not containing the required address: *unaddressed letters.*

un•ad•just•ed (ŭn′ə-jŭs′tĭd) *adj.* **1.** Not having been adjusted to conform to new data or information. **2.** Not having adapted to new conditions. **3.** Needing to be made operable or accurate by adjusting or regulating.

un•a•dopt•a•ble (ŭn′ə-dŏp′tə-bəl) *adj.* Difficult to place in an adoptive home.

un•a•dorned (ŭn′ə-dôrnd′) *adj.* Without adornment or embellishment; simple or plain.

un•a•dul•ter•at•ed (ŭn′ə-dŭl′tə-rā′tĭd) *adj.* **1.** Not mingled or diluted with extraneous matter; pure. See Syns at **pure.** **2.** Out-and-out; utter: *the unadulterated truth.*

un•af•fect•ed (ŭn′ə-fĕk′tĭd) *adj.* **1.** Not changed or affected. **2.** Marked by lack of affectation; genuine. See Syns at **naive.** —**un′af•fect′ed•ly** *adv.* —**un′af•fect′ed•ness** *n.*

un•af•fil•i•at•ed (ŭn′ə-fĭl′ē-ā′tĭd) *adj.* Not associated with another or others as a subordinate, subsidiary, or member; independent.

Un•a•las•ka Island (ŭn′ə-lăs′kə). An island of SW AK in the E Aleutian Is. SW of Unimak I.

un•al•ien•a•ble (ŭn-āl′yə-nə-bəl, -ā′lē-ə-) *adj.* Not to be separated, given away, or taken away; inalienable.

un•a•ligned (ŭn′ə-līnd′) *adj.* Nonaligned: *unaligned nations.*

un•al•loyed (ŭn′ə-loid′) *adj.* **1.** Not in mixture with other metals; pure. **2.** Complete; unqualified: *unalloyed blessings; unalloyed relief.* —**un′al•loy′ed•ly** (-loi′ĭd-lē) *adv.*

un-A•mer•i•can (ŭn′ə-mĕr′ĭ-kən) *adj.* Considered contrary to the institutions or principles of the United States.

U•na•mi (o͞o-nä′mē, yo͞o-năm′ē) *n., pl.* **Unami** or **-mis.** **1.** One of the two Algonquian languages of the Delaware peoples, originally spoken in central and southern New Jersey, eastern Pennsylvania, and northern Delaware. **2.** A speaker of this language.

U•na•mu•no (o͞o′nə-mo͞o′nō, -nä-). **Miguel de.** 1864–1936. Spanish philosopher whose works include *The Tragic Sense of Life* (1913).

unan. *abbr.* Unanimous.

un•a•neled (ŭn′ə-nēld′) *adj. Archaic.* Not having received extreme unction.

u•na•nim•i•ty (yo͞o′nə-nĭm′ĭ-tē) *n.* The condition of being unanimous.

u•nan•i•mous (yo͞o-năn′ə-məs) *adj.* **1.** Sharing the same opinions or views; being in complete harmony or accord. **2.** Based on or characterized by complete assent or agreement. [< Lat. *ūnanimus* : *ūnus*, one; see **oi-no-*** + *animus*, mind; see **anə-***.] —**u•nan′i•mous•ly** *adv.* —**u•nan′i•mous•ness** *n.*

un•an•swer•a•ble (ŭn-ăn′sər-ə-bəl) *adj.* Impossible to answer or refute; incontrovertible. —**un•an′swer•a•bil′i•ty, un•an′swer•a•ble•ness** *n.* —**un•an′swer•a•bly** *adv.*

un•an•tic•i•pat•ed (ŭn′ăn-tĭs′ə-pā′tĭd) *adj.* **1.** Not anticipated: *We had some unanticipated problems.* **2.** *Usage Problem.* Not having been expected; unexpected. —**un′an•tic′i•pat′ed•ly** *adv.*

un•ap•peal•a•ble (ŭn′ə-pē′lə-bəl) *adj.* Not subject to appeal: *an unappealable grievance.* —**un′ap•peal′a•bly** *adv.*

un•ap•peal•ing (un′ə-pē′lĭng) *adj.* Not appealing to the senses, as in taste or aroma. —**un′ap•peal′ing•ly** *adv.*

un•ap•pre•ci•at•ed (un′ə-prē′shē-ā′tĭd) *adj.* **1.** Not recognized, as to quality or worth: *an unappreciated favor.* **2.** Not having risen in price or value: *an unappreciated investment.*

un•apt (ŭn-ăpt′) *adj.* **1.** Not suitable or appropriate. **2.** Not likely or liable. —**un•apt′ly** *adv.* —**un•apt′ness** *n.*

un•armed (ŭn-ärmd′) *adj.* **1.a.** Lacking weapons or armor; defenseless. **b.** Not carrying, using, or displaying arms: *unarmed robbery.* **2.** *Biol.* Having no thorns, spines, teeth, claws, or other protective parts.

un•ar•tic•u•lat•ed (ŭn′är-tĭk′yə-lā′tĭd) *adj.* **1.a.** Not articulated: *our unarticulated fears.* **b.** Not carefully or thoroughly thought out. **2.** *Biol.* Not having joints or segments.

un•a•shamed (ŭn′ə-shāmd′) *adj.* **1.** Feeling or showing no remorse, shame, or need for apology. **2.** Exhibiting no embarrassment; unabashed: *lived in unashamed luxury.* —**un′a•sham′ed•ly** (-shā′mĭd-lē) *adv.* —**un′a•sham′ed•ness** *n.*

un•as•sail•a•ble (ŭn′ə-sā′lə-bəl) *adj.* **1.** Impossible to dispute or disprove; undeniable. **2.** Not subject to attack or sei-

---

un•a′ble *adj.*
un′ac•cept′a•bil′i•ty *n.*
un′ac•cept′a•ble *adj.*
un′ac•cept′a•bly *adv.*
un′ac•com′plished *adj.*
un′ac•count′a•bil′i•ty *n.*
un′ac•count′a•ble *adj.*
un′ac•count′a•ble•ness *n.*
un′ac•count′a•bly *adv.*
un′ac•cus′tomed *adj.*
un′ac•cus′tomed•ly *adv.*
un′ac•cus′tomed•ness *n.*
un′a•chiev′a•ble *adj.*
un′ac•knowl′edged *adj.*
un′ac•quaint′ed *adj.*
un′ad•ven′tur•ous *adj.*
un•ad′ver•tised′ *adj.*
un′ad•vised′ *adj.*
un′ad•vis′ed•ly *adv.*
un′ad•vis′ed•ness *n.*
un′af•ford′a•bil′i•ty *n.*
un′af•ford′a•ble *adj.*
un′af•ford′a•bly *adv.*
un′a•fraid′ *adj.*
un•aid′ed *adj.*
un′a•ligned′ *adj.*
un•al′ter•a•bil′i•ty *n.*
un•al′ter•a•ble *adj.*
un•al′ter•a•ble•ness *n.*
un•al′ter•a•bly *adv.*
un′am•big′u•ous *adj.*
un′am•big′u•ous•ly *adv.*
un•an′a•lyz′a•ble *adj.*
un•an′a•lyz′a•bly *adv.*
un′a•pol′o•get′ic *adj.*
un′a•pol′o•get′i•cal•ly *adv.*
un′ap•peas′a•ble *adj.*
un′ap•peas′a•bly *adv.*
un•ap′pe•tiz′ing *adj.*
un•ap′pe•tiz′ing•ly *adv.*
un′ap•pre′ci•at′ed *adj.*
un′ap•proach′a•bil′i•ty *n.*
un′ap•proach′a•ble *adj.*
un′ap•proach′a•ble•ness *n.*
un′ap•proach′a•bly *adv.*
un′ap•pro′pri•at′ed *adj.*
un′ap•proved′ *adj.*
un•ar′gu•a•ble *adj.*
un•ar′gu•a•bly *adv.*
un•arm′ *tr.v.*
un•asked′ *adj.*
un′as•ser′tive *adj.*
un′as•ser′tive•ly *adv.*
un′as•ser′tive•ness *n.*
un′as•sum′ing *adj.*
un′as•sum′ing•ly *adv.*
un′as•sum′ing•ness *n.*
un′at•tain′a•bil′i•ty *n.*
un′at•tain′a•ble *adj.*
un′at•tain′a•ble•ness *n.*
un′at•tain′a•bly *adv.*
un′at•test′ed *adj.*
un′at•trib′ut•ed *adj.*
un′a•vail′a•bil′i•ty *n.*
un′a•vail′a•ble *adj.*
un•baked′ *adj.*
un′be•liev′a•ble *adj.*
un′be•liev′a•bly *adv.*
un′be•liev′ing *adj.*
un′be•liev′ing•ly *adv.*
un′be•liev′ing•ness *n.*
un•bleached′ *adj.*
un•blem′ished *adj.*
un•blenched′ *adj.*
un•brand′ed *adj.*
un•breath′a•ble *adj.*
un•bri′dle *tr.v.*
un•bri′dled *adj.*
un•bri′dled•ly *adv.*
un•bur′den *tr.v.*
un•caged′ *adj.*
un•ceas′ing *adj.*
un•ceas′ing•ly *adv.*
un•ceas′ing•ness *n.*
un•cel′e•brat′ed *adj.*
un•cer′ti•fied′ *adj.*
un•chal′lenge•a•ble *adj.*
un•chal′lenge•a•bly *adv.*
un′char•ac•ter•is′tic *adj.*
un′char•ac•ter•is′ti•cal•ly *adv.*
un•char′i•ta•ble *adj.*
un•char′i•ta•ble•ness *n.*
un•char′i•ta•bly *adv.*
un•cir′cu•lat′ed *adj.*
un•civ′i•lized′ *adj.*
un•civ′i•liz′ed•ly *adv.*
un•civ′i•liz′ed•ness *n.*
un•clas′si•fied′ *adj.*
un•clench′ *tr. & intr.v.*
un•cloak′ *tr.v.*
un•clothe′ *tr.v.*
un•clut′tered *adj.*
un•coat′ed *adj.*
un•coil′ *tr. & intr.v.*
un′col•lect′ed *adj.*
un•com′pen•sat′ed *adj.*
un′com•pet′i•tive *adj.*
un′com•pet′i•tive•ly *adv.*
un′com•pet′i•tive•ness *n.*
un′com•plain′ing *adj.*
un′com•plain′ing•ly *adv.*
un′com•pli•men′ta•ry *adj.*
un′com•pre•hend′ing *adj.*
un′com•pre•hend′ing•ly *adv.*
un•com′pro•mis′ing *adj.*
un•com′pro•mis′ing•ly *adv.*
un′con•ceiv′a•ble *adj.*
un′con•ceiv′a•ble•ness *n.*
un′con•ceiv′a•bly *adv.*
un′con•di′tion•al *adj.*
un′con•di′tion•al′i•ty *n.*
un′con•di′tion•al•ly *adv.*
un′con•di′tion•al•ness *n.*
un′con•nect′ed *adj.*
un′con•nect′ed•ly *adv.*
un′con•nect′ed•ness *n.*
un•con′quer•a•ble *adj.*
un•con′quer•a•bly *adv.*
un′con•sol′i•dat′ed *adj.*
un′con•tam′i•nat′ed *adj.*
un′con•test′ed *adj.*
un′con•trol′la•bil′i•ty *n.*
un′con•trol′la•ble *adj.*
un′con•trol′la•ble•ness *n.*
un′con•trol′la•bly *adv.*
un′con•trolled′ *adj.*
un′con•trolled′ness *n.*
un′con•tro•ver′sial *adj.*
un′con•tro•ver′sial•ly *adv.*
un′con•ven′tion•al *adj.*
un′con•ven′tion•al′i•ty *n.*
un′con•ven′tion•al•ly *adv.*
un′con•vinc′ing *adj.*
un′con•vinc′ing•ly *adv.*
un′con•vinc′ing•ness *n.*
un•cooked′ *adj.*
un′co•op′er•a•tive *adj.*
un′co•op′er•a•tive•ly *adv.*
un′co•op′er•a•tive•ness *n.*
un′cor•rect′ed *adj.*
un′cor•rob′o•rat′ed *adj.*
un•crowd′ed *adj.*
un•cul′ti•vat′ed *adj.*
un•curl′ *tr. & intr.v.*
un•dam′aged *adj.*
un•dat′ed *adj.*
un′de•bat′a•ble *adj.*
un′de•bat′a•bly *adv.*
un′de•ceiv′a•ble *adj.*
un′de•ceiv′a•bly *adv.*
un′de•ceive′ *tr.v.*
un′de•cid′ed *adj. & n.*
un′de•cid′ed•ly *adv.*
un′de•cid′ed•ness *n.*
un′de•clared′ *adj.*
un′de•ni′a•ble *adj.*
un′de•ni′a•ble•ness *n.*
un′de•ni′a•bly *adv.*
un′de•pend′a•bil′i•ty *n.*
un′de•pend′a•ble *adj.*
un′de•served′ *adj.*

zure; impregnable. — **un′as•sail′a•bil′i•ty, un′as•sail′a•ble•ness** *n.* — **un′as•sail′a•bly** *adv.*

un•as•sem•bled (ŭn′ə-sĕm′bəld) *adj.* Made with parts or sections ready to be joined or fitted together before use.

un•as•sist•ed (ŭn′ə-sĭs′tĭd) *adj.* **1.** Not having assistance; unaided. **2.** *Baseball.* Of, relating to, or being a play handled by only one fielder.

un•at•tached (ŭn′ə-tăcht′) *adj.* **1.** Not joined, esp. to surrounding tissue. **2.a.** Not committed to or dependent on another person, group, or organization. **b.** Not engaged, married, or involved in a serious sexual or romantic relationship.

un•at•tend•ed (ŭn′ə-tĕn′dĭd) *adj.* **1.** Not being attended to, looked after, or watched. **2.** Having no attendants: *unattended counters.* **3.** Not being paid attention to or listened to.

un•a•vail•ing (ŭn′ə-vā′lĭng) *adj.* Not availing; ineffectual or useless. See Syns at **futile.** — **un′a•vail′ing•ly** *adv.* — **un′a•vail′ing•ness** *n.*

u•na vo•ce (yo͞o′nə vō′sē, o͞o′nə vō′kā) *adv.* With one voice; unanimously. [Lat. *ūnā vōce* : *ūnā*, fem. ablative of *ūnus*, one + *vōce*, ablative of *vōx*, voice.]

un•a•void•a•ble (ŭn′ə-voi′də-bəl) *adj.* Impossible to avoid; inevitable. — **un′a•void′a•bil′i•ty, un′a•void′a•ble•ness** *n.* — **un′a•void′a•bly** *adv.*

un•a•ware (ŭn′ə-wâr′) *adj.* Not aware or cognizant. — *adv.* Unawares. — **un′a•ware′ly** *adv.* — **un′a•ware′ness** *n.*

Usage Note: *Unaware,* followed by *of* (expressed or implied), is the usual adjectival form modifying a noun or pronoun or following a linking verb: *Unaware of the difficulty, I went ahead. He was unaware of my presence. Unawares* is the usual adverbial form: *The rain caught them unawares. They came upon it unawares.*

un•a•wares (ŭn′ə-wârz′) *adv.* **1.** By surprise; unexpectedly. **2.** Without forethought or plan. See Usage Note at **unaware.**

unb. *abbr.* Unbound.

un•backed (ŭn-băkt′) *adj.* **1.** Lacking backing or support. **2.** Not having a back. **3.** Never having been ridden.

un•bal•ance (ŭn-băl′əns) *tr.v.* **-anced, -anc•ing, -anc•es. 1.** To upset the balance, stability, or equilibrium of. **2.** To derange (the mind). — *n.* The condition of being unbalanced. — **un•bal′ance•a•ble** *adj.*

un•bal•anced (ŭn-băl′ənst) *adj.* **1.** Not in balance or in proper balance. **2.a.** Mentally deranged. **b.** Not exhibiting sound judgment; irrational. **3.** *Accounting.* Not satisfactorily adjusted so that debit and credit correspond.

un•bal•last•ed (ŭn-băl′ə-stĭd) *adj.* **1.** Not stabilized or properly stabilized by ballast. **2.** Unsteady; wavering.

un•bar (ŭn-bär′) *tr. & intr.v.* **-barred, -bar•ring, -bars.** To remove the bars from or become unbarred.

un•bat•ed (ŭn-bā′tĭd) *adj.* **1.** Unabated. **2.** *Archaic.* Not blunted by a guard on the tip, as a sword or fencing foil.

unbd. *abbr.* Unbound.

un•bear•a•ble (ŭn-bâr′ə-bəl) *adj.* So unpleasant, distasteful, or painful as to be intolerable: *unbearable heat.* — **un•bear′a•ble•ness** *n.* — **un•bear′a•bly** *adv.*

un•beat•a•ble (ŭn-bē′tə-bəl) *adj.* Impossible to defeat or surpass: *an unbeatable team.* — **un•beat′a•bly** *adv.*

un•beat•en (ŭn-bēt′n) *adj.* **1.** Not defeated: *an unbeaten team.* **2.** Not traversed before; untrodden: *an unbeaten path.* **3.** Not beaten or pounded, as in cooking: *unbeaten eggs.*

un•be•com•ing (ŭn′bĭ-kŭm′ĭng) *adj.* **1.** Not appropriate, attractive, or flattering. **2.** Not in accord with the standards implied by one's character or position. — **un′be•com′ing•ly** *adv.* — **un′be•com′ing•ness** *n.*

un•be•got•ten (ŭn′bĭ-gŏt′n) *adj.* **1.** Not yet begotten; as yet unborn. **2.** Self-existent; eternal.

un•be•known (ŭn′bĭ-nōn′) *adj.* Occurring or existing without the knowledge of; unknown: *a crisis unbeknown to us.* [UN-[1] + obsolete *beknown*, known (< ME *beknowen*, p.part. of *beknowen*, to get to know < OE *becnāwan* : *be-*, be- + *cnāwan*, to know; see KNOW).]

un•be•knownst (ŭn′bĭ-nōnst′) *adj.* Unbeknown. — *adv.* Without the knowledge of a specified party. Used with *to.* [UNBEKNOWN + *-st* (as in AMONGST).]

un•be•lief (ŭn′bĭ-lēf′) *n.* Lack of belief or faith, especially in religious matters.

un•be•liev•er (ŭn′bĭ-lē′vər) *n.* One who lacks belief or faith, esp. in a particular religion; a nonbeliever.

un•belt•ed (ŭn-bĕl′tĭd) *adj.* **1.** Made or designed to be worn without a belt. **2.** Not having or using a seat belt.

un•bend (ŭn-bĕnd′) *v.* **-bent** (-bĕnt′), **-bend•ing, -bends.** — *tr.* **1.** To release from mental tension, strain, or formality; relax. **2.** To release (a bow, for example) from flexure or tension. **3.** *Naut.* To untie or loosen (a knot or sail). **4.** To straighten (something crooked or bent): *unbend a paper clip.* — *intr.* **1.** To become less tense; relax. **2.** To become less strict. **3.** To become straight. — **un•bend′a•ble** *adj.*

un•bend•ing (ŭn-bĕn′dĭng) *adj.* **1.** Not yielding; inflexible: *an unbending will.* **2.** Aloof and often antisocial; extremely reserved: *an unbending manner.* — **un•bend′ing•ly** *adv.*

un•bi•ased also **un•bi•assed** (ŭn-bī′əst) *adj.* Without bias or prejudice; impartial. See Syns at **fair**[1]. — **un•bi′ased•ly** *adv.* — **un•bi′ased•ness** *n.*

---

un′de•serv′ed•ly *adv.*
un•dig′ni•fied′ *adj.*
un′dis•turbed′ *adj.*
un′e•mo′tion•al *adj.*
un′e•mo′tion•al•ly *adv.*
un′em•ploy′a•ble *adj.* & *n.*
un′em•ployed′ *adj.* & *n.*
un′em•ploy′ment *n.*
un′e•quiv′o•cal *adj.*
un′e•quiv′o•cal•ly *adv.*
un•err′ing *adj.*
un•err′ing•ly *adv.*
un•fad′ing *adj.*
un•fad′ing•ly *adv.*
un′fa•mil′iar *adj.*
un′fa•mil′iar′i•ty *n.*
un′fa•mil′iar•ly *adv.*
un•fash′ion•a•ble *adj.*
un•fash′ion•a•bly *adv.*
un•fas′ten *tr.* & *intr.v.*
un•fath′om•a•ble *adj.*
un•fa′vor•a•ble *adj.*
un•fa′vor•a•ble•ness *n.*
un•fa′vor•a•bly *adv.*
un•fet′ter *tr.v.*
un•fin′ished *adj.*
un′fore•seen′ *adj.*
un′for•get′ta•bil′i•ty *n.*
un′for•get′ta•ble *adj.*
un′for•get′ta•ble•ness *n.*
un′for•get′ta•bly *adv.*
un•friend′li•ness *n.*
un•friend′ly *adj.*
un•fund′ed *adj.*
un•fuss′y *adj.*
un•gen′er•ous *adj.*
un•gen′er•ous•ly *adv.*
un•grate′ful *adj.*
un•grate′ful•ly *adv.*
un•grate′ful•ness *n.*
un•hoped′-for′ *adj.*
un′im•por′tance *n.*
un′im•por′tant *adj.*
un′in•form′a•tive *adj.*
un′in•form′a•tive•ly *adv.*
un′in•hab′it•a•bil′i•ty *n.*
un′in•hab′it•a•ble *adj.*
un′in•hab′it•ed *adj.*
un′in•tel′li•gence *n.*
un′in•tel′li•gent *adj.*
un′in•tel′li•gent•ly *adv.*
un′in•tel′li•gi•bil′i•ty *n.*
un′in•tel′li•gi•ble *adj.*
un′in•tel′li•gi•ble•ness *n.*
un′in•tel′li•gi•bly *adv.*
un′in•ten′tion•al *adj.*
un′in•ten′tion•al•ly *adv.*
un′in•vit′ing *adj.*
un′in•vit′ing•ly *adv.*
un•latch′ *tr.* & *intr.v.*
un•leav′ened *adj.*
un•link′ *tr.* & *intr.v.*
un•looked′-for′ *adj.*
un•man′age•a•bil′i•ty *n.*
un•man′age•a•ble *adj.*
un•man′age•a•bly *adv.*
un•man′ner•li•ness *n.*
un•man′ner•ly *adj.* & *adv.*
un•marked′ *adj.*
un•mar′ried *adj.* & *n.*
un•mask′ *tr.* & *intr.v.*
un•meet′ *adj.*
un′mis•tak′a•ble *adj.*
un′mis•tak′a•bly *adv.*
un′mo•lest′ed *adj.*
un•mo′ti•vat′ed *adj.*
un•muf′fle *tr.* & *intr.v.*
un•my′e•lin•at′ed *adj.*
un•nec′es•sar′i•ly *adv.*
un•nec′es•sar′y *adj.*
un•no′tice•a•ble *adj.*
un•no′tice•a•bly *adv.*
un′ob•jec′tion•a•ble *adj.*
un′ob•struct′ed *adj.*
un•oc′cu•pied′ *adj.*
un′of•fi′cial *adj.*
un′of•fi′cial•ly *adv.*
un′op•posed′ *adj.*
un′o•rig′i•nal *adj.*
un•or′na•ment′ *tr.v.*
un•or′tho•dox′ *adj.*
un•or′tho•dox′ly *adv.*
un•or′tho•dox′y *n.*
un•pack′ *tr.* & *intr.v.*
un•pag′i•nat′ed *adj.*
un′pal•at•a•bil′i•ty *n.*
un•pal′at•a•ble *adj.*
un•pal′at•a•bly *adv.*
un•peo′ple *tr.v.*
un•peo′pled *adj.*
un′per•turbed′ *adj.*
un•pile′ *tr.v.*
un•planned′ *adj.*
un•pleas′ant *adj.*
un•pleas′ant•ly *adv.*
un•pleas′ant•ness *n.*
un′po•lit′i•cal *adj.*
un•pop′u•lar *adj.*
un′pop•u•lar′i•ty *n.*
un•prec′e•dent′ed *adj.*
un•prec′e•dent′ed•ly *adv.*
un′pre•dict′a•bil′i•ty *n.*
un′pre•dict′a•ble *adj.* & *n.*
un′pre•dict′a•bly *adv.*
un′pre•pos•sess′ing *adj.*
un′pre•pos•sess′ing•ly *adv.*
un•priced′ *adj.*
un•prin′ci•pled *adj.*
un•prin′ci•pled•ness *n.*
un•prof′it•a•bil′i•ty *n.*
un•prof′it•a•ble *adj.*
un•prof′it•a•ble•ness *n.*
un•prof′it•a•bly *adv.*
un•prom′is•ing *adj.*
un•prom′is•ing•ly *adv.*
un′pro•pi′tious *adj.*
un′pro•pi′tious•ly *adv.*
un•quench′a•ble *adj.*
un•quench′a•bly *adv.*
un•read′i•ly *adv.*
un•read′i•ness *n.*
un•read′y *adj.*
un•re′al•ized′ *adj.*
un′re•lent′ing *adj.*
un′re•lent′ing•ly *adv.*
un′re•li′a•bil′i•ty *n.*
un′re•li′a•ble *adj.*
un′re•li′a•ble•ness *n.*
un′re•li′a•bly *adv.*
un′re•lig′ious *adj.*
un′re•mark′a•ble *adj.*
un′re•mark′a•bly *adv.*
un′re•marked′ *adj.*
un′re•pent′ant *adj.*
un′re•pent′ant•ly *adv.*
un′re•proved′ *adj.*
un′re•quit′ed *adj.*
un′re•quit′ed•ly *adv.*
un′re•spon′sive *adj.*
un′re•spon′sive•ly *adv.*
un′re•spon′sive•ness *n.*
un′re•strained′ *adj.*
un′re•strain′ed•ly *adv.*
un′re•strain′ed•ness *n.*
un′re•straint′ *n.*
un•ripe′ *adj.*
un•ripe′ness *n.*
un•roof′ *tr.v.*
un•safe′ *adj.*
un•sat′is•fac•to′ri•ly *adv.*
un•sat′is•fac•to′ri•ness *n.*
un•sat′is•fac′to•ry *adj.*
un•scathed′ *adj.*
un•scru′pu•lous *adj.*
un•scru′pu•lous•ly *adv.*
un•scru′pu•lous•ness *n.*
un•seal′ *tr.v.*
un•seam′ *tr.v.*
un•search′a•ble *adj.*
un•search′a•bly *adv.*
un•self′ish *adj.*
un•self′ish•ly *adv.*
un•self′ish•ness *n.*
un•shack′le *tr.v.*

ă pat	oi boy
ā pay	ou out
âr care	o͝o took
ä father	o͞o boot
ĕ pet	ŭ cut
ē be	ûr urge
ĭ pit	th thin
ī pie	*th* this
îr pier	hw which
ŏ pot	zh vision
ō toe	ə about,
ô paw	item

Stress marks:
′ (primary);
′ (secondary), as in
dictionary (dĭk′shə-nĕr′ē)

un•bid•den (ŭn-bĭd′n) also **un•bid** (-bĭd′) *adj.* Not invited, asked, or requested; unasked: *unbidden guests.*

un•bind (ŭn-bīnd′) *tr.v.* **-bound** (-bound′), **-bind•ing, -binds. 1.** To untie or unfasten, as wrappings or bindings. **2.** To release from restraints or bonds; free.

un•blessed also **un•blest** (ŭn-blĕst′) *adj.* **1.** Deprived of a blessing. **2.** Evil. **—un•bless′ed•ness** (-blĕs′ĭd-nĭs) *n.*

un•blink•ing (ŭn-blĭng′kĭng) *adj.* **1.** Without blinking. **2.** Without visible emotion. **3.** Fearless in facing reality.

un•block (ŭn-blŏk′) *tr.v.* **-blocked, -block•ing, -blocks.** To remove or clear an obstruction from: *unblock a road.*

un•blush•ing (ŭn-blŭsh′ĭng) *adj.* **1.** Lacking or exhibiting a lack of shame or embarrassment. **2.** Not blushing. **—un•blush′ing•ly** *adv.* **—un•blush′ing•ness** *n.*

un•bod•ied (ŭn-bŏd′ēd) *adj.* **1.** Having no body or form; incorporeal. **2.** Being disembodied.

un•bolt (ŭn-bōlt′) *tr.v.* **-bolt•ed, -bolt•ing, -bolts.** To release the bolts of (a door, for example); unlock.

un•bolt•ed[1] (ŭn-bōl′tĭd) *adj.* Not bolted or fastened.

un•bolt•ed[2] (ŭn-bōl′tĭd) *adj.* Not sifted: *unbolted flour.*

un•born (ŭn-bôrn′) *adj.* **1.** Not yet born: *an unborn child.* **2.** Not yet appeared; future: *unborn inventions.*

un•bos•om (ŭn-bo͝oz′əm, -bo͞o′zəm) *v.* **-omed, -om•ing, -oms.** *—tr.* **1.** To confide (one's thoughts or feelings). **2.** To relieve (oneself) of troublesome thoughts or feelings. *—intr.* To reveal one's thoughts or feelings. **—un•bos′om•er** *n.*

un•bound (ŭn-bound′) *v.* P.t. and p.part. of **unbind.** *—adj.* **1.** Not bound: *an unbound book.* **2.** Freed from bonds or restraints; released: *an unbound captive.*

un•bound•ed (ŭn-boun′dĭd) *adj.* **1.** Having no boundaries or limits: *unbounded space.* **2.** Not kept within bounds; unrestrained: *unbounded enthusiasm.* **—un•bound′ed•ly** *adv.* **—un•bound′ed•ness** *n.*

un•bowed (ŭn-boud′) *adj.* **1.** Not bowed; unbent. **2.** Not subdued; unyielding.

un•brace (ŭn-brās′) *tr.v.* **-braced, -brac•ing, -brac•es. 1.** To set free by removing bands or braces. **2.** To release from tension; relax. **3.** To make slack; weaken.

un•break•a•ble (un-brā′kə-bəl) *adj.* **1.** Impossible to break; able to withstand rough usage: *unbreakable dinnerware.* **2.** Able to withstand an attempt to break. Used of a horse. *—n.* An article or object that is not easily broken. **—un•break′a•ble•ness** *n.* **—un•break′a•bly** *adv.*

un•bred (ŭn-brĕd′) *adj.* **1.** Not instructed; untaught. **2.** Not yet bred: *an unbred mare.* **3.** *Obsolete.* Ill-bred; impolite.

un•bridge•a•ble (ŭn-brĭj′ə-bəl) *adj.* Impossible to span. **—un•bridge′a•bly** *adv.*

un•bri•dled (ŭn-brīd′ld) *adj.* **1.** Unrestrained; uncontrolled: *unbridled anger.* **2.** Not wearing or being fitted with a bridle: *an unbridled pony.* **—un•bri′dled•ly** *adv.*

un•bro•ken (ŭn-brō′kən) *adj.* **1.** Not tampered with; intact: *an unbroken dozen.* **2.** Not violated or breached: *unbroken promises.* **3.** Uninterrupted; continuous. **4.** Not tamed or broken to harness. **5.** Not disordered or disturbed: *unbroken family ties.* **—un•bro′ken•ly** *adv.* **—un•bro′ken•ness** *n.*

un•buck•le (ŭn-bŭk′əl) *v.* **-led, -ling, -les.** *—tr.* To loosen or undo the buckle or buckles of. *—intr.* **1.** To undo buckles. **2.** *Informal.* To relax.

un•budg•ing (ŭn-bŭj′ĭng) *adj.* Not moving or willing to move from a position or place. **—un•budg′ing•ly** *adv.*

un•build (un-bĭld′) *v.* **-built** (-bĭlt′), **-build•ing, -builds.** *—tr.* To dismantle, take apart, or demolish; raze. *—intr.* To dismantle something built.

un•build•a•ble (ŭn-bĭl′də-bəl) *adj.* **1.** That cannot be built: *an unbuildable house.* **2.** Unsuitable to be built upon.

un•bun•dling (ŭn-bŭn′dlĭng) *n.* The separate pricing of goods and services.

un•but•ton (ŭn-bŭt′n) *v.* **-toned, -ton•ing, -tons.** *—tr.* **1.** To unfasten the buttons of. **2.** To free or remove (a button) from a buttonhole. **3.** To open as if by unbuttoning: *unbutton the hatches.* *—intr.* To undo buttons.

un•cal•cu•lat•ed (ŭn-kăl′kyə-lā′tĭd) *adj.* Not thought out in advance; spontaneous.

un•cal•cu•lat•ing (ŭn-kăl′kyə-lā′tĭng) *adj.* Not using or involving calculation: *an uncalculating answer.*

un•called-for (ŭn-kôld′fôr′) *adj.* **1.** Not required or requested; unwanted: *uncalled-for suggestions.* **2.** Not justified or deserved; unwarranted: *uncalled-for rudeness.*

un•can•ny (ŭn-kăn′ē) *adj.* **-ni•er, -ni•est. 1.** Peculiarly unsettling, as if of supernatural origin or nature; eerie. **2.** So keen and perceptive as to seem preternatural. **—un•can′ni•ly** *adv.* **—un•can′ni•ness** *n.*

un•cap (ŭn-kăp′) *v.* **-capped, -cap•ping, -caps.** *—tr.* To remove the cap or covering of. *—intr.* To remove one's head covering as a sign of deference.

un•cared-for (ŭn-kârd′fôr′) *adj.* Not looked after; neglected.

un•car•ing (ŭn-kâr′ĭng) *adj.* Devoid of concern or sympathy.

Un•cas (ŭng′kəs). 1588?–1683? Native American leader who rebelled against his father's leadership of the Pequot and with his followers formed the Mohegan tribe.

un•caused (ŭn-kôzd′) *adj.* Existing without a perceptible cause; spontaneous.

un•cen•sored (ŭn-sĕn′sərd) *adj.* Not examined, expurgated, or given a rating for inclusion of inappropriate material.

un•cer•e•mo•ni•ous (ŭn-sĕr′ə-mō′nē-əs) *adj.* **1.** Without the due formalities; abrupt: *an unceremonious departure.* **2.** Not ceremonious; informal. **—un•cer′e•mo′ni•ous•ly** *adv.* **—un•cer′e•mo′ni•ous•ness** *n.*

un•cer•tain (ŭn-sûr′tn) *adj.* **1.** Not known or established; questionable: *changes of uncertain consequences.* **2.** Not determined; undecided: *uncertain plans.* **3.** Not having sure knowledge: *an uncertain recollection of the events.* **4.a.** Subject to change; variable. **b.** Unsteady; fitful: *uncertain light.* **—un•cer′tain•ly** *adv.* **—un•cer′tain•ness** *n.*

un•cer•tain•ty (ŭn-sûr′tn-tē) *n., pl.* **-ties. 1.** The condition of being uncertain; doubt. **2.** Something uncertain: *the uncertainties of modern life.* **3.** *Statistics.* The estimated amount or percentage by which an observed or calculated value may differ from the true value.

Syns: *uncertainty, doubt, dubiety, skepticism, suspicion, mistrust.* These nouns all refer to the condition of being unsure about someone or something. *Uncertainty,* the least forceful, merely denotes a lack of assurance or conviction: *I regarded my decision with growing uncertainty. Doubt* and *dubiety* imply a questioning state of mind: *"Doubt is part of all religion"* (Isaac Bashevis Singer). *On this point there can be no dubiety. Skepticism* generally suggests an instinctive or habitual tendency to question and demand proof: *"A wise skepticism is the first attribute of a good critic"* (James Russell Lowell). *Suspicion* is doubt as to the innocence, truth, integrity, honesty, or soundness of someone or something: *His furtiveness aroused my suspicions. Mistrust* denotes lack of trust or confidence, as in a person's motives, arising from suspicion: *viewed the recommendations with mistrust.*

uncertainty principle *n.* A principle in quantum mechanics holding that increasing the accuracy of measurement of one observable quantity increases the uncertainty with which a related quantity may be known.

un•chain (ŭn-chān′) *tr.v.* **-chained, -chain•ing, -chains.** To release from or as if from chains or bonds; set free.

un•change•a•ble (ŭn-chān′jə-bəl) *adj* Not to be altered; immutable: *the unchangeable seasons.* **—un•change′a•bil′i•ty, un•change′a•ble•ness** *n.* **—un•change′a•bly** *adv.*

un•chang•ing (ŭn-chān′jĭng) *adj.* Remaining the same; showing or undergoing no change: *unchanging friendliness.* **—un•chang′ing•ly** *adv.* **—un•chang′ing•ness** *n.*

un•charged (ŭn-chärjd′) *adj.* **1.** Not loaded. Used of a weapon. **2.** Lacking electric charge.

un•chart•ed (ŭn-chär′tĭd) *adj.* **1.** Not charted or recorded on a map or plan. **2.** Unknown.

un•chaste (ŭn-chāst′) *adj.* **-chast•er, -chast•est.** Not chaste or modest. **—un•chaste′ly** *adv.* **—un•chaste′ness, un•chas′ti•ty** (-chăs′tĭ-tē) *n.*

un•checked (ŭn-chĕkt′) *adj.* **1.** Not held in check; unrestrained: *an unchecked temper.* **2.** Not checked for accuracy, efficiency, or flaws: *an unchecked list.*

un•chris•tian (ŭn-krĭs′chən) *adj.* **1.** Not in accord with the spirit or principles of Christianity. **2.** Not Christian. **3.** Uncivilized; barbaric.

un•church (ŭn-chûrch′) *tr.v.* **-churched, -church•ing, -church•es. 1.** To expel from a church or from church membership; excommunicate. **2.** To deprive (a congregation, sect, or building) of the status of a church.

un•ci (ŭn′sī) *n.* Pl. of **uncus.**

un•cial also **Un•cial** (ŭn′shəl, -sē-əl) *—adj.* Of or relating to a style of writing characterized by somewhat rounded capital letters and found esp. in Greek and Latin manuscripts of the fourth to the eighth century A.D. *—n.* **1.** A style of writing characterized by such letters. **2.** A capital letter written in this style. [< LLat. *unciālēs (litterae),* inch-high (letters), uncials,

---

un•sheathe′ *tr.v.*
un•skilled′ *adj.*
un′so•lic′it•ed *adj.*
un•sound′ *adj.*
un•sound′ly *adv.*
un•sound′ness *n.*
un•stint′ing *adj.*
un•stint′ing•ly *adv.*
un•strap′ *tr.v.*
un•strat′i•fied′ *adj.*
un•stri′at′ed *adj.*
un′sub•stan′tial *adj.*
un′sub•stan′ti•al′i•ty *n.*
un′sub•stan′tial•ly *adv.*
un′suc•cess′ *n.*
un′suc•cess′ful *adj.*
un′suc•cess′ful•ly *adv.*
un′suc•cess′ful•ness *n.*
un•suit′a•bil′i•ty *n.*
un•suit′a•ble *adj.*
un•suit′a•ble•ness *n.*
un•suit′a•bly *adv.*
un′sus•cep′ti•ble *adj.*
un•swathe′ *tr.v.*
un′sym•met′ri•cal *adj.*
un′sym•met′ri•cal•ly *adv.*
un•throne′ *tr.v.*
un•trou′bled *adj.*
un•trou′bled•ness *n.*
un•twine′ *tr. & intr.v.*
un•twist′ *tr. & intr.v.*
un•war′i•ly *adv.*
un•war′i•ness *n.*
un•war′y *adj.*
un•wed′ *adj.*
un•work′a•bil′i•ty *n.*
un•work′a•ble *adj.*
un•work′a•ble•ness *n.*
un•work′a•bly *adv.*
un•worn′ *adj.*

pl. of Lat. *unciālis*, inch-high < *uncia*, a twelfth part, ounce, inch. See **oi-no-***.]

un•ci•form (ŭn′sə-fôrm′) *adj.* Shaped like a hook. — *n.* See **hamate.** [Lat. *uncus*, hook + -FORM.]

un•ci•nar•i•a (ŭn′sə-nâr′ē-ə) *n.* See **hookworm.** [NLat. *Uncīnāria*, hookworm genus < Lat. *uncīnus*, barb. See UNCINATE.]

un•ci•nate (ŭn′sə-nāt′, -nĭt) *adj.* Bent at the end like a hook; unciform. [Lat. *uncīnātus* < *uncīnus*, barb < *uncus*, hook.]

un•cir•cum•cised (ŭn-sûr′kəm-sīzd′) *adj.* **1.** Not circumcised. **2.a.** Not Jewish; Gentile. **b.** Not Christian. — **un•cir′cum•ci′sion** (-sĭzh′ən) *n.*

un•civ•il (ŭn-sĭv′əl) *adj.* **1.** Discourteous. **2.** *Archaic.* Uncivilized; barbarous. — **un•civ′il•ly** *adv.* — **un•civ′il•ness** *n.*

un•clad (ŭn-klăd′) *adj.* Not wearing clothes; naked.

un•claimed (ŭn-klāmd′) *adj.* Not claimed as property.

un•clasp (ŭn-klăsp′) *v.* **-clasped, -clasp•ing, -clasps.** — *tr.* **1.** To release or loosen the clasp of. **2.** To release or loosen from a clasp or an embrace. — *intr.* **1.** To become unfastened. **2.** To release or relax a clasp or grasp; let go.

un•cle (ŭng′kəl) *n.* **1.a.** The brother of one's mother or father. **b.** The husband of one's aunt. **2.** Used as a form of address for an older man, esp. by children. **3.** A kindly counselor. **4.** *Slang.* A pawnbroker. **5. Uncle.** Uncle Sam. — ***idiom.* cry (or say) uncle.** *Informal.* To indicate a willingness to give up a fight or surrender. [ME < AN < Lat. *avunculus*, maternal uncle. See **awo-***.]

un•clean (ŭn-klēn′) *adj.* **-clean•er, -clean•est. 1.** Foul or dirty. **2.** Morally defiled; unchaste. **3.** Ceremonially impure. — **un•clean′ness** *n.*

un•clean•ly (ŭn-klĕn′lē) *adj.* **-li•er, -li•est.** Unclean. — *adv.* (-klēn′-). In an unclean manner. — **un•clean′li•ness** *n.*

un•clear (ŭn-klîr′) *adj.* **-clear•er, -clear•est.** Not clearly defined; not explicit.

Uncle Sam (săm) *n.* **1.** The government of the United States, often personified by a representation of a tall thin man having a white beard and wearing a blue swallow-tailed coat, red-and-white-striped trousers, and a tall hat with a band of stars. **2.** The American nation or its people. [< *U.S.*, abbr. of UNITED STATES.]

Uncle Tom (tŏm) *n. Offensive.* A Black person regarded as subservient or deferential to white people. [After *Uncle Tom*, a character in *Uncle Tom's Cabin* by Harriet Beecher Stowe.]

Uncle Tom•ism (tŏm′ĭz′əm) *n. Offensive.* Deferential, subservient behavior and attitudes believed typical of an Uncle Tom.

un•clog (ŭn-klŏg′) *tr.v.* **-clogged, -clog•ging, -clogs.** To clear a blockage from (a drain, for example).

un•close (ŭn-klōz′) *v.* **-closed, -clos•ing, -clos•es.** — *tr.* **1.** To open. **2.** To disclose. — *intr.* **1.** To be opened. **2.** To undergo disclosure.

un•co (ŭng′kō) *Scots.* — *adj.* So unusual as to be surprising; uncanny. — *n., pl.* **-cos. 1.** An unusual or amazing person. **2.** A stranger. **3. uncos.** News. — *adv.* To an excessive degree; remarkably. [ME *unkow*, var. of *uncouth*, strange. See UNCOUTH.]

un•com•fort•a•ble (ŭn-kŭm′fər-tə-bəl, -kŭmf′tə-) *adj.* **1.** Experiencing physical discomfort. **2.** Ill at ease; uneasy. **3.** Causing anxiety; disquieting. — **un•com′fort•a•ble•ness** *n.* — **un•com′fort•a•bly** *adv.*

un•com•mer•cial (ŭn′kə-mûr′shəl) *adj.* **1.** Not engaged in or involving trade or commerce. **2.** Not in accord with the spirit or methods of commerce. **3.** Uneconomical.

un•com•mit•ted (ŭn′kə-mĭt′ĭd) *adj.* Not pledged to a specific cause or course of action: *an uncommitted delegate.*

un•com•mon (ŭn-kŏm′ən) *adj.* **-er, -est. 1.** Not common; rare. **2.** Wonderful; remarkable. — **un•com′mon•ly** *adv.* — **un•com′mon•ness** *n.*

un•com•mu•ni•ca•tive (ŭn′kə-myo͞o′nĭ-kā′tĭv, -kə-tĭv) *adj.* Not disposed to be communicative. — **un′com•mu′ni•ca′tive•ly** *adv.* — **un′com•mu′ni•ca′tive•ness** *n.*

Un•com•pah•gre Peak (ŭn′kəm-pä′grē). A mountain, 4,364.2 m (14,309 ft), in the San Juan Mts. of SW CO.

un•com•plet•ed (ŭn′kəm-plē′tĭd) *adj.* As yet unfinished.

un•com•pli•cat•ed (ŭn-kŏm′plĭ-kā′tĭd) *adj.* **1.** Not complex or involved; simple. **2.** Not involving medical complications.

un•com•pro•mis•a•ble (ŭn-kŏm′prə-mī′zə-bəl) *adj.* That cannot be compromised: *uncompromisable honesty.*

un•com•put•er•ized (ŭn′kəm-pyo͞o′tə-rīzd′) *adj. Comp. Sci.* Not equipped with or using computers.

un•con•cern (ŭn′kən-sûrn′) *n.* **1.** Lack of interest; indifference. **2.** Lack of worry or apprehensiveness.

un•con•cerned (ŭn′kən-sûrnd′) *adj.* **1.** Not interested; indifferent. **2.** Not worried or apprehensive. — **un′con•cern′ed•ly** (-sûr′nĭd-lē) *adv.* — **un′con•cern′ed•ness** *n.*

un•con•di•tioned (ŭn′kən-dĭsh′ənd) *adj.* **1.** Unconditional; unrestricted. **2.** *Psychol.* Not dependent on or resulting from conditioning; unlearned or natural.

un•con•form•a•ble (ŭn′kən-fôr′mə-bəl) *adj.* **1.** Incapable of conformity; not conforming. **2.** *Geol.* Showing unconformity. — **un′con•form′a•bil′i•ty, un′con•form′a•ble•ness** *n.* — **un′con•form′a•bly** *adv.*

un•con•for•mi•ty (ŭn′kən-fôr′mĭ-tē) *n., pl.* **-ties. 1.** Lack of conformity; nonconformity. **2.** *Geol.* A surface of erosion between rock layers of different ages indicating that deposition was not continuous.

un•con•gen•ial (ŭn′kən-jēn′yəl) *adj.* **1.** Not compatible or sympathetic, as in character. **2.** Not appropriate; unsuitable. **3.** Not pleasing; disagreeable. — **un′con•ge′ni•al′ity** (-jē′nē-ăl′ĭ-tē) *n.*

un•con•scion•a•ble (ŭn-kŏn′shə-nə-bəl) *adj.* **1.** Not restrained by conscience; unscrupulous. **2.** Beyond prudence or reason; excessive: *unconscionable spending.* — **un•con′scion•a•ble•ness** *n.* — **un•con′scion•a•bly** *adv.*

un•con•scious (ŭn-kŏn′shəs) *adj.* **1.** Lacking awareness and the capacity for sensory perception; not conscious. **2.** Temporarily lacking consciousness. **3.** Occurring in the absence of conscious awareness or thought: *unconscious resentment.* **4.** Without conscious control; involuntary or unintended. — *n.* The division of the mind in psychoanalytic theory containing elements of psychic makeup that are not subject to conscious perception or control but that often affect conscious thoughts and behavior. — **un•con′scious•ly** *adv.* — **un•con′scious•ness** *n.*

un•con•sid•ered (ŭn′kən-sĭd′ərd) *adj.* Not reasoned or considered; rash: *an unconsidered remark.*

un•con•sti•tu•tion•al (ŭn′kŏn-stĭ-to͞o′shə-nəl, -tyo͞o′-) *adj.* Not in accord with the principles set forth in the constitution of a nation or state. — **un′con•sti•tu′tion•al′i•ty** (-shə-năl′ĭ-tē) *n.* — **un′con•sti•tu′tion•al•ly** *adv.*

un•con•struct•ed (ŭn′kən-strŭk′tĭd) *adj.* Designed or made with little or no interfacing, padding, or lining to produce a loose, soft shape. Used of apparel: *an unconstructed jacket.*

un•cool (ŭn-ko͞ol′) *adj. Slang.* **1.** Lacking assurance, self-control, or sophistication. **2.** Not in accord with the standards or mores of a specified group.

un•co•or•di•nat•ed (ŭn′kō-ôr′dn-ā′tĭd) *adj.* **1.** Lacking physical or mental coordination. **2.** Lacking planning, method, or organization. — **un′co•or′di•nat′ed•ly** *adv.*

un•cork (ŭn-kôrk′) *tr.v.* **-corked, -cork•ing, -corks. 1.** To draw the cork from. **2.** To free from a sealed or constrained condition.

un•count•a•ble (ŭn-koun′tə-bəl) *adj.* Too many to be counted; innumerable: *an uncountable number of tourists.*

un•count•ed (ŭn-koun′tĭd) *adj.* **1.** Not counted. **2.** Uncountable; innumerable.

un•cou•ple (ŭn-kŭp′əl) *v.* **-pled, -pling, -ples.** — *tr.* **1.** To disconnect: *uncouple the trailer.* **2.** To set loose or release from a couple. — *intr.* To come or break loose. — **un•cou′pler** *n.*

un•couth (ŭn-ko͞oth′) *adj.* **1.** Crude; unrefined. **2.** Awkward or clumsy; ungraceful. **3.** *Archaic.* Foreign; unfamiliar. [ME, unknown, strange < OE *uncūth* : *un-*, not; see UN-[1] + *cūth*, known; see **gnō-***.] — **un•couth′ly** *adv.* — **un•couth′ness** *n.*

un•cov•e•nant•ed (ŭn-kŭv′ə-nən-tĭd) *adj.* **1.** Not bound by a covenant. **2.** Not promised or guaranteed by a covenant.

un•cov•er (ŭn-kŭv′ər) *v.* **-ered, -er•ing, -ers.** — *tr.* **1.** To remove the cover from: *uncovered the saucepan.* **2.** To manifest or disclose; reveal: *uncovered new evidence.* **3.** To remove the hat from, as in respect or reverence. — *intr.* **1.** To remove a cover. **2.** To bare the head in respect or reverence.

un•cov•ered (ŭn-kŭv′ərd) *adj.* **1.** Having no cover or protection. **2.** Lacking the protection of insurance or collateral security. **3.** Bareheaded.

un•cre•at•ed (ŭn′krē-ā′tĭd) *adj.* **1.** Not having been created; not yet in existence. **2.** Existing of itself; uncaused.

un•cred•it•ed (ŭn-krĕd′ĭ-tĭd) *adj.* **1.** Not having been credited, as on a ledger: *an uncredited deposit.* **2.** Not having been accorded due recognition: *an uncredited discovery.*

un•crewed (ŭn-kro͞od′) *adj.* Not having a crew; crewless.

un•crit•i•cal (ŭn-krĭt′ĭ-kəl) *adj.* **1.** Not critical; undiscriminating or indulgent. **2.** Not using critical standards or methods, as in evaluation. — **un•crit′i•cal•ly** *adv.*

un•cross (ŭn-krôs′, -krŏs′) *tr.v.* **-crossed, -cross•ing, -cross•es.** To move (one's legs, for example) from a crossed position.

un•crowned (ŭn-kround′) *adj.* **1.** Yet to be crowned. **2.** Having the authority of a monarch or a similar figure but not the title: *the uncrowned king of espionage.*

unc•tion (ŭngk′shən) *n.* **1.** The act of anointing as part of a religious, ceremonial, or healing ritual. **2.** An ointment or oil; a salve. **3.** Something that serves to soothe; a balm. **4.** Affected or exaggerated earnestness, esp. in choice and use of language. [ME < Lat. *ūnctiō*, *ūnctiōn-* < *ūnctus*, p.part. of *unguere*, to anoint.]

unc•tu•ous (ŭngk′cho͞o-əs) *adj.* **1.** Characterized by affected, exaggerated, or insincere earnestness. **2.** Having the quality or characteristics of oil or ointment; slippery. **3.** Containing or composed of oil or fat. **4.** Abundant in organic materials; soft and rich: *unctuous soil.* [ME < OFr. *unctueus* < Med.Lat. *ūnctuōsus* < Lat. *ūnctum*, ointment < neut. p.part. of *unguere*, to anoint.] — **unc′tu•ous•ly** *adv.* — **unc′tu•ous•ness, unc′tu•os′i•ty** (-ŏs′ĭ-tē) *n.*

un•cul•tured (ŭn-kul′chərd) *adj.* Not cultured or cultivated: *an uncultured village.*

un•cus (ŭng′kəs) *n., pl.* **un•ci** (ŭn′sī). *Biol.* A hook-shaped part or process. [Lat., hook.]

un•cut (ŭn-kŭt′) *adj.* **1.** Not cut: *uncut hair.* **2.** *Print.* Having

Uncle Sam
World War I poster painted by James Montgomery Flagg

ă pat	oi boy
ā pay	ou out
âr care	o͝o took
ä father	o͞o boot
ĕ pet	ŭ cut
ē be	ûr urge
ĭ pit	th thin
ī pie	*th* this
îr pier	hw which
ŏ pot	zh vision
ō toe	ə about, item
ô paw	

Stress marks:
′ (primary);
′ (secondary), as in
dictionary (dĭk′shə-nĕr′ē)

the page edge not slit or trimmed. Used of a book. **3.** Not cut or ground to a specific shape. Used of a gemstone. **4.** Not condensed, abridged, or shortened, as by an editor or a censor: *the uncut version of the scandal.* — **un•cut′ta•ble** *adj.*

un•damped (ŭn′dămpt′) *adj.* **1.** *Phys.* Not tending toward a state of rest; not damped. Used of oscillations. **2.** Not stifled or discouraged; unchecked: *undamped ardor.*

un•daunt•a•ble (ŭn-dôn′tə-bəl, -dän′-) *adj.* Not admitting of discouragement: *undauntable optimism.*

un•daunt•ed (ŭn-dôn′tĭd, -dän′-) *adj.* Not discouraged or disheartened; resolutely courageous. See Syns at **brave.** — **un•daunt′ed•ly** *adv.* — **un•daunt′ed•ness** *n.*

un•decked¹ (ŭn-dĕkt′) *adj.* Not decorated; unornamented.

un•decked² (ŭn-dĕkt′) *adj. Naut.* Having no deck.

un•de•mon•stra•tive (ŭn′dĭ-mŏn′strə-tĭv) *adj.* Not disposed to expressions of feeling; reserved. — **un′de•mon′stra•tive•ly** *adv.* — **un′de•mon′stra•tive•ness** *n.*

un•der (ŭn′dər) *prep.* **1.a.** In a lower position or place than: *a rug under a chair.* **b.** To or into a lower position or place than: *rolled the ball under the couch.* **2.** Beneath the surface of: *swam under water.* **3.** Beneath the assumed surface or guise of: *traveled under a false name.* **4.** Less than; smaller than: *The jar's capacity is under three quarts.* **5.** Less than the required amount or degree of: *under voting age.* **6.** Inferior to in status or rank: *nine officers under me.* **7.** Subject to the authority, rule, or control of: *under a dictatorship.* **8.** Subject to the supervision, instruction, or influence of: *under parental guidance.* **9.** Undergoing or receiving the effects of: *under constant care.* **10.** Subject to the restraint or obligation of: *under contract.* **11.** Within the group or classification of: *listed under biology.* **12.** In the process of: *under discussion.* **13.** In view of; because of: *under these conditions.* **14.** With the authorization of. **15.** Sowed or planted with: *an acre under oats.* **16.** *Naut.* Powered or propelled by: *under sail.* **17.** During the time conventionally assigned to (a sign of the zodiac). —*adv.* **1.** In or into a place below or beneath. **2.** In or into a subordinate or inferior condition or position. **3.** So as to be covered or enveloped. **4.** So as to be less than the required amount or degree. —*adj.* **1.** Located or situated on a lower level or beneath something else. **2.** Lower in rank, power, or authority; subordinate. **3.** Less than is required or customary. [ME < OE. See **n̥dher-***.]

under– *pref.* **1.** Beneath or below in position: *underground.* **2.** Inferior or subordinate in rank or importance: *undersecretary.* **3.** Less in degree, rate, or quantity than normal or proper: *undersized.* [ME < OE. See **n̥dher-***.]

Usage Note: Many compounds other than those entered here may be formed with *under–*. In forming compounds, *under–* is joined with the following element without space or a hyphen: *underrate; undergrow.* Note, however, that the adjective *under* may combine with other words as a unit modifier. In such cases the words are joined by hyphens: *an under-the-table deal.*

un•der•act (ŭn′dər-ăkt′) *v.* **-act•ed, -act•ing, -acts.** —*tr.* **1.** To perform (a role) weakly or with insufficient expressiveness. **2.** To understate (a role) intentionally; underplay. —*intr.* To perform in an understated way.

un•der•age¹ (ŭn′dər-ĭj) *n.* **1.** An amount, as of money or goods actually on hand, that falls short of the listed amount in records or books of account. **2.** A deficient amount; a shortfall.

un•der•age² (ŭn′dər-āj′) also **un•der•aged** (-ājd′) *adj.* Below the customary or legal age, as for drinking or voting.

un•der•arm (ŭn′dər-ärm′) *adj.* **1.** Located, placed, or used under the arm. **2.** *Sports.* Executed with the hand brought forward and up from below the level of the shoulder; underhand. —*adv.* With an underarm motion or delivery. —*n.* The armpit.

un•der•bel•ly (ŭn′dər-bĕl′ē) *n., pl.* **-lies. 1.** The soft belly or underside of the body of an animal. **2.** The vulnerable or weak part.

un•der•bid (ŭn′dər-bĭd′) *v.* **-bid, -bid•ding, -bids.** —*tr.* To bid lower than (a competitor). —*intr.* **1.** To make an unnecessarily low bid. **2.** *Games.* To bid less than the full value of one's hand in bridge. — **un′der-bid′** *n.* — **un′der•bid′der** *n.*

un•der•bod•y (ŭn′dər-bŏd′ē) *n., pl.* **-ies. 1.** See **underbelly** 1. **2.** The under parts of the body of a motor vehicle.

un•der•bred (ŭn′dər-brĕd′) *adj.* **1.** Poorly brought up; ill-bred. **2.** Of mixed breed; not thoroughbred.

un•der•brush (ŭn′dər-brŭsh′) *n.* Small trees, shrubs, or similar plants growing beneath the taller trees in a forest.

un•der•buy (ŭn′dər-bī′) *v.* **-bought** (-bôt′), **-buy•ing, -buys.** —*tr.* **1.** To buy less (of something) than one wants or needs. **2.** To buy at a lower price than a competitor. **3.** To buy (something) at less than a proper or expected price. —*intr.* **1.** To buy less of something than what is wanted or needed. **2.** To buy something at less than a proper or expected price.

un•der•cap•i•tal•ize (ŭn′dər-kăp′ĭ-tl-īz′) *tr.v.* **-ized, -iz•ing, -iz•es.** To supply (a business or government, for example) with so little capital that operations are hindered. — **un′der•cap′i•tal•i•za′tion** (-ĭ-zā′shən) *n.*

un•der•car•riage (ŭn′dər-kăr′ĭj) *n.* **1.** A supporting framework or structure, as for the body of a motor vehicle. **2.** The landing gear of an aircraft.

un•der•charge (ŭn′dər-chärj′) *tr.v.* **-charged, -charg•ing, -charg•es. 1.** To charge (a customer, for example) less than is customary or required. **2.** To load (a firearm) with an insufficient charge. —*n.* (ŭn′dər-chärj′). An insufficient or improper charge.

un•der•class (ŭn′dər-klăs′) *n.* The lowest societal stratum, usu. composed of the disadvantaged.

un•der•class•man (ŭn′dər-klăs′mən) *n.* A student in the freshman or sophomore class at a secondary school or college.

un•der•clothes (ŭn′dər-klōz′, -klōthz′) *pl.n.* Clothes worn next to the skin, beneath one's outer clothing.

un•der•cloth•ing (ŭn′der-klō′thĭng) *n.* See **underclothes.**

un•der•coat (ŭn′dər-kōt′) *n.* **1.** A coat worn beneath another coat. **2.** A covering of short hairs lying underneath the longer outer hairs of an animal's coat. **3.** Also **un•der•coat•ing** (-kō′tĭng). **a.** A coat of sealing material applied to a surface before the outer coats, as of paint, are applied. **b.** The sealing material used for this purpose. **c.** A tarlike substance sprayed on the underside of a vehicle to prevent rusting. —*tr.v.* **-coat•ed, -coat•ing, -coats.** To apply an undercoat to.

un•der•cool (ŭn′dər-ko͞ol′) *tr.v.* **-cooled, -cool•ing, -cools.** To supercool.

un•der•count (ŭn′dər-kount′) *tr.v.* **-count•ed, -count•ing, -counts.** To record fewer than the actual number of (persons in a census, for example). — **un′der•count′** *n.*

un•der•cov•er (ŭn′dər-kŭv′ər) *adj.* **1.** Performed or occurring in secret: *an undercover investigation.* **2.** Engaged or employed in spying or secret investigation.

un•der•croft (ŭn′dər-krôft′, -krŏft′) *n.* A crypt, esp. for burial under a church. [ME : *under-*, under- + *croft*, crypt (< MDu. *crofte* < Med.Lat. *crupta* < Lat. *crypta*, crypt; see CRYPT).]

un•der•cur•rent (ŭn′dər-kûr′ənt, -kŭr′-) *n.* **1.** A current, as of air or water, below another current or beneath a surface. **2.** An underlying tendency, force, or influence often contrary to what is superficially evident; an intimation.

un•der•cut (ŭn′dər-kŭt′) *v.* **-cut, -cut•ting, -cuts.** —*tr.* **1.** To diminish or destroy the province or effectiveness of; undermine. **2.** To sell at a lower price than or to work for lower wages or fees than (a competitor). **3.** To make a cut under or below. **4.** To create an overhang by cutting material away from, as in carving. **5.** *Sports.* **a.** To impart backspin to (a ball) by striking downward as well as forward, as in golf. **b.** To cut or slice (a ball) with an underarm stroke, as in tennis. —*intr.* To engage in undercutting. —*n.* (ŭn′dər-kŭt′). **1.a.** A cut made in the under part to remove material. **b.** The material so removed. **2.** A notch cut in a tree to direct its fall and insure a clean break. **3.** *Chiefly British.* The tenderloin of beef; the fillet. **4.** *Sports.* **a.** A spin given to a ball opposite to its direction of flight; a backspin. **b.** A cut or slice imparting such a spin.

un•der•de•vel•oped (ŭn′dər-dĭ-vĕl′əpt) *adj.* **1.** Not adequately or normally developed; immature. **2.** Processed in too weak a developing solution, or for too short a time, or at too low a temperature to produce a normal degree of contrast. Used of film. **3.** Having a low level of economic productivity and technological sophistication; developing. — **un′der•de•vel′op•ment** *n.*

un•der•do (ŭn′dər-do͞o′) *tr.v.* **-did** (-dĭd′), **-done** (-dŭn′), **-do•ing, -does** (-dŭz′). To do to an insufficient degree, esp. to cook for too short a time.

un•der•dog (ŭn′dər-dôg′, -dŏg′) *n.* **1.** One that is expected to lose a contest or struggle, as in sports or politics. **2.** One that is at a disadvantage.

un•der•done (ŭn′dər-dŭn′) *adj.* Not sufficiently cooked.

un•der•draw•ers (ŭn′dər-drôrz′) *pl.n.* Undershorts; underpants.

un•der•dress (ŭn′dər-drĕs′) *n.* **1.** Apparel worn beneath outer garments; underclothing. **2.** An outer garment, such as a dress beneath a tunic or coat, that is worn as part of a costume or suit. —*intr.v.* (ŭn′dər-drĕs′) **-dressed, -dress•ing, -dress•es. 1.** To dress too informally for the occasion. **2.** To dress without sufficient warmth.

un•der•drive (ŭn′dər-drīv′) *n.* A gearing device that causes

---

un′der•a•chieve′ *intr.v.*
un′der•a•chieve′ment *n.*
un′der•ed′u•cat′ed *adj.*
un′der•em′pha•sis *n.*
un′der•em′pha•size′ *tr.v.*
un′der•en•dow′ *tr.v.*
un′der•en•dow′ment *n.*
un′der•fund′ *tr.v.*
un′der•pay′ *tr.v.*
un′der•pay′ment *n.*
un′der•priv′i•leged *adj. & n.*
un′der•pro•duce′ *tr. & intr.v.*
un′der•pro•duc′tion *n.*
un′der•pro•duc′tive *adj.*
un′der•rate′ *tr.v.*
un′der•re•act′ *intr.v.*
un′der•re•ac′tion *n.*
un′der•re•port′ *tr.v.*
un′der•sup•ply′ *n. & tr.v.*
un′der•val′u•a′tion *n.*
un′der•val′ue *tr.v.*

the output drive shaft to rotate at a slower rate than the engine input shaft.

un•der•em•ployed (ŭn′dər-ĕm-ploid′) *adj.* **1.** Employed only part-time when needing and wanting full-time employment. **2.** Inadequately employed, esp. employed at a low-paying job that requires less skill or training than one possesses. **3.** Not fully or adequately used or employed. —*n.* Underemployed persons considered as a group. —**un′der•em•ploy′ment** *n.*

un•der•es•ti•mate (ŭn′dər-ĕs′tə-māt′) *tr.v.* **-mat•ed, -mat•ing, -mates.** To make too low an estimate of the quantity, degree, or worth of. —*n.* (-ĕs′tə-mĭt). An estimate that is or proves to be too low. —**un′der•es′ti•ma′tion** *n.*

un•der•ex•pose (ŭn′dər-ĭk-spōz′) *tr.v.* **-posed, -pos•ing, -pos•es. 1.** To expose (film) to light for too short a time or to light or radiation insufficient to produce normal image contrast. **2.** To provide with too little publicity. —**un′der•ex•po′sure** (-ĭk-spō′zhər) *n.*

un•der•feed (ŭn′dər-fēd′) *tr.v.* **-fed** (-fĕd′), **-feed•ing, -feeds. 1.** To feed insufficiently. **2.** To supply (an engine) with fuel from the underside.

un•der•flow (ŭn′dər-flō′) *n. Comp. Sci.* A data-processing error arising when a computed quantity is a smaller number than the device is capable of displaying.

un•der•foot (ŭn′dər-fŏŏt′) *adv.* **1.** Below or under the foot or feet; against the ground: *trampled the beans underfoot.* **2.** At or under the foot or feet; on the ground. **3.** Hindering progress; in the way: *children underfoot.*

un•der•fur (ŭn′dər-fûr′) *n.* The soft fine undercoat of certain mammals, such as otters, beavers, and seals.

un•der•gar•ment (ŭn′dər-gär′mənt) *n.* A garment worn under outer garments, esp. one worn next to the skin.

un•der•gird (ŭn′dər-gûrd′) *tr.v.* **-gird•ed** or **-girt** (-gûrt′), **-gird•ing, -girds.** To support or strengthen from beneath.

un•der•glaze (ŭn′dər-glāz′) *n.* Coloring or decoration applied to pottery before glazing.

un•der•go (ŭn′dər-gō′) *tr.v.* **-went** (-wĕnt′), **-gone** (-gôn′, -gŏn′), **-go•ing, -goes** (-gōz′). **1.** To pass through; experience. **2.** To endure; suffer: *undergo great hardship.*

un•der•grad (ŭn′dər-grăd′) *n. & adj. Informal.* Undergraduate.

un•der•grad•u•ate (ŭn′dər-grăj′ōō-ĭt) *n.* **1.** A college or university student who has not yet received a bachelor's or similar degree. **2.** A high-school student who has not yet received a diploma. —*adj.* **1.** Of, relating to, or characteristic of undergraduates. **2.** Having the standing of an undergraduate.

un•der•ground (ŭn′dər-ground′) *adj.* **1.** Situated, occurring, or operating below the surface of the earth. **2.a.** Hidden or concealed; clandestine. **b.** Of or relating to an organization involved in secret or illegal activity. **3.** Of or relating to an avant-garde movement or its films, publications, and art. —*n.* **1.** A clandestine organization planning hostile activities against or the overthrow of a government. **2.** *Chiefly British.* A subway system. **3.** An avant-garde movement or publication. —*adv.* (ŭn′dər-ground′). **1.** Below the surface of the earth. **2.** In secret; stealthily.

Un•der•ground Railroad (ŭn′dər-ground′) *n.* A secret cooperative network that aided fugitive slaves in reaching sanctuary in the free states or Canada in the years before the abolition of slavery in the United States.

un•der•grown (ŭn′dər-grōn′) *adj.* **1.** Not fully grown; puny. **2.** Covered with undergrowth.

un•der•growth (ŭn′dər-grōth′) *n.* **1.** Low-growing plants, saplings, and shrubs beneath trees in a forest. **2.** A growth of short fine hairs underlying the longer and thicker outer hairs of an animal's coat; underfur or underwool. **3.** The condition of being less than fully grown.

un•der•hair (ŭn′dər-hâr′) *n.* A covering of soft downy hairs lying underneath the outer hairs of an animal's coat.

un•der•hand (ŭn′dər-hănd′) also **un•der•hand•ed** (ŭn′dər-hăn′dĭd) —*adj.* **1.** Marked by or done in a deceptive, secret, or sly manner; dishonest and sneaky. **2.** *Sports.* Underarm: *an underhand pitch.* —*adv.* **1.** With an underarm movement. **2.** In a sly and secret way. —**un′der•hand′** *n.* —**un′der•hand′ed•ly** *adv.* —**un′der•hand′ed•ness** *n.*

un•der•hung (ŭn′dər-hŭng′) *adj.* **1.a.** Protruding from beneath. **b.** Supported by or lying over something that projects. **2.** Resting on or mounted along a supporting track, as a sliding door on rollers. **3.** Underslung, as a machine. **4.** Having the lower jaw projecting beyond the upper jaw.

un•der•in•sure (ŭn′dər-ĭn-shŏŏr′) *tr.v.* **-sured, -sur•ing, -sures.** To insure under a policy that provides inadequate benefits. —**un′der•in•sur′ance** *n.*

un•der•kill (ŭn′dər-kĭl′) *n.* Insufficient force for the defeat of an enemy.

un•der•laid (ŭn′dər-lād′) *adj.* **1.** Placed or laid underneath. **2.** Supported or raised by something from beneath; having an underlay.

un•der•lay[1] (ŭn′dər-lā′) *tr.v.* **-laid** (-lād′), **-lay•ing, -lays. 1.** To put (one thing) under another. **2.** To provide with a base or support. **3.** *Print.* To raise or support (the level of a bed) by inserting a piece of paper or other material under the type. —*n.* (ŭn′dər-lā′). **1.** Something, such as felt under a carpet, that is underlaid. **2.** *Print.* Paper or other material used to underlay the level of a bed.

un•der•lay[2] (ŭn′dər-lā′) *v.* P.t. of **underlie.**

un•der•let (ŭn′dər-lĕt′) *tr.v.* **-let, -let•ting, -lets. 1.** To lease for less than the proper value. **2.** To sublet.

un•der•lie (ŭn′dər-lī′) *tr.v.* **-lay** (-lā′), **-lain** (-lān′), **-ly•ing, -lies. 1.** To be located under or below. **2.** To be the support or basis of; account for. **3.** To constitute a prior financial claim over.

un•der•line (ŭn′dər-līn′, ŭn′dər-līn′) *tr.v.* **-lined, -lin•ing, -lines. 1.** To draw a line under; emphasize or cause to stand out; underscore. **2.** To emphasize; stress. —*n.* (ŭn′dər-līn′). A line under something, such as a symbol, word, or phrase, used to indicate emphasis or italic type.

un•der•ling (ŭn′dər-lĭng) *n.* One of lesser rank or authority than another; a subordinate.

un•der•lin•ing (ŭn′dər-lī′nĭng) *n.* **1.** The act of drawing a line under; underscoring. **2.** Emphasis or stress, as in argument or rhetoric.

un•der•lip (ŭn′dər-lĭp′) *n.* The lower lip.

un•der•ly•ing (ŭn′dər-lī′ĭng) *adj.* **1.** Lying under or beneath something. **2.** Basic; fundamental. **3.** Present but not obvious; implicit: *an underlying meaning.* **4.** Taking precedence; prior.

un•der•mine (ŭn′dər-mīn′) *tr.v.* **-mined, -min•ing, -mines. 1.** To weaken by wearing away a base or foundation. **2.** To weaken, injure, or impair, often by degrees or imperceptibly; sap. **3.** To dig a mine or tunnel beneath.

un•der•most (ŭn′dər-mōst′) *adj.* Lowest in position, rank, or place; bottom. —*adv.* In or to the lowest place.

un•der•neath (ŭn′dər-nēth′) *adv.* **1.** In or to a place beneath; below. **2.** On the lower face or underside. —*prep.* **1.** Under; below; beneath. **2.** Under the power or control of. —*adj.* Lower; under. —*n.* The part or side below or under. [ME *undernethe* < OE *underneothan* : *under*, under; see UNDER + *neothan*, below; see BENEATH.]

un•der•nour•ish (ŭn′dər-nûr′ĭsh, -nŭr′-) *tr.v.* **-ished, -ish•ing, -ish•es.** To provide with insufficient quantity or quality of nourishment to sustain proper health and growth. —**un′der•nour′ish•ment** *n.*

un•der•pants (ŭn′dər-pănts′) *pl.n.* Briefs or shorts worn as underwear.

un•der•part (ŭn′dər-pärt′) *n.* **1.** A lower part or a portion of a lower part or underside, esp. of an animal's body. **2.** A subordinate role, as in a play.

un•der•pass (ŭn′dər-păs′) *n.* **1.** A passage underneath something, esp. a section of road that passes under another road or a railroad. **2.** An intersection formed in this way.

un•der•per•form (ŭn′dər-pər-fôrm′) *v.* **-formed, -form•ing, -forms.** —*tr.* **1.** To perform not as well as (something else): *stocks that underperformed the market.* **2.** To perform (a musical or theatrical work, for example) too seldom. —*intr.* To exhibit a level of performance that is below the standard. —**un′der•per•form′ance** *n.* —**un′der•per•form′er** *n.*

un•der•pin (ŭn′dər-pĭn′) *tr.v.* **-pinned, -pin•ning, -pins. 1.** To support from below, as with props, girders, or masonry. **2.** To give support or substance to.

un•der•pin•ning (ŭn′dər-pĭn′ĭng) *n.* **1.** Material or masonry used to support a structure, such as a wall. **2.** A support or foundation. Often used in the plural. **3.** *Informal.* The human legs. Often used in the plural.

un•der•play (ŭn′dər-plā′, ŭn′dər-plā′) *v.* **-played, -play•ing, -plays.** —*tr.* **1.** To act (a role) subtly or with restraint. **2.** To present or deal with subtly or with restraint; play down. —*intr.* **1.** To underplay a role. **2.** *Games.* To play a low card while holding a higher card in the same suit.

un•der•plot (ŭn′dər-plŏt′) *n.* See **subplot** 1.

un•der•pop•u•lat•ed (ŭn′dər-pŏp′yə-lā′tĭd) *adj.* Lacking the normal or required population density. —**un′der•pop•u•la′tion** *n.*

un•der•price (ŭn′dər-prīs′) *tr.v.* **-priced, -pric•ing, -pric•es. 1.** To price lower than the real, normal, or appropriate value. **2.** To sell at a lower price than (a competitor).

un•der•proof (ŭn′dər-prōōf′) *adj.* Having a smaller proportion of alcohol than proof spirit.

un•der•prop (ŭn′dər-prŏp′) *tr.v.* **-propped, -prop•ping, -props.** To prop (something) from below.

un•der•quote (ŭn′dər-kwōt′) *tr.v.* **-quot•ed, -quot•ing, -quotes. 1.** To offer (goods or services) for sale at a price lower than the official list or market price. **2.** To quote a lower price than that quoted by (another); undersell.

un•der•rep•re•sent (ŭn′dər-rĕp′rĭ-zĕnt′) *tr.v.* **-sent•ed, -sent•ing, -sents.** To imply or suggest a lower amount, quantity, quality, or degree of than is actually present. —**un′der•rep′re•sen•ta′tion** *n.*

un•der•rep•re•sent•ed (ŭn′dər-rĕp′rĭ-zĕn′tĭd) *adj.* Insufficiently or inadequately represented: *the underrepresented voters in the younger segment of the population.*

un•der•ruff (ŭn′dər-rŭf′) *intr.v.* **-ruffed, -ruf•fing, -ruffs.** *Games.* To play a trump lower than another card player's trump when trump has not been led.

un•der•run (ŭn′dər-rŭn′) *tr.v.* **-ran** (-răn′), **-run, -run•ning, -runs.** To run, pass, or go beneath. —*n.* **1.** Something that

underhand
Underhand softball pitch

ă pat	oi boy
ā pay	ou out
âr care	ŏŏ took
ä father	ōō boot
ĕ pet	ŭ cut
ē be	ûr urge
ĭ pit	th thin
ī pie	*th* this
îr pier	hw which
ŏ pot	zh vision
ō toe	ə about, item
ô paw	

Stress marks:
′ (primary);
′ (secondary), as in
dictionary (dĭk′shə-nĕr′ē)

runs under, as: **a.** An amount or a quantity produced that is less than what has been estimated. **b.** The difference between this amount or quantity and what has been estimated. **2.** An undercurrent.

un•der•score (ŭn′dər-skôr′, -skōr′) *tr.v.* **-scored, -scor•ing, -scores. 1.** To underline. **2.** To emphasize; stress. — *n.* An underline.

un•der•sea (ŭn′dər-sē′) *adj.* Existing, relating to, or created for use beneath the surface of the sea. — *adv.* (ŭn′dər-sē′) also **un•der•seas** (-sēz′). Beneath the surface of the sea.

un•der•sec•re•tar•y (ŭn′dər-sĕk′rə-tĕr′ē) *n., pl.* **-ies.** An official directly subordinate to a member of a cabinet. — **un′der•sec′re•tar′i•at** (-târ′ē-ĭt) *n.*

un•der•sell (ŭn′dər-sĕl′) *tr.v.* **-sold** (-sōld′), **-sell•ing, -sells. 1.** To sell goods for a lower price than (another seller). **2.** To sell (something) at a price less than the actual value. **3.** To present (an idea, for example) with little enthusiasm. — **un′der•sell′er** *n.*

un•der•set (ŭn′dər-sĕt′) *n.* An ocean undercurrent.

un•der•sexed (ŭn′dər-sĕkst′) *adj.* Having less sexual desire or potency than what is regarded as normal.

un•der•shirt (ŭn′dər-shûrt′) *n.* An upper undergarment, usu. having short or no sleeves, that is worn next to the skin under a shirt.

un•der•shoot (ŭn′dər-shōōt′) *v.* **-shot** (-shŏt′), **-shoot•ing, -shoots.** — *tr.* **1.** To shoot a projectile short of (a target). **2.a.** To start the approach of an aircraft to (a landing area) too low or too soon. **b.** To land an aircraft short of (a landing area). — *intr.* **1.** To shoot short of a target. **2.** To land short of a landing area.

un•der•shorts (ŭn′dər-shôrts′) *pl.n.* Shorts or briefs worn as undergarments, esp. by a man; underpants.

un•der•shot (ŭn′dər-shŏt′) *adj.* **1.** Driven by water passing from below, as a water wheel. **2.** Having the lower jaw or teeth projecting beyond the upper; underhung.

un•der•shrub (ŭn′dər-shrŭb′) *n.* A very low-growing shrub.

un•der•side (ŭn′dər-sīd′) *n.* **1.** The side or surface that is underneath; the bottom side. **2.** The side that is less desirable, reputable, or noble than the obverse.

un•der•sign (ŭn′dər-sīn′) *tr.v.* **-signed, -sign•ing, -signs.** To sign one's name at the bottom of (a letter or document).

un•der•signed (ŭn′dər-sīnd′) *adj.* **1.** Having signatures or a signature at the bottom or end. Used of documents. **2.** Signed at the bottom or end of a document: *the undersigned names.* **3.** Having placed one's signature at the bottom or end of a document. — *n., pl.* **undersigned.** A signer whose name appears at the bottom or end of a document.

un•der•sized (ŭn′dər-sīzd′) also **un•der•size** (-sīz′) *adj.* Of less than normal or sufficient size.

un•der•skirt (ŭn′dər-skûrt′) *n.* **1.** A skirt worn under another skirt; a petticoat. **2.** One skirt of a layered gown over which outer skirts are formed and draped.

un•der•sleeve (ŭn′dər-slēv′) *n.* **1.** A sleeve worn under another. **2.** An ornamental sleeve under another sleeve, extending below or showing through slashes in the outer sleeve.

un•der•slung (ŭn′dər-slŭng′) *adj.* **1.** Having springs attached to the axles from below. Used of a vehicle or of its frame. **2.** Supported from above. **3.** Having a low center of gravity.

un•der•soil (ŭn′dər-soil′) *n.* Soil below the ground surface.

un•der•sold (ŭn′dər-sōld′) *v.* P.t. and p.part. of **undersell.**

un•der•spin (ŭn′dər-spĭn′) *n.* A backspin.

un•der•staff (ŭn′dər-stăf′) *tr.v.* **-staffed, -staff•ing, -staffs.** To supply with fewer employees than required.

un•der•stand (ŭn′dər-stănd′) *v.* **-stood** (-stŏŏd′), **-stand•ing, -stands.** — *tr.* **1.** To perceive and comprehend the nature and significance of; grasp. See Syns at **apprehend. 2.** To know thoroughly by close contact or long experience with. **3.a.** To grasp or comprehend the meaning intended or expressed by (another). **b.** To comprehend the language, sounds, form, or symbols of. **4.** To know and be tolerant or sympathetic toward. **5.** To learn indirectly, as by hearsay: *I understand his departure was unexpected.* **6.** To infer: *Am I to understand you are staying the night?* **7.** To accept (something) as an agreed fact: *It is understood that the fee will be 50 dollars.* **8.** To supply or add (words or a meaning, for example) mentally. — *intr.* **1.a.** To have understanding, knowledge, or comprehension. **b.** To have sympathy or tolerance. **2.** To learn something indirectly or secondhand; gather. [ME *understanden* < OE *understandan* : *under-*, under- + *standan*, to stand; see **stā-***.] — **un′der•stand′a•bil′i•ty** *n.* — **un′der•stand′a•ble** *adj.* — **un′der•stand′a•bly** *adv.*

un•der•stand•ing (ŭn′dər-stăn′dĭng) *n.* **1.** The quality or condition of one who understands; comprehension. **2.** The faculty by which one understands; intelligence. **3.** Individual or specified judgment or outlook; opinion: *disagreed with the common understanding.* **4.a.** A compact implicit between two or more people or groups. **b.** The matter implicit in such a compact. **5.** A reconciliation of differences; a state of agreement. **6.** A disposition to appreciate or share the feelings and thoughts of others; sympathy. — *adj.* **1.** Marked by or having comprehension, good sense, or discernment. **2.** Compassionate; sympathetic. — **un′der•stand′ing•ly** *adv.*

un•der•state (ŭn′dər-stāt′) *v.* **-stat•ed, -stat•ing, -states.** — *tr.* **1.** To state with less completeness or truth than seems warranted by the facts. **2.** To express with restraint or lack of emphasis, esp. ironically. **3.** To state (a quantity, for example) that is too low. — *intr.* To give an understatement.

un•der•stat•ed (ŭn′dər-stā′tĭd) *adj.* Exhibiting restrained good taste: *an understated décor.* — **un′der•stat′ed•ly** *adv.*

un•der•state•ment (ŭn′dər-stāt′mənt, ŭn′dər-stāt′-) *n.* **1.** A disclosure or statement that is less than complete. **2.** Restraint or lack of emphasis in expression, as for rhetorical effect. **3.** Restraint in artistic expression.

un•der•steer (ŭn′dər-stîr′) *intr.v.* **-steered, -steer•ing, -steers.** To turn less sharply than the operator would expect. Used of vehicles. — *n.* **1.** An instance of understeering. **2.** A tendency to understeer.

un•der•stood (ŭn′dər-stŏŏd′) *adj.* **1.** Agreed on; assumed: *the understood conditions of troop withdrawal.* **2.** Not expressed in writing; implied.

un•der•stra•tum (ŭn′dər-strā′təm, -străt′əm) *n., pl.* **-stra•ta** (-strā′tə, -străt′ə) or **-stra•tums.** A substratum.

un•der•stud•y (ŭn′dər-stŭd′ē) *v.* **-ied** (-ēd), **-y•ing, -ies** (-ēz). — *tr.* **1.** To study or know (a role) so as to be able to replace the regular performer when required. **2.** To act as an understudy to. — *intr.* To be engaged in understudying a role. — *n., pl.* **-ies. 1.** A performer who understudies. **2.** A person trained to do the work of another.

un•der•sur•face (ŭn′dər-sûr′fəs) *n.* See **underside** 1.

un•der•take (ŭn′dər-tāk′) *v.* **-took** (-tŏŏk′), **-tak•en, -tak•ing, -takes.** — *tr.* **1.** To take upon oneself; decide or agree to do. **2.** To pledge or commit oneself: *undertake to care for an elderly relative.* **3.** To set about; begin. **4.** *Obsolete.* To accept combat with. — *intr. Archaic.* To make oneself responsible. Used with *for.*

un•der•tak•er (ŭn′dər-tā′kər) *n.* **1.** (ŭn′dər-tā′kər). See **funeral director. 2.** One that undertakes a task or job.

un•der•tak•ing (ŭn′dər-tā′kĭng) *n.* **1.** A task or an assignment undertaken; a venture. **2.** A guaranty, an engagement, or a promise. **3.** The profession or duties of a funeral director.

un•der-the-count•er (ŭn′dər-*th*ə-koun′tər) *adv. & adj.* Transacted, given, or sold illicitly.

un•der-the-ta•ble (ŭn′dər-*th*ə-tā′bəl) *adv. & adj.* Not straightforward; secret or underhand

un•der•things (ŭn′dər-thĭngz′) *pl.n.* Underwear, esp. of women or girls.

un•der•tint (ŭn′dər-tĭnt′) *n.* A slight or subtle tint.

un•der•tone (ŭn′dər-tōn′) *n.* **1.** An underlying or implied tendency or meaning; an undercurrent. **2.** A tone of low pitch or volume, esp. of spoken sound. **3.** *Color.* **a.** A pale or subdued color. **b.** A color applied under or seen through another.

un•der•tow (ŭn′dər-tō′) *n.* The seaward pull of receding waves after they break on a shore.

un•der•trick (ŭn′dər-trĭk′) *n. Games.* A trick in card games, the loss of which prevents a declarer from making a contract.

un•der•vest (ŭn′dər-vĕst′) *n. Chiefly British.* An undershirt.

un•der•wa•ter (ŭn′dər-wô′tər, -wŏt′ər) *adj.* **1.** Relating to, occurring, used, or performed beneath the surface of water. **2.** *Naut.* Below a vessel's water line. — **un′der•wa′ter** *adv.*

un•der way or **un•der•way** (ŭn′dər-wā′) *adv. & adj.* **1.** In motion or operation. **2.** Already commenced or initiated; in progress. **3.** *Naut.* Not anchored, aground, or moored to a fixed object.

un•der•wear (ŭn′dər-wâr′) *n.* See **underclothes.**

un•der•weight (ŭn′dər-wāt′) *adj.* Weighing less than is normal, healthy, or required. — *n.* Insufficiency of weight.

un•der•went (ŭn′dər-wĕnt′) *v.* P.t. of **undergo.**

un•der•whelm (ŭn′dər-hwĕlm′, -wĕlm′) *tr.v.* **-whelmed, -whelm•ing, -whelms.** To fail to excite, stimulate, or impress. [UNDER– + (OVER)WHELM.]

un•der•wing (ŭn′dər-wĭng′) *n.* **1.** One of a pair of hind wings of an insect, such as a moth. **2.** Any of various noctuid moths of the genus *Calocala,* having brightly colored hind wings visible only during flight.

un•der•wood (ŭn′dər-wŏŏd′) *n.* Shrubs and small trees growing beneath taller trees; underbrush.

un•der•wool (ŭn′dər-wŏŏl′) *n.* The soft woolly undercoat of certain animals, esp. sheep.

un•der•world (ŭn′dər-wûrld′) *n.* **1.** The part of society that is engaged in and organized for the purpose of crime and vice. **2.** A region, realm, or dwelling place conceived to be below the surface of the earth. **3.** The opposite side of the earth; the antipodes. **4.** *Gk. & Rom. Myth.* The world of the dead, located below the world of the living; Hades. **5.** *Archaic.* The world beneath the heavens; the earth.

un•der•write (ŭn′dər-rīt′) *v.* **-wrote** (-rōt′), **-writ•ten** (-rĭt′n), **-writ•ing, -writes.** — *tr.* **1.** To assume financial responsibility for; guarantee against failure. **2.a.** To sign (an insurance policy) so as to assume liability in case of specified losses. **b.** To insure. **c.** To insure against losses totaling (a given amount). **3.a.** To guarantee the purchase of (a full issue of stocks or bonds). **b.** To agree to buy the unsold part of (stock not yet sold publicly) at a fixed time and price. **4.a.** To write under or at the end of something. **b.** To subscribe to, esp. to sign or endorse (a document). **5.** To support or agree to (a decision, for example). — *intr.* To act as an underwriter, esp. to issue an insurance policy.

un•der•writ•er (ŭn′dər-rī′tər) *n.* One that underwrites, esp.: **a.** A person or firm engaged in the insurance business. **b.** An insurance agent who assesses the risk of enrolling an applicant for coverage or a policy. **c.** One that guarantees the purchase of a full issue of stocks or bonds.

un•de•scend•ed testicle (ŭn′dĭ-sĕn′dĭd) *n.* A testicle that has remained within the inguinal canal and has not descended to the scrotum.

un•de•sign•ing (ŭn′dĭ-zī′nĭng) *adj.* Having no ulterior motives; straightforward.

un•de•sir•a•ble (ŭn′dĭ-zīr′ə-bəl) *adj.* **1.** Not likely to please; objectionable. **2.** Not wanted: *undesirable aliens.* — *n.* A person regarded as undesirable. — **un′de•sir′a•bil′i•ty** *n.* — **un′de•sir′a•bly** *adv.*

un•de•ter•mined (ŭn′dĭ-tûr′mĭnd) *adj.* **1.** Not yet determined; undecided. **2.** Not specifically known or ascertained.

un•dies (ŭn′dēz) *pl.n. Informal.* Underwear, esp. for women or girls.

un•dine (ŭn-dēn′, ŭn′dēn′) *n.* According to Paracelsus, a female water spirit who could earn a soul by marrying a mortal and bearing his child. [NLat. *undīna* < Lat. *unda*, wave. See **wed-**[1]*.]

un•dip•lo•mat•ic (ŭn-dĭp′lə-măt′ĭk) *adj.* Not tactful or diplomatic. — **un•dip′lo•mat′i•cal•ly** *adv.*

un•di•rect•ed (ŭn′dĭ-rĕk′tĭd, -dī-) *adj.* **1.** Having no object or purpose; not guided. **2.** Having no prescribed destination. Used of mail.

un•dis•charged (ŭn′dĭs-chärjd′) *adj.* **1.** Not fulfilled: *an undischarged obligation.* **2.** Not paid: *an undischarged debt.* **3.** Not unloaded. Used of a ship's cargo.

un•dis•crim•i•nat•ing (ŭn′dĭ-skrĭm′ə-nā′tĭng) *adj.* **1.** Lacking sensitivity, taste, or judgment. **2.** Indiscriminate.

un•dis•posed (ŭn′dĭ-spōzd′) *adj.* **1.** Not settled, removed, or resolved: *undisposed assets.* **2.** Disinclined; unwilling.

un•dis•tin•guished (ŭn′dĭ-stĭng′gwĭsht) *adj.* **1.a.** Marked by no peculiar quality; not distinguished; ordinary. **b.** Lacking particularly good qualities; mediocre. **2.** Not separated from others into categories. **3.a.** Incapable of being noticed or perceived individually from others; indistinguishable. **b.** Unnoticed; unperceived.

un•do (ŭn-do͞o′) *v.* **-did** (-dĭd′), **-done** (-dŭn′), **-do•ing** (-do͞o′ĭng), **-does** (-dŭz′). — *tr.* **1.** To reverse or erase; annul. **2.** To untie, disassemble, or loosen: *undo a shoelace.* **3.** To open (a parcel, for example); unwrap. **4.a.** To cause the ruin or downfall of; destroy. **b.** To throw into confusion; unsettle. **5.** *Obsolete.* To solve or interpret; unravel. — *intr.* To come open or unfastened. — **un•do′er** *n.*

un•dock (ŭn-dŏk′) *tr.v.* **-docked, -dock•ing, -docks. 1.** *Naut.* To move (a ship) away from a dock. **2.** To uncouple (spacecraft).

un•doc•u•ment•ed (ŭn-dŏk′yə-mĕn′tĭd) *adj.* **1.** Not supported by written evidence: *undocumented accusations.* **2.** Not having the needed documents, as for permission to live or work in a foreign country. — *n.* A person not having proper documentation, esp. for immigration.

un•do•ing (ŭn-do͞o′ĭng) *n.* **1.** The act of unfastening or loosening. **2.a.** Ruin; destruction. **b.** The act of bringing to ruin. **c.** A cause or source of ruin; downfall. **3.** The act of reversing or annulling something accomplished; a cancellation.

un•dou•ble (ŭn-dŭb′əl) *tr.v.* **-bled, -bling, -bles.** To unfold, as a piece of paper money.

un•doubt•ed (ŭn-dou′tĭd) *adj.* Accepted as beyond question; undisputed. See Syns at **authentic.** — **un•doubt′ed•ly** *adv.*

un•draw (ŭn-drô′) *tr.v.* **-drew** (-dro͞o′), **-drawn** (-drôn′), **-draw•ing, -draws.** To draw to one side, as a curtain.

un•dreamed (ŭn-drēmd′) also **un•dreamt** (-drĕmt′) *adj.* Beyond what could be imagined; unimaginable. Often used with *of: a peaceful settlement undreamed of a generation ago.*

un•dress (ŭn-drĕs′) *v.* **-dressed, -dress•ing, -dress•es.** — *tr.* **1.** To remove the clothing of; disrobe. **2.** To remove the bandages from (a wound, for example). — *intr.* To take off one's clothing. — *n.* **1.** Informal attire or uniform. **2.a.** Nakedness or partial nakedness. **b.** Partial but incomplete dress.

un•dressed (ŭn-drĕst′) *adj.* **1.a.** Naked. **b.** Partially but not fully dressed. **2.** Not specially treated or processed: *undressed leather.* **3.a.** Not prepared for cooking or eating. Used of certain meats. **b.** Lacking sauce or dressing. Used of a salad. **4.** Not treated or bandaged: *an undressed wound.*

Und•set (o͝on′sĕt′), **Sigrid.** 1882–1949. Danish-born Norwegian writer who won the 1928 Nobel Prize for literature.

un•due (ŭn-do͞o′, -dyo͞o′) *adj.* **1.** Exceeding what is appropriate or normal; excessive. **2.** Not just, proper, or legal: *undue use of force.* **3.** Not yet payable or due: *an undue loan.*

un•du•lant (ŭn′jə-lənt, ŭn′dyə-, -də-) *adj.* Resembling waves in occurrence, appearance, or motion.

undulant fever *n.* See **brucellosis** 1.

un•du•late (ŭn′jə-lāt′, ŭn′dyə-, -də-) *v.* **-lat•ed, -lat•ing, -lates.** — *tr.* **1.** To cause to move in a smooth wavelike motion. **2.** To give a wavelike appearance or form to. — *intr.* **1.** To move in waves or with a smooth wavelike motion. **2.** To have a wavelike appearance or form. **3.** To increase and decrease in volume or pitch as if in waves. — *adj.* (-lĭt, -lāt′). Having a wavy outline or appearance. [< LLat. *undula*, small wave, dim. of Lat. *unda*, wave. See **wed-**[1]*.] — **un′du•la•to′ry** (-lə-tôr′ē, -tōr′ē) *adj.*

un•du•la•tion (ŭn′jə-lā′shən, ŭn′dyə-, -də-) *n.* **1.** A regular rising and falling or movement to alternating sides; movement in waves. **2.** A wavelike form, outline, or appearance. **3.** One of a series of waves or wavelike segments.

un•du•ly (ŭn-do͞o′lē, -dyo͞o′-) *adv.* Excessively; immoderately: *unduly familiar with strangers.*

un•du•ti•ful (ŭn-do͞o′tĭ-fəl, -dyo͞o′-) *adj.* **1.** Lacking a sense of duty. **2.** Unreliable or disobedient. — **un•du′ti•ful•ly** *adv.* — **un•du′ti•ful•ness** *n.*

un•dy•ing (ŭn-dī′ĭng) *adj.* Endless; everlasting; immortal.

un•earned (ŭn-ûrnd′) *adj.* **1.** Not gained by work or service: *unearned income.* **2.** Not deserved: *unearned luck.* **3.** Paid in anticipation of goods or services not yet rendered.

unearned increment *n.* The increase in property value resulting from factors independent of the owner, such as a general rise in demand for land.

un•earth (ŭn-ûrth′) *tr.v.* **-earthed, -earth•ing, -earths. 1.** To bring up out of the earth; dig up. **2.** To bring to public notice; uncover.

un•earth•ly (ŭn-ûrth′lē) *adj.* **-li•er, -li•est. 1.** Not of this earth; preternatural; supernatural. **2.** Unnaturally strange and frightening; eerie. **3.** Ridiculously unreasonable or uncustomary; absurd. — **un•earth′li•ness** *n.*

un•eas•y (ŭn-ē′zē) *adj.* **-i•er, -i•est. 1.** Lacking a sense of security; anxious or apprehensive. **2.** Affording no ease or reassurance: *an uneasy calm.* **3.a.** Awkward or unsure in manner; constrained: *uneasy with strangers.* **b.** Causing constraint or awkwardness: *an uneasy silence.* **4.** Not conducive to rest: *an uneasy sleep.* — **un•ease′, un•eas′i•ness** *n.* — **un•eas′i•ly** *adv.*

un•ed•it•ed (ŭn-ĕd′ĭ-tĭd) *adj.* **1.** Not edited or revised. **2.** Not adapted for a special audience or purpose.

un•ed•u•cat•ed (ŭn-ĕj′ə-kā′tĭd) *adj.* Not educated.

un•e•lect•a•ble (ŭn′ĭ-lĕk′tə-bəl) *adj.* Being such that election, as to high office, is difficult or impossible.

un•em•ploy•ment compensation (ŭn′ĕm-ploi′mənt) *n.* Financial compensation for unemployed workers, provided in the United States chiefly by state governments.

un-Eng•lish (ŭn-ĭng′glĭsh) *adj.* **1.** Not having the characteristics of British people or practices. **2.** Not in agreement with standard English usage.

un•e•qual (ŭn-ē′kwəl) *adj.* **1.** Not the same in any measurable aspect, such as extent or quantity. **2.** Not the same as another in rank or social position. **3.** Consisting of ill-matched opponents: *an unequal contest.* **4.** Having unbalanced sides or parts; asymmetrical. **5.** Not even or consistent; variable. **6.** Not having the required abilities. **7.** Not fair. — *n.* One that is not the equal of another. — **un•e′qual•ly** *adv.*

un•e•qualed also **un•e•qualled** (ŭn-ē′kwəld) *adj.* Not matched or paralleled by others of its kind; unrivaled.

un•e•quiv•o•cal (ŭn′ĭ-kwĭv′ə-kəl) *adj.* Admitting of no doubt or misunderstanding; clear and unambiguous: *an unequivocal success.* — **un′e•quiv′o•cal•ly** *adv.*

UNESCO *abbr.* United Nations Educational, Scientific, and Cultural Organization.

un•es•sen•tial (ŭn′ĭ-sĕn′shəl) *adj.* Not necessary or important; dispensable. — *n.* One that is unnecessary.

un•e•ven (ŭn-ē′vən) *adj.* **-er, -est. 1.a.** Not equal, as in size, length, or quality. **b.** Having ill-matched opponents: *an uneven contest.* **2.** Not consistent or uniform: *an uneven color.* **3.** Not smooth or level. **4.** Not straight or parallel. **5.** Of, relating to, or being an odd number. **6.** *Obsolete.* Not fair or equitable. — **un•e′ven•ly** *adv.* — **un•e′ven•ness** *n.*

un•e•vent•ful (ŭn′ĭ-vĕnt′fəl) *adj.* **1.** Lacking in significant events. **2.** Occurring without disruption. — **un′e•vent′ful•ly** *adv.* — **un′e•vent′ful•ness** *n.*

un•ex•am•pled (ŭn′ĭg-zăm′pəld) *adj.* Without precedent; unparalleled.

un•ex•cep•tion•a•ble (ŭn′ĭk-sĕp′shə-nə-bəl) *adj.* Beyond any reasonable objection; irreproachable. — **un′ex•cep′tion•a•ble•ness** *n.* — **un′ex•cep′tion•a•bly** *adv.*

Usage Note: *Unexceptionable* is derived from the word *exception* in the sense "objection," as in the idiom *take exception.* Thus *unexceptionable* means "not open to any objection," as in *A judge's ethical standards should be unexceptionable. Unexceptional,* in contrast, is related to the common sense of *exception* and generally means "not exceptional, not varying from the usual," as in *Some judges' ethical standards have unfortunately been unexceptional.*

un•ex•cep•tion•al (ŭn′ĭk-sĕp′shə-nəl) *adj.* **1.** Not varying from a norm; usual: *an unexceptional performance.* **2.** Not subject to exceptions; absolute. See Usage Note at **unexceptionable.** — **un′ex•cep′tion•al•ly** *adv.*

un•ex•pect•ed (ŭn′ĭk-spĕk′tĭd) *adj.* Coming without warning; unforeseen. — **un′ex•pect′ed•ly** *adv.* — **un′ex•pect′ed•ness** *n.*

ă pat	oi boy
ā pay	ou out
âr care	o͝o took
ä father	o͞o boot
ĕ pet	ŭ cut
ē be	ûr urge
ĭ pit	th thin
ī pie	*th* this
îr pier	hw which
ŏ pot	zh vision
ō toe	ə about, item
ô paw	

Stress marks:
′ (primary);
′ (secondary), as in dictionary (dĭk′shə-nĕr′ē)

un•ex•ploit•ed (ŭn′ĭk-sploi′tĭd) *adj.* Not exploited or developed: *unexploited oil reserves.*

un•ex•pres•sive (ŭn′ĭk-sprĕs′ĭv) *adj.* **1.** Not conveying the meaning intended or the emotion felt. **2.** *Obsolete.* Inexpressible. —**un′ex•pres′sive•ly** *adv.* —**un′ex•pres′sive•ness** *n.*

un•fail•ing (ŭn-fā′lĭng) *adj.* **1.** Always able to supply more; inexhaustible: *an unfailing source of good stories.* **2.** Constant; unflagging: *unfailing loyalty.* **3.** Incapable of error; infallible. —**un•fail′ing•ly** *adv.* —**un•fail′ing•ness** *n.*

un•fair (ŭn-fâr′) *adj.* **-er, -est. 1.** Not just or evenhanded; biased. **2.** Contrary to laws or conventions, esp. in commerce; unethical. —**un•fair′ly** *adv.* —**un•fair′ness** *n.*

un•faith (ŭn-fāth′) *n.* Absence of faith, esp. in religion.

un•faith•ful (ŭn-fāth′fəl) *adj.* **1.** Not adhering to promises, obligations, or allegiances; disloyal: *has never been unfaithful to her ideals.* **2.a.** Not true or constant to one's sexual partner. **b.** Not true to one's spouse; guilty of adultery. **3.** Not justly representing or reflecting the original; inaccurate. **4.** *Obsolete.* Deficient in or lacking religious faith; unbelieving. —**un•faith′ful•ly** *adv.* —**un•faith′ful•ness** *n.*

un•fa•thered (ŭn-fä′thərd) *adj.* **1.a.** Having no father; fatherless. **b.** Having no known father. **2.** Of uncertain origin or authenticity: *unfathered rumors.*

un•feel•ing (ŭn-fē′lĭng) *adj.* **1.** Having no physical feeling or sensation; insentient. **2.** Not sharing in the pleasures or pains of others; callous: *an unfeeling heart.* —**un•feel′ing•ly** *adv.* —**un•feel′ing•ness** *n.*

un•feigned (ŭn′fānd′) *adj.* Not feigned; genuine. —**un•feign′ed•ly** (ŭn-fā′nĭd-lē) *adv.*

un•fit (ŭn-fĭt′) *adj.* **1.** Not meant or adapted for a given purpose; inappropriate. **2.** Below the required standard; unqualified: *an unfit parent.* **3.** Not in good physical or mental health. —*tr.v.* **-fit•ted, -fit•ting, -fits.** To cause to be unsuited or unqualified. —**un•fit′ly** *adv.* —**un•fit′ness** *n.*

un•fix (ŭn-fĭks′) *tr.v.* **-fixed, -fix•ing, -fix•es. 1.** To detach from what secures; unfasten. **2.** To cause to leave a tranquil condition; disturb.

un•flag•ging (ŭn-flăg′ĭng) *adj.* Not flagging; untiring.

un•flap•pa•ble (ŭn-flăp′ə-bəl) *adj.* Persistently calm; not easily upset or excited. —**un•flap′pa•bil′i•ty** *n.* —**un•flap′pa•bly** *adv.*

un•flapped (ŭn-flăpt′) *adj.* Not upset or excited; calm.

un•flat•ter•ing (ŭn-flăt′ər-ĭng) *adj.* Acknowledging few or no good aspects; unfavorable. —**un•flat′ter•ing•ly** *adv.*

un•fledged (ŭn-flĕjd′) *adj.* **1.** Not having the feathers necessary to fly. Used of a young bird. **2.** Inexperienced, immature, or untried.

un•flinch•ing (ŭn-flĭn′chĭng) *adj.* Showing neither fear nor indecision; resolute. —**un•flinch′ing•ly** *adv.* —**un•flinch′ing•ness** *n.*

un•fo•cused also **un•fo•cussed** (ŭn-fō′kəst) *adj.* **1.** Not brought into focus: *an unfocused lens.* **2.** Not centered on anything specific: *unfocused thoughts.*

un•fold (ŭn-fōld′) *v.* **-fold•ed, -fold•ing, -folds.** —*tr.* **1.** To open and spread out (something folded); extend. **2.** To remove the coverings from; disclose to view. **3.** To reveal gradually by written or spoken explanation; make known. —*intr.* **1.a.** To become spread out; open out: *Spring flowers unfolded.* **b.** To develop, as if by spreading out: *A brilliant career unfolded.* **2.** To be revealed gradually to the understanding. —**un•fold′ment** *n.*

un•fore•seen (ŭn′fər-sēn′, -fôr-) *adj.* Not felt or realized beforehand; unexpected: *unforeseen difficulties.*

un•for•giv•ing (ŭn′fər-gĭv′ĭng) *adj.* **1.** Reluctant or refusing to forgive. **2.** Providing little or no opportunity to forestall undesired results or mistakes.

un•for•mat•ted (ŭn-fôr′măt′ĭd) *adj. Comp. Sci.* Of or relating to a disk that is not prepared for writing or reading.

un•formed (ŭn-fôrmd′) *adj.* **1.** Having no definite shape or structure; unorganized. **2.** Not yet developed to maturity. **3.** Not yet given a physical existence; uncreated.

un•for•tu•nate (ŭn-fôr′chə-nĭt) *adj.* **1.** Characterized by undeserved bad luck; unlucky. **2.** Causing misfortune; disastrous. **3.** Regrettable; deplorable. —*n.* A victim of bad luck. —**un•for′tu•nate•ly** *adv.* —**un•for′tu•nate•ness** *n.*

un•found•ed (ŭn-foun′dĭd) *adj.* **1.** Not based on fact or sound evidence; groundless. **2.** Not yet established. —**un•found′ed•ly** *adv.* —**un•found′ed•ness** *n.*

un•fre•quent•ed (ŭn-frē′kwən-tĭd, ŭn′frē-kwĕn′tĭd) *adj.* Receiving few or no travelers or visitors: *unfrequented inns.*

un•frock (ŭn-frŏk′) *tr.v.* **-frocked, -frock•ing, -frocks. 1.** To strip of priestly privileges and functions. **2.** To deprive of the right to practice a profession. **3.** To deprive of an honorary position.

un•fruit•ful (ŭn-fro͞ot′fəl) *adj.* **1.** Not bearing fruit or offspring. **2.** Not productive of a good or useful result. —**un•fruit′ful•ly** *adv.* —**un′fruit′ful•ness** *n.*

un•furl (ŭn-fûrl′) *tr. & intr.v.* **-furled, -furl•ing, -furls.** To spread or open (something) out or become spread or opened out: *an unfurled flag; with flags unfurled.*

un•gain•ly (ŭn-gān′lē) *adj.* **-li•er, -li•est. 1.** Lacking grace or ease of movement or form; clumsy. **2.** Difficult to move or use; unwieldy. [UN-[1] + *gainli,* proper (< ME < *gain* < ON *gegn,* direct).] —**un•gain′li•ness** *n.*

Un•ga•va Bay (ŭn-gā′və, -gä′-). An inlet of Hudson Strait in NE Quebec, Canada, between N Labrador and **Ungava Peninsula,** bordered on the W by Hudson Bay.

un•girt (ŭn-gûrt′) *adj.* **1.** Having the belt or girdle removed or loosened. **2.** Loose or free; slack.

un•glued (ŭn-glo͞od′) *adj.* **1.** Loosened or separated; unfastened. **2.** *Slang.* In confused distress; upset. —***idiom.* come unglued.** *Slang.* To lose one's composure.

un•god•ly (ŭn-gŏd′lē) *adj.* **-li•er, -li•est. 1.** Not revering God; impious. **2.** Sinful; wicked. **3.** Outrageous: *had to leave for work at an ungodly hour.* —**un•god′li•ness** *n.*

un•gov•ern•a•ble (ŭn-gŭv′ər-nə-bəl) *adj.* Incapable of being governed, restrained, or controlled. See Syns at **unruly.** —**un•gov′ern•a•ble•ness** *n.* —**un•gov′ern•a•bly** *adv.*

un•gra•cious (ŭn-grā′shəs) *adj.* **1.** Lacking social grace or graciousness; rude. **2.** Not welcome or acceptable; unattractive. **3.** *Archaic.* Evil; wicked. —**un•gra′cious•ly** *adv.* —**un•gra′cious•ness** *n.*

un•gram•mat•i•cal (ŭn′grə-măt′ĭ-kəl) *adj.* **1.** Not in accord with the rules of a prescriptive grammar. **2.** Not in accord with a language as used by a native speaker. —**un′gram•mat′i•cal′i•ty** (-kăl′ĭ-tē) *n.* —**un′gram•mat′i•cal•ly** *adv.*

un•gual (ŭng′gwəl) *adj.* **1.** Of, resembling, or bearing a hoof, nail, or claw. **2.** Of or relating to fingernails or toenails. [< Lat. *unguis,* nail. See UNGUIS.]

un•guard•ed (ŭn-gär′dĭd) *adj.* **1.** Lacking protection or a guard; vulnerable. **2.** Displaying, having, or feeling no wariness; incautious. —**un•guard′ed•ly** *adv.* —**un•guard′ed•ness** *n.*

un•guent (ŭng′gwənt) *n.* A salve for soothing or healing; an ointment. [ME < Lat. *unguentum* < *unguere,* to anoint.] —**un′guen•tar′y** (-tĕr′ē) *adj.*

un•guic•u•late (ŭng-gwĭk′yə-lĭt, -lāt′) also **un•guic•u•lat•ed** (-lā′tĭd) —*adj.* **1.** Having or resembling nails or claws. **2.** *Zool.* Having nails or claws, as opposed to hooves. Used of mammals. **3.** *Bot.* Having a claw-shaped base: *an unguiculate petal.* —*n. Zool.* A mammal having nails or claws. [NLat. *unguiculātus* < Lat. *unguiculus,* fingernail, dim. of *unguis.* See UNGUIS.]

un•guis (ŭng′gwĭs) *n., pl.* **-gues** (-gwēz). **1.** *Zool.* A nail, claw, or hoof. **2.** *Bot.* The clawlike base of some petals. [Lat. See **nogh-*.**]

un•gu•late (ŭng′gyə-lĭt, -lāt′) *adj.* **1.a.** Having hoofs. **b.** Resembling hoofs; hooflike. **2.** Of or belonging to the former order Ungulata, now divided into the orders Perissodactyla and Artiodactyla and composed of the hoofed mammals such as horses, cattle, deer, and elephants. —*n.* An ungulate mammal. [Lat. *ungulātus* < *ungula,* hoof, dim. of *unguis,* nail. See UNGUIS.]

un•hal•low (ŭn-hăl′ō) *tr.v.* **-lowed, -low•ing, -lows.** *Archaic.* To violate the holiness of; profane or desecrate.

un•hal•lowed (ŭn-hăl′ōd) *adj.* **1.** Not hallowed or consecrated. **2.a.** Lacking reverence; impious or irreligious. **b.** Not conforming to accepted ethical standards; immoral.

un•hand (ŭn-hănd′) *tr.v.* **-hand•ed, -hand•ing, -hands.** To remove one's hand from; let go.

un•hand•some (ŭn-hăn′səm) *adj.* **1.** Not attractive or beautiful; homely. **2.** Not courteous or in good taste; ungracious. —**un•hand′some•ly** *adv.* —**un•hand′some•ness** *n.*

un•hand•y (ŭn-hăn′dē) *adj.* **-i•er, -i•est. 1.** Difficult to handle or manage; unwieldy. **2.** Lacking manual skill or dexterity. —**un•hand′i•ly** *adv.* —**un•hand′i•ness** *n.*

un•hap•py (ŭn-hăp′ē) *adj.* **-pi•er, -pi•est. 1.** Not happy or joyful; sad or sorrowful. **2.** Not satisfied; displeased or discontented: *unhappy with her raise.* **3.** Not attended by or bringing good fortune; unlucky. **4.** Not suitable; inappropriate. —**un•hap′pi•ly** *adv.* —**un•hap′pi•ness** *n.*

un•har•ness (ŭn-här′nĭs) *tr.v.* **-nessed, -ness•ing, -ness•es. 1.** To remove the harness or similar equipment from. **2.** To release or liberate (energy or passions, for example). **3.** To remove the armor from (a wearer).

un•health•y (ŭn-hĕl′thē) *adj.* **-i•er, -i•est. 1.a.** Being in a state of ill health; sick. **b.** Characterized by or symptomatic of ill health. **c.** Causing or conducive to poor health; unwholesome. **2.** Harmful to character or moral health; corruptive. **3.** Characterized by or symptomatic of disturbed mental health: *an unhealthy interest in violence.* **4.** Of a risky nature; dangerous. —**un′health′i•ly** *adv.* —**un•health′i•ness** *n.*

un•heard (ŭn-hûrd′) *adj.* **1.** Not heard: *unheard pleas for help.* **2.** Not given a hearing; not listened to: *unheard objections.* **3.** *Archaic.* Not heard of; obscure.

un•heard-of (ŭn-hûrd′ŭv′, -ŏv′) *adj.* **1.** Not previously known; unknown. **2.** Without precedent; unparalleled. **3.** Highly offensive; outrageous or brazen.

un•hes•i•tat•ing (ŭn-hĕz′ĭ-tā′tĭng) *adj.* **1.** Prompt to act, move, or express oneself; ready: *I gave my unhesitating approval.* **2.** Unfaltering; steadfast. —**un•hes′i•tat′ing•ly** *adv.*

un•hinge (ŭn-hĭnj′) *tr.v.* **-hinged, -hing•ing, -hing•es. 1.** To remove from hinges. **2.** To remove the hinges from. **3.** To confuse; disrupt. **4.** To derange; unbalance.

un•his•tor•i•cal (ŭn′hĭ-stôr′ĭ-kəl, -stŏr′-) *adj.* Taking little or no account of history.

un•hitch (ŭn-hĭch′) *tr.v.* **-hitched, -hitch•ing, -hitch•es.** To release from or as if from a hitch; unfasten.

un•ho•ly (ŭn-hō′lē) *adj.* **-li•er, -li•est. 1.** Wicked; immoral. **2.** Not hallowed or consecrated. **3.** *Informal.* Outrageous: *took unholy risks.* **—un•ho′li•ly** *adv.* **—un•ho′li•ness** *n.*

un•hook (ŭn-ho͝ok′) *tr.v.* **-hooked, -hook•ing, -hooks. 1.** To release or remove from or as if from a hook. **2.** To unfasten the hooks of.

un•hoped (ŭn-hōpt′) *adj. Archaic.* Not hoped or looked for.

un•horse (ŭn-hôrs′) *tr.v.* **-horsed, -hors•ing, -hors•es. 1.** To cause to fall from a horse. **2.** To overthrow or dislodge; upset.

uni– *pref.* Single; one: *unicycle.* [Lat. *ūni-* < *ūnus*, one. See **oi-no-***.]

U•ni•at (yo͞o′nē-ăt′, -ĭt) also **U•ni•ate** (-ĭt, -āt′) *—adj.* Of or relating to any of several Eastern Christian churches that are in communion with the Roman Catholic Church but retain their own languages, rites, and canon law. *—n.* A member of any of these churches. [Russ. *uniyat* < Pol. *uniat*, the Union of Brest-Litovsk (1596) < *unija*, union < LLat. *ūniō, ūniōn-*. See UNION.]

u•ni•ax•i•al (yo͞o′nē-ăk′sē-əl) *adj.* **1.** Of, relating to, or affecting one axis. **2.** *Bot.* Of, relating to, or being a plant with one primary stem that has no branches and terminates in a flower. **3.** Having one direction along which double refraction of light does not take place. Used of a crystal.

u•ni•cam•er•al (yo͞o′nĭ-kăm′ər-əl) *adj.* Having or consisting of a single legislative chamber. [UNI– + Lat. *camera*, chamber; see CAMERA + –AL[1].] **—u′ni•cam′er•al•ly** *adv.*

UNICEF *abbr.* United Nations Children's Fund (formerly United Nations International Children's Emergency Fund).

u•ni•cel•lu•lar (yo͞o′nĭ-sĕl′yə-lər) *adj.* Having or consisting of one cell; one-celled: *unicellular organisms.* **—u′ni•cel′lu•lar′i•ty** (-lăr′ĭ-tē, -lâr′-) *n.*

u•ni•col•or (yo͞o′nĭ-kŭl′ər) *adj.* Monochromatic.

u•ni•corn (yo͞o′nĭ-kôrn′) *n.* A fabled creature symbolic of virginity and usu. represented as a horse with a single straight spiraled horn projecting from its forehead. [ME *unicorne* < OFr. < LLat. *ūnicornis* < Lat., having one horn : *ūnus*, one; see **oi-no-*** + *cornū*, horn; see **ker-**[1]*.]

U•ni•corn (yo͞o′nĭ-kôrn′) *n. Astron.* The constellation Monoceros.

u•ni•cos•tate (yo͞o′nĭ-kŏs′tāt′) *adj.* Having a single main costa, rib, or riblike part: *a unicostate leaf.*

u•ni•cy•cle (yo͞o′nĭ-sī′kəl) *n.* A vehicle consisting of a frame mounted over a single wheel, usu. propelled by pedals. [UNI– + *-cycle*, perh. on the model of BICYCLE.] **—u′ni•cy′clist** *n.*

un•i•den•ti•fied flying object (ŭn′ī-dĕn′tə-fīd′) *n.* A flying or apparently flying object of an unknown nature, esp. one suspected to have been sent by extraterrestrial beings.

u•ni•di•rec•tion•al (yo͞o′nĭ-dĭ-rĕk′shə-nəl, -dī-) *adj.* Having, operating, or moving in one direction only.

u•ni•fac•to•ri•al (yo͞o′nə-făk-tôr′ē-əl, -tōr′-) *adj.* Involving, dependent on, or controlled by a single gene.

u•ni•fied field theory (yo͞o′nə-fīd′) *n.* A physical theory that combines the treatment of two or more types of fields in order to discover interrelationships, esp. such a theory unifying the theories of nuclear, electromagnetic, and gravitational forces.

u•ni•fi•lar (yo͞o′nə-fī′lər) *adj.* Having or using only one filament, such as a thread or wire.

u•ni•fo•li•ate (yo͞o′nə-fō′lē-ĭt, -āt′) *adj. Bot.* Having a single leaf.

u•ni•fo•li•o•late (yo͞o′nĭ-fō′lē-ə-lāt′) *adj. Bot.* Compound in structure but having a single leaflet.

u•ni•form (yo͞o′nə-fôrm′) *adj.* **1.** Always the same, as in character or degree; unvarying. **2.** Conforming to one principle, standard, or rule; consistent. **3.** Being the same as or consonant with another or others. **4.** Unvaried in texture, color, or design. *—n.* A distinctive outfit intended to identify those who wear it as members of a specific group. *—tr.v.* **-formed, -form•ing, -forms. 1.** To make (something) uniform. **2.** To provide or dress with a uniform. [Lat. *ūniformis* : *ūni-*, uni- + *forma*, shape.] **—u′ni•for′mi•ty, u′ni•form′ness** *n.* **—u′ni•form′ly** *adv.*

u•ni•for•mi•tar•i•an•ism (yo͞o′nə-fôr′mĭ-târ′ē-ə-nĭz′əm) *n.* The theory that geologic phenomena may be explained as the result of existing forces operating uniformly from the origin of the earth to the present time. **—u′ni•for′mi•tar′i•an** *adj. & n.*

u•ni•fy (yo͞o′nə-fī′) *tr. & intr.v.* **-fied** (-fīd), **-fy•ing, -fies** (-fīz). To make into or become a unit; consolidate. [Fr. *unifier* < OFr. < LLat. *ūnificāre* : Lat. *ūni-*, uni- + Lat. *-ficāre*, -fy.] **—u′ni•fi′a•ble** *adj.* **—u′ni•fi•ca′tion** (-fĭ-kā′shən) *n.* **—u′ni•fi′er** *n.*

u•ni•lat•er•al (yo͞o′nə-lăt′ər-əl) *adj.* **1.** Of, on, relating to, involving, or affecting only one side. **2.** Performed or undertaken by only one side: *unilateral disarmament.* **3.** Obligating only one of two or more parties, nations, or persons, as a contract or an agreement. **4.** Emphasizing or recognizing only one side of a subject. **5.** Having only one side. **6.** Tracing the lineage of one parent only: *a unilateral genealogy.* **7.** *Bot.* Having leaves, flowers, or other parts on one side only. **—u′ni•lat′er•al•ism** *n.* **—u′ni•lat′er•a•list** *adj. & n.* **—u′ni•lat′er•al•ly** *adv.*

u•ni•lin•e•ar (yo͞o′nĭ-lĭn′ē-ər) *adj.* Of or developing in a progressive sequence usu. from the primitive to the advanced.

u•ni•lin•gual (yo͞o′nĭ-lĭng′gwəl) *adj.* Making use of or written in one language only.

u•ni•loc•u•lar (yo͞o′nə-lŏk′yə-lər) *adj. Bot.* Having a single compartment in the ovary or fruit, as in a melon.

U•ni•mak Island (yo͞o′nə-măk′). An island of SW AK in the E Aleutian Is.

un•im•pas•sioned (ŭn′ĭm-păsh′ənd) *adj.* Not impassioned; devoid of emotional influence or appeal.

un•im•peach•a•ble (ŭn′ĭm-pē′chə-bəl) *adj.* **1.** Difficult or impossible to impeach: *an unimpeachable witness.* **2.** Beyond reproach; blameless. **3.** Beyond doubt; unquestionable. **—un′im•peach′a•bly** *adv.*

un•im•proved (ŭn′ĭm-pro͞ovd′) *adj.* **1.** Not improved; not made better. **2.** Not made use of or put to advantage. **3.** Not built on or cultivated so as to increase in value. Used of land.

un•in•formed (ŭn′ĭn-fôrmd′) *adj.* Not having, showing, or making use of information; not informed: *uninformed voters.*

un•in•hab•it•ed (ŭn′ĭn-hăb′ĭ-tĭd) *adj.* Having no residents.

un•in•hib•it•ed (ŭn′ĭn-hĭb′ĭ-tĭd) *adj.* **1.** Open and unrestrained: *uninhibited laughter.* **2.** Free from traditional social or moral constraints. **—un′in•hib′it•ed•ly** *adv.* **—un′in•hib′it•ed•ness** *n.*

un•in•i•ti•ate (ŭn′ĭ-nĭsh′ē-ĭt) *adj.* Not experienced. **—un′in•i′ti•ate** *n.*

un•in•i•ti•at•ed (ŭn′ĭ-nĭsh′ē-ā′tĭd) *adj.* Not knowledgeable or skilled; inexperienced. *—n.* An uninformed, unskilled, or inexperienced person or group of people.

un•in•spired (ŭn′ĭn-spīrd′) *adj.* Having no intellectual, emotional, or spiritual excitement; dull.

un•in•struct•ed (ŭn′ĭn-strŭk′tĭd) *adj.* **1.** Not educated or informed: *an uninstructed young mind.* **2.** Not provided with directives on how to vote or proceed.

un•in•sured (ŭn′ĭn-sho͝ord′) *adj.* Not covered by insurance. *—n., pl.* **-sureds.** A party that is not insured.

un•in•tend•ed (ŭn′ĭn-tĕn′dĭd) *adj.* Not deliberate or intentional; unplanned: *an unintended slight.*

un•in•ter•est (ŭn-ĭn′trĭst, -tər-ĭst, -trĕst′) *n.* Lack of interest or concern; indifference.

un•in•ter•est•ed (ŭn-ĭn′trĭ-stĭd, -tər-ĭ-stĭd, -tə-rĕs′tĭd) *adj.* **1.a.** Without an interest: *uninterested parties.* **b.** Not having a financial interest. **2.** Marked by or exhibiting a lack of interest. See Usage Note at **disinterested. —un•in′ter•est•ed•ly** *adv.* **—un•in′ter•est•ed•ness** *n.*

un•in•ter•est•ing (ŭn-ĭn′trĭ-stĭng, -tər-ĭ-stĭng, -tə-rĕs′tĭng) *adj.* Boring. **—un•in′ter•est•ing•ly** *adv.*

u•ni•nu•cle•ate (yo͞o′nĭ-no͞o′klē-ĭt, -nyo͞o′-) *adj.* Having one nucleus.

un•in•vit•ed (ŭn′ĭn-vī′tĭd) *adj.* Not welcome or wanted: *uninvited guests.*

un•in•volved (ŭn′ĭn-vŏlvd′) *adj.* Feeling or showing no interest or involvement; unconcerned: *an uninvolved bystander.*

un•ion (yo͞on′yən) *n.* **1.a.** The act of uniting or the state of being united. **b.** A combination so formed, esp. an alliance or confederation of people, parties, or political entities for mutual interest or benefit. **2.** *Math.* A set, every member of which is an element of one or another of two or more given sets. **3.** Agreement or harmony resulting from the uniting of individuals; concord. **4.a.** The state of matrimony; marriage. **b.** Sexual intercourse. **5.a.** A combination of parishes for joint administration of relief for the poor in Great Britain. **b.** A workhouse maintained by such a union. **6.** A labor union. **7.** A coupling device for connecting parts, such as rods. **8.** A device on a flag or an ensign that signifies the union of two or more sovereignties. **9.** Often **Union. a.** An organization at a college or university that provides facilities for recreation; a student union. **b.** A building housing such facilities. **10. Union.** The United States of America regarded as a national unit, esp. during the Civil War. *—adj.* **1. Union.** Of, relating to, or loyal to the United States of America during the Civil War. **2.** Of or relating to a labor union or labor union organizing: *union negotiations.* [ME < OFr. < LLat. *ūniō, ūniōn-* < Lat. *ūnus*, one. See **oi-no-***.]

Union. A community of NE NJ WNW of Elizabeth; settled c. 1749. Pop. 50,024.

union catalog *n.* A library catalog combining in alphabetical sequence the contents of a number of catalogs or the contents of more than one library.

union church *n.* A local interdenominational church bringing together worshipers of different denominational backgrounds.

Union City. 1. A city of W CA SE of Oakland. Pop. 53,762. **2.** A city of NE NJ adjoining Jersey City. Pop. 58,012.

un•ion•ism (yo͞on′yə-nĭz′əm) *n.* **1.** The principle or theory of forming a union. **2.** The principles, theory, or system of a union, esp. a trade union. **3. Unionism.** Loyalty to the federal government during the Civil War.

un•ion•ist (yo͞on′yə-nĭst) *n.* **1.** One who believes in or supports a union or unionism. **2.** A member of a labor or trade

unicorn
Detail of late 18th- to early 19th-century American watercolor and ink drawing of rampant unicorn

unicycle

ă pat	oi boy
ā pay	ou out
âr care	o͝o took
ä father	o͞o boot
ĕ pet	ŭ cut
ē be	ûr urge
ĭ pit	th thin
ī pie	*th* this
îr pier	hw which
ŏ pot	zh vision
ō toe	ə about, item
ô paw	

Stress marks:
′ (primary);
′ (secondary), as in **dictionary** (dĭk′shə-nĕr′ē)

union. **3. Unionist.** One loyal to the federal government during the Civil War. **—un′ion•is′tic** *adj.*

un•ion•ize (yōōn′yə-nīz′) *v.* **-ized, -iz•ing, -iz•es.** *—tr.* **1.** To organize into a labor union. **2.** To cause to join a labor union. *—intr.* To organize or join a labor union. **—un′ion•i•za′tion** (-yə-nĭ-zā′shən) *n.* **—un′ion•iz′er** *n.*

union jack *n.* **1.** A flag consisting entirely of a union. **2. Union Jack.** The flag of the United Kingdom.

union label *n.* An identifying mark attached to a product indicating it has been produced by members of a trade union.

Union of So•vi•et Socialist Republics (sō′vē-ĕt′, -ĭt, sŏv′ē-, sō′vē-ĕt′). Commonly called **Soviet Union** or **Rus•sia** (rŭsh′ə) A former country of E Europe and N Asia with coastlines on the Baltic and Black seas and the Arctic and Pacific oceans; estab. in Dec. 1922. In Dec. 1991 it was officially dissolved into a number of independent republics.

Union Jack

union shop *n.* A business or industrial establishment whose employees are required either to be union members or to join the union within a specified time after being hired.

union suit *n.* A one-piece undergarment combining shirt and long pants.

u•nip•a•rous (yōō-nĭp′ər-əs) *adj.* **1.** Producing only one egg or offspring at a time. **2.** *Bot.* Forming a single axis at each branching, as certain flower clusters.

u•ni•per•son•al (yōō′nĭ-pûr′sə-nəl) *adj.* Manifested as or existent in the form of only one person: *a unipersonal spirit.*

u•ni•po•lar (yōō′nĭ-pō′lər) *adj.* **1.** Having, acting by means of, or produced by a single magnetic or electric pole. **2.** *Biol.* Having a single fibrous process. Used of a neuron. **—u′ni•po•lar′i•ty** (-pō-lăr′ĭ-tē, -pə-) *n.*

u•ni•po•tent (yōō-nĭp′ə-tənt) *adj.* Capable of developing into only one type of cell or tissue.

u•nique (yōō-nēk′) *adj.* **1.** Being the only one of its kind. **2.** Without an equal or equivalent; unparalleled. **3.a.** Characteristic of a particular category, condition, or locality: *a problem unique to coastal areas.* **b.** *Informal.* Unusual; extraordinary. [Fr. < OFr. < Lat. *ūnicus.* See **oi-no-***.] **—u•nique′ly** *adv.* **—u•nique′ness** *n.*

unitard

Usage Note: In the most recent survey the sentence *Her designs are quite unique in today's fashion scene* was unacceptable to 80 percent of the Usage Panel. Critical objections to the comparison and degree modification of absolute terms such as *unique* date to the 18th century and have been applied to a wide group of adjectives, including *equal, fatal, omnipotent, parallel, perfect,* and *unanimous.* According to the standard argument, such words denote properties that a thing either does or does not have but cannot have to a qualifiable degree. Thus if *unique* is properly used to mean "without equal or equivalent," something either is unique or it isn't, and phrases such as *very unique* and *more unique* can only betray a weakening of the sense to mean something like "unusual" or "distinctive." A reputable writer, however, might say that a painting is unique and mean that it is worthy of inclusion in a class by itself according to certain implicit but generally accepted criteria. Thus a legitimately unique painting might be one that realizes an unparalleled aesthetic vision but not one that is rendered only in pigments whose names begin with the letter *o.* Given this understanding, it is not inherently impossible to think of uniqueness as a matter of degree, in the sense that one painting may be more or less worthy of inclusion in a class by itself than some other. • What is troubling about the use of *unique* by copywriters, for example, is that in such writing uniqueness is claimed for a restaurant in virtue of some trivial properties of its decor or menu, for example. Though it may be true that such properties render a restaurant *logically* unique, they do not constitute legitimate grounds for putting it into a class by itself according to the criteria ordinarily invoked when things are sorted into classes. But it is not surprising that *unique* should lend itself to promiscuous modification and comparison; for once it is granted that uniqueness can be claimed for any product or service that is somehow distinctive from all its competitors, it is inevitable that an increase in uniqueness will be seen in every minor innovation. See Usage Note at **infinite.**

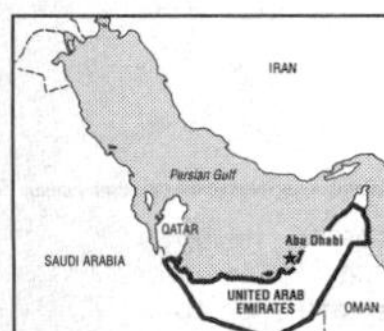

United Arab Emirates

u•ni•sex (yōō′nĭ-sĕks′) *adj.* **1.** Designed for or suitable to both sexes: *unisex clothing.* **2.** Not distinguished or distinguishable on the basis of sex: *a unisex look.* *—n.* Elimination or absence of sexual distinctions, esp. in dress.

u•ni•sex•u•al (yōō′nĭ-sĕk′shōō-əl) *adj.* **1.** Of or relating to only one sex. **2.** Having only one type of sexual organ; not a hermaphrodite. **3.** *Bot.* Having either stamens or pistils but not both. **4.** Unisex. **—u′ni•sex′u•al′i•ty** (-ăl′ĭ-tē) *n.* **—u′ni•sex′u•al•ly** *adv.*

u•ni•son (yōō′nĭ-sən, -zən) *n.* **1.** *Mus.* **a.** Identity of pitch; the interval of a perfect prime. **b.** The combination of parts at the same pitch or in octaves. **2.** The act or an instance of speaking the same words simultaneously by two or more speakers. **3.** An instance of agreement; concord. ***—idiom.* in unison. 1.** In complete agreement; harmonizing exactly. **2.** At the same time; at once. [ME < OFr. < Med.Lat. *ūnisonus,* in unison < LLat., monotonous : Lat. *ūni-,* uni- + Lat. *sonus,* sound; see **swen-***.]

u•nit (yōō′nĭt) *n.* **1.** An individual, a group, a structure, or other entity regarded as an elementary constituent of a whole. **2.** A group regarded as a distinct entity within a larger group. **3.a.** A mechanical part or module. **b.** An entire apparatus or the equipment that performs a specific function. **4.** A precise quantity in terms of which the magnitudes of other quantities of the same kind can be stated. **5.** *Medic.* The quantity of a drug or other agent necessary to produce a specific effect. **6.a.** A fixed amount of scholastic study used in calculating academic credits, usu. measured in hours of formal instruction or laboratory work. **b.** A section of an academic course focusing on a selected theme: *a unit on Native Americans.* **7.** The number immediately to the left of the decimal point in the Arabic numeral system. **8.** *Math.* The lowest positive whole number. [Back-formation < UNITY.]

Unit. *abbr.* **1.** Unitarian. **2.** Unitarianism.

u•ni•tard (yōō′nĭ-tärd′) *n.* A one-piece tight-fitting leotard and tights combination, sometimes with foot straps. [UNI- + (LEO)TARD.]

U•ni•tar•i•an (yōō′nĭ-târ′ē-ən) *n.* **1.** An adherent of Unitarian Universalism. **2.** A monotheist who is not a Christian. **3.** A Christian who is not a Trinitarian. [< NLat. *ūnitārius,* monotheist < Lat. *ūnitās,* unity. See UNITY.] **—U′ni•tar′i•an** *adj.* **—U′ni•tar′i•an•ism** *n.*

Unitarian Universalism *n.* A religious association of Christian origin that has no official creed and that considers God unipersonal, salvation universal, and reason and conscience the criteria for belief and practice. **—Unitarian Universalist** *adj. & n.*

u•ni•tar•y (yōō′nĭ-tĕr′ē) *adj.* **1.** Of or relating to a unit. **2.** Having the nature of a unit; whole. **3.** Based on or characterized by one or more units. **—u′ni•tar′i•ly** *adv.*

unit character *n.* *Genet.* A character inherited in accordance with Mendel's law of segregation.

unit cost *n.* The cost of a given unit of a product.

u•nite (yōō-nīt′) *v.* **u•nit•ed, u•nit•ing, u•nites.** *—tr.* **1.** To bring together so as to form a whole. **2.** To combine (people) in interest, attitude, or action. **3.** To join (a couple) in marriage. **4.** To cause to adhere. **5.** To have or demonstrate in combination: *She unites common sense with vision.* *—intr.* **1.** To become or seem to become joined, formed, or combined into a unit. **2.** To join and act together in a common purpose or endeavor. See Syns at **join. 3.** To be or become bound together by adhesion. [ME *uniten* < Lat. *ūnīre, ūnīt-* < *ūnus,* one. See **oi-no-***.]

u•nit•ed (yōō-nī′tĭd) *adj.* **1.** Combined into a single entity. **2.** Concerned with or resulting from mutual action. **3.** Being in harmony; agreed. **—u•nit′ed•ly** *adv.* **—u•nit′ed•ness** *n.*

U•nit•ed Ar•ab E•mir•ates (yōō-nī′tĭd ăr′əb ĭ-mîr′ĭts, ĕm′ər-). Formerly **Tru•cial O•man** (trōō′shəl ō-män′) A country of E Arabia, a federation of seven sheikdoms on the Persian Gulf and the Gulf of Oman; formed in 1971. Cap. Abu Dhabi. Pop. 980,000.

United Arab Republic. 1. A former union of Egypt and Syria from 1958 to 1961. Yemen joined the union in 1958, thus creating the **United Arab States. 2.** See **Egypt.**

United Kingdom or **United Kingdom of Great Brit•ain and Northern Ire•land** (brĭt′n; īr′lənd). Commonly called **Great Britain** or **Britain.** A country of W Europe comprising England, Scotland, Wales, and Northern Ireland. Beginning with the kingdom of England, it was created by three acts of union: with Wales (1536), Scotland (1707), and Northern Ireland (1800). Cap. London. Pop. 55,648,994.

United Nations. An international organization founded in 1945 to promote peace and economic development.

United States or **United States of A•mer•i•ca** (ə-mĕr′ĭ-kə). A country of central and NW North America with coastlines on the Atlantic and Pacific oceans. It includes the noncontiguous states of AK and HI and various island territories in the Caribbean Sea and Pacific Ocean. Cap. Washington DC. Pop. 249,632,692.

u•ni•tive (yōō′nĭ-tĭv, yōō-nī′-) *adj.* Serving to unite.

u•nit•ize (yōō′nĭ-tīz′) *tr.v.* **-ized, -iz•ing, -iz•es. 1.** To separate, classify, or package in discrete units. **2.** To make into a single unit. **—u′nit•i•za′tion** (yōō′nĭ-tĭ-zā′shən) *n.*

unit pric•ing (prī′sĭng) *n.* The pricing of goods on the basis of cost per unit of measure.

unit rule *n.* A rule holding that a state's entire vote must go to the candidate preferred by the majority of that state's delegates in a Democratic Party national convention.

u•ni•ty (yōō′nĭ-tē) *n., pl.* **-ties. 1.** The state or quality of being one; singleness. **2.** The state or quality of being in accord; harmony. **3.a.** The combination or arrangement of parts into a whole; unification. **b.** A combination or union thus formed. **4.** Singleness or constancy of purpose or action; continuity. **5.a.** An ordering of all elements in a work of art or literature so that each contributes to a unified aesthetic effect. **b.** The effect thus produced. **6.** One of the three principles of dramatic structure derived by French neoclassicists from Aristotle's *Poetics,* stating that a drama should have but one plot, which should take place in a single day and be confined to a single locale. **7.** *Math.* **a.** The number 1. **b.** See **identity el-**

ement. [ME *unite* < OFr. < Lat. *ūnitās* < *ūnus*, one. See **oi-no-***.]

univ. *abbr.* **1.** Universal. **2.** Or **Univ.** University.

u•ni•va•lent (yo͞o′nĭ-vā′lənt) *adj.* **1.** *Chem.* **a.** Having valence 1. **b.** Having only one valence. **2.** *Genet.* Of or relating to an unpaired chromosome.

u•ni•valve (yo͞o′nĭ-vălv′) *adj.* **1.** Having a shell consisting of a single valve or piece. Used of a mollusk. **2.** Composed of a single valve or piece. Used of a shell. —*n.* A univalve mollusk or shell.

u•ni•ver•sal (yo͞o′nə-vûr′səl) *adj.* **1.** Of, relating to, extending to, or affecting the entire world or all within the world; worldwide. **2.** Including, relating to, or affecting all members of the class or group under consideration: *the universal skepticism of philosophers.* See Syns at **general. 3.** Applicable or common to all purposes, conditions, or situations: *a universal remedy.* **4.** Of or relating to the universe or cosmos; cosmic. **5.** Knowledgeable about or constituting all or many subjects; comprehensively broad. **6.** Adapted or adjustable to many sizes or mechanical uses. **7.** *Logic.* Encompassing all of the members of a class or group. Used of a proposition. —*n.* **1.** *Logic.* **a.** A universal proposition. **b.** A general or abstract concept or term considered absolute or axiomatic. **2.** A general or widely held principle, concept, or notion. **3.** A trait or pattern of behavior characteristic of all the members of a particular culture or of all human beings. —**u′ni•ver′sal•ly** *adv.* —**u′ni•ver′sal•ness** *n.*

universal coupling *n.* See **universal joint.**

universal donor *n.* A person who has group O blood and is therefore able to serve as a donor to a person of any other blood group in the ABO system.

u•ni•ver•sal•ism (yo͞o′nə-vûr′sə-lĭz′əm) *n.* **1. Universalism. a.** *Theol.* The doctrine of universal salvation. **b.** Unitarian Universalism. **2.** The condition of being universal; universality. **3.** A universal scope or range, as of knowledge.

U•ni•ver•sal•ist (yo͞o′nə-vûr′sə-lĭst) *n.* An adherent of Unitarian Universalism. —**U′ni•ver′sal•ist** *adj.*

u•ni•ver•sal•is•tic (yo͞o′nə-vûr′sə-lĭs′tĭk) *adj.* Universal in character or scope: *universalistic values.*

u•ni•ver•sal•i•ty (yo͞o′nə-vər-săl′ĭ-tē) *n.*, *pl.* **-ties. 1.** The quality, fact, or condition of being universal. **2.** Universal inclusiveness in scope or range, esp. great versatility of the mind.

u•ni•ver•sal•ize (yo͞o′nə-vûr′sə-līz′) *tr.v.* **-ized, -iz•ing, -iz•es.** To make universal; generalize. —**u′ni•ver′sal•i•za′tion** (-sə-lĭ-zā′shən) *n.*

universal joint *n.* A joint or coupling that allows parts of a machine not in line with each other limited freedom of movement in any direction while transmitting rotary motion.

U•ni•ver•sal Product Code (yo͞o′nə-vûr′səl) *n.* A series of vertical bars of varying widths printed on consumer product packages and used esp. for computerized inventory control.

universal recipient *n.* A person who has group AB blood and is therefore able to receive blood from any other group in the ABO system.

universal set *n. Math.* A set containing all elements of a problem under consideration.

universal time *n.* The mean solar time for the meridian at Greenwich, England, used as a basis for calculating time throughout most of the world.

u•ni•verse (yo͞o′nə-vûrs′) *n.* **1.** All matter and energy, including Earth, the galaxies, and all the contents of intergalactic space, regarded as a whole. **2.a.** The earth together with all its inhabitants and created things. **b.** The human race. **3.** The realm where something exists or takes place. **4.** *Logic.* See **universe of discourse. 5.** *Statistics.* See **population** 5. [ME < OFr. *univers* < Lat. *ūniversum* < neut. of *ūniversus*, whole : *ūnus*, one; see **oi-no-*** + *versus*, p.part. of *vertere*, to turn; see **wer-[2]***.]

universe of discourse *n. Logic.* A class containing all the entities referred to in a discourse or an argument.

u•ni•ver•si•ty (yo͞o′nə-vûr′sĭ-tē) *n.*, *pl.* **-ties. 1.** An institution for higher learning with teaching and research facilities constituting graduate and professional schools that award master's degrees and doctorates and an undergraduate division that awards bachelor's degrees. **2.** The buildings and grounds of a university. **3.** The body of students and faculty of such an institution. [ME *universite* < OFr. < Med.Lat. *ūniversitās* < Lat., the whole, a corporate body < *ūniversus*, whole. See UNIVERSE.]

U•ni•ver•si•ty City (yo͞o′nə-vûr′sĭ-tē). A city of E MO, a suburb of St. Louis. Pop. 40,087.

University Park. A city of NE TX, a suburb surrounded by Dallas. Pop. 22,259.

u•niv•o•cal (yo͞o-nĭv′ə-kəl) *adj.* Having only one meaning; unambiguous. —*n.* A word or term having only one meaning. [< LLat. *ūnivōcus* : Lat. *ūni-*, uni- + Lat. *vōx*, *vōc-*, voice; see **wekʷ-***.] —**u•niv′o•cal•ly** *adv.*

UNIX (yo͞o′nĭks). A trademark used for a computer disk operating system.

un•joint (ŭn-joint′) *tr.v.* **-joint•ed, -joint•ing, -joints.** To dislocate a joint of; disjoint.

un•just (ŭn-jŭst′) *adj.* **1.** Violating principles of justice or fairness; unfair. **2.** *Archaic.* Faithless; dishonest. —**un•just′ly** *adv.* —**un•just′ness** *n.*

un•jus•ti•fi•a•ble (ŭn-jŭs′tə-fī′ə-bəl, ŭn′jŭs-tə-fī′-) *adj.* Impossible to excuse, pardon, or justify: *took an unjustifiable risk.* —**un•jus′ti•fi′a•bly** *adv.*

un•kempt (ŭn-kĕmpt′) *adj.* **1.a.** Not combed: *unkempt hair.* **b.** Not properly maintained; disorderly or untidy: *an unkempt garden.* See Syns at **sloppy. 2.** Unpolished; rude. [ME *unkemd* : *un-*, not; see UN-[1] + *kembed*, p.part. of *kemben*, to comb (< OE *cemban*; see **gembh-***).]

un•ken•nel (ŭn-kĕn′əl) *tr.v.* **-neled, -nel•ing, -nels** or **-nelled, -nel•ling, -nels. 1.a.** To drive from a lair or den. **b.** To loose from a kennel. **2.** To bring to light; uncover or disclose.

un•kept (ŭn-kĕpt′) *adj.* **1.** Unkempt: *an unkept cemetery plot.* **2.** Not kept or fulfilled: *an unkept promise.*

un•kind (ŭn-kīnd′) *adj.* **-er, -est. 1.** Lacking kindness; inconsiderate or unsympathetic. **2.** Harsh; severe: *unkind winters.* —**un•kind′ness** *n.*

un•kind•ly (ŭn-kīnd′lē) *adj.* **-li•er, -li•est.** Not kindly; unkind. —*adv.* In an unkind manner. —**un•kind′li•ness** *n.*

un•kink (ŭn-kĭngk′) *v.* **-kinked, -kink•ing, -kinks.** —*tr.* To remove kinks from; make straight. —*intr.* To become relaxed.

un•knit (ŭn-nĭt′) *tr. & intr.v.* **-knit** or **-knit•ted, -knit•ting, -knits.** To unravel or undo (something knit or tied) or become unraveled or undone.

un•know•a•ble (ŭn-nō′ə-bəl) *adj.* Impossible to know, esp. being beyond human experience or understanding: *unknowable mysteries.* —**un•know′a•bil′i•ty, un•know′a•ble•ness** *n.* —**un•know′a•ble** *n.* —**un•know′a•bly** *adv.*

un•know•ing (ŭn-nō′ĭng) *adj.* Not knowing; unaware. —**un•know′ing•ly** *adv.*

un•known (ŭn-nōn′) *adj.* **1.** Not known; unfamiliar: *a problem unknown earlier.* **2.a.** Not identified or ascertained: *flowers from an unknown admirer.* **b.** Not established or verified. **3.** Not well known or widely known: *an unknown artist.* —*n.* **1.a.** A person or thing that is unknown. **b.** A person who is not well known, as to the general public: *cast an unknown in the role.* **2.** *Math.* A quantity of unknown numerical value.

Un•known Soldier (ŭn′nōn′) *n.* An unidentified soldier killed in war and chosen to be interred with national honors as a representative of all those who died in a war.

un•la•bored (ŭn-lā′bərd) *adj.* **1.** Done with or requiring little effort; effortless. **2.** Not tilled or cultivated.

un•lace (ŭn-lās′) *tr.v.* **-laced, -lac•ing, -lac•es. 1.a.** To loosen or undo the lacing or laces of. **b.** To loosen or remove the clothing of. **2.** *Obsolete.* To disgrace.

un•lade (ŭn-lād′) *v.* **-lad•ed, -lad•ing, -lades.** —*tr.* **1.** To unload (cargo) from a ship. **2.** To unload (a ship). —*intr.* To discharge a cargo.

un•lash (ŭn-lăsh′) *tr.v.* **-lashed, -lash•ing, -lash•es.** To untie the lashing of; loose.

un•law•ful (ŭn-lô′fəl) *adj.* **1.** Not lawful; illegal. **2.** Contrary to accepted morality or convention; illicit. **3.** Of, relating to, or being a child or children born to parents not married to each other. —**un•law′ful•ly** *adv.* —**un•law′ful•ness** *n.*

un•lay (ŭn-lā′) *v.* **-laid** (-lād′), **-lay•ing, -lays.** —*tr.* To untwist the strands of (a rope). —*intr.* To untwist.

un•lead (ŭn-lĕd′) *tr.v.* **-lead•ed, -lead•ing, -leads. 1.** To remove the lead from. **2.** *Print.* To extricate the leads from between (lines of type).

un•lead•ed (ŭn-lĕd′ĭd) *adj.* **1.** Not containing tetraethyl lead. **2.** *Print.* Not spaced or separated with lead, as lines of type.

un•learn (ŭn-lûrn′) *tr.v.* **-learned** also **-learnt** (-lûrnt′), **-learn•ing, -learns. 1.** To put (something learned) out of the mind; forget. **2.** To undo the effect of; put aside the practice of: *tried to unlearn smoking.*

un•learn•ed (ŭn-lûr′nĭd) *adj.* **1.** Not educated; ignorant or illiterate. **2.** Not skilled or versed in a specified discipline. **3.** (-lûrnd′). Not acquired by training or studying: *an unlearned response.* —**un•learn′ed•ly** *adv.*

un•leash (ŭn-lēsh′) *tr.v.* **-leashed, -leash•ing, -leash•es.** To release or loose from or as if from a leash: *unleashed the dogs.*

un•less (ŭn-lĕs′) *conj.* Except on the condition that; except under the circumstances that. —*prep.* Except for; except. [ME *unlesse*, alteration (influenced by *un-*, not) of *onlesse* : *on*, on; see ON + *lesse*, less; see LESS.]

un•let•tered (ŭn-lĕt′ərd) *adj.* **1.a.** Not adept at reading and writing; deficient in the knowledge that can come from books. **b.** Illiterate. **2.** Having no lettering: *unlettered poster board.*

un•li•censed (ŭn-lī′sənst) *adj.* **1.** Having no official license. **2.** Done without permission; not authorized. **3.** Lacking moral restraint; unrestrained.

un•licked (ŭn-lĭkt′) *adj. Archaic.* **1.** Not licked clean. **2.** Not having proper shape or form.

un•like (ŭn-līk′) *adj.* **1.** Not alike; different: *For twins, they are very unlike.* **2.** Not equal, as in amount. —*prep.* **1.** Different from; not like: *She's unlike the rest of her family.* **2.** Not typical of: *It's unlike him not to call.*

un•like•li•hood (ŭn-līk′lē-ho͝od′) *n.* **1.** The state of being unlikely or improbable; improbability. **2.** Something unlikely.

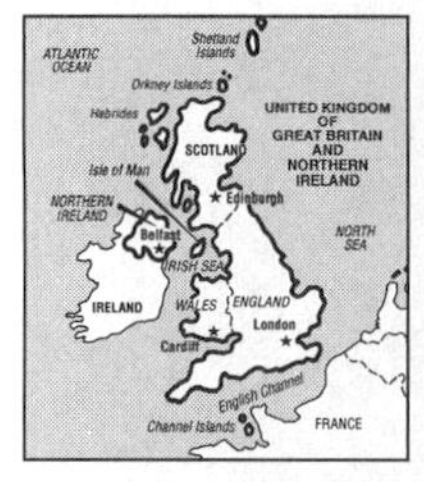

United Kingdom

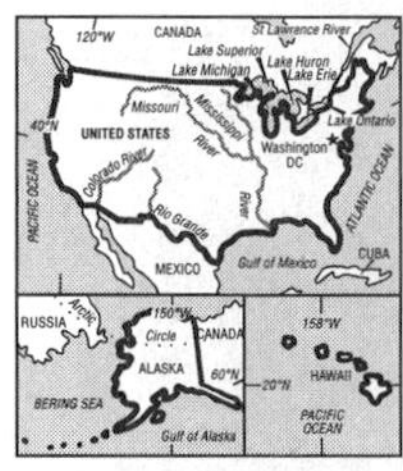

United States

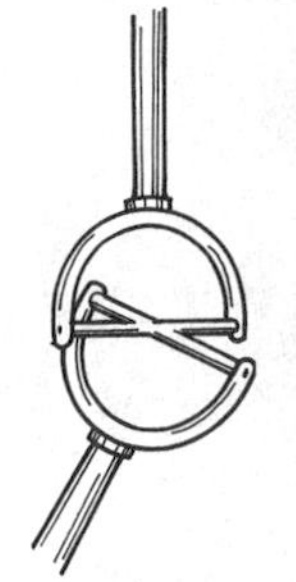

universal joint
Yoke and spider model

ă pat	oi boy
ā pay	ou out
âr care	o͝o took
ä father	o͞o boot
ĕ pet	ŭ cut
ē be	ûr urge
ĭ pit	th thin
ī pie	*th* this
îr pier	hw which
ŏ pot	zh vision
ō toe	ə about, item
ô paw	

Stress marks:
′ (primary);
′ (secondary), as in **dictionary** (dĭk′shə-nĕr′ē)

un•like•ly (ŭn-lĭk′lē) *adj.* **-li•er, -li•est. 1.** Not likely; improbable. **2.** Not promising; likely to fail. **—un•like′li•ness** *n.*

un•like•ness (ŭn-lĭk′nĭs) *n.* The quality or condition of being unlike. See Syns at **difference.**

un•lim•ber (ŭn-lĭm′bər) *v.* **-bered, -ber•ing, -bers.** *—tr.* **1.** To make ready for action. **2.** To detach (a gun or caisson) from its limber. *—intr.* To prepare something for action.

un•lim•it•ed (ŭn-lĭm′ĭ-tĭd) *adj.* **1.** Having no restrictions or controls: *an unlimited travel ticket.* **2.** Having or seeming to have no boundaries; infinite: *an unlimited horizon.* **3.** Without qualification or exception; absolute. **—un•lim′it•ed•ly** *adv.* **—un•lim′it•ed•ness** *n.*

un•list•ed (ŭn-lĭs′tĭd) *adj.* **1.** Not appearing on a list, esp. not listed in a telephone directory. **2.** Relating to or being stock or securities not listed on a stock exchange.

un•lis•ten•a•ble (ŭn-lĭs′ə-nə-bəl) *adj.* Being such that listening with comfort or pleasure is impossible.

un•liv•a•ble (ŭn-lĭv′ə-bəl) *adj.* Unfit for habitation.

un•live (ŭn-lĭv′) *tr.v.* **-lived, -liv•ing, -lives.** To undo the effects of; annul.

un•load (ŭn-lōd′) *v.* **-load•ed, -load•ing, -loads.** *—tr.* **1.a.** To remove the load or cargo from. **b.** To discharge (cargo or a load). **2.a.** To relieve of a burden; unburden: *unloaded the donkeys.* **b.** To give expression to (one's troubles or feelings); pour forth. **3.** To remove the charge from (a firearm). **4.** To dispose of, esp. by selling in great quantity; dump. *—intr.* To discharge a cargo or some other burden. **—un•load′er** *n.*

un•lock (ŭn-lŏk′) *v.* **-locked, -lock•ing, -locks.** *—tr.* **1.a.** To undo (a lock) by turning a key or corresponding part. **b.** To undo the lock of. **2.** To give access to; open. **3.** To set free; release. **4.** To provide a key to; disclose or reveal: *unlock a mystery.* *—intr.* To become unfastened, loosened, or freed from something.

un•loose (ŭn-lo͞os′) *tr.v.* **-loosed, -loos•ing, -loos•es. 1.** To unfasten; untie. **2.** To set free from or as if from restraints. **3.** To relax: *unloosed my grip on the handlebars.*

un•loos•en (ŭn-lo͞o′sən) *tr.v.* **-ened, -en•ing, -ens.** To unloose.

un•love•ly (ŭn-lŭv′lē) *adj.* **-li•er, -li•est. 1.** Not deemed visually attractive. **2.** Not pleasant; disagreeable.

un•luck•y (ŭn-lŭk′ē) *adj.* **-i•er, -i•est. 1.** Subjected to or marked by misfortune. **2.** Resulting or likely to result in misfortune; inauspicious. **3.** Not producing the desired outcome. **—un•luck′i•ly** *adv.* **—un•luck′i•ness** *n.*

un•made (ŭn-mād′) *adj.* Not made: *unmade plans.*

un•make (ŭn-māk′) *tr.v.* **-made** (-mād′), **-mak•ing, -makes. 1.** To deprive of position, rank, or authority; depose. **2.** To cause the ruin of; destroy. **3.** To alter the nature or characteristics of.

un•man (ŭn-măn′) *tr.v.* **-manned, -man•ning, -mans. 1.** To cause to give up manly courage or spirit. **2.** To take away virility from; emasculate.

un•man•ly (ŭn-măn′lē) *adj.* **-li•er, -li•est. 1.a.** Dishonorable; degrading. **b.** Lacking courage; cowardly. **2.** Regarded as unbecoming to a man. **—un•man′li•ness** *n.*

un•manned (ŭn-mănd′) *adj.* **1.** Not crewed: *an unmanned spacecraft.* **2.** *Obsolete.* Not trained. Used of a hawk.

un•man•nered (ŭn-măn′ərd) *adj.* **1.** Lacking good manners; rude. **2.** Natural and unaffected. **—un•man′nered•ly** *adv.*

un•matched (ŭn-măcht′) *adj.* **1.** Not matched: *unmatched socks.* **2.** Without equal or rival; peerless: *unmatched skill.*

un•mean•ing (ŭn-mē′nĭng) *adj.* **1.** Devoid of meaning or sense; meaningless. **2.** Lacking intelligence or liveliness of expression; vacant. **—un•mean′ing•ly** *adv.*

un•meant (ŭn-mĕnt′) *adj.* Not intentional.

un•me•chan•i•cal (ŭn′mĭ-kăn′ĭ-kəl) *adj.* Lacking ability or skill with machinery and tools. **—un′me•chan′i•cal•ly** *adv.*

un•men•tion•a•ble (ŭn-mĕn′shə-nə-bəl) *adj.* Not fit to be mentioned or discussed; unspeakable. *—n.* **1.** One that is not to be mentioned. **2. unmentionables.** Underwear. **—un•men′tion•a•ble•ness** *n.* **—un•men′tion•a•bly** *adv.*

un•mer•ci•ful (ŭn-mûr′sĭ-fəl) *adj.* **1.** Having or exhibiting no mercy; merciless. **2.** Exceeding a normal or reasonable limit; excessive: *unmerciful heat.* **—un•mer′ci•ful•ly** *adv.* **—un•mer′ci•ful•ness** *n.*

un•met (ŭn-mĕt′) *adj.* Not satisfied or fulfilled.

un•mind•ful (ŭn-mīnd′fəl) *adj.* Failing to give due heed, care, or attention; inattentive. **—un•mind′ful•ly** *adv.* **—un•mind′ful•ness** *n.*

un•mit•i•gat•ed (ŭn-mĭt′ĭ-gā′tĭd) *adj.* **1.** Not diminished or moderated in intensity or severity; unrelieved: *unmitigated suffering.* **2.** Without qualification or exception; absolute. **—un•mit′i•gat′ed•ly** *adv.* **—un•mit′i•gat′ed•ness** *n.*

un•mixed (ŭn-mĭkst′) *adj.* Free from other elements; pure: *unmixed pleasure.* **—un•mix′ed•ly** (-mĭk′sĭd-lē) *adv.*

un•mold (ŭn-mōld′) *tr.v.* **-mold•ed, -mold•ing, -molds.** To remove from a mold: *unmold a lemon mousse.*

un•moor (ŭn-mo͝or′) *v.* **-moored, -moor•ing, -moors.** *—tr.* **1.** To release from or as if from moorings. **2.** *Naut.* To release (a ship) from all but one anchor. *—intr.* To cast off moorings.

un•mor•al (ŭn-môr′əl, -mŏr′-) *adj.* **1.** Having no moral quality; amoral. **2.** Unrelated to moral or ethical considerations; nonmoral. **—un′mo•ral′i•ty** (-mə-răl′ĭ-tē, -mô-) *n.* **—un•mor′al•ly** *adv.*

un•mor•tise (ŭn-môr′tĭs) *tr.v.* **-tised, -tis•ing, -tis•es. 1.** To loosen a mortised joint of. **2.** To separate.

un•moved (ŭn-mo͞ovd′) *adj.* Emotionally unaffected.

un•mov•ing (ŭn-mo͞o′vĭng) *adj.* **1.** Not moving; motionless. **2.** Not affecting the emotions.

un•mu•si•cal (ŭn-myo͞o′zĭ-kəl) *adj.* **1.** Lacking in musical qualities, such as melody or harmony. **2.** Sounding harsh to the ear; dissonant. **3.** Not skilled or interested in music. **—un•mu′si•cal•ly** *adv.* **—un•mu′si•cal•ness** *n.*

un•muz•zle (ŭn-mŭz′əl) *tr.v.* **-zled, -zling, -zles. 1.** To remove a muzzle from: *unmuzzle a dog.* **2.** *Informal.* To free from restraint or censorship: *unmuzzle the press.*

un•name•a•ble or **un•nam•a•ble** (ŭn-nā′mə-bəl) *adj.* Not to be named or identified: *unnameable fears.*

un•nat•u•ral (ŭn-năch′ər-əl) *adj.* **1.** In violation of a natural law. **2.** Inconsistent with an individual pattern or custom. **3.** Deviating from a behavioral or social norm: *an unnatural attachment.* **4.** Contrived or constrained; artificial: *smiled in an unnatural manner.* **5.** In violation of natural feelings; inhuman. **—un•nat′u•ral•ly** *adv.* **—un•nat′u•ral•ness** *n.*

un•nerve (ŭn-nûrv′) *tr.v.* **-nerved, -nerv•ing, -nerves. 1.** To deprive of fortitude, strength, or firmness of purpose. **2.** To make nervous or upset. **—un•nerv′ing•ly** *adv.*

un•nil•quad•i•um (yo͞o′nĭl-kwŏd′ē-əm) *n.* Element 104. [Lat. *ūnus*, one; see UNION + *nīl*, nothing; see NIL + QUAD(RI)- + -IUM.]

un•nil•quin•ti•um (yo͞o′nĭl-kwĭn′tē-əm) *n.* Element 105. [Lat. *ūnus*, one; see UNION + *nīl*, nothing; see NIL + *quīntus*, fifth; see QUINTET + -IUM.]

un•num•bered (ŭn-nŭm′bərd) *adj.* **1.** Innumerable; countless: *the unnumbered stars.* **2.** Not marked with an identifying number: *unnumbered pages.*

un•ob•tru•sive (ŭn′əb-tro͞o′sĭv) *adj.* Not undesirably noticeable or blatant; inconspicuous. **—un′ob•tru′sive•ly** *adv.* **—un′ob•tru′sive•ness** *n.*

un•or•gan•ized (ŭn-ôr′gə-nīzd′) *adj.* **1.** Lacking order, system, or unity; disorganized. **2.** Having no organic qualities; inorganic. **3.** Not represented by a labor union.

un•os•ten•ta•tious (ŭn-ŏs′tĕn-tā′shəs, -tən-) *adj.* Not ostentatious; unpretentious. **—un•os′ten•ta′tious•ly** *adv.* **—un•os′ten•ta′tious•ness** *n.*

un•paid (ŭn-pād′) *adj.* **1.** Not yet paid: *unpaid bills.* **2.** Serving without pay; unsalaried: *unpaid research assistants.*

un•par•al•leled (ŭn-păr′ə-lĕld′) *adj.* Without parallel, equal, or match; unequaled.

un•par•lia•men•ta•ry (ŭn′pär-lə-mĕn′tə-rē, -mĕn′trē) *adj.* Not in accord with parliamentary procedure.

un•per•fo•rat•ed (ŭn-pûr′fə-rā′tĭd) *adj.* **1.** Lacking perforations. **2.** Imperforate. Used of a postage stamp.

un•per•son (ŭn′pûr′sən) *n.* A nonperson.

un•pick (ŭn-pĭk′) *tr.v.* **-picked, -pick•ing, -picks.** To undo (sewing) by removing stitches: *unpick a seam.*

un•pin (ŭn-pĭn′) *tr.v.* **-pinned, -pin•ning, -pins. 1.** To remove pins or a pin from. **2.a.** To open or unfasten by or as if by removing pins. **b.** To free.

un•pleas•ant•ry (ŭn-plĕz′ən-trē) *n., pl.* **-ries.** A disagreeable remark, situation, or act.

un•plug (ŭn-plŭg′) *tr.v.* **-plugged, -plug•ging, -plugs. 1.a.** To remove a plug from. **b.** To free from an obstruction. **2.a.** To remove (an electric plug) from an outlet. **b.** To disconnect (an electric appliance) by removing a plug from an outlet.

un•plumbed (ŭn-plŭmd′) *adj.* **1.** Not measured or sounded with a plumb: *unplumbed ocean depths.* **2.** Not fully examined or explored: *unplumbed ideas.*

un•pol•ished (ŭn-pŏl′ĭsht) *adj.* **1.** Not polished, as: **a.** Not smooth and shiny: *unpolished shoes.* **b.** Not elaborated, perfected, or completed: *an unpolished performance.* **c.** Not having attained a high degree of skill: *an unpolished tenor.* **2.** Lacking good manners, culture, or refinement. **3.** Natural and unsophisticated: *The service was friendly and unpolished.*

un•polled (ŭn-pōld′) *adj.* **1.** Not interviewed in a poll. **2.** Not registered at the polls: *unpolled voters.*

un•prac•ticed (ŭn-prăk′tĭst) *adj.* **1.** Not yet tested or tried. **2.** Lacking the benefit of experience; unskilled.

un•prej•u•diced (ŭn-prĕj′ə-dĭst) *adj.* Free from prejudice; impartial. See Syns at **fair[1].**

un•pre•med•i•tat•ed (ŭn′prĭ-mĕd′ĭ-tā′tĭd) *adj.* Not planned or thought out in advance. **—un′pre•med′i•tat′ed•ly** *adv.*

un•pre•pared (ŭn′prĭ-pârd′) *adj.* **1.** Having made no preparations. **2.** Not equipped to meet a contingency. **3.** Impromptu: *unprepared remarks.* **—un′pre•par′ed•ly** (-pâr′ĭd-lē) *adv.* **—un′pre•par′ed•ness** (-pâr′ĭd-nĭs, -pârd′nĭs) *n.*

un•pre•tend•ing (ŭn′prĭ-tĕn′dĭng) *adj.* Unpretentious.

un•pre•ten•tious (ŭn′prĭ-tĕn′shəs) *adj.* Lacking pretension or affectation; modest. **—un′pre•ten′tious•ly** *adv.* **—un′pre•ten′tious•ness** *n.*

un•print•a•ble (ŭn-prĭn′tə-bəl) *adj.* Not proper for publication for legal or social reasons: *unprintable remarks.*

un•pro•duc•tive (ŭn′prə-dŭk′tĭv) *adj.* **1.** Not productive;

idle. **2.** *Econ.* Adding nothing to exchangeable value. **— un′pro•duc′tive•ly** *adv.* **— un′pro•duc′tive•ness** *n.*

un•pro•fes•sion•al (ŭn′prə-fĕsh′ə-nəl) *adj.* **1.a.** Not in a profession. **b.** Not a qualified member of a professional group. **2.** Not conforming to the standards of a profession. **3.** Characteristic of an amateur; inexpert. **— un′pro•fes′sion•al•ism** *n.* **— un′pro•fes′sion•al•ly** *adv.*

un•pro•nounce•a•ble (ŭn′prə-noun′sə-bəl) *adj.* **1.** Difficult or impossible to pronounce correctly: *an unpronounceable last name.* **2.** Not fit to be mentioned.

un•pro•vid•ed (ŭn′prə-vī′dĭd) *adj.* Not supplied, furnished, or equipped. **— un′pro•vid′ed•ly** *adv.*

un•pro•voked (ŭn′prə-vōkt′) *adj.* Not provoked or prompted: *an unprovoked attack.*

un•pub•lish•a•ble (ŭn-pŭb′lĭ-shə-bəl) *adj.* Unfit for publication: *an unpublishable manuscript.*

un•qual•i•fied (ŭn-kwŏl′ə-fīd′) *adj.* **1.** Lacking the proper or required qualifications: *unqualified for the job.* **2.** Not modified by conditions or reservations; absolute: *an unqualified refusal.* **— un•qual′i•fied′ly** *adv.*

un•ques•tion•a•ble (ŭn-kwĕs′chə-nə-bəl) *adj.* Beyond question or doubt; indisputable. See Syns at **authentic. — un•ques′tion•a•bil′i•ty, un′ques′tion•a•ble•ness** *n.* **— un•ques′tion•a•bly** *adv.*

un•ques•tioned (ŭn-kwĕs′chənd) *adj.* **1.** Not subjected to questioning; not interrogated. **2.** Being such as to debar questioning or doubts; indisputable. **3.** Not called into question or examination; not doubted.

un•ques•tion•ing (ŭn-kwĕs′chə-nĭng) *adj.* Not marked by or exhibiting uncertainty or indecision: *unquestioning faith.*

un•qui•et (ŭn-kwī′ĭt) *adj.* **-er, -est. 1.** Emotionally or mentally restless or uneasy. **2.** Characterized by unrest or disorder; turbulent. **— un•qui′et•ly** *adv.* **— un•qui′et•ness** *n.*

un•quote (ŭn-kwōt′) *n.* Used by a speaker to indicate the end of a quotation.

un•raised (ŭn-rāzd′) *adj.* Containing no yeast; not leavened.

un•rav•el (ŭn-răv′əl) *v.* **-eled, -el•ing, -els** or **-elled, -el•ling, -els.** *— tr.* **1.a.** To undo or ravel the knitted fabric of. **b.** To separate (entangled threads). **2.** To separate and clarify the elements of (something mysterious or baffling); solve. See Syns at **solve.** *— intr.* To become unraveled.

un•reach•a•ble (ŭn-rē′chə-bəl) *adj.* Inaccessibly located or situated: *an unreachable canyon; an executive unreachable by telephone.* **— un•reach′a•bil′i•ty** *n.* **— un•reach′a•bly** *adv.*

un•read (ŭn-rĕd′) *adj.* **1.** Not read, studied, or perused: *an unread book.* **2.** Having read little; lacking in knowledge acquired by reading. **3.** Not versed in a specified subject.

un•read•a•ble (ŭn-rē′də-bəl) *adj.* **1.** Not legible or decipherable; illegible: *unreadable handwriting.* **2.** Unsuitable for or not worth reading: *unreadable prose.* **3.** Not interesting; dull. **4.** Incomprehensible; opaque. **— un•read′a•bil′i•ty** *n.*

un•re•al (ŭn-rē′əl, -rēl′) *adj.* **1.** Not real or substantial; illusory. **2.** *Slang.* So remarkable as to elicit disbelief; fantastic. **3.** Surreal.

un•re•al•is•tic (ŭn′rē-ə-lĭs′tĭk) *adj.* Not compatible with reality or fact; unreasonably idealistic: *unrealistic expectations.* **— un′re•al•is′ti•cal•ly** *adv.*

un•re•al•i•ty (ŭn′rē-ăl′ĭ-tē) *n., pl.* **-ties. 1.** The quality or state of being unreal. **2.** Something unreal, insubstantial, or imaginary. **3.** A lack of ability to deal with reality.

un•rea•son (ŭn-rē′zən) *n.* **1.** Absence or lack of reason; irrationality. **2.** Nonsense; absurdity.

un•rea•son•a•ble (ŭn-rē′zə-nə-bəl) *adj.* **1.** Not governed by reason: *an unreasonable attitude.* **2.** Exceeding reasonable limits; immoderate. See Syns at **excessive. — un•rea′son•a•ble•ness** *n.* **— un•rea′son•a•bly** *adv.*

un•rea•soned (ŭn-rē′zənd) *adj.* Not based on or guided by reason; unreasonable: *unreasoned prejudices.*

un•rea•son•ing (ŭn-rē′zə-nĭng) *adj.* Not governed or moderated by reason. **— un•rea′son•ing•ly** *adv.*

un•reck•on•a•ble (ŭn-rĕk′ə-nə-bəl) *adj.* Difficult or impossible to calculate or determine; incalculable.

un•re•con•struct•ed (ŭn′rē-kən-strŭk′tĭd) *adj.* Not reconciled to social, political, or economic change; maintaining outdated attitudes, beliefs, and practices.

un•reel (ŭn-rēl′) *tr. & intr.v.* **-reeled, -reel•ing, -reels.** To unwind (something) from or as if from a reel or become unwound.

un•reeve (ŭn-rēv′) *v.* **-reeved** or **-rove** (-rōv′), **-reeved** or **-rove** or **-ro•ven** (-rō′vən), **-reev•ing, -reeves.** *— tr.* To withdraw (a rope, for example) from an opening, such as a block or thimble. *— intr.* To become unreeved.

un•re•flect•ing (ŭn′rĭ-flĕk′tĭng) *adj.* Marked by or exhibiting a lack of serious thought or consideration: *unreflecting impulses.* **— un′re•flect′ing•ly** *adv.*

un•re•flec•tive (ŭn′rĭ-flĕk′tĭv) *adj.* Not reflective; unthinking. **— un′re•flec′tive•ly** *adv.*

un•re•gen•er•ate (ŭn′rĭ-jĕn′ər-ĭt) *adj.* **1.a.** Not spiritually renewed or reformed; not repentant. **b.** Sinful; dissolute. **2.a.** Not reconciled to change; unreconstructed. **b.** Stubborn; obstinate. **— un′re•gen′er•a•ble** *adj.* **— un′re•gen′er•a•cy** (-ə-sē) *n.* **— un′re•gen′er•ate•ly** *adv.*

un•re•hearsed (ŭn′rĭ-hûrst′) *adj.* Not rehearsed.

un•re•lieved (ŭn′rĭ-lēvd′) *adj.* Utter; complete: *unrelieved boredom.* **— un′re•liev′ed•ly** (-lē′vĭd-lē) *adv.*

un•re•mit•ting (ŭn′rĭ-mĭt′ĭng) *adj.* Never slackening; persistent. **— un′re•mit′ting•ly** *adv.* **— un′re•mit′ting•ness** *n.*

un•re•serve (ŭn′rĭ-zûrv′) *n.* Frankness of manner; candor.

un•re•served (ŭn′rĭ-zûrvd′) *adj.* **1.** Not held back for a particular person: *an unreserved seat.* **2.** Given without reservation; unqualified: *unreserved praise.* **3.** Exhibiting no reserve: *unreserved behavior.* **— un′re•serv′ed•ly** (-zûr′vĭd-lē) *adv.* **— un′re•serv′ed•ness** *n.*

un•rest (ŭn-rĕst′, ŭn′rĕst′) *n.* An uneasy or troubled condition: *social unrest.*

un•rid•dle (ŭn-rĭd′l) *tr.v.* **-dled, -dling, -dles.** To solve or explain (a riddle or mystery). **— un•rid′dler** *n.*

un•rig (ŭn-rĭg′) *tr.v.* **-rigged, -rig•ging, -rigs.** *Naut.* To strip (a vessel) of rigging.

un•right•eous (ŭn-rī′chəs) *adj.* **1.** Not righteous; wicked. **2.** Not right or fair; unjust. **— un•right′eous•ly** *adv.* **— un•right′eous•ness** *n.*

un•rip (ŭn-rĭp′) *tr.v.* **-ripped, -rip•ping, -rips.** To separate or detach by ripping; rip open.

un•ri•valed or **un•ri•valled** (ŭn-rī′vəld) *adj.* Having no rival or equal; incomparable.

un•roll (ŭn-rōl′) *v.* **-rolled, -roll•ing, -rolls.** *— tr.* **1.** To unwind and open (something rolled up). **2.** To unfold and present to view; reveal. *— intr.* To become unrolled.

un•root (ŭn-ro͞ot′, -ro͝ot′) *tr.v.* **-root•ed, -root•ing, -roots.** To uproot.

un•round (ŭn-round′) *tr.v.* **-round•ed, -round•ing, -rounds.** *Ling.* To pronounce (a sound) with the lips in a flattened or neutral position.

un•rove (ŭn-rōv′) *v. Naut.* A p.t. and p.part. of **unreeve.**

un•ro•ven (ŭn-rō′vən) *v. Naut.* A p.part. of **unreeve.**

UNRRA *abbr.* United Nations Relief and Rehabilitation Administration.

un•ruf•fled (ŭn-rŭf′əld) *adj.* **1.** Not agitated; calm. **2.** Regular and smooth, as the surface of water.

un•ru•ly (ŭn-ro͞o′lē) *adj.* **-li•er, -li•est.** Difficult or impossible to discipline, control, or rule. [ME *unreuli* : *un-*, not; see UN-[1] + *reuli*, easy to govern (< *reule*, rule; see RULE).] **— un•ru′li•ness** *n.*

Syns: *unruly, ungovernable, refractory, intractable, recalcitrant, willful, headstrong, wayward.* These adjectives all mean resistant or marked by resistance to control. *Unruly* implies failure to submit to rule or discipline: *unruly behavior in class.* One that is *ungovernable* is not capable of or amenable to being governed or restrained: *an ungovernable temper. Refractory* and *intractable* refer to what is obstinate and difficult to manage or control: *"Fox, as the less proud and intractable of the refractory pair, was preferred"* (Macaulay). One that is *recalcitrant* rebels against authority: *The university suspended the most recalcitrant demonstrators. Willful* and *headstrong* describe one obstinately bent on having his or her own way: *Willful people cannot tolerate such refusals. The headstrong senator ignored her constituency.* One who is *wayward* willfully and often perversely departs from what is desired, advised, expected, or required: *"a lively child, who had been spoilt and indulged, and therefore was sometimes wayward"* (Charlotte Brontë).

UNRWA *abbr.* United Nations Relief and Works Agency.

un•sad•dle (ŭn-săd′l) *v.* **-dled, -dling, -dles.** *— tr.* **1.** To remove a saddle from. **2.** To throw (a rider) from the saddle. Used of a horse. *— intr.* To remove a saddle from a horse.

un•said (ŭn-sĕd′) *adj.* Not said, esp. not uttered out loud.

un•san•i•tar•y (ŭn-săn′ĭ-tĕr′ē) *adj.* Not hygienic.

un•sat•u•rate (ŭn-săch′ə-rĭt) *n.* An unsaturated compound.

un•sat•u•rat•ed (ŭn-săch′ə-rā′tĭd) *adj.* **1.** Relating to or being a fat, usu. of plant origin, composed predominantly of fatty acids having one or more double bonds in the carbon chain. **2.** Capable of dissolving more of a solute at a given temperature.

un•sa•vor•y (ŭn-sā′və-rē) *adj.* **1.** Distasteful or disagreeable. **2.** Not savory: *an unsavory meal.* **3.** Morally offensive. **— un•sa′vor•i•ly** *adv.* **— un•sa′vor•i•ness** *n.*

un•say (ŭn-sā′) *tr.v.* **-said** (-sĕd′), **-say•ing, -says.** To retract (something said).

un•say•a•ble (ŭn-sā′ə-bəl) *adj.* Not readily spoken or expressed: *unsayable fears.* *— n.* **1.** Something not readily said. **2.** Something unfit to be said.

un•schooled (ŭn-sko͞old′) *adj.* **1.** Not educated or instructed; having little or no formal schooling. **2.** Not the result of training; natural: *an artist of unschooled talents.*

un•sci•en•tif•ic (ŭn′sī-ən-tĭf′ĭk) *adj.* **1.** Not adhering to the principles of science. **2.** Not knowledgeable about science or the scientific method. **— un′sci•en•tif′i•cal•ly** *adv.*

un•scram•ble (ŭn-skrăm′bəl) *tr.v.* **-bled, -bling, -bles. 1.** To straighten out or disentangle (a jumble or tangle); resolve. **2.** To restore (a scrambled message) to intelligible form. **— un•scram′bler** *n.*

un•screw (ŭn-skro͞o′) *v.* **-screwed, -screw•ing, -screws.** *— tr.* **1.** To take out the screw or screws from. **2.** To loosen, adjust,

ă pat	oi boy
ā pay	ou out
âr care	o͝o took
ä father	o͞o boot
ĕ pet	ŭ cut
ē be	ûr urge
ĭ pit	th thin
ī pie	*th* this
îr pier	hw which
ŏ pot	zh vision
ō toe	ə about, item
ô paw	

Stress marks:
′ (primary);
′ (secondary), as in
dictionary (dĭk′shə-nĕr′ē)

or remove by rotating. — *intr.* To become or allow to become unscrewed.

un•script•ed (ŭn-skrĭp′tĭd) *adj.* Not adhering to or in accordance with a script written beforehand: *an unscripted talk.*

un•sea•son•a•ble (ŭn-sē′zə-nə-bəl) *adj.* **1.** Not suitable to or appropriate for the season. **2.** Not characteristic of the time of year: *unseasonable weather.* **3.** Poorly timed; inopportune. — **un•sea′son•a•ble•ness** *n.* — **un•sea′son•a•bly** *adv.*

un•sea•soned (ŭn-sē′zənd) *adj.* **1.** Lacking experience and the knowledge gained from it; inexperienced. **2.** Inadequately aged or seasoned; not ripe or mature: *unseasoned wood.* **3.** Having no added seasoning: *unseasoned meat and carrots.*

un•seat (ŭn-sēt′) *tr.v.* **-seat•ed, -seat•ing, -seats. 1.** To remove from a seat, esp. from a saddle. **2.** To dislodge from a location or position, esp. to remove from office.

un•seem•ly (ŭn-sēm′lē) *adj.* **-li•er, -li•est. 1.** Not in accord with accepted standards of good taste; grossly improper. **2.** Not suited to the circumstances; inappropriate. — *adv.* In an improper or inappropriate manner. — **un•seem′li•ness** *n.*

un•seen (ŭn-sēn′) *adj.* **1.** Not directly evident; invisible. **2.** Recognized or grasped without previous study; understood or done as soon as seen.

un•seg•re•gat•ed (ŭn-sĕg′rĭ-gā′tĭd) *adj.* Not segregated, esp. not racially segregated.

un•se•lec•tive (ŭn′sĭ-lĕk′tĭv) *adj.* **1.** Not selective; indiscriminate. **2.** Marked by random selection.

un•self•cons•cious or **un•self-cons•cious** (ŭn′sĕlf-kŏn′shəs) *adj.* Not self-conscious; natural and genuine. — **un′self•cons′cious•ly** *adv.* — **un′self•cons′cious•ness** *n.*

un•sell (ŭn-sĕl′) *tr.v.* **-sold** (-sōld′), **-sell•ing, -sells.** To persuade not to believe in the advisability, worth, or truth of something.

un•set (ŭn-sĕt′) *adj.* **1.** Not yet firm or solidified: *unset cement.* **2.** Not mounted in a setting: *an unset gem.*

un•set•tle (ŭn-sĕt′l) *v.* **-tled, -tling, -tles.** — *tr.* **1.** To displace from a settled condition; disrupt. **2.** To make uneasy; disturb. — *intr.* To become unsettled. — **un•set′tle•ment** *n.* — **un•set′tling•ly** *adv.*

un•set•tled (ŭn-sĕt′ld) *adj.* **1.** Not in a state of order or calmness; disturbed: *these unsettled times.* **2.** Likely to change or vary; variable: *unsettled weather.* **3.a.** Not determined or resolved: *an unsettled issue.* **b.** Uncertain or doubtful: *unsettled with respect to their future plans.* **4.** Not paid or adjusted; outstanding: *an unsettled bill.* **5.** Not populated; uninhabited. **6.** Not fixed or established: *an unsettled way of life.*

un•sex (ŭn-sĕks′) *tr.v.* **-sexed, -sex•ing, -sex•es. 1.** To deprive of sexual capacity or sexual attributes. **2.** To castrate.

un•shak•a•ble (ŭn-shā′kə-bəl) *adj.* Incapable of being shaken: *unshakable faith.* — **un•shak′a•bly** *adv.*

un•shaped (ŭn-shāpt′) *adj.* **1.** Not shaped or formed. **2.** Imperfectly shaped or formed.

un•shap•en (ŭn-shā′pən) *adj.* Unshaped.

un•shell (ŭn-shĕl′) *tr.v.* **-shelled, -shell•ing, -shells.** To remove from a shell.

un•shift (ŭn-shĭft′) *intr.v.* **-shift•ed, -shift•ing, -shifts.** To release the shift key on a typewriter or computer keyboard.

un•ship (ŭn-shĭp′) *v.* **-shipped, -ship•ping, -ships.** — *tr. Naut.* **1.** To unload from a ship; discharge. **2.** To remove (a piece of gear) from its proper place; detach: *unship an oar.* — *intr.* To become or be capable of becoming removed or detached.

un•shod (ŭn-shŏd′) *adj.* Not having or wearing shoes or a shoe: *unshod horses.*

un•sight•ly (ŭn-sīt′lē) *adj.* **-li•er, -li•est.** Unpleasant or offensive to look at; unattractive. — **un′sight′li•ness** *n.*

un•skill•ful (ŭn-skĭl′fəl) *adj.* **1.** Unskilled; inexpert. **2.** *Obsolete.* Ignorant. — **un•skill′ful•ly** *adv.* — **un′skill′ful•ness** *n.*

un•sling (ŭn-slĭng′) *tr.v.* **-slung** (-slŭng′), **-sling•ing, -slings. 1.** To remove from a sling or a slung position: *unsling a bag.* **2.** *Naut.* To remove the slings of (a yard, for example).

un•snag (ŭn-snăg′) *tr.v.* **-snagged, -snag•ging, -snags.** To free of snags.

un•snap (ŭn-snăp′) *tr.v.* **-snapped, -snap•ping, -snaps.** To loosen, unfasten, or free by or as if by undoing snaps.

un•snarl (ŭn-snärl′) *tr.v.* **-snarled, -snarl•ing, -snarls.** To free of snarls; disentangle.

un•so•cia•ble (ŭn-sō′shə-bəl) *adj.* **1.** Not disposed to seek the company of others; reserved. **2.** Not congenial; incompatible. **3.** Not conducive to social exchange. — **un•so′cia•bil′i•ty, un•so′cia•ble•ness** *n.* — **un•so′cia•bly** *adv.*

un•so•cial (ŭn-sō′shəl) *adj.* Having or showing a lack of desire for the company of others. — **un•so′cial•ly** *adv.*

un•sold (ŭn-sōld′) *v.* P.t. of **unsell.**

un•so•phis•ti•cat•ed (ŭn′sə-fĭs′tĭ-kā′tĭd) *adj.* Not sophisticated. See Syns at **naive.** — **un′so•phis′ti•cat′ed•ly** *adv.* — **un′so•phis′ti•cat′ed•ness, un′so•phis′ti•ca′tion** *n.*

un•sought (ŭn-sôt′, ŭn′sôt′) *adj.* Not looked or asked for.

un•spar•ing (ŭn-spâr′ĭng) *adj.* **1.** Unmerciful; severe: *unsparing criticism.* **2.** Not frugal; generous. — **un•spar′ing•ly** *adv.* — **un•spar′ing•ness** *n.*

un•speak (ŭn-spēk′) *tr.v.* **-spoke** (-spōk′), **-spo•ken** (-spō′kən), **-speak•ing, -speaks.** *Obsolete.* To retract (something spoken); unsay.

un•speak•a•ble (ŭn-spē′kə-bəl) *adj.* **1.** Beyond description; inexpressible: *unspeakable joy.* **2.** Inexpressibly bad or objectionable: *unspeakable ills.* **3.** Not to be spoken: *unspeakable ideas.* — **un•speak′a•ble•ness** *n.* — **un•speak′a•bly** *adv.*

un•spe•cial•ized (ŭn-spĕsh′ə-līzd′) *adj.* Having no special function; without specialty or specialization.

un•sphere (ŭn-sfîr′) *tr.v.* **-sphered, -spher•ing, -spheres.** To remove from a sphere or position in the heavens.

un•spo•ken (ŭn-spō′kən) *adj.* Not orally articulated: *unspoken fears of failure.*

un•sports•man•like (ŭn-spôrts′mən-līk′, -spōrts′-) *adj.* Not displaying the qualities or behavior befitting a good sport.

un•spot•ted (ŭn-spŏt′ĭd) *adj.* **1.** Having no spots. **2.** Morally upright. — **un•spot′ted•ness** *n.*

un•sta•ble (ŭn-stā′bəl) *adj.* **-bler, -blest. 1.a.** Tending strongly to change: *unstable weather.* **b.** Not constant; fluctuating: *unstable vital signs.* **2.a.** Fickle. **b.** Lacking control of one's emotions; characterized by unpredictable behavior. **3.** Not firmly placed; unsteady. **4.** *Chem.* **a.** Decomposing readily. **b.** Highly or violently reactive. **5.** *Phys.* **a.** Decaying relatively quickly. Used of subatomic particles. **b.** Radioactive. — **un•sta′ble•ness** *n.* — **un•sta′bly** *adv.*

un•stead•y (ŭn-stĕd′ē) *adj.* **-i•er, -i•est. 1.** Not firm, solid, or securely in place; unstable. **2.** Marked by fluctuation or changeableness; inconstant: *an unsteady market.* **3.** Not even or regular; wavering: *an unsteady voice.* — *tr.v.* **-ied** (-ēd), **-y•ing, -ies** (-ēz). To cause to become unsteady. — **un•stead′i•ly** *adv.* — **un•stead′i•ness** *n.*

un•step (ŭn-stĕp′) *tr.v.* **-stepped, -step•ping, -steps.** *Naut.* To remove (a mast) from a step.

un•stick (ŭn-stĭk′) *tr.v.* **-stuck** (-stŭk′), **-stick•ing, -sticks.** To free from a condition of adhesion: *couldn't unstick the door.*

un•stop (ŭn-stŏp′) *tr.v.* **-stopped, -stop•ping, -stops. 1.** To remove a stopper from. **2.** To remove an obstruction from; open. **3.** *Mus.* To pull out the stops of (a pipe organ).

un•stop•pa•ble (ŭn-stŏp′ə-bəl) *adj.* Difficult or impossible to preclude or stop. — **un•stop′pa•bly** *adv.*

un•stopped (ŭn-stŏpt′) *adj.* **1.** Not stopped: *an era of unstopped progress in medicine.* **2.** *Ling.* Capable of being prolonged, as the consonants *z* and *l.*

un•stressed (ŭn-strĕst′) *adj.* **1.** *Ling.* Not stressed or accented: *an unstressed syllable.* **2.** Not subjected to stress.

un•string (ŭn-strĭng′) *tr.v.* **-strung** (-strŭng′), **-string•ing, -strings. 1.** To remove from a string. **2.** To unfasten or loosen the strings of. **3.** To deprive of composure or emotional stability; unnerve.

un•struc•tured (ŭn-strŭk′chərd) *adj.* **1.** Lacking a definite or formal structure or organization. **2.** Not regulated or regimented: *an unstructured environment.*

un•strung (ŭn-strŭng′) *adj.* **1.** Having a string or strings loosened or removed. **2.** Emotionally upset.

un•stuck (ŭn-stŭk′) *adj.* **1.** Freed from a condition of adhesion. **2.** Thrown into disorder or confusion. **3.** *Slang.* Emotionally upset or unbalanced.

un•stud•ied (ŭn-stŭd′ēd) *adj.* **1.** Not contrived; natural: *unstudied grace.* **2.** Not gained by study or instruction; unschooled.

un•sung (ŭn-sŭng′) *adj.* **1.** Not honored or praised; uncelebrated: *unsung heroines.* **2.** *Mus.* Not sung: *unsung hymns.*

un•sus•cep•ti•ble (ŭn′sə-sĕp′tə-bəl) *adj.* Not susceptible to or admitting of: *unsusceptible to illegal entry.*

un•sus•pect•ed (ŭn′sə-spĕk′tĭd) *adj.* **1.** Not under suspicion. **2.** Not known to exist: *an unsuspected disease.* — **un′sus•pect′ed•ly** *adv.*

un•sus•pect•ing (ŭn′sə-spĕk′tĭng) *adj.* Not suspicious; trusting. — **un′sus•pect′ing•ly** *adv.*

un•swear (ŭn-swâr′) *v.* **-swore** (-swôr′, -swōr′), **-sworn** (-swôrn′, -swōrn′), **-swear•ing, -swears.** — *tr.* To retract (an oath), often by swearing another oath. — *intr.* To recant or retract something sworn.

un•swerv•ing (ŭn-swûr′vĭng) *adj.* **1.** Not veering or turning aside. **2.** Constant; steady: *unswerving devotion.* — **un•swerv′ing•ly** *adv.*

un•sworn (ŭn-swôrn′, -swōrn′) *adj.* Not having been asserted as true under oath: *unsworn statements by witnesses.*

un•tan•gle (ŭn-tăng′gəl) *tr.v.* **-gled, -gling, -gles. 1.** To free from a tangle; disentangle. **2.** To straighten out (something puzzling or complicated); clarify or resolve.

un•tapped (ŭn-tăpt′) *adj.* **1.** Not having been tapped: *an untapped cask of wine.* **2.** Not utilized: *untapped resources.*

un•taught (ŭn-tôt′) *adj.* **1.** Not instructed; ignorant. **2.** Not acquired by instruction; natural.

un•teach (ŭn-tēch′) *tr.v.* **-taught** (-tôt′), **-teach•ing, -teach•es. 1.** To cause to forget or unlearn something. **2.** To teach the opposite or contrary of (something previously taught).

un•ten•a•ble (ŭn-tĕn′ə-bəl) *adj.* **1.** Being such that defense or maintenance is impossible: *an untenable position.* **2.** Being such that occupation or habitation is impossible. — **un•ten′a•bil′i•ty, un•ten′a•ble•ness** *n.* — **un•ten′a•bly** *adv.*

Un•ter•mey•er (ŭn′tər-mī′ər), **Louis.** 1885–1977. Amer. editor whose works include *Modern American Poetry* (1919).

un•thank•ful (ŭn-thăngk′fəl) *adj.* **1.** Not thankful; ungrateful. **2.** Not drawing thanks; unwelcome. — **un•thank′ful•ly** *adv.* — **un•thank′ful•ness** *n.*

un•think (ŭn-thĭngk′) *tr.v.* **-thought** (-thôt′), **-think•ing, -thinks.** To dismiss from the mind; disregard.

un•think•a•ble (ŭn-thĭng′kə-bəl) *adj.* **1.** Impossible to imagine; inconceivable. **2.** Contrary to what is plausible or probable. **3.** Not to be thought of or considered. — **un•think′a•bil′i•ty, un•think′a•ble•ness** *n.* — **un•think′a•bly** *adv.*

un•think•ing (ŭn′thĭng′kĭng) *adj.* **1.** Not taking due thought; thoughtless or heedless. **2.** Exhibiting a lack of thought: *unthinking bravado.* **3.** Incapable of the power of thought. — **un•think′ing•ly** *adv.* — **un•think′ing•ness** *n.*

un•thread (ŭn-thrĕd′) *tr.v.* **-thread•ed, -thread•ing, -threads. 1.** To draw out the thread from. **2.** To find one's way out of (a labyrinth, for example).

un•ti•dy (ŭn-tī′dē) *adj.* **-di•er, -di•est. 1.** Not neat and tidy; sloppy. **2.** Disorderly and unorganized: *untidy financial affairs.* — **un•ti′di•ly** *adv.* — **un•ti′di•ness** *n.*

un•tie (ŭn-tī′) *v.* **-tied, -ty•ing** (-tī′ĭng), **-ties.** — *tr.* **1.** To undo or loosen (a knot or something knotted). **2.** To free from something that binds or restrains. **3.** To straighten out (difficulties, for example); resolve. — *intr.* To become untied.

un•til (ŭn-tĭl′) *prep.* **1.** Up to the time of: *danced until dawn.* **2.** Before (a specified time): *can't leave until Friday.* **3.** *Scots.* Unto; to. — *conj.* **1.** Up to the time that: *walked until it got dark.* **2.** Before: *You cannot leave until you are finished.* **3.** To the point or extent that: *I talked until I was hoarse.* See Usage Note at **till**[2]. [ME : *un-*, up to (< ON *und*; see **ant-***) + *til*, till; see TILL[2].]

un•time•ly (ŭn-tīm′lē) *adj.* **-li•er, -li•est. 1.** Occurring or done at an inappropriate time; inopportune. **2.** Occurring too soon; premature: *an untimely death.* — *adv.* **1.** Inopportunely. **2.** Prematurely. — **un•time′li•ness** *n.*

un•tir•ing (ŭn-tīr′ĭng) *adj.* **1.** Not tiring; tireless. **2.** Not ceasing despite fatigue or frustration; indefatigable: *untiring efforts.* — **un•tir′ing•ly** *adv.*

un•ti•tled (ŭn-tīt′ld) *adj.* **1.** Not named. **2.** Not holding a title, as of nobility. **3.** Having no right or claim.

un•to (ŭn′to͞o) *prep.* **1.** To. **2.** Until: *unto death.* **3.** By: *a place unto itself.* [ME : *un-*, up to; see UNTIL + *to*, to; see TO.]

un•told (ŭn-tōld′) *adj.* **1.** Not told or revealed: *untold secrets.* **2.** Beyond description or enumeration: *untold suffering.*

un•touch•a•ble (ŭn-tŭch′ə-bəl) *adj.* **1.** Not to be touched. **2.** Out of reach; unobtainable. **3.** Being beyond the reach of criticism, impeachment, or attack. **4.** Loathsome or unpleasant to the touch. — *n.* also **Untouchable.** *Hinduism.* **1.** The class, comprising numerous subclasses, that is excluded from and considered ritually unclean and defiling by the four Hindu classes. **2.** A member of this class. — **un•touch′a•bil′i•ty** *n.* — **un•touch′a•bly** *adv.*

un•to•ward (ŭn-tôrd′, -tōrd′) *adj.* **1.** Not favorable; unpropitious. **2.** Troublesome; adverse. **3.** Hard to guide or control; unruly. **4.** Improper; unseemly. **5.** *Archaic.* Awkward. — **un•to•ward′ly** *adv.* — **un•to•ward′ness** *n.*

un•tram•meled (ŭn-trăm′əld) *adj.* Not limited or restricted.

un•trav•eled (ŭn-trăv′əld) *adj.* **1.** Not traveled on. **2.a.** Not having traveled. **b.** Provincial; narrow-minded.

un•tread (ŭn-trĕd′) *tr.v.* **-trod** (-trŏd′), **-trod•den** (-trŏd′n) or **-trod, -tread•ing, -treads.** *Archaic.* To go back over (one's course); retrace.

un•tried (ŭn-trīd′) *adj.* **1.** Not attempted, tested, or proved. **2.** *Law.* Not tried in court.

un•true (ŭn-tro͞o′) *adj.* **-tru•er, -tru•est. 1.** Contrary to fact; false. **2.** Deviating from a standard; not straight, even, level, or exact. **3.** Disloyal; unfaithful. — **un•tru′ly** *adv.*

un•truss (ŭn-trŭs′) *v.* **-trussed, -truss•ing, -truss•es.** — *tr.* **1.** To unfasten; undo. **2.** To undress. — *intr.* To remove one's clothes, esp. one's breeches.

un•truth (ŭn-tro͞oth′) *n.* **1.** Something untrue; a lie. **2.** The condition of being false; lack of truth. **3.** *Archaic.* Unfaithfulness.

un•truth•ful (ŭn-tro͞oth′fəl) *adj.* **1.** Contrary to truth. **2.** Given to falsehood; mendacious. — **un•truth′ful•ly** *adv.* — **un•truth′ful•ness** *n.*

un•tu•tored (ŭn-to͞o′tərd, -tyo͞o′-) *adj.* **1.** Having had no formal education or instruction. **2.** Unsophisticated; unrefined.

un•ty•ing (ŭn-tī′ĭng) *v.* Pr.part. of **untie.**

un•used (ŭn-yo͞ozd′, ŭn-yo͞ost′) *adj.* **1.** Not in use or put to use. **2.** Never having been used. **3.** Not accustomed.

un•u•su•al (ŭn-yo͞o′zho͞o-əl) *adj.* Not usual, common, or ordinary. — **un•u′su•al•ly** *adv.* — **un•u′su•al•ness** *n.*

un•ut•ter•a•ble (ŭn-ŭt′ər-ə-bəl) *adj.* **1.** That cannot or must not be uttered or expressed: *unutterable beauty.* **2.** Being such that pronunciation is impossible. — **un•ut′ter•a•ble•ness** *n.* — **un•ut′ter•a•bly** *adv.*

un•val•ued (ŭn-văl′yo͞od) *adj.* **1.** Not prized or valued; unappreciated. **2.** Not appraised or assayed: *an unvalued gemstone.* **3.** *Obsolete.* Inestimable; invaluable.

un•var•nished (ŭn′vär′nĭsht) *adj.* **1.** Not coated with varnish: *unvarnished floors.* **2.** Stated or otherwise presented without any effort to soften or disguise; plain.

un•veil (ŭn-vāl′) *v.* **-veiled, -veil•ing, -veils.** — *tr.* **1.** To remove a veil or covering from. **2.** To disclose; reveal. — *intr.* **1.** To take off one's veil. **2.** To reveal oneself.

un•voice (ŭn-vois′) *tr.v.* **-voiced, -voic•ing, -voic•es.** *Ling.* To devoice.

un•voiced (ŭn-voist′) *adj.* **1.** Not expressed or uttered: *unvoiced fears.* **2.** *Ling.* Voiceless: *unvoiced consonants.*

un•war•rant•a•ble (ŭn-wôr′ən-tə-bəl, -wŏr′-) *adj.* Not justifiable; inexcusable. — **un′war′rant•a•bly** *adv.*

un•war•rant•ed (ŭn-wôr′ən-tĭd, -wŏr′-) *adj.* Having no justification; groundless.

un•washed (ŭn-wŏsht′, -wôsht′) *adj.* **1.** Not washed; unclean. **2.** Plebeian: *the unwashed masses.*

un•wea•ried (ŭn-wîr′ēd) *adj.* **1.** Not tired. **2.** Never wearying; tireless. — **un•wea′ried•ly** *adv.*

un•well (ŭn-wĕl′) *adj.* **1.** Being in poor health; sick. **2.** Menstruating.

un•wept (ŭn-wĕpt′) *adj.* **1.** Not mourned or wept for: *the unwept dead.* **2.** Not yet shed: *unwept tears.*

un•whole•some (ŭn-hōl′səm) *adj.* **1.** Injurious to physical, mental, or moral health; unhealthy. **2.** Suggestive of disease or degeneracy. **3.** Offensive or loathsome. — **un•whole′some•ly** *adv.* — **un•whole′some•ness** *n.*

un•wield•y (ŭn-wēl′dē) *adj.* **-i•er, -i•est. 1.** Difficult to carry or manage because of bulk or shape. **2.** Clumsy; ungainly. — **un•wield′i•ly** *adv.* — **un•wield′i•ness** *n.*

un•willed (ŭn-wĭld′) *adj.* Involuntary; spontaneous.

un•will•ing (ŭn-wĭl′ĭng) *adj.* **1.** Not willing; hesitant or loath: *unwilling to face facts.* **2.** Done, given, or said reluctantly. — **un•will′ing•ly** *adv.* — **un•will′ing•ness** *n.*

un•wind (ŭn-wīnd′) *v.* **-wound** (-wound′), **-wind•ing, -winds.** — *tr.* **1.** To reverse the winding or twisting of: *unwind a ball of yarn.* **2.** To separate the tangled parts of; disentangle. **3.** To free of nervous tension or pent-up energy. — *intr.* **1.** To become unwound. **2.** To become free of nervous tension; relax.

un•wis•dom (ŭn-wĭz′dəm) *n.* Lack of wisdom; imprudence or recklessness.

un•wise (ŭn-wīz′) *adj.* **-wis•er, -wis•est.** Lacking or exhibiting a lack of wisdom; foolish or imprudent: *an unwise act.* — **un•wise′ly** *adv.*

un•wish (ŭn-wĭsh′) *tr.v.* **-wished, -wish•ing, -wish•es. 1.** To retract a wish for. **2.** *Obsolete.* To wish out of existence.

un•wit•ting (ŭn-wĭt′ĭng) *adj.* **1.** Not knowing; unaware: *an unwitting dupe.* **2.** Not intended; unintentional. [ME : *un-*, not; see UN-[1] + *witting*, pr.part. of *witten*, to know (< OE *witan*; see **weid-***).] — **un•wit′ting•ly** *adv.*

un•wont•ed (ŭn-wôn′tĭd, -wōn′-, -wŭn′-) *adj.* **1.** Not habitual or ordinary; unusual. **2.** Not accustomed; unused. — **un•wont′ed•ly** *adv.* — **un•wont′ed•ness** *n.*

un•world•ly (ŭn-wûrld′lē) *adj.* **-li•er, -li•est. 1.** Not of this world; spiritual. **2.** Concerned with matters of the spirit or soul. **3.** Not wise to the ways of the world; naive. — **un•world′li•ness** *n.*

un•wor•thy (ŭn-wûr′thē) *adj.* **-thi•er, -thi•est. 1.a.** Insufficient in worth; undeserving: *a plan unworthy of consideration.* **b.** Lacking value or merit; worthless. **2.** Not suiting or befitting. **3.** Vile; despicable. — **un•wor′thi•ly** *adv.* — **un•wor′thi•ness** *n.*

un•wrap (ŭn-răp′) *tr. & intr.v.* **-wrapped, -wrap•ping, -wraps.** To remove the wrapping or wrappings from or become unwrapped.

un•writ•ten (ŭn-rĭt′n) *adj.* **1.** Not written or recorded. **2.** Having authority based on custom, tradition, or usage rather than documentation. **3.** Not written on; blank.

un•yield•ing (ŭn-yēl′dĭng) *adj.* **1.** Not bending; inflexible. **2.** Not giving way to pressure or persuasion; obdurate. — **un•yield′ing•ly** *adv.* — **un•yield′ing•ness** *n.*

un•yoke (ŭn-yōk′) *v.* **-yoked, -yok•ing, -yokes.** — *tr.* **1.** To release from or as if from a yoke. **2.** To separate; disjoin. — *intr.* **1.** To remove a yoke. **2.** *Archaic.* To stop working.

un•zip (ŭn-zĭp′) *tr. & intr.v.* **-zipped, -zip•ping, -zips.** To open or unfasten by means of a zipper or become unzipped.

up (ŭp) *adv.* **1.a.** In or to a higher position: *looking up.* **b.** In a direction opposite to the center of the earth or a comparable gravitational center. **2.** In or to an upright position: *sat up in bed.* **3.a.** Above a surface: *coming up for air.* **b.** So as to detach or unearth: *pulling up weeds.* **c.** Above the horizon: *as the sun came up.* **4.** Into view or existence: *draw up a will.* **5.** Into consideration: *take up a new topic.* **6.** In or toward a position conventionally regarded as higher, as on a scale, chart, or map: *up in Canada.* **7.** To or at a higher price: *Stocks are going up.* **8.** So as to advance, increase, or improve: *Our spirits went up.* **9.** With or to a greater intensity, pitch, or volume: *turn the sound up.* **10.** Into a state of excitement or turbulence: *rouse up.* **11.** Completely; entirely: *fastened up the coat.* **12.** Used as an intensifier of the action of a verb: *typed up a list.* **13.** So as to approach; near: *came up and kissed me.* **14.** To a stop: *pulled up to the curb.* **15.** Each; apiece: *The score was tied at 11 up.* **16.** Apart; into pieces: *tore it up.* **17.** *Naut.* To windward. — *adj.* **1.** Being above a former position or level; higher: *My grades are up.* **2.a.** Out of bed: *was up by seven.* **b.** Standing; erect. **c.** Facing upward: *the up side of a tossed coin.* **3.** Raised; lifted: *a switch in the*

ă **pat**	oi **boy**
ā **pay**	ou **out**
âr **care**	o͝o **took**
ä **father**	o͞o **boot**
ĕ **pet**	ŭ **cut**
ē **be**	ûr **urge**
ĭ **pit**	th **thin**
ī **pie**	*th* **this**
îr **pier**	hw **which**
ŏ **pot**	zh **vision**
ō **toe**	ə **about,**
ô **paw**	**item**

Stress marks:
′ (primary);
′ (secondary), as in
dictionary (dĭk′shə-nĕr′ē)

John Updike
Photographed in 1988

up position. **4.** Moving or directed upward: *an up elevator.* **5.a.** Marked by increased excitement or agitation; aroused: *Our spirit was up.* **b.** *Informal.* Cheerful; optimistic; upbeat. **c.** *Slang.* Happily excited; euphoric. **6.** *Informal.* Taking place; going on: *what was up back home.* **7.** Being considered; under study: *a contract up for renewal.* **8.** Running as a candidate. **9.** On trial; charged: *The defendant is up for manslaughter.* **10.** Having been finished; over: *Your time is up.* **11.** *Informal.* **a.** Prepared; ready: *up for the game.* **b.** Well informed; abreast: *not up on sports.* **12.** Functioning or capable of functioning normally; operational: *Their computers are now up.* **13.** *Sports.* Being ahead of one's opponent: *up two strokes in golf.* **14.** *Baseball.* At bat. **15.** As a bet; at stake. **16.** *Naut.* Bound; headed: *a freighter up for Panama.* — *prep.* **1.** From a lower to or toward a higher point on: *up the hill.* **2.** Toward or at a point farther along: *two miles up the road.* **3.** In a direction toward the source of: *up the Mississippi.* **4.** *Naut.* Against: *up the wind.* — *n.* **1.** An upward slope; a rise. **2.** An upward movement or trend. **3.** *Slang.* A feeling of excitement or euphoria. — *v.* **upped, up•ping, ups.** — *tr.* **1.** To increase: *upped their fees.* **2.** To raise to a higher level, esp. to promote to a higher position. — *intr.* **1.** To get up; rise. **2.** *Informal.* To act suddenly or unexpectedly: *"She upped and perjured her immortal soul"* (Margery Allingham). — ***idioms.*** **on the up-and-up** (or **up and up**). *Informal.* Open and honest. **up against.** Confronted with; facing. **up to. 1.** Occupied with, esp. devising or scheming: *up to no good.* **2.** Able to do or deal with. **3.** Dependent on: *The success of this project is up to us.* **4.a.** As long as: *allowed up to two hours for the test.* **b.** As many as: *seed that yields up to 300 bushels per acre.* [ME *up*, upward, and *uppe*, on high, both < OE. See **upo***.]

up. *abbr.* Upper.

up– *pref.* **1.** Up; upward: *upheave.* **2.** Upper: *upland.* [ME < OE *ūp-*, *upp-*. See **upo***.]

up-and-com•ing (ŭp′ən-kŭm′ĭng) *adj.* Showing signs of advancement and ambitious development. — **up′-and-com′er** *n.*

up-and-down (ŭp′ən-doun′) *adj.* **1.** Characterized by or exhibiting an alternating upward and downward movement. **2.** Variable; changeable. **3.** Vertical.

U•pan•i•shad (o͞o-păn′ə-shăd′, o͞o-pä′nĭ-shäd′) *n.* Any of a group of philosophical treatises explicating Vedic theology. [Skt. *upaniṣad* : *upa*, under, near; see **upo*** + *ni-*, down + *sīdati*, *sad-*, he sits; see **sed-***.] — **U•pan′i•shad′ic** *adj.*

u•pas (yo͞o′pəs) *n.* **1.** A deciduous tree *(Antiaris toxicaria)* of tropical Africa and Asia that yields a latex used as an arrow poison. **2.** The poison obtained from this tree or from similar trees. [Malay *(pōhun) upas*, poison (tree), of Javanese orig.]

upland sandpiper
Bartramia longicauda

up•beat (ŭp′bēt′) *n. Mus.* An unaccented beat, esp. the last beat of a measure. — *adj. Informal.* **1.** Optimistic: *an upbeat business forecast.* **2.** Happy; cheerful.

up-bow (ŭp′bō′) *n. Mus.* A stroke on a stringed instrument in which the bow is moved across the strings from tip to heel.

up•braid (ŭp-brād′) *tr.v.* **-braid•ed, -braid•ing, -braids.** To reprove sharply; reproach. [ME *upbreiden* < OE *ūpbrēdan*, to bring forward as a ground for censure : *ūp-*, up- + *bregdan*, to turn, lay hold of.] — **up•braid′er** *n.*

up•bring•ing (ŭp′brĭng′ĭng) *n.* The rearing and training received during childhood.

up•build (ŭp-bĭld′) *tr.v.* **-built** (-bĭlt′), **-build•ing, -builds.** To build up; increase or enlarge. — **up•build′er** *n.*

UPC *abbr.* Universal Product Code.

up•cast (ŭp′kăst′) *adj.* Directed or thrown upward: *upcast volcanic ash.* — *n.* **1.** Something cast upward. **2.** A ventilating shaft, as in a mine.

up•chuck (ŭp′chŭk′) *tr. & intr.v.* **-chucked, -chuck•ing, -chucks.** *Slang.* To vomit or experience vomiting.

up•com•ing (ŭp′kŭm′ĭng) *adj.* Occurring soon; forthcoming.

up•coun•try (ŭp′kŭn′trē) *n.* An inland or upland region of a country. — *adj.* Of, located in, or coming from the upcountry. — *adv.* (*also* ŭp-kŭn′trē). In, to, or toward the upcountry.

up•date (ŭp-dāt′) *tr.v.* **-dat•ed, -dat•ing, -dates.** To bring up to date: *update the files.* — *n.* (ŭp′dāt′). **1.** Information that updates. **2.** The act or an instance of bringing up to date.

Up•dike (ŭp′dīk′), **John Hoyer.** b. 1932. Amer. writer noted for his tragicomic novels, such as *Rabbit, Run* (1960).

up•draft (ŭp′drăft′) *n.* An upward current of air.

up•end (ŭp-ĕnd′) *v.* **-end•ed, -end•ing, -ends.** — *tr.* **1.** To stand, set, or turn on one end: *upend an oblong box.* **2.** To overturn or overthrow. — *intr.* To be upended.

up-front or **up•front** (ŭp′frŭnt′) *adj. Informal.* **1.** Straightforward; frank. **2.** Paid or due in advance: *up-front cash.* — **up′front′** *adv.* — **up′-front′ness** *n.*

up•grade (ŭp′grād′) *v.* **-grad•ed, -grad•ing, -grades.** — *tr.* **1.** To raise to a higher grade or standard. **2.** To improve the quality of (livestock) by selective breeding. — *intr.* To exchange a possession for one of greater value or quality; trade up. — *n.* **1.** The act or an instance of upgrading. **2.** Something that upgrades. **3.** An upward incline. *adv., & adj.* Uphill. — ***idiom.*** **on the upgrade.** Improving or progressing.

up•growth (ŭp′grōth′) *n.* **1.** The process of growing upward. **2.** Upward development.

up•heav•al (ŭp-hē′vəl) *n.* **1.a.** The process of being heaved upward. **b.** An instance of being so heaved. **2.** A sudden violent disruption or upset. **3.** *Geol.* A raising of a part of the earth's crust.

up•heave (ŭp-hēv′) *v.* **-heaved, -heav•ing, -heaves.** — *tr.* To lift forcefully from beneath; heave upward. — *intr.* To be lifted or thrust upward.

up•hill (ŭp′hĭl′) *adj.* **1.** Located on high or higher ground: *an uphill mine entrance.* **2.** Going up a hill or slope. **3.** Marked by difficulty or strong resistance; laborious. — *adv.* (ŭp′hĭl′). **1.** To or toward higher ground; up a slope. **2.** Against adversity; with difficulty. — *n.* An upward slope or incline.

up•hold (ŭp-hōld′) *tr.v.* **-held** (-hĕld′), **-hold•ing, -holds. 1.** To hold aloft; raise: *upheld the banner.* **2.** To prevent from falling or sinking; support. **3.** To maintain or affirm against opposition. See Syns at **support.** — **up•hold′er** *n.*

up•hol•ster (ŭp-hōl′stər, ə-pōl′-) *tr.v.* **-stered, -ster•ing, -sters.** To supply (furniture) with stuffing, springs, cushions, and covering fabric. [Back-formation < UPHOLSTERER.]

up•hol•ster•er (ŭp-hōl′stər-ər, ə-pōl′-) *n.* One that upholsters furniture. [< obsolete *upholster* < ME *upholdester* : *upholden*, to repair (*up*, up; see UP + *holden*, to hold; see HOLD[1]) + *-ster*, -ster.]

up•hol•ster•y (ŭp-hōl′stə-rē, -strē, ə-pōl′-) *n., pl.* **-ies. 1.** Fabric, stuffing, and other materials used in upholstering. **2.** The craft, trade, or business of upholstering.

UPI or **U.P.I.** *abbr.* United Press International.

up•keep (ŭp′kēp′) *n.* **1.** Maintenance in proper operation, condition, and repair. **2.** The cost of such maintenance.

up•land (ŭp′lənd, -lănd′) *n.* **1.** Land or an area of land of high elevation, esp. when level. **2.** Land in the interior of a country. — *adj.* Of, relating to, or located in an upland.

Up•land (ŭp′lənd). A city of S CA E of Los Angeles. Pop. 63,374.

upland cotton *n.* A tropical American plant *(Gossypium hirsutum)* widely cultivated for the woolly lint around its seeds.

upland sandpiper *n.* A large brownish sandpiper *(Bartramia longicauda)* of fields and uplands of eastern North America.

up•lift (ŭp-lĭft′) *tr.v.* **-lift•ed, -lift•ing, -lifts. 1.** To raise; elevate. **2.** To raise to a higher social, intellectual, or moral level or condition. **3.** To raise to spiritual or emotional heights; exalt: *Music uplifts the spirit.* — *adj.* (ŭp′lĭft′). Uplifted. — *n.* (ŭp′lĭft′). **1.** The act, process, or result of raising or lifting up. **2.** An effort or a movement to improve social, moral, or intellectual standards. **3.** *Geol.* An upheaval.

up•link (ŭp′lĭngk′) *n.* A transmission path by which radio or other signals are sent to an aircraft or a communications satellite.

up•load (ŭp′lōd′) *v.* **-load•ed, -load•ing, -loads.** — *tr.* To transfer (data or programs), usu. from a peripheral computer or device to a central computer or bulletin board. — *intr.* To upload data or programs.

up•man•ship (ŭp′mən-shĭp′) *n.* One-upmanship.

up•mar•ket (ŭp′mär′kĭt) *adj.* Appealing to or designed for high-income consumers; upscale.

up•most (ŭp′mōst′) *adj.* Uppermost.

U•po•lu (o͞o-pō′lo͞o). A volcanic island of Western Samoa in the S Pacific; site of Apia, the country's capital.

up•on (ə-pŏn′, ə-pôn′) *prep.* On. See Usage Note at **on.**

up•per (ŭp′ər) *adj.* **1.** Higher in place, position, or rank: *the upper bunk.* **2.a.** Situated on higher ground: *upper regions.* **b.** Also **Upper.** Lying farther inland: *the upper Nile.* **c.** Also **Upper.** Northern: *the upper Midwest.* **3. Upper.** *Geol. & Archaeol.* Of, relating to, or being a later division of the period named. — *n.* **1.** The part of a shoe or boot above the sole. **2.** *Informal.* An upper berth. **3. uppers.** *Informal.* The upper teeth or a set of upper dentures. **4.** *Slang.* **a.** A drug, esp. an amphetamine, used as a stimulant. **b.** An exhilarating or euphoric experience. — ***idiom.*** **on (one's) uppers.** *Informal.* Impoverished; destitute.

Upper Ar•ling•ton (är′lĭng-tən). A city of central OH, a suburb of Columbus. Pop. 34,128.

upper atmosphere *n.* The part of the atmosphere above the troposphere.

Upper A•von (ā′vŏn, ā′vən, ăv′ən). See **Avon.**

upper bound *n. Math.* A number that is greater than or equal to every number in a given set of real numbers.

Upper Cal•i•for•ni•a (kăl′ĭ-fôr′nyə, -fôr′nē-ə). See **Alta California.**

Upper Can•a•da (kăn′ə-də). A historical region and province of British North America roughly coextensive with S Ontario; formed in 1791 and joined with Lower Canada in 1841.

Upper Carboniferous *adj. & n. Geol.* Pennsylvanian.

up•per•case (ŭp′ər-kās′) *Print.* — *adj.* Belonging to, set, or printed in capital letters; capital. — *tr.v.* **-cased, -cas•ing, -cas•es.** To print or set in uppercase letters.

upper class *n.* The highest socioeconomic class in a society. — **up′per-class′** (ŭp′ər-klăs′) *adj.*

up•per•class•man (ŭp′ər-klăs′mən) *n.* A student in the junior or senior class of a secondary school or college.

upper crust *n. Informal.* The highest social class or group. — **up′per-crust′** (ŭp′ər-krŭst′) *adj.*

up·per·cut (ŭp′ər-kŭt′) *n. Sports.* A swinging blow directed upward, as to a boxing opponent's chin.

Upper E·gypt (ē′jĭpt). A region of ancient Egypt in the valley of the Nile R. S of the delta area, which was known as Lower Egypt. The two regions were united c. 3100 B.C.

upper hand *n.* A position of control or advantage.

upper house *n.* The branch of a bicameral legislature that is smaller and less broadly representative of the population.

up·per·most (ŭp′ər-mōst′) *adv. & adj.* In the highest position, place, or rank.

Upper Pa·lat·i·nate (pə-lăt′n-ĭt). See **Palatinate.**

Upper Peninsula. The N part of MI between Lakes Superior and Michigan.

Upper Saint Clair (sānt clâr′). A community of SW PA, a suburb of Pittsburgh. Pop. 19,023.

Upper Tun·gus·ka (to͝ong-go͞o′skə, to͞on-). See **Tunguska.**

Upper Vol·ta (vŏl′tə, vōl′-). See **Burkina Faso.** — **Upper Vol′tan** *adj. & n.*

up·pish (ŭp′ĭsh) *adj. Informal.* Uppity. — **up′pish·ly** *adv.* — **up′pish·ness** *n.*

up·pi·ty (ŭp′ĭ-tē) *adj. Informal.* Taking liberties or assuming airs beyond one's station; presumptuous: *an uppity vassal.* [< UP.] — **up′pi·ty·ness** *n.*

Upp·sa·la (ŭp′sə-lə, -sä′-, o͝op′sä′lä). A city of E Sweden NNW of Stockholm; cap. of a pre-Christian kingdom in the early Middle Ages. Pop. 152,579.

up quark *n.* A quark with a charge of +⅔, a mass about 607 times that of the electron, and an upward spin. See table at **subatomic particle.**

up·raise (ŭp-rāz′) *tr.v.* **-raised, -rais·ing, -rais·es.** To raise or lift up; elevate.

up·rear (ŭp-rîr′) *v.* **-reared, -rear·ing, -rears.** — *tr.* To raise or lift up. — *intr.* To rise up: *The stallion upreared.*

up·right (ŭp′rīt′) *adj.* **1.a.** Being in a vertical position or direction: *an upright post.* **b.** Erect in posture or carriage. **2.** Adhering strictly to moral principles; righteous. — *adv.* Vertically: *walk upright.* — *n.* **1.** A perpendicular position; verticality. **2.** Something, such as a goal post, that stands upright. **3.** *Mus.* An upright piano. — **up′right′ly** *adv.* — **up′right′ness** *n.*

upright piano *n. Mus.* A piano having the strings mounted vertically in a rectangular case with the keyboard at a right angle to the case.

up·rise (ŭp-rīz′) *intr.v.* **-rose** (-rōz′), **-ris·en** (-rĭz′ən), **-ris·ing, -ris·es. 1.** To get up or stand up; rise. **2.** To go, move, or incline upward; ascend. **3.** To rise into view, esp. from below the horizon. **4.** To increase in pitch or volume; swell. — *n.* (ŭp′rīz′). **1.** The act or process of rising. **2.** An upward slope.

up·ris·ing (ŭp′rī′zĭng) *n.* **1.** A sometimes limited popular revolt against a government or its policies. See Syns at **rebellion. 2.** The act or an instance of rising or rising up.

up·riv·er (ŭp′rĭv′ər) *adv. & adj.* Toward or near the source of a river; in the direction opposite to that of the current.

up·roar (ŭp′rôr′, -rōr′) *n.* **1.** A state of noisy excitement and confusion; tumult. See Syns at **noise. 2.** A heated controversy. [Prob. by folk ety. < MLGer. *uprōr* : *up-*, up (< *up*); see **upo*** + *rōr*, motion; see **kerə-*.**]

up·roar·i·ous (ŭp-rôr′ē-əs, -rōr′-) *adj.* **1.** Causing or accompanied by an uproar. **2.** Loud and full; boisterous: *uproarious laughter.* **3.** Causing hearty laughter; hilarious: *uproarious stories.* — **up·roar′i·ous·ly** *adv.* — **up·roar′i·ous·ness** *n.*

up·root (ŭp-ro͞ot′, -ro͝ot′) *tr.v.* **-root·ed, -root·ing, -roots. 1.** To pull up (a plant and its roots) from the ground. **2.** To destroy or remove completely. **3.** To force to leave an accustomed or native location. — **up·root′ed·ness** *n.* — **up·root′er** *n.*

up·scale (ŭp′skāl′) *adj.* Of, intended for, or relating to high-income consumers: *upscale fashions.* — *tr.v.* (*also* ŭp-skāl′) **-scaled, -scal·ing, -scales. 1.** To raise to a higher level; upgrade. **2.** To redesign or market for higher-income consumers.

up·set (ŭp-sĕt′) *v.* **-set, -set·ting, -sets.** — *tr.* **1.** To cause to turn or tip over; capsize. **2.** To disturb the functioning, order, or course of: *upset the meeting by shouting.* **3.** To distress or perturb mentally or emotionally. **4.** To overthrow; overturn: *upset a will.* See Syns at **overthrow. 5.** (ŭp′sĕt′). To defeat unexpectedly (an opponent favored to win). **6.** To make (a heated metal bolt, for example) shorter and thicker by hammering on the end. — *intr.* **1.** To become overturned; capsize. **2.** To become disturbed. — *n.* (ŭp′sĕt′). **1.** The act of upsetting or the condition of being upset. **2.** A disturbance, disorder, or state of agitation. **3.** *Sports & Games.* A game or contest in which the favorite is defeated. **4.a.** A tool used for upsetting; a swage. **b.** An upset part or piece. — *adj.* **1.** Having been overturned; capsized. **2.** Exhibiting signs and symptoms of indigestion: *an upset stomach.* **3.** In a state of emotional or mental distress; distraught. [ME *upsetten*, to set up : *up-*, up- + *setten*, to set; see SET¹.] — **up·set′ter** *n.* — **up·set′ting·ly** *adv.*

upset price *n.* The lowest price at which an item of property may be auctioned or sold at public sale. [P.part. of UPSET, to establish (obsolete).]

up·shift (ŭp′shĭft′) *intr.v.* **-shift·ed, -shift·ing, -shifts.** To shift a motor vehicle into a higher gear. — **up′shift′** *n.*

up·shot (ŭp′shŏt′) *n.* The final result; the outcome. See Syns at **effect.** [Earlier *upshot*, the last shot in an archery contest.]

up·side (ŭp′sīd′) *n.* **1.** The upper side or portion. **2.** An advantageous aspect. **3.** An upward tendency, as in business profitability.

upside down *adv.* **1.** So that the upper or right side is down: *turned upside down.* **2.** In great disorder. [Alteration of ME *up so doun*, up as if down : *up*, up; see UP + *so*, as if; see so¹ + *doun*, down; see DOWN¹.] — **up′side-down′** (ŭp′sīd-doun′) *adj.*

upside-down cake *n.* A single-layer cake baked with sliced fruit at the bottom, then served with the fruit side up.

up·si·lon (ŭp′sə-lŏn′, yo͞op′-) *n.* The 20th letter of the Greek alphabet. [LGk. *u psilon*, simple u (< the fact that *oi* was given the same pronunciation in LGk. as *u*) < *psilon*, neut. of *psilos*, simple (written with one letter as opposed to two).]

up·spring (ŭp-sprĭng′) *intr. v.* **-sprang** (-sprăng′) or **-sprung** (-sprŭng′), **-sprung, -spring·ing, -springs. 1.** To spring up, as from the soil. **2.** To come into being; arise.

up·stage (ŭp′stāj′) *adv.* Toward, at, or on the rear part of a stage. — *adj.* **1.** Of or relating to the rear part of a stage. **2.** *Informal.* Haughty; aloof. — *n.* (ŭp′stāj′). The rear part of a stage, away from the audience. — *tr.v.* (ŭp-stāj′) **-staged, -stag·ing, -stag·es. 1.** To distract attention from (another performer) by moving upstage, thus forcing the other performer to face away from the audience. **2.** To divert attention or praise from. **3.** To treat haughtily. — **up·stag′er** *n.*

up·stairs (ŭp′stârz′) *adv.* **1.** Up the stairs: *raced upstairs.* **2.** To or on a higher floor: *went upstairs.* **3.** To or at a higher level: *was promoted upstairs.* — *adj.* (ŭp′stârz′). Of or located on an upper floor. — *n.* (ŭp′stârz′) (*used with a sing. v.*) The part of a building above the ground floor.

up·stand·ing (ŭp-stăn′dĭng, ŭp′stan′-) *adj.* **1.** Standing erect or upright. **2.** Morally upright. — **up·stand′ing·ness** *n.*

up·start (ŭp′stärt′) *n.* A person of humble origin who attains sudden wealth, power, or importance, esp. one made immodest or presumptuous by the change; a parvenu. — *adj.* **1.** Suddenly raised to a position of consequence. **2.** Self-important; presumptuous. — *intr.v.* (ŭp-stärt′) **-start·ed, -start·ing, -starts.** To spring or start up suddenly.

upright piano

up·state (ŭp′stāt′) *n.* The northerly section of a state in the United States. *adv., & adj.* To, from, or in the northerly section of a state. — **up′stat′er** *n.*

up·stream (ŭp′strēm′) *adv. & adj.* In the direction opposite to the current of a stream.

up·stroke (ŭp′strōk′) *n.* An upward stroke, as of a brush.

up·surge (ŭp-sûrj′) *intr.v.* **-surged, -surg·ing, -surg·es.** To surge up. — *n.* (ŭp′sûrj′). A rapid or abrupt rise.

up·sweep (ŭp′swēp′) *n.* **1.** An upward curve or sweep. **2.** A hairdo that is smoothed upward in the back and piled on top of the head. — *tr.v.* **-swept** (-swĕpt′), **-sweep·ing, -sweeps.** To brush, curve, or sweep upward.

up·swing (ŭp′swĭng′) *n.* **1.** An upward swing or trend. **2.** An increase, as in movement or business activity.

up·take (ŭp′tāk′) *n.* **1.** A passage for drawing up smoke or air. **2.** Understanding; comprehension: *quick on the uptake.*

up-tem·po also **up·tem·po** (ŭp′tĕm′pō) *Mus. n., pl.* **-pos.** A fast or lively tempo, as in jazz. — **up′-tem′po** *adj.*

up·throw (ŭp′thrō′) *n.* **1.** A throwing upward. **2.** *Geol.* An upward displacement of rock on one side of a fault.

up·tick (ŭp′tĭk′) *n.* **1.** An increase, esp. a small or incremental one. **2.** A transaction in a stock market security above the price of the previous transaction. [< the indication of a rise in price of a stock by a plus sign on boards above stock market stations.]

up·tight (ŭp′tīt′) *adj. Slang.* **1.** Tense; nervous. **2.** Financially pressed; destitute. **3.** Outraged; angry. **4.** Rigidly conventional, as in opinions. — **up′tight′ness** *n.*

up·time (ŭp′tīm′) *n.* The time during which a device, such as a computer, is functioning or available for use.

up-to-date (ŭp′tə-dāt′) *adj.* **1.** Informed of or reflecting the latest information or changes. **2.** Being in accord with the latest ideas, improvements, or styles. — **up′-to-date′ness** *n.*

up·town (ŭp′toun′) *n.* The upper part of a town or city. — *adv.* (ŭp′toun′). To, toward, or in the upper part of a town or city. — **up′town′** *adj.* — **up′town′er** *n.*

up·trend (ŭp′trĕnd′) *n.* An upward trend; an upturn.

up·turn (ŭp′tûrn′, ŭp-tûrn′) *v.* **-turned, -turn·ing, -turns.** — *tr.* **1.** To turn up or over: *upturn the soil.* **2.** To upset; overturn. **3.** To direct upward. — *intr.* To turn over or up. — *n.* (ŭp′tûrn′). An upward movement, curve, or trend.

up·ward (ŭp′wərd) *adv.* **1.** In, to, or toward a higher place, level, or position: *flying upward.* **2.** Toward a higher position in a hierarchy or on a socioeconomic scale. **3.** To or toward the source, origin, or interior. **4.** Toward the head or upper parts. **5.** Toward a higher amount, degree, or rank: *Prices soared upward.* **6.** Toward a later time or age: *from adolescence upward.* — *adj.* Directed toward a higher place or position. — ***idiom.* upward (or upwards) of.** More than; in excess of. — **up′ward·ly** *adv.* — **up′wards** *adv.*

ă pat	oi boy
ā pay	ou out
âr care	o͝o took
ä father	o͞o boot
ĕ pet	ŭ cut
ē be	ûr urge
ĭ pit	th thin
ī pie	*th* this
îr pier	hw which
ŏ pot	zh vision
ō toe	ə about,
ô paw	item

Stress marks:
′ (primary);
′ (secondary), as in
dictionary (dĭk′shə-nĕr′ē)

upwardly mobile *adj.* Advancing or likely to advance in economic and social standing.

up•well (ŭp-wĕl′) *intr.v.* **-welled, -well•ing, -wells.** To rise from a lower or inner source; well up.

up•well•ing (ŭp-wĕl′ĭng, ŭp′wĕl′-) *n.* **1.** The act or an instance of rising up from or as if from a lower source: *an upwelling of emotion.* **2.** The rising up of cold, often nutrient-rich waters from the ocean depths to the surface.

up•wind (ŭp′wĭnd′) *adv.* In or toward the direction from which the wind blows. **— up′wind′** *adj.*

Ur (ûr, o͝or). Known in biblical times as **Ur of the Chal•dees** (kăl′dēz′, kăl-dēz′). A city of ancient Sumer in S Mesopotamia on a site in present-day SE Iraq; an important center of Sumerian culture from c. 3000 B.C. until the 6th cent. B.C. and the birthplace of Abraham.

uraeus

ur–¹ *pref.* Var. of **uro–¹.**

ur–² *pref.* Var. of **uro–².**

URA *abbr.* Urban Renewal Administration.

u•ra•cil (yo͝or′ə-sĭl) *n.* A pyrimidine base, $C_4H_4N_2O_2$, that is an essential constituent of RNA. [UR(EA) + AC(ETIC) + *-il*, substance relating to.]

u•rae•mi•a (yo͞o-rē′mē-ə) *n.* Var. of **uremia.**

u•rae•us (yo͞o-rē′əs) *n.* The figure of the sacred serpent depicted on the headdress of ancient Egyptian rulers and deities. [NLat. < LGk. *ouraios*, cobra, perh. alteration (influenced by Gk. *ouraios*, of the tail < *oura*, tail; see URO–²) of Egypt. *y'rt.*]

U•ral-Al•ta•ic (yo͝or′əl-ăl-tā′ĭk) *n.* A hypothetical language group that comprises the Uralic and Altaic language families. **— U′ral-Al•ta′ic** *adj.*

U•ral•ic (yo͞o-răl′ĭk) also **U•ra•li•an** (yo͞o-rā′lē-ən) *n.* A language family that comprises the Finno-Ugric and Samoyedic subfamilies. [After the URAL (MOUNTAINS).] **— U•ral′ic** *adj.*

U•ral Mountains (yo͝or′əl). A range of W Russia forming the traditional boundary between Europe and Asia and extending c. 2,414 km (1,500 mi) from the Arctic Ocean to Kazakhstan.

Ural River. A river of W Russia and W Kazakhstan rising in the S Ural Mts. and flowing c. 2,533 km (1,574 mi) to the Caspian Sea.

Urania
Holding her attributes, a compass and globe

U•ralsk (yo͞o-rälsk′, o͞o-rälsk′). A city of NW Kazakhstan on the Ural R. WNW of Aktyubinsk; founded by Cossacks c. 1622. Pop. 192,000.

U•ra•ni•a (yo͞o-rā′nē-ə, -rān′yə) *n. Gk. Myth.* The muse of astronomy. [Lat. *Ūrania* < Gk. *Ourania* < *ouranos*, heaven.]

u•ran•ic¹ (yo͞o-răn′ĭk, -rā′nĭk) *adj.* Of or relating to the heavens; celestial. [< Gk. *ouranos*, heaven.]

u•ran•ic² (yo͞o-răn′ĭk, -rā′nĭk) *adj.* Of or relating to uranium, esp. with valence higher than in uranous compounds.

u•ra•ni•nite (yo͞o-rā′nə-nīt′) *n.* A complex brownish-black mineral, UO_2, forming the chief ore of uranium and containing radium, lead, thorium, and other elements. [Ger. *Uranin* (< NLat. *ūranium*, uranium; see URANIUM) + –ITE¹.]

u•ra•ni•um (yo͞o-rā′nē-əm) *n. Symbol* **U** An easily oxidized radioactive toxic metallic element having 14 known isotopes, of which U 238 is the most naturally abundant, occurring in several minerals, including uraninite and carnotite, and used in research, nuclear fuels, and nuclear weapons. Atomic number 92; atomic weight 238.03; melting point 1,132°C; boiling point 3,818°C; specific gravity 18.95; valence 2, 3, 4, 5, 6. See table at **element.** [After URANUS.]

Urban II
1592 Italian woodcut

uranium 235 *n.* A uranium isotope with mass number 235 and half-life 7.13 × 10^8 years, fissionable with slow neutrons and capable in a critical mass of sustaining a chain reaction.

uranium 238 *n.* A uranium isotope with mass number 238 and half-life 4.51 × 10^9 years, nonfissionable but irradiated with neutrons to produce fissionable plutonium 239.

urano– or **uran–** *pref.* Uranium: *uranyl.* [< URANIUM.]

u•ra•nous (yo͞o-rā′nəs, yo͝or′ə-nəs) *adj.* Of or relating to uranium, esp. with valence lower than in uranic compounds.

U•ra•nus (yo͝or′ə-nəs, yo͞o-rā′nəs) *n.* **1.** *Gk. Myth.* The earliest supreme god, who was the son and consort of Gaea and the father of the Cyclopes and Titans. **2.** The seventh planet from the sun, revolving about it every 84.07 years at a distance of approx. 2,869 million kilometers (1,790 million miles) and having a mean equatorial diameter of 52,290 kilometers (32,480 miles). [LLat. *Ūranus* < Gk. *ouranos*, heaven, Uranus.]

u•ra•nyl (yo͝or′ə-nĭl, yo͞o-rā′nəl) *n.* The divalent radical $UO_2{}_{++}$.

urn
c. 1450 Flemish

u•rate (yo͝or′āt′) *n.* A salt of uric acid. [UR(IC ACID) + –ATE².]

U•ra•wa (o͞o-rä′wə, -wä). A city of E-central Honshu, Japan, a suburb of Tokyo. Pop. 377,233.

ur•ban (ûr′bən) *adj.* **1.** Of or located in a city. **2.** Characteristic of the city or city life. [Lat. *urbānus* < *urbs, urb-*, city.]

Ur•ban II (ûr′bən). 1042?–99. Pope (1088–99) who promoted the First Crusade.

Urban VI. 1318?–89. Pope (1378–89) who precipitated the Great Schism by alienating the French cardinals, who in turn elected an antipope (1378).

Ur•ban•a (ûr-băn′ə). A city of E-central IL adjoining Champaign. Pop. 36,344.

Ur•ban•dale (ûr′bən-dāl′). A city of S-central IA, a suburb of Des Moines. Pop. 23,500.

urban district *n.* An administrative district of England, Wales, and Northern Ireland, usu. composed of several densely populated communities.

ur•bane (ûr-bān′) *adj.* **-ban•er, -ban•est.** Polite, refined, and often elegant in manner. [Lat. *urbānus*, of a city. See URBAN.] **— ur•bane′ly** *adv.*

urban forest *n.* A dense, widespread growth of trees and other plants covering an area of a city.

ur•ban•ism (ûr′bə-nĭz′əm) *n.* **1.** The culture or way of life of city dwellers. **2.** Urbanization.

ur•ban•ist (ûr′bə-nĭst) *n.* A specialist in the study and planning of cities. **— ur′ban•is′tic** *adj.*

ur•ban•ite (ûr′bə-nīt′) *n.* A city dweller.

ur•ban•i•ty (ûr-băn′ĭ-tē) *n., pl.* **-ties. 1.** Refinement and elegance of manner; polished courtesy. **2. urbanities.** Courtesies; civilities.

ur•ban•ize (ûr′bə-nīz′) *tr.v.* **-ized, -iz•ing, -iz•es.** To make urban in nature or character. **— ur′ban•i•za′tion** (-bə-nĭ-zā′shən) *n.*

ur•ban•ol•o•gist (ûr′bə-nŏl′ə-jĭst) *n.* A specialist in the problems of cities and urban life. **— ur′ban•ol′o•gy** *n.*

urban renewal *n.* Large-scale renovation or reconstruction of housing and public works in poor urban areas.

urban sprawl *n.* The unplanned, uncontrolled spreading of urban development into areas adjoining the edge of a city.

urban wind (wĭnd) *n.* A strong wind generated near or around a group of high-rise buildings, creating areas of intense air turbulence esp. at street level.

ur•ce•o•late (ûr-sē′ə-lĭt, ûr′sē-ə-lāt′) *adj.* Shaped like an urn: *an urceolate corolla.* [NLat. *urceolātus* < Lat. *urceolus*, dim. of *urceus*, jug.]

ur•chin (ûr′chĭn) *n.* **1.** A playful or mischievous youngster; a scamp. **2.** A sea urchin. **3.** A hedgehog. [ME *urchone*, hedgehog < OFr. *erichon* < VLat. **ēriciō, ēriciōn-* < Lat. *ēricius.*]

Ur•du (o͝or′do͞o, ûr′-) *n.* An Indic language, written in an Arabic alphabet, that is the official literary language of Pakistan and is also widely used in India. [Urdu *urdū*, short for *zabān-i urdū* : Pers. *zabān*, language, tongue + Pers. *urdū*, camp, court (< Old Turkic *ordu*, residence, court).] **— Ur′du** *adj.*

–ure *suff.* **1.** Act; process; condition: *erasure.* **2.a.** Function; office: *judicature.* **b.** Body performing a function: *legislature.* [ME < OFr. < Lat. *-ūra.*]

u•re•a (yo͞o-rē′ə) *n.* A water-soluble compound, $CO(NH_2)_2$, that is the major nitrogenous end product of protein metabolism and the chief nitrogenous component of the urine in mammals and other organisms. [NLat. < Fr. *urée* < *urine*, urine < OFr. < Lat. *ūrīna.* See URINE.]

u•re•a-for•mal•de•hyde resin (yo͞o-rē′ə-fôr-măl′də-hīd′) *n.* Any of various thermosetting resins made by combining urea and formaldehyde, widely used to make molded objects.

u•re•ase (yo͝or′ē-ās′, -āz′) *n.* An enzyme that promotes the hydrolysis of urea. [URE(A) + –ASE.]

u•re•din•i•um (yo͝or′ĭ-dĭn′ē-əm) also **u•re•di•um** (yo͞o-rē′dē-əm) *n., pl.* **-din•i•a** (-dĭn′ē-ə) also **-di•a** (-dē-ə). A reddish pustulelike structure that is formed on the tissue of a plant infected by a rust fungus and produces uredospores. [NLat. *ūrēdinium* < Lat. *ūrēdō, ūrēdin-*, blight < *ūrere*, to burn.]

u•re•do•spore (yo͞o-rē′də-spôr′, -spōr′) also **u•re•din•i•o•spore** (yo͝or′ĭ-dĭn′ē-ə-) *n.* A reddish spore that is produced in the uredinium of a rust fungus. [URED(INIUM) + SPORE.]

u•re•ide (yo͝or′ē-īd′) *n.* Any of various derivatives of urea.

u•re•mi•a also **u•rae•mi•a** (yo͞o-rē′mē-ə) *n.* A toxic condition resulting from kidney disease in which waste products normally excreted in the urine are retained in the bloodstream. **— u•re′mic** *adj.*

u•re•o•tel•ic (yo͞o-rē′ə-tĕl′ĭk, yo͝or′ē-ō-) *adj.* Excreting urea as the chief component of nitrogenous waste. [URE(A) + TELIC.] **— u•re′o•tel′ism** (yo͞o-rē′ə-tĕl′ĭz′əm, yo͝or′ē-ŏt′l-ĭz′əm) *n.*

u•re•ter (yo͞o-rē′tər, yo͝or′ĭ-tər) *n.* The long narrow duct that conveys urine from the kidney to the urinary bladder or cloaca. [NLat. *ūrētēr* < Gk. *ourētēr* < *ourein*, to urinate.] **— u•re′ter•al, u′re•ter′ic** (yo͝or′ĭ-tĕr′ĭk) *adj.*

u•re•thane (yo͝or′ĭ-thān′) also **u•re•than** (-thăn′) *n.* **1.** A colorless or white crystalline compound, $CO(NH_2)OC_2H_5$, used in organic synthesis and formerly as a palliative treatment for leukemia. **2.** Any of several esters, other than the ethyl ester, of carbamic acid. [UR(O)–¹ + ETH(YL) + –ANE.]

u•re•thra (yo͞o-rē′thrə) *n., pl.* **-thras** or **-thrae** (-thrē). The canal through which urine is discharged from the bladder in most mammals and through which semen is discharged in the male. [LLat. *ūrēthra* < Gk. *ourēthra* < *ourein*, to urinate.] **— u•re′thral** *adj.*

u•re•thri•tis (yo͝or′ĭ-thrī′tĭs) *n.* Inflammation of the urethra.

u•re•thro•scope (yo͞o-rē′thrə-skōp′) *n.* An instrument for examining the interior of the urethra. **— u′re•thros′co•py** (yo͝or′ə-thrŏs′kə-pē) *n.*

u•ret•ic (yo͞o-rĕt′ĭk) *adj.* Of or relating to urine; urinary. [LLat. *ūrēticus* < Gk. *ourētikos* < *ourein*, to urinate.]

U•rey (yo͝or′ē), **Harold Clayton.** 1893–1981. Amer. chemist who won a 1934 Nobel Prize.

Ur•fa (o͝or-fä′). A city of SE Turkey near the Syrian border; became part of the Ottoman Empire in 1637. Pop. 147,488.

urge (ûrj) *v.* **urged, urg•ing, urg•es.** —*tr.* **1.** To force or drive forward or onward; impel. **2.** To entreat earnestly and often repeatedly; exhort. **3.** To advocate earnestly the doing, consideration, or approval of; press for: *urge passage of the bill.* **4.** To stimulate; excite. **5.** To move or impel to action, effort, or speed; spur. —*intr.* **1.** To exert an impelling force; push vigorously. **2.** To present a forceful argument, claim, or case. —*n.* **1.** The act of urging. **2.a.** An impulse that prompts action or effort: *an urge to laugh.* **b.** An involuntary tendency to perform a given activity; an instinct. [Lat. *urgēre.*]

ur•gen•cy (ûr′jən-sē) *n., pl.* **-cies. 1.** The quality or condition of being urgent; pressing importance: *pleading with urgency.* **2.** A pressing necessity.

ur•gent (ûr′jənt) *adj.* **1.** Compelling immediate action or attention; pressing. **2.** Insistent or importunate: *urgent words.* **3.** Conveying a sense of pressing importance: *an urgent message.* [ME < OFr. < Lat. *urgēns, urgent-,* pr.part. of *urgēre,* to urge.] —**ur′gent•ly** *adv.*

Syns: *urgent, exigent, pressing, imperative.* These adjectives all mean compelling immediate attention. *Urgent* often implies that a matter takes precedence over others: *"My business is too urgent to waste time on apologies"* (John Buchan). *Exigent* and *pressing* suggest an urgency that requires prompt action: *"The danger now became too pressing to admit of longer delay"* (James Fenimore Cooper). *Her family's needs make exigent demands on her time and energy. Imperative* implies a need or demand whose fulfillment cannot be evaded or deferred: *It is imperative that we not procrastinate.*

–urgy *suff.* Technique or process for working with: *zymurgy.* [NLat. *-ūrgia* < Gk. *-ourgia* < *-ourgos,* working < *ergon,* work. See **werg-***.]

–uria *suff.* **1.** The condition of having a specified substance in the urine: *aciduria.* **2.** The condition of having a specified kind of urine: *polyuria.* [NLat. *-ūria* < Gk. *-ouria* < *ouron,* urine.]

U•ri•ah (yo͝o-rī′ə). In the Bible, the husband of Bathsheba who was sent to die in battle so that David could marry his wife.

u•ric (yo͝or′ĭk) *adj.* Of, contained in, or obtained from urine.

uric acid *n.* A semisolid compound, $C_5H_4N_4O_3$, that is the chief nitrogenous component of the urine in birds, terrestrial reptiles, and insects.

u•ri•co•sur•ic (yo͝or′ĭ-kə-so͝or′ĭk) *adj.* Promoting the excretion of uric acid in the urine. [< URIC + URIC.]

u•ri•co•tel•ic (yo͝or′ĭ-kō-tĕl′ĭk) *adj.* Excreting uric acid as the chief component of nitrogenous waste. —**u′ri•co•tel′•ism** (-kō-tĕl′ĭz′əm, -kŏt′l-) *n.*

u•ri•dine (yo͝or′ĭ-dēn′) *n.* A white odorless powder, $C_9H_{12}N_2O_6$, the nucleoside of uracil, important in carbohydrate metabolism and used in biochemical experiments.

U•ri•el (yo͝or′ē-əl) *n.* One of the archangels named in the Apocrypha and in Hebrew tradition.

U•rim and Thum•mim (yo͝or′ĭm ən thŭm′ĭm, o͞or′ĭm; to͞om′ĭm) *pl.n.* Sacred objects carried inside the breastplate of the high priest of ancient Israel and used to divine the will of God. [Partial transl. of Heb. *'ûrîm wĕtummîm.*]

u•ri•nal (yo͝or′ə-nəl) *n.* **1.a.** A fixture, typically upright, used by men for urinating. **b.** A room or other place containing facilities for urinating. **2.** A portable receptacle for urine. [ME, chamber pot < OFr. < LLat. *ūrīnāle,* neut. of *ūrīnālis,* pertaining to urine < Lat. *ūrīna,* urine. See URINE.]

u•ri•nal•y•sis (yo͝or′ə-năl′ĭ-sĭs) *n., pl.* **-ses** (-sēz′). *Medic.* Laboratory analysis of urine, used to aid in the diagnosis of disease or detect the presence of a specific substance, such as an illegal drug. [URIN(O)- + (AN)ALYSIS.]

u•ri•nar•y (yo͝or′ə-nĕr′ē) *adj.* **1.** Of or relating to urine, its production, function, or excretion. **2.** Of or relating to the organs involved in the formation and excretion of urine.

urinary bladder *n.* An elastic muscular sac, situated in the anterior part of the pelvic cavity, in which urine collects.

urinary calculus *n.* A hard mass of mineral salts in the urinary tract.

u•ri•nate (yo͝or′ə-nāt′) *intr.v.* **-nat•ed, -nat•ing, -nates.** To excrete urine. [Med.Lat. *ūrīnāre, ūrīnāt-* < Lat. *ūrīna,* urine. See URINE.] —**u′ri•na′tion** *n.* —**u′ri•na′tive** *adj.* —**u′ri•na′tor** *n.*

u•rine (yo͝or′ĭn) *n.* The waste product secreted by the kidneys that in mammals is a yellow to amber-colored, slightly acid fluid discharged from the body through the urethra. [ME < OFr. < Lat. *ūrīna.* See **wē-r-***.]

u•ri•nif•er•ous (yo͝or′ə-nĭf′ər-əs) *adj.* Conveying urine.

urino– or **urin–** *pref.* Urine: *urinalysis.* [< Lat. *ūrīna,* urine. See URINE.]

u•ri•no•gen•i•tal (yo͝or′ə-nō-jĕn′ĭ-tl) *adj.* Var. of **urogenital.**

u•ri•nom•e•ter (yo͝or′ə-nŏm′ĭ-tər) *n.* A hydrometer for measuring the specific gravity of urine.

u•ri•nous (yo͝or′ə-nəs) also **u•ri•nose** (-nōs) *adj.* Of, resembling, or containing urine.

Ur•mi•a (o͝or′mē-ə), **Lake.** A shallow saline lake of NW Iran between Tabriz and the Turkish border. The city of **Urmia** is the reputed birthplace of Zoroaster. Pop. 263,000.

urn (ûrn) *n.* **1.** A vase of varying size and shape, usu. having a footed base or pedestal. **2.** A closed metal vessel that has a spigot and is used for warming or serving tea or coffee. **3.** *Bot.* The spore-bearing part of a moss capsule. [ME *urne* < Lat. *urna.*]

uro–¹ or **ur–** *pref.* **1.** Urine: *uric.* **2.** Urinary tract: *urology.* **3.** Urea: *urethane.* [NLat. *ūro-* < Gk. *ouro-* < *ouron,* urine.]

uro–² or **ur–** *pref.* Tail: *urochord.* [NLat. *ūro-* < Gk. *ouro-* < *oura.* See **ors-***.]

u•ro•chord (yo͝or′ə-kôrd′) *n. Zool.* A notochord limited to the caudal region. [URO-² + CHORD².]

u•ro•chor•date (yo͝or′ə-kôr′dāt) *n.* A chordate marine animal of the subphylum Urochordata; a tunicate. —*adj.* Having a urochord.

u•ro•chrome (yo͝or′ə-krōm′) *n.* The yellow pigment responsible for the color of urine.

u•ro•dele (yo͝or′ə-dēl′) *n.* Any of various amphibians of the order Caudata, including the salamanders and newts, in which the larval tail persists in adult life. [< NLat. *Ūrodēla,* former order name : URO-² + Gk. *dēlos,* visible; see PSYCHEDELIC.]

u•ro•gen•i•tal (yo͝or′ō-jĕn′ĭ-tl) also **u•ri•no•gen•i•tal** (yo͝or′ə-nō-) *adj.* Of, relating to, or involving both the urinary and genital structures or functions.

u•ro•ki•nase (yo͝or′ō-kī′nās, -nāz) *n.* An enzyme in human urine that catalyzes the conversion of plasminogen to plasmin and is used in medicine to dissolve blood clots.

urol. *abbr.* **1.** Urological. **2.** Urology.

u•ro•lith (yo͝or′ə-lĭth′) *n.* See **urinary calculus.** —**u′ro•lith′•ic** *adj.*

u•ro•lith•i•a•sis (yo͝or′ə-lĭ-thī′ə-sĭs) *n.* A diseased condition resulting from the formation of urinary calculi.

u•rol•o•gy (yo͝o-rŏl′ə-jē) *n.* The branch of medicine that deals with the diagnosis and treatment of diseases of the urinary tract and urogenital system. —**ur′o•log′ic** (yo͝or′ə-lŏj′ĭk), **ur′o•log′i•cal** (-ĭ-kəl) *adj.* —**u•rol′o•gist** *n.*

–uronic *suff.* Connected with urine: *hyaluronic acid.* [< Gk. *ouron,* urine.]

u•ro•pod (yo͝or′ə-pŏd′) *n.* One of the last pair of posterior abdominal appendages of certain crustaceans, such as the lobster or shrimp. [URO-² + -POD.]

u•ro•py•gi•al gland (yo͝or′ə-pī′jē-əl, -pĭj′ē-) *n.* A gland at the base of a bird's tail that secretes an oil used in preening.

u•ro•py•gi•um (yo͝or′ə-pī′jē-əm, -pĭj′ē-) *n.* The posterior part of a bird's body, from which the tail feathers grow. [NLat. *ūropygium* < Gk. *ouropugion* : *ouro-,* tail; see URO-² + *pugē,* rump.] —**u′ro•py′gi•al** (-əl) *adj.*

u•ros•co•py (yo͝o-rŏs′kə-pē) *n., pl.* **-pies.** Examination of urine for diagnostic purposes.

–urous *suff.* Having a specified kind of tail: *anurous.* [< NLat. *-ūrus* < Gk. *-ouros* < *oura,* tail. See **ors-***.]

urp (ûrp) *intr.v.* **urped, urp•ing, urps.** *Mississippi River Delta.* To vomit. [Imit.]

Ur•quhart (ûr′kərt, -kärt′), Sir **Thomas.** 1611–60. Scottish writer and translator of the works of Rabelais.

Ur•sa Major (ûr′sə) *n.* A constellation in the region of the north celestial pole near Draco and Leo, containing the seven stars that form the Big Dipper. [ME < Lat. *Ursa Māior* : *ursa,* bear + *māior,* comp. of *magnus,* great.]

Ursa Minor *n.* A constellation having the shape of a ladle with Polaris at the tip of its handle. [< LLat. *minor Ursa* : *minor,* lesser + *ursa,* bear.]

ur•sine (ûr′sīn′) *adj.* Of or characteristic of bears or a bear. [Lat. *ursīnus* < *ursus,* bear. See **r̥tko-***.]

Ur•spra•che (o͞or′shprä′KHə) *n.* See **protolanguage.** [Ger. : *ur-,* original (< MHGer., out of < OHGer.; see **ud-***) + *Sprache,* language, speech (< MHGer. *sprāche* < OHGer. *sprāhha*).]

Ur•su•line (ûr′sə-lĭn, -līn′, -lēn′, ûr′syə-) *n.* A member of an order of nuns devoted to the education of girls. [After St. *Ursula,* legendary British princess and martyr.] —**Ur′su•line′** *adj.*

ur•ti•cant (ûr′tĭ-kənt) *adj.* Causing itching or stinging. —*n.* A substance that causes itching or stinging.

ur•ti•car•i•a (ûr′tĭ-kâr′ē-ə) *n.* See **hives.** [NLat. *urticāria* < Lat. *urtica,* nettle.] —**ur′ti•car′i•al** *adj.*

ur•ti•cate (ûr′tĭ-kāt′) *v.* **-cat•ed, -cat•ing, -cates.** —*tr.* To sting or whip with or as if with nettles. —*intr.* To produce a stinging or itching sensation. —*adj.* (-kĭt, -kāt′). Characterized by the presence of hives. [Med.Lat. *urticāre, urticāt-* < Lat. *urtica,* nettle.]

ur•ti•ca•tion (ûr′tĭ-kā′shən) *n.* **1.** The formation or development of hives. **2.** The sensation of having been stung by nettles. **3.** A lashing with nettles formerly used to treat a paralyzed part of the body.

U•rua•pan (o͞or-wä′pən, -pän). A city of SW-central Mexico W of Mexico City; founded 1540. Pop. 122,828.

U•ru•bam•ba (o͞o′ro͞o-bäm′bə). A river of Peru rising in the Andes and flowing c. 724 km (450 miles) NNW to join the Apurímac R. and form the Ucayali R.

Urug. *abbr.* Uruguay.

U•ru•guay (yo͝or′ə-gwī′, -gwā′, o͞o′ro͞o-gwī′). A country of SE South America on the Atlantic Ocean; gained independ-

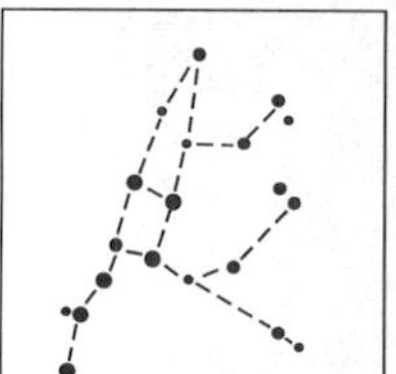

Ursa Major

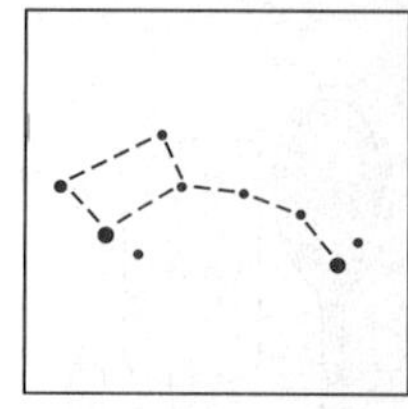

Ursa Minor

Uruguay

ă pat	oi boy
ā pay	ou out
âr care	o͝o took
ä father	o͞o boot
ĕ pet	ŭ cut
ē be	ûr urge
ĭ pit	th thin
ī pie	*th* this
îr pier	hw which
ŏ pot	zh vision
ō toe	ə about, item
ô paw	

Stress marks:
′ (primary);
′ (secondary), as in
dictionary (dĭk′shə-nĕr′ē)

ence from Spain in 1814. Cap. Montevideo. Pop. 2,788,429. **— U′ru•guay′an** *adj. & n.*

Uruguay River. A river of SE South America rising in S Brazil and flowing c. 1,609 km (1,000 mi) to the Río de la Plata.

Ü•rüm•qi also **U•rum•chi** (o͝o-ro͞om′chē, ü′rüm′chē′). A city of NW China in the Tien Shan. Pop. 947,000.

u•rus (yo͝or′əs) *n., pl.* **u•rus•es.** An extinct wild ox *(Bos primigenius)* of Europe, northern Africa, and western Asia, believed to be the ancestor of domestic cattle. [Lat. *ūrus*, of Gmc. orig.]

u•ru•shi•ol (o͞o-ro͞o′shē-ôl′, -ōl′, -ŏl′) *n.* A toxic substance present in plants of the genus *Rhus,* including poison ivy and the lacquer tree. [J. *urushi*, lacquer + -OL[1].]

us (ŭs) *pron.* The objective case of **we. 1.** Used as the direct object of a verb: *She saw us.* **2.** Used as the indirect object of a verb: *offered us free tickets.* **3.** Used as the object of a preposition: *This letter is addressed to us.* **4.** *Informal.* Used as a predicate nominative: *It's us.* See Usage Note at **we.** [ME < OE *ūs*. See **nes-[2]*.**]

u.s. *abbr. Lat.* **1.** Ubi supra (where mentioned above). **2.** Ut supra (as above).

U.S. or **US** *abbr.* **1.** Uncle Sam. **2.** Uniform System (of lens aperture). **3.** United States. **4.** United States highway.

USA *abbr.* **1.** Also **U.S.A.** United States Army. **2.** Or **U.S.A.** United States of America.

us•a•ble also **use•a•ble** (yo͞o′zə-bəl) *adj.* **1.** That can be used: *usable byproducts.* **2.** Fit for use; convenient to use: *usable parts.* **— us′a•bil′i•ty, us′a•ble•ness** *n.* **— us′a•bly** *adv.*

USAF also **U.S.A.F.** *abbr.* United States Air Force.

us•age (yo͞o′sĭj, -zĭj) *n.* **1.a.** The act, manner, or amount of using; use: *water usage.* **b.** The act or manner of treating; treatment. **2.** A usual, habitual, or accepted practice. See Syns at **habit. 3.** The way in which words or phrases are actually used, spoken, or written in a speech community. **4.** A particular expression in speech or writing: *a nonce usage.* [ME < OFr. < *us* < Lat. *ūsus* < p.part. of *ūtī*, to use.]

us•ance (yo͞o′zəns) *n.* **1.** The length of time, established by custom and varying between countries, allowed for payment of a foreign bill of exchange. **2.** Use. **3.** Usage; custom. **4.** Interest paid on borrowed money. [ME, usage < OFr., prob. < VLat. **ūsantia* < **ūsāns*, **ūsant-*, pr.part. of **ūsāre*, freq. of Lat. *ūtī*.]

USCG also **U.S.C.G.** *abbr.* United States Coast Guard.

USDA *abbr.* United States Department of Agriculture.

use (yo͞oz) *v.* **used, us•ing, us•es.** *— tr.* **1.** To put into service or apply for a purpose; employ. **2.** To avail oneself of; practice: *use caution.* **3.** To conduct oneself toward; treat or handle: *used his colleagues well.* **4.** To seek or achieve an end by means of; exploit: *felt he was being used.* **5.** To take or consume; partake of: *She rarely used alcohol.* *— intr.* Used in the past tense followed by *to* in order to indicate a former state, habitual practice, or custom: *Mail service used to be faster.* *— n.* (yo͞os). **1.a.** The act of using; the application or employment of something for a purpose: *with the use of a calculator.* **b.** The condition or fact of being used: *a chair in regular use.* **2.** The manner of using; usage: *learned the use of tools.* **3.a.** The permission, privilege, or benefit of using something. **b.** The power or ability to use something: *lost the use of one arm.* **4.** The need or occasion to use or employ: *no use for these old clothes.* **5.** The quality of being suitable or adaptable to an end; usefulness: *tried to be of use.* **6.** A purpose for which something is used: *a tool with several uses.* **7.** Gain or advantage; good: *There's no use in discussing it.* **8.** Accustomed or usual procedure or practice. **9.** *Law.* **a.** Enjoyment of property, as by occupying or exercising it. **b.** The benefit or profit of lands and tenements of which the legal title and possession are vested in another. **c.** The arrangement establishing the equitable right to such benefits and profits. **10.** A liturgical form practiced in a particular church, ecclesiastical district, or community. **11.** *Obsolete.* Usual occurrence or experience. **— *phrasal verb.* use up.** To consume completely: *used up all our money.* [ME *usen* < OFr. *user* < VLat. **ūsāre*, freq. of Lat. *ūtī*.]

used (yo͞ozd) *adj.* **1.** Not new; secondhand: *a used car.* **2.** (*also* yo͞ost). Accustomed; habituated: *used to the weather.*

use•ful (yo͞os′fəl) *adj.* **1.** Having a beneficial use; serviceable: *a useful gadget.* **2.** Being of practical use: *a useful job.* **— use′ful•ly** *adv.* **— use′ful•ness** *n.*

use•less (yo͞os′lĭs) *adj.* **1.** Having or being of no beneficial use; futile or ineffective. **2.** Incapable of functioning or assisting; ineffectual. See Syns at **futile. — use′less•ly** *adv.* **— use′less•ness** *n.*

us•er (yo͞o′zər) *n.* **1.** One that uses: *a user of public transportation.* **2.** *Law.* The exercise or enjoyment of a right or property. **3.** One who uses addictive drugs.

us•er-friend•ly (yo͞o′zər-frĕnd′lē) *adj.* **-li•er, -li•est.** Easy to use or learn to use. **— us′er-friend′li•ness** *n.*

ush•er (ŭsh′ər) *n.* **1.** One employed to escort people to their seats, as in a theater, church, or stadium. **2.** A man who attends a bridal party at a wedding. **3.** One who serves as official doorkeeper, as in a courtroom. **4.** An official whose duty is to make introductions between unacquainted persons or to precede persons of rank in a procession. **5.** *Archaic.* An assistant teacher in a school. *— v.* **-ered, -er•ing, -ers.** *— tr.* **1.** To serve as an usher to; escort **2.** To lead or conduct. **3.** To precede and introduce; inaugurate: *a celebration to usher in the new year.* *— intr.* To serve as an usher. [ME, doorkeeper < AN *usser* < VLat. **ūstiārius* < Lat. *ōstiārius* < *ōstium*, door. See **ōs-*.**]

ush•er•ette (ŭsh′ə-rĕt′) *n.* A girl or woman employed to escort people to their seats, as in a theater or stadium. See Usage Note at **-ette.**

USIA *abbr.* United States Information Agency.

U.S.M. *abbr.* United States Mail.

USMC also **U.S.M.C.** *abbr.* United States Marine Corps.

USN also **U.S.N.** *abbr.* United States Navy.

USNA also **U.S.N.A.** *abbr.* United States Naval Academy.

us•ne•a (ŭs′nē-ə, ŭz′-) *n.* Any of various common gray lichens of the genus *Usnea.* [< Ar. *'ušnah*, moss.]

USO or **U.S.O.** *abbr.* United Service Organizations.

U.S.P. *abbr.* United States Pharmacopoeia.

Us•pal•la•ta Pass (o͞o′spä-yä′tə, -tä). A pass, c. 3,813 m (12,500 ft), through the Andes between Mendoza, Argentina, and Santiago, Chile; site of a monumental sculpture of Christ.

USPO also **U.S.P.O.** *abbr.* United States Post Office.

USPS also **U.S.P.S.** *abbr.* United States Postal Service.

us•que•baugh (ŭs′kwĭ-bô′, -bä′) *n. Irish & Scots.* Whiskey. [Sc.Gael. *uisge beatha* and Ir.Gael. *uisce beatha*, water of life, whiskey (transl. of Med.Lat. *aqua vītae*) : OIr. *uisce*, water; see **wed-[1]*** + OIr. *bethad*, genitive of *bethu*, life; see **g[w]ei-*.**]

U.S.S. *abbr.* **1.** United States Senate. **2.** *Naut.* United States ship.

Ussh•er (ŭsh′ər), **James.** 1581–1656. Irish prelate and scholar who devised a scheme of biblical chronology.

U.S.S.R. or **USSR** *abbr.* Union of Soviet Socialist Republics.

U•sti•nov (o͞o-stĭn′ôf). See **Izhevsk.**

Ust-Ka•me•no•gorsk (o͞ost′kə-mĕn′ə-gôrsk′, -myĭ-nə-). A city of NE Kazakhstan SE of Semipalatinsk. Pop. 307,000.

usu. *abbr.* Usually.

u•su•al (yo͞o′zho͞o-əl) *adj.* **1.** Commonly encountered, experienced, or observed: *the usual summer heat.* **2.** Regularly or customarily used: *the usual expressions of thanks.* **3.** In conformity with regular practice or procedure: *Come at the usual time.* **— *idiom.* as usual.** As commonly or habitually happens: *As usual, I slept late.* [ME < OFr. *usuel* < LLat. *ūsuālis* < Lat. *ūsus*, use < p.part. of *ūtī*, to use.] **— u′su•al•ly** *adv.* **— u′su•al•ness** *n.*

Syns: *usual, habitual, customary, accustomed.* These adjectives apply to what is expected or familiar because it occurs frequently or recurs regularly. *Usual* describes what accords with normal, common, or ordinary practice or procedure: *"The parson said the usual things about the sea — its blueness . . . its beauty"* (George du Maurier). *Habitual* implies repetition and force of habit: *a habitual liar. Customary* and *accustomed* refer to conformity with the prevailing customs or conventions of a group or with an individual's own established practice: *"It is the customary fate of new truths to begin as heresies and to end as superstitions"* (Thomas H. Huxley). *She resolved the difficulty with her accustomed resourcefulness.*

u•su•fruct (yo͞o′zə-frŭkt′, -sə-) *n. Law.* The right to use and enjoy the profits and advantages of something belonging to another as long as the property is not damaged or altered in any way. [LLat. *ūsūfrūctus*, var. of Lat. *ūsusfrūctus* : *ūsus*, use; see USUAL + *frūctus*, enjoyment; see FRUIT.]

u•su•fruc•tu•ar•y (yo͞o′zə-frŭk′cho͞o-ĕr′ē, -sə-) *Law.* *— n., pl.* **-ies.** One that holds property by usufruct. *— adj.* Of or relating to the nature of a usufruct.

U•su•ma•cin•ta (o͞o′sə-mə-sĭn′tə, -so͞o-mä-sēn′tä). A river, c. 965 km (600 mi), of SE Mexico.

u•su•rer (yo͞o′zhər-ər) *n.* One who lends money at interest, esp. at an exorbitant or unlawfully high rate. [ME < AN < LLat. *ūsūrārius*, moneylender < Lat., interest-bearing < *ūsūra*, usury. See USURY.]

u•su•ri•ous (yo͞o-zho͝or′ē-əs) *adj.* **1.** Practicing usury. **2.** Of or constituting usury: *usurious interest rates.* **— u•su′ri•ous•ly** *adv.* **— u•su′ri•ous•ness** *n.*

u•surp (yo͞o-sûrp′, -zûrp′) *v.* **-surped, -surp•ing, -surps.** *— tr.* **1.** To seize and hold (the power or rights of another, for example) by force and without legal authority. **2.** To take over or occupy without right: *usurp land.* *— intr.* To seize another's place, authority, or possession wrongfully. [ME *usurpen* < OFr. *usurper* < Lat. *ūsūrpāre*, to take into use, usurp. See **reup-*.**] **— u•surp′er** *n.* **— u•surp′ing•ly** *adv.*

u•sur•pa•tion (yo͞o′sər-pā′shən, -zər-) *n.* **1.** The act of usurping, esp. the wrongful seizure of royal sovereignty. **2.** A wrongful seizure or exercise of authority or privilege belonging to another; an encroachment.

u•su•ry (yo͞o′zhə-rē) *n., pl.* **-ries. 1.** The practice of lending money and charging interest, esp. at an exorbitant or illegally high rate. **2.** An excessive or illegally high rate of interest charged. **3.** *Archaic.* Interest charged or paid on a loan. [ME < Med.Lat. *ūsūria*, alteration of Lat. *ūsūra* < *ūsus*, use. See USUAL.]

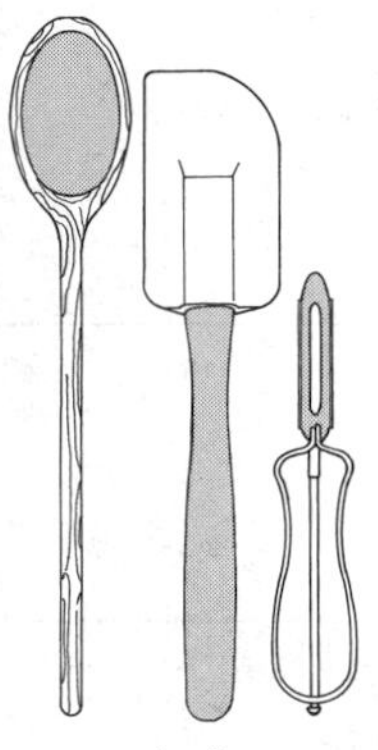

utensil
Left to right: Wooden spoon, spatula, and vegetable peeler

ut (ŭt, o͞ot) *n. Mus.* A syllable representing the tone C, otherwise represented by *do,* in the French system of solmization. [ME < Med.Lat. See GAMUT.]

UT *abbr.* **1.** Universal time. **2.** Or **Ut.** Utah.

U•tah (yo͞o′tô′, -tä′). A state of the W U.S.; admitted as the 45th state in 1896. The area was first explored by the Spanish in 1540 and settled in 1847 by Mormons led by Brigham Young. Cap. Salt Lake City. Pop. 1,727,784. **—U′tah•an** *adj. & n.*

UTC *abbr.* Universal time coordinated.

ut dict. *abbr. Lat.* Ut dictum (as directed).

Ute (yo͞ot) *n., pl.* **Ute** or **Utes. 1.** A member of a Native American people formerly inhabiting a large area of Colorado, Utah, and northern New Mexico, with present-day populations in northeast Utah and along the Colorado–New Mexico border. **2.** The Uto-Aztecan language of the Ute. [< *Utah,* Ute Indian < Am.Sp. *Yuta;* akin to Southern Paiute *yuuttaci.*]

u•ten•sil (yo͞o-tĕn′səl) *n.* An instrument, an implement, or a container used domestically, esp. in a kitchen. See Syns at **tool.** [ME < OFr. *utensile* < Lat. *ūtēnsilia,* utensils < neut. pl. of *ūtēnsilis,* fit for use < *ūtī,* to use.]

u•ter•ine (yo͞o′tər-ĭn, -tə-rīn′) *adj.* **1.** Of, relating to, or in the region of the uterus. **2.** Having the same mother but different fathers. [ME < LLat. *uterīnus* < Lat. *uterus,* uterus.]

u•ter•us (yo͞o′tər-əs) *n., pl.* **u•ter•i** (yo͞o′tə-rī′) or **u•ter•us•es. 1.** A hollow muscular organ located in the pelvic cavity of female mammals in which the fertilized egg implants and develops. **2.** A corresponding part in other animals. [ME < Lat.]

U Thant (o͞o thänt′, thănt′). See U **Thant.**

U•ther Pen•dra•gon (yo͞o′thər pĕn-drăg′ən, o͞o′-) *n.* In Arthurian legend, a king of Britain and the father of Arthur.

U•ti•ca (yo͞o′tĭ-kə). **1.** An ancient city of N Africa on the Mediterranean Sea NW of Carthage; destroyed by the Arabs c. A.D. 700. **2.** A city of central NY ENE of Syracuse; settled in 1773 on the site of a fort built in 1758. Pop. 68,637.

util. *abbr.* Utility.

u•tile (yo͞ot′l, yo͞o′tīl′) *adj.* Useful. [ME < OFr. < Lat. *ūtilis.* See UTILITY.]

u•til•i•tar•i•an (yo͞o-tĭl′ĭ-târ′ē-ən) *adj.* **1.** Of, relating to, or in the interests of utility. **2.** Exhibiting or stressing utility over other values; practical. **3.** Of, characterized by, or advocating utilitarianism. *—n.* One who advocates or practices utilitarianism. [UTILIT(Y) + -ARIAN.]

u•til•i•tar•i•an•ism (yo͞o-tĭl′ĭ-târ′ē-ə-nĭz′əm) *n.* **1.** The belief that the value of a thing or an action is determined by its utility. **2.** The ethical theory that all action should be directed toward achieving the greatest happiness for the greatest number of people. **3.** The quality of being utilitarian: *housing of bleak utilitarianism.*

u•til•i•ty (yo͞o-tĭl′ĭ-tē) *n., pl.* **-ties. 1.** The quality or condition of being useful; usefulness. **2.** A useful article or device. **3.a.** A public utility. **b.** A commodity or service, such as electricity or water, provided by a public utility. *—adj.* **1.** Used, serving, or working in several capacities as needed, esp.: **a.** Prepared to play any of the smaller theatrical roles on short notice: *a utility cast member.* **b.** Capable of playing as a substitute in any of several positions: *a utility infielder.* **2.** Designed for various often heavy-duty practical uses: *a utility knife.* **3.** Raised or kept for the production of a farm product rather than for show or as pets: *utility livestock.* **4.** Of the lowest U.S. Government grade: *utility beef.* [ME *utilite* < OFr. < Lat. *ūtilitās* < *ūtilis,* useful < *ūtī,* to use.]

u•til•ize (yo͞ot′l-īz′) *tr.v.* **-ized, -iz•ing, -iz•es.** To put to use, esp. to find a profitable or practical use for. [Fr. *utiliser* < Ital. *utilizzare* < *utile,* useful < Lat. *ūtilis* < *ūtī,* to use.] **—u′til•iz′a•ble** *adj.* **—u′til•i•za′tion** (-ĭ-zā′shən) *n.* **—u′til•iz′er** *n.*

Usage Note: It is true that many occurrences of *utilize* could be replaced by *use* with no loss to anything but pretentiousness. But *utilize* can mean "to find a profitable or practical use for." Thus the sentence *The teachers were unable to use the new computers* might mean only that the teachers were unable to turn the computers on, whereas *The teachers were unable to utilize the new computers* suggests that the teachers could not find ways to employ the computers in instruction.

ut•most (ŭt′mōst′) *adj.* **1.** Being or situated at the most distant limit or point; farthest: *the utmost tip of the peninsula.* **2.** Of the highest or greatest degree, amount, or intensity; most extreme: *of the utmost importance.* *—n.* The greatest possible amount, degree, or extent; the maximum: *worked to the utmost of her abilities.* [ME < OE *ūtmest* : *ūt,* out; see **ud-*** + *-mest,* -most.]

U•to-Az•tec•an (yo͞o′tō-ăz′tĕk′ən) *n.* **1.** A language phylum of North and Central America that includes Ute, Hopi, Nahuatl, and Shoshone. **2.** A member of a tribe speaking a Uto-Aztecan language. *—adj.* Of or relating to the Uto-Aztecans or to the languages spoken by them. [< UTE + AZTEC.]

u•to•pi•a (yo͞o-tō′pē-ə) *n.* **1.a.** Often **Utopia.** An ideally perfect place, esp. in its social, political, and moral aspects. **b.** A work of fiction describing a utopia. **2.** An impractical idealistic scheme for reform. [NLat. *Ūtopia,* imaginary island in *Utopia* (1516) by Sir Thomas More : Gk. *ou,* not, no + Gk. *topos,* place.]

u•to•pi•an (yo͞o-tō′pē-ən) *adj.* **1.** Often **Utopian.** Of, relating to, describing or having the characteristics of a Utopia: *a Utopian island.* **2.a.** Excellent or ideal but impracticable; visionary. **b.** Proposing impracticably ideal schemes. *—n.* A zealous but impractical reformer of human society.

u•to•pi•an•ism also **U•to•pi•an•ism** (yo͞o-tō′pē-ə-nĭz′əm) *n.* The ideals or principles of a utopian; idealistic and impractical social theory.

U•trecht (yo͞o′trĕkt′, ü′trĕKHt). A city of central Netherlands SSE of Amsterdam. The Treaty of Utrecht ended the War of the Spanish Succession (1701–13). Pop. 230,414.

u•tri•cle[1] (yo͞o′trĭ-kəl) *n.* **1.** A membranous sac contained within the labyrinth of the inner ear and connected with the semicircular canals. **2.** *Bot.* A small bladderlike one-seeded indehiscent fruit, as in the amaranth. [Lat. *utriculus,* dim. of *uter, utr-,* leather bottle, poss. < Gk. *hudria,* water vessel < *hudōr, hudr-,* water. See **wed-**[1]*.]

u•tri•cle[2] (yo͞o′trĭ-kəl) *n.* A small vestigial blind pouch of the prostate gland. [Lat. *utriculus,* sac, dim. of *uterus,* uterus.]

u•tric•u•lar[1] (yo͞o-trĭk′yə-lər) *adj.* **1.** Of, relating to, or resembling a utricle. **2.** Having one or more utricles.

u•tric•u•lar[2] (yo͞o-trĭk′yə-lər) *adj.* Relating to the uterus.

u•tric•u•lus (yo͞o-trĭk′yə-ləs) *n., pl.* **-li** (-lī′). A utricular sac.

U•tril•lo (yo͞o-trĭl′ō, ü-trē-ō′), **Maurice.** 1883–1955. French painter known esp. for his street scenes of Paris.

Maurice Utrillo
Photographed c. 1924

U•tsu•no•mi•ya (o͞ot′sə-nō′mē-ə, o͞o-tso͞o′nô-mē′yä). A city of central Honshu, Japan, N of Tokyo. Pop. 405,384.

ut•ter[1] (ŭt′ər) *tr.v.* **-tered, -ter•ing, -ters. 1.** To send forth with the voice. **2.** To articulate (words); pronounce or speak. See Syns at **vent**[1]. **3.** *Law.* To circulate (counterfeit money, for example). **4.** To publish (a book, for example). **5.** *Obsolete.* To sell or deliver (merchandise) in trading. [ME *utteren,* partly < MLGer. *uteren* (< *uter,* outer, comp. of *ūt,* out; see **ud-***) and partly alteration (influenced by *utter,* outer; see UTTER[2]) of ME *outen,* to disclose (< *out,* out; see OUT).] **—ut′ter•a•ble** *adj.* **—ut′ter•er** *n.*

ut•ter[2] (ŭt′ər) *adj.* Complete; absolute; entire: *utter darkness.* [ME < OE *ūtera,* outer. See **ud-***.]

ut•ter•ance[1] (ŭt′ər-əns) *n.* **1.a.** The act of uttering; vocal expression. **b.** The power of speaking; speech. **c.** A manner of speaking. **2.** Something uttered or expressed; a statement.

ut•ter•ance[2] (ŭt′ər-əns) *n.* The uttermost end or extremity; the bitter end. [ME < OFr. *outrance* < *outrer,* to go beyond limits < VLat. **ultrāre* < Lat. *ultrā,* beyond. See **al-**[1]*.]

ut•ter•ly (ŭt′ər-lē) *adv.* Completely; absolutely; entirely.

ut•ter•most (ŭt′ər-mōst′) *adj.* **1.** Utmost. **2.** Outermost. *—n.* The greatest amount or degree possible; the utmost. [ME : *utter,* outer; see UTTER[2] + *-most,* -most.]

U-turn (yo͞o′tûrn′) *n.* A turn, as by a vehicle, completely reversing the direction of travel.

UV also **U.V.** *abbr.* Ultraviolet.

u•va•rov•ite (yo͞o-vär′ə-vīt′, o͞o-) *n.* An emerald-green variety of garnet, $Ca_3Cr_2(SiO_4)_3$, found in chromium deposits. [After Count Sergei Semenovitch *Uvarov* (1785–1855), president of the St. Petersburg Academy.]

Uzbekistan

u•ve•a (yo͞o′vē-ə) *n.* The vascular middle layer of the eye constituting the iris, ciliary body, and choroid. [Med.Lat. *ūvea* < Lat. *ūva,* grape.] **—u′ve•al** *adj.*

u•ve•i•tis (yo͞o′vē-ī′tĭs) *n.* Inflammation of the uvea.

u•vu•la (yo͞o′vyə-lə) *n.* A small conical fleshy mass of tissue suspended from the center of the soft palate. [ME < LLat. *ūvula,* dim. of Lat. *ūva,* grape (< the organ's shape).]

u•vu•lar (yo͞o′vyə-lər) *adj.* **1.** Of, relating to, or associated with the uvula. **2.** *Ling.* Articulated by vibration of the uvula or with the back of the tongue near or touching the uvula.

UW *abbr.* Underwriter.

ux. *abbr. Lat.* Uxor (wife).

Ux•mal (o͞os-mäl′). An ancient ruined Mayan city of Yucatán in southeast Mexico; flourished from 600 to 900.

ux•o•ri•al (ŭk-sôr′ē-əl, -sōr′-, ŭg-zôr′-, -zōr′-) *adj.* Of a wife; regarded as befitting a wife. [< Lat. *uxōrius* < *uxor, uxōr-,* wife.] **—ux•o′ri•al•ly** *adv.*

ux•o•ri•cide (ŭk-sôr′ĭ-sīd′, -sōr′-, ŭg-zôr′-, -zōr′-) *n.* **1.** The killing of a wife by her husband. **2.** A man who kills his wife. [Med.Lat. *uxōricīdium* : Lat. *uxor, uxōr-,* wife + Lat. *-cīdium,* -cide.]

ux•o•ri•ous (ŭk-sôr′ē-əs, -sōr′-, ŭg-zôr′-, -zōr′-) *adj.* Excessively submissive or devoted to one's wife. [< Lat. *uxōrius* < *uxor, uxōr-,* wife.] **—ux•o′ri•ous•ly** *adv.* **—ux•o′ri•ous•ness** *n.*

Uz•bek (o͞oz′bĕk′, ŭz′-) *n., pl.* **Uzbek** or **-beks. 1.** A member of a Turkic people inhabiting Uzbekistan and neighboring areas. **2.** The Turkic language of the Uzbeks. [Russ. < Uzbek *ŭzbek.*]

Uz•bek•i•stan (o͞oz-bĕk′ĭ-stăn′, -stän′, ŭz-). A region and republic of W-central Asia; conquered by Alexander the Great, Genghis Khan, and Tamerlane and finally overrun by Uzbek peoples in the early 16th cent. It was a constituent republic of the U.S.S.R. from 1924 to 1991. Cap. Tashkent. Pop. 17,974,000.

ă pat	oi boy
ā pay	ou out
âr care	o͝o took
ä father	o͞o boot
ĕ pet	ŭ cut
ē be	ûr urge
ĭ pit	th thin
ī pie	*th* this
îr pier	hw which
ŏ pot	zh vision
ō toe	ə about, item
ô paw	

Stress marks:
′ (primary);
′ (secondary), as in
dictionary (dĭk′shə-nĕr′ē)

V v

v or **V** (vē) *n.*, *pl.* **v's** or **V's. 1.** The 22nd letter of the modern English alphabet. **2.** Any of the speech sounds represented by the letter *v*. **3.** The 22nd in a series. **4.** Something shaped like the letter V.

V[1] **1.** The symbol for the element **vanadium. 2.** *Elect.* The symbol for **potential** 5. **3.** Also **v.** The symbol for the Roman numeral 5.

V[2] *abbr.* **1.** *Phys.* Velocity. **2.** Victory. **3.** *Elect.* Volt. **4.** Volume (size or capacity).

V-1 (vē′wŭn′) *n.* A robot bomb deployed by the Germans in World War II. [Ger. *Vergeltungswaffe eins*, retaliation weapon (number) one.]

V-2 (vē′to͞o′) *n.* A long-range liquid-fuel rocket used by the Germans as a ballistic missile in World War II. [Ger. *Vergeltungswaffe zwei*, retaliation weapon (number) two.]

v. *abbr.* **1.** Verb. **2.** Verse. **3.** Version. **4.** *Print.* Verso. **5.** Versus. **6.** Or **V.** Very (in titles). **7.** Vide. **8.** Or **V.** Village. **9.** Violin. **10.** Vocative. **11.** Voice. **12.** Volume (book). **13.** Vowel.

V. *abbr.* **1.** Venerable (in titles). **2.** Viscount; viscountess.

VA or **Va.** *abbr.* Virginia.

V.A. *abbr.* **1.** Also **VA.** Veterans' Administration. **2.** Vicar apostolic.

Vaal (väl). A river rising in E South Africa and flowing c. 1,207 km (750 mi) to the Orange R.

VAB *abbr.* Voice answer back.

va•can•cy (vā′kən-sē) *n.*, *pl.* **-cies. 1.** The condition of being vacant or unoccupied. **2.** An empty or unoccupied space. **3.** A position, an office, or a place of accommodation that is unfilled or unoccupied. **4.** Emptiness of mind; inanity. **5.** A crystal defect caused by the absence of an atom, an ion, or a molecule in a crystal lattice. **6.** *Archaic.* A period of leisure; idleness.

va•cant (vā′kənt) *adj.* **1.** Containing nothing; empty. **2.** Without an incumbent or occupant; unfilled. **3.** Not occupied or put to use. **4.a.** Lacking intelligence or knowledge. **b.** Lacking expression; blank. **5.** Not filled with any activity. [ME < OFr. < Lat. *vacāns, vacant-*, pr.part. of *vacāre*, to be empty. See **eu-**[2*].] **—va′cant•ly** *adv.* **—va′cant•ness** *n.*

va•cate (vā′kāt′, vā-kāt′) *v.* **-cat•ed, -cat•ing, -cates.** *—tr.* **1.a.** To cease to occupy or hold; give up. **b.** To empty of occupants or incumbents. **2.** *Law.* To make void or annul; countermand. *—intr.* To leave a job, an office, or a lodging. [Lat. *vacāre, vacāt-*, to be empty. See **eu-**[2*].]

va•ca•tion (vā-kā′shən, və-) *n.* **1.** A period of time devoted to pleasure, rest, or relaxation, esp. one with pay granted to an employee. **2.a.** A holiday. **b.** A fixed period of holidays, esp. one during which a school, court, or business suspends activities. **3.** *Archaic.* The act or an instance of vacating. *—intr.v.* **-tioned, -tion•ing, -tions.** To take or spend a vacation. [Ult. < Lat. *vacātiō, vacātiōn-*, freedom from occupation < *vacātus*, p.part. of *vacāre*, to be empty, at leisure. See **eu-**[2*].] **—va•ca′tion•er, va•ca′tion•eer′** (-shə-nîr′) *n.*

va•ca•tion•ist (vā-kā′shə-nĭst, və-) *n.* One on vacation.

va•ca•tion•land (vā-kā′shən-lănd′) *n.* A place with special attractions for those on vacation.

Vac•a•ville (văk′ə-vĭl′). A city of central CA WSW of Sacramento. Pop. 71,479.

vac•ci•nal (văk′sə-nəl, văk-sē′-) *adj.* **1.** Of or relating to vaccination or a vaccine. **2.** Induced by vaccination.

vac•ci•nate (văk′sə-nāt′) *v.* **-nat•ed, -nat•ing, -nates.** *—tr.* To inoculate with a vaccine in order to produce immunity to an infectious disease, such as diphtheria or typhus. *—intr.* To perform vaccinations or a vaccination. **—vac′ci•na′tor** *n.*

vac•ci•na•tion (văk′sə-nā′shən) *n.* **1.** Inoculation with a vaccine in order to protect against a particular disease. **2.** A scar left on the skin by vaccinating.

vac•cine (văk-sēn′, văk′sēn′) *n.* **1.a.** A preparation of a weakened or killed pathogen, such as a bacterium or virus, or of a portion of the pathogen's structure that upon administration stimulates antibody production against the pathogen but is incapable of causing severe infection. **b.** A vaccine prepared from the cowpox virus and inoculated against smallpox. **2.** *Comp. Sci.* Software designed to detect and stop a computer virus. [< Lat. *vaccīnus*, of cows < *vacca*, cow.]

vac•ci•nee (văk′sə-nē′) *n.* One that has been vaccinated.

vac•cin•i•a (văk-sĭn′ē-ə) *n.* See **cowpox.** [NLat. *vaccinia* < Lat. *vaccīnus*, of cows. See VACCINE.] **—vac•cin′i•al** *adj.*

vac•il•lant (văs′ə-lənt) *adj.* Undergoing vacillation; wavering.

vac•il•late (văs′ə-lāt′) *intr.v.* **-lat•ed, -lat•ing, -lates. 1.** To sway from one side to the other; oscillate. **2.** To swing indecisively from one course of action or opinion to another. [Lat. *vacillāre, vacillāt-*, to waver.] **—vac′il•lat′ing•ly** *adv.* **—vac′il•la′tion** *n.* **—vac′il•la′tor** *n.*

vac•il•la•to•ry (văs′ə-lə-tôr′ē, -tōr′ē) *adj.* Inclined to waver.

va•cu•i•ty (vă-kyo͞o′ĭ-tē, və-) *n.*, *pl.* **-ties. 1.** Total absence of matter; emptiness. **2.** An empty space; a vacuum. **3.** Total lack of ideas; emptiness of mind. **4** Absence of meaningful occupation; idleness. **5.** The quality or fact of being devoid of something specified: *a vacuity of taste.* **6.** Something, esp. a remark, that is pointless or inane. [ME *vacuite* < OFr. < Lat. *vacuitās* < *vacuus*, empty. See VACUUM.]

vacuolar membrane *n.* See **tonoplast.**

vac•u•o•lat•ed (văk′yo͞o-ō-lā′tĭd) also **vac•u•o•late** (-lāt′, -lĭt) *adj.* Containing vacuoles or a vacuole.

vac•u•ole (văk′yo͞o-ōl′) *n.* A small cavity in cell cytoplasm, bound by a single membrane and containing water, food, or metabolic waste. [Fr. < Lat. *vacuus*, empty. See VACUUM.] **—vac′u•o′lar** (-ō′lər, -lär′) *adj.* **—vac′u•o•la′tion** *n.*

vac•u•ous (văk′yo͞o-əs) *adj.* **1.** Devoid of matter; empty. **2.a.** Lacking intelligence; stupid. **b.** Devoid of substance or meaning; inane: *a vacuous comment.* **c.** Devoid of expression; vacant. **3.** Lacking serious purpose or occupation; idle. [< Lat. *vacuus*, empty. See VACUUM.] **—vac′u•ous•ly** *adv.* **—vac′u•ous•ness** *n.*

vac•u•um (văk′yo͞o-əm, -yo͞om, -yəm) *n.*, *pl.* **-u•ums** or **-u•a** (-yo͞o-ə). **1.a.** Absence of matter. **b.** A space empty of matter. **c.** A space relatively empty of matter. **d.** A space in which the pressure is significantly lower than atmospheric pressure. **2.** A state of emptiness; a void. **3.** A state of being sealed off from external or environmental influences; isolation. **4.** *pl.* **-u•ums.** A vacuum cleaner. *—adj.* **1.** Of, relating to, or used to create a vacuum. **2.** Containing air or other gas at a reduced pressure. **3.** Operating by means of suction or by maintaining a partial vacuum. *—tr. & intr.v.* **-umed, -um•ing, -umes.** To clean with or use a vacuum cleaner. [Lat., empty space < neut. of *vacuus*, empty < *vacāre*, to be empty. See **eu-**[2*].]

vacuum bottle *n.* A bottle or flask having a vacuum between its inner and outer walls, designed to maintain the desired temperature of the contents.

vacuum cleaner *n.* An electrical appliance that cleans surfaces by suction.

vacuum gauge *n.* A device for measuring pressures below atmospheric pressure.

vac•u•um-packed (văk′yo͞o-əm-păkt′, -yo͞om-, văk′yəm-) *adj.* **1.** Packed in an airtight container. **2.** Sealed under low pressure or a partial vacuum.

vacuum pump *n.* **1.** A pump used to evacuate an enclosure. **2.** See **pulsometer.**

vacuum tube *n.* An electron tube from which all or most of the gas has been removed, permitting electrons to move with low interaction with any remaining gas molecules.

va•de me•cum (vā′dē mē′kəm, vä′dē mā′-) *n.*, *pl.* **va•de me•cums. 1.** A useful thing that one constantly carries about. **2.** A book, such as a guidebook, for ready reference. [Lat. *vāde mēcum*, go with me : *vāde*, sing. imper. of *vādere*, to go + *mē*, ablative sing. of *egō*, I + *cum*, with.]

V.Adm. or **VADM** *abbr.* Vice admiral.

va•dose (vā′dōs′) *adj.* Of, relating to, or being water located in the zone of aeration in the earth's crust above the ground water level. [Lat. *vadōsus*, shallow < *vadum*, a shallow, ford.]

Va•duz (vä-do͞ots′, fä-). The cap. of Liechtenstein, in the W part on the Rhine R. Pop. 4,927.

vag•a•bond (văg′ə-bŏnd′) *n.* **1.** A person without a permanent home who moves from place to place. **2.** A vagrant; a tramp. **3.** A wanderer; a rover. *—adj.* **1.** Of, relating to, or characteristic of a wanderer; nomadic. **2.** Aimless; drifting. **3.** Irregular in course or behavior; unpredictable. *—intr.v.* **-bond•ed, -bond•ing, -bonds.** To lead the life of a vagabond; roam about. [ME *vagabonde* < OFr. *vagabond* < LLat. *vagābundus*, wandering < Lat. *vagārī*, to wander < *vagus*, wandering.] **—vag′a•bond′age, vag′a•bond′ism** *n.*

va•gal (vā′gəl) *adj.* Of or relating to the vagus nerve.

va•ga•ry (vā′gə-rē, və-gâr′ē) *n.*, *pl.* **-ries.** An extravagant or erratic notion or action. [< Lat. *vagārī*, to wander < *vagus*, wandering.]

va•gi (vā′gī, -jī) *n.* Pl. of **vagus.**

vag•ile (văj′əl, -īl) *adj.* Able to move about or disperse in a given environment: *a vagile animal species.* [Lat. *vagus*, wandering + -ILE[1].] **—va•gil′i•ty** (və-jĭl′ĭ-tē, vă-) *n.*

va•gi•na (və-jī′nə) *n.*, *pl.* **-nas** or **-nae** (-nē). **1.** *Anat.* **a.** The passage leading from the opening of the vulva to the cervix of the uterus in female mammals. **b.** A similar part in some invertebrates. **2.** *Bot.* A sheathlike structure, such as the leaf of a grass that surrounds a stem. [Lat. *vāgīna*, sheath.]

vag•i•nal (văj′ə-nəl) *adj.* **1.** Of or relating to the vagina. **2.** Relating to or resembling a sheath. **—vag′i•nal•ly** *adv.*

vag•i•nate (văj′ə-nĭt, -nāt′) also **vag•i•nat•ed** (-nā′tĭd) *adj.* **1.** Forming or enclosed in a sheath. **2.** Resembling a sheath.

vag·i·nis·mus (văj′ə-nĭz′məs) *n.* A painful spasm of the vagina. [NLat. *vāgīnismus* : VAGIN(A) + Lat. *-ismus*, -ism.]

vag·i·ni·tis (văj′ə-nī′tĭs) *n.* Inflammation of the vagina.

va·got·o·my (vā-gŏt′ə-mē) *n., pl.* **-mies.** Surgical division of fibers of the vagus nerve, used to diminish acid secretion of the stomach and control a duodenal ulcer. [VAG(US) + -TOMY.]

va·go·to·ni·a (vā′gə-tō′nē-ə) *n.* Overactivity or irritability of the vagus nerve, adversely affecting function of the blood vessels, stomach, and muscles. [VAG(US) + -TONIA.] — **va′go·ton′ic** (-tŏn′ĭk) *adj.*

va·go·tro·pic (vā′gə-trō′pĭk, -trŏp′ĭk) *adj.* Affecting or acting on the vagus nerve. Used chiefly of a drug.

va·gran·cy (vā′grən-sē) *n., pl.* **-cies. 1.a.** The state of being a vagrant. **b.** The conduct or mode of existence of a vagrant. **c.** The offense of being a vagrant. **2.** A wandering in mind.

va·grant (vā′grənt) *n.* **1.** One who wanders from place to place without a permanent home or a means of livelihood. **2.** A wanderer; a rover. **3.** One who lives on the streets and constitutes a public nuisance. — *adj.* **1.** Wandering from place to place and lacking any means of support. **2.** Wayward; unrestrained: *a vagrant impulse.* **3.** Moving in a random fashion; not fixed in place. [ME *vagraunt*, prob. alteration of OFr. *wacrant*, pr.part. of *wacrer*, to wander, of Gmc. orig.] — **va′grant·ly** *adv.*

vague (vāg) *adj.* **vagu·er, vagu·est. 1.** Not clearly expressed; inexplicit. **2.** Not thinking or expressing oneself clearly. **3.** Lacking definite shape, form, or character; indistinct: *a vague outline.* **4.** Not clear in meaning or application. See Syns at **ambiguous. 5.** Indistinctly felt, perceived, understood, or recalled; hazy. [Fr. < OFr., wandering < Lat. *vagus.*] — **vague′ly** *adv.* — **vague′ness** *n.*

va·gus (vā′gəs) *n., pl.* **-gi** (-gī, -jī). The vagus nerve.

vagus nerve *n.* Either of the tenth and longest of the cranial nerves that innervate the neck, thorax, and abdomen with sensory and motor nerve fibers. [NLat. *(nervus) vagus*, wandering (nerve) < Lat.]

Váh (vä, väKH). A river of W Slovakia flowing c. 394 km (245 mi) W and S to the Danube R.

va·hi·ne (vä-hē′nē, -nā) *n.* Var. of **wahine.**

vail[1] (vāl) *v.* **vailed, vail·ing, vails.** — *tr.* **1.** To lower (a banner, for example). **2.** To doff (one's hat) as a token of respect or submission. — *intr.* **1.** To descend; lower. **2.** To doff one's hat. [ME *valen*, short for *avalen* < OFr. *avaler* < *aval*, downward < Lat. *ad vallem*, to the valley : *ad*, ad- + *vallem*, accusative of *vallēs*, valley; see **wel-**[2]*.]

vail[2] (vāl) *n. Obsolete.* Var. of **veil.**

vain (vān) *adj.* **vain·er, vain·est. 1.** Not yielding the desired outcome; fruitless: *a vain attempt.* **2.** Lacking substance or worth: *vain talk.* See Syns at **futile. 3.** Excessively proud of one's appearance or accomplishments; conceited. **4.** *Archaic.* Foolish. — ***idiom.* in vain. 1.** To no avail; without success. **2.** In an irreverent or disrespectful manner. [ME < OFr. < Lat. *vānus*, empty. See **eu-**[2]*.] — **vain′ly** *adv.* — **vain′ness** *n.*

vain·glo·ri·ous (vān-glôr′ē-əs, -glōr′-) *adj.* **1.** Marked by or showing excessive vanity; boastful. **2.** Proceeding from vainglory. — **vain·glo′ri·ous·ly** *adv.* — **vain·glo′ri·ous·ness** *n.*

vain·glo·ry (vān′glôr′ē, -glōr′ē, vān-glôr′ē, -glōr′ē) *n., pl.* **-ries. 1.** Boastful, unwarranted pride in one's accomplishments or qualities. **2.** Vain, ostentatious display. [ME *vein glory* < OFr. *vaine gloire* < Lat. *vāna glōria*, empty pride : *vānus*, empty; see VAIN + *glōria*, glory, pride.]

vair (vâr) *n.* **1.** A fur, probably squirrel, much used in medieval times to line and trim robes. **2.** *Her.* A representation of fur. [ME < OFr., variegated, vair < Lat. *varius*, variegated.]

Vaish·na·va (vīsh′nə-və) *n. Hinduism.* One who worships Vishnu. [< Skt. *vaiṣṇava-*, relating to Vishnu < *Viṣṇuḥ*, Vishnu.] — **Vaish′na·vism** (-vĭz′əm) *n.*

Vais·ya (vī′shə, vīsh′yə) *n.* **1.** The third of the four Hindu classes, comprising farmers, herders, artisans, merchants, and businessmen. **2.** A member of this caste. [Skt. *vaiśyaḥ*, settler, homesteader < *viśaḥ*, house. See **weik-**[1]*.]

val. *abbr.* **1.** Valley. **2.** Valuation; value.

val·ance (văl′əns, vā′ləns) *n.* **1.** An ornamental drapery hung across a top edge, as of a bed. **2.** A short drapery, decorative board, or metal strip mounted esp. across the top of a window to hide structural fixtures. — *tr.v.* **-anced, -anc·ing, -anc·es.** To supply with valances or a valance. [ME.]

Val·dai Hills also **Val·day Hills** (väl-dī′). An upland region of W Russia between St. Petersburg and Moscow.

Val·de·mar I (väl′də-mär′). See **Waldemar I.**

Val·dez (văl-dēz′). A city of S AK on Prince William Sound; S terminus of the oil pipeline from Prudhoe Bay. Pop. 4,068.

Val·do (văl′dō, väl′-), **Peter.** See Peter **Waldo.**

Val d'Or (văl′ dôr′, väl dôr′). A town of SW Quebec, Canada, near the Ontario border. Pop. 21,321.

Val·dos·ta (văl-dŏs′tə). A city of S GA near the FL border ENE of Tallahassee; settled in 1859. Pop. 39,806.

vale[1] (vāl) *n.* A valley, often coursed by a stream; a dale. [ME < OFr. *val* < Lat. *vallēs*. See **wel-**[2]*.]

va·le[2] (vä′lē, wä′lā) *interj.* Used to express leave-taking or farewell. — *n.* A farewell. [Lat. *valē*, sing. imper. of *valēre*, to be strong or well. See **wal-***.]

val·e·dic·tion (văl′ĭ-dĭk′shən) *n.* **1.** An act of bidding farewell; a leave-taking. **2.** A speech or statement made as a farewell. [< Lat. *valedictus*, p.part. of *valedīcere*, to say farewell : *valē*, farewell; see VALE[2] + *dīcere*, to say; see **deik-***.]

val·e·dic·to·ri·an (văl′ĭ-dĭk-tôr′ē-ən, -tōr′-) *n.* The student with the highest academic rank in a class who delivers the valedictory at graduation.

val·e·dic·to·ry (văl′ĭ-dĭk′tə-rē) *n., pl.* **-ries.** A closing or farewell statement or address, esp. one delivered at graduation exercises. — *adj.* Of, relating to, or expressing a valedictory.

va·lence (vā′ləns) also **va·len·cy** (-lən-sē) *n., pl.* **-lenc·es** also **-len·cies. 1.** *Chem.* **a.** The combining capacity of an atom or a radical determined by the number of electrons that it will lose, add, or share when it reacts with other atoms. **b.** A positive or negative integer used to represent this capacity. **2.** *Immunol.* The number of components of an antigen molecule to which an antibody molecule can bind. **3.** *Psychol.* The attraction or aversion that one feels toward a specific object or event. **4.** The capacity of something to unite, react, or interact with something else. [Lat. *valentia*, capacity < *valēns*, *valent-*, pr.part. of *valēre*, to be strong. See **wal-***.]

Va·lence (və-läNs′, vă-). A city of SE France S of Lyons; captured by the Visigoths in A.D. 413. Pop. 66,356.

valence electron *n.* An electron in an outer shell of an atom that can join in forming chemical bonds with other atoms.

valence shell *n.* The outermost shell of an atom consisting of the valence electrons.

Va·len·ci·a (və-lĕn′shē-ə, -chə, -sē-ə). **1.** (*also* bä-lĕn′thyä). A region and former kingdom of E Spain on the Mediterranean coast S of Catalonia; inhabited by Iberian peoples in early times and later colonized by Greek and Carthaginian traders. **2.** (*also* bä-lĕn′thyä). A city of E Spain on the **Gulf of Valencia,** a wide inlet of the Mediterranean Sea; captured by the Moors in 714. Pop. 785,273. **3.** (*also* bä-lĕn′syä). A city of N Venezuela WSW of Caracas on the W shore of **Lake Valencia;** founded 1555. Pop. 523,000.

Va·len·ci·ennes[1] (və-lĕn′sē-ĕnz′, vă-läN-syĕn′). A city of N France near the Belgian border SE of Lille; noted for its lace industry since the 15th century. Pop. 40,275.

Va·len·ci·ennes[2] (və-lĕn′sē-ĕn′, -ĕnz′, văl′ən-sē-) *n.* A fine lace with a floral pattern.

Va·lens (vā′lənz, -lĕnz′). A.D. 328?–378. Emperor of Rome in the East (364–378) who ruled jointly with his brother Valentinian I in the West.

-valent *suff.* Having a specified valence or valences: *polyvalent.* [< VALENCE.]

val·en·tine (văl′ən-tīn′) *n.* **1.a.** A sentimental or humorous greeting card sent, as to a sweetheart, on Saint Valentine's Day. **b.** A gift sent as a token of love to one's sweetheart on Saint Valentine's Day. **2.** A person singled out esp. as one's sweetheart on Saint Valentine's Day.

Word History: Geoffrey Chaucer should perhaps receive honor as the real Saint Valentine. Although reference books abound with mention of Roman festivals from which Valentine's Day — the day for lovers — may be derived, Jack B. Oruch has shown that no evidence exists to support these connections. No link between the day and lovers exists before the time of Chaucer and several literary contemporaries who also mention it, but after them the link becomes widespread. The fullest and perhaps earliest description of the tradition occurs in Chaucer's *Parlement of Foules,* composed around 1380, which takes place "on Seynt Valentynes day/Whan every foul cometh there to chese [choose] his make [mate]."

Val·en·tine (văl′ən-tīn′), Saint. fl. 3rd cent. A.D. Roman Christian who according to tradition was martyred during the persecution of Christians by Emperor Claudius II.

Val·en·tine's Day or **Val·en·tines Day** (văl′ən-tīnz′) *n.* See **Saint Valentine's Day.**

Val·en·tin·ian I (văl′ən-tĭn′ē-ən, -tĭn′yən). A.D. 321–375. Emperor of Rome in the West (364–375) who ruled jointly with his brother Valens in the East.

Valentinian II. A.D. 371?–392. Emperor of Rome (375–392) who ruled jointly with Gratian in the East (375–383).

Valentinian III. A.D. 419–455. Emperor of Rome in the West (425–455) whose reign was marked by numerous raids by Germanic tribes.

Val·en·ti·no (văl′ĭn-tē′nō), **Rudolf.** 1895–1926. Italian-born Amer. actor known for his romantic roles in silent films.

Rudolf Valentino

va·le·ri·an (və-lîr′ē-ən) *n.* **1.** A plant of the genus *Valeriana,* esp. *V. officinalis* of Eurasia, widely cultivated for its small fragrant white to pink or lavender flowers and for use in medicine. **2.** The dried rhizomes of this plant, used as a sedative. [ME < OFr. *valeriane* < Med.Lat. *valeriāna*, prob. < fem. of Lat. *Valeriānus*, of Valeria, Roman province.]

Va·le·ri·an (və-lîr′ē-ən). d. c. A.D. 260. Emperor of Rome (253–260) who was defeated by Persian forces (260) and died in captivity.

va·le·ric acid (və-lîr′ĭk, -lĕr′-) *n.* A colorless liquid, $C_5H_{10}O_2$, used in flavorings, perfumes, plasticizers, and pharmaceuticals. [< VALERIAN, < its occurrence in the plant's root.]

Va·lé·ry (văl′ə-rē′, vä-lā-rē′), **Paul Ambroise.** 1871–1945. French poet known for *Le Cimitière Marin* (1932).

ă pat	oi boy
ā pay	ou out
âr care	ŏŏ took
ä father	ōō boot
ĕ pet	ŭ cut
ē be	ûr urge
ĭ pit	th thin
ī pie	*th* this
îr pier	hw which
ŏ pot	zh vision
ō toe	ə about, item
ô paw	

Stress marks:
′ (primary);
′ (secondary), as in
dictionary (dĭk′shə-nĕr′ē)

Valhalla

vambrace
c. 1550 Spanish

vampire bat

Martin Van Buren

val•et (văl′ĭt, văl′ā, vă-lā′) *n.* **1.** A man's male servant, who takes care of his clothes and performs other personal services. **2.** An employee, as in a hotel or on a ship, who performs personal services for guests or passengers. **3.** A rack or stand for holding clothes. — *v.* **-et•ed, -et•ing, -ets.** — *tr.* To act as a personal servant to; attend. — *intr.* To work as a valet. [ME *valette* < OFr. *vaslet, valet*, servant, squire < VLat. **vassellitus*, dim. of **vassus*, vassal. See VASSAL.]

valet parking *n.* Parking provided to and done for patrons, as of a restaurant.

val•e•tu•di•nar•i•an (văl′ĭ-to͞od′n-âr′ē-ən, -tyo͞od′-) *n.* A sickly or weak person, esp. one constantly and morbidly concerned with his or her health. — *adj.* **1.** Chronically ailing; sickly. **2.** Constantly and morbidly concerned with one's health. [< Lat. *valētūdinārius* < *valētūdō, valētūdin-*, state of health < *valēre*, to be strong or well. See **wal-***.] — **val′e•tu′di•nar′i•an•ism** *n.*

val•e•tu•di•nar•y (văl′ĭ-to͞od′n-ĕr′ē, -tyo͞od′-) *adj.* Of, relating to, or typical of a valetudinarian. — **valetudinary** *n.*

val•gus (văl′gəs) *adj.* **1.** Characterized by an abnormal outward turning of a bone, esp. of the hip, knee, or foot. **2.** Knock-kneed. — *n.* A valgus bone. [< Lat., bowlegged.] — **val′goid′** (-goid′) *adj.*

Val•hal•la (văl-hăl′ə, väl-hä′lə) also **Wal•hal•la** (wăl-hăl′ə, văl-, wäl-hä′lə, väl-) *n. Myth.* The hall in which Odin received the souls of slain heroes. [ON *Valhöll* : *valr*, the slain in battle; see **welə-*** + *höll, hall*, hall; see **kel-¹***.]

val•iant (văl′yənt) *adj.* **1.** Possessing valor; brave. **2.** Marked by or done with valor. See Syns at **brave.** — *n.* A brave person. [ME < OFr. *vaillant* < Lat. *valēns, valent-*, pr.part. of *valēre*, to be strong. See **wal-***.] — **val′ian•cy, val′iance, val′iant•ness** *n.* — **val′iant•ly** *adv.*

val•id (văl′ĭd) *adj.* **1.** Well grounded; just: *a valid objection.* **2.** Producing the desired results; efficacious: *valid methods.* **3.** Having legal force; effective or binding: *a valid title.* **4.** *Logic.* **a.** Containing premises from which the conclusion may logically be derived. **b.** Correctly inferred or deduced from a premise. **5.** *Archaic.* Of sound health; robust. [Fr. *valide* < OFr. < Lat. *validus*, strong < *valēre*, to be strong. See **wal-***.] — **va•lid′i•ty, val′id•ness** *n.* — **val′id•ly** *adv.*

Syns: valid, sound, cogent, convincing, telling. These adjectives describe assertions, arguments, conclusions, reasons, or intellectual processes that are persuasive because they are well founded. What is *valid* is based on or borne out by truth or fact or has legal force: *a valid excuse; a valid claim.* What is *sound* is free from logical flaws or is based on valid reasoning: *sound principles.* Something *cogent* is both sound and compelling: *cogent testimony; a cogent explanation. Convincing* implies the power to dispel doubt or overcome resistance or opposition: *convincing proof. Telling* means strikingly effective: *The attorney's summation was telling.*

val•i•date (văl′ĭ-dāt′) *tr.v.* **-dat•ed, -dat•ing, -dates. 1.** To declare or make legally valid. **2.** To mark with an indication of official sanction. **3.** To establish the soundness of; corroborate. — **val′i•da′tion** *n.*

val•ine (văl′ēn′, vā′lēn′) *n.* An essential amino acid, $C_5H_{11}NO_2$. [VAL(ERIC ACID) + -INE².]

va•lise (və-lēs′) *n.* A small piece of hand luggage. [Fr. < Ital. *valigia.*]

Val•i•um (văl′ē-əm). A trademark used for diazepam.

Val•kyr•ie (văl-kîr′ē, -kī′rē, văl′kə-rē) also **Wal•kyr•ie** (wäl-kîr′ē, -kī′rē, väl-, wäl′kə-rē, väl′-) *n. Myth.* Any of Odin's handmaidens who conducted the souls of slain heroes to Valhalla. [ON *Valkyrja.* See **welə-***.]

Val•la•do•lid (văl′ə-də-lĭd′, bä′lyä-*th*ô-lē*th*′). A city of NW-central Spain NNW of Madrid. Pop. 331,404.

val•la•tion (vă-lā′shən) *n.* **1.** An earthwork wall used for military defense; a rampart. **2.** The process of planning or erecting earth fortifications. [LLat. *vallātiō, vallātiōn-* < Lat. *vallātus*, p.part. of *vallāre*, to surround with a rampart < *vallum*, rampart < *vallus*, stake.]

val•lec•u•la (vă-lĕk′yə-lə, və-) *n., pl.* **-lae** (-lē′). A shallow groove, depression, or furrow, as between the hemispheres of the brain. [LLat., dim. of Lat. *vallēs*, valley.] — **val•lec′u•lar, val•lec′u•late** (-lĭt, -lāt′) *adj.*

Val•le d'A•os•ta (vä′lā dä-ō′stə, -ô′stâ). A region of NW Italy bordering on France and Switzerland.

Val•le•jo (və-lā′ō, -hō). A city of W CA on San Pablo Bay N of Oakland. Pop. 109,199.

Val•let•ta (və-lĕt′ə). The cap. of Malta, on the NE coast of the main island; founded in the 16th cent. Pop. 14,013.

val•ley (văl′ē) *n., pl.* **-leys. 1.** An elongated lowland between ranges of mountains, hills, or other uplands, often having a river or stream. **2.** An extensive area of land drained or irrigated by a river system. **3.** A depression or hollow resembling or suggesting a valley, as the point at which the two slopes of a roof meet. [ME *valey* < OFr. *valee* < VLat. **vallāta* < Lat. *vallēs.* See **wel-²***.] — **val′leyed** *adj.*

Val•ley East (văl′ē). A town of central Ontario, Canada, a suburb of Sudbury. Pop. 20,433.

valley fever *n.* See **coccidioidomycosis.**

Val•ley•field (văl′ē-fēld′). A city of S Quebec, Canada, on the St. Lawrence R. SW of Montreal. Pop. 29,574.

Valley Forge. A village of SE PA on the Schuylkill R. NW of Philadelphia; site of the Continental Army headquarters (Dec. 1777–Jun. 1778).

Valley of Ten Thou•sand Smokes (tĕn′ thou′zənd smōks′). A volcanic region of SW AK at the upper end of the Alaska Peninsula; formed by the eruption of Mt. Katmai in 1912.

Valley of the Kings (kĭngz). A narrow valley of E-central Egypt surrounding the site of ancient Thebes between Karnak and Luxor. The valley contains the tombs of numerous pharaohs of the XVIII, XIX, and XX Dynasties.

Valley Stream. A village of SE NY on SW Long I. Pop. 33,946.

Va•lois¹ (văl′wä, väl-wä′). A French ruling dynasty (1328–1589) that succeeded the Capetian line.

Va•lois² (văl′wä′, väl-wä′). A historical region and former duchy of N France; an appanage of the royal house of Valois after 1285.

va•lo•ni•a (və-lō′nē-ə, -lōn′yə) *n.* The dried acorn cups of an oak tree *(Quercus aegilops)* of the eastern Mediterranean, used chiefly in tanning and dyeing. [Ital. *vallonia* < Mod.Gk. *balania*, pl. of *balani*, acorn < Gk. *balanos.*]

val•or (văl′ər) *n.* Courage and boldness, as in battle; bravery. [ME *valour* < OFr. < LLat. *valor* < Lat. *valēre*, to be strong. See **wal-***.]

val•or•ize (văl′ə-rīz′) *tr.v.* **-ized, -iz•ing, -iz•es. 1.** To establish and maintain the price of (a commodity) by governmental action. **2.** To give or assign a value to. [Port. *valorizar* < *valor*, value < LLat. See VALOR.] — **val′or•i•za′tion** (-ər-ĭ-zā′shən) *n.*

val•or•ous (văl′ər-əs) *adj.* Marked by or possessing great personal bravery; valiant. — **val′or•ous•ly** *adv.* — **val′or•ous•ness** *n.*

val•our (văl′ər) *n. Chiefly British.* Var. of **valor.**

Val•pa•rai•so (văl′pə-rī′zō). **1.** Also **Val•pa•ra•í•so** (bäl′pä-rä-ē′sô). A city of central Chile on the Pacific Ocean WNW of Santiago; founded 1536. Pop. 265,355. **2.** A city of NW IN SE of Gary. Pop. 24,414.

Val•sal•va maneuver (văl-săl′və) *n.* Expiratory effort when the mouth is closed and the nostrils are pinched shut, which forces air into the eustachian tubes and increases pressure on the inside of the eardrum. [After Antonio Maria *Valsalva* (1666–1723), Italian anatomist.]

val•u•a•ble (văl′yo͞o-ə-bəl, văl′yə-) *adj.* **1.** Having considerable monetary or material value for use or exchange. **2.** Of great importance, use, or service. **3.** Having admirable or esteemed qualities or characteristics. — *n.* A personal possession with a relatively high monetary value. Often used in the plural. — **val′u•a•ble•ness** *n.* — **val′u•a•bly** *adv.*

val•u•ate (văl′yo͞o-āt′) *tr.v.* **-at•ed, -at•ing, -ates.** To set a value for; appraise. [Back-formation < VALUATION.]

val•u•a•tion (văl′yo͞o-ā′shən) *n.* **1.** The act or process of assessing value or price; an appraisal. **2.** Assessed value or price. **3.** An estimation or appreciation of worth, merit, or character. — **val′u•a′tion•al** *adj.*

val•u•a•tor (văl′yo͞o-ā′tər) *n.* One that estimates values.

val•ue (văl′yo͞o) *n.* **1.** An amount, as of goods, services, or money, considered to be a fair and suitable equivalent for something else; a fair price or return. **2.** Monetary or material worth: *the value of gold.* **3.** Worth in usefulness or importance to the possessor; utility or merit. **4.** A principle, standard, or quality considered worthwhile or desirable: *family values.* **5.** Precise meaning or import, as of a word. **6.** *Math.* An assigned or calculated numerical quantity. **7.** *Mus.* The relative duration of a tone or rest. **8.** *Color.* The relative darkness or lightness of a color. **9.** *Ling.* The sound quality of a letter or diphthong. **10.** One of a series of specified values: *issued a stamp of new value.* — *tr.v.* **-ued, -u•ing, -ues. 1.** To determine or estimate the worth or value of; appraise. **2.** To regard highly; esteem. See Syns at **appreciate. 3.** To rate according to relative estimate of worth or desirability; evaluate. **4.** To assign a value to (a unit of currency, for example). [ME < OFr. < fem. p.part. of *valoir*, to be strong, be worth < Lat. *valēre.* See **wal-***.] — **val′u•er** *n.*

val•ue-add•ed tax (văl′yo͞o-ăd′ĭd) *n.* A tax on the estimated market value added to a product or material at each stage of its manufacture or distribution, ultimately passed on to the consumer.

value judgment *n.* A judgment that assigns a value, as to an object or action; a subjective evaluation.

val•var (văl′vər) *adj.* Valvular.

val•vate (văl′vāt′) *adj.* **1.** Having valvelike parts. **2.** *Bot.* **a.** Meeting at the edges without overlapping, as some petals. **b.** Opening by valves, as the capsule of a lily or iris.

valve (vălv) *n.* **1.** *Anat.* A membranous structure in a hollow organ or passage, as in an artery or a vein, that folds or closes to prevent the return flow of the body fluid passing through it. **2.a.** Any of various devices that regulate the flow of gases, liquids, or loose materials through piping or apertures by opening, closing, or obstructing ports or passageways. **b.** The movable control element of such a device. **c.** *Mus.* A device in a brass wind instrument that permits change in pitch by a rapid varying of the air column in a tube. **3.** *Biol.* **a.** One of the paired hinged shells of certain mollusks and of brachiopods. **b.** One of the two silicified halves of the cell wall of a diatom. **c.** The entire one-piece shell of certain mollusks. **4.** *Bot.* **a.** One of the sections into which the wall of a seedpod or other dehiscent fruit splits. **b.** A lidlike covering of an anther. **5.** *Chiefly British.* An electron tube or a vacuum tube. **6.** *Archaic.* Either half of a double or folding door. — *tr.v.* **valved, valv•ing, valves. 1.** To provide with a valve. **2.** To control by means of a valve. [ME, leaf of a door < Lat. *valva.* See **wel-²*.**] — **valve′less** *adj.*

valve-in-head engine (vălv′ĭn-hĕd′) *n.* An internal-combustion engine that has the inlet and exhaust valves in the cylinder head instead of in the engine block.

val•vu•lar (văl′vyə-lər) *adj.* Relating to, having, or operating by means of valves or valvelike parts.

val•vule (văl′vyo͞ol′) also **val•vu•la** (-vyə-lə) *n., pl.* **-vules** also **-vu•lae** (-vyə-lē′). A small valve or valvelike structure.

val•vu•li•tis (văl′vyə-lī′tĭs) *n.* Inflammation of a valve, esp. a cardiac valve.

vam•brace (văm′brās′) *n.* Armor used to protect the forearm. [ME *vambras* < AN *vauntbras* : *vaunt* (var. of OFr. *avaunt,* before; see VANGUARD) + *bras,* arm; see BRACER².]

va•moose (vă-mo͞os′, və-) *intr.v.* **-moosed, -moos•ing, -moos•es.** *Slang.* To leave hurriedly. [< Sp. *vamos,* let's go < Lat. *vādāmus,* first pers. pl. subjunctive of *vādere,* to go.]

vamp¹ (vămp) *n.* **1.** The upper part of a boot or shoe covering the instep and sometimes extending over the toe. **2.a.** Something patched up or refurbished. **b.** Something rehashed, as a book based on old material. **3.** *Mus.* An improvised accompaniment. — *v.* **vamped, vamp•ing, vamps.** — *tr.* **1.** To provide (a shoe) with a new vamp. **2.** To patch up (something old); refurbish. **3.** To put together; fabricate or improvise: *Reporters vamped up questions.* **4.** *Mus.* To improvise (an accompaniment, for example) for a solo. — *intr. Mus.* To improvise simple accompaniment or variation of a tune. [ME *vampe,* sock < OFr. *avanpie* : *avaunt,* before; see VANGUARD + *pie,* foot (< Lat. *pēs;* see **ped-***).] — **vamp′er** *n.*

vamp² (vămp) *Informal.* — *n.* A seductive woman who entraps and exploits men. — *v.* **vamped, vamp•ing, vamps.** — *tr.* To seduce or exploit (someone) in the manner of a vamp. — *intr.* To play the part of a vamp. [Short for VAMPIRE.] — **vamp′ish** *adj.* — **vamp′ish•ly** *adv.* — **vamp′y** *adj.*

vam•pire (văm′pīr′) *n.* **1.** A reanimated corpse that is believed to rise from the grave at night to suck blood from people in their sleep. **2.** A person who preys upon others. **3.** A vampire bat. [Fr. < Ger. *Vampir,* of Slav. orig.] — **vam•pir′ic** (văm-pĭr′ĭk), **vam•pir′i•cal** (-ĭ-kəl), **vam′pir′ish** (-ĭsh) *adj.*

vampire bat *n.* **1.** Any of various tropical American bats of the family Desmodontidae that bite mammals and birds to feed on their blood and often carry diseases such as rabies. **2.** Any of various other bats, as those of the family Megadermatidae, erroneously believed to feed on blood.

vam•pir•ism (văm′pīr-ĭz′əm) *n.* **1.** Belief in vampires. **2.** The behavior of a vampire.

van¹ (văn) *n.* **1.a.** A boxlike motor vehicle having rear or side doors and side panels esp. for transporting people. **b.** A covered or enclosed truck or wagon often used for transporting goods or livestock. **2.** *Chiefly British.* A closed railroad car used for carrying baggage or freight. — *v.* **vanned, van•ning, vans.** — *tr.* To transport by van. — *intr.* To drive or travel in a van. [Short for CARAVAN.]

van² (văn) *n.* The vanguard; the forefront. [Short for VANGUARD.]

van³ (văn) *n.* **1.** A wing. **2.** *Archaic.* A winnowing device, such as a fan. [ME < OE *fann* and OFr. *van,* both < Lat. *vannus.* See **wet-¹*.**]

Van (văn, vän), **Lake.** A salt lake of E Turkey having no known outlet.

van•a•date (văn′ə-dāt′) *n.* Any of three anions, VO_3, VO_4, or V_2O_7, containing pentavalent vanadium.

va•na•dic acid (və-nā′dĭk, -năd′ĭk) *n.* An acid containing a vanadate group, esp. HVO_3, H_3VO_4, or $H_4V_2O_7$, not existing in a pure state.

va•na•di•nite (və-năd′n-īt′, -năd′-, văn′ə-dē′nīt′) *n.* A red, yellow, or brown mineral that is an ore of vanadium and lead.

va•na•di•um (və-nā′dē-əm) *n. Symbol* **V** A soft ductile metallic element found in several minerals, notably vanadinite and carnotite, and used in rust-resistant high-speed tools, as a carbon stabilizer in some steels, and as a catalyst. Atomic number 23; atomic weight 50.942; melting point 1,890°C; boiling point 3,000°C; specific gravity 6.11; valence 2, 3, 4, 5. See table at **element.** [< ON *Vanadīs,* the goddess Freya. See **wen-¹*.**]

vanadium pentoxide *n.* A crystalline powder, V_2O_5, used as a catalyst in various organic reactions.

vanadium steel *n.* Steel alloyed with vanadium for added strength, hardness, and high-temperature stability.

Van Al•len belt (văn ăl′ən) *n.* Either of two zones of high-intensity particulate radiation trapped in Earth's magnetic field and surrounding the planet, beginning at an altitude of about 800 kilometers (500 miles) and extending into space. [After James Alfred *Van Allen* (b. 1914), Amer. physicist.]

Van Bu•ren (văn byo͝or′ən), **Martin.** 1782–1862. The 8th President of the U.S. (1837–41), who also served in the U.S. Senate (1821–28) and as Vice President (1833–37).

Van•cou•ver (văn-ko͞o′vər). **1.** A city of SW British Columbia, Canada, on the Strait of Georgia opposite Vancouver I. Pop. 414,281. **2.** A city of SW WA on the Columbia R. opposite Portland, OR; founded as Fort Vancouver by the Hudson's Bay Company in the 1820's. Pop. 46,380.

Vancouver, George. 1757–98. British navigator who led expeditions to Australia, New Zealand, and the Hawaiian Is. (1791–92) and the coast of North America (1792–94).

Vancouver, Mount. A peak, 4,873.6 m (15,979 ft), in the St. Elias Mts. of SW Yukon Terr., Canada.

Vancouver Island. An island of southwest British Columbia, Canada, in the Pacific Ocean separated from the mainland by the Strait of Georgia and Queen Charlotte Strait.

Van•dal (văn′dl) *n.* **1. vandal.** One who willfully or maliciously defaces or destroys public or private property. **2.** A member of a Germanic people that overran Gaul, Spain, and northern Africa in the fourth and fifth centuries A.D. and sacked Rome in 455. [Lat. *Vandalus,* a Vandal, prob. of Gmc. orig.] — **Van•dal′ic** (văn-dăl′ĭk) *adj.*

van•dal•ism (văn′dl-ĭz′əm) *n.* Willful or malicious destruction of public or private property. — **van′dal•is′tic** *adj.*

van•dal•ize (văn′dl-īz′) *tr.v.* **-ized, -iz•ing, -iz•es.** To destroy or deface (public or private property) willfully or maliciously. — **van′dal•i•za′tion** (-ĭ-zā′shən) *n.*

Van de Graaff generator (văn′ də grăf′) *n.* An electrostatic generator in which an electric charge is transferred to a large hollow spherical electrode by a rapidly moving belt, producing potentials of millions of volts. [After Robert Jemison *Van de Graaff* (1901–67), Amer. physicist.]

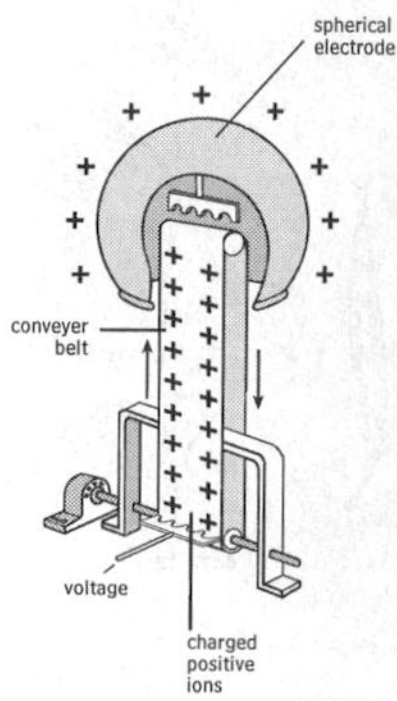

Van de Graaff generator

Van•der•bilt (văn′dər-bĭlt′), **Cornelius.** 1794–1877. Amer. transportation promoter and financier who amassed a great fortune through railroad and shipping interests.

Van Der Ro•he (văn dər rō′ə, fän). See Ludwig **Mies Van Der Rohe.**

van der Waals force (văn′ dər wôlz′, wälz′) *n.* A weak attractive force between atoms or nonpolar molecules caused by a temporary change in dipole moment of one atom or molecule and inducing a similar change in adjacent atoms or molecules. [After Johannes Diderik *van der Waals* (1837–1923), Dutch physicist.]

Van De•van•ter (văn′ də-văn′tər), **Willis.** 1859–1941. Amer. jurist; associate justice of the U.S. Supreme Court (1910–37).

Van Die•men's Land (văn dē′mənz, vän). See **Tasmania.**

van Dong•en (văn dŏng′ən, vän dông′ən), **Kees.** 1877–1968. Dutch artist best known for his fauvist paintings.

Van Dor•en (văn dôr′ən, dōr′-), **Carl Clinton.** 1885–1950. Amer. literary critic, editor, and biographer. His brother **Mark** (1894–1972) is best known for his poetry.

Van•dyke (văn-dīk′) *n.* **1.** A Vandyke beard. **2.** A Vandyke collar. **3.a.** A V-shaped point that is part of a decorative border or edging. **b.** A border made up of such points.

Vandyke or **Van Dyck** (văn dīk′), Sir **Anthony.** 1599–1641. Flemish painter known for his idealized portraits.

Vandyke beard *n.* A short pointed beard.

Vandyke brown *n. Color.* A moderate to grayish brown. — **Van•dyke′-brown′** (văn-dīk′broun′) *adj.*

Vandyke collar *n.* A large collar of linen or lace having a deeply indented or scalloped edge. [After Sir Anthony VANDYKE.]

vane (vān) *n.* **1.** A weathervane. **2.** Any of several usu. relatively thin, rigid, flat, or sometimes curved surfaces radially mounted along an axis, as a sail on a windmill, that is turned by or used to turn a fluid. **3.** The flattened weblike part of a feather, consisting of a series of barbs on either side of the shaft. **4.a.** The movable target on a leveling rod. **b.** A sight on a quadrant or compass. **5.** One of the metal guidance or stabilizing fins attached to the tail of a bomb or other missile. [ME, var. of obsolete *fane* < OE *fana,* flag. See **pan-*.**]

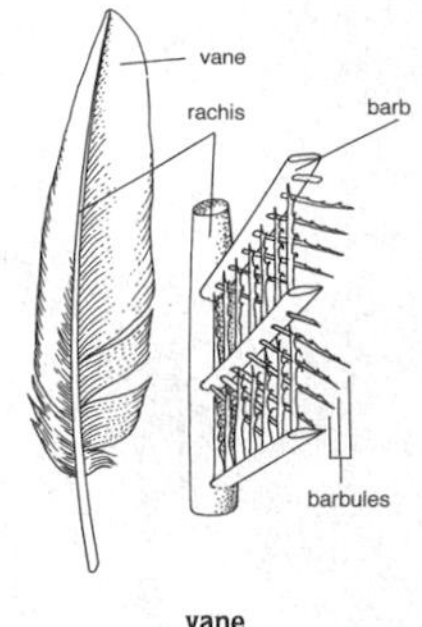

vane

Vane (vān), Sir **Henry** or **Harry.** 1613–62. English politician and leading Parliamentarian during the English Civil War.

Vä•nern (vā′nərn, vĕ′-). A lake of SW Sweden; navigable for small oceangoing ships via the Göta Canal.

van Eyck (văn īk′), **Jan.** 1390?–1441. Flemish painter whose works include the Altarpiece of the Lamb (1432), begun by his brother **Hubert** (1366?–1426).

vang (văng) *n. Naut.* **1.** A tackle or an adjuster that prevents a boom from lifting when sailing downwind. **2.** A guy running from the peak of a gaff or derrick to the deck. [Du., a catch < *vangen,* to catch. See **pag-*.**]

van Gogh (văn gō′, gôKH′, vän KHôKH′), **Vincent.** 1853–90. Dutch postimpressionist painter whose works include numerous self-portraits and a series of sunflower paintings (1888).

van•guard (văn′gärd) *n.* **1.** The foremost position in an army or a fleet advancing into battle. **2.a.** The foremost or leading position in a trend or movement. **b.** Those occupying a foremost position. [ME *vandgard* < *avaunt garde* < OFr. : *avaunt,* before (< Lat. *abante;* see ADVANCE) + *garde,* guard (< *garder,* to guard; see GUARD).] — **van′guard•ism** *n.* — **van′guard•ist** *n.*

Va•nier (văn-yā′). A city of SE Ontario, Canada, a suburb of Ottawa on the Ottawa R. Pop. 18,792.

ă pat	oi boy
ā pay	ou out
âr care	o͝o took
ä father	o͞o boot
ĕ pet	ŭ cut
ē be	ûr urge
ĭ pit	th thin
ī pie	*th* this
îr pier	hw which
ŏ pot	zh vision
ō toe	ə about, item
ô paw	

Stress marks:
′ (primary);
′ (secondary), as in
dictionary (dĭk′shə-nĕr′ē)

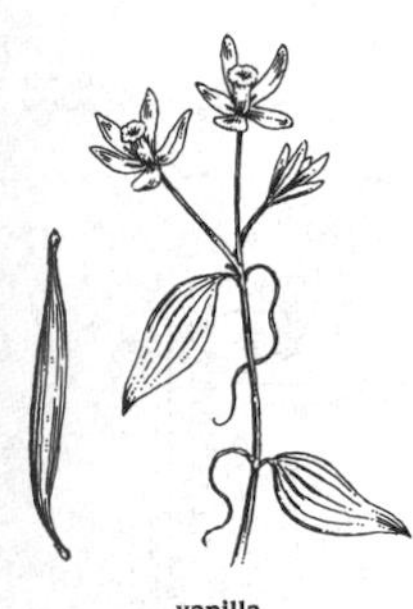
vanilla

va•nil•la (və-nĭl′ə) *n.* **1.** Any of various tropical American vines of the genus *Vanilla* in the orchid family, esp. *V. planifolia,* cultivated for their long narrow seedpods from which a flavoring agent is obtained. **2.** This seedpod. **3.** A flavoring extract prepared from the cured seedpods of this plant or produced synthetically. —*adj.* **1.** Flavored with vanilla. **2.** Relatively unoriginal, unexciting, or uninspiring. [Obsolete Sp. *vainilla,* dim. of *vaina,* sheath < Lat. *vāgīna.*]

vanilla bean *n.* See **vanilla** 2.

vanilla plant *n.* A fragrant perennial herb *(Carphephorus odoratissimus)* of the southeast United States having numerous lavender to purple flower heads.

va•nil•lic (və-nĭl′ĭk) *adj.* Of, relating to, or derived from vanilla or vanillin.

va•nil•lin (və-nĭl′ĭn, văn′ə-lĭn) *n.* A white or yellowish crystalline compound, $C_8H_8O_3$, found in vanilla beans and certain balsams and resins and used in perfumes, flavorings, and pharmaceuticals.

Va•nir (vä′nîr′) *pl.n. Myth.* An early race of Norse gods who dwelt with the Aesir in Asgard. [ON. See **wen-**[1]*.]

van•ish (văn′ĭsh) *intr.v.* **-ished, -ish•ing, -ish•es. 1.a.** To pass out of sight, esp. quickly; disappear. See Syns at **disappear. b.** To pass out of existence. **2.** *Math.* To become zero. Used of a function or variable. [ME *vanisshen,* alteration of OFr. *esvanir, esvaniss-* < VLat. **exvanīre,* alteration of Lat. *ēvānēscere* : *ē-, ex-,* ex- + *vānēscere,* to vanish (< *vānus,* empty; see **eu-**[2]*).] —**van′ish•er** *n.* —**van′ish•ment** *n.*

van•ish•ing point (văn′ĭ-shĭng) *n.* **1.** A point at which parallel lines drawn in perspective converge or seem to converge. **2.** A point at which a thing disappears or ceases to exist.

van•i•ty (văn′ĭ-tē) *n., pl.* **-ties. 1.** The quality or condition of being vain. **2.** Excessive pride in one's appearance or accomplishments; conceit. **3.** Lack of usefulness, worth, or effect; worthlessness. **4.a.** Something that is vain, futile, or worthless. **b.** Something about which one is vain or conceited. **5.** A vanity case. **6.** See **dressing table. 7.** A bathroom cabinet with storage space that encloses a basin and its water lines and drain. [ME *vanite* < OFr. < Lat. *vānitās* < *vānus,* empty. See **eu-**[2]*.]

vanity case *n.* **1.** A small handbag or case used by women for carrying cosmetics or toiletries. **2.** A woman's compact.

Van•i•ty Fair also **van•i•ty fair** (văn′ĭ-tē) *n.* A place or scene of ostentation or empty, idle amusement and frivolity. [From *Vanity Fair,* the fair in *Pilgrim's Progress* by John Bunyan.]

vanity plate *n.* A license plate for a motor vehicle bearing a combination of letters or numbers selected by the purchaser.

vanity press *n.* A publisher that publishes a book at the expense of the author.

van•load (văn′lōd′) *n.* The quantity, as of passengers or goods, that a van can carry.

van•quish (văng′kwĭsh, văn′-) *tr.v.* **-quished, -quish•ing, -quish•es. 1.a.** To defeat or conquer in battle; subjugate. **b.** To defeat in a contest, conflict, or competition. **2.** To overcome or subdue (an emotion, for example); suppress. See Syns at **defeat.** [ME *vaynquisshen* < OFr. *vainquir, vainquiss-* < Lat. *vincere.* See **weik-**[3]*.] —**van′quish•a•ble** *adj.* —**van′quish•er** *n.* —**van′quish•ment** *n.*

Van Rens•se•laer (văn rĕn′sə-lîr′, rĕn′sə-lər, vän rĕn′sə-lär′), **Killian** or **Kiliaen.** 1595–1644. Dutch merchant who established Rensselaerswyck (1635), the only successful privately held colony in America, in present-day upstate NY.

Van Rensselaer, Stephen. 1764–1839. Amer. army officer and politician who was an early advocate of the Erie Canal.

van•tage (văn′tĭj) *n.* **1.a.** An advantage in a competition or conflict; superiority. **b.** A position, a condition, or an opportunity that is likely to provide superiority or an advantage. **2.** A position that affords a broad overall view or perspective, as of a place. **3.** *Sports.* An advantage. [ME < AN, short for OFr. *avantage,* advantage. See ADVANTAGE.]

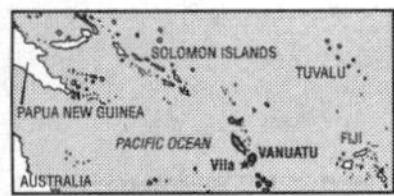

Vanuatu

Va•nu•a Le•vu (və-no͞o′ə lĕv′o͞o). A volcanic island of Fiji in the S Pacific NE of Viti Levu.

Va•nu•a•tu (vä′no͞o-ä′to͞o). Formerly **New Heb•ri•des** (no͞o hĕb′rĭ-dēz′, nyo͞o). An island country of the S Pacific E of N Australia; under joint French and British control after 1906 and independent since 1980. Cap. Vila. Pop. 138,000. —**Va′nu•a′tu•an** *adj. & n.*

Van Vleck (văn vlĕk′), **John Hasbrouck.** 1899–1980. Amer. physicist who shared a 1977 Nobel Prize.

Van•zet•ti (văn-zĕt′ē, vän-dzĕt′tē), **Bartolomeo.** 1888–1927. Italian-born Amer. anarchist who with Nicola Sacco was convicted of murder and sentenced to death (1921). Despite the circumstantial nature of the evidence against them, the two were executed in 1927.

vap•id (văp′ĭd, vā′pĭd) *adj.* **1.** Lacking liveliness, animation, or interest; dull. **2.** Lacking taste, zest, or flavor; flat. [Lat. *vapidus.*] —**va•pid′i•ty, vap′id•ness** *n.* —**vap′id•ly** *adv.*

va•por (vā′pər) *n.* **1.** Barely visible or cloudy diffused matter, such as mist or smoke, suspended in the air. **2.a.** A gas that is below its critical temperature and can be liquefied by pressure. **b.** The gaseous state of a substance that is liquid or solid under ordinary conditions. **3.a.** The vaporized form of a substance for use in industrial, military, or medical processes. **b.** A mixture of a vapor and air, as the explosive gasoline-air mixture burned in an internal-combustion engine. **4.** *Archaic.* **a.** Something insubstantial, worthless, or fleeting. **b.** A fantastic or foolish idea. **5. vapors.** *Archaic.* **a.** Exhalations within a bodily organ, esp. the stomach, supposed to affect one's condition. **b.** A nervous disorder such as depression or hysteria. —*v.* **-pored, -por•ing, -pors.** —*tr.* To vaporize. —*intr.* **1.** To give off vapor. **2.** To evaporate. **3.** To engage in idle, boastful talk. [ME *vapour* < AN < Lat. *vapor, vapōr-.*] —**va′por•er** *n.*

va•por•es•cence (vā′pə-rĕs′əns) *n.* Formation of vapor.

va•por•if•ic (vā′pə-rĭf′ĭk) *adj.* **1.** Producing or turning to vapor. **2.** Having the nature of vapor; vaporous.

va•por•ing (vā′pər-ĭng) *n.* Boastful or bombastic talk or behavior. —**va′por•ing** *adj.* —**va′por•ing•ly** *adv.*

va•por•ish (vā′pər-ĭsh) *adj.* **1.** Suggestive of or resembling vapor. **2.** *Archaic.* Affected by the vapors; given to spells of hysteria or low spirits. —**va′por•ish•ness** *n.*

va•por•ize (vā′pə-rīz′) *tr. & intr.v.* **-ized, -iz•ing, -iz•es.** To convert or be converted into vapor. —**va′por•iz′a•ble** *adj.* —**va′por•i•za′tion** (-ĭ-zā′shən) *n.*

va•por•iz•er (vā′pə-rī′zər) *n.* One that vaporizes, esp. a device used to vaporize medicine for inhalation.

vapor lock *n.* A pocket of vaporized gasoline in the fuel line of an internal-combustion engine that obstructs the normal flow of fuel. —**va′por-lock′** (vā′pər-lŏk′) *v.*

va•por•ous (vā′pər-əs) *adj.* **1.** Of or resembling vapor. **2.a.** Producing vapors; volatile. **b.** Full of vapors. **3.** Insubstantial, vague, or ethereal. See Syns at **airy. 4.** Extravagantly fanciful; high-flown. —**va′por•os′i•ty** (vā′pə-rŏs′ĭ-tē), **va′por•ous•ness** (-pər-əs-nĭs) *n.* —**va′por•ous•ly** *adv.*

vapor pressure *n.* The pressure exerted by a vapor in equilibrium with its solid or liquid phase.

vapor trail *n.* See **contrail.**

va•por•y (vā′pə-rē) *adj.* Vaporous.

va•pour (vā′pər) *n. & v. Chiefly British.* Vapor.

va•que•ro (vä-kâr′ō) *n., pl.* **-ros.** *Chiefly Texas.* See **cowboy** 1. [Sp. < *vaca,* cow < Lat. *vacca.*]

Regional Note: Used chiefly in southwest and central Texas to mean a ranch hand or cowboy, the word *vaquero* is a direct loan from Spanish. In California, however, the same word was Anglicized to *buckaroo.* Craig M. Carver, author of *American Regional Dialects,* points out that the two words reflect cultural differences between cattlemen in Texas and California. The Texas vaquero was typically a bachelor who hired on with different outfits, while the California buckaroo usually married and stayed on the same ranch where he was born or had grown up.

var. *abbr.* **1.** Variable. **2.** Variant. **3.** Variation. **4.** Variety. **5.** Various.

va•ra (vär′ə) *n.* **1.** A Spanish, Portuguese, and Latin-American unit of linear measure varying from about 81 to 109 centimeters (32 to 43 inches). **2.** A square vara. [Sp. and Port., rod, both < Lat. *vāra,* forked pole < *vārus,* bent.]

va•rac•tor (və-răk′tər, vă-) *n.* A semiconductor device in which the capacitance varies with the applied voltage. [VAR(YING) + (RE)ACT(ANCE) + -OR[1].]

Va•ra•na•si (və-rä′nə-sē) also **Be•na•res** (bə-när′əs, -ēz) or **Ba•na•ras** (bə-när′əs). A city of NE-central India on the Ganges R. SE of Lucknow. Pop. 708,647.

Var•dar (vär′där′). A river rising in NW Macedonia and flowing c. 386 km (240 mi) to an arm of the Aegean Sea.

Va•re•se (və-rā′sē, vä-rĕ′zĕ). A city of N Italy NW of Milan. Pop. 90,285.

Va•rèse (və-rĕz′, vä-rĕz′), **Edgard.** 1883–1965. French-born Amer. composer of arrhythmic and atonal works.

Var•gas (vär′gəs), **Getulio Dornelles.** 1883–1954. Brazilian politician who led a successful revolution (1930) and served as president (1930–45 and 1951–54).

Var•gas Llo•sa (vär′gəs yō′sə, bär′gäs yô′sä), **Mario.** b. 1936. Peruvian writer known for his stylistically innovative and complex novels, such as *The Green House* (1966).

vari– *pref.* Var. of **vario–.**

var•i•a (vâr′ē-ə, văr′-) *n.* A miscellany, esp. of literary works. [Lat. < neut. pl. of *varius,* various.]

var•i•a•bil•i•ty (vâr′ē-ə-bĭl′ĭ-tē, văr′-) *n., pl.* **-ties.** The quality, state, or degree of being variable or changeable.

var•i•a•ble (vâr′ē-ə-bəl, văr′-) *adj.* **1.a.** Likely to change or vary; subject to variation. **b.** Inconstant; fickle. **2.** *Biol.* Tending to deviate, as from a normal or recognized type; aberrant. **3.** *Math.* Having no fixed quantitative value. —*n.* **1.** Something that varies or is prone to variation. **2.** *Astron.* A variable star. **3.** *Math.* **a.** A quantity capable of assuming any of a set of values. **b.** A symbol representing such a quantity. —**var′i•a•ble•ness** *n.* —**var′i•a•bly** *adv.*

var•i•a•ble-rate mortgage (vâr′ē-ə-bəl-rāt′, văr′-) *n.* A mortgage that is renegotiable at periodic intervals, with a variable interest rate that is indexed to market rates.

variable star *n.* A star whose brightness varies because of internal changes or periodic eclipsing by a mutually revolving star.

var•i•ance (vâr′ē-əns, văr′-) *n.* **1.a.** The act of varying. **b.** The state or quality of being variant or variable. **c.** A difference between what is expected and what actually occurs. **2.** The state or fact of differing or of being in conflict. **3.** *Law.* **a.** A discrepancy between two statements or documents in a proceeding. **b.** License to engage in an act contrary to a usual rule: *a zoning variance.* **4.** *Statistics.* The square of the standard deviation. **5.** *Chem.* The number of thermodynamic variables, such as temperature and pressure, required to specify a state of equilibrium of a system. **—*idiom.* at variance.** In a state of discrepancy; differing.

var•i•ant (vâr′ē-ənt, văr′-) *adj.* **1.** Having or exhibiting variation; differing. **2.** Tending or liable to vary; variable. **3.** Deviating from a standard, usu. by only a slight difference. —*n.* Something that differs in form only slightly from something else, as a different spelling of the same word. [ME < OFr. < Lat. *variāns, variant-,* pr.part. of *variāre,* to vary. See VARY.]

var•i•ate (vâr′ē-ĭt, -āt′, văr′-) *n. Statistics.* A random variable with a numerical value defined for a given sample. [< Lat. *variātus,* p.part. of *variāre,* to vary. See VARY.]

var•i•a•tion (vâr′ē-ā′shən, văr′-) *n.* **1.a.** The act, process, or result of varying. **b.** The state or fact of being varied. See Syns at **difference. 2.** The extent or degree to which something varies. **3.** Magnetic declination. **4.** Something slightly different from another of the same type. **5.** *Biol.* **a.** Marked difference or deviation from the normal or recognized form, function, or structure. **b.** An organism or a plant exhibiting such difference or deviation. **6.** *Math.* A function that relates the values of one variable to those of other variables. **7.** *Mus.* **a.** A form that is an altered version of a given theme. **b.** One of a series of forms based on a single theme. **8.** A solo dance, esp. as part of a larger work. **—var′i•a′tion•al** *adj.*

var•i•cel•la (văr′ĭ-sĕl′ə) *n.* See **chickenpox.** [NLat., dim. of *variola,* variola. See VARIOLA.]

var•i•cel•late (văr′ĭ-sĕl′ĭt, -āt) *adj.* Having small varices, as certain gastropod shells.

var•i•cel•la-zos•ter virus (văr′ĭ-sĕl′ə-zŏs′tər) *n.* A herpesvirus that causes chickenpox and shingles.

var•i•ces (văr′ĭ-sēz′) *n.* Pl. of **varix.**

varico– or **varic–** *pref.* Varix; varicose vein: *varicosis.* [< Lat. *varix, varic-,* varix.]

var•i•co•cele (văr′ĭ-kō-sēl′) *n.* A varicose condition of veins of the spermatic cord or the ovaries, forming a soft tumor.

var•i•col•ored (vâr′ĭ-kŭl′ərd, văr′-) *adj.* Having a variety of colors; variegated.

var•i•cose (văr′ĭ-kōs′) *adj.* **1.** Abnormally swollen or knotted: *varicose veins.* **2.** Relating to or causing unusual swelling. **3.** Resembling a varix on the surface of a shell. [Lat. *varicōsus* < *varix, varic-,* swollen vein.]

var•i•co•sis (văr′ĭ-kō′sĭs) *n., pl.* **-ses** (-sēz). **1.** The condition of being varicose. **2.** Formation of varices.

var•i•cos•i•ty (văr′ĭ-kŏs′ĭ-tē) *n., pl.* **-ties. 1.** Varicosis. **2.** A varicose enlargement or swelling. **3.** The condition of having varicose veins.

var•i•cot•o•my (văr′ĭ-kŏt′ə-mē) *n., pl.* **-mies.** Surgical removal of varicose veins.

var•ied (vâr′ēd, văr′-) *adj.* **1.** Having or consisting of various kinds or forms; diverse. See Syns at **miscellaneous. 2.** Having been modified or altered. **3.** Of several colors; varicolored or variegated. **—var′ied•ly** *adv.*

var•i•e•gate (vâr′ē-ĭ-gāt′, vâr′ĭ-gāt′, văr′-) *tr.v.* **-gat•ed, -gat•ing, -gates. 1.** To change the appearance of, esp. by marking with different colors; streak. **2.** To give variety to; make varied. [< LLat. *variegātus,* p.part. of *variegāre* : Lat. *varius,* various + Lat. *agere,* to do, drive; see **ag-*.**] **—var′i•e•ga′tor** *n.*

var•i•e•gat•ed (vâr′ē-ĭ-gā′tĭd, vâr′ĭ-gā′-, văr′-) *adj.* **1.** Having streaks, marks, or patches of a different color or colors; varicolored. **2.** Distinguished or characterized by variety.

var•i•e•ga•tion (vâr′ē-ĭ-gā′shən, vâr′ĭ-gā′-, văr′-) *n.* The state of being variegated; diversified coloration.

va•ri•e•tal (və-rī′ĭ-tl) *adj.* Of, indicating, or characterizing a variety, esp. a biological variety. —*n.* A wine made principally from one variety of grape and carrying the name of that grape. [< VARIETY.] **—va•ri′e•tal•ly** *adv.*

va•ri•e•ty (və-rī′ĭ-tē) *n., pl.* **-ties. 1.** The quality or condition of being various or varied; diversity. **2.** A number or collection of varied things, esp. of a particular group; an assortment. **3.** A group distinguished from other groups by a specific characteristic or set of characteristics. **4.** *Biol.* **a.** A taxonomic subdivision of a species consisting of groups or individuals that differ from the remainder of the species in certain minor characteristics. **b.** An organism, esp. a plant, belonging to such a subdivision. **5.** A variety show. [Fr. *variété* < OFr. < Lat. *varietās, varietāt-* < *varius,* various.]

variety meat *n.* **1.** Meat taken from a part other than skeletal muscles. **2.** Meat, such as sausage, that has been processed.

variety show *n.* A theatrical entertainment consisting of successive unrelated acts, such as songs and comedy skits.

variety store *n.* A retail store that carries a large variety of usu. inexpensive merchandise.

var•i•form (vâr′ə-fôrm′, văr′-) *adj.* Having a variety of forms; diversiform.

vario– or **vari–** *pref.* Variety; difference; variation: *variometer.* [< Lat. *varius,* speckled.]

va•ri•o•la (və-rī′ə-lə, vâr′ē-ō′lə, văr′-) *n.* See **smallpox.** [NLat. < Med.Lat., pustule < Lat. *varius,* speckled.]

var•i•o•late (vâr′ē-ə-lāt′, văr′-) *adj.* Having pustules or marks like those of smallpox. —*tr.v.* **-lat•ed, -lat•ing, -lates.** To inoculate with the smallpox virus.

var•i•ole (vâr′ē-ōl′) *n.* A small pocklike mark, as on an insect.

var•i•o•lite (vâr′ē-ə-līt′, văr′-) *n.* A basic rock whose pockmarked appearance is caused by the presence of numerous white rounded embedded spherules. **—var′i•o•lit′ic** *adj.*

var•i•o•loid (vâr′ē-ə-loid′, văr′-, və-rī′ə-loid′) *n.* A mild form of smallpox occurring in people who have been previously vaccinated or who have had the disease.

va•ri•o•lous (və-rī′ə-ləs, vâr′ē-ō′-, văr′-) *adj.* Of, relating to, or affected with smallpox.

var•i•om•e•ter (vâr′ē-ŏm′ĭ-tər, văr′-) *n.* A variable inductor used to measure variations in terrestrial magnetism.

var•i•o•rum (vâr′ē-ôr′əm, -ōr′-, văr′-) *n.* **1.** An edition of the works of an author with notes by various scholars or editors. **2.** An edition containing various versions of a text. —*adj.* Of or relating to a variorum edition or text. [< Lat. *(ēditiō cum notīs) variōrum,* (edition with the notes) of various persons, genitive pl. of *varius,* various.]

var•i•ous (vâr′ē-əs, văr′-) *adj.* **1.a.** Of diverse kinds: *for various reasons.* **b.** Unlike; different. **2.** Being more than one; several. **3.** Many-sided; versatile. **4.** Having a variegated nature or appearance. **5.** Being an individual or separate member of a class or group: *The various reports all agreed.* **6.** *Archaic.* Changeable; variable. —*pron. (used with a pl. v.) Usage Problem.* Several different individuals. [< Lat. *varius.*] **—var′i•ous•ly** *adv.* **—var′i•ous•ness** *n.*

Usage Note: *Various* is sometimes used as a pronoun, as in *He spoke to various of the members.* This usage is supported by analogy to the uses of quantifiers such as *few, many,* and *several.* But it has occasioned widespread critical objections; in an earlier survey the usage was found unacceptable by 91 percent of the Usage Panel.

var•i•sized (vâr′ĭ-sīzd′, văr′-) *adj.* Of different sizes.

var•ix (văr′ĭks) *n., pl.* **-i•ces** (-ĭ-sēz′). **1.** An abnormally dilated or swollen vein, artery, or lymph vessel. **2.** One of the longitudinal ridges on a gastropod shell. [Lat., swollen vein.]

var•let (vär′lĭt) *n.* **1.** An attendant or a servant. **2.** A knight's page. **3.** A rascal; a knave. [ME < OFr., var. of *vaslet.* See VALET.]

var•let•ry (vär′lĭ-trē) *n., pl.* **-tries.** *Archaic.* **1.** A crowd of attendants or menials. **2.** A disorderly crowd; a rabble.

var•mint (vär′mĭnt) *n. Informal.* One that is considered undesirable, obnoxious, or troublesome. [Var. of VERMIN.]

Var•na (vär′nə). A city of E Bulgaria on the Black Sea NNE of Burgas; founded in the 6th cent. B.C. Pop. 297,000.

var•nish (vär′nĭsh) *n.* **1.a.** A paint containing a solvent and an oxidizing or evaporating binder, used to coat a surface with a hard, glossy transparent film. **b.** The smooth coating or gloss resulting from the application of this paint. **2.a.** Something suggestive of or resembling varnish. **b.** A deceptively attractive external appearance; an outward show. —*tr.v.* **-nished, -nish•ing, -nish•es. 1.** To cover with varnish. **2.** To give a smooth and glossy finish to. **3.** To give a deceptively attractive appearance to; gloss over. [ME *vernisshe* < OFr. *vernis* < Med.Lat. *veronix, vernix,* sandarac resin < LGk. *verenikē* < Gk. *Berenikē,* Berenice (Benghazi), an ancient city of Cyrenaica.] **—var′nish•er** *n.*

varnish tree *n.* Any of several trees having milky juice used to make varnish.

va•room (və-ro͞om′, -ro͝om′) *n. & v.* Var. of **vroom.**

var•si•ty (vär′sĭ-tē) *n., pl.* **-ties. 1.** The principal team representing a university, college, or school in competitions. **2.** *Chiefly British.* A university. [Alteration of UNIVERSITY.]

var•us (vâr′əs, văr′-) *n.* An abnormal position of a bone of the leg or foot. [< Lat. *vārus,* crooked.]

varve (värv) *n. Geol.* A layer or series of layers of sediment deposited in a body of still water in one year. [Swed. *varv,* layer < *varva,* to bend < ON *hverfa.*]

var•y (vâr′ē, văr′ē) *v.* **-ied** (-ēd), **-y•ing, -ies** (-ēz). —*tr.* **1.** To make or cause changes in the characteristics or attributes of; modify or alter. **2.** To give variety to; make diverse. **3.** To introduce under new aspects; express in a different manner: *vary a tempo.* —*intr.* **1.** To undergo or show change. **2.** To be different; deviate. **3.** To undergo successive or alternate changes in attributes or qualities. [ME *varien,* to undergo change < OFr. *varier* < Lat. *variāre* < *varius,* various.]

var•y•ing hare (vâr′ē-ĭng, văr′-) *n.* See **snowshoe rabbit.**

vas (văs) *n., pl.* **va•sa** (vā′zə). *Anat.* A vessel or duct. [Lat. *vās,* vessel.]

vas– *pref.* Var. of **vaso–.**

vasa ef•fer•en•ti•a (ĕf′ə-rĕn′shē-ə) *n.* Pl. of **vas efferens.**

va•sal (vā′səl, -zəl) *adj.* Of, relating to, or connected with a vessel or duct of the body.

Va•sa•ri (və-zär′ē, -sär′ē, vä-zä′rē), **Giorgio.** 1511–74. Italian painter and architect known for his history of Italian Renaissance art (1550).

ă pat	oi boy
ā pay	ou out
âr care	o͝o took
ä father	o͞o boot
ĕ pet	ŭ cut
ē be	ûr urge
ĭ pit	th thin
ī pie	*th* this
îr pier	hw which
ŏ pot	zh vision
ō toe	ə about, item
ô paw	

Stress marks:
′ (primary);
′ (secondary), as in dictionary (dĭk′shə-nĕr′ē)

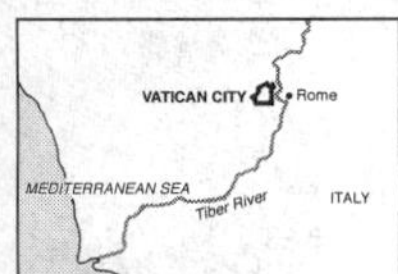

Vatican City

Sarah Vaughan
Photographed in 1960

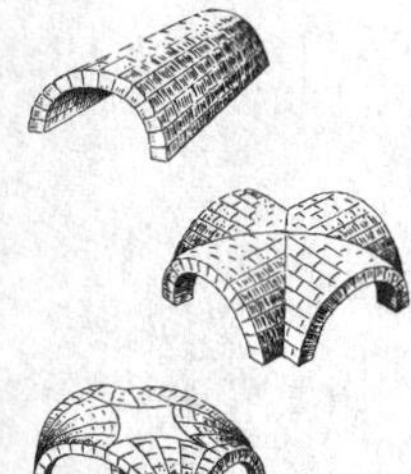
vault[1]
Top: Barrel vault
Center: Groin vault
Bottom: Fan vault

VDT

vas•cu•lar (văs′kyə-lər) *adj. Biol.* Of, characterized by, or containing vessels that carry or circulate fluids, such as blood or sap, through the body of an animal or a plant. [< Lat. *vāsculum*, dim. of *vās*, vessel.] **—vas′cu•lar′i•ty** (-lăr′ĭ-tē) *n.*

vascular bundle *n. Bot.* A strand of primary conductive plant tissue consisting essentially of xylem and phloem.

vas•cu•lar•i•za•tion (văs′kyə-lər-ĭ-zā′shən) *n.* **1.** The process of making or becoming vascular; the formation of vessels. **2.** *Medic.* An abnormal or pathological formation of blood vessels.

vascular plant *n.* Any of various plants, such as the ferns and seed-bearing plants, in which the phloem transports sugar and the xylem transports water and salts.

vascular tissue *n.* The supportive and conductive tissue in plants, consisting of xylem and phloem.

vas•cu•lum (văs′kyə-ləm) *n., pl.* **-la** (-lə). A small box or case used for carrying collected plant specimens. [Lat. *vāsculum*, small vessel. See VASCULAR.]

vas def•er•ens (văs′ dĕf′ər-ənz, -ə-rĕnz′) *n., pl.* **va•sa def•er•en•ti•a** (vā′zə dĕf′ə-rĕn′shē-ə). The main duct through which semen is carried from the epididymis to the ejaculatory duct. [NLat. *vās dēferēns* : *vās*, duct + Lat. *dēferēns*, carrying away.]

vase (vās, vāz, väz) *n.* An open container used for holding flowers or for ornamentation. [Fr. < Lat. *vās*, vessel.]

va•sec•to•my (və-sĕk′tə-mē, vā-zĕk′-) *n., pl.* **-mies.** Surgical removal of all or part of the vas deferens, usu. as a means of sterilization. **—va•sec′to•mize′** *v.*

vas ef•fer•ens (văs′ ĕf′ər-ənz, -ə-rĕnz′) *n., pl.* **va•sa ef•fer•en•ti•a** (vā′zə ĕf′ə-rĕn′shē-ə). Any of a number of small ducts that carry semen from the testis to the epididymis. [NLat. *vās efferēns* : *vās*, duct + Lat. *efferēns*, carrying out.]

Vas•e•line (văs′ə-lēn′, văs′ə-lēn′). A trademark used for a brand of petroleum jelly.

vaso– or **vas–** *pref.* **1.** Blood vessel: *vasoconstriction.* **2.** Vas deferens: *vasectomy.* [< Lat. *vās*, vessel.]

va•so•ac•tive (vā′zō-ăk′tĭv) *adj.* Causing constriction or dilation of blood vessels. **—va′so•ac•tiv′i•ty** *n.*

va•so•con•stric•tion (vā′zō-kən-strĭk′shən) *n.* Constriction of a blood vessel. **—vas′o•con•stric′tive** *adj.*

va•so•con•stric•tor (vā′zō-kən-strĭk′tər) *n.* Something, such as a nerve or drug, that causes vasoconstriction.

va•so•dil•a•tion (vā′zō-dī-lā′shən, -dĭ-) also **va•so•dil•a•ta•tion** (-dĭl′ə-tā′shən, -dī′lə-) *n.* Dilation of a blood vessel, as by the action of a nerve or drug.

va•so•di•la•tor (vā′zō-dī-lā′tər, -dĭ-, -dī′lā-) *n.* Something, such as a nerve or drug, that causes vasodilation.

va•so•mo•tor (vā′zō-mō′tər) *adj.* Relating to, causing, or regulating constriction or dilation of blood vessels.

va•so•pres•sin (vā′zō-prĕs′ĭn) *n.* A hormone secreted by the posterior lobe of the pituitary gland that constricts blood vessels, raises blood pressure, and reduces excretion of urine.

va•so•pres•sor (vā′zō-prĕs′ər) *adj.* Of or causing constriction of blood vessels. *—n.* A vasopressor agent.

va•so•spasm (vā′zō-spăz′əm) *n.* A sudden constriction of a blood vessel. **—va′so•spas′tic** (-spăs′tĭk) *adj.*

va•so•va•gal (vā′zō-vā′gəl) *adj.* Relating to or involving blood vessels and the vagus nerve.

vas•sal (văs′əl) *n.* **1.** A person who held land from a feudal lord and received protection in return for homage and allegiance. **2.** A bondman; a slave. **3.** A subordinate or dependent. [ME < OFr. < VLat. **vassallus* < **vassus*, of Celt. orig. See **upo*.**]

vas•sal•age (văs′ə-lĭj) *n.* **1.** The condition of being a vassal. **2.** The service, homage, and fealty required of a vassal. **3.** A position of subordination or subjection; servitude.

vast (văst) *adj.* **vast•er, vast•est. 1.** Very great in size, number, amount, or quantity. **2.** Very great in area or extent. **3.** Very great in degree or intensity. *—n. Archaic.* An immense space. [Lat. *vastus*.] **—vast′ly** *adv.* **—vast′ness** *n.*

Väs•ter•ås (vĕs′tə-rōs′). A city of E Sweden WNW of Stockholm. Pop. 117,658.

vas•ti•tude (văs′tĭ-to͞od′, -tyo͞od′) also **vas•ti•ty** (-tē) *n.* Immensity. [Lat. *vastitūdō* < *vastus*, vast.]

vast•y (văs′tē) *adj.* **-i•er, -i•est.** *Archaic.* Vast.

vat (văt) *n.* A large vessel, such as a tub or barrel, used to hold or store liquids. *—tr.v.* **vat•ted, vat•ting, vats.** To put into or treat in a vat. [ME, var. of *fat* < OE *fæt*.]

VAT or **V.A.T.** *abbr.* Value-added tax.

vat dye *n.* A dye, such as indigo, that produces a fast color by impregnating fiber with a reduced soluble form that is then oxidized to an insoluble form. **—vat′-dyed′** (văt′dīd′) *adj.*

vat•ic (văt′ĭk) also **vat•i•cal** (-ĭ-kəl) *adj.* Of or characteristic of a prophet; oracular. [< Lat. *vātēs*, seer. See **wet-¹*.**]

Vat•i•can (văt′ĭ-kən) *n.* **1.** The official residence of the pope in Vatican City. **2.** The papal government; the papacy. [Lat. *Vaticānus (mōns)*, the Vatican (Hill).]

Vatican City. An independent papal state on the Tiber R. within Rome, Italy; created by the Lateran Treaty signed by Pope Pius XI and Victor Emmanuel III of Italy in 1929. Pop. 736.

Vat•i•can•ism (văt′ĭ-kə-nĭz′əm) *n.* The policies and authority of the papacy.

va•tic•i•nal (vă-tĭs′ə-nəl, və-) *adj.* Prophetic.

va•tic•i•nate (vă-tĭs′ə-nāt′, və-) *v.* **-nat•ed, -nat•ing, -nates.** *—tr.* To prophesy; foretell. *—intr.* To be a prophet. [Lat. *vāticinārī, vāticināt-* < *vātēs*, seer. See VATIC.] **—va•tic′i•na′tor** *n.*

va•tic•i•na•tion (vă-tĭs′ə-nā′shən, və-) *n.* **1.** The act of prophesying. **2.** A prediction; a prophecy.

Vät•tern (vĕt′ərn). A lake of S-central Sweden SE of Lake Vänern; connected with the Baltic Sea by the Göta Canal.

va•tu (vä′to͞o) *n.* See table at **currency.** [Native word in Vanuatu.]

vau (väv, vôv) *n.* Var. of **vav.**

vaude•ville (vôd′vĭl′, vōd′-, vô′də-) *n.* **1.a.** Stage entertainment offering a variety of short acts such as song-and-dance routines and juggling performances. **b.** A theatrical performance of this kind; a variety show. **2.** A light comic play that often includes songs and pantomime. **3.** *Mus.* A popular, often satirical song. [Fr., alteration of OFr. *vaudevire*, occasional or topical light popular song, poss. short for *chanson du Vau de Vire*, song of Vau de Vire, a valley of NW France, or perh. : dial. *vauder*, to go + *virer*, to turn; see VEER¹.]

vaude•vil•lian (vôd-vĭl′yən, vōd-, vô′də-) *n.* One, esp. a performer, who works in vaudeville. **—vaude•vil′lian** *adj.*

Vau•dois (vō-dwä′) *pl.n.* See **Waldenses.** [Fr. < OFr. *vaudeis* < Med.Lat. *Waldēnsēs*. See WALDENSES.]

Vaughan (vôn, văn). A town of SE Ontario, Canada, a suburb of Toronto. Pop. 29,674.

Vaughan (vôn), **Henry.** "the Silurist." 1622–95. Welsh poet whose works include *Silex Scintillans* (1650–55).

Vaughan, Sarah. 1924–90. Amer. jazz singer known for her complex bebop phrasing and her scat-singing virtuosity.

Vaughan Wil•liams (wĭl′yəmz), **Ralph.** 1872–1958. British composer whose works include the ballet *Job* (1930).

vault¹ (vôlt) *n.* **1.a.** An arched structure, usu. of stone, brick, or concrete, forming the supporting structure of a ceiling or roof. **b.** An arched overhead covering, such as the sky, that resembles a vault in form. **2.** A room or space, such as a cellar or storeroom, with arched walls and ceiling, esp. when underground. **3.** A room or compartment, often built of steel, for the safekeeping of valuables. **4.** A burial chamber, esp. when underground. **5.** *Anat.* An arched part of the body, esp. the top part of the skull. *—tr.v.* **vault•ed, vault•ing, vaults. 1.** To construct or supply with an arched ceiling; cover with a vault. **2.** To build or make in the shape of a vault; arch. [ME *vaute* < OFr. < VLat. **volvita, *volta* < fem. of **volvitus*, arched, alteration of Lat. *volūtus*, p.part. of *volvere*, to roll. See **wel-²*.**]

vault² (vôlt) *v.* **vault•ed, vault•ing, vaults.** *—tr.* To vault over. *—intr.* **1.** To jump or leap, esp. with the use of the hands or a pole. **2.** To do something as if by leaping suddenly or vigorously. *—n.* The act of vaulting; a jump. [Obsolete Fr. *volter* < OFr. < OItal. *voltare* < VLat. **volvitāre*, freq. of Lat. *volvere*, to turn, roll. See **wel-²*.**] **—vault′er** *n.*

vault•ing¹ (vôl′tĭng) *n.* Something vaulted or arched.

vault•ing² (vôl′tĭng) *adj.* **1.** Leaping upward or over. **2.** Reaching too far; exaggerated: *his vaulting ambition.* **3.** Employed in leaping over: *a vaulting pole.*

vaunt (vônt, vŏnt) *v.* **vaunt•ed, vaunt•ing, vaunts.** *—tr.* To speak boastfully of; brag about. *—intr.* To speak boastfully; brag. *—n.* **1.** A boastful remark. **2.** Speech of extravagant self-praise. [ME *vaunten* < OFr. *vanter* < LLat. *vānitāre*, to talk frivolously, freq. of Lat. *vānāre* < *vānus*, empty. See **eu-²*.**] **—vaunt′er** *n.* **—vaunt′ing•ly** *adv.*

vaunt-cour•i•er (vônt′ko͝or′ē-ər, -kûr′-, kŭr′-, vŏnt′-) *n. Archaic.* A person, such as a herald, sent in advance. [Short for obsolete Fr. *avaunt-courier* : OFr. *avaunt*, in front; see VANGUARD + OFr. *courrier*, messenger; see COURIER.]

Vau•pés (vou-pās′, -pĕs′). See **Uaupés.**

vav also **vau** or **waw** (väv, vôv) *n.* The sixth letter of the Hebrew alphabet. [Heb. *wāw*, hook.]

vav•a•sor also **vav•a•sour** (văv′ə-sôr′, -sōr′, -so͝or′) *n.* A feudal tenant ranking directly below a baron or peer. [ME *vavasour* < OFr. < Med.Lat. *vavassor*, poss. contraction of *vassus vassōrum*, vassal of vassals : *vassus*, vassal (< VLat. **vassus*; see VASSAL) + *vassōrum*, genitive pl. of *vassus*, vassal.]

vb. *abbr.* Verb; verbal.

VC also **V.C.** *abbr.* Vietcong.

V.C. *abbr.* **1.** Vice-chairman; vice-chairperson. **2.** Vice chancellor. **3.** Vice consul. **4.** Victoria Cross.

VCR (vē′sē-är′) *n., pl.* **VCR's.** An electronic device for recording and playing back video images and sound on a videocassette. [*V(ideo)c(assette) r(ecorder).*]

VD also **V.D.** *abbr.* Venereal disease.

v.d. *abbr.* **1.** Vapor density. **2.** Various dates.

V-day (vē′dā′) *n.* A day of victory, as at war's end.

VDT (vē′dē-tē′) *n., pl.* **VDT's.** *Comp. Sci.* An output device using the screen of a cathode-ray tube to display data and graphic images. [*V(ideo) d(isplay) t(erminal).*]

've. Have: *I've been invited.*

veal (vēl) *n.* **1.** The meat of a calf. **2.** Also **veal•er** (vē′lər). A calf raised to be slaughtered for food. [ME *veel* < OFr. < Lat. *vitellus*, dim. of *vitulus*, calf. See **wet-²*.**]

Veb•len (vĕb′lən), **Thorstein Bunde.** 1857–1929. Amer. economist who described a fundamental conflict between the provision of goods and the making of money.

vec•tor (vĕk′tər) *n.* **1.** *Math.* **a.** A quantity, such as velocity, completely specified by a magnitude and a direction. **b.** A one-dimensional array. **c.** An element of a vector space. **2.** *Pathol.* An organism, such as a tick, that carries disease-causing microorganisms from one host to another. **3.** *Genet.* A bacteriophage or another agent that transfers genetic material from one location to another. **4.** A force or an influence. —*tr.v.* **-tored, -tor•ing, -tors.** To guide (a pilot or an aircraft, for example) by means of radio communication according to vectors. [Lat., carrier < *vehere, vect-*, to carry. See **wegh-*.**] —**vec•to′ri•al** (vĕk-tôr′ē-əl, -tōr′-) *adj.*

vector product *n. Math.* A vector ***C*** that has magnitude equal to the product of the magnitudes of two vectors ***A*** and ***B*** and the sine of the angle between ***A*** and ***B*** and is directed perpendicular to the plane of ***A*** and ***B*** so that a right-handed rotation about ***C*** carries ***A*** into ***B*** through an angle not greater than 180°.

vector space *n. Math.* A set of generalized vectors and a field of scalars, having the same rules for vector addition and scalar multiplication as physical vectors and scalars.

Ve•da (vā′də, vē′-) *n. Hinduism.* Any of the oldest Hindu sacred texts, composed in Sanskrit and gathered into four collections. [Skt. *vedaḥ*, sacred lore, knowledge, Veda. See **weid-*.**]

Ve•dan•ta (vĭ-dän′tə, -dăn′-) *n. Hinduism.* The system of philosophy that further develops the implications in the Upanishads that all reality is a single principle, Brahman, and teaches that the believer's goal is to transcend the limitations of self-identity and realize one's unity with Brahman. [Skt. *vedāntaḥ*, complete knowledge of the Veda : *vedaḥ*, Veda; see VEDA + *antaḥ*, end; see **ant-*.**] —**Ve•dan′tic** *adj.* —**Ve•dan′tism** *n.* —**Ve•dan′tist** *n.*

V-E Day (vē′ē′) *n.* May 8, 1945, on which the Allies announced the surrender of German forces in Europe. [*V(ictory) in) E(urope) Day.*]

Ved•da also **Ved•dah** (vĕd′ə) *n., pl.* **Vedda** or **-das** also **Veddah** or **-dahs.** A member of the earliest people of Sri Lanka, originally forest-dwelling hunters but now almost completely assimilated into the Singhalese population. [Singhalese, hunter.]

ve•dette also **vi•dette** (vĭ-dĕt′) *n.* A mounted sentinel stationed in advance of an outpost. [Fr. < Ital. *vedetta*, alteration of *veletta*, prob. < Sp. *vela*, watch < *velar*, to watch < Lat. *vigilāre*, to watch by night < *vigil*, awake. See **weg-*.**]

Ve•dic (vā′dĭk, vē′-) *adj.* Of or relating to the Veda or Vedas, the variety of Sanskrit in which they are written, or the Hindu culture that produced them. —*n.* This early Sanskrit.

vee (vē) *n.* The letter *v.*

vee-jay (vē′jā′) *n.* A video jockey. [V(IDEO) + (D)EEJAY.]

vee•na (vē′nə) *n. Mus.* Var. of **vina.**

veep (vēp) *n. Slang.* A vice president. [Pronunciation of *V.P.*]

veer¹ (vîr) *v.* **veered, veer•ing, veers.** —*intr.* **1.** To turn aside from a course, direction, or purpose; swerve. See Syns at **swerve. 2.** To shift clockwise in direction, as from north to northeast. Used of the wind. **3.** *Naut.* To veer a ship. —*tr.* **1.** To alter the direction of; turn. **2.** *Naut.* To change the course of (a ship) upwind by turning the stern through the wind. —*n.* A change in direction; a swerve. [Fr. *virer* < OFr.]

veer² (vîr) *tr.v.* **veered, veer•ing, veers.** *Naut.* To let out or release (a line or an anchor chain). [ME *veren* < MDu. *vieren.* See **per¹*.**]

vee•ry (vîr′ē) *n., pl.* **-ries.** A New World thrush *(Hylocichla fuscescens)* having a reddish-brown head, back, and tail and an indistinctly spotted breast. [Poss. imit. of its song.]

veg. *abbr.* Vegetable.

Ve•ga (vē′gə, vā′-) *n.* The brightest star in Lyra. [Med.Lat. < Ar. *(al nasr) al wāqi'*, the falling (vulture), Vega.]

Vega (vā′gə, bĕ′gä), **Lope de.** 1562–1635. Spanish playwright whose works include *Fuenteovejuna* (c. 1619).

veg•an (vē′gən, vĕj′ən) *n.* A vegetarian whose diet consists of plant products only. [Short for VEGETARIAN.] —**veg′an•ism** *n.*

veg•e•ta•ble (vĕj′tə-bəl, vĕj′ĭ-tə-) *n.* **1.a.** A plant cultivated for an edible part, such as the leaf of spinach. **b.** This edible part. **c.** A member of the vegetable kingdom; a plant. **2.** A person regarded as dull, passive, or unresponsive. —*adj.* **1.** Of or derived from plants or a plant. **2.** Suggestive of or resembling a plant. **3.** Growing or multiplying like plants. [< ME, living and growing as plants do < OFr. < Med.Lat. *vegetābilis* < LLat., enlivening < Lat. *vegetāre*, to enliven < *vegetus*, lively < *vegēre*, to enliven. See **weg-*.**]

Word History: When the speaker in Andrew Marvell's "To his Coy Mistress" tells his mistress that "Had we but world enough, and time . . . /My vegetable love should grow/ Vaster than empires and more slow," he uses *vegetable* figuratively to mean "having the property of life and growth, as does a plant." This use is based on the ancient religious and philosophical notion of the tripartite soul as interpreted by the Scholastics: the *vegetative* soul common to plants, animals, and humans; the *sensitive* soul common to animals and humans; and the *rational* soul, found only in humans. "Vegetable love" in Marvell's poem is thus a love that grows, takes nourishment, and reproduces, although it grows slowly. Marvell's use illustrates the original sense of *vegetable,* first recorded in the 15th century. In a work published in 1582 we first find the adjective use "having to do with plants." In a work of the same date appears the noun, meaning "a plant." But not until the 18th century could we say "Eat your vegetables."

vegetable ivory *n.* A hard ivorylike material obtained from the ivory nut, used for small objects such as buttons.

vegetable marrow *n. Chiefly British.* Marrow squash.

vegetable oil *n.* Any of various oils obtained from plants and used in food products and industrially.

vegetable oyster *n.* See **salsify.**

vegetable silk *n.* Any of several silky fibers from the seedpods of certain plants, such as the kapok.

vegetable sponge *n.* See **loofa** 2.

vegetable tallow *n.* **1.** Any of various waxy fats obtained from certain plants, such as the bayberry, and used in making soap and candles. **2.** See **Chinese tallow tree.**

vegetable wax *n.* A waxy substance of plant origin.

veg•e•tal (vĕj′ĭ-tl) *adj.* **1.** Of, relating to, or characteristic of plants. **2.** Relating to growth rather than to sexual reproduction; vegetative. [ME < Med.Lat. *vegetālis* < Lat. *vegetāre*, to enliven. See VEGETABLE.]

vegetal pole *n. Embryol.* The portion of an egg opposite the animal pole that contains most of the yolk.

veg•e•tar•i•an (vĕj′ĭ-târ′ē-ən) *n.* **1.** One who practices vegetarianism. **2.** A herbivore. —*adj.* **1.** Of or relating to vegetarianism or vegetarians. **2.** Consisting primarily or wholly of vegetables and vegetable products. [VEGET(ABLE) + –ARIAN.]

veg•e•tar•i•an•ism (vĕj′ĭ-târ′ē-ə-nĭz′əm) *n.* The practice of subsisting on a diet composed of vegetables, grains, fruits, nuts, and seeds, with or without eggs and dairy products.

veg•e•tate (vĕj′ĭ-tāt′) *intr.v.* **-tat•ed, -tat•ing, -tates. 1.** To grow or sprout as a plant does. **2.** *Pathol.* To grow in size or spread abnormally. **3.** To exist in a state of inactivity or insensibility. [Lat. *vegetāre, vegetāt-*, to enliven. See VEGETABLE.]

veg•e•ta•tion (vĕj′ĭ-tā′shən) *n.* **1.** The act or process of vegetating. **2.** The plants of an area or a region; plant life: *lush vegetation.* **3.** *Pathol.* An abnormal growth on the body. —**veg′e•ta′tion•al** *adj.*

veg•e•ta•tive (vĕj′ĭ-tā′tĭv) also **veg•e•tive** (-ĭ-tĭv) *adj.* **1.** Of or characteristic of plants or their growth. **2.** *Biol.* **a.** Of or capable of growth. **b.** Of or functioning in processes such as growth or nutrition rather than sexual reproduction. **c.** Of or relating to asexual reproduction, such as fission.

veg•gie also **veg•ie** (vĕj′ē) *n. Informal.* A vegetable.

ve•he•ment (vē′ə-mənt) *adj.* **1.** Forceful or intense in expression, emotion, or conviction; fervid. **2.** Vigorous or energetic; strong: *a vehement storm.* [ME < OFr. < Lat. *vehemēns, vehement-*, perh. < *vehere*, to carry. See **wegh-*.**] —**ve′he•mence, ve′he•men•cy** *n.* —**ve′he•ment•ly** *adv.*

ve•hi•cle (vē′ĭ-kəl) *n.* **1.a.** A device or structure for transporting persons or things; a conveyance: *a space vehicle.* **b.** A self-propelled conveyance that runs on tires; a motor vehicle. **2.** A medium through which something is transmitted, expressed, or accomplished. **3.** The concrete or specific word or phrase that is applied to the tenor of a metaphor and gives the metaphor its figurative power, as *walking shadow* in *"Life's but a walking shadow"* (Shakespeare). **4.** A play, role, or piece of music used to display the special talents of one performer or company. **5.** A substance of no therapeutic value used to convey an active medicine. **6.** A substance in which paint pigments are mixed for application. [Lat. *vehiculum* < *vehere*, to carry. See **wegh-*.**]

ve•hic•u•lar (vē-hĭk′yə-lər) *adj.* **1.** Of, relating to, or intended for vehicles, esp. motor vehicles. **2.** Serving as a vehicle.

Ve•ii (vē′ī). An ancient city of Etruria N of modern-day Rome, Italy; conquered by Rome in 396 B.C.

veil (vāl) *n.* **1.** A cloth worn, usu. by women, over the head, shoulders, and often the face. **2.** A length of netting attached to a woman's hat or headdress, worn for decoration or to protect the head and face. **3.a.** The part of a nun's headdress that frames the face and falls over the shoulders. **b.** The life or vows of a nun. **4.a.** A piece of light fabric hung to serve as a curtain. **b.** Something that conceals, separates, or screens like a curtain: *a veil of secrecy.* **5.** *Biol.* A membranous covering or part; a velum. —*tr.v.* **veiled, veil•ing, veils. 1.** To cover with or as if with a veil. **2.** To conceal or disguise. [ME < ONFr. < Lat. *vēla*, pl. of *vēlum*, a covering.]

veiled (vāld) *adj.* **1.** Covered with a veil. **2.** Concealed or disguised as if with a veil.

veil•ing (vā′lĭng) *n.* **1.** A veil. **2.** Sheer material used for veils.

vein (vān) *n.* **1.a.** *Anat.* Any of a branching system of membranous tubes that carry blood to the heart. **b.** A blood vessel. **2.** *Bot.* One of the vascular bundles or ribs that form the branching framework of conducting and supporting tissues in a leaf. **3.** *Zool.* One of the horny ribs that stiffen and support the wing of an insect. **4.** *Geol.* A regularly shaped and lengthy occurrence of an ore; a lode. **5.** A long wavy strip of a different shade or color, as in marble. **6.** A fissure, crack, or

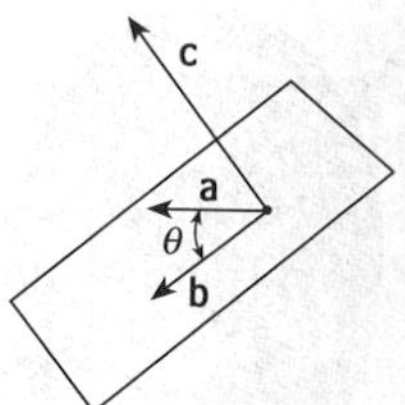

vector product
c = a × b

veil

ă pat	oi boy
ā pay	ou out
âr care	o͝o took
ä father	o͞o boot
ĕ pet	ŭ cut
ē be	ûr urge
ĭ pit	th thin
ī pie	*th* this
îr pier	hw which
ŏ pot	zh vision
ō toe	ə about, item
ô paw	

Stress marks:
′ (primary);
′ (secondary), as in
dictionary (dĭk′shə-nĕr′ē)

cleft. **7.** A pervading character or quality; a streak. **8.a.** A transient attitude or mood. **b.** A particular turn of mind: *in a serious vein.* —*tr.v.* **veined, vein•ing, veins. 1.** To supply or fill with veins. **2.** To mark or decorate with veins. [ME *veine* < OFr. < Lat. *vēna.*] —**vein′al** *adj.*

veined (vānd) *adj.* Having veins or showing veinlike markings.

vein•ing (vā′nĭng) *n.* Distribution or arrangement of veins or veinlike markings.

vein•let (vān′lĭt) *n.* A small or secondary vein, as on the wing of an insect.

vein•stone (vān′stōn′) *n.* Mineral matter in a vein exclusive of the ore; gangue.

vein•ule (vān′yo͞ol) *n.* A small vein.

vein•y (vā′nē) *adj.* **-i•er, -i•est.** Full of or exhibiting veins; veined.

vel. *abbr.* **1.** Vellum. **2.** Velocity.

ve•la (vē′lə) *n. Biol., Anat., & Zool.* Pl. of **velum.**

Ve•la (vē′lə, vā′-) *n.* A Southern constellation near Pyxis and Carina. [Lat. *vēla*, pl. of *vēlum*, a covering.]

ve•la•men (və-lā′mən) *n., pl.* **-lam•i•na** (-lăm′ə-nə). **1.** *Anat.* A membranous covering or partition; velum. **2.** *Bot.* The spongy multiple epidermis that covers the aerial roots of certain plants and is capable of absorbing atmospheric moisture. [Lat., covering < *vēlāre*, to cover < *vēlum*, a covering.] —**vel′a•men′tous** (vĕl′ə-mĕn′təs) *adj.*

ve•lar (vē′lər) *adj.* **1.a.** Of or relating to a velum. **b.** Of or using the soft palate. **2.** *Ling.* Articulated with the back of the tongue touching or near the velum, as (g) in *good.* —*n. Ling.* A velar sound. —**ve′lar•ize′** *v.* —**ve′lar•i•za′tion** *n.*

velocipede
1869 Pickering velocipede

ve•late (vē′lāt′, -lĭt) *adj. Biol.* Having or covered by a velum or veil.

Ve•láz•quez (və-läs′kĕ, bĕ-läth′kĕth), **Diego Rodríguez de Silva y.** 1599–1660. Spanish painter whose works include *The Surrender of Breda* (1635).

Vel•bert (fĕl′bərt). A city of W-central Germany in the Ruhr Valley NE of Düsseldorf. Pop. 89,261.

Vel•cro (vĕl′krō). A trademark used for a fastening tape consisting of a strip of nylon with a surface of minute hooks that fasten to a corresponding strip with a surface of uncut pile, used esp. on cloth products.

veldt also **veld** (vĕlt, fĕlt) *n.* Any of the open grazing areas of southern Africa. [Afr. *veld* < MDu., field. See **pelə-[2]*.**]

Ve•li•a (vē′lē-ə). See **Elea.**

ve•li•ger (vē′lə-jər, vĕl′ə-) *n.* A larval stage of a mollusk characterized by the presence of a velum. [NLat. *vēliger* : *vēlum*, velum; see VELUM + Lat. *gerere*, to bear.]

vel•le•i•ty (vĕ-lē′ĭ-tē, və-) *n., pl.* **-ties. 1.** Volition at its lowest level. **2.** A mere wish or inclination. [NLat. *velleitās* < Lat. *velle*, to wish. See **wel-[1]*.**]

vel•lum (vĕl′əm) *n.* **1.a.** A fine parchment made from calfskin, lambskin, or kidskin and used for the pages and binding of books. **b.** A work written or printed on this parchment. **2.** A heavy off-white fine-quality paper resembling this parchment. [ME *velim* < OFr. *velin* < *veel*, calf. See VEAL.]

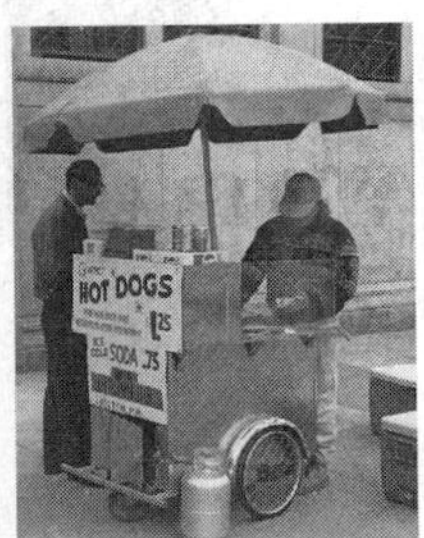

vender

ve•lo•ce (vā-lō′chā) *adv. Mus.* Rapidly. [Ital. < Lat. *vēlōx*, *vēlōc-*, rapid. See VELOCITY.]

ve•lo•cim•e•ter (vē′lō-sĭm′ĭ-tər, vĕl′ō-) *n.* A device for measuring the speed of sound in water. [VELOCI(TY) + -METER.]

ve•loc•i•pede (və-lŏs′ə-pēd′) *n.* **1.** A tricycle. **2.a.** Any of several early bicycles with pedals on the front wheel. **b.** An early bicycle propelled by the feet. [Fr. *vélocipède* : Lat. *vēlōx*, *vēlōc-*, fast; see VELOCITY + Lat. *pēs*, *ped-*, foot; see -PED.]

ve•loc•i•ty (və-lŏs′ĭ-tē) *n., pl.* **-ties. 1.** Rapidity or speed of motion; swiftness. **2.** *Phys.* A vector quantity whose magnitude is a body's speed and whose direction is the body's direction of motion. **3.** The rate of speed of action or occurrence. [ME *velocite* < OFr. < Lat. *vēlōcitās* < *vēlōx*, *vēlōc-*, fast. See **weg-*.**]

ve•lour or **ve•lours** (və-lo͝or′) *n., pl.* **-lours** (-lo͝orz′). **1.** A closely napped fabric resembling velvet. **2.** A felt resembling velvet, used in making hats. [Alteration of Fr. *velours*, velvet < OFr. *velour*, alteration of *velous* < OProv. *velos* < Lat. *villōsus*, hairy < *villus*, shaggy hair. See VELVET.]

ve•lou•té (və-lo͞o-tā′) *n.* A white sauce made of chicken, veal, or fish stock thickened with a roux of flour and butter. [Fr. < OFr. *vellute*, velvety < *velous*, velvet. See VELOUR.]

ve•lum (vē′ləm) *n., pl.* **-la** (-lə). **1.** *Biol.* A covering or partition of thin membranous tissue, such as the veil of a mushroom or a membrane of the brain. **2.** *Anat.* The soft palate. **3.** *Zool.* A ciliated swimming organ that develops in certain larval stages of most marine gastropod mollusks. [Lat., veil.]

ve•lure (vĕ-lo͝or′, vĕl′yər) *n. Obsolete.* Velvet or a velvetlike fabric. [Alteration of Fr. *velours.* See VELOUR.]

ve•lu•ti•nous (və-lo͞ot′n-əs) *adj.* Covered with dense soft silky hairs. [< NLat. *velūtīnus* < Med.Lat. *velūtum*, velvet < VLat. **villūtus.* See VELVET.]

vel•vet (vĕl′vĭt) *n.* **1.** A soft fabric, such as silk, rayon, or nylon, having a smooth dense pile and a plain underside. **2.** Something suggesting the smooth surface of velvet. **3.** The soft furry covering on the developing antlers of deer. **4.** *Informal.* **a.** The winnings of a gambler. **b.** A profit or gain beyond what is expected or due. **5.** *New England.* See **milk shake** 1. See Regional Note at **milk shake.** [ME *veluet*, prob. < OProv. < VLat. **villūtittus*, dim. of **villūtus* < Lat. *villus*, shaggy hair, nap.]

velvet ant *n.* Any of various wasps of the family Mutillidae, the females of which are wingless and have a coat of velvety hair.

vel•vet•een (vĕl′vĭ-tēn′) *n.* A cotton pile fabric resembling velvet. [< VELVET.]

velvet plant *n.* See **mullein.** [< its dense, velvety hairs.]

vel•vet•y (vĕl′vĭ-tē) *adj.* **-i•er, -i•est. 1.** Suggestive of the texture of velvet; soft and smooth: *velvety skin.* **2.** Smooth-tasting; mellow: *a velvety sherry.*

Ven. *abbr.* **1.** Venerable. **2.** Venezuela.

ven– *pref.* Var. of **veno–.**

ve•na (vē′nə) *n., pl.* **-nae** (-nē). *Anat.* A vein. [ME < Lat. *vēna.*]

vena ca•va (kā′və) *n., pl.* **venae ca•vae** (kā′vē). Either of two large veins that drain blood from the upper body and the lower body and empty into the right atrium of the heart. [NLat. *vēna cava* : Lat. *vēna*, vein + Lat. *cava*, hollow.]

ve•nal (vē′nəl) *adj.* **1.a.** Open to bribery; mercenary: *a venal police officer.* **b.** Capable of betraying honor, duty, or scruples for a price; corruptible. **2.** Marked by corrupt dealings, esp. bribery: *a venal administration.* **3.** Obtainable for a price. [Lat. *vēnālis* < *vēnum*, sale. See **wes-[3]*.**] —**ve′nal•ly** *adv.*

ve•nal•i•ty (vē-năl′ĭ-tē) *n., pl.* **-ties.** Susceptibility to bribery or corruption.

ve•na•tion (vē-nā′shən, vĕ-) *n.* **1.** Distribution or arrangement of a system of veins, as in a leaf blade. **2.** The veins of such a system considered as a group. —**ve•na′tion•al** *adj.*

vend (vĕnd) *v.* **vend•ed, vend•ing, vends.** —*tr.* **1.a.** To sell by means of a vending machine. **b.** To sell, esp. by peddling. **2.** To offer (an idea, for example) for public consideration. —*intr.* To sell. [Lat. *vendere*, alteration of *vēnumdare* : *vēnum*, sale; see **wes-[3]*** + *dare*, to give; see **dō-*.**]

Ven•da (vĕn′də). An internally self-governing Black African homeland in NE South Africa; granted nominal independence in 1979. Cap. Thohoyandou. Pop. 374,000.

vend•ee (vĕn-dē′) *n.* One to whom something is sold; a buyer.

vend•er or **ven•dor** (vĕn′dər) *n.* **1.** One that sells or vends: *a street vender.* **2.** A vending machine.

ven•det•ta (vĕn-dĕt′ə) *n.* **1.** A feud between two families or clans that arises out of a slaying and is perpetuated by retaliatory acts of revenge; a blood feud. **2.** A bitter, destructive feud. [Ital. < Lat. *vindicta*, revenge. See VINDICTIVE.]

vend•i•ble also **vend•a•ble** (vĕn′də-bəl) —*adj.* **1.** Suitable or fit for sale; salable: *vendible items of food.* **2.** *Obsolete.* Venal. —*n.* Something that can be sold.

vend•ing machine (vĕn′dĭng) *n.* A coin-operated machine that dispenses merchandise.

Ven•dôme (väɴ-dōm′), Duc de. Louis Joseph de Bourbon. 1654–1712. French general who commanded Spanish troops in Italy (1710) during the War of the Spanish Succession.

ven•due (vĕn′do͞o, -dyo͞o, vĕn-do͞o′, -dyo͞o′) *n.* A public sale; an auction. [Du. *vendu* < obsolete Fr. *vendue*, sale < OFr., fem. p.part. of *vendre*, to sell < Lat. *vendere.* See VEND.]

ve•neer (və-nîr′) *n.* **1.** A thin surface layer, as of wood, glued to a base of inferior material. **2.** Any of the thin layers glued together to make plywood. **3.** A decorative facing, as of brick. **4.** A deceptive superficial show; a façade. —*tr.v.* **-neered, -neer•ing, -neers. 1.** To overlay (a surface) with a thin layer of a fine or decorative material. **2.** To glue together (layers of wood) to make plywood. **3.** To conceal, as something crude, with a deceptively attractive outward show. [Alteration of obsolete *faneering* < Ger. *Furnierung* < *furnieren*, to furnish, veneer < Fr. *fournir*, to furnish < OFr. *furnir*, of Gmc. orig. See **per[1]*.**] —**ve•neer′er** *n.*

ven•e•na•tion (vĕn′ə-nā′shən) *n.* **1.** Introduction of a venom into animal tissue. **2.** The poisoned condition produced by a venom. [< Lat. *venēnātus*, p.part. of *venēnāre*, to poison < *venēnum*, venom. See VENOM.]

ve•nene (və-nēn′, vĕn′ēn) *n.* **1.** A preparation of snake venoms used in medicine, esp. in the treatment of epilepsy. **2.** Var. of **venin.** [< Lat. *venēnum*, venom. See VENOM.]

ve•ne•punc•ture (vē′nĭ-pŭngk′chər, vĕn′ĭ-) *n.* Var. of **venipuncture.**

ven•er•a•ble (vĕn′ər-ə-bəl) *adj.* **1.** Commanding respect by virtue of age, dignity, character, or position. **2.** Worthy of reverence, esp. by religious or historical association. **3. Venerable. a.** *Rom. Cath. Ch.* Used as a form of address for a person who has reached the first stage of canonization. **b.** Used as a form of address for an archdeacon in the Anglican Church or the Episcopal Church. —**ven′er•a•ble•ness, ven′er•a•bil′i•ty** *n.* —**ven′er•a•bly** *adv.*

ven•er•ate (vĕn′ə-rāt′) *tr.v.* **-at•ed, -at•ing, -ates.** To regard with respect, reverence, or heartfelt deference. See Syns at **revere[1].** [Lat. *venerārī*, *venerāt-*, to venerate < *venus*, *vener-*, love, desire. See **wen-[1]*.**] —**ven′er•a′tor** *n.*

ven•er•a•tion (vĕn′ə-rā′shən) *n.* **1.** The act of venerating. **2.** Profound respect or reverence. **3.** The condition or status of one who is venerated. —**ven′er•a′tion•al** *adj.*

ve•ne•re•al (və-nîr′ē-əl) *adj.* **1.a.** Transmitted by sexual intercourse. **b.** Of or relating to a sexually transmitted disease.

2. Of or relating to sexual intercourse. **3.** Of or relating to the genitals. [ME *venerealle* < Lat. *venereus* < *venus, vener-*, desire, love. See **wen-**[1]*.]

venereal disease *n.* Any of several contagious diseases, such as syphilis and gonorrhea, contracted through sexual intercourse; a sexually transmitted disease.

venereal wart *n.* See **genital wart.**

ven•er•y[1] (vĕn′ə-rē) *n., pl.* **-ies.** *Archaic.* **1.** Indulgence in or pursuit of sexual activity. **2.** The act of sexual intercourse. [ME *venerie* < OFr. < Med.Lat. *veneria* < Lat. *venus, vener-*, desire, love. See **wen-**[1]*.]

ven•er•y[2] (vĕn′ə-rē) *n., pl.* **-ies.** *Archaic.* The act or sport of hunting; the chase. [ME *venerie* < OFr. < *vener*, to hunt < Lat. *vēnārī*. See **wen-**[1]*.]

ven•e•sec•tion (vĕn′ĭ-sĕk′shən, vē′nĭ-) *n.* See **phlebotomy.** [NLat. *venae sectiō, venae sectiōn-* : Lat. *vēnae*, genitive sing. of *vēna*, vein + Lat. *sectiō*, cutting; see SECTION.]

Ve•ne•ti•a (və-nē′shē-ə, -shə). A historical region including Istria and the lands between the Po R. and the Alps.

Ve•ne•tian (və-nē′shən) *adj.* Of or relating to Venice, Italy, or its people, language, or culture. — *n.* **1.** A native or inhabitant of Venice. **2.** The variety of Italian spoken in Venice. [Med.Lat. *Venetiānus* < Lat. *Venetia*, region of NE Italy.]

ve•ne•tian blind or **Ve•ne•tian blind** (və-nē′shən) *n.* A window blind consisting of a number of thin horizontal adjustable slats that overlap when closed.

venetian blue *n. Color.* A strong blue to greenish blue.

Venetian glass *n.* A fine, often colored and ornamented glassware made in or near Venice.

venetian red *n. Color.* A deep to strong reddish brown.

Ve•ne•to (vĕn′ĕ-tō′). A region of NE Italy bordering on the Adriatic Sea; passed to Austria in 1797 and became part of Italy in 1866.

Venez. *abbr.* Venezuela.

Ven•e•zue•la (vĕn′ə-zwā′lə, -zwē′-). A country of N South America on the Caribbean Sea; liberated from Spain in 1821 but not formally separated from Colombia until 1830. Cap. Caracas. Pop. 14,515,885. — **Ven′e•zue′lan** *adj. & n.*

Venezuela, Gulf of. An inlet of the Caribbean Sea between NW Venezuela and N Colombia.

venge (vĕnj) *tr.v.* **venged, veng•ing, veng•es.** *Archaic.* To avenge. [ME *vengen* < OFr. *vengier*. See VENGEANCE.]

ven•geance (vĕn′jəns) *n.* Infliction of punishment in return for a wrong; retribution. — ***idiom.* with a vengeance. 1.** With great violence or force. **2.** To an extreme degree. [ME < OFr. < *vengier*, to avenge < Lat. *vindicāre*. See VINDICATE.]

venge•ful (vĕnj′fəl) *adj.* **1.** Desiring vengeance; vindictive. **2.** Indicating or proceeding from a desire for revenge. **3.** Serving to exact vengeance. — **venge′ful•ly** *adv.* — **venge′ful•ness** *n.*

V-en•gine (vē′ĕn′jən) *n.* An internal-combustion engine having cylinders arranged so that pairs form V shapes.

ve•ni•al (vē′nē-əl, vēn′yəl) *adj.* Easily excused or forgiven; pardonable: *a venial offense.* [ME < OFr. < LLat. *veniālis* < Lat. *venia*, forgiveness. See **wen-**[1]*.] — **ve′ni•al′i•ty** (vē′nē-ăl′ĭ-tē, vēn-yăl′-), **ve′ni•al•ness** (vē′nē-əl-nĭs, vēn′yəl-) *n.* — **ve′ni•al•ly** *adv.*

Ven•ice (vĕn′ĭs). A city of NE Italy on islets within a lagoon in the **Gulf of Venice,** a wide inlet of the N Adriatic Sea. Founded in the 5th cent. A.D., it became a major maritime power by the 13th cent. and was ceded to Italy in 1866. Pop. 332,775.

ven•in (vĕn′ĭn, vē′nĭn) also **ve•nene** (və-nēn′, vĕn′ēn) *n.* Any of various toxic substances found in the venom of snakes.

ve•ni•punc•ture also **ve•ne•punc•ture** (vē′nĭ-pŭngk′chər, vĕn′ĭ-) *n.* Puncture of a vein, as for drawing blood, intravenous feeding, or administration of medicine.

ven•i•son (vĕn′ĭ-sən, -zən) *n.* **1.** The flesh of a deer used as food. **2.** *Archaic.* The flesh of a game animal used as food. [ME *veneson* < OFr. < Lat. *vēnātiō, vēnātiōn-*, hunting < *vēnātus*, p.part. of *vēnārī*, to hunt. See **wen-**[1]*.]

Venn diagram (vĕn) *n.* A diagram using circles to represent an operation in set theory, with the position and overlap of the circles indicating the relationships between the sets. [After John *Venn* (1834–1923), British logician.]

veno– or **veni–** or **ven–** *pref.* Vein: *venipuncture.* [< Lat. *vēna*.]

ve•no•gram (vē′nə-grăm′) *n.* A radiograph of a vein after injection of a radiopaque substance.

ve•nog•ra•phy (vĭ-nŏg′rə-fē) *n.* Radiography of veins or a vein after injection of a radiopaque substance.

ven•om (vĕn′əm) *n.* **1.** A poisonous secretion of an animal, such as a snake, spider, or scorpion, usu. transmitted by a bite or sting. **2.** A poison. **3.** Malice; spite. [ME *venim* < OFr. < VLat. **venīmen* < Lat. *venēnum*, poison. See **wen-**[1]*.]

ven•om•ous (vĕn′ə-məs) *adj.* **1.a.** Secreting and transmitting venom: *a venomous snake.* **b.** Full of or containing venom. **2.** Malicious; spiteful: *a venomous remark.* — **ven′om•ous•ly** *adv.* — **ven′om•ous•ness** *n.*

ve•nose (vē′nōs′) *adj.* **1.** Having noticeable veins or veinlike markings. **2.** Venous. [Lat. *vēnōsus* < *vēna*, vein.]

ve•nos•i•ty (vē-nŏs′ĭ-tē) *n.* The quality or condition of being venous or venose.

ve•nous (vē′nəs) *adj.* **1.** *Physiol.* Of, relating to, or contained in the veins: *venous blood.* **2.** Having numerous veins, as a leaf or the wings of an insect. [< Lat. *vēnōsus* < *vēna*, vein.] — **ve′nous•ly** *adv.* — **ve′nous•ness** *n.*

vent[1] (vĕnt) *n.* **1.** A means of escape or release from confinement; an outlet: *give vent to anger.* **2.** An opening permitting the escape of fumes, a liquid, a gas, or steam. **3.** The small hole at the breech of a gun through which the charge is ignited. **4.** *Zool.* The external opening of the cloaca. **5.** *Geol.* **a.** The opening of a volcano in the earth's crust. **b.** An opening on the ocean floor that emits hot water and dissolved minerals. — *tr.v.* **vent•ed, vent•ing, vents. 1.** To give often forceful expression or utterance to. **2.** To release or discharge (steam, for example) through an opening. **3.** To provide with a vent. [Partly < Fr. *vent* (< OFr.) and partly alteration of Fr. *évent* (< OFr. *esvent* < *esventer*, to let out air < VLat. **exventāre* : Lat. *ex-*; see EX– + Lat. *ventus*, wind; see **wē-***).] — **vent′er** *n.*

Syns: *vent, air, express, voice, utter.* These verbs mean to give outlet to thoughts or emotions. To *vent* is to unburden oneself of a strong pent-up emotion: *"She was jealous . . . and glad of any excuse to vent her pique"* (Edward G.E.L. Bulwer-Lytton). To *air* is to give vent to and often to show off one's feelings, beliefs, or ideas: *time to air our differences. Express* refers to communication by both verbal and nonverbal means: *"expressing emotion in the form of art"* (T.S. Eliot). *Voice* denotes the expression of an outlook or a viewpoint: *voiced her satisfaction with the verdict. Utter* involves vocal expression: *"The words were uttered in the hearing of Montezuma"* (William Hickling Prescott).

vent[2] (vĕnt) *n.* A slit in a garment, as in the back seam of a pocket. [ME *vente*, alteration of *fente* < OFr., slit < *fendre*, to split open < Lat. *findere*. See FISSION.]

vent•age (vĕn′tĭj) *n.* A small opening; a vent.

ven•tail (vĕn′tāl′) *n.* The lower movable part of the front of a medieval helmet, fitting over the mouth or neck. [ME < OFr. *vantail* < *vent*, wind < Lat. *ventus*. See **wē-***.]

ven•ter (vĕn′tər) *n.* **1.** *Anat.* **a.** The abdomen. **b.** The prominent fleshy portion of a muscle. **c.** A cavity or hollowed surface, esp. of a bone. **2.** *Zool.* A part in lower forms of animal life corresponding to the abdomen of mammals. **3.** *Bot.* The swollen lower portion of an archegonium containing the egg. [AN < Lat.]

ven•ti•fact (vĕn′tə-făkt′) *n.* A stone that has been shaped, polished, or faceted by wind-driven sand. [Lat. *ventus*, wind; see VENT[1] + (ARTI)FACT.]

ven•ti•late (vĕn′tl-āt′) *tr.v.* **-lat•ed, -lat•ing, -lates. 1.** To admit fresh air into (a mine, for example) to replace stale or noxious air. **2.** To circulate through and freshen. **3.** To provide with a vent, as for airing. **4.** To expose (a substance) to fresh air, as to retard spoilage. **5.** To expose to public discussion or examination: *ventilated their grievances.* **6.** To aerate or oxygenate (blood). [ME *ventilaten*, to blow away < Lat. *ventilāre, ventilāt-*, to fan < *ventulus*, dim. of *ventus*, wind. See **wē-***.] — **ven′ti•la′tion** *n.*

ven•ti•la•tor (vĕn′tl-ā′tər) *n.* **1.** A device that circulates fresh air and expels stale or foul air. **2.** *Medic.* A respirator. — **ven′ti•la•to′ry** (vĕn′tl-ə-tôr′ē, -tōr′ē) *adj.*

ven•tral (vĕn′trəl) *adj.* **1.** *Anat.* **a.** Of or situated on or close to the abdomen; abdominal. **b.** Of or situated on or close to the anterior aspect of the human body or the lower surface of the body of an animal. **2.** *Bot.* Of or on the lower or inner surface of an organ that faces the axis. — *n.* **1.** A ventral fin. **2.** The abdominal segment of an insect. [LLat. *ventrālis* < Lat. *venter, ventr-*, belly.] — **ven′tral•ly** *adv.*

ventral fin *n. Zool.* A fin, such as a pelvic fin or an anal fin, that is found on the ventral side of a fish.

ven•tri•cle (vĕn′trĭ-kəl) *n.* A small cavity or chamber within a body or an organ, esp.: **a.** The chamber on the left side of the heart that receives arterial blood from the left atrium and contracts to force it into the aorta. **b.** The chamber on the right side of the heart that receives venous blood from the right atrium and forces it into the pulmonary artery. **c.** Any of the interconnecting cavities of the brain. [ME < OFr. *ventricule* < Lat. *ventriculus*, dim. of *venter*, belly.]

ven•tri•cose (vĕn′trĭ-kōs′) also **ven•tri•cous** (-kəs) *adj.* Inflated, swollen, or distended, esp. on one side: *the ventricose gullet of an insect.* [NLat. *ventricōsus* < Lat. *venter, ventr-*, belly.] — **ven′tri•cos′i•ty** (-kŏs′ĭ-tē) *n.*

ven•tric•u•lar (vĕn-trĭk′yə-lər) *adj.* Of or relating to a ventricle or ventriculus.

ven•tric•u•lus (vĕn-trĭk′yə-ləs) *n., pl.* **-li** (-lī′). **1.** A hollow digestive organ, esp. the stomach of certain insects or the gizzard of a bird. **2.** The digestive cavity in the body of a sponge. [Lat., dim. of *venter, ventr-*, belly.]

ven•tri•lo•qui•al (vĕn′trə-lō′kwē-əl) *adj.* Of, relating to, or practicing ventriloquism. — **ven′tri•lo′qui•al•ly** *adv.*

ven•tril•o•quism (vĕn-trĭl′ə-kwĭz′əm) also **ven•tril•o•quy** (-kwē) *n.* The art of projecting one's voice so that it seems to come from another source, as from a wooden figure. [< Lat. *ventriloquus*, speaking from the belly : *venter, ventr-*, belly + *loquī*, to speak; see **tolkʷ-***.] — **ven•tril′o•quist** *n.* — **ven•**

Venezuela

ă pat	oi boy
ā pay	ou out
âr care	ŏŏ took
ä father	ōō boot
ĕ pet	ŭ cut
ē be	ûr urge
ĭ pit	th thin
ī pie	*th* this
îr pier	hw which
ŏ pot	zh vision
ō toe	ə about, item
ô paw	

Stress marks:
′ (primary);
′ (secondary), as in dictionary (dĭk′shə-nĕr′ē)

tril′o•quis′tic *adj.* — **ven•tril′o•quize′** (-kwīz′) *v.*

ventro– or **ventr–** *pref.* Ventral: *ventrolateral.* [< Lat. *venter, ventr-*, belly.]

ven•tro•dor•sal (vĕn′trō-dôr′səl) *adj.* Both ventral and dorsal; extending from a ventral to a dorsal surface. — **ven′tro•dor′sal•ly** *adv.*

ven•tro•lat•er•al (vĕn′trō-lăt′ər-əl) *adj.* Both ventral and lateral; extending from a ventral to a lateral surface. — **ven′tro•lat′er•al•ly** *adv.*

ven•tro•me•di•al (vĕn′trō-mē′dē-əl) *adj.* Both ventral and medial; extending toward the median line of the ventral surface. — **ven′tro•me′di•al•ly** *adv.*

Ven•tu•ra (vĕn-tŏŏr′ə). A city of S CA on the Pacific Ocean W of Los Angeles; founded 1782. Pop. 92,575.

ven•ture (vĕn′chər) *n.* **1.** A dangerous, daring, or dubious undertaking. **2.** A business enterprise involving some risk in expectation of gain. **3.** Something, such as cargo, at hazard in a risky enterprise. — *v.* **-tured, -tur•ing, -tures.** — *tr.* **1.** To expose to danger or risk. **2.** To brave the dangers of. **3.** To express at the risk of denial, criticism, or censure. — *intr.* **1.** To take a risk; dare. **2.** To proceed despite possible danger or risk. — ***idiom.* at a venture.** By mere chance or fortune; at random. [ME, chance, short for *aventure*, adventure. See ADVENTURE.] — **ven′tur•er** *n.*

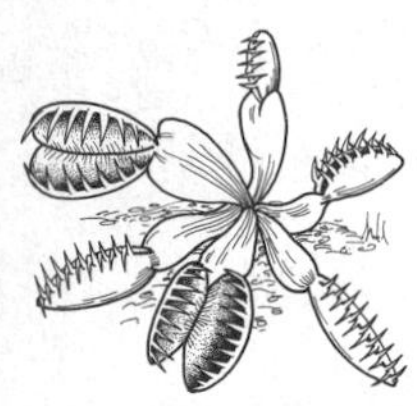

Venus's-flytrap
Dionaea muscipula

venture capital *n.* Money for investment in innovative enterprises or research in which both the risk of loss and the potential for profit may be considerable. — **venture capitalist** *n.*

ven•ture•some (vĕn′chər-səm) *adj.* **1.** Disposed to venture or to take risks; daring. **2.** Involving risk or danger; hazardous.

ven•tu•ri (vĕn-tŏŏr′ē) *n., pl.* **-ris. 1.** A short tube with a constricted throat used to determine fluid pressures and velocities by measurement of differential pressures generated at the throat as a fluid traverses the tube. **2.** A constricted throat in the air passage of a carburetor, causing a reduction in pressure that results in fuel vapor being drawn out of the carburetor bowl. [After Giovanni Battista *Venturi* (1746–1822), Italian physicist.]

ven•tur•ous (vĕn′chər-əs) *adj.* Venturesome. — **ven′tur•ous•ly** *adv.* — **ven′tur•ous•ness** *n.*

Giuseppe Verdi
1886 pastel portrait by Giovanni Boldini (1845–1931)

ven•ue (vĕn′yōō) *n.* **1.** *Law.* **a.** The locality where a crime is committed or a cause of action occurs. **b.** The locality or political division from which a jury is called and in which a trial is held. **c.** The clause within a declaration naming the locality in which a trial will be held. **d.** The clause in an affidavit naming the place where it was sworn to. **2.** The scene or setting in which something takes place; a locale. [ME, attack < OFr., a coming, attack < fem. p.part. of *venir*, to come < Lat. *venīre.* See **gʷā-***.]

ven•ule (vĕn′yōōl, vēn′-) *n.* A small vein, esp. one joining capillaries to larger veins. [Lat. *vēnula*, dim. of *vēna*, vein.] — **ven′u•lar** (-yə-lər) *adj.*

Ve•nus (vē′nəs) *n.* **1.** *Rom. Myth.* The goddess of sexual love and physical beauty. **2.** The second planet from the sun, having an average radius of 6,052 kilometers (3,760 miles) and a sidereal period of revolution about the sun of 224.7 days at a mean distance of approx. 108.1 million kilometers (67.2 million miles). [ME < OE < Lat., love, Venus. See **wen-¹***.]

Ve•nu•sian (vĭ-nōō′zhən, -shē-ən, -nyōō′-) *adj.* Of, relating to, or characteristic of the planet Venus. — *n.* A hypothetical inhabitant of the planet Venus.

Ve•nus's-fly•trap (vē′nəs-flī′trăp′, vē′nə-sĭz-) or **Venus fly•trap** *n.* An insectivorous plant *(Dionaea muscipula)* of the Carolinas having sensitive, hinged, marginally bristled two-lobed leaf blades that close and entrap insects.

Ve•nus's-hair (vē′nə-sĭz-hâr′) *n.* A maidenhair fern *(Adiantum capillus-veneris)* of warm moist regions having slender blackish stalks, bipinnately compound fronds, and marginal sori.

ver. *abbr.* **1.** Verse. **2.** Version.

ve•ra•cious (və-rā′shəs) *adj.* **1.** Honest; truthful. **2.** Accurate; precise. [< Lat. *vērāx, vērāc-* < *vērus*, true. See **wēro-***.] — **ve•ra′cious•ly** *adv.* — **ve•ra′cious•ness** *n.*

ve•rac•i•ty (və-răs′ĭ-tē) *n., pl.* **-ties. 1.** Adherence to the truth; truthfulness. **2.** Conformity to fact or truth; accuracy or precision. **3.** Something that is true. [Med.Lat. *vērācitās* < Lat. *vērāx, vērāc-*, true. See VERACIOUS.]

Ve•ra•cruz (vĕr′ə-krōōz′, bă′rä-krōōs′). A city of E-central Mexico on the Gulf of Mexico E of Puebla; founded 1599 on a site visited by Cortés in 1519. Pop. 284,822.

ve•ran•da or **ve•ran•dah** (və-răn′də) *n.* A porch or balcony, usu. roofed and often partly enclosed, extending along the outside of a building. Also called regionally *gallery.* [Hindi *varaṇḍā* < Pers. *bar āmadah*, coming out, or < Port. *varanda* (perh. ult. < VLat. **barra*, barrier, bar).]

ve•rat•ri•dine (və-răt′rĭ-dēn′) *n.* A yellowish-white amorphous powdered alkaloid, $C_{36}H_{51}NO_{11}$, obtained from sabadilla seeds and the rhizome of hellebore. [VERATR(INE) + -ID(E) + -INE².]

ver•a•trine (vĕr′ə-trēn′, -trĭn) *n.* A poisonous mixture of colorless crystalline alkaloids extracted from sabadilla seeds and formerly used medicinally as a counterirritant. [NLat. *vērātrīna* < *Vērātrum*, genus name of a hellebore < Lat. *vērātrum*, hellebore.]

verb (vûrb) *n.* **1.a.** The part of speech that expresses existence, action, or occurrence in most languages. **b.** Any of the words within this part of speech, as *be, run,* or *conceive.* **2.** A phrase or other construction used as a verb. [ME *verbe* < OFr. < Lat. *verbum*, word, verb. See **wer-⁵***.]

ver•bal (vûr′bəl) *adj.* **1.** Of, relating to, or associated with words. **2.a.** Concerned with words only rather than with content or ideas. **b.** Consisting of words alone without action. **3.** Spoken rather than written; oral: *a verbal contract.* **4.** Corresponding word for word; literal. **5.** *Gram.* **a.** Relating to, having the nature or function of, or derived from a verb. **b.** Used to form verbs: *a verbal suffix.* **6.** Of or relating to proficiency in the use and understanding of words: *verbal aptitude.* — *n. Gram.* A verbal noun or adjective. [ME < OFr. < LLat. *verbālis* < Lat. *verbum*, word. See VERB.] — **ver′bal•ly** *adv.*

Usage Note: *Verbal* has been used to refer to spoken, as opposed to written, communication by reputable writers since the 16th century, and the usage cannot be considered incorrect. But critics are right to observe that this use of *verbal* may sometimes invite confusion with the use meaning "by linguistic means." Thus the phrase *modern technologies for verbal communication* may refer only to devices such as radio or may also refer to devices such as the fax machine. In such contexts the word *oral* is always available to convey the narrower sense of communication by spoken means.

verbal adjective *n.* An adjective that is derived from a verb and that in some constructions preserves the verb's syntactic features, such as transitivity.

ver•bal•ism (vûr′bə-lĭz′əm) *n.* **1.a.** An expression in words; a word or phrase. **b.** The manner in which something is phrased; wording. **2.** A wordy phrase or sentence with little meaning. **3.** Abundant use of words without conveying much meaning.

ver•bal•ist (vûr′bə-lĭst) *n.* **1.** One skilled in the use of words. **2.** One who favors words over ideas or substance. — **ver′bal•is′tic** *adj.*

ver•bal•ize (vûr′bə-līz′) *v.* **-ized, -iz•ing, -iz•es.** — *tr.* **1.** To express in words. **2.** *Gram.* To convert to use as a verb: *verbalized the noun* contact. — *intr.* **1.** To express oneself in words. **2.** To be verbose. — **ver′bal•i•za′tion** (-bə-lĭ-zā′shən) *n.* — **ver′bal•iz′er** *n.*

verbal noun *n.* A noun that is derived from a verb and usu. preserves the verb's syntactic features, such as transitivity.

ver•ba•tim (vər-bā′tĭm) *adj.* Using exactly the same words; corresponding word for word: *a verbatim report of the conversation.* — *adv.* In exactly the same words; word for word. [ME < Med.Lat. *verbātim* < Lat. *verbum*, word. See VERB.]

ver•be•na (vər-bē′nə) *n.* **1.** Any of various New World plants of the genus *Verbena*, esp. one of several species having spikes of showy flowers. **2.** Any of several similar plants, such as the lemon verbena. [Lat. *verbēna*, sacred foliage. See **wer-²***.]

ver•bi•age (vûr′bē-ĭj, -bĭj) *n.* **1.** An excess of words for the purpose; wordiness. **2.** The manner in which something is expressed in words: *software verbiage.* [Fr. < OFr. *verbier*, to chatter < *verbe*, word < Lat. *verbum.* See VERB.]

verb•i•fy (vûr′bə-fī′) *tr.v.* **-fied** (-fīd′), **-fy•ing, -fies** (-fīz′). To use (a noun, for example) as a verb.

ver•big•er•a•tion (vər-bĭj′ə-rā′shən) *n.* Obsessive repetition of meaningless words and phrases, esp. due to mental illness. [< Lat. *verbigerātus*, p.part. of *verbigerāre*, to chat, dispute : *verbum*, word; see VERB + *-gerāre*, freq. of *gerere*, to carry.]

ver•bose (vər-bōs′) *adj.* Using or containing a great and usu. an excessive number of words; wordy. [ME **verbous* < Lat. *verbōsus* < *verbum*, word. See VERB.] — **ver•bose′ly** *adv.* — **ver•bose′ness, ver•bos′i•ty** (-bŏs′ĭ-tē) *n.*

ver•bo•ten (vər-bōt′n, fĕr-) *adj.* Forbidden; prohibited. [Ger., p.part. of *verbieten*, to forbid < MHGer. < OHGer. *farbiotan.* See **bheudh-***.]

ver•dant (vûr′dnt) *adj.* **1.** Green with vegetation; covered with green growth. **2.** *Color.* Green in hue. **3.** Lacking experience or sophistication; naive. [Fr. *verdoyant* < OFr., pr.part. of *verdoyer*, to become green < VLat. **viridiāre* < Lat. *viridis*, green.] — **ver′dan•cy** *n.* — **ver′dant•ly** *adv.*

verd antique also **verde antique** (vûrd) *n.* A dull green mottled or veined serpentine used in interior decoration. [Obsolete Fr. < Ital. *verde antico* : *verde*, green + *antico*, antique.]

Verde (vûrd), **Cape.** A peninsula of W Senegal projecting into the Atlantic Ocean; the westernmost point of Africa.

ver•der•er also **ver•der•or** (vûr′dər-ər) *n.* A man serving as an official in charge of the royal forests of medieval England. [AN < *verd*, green < Lat. *viridis.*]

Ver•di (vâr′dē), **Giuseppe.** 1813–1901. Italian composer whose operas include *La Traviata* (1853).

ver•dict (vûr′dĭkt) *n.* **1.** *Law.* The finding of a jury in a trial. **2.** An expressed conclusion; a judgment or an opinion: *the verdict of history.* [ME *verdit* < AN : *ver*, true (< Lat. *vērus*; see **wēro-***) + *dit*, speech (< Lat. *dictum* < neut. p.part. of *dīcere*, to say; see **deik-***).]

ver•di•gris (vûr′dĭ-grēs′, -grĭs′, -grē′) *n.* **1.** A blue or green powder consisting of basic cupric acetate used as a paint pigment and fungicide. **2.** A green patina or crust of copper sulfate or copper chloride formed on copper, brass, and bronze exposed to air or seawater for long periods of time. [ME *vertegrez* < OFr. *verte grez*, alteration of *vert-de-Grice* : *verd*, green; see VERDURE + *de*, of (< Lat. *dē*; see DE-) + *Grice*, Greece.]

Ver•di•gris (vûr′dĭ-grĭs). A river, c. 451 km (280 mi), of SE KS and NE OK flowing generally S to the Arkansas R.

ver•din (vûr′dn) *n.* A small grayish bird *(Auriparus flaviceps)* of Mexico and the southwest United States having a yellowish head and throat. [Fr., bunting < *vert*, green < OFr. *verd*. See VERDURE.]

ver•di•ter (vûr′dĭ-tər) *n.* Either of two basic carbonates of copper, used as a blue or green pigment. [ME, alteration of OFr. *verd de terre*, green of earth : *verd*, green; see VERDURE + *de*, of; see VERDIGRIS + *terre*, earth (< Lat. *terra*; see **ters-***).]

Ver•dun (vər-dŭn′, vĕr-dœn′). **1.** A city of S Quebec, Canada, a suburb of Montreal on Montreal I. Pop. 61,287. **2.** A city of NE France on the Meuse R. W of Metz; site of a prolonged World War I battle (Feb.–Dec. 1916). Pop. 21,516.

ver•dure (vûr′jər) *n.* **1.a.** The lush greenness of flourishing vegetation. **b.** Vigorous greenery. **2.** A fresh or flourishing condition. [ME < OFr. < *verd*, green < Lat. *viridis*.] —**ver′dur•ous** *adj.* —**ver′dur•ous•ness** *n.*

verge[1] (vûrj) *n.* **1.** The extreme edge or margin; a border. See Syns at **border. 2.a.** An enclosing boundary. **b.** The space enclosed by such a boundary. **3.** The point beyond which an action, a state, or a condition is likely to begin or occur; the brink: *on the verge of prosperity.* **4.** *Archit.* The edge of the tiling that projects over a roof gable. **5.** *Chiefly British.* The shoulder of a road. **6.** A rod, wand, or staff carried as an emblem of authority or office. **7.** *Obsolete.* The rod held by a feudal tenant while swearing fealty to a lord. **8.** The spindle of a balance wheel in a clock or watch, esp. such a spindle in a clock with vertical escapement. **9.** The male organ of copulation in certain invertebrates. —*intr.v.* **verged, verg•ing, verg•es. 1.** To approach the nature or condition of something specified; come close. Used with *on*: *a brilliance verging on genius.* **2.** To be on the edge or border: *Her land verges on state forest.* [ME < OFr., rod, ring < Lat. *virga*, rod, strip.]

verge[2] (vûrj) *intr.v.* **verged, verg•ing, verg•es. 1.** To slope or incline. **2.** To tend to move in a particular direction. **3.** To pass or merge gradually. [Lat. *vergere*. See **wer-**[2]***.]

verg•er (vûr′jər) *n. Chiefly British.* **1.** One who carries the verge or other emblem of authority before a scholastic, legal, or religious dignitary in a procession. **2.** One who takes care of the interior of a church and acts as an attendant during ceremonies.

Ver•gil (vûr′jəl). See **Virgil.**

ve•rid•i•cal (və-rĭd′ĭ-kəl) also **ve•rid•ic** (-rĭd′ĭk) *adj.* **1.** Truthful; veracious. **2.** Coinciding with fact or reality; genuine or real. [< Lat. *vēridicus* : *vērus*, true; see **wēro-*** + *dīcere*, to say; see **deik-***.] —**ve•rid′i•cal′i•ty** (-kăl′ĭ-tē) *n.*

ver•i•fi•a•ble (vĕr′ə-fī′ə-bəl) *adj.* Possible to verify. —**ver′i•fi′a•bil′i•ty, ver′i•fi′a•ble•ness** *n.* —**ver′i•fi′a•bly** *adv.*

ver•i•fi•ca•tion (vĕr′ə-fĭ-kā′shən) *n.* **1.** The act of verifying or the state of being verified. **2.a.** A confirmation of truth or authority. **b.** The evidence for such a confirmation. **c.** A formal assertion of validity. **3.** *Law.* An affidavit that attests to the truth of a pleading. —**ver′i•fi•ca′tive** *adj.*

ver•i•fy (vĕr′ə-fī′) *tr.v.* **-fied** (-fīd′), **-fy•ing, -fies** (-fīz′). **1.** To prove the truth of with evidence or testimony; substantiate. **2.** To determine or test the truth or accuracy of, as by comparison or investigation. **3.** *Law.* **a.** To affirm formally or under oath. **b.** To append a verification to (a pleading); conclude with a verification. [ME *verifien* < OFr. *verifier* < Med. Lat. *vērificāre* : Lat. *vērus*, true; see **wēro-*** + Lat. *-ficāre*, -fy.] —**ver′i•fi′er** *n.*

ver•i•ly (vĕr′ə-lē) *adv.* **1.** In truth; in fact. **2.** With confidence; assuredly. [ME *verraily* < *verrai*, true. See VERY.]

ver•i•sim•i•lar (vĕr′ə-sĭm′ə-lər) *adj.* Appearing to be true or real; probable. [< Lat. *vērīsimilis* : *vērī*, genitive of *vērum*, truth < neut. sing. of *vērus*, true; see **wēro-*** + *similis*, similar; see SIMILAR.] —**ver′i•sim′i•lar•ly** *adv.*

ver•i•si•mil•i•tude (vĕr′ə-sĭ-mĭl′ĭ-to͞od′, -tyo͞od′) *n.* **1.** The quality of appearing to be true or real. **2.** Something that has the appearance of being true or real. [Lat. *vērīsimilitūdō* < *vērīsimilis*, verisimilar. See VERISIMILAR.] —**ver′i•si•mil′i•tu′di•nous** (-to͞od′n-əs, -tyo͞od′-) *adj.*

ver•ism (vĕr′ĭz′əm) *n.* Realism in art and literature. [Ital. *verismo* : *vero*, true (< Lat. *vērus*; see **wēro-***) + *-ismo*, system of principles (< Lat. *-ismus*, -ism).] —**ver′ist** *n.* —**ve•ris′tic** (və-rĭs′tĭk) *adj.*

ve•ris•mo (və-rĭz′mō) *n.* **1.** Verism. **2.** An artistic movement of the late 19th century, originating in Italy and influential esp. in grand opera, marked by the use of common themes often treated in a melodramatic manner. [Ital. See VERISM.]

ver•i•ta•ble (vĕr′ĭ-tə-bəl) *adj.* Being truly so called; real or genuine. [ME < OFr. < *verite*, truth. See VERITY.] —**ver′i•ta•ble•ness** *n.* —**ver′i•ta•bly** *adv.*

vé•ri•té (vā-rē-tā′) *n.* Cinéma vérité.

ver•i•ty (vĕr′ĭ-tē) *n., pl.* **-ties. 1.** The quality or state of being true, factual, or real. **2.** Something, such as a statement or principle, that is true, esp. an enduring truth. [ME *verite*, truth < OFr. < Lat. *vēritās* < *vērus*, true. See **wēro-***.]

ver•juice (vûr′jo͞os′) *n.* **1.** The acidic juice of crab apples or other sour fruit. **2.** Sourness, as of disposition. [ME *verjus* < OFr. *vertjus* : *verd*, unripe; see VERDURE + *jus*, juice; see JUICE.]

Ver•kho•yansk Range (vĕr′kə-yänsk′, vĭr-KHô-). A mountain chain of NE Russia parallel to and E of the lower Lena R.

Ver•laine (vĕr-lān′, -lĕn′), **Paul.** 1844–96. French symbolist poet whose works include *Romances sans Paroles* (1874).

Ver•meer (vər-mîr′, -mâr′), **Jan.** 1632–75. Dutch painter noted for interior genre scenes.

ver•meil (vûr′məl, -māl′) *n.* **1.** *Color.* Vermilion or a similar bright red color. **2.** (vĕr-mā′). Gilded silver, bronze, or copper. —*adj. Color.* Bright red in color. [ME *vermail* < OFr. *vermeil* < LLat. *vermiculus*, a kind of red worm < Lat., grub, dim. of *vermis*, worm. See **wer-**[2]***.]

vermi– *pref.* Worm: *vermicide.* [< Lat. *vermis*, worm. See **wer-**[2]***.]

ver•mi•cel•li (vûr′mĭ-chĕl′ē, -sĕl′ē) *n.* Pasta made in long strands thinner than spaghetti. [Ital., pl. of *vermicello*, dim. of *verme*, worm < Lat. *vermis*. See **wer-**[2]***.]

ver•mi•cide (vûr′mĭ-sīd′) *n.* An agent used to kill worms. —**ver′mi•cid′al** (-sīd′l) *adj.*

ver•mic•u•lar (vər-mĭk′yə-lər) *adj.* **1.** Having the shape or motion of a worm. **2.** Having wormlike markings; vermiculate. **3.** Caused by or relating to worms. [Med.Lat. *vermiculāris* < Lat. *vermiculus*, dim. of *vermis*, worm. See **wer-**[2]***.] —**ver•mic′u•lar•ly** *adv.*

ver•mic•u•late (vər-mĭk′yə-lāt′) *tr.v.* **-lat•ed, -lat•ing, -lates.** To adorn with wavy or winding lines. —*adj.* (-lĭt, -lāt′). **1.** Bearing wavy wormlike lines. **2.** Wormlike in motion; twisting or wriggling. **3.** Sinuous; tortuous. **4.** Infested with worms; worm-eaten. [Lat. *vermiculārī*, *vermiculāt-* < *vermiculus*, dim. of *vermis*, worm. See VERMICULAR.]

ver•mic•u•la•tion (vər-mĭk′yə-lā′shən) *n.* **1.** Motion resembling that of a worm, esp. the wavelike contractions of the intestine; peristalsis. **2.** Wormlike marks or carvings, as in a mosaic or masonry. **3.** The condition of being worm-eaten.

ver•mic•u•lite (vər-mĭk′yə-līt′) *n.* Any of a group of micaceous hydrated silicate minerals related to the chlorites and used in heat-expanded form as insulation and as a planting medium.

ver•mi•form (vûr′mə-fôrm′) *adj.* Resembling or having the long, thin, cylindrical shape of a worm.

vermiform appendix *n.* A narrow vestigial process projecting from the cecum in the lower right-hand part of the abdomen of some mammals, including human beings.

ver•mi•fuge (vûr′mə-fyo͞oj′) *n.* A medicine that expels intestinal worms. —*adj.* Causing expulsion of intestinal worms.

ver•mil•ion also **ver•mil•lion** (vər-mĭl′yən) —*n.* **1.** A bright red mercuric sulfide used as a pigment. **2.** *Color.* A vivid red to reddish orange. —*adj. Color.* Of the color vermilion. —*tr.v.* **-ioned, -ion•ing, -ions** also **-lioned, -lion•ing, -lions.** To color or dye (something) in the hue vermilion. [ME *vermelion* < OFr. *vermeillon* < *vermeil*. See VERMEIL.]

ver•min (vûr′mĭn) *n., pl.* **vermin. 1.** Various small animals or insects, such as rats or cockroaches, that are destructive, annoying, or injurious to health. **2.** Animals that prey on game, such as foxes. **3.a.** A person considered loathsome or highly offensive. **b.** Such people considered as a group. [ME < OFr. < VLat. *verminum < Lat. *vermis*, worm. See **wer-**[2]***.]

ver•mi•na•tion (vûr′mə-nā′shən) *n.* Infestation by vermin, esp. parasitic vermin.

ver•min•ous (vûr′mə-nəs) *adj.* **1.** Of, relating to, or caused by vermin: *verminous diseases.* **2.** Infested with vermin. **3.** Of the nature of vermin; repulsive. —**ver′min•ous•ly** *adv.*

ver•miv•o•rous (vər-mĭv′ər-əs) *adj.* Feeding on worms or insect vermin. Used of a bird.

Ver•mont (vər-mŏnt′). A state of the NE U.S. bordering on Canada; admitted as the 14th state in 1791. Cap. Montpelier. Pop. 564,964. —**Ver•mont′er** *n.*

ver•mouth (vər-mo͞oth′) *n.* A sweet or dry wine flavored with aromatic herbs and often used in mixed drinks. [Fr. *vermout* < Ger. *Wermut* < MHGer. *wermuot*, wormwood < OHGer. *wermuota*.]

ver•nac•u•lar (vər-năk′yə-lər) *n.* **1.** The standard native language of a country or locality. **2.** The everyday language spoken by a people as distinguished from the literary language. **3.** The idiom of a particular trade or profession. **4.** An idiomatic word, phrase, or expression. **5.** The common nonscientific name of a plant or an animal. —*adj.* **1.** Native to or commonly spoken by the members of a particular country or region. **2.** Using the native language of a region, esp. as distinct from the literary language. **3.** Relating to or expressed in the native language or dialect. **4.** Of, relating to, or characteristic of the style of architecture and decoration common in a particular region, culture, or period. **5.** Occurring or existing in a particular locality; endemic. **6.** Relating to or being the common nonscientific name of a plant or an animal. [< Lat. *vernāculus*, native < *verna*, native slave, perh. of Etruscan orig.] —**ver•nac′u•lar•ly** *adv.*

verdin
Auriparus flaviceps

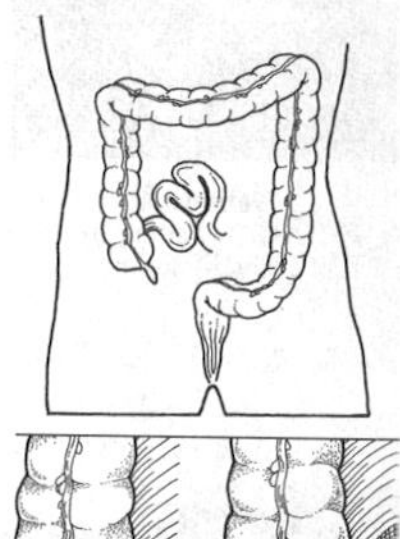

vermiform appendix

ă pat	oi boy
ā pay	ou out
âr care	o͝o took
ä father	o͞o boot
ĕ pet	ŭ cut
ē be	ûr urge
ĭ pit	th thin
ī pie	*th* this
îr pier	hw which
ŏ pot	zh vision
ō toe	ə about, item
ô paw	

Stress marks:
′ (primary);
′ (secondary), as in
dictionary (dĭk′shə-nĕr′ē)

ver•nac•u•lar•ism (vər-năk′yə-lə-rĭz′əm) *n.* A vernacular word or expression.

ver•nac•u•lar•ize (vər-năk′yə-lə-rīz′) *tr.v.* **-ized, -iz•ing, -iz•es.** To translate into everyday language.

ver•nal (vûr′nəl) *adj.* **1.** Of, relating to, or occurring in the spring. **2.** Characteristic of or resembling spring. **3.** Fresh and young; youthful. [Lat. *vērnālis* < *vērnus* < *vēr*, spring. See **wes̱r***.] — **ver′nal•ly** *adv.*

vernal equinox *n.* **1.** The point at which the ecliptic intersects the celestial equator, the sun having a northerly motion. **2.** The moment at which the sun passes through the vernal equinox, marking the beginning of spring.

ver•nal•i•za•tion (vûr′nə-lĭ-zā′shən) *n.* Subjection of seeds or seedlings to low temperature to hasten plant development.

ver•na•tion (vər-nā′shən) *n.* The arrangement of the young leaves within a bud. [NLat. *vērnātiō*, *vērnātiōn-* < Lat. *vērnātus*, p.part. of *vērnāre*, to flourish < *vērnus*, vernal. See VERNAL.]

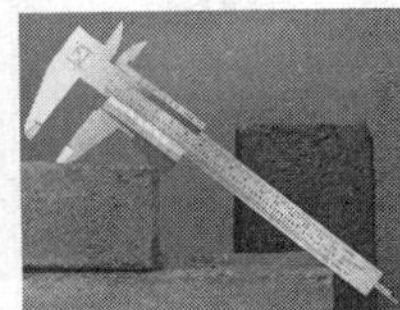
vernier caliper

Verne (vûrn, vĕrn), **Jules.** 1828–1905. French writer whose novels include *Journey to the Center of the Earth* (1864).

Ver•ner's Law (vûr′nərz, vĕr′-) *n. Ling.* A law stating essentially that Proto-Germanic noninitial voiceless fricatives in voiced environments became voiced when the previous syllable was unstressed in Proto-Indo-European. [After Karl Adolph *Verner* (1846–96), Danish philologist.]

ver•ni•er (vûr′nē-ər) *n.* **1.** A small movable auxiliary graduated scale attached parallel to a main graduated scale, calibrated to indicate fractional parts of the subdivisions of the larger scale and used to increase accuracy in measurement. **2.** An auxiliary device designed to facilitate fine adjustments or measurements on precision instruments. — *adj.* Of or relating to a vernier. [After Pierre *Vernier* (1580?–1637), French mathematician.]

vernier caliper *n.* A measuring instrument consisting of an L-shaped frame with a linear scale along its longer arm and an L-shaped sliding attachment with a vernier scale, used to read directly the thickness or diameter of an object.

vernier scale *n.* See **vernier.**

veronica²
c. 1480 painting by Hans Memling

ver•nis•sage (vĕr′nĭ-säzh′) *n.* A private showing before an art exhibition opens. [Fr. < *vernis*, varnish < OFr. See VARNISH.]

ver•nix (vûr′nĭks) *n.* A waxy white protective substance covering the skin of a fetus. [Short for VERNIX CASEOSA.]

vernix ca•se•o•sa (kā′sē-ō′sə) *n.* Vernix. [NLat. *vernix cāseōsa* : *vernix*, varnish + *cāseōsa*, cheeselike.]

Ver•non (vûr′nən). **1.** A city of S British Columbia, Canada, near the N end of Okanagan Lake. Pop. 19,987. **2.** A town of N CT NE of Hartford; settled c. 1726. Pop. 29,841.

Ve•ro Beach (vîr′ō). A city of E FL on the Indian R. lagoon NNW of West Palm Beach. Pop. 17,350.

Ve•ro•na (və-rō′nə). A city of N Italy on the Adige R. W of Venice; became an independent republic in A.D. 1107 and formed the powerful Veronese League in 1164. Pop. 261,208. — **Ve′ro•nese′** (vĕr′ə-nēz′, -nēs′) *adj.* & *n.*

Ve•ro•ne•se (vĕr′ə-nā′sē, -zē, vĕ′rô-nĕ′zĕ), **Paolo.** 1528–88. Italian painter whose works include *Rape of Europa* (1576).

Giovanni da Verrazano

ve•ron•i•ca¹ (və-rŏn′ĭ-kə) *n.* Any of various plants of the genus *Veronica*, which includes the speedwells. [NLat. *Veronica*, genus name.]

ve•ron•i•ca² (və-rŏn′ĭ-kə) *n.* **1.a.** According to legend, an image of the face of Jesus impressed on the handkerchief offered to him by Saint Veronica on his way to Calvary. **b.** The handkerchief itself. **2.** A cloth bearing an image of Jesus's face. [Med.Lat., perh. alteration of *vēra īconica*, true image : Lat. *vēra*, fem. of *vērus*, true; see VERY + Lat. *īconica*, fem. of *īconicus*, of an image (< Gk. *eikonikos* < *eikōn*, image; see ICON).]

ve•ron•i•ca³ (və-rŏn′ĭ-kə) *n.* A maneuver in bullfighting in which the matador stands with both feet fixed in position and swings the cape slowly away from the charging bull. [Sp. < *veronica*, the veronica (< the gesture St. Veronica made) < Med.Lat. See VERONICA².]

Ver•ra•za•no or **Ver•raz•za•no** (vĕr′ə-zä′nō, -rä-tsä′nô), **Giovanni da.** 1485?–1528? Italian explorer of the Atlantic coast of North America.

Ver•roc•chio (və-rō′kē-ō, vĕr-rôk′kyô), **Andrea del.** 1435–88. Florentine artist who tutored Leonardo da Vinci.

vervet
Cercopithecus aethiops

ver•ru•ca (və-ro͞o′kə) *n.*, *pl.* **-cae** (-kē). **1.** *Medic.* A wart. **2.** *Biol.* A wartlike projection. [Lat. *verrūca*.]

ver•ru•cose (və-ro͞o′kōs′) also **ver•ru•cous** (-kəs) *adj.* Covered with warts or wartlike projections. [Lat. *verrūcōsus* < *verrūca*, wart.]

vers *abbr. Math.* Versed sine.

Ver•sailles (vər-sī′, vĕr-). A city of N-central France WSW of Paris; known for its magnificent palace, built by Louis XIV in the mid-17th cent. Pop. 91,494.

ver•sant (vûr′sənt) *n.* **1.** The slope of a side of a mountain or mountain range. **2.** The general slope of a region. [Fr., pr.part. of *verser*, to turn < OFr. < Lat. *versāre*, to turn frequently. See VERSATILE.]

ver•sa•tile (vûr′sə-təl, -tīl′) *adj.* **1.** Capable of doing many things competently. **2.** Having varied uses or serving many functions. **3.** Variable or inconstant; changeable. **4.** *Biol.* Capable of moving freely in all directions, as the toe of an owl. [Lat. *versātilis* < *versātus*, p.part. of *versāre*, to turn. See **wer-²***.] — **ver′sa•tile•ly** *adv.* — **ver′sa•til′i•ty** (-tĭl′ĭ-tē), **ver′sa•tile•ness** (-təl-nĭs, -tīl′-) *n.*

verse¹ (vûrs) *n.* **1.a.** A single metrical line in a poetic composition; one line of poetry. **b.** A division of a metrical composition, such as a stanza of a poem. **c.** A poem. **2.** Metrical or rhymed composition as distinct from prose; poetry. **3.a.** The art or work of a poet. **b.** A group of poems: *a book of verse.* **4.** Metrical writing that lacks depth or artistic merit. **5.** A particular type of metrical composition, such as blank verse. **6.** One of the numbered subdivisions of a chapter in the Bible. — *tr.* & *intr.v.* **versed, vers•ing, vers•es.** To versify. [ME *vers* < OE *fers* and < OFr. *vers*, both < Lat. *versus* < p.part. of *vertere*, to turn. See **wer-²***.]

verse² (vûrs) *tr.v.* **versed, vers•ing, vers•es.** To familiarize by study or experience. [Lat. *versāre*. See VERSATILE.]

versed (vûrst) *adj.* Acquainted through study or experience; knowledgeable or skilled: *She is well versed in languages.*

versed cosine *n. Math.* A trigonometric function of an angle equal to one minus the sine of that angle. [VERSED (SINE) + COSINE.]

versed sine *n. Math.* A trigonometric function of an angle equal to one minus the cosine of that angle. [Transl. of NLat. *sinus versus* : *sinus*, sine + Lat. *versus*, p.part. of *vertere*, to turn.]

ver•si•cle (vûr′sĭ-kəl) *n.* **1.** A short verse. **2.** A short sentence spoken or chanted in a Christian liturgy. [ME < Lat. *versiculus*, dim. of *versus*, verse. See VERSE¹.]

ver•si•col•or (vûr′sĭ-kŭl′ər) also **ver•si•col•ored** (-kŭl′ərd) *adj.* **1.** Having a variety of colors; variegated. **2.** Changing in color; iridescent. [Lat. : *versus*, p.part. of *vertere*, to turn; see VERSE¹ + *color*, color; see COLOR.]

ver•si•fi•er (vûr′sə-fī′ər) *n.* One who versifies.

ver•si•fy (vûr′sə-fī′) *v.* **-fied** (-fīd′), **-fy•ing, -fies** (-fīz′). — *tr.* **1.** To change from prose into metrical form. **2.** To treat or tell in verse. — *intr.* To write verses. [ME *versifien* < OFr. *versifier* < Lat. *versificāre* : *versus*, verse; see VERSE¹ + *-ficāre*, -fy.] — **ver′si•fi•ca′tion** (-fĭ-kā′shən) *n.*

ver•sine (vûr′sīn′) *n. Math.* See **versed sine.** [Contraction of VERSED SINE.]

ver•sion (vûr′zhən, -shən) *n.* **1.** An account from one point of view, esp. as opposed to another. **2.a.** A translation from another language. **b.** Often **Version.** A translation of the entire Bible or a part of it. **3.** A particular form or variation of an earlier or original type. **4.** An adaptation of a work of art or literature into another medium or style. **5.** *Medic.* **a.** Manipulation of a fetus in the uterus to bring it into a desirable position for delivery. **b.** Deflection of an organ, such as the uterus, from its normal position. [Fr. < OFr., act of turning < Med.Lat. *versiō*, *versiōn-* < Lat. *versus*, p.part. of *vertere*, to turn. See **wer-²***.] — **ver′sion•al** *adj.*

vers li•bre (vĕr lē′brə) *n.* Free verse. [Fr.]

ver•so (vûr′sō) *n.*, *pl.* **-sos. 1.** *Print.* A left-hand page of a book or the reverse side of a leaf, as opposed to the recto. **2.** The back of a coin or medal. [NLat. *versō (foliō)*, (with the page) turned, verso < Lat. *versō*, ablative of *versus*, p.part. of *vertere*, to turn. See VERSION.]

verst (vûrst) *n.* A Russian measure of linear distance equivalent to about two thirds of a mile. [Fr. *verste* or Ger. *Werst*, both < Russ. *versta*. See **wer-²***.]

ver•sus (vûr′səs, -səz) *prep.* **1.** Against: *the plaintiff versus the defendant.* **2.** As the alternative to or in contrast with. [ME < Med.Lat. < Lat., turned, toward < p.part. of *vertere*, to turn. See **wer-²***.]

vert (vûrt) *n.* **1.** *Her.* The color green. **2.a.** Green vegetation that can serve as cover for deer. Used in English forest law. **b.** The right to cut such vegetation. [ME *verte* < AN, fem. of *verd*. See VERDERER.]

vert. *abbr.* **1.** Vertebrate. **2.** Vertical.

ver•te•bra (vûr′tə-brə) *n.*, *pl.* **-brae** (-brā′, -brē′) or **-bras.** Any of the bones or cartilaginous segments forming the spinal column. [ME < Lat. < *vertere*, to turn. See **wer-²***.]

ver•te•bral (vûr′tə-brəl, vər-tē′brəl) *adj.* **1.** Of, relating to, or of the nature of a vertebra. **2.** Having or consisting of vertebrae. **3.** Having a spinal column. — **ver′te•bral•ly** *adv.*

vertebral canal *n.* See **spinal canal.**

vertebral column *n.* See **spinal column.**

ver•te•brate (vûr′tə-brĭt, -brāt′) *adj.* **1.** Having a backbone or spinal column. **2.** Of or characteristic of vertebrates or a vertebrate. — *n.* A member of the subphylum Vertebrata, a primary division of the phylum Chordata that includes the fishes, amphibians, reptiles, birds, and mammals, all of which are characterized by a segmented spinal column and a distinct, well-differentiated head. [Lat. *vertebrātus*, having joints < *vertebra*, vertebra. See VERTEBRA.]

ver•te•bra•tion (vûr′tə-brā′shən) *n.* Division into segments like those of the spinal column; vertebral formation.

ver•tex (vûr′tĕks′) *n.*, *pl.* **-tex•es** or **-ti•ces** (-tĭ-sēz′). **1.** The highest point; the apex or summit: *the vertex of a mountain.* **2.** *Anat.* **a.** The highest point of the skull. **b.** The top of the head. **3.** *Astron.* The highest point reached in the apparent motion of a celestial body. **4.** *Math.* **a.** The point at which the sides of an angle intersect. **b.** The point on a triangle or pyramid opposite to and farthest away from its base. **c.** A point on a polyhedron common to three or more sides. [Lat., whirling column, vertex < *vertere*, to turn. See **wer-**[2]*.]

ver•ti•cal (vûr′tĭ-kəl) *adj.* **1.** Being or situated at right angles to the horizon; upright. **2.** Situated at the vertex or highest point; directly overhead. **3.** *Anat.* Of or relating to the vertex of the head. **4.** *Econ.* Relating to or involving all stages from production to sale: *vertical integration.* **5.** Relating to or composed of elements at different levels, as of society. —*n.* **1.** Something vertical, as a line, plane, or circle. **2.** A vertical position. [LLat. *verticālis*, overhead < Lat. *vertex, vertic-*, highest point. See VERTEX.] —**ver′ti•cal′i•ty** (-kăl′ĭ-tē), **ver′ti•cal•ness** (-kəl-nĭs) *n.* —**ver′ti•cal•ly** *adv.*

vertical angle *n. Math.* Either of two angles formed by two intersecting lines and lying on opposite sides of the point of intersection.

vertical circle *n.* A great circle on the celestial sphere that passes through the zenith and the nadir and thus is perpendicular to the horizon.

vertical file *n.* A collection of resource materials, such as pamphlets and photographs, for ready reference, as in a library.

vertical union *n.* An industrial union.

ver•ti•cil (vûr′tĭ-sĭl′) *n.* A circular arrangement, as of flowers, leaves, or hairs, growing about a central point; a whorl. [Lat. *verticillus*, the whorl of a spindle, dim. of *vertex, vertic-*, highest point. See VERTEX.]

ver•ti•cil•las•ter (vûr′tĭ-sə-lăs′tər) *n.* A cymose inflorescence resembling a whorl but actually arising in the axils of opposite bracts, as in most mints. [NLat. *verticillastēr* : Lat. *verticillus*, whorl; see VERTICIL + Lat. *astēr*, star; see ASTER.]

ver•ti•cil•late (vûr′tĭ-sĭl′ĭt, -āt′) also **ver•ti•cil•lat•ed** (-sĭl′ā′tĭd) *adj.* Arranged in or forming whorls or a whorl.

ver•tig•i•nous (vər-tĭj′ə-nəs) *adj.* **1.** Turning about an axis; revolving or whirling. **2.** Affected by vertigo; dizzy. **3.** Tending to produce vertigo. **4.** Inclined to change quickly. [< Lat. *vertīgō, vertīgin-*, a whirling < *vertere*, to turn. See VERSION.] —**ver•tig′i•nous•ly** *adv.* —**ver•tig′i•nous•ness** *n.*

ver•ti•go (vûr′tĭ-gō′) *n., pl.* **-goes** or **-gos. 1.a.** The sensation of dizziness. **b.** An instance of such a sensation. **2.** A confused, disoriented state of mind. [ME < Lat. *vertīgō* < *vertere*, to turn. See **wer-**[2]*.]

ver•tu (vər-to͞o′) *n.* Var. of **virtu.**

ver•vain (vûr′vān′) *n.* See **verbena** 1. [ME *verveine* < OFr. < Lat. *verbēna*, leafage. See VERBENA.]

verve (vûrv) *n.* **1.** Energy and enthusiasm in the expression of ideas, esp. in artistic performance or composition. **2.** Vitality; liveliness. **3.** *Archaic.* Aptitude; talent. [Fr. < OFr., fanciful expression, prob. < VLat. **verva* < Lat. *verba*, pl. of *verbum*, word. See **wer-**[5]*.]

ver•vet (vûr′vĭt) *n.* A small African monkey *(Cercopithecus aethiops)* having a yellowish-brown or greenish coat. [Fr. : *vert*, green (< OFr. *verd*; see VERDURE) + *grivet*, grivet.]

ver•y (vĕr′ē) *adv.* **1.** In a high degree; extremely: *very happy.* **2.** Truly; absolutely: *the very best advice.* **3. Very.** Used in titles: *the Very Reverend Jane Smith.* —*adj.* **-i•er, -i•est. 1.** Complete; absolute: *the very opposite.* **2.** Being the identical one; selfsame: *the very question she asked.* **3.** Used to emphasize the importance of the thing named: *the very basis of poetry.* **4.** Being particularly suitable or appropriate: *the very item needed.* **5.** Being precisely as stated: *the very center.* **6.** Mere: *The very thought is frightening.* **7.** Actual: *caught in the very act.* **8.** Genuine; true. [ME *verrai* < OFr. *verai*, true < VLat. **vērācus* < Lat. *vērāx, vērāc-*, truthful < *vērus*, true. See **wēro-***.]

Usage Note: In general usage *very* is not used alone to modify a past participle. Thus we may say of a book, for example, that it has been *very much praised* but not that it has been *very praised.* However, many past participle forms do double duty as adjectives, in which case modification by a bare *very*, or by analogous adverbs such as *quite*, is acceptable: there can be no objection to phrases such as *a very celebrated singer* or *a very polished performance.* In some cases there is disagreement as to whether a particular participle can be used properly as an adjective. What is more, some participles allow treatment as adjectives in one sense but not another: one may speak of *a very inflated reputation,* for example, but not, ordinarily, of *a very inflated balloon.* As a result, there is no sure way to tell which participles may be modified by a bare *very* — syntactic tests such as the use of the participle as an attributive adjective will themselves yield different judgments for different speakers — and writers must trust their ears. When in doubt, the use of *very much* is generally the safer alternative.

very close veins *pl.n. Chiefly Southern U.S.* Varicose veins. [By folk ety. < *varicose veins.*]

very high frequency *n.* A band of radio frequencies falling between 30 and 300 megahertz.

very large scale integration *n. Electron.* Technology that enables the placement of more than 100,000 integrated circuits on a single semiconductor chip.

very low frequency *n.* A band of radio frequencies falling between 3 and 30 kilohertz.

Ver•y pistol (vĕr′ē, vîr′ē) *n.* A pistol used for firing colored signal flares. [After Edward Wilson *Very* (1847–1910), Amer. naval officer.]

Ve•sa•li•us (vĭ-sā′lē-əs, -zā′-), **Andreas.** 1514–64. Flemish anatomist considered the founder of modern anatomy.

ve•si•ca (və-sī′kə, -sē′-) *n., pl.* **-cae** (-kē, -sē). A bladder, esp. the urinary bladder or the gallbladder. [Lat. *vēsīca.*] —**ves′i•cal** (vĕs′ĭ-kəl) *adj.*

ves•i•cant (vĕs′ĭ-kənt) *n.* A blistering agent, esp. mustard gas, used in chemical warfare. —*adj.* Causing blisters.

ves•i•cate (vĕs′ĭ-kāt′) *tr. & intr.v.* **-cat•ed, -cat•ing, -cates.** To blister or become blistered. [NLat. *vēsīcāre, vēsīcāt-* < Lat. *vēsīca*, bladder, blister.] —**ves′i•ca′tion** *n.*

ves•i•ca•to•ry (vĕs′ĭ-kə-tôr′ē, -tōr′ē) *adj.* Vesicant. —*n., pl.* **-ries.** A vesicant.

ves•i•cle (vĕs′ĭ-kəl) *n.* **1.** A small bladderlike cell or cavity. **2.** *Anat.* A small sac or cyst, esp. one containing fluid. **3.** *Pathol.* A serum-filled blister formed in or beneath the skin. **4.** *Geol.* A small cavity formed in volcanic rock by entrapment of a gas bubble during solidification. [ME < OFr. *vesicule* < Lat. *vēsīcula*, dim. of *vēsīca*, bladder, blister.]

ve•sic•u•lar (vĕ-sĭk′yə-lər, və-) *adj.* **1.** Of or relating to vesicles. **2.** Composed of or containing vesicles. **3.** Having the form of a vesicle. —**ve•sic′u•lar•ly** *adv.*

vesicular exanthema *n.* An acute, highly infectious viral disease of swine characterized by formation of vesicles on the snout, the mucous membranes of the mouth, and the feet.

vesicular stomatitis *n.* An acute viral disease of cattle, swine, and horses, transmitted by insects and having symptoms resembling those of vesicular exanthema.

ve•sic•u•late (vĕ-sĭk′yə-lāt′, və-) *tr. & intr.v.* **-lat•ed, -lat•ing, -lates.** To make or become vesicular. —*adj.* (-lĭt, -lāt′). Full of or bearing vesicles; vesicular. —**ve•sic′u•la′tion** *n.*

Ves•pa•sian (vĕs-pā′zhən, -zhē-ən). A.D. 9–79. Emperor of Rome (69–79) who reformed the army.

ves•per (vĕs′pər) *n.* **1.** A bell that summons worshipers to vespers. **2. Vesper.** The evening star, esp. Venus. **3.** *Archaic.* Evening. [ME, evening star < Lat., evening. See **wes-pero-***.]

ves•per•al (vĕs′pər-əl) *Eccles.* —*n.* **1.** A book containing the vespers liturgy. **2.** A covering used to protect an altar cloth. —*adj.* Of or relating to vesper or vespers.

ves•pers also **Ves•pers** (vĕs′pərz) *pl.n. (used with a sing. or pl. v.) Eccles.* **1.a.** The sixth of the seven canonical hours. **b.** The evening office of many Western Christian churches. **c.** The time of day appointed for this service. **2.** Evening Prayer. [Obsolete Fr. *vespres* < OFr. < Med.Lat. *vesperās*, evening service < Lat., accusative pl. of *vespera*, evening, var. of *vesper.* See VESPER.]

vesper sparrow *n.* A North American sparrow *(Pooecetes gramineus)* having white markings on its outer tail feathers.

ves•per•til•i•o•nid (vĕs′pər-tĭl′ē-ə-nĭd) *n.* Any of various widely distributed insect-eating bats of the family Vespertilionidae, characterized by a long tail. [< NLat. *Vespertiliōnidae*, family name < *Vespertiliō, Vespertiliōn-*, type genus < Lat. *vespertiliō*, bat < *vesper*, evening. See **wes-pero-***.] —**ves′per•til′i•o•nid** *adj.*

ves•per•tine (vĕs′pər-tīn′) also **ves•per•ti•nal** (vĕs′pər-tī′nəl) *adj.* **1.** Of, relating to, or occurring in the evening. **2.** *Bot.* Opening or blooming in the evening. **3.** *Zool.* Becoming active in the evening, as bats and owls; crepuscular. [Lat. *vespertīnus* < *vesper*, evening. See VESPER.]

ves•pi•ar•y (vĕs′pē-ĕr′ē) *n., pl.* **-ies.** A nest or colony of wasps or hornets. [Lat. *vespa*, wasp + (AP)IARY.]

ves•pid (vĕs′pĭd) *n.* Any of various widely distributed social insects of the family Vespidae, which includes certain wasps and yellow jackets. [< NLat. *Vespidae*, family name < *Vespa*, type genus < Lat. *vespa*, wasp.] —**ves′pid** *adj.*

ves•pine (vĕs′pīn′) *adj.* Of, relating to, or resembling a wasp. [< Lat. *vespa*, wasp.]

Ves•puc•ci (vĕs-po͞o′chē, -pyo͞o′-), **Amerigo.** Latin name Americus Vespucius. 1454–1512. Italian explorer of the South American coast. America was named in his honor.

ves•sel (vĕs′əl) *n.* **1.** A hollow utensil, such as a cup, vase, or pitcher, used as a container, esp. for liquids. **2.a.** *Naut.* A craft, esp. one larger than a rowboat, designed to navigate on water. **b.** An airship. **3.** *Anat.* A duct, canal, or other tube that contains or conveys a body fluid: *a blood vessel.* **4.** *Bot.* One of the tubular conductive structures of xylem, consisting of dead cylindrical cells attached end to end and connected by perforations. **5.** A person seen as the agent or embodiment, as of a quality: *a vessel of mercy.* [ME < OFr. < LLat. *vāscellum*, dim. of Lat. *vāsculum*, dim. of *vās*, vessel.]

vest (vĕst) *n.* **1.** A sleeveless garment, often having buttons down the front, worn usu. over a shirt or blouse. **2.** A waist-length sleeveless garment worn for protection: *a thick down vest.* **3.** A fabric trim worn to fill in the neckline of a woman's garment; a vestee. **4.** *Chiefly British.* An undershirt. **5.a.** *Archaic.* Clothing; raiment. **b.** *Obsolete.* An ecclesiastical vestment. —*v.* **vest•ed, vest•ing, vests.** —*tr.* **1.** To place (authority, property, or rights, for example) in the control of a

vesper sparrow
Pooecetes gramineus

Amerigo Vespucci
Portrait by
an unknown artist

vest

ă pat	oi boy
ā pay	ou out
âr care	o͝o took
ä father	o͞o boot
ĕ pet	ŭ cut
ē be	ûr urge
ĭ pit	th thin
ī pie	*th* this
îr pier	hw which
ŏ pot	zh vision
ō toe	ə about, item
ô paw	

Stress marks:
′ (primary);
′ (secondary), as in
dictionary (dĭk′shə-nĕr′ē)

person or group, esp. to give someone an immediate right to present or future possession or enjoyment of (an estate, for example). Used with *in*: *vested his estate in his daughter.* **2.** To invest or endow (a person or group) with something, such as power or rights. Used with *with*: *vested the council with broad powers.* **3.** To clothe or robe, as in ecclesiastical vestments. —*intr.* **1.** To become legally vested. **2.** To dress oneself, esp. in ecclesiastical vestments. [Fr. *veste*, robe < Ital. *vesta* < Lat. *vestis*, garment. See **wes-²***.]

Ves•ta (vĕs′tə) *n.* **1.** *Rom. Myth.* The goddess of the hearth, worshiped in a temple containing the sacred fire tended by the vestal virgins. **2.** The brightest asteroid. [Lat. See **wes-¹***.]

ves•tal (vĕs′təl) *adj.* **1.** *Rom. Myth.* **a.** Of or relating to Vesta. **b.** Relating to or characteristic of the vestal virgins. **2.** Chaste; pure. —*n.* **1.** *Rom. Myth.* A vestal virgin. **2.** A woman who is a virgin. **3.** A nun.

vestal virgin *n. Rom. Myth.* One of the girls or women who tended the fire in the temple of Vesta in Rome, remaining virgins during their office.

vest•ed (vĕs′tĭd) *adj.* **1.** *Law.* Settled, fixed, or absolute; being without contingency: *a vested right.* **2.** Dressed or clothed, esp. in ecclesiastical vestments.

vested interest *n.* **1.** *Law.* A right or title, as to present or future possession of an estate, that can be conveyed to another. **2.** A fixed right granted to an employee under a pension plan. **3.** A special interest in protecting or promoting that which is to one's own personal advantage. **4. vested interests.** Those groups that seek to maintain or control an existing system or activity from which they derive private benefit.

vetch
Cow vetch
Vicia cracca

vest•ee (vĕ-stē′) *n.* A garment worn by women as a blouse front under a sweater or jacket. [< VEST.]

ves•ti•ar•y (vĕs′tē-ĕr′ē, -chē-) *adj.* Of or relating to clothes. —*n.*, *pl.* **-ies.** A dressing room, cloakroom, or vestry. [Lat. *vestiārius* < *vestis*, garment. See VEST.]

ves•tib•u•lar (vĕ-stĭb′yə-lər) *adj.* Of or serving as a vestibule.

vestibular nerve *n.* A division of the acoustic nerve that conducts impulses related to maintaining balance to the brain.

ves•ti•bule (vĕs′tə-byo͞ol′) *n.* **1.** A small entrance hall or passage between the outer door and the interior of a house or building. **2.** An enclosed area at the end of a passenger car on a railroad train. **3.** *Anat.* A cavity, chamber, or channel that leads to or is an entrance to another cavity. [Lat. *vestibulum.*]

ves•tige (vĕs′tĭj) *n.* **1.** A visible trace, evidence, or sign of something that exists or appears no longer. **2.** *Biol.* A rudimentary or degenerate, usu. nonfunctioning structure that is the remnant of a formerly fully developed or functioning organ or part. [Fr. < OFr. < Lat. *vestīgium.*]

ves•tig•i•al (vĕ-stĭj′ē-əl, -stĭj′əl) *adj.* **1.** Of, relating to, or constituting a vestige. **2.** *Biol.* Occurring or persisting as a rudimentary or degenerate structure. —**ves•tig′i•al•ly** *adv.*

ves•tig•i•um (vĕ-stĭj′ē-əm) *n.*, *pl.* **-i•a** (-ē-ə). *Biol.* A vestige. [Lat. *vestīgium*, footprint.]

vest•ing (vĕs′tĭng) *n.* The granting to an employee of credits toward a pension even if separated from the job before retirement.

vest•ment (vĕst′mənt) *n.* **1.** A garment, esp. a robe or gown of office or state. **2.** *Eccles.* Any of the liturgical robes worn by celebrants or assistants, esp. at the celebration of the Eucharist. [ME *vestement* < OFr. *vestment* < Lat. *vestīmentum* < *vestīre*, to clothe < *vestis*, garment. See VEST.]

vest-pock•et (vĕst′pŏk′ĭt) *adj.* **1.** Small enough to fit into a vest pocket: *a vest-pocket book.* **2.** Very small; diminutive.

ves•try (vĕs′trē) *n.*, *pl.* **-tries.** **1.** A room in or attached to a church where clergy put on their vestments and where sacred objects are stored; a sacristy. **2.** A room in a church used for meetings and classes. **3.** A committee of members elected to administer the temporal affairs of a parish. **4.** A business meeting of parishioners in a parish. [ME *vestrie*, ult. < Lat. *vestiārius*, of clothes.]

ves•try•man (vĕs′trē-mən) *n.* A man who is a member of a vestry.

ves•try•wom•an (vĕs′trē-wo͝om′ən) *n.* A woman who is a member of a vestry.

ves•ture (vĕs′chər) *n.* **1.** Clothing; apparel. **2.** Something that covers or cloaks: *hills in a vesture of mist.* —*tr.v.* **-tured, -tur•ing, -tures.** To cover with vesture; clothe. [ME < OFr. < VLat. **vestītūra* < Lat. *vestītus*, p.part. of *vestīre*, to clothe < *vestis*, garment. See VEST.]

ve•su•vi•an (vĭ-so͞o′vē-ən) *n.* A friction match with a phosphorus tip. —*adj.* Marked by sudden or violent outbursts. [After Mt. VESUVIUS.]

ve•su•vi•an•ite (vĭ-so͞o′vē-ə-nīt′) *n.* A green, brown, or yellow metamorphic silicate mineral, $Ca_{10}Mg_2Al_4Si_9O_{34}(OH)_4$.

Ve•su•vi•us (vĭ-so͞o′vē-əs), **Mount.** An active volcano, 1,281 m (4,200 ft), of S Italy on the E shore of the Bay of Naples. A violent eruption in A.D. 79 destroyed the nearby city of Pompeii. —**Ve•su′vi•an** *adj.*

vet¹ (vĕt) *Informal.* —*n.* A veterinarian. —*v.* **vet•ted, vet•ting, vets.** —*tr.* **1.** To subject to veterinary evaluation, examination, medication, or surgery. **2.** To subject to thorough examination or evaluation: *vet a manuscript.* —*intr.* To engage in the practice of veterinary medicine.

vet² (vĕt) *n. Informal.* A veteran.

vet. *abbr.* Veteran.

vetch (vĕch) *n.* Any of various herbs of the genus *Vicia*, having pinnately compound leaves that terminate in tendrils and small, variously colored flowers. [ME *vetche* < ONFr. *veche* < Lat. *vicia*. See **weik-²***.]

vetch•ling (vĕch′lĭng) *n.* Any of several plants of the genus *Lathyrus*, having pinnately compound leaves, slender tendrils, and variously colored flowers.

veter. *abbr.* Veterinary.

vet•er•an (vĕt′ər-ən, vĕt′rən) *n.* **1.** A person who is long experienced or practiced in an activity or a capacity. **2.** One who has served in the armed forces. **3.** An old soldier who has seen long service. —*adj.* **1.** Having had long experience or practice. **2.** Of or relating to former members of the armed forces. [Lat. *veterānus* < *vetus*, *veter-*, old. See **wet-²***.]

Vet•er•ans Day (vĕt′ər-ənz, vĕt′rənz) *n.* November 11, observed in honor of veterans of the armed services and in commemoration of the armistice that ended World War I in 1918.

vet•er•i•nar•i•an (vĕt′ər-ə-nâr′ē-ən, vĕt′rə-) *n.* A person who practices veterinary medicine.

vet•er•i•nar•y (vĕt′ər-ə-nĕr′ē, vĕt′rə-) *adj.* Of or relating to veterinary medicine; concerned or connected with the medical or surgical treatment of animals, esp. domestic animals. —*n.*, *pl.* **-ies.** A veterinarian. [Lat. *veterīnārius*, ult. < *veterīnus*, of beasts of burden. See **wet-²***.]

veterinary medicine *n.* The branch of medicine that deals with the causes, diagnosis, and treatment of diseases and injuries of animals, esp. domestic animals.

veterinary surgeon *n.* A veterinarian.

vet•i•ver (vĕt′ə-vər) *n.* **1.** A grass *(Vetiveria zizanioides)* of tropical India cultivated for its aromatic roots that yield an oil used in perfumery. **2.** The root of this plant. [Fr. *vétiver* < Tamil *veṭṭivēr* : *veṭṭi*, worthless + *vēru*, useless.]

vet•i•vert (vĕt′ə-vûrt′) *n.* The essential oil of the vetiver.

Vet•lu•ga (vĕt-lo͞o′gə). A river of W Russia flowing c. 850 km (528 mi) generally S to the Volga R.

ve•to (vē′tō) *n.*, *pl.* **-toes.** **1.a.** The vested power or constitutional right of one branch or department of government to refuse approval of measures proposed by another department, esp. the power of a chief executive to reject a bill passed by the legislature and thus prevent or delay its enactment into law. **b.** Exercise of this right. **c.** An official document or message from a chief executive stating the reasons for rejection of a bill. **2.** An authoritative prohibition or rejection of a proposed or intended act. —*tr.v.* **-toed, -to•ing, -toes.** **1.** To prevent (a legislative bill) from becoming law by veto. **2.** To forbid or prohibit authoritatively. [< Lat. *vetō*, first pers. sing. pr.t. of *vetāre*, to forbid.] —**ve′to•er** *n.*

vex (vĕks) *tr.v.* **vexed, vex•ing, vex•es.** **1.** To annoy, as with petty importunities; bother. **2.** To cause perplexity in; puzzle. **3.** To bring distress or suffering to; plague or afflict. **4.** To debate or discuss (a question, for example) at length. **5.** To toss about or shake up. [ME *vexen* < OFr. *vexer* < Lat. *vexāre*. See **wegh-***.] —**vex′ed•ly** (vĕk′sĭd-lē) *adv.* —**vex′er** *n.* —**vex′ing•ly** *adv.*

vex•a•tion (vĕk-sā′shən) *n.* **1.** The act of annoying, irritating, or vexing. **2.** The quality or condition of being vexed; annoyance. **3.** A source of irritation or annoyance.

vex•a•tious (vĕk-sā′shəs) *adj.* **1.** Causing or creating vexation; annoying. **2.** Full of annoyance or distress; harassed. **3.** Intended to vex or annoy. —**vex•a′tious•ly** *adv.* —**vex•a′tious•ness** *n.*

vexed (vĕkst) *adj.* **1.** Irritated, distressed, or annoyed. **2.** Much discussed or debated: *a vexed question.*

vex•il•lar•y (vĕk′sə-lĕr′ē) *n.*, *pl.* **-ies.** **1.** A member of the oldest class of army veterans who served under a special standard in ancient Rome. **2.** A standard-bearer. —*adj.* Of or relating to a vexillum. [Lat. *vexillārius* < *vexillum*, flag. See VEXILLUM.]

vex•il•late (vĕk′sə-lĭt, -lāt′) *adj.* Having a vexillum.

vex•il•lol•o•gy (vĕk′sə-lŏl′ə-jē) *n.* The study of flags. —**vex•il′lo•log′ic** (vĕk-sĭl′ə-lŏj′ĭk), **vex•il′lo•log′i•cal** (-ĭ-kəl) *adj.* —**vex′il•lol′o•gist** *n.*

vex•il•lum (vĕk-sĭl′əm) *n.*, *pl.* **vex•il•la** (vĕk-sĭl′ə). **1.** *Bot.* See **standard** 8. **2.** *Zool.* The weblike part of a feather; the vane. [Lat., flag, dim. of *vēlum*, a covering.]

V.F. *abbr.* **1.** Also **VF.** Video frequency. **2.** Also **VF.** Visual field.

VFD *abbr.* Volunteer fire department.

VFR *abbr.* Visual flight rules.

VFW also **V.F.W.** *abbr.* Veterans of Foreign Wars.

V.G. *abbr. Rom. Cath. Ch.* Vicar general.

vhf or **VHF** *abbr.* Very high frequency.

VI or **V.I.** *abbr.* Virgin Islands.

v.i. *abbr. Lat.* Vide infra (see below).

vi•a (vī′ə, vē′ə) *prep.* **1.** By way of: *to Pittsburgh via Philadelphia.* **2.** By means of: *sent the letter via airmail.* [Lat. *viā*, ablative of *via*, road. See **wegh-***.]

vi•a•ble (vī′ə-bəl) *adj.* **1.** Able to live, develop, or germinate under favorable conditions. **2.** Able to live outside the uterus. Used of a fetus or newborn. **3.** Capable of success or continuing effectiveness; practicable. [Fr. < *vie*, life < OFr. < Lat.

vīta. See **g^{w}ei-***.] — **vi′a•bil′i•ty** *n.* — **vi′a•bly** *adv.*

vi•a•duct (vī′ə-dŭkt′) *n.* A series of spans or arches used to carry a road or railroad over a wide valley or over other roads or railroads. [Lat. *via,* road; see VIA + (AQUE)DUCT.]

vi•al (vī′əl) *n.* A small container, usu. with a closure, esp. for liquids. — *tr.v.* **-aled, -al•ing, -als** or **-alled, -al•ling, -als.** To put or keep in or as if in a vial. [ME *viole,* var. of *fiol.* See PHIAL.]

via me•di•a (mē′dē-ə, mĕd′ē-ə, mā′dē-ə) *n.* The middle course or way. [Lat. : *via,* way + *media,* middle.]

vi•and (vī′ənd) *n.* **1.a.** An item of food. **b.** A very choice or delicious dish. **2. viands.** Provisions; victuals. [ME *viaunde* < OFr. *viande* < VLat. **vīvanda,* alteration of Lat. *vīvenda,* neut. pl. gerundive of *vīvere,* to live. See **g^{w}ei-***.]

vi•at•ic (vī-ăt′ĭk) also **vi•at•i•cal** (-ĭ-kəl) *adj.* Of or relating to traveling, a road, or a way. [Lat. *viāticus* < *via,* road. See VIA.]

vi•at•i•cum (vī-ăt′ĭ-kəm, vē-) *n., pl.* **-ca** (-kə) or **-cums.** **1.** *Eccles.* The Eucharist given to a dying person or one in danger of death. **2.** Journey supplies. [LLat. *viāticum* < Lat., traveling provisions < neut. of *viāticus,* viatic. See VIATIC.]

vibe (vīb) *n. Slang.* A vibration. Often used in the plural: *good vibes; bad vibes.* [Short for VIBRATION.]

vibes (vībz) *pl.n. Mus.* A vibraphone. — **vib′ist** (vī′bĭst) *n.*

vi•brac•u•lum (vī-brăk′yə-ləm) *n., pl.* **-la** (-lə). One of the long, whiplike, modified zooids on the surface of certain bryozoan colonies. [NLat. *vibrāculum* < Lat. *vibrāre,* to shake. See VIBRATE.] — **vi•brac′u•lar** (-lər) *adj.*

vi•bra•harp (vī′brə-härp′) *n. Mus.* See **vibraphone.** — **vi′bra•harp′ist** *n.*

vi•brant (vī′brənt) *adj.* **1.a.** Pulsing or throbbing with energy or activity: *vibrant city streets.* **b.** Vigorous, lively, and vital. **2.** Exhibiting or characterized by rapid, rhythmic movement back and forth or to and fro; vibrating. **3.** Produced as a result of vibration; resonant or resounding: *vibrant voices.* **4.** *Color.* Relatively high on the scale of brightness: *a vibrant hue.* — **vi′bran•cy, vi′brance** *n.* — **vi′brant•ly** *adv.*

vi•bra•phone (vī′brə-fōn′) *n. Mus.* An instrument similar to a marimba but having metal bars and rotating disks in the resonators to produce a vibrato. [Lat. *vibrāre,* to shake; see VIBRATE + -PHONE.] — **vi′bra•phon′ist** *n.*

vi•brate (vī′brāt′) *v.* **-brat•ed, -brat•ing, -brates.** — *intr.* **1.** To move back and forth or to and fro, esp. rhythmically and rapidly. **2.** To feel a quiver of emotion. **3.** To shake or move with or as if with a slight quivering or trembling motion. **4.** To produce a sound; resonate. **5.** To fluctuate or waver in making choices; vacillate. — *tr.* **1.** To cause to tremble or quiver. **2.** To cause to move back and forth rapidly. **3.** To produce (sound) by vibration. [Lat. *vibrāre, vibrāt-.* See **weip-***.]

vi•bra•tile (vī′brə-tl, -tīl′) *adj.* **1.** Characterized by vibration. **2.** Capable of or adapted to vibratory motion. [Fr. < Lat. *vibrātus,* p.part. of *vibrāre,* to vibrate. See VIBRATE.] — **vi′bra•til′i•ty** (-tĭl′ĭ-tē) *n.*

vi•bra•tion (vī-brā′shən) *n.* **1.a.** The act of vibrating. **b.** The condition of being vibrated. **2.** *Phys.* **a.** A rapid linear motion of a particle or of an elastic solid about an equilibrium position. **b.** An oscillation. **3.** A single complete vibrating motion; a quiver. **4.** *Slang.* A distinctive aura or atmosphere held to be instinctively sensed. Often used in the plural. — **vi•bra′tion•al** *adj.*

vi•bra•to (və-brä′tō, vī-) *n., pl.* **-tos.** *Mus.* A tremulous or pulsating effect produced in an instrumental or vocal tone by minute and rapid variations in pitch. [Ital. < LLat. *vibrātus,* a quivering < Lat., p.part. of *vibrāre,* to vibrate. See VIBRATE.]

vi•bra•tor (vī′brā′tər) *n.* **1.** Something that vibrates. **2.** An electrically operated massage device. **3.** An electrical device consisting of a vibrating conductor interrupting a current.

vi•bra•to•ry (vī′brə-tôr′ē, -tōr′ē) also **vi•bra•tive** (-tĭv) *adj.* **1.** Of, characterized by, or consisting of vibration. **2.** Causing vibration. **3.** Vibrating or capable of vibration.

vib•ri•o (vĭb′rē-ō′) *n., pl.* **-os.** Any of various short motile S-shaped or comma-shaped bacteria of the genus *Vibrio,* esp. *V. cholerae,* which causes cholera. [NLat. *Vibriō,* genus name < Lat. *vibrāre,* to vibrate (< their vibratory motion). See VIBRATE.] — **vib′ri•oid′** (-oid′) *adj.*

vib•ri•o•sis (vĭb′rē-ō′sĭs) *n., pl.* **-ses** (-sēz). **1.** Infection with the bacterium *Vibrio parahaemolyticus,* often from eating undercooked seafood from contaminated waters. **2.** A venereal infection in cattle and sheep caused by the bacterium *Vibrio fetus,* often producing infertility or spontaneous abortion.

vi•bris•sa (vī-brĭs′ə, və-) *n., pl.* **-bris•sae** (-brĭs′ē). **1.** Any of the long, stiff hairs that project from the snout or brow of most mammals, as the whiskers of a cat. **2.** One of several long modified feathers that grow along the gape of the mouth of insect-eating birds. [< LLat. *vibrissae,* nostril hairs < *vibrāre,* to vibrate. See VIBRATE.]

vi•bron•ic (vī-brŏn′ĭk) *adj.* Of or relating to changes in molecular energy states associated with the vibrational energy of atoms. [VIBR(ATION) + (ELECTR)ONIC.]

vi•bur•num (vī-bûr′nəm) *n.* Any of various shrubs or trees of the genus *Viburnum,* having opposite leaves, white or pink flowers, and red or black drupes. [Lat. *vīburnum,* a shrub.]

vic. *abbr.* **1.** Vicar. **2.** Vicinity.

vic•ar (vĭk′ər) *n.* **1.a.** A parish priest in the Church of England who receives a stipend or salary but no tithes. **b.** A cleric in charge of a chapel in the Episcopal Church. **c.** A cleric acting in the place of a rector or bishop in the Anglican Communion. **2.** *Rom. Cath. Ch.* A priest who acts for or represents another cleric. [ME < OFr. *vicaire* < Lat. *vicārius,* vicarious, a substitute < *vicis,* genitive of **vix,* change. See **weik-**[2]***.] — **vic′ar•ship′** *n.*

vic•ar•age (vĭk′ər-ĭj) *n.* **1.** The residence of a vicar. **2.** The benefice of a vicar. **3.** The duties or office of a vicar; a vicariate.

vicar apostolic *n., pl.* **vicars apostolic.** *Rom. Cath. Ch.* A titular bishop who administers a region that is not yet a diocese or in which the ordinary episcopal jurisdiction is impeded.

vicar general *n., pl.* **vicars general.** **1.** *Rom. Cath. Ch.* **a.** A priest acting as deputy to a bishop. **b.** The head of a religious order. **2.** An official in the Church of England, usu. a layperson, who assists a bishop.

vi•car•i•al (vī-kâr′ē-əl, -kăr′-, vĭ-) *adj.* **1.** Of or relating to a vicar. **2.** Acting as or having the position of a vicar. **3.** Serving in the place of someone or something else.

vi•car•i•ate (vī-kâr′ē-ĭt, -āt′, -kăr′-, vĭ-) *n.* **1.** The office or authority of a vicar. **2.** The district under a vicar.

vi•car•i•ous (vī-kâr′ē-əs, -kăr′-, vĭ-) *adj.* **1.** Felt or undergone as if one were taking part in the experience or feelings of another. **2.** Endured or done by one person substituting for another. **3.a.** Acting or serving in place of someone or something else; substituted. **b.** Committed or entrusted to another, as powers or authority; delegated. **4.** *Physiol.* Occurring in or performed by a part of the body not normally associated with a certain function. [< Lat. *vicārius.* See VICAR.] — **vi•car′i•ous•ly** *adv.* — **vi•car′i•ous•ness** *n.*

Vic•ar of Christ (vĭk′ər) *n. Rom. Cath. Ch.* The pope.

vice[1] (vīs) *n.* **1.a.** An evil, degrading, or immoral practice or habit. **b.** A serious moral failing. **c.** Wicked or evil conduct or habits; corruption. **2.** Sexual immorality, esp. prostitution. **3.a.** A slight personal failing; a foible. **b.** A flaw; a defect. **4.** A physical defect or weakness. **5.** An undesirable habit in a domestic animal. **6. Vice. a.** A character representing generalized or particular vice in English morality plays. **b.** A jester or buffoon. [ME < OFr. < Lat. *vitium.*]

vice[2] (vīs) *n. & v.* Var. of **vise.**

vi•ce[3] (vī′sē, -sə) *prep.* In place of; replacing. [Latin, ablative of **vix,* change. See VICE-.]

vice- *pref.* One who acts in the place of another; deputy: *vicechairman.* [ME < OFr. < LLat. < Lat. *vice,* ablative of **vix,* change. See **weik-**[2]***.]

vice admiral (vīs) *n.* A commissioned officer in the U.S. Navy or Coast Guard ranking above rear admiral and below admiral.

vice-ad•mir•al•ty (vīs-ăd′mər-əl-tē) *n., pl.* **-ties.** The office, rank, or command of a vice admiral.

vice chancellor (vīs) *n.* **1.** A deputy or an assistant chancellor in a university. **2.** A deputy to or a substitute for a head of state or an official bearing the title chancellor. **3.** *Law.* A judge in equity courts ranking below a chancellor. — **vice-chan′cel•lor•ship′** (vīs-chăn′sə-lər-shĭp′, -chăns′lər-) *n.*

vice consul (vīs) *n.* A consular officer who is subordinate to and a deputy of a consul or consul general. — **vice-con′su•lar** (vīs-kŏn′sə-lər) *adj.* — **vice-con′su•late** (-sə-lĭt), **vice-con′sul•ship′** (-səl-shĭp′) *n.*

vice•ge•ren•cy (vīs-jîr′ən-sē) *n., pl.* **-cies.** **1.** The position, function, or authority of a vicegerent. **2.** A district under a vicegerent's jurisdiction.

vice•ge•rent (vīs-jîr′ənt) *n.* A person appointed by a ruler or head of state to act as an administrative deputy. [Med.Lat. *vicegerēns, vicegerent-* : Lat. *vice,* ablative of **vix,* change; see VICE[3] + Lat. *gerēns,* governing; see GERENT.] — **vice•ge′ral** (-jîr′əl) *adj.*

vic•e•nar•y (vĭs′ə-nĕr′ē) *adj.* Consisting of, relating to, or based on 20. [Lat. *vīcēnārius* < *vīcēnī,* twenty each < *vīgintī,* twenty. See **wīkm̥tī***.]

vi•cen•ni•al (vī-sĕn′ē-əl) *adj.* **1.** Happening once every 20 years. **2.** Existing or lasting for 20 years. [< LLat. *vīcennium,* period of twenty years : Lat. *vīciēns,* twenty times (< *vīgintī,* twenty; see VICENARY) + Lat. *annus,* year; see **at-***.]

Vi•cen•za (vĭ-chĕn′sə, vē-chĕn′dzä). A city of NE Italy W of Venice; founded by Ligurians c. 1st cent. B.C.

vice pres•i•dent or **vice-pres•i•dent** (vīs′prĕz′ĭ-dənt, -dĕnt′) *n.* **1.** An officer ranking next below a president, usu. empowered to assume the president's duties under conditions such as absence or death. **2.** A deputy to a president, esp. in a corporation, in charge of a specific department or location: *vice president of sales.* — **vice-pres′i•den•cy** (vīs-prĕz′ĭ-dən-sē, -dĕn′-) *n.* — **vice-pres′i•den′tial** (-dĕn′shəl) *adj.*

vice•re•gal (vīs-rē′gəl) *adj.* Of or relating to a viceroy. — **vice•re′gal•ly** *adv.*

vice regent (vīs) *n.* One who acts as a regent's deputy. — **vice-re′gen•cy** (vīs-rē′jən-sē) *n.*

vice•reine (vīs′rān′) *n.* **1.** The wife of a viceroy. **2.** A woman who governs a country, province, or colony as the represen-

viaduct

ă pat	oi boy
ā pay	ou out
âr care	o͝o took
ä father	o͞o boot
ĕ pet	ŭ cut
ē be	ûr urge
ĭ pit	th thin
ī pie	*th* this
îr pier	hw which
ŏ pot	zh vision
ō toe	ə about, item
ô paw	

Stress marks:
′ (primary);
′ (secondary), as in
dictionary (dĭk′shə-nĕr′ē)

tative of a sovereign. [Fr. : *vice-*, vice (< OFr.; see VICE[3]) + *reine*, queen (< Lat. *rēgīna*, fem. of *rēx*, *rēg-*, king; see **reg-***).]

vice•roy (vīs′roi′) *n.* **1.** A man who governs a country, province, or colony as the representative of a sovereign. **2.** An orange and black North American butterfly *(Limenitis archippus)* resembling the monarch. [Fr. : *vice-*, vice; see VICEREINE + *roi*, king (< Lat. *rēx*, *rēg-*; see **reg-***).]

vice•roy•al•ty (vīs′roi′əl-tē, vīs-roi′-) *n., pl.* **-ties. 1.** The office, authority, or term of service of a viceroy. **2.** A district or province governed by a viceroy.

vice squad (vīs) *n.* A police division charged with law enforcement in areas such as gambling and prostitution.

vi•ce ver•sa (vī′sə vûr′sə, vīs′) *adv.* With the order or meaning reversed; conversely. [Lat. *vice versā* : *vice*, ablative of **vix*, position + *versā*, fem. ablative of *versus*, p.part. of *vertere*, to turn.]

victoria

Vi•chy (vĭsh′ē, vē′shē). A city of central France SSE of Paris; cap. of unoccupied France from Jul. 1940 until Nov. 1942 during World War II. Pop. 30,527.

vi•chys•soise (vĭsh′ē-swäz′, vē′shē-) *n.* A thick creamy potato soup flavored with leeks and onions, usu. served cold. [Fr. < fem. of *vichyssois*, of Vichy.]

Vichy water *n.* **1.** A naturally effervescent mineral water from the springs at Vichy. **2.** A sparkling mineral water resembling this effervescent beverage.

vic•i•nage (vĭs′ə-nĭj) *n.* **1.a.** A limited region around a particular area; a vicinity. **b.** A number of places near each other, considered as a group. **2.** The residents of a given neighborhood. **3.** The state of living in a neighborhood; proximity. [ME *vesinage* < OFr. < *vesin*, neighboring < Lat. *vīcīnus*. See VICINITY.]

Victoria[1]

vic•i•nal (vĭs′ə-nəl) *adj.* **1.** Of, belonging to, or restricted to a limited area or neighborhood; local. **2.** Relating to or being a local road. **3.** *Mineral.* Approximating, resembling, or taking the place of a fundamental crystalline form or face. **4.** *Chem.* Of or relating to consecutive positions on a benzene ring. [Lat. *vīcīnālis* < *vīcīnus*, neighboring. See VICINITY.]

vi•cin•i•ty (vĭ-sĭn′ĭ-tē) *n., pl.* **-ties. 1.** The state of being near in space or relationship; proximity. **2.** A nearby, surrounding, or adjoining region; a neighborhood. **3.** An approximate degree or amount. [Lat. *vīcīnitās* < *vīcīnus*, neighboring < *vīcus*, neighborhood. See **weik-**[1]*.]

vi•cious (vĭsh′əs) *adj.* **1.** Having the nature of vice; evil, immoral, or depraved. **2.** Given to vice, immorality, or depravity. **3.** Spiteful; malicious. **4.** Disposed to or characterized by violent or destructive behavior. See Syns at **cruel. 5.** Marked by an aggressive disposition; savage. Used chiefly of animals. **6.** Faulty, imperfect, or otherwise impaired by defects or a defect. **7.** Impure; foul. [ME < OFr. *vicieus* < Lat. *vitiōsus* < *vitium*, vice.] **—vi′cious•ly** *adv.* **—vi′cious•ness** *n.*

vicious circle *n.* **1.** A situation in which the apparent solution of one problem in a chain of circumstances creates a new problem. **2.** A condition in which a disorder or disease gives rise to another. **3.** *Logic.* A fallacy in reasoning in which the premise is used to prove the conclusion and the conclusion used to prove the premise. [Transl. of NLat. *circulus vitiōsus*, circular argument : Med.Lat. *circulus*, circular argument + Lat. *vitiōsus*, flawed, faulty.]

vicuña
Vicugna vicugna

vi•cis•si•tude (vĭ-sĭs′ĭ-to͞od′, -tyo͞od′) *n.* **1.a.** A change or variation. **b.** The quality of being changeable; mutability. **2.** One of the sudden or unexpected changes or shifts often encountered in one's life, activities, or surroundings. Often used in the plural. See Syns at **difficulty.** [Lat. *vicissitūdō* < *vicissim*, in turn, prob. < *vicēs*, pl. of **vix*, change. See **weik-**[2]*.]

vi•cis•si•tu•di•nar•y (vĭ-sĭs′ĭ-to͞od′n-ĕr′ē, -tyo͞od′-) also **vi•cis•si•tu•di•nous** (-to͞od′n-əs, -tyo͞od′-) *adj.* Characterized by, full of, or subject to vicissitudes.

Vicks•burg (vĭks′bûrg′). A city of W MS on bluffs above the Mississippi R. W of Jackson; besieged and captured (1862–63) by Union troops in the Civil War. Pop. 20,908.

vic•tim (vĭk′tĭm) *n.* **1.** One who is harmed or killed by another. **2.** A living creature slain and offered as a sacrifice during a religious rite. **3.** One harmed by or made to suffer from an act, circumstance, agency, or condition. **4.** One who suffers injury, loss, or death as a result of a voluntary undertaking. **5.** One who is tricked, swindled, or taken advantage of. [Lat. *victima.*] **—vic′tim•hood′** (-ho͝od′) *n.*

video game

vic•tim•ize (vĭk′tə-mīz′) *tr.v.* **-ized, -iz•ing, -iz•es. 1.** To subject to swindle or fraud. **2.** To make a victim of. **—vic′tim•i•za′tion** (-tə-mĭ-zā′shən) *n.* **—vic′tim•iz′er** *n.*

vic•tim•less crime (vĭk′tĭm-lĭs) *n.* An illegal act that is felt to have no direct or identifiable victim.

vic•tor (vĭk′tər) *n.* One who defeats an adversary; the winner in a fight, contest, or struggle. [Ult. < Lat. *victor*, *victōr-* < *victus*, p.part. of *vincere*, to conquer. See **weik-**[3]*.]

Vic•tor Em•man•u•el II (vĭk′tər ĭ-măn′yo͞o-əl). 1820–78. Italian king (1861–78) who completed the unification of Italy by acquiring Venice (1866) and Rome (1870).

Victor Emmanuel III. 1869–1947. Italian king (1900–46) who appointed Benito Mussolini prime minister in 1922 and abdicated in 1946.

vic•to•ri•a (vĭk-tôr′ē-ə, -tōr′-) *n.* **1.** A low light four-wheeled carriage for two with a folding top and an elevated driver's seat in front. **2.** A touring car with a folding top usu. covering only the rear seat. [After VICTORIA[1].]

Vic•to•ri•a[1] (vĭk-tôr′ē-ə, -tōr′-). 1819–1901. Queen of Great Britain and Ireland (1837–1901) and empress of India (1876–1901).

Vic•to•ri•a[2] (vĭk-tôr′ē-ə, -tōr′-). **1.** The cap. of British Columbia, Canada, on SE Vancouver I. at the E end of the Strait of Juan de Fuca; founded in 1843 as a Hudson's Bay Company outpost. Pop. 64,379. **2.** The cap. of Hong Kong, on the NW coast of Hong Kong I. Pop. 1,183,621. **3.** The cap. of Seychelles, on the NE coast of Mahé I. on the Indian Ocean. Pop. 23,000. **4.** A city of SE TX SE of San Antonio. Pop. 55,076.

Victoria, Lake. Also **Victoria Ny•an•za** (nī-ăn′zə, nyän′-). A lake of E-central Africa bordered by Uganda, Kenya, and Tanzania.

Victoria Cross *n.* A bronze Maltese cross, Britain's highest military award for conspicuous valor. [After VICTORIA[1].]

Victoria Day *n.* The last Monday before May 25, observed in Canada in commemoration of the birthday of Queen Victoria.

Victoria Falls. A waterfall, 108.3 m (355 ft), of S-central Africa in the Zambezi R. between SW Zambia and NW Zimbabwe.

Victoria Island. An island of N-central Northwest Terrs., Canada, in the Arctic Archipelago E of Banks I.

Victoria Land. A region of Antarctica bounded by Ross Sea and Wilkes Land; discovered by Sir James Clark Ross during his 1839–43 expedition.

Vic•to•ri•an (vĭk-tôr′ē-ən, -tōr′-) *adj.* **1.** Of or relating to the period of the reign of Queen Victoria. **2.** Relating to or displaying the standards of morality regarded as characteristic of the time of Queen Victoria. **3.** Being in the highly ornamented massive style of architecture, decor, and furnishings popular in 19th-century England. — *n.* One belonging to or exhibiting characteristics typical of the Victorian period. **—Vic•to′ri•an•ism** *n.* **—Vic•to′ri•an•ize′** *v.*

Vic•to•ri•an•a (vĭk-tôr′ē-ăn′ə, -ä′nə, -tōr′-) *n.* Material or a collection of materials of, relating to, or characteristic of the Victorian era.

Victoria Nile (nīl). A section of the Nile R., c. 418 km (260 mi), between Lake Victoria and Lake Albert in central Uganda.

Vic•to•ri•a•ville (vĭk-tôr′ē-ə-vĭl′, -tōr′-). A town of S Quebec, Canada, SE of Trois Rivières. Pop. 21,838.

vic•to•ri•ous (vĭk-tôr′ē-əs, -tōr′-) *adj.* **1.** Being the winner in a contest or struggle: *the victorious army.* **2.** Characteristic of or expressing a sense of victory or fulfillment: *a victorious cheer.* **—vic•to′ri•ous•ly** *adv.* **—vic•to′ri•ous•ness** *n.*

vic•to•ry (vĭk′tə-rē) *n., pl.* **-ries. 1.** Defeat of an enemy or opponent. **2.** Success in a struggle against difficulties or an obstacle. **3.** The state of having triumphed. [ME < OFr. *victorie* < Lat. *victōria* < *victor*, *victōr-*, victor. See VICTOR.]

vict•ual (vĭt′l) *n.* **1.** Food fit for human consumption. **2. victuals.** Food supplies; provisions. — *v.* **-ualed, -ual•ing, -uals** or **-ualled, -ual•ling, -uals.** — *tr.* To provide with food. — *intr.* **1.** To lay in food supplies. **2.** To eat. [Alteration of ME *vitaille* < OFr. < LLat. *vīctuālia*, provisions < Lat., neut. pl. of *vīctuālis*, of nourishment < *vīctus*, nourishment < p.part. of *vīvere*, to live. See **g**ʷ**ei-***.]

vict•ual•er also **vict•ual•ler** (vĭt′l-ər) *n.* **1.** A supplier of victuals; a sutler. **2.** *Chiefly British.* An innkeeper. **3.** *Naut.* A supply ship.

vi•cu•ña also **vi•cu•na** (vī-ko͞on′yə, -ko͞o′nə, -kyo͞o′nə, vĭ-) *n.* **1.** A llamalike ruminant mammal *(Vicugna vicugna)* of the central Andes having fine silky fleece. **2.** This fleece. **3.** Fabric made from vicuña fleece. [Sp. < Quechua *wikuña.*]

Vi•dal (vĭ-däl′), **Gore.** Born 1925. Amer. writer whose works include the novel *Myra Breckinridge* (1968).

vi•de (vī′dē, vē′dā′, wē′-) *v.* See. Used to direct a reader's attention. [Lat., sing. imper. of *vidēre*, to see. See **weid-***.]

vi•del•i•cet (vĭ-dĕl′ĭ-sĕt′, vī-, wĭ-dā′lĭ-kĕt′) *adv.* That is; namely. Used to introduce examples, lists, or items. [Lat. *vidēlicet*, contraction of *vidēre licet*, it is permitted to see : *vidēre*, to see; see VIDE + *licet*, it is permitted, third pers. sing. pr.t. of *licēre*, to be permitted.]

vid•e•o (vĭd′ē-ō′) *adj.* **1.** Of or relating to television, esp. televised images. **2.** Of or relating to videotaped productions or videotape equipment and technology. — *n., pl.* **-os. 1.** The visual portion of a televised broadcast. **2.** Television: *a star of video.* **3.** A videocassette or videotape, esp. one containing a recording for playback on a television set. [< Lat. *videō*, first pers. sing. pr.t. of *vidēre*, to see. See VIDE.]

video camera *n.* A portable camera that records on videocassettes for playback on a television set.

vid•e•o•cas•sette (vĭd′ē-ō-kə-sĕt′, -kă-) *n.* A cassette containing blank or prerecorded videotape.

videocassette recorder *n.* A VCR.

vid•e•o•con•fer•ence (vĭd′ē-ō-kŏn′fər-əns, -frəns) *n.* A teleconference conducted via closed-circuit television. **—vid′e•o•con′fer•enc•ing** *n.*

vid•e•o•disk also **vid•e•o•disc** (vĭd′ē-ō-dĭsk′) *n.* A recording on disk of sounds and images that can be played back on a television receiver. [Originally a Ger. trademark.]

video display terminal *n.* A VDT.

video game *n.* An electronic or computerized game played by manipulating images on a display screen.

vid•e•og•ra•phy (vĭd′ē-ŏg′rə-fē) *n.* The art or practice of making video shows or movies with a video camera. — **vid′e•og′ra•pher** *n.*

video jockey *n.* One who announces, plays, and provides commentary on videotaped programs, esp. music videos.

vid•e•o•phone (vĭd′ē-ō-fōn′) *n.* A telephone equipped for both audio and video transmission.

vid•e•o•tape (vĭd′ē-ō-tāp′) *n.* **1.** A magnetic tape used to record visual images and associated sound for playback or broadcasting. **2.** A recording made on such a tape. — *tr.v.* **-taped, -tap•ing, -tapes.** To make a videotape recording of.

videotape recorder *n.* A device for making a videotape.

video terminal *n.* A VDT.

vid•e•o•tex (vĭd′ē-ō-tĕks′) also **vid•e•o•text** (-tĕkst′) *n.* A system that transmits computer-stored information over television cables or telephone lines for display on home television screens or computer terminals.

video vérité *n.* A documentary television filming or videotaping technique in which the subjects are portrayed with frank, unbiased realism. [VIDEO + (CINÉMA) VÉRITÉ.]

vi•dette (vĭ-dĕt′) *n.* Var. of **vedette.**

vid•i•con (vĭd′ĭ-kŏn′) *n.* A small television camera tube that forms a charge-density image on a photoconductive surface for subsequent electron-beam scanning. [VID(EO) + ICON(OSCOPE).]

vie (vī) *v.* **vied, vy•ing** (vī′ĭng), **vies.** — *intr.* To strive for victory or superiority; contend. — *tr.* **1.** *Archaic.* To offer in competition; match. **2.** *Obsolete.* To wager or bet. [Short for ME *envien* < OFr. *envier* < Lat. *invītāre*, to invite, give occasion for. See INVITE.]

Vi•en•na (vē-ĕn′ə). The cap. of Austria, in the NE part of the country on the Danube R.; became the official residence of the house of Hapsburg in 1278. Pop. 1,524,510.

Vienna sausage *n.* A small sausage resembling a frankfurter, often served as an hors d'oeuvre. [After VIENNA.]

Vienne (vyĕn). A river of SW-central France flowing c. 349 km (217 mi) generally NW to the Loire R.

Vi•en•nese (vē′ə-nēz′, -nēs′) *adj.* Relating to or characteristic of Vienna. — *n., pl.* **Viennese. 1.** A native or inhabitant of Vienna. **2.** The variety of German spoken in Vienna.

Vien•tiane (vyĕn-tyän′). The cap. of Laos, in the N-central part of the country on the Mekong R. Pop. 210,000.

Vier•sen (fîr′zən). A city of W-central Germany W of Düsseldorf. Pop. 78,784.

Viet. *abbr.* **1.** Vietnam. **2.** Vietnamese.

Vi•et•cong also **Vi•et Cong** (vē-ĕt′kŏng′, -kông′, vē′ĭt-, vyĕt′-) *n., pl.* **Vietcong** also **Viet Cong.** A Vietnamese belonging to or supporting the National Liberation Front of South Vietnam. [Vietnamese, short for *Viet Nam Cong San*, Vietnamese Communist.]

Vi•et•minh also **Vi•et Minh** (vē-ĕt′mĭn′, vyĕt′-, vē′ĭt-) *n., pl.* **Vietminh** also **Viet Minh.** A member of the Vietnamese army that defeated the Japanese and the French between 1941 and 1954. [Vietnamese, short for *Viet Nam Doc Lap Dong Minh Hoi*, Vietnam Federation of Independence.]

Vi•et•nam (vē-ĕt′näm′, -năm′, vē′ĭt-, vyĕt′-). A country of SE Asia in E Indochina on the South China Sea. Occupied by the French in the 19th cent., it was partitioned into **North Vietnam** and **South Vietnam** after 1954 and reunited in Jul. 1976 after the end of the Vietnam War (1954–75). Cap. Hanoi. Pop. 52,741,766.

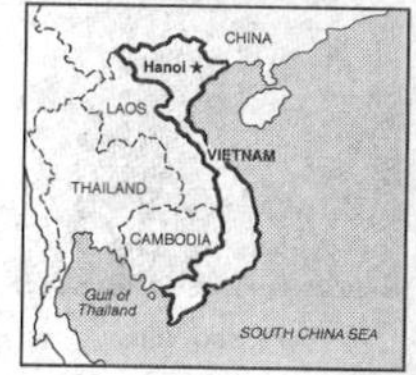

Vietnam

Vi•et•nam•ese (vē-ĕt′nə-mēz′, -mēs′, vē′ĭt-, vyĕt′-) *adj.* Of or relating to Vietnam or its people, language, or culture. — *n., pl.* **Vietnamese. 1.** A native or inhabitant of Vietnam. **2.** The language of the largest ethnic group in Vietnam and the official language of the nation.

view (vyo͞o) *n.* **1.a.** An examination or inspection. **b.** A sight; a look. **2.** A systematic survey; coverage. **3.** An individual and personal perception, judgment, or interpretation; an opinion. **4.** Field of vision. **5.** A scene or vista. **6.** A picture of a landscape. **7.** A way of showing or seeing something, as from a particular angle. **8.** Something kept in sight as an aim or intention. **9.** Expectation; chance. — *tr.v.* **viewed, view•ing, views. 1.** To look at; watch. **2.a.** To examine or inspect. **b.** To survey or study mentally; consider. **3.** To think of in a particular way; regard. See Syns at **see**[1]. — ***idioms.* in view of.** Taking into account; in consideration of. **on view.** Placed so as to be seen; exhibited. [ME *vewe* < AN < fem. p.part. of *veoir*, to see < Lat. *vidēre*. See **weid-***.] — **view′a•ble** *adj.*

view•da•ta (vyo͞o′dā′tə, -dăt′ə, dä′tə) *n.* An interactive videotex system.

view•er (vyo͞o′ər) *n.* **1.** One that views, esp. an onlooker or a spectator. **2.** Any of various optical devices used to facilitate the viewing of photographic transparencies. **3.** One who watches television: *viewers of prime-time shows.*

view•er•ship (vyo͞o′ər-shĭp′) *n.* A television audience, esp. of a particular kind or extent.

view•find•er (vyo͞o′fīn′dər) *n.* A device on a camera that indicates what will appear in the field of view of the lens.

view hal•loo (vyo͞o′ hə-lo͞o′) *n.* A strident call given during a fox hunt to indicate that the fox has been seen breaking cover.

view•ing (vyo͞o′ĭng) *n.* **1.** The act of seeing, watching, or examining. **2.** The act or an instance of watching a movie or television. **3.** *Pennsylvania.* See **wake**[1] 2. — *adj.* Engaged in watching a movie or television.

view•less (vyo͞o′lĭs) *adj.* **1.** Providing no view. **2.** Not having or expressing opinions or views. — **view′less•ly** *adv.*

view•point (vyo͞o′point′) *n.* A position from which something is observed or considered; a point of view.

view•y (vyo͞o′ē) *adj.* **-i•er, -i•est. 1.** Exhibiting extravagant or visionary opinions. **2.** Conspicuous or striking; showy.

Vi•gée-Le•brun (vē-zhā′lə-brœN′), **(Marie Louise) Elisabeth.** 1755–1842. French painter noted for her portraits.

vi•ges•i•mal (vī-jĕs′ə-məl) *adj.* **1.** Twentieth. **2.** Proceeding or occurring in intervals of 20. **3.** Based on or relating to 20. [< Lat. *vīgēsimus*, var. of *vīcēsimus*, twentieth < *vīgintī*, twenty. See **wīkmtī***.]

vig•il (vĭj′əl) *n.* **1.a.** A watch kept during normal sleeping hours. **b.** The act or a period of observing; surveillance. **2.** The eve of a religious festival as observed by devotional watching. **3.** Ritual devotions observed on the eve of a holy day. Often used in the plural. [ME *vigile*, a devotional watching < OFr. < Lat. *vigilia*, wakefulness, watch < *vigil*, awake. See **weg-***.]

vig•i•lance (vĭj′ə-ləns) *n.* Alert watchfulness.

vigilance committee *n.* A group that without authority assumes powers such as punishing those suspected of crime.

vig•i•lant (vĭj′ə-lənt) *adj.* On the alert; watchful. See Syns at **aware.** [ME < OFr. < Lat. *vigilāns, vigilant-*, pr.part. of *vigilāre*, to be watchful. See VIGILANTE.] — **vig′i•lant•ly** *adv.*

vig•i•lan•te (vĭj′ə-lăn′tē) *n.* **1.** One who takes or advocates the taking of law enforcement into one's own hands. **2.** A member of a vigilance committee. [Sp., watchman, vigilante < Lat. *vigilāns, vigilant-*, pr.part. of *vigilāre*, to be watchful < *vigil*, watchful. See **weg-***.] — **vig′i•lan′tism** (-lăn′tĭz-əm), **vig′i•lan′te•ism** (-tē-ĭz′əm) *n.*

vigil light *n.* **1.** A candle kept burning in the chancel of Christian churches to symbolize the Holy Sacrament; an altar light. **2.** A candle lit by a worshiper for a devotional purpose. **3.** A light or candle kept burning at a shrine or before an icon.

vi•gnette (vĭn-yĕt′) *n.* **1.** A decorative design placed at the beginning or end of a book or chapter or along the border of a page. **2.** An unbordered picture that shades off into the surrounding color at the edges. **3.a.** A short, usu. descriptive literary sketch. **b.** A short scene or incident, as from a movie. — *tr.v.* **-gnet•ted, -gnet•ting, -gnettes. 1.** To soften the edges of (a picture) in vignette style. **2.** To describe in a brief way. [Fr. < OFr., dim. of *vigne*, vine (from the use of vine tendrils in decorative borders). See VINE.]

vi•gnet•ter (vĭn-yĕt′ər) *n.* **1.** A device used to print photographs and illustrations with borders that fade gradually into the background. **2.** Also **vi•gnet•tist** (-ĭst). One who makes or specializes in the making of vignettes.

Vi•gny (vēn-yē′), Comte **Alfred Victor de.** 1797–1863. French writer whose works include *Les Destinées* (1864).

Vi•go (vē′gō, bē′gô). A city of NW Spain on the **Bay of Vigo,** an inlet of the Atlantic Ocean. Pop. 277,460.

Élisabeth Vigée-Lebrun
Detail of a c. 1781 oil on canvas self-portrait (25½″ × 21¼″)

vig•or (vĭg′ər) *n.* **1.** Physical or mental strength, energy, or force. **2.** The capacity for natural growth and survival, as of plants or animals. **3.** Strong feeling; enthusiasm or intensity. **4.** Legal effectiveness or validity. [ME < OFr. < Lat. *vigor, vigōr-* < *vigēre*, to be lively. See **weg-***.]

vig•o•rish (vĭg′ər-ĭsh) *n. Slang.* **1.a.** A charge taken on bets, as by a bookie or gambling establishment. **b.** The rate or amount of such a charge. **2.** Interest, esp. excessive interest, paid to a moneylender. [Yiddish slang < Russ. *vyigrysh*, winnings : *vy-*, out; see **ud-*** + *-igrysh*, as in *proigrysh*, a loss (< *igrat'*, to play).]

vig•o•ro•so (vĭg′ə-rō′sō, -zō, vē′gə-) *adv. & adj. Mus.* With emphasis and spirit. [Ital. < Med.Lat. *vigōrōsus* < Lat. *vigor, vigōr-*, vigor. See VIGOR.]

vig•or•ous (vĭg′ər-əs) *adj.* **1.** Strong, energetic, and active in mind or body; robust. See Syns at **healthy. 2.** Marked by or done with force and energy. — **vig′or•ous•ly** *adv.* — **vig′or•ous•ness** *n.*

vig•our (vĭg′ər) *n. Chiefly British.* Var. of **vigor.**

Vi•ja•ya•wa•da (vĭj′ə-yə-wä′də, vē′jə-). Formerly **Bez•wa•da** (bĕz-wä′də). A city of SE India ESE of Hyderabad. Pop. 454,577.

Vi•king (vī′kĭng) *n.* **1.** One of a seafaring Scandinavian people who plundered the coasts of northern and western Europe from the eighth through the tenth century. **2.** A Scandinavian. [ON *víkingr*, perh. < *vík*, creek, inlet.]

vil. *abbr.* Village.

Vi•la (vē′lə). The cap. of Vanuatu, in the SW Pacific. Pop. 13,067.

vi•la•yet (vē′lä-yĕt′) *n.* An administrative division of Turkey. [Turk. *vilâyet*, administrative district < Ar. *wilāyah*, province < *waliya*, to administer.]

vile (vīl) *adj.* **vil•er, vil•est. 1.** Loathsome; disgusting: *vile lan-*

ă pat	oi boy
ā pay	ou out
âr care	o͝o took
ä father	o͞o boot
ĕ pet	ŭ cut
ē be	ûr urge
ĭ pit	th thin
ī pie	*th* this
îr pier	hw which
ŏ pot	zh vision
ō toe	ə about,
ô paw	item

Stress marks:
′ (primary);
′ (secondary), as in dictionary (dĭk′shə-nĕr′ē)

guage. **2.** Unpleasant or objectionable. **3.a.** Contemptibly low in worth or account; second-rate. **b.** Of mean or low condition. **4.** Miserably poor and degrading; wretched: *a vile existence.* **5.** Morally depraved; ignoble or wicked. [ME < OFr. < Lat. *vīlis.*] —**vile′ly** *adv.* —**vile′ness** *n.*

vil•i•fy (vĭl′ə-fī′) *tr.v.* **-fied** (-fīd′), **-fy•ing, -fies** (-fīz′). To make vicious and defamatory statements about. [ME *vilifien* < LLat. *vīlificāre,* to hold cheap : Lat. *vīlis,* worthless + Lat. *-ficāre,* -fy.] —**vil′i•fi•ca′tion** *n.* —**vil′i•fi′er** *n.*

vil•i•pend (vĭl′ə-pĕnd′) *tr.v.* **-pend•ed, -pend•ing, -pends.** **1.** To view or treat with contempt; despise. **2.** To speak ill of; disparage. [Ult. < Lat. *vīlipendere* : *vīlis,* worthless + *pendere,* to consider, weigh; see **(s)pen-*.**]

Pancho Villa

vil•la (vĭl′ə) *n.* **1.** The often large luxurious country house of a well-to-do person. **2.** A country estate with a substantial house. **3.** *Chiefly British.* A house in a middle-class suburb. [Ital. < Lat. *villa.* See **weik-¹*.**]

Vil•la (vē′ə, bē′yä), **Francisco.** "Pancho." 1877?–1923. Mexican revolutionary leader who ran unsuccessfully for the presidency after the Mexican Revolution (1910).

vil•lage (vĭl′ĭj) *n.* **1.** A small group of dwellings in a rural area, usu. ranking in size between a hamlet and a town. **2.** In some U.S. states, an incorporated community smaller in population than a town. **3.** The inhabitants of a village. **4.** A group of bird or animal habitations suggesting a village. [ME < OFr. < Lat. *vīllāticum,* farmstead < neut. of *vīllāticus,* of a farmstead < *vīlla,* country house, farm. See **weik-¹*.**]

vil•lag•er (vĭl′ə-jər) *n.* An inhabitant of a village.

Vil•la•her•mo•sa (vē′ə-ĕr-mō′sə, bē′yä-). A city of SE Mexico E of the Isthmus of Tehuantepec. Pop. 158,216.

vil•lain (vĭl′ən) *n.* **1.** A wicked or evil person; a scoundrel. **2.** A dramatic or fictional character typically at odds with the hero. **3.** (*also* vĭl′ān′, vĭ-lān′). Var. of **villein. 4.** Something said to be the cause of particular trouble or an evil. **5.** *Obsolete.* A peasant regarded as vile and brutish. [ME *vilein,* person of coarse feelings < OFr. < VLat. **vīllānus,* feudal serf < Lat. *vīlla,* country house. See **weik-¹*.**]

vil•lain•age (vĭl′ə-nĭj) *n.* Var. of **villeinage.**

vil•lain•ess (vĭl′ə-nĭs) *n.* A woman who is a villain.

vil•lain•ous (vĭl′ə-nəs) *adj.* **1.a.** Appropriate to a villain, as in wickedness or depravity. **b.** Being or manifesting the nature of a villain. **2.** Highly undesirable or offensive; obnoxious. —**vil′lain•ous•ly** *adv.* —**vil′lain•ous•ness** *n.*

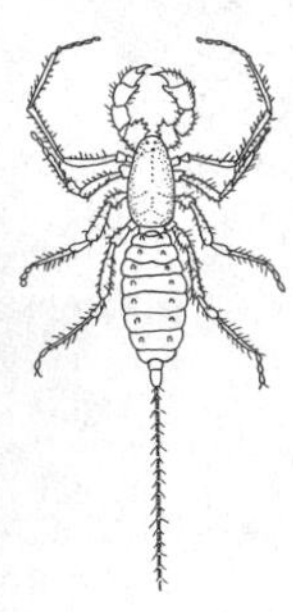

vinegarroon
Mastigoproctus giganteus

vil•lain•y (vĭl′ə-nē) *n., pl.* **-ies. 1.** Baseness of mind or character. **2.** Viciousness of conduct or action. **3.** A treacherous or vicious act.

Vil•la-Lo•bos (vē′lə-lō′bōs, vē′lä-lô′bo͞os), **Heitor.** 1887–1959. Brazilian composer influenced by folk traditions.

vil•la•nelle (vĭl′ə-nĕl′) *n.* A 19-line poem of fixed form consisting of five tercets and a final quatrain on two rhymes, with the first and third lines of the first tercet repeated alternately to close the succeeding tercets and joined as the final couplet of the quatrain. [Fr. < Ital. *villanella* < fem. of *villanello,* rustic < *villano,* peasant < VLat. **vīllānus* < Lat. *vīlla,* country house. See **weik-¹*.**]

Vil•la Park (vĭl′ə). A village of NE IL, a suburb of Chicago. Pop. 22,253.

Vil•lard (vĭ-lär′, -lärd′), **Oswald Garrison.** 1872–1949. Amer. journalist who was president of the *New York Evening Post* (1900–18) and owner of *The Nation* (1918–35).

vil•lat•ic (vĭ-lăt′ĭk) *adj.* Rustic; rural. [Lat. *vīllāticus,* of a farmstead. See VILLAGE.]

Vil•la•vi•cen•ci•o (vē′ə-vĭ-sĕn′sē-ō′, bē′yä-vē-sĕn′syô). A city of central Colombia SE of Bogotá. Pop. 159,808.

vil•lein also **vil•lain** (vĭl′ən, -ān′, vĭ-lān′) *n.* One of a class of feudal serfs who held the legal status of freemen in their dealings with all people except their lord. [ME *vilein.* See VILLAIN.]

vil•lein•age also **vil•lain•age** (vĭl′ə-nĭj) *n.* **1.** The legal status or condition of a villein. **2.** The legal tenure by which a villein held land.

Ville•ur•banne (vē′lər-băn′, vēl-ür-băn′). A city of SE France, a suburb of Lyons. Pop. 115,960.

Vil•liers (vĭl′ərz, -yərz), **George.** See **Buckingham.**

vil•li•form (vĭl′ə-fôrm′) *adj.* Having the form of villi.

Vil•ling•en-Schwen•ning•en (fĭl′ĭng-ən-shvĕn′ĭng-ən). A city of SW Germany SSW of Stuttgart. Pop. 76,600.

viola da gamba
18th-century Swedish

Vil•lon (vē-yôɴ′), **François.** 1431–63? French poet whose satirical works include *Le Testament* (c. 1461).

vil•los•i•ty (vĭ-lŏs′ĭ-tē) *n., pl.* **-ties. 1.** The condition of being villous. **2.** A villous surface or coating. **3.** A villus.

vil•lous (vĭl′əs) also **vil•lose** (-ōs′) *adj.* **1.** *Biol.* Of, resembling, or covered with villi. **2.** *Bot.* Covered with villi. [< Lat. *villōsus,* hairy < *villus,* shaggy hair.] —**vil′lous•ly** *adv.*

vil•lus (vĭl′əs) *n., pl.* **vil•li** (vĭl′ī). **1.** *Biol.* A minute projection arising from a mucous membrane, esp.: **a.** One of the numerous vascular projections of the small intestine. **b.** One of the fingerlike projections of the chorion that forms the placenta in mammals. **2.** *Bot.* A fine hairlike epidermal outgrowth. [Lat., shaggy hair.]

Vil•ni•us (vĭl′nē-əs) or **Vil•na** (-nə). The cap. of Lithuania, in the SE part ESE of Kaunas; founded in the 10th cent. Pop. 544,000.

Vil•yu•i (vĭl-yo͞o′ē). A river of E Russia flowing c. 2,446 km (1,520 mi) to the Lena R.

vim (vĭm) *n.* Ebullient vitality and energy. [Lat., accusative of *vīs.* See **weiə-*.**]

Vim•i•nal (vĭm′ə-nəl). One of the seven hills of ancient Rome. —**Vim′i•nal** *adj.*

vin– *pref.* Var. of **vini–.**

vi•na also **vee•na** (vē′nə) *n. Mus.* A stringed instrument of India that has a long fretted fingerboard with resonating gourds at each end. [Hindi *vīṇā* < Skt.]

vi•na•ceous (vī-nā′shəs, vĭ-) *adj.* Having the color of red wine. [< Lat. *vīnāceus,* refuse from wine pressing < *vīnum,* wine.]

Vi•ña del Mar (vēn′yə dĕl mär′, bē′nyä *thĕl*). A city of central Chile, a suburb of Valparaiso. Pop. 244,899.

vin•ai•grette (vĭn′ĭ-grĕt′) *n.* **1.** A small decorative bottle or container with a perforated top, used for holding an aromatic preparation such as smelling salts. **2.** A cold sauce or dressing made of vinegar or lemon juice and oil flavored with seasonings. [Fr. < OFr., dim. of *vinaigre,* vinegar. See VINEGAR.]

vi•nasse (vĭ-năs′, vĭ-) *n.* The residue left in a still after the process of distillation. [Fr. < Prov. *vinassa* < Lat. *vīnācea* < fem. of *vīnāceus.* See VINACEOUS.]

vin•blas•tine (vĭn-blăs′tēn′) *n.* An alkaloid, $C_{46}H_{58}N_4O_9$, obtained from the Madagascar periwinkle and used as an antineoplastic drug. [NLat. *Vinca,* periwinkle genus (short for Lat. *pervinca,* periwinkle; see PERIWINKLE²) + E. *leukoblast,* a developing leukocyte (LEUKO– + –BLAST) + –INE².]

Vin•cennes. (vĭn-sĕnz′). A city of SW IN on the Wabash R. S of Terre Haute; founded in the early 18th cent. Pop. 19,859.

Vin•cent de Paul (vĭn′sənt də pôl), **Saint.** 1581–1660. French ecclesiastic who founded the Congregation of the Mission (1625) and the Daughters of Charity (1633).

Vin•cent's angina (vĭn′sənts) *n.* See **trench mouth.** [After Jean Hyacinthe *Vincent* (1862–1950), French physician.]

vin•ci•ble (vĭn′sə-bəl) *adj.* Capable of being overcome or defeated: *a vincible army.* [Lat. *vincibilis* < *vincere,* to conquer. See **weik-³*.**] —**vin′ci•bil′i•ty** *n.* —**vin′ci•bly** *adv.*

vin•cris•tine (vĭn-krĭs′tēn′) *n.* An alkaloid, $C_{46}H_{56}N_4O_{10}$, obtained from the Madagascar periwinkle and used to treat acute leukemia. [NLat. *Vinca,* periwinkle genus; see VINBLASTINE + Lat. *crista,* crest; see CREST + –INE².]

vin•cu•lum (vĭng′kyə-ləm) *n., pl.* **-lums** or **-la** (-lə). **1.** *Math.* A bar drawn over two or more algebraic terms to indicate that they are to be treated as a single term. **2.** *Anat.* A ligament that limits the movement of an organ or a part. **3.** A bond or tie. [Lat., bond, tie < *vincīre,* to tie.]

Vin•dhya Range (vĭn′dyə). A chain of hills in central India rising to c. 915 m (3,000 ft).

vin•di•ca•ble (vĭn′dĭ-kə-bəl) *adj.* Possible to vindicate.

vin•di•cate (vĭn′dĭ-kāt′) *tr.v.* **-cat•ed, -cat•ing, -cates. 1.** To clear of accusation, blame, suspicion, or doubt with supporting arguments or proof. **2.** To provide justification or support for: *vindicate one's claim.* **3.** To justify or prove the worth of, esp. in light of later developments. **4.** To defend, maintain, or insist on the recognition of (one's rights, for example). **5.** To exact revenge for; avenge. [Lat. *vindicāre, vindicāt-* < *vindex, vindic-,* surety, avenger. See **deik-*.**] —**vin′di•ca′tor** *n.*

vin•di•ca•tion (vĭn′dĭ-kā′shən) *n.* **1.** The act of vindicating or condition of being vindicated. **2.** The defense, such as evidence or argument, that serves to justify a claim or deed.

vin•di•ca•to•ry (vĭn′dĭ-kə-tôr′ē, -tōr′ē) *adj.* **1.** Affording vindication; justifying. **2.** Exacting retribution; punitive.

vin•dic•tive (vĭn-dĭk′tĭv) *adj.* **1.** Disposed to seek revenge. **2.** Marked by or resulting from a desire to hurt; spiteful. [< Lat. *vindicta,* vengeance < *vindex, vindic-,* surety, avenger. See VINDICATE.] —**vin•dic′tive•ly** *adv.* —**vin•dic′tive•ness** *n.*

vine (vīn) *n.* **1.a.** A weak-stemmed plant that derives its support from climbing, twining, or creeping along a surface. **b.** The stem of such a plant. **2.a.** A grapevine. **b.** Grapevines considered as a group: *products of the vine.* —*intr.v.* **vined, vin•ing, vines.** To form or develop like a vine. [ME < OFr. *vigne* < Lat. *vīnea* < fem. of *vīneus,* of wine < *vīnum,* wine.]

vine•dress•er (vīn′drĕs′ər) *n.* One that cultivates and prunes grapevines.

vin•e•gar (vĭn′ĭ-gər) *n.* **1.** An impure dilute solution of acetic acid obtained by fermentation beyond the alcohol stage and used as a condiment and preservative. **2.** Sourness of speech or mood; ill temper. **3.** Liveliness and enthusiasm; vim. [ME *vinegre* < OFr. *vinaigre* : *vin,* wine (< Lat. *vīnum*) + *aigre,* sour (< VLat. **acrus* < Lat. *ācer;* see **ak-*.**)]

vinegar eel *n.* A minute nematode worm *(Anguillula aceti)* that feeds on the organisms causing fermentation in vinegar.

vinegar fly *n.* See **fruit fly** 1.

vin•e•gar•roon (vĭn′ĭ-gə-ro͞on′) also **vin•e•ga•rone** (-rōn′) *n.* A large whip scorpion *(Mastigoproctus giganteus)* of the southern United States and Mexico that emits a strong odor of vinegar when disturbed. [Am.Sp. *vinagrón* < Sp. *vinagre,* vinegar < OSp. < OFr. *vinaigre.* See VINEGAR.]

vinegar worm *n.* See **vinegar eel.**

vin•e•gar•y (vĭn′ĭ-gə-rē, -grē) also **vin•e•gar•ish** (-gər-ĭsh, -grĭsh) *adj.* **1.** Having the taste, smell, or nature of vinegar. **2.** Unpleasant and irascible.

Vine•land (vĭn′lənd). A city of S NJ SSW of Camden. Pop. 54,780.
vin•er•y (vī′nə-rē) *n., pl.* **-ies.** An area or a greenhouse for growing vines.
vine•yard (vĭn′yərd) *n.* **1.** Ground planted with cultivated grapevines. **2.** A sphere of spiritual, mental, or physical endeavor. **—vine′yard•ist** *n.*
vingt-et-un (văN′tā-oeN′) *n. Games.* See **blackjack** 3. [Fr., twenty-one : *vingt,* twenty + *et,* and + *un,* one.]
vini– or **vino–** or **vin–** *pref.* Wine: *vinic.* [< Lat. *vīni-* < *vīnum.*]
vi•nic (vī′nĭk) *adj.* Of, contained in, or derived from wine.
vin•i•cul•ture (vĭn′ĭ-kŭl′chər, vī′nĭ-) *n.* Cultivation of grapes. **—vin′i•cul′tur•al** *adj.* **—vin′i•cul′tur•ist** *n.*
vin•i•fy (vĭn′ə-fī′) *tr.v.* **-fied** (-fīd′), **-fy•ing, -fies** (-fīz′). To convert (the juice of grapes, for example) into wine by the process of fermentation. **—vin′i•fi•ca′tion** (-fĭ-kā′shən) *n.*
Vin•land (vĭn′lənd). An unidentified coastal region of NE North America visited by Norse voyagers as early as c. 1000.
Vin•ni•tsa (vĭn′ĭ-tsə, vyē′nĭ-). A city of W Ukraine SW of Kiev; founded in the 14th cent. Pop. 367,000.
vi•no (vē′nō) *n., pl.* **-nos.** Wine. [Ital. and Sp., both < Lat. *vīnum.*]
vin or•di•naire (văN′ ôr-dē-nâr′) *n., pl.* **vins or•di•naires** (văNz′ ôr-dē-nâr′). An inexpensive red table wine. [Fr.]
vi•nos•i•ty (vī-nŏs′ĭ-tē) *n., pl.* **-ties.** The distinctive body, color, and taste of wine. [LLat. *vīnōsitās* < Lat. *vīnōsus,* vinous. See VINOUS.]
vi•nous (vī′nəs) *adj.* **1.** Of or made with wine. **2.** Affected or caused by the consumption of wine. **3.** Of the color of wine. [Lat. *vīnōsus* < *vīnum,* wine.] **—vi′nous•ly** *adv.*
Vin•son (vĭn′sən), **Frederick Moore.** 1890–1953. Amer. jurist; chief justice of the U.S. Supreme Court (1946–53).
vin•tage (vĭn′tĭj) *n.* **1.** The yield of wine or grapes from a vineyard or district during one season. **2.** Wine, usu. of high quality, identified as to year and vineyard or district of origin. **3.** The year or place in which a wine is bottled. **4.a.** The harvesting of a grape crop. **b.** The initial stages of winemaking. **5.** *Informal.* **a.** A group of people or things sharing certain characteristics. **b.** A year or period of origin. **c.** Length of existence; age. —*adj.* **1.** Of or relating to a vintage. **2.** Characterized by excellence, maturity, and enduring appeal; classic. **3.** Old or outmoded. **4.a.** Of the best. **b.** Of the most distinctive. [ME < AN, alteration of OFr. *vendange* < Lat. *vīndēmia* : *vīnum,* grapes + *dēmere,* to take off (*dē,* de- + *emere,* to obtain; see **em-***).]
vin•tag•er (vĭn′tə-jər) *n.* A producer or harvester of wine grapes.
vintage year *n.* **1.** The year in which a vintage wine is produced. **2.** A year of outstanding achievement or success.
vint•ner (vĭnt′nər) *n.* **1.** A wine merchant. **2.** One who makes wine. [ME *vineter* < OFr. *vinetier* < Med.Lat. *vīnētārius* < Lat. *vīnētum,* vineyard < *vīnum,* wine.]
vin•y (vī′nē) *adj.* **-i•er, -i•est. 1.** Of, relating to, or having the nature of vines. **2.** Overgrown with or abounding in vines.
vi•nyl (vī′nəl) *n.* **1.** The univalent chemical radical CH_2CH. **2.** Any of various easily polymerized compounds containing the vinyl radical, used as basic materials for plastics. **3.** Any of various tough flexible shiny plastics used for coverings and clothing. [VIN(I)– + –YL.] **—vi•nyl′ic** (-nĭl′ĭk) *adj.*
vinyl chloride *n.* A flammable gas, $CH_2{:}CHCl$, used as a monomer for polyvinyl chloride.
vi•ol (vī′əl) *n. Mus.* **1.** Any of a family of stringed instruments, chiefly of the 16th and 17th centuries, having a fretted fingerboard, usu. six strings, and a flat back and played with a curved bow. **2.** See **viola da gamba.** [Alteration of ME *viel* < OFr. *viole, vielle* < OProv. *viola.* See VIOLA[1].]
vi•o•la[1] (vē-ō′lə) *n. Mus.* A stringed instrument of the violin family, slightly larger than a violin, tuned a fifth lower, and having a deeper, more sonorous tone. [Ital. < OProv., viola, prob. of imit. orig.] **—vi•o′list** *n.*
vi•o•la[2] (vī-ō′lə, vē-, vī′ə-lə) *n.* A plant of the genus *Viola,* which includes the violets and pansies. [ME < Lat.]
vi•o•la•ble (vī′ə-lə-bəl) *adj.* That can be violated. **—vi′o•la•bil′i•ty, vi′o•la•ble•ness** *n.* **—vi′o•la•bly** *adv.*
vi•o•la da brac•cio (vē-ō′lə də brä′chō) *n., pl.* **viola da braccios.** *Mus.* A stringed instrument of the viol family with approximately the range of the viola. [Ital. : *viola,* viol + *da,* of, for + *braccio,* arm.]
viola da gam•ba (gäm′bə, găm′-) *n. Mus.* A stringed instrument, the bass of the viol family, with approximately the cello's range. [Ital. : *viola,* viol + *da,* of, for + *gamba,* leg.]
viola d'a•mo•re (dä-môr′ā, -môr′ā, -môr′ē, -môr′ē) *n. Mus.* A stringed instrument, the tenor of the viol family, having six or seven stopped strings and an equal number of sympathetic strings that produce a characteristic silvery tone. [Ital. : *viola,* viol + *da,* of + *amore,* love.]
vi•o•late (vī′ə-lāt′) *tr.v.* **-lat•ed, -lat•ing, -lates. 1.** To break or disregard (a law, for example). **2.** To assault (a person) sexually. **3.** To do harm to (property or qualities seen as sacred); desecrate or defile. **4.** To disturb rudely or improperly; interrupt. [ME *violaten* < Lat. *violāre, violāt-* < *vīs, vi-,* force. See **weiə-***.] **—vi′o•la′tive** *adj.* **—vi′o•la′tor** *n.*
vi•o•la•tion (vī′ə-lā′shən) *n.* The act or an instance of violating or the condition of being violated. See Syns at **breach.**
vi•o•lence (vī′ə-ləns) *n.* **1.** Physical force exerted for the purpose of violating, damaging, or abusing: *crimes of violence.* **2.** The act or an instance of violent action or behavior. **3.** Intensity or severity, as in natural phenomena; untamed force. **4.** Abusive or unjust exercise of power. **5.** Abuse or injury to meaning, content, or intent. **6.** Vehemence of feeling or expression; fervor.
vi•o•lent (vī′ə-lənt) *adj.* **1.** Marked by, acting with, or resulting from great force: *a violent attack.* **2.** Having or showing great emotional force. **3.** Marked by intensity; extreme. **4.** Caused by unexpected force or injury rather than by natural causes: *a violent death.* **5.** Tending to distort or injure meaning, phrasing, or intent. [ME < OFr. < Lat. *violentus* < *vīs, vi-,* force. See **weiə-***.] **—vi′o•lent•ly** *adv.*
vi•o•let (vī′ə-lĭt) *n.* **1.a.** Any of various low-growing herbs of the genus *Viola,* having short-spurred irregular flowers that are typically purplish-blue. **b.** Any of several similar plants, such as the African violet. **2.** *Color.* The hue of the short-wave end of the visible spectrum, evoked in the human observer by radiant energy with wavelengths of approx. 380 to 420 nanometers; any of a group of colors that are reddish-blue in hue. [ME < OFr. *violete,* dim. of *viole* < Lat. *viola.*]
vi•o•lin (vī′ə-lĭn′) *n. Mus.* A stringed instrument that is played with a bow, having four strings that are tuned at intervals of a fifth, an unfretted fingerboard, a shallower body than the viol, and a flexible range, tone, and dynamics. [Ital. *violino,* dim. of *viola,* viola. See VIOLA[1].] **—vi′o•lin′ist** *n.* **—vi′o•lin•is′tic** *adj.*
Viol•let-le-Duc (vē′ə-lā′lə-do͞ok′, -dyo͞ok′, vyô-lĕ′lə-dük′), **Eugène Emmanuel.** 1814–79. French architect who was a leader of the Gothic revival in France.
vi•o•lon•cel•lo (vē′ə-lən-chĕl′ō, vī′ə-) *n., pl.* **-los.** *Mus.* A cello. [Ital., dim. of *violone,* a very low-pitched viol, aug. of *viola,* viola. See VIOLA[1].] **—vi′o•lon•cel′list** *n.*
VIP (vē′ī-pē′) *n., pl.* **VIPs.** *Informal.* A person of great importance or influence, esp. a dignitary who commands special treatment. [*v(ery) i(mportant) p(erson).*]
vi•per (vī′pər) *n.* **1.** Any of several venomous Old World snakes of the family Viperidae, having a pair of long hollow fangs and a thick heavy body. **2.** A pit viper. **3.** A venomous or supposedly venomous snake. **4.** A person regarded as malicious or treacherous. [ME *vipere* < OFr. < Lat. *vīpera,* snake, contraction of **vīvipera* : *vīvus,* alive; see **gʷei-*** + *parere,* to give birth; see **perə-**[1]*.]
vi•per•fish (vī′pər-fĭsh′) *n., pl.* **viperfish** or **-fish•es.** Any of various small deep-sea fish of the family Chauliodontidae, having fanglike teeth and a long first ray of the dorsal fin.
vi•per•ine (vī′pə-rīn′) *adj.* Of, resembling, or characteristic of a viper.
vi•per•ish (vī′pər-ĭsh) *adj.* Spiteful or malicious; venomous.
vi•per•ous (vī′pər-əs) *adj.* **1.** Suggestive of or related to a viper. **2.** Venomous; malicious. **—vi′per•ous•ly** *adv.*
vi•per's bugloss (vī′pərz) *n.* Any of various Eurasian plants of the genus *Echium,* including the blueweed, having bright blue to white flowers, bristly foliage, and a dense scorpioid inflorescence.
vir– *pref.* Var. of **viro–.**
vi•ra•go (və-rä′gō, -rā′-, vîr′ə-gō′) *n., pl.* **-goes** or **-gos. 1.** A woman regarded as noisy, scolding, or domineering. **2.** A large, strong, courageous woman. [Lat. *virāgō* < *vir,* man. See **wī-ro-***.] **—vi•rag′i•nous** (və-răj′ə-nəs) *adj.*
vi•ral (vī′rəl) *adj.* Of, relating to, or caused by a virus. **—vi′ral•ly** *adv.*
vir•e•lay (vîr′ə-lā′) *n.* Any of several medieval French verse and song forms, esp. one in which each stanza has two rhymes, the end rhyme recurring as the first rhyme of the following stanza. [ME *virelai* < OFr., alteration (influenced by *lai,* lay) of *vireli,* song refrain.]
vi•re•mi•a (vī-rē′mē-ə) *n.* The presence of viruses in the bloodstream. **—vi•re′mic** (-mĭk) *adj.*
vir•e•o (vîr′ē-ō′) *n., pl.* **-os.** Any of various small insect-eating New World songbirds of the genus *Vireo,* having grayish or greenish plumage. [Lat. *vireō,* a bird < *virēre,* to be green.]
vi•res•cence (və-rĕs′əns, vī-) *n.* The state or process of becoming green, esp. the abnormal development of green coloration in plant parts normally not green.
vi•res•cent (və-rĕs′ənt, vī-) *adj.* **1.** Becoming green. **2.** Somewhat green; greenish. [Lat. *virēscēns, virēscent-,* pr.part. of *virēscere,* to become green, inchoative of *virēre,* to be green.]
vir•ga (vûr′gə) *n.* Wisps of precipitation streaming from a cloud but evaporating before reaching the ground. [Lat., twig, virga.]
vir•gate[1] (vûr′gāt′) *adj.* Shaped like a wand or rod. [Lat. *virgātus,* made of twigs < *virga,* twig.]
vir•gate[2] (vûr′gĭt) *n.* An early English measure of land area of varying value, often equal to about 30 acres (12 hectares). [Med.Lat. *virgāta* < fem. of Lat. *virgātus,* relating to a rod. See VIRGATE[1].]
Vir•gil also **Ver•gil** (vûr′jəl). 70–19 B.C. Roman poet best

violet
Marsh blue violet
Viola cucullata

violin

vireo
Philadelphia vireo
Vireo philadelphicus

ă pat	oi boy
ā pay	ou out
âr care	o͝o took
ä father	o͞o boot
ĕ pet	ŭ cut
ē be	ûr urge
ĭ pit	th thin
ī pie	*th* this
îr pier	hw which
ŏ pot	zh vision
ō toe	ə about,
ô paw	item

Stress marks:
′ (primary);
′ (secondary), as in dictionary (dĭk′shə-nĕr′ē)

known for the epic poem *Aeneid*. **— Vir•gil′i•an** (vûr-jĭl′ē-ən, -jĭl′yən) *adj.*

vir•gin (vûr′jĭn) *n.* **1.** A person who has not experienced sexual intercourse. **2.** A chaste or unmarried woman; a maiden. **3.** An unmarried woman who has taken religious vows of chastity. **4. Virgin.** The Virgin Mary. **5.** *Zool.* **a.** A female animal that has not copulated. **b.** A female bee, wasp, or other insect that produces fertile eggs without copulating. *— adj.* **1.** Of, relating to, or being a virgin; chaste. **2.** Being in a pure or natural state; unsullied: *virgin snow.* **3.** Unused, uncultivated, or unexplored. **4.** Existing in native or raw form; not processed or refined. **5.** Happening for the first time; initial. **6.** Obtained directly from the first pressing: *virgin olive oil.* [ME < OFr. *virgine* < Lat. *virgō, virgin-.*]

Virgin *n.* See **Virgo** 1, 2a.

vir•gin•al¹ (vûr′jə-nəl) *adj.* **1.** Relating to, characteristic of, or befitting a virgin; chaste. **2.** Remaining in a state of virginity. **3.** Untouched or unsullied; fresh. **4.** *Zool.* Virgin. **— vir′gin•al•ly** *adv.*

virginal²
Early 17th-century Flemish by Andries Ruckers (1579 – 1640?)

vir•gin•al² (vûr′jə-nəl) *n. Mus.* A small legless rectangular harpsichord popular in the 16th and 17th centuries. Often used in the plural. [< VIRGIN (perh. < its being associated with female performers).]

virgin birth *n. Theol.* The doctrine that Jesus was born of Mary, whose virginity remained intact.

Vir•gin•ia (vər-jĭn′yə). A state of the E U.S. on Chesapeake Bay and the Atlantic Ocean; admitted as one of the original Thirteen Colonies in 1788. The first permanent settlement in the region was at Jamestown in 1607. Cap. Richmond. Pop. 6,216,568. **— Vir•gin′ian** *adj. & n.*

Virginia Algonquian *n.* The extinct Eastern Algonquian language of eastern Virginia.

Virginia Beach. An independent city of SE VA on the Atlantic Ocean E of Norfolk. Pop. 393,069.

Virginia bluebell *n.* See **Virginia cowslip.**

Virginia City. A town of SW MT S of Helena; founded 1863 after the discovery of gold. Pop. 142.

Virginia cowslip *n.* An eastern North American plant *(Mertensia virginica)* having clusters of nodding blue flowers.

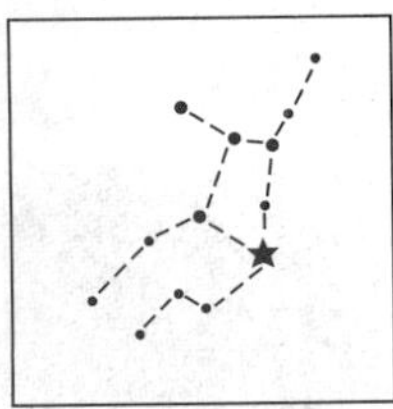

Virgo

Virginia creeper *n.* A North American climbing vine *(Parthenocissus quinquefolia)* having palmately compound leaves with five leaflets and bluish-black berries.

Virginia fence *n.* See **worm fence.**

Virginia ham *n.* A lean hickory-smoked ham.

Virginia rail *n.* A small reddish-brown American rail *(Rallus limicola)* having a long slender bill.

Virginia reel *n.* An American country-dance in which couples perform various steps together to the instructions of a caller.

Virgin Islands. 1. A group of islands of the NE West Indies E of Puerto Rico divided into the **British Virgin Islands** to the NE and the Virgin Islands of the U.S. to the SW. **2.** Officially **Virgin Islands of the United States.** A U.S. territory constituting the SW group of the Virgin Is.; purchased from the Dutch in 1917. Cap. Charlotte Amalie. Pop. 96,569.

vir•gin•i•ty (vər-jĭn′ĭ-tē) *n., pl.* **-ties. 1.** The quality or condition of being a virgin. **2.** The state of being pure, unsullied, or untouched.

Virgin Mary *n.* The mother of Jesus.

vir•gin's bower (vûr′jĭnz) *n.* Any of several climbing plants of the genus *Clematis,* esp. *C. virginiana* of eastern North America, having white flowers and a cluster of seedlike fruits, each with a feathery persistent style.

virgin wool *n.* Wool not previously used in manufacture.

Vir•go (vûr′gō) *n.* **1.** A constellation in the region of the celestial equator between Leo and Libra. **2.a.** The sixth sign of the zodiac in astrology. **b.** *pl.* **-gos.** One who is born under this sign. [ME < Lat., virgin, the constellation Virgo.]

Vishnu
Tenth-century bronze

vir•gu•late (vûr′gyə-lĭt, -lāt′) *adj.* Shaped like a small rod. [< Lat. *virgula,* small rod < *virga,* rod.]

vir•gule (vûr′gyo͞ol) *n. Print.* A diagonal mark (/) used esp. to separate alternatives, as in *and/or,* to represent the word *per,* as in *miles/hour,* and to indicate the ends of verse lines printed continuously, as in *Old King Cole/Was a merry old soul.* [Fr., comma, obelus < LLat. *virgula,* accentual mark < Lat., obelus, dim. of *virga,* rod.]

vi•ri•cide (vī′rĭ-sīd′) also **vi•ru•cide** (vī′rə-) *n.* An agent that inhibits or destroys viruses. **— vi′ri•cid′al** (-sīd′l) *adj.*

vir•id (vîr′ĭd) *adj.* Bright green with or as if with vegetation; verdant. [Lat. *viridis* < *virēre,* to be green.]

vir•i•des•cent (vîr′ĭ-dĕs′ənt) *adj.* Green or slightly green. **— vir′i•des′cence** *n.*

vi•rid•i•an (və-rĭd′ē-ən) *n.* A durable bluish-green pigment.

vi•rid•i•ty (və-rĭd′ĭ-tē) *n.* **1.a.** The quality or condition of being green; greenness. **b.** The green color of vegetation or leaves. **2.** Innocence or inexperience.

vir•ile (vîr′əl, -īl′) *adj.* **1.** Of, relating to, or having the characteristics of an adult male. **2.** Having or showing masculine spirit, strength, vigor, or power. **3.** Capable of performing sexually as a male; potent. [ME < OFr. *viril* < Lat. *virīlis* < *vir,* man. See **wī-ro-*.**]

vir•il•ism (vîr′ə-lĭz′əm) *n.* The presence of male secondary sexual characteristics in a female.

vi•ril•i•ty (və-rĭl′ĭ-tē) *n.* **1.** The quality or state of being virile; manly character. **2.** Masculine vigor; potency.

vir•i•li•za•tion (vîr′ə-lĭ-zā′shən) *n.* Development of male secondary sexual characteristics. **— vir′il•ize′** (-ə-līz′) *v.*

vi•ri•on (vī′rē-ŏn′, vîr′ē-) *n.* A complete viral particle, consisting of RNA or DNA surrounded by a protein shell and constituting the infective form of a virus. [VIR(US) + -ON¹.]

viro– or **vir–** *pref.* Virus: *virology.* [< VIRUS.]

vi•roid (vī′roid′) *n.* A viruslike infectious particle that consists solely of a strand of RNA and causes disease in plants.

vi•rol•o•gy (vī-rŏl′ə-jē) *n.* The study of viruses and viral diseases. **— vi′ro•log′i•cal** (vī′rə-lŏj′ĭ-kəl), **vi′ro•log′ic** (-ĭk) *adj.* **— vi•rol′o•gist** *n.*

vir•tu (vər-to͞o′, vîr-) also **ver•tu** (vər-) *n.* **1.** A knowledge of or taste for the fine arts. **2.** The quality of being beautiful, rare, or collectible. **3.** Such artistic objects. [Ital. *virtù,* virtue, virtu < Lat. *virtūs,* excellence, virtue. See VIRTUE.]

vir•tu•al (vûr′cho͞o-əl) *adj.* Existing or resulting in essence or effect though not in actual fact, form, or name. [ME *virtuall,* effective < Med.Lat. *virtuālis* < Lat. *virtūs,* excellence. See VIRTUE.] **— vir′tu•al′i•ty** (-ăl′ĭ-tē) *n.*

virtual focus *n.* The point from which divergent rays of reflected or refracted light seem to have emanated.

virtual image *n.* An image from which rays of reflected or refracted light appear to diverge.

vir•tu•al•ly (vûr′cho͞o-ə-lē) *adv.* **1.** In fact or to all purposes; practically. **2.** Almost but not quite; nearly.

virtual memory *n. Comp. Sci.* Computer memory, separate from the main memory of a specific machine, that can be used as an extension of the machine's main memory.

virtual reality *n. Comp. Sci.* A computer simulation of a real or imaginary system that enables a user to perform operations on the simulated system and shows the effects in real time.

vir•tue (vûr′cho͞o) *n.* **1.a.** Moral excellence and righteousness; goodness. **b.** An example or kind of moral excellence: *the virtue of patience.* **2.** Chastity, esp. in a girl or woman. **3.** A particularly efficacious, good, or beneficial quality; advantage. **4.** Effective force or power. **5. virtues.** *Theol.* The fifth of the nine orders of angels. **6.** *Obsolete.* Manly courage; valor. **— *idiom.* by (or in) virtue of.** On the grounds or basis of; by reason of. [ME *vertu* < OFr. < Lat. *virtūs,* manliness, excellence, goodness < *vir,* man. See **wī-ro-*.**]

vir•tu•o•sa (vûr′cho͞o-ō′sə, -zə) *n.* A woman who is a virtuoso. [Ital., fem. of *virtuoso,* virtuoso. See VIRTUOSO.]

vir•tu•os•i•ty (vûr′cho͞o-ŏs′ĭ-tē) *n., pl.* **-ties. 1.** The technical skill, fluency, or style exhibited by a virtuoso. **2.** An appreciation for or interest in fine objects of art.

vir•tu•o•so (vûr′cho͞o-ō′sō, -zō) *n., pl.* **-sos** or **-si** (-sē). **1.** A musician with outstanding ability, technique, or personal style. **2.** One with outstanding skill or technique in the arts. **3.** One who experiments or investigates in the arts and sciences; a savant. *— adj.* Exhibiting the ability, technique, or personal style of a virtuoso. [Ital., skilled, of great worth, virtuoso < LLat. *virtuōsus,* virtuous < Lat. *virtūs,* excellence. See VIRTUE.] **— vir′tu•o′sic** (-ō′sĭk, -zĭk) *adj.*

vir•tu•ous (vûr′cho͞o-əs) *adj.* **1.** Having or showing virtue, esp. moral excellence: *led a virtuous life.* **2.** Possessing or characterized by chastity; pure. See Syns at **moral. — vir′tu•ous•ly** *adv.* **— vir′tu•ous•ness** *n.*

vi•ru•cide (vī′rə-sīd′) *n.* Var. of **viricide.**

vir•u•lent (vîr′yə-lənt, vîr′ə-) *adj.* **1.a.** Extremely infectious, malignant, or poisonous. Used of a disease or toxin. **b.** Capable of causing disease by breaking down protective mechanisms of the host. Used of a pathogen. **2.** Bitterly hostile or antagonistic; hateful: *virulent criticism.* **3.** Intensely irritating, obnoxious, or harsh. [ME < Lat. *vīrulentus* < *vīrus,* poison.] **— vir′u•lence, vir′u•len•cy** *n.* **— vir′u•lent•ly** *adv.*

vir•u•lif•er•ous (vîr′yə-lĭf′ər-əs, vîr′ə-) *adj.* Carrying or containing a virus: *viruliferous aphids.* [VIRUL(ENCE) + -FEROUS.]

vi•rus (vī′rəs) *n., pl.* **-rus•es. 1.a.** Any of various simple submicroscopic infectious agents that often cause disease in plants, animals, and bacteria and that consist essentially of a core of RNA or DNA surrounded by a protein coat, are unable to replicate without a host cell, and are typically not considered living organisms. **b.** A disease caused by a virus. **2.** Something that poisons one's soul or mind. **3.** *Comp. Sci.* A computer virus. [Lat. *vīrus,* poison.]

vis. *abbr.* **1.** Visibility. **2.** Visual.

Vis. *abbr.* **1.** Viscount. **2.** Viscountess.

vi•sa (vē′zə) *n.* An official authorization appended to a passport, permitting entry into and travel within a particular country or region. *— tr.v.* **-saed, -sa•ing, -sas. 1.** To endorse or ratify (a passport). **2.** To give a visa to. [Fr., short for Lat. *(carta) vīsa,* (the document has been) seen < fem. p.part. of *vidēre,* to see. See **weid-*.**]

vis•age (vĭz′ĭj) *n.* **1.** The face or facial expression of a person; countenance. **2.** Appearance; aspect: *the bleak visage of winter.* [ME < OFr. < *vis* < Lat. *vīsus,* appearance < p.part. of *vidēre,* to see. See **weid-*.**]

Vi•sa•kha•pat•nam (vĭ-sä′kə-pŭt′nəm) also **Vi•za•ga•pa•tam** (vĭ-zä′gə-pŭt′əm). A city of E India on the Bay of Bengal NE of Madras. Pop. 565,321.

Vi•sa•lia (vĭ-sāl′yə). A city of S-central CA SE of Fresno. Pop. 75,636.

vis•ard (vĭz′ərd, -ärd′) *n.* Var. of **vizard.**

vis-à-vis (vē′zə-vē′) *prep.* **1.** Face to face with; opposite to. **2.** Compared with. **3.** In relation to. —*adv.* Face to face. —*n., pl.* **vis-à-vis** (-vēz′, -vē′). **1.** One that is face to face with or opposite to another. **2.** A date or an escort. **3.** One that has the same functions and characteristics as another; a counterpart. [Fr. : *vis,* face + *à,* to.] —**vis′-à-vis′** *adj.*

Vi•sa•yan (vĭ-sī′ən) *n.* **1.** A member of the largest ethnic group indigenous to the Philippines, found in the Visayan Islands. **2.** Their Austronesian language. —**Vi•say′an** *adj.*

Visayan Islands. An island group of the central Philippines in and around the **Visayan Sea** between Luzon and Mindanao.

vis•ca•cha (vĭ-skä′chə) *n.* Any of several gregarious burrowing South American rodents of the genera *Lagostomus* and *Lagidium,* related to and resembling the chinchilla. [Sp. *vizcacha* < Quechua *wiskácha.*]

vis•cer•a (vĭs′ər-ə) *pl.n.* **1.** The soft internal organs of the body, esp. those contained within the abdominal and thoracic cavities. **2.** The intestines. [Lat. *vīscera,* pl. of *vīscus.*]

vis•cer•al (vĭs′ər-əl) *adj.* **1.** Relating to, situated in, or affecting the viscera. **2.** Perceived in or as if in the viscera; profound. **3.** Instinctive: *visceral needs.* —**vis′cer•al•ly** *adv.*

vis•cer•o•mo•tor (vĭs′ər-ə-mō′tər) *adj.* Producing or related to movements of the viscera.

vis•cid (vĭs′ĭd) *adj.* **1.** Thick and adhesive. Used of a fluid. **2.** Covered with a sticky or clammy coating. [LLat. *viscidus* < Lat. *viscum,* mistletoe, birdlime made from mistletoe berries.] —**vis•cid′i•ty, vis′cid•ness** *n.* —**vis′cid•ly** *adv.*

vis•com•e•ter (vĭ-skŏm′ĭ-tər) *n.* An instrument used to measure viscosity. [Short for VISCOSIMETER.] —**vis′co•met′ric** (vĭs′kə-mĕt′rĭk) *adj.* —**vis•com′e•try** *n.*

vis•cose (vĭs′kōs′) *n.* **1.** A thick golden-brown viscous solution of cellulose xanthate, used in making rayon and cellophane. **2.** Viscose rayon. —*adj.* **1.** Viscous. **2.** Of, relating to, or made from viscose. [VISC(OUS) + -OSE[2]. Adj., sense 1, ME, viscous < LLat. *viscōsus* < Lat. *viscum,* mistletoe, birdlime made from mistletoe berries.]

viscose rayon *n.* A rayon made by reconverting cellulose from a soluble xanthate form to tough fibers by washing in acid.

vis•co•sim•e•ter (vĭs′kə-sĭm′ĭ-tər) *n.* See **viscometer.** —**vis•cos′i•met′ric** (vĭ-skŏs′ə-mĕt′rĭk) *adj.*

vis•cos•i•ty (vĭ-skŏs′ĭ-tē) *n., pl.* **-ties. 1.** The condition or property of being viscous. **2.** *Phys.* A numerical measure of the degree to which a fluid resists flow under an applied force.

vis•count (vī′kount′) *n.* **1.** A nobleman ranking below an earl or a count and above a baron. **2.** Used as a title for such a nobleman. [ME < OFr. *visconte* < Med.Lat. *vicecomes, vicecomit-* : LLat. *vice-,* vice- + LLat. *comes,* occupant of any state office; see COUNT[2].]

vis•count•cy (vī′kount′sē) *n., pl.* **-cies.** The rank, title, or dignity of a viscount.

vis•count•ess (vī′koun′tĭs) *n.* **1.** The wife or widow of a viscount. **2.** A noblewoman holding a viscountcy in her own right.

Vis•count Mel•ville Sound (vī′kount mĕl′vĭl′, -vəl). An arm of the Arctic Ocean between Victoria and Melville islands in N Northwest Terrs., Canada.

vis•count•y (vī′koun′tē) *n., pl.* **-ies.** See **viscountcy.**

vis•cous (vĭs′kəs) *adj.* **1.** Having relatively high resistance to flow. **2.** Viscid. [ME < OFr. < LLat. *viscōsus.* See VISCOSE.] —**vis′cous•ly** *adv.* —**vis′cous•ness** *n.*

vis•cus (vĭs′kəs) *n.* Singular of **viscera.**

vise also **vice** (vīs) —*n.* A clamping device of metal or wood, usu. consisting of two jaws closed or opened by a screw or lever and used in carpentry or metalworking to hold a piece in position. —*tr.v.* **vised, vis•ing, vis•es** also **viced, vic•ing, vic•es.** To hold or compress in or as if in a vise. [ME *vis,* screwlike device < OFr., screw < Lat. *vītis,* vine (< its spiral wrappings). See **wei-*.**]

Vish•nu (vĭsh′nōō) *n. Hinduism.* One of the principal Hindu deities, a member of the triad including also Brahma and Shiva and worshiped as the protector and preserver of worlds.

vis•i•bil•i•ty (vĭz′ə-bĭl′ĭ-tē) *n., pl.* **-ties. 1.** The fact, state, or degree of being visible. **2.** The greatest distance under given weather conditions to which it is possible to see without instrumental assistance. **3.a.** The capability of being easily observed. **b.** The capability of providing a clear unobstructed view: *a windshield with good visibility.*

vis•i•ble (vĭz′ə-bəl) *adj.* **1.** Possible to see; perceptible to the eye. **2.a.** Obvious to the eye: *a visible change of expression.* **b.** Being often in the public view; conspicuous. **3.** Manifest; apparent: *no visible solution.* **4.** On hand; available. **5.** Constructed or designed to keep important parts in easily accessible view: *a visible file.* **6.** Represented visually, as by symbols. [ME < OFr. < Lat. *vīsibilis* < *vīsus,* p.part. of *vidēre,* to see. See VISION.] —**vis′i•ble•ness** *n.* —**vis′i•bly** *adv.*

visible speech *n.* A system of phonetic notation used in teaching speech to hearing-impaired people and consisting of diagrams of the speech organs in the positions required to articulate sounds.

Vis•i•goth (vĭz′ĭ-gŏth′) *n.* A member of the western Goths that invaded the Roman Empire in the fourth century A.D. and settled in France and Spain, establishing a monarchy that lasted until the early eighth century. [LLat. *Visigothī,* the Visigoths. See **wes-pero-*.**] —**Vis′i•goth′ic** *adj.*

vi•sion (vĭzh′ən) *n.* **1.a.** The faculty of sight; eyesight: *poor vision.* **b.** Something that is or has been seen. **2.** Unusual competence in discernment or perception; intelligent foresight. **3.** The manner in which one sees or conceives of something. **4.** A mental image produced by the imagination. **5.** The mystical experience of seeing as if with the eyes the supernatural or a supernatural being. **6.** A person or thing of extraordinary beauty. —*tr.v.* **-sioned, -sion•ing, -sions.** To see in or as if in a vision; envision. [ME < OFr. < Lat. *vīsiō, vīsiōn-* < *vīsus* < p.part. of *vidēre,* to see. See **weid-*.**] —**vi′sion•al** *adj.* —**vi′sion•al•ly** *adv.*

vi•sion•ar•y (vĭzh′ə-nĕr′ē) *adj.* **1.** Characterized by vision or foresight. **2.a.** Having the nature of fantasies or dreams; illusory. **b.** Existing in imagination only; imaginary. **3.a.** Characterized by or given to apparitions, prophecies, or revelations. **b.** Given to daydreams or reverie; dreamy. **4.a.** Not practicable or realizable; utopian. **b.** Tending to envision things in perfect but unrealistic form; idealistic. —*n., pl.* **-ies. 1.** One who is given to impractical or speculative ideas; a dreamer. **2.** One who has visions; a seer. —**vi′sion•ar′i•ness** *n.*

vi•sion•less (vĭzh′ən-lĭs) *adj.* **1.** Lacking the faculty of sight; blind. **2.** Lacking intelligent foresight or imagination.

vis•it (vĭz′ĭt) *v.* **-it•ed, -it•ing, -its.** —*tr.* **1.a.** To call on socially. **b.** To go to see or spend time at (a place) with a certain intent. **c.** To stay with as a guest. **d.** To go to see in an official or professional capacity: *visited the dentist.* **2.** To go or come to: *visits the bank on Fridays.* **3.** To go to see in order to aid or console. **4.** To make itself known to or seize fleetingly: *visited by a bizarre thought.* **5.a.** To afflict or assail: *A plague visited the village.* **b.** To inflict punishment on or for; avenge. —*intr.* **1.** To make a visit. **2.** *Informal.* To converse or chat. —*n.* **1.** The act or an instance of visiting a person, place, or thing. **2.** A stay or sojourn as a guest. **3.** The act of visiting in a professional capacity. **4.** The act of visiting in an official capacity, such as an inspection. [ME *visiten* < OFr. *visiter* < Lat. *vīsitāre,* freq. of *vīsere,* freq. of *vidēre,* to see. See VISION.]

vis•it•a•ble (vĭz′ĭ-tə-bəl) *adj.* **1.** Subject to inspection or visitation. **2.** Accessible or open.

vis•i•tant (vĭz′ĭ-tənt) *n.* **1.** A visitor; a guest. **2.** A supernatural being; a ghost. **3.** A migratory bird that stops in a particular place for a limited period of time. —*adj.* Visiting.

vis•i•ta•tion (vĭz′ĭ-tā′shən) *n.* **1.** The act or an instance of visiting or an instance of being visited. **2.** An official visit for the purpose of inspection or examination. **3.** The right of a parent to visit a child as specified in a divorce or separation order. **4.a.** A visit of punishment or affliction or of comfort and blessing regarded as ordained by God. **b.** A calamitous event or experience; a grave misfortune. **5.** The appearance or arrival of a supernatural being. **6. Visitation.** *Rom. Cath. Ch.* **a.** The visit of the Virgin Mary to her cousin Elizabeth. **b.** The Christian feast commemorating this event, traditionally observed on May 31. —**vis′i•ta′tion•al** *adj.*

vis•i•ta•to•ri•al (vĭz′ĭ-tə-tôr′ē-əl, -tōr′-) *adj.* **1.** Of or relating to an official visitor or visit. **2.** Having the right or power of visitation.

vis•it•ing card (vĭz′ĭ-tĭng) *n.* See **calling card.**

visiting fireman *n. Informal.* **1.** An important visitor who is entertained impressively. **2.** A visitor, esp. a tourist or conventioneer, thought to be a free spender.

visiting nurse *n.* A registered nurse employed by a public health agency or hospital to promote community health and esp. to visit and treat sick people in their homes.

visiting professor *n.* A professor invited to serve on the faculty of another college or university for a limited period of time.

visiting teacher *n.* A teacher affiliated with a public school system who visits and instructs sick or handicapped children.

vis•i•tor (vĭz′ĭ-tər) *n.* One that visits: *evening visitors.*

vi•sor also **vi•zor** (vī′zər) —*n.* **1.** A piece projecting from the front of a cap to shade or protect the eyes. **2.** A shield against glare attached above the windshield of an automotive vehicle. **3.** The front piece of the helmet of a suit of armor, capable of being raised and lowered and designed to protect the eyes, nose, and forehead. **4.** A means of concealment or disguise; a mask. —*tr.v.* **-sored, -sor•ing, -sors** also **-zored, -zor•ing, -zors.** To provide or protect with a visor. [Alteration of ME *viser* < AN < *vis,* face < Lat. *vīsus,* appearance. See VISAGE.]

vis•ta (vĭs′tə) *n.* **1.a.** A distant view or prospect, esp. one seen through an opening, as between rows of trees. **b.** An avenue or other passage affording such a view. **2.** An awareness of a range of time, events, or subjects; a broad mental view. [Ital. < fem. p.part. of *vedere,* to see < Lat. *vidēre.* See **weid-*.**]

VISTA *abbr.* Volunteers In Service To America.

Vis•tu•la (vĭs′chə-lə, -chōō-). A river of Poland rising in the W Beskids and flowing c. 1,091 km (678 mi) in an arc to the Gulf of Gdańsk.

vi•su•al (vĭzh′ōō-əl) *adj.* **1.** Of or relating to the sense of sight.

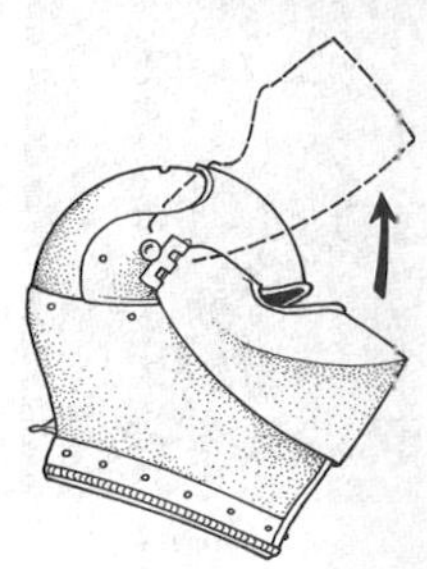

visor
Top: Of a cap
Bottom: Of a helmet

ă pat	oi boy
ā pay	ou out
âr care	ŏŏ took
ä father	ōō boot
ĕ pet	ŭ cut
ē be	ûr urge
ĭ pit	th thin
ī pie	*th* this
îr pier	hw which
ŏ pot	zh vision
ō toe	ə about, item
ô paw	

Stress marks:
′ (primary);
′ (secondary), as in
dictionary (dĭk′shə-nĕr′ē)

2. Seen or able to be seen by the eye; visible. **3.** Optical. **4.** Done, maintained, or executed by sight only. **5.** Having the nature of or producing an image in the mind: *a visual memory.* **6.** Of or relating to a method of instruction involving sight. —*n.* A picture, chart, or other presentation that appeals to the sense of sight, used in promotion or for illustration or narration. Often used in the plural. [ME < LLat. *vīsuālis* < Lat. *vīsus*, sight. See VISION.] —**vi′su•al•ly** *adv.* —**vi′su•al•ness, vi′su•al′i•ty** (-ăl′ĭ-tē) *n.*

visual acuity *n.* Sharpness of vision, esp. as tested with a Snellen chart, according to which normal visual acuity is 20/20.

visual aid *n.* An instructional aid, such as a scale model, filmstrip, or videotape, that presents information visually.

visual field *n.* The space or range within which objects are visible to the immobile eyes at a given time.

vi•su•al•ize (vĭzh′o͞o-ə-līz′) *v.* **-ized, -iz•ing, -iz•es.** —*tr.* **1.** To form a mental image of. **2.** To make visible. —*intr.* To form a mental image. —**vi′su•al•i•za′tion** (-ə-lĭ-zā′shən) *n.* —**vi′su•al•iz′er** *n.*

visual purple *n.* See **rhodopsin.**

vi•su•o•spa•tial (vĭsh′o͞o-ō-spā′shəl) *adj.* Of or relating to visual perception of spatial relationships among objects.

vi•ta (vī′tə, vē′-) *n., pl.* **vi•tae** (vī′tē, vē′tī). **1.** A short biographical or autobiographical account. **2.** A curriculum vitae. [Lat. *vīta*, life. See VITAL.]

vi•tal (vīt′l) *adj.* **1.** Of, relating to, or characteristic of life. **2.** Necessary to the continuation of life; life-sustaining: *a vital organ.* **3.** Full of life; animated. **4.** Imparting life or animation; invigorating: *the sun's vital rays.* **5.** Necessary to continued existence or effectiveness; essential. **6.** Concerned with or recording data pertinent to lives. **7.** *Biol.* Used or done on a living cell or tissue. **8.** Destructive to life; fatal: *a vital injury.* [ME < OFr. < Lat. *vītālis* < *vīta*, life. See **gʷei-*.**] —**vi′tal•ly** *adv.* —**vi′tal•ness** *n.*

vital capacity *n.* The amount of air that can be forcibly expelled from the lungs after breathing in as deeply as possible.

vi•tal•ism (vīt′l-ĭz′əm) *n.* The theory or doctrine that life processes arise from or contain a nonmaterial vital principle and cannot be explained entirely as physical and chemical phenomena. —**vi′tal•ist** *adj. & n.* —**vi′tal•is′tic** *adj.*

vi•tal•i•ty (vī-tăl′ĭ-tē) *n., pl.* **-ties. 1.** The capacity to live, grow, or develop. **2.** Physical or intellectual vigor; energy. **3.** The characteristic, principle, or force that distinguishes living things from nonliving things. **4.** Power to survive.

vi•tal•ize (vīt′l-īz′) *tr.v.* **-ized, -iz•ing, -iz•es. 1.** To endow with life; animate. **2.** To make more lively or vigorous; invigorate. —**vi′tal•i•za′tion** (-ĭ-zā′shən) *n.* —**vi′tal•iz′er** *n.*

vi•tals (vīt′lz) *pl.n.* **1.** The vital body organs. **2.** The parts essential to continued functioning, as of a system.

vital signs *pl.n.* The pulse rate, temperature, and respiratory rate of an individual.

vital statistics *pl.n.* Statistics concerning the important events in human life, such as births, deaths, and marriages.

vi•ta•min (vī′tə-mĭn) *n.* Any of various fat-soluble or water-soluble organic substances essential in minute amounts for normal growth and activity of the body and obtained naturally from plant and animal foods. [Alteration of *vitamine* : Lat. *vīta*, life; see **gʷei-*** + AMINE (so called because they were originally thought to be amines).] —**vi′ta•min′ic** *adj.*

vitamin A *n.* A fat-soluble vitamin or a mixture of vitamins, esp. vitamin A_1 or a mixture of vitamins A_1 and A_2, occurring principally in fish-liver oils, milk, and some yellow and dark green vegetables and functioning in normal cell growth, the maintenance of epithelial tissue, and the prevention of night blindness.

vitamin A_1 *n.* A yellow crystalline compound, $C_{20}H_{30}O$, extracted from egg yolks, milk, and cod-liver oil.

vitamin A_2 *n.* A golden yellow oil, $C_{20}H_{28}O$, occurring chiefly in the livers of freshwater fish.

vitamin B *n.* **1.** Vitamin B complex. **2.** A member of the vitamin B complex, esp. thiamine.

vitamin B_1 *n.* See **thiamine.**

vitamin B_2 *n.* See **riboflavin.**

vitamin B_6 *n.* See **pyridoxine.**

vitamin B_{12} *n.* A complex compound containing cobalt, found esp. in liver and widely used to treat pernicious anemia.

vitamin B_c *n.* See **folic acid.**

vitamin B complex *n.* A group of water-soluble vitamins including thiamine, riboflavin, niacin, pantothenic acid, biotin, pyridoxine, folic acid, inositol, and vitamin B_{12} and occurring chiefly in yeast, liver, eggs, and some vegetables.

vitamin C *n.* See **ascorbic acid.**

vitamin D *n.* A fat-soluble vitamin occurring in several forms, esp. vitamin D_2 or vitamin D_3, required for normal growth of teeth and bones and produced in general by ultraviolet irradiation of sterols found in milk, fish, and eggs.

vitamin D_2 *n.* A white crystalline compound, $C_{28}H_{44}O$, produced by ultraviolet irradiation of ergosterol.

vitamin D_3 *n.* A colorless crystalline compound, $C_{27}H_{44}O$, found in fish-liver oils.

vitamin E *n.* A fat-soluble vitamin, $C_{29}H_{50}O_2$, found chiefly in plant leaves and wheat germ oil and used to treat sterility and abnormalities of the muscles, red blood cells, liver, and brain.

vitamin G *n.* Riboflavin.

vitamin H *n.* Biotin.

vitamin K *n.* A fat-soluble vitamin existing in several related forms, occurring in leafy green vegetables, tomatoes, and egg yolks and functioning to promote blood clotting and prevent hemorrhaging.

vitamin K_1 *n.* A yellow viscous oil, $C_{31}H_{46}O_2$, found in leafy green vegetables and used by the body to form prothrombin.

vitamin K_2 *n.* A crystalline compound, $C_{41}H_{56}O_2$, found in various intestinal bacteria and used to stop hemorrhaging.

vitamin P *n.* A water-soluble vitamin found as a crystalline substance esp. in citrus juices and functioning as a bioflavonoid in promoting capillary resistance to hemorrhaging.

Vi•tebsk (vē′tĕpsk′, vyĕ′tyĭpsk). A city of NE Belorussia on the Western Dvina R. NE of Minsk. Pop. 335,000.

vi•tel•lin (vĭ-tĕl′ĭn, vī-) *n.* A protein found in egg yolk.

vi•tel•line (vĭ-tĕl′ĭn, -ēn′, vī-) *adj.* **1.** Of, relating to, or associated with the yolk of an egg: *the vitelline membrane.* **2.** *Color.* Having the yellow hue of an egg yolk; dull yellow. —*n.* The yolk of an egg. [VITELL(US) + -INE[1].]

vi•tel•lo•gen•e•sis (vĭt′l-ō-jĕn′ĭ-sĭs, vīt′-) *n.* Formation of the yolk of an egg. [VITELL(US) + -GENESIS.] —**vi′tel•lo•ge•net′ic** (-jə-nĕt′ĭk), **vi′tel•lo•gen′ic** (-jĕn′ĭk) *adj.*

vi•tel•lus (vĭ-tĕl′əs, vī-) *n., pl.* **-lus•es.** The yolk of an egg. [Lat., prob. dim. of *vitulus*, calf. See **wet-²*.**]

vi•ti•ate (vĭsh′ē-āt′) *tr.v.* **-at•ed, -at•ing, -ates. 1.** To reduce the value or impair the quality of. **2.** To corrupt morally; debase. **3.** To make ineffective; invalidate. [Lat. *vitiāre, vitiāt-* < *vitium*, fault.] —**vi′ti•a•ble** (vĭsh′ē-ə-bəl) *adj.* —**vi′ti•a′tion** *n.* —**vi′ti•a′tor** *n.*

vit•i•cul•ture (vĭt′ĭ-kŭl′chər, vī′tĭ-) *n.* The cultivation of grapes. [Lat. *vītis*, vine; see **wei-*** + CULTURE.] —**vit′i•cul′tur•al** *adj.* —**vit′i•cul′tur•ist** *n.*

Vi•ti Le•vu (vē′tē lĕv′o͞o). The largest of the Fiji Is., in the SW Pacific Ocean.

vit•i•li•go (vĭt′l-ī′gō, -ē′gō) *n., pl.* **-gos.** See **leukoderma.** [Lat. *vitilīgō*, tetter.]

Vi•tim (vĭ-tēm′). A river of SE Russia flowing c. 1,834 km (1,140 mi) generally NE and N to the Lena R.

Vi•to•ri•a (vĭ-tôr′ē-ə, -tōr′-, bē-tô′ryä). A city of N-central Spain SSE of Bilbao; probably founded by the Visigoths in the 6th cent. A.D. Pop. 199,239.

Vi•tó•ri•a (vĭ-tôr′ē-ə, -tōr′-, vē-tôr′yä). A city of E Brazil on the Atlantic Ocean NE of Rio de Janeiro. Pop. 165,090.

vit•rec•to•my (vĭ-trĕk′tə-mē) *n., pl.* **-mies.** Surgical removal of the vitreous humor from the eyeball.

vit•re•ous (vĭt′rē-əs) *adj.* **1.** Of, relating to, resembling, or having the nature of glass; glassy. **2.** Obtained or made from glass. **3.** Of or relating to the vitreous humor. —*n.* The vitreous humor. [< Lat. *vitreus* < *vitrum*, glass.] —**vit′re•os′i•ty** (-ŏs′ĭ-tē), **vit′re•ous•ness** (-əs-nĭs) *n.*

vitreous humor *n.* The clear gelatinous substance that fills the eyeball between the retina and the lens.

vit•ri•fy (vĭt′rə-fī′) *v.* **-fied** (-fīd′), **-fy•ing, -fies** (-fīz′). —*tr.* To change or make into glass or a glassy substance, esp. through heat fusion. —*intr.* To become vitreous. [Fr. *vitrifier* < Med.Lat. *vitrificāre* : Lat. *vitrum*, glass + Lat. *-ficāre*, -fy.] —**vit′ri•fi′a•bil′i•ty** *n.* —**vit′ri•fi′a•ble** *adj.* —**vit′ri•fi•ca′tion** (-fĭ-kā′shən) *n.*

vi•trine (vē-trēn′) *n.* A glass-paneled cabinet or case for displaying articles such as china, objects d'art, or fine merchandise. [Fr. < *vitre*, pane of glass < OFr., glass, window with multiple lights < Lat. *vitrum.*]

vitrine

vit•ri•ol (vĭt′rē-ōl′, -əl) *n.* **1.a.** See **sulfuric acid. b.** Any of various sulfates of metals, such as zinc sulfate. **2.** Bitterly abusive feeling or expression. —*tr.v.* **-oled, -ol•ing, -ols** or **-olled, -ol•ling, -ols.** To expose or subject to vitriol. [ME < OFr. < Med.Lat. *vitriolum* < LLat. *vitreolum*, neut. of *vitreolus*, of glass < Lat. *vitreus*. See VITREOUS.]

vit•ri•ol•ic (vĭt′rē-ŏl′ĭk) *adj.* **1.** Of, similar to, or derived from a vitriol. **2.** Bitterly scathing; caustic: *vitriolic criticism.*

Vi•tru•vi•us (vĭ-tro͞o′vē-əs). fl. 1st cent. B.C. Roman architect known for his *De Architectura.*

Vi•try-sur-Seine (vē-trē′so͝or-sĕn′, -sür-). A city of N-central France, a suburb of Paris. Pop. 85,263.

vit•ta (vĭt′ə) *n., pl.* **vit•tae** (vĭt′ē). **1.** *Zool.* A streak or band of color, as on the bill of a bird. **2.** *Bot.* An oil tube in the fruit of certain plants, such as the carrot or parsley. [Lat., headband, ribbon. See **wei-*.**] —**vit′tate′** (vĭt′āt′) *adj.*

vit•tle (vĭt′əl) *n. & v. Non-Standard.* Var. of **victual** 2.

vi•tu•per•ate (vī-to͞o′pə-rāt′, -tyo͞o′-, vĭ-) *v.* **-at•ed, -at•ing, -ates.** —*tr.* To rebuke or criticize harshly or abusively; berate. —*intr.* To use harshly abusive language; rail. [Lat. *vituperāre, vituperāt-.*] —**vi•tu′per•a′tor** *n.*

vi•tu•per•a•tion (vī-to͞o′pə-rā′shən, -tyo͞o′-, vĭ-) *n.* **1.** The act or an instance of vituperating; abusive censure. **2.** Sustained, harshly abusive language; invective.

vi•tu•per•a•tive (vī-to͞o′pər-ə-tĭv, -tyo͞o′-, -pə-rā′-, vĭ-) *adj.* Using, containing, or marked by harshly abusive censure. —**vi•tu′per•a•tive•ly** *adv.* —**vi•tu′per•a•tive•ness** *n.*

vi•va (vē′və, -vä′) *interj.* Used to express acclamation, salute, or applause. [Ital. and Sp., (long) live, both < Lat. *vīva*, third pers. sing. pr. subjunctive of *vīvere*, to live. See **gʷei-***.]

vi•va•ce (vē-vä′chā) *adv. & adj. Mus.* In a vivacious manner. [Ital. < Lat. *vīvāx*, *vīvāc-*, vivacious. See VIVACIOUS.]

vi•va•cious (vĭ-vā′shəs, vī-) *adj.* Full of animation and spirit; lively. [< Lat. *vīvāx*, *vīvāc-* < *vīvere*, to live. See **gʷei-***.] —**vi•va′cious•ly** *adv.* —**vi•va′cious•ness** *n.*

vi•vac•i•ty (vĭ-văs′ĭ-tē, vī-) *n.* The quality or condition of being vivacious; liveliness.

Vi•val•di (vĭ-väl′dē, -vôl′-), **Antonio Lucio.** 1675?–1741. Italian composer whose works include *The Four Seasons* (1725).

vi•var•i•um (vī-vâr′ē-əm) *n., pl.* **-i•ums** or **-i•a** (-ē-ə). A place, esp. an indoor enclosure, for keeping and raising living animals and plants under natural conditions for observation or research. [Lat. *vīvārium* < neut. of *vīvārius*, of living creatures < *vīvus*, alive. See VIVIFY.]

vi•va vo•ce (vī′və vō′sē, vē′və) *adv. & adj.* By word of mouth: *a report submitted viva voce.* [Med.Lat. *vīvā vōce*, with the living voice : Lat. *vīvā*, fem. ablative sing. of *vīvus*, living + Lat. *vōce*, ablative of *vōx*, voice.]

vi•ver•rid (vī-vĕr′ĭd) *adj.* Of or belonging to the family Viverridae, which includes small carnivorous mammals such as the civets and mongooses. [< NLat. *Vīverridae*, family name < *Vīverra*, type genus < Lat. *vīverra*, ferret.] —**viverrid** *n.*

viv•id (vĭv′ĭd) *adj.* **-er, -est. 1.** Perceived as bright and distinct; brilliant. **2.a.** Having intensely bright colors: *a vivid tapestry.* **b.** Having a very high degree of saturation: *a vivid purple.* **3.** Full of the vigor and freshness of immediate experience. **4.a.** Evoking lifelike images within the mind; heard, seen, or felt as if real. See Syns at **graphic. b.** Active in forming lifelike images: *a vivid imagination.* [Lat. *vīvidus* < *vīvere*, to live. See **gʷei-***.] —**viv′id•ly** *adv.* —**viv′id•ness** *n.*

viv•i•fy (vĭv′ə-fī′) *tr.v.* **-fied, -fy•ing, -fies. 1.** To give or bring life to; animate. **2.** To make more lively, intense, or striking; enliven. [ME *vivifien* < OFr. *vivifier* < LLat. *vīvificāre* : Lat. *vīvus*, alive; see **gʷei-*** + Lat. *-ficāre*, -fy.] —**viv′i•fi•ca′tion** (-fĭ-kā′shən) *n.* —**viv′i•fi′er** *n.*

vi•vip•a•rous (vī-vĭp′ər-əs, vĭ-) *adj.* **1.** *Zool.* Giving birth to living offspring that develop within the mother's body. **2.** *Bot.* **a.** Germinating or producing seeds that germinate before becoming detached from the parent plant. **b.** Producing bulbils or new plants rather than seed. [< Lat. *vīviparus* : *vīvus*, alive; see **gʷei-*** + *-parus*, -parous.] —**vi′vi•par′i•ty** (vī′və-păr′ĭ-tē, vĭv′ə-) *n.* —**vi•vip′a•rous•ly** *adv.*

viv•i•sect (vĭv′ĭ-sĕkt′) *v.* **-sect•ed, -sect•ing, -sects.** —*tr.* To perform vivisection on (an animal). —*intr.* To practice vivisection. [Back-formation < VIVISECTION.] —**viv′i•sec′tor** *n.*

viv•i•sec•tion (vĭv′ĭ-sĕk′shən, vĭv′ĭ-sĕk′-) *n.* The act or practice of cutting into or otherwise injuring living animals, esp. for the purpose of scientific research. [Lat. *vīvus*, alive; see VIVIFY + (DIS)SECTION.] —**viv′i•sec′tion•al** *adj.* —**viv′i•sec′tion•al•ly** *adv.* —**viv′i•sec′tion•ist** *n.*

vix•en (vĭk′sən) *n.* **1.** A female fox. **2.** A woman regarded as quarrelsome, shrewish, or malicious. [ME *fixen* < OE *fyxe*.] —**vix′en•ish** *adj.* —**vix′en•ish•ness** *n.*

viz. *abbr.* Videlicet.

Vi•za•ga•pa•tam (vĭ-zä′gə-pŭt′əm). See **Visakhapatnam.**

viz•ard also **vis•ard** (vĭz′ərd, -ärd′) *n.* **1.** A visor or mask. **2.** A disguise. [Alteration of obsolete *vizar* < ME *viser*. See VISOR.]

vi•zier (vĭ-zîr′, vĭz′yər) *n.* A high officer in a Muslim government, esp. in the Ottoman Empire. [Turk. *vezīr* < Ar. *wazīr*, minister < *wazara*, to bear, carry.] —**vi•zier′ate** (vĭ-zîr′ĭt, -āt′, vĭz′yər-ĭt, -yə-rāt′) *n.* —**vi•zier′i•al** *adj.*

vi•zor (vī′zər) *n. & v.* Var. of **visor.**

vizs•la (vĭzh′lä) *n.* Any of a Hungarian breed of shorthaired medium-sized hunting dogs having a deep rust-gold coat and a docked tail. [Prob. < Czech *vyžle*, a hunting dog.]

VJ *abbr.* Video jockey.

V-J Day (vē′jā′) *n.* August 15, 1945, on which the Allies announced the surrender of Japanese forces during World War II. [*V(ictory in) J(apan) Day.*]

VL *abbr.* Vulgar Latin.

Vlaar•ding•en (vlär′dĭng-ən). A city of SW Netherlands, a suburb of Rotterdam. Pop. 76,466.

Vla•di•mir (vlăd′ə-mîr′, vlə-dyē′mĭr). A city of W-central Russia E of Moscow; founded c. 10th cent. Pop. 331,000.

Vlad•i•vos•tok (vlăd′ə-və-stŏk′, -vŏs′tŏk′, vlə-dyə-və-stôk′). A city of extreme SE Russia on an arm of the Sea of Japan; a naval base since 1872. Pop. 600,000.

Vla•minck (vlä-măɴk′), **Maurice de.** 1876–1958. French artist who was a leading exponent of fauvism.

vlf or **VLF** *abbr.* Very low frequency.

Vlis•sing•en (vlĭs′ĭng-ən) also **Flush•ing** (flŭsh′ĭng). A city of SW Netherlands on an island in the Schelde estuary and the North Sea; chartered 1247. Pop. 26,500.

Vlo•rë (vlôr′ə, vlōr′ə) **Vlo•ne** (vlō′nə). A city of SW Albania on **Vlorë Bay,** an inlet of the Adriatic Sea; site of the proclamation of Albania's independence in 1912. Pop. 61,100.

VLSI *abbr. Electron.* Very large scale integration.

Vl•ta•va (vŭl′tə-və, vəl′tä-vä). A river of W Czech Republic flowing c. 434 km (270 mi) to the Elbe R.

V.M.D. *abbr. Lat.* Veterinariae Medicinae Doctor (Doctor of Veterinary Medicine).

V-neck (vē′nĕk′) *n.* A V-shaped neckline, as of a sweater.

vo. *abbr. Print.* Verso.

VOA *abbr.* Voice of America.

voc. *abbr.* **1.** Vocational. **2.** Vocative.

vocab. *abbr.* Vocabulary.

vo•ca•ble (vō′kə-bəl) *Ling.* —*n.* A word considered only as a sequence of sounds or letters rather than as a unit of meaning. —*adj.* Capable of being voiced or spoken. [Fr. < OFr. < Lat. *vocābulum*, name < *vocāre*, to call. See **wekʷ-***.]

vo•cab•u•lar•y (vō-kăb′yə-lĕr′ē) *n., pl.* **-ies. 1.** All the words of a language. **2.** The sum of words used by, understood by, or at the command of a particular person or group. **3.** A list of words and often phrases, usu. arranged alphabetically and defined or translated; a lexicon or glossary. **4.** A supply of expressive means; a repertoire of communication: *a dancer's vocabulary of movement.* [Fr. *vocabulaire* < OFr. < Med.Lat. *vocābulārium* < neut. of *vocābulārius*, of words < Lat. *vocābulum*, name. See VOCABLE.]

vo•cal (vō′kəl) *adj.* **1.** Of or relating to the voice: *vocal organs.* **2.** Uttered or produced by the voice. **3.** Having a voice; capable of emitting sound or speech. **4.** Full of voices; resounding. **5.** Tending to express oneself often or freely; outspoken: *a vocal critic.* **6.** *Ling.* **a.** Of or resembling vowels; vocalic. **b.** Voiced. **7.** *Mus.* Of, relating to, or performed by singing: *vocal music.* —*n.* **1.** A vocal sound. **2.** *Mus.* A popular composition for a singer, often with instrumental accompaniment. [ME < OFr. < Lat. *vōcālis* < *vōx*, *vōc-*, voice. See **wekʷ-***.] —**vo′cal•ly** *adv.* —**vo′cal•ness** *n.*

vocal cords *pl.n.* Either of two pairs of bands or folds of mucous membrane in the throat that project into the larynx, the lower pair of which produces sound when air is passed up from the lungs.

vocal folds *pl.n.* Vocal cords.

vo•cal•ic (vō-kăl′ĭk) *adj. Ling.* **1.** Containing, marked by, or consisting of vowels. **2.** Of, relating to, or having the nature of a vowel. —**vo•cal′i•cal•ly** *adv.*

vo•cal•ise¹ (vō′kə-lēz′) *n. Mus.* An exercise, a composition, or an arrangement in which a performer sings sol-fa syllables or other meaningless vocal sounds rather than a text. [Fr. < *vocaliser*, to vocalize < *vocal*, vocal < OFr. See VOCAL.]

vo•cal•ise² (vō′kə-līz′) *v. Chiefly British.* Var. of **vocalize.**

vo•cal•ism (vō′kə-lĭz′əm) *n.* **1.** Use of the voice in speaking or singing. **2.** *Mus.* The act, technique, or art of singing. **3.** *Ling.* **a.** A vowel sound. **b.** A system of vowels used in a language or dialect. —**vo′cal•is′tic** *adj.*

vo•cal•ist (vō′kə-lĭst) *n. Mus.* A singer. —**vo′ca•lis′tic** *adj.*

vo•cal•ize (vō′kə-līz′) *v.* **-ized, -iz•ing, -iz•es.** —*tr.* **1.** To produce with the voice. **2.** To give voice to; articulate. **3.** To mark (a vowelless Hebrew text, for example) with vowel points. **4.** *Ling.* **a.** To change (a consonant) into a vowel during articulation. **b.** To voice. —*intr.* **1.a.** To use the voice. **b.** *Mus.* To sing. **2.** *Ling.* To be changed into a vowel. —**vo′cal•i•za′tion** (-kə-lĭ-zā′shən) *n.* —**vo′cal•iz′er** *n.*

vo•ca•tion (vō-kā′shən) *n.* **1.** A regular occupation, esp. one for which a person is particularly suited or qualified. **2.** An inclination, as if in response to a summons, to undertake a certain kind of work, esp. a religious career; a calling. [Ult. < Lat. *vocātiō*, *vocātiōn-*, a calling < *vocātus*, p.part. of *vocāre*, to call. See **wekʷ-***.]

vo•ca•tion•al (vō-kā′shə-nəl) *adj.* **1.** Of or relating to a vocation or vocations: *vocational counseling.* **2.** Relating to, providing, or undergoing training in a special skill to be pursued in a trade: *vocational students.* —**vo•ca′tion•al•ly** *adv.*

vo•ca•tion•al•ism (vō-kā′shə-nə-lĭz′əm) *n.* The stressing of vocational training in education. —**vo•ca′tion•al•ist** *n.*

vocational school *n.* A school, esp. one on a secondary level, that offers instruction and practical introductory experience in skilled trades such as mechanics, carpentry, and plumbing.

voc•a•tive (vŏk′ə-tĭv) *adj.* **1.** Relating to, characteristic of, or used in calling. **2.** Relating to or being a grammatical case used to indicate the person or thing being addressed. —*n.* **1.** The vocative case. **2.** A word in the vocative case. [ME *vocatif* < OFr. < Lat. *vocātīvus (cāsus)*, vocative (case) < *vocātus*, p.part. of *vocāre*, to call. See VOCATION.] —**voc′a•tive•ly** *adv.*

vo•cif•er•ant (vō-sĭf′ər-ənt) *adj.* Vociferous.

vo•cif•er•ate (vō-sĭf′ə-rāt′) *tr. & intr.v.* **-at•ed, -at•ing, -ates.** To utter (something) or cry out loudly and vehemently, esp. in protest. [Lat. *vōciferārī*, *vōciferāt-* : *vōx*, *vōc-*, voice; see VOICE + *ferre*, to carry; see **bher-¹***.] —**vo•cif′er•a′tion** *n.* —**vo•cif′er•a′tor** *n.*

vo•cif•er•ous (vō-sĭf′ər-əs) *adj.* Making, given to, or marked by noisy and vehement outcry. —**vo•cif′er•ous•ly** *adv.* —**vo•cif′er•ous•ness** *n.*

vo•cod•er (vō′kō′dər) *n.* An electronic device or system for synthesizing speech. [VO(ICE) + COD(E) + -ER¹.]

vod•ka (vŏd′kə) *n.* An alcoholic liquor originally distilled from fermented wheat mash but now also made from a mash of rye, corn, or potatoes. [Russ., dim. of *voda*, water. See **wed-¹***.]

ă pat	oi boy
ā pay	ou out
âr care	o͝o took
ä father	o͞o boot
ĕ pet	ŭ cut
ē be	ûr urge
ĭ pit	th thin
ī pie	*th* this
îr pier	hw which
ŏ pot	zh vision
ō toe	ə about, item
ô paw	

Stress marks:
′ (primary);
′ (secondary), as in dictionary (dĭk′shə-nĕr′ē)

vo•doun or **vo•dun** (vō-do͞on′) *n.* See **voodoo** 1. [Haitian Creole < Ewe *vodu* or Fon *vodun.*]

vogue (vōg) *n.* **1.** The prevailing fashion, practice, or style: *Hoop skirts were once the vogue.* **2.** Popular acceptance or favor; popularity: *a game no longer in vogue.* [Fr. < OFr., prob. < *voguer,* to sail, row. See **wegh-*.**]

vogu•ish (vō′gĭsh) *adj.* **1.** Fashionable; chic: *a suit of voguish cut.* **2.** Temporarily in frequent use; faddish: *voguish terminology.* **—vogu′ish•ly** *adv.* **—vogu′ish•ness** *n.*

Vo•gul (vō′go͝ol) *n., pl.* **Vogul** or **-guls. 1.** A member of a people inhabiting the region of the Ob River in western Siberia, related to the Ostyak. **2.** Their Ugric language.

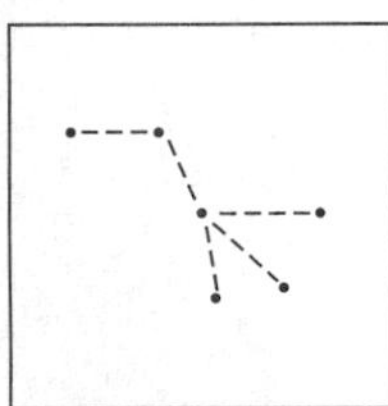

Volans

voice (vois) *n.* **1.a.** The sound produced by the vocal organs of a vertebrate, esp. a human being. **b.** The ability to produce such sounds. **2.** A specified quality, condition, or pitch of vocal sound. **3.** *Ling.* Expiration of air through vibrating vocal cords, used in the production of vowels and voiced consonants. **4.** A sound resembling or reminiscent of vocal utterance. **5.** *Mus.* **a.** Musical sound produced by vibration of the human vocal cords and resonated within the throat and head cavities. **b.** The quality or condition of a person's singing. **c.** A singer. **d.** One of the individual parts or strands in a composition. **6.a.** Expression; utterance. **b.** A medium or an agency of expression. **c.** The right or opportunity to express a choice or an opinion. **7.** *Gram.* A property of verbs or a set of verb inflections indicating the relation between the subject and the action expressed by the verb: *"Birds build nests" uses the active voice; "nests built by birds" uses the passive voice.* **8.** The distinctive style or manner of expression of an author or a character in a book. **—***tr.v.* **voiced, voic•ing, voic•es. 1.** To give voice to; utter. See Syns at **vent[1]**. **2.** *Ling.* To pronounce with vibration of the vocal cords. **3.** *Mus.* **a.** To provide (a composition) with voice parts. **b.** To regulate the tone of (the pipes of an organ, for example). **—*idiom.* with one voice.** In complete agreement; unanimously. [ME < OFr. *vois* < Lat. *vōx, vōc-.* See **wek[w]-*.**]

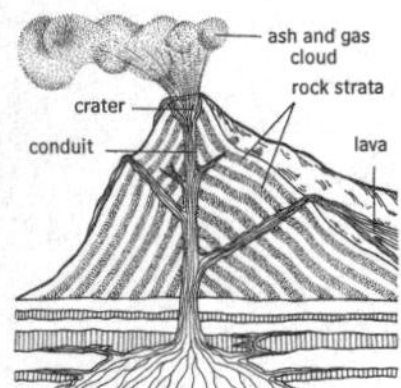

volcano
Cutaway view of an erupting volcano

voice box *n.* The larynx.

voiced (voist) *adj.* **1.** Having a voice or a specified kind of voice. Often used in combination: *harsh-voiced.* **2.** *Ling.* Uttered with vibration of the vocal cords, as the consonants *b* and *d.* **—voiced′ness** (voist′nĭs, voi′sĭd-) *n.*

voice•ful (vois′fəl) *adj.* Having a voice, esp. a loud voice; resounding. **—voice′ful•ness** *n.*

voice•less (vois′lĭs) *adj.* **1.** Having no voice; mute. **2.** *Ling.* Uttered without vibration of the vocal cords, as the consonants *t* and *p.* **—voice′less•ly** *adv.* **—voice′less•ness** *n.*

voice mail *n.* An interactive computerized system for answering and routing telephone calls, for recording, saving, and relaying messages, and sometimes for paging the user.

voice-o•ver or **voice•o•ver** (vois′ō′vər) *n.* The voice of an unseen narrator or of an on-screen character not seen speaking in a movie or a television broadcast.

voice part *n. Mus.* **1.** A part or strand of a composition written for the human voice. **2.** See **voice** 5d.

volleyball

voice•print (vois′prĭnt′) *n.* An electronically recorded graphic representation of a person's voice, in which the configuration for an utterance is uniquely characteristic of the speaker.

voic•er (voi′sər) *n.* **1.** One that voices: *a voicer of criticism.* **2.** *Mus.* A specialist in regulating the tone of organ pipes.

voic•ing (voi′sĭng) *n.* **1.** The act, practice, or production of one that voices. **2.** *Mus.* Tonal quality of an instrument in an ensemble, esp. a jazz ensemble, or of the ensemble as a whole.

void (void) *adj.* **1.** Containing no matter; empty. **2.** Not occupied; unfilled. **3.** Completely lacking; devoid: *void of understanding.* **4.** Ineffective; useless. **5.** Having no legal force or validity; null: *a contract rendered void.* **6.** *Games.* Lacking cards of a particular suit in a hand. **—***n.* **1.a.** An empty space. **b.** A vacuum. **2.** An open space or a break in continuity; a gap. **3.** A feeling or state of emptiness, loneliness, or loss. **4.** *Games.* Absence of cards of a particular suit in a hand. **—***v.* **void•ed, void•ing, voids. —***tr.* **1.** To take out (the contents of something); empty. **2.** To excrete (body wastes). **3.** To leave; vacate. **4.** To make void; invalidate. **—***intr.* To excrete body wastes. [ME < OFr. *voide,* fem. of *voit* < VLat. **vocitus,* alteration of Lat. *vacīvus, vocīvus,* var. of *vacuus* < *vacāre,* to be empty. See **eu-[2]*.**] **—void′er** *n.*

void•a•ble (voi′də-bəl) *adj.* That can be voided or esp. annulled: *voidable contracts.* **—void′a•ble•ness** *n.*

void•ance (void′ns) *n.* **1.** The act of voiding. **2.** The condition of being vacant; emptiness.

void•ed (voi′dĭd) *adj. Her.* Having the central area cut out or left vacant, leaving a narrow border or an outline.

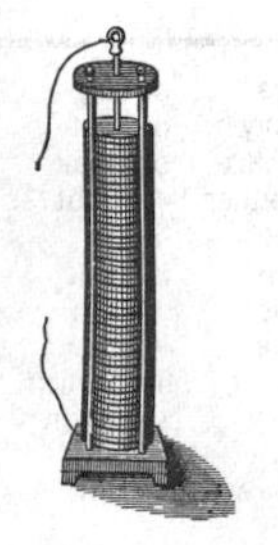

voltaic pile

voi•là (vwä-lä′) *interj.* Used to call attention to or express satisfaction with a thing shown or accomplished. [Fr. : *voi,* second pers. sing. imper. of *voir,* to see (< OFr.; see VOYEUR) + *là,* there (< OFr. *la, lai,* prob. < Lat. *illāc,* by that way : *illa,* that, fem. of *ille;* see **al-[1]*** + *-ce,* deictic particle).]

voile (voil) *n.* A light plain-weave sheer fabric of cotton, rayon, silk, or wool used esp. for making dresses and curtains. [Fr. < OFr. *veile,* veil < Lat. *vēla,* neut. pl. of *vēlum,* covering.]

voir dire (vwär dîr′) *n. Law.* A preliminary examination of prospective jurors or witnesses under oath to determine their competence or suitability. [AN, to speak the truth : Lat. *vērus,* true; see **wēro-*** + Lat. *dīcere,* to say; see **deik-*.**]

Voj•vod•i•na (voi′və-dē′nə). A region of N Serbia; formerly part of Hungary and an autonomous region of Yugoslavia after 1946.

vol. *abbr.* **1.** Volcano. **2.** Volume. **3.** Volunteer.

Vo•lans (vō′lănz′) *n.* A constellation in the polar region of the celestial Southern Hemisphere near Carina and Dorado. [Lat. *volāns,* pr.part. of *volāre,* to fly.]

vo•lant (vō′lənt) *adj.* **1.** Flying or capable of flying. **2.** Moving quickly or nimbly. **3.** *Her.* Depicted with the wings extended as in flying. [Lat. *volāns, volant-,* pr.part. of *volāre,* to fly. Sense 3 < Fr. < OFr., pr.part. of *voler,* to fly < Lat. *volāre.*]

Vo•la•pük (vō′lə-po͝ok′, -pük′, vŏl′ə-) *n.* An artificial international language based on English. [Volapük : *vol,* world (alteration of E. WORLD) + *pük,* speech (alteration of E. SPEECH).]

vo•lar (vō′lər) *adj.* Of or relating to the sole of the foot or the palm of the hand. [< Lat. *vola,* sole, palm.]

vol•a•tile (vŏl′ə-tl, -tīl′) *adj.* **1.** *Chem.* **a.** Evaporating readily at normal temperatures and pressures. **b.** That can be readily vaporized. **2.a.** Tending to vary often or widely, as in price. **b.** Inconstant; fickle. **c.** Lighthearted; flighty. **d.** Ephemeral; fleeting. **3.** Tending to violence; explosive. **4.** Flying or capable of flying; volant. [Fr. < OFr. < Lat. *volātilis,* flying < *volātus,* p.part. of *volāre,* to fly.] **—vol′a•tile** *n.* **—vol′a•til′i•ty** (-tĭl′ĭ-tē), **vol′a•tile•ness** (-tl-nĭs, -tīl′-) *n.*

volatile oil *n.* A rapidly evaporating oil, esp. an essential oil.

vol•a•til•ize (vŏl′ə-tl-īz′) *intr. & tr.v.* **-ized, -iz•ing, -iz•es. 1.** To become or make volatile. **2.** To evaporate or cause to evaporate. **—vol′a•til•iz′a•ble** *adj.* **—vol′a•til•i•za′tion** (-ĭ-zā′shən) *n.* **—vol′a•til•iz′er** *n.*

vol-au-vent (vô′lō-väN′) *n.* A light pastry shell filled with a ragout. [Fr. : *vol,* flight + *à,* with + *le,* the + *vent,* wind.]

vol•can•ic (vŏl-kăn′ĭk, vôl-) *adj.* **1.** Of, resembling, or caused by a volcano or volcanoes. **2.** Produced by or discharged from a volcano. **3.** Characterized by the presence of volcanoes. **4.** Powerfully explosive. **—vol•can′i•cal•ly** *adv.*

volcanic glass *n.* Natural glass produced by the cooling of molten lava too quickly to permit crystallization.

vol•ca•nism (vŏl′kə-nĭz′əm) also **vul•ca•nism** (vŭl′-) *n.* **1.** Volcanic force or activity. **2.** The phenomena associated with volcanic activity.

vol•ca•nize (vŏl′kə-nīz′) *tr.v.* **-nized, -niz•ing, -niz•es.** To subject to or change by the effects of volcanic heat. **—vol′ca•ni•za′tion** (-nĭ-zā′shən) *n.*

vol•ca•no (vŏl-kā′nō) *n., pl.* **-noes** or **-nos. 1.a.** An opening in the earth's crust through which molten lava, ash, and gases are ejected. **b.** A similar opening on the surface of another planet. **2.** A mountain formed by the materials ejected from a volcano. [Ital. < Sp. *volcán* or Port. *volcão,* both prob. < Lat. *vulcānus,* fire < *Volcānus,* Vulcan.]

Vol•ca•no Islands (vŏl-kā′nō). A group of Japanese islands in the NW Pacific N of the Mariana Is.

vol•ca•nol•o•gy (vŏl′kə-nŏl′ə-jē, vôl′-) also **vul•ca•nol•o•gy** (vŭl′-) *n.* The scientific study of volcanoes. **—vol′ca•no•log′i•cal** (-nə-lŏj′ĭ-kəl) *adj.* **—vol′ca•nol′o•gist** *n.*

vole[1] (vōl) *n.* Any of various rodents of the genus *Microtus* and related genera, resembling rats or mice but having a shorter tail and limbs and a heavier body. [Short for obsolete *volemouse,* perh. < Norw. **vollmus* : ON *vǫllr,* field + ON *mūs,* mouse.]

vole[2] (vōl) *n. Games.* The winning of all the tricks during the play of one hand; a grand slam. [Fr., prob. < *voler,* to fly < OFr. < Lat. *volāre,* to fly.]

Vol•ga (vŏl′gə, vôl′-, vōl′-). A river of W Russia rising in the Valdai Hills NW of Moscow and flowing c. 3,701 km (2,300 mi) to the Caspian Sea.

Vol•go•grad (vŏl′gə-grăd′, vōl′-, vŭl-gə-grät′). Formerly **Sta•lin•grad** (stä′lĭn-grăd′, stə-lyĭn-grät′). A city of SW Russia E of Voroshilovgrad; founded 1589. Pop. 974,000.

vol•i•tant (vŏl′ĭ-tnt) *adj.* **1.** Flying or capable of flying. **2.** Moving about rapidly. [Lat. *volitāns, volitant-,* pr.part. of *volitāre,* to fly to and fro, freq. of *volāre,* to fly.]

vol•i•ta•tion (vŏl′ĭ-tā′shən) *n.* **1.** The act of flying; flight. **2.** The ability to fly. **—vol′i•ta′tion•al** *adj.*

vo•li•tion (və-lĭsh′ən) *n.* **1.** The act or an instance of making a conscious choice or decision. **2.** A conscious choice or decision. **3.** The power or faculty of choosing; the will. [Fr. < Med.Lat. *volitiō, volitiōn-* < Lat. *velle, vol-,* to wish. See **wel-[1]*.**] **—vo•li′tion•al** *adj.* **—vo•li′tion•al•ly** *adv.*

vol•i•tive (vŏl′ĭ-tĭv) *adj.* **1.** Of, relating to, or originating in the will. **2.** Expressing a wish or permission.

volks•lied (fōks′lēt′, fōlk′s-) *n., pl.* **-lie•der** (-lē′dər). *Mus.* A folk song. [Ger. : *Volks,* genitive of *Volk,* people (< MHGer. *volc* < OHGer. *folc;* see **pelə-[1]***) + *Lied,* song; see LIED.]

vol•ley (vŏl′ē) *n., pl.* **-leys. 1.a.** A simultaneous discharge of a number of missiles. **b.** The missiles thus discharged. **2.** A bursting forth of many things together: *a volley of oaths.* **3.** *Sports.* **a.** The flight of a ball before it touches the ground. **b.** A shot, esp. in tennis, made by striking the ball before it touches the ground. **—***v.* **-leyed, -ley•ing, -leys. —***tr.* **1.** To discharge in or as if in a volley. **2.** *Sports.* To strike (a tennis ball, for example) before it touches the ground. —*intr.* **1.** To be discharged in or as if in a volley. **2.** *Sports.* To make a volley, esp. in tennis. **3.** To move rapidly, forcefully, or loudly like missiles: *The hailstones volleyed down.* [Fr. *volée* < OFr. < *voler*, to fly < Lat. *volāre*, to fly.] —**vol′ley•er** *n.*

vol•ley•ball (vŏl′ē-bôl′) *n. Sports.* **1.** A game played on a rectangular court divided by a high net, in which each of two teams tries to ground the ball on the other team's side of the net. **2.** The ball used in this game. —**vol′ley•ball′er** *n.*

Vo•log•da (vô′ləg-də). A city of W Russia NNE of Moscow; founded in the mid-12th cent. Pop. 269,000.

Vó•los (vō′lŏs′, vô′lôs). A city of E Greece in Thessaly on the **Gulf of Vólos,** an inlet of the Aegean Sea. Pop. 171,378.

vol•plane (vŏl′plān′, vôl′-) *intr.v.* **-planed, -plan•ing, -planes. 1.a.** To glide toward the earth in an airplane with the engine cut off. **b.** To glide toward the earth with the engine cut off. Used of an airplane. **2.** To make one's way or go by gliding. —*n.* The act or an instance of volplaning. [< Fr. *vol plané*, gliding flight : *vol*, flight (< OFr. < *voler*, to fly; see VOLLEY) + *plané*, gliding, p.part. of *planer*, to glide; see PLANE³.]

Vol•sci (vôl′skē, vŏl′sī, -sē, -shē) *pl.n.* A people of ancient Italy whose land was conquered by Rome in the fourth century B.C.

Vol•scian (vŏl′shən, vôl′skē-ən) *adj.* Of or relating to the Volsci or their language. —*n.* **1.** The Italic language of the Volsci. **2.** A member of the Volsci.

Vol•stead (vŏl′stĕd′, vôl′-, vōl′-), **Andrew John.** 1860–1947. Amer. legislator who sponsored the Volstead Act (1919), prohibiting the sale, manufacture, and transportation of alcoholic beverages.

volt¹ (vōlt) *n.* The International System unit of electric potential and electromotive force, equal to the difference of electric potential between two points on a conducting wire carrying a constant current of one ampere when the power dissipated between the points is one watt. See table at **measurement.** [After Count Alessandro VOLTA.]

volt² (vōlt, vôlt) *n. Sports.* A sudden movement made in avoiding a thrust in fencing. [Fr. *volte* < Ital. *volta*, turn < *voltare*, to turn, leap. See VAULT².]

Vol•ta (vŏl′tə, vōl′-, vôl′-). A river formed in central Ghana by the confluence of the White Volta and the Black Volta and flowing c. 467 km (290 mi) through artificial **Lake Volta** to the Bight of Benin in the Gulf of Guinea.

Vol•ta (vōl′tə, vôl′tä), Count **Alessandro.** 1745–1827. Italian physicist who invented the first electric battery (1800).

volt•age (vōl′tĭj) *n.* Electromotive force or potential difference, usu. expressed in volts.

voltage divider *n.* A number of resistors in series provided with taps at certain points to make available a fixed or variable fraction of the applied voltage.

vol•ta•ic (vŏl-tā′ĭk, vōl-, vôl-) *adj.* **1.** Of, relating to, or being electricity or electric current produced by chemical action; galvanic. **2.** Producing electricity by chemical action. [After Count Alessandro VOLTA.]

voltaic cell *n.* See **primary cell.**

voltaic pile *n.* A source of electricity consisting of a number of alternating disks of two different metals separated by acid-moistened pads, forming primary cells connected in series.

Vol•taire (vōl-târ′, vŏl-, vôl-tĕr′). François Marie Arouet. 1694–1778. French philosopher and writer whose works include *Candide* (1759).

Voltaire
1778 bust by
Jean Antoine Houdon

vol•ta•ism (vŏl′tə-ĭz′əm, vōl′-, vôl′-) *n.* See **galvanism** 1.

volt•am•me•ter (vōl-tăm′mē′tər, vōlt′ăm′-) *n.* An instrument for measuring electrical current or potential.

volt-am•pere (vōlt′ăm′pîr′) *n.* A unit of electric power in an alternating current circuit, equivalent to one watt.

Vol•ta Re•don•da (vôl′tä rĭ-dŏn′də, -dôn′dä). A city of E Brazil on the Paraíba R. WNW of Rio de Janeiro; founded 1941. Pop. 180,126.

volte-face (vôlt-fäs′, vôl′tə-) *n.* A reversal, as in policy; an about-face. [Fr. < Ital. *voltafaccia* : *volta* (< *voltare*, to turn; see VAULT²) + *faccia*, face (< VLat. **facia*; see FACE).]

volt•me•ter (vōlt′mē′tər) *n.* An instrument, such as a galvanometer, for measuring potential differences in volts.

vol•u•ble (vŏl′yə-bəl) *adj.* **1.** Marked by a ready flow of speech; fluent. **2.a.** Turning easily on an axis; rotating. **b.** *Bot.* Twining or twisting. [ME, moving easily < OFr. < Lat. *volūbilis*, revolving, fluent < *volvere*, to roll. See **wel-²*.**] —**vol′u•bil′i•ty, vol′u•ble•ness** *n.* —**vol′u•bly** *adv.*

vol•ume (vŏl′yo͞om, -yəm) *n.* **1.a.** A collection of written or printed sheets bound together; a book. **b.** One of the books of a work printed and bound in more than one book. **c.** A series of issues of a periodical, usu. covering one calendar year. **d.** A unit of written material assembled together and cataloged in a library. **2.** A roll of parchment; a scroll. **3.a.** The amount of space occupied by a three-dimensional object or region of space, expressed in cubic units. **b.** The capacity of such a region or of a specified container, expressed in cubic units. **4.a.** Amount; quantity: *a low volume of business.* **b.** A large amount. Often used in the plural: *volumes of praise.* **5.a.** The amplitude or loudness of a sound. **b.** A control, as on a radio, for adjusting amplitude or loudness. [ME < OFr. < Lat. *volūmen*, roll of writing < *volvere*, to roll. See **wel-²*.**]

vol•umed (vŏl′yo͞omd, -yəmd) *adj.* **1.** Consisting of a volume or volumes. Often used in combination: *a large-volumed edition.* **2.** Formed or moving in rolling or rounded masses.

vol•u•me•ter (vŏl′yo͞o-mē′tər) *n.* Any of several instruments for measuring volume.

vol•u•met•ric (vŏl′yo͞o-mĕt′rĭk) *adj.* Of or relating to measurement by volume. —**vol′u•met′ri•cal•ly** *adv.*

volumetric analysis *n.* **1.** Quantitative analysis using accurately measured titrated volumes of standard chemical solutions. **2.** Analysis of a gas by volume.

vo•lu•mi•nous (və-lo͞o′mə-nəs) *adj.* **1.** Having great volume, fullness, size, or number. **2.** Filling or capable of filling a large volume or many volumes. **3.** Ample or lengthy in speech or writing. **4.** Having many coils; winding. [LLat. *volūminōsus*, having many folds < Lat. *volūmen*, *volūmin-*, roll of writing. See VOLUME.] —**vo•lu′mi•nos′i•ty** (-nŏs′ĭ-tē), **vo•lu′mi•nous•ness** (-nəs-nĭs) *n.* —**vo•lu′mi•nous•ly** *adv.*

vol•un•ta•rism (vŏl′ən-tə-rĭz′əm) *n.* **1.** The use of or reliance on voluntary action. **2.** A theory or doctrine that regards the will as the fundamental principle of the individual or of the universe. —**vol′un•ta•rist** *n.* —**vol′un•ta•ris′tic** *adj.*

vol•un•tar•y (vŏl′ən-tĕr′ē) *adj.* **1.** Arising from or acting on one's own free will. **2.** Acting, serving, or done willingly and without constraint or expectation of reward. **3.** Normally controlled by or subject to individual volition. **4.** Capable of making choices; having the faculty of will. **5.** Supported by contributions or charitable donations rather than by government appropriations. —*n., pl.* **-ies. 1.** *Mus.* **a.** A short piece of music played as an introduction to a larger work. **b.** A piece for solo organ played before, during, or after a religious service. **2.** A volunteer. [ME < Lat. *voluntārius* < *voluntās*, choice < *velle, vol-*, to wish. See **wel-¹*.**] —**vol′un•tar′i•ly** (-târ′ə-lē) *adv.* —**vol′un•tar′i•ness** *n.*

Syns: *voluntary, intentional, deliberate, willful, willing.* These adjectives mean being or resulting from one's own free will. *Voluntary* implies the operation of unforced choice: *"Ignorance, when it is voluntary, is criminal"* (Samuel Johnson). *Intentional* applies to something undertaken to further a plan or realize an aim: *"I will abstain from all intentional wrong-doing and harm"* (Hippocratic Oath). *Deliberate* stresses premeditation and full awareness of the character and consequences of one's acts: *taking deliberate and decisive action. Willful* implies deliberate, headstrong persistence in a self-determined course of action: *a willful waste of time. Willing* suggests ready or cheerful acquiescence in the proposals or requirements of another: *"The first requisite of a good citizen . . . is that he shall be able and willing to pull his weight"* (Theodore Roosevelt).

vol•un•tar•y•ism (vŏl′ən-tĕr′ē-ĭz′əm) *n.* Reliance on voluntary contributions rather than government funds, as for churches or schools; voluntarism. —**vol′un•tar′y•ist** *n.*

voluntary muscle *n.* Muscle normally controlled by individual volition.

vol•un•teer (vŏl′ən-tîr′) *n.* **1.** A person who performs or offers to perform a service of his or her own free will. **2.** *Bot.* A cultivated plant growing from self-sown or accidentally dropped seed. —*adj.* **1.** Being, consisting of, or done by volunteers. **2.** *Bot.* Growing from self-sown or accidentally dropped seed. Used of a cultivated plant or crop. —*v.* **-teered, -teer•ing, -teers.** —*tr.* To give or offer to give voluntarily: *volunteer to give blood.* —*intr.* **1.** To perform or offer to perform a service of one's own free will. **2.** To do charitable or helpful work without pay. [Obsolete Fr. *voluntaire* < OFr., voluntary < Lat. *voluntārius*. See VOLUNTARY.]

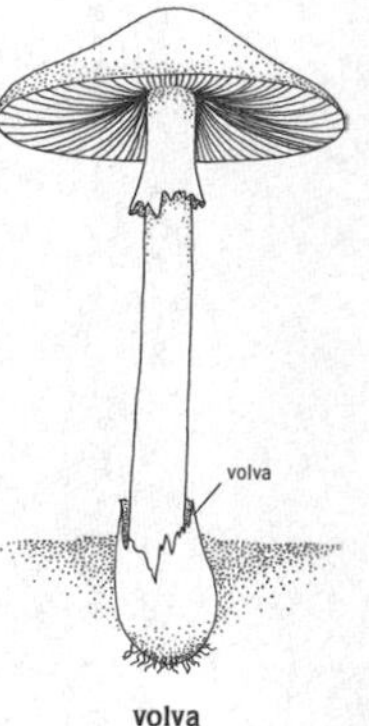

volva

vol•un•teer•ism (vŏl′ən-tîr′ĭz′əm) *n.* Use of or reliance on volunteers, esp. to perform social or educational work.

vo•lup•tu•ar•y (və-lŭp′cho͞o-ĕr′ē) *n., pl.* **-ies.** A person whose life is given over to luxury and sensual pleasures; a sensualist. [Fr. *voluptuaire* < OFr. < LLat. *voluptuārius*, var. of Lat. *voluptārius*, devoted to pleasure < *voluptās*, pleasure. See **wel-¹*.**] —**vo•lup′tu•ar′y** *adj.*

vo•lup•tu•ous (və-lŭp′cho͞o-əs) *adj.* **1.** Giving, characterized by, or suggesting ample, unrestrained pleasure to the senses: *a voluptuous ripe fruit.* **2.a.** Devoted to or indulging in sensual pleasures. **b.** Directed toward or anticipating sensual pleasure: *voluptuous thoughts.* **c.** Arising from or contributing to the satisfaction of sensuous or sensual desires. [ME < OFr. *voluptueux* < Lat. *voluptuōsus*, full of pleasure < *voluptās*, pleasure. See **wel-¹*.**] —**vo•lup′tu•ous•ly** *adv.* —**vo•lup′tu•ous•ness** *n.*

vo•lute (və-lo͞ot′) *n.* **1.** A spiral scroll-like ornament such as that on an Ionic capital. **2.a.** A spiral formation, such as a whorl of a gastropod shell. **b.** Any of various marine gastropod mollusks of the family Volutidae, having a spiral, often colorfully marked shell. [Fr. < Ital. *voluta* < Lat. *volūta* < fem. p.part. of *volvere*, to turn, roll. See **wel-²*.**] —**vo•lut′ed** (-lo͞o′tĭd) *adj.*

vo•lu•tion (və-lo͞o′shən) *n.* **1.** A turn or twist about a center; a spiral. **2.** *Zool.* One of the whorls of a spiral gastropod shell. [< Lat. *volūtus*, p.part. of *volvere*, to turn. See VOLUTE.]

vol•va (vŏl′və, vôl′-) *n.* A cuplike structure around the base of

ă pat	oi boy
ā pay	ou out
âr care	o͝o took
ä father	o͞o boot
ĕ pet	ŭ cut
ē be	ûr urge
ĭ pit	th thin
ī pie	*th* this
îr pier	hw which
ŏ pot	zh vision
ō toe	ə about,
ô paw	item

Stress marks:
′ (primary);
′ (secondary), as in
dictionary (dĭk′shə-nĕr′ē)

the stalk of certain fungi. [Lat., a covering. See **wel-**[2]*.] **—vol′vate′** (-vāt′) *adj.*

vol•vox (vŏl′vŏks′, vôl′-) *n.* Any of various freshwater algae of the genus *Volvox* that form spherical multicellular colonies. [NLat. *Volvox*, genus name < Lat. *volvere*, to roll. See **wel-**[2]*.]

vol•vu•lus (vŏl′vyə-ləs, vôl′-) *n.* Abnormal twisting of the intestine causing obstruction. [NLat. < Lat. *volvere*, to turn. See VOLVOX.]

Volzh•skiy (vôlzh′skē, vôlsh′-). A city of SW Russia on the Volga R., a suburb of Volgograd. Pop. 245,000.

vo•mer (vō′mər) *n.* A thin flat bone forming the inferior and posterior part of the nasal septum and dividing the nostrils in most vertebrates. [Lat. *vōmer*, plowshare.] **—vo′mer•ine′** (-mə-rīn′) *adj.*

V sign
Sir Winston Churchill in 1953

vom•it (vŏm′ĭt) *v.* **-it•ed, -it•ing, -its.** *—intr.* **1.** To eject part or all of the contents of the stomach through the mouth, usu. in a series of involuntary spasmic movements. **2.** To be discharged forcefully and abundantly; spew or gush. *—tr.* **1.** To eject (contents of the stomach) through the mouth. **2.** To eject or discharge in a gush; spew out. *—n.* **1.** The act or an instance of vomiting from the stomach. **2.** Matter ejected in vomiting. **3.** An emetic. [ME *vomiten* < Lat. *vomitāre*, freq. of *vomere*. See **wemə-***.] **—vom′it•er** *n.* **—vom′i•tive** *adj. & n.*

vom•i•to•ry (vŏm′ĭ-tôr′ē, -tōr′ē) *adj.* Relating to or inducing vomiting. *—n., pl.* **-ries. 1.** Something that induces vomiting. **2.** An aperture through which matter is discharged. **3.** One of the passageways of an amphitheater or a stadium leading from the outside wall or passageway to the seats.

vom•i•tus (vŏm′ĭ-təs) *n.* Vomited matter. [Lat. < p.part. of *vomere*, to vomit. See VOMIT.]

Von•ne•gut (vŏn′ĭ-gət), **Kurt, Jr.** b. 1922. Amer. writer whose novels include *Slaughterhouse Five* (1969).

Von Neu•mann (vŏn noi′män′), **John.** 1903–57. Hungarian-born Amer. mathematician noted for his contributions to game theory and quantum theory.

von Wil•le•brand's disease (vŏn wĭl′ə-brăndz′, fôn vĭl′ə-bränts′) *n.* A hereditary disease characterized by prolonged bleeding from the skin and mucous surfaces caused by abnormalities of the capillaries. [After Erik Adolf *von Willebrand* (1870–1949), Finnish physician.]

voo•doo (vo͞o′do͞o) *n., pl.* **-doos. 1.** A religion practiced chiefly in Caribbean countries, esp. Haiti, based on West African spiritual traditions with elements of Roman Catholicism incorporated and marked by monism and a belief in spirits who communicate with believers in dreams, trances, and ritual possessions. **2.** A charm, fetish, spell, or curse holding magic power for adherents of voodoo. **3.** A practitioner, priest, or priestess of voodoo. *—tr.v.* **-dooed, -doo•ing, -doos.** To place under the influence of a spell or curse; bewitch. [Louisiana Fr. *voudou* < Ewe *vodu* and Fon *vodun*.] **—voo′doo** *adj.*

voo•doo•ism (vo͞o′do͞o-ĭz′əm) *n.* **1.** The practice and doctrines of voodoo. **2.** The practice of sorcery or witchcraft. **—voo′doo•ist** *n.* **—voo′doo•is′tic** *adj.*

vo•ra•cious (vô-rā′shəs, və-) *adj.* **1.** Consuming or eager to consume great amounts of food; ravenous. **2.** Having or marked by an insatiable appetite for an activity or a pursuit; greedy: *a voracious reader.* [< Lat. *vorāx, vorāc-* < *vorāre*, to swallow, devour.] **—vo•ra′cious•ly** *adv.* **—vo•rac′i•ty** (-răs′ĭ-tē), **vo•ra′cious•ness** (-rā′shəs-nĭs) *n.*

vor•la•ge (fôr′lä′gə, fōr′-) *n. Sports.* A posture in skiing in which the skier leans forward from the ankles, usu. without lifting the heels. [Ger. : *vor*, forward, before (< MHGer. < OHGer. *fora*; see **per**[1]*) + *Lage*, stance (< MHGer. *lāge* < OHGer. *lāga*, act of laying; see **legh-***).]

Vo•ro•nezh (və-rô′nĭsh). A city of W Russia on the Don R. SW of Lipetsk; founded 1586. Pop. 850,000.

Vo•ro•shi•lov (vôr′ə-shē′lôf′, -ləf), **Kliment Efremovich.** 1881–1969. Soviet commissar for defense (1925–40).

Vo•ro•shi•lov•grad (vôr′ə-shē′ləf-grăd′, və-rə-shē-ləf-grät′). A city of W Ukraine in the Donets Basin SE of Kharkov; founded c. 1795. Pop. 497,000.

-vorous *suff.* Eating; feeding on: *vermivorous.* [< Lat. *-vorus* < *vorāre*, to swallow, devour.]

Vor•ster (fôr′stər), **Balthazar Johannes.** 1915–83. South African prime minister (1966–78).

vor•tex (vôr′tĕks′) *n., pl.* **-tex•es** or **-ti•ces** (-tĭ-sēz′). **1.** A spiral motion of fluid within a limited area, esp. a whirling mass of water or air that sucks everything near it toward its center. **2.** A place or situation regarded as drawing into its center all that surrounds it. [Lat. *vortex, vortic-*, var. of *vertex* < *vertere*, to turn. See **wer-**[2]*.]

vor•ti•cal (vôr′tĭ-kəl) *adj.* Of, relating to, or moving in a vortex; whirling. **—vor′ti•cal•ly** *adv.*

vor•ti•cel•la (vôr′tĭ-sĕl′ə) *n., pl.* **-cel•lae** (-sĕl′ē) or **-cel•las.** Any of various stalked bell-shaped ciliate protozoans of the genus *Vorticella*, living underwater often attached to a plant or other object. [NLat. *Vorticella*, genus name < Lat. *vortex, vortic-*, vortex. See VORTEX.]

vor•ti•cism (vôr′tĭ-sĭz′əm) *n.* A short-lived English movement in art and literature that arose in 1914 and was heavily influenced by cubism and futurism.

vor•ti•cose (vôr′tĭ-kōs′) *adj.* Vortical.

vor•tig•i•nous (vôr-tĭj′ə-nəs) *adj.* Vortical. [Blend of VORTEX and VERTIGINOUS.]

Vosges (vōzh). A mountain range of NE France extending c. 193 km (120 mi) parallel to the Rhine R.

vo•ta•ry (vō′tə-rē) *n., pl.* **-ries. 1.a.** One bound by vows to a life of religious worship or service. **b.** A devout adherent of a cult or religion; a committed worshiper: *the votaries of Isis.* **2.** One who is fervently devoted, as to a leader or an ideal; a faithful follower. **3.** One who is filled with enthusiasm, as for a pursuit; an enthusiast. [< Lat. *vōtum*, vow. See VOTE.]

vote (vōt) *n.* **1.a.** A formal expression of preference for a candidate for office or a proposed resolution of an issue. **b.** A means by which such a preference is made known, such as a marked ballot. **2.** The number of votes cast in an election or to resolve an issue: *a heavy vote.* **3.** A group of voters alike in some way. **4.** The act or process of voting: *took a vote.* **5.** The result of an election or a referendum. **6.** The right to participate as a voter; suffrage. *—v.* **vot•ed, vot•ing, votes.** *—intr.* **1.** To express one's preference for a candidate or for a proposed resolution of an issue; cast a vote. **2.** To express a choice or an opinion. *—tr.* **1.** To express one's preference for by vote. **2.** To decide the disposition of by vote, as by electing or defeating: *vote in a new mayor.* **3.** To bring into existence or make available by vote. **4.** To be guided by in voting: *vote one's conscience.* **5.** To declare or pronounce by general consent. **6.** *Informal.* To state as a preference or an opinion. [ME, vow < Lat. *vōtum* < neut. p.part. of *vovēre*, to vow.] **—vot′a•ble, vote′a•ble** *adj.* **—vot′er** *n.*

vote•less (vōt′lĭs) *adj.* Having no vote; denied a vote or the right to vote.

vot•ing machine (vō′tĭng) *n.* An apparatus for use in polling places that mechanically records and counts votes.

vo•tive (vō′tĭv) *adj.* **1.** Given or dedicated in fulfillment of a vow or pledge: *a votive offering.* **2.** Expressing or symbolizing a wish, desire, or vow: *a votive prayer.* [Lat. *vōtīvus* < *vōtum*, vow. See VOTE.] **—vo′tive•ly** *adv.*

votive Mass *n. Rom. Cath. Ch.* A Mass differing from the one prescribed for the day, said for a special intention.

vou. *abbr.* Voucher.

vouch (vouch) *v.* **vouched, vouch•ing, vouch•es.** *—intr.* **1.** To give personal assurances; give a guarantee. **2.** To constitute supporting evidence; substantiate. *—tr.* **1.** To substantiate by supplying evidence; prove. **2.** To refer to (an authority, for example) in support or corroboration; cite. **3.** To assert; declare. *—n. Obsolete.* A declaration of opinion; an assertion. [ME *vouchen*, to summon to court, warrant < AN *voucher*, prob. < VLat. **voticāre*, alteration of Lat. *vocitāre*, freq. of *vocāre*, to call. See **wek^w-***.]

vouch•er (vou′chər) *n.* **1.** A piece of substantiating evidence; a proof. **2.** A written record of an expenditure, a disbursement, or a completed transaction. **3.** A written authorization or certificate, esp. one exchangeable for cash or representing a credit against future expenditures. *—tr.v.* **-ered, -er•ing, -ers. 1.** To substantiate or authenticate with evidence. **2.** To prepare a voucher for. **3.** To issue a voucher to.

vouch•safe (vouch-sāf′, vouch′sāf′) *tr.v.* **-safed, -saf•ing, -safes.** To condescend to grant or bestow (a privilege, for example); deign. [ME *vouchen sauf*, to warrant as safe : *vouchen*, to warrant; see VOUCH + *sauf*, safe; see SAFE.] **—vouch•safe′ment** *n.*

vous•soir (vo͞o-swär′) *n.* One of the wedge-shaped stones forming the curved parts of an arch or a vaulted ceiling. [Fr. < OFr. *vossoir* < VLat. **volsōrium* < **volsus*, p.part. of Lat. *volvere*, to turn, roll. See **wel-**[2]*.]

Vou•vray (vo͞o-vrā′) *n.* A dry white table wine from central France. [After *Vouvray*, a village of W-central France.]

vow[1] (vou) *n.* **1.** An earnest promise to perform a specified act or behave in a certain manner, esp. a promise to live by the rules of a religious order. **2.** A declaration or an assertion. *—v.* **vowed, vow•ing, vows.** *—tr.* **1.** To promise solemnly; pledge. **2.** To make a pledge or threat to undertake: *vowing revenge.* *—intr.* To make a vow; promise. [ME *vou* < OFr. < Lat. *vōtum*. See VOTE.] **—vow′er** *n.*

vow[2] (vou) *tr.v.* To declare or assert. [Short for AVOW.]

vow•el (vou′əl) *n.* **1.** A speech sound created by the relatively free passage of breath through the larynx and oral cavity, usu. forming the most prominent and central sound of a syllable. **2.** A letter, such as *a* or *e* in the English alphabet, that represents a vowel. [ME *vowelle* < OFr. *vouel* < Lat. *(littera) vōcālis*, sounding (letter) < *vōx, vōc-*, voice. See **wek^w-***.]

vow•el•ize (vou′ə-līz′) *tr.v.* **-ized, -iz•ing, -iz•es.** To provide with vowel points. **—vow′el•i•za′tion** (-ə-lĭ-zā′shən) *n.*

vowel mutation *n. Ling.* See **umlaut** 1.

vowel point *n.* Any of a number of diacritical marks written above or below consonants to indicate a vowel in languages usu. written without vowel letters, as Hebrew and Arabic.

vox pop•u•li (pŏp′yə-lī′, -lē) *n.* Popular opinion. [Lat. *vōx populī* : *vōx*, voice + *populī*, genitive of *populus*, people.]

voy•age (voi′ĭj) *n.* **1.** A long journey, as: **a.** A journey by sea to a foreign or distant land. **b.** A journey by land to distant parts. **c.** A journey through outer space. **2.a.** The events of a journey of exploration or discovery considered as material for a narrative. **b.** Such a narrative. In both senses often used in the plural. — *v.* **-aged, -ag•ing, -ag•es.** — *intr.* To make a voyage. — *tr.* To sail across; traverse: *voyaged the western ocean.* [ME < OFr. *veyage* < LLat. *viāticum*, a journey < Lat., provisions for a journey < neut. of *viāticus*, of a journey < *via*, road. See **wegh-***.] — **voy′ag•er** *n.*

voy•a•geur (voi′ə-zhûr′, vwä′yä-zhœr′) *n.*, *pl.* **-geurs** (-zhûr′, -zhœr′). A workman, boatman, or guide employed by a fur company to transport goods and supplies between remote stations in Canada or the U.S. Northwest. [Fr., traveler < *voyager*, to travel < *voyage*, journey < OFr. *veyage*. See VOYAGE.]

voy•eur (voi-yûr′) *n.* **1.** A person who derives sexual gratification from observing the naked bodies or sexual acts of others, esp. secretly. **2.** An obsessive observer of sordid or sensational subjects. [Fr. < OFr., one who lies in wait < *voir*, to see < Lat. *vidēre*, to see. See **weid-***.] — **voy•eur′ism** *n.* — **voy′eur•is′tic** *adj.* — **voy′eur•is′ti•cal•ly** *adv.*

Voz•ne•sen•ski (vŏz′nə-sĕn′skē), **Andrei.** b. 1933. Soviet poet whose collections of verse include *Parabola* (1960).

VP *abbr.* **1.** Variable pitch. **2.** Verb phrase. **3.** Or **V.P.** Vice president.

Vree•land (vrē′lənd), **Diana Dalziel.** 1903–89. French-born Amer. editor of *Vogue* (1963–71).

vroom (vrōōm, vrŏŏm) also **va•room** (və-rōōm′, -rŏŏm′) — *n.* The loud, roaring noise of an engine operating at high speed. — *intr.v.* **vroomed, vroom•ing, vrooms** also **va•roomed, va•room•ing, va•rooms.** To move noisily at high speed in or as if in a motor vehicle. [Imit.]

vs. *abbr.* Versus.

v.s. *abbr. Lat.* Vide supra (see above).

V.S. *abbr.* Veterinary surgeon.

V sign *n.* A hand sign indicating victory, solidarity, or approval, formed by holding the raised index and middle fingers in the shape of a V.

vss. *abbr.* **1.** Verses. **2.** Versions.

V/STOL *abbr.* Vertical or short takeoff and landing.

VT *abbr.* **1.** Vacuum tube. **2.** Variable time. **3.** Also **Vt.** Vermont.

VTOL *abbr.* Vertical takeoff and landing.

VTR *abbr.* Videotape recorder.

vug (vŭg, vŏŏg) *n.* A small cavity in a rock or vein, often with a mineral lining of different composition from that of the surrounding rock. [Cornish *vooga*.]

Vuil•lard (vwē-yär′), **(Jean) Edouard.** 1868–1940. French painter whose works include *Public Gardens* (1894).

Vul. *abbr.* Vulgate.

Vul•can (vŭl′kən) *n. Rom. Myth.* The god of fire and metalworking. [Lat. *Volcānus, Vulcānus.*]

vul•ca•ni•an (vŭl-kā′nē-ən) *adj.* **1.** *Geol.* Of, relating to, or originating from an explosive volcanic eruption. **2. Vulcanian.** *Rom. Myth.* Of or relating to Vulcan. **3.** Of or relating to metalworking or craft.

vul•ca•nism (vŭl′kə-nĭz′əm) *n.* Var. of **volcanism.**

vul•ca•nite (vŭl′kə-nīt′) *n.* A hard vulcanized rubber.

vul•ca•nize (vŭl′kə-nīz′) *tr.v.* **-nized, -niz•ing, -niz•es.** To improve the strength, resiliency, and freedom from stickiness of (rubber, for example) by combining with sulfur or other additives under heat and pressure. — **vul′ca•niz′a•ble** *adj.* — **vul′ca•ni•za′tion** (-nĭ-zā′shən) *n.* — **vul′ca•niz′er** *n.*

vul•ca•nol•o•gy (vŭl′kə-nŏl′ə-jē) *n.* Var. of **volcanology.**

vulg. *abbr.* Vulgar.

Vulg. *abbr.* Vulgate.

vul•gar (vŭl′gər) *adj.* **1.** Of or associated with the great masses of people; common. **2.** Spoken by or expressed in language spoken by the common people; vernacular: *technical and vulgar names for an animal.* **3.a.** Deficient in taste, delicacy, or refinement. **b.** Marked by a lack of good breeding; boorish. **c.** Offensively excessive in self-display or expenditure; ostentatious. **4.** Crudely indecent. [ME < Lat. *vulgāris* < *vulgus*, the common people.] — **vul′gar•ly** *adv.* — **vul′gar•ness** *n.*

vul•gar•i•an (vŭl-gâr′ē-ən) *n.* A vulgar person, esp. one who makes a conspicuous display of wealth.

vul•gar•ism (vŭl′gə-rĭz′əm) *n.* **1.** Vulgarity. **2.a.** A crudely indecent word or phrase; an obscenity. **b.** A word, phrase, or manner of expression used chiefly by uneducated people.

vul•gar•i•ty (vŭl-găr′ĭ-tē) *n.*, *pl.* **-ties. 1.** The quality or condition of being vulgar. **2.** Something, such as an act or expression, that offends good taste or propriety.

vul•gar•ize (vŭl′gə-rīz′) *tr.v.* **-ized, -iz•ing, -iz•es. 1.** To make vulgar; debase. **2.** To disseminate widely; popularize. — **vul′gar•i•za′tion** (-gər-ĭ-zā′shən) *n.* — **vul′gar•iz′er** *n.*

Vul•gar Latin (vŭl′gər) *n.* The common speech of the ancient Romans, which is distinguished from standard literary Latin and is the ancestor of the Romance languages.

vul•gate (vŭl′gāt′, -gĭt) *n.* **1.** The common speech of a people; the vernacular. **2.** A widely accepted text or version of a work. **3. Vulgate.** The Latin edition of the Bible made by Saint Jerome at the end of the fourth century A.D. [Med.Lat. *Vulgāta* < LLat. *vulgāta (ēditiō)*, popular (edition) < Lat., fem. p.part. of *vulgāre*, to make known to all < *vulgus*, the common people.]

vul•ner•a•ble (vŭl′nər-ə-bəl) *adj.* **1.a.** Susceptible to physical injury. **b.** Susceptible to attack. **c.** Open to censure or criticism; assailable. **2.a.** Liable to succumb, as to persuasion or temptation. **b.** *Games.* In a position to receive greater penalties or bonuses in a hand of bridge. [LLat. *vulnerābilis*, wounding < Lat. *vulnerāre*, to wound < *vulnus, vulner-*, wound. See **welə-***.] — **vul′ner•a•bil′i•ty, vul′ner•a•ble•ness** *n.* — **vul′ner•a•bly** *adv.*

vul•ner•ar•y (vŭl′nə-rĕr′ē) *adj.* Used in the healing or treating of wounds. — *n.*, *pl.* **-ies.** A remedy used in healing or treating wounds. [Lat. *vulnerārius* < *vulnus, vulner-*, wound. See VULNERABLE.]

Vul•pec•u•la (vŭl-pĕk′yə-lə) *n.* A constellation in the celestial Northern Hemisphere near Cygnus and Sagitta. [NLat. < Lat. *vulpēcula*, dim. of *vulpēs*, fox. See VULPINE.]

vul•pec•u•lar (vŭl-pĕk′yə-lər) *adj.* Vulpine.

vul•pine (vŭl′pīn′) *adj.* **1.** Of, resembling, or characteristic of a fox. **2.** Cunning. [Lat. *vulpīnus* < *vulpēs*, fox. See **wl̥p-ē-***.]

vul•ture (vŭl′chər) *n.* **1.** Any of various large birds of prey of the New World family Cathartidae or the Old World family Accipitridae, characteristically having dark plumage and a featherless head and neck and generally feeding on carrion. **2.** A person of a rapacious, predatory, or profiteering nature. [ME < OFr. *voltour* < Lat. *vultur.*]

vul•tur•ine (vŭl′chə-rīn′) also **vul•tur•ous** (-chər-əs) *adj.* **1.** Of or characteristic of a vulture. **2.** Predatory.

vul•va (vŭl′və) *n.*, *pl.* **-vae** (-vē). The external genital organs of the female, including the labia majora, labia minora, clitoris, and vestibule of the vagina. [Lat., womb, covering. See **wel-**[2]***.] — **vul′val, vul′var** (-vər, -vär′) *adj.* — **vul′vate′** (-vāt′, -vĭt) *adj.* — **vul′vi•form′** (-və-fôrm′) *adj.*

vul•vi•tis (vŭl-vī′tĭs) *n.* Inflammation of the vulva.

vul•vo•vag•i•ni•tis (vŭl′vō-văj′ə-nī′tĭs) *n.* Inflammation of the vulva and vagina.

vum (vŭm) *interj. New England.* Used to express surprise. [Alteration of vow[2].]

Regional Note: A surprised New Englander might say, *"Well, I vum!" Vum* is in fact an alteration of the verb *vow* that goes back to the days of the American Revolution. It is also heard simply as *"Vum!"* or in *"I'll be vummed!"* A southern equivalent is *swanny,* also meaning "swear": *Now, I swanny!* According to the *Oxford English Dictionary,* the word *swanny* derives from the dialect of the North of England: *Is' wan ye,* "I shall warrant ye."

vv. *abbr.* Verses.

v.v. *abbr.* Vice versa.

Vyat•ka (vyät′kə). A river of W Russia rising in the Ural Mts. and flowing c. 1,368 km (850 mi) to the Kama R.

Vy•borg (vē′bôrg′, -bərk). A city of NW Russia NW of St. Petersburg on the Gulf of Finland. Pop. 80,000.

Vy•cheg•da (vĭch′ĭg-də). A river of NW Russia flowing c. 1,126 km (700 mi) to the Northern Dvina R.

vy•ing (vī′ĭng) *v.* Pr.part. of **vie.**

Vulcan

vulture
Rüppell's griffon vulture
Gyps rueppellii

ă pat | oi boy
ā pay | ou out
âr care | ŏŏ took
ä father | ōō boot
ĕ pet | ŭ cut
ē be | ûr urge
ĭ pit | th thin
ī pie | *th* this
îr pier | hw which
ŏ pot | zh vision
ō toe | ə about, item
ô paw

Stress marks:
′ (primary);
′ (secondary), as in
dictionary (dĭk′shə-nĕr′ē)

w[1] or **W** (dŭb′əl-yōō, -yŏŏ) *n.*, *pl.* **w's** or **W's. 1.** The 23rd letter of the modern English alphabet. **2.** Any of the speech sounds represented by the letter *w*. **3.** The 23rd in a series. **4.** Something shaped like the letter W.

w[2] *abbr. Phys.* Work.

W[1] The symbol for the element **tungsten.** [Ger. *Wolfram.* See WOLFRAM.]

W[2] *abbr.* **1.** *Elect.* Watt. **2.** Also **W.** or **w** or **w.** West; western.

w. *abbr.* **1.** Week. **2.** Weight. **3.** Wide. **4.** Width. **5.** Wife. **6.** With.

W. *abbr.* **1.** Wednesday. **2.** Welsh.

WA *abbr.* **1.** Washington. **2.** With average.

Waal (väl). The S branch of the Lower Rhine R. in S Netherlands flowing c. 84 km (52 mi) to the Maas R.

Wa•ba•na•ki (wä′bə-nä′kē) *n., pl.* **Wabanaki** or **-kis.** See **Abenaki.**

Wa•bash (wô′băsh′). A river of the E-central U.S. rising in W OH and flowing c. 764 km (475 mi) to the Ohio R.

wab•ble (wŏb′əl) *v. & n.* Var. of **wobble.**

Wace (wās, wäs). fl. 12th cent. Anglo-Norman poet who adapted Arthurian legend in his *Roman de Brut* (1155).

wack (wăk) *n. Slang.* A person regarded as eccentric.

wack•o (wăk′ō) also **whack•o** (hwăk′ō, wăk′ō) *n., pl.* **-os.** *Slang.* A person regarded as eccentric. —**wack′o** *adj.*

wack•y (wăk′ē) also **whack•y** (hwăk′ē, wăk′ē) *adj.* **-i•er, -i•est.** *Slang.* **1.** Eccentric: *a wacky person.* **2.** Crazy; silly: *a wacky outfit.* [Var. of *whacky*, prob. < the phrase *out of whack.* See WHACK.] —**wack′i•ly** *adv.* —**wack′i•ness** *n.*

waders

Wa•co (wā′kō). A city of E-central TX S of Dallas–Fort Worth. Pop. 103,590.

wad (wŏd) *n.* **1.** A small mass of soft material, often folded or rolled, used for padding, stuffing, or packing. **2.** A compressed ball, roll, or lump, as of tobacco. **3.a.** A plug, as of cloth or paper, used to retain a powder charge in a muzzleloading gun or cannon. **b.** A disk, as of felt or paper, used to keep the powder and shot in place in a shotgun cartridge. **4.** *Informal.* A large amount: *a wad of troubles.* **5.** *Informal.* **a.** A sizable roll of paper money. **b.** A considerable amount of money. —*v.* **wad•ded, wad•ding, wads.** —*tr.* **1.** To compress into a wad. **2.** To pad, pack, line, or plug with wadding. **3.a.** To hold (shot or powder) in place with a wad. **b.** To insert a wad into (a firearm). —*intr.* To form into a wad. [?]

Wad•den•zee (väd′n-zā′). An inlet of the North Sea off N Netherlands between the Ijsselmeer and the West Frisian Is.

wad•die (wŏd′ē) *n. Western U.S.* Var. of **waddy[2].**

wad•ding (wŏd′ĭng) *n.* **1.a.** A wad. **b.** Wads considered as a group. **2.** A soft layer of fibrous cotton or wool used for padding or stuffing. **3.** Material for gun wads.

wad•dle (wŏd′l) *intr.v.* **-dled, -dling, -dles. 1.** To walk with short steps that tilt the body from side to side. **2.** To walk heavily and clumsily with a pronounced sway. —*n.* A swaying gait. [Freq. of WADE.] —**wad′dler** *n.*

wad•dy[1] (wŏd′ē) *Australian.* —*n., pl.* **-dies.** A heavy straight stick or club thrown as a weapon by aborigines. —*tr.v.* **-died** (wŏd′ēd), **-dy•ing, -dies** (wŏd′ēz). To strike with a waddy. [Dharuk (Aboriginal language of SE Australia) *wadi.*]

Richard Wagner
Photographed in 1865

wad•dy[2] also **wad•die** (wŏd′ē) *n., pl.* **-dies.** *Western U.S.* **1.** See **cowboy** 1. **2.** A cattle rustler. [?]

wade (wād) *v.* **wad•ed, wad•ing, wades.** —*intr.* **1.** To walk in or through water or something else that similarly impedes normal movement. **2.** To make one's way arduously. —*tr.* To cross or pass through (water, for example) with difficulty. —*n.* The act or an instance of wading. —***phrasal verb.*** **wade in** (or **into**). To plunge into, begin, or attack resolutely and energetically. [ME *waden* < OE *wadan.*]

wad•er (wā′dər) *n.* **1.** See **wading bird. 2. waders.** Waterproof hip boots or trousers worn esp. by people while fishing.

wa•di also **wa•dy** (wä′dē) *n., pl.* **-dis** also **-dies. 1.a.** A valley, gully, or streambed in northern Africa and southwest Asia that remains dry except during the rainy season. **b.** A stream that flows through such a channel. **2.** An oasis. [Ar. *wādī.*]

wad•ing bird (wā′dĭng) *n.* A long-legged bird, such as a crane or stork, that frequents shallow water in search of food.

wa•fer (wā′fər) *n.* **1.** A small thin crisp cake, biscuit, or candy. **2.** *Eccles.* A small thin disk of unleavened bread used in the Eucharist. **3.** A small disk of adhesive material used as a seal for papers. **4.** *Electron.* A small thin circular slice of a semiconducting material, such as pure silicon, on which an integrated circuit can be formed. —*tr.v.* **-fered, -fer•ing, -fers. 1.** To seal or fasten together with a disk of adhesive material. **2.** *Electron.* To divide into wafers. [ME *wafre* < AN, var. of ONFr. *waufre*, of Gmc. orig. See **webh-*.**]

waff (wăf, wäf) *Scots.* —*v.* **waffed, waff•ing, waffs.** *intr. & tr.v.* To wave or flutter or cause to do so. —*n.* **1.** A waving or fluttering motion. **2.** A gust of air; a waft. [ME *waffen*, to wave, alteration of *waven.* See WAVE.]

waf•fle[1] (wŏf′əl) *n.* A light crisp battercake baked in a waffle iron. [Du. *wafel* < MDu. *wāfel.* See **webh-*.**]

waf•fle[2] (wŏf′əl) *Informal.* —*v.* **-fled, -fling, -fles.** —*intr.* To speak or write evasively. —*tr.* To speak, write, or act evasively about. —*n.* Evasive or vague speech or writing. [Prob. freq. of obsolete *waff*, to yelp, prob. of imit. orig.] —**waf′fler** *n.* —**waf′fling•ly** *adv.* —**waf′fly** *adj.*

waffle iron *n.* An appliance having hinged indented plates that impress a grid pattern into waffle batter as it bakes.

waft (wäft, wăft) *v.* **waft•ed, waft•ing, wafts.** —*tr.* **1.** To cause to go gently and smoothly through the air or over water. **2.** To convey or send floating through the air or over water. —*intr.* To float gently; drift. —*n.* **1.** Something, such as an odor, carried through the air. **2.** A light breeze; a rush of air. **3.** The act of fluttering or waving. **4.** *Naut.* **a.** A flag used for signaling or indicating wind direction. **b.** A signal with a flag. [Back-formation < *wafter*, convoy ship, alteration of ME *waughter* < MDu. or MLGer. *wachter*, a guard < *wachten*, to guard. See **weg-*.**] —**waft′er** *n.*

wag[1] (wăg) *v.* **wagged, wag•ging, wags.** —*intr.* **1.** To move briskly and repeatedly from side to side, to and fro, or up and down. **2.** To move rapidly in talking. Used of the tongue. **3.** To walk with a clumsy sway; waddle. **4.** *Archaic.* To be on one's way; depart. —*tr.* To move (a body part) rapidly from side to side or up and down, as in playfulness, admonition, or chatter. —*n.* The act or motion of wagging: *a wag of the hand.* [ME *waggen.* See **wegh-*.**] —**wag′ger** *n.*

wag[2] (wăg) *n.* A humorous or droll person; a wit. [Perh. < WAG[1].]

wage (wāj) *n.* **1.** Payment for labor or services to a worker, esp. remuneration on an hourly, daily, or weekly basis or by the piece. **2. wages.** The portion of the national product that represents the aggregate paid for all contributing labor and services. **3.** A fitting return; a recompense. Often used in the plural with a singular or plural verb: *the wages of sin.* —*tr.v.* **waged, wag•ing, wag•es.** To engage in (a war or campaign, for example). [ME < ONFr., of Gmc. orig.]

wage earner *n.* **1.** One who works for wages. **2.** One whose earnings support or help support a household.

wa•ger (wā′jər) *n.* **1.** *Games.* **a.** An agreement under which each bettor pledges something against the outcome of an unsettled matter. **b.** A matter bet on; a gamble. **2.** Something staked on an uncertain outcome; a bet. See Syns at **bet. 3.** *Archaic.* A pledge of personal combat to resolve an issue or a case. —*v.* **-gered, -ger•ing, -gers.** —*tr.* To risk or stake (an amount or a possession) on an uncertain outcome; bet. —*intr.* To make a bet. [ME < AN *wageure* < ONFr. *wagier*, to pledge < *wage*, pledge. See WAGE.] —**wa′ger•er** *n.*

wage scale *n.* The scale of wages paid to employees for the various jobs within an industry, a factory, or a company.

wage•work•er (wāj′wûr′kər) *n.* A wage earner.

wag•ger•y (wăg′ə-rē) *n., pl.* **-ies. 1.** Waggish behavior or spirit; drollery. **2.** A droll remark or act.

wag•gish (wăg′ĭsh) *adj.* Characteristic of or resembling a wag; jocular or witty. —**wag′gish•ly** *adv.* —**wag′gish•ness** *n.*

wag•gle (wăg′əl) *v.* **-gled, -gling, -gles.** —*tr.* To move (an attached part, for example) with short quick motions. —*intr.* To move shakily; wobble. —*n.* A wobbling motion. [ME *wagelen*, freq. of *waggen.* See WAG[1].] —**wag′gly** *adj.*

Wag•ner (väg′nər), **Richard.** 1813–83. German composer known esp. for *Der Ring des Nibelungen* (1853–74). —**Wag•ner′i•an** (-nîr′ē-ən) *adj. & n.*

wag•on (wăg′ən) *n.* **1.** A four-wheeled, usu. horse-drawn vehicle with a large rectangular body, used to transport loads. **2.a.** A light automotive transport or delivery vehicle. **b.** A station wagon. **c.** A police patrol wagon. **3.** A child's low four-wheeled cart pulled by a long handle. **4.** A small table or tray on wheels used for serving drinks or food. **5.** *Chiefly British.* An open railway freight car —*v.* **-oned, -on•ing, -ons.** —*tr. & intr.v.* To transport or undergo transportation by wagon. —***idioms.*** **off the wagon.** *Slang.* No longer abstaining from alcoholic beverages. **on the wagon.** *Slang.* Abstaining from alcoholic beverages. [ME *waggin* < MDu. *wagen.* See **wegh-*.**]

Wag•on (wăg′ən) *n.* The Big Dipper.

wag•on•er (wăg′ə-nər) *n.* One who drives a wagon.

Wag•on•er (wăg′ə-nər) *n.* Auriga.

wa•gon-lit (vä′gôN-lē′) *n., pl.* **wa•gons-lits** or **wa•gon-lits** (vä′gôN-lē′). A sleeping car on a European railroad train. [Fr. : *wagon*, railroad car (< E. WAGON) + *lit*, bed (< OFr. < Lat. *lectus*; see **legh-*).**]

wag•on•load (wăg′ən-lōd′) *n.* The amount a wagon holds.

wagon train *n.* A line or train of wagons that are traveling cross-country.

Wa•gram (vä′gräm′). A town of NE Austria NE of Vienna; site of Napoleon's defeat of the Austrians in Jul. 1809.

wag•tail (wăg′tāl′) *n.* Any of various chiefly Old World birds of the family Motacillidae, having a slender body with a long tail that constantly wags.

Wah•ha•bi or **Wa•ha•bi** (wä-hä′bē) *n., pl.* **-bis.** A member of a Muslim sect founded by Abdul Wahhab (1703–1792), known for its strict observance of the Koran.

Wa•hi•a•wa (wä′hē-ə-wä′). A city of central Oahu, HI, NW of Honolulu. Pop. 17,386.

wa•hi•ne (wä-hē′nē, -nā′) also **va•hi•ne** (vä-) *n.* A Polynesian woman or wife. [Hawaiian.]

wa•hoo[1] (wä-ho͞o′, wä′ho͞o) *n., pl.* **-hoos.** A deciduous shrub or small tree *(Euonymus atropurpurea)* of eastern North America having purplish flowers. [Dakota *wāhu.*]

wa•hoo[2] (wä-ho͞o′, wä′ho͞o) *n., pl.* **-hoos. 1.** An elm tree *(Ulmus alata)* of the southeast United States having twigs with winged corky edges. **2.** Any of several similar trees. [?]

wa•hoo[3] (wä-ho͞o′, wä′ho͞o) *n., pl.* **wahoo** or **-hoos.** A tropical marine food and game fish *(Acanthocybium solanderi)* of the mackerel family, having a pointed snout, narrow body, and long dorsal fin. [?]

wa•hoo[4] (wä′ho͞o′) *Chiefly Western U.S.* —*interj.* Used to express exuberance. —*n., pl.* **-hoos.** An exuberant cry. Also called regionally *rebel yell.*

Wah•pe•ku•te (wä′pə-ko͞o′tē) *n., pl.* **Wahpekute** or **-tes.** A member of a Native American people of the Santee branch of the Sioux.

Wah•pe•ton (wôʹpĭ-tn) *n., pl.* **Wahpeton** or **-tons.** A member of a Native American people of the Santee branch of the Sioux.

wah-wah also **wa-wa** (wäʹwäʹ) *n. Mus.* A wavering sound produced by an instrument, as by alternately muting and uncovering a trumpet or trombone. [Imit.] **—wahʹ-wahʹ** *adj.*

waif¹ (wāf) *n.* **1.a.** A homeless person, esp. a forsaken or orphaned child. **b.** An abandoned young animal. **2.** Something found and unclaimed, as an object cast up by the sea. [ME, stray animal < AN, prob. of Scand. orig. See **weip-*.**]

waif² (wāf) *n. Naut.* See **waft** 4. [Prob. of Scand. orig. See **weip-*.**]

Wai•ki•ki (wīʹkĭ-kēʹ). A beach and resort district of Oahu I., HI, SE of Honolulu.

wail (wāl) *v.* **wailed, wail•ing, wails.** *—intr.* **1.** To grieve or protest loudly and bitterly; lament. See Syns at **cry. 2.** To make a prolonged high-pitched sound suggestive of a cry. *—tr. Archaic.* To lament over; bewail. *—n.* **1.** A long loud high-pitched cry, as of grief or pain. **2.** A long loud high-pitched sound. **3.** A loud bitter protest. [ME *wailen*, prob. of Scand. orig.] **—wailʹer** *n.* **—wailʹing•ly** *adv.*

wail•ful (wālʹfəl) *adj.* **1.** Resembling a wail; mournful. **2.** Issuing a sound resembling a wail. **—wailʹful•ly** *adv.*

Wail•ing Wall (wāʹlĭng). See **Western Wall.**

wain (wān) *n.* A large open farm wagon. [ME < OE *wǣn, wægn.* See **wegh-*.**]

Wain (wān) *n.* The Big Dipper.

wain•scot (wānʹskət, -skŏtʹ, -skōtʹ) *n.* **1.** A facing or paneling, usu. of wood, applied to the walls of a room. **2.** The lower part of an interior wall when finished in a material different from that of the upper part. *—tr.v.* **-scot•ed, -scot•ing, -scots** or **-scot•ted, -scot•ting, -scots.** To line or panel (a room or wall) with wainscoting. [ME < MDu. *waghenscot* : perh. *waghen, wagen*, wagon (< the quality of wood used for carriagework); see WAGON + *scot*, partition; see **skeud-*.**]

wain•scot•ing or **wain•scot•ting** (wānʹskə-tĭng, -skŏtʹĭng, -skōʹtĭng) *n.* **1.** A wainscoted wall or walls; paneling. **2.** Material, such as wood, used for wainscoting.

wain•wright (wānʹrītʹ) *n.* A wagon builder and repairer.

Wai•pa•hu (wī-päʹhōō). A city of S Oahu, HI, on the NW shore of Pearl Harbor. Pop. 31,435.

waist (wāst) *n.* **1.a.** The part of the human trunk between the bottom of the rib cage and the pelvis. **b.** The narrow part of the abdomen of an insect. **2.a.** The part of a garment that encircles the waist of the body. **b.** The upper part of a garment, extending from the shoulders to the waistline, esp. the bodice of a dress. **c.** A blouse. **d.** A child's undershirt. **3.** The middle section or part of an object, esp. when narrower than the rest. **4.** *Naut.* The middle part of the deck of a ship between the forecastle and the quarterdeck. [ME *wast*, perh. < OE **wæst*, growth, size. See **aug-*.**] **—waistʹless** *adj.*

waist•band (wāstʹbăndʹ) *n.* A band of material encircling and fitting the waist of a garment, such as trousers or a skirt.

waist•cloth (wāstʹklôthʹ, -klŏthʹ) *n.* A loincloth.

waist•coat (wĕsʹkĭt, wāstʹkōtʹ) *n.* **1.** A garment formerly worn by men under a doublet. **2.** *Chiefly British.* A short sleeveless collarless garment worn esp. over a shirt and often under a suit jacket; a vest. **—waistʹcoatʹed** *adj.*

waist•line (wāstʹlīnʹ) *n.* **1.a.** A line thought of as encircling the body at the waist. **b.** The measurement of this line. **2.a.** The line at which the skirt and bodice of a dress join. **b.** The part of a garment that lies at or according to fashion above or below the narrowest part of the waist.

wait (wāt) *v.* **wait•ed, wait•ing, waits.** *—intr.* **1.a.** To remain or rest in expectation. See Syns at **stay¹. b.** To tarry until another catches up. **2.** To remain or be in readiness. **3.** To remain temporarily neglected, unattended to, or postponed. **4.** To work as a waiter or waitress. *—tr.* **1.** To remain or stay in expectation of; await. **2.** *Informal.* To delay (a meal or an event); postpone. **3.** To be a waiter or waitress at. *—n.* **1.** The act of waiting or the time spent waiting. **2.** *Chiefly British.* **a.** One of a group of musicians employed to play in parades or public ceremonies. **b.** One of a group of musicians or carolers who perform in the streets at Christmastime. ***—phrasal verbs.*** **wait on** (or **upon**). **1.** To serve the needs of; be in attendance on. **2.** To make a formal call on; visit. **3.** To follow as a result; depend on. **4.** To await. **wait out.** To delay until the termination of. **wait up. 1.** To postpone going to bed in anticipation of something or someone. **2.** *Informal.* To stop or pause so that another can catch up. [ME *waiten* < ONFr. *waitier*, to watch, of Gmc. orig. See **weg-*.**]

wait-a-bit (wātʹə-bĭtʹ) *n.* Any of several plants having sharp, often hooked thorns. [Transl. of Afr. *wag-'n-bietjie.*]

Waite (wāt), **Morrison Remick.** 1816–88. Amer. jurist; chief justice of the U.S. Supreme Court (1874–88).

wait•er (wāʹtər) *n.* **1.** One who serves at a table, as in a restaurant. **2.** A tray or salver.

wait•ing (wāʹtĭng) *n.* **1.** The act of remaining inactive or stationary. **2.** A period of time spent waiting. ***—idiom.*** **in waiting.** In attendance, esp. at a royal court.

waiting game *n.* The stratagem of deferring action and allowing the passage of time to work in one's favor.

waiting list *n.* A list of persons waiting, as for an appointment.

waiting room *n.* A room for the use of people waiting.

wait•per•son (wātʹpûrʹsən) *n.* A waiter or waitress.

wait•ress (wāʹtrĭs) *n.* A woman who serves at a table, as in a restaurant. See Usage Note at **-ess.**

wait•ron (wāʹtrən) *n.* A waiter or waitress.

waive (wāv) *tr.v.* **waived, waiv•ing, waives. 1.** To give up (a claim or right) voluntarily; relinquish. See Syns at **relinquish. 2.** To refrain from insisting on or enforcing (a rule, for example); dispense with. **3.** To put aside or off temporarily; defer. [ME *weiven*, to abandon < AN *weyver* < *waif*, ownerless property. See WAIF¹.]

waiv•er (wāʹvər) *n.* **1.a.** Intentional relinquishment of a right, claim, or privilege. **b.** The document that evidences such relinquishment. **2.** A dispensation, as from a rule. **3.** A deferment. [AN *weyver* < *weyver*, to abandon. See WAIVE.]

Wa•kash•an (wä-kăshʹən, wôʹkə-shănʹ) *n.* A family of North American Indian languages spoken by the Nootka and other peoples of Washington and British Columbia. [Ult. < Nootka *waakaash*, bravo!] **—Wa•kashʹan** *adj.*

Wa•ka•ya•ma (wäʹkə-yäʹmə). A city of S Honshu, Japan, SSW of Osaka on the Inland Sea. Pop. 401,357.

wake¹ (wāk) *v.* **woke** (wōk) or **waked** (wākt), **waked** or **wok•en** (wōʹkən), **wak•ing, wakes.** *—intr.* **1.a.** To cease to sleep; become awake. **b.** To stay awake. **c.** To be brought into a state of awareness or alertness. **2.** To keep watch or guard, esp. over a corpse. *—tr.* **1.** To rouse from sleep; awaken. **2.** To stir, as from a dormant or inactive condition; rouse. **3.** To make aware of; alert. **4.a.** To keep a vigil over. **b.** To hold a wake over. *—n.* **1.** A watch; a vigil. **2.** A watch over a corpse before burial. Also called regionally *viewing.* **3. wakes.** *(used with a sing. or pl. v.) Chiefly British.* **a.** A parish festival, often in honor of a patron saint. **b.** An annual vacation. [ME *wakien, waken* < OE *wacan*, to wake up, and *wacian*, to be awake, keep watch; see **weg-*.**] **—wakʹer** *n.*

Usage Note: The pairs *wake, waken* and *awake, awaken* have formed a bewildering array since the Middle English period. All four words have similar meanings, though there are some differences in use. Only *wake* is used in the sense "to be awake," as in expressions such as *waking* (not *wakening*) *and sleeping, every waking hour. Wake* is also more common than *waken* when used together with *up*; and *awake* and *awaken* never occur in this context: *She woke up* (rarely *wakened up*; never *awakened up* or *awoke up*). Some writers have suggested that *waken* should be used only transitively and *awaken* only intransitively, but there is ample literary precedent for usages such as *He wakened early* and *They did not awaken her.* In figurative senses *awake* and *awaken* are more prevalent: *awoke to the danger; awakened my memory.*

Regional Note: Regional American dialects vary in the way that certain verbs form their principal parts. Northern dialects seem to favor forms that change the internal vowel in the verb — hence *dove* for the past tense of *dive*, and *woke* for *wake*: *They woke up with a start.* Southern dialects, on the other hand, tend to prefer forms that add an *-ed* to form the past tense and the past participle of these same verbs: *The children dived into the pool. The baby waked up early.*

wake² (wāk) *n.* **1.** The visible track of turbulence left by something moving through water: *the wake of a ship.* **2.** A track, course, or condition left behind. ***—idiom.*** **in the wake of. 1.** Following directly on. **2.** In the aftermath of; as a consequence of. [Poss. < MLGer., hole in the ice, of Scand. orig.]

Wake•field (wākʹfēldʹ). **1.** A borough of N-central England ENE of Manchester; site of the Battle of Wakefield (1460), in which Richard Plantagenet, the 3rd duke of York (1411–60), was slain by Lancastrian forces in the Wars of the Roses. **2.** A town of E MA, a suburb of Boston. Pop. 24,825.

wake•ful (wākʹfəl) *adj.* **1.a.** Not sleeping or not able to sleep. **b.** Without sleep; sleepless. **2.** Watchful; alert. **—wakeʹful•ly** *adv.* **—wakeʹful•ness** *n.*

Wake Island (wāk). An island of the W Pacific between HI and Guam; annexed by the U.S. in 1898.

wake•less (wākʹlĭs) *adj.* Unbroken. Used of sleep.

wak•en (wāʹkən) *v.* **-ened, -en•ing, -ens.** *—tr.* **1.** To rouse from sleep; awake: *The noise wakened me.* **2.** To rouse from a quiescent or inactive state; stir. *—intr.* To become awake; wake up. See Usage Note at **wake¹.** [ME *wakenen* < OE *wæcnan.* See **weg-*.**] **—wakʹen•er** *n.*

wake-rob•in (wākʹrŏbʹĭn) *n.* **1.** See **trillium. 2.** Any of various North American aroid plants that bloom early in the spring.

wak•ing (wāʹkĭng) *adj.* Marked by full consciousness, awareness, and alertness: *worked all of my waking hours.*

Waks•man (wăksʹmən), **Selman Abraham.** 1888–1973. Russian-born microbiologist who won a 1952 Nobel Prize.

Wa•la•chi•a (wə-lāʹkē-ə, wŏ-). See **Wallachia.**

Wa•la•pai (wäʹlə-pīʹ) *n.* Var. of **Hualapai.**

Wał•brzych (välbʹzhĭkʹ, -zhĭKHʹ). A city of SW Poland SW of Wroclaw. Pop. 138,000.

Wal•cott (wôlʹkŏt, wŏlʹ-), **Derek.** b. 1930. West Indian-born writer best known for his epic poem *Omeros* (1990). He won the 1992 Nobel Prize for literature.

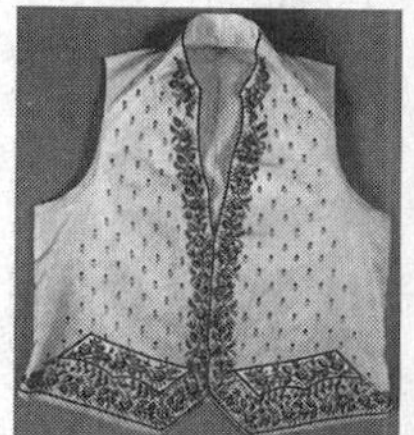

waistcoat

wake²

ă pat	oi boy
ā pay	ou out
âr care	ŏŏ took
ä father	ōō boot
ĕ pet	ŭ cut
ē be	ûr urge
ĭ pit	th thin
ī pie	*th* this
îr pier	hw which
ŏ pot	zh vision
ō toe	ə about, item
ô paw	

Stress marks:
ʹ (primary);
ʹ (secondary), as in
dictionary (dĭkʹshə-nĕrʹē)

Alice Walker

walkie-talkie

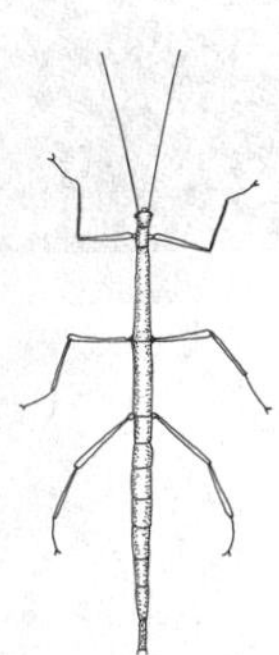
walking stick
Diapheromera femorata

Wald (wôld), **Lillian D.** 1867–1940. Amer. nurse and social reformer who founded a public-health service, the Henry Street Settlement, in New York City (1893).

Wal•de•mar I (wôl′də-mär′, väl′-) or **Val•de•mar I** (väl′-). 1131–82. Danish king (1157–82) who gained recognition for the hereditary rule of his family.

Wal•den Pond (wôl′dən). A pond of NE MA near Concord. Henry David Thoreau lived in a cabin near the pond from 1845 to 1847.

Wal•den•ses (wŏl-dĕn′sēz, wôl-) *pl.n.* A Christian schismatic sect that originated in southern France in the late 12th century and adopted Calvinist doctrines in the 16th century. [Med. Lat. *Waldēnsēs*, after Peter WALDO.] **—Wal•den′sian** (-shən) *adj. & n.*

Wald•heim (wôld′hīm′, vält′-), **Kurt.** b. 1918. Austrian diplomat who served as secretary-general of the United Nations (1972–81) and president of Austria (1986–92).

Wal•do (wôl′dō, wäl′-) or **Val•do** (văl′-, väl′-), **Peter.** fl. 12th cent. French religious leader who founded the Waldenses and was excommunicated in 1184.

Wal•dorf salad (wôl′dôrf′) *n.* A salad of diced raw apples, celery, and walnuts mixed with mayonnaise. [After the *Waldorf*-Astoria Hotel in New York City.]

wale (wāl) *n.* **1.** A mark raised on the skin, as by a whip; a weal or welt. **2.a.** One of the parallel ribs or ridges in the surface of a fabric such as corduroy. **b.** The texture or weave of such a fabric: *a wide wale.* **3.** *Naut.* **a.** A gunwale. **b.** One of the heavy planks or strakes extending along the sides of a wooden ship. *—tr.v.* **waled, wal•ing, wales.** To raise marks on (the skin), as by whipping. [ME < OE, var. of *walu.* See **wel-**[2]*.]

Wal•er also **wal•er** (wā′lər) *n.* A saddle horse developed in Australia and formerly exported to the British military forces in India. [After New S *Wales* in Australia.]

Wales (wālz). A principality of the United Kingdom on the W peninsula of Great Britain; incorporated with England since the Act of Union of 1536. Cap. Cardiff. Pop. 2,790,462.

Wa•le•sa (wä-lĕn′sə, vä-wĕn′sä), **Lech.** b. 1943. Polish politician who won the 1983 Nobel Peace Prize and was elected president of Poland in 1990.

Wal•hal•la (wăl-hăl′ə, văl-, wäl-hä′lə, väl-) *n. Myth.* Var. of **Valhalla.**

walk (wôk) *v.* **walked, walk•ing, walks.** *—intr.* **1.** To move over a surface by taking steps with the feet at a pace slower than a run. **2.a.** To go or travel on foot. **b.** To go on foot for pleasure or exercise; stroll. **c.** To move in a manner suggestive of walking. **3.** To conduct oneself or behave in a particular manner; live. **4.** To appear as a supernatural being. **5.** *Slang.* **a.** To go out on strike. **b.** To resign from one's job abruptly; quit. **6.a.** *Baseball.* To go to first base after the pitcher has thrown four balls. **b.** *Basketball.* To move illegally while holding the ball; travel. **7.** *Obsolete.* To be in constant motion. *—tr.* **1.** To go or pass over, on, or through by walking. **2.** To bring to a specified condition by walking. **3.** To cause to walk or proceed at a walk. **4.** To accompany in walking; escort on foot. **5.** To traverse on foot in order to survey or measure; pace off. **6.** To move (a heavy or cumbersome object) in a manner suggestive of walking. **7.** *Baseball.* To allow (a batter) to go to first base by pitching four balls. *—n.* **1.a.** The gait of a human being or other biped in which the feet are lifted alternately with one foot always on the ground. **b.** The gait of a quadruped in which at least two feet are always touching the ground, esp. this gait in a horse. **c.** The extravehicular movement in space of an astronaut. **2.** The act or an instance of walking, esp. a stroll for pleasure or exercise. **3.a.** The rate at which one walks; a walking pace. **b.** The characteristic way in which one walks. **4.** The distance covered or to be covered in walking. **5.** A place, such as a sidewalk, on which one may walk. **6.** A route or circuit particularly suitable for walking. **7.a.** *Baseball.* Base on balls. **b.** *Basketball.* The act or an instance of moving illegally with the ball; traveling. **8.** *Sports.* **a.** A track event in which contestants compete in walking a specified distance. **b.** Race walking. **9.** An enclosed area designated for the exercise or pasture of livestock. **10.a.** An arrangement of trees or shrubs planted in widely spaced rows. **b.** The space between such rows. *—**phrasal verbs.*** **walk out. 1.** To go on strike. **2.** To leave suddenly, often as a signal of disapproval. **walk over.** *Informal.* **1.** To treat badly or contemptuously. **2.** To gain an easy or uncontested victory over. **walk through.** To perform (a play, for example) in a perfunctory fashion, as at a first rehearsal. *—**idioms.*** **walk away from. 1.** To outdo, outrun, or defeat with little difficulty. **2.** To survive (an accident) with very little injury. **walk off with. 1.** To win easily or unexpectedly. **2.** To steal. **walk on air.** To feel elated. **walk out on.** To desert or abandon. **walk the plank.** To be forced, as by pirates, to walk off a plank extended over the side of a ship so as to drown. [ME *walken* < OE *wealcan*, to roll. See **wel-**[2]*.] **—walk′a•bil′i•ty** *n.* **—walk′a•ble** *adj.*

walk•a•bout (wôk′ə-bout′) *n.* **1.** *Australian.* A temporary return to traditional aboriginal life, usu. involving time spent in the bush. **2.** A walking trip. **3.** *Chiefly British.* A public stroll taken by an important person, such as a monarch.

walk•a•way (wôk′ə-wā′) *n.* **1.** An easily won contest or victory. **2.** Something that is easy and presents no difficulties.

walk•er (wô′kər) *n.* **1.** One that walks, esp. a contestant in a footrace. **2.** A frame device used to support someone walking, such as an infant or a convalescent. **3.** A shoe designed for walking comfortably. Often used in the plural.

Wal•ker (wô′kər), **Alice.** b. 1944. Amer. writer whose works include the novel *The Color Purple* (1982).

Walker, James John ("Jimmy"). 1881–1946. Amer. politician who was the mayor of New York City from 1926 to 1932.

walk•ie-talk•ie also **walk•y-talk•y** (wô′kē-tô′kē) *n., pl.* **-ies.** A hand-held battery-powered radio transceiver.

walk-in (wôk′ĭn′) *adj.* **1.** Large enough to admit entrance. **2.** Located so as to be entered directly from the street. *—n.* **1.** A room, such as a closet, large enough to admit entrance. **2.** An easily won victory, esp. in an election. **3.** *Slang.* One who walks in without having an appointment.

walk•ing (wô′kĭng) *adj.* Regarded as having the capabilities or qualities of a specified object: *a walking dictionary.*

walking bass (bās) *n. Mus.* A repetitive bass figure composed of nonsyncopated eighth notes, used in jazz.

walking catfish *n.* A freshwater catfish *(Clarius batrachus)* of southeast Asia that is able to travel short distances on land.

walking delegate *n.* A trade union official appointed to inspect and confer with local unions or to serve as a representative of a union in dealings with an employer.

walking fern *n.* An eastern North American fern *(Camptosorus rhizophyllus)* having fronds that often take root at the tip.

walking leaf *n.* **1.** A walking fern. **2.** See **leaf insect.**

walking papers *pl.n. Slang.* A notice of discharge or dismissal.

walking stick *n.* **1.** A cane or staff used as an aid in walking. **2.** A stick insect, esp. the widely distributed brown to green North American species *Diapheromera femorata.*

Walk•man (wôk′măn′, -mən). A trademark used for a pocket-sized audiocassette player, radio, or combined unit with lightweight earphones.

walk of life *n., pl.* **walks of life.** An occupation, a profession, or a social class: *people from all walks of life.*

walk-on (wôk′ŏn′, -ôn′) *n.* **1.** A minor role in a theatrical production. **2.** A performer playing such a role.

walk•out (wôk′out′) *n.* **1.** A labor strike. **2.** The act of leaving or quitting a meeting or an organization, esp. in protest.

walk•o•ver (wôk′ō′vər) *n.* **1.** *Sports.* **a.** An easy or uncontested win in a competition. **b.** A horserace with only one horse entered. **2.** A walkaway.

walk-through (wôk′thro͞o′) *n.* **1.** A brief rehearsal, as of a play or role, performed usu. in an early stage of production. **2.** A television rehearsal during which no cameras are used.

walk•up also **walk-up** (wôk′ŭp′) *n.* **1.** An apartment house or office building with no elevator. **2.** An apartment or office in a building with no elevator.

walk•way (wôk′wā′) *n.* A passage or path for walking.

Wal•kyr•ie (wäl-kîr′ē, -kī′rē, väl-, wäl′kə-rē, väl′-) *n.* Var. of **Valkyrie.**

walk•y-talk•y (wô′kē-tô′kē) *n.* Var. of **walkie-talkie.**

wall (wôl) *n.* **1.** An upright structure, as of masonry, serving to enclose, divide, or protect an area, esp. a vertical construction forming an inner partition or exterior siding of a building. **2.** A continuous structure, as of masonry, forming a rampart and built for defensive purposes. Often used in the plural. **3.** A structure of stonework, cement, or other material built to retain a flow of water. **4.a.** Something resembling a wall in appearance, function, or construction, as the surface of a body organ. **b.** Something resembling a wall in impenetrability or strength. **c.** An extreme or desperate condition or position, such as defeat or ruin. **5.** *Sports.* The vertical surface of an ocean wave in surfing. *—tr.v.* **walled, wall•ing, walls. 1.** To enclose, surround, or fortify with or as if with a wall. **2.** To divide or separate with or as if with a wall: *wall off half a room.* **3.** To enclose within a wall; immure. **4.** To block or close (an opening or a passage, for example) with or as if with a wall. *—**idioms.*** **off the wall.** *Slang.* **1.** Extremely unconventional. **2.** Without foundation; ridiculous. **up the wall.** *Slang.* Into a state of extreme frustration, anger, or distress. **writing** (or **handwriting**) **on the wall.** An ominous indication of the course of future events. [ME < OE *weall* < Lat. *vallum*, palisade < *vallus*, stake.]

wal•la•by (wŏl′ə-bē) *n., pl.* **-bies** or **wallaby.** Any of various marsupials of the genus *Wallabia* and related genera of Australia and adjacent islands, related to the kangaroos but generally smaller and often having a colorful coat. [Dharuk (Aboriginal language of SE Australia) *walaba.*]

Wal•lace (wŏl′ĭs), **Alfred Russel.** 1823–1913. British naturalist whose concept of evolution paralleled that of Darwin.

Wallace, George Corley. b. 1919. Amer. politician who ran unsuccessfully for the presidency in 1968 and 1972.

Wallace, Henry Agard. 1888–1965. Vice President of the U.S. (1941–45) who ran unsuccessfully for President in 1948.

Wallace, Lew(is). 1827–1905. Amer. general, diplomat, and writer known esp. for his novel *Ben Hur* (1880).

Wallace, Sir **William.** 1272?–1305. Scottish patriot who briefly gained control of Scotland in 1298.

Wal•la•chi•a also **Wa•la•chi•a** (wə-lā′kē-ə, wŏ-). A historical region of SE Romania between the Transylvanian Alps and the Danube R.; united with Moldavia to form Romania in 1861. — **Wal•la′chi•an** *adj. & n.*

wal•lah also **wal•la** (wä′lä, wŏl′ə) *n.* **1.** One employed or engaged in a particular occupation or activity. **2.** *Chiefly British.* A man; a chap. [< Hindi *-wālā*, connected with.]

wal•la•roo (wŏl′ə-ro͞o′) *n., pl.* **-roos** or **wallaroo.** A large kangaroo *(Macropus robustus)* having reddish or gray fur. [Dharuk (Aboriginal language of SE Australia) *walaru.*]

Wal•la Wal•la (wŏl′ə wŏl′ə). A city of SE WA near the OR border SSW of Spokane; founded 1856. Pop. 26,478.

wall•board (wôl′bôrd′, -bōrd′) *n.* See **plasterboard.**

wall creeper *n.* A long-billed crimson and gray Old World bird *(Tichodroma muraria)* of alpine regions that feeds on insects.

Wal•len•stein (wŏl′ən-stīn′, väl′ən-shtīn′), **Albrecht Eusebius Wenzel von.** 1583–1634. Austrian military leader who fought for the Hapsburgs during the Thirty Years' War (1618–48).

Wal•ler (wŏl′ər), **Edmund.** 1606–87. English poet known for his love lyrics, including "Go, Lovely Rose" (1645).

Waller, Thomas Wright. "Fats." 1904–43. Amer. jazz musician whose songs include "Ain't Misbehavin" (1929).

wal•let (wŏl′ĭt) *n.* A flat pocket-sized folding case, usu. made of leather, for holding paper money, cards, or photographs; a billfold. [ME *walet*, knapsack, poss. < ONFr. **walet*, roll, knapsack. See **wel-²*.**]

wall•eye (wôl′ī′) *n.* **1.** An eye with a light-colored iris or a white or opaque cornea. **2.** *Pathol.* **a.** The condition of having a dense white opacity of the cornea. **b.** A form of strabismus in which the visual axis of one eye deviates from that of the other. **3.** *pl.* **walleye** or **-eyes.** A freshwater food and game fish *(Stizostedium vitreum)* of North America having large staring eyes. [Back-formation < WALLEYED.]

wall•eyed (wôl′īd′) *adj.* **1.** Having a walleye. **2.** *Pathol.* Affected with walleye. **3.a.** Having large bulging or staring eyes. **b.** *Slang.* Having eyes with greatly distended pupils. **4.** *Slang.* Intoxicated; drunk. [ME *wawileyed* < ON *vagl-eygr* : *vagl*, film over the eye; see **wegh-*** + *auga*, eye; see **okʷ-*.**]

walleyed pike *n.* See **walleye** 3.

wall fern *n.* A low-growing Eurasian fern *(Polypodium vulgare)* characterized by creeping stems that form dense mats.

wall•flow•er (wôl′flou′ər) *n.* **1.a.** Any of numerous herbs of the genus *Erysimum* of the mustard family, having fragrant yellow, orange, or brownish flowers. **b.** Any of several perennial herbs of the genus *Cheiranthus*, esp. *C. cheiri.* **2.** One whose shyness or unpopularity prevents participation at a social event.

wall hanging *n.* A flat decorative object, such as a tapestry, hung against a wall.

Wal•ling•ford (wŏl′ĭng-fərd). A town of S CT NNE of New Haven. Pop. 40,822.

Wal•lis and Fu•tu•na Islands (wŏl′ĭs; fo͞o-to͞o′nə). A French overseas territory in the SW Pacific W of Samoa.

Wal•lo•ni•a (wä-lō′nē-ə). A French-speaking region of S Belgium; granted limited autonomy in 1980.

Wal•loon (wŏ-lo͞on′) *n.* **1.** One of a French-speaking people of Celtic descent inhabiting southern and southeast Belgium and adjacent regions of France. **2.** The dialect of French spoken by this people. [Fr. *Wallon* < OFr., of Gmc. orig.]

wal•lop (wŏl′əp) *Informal.* — *v.* **-loped, -lop•ing, -lops.** — *tr.* **1.** To beat soundly; thrash. **2.** To strike with a hard blow. **3.** To defeat thoroughly. — *intr.* **1.** To move in a rolling, clumsy manner; waddle. **2.** To boil noisily. Used of a liquid. — *n.* **1.** A hard or severe blow. **2.a.** The ability to strike a powerful blow. **b.** The capacity to create a forceful effect. [ME *walopen*, to gallop < ONFr. **waloper*. See **wel-¹*.**] — **wal′lop•er** *n.*

wal•lop•ing (wŏl′ə-pĭng) *Informal.* — *adj.* **1.** Very large; huge. **2.** Very fine; impressive. — *adv.* Used as an intensive: *a walloping huge lie.* — *n.* A sound thrashing or defeat.

wal•low (wŏl′ō) *intr.v.* **-lowed, -low•ing, -lows. 1.** To roll the body about indolently or clumsily in or as if in water, snow, or mud. **2.** To luxuriate; revel. **3.** To be plentifully supplied. **4.** To move with difficulty in a clumsy or rolling manner; flounder. **5.** To swell or surge forth; billow. — *n.* **1.** The act or an instance of wallowing. **2.a.** A pool of water or mud where animals go to wallow. **b.** The depression, pool, or pit produced by wallowing animals. **3.** A condition of degradation or baseness. [ME *walowen* < OE *wealwian*. See **wel-²*.**] — **wal′low•er** *n.*

wall•pa•per (wôl′pā′pər) *n.* Paper often printed with designs that is pasted to a wall as a decorative covering. — *v.* **-pered, -per•ing, -pers.** — *tr.* To cover with or as if with wallpaper. — *intr.* To decorate a wall or room with wallpaper.

wall plate *n.* **1.** A timber situated along the top of a wall at the level of the eaves for bearing the ends of joists or rafters. **2.** A plate used to attach a bracket or similar device to a wall.

wall plug *n.* An electric socket, usu. located in a wall.

wall rock *n.* The rock that forms the walls of a vein or lode.

wall rue *n.* A small delicate fern *(Asplenium ruta-muraria)* that grows on rocks or in rocky crevices.

Wall Street (wôl) *n.* The controlling financial interests of the United States. [After *Wall Street* in New York City.] — **Wall′-Street′er** (wôl′strē′tər) *n.*

wall-to-wall (wôl′tə-wôl′) *adj.* **1.** Completely covering a floor. **2.** *Informal.* **a.** Present or spreading throughout an entire area. **b.** Found everywhere or including everything; pervasive. — *n.* A carpet that completely covers a floor.

wal•nut (wôl′nŭt′, -nət) *n.* **1.a.** Any of several deciduous trees of the genus *Juglans*, having pinnately compound leaves and a round sticky outer fruit wall that encloses a nutlike stone with an edible seed. **b.** The stone or the ridged or corrugated seed of such a tree. **2.** The hard, dark brown wood of any of these trees. [ME *walnot* < OE *wealhhnutu* : *wealh*, Celt, foreigner + *hnutu*, nut.] — **wal′nut** *adj.*

Wal•nut Creek (wôl′nŭt′, -nət). A city of W CA NE of Oakland. Pop. 60,569.

Wal•pole (wôl′pōl′, wŏl′-). A town of E MA SW of Boston; settled in 1659. Pop. 20,212.

Walpole, Horace or **Horatio.** 4th Earl of Orford. 1717–97. British writer and historian noted for his correspondence and memoirs and the Gothic novel *The Castle of Otranto* (1764).

Walpole, Sir **Hugh Seymour.** 1884–1941. New Zealand-born writer whose works include *The Herries Chronicle* (1930–33).

Walpole, Sir **Robert.** 1st Earl of Orford. 1676–1745. English politician who as first lord of the treasury and Chancellor of the Exchequer (1715–17 and 1721–42) was regarded as Britain's first prime minister.

Wal•pur•gis Night (väl-po͝or′gĭs) *n.* **1.a.** The eve of May Day, observed in some areas in celebration of spring. **b.** The eve of Beltane, believed by medieval Christians to be the occasion of a witches' Sabbath. **2.** An episode or a situation having the quality of nightmarish wildness. [Partial transl. of Ger. *Walpurgisnacht* : *Walpurgis*, St. Walpurga (died 779) + *Nacht*, night.]

wal•rus (wôl′rəs, wŏl′-) *n., pl.* **walrus** or **-rus•es.** A large marine mammal *(Odobenus rosmarus)* of Arctic regions, related to the seals and having two long tusks, tough wrinkled skin, and four flippers. [Du., of Scand. orig.]

walrus mustache *n.* A bushy, drooping mustache.

Wal•sall (wôl′sôl′, -səl). A borough of W-central England NW of Birmingham. Pop. 267,500.

Wal•ter (väl′tər), **Bruno.** 1876–1962. German conductor noted for his interpretations of Mozart and Mahler.

Wal•ter Mit•ty (wôl′tər mĭt′ē) *n.* An ordinary, often ineffectual person who daydreams of fantastic personal triumphs. [After "The Secret Life of *Walter Mitty*" (1939) by James Thurber.]

Wal•tham (wôl′thăm′, -thəm). A city of E MA W of Boston; seat of Brandeis University (estab. 1947). Pop. 57,878.

Wal•ther von der Vo•gel•wei•de (väl′tər fôn der fō′gəl-vī′də). 1170?–1230? German minnesinger. The German national anthem is based on one of his songs.

Wal•ton (wôl′tən), **Ernest Thomas Sinton.** b. 1903. Irish physicist who shared a 1951 Nobel Prize.

Walton, Izaak. 1593–1683. English writer primarily known for *The Compleat Angler* (1653), a literary treatise on fishing.

Walton, Sir **William Turner.** 1902–83. British composer of orchestral works and chamber music, including *Façade* (1923).

waltz (wôlts, wôls) *n.* **1.a.** A ballroom dance in triple time with a strong accent on the first beat. **b.** A piece of music for this dance. **c.** An instrumental or vocal composition in triple time. **2.** *Informal.* Something that can be accomplished with little effort. — *v.* **waltzed, waltz•ing, waltz•es.** — *intr.* **1.** To dance the waltz. **2.** *Slang.* To move unhesitantly, briskly, and with aplomb. **3.** *Informal.* To accomplish a task with little effort. — *tr.* **1.** To dance the waltz with. **2.** *Slang.* To lead or force to move briskly and purposefully; march. [Ger. *Walzer* < *walzen*, to turn about < MHGer., to roll < OHGer. *walzan*. See **wel-²*.**] — **waltz′er** *n.*

Wal•vis Bay (wôl′vĭs). An inlet of the Atlantic Ocean on the W coast of Namibia. The town of **Walvis Bay** (pop. 11,600) and the surrounding area constitute an exclave of South Africa.

wam•ble (wŏm′bəl, wăm′-) *intr.v.* **-bled, -bling, -bles. 1.** To move in a weaving, wobbling, or rolling manner. **2.** To turn or roll. Used of the stomach. — *n.* **1.** A wobble or roll. **2.** An upset stomach. [ME *wamelen*, to feel nausea. See **wemə-*.**] — **wam′bli•ness** *n.* — **wam′bling•ly** *adv.* — **wam′bly** *adj.*

Wam•pa•no•ag (wäm′pə-nō′ăg) *n., pl.* **Wampanoag** or **-ags. 1.** A member of a Native American people formerly inhabiting Rhode Island and Massachusetts, with present-day descendants in this same area. **2.** The Algonquian language of the Wampanoag. [Narragansett, those of the east.]

wam•pum (wŏm′pəm, wôm′-) *n.* **1.** Small cylindrical beads made from polished shells, formerly used by certain Native American peoples as currency and jewelry or for ceremonial purposes. **2.** *Informal.* Money. [Short for WAMPUMPEAG.]

wam•pum•peag (wŏm′pəm-pēg′, wôm′-) *n.* White shell beads used as wampum. [Massachusett.]

wan (wŏn) *adj.* **wan•ner, wan•nest. 1.** Unnaturally pale, as from distress. **2.** Suggestive or indicative of weariness, illness, or unhappiness; melancholy. — *intr.v.* **wanned, wan•ning,**

wallaby

walnut

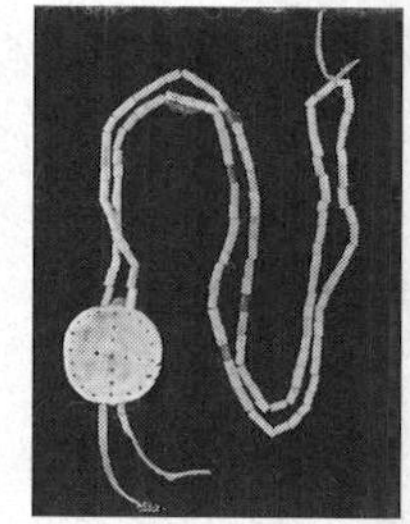

wampum
Huron wampum necklace

ă pat	oi boy
ā pay	ou out
âr care	o͝o took
ä father	o͞o boot
ĕ pet	ŭ cut
ē be	ûr urge
ĭ pit	th thin
ī pie	*th* this
îr pier	hw which
ŏ pot	zh vision
ō toe	ə about, item
ô paw	

Stress marks:
′ (primary);
′ (secondary), as in
dictionary (dĭk′shə-nĕr′ē)

wans. To become pale. [ME, pale, gloomy < OE *wann,* gloomy, dark.] — **wan′ly** *adv.* — **wan′ness** *n.*

Wan·a·ma·ker (wŏn′ə-mā′kər), **John.** 1838–1922. Amer. merchant who founded one of the first department stores.

wand (wŏnd) *n.* **1.** A thin supple rod, twig, or stick. **2.** A slender rod carried as a symbol of office; a scepter. **3.** *Mus.* A conductor's baton. **4.** A stick or baton used by a magician, conjurer, or diviner. **5.** A pipelike attachment that lengthens the handle of a device or tool. **6.** *Sports.* A six-foot by two-foot slat used as an archery target. [ME < ON *vöndr.*]

wan·der (wŏn′dər) *v.* **-dered, -der·ing, -ders.** — *intr.* **1.** To move about without a definite destination or purpose. **2.** To go by an indirect route or at no set pace; amble. **3.** To proceed in an irregular course; meander. **4.** To go astray. **5.** To lose clarity or coherence of thought or expression. — *tr.* To wander across or through. — *n.* The act or an instance of wandering; a stroll. [ME *wanderen* < OE *wandrian.*] — **wan′der·er** *n.* — **wan′der·ing·ly** *adv.*

wapiti
Cervus canadensis

Syns: *wander, ramble, roam, rove, range, meander, stray, gallivant, gad.* These verbs mean to move about at random or without destination or purpose. *Wander* and *ramble* stress the absence of a fixed course or goal: *She wandered into the room. "They would go off together, rambling along the river"* (John Galsworthy). *Roam* and *rove* emphasize freedom of movement, often over a wide area: *"Herds of horses and cattle roamed at will over the plain"* (George W. Cable). *"For ten long years I roved about, living first in one capital, then another"* (Charlotte Brontë). *Range* suggests wandering in all directions: *"a large hunting party known to be ranging the prairie"* (Francis Parkman). *Meander* suggests leisurely, sometimes aimless wandering over an irregular or winding course: *"He meandered to and fro . . . observing the manners and customs of Hillport society"* (Arnold Bennett). *Stray* refers to deviation from a proper course: *"I ask pardon, I am straying from the question"* (Oliver Goldsmith). *Gallivant* refers to wandering in search of pleasure: *gallivanted all over the city during the class trip. Gad* suggests restless, pointless wandering: *gadding about unaccompanied in foreign places.*

wan·der·ing albatross (wŏn′dər-ĭng) *n.* A large, mostly white albatross *(Diomedea exulans)* of southern seas.

wandering Jew *n.* Any of three trailing plants, *Tradescantia albiflora, T. fluminensis,* or *Zebrina pendula,* native to tropical America and having usu. variegated foliage.

warbler
Yellow-throated warbler
Dendroica dominica

Wan·der·ing Jew (wŏn′dər-ĭng) *n.* A Jew of medieval legend condemned to wander until the Day of Judgment for having mocked Jesus on the day of the Crucifixion.

wan·der·lust (wŏn′dər-lŭst′) *n.* A very strong or irresistible impulse to travel. [Ger. : *wandern,* to wander (< MHGer.) + *Lust,* desire (< MHGer. < OHGer.; see **las-***).]

wane (wān) *intr.v.* **waned, wan·ing, wanes. 1.** To decrease gradually in size, amount, intensity, or degree; decline. **2.** To exhibit a decreasing illuminated area from full moon to new moon. **3.** To approach an end. — *n.* **1.** The act or process of gradually declining or diminishing. **2.a.** A time or phase of gradual decrease. **b.** The period of the decrease of the moon's illuminated visible surface. **3.** A defective edge of a board caused by remaining bark or a beveled end. — ***idiom.* on the wane.** In a period of decline or decrease. [ME *wanen* < OE *wanian.* See **eu-²***.]

wan·gle (wăng′gəl) *v.* **-gled, -gling, -gles.** — *tr.* **1.** To make, achieve, or get by contrivance. **2.** To manipulate or juggle, esp. fraudulently. **3.** To extricate (oneself) from difficulty. — *intr.* **1.** To use indirect, tricky, or fraudulent methods. **2.** To extricate oneself by subtle or indirect means, as from difficulty; wriggle. [?] — **wang′le** *n.* — **wang′ler** *n.*

war bonnet

wan·i·gan or **wan·ni·gan** (wŏn′-ĭ-gən) also **wan·gun** (wŏn′gən, wăng′-) *n.* **1.** *New England & Upper Northern U.S.* **a.** A boat or small chest equipped with supplies for a lumber camp. **b.** Provisions for a camp or cabin. **2.** *Alaska.* **a.** A small building mounted on skids and towed behind a tractor train as eating and sleeping quarters for a work crew. **b.** An addition built onto a trailer house for extra living or storage space. [Ojibwa *waanikaan,* storage pit.]

Wan·kel engine (väng′kəl, wäng′-, wăng′-) *n.* A rotary internal-combustion engine in which a triangular rotor performs the functions allotted to the pistons of a conventional engine. [After Felix *Wankel* (1902–88), German engineer.]

want (wŏnt, wônt) *v.* **want·ed, want·ing, wants.** — *tr.* **1.** To desire greatly; wish for. **2.** To be without; lack. See Syns at **lack. 3.** To be in need of; require. **4.a.** To request the presence or assistance of. **b.** To seek with intent to capture. **5.a.** To have a desire for. See Syns at **desire. b.** To have an inclination toward; like. — *intr.* **1.** To have need. **2.** To be destitute or needy. **3.** To be disposed; wish. — *n.* **1.** The condition or quality of lacking something usual or necessary. **2.** Pressing need; destitution. **3.** Something desired. **4.** A defect of character; a fault. — ***phrasal verbs.* want in.** *Slang.* **1.** To desire greatly to enter. **2.** To wish to join a project, business, or other undertaking. **want out.** *Slang.* **1.** To desire greatly to leave. **2.** To wish to leave a project, a business, or other undertaking. [ME *wanten,* to be lacking < ON *vanta.* See **eu-²***.] — **want′er** *n.*

Usage Note: When *want* is followed immediately by an infinitive construction, it does not take *for: I want you to go* (not *want for you*). When *want* and the infinitive are separated in the sentence, however, *for* is used: *What I want is for you to go.* See Usage Note at **wish.**

want ad *n. Informal.* A classified advertisement.

Wan·tagh (wŏn′tô′). A town of SE NY on the S shore of Long I. Pop. 18,567.

want·ing (wŏn′tĭng, wôn′-) *adj.* **1.** Absent; lacking. **2.** Not measuring up to standards or expectations. — *prep.* **1.** Without. **2.** Minus; less: *an hour wanting 15 minutes.*

wan·ton (wŏn′tən) *adj.* **1.** Immoral or unchaste; lewd. **2.a.** Gratuitously cruel; merciless. **b.** Marked by unprovoked, gratuitous maliciousness; capricious and unjust. **3.** Unrestrainedly excessive. **4.** Luxuriant; overabundant. **5.** Frolicsome; playful. **6.** Undisciplined; spoiled. **7.** *Obsolete.* Rebellious; refractory. — *v.* **-toned, -ton·ing, -tons.** — *intr.* To act, grow, or move in a wanton manner; be wanton. — *tr.* To waste or squander extravagantly. — *n.* **1.** One who is immoral, lewd, or licentious. **2.** One that is playful or frolicsome. **3.** One that is undisciplined or spoiled. [ME *wantowen* : *wan-,* not, lacking (< OE; akin to *wana,* lack; see WANE) + *towen,* p.part. of *teen,* to bring up (< OE *tēon,* to lead, draw; see **deuk-***).] — **wan′ton·ly** *adv.* — **wan′ton·ness** *n.*

wap·en·take (wŏp′ən-tāk′, wăp′-) *n.* A historical subdivision of some northern counties in England, corresponding roughly to the hundred. [ME < OE *wæpengetæc* < ON *vāpnatak,* act of taking weapons : *vāpna,* genitive pl. of *vāpn,* weapon + *tak,* act of taking (< *taka,* to take).]

wap·i·ti (wŏp′ĭ-tē) *n., pl.* **wapiti** or **-tis.** A large light brown or grayish-brown North American deer *(Cervus canadensis)* having long branching antlers. [Shawnee *waapiti.*]

Wap·pin·ger (wä′pĭn-jər) *n., pl.* **Wappinger** or **-gers.** A member of a Native American people formerly inhabiting the lower east bank of the Hudson River. [Of Algonquian orig.]

Wap·si·pin·i·con (wŏp′sə-pĭn′ĭ-kən). A river rising in S MN and flowing c. 410 km (255 mi) to the Mississippi R.

war (wôr) *n.* **1.a.** A state of open, armed conflict between nations, states, or parties. **b.** The period of such conflict. **c.** The techniques and procedures of war; military science. **2.a.** A condition of active antagonism or contention. **b.** A concerted effort to combat something injurious. — *intr.v.* **warred, war·ring, wars. 1.** To wage or carry on warfare. **2.** To be in a state of hostility or rivalry; contend. — ***idiom.* at war.** In an active state of conflict or contention. [ME *warre* < ONFr. *werre,* of Gmc. orig. See **wers-***.]

war. *abbr.* Warrant.

Wa·ran·gal (wə-rŭng′gəl, wôr′əng-). A city of SE India NE of Hyderabad. Pop. 335,150.

war baby *n.* A child born during wartime, esp. during World War I or World War II.

War Between the States (wôr) *n.* See **civil war** 3.

war·ble¹ (wôr′bəl) *v.* **-bled, -bling, -bles.** — *tr. Mus.* To sing (a note, for example) with trills or other melodic embellishments. — *intr.* **1.** *Mus.* To sing with trills, runs, or quavers. **2.** To be sounded in a trilling or quavering manner. — *n. Mus.* The act or an instance of warbling. [ME *werbelen* < ONFr. *werbler,* of Gmc. orig.]

war·ble² (wôr′bəl) *n.* **1.a.** An abscessed boillike swelling on the back of cattle, deer, and certain other animals, caused by the larva of a warble fly. **b.** The warble fly, esp. in its larval stage. **2.** A hard lump of tissue on a riding horse's back caused by the saddle. [Prob. of Scand. orig.]

warble fly *n.* Any of several large hairy flies of the family Oestridae, having larvae that form warbles.

war·bler (wôr′blər) *n.* **1.** Any of various small New World songbirds of the family Parulidae, such as the redstart, many of which are brightly colored. **2.** Any of various small, often brownish or grayish Old World songbirds of the family Silviidae, such as the blackcap. **3.** One that warbles; a singer.

war bonnet *n.* A ceremonial headdress used by some Plains Indians consisting of a cap or band and a trailing extension and decorated with erect feathers.

war bride *n.* A woman who marries a serviceman during war.

War·burg (wôr′bərg′, vär′bo͝ork′), **Otto Heinrich.** 1883–1970. German biochemist who won a 1931 Nobel Prize.

war chest *n.* **1.** An accumulation of funds to finance a war effort. **2.** A fund reserved for a particular purpose.

war correspondent *n.* A journalist, reporter, or commentator assigned to report directly from a war or combat zone.

war crime *n.* Any of various crimes, such as genocide or the mistreatment of prisoners of war, considered in violation of the conventions of warfare. — **war criminal** *n.*

war cry *n.* **1.** A cry uttered by combatants as they attack; a battle cry. **2.** A phrase used to rally people to a cause.

ward (wôrd) *n.* **1.** A division of a city or town, esp. an electoral district, for administrative and representative purposes. **2.** A district of some English and Scottish counties corresponding roughly to the hundred or the wapentake. **3.a.** A room in a hospital usu. holding six or more patients. **b.** A division in a hospital for the care of a particular group of patients: *a maternity ward.* **4.** One of the divisions of a penal institution, such as a prison. **5.** An open court or area of a castle or fortification enclosed by walls. **6.a.** *Law.* A minor or incompetent person placed under the care or protection of a guardian or court. **b.** A person under the protection or care of another. **7.** The state of being under guard; custody. **8.** The act of guarding or protecting; guardianship. **9.** A means of protection; a defense. **10.** A defensive movement or attitude, esp. in fencing; a guard. **11.a.** The projecting ridge of a lock or keyhole that prevents the turning of a key other than the proper one. **b.** The notch cut into a key that corresponds to such a ridge. — *tr.v.* **ward•ed, ward•ing, wards.** To guard; protect. — ***phrasal verb.* ward off. 1.** To turn aside; parry: *ward off blows.* **2.** To try to prevent; avert. [ME, action of guarding < OE *weard,* a watching, keeper. See **wer-[3]*.**]

Ward (wôrd), **Artemus[1].** 1727–1800. Amer. Revolutionary general who directed the siege of Boston until 1776.

Ward, Artemus[2]. See Charles Farrar **Browne.**

Ward, Barbara. Baroness Jackson of Lodsworth. 1914–81. British economist, conservationist, and writer whose works include *Spaceship Earth* (1966).

Ward, Mary Augusta Arnold. "Mrs. Humphry Ward." 1851–1920. British writer of *Robert Elsmere* (1888).

-ward or **-wards** *suff.* **1.a.** In a specified direction in time or space: *downward.* **b.** Toward a specified place or position: *skyward.* **2.a.** Occurring or situated in a specified direction: *leftward.* **b.** Having a direction toward a specified place or position: *landward.* [ME < OE *-weard.* See **wer-[2]*.**]

ward•ed (wôr′dĭd) *adj.* Having notches or ridges. Used of a key or lock.

war•den (wôrd′n) *n.* **1.** The chief administrative official of a prison. **2.** An official charged with enforcing certain laws and regulations. **3.** *Chiefly British.* **a.** The chief executive official in charge of a port or market. **b.** Any of various crown officers having administrative duties. **c.** One of the governing officials of certain schools, guilds, or hospitals; a trustee. **4.** The chief executive of a borough in certain states. **5.** A churchwarden. [ME *wardein* < ONFr. < *warder,* to guard, of Gmc. orig. See **wer-[3]*.**] — **war′den•ship′** *n.*

war•den•ry (wôrd′n-rē) *n., pl.* **-ries.** The office, duties, or jurisdiction of a warden.

ward•er[1] (wôr′dər) *n.* **1.** A guard, porter, or watcher of a gate or tower. **2.** *Chiefly British.* A prison guard. [ME < AN *wardere* < ONFr. *warder,* to guard. See WARDEN.] — **war′der•ship′** *n.*

ward•er[2] (wôr′dər) *n.* A baton formerly used by a ruler or commander as a symbol of authority and to signal orders. [ME, poss. < *warden,* to ward < OE *weardian.* See **wer-[3]*.**]

ward heeler *n. Informal.* A worker for the ward organization of a political machine.

ward•robe (wôr′drōb′) *n.* **1.** A tall cabinet, closet, or small room built to hold clothes. **2.** Garments considered as a group, esp. all the clothing belonging to one person. **3.a.** The costumes belonging to a theater or theatrical troupe. **b.** The place in which theatrical costumes are kept. **4.** The department in charge of wearing apparel, jewelry, and accessories in a royal or noble household. [ME *warderobe* < ONFr. : *warder,* to guard; see **wer-[3]*** + *robe,* garment; see ROBE.]

ward•room (wôrd′ro͞om′, -ro͝om′) *n.* **1.** The common recreation area and dining room for the commissioned officers on a warship. **2.** The commissioned officers serving together on a warship.

-wards *suff.* Var. of **-ward.**

ward•ship (wôrd′shĭp′) *n.* **1.** The state of being in the charge of a guardian. **2.** Custody; guardianship.

ware[1] (wâr) *n.* **1.** Articles of the same general kind, made of a specified material or used in a specific application. Often used in combination: *silverware.* **2.a.** An article of commerce. **b.** An immaterial asset or benefit regarded as an article of commerce. [ME < OE *waru,* goods. See **wer-[3]*.**]

ware[2] (wâr) *tr.v.* **wared, war•ing, wares.** *Archaic.* To beware of. — *adj. Obsolete.* **1.** Watchful; wary. **2.** Aware. [ME *waren* < OE *warian.* See **wer-[3]*.** Adj., ME. See WARY.]

Ware•ham (wâr′əm, -hăm′). A town of SE MA on Buzzards Bay NE of New Bedford. Pop. 19,232.

ware•house (wâr′hous′) *n.* **1.** A place in which goods or merchandise are stored; a storehouse. **2.** A large, usu. wholesale shop. — *tr.v.* (*also* -houz′) **-housed, -hous•ing, -hous•es. 1.** To place or store in a warehouse, esp. in a bonded or government warehouse. **2.** To institutionalize (people) in usu. deficient housing and in substandard conditions. — **ware′hous′er** (-hou′zər) *n.*

ware•room (wâr′ro͞om′, -ro͝om′) *n.* A room used for the storage or display of goods or wares.

war•fare (wôr′fâr′) *n.* **1.a.** The waging of war against an enemy; armed conflict. **b.** Military operations marked by a specific characteristic: *guerrilla warfare.* **2.** A state of disharmony or conflict; strife. **3.** Acts undertaken to destroy or undermine the strength of another. [ME : *warre,* war; see WAR + *fare,* journey (< OE *faru* < *faran,* to journey; see FARE).]

war•fa•rin (wôr′fər-ĭn) *n.* A white crystalline compound, $C_{19}H_{16}O_4$, that is used as an anticoagulant. [*W(isconsin) A(lumni) R(esearch) F(oundation)* + (COUM)ARIN.]

war game *n.* **1.** A simulation of a military operation. **2.** A simulation of a proposed plan of action or strategy to test its validity. — **war′-game′** *v.*

war hawk *n.* **1.** A member of the 12th U.S. Congress (1811–1813) who advocated war with Great Britain. **2.** One who advocates war; a hawk.

war•head (wôr′hĕd′) *n.* A part of the armament system usu. in the forward part of a projectile that contains the explosive or other agent intended to inflict damage on a target.

War•hol (wôr′hôl′, -hōl′), **Andy.** 1930?–87. Amer. artist who was a leader of the pop art movement.

Andy Warhol

war•horse also **war-horse** (wôr′hôrs′) *n.* **1.** A horse used in combat; a charger. **2.** *Informal.* One who has been through many battles or struggles. **3.** *Informal.* A musical or dramatic work that has become hackneyed.

war•like (wôr′līk′) *adj.* **1.** Belligerent; hostile. **2.a.** Of or relating to war; martial. **b.** Indicative of or threatening war.

war•lock (wôr′lŏk′) *n.* A male witch, sorcerer, wizard, or demon. [ME *warloghe* < OE *wǣrloga,* oath-breaker : *wǣr,* pledge; see **wēro-*** + *-loga,* liar (< *lēogan,* to lie; see **leugh-***).]

war•lord (wôr′lôrd′) *n.* A military commander exercising civil power in a region, whether in nominal allegiance to the national government or in defiance of it. — **war′lord′ism** *n.*

warm (wôrm) *adj.* **warm•er, warm•est. 1.** Somewhat hotter than temperate; moderately, often comfortably hot. **2.** Having the natural heat of living beings: *a warm body.* **3.** Preserving or imparting heat: *a warm overcoat.* **4.** Having or causing a sensation of unusually high body heat, as from exercise; overheated. **5.** Marked by enthusiasm; ardent. **6.** Marked by liveliness, excitement, or disagreement; heated: *a warm debate.* **7.** Marked by or revealing friendliness or sincerity; cordial. **8.** Loving; passionate. **9.** Excitable, impetuous, or quick to be aroused. **10.** *Color.* Predominantly red or yellow in tone. **11.** Recently made; fresh. **12.** Close to guessing or finding something, as in certain games. **13.** *Informal.* Uncomfortable because of danger or annoyance. — *v.* **warmed, warm•ing, warms.** — *tr.* **1.** To raise slightly in temperature; make warm: *warm up the house.* **2.** To make zealous or ardent; enliven. **3.** To fill with pleasant emotions. — *intr.* **1.** To become warm. **2.** To become ardent, enthusiastic, or animated. **3.** To become kindly disposed or friendly. — *n. Informal.* A warming or heating. — ***phrasal verb.* warm up. 1.** *Sports.* To prepare for an athletic event by exercising, stretching, or practicing. **2.** To make or become ready for an event or operation. **3.** To make more enthusiastic, excited, or animated. **4.** To approach a state of confrontation or violence. [ME < OE *wearm.*] — **warm′er** *n.* — **warm′ish** *adj.* — **warm′ly** *adv.* — **warm′ness** *n.*

warm-blood•ed (wôrm′blŭd′ĭd) *adj.* **1.** *Zool.* Maintaining a relatively constant and warm body temperature independent of environmental temperature; homeothermic. **2.** Ardent; passionate. — **warm′-blood′ed•ness** *n.*

warmed-o•ver (wôrmd′ō′vər) *adj.* **1.** Warmed up; reheated. **2.** Not new, fresh, or spontaneous; stale.

warm front *n.* A front along which an advancing mass of warm air rises over a mass of cold air.

warm-heart•ed (wôrm′här′tĭd) *adj.* Marked by kindness, sympathy, and generosity. — **warm′heart′ed•ness** *n.*

warm•ing pan (wôr′mĭng) *n.* A metal pan with a cover and a long handle, designed to hold hot liquids or coals and used to warm a bed.

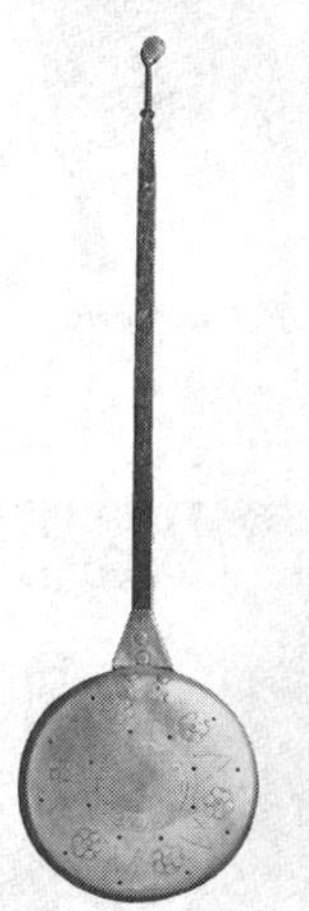

warming pan
c. 1700–1750 Scandinavian

war•mon•ger (wôr′mŭng′gər, -mŏng′-) *n.* One who advocates or tries to stir up war. — **war′mon′ger•ing** *adj. & n.*

war•mouth (wôr′mouth′) *n., pl.* **-mouths** (-mouthz′, -mouths′) or **warmouth.** A freshwater sunfish *(Lepomis gulosus)* of the eastern and Midwestern United States having a large mouth and minute teeth on its tongue. [?]

warmth (wôrmth) *n.* **1.** The state, sensation, or quality of producing or having a moderate degree of heat. **2.a.** Friendliness, kindness, or affection. **b.** Excitement or intensity, as of love; ardor. **3.** *Color.* The glowing effect produced by using warm hues. [ME < OE **wiermthu* < *wearm,* warm.]

warm-up or **warm•up** (wôrm′ŭp′) *n.* **1.a.** The act or procedure of warming up. **b.** A period spent in warming up. **2.** Clothing, such as a sweat suit, designed to be worn before or after an athletic event. Often used in the plural.

warn (wôrn) *v.* **warned, warn•ing, warns.** — *tr.* **1.** To make aware in advance of actual or potential harm, danger, or evil. **2.** To admonish as to action or manners. **3.** To notify (a person) to go or stay away: *warned them off the property.* **4.** To notify or apprise in advance. — *intr.* To give a warning. [ME *warnen* < OE *warnian.* See **wer-[4]*.**] — **warn′er** *n.*

War•ner (wôr′nər), **Harry Morris.** 1881–1958. Amer. filmmaker who with his brothers **Albert** (1884–1967), **Samuel Louis** (1887–1927), and **Jack** (1892–1978) founded Warner Brothers Pictures.

Warner Rob•ins (rŏb′ĭnz). A city of central GA S of Macon; incorp. 1943. Pop. 43,726.

warn•ing (wôr′nĭng) *n.* **1.** An intimation, a threat, or a sign of impending danger or evil. **2.a.** Advice to beware. **b.** Counsel to desist from a specified course of action. **3.** A cautionary or

ă pat	oi boy
ā pay	ou out
âr care	o͝o took
ä father	o͞o boot
ĕ pet	ŭ cut
ē be	ûr urge
ĭ pit	th thin
ī pie	*th* this
îr pier	hw which
ŏ pot	zh vision
ō toe	ə about, item
ô paw	

Stress marks:
′ (primary);
′ (secondary), as in
dictionary (dĭk′shə-nĕr′ē)

wart hog
Phacochoerus aethiopicus

washboard

Booker T. Washington
c. 1895 photograph
by Elmer Chickering
(died 1915)

ă pat oi boy
ā pay ou out
âr care o͝o to͝ok
ä father o͞o bo͞ot
ĕ pet ŭ cut
ē be ûr urge
ĭ pit th thin
ī pie *th* this
îr pier hw which
ŏ pot zh vision
ō toe ə about, item
ô paw

Stress marks:
ʹ (primary);
ʹ (secondary), as in
dictionary (dĭkʹshə-nĕrʹē)

deterrent example. **4.** Something, such as a signal, that warns. See Syns at **alarm.** — *adj.* Acting or serving to warn.

warning coloration *n.* The conspicuous markings of an animal, such as a skunk, that serve to warn off predators.

war of nerves *n., pl.* **wars of nerves.** A conflict marked by psychological tactics, such as intimidation and threats, intended to confuse and erode the morale of one's enemy.

warp (wôrp) *v.* **warped, warp•ing, warps.** — *tr.* **1.** To turn or twist (wood, for example) out of shape. **2.** To turn from a correct or proper course; deflect. **3.** To affect unfavorably, unfairly, or wrongly; bias. **4.** To arrange (strands of yarn or thread) so that they run lengthwise in weaving. **5.** *Naut.* To move (a vessel) by hauling on a line that is fastened to or around a piling, an anchor, or a pier. — *intr.* **1.** To become bent or twisted out of shape. **2.** To turn aside from a true, correct, or natural course; go astray. **3.** *Naut.* To warp a vessel. — *n.* **1.** The state of being twisted or bent out of shape. **2.** A distortion or twist, esp. in a piece of wood. **3.** A mental or moral twist, aberration, or deviation. **4.** The threads that run lengthwise in a woven fabric, crossed at right angles to the weft. **5.** Warp and weft. **6.** *Naut.* A towline used in warping a vessel. [ME *werpen* < OE *weorpan*, to throw away. See **wer-**[2]*.] — **warpʹer** *n.*

war paint *n.* **1.** Pigments applied to the face or body in preparation for battle, as in certain tribal societies. **2.** *Informal.* Cosmetics such as lipstick, rouge, or mascara.

warp and woof *n.* The underlying structure on which something is built; a base or foundation.

war party *n.* **1.** A band of warriors engaged in fighting or raiding an enemy. Used esp. of Native Americans. **2.** A usu. blatantly patriotic political party supporting a war.

war•path (wôrʹpăthʹ, -päthʹ) *n.* **1.** A course that leads to warfare or battle. **2.** A hostile course or mood.

war•plane (wôrʹplānʹ) *n.* A combat aircraft.

war•rant (wôrʹənt, wŏrʹ-) *n.* **1.** Authorization or certification; sanction, as given by a superior. **2.** Justification for an action or a belief; grounds. **3.** Something that provides assurance or confirmation; a guarantee or proof: *a warrant of authenticity.* **4.** An order that serves as authorization, esp.: **a.** A voucher authorizing payment or receipt of money. **b.** *Law.* A judicial writ authorizing an officer to make a search, a seizure, or an arrest or to execute a judgment. **5.a.** A warrant officer. **b.** A certificate of appointment given to a warrant officer. — *tr.v.* **-rant•ed, -rant•ing, -rants. 1.** To guarantee or attest to the quality, accuracy, or condition of. **2.** To guarantee or attest to the character or reliability of; vouch for. **3.a.** To guarantee (a product). **b.** To guarantee (a purchaser) indemnification against damage or loss. **4.** To guarantee the immunity or security of. **5.** To provide adequate grounds for; justify. **6.** To grant authorization or sanction to (someone); authorize or empower. **7.** *Law.* To guarantee clear title to (real property). [ME *warant* < ONFr., of Gmc. orig. See **wer-**[4]*.] — **warʹrant•a•bilʹi•ty, warʹrant•a•ble•ness** *n.* — **warʹrant•a•ble** *adj.* — **warʹrant•a•bly** *adv.*

war•ran•tee (wôrʹən-tēʹ, wŏrʹ-) *n.* One to whom a warranty is made or a warrant is given.

warrant officer *n.* A military officer, usu. a skilled technician or a helicopter pilot, intermediate in rank between a noncommissioned officer and a commissioned officer and having authority by virtue of a warrant.

war•ran•tor (wôrʹən-tər, -tôrʹ, wŏrʹ-) also **war•rant•er** (-tər) *n.* One that makes a warrant or gives a warranty.

war•ran•ty (wôrʹən-tē, wŏrʹ-) *n., pl.* **-ties. 1.** Official authorization, sanction, or warrant. **2.** Justification or valid grounds for an act or a course of action. **3.** *Law.* **a.** An assurance by the seller of property that the goods or property are as represented or will be as promised. **b.** The insured's guarantee that the facts are as stated in reference to an insurance risk or that specified conditions will be fulfilled to keep the contract effective. **c.** A covenant by which the seller of land binds himself or herself and his or her heirs to defend the security of the estate conveyed. **d.** A judicial writ; a warrant. **4.** A guarantee given to a purchaser stating that a product is reliable and free from known defects and that the seller will repair or replace defective parts. [ME *warantie* < ONFr. < fem. p.part. of *warantir*, to guarantee < *warant*, warrant. See **wer-**[4]*.]

war•ren (wôrʹən, wŏrʹ-) *n.* **1.a.** An area where rabbits live in burrows. **b.** A colony of rabbits. **2.** An enclosure for small game animals. **3.a.** An overcrowded living area. **b.** A mazelike place where one may easily become lost. [ME *warenne* < ONFr., enclosure. See **wer-**[4]*.]

War•ren (wôrʹən, wŏrʹ-). **1.** A city of SE MI, a suburb of Detroit. Pop. 144,864. **2.** A city of NE OH NW of Youngstown. Pop. 50,793.

Warren, Earl. 1891–1974. Amer. jurist; chief justice of the U.S. Supreme Court (1953–69).

Warren, Mercy Otis. 1728–1814. Amer. writer whose satirical plays include *The Adulateur* (1773).

Warren, Robert Penn. 1905–89. Amer. writer and critic known for his novel *All the King's Men* (1946).

war•ren•er (wôrʹə-nər, wŏrʹ-) *n.* **1.** One who owns or keeps a rabbit warren. **2.** A gamekeeper.

War•ring•ton (wôrʹĭng-tən, wŏrʹ-). A borough of W-central England E of Liverpool on the Mersey R. Pop. 168,600.

war•ri•or (wôrʹē-ər, wŏrʹ-) *n.* One who is engaged in or experienced in battle. [ME *werreour* < ONFr. *werreieur* < *werreier*, to make war < *werre*, war. See WAR.]

war•saw (wôrʹsô) *n.* A large Caribbean grouper *(Epinephelus nigritus).* [Perh. alteration of Am.Sp. *guasa*, a sea bass.]

War•saw (wôrʹsôʹ). The cap. of Poland, in the E-central part of the country on the Vistula R.; founded in the 13th cent. Pop. 1,649,000.

war•ship (wôrʹshĭpʹ) *n.* A combat ship.

wart (wôrt) *n.* **1.a.** A hard rough skin growth caused by viral infection, typically on the hands or feet. **b.** A similar growth or protuberance, as on a plant. **2.** A genital wart. **3.a.** One that resembles or is likened to a wart, esp. in unattractiveness. **b.** An imperfection; a flaw. — ***idiom.*** **warts and all.** *Slang.* All defects and imperfections notwithstanding. [ME < OE *wearte.*] — **wartʹed, wartʹy** *adj.*

War•ta (värʹtə, -tä). A river rising in S-central Poland NW of Cracow and flowing c. 764 km (475 mi) to the Oder R.

wart hog also **wart•hog** (wôrtʹhôgʹ, -hŏgʹ) *n.* A wild African hog *(Phacochoerus aethiopicus)* that has a pair of prominent tusks and wartlike growths on the face.

war•time (wôrʹtīmʹ) *n.* A period during a war.

War•wick (wôrʹwĭk). A city of E-central RI on Narragansett Bay S of Providence; settled in 1643. Pop. 85,427.

War•wick (wŏrʹĭk), Earl of. Richard Neville. "the Kingmaker." 1428–71. English military and political leader who fought for the Yorkists during the Wars of the Roses and secured the throne for Edward IV (1461). He then changed allegiance and restored Henry VI to the throne (1470).

war•y (wârʹē) *adj.* **-i•er, -i•est. 1.** On guard; watchful. **2.** Characterized by caution. [ME *ware* < OE *wær.* See **wer-**[3]*.] — **warʹi•ly** *adv.* — **warʹi•ness** *n.*

was (wŭz, wŏz; wəz *when unstressed*) *v.* First and third pers. sing. p. indic. of **be.** [ME < OE *wæs.* See **wes-**[1]*.]

wa•sa•bi (wäʹsä-bē) *n.* A pungent green Oriental horseradish usu. served as a condiment. [J.]

Wa•satch Range (wôʹsăchʹ). A range of the Rocky Mts. in SE ID and central UT rising to 3,662.4 m (12,008 ft).

wash (wŏsh, wôsh) *v.* **washed, wash•ing, wash•es.** — *tr.* **1.a.** To cleanse, using water or other liquid, usu. with soap, detergent, or bleach, by immersing, dipping, rubbing, or scrubbing. **b.** To soak, rinse out, and remove (dirt or stain) with or as if with water. **2.** To make moist or wet; drench. **3.** To flow over, against, or past. **4.** To carry, erode, remove, or destroy by the action of moving water. **5.** To rid of corruption or guilt; cleanse or purify. **6.** To cover or coat with a watery layer of paint or other coloring substance. **7.** *Chem.* **a.** To purify (a gas) by passing through or over a liquid, as to remove soluble matter. **b.** To pass a solvent through (a precipitate). **8.** To separate constituents of (an ore) by immersion in or agitation with water. **9.** To cause to undergo a swirling action. — *intr.* **1.** To cleanse something in or by means of water or other liquid. **2.a.** To undergo washing without fading or other damage. **b.** *Informal.* To hold up under examination; be convincing. **3.** To flow, sweep, or beat with a characteristic lapping sound. **4.** To be carried away, removed, or drawn by the action of water. — *n.* **1.** The act or process of washing or cleansing. **2.** A quantity of articles washed or intended for washing. **3.** Waste liquid; swill. **4.** Fermented liquid from which liquor is distilled. **5.** A preparation or product used in washing or coating. **6.** A cosmetic or medicinal liquid, such as a mouthwash. **7.a.** A thin layer of water color or India ink spread on a drawing. **b.** A light tint or hue. **8.a.** A rush or surge of water or waves. **b.** The sound of this rush or surge. **9.a.** Removal or erosion of soil by the action of moving water. **b.** A deposit of recently eroded debris. **10.a.** Low or marshy ground washed by tidal waters. **b.** A stretch of shallow water. **11.** *Western U.S.* The dry bed of a stream. **12.** Turbulence in air or water caused by the motion or action of an oar, propeller, jet, or airfoil. **13.** *Informal.* An activity, action, or enterprise that yields neither marked gain nor marked loss. — *adj.* **1.** Used for washing. **2.** Being such that washing is possible; washable. — ***phrasal verbs.*** **wash down. 1.** To clean by washing with water from top to bottom. **2.** To follow the ingestion of (food, for example) with the ingestion of a liquid. **wash out. 1.a.** To remove or be removed by washing. **b.** To cause to fade by laundering. **2.** To carry or wear away or be carried or worn away by the action of moving water. **3.** To deplete or become depleted of vitality. **4.** To eliminate or be eliminated as unsatisfactory. **5.** To cause (an event) to be rained out. **wash up. 1.** To wash one's hands and face. **2.** *Chiefly British.* To wash dishes after a meal. **3.** To bring about the end or ruin of; finish. — ***idioms.*** **come out in the wash.** *Slang.* **1.** To be revealed eventually. **2.** To turn out well in the end. **wash (one's) hands of. 1.** To refuse to accept responsibility for. **2.** To abandon; renounce. [ME *washen* < OE *wacsan, wæscan.* See **wed-**[1]*.]

Wash (wŏsh, wôsh). An inlet of the North Sea off E-central England.

Wash. *abbr.* Washington.

wash•a•ble (wŏsh′ə-bəl, wôsh′-) *adj.* Capable of being washed without injury. — **wash′a•bil′i•ty** *n.*

wash-and-wear (wŏsh′ən-wâr′, wôsh′-) *adj.* Treated so as to be easily or quickly washed or rinsed clean and to require little or no ironing. Used of clothes and linens.

wash•ba•sin (wŏsh′bā′sən, wôsh′-) *n.* See **washbowl.**

wash•board (wŏsh′bôrd′, -bōrd′, wôsh′-) *n.* **1.a.** A board having a corrugated surface on which clothes can be rubbed in the process of laundering. **b.** *Mus.* A similar board used as a percussion instrument. **2.** A board fastened to a wall at the floor; a baseboard. **3.** *Naut.* A thin plank fastened to the side of a boat or the sill of a port to keep out the sea.

wash•bowl (wŏsh′bōl′, wôsh′-) *n.* A basin that can be filled with water for use in washing oneself.

wash•cloth (wŏsh′klôth′, -klŏth′, wôsh′-) *n.* A small, usu. square cloth used for washing the face or body.

wash•day (wŏsh′dā′, wôsh′-) *n.* A day set aside for doing household washing.

wash drawing *n.* A drawing or painting in which washes of color are used.

washed-out (wŏsht′out′, wôsht′-) *adj.* **1.** Lacking color or intensity; faded. **2.** Exhausted or tired-looking. **3.** Having dropped an enterprise or having been dropped from one.

washed-up (wŏsht′ŭp′, wôsht′-) *adj.* **1.** No longer successful or needed; finished. **2.** Ready to give up in disgust.

wash•er (wŏsh′ər, wô′shər) *n.* **1.** One who washes. **2.** An appliance used for washing, esp.: **a.** A washing machine. **b.** An automatic dishwasher. **3.** A flat disk, as of metal, placed beneath a nut or at an axle bearing or a joint to relieve friction, prevent leakage, or distribute pressure.

wash•er•wom•an (wŏsh′ər-wo͝om′ən, wô′shər-) also **wash•wom•an** (wŏsh′wo͝om′ən, wôsh′-) *n.* A woman who washes clothes and linens for a living.

wash•ing (wŏsh′ĭng, wô′shĭng) *n.* **1.** The act or process of one that washes. **2.** Articles washed or intended to be washed at one time. **3.** The residue after an ore or other material has been washed. **4.** The liquid used to wash something. Often used in the plural.

washing machine *n.* A usu. automatic machine for washing clothes and linens.

washing soda *n.* A hydrated sodium carbonate used as a general cleanser.

Wash•ing•ton (wŏsh′ĭng-tən, wô′shĭng-). **1.** A state of the NW U.S. on the Pacific Ocean; admitted as the 42nd state in 1889. Cap. Olympia. Pop. 4,887,941. **2.** The cap. of the U.S., on the Potomac R. between VA and MD and coextensive with the District of Columbia; designated as cap. in 1800. Pop. 609,909. — **Wash′ing•to′ni•an** (wŏsh′ĭng-tō′nē-ən, wô′-shĭng-) *adj. & n.*

Washington, Booker T(aliaferro). 1856–1915. Amer. educator and principal of Tuskegee Institute from 1881 to 1915.

Washington, Bushrod. 1762–1829. Amer. jurist; associate justice of the U.S. Supreme Court (1798–1829).

Washington, George. 1732–99. Amer. military leader and the first President of the U.S. (1789–97).

Washington, Lake. A lake in W-central WA on the E boundary of Seattle.

Washington, Martha Dandridge Custis. 1731–1802. First Lady of the U.S. (1789–97).

Washington, Mount. A mountain, 1,917.8 m (6,288 ft), in the White Mts. of E NH.

Wash•ing•ton's Birthday (wŏsh′ĭng-tənz, wô′shĭng-) *n.* February 22, formerly observed to commemorate the birth of George Washington in 1732.

Wash•i•ta (wŏsh′ĭ-tô′, wô′shĭ-). A river rising in NW TX and flowing c. 724 km (450 mi) across OK to the Red R.

wash•out (wŏsh′out′, wôsh′-) *n.* **1.a.** Erosion of a relatively soft surface by a sudden gush of water, as from a downpour. **b.** A channel thus produced. **2.a.** A total failure or disappointment. **b.** One who fails to measure up to a standard, as by failing a course of training or study.

wash•rag (wŏsh′răg′, wôsh′-) *n.* See **washcloth.**

wash•room (wŏsh′ro͞om′, -ro͝om′, wôsh′-) *n.* A bathroom.

wash•stand (wŏsh′stănd′, wôsh′-) *n.* **1.** A stand designed to hold a basin and pitcher of water for washing. **2.** A stationary bathroom sink.

wash•tub (wŏsh′tŭb′, wôsh′-) *n.* A tub used for washing clothes.

wash•wom•an (wŏsh′wo͝om′ən, wôsh′-) *n.* Var. of **washerwoman.**

wash•y (wŏsh′ē, wô′shē) *adj.* **-i•er, -i•est. 1.** Watery; diluted. **2.** Lacking strength or intensity. — **wash′i•ness** *n.*

was•n't (wŭz′ənt, wŏz′-). Was not.

wasp (wŏsp, wôsp) *n.* Any of numerous social or solitary insects, chiefly of the superfamilies Vespoidea and Sphecoidea, having two pairs of membranous wings, mouths adapted for biting or sucking, and in the females an ovipositor often modified as a sting. [ME *waspe* < OE *wæps, wæsp.*]

Wasp or **WASP** (wŏsp, wôsp) *n.* A white Protestant of Anglo-Saxon ancestry. [*W(hite) A(nglo-Saxon) P(rotestant).*]

wasp•ish (wŏs′pĭsh) *adj.* **1.** Of, relating to, or suggestive of a wasp. **2.** Easily irritated or annoyed; irascible. **3.** Indicative of irritation, annoyance, or spite: *a waspish remark.* — **wasp′ish•ly** *adv.* — **wasp′ish•ness** *n.*

wasp waist *n.* A very slender waist or one that is tightly corseted. — **wasp′-waist′ed** (wŏsp′wās′tĭd, wôsp′-) *adj.*

wasp•y (wŏs′pē) *adj.* **-i•er, -i•est.** Characteristic of a wasp.

was•sail (wŏs′əl, wŏ-sāl′) *n.* **1.a.** A salutation or toast given in drinking someone's health or as an expression of good will. **b.** The drink used in such toasting, commonly ale or wine spiced with roasted apples and sugar. **2.** A festivity characterized by much drinking. — *v.* **-sailed, -sail•ing, -sails.** — *tr.* To drink to the health of; toast. — *intr.* To engage in or drink a wassail. [ME, contraction of *wæshæil*, be healthy < ON *ves heill* : *ves*, imper. sing. of *vera*, to be; see **wes-**[1]* + *heill*, healthy; see **kailo-*.**] — **was′sail•er** *n.*

Was•ser•mann reaction (wä′sər-mən) *n.* A complement-fixing reaction to the Wassermann test.

Wassermann test *n.* A diagnostic test for syphilis involving the fixation or inactivation of a complement by an antibody in a blood serum sample. [After August von *Wassermann* (1866–1925), German bacteriologist.]

wast (wŏst; wəst *when unstressed*) *v. Archaic.* A second pers. sing. p.t. of **be.**

wast•age (wā′stĭj) *n.* **1.** Loss by deterioration, wear, or destruction. **2.** The gradual process of wasting. **3.** An amount that is wasted or lost by wear.

waste (wāst) *v.* **wast•ed, wast•ing, wastes.** — *tr.* **1.** To use, consume, spend, or expend thoughtlessly or carelessly. **2.** To cause to lose energy, strength, or vigor; exhaust, tire, or enfeeble. **3.** To fail to take advantage of or use for profit; lose. **4.a.** To destroy completely. **b.** *Slang.* To kill; murder. — *intr.* **1.** To lose energy, strength, weight, or vigor; become weak or enfeebled: *wasting away.* **2.** To pass without being put to use. — *n.* **1.** The act or an instance of wasting or the condition of being wasted. **2.** A place, region, or land that is uninhabited or uncultivated; a desert or wilderness. **3.** A devastated or destroyed region, town, or building; a ruin. **4.a.** A useless or worthless byproduct, as in manufacturing. **b.** Something, such as steam, that escapes without being used. **5.** Garbage; trash. **6.** The undigested residue of food eliminated from the body; excrement. — *adj.* **1.** Regarded or discarded as worthless or useless. **2.** Used as a conveyance or container for refuse. **3.** Excreted from the body. — ***idiom.* waste (one's) breath.** To gain or accomplish nothing by speaking. [ME *wasten* < ONFr. *waster* < Lat. *vāstāre*, to make empty < *vāstus*, empty. See **eu-**[2]*.]

waste•bas•ket (wāst′băs′kĭt) *n.* An open-topped container for rubbish.

wast•ed (wā′stĭd) *adj.* **1.** Not profitably used or maintained. **2.** Needless or superfluous. **3.** Deteriorated; ravaged. **4.** Frail and enfeebled, as from prolonged illness; emaciated. **5.** *Slang.* Under the influence of a mind-altering drug. **6.** *Archaic.* Having elapsed.

waste•ful (wāst′fəl) *adj.* Marked by or inclined to waste; extravagant. — **waste′ful•ly** *adv.* — **waste′ful•ness** *n.*

waste•land (wāst′lănd′) *n.* **1.** Land that is desolate, barren, or ravaged. **2.** A place, an era, or an aspect of life considered as lacking in spiritual, aesthetic, or other humanizing qualities.

waste•pa•per (wāst′pā′pər) *n.* Discarded paper.

waste pipe *n.* A pipe that carries off liquid waste.

wast•er (wā′stər) *n.* **1.** One that wastes. **2.** One that destroys.

waste•wa•ter (wāst′wô′tər, -wŏt′ər) *n.* Water that has been used, as for washing or flushing or in a manufacturing process, and so contains waste products; sewage.

wast•ing (wā′stĭng) *adj.* **1.** Gradually deteriorating; declining. **2.** Sapping the strength, energy, or substance of the body; emaciating: *a wasting disease.* — **wast′ing•ly** *adv.*

wast•rel (wā′strəl) *n.* **1.** One who wastes, esp. one who wastes money; a profligate. **2.** An idler or a loafer. [WAST(E) + *-rel* (as in SCOUNDREL).]

watch (wŏch) *v.* **watched, watch•ing, watch•es.** — *intr.* **1.** To look or observe attentively or carefully; be closely observant. **2.** To look and wait expectantly or in anticipation. **3.** To act as a spectator; look on. **4.** To stay awake at night while serving as a guard, sentinel, or watcher. **5.** To stay alert as a devotional or religious exercise; keep vigil. — *tr.* **1.** To look at steadily; observe carefully or continuously. **2.** To keep a watchful eye on; guard. **3.** To observe the course of mentally; keep informed about. **4.** To tend (a flock, for example). See Syns at **tend**[2]. — *n.* **1.** The act or process of keeping awake or mentally alert, esp. for the purpose of guarding. **2.a.** The act of observing closely or the condition of being closely observed; surveillance. **b.** A period of close observation. **3.** A person or group of people serving to guard or protect. **4.** The post or period of duty of a guard, sentinel, or watcher. **5.** Any of the periods into which the night is divided; a part of the night. **6.** *Naut.* **a.** Any of the periods of time aboard ship into which the day is divided and during which the crew is assigned to duty. **b.** The members of a ship's crew on duty during a specific watch. **c.** A chronometer on a ship. **7.a.** A period of wakefulness, esp. one observed as a religious vigil. **b.** A funeral wake. **8.** A small portable timepiece, esp. one worn on the wrist or carried in the pocket. **9.** A flock of

George Washington
1795 portrait by Rembrandt Peale

Martha Washington
Early 19th-century portrait by an unknown artist

wasp

wasp waist
c. 1900 photograph of Anna Held

nightingales. — ***phrasal verbs.*** **watch out.** To be careful or on the alert; take care. **watch over.** To be in charge of; superintend. — ***idioms.*** **watch it.** To be careful. **watch (one's) step. 1.** To act or proceed with care and caution. **2.** To behave as is demanded, required, or appropriate. [ME *wacchen* < OE *wæccan*, to watch, be awake. See **weg-***.]

watch•band (wŏch′bănd′) *n.* A band, as of leather, that holds a wristwatch in place.

watch cap *n.* A dark blue knitted cap worn in cold weather, esp. by enlisted naval personnel.

watch•case (wŏch′kās′) *n.* The casing for the mechanism of a watch.

watch•dog (wŏch′dôg′, -dŏg′) *n.* **1.** A dog trained to guard people or property. **2.** A guardian or protector against waste, loss, or illegal practices. —**watch′dog′** *v.*

waterbuck

watch•er (wŏch′ər) *n.* **1.** One that watches or observes. **2.** One who keeps vigil, as at a sick person's bedside.

watch•eye (wŏch′ī′) *n.* Walleye, esp. in dogs.

watch fire *n.* A fire kept burning at night, as for a signal.

watch•ful (wŏch′fəl) *adj.* **1.** Closely observant or alert; vigilant. See Syns at **aware, careful. 2.** *Archaic.* Not sleeping; awake. —**watch′ful•ly** *adv.* —**watch′ful•ness** *n.*

watch glass *n.* **1.** A shallow glass dish used as a beaker cover or an evaporating surface. **2.** A concavo-convex glass or plastic disk used to cover the face of a watch.

watch•mak•er (wŏch′mā′kər) *n.* One that makes or repairs watches.

watch•man (wŏch′mən) *n.* A man who is employed to stand guard or keep watch.

watch night *n.* **1.** New Year's Eve. **2.** A religious service held on New Year's Eve.

watch•tow•er (wŏch′tou′ər) *n.* An observation tower on which a guard or lookout is stationed to keep watch.

watch•word (wŏch′wûrd′) *n.* **1.** A prearranged reply to a challenge, as from a guard; a password. **2.** A rallying cry.

wa•ter (wô′tər, wŏt′ər) *n.* **1.** A clear, colorless, odorless, and tasteless liquid, H_2O, essential for most plant and animal life and the most widely used of all solvents. Freezing point 0°C (32°F); boiling point 100°C (212°F); specific gravity (4°C) 1.0. **2.a.** Any of various forms of water. **b.** Naturally occurring mineral water, as at a spa. Often used in the plural. **3.a.** A body of water such as a sea, lake, river, or stream. **b. waters.** A particular stretch of sea or ocean, esp. that of a state or country. **4.a.** A supply of water. **b.** A water supply system. **5.a.** Any of the liquids present in or passed out of the body, such as urine or saliva. **b.** The fluid surrounding a fetus in the uterus; amniotic fluid. **6.** An aqueous solution of a substance, esp. a gas: *ammonia water.* **7.** A wavy finish or sheen, as of a fabric. **8.a.** The valuation of the assets of a business firm beyond their real value. **b.** Stock issued in excess of paid-in capital. **9.a.** The transparency and luster of a gem. **b.** A level of excellence. — *v.* **-tered, -ter•ing, -ters.** — *tr.* **1.** To pour or sprinkle water on; make wet. **2.a.** To give drinking water to. **b.** To lead (an animal) to drinking water. **3.** To dilute or weaken by adding water. **4.** To give a sheen to the surface of (silk, linen, or metal). **5.** To increase (the number of shares of stock) without increasing the value of the assets represented. **6.** To irrigate (land). — *intr.* **1.** To produce or discharge fluid, as from the eyes. **2.** To salivate in anticipation of food. **3.** To take on a supply of water, as a ship. **4.** To drink water, as an animal. — ***phrasal verb.*** **water down.** To reduce the strength or effectiveness of. — ***idioms.*** **above water.** Out of difficulty or trouble. **water under the bridge.** A past occurrence that cannot be undone or rectified. [ME < OE *wæter.* See **wed-¹***.] —**wa′ter•er** *n.*

water lily

water bag *n.* The membranous sac filled with amniotic fluid that protects a fetus during pregnancy.

water ballet *n.* **1.** Dancelike movement in water; synchronized swimming. **2.** A performance or competition of this.

water bear *n.* See **tardigrade.**

Wa•ter Bearer (wô′tər, wŏt′ər) *n.* See **Aquarius** 1, 2a.

wa•ter•bed (wô′tər-bĕd′, wŏt′ər-) *n.* A bed with a mattress made of a tough plastic that is filled with water.

water beetle *n.* Any of various aquatic beetles, esp. of the family Dytiscidae, having a smooth oval body and flattened and fringed hind legs adapted for swimming.

water polo

water bird *n.* A swimming or wading bird.

water biscuit *n.* A biscuit made of flour and water.

water blister *n.* A blister having watery contents without blood or pus.

water bloom *n.* A growth of algae at or near the surface of a body of water, such as a pond.

water boatman *n.* Any of various aquatic insects of the families Corixidae and Notonectidae, having long oarlike hind legs adapted for swimming.

wa•ter•borne (wô′tər-bôrn′, -bōrn′, wŏt′ər-) *adj.* **1.** Floating on or supported by water; afloat. **2.** Transported by water. **3.** Transmitted in water: *waterborne disease.*

wa•ter•buck (wô′tər-bŭk′, wŏt′ər-) *n., pl.* **waterbuck** or **-bucks.** Any of several African antelopes of the genus *Kobus,* having curved ridged horns and frequenting swamps, rivers, and other bodies of water. [Transl. of Afr. *waterbok.*]

water buffalo *n.* A widely domesticated buffalo *(Bubalus bubalis)* of Asia having large spreading horns.

water bug *n.* **1.** Any of various aquatic insects, esp. the water boatman and certain backswimmers. **2.** A large cockroach.

Wat•er•bury (wô′tər-bĕr′ē, wŏt′ər-) A city of W-central CT NNW of New Haven. Pop. 108,961.

wa•ter•bus (wô′tər-bŭs′, wŏt′ər-) *n., pl.* **-bus•es** or **-bus•ses.** *Naut.* A large motorboat used for carrying passengers on rivers or canals.

water cal•trop (kăl′trəp) *n.* See **water chestnut** 1.

water cannon *n.* A truck-mounted apparatus that fires water at high pressure, used esp. to control crowds.

water chestnut *n.* **1.** A floating aquatic plant *(Trapa natans)* native to Eurasia and Africa and bearing four-pronged nutlike fruit. **2.a.** A tropical Asian aquatic sedge *(Eleocharis dulcis)* having an edible corm and cylindrical leaves. **b.** This corm.

water chinquapin *n.* A North American aquatic plant *(Nelumbo lutea)* related to the lotus and having shield-shaped aerial leaves, pale-yellow flowers, and edible nutlike seeds.

water clock *n.* A clepsydra.

water closet *n.* A room or booth containing a toilet and often a washbowl.

wa•ter•col•or (wô′tər-kŭl′ər, wŏt′ər-) *n.* **1.a.** A paint composed of a water-soluble pigment. **b.** A work that is executed through the use of this paint. **2.** The art of using watercolors. —**wa′ter•col′or** *adj.* —**wa′ter•col′or•ist** *n.*

wa•ter-cool (wô′tər-ko͞ol′, wŏt′ər-) *tr.v.* **-cooled, -cool•ing, -cools.** To cool (an engine) with water, esp. circulating water.

water cooler *n.* A device for cooling and dispensing drinking water.

wa•ter•course (wô′tər-kôrs′, -kōrs′, wŏt′ər-) *n.* **1.** A natural or artificial channel for flowing water. **2.** A stream or river.

wa•ter•craft (wô′tər-krăft′, wŏt′ər-) *n.* **1.** *Sports.* Skill in boating, swimming, or other water-related sports. **2.** *Naut.* **a.** A boat or ship. **b.** Water vehicles considered as a group.

wa•ter•cress (wô′tər-krĕs′, wŏt′ər-) *n.* **1.** A pungent perennial Eurasian herb *(Rorippa nasturtium-aquaticum)* of the mustard family, growing in ponds and streams and often used as a garnish. **2.** Any of several related aquatic plants.

water cure *n.* Hydropathy or hydrotherapy.

water cycle *n.* The cycle that controls the distribution of Earth's water as it evaporates from bodies of water, condenses, precipitates, and returns to those bodies of water.

water dog *n.* **1.** A dog that takes easily to the water, esp. one trained for hunting waterfowl. **2.** *Informal.* A person who feels at home in or on the water. **3.** Often **wa•ter•dog** (wô′tər-dôg′, -dŏg′, wŏt′ər-). See **mud puppy** 1. **4.** *Western U.S.* Any of several large salamanders.

wa•tered-down (wô′tərd-doun′, wŏt′ərd-) *adj.* Diminished in force or effect.

Wa•ter•ee (wô′tə-rē, wŏt′ə-). A river of central SC flowing c. 233 km (145 mi) S to form the Santee R. Its upper course in NC is called the Catawba R.

water elm *n.* See **planer tree.**

wa•ter•fall (wô′tər-fôl′, wŏt′ər-) *n.* A steep descent of water from a height; a cascade.

wa•ter•find•er (wô′tər-fīn′dər, wŏt′ər-) *n.* A dowser.

water flea *n.* Any of various small active aquatic crustaceans of the order Cladocera, esp. the daphnid.

Wa•ter•ford (wô′tər-fərd, wŏt′ər-). **1.** A borough of SE Ireland SSW of Dublin. Pop. 38,473. **2.** A town of SE CT on Long Island Sound; settled c. 1653. Pop. 17,930.

wa•ter•fowl (wô′tər-foul′, wŏt′ər-) *n., pl.* **waterfowl** or **-fowls. 1.** A water bird, esp. a swimming bird. **2.** Swimming game birds, such as ducks and geese, considered as a group.

wa•ter•front (wô′tər-frŭnt′, wŏt′ər-) *n.* **1.** Land abutting a body of water. **2.** The part of a town or city that abuts water, esp. a district of wharves where ships dock.

water gap *n.* A transverse cleft in a mountain ridge through which a stream flows.

water gas *n.* A fuel gas, chiefly carbon monoxide and with some hydrogen, methane, carbon dioxide, and nitrogen, made from coke, air, and steam.

water gate *n.* **1.** See **floodgate** 1. **2.** A gate that provides access to a body of water.

Wa•ter•gate (wô′tĕr-gāt′, wŏt′ər-) *n.* A scandal involving abuse of power by public officials, violation of the public trust, bribery, and attempted obstruction of justice. [After *Watergate,* a building complex in Washington DC, the site of illegal activities (1972).]

water gauge *n.* An instrument indicating the level of water, as in a boiler, tank, reservoir, or stream.

water glass *n.* **1.** A drinking glass or goblet. **2.** An open tube or box having a glass bottom for making observations below the surface of the water. **3.** See **sodium silicate. 4.** A water gauge made of glass. **5.** See **clepsydra.**

water gun *n.* See **squirt gun.**

water hammer *n.* **1.** A banging noise heard in a water pipe following an abrupt alteration of the flow with resultant pressure surges. **2.** A banging noise in steam pipes, caused by steam bubbles entering a cold pipe partially filled with water.

water hemlock *n.* Any of several poisonous perennial herbs of the genus *Cicuta,* esp. *C. maculata* of marshy areas of North America, having bipinnately compound leaves.

water hen *n.* Any of various water birds of the family Rallidae, as the gallinule, rail, or coot, that inhabit marshland.

water hole *n.* **1.** A small natural depression in which water collects, esp. a pool where animals come to drink. **2.** *Informal.* A watering hole.

water hyacinth *n.* An aquatic tropical American herb *(Eichhornia crassipes)* forming dense floating masses and having bluish-purple flowers.

water ice *n.* A dessert made of finely crushed ice that has been sweetened and flavored.

wa•ter•ing can (wô′tər-ĭng, wŏt′ər-) *n.* See **watering pot.**

watering hole *n.* *Informal.* A social gathering place, such as a bar or saloon, where drinks are served.

watering place *n.* **1.** A place where animals find water to drink. **2.** A health resort with mineral springs; a spa. **3.** *Informal.* A watering hole.

watering pot *n.* A vessel, usu. having a long spout with a perforated nozzle, used to water plants.

wa•ter•ish (wô′tər-ĭsh, wŏt′ər-) *adj.* Resembling water; watery.

water jacket *n.* A casing containing water circulated by a pump, used around a part to be cooled, esp. in water-cooled internal-combustion engines. **— wa′ter-jack′et** *v.*

wa•ter•leaf (wô′tər-lēf′, wŏt′ər-) *n., pl.* **-leafs.** Any of various North American herbs of the genus *Hydrophyllum,* having pinnately lobed leaves and white or purplish flowers.

wa•ter•less (wô′tər-lĭs, wŏt′ər-) *adj.* **1.** Lacking water; dry. **2.** Not requiring water, as a cooling system.

water level *n.* **1.** The level of the surface of a body of water. **2.** *Geol.* See **water table** 2. **3.** The water line of a ship.

water lily *n.* Any of various cosmopolitan aquatic herbs of the genus *Nymphaea,* having floating leaves and showy, variously colored flowers, esp. *N. odorata.*

water line *n.* **1.** *Naut.* **a.** The line on the hull of a ship to which the surface of the water rises. **b.** Any of several lines parallel to this line, marked on the hull of a ship to indicate the depth at which the ship is submerged under various loads. **2.** A line or stain, as one left on a sea wall, indicating the height to which water has risen or may rise; a watermark.

wa•ter•log (wô′tər-lôg′, -lŏg′, wŏt′ər-) *tr.v.* **-logged, -log•ging, -logs. 1.** To make (a boat, for example) heavy and unwieldy by flooding with water. **2.** To saturate with water and make soggy or unusable. [Back-formation < WATERLOGGED.]

wa•ter•logged (wô′tər-lôgd′, -lŏgd′, wŏt′ər-) *adj.* **1.** *Naut.* Heavy and sluggish in the water because of flooding, as in the hold. **2.** Soaked or saturated with water. [WATER + LOGGED, p.part. of LOG[1], to accumulate in a ship: used of water.]

wa•ter•loo (wô′tər-lo͞o′, wŏt′ər-, wô′tər-lo͞o′, wŏt′ər-) *n., pl.* **-loos.** A final, crushing defeat. [After WATERLOO, Belgium.]

Wa•ter•loo (wô′tər-lo͞o′, wŏt′ər-, wô′tər-lo͞o′, wŏt′ər-). **1.** A town of central Belgium near Brussels; site of Napoleon's final defeat (Jun. 18, 1815). **2.** A city of SE Ontario, Canada, a suburb of Kitchener. Pop. 24,933. **3.** A city of NE IA NW of Cedar Rapids; first settled in 1845. Pop. 66,467.

wa•ter•man (wô′tər-mən, wŏt′ər-) *n.* A boatman.

wa•ter•mark (wô′tər-märk′, wŏt′ər-) *n.* **1.a.** A mark showing the greatest height to which water has risen. **b.** A line showing the heights of high and low tide. **2.a.** A translucent design impressed on paper during manufacture and visible when the paper is held to the light. **b.** The metal pattern that produces this design. *— tr.v.* **-marked, -mark•ing, -marks. 1.** To mark (paper) with a watermark. **2.** To impress (a design) as a watermark.

wa•ter•mel•on (wô′tər-mĕl′ən, wŏt′ər-) *n.* **1.** An African vine *(Citrullus lanatus)* cultivated for its large edible fruit. **2.** The fruit of this plant, having a hard green rind and sweet watery pink or reddish flesh.

water milfoil *n.* Any of various aquatic herbs of the genus *Myriophyllum,* having finely dissected submersed leaves and entire or toothed emersed leaves.

water mill *n.* A mill with machinery that is driven by water.

water moccasin *n.* **1.** A semiaquatic pit viper *(Agkistrodon piscivorus)* of the southern United States. **2.** Any of various similar but harmless water snakes.

water mold *n.* Any of various parasitic or saprobic fungi of the phylum Oomycota, living chiefly in fresh water or moist soil.

water nymph *n.* *Myth.* A nymph, such as a naiad or Nereid, living in or near water.

water oak *n.* Any of various oak trees that grow in wetlands, esp. *Quercus nigra* of eastern North America.

water of crystallization *n.* Water in chemical combination with a crystal, capable of being removed by sufficient heat.

water of hydration *n.* Water combined with a substance in such a way that it can be removed without substantially changing the chemical composition of the substance.

water ouzel *n.* See **dipper** 2.

water parting *n.* See **watershed** 1.

water pepper *n.* A North American perennial herb *(Polygonum hydropiperoides)* of marshes and bogs, having reddish stems, small greenish flowers, and acrid-tasting leaves.

water pipe *n.* **1.** A pipe that is a conduit for water. **2.** An apparatus for smoking in which the smoke is drawn through a container of water or ice and cooled before inhaling.

water pistol *n.* See **squirt gun.**

water plantain *n.* Any of various aquatic herbs of the genus *Alisma,* having small three-petaled white or pinkish flowers.

water polo *n.* *Sports.* A water sport with two teams of swimmers each of which tries to pass a ball into the other's goal.

wa•ter•pow•er (wô′tər-pou′ər, wŏt′ər-) *n.* **1.a.** The energy produced by running or falling water that is used for driving machinery, esp. for generating electricity. **b.** A source of such energy, as a waterfall. **2.** A water right owned by a mill.

wa•ter•proof (wô′tər-pro͞of′, wŏt′ər-) *adj.* **1.** Impervious to or unaffected by water. **2.** Made of or coated or treated with rubber, plastic, or a sealing agent to prevent penetration by water. *— n.* **1.** A material or fabric impervious to water. **2.** *Chiefly British.* A raincoat or other such garment. *— tr.v.* **-proofed, -proof•ing, -proofs.** To make impervious to water.

water rat *n.* **1.a.** Any of various semiaquatic rodents, esp. *Neofiber alleni* of Florida and southern Georgia, closely related to and resembling the muskrat. **b.** See **muskrat** 1. **2.** *Slang.* A petty thief or ruffian who frequents waterfronts.

wa•ter-re•pel•lent (wô′tər-rĭ-pĕl′ənt, wŏt′ər-) *adj.* Resistant to penetration by water but not entirely waterproof.

wa•ter-re•sis•tant (wô′tər-rĭ-zĭs′tənt, wŏt′ər-) *adj.* Water-repellent.

water right *n.* **1.** The right to draw water from a particular source, such as a lake, a canal, or a stream. Often used in the plural. **2.** *Naut.* The right to navigate on particular waters.

Wa•ters (wô′tərz, wŏt′ərz), **Ethel.** 1896–1977. Amer. actress and singer who appeared on Broadway and in films such as *The Sound and the Fury* (1959).

water sapphire *n.* A clear blue cordierite often used as a gemstone.

wa•ter•scape (wô′tər-skāp′, wŏt′ər-) *n.* A seascape.

water scorpion *n.* Any of various aquatic insects of the family Nepidae, having a large breathing tube projecting from the posterior part of the abdomen and inflicting a painful sting.

wa•ter•shed (wô′tər-shĕd′, wŏt′ər-) *n.* **1.** A ridge of high land dividing two areas that are drained by different river systems. **2.** The region draining into a river, river system, or other body of water. **3.** A critical point that marks a division or a change of course; a turning point. [Prob. transl. of Ger. *Wasserscheide* : *Wasser,* water + *Scheide,* divide, parting.]

water shield *n.* **1.** A cosmopolitan aquatic herb *(Brasenia schreberi)* having floating elliptic or ovate leaves and purplish flowers. **2.** Any of several New World aquatic herbs of the genus *Cabomba,* having alternate floating leaves and finely divided opposite or whorled submersed leaves.

wa•ter-sick (wô′tər-sĭk′, wŏt′ər-) *adj.* Unproductive because of excessive irrigation: *water-sick soil.*

wa•ter•side (wô′tər-sīd′, wŏt′ər-) *n.* Land bordering a body of water; a bank or shore. *— adj.* **1.** Of or situated at the waterside. **2.** Living or working along the waterside.

water ski *n.* *Sports.* A broad ski used for skiing on water.

wa•ter-ski (wô′tər-skē′, wŏt′ər-) *intr.v.* **-skied, -ski•ing, -skis.** *Sports.* To ski on water while being towed by a motorboat. **— wa′ter-ski′er** *n.* **— wa′ter-ski′ing** *n.*

water snake *n.* **1.** Any of various nonvenomous snakes of the genus *Natrix,* living in or frequenting freshwater streams and ponds. **2.** Any of various aquatic or semiaquatic snakes.

water spaniel *n.* A large spaniel having a curly water-resistant coat, often used in hunting to retrieve waterfowl.

wa•ter•spout (wô′tər-spout′, wŏt′ər-) *n.* **1.** A tornado or lesser whirlwind occurring over water. **2.** A hole or pipe from which water is discharged.

water sprite *n.* A sprite or nymph that inhabits or haunts a body of water.

water strider *n.* Any of various insects of the family Gerridae, having long slender legs to support themselves on water.

water supply *n.* **1.** The water available for a community or region. **2.** The source and delivery system of such water.

water system *n.* **1.** A river and all its tributaries. **2.** A water supply.

water table *n.* **1.** A projecting ledge, molding, or stringcourse along the side of a building, designed to divert rainwater. **2.** The level below which the ground is completely saturated with water.

water thrush *n.* Either of two New World warblers *(Seiurus noveboracensis* or *S. motacilla)* living near streams and ponds.

wa•ter•tight (wô′tər-tīt′, wŏt′ər-) *adj.* **1.** Made so that water cannot enter or escape. **2.** Having no flaws or loopholes; impossible to fault, refute, or evade.

water tower *n.* **1.** A standpipe or elevated tank used as a reservoir or for keeping equal pressure in a water system. **2.** A firefighting apparatus for lifting hoses to high levels.

Wa•ter•town (wô′tər-toun′, wŏt′ər-). **1.** A town of W CT near Waterbury. Pop. 20,456. **2.** A town of E MA, a suburb of Boston. Pop. 33,284. **3.** A city of N NY N of Syracuse; settled c. 1800. Pop. 29,429. **4.** A city of SE WI ENE of Madison. Pop. 19,142.

water turkey *n.* See **anhinga.**

water spaniel
Irish water spaniel

water tower

ă pat	oi boy
ā pay	ou out
âr care	o͝o took
ä father	o͞o boot
ĕ pet	ŭ cut
ē be	ûr urge
ĭ pit	th thin
ī pie	*th* this
îr pier	hw which
ŏ pot	zh vision
ō toe	ə about, item
ô paw	

Stress marks:
′ (primary);
′ (secondary), as in
dictionary (dĭk′shə-nĕr′ē)

water vapor *n.* Water in a gaseous state, esp. diffused in the atmosphere and at a temperature below boiling point.

wa•ter-vas•cu•lar system (wô′tər-văs′kyə-lər, wŏt′ər-) *n.* A system of water-filled canals derived from the coelom that connects the tube feet of echinoderms.

Wa•ter•ville (wô′tər-vĭl′, wŏt′ər-). A city of S ME N of Augusta; settled in 1754. Pop. 17,173.

wa•ter•way (wô′tər-wā′, wŏt′ər-) *n. Naut.* **1.** A navigable body of water, such as a river, channel, or canal. **2.** A channel at the edge of a ship's deck to drain away water.

wa•ter•weed (wô′tər-wēd′, wŏt′ər-) *n.* Any of various submersed aquatic herbs of the genus *Elodea,* native to the New World and having narrow leaves and small axillary flowers.

water wheel *n.* **1.** A wheel propelled by falling or running water and used to power machinery. **2.** A wheel with buckets attached to its rim for raising water.

water wings *pl.n.* A pair of joined inflatable waterproof bags that fit under the arms to provide buoyancy.

water witch *n.* One who claims to be able to find underground water by means of a divining rod; a dowser.

wa•ter•works (wô′tər-wûrks′, wŏt′ər-) *pl.n.* **1.a.** *(used with a sing. or pl. v.)* The water system, including reservoirs, pumps, and pipes, that supplies water to a municipality. **b.** *(used with a sing. v.)* A single unit, such as a pumping station, within such a system. **2.** *(used with a sing. v.)* An exhibition of moving water, such as a fountain.

wa•ter•y (wô′tə-rē, wŏt′ə-) *adj.* **-i•er, -i•est. 1.** Filled with, consisting of, or soaked with water; wet or soggy: *watery soil.* **2.** Containing too much water; diluted: *watery soup.* **3.** Suggestive of water, as in being thin, pale, or liquid: *watery sunshine.* **4.** Lacking force or substance; weak or insipid: *watery prose.* **5.** Secreting or discharging water or watery fluid, esp. as a symptom of disease. —**wa′ter•i•ness** *n.*

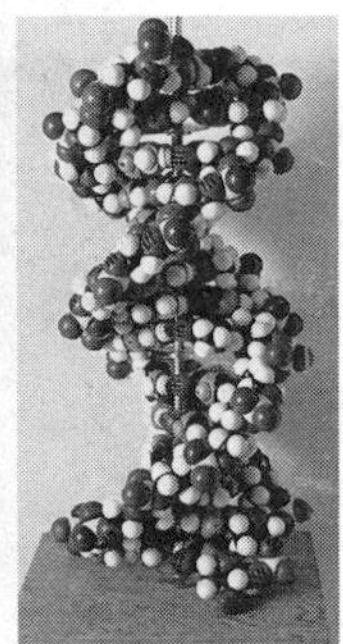

Watson-Crick model

Wat•lings Island (wät′lĭngz). See **San Salvador**[1].

WATS *abbr.* Wide-Area Telecommunications Service.

Wat•son (wŏt′sən), **James Dewey.** b. 1928. Amer. biologist who with Francis Crick proposed the double helix for the molecular structure of DNA and shared a 1962 Nobel Prize.

Wat•son-Crick model (wät′sən-krĭk′) *n.* A three-dimensional model of the DNA molecule, consisting of two polynucleotide strands wound in the form of a double helix and joined in a ladderlike fashion by hydrogen bonds between the purine and pyrimidine bases. [After James WATSON and Francis CRICK.]

Wat•son•ville (wŏt′sən-vĭl′). A city of W CA ESE of Santa Cruz; founded 1852. Pop. 31,099.

watt (wŏt) *n. Elect.* An International System unit of power equal to one joule per second. See table at **measurement.** [After James WATT.]

Watt (wŏt), **James.** 1736–1819. British engineer and inventor who made fundamental improvements in the steam engine.

watt•age (wŏt′ĭj) *n.* **1.** An amount of power, esp. electric power, expressed in watts or kilowatts. **2.** The electric power required by an appliance or a device.

wattle

Wat•teau (wŏ-tō′, vä-), **Jean Antoine.** 1684–1721. French painter noted for his scenes of festive gatherings.

watt-hour (wŏt′our′) *n.* A unit of energy, esp. electrical energy, equal to the work done by one watt acting for one hour and equivalent to 3,600 joules.

wat•tle (wŏt′l) *n.* **1.a.** A construction of poles intertwined with twigs, reeds, or branches, used for walls, fences, and roofs. **b.** Material used for such construction. **2.** A fleshy, wrinkled, often brightly colored fold of skin hanging from the neck or throat, characteristic of certain birds, such as chickens or turkeys, and some lizards. **3.** *Bot.* Any of various Australian trees or shrubs of the genus *Acacia.* —*tr.v.* **-tled, -tling, -tles. 1.** To construct from wattle. **2.** To weave into wattle. [ME *wattel* < OE *watel,* hurdle.] —**wat′tled** *adj.*

wattle and daub *n.* An interweaving of rods and twigs overlaid with clay and used as a building material.

wat•tle•bird (wŏt′l-bûrd′) *n.* Any of several honeyeaters of the genus *Anthochaera,* having wattles on either side.

watt•me•ter (wŏt′mē′tər) *n.* An instrument for measuring in watts the power flowing in a circuit.

Evelyn Waugh
Photographed in the 1950's

Watts (wŏts). A district of Los Angeles, CA; site of severe racial tensions and violence in 1965.

Watts, Isaac. 1674–1748. English poet and theologian whose poems include *The Psalms of David Imitated* (1719).

Waugh (wô), **Evelyn (Arthur Saint John).** 1903–66. British writer whose satirical novels include *Decline and Fall* (1928).

Wau•ke•gan (wô-kē′gən). A city of NE IL on Lake Michigan N of Chicago. Pop. 69,392.

Wau•ke•sha (wô′kə-shô′). A city of SE WI W of Milwaukee. Pop. 56,958.

Wau•sau (wô′sô′). A city of N-central WI WNW of Green Bay; settled in 1839. Pop. 37,060.

Wau•wa•to•sa (wô′wə-tō′sə). A city of SE WI, a suburb of Milwaukee. Pop. 49,366.

wave (wāv) *v.* **waved, wav•ing, waves.** —*intr.* **1.** To move freely back and forth or up and down in the air, as branches in the wind. **2.** To make a signal with an up-and-down or back-and-forth hand movement or hand-held object. **3.** To have an undulating or wavy form; curve or curl. —*tr.* **1.** To cause to move back and forth or up and down, either once or repeatedly. **2.a.** To move or swing as in giving a signal: *He waved his hand.* See Syns at **flourish. b.** To signal or express by waving. **c.** To signal (a person) to move in a specified direction. **3.** To arrange into curves, curls, or undulations. —*n.* **1.a.** A ridge or swell moving through or along the surface of a large body of water. **b.** A small ridge or swell moving across the interface of two fluids and dependent on surface tension. **2.** The sea. Often used in the plural. **3.** Something that suggests the form and motion of a wave in the sea, esp.: **a.** A moving curve or succession of curves in or on a surface; an undulation. **b.** A curve or succession of curves, as in the hair. **c.** A curved shape, outline, or pattern. **4.** A movement up and down or back and forth. **5.a.** A surge or rush, as of sensation. **b.** A sudden great rise, as in activity or intensity. **c.** A rising trend that involves large numbers of individuals. **d.** One of a succession of mass movements: *the first wave of settlers.* **e.** A maneuver in which fans at a sports event simulate an ocean wave by rising quickly in sequence with arms upraised and then quickly sitting down again in a continuous rolling motion. **6.** A widespread persistent meteorological condition, esp. of temperature: *a heat wave.* **7.** *Phys.* **a.** A disturbance traveling through a medium by which energy is transferred from one particle of the medium to another without causing any permanent displacement of the medium itself. **b.** A graphic representation of the variation of such a disturbance with time. **c.** A single cycle of such a disturbance. [ME *waven* < OE *wafian.* See **webh-*.**] —**wav′er** *n.*

wave•band (wāv′bănd′) *n.* A range of frequencies, esp. radio frequencies, such as those assigned to broadcasting.

wave equation *n.* **1.** A partial differential equation used to represent wave motion. **2.** The fundamental equation of wave mechanics.

wave•form (wāv′fôrm′) *n.* The mathematical representation of a wave, esp. a graph obtained by plotting a characteristic of the wave against time.

wave front *n.* The continuous line or surface including all the points in space reached by a wave or vibration at the same instant as it travels through a medium.

wave function *n.* A mathematical function used in quantum mechanics to describe the propagation of the wave associated with any particle or group of particles.

wave-guide (wāv′gīd′) *n.* A solid dielectric rod or dielectric-filled tubular conductor capable of guiding high-frequency electromagnetic waves.

wave•length (wāv′lĕngkth′, -lĕngth′) *n.* The distance between one peak or crest of a wave and the next corresponding peak or crest. —***idiom.* on the same wavelength.** *Informal.* In complete accord.

wave•let (wāv′lĭt) *n.* A small wave; a ripple.

Wa•vell (wā′vəl), **Archibald Percival.** 1st Earl Wavell. 1883–1950. British field marshal in North Africa (1940–41) and viceroy of India (1943–47).

wave mechanics *n. (used with a sing. or pl. v.)* A theory that ascribes characteristics of waves to subatomic particles and attempts to interpret physical phenomena on this basis.

wave number *n.* The reciprocal of the wavelength of a wave.

wa•ver (wā′vər) *intr.v.* **-vered, -ver•ing, -vers. 1.** To move unsteadily back and forth. **2.a.** To exhibit irresolution or indecision; vacillate. **b.** To become unsteady or unsure; falter. **3.** To tremble or quaver in sound, as of the voice. **4.** To flicker or glimmer, as light. —*n.* The act of wavering. [ME *waveren.* See **webh-*.**] —**wa′ver•er** *n.*

wave train *n. Phys.* A succession of similar wave pulses.

wav•y (wā′vē) *adj.* **-i•er, -i•est. 1.** Abounding or rising in waves: *a wavy sea.* **2.** Marked by or moving in a wavelike form or motion; sinuous. **3.** Having curls, curves, or undulations: *wavy hair.* **4.** Characteristic or suggestive of waves. **5.** Wavering; unstable. —**wav′i•ly** *adv.* —**wav′i•ness** *n.*

waw (väv, vôv) *n.* Var. of **vav.**

wa-wa (wä′wä′) *n. Mus.* Var. of **wah-wah.**

wax[1] (wăks) *n.* **1.a.** Any of various natural, oily or greasy heat-sensitive substances, consisting of hydrocarbons or esters of fatty acids. **b.** Beeswax. **c.** Cerumen. **2.a.** A plastic solid or semisolid, such as paraffin, originating from petroleum and used in coatings, as insulation, and in crayons. **b.** A preparation containing wax used for polishing floors and other surfaces. **3.** A resinous mixture used by shoemakers to rub on thread. **4.** A phonograph record. **5.** Something suggestive of wax in being impressionable or readily molded. —*adj.* Made of wax. —*tr.v.* **waxed, wax•ing, wax•es. 1.** To coat, treat, or polish with wax. **2.** *Informal.* To make a phonograph record of. [ME < OE *weax.*]

wax[2] (wăks) *intr.v.* **waxed, wax•ing, wax•es. 1.** To increase gradually in size, number, strength, or intensity. **2.** To show a progressively larger illuminated area, as the moon does in passing from new to full. **3.** To grow or become as specified: *waxed poetic.* [ME *waxen* < OE *weaxan.* See **aug-*.**]

wax bean *n.* A variety of string bean having yellow pods. Also called regionally *butter bean.*

wax•ber•ry (wăks′bĕr′ē) *n.* The waxy fruit of the wax myrtle or the snowberry.

wax•bill (wăks′bĭl′) *n.* Any of various tropical Old World birds of the genus *Estrilda* and related genera, having a short, often brightly colored waxy beak.

waxed paper (wăkst) *n.* Wax paper.

wax•en (wăk′sən) *adj.* **1.** Made of or covered with wax. **2.** Pale or smooth as wax: *waxen skin.* **3.** Weak, pliable, or impressionable.

wax•er (wăk′sər) *n.* One that polishes with or applies wax.

wax insect *n.* Any of various scale insects that secrete a waxy substance, esp. a Chinese species *(Ericerus pe-la)* bred commercially for the production of candles.

wax moth *n.* See **bee moth.**

wax museum *n.* A place where life-size wax figures, usu. of famous people, are exhibited.

wax myrtle *n.* An evergreen shrub *(Myrica cerifera)* of the southeast United States having usu. serrate leaves and small berrylike fruit with a waxy coating.

wax palm *n.* Any of several palm trees that yield wax, as *Copernica prunifera,* the source of carnauba wax, or *Ceroxylon alpinum* of South America.

wax paper *n.* Paper that has been made moistureproof by treatment with wax, used esp. in cooking and in food storage.

wax•wing (wăks′wĭng′) *n.* Any of several birds of the genus *Bombycilla,* having crested heads, grayish-brown plumage, and waxy red tips on the wing feathers.

wax•work (wăks′wûrk′) *n.* **1.** The art of modeling in wax. **2.** A figure made of wax, esp. a life-size wax effigy of a famous person. **3. waxworks.** *(used with a sing. or pl. v.)* An exhibition of wax figures in a museum.

wax•y (wăk′sē) *adj.* **-i•er, -i•est. 1.** Resembling wax, esp.: **a.** Pale. **b.** Smooth and lustrous. **c.** Pliable or impressionable. **2.** Consisting of, abounding in, or covered with wax. **3.** *Pathol.* Containing amyloid deposits, as an organ.

way (wā) *n.* **1.a.** A road, path, or highway affording passage from one place to another. **b.** An opening affording passage: *the only way into the attic.* **2.a.** Space to proceed. **b.** Opportunity to advance: *the way to peace.* **3.** A course that is or may be used in going from one place to another: *the shortest way home.* **4.** Progress or travel along a certain route or in a specific direction. **5.** A course of conduct or action. **6.** A manner or method of doing: *no way to reach her.* **7.** A usual or habitual manner or mode of being, living, or acting. **8.** An individual or personal manner of behaving, acting, or doing. **9.** Also **ways** (wāz). *(used with a sing. v.) Informal.* Distance: *a long way.* **10.a.** A specific direction: *He glanced my way.* **b.** A participant. Often used in combination: *a three-way conversation.* **11.a.** An aspect, particular, or feature: *in no way comparable.* **b.** Nature or category: *not much in the way of a plot.* **12.** Freedom to do as one wishes. **13.** An aptitude or a facility: *a way with words.* **14.** A state or condition. **15.** Vicinity. **16.** A longitudinal strip on a surface that serves to guide a moving machine part. Often used in the plural. **17. ways.** *(used with a sing. or pl. v.) Naut.* The timbered structure on which a ship is built and from which it slides when launched. **18.** *Naut.* Motion through the water: *The ship had too much way on.* —*adv. Informal.* **1.** By a great distance or to a great degree; far. **2.** From this place; away: *Go way.* —***idioms.*** **by way of. 1.** Through; via. **2.** As a means of. **go out of one's (or the) way.** To inconvenience oneself in doing something beyond what is required. **in a way. 1.** To a certain extent; with reservations. **2.** From one point of view. **in the way.** In a position to obstruct, hinder, or interfere. **on one's (or the) way.** In the process of coming, going, or traveling. **on the way.** On the route of a journey. **out of the way. 1.** In such a position as not to obstruct, hinder, or interfere. **2.** Taken care of; disposed of. **3.** In a remote location. **4.** Of an unusual character; remarkable. **5.** Improper; amiss. [ME < OE *weg.* See **wegh-***.]

Syns: *way, route, course, passage, pass, artery.* These nouns refer to paths leading or going from one place or point to another. *Way* is the least specific: *"Many ways meet in one town"* (Shakespeare). *Route* refers to a planned, well-established, or regularly traveled way: *"Their one purpose of speed over the great ocean routes was achieved by perfect balance of spars and sails to the curving lines of the smooth black hull"* (Samuel Eliot Morison). *Course* suggests the path or channel taken by something that moves: *"earth's diurnal course"* (William Wordsworth). *Passage* denotes a traversal over, across, or through something: *The yacht continued its passage with favorable winds. Pass* usually refers to a way affording passage around, over, or through a barrier: *"They had reached one of those very narrow passes between two tall stones"* (George Eliot). An *artery* is a main route for the circulation of traffic: *The central artery is closed for extensive repairs.* See also Syns at **method.**

Usage Note: In American English *ways* is often used as an equivalent of *way* in phrases such as *a long ways to go.* The usage is not incorrect but is widely regarded as informal.

way•bill (wā′bĭl′) *n.* A document giving details and instructions relating to a shipment of goods.

Way•cross (wā′krôs′, -krŏs′). A city of SE GA SW of Savannah. Pop. 16,410.

way•far•er (wā′fâr′ər) *n.* One who travels, esp. on foot. [ME *weifarere* : *wei,* way; see WAY + *faren,* to go on a journey (< OE *faran*; see **per-[2]***).]

way•far•ing (wā′fâr′ĭng) *n.* Traveling, esp. on foot. [< ME *waifaringe,* journeying < OE *wegfarende* : *weg,* way; see WAY + *farende,* pr.part. of *faran,* to go on a journey; see **per-[2]***.] —**way′far′ing** *adj.*

way•lay (wā′lā′) *tr.v.* **-laid** (-lād′), **-lay•ing, -lays. 1.** To lie in wait for and attack from ambush. **2.** To accost or intercept unexpectedly. —**way′lay′er** *n.*

Wayne (wān). **1.** A city of SE MI, a suburb of Detroit. Pop. 19,899. **2.** A town of N NJ W of Paterson. Pop. 47,025.

Wayne, Anthony. "Mad Anthony." 1745–96. Amer. Revolutionary general at Brandywine (1777) and Monmouth (1778).

Wayne, James Moore. 1790–1867. Amer. jurist; associate justice of the U.S. Supreme Court (1835–67).

Wayne, John. 1907–79. Amer. film actor who played tough heroes in Westerns such as *Red River* (1948).

John Wayne

way-out (wā′out′) *adj. Slang.* Very unconventional, unusual, or strange.

way•point (wā′point′) *n.* A point between major points on a route, as along a track.

ways (wāz) *n. (used with a sing. v.) Informal.* Var. of **way** 9. See Usage Note at **way.**

-ways *suff.* In a specified way, manner, direction, or position: *sideways.* [ME < *weies, wais,* in such a way < OE *weges* : *weg,* way; see WAY + *-es,* gen. sing. suff.; see -s[3].]

ways and means *pl.n.* **1.** Methods and resources available to accomplish an end, esp. to meet expenses. **2.** Methods and means, esp. legislation, for raising government revenue.

way•side (wā′sīd′) *n.* The side or edge of a road, way, path, or highway. —*adj.* Situated at or near a wayside. —***idioms.*** **fall by the wayside.** To fail to continue; give up. **go by the wayside.** To be set aside or discarded because of other considerations.

way station *n.* A station between principal stations on a route.

way•ward (wā′wərd) *adj.* **1.** Given to or marked by willful, often perverse deviation from what is desired, expected, or required in order to gratify one's own impulses or inclinations. See Syns at **unruly. 2.** Swayed or prompted by caprice; unpredictable. [ME, short for *awaiward,* turned away, perverse : *awai,* away; see AWAY + *-ward,* -ward.] —**way′ward•ly** *adv.* —**way′ward•ness** *n.*

way•worn (wā′wôrn′, -wōrn′) *adj.* Wearied by traveling.

Wa•zir•i•stan (wə-zîr′ĭ-stăn′, -stän′). A mountainous region of NW Pakistan on the Afghanistan border, divided into **North Waziristan** and **South Waziristan.**

Wb *abbr. Phys.* Weber.

w.b. *abbr.* **1.** Water ballast. **2.** Also **W.B.** Waybill. **3.** Westbound.

W.B. *abbr.* Weather bureau.

WBC *abbr.* White blood cell.

WbN *abbr.* West by north.

WbS *abbr.* West by south.

W.C. *abbr.* **1.** Water closet. **2.** Without charge.

WCTU also **W.C.T.U.** *abbr.* Woman's Christian Temperance Union.

WD also **W.D.** *abbr.* War Department.

wd. *abbr.* **1.** Wood. **2.** Word.

we (wē) *pron.* **1.** Used by the speaker or writer to indicate the speaker or writer along with another or others as the subject: *We made it on time.* **2.** Used instead of *I,* esp. by a sovereign or by a writer wishing to maintain an impersonal tone. **3.** Used to refer to people in general, including the speaker or writer. **4.** Used instead of *you* in direct address, esp. to imply a patronizing camaraderie with the addressee: *How are we feeling today?* [ME < OE *wē.* See **we-***.]

Usage Note: When the pronoun is followed by an appositive noun phrase, the form *us* is frequently encountered where grammatical correctness would require *we,* as in *Us owners* (properly *We owners*) *will have something to say.* Less frequently, *we* is substituted for *us,* as in *For we students, it's a no-win situation.* Both usages should be avoided. See Usage Notes at **be, I[1].**

weak (wēk) *adj.* **weak•er, weak•est. 1.** Lacking physical strength, energy, or vigor; feeble. **2.** Likely to fail under pressure, stress, or strain; lacking resistance: *a weak link in a chain.* **3.** Lacking firmness of character or strength of will. **4.** Lacking the proper strength or amount of ingredients. **5.** Lacking the ability to function normally or fully: *a weak heart.* **6.** Lacking aptitude or skill. **7.** Lacking or resulting from a lack of intelligence. **8.** Lacking persuasiveness; unconvincing. **9.** Lacking authority or the power to govern. **10.** Lacking potency or intensity: *weak sunlight.* **11.** *Ling.* **a.** Of, relating to, or being those verbs in Germanic languages that form a past tense and past participle by means of a dental suffix, as *start, started.* **b.** Of, relating to, or being the inflection of nouns or adjectives in Germanic languages with a declensional suffix that historically contained an *n.* **12.** Unstressed or unaccented in pronunciation or poetic meter. Used of a word or syllable. **13.** Being a verse ending in which the metrical stress falls on a word or syllable that is unstressed in

ă pat	oi boy
ā pay	ou out
âr care	o͝o took
ä father	o͞o boot
ĕ pet	ŭ cut
ē be	ûr urge
ĭ pit	th thin
ī pie	*th* this
îr pier	hw which
ŏ pot	zh vision
ō toe	ə about, item
ô paw	

Stress marks:
′ (primary);
′ (secondary), as in
dictionary (dĭk′shə-nĕr′ē)

normal speech, such as a preposition. **14.** Tending downward in price. [ME *weike* < ON *veikr*, pliant. See **weik-**[2]***.**]

weak·en (wē′kən) *tr. & intr.v.* **-ened, -en·ing, -ens.** To make or become weak or weaker. **—weak′en·er** *n.*

weak·fish (wēk′fĭsh′) *n., pl.* **weakfish** or **-fish·es.** A marine food and game fish *(Cynoscion regalis)* of North American Atlantic waters. [Obsolete Du. *weekvis* : *week*, soft (< MDu. *weec*; see **weik-**[2]***) + Du. *vis*, fish (< MDu.).]

weak interaction *n.* A fundamental interaction between elementary particles that is several orders of magnitude weaker than the electromagnetic interaction and is responsible for nuclear beta decay and neutrino interaction.

weak-kneed (wēk′nēd′) *adj.* Lacking strength of character or purpose.

weasel

weak·ling (wēk′lĭng) *n.* One of weak constitution or character: *a weakling in enforcing discipline.*

weak·ly (wēk′lē) *adj.* **-li·er, -li·est.** Delicate in constitution; frail or sickly. *—adv.* **1.** With little physical strength or force. **2.** With little strength of character. **—weak′li·ness** *n.*

weak-mind·ed (wēk′mīn′dĭd) *adj.* **1.** Having or exhibiting a lack of judgment or conviction. **2.** Foolish; silly. **3.** *Offensive.* Of less than normal intellect. **—weak′-mind′ed·ness** *n.*

weak·ness (wēk′nĭs) *n.* **1.** The condition or quality of being weak. **2.** A personal defect or failing. **3.a.** A special fondness or inclination: *has a weakness for fast cars.* **b.** Something of which one is excessively fond or desirous.

weak·on (wē′kŏn′) *n.* Either of two bosons, the W particle or the Z particle, that are quanta of the weak interaction. See table at **subatomic particle.**

weak sister *n. Slang.* **1.** A weak or undependable member of a group. **2.** A person regarded as timid or indecisive.

weathering

weal[1] (wēl) *n.* **1.** Prosperity; happiness: *in weal and woe.* **2.** The welfare of the community; the general good: *the public weal.* [ME *wele* < OE *wela.* See **wel-**[1]***.**]

weal[2] (wēl) *n.* A ridge on the flesh raised by a blow; a welt. [Alteration (influenced by WHEAL) of WALE.]

weald (wēld) *n. Chiefly British.* **1.** A woodland. **2.** An area of open rolling upland. [< *Weald*, a once-forested area in SE England < OE *wald, weald*, forest.]

wealth (wĕlth) *n.* **1.a.** An abundance of valuable material possessions or resources; riches. **b.** The state of being rich; affluence. **2.** All goods and resources having value in terms of exchange or use. **3.** A great amount; a profusion: *a wealth of advice.* [ME *welthe* < *wele* < OE *wela.* See **wel-**[1]***.**]

wealth·y (wĕl′thē) *adj.* **-i·er, -i·est.** **1.** Having wealth; rich. **2.** Marked by abundance: *a wealthy land.* **3.** Well supplied: *wealthy in love.* **—wealth′i·ly** *adv.* **—wealth′i·ness** *n.*

wean (wēn) *tr.v.* **weaned, wean·ing, weans.** **1.** To accustom (the young of a mammal) to take nourishment other than by suckling. **2.** To detach from that to which one is strongly habituated or devoted: *She weaned herself from cigarettes.* **3.** To be raised on. [ME *wenen* < OE *wenian.* See **wen-**[1]***.**]

wean·ling (wēn′lĭng) *n.* A newly weaned child or young animal. *—adj.* Newly weaned.

weathervane

weap·on (wĕp′ən) *n.* **1.** An instrument of attack or defense in combat, as a gun or sword. **2.** *Zool.* A part or an organ, such as a claw, used by an animal in attack or defense. **3.** A means used to defend against or defeat another: *Logic was her weapon.* *—tr.v.* **-oned, -on·ing, -ons.** To supply with weapons or a weapon; arm. [ME *wepen* < OE *wǣpen.*]

weap·on·eer (wĕp′ə-nîr′) *n.* **1.** One who prepares a nuclear weapon for release. **2.** One who designs weapons, esp. nuclear weapons. **—weap′on·eer′ing** *n.*

weap·on·ry (wĕp′ən-rē) *n.* **1.** Weapons considered as a group. **2.** The design and production of weapons.

weap·ons system (wĕp′ənz) *n.* One or more weapons and the materiel necessary for their targeting and delivery.

wear (wâr) *v.* **wore** (wôr, wōr), **worn** (wôrn, wōrn), **wear·ing, wears.** *—tr.* **1.** To carry or have on the person as covering, adornment, or protection: *wearing a seat belt.* **2.** To carry or have habitually on the person, esp. as an aid: *wears glasses.* **3.** To display in one's appearance: *always wears a smile.* **4.** To bear, carry, or maintain in a particular manner: *wears her hair long.* **5.** To fly or display (colors). Used of a ship, jockey, or knight. **6.** To damage, diminish, erode, or consume by long or hard use, attrition, or exposure. Often used with *away, down,* or *off.* **7.** To produce by constant use, attrition, or exposure: *wore hollows in the stone steps.* **8.** To bring to a specified condition by long use or attrition: *pebbles worn smooth.* **9.** To fatigue, weary, or exhaust. **10.** *Naut.* To make (a sailing ship) change course from close-hauled on one tack to close-hauled on the other by turning the stern to windward. *—intr.* **1.a.** To last under continual or hard use. **b.** To last through the passage of time. **2.** To break down or diminish through use or attrition. **3.** To pass gradually or tediously: *The hours wore on.* **4.** *Naut.* To wear a sailing ship. *—n.* **1.** The act of wearing or the state of being worn; use. **2.** Clothing, esp. of a particular kind or for a particular use. Often used in combination: *footwear.* **3.** Gradual impairment or diminution resulting from use or attrition. **4.** The ability to withstand impairment from use or attrition. ***—phrasal verbs.*** **wear down.** To break down or exhaust by relentless pressure or resistance. **wear off.** To diminish gradually in effect. **wear out.** **1.** To make or become unusable through long or heavy use. **2.** To use up or consume gradually. **3.** To exhaust; tire. **4.** *Chiefly Southern U.S.* To punish by spanking. ***—idioms.*** **wear the pants** (or **trousers**). *Informal.* To exercise controlling authority in a household. **wear thin.** **1.** To be weakened or eroded gradually. **2.** To become less convincing, acceptable, or popular, as through repeated use. [ME *weren* < OE *werian.* See **wes-**[2]***.**] **—wear′er** *n.*

wear·a·bil·i·ty (wâr′ə-bĭl′ĭ-tē) *n.* The ability of a garment to withstand prolonged wear.

wear·a·ble (wâr′ə-bəl) *adj.* **1.** Suitable for wear. **2.** Suitable for easy wear. *—n.* Something that can be worn, esp. a garment. Often used in the plural.

wear and tear (târ) *n.* Loss, damage, or depreciation resulting from ordinary use and exposure.

wea·ri·ful (wîr′ē-fəl) *adj.* **1.** Causing weariness; tedious. **2.** Fatigued; exhausted. **—wea′ri·ful·ly** *adv.* **—wea′ri·ful·ness** *n.*

wea·ri·less (wîr′ē-lĭs) *adj.* Displaying or feeling no fatigue; tireless. **—wea′ri·less·ly** *adv.* **—wea′ri·less·ness** *n.*

wear·ing[1] (wâr′ĭng) *adj.* Intended to be worn.

wear·ing[2] (wâr′ĭng) *adj.* Causing fatigue; tiring.

wea·ri·some (wîr′ē-səm) *adj.* Causing physical or mental fatigue; tedious or tiresome. **—wea′ri·some·ly** *adv.* **—wea′ri·some·ness** *n.*

wea·ry (wîr′ē) *adj.* **-ri·er, -ri·est.** **1.** Physically or mentally fatigued. **2.** Expressive of or prompted by fatigue: *a weary smile.* **3.** Having one's interest, forbearance, or indulgence worn out: *weary of delays.* **4.** Causing fatigue; tiresome: *a weary wait.* *—tr. & intr.v.* **wea·ried** (wîr′ēd), **wea·ry·ing, wea·ries** (wîr′ēz). To make or become weary. [ME *weri* < OE *wērig.*] **—wea′ri·ly** *adv.* **—wea′ri·ness** *n.*

wea·sand (wē′zənd) *n.* The gullet or throat. [ME *wesand*, perh. < OE **wǣsend*, var. of *wāsand.*]

wea·sel (wē′zəl) *n.* **1.** Any of various carnivorous mammals of the genus *Mustela,* having a long slender body, a long tail, short legs, and brownish fur that in many species turns white in winter. **2.** A person regarded as sneaky or treacherous. *—intr.v.* **-seled, -sel·ing, -sels** also **-selled, -sel·ling, -sels.** To be evasive; equivocate. ***—phrasal verb.*** **weasel out.** *Informal.* To back out of a situation or commitment in a sneaky or cowardly manner. [ME *wesele* < OE *wesle.*]

weasel word *n.* A word of an equivocal nature used to deprive a statement of its force or evade a direct commitment. [< the weasel's habit of sucking the contents out of an egg without breaking the shell.]

weath·er (wĕth′ər) *n.* **1.** The state of the atmosphere at a given time and place, with respect to variables such as temperature, humidity, and wind velocity. **2.a.** Adverse or destructive atmospheric conditions, such as high winds or heavy rain. **b.** The unpleasant or destructive effects of such atmospheric conditions. **3.** **weathers.** Changes of fortune. *—v.* **-ered, -er·ing, -ers.** *—tr.* **1.** To expose to the action of the elements, as for drying, seasoning, or coloring. **2.** To discolor, disintegrate, wear, or otherwise affect adversely by exposure. **3.** To come through (something) safely; survive. **4.** To slope (a roof, for example) so as to shed water. **5.** *Naut.* To pass to windward of. *—intr.* **1.** To show the effects, such as discoloration, of exposure to the elements. **2.** To withstand the effects of weather. *—adj.* **1.** *Naut.* Of or relating to the windward side of a ship; windward. **2.** Relating to or used in weather forecasting. ***—idioms.*** **make heavy weather of.** To exaggerate the difficulty of something to be done. **under the weather.** **1.** Somewhat indisposed; slightly ill. **2.** *Informal.* **a.** Intoxicated; drunk. **b.** Suffering from a hangover; crapulous. [ME *weder, wether* < OE *weder.* See **wē-*****.**]

weather balloon *n.* A balloon used to carry instruments aloft to gather meteorological data in the atmosphere.

weath·er-beat·en (wĕth′ər-bēt′n) *adj.* **1.** Worn by exposure to weather. **2.** Tanned and coarsened from the outdoors.

weath·er·board (wĕth′ər-bôrd′, -bōrd′) *n.* See **clapboard.**

weath·er·board·ing (wĕth′ər-bôr′dĭng, -bōr′-) *n.* Clapboards considered as a group; siding.

weath·er-bound (wĕth′ər-bound′) *adj.* Delayed, halted, or kept indoors by bad weather.

weather bureau *n.* An agency that gathers and interprets meteorological data for weather study and forecasts.

weath·er·cast (wĕth′ər-kăst′) *n.* A broadcast of weather conditions. [WEATHER + (FORE)CAST.] **—weath′er·cast′er** *n.*

weath·er·cock (wĕth′ər-kŏk′) *n.* **1.** A weathervane, esp. one in the form of a rooster. **2.** One that is very changeable or fickle. *—intr.v.* **-cocked, -cock·ing, -cocks.** To have a tendency to veer in the direction of the wind. Used of an aircraft or a missile.

weather deck *n. Naut.* A ship's deck that is open to the sky.

weath·ered (wĕth′ərd) *adj.* **1.** Worn, stained, or warped by or as if by exposure to weather; seasoned. **2.** *Archit.* Sloped to shed water.

weather eye *n.* An eye quick to recognize signs of changes in the weather. ***—idiom.*** **keep a** (or **one's**) **weather eye open.** To keep watch; stay alert.

ă pat	oi boy
ā pay	ou out
âr care	o͝o took
ä father	o͞o boot
ĕ pet	ŭ cut
ē be	ûr urge
ĭ pit	th thin
ī pie	*th* this
îr pier	hw which
ŏ pot	zh vision
ō toe	ə about,
ô paw	item

Stress marks:
′ (primary);
′ (secondary), as in
dictionary (dĭk′shə-nĕr′ē)

weath•er•glass (wĕ*th*′ər-glăs′) *n.* An instrument, such as a barometer, that indicates changes in atmospheric conditions.
weath•er•ing (wĕ*th*′ər-ĭng) *n.* Any of the chemical or mechanical processes by which rocks exposed to the weather undergo changes in character and break down.
weath•er•ize (wĕ*th*′ə-rīz′) *tr.v.* **-ized, -iz•ing, -iz•es.** To protect (a structure) against cold weather, as with insulation.
weath•er•ly (wĕ*th*′ər-lē) *adj. Naut.* Able to sail close to the wind with little drift to leeward. **—weath′er•li•ness** *n.*
weather map *n.* A map or chart depicting the meteorological conditions over a specific geographic area at a specific time.
weath•er•proof (wĕ*th*′ər-pro͞of′) *adj.* Capable of withstanding exposure to weather without damage. *—tr.v.* **-proofed, -proof•ing, -proofs.** To make weatherproof. **—weath′er•proof′ness** *n.*
weather ship *n. Naut.* An oceangoing vessel equipped to make meteorological observations.
weather station *n.* A facility or location where meteorological data is gathered, recorded, and released.
weath•er-strip (wĕ*th*′ər-strĭp′) *tr.v.* **-stripped, -strip•ping, -strips.** To fit or equip with weather stripping.
weather strip•ping (strĭp′ĭng) *n.* **1.** A narrow piece of material, such as plastic, rubber, felt, or metal, installed around doors and windows to protect an interior from external extremes in temperature. **2.** This material considered as a unit.
weath•er•vane (wĕ*th*′ər-vān′) *n.* A wind direction indicator.
weath•er-wise (wĕ*th*′ər-wīz′) *adj.* Skilled in predicting shifts, as in the weather or public opinion.
weath•er•worn (wĕ*th*′ər-wôrn′, -wōrn′) *adj.* Weather-beaten.
weave (wēv) *v.* **wove** (wōv), **wo•ven** (wō′vən), **weav•ing, weaves.** *—tr.* **1.a.** To make (cloth) by interlacing the threads of the weft and the warp on a loom. **b.** To interlace (threads, for example) into cloth. **2.** To construct by interlacing or interweaving strips or strands of material. **3.a.** To interweave or combine (elements) into a complex whole. **b.** To contrive (something complex or elaborate) in this way. **4.** To introduce (another element) into a complex whole; work in. **5.** To spin (a web, for example). **6.** *p.t.* **weaved.** To make (a path or way) by winding in and out or from side to side. *—intr.* **1.a.** To engage in weaving; make cloth. **b.** To work at a loom. **2.** *p.t.* **weaved.** To move in and out or sway from side to side. *—n.* The pattern, method of weaving, or construction of a fabric: *a loose weave.* [ME *weven* < OE *wefan.* See **webh-*.**]
weav•er (wē′vər) *n.* **1.** One that weaves. **2.** A weaverbird.
weav•er•bird (wē′vər-bûrd′) *n.* Any of various chiefly tropical Old World birds of the family Ploceidae, marked by the ability to build complex woven communal nests.
wea•ver's knot (wē′vərz) *n. Naut.* A sheet bend.
web (wĕb) *n.* **1.a.** A woven fabric, esp. one on a loom or just removed from it. **b.** The structural part of cloth. **2.** A latticed or woven structure: *A web of palm branches.* **3.** A structure of delicate threadlike filaments characteristically spun by spiders or certain insect larvae. **4.** Something intricately contrived, esp. something that ensnares or entangles: *caught in a web of lies.* **5.** A complex interconnected structure or arrangement: *a web of telephone wires.* **6.** A radio or television network. **7.** A membrane or fold of skin connecting the toes, as of certain amphibians, birds, and mammals. **8.** The barbs on each side of the shaft of a bird's feather; a vane. **9.** *Archit.* The surface between the ribs of a ribbed vault. **10.** A metal sheet or plate connecting the heavier sections, ribs, or flanges of a structural element. **11.** A thin metal plate or strip, as the bit of a key or the blade of a saw. **12.** A large continuous roll of paper, such as newsprint, either in the process of manufacture or as it is fed into a web press. *—tr.v.* **webbed, web•bing, webs. 1.** To provide with a web. **2.** To cover or envelop with a web. **3.** To ensnare in a web. [ME < OE. See **webh-*.**]
Webb (wĕb), **Sidney James.** 1st Baron Passfield. 1859–1947. British sociologist and a founder of the London School of Economics (1895). He and his wife, **Beatrice Potter Webb** (1858–1943), were key members of the Fabian Society.
webbed (wĕbd) *adj.* Having or connected by a web.
web•bing (wĕb′ĭng) *n.* **1.** A strong, narrow, closely woven fabric used esp. for seat belts and harnesses or in upholstery. **2.** Something forming a web.
web•by (wĕb′ē) *adj.* **-bi•er, -bi•est.** Consisting of, resembling, or having webs or a web.
web•er (wĕb′ər, vā′bər) *n. Phys.* The SI unit of magnetic flux equal to the magnetic flux that in linking a circuit of one turn produces in it an electromotive force of one volt as it is uniformly reduced to zero within one second. See table at **measurement.** [After Wilhelm Eduard WEBER.]
We•ber (vā′bər), **Ernst Heinrich.** 1795–1878. German physiologist considered a founder of experimental psychology.
Weber, Baron **Karl Maria Friedrich Ernst von.** 1786–1826. German composer of *Der Freischütz* (1821).
We•ber (vā′bər), **Max¹.** 1864–1920. German sociologist and a pioneer of the modern analytical method of sociology.
We•ber (wĕb′ər), **Max².** 1881–1961. Russian-born Amer. painter known for his avant-garde abstract works.
We•ber (vā′bər), **Wilhelm Eduard.** 1804–91. German physicist noted for his study of terrestrial magnetism.
We•bern (vā′bərn), **Anton Friedrich Wilhelm von.** 1883–1945. Austrian composer whose works are characterized by brevity and tonal dissonance.
web•foot (wĕb′fo͝ot′) *n., pl.* **-feet** (-fēt′). **1.** A foot with webbed toes. **2.** An animal with webbed feet.
web-foot•ed (wĕb′fo͝ot′ĭd) *adj.* Having webbed toes.
web member *n.* One of the structural elements connecting the top and bottom flanges of a lattice girder or the outside members of a truss.
web press *n. Print.* A rotary press that prints on a web.
web spinner *n.* Any of various social insects of the order Embioptera, producing silk from glands in the front legs.
web•ster (wĕb′stər) *n. Obsolete.* A weaver of cloth. [ME < OE *webbestre,* fem. of *webba,* weaver < *webb,* web. See **webh-*.**]
Web•ster (wĕb′stər), **Daniel.** 1782–1852. Amer. legislator and public official noted for his oratory.
Webster, John. 1580?–1625? English playwright whose works include *The White Devil* (published 1612).
Webster, Noah. 1758–1843. Amer. lexicographer whose *American Dictionary of the English Language* was first published in 1828.
Webster Groves. A city of E MO, a suburb of St. Louis. Pop. 22,987.
web-toed (wĕb′tōd′) *adj.* Web-footed.
web•worm (wĕb′wûrm′) *n.* Any of various usu. destructive caterpillars that construct webs.
weck (wĕk) *n. Buffalo.* See **kümmelweck.** [Ger. dial., wedge-shaped roll < MHGer. *wecke* < OHGer., wedge.]
wed (wĕd) *v.* **wed•ded, wed** or **wed•ded, wed•ding, weds.** *—tr.* **1.** To take as a spouse; marry. **2.** To perform the marriage ceremony for. **3.** To unite closely. *—intr.* To take a spouse; marry. [ME *wedden* < OE *weddian.*]
Wed. *abbr.* Wednesday.
we'd (wēd). **1.** We had. **2.** We should. **3.** We would.
wed•ded (wĕd′ĭd) *adj.* **1.** Joined in marriage. **2.** Of or relating to marriage. **3.** Closely attached or devoted.
Wed•dell Sea (wĭ-dĕl′, wĕd′l). A sea of the S Atlantic off W Antarctica E of the Antarctic Peninsula.
wed•ding (wĕd′ĭng) *n.* **1.a.** The act of marrying. **b.** The ceremony or celebration of a marriage. **2.** The anniversary of a marriage. **3.** The act or an instance of joining closely.
wedding band *n.* See **wedding ring.**
wedding cake *n.* An elaborately decorated cake usu. arranged in tiers and having white icing, served at a wedding.
wed•ding-cake (wĕd′ĭng-kāk′) *adj.* Of, relating to, or having a highly ornate architectural style.
wedding ring *n.* A ring, often one of a pair of plain gold or platinum bands, given during the wedding ceremony by the groom or bride to his or her future spouse.
we•del (vād′l) *intr.v.* **-deled, -del•ling, -dels.** *Sports.* To ski on snow by means of wedeln. [Back-formation < WEDELN.]
we•deln (vād′ln) *n. Sports.* A snow skiing style in which the skier executes a series of short quick parallel turns by moving the backs of the skis from side to side at a constant speed. [Ger. < *wedeln,* to wag the tail, fan < MHGer. *wadelen, wedelen* < *wadel, wedel,* fan, tuft of hair < OHGer. *wadal, wedil.* See **wet-¹*.**]
wedge (wĕj) *n.* **1.** A piece of material, such as metal, thick at one edge and tapered to a thin edge at the other for insertion in a narrow crevice, used for splitting, tightening, securing, or levering. **2.a.** Something shaped like a wedge. **b.** *Downstate New York.* See **submarine** 2. See Regional Note at **submarine. c.** A wedge-shaped formation, as in football or ground warfare. **3.a.** Something that intrudes and causes division or disruption. **b.** Something that forces an opening or a beginning. **4.** *Sports.* An iron golf club with a very slanted face, used to lift the ball, as from sand. **5.** One of the triangular characters of cuneiform writing. *—v.* **wedged, wedg•ing, wedg•es.** *—tr.* **1.** To split or force apart with or as if with a wedge. **2.** To fix in place or tighten with a wedge. **3.** To crowd or squeeze into a limited space. *—intr.* To become lodged or jammed. [ME *wegge* < OE *wecg.*]
wedg•ie (wĕj′ē) *n.* A shoe having a wedge-shaped heel joined to a half sole so as to form a continuous undersurface. Often used in the plural. [Originally a trademark.]
Wedg•wood (wĕj′wo͝od′). A trademark used for a type of pottery made by Josiah Wedgwood and his successors.
Wedgwood, Josiah. 1730–95. British potter who produced some of the finest examples of British earthenware.
wed•lock (wĕd′lŏk′) *n.* The state of being married; matrimony. *—idiom.* **out of wedlock.** Of parents not legally married to each other: *born out of wedlock.* [ME *wedlocke* < OE *wedlāc* : *wedd,* pledge + *-lāc,* n. suff. expressing activity.]
Wednes•day (wĕnz′dē, -dā′) *n.* The fourth day of the week. [ME < OE *Wōdnesdæg,* Woden's day. See **wet-¹*.**]
Word History: The names of the days of our week are based on the ancient astrological notion that the seven celestial bodies (the sun, the moon, Mars, Mercury, Jupiter, Venus, and Saturn) revolving around stationary Earth influence what happens on it and that each of these celestial bodies controls

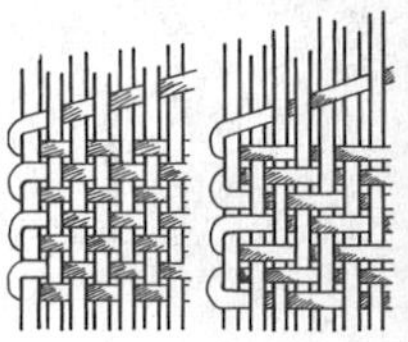

weave
Top: Weaving a tapestry
Bottom: Plain weave design (*left*) and twilled weave design (*right*)

Daniel Webster
20th-century portrait by Adrian Lamb

wedge

the first hour of the day named after it. This system was brought into Hellenistic Egypt from Mesopotamia. In A.D. 321 the Emperor Constantine the Great grafted this astrological system onto the Roman calendar, made the first day of this new week a day of rest and worship for all, and imposed the following sequence and names to the days of the week: *Diēs Sōlis,* "Sun's Day"; *Diēs Lūnae,* "Moon's Day"; *Diēs Martis,* "Mars's Day"; *Diēs Mercuriī,* "Mercury's Day"; *Diēs Iovis,* "Jove's Day" or "Jupiter's Day"; *Diēs Veneris,* "Venus's Day"; and *Diēs Saturnī,* "Saturn's Day." This new Roman system was adopted with modifications throughout most of western Europe: in the Germanic languages, such as Old English, the names of four of the Roman gods were converted into those of the corresponding Germanic gods. Therefore in Old English we have the following names (with their Modern English developments): *Sunnandæg,* Sunday; *Mōnandæg,* Monday; *Tīwesdæg,* Tuesday (the god Tiu, like Mars, was a god of war); *Wōdnesdæg,* Wednesday (the god Woden, like Mercury, was quick and eloquent); *Thunresdæg,* Thursday (the god Thunor in Old English or Thor in Old Norse, like Jupiter, was lord of the sky; Old Norse *Thōrsdagr* influenced the English form); *Frīgedæg,* Friday (the goddess Frigg, like Venus, was the goddess of love); and *Sæternesdæg,* Saturday.

weeping willow
Salix babylonica

wee (wē) *adj.* **we•er, we•est. 1.** Very small; tiny. See Syns at **small. 2.** Very early: *the wee hours of the morning.* —*n. Scots.* A short time; a little bit. [ME *wei, we,* a small amount, small < OE *wǣge, wēg,* weight. See **wegh-*.**]

weed[1] (wēd) *n.* **1.a.** A plant considered undesirable, unattractive, or troublesome, esp. one growing where it is not wanted, as in a garden. **b.** Rank growth of such plants. **2.** A water plant, esp. seaweed. **3.** The leaves or stems of a plant as distinguished from the seeds: *dill weed.* **4.** Something useless, detrimental, or worthless, esp. an animal unfit for breeding. **5.** *Slang.* **a.** Tobacco. **b.** A cigarette. **c.** Marijuana. —*v.* **weed•ed, weed•ing, weeds.** —*tr.* **1.** To clear of weeds. **2.** To remove (weeds). Often used with *out.* **3.** To eliminate as unsuitable or unwanted. Often used with *out.* —*intr.* To remove weeds. [ME < OE *wēod,* herb, grass, weed.]

weed[2] (wēd) *n.* **1.** A token of mourning, as a black band worn on a man's hat or sleeve. **2. weeds.** The black mourning clothes of a widow. **3.** An article of clothing; a garment. Often used in the plural. [ME *wede,* garment < OE *wǣd.*]

weed•er (wē′dər) *n.* One that removes weeds.

weed•y (wē′dē) *adj.* **-i•er, -i•est. 1.** Full of or consisting of weeds: *a weedy lawn.* **2.** Resembling or characteristic of a weed: *a weedy plant.* **3.** Of a scrawny build; spindly or gawky. —**weed′i•ly** *adv.* —**weed′i•ness** *n.*

week (wēk) *n.* **1.a.** A period of seven days: *a week of rain.* **b.** A seven-day calendar period, esp. one starting with Sunday and continuing through Saturday: *this week.* **2.a.** A week designated by an event or a holiday occurring within it. **b.** A week dedicated to a particular cause or institution. **3.** The part of a calendar week devoted to work, school, or business: *working a three-day week.* **4.a.** One week from a specified day: *I'll see you Friday week.* **b.** One week ago from a specified day: *It was Friday week that we last met.* [ME *weke* < OE *wicu.* See **weik-[2]*.**]

week•day (wēk′dā′) *n.* Any day of the week except Sunday, or often except Saturday and Sunday.

week•end (wēk′ĕnd′) *n.* The end of the week, esp. the period from Friday evening through Sunday evening. —*intr.v.* **-end•ed, -end•ing, -ends.** To spend weekends or a weekend.

week•end•er (wēk′ĕn′dər) *n.* **1.** One who vacations or visits on a weekend. **2.** A small suitcase or bag for carrying clothing and toiletries for a weekend.

week•long (wēk′lông′, -lŏng′) *adj.* Continuing through the week: *a weeklong conference.*

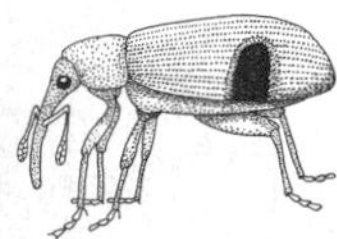
weevil
Strawberry weevil
Anthonomus signatus

week•ly (wēk′lē) *adv.* **1.** Once a week. **2.** Every week. **3.** By the week. —*adj.* **1.** Of or relating to a week. **2.** Occurring, appearing, or done once a week or every week. **3.** Computed by the week. —*n., pl.* **-lies.** A weekly publication.

week•night (wēk′nīt′) *n.* A night of the week exclusive of Saturday and Sunday.

Weems (wēmz), **Mason Locke.** "Parson Weems." 1759–1825. Amer. cleric known for his fictionalized biography of George Washington (1800).

ween (wēn) *tr.v.* **weened, ween•ing, weens.** *Archaic.* To think; suppose. [ME *wenen* < OE *wēnan.* See **wen-[1]*.**]

ween•ie (wē′nē) *n.* **1.** *Informal.* A wiener. **2.** *Slang.* A person, esp. a man, who is regarded as being weak and ineffectual.

wee•ny (wē′nē) *adj.* **-ni•er, -ni•est.** *Informal.* Very small; tiny. [Perh. blend of WEE and TINY.]

weep (wēp) *v.* **wept** (wĕpt), **weep•ing, weeps.** —*tr.* **1.** To shed (tears) as an expression of emotion. **2.** To express grief or anguish for; lament. **3.** To bring to a specified condition by weeping. **4.** To exude or let fall (drops of liquid). —*intr.* **1.** To express emotion, such as grief or sadness, by shedding tears. See Syns at **cry. 2.** To mourn or grieve. **3.** To emit or run with drops of liquid. —*n.* A period or fit of weeping. Often used in the plural. [ME *wepen* < OE *wēpan.*]

weep•er (wē′pər) *n.* **1.** One that weeps. **2.** A hired mourner. **3.** A badge of mourning, such as a black veil. **4.** A hole or pipe in a wall to allow water to run off. **5.** *Informal.* A highly sentimental artistic, cinematic, or dramatic work.

weep•ie (wē′pē) *n. Informal.* A work, esp. a film or play, that is excessively sentimental.

weep•ing (wē′pĭng) *adj.* **1.** Shedding tears; tearful. **2.** Dropping rain. **3.** Having slender drooping branches.

weeping willow *n.* A widely cultivated deciduous tree *(Salix babylonica)* native to China and having long slender drooping branches and narrow leaves.

weep•y (wē′pē) *adj.* **-i•er, -i•est.** Weeping or inclined to weep.

wee•vil (wē′vəl) *n.* Any of numerous beetles of the superfamily Curculionoidea, esp. the snout beetle, that have a downward-curving snout and are destructive to nuts, fruits, stems, and roots. [ME *wevel* < OE *wifel.* See **webh-*.**]

weft (wĕft) *n.* **1.a.** The horizontal threads interlaced through the warp in a woven fabric; woof. **b.** Yarn used for the weft. **2.** Woven fabric. [ME < OE *wefta.* See **webh-*.**]

Wei (wā). Name of several Chinese dynasties ruling from A.D. 220 to 265 and 386 to 556.

wei•ge•la (wī-gē′lə, -jē′-, wī′jə-) *n.* Any of various deciduous shrubs of the genus *Weigela* of Asia, esp. *W. florida,* widely cultivated for its pink, white, or red flowers. [NLat., genus name, after C.E. *Weigel* (1748–1831), German physician.]

weigh[1] (wā) *v.* **weighed, weigh•ing, weighs.** —*tr.* **1.** To determine the weight of by or as if by using a scale or balance. **2.** To measure or apportion (a certain quantity) by or as if by weight. Often used with *out.* **3.a.** To balance in the mind in order to make a choice; ponder or evaluate. **b.** To choose carefully or deliberately. **4.** *Naut.* To raise (anchor). —*intr.* **1.** To be of a specific weight. **2.** To have consequence or importance. See Syns at **count[1]. 3.** To press heavily. Used with *on* or *upon*: *Guilt weighed on him.* **4.** *Naut.* To raise anchor. —***phrasal verbs.* weigh down. 1.** To cause to bend down with added weight. **2.** To burden or oppress. **weigh in. 1.** *Sports.* To be weighed before or after an athletic contest. **2.** To have one's baggage weighed, as at an airport. **3.** *Slang.* To enter as a participant. [ME *weien* < OE *wegan.* See **wegh-*.**] —**weigh′er** *n.*

weigh[2] (wā) *n. Naut.* Way. Used in the phrase *under weigh.* [Var. of WAY (influenced by WEIGH[1]).]

weight (wāt) *n.* **1.** The relative heaviness of an object. **2.** The force with which a body is attracted to Earth or another celestial body, equal to the product of the object's mass and the acceleration of gravity. **3.a.** A unit measure of gravitational force: *a table of weights and measures.* **b.** A system of such measures: *avoirdupois weight.* **4.** The measured heaviness of a specific object: *a two-pound weight.* **5.** An object used principally to exert a force by virtue of its gravitational attraction to Earth, esp.: **a.** A metallic solid used as a standard of comparison in weighing. **b.** An object used to hold something else down. **c.** A counterbalance in a machine. **d.** *Sports.* A heavy object, such as a dumbbell, lifted for exercise or in athletic competition. **6.** *Statistics.* A factor assigned to a number in a computation, as in determining an average, to make the number's effect on the computation reflect its importance. **7.** Burden; oppressiveness. **8.** The greater part; preponderance. **9.a.** Influence, importance, or authority. See Syns at **importance. b.** Ponderous quality. **10.** *Sports.* A classification according to comparative lightness or heaviness. Often used in combination: *a heavyweight boxer.* **11.** The heaviness or thickness of a fabric in relation to a particular season or use. Often used in combination: *a summerweight jacket.* —*tr.v.* **weight•ed, weight•ing, weights. 1.** To add to by or as if by attaching a weight; make heavy or heavier. **2.** To load down, burden, or oppress. **3.** To increase the weight or body of (fabrics) by treating with chemicals. **4.** *Math. & Statistics.* To assign weights or a weight to. **5.** To cause to have a slant or bias. **6.** *Sports.* To assign to (a horse) the weight it must carry as a handicap in a race. —***idiom.* by weight.** According to weight rather than volume or other measure. [ME *wight* < OE *wiht.* See **wegh-*.**]

weight•ed (wā′tĭd) *adj. Statistics.* Adjusted to reflect value or proportion: *a weighted average.*

weight•less (wāt′lĭs) *adj.* **1.** Having little or no weight. **2.** Not experiencing the effects of gravity; being in a state of free fall. —**weight′less•ly** *adv.* —**weight′less•ness** *n.*

weight lift•er or **weight•lift•er** (wāt′lĭf′tər) *n. Sports.* One who engages in weightlifting.

weight•lift•ing (wāt′lĭf′tĭng) *n. Sports.* The lifting of weights in a prescribed manner.

weight•y (wā′tē) *adj.* **-i•er, -i•est. 1.** Having considerable weight; heavy. **2.** Burdensome; oppressive: *weighty problems.* **3.** Of great consequence; momentous: *weighty matters before the delegates.* **4.** Having great power or influence. **5.** Solemn; serious. —**weight′i•ly** *adv.* —**weight′i•ness** *n.*

Wei He (wā′ hə′). A river of central China flowing c. 724 km (450 mi) to the Huang He (Yellow R.).

Weil (vāl), **Simone.** 1909–43. French philosopher and mystic whose works include *Waiting for God.*

Weill (wīl, vīl), **Kurt.** 1900–50. German-born composer who collaborated with Brecht on *The Threepenny Opera* (1928).

Wei•mar (wī′mär′, vī′-). A city of central Germany SW of

Leipzig. The **Weimar Republic** lasted from 1919 to 1933. Pop. 64,007.

Wei•mar•an•er (vī′mə-rä′nər, wī′-) *n.* Any of a large breed of hunting dog that originated in Germany, having a smooth grayish coat. [Ger., after WEIMAR.]

weir (wîr) *n.* **1.** A fence or wattle placed in a stream to catch or retain fish. **2.** A dam placed across a river or canal to raise or divert the water, as for a millrace, or regulate or measure the flow. [ME *were* < OE *wer.* See **wer-⁴*.**]

weird (wîrd) *adj.* **weird•er, weird•est. 1.** Of, relating to, or suggestive of the preternatural or supernatural. **2.** Of a strikingly odd or unusual character; strange. **3.** *Archaic.* Of or relating to fate or the Fates. —*n.* **1.a.** Fate; destiny. **b.** One's assigned lot or fortune, esp. when evil. **2.** Often **Weird.** *Gk. & Rom. Myth.* One of the Fates. [ME *werde,* fate, having power to control fate < OE *wyrd,* fate. See **wer-²*.**] —**weird′ly** *adv.* —**weird′ness** *n.*

weird•ie also **weird•y** (wîr′dē) *n., pl.* **-ies.** *Slang.* A strange person, event, or thing.

weird•o (wîr′dō) *n., pl.* **-oes.** *Slang.* **1.** A person regarded as being very strange or eccentric. **2.** A deranged, potentially dangerous person.

Weir•ton (wîr′tn). A city of N WV in the Panhandle on the Ohio R. NNE of Wheeling. Pop. 22,124.

weis•en•hei•mer (wīz′ən-hī′mər) *n. Informal.* Var. of **wisenheimer.**

Weis•mann (vīs′män′), **August Friedrich Leopold.** 1834–1914. German biologist who asserted that hereditary characteristics are transmitted by a germinal plasm.

Weis•mann•ism (wīs′mə-nĭz′əm, vīs′män-ĭz′əm) *n. Genet.* The theory that all heritable characteristics arise in the germ plasm and that acquired characteristics cannot be inherited. [After August Friedrich Leopold WEISMANN.]

Weiz•mann (wīts′mən, vīts′män), **Chaim Azriel.** 1874–1952. Polish-born chemist and first president of Israel (1948–52).

we•ka (wē′kə, wā′-) *n.* A flightless bird *(Gallirallus australis)* of New Zealand having mottled brown plumage. [Maori.]

welch (wĕlch) *v.* Var. of **welsh.**

wel•come (wĕl′kəm) *adj.* **1.** Received with pleasure and hospitality into one's company or home. **2.** Giving pleasure or satisfaction; agreeable or gratifying. **3.** Cordially or willingly permitted or invited. **4.** Freely granted one's courtesy. Used to acknowledge an expression of gratitude. —*n.* **1.** A cordial greeting or hospitable reception given to an arriving person. **2.** A reception upon arrival. **3.** The state of being welcome. —*tr.v.* **-comed, -com•ing, -comes. 1.** To greet, receive, or entertain (another or others) cordially or hospitably. **2.** To receive or accept gladly. —*interj.* Used to greet cordially a visitor or recent arrival. —***idiom.* wear out (one's) welcome.** To visit so often or stay so long as to become a nuisance. [ME, alteration (influenced by *wel,* well) of OE *wilcuma,* welcome guest, welcome. See **gʷā-*.**] —**wel′come•ly** *adv.* —**wel′come•ness** *n.* —**wel′com•er** *n.*

weld¹ (wĕld) *v.* **weld•ed, weld•ing, welds.** —*tr.* **1.** To join (metals) by applying heat and pressure. **2.** To bring into close association or union. —*intr.* To be capable of being welded. —*n.* **1.** The union of two metal parts by welding. **2.** The joint formed by welding. [Alteration (prob. influenced by WELLED, p.part. of WELL¹) of WELL¹, to weld (obsolete and dialectal).] —**weld′er, wel′dor** *n.*

weld² (wĕld) also **wold** (wōld) *n.* **1.** See **dyer's rocket. 2.** The yellow dye obtained from dyer's rocket. [ME *welde.*]

weld•ment (wĕld′mənt) *n.* A unit composed of an assemblage of pieces welded together.

wel•fare (wĕl′fâr′) *n.* **1.a.** Health, happiness, and good fortune; well-being. **b.** Prosperity. **2.** Welfare work. **3.** Financial or other aid provided, esp. by the government, to people in need. —***idiom.* on welfare.** Receiving regular assistance from the government or private agencies because of need. [ME < *wel faren,* to fare well < OE *wel faran* : *wel,* well; see WELL² + *faran,* to get along; see FARE.]

Wel•fare Island (wĕl′fâr′). See **Roosevelt Island** 1.

welfare state *n.* **1.** A social system whereby the state assumes primary responsibility for the welfare of its citizens, as in matters of health care, education, employment, and social security. **2.** A nation in which such a system operates.

welfare work *n.* Organized efforts by a community, an organization, or an agency to improve the socioeconomic conditions of disadvantaged groups in society. —**welfare worker** *n.*

wel•kin (wĕl′kĭn) *n.* **1.** The vault of heaven; the sky. **2.** The upper air. [ME *welken* < OE *wolcen, weolcen,* cloud.]

well¹ (wĕl) *n.* **1.** A deep hole or shaft sunk into the earth to obtain water, oil, gas, or brine. **2.** A container or reservoir for a liquid, such as ink. **3.a.** A place where water issues from the earth; a spring or fountain. **b.** A mineral spring. **c. wells.** A watering place; a spa. **4.** An abundant source. **5.** An open space extending vertically through the floors of a building, as for stairs or ventilation. **6.** *Naut.* An enclosure in a ship's hold for the pumps. **7.** A cistern with a perforated bottom in the hold of a fishing vessel for keeping fish alive. **8.** An enclosed space for receiving and holding something, such as the wheels of an airplane when retracted. **9.** *Chiefly British.* The central space in a law court, directly in front of the judge's bench, where the counsel or solicitor sits. —*v.* **welled, well•ing, wells.** —*intr.* **1.** To rise to the surface, ready to flow. **2.** To rise or surge from an inner source: *Anger welled up.* —*tr.* To pour forth. [ME *welle* < OE. See **wel-²*.**]

well² (wĕl) *adv.* **bet•ter** (bĕt′ər), **best** (bĕst). **1.** In a good or proper manner. **2.** Skillfully or proficiently. **3.** Satisfactorily or sufficiently: *slept well.* **4.** Successfully or effectively. **5.** In a comfortable or affluent manner. **6.** In a manner affording benefit or gain; advantageously: *married well.* **7.** With reason or propriety; reasonably: *can't very well say no.* **8.** In all likelihood; indeed. **9.** In a prudent or sensible manner: *do well to say no more.* **10.** In a close or familiar manner. **11.** In a favorable or approving manner. **12.** Thoroughly; completely. **13.** Perfectly; clearly. **14.** To a suitable or appropriate degree: *well pleased.* **15.** To a considerable extent or degree. **16.** With care or attention. **17.** Entirely; fully. —*adj.* **better, best. 1.** In a satisfactory condition; right or proper. **2.a.** Not ailing, infirm, or diseased; healthy. See Syns at **healthy. b.** Cured or healed, as a wound. **3.a.** Advisable; prudent. **b.** Fortunate; good: *It is well that you stayed.* —*interj.* **1.** Used to introduce a remark, resume a narrative, or fill a pause during conversation. **2.** Used to express surprise. —***idioms.* as well. 1.** In addition; also. **2.** With equal effect: *I might as well go.* **in well with.** *Informal.* In a position to influence or be favored by. [ME *wel* < OE. See **wel-¹*.**]

Usage Note: Used as an adjective applied to people, *well* usually refers to a state of health, whereas *good* has a much wider range of senses. It is true that there is a distinction between *feel well* and *feel good,* but both can be applied to a state of health. Thus a patient suffering from a chronic disease might appropriately say to a doctor *I feel good today,* which implies a relative lack of physical discomfort. By contrast, *I feel well today* would be appropriate if the patient believes that the ailment has disappeared. See Usage Note at **good.**

we'll (wēl). **1.** We will. **2.** We shall.

well•a•day (wĕl′ə-dā′) *interj. & n. Archaic.* Var. of **wellaway.**

Wel•land (wĕl′ənd). A city of SE Ontario, Canada, on the **Welland Ship Canal,** 44.4 km (27.6 mi), which connects Lake Erie with Lake Ontario. Pop. 45,448.

well-ap•point•ed (wĕl′ə-poin′tĭd) *adj.* Having a full array of suitable equipment or furnishings: *a well-appointed kitchen.*

well•a•way (wĕl′ə-wā′) *Archaic.* —*interj.* Used to express woe or distress. —*n., pl.* **-ways.** A lamentation. [ME, alteration of OE *weilāwei,* alteration of *wā lā wā* : *wā,* woe; see WOE + *lā,* lo; see LO.]

well-bal•anced (wĕl′băl′ənst) *adj.* **1.** Evenly proportioned, balanced, or regulated. **2.** Mentally stable; sensible or sound.

well-be•ing (wĕl′bē′ĭng) *n.* The state of being healthy, happy, or prosperous; welfare.

well•born (wĕl′bôrn′) *adj.* Of good lineage or stock.

well-bred (wĕl′brĕd′) *adj.* **1.** Of good upbringing; well-mannered and refined. **2.** Of good breed. Used of animals.

well-de•fined (wĕl′dĭ-fīnd′) *adj.* **1.** Having definite and distinct lines or features. **2.** Accurately and unambiguously stated or described: *a well-defined argument.*

well-dis•posed (wĕl′dĭ-spōzd′) *adj.* Disposed to be kindly, friendly, or sympathetic.

well-done (wĕl′dŭn′) *adj.* Cooked all the way through.

Welles (wĕlz), **(George) Orson.** 1915–85. Amer. filmmaker and actor who directed and starred in *Citizen Kane* (1941).

Welles•ley (wĕlz′lē). A town of E MA WSW of Boston; seat of Wellesley College (estab. 1875). Pop. 26,615.

well-fa•vored (wĕl′fā′vərd) *adj.* Handsome; attractive.

well-fed (wĕl′fĕd′) *adj.* **1.** Adequately or properly nourished. **2.** Overfed; fat.

well-fixed (wĕl′fĭkst′) *adj. Informal.* Financially secure; well-to-do; well-off.

well-found (wĕl′found′) *adj.* Properly furnished or equipped.

well-found•ed (wĕl′foun′dĭd) *adj.* Based on sound judgment, reasoning, or evidence; adequately substantiated.

well-groomed (wĕl′gro͞omd′) *adj.* **1.** Attentive to details of dress; meticulously neat. **2.** Carefully tended or curried: *a well-groomed horse.* **3.** Trim and tidy: *a well-groomed lawn.*

well-ground•ed (wĕl′groun′dĭd) *adj.* **1.** Adequately versed in a subject. **2.** Having a sound basis; well-founded.

well-han•dled (wĕl′hăn′dəld) *adj.* **1.** Managed well. **2.** Showing signs of much handling.

well•head (wĕl′hĕd′) *n.* **1.** The source of a well or stream. **2.** A principal source. **3.** The structure built over a well.

well-heeled (wĕl′hēld′) *adj.* Having plenty of money; prosperous; well-to-do.

Wel•ling•ton (wĕl′ĭng-tən). The cap. of New Zealand, on an inlet of Cook Strait in extreme S North I.; founded in 1840 and supplanted Auckland as capital in 1865. Pop. 133,200.

Wellington, 1st Duke of. Arthur Wellesley. "the Iron Duke." 1769–1852. British general who defeated Napoleon at Waterloo (1815) and served as prime minister (1828–30).

Wellington boot *n.* **1.** A boot extending to the top of the knee in front but cut low in back. **2.** *Chiefly British.* A waterproof rubber or leather boot reaching to below the knee. [After the Duke of WELLINGTON.]

Weimaraner

Orson Welles

Duke of Wellington

ă pat	oi boy
ā pay	ou out
âr care	o͝o took
ä father	o͞o boot
ĕ pet	ŭ cut
ē be	ûr urge
ĭ pit	th thin
ī pie	*th* this
îr pier	hw which
ŏ pot	zh vision
ō toe	ə about,
ô paw	item

Stress marks:
′ (primary);
′ (secondary), as in
dictionary (dĭk′shə-nĕr′ē)

Welsh corgi

Welsh terrier

Mae West
Photographed in the 1930's

well-in•ten•tioned (wĕl′ĭn-tĕn′shənd) *adj.* Marked by or having good intentions.
well-knit (wĕl′nĭt′) *adj.* Strongly knit, esp. strongly and firmly constructed: *a well-knit body; a well-knit plot.*
well-known (wĕl′nōn′) *adj.* **1.** Widely known; familiar or famous. **2.** Fully known.
well-man•nered (wĕl′măn′ərd) *adj.* Polite; courteous.
well-mean•ing (wĕl′mē′nĭng) *adj.* Well-intentioned.
well-meant (wĕl′mĕnt′) *adj.* Kindly or honestly intended.
well•ness (wĕl′nĭs) *n.* The condition of good physical and mental health, esp. when properly maintained.
well-nigh (wĕl′nī′) *adv.* Nearly; almost.
well-off (wĕl′ôf′, -ŏf′) *adj.* **1.** Well-to-do. **2.** In fortunate circumstances. [OFF, circumstanced, prob. < the phrase *to come well off,* to emerge from in good circumstances.]
well-read (wĕl′rĕd′) *adj.* Knowledgeable through having read extensively.
well-round•ed (wĕl′roun′dĭd) *adj.* **1.** Comprehensively developed and well-balanced in a range or variety of aspects. **2.** Having a fully developed or shapely figure.
Wells (wĕlz), **H(erbert) G(eorge).** 1866–1946. British writer whose novels include *The War of the Worlds* (1898).
Wells, Ida Bell. 1862–1931. Amer. journalist and reformer who founded the Negro Fellowship League in 1910.
well-spo•ken (wĕl′spō′kən) *adj.* **1.** Chosen or expressed with aptness or propriety. **2.** Courteous in speech.
well•spring (wĕl′sprĭng′) *n.* **1.** The source of a stream or spring. **2.** A source: *a wellspring of ideas.*
well-thought-of (wĕl-thôt′ŭv′, -ŏv′) *adj.* Regarded with respect; esteemed.
well-tim•bered (wĕl′tĭm′bərd) *adj.* **1.** Having a good framework or structure. **2.** Covered with a good growth of timber.
well-timed (wĕl′tīmd′) *adj.* Occurring or done opportunely.
well-to-do (wĕl′tə-do͞o′) *adj.* Prosperous; affluent; well-off. [< the phrase *well to do in the world* : WELL[2], prosperous, affluent + TO, for + DO[1], doing.]
well-turned (wĕl′tûrnd′) *adj.* **1.** Shapely: *a well-turned ankle.* **2.** Concisely or aptly expressed: *a well-turned phrase.* **3.** Expertly rounded or turned: *a well-turned bedpost.*
well-wish•er (wĕl′wĭsh′ər) *n.* One who extends good wishes to another. **—well′-wish′ing** *adj. & n.*
well-worn (wĕl′wôrn′, -wōrn′) *adj.* **1.** Showing signs of much wear or use. **2.** Repeated too often; trite or hackneyed. **3.** Carried or worn in a becoming manner: *well-worn fame.*
welsh (wĕlsh, wĕlch) also **welch** (wĕlch) *intr.v.* **welshed, welsh•ing, welsh•es** also **welched, welch•ing, welch•es.** *Informal.* **1.** To swindle a person by not paying a debt or wager: *He welshed on his debts.* **2.** To fail to fulfill an obligation. [?] **—welsh′er** *n.*
Welsh (wĕlsh, wĕlch) *adj.* Of or relating to Wales or its people, language, or culture. —*n.* **1.** The people of Wales. **2.** The Celtic language of Wales. [ME *Walische* < OE *Wælisc* < *Wealh,* Welshman, Celt, perh. of Celt. orig.]
Welsh corgi *n.* Either of two breeds of dog originating in Wales and having a long body, short legs, and a foxlike head.
Welsh•man (wĕlsh′mən, wĕlch′-) *n.* A man who is a native or inhabitant of Wales.
Welsh rabbit *n.* A dish made of cheese, milk or cream, seasonings, and sometimes ale, served hot over toast or crackers.
Welsh rare•bit (râr′bĭt) *n.* Welsh rabbit.
Welsh springer spaniel *n.* Any of a breed of medium-sized hunting dog of Welsh origin, having a red and white coat.
Welsh terrier *n.* Any of a breed of terrier originating in Wales and having a wiry black and tan coat.
Welsh•wom•an (wĕlsh′wo͝om′ən, wĕlch′-) *n.* A woman who is a native or inhabitant of Wales.
welt (wĕlt) *n.* **1.** A strip, as of leather, stitched into a shoe between the sole and the upper. **2.** A tape or covered cord sewn into a seam as reinforcement or trimming. **3.a.** A ridge or bump on the skin, esp. one caused by a lash or blow. **b.** A lash or blow producing such a mark. —*tr.v.* **welt•ed, welt•ing, welts. 1.** To reinforce or trim with a welt. **2.** To beat severely; flog. **3.** To raise welts or a welt on. [ME *welte.*]
Welt•an•schau•ung (vĕlt′än′shou′o͝ong) *n., pl.* **-ungs** or **-ung•en** (-o͝ong-ən). A comprehensive philosophy of the world or of human life. [Ger. : *Welt,* world (< MHGer. *wërlt* < OHGer. *weralt*; see **wī-ro-***) + *Anschauung,* view (< MHGer. *anschouwunge,* observation, mystical contemplation : *an-,* on, at < OHGer. *ana-*; see ANLAGE + *schouwunge,* look < *schouwen,* to look at < OHGer. *scouwōn*; see **keu-***).]
wel•ter (wĕl′tər) *n.* **1.** A confused mass; a jumble. **2.** Confusion; turmoil. —*intr.v.* **-tered, -ter•ing, -ters. 1.** To wallow, roll, or toss about, as in mud or high seas. **2.** To lie soaked in a liquid. **3.** To roll and surge, as the sea. [< ME *welteren,* to toss about < MLGer. or MDu., to roll; see **wel-[2]***.]
wel•ter•weight (wĕl′tər-wāt′) *n. Sports.* **1.** A professional boxer weighing more than 135 and not more than 147 pounds (approx. 61–66.5 kilograms), heavier than a lightweight and lighter than a middleweight. **2.** A contestant in various other sports in a similar weight class. [< *welter,* heavyweight boxer, perh. < WELT.]
Welt•schmerz (vĕlt′shmĕrts′) *n.* Sadness over the evils of the world, esp. as an expression of romantic pessimism. [Ger. : *Welt,* world; see WELTANSCHAUUNG + *Schmerz,* pain (< MHGer. *smërze* < OHGer. *smerzo*).]
Wel•ty (wĕl′tē), **Eudora.** b. 1909. Amer. writer known esp. for her tales of rural Southern life.
wen[1] (wĕn) *n.* A harmless cyst containing the fatty secretion of a sebaceous gland. [ME < OE. See **wen-[2]***.]
wen[2] (wĕn) *n.* Var. of **wynn.**
We•natch•ee (wə-năch′ē). A city of central WA on the Columbia R. NNE of Yakima. Pop. 21,756.
Wen•ces•laus (wĕn′sĭ-slôs′) or **Wen•zel** (vĕn′tsəl). 1361–1419. Holy Roman emperor and king of Germany (1378–1400) and Bohemia (1378–1419).
wench (wĕnch) *n.* **1.** A young woman or girl, esp. a peasant girl. **2.** A woman servant. **3.** *Archaic.* A wanton woman. —*intr.v.* **wenched, wench•ing, wench•es. 1.** To engage in promiscuous sex with women. Used of a man. **2.** To consort with women prostitutes. Used of a man. [ME, short for *wenchel,* child < OE *wencel.*] **—wench′er** *n.*
wend (wĕnd) *v.* **wend•ed, wend•ing, wends.** —*tr.* To proceed on or along; go: *wend one's way home.* —*intr.* To go one's way; proceed. [ME *wenden* < OE *wendan.*]
Wend (wĕnd) *n.* One of a Slavic people inhabiting Saxony and Brandenburg. [Ger. *Wende* < MHGer. *Winde, Wende* < OHGer. *Winid.* See **wen-[1]***.] **—Wend** *adj.*
Wend•ish (wĕn′dĭsh) *adj.* Of or relating to the Wends or their language. —*n.* The Slavic language of the Wends.
went (wĕnt) *v.* **1.** P.t. of **go[1]**. **2.** *Archaic.* A p.t. and p.part. of **wend.** [ME < OE *wende,* p.t. and p.part. of *wendan,* to go.]
wen•tle•trap (wĕnt′l-trăp′) *n.* Any of various marine snails of the family Epitoniidae, having a tapering, usu. white spiral shell. [Du. *wenteltrap* < MDu. *wendeltrappe* : *wendel,* winding (< *wenden,* to wind) + *trappe,* stairs.]
wept (wĕpt) *v.* P.t. and p.part. of **weep.**
were (wûr) *v.* **1.** Second pers. sing. and pl. and first and third pers. pl. p. indic. of **be. 2.** P. subjunctive of **be.** See Usage Notes at **if, wish.** [ME *were, weren* < OE *wǣre, wǣren, wǣron.* See **wes-[1]***.]
we're (wîr). We are.
were•n't (wûrnt, wûr′ənt). Were not.
were•wolf also **wer•wolf** (wâr′wo͝olf′, wîr′-, wûr′-) *n.* A person transformed into a wolf or capable of assuming the form of a wolf. [ME < OE *werewulf* : *wer,* man; see **wī-ro-*** + *wulf,* wolf; see WOLF.]
Wer•fel (vĕr′fəl), **Franz.** 1890–1945. Austrian writer whose works include the novel *Song of Bernadette* (1941).
wer•geld (wûr′gĕld′) also **wer•gild** or **were•gild** (-gĭld′) *n.* In Anglo-Saxon and Germanic law, a price set upon a person's life on the basis of rank and paid by the family of a slayer to the kindred or lord of a slain person. [ME *wargeld* < OE *wergeld* : *wer,* man; see **wī-ro-*** + *geld,* payment.]
wer•ner•ite (wûr′nə-rīt′) *n.* See **scapolite.** [After Abraham Gottlob *Werner* (1750–1817), German mineralogist.]
Wer•nick•e's encephalopathy (vĕr′nĭ-kēz, -kəz) *n.* A disease of the brain caused by a deficiency of thiamine, usu. associated with alcoholism and marked by loss of muscular coordination, abnormal eye movements, and forgetfulness. [After Karl *Wernicke* (1848–1905), German neurologist.]
wert (wûrt) *v. Archaic.* A second pers. sing. p. indic. and p. subjunctive of **be.** [Blend of WERE and WAST.]
We•ser (vā′zər). A river of central and NW Germany flowing c. 483 km (300 mi) to the North Sea.
wes•kit (wĕs′kĭt) *n.* A waistcoat; a vest. [Var. of WAISTCOAT.]
Wes•la•co (wĕs′lə-kō′). A city of extreme S TX NW of Brownsville. Pop. 21,877.
Wes•ley (wĕs′lē, wĕz′-), **John.** 1703–91. British cleric who founded Methodism (1738). His brother **Charles** (1707–88) wrote the hymn "Hark, the Herald Angels Sing."
Wes•ley•an (wĕs′lē-ən, wĕz′-) *adj.* Of or relating to John or Charles Wesley or to Methodism. —*n.* A Methodist. **—Wes′ley•an•ism** *n.*
Wes•sex (wĕs′ĭks). A region and ancient Anglo-Saxon kingdom of S England; traditionally founded by the Saxon conquerors of Britain.
west (wĕst) *n.* **1.a.** The cardinal point on the compass 270° clockwise from due north and directly opposite east. **b.** The direction opposite to the direction of the earth's axial rotation. **2.** An area or a region lying in the west. **3.** Often **West. a.** The western part of the earth, esp. Europe and the Western Hemisphere. **b.** The western part of a region or country. **4.** Often **West. a.** A historical region of the United States west of the Allegheny Mountains. **b.** The region of the United States west of the Mississippi River. **c.** The noncommunist countries of Europe and the Americas. —*adj.* **1.** To, toward, of, facing, or in the west. **2.** Originating in or coming from the west: *a west wind.* —*adv.* In, from, or toward the west. [ME < OE. See **wes-pero-***.]
West, Benjamin. 1738–1820. Amer. painter who was the first American to study art in Italy (1760–63).
West, Mae. 1892?–1980. Amer. actress whose films include *I'm No Angel* (1933).
West, Nathanael. 1903–40. Amer. writer known for his novels

of dark comedy, such as *Miss Lonelyhearts* (1933).

West, Dame **Rebecca.** 1892–1983. British writer and critic whose works include *The Judge* (1922).

West Af•ri•ca (ăf′rĭ-kə). A region of W Africa between the Sahara and the Gulf of Guinea. **—West Af′ri•can** *adj. & n.*

West Al•lis (ăl′ĭs). A city of SE WI, a suburb of Milwaukee. Pop. 63,221.

West Atlantic *n.* The westernmost branch of the Niger-Congo language family.

West Bank (băngk). A disputed territory of SW Asia between Israel and Jordan W of the Jordan R.

West Bend (bĕnd). A city of SE WI NNW of Milwaukee. Pop. 23,916.

West Ber•lin (bər-lĭn′). See **Berlin.** **—West Ber•lin′er** *n.*

West Bes•kids (bĕs′kĭdz, bĕs-kēdz′). See **Beskids.**

west•bound (wĕst′bound′) *adj.* Going toward the west.

west by north *n.* The direction or point on the compass halfway between due west and west-northwest, or 78°45′ west of due north. *—adv. & adj.* Toward or from west by north.

west by south *n.* The direction or point on the compass halfway between due west and west-southwest, or 101°15′ west of due north. *—adv. & adj.* Toward or from west by south.

West•ches•ter (wĕst′chĕs′tər). A village of NE IL, a suburb of Chicago. Pop. 17,301.

West Ches•ter (chĕs′tər). A borough of SE PA W of Philadelphia. Pop. 18,041.

West Coast. A region of the W U.S. bordering on the Pacific and including WA, OR, and CA.

West Co•vi•na (kō-vē′nə). A city of S CA E of Los Angeles. Pop. 96,086.

West Des Moines (dĭ moin′). A city of S-central IA, a suburb of Des Moines. Pop. 31,702.

West End. The W section of central London, England, noted for its fashionable districts and its shops and theaters.

west•er (wĕs′tər) *n.* A strong wind coming from the west. *—intr.v.* **-ered, -er•ing, -ers.** To move westward. Used of the sun, the moon, or a star. [ME *westren* < *west*, west. See WEST.]

west•er•ly (wĕs′tər-lē) *adj.* **1.** Situated toward the west. **2.** Coming or being from the west: *westerly winds.* *—n., pl.* **-lies.** A storm or wind coming from the west. [ME < *wester*, western < OE *westra*. See **wes-pero-*.**] **—west′er•ly** *adv.*

Wes•ter•ly (wĕs′tər-lē). A town of extreme SW RI on the border of CT E of New London; settled in 1648. Pop. 21,605.

west•ern (wĕs′tərn) *adj.* **1.** Situated in, toward, or facing the west. **2.** Coming from the west: *western breezes.* **3.** Native to or growing in the west. **4.** Often **Western.** Of, relating to, or characteristic of western regions or the West. **5. Western.** Of, relating to, or descended from those Christian churches that use or formerly used Latin as their liturgical language. *—n.* Often **Western.** A novel, film, or television or radio program about frontier life in the American West. [ME < OE *westerne.* See **wes-pero-*.**] **—west′ern•ness** *n.*

Western Bug (bo͝og, bo͞ok). See **Bug** 1.

Western Dvi•na (dvē-nä′). See **Dvina** 2.

Western Empire or **Western Ro•man Empire** (rō′mən). The W section of the Roman Empire, set apart in A.D. 286 by Emperor Diocletian and lasting until 476.

west•ern•er also **West•ern•er** (wĕs′tər-nər) *n.* A native or inhabitant of the west, esp. the western United States.

Western Eu•rope (yo͝or′əp). The countries of W Europe, esp. those allied with the U.S. and Canada.

Western Ghats (gôts). See **Ghats.**

Western Hemisphere. The half of the earth comprising North America, Mexico, Central America, and South America.

western honey mesquite *n.* See **mesquite** a.

Western Islands. See **Hebrides.**

west•ern•ize (wĕs′tər-nīz′) *tr.v.* **-ized, -iz•ing, -iz•es.** To convert to the customs of Western civilization. **—west′ern•i•za′tion** (wĕs′tər-nĭ-zā′shən) *n.*

west•ern•most (wĕs′tərn-mōst′) *adj.* Farthest west.

western omelet *n.* An omelet cooked with diced ham, chopped green pepper, and onion.

Western Reserve. A historical region of NE OH.

Western Ro•man Empire (rō′mən). See **Western Empire.**

western saddle *n.* See **stock saddle.**

Western Sa•ha•ra (sə-hâr′ə, -hăr′ə, -hä′rə) also **Span•ish Sahara** (spăn′ĭsh). A region of NW Africa on the Atlantic coast; claimed as a protectorate by Spain in 1884 and partly annexed (1976) and occupied (1979) by Morocco.

Western Sa•mo•a (sə-mō′ə). An island country of the S Pacific comprising the W Samoa Is.; achieved independence in 1962. Cap. Apia, on Upolu I. Pop. 156,349.

Western Shoshone *n.* See **Shoshone** 1b.

western tanager *n.* A tanager *(Piranga ludoviciana)* of western North America, the male of which is yellow with a red head and a black back.

Western Wall also **Wail•ing Wall** (wā′lĭng). A remnant of the wall of the second Temple in Jerusalem; a site of pilgrimage, lamentation, and prayer.

Wes•ter•ville (wĕs′tər-vĭl′). A city of central OH, a suburb of Columbus. Pop. 30,269.

West•field (wĕst′fēld′). **1.** A city of SW MA, a suburb of Springfield. Pop. 38,372. **2.** A town of NE-central NJ SW of Newark. Pop. 28,870.

West Fri•sian Islands (frĭzh′ən, frē′zhən). See **Frisian Islands.**

West Germanic *n.* A subdivision of the Germanic languages that includes High German, Low German, Yiddish, Dutch, Afrikaans, Flemish, Frisian, and English.

West Ger•ma•ny (jûr′mə-nē). A former country of central Europe bordering on the North Sea; part of Germany until 1945, when the country was divided into U.S., French, British, and Soviet zones of occupation. In 1949 the three W zones were reconstituted as West Germany; the Soviet zone became East Germany. The two countries were reunified in Oct. 1990. **—West Ger′man** *adj. & n.*

West Hart•ford (härt′fərd). A town of central CT, a suburb of Hartford. Pop. 60,110.

West Ha•ven (hā′vən). A city of S CT, a suburb of New Haven. Pop. 54,021.

West Highland white terrier *n.* A small white terrier with upright ears and tail, developed in Scotland.

West Hol•ly•wood (hŏl′ē-wo͝od′). A community of S CA NE of Beverly Hills. Pop. 36,118.

West In•dies (ĭn′dēz). An archipelago between SE North America and N South America, separating the Caribbean Sea from the Atlantic and including the Greater Antilles, the Lesser Antilles, and the Bahama Is. **—West In′di•an** *adj. & n.*

West Indies Federation. A group of ten former British colonies in the West Indies, including Jamaica, Trinidad and Tobago, and Barbados, that lasted from 1958 to 1962. Some of the islands later formed the British-sponsored **West Indies Associated States,** which was gradually disbanded as the islands achieved independence in the 1970's and 1980's.

west•ing (wĕs′tĭng) *n.* **1.** The difference in longitude between two positions as a result of a movement to the west. **2.** Progress toward the west. [< WEST.]

West•ing•house (wĕs′tĭng-hous′), **George.** 1846–1914. Amer. engineer who received more than 400 patents for his inventions, including the air brake (1869).

West Jor•dan (jôr′dn). A city of N-central UT, a suburb of Salt Lake City. Pop. 42,892.

West La•fay•ette (lä′fē-ĕt′, lăf′ē-). A city of W IN on the Wabash R. opposite Lafayette. Pop. 25,907.

West•lake (wĕst′lāk′). A city of NE OH, a suburb of Cleveland. Pop. 27,018.

West•land (wĕst′lənd). A city of SE MI, a suburb of Detroit. Pop. 84,724.

West Mem•phis (mĕm′fĭs). A city of E AR near the Mississippi R. W of Memphis TN. Pop. 28,259.

West Mif•flin (mĭf′lĭn). A borough of SW PA, a suburb of Pittsburgh on the Monongahela R. Pop. 23,644.

West•min•ster (wĕst′mĭn′stər). **1.** Officially **City of Westminster.** A borough of Greater London in SE England on the Thames R.; site of Buckingham Palace. **2.** A city of S CA, a suburb of Long Beach. Pop. 78,118. **3.** A city of N-central CO, a suburb of Denver. Pop. 74,625.

West•mont (wĕst′mŏnt′). **1.** A community of S CA, a suburb between Los Angeles and Long Beach. Pop. 31,044. **2.** A village of NE IL, a suburb of Chicago. Pop. 21,228.

West•mount (wĕst′mount′). A city of S Quebec, Canada, a suburb of Montreal on Montreal I. Pop. 20,480.

West New York (no͞o yôrk′, nyo͞o). A town of NE NJ on the Hudson R. opposite Manhattan. Pop. 38,125.

west-north•west (wĕst′nôrth′wĕst′, -nôr-wĕst′) *n.* The direction or point on the compass halfway between due west and northwest, or 67°30′ west of due north. *—adj.* To, toward, of, facing, or in the west-northwest. *—adv.* In, from, or toward the west-northwest.

Wes•ton (wĕs′tən), **Edward.** 1886–1958. Amer. photographer known esp. for his stark images of landscapes.

West Or•ange (ôr′ĭnj, ŏr′-). A town of NE NJ, a suburb of Newark. Pop. 39,103.

West Pak•i•stan (păk′ĭ-stăn′, pä′kĭ-stän′). A former region of Pakistan (after 1947) separated by c. 1,609 km (1,000 mi) from East Pakistan, formerly East Bengal. In 1971 East Pakistan declared its independence as Bangladesh, and West Pakistan became the sole territory governed by Pakistan.

West Palm Beach (päm). A city of SE FL opposite Palm Beach. Pop. 67,643.

West Pen•sa•co•la (pĕn′sə-kō′lə). A community of NW FL, a suburb of Pensacola in the Florida Panhandle. Pop. 22,107.

West•pha•lia (wĕst-fāl′yə, -fā′lē-ə). A historical region and former duchy of W-central Germany E of the Rhine R. The Peace of Westphalia (1648) marked the end of the Thirty Years' War. **—West•pha′lian** *adj. & n.*

West Point. A U.S. military installation in SE NY on the W bank of the Hudson R. N of New York City.

West•port (wĕst′pôrt′, -pōrt′). A town of SW CT on Long Island Sound; settled in 1645. Pop. 24,410.

West Prus•sia (prŭsh′ə). A historical region of NE Germany between Pomerania and East Prussia S of the Baltic Sea.

West Saint Paul (sānt pôl′). A city of SE MN, a suburb of St. Paul. Pop. 19,248.

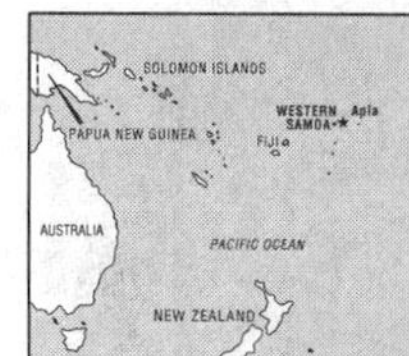

Western Samoa

Western Wall

West Highland white terrier

ă pat	oi boy
ā pay	ou out
âr care	o͝o took
ä father	o͞o boot
ĕ pet	ŭ cut
ē be	ûr urge
ĭ pit	th thin
ī pie	*th* this
îr pier	hw which
ŏ pot	zh vision
ō toe	ə about, item
ô paw	

Stress marks:
′ (primary);
′ (secondary), as in
dictionary (dĭk′shə-nĕr′ē)

wet suit

Phillis Wheatley
1773 engraving by an unknown artist

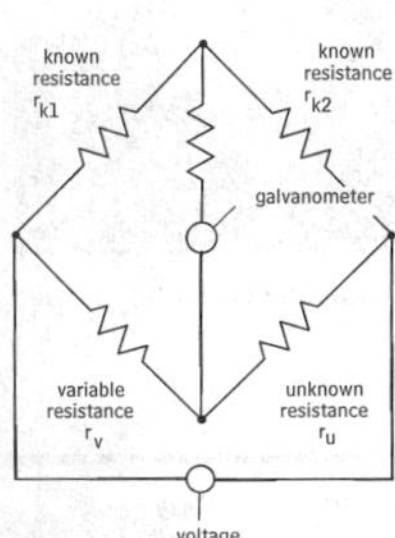

Wheatstone bridge

West Saxon *n.* **1.** The dialect of Old English used in southern England that was the chief literary dialect of England before the Norman Conquest. **2.** One of the Saxons inhabiting Wessex before the Norman Conquest.

west-south•west (wĕst′south′wĕst′, -sou-wĕst′) *n.* The direction or point on the compass halfway between due west and southwest, or 112°30′ west of due north. —*adj.* To, toward, of, facing, or in the west-southwest. —*adv.* In, from, or toward the west-southwest.

West Spring•field (sprĭng′fēld′). **1.** A town of SW MA, a suburb of Springfield. Pop. 27,537. **2.** A community of NE VA, a suburb of Alexandria. Pop. 28,126.

West Van•cou•ver (văn-ko͞o′vər). A city of SW British Columbia, Canada, a suburb of Vancouver. Pop. 35,728.

West Vir•gin•ia (vər-jĭn′yə). A state of the E-central U.S.; admitted as the 35th state in 1863. It was part of VA until the area refused to endorse secession in 1861. Cap. Charleston. Pop. 1,801,625. —**West Vir•gin′ian** *adj. & n.*

west•ward (wĕst′wərd) *adv. & adj.* Toward, to, or in the west. —*n.* A westward direction, point, or region. —**west′ward•ly** *adv. & adj.* —**west′wards** *adv.*

West War•wick (wŏr′ĭk, wôr′wĭk). A town of E-central RI SSW of Providence. Pop. 29,268.

wet (wĕt) *adj.* **wet•ter, wet•test. 1.** Covered or soaked with a liquid, such as water. **2.** Not yet dry or firm. **3.** Stored or preserved in liquid. **4.** Used or prepared with water or other liquids. **5.a.** Rainy, humid, or foggy. **b.** Marked by frequent or heavy precipitation. **6.** *Informal.* Allowing the sale of alcoholic beverages. —*n.* **1.** Something that wets; moisture. **2.** Rainy or snowy weather. **3.** *Informal.* One who supports the legality of alcoholic beverages. **4. wets.** *Chicago.* French fries served with gravy. —*v.* **wet** or **wet•ted, wet•ting, wets.** —*tr.* **1.** To make wet; dampen. **2.** To make (a bed or one's clothes) wet by urinating. —*intr.* To become wet. —***idioms.* all wet.** *Slang.* Entirely mistaken. **wet behind the ears.** Inexperienced; green. **wet (one's) whistle.** *Informal.* To take a drink. [ME < OE *wǣt.* See **wed-**[1*].]

Syns: *wet, damp, moist, dank, humid.* These adjectives mean covered with or saturated with liquid. *Wet* describes not only what is covered or soaked (*a wet sponge*) but also what is not yet dry (*wet paint*). *Damp* and *moist* both mean slightly wet, but *damp* often implies an unpleasant clamminess: *a cold, damp cellar; a moist breeze. Dank* emphasizes disagreeable, often unhealthful wetness: *a dank cave. Humid* refers to an unpleasantly high degree of moisture in the atmosphere: *hot, humid weather.*

wet•back (wĕt′băk′) *n. Offensive Slang.* Used as a disparaging term for a Mexican, esp. one who enters the U.S. illegally. [< the fact that the Rio Grande is a common entry point.]

wet blanket *n. Informal.* One that discourages enjoyment or enthusiasm.

wet cell *n. Elect.* A primary cell with a liquid electrolyte.

wet dream *n.* An erotic dream accompanied by ejaculation.

wet fly *n.* An artificial fly used in fishing that sinks below the surface of the water.

weth•er (wĕ*th*′ər) *n.* A castrated ram. [ME < OE. See **wet-**[2*].]

Weth•ers•field (wĕ*th*′ərz-fēld′). A town of central CT, a suburb of Hartford; settled in 1634. Pop. 25,651.

wet•land (wĕt′lănd′) *n.* A lowland area, such as a marsh or swamp, that is saturated with moisture.

wet•ness (wĕt′nĭs) *n.* **1.** The condition of being wet. **2.** Moisture. **3.** Rainy or persistently damp weather.

wet nurse *n.* **1.** A woman who suckles another woman's child. **2.** One who treats another with excessive care or solicitude. —**wet′-nurse′** (wĕt′nûrs′) *v.*

wet suit *n.* A tight-fitting permeable suit worn in cold water, as by skin divers, to retain body heat.

wet•ter (wĕt′ər) *n.* One that wets.

Wet•ter•horn Peak (vĕt′ər-hôrn′). A mountain, 4,274.6 m (14,015 ft), in the San Juan Mts. of SW CO.

wet•ting agent (wĕt′ĭng) *n.* A substance that reduces the surface tension of a liquid, causing the liquid to spread across or penetrate more easily the surface of a solid.

we've (wēv). We have.

Wey•den (wīd′n, vīd′n), **Rogier van der.** 1400?–64. Flemish painter whose works include *The Deposition* (c. 1435).

Wey•mouth (wā′məth). A town of E MA, a suburb of Boston. Pop. 54,063.

wf or **w.f.** *abbr. Print.* Wrong font.

WFTU *abbr.* World Federation of Trade Unions.

WH *abbr.* Watt-hour.

wh. *abbr.* White.

whack (hwăk, wăk) *v.* **whacked, whack•ing, whacks.** —*tr.* To strike with a sharp blow; slap. —*intr.* To deal a sharp resounding blow. —*n.* **1.** A sharp swift blow. **2.** The sound made by a sharp swift blow. —***phrasal verb.* whack off.** *Vulgar Slang.* To masturbate. —***idioms.* have (**or **take) a whack at.** *Informal.* To try out; attempt. **out of whack.** *Informal.* Improperly ordered or balanced; not functioning correctly. **whacked out.** *Slang.* **1.** Exhausted. **2.** Crazy. **3.** Under the influence of a mind-altering drug. [Prob. imit.]

whack•ing (hwăk′ĭng, wăk′-) *Chiefly British.* —*adj.* Superlative; excellent. —*adv.* Used as an intensive.

whack•o (hwăk′ō, wăk′ō) *n. Slang.* Var. of **wacko.**

whack•y (hwăk′ē, wăk′ē) *adj. Slang.* Var. of **wacky.**

whale[1] (hwāl, wāl) *n.* **1.** Any of various marine mammals of the order Cetacea, having the general shape of a fish with forelimbs modified to form flippers, a tail with horizontal flukes, and one or two blowholes for breathing, esp. one of the very large species. **2.** *Informal.* An impressive example: *a whale of a story.* —*intr.v.* **whaled, whal•ing, whales.** To engage in the hunting of whales. [ME < OE *hwæl.*]

whale[2] (hwāl, wāl) *v.* **whaled, whal•ing, whales.** —*tr.* To strike or hit repeatedly and forcefully; thrash. —*intr.* To attack vehemently. [?]

whale•back (hwāl′băk′, wāl′-) *n. Naut.* A steamship with the bow and upper deck rounded so as to shed water.

whale•boat (hwāl′bōt′, wāl′-) *n. Naut.* **1.** A long rowboat, pointed at both ends and designed to move and turn swiftly, formerly used in the pursuit and harpooning of whales. **2.** A boat similar to such a rowboat in size and shape; a whaler.

whale•bone (hwāl′bōn′, wāl′-) *n.* **1.** The elastic horny material forming the fringed plates that hang from the upper jaw of baleen whales and strain plankton from the water. **2.** An object made of this material.

whalebone whale *n.* See **baleen whale.**

whale oil *n.* An oil obtained from whale blubber, formerly used in making soap and candles and as a lubricating oil.

whal•er (hwā′lər, wā′-) *n.* **1.** One that hunts or processes whales. **2.** *Naut.* A whaling ship. **3.** *Naut.* A whaleboat.

Whales (hwālz, wālz), **Bay of.** An inlet of the Ross Sea in the Ross Ice Shelf of Antarctica.

whale shark *n.* A very large shark (*Rhincodon typus*) of warm marine waters having a network of rakelike sieves extending from its gills for straining plankton from the water.

whal•ing (hwā′lĭng, wā′-) *n.* The business or practice of hunting, killing, and processing whales.

wham (hwăm, wăm) *n.* **1.** A forceful, resounding blow. **2.** The sound of such a blow; a thud. —*v.* **whammed, wham•ming, whams.** —*tr.* To strike or smash into with resounding impact. —*intr.* To smash with great force. [Imit.]

wham•mo (hwăm′ō, wăm′ō) *interj. Slang.* Used to indicate the startling abruptness of a sound, an action, or an event.

wham•my (hwăm′ē, wăm′ē) *n., pl.* **-mies.** *Slang.* A supernatural spell for subduing an adversary; a hex. [Perh. < WHAM.]

whang[1] (hwăng, wăng) *n.* **1.** A thong or whip of hide or leather. **2.a.** A lashing blow, as of a whip. **b.** The sound of such a blow. —*tr.v.* **whanged, whang•ing, whangs. 1.** To beat or whip with a thong. **2.** To beat with a sharp blow or blows. [Dialectal var. of ME *thong, thwang,* thong. See THONG.]

whang[2] (hwăng, wăng) *Informal.* —*v.* **whanged, whang•ing, whangs.** —*tr.* To strike so as to produce a loud reverberant noise. —*intr.* To produce a loud reverberant noise. —*n.* A loud reverberant noise. [Imit.]

whang•ee (hwăng-gē′, wăng′-) *n.* **1.** Any of several Asian bamboos of the genus *Phyllostachys.* **2.** A walking stick made from the woody stem of any of these bamboos. [Chin. (Mandarin) *huáng lí* : *huáng* (short for *huáng zhú* : *huáng,* yellow + *zhú,* bamboo) + *lí,* a kind of bramble.]

wharf (hwôrf, wôrf) *n., pl.* **wharves** (hwôrvz, wôrvz) or **wharfs. 1.** A landing place or pier where ships may tie up and load or unload. **2.** *Obsolete.* A shore or riverbank. —*v.* **wharfed, wharf•ing, wharfs.** —*tr.* **1.** To moor (a vessel) at a wharf. **2.** To take to or store on a wharf. **3.** To furnish, equip, or protect with wharves or a wharf. —*intr.* To berth at a wharf. [ME < OE *hwearf.*]

wharf•age (hwôr′fĭj, wôr′fĭj) *n.* **1.a.** The use of wharves or a wharf. **b.** The charges for this usage. **2.** A group of wharves.

wharf•in•ger (hwôr′fĭn-jər, wôr′-) *n.* One who owns or manages a wharf. [Alteration of WHARFAGE + -ER[1].]

wharf rat *n.* **1.** A rat that infests wharves and ships. **2.** *Slang.* A person who frequents wharves.

Whar•ton (hwôr′tn, wôr′-), **Edith Newbold Jones.** 1862–1937. Amer. writer of *Ethan Frome* (1911).

what (hwŏt, hwŭt, wŏt, wŭt; hwət, wət *when unstressed*) *pron.* **1.a.** Which thing or which particular one of many: *What do you want?* See Usage Note at **which. b.** Which kind, character, or designation: *What are these objects?* **c.** One of how much value or significance: *What are possessions to a dying man?* **2.a.** That which; the thing that: *Listen to what I tell you.* **b.** Whatever thing that: *come what may.* **3.** *Informal.* Something: *I'll tell you what.* **4.** *Non-Standard.* Which, who, or that: *It's the poor what gets the blame.* —*adj.* **1.** Which one or ones of several or many: *What musical is that song from?* **2.** Whatever: *Repair what damage has been done.* **3.** How great; how astonishing: *What a fool!* —*adv.* How much; in what respect; how: *What does it matter?* —*conj.* That: *I don't know but what I'll go.* —*interj.* **1.** Used to express surprise, incredulity, or other strong and sudden excitement. **2.** *Chiefly British.* Used as a tag question, often to solicit agreement. —***idioms.* what for.** *Informal.* A scolding or strong reprimand. **what have you.** What remains and need not be mentioned. **what if. 1.** What would occur if; suppose that. **2.** What does it matter if. **what it takes.** The necessary expertise or qualities for success. **what's what.** *Informal.* The fundamentals and details of a situation or process; the true state. **what with.** Taking into consideration; because of. [ME < OE *hwæt.* See **kʷo-***.]

what•cha•ma•call•it (hwŏch′ə-mə-kôl′ĭt, hwŭch′-, wŏch′-, wŭch′-) also **what•cha•ma•call•um** (-əm) *n.* An item or a thing that is unnamed or unnamable. [Alteration of *what you may call it.*]

what•ev•er (hwŏt-ĕv′ər, hwŭt-, wŏt-, wŭt-) *pron.* **1.** Everything or anything that: *Do whatever you please.* **2.** What amount that; the whole of what: *Whatever is left is yours.* **3.** No matter what: *Whatever happens, we'll meet tonight.* **4.** *Informal.* Which thing or things; what: *Whatever does he mean?* —*adj.* **1.** Of any number or kind; any: *whatever requests you make.* **2.** All of; the whole of: *whatever strength she had.* **3.** Of any kind at all: *no campers whatever.*

Usage Note: Both *whatever* and *what ever* can be used in sentences such as *Whatever* (or *What ever*) *made her say that?* Critics have occasionally objected to the one-word form, but it is supported by extensive precedent in reputable writing. The same is true of the forms *whoever, whenever, wherever,* and *however* when these expressions are used similarly. In adjectival uses only the one-word form is used: *Take whatever books you need.* • It is regarded as incorrect to write *whatever book that you want to look at*; one should write instead *Whatever book you want to look at will be sent to your office* or *Whichever book costs less is fine with us.* See Usage Notes at **however, that.**

what•not (hwŏt′nŏt′, hwŭt′-, wŏt′-, wŭt′-) *n.* **1.** A minor or unspecified object or article. **2.** A set of light, open shelves for ornaments. —*pron.* Any of various additional or unspecified things or items.

what•so•ev•er (hwŏt′sō-ĕv′ər, hwŭt′-, wŏt′-, wŭt′-) *pron.* Whatever. —*adj.* Whatever: *no power whatsoever.*

wheal (hwēl, wēl) *n.* A small swelling on the skin that usu. itches or burns. [Prob. alteration of WALE.]

wheat (hwēt, wēt) *n.* **1.** Any of various annual cereal grasses of the genus *Triticum* of the Mediterranean region and southwest Asia, esp. *T. aestivum,* widely cultivated in temperate regions for their edible grain. **2.** The grain of any of these grasses, ground to produce flour used in breadstuffs and pasta. [ME *whete* < OE *hwǣte.* See **kweit-***.]

wheat bread *n.* A bread made from a mixture of white and whole-wheat flours.

wheat•ear (hwēt′îr′, wēt′-) *n.* A small thrush *(Oenanthe oenanthe)* of northern regions having a gray back, buff breast, and white rump. [Back-formation < earlier *wheatears* (taken as pl.) : prob. by folk ety. < WHITE + ARSE.]

wheat•en (hwēt′n, wēt′n) *adj.* Of or derived from wheat.

wheat germ *n.* The vitamin-rich embryo of the wheat kernel separated in milling for use as a cereal or food supplement.

Wheat•ley (hwēt′lē, wēt′-), **Phillis.** 1753?–84. African-born Amer. poet whose works include *Poems on Various Subjects* (1773).

Whea•ton (hwēt′n, wēt′n). A city of NE IL W of Chicago; settled in the 1830's. Pop. 51,464.

Wheat Ridge (hwēt′, wēt′). A city of N-central CO, a suburb of Denver. Pop. 29,419.

wheat rust *n.* **1.** A destructive disease of wheat caused by a rust fungus. **2.** Any of several rust fungi of the genus *Puccinia* that cause this disease.

Wheat•stone bridge (hwēt′stōn′, wēt′-) also **Wheat•stone's bridge** (-stōnz′) *n.* An instrument or a circuit used to determine the value of an unknown resistance in terms of three known resistances. [After Sir Charles *Wheatstone* (1802–75), British physicist.]

wheat•worm (hwēt′wûrm′, wēt′-) *n.* A small nematode worm *(Anguina tritici)* that is destructive to wheat.

whee (hwē, wē) *interj.* Used to express extreme pleasure or enthusiasm.

whee•dle (hwēd′l, wēd′l) *v.* **-dled, -dling, -dles.** —*tr.* **1.** To persuade or attempt to persuade by flattery or guile; cajole. **2.** To obtain through the use of flattery or guile. —*intr.* To use flattery or cajolery for one's ends. [?] —**whee′dler** *n.*

wheel (hwēl, wēl) *n.* **1.** A solid disk or a rigid circular frame, designed to turn around a central axle. **2.** Something resembling such a wheel in appearance or movement or having a wheel as its principal part or characteristic, as: **a.** The steering device on a vehicle. **b.** A potter's wheel. **c.** A water wheel. **d.** A spinning wheel. **e.** *Games.* A device used in roulette and other games of chance. **f.** A firework that rotates while burning. **g.** *Informal.* A bicycle. **h.** An instrument to which a victim was bound for torture during the Middle Ages. **3. wheels.** Forces that provide energy, movement, or direction. **4.** The act or process of turning; revolution or rotation. **5. wheels.** *Slang.* A motor vehicle or access thereto. **6.** *Slang.* A person with a great deal of power or influence. —*v.* **wheeled, wheel•ing, wheels.** —*tr.* **1.** To roll, move, or transport on wheels or a wheel. **2.** To cause to turn around or as if around a central axis; revolve or rotate. **3.** To provide with wheels or a wheel. —*intr.* **1.** To turn around or as if around a central axis; revolve or rotate. **2.** To roll or move on or as if on wheels or a wheel. **3.** To fly in a curving or circular course. **4.** To turn or whirl around in place; pivot. **5.** To reverse one's opinion or practice: *wheel about on a subject.* —*idioms.* **at** (or **behind**) **the wheel. 1.** Operating the steering mechanism of a vehicle; driving. **2.** Directing or controlling; in charge. **wheel and deal.** *Informal.* To engage in the advancement of one's own interests, esp. in a canny, aggressive, or unscrupulous way. [ME < OE *hwēol.* See **kʷel-[1]***.]

wheel and axle *n.* A machine consisting of an axle to which a wheel is fastened so that torque applied to the wheel winds a rope or chain onto the axle.

wheel•bar•row (hwēl′băr′ō, wēl′-) *n.* A one- or two-wheeled vehicle with handles at the rear, used for small loads.

wheel•base (hwēl′bās′, wēl′-) *n.* The distance between front wheel and rear wheel centers in a motor vehicle.

wheel bug *n.* A large assassin bug *(Arilus cristatus)* of North America that has a notched wheellike projection on the back of the thorax and preys on other insects.

wheel•chair also **wheel chair** (hwēl′châr′, wēl′-) *n.* A chair with large wheels for a sick or disabled person.

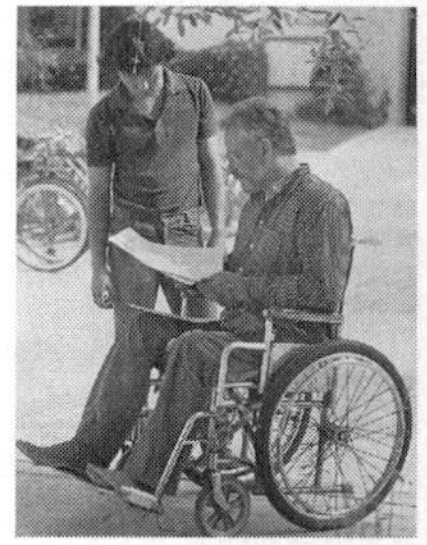

wheelchair

wheeled (hwēld, wēld) *adj.* Having wheels or a wheel. Often used in combination: *a three-wheeled bike.*

wheel•er (hwē′lər, wē′-) *n.* **1.** One that wheels. **2.** A thing that moves on or is equipped with wheels or a wheel. Often used in combination: *a three-wheeler.* **3.** A wheel horse.

Whee•ler (hwē′lər, wē′-), **William Almon.** 1819–87. Vice President of the U.S. (1877–81).

wheel•er-deal•er (hwē′lər-dē′lər, wē′-) *n.* *Informal.* One who advances his or her own interests by canny, aggressive, or unscrupulous behavior.

wheel horse *n.* **1.** The horse in a team that follows the leader and is harnessed nearest the front wheels. **2.** A diligent dependable worker, esp. in a political organization.

wheel•house (hwēl′hous′, wēl′-) *n.* *Naut.* See **pilothouse.**

wheel•ie (hwē′lē, wē-) *n.* A stunt in which the front wheel or wheels of a vehicle, such as a bicycle, are raised so that the vehicle is balanced momentarily on its rear wheel or wheels.

wheelie

Wheel•ing (hwē′lĭng, wē′-). **1.** A village of NE IL, a suburb of Chicago. Pop. 29,911. **2.** A city of NW WV in the Panhandle SW of Pittsburgh PA; settled in 1769. Pop. 34,882.

wheel lock *n.* **1.** A firing mechanism in certain obsolete small arms, in which a small wheel produces sparks by revolving against a flint. **2.** A firearm using such a mechanism.

wheel•man (hwēl′mən, wēl′-) *n.* **1.** *Naut.* One who steers a ship; a helmsman. **2.** The driver of an automobile, esp. of a getaway car. **3.** A bicyclist.

wheels•man (hwēlz′mən, wēlz′-) *n.* A wheelman.

wheel•work (hwēl′wûrk′, wēl′-) *n.* An arrangement of gears or wheels in a mechanical device.

wheel•wright (hwēl′rīt′, wēl′-) *n.* One who builds and repairs wheels.

wheeze (hwēz, wēz) *v.* **wheezed, wheez•ing, wheez•es.** —*intr.* **1.** To breathe with difficulty, producing a hoarse whistling sound. **2.** To make a sound resembling wheezing. —*tr.* To produce or utter with a hoarse whistling sound. —*n.* **1.** A wheezing sound. **2.** *Informal.* An old joke. [ME *whesen,* prob. < ON *hvæsa,* to hiss. See **kwes-***.] —**wheez′er** *n.*

wheez•y (hwē′zē, wē′-) *adj.* **-i•er, -i•est. 1.** Given to wheezing. **2.** Producing a wheezing sound. —**wheez′i•ly** *adv.* —**wheez′i•ness** *n.*

whelk[1] (hwĕlk, wĕlk) *n.* Any of various large, mostly edible marine snails of the family Buccinidae, esp. *Buccinum undatum,* having a pointed spiral shell. [ME *welke, whelke* < OE *weoloc.* See **wel-[2]***.]

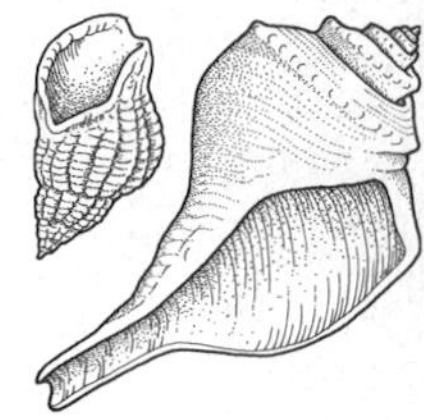

whelk[1]
Left: Waved whelk
Buccinum undatum
Right: Channeled whelk
Busycon canaliculatum

whelk[2] (hwĕlk, wĕlk) *n.* An inflamed swelling, such as a pimple or pustule. [ME *whelke* < OE *hwylca.*] —**whelk′y** *adj.*

whelm (hwĕlm, wĕlm) *tr.v.* **whelmed, whelm•ing, whelms. 1.** To cover with water; submerge. **2.** To overwhelm. [ME *whelmen,* to overturn, prob. alteration of *whelven* < OE *-hwelfan,* as in *āhwelfan,* to cover over.]

whelp (hwĕlp, wĕlp) *n.* **1.** A young offspring of a mammal, such as a dog or wolf. **2.a.** A child; a youth. **b.** An impudent young fellow. See Usage Note at **adage. 3.a.** A tooth of a sprocket wheel. **b.** *Naut.* Any of the ridges on the barrel of a windlass or capstan. —*v.* **whelped, whelp•ing, whelps.** —*intr.* To give birth to whelps or a whelp. —*tr.* To give birth to (whelps or a whelp). [ME < OE *hwelp.*]

when (hwĕn, wĕn) *adv.* At what time: *When will we leave?* —*conj.* **1.** At the time that: *in the spring when the snow melts.* **2.** As soon as: *I'll call when I arrive.* **3.** Whenever: *When the wind blows, the doors rattle.* **4.** During the time at which; while: *When I was young, I was happy.* **5.** Whereas; although: *She stopped when she should have continued.* **6.** Considering that; if: *How can he get paid when he won't work?* —*pron.* What or which time: *Since when has this been going on?* —*n.* The time or date: *Have they decided the where and when?* [ME < OE *hwenne.* See **kʷo-***.]

Usage Note: In informal style *when* is often used after *be* in definitions: *A dilemma is when you don't know which way to turn.* The construction is useful, but it is widely regarded as incorrect or unsuitable for formal discourse. In formal style

ă **pat**	oi **boy**
ā **pay**	ou **out**
âr **care**	o͝o **took**
ä **father**	o͞o **boot**
ĕ **pet**	ŭ **cut**
ē **be**	ûr **urge**
ĭ **pit**	th **thin**
ī **pie**	*th* **this**
îr **pier**	hw **which**
ŏ **pot**	zh **vision**
ō **toe**	ə **about, item**
ô **paw**	

Stress marks:
′ (primary);
′ (secondary), as in
dictionary (dĭk′shə-nĕr′ē)

rephrase such definitions to avoid *is when*: *A dilemma is a situation in which you don't know which way to turn. You are in a dilemma when you don't know which way to turn.*

when•as (hwĕn-ăz′, wĕn-) *conj. Archaic.* **1.** When. **2.** Whereas.

whence (hwĕns, wĕns) *adv.* **1.** From where; from what place: *Whence came you?* **2.** From what origin or source. — *conj.* **1.** Out of which place; from or out of which. **2.** By reason of which; from which: *The dog was black, whence the name Shadow.* [ME *whennes* : *whenne,* whence (< OE *hwanon*; see **kʷo-***) + *-es,* genitive sing. suff.; see -s³.]

Usage Note: The construction *from whence* has been criticized as redundant since the 18th century. It is true that *whence* incorporates the sense of *from*: *a remote village, whence little news reached the wider world.* But *from whence* has been used steadily by reputable writers since the 14th century. Still, *whence* (like *thence*) is most often used nowadays to impart an archaic or highly formal tone to a passage, an effect better realized if the archaic syntax of the word — without *from* — is preserved as well.

whence•so•ev•er (hwĕns′sō-ĕv′ər, wĕns′-) *adv.* From whatever place or source. — *conj.* From any place or source that.

when•ev•er (hwĕn-ĕv′ər, wĕn-) *adv.* **1.** At whatever time. **2.** When. See Usage Note at **whatever.** — *conj.* **1.** At whatever time that: *We'll go whenever you're ready.* **2.** Every time that: *He smiles whenever the puppy appears.*

when•so•ev•er (hwĕn′sō-ĕv′ər, wĕn′-) *adv.* At whatever time at all; whenever. — *conj.* Whenever.

where (hwâr, wâr) *adv.* **1.** At or in what place: *Where is the phone?* **2.** In what situation or position: *Where would we be without you?* **3.** From what place or source: *Where did you get this idea?* **4.** To what place; toward what end: *Where is this argument leading?* — *conj.* **1.** At what or which place: *She moved to the city, where jobs are available.* **2.a.** In a place in which: *He lives where the climate is mild.* **b.** In any place or situation in which; wherever: *Where there's smoke, there's fire.* **3.a.** To a place in which: *Go where it is quieter.* **b.** To a place or situation in which: *Go where you are happy.* — *n.* **1.** The place or occasion: *We know the when but not the where of it.* **2.** What place, source, or cause: *Where are you from?* [ME < OE *hwǣr.* See **kʷo-***.]

Usage Note: When *where* is used to refer to a point of origin, the preposition *from* is required: *Where did she come from?* When it is used to refer to a point of destination, the preposition *to* is generally superfluous: *Where is she going?* (preferable to *Where is she going to?*). When it is used to refer to the place at which an event or a situation is located, the use of *at* is widely regarded as regional or colloquial: *Where is the station?* (not *Where is the station at?*). See Usage Note at **why.**

whippet

where•a•bouts (hwâr′ə-bouts′, wâr′-) *adv.* About where; in, at, or near what location: *Whereabouts do you live?* — *n.* *(used with a sing. or pl. v.)* Approximate location.

where•as (hwâr-ăz′, wâr-) *conj.* **1.** It being the fact that; inasmuch as. **2.** While at the same time. **3.** While on the contrary. — *n.* **1.** An introductory statement to a formal document; a preamble. **2.** A conditional statement.

where•at (hwâr-ăt′, wâr-) *conj.* **1.** Toward or at which. **2.** As a result or consequence of; whereupon.

where•by (hwâr-bī′, wâr-) *conj.* In accordance with which; by or through which.

where•fore (hwâr′fôr′, -fōr′, wâr′-) *adv.* **1.** For what purpose or reason; why. **2.** Therefore. — *n.* A purpose or cause.

where•from (hwâr′frŭm′, -frŏm′, wâr′-) *conj.* From which.

where•in (hwâr-ĭn′, wâr-) *adv.* In what way; how: *Wherein have we sinned?* — *conj.* **1.** In which location; where. **2.** During which. **3.** In what way; how.

where•in•to (hwâr-ĭn′to͞o, wâr-) *conj.* Into which.

where•of (hwâr-ŏv′, -ŭv′, wâr-) *conj.* **1.** Of what: *I know whereof I speak.* **2.a.** Of which: *pottery whereof many examples are lost.* **b.** Of whom. — *adv. Archaic.* Of what.

where•on (hwâr-ŏn′, -ôn′, wâr-) *adv. Archaic.* On which or what: *"the ground whereon she trod"* (John Milton).

where•so•ev•er (hwâr′sō-ĕv′ər, wâr′-) *conj.* In, to, or from whatever place at all; wherever.

where•through (hwâr′thro͞o′, wâr′-) *conj.* Through, because of, or during which.

where•to (hwâr′to͞o′, wâr′-) *adv.* To what place; toward what end. — *conj.* To which.

where•un•to (hwâr-ŭn′to͞o, wâr-) *adv. & conj.* Whereto.

where•up•on (hwâr′ə-pŏn′, -pôn′, wâr′-) *conj.* **1.** On which. **2.** In close consequence of which.

wher•ev•er (hwâr-ĕv′ər, wâr-) *adv.* **1.** In or to whatever place: *used red pencil wherever needed.* **2.** Where: *Wherever have you been so long?* See Usage Note at **whatever.** — *conj.* In or to whichever place or situation.

where•with (hwâr′wĭth′, -wĭth′, wâr′-) *pron.* The thing or things with which. — *conj.* By means of which. — *adv. Obsolete.* With what or which.

where•with•al (hwâr′wĭth-ôl′, -wĭth-, wâr′-) *n.* The necessary means, esp. financial means: *the wherewithal to survive.* — *conj.* Wherewith. — *pron.* Wherewith.

wher•ry (hwĕr′ē, wĕr′ē) *n., pl.* **-ries.** *Naut.* **1.** A light, swift rowboat built for one person and often used in racing. **2.** A sailing barge used in East Anglia. [ME *whery.*]

whet (hwĕt, wĕt) *tr.v.* **whet•ted, whet•ting, whets. 1.** To sharpen (a knife, for example); hone. **2.** To make more keen; stimulate: *The smell whetted my appetite.* — *n.* **1.** The act of whetting. **2.** Something that whets. **3.** *Informal.* An appetizer. [ME *whetten* < OE *hwettan.*]

wheth•er (hwĕth′ər, wĕth′-) *conj.* **1.** Used in indirect questions to introduce one alternative: *Find out whether the museum is open.* See Usage Note at **if. 2.** Used to introduce alternative possibilities: *whether she wins or whether she loses.* **3.** Either: *He passed the test, whether by skill or luck.* — *pron. Archaic.* Which. — ***idiom.* whether or no.** Regardless of circumstances. [ME < OE *hwether.* See **kʷo-***.]

whet•stone (hwĕt′stōn′, wĕt′-) *n.* A hard, fine-grained stone for honing tools.

whew (hwyo͞o, hwo͞o, hwyo͞o *unvoiced*) *interj.* Used to express strong emotion, such as relief or amazement.

whey (hwā, wā) *n.* The watery part of milk that separates from the curds, as in the process of making cheese. [ME < OE *hwæg.*] — **whey′ey** *adj.*

whey-face (hwā′fās′, wā′-) *n.* A person with a pallid face.

which (hwĭch, wĭch) *pron.* **1.** What particular one or ones: *Which is yours?* **2.** The one or ones previously mentioned or implied, specifically: **a.** Used as a relative pronoun in a clause that provides additional information about the antecedent: *my house, which is old.* **b.** Used as a relative pronoun preceded by *that* or a preposition in a clause that defines or restricts the antecedent: *that which he needed.* **c.** Used instead of *that* as a relative pronoun in a clause that defines or restricts the antecedent: *The movie which was shown later was better.* **3.** Any of the things, events, or people designated or implied; whichever: *Choose which you like best.* **4.** A thing or circumstance that: *He left early, which was wise.* — *adj.* **1.** What particular one or ones of a number of things or people: *Which part of town is it?* **2.** Any one or any number of; whichever: *Use which door you please.* **3.** Being the one or ones previously mentioned or implied: *It blew up, at which point we ran.* [ME < OE *hwilc.* See **kʷo-***.]

Usage Note: The antecedent of *which* can sometimes be a sentence or clause, as in *She ignored him, which proved to be unwise.* Care should be taken that this usage does not cause ambiguities. The sentence *It emerged that Edna made the complaint, which surprised everybody* may mean either that the complaint was surprising or that it was surprising that Edna made it. The ambiguity can be avoided with paraphrases such as *It emerged that Edna made the complaint, a revelation that surprised everybody.* • In its use to refer to the contents of sentences and clauses, *which* should be used only when it is preceded by its antecedent. When the antecedent follows, *what* should be used, particularly in formal style: *Still, what is more surprising, he has spoken since.* See Usage Notes at **that, whose.**

which•ev•er (hwĭch-ĕv′ər, wĭch-) *pron.* Whatever one or ones. — *adj.* Being any one or any number of a group: *Read whichever books you please.* See Usage Note at **whatever.**

which•so•ev•er (hwĭch′sō-ĕv′ər, wĭch′-) *pron. & adj.* Whichever.

whick•er (hwĭk′ər, wĭk′-) *intr.v.* **-ered, -er•ing, -ers.** To whinny. — *n.* A whinny. [Imit.]

whid•ah (hwĭd′ə, wĭd′ə) *n.* Var. of **whydah.**

Whid•bey Island (hwĭd′bē, wĭd′-). An island of NW WA in Puget Sound NW of Everett.

whiff (hwĭf, wĭf) *n.* **1.** A slight, gentle gust of air; a waft. **2.a.** A brief passing odor carried in the air. **b.** A minute trace. **3.** An inhalation, as of air or smoke. **4.** *Baseball.* A strikeout. — *v.* **whiffed, whiff•ing, whiffs.** — *intr.* **1.** To be carried in brief gusts; waft. **2.** *Sports.* To swing at and miss a ball or puck. **3.** *Baseball.* To strike out. Used of a batter. — *tr.* **1.** To blow or convey in whiffs. **2.** To inhale through the nose; sniff. **3.** *Baseball.* To strike out (a batter). [Perh. alteration of ME *weffe,* offensive smell.] — **whiff′er** *n.*

whif•fle (hwĭf′əl, wĭf′-) *v.* **-fled, -fling, -fles.** — *intr.* **1.** To move or think erratically; vacillate. **2.** To blow in fitful gusts; puff. **3.** To whistle lightly. — *tr.* To blow, displace, or scatter with gusts of air. [Perh. freq. of WHIFF.]

whif•fle•tree (hwĭf′əl-trē, wĭf′-) *n. Northeastern U.S.* The pivoted horizontal crossbar to which the harness traces of a draft animal are attached and which is in turn attached to a vehicle or an implement. Also called regionally *whippletree.* [Var. of WHIPPLETREE.]

Whig (hwĭg, wĭg) *n.* **1.** A member of an 18th- and 19th-century British political party opposed to the Tories. **2.** A supporter of the war against England during the American Revolution. **3.** A 19th-century American political party formed to oppose the Democratic Party and favoring high tariffs and a loose interpretation of the Constitution. [Prob. short for *Whiggamore,* a member of a body of 17th-cent. Scottish Presbyterian rebels.] — **Whig′ger•y** *n.* — **Whig′gish** *adj.* — **Whig′gism** *n.*

while (hwīl, wīl) *n.* **1.** A period of time: *stayed for a while.* See Usage Note at **awhile. 2.** The time, effort, or trouble taken in doing something: *The project wasn't worth my while.* — *conj.*

1. As long as; during the time that: *It was lovely while it lasted.* 2. At the same time that; although: *While we love the children, we are strict with them.* 3. Whereas; and: *The soles are leather, while the uppers are canvas.* — *tr.v.* **whiled, whil•ing, whiles.** To spend (time) idly or pleasantly: *while the hours away.* [ME < OE *hwīl.* See **kʷeiə-***.]

whiles (hwīlz, wīlz) *conj. Archaic.* While. [ME : *while,* while; see WHILE + *-es,* genitive sing. suff.; see *-s*³.]

whi•lom (hwī′ləm, wī′-) *adj.* Having once been; former. — *adv. Archaic.* At a past time; formerly. [ME, at times < OE *hwīlum,* dative pl. of *hwīl,* time, while. See **kʷeiə-***.]

whilst (hwīlst, wīlst) *conj. Chiefly British.* While. [ME *whilest,* alteration of *whiles,* whiles. See WHILES.]

whim (hwĭm, wĭm) *n.* 1. A sudden or capricious idea; a fancy. 2. Arbitrary thought or impulse: *governed by whim.* 3. A vertical horse-powered drum used as a hoist in a mine. [Short for *whim-wham,* fanciful object.]

whim•brel (hwĭm′brəl, wĭm′-) *n.* A grayish-brown wading bird *(Numenius phaeopus)* having a white, heavily streaked breast. [Perh. alteration of WHIMPER (< its cry).]

whim•per (hwĭm′pər, wĭm′-) *v.* **-pered, -per•ing, -pers.** — *intr.* 1. To cry or sob with soft intermittent sounds; whine. See Syns at **cry.** 2. To complain. — *tr.* To utter in a whimper. — *n.* A low, broken, sobbing sound; a whine. [Prob. imit.] — **whim′per•er** *n.* — **whim′per•ing•ly** *adv.*

whim•si•cal (hwĭm′zĭ-kəl, wĭm′-) *adj.* 1. Determined by, arising from, or marked by whim or caprice. 2. Erratic in behavior or degree of unpredictability. [< WHIMSY.]

whim•si•cal•i•ty (hwĭm′zĭ-kăl′ĭ-tē, wĭm′-) *n., pl.* **-ties.** 1. The quality or state of being whimsical. 2. A whimsical idea or its expression; a caprice.

whim•sy also **whim•sey** (hwĭm′zē, wĭm′-) *n., pl.* **-sies** also **-seys.** 1. An odd or fanciful idea; a whim. 2. A quaint or fanciful quality. [Prob. < *whim-wham,* fanciful object.]

whin¹ (hwĭn, wĭn) *n. Bot.* See **gorse.** [ME *whinne,* prob. of Scand. orig.]

whin² (hwĭn, wĭn) *n.* A whinstone. [ME *quin.*]

whin•chat (hwĭn′chăt′, wĭn′-) *n.* A small brownish Old World songbird *(Saxicola rubetra)* found in open country.

whine (hwīn, wīn) *v.* **whined, whin•ing, whines.** — *intr.* 1. To utter a plaintive, high-pitched, protracted sound, as in pain or complaint. 2. To complain or protest in a childish fashion. 3. To produce a sustained noise of relatively high pitch. — *tr.* To utter with a whine. — *n.* 1. The act of whining. 2. A whining sound. 3. A complaint uttered in a plaintive tone. [ME *whinen* < OE *hwīnan,* to make a whizzing sound.] — **whin′er** *n.* — **whin′ing•ly** *adv.* — **whin′y, whin′ey** *adj.*

whin•ny (hwĭn′ē, wĭn′ē) *v.* **whin•nied** (hwĭn′ēd, wĭn′-), **whin•ny•ing, whin•nies** (hwĭn′ēz, wĭn′-). — *intr.* To neigh, esp. in a gentle tone. — *tr.* To express in a whinny. — *n., pl.* **-nies.** The sound made in whinnying; a neigh. [Prob. akin to WHINE, to whinny.]

whip (hwĭp, wĭp) *v.* **whipped** or **whipt** (hwĭpt, wĭpt), **whip•ping, whips.** — *tr.* 1. To strike with repeated strokes, as with a strap; lash. 2.a. To punish or chastise by repeated striking with a strap or rod; flog. b. To afflict, castigate, or reprove severely. 3. To drive, force, or compel by flogging, lashing, or other means. 4. To strike or affect in a manner similar to whipping or lashing. 5. To beat (eggs, for example) into a froth or foam. 6. *Informal.* To snatch, pull, or remove in a sudden manner. 7. To sew with a loose overcast or overhand stitch. 8. To wrap or bind (a rope, for example) with thread or twine to prevent unlaying; seize. 9. *Naut.* To hoist by means of a rope passing through a single block. 10. *Informal.* To defeat; outdo. — *intr.* 1. To move in a sudden quick manner; dart. 2. To move in a manner similar to a whip; thrash or snap about. — *n.* 1. An instrument, either a flexible rod or a flexible thong or lash attached to a handle, used for whipping. 2. A whipping or lashing motion or stroke; a whiplash. 3. A blow, wound, or cut made by or as if by whipping. 4. Something similar to a whip in form or flexibility. 5. *Sports.* Flexibility, as in the shaft of a golf club. 6.a. A member of a legislative body in charge of enforcing party discipline and ensuring attendance. b. A call issued to party members in a lawmaking body to ensure attendance at a particular time. 7. A dessert made of sugar and stiffly beaten egg whites or cream, often with fruit. 8. An arm on a windmill. 9. *Naut.* A hoist consisting of a single rope passing through an overhead block. 10. A ride in an amusement park, consisting of small cars that move in a rapid, whipping motion along an oval track. — ***phrasal verbs.*** **whip in.** To keep together, as members of a political party or hounds in a pack. **whip up.** 1. To arouse; excite. 2. *Informal.* To prepare quickly. — ***idiom.*** **whip into shape.** *Informal.* To bring to a specified state or condition, vigorously and often forcefully. [ME *wippen, whippen.* See **weip-***.] — **whip′per** *n.*

whip•cord (hwĭp′kôrd′, wĭp′-) *n.* 1. A worsted fabric with a distinct diagonal rib. 2. A strong twisted or braided cord sometimes used in making whiplashes. 3. Catgut.

whip hand *n.* 1. A dominating position; an advantage. 2. The hand in which a whip is held.

whip•lash (hwĭp′lăsh′, wĭp′-) *n.* 1. The lash of a whip. 2. An injury to the cervical spine caused by an abrupt jerking motion of the head, either backward or forward.

whip•per•snap•per (hwĭp′ər-snăp′ər, wĭp′-) *n.* A person regarded as insignificant and pretentious. [Alteration (influenced by WHIP) of dial. *snippersnapper.*]

whip•pet (hwĭp′ĭt, wĭp′-) *n.* Any of a breed of swift short-haired dog developed in England for racing, resembling the greyhound but smaller. [Prob. < WHIP.]

whip•ping (hwĭp′ĭng, wĭp′-) *n.* 1. The act of one that whips. 2. A thrashing administered esp. as punishment. 3. Material, such as cord or thread, used to lash or bind parts.

whipping boy *n.* 1. A scapegoat. 2. A boy formerly raised with a nobleman and whipped for the latter's misdeeds.

Whip•ple (hwĭp′əl, wĭp′-), **George Hoyt.** 1878–1976. Amer. pathologist who shared a 1934 Nobel Prize.

whip•ple•tree (hwĭp′əl-trē′, wĭp′-) *n. Upper Northern U.S.* See **whiffletree.** [Perh. blend of dial. *whippin,* whippletree, and SWINGLETREE.]

whip•poor•will (hwĭp′ər-wĭl′, wĭp′-, hwĭp′ər-wĭl′, wĭp′-) *n.* A nocturnal North American bird *(Caprimulgus vociferus)* of the goatsucker family, having spotted brown feathers that blend with its woodland habitat. [Imit. of its call.]

whip•saw (hwĭp′sô′, wĭp′-) *n.* A narrow two-person crosscut saw. — *tr.v.* **-sawed, -sawed** or **-sawn** (-sôn′), **-saw•ing, -saws.** 1. To cut with a whipsaw. 2. *Games.* To win two bets from (a person) at one time, as in faro. 3. To defeat or best in two ways at once.

whip scorpion *n.* Any of various arachnids of the order Pedipalpi that resemble scorpions but have a whiplike process on the abdomen and no poisonous sting.

whip snake *n.* 1. Any of several slender nonvenomous New World snakes of the genus *Masticophis,* having a long tail that resembles a whip. 2. Any of several similar or related snakes.

whip•stall (hwĭp′stôl′, wĭp′-) *n.* A usu. intentional stall in which a small aircraft enters a vertical climb, pauses, slips backward momentarily, then drops nose downward.

whip•stitch (hwĭp′stĭch′, wĭp′-) *tr.v.* **-stitched, -stitch•ing, -stitch•es.** To sew with overcast stitches, as in finishing or binding fabric. — *n.* A stitch made in this manner.

whipt (hwĭpt, wĭpt) *v.* A p.t. and p.part. of **whip.**

whip•tail (hwĭp′tāl′) *n.* Any of various New World lizards of the genus *Cnemidophorus,* having a long slender tail.

whip•worm (hwĭp′wûrm′, wĭp′-) *n.* A slender whip-shaped parasitic nematode worm *(Trichuris trichiura)* that often infests the intestine of human beings.

whir (hwûr, wûr) *v.* **whirred, whir•ring, whirs.** — *intr.* To move so as to produce a vibrating or buzzing sound. — *tr.* To cause to make a vibratory sound. — *n.* 1. A sound of buzzing or vibration. 2. Excited noisy activity; bustle. [ME *whirren,* prob. of Scand. orig.]

whirl (hwûrl, wûrl) *v.* **whirled, whirl•ing, whirls.** — *intr.* 1. To revolve rapidly about a center or an axis. 2. To rotate or spin rapidly. 3. To turn rapidly, changing direction; wheel. 4. To have the sensation of spinning; reel. 5. To move circularly and rapidly in varied, random directions. — *tr.* 1. To cause to rotate or turn rapidly. 2. To move or drive in a circular or curving course. 3. To drive at high speed. 4. *Obsolete.* To hurl. — *n.* 1. The act of rotating or revolving rapidly. 2. Something, such as a cloud of dust, that whirls or is whirled. 3. A state of confusion; tumult. 4. A swift succession or round of events. 5. A state of mental confusion or giddiness; dizziness. 6. *Informal.* A short trip or ride. 7. *Informal.* A brief or experimental try. [ME *whirlen,* prob. < ON *hvirfla.*] — **whirl′er** *n.*

whirl•i•gig (hwûr′lĭ-gĭg′, wûr′-) *n.* 1. Any of various spinning toys. 2. A carousel; a merry-go-round. 3. Something that continuously whirls. 4. The whirligig beetle. [ME *whirlegigge* : *whirlen,* whirl; see WHIRL + *-gigge,* something that rotates, poss. of Scand. orig.; akin to GIG¹.]

whirligig beetle *n.* Any of various gregarious beetles of the family Gyrinidae that circle about rapidly on water.

whirl•pool (hwûrl′po͞ol′, wûrl′-) *n.* 1. A rapidly rotating current of water; a vortex. 2.a. Turmoil; whirl. b. A magnetic impelling force into which one may be pulled. 3. A bathtub or pool having jets of warm water.

whirl•wind (hwûrl′wĭnd′, wûrl′-) *n.* 1. A rapidly rotating, generally vertical column of air, such as a tornado. 2.a. A tumultuous confused rush. b. A destructive force or thing. — *adj.* Tumultuous or rapid: *a whirlwind political campaign.*

whirl•y•bird (hwûr′lē-bûrd′, wûr′-) *n. Informal.* A helicopter.

whirr (hwûr, wûr) *v. & n. Chiefly British.* Var. of **whir.**

whisk (hwĭsk, wĭsk) *v.* **whisked, whisk•ing, whisks.** — *tr.* 1. To move or cause to move with quick light sweeping motions. 2. To whip (eggs or cream). — *intr.* To move lightly, nimbly, and rapidly. — *n.* 1. A quick light sweeping motion. 2. A whiskbroom. 3. A small bunch, as of twigs, attached to a handle and used in brushing. 4. A kitchen utensil for whipping foodstuffs. [ME *wisken,* of Scand. orig.]

whisk•broom (hwĭsk′bro͞om′, -bro͝om′, wĭsk′-) *n.* A small short-handled broom used esp. to brush clothes.

whisk•er (hwĭs′kər, wĭs′-) *n.* 1.a. **whiskers.** The hair on a

whisk

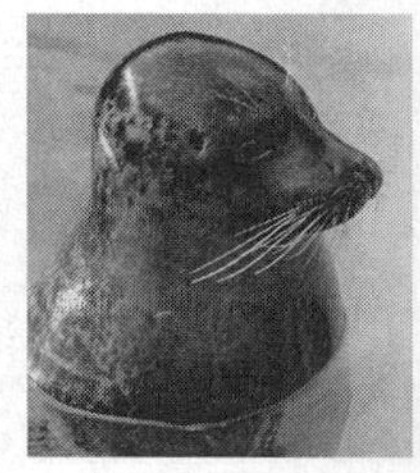

whisker
On a sea lion

ă pat	oi boy
ā pay	ou out
âr care	o͝o took
ä father	o͞o boot
ĕ pet	ŭ cut
ē be	ûr urge
ĭ pit	th thin
ī pie	*th* this
îr pier	hw which
ŏ pot	zh vision
ō toe	ə about, item
ô paw	

Stress marks:
′ (primary);
′ (secondary), as in
dictionary (dĭk′shə-nĕr′ē)

man's cheeks and chin. **b.** A single hair of a beard or mustache. **2.** One of the long stiff tactile bristles or hairs that grow near the mouth and elsewhere on the head of most mammals; a vibrissa. **3.** *Informal.* A narrow margin; a hairsbreadth. **4.** *Naut.* One of two spars or booms projecting from the side of a bowsprit for spreading the jib or flying-jib guys. **5.** *Chem.* An extremely fine filamentary crystal with extraordinary shear strength and unusual electrical or surface properties. [ME *wisker*, anything that wisks < *wisken*, to whisk. See WHISK.] **—whisk′ered, whisk′er•y** *adj.*

whis•key also **whis•ky** (hwĭs′kē, wĭs′-) *n., pl.* **-keys** also **whis•kies. 1.** An alcoholic liquor distilled from grain, such as corn, rye, or barley. **2.** A drink of such liquor. [< USQUEBAUGH.]

Usage Note: Either *whiskey* or, less frequently, *whisky* can be used to refer to spirits distilled in the United States. Some writers prefer to reserve *whisky* for spirits distilled in Great Britain, but no widespread agreement on this exists.

whiskey jack *n.* See **gray jay.** [Alteration of *whiskey-john*, by folk ety. < Cree dial. *wiiskachaan.*]

whiskey sour *n.* A cocktail made with whiskey, lemon juice, and sugar.

white admiral
Limenitis arthemis

whis•per (hwĭs′pər, wĭs′-) *n.* **1.** Soft speech produced without full voice. **2.** Something uttered very softly. **3.** A secretly or surreptitiously expressed belief, rumor, or hint: *whispers of scandal.* **4.** A low rustling sound. **—*v.* -pered, -per•ing, -pers. —*intr.* 1.** To speak softly. **2.** To speak quietly and privately, as by way of gossip or intrigue. **3.** To make a soft rustling sound. **—*tr.* 1.** To utter very softly. **2.** To say or tell privately or secretly. [< ME *whisperen*, to whisper < OE *hwisprian.*] **—whis′per•er** *n.* **—whis′per•y** *adj.*

whist (hwĭst, wĭst) *n. Games.* A card game played with a full deck by two teams of two players, in which the last card dealt indicates trump and the object of play is to win the majority of the tricks. [Alteration of dial. *whisk*, perh. < WHISK.]

whis•tle (hwĭs′əl, wĭs′-) *v.* **-tled, -tling, -tles. —*intr.* 1.** To produce a clear musical sound by forcing air through the teeth or through an aperture formed by pursing the lips. **2.** To produce a clear, shrill, sharp musical sound by blowing on or through a device. **3.a.** To produce a high-pitched sound when moving swiftly through the air. **b.** To produce a high-pitched sound by the rapid movement of air through an opening or past an obstruction. **4.** To emit a shrill, sharp, high-pitched cry, as some birds and other animals. **5.** To summon by whistling. **—*tr.* 1.** To produce by whistling. **2.** To summon, signal, or direct by whistling. **3.** To cause to move with a whistling noise. **—*n.* 1.a.** A small wind instrument for making whistling sounds by means of the breath. **b.** A device for making whistling sounds by means of forced air or steam. **2.** A sound produced by a whistling device or by whistling through the lips. **3.** A whistling sound, as of an animal or a projectile. **4.** The act of whistling. **5.** A whistling sound used to summon or command. **—*idioms.* blow the whistle.** *Slang.* To expose a wrongdoing in the hope of bringing it to a halt. **whistle in the dark.** To attempt to keep one's courage up. [ME *whistlen* < OE *hwistlian.*]

White House
Top: North Portico, facing Pennsylvania Avenue
Bottom: South Portico

whistle blower or **whis•tle-blow•er** or **whis•tle•blow•er** (hwĭs′əl-blō′ər, wĭs′-) *n. Slang.* One who brings wrongdoing within an organization to light. **—whis′tle-blow′ing** *n.*

whistle pig *n. Appalachian Mountains.* See **woodchuck.** See Regional Note at **woodchuck.**

whis•tler (hwĭs′lər, wĭs′-) *n.* **1.** One that whistles. **2.a.** A marmot *(Marmota caligata)* of the mountains of northwest North America having a grayish coat and a shrill whistling cry. **b.** Any of various birds that produce a whistling sound. **c.** A horse having a respiratory disease characterized by wheezing. **3.** *Phys.* An electromagnetic wave of audio frequency produced by atmospheric disturbances such as lightning, having a characteristic whistling sound in detection equipment.

Whis•tler (hwĭs′lər, wĭs′-), **James Abbott McNeill.** 1834–1903. Amer. painter whose subtle coloring and tonal harmony were influenced by musical aesthetics and Japanese art.

whistle stop *n.* **1.** A town or station at which a train stops only if signaled. **2.** A brief appearance of a political candidate in a small town, traditionally on a train observation platform.

whis•tle-stop (hwĭs′əl-stŏp′, wĭs′-) *intr.v.* **-stopped, -stop•ping, -stops.** To conduct a political campaign by making brief appearances or speeches in a series of small towns.

whis•tling swan (hwĭs′lĭng, wĭs′-) *n.* A white North American swan *(Olor columbianus)* having a soft, musical trumpeting voice and a black beak with a yellow spot at the base.

whit (hwĭt, wĭt) *n.* The least bit; an iota: *not a whit afraid.* [ME, amount < OE *wiht.* See WIGHT[1].]

Whit•by (hwĭt′bē, wĭt′-). A town of SE Ontario, Canada, on Lake Ontario NE of Toronto. Pop. 36,698.

white (hwīt, wīt) *n.* **1.** *Color.* The achromatic color of maximum lightness; the color of objects that reflect nearly all light of all visible wavelengths; the complement or antagonist of black. **2.** The white or nearly white part, as: **a.** The albumen of an egg. **b.** The white part of an eyeball. **c.** A blank unprinted area, as of an advertisement. **3.** One that is white or nearly white, as: **a. whites.** White trousers or a white outfit of a special nature. **b. whites.** The white dress uniform of the U.S. Navy or Coast Guard. **c.** A white wine. **d.** A white pigment. **e.** A white breed, species, or variety of animal. **f.** Also **White.** A member of a racial group of people having light skin coloration, esp. one of European origin. See Usage Note at **black. g.** A product of a white color, such as flour, salt, and sugar. Often used in the plural. **4.** *Games.* **a.** The white or light-colored pieces, as in chess. **b.** The player using these pieces. **5.a.** The outermost ring of an archery target. **b.** A hit in this ring. **6. whites.** *Pathol.* Leukorrhea. **7.** A politically ultraconservative or reactionary person. **—*adj.* whit•er, whit•est. 1.** Being of the color white; devoid of hue, as new snow. **2.** Approaching the color white, as: **a.** Weakly colored; almost colorless; pale. **b.** Pale gray; silvery and lustrous. **c.** Bloodless; blanched. **3.** Light or whitish in color or having light or whitish parts. Used with animal and plant names. **4.** Also **White.** Of or belonging to a racial group having light skin coloration, esp. one of European origin. **5.** Not written or printed on; blank. **6.** Unsullied; pure. **7.** Habited in white. **8.** Accompanied by or mantled with snow. **9.a.** Incandescent. **b.** Intensely heated; impassioned. **10.** Ultraconservative or reactionary. **11.** With milk added. Used of tea or coffee. **—*tr.v.* whit•ed, whit•ing, whites. 1.** *Print.* To create or leave blank spaces in (printed or illustrated matter). Often used with *out.* **2.** *Archaic.* **a.** To whiten; whitewash. **b.** To blanch. [ME < OE *hwīt.* See **kweit-*.**] **—white′ness** *n.*

White, Byron Raymond. b. 1917. Amer. jurist; associate justice of the U.S. Supreme Court (1962–93).

White, Edward Douglass. 1845–1921. Amer. jurist; associate justice (1894–1910) and chief justice (1910–21) of the U.S. Supreme Court.

White, E(lwyn) B(rooks). 1899–1985. Amer. writer known for his children's books, such as *Charlotte's Web* (1952), and his revision of a 1918 writing manual, *The Elements of Style* (1959).

White, John. d. 1593? English painter and cartographer at Roanoke I. (1585–86) who executed paintings of native inhabitants and local flora and fauna.

White, Patrick. 1912–90. Australian writer who won the 1973 Nobel Prize for literature.

White, Stanford. 1853–1906. Amer. architect particularly noted for his interior designs and ornate eclectic buildings.

White, T(erence) H(anbury). 1906–64. British writer best known for the novel *The Once and Future King* (1958).

White, William Allen. 1868–1944. Amer. newspaper editor and writer noted for his politically influential editorials.

white admiral *n.* A nymphalid butterfly *(Limenitis arthemis)* of eastern North America having a broad white band on blue-black wings.

white ant *n.* See **termite.**

white•bait (hwīt′bāt′, wīt′-) *n.* **1.** The young of various fishes, esp. the herring, considered a delicacy when fried. **2.** Any of various similar or related small edible fishes.

white bass (băs) *n.* A North American freshwater food fish *(Morone chrysops)* having a silvery color and blackish stripes.

White Bear Lake (bâr′). A city of E MN, a suburb of St. Paul. Pop. 24,704.

white birch *n.* Any of several birch trees having white bark, as the paper birch of North America.

white blood cell *n.* Any of the colorless or white cells in the blood that have a nucleus and cytoplasm and help protect the body from infection and disease through specialized neutrophils, lymphocytes, and monocytes.

white book *n.* An official publication of a national government. [< its formerly being bound in white.]

white bread *n.* Bread made from finely ground, usu. bleached wheat flour. Also called regionally *light bread.*

white•cap (hwīt′kăp′, wīt′-) *n.* A wave with a crest of foam.

white cedar *n.* Either of two North American evergreen trees *(Thuja occidentalis* or *Chamaecyparis thyoides)* having light-colored wood.

white cell *n.* See **white blood cell.**

White Center. A community of W-central WA, a suburb of Seattle. Pop. 20,531.

white chip *n.* **1.** *Games.* A white disk used in poker as a betting token of minimal value. **2.** Something of minimal value.

white cloud *n.* A small, brightly colored freshwater fish *(Tanichthys albonubes)* popular in aquariums.

white clover *n.* A common European clover *(Trifolium repens)* having rounded white flower heads.

white-col•lar (hwīt′kŏl′ər, wīt′-) *adj.* Of or relating to workers whose work usu. does not involve manual labor.

white corpuscle *n.* See **white blood cell.**

white crappie *n.* A silvery edible North American freshwater fish *(Pomoxis annularis)* related to the sunfish.

whit•ed sepulcher (hwī′tĭd, wī′-) *n.* An evil person who pretends to be holy or good; a hypocrite. [From the simile applied by Jesus to hypocrites (Matthew 23:27).]

white dwarf *n.* A whitish star in a latter stage of development, having low luminosity, small size, and very great density.

white elephant *n.* **1.a.** A rare expensive possession that is a financial burden to maintain. **b.** Something of dubious or limited value. **2.** An article no longer wanted by its owner. **3.** An endeavor or a venture that fails conspicuously. **4.** A rare whitish or light-gray form of the Asian elephant, venerated in regions of southeast Asia and India.

white-eye (hwīt′ī′, wīt′ī′) *n.* Any of various small, greenish, chiefly tropical Old World birds of the genus *Zosterops,* having a narrow ring of white feathers around each eye.

white•face (hwīt′fās′, wīt′-) *n.* **1.** White facial makeup. **2.** A white-faced animal, esp. a Hereford.

white-faced (hwīt′fāst′, wīt′-) *adj.* **1.** Having a pale face; pallid. **2.** Having a white face or a white patch extending from the muzzle to the forehead: *a white-faced antelope.*

white feather *n.* A sign of cowardice. **—*idiom.* show the white feather.** To act like a coward. [< the belief that a gamecock with a white feather in its tail was a poor fighter.]

White•field (hwĭt′fēld′, wĭt′-, hwīt′-, wīt′-), **George.** 1714–70. British religious leader who was a central figure in the establishment of Methodism in America.

white•fish (hwīt′fĭsh′, wīt′-) *n., pl.* **whitefish** or **-fish•es. 1.a.** Any of various chiefly North American freshwater food fishes of the genus *Coregonus,* having a generally white or silvery color. **b.** Any of various similar or related fishes, such as the lake herring, whiting, or menhaden. **2.** See **beluga** 2.

white flag *n.* A white cloth or flag signaling truce or surrender.

white•fly (hwīt′flī′, wīt′-) *n.* Any of various small whitish homopterous insects of the family Aleyrodidae, having long wings and a white waxy body and often injurious to plants.

white-foot•ed mouse (hwīt′fo͝ot′ĭd, wīt′-) *n.* A semidesert mouse *(Peromyscus leucopus)* of New Mexico that feeds on crop-damaging insects.

white fox *n.* The arctic fox in its winter color phase.

White Friar *n.* See **Carmelite** 1. [< the color of the habit.]

white frost *n.* See **hoarfrost.**

white gasoline *n.* Gasoline containing no tetraethyl lead.

white gold *n.* An alloy of gold and nickel, sometimes also containing palladium or zinc, having a pale platinumlike color.

White•hall[1] (hwīt′hôl′, wīt′-). A wide thoroughfare in London, England, running N and S between Trafalgar Square and the Houses of Parliament; site of many government offices.

White•hall[2] (hwīt′hôl′, wīt′-). A city of central OH, a suburb of Columbus. Pop. 20,572.

White•hall[3] (hwīt′hôl′, wīt′-) *n.* The British civil service.

white•head (hwīt′hĕd′, wīt′-) *n.* See **milium.**

White•head (hwīt′hĕd′, wīt′-), **Alfred North.** 1861–1947. British philosopher and a founder of mathematical logic.

white-head•ed (hwīt′hĕd′ĭd, wīt′-) *adj.* **1.** Having white hair, fur, or plumage on the head. **2.** *Irish.* Favorite; darling.

white heat *n.* **1.** The temperature or physical condition of a white-hot substance. **2.** Intense emotion or excitement.

white hole *n.* A hypothetical hole in outer space from which energy and matter emerge. [WHITE + (BLACK) HOLE.]

white hope *n.* **1.** Someone, esp. a beginning competitor, whom supporters hope will gain success. **2.** A white prizefighter believed to have a chance of defeating a Black champion.

White•horse (hwīt′hôrs′, wīt′-). The cap. of Yukon Terr., Canada, in the S part on the Yukon R. Pop. 14,814.

white-hot (hwīt′hŏt′, wīt′-) *adj.* **1.** So hot as to glow with a bright white light. **2.** Zealous; fervid.

White House *n.* **1.** The executive branch of the U.S. government. **2.** The executive mansion of the President of the United States.

white iron pyrites *n.* See **marcasite** 1.

white knight *n.* One that comes to the rescue; a savior.

white-knuck•le (hwīt′nŭk′əl, wīt′-) *adj. Slang.* Characterized by tense nervousness or apprehension.

white lead (lĕd) *n.* A heavy white poisonous powder, essentially basic lead carbonate, used in paint pigments.

white leather also **whit•leath•er** (hwĭt′lĕ*th*′ər, wĭt′-) *n.* A soft leather specially treated with salt and alum.

white lie *n.* A trivial, harmless, or well-intentioned untruth.

white lightning *n. Chiefly Southern U.S.* See **moonshine** 3.

white-liv•ered (hwīt′lĭv′ərd, wīt′-) *adj.* Cowardly.

white magic *n.* Magic or incantation practiced for good purposes or as a counter to evil.

white mahogany *n.* See **primavera**[1] 2.

white man's burden (mănz) *n.* The supposed responsibility of white people to govern and impart their culture to nonwhite people. [< *"The White Man's Burden"* by Kipling.]

white marriage *n.* A marriage without sexual relations.

white matter *n.* Whitish nerve tissue, esp. of the brain and spinal cord, consisting chiefly of myelinated nerve fibers.

white meat *n.* Light-colored meat, esp. of poultry.

white metal *n.* Any of various whitish alloys, such as pewter, that contain high percentages of tin or lead.

white mica *n.* See **muscovite.**

White Mountain. A peak, 4,345 m (14,246 ft), in the Sierra Nevada of E-central CA.

White Mountains. A section of the Appalachian Mts. in N NH rising to 1,917.8 m (6,288 ft).

whit•en (hwīt′n, wīt′n) *tr. & intr.v.* **-ened, -en•ing, -ens.** To make or become white, esp. by bleaching. **—whit′en•er** *n.*

white night *n.* **1.** A night without sleep. **2.** A night without full darkness, as during the summer in high latitudes.

White Nile (nīl). A section of the Nile R. in E Africa flowing to Khartoum, where it joins the Blue Nile to form the Nile R. proper.

white noise *n.* Acoustical or electrical noise with equal intensity at all frequencies within a given band. [< white light, which contains all visible spectrum frequencies.]

white oak *n.* **1.** A large oak *(Quercus alba)* of eastern North America, having light-colored wood. **2.** See **roble** 1.

white•out (hwīt′out′, wīt′-) *n.* A polar weather condition caused by a heavy cloud cover over the snow, characterized by absence of shadow, invisibility of the horizon, and discernibility of only very dark objects.

white paper *n.* **1.** A government report. **2.** An authoritative report on a major issue, as by a team of journalists.

white pepper *n.* Pepper ground from peppercorns from which the outer black layer has been removed.

white perch *n.* A small silvery food fish *(Roccus americanus)* of the coast and freshwater streams of eastern North America.

white pine *n.* **1.** A timber tree *(Pinus strobus)* of eastern North America having needles in clusters of five and durable, easily worked wood. **2.** The wood of this tree. **3.** Any of several other pines having needles in clusters of five.

White Plains. A city of SE NY, a suburb of New York City. Pop. 48,718.

white poplar *n.* A deciduous Eurasian tree *(Populus alba)* having palmately lobed leaves with whitish undersides.

white potato *n.* The edible tuber of the common potato.

white•print (hwīt′prĭnt′, wīt′-) *n.* A photomechanical copy, usu. of a line drawing, in which black or colored lines appear on a white background.

White River. 1. A river of N AR and S MO flowing c. 1,110 km (690 mi) to the Mississippi R. **2.** A river of NW NE and S SD flowing c. 523 km (325 mi) to the Missouri R.

white room *n.* See **clean room.**

White Rus•sia (rŭsh′ə). See **Belorussia.**

white sauce *n.* A sauce made with butter, flour, and milk, cream, or stock, used as a base for other sauces.

White Sea. A sea of NW Russia, an inlet of the Barents Sea.

white shark *n.* The great white shark.

white slave *n.* A woman held unwillingly for prostitution.

white slaver *n.* A procurer of or trafficker in white slaves.

white slavery *n.* Forced prostitution.

white•smith (hwīt′smĭth′, wīt′-) *n.* **1.** One who works white metal. **2.** One who does finish work, such as polishing, on iron. [WHITE + (BLACK)SMITH.]

white snakeroot *n.* A poisonous eastern North American plant *(Eupatorium rugosum)* having opposite, heart-shaped leaves and flat-topped clusters of small white flower heads.

white space *n.* Space on a page or poster not covered by print or graphic matter.

white squall *n.* A sudden squall occurring in tropical or subtropical waters, characterized by the absence of a dark cloud and the presence of white-capped waves or broken water.

white stork *n.* The common stork *(Ciconia ciconia)* of Europe and Asia, having black and white plumage, a dark red bill, and pinkish-red legs.

white supremacy *n.* The belief or theory that the white race is inherently superior to and therefore entitled to rule over all other races. **—white supremacist** *n.*

white•tail (hwīt′tāl′, wīt′-) *n.* See **white-tailed deer.**

white-tailed deer (hwīt′tāld′, wīt′-) *n.* A common North American deer *(Odocoileus virginianus)* having a tail that is white on the underside.

white•throat (hwīt′thrōt′, wīt′-) *n.* **1.** Either of two Old World songbirds *(Sylvia communis* or *S. curruca)* having a white throat and belly. **2.** See **white-throated sparrow.**

white-throat•ed sparrow (hwīt′thrō′tĭd, wīt′-) *n.* A large North American sparrow *(Zonotrichia albicollis)* having a white patch on the throat and a striped crown.

white tie *n.* **1.** A white bow tie worn as a part of men's formal evening dress. **2.** Men's formal evening dress. **—white′-tie′** (hwīt′tī′, wīt′-) *adj.*

white trash *n. Offensive Slang.* Used as a disparaging term for a poor white person or poor white people.

white vitriol *n.* See **zinc sulfate.**

White Vol•ta (vŏl′tə, vōl′-, vôl′-). A river of Burkina Faso and N Ghana flowing c. 885 km (550 mi) to join the Black Volta and form the Volta R.

white•wall tire (hwīt′wôl′, wīt′-) *n.* A vehicular tire having a white sidewall.

white walnut *n.* See **butternut** 1a.

white•wash (hwīt′wŏsh′, -wôsh′, wīt′-) *n.* **1.** A mixture of lime and water, often with whiting, size, or glue added, that is used to whiten walls, fences, or other structures. **2.** Concealment or palliation of flaws or failures. **3.** *Sports & Games.* A defeat in a game in which the loser scores no points. **—*tr.v.* -washed, -wash•ing, -wash•es. 1.** To paint or coat with or as if with whitewash. **2.** To conceal or gloss over (wrongdoing, for example). **—white′wash′er** *n.*

white water *n.* Turbulent or frothy water, as in rapids or surf.

white-wa•ter (hwīt′wô′tər, -wŏt′ər, wīt′-) *adj.* Of, intended for, or taking place on white water, esp. in river rapids.

white pine
Pinus strobus

white snakeroot
Eupatorium rugosum

whitewall tire

ă pat	oi boy
ā pay	ou out
âr care	o͝o took
ä father	o͞o boot
ĕ pet	ŭ cut
ē be	ûr urge
ĭ pit	th thin
ī pie	*th* this
îr pier	hw which
ŏ pot	zh vision
ō toe	ə about, item
ô paw	

Stress marks:
′ (primary);
′ (secondary), as in
dictionary (dĭk′shə-nĕr′ē)

Eli Whitney

white whale *n.* A small toothed whale *(Delphinapterus leucas),* chiefly of northern waters, that is white when full-grown.

white•wood (hwīt′wo͝od′, wīt′-) *n.* **1.** Any of various deciduous trees such as the tulip tree, basswood, or cottonwood. **2.** The soft light-colored wood of any of these trees.

whit•ey also **Whit•ey** (hwī′tē, wī′-) *n., pl.* **-eys.** *Offensive Slang.* Used as a disparaging term for a white person or white people.

whith•er (hwĭth′ər, wĭth′-) *adv.* To what place, result, or condition: *Whither are we wandering?* — *conj.* **1.** To which specified place or position. **2.** To whatever place, result, or condition. [ME < OE *hwider.* See **kʷo-***.]

whith•er•so•ev•er (hwĭth′ər-sō-ĕv′ər, wĭth′-) *adv.* To whatever place; to any place whatsoever.

whit•ing¹ (hwī′tĭng, wī′-) *n.* A pure white grade of chalk that has been ground and washed for use in paints, ink, and putty. [ME *whityng* < *whiten,* to whiten < *white,* white. See WHITE.]

whit•ing² (hwī′tĭng, wī′-) *n., pl.* **whiting** or **-ings. 1.** A food fish *(Merlangus merlangus)* of European Atlantic waters, related to the cod. **2.** Any of several marine food fishes of the genera *Menticirrhus* and *Merluccius* of North American coastal waters, including the corbina and the silver hake. [ME *whitynge* < MDu. *wijting.* See **kweit-***.]

whit•ish (hwī′tĭsh, wī′-) *adj.* Somewhat white.

whit•leath•er (hwĭt′lĕth′ər, wĭt′-) *n.* Var. of **white leather.**

whit•low (hwĭt′lō, wĭt′-) *n.* See **felon².** [Alteration of ME *whitflawe* : *white,* white (perh. alteration of MDu. *vijt,* abscess) + *flaue,* splinter, flaw; see FLAW¹.]

Whit•man (hwĭt′mən, wĭt′-), **Marcus.** 1802–47. Amer. missionary who with his wife **Narcissa Prentiss** (1808–47) established a post in the Oregon region (1836).

Whitman, Walt. 1819–92. Amer. poet known esp. for his collection *Leaves of Grass* (first published 1855).

Whit•mon•day also **Whit-Mon•day** (hwĭt′mŭn′dē, -dā′, wĭt′-) *n.* The day after Whitsunday.

Whit•ney (hwĭt′nē, wĭt′-), **Eli.** 1765–1825. Amer. inventor and manufacturer who invented the cotton gin (1793) and developed the first factory to use mass-production techniques.

Whitney, Mount. A peak, 4,420.7 m (14,494 ft), in the Sierra Nevada of E-central CA.

Whit•sun (hwĭt′sən, wĭt′-) *adj.* Of, relating to, or observed on Whitsunday or at Whitsuntide.

Whit•sun•day (hwĭt′sən-dē, -dā′, wĭt′-) *n.* See **Pentecost** 1. [ME *whitsonday* < OE *hwīta sunnandæg,* White Sunday (< the white vestments worn on this day).]

Whit•sun•tide also **Whit•sun Tide** (hwĭt′sən-tīd′, wĭt′-) *n.* The week starting on Whitsunday, esp. its first three days.

Whit•ta•ker (hwĭt′ə-kər, wĭt′-), **Charles Evans.** 1901–73. Amer. jurist; associate justice of the U.S. Supreme Court (1957–62).

Whit•ti•er (hwĭt′ē-ər, wĭt′-). A city of S CA ESE of Los Angeles; founded by Quakers in 1887. Pop. 77,671.

Whittier, John Greenleaf. 1807–92. Amer. poet whose poems about New England include *Snow-Bound* (1866).

Whit•ting•ton (hwĭt′ĭng-tən, wĭt′-), **Richard.** 1358?–1423. English merchant and mayor of London who loaned large sums of money to Henry IV and Henry V.

whit•tle (hwĭt′l, wĭt′l) *v.* **-tled, -tling, -tles.** — *tr.* **1.a.** To cut small bits or pare shavings from (a piece of wood). **b.** To fashion or shape in this way: *whittle a toy boat.* **2.** To reduce or eliminate gradually, as if by whittling with a knife: *whittled down the debt.* — *intr.* To cut or shape wood with a knife. [< ME *whyttel,* knife, var. of *thwitel* < *thwiten,* to whittle < OE *thwītan,* to strike, whittle down.] — **whit′tler** *n.*

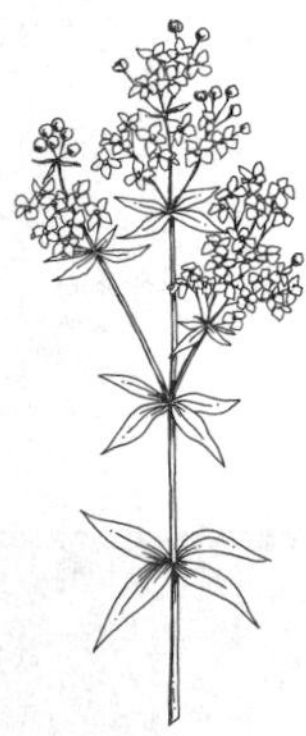
whorl
Whorled leaves of northern bedstraw *Galium boreale*

whiz also **whizz** (hwĭz, wĭz) — *v.* **whizzed, whiz•zing, whiz•zes.** — *intr.* **1.** To make a whirring or hissing sound, as of an object speeding through air. **2.** To move swiftly with or as if with such a sound; rush. — *tr.* To throw or spin rapidly. — *n.* **1.** A whirring or hissing sound. **2.** A rapid passage or journey. **3.** *Informal.* One who has remarkable skill. [Imit.]

whiz-bang also **whizz-bang** (hwĭz′băng′, wĭz′-) *Informal.* — *n.* One that is conspicuously effective, successful, or skillful. — *adj.* **1.** Conspicuously effective, successful, or skillful. **2.** Very rapid and eventful; rushed. [< *whizzbang,* a shell heard only an instant before landing and exploding.]

whiz kid *n. Informal.* A young person who is exceptionally intelligent, innovatively clever, or precociously successful. [Alteration of *Quiz Kid,* a panelist on an early game show.]

who (ho͞o) *pron.* **1.** What or which person or persons: *Who left?* **2.** Used as a relative pronoun to introduce a clause when the antecedent is a person or persons or one to whom personality is attributed: *the visitor who came yesterday.* **3.** The person or persons that; whoever: *Who believes that will believe anything.* [ME < OE *hwā.* See **kʷo-***.]

Usage Note: The traditional rules that determine the use of *who* and *whom* are relatively simple: *who* is used for a grammatical subject, where a nominative pronoun such as *I* or *he* would be appropriate, and *whom* is used elsewhere. Thus, we write *The actor who played Hamlet was there,* since *who* stands for the subject of *played Hamlet*; and *Who do you think is the best candidate?* where *who* stands for the subject of *is the best candidate.* But we write *The man whom the papers criticized did not show up,* since *whom* is the object of the verb *criticized.* • Considerable effort and attention are required to apply the rules correctly in complicated sentences. It is thus not surprising that writers from Shakespeare onward should often have interchanged *who* and *whom.* • We may say either *The scientist who discovers a cure for cancer will be immortalized,* where the restrictive clause *who discovers a cure for cancer* indicates which scientist will be immortalized, or *The mathematician over there, who solved the four-color theorem, is widely known,* where the nonrestrictive clause *who solved the four-color theorem* adds information about a person already identified by the phrase *the mathematician over there.* • It is entirely acceptable to write either *the man that wanted to talk to you* or *the man who wanted to talk to you.* • The grammatical rules governing the use of *who* and *whom* apply equally to *whoever* and *whomever.* See Usage Notes at **else, that, whose.**

WHO *abbr.* World Health Organization.

whoa (hwō, wō) *interj.* Used to order a halt, as by a horse.

who'd (ho͞od). **1.** Who would. **2.** Who had.

who•dun•it (ho͞o-dŭn′ĭt) *n. Informal.* A detective story.

who•ev•er (ho͞o-ĕv′ər) *pron.* **1.** Whatever person or persons: *Whoever comes will be welcomed.* **2.** Who: *Whoever could have dreamed of it?* See Usage Notes at **whatever, who.**

whole (hōl) *adj.* **1.** Containing all components; complete. **2.** Not divided or disjoined; in one unit. **3.** Constituting the full amount, extent, or duration. **4.a.** Not wounded, injured, or impaired; sound or unhurt. **b.** Having been restored; healed. **5.** Having the same parents. **6.** *Math.* Not fractional; integral. — *n.* **1.** A number, group, set, or thing lacking no part or element; a complete thing. **2.** An entity or a system made up of interrelated parts. — *adv. Informal.* Entirely; wholly. — ***idioms.*** **as a whole.** All parts or aspects considered; altogether. **on the whole. 1.** Considering everything. **2.** In most instances or cases; as a rule. [ME *hole,* unharmed < OE *hāl.* See **kailo-***.] — **whole′ness** *n.*

Syns: *whole, all, entire, gross, total.* The central meaning shared by these adjectives is "including every constituent or individual": *a whole town devastated by an earthquake; all the class going on a field trip; the entire group; gross income; the total cost.* ***Ant:*** *partial.*

whole blood *n.* Blood drawn from the body from which no constituent, such as plasma or platelets, has been removed.

whole cloth *n.* Pure fabrication or fiction. [< the fabrication of garments out of new full-sized pieces of cloth.]

whole•heart•ed (hōl′här′tĭd) *adj.* Marked by unconditional commitment, unstinting devotion, or unreserved enthusiasm. — **whole′heart′ed•ly** *adv.* — **whole′heart′ed•ness** *n.*

whole hog *Slang.* — *n.* The whole way; the fullest extent. — *adv.* Completely; unreservedly.

whole life insurance *n.* Life insurance that provides protection for the entire lifetime of the insured in return for constant premiums as long as the insured owns the policy.

whole milk *n.* Milk from which no constituent, such as fat, has been removed.

whole note *n. Mus.* A note having, in common time, the value of four beats.

whole number *n. Math.* Any of the set of numbers including 0 and all negative and positive multiples of 1.

whole•sale (hōl′sāl′) *n.* The sale of goods in large quantities, as for resale by a retailer. — *adj.* **1.** Of, relating to, or engaged in the sale of goods in large quantities for resale. **2.** Made or accomplished extensively and indiscriminately; blanket. — *adv.* **1.** In large bulk or quantity. **2.** Extensively; indiscriminately. — *v.* **-saled, -sal•ing, -sales.** — *tr.* To sell in large quantities for resale. — *intr.* **1.** To engage in wholesale selling. **2.** To be sold wholesale. — **whole′sal′er** *n.*

whole•some (hōl′səm) *adj.* **-som•er, -som•est. 1.** Conducive to sound health or well-being; salutary. **2.** Promoting mental, moral, or social health. **3.** Enjoying or marked by physical, mental, or moral soundness; healthy. See Syns at **healthy.** [ME *holsom* < OE **hālsum.* See **kailo-***.] — **whole′some•ly** *adv.* — **whole′some•ness** *n.*

whole-wheat (hōl′hwēt′, -wēt′) *adj.* **1.** Made from the entire grain of wheat, including the bran: *whole-wheat flour.* **2.** Made with whole-wheat flour: *whole-wheat bread.*

who'll (ho͞ol). **1.** Who will. **2.** Who shall.

whol•ly (hō′lē, hōl′lē) *adv.* **1.** Completely; entirely. **2.** Exclusively; solely.

whom (ho͞om) *pron.* The objective case of **who.** See Usage Note at **who.** [ME < OE *hwǣm, hwām.* See **kʷo-***.]

whom•ev•er (ho͞om-ĕv′ər) *pron.* The objective case of **whoever.** See Usage Note at **who.**

whom•so•ev•er (ho͞om′sō-ĕv′ər) *pron.* The objective case of **whosoever.**

whoop (ho͞op, hwo͞op, wo͞op) *n.* **1.a.** A loud cry of exultation or excitement. **b.** A shout uttered by a hunter or warrior. **2.** A hooting cry, as of a bird. **3.** The paroxysmal gasp characteristic of whooping cough. — *v.* **whooped, whoop•ing, whoops.** — *intr.* **1.** To utter a loud shout or cry. See Syns at **shout. 2.** To utter a hooting cry. **3.** To make the paroxysmal gasp characteristic of whooping cough. — *tr.* **1.** To utter with a whoop. **2.** To chase, call, urge on, or drive with a whoop. **—*idiom.* whoop it up.** *Slang.* **1.** To have a jolly, noisy celebration. **2.** To express or arouse enthusiasm; cheer: *conventioneers whooping it up for their candidate.* [< ME *whopen,* to whoop, var. of *hopen* < OFr. *hopper,* of imit. orig.]

whoop•ee (hwo͝op′ē, hwo͞o′pē, wo͝o′-) *Slang. interj.* Used to express jubilance. **—*idiom.* make whoopee.** *Slang.* **1.** To engage in a noisy boisterous celebration. **2.** To make love. [Alteration of WHOOP.]

whoop•er (ho͞o′pər, hwo͞o′-, wo͞o′-) *n.* A whooping crane.

whoop•ing cough (ho͞o′pĭng, hwo͞o′-, wo͞o′-, ho͝op′ĭng) *n.* A highly contagious disease, usu. affecting children, that is caused by the bacterium *Bordetella pertussis* and marked by spasms of coughing interspersed with deep noisy inhalations.

whooping crane *n.* A large, long-legged North American bird *(Grus americana),* now very rare, having predominantly white plumage and a loud trumpeting cry.

whoops (hwo͝ops, wo͝ops, hwo͞ops, wo͞ops) also **woops** (wo͝ops, wo͞ops) *interj.* Used to express apology or mild surprise.

whoosh (hwo͞osh, wo͞osh, hwo͝osh, wo͝osh) *n.* **1.** A sibilant sound. **2.** A swift movement or flow; a rush or spurt. *—intr.v.* **whooshed, whoosh•ing, whoosh•es. 1.** To make a soft sibilant sound. **2.** To move or flow swiftly with or as if with such a sound. [Imit.]

whop (hwŏp, wŏp) *tr.v.* **whopped, whop•ping, whops. 1.** To strike with a heavy blow. **2.** To defeat soundly; thrash. *—n.* A heavy blow; a sharp thud. [ME *whappen,* var. of *wappen,* to throw violently.]

whop•per (hwŏp′ər, wŏp′-) *n. Slang.* **1.** Something exceptionally big or remarkable. **2.** A gross untruth. [< WHOPPING.]

whop•ping (hwŏp′ĭng, wŏp′-) *Slang. —adj.* Exceptionally large. *—adv.* Used as an intensive: *a whopping good joke.* [Pr.part. of WHOP.]

whore (hôr, hōr) *n.* **1.** A prostitute. **2.** A person considered sexually promiscuous. **3.** A person considered as having compromised principles for personal gain. *—intr.v.* **whored, whor•ing, whores. 1.** To associate or have sexual relations with prostitutes or a prostitute. **2.** To accept payment in exchange for sexual relations. **3.** To compromise one's principles for personal gain. [ME *hore* < OE *hōre.* See **kā-*.**]

whore•dom (hôr′dəm, hōr′-) *n.* **1.** Prostitution. **2.a.** Unlawful sexual relations. **b.** Promiscuous sex. **3.** *Bible.* Unfaithfulness to God; idolatry. [ME *hordom* < ON *hōrdōmr.* See **kā-*.**]

whore•house (hôr′hous′, hōr′-) *n.* A house of prostitution.

whore•mas•ter (hôr′măs′tər, hōr′-) *n.* **1.** A man who associates with or pays for sexual relations with prostitutes or a prostitute. **2.** A pimp.

whore•mong•er (hôr′mŭng′gər, -mŏng′-, hōr′-) *n.* A whoremaster.

whore•son (hôr′sən, hōr′-) *n.* A child born to parents not married to each other. *—adj.* Abominable.

whor•ish (hôr′ĭsh, hōr′-) *adj.* Of or characteristic of whores or a whore; lewd. **—whor′ish•ly** *adv.* **—whor′ish•ness** *n.*

whorl (hwôrl, wôrl, hwûrl, wûrl) *n.* **1.** A form that coils or spirals; a curl or swirl. **2.** *Bot.* An arrangement of three or more leaves, petals, or other organs radiating from a single node. **3.** *Zool.* A single turn or volution of a spiral shell. **4.** One of the circular ridges or convolutions of a fingerprint. **5.** *Archit.* An ornamental device, as in stonework or weaving, consisting of stylized vine leaves and tendrils. **6.** A small flywheel that regulates the speed of a spinning wheel. [ME *whorle,* alteration of *whirle,* whirl < *whirlen,* to whirl. See WHIRL.]

whorled (hwôrld, wôrld, hwûrld, wûrld) *adj.* Having or forming whorls or a whorl: *whorled flower parts.*

whort (hwûrt, wûrt) also **whor•tle** (hwûrt′l, wûrt′l) *n.* The whortleberry or its fruit. [Var. of dial. *hurt.*]

whor•tle•ber•ry (hwûrt′l-bĕr′ē, wûrt′-) *n.* **1.** Either of two deciduous shrubs, *Vaccinium myrtillus* of Eurasia or *V. corymbosum* of eastern North America, having edible blackish berries. **2.** Their fruit. [Dial., var. of *hurtleberry.*]

who's (ho͞oz). **1.** Who is. **2.** Who has.

whose (ho͞oz) *adj.* **1.** The possessive form of **who. 2.** The possessive form of **which.** [ME *whos* < OE *hwæs.* See **kʷo-*.**]

Usage Note: There is extensive literary precedent for the use of *whose* as the possessive of *which,* as in *The play, whose style is rigidly formal, is typical of the period.* In an earlier survey this example was acceptable to a large majority of the Usage Panel. One, of course, may also write *The play, the style of which is rigidly formal, is typical of the period.* But, as in this example, substituting *of which* for *whose* may result in stiltedness. See Usage Notes at **else, which, who.**

who•so•ev•er (ho͞o′sō-ĕv′ər) *pron.* Whoever.

who's who or **Who's Who** *n.* **1.** A reference work containing short biographical sketches of outstanding persons in a field. **2.** The outstanding or best-known persons of a group.

W-hr *abbr.* Watt-hour.

whs. *abbr.* Warehouse.

whsle. *abbr.* Wholesale.

whup (hwŭp, wŭp, hwo͝op, wo͝op) *v. Chiefly Southern U.S.* Var. of **whip.** [Sc., var. of WHIP.]

why (hwī, wī) *adv.* For what purpose, reason, or cause; with what intention, justification, or motive: *Why do birds sing?* *—conj.* **1.** The reason, cause, or purpose for which: *I know why you left.* **2.** *Usage Problem.* On account of which; for which: *The reason why he failed the exam is unclear.* *—n., pl.* **whys. 1.** The cause or intention underlying a given action or situation. **2.** A difficult problem or question. *—interj.* Used to express mild surprise, indignation, or impatience. [ME < OE *hwȳ.* See **kʷo-*.**]

Usage Note: *Why* could be eliminated in *The reason why he accepted the nomination is not clear* with no loss to the sense, but the construction has been used by reputable English writers since the Renaissance. See Usage Note at **where.**

whyd•ah also **whid•ah** (hwĭd′ə, wĭd′ə) *n.* Any of several African weaverbirds of the genus *Vidua,* the male of which grows long, drooping, predominantly black tail feathers during the breeding season. [Prob. alteration of WIDOW (BIRD).]

WI *abbr.* Wisconsin.

w.i. *abbr. Bus.* When issued (financial stock).

W.I. *abbr.* **1.** West Indian. **2.** West Indies.

WIA *abbr.* Wounded in action.

Wic•ca (wĭk′ə) *n.* **1.** A pagan nature religion having its roots in pre-Christian western Europe and undergoing a 20th-century revival. **2.** A group or community of Wiccans. [OE *wicca,* necromancer. See WITCH.] **—Wic′can** *adj. & n.*

Wich•i•ta[1] (wĭch′ĭ-tô′) *n., pl.* **Wichita** or **-tas. 1.** A member of a Native American confederacy formerly inhabiting Kansas, Oklahoma, and Texas, with a present-day population in southwest Oklahoma. **2.** Their Caddoan language. [Caddo *wiíc'ita.*]

Wich•i•ta[2] (wĭch′ĭ-tô′). A city of S-central KS SW of Kansas City; founded in the 1860's. Pop. 304,011.

Wichita Falls. A city of N-central TX near the OK border NW of Fort Worth. Pop. 96,259.

wick (wĭk) *n.* **1.** A cord or strand of loosely woven, twisted, or braided fibers, as on a candle or an oil lamp, that draws up fuel to the flame by capillary action. **2.** A piece of material that conveys liquid by capillary action. *—tr. & intr.v.* **wicked** (wĭkt), **wick•ing, wicks.** To convey or be conveyed by capillary action. [ME *wike* < OE *wēoce.*]

wick•ed (wĭk′ĭd) *adj.* **-er, -est. 1.** Evil by nature and in practice. See Syns at **bad[1]. 2.** Playfully malicious or mischievous. **3.** Severe and distressing. **4.** Highly offensive; obnoxious. **5.** *Slang.* Strikingly good, effective, or skillful. *—adv. Slang.* Used as an intensive. [ME, alteration of *wicke,* ult. < OE *wicca,* sorcerer. See WITCH.] **—wick′ed•ly** *adv.* **—wick′ed•ness** *n.*

wick•er (wĭk′ər) *n.* **1.** A flexible plant branch or twig, as of a willow, used in weaving baskets or furniture. **2.** Wickerwork. [ME *wiker,* of Scand. orig. See **weik-[2]*.**]

wick•er•work (wĭk′ər-wûrk′) *n.* Work made of interlaced plant branches or twigs.

wick•et (wĭk′ĭt) *n.* **1.** A small door or gate, esp. one built into or near a larger one. **2.** A small window or opening, often fitted with glass or a grating. **3.** A sluice gate for regulating the amount of water in a millrace or a canal or for emptying a lock. **4.** *Sports.* In cricket: **a.** Either of the two sets of three stumps, topped by bails, that forms the target of the bowler and is defended by the batsman. **b.** A batsman's innings, which may be terminated by the ball knocking the bails off the stumps. **c.** The termination of a batsman's innings. **d.** The period during which two batsmen are in together. **e.** See **pitch[2]** 3. **5.** *Games.* Any of the small arches, usu. made of wire, through which players try to drive their ball in croquet. [ME < ONFr. *wiket,* nook, wicket. See **weik-[2]*.**]

wick•i•up also **wik•i•up** (wĭk′ē-ŭp′) *n.* A frame hut covered with matting, as of bark or brush, used by nomadic Native Americans of North America. [Fox *wiikiyaapi,* wigwam.]

Wick•liffe or **Wic•lif** (wĭk′lĭf), **John.** See John **Wycliffe.**

wic•o•py (wĭk′ə-pē) *n., pl.* **-pies.** See **leatherwood.** [Eastern Abenaki *wikəpi,* inner bark used for cordage.]

wid. *abbr.* **1.** Widow. **2.** Widower.

wid•der•shins (wĭd′ər-shĭnz′) or **with•er•shins** (wĭth′-) *adv.* In a contrary or counterclockwise direction. [MLGer. *weddersinnes* < MHGer. *widersinnes* : *wider,* back (< OHGer. *widar;* see **wi-***) + *sinnes,* in the direction of (< *sin,* direction < OHGer.; see **sent-***).]

wide (wīd) *adj.* **wid•er, wid•est. 1.a.** Having a specified extent from side to side. **b.** Extending over a great distance from side to side; broad. **2.** Having great extent or range; including much or many. **3.** Fully open or extended. **4.a.** Being at a distance from a desired goal or point. **b.** *Baseball.* Outside. **5.** *Ling.* Lax. *—adv.* **wider, widest. 1.** Over a great distance; extensively. **2.** To the full extent; completely. **3.** So as to miss a target; astray. *—n. Sports.* A ball bowled outside of the batsman's reach, counting as a run for the batting team in cricket. [ME < OE *wīd.* See **wi-*.**] **—wide′ly** *adv.* **—wide′ness** *n.*

-wide *suff.* Extending or effective throughout a specified area or region: *statewide.* [< WIDE.]

wide-an•gle (wīd′ăng′gəl) *adj.* Of, having, or being a camera lens with a relatively short focal length that permits an angle of view wider than approx. 70°.

wide-a•wake (wīd′ə-wāk′) *adj.* **1.** Completely awake.

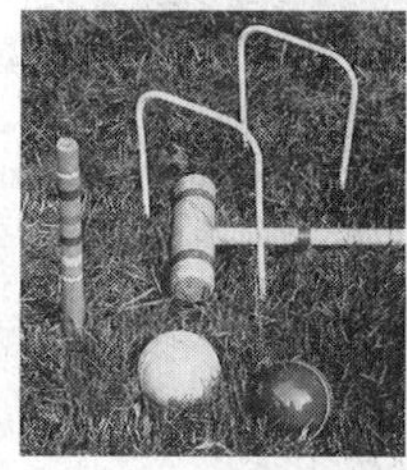

wicket

wickiup
1905 Apache

ă pat	oi boy
ā pay	ou out
âr care	o͝o took
ä father	o͞o boot
ĕ pet	ŭ cut
ē be	ûr urge
ĭ pit	th thin
ī pie	*th* this
îr pier	hw which
ŏ pot	zh vision
ō toe	ə about, item
ô paw	

Stress marks:
′ (primary);
′ (secondary), as in
dictionary (dĭk′shə-nĕr′ē)

widow's walk

Elie Wiesel

wigwam
Birch bark wigwam

Oscar Wilde
Photographed in 1882

2. Alert. —*n.* See **sooty tern.** —**wide′a•wake′ness** *n.*

wide-bod•ied (wīd′bŏd′ēd) *adj.* Being or relating to a jet aircraft having a wide fuselage with passenger seats divided by two lengthwise aisles.

wide-eyed (wīd′īd′) *adj.* **1.** Having the eyes completely opened, as in wonder. **2.** Innocent; credulous.

wid•en (wīd′n) *tr. & intr.v.* **wid•ened, wid•en•ing, wid•ens.** To make or become wide or wider. —**wid′en•er** *n.*

wide-o•pen (wīd′ō′pən) *adj.* **1.** Completely open: *a wide-open door.* **2.** Being without laws or law enforcement.

wide receiver *n. Football.* A receiver who usu. lines up several yards to the side of the offensive formation.

wide•spread (wīd′sprĕd′) *adj.* **1.** Spread or scattered over a considerable extent. **2.** Occurring or accepted widely.

wid•geon also **wi•geon** (wĭj′ən) *n., pl.* **widgeon** also **wigeon** or **-geons.** Either of two wild freshwater ducks (*Anas americana* of North America or *A. penelope* of Europe) having a grayish or brownish back and a white belly. [?]

widg•et (wĭj′ĭt) *n.* **1.** A small mechanical device or control; a gadget. **2.** An unnamed or hypothetical manufactured article. [Perh. alteration of GADGET.]

Wid•nes (wĭd′nĭs). A municipal borough of NW England on the Mersey R. ESE of Liverpool. Pop. 122,500.

wid•ow (wĭd′ō) *n.* **1.** A woman whose husband has died and who has not remarried. **2.** *Informal.* A woman whose husband is often away pursuing a sport or hobby. **3.** *Games.* An additional hand of cards dealt face down in some card games, to be used by the highest bidder. **4.** *Print.* **a.** A single, usu. short line of type, as one ending a paragraph, carried over to the top of the next page or column. **b.** A short line at the bottom of a page, column, or paragraph. —*tr.v.* **-owed, -ow•ing, -ows.** To make a widow or widower of. [ME *widewe* < OE *widuwe.*] —**wid′ow•hood′** *n.*

widow bird *n.* See **whydah.** [< its black plumage.]

wid•ow•er (wĭd′ō-ər) *n.* A man whose wife has died and who has not remarried. [ME *widewer* < *widewe,* widow. See WIDOW.] —**wid′ow•er•hood′** *n.*

wid•ow's mite (wĭd′ōz) *n.* A small contribution made by one who has little. [< the widow who gave two small coins to the Temple treasury (Mark 12:41–44).]

widow's peak *n.* A V-shaped point formed by the hair at the middle of the forehead. [< the superstition that it is a sign of early widowhood.]

widow's walk *n.* A railed rooftop platform typically on a coastal house, originally designed to observe vessels at sea.

width (wĭdth, wĭth, wĭtth) *n.* **1.** The state, quality, or fact of being wide. **2.** The measurement of the extent of something from side to side. **3.** A piece of material measured along the crosswise grain, esp. a piece of fabric measured from selvage to selvage in sewing. [WIDE + -TH².]

width•wise (wĭdth′wīz′, wĭth′-, wĭtth-) *adv.* From side to side; in terms of width.

wield (wēld) *tr.v.* **wield•ed, wield•ing, wields. 1.** To handle (a weapon or tool, for example) with skill and ease. **2.** To exercise (authority or influence, for example) effectively. [ME *welden* < OE *wealdan,* to rule, and *wieldan,* to govern; see **wal-*.**] —**wield′a•ble** *adj.* —**wield′er** *n.*

wield•y (wēl′dē) *adj.* **-i•er, -i•est.** Easily wielded or managed.

wie•ner (wē′nər) *n.* **1.** Wienerwurst. **2.** A frankfurter. [Ger., short for *Wienerwurst.* See WIENERWURST.]

Wie•ner (wē′nər), **Norbert.** 1894–1964. Amer. mathematician who founded cybernetics.

Wie•ner schnit•zel (vē′nər shnĭt′səl) *n.* A breaded veal cutlet. [Ger. : *Wiener,* of Vienna, Austria + *schnitzel,* cutlet.]

wie•ner•wurst (wē′nər-wûrst′, -wŏŏrst′) *n.* A smoked pork or beef sausage similar to a frankfurter. [Ger. : *Wiener,* of Vienna, Austria + *Wurst,* sausage; see WURST.]

Wies•ba•den (vēs′bäd′n). A city of W-central Germany on the Rhine R. W of Frankfurt; founded as a Celtic settlement in the 3rd cent. B.C. Pop. 267,467.

Wie•sel (vē′səl), **Elie(zer).** b. 1928. Romanian-born writer and lecturer who won the 1986 Nobel Peace Prize.

wife (wīf) *n., pl.* **wives** (wīvz). A woman joined to a man in marriage; a female spouse. [ME < OE *wīf.*] —**wife′hood′** *n.*

wife•ly (wīf′lē) *adj.* Of or befitting a wife. —**wife′li•ness** *n.*

wig (wĭg) *n.* A covering of human or synthetic hair worn on the head for adornment, as part of a costume, or to conceal baldness. —*tr.v.* **wigged, wig•ging, wigs.** To scold or censure. —***phrasal verb.* wig out.** *Slang.* To make or become wildly excited or enthusiastic. [Short for PERIWIG.]

wig•an (wĭg′ən) *n.* A stiff fabric used for stiffening.

Wig•an (wĭg′ən). A borough of NW England NE of Liverpool. Pop. 310,000.

wi•geon (wĭj′ən) *n.* Var. of **widgeon.**

Wig•gin (wĭg′ĭn), **Kate Douglas Smith.** 1856–1923. Amer. writer of *Rebecca of Sunnybrook Farm* (1903).

wig•gle (wĭg′əl) *intr. & tr.v.* **-gled, -gling, -gles.** To move or cause to move from side to side with short irregular twisting motions: *wiggled restlessly in her chair.* —*n.* A wiggling movement or course. —***idiom.* get a wiggle on.** *Slang.* To hurry or hurry up. [ME *wiglen,* prob. < MLGer. *wiggelen,* to totter. See **wegh-*.**] —**wig′gly** *adj.*

wig•gler (wĭg′lər) *n.* **1.** One that wiggles: *The toddler was a real wiggler on trips.* **2.** The larva or pupa of a mosquito.

Wig•gles•worth (wĭg′əlz-wûrth′), **Michael.** 1631–1705. English-born Amer. cleric and poet whose works include the popular poem *The Day of Doom* (1662).

wight¹ (wīt) *n. Obsolete.* A living being; a creature. [ME < OE *wiht.* See **wekti-*.**]

wight² (wīt) *adj. Archaic.* Valorous; brave. [ME < ON *vīgt,* neut. of *vīgr,* able to fight. See **weik-³*.**]

Wight (wīt), **Isle of.** An island in the English Channel off S-central England.

Wig•ner (wĭg′nər), **Eugene Paul.** b. 1902. Hungarian-born Amer. physicist who shared a 1963 Nobel Prize.

wig•wag (wĭg′wăg′) *v.* **-wagged, -wag•ging, -wags.** —*intr.* **1.** To move back and forth; wag steadily or rhythmically. **2.** To signal by waving an upraised arm, a flag, or a light, esp. in accordance with a code. —*tr.* **1.** To move (something) back and forth steadily or rhythmically. **2.** To convey (a message or signal) by waving an upraised arm, a flag, or a light. —*n.* **1.** The act or practice of wigwagging. **2.** A message thus sent. [Dial. *wig,* to move + WAG¹.] —**wig′wag′ger** *n.*

wig•wam (wĭg′wŏm′) *n.* A Native American dwelling commonly having an arched or conical framework overlaid with bark, hides, or mats. [Eastern Abenaki *wikəwαm.*]

wik•i•up (wĭk′ē-ŭp′) *n.* Var. of **wickiup.**

Wil•ber•force (wĭl′bər-fôrs′, -fōrs′), **William.** 1759–1833. British politician who as a member of Parliament (1780–1825) campaigned for the abolition of slavery.

Wil•bur (wĭl′bər), **Richard Purdy.** b. 1921. Amer. poet whose works include *Things of This World* (1956).

wild (wīld) *adj.* **wild•er, wild•est. 1.** Occurring, growing, or living in a natural state; not domesticated, cultivated, or tamed. **2.** Not inhabited or farmed. **3.** Uncivilized or barbarous; savage. **4.a.** Lacking restraint; unruly. **b.** Characterized by a lack of moral restraint; dissolute or licentious. **5.** Disorderly; disarranged. **6.** Full of, marked by, or suggestive of strong, uncontrolled emotion. **7.** Extravagant; fantastic. **8.** Furiously disturbed or turbulent; stormy. **9.** Risky; imprudent. **10.a.** Impatiently eager. **b.** *Informal.* Highly enthusiastic. **11.** Based on little or no evidence or probability; unfounded. **12.** Deviating greatly from an intended course; erratic. **13.** *Games.* Having an equivalence or value determined by the cardholder's choice. —*adv.* In a wild manner. —*n.* **1.** A natural or undomesticated state. **2.** An uninhabited or uncultivated region. [ME *wilde* < OE.] —**wild′ly** *adv.* —**wild′ness** *n.*

wild bergamot *n.* See **horsemint** 1.

wild boar *n.* An Old World wild pig *(Sus scrofa)* with dark dense bristles that is the ancestor of the domestic hog.

wild card *n.* **1.** *Games.* A card assigned specific values that may vary during a game and acquire any value assigned by its holder. **2.** *Slang.* An unpredictable or unforeseeable factor.

wild carrot *n.* See **Queen Anne's lace.**

wild•cat (wīld′kăt′) *n.* **1.** Any of various wild felines of small to medium size, esp. of the genus *Lynx,* including the bobcat and the caracal. **2.** Either of two small felines *(Felis silvestris* subsp. *silvestris* or subsp. *lybica)* of Europe, Asia, and Africa, often regarded as being the ancestor of the domestic cat. **3.a.** A quick-tempered person. **b.** A fierce person. **4.** A wildcat oil or natural-gas well. **5.** A wildcat strike. —*adj.* **1.a.** Risky or unsound, esp. financially. **b.** Issued by a financially irresponsible bank. **c.** Operating or accomplished outside business procedural and ethical norms. **2.** Of or being an oil or natural-gas well drilled speculatively in a supposedly unproductive area. **3.** Undertaken by workers without approval of union officials. —*v.* **-cat•ted, -cat•ting, -cats.** —*tr.* To prospect for (oil, for example) as a wildcatter. —*intr.* **1.** To wildcat for oil or other minerals. **2.** To go out on a wildcat strike.

wild•cat•ter (wīld′kăt′ər) *n.* **1.** One who is engaged in speculative mining or well drilling in areas not known to be productive. **2.** A promoter of speculative or fraudulent enterprises. **3.** A worker who participates in a wildcat strike.

Wilde (wīld), **Oscar (Fingal O'Flahertie Wills).** 1854–1900. Irish-born writer whose works include *The Picture of Dorian Gray* (1891) and *The Importance of Being Earnest* (1895).

wil•de•beest (wĭl′də-bēst′, vĭl′-) *n., pl.* **-beests** or **wildebeest.** See **gnu.** [Obsolete Afr. : Du. *wild,* wild (< MDu. *wilt*) + Du. *beest,* beast (< MDu. *beeste* < OFr. *beste;* see BEAST).]

wil•der (wĭl′dər) *v.* **-dered, -der•ing, -ders.** —*tr.* **1.** To lead astray; mislead. **2.** To bewilder; perplex. —*intr.* **1.** To lose one's way. **2.** To become bewildered. [Perh. ME **wildren,* blend of *wilden,* to be wild (< *wilde,* wild; see WILD) and *wanderen,* to wander; see WANDER.] —**wil′der•ment** *n.*

Wil•der (wīl′dər), **Billy.** b. 1906. Austrian-born Amer. filmmaker whose works include *Some Like It Hot* (1959).

Wilder, Laura Ingalls. 1867–1957. Amer. writer whose novels include *Little House on the Prairie* (1935).

Wilder, Thornton (Niven). 1897–1975. Amer. writer best known for the drama *Our Town* (1938).

wil•der•ness (wĭl′dər-nĭs) *n.* **1.** An unsettled, uncultivated region left in its natural condition, esp.: **a.** A large wild tract of land covered with dense vegetation or forests. **b.** An extensive area, such as a desert or an ocean, that is barren or empty; a waste. **c.** A piece of land set aside to grow wild. **2.** Something characterized by bewildering vastness, perilousness, or unchecked profusion. [ME < OE *wilddēornes*, prob. < *wild-dēor*, wild beast : *wilde*, wild + *dēor*, wild animal.]

Wil•der•ness Road (wĭl′dər-nĭs). The principal route for westward migration in the U.S. from c. 1790 to 1840, stretching from VA to the Ohio R.

wild-eyed (wīld′īd′) *adj.* **1.** Glaring in or as if in anger, terror, or madness. **2.** Extreme and passionate in belief or advocacy.

wild•fire (wīld′fīr′) *n.* **1.** A raging, rapidly spreading fire. **2.** Something that acts very quickly and intensely. **3.** Lightning occurring without audible thunder. **4.** A luminosity that appears over swamps or marshes at night; ignis fatuus. **5.** A highly flammable material once used in warfare.

wild•flow•er also **wild flow•er** (wīld′flou′ər) *n.* **1.** A flowering plant that grows in a natural uncultivated state. **2.** The flower of such a plant.

wild•fowl (wīld′foul′) *n., pl.* **wildfowl** or **-fowls.** A wild game bird, such as a duck, goose, or quail.

wild geranium *n.* A North American woodland plant *(Geranium maculatum)* having rose-purple flowers.

wild ginger *n.* Any of various plants of the genus *Asarum,* esp. *A. canadense* of North America, having broad leaves, a solitary brownish flower, and an aromatic root.

wild-goose chase (wīld′go͞os′) *n.* A futile pursuit or search.

wild indigo *n.* Any of several North American plants of the genus *Baptisia,* esp. *B. tinctoria,* having bright yellow flowers.

wild•ing (wīl′dĭng) *n.* **1.** A plant that grows wild or has escaped from cultivation, esp. a wild apple tree or its fruit. **2.** A wild animal. — *adj.* **1.** Growing wild; not cultivated. **2.** Undomesticated. [< WILD.]

wild•life (wīld′līf′) *n.* Wild animals and vegetation, esp. animals living in a natural undomesticated state.

wild•ling (wīld′lĭng) *n.* A wild plant or animal, esp. a wild plant transplanted to a cultivated spot.

wild oat *n.* **1.** An annual Eurasian grass *(Avena fatua)* related to the cultivated oat. Often used in the plural. **2. wild oats.** Misdeeds and indiscretions committed when young.

wild olive *n.* See **devilwood.**

wild pansy *n.* The heartsease.

wild pink *n.* A perennial herb *(Silene caroliniana)* of eastern North America having pink or white flowers.

wild pitch *n. Baseball.* An erratic pitch that the catcher cannot be expected to catch and that enables a base runner to advance.

wild rice *n.* **1.** A tall aquatic annual grass *(Zizania aquatica)* of North America bearing edible grain. **2.** This grain.

wild rye *n.* Any of various grasses of the genus *Elymus* of the Northern Hemisphere.

wild turkey *n.* A wild variety of turkey, esp. the ancestor of the common domesticated North American turkey.

wild type *n.* The typical form of an organism, strain, gene, or characteristic as it occurs in nature, as distinguished from mutant forms that may result from selective breeding.

Wild West (wīld) *n.* The western United States during the period of its settlement, esp. with reference to its lawlessness.

wild•wood (wīld′wo͝od′) *n.* A forest or wooded area in its natural state.

wile (wīl) *n.* **1.** A stratagem or trick intended to deceive or ensnare. **2.** A disarming or seductive manner, device, or procedure. **3.** Trickery; cunning. — *tr.v.* **wiled, wil•ing, wiles. 1.** To influence or lead by means of wiles; entice. **2.** To pass (time) agreeably: *wile away an afternoon.* [ME *wil* < ONFr. < ON *vēl*, trick, or of LGer. orig.]

wil•ful (wĭl′fəl) *adj.* Var. of **willful.**

Wil•helm (vĭl′hĕlm). See **William.**

Wil•hel•mi•na (wĭl′ə-mē′nə, vĭl′hĕl-). 1880–1962. Queen of the Netherlands (1890–1948) who sought refuge in England during World War II.

Wil•helms•ha•ven (vĭl′hĕlmz-hä′fən). A city of NW Germany on an inlet of the North Sea; a major naval base during World Wars I and II. Pop. 97,495.

Wilkes (wĭlks), **Charles.** 1798–1877. Amer. naval officer who explored Antarctica and the W coast of North America.

Wilkes, John. 1727–97. British political reformer noted for his support of the rights of American colonists.

Wilkes-Bar•re (wĭlks′băr′ē, -băr′ə). A city of NE PA SW of Scranton; settled in 1769. Pop. 47,523.

Wilkes Land. A coastal region of Antarctica S of Australia; mainly claimed by Australia.

Wil•kins (wĭl′kĭnz), Sir **George Hubert.** 1888–1958. Australian explorer and aviator who was the first to explore the Arctic by air (1928).

Wilkins, Maurice Hugh Frederick. b. 1916. British biophysicist who shared a 1962 Nobel Prize.

Wilkins, Roy. 1901–81. Amer. civil rights leader who asserted that racial equality should be achieved through the democratic process.

Wil•kins•burg (wĭl′kĭnz-bûrg′). A borough of SW PA, a suburb of Pittsburgh. Pop. 21,080.

Wil•kin•son (wĭl′kĭn-sən), Sir **Geoffrey.** b. 1921. British chemist who shared a 1973 Nobel Prize.

will[1] (wĭl) *n.* **1.a.** The mental faculty by which one deliberately chooses or decides upon a course of action; volition. **b.** The act of exercising the will. **2.a.** Diligent purposefulness; determination. **b.** Self-control; self-discipline. **3.** A desire, purpose, or determination, esp. of one in authority. **4.** Deliberate intention or wish: *against my will.* **5.** Free discretion; inclination or pleasure. **6.** Bearing or attitude toward others; disposition. **7.a.** A legal declaration of how a person wishes his or her possessions to be disposed of after death. **b.** A legally executed document containing this declaration. — *v.* **willed, will•ing, wills.** — *tr.* **1.** To decide on; choose. **2.** To yearn for; desire. **3.** To decree, dictate, or order. **4.** To resolve with a forceful will; determine. **5.** To induce or try to induce by sheer force of will. **6.** To grant in a legal will; bequeath. — *intr.* **1.** To exercise the will. **2.** To make a choice; choose. — ***idiom.*** **at will.** Just as or when one wishes. [ME < OE *willa.* See **wel-**[1]*.]

will[2] (wĭl) *aux.v.* P.t. **would** (wo͝od). **1.** Used to indicate simple futurity: *They will appear later.* **2.** Used to indicate likelihood or certainty: *You will regret this.* **3.** Used to indicate willingness: *Will you help me?* **4.** Used to indicate requirement or command: *You will report to me.* **5.** Used to indicate intention: *I will go if I feel like it.* **6.** Used to indicate customary or habitual action: *People will talk.* **7.** Used to indicate capacity or ability: *This metal will not crack.* **8.** Used to indicate probability or expectation: *That will be the dog.* — *tr. & intr.v.* To wish; desire: *Sit here if you will.* See Usage Note at **shall.** [ME *willen*, to intend to < OE *willan.* See **wel-**[1]*.]

Wil•lam•ette (wə-lăm′ĭt). A river of NW OR flowing c. 473 km (294 mi) to the Columbia R. near Portland.

Wil•lard (wĭl′ərd), **Emma Hart.** 1787–1870. Amer. educator who was an early proponent of higher education for women.

Willard, Frances Elizabeth Caroline. 1839–98. Amer. reformer who was president of the Woman's Christian Temperance Union (1879–98).

willed (wĭld) *adj.* **1.** Having a will of a specified kind. Often used in combination: *weak-willed.* **2.** Determined by or proceeding from the will; deliberate.

wil•lem•ite (wĭl′ə-mīt′) *n.* A colorless often fluorescent mineral, Zn_2SiO_4, a minor ore of zinc. [Du. *willemit*, after *Willem* I (1772–1843), king of the Netherlands.]

Wil•lem•stad (vĭl′əm-stät′). The cap. of the Netherlands Antilles, on the S coast of Curaçao; founded 1634. Pop. 43,547.

wil•let (wĭl′ĭt) *n.* A large grayish shore bird *(Catoptrophorus semipalmatus)* of North America having black wings with a broad white stripe. [Imit. of its call.]

will•ful also **wil•ful** (wĭl′fəl) *adj.* **1.** Said or done on purpose; deliberate. See Syns at **voluntary. 2.** Obstinately bent on having one's own way. See Syns at **unruly.** — **will′ful•ly** *adv.* — **will′ful•ness** *n.*

Wil•liam (wĭl′yəm) also **Wil•helm** (vĭl′hĕlm). 1882–1951. German crown prince who renounced the crown at the close of World War I.

William I[1]. "William the Conqueror." 1027?–87. King of England (1066–87) and duke of Normandy (1035–87) who led the Norman invasion of England (1066) and defeated Harold at the Battle of Hastings.

William I[2]. Prince of Orange. "William the Silent." 1533–84. Dutch stadholder (1579–84) who was made governor of Holland, Zeeland, and Utrecht (1559) by Phillip II of Spain and later led a revolt (1568–76) against Spanish rule.

William I[3] also **Wilhelm I** 1797–1888. King of Prussia (1861–88) and emperor of Germany (1871–88) whose reign was marked by the Franco-Prussian War (1870–71).

William II[1]. "William Rufus." 1056?–1100. King of England (1087–1100) who was the second son of William the Conqueror, on whose death he succeeded to the throne.

William II[2] also **Wilhelm II** 1859–1941. Emperor of Germany and king of Prussia (1888–1918).

William III. "William of Orange." 1650–1702. King of England, Scotland, and Ireland (1689–1702), Dutch stadholder (1672–1702), and prince of Orange. Married to Mary, daughter of James II, he invaded England (1688) and was proclaimed joint monarch with Mary (1689) after James fled.

William IV. 1765–1837. King of Great Britain and Ireland (1830–37). Son of George III and brother of George IV, he was succeeded by his niece Victoria.

William of Malmes•bur•y (mämz′bĕr′ē, -bə-rē, -brē). 1090?–1143? English monk and historian whose works include *Chronicle of the Kings of England.*

Wil•liams (wĭl′yəmz), **Elizabeth ("Betty").** b. 1943. Irish peace activist who shared the 1976 Nobel Peace Prize.

Williams, Roger. 1603?–83. English cleric in America who founded Providence (1636) and obtained a royal charter for Rhode Island (1663).

Williams, Tennessee. Thomas Lanier Williams. 1911–83. Amer. playwright whose works include *A Streetcar Named Desire* (1947).

Williams, William Carlos. 1883–1963. Amer. poet whose verse is marked by a lucid spare style.

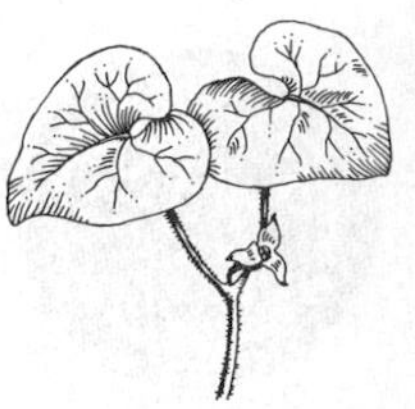

wild ginger

wild turkey

Tennessee Williams

ă pat	oi boy
ā pay	ou out
âr care	o͝o took
ä father	o͞o boot
ĕ pet	ŭ cut
ē be	ûr urge
ĭ pit	th thin
ī pie	*th* this
îr pier	hw which
ŏ pot	zh vision
ō toe	ə about, item
ô paw	

Stress marks:
′ (primary);
′ (secondary), as in
dictionary (dĭk′shə-nĕr′ē)

willowware
c. 1820 English ceramic plate

Edith Wilson

Ellen Wilson

Woodrow Wilson

Wil•liams•burg (wĭl′yəmz-bûrg′). A city of SE VA NW of Newport News; settled c. 1632 and site of a large-scale restoration project begun in 1926. Pop. 11,530.

Wil•liam•son (wĭl′yəm-sən), **Mount.** A peak, 4,382.9 m (14,370 ft), in the Sierra Nevada of E-central CA.

Wil•liams•port (wĭl′yəmz-pôrt′, -pōrt′). A city of central PA N of Harrisburg. Pop. 31,933.

William the Conqueror. See **William I¹.**

wil•lies (wĭl′ēz) *pl.n. Slang.* Feelings of uneasiness. Often used with *the: They gave me the willies.* [Perh. < dial. *will*, desolate, gone astray, bewildered < ON *villr* or *villi-*, wild, bewildering; akin to OE *wilde*, wild.]

will•ing (wĭl′ĭng) *adj.* **1.** Disposed or inclined; prepared. **2.** Acting or ready to act gladly; eagerly compliant. **3.** Done, given, accepted, or borne voluntarily or ungrudgingly. See Syns at **voluntary. 4.** Of or relating to exercise of the will; volitional. **—will′ing•ly** *adv.* **—will′ing•ness** *n.*

Wil•ling•bo•ro (wĭl′ĭng-bûr′ō, -bŭr′ō). A community of S-central NJ NE of Camden. Pop. 36,291.

wil•li•waw (wĭl′ē-wô′) *n.* **1.** A violent gust of cold wind blowing seaward from a mountainous coast, esp. in the Straits of Magellan. **2.** A sudden gust of wind; a squall. [?]

Will•kie (wĭl′kē), **Wendell Lewis.** 1892–1944. Amer. politician who was the Republican nominee for President in 1940.

will-o'-the-wisp (wĭl′ə-*thə*-wĭsp′) *n.* **1.** See **ignis fatuus** 1. **2.** A delusive or misleading hope. [< the name *Will*.]

Wil•lough•by (wĭl′ə-bē). A city of NE OH on Lake Erie NE of Cleveland. Pop. 20,510.

wil•low (wĭl′ō) *n.* **1.a.** Any of various deciduous trees or shrubs of the genus *Salix*, having usu. narrow leaves and strong lightweight wood. **b.** The wood of any of these trees. **2.** Something, such as a cricket bat, that is made from willow. **3.** A textile machine consisting of a spiked drum revolving inside a chamber fitted internally with spikes, used to open and clean unprocessed cotton or wool. *—tr.v.* **-lowed, -low•ing, -lows.** To open and clean (textile fibers) with a willow. [ME *wilowe* < OE *welig*. See **wel-²*.**]

Wil•low Grove (wĭl′ō). A community of SE PA, a suburb of Philadelphia. Pop. 16,325.

willow herb *n.* See **fireweed** 1.

willow oak *n.* A deciduous timber tree *(Quercus phellos)* of southern and central North America having willowlike leaves.

wil•low•ware (wĭl′ō-wâr′) *n.* Household china with a blue-on-white design depicting a willow tree and often a river.

wil•low•y (wĭl′ō-ē) *adj.* **-i•er, -i•est. 1.** Planted with or abounding in willows. **2.** Resembling a willow tree, esp.: **a.** Flexible; pliant. **b.** Tall, slender, and graceful.

will•pow•er or **will pow•er** (wĭl′pou′ər) *n.* The strength of will to carry out one's decisions, wishes, or plans.

wil•ly-nil•ly (wĭl′ē-nĭl′ē) *adv.* **1.** Whether desired or not. **2.** Without order or plan; haphazardly. *—adj.* **1.** Being or occurring whether desired or not. **2.** Disordered; haphazard. [Alteration of *will ye (or he), nill ye (or he), be you (or he) willing, be you (or he) unwilling.*]

Wil•mette (wĭl-mĕt′). A village of NE IL, a residential suburb of Chicago on Lake Michigan. Pop. 26,690.

Wil•ming•ton (wĭl′mĭng-tən). **1.** A city of NE DE on the Delaware R. SW of Philadelphia PA; founded as Fort Christina by Swedish settlers in 1638. Pop. 71,529. **2.** A town of NE MA, a suburb of Boston. Pop. 17,654. **3.** A city of SE NC on the Cape Fear R. SSE of Raleigh; settled c. 1730. Pop. 55,530.

Wil•son (wĭl′sən). A city of E-central NC E of Raleigh. Pop. 36,930.

Wilson, Charles Thomson Rees. 1869–1959. British physicist who shared a 1927 Nobel Prize.

Wilson, Edith Bolling. 1872–1961. First Lady of the U.S. (1915–21) as the second wife of President Woodrow Wilson.

Wilson, Edmund. 1895–1972. Amer. literary critic whose works include *Axel's Castle* (1931) and *Patriotic Gore* (1962).

Wilson, Ellen Louise Axson. 1860–1914. First Lady of the U.S. (1913–14) as the first wife of President Woodrow Wilson.

Wilson, Henry. Orig. Jeremiah Jones Colbath. 1812–75. Vice President of the U.S. (1873–75).

Wilson, James. 1742–98. Amer. jurist who signed the Declaration of Independence and later served as an associate justice of the U.S. Supreme Court (1789–98).

Wilson, (James) Harold. Baron Wilson of Rievaulx. b. 1916. British prime minister (1964–70 and 1974–76).

Wilson, Mount. 1. A mountain, 1,741.6 m (5,710 ft), in the San Gabriel Mts. of SW CA NE of Pasadena; site of an observatory (estab. 1904). **2.** A peak, 4,345 m (14,246 ft), in the San Juan Mts. of SW CO.

Wilson, Robert Woodrow. b. 1936. Amer. physicist and radio astronomer who shared a 1978 Nobel Prize.

Wilson, (Thomas) Woodrow. 1856–1924. The 28th President of the U.S. (1913–21), who won the 1919 Nobel Peace Prize. **—Wil•so′ni•an** (-sō′nē-ən) *adj.*

Wil•son's disease (wĭl′sənz) *n.* A rare hereditary disease marked by an accumulation of copper deposits in organs such as the brain, liver, and kidneys. [After Samuel A.K. *Wilson* (1878–1937), British neurologist.]

Wilson's phalarope *n.* A grayish American wading bird *(Phalaropus tricolor)* with white underparts and a needlelike bill. [After Alexander *Wilson* (1766–1813), Scottish-born Amer. ornithologist.]

Wilson's snipe *n.* A common North American snipe *(Capella gallinago* subsp. *delicata.)*

Wilson's thrush *n.* See **veery.**

Wilson's warbler *n.* A North American warbler *(Wilsonia pusilla)* with olive-green plumage, yellow underparts, and a black patch on top of the head.

wilt¹ (wĭlt) *v.* **wilt•ed, wilt•ing, wilts.** *—intr.* **1.** To become limp or flaccid; droop. **2.** To feel or exhibit the effects of fatigue or exhaustion; weaken markedly. *—tr.* **1.** To cause to droop or lose freshness. **2.** To deprive of energy or vigor; fatigue or exhaust. *—n.* **1.** The act of wilting or the state of being wilted. **2.** Any of various plant diseases characterized by slow or rapid collapse of terminal shoots, branches, or entire plants. [Poss. alteration of dial. *welk* < ME *welken*.]

wilt² (wĭlt) *aux.v. Archaic.* A second pers. sing. pr.t. of **will².**

Wil•ton² (wĭl′tən) *n.* A carpet woven on a jacquard loom and having a velvety surface formed by the cut loops of a pile. [After *Wilton*, a municipal borough of S-central England.]

Wilt•shire (wĭlt′shîr, -shər) *n.* A white sheep of a breed originating in England, characterized by a long head with spiraling horns. [After *Wiltshire*, a county of S-central England.]

wi•ly (wī′lē) *adj.* **-li•er, -li•est.** Full of wiles; cunning. **—wi′li•ly** *adv.* **—wi′li•ness** *n.*

wim•ble (wĭm′bəl) *n.* Any of numerous hand tools for boring holes. [ME < AN, prob. < MDu. *wimmel*. See **weip-*.**] **—wim′ble** *v.*

Wim•ble•don (wĭm′bəl-dən). A district of S Greater London, England; site of a major annual tennis tournament.

wimp (wĭmp) *n. Slang.* A person who is regarded as weak or ineffectual. [Perh. < WHIMPER.] **—wimp′ish, wimp′y** *adj.*

wim•ple (wĭm′pəl) *n.* **1.** A cloth wound around the head, framing the face, and drawn into folds beneath the chin, worn by women in medieval times and as part of the habit of certain orders of nuns. **2.a.** A fold or pleat in cloth. **b.** A ripple, as on the surface of water. **c.** A curve or bend. *—v.* **-pled, -pling, -ples.** *—tr.* **1.** To cover with or dress in a wimple. **2.** To cause to form folds, pleats, or ripples. *—intr.* **1.** *Archaic.* To form or lie in folds. **2.** To ripple. [ME *wimpel* < OE. See **weip-*.**]

win (wĭn) *v.* **won** (wŭn), **win•ning, wins.** *—intr.* **1.** To achieve victory or finish first in a competition. **2.** To achieve success in an effort or a venture. *—tr.* **1.** To achieve victory or finish first in. **2.** To receive as a prize or reward for performance. **3.a.** To achieve or attain by effort. **b.** To obtain or earn (a livelihood, for example). See Syns at **earn¹. 4.** To make (one's way) with effort. **5.** To reach with difficulty. **6.** To take in battle; capture. **7.** To succeed in gaining the favor or support of; prevail on. **8.a.** To gain the affection or loyalty of. **b.** To appeal successfully to (someone's sympathy, for example). **c.** To persuade (another) to marry one. **9.a.** To discover and open (a vein or deposit) in mining. **b.** To extract from a mine or from mined ore. *—n.* **1.a.** A victory, esp. in a competition. **b.** First place in a competition. **2.** An amount won or earned. **—*phrasal verbs.* win out.** To succeed or prevail. **win through.** To overcome difficulties and attain a desired goal or end. **—*idiom.* win the day.** To be successful. [ME *winnen* < OE *winnan*, to fight, strive. See **wen-¹*.**]

wince (wĭns) *intr.v.* **winced, winc•ing, winc•es.** To shrink or start involuntarily, as in pain or distress; flinch. *—n.* A shrinking or startled movement or gesture. [ME *wincen*, to kick < ONFr. **wencier*, var. of Old French *guencir*, of Gmc. orig.] **—winc′er** *n.*

winch (wĭnch) *n.* **1.** A stationary hoisting or hauling machine having a drum around which is wound a rope or chain. **2.** The crank used to give motion to a grindstone or similar device. *—tr.v.* **winched, winch•ing, winch•es.** To move with or as if with a winch. [ME *winche*, pulley < OE *wince*, reel, roller.] **—winch′er** *n.*

Win•ches•ter¹ (wĭn′chĕs′tər, -chĭ-stər). **1.** A municipal borough of S-central England SW of London. Pop. 32,100. **2.** A town of NE MA, a suburb of Boston. Pop. 20,267. **3.** A community of SE NV, a suburb of Las Vegas. Pop. 23,365. **4.** An independent city of N VA WNW of Washington DC; settled c. 1744. Pop. 21,947.

Win•ches•ter² (wĭn′chĕs′tər, -chə-stər). A trademark used for a shoulder firearm.

Winck•el•mann (vĭng′kəl-män′), **Johann Joachim.** 1717–68. German archaeologist and antiquary who was the first to study ancient art as history.

wind¹ (wĭnd) *n.* **1.a.** Moving air, esp. a natural and perceptible movement of air parallel to or along the ground. **b.** A movement of air generated artificially, as by bellows or a fan. **2.a.** The direction from which a movement of air comes. **b.** A movement of air coming from one of the four cardinal points of the compass. **3.** Moving air carrying sound, an odor, or a scent. **4.a.** Breath, esp. normal or adequate breathing; respiration. **b.** Gas produced in the stomach or intestines during digestion; flatulence. **5.** *Mus.* **a.** The brass and woodwinds sections of a band or an orchestra. **b.** Wind instruments or their players considered as a group. In both senses often used in the plural. **6.a.** Something that disrupts or destroys. **b.** A tendency; a trend. **7.** Information, esp. of something concealed; intimation. **8.a.** Speech or writing empty of meaning; verbiage. **b.** Futile or idle labor or thought. — *tr.v.* **wind•ed, wind•ing, winds. 1.** To expose to free movement of air; ventilate or dry. **2.a.** To detect the smell of; catch a scent of. **b.** To pursue by following a scent. **3.** To cause to be out of or short of breath. **4.** To afford a recovery of breath. — ***idioms.*** **before the wind.** *Naut.* In the same direction as the wind. **close to the wind.** *Naut.* As close as possible to the direction from which the wind is blowing. **in the wind.** Likely to occur; in the offing. **near the wind. 1.** *Naut.* Close to the wind. **2.** Close to danger. **off the wind.** *Naut.* In a direction away from the wind. **on (or into or down) the wind.** *Naut.* In the same or nearly the same direction as the wind. **under the wind. 1.** *Naut.* To the leeward. **2.** In a location protected from the wind. **up the wind.** *Naut.* In a direction opposite or nearly opposite the wind. [ME < OE. See **wē-*.**]

wind² (wīnd) *v.* **wound** (wound), **wind•ing, winds.** — *tr.* **1.** To wrap (something) around a center or another object once or repeatedly. **2.** To wrap or encircle (an object) in a series of coils; entwine. **3.a.** To go along (a curving or twisting course). **b.** To proceed on (one's way) with a curving or twisting course. **4.** To introduce in a disguised or devious manner; insinuate. **5.** To turn (a crank, for example) in a series of circular motions. **6.a.** To coil the spring of (a mechanism) by turning a stem or cord, for example. **b.** To coil (thread, for example), as onto a spool or into a ball. **c.** To remove or unwind (thread, for example), as from a spool. **7.** To lift or haul by means of a windlass or winch. — *intr.* **1.** To move in or have a curving or twisting course. **2.a.** To move in or have a spiral or circular course. **b.** To be coiled or spiraled. **3.** To be twisted or whorled into curved forms. **4.** To proceed misleadingly or insidiously in discourse or conduct. **5.** To become wound. — *n.* **1.** The act of winding. **2.** A single turn, twist, or curve. — ***phrasal verbs.*** **wind down.** *Informal.* **1.** To diminish gradually in energy, intensity, or scope. **2.** To relax; unwind. **wind up. 1.** To come or bring to a finish; end. **2.** To put in order; settle. **3.** *Informal.* To arrive in a place or situation after or because of a course of action. **4.** *Baseball.* To swing back the arm and raise the foot in preparation for pitching the ball. [ME *winden* < OE *windan.*]

wind³ (wīnd, wĭnd) *tr.v.* **wind•ed** (wīn′dĭd, wĭn′-) or **wound** (wound), **wind•ing, winds.** *Mus.* **1.** To blow (a wind instrument). **2.** To sound by blowing. [< WIND¹.] — **wind′er** *n.*

wind•age (wĭn′dĭj) *n.* **1.a.** The effect of wind on the course of a projectile. **b.** The point or degree at which the wind gauge or sight of a rifle or gun must be set to compensate for the effect of the wind. **c.** The difference in a given firearm between the diameter of the projectile fired and the diameter of the bore of the firearm. **2.** The disturbance of air caused by the passage of a fast-moving object. **3.** *Naut.* The part of the surface of a ship left exposed to the wind.

Win•daus (vĭn′dous′), **Adolf.** 1876–1959. German chemist who won a 1928 Nobel Prize.

wind•bag (wĭnd′băg′) *n.* **1.** *Mus.* The flexible air-filled chamber of a bagpipe, an accordion, or a similar wind instrument. **2.** *Slang.* A talkative person who communicates nothing of substance or interest.

wind-bell (wĭnd′bĕl′) *n.* **1.** A light bell that can be sounded by the wind. **2. wind-bells.** See **wind chimes.**

wind•blast (wĭnd′blăst′) *n.* **1.** An exceedingly strong gust of wind. **2.** The damaging effect of air friction on a pilot ejected from a high-speed aircraft.

wind•blown (wĭnd′blōn′) *adj.* **1.** Blown or dispersed by the wind: *windblown pollen.* **2.** Growing or shaped in a manner governed by the prevailing winds: *windblown pines.* **3.** Cut short and curled or combed toward the front of the head.

wind•break (wĭnd′brāk′) *n.* A hedge, fence, or row of trees serving to lessen or break the force of the wind.

Wind•break•er (wĭnd′brā′kər). A trademark used for a warm outer jacket having close-fitting cuffs and waistband.

wind-bro•ken (wĭnd′brō′kən) *adj.* Suffering from the heaves or other impairment of breathing. Used of a horse.

wind•burn (wĭnd′bûrn′) *n.* A reddened irritation of the skin caused by long exposure to the wind. — **wind′burned′** *adj.*

wind-chill factor (wĭnd′chĭl′) *n.* The temperature of windless air that would have the same effect on exposed human skin as a given combination of wind speed and air temperature.

wind chimes (wĭnd) *pl.n.* An arrangement of small suspended pieces, as of glass, metal, or ceramic, hung loosely together so that they tinkle pleasingly when blown by the wind.

wind cone (wĭnd) *n.* See **windsock.**

wind•ed (wĭn′dĭd) *adj.* **1.** Having breath or respiratory power of a specified kind. Often used in combination: *short-winded.* **2.** Out of breath: *a winded runner.*

wind•er¹ (wīn′dər) *n.* **1.** One that winds, esp. a textile worker or machine that winds cloth or materials. **2.** An object, such as a spool or barrel, around which material is wound. **3.** A device, such as a key, for winding up a spring-driven mechanism. **4.** One of the steps of a winding staircase.

win•der² (wĭn′dər) *n. Upper Southern U.S.* Var. of **window.** See Regional Note at **holler².**

Win•der•mere (wĭn′dər-mîr′), **Lake.** A lake of NW England.

wind•fall (wĭnd′fôl′) *n.* **1.** A sudden unexpected piece of good fortune or personal gain. **2.** Something, such as a ripened fruit, that has been blown down by the wind.

wind•flaw (wĭnd′flô′) *n.* A sudden gust or blast of wind.

wind•flow•er (wĭnd′flou′ər) *n.* See **anemone** 1.

wind gap (wĭnd) *n.* A shallow notch in the crest of a mountain ridge.

Wind•ham (wĭn′dəm). A town of E-central CT NNW of Norwich. Pop. 22,039.

wind harp (wĭnd) *n.* See **Aeolian harp.**

Wind•hoek (vĭnt′ho͝ok′). The cap. of Namibia, in the central part of the country. Pop. 88,700.

wind•ing (wīn′dĭng) *n.* **1.a.** Something wound about a center or an object. **b.** The way in which something is wound. **c.** One complete turn of something wound. **2.** A curve or bend, as of a road. — *adj.* **1.** Twisting or turning; sinuous. **2.** Spiral. — **wind′ing•ly** *adv.*

wind•ing-sheet (wīn′dĭng-shēt′) *n.* A sheet for wrapping a corpse; a shroud.

wind instrument (wĭnd) *n. Mus.* An instrument, such as a clarinet or harmonica, in which sound is produced by the movement of an enclosed column of air, esp. the breath.

wind•jam•mer (wĭnd′jăm′ər) *n. Naut.* A large sailing ship.

wind•lass (wĭnd′ləs) *n.* Any of numerous hauling or lifting machines consisting essentially of a horizontal cylinder turned by a crank or a motor so that a line attached to the load is wound around the cylinder. — *tr.v.* **-lassed, -lass•ing, -lass•es.** To raise with a windlass. [ME *wyndlas*, alteration of *windas* < ON *vindāss* : *vinda*, to wind + *āss*, pole.]

win•dle•straw (wĭn′dl-strô′) *n. Chiefly British.* A thin dried stalk of grass. [OE *windelstrēaw* : *windel*, basket (< *windan*, to wind) + *strēaw*, straw; see STRAW.]

wind•mill (wĭnd′mĭl′) *n.* **1.** A machine that runs on the energy generated by a wheel of adjustable blades or slats rotated by the wind. **2.** Something, such as a toy pinwheel, similar to a windmill in appearance or operation. — *intr. & tr.v.* **-milled, -mill•ing, -mills.** To move or cause to move like the wheel of a windmill. — ***idiom.*** **tilt at windmills.** To confront and engage in conflict with an imagined opponent or threat.

Win•dom Peak (wĭn′dəm). A mountain, 4,295 m (14,082 ft), in the San Juan Mts. of SW CO.

win•dow (wĭn′dō) *n.* **1.a.** An opening constructed in a wall or roof that admits light or air to an enclosure and is often framed and spanned with glass mounted to permit opening and closing. **b.** A framework enclosing a pane of glass for such an opening; a sash. **c.** A pane of glass or similar material in such a framework. **2.a.** An opening that resembles a window in function or appearance. **b.** The transparent panel on a window envelope. **3.** The area or space behind a window, esp. at the front of a shop. **4.** A means of access or observation. **5.** An interval of time during which an activity can or must take place. **6.** Strips of foil dropped from an aircraft to confuse enemy radar; chaff. **7.** A range of electromagnetic frequencies that pass unobstructed through a planetary atmosphere. **8.** *Comp. Sci.* A small area on a screen in which a file or a part of a file can be displayed. **9.** *Aerospace.* A launch window. [ME < ON *vindauga* : *vindr*, air, wind; see **wē-*** + *auga*, eye; see **okʷ-*.**]

window box *n.* **1.** A usu. long narrow box for growing plants, placed on a windowsill or ledge. **2.** One of the vertical grooves on the inner sides of a window frame for the weights that counterbalance the sash.

win•dow-dress•ing also **win•dow dress•ing** (wĭn′dō-drĕs′ĭng) *n.* **1.a.** Decorative exhibition of retail merchandise in store windows. **b.** Goods and trimmings used in such displays. **2.** A means of improving appearances or creating a falsely favorable impression. — **win′dow-dress′er** *n.*

win•dow•pane (wĭn′dō-pān′) *n.* A piece of glass in a window.

window shade *n.* An opaque fabric mounted to cover or expose a window.

win•dow-shop (wĭn′dō-shŏp′) *intr.v.* **-shopped, -shop•ping, -shops.** To look at merchandise in store windows or showcases without making purchases. — **win′dow-shop′per** *n.*

win•dow•sill (wĭn′dō-sĭl′) *n.* The horizontal member at the base of a window opening.

wind•pipe (wĭnd′pīp′) *n. Anat.* See **trachea** 1.

Wind River Range (wĭnd). A section of the Rocky Mts. in W-central WY rising to 4,210.2 m (13,804 ft).

Wind River Shoshone *n.* See **Shoshone** 1c.

wind rose (wĭnd) *n.* A meteorological diagram depicting the distribution of wind direction and speed at a location over a period of time. [Transl. of Ger. *Windrose*, compass card : *Wind*, wind, air + *Rose*, rose.]

wind•row (wĭnd′rō′) *n.* **1.** A row, as of snow, heaped up by the wind. **2.** A long row of cut hay or grain left to dry in a field before bundling. — *tr.v.* **-rowed, -row•ing, -rows.** To shape or arrange into a windrow. — **wind′row′er** *n.*

wind•screen (wĭnd′skrēn′) *n.* **1.** A screen for protection

winch

windmill
Top: Water-pumping windmill in Colorado
Bottom: Grain-grinding windmill in La Mancha, Spain

ă pat	oi boy
ā pay	ou out
âr care	o͝o took
ä father	o͞o boot
ĕ pet	ŭ cut
ē be	ûr urge
ĭ pit	th thin
ī pie	*th* this
îr pier	hw which
ŏ pot	zh vision
ō toe	ə about, item
ô paw	

Stress marks:
′ (primary);
′ (secondary), as in
dictionary (dĭk′shə-nĕr′ē)

against the wind. **2.** *Chiefly British.* The windshield of a motor vehicle.

wind•shake (wĭnd′shāk′) *n.* A crack or separation between growth rings in timber, attributed to the straining of tree trunks in high winds.

wind shear (wĭnd) *n.* A change in wind direction and speed between slightly different altitudes, esp. a sudden downdraft.

wind•shield (wĭnd′shēld′) *n.* **1.** A framed pane of usu. curved glass or other transparent shielding located in front of the occupants of a vehicle to protect them from the wind. **2.** A shield placed to protect an object from the wind.

wind•sock (wĭnd′sŏk′) *n.* A tapered open-ended sleeve pivotally attached to a standard to indicate wind direction.

Wind•sor[1] (wĭn′zər). Ruling house of Great Britain (since 1917), including George V, who adopted the name.

Wind•sor[2] (wĭn′zər). **1.** A city of SE Ontario, Canada, on the Detroit R. opposite Detroit MI; settled by the French after 1701. Pop. 192,083. **2.** A municipal borough of S-central England on the Thames R. SW of London; site of Windsor Castle, a royal residence since the time of William the Conqueror. Pop. 28,700. **3.** A town of N CT N of Hartford; settled c. 1635. Pop. 27,817.

Duchess of Windsor
Photographed by
Cecil Beaton

Windsor, Duke of. See **Edward VIII.**

Windsor, Wallis Warfield. Duchess of Windsor. 1896–1986. Amer. who married the Duke of Windsor in 1937.

Windsor chair *n.* A wooden chair having a high spoked back, outward-slanting legs connected by crossbars, and a saddle seat. [After WINDSOR[2], England.]

Windsor knot *n.* A wide triangular slipknot used to tie a four-in-hand necktie. [Perh. after the Duke of WINDSOR.]

Windsor tie *n.* A wide silk necktie tied in a loose bow.

wind sprint (wĭnd) *n. Sports.* A sprint run repeatedly to develop breath and endurance.

wind•storm (wĭnd′stôrm′) *n.* A storm with high winds or violent gusts but little or no rain.

wind•suck•ing (wĭnd′sŭk′ĭng) *n.* The injurious habit of horses of drawing in and swallowing air. — **wind′suck•er** *n.*

wind•surf (wĭnd′sûrf′) *intr.v.* **-surfed, -surf•ing, -surfs.** *Sports.* To engage in windsurfing.

Wind•surf•er (wĭnd′sûr′fər). A trademark used for a brand of sailboard.

wind•surf•ing (wĭnd′sûr′fĭng) *n. Sports.* The sport of sailing while standing on a sailboard.

wind•swept (wĭnd′swĕpt′) *adj.* Exposed to or swept by winds: *windswept moors.*

wind tee (wĭnd) *n.* A large weathervane with a horizontal T-shaped wind indicator, commonly found at airfields.

wind tunnel (wĭnd) *n.* A chamber through which air is forced at controlled velocities in order to study the effects of aerodynamic flow around airfoils, scale models, or other objects.

wind-up or **wind•up** (wīnd′ŭp′) — *n.* **1.a.** The act of bringing something to an end. **b.** A concluding part; a conclusion. **2.** *Baseball.* The movements of a pitcher, including the swinging back of the arm and the raising of the forward foot, preparatory to pitching the ball. — *adj.* Operated by a spring that is wound up by hand.

wind•ward (wĭnd′wərd) *adj.* **1.** Of or moving toward the quarter from which the wind blows. **2.** Of or on the side exposed to the wind or to prevailing winds. — *adv.* In a direction from which the wind blows; against the wind. — *n.* The direction from which the wind blows. — ***idiom.* to windward.** Into or to an advantageous posture or position.

Windsor chair
c. 1795 American

Wind•ward Islands (wĭnd′wərd). An island group of the SE West Indies, including the S group of the Lesser Antilles from Martinique S to Grenada.

Windward Passage. A channel between E Cuba and NW Haiti connecting the Atlantic with the Caribbean Sea.

wind•y (wĭn′dē) *adj.* **-i•er, -i•est. 1.** Characterized by or abounding in wind. **2.** Open to the wind; unsheltered. **3.** Swift, forceful, or variable. **4.a.** Lacking substance; empty. **b.** Given to or characterized by prolonged talk; verbose. **5.** Flatulent. — **wind′i•ly** *adv.* — **wind′i•ness** *n.*

wine (wīn) *n.* **1.a.** A beverage made of the fermented juice of any of various kinds of grapes, usu. containing from 10 to 15 percent alcohol by volume. **b.** A beverage made of the fermented juice of any of various other fruits or plants. **2.** Something that intoxicates or exhilarates. **3.** *Color.* The color of red wine. — *v.* **wined, win•ing, wines.** — *tr.* To provide or entertain with wine. — *intr.* To drink wine. [ME < OE *wīn* < Lat. *vīnum.*]

wine•bib•bing (wīn′bĭb′ĭng) *adj.* Given to much drinking of wine. — *n.* Habitual drinking of wine. — **wine′bib′ber** *n.*

wine cellar *n.* **1.** A place for storing wine. **2.** A stock of wines.

wine cooler *n.* **1.** A container, such as an ice-filled bucket or chest, for cooling wine. **2.** A bottled mixture of wine, fruit juice, and sometimes soda water.

wine•glass (wīn′glăs′) *n.* A glass, usu. with a stem, from which wine is drunk.

wine•grow•er (wīn′grō′ər) *n.* One that owns a vineyard and produces wine.

wine•mak•ing (wīn′mā′kĭng) *n.* The art and science of making wine. — **wine′mak′er** *n.* — **wine′mak′ing** *adj.*

wine palm *n.* Any of various palm trees having sap or juice from which wine is made.

wine•press (wīn′prĕs′) *n.* **1.** A vat in which the juice is pressed from grapes. **2.** A machine or device that presses the juice from grapes.

win•er•y (wī′nə-rē) *n., pl.* **-ies.** An establishment at which wine is made.

Wine•sap (wīn′săp′) *n.* A variety of apple having fruit with dark red skin.

wine•skin (wīn′skĭn′) *n.* A bag made from the skin of a goat, for example, and used for holding and dispensing wine.

wine taster *n.* **1.** One who evaluates the quality of wine by tasting it, esp. on a professional basis. **2.** A small bowl used to hold wine for tasting.

wine•tast•ing (wīn′tā′stĭng) *n.* A gathering of people to taste and compare a number of wines.

wine•y (wī′nē) *adj.* Var. of **winy.**

wing (wĭng) *n.* **1.** One of a pair of movable organs for flying, as the feather-covered modified forelimb of a bird. **2.** Any of usu. four membranous organs for flying that extend from the thorax of an insect. **3.** A winglike organ or structure used for flying, as the folds of skin of a flying squirrel. **4.** *Bot.* **a.** A thin or membranous extension, as of the fruit of the elm. **b.** One of the lateral petals of the flower of a pea or of most plants in the pea family. **5.** *Informal.* An arm of a human being. **6.** An airfoil whose principal function is providing lift, esp. either of two such airfoils symmetrically positioned on each side of the fuselage of an aircraft. **7.** Something that resembles a wing in appearance, function, or position relative to a main body. **8.a.** The act or manner of flying. **b.** A means of flight or of rapid ascent. **9.a.** Something, such as a weathervane, that is moved by or moves against the air. **b.** The sail of a ship. **10.** *Chiefly British.* The fender of a motor vehicle. **11.** A folding section, as of a double door. **12.** Either of the two side projections on the back of a wing chair. **13.a.** A flat of theatrical scenery projecting onto the stage from the side. **b. wings.** The unseen backstage area on either side of the stage of a proscenium theater. **14.** A structure attached to and connected internally with the side of a main building. **15.** A section of a large building devoted to a specific purpose. **16.** A group affiliated with or subordinate to an older or larger organization. **17.a.** Either of two groups with opposing views within a larger group; a faction. **b.** A section of a party, legislature, or community holding distinct, esp. dissenting, political views. **18.a.** Either the left or right flank of an army or a naval fleet. **b.** An air force unit larger than a group but smaller than a division. **19.** *Sports.* Either of the forward positions played near the sideline, esp. in hockey. **20. wings.** An outspread pair of stylized bird's wings worn as insignia by qualified pilots or air crew members. — *v.* **winged, wing•ing, wings.** — *intr.* To move on or as if on wings; fly. — *tr.* **1.a.** To furnish with wings. **b.** To cause or enable to fly or speed swiftly along. **2.** To feather (an arrow). **3.a.** To pass over or through with or as if with wings. **b.** To carry or transport by or as if by flying. **c.** To effect by flying. **4.** To throw or dispatch (a ball, for example). **5.a.** To wound the wing of (a game bird, for example). **b.** To wound superficially. **6.** To furnish with side or subordinate extensions, as a building. — ***idioms.* in the wings. 1.** In the stage wings, unseen by the audience. **2.** Close by in the background; available at short notice. **on the wing.** In flight; flying. **take wing.** To fly off; soar away. **under (one's) wing.** Under one's protection; in one's care. **wing it.** *Informal.* To improvise. [ME *wenge, winge,* of Scand. orig. See **wē-*.**]

wing and wing *adv. Naut.* With sails extended on both sides.

wing•back (wĭng′băk′) *n. Football.* **1.** A back positioned on offense behind or outside of an end. **2.** This position.

wing•bow (wĭng′bō′) *n.* A distinctive mark of color on the bend of a bird's wing, esp. in domestic fowl.

wing case *n.* See **elytron.**

wing chair also **wing•chair** (wĭng′châr′) *n.* An armchair with a high back from which large enclosing side pieces project.

wing•ding (wĭng′dĭng′) *n. Informal.* A lavish or lively party or celebration. [?]

winged (wĭngd, wĭng′ĭd) *adj.* **1.a.** Having wings or winglike appendages. **b.** Having wings of a specified kind. Often used in combination: *big-winged.* **2.** Moving on or as if on wings; flying. **3.** Soaring as if with wings; elevated or sublime. **4.** Swift; fleet.

wing-foot•ed (wĭng′fo͝ot′ĭd) *adj.* **1.** Having winged feet. **2.** Swift; fleet.

wing•less (wĭng′lĭs) *adj.* Having no wings or only rudimentary wings. — **wing′less•ness** *n.*

wing•let (wĭng′lĭt) *n.* **1.** A small or rudimentary wing. **2.** A short, almost vertical stabilizing fin projecting from the tip of an aircraft wing.

wing loading *n.* The gross weight of an airplane divided by the wing area. Used in stress analysis.

wing•man (wĭng′mən) *n.* A pilot whose plane is positioned behind and outside the leader in a formation of flying aircraft.

wing nut *n.* A nut with winglike projections for thumb and forefinger leverage in turning.

wing·o·ver (wĭng′ō′vər) *n.* A flight maneuver or stunt in which an airplane enters a climbing turn until almost stalled and is allowed to fall while the turn is continued until normal flight is attained in a direction opposite the original heading.

wing·span (wĭng′spăn′) *n.* **1.** The linear distance between the extremities of an airfoil. **2.** Wingspread.

wing·spread (wĭng′sprĕd′) *n.* The distance between the tips of the wings, as of a bird or an insect, when fully extended.

wing·tip also **wing tip** (wĭng′tĭp′) *n.* **1.a.** An often perforated shoe part that covers the toe and extends backward along the sides of the shoe from a point at the center. **b.** A style of shoe having such a tip. **2.** The tip of the wing of a bird or another animal. **3.** The extreme edge of a wing, as of an aircraft.

wink (wĭngk) *v.* **winked, wink·ing, winks.** —*intr.* **1.** To close and open the eyelid of one eye deliberately, as to convey a message, signal, or suggestion. **2.** To close and open the eyelids of both eyes; blink. **3.** To shine fitfully; twinkle. —*tr.* **1.** To close and open (an eye or the eyes) rapidly. **2.** To signal or express by winking. —*n.* **1.a.** The act of winking. **b.** A signal or hint conveyed by winking. **2.** The very brief time required for a wink; an instant. **3.** A quick closing and opening of the eyelids; a blink. **4.** A gleam or twinkle. **5.** *Informal.* A brief period of sleep. —***phrasal verb.*** **wink at.** To pretend not to see. [ME *winken,* to close one's eyes < OE *wincian.*]

wink·er (wĭng′kər) *n.* One that winks, as: **a.** A blinder for a horse. **b.** *Informal.* An eye. **c.** *Informal.* An eyelash.

win·kle[1] (wĭng′kəl) *n. Zool.* A periwinkle.

win·kle[2] (wĭng′kəl) *tr.v.* **-kled, -kling, -kles.** *Chiefly British.* To pry, extract, or force from a place or position. Often used with *out.* [< WINKLE[1] (< extracting periwinkles).]

win·na·ble (wĭn′ə-bəl) *adj.* Possible to win or achieve. —**win′na·bil′i·ty** *n.*

Win·ne·ba·go (wĭn′ə-bā′gō) *n., pl.* **Winnebago** or **-gos** or **-goes. 1.** A member of a Native American people formerly inhabiting the Green Bay area of Wisconsin, with present-day populations in Wisconsin and Nebraska. **2.** Their Siouan language. [Fox *wiinepyeekooha,* those of the dirty water.]

Winnebago, Lake. A lake of E WI traversed by the Fox R.

win·ner (wĭn′ər) *n.* One that wins, esp. a victor in sports or a notably successful person.

win·ner's circle (wĭn′ərz) *n., pl.* **winners' circles.** *Sports.* An enclosed area at a racetrack where the winning horse and jockey are brought for awards and publicity.

win·ning (wĭn′ĭng) *adj.* **1.a.** Of or relating to the act of winning. **b.** Successful; victorious. **2.** Attractive; charming. —*n.* **1.** The act of one that wins; victory. **2.** Something won, esp. money. Often used in the plural. **3.** A section of a mine that has been recently prepared or opened for working. —**win′ning·ly** *adv.* —**win′ning·ness** *n.*

Win·ni·peg (wĭn′ə-pĕg′). The cap. of Manitoba, Canada, in the SE part at the confluence of the Red and Assiniboine rivers. Pop. 564,473.

Winnipeg, Lake. A lake of S-central Manitoba, Canada; a remnant of the glacial Lake Agassiz.

Win·ni·pe·go·sis (wĭn′ə-pĭ-gō′sĭs), **Lake.** A lake of SW Manitoba, Canada, W of Lake Winnipeg.

Winnipeg River. A river of SW Ontario and SE Manitoba, Canada, flowing c. 322 km (200 mi) to Lake Winnipeg.

Win·ni·pe·sau·kee (wĭn′ə-pĭ-sô′kē), **Lake.** A lake of E-central NH.

win·now (wĭn′ō) *v.* **-nowed, -now·ing, -nows.** —*tr.* **1.a.** To separate the chaff from (grain) by means of a current of air. **b.** To rid of undesirable parts. **2.** To blow (chaff) off or away. **3.** To blow away; scatter. **4.** To blow on; fan. **5.** To examine closely in order to separate the good from the bad; sift. **6.a.** To separate or get rid of (an undesirable part); eliminate: *winnowing out errors.* **b.** To sort or select (a desirable part); extract. —*intr.* **1.** To separate grain from chaff. **2.** To separate the good from the bad. —*n.* **1.** A device for winnowing grain. **2.** An act of winnowing. [ME *winnewen,* alteration of *windwen* < OE *windwian* < *wind,* wind. See WIND[1].] —**win′now·er** *n.*

win·o (wī′nō) *n., pl.* **-os.** *Slang.* An indigent wine-drinking alcoholic.

Wi·no·na (wĭ-nō′nə). A city of SE MN on the Mississippi R. SE of St. Paul. Pop. 25,399.

Win·slow (wĭnz′lō), **Edward.** 1595–1655. English colonial administrator who served as governor of Plymouth Colony (1633, 1636, and 1644).

win·some (wĭn′səm) *adj.* Charming, often in a childlike or naive way. [ME *winsum* < OE *wynsum* : < *wynn,* joy; see **wen-[1]*** + *-sum,* characterized by; see -SOME[1].] —**win′some·ly** *adv.* —**win′some·ness** *n.*

Win·ston-Sa·lem (wĭn′stən-sā′ləm). A city of N-central NC NNE of Charlotte. Salem was founded by Moravians in 1766, and Winston was estab. in 1849; the cities were consolidated in 1913. Pop. 143,485.

win·ter (wĭn′tər) *n.* **1.** The usu. coldest season of the year, occurring between autumn and spring and comprising December, January, and February in the Northern Hemisphere or, as calculated astronomically, extending from the winter solstice to the vernal equinox. **2.** A year as expressed through the recurrence of the winter season. **3.** A period of time characterized by coldness, misery, barrenness, or death. —*adj.* **1.** Of, relating to, occurring in, or appropriate to the season of winter. **2.** Grown during the season of winter. —*v.* **-tered, -ter·ing, -ters.** —*intr.* **1.** To spend the winter. **2.** To feed in winter. Used with *on: deer wintering on cedar bark.* —*tr.* To lodge, keep, or care for during the winter. [ME < OE. See **wed-[1]***.] —**win′ter·ish** *adj.*

winter aconite *n.* Any of various Eurasian herbs of the genus *Eranthis,* esp. *E. hyemalis,* having palmately dissected leaves and a yellow flower that blooms in winter or early spring.

win·ter·ber·ry (wĭn′tər-bĕr′ē) *n.* **1.** Any of several North American shrubs of the genus *Ilex,* having showy red berries. **2.** See **black alder** 1.

win·ter-feed (wĭn′tər-fēd′) *tr.v.* **-fed** (-fĕd′), **-feed·ing, -feeds.** To feed (livestock) when grazing is not possible.

winter flounder *n.* A dark rusty brown flounder *(Pseudopleuronectes americanus)* of the North American Atlantic coast, prized esp. in winter as a food fish.

win·ter·green (wĭn′tər-grēn′) *n.* **1.a.** A low-growing creeping evergreen plant *(Gaultheria procumbens)* of North America having solitary nodding white flowers, aromatic leaves, and spicy edible scarlet berries. **b.** An oil or a flavoring obtained from this plant. **2.** Any of several similar or related plants, such as the pipsissewa. [Transl. of Du. *wintergroen.*]

Win·ter Ha·ven (wĭn′tər hā′vən). A city of central FL E of Lakeland. Pop. 24,725.

win·ter·ize (wĭn′tə-rīz′) *tr.v.* **-ized, -iz·ing, -iz·es.** To prepare or equip (an automobile or a house, for example) for winter weather. —**win′ter·i·za′tion** (-tĕr-ĭ-zā′shən) *n.*

win·ter·kill (wĭn′tər-kĭl′) *v.* **-killed, -kill·ing, -kills.** —*tr.* To kill (plants, for example) by exposing to extremely cold winter weather. —*intr.* To die from exposure to cold winter weather. Used esp. of plants. —*n.* Death, as of plants, resulting from exposure to winter weather.

winter melon *n.* See **honeydew melon.** [Transl. of Chin. *dōng guā* : *dōng,* winter + *guā,* melon.]

Winter Park. A city of central FL N of Orlando. Pop. 22,242.

winter savory *n.* See **savory[2]** 2.

winter solstice *n.* In the Northern Hemisphere, the solstice that occurs on or about December 22.

winter squash *n.* Any of several thick-rinded varieties of squash that can be stored for long periods.

Win·ter·thur (vĭn′tər-to͝or′). A city of N Switzerland NE of Zurich; became a free imperial city in 1415. Pop. 84,600.

win·ter·time (wĭn′tər-tīm′) *n.* The season of winter.

winter wheat *n.* Wheat planted in the autumn and harvested the following spring or early summer.

Win·throp (wĭn′thrəp). A town of E MA, a suburb of Boston. Pop. 18,127.

Winthrop, John[1]. 1588–1649. English colonial administrator who was the first governor of Massachusetts Bay Colony, serving seven terms between 1629 and 1649. His son **John** (1606–76) was governor of Connecticut (1636, 1657, and 1659–76).

Winthrop, John[2]. 1714–79. Amer. scientist who founded the first physics laboratory in the U.S. (1646).

win·try (wĭn′trē) also **win·ter·y** (wĭn′tə-rē) *adj.* **-tri·er, -tri·est** also **-ter·i·er, -ter·i·est. 1.** Belonging to or characteristic of winter; cold. **2.** Suggestive of winter, as in cheerlessness. —**win′tri·ly** *adv.* —**win′tri·ness** *n.*

win·y or **wine·y** (wī′nē) *adj.* **-i·er, -i·est.** Having the qualities or taste of wine; heady or intoxicating.

winze (wĭnz) *n.* An inclined or vertical shaft or passage between levels in a mine. [Alteration of obsolete *winds,* prob. < WIND[2], apparatus for winding.]

wipe (wīp) *tr.v.* **wiped, wip·ing, wipes. 1.a.** To subject to light rubbing or friction, as with a cloth, in order to clean or dry. **b.** To clean or dry by rubbing. **c.** To rub, move, or pass (a cloth, for example) over a surface. **2.a.** To remove by or as if by rubbing. **b.** To blot out completely, as from the memory. **3.a.** To spread or apply by or as if by wiping. **b.** To form (a joint) in plumbing by spreading solder with a piece of cloth or leather. —*n.* **1.** The act or an instance of wiping. **2.** Something used for wiping. **3.** A cam that activates another part; a wiper. **4.a.** A blow or swipe. **b.** *Informal.* A jeer; a gibe. **5.** A replacement of one scene in a film by another, in which the new scene appears to wipe the old off the screen. —***phrasal verb.*** **wipe out. 1.** To destroy or be destroyed completely. **2.** *Slang.* To murder. **3.** *Sports.* To lose one's balance and fall or jump off a surfboard. [ME *wipen* < OE *wīpian.* See **weip-***.]

wiped-out (wīpt′out′) *adj. Slang.* Totally exhausted.

wipe·out (wīp′out′) *n.* **1.a.** The act or an instance of wiping out. **b.** Complete destruction. **2.** *Sports.* A fall from a surfboard.

wip·er (wī′pər) *n.* **1.** One that wipes. **2.** Something, such as a towel, used for wiping. **3.** A device designed for wiping, as on an automobile windshield. **4.** A projecting cam that activates another machine part. **5.** *Elect.* A movable electrical contact.

wire (wīr) *n.* **1.** A usu. pliable metallic strand or rod made in many lengths and diameters and often electrically insulated,

windsurfing

wing chair
c. 1750–1770 American

ă pat	oi boy
ā pay	ou out
âr care	o͝o took
ä father	o͞o boot
ĕ pet	ŭ cut
ē be	ûr urge
ĭ pit	th thin
ī pie	*th* this
îr pier	hw which
ŏ pot	zh vision
ō toe	ə about, item
ô paw	

Stress marks:
′ (primary);
′ (secondary), as in
dictionary (dĭk′shə-nĕr′ē)

used chiefly for structural support or to conduct electricity. **2.** A group of wire strands bundled or twisted together as a functional unit; a cable. **3.** Something resembling a wire, as in slenderness. **4.** An open telephone connection. **5.** *Slang.* A hidden microphone, as on a person's body. **6.a.** A telegraph service. **b.** A telegram or cablegram. **7.** *Comp. Sci.* A pin in the print head of a computer printer. **8.** The screen on which sheets of paper are formed in a papermaking machine. **9.** *Sports.* The finish line of a racetrack. **10. wires. a.** The system of strings for manipulating puppets in a show. **b.** Hidden controlling influences. **11.** *Slang.* A pickpocket. **12.** Fencing usu. made of barbed wire. —*v.* **wired, wir•ing, wires.** —*tr.* **1.** To bind, connect, or attach with wires or a wire. **2.** To string (beads, for example) on wire. **3.** To equip with a system of electrical wires. **4.** *Slang.* To install electronic eavesdropping equipment in (a room, for example). **5.** To send by telegraph. **6.** To send a telegram to. —*intr.* To send a telegram. —***idioms.*** **down to the wire.** *Informal.* To the very end, as in a contest. **under the wire. 1.** *Sports.* At the finish line. **2.** *Informal.* Just in the nick of time. [ME, slender metal rod < OE *wīr.* See **wei-*.**] —**wir′a•ble** *adj.*

wired (wīrd) *adj.* **1.** Equipped with a system of wires, as for electric connections. **2.** *Slang.* Equipped with hidden electronic eavesdropping devices. **3.a.** Reinforced or supported by wires. **b.** Tied or bound up with wire. **4.** *Slang.* Well connected, as with high-ranking members of an organization. **5.** *Slang.* Very stimulated or excited, as from a stimulant.

wire•draw (wīr′drô′) *tr.v.* **-drew** (-dro͞o′), **-drawn** (-drôn′), **-draw•ing, -draws. 1.** To draw (metal) into wire. **2.** To treat (a subject, for example) with great length, excessive detail, or overrefinement; spin out. —**wire′draw′er** *n.*

wire•drawn (wīr′drôn′) *adj.* Overly subtle and particularized.

wire fox terrier *n.* Any of a breed of small fox terrier developed in northern England and having a rough wiry coat.

wire gauge *n.* **1.** A gauge for measuring the diameter of wire, usu. consisting of a disk having variously sized slots in its periphery or a long graduated plate with similar slots along its edge. **2.** A standardized system of wire sizes.

wire glass *n.* Sheet glass reinforced with wire netting.

wire•grass (wīr′grăs′) *n.* Any of various grasses, such as Bermuda grass, having tough wiry roots or rootstocks.

wire•hair (wīr′hâr′) *n.* See **wire fox terrier.**

wire•haired (wīr′hârd′) *adj.* Having a coat of stiff wiry hair. Used esp. of breeds of dogs.

wire fox terrier

wirehaired point•ing griffon (poin′tĭng) *n.* Any of a breed of medium-sized hunting dog originating in the Netherlands and having a rough steel-gray coat with patches of chestnut.

wirehaired terrier *n.* See **wire fox terrier.**

wire•less (wīr′lĭs) *adj.* **1.** Having no wires: *a wireless security system.* **2.** *Chiefly British.* Of or relating to radio communication. —*n.* *Chiefly British.* **1.** A message transmitted by wireless telegraph or telephone. **2.** Radio. —*tr. & intr.v.* **-lessed, -less•ing, -less•es.** *Chiefly British.* To communicate with or send communications by wireless.

wireless telegraphy *n.* Telegraphy by radio rather than by long-distance transmission lines.

wireless telephone *n.* See **radiotelephone.**

wire•man (wīr′mən) *n.* **1.** One who works with electric wiring. **2.** *Slang.* One who taps telephone lines; a wiretapper.

Wire•pho•to (wīr′fō′tō). A trademark used for a photograph electrically transmitted over telephone wires.

wire•pull•er (wīr′po͝ol′ər) *n.* **1.** *Slang.* One who uses private influence or underhand means to reach a goal. **2.** One who pulls wires or strings, as of puppets. —**wire′pull′ing** *n.*

wire rope *n.* Rope made of twisted strands of wire.

wire service *n.* A news-gathering organization that distributes syndicated copy electronically to subscribers.

wire•tap (wīr′tăp′) *n.* **1.** A concealed listening or recording device connected to a communications circuit. **2.** The act of installing such a device. —*v.* **-tapped, -tap•ping, -taps.** —*tr.* **1.** To connect a wiretap to. **2.** To monitor (a telephone line) with a wiretap. —*intr.* To install a wiretap or use it to monitor communications. —**wire′tap′per** *n.*

wire•worm (wīr′wûrm′) *n.* **1.** The yellowish hard-bodied larva of various click beetles that feeds on the roots and seedlings of many crop plants. **2.** Any of various millipedes.

wir•ing (wīr′ĭng) *n.* **1.** The act of attaching, connecting, or installing electric wires. **2.** A system of electric wires.

wir•ra (wĭr′ə) *interj.* *Irish.* Used to express sorrow or anxious concern. [< Ir.Gael. *a Muire,* Virgin Mary : *a,* O + *Muire,* Mary.]

wir•y (wīr′ē) *adj.* **-i•er, -i•est. 1.** Of or relating to wire. **2.** Resembling wire in form or quality, esp. in stiffness. **3.** Sinewy and lean. **4.** Produced by or as if by wire being vibrated. Used of sounds. —**wir′i•ly** *adv.* —**wir′i•ness** *n.*

Wis. *abbr.* Wisconsin.

Wis•con•sin[1] (wĭs-kŏn′sĭn). A state of the N-central U.S.; admitted as the 30th state in 1848. The region became part of the Northwest Terr. in 1787. Cap. Madison. Pop. 4,906,745. —**Wis•con′sin•ite′** *n.*

Wis•con•sin[2] (wĭs-kŏn′sĭn) *adj.* *Geol.* Of the fourth glacial stage of the Pleistocene Epoch in North America.

Wisconsin Rapids. A city of central WI S of Wausau on the Wisconsin R.. Pop. 18,245.

Wisconsin River. A river of central and SW WI flowing c. 692 km (430 mi) to the Mississippi R.

wis•dom (wĭz′dəm) *n.* **1.** Understanding of what is true, right, or lasting; insight. **2.** Common sense; good judgment. **3.a.** The sum of scholarly learning through the ages; knowledge. **b.** Wise teachings of the ancient sages. **4.** A wise outlook, plan, or course of action. **5. Wisdom.** Wisdom of Solomon. [ME < OE *wīsdōm.* See **weid-*.**]

Wisdom of Jesus, the Son of Si•rach (sī′răk′) *n.* Ecclesiasticus.

Wisdom of Solomon *n.* See table at **Bible.**

wisdom tooth *n.* One of four rearmost molars on each side of both jaws in human beings.

wise[1] (wīz) *adj.* **wis•er, wis•est. 1.** Having understanding or discernment of what is true, right, or lasting; sagacious. **2.a.** Exhibiting common sense; prudent. **b.** Shrewd; crafty. **3.** Having great learning; erudite. **4.** Provided with information; informed. Used with *to.* **5.** *Slang.* Rude and disrespectful; impudent. —***phrasal verb.*** **wise up.** *Slang.* To make or become aware, informed, or sophisticated. [ME < OE *wīs.* See **weid-*.**] —**wise′ly** *adv.* —**wise′ness** *n.*

wise[2] (wīz) *n.* Method or manner of doing; way: *in no wise; in any wise.* [ME < OE *wīse.* See **weid-*.**]

Wise (wīz), **Isaac Mayer.** 1819–1900. Bohemian-born religious leader who united U.S. Reform Jewish organizations.

Wise, Stephen Samuel. 1874–1949. Hungarian-born Amer. founder of the World Jewish Congress (1936).

–wise *suff.* **1.** In a specified manner, direction, or position: *clockwise.* **2.** *Usage Problem.* With reference to; in regard to: *profitwise.* [ME < OE *-wīsan* < *-wīse,* manner. See WISE[2].]

Usage Note: The suffix *–wise* has a long history of use to mean "in the manner or direction of," as in *clockwise, otherwise,* and *slantwise.* Since the 1930's, however, the suffix has been widely used in the vaguer sense of "with reference to," as in *This has not been a good year saleswise.* The suffix may save a few syllables, but in most writing there is no alternative to paraphrases such as *This has not been a good year with respect to sales.*

wise•a•cre (wīz′ā′kər) *n.* *Slang.* A person regarded as disagreeably egotistical and self-assured. [Alteration of MDu. *wijsseggher,* soothsayer, transl. of MHGer. *wīssage* < OHGer. *wīssago, wīzzago,* seer. See **weid-*.**]

wise•ass also **wise-ass** (wīz′ăs′) *n.* *Vulgar Slang.* A smart aleck.

wise•crack (wīz′krăk′) *Slang.* —*n.* A flippant, usu. sardonic remark. —*intr.v.* **-cracked, -crack•ing, -cracks.** To make or utter a wisecrack. —**wise′crack′er** *n.*

wise guy *n.* *Slang.* A smart aleck.

wise man *n.* **1.** One of the magi who paid homage to the baby Jesus; a magus. **2.** A sage.

wis•en•heim•er also **weis•en•heim•er** (wī′zən-hī′mər) *n.* *Informal.* A smart aleck. [WISE[1] + Ger. *-enheimer* (as in surnames such as *Oppenheimer*).]

wi•sent (vē′zənt) *n.* The European bison *(Bison bonasus)* having a smaller and higher head than the North American bison. [Ger. < MHGer. < OHGer. *wisunt.*]

wish (wĭsh) *n.* **1.** A desire, longing, or strong inclination for a specific thing. **2.** An expression of a wish; a petition. **3.** Something desired or longed for. —*v.* **wished, wish•ing, wish•es.** —*tr.* **1.** To long for; want. See Syns at **desire. 2.** To entertain or express wishes for; bid. **3.** To call or invoke upon. **4.** To order or entreat. **5.** To impose or force; foist. —*intr.* **1.** To have or feel a desire. **2.** To express a wish. [ME *wissh* < *wisshen,* to wish < OE *wȳscan.* See **wen-[1]*.**] —**wish′er** *n.*

Usage Note: *Wish* is widely used as a polite formal substitute for *want* with infinitives: *Do you wish to sit at a table on the terrace?* The corresponding use of *wish* with a noun-phrase object is less frequent, though it cannot be regarded as incorrect: *Anyone who wishes an aisle seat should see an attendant.* • When *wish* precedes a subordinate clause containing a contrary-to-fact statement, strict grammatical correctness requires that one use *were* rather than *was: I wish I were lighter on my feet.* However, precedent for using the indicative *was* in such clauses can be found in the works of many good writers. See Usage Notes at **if, want.**

wish•bone (wĭsh′bōn′) *n.* **1.** The forked bone anterior to the breastbone of most birds, formed by the fusion of the clavicles. **2.** *Football.* An offensive formation in which the halfbacks are positioned behind and to the left and right of the fullback. [< the superstition that when two people pull the bone apart, the one with the longer part will get a wish.]

wish•ful (wĭsh′fəl) *adj.* Having or expressing a wish or longing. —**wish′ful•ly** *adv.* —**wish′ful•ness** *n.*

wish fulfillment *n.* **1.** Gratification of a desire. **2.** In psychoanalytic theory, the satisfaction of a desire, a need, or an impulse through a dream or other exercise of the imagination.

wishful thinking *n.* Identification of one's wishes or desires with reality.

wish list *n.* *Informal.* An often mental list of things wanted.

wish-wash (wĭsh′wŏsh′, -wôsh′) *n.* *Informal.* **1.** Speech or writing deemed banal or foolish. **2.** A thin watery drink. [Redup. of WASH.]

wish•y-wash•y (wĭsh′ē-wŏsh′ē, -wô′shē) *adj.* **-i•er, -i•est.** *Informal.* **1.** Thin and watery, as tea or soup; insipid. **2.** Lacking in strength of character or purpose; ineffective. [Redup. of *washy*, thin, watery < WASH.] **—wish′y-wash′i•ness** *n.*

wisp (wĭsp) *n.* **1.** A small bunch or bundle, as of straw, hair, or grass. **2.a.** One that is thin, frail, or slight. **b.** A thin or faint streak or fragment, as of smoke or clouds. **3.** A fleeting trace or indication; a hint. **4.** A flock of birds, esp. snipe. **5.** See **ignis fatuus** 1. *—v.* **wisped, wisp•ing, wisps.** *—tr.* To twist into wisps or a wisp. *—intr.* To drift in wisps. [ME.] **—wisp′i•ly** *adv.* **—wisp′i•ness** (wĭs′pē-nĭs) *n.* **—wisp′y** *adj.*

wist (wĭst) *v. Archaic.* P.t. and p.part. of **wit²**.

Wis•ter (wĭs′tər), **Owen.** 1860–1938. Amer. writer known esp. for his novel *The Virginian* (1902).

wis•ter•i•a (wĭ-stîr′ē-ə) also **wis•tar•i•a** (wĭ-stâr′-) *n.* Any of several climbing vines of the genus *Wisteria* in the pea family, having pinnately compound leaves and drooping racemes of purplish or white flowers. [NLat. *Wisteria*, genus name, after Caspar *Wistar* (1761–1818), Amer. physician.]

wist•ful (wĭst′fəl) *adj.* **1.** Full of wishful yearning. **2.** Pensively sad; melancholy. [< obsolete *wistly*, intently.] **—wist′ful•ly** *adv.* **—wist′ful•ness** *n.*

wit¹ (wĭt) *n.* **1.** The natural ability to perceive and understand; intelligence. **2.a.** Keenness and quickness of perception or discernment; ingenuity. Often used in the plural. **b. wits.** Sound mental faculties; sanity. **3.a.** The ability to perceive and express in an ingeniously humorous manner the relationship between seemingly incongruous or disparate things. **b.** One noted for this ability, esp. one skilled in repartee. **c.** A person of exceptional intelligence. ***—idioms.*** **at (one's) wits' end.** At the limit of one's mental resources; utterly at a loss. **have** (or **keep) (one's) wits about (one).** To remain alert or calm, esp. in a crisis. [ME < OE. See **weid-***.]

wit² (wĭt) *v.* **wist** (wĭst), **wit•ting** (wĭt′ĭng), first and third pers. sing. pr.t. **wot** (wŏt). *—tr.* To be or become aware of; learn. *—intr.* To know. ***—idiom.*** **to wit.** That is to say; namely. [ME < OE *witan*. See **weid-***.]

wit•an (wĭt′än) *pl.n.* **1.** The members of the witenagemot in Anglo-Saxon England. **2.** The witenagemot. [OE, pl. of *wita*, councilor. See WITENAGEMOT.]

witch (wĭch) *n.* **1.** A woman popularly believed to have supernatural powers and practice sorcery and often believed to be aided by spirits or a familiar. **2.** A believer or follower of Wicca; a Wiccan. **3.** *Offensive.* An elderly woman perceived as ugly and frightful. **4.** *Informal.* A woman or girl considered bewitching. **5.** One particularly skilled or competent at one's craft. *—v.* **witched, witch•ing, witch•es.** *—tr.* **1.** To work or cast a spell on; bewitch. **2.** To cause, bring, or effect by witchcraft. *—intr.* To dowse. [ME *wicche* < OE *wicce*, witch, and *wicca*, wizard, sorcerer; see **weg-***.] **—witch′er•y** (-ə-rē) *n.* **—witch′y** *adj.*

witch•craft (wĭch′krăft′) *n.* **1.** Magic; sorcery. **2.** Wicca. **3.** A magical or irresistible influence, attraction, or charm.

witch doctor *n. Anthro.* A shamanistic healer, a sorcerer, or a prophet, esp. among African peoples. Not in scientific use.

witch elm *n.* Var. of **wych elm.** [Alteration of WYCH ELM.]

witch•es' brew (wĭch′ĭz) *n.* A powerful or terrifying concoction.

witches' broom *n.* An abnormal brushlike growth of shoots or branches on a tree, caused by fungi or viruses.

witches' Sabbath *n.* A meeting of witches, supposed by medieval Christians to be a demonic orgy.

witch grass *n.* **1.** An annual North American grass *(Panicum capillare)* having branching purplish panicles. **2.** See **couch grass.** [Prob. alteration of QUITCH GRASS.]

witch hazel *n.* **1.** Any of several deciduous shrubs or small trees of the genus *Hamamelis*, esp. *H. virginiana* of eastern North America, having yellow flowers. **2.** An alcoholic solution containing an extract of the bark and leaves of this plant, used as a mild astringent. [Alteration of obsolete *wych*, wych elm; see WYCH ELM + HAZEL.]

witch-hunt (wĭch′hŭnt′) *n.* An investigation carried out ostensibly to uncover subversive activities but actually used to harass and undermine those with differing views. **—witch′-hunt′er** *n.* **—witch′-hunt′ing** *adj. & n.*

witch•ing (wĭch′ĭng) *adj.* **1.** Of or characteristic of witchcraft. **2.** Having the power to charm or enchant; bewitching. *—n.* Witchcraft; sorcery. **—witch′ing•ly** *adv.*

witch moth *n.* Any of several large noctuid moths of the genus *Erebus* of the southern United States and tropical America.

wite (wīt) *n. Scots.* Blame; fault. [ME < OE *wīte*, penalty. See **weid-***.]

wit•e•na•ge•mot (wĭt′n-ə-gə-mōt′) *n.* An Anglo-Saxon advisory council to the king, convened at intervals to discuss administrative and judicial affairs. [OE *witena gemōt*, meeting of councilors : *witena*, genitive pl. of *wita*, councilor; see **weid-*** + *gemōt*, meeting (*ge-*, collective pref.; see **kom*** + *mōt*, meeting).]

with (wĭth, wĭ*th*) *prep.* **1.** In the company of; accompanying: *Did you go with her?* **2.** Next to; alongside of: *sat with them.* **3.a.** Having as a possession, an attribute, or a characteristic: *a man with a moustache.* **b.** Used as a function word to indicate accompanying detail or condition: *sat with his mouth open.* **4.a.** In a manner characterized by: *performed with skill.* **b.** In the performance, use, or operation of: *trouble with the car.* **5.** In the charge or keeping of: *left the cat with the neighbors.* **6.** In the opinion or estimation of: *if it's all right with you.* **7.a.** In support of; on the side of: *I'm with you.* **b.** Of the same opinion or belief as: *with us on that issue.* **8.** In the same group or mixture as; among: *planted onions with the carrots.* **9.** In the membership or employment of: *is with a small company.* **10.a.** By the means or agency of: *eat with a fork.* **b.** By the presence or use of: *a pillow stuffed with feathers.* **11.** In spite of: *With all her experience, she failed.* **12.** In the same direction as: *sail with the wind.* **13.** At the same time as: *gets up with the birds.* **14.a.** In regard to: *pleased with her decision.* **b.** Used as a function word to indicate a party to an action, a communicative activity, or an informal agreement or settlement: *lives with an aunt.* **15.** In comparison or contrast to: *pants identical with her sister's.* **16.** Having received: *With her permission, he left.* **17.a.** And; plus: *My books, with my brother's, are here.* **b.** Inclusive of; including: *$29.95 with postage.* **18.** In opposition to; against: *wrestling with him.* **19.** As a result or consequence of: *sick with the flu.* **20.** So as to be touching or joined to: *linked arms with their partners.* **21.** So as to be free of or separated from: *parted with them.* **22.** In the course of: *We grow older with the hours.* **23.** In proportion to: *improves with age.* **24.** In relationship to: *at ease with my peers.* **25.** As well as; in favorable comparison to: *sang with the best.* **26.** According to the experience or practice of: *With me, it is all the same.* **27.** Used as a function word to indicate close association: *With the advent of the rockets, the Space Age began.* ***—idiom.*** **in with.** *Informal.* In league or association with. [ME, with, against, from < OE. See **wi-***.]

Usage Note: *With* does not have the conjunctive force of *and*. Consequently, in the following example the verb is governed by the singular subject and remains singular: *The governor, with his aides, is here.* See Usage Note at **and.**

with•al (wĭ*th*-ôl′, wĭth-) *adv.* **1.** In addition; besides. **2.** Despite that; nevertheless. **3.** *Archaic.* Therewith. *—prep. Archaic.* With. Used after its object at the end of a sentence or clause. [ME : *with*, with; see WITH + *al*, all; see ALL.]

wisteria

with•draw (wĭ*th*-drô′, wĭth-) *v.* **-drew** (-dro͞o′), **-drawn** (-drôn′), **-draw•ing, -draws.** *—tr.* **1.a.** To take back or away; remove. **b.** To remove (money) from an account. **c.** To turn away (one's gaze, for example). **d.** To draw aside. **2.a.** To remove from consideration or participation. **b.** To recall or retract. *—intr.* **1.a.** To move or draw back; retire. **b.** To retreat from a battlefield. **2.a.** To remove oneself from active participation. **b.** To become detached from social or emotional involvement. **3.** To recall or remove a motion from consideration in parliamentary procedure. **4.** To discontinue the use of an addictive substance. [ME *withdrawen* : *with*, away from; see WITH + *drawen*, to pull; see DRAW.] **—with•draw′a•ble** *adj.* **—with•draw′er** *n.*

with•draw•al (wĭ*th*-drô′əl, wĭth-) *n.* **1.** The act or process of withdrawing, as: **a.** A retreat or retirement. **b.** Retreat of a military force in the face of enemy attack or after a defeat. **c.** Detachment, as from emotional involvement. **d.** A removal from a place or position of something that has been deposited. **2.a.** Discontinuation of the use of an addictive substance. **b.** The physiological and mental readjustment that accompanies such discontinuation. **3.** The act or an instance of retracting or revoking.

with•drawn (wĭ*th*-drôn′, wĭth-) *adj.* **1.** Not readily approached; remote. **2.a.** Not friendly or sociable; aloof. **b.** Emotionally unresponsive and detached; introverted. **—with•drawn′ness** *n.*

withe (wĭth, wĭ*th*, wī*th*) *n.* A tough supple twig, esp. of willow, used to bind things together. [ME < OE *withthe*. See **wei-***.]

with•er (wĭ*th*′ər) *v.* **-ered, -er•ing, -ers.** *—intr.* **1.** To dry up or shrivel from or as if from loss of moisture. **2.** To lose freshness; droop. *—tr.* **1.** To cause to shrivel or fade. **2.** To render speechless or incapable of action; stun. [Alteration of ME *widderen*, perh. var. of *wederen*, to weather < *weder*, weather. See WEATHER.]

with•ered (wĭ*th*′ərd) *adj.* Shriveled, shrunken, or faded from or as if from loss of moisture or sustenance.

with•er•ing (wĭ*th*′ər-ĭng) *adj.* Tending to overwhelm or destroy; devastating: *withering sarcasm.* **—with′er•ing•ly** *adv.*

with•er•ite (wĭ*th*′ə-rīt′) *n.* A white, yellow, or gray mineral, chiefly $BaCO_3$. [Ger. *Witherit*, after William *Withering* (1741–99), British physician.]

withe rod *n.* An eastern North American deciduous shrub *(Viburnum cassinoides)* having clusters of small white flowers and bluish-black edible fruit.

with•ers (wĭ*th*′ərz) *pl.n.* The high part of the back of a horse or similar animal, located between the shoulder blades. [Poss. < obsolete *wither-*, against (< the strain exerted on them when a horse draws a load) < ME < OE *wither-*. See **wi-***.]

ă pat	oi boy
ā pay	ou out
âr care	o͝o took
ä father	o͞o boot
ĕ pet	ŭ cut
ē be	ûr urge
ĭ pit	th thin
ī pie	*th* this
îr pier	hw which
ŏ pot	zh vision
ō toe	ə about, item
ô paw	

Stress marks:
′ (primary);
′ (secondary), as in
dictionary (dĭk′shə-nĕr′ē)

with•er•shins (wĭth′ər-shĭnz′) *adv.* Var. of **widdershins.**

With•er•spoon (wĭth′ər-spo͞on′), **John.** 1723–94. Scottish-born Amer. cleric and Revolutionary leader who was a signer of the Declaration of Independence.

with•hold (wĭth-hōld′, wĭth-) *v.* **-held** (-hĕld′), **-hold•ing, -holds.** —*tr.* **1.** To keep in check; restrain. **2.** To refrain from giving, granting, or permitting. See Syns at **keep. 3.** To deduct (withholding tax) from an employee's salary. —*intr.* To refrain or forbear. [ME *witholden* : *with*, away from; see WITH + *holden*, to hold; see HOLD[1].] —**with•hold′er** *n.*

with•hold•ing tax (wĭth-hōl′dĭng, wĭth-) *n.* A portion of an employee's wages or salary withheld by the employer as partial payment of the employee's income tax.

with•in (wĭth-ĭn′, wĭth-) *adv.* **1.** In or into the inner part; inside. **2.** Inside the mind, heart, or soul; inwardly. —*prep.* **1.** In the inner part or parts of; inside. **2.a.** Inside the limits or extent of in time or distance. **b.** Inside the fixed limits of; not beyond. **c.** In the scope or sphere of. **d.** Inside a specified amount or degree. —*n.* An inner position, place, or area. [ME *withinne* < OE *withinnan* : *with*, with; see WITH + *innan*, from within (< *in*, in; see IN[1]).]

with•in•doors (wĭth-ĭn′dôrz′, -dōrz′, wĭth-) *adv.* Into or inside a house or other building; indoors.

with-it (wĭth′ĭt′, wĭth-) *adj. Slang.* **1.** Interested in and sensitive to the latest styles and trends; up-to-date. **2.** Streetwise and knowing; savvy.

with•out (wĭth-out′, wĭth-) *adv.* **1.** On the outside. **2.** With something absent or lacking. —*prep.* **1.a.** Not having; lacking. **b.** Not accompanied by; in the absence of. **2.** At, on, to, or toward the outside or exterior of: *standing without the door.* —*conj. Regional.* Unless. [ME *withoute* < OE *withūtan* : *with*, with; see WITH + *ūtan*, from without (< *ūt*, out; see OUT).]

with•out•doors (wĭth-out′dôrz′, -dōrz′, wĭth-) *adv.* Outside a house or other building; outdoors.

with•stand (wĭth-stănd′, wĭth-) *v.* **-stood** (-sto͝od′), **-stand•ing, -stands.** —*tr.* **1.** To oppose with force or resolution. **2.** To be successful in resisting. See Syns at **oppose.** —*intr.* To resist or endure successfully. [ME *withstanden* < OE *withstandan* : *with*, against; see WITH + *standan*, to stand; see STAND.] —**with•stand′er** *n.*

wolf
Tundra wolf
Canis lupus tundarum

with•y (wĭth′ē, wĭth′ē) *adj.* **1.** Made of or as flexible as withes; tough. **2.** Wiry and agile. —*n., pl.* **-ies. 1.** A rope or band made of withes. **2.a.** A long flexible twig, as that of an osier. **b.** A tree or shrub having such twigs. [WITHE + -Y[1]. N. < ME *withye*, willow branch < OE *wīthig*, willow. See **wei-***.]

wit•less (wĭt′lĭs) *adj.* Lacking intelligence or wit; foolish. —**wit′less•ly** *adv.* —**wit′less•ness** *n.*

wit•ling (wĭt′lĭng) *n.* **1.** One who aspires to wittiness. **2.** One who has little wit.

wit•loof (wĭt′lōf′) *n.* See **endive** 2. [Du. dial. : *wit*, white (< MDu.; see **kweit-***) + *loof*, leaf (< MDu.).]

wit•ness (wĭt′nĭs) *n.* **1.a.** One who can give a firsthand account of something. **b.** One who furnishes evidence. **2.** Something that serves as evidence; a sign. **3.** *Law.* **a.** One who is called on to testify before a court. **b.** One who is called on to attest to what takes place at a transaction. **c.** One who signs one's name to a document to attest to its authenticity. **4.** An attestation to a fact, a statement, or an event; testimony. **5. Witness.** A member of the Jehovah's Witnesses. —*v.* **-nessed, -ness•ing, -ness•es.** —*tr.* **1.a.** To be present at or have personal knowledge of. **b.** To take note of; observe. **2.** To provide or serve as evidence of. **3.** To testify to; bear witness. **4.** To be the setting or site of. **5.** To attest to the legality or authenticity of by signing one's name to. —*intr.* **1.** To furnish or serve as evidence; testify. **2.** To testify to one's religious beliefs. [ME < OE < *wit*, knowledge. See WIT[1].] —**wit′ness•er** *n.*

witness box *n. Chiefly British.* A witness stand.

witness stand *n. Law.* A stand or an enclosed area in a courtroom from which a witness presents testimony.

wit•ted (wĭt′ĭd) *adj.* Having wit or intellectual comprehension. Often used in combination: *keen-witted.* —**wit′ted•ness** *n.*

Wit•ten (vĭt′n). A city of W-central Germany on the Ruhr R. ESE of Essen. Pop. 102,195.

Wit•ten•berg (wĭt′n-bûrg′, vĭt′n-bĕrk′). A city of E-central Germany E of Dessau; center of the Protestant Reformation after Martin Luther nailed his 95 theses to the door of the Schlosskirche in 1517. Pop. 54,306.

Witt•gen•stein (vĭt′gən-shtīn′, -stīn), **Ludwig.** 1889–1951. Austrian-born British philosopher noted for his analyses of language and meaning.

wit•ti•cism (wĭt′ĭ-sĭz′əm) *n.* A witty remark. [WITT(Y) + (CRIT)ICISM.]

wit•ting (wĭt′ĭng) *adj.* **1.** Aware or conscious of something. **2.** Done intentionally or with premeditation; deliberate. —*v. Archaic.* Pr.part. of **wit[2].** —*n. Chiefly British.* **1.** Knowledge or awareness; cognizance. **2.** Information obtained and passed on; news. —**wit′ting•ly** *adv.*

wit•tol (wĭt′l) *n. Archaic.* A man who knows of and tolerates his wife's infidelity. [ME *wetewold* : *weten*, to know (< OE *witan*; see WIT[2]) + *(coke)wold*, cuckold; see CUCKOLD.]

wit•ty (wĭt′ē) *adj.* **-ti•er, -ti•est. 1.** Possessing or demonstrating wit in speech or writing; very clever and humorous. **2.** Marked by or having the nature of wit; funny. **3.** Quick to discern and express amusing insights or relationships. **4.** Entertainingly and strikingly clever or original in concept, design, or performance. —**wit′ti•ly** *adv.* —**wit′ti•ness** *n.*

Wit•wa•ters•rand (wĭt-wô′tərz-rănd′, -ränd′, -wŏt′ərz-). Often **Rand** (rănd). A region of NE South Africa between the Vaal R. and Johannesburg; one of the richest gold-mining areas in the world since the discovery of gold in 1886.

wive (wīv) *v.* **wived, wiv•ing, wives.** —*tr.* **1.** To marry as a wife. **2.** To provide a wife for. —*intr.* To marry a woman. [ME *wiven* < OE *wīfian* < *wīf*, woman.]

wi•vern (wī′vərn) *n. Her.* Var. of **wyvern.**

wives (wīvz) *n.* Pl. of **wife.**

wiz (wĭz) *n. Informal.* A person considered exceptionally gifted or skilled. [Short for WIZARD.]

wiz•ard (wĭz′ərd) *n.* **1.** One who practices magic; a sorcerer or magician. **2.** A skilled or clever person: *a wizard at math.* **3.** *Archaic.* A sage. —*adj.* **1.** *Chiefly British.* Excellent. **2.** *Archaic.* Of or relating to wizards or wizardry. [ME *wisard* : *wise*, wise; see WISE[1] + *-ard*, pejorative suff.; see -ARD.]

wiz•ard•ly (wĭz′ərd-lē) *adj.* **1.** Having the qualities or attributes of a wizard. **2.** Astonishing in design, performance, or execution; fabulous: *wizardly lighting.*

wiz•ard•ry (wĭz′ər-drē) *n., pl.* **-ries. 1.** The art, skill, or practice of a wizard; sorcery. **2.** A power or an effect that appears magical by its capacity to transform: *computer wizardry.* **3.** Great ability or adroitness in a pursuit: *artistic wizardry.*

wiz•en (wĭz′ən) *v.* **-ened, -en•ing, -ens.** —*intr.* To dry up; wither or shrivel. —*tr.* To cause to wither or shrivel. —*adj.* Shriveled or dried up; withered. [ME *wisenen* < OE *wisnian.*]

wiz•ened (wĭz′ənd) *adj.* Withered; wizen.

wk. *abbr.* **1.** Week. **2.** Work.

wkly. *abbr.* Weekly.

WL *abbr.* **1.** Or **w.l.** Water line. **2.** Wavelength.

Wlo•cla•wek (vlôt-slä′vĕk). A city of central Poland WNW of Warsaw; founded in the 12th cent. Pop. 115,300.

WNW *abbr.* West-northwest.

wo (wō) *n. Archaic.* Var. of **woe.**

w/o *abbr.* Without.

woad (wōd) *n.* **1.** An annual Old World plant *(Isatis tinctoria)* in the mustard family, having leaves that yield a blue dye. **2.** The dye obtained from this plant. [ME *wode* < OE *wād.*]

woad•wax•en (wōd′wăk′sən) *n.* See **dyer's greenweed.** [Alteration of WOODWAXEN.]

wob•ble also **wab•ble** (wŏb′əl) —*v.* **-bled, -bling, -bles.** —*intr.* **1.** To move or rotate with an uneven or rocking motion from side to side. **2.** To tremble or quaver. **3.** To waver in one's views or feelings. —*tr.* To cause to wobble. —*n.* **1.** The act or an instance of wobbling; unsteady motion. **2.** A tremulous, uncertain tone or sound: *a vocal wobble.* [Prob. < LGer. *wabbeln.* See **webh-***.] —**wob′bler** *n.*

wob•bly (wŏb′lē) *adj.* **-bli•er, -bli•est.** Tending to wobble; unsteady. —**wob′bli•ness** *n.*

Wo•burn (wo͞o′bərn). A city of NE MA, a suburb of Boston. Pop. 35,943.

w.o.c. *abbr.* Without compensation.

Wode•house (wo͝od′hous′), **P(elham) G(renville).** 1881–1975. British writer known for his humorous works featuring the aristocrat Bertie Wooster and his butler Jeeves.

Wo•den also **Wo•dan** (wōd′n) *n. Myth.* An Anglo-Saxon god identified with Odin. [ME < OE *Wōden.* See **wet-[1]***.]

Wod•zi•slaw Sla•ski (vô-jē′swäf shlôN′skē). A city of S Poland SW of Katowice. Pop. 107,700.

woe (wō) *n.* **1.** Deep distress or misery, as from grief. See Syns at **regret. 2.** Misfortune; calamity. —*interj.* Used to express sorrow or dismay. [ME *wa, wo* < OE *wā*, woe!]

woe•be•gone (wō′bĭ-gôn′, -gŏn′) *adj.* **1.** Affected with or marked by deep sorrow, grief, or wretchedness. See Syns at **sad. 2.** Of an inferior or deplorable condition: *a woebegone old shack.* [ME *wo begon*, beset with woe : *wo*, woe; see WOE + *begon*, p.part. of *begon*, to beset (< OE *begān* : *bī*, *be-*, be- + *gān*, to go; see GO[1]).] —**woe′be•gone′ness** *n.*

woe•ful also **wo•ful** (wō′fəl) *adj.* **1.** Affected by or full of woe. **2.** Causing or involving woe. **3.** Deplorably bad or wretched. —**woe′ful•ly** *adv.* —**woe′ful•ness** *n.*

wog (wŏg) *n. Chiefly British & Offensive Slang.* Used as a disparaging term for a person of color, esp. a foreigner from the Middle East or Asia. [Prob. short for GOLLIWOG.]

wok (wŏk) *n.* A metal pan having a rounded bottom, used esp. in Asian cooking. [Chin. (Cantonese).]

woke (wōk) *v.* A p.t. of **wake[1].** See Regional Note at **wake[1].**

wok•en (wō′kən) *v.* A p.part. of **wake[1].**

wold[1] (wōld) *n.* An unforested rolling plain; a moor. [ME < OE *weald*, forest.]

wold[2] (wōld) *n.* Var. of **weld[2].**

Wolds (wōldz). A range of chalk hills in NE England along both banks of the Humber R.

wolf (wo͝olf) *n., pl.* **wolves** (wo͝olvz). **1.a.** Either of two carnivorous mammals of the family Canidae, esp. the gray wolf of northern regions, that typically live and hunt in hierarchical packs. **b.** The fur of such an animal. **c.** Any of various similar or related mammals, such as the hyena. **2.** The destructive larva of any of various moths, beetles, or flies. **3.** One that is regarded as predatory, rapacious, and fierce. **4.** *Slang.* A man given to paying unwanted sexual attention to women. **5.** *Mus.* **a.** A harshness in some tones of a bowed stringed instrument due to defective vibration. **b.** Dissonance in some intervals of a keyboard instrument tuned to a system of unequal temperament. — *tr.v.* **wolfed, wolf•ing, wolfs.** To eat greedily or voraciously: *wolfing down food.* — ***idioms.*** **keep the wolf from the door.** *Slang.* To avoid the privation and suffering due to lack of money. **wolf at the door.** Creditors or a creditor. **wolf in sheep's clothing.** One with malevolent intentions who feigns congeniality. [ME < OE *wulf.* See **wl̥kʷo-***.]

Wolf (vôlf), **Friedrich August.** 1759–1824. German classical scholar who proposed that the *Iliad* and the *Odyssey* are the work of several authors.

Wolf, Hugo. 1860–1903. Austrian composer known for his opera *Der Corregidor* (1895).

wolf•ber•ry (wo͝olf′bĕr′ē) *n.* A deciduous shrub *(Symphoricarpos occidentalis)* of western North America having white berries and pinkish bell-shaped flowers.

wolf dog *n.* **1.** A dog trained to hunt wolves. **2.** The hybrid offspring of a dog and a wolf.

Wolfe (wo͝olf), **James.** 1727–59. British general who defeated the French at Quebec (1759) but was mortally wounded in the battle.

Wolfe, Thomas (Clayton). 1900–38. Amer. writer who is best known for his two autobiographical novels, *Look Homeward, Angel* (1929) and *You Can't Go Home Again* (1940).

Wolff (vôlf), **Kaspar Friedrich.** 1733–94. German anatomist noted for his pioneering work in embryology.

Wolff•i•an body (wo͝ol′fē-ən) *n. Biol.* See **mesonephros.**

wolf fish *n.* Any of several northern marine fishes of the genus *Anarhichas,* having sharp teeth and a voracious appetite.

wolf•hound (wo͝olf′hound′) *n.* Any of various large dogs, such as the borzoi, trained to hunt wolves or other large game.

wolf•ish (wo͝ol′fĭsh) *adj.* **1.** Of or relating to wolves. **2.a.** Suggestive of or resembling a wolf. **b.** Fierce or rapacious. — **wolf′ish•ly** *adv.* — **wolf′ish•ness** *n.*

wolf•ram (wo͝ol′frəm) *n.* See **tungsten.** [Ger., wolframite, tungsten : prob. *Wolf,* wolf (< MHGer. < OHGer.; see **wl̥kʷo-***) + *-ram* (< MHGer. *rām,* dirt).]

wolf•ram•ite (wo͝ol′frə-mīt′) *n.* Any of several red-brown to black minerals with the general formula $(Fe,Mn)WO_4$, constituting a major source of tungsten.

wolfs•bane (wo͝olfs′bān′) *n.* **1.** See **monkshood** 2. **2.** Any of several poisonous perennial herbs of the genus *Aconitum,* esp. *A. lycoctonum,* having rounded leaves and purplish flowers.

Wolfs•burg (wo͝olfs′bûrg′, vôlfs′bo͝ork′). A city of N-central Germany NE of Brunswick. Pop. 122,099.

wolf spider *n.* Any of various spiders of the family Lycosidae that stalk prey on the ground and do not spin webs, esp. a common small species *(Lycosa tarentula)* of southern Europe.

wolf whistle *n.* A typically two-note whistle made by a boy or man as an expression of sexual attention, often unsolicited, to a girl or woman. — **wolf whistle** *v.*

Wol•las•ton (wo͝ol′ə-stən), **William Hyde.** 1766–1828. British chemist who discovered palladium (1803) and rhodium (1804).

wol•las•ton•ite (wo͝ol′ə-stə-nīt′) *n.* A white to gray mineral, essentially $CaSiO_3$, found in metamorphic rocks and used in ceramics, paints, plastics, and cements.

Wol•lon•gong (wo͝ol′ən-gŏng′, -gông′). A city of SE Australia on the Tasman Sea SSW of Sydney. Pop. 176,500.

Woll•stone•craft (wo͝ol′stən-krăft′, -kräft′), **Mary.** Mary Wollstonecraft Godwin. 1759–97. British writer and reformer noted for *A Vindication of the Rights of Woman* (1792).

Wo•lof (wō′lŏf′) *n.* **1.** A member of a West African people primarily inhabiting coastal Senegal. **2.** Their West Atlantic language, widely used as a lingua franca in Senegal.

Wol•sey (wo͝ol′zē), **Thomas.** 1475?–1530. English prelate who fell from favor after failing to secure papal approval for Henry VIII's divorce from Catherine of Aragon (1529).

Wol•ver•hamp•ton (wo͝ol′vər-hămp′tən, -hăm′-). A borough of W-central England NW of Birmingham. Pop. 256,500.

wol•ver•ine (wo͝ol′və-rēn′, wo͝ol′və-rēn′) *n.* A solitary burrowing carnivorous mammal *(Gulo gulo)* of northern forest regions, related to the weasel and having a heavyset body, short legs, and dark fur with a bushy tail. [Prob. < WOLF.]

wolves (wo͝olvz) *n.* Pl. of **wolf.**

wom•an (wo͝om′ən) *n., pl.* **wom•en** (wĭm′ĭn). **1.** An adult female human being. **2.** Women considered as a group; womankind. **3.** An adult female human being belonging to a specified occupation, group, nationality, or other category. Often used in combination: *congresswoman.* **4.** Feminine quality or aspect; womanliness. **5.** A female servant or subordinate. **6.** *Informal.* **a.** A wife. **b.** A lover or sweetheart. **7.** A representative, as of a company. — ***idiom.*** **(one's) own woman.** Independent in judgment or action. [ME < OE *wimman,* var. of *wīfman* : *wīf,* woman + *man,* person; see MAN.]

woman about town *n., pl.* **women about town.** A sophisticated and socially active woman who frequents fashionable places.

wom•an•ful•ly (wo͝om′ən-fo͝ol′ē) *adv.* With the characteristic grace, strength, or purposefulness of a woman.

wom•an•hood (wo͝om′ən-ho͝od′) *n.* **1.** The state of being a woman. **2.** The composite of qualities deemed appropriate to or representative of women. **3.** Women considered as a group.

wom•an•ish (wo͝om′ə-nĭsh) *adj.* **1.** Of, characteristic of, or natural to a woman. **2.** Resembling or suggestive of a woman. — **wom′an•ish•ly** *adv.* — **wom′an•ish•ness** *n.*

wom•an•ist (wo͝om′ən-ĭst) *adj.* Having or expressing a belief in or respect for women and their talents and abilities beyond the boundaries of race and class; exhibiting a feminism that is inclusive esp. of Black American culture. — *n.* One informed by womanist ideals. — **wom′an•ism** *n.*

wom•an•ize (wo͝om′ə-nīz′) *v.* **-ized, -iz•ing, -iz•es.** — *intr.* To pursue women lecherously. — *tr.* To give female characteristics to; feminize. — **wom′an•iz′er** *n.*

wom•an•kind (wo͝om′ən-kīnd′) *n.* Women considered as a group.

wom•an•like (wo͝om′ən-līk′) *adj.* **1.** Resembling a woman: *a womanlike image.* **2.** Belonging to or befitting a woman.

wom•an•ly (wo͝om′ən-lē) *adj.* **-li•er, -li•est. 1.** Having qualities generally attributed to a woman. **2.** Of or representative of a woman; feminine. — **wom′an•li•ness** *n.*

woman of the house *n., pl.* **women of the house.** The primary woman of a household.

woman of the world *n., pl.* **women of the world.** A sophisticated, worldly woman.

wom•an•pow•er (wo͝om′ən-pou′ər) *n.* Power in terms of the women available to a particular group or required for a particular task.

woman suffrage *n.* **1.** The right of women to vote. **2.** A movement to promote and secure such rights.

wom•an-to-wom•an (wo͝om′ən-tə-wo͝om′ən) *adj.* Characterized by direct interaction between or among women.

womb (wo͞om) *n.* **1.** See **uterus** 1. **2.a.** A place where something is generated. **b.** An encompassing, protective hollow or space. **3.** *Obsolete.* The belly. [ME < OE *wamb.*]

wom•bat (wŏm′băt′) *n.* Any of several small bear-like burrowing Australian marsupials of the family Vombatidae. [Dharuk (Aboriginal language of SE Australia) *wambatʸ.*]

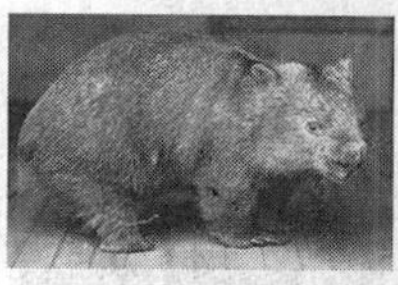

wombat
Common wombat
Vombatus ursinus

wom•en (wĭm′ĭn) *n.* Pl. of **woman.**

wom•en•folk (wĭm′ĭn-fōk′) also **wom•en•folks** (-fōks′) *pl.n.* **1.** Women considered as a group. **2.** The women of a community or family.

wom•en•kind (wĭm′ən-kīnd′) *n.* Womankind.

wom•en's movement (wĭm′ĭnz) *n.* A movement in the United States focusing primarily on women's roles as wage earners, women's sexuality, an end to violence against women, and ratification of the Equal Rights Amendment.

women's rights *pl.n.* **1.** Socioeconomic, political, and legal rights for all women equal to those of men. **2.** A movement in support of these rights.

women's room *n.* A restroom for women.

wom•en's studies also **Wom•en's Studies** (wĭm′ĭnz) *n. (used with a sing. or pl. v.)* An academic curriculum focusing on the roles and contributions of women in fields such as literature, history, and the social sciences.

women's wear *n.* Clothing for women.

wom•er•a (wŏm′ər-ə) *n.* Var. of **woomera.**

won¹ (wŭn, wōn) *intr.v.* **wonned, won•ning, wons.** *Archaic.* To dwell or abide. [ME *wonen* < OE *wunian.* See **wen-¹***.]

won² (wôn) *n., pl.* **won.** See table at **currency.** [Korean.]

won³ (wŭn) *v.* P.t. and p.part. of **win.**

won•der (wŭn′dər) *n.* **1.a.** One that arouses awe, astonishment, surprise, or admiration; a marvel. **b.** The emotion aroused by a wonder. **2.** An event inexplicable by the laws of nature; a miracle. **3.** A feeling of puzzlement or doubt. **4.** Often **Wonder.** A monumental human creation regarded with awe, esp. one of seven monuments of the ancient world that appeared on various lists of late antiquity. — *v.* **-dered, -der•ing, -ders.** — *intr.* **1.a.** To have a feeling of awe or admiration; marvel. **b.** To have a feeling of surprise. **2.** To be filled with curiosity or doubt. — *tr.* To feel curiosity or be in doubt about. — *adj.* **1.a.** Arousing awe or admiration. **b.** Wonderful. **2.** Far superior to anything formerly recognized or foreseen. — ***idiom.*** **for a wonder.** As a cause for surprise; surprisingly. [ME < OE *wundor.*] — **won′der•er** *n.*

Syns: *wonder, marvel, miracle, phenomenon, prodigy, sensation.* The meaning shared by these nouns is "one that evokes amazement or admiration": *the wonders of Paris; a marvel of technology; a miracle of culinary art; a phenomenon of science; a musical prodigy; a theatrical sensation.*

wonder drug *n.* See **miracle drug.**

won•der•ful (wŭn′dər-fəl) *adj.* **1.** Capable of eliciting wonder; astonishing. **2.** Admirable; excellent. — **won′der•ful•ly** *adv.* — **won′der•ful•ness** *n.*

won•der•ing (wŭn′dər-ĭng) *adj.* Feeling or expressing awe, admiration, amazement, or surprise. — **won′der•ing•ly** *adv.*

ă pat	oi boy
ā pay	ou out
âr care	o͝o took
ä father	o͞o boot
ĕ pet	ŭ cut
ē be	ûr urge
ĭ pit	th thin
ī pie	*th* this
îr pier	hw which
ŏ pot	zh vision
ō toe	ə about, item
ô paw	

Stress marks:
′ (primary);
′ (secondary), as in
dictionary (dĭk′shə-nĕr′ē)

woodchuck
Marmota monax

Victoria Woodhull

woodpecker
Common flicker
Colaptes auratus

won•der•land (wŭn′dər-lănd′) *n.* **1.** A marvelous imaginary realm. **2.** A marvelous real place or scene.
won•der•ment (wŭn′dər-mənt) *n.* **1.** Astonishment, awe, or surprise. **2.** Something that produces wonder; a marvel. **3.** Puzzlement or curiosity.
won•der•work (wŭn′dər-wûrk′) *n.* A marvelous or miraculous act, work, or achievement; a marvel. **—won′der•work′er** *n.* **—won′der•work′ing** *adj.*
won•drous (wŭn′drəs) *adj.* Remarkable or extraordinary; wonderful. *—adv. Archaic.* To a wonderful or remarkable extent. **—won′drous•ly** *adv.* **—won′drous•ness** *n.*
wonk (wŏngk) *n. Slang.* A student who studies excessively. [?]
won•ky (wŏng′kē) *adj.* **-ki•er, -ki•est.** *Chiefly British.* **1.** Shaky; feeble. **2.** Wrong; awry. [Prob. alteration of dial. *wanky,* alteration of *wankle* < ME *wankel* < OE *wancol,* unsteady.]
Won•san (wŭn′sän′). A city of SE North Korea on the Sea of Japan E of Pyongyang. Pop. 350,000.
wont (wônt, wōnt, wŭnt) *adj.* **1.** Accustomed or used. **2.** Likely. *—n.* Customary practice; usage. *—v.* **wont** or **wont•ed, wont•ing, wonts.** *—tr.* To make accustomed to. *—intr.* To be in the habit of doing something. [ME, p.part. of *wonen,* to be used to, dwell. See WON[1].]
won't (wōnt). Will not.
wont•ed (wôn′tĭd, wōn′-, wŭn′-) *adj.* Accustomed; usual. **—wont′ed•ly** *adv.* **—wont′ed•ness** *n.*
won ton or **won•ton** (wŏn′tŏn′) *n.* **1.** A noodle-dough dumpling filled typically with spiced minced pork or other ground meat. **2.** Soup containing won tons. [Chin. (Cantonese) *wan tan.*]
woo (wo͞o) *v.* **wooed, woo•ing, woos.** *—tr.* **1.** To seek the affection of with romantic intentions. **2.a.** To seek to achieve; try to gain. **b.** To tempt or invite. **3.** To entreat, solicit, or importune. *—intr.* To court a woman. Used of a man. [ME *wowen* < OE *wōgian.*] **—woo′er** *n.*
wood[1] (wo͝od) *n.* **1.a.** The secondary xylem of trees and shrubs, lying beneath the bark and consisting largely of cellulose and lignin. **b.** This tissue, often cut and dried esp. for use as building material and fuel. **2.** A dense growth of trees; a forest. Often used in the plural. **3.** An object made of wood, esp.: **a.** *Mus.* A woodwind. **b.** *Sports.* A golf club used to hit long shots, having a wooden head numbered one to five in order of increasing loft. *—v.* **wood•ed, wood•ing, woods.** *—tr.* **1.** To fuel with wood. **2.** To cover with trees; forest. *—intr.* To gather or be supplied with wood. *—adj.* **1.** Made or consisting of wood; wooden. **2.** Used or suitable for cutting, storing, or working with wood. **3. woods.** Living, growing, or present in forests. **—*idiom.* out of the woods.** *Informal.* Free of a difficult or hazardous situation; safe or secure. [ME *wode* < OE *wudu.*]
wood[2] (wo͝od) *adj. Archaic.* Mentally unbalanced; insane. [ME < OE *wōd.* See **wet-[1]***.]
Wood (wo͝od), **Grant.** 1892–1942. Amer. artist whose paintings include *American Gothic* (1930).
Wood, Leonard. 1860–1927. Amer. military leader who was governor-general of the Philippines (1921–27).
wood alcohol *n.* See **methanol.**
wood anemone *n.* Either of two plants, *Anemone quinquefolia* of eastern North America or *A. nemorosa* of Eurasia, with deeply divided leaves and a solitary white to crimson flower.
wood betony *n.* See **lousewort.**
wood•bin (wo͝od′bĭn′) *n.* A box for holding firewood.
wood•bine (wo͝od′bīn′) *n.* **1.** Any of various climbing vines, esp. a Mediterranean honeysuckle *(Lonicera periclymenum)* having yellowish flowers. **2.** See **Virginia creeper.** [ME *wodebinde* < OE *wudubinde* : *wudu,* wood + *binde,* wreath (< *bindan,* to bind; see **bhendh-***).]
wood•block (wo͝od′blŏk′) *n.* **1.** See **woodcut. 2.** Also **wood block.** *Mus.* A hollow block of wood struck with a drumstick to produce percussive effects in an orchestra.
wood•bor•er (wo͝od′bôr′ər, -bōr′ər) *n.* Any of various insects, insect larvae, or mollusks that bore into wood. **—wood′bor′ing** *adj.*
Wood•bridge (wo͝od′brĭj′). **1.** A city of NE NJ SSW of Elizabeth; settled in 1665. Pop. 90,074. **2.** A community of NW VA, a suburb of Alexandria and Washington DC. Pop. 26,401.
Wood•bury (wo͝od′bĕr′ē, -bə-rē), **Levi.** 1789–1851. Amer. jurist; associate justice of the U.S. Supreme Court (1845–51).
wood•carv•ing (wo͝od′kär′vĭng) *n.* **1.** The art or process of creating or decorating objects of wood by carving with a sharp hand-held tool. **2.** A carved wood object. **—wood′carv′er** *n.*
wood•chat (wo͝od′chăt′) *n.* An Old World shrike *(Lanius senator)* with black and white plumage and a reddish crown.
wood•chuck (wo͝od′chŭk′) *n.* A common burrowing rodent *(Marmota monax)* of northern and eastern North America having a short-legged heavy-set body and grizzled brownish fur. Also called regionally *whistle pig.* [By folk ety., prob. of New England Algonquian orig.]
Regional Note: The woodchuck goes by several names in the United States. The most famous of these is *groundhog,* under which name all the legends about the animal's hibernation have accrued. In the Appalachian Mountains the woodchuck is known as a *whistle pig.*
wood coal *n.* **1.** Charcoal. **2.** Lignite.
wood•cock (wo͝od′kŏk′) *n., pl.* **woodcock** or **-cocks.** Either of two related game birds, *Scolopax rusticola* of the Old World or *Philohela minor* of North America, having brownish plumage, short legs, and a long bill.
wood•craft (wo͝od′krăft′) *n.* **1.** Skill and experience in matters relating to the woods, as hunting or fishing. **2.** The act, process, or art of carving or fashioning objects from wood.
wood•cut (wo͝od′kŭt′) *n.* **1.** A block of wood on which a design for printing is engraved. **2.** A print made from a woodcut.
wood•cut•ting (wo͝od′kŭt′ĭng) *n.* **1.** The act, activity, or job of cutting wood. **2.** The art or process of making woodcuts.
wood duck *n.* A brightly colored American duck *(Aix sponsa)* that nests in hollow trees, the male of which has a large crest.
wood•ed (wo͝od′ĭd) *adj.* Covered with trees or woods.
wood•en (wo͝od′n) *adj.* **1.** Made or consisting of wood. **2.** Stiff and unnatural; without spirit: *a wooden smile.* **3.** Clumsy and awkward; ungainly. **—wood′en•ly** *adv.* **—wood′en•ness** *n.*
wood engraving *n.* **1.a.** A block of wood on whose surface a design for printing is engraved across the end grain. **b.** A print made from a wood engraving. **2.** The art or process of making wood engravings.
wood•en•head (wo͝od′n-hĕd′) *n.* A stupid person.
wood•en•ware (wo͝od′n-wâr′) *n.* Articles made of wood.
Wood•hull (wo͝od′hŭl′), **Victoria Claflin.** 1838–1927. Amer. reformer who ran for the U.S. presidency (1872).
wood ibis *n.* Any of several large, mainly white wading birds of the subfamily Mycteriinae, related to the storks.
wood•ie (wo͝od′ē) *n.* Var. of **woody[2].**
wood•land (wo͝od′lənd, -lănd′) *n.* Land having a cover of trees and shrubs. *—adj.* **1.** Of, relating to, or constituting woodland. **2.** Living, growing, or present in woodland: *woodland flowers.* **—wood′land•er** (-lən-dər) *n.*
Wood•land (wo͝od′lənd). A city of N-central CA WNW of Sacramento. Pop. 39,802.
wood lot or **wood•lot** (wo͝od′lŏt′) *n.* A usu. private area restricted to the growing of forest trees, esp. for building material or fuel.
wood louse *n.* See **sow bug.**
wood•man (wo͝od′mən) *n.* A woodsman.
wood•note (wo͝od′nōt′) *n.* **1.** A song or call characteristic of a woodland bird. **2.** Natural spontaneous verbal utterance.
wood nymph *n.* **1.** A nymph of the forest; a dryad. **2.** Any of several tropical hummingbirds of the genera *Thalurania* and *Cyanophaia.* **3.** Any of various butterflies of the family Satyridae, esp. *Cercyonis pegala,* having brownish wings with dark eyespots.
wood•peck•er (wo͝od′pĕk′ər) *n.* Any of various usu. brightly colored birds of the family Picidae, having strong claws and a stiff tail for climbing trees and a chisellike bill for drilling into bark and wood. Also called regionally *peckerwood.*
wood pigeon *n.* A large pigeon *(Columba palumbus)* of Europe and Asia having a white band on each wing.
wood•pile (wo͝od′pīl′) *n.* A pile of wood, esp. for fuel.
wood pulp *n.* Pulp made from wood, used esp. to make paper.
wood pussy *n. Slang.* A skunk.
wood rat *n.* See **pack rat** 1.
Wood•ridge (wo͝od′rĭj′). A village of NE IL W of Chicago. Pop. 26,256.
wood•ruff (wo͝od′rəf, -rŭf′) *n.* **1.** A perennial herb *(Galium odoratum)* of Eurasia and North Africa having small white flowers and narrow leaves used for flavoring wine and in sachets. **2.** Any of various plants of the genus *Asperula,* having whorled leaves and small funnel-shaped flowers. [ME *woderofe* < OE *wudurofe* : *wudu,* wood + *-rofe.*]
Woods (wo͝odz), **Lake of the.** A lake of SW Ontario and SW Manitoba, Canada, and N Minnesota.
Woods, William Burnham. 1824–87. Amer. jurist; associate justice of the U.S. Supreme Court (1880–87).
woods colt (wo͝odz) *n. Chiefly Southern U.S.* See **old-field colt.**
wood•shed (wo͝od′shĕd′) *n.* A shed in which firewood is stored. *—intr.v.* **-shed•ded, -shed•ding, -sheds.** *Slang.* To practice on a musical instrument.
woods•man (wo͝odz′mən) *n.* A man who works or lives in the woods or is versed in woodcraft; a forester.
wood sorrel *n.* See **oxalis.**
wood spirits *pl.n. (used with a sing. or pl. v.)* See **methanol.**
Wood•stock (wo͝od′stŏk′). A city of S Ontario, Canada, on the Thames R. WSW of Toronto. Pop. 26,603.
wood sugar *n.* See **xylose.**
woods•y (wo͝od′zē) *adj.* **-i•er, -i•est.** Of, relating to, characteristic of, or suggestive of the woods.
wood tar *n.* A viscous black fluid that is a byproduct of the destructive distillation of wood and is used in pitch, preservatives, and medicines.
wood thrush *n.* A large plump thrush *(Hylocichla mustelina)* of wooded areas of eastern North America having a reddish-brown head and a spotted cream-colored breast.
wood tick *n.* Any of various ticks of the genus *Dermacentor*

that transmit the microorganism causing Rocky Mountain spotted fever and tularemia in human beings.

wood•turn•ing (wo͝od′tûr′nĭng) *n.* The art or process of shaping wood into forms on a lathe. — **wood′turn′er** *n.*

wood vinegar *n.* See **pyroligneous acid.**

wood warbler *n.* See **warbler** 1.

Wood•ward (wo͝od′wərd), **Robert Burns.** 1917–79. Amer. chemist who won a 1965 Nobel Prize.

wood•wax•en (wo͝od′wăk′sən) *n.* See **dyer's greenweed.** [ME *wodewaxen* < OE *wuduweaxe* : *wudu*, wood + *weaxan*, to grow; see WAX².]

wood•wind (wo͝od′wĭnd′) *n. Mus.* **1.** A wind instrument in which sound is produced by the vibration of reeds in or by the passing of air across the mouthpiece. **2. woodwinds. a.** Woodwind instruments or their players considered as a group. **b.** The section of a band or an orchestra composed of woodwinds.

wood•work (wo͝od′wûrk′) *n.* Objects made of or work done in wood, esp. wooden interior fittings in a house, as moldings, doors, staircases, or windowsills. — ***idiom.* out of the woodwork.** Out of obscurity or a place of seclusion.

wood•work•ing (wo͝od′wûr′kĭng) *n.* The act, art, or trade of working with wood. — **wood′work′er** *n.*

wood•y¹ (wo͝od′ē) *adj.* **-i•er, -i•est. 1.** Forming or consisting of wood; ligneous. **2.** Marked by the presence of wood or xylem: *woody plants.* **3.** Characteristic or suggestive of wood. **4.** Abounding in trees; wooded. — **wood′i•ness** *n.*

wood•y² Also **wood•ie** (wo͝od′ē) *n., pl.* **-ies.** A station wagon with exterior wood paneling.

woof¹ (wo͝of, wo͞of) *n.* **1.** The threads that run crosswise in a woven fabric, at right angles to the warp threads. **2.** The texture of a fabric. [Alteration (influenced by WARP) of ME *oof* < OE *ōwef* : *ō-*, *on*, on; see ON + *wefan*, to weave; see **webh-*.**]

woof² (wo͝of) *n.* **1.** The characteristically deep gruff bark of a dog. **2.** A sound similar to a woof. — *intr.v.* **woofed, woof•ing, woofs.** To make this sound. [Imit.]

woof•er (wo͝of′ər) *n.* A loudspeaker designed to reproduce bass frequencies. [< WOOF².]

wool (wo͝ol) *n.* **1.a.** The dense, soft, often curly hair forming the coat of sheep and certain other mammals, consisting of cylindrical fibers of keratin covered by minute overlapping scales and used as a textile fabric. **b.** A material or garment of wool. **2.** The furry hair of some insect larvae. **3.** A filamentous or fibrous covering or substance suggestive of the texture of true wool. [ME *wolle* < OE *wull.*] — **wool** *adj.*

wool•en also **wool•len** (wo͝ol′ən) — *adj.* **1.** Made or consisting of wool. **2.** Of or relating to the production or marketing of woolen goods. — *n.* Fabric or clothing made from wool. Often used in the plural.

Woolf (wo͝olf), **(Adeline) Virginia (Stephen).** 1882–1941. British writer whose works include *To the Lighthouse* (1927).

wool fat *n.* **1.** See **wool grease. 2.** See **lanolin.**

wool•gath•er (wo͝ol′găth′ər) *intr.v.* **-ered, -er•ing, -ers.** To engage in fanciful daydreaming. — **wool′gath′er•er** *n.*

wool•gath•er•ing (wo͝ol′găth′ər-ĭng) *n.* Indulgence in fanciful daydreams. — **wool′gath′er•ing** *adj.*

wool grease *n.* A fatty, pale yellow wax that coats the fibers of sheep's wool and yields lanolin.

wool•grow•er (wo͝ol′grō′ər) *n.* One that raises sheep or other animals for the production of wool. — **wool′grow′ing** *n.*

wool•ly also **wool•y** (wo͝ol′ē) — *adj.* **-li•er, -li•est** also **-i•er, -i•est. 1.a.** Of, relating to, or covered with wool. **b.** Resembling wool. **2.a.** Lacking sharp detail or clarity. **b.** Mentally or intellectually disorganized or unclear. **3.** Having the characteristics of the rough, generally lawless atmosphere of the American frontier. — *n., pl.* **-lies** also **-ies. 1.** A garment made of wool, esp. a knitted undergarment. **2.** *Australia.* A sheep. — **wool′li•ness** *n.*

woolly bear *n.* The hairy caterpillar of any of various moths, esp. that of the North American tiger moth *Isia isabella.*

wool•ly-head•ed (wo͝ol′ē-hĕd′ĭd) *adj.* **1.** Having hair that looks or feels like wool. **2.** Vague or muddled.

wool•sack (wo͝ol′săk′) *n.* **1.** A sack for wool. **2.** The official seat of the Lord Chancellor in the House of Lords.

wool shed *n.* A building or buildings in which sheep are sheared and wool is prepared for shipment to market.

wool•skin (wo͝ol′skĭn′) *n.* A sheepskin with the wool attached.

wool-sort•er's disease (wo͝ol′sôr′tərz) *n.* A pulmonary form of anthrax that results from the inhalation of spores of the bacterium *Bacillus anthracis* in the wool of contaminated sheep.

wool-sta•pler (wo͝ol′stā′plər) *n.* **1.** A dealer in wool. **2.** One who sorts wool by the quality of the staple or fiber. — **wool′-sta′pling** *adj. & n.*

Wool•worth (wo͝ol′wûrth′), **Frank Winfield.** 1852–1919. Amer. merchant who built a successful national chain of five-and-tens after 1879.

woom•er•a (wo͞om′ər-ə) also **wom•er•a** (wŏm′-) *n.* A hooked wooden stick used by aboriginal peoples of Australia for hurling a spear or dart. [Dharuk (Aboriginal language of SE Australia) *wumara.*]

Woon•sock•et (wo͞on-sŏk′ĭt, wo͞on′sŏk′-). A city of N RI NNW of Providence; settled c. 1666. Pop. 43,877.

woops (wo͝ops, wo͞ops) *interj.* Var. of **whoops.**

Woo•ster (wo͝os′tər). A city of N-central Ohio SW of Akron. Pop. 22,191.

wooz•y (wo͞o′zē, wo͝oz′ē) *adj.* **-i•er, -i•est. 1.** Dazed or confused. **2.** Dizzy or queasy. [Poss. < alteration of *boozy*, drunken < BOOZE.] — **wooz′i•ly** *adv.* — **wooz′i•ness** *n.*

wop (wŏp) *n. Offensive Slang.* Used as a disparaging term for an Italian. [Ital. dial. *guappo*, thug < Sp. *guapo*, handsome, dashing, braggart, bully < Fr. dial. *wape*, rogue < Lat. *vappa*, flat wine, scoundrel.]

Worces•ter¹ (wo͝os′tər). **1.** A borough of W-central England on the Severn River SSW of Birmingham; site of Cromwell's final victory over Charles II and the Scottish army (Sep. 3, 1651). Pop. 73,900. **2.** A city of central MA W of Boston. Pop. 169,759.

Worces•ter² (wo͝os′tər). A trademark used for a fine porcelain made in Worcester, England.

Worcester, Joseph Emerson. 1784–1865. Amer. lexicographer noted for his *Comprehensive Pronouncing and Explanatory Dictionary of the English Language* (1830).

Worces•ter•shire (wo͝os′tər-shîr, -shər) *n.* A piquant sauce of soy, vinegar, and spices.

word (wûrd) *n.* **1.** A sound or a combination of sounds, or its representation in writing or printing, that symbolizes and communicates a meaning and may consist of a single morpheme or of a combination of morphemes. **2.** Something said; an utterance, a remark, or a comment. **3.** *Comp. Sci.* A set of bits constituting the smallest unit of addressable memory. **4. words.** Discourse or talk; speech. **5. words.** *Mus.* The text of a vocal composition; lyrics. **6.** An assurance or a promise; sworn intention. **7.a.** A command or direction; an order. **b.** A verbal signal; a password or watchword. **8.a.** News. **b.** Rumor. **9. words.** Hostile or angry remarks made back and forth. **10. Word. a.** See **Logos** 3. **b.** The Scriptures; the Bible. — *tr.v.* **word•ed, word•ing, words.** To express in words. — ***idioms.* at a word.** In immediate response. **good word. 1.** A favorable comment. **2.** Favorable news. **have no words for.** To be unable to describe or talk about. **in a word.** In short; in summary. **in so many words. 1.** In precisely those words; exactly. **2.** Speaking candidly and straightforwardly. **of few words.** Not conversational or loquacious; laconic. **of (one's) word.** Displaying personal dependability. **take at (one's) word.** To be convinced of another's sincerity and act in accord with his or her statement. **upon my word.** Indeed; really. [ME < OE. See **wer-⁵*.**]

word•age (wûr′dĭj) *n.* **1.** Words considered as a group. **2.** The use of an excessive number of words; verbiage. **3.** The number of words used, as in a novel. **4.** Wording.

word association test *n. Psychol.* A test in which the subject is asked to respond to a given word with the first word that comes to mind or with a predetermined type of word.

word blindness *n.* See **alexia.** — **word′-blind′** (wûrd′blīnd′) *adj.*

word•book (wûrd′bo͝ok′) *n.* A lexicon, vocabulary, or dictionary.

word deafness *n.* A form of aphasia in which the meaning of ordinary spoken words becomes incomprehensible.

word for word *adv.* In exactly the same words; verbatim. — **word′-for-word′** (wûrd′fər-wûrd′) *adj.*

word-hoard (wûrd′hôrd′, -hōrd′) *n.* The sum of words one uses or understands; a vocabulary.

word•ing (wûr′dĭng) *n.* The act or style of expressing in words.

word•less (wûrd′lĭs) *adj.* **1.** Not expressed in words; unspoken: *wordless animosity.* **2.** Inarticulate; silent: *wordless spectators.* — **word′less•ly** *adv.* — **word′less•ness** *n.*

word•mon•ger (wûrd′mŭng′gər, -mŏng′-) *n.* A writer or speaker who uses language pretentiously or carelessly.

word of mouth *n.* Spoken communication. — **word′-of-mouth′** (wûrd′əv-mouth′) *adj.*

word order *n.* The syntactic arrangement of words in a sentence, clause, or phrase.

word•play or **word play** (wûrd′plā′) *n.* **1.** Witty or clever verbal exchange; repartee. **2.** The act or an instance of playing on words.

word proc•ess•ing (prŏs′ĕs′ĭng, prō′sĕs′-) *n. Comp. Sci.* The creation, input, editing, and production of documents and texts using computer systems. — **word′-proc′ess** (wûrd′prŏs′ĕs, -prō′sĕs) *v.* — **word′-proc′ess•ing** *adj.*

word processor *n. Comp. Sci.* A computer system designed for or capable of word processing.

word•smith (wûrd′smĭth′) *n.* **1.** A fluent and prolific writer, esp. one who writes professionally. **2.** An expert on words.

word square *n. Games.* A set of words arranged in a square such that they read the same horizontally and vertically.

Words•worth (wûrdz′wûrth′), **William.** 1770–1850. British poet whose most important collection, *Lyrical Ballads* (1798), published jointly with Samuel Taylor Coleridge, helped establish romanticism in England. — **Words•worth′i•an** *adj.*

word•y (wûr′dē) *adj.* **-i•er, -i•est. 1.** Relating to or consisting

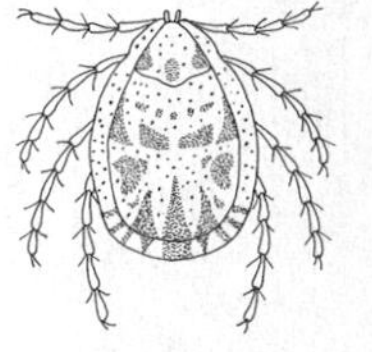

wood tick
Rocky Mountain wood tick
Dermacentor andersoni

Virginia Woolf
Photographed in 1902 by George Charles Beresford (1864–1938)

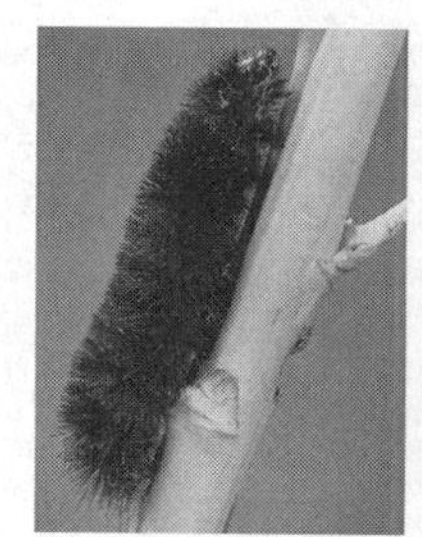

woolly bear
Isabella tiger moth caterpillar
Pyrrharctia isabella

ă **pat**	oi **boy**
ā **pay**	ou **out**
âr **care**	o͝o **took**
ä **father**	o͞o **boot**
ĕ **pet**	ŭ **cut**
ē **be**	ûr **urge**
ĭ **pit**	th **thin**
ī **pie**	*th* **this**
îr **pier**	hw **which**
ŏ **pot**	zh **vision**
ō **toe**	ə **about,**
ô **paw**	**item**

Stress marks:
′ (primary);
′ (secondary), as in **dictionary** (dĭk′shə-nĕr′ē)

of words; verbal. **2.** Tending to use, using, or expressed in more words than are necessary to convey meaning. **—word′i•ly** *adv.* **—word′i•ness** *n.*

wore (wôr, wōr) *v.* P.t. of **wear.**

work (wûrk) *n.* **1.** Physical or mental effort or activity directed toward the production or accomplishment of something. **2.a.** A job; employment. **b.** A trade, profession, or other means of livelihood. **3.a.** Something that one is doing, making, or performing, esp. as an occupation or undertaking; a duty or task. **b.** An amount of such activity either done or required. **4.a.** The part of a day devoted to an occupation or undertaking. **b.** One's place of employment. **5.a.** Something produced or accomplished through the effort, activity, or agency of a person or thing. **b.** Full action or effect of an agency. **c.** An act; a deed. **6.a.** An artistic creation, such as a painting, or musical composition; a work of art. **b. works.** The output of a writer, an artist, or a musician considered or collected as a whole. **7.a. works.** Engineering structures, such as bridges or dams. **b.** A fortified structure, such as a trench or fortress. **8.a.** Needlework, weaving, lacemaking, or a similar textile art. **b.** A piece of such textile art. **9.** A material or piece of material being processed in a machine during manufacture. **10. works.** *(used with a sing. or pl. v.)* A factory or similar building or complex of buildings where a specific type of business or industry is carried on. Often used in combination: *a steelworks.* **11. works.** Internal mechanism. **12.** The manner, style, or quality of working or treatment; workmanship. **13.** *Phys.* The transfer of energy from one physical system to another, esp. the transfer of energy to a body by the application of a force that moves the body in the direction of the force. **14. works.** *Theol.* Moral or righteous acts or deeds. **15. works. a.** *Informal.* The full range of possibilities; everything. Used with *the.* **b.** *Slang.* A thorough beating or other severe treatment. Used with *the.* *—adj.* Of, relating to, designed for, or engaged in work. *—v.* **worked** also **wrought** (rôt), **work•ing, works.** *—intr.* **1.** To exert oneself physically or mentally to do, make, or accomplish something. **2.** To be employed; have a job. **3.a.** To function; operate. **b.** To function or operate in the desired or required way. **4.a.** To have a given effect or outcome. **b.** To have the desired effect or outcome; prove successful. **5.** To exert an influence. Used with *on* or *upon.* **6.** To arrive at a specified condition through gradual or repeated movement: *The stitches worked loose.* **7.** To proceed or progress slowly and laboriously. **8.** To move in an agitated manner, as with emotion: *Her mouth worked with fear.* **9.** To behave in a specified way when handled or processed. **10.** To ferment. **11.** *Naut.* **a.** To strain in heavy seas so that the joints give slightly and the fastenings become slack. Used of a boat or ship. **b.** To sail against the wind. **12.** To undergo small motions that result in friction and wear: *The gears work against each other.* *—tr.* **1.** To cause or effect; bring about. **2.** To cause to operate or function; actuate, use, or manage. **3.** To shape or forge. **4.** To make or decorate by needlework. **5.** To solve (a problem) by calculation and reasoning. **6.** To knead, stir, or otherwise manipulate in preparation. **7.** To bring to a specified condition by gradual or repeated effort. **8.** To make, achieve, or pay for by work or effort. **9.** *Informal.* To arrange or contrive. Often used with *it.* **10.** To make productive; cultivate: *work a farm.* **11.** To cause to work: *works his laborers hard.* **12.** To excite or provoke. **13.** *Informal.* **a.** To gratify, cajole, or enchant artfully, esp. for influencing: *The politician worked the crowd.* **b.** To use or manipulate to one's own advantage; exploit. **14.** To carry on an operation or a function in or through. **15.** To ferment (liquor, for example). ***—phrasal verbs.*** **work in. 1.** To insert or introduce. **2.** To make an opening for, as in a schedule. **3.** To cause to be inserted by repeated or continuous effort. **work into. 1.** To insert or introduce into. **2.** To make an opening for (someone or something) in. **3.** To cause to be inserted in by repeated or continuous effort. **work off.** To get rid of by work or effort. **work out. 1.** To accomplish by work or effort. **2.** To find a solution for; solve. **3.** To formulate or develop. **4.** To discharge (an obligation or a debt) with labor in place of money. **5.** To prove successful, effective, or satisfactory. **6.** To have a specified result. **7.** To engage in strenuous exercise for physical conditioning. **8.** To exhaust (a mine, for example). **work over. 1.** To do for a second time; rework. **2.** *Slang.* To inflict severe physical damage on; beat up. **work up. 1.** To arouse the emotions of; excite. **2.a.** To increase one's skill, responsibility, efficiency, or status through work. **b.** To intensify gradually. **3.** To develop or produce by mental or physical effort. ***—idioms.*** **at work. 1.** Engaged in labor; working. **2.** In operation. **in the works.** In preparation; under development. **out of work.** Without a job; unemployed. **put in work.** To perform labor or duties, as on a specified project. **work both sides of the street.** To engage in double-dealing; be duplicitous. **work like a charm.** To function very well or have a very good effect or outcome. **work (one's) fingers to the bone.** To labor extremely hard; toil or travail. [ME < OE *weorc.* See **werg-*.**]

Work (wûrk), **Henry Clay.** 1832–84. Amer. songwriter noted for his Union compositions during the Civil War.

worktable
c. 1790–1810 sewing table

work•a•ble (wûr′kə-bəl) *adj.* **1.** Capable of being worked, dealt with, or handled. **2.** Capable of being put into effective operation; practicable or feasible. **—work′a•bil′i•ty, work′a•ble•ness** *n.* **—work′a•bly** *adv.*

work•a•day (wûr′kə-dā′) *adj.* **1.** Relating to or suited for working days; everyday. **2.** Mundane; commonplace. [< ME *werkeday,* workday : *work;* see WORK + *day;* see DAY.]

work•a•hol•ic (wûr′kə-hô′lĭk, -hŏl′ĭk) *n.* One who compulsively needs to work. **—work′a•hol′ism** *n.*

work•bench (wûrk′bĕnch′) *n.* A sturdy table or bench at which manual work is done, as by a machinist or a jeweler.

work•book (wûrk′bo͝ok′) *n.* **1.** A booklet containing problems and exercises that a student may do directly on the pages. **2.** A manual containing operating instructions, as for an appliance or a machine. **3.** A book in which a record is kept of work proposed or accomplished.

work camp *n.* **1.** See **prison camp** 2. **2.** A camp where volunteers work together on community service projects.

work•day (wûrk′dā′) *n.* **1.** A day on which work is usu. done. **2.** The part of the day during which one works: *an eight-hour workday.* *—adj.* Workaday.

work•er (wûr′kər) *n.* **1.a.** One who works at a particular occupation or activity. **b.** One who does manual or industrial labor. **2.** A member of the working class. **3.** A member of a colony of social insects such as ants, usu. a sterile female, that performs specialized work such as building the nest.

work•ers' compensation (wûr′kərz) *n.* Payments required by law to be made to an employee who is injured or disabled in connection with work.

work ethic *n.* A set of values based on the moral virtues of hard work and diligence.

work•fare (wûrk′fâr′) *n.* A form of welfare in which able-bodied adults receiving aid are required to perform public-service work. [WORK + (WEL)FARE.]

work farm *n.* A correctional facility that operates as a farm worked by prisoners.

work•flow (wûrk′flō′) *n.* **1.** The flow or progress of work done by a company, an industry, a department, or a person. **2.** The rate at which such flow or progress takes place.

work•folk (wûrk′fōk′) also **work•folks** (-fōks′) *n.* Laborers, esp. farm workers.

work force or **work•force** (wûrk′fôrs′, -fōrs′) *n.* **1.** The workers employed in a specific project or activity. **2.** All the people working or available to work, as in a nation or a company.

work function *n.* The minimum amount of energy required to remove an electron from the surface of a metal.

work hardening *n.* The increase in strength that accompanies plastic deformation of a metal.

work•horse (wûrk′hôrs′) *n.* **1.** Something, such as a machine, that performs dependably under heavy or prolonged use. **2.** A horse used for labor rather than for racing or riding. **3.** *Informal.* A person who works tirelessly.

work•house (wûrk′hous′) *n.* **1.** A prison in which limited sentences are served at manual labor. **2.** *Chiefly British.* A poorhouse.

work•ing (wûr′kĭng) *adj.* **1.a.** Performing work: *a working committee.* **b.** Operating or functioning as required. **2.** Having a paying job; employed. **3.a.** Spent at work. **b.** Taken while continuing to work: *a working vacation.* **4.a.** Sufficient to allow action: *a working majority.* **b.** Adequate for practical use. **5.** Serving as a basis or guide for further work. *—n.* **1.** The manner in which something operates or functions. Often used in the plural: *the workings of the mind.* **2.** The parts of a mine or quarry that have been or are being excavated. Often used in the plural.

working capital *n.* **1.** The assets of a business that can be applied to its operation. **2.** The amount of current assets that exceeds current liabilities.

working class *n.* The part of society consisting of those who work for wages, esp. manual or industrial laborers. **—work′ing-class′** (wûr′kĭng-klăs′) *adj.*

working dog *n.* Any of various breeds of dogs developed or trained to do useful work, such as herding animals.

working girl *n.* **1.** A young woman who works. **2.** *Slang.* A woman prostitute.

work•ing•man (wûr′kĭng-măn′) *n.* **1.** A man who works for wages. **2.** A man who performs heavy manual or industrial labor.

working papers *pl.n.* Legal documents certifying the right to employment of a minor or an alien.

working storage *n. Comp. Sci.* The section of computer storage reserved for data to be temporarily stored during the running of a program.

working substance *n.* A substance, such as a fluid, used to effect a thermodynamic or other change in a system.

work•ing•wom•an (wûr′kĭng-wo͝om′ən) *n.* A woman who works for wages.

work in progress *n., pl.* **works in progress.** A yet incomplete artistic, theatrical, or musical work, often made available for public viewing or listening.

work•load (wûrk′lōd′) *n.* **1.** The amount of work assigned to or expected from a worker in a specified time period. **2.** The amount of work that a machine produces or can produce in a specified time period.

work•man (wûrk′mən) *n.* **1.** A man who performs manual or industrial labor for wages. **2.** A craftsman or an artisan.

work•man•like (wûrk′mən-līk′) *adj.* Befitting a skilled artisan or craftsperson; skillfully done.

work•man•ship (wûrk′mən-shĭp′) *n.* **1.** The skill of a craftsperson or an artisan. **2.** The quality of something made, as by an artisan. **3.** Something made or produced by a workman. **4.** The product of effort or endeavor.

work•men's compensation (wûrk′mənz) *n.* Workers' compensation.

work of art *n., pl.* **works of art. 1.** A product of the fine arts, esp. a painting or sculpture. **2.** Something likened to a fine artistic work, as by reason of beauty or craft.

work•out (wûrk′out′) *n.* **1.** A session of exercise or practice to improve fitness, as for athletic competition. **2.** A strenuous test of ability and endurance.

work•peo•ple (wûrk′pē′pəl) *n. Chiefly British.* Those who work for wages; workers.

work•place also **work place** (wûrk′plās′) *n.* **1.** A place where people are employed. **2.** The work setting in general.

work release *n.* A correctional program under which prisoners are permitted employment outside a prison while serving their sentences. **—work′-re•lease′** (wûrk′rĭ-lēs′) *adj.*

work•room (wûrk′ro͞om′, -ro͝om′) *n.* A room for work.

work sheet or **work•sheet** (wûrk′shēt′) *n.* **1.** A sheet of paper on which work records are kept. **2.** A sheet of paper on which preliminary notes or computations are set down.

work•shop (wûrk′shŏp′) *n.* **1.** A room, an area, or a small establishment where manual or light industrial work is done. **2.** An educational seminar or series of meetings, usu. for a small group, emphasizing interaction.

work song *n. Mus.* A song sung to accompany work, typically having a steady rhythm.

work•space (wûrk′spās′) *n.* An area for one's work.

work•sta•tion (wûrk′stā′shən) *n.* An area, as in an office, outfitted with equipment and furnishings for one worker, often including a computer or computer terminal.

work stoppage *n.* A cessation of work by a group of employees as a means of protest.

work-stud•y (wûrk′stŭd′ē) *adj.* Of, relating to, or being an academic program that enables students to gain work experience and make money while continuing their studies.

work•ta•ble (wûrk′tā′bəl) *n.* A table designed for a specific kind of task or activity, such as needlework.

work•up (wûrk′ŭp′) *n.* A thorough medical examination for diagnostic purposes.

work•week (wûrk′wēk′) *n.* The hours or days worked in a week: *a four-day workweek.*

work•wom•an (wûrk′wo͝om′ən) *n.* A woman who performs manual or industrial labor for wages.

world (wûrld) *n.* **1.** The earth. **2.** The universe. **3.** The earth with its inhabitants. **4.** The inhabitants of the earth; the human race. **5.a.** Humankind considered as social beings; human society. **b.** People as a whole; the public. **6.** Often **World.** A specified part of the earth. **7.** A part of the earth and its inhabitants as known at a given period in history: *the ancient world.* **8.** A realm or domain: *the animal world.* **9.a.** A sphere of human activity or interest. **b.** A class or group of people with common characteristics or pursuits. **10.** A particular way of life. **11.** All that relates to or affects the life of a person: *He saw his world collapse.* **12.** Secular life and its concerns. **13.a.** Human existence; life: *brought a child into the world.* **b.** A state of existence: *the next world.* **14.** A large amount; much. Often used in the plural: *worlds of good.* **15.** A celestial body such as a planet. *—adj.* **1.** Of or relating to the world: *a world champion.* **2.** Involving or extending throughout the entire world. ***—idioms.* for all the world.** In all respects; precisely. **in the world.** Used as an intensive: *How in the world did they manage?* **out of this world.** *Informal.* Extraordinary; superb. **the world over.** Throughout the world. **world without end.** Forever. [ME < OE *weorold.* See **wī-ro-***.]

world-class (wûrld′klăs′) *adj.* Ranking among the foremost in the world; of an international standard of excellence; of the highest order: *a world-class figure skater.*

world line *n.* The path in space-time traveled by an elementary particle for the time and distance that it retains its identity.

world•ling (wûrld′lĭng) *n.* One who is absorbed by worldly pursuits and pleasures.

world•ly (wûrld′lē) *adj.* **-li•er, -li•est. 1.** Of, relating to, or devoted to the temporal world; earthly. **2.** Sophisticated; cosmopolitan. **—world′li•ness** *n.* **—world′ly** *adv.*

world•ly-mind•ed (wûrld′lē-mīn′dĭd) *adj.* Absorbed in the affairs of this world. **—world′ly-mind′ed•ness** *n.*

world•ly-wise (wûrld′lē-wīz′) *adj.* Experienced in the ways of the world.

World Series *n. Baseball.* A series of baseball games played each fall between the winning teams of the American League and the National League for the major-league championship.

world's fair (wûrldz) *n.* A large exposition featuring exhibits, as of arts and crafts, scientific discoveries, and industrial products, provided by countries from around the world.

world soul *n.* A spiritual principle having the same relation to the physical world as the human soul does to the body; the animating force of the world.

world-view or **world•view** (wûrld′vyo͞o′) *n.* **1.** The overall perspective from which one sees and interprets the world. **2.** A collection of beliefs about life and the universe held by an individual or a group. [Transl. of Ger. *Weltanschauung.*]

World War I *n.* A war fought from 1914 to 1918, in which Great Britain, France, Russia, Belgium, Italy, Japan, the United States, and other allies defeated Germany, Austria-Hungary, Turkey, and Bulgaria.

World War II *n.* A war fought from 1939 to 1945, in which Great Britain, France, the Soviet Union, the United States, China, and other allies defeated Germany, Italy, and Japan.

world-wea•ry (wûrld′wîr′ē) *adj.* **-ri•er, -ri•est.** Tired of the world; bored with life. **—world′-wea′ri•ness** *n.*

world•wide (wûrld′wīd′) *adj.* Involving or extending throughout the entire world; universal. **—world′wide′** *adv.*

worm (wûrm) *n.* **1.** Any of various invertebrates, as those of the phyla Annelida, Nematoda, Nemertea, or Platyhelminthes, having a long flexible rounded or flattened body, often without obvious appendages. **2.** Any of various crawling insect larvae, such as a grub or a caterpillar, having a soft elongated body. **3.** Any of various unrelated animals, such as the shipworm, resembling a worm in habit or appearance. **4.a.** Something, such as the thread of a screw, that resembles a worm in form or appearance. **b.** The spirally threaded shaft of a worm gear. **5.** An insidiously tormenting or devouring force. **6.** A person regarded as pitiable or contemptible. **7. worms.** *Pathol.* Infestation of the intestines or other parts of the body with worms or wormlike parasites; helminthiasis. **8.** *Comp. Sci.* A program that replicates itself and interferes with software function or destroys stored information. *—v.* **wormed, worm•ing, worms.** *—tr.* **1.** To make (one's way) with or as if with the sinuous crawling motion of a worm. **2.** To work (one's way or oneself) subtly or gradually; insinuate. **3.** To elicit by artful or devious means. Usually used with *out of.* **4.** To cure of intestinal worms. **5.** *Naut.* To wrap yarn or twine spirally around (rope). *—intr.* **1.** To move in a manner suggestive of a worm. **2.** To make one's way by artful or devious means. [ME < OE *wurm,* var. of *wyrm.* See **wer-**[2]*.]

worm-eat•en (wûrm′ēt′n) *adj.* **1.** Bored through or gnawed by worms. **2.** Decayed; rotten. **3.** Antiquated; decrepit.

worm fence *n.* A fence of crossed rails supporting one another and forming a zigzag pattern.

worm gear *n.* **1.** A gear consisting of a spirally threaded shaft and a wheel with marginal teeth that mesh into it. **2.** The toothed wheel of this gear; a worm wheel.

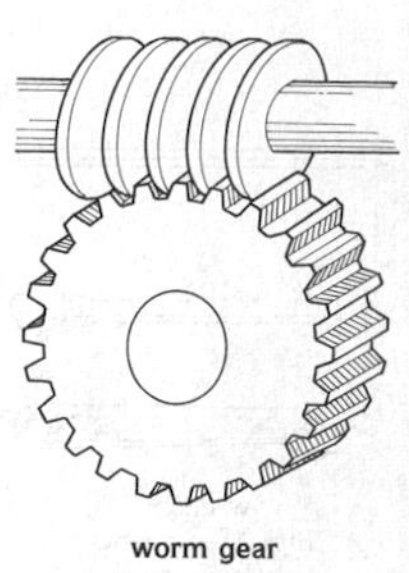
worm gear

worm•hole (wûrm′hōl′) *n.* A hole made by a worm.

Worms (wûrmz, vôrms). A city of SW Germany on the Rhine R. NNW of Mannheim; site of the Diet of Worms (1521) in which Martin Luther refused to recant his beliefs and was outlawed by the Roman Catholic Church. Pop. 72,610.

worm•seed (wûrm′sēd′) *n.* **1.** A tropical American plant *(Chenopodium ambrosioides)* yielding an oil used as an anthelmintic. **2.** Any of several other plants used thus.

worm's-eye view (wûrmz′ī′) *n.* A view from below or from an inferior position.

worm snake *n.* A small harmless burrowing snake *(Carphophis amoena)* of the central and eastern United States, usu. living under stones or logs and feeding chiefly on earthworms.

worm wheel *n.* The toothed wheel of a worm gear.

worm•wood (wûrm′wo͝od′) *n.* **1.** Any of several aromatic plants of the genus *Artemisia,* esp. *A. absinthium* of Europe, yielding a bitter extract used in making absinthe and in flavoring certain wines. **2.** Something harsh or embittering. [ME, alteration of *wermod* < OE *wermōd.*]

worm•y (wûr′mē) *adj.* **-i•er, -i•est. 1.** Infested with or damaged by worms. **2.** Suggestive of a worm. **—worm′i•ness** *n.*

worn (wôrn, wōrn) *v.* P.part. of **wear.** *—adj.* **1.** Affected by wear or use. **2.** Impaired or damaged by wear or use. **3.** Showing the wearing effects of overwork, care, worry, or suffering. [ME, p.part. of *weren,* to wear. See WEAR.]

worn-out (wôrn′out′, wōrn′-) *adj.* **1.** Worn or used until no longer usable or effective. **2.** Thoroughly exhausted; spent.

wor•ri•ment (wûr′ē-mənt, wŭr′-) *n.* **1.** The act or an instance of worrying. **2.** A source of anxiety; a worry.

wor•ri•some (wûr′ē-səm, wŭr′-) *adj.* **1.** Causing worry or anxiety. **2.** Tending to worry. **—wor′ri•some•ly** *adv.*

wor•ry (wûr′ē, wŭr′ē) *v.* **wor•ried** (wûr′ēd, wŭr′-), **wor•ry•ing, wor•ries** (wûr′ēz, wŭr′-). *—intr.* **1.** To feel uneasy or concerned about something; be troubled. See Syns at **brood. 2.** To pull or tear at something with or as if with the teeth. **3.** To proceed doggedly in the face of difficulty or hardship; struggle. *—tr.* **1.** To cause to feel anxious, distressed, or troubled. See Syns at **trouble. 2.** To bother or annoy, as with petty complaints. **3.a.** To seize with the teeth and shake or tug at repeatedly. **b.** To attack roughly and repeatedly; harass. **c.** To touch, move, or handle idly; toy with. *—n., pl.* **-ries. 1.** The act of worrying or the condition of being worried;

ă pat	oi boy
ā pay	ou out
âr care	o͝o to͝ok
ä father	o͞o bo͞ot
ĕ pet	ŭ cut
ē be	ûr urge
ĭ pit	th thin
ī pie	*th* this
îr pier	hw which
ŏ pot	zh vision
ō toe	ə about, item
ô paw	

Stress marks:
′ (primary);
′ (secondary), as in
dictionary (dĭk′shə-nĕr′ē)

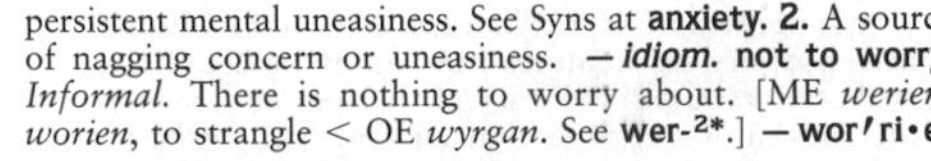

persistent mental uneasiness. See Syns at **anxiety. 2.** A source of nagging concern or uneasiness. **—*idiom.* not to worry.** *Informal.* There is nothing to worry about. [ME *werien, worien,* to strangle < OE *wyrgan.* See **wer-²*.**] **—wor′ri·er** *n.*

worry beads *pl.n.* A string of beads for fingering in times of worry, boredom, or tension.

wor·ry·wart (wûr′ē-wôrt′, wŭr′-) *n.* One who worries excessively and needlessly.

worse (wûrs) *adj.* Comp. of **bad¹, ill. 1.** More inferior, as in quality, condition, or effect. **2.** More severe or unfavorable. **3.** Being further from a standard; less desirable or satisfactory. **4.** Being in poorer health; more ill. *—n.* Something that is worse. *—adv.* Comp. of **badly, ill.** In a worse manner; to a worse degree. **—*idiom.* for better or (for) worse.** Whether the situation or consequences be good or ill. [ME < OE *wyrsa.* See **wers-*.**]

Christopher Wren
Detail of a 1711 painting by Sir Godfrey Kneller

wors·en (wûr′sən) *tr. & intr.v.* **-ened, -en·ing, -ens.** To make or become worse.

wors·er (wûr′sər) *adv. & adj. Non-Standard.* Worse.

wor·ship (wûr′shĭp) *n.* **1.a.** The reverent love and devotion accorded a deity, an idol, or a sacred object. **b.** The ceremonies, prayers, or other religious forms by which this love is expressed. **2.** Ardent devotion; adoration. **3.** Often **Worship.** *Chiefly British.* Used as a form of address for magistrates, mayors, and certain other dignitaries: *Your Worship.* *—v.* **-shiped, -ship·ing, -ships** or **-shipped, -ship·ping, -ships.** *—tr.* **1.** To honor and love as a deity. **2.** To regard with ardent or adoring esteem or devotion. See Syns at **revere¹.** *—intr.* **1.** To participate in religious rites of worship. **2.** To perform an act of worship. [ME *worshipe,* worthiness, honor < OE *weorthscipe* : *weorth,* worth; see WORTH¹ + *-scipe,* -ship.] **—wor′ship·er, wor′ship·per** *n.*

wor·ship·ful (wûr′shĭp-fəl) *adj.* **1.** Given to or expressive of worship; reverent or adoring. **2.** *Chiefly British.* Used as a respectful form of address. **—wor′ship·ful·ly** *adv.* **—wor′ship·ful·ness** *n.*

worst (wûrst) *adj.* Superl. of **bad¹, ill. 1.** Most inferior, as in quality, condition, or effect. **2.** Most severe or unfavorable. **3.** Being furthest from an ideal or a standard; least desirable or satisfactory. *—adv.* Superl. of **badly, ill.** In the worst manner or degree. *—tr.v.* **worst·ed, worst·ing, worsts.** To gain the advantage over; defeat. *—n.* Something that is worst. **—*idioms.* at (the) worst.** Under the most negative circumstances, estimation, or interpretation. **get (or have) the worst of it.** To suffer a defeat or disadvantage. **if (the) worst comes to (the) worst.** If the very worst thing happens. **in the worst way.** *Informal.* Very much; a great deal. [ME < OE *wyrsta.* See **wers-*.**]

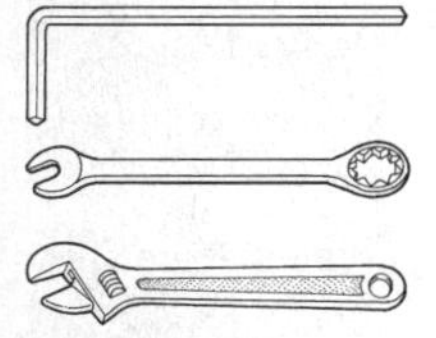

wrench
Top: Allen wrench
Center: Open-end box wrench
Bottom: Adjustable wrench

worst-case (wûrst′kās′) *adj.* Most unfavorable; being or involving the worst possibility.

wor·sted (wo͝os′tĭd, wûr′stĭd) *n.* **1.** Firm-textured, compactly twisted woolen yarn made from long-staple fibers. **2.** Fabric made from such yarn. [ME, var. of *worthstede,* after *Worthstede* (Worstead) in E England.] **—wor′sted** *adj.*

wort¹ (wûrt, wôrt) *n.* A plant. Often used in combination: *liverwort; milkwort.* [ME < OE *wyrt.* See **wrād-*.**]

wort² (wûrt, wôrt) *n.* An infusion of malt that is fermented to make beer. [ME < OE *wyrt.* See **wrād-*.**]

worth¹ (wûrth) *n.* **1.** The quality that renders something desirable, useful, or valuable. **2.** Material or market value. **3.** A quantity of something that may be purchased for a specified sum or by a specified means: *wanted their money's worth.* **4.** Wealth; riches: *her net worth.* **5.** Quality that commands esteem or respect; merit. *—adj.* **1.** Equal in value to something specified. **2.** Deserving of; meriting. **3.** Having wealth or riches amounting to. **—*idioms.* for all (one) is worth.** To the utmost of one's powers or ability. **for what it's worth.** Even though it may not be important or valuable. [ME < OE *weorth.* See **wer-²*.**]

worth² (wûrth) *intr.v.* **worthed, worth·ing, worths.** *Archaic.* To befall; betide. [ME *worthen* < OE *weorthan.* See **wer-²*.**]

Wor·thing (wûr′*th*ĭng). A borough of SE England on the English Channel SSW of London. Pop. 92,600.

wrestling

worth·less (wûrth′lĭs) *adj.* **1.** Lacking worth; of no use or value. **2.** Low; despicable. **—worth′less·ly** *adv.* **—worth′less·ness** *n.*

worth·while (wûrth′hwīl′, -wīl′) *adj.* Sufficiently valuable or important to be worth one's time, effort, or interest. **—worth′while′ness** *n.*

wor·thy (wûr′*th*ē) *adj.* **-thi·er, -thi·est. 1.** Having worth, merit, or value; useful or valuable. **2.** Honorable; admirable: *a worthy fellow.* **3.** Having sufficient worth; deserving: *worthy of acclaim.* *—n., pl.* **-thies.** An eminent or distinguished person. **—wor′thi·ly** *adv.* **—wor′thi·ness** *n.*

-worthy *suff.* **1.** Of sufficient worth for: *creditworthy.* **2.** Suitable or safe for: *crashworthy.* [< WORTHY.]

wot (wŏt) *v. Archaic.* First and third pers. sing. pr.t. of **wit².**

Wo·tan (vō′tän′) *n. Myth.* A German god identified with Odin. [Ger. < MHGer. < OHGer. *Wuotan.* See **wet-¹*.**]

Wouk (wōk), **Herman.** b. 1915. Amer. writer whose novels include *The Caine Mutiny* (1951).

would (wo͝od) *aux.v.* P.t. of **will². 1.** Used after a statement of desire, request, or advice: *I wish you would stay.* **2.** Used to make a polite request: *Would you go?* **3.** Used to indicate uncertainty: *It would seem so.* See Usage Note at **if.**

would-be (wo͝od′bē′) *adj.* Desiring, attempting, or professing to be: *a would-be pilot.*

would·n't (wo͝od′nt). Would not.

wouldst (wo͝odst) or **would·est** (wo͝od′ĭst) *v. Archaic.* Second pers. sing. p.t. of **will².**

wound¹ (wo͞ond) *n.* **1.** An injury, esp. one in which the skin or other external surface is torn, pierced, cut, or otherwise broken. **2.** An injury to the feelings. *—v.* **wound·ed, wound·ing, wounds.** *—tr.* To inflict wounds or a wound on. *—intr.* To inflict wounds or a wound. [ME < OE *wund.* See **wen-²*.**] **—wound′ed·ly** *adv.* **—wound′ing·ly** *adv.*

wound² (wound) *v.* P.t. and p.part. of **wind².**

wound³ (wound) *v. Mus.* A p.t. and p.part. of **wind³.**

Wound·ed Knee (wo͞on′dĭd nē′). A creek of SW SD. Almost 200 Native Americans were massacred here by U.S. troops on Dec. 29, 1890.

wound·wort (wo͞ond′wûrt′, -wôrt′) *n.* **1.** See **betony** 1. **2.** Any of several plants formerly used to treat wounds.

wove (wōv) *v.* P.t. of **weave.**

wo·ven (wō′vən) *v.* P.part. of **weave.** *—adj.* Made by weaving. *—n.* Material or a fabric made by weaving.

wove paper *n.* Paper made on a closely woven wire roller or mold and having a faint mesh pattern. [Var. p.part. of WEAVE.]

Wo·vo·ka (wō-vō′kə). 1858?–1932. Paiute religious leader who founded the Ghost Dance movement.

wow¹ (wou) *Informal.* *—interj.* Used to express wonder, amazement, or great pleasure. *—n.* An outstanding success. *—tr.v.* **wowed, wow·ing, wows.** To have a strong, usu. pleasurable effect on.

wow² (wou) *n.* Slow variation in the pitch of a sound reproduction resulting from variations in the speed of the recording or reproducing equipment. [Imit.]

wow·ser (wou′zər) *n. Australian & New Zealand.* A person regarded as obnoxiously puritanical. [Poss. < dial. *wow,* to howl, complain, of imit. orig.]

WP *abbr.* **1.** Weather permitting. **2.** *Comp. Sci.* Word processing; word processor.

WPA *abbr.* Work Projects Administration.

W particle *n.* A massive charged elementary particle, the quantum of weak interactions in which the charges of participating particles change. See table at **subatomic particle.**

wpm or **w.p.m.** *abbr.* Words per minute.

wpn. *abbr.* Weapon.

wrack¹ also **rack** (răk) *n.* **1.** Destruction or ruin. **2.** A remnant or vestige of something destroyed. [ME < OE *wræc,* punishment (influenced by MDu. *wrak,* shipwreck).]

wrack² also **rack** (răk) *—n.* **1.a.** Wreckage, esp. of a ship cast ashore. **b.** *Chiefly British.* Violent destruction of a building or vehicle. **2.a.** Dried seaweed. **b.** Marine vegetation, esp. kelp. *—v.* **wracked, wrack·ing, wracks** also **racked, rack·ing, racks.** *—tr.* To cause the ruin of; wreck. *—intr.* To be wrecked. [ME *wrak* < MDu.]

wraith (rāth) *n.* **1.** An apparition of a living person that appears as a portent just before that person's death. **2.** The ghost of a dead person. **3.** Something shadowy and insubstantial. [?]

Wran·gel Island (răng′gəl, vrăn′gyĭl). An island of NE Russia in the Arctic Ocean NW of the Bering Strait.

Wran·gell (răng′gəl), **Mount.** A peak, 4,319.7 m (14,163 ft), of the central Wrangell Mts. in S AK.

Wrangell Mountains. A mountain range of S AK extending c. 161 km (100 mi) and rising to 5,032.5 m (16,500 ft).

wran·gle (răng′gəl) *v.* **-gled, -gling, -gles.** *—intr.* To quarrel noisily or angrily; bicker. *—tr.* **1.** To win or obtain by argument. **2.** To herd (horses or other livestock). *—n.* **1.** The act of wrangling. **2.** An angry noisy argument or dispute. [ME *wranglen,* of MLGer. orig. See **wer-²*.**]

wran·gler (răng′glər) *n.* **1.** One who wrangles or quarrels. **2.** A cowboy or cowgirl, esp. one who tends saddle horses.

wrap (răp) *v.* **wrapped** or **wrapt** (răpt), **wrap·ping, wraps.** *—tr.* **1.** To arrange or fold (something) about as cover or protection. **2.** To cover, envelop, or encase, as by folding or coiling something about. **3.** To enclose, esp. in paper, and fasten. **4.** To clasp, fold, or coil about something. **5.** To envelop and obscure. **6.** To surround or involve in a specified quality or atmosphere: *wrapped in secrecy.* **7.** To engross: *wrapped in thought.* *—intr.* **1.** To coil or twist about or around something. **2.** To put on warm clothing. Usu. used with *up.* **3.** To conclude filming. *—n.* **1.** A garment to be wrapped or folded about a person, esp. an outer garment such as a robe or coat. **2.** A blanket. **3.** A wrapping or wrapper. **4.** The completion of filming on a movie. **—*phrasal verb.* wrap up. 1.** To bring to a conclusion; settle finally or successfully. **2.** To summarize; recapitulate. **—*idioms.* under wraps.** *Informal.* Secret or concealed. **wrapped up in. 1.** Completely immersed or absorbed in. **2.** Involved in. [ME *wrappen.* See **wer-²*.**]

wrap·a·round (răp′ə-round′) *adj.* **1.** Designed to be wrapped around the body and fastened: *a wraparound skirt.* **2.** Shaped to curve around the sides: *a wraparound windshield.* —*n.* **1.** A garment open to the side and wrapped around the body. **2.** Something that encompasses or laps over something else.

wrap•per (răp′ər) *n.* **1.** That in which an object is wrapped or covered, as: **a.** The material, such as paper, in which something is wrapped. **b.** The material encircling a magazine or newspaper sent by mail. **c.** A book jacket. **d.** The tobacco leaf covering a cigar. **2.** A loose dressing gown or negligee. **3.** One that wraps, as a store employee who wraps parcels.

wrap•ping (răp′ĭng) also **wrap•pings** (-ĭngz) *n.* The material in which something is wrapped.

wrap-up (răp′ŭp′) *n.* **1.** A brief final summary, as of the news. **2.** A concluding or final action: *the wrap-up of a campaign.*

wrasse (răs) *n.* Any of numerous chiefly tropical, often brightly colored marine fishes of the family Labridae, having spiny fins, thick lips, and powerful jaws and often valued for food. [Cornish *gwragh* and Welsh *gwrach*, old woman.]

wrath (răth, räth) *n.* **1.** Forceful, often vindictive anger. See Syns at **anger. 2.a.** Punishment or vengeance as a manifestation of anger. **b.** Divine retribution for sin. —*adj. Archaic.* Wrathful. [ME < OE *wrǣththu* < *wrāth*, angry. See **wer-**[2]*.]

wrath•ful (răth′fəl, räth′-) *adj.* **1.** Full of wrath; fiercely angry. **2.** Proceeding from or expressing wrath. —**wrath′ful•ly** *adv.* —**wrath′ful•ness** *n.*

wreak (rēk) *tr.v.* **wreaked, wreak•ing, wreaks. 1.** To inflict (vengeance or punishment) upon a person. **2.** To express or gratify (anger, malevolence, or resentment); vent. **3.** To bring about; cause: *wreak havoc.* **4.** *Archaic.* To take vengeance for; avenge. [ME *wreken* < OE *wrecan.*]

Usage Note: *Wreak* is sometimes confused with *wreck,* perhaps because the wreaking of damage may leave a wreck: *The storm wreaked havoc along the coast.* The past tense and past participle of *wreak* is *wreaked,* not *wrought,* which is an alternative past tense and past participle of *work.*

wreath (rēth) *n., pl.* **wreaths** (rēthz, rēths). **1.a.** A ring or circlet of flowers, boughs, or leaves worn on the head, placed on a memorial, or hung as a decoration. **b.** A representation of this ring or circlet, as in woodwork. **2.** A curling or circular form. [ME *wrethe* < OE *writha*, band. See **wer-**[2]*.]

wreathe (rē*th*) *v.* **wreathed, wreath•ing, wreathes.** —*tr.* **1.** To twist or entwine into a wreath. **2.** To twist or curl into a wreathlike shape. **3.** To crown, decorate, or encircle with or as if with a wreath. **4.** To coil or curl. **5.** To form a wreath or wreathlike shape around. —*intr.* **1.** To assume the form of a wreath. **2.** To curl, writhe, or spiral. [< WREATH.]

wreck (rĕk) *n.* **1.** The act of wrecking or the state of being wrecked; destruction. **2.** Accidental destruction of a ship; a shipwreck. **3.a.** The stranded hulk of a severely damaged ship. **b.** Fragments of a ship or its cargo cast ashore by the sea after a shipwreck; wreckage. **4.** The remains of something wrecked or ruined. **5.** Something shattered or dilapidated. **6.** A person who is broken down or worn out. —*v.* **wrecked, wreck•ing, wrecks.** —*tr.* **1.** To cause the destruction of in or as if in a collision. **2.** To dismantle or raze; tear down. **3.** To cause to undergo ruin or disaster. See Syns at **ruin.** See Usage Note at **wreak.** —*intr.* **1.** To suffer destruction or ruin; become wrecked. **2.** To work as a wrecker. [ME *wrek* < AN *wrec*, of Scand. orig.; akin to ON *rec*, wreckage.]

wreck•age (rĕk′ĭj) *n.* **1.** The act of wrecking or the state of being wrecked. **2.** Something wrecked. **3.** The debris of something wrecked.

wreck•er (rĕk′ər) *n.* **1.** One that wrecks or destroys: *a wrecker of dreams.* **2.a.** One who is in the business of demolishing old buildings. **b.** One who dismantles cars for salvage. **3.a.** A person, vehicle, or piece of equipment employed in recovering or removing wrecks. **b.** One that salvages wrecked cargo or parts. **4.a.** One who lures a vessel to destruction, as by a display of lights on a rocky coastline, in order to plunder it. **b.** A plunderer.

wreck•ing bar (rĕk′ĭng) *n.* A small crowbar with a claw at one end and a slight curve at the other end.

wren (rĕn) *n.* **1.** Any of various small brownish songbirds of the family Troglodytidae, having rounded wings, a slender bill, and a short, often erect tail. **2.** Any of various similar unrelated songbirds. [ME *wrenne* < OE *wrenna.*]

Wren (rĕn), Sir **Christopher.** 1632–1723. English architect who designed more than 50 London churches, most notably Saint Paul's Cathedral (1675–1710).

wrench (rĕnch) *n.* **1.** A sudden sharp, forcible twist or turn. **2.** An injury produced by twisting or straining. **3.** A sudden tug at one's emotions; a surge of compassion, sorrow, or anguish. **4.a.** A break or parting that causes emotional distress. **b.** The pain so associated. **5.** A distortion in the original form or meaning of something written or spoken; twisted interpretation. **6.** Any of various hand or power tools with fixed or adjustable jaws for gripping, turning, or twisting objects such as nuts, bolts, or pipes. —*v.* **wrenched, wrench•ing, wrench•es.** —*tr.* **1.a.** To twist or turn suddenly and forcibly. **b.** To twist and sprain. **2.a.** To force free by pulling at; yank. **b.** To pull with a wrench. **3.** To pull at the feelings or emotions of; distress. **4.** To distort or twist the original character or import of. —*intr.* To give a wrench, twist, or turn. [< ME *wrenchen*, to twist < OE *wrencan.* See **wer-**[2]*.]

wrest (rĕst) *tr.v.* **wrest•ed, wrest•ing, wrests. 1.** To obtain by or as if by pulling with violent twisting movements. **2.** To usurp forcefully. **3.** To extract by or as if by force, twisting, or persistent effort; wring. **4.a.** To distort or twist the nature or meaning of. **b.** To divert to an improper use; misapply. —*n.* **1.** The act of wresting. **2.** *Mus.* A small tuning key for the wrest pins of a stringed instrument. [ME *wresten* < OE *wrǣstan*, to twist. See **wer-**[2]*.] —**wrest′er** *n.*

wres•tle (rĕs′əl) *v.* **-tled, -tling, -tles.** —*intr.* **1.** To contend by grappling and attempting to throw or immobilize one's opponent, esp. under contest rules. **2.** To contend or struggle. **3.** To strive in an effort to master something. —*tr.* **1.a.** To take part in (a wrestling match). **b.** To take part in a wrestling match with. **2.** To move or lift with great effort and force. **3.** To throw (a calf or other animal) for branding. —*n.* **1.** The act or a bout of wrestling. **2.** A struggle. [ME *wrestlen* < OE **wrǣstlian*, freq. of *wrǣstan*, to twist. See **wer-**[2]*.] —**wres′tler** *n.*

wres•tling (rĕs′lĭng) *n. Sports.* A sport in which two competitors attempt to throw or immobilize each other by grappling.

wrest pin *n. Mus.* One of the pins to which the strings of a musical instrument, esp. of a keyboard instrument, are attached and by turning which they are tuned.

wretch (rĕch) *n.* **1.** A miserable, unfortunate, or unhappy person. **2.** A person regarded as base, mean, or despicable. [ME *wrecche* < OE *wrecca*, exile, wretch.]

wretch•ed (rĕch′ĭd) *adj.* **-er, -est. 1.** In a deplorable state of distress or misfortune; miserable. **2.** Characterized by or attended with misery or woe. **3.** Of a poor or mean character; dismal. **4.** Contemptible; despicable. **5.** Of very inferior quality. [ME *wrecched* < *wrecche*, wretch. See WRETCH.] —**wretch′ed•ly** *adv.* —**wretch′ed•ness** *n.*

wri•er (rī′ər) *adj.* A comp. of **wry.**

wri•est (rī′ĭst) *adj.* A superl. of **wry.**

wrig•gle (rĭg′əl) *v.* **-gled, -gling, -gles.** —*intr.* **1.** To turn or twist the body with sinuous writhing motions; squirm. **2.** To proceed with writhing motions. **3.** To worm one's way into or out of a situation; insinuate or extricate oneself by sly or subtle means. —*tr.* **1.** To move with a wriggling motion. **2.** To make (one's way, for example) by or as if by wriggling. —*n.* **1.** A wriggling movement. **2.** A sinuous path, line, or marking. [ME *wrigglen*, perh. < MLGer. *wriggeln.* See **wer-**[2]*.] —**wrig′gly** *adj.*

wrig•gler (rĭg′lər) *n.* **1.** The larva of a mosquito. **2.** One that wriggles or squirms.

wright (rīt) *n.* One that constructs or repairs something. Often used in combination: *a playwright; a shipwright.* [ME < OE *wryhta.* See **werg-***.]

Wright (rīt), **Frank Lloyd.** 1869–1959. Amer. architect whose distinctive style was based on natural forms.

Wright, Orville. 1871–1948. Amer. aviation pioneer who with his brother **Wilbur** (1867–1912) made the first controlled sustained flights in a powered heavier-than-air vehicle on Dec. 17, 1903, near Kitty Hawk NC.

Wright, Richard. 1908–60. Amer. writer whose works include *Native Son* (1940) and *Black Boy* (1945).

wring (rĭng) *v.* **wrung** (rŭng), **wring•ing, wrings.** —*tr.* **1.** To twist, squeeze, or compress, esp. to extract liquid. Often used with *out.* **2.** To extract (liquid) by twisting or compressing. Often used with *out.* **3.** To wrench or twist forcibly or painfully. **4.** To clasp and twist or squeeze (one's hands), as in distress. **5.** To clasp firmly and shake (another's hand), as in congratulation. **6.** To cause distress to; affect with painful emotion. **7.** To obtain or extract by applying force or pressure. —*intr.* To writhe or squirm, as in pain. —*n.* The act or an instance of wringing; a squeeze or twist. [ME *wringen* < OE *wringan.* See **wer-**[2]*.]

wring•er (rĭng′ər) *n.* One that wrings, esp. a device in which laundry is pressed between rollers to extract water. —***idiom.* put (someone) through the wringer.** *Slang.* To subject to a severe trial or ordeal.

wrin•kle (rĭng′kəl) *n.* **1.** A small furrow, ridge, or crease on a normally smooth surface, caused by crumpling, folding, or shrinking. **2.** A line or crease in the skin, as from age. **3.** *Informal.* A clever trick, method, or device, esp. one that is new and different; an innovation. —*v.* **-kled, -kling, -kles.** —*tr.* **1.** To make wrinkles or a wrinkle in. **2.** To draw up into wrinkles; pucker: *wrinkled her nose.* —*intr.* To form wrinkles. [ME, back-formation < *wrinkled*, wrinkled, prob. < OE *gewrinclod*, p.part. of *gewrinclian*, to wind, crease. See **wer-**[2]*.] —**wrin′kly** *adj.*

wrist (rĭst) *n.* **1.a.** The joint between the hand and the forearm. **b.** See **carpus** 1. **2.** The part of a sleeve or glove that encircles the wrist. [ME < OE. See **wer-**[2]*.]

wrist•band (rĭst′bănd′) *n.* A band, as on a long sleeve or a wristwatch, that encircles the wrist.

wrist•let (rĭst′lĭt) *n.* **1.** A band of material worn round the wrist for warmth or support. **2.** A bracelet.

wrist•lock (rĭst′lŏk′) *n. Sports.* A wrestling hold in which an opponent's wrist is gripped and twisted to immobilize the opponent.

Frank Lloyd Wright

Wright Brothers
Top: Orville Wright
Bottom: Wilbur Wright

ă pat	oi boy
ā pay	ou out
âr care	o͝o took
ä father	o͞o boot
ĕ pet	ŭ cut
ē be	ûr urge
ĭ pit	th thin
ī pie	*th* this
îr pier	hw which
ŏ pot	zh vision
ō toe	ə about, item
ô paw	

Stress marks:
′ (primary);
′ (secondary), as in dictionary (dĭk′shə-nĕr′ē)

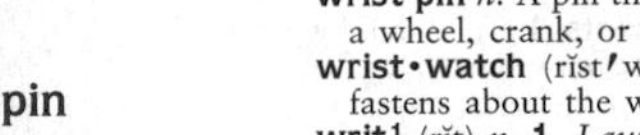

wrist pin *n.* A pin that attaches one end of a connecting rod to a wheel, crank, or piston.

wrist•watch (rĭst′wŏch′) *n.* A watch worn on a band that fastens about the wrist.

writ[1] (rĭt) *n.* **1.** *Law.* A written order issued by a court, commanding the party to whom it is addressed to perform or cease performing a specified act. **2.** Writings. [ME < OE.]

writ[2] (rĭt) *v.* A p.t. and p.part. of **write.**

write (rīt) *v.* **wrote** (rōt), **writ•ten** (rĭt′n) also **writ** (rĭt), **writ•ing, writes.** —*tr.* **1.a.** To form (letters, words, or symbols) on a surface such as paper with an instrument such as a pen. **b.** To spell. **2.** To form (letters or words) in cursive style. **3.** To compose and set down, esp. in literary or musical form. **4.** To draw up in legal form; draft. **5.** To fill in or cover with writing. **6.** To express in writing; set down. **7.** To communicate by correspondence. **8.** To underwrite, as an insurance policy. **9.** To mark: *sadness written on his face.* **10.** To ordain or prophesy. **11.** *Comp. Sci.* To record (data) on a storage device. —*intr.* **1.** To trace or form letters, words, or symbols on paper or another surface. **2.** To produce written material, such as articles or books. **3.** To compose a letter; communicate by mail. —***phrasal verbs.* write down. 1.** To set down in writing. **2.** To reduce in rank, value, or price. **3.** To disparage in writing. **4.** To write in a conspicuously simple or condescending style. **write in. 1.** To cast a vote by inserting (a name not listed on a ballot). **2.** To insert in a text or document. **3.** To communicate with an organization by mail. **write off. 1.** To reduce to zero the book value of (an asset that has become worthless). **2.** To cancel from accounts as a loss. **3.** To consider as a loss or failure. **write out. 1.** To express or compose in writing. **2.** To write in full or expanded form. **write up. 1.** To write a report or description of, as for publication. **2.** To bring (a journal, for example) up to date. **3.** To overstate the value of (assets). **4.** To report (someone) in writing, as for breaking the law. —***idioms.* write (one's) own ticket.** To set one's own terms or course of action entirely according to one's own needs or wishes. **writ large.** Signified, expressed, or embodied in a greater or more prominent magnitude or degree. [ME *writen* < OE *wrītan.*]

wrought iron

write-down (rīt′doun′) *n. Accounting.* A reduction of the entered value of an asset.

write-in (rīt′ĭn′) *n.* **1.** A vote cast by writing in the name of a candidate not on the ballot. **2.** A candidate thus voted for.

write-off (rīt′ôf′, -ŏf′) *n. Accounting.* **1.a.** A cancellation of an item in account books. **b.** The amount canceled or lost. **2.** A reduction to zero of the entered value of an item.

writ•er (rī′tər) *n.* One who writes, esp. as an occupation.

writ•er's block (rī′tərz) *n.* A usu. temporary psychological inability to begin or continue work on a piece of writing.

writer's cramp *n., pl.* **writers' cramps.** A cramp or spasm of the muscles of the fingers, hand, and forearm during writing.

write-up (rīt′ŭp′) *n.* **1.** A published account, review, or notice, esp. a favorable one. **2.** *Accounting.* An intentional overevaluation of a corporation's assets.

writhe (rīth) *v.* **writhed, writh•ing, writhes.** —*intr.* **1.** To twist, as in pain or embarrassment. **2.** To move with a twisting or contorted motion. **3.** To suffer acutely. —*tr.* To cause to twist or squirm; contort. —*n.* The act or an instance of writhing; a contortion. [ME *writhen* < OE *wrīthan.* See **wer-**[2]***.**] —**writh′er** *n.*

Wyandotte[2]
Columbian Wyandotte hen

writ•ing (rī′tĭng) *n.* **1.** The act of one who writes. **2.** Written form. **3.** Handwriting; penmanship. **4.** Something written, esp.: **a.** Meaningful letters or characters that constitute readable matter. **b.** A written work, esp. a literary composition. **5.** The occupation or style of a writer. **6. Writings.** *(used with a sing. or pl. v.)* The third of the three divisions of the Hebrew Bible, usu. composed of Psalms, Proverbs, Job, Song of Solomon, Ruth, Lamentations, Ecclesiastes, Esther, Daniel, Ezra, Nehemiah, and Chronicles. See table at **Bible.**

writ of election *n., pl.* **writs of election.** A writ issued by a governor or other executive authority requiring that an election be held, esp. a special election to fill a vacancy.

writ of error *n., pl.* **writs of error.** *Law.* A writ commissioning an appellate court to review the proceedings of another court and correct the judgment given if deemed necessary.

writ of prohibition *n., pl.* **writs of prohibition.** *Law.* An order issued by a higher court commanding a lower court to cease from proceeding in some matter not within its jurisdiction.

writ of summons *n., pl.* **writs of summons.** *Law.* A writ directing a person to appear in court to answer a complaint.

writ•ten (rĭt′n) *v.* P.part. of **write.**

wrnt. *abbr.* Warrant.

Wro•claw (vrôt′släf′) also **Bres•lau** (brĕs′lou). A city of SW Poland on the Oder R.; assigned to Poland by the Potsdam Conference (1945). Pop. 636,000.

wrong (rông, rŏng) *adj.* **1.** Not in conformity with fact or truth; incorrect or erroneous. **2.a.** Contrary to conscience, morality, or law; immoral or wicked. **b.** Unfair; unjust. **3.** Not required, intended, or wanted: *took a wrong turn.* **4.** Not fitting or suitable; inappropriate or improper. **5.** Not in accord with established usage, method, or procedure. **6.** Not functioning properly; out of order. **7.** Unacceptable or undesirable according to social convention. **8.** Being the side, as of a garment, that is less finished and not intended to show. —*adv.* **1.** In a wrong manner; mistakenly or erroneously. **2.** In a wrong course or direction. **3.** Immorally or unjustly. **4.** In an unfavorable way. See Syns at **amiss.** —*n.* **1.a.** An unjust or injurious act. **b.** Something contrary to ethics or morality. **2.a.** An invasion or a violation of another's legal rights. **b.** *Law.* A tort. **3.** The condition of being in error or at fault. —*tr.v.* **wronged, wrong•ing, wrongs. 1.** To treat unjustly or injuriously. **2.** To discredit unjustly; malign. **3.** To treat dishonorably; violate. —***idioms.* do (someone) wrong.** *Informal.* To be unfaithful or disloyal. **go wrong. 1.** To take a wrong turn or make a wrong move. **2.** To go astray morally. **3.** To go amiss; turn out badly. [ME, of Scand. orig. See **wer-**[2]***.**] —**wrong′er** *n.* —**wrong′ly** *adv.* —**wrong′ness** *n.*

wrong•do•er (rông′dōō′ər, rŏng′-) *n.* One who does wrong, esp. morally or ethically. —**wrong′do′ing** *n.*

wrong•ful (rông′fəl, rŏng′-) *adj.* **1.** Wrong; unjust. **2.** Unlawful. —**wrong′ful•ly** *adv.* —**wrong′ful•ness** *n.*

wrong-head•ed (rông′hĕd′ĭd, rŏng′-) *adj.* Stubbornly defiant of what is right or reasonable; obstinately perverse in judgment or opinion. —**wrong′-head′ed•ly** *adv.* —**wrong′-head′ed•ness** *n.*

wrote (rōt) *v.* P.t. of **write.**

wroth (rôth) *adj.* Wrathful; angry. [ME < OE *wrāth.* See **wer-**[2]***.**]

wrought (rôt) *v.* A p.t. and p.part. of **work.** —*adj.* **1.** Put together; created: *a carefully wrought plan.* **2.** Shaped by hammering with tools. Used chiefly of metals or metalwork. **3.** Made delicately or elaborately. [ME *wroght* < OE *geworht,* p.part. of *wyrcan,* to work. See **werg-*.**]

wrought iron *n.* An easily worked iron that is a mixture of refined metallic iron with 1 to 3 percent siliceous slag.

wrought-up also **wrought up** (rôt′ŭp′) *adj.* Agitated; excited.

wrung (rŭng) *v.* P.t. and p.part. of **wring.**

wry (rī) *adj.* **wri•er** (rī′ər), **wri•est** (rī′ĭst) or **wry•er** or **wry•est. 1.** Dryly humorous, often with a touch of irony. **2.** Temporarily twisted in an expression of distaste or displeasure: *a wry face.* **3.** Abnormally twisted or bent to one side; crooked: *a wry nose.* **4.** Being at variance with what is right, proper, or suitable; perverse. [< ME *wrien,* to turn < OE *wrīgian.* See **wer-**[2]***.**] —**wry′ly** *adv.* —**wry′ness** *n.*

wry•neck (rī′nĕk′) *n.* **1.** Either of two small Old World woodpeckers, *Jynx torquilla* or *J. ruficollis,* having a sharply pointed bill and the habit of twisting the head and neck into contortions. **2.a.** See **torticollis. b.** A person with torticollis.

WSW *abbr.* West-southwest.

wt. *abbr.* Weight.

Wu•han (wōō′hän′). A city of E-central China on the Yangtze R. (Chang Jiang); cap. of Hubei province. Pop. 3,400,000.

Wu•hu (wōō′hōō′). A city of E-central China on the Yangtze R. (Chang Jiang) SSW of Nanjing. Pop. 360,000.

Wu Jiang (wōō′ jyäng′). A river rising in S-central China and flowing c. 805 km (500 mi) E and N to the Yangtze R. (Chang Jiang).

wul•fen•ite (wŏŏl′fə-nīt′) *n.* A usu. yellow to orange-brown mineral, $PbMoO_4$, a molybdenum ore. [Ger. *Wulfenit,* after Franz X. von *Wulfen* (1728–1805), Austrian mineralogist.]

wun•der•kind (vŏŏn′dər-kĭnd′, wŭn′-) *n., pl.* **-kin•der** (-kĭn′dər). **1.** A child prodigy. **2.** A person of remarkable talent or ability who achieves great success or acclaim at an early age. [Ger. : *Wunder,* wonder, prodigy (< MHGer. < OHGer. *wuntar*) + *Kind,* child; see KINDERGARTEN.]

Wup•per•tal (vŏŏp′ər-täl′). A city of W-central Germany NNE of Düsseldorf. Pop. 379,393.

wurst (wûrst, wŏŏrst) *n.* Sausage. [Ger. < MHGer. < OHGer. See **wers-*.**]

Würt•tem•berg (wûr′təm-bûrg′, vür′təm-bĕrk′). A historical region and kingdom (1806–1918) of SW Germany.

Würz•burg (wûrts′bûrg′, vürts′bŏŏrk′). A city of S-central Germany on the Main R. Pop. 129,995.

wu•shu also **wu shu** (wōō′shōō′) *n.* The Chinese martial arts. [Chin. (Mandarin) *wǔ shù* : *wǔ,* martial + *shù,* skill, art.]

Wu•xi also **Wu•sih** (wōō′shē′). A city of E China between Shanghai and Nanjing. Pop. 696,300.

WV *abbr.* West Virginia.

W.Va. *abbr.* West Virginia.

WWI *abbr.* World War I.

WWII *abbr.* World War II.

WY *abbr.* Wyoming.

Wy•an•dot also **Wy•an•dotte** (wī′ən-dŏt′) *n., pl.* **Wyandot** or **-dots** also **Wyandotte** or **-dottes. 1.** A member of a Native American people formerly located in Ohio and the upper Midwest and now living in northeast Oklahoma. **2.** Their Iroquoian language. [Wyandot *wădát,* tribal name.]

Wy•an•dotte[1] (wī′ən-dŏt′). A city of SE MI, a suburb of Detroit. Pop. 30,938.

Wy•an•dotte[2] (wī′ən-dŏt′) *n.* **1.** A medium-sized domestic chicken of a breed developed in North America for its eggs and meat. **2.** Var. of **Wyandot.**

Wy•att or **Wy•at** (wī′ət), Sir **Thomas.** 1503–42. English poet noted for introducing the sonnet form into English literature.

wych elm also **witch elm** (wĭch) *n.* A Eurasian elm *(Ulmus glabra) often planted as a shade tree.* [< ME *wiche* < OE *wice.* See **weik-²*.**]

Wych•er•ley (wĭch′ər-lē), **William.** 1640?–1716. English satirist whose plays include *The Country Wife* (1675).

Wyc•liffe also **Wick•liffe** or **Wyc•lif** or **Wic•lif** (wĭk′lĭf), **John.** 1328?–84. English theologian and religious reformer whose rejection of the biblical basis of papal power and dispute with the doctrine of the transubstantiation of the host anticipated the Protestant Reformation.

wye (wī) *n.* **1.** The letter *y.* **2.** An object shaped like a Y.

Wy•eth (wī′ĭth), **Andrew.** b. 1917. Amer. artist whose realistic paintings, such as *Christina's World* (1948), depict stark rural scenes. His father, **Newell Convers Wyeth** (1882–1945), was also a painter and a book illustrator.

Wy•lie (wī′lē), **Elinor Morton Hoyt.** 1885–1928. Amer. writer whose works include *Nets to Catch the Wind* (1921).

wynn (wĭn) or **wen** (wĕn) *n.* An Old English rune having the sound (w) and used in Old English and Middle English writing. [OE. See **wen-¹*.**]

Wyo. *abbr.* Wyoming.

Wy•o•ming (wī-ō′mĭng). **1.** A state of the W U.S.; admitted as the 44th state in 1890. The region was acquired by the U.S. as part of the Louisiana Purchase (1803). Cap. Cheyenne. Pop. 455,975. **2.** A city of W-central MI, a suburb of Grand Rapids. Pop. 63,891.

WYSIWYG (wĭz′ē-wĭg′) *Comp. Sci.* — *adj.* Relating to or being a word-processing or desktop publishing system in which the screen displays text exactly as it will be printed. — *n.* A WYSIWYG system, effect, or screen display. [*w(hat) y(ou) s(ee) i(s) w(hat) y(ou) g(et).*]

wy•vern also **wi•vern** (wī′vərn) *n. Her.* A two-legged dragon having wings and a barbed tail. [Alteration of ME *wyvere,* viper < ONFr. *wivre* < Lat. *vīpera.* See VIPER.]

Andrew Wyeth
Photographed in 1987

X x

x¹ or **X** (ĕks) — *n., pl.* **x's** or **X's. 1.** The 24th letter of the modern English alphabet. **2.** Any of the speech sounds represented by the letter *x.* **3.** The 24th in a series. **4.** Something shaped like the letter X. **5.** A mark inscribed in lieu of the signature of one who is unable to sign one's name. **6.** An unknown or unnamed factor, thing, or person. — *tr.v.* **x'd, x'ing, x's** or **X'd, X'ing, X's. 1.** To mark or sign with an X. **2.** To delete, cancel, or obliterate with a series of X's. Often used with *out.*

x² *Math.* The symbol for **abscissa.**

X¹ (ĕks) *n.* A movie rating that admits no one under 17.

X² 1. *Elect.* The symbol for **reactance. 2.** Also **x** The symbol for the Roman numeral 10.

X³ *abbr.* **1.** Christ (Greek Χριστοσ, Christos). **2.** Christian. **3.** Or **x** Experimental. **4.** Extra.

x. *abbr. Bus.* Ex.

Xan•a•du (zăn′ə-do͞o′, -dyo͞o′) *n.* An idyllic beautiful place. [After *Xanadu* in "Kubla Khan" by Samuel Taylor Coleridge.]

xan•than gum (zăn′thən) *n.* A natural gum produced by culture fermentation of glucose and used as a stabilizer in commercial food preparation. [< NLat. *Xanthomonas (campestris),* name of the bacterium used to produce it : Gk. *xanthos,* yellow (< its color) + Gk. *monas,* monad; see MONAD.]

xan•thate (zăn′thāt′) *n.* A salt of a xanthic acid, esp. a simple xanthic acid salt, as of sodium or potassium, used as a flotation collector for copper, silver, and gold.

xan•thene (zăn′thēn′) *n.* A yellow crystalline compound, $CH_2(C_6H_4)_2O$, used as a fungicide and in organic synthesis.

xan•thic acid (zăn′thĭk) *n.* Any of various unstable acids of the form ROC(S)SH, in which R is usu. an alkyl radical.

xan•thine (zăn′thēn′, -thĭn) *n.* **1.** A yellowish-white crystalline purine base, $C_5H_4N_4O_2$, that is a precursor of uric acid and is found in blood, urine, muscle tissue, and certain plants. **2.** Any of several derivatives of this compound.

Xan•thip•pe (zăn-thĭp′ē, -tĭp′ē) or **Xan•tip•pe** (-tĭp′ē). 5th cent. B.C. Wife of Socrates traditionally described as shrewish.

xantho– or **xanth–** *pref.* **1.** Yellow: *xanthine.* **2.** Xanthic acid: *xanthate.* [Gk., yellow < *xanthos.*]

xan•tho•chroid (zăn′thə-kroid′) *adj.* Having a light complexion and light hair. — *n.* A person having a light complexion and light hair. [NLat. *xanthŏchroi,* yellow-haired, fair-skinned people (Gk. *xantho-,* xantho- + Gk. *ōkhroi,* pl. of *ōkhros,* pale) + -OID.] — **xan′tho•chro′ic** (-krō′ĭk) *adj.*

xan•tho•ma (zăn-thō′mə) *n., pl.* **-mas** or **-ma•ta** (-mə-tə). A yellowish-orange lipid-filled nodule or papule in the skin, often on an eyelid or over a joint.

xan•tho•phyll (zăn′thə-fĭl′) *n.* **1.** A yellow carotenoid pigment, $C_{40}H_{56}O_2$, found with chlorophyll in green plants and identical with lutein. **2.** Any of various related yellow pigments. — **xan′tho•phyl′lic, xan′tho•phyl′lous** *adj.*

xan•thous (zăn′thəs) *adj.* **1.** *Color.* Yellow. **2.** Having light brown or yellowish skin.

Xan•thus (zăn′thəs). An ancient city of Lycia in present-day SW Turkey; besieged and taken by the Persians (c. 546 B.C.) and the Romans (c. 42 B.C.).

Xa•vi•er (zā′vē-ər, zăv′ē-), Saint **Francis.** 1506–52. Spanish missionary who was a cofounder of the Jesuit order (1534).

x-ax•is (ĕks′ăk′sĭs) *n., pl.* **x-ax•es** (-ăk′sēz). *Math.* **1.** The horizontal axis of a two-dimensional Cartesian coordinate system. **2.** One of three axes in a three-dimensional Cartesian coordinate system.

XC or **X-C** *abbr. Sports.* Cross-country.

X-chro•mo•some (ĕks′krō′mə-sōm′) *n.* The sex chromosome associated with female characteristics, occurring paired in the female and single in the male sex-chromosome pair.

XD *abbr.* Ex dividend.

x-div. *abbr.* Ex dividend.

Xe The symbol for the element **xenon.**

xe•bec also **ze•bec** or **ze•beck** (zē′bĕk′) *n. Naut.* A small three-masted Mediterranean vessel with both square and triangular sails. [Fr. *chebec,* prob. < Catalan *xabec* < Ar. dial. *šabbāk.*]

xe•ni•a (zē′nē-ə, zēn′yə) *n. Bot.* The direct effect on a hybrid plant produced by the transfer of pollen from one strain to the endosperm of a different strain. [NLat. < Gk., hospitality < *xenos,* guest, stranger. See XENO–.]

Xen•ia (zēn′yə, zē′nē-ə). A city of SW-central OH ESE of Dayton. Pop. 24,664.

xeno– or **xen–** *pref.* **1.** Stranger; foreigner: *xenophobia.* **2.** Strange; foreign; different: *xenolith.* [NLat. < Gk. < *xenos,* stranger. See **ghos-ti-*.**]

xen•o•bi•ot•ic (zĕn′ə-bī-ŏt′ĭk, zē′nə-) *adj.* Foreign to the body or to living organisms. Used of chemical compounds. — *n.* A xenobiotic chemical, such as a pesticide.

xen•o•blast (zĕn′ə-blăst′, zē′nə-) *n.* A mineral deposit that has developed during metamorphism without developing crystalline faces.

xen•o•cryst (zĕn′ə-krĭst′, zē′nə-) *n.* A crystal foreign to the igneous rock in which it occurs. [XENO– + CRYST(AL).]

xen•o•gen•e•sis (zĕn′ə-jĕn′ĭ-sĭs, zē′nə-) *n.* **1.** The production of offspring markedly different from either parent. **2.** See **alternation of generations.** — **xen′o•ge•net′ic** (-jə-nĕt′ĭk), **xen′o•gen′ic** (-jĕn′ĭk) *adj.*

xen•o•graft (zĕn′ə-grăft′, zē′nə-) *n.* See **heterograft.**

xen•o•lith (zĕn′ə-lĭth′, zē′nə-) *n.* A rock fragment foreign to the igneous mass in which it occurs.

xe•non (zē′nŏn′) *n. Symbol* **Xe** A colorless, odorless, highly unreactive gaseous element found in minute quantities in the atmosphere, extracted commercially from liquefied air and used in stroboscopic, bactericidal, and laser-pumping lamps. Atomic number 54; atomic weight 131.30; melting point −111.9°C; boiling point −107.1°C; density (gas) 5.887 grams per liter; specific gravity (liquid) 3.52 (−109°C). See table at **element.** [< Gk., neut. of *xenos,* foreign, strange. See XENO–.]

Xe•noph•a•nes (zə-nŏf′ə-nēz′). 560?–478? B.C. Greek philosopher who was a founder of the Eleatic school.

xen•o•phile (zĕn′ə-fīl′, zē′nə-) *n.* A person attracted to that which is foreign, esp. to foreign peoples, manners, or cultures. — **xen′o•phil′i•a** (-fĭl′ē-ə) *n.* — **xe•noph′i•lous** (zĕ-nŏf′ə-ləs, zē-) *adj.*

xen•o•phobe (zĕn′ə-fōb′, zē′nə-) *n.* A person unduly fearful or contemptuous of that which is foreign, esp. of strangers or foreign peoples. — **xen′o•pho′bi•a** *n.* — **xen′o•pho′bic** *adj.*

Xen•o•phon (zĕn′ə-fən, -fŏn′). 430?–355? B.C. Greek soldier who after a failed attack on Persia (401 B.C.) led Greek troops to the Black Sea, an ordeal recounted in *Anabasis.*

Xer (ĕk′sər) *n.* A member of Generation X.

xer•ic (zĕr′ĭk, zîr′-) *adj.* Of, characterized by, or adapted to an extremely dry habitat. — **xer′i•cal•ly** *adv.*

xero– or **xer–** *pref.* Dry; dryness: *xeroderma.* [Gk. *xēro-* < *xēros,* dry.]

xer•o•der•ma (zîr′ō-dûr′mə) also **xe•ro•der•mi•a** (-mē-ə) *n.* Excessive or abnormal dryness of the skin, as in ichthyosis.

xe•rog•ra•phy (zĭ-rŏg′rə-fē) *n.* A dry photographic or photocopying process in which a negative image formed by a resinous powder on an electrically charged plate is electrically transferred to and thermally fixed as positive on a paper or other copying surface. — **xe•rog′ra•pher** *n.* — **xer′o•**

Saint Francis Xavier
17th-century
Hispano-Philippine
carved ivory head

ă pat	oi boy
ā pay	ou out
âr care	o͝o took
ä father	o͞o boot
ĕ pet	ŭ cut
ē be	ûr urge
ĭ pit	th thin
ī pie	*th* this
îr pier	hw which
ŏ pot	zh vision
ō toe	ə about, item
ô paw	

Stress marks:
′ (primary);
′ (secondary), as in
dictionary (dĭk′shə-nĕr′ē)

graph′ic (zîr′ə-grăf′ĭk) *adj.* **—xer′o•graph′i•cal•ly** *adv.*

xe•roph•i•lous (zĭ-rŏf′ə-ləs) *adj.* Flourishing in or adapted to a dry hot environment. **—xe•roph′i•ly** *n.*

xer•oph•thal•mi•a (zîr′əf-thăl′mē-ə) *n.* Extreme dryness and thickening of the conjunctiva, often resulting from a deficiency of vitamin A. **—xer′oph•thal′mic** *adj.*

xer•o•phyte (zîr′ə-fīt′) *n.* A plant adapted to living in an arid habitat; a desert plant. **—xer′o•phyt′ic** (-fĭt′ĭk) *adj.* **—xer′o•phyt′ism** (-fī′tĭz-əm, -fĭ-tĭz′-) *n.*

xe•ro•sis (zĭ-rō′sĭs) *n., pl.* **-ses** (-sēz). **1.** Abnormal dryness, esp. of the skin, eyes, or mucous membranes. **2.** The normal hardening of aging tissue.

Xerxes I
Fifth-century B.C. low relief from Persepolis, widely recognized as Xerxes the Great

xer•o•ther•mic (zîr′ə-thûr′mĭk) *adj.* **1.** Both dry and hot: *a xerothermic climate.* **2.** Adapted to or flourishing in an environment that is both dry and hot: *xerothermic organisms.*

Xer•ox (zîr′ŏks). A trademark used for a xerographic photocopying process or machine.

Xer•xes I (zûrk′sēz). "Xerxes the Great." 519?–465 B.C. King of Persia (486–465) who organized a vast army that defeated the Greeks at Thermopylae and destroyed Athens (480).

x-height (ĕks′hīt′) *n. Print.* The height of a lowercase x.

Xho•sa also **Xo•sa** (kō′sä, -zə) *n., pl.* **Xhosa** or **-sas** also **Xosa** or **-sas. 1.** A member of a Bantu people inhabiting the eastern part of Cape Province, South Africa. **2.** The Nguni language of this people, closely related to Zulu.

xi (zī, sī, ksē) *n.* **1.** The 14th letter of the Greek alphabet. **2.** See **xi hyperon.** [Gk. *xei.*]

XI *abbr. Bus.* Ex interest.

Xia•men (shyä′mən) also **A•moy** (ä-moi′). A city of E China ENE of Guangzhou; an early center of European commercial activity. Pop. 350,000.

Xi'an (shē′än′, shyän) also **Si•an** (sē′än′, shē′-) or **Hsian** (shyän). A city of central China SW of Beijing; cap. (221–206 B.C.) of the Qin dynasty. Pop. 1,730,000.

Xiang Jiang (shyäng′ jyäng′) also **Siang Kiang** (syäng′ kyäng′, shyäng′) or **Hsiang Kiang** (shyäng′). A river, c. 1,150 km (715 mi), flowing generally N from SE China.

Xiang•tan (shyäng′tän′) also **Siang•tan** (syäng′-, shyäng′-). A city of S-central China on the Xiang Jiang SSW of Changsha. Pop. 350,000.

xi hyperon *n.* Either of two subatomic particles in the baryon family, one neutral and one negatively charged, with masses of 2,573 and 2,585 times that of the electron. See table at **subatomic particle.**

Xi Jiang (shē′ jyäng′) also **Si Kiang** (sē′ kyäng′, shē′). A river rising in SE China and flowing c. 2,011 km (1,250 mi) generally E to the South China Sea near Guangzhou.

Xin•gu (shēng-gōō′). A river of central and N Brazil flowing c. 1,979 km (1,230 mi) to the Amazon R.

Xi•ning (shē′nĭng′). A city of central China NNE of Chengdu; cap. of Qinghai province. Pop. 400,000.

Xin•jiang Uy•gur (shĭn′jyäng′ wē′gər) also **Sin•kiang Ui•ghur** or **Sin•kiang Ui•gur** (sĭn′kyäng′ wē′gər, shĭn′jyäng′). An autonomous region of extreme W China; came under Chinese control in the 16th cent. Cap. Ürümqi. Pop. 13,610,000.

Xin•xiang (shĭn′shyäng′). A city of E China SSE of Taiyuan. Pop. 325,000.

xiph•i•ster•num (zĭf′ĭ-stûr′nəm) *n., pl.* **-na** (-nə). The posterior and smallest of the three divisions of the sternum, below the gladiolus and the manubrium. [< Gk. *xiphos,* sword.]

xiph•oid (zĭf′oid′) *adj.* **1.** Shaped like a sword. **2.** Of or relating to the xiphisternum. **—***n.* See **xiphisternum.** [Gk. *xiphoeidēs* : *xiphos,* sword + *-oeidēs,* -oid.]

xiphoid process *n.* See **xiphisternum.**

xiph•o•su•ran (zĭf′ə-sŏŏr′ən) *n.* An arthropod of the order Xiphosura, which includes the horseshoe crab and many extinct forms. [< NLat. *Xiphosūra,* order name : Gk. *xiphos,* sword + Gk. *-oura,* neut. pl. of *-ouros,* -urous.] **—xiph′o•su′ran** *adj.*

Xi•zang (shē′dzäng′) or **Ti•bet** (tə-bĕt′). An autonomous region of SW China N and W of the Himalaya Mts.; controlled by China since 1720 and formally proclaimed an autonomous region in 1965. Cap. Lhasa. Pop. 1,990,000.

XL *abbr.* **1.** Extra large. **2.** Extra long.

X•mas (krĭs′məs, ĕks′məs) *n. Usage Problem.* Christmas. [< X, the Gk. letter chi, abbreviation of *Khristos,* Christ. See CHRIST.]

Usage Note: *Xmas* has been used for hundreds of years in religious writing, where the *X* is understood to represent a Greek chi, the first letter of Χριστος, "Christ"; in this use it is parallel to other forms like *Xtian,* "Christian." But the letter *X,* or especially *x,* is nowadays more frequently interpreted as a mathematical variable than as a Greek letter, as indicated by the common pronunciation of the form *Xmas* as (ĕks′məs). Thus, while the word is etymologically innocent of the charge that it omits Christ from Christmas, it is now generally understood only as an informal shortening.

Xo•sa (kō′sä, -zə) *n.* Var. of **Xhosa.**

x-ra•di•a•tion (ĕks′rā′dē-ā′shən) *n.* **1.** Treatment with or exposure to x-rays. **2.** Radiation composed of x-rays.

X-rat•ed (ĕks′rā′tĭd) *adj.* **1.** Having the rating X: *an X-rated movie.* **2.** Vulgar, obscene, or explicit in the treatment of sex.

x-ray also **X-ray** (ĕks′rā′) **—***n.* also **x ray.** or **X ray 1.a.** A relatively high-energy photon with wavelength in the approximate range from 0.01 to 10 nanometers. **b.** A stream of such photons, used for their penetrating power in radiography, radiology, radiotherapy, and scientific research. Often used in the plural. **2.** A photograph taken with x-rays. **—***tr.v.* **x-rayed, x-ray•ing, x-rays** also **X-rayed, X-ray•ing, X-rays. 1.** To irradiate with x-rays. **2.** To photograph with x-rays.

x-ray astronomy *n.* The branch of astronomy that deals with the properties of celestial sources of x-rays.

x-ray diffraction *n.* The scattering of x-rays by crystal atoms, producing a diffraction pattern that yields information about the structure of the crystal.

x-ray star *n.* A celestial object, esp. a star, that emits a major portion of its radiation in x-rays.

x-ray therapy *n.* Medical treatment using controlled doses of x-ray radiation.

x-ray tube *n.* A vacuum tube containing electrodes that accelerate electrons and direct them to a metal anode, where their impacts produce x-rays.

Xu•zhou (shōō′jō′) also **Sü•chow** (sōō′chou′, sü′jō′). A city of E China NNW of Nanjing. Pop. 806,400.

xy•lan (zī′lən) *n.* A yellow water-soluble gummy polysaccharide found in plant cell walls and yielding xylose upon hydrolysis.

xy•lem (zī′ləm) *n.* The supporting and water-conducting tissue of vascular plants, consisting primarily of tracheids and vessels; woody tissue. [Ger. < Gk. *xulon,* wood.]

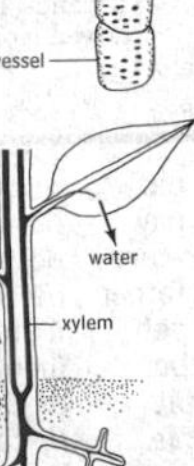

xylem

xy•lene (zī-lēn′, zī′lēn′) also **xy•lol** (zī′lôl′, -lōl′) *n.* **1.** Any of three flammable isomeric hydrocarbons, $C_6H_4(CH_3)_2$, obtained from wood and coal tar. **2.** A mixture of xylene isomers used as a solvent in making lacquers and rubber cement.

xy•li•dine (zī′lĭ-dēn′, -dĭn, zĭl′ĭ-) *n.* **1.** Any of six isomers, $(CH_3)_2C_6H_3NH_2$, derived from xylene and used as dye intermediates. **2.** Any of various mixtures of xylidine isomers.

xylo– or **xyl–** *pref.* **1.** Wood: *xylograph.* **2.** Xylene: *xylidine.* [Gk. *xulo-* < *xulon,* wood.]

xy•lo•graph (zī′lə-grăf′) *n.* **1.** An engraving on wood. **2.** An impression from a woodblock. **—***tr.v.* **-graphed, -graph•ing, -graphs.** To print from a wood engraving. **—xy•log′ra•pher** (-lŏg′rə-fər) *n.*

xy•log•ra•phy (zī-lŏg′rə-fē) *n.* **1.** Wood engraving, esp. of an early period. **2.** The art of printing texts or illustrations, sometimes with color, from woodblocks, as distinct from typography. **—xy′lo•graph′ic** (-lə-grăf′ĭk), **xy′lo•graph′i•cal** (-ĭ-kəl) *adj.* **—xy′lo•graph′i•cal•ly** *adv.*

xy•loid (zī′loid′) *adj.* Of or similar to wood.

xy•loph•a•gous (zī-lŏf′ə-gəs) *adj.* **1.** Feeding on wood, as certain insects or insect larvae. **2.** Destructive to wood, as certain crustaceans or fungi. **—xy′lo•phage′** (zī′lə-fāj′) *n.*

xy•lo•phone (zī′lə-fōn′) *n. Mus.* A percussion instrument consisting of a mounted row of wooden bars graduated in length to sound a chromatic scale, played with two small mallets. **—xy′lo•phon′ist** *n.*

xy•lose (zī′lōs′) *n.* A white crystalline sugar, $C_5H_{10}O_5$, used in dyeing and tanning and in diabetic diets.

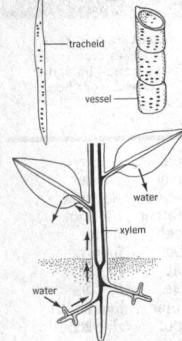

Y y

y[1] or **Y** (wī) *n., pl.* **y's** or **Y's. 1.** The 25th letter of the modern English alphabet. **2.** Any of the speech sounds represented by the letter *y.* **3.** Something shaped like the letter Y. **4.** The 25th in a series.

y[2] *Math.* The symbol for **ordinate.**

y[3] or **Y** *abbr.* Yen.

Y[1] **1.** The symbol for the element **yttrium. 2.** *Elect.* The symbol for **admittance** 3. **3.** *Phys.* The symbol for **hypercharge.**

Y[2] *abbr.* Yeoman.

y. *abbr.* Year.

–y[1] or **–ey** *suff.* **1.** Characterized by; consisting of: *clayey.* **2.a.** Like: *summery.* **b.** To some degree; somewhat: *chilly.* **3.** Tending toward; inclined toward: *sleepy.* [ME < OE *-ig.*]

–y[2] *suff.* **1.** Condition; state; quality: *jealousy.* **2.a.** Activity:

cookery. **b.** Instance of a specified action: *entreaty.* **3.a.** Place for an activity: *cannery.* **b.** Result or product of an activity: *laundry.* **4.** Collection; body; group: *soldiery.* [ME *-ie* < OFr. < Lat. *-ia.* Sense 2b, ult. < Lat. *-ium.*]

–y[3] or **–ie** *suff.* **1.** Small one: *doggy.* **2.** Dear one: *sweetie.* **3.** One having to do with or characterized by: *townie.* [ME *-ie, -y.*]

yab•ber (yăb**′**ər) *Australian.* —*n.* Jabber. —*tr. & intr.v.* **-bered, -ber•ing, -bers.** To jabber (something) or engage in jabbering. [< Australian pidgin, prob. < Wuywurung, Aboriginal language of SE Australia *yaba,* to talk.]

Ya•blo•no•vy Range (yä**′**blə-nə-vē**′**). A mountain chain of SE Russia extending NE from near the Mongolian border.

yacht (yät) *Naut.* —*n.* Any of various relatively small sailing or motor-driven vessels, used for pleasure cruises or racing. —*intr.v.* **yacht•ed, yacht•ing, yachts.** To sail, cruise, or race in a yacht. [Prob. obsolete Norw. *jagt* < MLGer. *jacht,* short for *jachtschip* : *jagen,* to chase (< OHGer. *jagōn*) + *schip,* ship.]

yacht•ing (yä**′**tĭng) *n. Naut.* The activity of sailing in yachts.

yachts•man (yäts**′**mən) *n. Naut.* A man who owns or sails a yacht.

yachts•wom•an (yäts**′**wo͝om′ən) *n.* A woman who owns or sails a yacht.

yack (yăk) *v. & n. Slang.* Var. of **yak[2].**

yack•e•ty-yak (yăk**′**ĭ-tē-yăk**′**) *n. Slang.* Prolonged, sometimes senseless talk. [Imit.]

YAG (yăg) *n.* A hard synthetic yttrium aluminum garnet used in laser technology.

ya•gi (yä**′**gē, yăg**′**ē) *n., pl.* **-gis.** A directional radio and television antenna consisting of a horizontal conductor with several insulated dipoles parallel to and in the plane of the conductor. [After Hidetsugu *Yagi* (1886–1976), Japanese electrical engineer.]

ya•hoo (yä**′**ho͞o, yā**′**-) *n., pl.* **-hoos.** A person regarded as crude or brutish. [From *Yahoo,* member of a race of brutes having human form in *Gulliver's Travels* by Jonathan Swift.] **—ya′hoo•ism** *n.*

Yah•weh (yä**′**wā, -wĕ) also **Yah•veh** (-vā, -vĕ) or **Jah•veh** (yä**′**vā, -vĕ) or **Jah•weh** (yä**′**wā, -wĕ) *n.* A convention for pronouncing the Tetragrammaton. [Heb.]

Yah•wist (yä**′**wĭst) also **Yah•vist** (-vĭst) *n.* The author of the earliest sources of the Hexateuch, in which God is consistently referred to by the Tetragrammaton. **—Yah•wis′tic** *adj.*

yak[1] (yăk) *n.* **1.** A wild shaggy-haired ox *(Bos grunniens)* of the mountains of central Asia. **2.** A domesticated yak, used as a work animal or raised for meat and milk. [Tibetan *gyag.*]

yak[2] also **yack** (yăk) *Slang.* —*intr.v.* **yakked, yak•king, yaks** also **yacked, yack•ing, yacks.** To talk persistently and meaninglessly. —*n.* Prolonged, sometimes senseless talk. [Imit.]

Ya•ki•ma[1] (yăk**′**ə-mô, -mə) *n., pl.* **Yakima** or **-mas. 1.** A member of a Native American people inhabiting south-central Washington. **2.** Their Sahaptin dialect.

Ya•ki•ma[2] (yăk**′**ə-mô′, -mə). A city of S-central WA SE of Seattle. Pop. 54,827.

Yakima River. A river of central and SE WA flowing c. 327 km (203 mi) to the Columbia R.

ya•ki•to•ri (yä′kĭ-tôr**′**ē, -tōr**′**ē) *n.* A dish consisting of bite-sized marinated chicken pieces that are grilled on small skewers. [J. : *yaki,* roasting + *tori,* bird.]

Ya•kut (yä-ko͞ot**′**) *n., pl.* **Yakut** or **-kuts. 1.** A member of a people inhabiting the region of the Lena River in eastern Siberia. **2.** The Turkic language of the Yakut. **—Ya•kut′** *adj.*

Ya•kutsk (yə-ko͞otsk**′**). A city of E-central Russia on the Lena R.; founded as a fort in 1632. Pop. 180,000.

ya•ku•za (yä**′**ko͞o-zä′) *n., pl.* **yakuza. 1.** A loose alliance of Japanese criminal organizations and illegal enterprises. **2.** A Japanese gangster. [J., good-for-nothing, gambler, racketeer.]

Yale (yāl), **Elihu.** 1649–1721. Colonial-born English merchant who made a series of contributions to the Collegiate School, which was renamed in Yale's honor (1718).

Yale, Mount. A peak, 4,329.8 m (14,196 ft), in the Sawatch Range of the Rocky Mts. in central CO.

y'all (yôl) *pron. Chiefly Southern U.S.* Var. of **you-all.** See Regional Note at **you-all.**

Ya•long Jiang (yä**′**lo͝ong**′** jyäng**′**). A river of S-central China flowing c. 1,287 km (800 mi) to the Yangtze R. (Chang Jiang).

Yal•ow (yăl**′**ō), **Rosalyn Sussman.** b. 1921. Amer. medical physicist who shared a 1977 Nobel Prize.

Yal•ta (yôl**′**tə). A city of SE Ukraine in the S Crimea; site of an Allied conference in Feb. 1945. Pop. 86,000.

Ya•lu Jiang (yä**′**lo͞o**′** jyäng**′**). A river, c. 805 km (500 mi), forming part of the North Korea–China border.

yam (yăm) *n.* **1.** Any of numerous chiefly tropical vines of the genus *Dioscorea,* many of which have edible tuberous roots. **2.** The starchy root of any of these plants, used as food. **3.** *Chiefly Southern U.S.* See **sweet potato** 1. See Regional Note at **goober.** [Port. *inhame* or obsolete Sp. *igname, ñame,* both < Port. and E. Creole *nyam,* to eat, of West African orig.; akin to Fulani *nyami,* to eat, Wolof *ñam,* food, to eat, or Mandingo (Bambara) *ñambu,* manioc.]

Ya•ma•see (yä**′**mə-sē′) *n., pl.* **Yamasee** or **-sees.** A member of a Native American people formerly inhabiting parts of coastal Georgia and South Carolina.

Yam•bol (yäm**′**bōl′). A city of SE Bulgaria E of Stara Zagora; under Turkish rule from the 15th to the 19th cent. Pop. 91,000.

ya•men (yä**′**mən) *n.* The office or residence of an official in the Chinese Empire. [Chin. (Mandarin) *yámen* : *yá,* magistracy (< *yá,* tooth, flag with a serrated edge) + *mén,* gate.]

yam•mer (yăm**′**ər) *Informal.* —*v.* **-mered, -mer•ing, -mers.** —*intr.* **1.** To complain peevishly or whimperingly; whine. **2.** To talk volubly and loudly. —*tr.* To utter or say in a complaining or clamorous tone. —*n.* The act of yammering. [ME *yameren,* to lament, prob. < MFlem. *jammeren,* to be sorrowful.] **—yam′mer•er** *n.*

Yam•pa (yăm**′**pə). A river of NW CO flowing c. 402 km (250 mi) to the Green R. near the UT border.

Ya•na (yä**′**nə). A river of NE Russia flowing c. 1,207 km (750 mi) to the Laptev Sea.

yang (yăng) *n.* The active, masculine cosmic principle in Chinese dualistic philosophy. [Chin. (Mandarin) *yáng,* sun, light, masculine element.]

Yang Chen Ning (yăng**′** chĕn**′** nĭng**′**, jœn**′**). b. 1922. Chinese-born Amer. physicist who shared a 1957 Nobel Prize.

Yan•gon (yäɴ**′**gôɴ**′**). See **Rangoon.**

Yang•tze River (yăng**′**sē**′**, -tsē**′**, yäng**′**dzə**′**) or **Chang Jiang** (chäng**′** jyäng**′**). The longest river of China and of Asia, flowing c. 5,551 km (3,450 mi) from Xizang (Tibet) to the East China Sea.

Yang•zhou also **Yang•chow** (yäng**′**jō**′**). A city of E-central China on the Grand Canal; a cap. of China in the 6th cent. A.D. Pop. 255,000.

yank (yăngk) *v.* **yanked, yank•ing, yanks.** —*tr.* **1.** To pull with a quick, strong movement; jerk. **2.** *Slang.* To extract or remove abruptly. —*intr.* To pull on something suddenly. —*n.* A sudden vigorous pull; a jerk. [?]

Yank (yăngk) *n. Informal.* A Yankee.

Yan•kee (yăng**′**kē) *n.* **1.** A native or inhabitant of New England. **2.** A native or inhabitant of a northern U.S. state, esp. a Union soldier during the Civil War. **3.** A native or inhabitant of the United States. [?] **—Yan′kee•dom** *n.*

Word History: *Yankee* is an excellent example of a widely known word whose origins cannot be determined. The best hypothesis is that *Yankee* comes from Dutch *Janke,* a nickname for *Jan,* "John." Evidence can be found in the *Oxford English Dictionary* that the forms *Yankey, Yanky,* and *Yankee* were used as surnames or nicknames in the 17th century. The word *Yankee* is first found in one of our modern senses in 1758, the sense being "a New Englander." The 17th-century nickname for *Jan* was derisive, and the first instances of our word show the term being used derisively by the British for New Englanders. After the Battle of Lexington (1775) New Englanders dignified the name. The British were responsible for application of the term to all Americans (a use first recorded around 1784); and Southerners, for application of the term to Northerners (first recorded in 1817).

Yankee Doodle *n.* A Yankee. [< the title of a song popular during the Revolutionary War.]

Yan•kee•ism (yăng**′**kē-ĭz′əm) *n.* A Yankee custom, characteristic, usage, or pronunciation.

Yank•ton (yăngk**′**tən) *n., pl.* **Yankton** or **-tons.** A member of a division of the Sioux people formerly inhabiting northern Minnesota, now located mainly in the eastern Dakotas.

Yank•to•nai (yăngk′tə-nī**′**) *n., pl.* **Yanktonai** or **-nais.** A member of a division of the Sioux people formerly inhabiting northern Minnesota, now located in the Dakotas and eastern Montana.

Yao[1] (you) *n., pl.* **Yao** or **Yaos. 1.** A member of a people related to the Hmong and inhabiting southern China, Laos, Thailand, and Vietnam. **2.** The Miao-Yao language of the Yao.

Yao[2] (you). A city of S Honshu, Japan, a suburb of Osaka. Pop. 276,397.

Ya•oun•dé (yä-o͞on-dā**′**). The cap. of Cameroon, in the S-central part; founded 1888. Pop. 561,000.

yap (yăp) *v.* **yapped, yap•ping, yaps.** —*intr.* **1.** To bark sharply or shrilly; yelp. **2.** *Slang.* To talk noisily or stupidly; jabber. —*tr.* To utter by yapping. —*n.* **1.** A sharp, shrill bark; a yelp. **2.** *Slang.* Noisy stupid talk; jabber. **3.** *Slang.* The mouth: *Shut your yap.* **4.** *Slang.* A person regarded as stupid, crude, or loud. [Prob. imit.] **—yap′per** *n.*

Yap (yăp, yäp). An island group in the W Caroline Is. of the western Pacific; part of a Japanese mandate after 1920.

ya•pok (yə-pŏk**′**) *n.* An aquatic opossum *(Chironectes minimus)* of tropical America having webbed hind feet and a long tail. [After the *Oyapock,* a river of N South America.]

Ya•qui (yä**′**kē) *n., pl.* **Yaqui** or **-quis. 1.** A member of a Native American people of Sonora, a state of northwest Mexico, now also located in southern Arizona. **2.** The Uto-Aztecan language of the Yaqui. [Sp. < Yaqui *hiaki.*]

yar•bor•ough (yär**′**bûr′ō, -bŭr′ō, -bər-ə) *n. Games.* A bridge or whist hand containing no honor cards. [After Charles Anderson Worsley, 2nd Earl of *Yarborough* (1809–97), said to

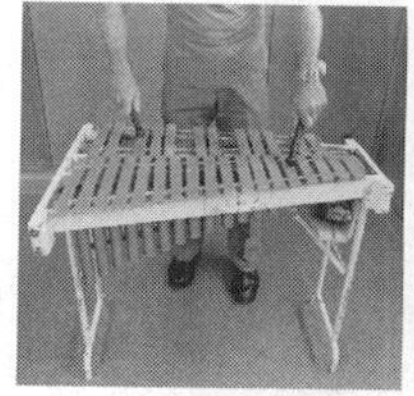

xylophone

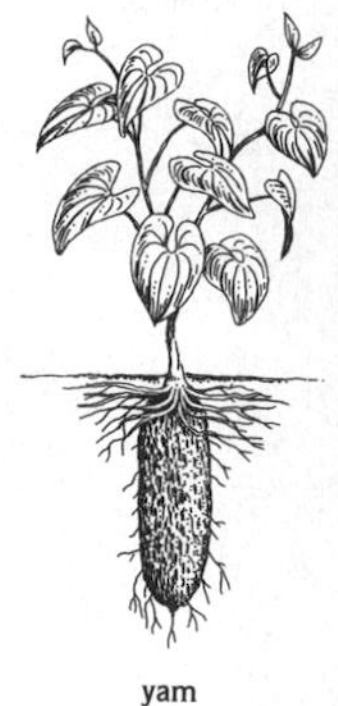

yam

yang
Yang (*left*) and yin (*right*)

ă **pat**	oi **boy**
ā **pay**	ou **out**
âr **care**	o͝o **took**
ä **father**	o͞o **boot**
ĕ **pet**	ŭ **cut**
ē **be**	ûr **urge**
ĭ **pit**	th **thin**
ī **pie**	*th* **this**
îr **pier**	hw **which**
ŏ **pot**	zh **vision**
ō **toe**	ə **about,**
ô **paw**	**item**

Stress marks:
′ (primary);
′ (secondary), as in
dictionary (dĭk**′**shə-nĕr′ē)

have bet 1,000 to 1 that such a hand would not occur.]

yard[1] (yärd) *n.* **1.** A fundamental unit of length in both the U.S. Customary System and the British Imperial System, equal to 3 feet, or 36 inches (0.9144 meter). See table at **measurement.** **2.** *Naut.* A long tapering spar slung to a mast to support and spread the head of a square sail, lugsail, or lateen. [ME *yerde,* stick, unit of measure < OE *gerd.*]

yard[2] (yärd) *n.* **1.** A tract of ground adjacent to, surrounding, or surrounded by a building or group of buildings. **2.** A tract of ground, often enclosed, used for a specific work, business, or other activity. **3.** An area where railroad trains are made up and cars are switched, stored, and serviced on tracks and sidings. **4.a.** A winter pasture for deer or other grazing animals. **b.** An enclosed tract of ground in which animals are kept. —*v.* **yarded, yard•ing, yards.** —*tr.* To enclose, collect, or put into or as if into a yard. —*intr.* To be gathered into or as if into a yard. [ME < OE *geard.* See **gher-**[1]***.**]

yashmak

yard•age[1] (yär′dĭj) *n.* **1.** An amount or length measured in yards. **2.** Cloth sold by the yard.

yard•age[2] (yär′dĭj) *n.* **1.** The use of a livestock yard at a station in the process of transporting cattle by railroad. **2.** A fee paid for such usage.

yard•arm (yärd′ärm′) *n. Naut.* Either end of a yard of a square sail.

yard bird *n. Slang.* **1.a.** An untrained military recruit. **b.** A soldier confined to a restricted area or assigned menial tasks as a punishment. **2.** A convict; a prisoner.

yard goods *pl.n.* See **piece goods.**

yard•man (yärd′mən) *n.* A man employed in a yard, esp. a railroad yard.

yard•mas•ter (yärd′măs′tər) *n.* A railroad employee in charge of a yard.

yard sale *n.* A sale of used household belongings on the front or back lawn of a house.

yard•stick (yärd′stĭk′) *n.* **1.** A graduated measuring stick one yard in length. **2.** A test or standard used in measurement, comparison, or judgment.

yare (yâr) *adj.* **1.** Agile; lively. **2.** *Naut.* Responding easily; maneuverable. Used of a vessel. **3.** *Archaic.* Ready; prepared. —*adv. Archaic.* Soon; quickly. [ME < OE *gearo,* ready.] —**yare′ly** *adv.*

Yar•kant He (yär-kănt′ hə′, -känt′) also **Yar•kand River** (-kănd′, -känd′). A river of NW China flowing c. 805 km (500 mi) to the Tarim He.

Yar•mouth (yär′məth). A town of SE MA on S-central Cape Cod east of Barnstable. Pop. 21,174.

yar•mul•ke also **yar•mel•ke** (yär′məl-kə, yä′məl-) *n.* A skullcap worn by certain observant Jews, esp. at prayer. [Yiddish < Pol. and Ukranian *yarmulka,* poss. < Turk. *yağmurluk,* rain clothing < *yağmur,* rain.]

yarn (yärn) *n.* **1.** A continuous strand of twisted threads of natural or synthetic material, such as wool or nylon, used in weaving or knitting. **2.** *Informal.* A narrative of real or fictitious adventures; an entertaining tale. —*intr.v.* **yarned, yarn•ing, yarns.** *Informal.* To tell a yarn or series of yarns. [ME < OE *gearn.* See **gherə-*.**]

William Butler Yeats
Photographed in 1932

Ya•ro•slavl (yär′ə-slä′vəl, yə-rə-). A city of W-central Russia on the Volga R. NE of Moscow; annexed by Moscow in 1463. Pop. 626,000.

yar•row (yăr′ō) *n.* Any of several plants of the genus *Achillea* of the composite family, esp. *A. millefolium,* native to Eurasia, having finely dissected foliage and flat, usu. white flower heads. [ME *yarowe* < OE *gearwe.*]

yash•mak also **yash•mac** (yäsh-mäk′, yăsh′măk) *n.* A veil worn by Muslim women to cover the face in public. [Turk.]

yat•a•ghan also **yat•a•gan** (yăt′ə-găn′, -gən) *n.* A Turkish sword or scimitar having a double-curved blade but lacking a handle guard. [Turk. *yatağan.*]

yau•pon (yô′pən) *n.* An evergreen holly *(Ilex vomitoria)* of the southeast United States having dried leaves used to make a bitter tea. [Catawba *yă′pă.*]

Ya•va•pai (yăv′ə-pī′, yä′və-) *n., pl.* **Yavapai** or **-pais. 1.** A member of a Native American people inhabiting western Arizona. **2.** The Yuman language of the Yavapai.

yaw (yô) *v.* **yawed, yaw•ing, yaws.** —*intr.* **1.** *Naut.* To swerve off course momentarily or temporarily. **2.** To turn about the vertical axis. Used of an aircraft, a spacecraft, or a projectile. **3.** To move unsteadily; weave. —*tr.* To cause to yaw. —*n.* **1.** The act of yawing. **2.** Extent of yawing, measured in degrees. [Perhaps of Scand. orig.]

yawl (yôl) *n. Naut.* **1.** A two-masted fore-and-aft-rigged sailing vessel similar to the ketch but having a smaller jigger mast stepped abaft the rudder. **2.** A ship's small boat, crewed by rowers. [Du. *jol,* poss. < LGer. *jolle.*]

yawn (yôn) *v.* **yawned, yawn•ing, yawns.** —*intr.* **1.** To open the mouth wide with a deep inhalation, usu. involuntarily from drowsiness, fatigue, or boredom. **2.** To open wide; gape. —*tr.* To utter wearily, while or as if while yawning. —*n.* **1.** The act of yawning. **2.** A fatigued or bored response. **3.** *Informal.* One that provokes yawns; a bore. [ME *yanen,* alteration of *yonen, yenen* < OE *geonian.*] —**yawn′er** *n.*

yawn•ing (yô′nĭng) *adj.* Gaping open; cavernous.

yawp also **yaup** (yôp) —*intr.v.* **yawped, yawp•ing, yawps** also **yauped, yaup•ing, yaups. 1.** To utter a sharp cry; yelp. **2.** To talk loudly, raucously, or coarsely. —*n.* **1.** A bark; a yelp. **2.** Loud or coarse talk or utterance. [ME *yolpen,* possible var. of *yelpen.* See YELP.] —**yawp′er** *n.*

yaws (yôz) *pl.n. (used with a sing. or pl. v.)* A highly contagious tropical disease that chiefly affects children, caused by the spirochete *Treponema pertenue* and characterized by raspberrylike sores. [< Am.Sp. *yaya,* sore < Carib *yaya,* disease.]

y-ax•is (wī′ăk′sĭs) *n., pl.* **y-ax•es** (wī′ăk′sēz). *Math.* **1.** The vertical axis of a two-dimensional Cartesian coordinate system. **2.** One of three axes in a three-dimensional Cartesian coordinate system.

Ya•zoo (yə-zo͞o′, yăz′o͞o). A river of W-central MS flowing 302.5 km (188 mi) to the Mississippi R. above Vicksburg.

Yb The symbol for the element **ytterbium.**

YB *abbr.* Yearbook.

Y-chro•mo•some (wī′krō′mə-sōm′) *n.* The sex chromosome associated with male characteristics, occurring with one X-chromosome in the male sex-chromosome pair.

y•clept (ĭ-klĕpt′) or **y•cleped** (ĭ-klĕpt′, ĭ-klĕpt′) *v.* A p.part. of **clepe.** [ME *icleped* < OE *geclepod,* p.part. of *gecleopian,* to call : *ge-,* participial pref.; see **kom*** + *cleopian,* to call.]

yd *abbr.* Yard (measurement).

ye[1] (*th*ē) *def.art. Archaic.* The. [Misreading of *ye* < ME *þe,* spelling of *the,* the (using the letter thorn).]

ye[2] (yē) *pron.* **1.** *(used with a pl. v.) Archaic.* You. **2.** *(used with a sing. v.) Archaic.* You. [ME < OE *gē.* See **yu-*.**]

yea (yā) *adv.* **1.** Yes; aye. **2.** Indeed; truly. —*n.* **1.** An affirmative statement or vote. **2.** One who votes affirmatively. [ME < OE *gēa.* See **i-*.**]

yeah (yĕ′ə, yă′ə, yā′ə) *adv. Informal.* Yes. [Var. of YEA.]

yean (yēn) *v.* **yeaned, yean•ing, yeans.** —*intr.* To bear young. Used of sheep and goats. —*tr.* To give birth to; bear. Used of sheep and goats. [ME *iyenen, yenen* < OE **geēanian : ge-,* verb pref.; see YCLEPT + *ēanian,* to bear young.]

yean•ling (yēn′lĭng) *n.* The young of a sheep or goat; a lamb or kid. —*adj.* Newly born; infant.

year (yîr) *n.* **1.a.** The period of time during which the earth completes a single revolution around the sun, consisting of 365 days, 5 hours, 49 minutes, and 12 seconds of mean solar time, beginning in the Gregorian calendar on January 1 and ending on December 31. **b.** A period approximately equal to a year in other calendars. **c.** A period of approximately the duration of a calendar year: *We were married a year ago.* **2.** A sidereal year. **3.** A solar year. **4.** A period equal to the calendar year but beginning on a different date: *a fiscal year.* **5.** A specific period of time, usu. shorter than 12 months, devoted to a special activity: *the academic year.* **6. years.** Age, esp. old age. **7. years.** An indefinitely long period of time: *years since we saw her.* [ME *yere* < OE *gēar.* See **yēr-*.**]

year•book (yîr′bo͝ok′) *n.* **1.** A documentary, memorial, or historical book published every year, containing information about the previous year. **2.** A publication compiled by the graduating class of a school or college, recording the year's events and typically containing photographs of students.

year-end also **year•end** (yîr′ĕnd′) —*n.* The end of a year. —*adj.* Occurring or done at the end of the year.

year•ling (yîr′lĭng) *n.* **1.** An animal that is one year old or has not completed its second year. **2.** A thoroughbred racehorse one year old dating from January 1 of the year in which it was foaled. —*adj.* Being one year old.

year•long (yîr′lông′, -lŏng′) *adj.* Lasting one year.

year•ly (yîr′lē) *adj.* Occurring once a year or every year; annual. —*adv.* Once a year; annually. —*n., pl.* **-lies.** A publication issued once a year.

yearn (yûrn) *intr.v.* **yearned, yearn•ing, yearns. 1.** To have a strong, often melancholy desire. **2.** To feel deep pity, sympathy, or tenderness. [ME *yernen* < OE *geornan, giernan.* See **gher-**[2]***.**] —**yearn′er** *n.* —**yearn′ing•ly** *adv.*

yearn•ing (yûr′nĭng) *n.* A persistent, often wistful or melancholy desire; a longing.

year-round (yîr′round′) *adj.* Existing, active, or continuous throughout the year: *a year-round resort.*

yea-say•er (yā′sā′ər) *n.* **1.** One who is confidently affirmative in attitude. **2.** One who uncritically agrees.

yeast (yēst) *n.* **1.a.** Any of various unicellular fungi of the genus *Saccharomyces,* esp. *S. cerevisiae,* reproducing by budding and from ascospores and capable of fermenting carbohydrates. **b.** Any of various similar fungi. **2.** Froth consisting of yeast cells together with the carbon dioxide they produce in the process of fermentation, present in or added to fruit juices and other substances in the production of alcoholic beverages. **3.** A commercial preparation in either powdered or compressed form, containing yeast cells and inert material such as meal and used esp. as a leavening agent or as a dietary supplement. **4.** Foam; froth. **5.** An agent of ferment or activity. —*intr.v.* **yeast•ed, yeast•ing, yeasts. 1.** To ferment. **2.** To froth or foam. [ME *yeest* < OE *gist.* See **yes-*.**]

yeast•y (yē′stē) *adj.* **-i•er, -i•est. 1.** Of, similar to, or containing yeast. **2.** Causing or characterized by unrest or agitation; turbulent. **3.** Frothy; frivolous: *a yeasty comedy.* **4.** Full of productivity or vitality; exuberantly creative. —**yeast′i•ly** *adv.* —**yeast′i•ness** *n.*

Yeats (yāts), **William Butler.** 1865–1939. Irish writer who won the 1923 Nobel Prize for literature. —**Yeats′i•an** *adj.*

yech or **yecch** (yĕkн, yŭkн, yĕk) *interj.* Used to express contempt or disgust. [Imit.]

yegg (yĕg) *n. Slang.* A thief, esp. a burglar or safecracker. [?]

Ye•ka•te•rin•burg (yĭ-kăt′ər-ĭn-bûrg′). See **Sverdlovsk.**

yel. *abbr. Color.* Yellow.

yell (yĕl) *v.* **yelled, yell•ing, yells.** —*intr.* To cry out loudly, as in pain, fright, surprise, or enthusiasm. —*tr.* To utter or express with a loud cry; shout. See Syns at **shout.** —*n.* **1.** A loud cry; a shout. **2.** A rhythmic cheer uttered or chanted in unison by a group. [ME *yellen* < OE *giellan, geilan.* See **ghel-**[1]*.] —**yell′er** *n.*

yel•low (yĕl′ō) *n.* **1.a.** *Color.* The hue of that portion of the visible spectrum lying between orange and green, evoked in the human observer by radiant energy with wavelengths of approx. 570 to 590 nanometers; any of a group of colors of a hue resembling that of ripe lemons; one of the subtractive primaries; one of the psychological primary hues. **b.** A pigment or dye having this hue. **c.** Something that has this hue. **2.** *Chiefly Southern U.S.* The yolk of an egg. **3.** *Western U.S.* Gold. Used formerly by prospectors. **4. yellows.** Any of various plant diseases usu. caused by fungi of the genus *Fusarium* or viruses of the genus *Chlorogenus* and characterized by yellow or yellowish discoloration. —*adj.* **-er, -est. 1.** *Color.* Of the color yellow. **2.a.** Having a yellow-brown skin color. **b.** *Offensive.* Of or being a person of Asian origin. **3.** *Slang.* Cowardly. —*tr. & intr.v.* **-lowed, -low•ing, -lows.** To make or become yellow. [ME *yelow* < OE *geolu.* See **ghel-**[2]*.] —**yel′low•ness** *n.*

yel•low-bel•lied (yĕl′ō-bĕl′ēd) *adj.* **1.** Having a belly that is yellow or yellowish. Used of certain birds, for example. **2.** *Slang.* Cowardly. —**yel′low-bel′ly** *n.*

yellow-bellied sapsucker *n.* A showy sapsucker *(Sphyrapicus varius)* having a yellowish belly and in the male a bright scarlet crown and throat.

yellow bile *n. Archaic.* Choler.

yellow birch *n.* A North American deciduous tree *(Betula alleghaniensis)* having aromatic twigs, yellowish bark, and hard light-colored wood used for furniture and flooring.

yel•low•bird (yĕl′ō-bûrd′) *n.* Any of various yellow or mostly yellow birds, such as the yellow warbler.

yel•low•cake (yĕl′ō-kāk′) *n.* The concentrated oxide of uranium formed in the milling of uranium ore.

yel•low-dog contract (yĕl′ō-dôg′, -dŏg′) *n.* An employer-employee contract, no longer legal, by which the employee agrees not to join a union while employed.

yellow fever *n.* An infectious tropical disease caused by an arbovirus transmitted by mosquitoes of the genera *Aedes,* esp. *A. aegypti,* and *Haemagogus,* characterized by high fever and jaundice.

yel•low-fe•ver mosquito (yĕl′ō-fē′vər) *n.* See **aedes.**

yel•low•fin tuna (yĕl′ō-fĭn′) *n.* A tuna *(Thunnus albacares)* with bright yellow fins and many scales, found in warm parts of the Atlantic and Pacific oceans.

yel•low-green alga (yĕl′ō-grēn′) *n.* An alga of the division Chrysophyta, plastids of which contain golden yellow pigments that mask the chlorophyll.

yel•low•ham•mer (yĕl′ō-hăm′ər) *n.* **1.** A small bunting *(Emberiza citrinella)* of Europe and western Asia having bright yellow plumage on the head, neck, and breast. **2.** See **yellow-shafted flicker.** [By folk ety. < earlier *yelambre,* perh. < ME **yelwambre* : *yelow,* yellow; see YELLOW + OE *amore,* a kind of bird.]

yel•low•ish (yĕl′ō-ĭsh) *adj. Color.* Somewhat yellow; tinged with yellow. —**yel′low•ish•ness** *n.*

yellow jack *n.* **1.** A yellowish-silver carangid food fish *(Caranx bartholomaei)* of western Atlantic and Caribbean waters. **2.** *Naut.* A yellow flag hoisted on a ship to request pratique or warn of disease on board. **3.** See **yellow fever.**

yellow jacket *n.* Any of several small social wasps of the family Vespidae, having yellow and black markings.

yellow jessamine *n.* See **Carolina jasmine.**

yellow journalism *n.* Journalism that exploits, distorts, or exaggerates the news to create sensations. [< the use of yellow ink in printing "Yellow Kid," a cartoon strip in the *New York World,* a newspaper noted for sensationalism.]

Yel•low•knife (yĕl′ō-nīf′). The cap. of Northwest Terrs., Canada, on the N shore of Great Slave Lake; founded in 1935 and the provincial cap. since 1967. Pop. 9,483.

yel•low•legs (yĕl′ō-lĕgz′) *n., pl.* **yellowlegs.** Either of two North American wading birds *(Tringa melanoleuca* or *T. flavipes)* having yellow legs and a long narrow bill.

yellow ocher *n.* **1.** A yellow pigment, usu. containing limonite. **2.** *Color.* A moderate orange with yellow overtones.

yellow pages or **Yellow Pages** *pl.n.* A volume or section of a telephone directory listing businesses, services, or products alphabetically by field. [Usu. printed on yellow paper.]

yellow perch *n.* A North American perch *(Perca flavescens)* having golden yellow sides marked by dark vertical bars.

yellow peril or **Yellow Peril** *n. Offensive.* Threatened expansion of Asian populations as imagined in the West.

yellow pine *n.* **1.** See **shortleaf pine. 2.** See **longleaf pine. 3.** The wood of either of these pines.

yellow poplar *n.* The tulip tree.

yellow rain *n.* A powdery poisonous yellow substance reported as dropping from the air in southeast Asia and found to be the excrement of wild honeybees contaminated by a fungal toxin.

Yellow River. See **Huang He.**

Yellow Sea. An arm of the Pacific between the Chinese mainland and the Korean Peninsula.

yel•low-shaft•ed flicker (yĕl′ō-shăf′tĭd) *n.* A large woodpecker *(Colaptes auratus)* of eastern North America having a black crescent on the breast, a conspicuous white rump, and yellow shafts in the wing and tail feathers.

yellow spot *n.* See **macula lutea.**

Yel•low•stone (yĕl′ō-stōn′). A river, c. 1,080 km (671 mi), of NW WY and S and E MT flowing through **Yellowstone Lake** and **Yellowstone National Park** to the Missouri R.

yel•low•tail (yĕl′ō-tāl′) *n.* **1.** Any of several large marine game fishes of the genus *Seriola,* having a yellow or yellowish tail. **2.** Any of several other fishes having a yellowish tail, as the silver perch.

yel•low•throat (yĕl′ō-thrōt′) *n.* Any of several small New World warblers of the genus *Geothlypis,* esp. *G. trichas,* having a yellow throat and a black facial mask in the male.

yel•low-throat•ed warbler (yĕl′ō-thrō′tĭd) *n.* A warbler *(Dendroica dominica)* of the southern United States having a gray back, yellow throat and breast, and a white belly.

yellow warbler *n.* A small New World warbler *(Dendroica petechia)* having mostly yellow plumage with chestnut streaks along the sides.

yel•low•wood (yĕl′ō-wo͝od′) *n.* **1.a.** A deciduous tree *(Cladrastis lutea)* of southeast North America having drooping clusters of white flowers and wood yielding a yellow dye. **b.** This wood. **2.** Any of various trees having yellow wood.

yel•low•y (yĕl′ō-ē) *adj.* Somewhat yellow; yellowish.

yelp (yĕlp) *v.* **yelped, yelp•ing, yelps.** —*intr.* To utter a short sharp bark or cry. —*tr.* To utter by yelping. —*n.* A short sharp cry or bark. [ME *yelpen,* to cry aloud < OE *gelpan, gielpan,* to boast. See **ghel-**[1]*.] —**yelp′er** *n.*

Yel•tsin (yĕlt′sĭn), **Boris Nikolayevich.** b. 1931. Russian politician who was elected president of the republic of Russia in 1991.

Yem•en (yĕm′ən, yā′mən). A country of SW Asia at the S tip of Arabia; formed when Yemen (or North Yemen) merged with Southern Yemen in May 1990. Cap. Sana. Pop. 8,959,000. —**Yem′en•ite′, Yem′e•ni** (-ə-nē) *adj. & n.*

yen[1] (yĕn) *n.* A strong desire or inclination; a yearning or craving. —*intr.v.* **yenned, yen•ning, yens.** To have a yen. [Cantonese *yem.*]

yen[2] (yĕn) *n., pl.* **yen.** See table at **currency.** [J. *en* < Chin. (Mandarin) *yuán,* dollar.]

Ye•ni•sei (yĕn′ĭ-sā′, yĭ-nĭ-syā′). A river of central Russia flowing c. 4,023 km (2,500 mi) to the Kara Sea through **Yenisei Bay,** a long estuary.

yen•ta (yĕn′tə) *n. Slang.* A person, esp. a woman, who is regarded as meddlesome or gossipy. [Yiddish *yente,* back-formation < the woman's name *Yente,* alteration of *Yentl* < OItal. *Gentile* < *gentile,* amiable, highborn < Lat. *gentilis,* of the same clan. See GENTLE.]

yeo. *abbr.* Yeoman; yeomanry.

yeo•man (yō′mən) *n.* **1.a.** An attendant, a servant, or a lesser official in a royal or noble household. **b.** A yeoman of the guard. **2.** A petty officer performing chiefly clerical duties in the U.S. Navy. **3.** An assistant or other subordinate, as of a sheriff. **4.** A diligent dependable worker. **5.** A farmer who cultivates his own land, esp. a member of a former class of small freeholding farmers in England. —*adj.* **1.** Of, relating to, or ranking as a yeoman. **2.** Sturdy, staunch, or workmanlike: *yeoman service.* [ME *yoman,* perh. < OE **gēaman* < Old Frisian *gāman,* villager.]

yeoman of the guard *n., pl.* **yeomen of the guard.** A member of a ceremonial guard attending the British sovereign and royal family and also guarding the Tower of London.

yeo•man•ry (yō′mən-rē) *n., pl.* **-ries. 1.** The class of yeomen; small freeholding farmers. **2.** A British volunteer cavalry force organized in 1761 to serve as a home guard and later incorporated into the Territorial Army.

yep (yĕp) *adv. Informal.* Yes. [Alteration of YES.]

yer•ba ma•té or **yer•ba ma•te** (yâr′bə mä′tā, yûr′bə mä-tā′) *n.* See **maté** 2. [Am.Sp. *yerba mate* : *yerba,* herb + *mate,* maté.]

Ye•re•van also **E•re•van** or **E•ri•van** (yĕ′rĭ-vän′). The cap. of Armenia, in the W-central part. Pop. 1,133,000.

Yer•kes (yûr′kēz), **Charles Tyson.** 1837–1905. Amer. financier whose syndicate developed the Chicago transit system.

Yerkes, Robert Mearns. 1876–1956. Amer. psychobiologist who studied the intelligence of humans and primates.

yes (yĕs) *adv.* It is so; as you say or ask. Used to express affirmation, agreement, positive confirmation, or consent. —*n., pl.* **yes•es. 1.** An affirmative or consenting reply. **2.** An af-

yellow jacket
Vespula maculifrons

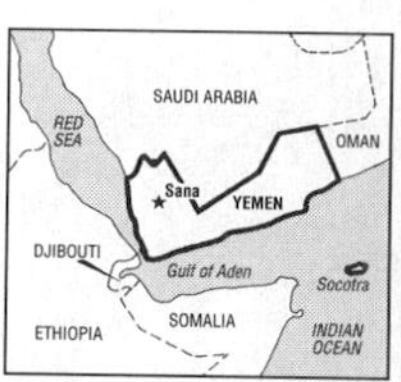

Yemen

ă **pat**	oi **boy**
ā **pay**	ou **out**
âr **care**	o͝o **took**
ä **father**	o͞o **boot**
ĕ **pet**	ŭ **cut**
ē **be**	ûr **urge**
ĭ **pit**	th **thin**
ī **pie**	*th* **this**
îr **pier**	hw **which**
ŏ **pot**	zh **vision**
ō **toe**	ə **a**bout,
ô **paw**	it**e**m

Stress marks:
′ (primary);
′ (secondary), as in
dictionary (dĭk′shə-nĕr′ē)

firmative vote or voter. — *tr.v.* **yessed, yes•sing, yes•es.** To give an affirmative reply to. [ME < OE *gēse*, so be it! : prob. *gēa*, so; see **i-*** + *sīe*, may it be so; see **es-***.]

ye•shi•va or **ye•shi•vah** (yə-shē′və) *n. Judaism.* **1.** An institute of learning where students study sacred texts. **2.** An elementary or secondary school with a curriculum that includes religion and culture. [Heb. *yĕšîbâ* < *yāšab*, to sit down.]

yes man *n. Informal.* One who slavishly agrees with a superior; a sycophant.

yester– *pref.* Yesterday: *yestermorning.* [ME < OE *geostran.* See **dhgh(y)es-***.]

yes•ter•day (yĕs′tər-dā′, -dē) *n.* **1.** The day before the present day. **2.** Also **yesterdays.** Time in the past, esp. the recent past. — *adv.* **1.** On the day before the present day. **2.** A short while ago. [ME < OE *geostran dæg* : *geostran*, yesterday; see YESTER– + *dæg*, day; see DAY.]

yes•ter•eve•ning (yĕs′tər-ēv′nĭng) also **yes•ter•eve** (-ēv′) or **yes•ter•e•ven** (-ē′vən) *n.* The evening of yesterday. — **yes′ter•eve′ning** *adv.*

yes•ter•morn•ing (yĕs′tər-môr′nĭng) also **yes•ter•morn** (-môrn′) *n.* Yesterday morning. — **yes′ter•morn′ing** *adv.*

yes•ter•night (yĕs′tər-nīt′) *n.* Last night. — **yes′ter•night′** *adv.*

yes•ter•year (yĕs′tər-yîr′) *n.* **1.** The year before the present year. **2.** Time past; yore. — **yes′ter•year′** *adv.*

yes•treen (yĕs-trēn′) *n. Scots.* Yesterday evening.

yet (yĕt) *adv.* **1.** At this time; for the present: *isn't ready yet.* **2.** Up to a specified time; thus far: *The end had not yet come.* **3.** At a future time; eventually: *may yet change his mind.* **4.** Besides; in addition: *returned for yet another helping.* **5.** Still more; even: *a yet sadder tale.* **6.** Nevertheless: *young yet wise.* — *conj.* And despite this; nevertheless: *She said she would be late, yet she arrived on time.* — ***idiom.*** **as yet.** Up to the present time; up to now. [ME < OE *gīet*, *gēt*. See **i-***.]

Usage Note: In formal style *yet* in the sense "up to now" requires that the accompanying verb be in the present perfect, rather than in the simple past: *He hasn't started yet,* not *He didn't start yet.*

yew

ye•ti (yĕt′ē) *n., pl.* **-tis.** See **abominable snowman.** [Alteration of Tibetan *miti* : *mi*, person + *ti*, a kind of animal.]

Yev•tu•shen•ko (yĕv′tə-shĕng′kō, yĭf-to͞o-shĕn′kə), **Yevgeny Aleksandrovich.** b. 1933. Soviet poet whose works include "Babi Yar" (1961).

yew (yo͞o) *n.* **1.** Any of several poisonous evergreen trees or shrubs of the genus *Taxus,* having scarlet cup-shaped seeds and flat needles. **2.** Their wood. [ME < OE *īw.*]

Ygg•dra•sil also **Yg•dra•sil** (ĭg′drə-sĭl, üg′-) *n. Myth.* In Norse mythology, the great ash tree that holds together earth, heaven, and hell by its roots and branches.

YHWH also **YHVH** or **JHVH** or **JHWH** (yo͝od′hä′väv′hä′, yä′wā, yä′wĕ) *n.* A transliteration of the Tetragrammaton.

yid (yĭd) *n. Offensive Slang.* Used as a disparaging term for a Jew. [Yiddish < MHGer. *jüde.* See YIDDISH.]

Yid•dish (yĭd′ĭsh) *n.* The language historically of Ashkenazic Jews of Central and Eastern Europe, resulting from a fusion of elements derived principally from medieval German dialects and secondarily from Hebrew and Aramaic, various Slavic languages, and Old French and Old Italian. [Yiddish *yidish*, Jewish, Yiddish < MHGer. *jüdisch*, Jewish < *jude, jüde*, Jew < OHGer. *judo* < Lat. *Jūdaeus.* See JEW.] — **Yid′dish** *adj.* — **Yid′dish•ism** *n.*

yield (yēld) *v.* **yield•ed, yield•ing, yields.** — *tr.* **1.a.** To give forth by or as if by a natural process, esp. by cultivation. **b.** To furnish as return for effort or investment; be productive of. **2.a.** To give over possession of, as in deference or defeat; surrender. **b.** To give up (an advantage, for example) to another; concede. — *intr.* **1.a.** To give forth a natural product; be productive. **b.** To produce a return for effort or investment. **2.a.** To give up, as in defeat; surrender or submit. **b.** To give way to pressure or force. **c.** To give way to argument, persuasion, influence, or entreaty. **d.** To give place, as to one that is superior. — *n.* **1.a.** An amount yielded or produced; a product. **b.** A profit obtained from an investment; a return. **2.** The energy released by a nuclear explosion, expressed in units of weight of TNT required to produce an equivalent release. [ME *yielden* < OE *geldan*, to pay.] — **yield′er** *n.*

Syns: *yield, bow, defer, submit, succumb.* These verbs all mean to give in to what one can no longer oppose or resist. *Yield* has the widest application: *"The child . . . soon yielded to the drowsiness"* (Charles Dickens). *Bow* suggests giving way in defeat or through courtesy: *"Bow and accept the end/ Of a love"* (Robert Frost). To *defer* is to yield out of respect or in recognition of another's authority, knowledge, or judgment: *"Philip . . . had the good sense to defer to the long experience and the wisdom of his father"* (William Hickling Prescott). *Submit* implies giving way out of necessity, as after futile or unsuccessful resistance: *"obliged to submit to those laws which are imposed upon us"* (Abigail Adams). *Succumb* strongly suggests submission to something overpowering or overwhelming: *"I didn't succumb without a struggle to my uncle's allurements"* (H.G. Wells). See also Syns at **produce, relinquish.**

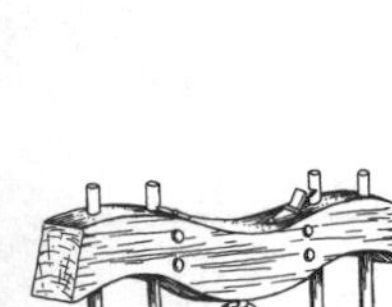

yoke

yield•ing (yēl′dĭng) *adj.* Inclined to give way to pressure, argument, or influence; docile. — **yield′ing•ness** *n.*

yin (yĭn) *n.* The passive, female cosmic principle in Chinese dualistic philosophy. [Chin. (Mandarin) *yīn*, moon, shade, femininity.]

Yin•chuan also **Yin•chwan** (yĭn′chwän′). A city of N-central China WSW of Beijing; cap. of Ningxia Hiuzu province. Pop. 200,000.

yip (yĭp) *n.* A sharp high-pitched bark; a yelp. — *intr.v.* **yipped, yip•ping, yips.** To emit a yip. [Perh. ME *yippe*, a cheeping sound < *yippen*, to cheep, of imit. orig.]

yipe (yīp) also **yipes** (yīps) *interj. Informal.* Used to express surprise, fear, or dismay.

yip•pee (yĭp′ē) *interj. Informal.* Used to express joy or elation.

–yl *suff.* An organic acid radical: *carbonyl.* [Fr. *-yle* < Gk. *hulē*, wood, matter.]

y•lang-y•lang or **i•lang-i•lang** (ē′läng-ē′läng) *n.* **1.** An Asian tree *(Cananga odorata)* having fragrant greenish-yellow flowers that yield an oil used in perfumery. **2.** An oil or a perfume obtained from the flowers of this tree. [Tagalog *ilang-ilang.*]

y•lem (ī′ləm) *n.* A form of matter hypothesized by proponents of the big bang theory to have existed before the formation of the chemical elements. [ME, universal matter < OFr. *ilem* < Med.Lat. *hȳlem*, accusative of *hȳlē*, matter < Gk. *hulē.*]

YMCA or **Y.M.C.A.** *abbr.* Young Men's Christian Association.

YMHA or **Y.M.H.A.** *abbr.* Young Men's Hebrew Association.

yo (yō) *interj. Slang.* Used as a greeting or to attract someone's attention.

yob (yŏb) *n. Chiefly British.* A rowdy, destructive youth; a hooligan or ruffian. [Alteration of BOY (spelled backward).]

yock (yŏk, yŭk) *Slang.* — *intr.v.* **yocked, yock•ing, yocks.** To laugh or joke, esp. loudly. — *n.* A loud laugh or joke. [Imit.]

yo•del (yōd′l) *Mus.* — *v.* **-deled, -del•ing, -dels** or **-delled, -del•ling, -dels.** — *intr.* To sing so that the voice fluctuates rapidly between the normal chest voice and a falsetto. — *tr.* To sing (a song) by yodeling. — *n.* A song or cry that is yodeled. [Ger. *jodeln* < Ger. dial. *jo*, exclamation of delight, of imit. orig.] — **yo′del•er** *n.*

yodh (yo͝od, yôd) *n.* The tenth letter of the Hebrew alphabet. [Heb. *yôd* < *yād*, hand.]

yo•ga (yō′gə) *n.* **1.** Also **Yoga.** A Hindu discipline aimed at training the consciousness for a state of perfect spiritual insight and tranquillity. **2.** A system of exercises practiced as part of this discipline to promote control of the body and mind. [Skt. *yogaḥ*, union, joining. See **yeug-***.] — **yo′gic** (-gĭk) *adj.*

yogh (yōKH) *n.* The Middle English letter ȝ [ME, poss. < OE *īw, ēoh*, yew.]

yo•gi (yō′gē) *n., pl.* **-gis.** One who practices yoga. [Skt. *yogī* < *yogaḥ*, union. See YOGA.]

yo•gurt also **yo•ghurt** or **yo•ghourt** (yō′gərt) *n.* A custardlike tart-flavored food prepared from milk curdled by bacteria, esp. *Lactobacillus bulgaricus* and *Streptococcus thermophilus,* often sweetened or flavored. [Turk. *yoğurt.*]

Yog•ya•kar•ta (yŏg′yə-kär′tə, jôk′jä-, jŏk′yə-). See **Jogjakarta.**

yo•him•bine (yō-hĭm′bēn′) *n.* A poisonous alkaloid, $C_{21}H_{26}N_2O_3$, derived from the bark of a tree, *Corynanthe yohimbe,* and formerly used as an aphrodisiac, a local anesthetic, and a mydriatic. [NLat. *yohimbe*, specific epithet of *Corynanthe yohimbe*, species of tree from which it is derived (of Cameroonian Bantu orig.; akin to Duala *djombe*) + -INE[2].]

yoicks (yoiks) also **hoicks** (hoiks) *interj.* Used as a hunting cry to urge hounds after a fox.

yoke (yōk) *n.* **1.a.** A crossbar with two U-shaped pieces that encircle the necks of a pair of oxen or other draft animals working together. **b.** *pl.* **yoke** or **yokes.** A pair of draft animals, such as oxen, joined by a yoke. **c.** A bar used with a double harness to connect the collar of each horse to the pole of a wagon or coach. **2.** A frame designed to be carried across a person's shoulders with equal loads suspended from each end. **3.** *Naut.* A crossbar on a ship's rudder to which the steering cables are connected. **4.** A clamp or vise that holds a machine part in place or controls its movement or that holds two such parts together. **5.** A piece of a garment that is closely fitted, either around the neck and shoulders or at the hips, and from which an unfitted or gathered part of the garment is hung. **6.** Something that connects or joins together; a bond or tie. **7.** *Electron.* A series of two or more magnetic recording heads fastened securely together for playing or recording on more than one track simultaneously. **8.a.** Any of various emblems of subjugation, such as a structure made of two upright spears with a third laid across them, under which conquered enemies of ancient Rome were forced to march. **b.** The condition of being subjugated by or as if by a conqueror; subjugation or bondage. — *v.* **yoked, yok•ing, yokes.** — *tr.* **1.** To fit or join with a yoke. **2.a.** To harness a draft animal to. **b.** To harness (a draft animal) to a vehicle or an implement. **3.** To join securely as if with a yoke; bind. **4.** To force into heavy labor, bondage, or subjugation. — *intr.* To become joined securely. [ME < OE *geoc.* See **yeug-***.]

yo•kel (yō′kəl) *n.* A rustic; a bumpkin. [?]
Yo•ko•ha•ma (yō′kə-hä′mə, yô′kô-hä′mä). A city of SE Honshu, Japan, on W Tokyo Bay. Pop. 2,992,644.
Yo•ko•su•ka (yō′kə-so͞o′kə, yô′kô-so͞o′kä). A city of SE Honshu, Japan, on Tokyo Bay. Pop. 427,087.
Yo•kuts (yō′ko͝ots) *n., pl.* **Yokuts. 1.** A member of a group of Native American peoples inhabiting the southern San Joaquin Valley and adjacent foothills of the Sierra Nevada. **2.** Any or all of the languages of the Yokuts peoples.
yolk (yōk) *n.* **1.a.** The yellow, usu. spherical portion of an egg of a bird or reptile, surrounded by the albumen and serving as nutriment for the developing young. **b.** A corresponding portion of the egg of other animals, consisting of protein and fat that serve as the primary source of nourishment for the early embryo. **2.** A greasy substance found in unprocessed sheep's wool. [ME *yolke* < OE *geolca* < *geolu*, yellow. See YELLOW.] **—yolk′y** *adj.*
yolk sac *n.* A membranous sac attached to an embryo, enclosing yolk in bony fishes, sharks, reptiles, birds, and primitive mammals and functioning as the circulatory system of the human embryo before internal circulation begins.
yolk stalk *n.* A narrow ductlike part that connects the yolk sac to the middle of the digestive tract of an embryo.
Yom Kip•pur (yôm′ kĭp′ər, yōm′, yŏm′, yôm′ kē-po͝or′) *n. Judaism.* A holy day observed on the tenth day of Tishri and marked by fasting and prayer for the atonement of sins. [Heb. *yôm kippûr* : *yôm*, day + *kippûr*, atonement (< *kippēr*, to cover, atone).]
yon (yŏn) *adv. & adj.* Yonder. *—pron. Regional.* That one or those yonder. [ME, short for *yond*, yond; see YOND, and *yonder*, yonder; see YONDER. Pron., ME < OE *geon*. See **i-***.]
yond (yŏnd) *adv. & adj. Archaic.* Yonder. [ME < OE *geond*. See **i-***.]
yon•der (yŏn′dər) *adv.* In or at that indicated place: *the house over yonder.* *—adj.* Being at an indicated distance, usu. within sight. *—pron.* One that is at an indicated place, usu. within sight. [ME < *yond*, yond. See YOND.]
yo•ni (yō′nē) *n., pl.* **-nis.** *Hinduism.* A stylized vulva worshiped as a symbol of a goddess or Shakti. [Skt. *yoniḥ*, womb, abode, source.]
Yon•kers (yŏng′kərz). A city of SE NY N of New York City; settled by the Dutch in the mid-1600's. Pop. 188,082.
yoo-hoo (yo͞o′ho͞o′) *interj.* Used to call someone at a distance or to gain someone's attention.
Yor•ba Lin•da (yôr′bə lĭn′də). A city of S CA SE of Los Angeles. Pop. 52,422.
yore (yôr, yōr) *n.* Time long past: *days of yore.* [ME, long ago, time long past < OE *gēara*, *geāra*, long ago < genitive pl. of *gēar*, year. See YEAR.]
York¹ (Yôrk). Ruling house of England (1461–85), including Edward IV, Edward V, and Richard III. During the Wars of the Roses its symbol was a white rose. **—York′ist** *adj. & n.*
York². **1.** A borough of N England on the Ouse R. ENE of Leeds; orig. a Celtic settlement. Pop. 101,600. **2.** A city of S PA SSE of Harrisburg; settled in 1735. Pop. 42,192.
York, Alvin Cullum. "Sergeant York." 1887–1964. Amer. World War I hero famed for his single-handed attack on a German post.
York, Cape. 1. The northernmost point of Australia, on Torres Strait at the tip of Cape York Peninsula. **2.** A cape of NW Greenland in N Baffin Bay; used as a base by Robert E. Peary.
Yorke Peninsula (yôrk). A narrow peninsula of S Australia bounded by Spencer Gulf.
York River. An estuary, c. 64 km (40 mi), of E VA flowing SE into Chesapeake Bay.
York•shire (yôrk′shîr, -shər). A historical region and former county of N England; an important area during Roman times and later part of the kingdom of Northumbria.
Yorkshire pudding *n.* A popoverlike quick bread served with roast beef, made by baking a batter of eggs, flour, and milk in the drippings of the beef. [After YORKSHIRE.]
Yorkshire terrier *n.* Any of a breed of toy terrier developed in Yorkshire and having a long silky bluish-gray coat.
York•town (yôrk′toun′). A village of SE VA on the York R. N of Newport News; site of important battles during the American Revolution and the Civil War.
Yo•ru•ba (yôr′ə-bə, yō′ro͞o-bä′) *n., pl.* **Yoruba** or **-bas. 1.** A member of a West African people living chiefly in southwest Nigeria. **2.** Their South Central Niger-Congo language.
Yo•sem•i•te Valley (yō-sĕm′ĭ-tē). A valley of E-central CA along the Merced R. It is surrounded by **Yosemite National Park** and includes many noted waterfalls, such as **Yosemite Falls**, with a total drop of 739.6 m (2,425 ft).
Yo•shi•hi•to (yō′shĭ-hē′tō, yô′shē-hē′tô). 1879–1926. Emperor of Japan (1912–26).
you (yo͞o) *pron.* **1.** Used to refer to the one or ones being addressed: *I'll lend you the book.* See Regional Note at **you-all. 2.** Used to refer to an indefinitely specified person; one: *You can't win them all.* [ME < OE *ēow*, dative and accusative of *gē*, ye, you. See **yu-***.]
you-all (yo͞o′ôl′) also **y'all** (yôl) *pron. Chiefly Southern U.S.* You. Used when addressing two or more people or when referring to two or more people, one of whom is addressed.
Regional Note: The single most famous feature of southern United States dialects is the pronoun *you-all,* probably heard more often in its variant *y'all.* *You* and *you-all* preserve the singular/plural distinction that English used to have in *thou/you.* A single person may only be addressed as *you-all* if the speaker implies in the reference other persons not present: *Did you-all* (that is, you and others) *have dinner yet?*
you'd (yo͞od). **1.** You had. **2.** You would.
you'll (yo͞ol, yo͞ol; yəl *when unstressed*). **1.** You will. **2.** You shall.
young (yŭng) *adj.* **young•er, young•est. 1.** Being in an early period of life, development, or growth. **2.** Newly begun or formed; not advanced. **3.** Of, belonging to, or suggestive of youth or early life. **4.** Vigorous or fresh; youthful. **5.** Lacking experience; immature. **6.** Being the junior of two people having the same name. **7.** *Geol.* Being of an early stage in a geologic cycle. Used of bodies of water and land formations. *—n.* **1.** Young persons considered as a group; youth. **2.** Offspring; brood. **—*idiom.* with young.** Pregnant. [ME *yong* < OE *geong*. See **yeu-***.] **—young′ness** *n.*

Yorkshire terrier

Young (yŭng), **Andrew Jackson, Jr.** b. 1932. Amer. politician who was U.S. ambassador to the United Nations (1977–79) and mayor of Atlanta (1981–89).
Young, Brigham. 1801–77. Amer. religious leader who directed the Mormon Church after the assassination (1884) of its founder, Joseph Smith, and led an exodus of the Mormons from IL to the site of present-day Salt Lake City UT.
Young, Denton True ("Cy"). 1867–1955. Amer. baseball player who pitched the first perfect game (1904).
Young, Edward. 1683–1765. English poet known for *Night Thoughts on Life, Death, and Immortality* (1742–45).
Young, Lester Willis ("Pres"). 1909–59. Amer. jazz musician who greatly influenced jazz improvisation.
Young, Thomas. 1773–1829. British physician, physicist, and Egyptologist who helped decipher the Rosetta Stone.

Andrew Young
Photographed in the late 1980's

young•ber•ry (yŭng′bĕr′ē) *n.* **1.** A trailing prickly hybrid between a blackberry and a dewberry *(Rubus ursinus* cv. *Young)* of the rose family. **2.** The edible dark red berry of this plant. [After B.M. *Young* (fl. 1905), Amer. fruit grower.]
young•ish (yŭng′ĭsh) *adj.* Somewhat young.
young•ling (yŭng′lĭng) *n.* A young person, animal, or plant.
young•ster (yŭng′stər) *n.* **1.** A young person; a child or youth. **2.** A young animal. **3.** A member of the second-year class in the U.S. Naval Academy.
Youngs•town (yŭngz′toun′). A city of NE OH E of Akron. Pop. 95,732.
Young Turk *n.* **1.** A young progressive or insurgent member of a collective enterprise, such as a political party. **2.** A member of a Turkish reformist and nationalist political party active in the early 20th century. [After the *Young Turks*, a late 19th- and early 20th-cent. revolutionary party in Turkey.]
young•'un (yŭng′ən) *n. Informal.* A young one; a child.
youn•ker (yŭng′kər) *n.* **1.** A young man. **2.** A child. [Obsolete Du. *jonchere*, young nobleman < MDu. : *jonc*, young; see **yeu-*** + *here*, lord.]
your (yo͝or, yôr, yōr; yər *when unstressed*) *adj.* The possessive form of **you. 1.** Used as a modifier before a noun: *your boots.* **2.** A person's; one's: *The light switch is on your right.* **3.** *Informal.* Used with little or no sense of possession to indicate a type familiar to the listener: *your basic frame house.* [ME < OE *ēower*, genitive of *gē*, ye. See YOU.]
you're (yo͝or; yər *when unstressed*). You are.
yours (yo͝orz, yôrz, yōrz) *pron. (used with a sing. or pl. v.)* **1.** Used to indicate the one or ones belonging to you: *The larger boots are yours.* **2.** Used often with an adverbial modifier in the complimentary close of a letter: *Sincerely yours.* **—*idiom.* yours truly.** I, myself, or me. [ME < *your*, your. See YOUR.]

Brigham Young

your•self (yo͝or-sĕlf′, yôr-, yōr-, yər-) *pron., pl.* **-selves. 1.** That one identical with you. **a.** Used reflexively as the direct or indirect object of a verb or as the object of a preposition: *Did you buy yourself a gift?* **b.** Used for emphasis: *You yourself were certain of the facts.* **c.** Used in an absolute construction: *In office yourself, you helped push the bill along.* **2.** Your normal or healthy condition: *Are you feeling yourself again?* See Usage Note at **myself.**
your•selves (yo͝or-sĕlvz′, yôr-, yōr-, yər-) *pron.* Pl. of **yourself.** See Usage Note at **myself.**
youth (yo͞oth) *n., pl.* **youths** (yo͞oths, yo͞othz). **1.a.** The condition or quality of being young. **b.** An early period of development or existence. **2.** The time of life between childhood and maturity. **3.a.** A young person, esp. a young male in late adolescence. **b.** *(used with a sing. or pl. v.)* Young people considered as a group. **4.** *Geol.* The first stage in the erosion cycle. [ME *youthe* < OE *geoguth*. See **yeu-***.]
youth•ful (yo͞oth′fəl) *adj.* **1.** Characterized by youth; young. **2.** Of, relating to, or characteristic of youth. **3.** Marked by or possessing characteristics, such as vigor, freshness, or enthusiasm, that are associated with youth. **4.** In an early stage of development; new. **5.** *Geol.* Young: *a youthful streambed.* **—youth′ful•ly** *adv.* **—youth′ful•ness** *n.*

ă pat	oi boy
ā pay	ou out
âr care	o͝o took
ä father	o͞o boot
ĕ pet	ŭ cut
ē be	ûr urge
ĭ pit	th thin
ī pie	*th* this
îr pier	hw which
ŏ pot	zh vision
ō toe	ə about, item
ô paw	

Stress marks:
′ (primary);
′ (secondary), as in dictionary (dĭk′shə-nĕr′ē)

youth hostel *n.* A supervised inexpensive lodging place for young travelers.
you-uns (yo͞o′ənz) *pron. Upper Southern U.S.* You. Used in addressing two or more people. [YOU + dial. *uns*, people, var. of *ones*, pl. of ONE.]
you've (yo͞ov). You have.
yow (you) *interj.* Used to express alarm, pain, or surprise.
yowl (youl) *v.* **yowled, yowl•ing, yowls.** —*intr.* To utter a yowl. —*tr.* To say or utter with a yowl. —*n.* A long loud mournful cry; a wail. [ME *yowlen*, prob. of imit. origin.]
yo-yo (yō′yō′) *n., pl.* **-yos. 1.** A toy consisting of a flattened spool wound with string that is spun down from and reeled up to the hand by motions of the wrist. **2.** *Informal.* One that undergoes frequent shifts or reversals, as of opinion; a vacillator. **3.** *Slang.* A stupid or objectionable person. —*intr.v.* **-yoed, -yo•ing, -yos.** *Informal.* To undergo frequent shifts or reversals, as of opinion; vacillate. [Originally a trademark.]

yucca
Yucca rigida

Y•pres (ē′prə). See **leper.**
Yp•si•lan•ti (ĭp′sə-lăn′tē). A city of SE MI WSW of Detroit. Pop. 24,846.
Y•quem (ē-kĕm′) *n.* A sweet white wine from the Sauternes region of southwest France. [After Château d'*Yquem*, an estate in SW France.]
yr. *abbr.* **1.** Year. **2.** Younger. **3.** Your.
Y.T. *abbr.* Yukon Territory.
yt•ter•bi•um (ĭ-tûr′bē-əm) *n. Symbol* **Yb** A soft bright allotropic rare-earth element used as an x-ray source, in some laser materials, and in some special alloys. Atomic number 70; atomic weight 173.04; melting point 824°C; boiling point 1,196°C; specific gravity 6.972 or 6.54 (25°C) depending on allotropic form; valence 2, 3. See table at **element.** [After *Ytterby*, a town in Sweden.] —**yt•ter′bic** (-bĭk) *adj.*
yt•tri•a (ĭt′rē-ə) *n.* See **yttrium oxide.** [NLat., after *Ytterby*, a town in Sweden.]
yt•tri•um (ĭt′rē-əm) *n. Symbol* **Y** A metallic element, not a rare earth but occurring in nearly all rare-earth minerals, used in various alloys, esp. to strengthen magnesium and aluminum alloys. Atomic number 39; atomic weight 88.905; melting point 1,522°C; boiling point 3,338°C; specific gravity 4.45 (25°C); valence 3. See table at **element.** —**yt′tric** (ĭt′rĭk) *adj.*

yurt
In the Gobi Desert

yttrium oxide *n.* A yellowish powder, Y_2O_3, used in optical glasses, ceramics, and color-television tubes.
yu•an (yo͞o-än′, yüän) *n., pl.* **yuan** or **-ans.** See table at **currency.** [Chin. (Mandarin) *yuán*, dollar.]
Yu•an (yo͞o′än′, yüän). A Chinese dynasty (1271–1368) founded by Kublai Khan at Peking (Beijing).
Yuan Jiang (jyäng′). See **Red River** 1.
Yu•ba City (yo͞o′bə). A city of N-central CA N of Sacramento. Pop. 27,437.
Yu•cai•pa (yo͞o-kī′pə). A community of S CA in the foothills of the San Bernardino Mts. E of Los Angeles. Pop. 32,824.
Yu•ca•tán (yo͞o′kə-tăn′, -tän′). A peninsula mostly in SE Mexico between the Caribbean Sea and the Gulf of Mexico and separated from W Cuba by the **Yucatán Channel.**
Yuc•a•tec (yo͞o′kə-tĕk′) *n., pl.* **Yucatec** or **-tecs. 1.** A member of a Mayan people inhabiting the Yucatán Peninsula. **2.** The Mayan language of the Yucatec.
yuc•ca (yŭk′ə) *n.* Any of various evergreen plants of the genus *Yucca*, native to the warmer regions of North America and having often tall stout stems and white flowers. [< NLat. *Iucca*, genus name < Sp. *yuca*, cassava < Taino.]
Yu•chi (yo͞o′chē) *n., pl.* **Yuchi** or **-chis. 1.** A member of a Native American people formerly inhabiting northern Georgia and eastern Tennessee. **2.** Their language. [Prob. Cherokee *yutsi*.]
yuck (yŭk) *interj. Slang.* Used to express rejection or strong disgust.
yuck•y (yŭk′ē) *adj.* **-i•er, -i•est.** *Slang.* Repugnant; disgusting. —**yuck′i•ness** *n.*
Yug. *abbr.* Yugoslavian.
yu•ga (yo͝og′ə) *n. Hinduism.* One of the four ages constituting a cycle of history. [Skt. *yugam*, yoke, pair, era. See **yeug-*.**]
Yugo. *abbr.* Yugoslavian.
Yu•go•sla•vi•a (yo͞o′gō-slä′vē-ə). A country (since 1992) of SE Europe comprising Serbia and Montenegro. It was orig. formed in 1918 as the Kingdom of Serbs, Croats, and Slovenes and renamed Yugoslavia in 1929. After 1946 the country included six constituent republics, four of which declared independence in 1991. Cap. Belgrade. Pop. 12,098,779. —**Yu′go•sla′vi•an** *adj. & n.*
Yu•ka•wa (yo͞o-kä′wä), **Hideki.** 1907–81. Japanese physicist who won a 1949 Nobel Prize.
Yu•kon (yo͞o′kŏn′). A city of central OK W of Oklahoma City. Pop. 20,935.
Yukon River. A river flowing c. 3,218 km (2,000 mi) from S Yukon Terr., Canada, through AK to the Bering Sea; a major route to the Klondike during the gold rush of 1897–98.
Yukon Territory. A territory of NW Canada E of AK; joined the Confederacy in 1898. Cap. Whitehorse. Pop. 23,153.
Yukon Time *n.* Alaska Standard Time.
Yule (yo͞ol) *n.* Christmas, or the season or feast celebrating Christmas. [ME *yole* < OE *geōl*.]
yule log (yo͞ol) *n.* A large log traditionally burned in a fireplace at Christmas.
Yule•tide (yo͞ol′tīd′) *n.* The Christmas season.
Yu•ma[1] (yo͞o′mə) *n., pl.* **Yuma** or **-mas. 1.** A member of a Native American people inhabiting an area along the lower Colorado River. **2.** Their Yuman language. [Sp. < Papago *yuumi*.]
Yu•ma[2] (yo͞o′mə). A city of SW AZ on the Colorado R. and the CA border. Pop. 54,923.
Yu•man (yo͞o′mən) *n.* A language family constituting the languages of the Yuma and Mohave peoples and other Native American languages of western Arizona and adjacent parts of California and Mexico. —**Yu′man** *adj.*
yum•my (yŭm′ē) *adj.* **-mi•er, -mi•est. 1.** Very pleasing to the taste or smell; delicious. **2.** Delightful; delicious. [< *yum*, the sound of smacking the lips.] —**yum′mi•ness** *n.*
Yun•nan (yo͞o′nän′). A province of S-central China bordering on Vietnam, Laos, and Burma; became part of China in the 17th cent. Cap. Kunming. Pop. 34,060,000.
Yu•pik (yo͞o′pĭk) *n., pl.* **Yupik** or **-piks. 1.** A member of a group of Eskimoan peoples inhabiting coastal areas of western Alaska and northeast Siberia. **2.** The group of Eskimoan languages spoken by the Yupik.
yup•pie also **Yup•pie** (yŭp′ē) *n. Informal.* A young city or suburban resident with a well-paid job and a materialistic lifestyle. [Y(OUNG) + U(RBAN) + P(ROFESSIONAL), influenced by *yippie*, politically active hippie.] —**yup′pie•dom** *n.*
Yu•rok (yo͝or′ŏk) *n., pl.* **Yurok** or **-roks. 1.** A member of a Native American people inhabiting northwest California along the Pacific coast and lower Klamath River. **2.** The language of this people.
yurt (yûrt) *n.* A circular domed portable tent used by the nomadic Mongols of central Asia. [Russ. *yurta*, of Turkic orig.]
YWCA or **Y.W.C.A.** *abbr.* Young Women's Christian Association.
YWHA or **Y.W.H.A.** *abbr.* Young Women's Hebrew Association.
y•wis (ĭ-wĭs′) *adv.* Var. of **iwis.**

Z z

Zaire

z or **Z** (zē) *n., pl.* **z's** or **Z's. 1.** The 26th letter of the modern English alphabet. **2.** Any of the speech sounds represented by the letter *z*. **3.** The 26th in a series. **4.** Something shaped like the letter Z.
Z 1. The symbol for **atomic number. 2.** The symbol for **impedance.**
z. *abbr.* **1.** Zero. **2.** Zone.
Zaan•dam (zän-dăm′, -däm′). A city of W Netherlands WNW of Amsterdam. Pop. 128,413.
za•ba•glio•ne (zä′bəl-yō′nē, -bäl-yô′nĕ) *n.* A dessert or sauce consisting of egg yolks, sugar, and wine beaten until thick. [Ital., var. of *zabaione*, ult. < Illyrian *sabaium*, beer.]
Zab•rze (zäb′zhĕ). A city of S-central Poland W of Katowice; founded in the 13th cent. Pop. 198,000.
Zach•a•rias (zăk′ə-rī′əs) also **Zech•a•ri•ah** (zĕk′ə-rī′ə). In the Bible, the father of John the Baptist.
zaf•fer also **zaf•fre** (zăf′ər) *n.* An impure oxide of cobalt, used to produce a blue color in enamel and in the making of smalt. [Ital. *zaffera* < OFr. *safre*, perh. alteration of *safir*, sapphire; see SAPPHIRE or < Ar. *ṣufr*, yellow copper, brass.]
zaf•tig or **zof•tig** (zăf′tĭk, -tĭg) *adj.* **1.** Full-bosomed. **2.** Having a full shapely figure. [Yiddish *zaftik*, juicy < MHGer. *saftec* < *saft*, juice < OHGer. *saf*.]
zag (zăg) *n.* One of a series of sharp turns or reversals: *zigs and zags.* —*intr.v.* **zagged, zag•ging, zags. 1.** To turn or change direction suddenly. Usu. used in contrast to *zig*: *The runner zigged when he should have zagged.* **2.** To behave erratically or indecisively. Usu. used with *zig*. [< ZIGZAG.]
Za•gorsk (zə-gôrsk′). A city of W-central Russia NE of Moscow; on the site of a monastery built in 1340. Pop. 112,000.
Za•greb (zä′grĕb). The cap. of Croatia, in the N part on the Sava R. Pop. 768,700.

Zag•ros Mountains (zăg′rəs). A range of W Iran forming the W and S borders of the central Iranian plateau and rising to 4,550.6 m (14,920 ft).

Za•har•i•as (zə-hăr′ē-əs), **Mildred Ella Didrikson.** See Mildred Ella **Didrikson.**

zai•bat•su (zī′bät-so͞o′) *n.*, *pl.* **zaibatsu. 1.** A powerful family-controlled commercial combine of Japan. **2.** A Japanese conglomerate or cartel. [J. : *zai*, wealth (< Chin. *cái*) + *batsu*, powerful person or family (< Chin. *fá*).]

zaire (zī′îr, zä-îr′) *n.* See table at **currency.** [Port., the Congo River < Kongo *n-zadi*, large river.]

Zaire (zī′îr, zä-îr′). Formerly (1885–1908) **Con•go Free State** (kŏng′gō) and (1908–60) **Bel•gian Congo** (bĕl′jən) and (1960–71) **Congo.** A country of central Africa astride the equator; achieved full independence from Belgium in 1960. Cap. Kinshasa. Pop. 29,671,407. **—Za•ir′e•an, Za•ir′i•an** *adj.* & *n.*

Zaire River. See **Congo River.**

za•kat (zə-kät′) *n.* The alms tax required of all Muslims by the sharī'a.

Za•ma (zā′mə, zä′mä). An ancient town of N Africa SW of Carthage in present-day N Tunisia; site of the Roman defeat of Hannibal, which ended the Second Punic War (202 B.C.).

Zam•be•zi (zăm-bē′zē). A river of central and S Africa rising in NW Zambia and flowing c. 2,735 km (1,700 mi) to the Mozambique Channel.

Zam•bi•a (zăm′bē-ə). A country of S-central Africa; gained independence from Great Britain in 1964. Cap. Lusaka. Pop. 5,661,801. **—Zam′bi•an** *adj.* & *n.*

za•mi•a (zā′mē-ə) *n.* Any of various chiefly tropical American cycads of the genus *Zamia*, having a thick trunk, palmlike terminal leaves, and seeds borne in woody cones. [NLat. *Zamia*, genus name < misreading of *(nucēs) azāniae*, pine cone (nuts), prob. < Gk. *azainein*, to dry up < *azein*, to dry. See **as-*.**]

zam•in•dar also **zem•in•dar** (zăm′ən-där′, zĕm′-, zə-mēn-där′) *n.* **1.** An official in precolonial India assigned to collect the land taxes of his district. **2.** A landholder in British colonial India responsible for collecting and paying to the government the taxes on the land under his jurisdiction. [Hindi *zamīndār* < Pers. : *zamīn*, earth; see **dhghem-*** + *-dār*, -holder; see **dher-*.**]

zan•der (zăn′dər) *n.*, *pl.* **zander** or **-ders.** A common European pikeperch *(Stizostedion lucioperca)* valued as a food fish. [Ger. < LGer. *Sander.*]

Zanes•ville (zānz′vĭl′). A city of E-central Ohio E of Columbus; a former state cap. (1810–12). Pop. 26,778.

Zan•gwill (zăng′gwĭl′, -wĭl′), **Israel.** 1864–1926. British writer whose works include *Children of the Ghetto* (1892).

za•ny (zā′nē) *n.*, *pl.* **-nies. 1.** A comic performer who assists or imitates a clown, acrobat, or mountebank. **2.** A comical person given to extravagant or outlandish behavior. *—adj.* **-ni•er, -ni•est. 1.** Ludicrously comical; clownish. **2.** Comical because of incongruity or strangeness; bizarre. [Fr. *zani* < Ital. dial. *zanni* < *Zanni*, var. of Ital. *Gianni*, nickname for *Giovanni*, John, the name of servants who act as clowns in commedia dell'arte.] **—za′ni•ly** *adv.* **—za′ni•ness** *n.*

Zan•zi•bar (zăn′zə-bär′). **1.** A region of E Africa, comprising **Zanzibar Island** and several adjacent islands; became an independent sultanate in 1963 and in 1964 joined Tanganyika to form Tanzania. **2.** A city of Tanzania on the W coast of Zanzibar I.; founded in the 16th cent. Pop. 110,699.

zap (zăp) *Slang.* *—v.* **zapped, zap•ping, zaps.** *—tr.* **1.a.** To destroy or kill with a burst of gunfire, flame, or electric current. **b.** To kill or destroy as if by shooting. **c.** To strike suddenly and forcefully as if with a projectile or weapon. **d.** To expose to radiation; irradiate. **2.** To attack (an enemy) with heavy firepower; strafe or bombard. **3.** To use a remote control device to switch (channels on a television) or to turn off (a television set). *—intr.* To move swiftly; zoom. *—n.* Something that imparts excitement or great interest. *—interj.* **1.** Used to imitate a sound made by a gun when fired. **2.** Used to indicate a sudden occurrence. [Imit.]

Za•pa•ta (zə-pä′tə, sä-pä′tä), **Emiliano.** 1879?–1919. Mexican revolutionary who led an agrarian revolt (1910–19).

za•pa•te•a•do (zä′pə-tä-ä′dō, thä′pä-tä-ä′*th*ô, sä′-) *n.*, *pl.* **-dos.** A Spanish flamenco dance in which the performer stamps and taps rhythmically with the heels. [Sp. < *zapatear*, to tap with the shoe < *zapato*, shoe.]

Za•po•pan (zä′pō-pän′, sä′pô-). A city of SW Mexico W of Guadalajara. Pop. 345,390.

Za•po•ro•zhe (zä′pə-rô′zhə, zə-pə-rô′zhyĕ). Formerly **A•lek•san•drovsk** (ăl′ĭk-săn′drəfsk, ə-lĭk-sän′-). A city of S Ukraine W of Donetsk; founded 1770. Pop. 852,000.

Za•po•tec (zä′pə-tĕk′, sä′pô-) *n.*, *pl.* **Zapotec** or **-tecs. 1.a.** A member of a Mesoamerican Indian people of southern Mexico, whose civilization reached its height around A.D. 300–900. **b.** A modern-day descendant of this people. **2.** Any of a group of related languages spoken in southern Mexico. [Sp. *Zapoteco* < Nahuatl *tzapotēcah*, pl. of *tzapotēcatl*, person from Tzapotlan < *Tzapotlān*, place name : *tzapotl*, sapodilla + *tlān*, place.] **—Za′po•tec′** *adj.*

zap•py (zăp′ē) *adj.* **-pi•er, -pi•est.** *Slang.* Lively.

Za•ra•go•za (zăr′ə-gō′zə, thä′rä-gô′thä). See **Saragossa.**

Zar•a•thu•stra (zăr′ə-tho͞o′strə). See **Zoroaster.**

za•re•ba also **za•ree•ba** (zə-rē′bə) *n.* **1.** An enclosure of bushes or stakes protecting a campsite or village in northeast Africa. **2.** A campsite or village protected by such an enclosure. [Ar. *zarībah*, pen for cattle.]

zarf (zärf) *n.* A chalicelike holder for a hot coffee cup, typically made of ornamented metal, used in the Middle East. [Ar. *ẓarf*, container.]

zas•tru•ga (ză-stro͞o′gə, zä-) *n.* Var. of **sastruga.**

z-ax•is (zē′ăk′sĭs) *n.*, *pl.* **z-ax•es** (zē′ak′sēz). *Math.* One of three axes in a three-dimensional Cartesian coordinate system.

za•yin (zä′yĭn) *n.* The seventh letter of the Hebrew alphabet. [Heb. < Aram.]

Zc *abbr. Bible.* Zechariah.

zeal (zēl) *n.* Enthusiastic devotion to a cause, an ideal, or a goal and tireless diligence in its furtherance. [ME *zele* < OFr. *zel* < LLat. *zēlus* < Gk. *zēlos.*]

Zea•land (zē′lənd). See **Sjaelland.**

zeal•ot (zĕl′ət) *n.* **1.a.** One who is zealous, esp. excessively so. **b.** A fanatically committed person. **2. Zealot.** A member of a Jewish movement of the first century A.D. that fought against Roman rule in Palestine as incompatible with strict monotheism. [ME *zelote* < Lat. *zēlōtēs* < Gk. < *zēlos*, zeal.]

zeal•ot•ry (zĕl′ə-trē) *n.* Excessive zeal; fanaticism.

zeal•ous (zĕl′əs) *adj.* Filled with or motivated by zeal; fervent. **—zeal′ous•ly** *adv.* **—zeal′ous•ness** *n.*

ze•a•tin (zē′ə-tĭn) *n.* A cytokinin originally isolated from young corn kernels. [NLat. *Zea*, corn genus; see ZEIN + -IN.]

ze•bec or **ze•beck** (zē′bĕk′) *n. Naut.* Var. of **xebec.**

Zeb•e•dee (zĕb′ĭ-dē′). In the Bible, a fisherman whose sons James and John became disciples of Jesus.

ze•bra (zē′brə) *n.* Any of several swift, wild, horselike African mammals of the genus *Equus*, having distinctive overall markings of alternating white and black or brown stripes. [Ital. < OPort. *zevro, zevra*, wild ass.] **—ze′brine′** (zē′brīne′) *adj.*

zebra crossing *n. Chiefly British.* A pedestrian crosswalk.

zebra finch *n.* A small Australian bird *(Poephila guttata)* having black and white markings and popular as a cage bird.

zebra fish *n.* A small freshwater tropical fish *(Brachydanio rerio)* of India having horizontal dark blue and silvery stripes.

ze•bra•wood (zē′brə-wo͝od′) *n.* **1.** Any of several African or tropical American trees having striped wood. **2.** The wood of any of these trees, used in cabinetmaking.

ze•bu (zē′bo͞o, -byo͞o) *n.* A domesticated ox *(Bos indicus)* of Asia and eastern Africa having a prominent hump on the back and a large dewlap. [Fr. *zébu.*]

Zeb•u•lon also **Zeb•u•lun** (zĕb′yə-lən). In the Bible, a son of Jacob and Leah and the forebear of one of the tribes of Israel.

zec•chi•no (zĕ-kē′nō) also **zec•chin** or **zech•in** (zĕk′ĭn) *n.*, *pl.* **-ni** (-nē) or **-nos** also **-chins** or **-ins.** See **sequin** 2. [Ital. See SEQUIN.]

Zech•a•ri•ah[1] (zĕk′ə-rī′ə) *n. Bible.* **1.** A Hebrew prophet of the 6th cent. B.C. **2.** See table at **Bible.** [Heb. *Zĕkaryāh* : *zekar'*, remembrance + *Yāh*, God.]

Zech•a•ri•ah[2] (zĕk′ə-rī′ə). See **Zacharias.**

zed (zĕd) *n. Chiefly British.* The letter *z.* [ME < OFr. *zede* < LLat. *zēta*, zeta < Gk. See ZETA.]

Zed•e•ki•ah (zĕd′ĭ-kī′ə). 6th cent. B.C. The last king of Judah (597–586 B.C.), who led an unsuccessful uprising (588–586) against Nebuchadnezzar II and was sent to captivity in Babylon.

zed•o•ar•y (zĕd′ō-ĕr′ē) *n.*, *pl.* **-ies. 1.** An Indian plant *(Curcuma zedoaria)* having yellow flowers and starchy tuberous rhizomes. **2.** The dried rhizomes of this plant, used as a condiment and in perfumes, medicines, and cosmetics. [ME *zeduarie* < Med.Lat. *zeduāria* < Ar. *zadwār* < Pers.]

zee (zē) *n.* The letter *z.*

Zee•land (zē′lənd, zā′länt). A historical region of SW Netherlands bordering on Belgium and the North Sea; part of Holland after the 10th cent.

Zee•man (zā′män′), **Pieter.** 1865–1943. Dutch physicist who shared a 1902 Nobel Prize.

Zeeman effect *n.* The splitting of single spectral lines of an emission spectrum into three or more polarized components when the radiation source is in a magnetic field.

ze•in (zē′ĭn) *n.* A prolamine protein derived from corn, used in the manufacture of various plastics, coatings, and lacquers. [NLat. *Zea*, corn genus (< Lat. *zēa*, emmer < Gk. *zeia*, one-seeded wheat, barley; see **yewo-***) + -IN.]

Zeist (zīst). A city of central Netherlands E of Utrecht. Pop. 60,478.

Zeit•geist (tsīt′gīst′, zīt′-) *n.* The spirit of the time; the taste and outlook characteristic of a period or generation. [Ger. : *Zeit*, time (< MHGer. *zīt* < OHGer.; see **dā-***) + *Geist*, spirit; see POLTERGEIST.]

zem•in•dar (zăm′ən-där′, zĕm′-, zə-mēn-där′) *n.* Var. of **zamindar.**

zemst•vo (zĕmst′vō, zyĕm′stvə) *n.*, *pl.* **-vos.** An elective council responsible for the local administration of a provincial dis-

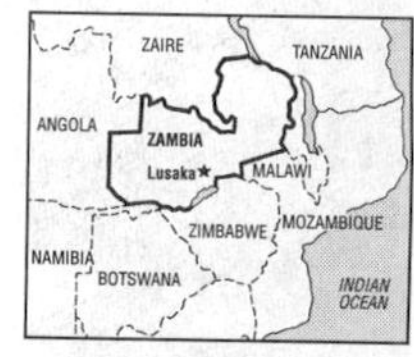

Zambia

Emiliano Zapata

zebra
Grevy's zebra
Equus grevyi

ă pat	oi boy
ā pay	ou out
âr care	o͝o took
ä father	o͞o boot
ĕ pet	ŭ cut
ē be	ûr urge
ĭ pit	th thin
ī pie	*th* this
îr pier	hw which
ŏ pot	zh vision
ō toe	ə about, item
ô paw	

Stress marks:
′ (primary);
′ (secondary), as in dictionary (dĭk′shə-nĕr′ē)

trict in czarist Russia. [Russ. < ORuss. *zemĭ*, land. See **dhghem-***.]

Zen (zĕn) *n.* Zen Buddhism.

ze•na•na (zə-näʹnə) *n.* The part of a house in southwest Asia reserved for the women of the household. [Hindi *zenāna* < Pers. < *zan*, woman. See **gʷen-***.]

Zen Buddhism *n.* A Chinese and Japanese school of Mahayana Buddhism that asserts that enlightenment can be attained through meditation, self-contemplation, and intuition rather than through faith and devotion. [J. *zen* < Chin. (Mandarin) *chán*, meditation < Pali *jhānaṃ* < Skt. *dhyānam* < *dhyāti*, he meditates.] **—Zen Buddhist** *n.*

Zend (zĕnd) *n.* The Zend-Avesta.

Zend-A•ves•ta (zĕnʹdə-vĕsʹtə) *n.* The entire body of sacred writings of the Zoroastrian religion. [Fr. < Pers. *zandavastā* < *Avesta-va-zend*, Avesta with an interpretation : MPers. *apastāk*, text + MPers. *va*, with + MPers. *zend*, interpretation.] **—Zendʹ-A•ves•taʹic** (-vĕs-tāʹĭk) *adj.*

ze•ner diode or **Ze•ner diode** (zēʹnər) *n.* A silicon semiconductor device used as a voltage regulator because of its ability to maintain an almost constant voltage with a wide range of currents. [After C.M. *Zener* (b. 1905), Amer. physicist.]

Zhou Enlai

Zeng•er (zĕngʹgər, -ər), **John Peter.** 1697–1746. German-born colonial printer and journalist whose acquittal (1735) of libel charges set a legal precedent for freedom of the press.

ze•nith (zēʹnĭth) *n.* **1.** The point on the celestial sphere that is directly above the observer. **2.** The upper region of the sky. **3.** The highest point above the observer's horizon attained by a celestial body. **4.** The point of culmination; the peak: *the zenith of her career.* [ME *senith* < OFr. *cenith* < Med.Lat. < Ar. *samt (ar-ra's)*, path (over the head).]

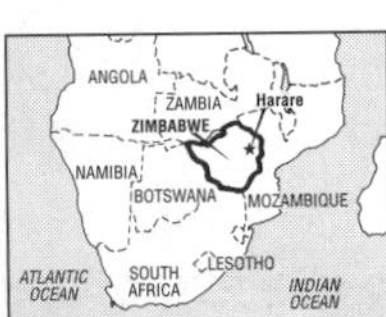

Zimbabwe[2]

Ze•no of Cit•i•um (zēʹnō, sĭtʹē-əm). 335?–263? B.C. Greek philosopher who founded the Stoic school.

Zeno of E•le•a (ē-lēʹə). 495?–430? B.C. Greek philosopher who formulated numerous paradoxes that challenged the ideas of pluralism and the existence of motion and change.

ze•o•lite (zēʹə-lītʹ) *n.* Any one of a family of hydrous aluminum silicate minerals, whose molecules enclose cations of sodium, potassium, calcium, strontium, or barium, or a corresponding synthetic compound, used as molecular filters and ion-exchange agents. [Swed. *zeolit* < Gk. *zein*, to boil (< swelling and boiling under the blowpipe). See **yes-***.]

zep (zĕp) *n. Chiefly New Jersey.* See **submarine** 2. See Regional Note at **submarine.** [Poss. short for ZEPPELIN (< its shape).]

Zeph•a•ni•ah (zĕfʹə-nīʹə) *n. Bible.* **1.** A Hebrew prophet of the 7th cent. B.C. **2.** See table at **Bible.**

zeph•yr (zĕfʹər) *n.* **1.** The west wind. **2.** A gentle breeze. **3.** Any of various soft light fabrics, yarns, or garments. **4.** Something that is airy, insubstantial, or passing. [ME *Zephirus*, Zephyrus < Lat. *Zephyrus* < Gk. *Zephuros.*]

zinnia

Zeph•y•rus (zĕfʹər-əs) *n. Gk. Myth.* A god personifying the west wind.

zep•pe•lin also **Zep•pe•lin** (zĕpʹə-lĭn) *n.* A rigid airship having a long cylindrical body supported by internal gas cells.

Zep•pe•lin (zĕpʹə-lĭn, zĕpʹlĭn, tsĕpʹə-lēnʹ), Count **Ferdinand von.** 1838–1917. German inventor who designed the first motorized rigid-frame dirigible balloon (1900).

ze•ro (zîrʹō, zēʹrō) *n., pl.* **-ros** or **-roes. 1.** The numerical symbol 0; a cipher. **2.** *Math.* **a.** An element of a set that when added to any other element in the set produces a sum identical with the element to which it is added. **b.** A cardinal number indicating the absence of any or all units under consideration. **c.** An ordinal number indicating an initial point or origin. **d.** An argument at which the value of a function vanishes. **3.** The temperature indicated by the numeral 0 on a thermometer. **4.** A sight setting that enables a firearm to shoot on target. **5.** *Informal.* One having no influence or importance; a nonentity. **6.** The lowest point: *Prospects approached zero.* **7.** A zero-coupon bond. **8.** *Informal.* Nothing; nil. **—*adj.*** **1.** Of, relating to, or being zero. **2.a.** Having no determinable value. **b.** *Informal.* Absent, inoperative, or irrelevant in specified circumstances. **3.** *Meteorol.* **a.** Being a ceiling not more than 16 meters (52 feet) high. **b.** Limited in horizontal visibility to no more than 55 meters (180 feet). **—*tr.v.*** **-roed, -ro•ing, -roes.** To adjust (an instrument or a device) to zero value. **—*phrasal verb.* zero in. 1.a.** To aim or concentrate firepower on an exact target location. **b.** To adjust the aim or sight of by repeated firings. **2.** To converge intently; close in: *The children zeroed in on the toys.* [Ital. < alteration of Med. Lat. *zephirum* < Ar. *ṣifr*, nothing, cipher.]

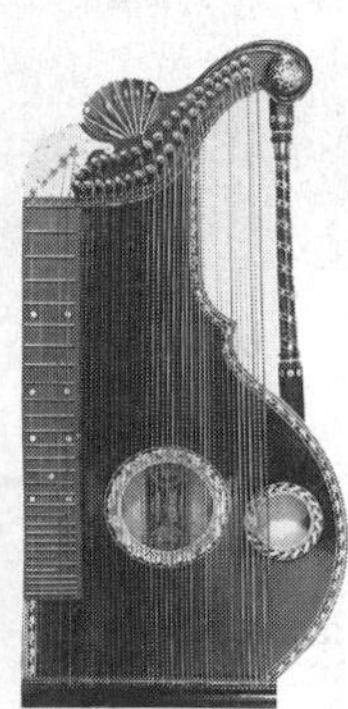
zither

ze•ro-base (zîrʹō-bās', zēʹrō-) or **ze•ro-based** (-bāstʹ) *adj.* Having each expenditure or item justified as to need or cost.

ze•ro-cou•pon (zîrʹō-kōōʹpŏn, -kyōōʹ-, zēʹrō-) *adj.* Paying no interest until maturity or sale: *a zero-coupon bond.*

zero gravity *n.* The condition of apparent weightlessness occurring when the centrifugal force on a body exactly counterbalances the gravitational attraction on it.

zero hour *n.* The scheduled time for the start of an operation or action, esp. a combat operation of great size.

ze•ro-point energy (zîrʹō-pointʹ, zēʹrō-) *n.* The irreducible minimum energy possessed by a substance at absolute zero temperature.

zero population growth *n.* The limiting of population increase to the number of live births needed to replace the existing population.

ze•ro-sum game (zîrʹō-sŭmʹ, zēʹrō-) *n.* A situation in which a gain by one must be matched by a loss by another.

zest (zĕst) *n.* **1.a.** Flavor or interest; piquancy. **b.** The outermost part of the rind of an orange or a lemon, used as flavoring. **2.** Spirited enjoyment; gusto. **—*tr.v.*** **zest•ed, zest•ing, zests.** To give zest, charm, or spirit to. [Obsolete Fr., orange or lemon peel.] **—zestʹful** *adj.* **—zestʹful•ly** *adv.* **—zestʹful•ness** *n.*

ze•ta (zāʹtə, zēʹ-) *n.* The sixth letter of the Greek alphabet. [Gk. *zēta*, of Phoenician orig.; akin to Heb. *zayin.*]

Ze•thus also **Ze•thos** (zēʹthəs) *n. Gk. Myth.* The twin brother of Amphion.

zeug•ma (zōōgʹmə) *n.* **1.** A construction in which a single word, esp. a verb or an adjective, is applied to two or more nouns when its sense is appropriate to only one of them or to both in different ways, as in *He took my advice and my wallet.* **2.** Syllepsis. [Lat. < Gk., a joining, bond. See **yeug-***.]

Zeus (zōōs) *n. Gk. Myth.* The principal god of the Greek pantheon, ruler of the heavens and father of other gods and mortal heroes. [Gk. See **deiw-***.]

Zeux•is (zōōkʹsĭs). 5th cent. B.C. Greek artist who was among the first Athenians to use shading.

Ze•ya (zāʹyə, zyĕʹ-). A river of SE Russia flowing c. 1,287 km (800 mi) to the Amur R.

Zhang•jia•kou (jängʹjyäʹkōʹ) also **Kal•gan** (kälʹgänʹ). A city of NE China NW of Beijing. Pop. 350,000.

Zhan•jiang also **Chan•chiang** (jänʹjyängʹ) or **Chan•kiang** (chänʹkyängʹ). A city of SE China SW of Guangzhou on an inlet of the South China Sea. Pop. 300,000.

Zhao Kuang•yin or **Chao K'uang-yin** (jouʹ kwängʹyĭnʹ). 927–976. Emperor of China (960–976) who founded the Song dynasty and unified much of China.

Zhao Zi•yang (jouʹ dzē-yängʹ) or **Chao Tzu-yang** (jouʹ dzōō-yängʹ). b. 1919. Chinese premier (1980–87) and general secretary of the Communist Party (1987–89).

Zhda•nov (zhdäʹnəf). A city of SE Ukraine on the Sea of Azov; founded 1779. Pop. 522,000.

Zhe•jiang (jœʹjyängʹ) also **Che•kiang** (chŭʹkyängʹ, jəʹ-gyängʹ). A province of E China on the East China Sea. Cap. Hangzhou. Pop. 40,300,000.

Zheng•zhou also **Cheng•chow** (jŭngʹjōʹ, jœngʹ-). A city of E-central China SSW of Beijing; cap. of Henan province. Pop. 1,000,000.

Zhen•jiang (jŭnʹjyängʹ, jœnʹ-) also **Chin•kiang** (chĭnʹ-kyăngʹ, jĭnʹgyängʹ). A city of E China on the Grand Canal E of Nanjing. Pop. 250,000.

Zhi•to•mir (zhĭ-tôʹmîr). A city of W Ukraine W of Kiev; first mentioned in 1240. Pop. 275,000.

Zhou or **Chou** or **Chow** (jō). A Chinese dynasty (traditionally dated 1122–221 B.C.) characterized by great intellectual achievements, including the rise of Confucianism and Taoism.

Zhou En•lai or **Chou En-lai** (jōʹ ĕn-līʹ). 1898–1976. Chinese revolutionary who was the first prime minister (1949–76) and foreign minister (1949–58) of China.

Zhu Jiang (jōōʹ jyängʹ) also **Can•ton River** (kănʹtŏnʹ, kănʹ-tŏnʹ) or **Chu Kiang** (chōōʹ kyängʹ, jōōʹ gyängʹ). A river of SE China flowing 177 km (110 mi) to the South China Sea.

Zhu•kov (zhōōʹkəf), **Georgi Konstantinovich.** 1896–1974. Soviet army officer who relieved the siege of Leningrad (1942–43) and captured Berlin (1945).

Zi•a ul-Haq (zēʹə ōōl-hăkʹ, -häkʹ), **Mohammad.** 1924–88. Pakistani politician who overthrew Ali Bhutto (1977) and as president (1978–88) introduced strict Islamic law.

zib•e•line or **zib•el•line** (zĭbʹə-lēnʹ, -līnʹ) *n.* **1.** A thick, lustrous, silky fabric of wool and other animal hair. **2.** The sable or its fur. [Fr., sable < Ital. *zibellino*, of Slav. orig.]

Zi•bo (dzēʹbōʹ) also **Tze•po** (tsŭʹpōʹ, dzŭʹbōʹ). A city of E China E of Jinan. Pop. 762,500.

zi•do•vu•dine (zĭ-dōʹvyōō-dēnʹ) *n.* See **azidothymidine.** [Alteration of (A)ZIDO(THYMI)DINE.]

Zieg•feld (zĭgʹfĕldʹ, -fēldʹ, zēgʹ-), **Florenz.** 1869–1932. Amer. theatrical producer famed for his extravagant revues known as the *Ziegfeld Follies* (1907–31).

Zie•gler (zēʹglər, tsēʹ-), **Karl Waldemar.** 1898–1973. German chemist who shared a 1963 Nobel Prize.

Zie•lo•no Gó•ra (zhĕ-lôʹnə gōōrʹə). A city of W Poland W of Łódź; founded in the 13th cent. Pop. 109,400.

zig (zĭg) *n.* One of a series of sharp turns or reversals. **—*intr.v.*** **zigged, zig•ging, zigs. 1.** To turn or change direction suddenly. Usu. used in contrast to *zag*: *When your opponent zigs, zag!* **2.** To behave erratically or indecisively. Usu. used with *zag.* [< ZIGZAG.]

zig•gu•rat (zĭgʹə-rătʹ) *n.* A temple tower of the ancient Assyrians and Babylonians, having the form of a terraced pyramid of successively receding stories. [Assyrian *ziggurratu*, summit.]

Zi•gong (dzēʹgōōngʹ) also **Tze•kung** (tsŭʹkōōngʹ, dzŭʹ-gōōngʹ). A city of S-central China W of Chongqing. Pop. 450,000.

zig•zag (zĭg′zăg′) *n.* **1.a.** A line or course that proceeds by sharp turns in alternating directions. **b.** One of a series of zigzags. **2.** Something that exhibits one or a series of sharp turns. —*adj.* Moving in or having a zigzag. —*adv.* In a zigzag manner or pattern. —*v.* **-zagged, -zag•ging, -zags.** —*intr.* To move in or form a zigzag. —*tr.* To cause to zigzag. [Fr., alteration of *zic-zac* < Ger. *Zickzack*, perh. redup. of *Zacke*, tooth, cog < MHGer. *zacke*, point, nail.]

zilch (zĭlch) *Slang.* —*n.* **1.** Zero; nothing. **2.** A person regarded as insignificant; a nonentity. —*adj.* Amounting to nothing; nil. [?]

zil•lion (zĭl′yən) *n. Informal.* An extremely large indefinite number. [On the model of MILLION, BILLION, etc.]

Zim•bab•we¹ (zĭm-bäb′wē, -wā). A ruined city of SE Zimbabwe S of Harare; first occupied in the 3rd cent. A.D.

Zim•bab•we² (zĭm-bäb′wē, -wā). Formerly **Rho•de•sia** (rō-dē′zhə). A country of S Africa. Administered by the British South Africa Company (1889–1923), it declared itself independent in 1965, although independence was not formally granted by Great Britain until 1980. Cap. Harare. Pop. 7,539,000. —**Zim•bab′we•an** *adj. & n.*

zinc (zĭngk) *n. Symbol* **Zn** A lustrous metallic element that is brittle at room temperature but malleable with heating, used to form a wide variety of alloys including brass, bronze, and nickel silver, in galvanizing metals, for electric fuses and meter cases, and in roofing, gutters, and various household objects. Atomic number 30; atomic weight 65.37; melting point 419.4°C; boiling point 907°C; specific gravity 7.133 (25°C); valence 2. See table at **element.** —*tr.v.* **zinced, zinc•ing, zincs** or **zincked, zinck•ing, zincks.** To coat or treat with zinc; galvanize. [Ger. *Zink*, poss. < *Zinke*, spike (< becoming jagged in the furnace) < MHGer. *zinke* < OHGer. *zinko.*]

zinc•ate (zĭng′kāt′) *n.* A salt of zinc hydroxide.

zinc blende *n.* See **sphalerite.**

zinc•ite (zĭng′kīt′) *n.* A red to yellow-orange zinc ore, ZnO.

zinc•og•ra•phy (zĭng-kŏg′rə-fē) *n.* The process of engraving zinc printing plates. —**zinc•og′ra•pher** *n.* —**zinc′o•graph′ic** (zĭng′kə-grăf′ĭk), **zinc′o•graph′i•cal** (-ĭ-kəl) *adj.*

zinc ointment *n.* A salve consisting of about 20 percent zinc oxide with beeswax or paraffin and petrolatum, used in the treatment of skin disorders.

zinc oxide *n.* An amorphous white or yellowish powder, ZnO, used as a pigment, in compounding rubber, in the manufacture of plastics, and in pharmaceuticals and cosmetics.

zinc spinel *n.* See **gahnite.**

zinc sulfate *n.* A crystalline compound, $ZnSO_4 \cdot 7H_2O$, used medicinally as an emetic and astringent, as a fungicide, and in wood and skin preservatives.

zinc white *n.* See **zinc oxide.**

zin•fan•del also **Zin•fan•del** (zĭn′fən-dĕl′) *n.* A dry red California table wine similar to claret. [?]

zing (zĭng) *n.* A brief high-pitched humming or buzzing sound, such as that made by a swiftly passing object or a taut vibrating string. —*v.* **zinged, zing•ing, zings.** —*intr.* **1.** To make a zing. **2.** To move swiftly with or as if with a zing: *an arrow zinging toward its target.* **3.** *Informal.* To be vivacious or lively: *a conversation zinging along.* —*tr. Informal.* **1.** To attack verbally; criticize sharply. **2.** To strike suddenly. [Imit.]

zing•er (zĭng′ər) *n. Informal.* **1.** A witty, often caustic remark. **2.** A sudden shock, revelation, or turn of events.

zing•y (zĭng′ē) *adj.* **-i•er, -i•est.** *Informal.* **1.** Pleasantly stimulating. **2.** Exceptionally attractive or appealing.

zin•ni•a (zĭn′ē-ə) *n.* Any of various plants of the genus *Zinnia* of tropical America, esp. *Z. elegans,* widely cultivated for their showy, rayed, variously colored flower heads. Also called regionally *old maid, old maid flower.* [NLat. *Zinnia*, genus name, after J.G. *Zinn* (1727–59), German botanist.]

Zi•nov•iev (zĭ-nō′vē-ĕf′, zyĭ-nôf′yĭf), **Grigori Evseyevich.** 1883–1936. Soviet politician who briefly shared power with Kamenev and Stalin after Lenin's death (1924).

Zins•ser (zĭn′sər), **Hans.** 1878–1940. Amer. bacteriologist and pioneer immunologist who helped develop immunization against varieties of typhus fever (1930).

Zin•zen•dorf (zĭn′zən-dôrf′, tsĭn′tsən-), Count **Nikolaus Ludwig von.** 1700–60. German theologian who founded the Moravian Church (1722).

Zi•on¹ (zī′ən). A city of NE IL on Lake Michigan N of Waukegan; founded 1901. Pop. 19,775.

Zi•on² (zī′ən) also **Si•on** (sī′ən) *n.* **1.a.** The historic land of Israel as a symbol of the Jewish people. **b.** The Jewish people; Israel. **2.** A place or religious community regarded as sacredly devoted to God. **3.** An idealized harmonious community; utopia. [ME *Sion* < OE < LLat. *Siōn* < Gk. *Seiōn* < Heb. *ṣîyôn.*]

Zi•on•ism (zī′ə-nĭz′əm) *n.* A Jewish movement that arose in the late 19th century in response to growing anti-Semitism and sought to reestablish a Jewish homeland in Palestine and that now concerns itself with the survival and development of the state of Israel. —**Zi′on•ist** *adj. & n.* —**Zi′on•is′tic** *adj.*

zip (zĭp) *n.* **1.** A brief sharp hissing sound. **2.** Energy; vim. **3.** A zipper. **4.** *Slang.* Nothing; nil; zero. —*v.* **zipped, zip•ping, zips.** —*intr.* **1.a.** To move with a sharp hissing sound. **b.** To move or act with a speed that suggests such a sound. **2.** To act or proceed swiftly and energetically: *zipped through her homework.* **3.** To become fastened or unfastened by a zipper. —*tr.* **1.** To give speed and force to. **2.** To impart life or zest to. **3.** To fasten or unfasten with a zipper. [Imit.]

ZIP code (zĭp). A service mark used for a system designed to expedite the sorting and delivery of mail by assigning a series of numbers to each delivery area in the United States.

zip gun *n. Slang.* A crude homemade pistol.

zip•per (zĭp′ər) *n.* A fastening device consisting of parallel rows of metal, plastic, or nylon teeth on adjacent edges of an opening that are interlocked by a sliding tab. [< ZIP.]

zip•py (zĭp′ē) *adj.* **-pi•er, -pi•est.** Full of energy; lively.

zir•ca•loy (zûr′kə-loi′) *n.* A stable corrosion-resistant zirconium alloy. [ZIRC(ONIUM) + AL(L)OY.]

zir•con (zûr′kŏn′) *n.* A brown to colorless mineral, $ZrSiO_4$, that is heated, cut, and polished to form a brilliant blue-white gem. [Ger. *Zirkon* < Ar. *zarqūn*, minium < Aram. *sīrīqūn* < Gk. *surikon* < Pers. *āzargūn*, fire color < *zar*, gold.]

zir•co•ni•a (zûr-kō′nē-ə) *n.* Cubic zirconia. [NLat. < ZIRCON.]

zir•co•ni•um (zûr-kō′nē-əm) *n. Symbol* **Zr** A lustrous strong ductile metallic element obtained primarily from zircon and used chiefly in ceramic and refractory compounds, as an alloying agent, and in nuclear reactors as a highly corrosion-resistant alloy. Atomic number 40; atomic weight 91.22; melting point 1,852°C; boiling point 3,578°C; specific gravity 6.56 (20°C); valence 2, 3, 4. See table at **element.**

zirconium oxide *n.* A hard white amorphous powder, ZrO_2, derived from zirconium and also found naturally, used chiefly in pigments, refractories, and ceramics and as an abrasive.

zit (zĭt) *n. Slang.* A pimple. [?]

zith•er (zĭth′ər, zĭth′-) also **zith•ern** (-ərn) *n. Mus.* An instrument composed of a flat sound box with about 30 to 40 strings and played horizontally with the fingertips or a plectrum. [Ger. < MHGer. **zitter* < OHGer. *zitera* < Lat. *cithara*, cithara < Gk. *kithara.*] —**zith′er•ist** *n.*

zi•ti (zē′tē) *n.* Medium-sized tubular pasta. [Ital. < pl. of *zito*, boy.]

zi•zith (tsē-tsēt′, tsĭt′sĭs) *pl.n. Judaism.* The ritually knotted fringes attached to the corners of a garment, esp. a tallith, to symbolize the mitzvot. [Heb. *ṣîṣit.*]

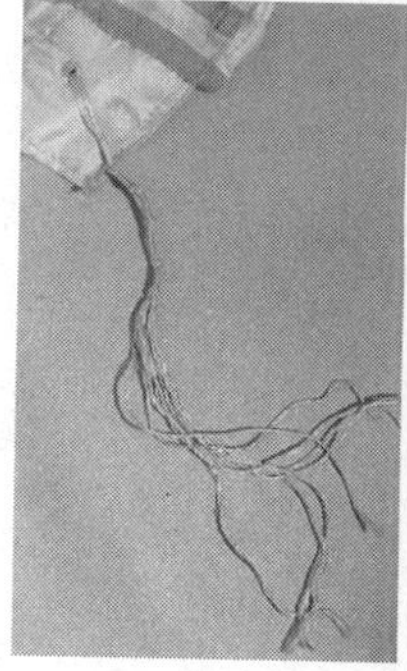

zizith

Žiž•ka (zhĭsh′kə, -kä), Count **Jan.** 1376?–1424. Bohemian military leader who commanded the Hussites (1420–24) during the Hussite Wars against Catholic forces.

Zl *abbr.* Zloty.

Zla•to•ust (zlä′tə-o͞ost′, zlə-). A city of W Russia in the S Ural Mts. W of Chelyabinsk. Pop. 204,000.

zlo•ty (zlô′tē) *n., pl.* **zloty** or **-tys.** See table at **currency.** [Pol. *złoty*, golden, zloty < *złoto*, gold. See **ghel-²*.**]

Zn The symbol for the element **zinc.**

zo– *pref.* Var. of **zoo–.**

zo•a (zō′ə) *n.* Pl. of **zoon¹.**

zo•di•ac (zō′dē-ăk′) *n.* **1.a.** *Astron.* A band of the celestial sphere extending about 8° to either side of the ecliptic that represents the path of the principal planets, the moon, and the sun. **b.** In astrology, this band divided into 12 equal parts called signs, each 30° wide, bearing the name of a constellation for which it was originally named but with which it no longer coincides owing to the precession of the equinoxes. **c.** A diagram or figure representing the zodiac. **2.** A complete circuit; a circle. [ME < OFr. *zodiaque* < Lat. *zōdiacus* < Gk. *zōidiakos (kuklos)*, (circle) of the zodiac < *zōidion*, small represented figure, zodiacal sign, dim. of *zōion*, living being. See ZOON¹.] —**zo•di′a•cal** (-dī′ə-kəl) *adj.*

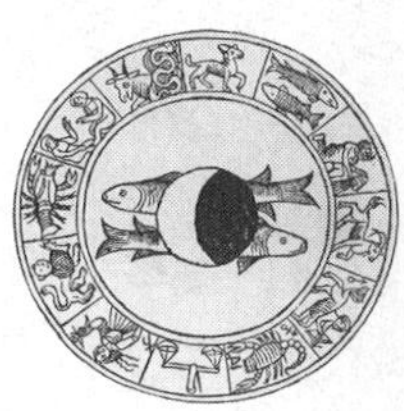

zodiac
16th-century German

zodiacal light *n.* A faint hazy cone of light, apparently caused by the reflection of sunlight from meteoric particles in the plane of the ecliptic.

zo•e•a (zō-ē′ə) *n., pl.* **-e•ae** (-ē′ē) or **-e•as.** A larval form of crabs and other decapod crustaceans, characterized by one or more spines on the carapace and rudimentary limbs on the abdomen and thorax. [NLat. < Gk. *zōē*, life. See AZO–.]

zof•tig (zäf′tĭk, -tĭg) *adj.* Var. of **zaftig.**

–zoic *suff.* **1.** Relating to a specified manner of animal existence: *holozoic.* **2.** Of or relating to a specified geologic era: *Archeozoic.* [< Gk. *zōikos*, of animals < *zōion*, living being. See **gʷei-*.**]

zoi•site (zoi′sīt′) *n.* A gray, brown, or pink mineral, $Ca_2Al_3(SiO_4)_3(OH)$, used in ornamental stonework. [Ger. *Zoisit*, after Baron Sigismund *Zois* von Edelstein (1747–1819), Slovenian noble.]

Zo•la (zō′lə, zō-lä′), **Emile.** 1840–1902. French writer and critic whose works include *Nana* (1880) and "J'Accuse" (1898), a letter in defense of Alfred Dreyfus.

Émile Zola

zom•bie also **zom•bi** (zŏm′bē) *n., pl.* **zom•bies** also **zom•bis.** **1.** A voodoo snake spirit. **2.a.** A supernatural power or spell that according to voodoo can enter into and reanimate a corpse. **b.** A corpse revived in this way. **3.** One who looks or behaves like an automaton. **4.** A tall mixed drink made of various rums, liqueur, and fruit juice. [Caribbean Fr. and E. Creole < Kimbundu *n-zumbi*, ghost, departed spirit.]

zon•al (zō′nəl) also **zo•na•ry** (-nə-rē) *adj.* **1.** Of or associated with a zone. **2.** Divided into zones. —**zon′al•ly** *adv.*

zo•na pel•lu•ci•da (zō′nə pə-lo͞o′sĭ-də, pĕl-yo͞o′-) *n.* The

ă pat	oi boy
ā pay	ou out
âr care	o͝o took
ä father	o͞o boot
ĕ pet	ŭ cut
ē be	ûr urge
ĭ pit	th thin
ī pie	*th* this
îr pier	hw which
ŏ pot	zh vision
ō toe	ə about, item
ô paw	

Stress marks:
′ (primary);
′ (secondary), as in
dictionary (dĭk′shə-nĕr′ē)

thick solid transparent outer membrane of a developed mammalian ovum. [NLat. *zōna pellūcida* : Lat. *zōna*, belt, girdle + Lat. *pellūcidus*, transparent.]

zo•nate (zō′nāt′) also **zo•nat•ed** (-nā′tĭd) *adj.* Having zones; belted, striped, or ringed.

zo•na•tion (zō-nā′shən) *n.* **1.** Arrangement or formation in zones; zonate structure. **2.** *Ecol.* The distribution of organisms in biogeographic zones.

zone (zōn) *n.* **1.** An area distinguished from adjacent parts by a distinctive feature or characteristic. **2.a.** Any of the five regions of the surface of the earth that are loosely divided according to prevailing climate and latitude, including the Torrid Zone, the North and South Temperate zones, and the North and South Frigid zones. **b.** A similar division on any other planet. **c.** *Math.* A portion of a sphere bounded by the intersections of two parallel planes with the sphere. **3.** *Ecol.* An area characterized by distinct physical conditions and populated by communities of certain kinds of organisms. **4.** *Anat.* A ringlike or cylindrical growth or structure. **5.** *Geol.* A region or stratum distinguished by composition or content. **6.** A section of an area or a territory established for a specific purpose, as a section of a city restricted to a particular type of building, enterprise, or activity: *a residential zone.* **7.** An area of a given radius within which a uniform rate is charged, as for shipping. **8.** *Comp. Sci.* **a.** A region on a punch card or on magnetic tape in which nondigital information is recorded. **b.** A section of storage to be used for a particular purpose. **9.** *Archaic.* A belt or girdle. —*tr.v.* **zoned, zon•ing, zones. 1.** To divide into zones. **2.** To designate or mark off into zones. **3.** To surround or encircle with or as if with a belt or girdle. [Lat. *zōna*, girdle < Gk. *zōnē*.]

zone melting *n.* A purification technique for crystalline substances in which a heating system passes slowly over a bar of the material to be refined, creating a molten region that carries impurities with it across the bar.

zone of accumulation *n. Geol.* See **B-horizon.**

zone of illuviation *n. Geol.* See **B-horizon.**

zone of leach•ing (lē′chĭng) *n. Geol.* See **A-horizon.**

zone re•fin•ing (rĭ-fī′nĭng) *n.* See **zone melting.**

zone•time (zōn′tīm′) *n. Naut.* The standard time throughout a time zone that is the actual time at the meridian on which the time zone is based.

zonk (zôngk, zŏngk) *v.* **zonked, zonk•ing, zonks.** —*tr.* **1.** To stupefy; stun. **2.** To intoxicate with drugs or alcohol. —*intr.* To become intoxicated with drugs or alcohol. [?]

zon•ule (zōn′yo͞ol) *n.* A small zone, as of a ligament.

zucchini

zoo (zo͞o) *n., pl.* **zoos. 1.** A park or an institution in which living animals are kept and usu. exhibited to the public. **2.** *Slang.* A place or situation marked by confusion or disorder. [Short for ZOOLOGICAL GARDEN.]

zoo– or **zo–** *pref.* **1.** Animal; animal kingdom: *zoography.* **2.** Motile: *zoospore.* [Gk. *zōo-*, *zōio-* < *zōion*, living being. See **g^{w}ei-***.]

zo•o•chore (zō′ə-kôr′, -kōr′) *n.* A plant dispersed by animals.

zo•o•flag•el•late (zō′ə-flăj′ə-lĭt, -lāt′) *n.* A flagellated protist that ingests food and lacks chlorophyll.

zo•o•gen•ic (zō′ə-jĕn′ĭk) also **zo•og•e•nous** (zō-ŏj′ə-nəs) *adj.* Originating in or produced by animals.

zo•o•ge•og•ra•phy (zō′ə-jē-ŏg′rə-fē) *n.* The biological study of the geographic distribution of animals, esp. its causes and effects. —**zo′o•ge•og′ra•pher** *n.* —**zo′o•ge′o•graph′ic** (-ə-grăf′ĭk), **zo′o•ge′o•graph′i•cal** (-ĭ-kəl) *adj.*

zo•o•gle•a also **zo•o•gloe•a** (zō′ə-glē′ə) *n., pl.* **-gle•ae** (-glē′ē′) or **-gle•as** also **-gloe•ae** (-glē′ē′) or **-gloe•as.** An aggregate of bacteria forming a jellylike mass. [ZOO– + NLat. *gloea*, gum (< Med.Gk. *gloia*, *glia*, gum, glue < Gk. *gloios*).]

zo•og•ra•phy (zō-ŏg′rə-fē) *n.* The biological description of animals and their habitats. —**zo′o•graph′ic** (-ə-grăf′ĭk), **zo′o•graph′i•cal** (-ĭ-kəl) *adj.*

zo•oid (zō′oid′) *n.* **1.** *Biol.* **a.** An organic cell or organized body that has independent movement within a living organism, esp. a motile gamete such as a spermatozoon. **b.** An independent animallike organism produced asexually. **2.** *Zool.* One of the distinct individuals forming a colonial animal such as a bryozoan or hydrozoan. —**zo•oid′al** (-oid′l) *adj.*

zoo•keep•er (zo͞o′kē′pər) *n.* One who takes care of animals in a zoo.

zool. *abbr.* Zoological; zoology.

zo•ol•a•try (zō-ŏl′ə-trē) *n.* Worship of animals. —**zo•ol′a•ter** *n.* —**zo•ol′a•trous** *adj.*

zo•o•log•i•cal (zō′ə-lŏj′ĭ-kəl) also **zo•o•log•ic** (-lŏj′ĭk) *adj.* **1.** Of or relating to animals or animal life. **2.** Of or relating to the science of zoology. —**zo′o•log′i•cal•ly** *adv.*

zoological garden *n.* See **zoo** 1.

zo•ol•o•gy (zō-ŏl′ə-jē) *n., pl.* **-gies. 1.** The branch of biology that deals with the study of the structure, physiology, development, and classification of animals. **2.** The animal life of a particular area or period: *the zoology of the Pleistocene.* **3.** The characteristics of a particular animal group or category: *the zoology of mammals.* —**zo•ol′o•gist** *n.*

zoom (zo͞om) *v.* **zoomed, zoom•ing, zooms.** —*intr.* **1.a.** To buzz or hum at a continuous low pitch. **b.** To move while making such a sound. **2.** To climb suddenly and sharply. Used of an airplane. **3.** To move about rapidly; swoop. **4.a.** To move a camera lens rapidly toward or away from a subject. **b.** To simulate such a movement, as with a zoom lens. —*tr.* To cause to zoom. —*n.* The act or sound of zooming. [Imit.]

zoom lens *n.* A camera lens whose focal length can be rapidly changed, allowing rapid change in the size of an image or the illusion of camera movement.

zo•o•mor•phism (zō′ə-môr′fĭz′əm) *n.* **1.** Attribution of animal traits or qualities to a god. **2.** Use of animal forms in symbolism, literature, or graphics. —**zo′o•mor′phic** *adj.*

zo•on[1] (zō′ŏn′) *n., pl.* **zo•ons** or **zo•a** (zō′ə). **1.** An animal developed from a fertilized egg. **2.** One of the distinct individuals that join to form a compound or colonial animal; a zooid. [NLat. *zōon* < Gk. *zōion*, *zōon*, living being. See **g^{w}ei-***.]

zoon[2] (zo͞on) *intr.v.* **zooned, zoon•ing, zoons.** *Chiefly Southern U.S.* To fly with a humming or buzzing sound. [Prob. imit.]

–zoon *suff.* Animal; independently moving organic unit: *spermatozoon.* [NLat. *-zōon* < Gk. *zōion*, *zōon*, living being. See **g^{w}ei-***.]

zo•on•o•sis (zō-ŏn′ə-sĭs) *n., pl.* **-ses** (-sēz′). A disease of animals, such as rabies or psittacosis, that can be transmitted to human beings. [NLat. : zoo– + *-nosis*, alteration (influenced by –OSIS) of Gk. *nosos*, disease.]

zo•oph•a•gous (zō-ŏf′ə-gəs) *adj.* Feeding on animal matter.

zo•oph•i•lism (zō-ŏf′ə-lĭz′əm) also **zo•oph•i•ly** (-ə-lē) or **zo•o•phil•i•a** (zō′ə-fĭl′ē-ə) *n.* Attraction to or affinity for animals. —**zo′o•phil′ic** (zō′ə-fĭl′ĭk) *adj.*

zo•oph•i•lous (zō-ŏf′ə-ləs) *adj. Bot.* Pollinated by animals.

zo•o•pho•bi•a (zō′ə-fō′bē-ə) *n.* An abnormal fear of animals. —**zo′o•phobe′** (-fōb′) *n.*

zo•o•phyte (zō′ə-fīt′) *n.* Any of various invertebrate animals, such as a sea anemone or sponge, that attach to surfaces and superficially resemble plants. —**zo′o•phyt′ic** (-fĭt′ĭk), **zo′o•phyt′i•cal** (-ĭ-kəl) *adj.*

zo•o•plank•ton (zō′ə-plăngk′tən) *n.* Plankton that consists of animals, including the corals, rotifers, sea anemones, and jellyfish. —**zo′o•plank•ton′ic** (-tŏn′ĭk) *adj.*

zo•o•spo•ran•gi•um (zō′ə-spə-răn′jē-əm) *n., pl.* **-gi•a** (-jē-ə). A sporangium in which zoospores develop.

zo•o•spore (zō′ə-spôr′, -spōr′) *n.* A motile flagellated asexual spore, as of certain algae and fungi. —**zo′o•spor′ic** (-spôr′ĭk, -spŏr′-), **zo′o•spor′ous** (zō′ə-spôr′əs, -spōr′-, zō-ŏs′pər-əs) *adj.*

zo•os•ter•ol (zō-ŏs′tə-rôl′, -rōl′, -rŏl′) *n.* A sterol, such as cholesterol, that is produced by animals rather than plants.

zo•ot•o•my (zō-ŏt′ə-mē) *n., pl.* **-mies. 1.** The anatomy of animals. **2.** Dissection of animals. —**zo′o•tom′ic** (zō′ə-tŏm′ĭk), **zo′o•tom′i•cal** (-ĭ-kəl) *adj.* —**zo•ot′o•mist** *n.*

zoot suit (zo͞ot) *n. Slang.* A man's suit popular during the early 1940's, marked by full-legged tight-cuffed trousers and a long coat with wide lapels and padded shoulders. [Prob. < an alteration of SUIT.] —**zoot′-suit′er** (zo͞ot′so͞o′tər) *n.*

zo•ri (zôr′ē, zōr′ē) *n., pl.* **zori** or **-ris.** A flat sandal with thongs, usu. made of straw or leather. [J. *zōri* : *sō*, grass, straw + *ri*, sole.]

zor•ille also **zor•il** (zôr′ĭl, zŏr′-) or **zo•ril•la** (zə-rĭl′ə) *n.* A skunklike carnivorous African mammal *(Ictonyx striatus)* related to the weasel. [Fr. < Sp. *zorrillo*, skunk, dim. of *zorro*, fox < OSp., idler, vagabond, fox.]

Zo•ro•as•ter (zôr′ō-ăs′tər, zōr′-) also **Zar•a•thu•stra** (zăr′ə-tho͞o′strə). 6th cent. B.C. Persian prophet.

Zo•ro•as•tri•an•ism (zôr′ō-ăs′trē-ə-nĭz′əm) *n.* The religious system founded in Persia by Zoroaster and set forth in the Zend-Avesta, teaching the worship of Ormazd in the context of a universal struggle between the forces of light and of darkness. —**Zo′ro•as′tri•an** *adj. & n.*

Zor•ril•la y Mo•ral (zə-rē′ə ē mə-räl′, thô-rē′lyä ē mô-räl′), **José.** 1817–93. Spanish writer whose romantic works include the play *Don Juan Tenorio* (1844).

zos•ter (zŏs′tər) *n.* **1.** A belt or girdle worn by men in ancient Greece. **2.** Herpes zoster. [Gk. *zōstēr*, girdle.]

Zou•ave (zo͞o-äv′, zwäv) *n.* **1.** A member of a French infantry unit, formerly composed of Algerian recruits. **2.** A member of a group patterned after the French Zouaves, esp. a member of such a unit of the Union Army during the U.S. Civil War. [Fr. < Berber *Zwāwa*, an Algerian tribe.]

zounds (zoundz) *interj.* Used to express anger, surprise, or indignation. [Shortening and alteration of *God's wounds!*]

zoy•sia (zoi′shə, -zhə, -sē-ə, -zē-ə) *n.* Any of several creeping lawn grasses of the genus *Zoysia*, native to southeast Asia and New Zealand. [NLat. *Zoysia*, genus name, after Karl von Zoys zu Laubach (1756–1800?), Austrian botanist.]

Zp *abbr. Bible.* Zephaniah.

Z particle *n.* A massive elementary particle, electrically neutral, that is the quantum of weak interactions in which the charges of participating particles do not change. See table at **subatomic particle.**

ZPG *abbr.* Zero population growth.

Zr The symbol for the element **zirconium.**

Z score *n. Statistics.* A measure of the distance in standard deviations of a sample from the mean.

zuc•chet•to (zo͞o-kĕt′ō, tso͞ok-kĕt′tô) *n., pl.* **-tos.** *Rom. Cath. Ch.* A skullcap worn by clerics, varying in color with the rank of the wearer. [Ital., var. of *zucchetta*, dim. of *zucca*, gourd, head. See ZUCCHINI.]

zuc•chi•ni (zo͞o-kē′nē) *n., pl.* **zucchini** or **-nis.** A variety of squash having an elongated shape and a smooth thin green rind. [Ital., pl. of *zucchino*, dim. of *zucca*, gourd < LLat. *cucutia.*]

zug•zwang (tso͞ok′tsväng′) *n. Games.* A situation in a chess game in which a player is forced to make an undesirable or disadvantageous move. [Ger. *Zugzwang* : *Zug*, pull, move (< MHGer. *zuc*, pull < OHGer. < *ziohan*, to pull; see **deuk-***) + *Zwang*, compulsion (< MHGer. *twanc* < OHGer.).]

Zui•der Zee (zī′dər zē′, zā′, zoi′dər zā′). A former shallow inlet of the North Sea in NE Netherlands.

Zu•lu (zo͞o′lo͞o) *n., pl.* **Zulu** or **-lus. 1.** A member of a Bantu people of southeast Africa, primarily inhabiting northeast Natal province in South Africa. **2.** The Nguni language of this people, closely related to Xhosa.

Zu•lu•land (zo͞o′lo͞o-lănd′). A historical region of NE South Africa; settled by members of a Bantu nation.

Zu•ni (zo͞o′nē) also **Zu•ñi** (-nyē, -nē) *n., pl.* **Zuni** or **-nis** also **Zuñi** or **-ñis. 1.** A member of a Pueblo people located in western New Mexico. **2.** The language of the Zuni.

Zu•ni•an (zo͞o′nē-ən) or **Zu•ñi•an** (zo͞on′yē-) *n.* A language family consisting only of Zuni. **—Zu′ni•an, Zu′ñi•an** *adj.*

Zur•ba•rán (zo͝or′bä-rän′, tho͝or′-), **Francisco de.** 1598–1664. Spanish painter whose works include *The Adoration of the Shepherds* (1638).

Zu•rich (zo͝or′ĭk). A city of NE Switzerland on the **Lake of Zurich;** joined the Swiss Confederation in 1351. Pop. 354,500.

Zweig (zwīg, swīg, tsvīk), **Arnold.** 1887–1968. German-born writer best known for *The Case of Sergeant Grischa* (1927).

Zweig, Stefan. 1881–1942. Austrian writer whose works include *Three Masters* (1920).

Zwick•au (zwĭk′ou, tsvĭk′-). A city of E-central Germany S of Leipzig; chartered in the early 13th cent. Pop. 120,486.

zwie•back (swē′băk′, -bäk′, swī′-, zwē′-, zwī′-) *n.* A usu. sweetened bread baked first as a loaf and later cut into slices and toasted. [Ger. : *zwie-*, twice (< MHGer. *zwi-* < OHGer.; see **dwo-***) + *backen*, to bake (< MHGer. < OHGer. *bahhan, backan*).]

Zwing•li (zwĭng′lē, swĭng′-, tsvĭng′-), **Ulrich** or **Huldreich.** 1484–1531. Swiss religious reformer whose sermons on the absolute authority of the Bible (1519) marked the beginning of the Reformation in Switzerland.

Zwing•li•an (zwĭng′lē-ən, swĭng′-, tsvĭng′-) *adj.* Of or relating to Ulrich Zwingli or to his theology, esp. that Jesus is not physically present in the Eucharist. —*n.* A follower of Zwingli. **—Zwing′li•an•ism** *n.*

zwit•ter•i•on (zwĭt′ər-ī′ən, swĭt′-, tsvĭt′-) *n. Phys.* A molecule carrying both a positive and a negative charge. [Ger. : *Zwitter*, hybrid (< MHGer. *zwitarn* < OHGer. < *zwi-*, twice; see **dwo-***) + *ion*, ion (< Gk.; see ION).] **—zwit′ter•i•on′ic** (-ī-ŏn′ĭk) *adj.*

Zwol•le (zwôl′ə, zvôl′ə). A city of N Netherlands on the Ijssel R. Pop. 87,340.

Zwor•y•kin (zwôr′ĭ-kĭn, zvôr′yə-), **Vladimir Kosma.** 1889–1982. Russian-born Amer. physicist and inventor of the iconoscope (1923), the first practical television camera.

zy•de•co (zī′dĭ-kō′) *n. Mus.* Popular music of southern Louisiana that combines elements of French and Caribbean music and the blues, played on the guitar, the accordion, and a washboard. [< Louisiana Fr., poss. alteration of *Les haricots (sont pas salé)*, name of a song, pl. of Fr. *haricot*, bean. See HARICOT[1].]

zyg•a•poph•y•sis (zĭg′ə-pŏf′ĭ-sĭs, zī′gə-) *n., pl.* **-ses** (-sēz′). One of two usu. paired processes of the neural arch of a vertebra that articulates with corresponding parts of adjacent vertebrae.

zygo– or **zyg–** *pref.* **1.** Yoke; pair: *zygodactyl.* **2.** Union: *zygospore.* [NLat. < Gk. *zugo-* < *zugon*, yoke. See **yeug-***.]

zy•go•dac•tyl (zī′gə-dăk′tĭl, zĭg′ə-) *adj.* Having two toes projecting forward and two projecting backward, as certain climbing birds. —*n.* A zygodactyl bird, such as a parrot.

zy•go•gen•e•sis (zī′gō-jĕn′ĭ-sĭs) *n., pl.* **-ses** (-sēz′). Reproduction involving the formation of a zygote. **—zy′go•ge•net′ic** (-jə-nĕt′ĭk) *adj.*

zy•go•ma (zī-gō′mə, zĭ-) *n., pl.* **-ma•ta** (-mə-tə) or **-mas. 1.** The zygomatic bone. **2.** The zygomatic arch. **3.** The zygomatic process. [NLat. *zygōma, zygōmat-* < Gk. *zugōma*, bolt < *zugoun*, to join. See **yeug-***.]

zy•go•mat•ic (zī′gə-măt′ĭk, zĭg′ə-) *adj.* Of, relating to, or located in the area of the zygoma: *a zygomatic muscle.*

zygomatic arch *n.* The bony arch in vertebrates that extends along the side or front of the skull beneath the eye socket and that is formed by the zygomatic bone and the zygomatic process of the temporal bone.

zygomatic bone *n.* A small bone in vertebrates on each side of the face socket, forming the prominence of the cheek.

zygomatic process *n.* Any of three processes that articulate with the zygomatic bone, esp. the process from the temporal bone that articulates to form the zygomatic arch.

zy•go•mor•phic (zī′gə-môr′fĭk, zĭg′ə-) also **zy•go•mor•phous** (-fəs) *adj.* Bilaterally symmetrical. Used of organisms or parts. **—zy′go•mor′phism** *n.*

zy•gos•i•ty (zī-gŏs′ĭ-tē) *n.* The genetic condition of a zygote, esp. with respect to its being a homozygote or a heterozygote.

zy•go•spore (zī′gə-spôr′, -spōr′, zĭg′ə-) *n.* A large multinucleate spore formed by union of similar gametes, as in algae.

zy•gote (zī′gōt′) *n.* **1.** The cell formed by the union of two gametes, esp. a fertilized ovum before cleavage. **2.** The organism that develops from a zygote. [< Gk. *zugōtos*, yoked < *zugoun*, to yoke. See **yeug-***.] **—zy•got′ic** (-gŏt′ĭk) *adj.* **—zy•got′i•cal•ly** *adv.*

zy•go•tene (zī′gə-tēn′) *n.* The stage in prophase of meiosis during which homologous chromosomes become paired. [Fr. *zygotène* : *zygo-*, pair (< NLat.; see ZYGO–) + *-tène*, ribbon (< Lat. *taenia*; see TAENIA).]

–zygous *suff.* Having a zygotic constitution of a specified kind: *heterozygous.* [< Gk. *-zugos*, yoked < *zugon*, yoke. See **yeug-***.]

zy•mase (zī′mās′, -māz′) *n.* The enzyme complex in yeasts that catalyzes the breakdown of sugar into alcohol and carbon dioxide.

–zyme *suff.* Enzyme: *lysozyme.* [< Gk. *zumē*, leaven.]

zymo– or **zym–** *pref.* **1.** Fermentation: *zymurgy.* **2.** Enzyme: *zymase.* [NLat. < Gk. *zumē*, leaven.]

zy•mo•gen (zī′mə-jən) *n.* See **proenzyme.**

zy•mol•o•gy (zī-mŏl′ə-jē) *n.* The chemistry of fermentation. **—zy′mo•log′ic** (-mə-lŏj′ĭk) *adj.* **—zy•mol′o•gist** *n.*

zy•mol•y•sis (zī-mŏl′ĭ-sĭs) *n.* Fermentation. **—zy′mo•lyt′ic** (-mə-lĭt′ĭk) *adj.*

zy•mom•e•ter (zī-mŏm′ĭ-tər) *n.* An instrument used to determine fermentation efficiency.

zy•mo•sis (zī-mō′sĭs) *n., pl.* **-ses** (-sēz). **1.** Fermentation. **2.** *Medic.* **a.** The process of infection. **b.** An infectious disease, esp. one caused by a fungus. [Gk. *zumōsis* < *zumoun*, to leaven < *zumē*, leaven.] **—zy•mot′ic** (-mŏt′ĭk) *adj.*

zy•mur•gy (zī′mûr′jē) *n.* The branch of chemistry that deals with fermentation processes, as in brewing.

zyz•zy•va (zĭz′ə-və) *n.* Any of various tropical American weevils of the genus *Zyzzyva,* often destructive to plants. [NLat. *Zyzzyva*, genus name, prob. < *Zyzza*, former genus of leafhoppers.]

Ulrich Zwingli

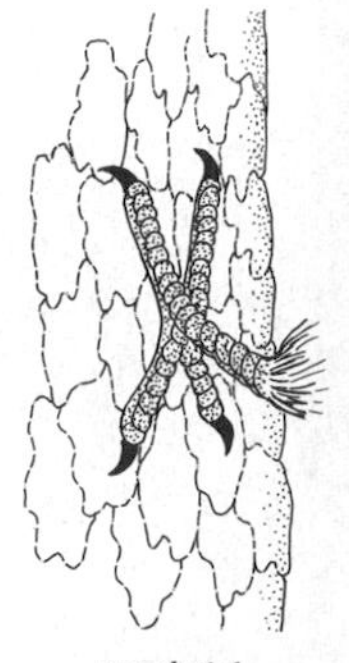
zygodactyl

ă pat	oi boy
ā pay	ou out
âr care	o͝o took
ä father	o͞o boot
ĕ pet	ŭ cut
ē be	ûr urge
ĭ pit	th thin
ī pie	*th* this
îr pier	hw which
ŏ pot	zh vision
ō toe	ə about, item
ô paw	

Stress marks:
′ (primary);
′ (secondary), as in
dictionary (dĭk′shə-nĕr′ē)

Indo-European and the Indo-Europeans

Calvert Watkins

The name *Indo-European* is given for geographic reasons to the large and well-defined linguistic family that includes most of the languages of Europe, past and present, as well as those found in a vast area extending across Iran and Afghanistan to the northern half of the Indian subcontinent. In modern times the family has spread by colonization throughout the Western Hemisphere.

A curious byproduct of the age of colonialism and mercantilism was the introduction of Sanskrit in the 18th century to European intellectuals and scholars long familiar with Latin and Greek and with the European languages of culture—Romance, Germanic, and Slavic. The comparison of this ancient tongue with the two classical languages revolutionized the perception of linguistic relationships.

Speaking to the Asiatick Society in Calcutta on February 2, 1786, the English Orientalist and jurist Sir William Jones (1746–1794) observed of the Sanskrit, Greek, and Latin languages, that

> no philologer could examine them all three, without believing them to have sprung from some common source, which, perhaps, no longer exists.

Jones was content with the assertion of a common original language, without exploring the details. Others took up the cause, but it remained for the German philologist Franz Bopp (1791–1867) to found the new science of comparative grammar, with the publication in 1816 of his work *On the Conjugational System of the Sanskrit Language, in Comparison with that of the Greek, Latin, Persian, and Germanic Languages.* He was 25 years old when it appeared.

It has been rightly said that the comparatist has one fact and one hypothesis. The one fact is that certain languages present similarities among themselves which are so numerous and so precise that they cannot be attributed to chance and which are such that they cannot be explained as borrowings or as universal features. The one hypothesis is that these languages must then be the result of descent from a common original.

In the early part of the 19th century scholars set about systematically exploring the similarities observable among the principal languages spoken now or formerly from Iceland and Ireland to India. They were able to group these languages into a *family* that they called *Indo-European.*

Those dialects or branches of Indo-European still represented today by one or more languages are Indic and Iranian, Greek, Armenian, Slavic, Baltic, Albanian, Celtic, Italic, and Germanic. The present century has seen the addition of two branches to the family, neither of which has left any living trace: Hittite and the other Anatolian languages and Tocharian.

English is thus one of many direct descendants of Indo-European: one of the dialects of the parent language became prehistoric Common Germanic, which subdivided into dialects of which one was West Germanic; this in turn broke up into further dialects, one of which emerged into documentary attestation as Old English. From Old English we can follow the development of the language directly, in texts, down to the present day. This history is our linguistic heritage; our ancestors, in a real cultural sense, are our linguistic ancestors. Indeed, languages have perhaps the longest uninterrupted histories of all the cultural phenomena that we can study.

The comparative method—what we have called the comparatist's "one fact and one hypothesis"—remains today the most powerful device for elucidating linguistic history. When it is carried to a successful conclusion, the comparative method leads not merely to the assumption of the previous existence of an antecedent common language but to a reconstruction of all the salient features of that language. In the best circumstances, as with Indo-European, we can reconstruct the sounds, forms, words, even the structure of sentences—in short, both grammar and lexicon—of a language spoken before the human race had invented the art of writing. It is worth reflecting on this accomplishment. A reconstructed grammar and dictionary cannot claim any sort of completeness, to be sure, and the reconstruction may always be changed because of new data or better analysis. But it remains true, as the distinguished scholar Mary R. Haas has put it, that a reconstructed protolanguage is "a glorious artifact, one which is far more precious than anything an archaeologist can ever hope to unearth."

Proto-Indo-European Grammar: Sounds and Forms

A large part of the success of the comparative method with the Indo-European family is due to the number and the precision of the agreements among the languages, not only in the regular sound correspondences of the roots but even more strikingly so in the particulars of morphology, the forms of language in their grammatical function. Consider the partial paradigms of the words for "dog" *(*kwon-)* and "to kill" *(*g^{w}hen-)*:

	Hittite	Greek	Vedic
nominative	*kuwas*	*kúōn*	*ś(u)vā́*
accusative	*kuwanan*	*kúna*	*śvā́nam*
genitive	*kūnas*	*kunós*	*śúnas*

	Lithuanian	Old Irish	Proto-Indo-European
nominative	*šuõ*	*cú*	**k(u)wō(n)*
accusative	*šùnį*	*coin*	**kwónm̥*
genitive	*šuñs*	*con*	**kunés*

	Hittite	Vedic	PIE
third singular present indicative	*kuenzi*	*hánti*	**g^{w}hén-ti*
third plural present indicative	*kunanzi*	*ghnánti*	**g^{w}hn-énti*

The agreement of detail in sound correspondences, in vowel alternations and their distribution, in the accent, in the grammatical forms (endings), and in the syntactic functions is little short of astounding.

Speech Sounds and their Alternations. The system of *sounds* in Proto-Indo-European was rich in stop consonants. There was an unvoiced series, *p, t, k, k^w* (like the *qu* of *quick*), a voiced series, *b, d, g, g^w*, and a voiced aspirate or "murmured" series, *bh, dh, gh, g^{w}h*, pronounced like the voiced series but followed by a puff of breath. The language had a single continuant *s*, which was voiced to *z* before voiced stop consonants. It had as well three so-called *laryngeals* or *h*-like sounds, all of which are written here as schwa, or *ə* (equivalent notations are *H* or *h*).

Proto-Indo-European had two nasals, *m* and *n*, two liquids, *r* and *l*, and the glides *w* and *y*. A salient characteristic of Indo-European was that these sounds could function both as consonants and as vowels. Their consonantal value was as in English. As vowels, symbolized *m̥, n̥, l̥,* and *r̥*, the liquids and nasals sounded much like the final syllables of English *bottom, button, bottle,* and *butter*. The vocalic counterparts of *w* and *y* were the vowels *u* and *i*. The laryngeals too could function both as consonants and as vowels: their consonantal value was that of *h*-like sounds, while as vowels they were varieties of schwa, much like the final syllable of English *sofa*; hence the choice of schwa to represent laryngeals in this Appendix.

The other vowels of Indo-European were *e, o,* and *a*. These, as well as *i* and *u*, occurred both long and short, as did the diphthongs *ei, oi, ai, eu, ou, au.* (All vowels are pronounced as in Latin or Italian.) A number of the long vowels of later Indo-European resulted from the contraction of early Indo-European short vowels with a following *ə*. Already in Proto-Indo-European itself two of the three laryngeals had the property of "coloring" an adjacent fundamental vowel *e* to *a* and *o*, respectively, before the contractions took place. Thus the root **pā-**, "to protect," is contracted from older **paə-*, with "a-coloring"; the root **dō-**, "to give," is contracted from older **doə-*, with "o-coloring"; and the root **dhē-**, "to set, put," is contracted from older **dheə-*, without coloring. The fundamental vowel in each of these roots, as in most Indo-European roots, was originally *e*. In scholarly usage it is now customary to write the noncoloring laryngeal as $ə_1$ (or h_1), thus **dheə$_1$-*; the a-coloring laryngeal as $ə_2$ (or h_2), thus **paə$_2$-*; and the o-coloring laryngeal as $ə_3$ (or h_3), thus **doə$_3$-*. This typographically cumbersome notation has been simplified in the Appendix, since the vowel before the schwa is sufficient to distinguish the three in the cases of contraction to a long vowel, and in other positions in most languages other than Greek the three merge to one. No systematic notice has been taken in this Appendix of word-initial laryngeals before vowels (amply attested in Hittite), since the root forms with initial vowel are readily convertible by the reader. Thus **ant-**, "front, forehead," from **ə$_2$ant-, *əant-* (Hittite *hant-*, "front, forehead"); **op-**, "to work, produce in abundance," from **ə$_3$op-, *əop-* (Hittite *happ-in-ant-*, "rich"); and **ed-**, "to eat," from **ə$_1$ed-, *əed-* (Hittite *ed-*, "to eat").

A characteristic feature of Indo-European was the system of vocalic *alternations* termed *apophony* or *ablaut*. This was a set of internal vowel changes expressing different morphological functions. A clear reflex of this feature is preserved in the English strong verbs, where, for example, the vocalic alternations between *write* and *wrote, give* and *gave,* express the present and past tenses. Ablaut in Indo-European affected the vowels *e* and *o*. The fundamental form was *e*; this *e* could appear as *o* under certain conditions, and in other conditions both *e* and *o* could disappear entirely. On this basis we speak of given forms in Indo-European as exhibiting, respectively, the *e-grade* (or *full grade*), the *o-grade,* or the *zero grade*. The *e* and the *o* might furthermore occur as long *ē* or *ō*, termed the *lengthened grade*.

To illustrate: the Indo-European root **ped-**, "foot," appears in the e-grade in Latin *ped-* (PEDAL), but in the o-grade in Greek *pod-* (PODIATRIST). Germanic **fōtuz* (FOOT) reflects the lengthened o-grade **pōd-*. The zero grade of the same root shows no vowel at all: **pd-*, a form attested in Greek and Sanskrit.

When the zero grade involved a root with one of the sounds *m, n, r, l, w,* or *y* (collectively termed *resonants*), the resonant would regularly appear in its vocalic function, forming a syllable. We have the e-grade root **senkʷ-** in English SINK, the o-grade form **sonkʷ-* in SANK, and the zero-grade form **sn̥kʷ-* in SUNK. Compare the different forms of the words for "dog" and "kill"in the paradigms cited earlier.

In the case of roots with long vowels arising from contraction with *ə*, the ablaut can be most clearly understood by referring to the older, uncontracted forms. Thus **pā-**, "to protect," contracted from **paə-*, has a zero grade **pə-*; **dō-**, "to give," contracted from **doə-*, has a zero grade **də-*; **dhē-**, "to place," contracted from **dheə-*, has a zero grade **dhə-*. The fundamental vowel of the full grade disappears in the zero grade, and only the *ə* remains. Long *ū* and long *ī* could also arise from contraction: full grade **peuə-**, "to purify," has a zero grade **puə-* contracted to **pū-* (PURE).

Grammatical Forms and Syntax. Proto-Indo-European was a highly inflected language. Grammatical relationships and the syntactic function of words in the sentence were indicated primarily by variations in the endings of the words.

The structure of all inflected words, regardless of part of speech, was the same: *root* plus one or more *suffixes* plus *ending*. Thus the word **ker-wo-s*, "a stag," is composed of the root **ker-[1]**, "horn," plus the noun suffix *-wo-*, plus the nominative singular ending *-s*. The root contained the basic semantic kernel, the underlying notion, which the suffix could modify in various ways. It was primarily the suffix that determined the part of speech of the word. Thus a single root like **prek-**, "to ask," could, depending on the suffix, form a verb **pr̥k-sko-*, "to ask" (Latin *poscere*), a noun **prek-*, "prayer" (Latin *precēs*), and an adjective **prok-o-*, "asking" (underlying Latin *procus*, "suitor").

The root plus the suffix or suffixes constituted the *stem*. The stems represented the basic lexical stock of Indo-European, the separate words of its dictionary. Yet a single root would commonly furnish a large number of derivative stems with different suffixes, both nominal and verbal, much as English *love* is both noun and verb as well as the base of such derivatives as *lovely, lover,* and *beloved*. For this reason it is customary to group such collections of derivatives, in a variety of Indo-European languages, under the root on which they are built. The root entries of the Appendix are arranged in this way, with derivatives that exhibit similar suffixes forming subgroups consisting of Indo-European stems or words.

An important technique of word formation in Indo-European was *composition*, the combining of two separate words or notions into a single word. It is in the area of composition that English has most faithfully preserved the ancient Indo-European patterns of word formation, by continuously forming them anew, re-creating them.

Lexicon and Culture

The reconstruction of a *protolanguage* — the common ancestor of a family of spoken or attested languages — has a further implication. When we have reconstructed a protolanguage, we have also necessarily established the existence of a prehistoric society, a speech community that used that protolanguage. The existence of Proto-Indo-European thus presupposes the existence, in some fashion, of a society of Indo-Europeans.

Though by no means a perfect mirror, the lexicon of a language remains the single most effective way of approaching and understanding the culture of its speakers. As such, the contents of the Indo-European lexicon provide a remarkably clear view of the whole culture of an otherwise unknown prehistoric society.

We are able to examine the contents of this Indo-European lexicon, which aside from its inherent interest permits us to ascertain many characteristics of Indo-European society. It is remarkable how much of this reconstructed vocabulary is preserved in native or borrowed derivatives in Modern English.

General Terms. It is appropriate to begin with a sampling of basic terms in the lexicon, which have no special cultural value but attest to the richness of the tradition. All are widespread in the family. There are two verbs expressing existence, **es-** and **bheuə-**, found in English IS, Latin *esse*, and English BE, Latin *fu-tūrus* (FUTURE), respectively.

A number of qualitative adjectives are attested that go back to the protolanguage. Some come in semantic pairs: **sen-**, "old," and **newo-**, "new"; also **sen-**, "old," and **yeu-**, "youthful vigor"; **tenu-*, "thin" (under **ten-**), and **tegu-**, "thick"; **gʷerə-[1]**, "heavy," and **legʷh-**, "light." There are also the two prefixes **su-**, "good, well-," and **dus-**, "bad, ill-," in the Greek forms borrowed as EU- and DYS- .

The personal pronouns belong to the very earliest layer of Indo-European that can be reached by reconstruction. The lack of any formal resemblance in English between the subject case (nominative) I and the object case (accusative) ME is a direct and faithful reflection of the same disparity in Proto-Indo-European, respectively **eg** *(*egō)* and **me-[1]**. The other pronouns are **tu-** *(*te-)*, "thou," **nes-[2]** or **we-**, "we," and **yu-**, "you." No pronouns for the third person were in use.

The most persistent and widespread pronominal stems are **to-** and **k^{w}o-**, which are preserved in the English demonstrative and interrogative-relative pronouns and adverbs beginning with *th-* (THIS, THEN) and *wh-* (WHO, WHICH, WHEN).

All the languages of the family show some or all of the Indo-European numerals. The language had a decimal system. There is complete agreement on the numerals from two to ten: **dwo-** *(*duwō)*, **trei-** *(*treyes)*, **k^{w}etwer-** *(*k^{w}etwores)*, **penk^{w}e**, **s(w)eks**, **septm̥**, **oktō(u)**, **newn̥**, **dekm̥**. For the numeral "one" the dialects vary. We have a root **sem-**^{1} in some derivatives, while the western Indo-European languages Germanic, Celtic, and Latin share the form **oi-no-**. The word for "hundred," formed from **dekm̥**, "ten," was **(d)km̥tom*. No common form for "thousand" or any other higher number can be reconstructed for the protolanguage.

Nature and the Physical Environment. In Indo-European "moon/month" is a derivative of the verb "to measure," **mē-**^{2}. The other celestial bodies recognized were the sun, **sāwel-**, and the stars, **ster-**^{3}. The movement of the sun dictated the names for the points of the compass. The word for "east" is derived from the verbal root **aus-**, "to shine." The setting sun furnished the word for "evening" and "west": **wes-pero-**. The most widespread of the words for "night" was **nek^{w}-t-**.

The Indo-Europeans knew snow in their homeland; the word **sneig^{w}h-** is nearly ubiquitous. However, the word for "rain" varies among the separate branches: we have words of differing distribution such as **seuə-**^{2}.

The root **deiw-** occurs widely as the divine bright sky (ZEUS). Another divine natural phenomenon is illustrated by the root **(s)tenə-**, "thunder," and the name of the Germanic god THOR.

A word for the earth can be reconstructed as **dhghem-** *(*dheghom)*. The root **mori-** is attested dialectally (MERE), but it may well have referred to a lake or other smaller body of water. Transportation by or across water was known to the Indo-Europeans, since most of the languages attest an old word for "boat" or "ship," **nāu-**, probably propelled by oars or a pole (**erə-**, "to row").

The names for a number of different trees are widely enough attested to be viewed as Proto-Indo-European in date. The general term for "tree" and "wood" was **deru-**. The original meaning of the root was doubtless "to be firm, solid," and from it is derived not only the family of English TREE but also that of English TRUE.

Indo-European had a generic term for "wild animal," **ghwer-** (FERAL). The wolf was known and evidently feared; its name is subject to taboo deformation (the conscious alteration of the form of a tabooed word, as in English *gol-derned, dad-burned*). The variant forms **wl̥k^{w}o-**, **lupo-*, and **wl̥p-** (also "fox") are all found. The name of the bear was likewise subject to

Reconstructed female and male heads (Dnieper-Donets culture, c. 4000 B.C.)

a hunter's taboo: the animal could not be mentioned by its real name on the hunt. The southern Indo-European languages have the original form, **r̥tko-** (Latin *ursus*, Greek *arktos*), but all the northern languages have a substitute term. In Slavic the bear is the "honey-eater," in Germanic the "brown one" (BEAR^{2}, and note also BRUIN).

A generic term for "fish" existed, **dhghū-* (also **peisk-* in Europe). The salmon (**laks-**) and the eel *(*ang^{w}i-)* were known, the latter also in the meaning "snake." Several birds were known, including the crane (**gerə-**^{2}) and the eagle (**or-**).

The names for a number of insects can be reconstructed in the protolanguage, including the wasp *(*wopsā)*, the hornet (**krəs-r̥o-*, a derivative of **ker-**^{1}, "head," from the shape of the insect), and the fly *(*mū-)*. The bee (**bhei-**) was particularly important as the producer of honey, for which we have the common Indo-European name **melit-** (MILDEW). Honey was the only source of sugar and sweetness (**swād-**, "sweet," is ancient), and notably was the base of the only certain Indo-European alcoholic beverage, **medhu-**, which in different dialects meant both MEAD ("wine" in Greece and Anatolia) and "honey."

People and Society. For human beings themselves, a number of terms were employed, with different nuances of meaning. The usual terms for "man" and "woman" are **wī-ro-** (VIRILE) and **g^{w}enā-* from **g^{w}en-** (GYNECOLOGY). For "person" in general, the oldest word was apparently **manu-* (**man-**^{1}), as preserved in English MAN and in Slavic and Sanskrit. In other dialects we find interesting metaphorical expressions, which attest a set of religious concepts opposing the gods as immortal and celestial to humankind as mortal and terrestrial. Humans are either **mortos*, "mortal" (**mer-**, "to die"), or **dhghomyo-*, "earthling" (**dhghem-**, "earth").

The parts of the body belong to the basic layer of vocabulary and are for the most part faithfully preserved in Indo-European languages. The word for "foot" is attested everywhere (**ped-**), while that for "hand" differs according to dialect; the most widespread is **ghes-r̥-* (CHIRO-). Internal organs named in

Indo-European times include the heart (**kerd-**), womb (**gʷelbh-*), gall (**ghel-**[2]), and liver (**yĕkʷr̥**). The male sexual organs, **pes-** and **ergh-*, are common patrimony, as is **ors-**, "backside."

A large number of kinship terms have been reconstructed. They are agreed in pointing to a society that was patriarchal, patrilocal (the bride leaving her household to join that of her husband's family), and patrilineal (descent reckoned by the male line). "Father" and "head of the household" are one: **pəter-**, with his spouse, the **māter-**. Related terms are found for the grandfather (**awo-**) and the maternal uncle (**awon-*), and correspondingly the term **nepōt-** (feminine **neptī-*) applied to both grandson (perhaps originally "daughter's son") and nephew ("sister's son"). The English words SON and DAUGHTER clearly reflect Indo-European **sūnu-* (from **seuə-**[1]) and **dhughəter-**.

Male blood relations were designated as **bhrāter-** (BROTHER), which doubtless extended beyond those with a common father or mother; the Greek cognate means "fellow member of a clanlike group." The female counterpart was **swesor-** (SISTER), probably literally "the female member of the kin group," with an old word for "woman" **-sor-* and the root **s(w)e-**, designating the self, one's own group.

Reconstructed hillfort at Vučedol in eastern Croatia (c. 3000 B.C.)

The root **dem-** denoted both the house (Latin *domus*) and the household as a social unit. The father of the family (Latin *pater familias*) was the "master of the house" (Greek *despotēs*) or simply "he of the house" (Latin *dominus*). A larger unit was the village, designated by the word **weik-**[1]. Human settlements were frequently built on the top of high places fortified for defense. Words for such fortified high places vary; there are **pelə-**[3], variant **poli-* (ACROPOLIS), the Celtic word for "ring fort," **dhūno-** (TOWN), and **bhergh-**[2] (*-burg* in place names).

Economic Life and Technology. A characteristic of Indo-European and other archaic societies was the principle of exchange and reciprocal gift-giving. The presentation of a gift entailed the obligation of a countergift, and the acts of giving and receiving were equivalent. They were simply facets of a single process of generalized exchange, which assured the circulation of wealth throughout the society.

Clay model of wagon from Budakalász, Hungary (c. 2800 B.C.)

This principle has left clear traces in the Indo-European vocabulary. The root **dō-** of Latin *dōnāre* means "to give" in most dialects but in Hittite means "to take." The GUEST (**ghos-ti-**) in Indo-European times was the person with whom one had mutual obligations of hospitality. But he was also the stranger, and the stranger in an uncertain and warring tribal society may well be hostile: the Latin cognate *hostis* means "enemy."

The Indo-Europeans practiced agriculture and the cultivation of cereals. We have several terms of Indo-European antiquity for grain: **gr̥ə-no-** (CORN), **yewo-**, and **pūro-*, which may have designated wheat or spelt. Of more restricted distribution is **bhares-**, "barley." A root for grinding is attested, **melə-** (MEAL[2], MILL). The verb "to plow" is **arə-*, again a common European term, with the name of the plow, **arə-trom.*

Stockbreeding and animal husbandry were an important part of Indo-European economic life. The names for all the familiar domesticated animals are present throughout the family. The common Indo-European name of the horse, **ekwo-**, is probably derived from the adjective **ōku-**, "swift." The expansion and migration of the Indo-European-speaking peoples in the later third and early second millenniums B.C. is intimately bound up with the diffusion of the horse. The verbal root **demə-**, "to force," acquired the special sense of "to tame horses," whence English TAME.

Stock was a source and measure of wealth. The original sense of **peku-** was probably "wealth, riches," as in Latin *pecunia,* which came to mean "wealth in cattle" and finally "cattle" proper.

The verbal roots **pā-**, "to protect," and **kʷel-**[1], "to revolve, move around," are widely used for the notion of herding or watching over stock.

Roots indicating a number of technical operations are attested in most of the languages of the family. One such is **teks-**, which in some dialects means "to fabricate, especially by working with an ax," but in others means "to weave" (TEXTILE). The root **dheigh-**, meaning "to mold, shape," is applied both to bread

(DOUGH) and to mud or clay, whence words for both pottery and mud walls (Iranian **pari-daiza-*, "walled around," borrowed into Greek as the word that became English PARADISE.)

The house (**dem-**) included a **dhwer-** (DOOR), which probably referred originally to the gateway into the enclosure of the household. The house would have had a central hearth, denoted in some languages by **as-** (properly a verb, "to burn"). Fire itself was known by two words, one of animate gender (**egni-*, Latin *ignis*) and one neuter (**pūr-**, Greek *pur*).

The Indo-Europeans knew metal and metallurgy, to judge from the presence of the word **ayes-* in Sanskrit, Germanic, and Latin. The term designated copper and perhaps bronze. Iron is a latecomer, technologically, and the terms for it vary from dialect to dialect. Latin has *ferrum,* while the Germanic and Celtic term was **isarno-*, properly "holy (metal)," from **eis-**, doubtless so called because the first iron was derived from small meteorites. Gold, **ghel-²**, probably "yellow (metal)," was known from ancient times, though the names for it vary. Silver was **arg-**, with various suffixes, doubtless meaning "white (metal)."

It was probably not long before the dispersal of the Proto-Indo-European community that the use of the wheel and wheeled transport was adopted. Despite the existence of widespread word families, most terms relating to wheeled vehicles seem to be metaphors formed from already existing words, rather than original, unanalyzable ones. So NAVE, or hub of the wheel (**nobh-**), is the same word as NAVEL. This is clearly the case with WHEEL itself, where the widespread **kʷ(e)kʷl-o-* is an expressive derivative of a verb (**kʷel-¹**) meaning "to revolve or go around." Other words for "wheel" are dialectal and again derivative, such as Latin *rota* from a verbal root **ret-**, "to run." The root **wegh-**, "to go, transport in a vehicle" (WAGON), is attested quite early, though not in Hittite. This evidence for the late appearance of the wheel agrees with archaeological findings that date the distribution of the wheel in Europe to the latter part of the fifth millennium B.C., the latest possible date for the community of Proto-Indo-European proper.

Ideology. A number of verbs denoting mental activity are found. The most widespread is **men-¹**, preserved in English MIND. Other derivatives refer to remembering, warning (putting in mind), and thinking in general.

The notions of government and sovereignty were well represented. The presence of the old word for tribal king, **reg-* (**reg-**), only in the extreme east (RAJAH) and the extreme west (Latin *rēx,* Celtic *-rīx*) virtually guarantees its presence in the earliest Indo-European society. Another aspect of the function of sovereignty is the sphere of the law. There is an old word, **yewes-**, probably for "religious law," in Latin

Stele from Kernosovka in the Crimea

iūs. Latin *lēx* is also ancient (**leg-** or **legh-**), though the details of its etymology are uncertain. In a society that emphasized the principle of exchange and reciprocity, it is scarcely surprising that the notion of contractual obligation should be well represented. Several roots specify the notion of "bond": **bhendh-**, **ned-**, and **leig-**, all of which have derivatives with technical legal meanings in various languages.

Indo-European is particularly rich in religious vocabulary. An important form, which is also found only in the peripheral languages Sanskrit, Latin, and Celtic, is the two-word metaphoric phrase **kred-dhē-*, literally "to put (**dhē-**) heart (**kerd-**)." The two words have been joined together in the western languages, as in Latin *crēdō,* "I believe."

Oral prayers, requests of the deity, and other ritual utterances must have played a significant role in Indo-European religion. We have already seen **prek-** (PRAY), and note also **sengʷh-** (SING), and **gwerə-²**, which in Latin *grātia* (GRACE) has had a new life in Christianity. The root **spend-** has the basic meaning of "to make an offering or perform a rite," whence "to engage oneself by a ritual act." Its Latin derivative *spondēre* means "to promise" (SPOUSE).

It is noteworthy that the idea of "holy" is intimately bound up with that of "whole, healthy," in a number of forms: **kailo-** (WHOLE and HOLY) and **solə-**, whence Latin *salvus* (SALVATION). An ancient root relating solely to religion is **sak-** (SACRED).

We may also add that poetry and a tradition of poetics are common patrimony in most of the Indo-European traditions. The hymns of the Rig-Veda are composed in meters related to those used by the Greek poets. Furthermore, one securely reconstructible Indo-European place name rests squarely on a metaphor: **Pīwer-iā* in Greek *Pieria* (PIERIAN SPRING) and *Īwer-ion-*, the prehistoric Celtic name for Ireland (Gaelic *Éire, Érin*), both continue an Indo-European feminine adjective *pīwer-iə, "fat," metaphorically "fertile," from **peiə-**, the same root that gives English FAT.

Most interesting are the cases where it is possible to reconstruct from two or more traditions (usually including Homer and the Rig-Veda) a poetic phrase or formula consisting of two members. One such example is the expression "imperishable fame," **klewos n̥dhgʷhitom* (**kleu-**). The immortality of the gods (**n̥-mrto-*, from **mer-**) is emphasized anew by the vivid verb phrase **nek-**[1] **terə-**[2], "to overcome death," appearing in the Greek word *nektar*, the drink of the gods. And at least one three-member formula can be reconstructed for the poetic language of prayer on the combined evidence of Latin, Umbrian, Avestan, and Sanskrit: "Protect man and cattle!" (**pā- wī-ro- peku**).

Conclusion

By far the greatest part of the information about Indo-European culture and society is furnished by language and lexicon alone. Other disciplines ideally serve to fill out and complete the picture to be gathered from the study of vocabulary: archaeology, prehistory, comparative religion, and the history of institutions.

Archaeologists have not in fact succeeded in locating the Indo-Europeans. The so-called Kurgan peoples, named after the Russian word for their characteristic "barrow" or "tumulus" grave structure, may well have spoken an Indo-European language. The correlation between the Kurgan cultural features described by archaeologists and the Indo-European lexicon are striking, down to architectural features such as a small subterranean or aboveground rectangular hut (**dom-*, **dem-**) of timber uprights (**kli-t-*, **klei-**, and **stu-t-*, **stā-**, still with us in English STUD).

Some time around the middle of the fifth millennium B.C., these people expanded from the steppe zone north of the Black Sea and beyond the Volga into the Balkans and adjacent areas. These Kurgan peoples bore a new mobile and aggressive culture into Neolithic Europe, and it is not unreasonable to associate them with the coming of the Indo-Europeans. We should perhaps be content to recognize the Kurgan peoples as speakers of certain Indo-European languages and as sharing a common Indo-European cultural patrimony. The ultimate "cradle" of the Indo-Europeans may well never be known, and language remains the best and fullest evidence for prehistoric Indo-European society. It is the comparative method in historical linguistics that can illumine not only ancient ways of life but also ancient modes of thought.

Guide to the Appendix

This Dictionary carries the etymology of the English language to its logical and natural conclusion, for if the documentary history of words is of interest and value, so is their reconstructed prehistory. The historical component is given in the etymologies, after the definitions in the main body of the Dictionary. This Appendix supplies the prehistoric component, tracing the ultimate Indo-European derivations of those English words that are descended from a selected group of Indo-European roots.

The form that is given in **boldface** type at the head of each entry is, unless otherwise identified, an Indo-European root in its basic form; this is followed by a list of some of its more important Modern English descendants. The entry proper begins with a repetition of the basic root form, followed in some cases by one or more variants, also in boldface type. The basic meaning or meanings of the root are given immediately after the entry form and its variants. Meanings that are different parts of speech are separated by a semicolon:

kei-[1]. To lie; bed, couch; beloved, dear.
pelə-[2]. Flat; to spread.
leg-. To collect; with derivatives meaning "to speak."

After the basic meaning there may appear further information about the phonological shape or nature of the root:

skei-. To cut, split. Extension of **sek-**.
kʷr̥mi-. Worm. Rhyme word to **wr̥mi-*, worm (see **wer-**[2]).
pā-. To protect, feed. Contracted from **paə-*.
līk-. Body, form; like, same. Germanic root.

Most, but not all, of the additional information is self-explanatory. In the first two examples, the boldface forms **sek-** and **wer-**[2] are cross-references to those roots, which are main entries in this Appendix. Every boldface form appearing in the text of an entry is such a cross-reference. In the example **pā-** the form **paə-* represents an older root form; the nature of these contractions is explained in the preceding essay under "Speech Sounds and their Alternations." The entries **līk-**, **nēhw-iz**, and **re-** are not, strictly speaking, Indo-European, since they are represented in only one branch of the family, but they are included within boldface brackets because of the number of English words among their descendants.

The text of each entry describes in detail the development of Modern English words from the root. Each section of an entry begins with a list, in SMALL CAPITALS, of the Modern English words derived from a particular form of the root. The simple (uncompounded) derivatives are given first; the compounds follow, separated from them by a semicolon. Parentheses indicate that the etymology of a word in the body of the Dictionary contains a cross-reference to the etymology at another entry. In some cases no further semantic or morphological development needs to be explained, and the *lemma,* the historically attested representative of the root, is immediately given:

awi-. Bird. **I. 1.** AVIAN . . . from Latin *avis,* bird.

Much more commonly, however, intermediate developments require explanation. These intermediate stages are reconstructions representing a word stem in Indo-European that is necessary to explain the lemma following it (see the section "Grammatical Forms and Syntax" in the preceding essay). The reconstructed forms are not historically attested; they are preceded by an asterisk (*) to note this fact. Sometimes earlier or later developments of the intermediate forms are given in parentheses, as in the example of **stā-** below. In these cases the symbol < is used to mean "derived from" and the symbol > is used to mean "developed into." The following terms are used to describe typical morphological processes of Indo-European:

Full-grade form: A form with e-vocalism (the basic form); so identified for descriptive contrast.

O-grade form: A form with o-vocalism:

nekʷ-t-. . . . O-grade form **nokʷ-t-*.

Zero-grade form: A form with zero-vocalism:

men-[1]. . . . **I.** Zero-grade form **mn̥-*.

Lengthened-grade form: A form with lengthened vocalism:

ked-. . . . **1.** Lengthened-grade form **kēd-*.

Secondary full-grade form: A new full-grade form created by inserting the fundamental vowel *e* in the zero-grade form of an extended root:

stā-. . . . **V.** Zero-grade extended root **stū-* (< **stuə-*). . . . **VI.** Secondary full-grade form **steuə-*.

Basic form: The unchanged root; so identified for descriptive contrast.

Suffixed form: A form with one or more suffixes, written with an internal hyphen:

laks-. . . . Suffixed form **laks-o-*.
maghu-. . . . Suffixed form **magho-ti-*.
mel-[2]. . . . **1.** Suffixed (comparative) form **mel-yos-*.

Prefixed form: A form with a prefix, written with an internal hyphen:

op-. . . . **6.** . . . from prefixed form **co-op-*.

Extended form: A form with an extension or enlargement, written without internal hyphens:

pel-[5]. . . . **II.** Extended form **pelə-*.

Nasalized form: A form with a nasal infix, written with internal hyphens:

tag-. . . . **1.** Nasalized form **ta-n-g-*.

Reduplicated form: A form prefixed by its own initial consonant followed by a vowel:

segh-. . . . **5.** Reduplicated form **si-sgh-*.

Expressive form: A form with "expressive gemination" (doubling of the final consonant), written without internal hyphens:

gal-. . . . **3.** Expressive form **gall-*.

Compound Form: A form compounded with a form of another root, written with internal hyphens:

dem-. . . . **3.** Compound **dems-pot-*.

Shortened form: A form with shortened vocalism:

syū-. . . . **III.** Suffixed shortened form **syu-men-*.

Reduced form: A form with loss of one or more sounds:

ghesor-. . . . Reduced form **ghesr-*.

Oldest root form: A root form showing a laryngeal (*ə*) in a position, typically at the beginning or end of a root, where it is preserved in only a few Indo-European languages, such as Greek or Hittite:

ster-[3]. . . . **3.** Oldest root form **əster-*.

Variant form: A form altered in any way other than those described in the above categories:

deru-. . . . **2.** Variant form *dreu-*.

These terms can be combined freely to describe in as much detail as necessary the development from the root to the lemma.

dhē(i)-. . . . **1.** Suffixed reduced form **dhē-mnā-*. FEMALE, FEMININE; EFFEMINATE, from Latin *fēmina,* woman (< "she who suckles").

gerə-[1]. . . . **1.** Suffixed lengthened-grade form **gērə-s-*. AGERATUM, GERIATRICS, from Greek *gēras,* old age.

petə-. . . . **2.** Suffixed (stative) variant zero-grade form **pat-ē-*. PATENT, PATULOUS, from Latin *patēre,* to be open.

In order to emphasize the fact that English belongs to the Germanic branch of Indo-European and give precedence to directly inherited words in contrast to words borrowed from other branches, the intermediate stages in Germanic etymologies are covered in fuller detail. The Common or Proto-Germanic (here called simply Germanic) forms underlying English words are always given. Where no other considerations intervene, Germanic is given first of the Indo-European groups, and Old English is given first within Germanic, although this order of precedence is not rigidly applied.

The final item in most entries is an abbreviated reference, in brackets, to Julius Pokorny's *Indogermanisches Etymologisches Wörterbuch* (Bern, 1959). This, the standard work of reference and synthesis in the Indo-European field, carries a full range of the actual comparative material on which the roots are reconstructed. Our Appendix presents only those aspects of the material that are directly relevant to English. For example, the English word MANY is found at the root **menegh-**, "copious." This entry describes the transition of the Indo-European form through Germanic **managa-* to Old English *manig, mænig,* "many." It does not cite the evidence on which this assertion is based, but it refers to "Pokorny *men(e)gh-* 730." The entry *men(e)gh-* on page 730 in Pokorny's dictionary cites, in addition to the Old English word, the forms attested in Sanskrit, Celtic, Gothic, Old High German, Old Norse, Slavic, and Lithuanian, from which the reconstruction of the root was made. These references should serve as a reminder that the information given in this Appendix is assertive rather than expository and that the evidence and evaluation upon which its assertions are based are not presented here.

Symbols: * unattested
< derived from
> developed into

INDO-EUROPEAN SOUND CORRESPONDENCES

Probably the most basic element of language change is a gradual shift in the way individual speech sounds are pronounced. As the Indo-European speech community expanded over the centuries into new territories, local dialectal variations gave rise to increasingly divergent language families. This table shows the historical development of sounds from Proto-Indo-European to the principal older Indo-European languages. For example, reading down the first column, it can be seen that Proto-Indo-European initial **p** remains **p** in Latin, but it is lost entirely in Old Irish and becomes **f** in Germanic and consequently in Old English: thus Indo-European ***pəter-**, meaning "father," becomes Latin *pater*, Old Irish *athir*, and Common Germanic ***fadar**, Old English *fæder*. A more precise way of describing this relationship is to say that initial **p** in Proto-Indo-European corresponds to **p** in Latin, to **f** in Germanic and Old English, and to

	CONSONANTS															
	STOPS												CONTINUANT	LARYNGEALS		
	UNVOICED				VOICED				VOICED ASPIRATE							
INDO-EUROPEAN	p	t	k	k^w	b	d	g	g^w	bh	dh	gh	g^wh	s	ə$_1$	ə$_2$	ə$_3$
HITTITE	p	t	k	ku	p	t	k	ku	p	t	k	ku	s	—*	h	h
TOCHARIAN	p	t/c/ts	k/ś	k/ś	p	t/c/ts	k/ś	k/ś	p	t/c/ts	k/ś	k/ś	s/ṣ	—	—	—
SANSKRIT	p	t	ś	k/c	b	d	j	g/j	bh	dh	h	gh/h	s/ṣ	—	—	—
AVESTAN	p	t	s	k/c	b	d	z	g/j	b	d	g/z	g/j	h	—	—	—
OLD PERSIAN	p	t	th	k	b	d	d/z	g/j	b	d	g/d	g/j	h	—	—	—
OLD CHURCH SLAVONIC	p	t	s	k/č/c	b	d	z	g/ž/z	b	d	z	g/ž/z	s	—	—	—
LITHUANIAN	p	t	s	k	b	d	z	g	b	d	z	g	s	—	—	—
ARMENIAN	h	th	s	kh	p	t	c	k	b	d	z(j)	g	h	—	—	—
GREEK	p	t	k	p/t/k	b	d	g	b/d/g	ph	th	kh	ph/th/kh	h	—	—	—
LATIN	p	t	c	qu	b	d	g	v	f(b)	f(d)	h	f	s	—	—	—
OLD IRISH	–*	t	c	c	b	d	g	b	b	d	g	g	s	—	—	—
COMMON GERMANIC	f	th	h	hw	p	t	k	kw/k	b	d	g	b/g	s	—	—	—
GOTHIC	f	th	h(j)	hw/w	p	t	k	q	b	d	g	b/g	s	—	—	—
OLD NORSE†	f	th	h	hv	p	t	k	kv	b	d	g	b/g	s	—	—	—
OLD HIGH GERMAN†	f	d	h	hw/w	p/pf	z	k	qu	b	t/d	g	b/g	s	—	—	—
MIDDLE DUTCH†	v	th/d	h	w	p	t	k	qu	b	d	g	b/g	s	—	—	—
OLD ENGLISH†	f	th	h	hw	p	t	c	cw/c	b	d	g	b/g	s	—	—	—

zero in Old Irish. The correspondences shown in the table are regular: they always occur as stated unless specific factors intervene. This table shows only the initial consonants and vowels in initial syllables, which are generally the simplest elements involved in sound change. All other phonetic elements including stress and environment also show regular correspondences, but often with considerable complexity.

NOTES:
*— equals zero: p was lost in Old Irish.
w was lost in Greek.
y was lost in Old Irish, Old Norse.
Initial laryngeals are preserved only in Hittite.

†The effects of umlaut are not considered.

SONORANTS						**VOWELS**													
NASALS		**LIQUIDS**		**GLIDES**		**SHORT**					**LONG**					**SYLLABIC SONORANTS**			
m	n	r	l	y/i	w/u	e	o	a	i	u	ē (eə)	ō (oə)	ā (aə)	ī (iə)	ū (uə)	m̥	n̥	r̥	l̥
m	n	r	l	y	w	ei	a/ha	a/ha	i	u	e/i	a	a/ah	i	u/uh	am	an	ar	al
m	n	r	l	y	w	ä	e	ā	ä/i	ä/u	e	o,ā	o,ā	i	u	äm	än	är	äl
m	n	r/l	l/r	y	v	a	a/ā	a	i	u	ā	ā	ā	ī	ū	a	a	ṛ	ṛ
m	n	r	l	y	v	a	a/ā	a	i	u	ā	ā	ā	ī	ū	a	a	ərə	ərə
m	n	r	l	y	v	a	a/ā	a	i	u	ā	ā	ā	ī	ū	a	a	(a)r	(a)r
m	n	r	l	j	v	e	o	o	ĭ	ŭ	e	a	a	i	u	ę	e	rŭ	lŭ
m	n	r	l	j	v	e	a	a	i	u	ė	uo	o	y	u	im	in	ir	il
m	n	r	l	y	g/v	e	o	a	i	u	i	u	a	i	u	am	an	ar	ał
m	n	r	l	h/z	–*	e	o	a	i	u	ē	ō	ā/ē	ī	ū	a	a	ar/ra	al/la
m	n	r	l	i/j	v	e	o	a	i	u	ē	ō	ā	ī	ū	em	en	or	ul
m	n	r	l	–*	f	e/i	o/u	a	i/e	u/o	ī	ā	ā	ī	ū	(*am)e	(*an)e	ri	li
m	n	r	l	j	w	e	a	a	i	u	ē	ō	ā	ī	ū	um	un	ur	ul
m	n	r	l	j	w	i/ai	a	a	i/e	u	ē	ō	ō	ī	ū	um	un	aur	ul
m	n	r	l	–*	v	e	a	a	i/e	u/o	ā	ō	ō	ī	ū	um	un	ur/or	ul/ol
m	n	r	l	j	w	e	a	a	i/e	u/o	ā	uo	uo	ī	ū	um	un	ur/or	ul/ol
m	n	r	l	g	w	e	a	a	i/e	u/o	ē	ō	ō	ī	ū	um	un	ur/or	ul/ol
m	n	r	l	g(y)	w	e	æ/a	æ/a	i/e	u/o	ǣ	ō	ō	ī	ū	um	un	ur/or	ul/ol

Indo-European Roots

ad-. Important derivatives are *at*[1] and *aid*.

ad-. To, near, at. **1.** ADO, AT[1], from Old English *æt*, near, by, at, and from Middle English *at*, "to," from Old Norse *at*, both from Germanic **at*. **2.** AD-, -AD; (ADJUVANT), AID, AMOUNT, (PARAMOUNT), from Latin *ad, ad-*, to, toward. [Pokorny 1. *ad-* 3.]

ag-. Important derivatives are *act, agent, agile, ambiguous, essay, exact, navigate,* and *agony*.

ag-. To drive, draw, move. **1.** ACT, ACTIVE, ACTOR, ACTUAL, ACTUARY, AGENDUM, AGENT, AGILE, AGITATE; (ALLEGE), AMBAGE, AMBIGUOUS, (ASSAY), (CACHE), COAGULUM, COGENT, ESSAY, EXACT, (EXAMINE), (EXIGENT), FUMIGATE, FUSTIGATE, INTRANSIGENT, LEVIGATE, LITIGATE, NAVIGATE, OBJURGATE, PRODIGALITY, RETROACTIVE, SQUAT, TRANSACT, VARIEGATE, from Latin *agere*, to do, act, drive, conduct, lead, weigh. **2.** -AGOGUE, AGONY; ANAGOGE, (ANTAGONIZE), CHORAGUS, DEMAGOGUE, EPACT, GLUCAGON, HYPNAGOGIC, MYSTAGOGUE, PEDAGOGUE, PROTAGONIST, STRATAGEM, SYNAGOGUE, from Greek *agein*, to drive, lead, weigh. **3.** Suffixed form **ag-to-*. AMBASSADOR, EMBASSAGE, (EMBASSY), from Latin *ambactus*, servant, from Celtic **amb(i)-ag-to-*, "one who goes around" (**ambi*, around; see **ambhi**). **4.** Suffixed form **ag-ti-*, whence adjective **ag-ty-o-*, "weighty." AXIOM; AXIOLOGY, CHRONAXIE, from Greek *axios*, worth, worthy, of like value, weighing as much. **5.** Possibly suffixed form **ag-ro-*, driving, pursuing, grabbing. PELLAGRA, PODAGRA, from Greek *agra*, a seizing. [Pokorny *aĝ-* 4.] Derivative **agro-**.

agh-. Important derivatives are *day, today,* and *dawn*.

agh-. A day (considered as a span of time). **a.** DAY; DAISY, TODAY, from Old English *dæg*, day; **b.** LANDTAG, from Old High German *tag*, day; **c.** DAWN, from Old English denominative *dagian*, to dawn. **a, b,** and **c** all from Germanic **dagaz* (with initial *d-* of obscure origin), day. [Pokorny *agher-* 7.]

agro-. Important derivatives are *acre* and *pilgrim*.

agro-. Field. Probably a derivative of **ag-**, "to drive." **1.** ACRE, from Old English *æcer*, field, acre, from Germanic **akraz*. **2.** AGRARIAN; AGRICULTURE, PEREGRINE, (PILGRIM), from Latin *ager* (genitive *agrī*), earlier **agros*, district, property, field. **3.** AGRIA, AGRO-; (AGROSTOLOGY), ONAGER, STAVESACRE, from Greek *agros*, field, and *agrios*, wild. [In Pokorny *aĝ-* 4.]

ais-. An important derivative is *ask*.

ais-. To wish, desire. Suffixed form **ais-sk-*. ASK, from Old English *āscian, ācsian*, to ask, seek, from Germanic **aiskōn*. [Pokorny 1. *ais-* 16.]

aiw-. Important derivatives are *no*[1], *ever, every, never, medieval, age, eternal,* and *eon*.

aiw-. Vital force, life, long life, eternity; also "endowed with the acme of vital force, young." **1.a.** NO[1], from Old English *ā*, ever; **b.** AUGHT[1], from Old English *āwiht, āuht*, anything, "ever a creature"; **c.** EVER; EVERY, NEVER, from Old English *ǣfre* (second element obscure), ever; **d.** AYE[2]; NAY, from Old Norse *ei*, ever. **a, c,** and **d** all from extended form in Germanic **aiwi;* **b** from Germanic **aiwi* + **wihti*, "ever a thing, anything" (**wihti-*, thing; see **wekti-**). **2.a.** Suffixed form **aiw-o-*. COEVAL, LONGEVITY, MEDIEVAL, PRIMEVAL, from Latin *aevum*, age, eternity; **b.** suffixed form **aiwo-tā(ti)-*. AGE; COETANEOUS, from Latin *aetās* (stem *aetāti-*), age; **c.** suffixed form **aiwo-t-erno-*. ETERNAL; SEMPITERNAL, from Latin *aeternus*, eternal. **3.** Suffixed form **aiw-en-*. EON, from Greek *aiōn*, age, vital force. [Pokorny *aiu̯-* 17.] See also **yuwen-* under **yeu-**.

ak-. Important derivatives are *edge, acute, hammer, heaven, acrid, eager*[1], *vinegar, acid, acme, acne, acro-,* and *oxygen*.

ak-. Sharp. **1.** Suffixed form **ak-yā-*. **a.** EDGE, from Old English *ecg*, sharp side, from Germanic **agjō;* **b.** EGG[2], from Old Norse *eggja*, to incite, goad, from Germanic **agjan*. **2.** Suffixed form **ak-u-*. **a.** EAR[2], from Old English *æhher, ēar*, spike, ear of grain, from Germanic **ahuz-;* **b.** ACICULA, (ACUITY), ACUMEN, ACUPUNCTURE, ACUTE, AGLET, EGLANTINE, from Latin *acus*, needle; **c.** ACEROSE, from Latin *acus*, chaff. **3.** Suffixed form **ak-i-*. ACIDANTHERA, from Greek *akis*, needle. **4.** Suffixed form **ak-men-*, stone, sharp stone used as a tool, with metathetic variant **ka-men-*, with variants: **a.** **ka-mer-*. HAMMER, from Old English *hamor*, hammer, from Germanic **hamaraz;* **b.** **ke-men-* (probable variant). HEAVEN, from Old English *heofon, hefn*, heaven, from Germanic **hibin-*, "the stony vault of heaven," dissimilated form of **himin-*. **5.** Suffixed form **ak-onā-*, independently created in: **a.** AWN, from Old Norse *ögn*, ear of grain, and Old English *agen*, ear of grain, from Germanic **aganō*, and **b.** PARAGON, from Greek *akonē*, whetstone. **6.** Suffixed lengthened form **āk-ri-*. ACERATE, ACRID, ACRIMONY, EAGER[1]; CARVACROL, VINEGAR, from Latin *ācer*, sharp, bitter. **7.** Suffixed form **ak-ri-bhwo-*. ACERBIC, EXACERBATE, from Latin *acerbus*, bitter, sharp, tart. **8.** Suffixed (stative) form **ak-ē-*. ACID, from Latin *acēre*, to be sharp. **9.** Suffixed form **ak-ēto-*. (ACETABULUM), (ACETIC), ACETUM; ESTER, from Latin *acētum*, vinegar. **10.** Suffixed form **ak-mā-*. ACME, (ACNE), from Greek *akmē*, point. **11.** Suffixed form **ak-ro-*. ACRO-; (ACROBAT), ACROMION, from Greek *akros*, topmost. **12.** Suffixed o-grade form **ok-ri-*. MEDIOCRE, from Latin *ocris*, rugged mountain. **13.** Suffixed o-grade form **ok-su-*. AMPHIOXUS, OXALIS, OXYGEN, OXYURIASIS, PAROXYSM, from Greek *oxus*, sharp, sour. [Pokorny 2. *ak̂-* 18, 3. *k̂em-* 556.]

akʷ-ā-. Important derivatives are *island, aquatic, ewer,* and *sewer*[1].

akʷ-ā-. Water. **1.** ISLAND, from Old English *īg, īeg*, island, from Germanic **aujō*, "thing on the water," from **agwjō*. **2.** AQUA, AQUARELLE, AQUARIUM, AQUATIC, AQUI-, EWER, GOUACHE; SEWER[1], from Latin *aqua*, water. [Pokorny *aku̯ā-* 23.]

al-[1]. Important derivatives are *alarm, alert, ultimate, ultra-, alternate, adulterate, other, else, alien, alibi,* and *parallel*.

al-[1]. Beyond. **1.** Variant **ol-*, "beyond." **a.** Suffixed forms **ol-se-, *ol-so-*. ALARM, ALERT, ALLIGATOR, EL NIÑO, VOILÀ, from Latin *ille* (feminine *illa*, neuter *illud*), "yonder," that, from Old Latin *ollus;* **b.** suffixed forms **ol-s, *ol-tero-*. OUTRÉ, ULTERIOR, ULTIMATE, ULTRA-, UTTERANCE[2], from Latin *uls, *ulter, ultrā*, beyond. **2.** Suffixed form **al-tero-*, "other of two." **a.** ALTER, ALTERCATE, ALTERNATE, ALTRUISM; SUBALTERN, from Latin *alter*, other, other of two; **b.** ADULTERATE, (ADULTERINE), (ADULTERY), from Latin *adulterāre*, to commit adultery with, pollute, probably from the phrase *ad alterum*, "(approaching) another (unlawfully)" (*ad-*, to; see **ad-**); **c.** variant suffixed form **an-tero-*, "other (of two)." OTHER, from Old English *ōther*, other, from Germanic **antharaz*. **3.** Extended form **alyo-*, "other of more than two." **a.** ELSE; ELDRITCH, from Old English *el-, elles*, else, otherwise, from Germanic **aljaz* (with adverbial suffix); **b.** ALIAS, ALIEN; ALIBI, ALIQUOT, HIDALGO, from Latin *alius*, other of more than two; **c.** ALLO-; ALLEGORY, ALLELOMORPH, ALLELOPATHY, MORPHALLAXIS, PARALLAX, PARALLEL, TROPHALLAXIS, from Greek *allos*, other. [Pokorny 1. *al-* 24, 2. *an-* 37.]

al-[2]. Important derivatives are *old, elder*[1], *haughty, altitude, enhance, exalt, adolescent, alumnus, coalesce,* and *prolific*.

al-[2]. To grow, nourish.

I. Suffixed (participial) form **al-to-*, "grown." **1.a.** ALDERMAN, OLD, from Old English *eald, ald*, old; **b.** ELDER[1], from Old English (comparative) *ieldra, eldra*, older, elder; **c.** ELDEST, from Old English (superlative) *ieldesta, eldesta*, eldest; **d.** (see **wī-ro-**) Germanic compound **wer-ald-*, "life or age of man." **a, b, c,** and **d** all from Germanic **alda-*. **2.** ALT, ALTO, HAUGHTY, HAWSER; ALTIMETER, ALTIPLANO, ALTITUDE, ALTOCUMULUS, ALTOSTRATUS, ENHANCE, EXALT, (HAUTBOY), from Latin *altus*, high, deep.

II. ADOLESCENT, (ADULT), ALIBLE, ALIMENT, ALIMONY, ALTRICIAL, ALUMNUS; COALESCE, from Latin *alere*, to nourish.

III. Suffixed (causative) form **ol-eye-*. ABOLISH, from Latin *abolēre*, to retard the growth of, abolish (*ab-*, from; see **apo-**).

IV. Compound form **pro-al-* (*pro-*, forth; see **per**[1]). PROLETARIAN, PROLIFEROUS, PROLIFIC, from Latin *prōlēs*, offspring.

V. Extended form **aldh-*. ALTHEA, from Greek *althein, althainein*, to get well. [Pokorny 2. *al-* 26.]

al-[3]. Important derivatives are *all* and *also*.

al-[3]. All. Germanic and Celtic root. **1.** Suffixed form **al-na-*. ALL; ALSO, from Old English *all, eall, eal-, al-*, all, from Germanic **allaz*. **2.** (see **man-**[1]) Germanic prefix **ala-*, all, in **Alamanniz*, "all men."

albho-. Important derivatives are *elf, oaf, albino, album, auburn,* and *daub*.

albho-. White. **1.a.** ELF, from Old English *ælf*, elf; **b.** OAF, from Old Norse *alfr*, elf; **c.** OBERON, from Old French *Auberon*, from a source akin to Old High German *Alberich*. **a, b,** and **c** all possibly from Germanic **albiz, *albaz*, if meaning "white ghostly apparitions." **2.** ELFIN, from Old English *-elfen*, elf, possibly from Germanic **albinjō*. **3.** ABELE, ALB, ALBEDO, ALBESCENT, ALBINO, ALBITE, ALBUM, ALBUMEN, AUBADE, AUBURN; DAUB, from Latin *albus*, white. [Pokorny *albho-* 30.]

alu-. An important derivative is *ale*.

alu-. In words related to sorcery, magic, possession, and intoxication. Suffixed form **alu-t-*. ALE, from Old English *(e)alu*, ale, from Germanic **aluth-*. [Pokorny *alu-* 33.]

ambhi. Important derivatives are *by*[1], *be-, ambi-,* and *amphi-*.

ambhi. Also **m̥bhi**. Around. Probably derived from *ant-bhi*. See **ant-**. **1.** Reduced form **bhi*. **a.** BY[1]; ABAFT, BUT, from Old English *bi, bī, be*, by; **b.** BE-, from Old English *be-*, on all sides, be-, also intensive prefix; **c.** BELEAGUER, from Middle Dutch *bie*, by; **d.** BIVOUAC, from Old High German *bi*, by, at. **a, b, c,** and **d** all from Germanic **bi, *bi-* (intensive prefix). **2.a.** EMBER DAY, from Old English *ymbe*, around; **b.** OMBUDSMAN, from Old Norse *um(b)*, about, around; **c.** UMLAUT, from Old High German *umbi*, around. **a, b,** and **c** all from Germanic **umbi*. **3.a.** AMBI-, from Latin *ambi-*, around, about; **b.** (ALLEY[1]); AMBULATE, FUNAMBULIST, (PREAMBLE), from Latin *amb-*, around, about, in *ambulāre*, to go about, walk (**alāre*, to go). **4.** AMPHI-, from Greek *amphi*, around, about. **5.** (see **ag-**) Celtic **ambi*. [Pokorny *ambhi* 34.]

an-. Important derivatives are *on, acknowledge, alike, aloft, onslaught,* and *ana-*.

an-. On. Extended form **ana*. **1.a.** ON; (ACKNOWLEDGE), ALIKE, from Old English *an, on, a, on*, and prefixed *on-;* **b.** ALOFT, AMISS, from Old Norse *ā*, in, on; **c.** ANLAGE, ANSCHLUSS, from Old High German *ana-*, on; **d.** ONSLAUGHT, from Middle Dutch *aen*, on. **a, b, c,** and **d** all from Germanic **ana, *anō.* **2.** ANA[2], ANA-, from Greek *ana*, on, up, at the rate of. [Pokorny 4. *an* 39.]

---

anə-. Important derivatives are *anima, animal, animus, equanimity,* and *unanimous.*

anə-. To breathe. Suffixed form **anə-mo-.* **a.** ANIMA, ANIMADVERT, ANIMAL, ANIMATE, (ANIMATO), ANIMISM, ANIMOSITY, ANIMUS; EQUANIMITY, LONGANIMITY, MAGNANIMOUS, PUSILLANIMOUS, UNANIMOUS, from Latin *animus*, reason, mind, spirit, and *anima*, soul, spirit, life, breath; **b.** ANEMO-, from Greek *anemos*, wind. [Pokorny 3. *an(ə)-* 38.]

---

angh-. Important derivatives are *anger, anxious, anguish,* and *angina.*

angh-. Tight, painfully constricted, painful. **1.** AGNAIL, (HANGNAIL), from Old English *ang-nægl*, "painful spike (in the flesh)," corn, excrescence (*nægl*, spike; see **nogh-**), from Germanic **ang-*, compressed, hard, painful. **2.** Suffixed form **angh-os-.* ANGER, from Old Norse *angr*, sorrow, grief, from Germanic **angaz.* **3.** Suffixed form **angh-os-ti-.* ANGST[1], from Old High German *angust*, anxiety, from Germanic **angusti-.* **4.** ANXIOUS, from Latin *angere*, to strangle, torment. **5.** Suffixed form **angh-os-to-.* ANGUISH, from Latin *angustus*, narrow. **6.** QUINSY, from Greek *ankhein*, to squeeze, embrace. **7.** ANGINA, from Greek *ankhonē*, a strangling. [Pokorny *anĝh-* 42.]

---

ansu-. Important derivatives are *Aesir* and *Ormazd.*

ansu-. Spirit, demon. **1.** AESIR, from Old Norse *āss*, god, from Germanic **ansu-.* **2.** Suffixed reduced form **n̥su-ro-.* AHURA MAZDA, (ORMAZD), from Avestan *ahura-*, spirit, lord. [Pokorny *ansu-* 48.]

---

ant-. Important derivatives are *along, end, ante-, advance, anti-, antic, antique,* and *until.*

ant-. Front, forehead.
I. Inflected form (locative singular) **anti*, "against," with derivatives meaning in front of, before; also end. **1.** UN-[2]; ALONG, from Old English *and-*, indicating opposition, from Germanic **andi-* and **anda-.* **2.** END, from Old English *ende*, end, from Germanic **andja-.* **3.** ANCIENT[1], ANTE, ANTE-, ANTERIOR; ADVANCE, from Latin *ante*, before, in front of, against. **4.** ANTI-; ENANTIOMER, ENANTIOMORPH, from Greek *anti*, against, and *enantios*, opposite. **5.** Compound form **anti-ək^{w}o-*, "appearing before, having prior aspect" (**ək^{w}-*, appearance; see **ok^{w}-**). ANTIC, ANTIQUE, from Latin *antīquus*, former, antique. **6.** Reduced form **n̥ti-.* **a.** UNTIL, from Old Norse *und*, until, unto; **b.** ELOPE, from Middle Dutch *ont-*, away from. Both **a** and **b** from Germanic **und-.* **7.** Variant form **anto-.* VEDANTA, from Sanskrit *antaḥ*, end.
II. Probable inflected form (ablative plural) **ant-bhi*, "from both sides," whence **ambhi.* See **ambhi-.** [Pokorny *ant-s* 48.]

---

apo-. Important derivatives are *of, off, ebb, apo-, after, post-, deposit, dispose, impose, oppose, position, positive, post*[2], *post*[3], and *suppose.*

apo-. Also **ap-.** Off, away. **1.a.** OF, OFF, OFFAL, from Old English *of, æf*, off; **b.** EBB, from Old English *ebba*, low tide; **c.** ABLAUT, from Old High German *aba*, off, away from; **d.** AFT; ABAFT, from Old English *æftan*, behind, from Germanic **aftan-.* **a, b, c,** and **d** all from Germanic **af.* **2.** AB-[1], from Latin *ab, ab-*, away from. **3.** APO-, from Greek *apo*, away from, from. **4.** Suffixed (comparative) form **ap(o)-tero-.* AFTER, from Old English *æfter*, after, behind, from Germanic **aftar-.* **5.** Suffixed form **ap-t-is-.* EFTSOONS, from Old English *eft*, again, from Germanic **aftiz.* **6.** Suffixed form **apu-ko-.* AWKWARD, from Old Norse *öfugr*, turned backward, from Germanic **afug-.* **7.** Possible variant root form **po(s)*, on, in. **a.** POGROM, from Russian *po*, at, by, next to; **b.** POST-, POSTERIOR; (POSTMORTEM), PREPOSTEROUS, PUISNE, (PUNY), from Latin *post*, behind, back, afterward; **c.** APPOSITE, (APPOSITION), COMPONENT, (COMPOSE), (COMPOSITE), (COMPOSITION), (COMPOUND), CONTRAPPOSTO, DEPONE, DEPOSIT, DISPOSE, EXPOUND, IMPOSE, INTERPOSE, OPPOSE, POSITION, POSITIVE, POST[2], POST[3], POSTICHE, POSTURE, PREPOSITION, PROPOSE, PROVOST, PUNT[3], REPOSIT, SUPPOSE, TRANSPOSE, from Latin *pōnere*, to put, place, from **po-sinere* (*sinere*, to leave, let; of obscure origin). [Pokorny *apo-* 53.]

---

ar-. Important derivatives are *arm*[1], *arm*[2], *army, alarm, disarm, harmony, art*[1], *artist, inert, article, aristocracy, order, ordinary, ornate, adorn, rate*[1], *ratio, reason, read, hatred, riddle*[2], *rite, arithmetic,* and *rhyme.*

ar-. Also **arə-.** To fit together.
I. Basic form **arə-.* **1.** Suffixed form **ar(ə)-mo-.* **a.** ARM[1], from Old English *earm*, arm, from Germanic **armaz;* **b.** ARM[2], (ARMADA), ARMADILLO, ARMATURE, ARMOIRE, ARMY; ALARM, DISARM, from Latin *arma*, tools, arms; **c.** ARMILLARY SPHERE, from Latin *armus*, upper arm. **2.** Suffixed form **ar(ə)-smo-.* HARMONY, from Greek *harmos*, joint, shoulder. **3.** Suffixed form **ar(ə)-ti-.* **a.** ART[1], ARTISAN, ARTIST; INERT, (INERTIA), from Latin *ars* (stem *art-*), art, skill, craft; **b.** further suffixed form **ar(ə)-ti-o-.* ARTIODACTYL, from Greek *artios*, fitting, even. **4.** Suffixed form **ar(ə)-tu-.* ARTICLE, from Latin *artus*, joint. **5.** Suffixed form **ar(ə)-to-.* COARCTATE, from Latin *artus*, tight. **6.** Suffixed form **ar(ə)-dhro-.* ARTHRO-; ANARTHROUS, DIARTHROSIS, ENARTHROSIS, SYNARTHROSIS, from Greek *arthron*, joint. **7.** Suffixed (superlative) form **ar(ə)-isto-.* ARISTOCRACY, from Greek *aristos*, best.
II. Possibly suffixed variant form (or separate root) **ōr-dh-.* **1.** ORDAIN, ORDER, ORDINAL, ORDINANCE, ORDINARY, ORDINATE, ORDO; COORDINATION, INORDINATE, SUBORDINATE, from Latin *ōrdō*, order (originally a row of threads in a loom). **2.** EXORDIUM, PRIMORDIAL, from Latin *ōrdīrī*, to begin to weave. **3.** ORNAMENT, ORNATE; ADORN, SUBORN, from Latin *ōrnāre*, to adorn.
III. Variant or separate root **rē-* (< **reə-*). **1.** RATE[1], RATIO, REASON; (ARRAIGN), from Latin *rērī*, to consider, confirm, ratify. **2.** Suffixed form **rē-dh-.* **a.** *(i)* READ, REDE, from Old English *rǣdan*, to advise; *(ii)* HATRED, KINDRED, from Old English *rǣden*, condition. Both *(i)* and *(ii)* from Germanic **rēdan;* **b.** *(i)* RATHSKELLER, from Old High German *rāt*, counsel; *(ii)* RIDDLE[2], from Old English *rǣdels(e)*, opinion, riddle. Both *(i)* and *(ii)* from Germanic **rēdaz.* **3.** Zero-grade form **rə-.* (see **dekm̥**) Germanic **radam*, number.
IV. Variant (or separate root) **rī-.* **1.** Suffixed form **rī-tu-.* RITE, from Latin *rītus*, rite, custom, usage. **2.** Suffixed form **(a)rī-dhmo-.* ARITHMETIC, LOGARITHM, from Greek *arithmos*, number, amount. **3.** RHYME, from a Germanic source akin to Old High German *rīm*, number, series. [Pokorny 1. *ar-* 55.]

---

arg-. An important derivative is *argue.*

arg-. To shine; white; the shining or white metal, silver. **1.** Suffixed form **arg-ent-.* ARGENT, ARGENTINE, from Latin *argentum*, silver. **2.** Suffixed form **arg-i-l(l)-.* ARGIL, from Greek *argillos*, white clay. **3.** Suffixed form **arg-u-ro-.* LITHARGE, (PYRARGYRITE), from Greek *arguros*, silver. **4.** Suffixed form **arg-i-n-.* ARGININE, from Greek *arginoeis*, brilliant, bright-shining. **5.** Extended form **argu-*, brilliance, clarity. ARGUE, from Latin denominative *arguere*, to make clear, demonstrate. **6.** Suffixed form **arg-ro-.* **a.** (see **pel-**[1]). Greek *argos* (< **argros*), white; **b.** AGRIMONY, possibly from Greek *argos*, white. [Pokorny *ar(e)ĝ-* 64.]

---

as-. Important derivatives are *ash*[1], *arid, ardent, arson,* and *azalea.*

as-. To burn, glow. **1.** Extended form **asg-.* ASH[1], from Old English *æsce, asce*, ash, from Germanic **askōn-.* **2.** Suffixed form **ās-ā-.* ARA, from Latin *āra*, altar, hearth. **3.** Suffixed (stative) form **ās-ē-.* **a.** ARID, from Latin *āridus*, dry, parched, from *ārēre*, to be dry; **b.** ARDENT, ARDOR, ARSON, from Latin *ārdēre*, to burn, be on fire, from *āridus*, parched. **4.** Extended form **asd-.* **a.** ZAMIA, from Greek *azein*, to dry; **b.** AZALEA, from Greek *azaleos*, dry. [Pokorny *as-* 68.]

---

at-. Important derivatives are *annual, anniversary, millennium,* and *perennial.*

at-. To go; with Germanic and Latin derivatives meaning a year (conceived as "the period gone through, the revolving year"). Suffixed form **at-no-.* ANNALS, ANNUAL, ANNUITY; ANNIVERSARY, BIENNIUM, DECENNIUM, MILLENNIUM, PERENNIAL, QUADRENNIUM, QUINDECENNIAL, QUINQUENNIUM, SEPTENNIAL, SEXENNIAL, SUPERANNUATED, TRIENNIUM, VICENNIAL, from Latin *annus*, year. [Pokorny *at-* 69.]

āter-. Important derivatives are *atrium* and *atrocious.*

āter-. Fire. **1.** Suffixed zero-grade form **ātr-o-.* ATRABILIOUS, from Latin *āter* (feminine *ātra*), black (< "blackened by fire"). **2.** Suffixed zero-grade form **ātr-yo-.* ATRIUM, from Latin *ātrium*, forecourt, hall, atrium (perhaps originally the place where the smoke from the hearth escaped through a hole in the roof). **3.** Compound shortened zero-grade form **atro-ək^{w}-* (**ək^{w}-*, "looking"; see **ok^{w}-**). ATROCIOUS, from Latin *ătrōx*, "black-looking," frightful. [Pokorny *āt(e)r-* 69.]

---

au-. Important derivatives are *audible, audience, audio-, audit, auditorium, obey, aesthetic,* and *anesthesia.*

au-. To perceive. Compound forms **aw-dh-, *awis-dh-*, "to place perception" (see **dhē-**). **1.** Suffixed form **awisdh-yo-* or **awdh-yo-.* AUDIBLE, AUDIENCE, AUDILE, AUDIO-, AUDIT, AUDITION, AUDITOR, AUDITORIUM, AUDITORY, OYEZ; OBEY, SUBAUDITION, from Latin *audīre*, to hear. **2.** AESTHETIC; ANESTHESIA, from Greek *aisthanesthai*, to feel. [Pokorny 8. *au̯-* 78.]

---

aug-. Important derivatives are *nickname, wax*[2], *auction, augment, author, inaugurate,* and *auxiliary.*

aug-. To increase. Variant **(a)weg-* (< **əweg-*). **1.** EKE[1], from Old English *ēacan, ēcan*, to increase; **b.** NICKNAME, from Old English *ēaca*, an addition. Both **a** and **b** from Germanic **aukan.* **2.** Variant extended forms **wogs-, *wegs-.* **a.** WAX[2], from Old English *weaxan*, to grow, from Germanic **wahsan;* **b.** WAIST, from Old English **wæst*, growth, hence perhaps waist, size, from Germanic **wahs-tu-.* **3.** Form **aug-ē-.* AUCTION, AUGEND, AUGMENT, AUTHOR, (AUTHORIZE), from Latin *augēre*, to increase. **4.** AUGUR; INAUGURATE, from Latin *augur*, diviner (< "he who obtains favorable presage" < "divine favor, increase"). **5.** AUGUST, from Latin *augustus*, majestic, august. **6.** Suffixed form **aug-s-.* **a.** AUXILIARY, from Latin *auxilium*, aid, support, assistance; **b.** AUXIN, AUXESIS from Greek *auxein, auxanein*, to increase. [Pokorny *au̯eg-* 84.]

---

aus-. Important derivatives are *east, Easter,* and *aurora.*

aus-. To shine. **1.a.** EAST, from Old English *ēast*, east (< "the direction of the sunrise"); **b.** OSTMARK, from Old High German *ōstan*, east. Both **a** and **b** from Germanic **aust-.* **2.a.** EASTERN, from Old English *ēasterne*, eastern; **b.** OSTROGOTH, from Late Latin *ostro-*, eastern. Both **a** and **b** from Germanic **austra-.* **3.** EASTER, from Old English *ēastre*, Easter, from Germanic **austrōn-*, a dawn-goddess whose holiday was celebrated at the vernal equinox. **4.** Possibly in AUSTRO-[1], from Latin *auster*, the south wind, formally identical to the Germanic forms in **2** and **3**, but the semantics are unclear. **5.** Probably suffixed form **ausōs-*, dawn, also Indo-European goddess of the dawn. **a.** AURORA, from Latin *aurōra*, dawn; **b.** EO-, EOS; EOSIN, from Greek *ēōs*, dawn. [Pokorny *au̯es-* 86.]

---

awi-. Important derivatives are *aviation, bustard, osprey, ostrich, auspice, cockney, oval, ovary, ovum,* and *caviar.*

awi-. Bird.
I. 1. AVIAN, AVIARY, AVIATION; AVICULTURE, AVIFAUNA, BUSTARD, OCARINA, OSPREY, OSTRICH, from Latin *avis*, bird. **2.** Compound **awi-spek-*, "observer of birds" (**spek-*, to see; see **spek-**). AUSPICE, from Latin *auspex*, augur.
II. Possible derivatives are the Indo-European words for egg, **ōwyo-, *əyo-.* **1.a.** COCKNEY, from Old English *ǣg*, egg; **b.** EGG[1], from Old Norse *egg*, egg. Both **a** and **b** from Germanic **ajja(m).* **2.** OVAL, OVARY, OVATE, OVI-, OVOLO, OVULE, OVUM, from Latin *ōvum*, egg. **3.** OO-, from Greek *ōion*, egg. **4.** CAVIAR, from a source akin to Middle Persian *khāyak*, egg, from Old Iranian **āvyaka-*, diminutive of **avya-.* [Pokorny *au̯ei-* 86.]

awo-. Important derivatives are *avuncular* and *uncle.*

awo-. An adult male relative other than one's father. **1.** ATAVISM, from Latin *avus,* grandfather. **2.** AVUNCULAR, UNCLE, from Latin *avunculus,* maternal uncle. **3.** AYAH, from Latin *avia,* grandmother. [Pokorny *au̯o-s* 89.]

ayer-. Important derivatives are *early* and *ere.*

ayer-. Day, morning. **1.a.** EARLY, ERE, OR[2], from Old English *ǣr,* before; **b.** OR[2], from Old Norse *ār,* before. Both **a** and **b** from Germanic *airiz. **2.** ERST, from Old English *ǣrest,* earliest, from Germanic (superlative) *airistaz. [Pokorny *ai̯er-* 12.]

ayes-. An important derivative is *era.*

ayes-. A metal, copper or bronze. AENEOUS, ERA, from Latin *aes,* bronze, money. [Pokorny *ai̯os-* 15.]

bak-. Important derivatives are *imbecile* and *bacterium.*

bak-. Staff used for support. **1.** BACILLUS, BAGUETTE, (BAIL[4]), (BAILEY); BACULIFORM, DEBACLE, IMBECILE, possibly from Latin *baculum,* rod, walking stick. **2.** BACTERIUM; (CORYNEBACTERIUM), from Greek *baktron,* staff. [Pokorny *bak-* 93.]

bel-. Derivatives are *Bolshevik* and *debilitate.*

bel-. Strong. **1.** Suffixed o-grade form *bol-iyo-. BOLSHEVIK, from Russian *bol'shoĭ,* large. **2.** Prefixed form *dē-bel-i-, "without strength" (*dē-,* privative prefix; see **de-**). DEBILITATE, DEBILITY, from Latin *dēbilis,* weak. [Pokorny 2. *bel-* 96.]

bhā-[1]. Important derivatives are *beacon, beckon, berry, banner, photo-, fantasy,* and *phase.*

bhā-[1]. To shine. Contracted from *bhaə-. **1.** Suffixed zero-grade form *bhə-w-. **a.** BEACON, from Old English *bēac(e)n,* beacon; **b.** BECKON, from Old English denominative *bēcnan, bēcnian,* to make a sign, beckon; **c.** BUOY, from Old French *boue,* buoy. **a, b,** and **c** all from Germanic *baukna-, beacon, signal. **2.a.** BERRY; MULBERRY, from Old English *berie, berige,* berry, and Old High German *beri,* berry; **b.** FRAMBESIA, from Old French *framboise,* raspberry, alteration of Frankish *brām-besi, "bramble berry." Both **a** and **b** from Germanic *bazja-, berry (< "bright-colored fruit"), perhaps from **bhā-[1]**. **3.a.** BANDOLEER, from Spanish *banda,* sash; **b.** BANNER, (BANNERET[1]), (BANNERET[2]), from Late Latin *bandum,* banner, standard. Both **a** and **b** from Germanic *bandwa-, "identifying sign," banner, standard, sash, also "company united under a (particular) banner." **4.** Suffixed form *bhə-w-es-. PHOS-, PHOT, PHOTO-; PHOSPHORUS, from Greek *phōs* (stem *phōt-*), light. **5.** Extended and suffixed form *bhə-n-yo-. FANTASY, (PANT), -PHANE, PHANTASM, (PHANTOM), PHASE, PHENO-, PHENOMENON; DIAPHANOUS, EMPHASIS, EPIPHANY, HIEROPHANT, PHANEROGAM, (PHANTASMAGORIA), PHOSPHENE, SYCOPHANT, THEOPHANY, (TIFFANY), from Greek *phainein,* "to bring to light," cause to appear, show, and *phainesthai* (passive), "to be brought to light," appear, with zero-grade noun *phasis* (*bhə-ti-), an appearance. [Pokorny 1. *bhā-* 104.]

bhā-[2]. Important derivatives are *fable, fate, infant, preface, prophet, abandon, banish, bandit, fame, phono-, symphony, confess,* and *blame.*

bhā-[2]. To speak. Contracted from *bhaə-. **1.** FABLE, FATE; AFFABLE, (FANTOCCINI), INEFFABLE, INFANT, (INFANTRY), PREFACE, from Latin *fārī,* to speak. **2.** -PHASIA; APOPHASIS, PROPHET, from Greek *phanai,* to speak. **3.a.** BAN[1], from Old English *bannan,* to summon, proclaim, and Old Norse *banna,* to prohibit, curse; **b.** BANAL, BANNS; ABANDON, from Old French *ban,* feudal jurisdiction, summons to military service, proclamation, Old French *bandon,* power, and Old English *gebann,* proclamation; **c.** BANISH, from Old French *banir,* to banish; **d.** CONTRABAND, from Late Latin *bannus, bannum,* proclamation; **e.** BANDIT, from Italian *bandire,* to muster, band together (< "to have been summoned"). **a, b, c, d,** and **e** all from Germanic suffixed form *ban-wan, *bannan, to speak publicly (used of particular kinds of proclamation in feudal or prefeudal custom; "to proclaim under penalty, summon to the levy, declare outlaw"). **4.** Suffixed form *bhā-ni-. **a.** BOON[1], from Old Norse *bōn,* prayer, request; **b.** BEE[1], perhaps from Old English *bēn,* prayer, from a Scandinavian source akin to Old Norse *bōn,* prayer. Both **a** and **b** from Germanic *bōni-. **5.** Suffixed form *bhā-ma. **a.** FAME, FAMOUS; DEFAME, INFAMOUS, from Latin *fāma,* talk, reputation, fame; **b.** EUPHEMISM, from Greek *phēmē,* saying, speech. **6.** Suffixed o-grade form *bhō-nā. PHONE[2], -PHONE, PHONEME, PHONETIC, PHONO-, -PHONY; ANTHEM, (ANTIPHON), APHONIA, CACOPHONOUS, EUPHONY, SYMPHONY, from Greek *phōnē,* voice, sound, and (denominative) *phōnein,* to speak. **7.** Suffixed zero-grade form *bhə-to-. CONFESS, PROFESS, from Latin *fatērī,* to acknowledge, admit. **8.** (BLAME), BLASPHEME, from Greek *blasphēmos,* evil-speaking, blas-phemous (first element obscure). [Pokorny 2. *bhā-* 105.]

bha-bhā-. An important derivative is *bean.*

bha-bhā-. Broad bean. **1.** FAVA BEAN, from Latin *faba,* broad bean. **2.** Variant form *bha-un-. BEAN, from Old English *bēan,* broad bean, bean of any kind, from Germanic *baunō. **3.** Possible suffixed form *bha-ko-. PHACOEMULSIFICATION, from Greek *phakos,* lentil. [Pokorny *bhabhā* 106.]

bhad-. Important derivatives are *better* and *best.*

bhad-. Good. **1.** BETTER, from Old English *betera,* better, from Germanic (comparative) *batizō. **2.** BEST, from Old English *bet(e)st,* best, from Germanic (superlative) *batistaz. **3.** BOOT[2], from Old English *bōt,* remedy, aid, from Germanic noun *bōtō. **4.** BATTEN[1], ultimately from Old Norse *batna,* to improve, from Germanic verb *batnan, to become better. [Pokorny *bhād-* 106.]

bhag-. Derivatives are *phago-* and *-phagous.*

bhag-. To share out, apportion, also to get a share. **1.** -PHAGE, -PHAGIA, PHAGO-, -PHAGOUS, from Greek *phagein,* to eat (< "to have a share of food"). **2.** NEBBISH, from a Slavic source akin to Czech *neboh,* poor, unfortunate, from Common Slavic *ne-bogŭ, poor ("un-endowed"). **3.** PAGODA; BHAGAVAD-GITA, from Sanskrit *bhagaḥ,* good fortune. **4.** Extended form *bhags-. BAKSHEESH, (BUCKSHEE), from Persian *bakhshīdan,* to give, from Avestan *bakhsh-.* [Pokorny 1. *bhag-* 107.]

bhāghu-. An important derivative is *bough.*

bhāghu-. Arm. BOUGH, from Old English *bōg, bōh,* bough, from Germanic *bōguz. [Pokorny *bhāghú-s* 108.]

bhāgo-. Important derivatives are *book, buckwheat,* and *beech.*

bhāgo-. Beech tree. **1.a.** BOOK, from Old English *bōc,* written document, composition; **b.** BUCKWHEAT, from Middle Dutch *boek,* beech; **c.** BOKMÅL, from Norwegian *bok,* book. **a, b,** and **c** all from Germanic *bōkō, beech, also "beech staff for carving runes on" (an early Germanic writing device). **2.** BEECH, from Old English *bēce,* beech, from Germanic *bōkjōn-. [Pokorny *bhāgo-s* 107.]

bhardh-ā-. Important derivatives are *beard, barb[1],* and *barber.*

bhardh-ā-. Beard. **1.** BEARD, from Old English *beard,* beard, from Germanic *bardaz. **2.** HALBERD, from Old High German *barta,* beard, ax, from Germanic *bardō, beard, also hatchet, broadax. **3.** BARB[1], BARBEL[1], BARBELLATE, BARBER, (BARBETTE), BARBICEL, BARBULE; REBARBATIVE, from Latin *barba,* beard. [Pokorny *bhardhā* 110.]

bhares-. Important derivatives are *barley, barn,* and *farina.*

bhares-. Also **bhars-.** Barley. **1.a.** BARN, from Old English *bere,* barley, from Germanic *bariz-; **b.** BARLEY, from Old English *bærlic,* barley-like, barley, from Germanic *barz-. **2.** FARINA, (FARINACEOUS), (FARRAGINOUS), FARRAGO, from Latin *far* (stem *farr-*), spelt, grain. [Pokorny *bhares-* 111.]

bhau-. Important derivatives are *beat, buttock, halibut, butt[1], button,* and *refute.*

bhau-. To strike. Contracted from *bhaəu-. **1.** BEAT, from Old English *bēatan,* to beat, from Germanic *bautan. **2.** BEETLE[3], from Old English *bȳtl,* hammer, mallet, from Germanic *bautilaz, hammer. **3.** BASTE[3], probably from a Scandinavian source akin to Old Norse *beysta,* to beat, denominative from Germanic *baut-sti-. **4.** BUTTOCK, from Old English diminutive *buttuc,* end, strip of land, from Germanic *būtaz. **5.a.** HALIBUT, from Middle Dutch *butte,* flatfish; **b.** TURBOT, from a Scandinavian source akin to Old Swedish *but,* flatfish. Both **a** and **b** from Germanic *butt-, name for a flatfish. **6.** (BOUTON), BUTT[1], BUTTON, BUTTRESS; ABUT, REBUT, SACKBUT, from Old French *bo(u)ter,* to strike, push, from Germanic *buttan. **7.** Zero-grade form *bhū- (*bhuə-) with verbal suffix *-tā-.* **a.** CONFUTE, from Latin *cōnfūtāre,* to check, suppress, restrain (*com-,* intensive prefix; see **kom**); **b.** REFUTE, from Latin *refūtāre,* to drive back, rebut (*re-,* back; see **re-**). **8.** Possibly reduced suffixed form *bhu-tu- (*bhəu-). FOOTLE, from Latin *futuere,* to have intercourse with (a woman). [Pokorny 1. *bhau-* 112.]

bheg^{w}-. Derivatives are *-phobe* and *-phobia.*

bheg^{w}-. To run. **1.** BECK[2], from Old Norse *bekkr,* a stream, from Germanic *bakjaz, a stream. **2.** -PHOBE, -PHOBIA, from Greek *phobos,* panic, flight, fear, from *phebesthai,* to flee in terror. [Pokorny *bheg^{u}-* 116.]

bhei-. An important derivative is *bee[1].*

bhei-. A bee. BEE[1], from Old English *bēo,* a bee, from Germanic suffixed form *bīōn-. [Pokorny *bhei-* 116.]

bheid-. Important derivatives are *beetle[1], bite, bit[1], bitter, bait[1], boat,* and *fission.*

bheid-. To split; with Germanic derivatives referring to biting (hence also to eating and to hunting) and woodworking. **1.a.** BEETLE[1], BITE, from Old English *bītan,* to bite; **b.** TSIMMES, from Old High German *bīzan, bizzan,* to bite. Both **a** and **b** from Germanic *bītan. **2.** Zero-grade form *bhid-. **a.** BIT[2], from Old English *bite,* a bite, sting, from Germanic *bitiz; **b.** (*i*) BIT[1], from Old English *bita,* a piece bitten off, morsel; (*ii*) BITT, from a Germanic source akin to Old Norse *biti,* bit, crossbeam. Both (*i*) and (*ii*) from Germanic *bitōn-; **c.** suffixed form *bhid-ro-. BITTER, from Old English *bit(t)er,* "biting," sharp, bitter. **3.** O-grade form *bhoid-. **a.** BAIT[1], from Old Norse *beita* (verb), to hunt with dogs, and *beita* (noun), pasture, food; **b.** ABET, from Old French *beter,* to harass with dogs. Both **a** and **b** from Germanic *baitjan. **4.** BATEAU, BOAT; (BOATSWAIN), from Old English *bāt,* boat, from Germanic *bait-, a boat (< "dugout canoe" or "split planking"). **5.** Nasalized zero-grade form *bhi-n-d-. -FID, FISSI-, (FISSILE), (FISSION), (FISSURE), from Latin *findere,* to split. [Pokorny *bheid-* 116.]

bheidh-. Important derivatives are *bide, abide, fiancé, affidavit, confide, confident, defy, federal, faith, fidelity,* and *infidel.*

bheidh-. To trust, confide, persuade. **1.** BIDE; ABIDE, (ABODE), from Old English *bīdan,* to wait, stay, from Germanic *bīdan, to await (< "to await trustingly, expect, trust"), probably from **bheidh-.** **2.** FIANCÉ, FIDUCIAL, (FIDUCIARY); AFFIANCE, (AFFIANT), (AFFIDAVIT), (CONFIDANT), CONFIDE, (CONFIDENT), (DEFIANCE), DEFY, DIFFIDENT, from Latin *fīdere,* to trust, confide, and *fīdus,* faithful. **3.** Suffixed o-grade form *bhoidh-es-. FEDERAL, FEDERATE; CONFEDERATE, from Latin *foedus* (stem *foeder-*), treaty, league. **4.** Zero-grade form *bhidh-. FAITH, FEALTY, FIDELITY; INFIDEL, PERFIDY, from Latin *fidēs,* faith, trust. [Pokorny *bheidh-* 117.]

bhel-[1]. Important derivatives are *blue, bleach, bleak[1], blaze[1], blemish, blind, blend, blond, blank, blanket, blush, black, flagrant,* and *flame.*

bhel-[1]. To shine, flash, burn; shining white and various bright colors.

I. 1. BELUGA, from Russian *belyĭ,* white. **2.** PHALAROPE, from Greek *phalaros,* having a white spot.

II. 1. Suffixed variant form *bhlē-wo-. BLUE, from Old French *bleu,* blue, from Germanic *blēwaz, blue. **2.** Suffixed zero-grade form *bhlə-wo-. FLAVESCENT, FLAVO-; (FLAVIN), (FLAVONE), (FLAVOPROTEIN), from Latin *flāvus,* golden or reddish yellow.

III. Various extended Germanic forms. **1.** BLEACH, from Old English *blǣcan,* to bleach, from Germanic *blaikjan, to make white. **2.** BLEAK[1], from Old Norse *bleikr,* shining, white, from Germanic **blaikaz,* shining, white. **3.** BLITZKRIEG, from Old High German *blëcchazzen,* to flash, lighten, from Germanic **blikkatjan.* **4.a.** BLAZE[1], from Old English *blæse,* torch, bright fire; **b.** BLESBOK, from Middle Dutch *bles,* white spot; **c.** BLEMISH, from Old French *ble(s)mir,* to make pale. **a, b,** and **c** all from Germanic **blas-,* shining, white. **5.a.** BLIND; (BLINDFOLD), (PURBLIND), from Old English *blind,* blind; **b.** BLENDE, from Old High German *blentan,* to blind, deceive; **c.** BLEND, from Old Norse *blanda,* to mix; **d.** BLOND, from Old French *blond,* blond. **a, b, c,** and **d** all from Germanic **blendaz,* clouded, and **bland-, *bland-ja-,* to mix, mingle (< "make cloudy"). **6.a.** BLENCH[1], from Old English *blencan,* to deceive; **b.** BLANCH, BLANK, BLANKET; BLANCMANGE, from Old French *blanc,* white. Both **a** and **b** from Germanic **blenk-, *blank-,* to shine, dazzle, blind. **7.** BLUSH, from Old English *blyscan,* to glow red, from Germanic **blisk-,* to shine, burn. **IV.** Extended form **bhleg-,* to shine, flash, burn. **1.** O-grade form *bhlog-.* BLACK, from Old English *blæc,* black, from Germanic **blakaz,* burned. **2.** Zero-grade form **bhḷg-.* **a.** FULGENT, FULGURATE; EFFULGENT, FOUDROYANT, REFULGENT, from Latin *fulgēre,* to flash, shine, and *fulgur,* lightning; **b.** FULMINATE, from Latin *fulmen* (< **fulg-men*), lightning, thunderbolt. **3.a.** FLAGRANT; CONFLAGRANT, (CONFLAGRATION), DEFLAGRATE, from Latin *flagrāre,* to blaze; **b.** (FLAMBÉ), (FLAMBEAU), (FLAMBOYANT), FLAME, FLAMINGO, FLAMMABLE; INFLAME, from Latin *flamma* (< **flag-ma*), a flame. **4.** PHLEGM, PHLEGMATIC, PHLEGETHON, from Greek *phlegein,* to burn. **5.** O-grade form **bhlog-.* PHLOGISTON, PHLOX; PHLOGOPITE, from Greek *phlox,* a flame, also a wallflower. [Pokorny 1. *bhel-* 118, *bheleg-* 124, *bhleu-(k)-* 159.]

bhel-[2]. Important derivatives are *bowl[1], bulk[1], boulevard, boulder, bull[1], phallus, ball[1], balloon, ballot, bold,* and *fool.*

bhel-[2]. To blow, swell; with derivatives referring to various round objects and to the notion of tumescent masculinity. **1.** Zero-grade form *bhḷ-.* **a.** BOWL[1], from Old English *bolla,* pot, bowl; **b.** BOLE, from Old Norse *bolr,* tree trunk; **c.** BULK, from Old Norse *bulki,* cargo (< "rolled-up load"); **d.** ROCAMBOLE, from Old High German *bolla,* ball; **e.** (BOULEVARD), BULWARK, from Middle High German *bole,* beam, plank; **f.** BOLL, from Middle Dutch *bolle,* round object; **g.** BILTONG, from Middle Dutch *bille,* buttock; **h.** BOULDER, from a Scandinavian source akin to Swedish *bullersten,* "rounded stone," boulder, from **buller-,* "round object." **a, b, c, d, e, f, g,** and **h** all from Germanic **bul-.* **2.** Suffixed zero-grade form **bhḷ-n-.* **a.** BULL[1], from Old Norse *boli,* bull, from Germanic **bullōn-,* bull; **b.** BULLOCK, from Old English *bulluc,* bull, from Germanic **bulluka-;* **c.** PHALLUS; ITHYPHALLIC, from Greek *phallos,* phallus; **d.** FULL[2], from Latin *fullō,* a fuller, possibly from **bhel-[2]**. **3.** O-grade form **bhol-.* **a.** BOLLIX, from Old English *beallucas,* testicles; **b.** BALL[1], from Old English **beall,* ball; **c.** BILBERRY, probably from a Scandinavian source akin to Danish *bolle,* round roll; **d.** BALLOON, BALLOT, (BALLOTTEMENT), from Italian dialectal *balla,* ball; **e.** PALL-MALL, from Italian *palla,* ball; **f.** BALE[1], from Old French *bale,* rolled-up bundle. **a, b, c, d, e,** and **f** all from Germanic **ball-.* **4.** Possibly suffixed o-grade form **bhol-to-.* **a.** BOLD, from Old English *bald, beald,* bold; **b.** BAWD, from Old Low German *bald,* bold. Both **a** and **b** from Germanic **balthaz,* bold. **5.** Suffixed o-grade form **bhol-n-.* FILS[2], FOLLICLE, FOOL; (FOLLICULITIS), from Latin *follis,* bellows, inflated ball. **6.** BALEEN, from Greek *phal(l)aina,* whale, possibly from **bhel-[2]**. **7.** PHELLEM; PHELLODERM, PHELLOGEN, from Greek *phellos,* cork, cork oak, conceivably from **bhel-[2]** (but more likely unrelated). [Pokorny 3. *bhel-* 120.] (The following derivatives of this root are entered separately: **bhel-[3]**, **bhelgh-**, **bhleu-**.)

bhel-[3]. Important derivatives are *foliage, folio, bloom[1], blossom, flora, flour, flourish, flower, bleed, blood, bless,* and *blade.*

bhel-[3]. To thrive, bloom. Possibly from **bhel-[2]**. **I.** Suffixed o-grade form **bhol-yo-,* leaf. **1.** FOIL[2], (FOLIAGE), FOLIO, FOLIUM; (CINQUEFOIL), DEFOLIATE, EXFOLIATE, FEUILLETON, MILFOIL, PERFOLIATE, PORTFOLIO, TREFOIL, from Latin *folium,* leaf. **2.** (-PHYLL), PHYLLO-, -PHYLLOUS; CHERVIL, GILLYFLOWER, PODOPHYLLIN, from Greek *phullon,* leaf. **II.** Extended form **bhlē-* (< **bhleə-*). **1.** O-grade form **bhlō-.* **a.** suffixed form **bhlō-w-.* BLOW[3], from Old English *blōwan,* to flower, from Germanic **blō-w-;* **b.** *(i)* BLOOM[1], from Old Norse *blōm, blōmi,* flower, blossom; *(ii)* BLOOM[2], from Old English *blōma,* a hammered ingot of iron (semantic development obscure). Both *(i)* and *(ii)* from Germanic suffixed form **blō-mōn-;* **c.** BLOSSOM, from Old English *blōstm, blōstma,* flower, blossom, from Germanic suffixed form **blō-s-;* **d.** FERRET[2], (FLORA), FLORA, (FLORAL), FLORIATED, FLORID, FLORIN, FLORIST, -FLOROUS, (FLOUR), FLOURISH, FLOWER; (CAULIFLOWER), DEFLOWER, EFFLORESCE, ENFLEURAGE, FLORIGEN, from Latin *flōs* (stem *flōr-*), flower, from Italic suffixed form **flō-s-;* **e.** suffixed form *bhlō-to-;* *(i)* BLEED, BLOOD, from Old English *blōd,* blood; *(ii)* BLESS, from Old English *bloedsian, blētsian,* to consecrate, from Germanic **blōdisōn,* to treat or hallow with blood. Both *(i)* and *(ii)* from Germanic **blō-dam,* possibly from **bhel-[3]** in the meaning "swell, gush, spurt." **2.** EMBLEMENTS, from Medieval Latin *blādum, bladium,* produce of the land, grain, from Germanic suffixed form **blē-da-.* **3.** Suffixed zero-grade form **bhlə-to-.* BLADE, from Old English *blæd,* leaf, blade, from Germanic **bladaz.* [Pokorny 4. *bhel-* 122.]

bhelgh-. Important derivatives are *bellows, belly, billow, budget,* and *bulge.*

bhelgh-. To swell. Extension of **bhel-[2]**. **1.** O-grade form **bholgh-.* BELLOWS, BELLY, from Old English *bel(i)g, bælig,* bag, bellows, from Germanic **balgiz.* **2.** Zero-grade form **bhḷgh-.* BILLOW, from Old Norse *bylgja,* a wave, from Germanic **bulgjan.* **3.** Zero-grade form **bhḷgh-.* BOLSTER, from Old English *bolster,* cushion, from Germanic **bulgstraz.* **4.** O-grade form **bholgh-.* BUDGET, BULGE, from Latin *bulga,* leather sack, from Celtic **bolg-.* [Pokorny *bhelgh-* 125.]

bhendh-. Important derivatives are *bind, bend[1], band[1], bond,* and *bundle.*

bhendh-. To bind. **1.a.** BIND; WOODBINE, from Old English *bindan,* to bind; **b.** BINDLESTIFF, from Old High German *binten,* to bind. Both **a** and **b** from Germanic **bindan.* **2.** BANDANNA, from Sanskrit *bandhati,* he ties. **3.** O-grade form **bhondh-.* **a.** BEND[2]; RIBBON, from Old English *bend,* band, and Old French *bende,* band; **b.** BEND[1], from Old English *bendan,* to bend; **c.** BAND[1], BOND, from Old Norse *band,* band, fetter; **d.** BAND[1], from Old French *bande,* bond, tie, link. **a, b, c,** and **d** all from Germanic **band-.* **4.** Suffixed form **bhond-o-.* BUND[1]; (CUMMERBUND), from Old Iranian *banda-,* bond, fetter. **5.** Zero-grade form **bhṇdh-.* **a.** BUND[2], from Middle High German *bunt,* league; **b.** BUNDLE, from Middle Dutch *bondel,* sheaf of papers, bundle. Both **a** and **b** from Germanic **bund-.* [Pokorny *bhendh-* 127.]

bher-[1]. Important derivatives are *bear[1], burden[1], birth, bring, fertile, differ, offer, prefer, suffer, transfer, furtive,* and *metaphor.*

bher-[1]. To carry; also to bear children. **1.a.** *(i)* BEAR[1], from Old English *beran,* to carry; *(ii)* FORBEAR[1], from Old English *forberan,* to bear, endure (*for-,* for-; see **per[1]**). Both *(i)* and *(ii)* from Germanic **beran;* **b.** BIER, from Old English *bēr, bǣr,* bier, and Old French *biere* bier, both from Germanic **bērō;* **c.** BORE[3], from Old Norse *bāra,* wave, billow, from Germanic **bēr-.* **2.a.** BAIRN, from Old English *bearn,* child, from Germanic **barnam;* **b.** BARROW[1], from Old English *bearwe,* basket, wheelbarrow, from Germanic **barwōn-.* **3.a.** BURLY, from Old English **borlic,* excellent, exalted (< "borne up"), from Germanic **bur-;* **b.** BURDEN[1], from Old English *byrthen,* burden, from Germanic **burthinja;* **c.** BIRTH, from a source akin to Old Norse *burdhr,* birth, from Germanic **burthiz;* **d.** BIRR[1], from Old Norse *byrr,* favorable wind, perhaps from Germanic **burja-.* **4.** Compound root **bhrenk-,* to bring (< **bher-* + **enk-,* to reach; see **nek-[2]**). BRING, from Old English *bringan,* to bring, from Germanic **brengan.* **5.** -FER, FERTILE; AFFERENT, CIRCUMFERENCE, CONFER, (DEFER[1]), DEFER[2], DIFFER, EFFERENT, INFER, OFFER, PREFER, (PROFFER), REFER, SUFFER, TRANSFER, VOCIFERATE, from Latin *ferre,* to carry. **6.** OPPROBRIUM, from Latin *probrum,* a reproach (< **pro-bhr-o-,* "something brought before one"; *pro-,* before; see **per[1]**). **7.** Probably lengthened o-grade form **bhōr-.* FERRET[1], FURTIVE, FURUNCLE; (FURUNCULOSIS), from Latin *fūr,* thief. **8.** FERETORY, -PHORE, -PHORESIS, -PHOROUS; AMPHORA, ANAPHORA, DIAPHORESIS, EUPHORIA, METAPHOR, PERIPHERY, PHEROMONE, TELPHER, TOCOPHEROL, from Greek *pherein,* to carry, with o-grade noun *phoros,* a carrying. **9.** PARAPHERNALIA, from Greek *phernē,* dowry ("something brought by a bride"). **10.** SAMBAL, from Sanskrit *bharati,* he carries, brings. [Pokorny 1. *bher-* 128.]

bher-[2]. Important derivatives are *brown, burnish, beaver[1],* and *bear[2].*

bher-[2]. Bright, brown. **1.** Suffixed variant form **bhrū-no-.* **a.** BROWN, from Old English *brūn,* brown; **b.** BRUIN, from Middle Dutch *bruun;* **c.** BRUNET, BURNET, BURNISH, from Old French *brun,* shining, brown. **a, b,** and **c** all from Germanic **brūnaz.* **2.** Reduplicated form **bhibhru-, *bhebhru-,* "the brown animal," beaver. BEAVER[1], from Old English *be(o)for,* beaver, from Germanic **bebruz.* **3.** BEAR[2], from Old English *bera,* bear, from Germanic **berō,* "the brown animal," bear. **4.** BERSERKER, from Old Norse *björn,* bear, from Germanic **bernuz.* [Pokorny 5. *bher-* 136.]

bherəg-. Important derivatives are *bright* and *birch.*

bherəg-. To shine; bright, white. **1.** BRIGHT, from Old English *beorht,* bright, from Germanic **berhtaz,* bright. **2.** "The white tree," the birch (also the ash). **a.** BIRCH, (BIRK), from Old English *birc(e),* birch, from Germanic **birkjōn-;* **b.** probably suffixed zero-grade form **bhrag-s-.* FRAXINELLA, from Latin *fraxinus,* ash tree. [Pokorny *bherəg-* 139.]

bhergh-[1]. Important derivatives are *bury, burial, borrow,* and *bargain.*

bhergh-[1]. To hide, protect. **1.a.** (see **kʷel-[1]**) Germanic compound **h(w)als-berg-,* "neck-protector," gorget (**h(w)alsaz,* neck); **b.** (see **sker-[1]**) Germanic compound **skēr-berg-,* "sword-protector," scabbard (**skēr-,* sword). Both **a** and **b** from Germanic **bergan.* **2.** Zero-grade form **bhṛgh-.* **a.** BURY, from Old English *byrgan,* to bury, from Germanic **burgjan;* **b.** BURIAL, from Old English *byrgels,* burial, from Germanic derivative **burgisli-.* **3.a.** BORROW, from Old English *borgian,* to borrow, from Germanic **borgēn,* to pledge, lend, borrow; **b.** BARGAIN, from Old French *bargaignier,* to haggle, from Germanic derivative **borganjan.* [Pokorny *bhergh-* 145.]

bhergh-[2]. Important derivatives are *iceberg, bourgeois, burglar, force, fort, comfort, effort, enforce,* and *fortify.*

bhergh-[2]. High; with derivatives referring to hills and hill-forts. **1.a.** BARROW[2], from Old English *beorg,* hill; **b.** ICEBERG, from Middle Dutch *bergh,* mountain. Both **a** and **b** from Germanic **bergaz,* hill, mountain. **2.** (see **koro-**) Germanic compound **harja-bergaz,* "army-hill," hill-fort (**harjaz,* army). **3.** BELFRY, from Old French *berfroi,* tower, from Germanic compound **berg-frij-,* "high place of safety," tower (**frij-,* peace, safety; see **prī-**). **4.** Zero-grade form **bhṛgh-.* **a.** BOROUGH, BURG, from Old English *burg, burh, byrig,* (fortified) town; **b.** BURGHER, from Old High German *burg,* fortress; **c.** BURGOMASTER, from Middle Dutch *burch,* town; **d.** BOURG, (BOURGEOIS), BURGESS, BURGLAR; FAUBOURG, from Late Latin *burgus,* fortified place, and Old French *burg,* borough. **a, b, c,** and **d** all from Germanic **burgs,* hill-fort. **5.** Possibly suffixed zero-grade form **bhṛgh-to-.* FORCE, FORT, (FORTALICE), FORTE[1], FORTE[2], FORTIS, (FORTISSIMO), FORTITUDE, FORTRESS; COMFORT, DEFORCE, EFFORT, (ENFORCE), FORTIFY, (PIANOFORTE), (REINFORCE), from Latin *fortis,* strong (but this is also possibly from **dher-**). [Pokorny *bheregh-* 140.]

bhes-. Important derivatives are *psyche, psychic,* and *psycho-.*

bhes-. To breathe. Probably imitative. Zero-grade form **bhs-*. PSYCHE, PSYCHIC, PSYCHO-; METEMPSYCHOSIS, from Greek *psukhē,* spirit, soul, from *psukhein* (< **bhs-ū-kh-*), to breathe. [Pokorny 2. *bhes-* 146.]

---

bheudh-. Important derivatives are *bid, forbid, bode*[1], and *Buddha*[2].

bheudh-. To be aware, to make aware. **1.a.** BID, from Old English *bēodan,* to proclaim; **b.** FORBID, from Old English *forbēodan,* to forbid; **c.** VERBOTEN, from Old High German *farbiotan,* to forbid. **a, b,** and **c** all from Germanic **(for)beudan* (**for,* before; see **per**[1]). **2.** BODE[1], from Old English *bodian,* to announce, from *boda,* messenger, from Germanic **budōn-*. **3.** BEADLE, from Old English *bydel,* herald, messenger, and Old High German *butil,* herald, both from Germanic **budilaz,* herald. **4.** OMBUDSMAN, from Old Norse *bodh,* command, from Germanic **budam.* **5.** BUDDHA[2]; BODHISATTVA, BO TREE, from Sanskrit *bodhati,* he awakes, is enlightened, becomes aware, and *bodhiḥ,* perfect knowledge. [Pokorny *bheudh-* 150.]

---

bheuə-. Important derivatives are *be, husband, booth, build, future, neighbor,* and *beam.*

bheuə-. Also **bheu-**. To be, exist, grow.
I. Extended forms **bhwiy(o)-, *bhwī-*. **1.** BE, from Old English *bēon,* to be, from Germanic **biju,* I am, will be. **2.** FIAT, from Latin *fierī,* to become. **3.** Possibly suffixed form **bhwī-lyo-*. (see **dhē(i)-**) Latin *fīlius,* son.
II. Lengthened o-grade form **bhōw-*. **a.** BONDAGE, BOUND[4]; BUSTLE[1], HUSBAND, from Old Norse *būa,* to live, prepare, and *būask,* to make oneself ready (*-sk,* reflexive suffix; see **s(w)e-**); **b.** BOOTH, from Middle English *bothe,* market stall, from a Scandinavian source akin to Old Danish *bōth,* dwelling, stall. Both **a** and **b** from Germanic **bōwan.*
III. Zero-grade form **bhu-*. **1.a.** BUILD, from Old English *byldan,* to build, from *bold,* dwelling, house, from Germanic **buthla;* **b.** BOODLE, from Middle Dutch *bōdel,* riches, property, from alternate Germanic form **bōthla.* **2.** PHYSIC, PHYSICS, PHYSIO-, PHYSIQUE, -PHYTE, PHYTO-, (PHYTON); APOPHYSIS, DIAPHYSIS, DIPHYODONT, EPIPHYSIS, EUPHUISM, HYPOPHYSIS, IMP, MONOPHYSITE, NEOPHYTE, PERIPHYTON, SYMPHYSIS, TRACHEOPHYTE, from Greek *phuein,* to bring forth, make grow, *phutos, phuton,* a plant, and *phusis,* growth, nature. **3.** Suffixed form **bhu-tā-*. EISTEDDFOD, from Welsh *bod,* to be. **4.** Suffixed form **bhu-tu-*. FUTURE, from Latin *futūrus,* "that is to be," future.
IV. Zero-grade form **bhū-* (< **bhuə-*). **1.a.** BOWER[1], from Old English *būr,* "dwelling space," bower, room; **b.** NEIGHBOR, from Old English *gebūr,* dweller (*ge-,* collective prefix; see **kom**); **c.** BOER, BOOR, from Middle Dutch *gheboer, ghebuer,* peasant. **a, b,** and **c** all from Germanic **būram,* dweller, especially farmer. **2.** BYRE, from Old English *bȳre,* stall, hut, from Germanic **būrjam,* dwelling. **3.** BYLAW, from a Scandinavian source akin to Old Norse *bȳr,* settlement, from Germanic **būwi-*. **4.** Suffixed form **bhū-lo-*. PHYLE, PHYLETIC, PHYLUM; PHYLOGENY, from Greek *phulon,* tribe, class, race, and *phulē,* tribe, clan.
V. Suffixal forms in Latin. **1.** (see **dwo-**) Latin *dubius,* doubtful, and *dubitāre,* to doubt, from **du-bhw-io-*. **2.** (see **per**[1]) Latin *probus,* upright, from **pro-bhw-o-*, "growing well or straightforward." **3.** (see **uper**) Latin *superbus,* superior, proud, from **super-bhw-o-*, "being above."
VI. a. BEAM, from Old English *bēam,* tree, beam; **b.** BOOM[2], from Middle Dutch *boom,* tree; **c.** BUMPKIN[1], from Flemish *boom,* tree. **a, b** and **c** all from Germanic **baumaz* (and **bagmaz*), tree (? < "growing thing"), possibly from **bheuə-**. [Pokorny *bheu-* 146.]

---

bheug-. Important derivatives are *bow*[3], *bow*[2], and *bog.*

bheug-. To bend; with derivatives referring to bent, pliable, or curved objects.
I. Variant form **bheugh-* in Germanic **beug-*. **1.a.** BEE[2], from Old English *bēag,* a ring; **b.** BAGEL, from Old High German *boug,* a ring. Both **a** and **b** from Germanic **baugaz.* **2.a.** BOW[3], from Old English *boga,* a bow, arch; **b.** (see **el-**) Germanic compound **alino-bugōn-*, "bend of the forearm," elbow (**alino-,* forearm); **c.** BOW[1], from a source akin to Middle Low German *boog,* bow of a boat. **a, b,** and **c** all from Germanic **bugōn-*. **3.** BOW[2], BUXOM, from Old English *būgan,* to bend, from Germanic *būgan.* **4.** BAIL[3], from Middle English *beil,* a handle, perhaps from Old English **bēgel* or from a Scandinavian source akin to Old Swedish **bøghil,* both from Germanic **baugil-*. **5.** BIGHT, from Old English *byht,* a bend, angle, from Germanic **buhtiz.*
II. BOG, from Scottish and Irish Gaelic *bog,* soft, from Celtic **buggo-*, "flexible." [Pokorny 3. *bheug-* 152.]

---

bhlē-. Important derivatives are *blow*[1], *bladder, blast, flavor,* and *inflate.*

bhlē-. Also **bhlā-**. To blow. Possibly identical to **bhel-**[3] II **bhlē-* above. **1.** BLOW[1], from Old English *blāwan,* to blow, from Germanic suffixed form **blē-w-*. **2.a.** BLADDER, from Old English *blǣdre,* blister, bladder; **b.** BLATHER, from Old Norse *bladhra* (noun), bladder, and *bladhra* (verb), to prattle. Both **a** and **b** from Germanic suffixed form **blēdram,* "something blown up." **3.a.** BLAST, from Old English *blǣst,* a blowing, blast; **b.** ISINGLASS, from Middle Dutch *blas(e),* a bladder; **c.** BLASÉ, BLAZE[3], from Middle Dutch *blāsen,* to blow up, swell. **a, b** and **c** all from Germanic extended form **blēs-*. **4.** Variant form **bhlā-*. FLABELLUM, FLATUS, FLAVOR; AFFLATUS, CONFLATE, (DEFLATE), INFLATE, SOUFFLÉ, from Latin *flāre,* to blow. [In Pokorny 3. *bhel-* 120.]

---

bhleu-. Important derivatives are *bloat, fluctuate, fluent, fluid, affluent,* and *influence.*

bhleu-. To swell, well up, overflow. Extension of **bhel-**[2]. **1.** BLOAT, from Old Norse *blautr,* soft, wet, from Germanic **blaut-*, possibly from **bhleu-**. **2.** Extended form **bhleug^w-*. FLUCTUATE, FLUENT, FLUERIC, FLUID, FLUME, FLUOR, (FLUORO-), (FLUSH[2]), FLUVIAL, FLUX; AFFLUENT, CONFLUENT, EFFLUENT, (EFFLUVIUM), (EFFLUX), (FLUORIDE), FLUVIOMARINE, INFLUENCE, (INFLUENZA), MELLIFLUOUS, REFLUX, SUPERFLUOUS, from Latin *fluere,* to flow, and *-fluus,* flowing. **3.** Zero-grade form **bhlu-*. PHLYCTENA, from Greek *phluein, phluzein,* to boil over. **4.** PHLOEM, from Greek *phloos, phloios,* tree bark (< "swelling with growth"), possibly from **bhleu-**. [Pokorny *bhleu-* 158.]

---

bhoso-. An important derivative is *bare*[1].

bhoso-. Naked. **a.** BARE[1], from Old English *bær,* bare; **b.** BALLAST, from Old Swedish and Old Danish *bar,* bare. Both **a** and **b** from Germanic **bazaz.* [Pokorny *bhoso-s* 163.]

---

bhrāter-. Important derivatives are *brother, fraternal,* and *pal.*

bhrāter-. Brother, male agnate. **1.a.** BROTHER, from Old English *brōthor,* brother; **b.** BULLY[1], from Middle Dutch *broeder,* brother. Both **a** and **b** from Germanic **brōthar-*. **2.** FRA, FRATERNAL, FRIAR; CONFRERE, FRATRICIDE, from Latin *frāter,* brother. **3.** PHRATRY, from Greek *phratēr,* fellow member of a clan. **4.** PAL, from Sanskrit *bhrātā, bhrātar-*, brother. [Pokorny *bhrāter-* 163.]

---

bhreg-. Important derivatives are *break, breach, fraction, fracture, fragile, fragment, frail*[1], *infringe,* and *suffrage.*

bhreg-. To break. **1.a.** BREAK, from Old English *brecan,* to break; **b.** BREACH, from Old English *brēc,* a breaking; **c.** (BRASH[2]), BRECCIA, from Italian *breccia,* breccia, rubble, breach in a wall, from Old High German **brehha,* from *brehhan,* to break; **d.** BRAY[2], from Old French *breier,* to break; **e.** BRIOCHE, from Old French *brier,* dialectal variant of *broyer,* to knead. **a, b, c, d,** and **e** all from Germanic **brekan.* **2.** BRACKEN, (BRAKE[4]), from Middle English *brake(n),* bracken, probably from a Scandinavian source akin to Old Norse **brakni,* undergrowth; **b.** BRAKE[5], from Middle Low German *brake,* thicket. Both **a** and **b** from Germanic **brak-*, bushes (< "that which impedes motion"). **3.** BRAKE[2], from Middle Low German *brake,* flax brake, from Germanic **brāk-*, crushing instruments. **4.** Nasalized zero-grade form **bhr̥-n-g-*. (FRACTED), FRACTION, (FRACTIOUS), FRACTURE, FRAGILE, FRAGMENT, FRAIL[1], FRANGIBLE; ANFRACTUOUS, CHAMFER, DEFRAY, DIFFRACTION, (INFRACT), INFRANGIBLE, INFRINGE, OSSIFRAGE, REFRACT, (REFRAIN[2]), (REFRINGENT), SAXIFRAGE, SEPTIFRAGAL, from Latin *frangere,* to break. **5.a.** SUFFRAGAN, SUFFRAGE, from Latin *suffrāgium,* the right to vote, from *suffrāgārī,* to vote for (? < "to use a broken piece of tile as a ballot"); **b.** IRREFRAGABLE, from Latin *refrāgārī,* to vote against. [Pokorny 1. *bhreĝ-* 165.]

---

bhreu-. Important derivatives are *brew, bread, broth, brood, breed, ferment,* and *fervent.*

bhreu-. To boil, bubble, effervesce, burn; with derivatives referring to cooking and brewing.
I. 1. BREW, from Old English *brēowan,* to brew, from Germanic **breuwan,* to brew. **2.** BREAD, from Old English *brēad,* piece of food, bread, from Germanic **braudam,* (cooked) food, (leavened) bread. **3.a.** BROTH, from Old English *broth,* broth; **b.** BREWIS, BROIL[2], from Vulgar Latin **brodum,* broth. Both **a** and **b** from Germanic **brudam,* broth.
II. Variant form **bhrē-* **1.a.** BROOD, from Old English *brōd,* offspring, brood; **b.** BREED, from Old English *brēdan,* to beget or cherish offspring, breed, from Germanic denominative **brōdjan,* to rear young. Both **a** and **b** from Germanic derivative **brōd-ō,* "a warming," hatching, rearing of young. **2.a.** BRATWURST, SAUERBRATEN, from Old High German *brāt, brāto,* roast meat; **b.** BRAWN, from Old French *braon,* meat. Both **a** and **b** from Germanic derivative **brēd-ōn-*, roast flesh. Both **1** and **2** from Germanic **brēdan,* to warm.
III. a. Variant form **bhres-*. BRAISE, BRAZE[2], (BRAZIER[2]), BREEZE[2], from Old French *brese,* burning coal, ember; **b.** BRACIOLA, from Italian dialectal *bras'a,* burning coal. Both **a** and **b** from Germanic **bres-*.
IV. Reduced form **bher-*, especially in derivatives referring to fermentation. **1.a.** Suffixed form **bher-men-*, yeast. BARM, (BARMY), from Old English *beorma,* yeast, from Germanic **bermōn-;* **b.** further suffixed form **bhermen-to-*. FERMENT, from Latin *fermentum,* yeast. **2.** Extended form **bherw-*. FERVENT, FERVID, FERVOR; DEFERVESCENCE, EFFERVESCE, from Latin *fervēre,* to be boiling or fermenting.
V. As a very archaic word for a spring. **1.** Suffixed zero-grade form **bhru-n(e)n-*. BOURN[1], BURN[2], from Old English *burn, burna,* spring, stream, from Germanic **brunnōn-*. **2.** Suffixed form **bhrēw-r̥-*. PHREATIC, from Greek *phrear,* spring. [Pokorny *bh(e)reu-* 143, 2. *bher-* 132.]

---

bhrū-. Important derivatives are *brow* and *bridge*[1].

bhrū-. Eyebrow. Contracted from **bhruə-*. **1.** BROW, from Old English *brū-*, eyebrow, eyelid, eyelash, from Germanic **brūs.* **2.** Possibly in the sense of a beam of wood, and perhaps a log bridge. BRIDGE[1], from Old English *brycg(e),* bridge, from Germanic **brugjō* (with cognates in Celtic and Slavic). [Pokorny 1. *bhrū-* 172, 2. *bhrū-* 173.]

---

dā-. Important derivatives are *democracy, epidemic, demon, tide*[1], and *time.*

dā-. To divide. Contracted from **daə-*.
I. Suffixed form **dā-mo-*, perhaps "division of society." DEME, DEMOS, DEMOTIC; DEMAGOGUE, DEMIURGE, DEMOCRACY, DEMOGRAPHY, ENDEMIC, EPIDEMIC, PANDEMIC, from Greek *dēmos,* people, land.
II. Variants **dai-, *dī-*, from extended root **daəi-*. **1.** Root form **dai-*. GEODESY, from Greek *daiesthai,* to divide. **2.** Suffixed form **daimon-*, divider, provider. DEMON, from Greek *daimōn,* divinity. **3.** Suffixed variant form **dī-ti-*. **a.** TIDE[1]; EVENTIDE, from Old English *tīd,* time, season; **b.** TIDE[2], from Old English denominative *tīdan,* to happen (< "to occur in time"); **c.** TIDING, from Old Norse *tīdhr,* occurring; **d.** ZEITGEIST, from Old High German *zīt,* time. **a, b, c,** and **d** all from Germanic **tīdiz,* division of time. **4.** Suffixed variant form **dī-mon-*. TIME, from Old English *tīma,* time, period, from Germanic **tīmōn-*. [Pokorny *dā-* 175.]

---

dail-. Important derivatives are *deal*[1] and *ordeal.*

dail-. To divide. Northern Indo-European root extended from **da(ə)i-* (see **dā-**). **1.** DEAL[1], from Old English *dǣlan,* to share, from Germanic **dailjan.* **2.** DOLE[1], from Old English *dāl,* portion, lot, from Germanic **dailaz.* **3.** ORDEAL, from Old English *ordāl,* trial by ordeal, from Germanic prefixed form **uz-dailjam,* "a portioning out," judgment (**uz-,* out; see **ud-**). **4.** FIRKIN, from Middle Dutch *deel,* part, from Germanic **dailiz.* [In Pokorny *dā-* 175.]

daiwer-. A derivative is *levirate.*

daiwer-. Husband's brother. LEVIRATE, from Latin *lēvir,* husband's brother. [Pokorny *dāiu̯ēr* 179.]

dakru-. An important derivative is *tear*[2].

dakru-. Tear. **1.a.** TEAR[2], from Old English *tēar, tehher,* tear; **b.** TRAIN OIL, from Middle Dutch *trane,* tear, drop. Both **a** and **b** from Germanic **tahr-, *tagr-.* **2.** Suffixed form **dakru-mā.* LACHRYMAL, from Latin *lacrima* (Old Latin *dacruma*), tear. [Pokorny *dakru-* 179.]

de-. Important derivatives are *to, too, de-,* and *deteriorate.*

de-. Demonstrative stem, base of prepositions and adverbs. **1.a.** TO, TOO, from Old English *tō,* to; **b.** TSIMMES, from Old High German *zuo, ze,* to; **c.** TATTOO[1], from Middle Dutch *toe,* to, shut. **a, b,** and **c** all from Germanic **tō.* **2.** DE-, from Latin *dē, dē-,* from, perhaps from **de-**. **3.** (see **kʷo-**) Latin *quandō,* when. **4.** DETERIORATE, from Latin *dēterior,* worse. **5.** (see **bel-**) Latin *dēbilis,* weak. **6.** EISTEDDFOD, from Welsh *eistedd,* sitting, from Celtic **eks-dī-sedo-* (**dī-* from **dē-*). [Pokorny *de-, do-* 181.]

deik-. Important derivatives are *teach, token, digit, toe, dictate, addict, condition, predict, preach, index, indicate, judge, prejudice, revenge,* and *disk.*

deik-. To show, pronounce solemnly; also in derivatives referring to the directing of words or objects.

I. Variant **deig-.* **1.** O-grade form **doig-.* **a.** TEACH, from Old English *tǣcan,* to show, instruct, from Germanic **taikjan,* to show; **b.** *(i)* TOKEN, from Old English *tācen, tācn,* sign, mark; *(ii)* BETOKEN, from Old English *tācnian,* to signify; *(iii)* TETCHY, from Gothic *taikns,* sign; *(iv)* TACHISME, from Old French *tache, teche,* mark, stain. *(i), (ii), (iii),* and *(iv)* all from Germanic **taiknam.* **2.** DIGIT, from Latin *digitus,* finger (< "pointer," "indicator").

II. Basic form **deik-.* **1.** Possibly o-grade form **doik-.* TOE, from Old English *tā, tahe,* toe, from Germanic **taihwō.* **2.** Basic form **deik-.* DICTATE, DICTION, DICTUM, DITTO, DITTY; ADDICT, BENEDICTION, CONDITION, CONTRADICT, EDICT, FATIDIC, (INDICT), INDITE, INTERDICT, JURIDICAL, JURISDICTION, MALEDICT, PREDICT, VALEDICTION, VERDICT, VERIDICAL, VOIR DIRE, from Latin *dīcere,* to say, tell. **3.** Zero-grade form **dik-ā-.* ABDICATE, DEDICATE, PREACH, PREDICATE, from Latin *dicāre,* to proclaim. **4.** Agential suffix **-dik-.* **a.** INDEX, INDICATE, from Latin *index,* indicator, forefinger (*in-,* toward; see **en**); **b.** JUDGE, JUDICIAL; PREJUDICE, from Latin *iūdex* (< **yewes-dik-*), judge, "one who shows or pronounces the law" (*iūs,* law; see **yewes-**); **c.** (VENDETTA), VINDICATE; (AVENGE), REVENGE, from Latin *vindex* (first element obscure), surety, claimant, avenger. **5.** DEICTIC; APODICTIC, PARADIGM, POLICY[2], from Greek *deiknunai,* to show, with *deigma* (**deik-mn̥*), sample, pattern. **6.** Zero-grade form **dik-.* DISK; DICTYOSOME, from suffixed form **dikskos,* from Greek *dikein,* to throw (< "to direct an object"). **7.** Form **dikā.* DICAST; SYNDIC, THEODICY, from Greek *dikē,* justice, right, court case. [Pokorny *deik̑-* 188.]

deiw-. Important derivatives are *Tuesday, deity, divine, jovial, July, Jupiter, Zeus, dial, diary, dismal, journey,* and *psychedelic.*

deiw-. To shine (and in many derivatives, "sky, heaven, god").

I. Noun **deiwos,* god. **1.a.** TIU, (TUESDAY), from Old English *Tīw* (genitive *Tīwes*), god of war and sky; **b.** TYR, from Old Norse *Týr,* sky god. Both **a** and **b** from Germanic **Tīwaz.* **2.** DEISM, DEITY, JOSS; ADIEU, DEIFIC, from Latin *deus,* god. **3.** DIVA, DIVINE, from Latin *dīvus,* divine, god. **4.** DIVES, from Latin *dīves,* rich (< "fortunate, blessed, divine"). **5.** Suffixed zero-grade form **diw-yo-,* heavenly. DIANA, from Latin *Diāna,* moon goddess. **6.** DEVI; DEODAR, DEVANAGARI, from Sanskrit *de-vaḥ,* god, and *deva-,* divine.

II. Variant **dyeu-,* Jove, the name of the god of the bright sky, head of the Indo-European pantheon. **1.** JOVE, JOVIAL, from Latin *Iovis,* Jupiter, or *Iov-,* stem of *Iuppiter,* Jupiter. **2.** JULY, from Latin *Iūlius,* "descended from Jupiter" (name of a Roman gens), from derivative **iou-il-.* **3.** Vocative compound **dyeu-pəter-,* "O father Jove" (**pəter-,* father; see **pəter-**). JUPITER, from Latin *Iuppiter, Iūpiter,* head of the Roman pantheon. **4.** DIONE, ZEUS; DIOSCURI, from Greek *Zeus* (genitive *Dios*), Zeus.

III. Variant **dyē-* (< **dyeə-*). DIAL, DIARY, DIET[2], DISMAL, DIURNAL; ADJOURN, CIRCADIAN, (JOURNAL), (JOURNEY), MERIDIAN, (POSTMERIDIAN), QUOTIDIAN, SOJOURN, from Latin *diēs,* day.

IV. Variant **deiə-.* PSYCHEDELIC, from Greek *dēlos,* (< **deyalos*), clear. [Pokorny 1. *dei-* 183.]

dek-. Important derivatives are *decent, doctor, doctrine, document, dogma, paradox, decorate, dainty, dignity, disdain, indignant, disciple,* and *discipline.*

dek-. To take, accept. **1.** Suffixed (stative) form **dek-ē-.* DECENT, from Latin *decēre,* to be fitting (< "to be acceptable"). **2.** Suffixed (causative) o-grade form **dok-eye-.* **a.** DOCENT, DOCILE, DOCTOR, DOCTRINE, DOCUMENT, from Latin *docēre,* to teach (< "to cause to accept"); **b.** DOGMA, (DOGMATIC); DOCETISM, DOXOLOGY, HETERODOX, ORTHODOX, PARADOX, from Greek *dokein,* to appear, seem, think (< "to cause to accept or be accepted"). **3.** Suffixed form **dek-es-.* **a.** (DÉCOR), DECORATE, from Latin *decus,* grace, ornament; **b.** DECOROUS, from Latin *decor,* seemliness, elegance, beauty. **4.** Suffixed form **dek-no-.* DAINTY, DEIGN, DIGNITY, CONDIGN, DIGNIFY, DISDAIN, INDIGN, (INDIGNANT), (INDIGNATION), from Latin *dignus,* worthy, deserving, fitting. **5.** Reduplicated form **di-dk-ske-.* DISCIPLE, (DISCIPLINE), from Latin *discere,* to learn. **6.** (DOWEL), PANDECT, SYNECDOCHE, from Greek *dekhesthai,* to accept. **7.** DIPLODOCUS, from Greek *dokos,* beam, support. [Pokorny 1. *dek̑-* 189.]

dekm̥. Important derivatives are *ten, December, decimal, dime, dozen, dean, decade, tenth, hundred, cent, century,* and *percent.*

dekm̥. Ten.

I. Basic form **dekm̥.* **1.a.** TEN, from Old English *tīen,* ten; **b.** (see **oktō(u)**) Old Norse *tjan,* ten. Both **a** and **b** from Germanic **tehun.* **2.** EIGHTEEN, FIFTEEN, FOURTEEN, NINETEEN, SEVENTEEN, SIXTEEN, THIRTEEN, from Old English suffix *-tēne, -tīne, -týne,* ten, -teen, from Germanic **tehan.* **3.** DECEMBER, DECEMVIR, DECI-, DECIMAL, DECIMATE, DECUPLE, DICKER, DIME; (DECENNARY), DECENNIUM, DECUSSATE, DOZEN, DUODECIMAL, OCTODECIMO, SEXTODECIMO, from Latin *decem,* ten. **4.** (DENARIUS), DENARY, (DENIER[2]), from irregular Latin distributive *dēnī,* by tens, ten each (formed by analogy with *nōnī,* nine each). **5.** DEAN, DECA-, DECADE, (DOYEN); DECAGON, DECALOGUE, DODECAGON, from Greek *deka,* ten.

II. Extended form **dekm̥t-.* (see **dwo-**) Old English *-tig,* ten, from Germanic **-tig.*

III. Ordinal number **dekm̥to-.* TENTH, (TITHE), from Old English *teogotha, tēotha,* tenth, from Germanic **teguntha-.*

IV. Suffixed zero-grade form **-dkm̥-tă,* reduced to **-km̥tă,* and lengthened o-grade form **-dkōmtă,* reduced to **-kontă.* **1.** NONAGENARIAN, OCTOGENARIAN, SEPTUAGINT, SEXAGENARY, from Latin *-gintā,* ten times. **2.** PENTECOST, from Greek **-konta,* ten times.

V. Suffixed zero-grade form **dkm̥-tom,* hundred, reduced to **km̥tom.* **1.** HUNDRED, from Old English *hundred,* hundred (*-red,* from Germanic **radam,* number; see **ar-**), from Germanic **hundam,* hundred. **2.** (see **teuə-**) Germanic **thūs-hundi,* "swollen hundred," thousand. **3.** CENT, CENTAL, CENTAVO, (CENTENARIAN), CENTENARY, CENTESIMAL, CENTI-, CENTIME, (CENTNER), CENTUM, CENTURY; CENTENNIAL, CINQUECENTO, PERCENT, QUATTROCENTO, SEICENTO, (SEN[2]), (SENITI), SEXCENTENARY, TRECENTO, from Latin *centum,* hundred. **4.** HECATOMB, HECTO-, from Greek *hekaton,* a hundred (? dissimilated from **hem-katon,* one hundred; see **sem-**[1]). **5.** STOTINKA, from Old Church Slavonic *sŭto,* hundred. **6.** SATEM, from Avestan *satəm,* hundred. [Pokorny *dek̑m̥* 191.] See also compound root **wīkm̥tī.**

del-[1]**.** Important derivatives are *linger, long*[1]*, long*[2]*, length, Lent, longitude, lunge,* and *prolong.*

del-[1]**.** Long. Probably extended and suffixed zero-grade form **dlon-gho-.* **1.a.** LONG[1], from Old English *lang, long,* long; **b.** LANGLAUF, from Old High German *lang,* long; **c.** BELONG, from Old English *gelang,* along; **d.** LONG[2], from Old English denominative *langian,* to grow longer, yearn for, from Germanic **langōn;* **e.** LINGER, from Old English *lengan,* to prolong (possibly influenced by Old Norse *lengja,* to lengthen), from Germanic **langjan,* to make long; **f.** LOMBARD, from Latin compound *Longobardus, Langobardus* (with Germanic ethnic name **Bardi*). **a, b, c, d, e,** and **f** all from Germanic **langaz,* long. **2.a.** LENGTH, from Old English *lengthu,* length; **b.** LENT, from Old English *lengten, lencten,* spring, Lent, from West Germanic **langitinaz,* lengthening of day; **c.** LING[1], from Middle English *lenge, ling,* ling, from a Low German source akin to Dutch *lenghe, linghe,* "long one." **a, b,** and **c** all from Germanic abstract noun **langithō.* **3.** LONGERON, LONGITUDE; ELOIGN, (ELONGATE), LONGEVITY, LUNGE, OBLONG, PROLONG, PURLOIN, from Latin *longus,* long. **4.** Possibly suffixed variant **dl̥əgho-.* DOLICHOCEPHALIC, DOLICHOCRANIAL, from Greek *dolikhos,* long. [Pokorny 5. *del-* 196.]

del-[2]**.** Important derivatives are *tell, tale,* and *talk.*

del-[2]**.** To recount, count. **1.** TELL, from Old English *tellan,* to count, recount, from Germanic **taljan.* **2.** TALL, from Old English *getæl,* quick, ready, from West Germanic **(ge-)tala-.* **3.a.** TALE, from Old English *talu,* story; **b.** TAAL[2], from Middle Dutch *tāle,* speech, language. Both **a** and **b** from Germanic **talō.* **4.** TALK, from Middle English *talken,* to talk, from a source probably akin to Old English denominative *talian,* to tell, relate. **5.** DOLERITE, SEDULOUS, from Greek *dolos,* ruse, snare, perhaps from **del-**[2]. [Pokorny 1. *del-* 193.]

dem-. Important derivatives are *dome, domestic, danger, domain, dominate,* and *timber.*

dem-. House, household. **1.** Suffixed o-grade form **dom-o-, dom-u-,* house. **a.** DOME, DOMESTIC, DOMICILE; MAJOR-DOMO, from Latin *domus,* house; **b.** suffixed form **dom-o-no-.* DAME, DAN[2], DANGER, DOM, DOMAIN, DOMINATE, DOMINICAL, DOMINIE, DOMINION, (DOMINO[1]), DOMINO[2], DON[1], DUNGEON; (MADAM), MADAME, MADEMOISELLE, MADONNA, PREDOMINATE, from Latin *dominus,* master of a household (feminine *domina*). **2.** Possibly lengthened-grade form **dōm-m̥.* DOME, from Greek *dōma,* house. **3.** Compound **dems-pot-,* "house-master" (**-pot-,* powerful; see **poti-**). DESPOT, from Greek *despotēs,* master, lord. **4.** Root form **dem(ə)-,* to build (possibly a separate root). **a.** TIMBER, from Old English *timber,* building material, lumber, from Germanic **timram;* **b.** TOFT, from Old Norse *topt,* homestead, from Germanic **tumftō.* [Pokorny *dem-* 198.]

demə-. Important derivatives are *tame, daunt, adamant,* and *diamond.*

demə-. To constrain, force, especially to break in (horses). **1.** Suffixed o-grade form **dom(ə)-o-.* TAME, from Old English *tam,* domesticated, from Germanic **tamaz.* **2.** O-grade form **domə-.* DAUNT; INDOMITABLE, from Latin *domāre,* to tame, subdue. **3.** Zero-grade form **dm̥ə-.* ADAMANT, (DIAMOND), from Greek *daman,* to tame (> *adamas,* unconquerable, from **n̥-dm̥ə-nt-*). [Pokorny *(demə-), domə-* 199.]

dent-. Important derivatives are *tooth, tusk, dental, dandelion,* and *indent*[1].

dent-. Tooth. (Originally participle of **ed-** in the earlier meaning "to bite".) **1.** O-grade form **dont-.* TOOTH, from Old English *tōth,* tooth, from Germanic **tanthuz.* **2.** Zero-grade form **dn̥t-.* TUSK, from Old English *tūsc, tūx,* canine tooth, from Germanic **tunth-sk-.* **3.** Full-grade form **dent-.* DENTAL, DENTATE, DENTI-, DENTICLE, DENTIST; DANDELION, EDENTATE, EDENTULOUS, INDENT[1], (INDENTURE), TRIDENT, from Latin *dēns* (stem *dent-*), tooth.

4. O-grade variant form *(o)dont-. -ODON, -ODONT, ODONTO-; CERATODUS, MASTODON, from Greek *odōn, odous,* tooth. [In Pokorny *ed-* 287.]

der-. Important derivatives are *tear*[1], *tart*[2], *turd, epidermis, drab*[1], and *drape.*

der-. To split, peel, flay; with derivatives referring to skin and leather. **1.** TEAR[1], from Old English *teran,* to tear, from Germanic *teran. **2.** TART[1], from Old English *teart,* sharp, severe, from Germanic *ter-t. **3.** Suffixed zero-grade form *dr̥-tom, "something separated or discarded." TURD, from Old English *tord,* turd, from Germanic *turdam, turd. **4.** Reduplicated form *de-dr-u-. TETTER, from Old English *tet(e)r,* eruption, skin disease. **5.** DERRIS, from Greek *derris,* leather covering. **6.** Suffixed form *der-mn̥. -DERM, DERMA[1], -DERMA, DERMATO-; EPIDERMIS, from Greek *derma,* skin. [Pokorny 4. *der-* 206.]

deru-. Important derivatives are *tree, truce, true, truth, trust, tray, trough, trim, tar*[1], *endure,* and *druid.*

deru-. Also **dreu-**. To be firm, solid, steadfast; hence specialized senses "wood," "tree," and derivatives referring to objects made of wood. **1.** Suffixed variant form *drew-o-. **a.** TREE, from Old English *trēow,* tree, from Germanic *trewam; **b.** TRUCE, from Old English *trēow,* pledge, from Germanic *treuwō. **2.** Variant form *dreu-.* **a.** TRUE, from Old English *trēowe,* firm, true; **b.** TROW, from Old English *trēowian, trūwian,* to trust; **c.** TRIG[1], from Old Norse *tryggr,* firm, true; **d.** TROTH, TRUTH; BETROTH, from Old English *trēowth* faith, loyalty, truth, from Germanic abstract noun *treuwithō; **e.** TRUST, from Old Norse *traust,* confidence, firmness, from Germanic abstract noun *traustam; **f.** TRYST, from Old French *triste,* waiting place (< "place where one waits trustingly"), probably from a source akin to Old Norse denominative *treysta,* to trust, make firm. **a, b, c, d, e,** and **f** all from Germanic *treuwaz. **3.** Variant form *drou-. TRAY, from Old English *trēg, trīg,* wooden board, from Germanic *traujam. **4.** Suffixed zero-grade form *dru-ko-. TROUGH, from Old English *trog,* wooden vessel, tray, from Germanic *trugaz. **5.** Suffixed zero-grade form *dru-mo-. **a.** TRIM, from Old English *trum,* firm, strong; **b.** SHELTER, from Old English *truma,* troop. Both **a** and **b** from Germanic *trum-. **6.** Variant form *derw-. TAR[1], from Old English *te(o)ru,* resin, pitch (obtained from the pine tree), from Germanic *terw-. **7.** Suffixed variant form *drū-ro-. DOUR, DURAMEN, DURESS, DURUM; (DURA MATER), ENDURE, INDURATE, OBDURATE, from Latin *dūrus,* hard (many of whose English derivatives represent a semantic cross with Latin *dūrāre,* to last long; see **deuə-**). **8.** Lengthened zero-grade form *drū-. DRUPE, DRYAD; DRYOPITHECINE, GERMANDER, HAMADRYAD, from Greek *drus,* oak. **9.** Reduplicated form *der-drew-, dissimilated with suffix in *der-drew-on. DENDRO-, DENDRON; PHILODENDRON, RHODODENDRON, from Greek *dendron,* tree. **10.** DRUID, from Latin *druides,* druids, probably from Celtic compound *dru-wid-, "strong seer" (*wid-, seeing; see **weid-**), the Celtic priestly caste. **11.** O-grade form *doru-. DEODAR, from Sanskrit *dāru,* wood, timber. [Pokorny *deru-* 214.]

deu-[1]. An important derivative is *tire*[1].

deu-[1]. To lack, be wanting. **1.** Possibly suffixed form *deu-s-. **a.** TIRE[1], from Old English *tēorian, tyrian,* to fail, tire (< "to fall behind"), from Germanic *teuzōn; **b.** DEONTOLOGY, from Greek *dein,* to lack, want. **2.** Suffixed form *deu-tero-. DEUTERO- ; DEUTERAGONIST, (DEUTERIUM), DEUTERONOMY, from Greek *deuteros,* "missing," next, second. [Pokorny 3. *deu-* 219.] (For suffixed zero-grade form *du-s-, combining form of *dew-es-, a lack, see **dus-**.)

deu-[2]. Important derivatives are *bonus, bounty, benefactor, benefit, benign, beauty, embellish, dynamic, dynamite,* and *dynasty.*

deu-[2]. To do, perform, show favor, revere. **1.** Suffixed form *dw-enos. BONBON, BONITO, BONUS, BOON[2], BOUNTY; BONANZA, BONHOMIE, DEBONAIR, from Latin *bonus,* good (< "useful, efficient, working"). **2.** Adverbial form *dw-enē. BENEDICTION, BENEFACTION, (BENEFACTOR), (BENEFIC), (BENEFICENCE), (BENEFIT), BENEVOLENT, (BENIGN), (HERB BENNET), from Latin *bene,* well. **3.** Diminutive *dw-en-elo-. BEAU, BEAUTY, BELLE; BELDAM, BELLADONNA, BELVEDERE, EMBELLISH, from Latin *bellus,* handsome, pretty, fine. **4.** Possibly suffixed zero-grade form *dw-eye-. (BEATITUDE); BEATIFIC, (BEATIFY), from Latin *beāre,* to make blessed. **5.** Possible (but unlikely for formal and semantic reasons) suffixed zero-grade form *du-nə-. DYNAMIC, (DYNAMITE), DYNAST, (DYNASTY); AERODYNE, from Greek *dunasthai,* to be able. [Pokorny 2. *deu-* 218.]

deuə-. Important derivatives are *durable, duration,* and *during.*

deuə-. Also **dwaə-**. Long (in duration). Suffixed zero-grade form *dū-ro- (< *duə-ro-). DURABLE, DURANCE, DURATION, DURING; PERDURABLE, THERMODURIC, from Latin *dūrāre,* to last. [In Pokorny 3. *deu-* 219.]

deuk-. Important derivatives are *tug, wanton, tow*[1], *tie, team, dock*[1], *duct, duke, abduct, conduct, deduce, introduce, produce, reduce, subdue,* and *educate.*

deuk-. To lead. **1.** TUG; WANTON, from Old English *tēon,* to pull, draw, lead, from Germanic *teuhan. **2.** Suffixed zero-grade form *duk-ā-. TOW[1], from Old English *togian,* to draw, drag, from Germanic *tugōn. **3.** Suffixed o-grade form *douk-eyo-. TIE, from Old English *tīegan, tīgan, to bind. **4.** Suffixed o-grade form *douk-mo-. TEAM, from Old English *tēam,* descendant, family, race, brood, team, from Germanic *tau(h)maz. **5.** TEEM[1], from Old English *tēman, tīeman,* to beget, from Germanic denominative *tau(h)mjan. **6.** Basic form *deuk-. DOGE, DOUCHE, (DUCAL), (DUCAT), (DUCE), (DUCHESS), (DUCHY), DUCT, DUCTILE, DUKE; (ABDUCENS), ABDUCT, ADDUCE, CIRCUMDUCTION, (CON[3]), (CONDOTTIERE), CONDUCE, (CONDUCT), DEDUCE, (DEDUCT), EDUCE, (ENDUE), INDUCE, INTRODUCE, PRODUCE, (REDOUBT), REDUCE, SEDUCE, SUBDUCTION, SUBDUE, TRADUCE, TRANSDUCER, from Latin *dūcere,* to lead. **7.** Suffixed zero-grade form *duk-ā-. EDUCATE, from Latin *ēducāre,* to lead out, bring up (*ē-* < *ex-,* out; see **eghs**). [Pokorny *deuk-* 220.]

dhē-. Important derivatives are *do*[1], *deed, doom, -dom, deem, fact, factor, fashion, feat*[1], *feature, affair, affect*[1], *affection, amplify, benefit, defeat, defect, effect, efficient, infect, justify, modify, notify, perfect, profit, qualify, sacrifice, face, surface, difficulty, thesis,* and *theme.*

dhē-. To set, put. Contracted from *dheə-. **1.** O-grade form *dhō-. DO[1]; FORDO, from Old English *dōn,* to do, from Germanic *dōn. **2.** Suffixed form *dhē-ti-, "thing laid down or done, law, deed." DEED, from Old English *dǣd,* doing, deed, from Germanic *dēdiz. **3.** Suffixed o-grade form *dhō-mo-. **a.** DOOM, from Old English *dōm,* judgment (< "thing set or put down"); **b.** -DOM, from Old English *-dōm,* abstract suffix indicating state, condition, or power; **c.** (see **kā-**) Old Norse *-dōmr,* condition; **d.** DUMA, from Russian *Duma,* Duma, from a Germanic source akin to Gothic *dōms,* judgment; **e.** DEEM, from Old English *dēman,* to judge, from Germanic denominative *dōmjan.* **a, b, c, d,** and **e** all from Germanic *dōmaz.* **4.** Suffixed o-grade form *dhō-t-. (see **sak-**) Latin *sacerdōs,* priest, "performer of sacred rites." **5.** Zero-grade form *dhə-. **a.** prefixed form *kom-dhə-. ABSCOND, INCONDITE, RECONDITE, SCONCE[2], from Latin *condere,* to put together, establish, preserve (*kom, together; see **kom**); **b.** prefixed and suffixed form *kom-dh(ə)-yo-. CONDIMENT, from Latin *condīre,* to season, flavor; **c.** compound *kred-dhə-. (see **kerd-**) **6.** Suffixed zero-grade form *dhə-k-.* **a.** -FACIENT, FACT, FACTION[1], -FACTION, FACTITIOUS, FACTITIVE, FACTOR, FASHION, FEASIBLE, FEAT[1], FEATURE, (FETISH), -FIC, (-FY), HACIENDA; AFFAIR, AFFECT[1], (AFFECT[2]), (AFFECTION), (AMPLIFY), ARTIFACT, ARTIFICE, (BEATIFIC), BENEFACTION, (BENEFIC), (BENEFICE), (BENEFICENCE), (BENEFIT), CHAFE, COMFIT, CONFECT, (CONFETTI), COUNTERFEIT, (DEFEASANCE), DEFEAT, DEFECT, (DEFICIENT), (DISCOMFIT), (EDIFICE), (EDIFY), EFFECT, (EFFICACIOUS), (EFFICIENT), FACSIMILE, FACTOTUM, FORFEIT, INFECT, (JUSTIFY), MALEFACTOR, (MALFEASANCE), MANUFACTURE, MISFEASANCE, (MODIFY), (MOLLIFY), (NIDIFY), (NOTIFY), (NULLIFY), OFFICINAL, ORIFICE, PERFECT, (PETRIFY), (PLUPERFECT), PONTIFEX, PREFECT, (PROFICIENT), PROFIT, PUTREFY, (QUALIFY), RAREFY, (RECTIFY), REFECT, (REFECTORY), RUBEFACIENT, SACRIFICE, SATISFY, SPINIFEX, SUFFICE, (SUFFICIENT), SURFEIT, TUBIFEX, TUMEFACIENT, (VIVIFY), from Latin *facere* (< *fak-yo-), to do, make, and Latin combining form *-fex* (< *-fak-s), "maker"; **b.** FAÇADE, FACE, (FACET), (FACIAL), FACIES; (DEFACE), EFFACE, (SURFACE), from Latin derivative *faciēs,* shape, face (< "form imposed on something"); **c.** OFFICE, from Latin compound *officium* (< *opi-fici-om), service, duty, business, performance of work (*opi-, work; see **op-**); **d.** further suffixed form *dhə-k-li-. FACILE, (FACILITATE), FACULTY, DIFFICULTY, from Latin *facilis* (< Old Latin *facul*), feasible, easy. **7.** Suffixed zero-grade form *dhə-s- (probably identical with zero-grade of **dhēs-**). NEFARIOUS, from Latin *fās,* divine law, right. **8.** MULTIFARIOUS, OMNIFARIOUS, from Latin *-fāriam,* adverbial suffix, as in *bifāriam,* in two places, parts, double, from *dwi-dh(ə)-, "making two" (*dwi-, two; see **dwo-**). **9.** Reduplicated form *dhi-dhə-. THESIS, THETIC; ANATHEMA, ANTITHESIS, DIATHESIS, EPENTHESIS, EPITHET, HYPOTHESIS, METATHESIS, PARENTHESIS, PROSTHESIS, PROTHESIS, SYNTHESIS, from Greek *tithenai,* to put, with zero-grade noun *thesis* (*dhə-ti-), a placing, and verbal adjective *thetos* (*dhə-to-), placed. **10.** Suffixed form *dhē-k-. THECA, TICK[3]; AMPHITHECIUM, APOTHECARY, (APOTHECIUM), BIBLIOTHECA, (BODEGA), (BOUTIQUE), CLEISTOTHECIUM, ENDOTHECIUM, PERITHECIUM, from Greek *thēkē,* receptacle. **11.** Suffixed zero-grade form *dhə-mn̥. (THEMATIC), THEME, from Greek *thema,* "thing placed," proposition. **12.** Reduplicated form *dhe-dhē-. SANDHI, from Sanskrit *dadhāti,* he places. **13.** Basic form *dhē-. PURDAH, from Old Persian *dā-,* to place. **14.** Suffixed form *dhē-to-, set down, created. (see **s(w)e-**) Old Iranian compound *khvatō-dāta-, created from oneself. **15.** Reduced form *dh-. (see **au-**) [Pokorny 2. *dhē-* 235.]

dhē(i)-. Important derivatives are *female, feminine, fawn*[2], *fetus, fennel,* and *affiliate.*

dhē(i)-. To suck. Contracted from *dheə(i)-. **1.** Suffixed reduced form *dhē-mnā-. FEMALE, FEMININE; EFFEMINATE, from Latin *fēmina,* woman (< "she who suckles"). **2.** Suffixed reduced form *dhē-to-. FAWN[2], (FETAL), FETUS; EFFETE, (FETICIDE), SUPERFETATE, from Latin *fētus,* pregnancy, childbearing, offspring, with adjective *fētus, fēta,* pregnant. **3.** Suffixed reduced form *dhē-kwondo-. FECUND, from Latin *fēcundus,* fruitful. **4.** Suffixed reduced form *dhē-no-. FENNEL, FINOCCHIO; (FENUGREEK), SAINFOIN, from Latin *fēnum, faenum,* hay (< "produce"). **5.** Perhaps suffixed zero-grade form *dhī-lyo- (< *dhiə-lyo-). FILIAL; FILS[1]; AFFILIATE, HIDALGO, from Latin *fīlius,* son, and *fīlia,* daughter (but these are equally possibly from the root **bheuə-**). **6.** Suffixed reduced form *dhē-lo-. FELLATIO, from Latin *fēlāre, fellāre,* to suck. **7.** Suffixed reduced form *dhē-l-īk-. FELICITATE, FELICITY; FELICIFIC, INFELICITY, from Latin *fēlīx,* fruitful, fertile, lucky, happy. **8.** Suffixed reduced form *dhē-lā-. ENDOTHELIUM, EPITHELIUM, (MESOTHELIUM), from Greek *thēlē,* nipple. **9.** Suffixed reduced form *dhē-l-u-. THEELIN, from Greek *thēlus,* female. [Pokorny *dhē(i)-* 241.]

dheigh-. Important derivatives are *dairy, lady, dough, figure, faint, fiction, effigy,* and *paradise.*

dheigh-. To form, build. **1.** DAIRY, from Old English *dǣge,* bread kneader, from Germanic *daigjōn-. **2.** LADY, from Old English compound *hlǣfdige,* mistress of a household (< "bread kneader"; *hlāf,* bread, loaf), from Germanic *dīg-. **3.** Suffixed o-grade form *dhoigh-o-. **a.** DOUGH, from Old English *dāg,* dough, from Germanic *daigaz. **4.** Suffixed zero-grade form *dhigh-ūrā. FIGURE; CONFIGURE, DISFIGURE, PREFIGURE, TRANSFIGURE, from Latin *figūra,* form, shape (< "result of kneading"). **5.** Nasalized zero-grade form *dhi-n-gh-. (FAINT), FEIGN, (FEINT), FICTILE, FICTION, FIGMENT; EFFIGY, from Latin *fingere,* to shape. **6.** Probable nasalized zero-grade form *dhi-n-g(h)-. THIGMOTAXIS, THIXOTROPY, from Greek *thinganein,* to touch. **7.** Suffixed o-grade form *dhoigh-o-. PARADISE, from Avestan *daēza-,* wall (originally made of clay or mud bricks). [Pokorny *dheigh-* 244.]

dher-. Important derivatives are *farm, firm*[1], *confirm,* and *throne.*

dher-. To hold firmly, support. **1.** Suffixed form **dher-mo-*. FARM, FERMATA, FIRM[1], FIRM[2], (FIRMAMENT); AFFIRM, CONFIRM, INFIRM, (INFIRMARY), from Latin *firmus,* firm, strong. **2.** Perhaps extended form **dhergh-*. (see **bhergh-**[2]) Latin *fortis,* strong (but this is also possibly from **bhergh-**[2]). **3.** Suffixed zero-grade form **dhr-ono-*. THRONE, from Greek *thronos,* seat, throne (< "support"). **4.** Suffixed form **dher-mn̥*. DHARMA, from Sanskrit *dharma,* statute, law (< "that which is established firmly"). **5.** Suffixed form **dher-eno-*. DHARNA, from Prakrit *dharaṇa,* a holding firm. **6.** Suffixed o-grade form **dhor-o-*. SIRDAR, TAHSILDAR, ZAMINDAR, from Iranian *dāra-,* holding, whence Persian *-dār.* [Pokorny 2. *dher-* 252.]

dhers-. An important derivative is *dare.*

dhers-. To venture, be bold. O-grade form **dhors-* and zero-grade form **dhr̥s-*. DARE, (DURST), from Old English *dearr* and *durst,* first and third person singular present and past indicative of *durran,* to venture, respectively from Germanic **dors-* and **durs-*. [Pokorny *dhers-* 259.]

dhēs-. Important derivatives are *fair*[2], *feast, festival, fanatic, profane, atheism,* and *enthusiasm.*

dhēs-. Root of words in religious concepts. Contracted from *dheəs-*. Possibly an extension of **dhē-**. **1.** Suffixed form **dhēs-yā*. FAIR[2], FERIA, from Latin *fēriae* (< Old Latin *fēsiae*), holidays. **2.** Suffixed form **dhēs-to-*. FEAST, (-FEST), (FESTAL), FESTIVAL, FESTIVE, (FESTOON), (FETE), (FIESTA); (GABFEST), OKTOBERFEST, from Latin *fēstus,* festive. **3.** Suffixed zero-grade form **dhəs-no-*. FANATIC; PROFANE, from Latin *fānum,* temple. **4.** Suffixed zero-grade form **dhəs-o-*. THEO-; APOTHEOSIS, ATHEISM, ENTHUSIASM, PANTHEON, POLYTHEISM, from Greek *theos* (< **thes-os*), god. [Pokorny *dhēs-* 259.]

dheu-[1]. An important derivative is *dew.*

dheu-[1]. To flow. **a.** DEW, from Old English *dēaw,* dew; **b.** SUNDEW, from Middle Dutch *dau,* dew; **c.** (see **melit-**) Germanic compound **melith-dauwaz,* "honeydew." **a, b,** and **c** all from Germanic **dauwaz,* dew. [Pokorny 1. *dheu-* 259.]

dheu-[2]. Important derivatives are *dead, death, die*[1], and *dwindle.*

dheu-[2]. To die. **1.** Suffixed o-grade form **dhou-to-*. DEAD, from Old English *dēad,* dead, from Germanic **daudaz.* **2.** Suffixed o-grade form **dhou-tu-*. DEATH, from Old English *dēath,* death, from Germanic **dauthuz.* **3.** Suffixed o-grade form **dhow-yo-*. DIE[1], from Old Norse *deyja,* to die. **4.** Suffixed extended zero-grade form **dhwī-no-*. DWINDLE, from Old English *dwīnan,* to diminish, languish, from Germanic **dwīnan.* [Pokorny 2. *dheu-* 260.] See **dhū-no-**.

dheub-. Important derivatives are *deep, depth, dip,* and *dive.*

dheub-. Deep, hollow. **1.** DEEP, (DEPTH), from Old English *dēop,* deep, from Germanic **deupaz.* **2.** DIP, from Old English *dyppan,* to immerse, dip, from Germanic expressive denominative **duppjan.* **3.** Parallel root form **dheubh-*. DIVE, from Old English *dȳfan,* to dip, and *dūfan,* to sink, dive, from Germanic verb **dūbjan,* from **deub-, *dub-*. [Pokorny *dheu-b-* 267.]

dheugh-. Derivatives are *doughty* and *Pentateuch.*

dheugh-. To produce something of utility. **1.** DOUGHTY, from Old English *dyhtig, dohtig,* strong (< "productive"), from Germanic extended form **duht-*. **2.** Suffixed form **dheugh-os-*. HEPTATEUCH, (HEXATEUCH), PENTATEUCH, from Greek *teukhos* (< **theukhos*), gear, anything produced, tool, container, scroll. [Pokorny *dheugh-* 271.]

dhghem-. Important derivatives are *bridegroom, chamomile, humble, homage, homicide,* and *human.*

dhghem-. Earth. **1.** Suffixed zero-grade form **(dh)ghm̥-on-,* "earthling." BRIDEGROOM, from Old English *guma,* man, from Germanic **gumōn-*. **2.** O-grade form **dh(e)ghom-*. CHTHONIC; AUTOCHTHON, from Greek *khthōn,* earth. **3.** Zero-grade form **dhghm̥-*. CHAMAEPHYTE, CHAMELEON, CHAMOMILE, GERMANDER, from Greek *khamai,* on the ground. **4.** Suffixed o-grade form **(dh)ghom-o-*. HUMBLE, (HUMILIATE), (HUMILITY), HUMUS[1]; EXHUME, INHUME, TRANSHUMANCE, from Latin *humus,* earth. **5.** Suffixed o-grade form **(dh)ghom-on-,* "earthling." **a.** HOMAGE, HOMBRE[1], HOMINID, HOMO[1], HOMUNCULUS, OMBRE; BONHOMIE, HOMICIDE, from Latin *homō,* human being, man; **b.** HUMAN, (HUMANE), from Latin *hūmānus,* human, kind, humane (in part from **dhghem-**). **6.** Suffixed form **(dh)ghem-yā.* CHERNOZEM, ZEMSTVO, from Old Russian *zemĭ,* land, earth. **7.** Full-grade form **(dh)ghem-*. ZAMINDAR, from Persian *zamīn,* earth, land. [Pokorny *ĝhwem-* 414.]

dhgh(y)es-. An important derivative is *yesterday.*

dhgh(y)es-. Yesterday. Suffixed (comparative) form **(dh)ghes-ter-*. YESTER-, (YESTERDAY), from Old English *geostran, giestran,* "yester-," from Germanic **ges-ter-*. [Pokorny *ĝhwi̯es* 416.]

dhīg^{w}-. Important derivatives are *dike*[1], *ditch, dig, fix,* and *prefix.*

dhīg^{w}-. To stick, fix. **1.a.** DIKE[1], DITCH, from Old English *dīc,* trench, moat; **b.** DIG, from Middle English *diggen,* to dig, from a source perhaps akin to Old French *digue,* trench. Both **a** and **b** from Germanic **dīk-*. **2.** FIBULA, FICHU, FINCA, FIX, (FIXATE), (FIXITY), (FIXTURE); AFFIX, ANTEFIX, CRUCIFY, INFIX, MICROFICHE, PREFIX, SUFFIX, TRANSFIX, from Latin *fīgere,* to fasten, fix. [Pokorny *dhēig^{u}-* 243.]

dhreg-. Important derivatives are *drink, drench,* and *drown.*

dhreg-. To draw, glide. **1.** DRINK, from Old English *drincan,* to drink, from nasalized Germanic form **drenkan,* to draw into the mouth, drink. **2.** DRENCH, from Old English *drencan,* to soak, from nasalized o-grade Germanic causative form **drankjan,* "to cause to drink." **3.** DROWN, from a Scandinavian or late Old English source similar to Old Norse *drukkna,* to drown, from Germanic zero- grade suffixed form **drunk-nōn.* [Pokorny *dhreĝ-* 273.]

dhreibh-. Important derivatives are *drive* and *drift.*

dhreibh-. To drive, push; snow. **1.** DRIVE, DROVE[2], from Old English *drīfan,* to drive, rush, from Germanic **drīban.* **2.** DRIFT, from Middle English *drift,* drove, herd, akin to Old Norse *drift,* snowdrift, and Middle Dutch *drift,* herd, from Germanic zero-grade suffixed form **driftiz.* [Pokorny *dhreibh-* 274.]

dhreu-. Important derivatives are *drizzle, dreary, drowse, drop, droop,* and *drip.*

dhreu-. To fall, flow, drip, droop. **1.** Extended form **dhreus-*. DRIZZLE, from Old English *-drysnian* (in *gedrysnian,* to pass away, vanish), from zero-grade Germanic derived verb **drusinōn.* **2.** Extended o-grade form **dhrous-*. **a.** DREARY, from Old English *drēor,* flowing blood, from Germanic **drauzaz;* **b.** DROWSE, from Old English *drūsian,* to be sluggish, from Germanic **drūsjan.* **3.** Extended zero-grade form **dhrub-*. **a.** DROP, from Old English *dropa,* drop, from Germanic **drupan;* **b.** DROOP, from Old Norse *drūpa,* to hang down, from Germanic **drūpōn,* to let fall; **c.** DRIP, from Middle English *drippen,* to drip, drop, from an unattested Old English **dryppan* or another source akin to Old English *droppa,* drop, from Germanic geminated **drupp-*. **4.** Suffixed zero-grade form **dhrubh-yo-*. LITHOTRIPTER, (LITHOTRITY), from Greek *thruptein,* to crumble. [Pokorny *dhreu-* 274.]

dhughəter-. An important derivative is *daughter.*

dhughəter-. Daughter. DAUGHTER, from Old English *dohtor,* daughter, from Germanic **dohtēr.* [Pokorny *dhug(h)əter-* 277.]

dhū-no-. Important derivatives are *down*[1], *dune,* and *town.*

dhū-no-. Enclosed, fortified place. Derivative of a verb **dhuə-,* "to close, finish," probably related to **dheu-**[2], "to die." **1.a.** DOWN[1], DOWN[3], from Old English *dūn,* hill; **b.** DUNE, from Middle Dutch *dūne,* sandy hill. Both **a** and **b** from Germanic **dūnaz,* possibly from **dhū-no-**. **2.** TOWN, from Old English *tūn,* enclosed place, homestead, village, from Germanic **tūnaz,* fortified place, borrowed from Celtic **dūn-o-,* hill, stronghold. [In Pokorny 4. *dheu-* 261.]

dhwer-. Important derivatives are *door, foreign, forest, forfeit,* and *forum.*

dhwer-. Door, doorway (usually in plural). Originally an apophonic noun **dhwor, *dhur-,* in the plural, designating the entrance to the enclosure (**dhwor-o-*) surrounding the house proper. **1.** Zero-grade form **dhur-* in suffixed forms **dhur-n̥s* (accusative plural) and **dhur-o-* (neuter). DOOR, from Old English *duru,* door (feminine, originally plural), and *dor,* door (neuter), respectively from Germanic **durunz* and **duram.* **2.** Suffixed o-grade form **dhwor-āns* (accusative plural). FOREIGN, from Latin *forās,* (toward) out of doors, outside. **3.** Suffixed o-grade form **dhwor-ois* (locative plural). FOREST; (AFFOREST), FAUBOURG, FORECLOSE, FORFEIT, from Latin *forīs,* (being) out of doors. **4.** Suffixed o-grade form **dhwor-o-*. FORENSIC, FORUM, from Latin *forum,* marketplace (originally the enclosed space around a home). **5.** DURBAR, from Old Persian *duvara-,* door, gate. **6.** Zero-grade form **dhur-*. THYROID, from Greek *thura,* door. [Pokorny *dhu̯er-* 278.]

dn̥ghū-. Important derivatives are *tongue, language,* and *linguist.*

dn̥ghū-. Tongue. **1.a.** TONGUE, from Old English *tunge,* tongue; **b.** BILTONG, from Middle Dutch *tonghe,* tongue. Both **a** and **b** from Germanic **tungōn-*. **2.** LANGUAGE, LANGUET, LIGULA, LIGULE, LINGO, LINGUA, LINGUIST; (BILINGUAL), from Latin *lingua* (< Old Latin *dingua*), tongue, language. [Pokorny *dn̥ĝhū* 223.]

dō-. Important derivatives are *date, add, betray, edition, rent*[1], *surrender, tradition, traitor, vend, donation, pardon, endow, dose,* and *antidote.*

dō-. To give. Contracted from **doə-*. **1.a.** Zero-grade form **də-*. DADO, DATE[1], DATIVE, DATUM, DIE[2]; ADD, (BETRAY), EDITION, PERDITION, RENDER, (RENT[1]), (SURRENDER), TRADITION, (TRAITOR), (TREASON), VEND, from Latin *dare,* to give; **b.** (see **4**) Greek *dosis,* something given. **2.** Suffixed form **dō-no-*. DONATION, (DONATIVE), (DONOR); CONDONE, PARDON, from Latin *dōnum,* gift. **3.** Suffixed form **dō-t(i)-*. **a.** DOT[2], DOWAGER, DOWER, (DOWRY); ENDOW, from Latin *dōs* (genitive *dōtis*), dowry; **b.** DACHA, from Russian *dacha,* gift, dacha, from Slavic **datja;* **c.** SAMIZDAT, from Russian *samizdat,* samizdat, from *dat',* to give. **4.** Suffixed form **dō-ro-*. LOBSTER THERMIDOR, from Greek *dōron,* gift. **5.** Reduplicated form **di-dō-*. DOSE; ANECDOTE, ANTIDOTE, APODOSIS, EPIDOTE, from Greek *didonai,* to give, with zero-grade noun *dosis* (< **də-ti-*), something given. [Pokorny *dō-* 223.]

dus-. A derivative is *dys-.*

dus-. Bad, evil; mis- (used as a prefix). Derivative of **deu-**[1]. DYS-, from Greek *dus-,* bad. [Pokorny *dus-* 227.]

dwo-. Important derivatives are *two, twelve, twilight, biscuit, twist, twice, twenty, twine, between, twin, binary, combine, twig*[1], *diploma, deuce*[1], *dozen, dual, duet, double, duplicate, doubt,* and *dubious.*

dwo-. Two.

I. Variant form **duwo.* **1.a.** TWO, from Old English *twā,* two (nominative feminine and neuter); **b.** TWAIN, from Old English *twēgen,* two (nominative and accusative masculine). Both **a** and **b** from Germanic **twa,* two. **2.** TWELFTH, TWELVE, from Old English *twelf,* twelve, and *twelfta,* twelfth, from Germanic compound **twa-lif-,* "two left (over from ten)," twelve (**-lif-,* left; see **leik^{w}-**).

II. Adverbial form **dwis* and combining form **dwi-*. **1.a.** TWIBILL, TWILIGHT, from Old English *twi-,* two; **b.** ZWIEBACK, ZWITTERION, from Old High German *zwi-,* twice. Both **a** and **b** from Germanic **twi-*. **2.** BI-[1], BIS; BALANCE, BAROUCHE, BEZEL, BISCUIT, from Latin *bis* (combining form *bi-*), twice. **3.** DI-[1], from Greek *dis* (combining form *di-*), twice. **4.** TWIST, from Old English *-twist,* divided object, fork, rope, from Germanic **twis.* **5.** TWICE, from Old English *twige, twiga,* twice, from Germanic **twiyes.* **6.** TWENTY, from Old English *twēntig,* twenty, from Germanic compound **twēgentig,* "twice ten" (**-tig,* ten; see **dekm̥**). **7.** TWINE, from Old English *twīn,* double thread, from Germanic **twīhna,* double thread, twisted thread. **8.** BETWEEN, BETWIXT, (TWIXT), from Old English *betwēonum* and *betweox, betwix,* between, from Germanic compounds **bi-twīhna* and **bi-twisk,* "at the middle point of two" (*bi,* at, by; see **ambhi**). **9.** TWILL, from Old English *twilic,* woven of double thread, from Germanic compound **twilic-,* "two-threaded fabric." **10.** Suffixed form **dwis-no-.* **a.** TWIN, from Old English *twinn, getwinn,* two by two, twin, from Germanic **twisnaz,* double; **b.** BI-, BINAL, BINARY; COMBINE, from Latin *bīnī,* two by two, two each. **11.** Suffixed form **dwi-ko-.* TWIG[1], from Old English *twigge,* a branch, from Germanic **twig(g)a,* a fork. **12.** Compound **dwi-plo-,* twofold (**-plo-,* -fold; see **pel-[2]**). DIPLO-, DIPLOE, DIPLOID, DIPLOMA; ANADIPLOSIS, from Greek *diploos, diplous,* twofold. **13.** Suffixed reduplicated form **dwi-du-mo-.* DIDYMIUM, DIDYMOUS; EPIDIDYMIS, from Greek *didumos,* double, the testicles. **14.** Suffixed form **dwi-gha.* DICHASIUM, DICHO-, from Greek *dikha,* in two.

III. Inflected form **duwō.* **1.** DEUCE[1], DOZEN, DUAL, DUET, DUO, DUO-; DUODECIMAL, from Latin *duo,* two. **2.** DUAD, DYAD; DODECAGON, HENDIADYS, from Greek *duo, duō,* two.

IV. Variant form **du-.* **1.** Compound **du-plo-,* twofold (**-plo-,* -fold; see **pel-[2]**). DOUBLE, (DOUBLET), DOUBLOON, DUPLE, from Latin *duplus,* double. **2.** Compound **du-plek-,* twofold (**-plek-,* -fold; see **plek-**). DUPLEX, DUPLICATE, DUPLICITY; CONDUPLICATE, from Latin *duplex,* double. **3.** Suffixed form **du-bhw-io-.* DOUBT, DUBIOUS; (REDOUBTABLE), from Latin *dubius,* doubtful (< "hesitating between two alternatives"), and *dubitāre,* to be in doubt. [Pokorny *du̯ō(u)-* 228.]

---

ed-. Important derivatives are *eat, etch,* and *edible.*

ed-. To eat; original meaning "to bite." See **dent-.** **1.a.** EAT, from Old English *etan,* to eat; **b.** ETCH, from Old High German *ezzen,* to feed on, eat; **c.** ORT, from Middle Dutch *eten,* to eat; **d.** FRET[1], from Old English *fretan,* to devour, from Germanic compound **fra-etan,* to eat up (**fra-,* completely; see **per[1]**). **a, b, c,** and **d** all from Germanic **etan.* **2.** EDACIOUS, EDIBLE, ESCAROLE, ESCULENT, ESURIENT; COMEDO, COMESTIBLE, OBESE, from Latin *edere,* to eat. **3.** PRANDIAL, from Latin compound *prandium* (syncopated from **pram-edium*), "first meal," lunch (**pram-,* first; see **per[1]**). **4.** Suffixed form **ed-un-ā.* ANODYNE, PLEURODYNIA, from Greek *odunē,* pain (< "gnawing care"). **5.** SAMOYED, from Russian *-ed,* eater. [Pokorny *ed-* 287.]

---

eg. Important derivatives are *I* and *ego.*

eg. I. Nominative form of the personal pronoun of the first person singular. For oblique forms see **me-[1]**. **1.** I, from Old English *ic,* I, from Germanic **ek.* **2.** Extended form **egō.* EGO, (EGOIST), (EGOTISM), from Latin *ego,* I. [Pokorny *eĝ-* 291.]

---

eghs. Important derivatives are *ex-, exotic, external, extra-, strange,* and *extreme.*

eghs. Out. **1.** Variant **eks.* **a.** EX[1], EX-, from Latin *ex, ex-,* out of, away from; **b.** ECTO-, EXO-, EXOTERIC, EXOTIC; ELECTUARY, SYNECDOCHE, from Greek *ex, ek,* out of, from. **2.** Suffixed (comparative) variant form **eks-tero-.* EXTERIOR, EXTERNAL, EXTRA-, STRANGE, from Latin *exter,* outward (feminine ablative *exterā, extrā,* on the outside). **3.** Suffixed (superlative) form. EXTREME, from Latin *extrēmus,* outermost (**-mo-,* superlative suffix). **4.** Suffixed form **eghs-ko-.* ESCHATOLOGY, from Greek *eskhatos,* outermost, last. **5.** EISTEDDFOD, from Welsh *eistedd,* sitting, from Celtic **eks-dī-sedo-.* **6.** SAMIZDAT, from Russian *iz,* from, out of, from Balto-Slavic **iz.* [Pokorny *eĝhs* 292.]

ēgʷh-. A derivative is *inebriate.*

ēgʷh-. To drink. Suffixed form **ēgʷh-r-yo-.* **a.** INEBRIATE, from Latin *ēbrius,* drunk; **b.** (see **s(w)e-**) Latin compound *sōbrius* (*sē,* without).

---

ei-. Important derivatives are *ambition, circuit, exit[2], issue, perish, sudden, transit, ion, commence, initial, janitor,* and *January.*

ei-. To go. **1.** Full-grade form **ei-.* **a.** ADIT, AMBIENT, (AMBITION), CIRCUIT, COITUS, COMITIA, EXIT, INTROIT, ISSUE, OBITUARY, PERISH, PRAETOR, PRETERIT, SEDITION, (SUBITO), SUDDEN, (TRANCE), TRANSIENT, (TRANSIT), (TRANSITIVE), from Latin *īre,* to go; **b.** ION; ANION, CATION, DYSPROSIUM, from Greek *ienai,* to go. **2.** Suffixed zero-grade form **i-t-.* **a.** further suffixed form **i-t-yo-.* COMMENCE, INITIAL, INITIATE, from Latin *initium,* entrance, beginning (*in-,* in; see **en**); **b.** COUNT[2], COUNTY; CONCOMITANT, CONSTABLE, (VISCOUNT), from Latin *comes* (stem *comit-*), companion (< "one who goes with another"; *com-,* with; see **kom**). **3.** Suffixed form **i-ter.* ERRANT, EYRE, ITINERANT, ITINERARY, from Latin *iter,* journey. **4.** Extended form **yā-* (< **yaə-*) in suffixed forms **yā-no-, *yā-nu-.* **a.** JANITOR, JANUARY, JANUS, from Latin *iānus,* archway, and *Iānus,* god of doors and of the beginning of a year; **b.** HINAYANA, MAHAYANA, from Sanskrit *yānam,* way (in Buddhism, "mode of knowledge," "vehicle"). [Pokorny 1. *ei-* 293.]

ēik-. Important derivatives are *ought[1], owe, own,* and *freight.*

ēik-. To be master of, possess. **1.** OUGHT[1], OWE, from Old English *āgan,* to possess, from Germanic **aigan,* to possess. **2.** OWN, from Old English *āgen,* one's own, from Germanic participial form **aiganaz,* possessed, owned. **3.** FRAUGHT, FREIGHT, from Middle Low German and Middle Dutch *vrecht, vracht,* "earnings," hire for a ship, freight, from Germanic prefixed form **fra-aihtiz,* absolute possession, property (**fra-,* intensive prefix; see **per[1]**). [Pokorny *ēik-* 298.]

---

eis-. Important derivatives are *irate, hierarchy,* and *iron.*

eis-. In words denoting passion. **1.** Suffixed form **eis-ā-.* IRASCIBLE, IRATE, IRE, from Latin *īra,* anger. **2.** Suffixed zero-grade form **is-(ə)ro-,* powerful, holy. HIERATIC, HIERO-; HIERARCH, (HIERARCHY), HIEROGLYPHIC, HIEROPHANT, from Greek *hieros,* "filled with the divine," holy. **3.a.** IRON, from Old English *īse(r)n, īren,* iron; **b.** GISARME, SPIEGELEISEN, from Old High German *īsarn, īsan,* iron. Both **a** and **b** from Germanic **īsarno-,* "holy metal" (possibly from Celtic). **4.** Suffixed o-grade form **ois-tro-,* madness. ESTRUS; (ESTRONE), from Greek *oistros,* gadfly, goad, anything causing madness. [Pokorny 1. *eis-* 299.]

---

ekwo-. Derivatives are *equestrian* and *hippopotamus.*

ekwo-. Horse. Probably originally derived from **ōku-. 1.** EQUESTRIAN, EQUINE, EQUITANT, (EQUITATION); EQUISETUM, from Latin *equus,* horse. **2.** EOHIPPUS, HIPPOCAMPUS, HIPPOCRENE, HIPPODROME, HIPPOGRIFF, HIPPOPOTAMUS, from Greek *hippos,* horse. [Pokorny *eku̯o-s* 301.]

---

el-. An important derivative is *elbow.*

el-. Elbow, forearm. Extended o-grade form **olinā,* elbow. **a.** ELL[2], from Old English *eln,* forearm, cubit, from Germanic **alinō;* **b.** ELBOW, from Old English *elnboga,* elbow, from Germanic compound **alino-bugōn-,* "bend of the forearm," elbow (**bugōn-,* bend, bow; see **bheug-**); **c.** ULNA, from Latin *ulna,* forearm; **d.** lengthened variant form **ōlenā-.* OLECRANON, from Greek *ōlenē,* elbow. [Pokorny 8. *el-* 307.]

---

em-. Important derivatives are *example, exempt, premium, prompt, ransom, redeem, sample, vintage, assume, consume,* and *resume.*

em-. To take, distribute. **1.** ADEMPTION, EXAMPLE, (EXEMPLARY), (EXEMPLIFY), (EXEMPLUM), (EXEMPT), (IMPROMPTU), PEREMPTORY, PREEMPTION, PREMIUM, PROMPT, (RANSOM), REDEEM, (REDEMPTION), (SAMPLE), VINTAGE, from Latin *emere,* to obtain, buy. **2.** SUMPTUARY, (SUMPTUOUS); ASSUME, CONSUME, PRESUME, RESUME, SUBSUME, from Latin *sūmere* (< **sus(e)m-*), to take, obtain, buy (*sus-,* variant of *sub-,* up from under; see **upo**). [Pokorny *em-* 310.]

---

en. Important derivatives are *in[1], inner, en-[1], intro-, enter, intimate[2], industry, episode,* and *and.*

en. In. **1.a.** IN[1] (preposition), from Old English *in,* in; **b.** IN[1] (adverb), from Old English *inn,* into, *inne,* inside; **c.** INN, from Old English *inn,* habitation, inn; **d.** TSIMMES, from Old High German *in,* in; **e.** INNER, from Old English *innera,* farther in, inner, from Germanic (comparative) **inn(e)ra;* **f.** BEN, from Old English *binnan,* within, from Germanic **innan.* **a, b, c, d, e,** and **f** all from Germanic **in.* **2.** EN-[1], IN-[2], from Latin *in, in-,* in, into. **3.** EN-[2]; ENKEPHALIN, PARENCHYMA, PARENTHESIS, from Greek *en, en-.* **4.** Suffixed form **en-t(e)ro-.* **a.** INTRO-; INTRODUCE, INTROIT, INTROMIT, INTRORSE, INTROSPECT, from Latin *intrō,* inward, within; **b.** ENTER, INTRA-; (INTRADOS), from Latin *intrā,* inside, within; **c.** INTERIM, INTRINSIC, from Latin *interim,* meanwhile, with ablative suffix *-im; intrīnsecus,* on the inside, from *int(e)rim* + *secus,* alongside (see **sekʷ-[1]**). **5.** Suffixed form **en-ter.* ENTRAILS, INTER-, INTERIOR, INTERNAL, from Latin *inter, inter-,* between, among. **6.** INTIMA, INTIMATE[2], from Latin (superlative) *intimus,* innermost (**-mo-,* superlative suffix). **7.** Extended form **en-do.* **a.** INDUSTRY, from Latin *industrius,* diligent (**stru-,* to construct; see **ster-[2]**); **b.** INDIGENT, from Latin *indigēre,* to be in need (*egēre,* to be in need). Both **a** and **b** from *indu-,* within, from Old Latin *endo;* **c.** ENDO-, from Greek *endo, endo-,* within. **8.** Suffixed form **en-tos.* **a.** DEDANS, INTESTINE, INTINE, INTUSSUSCEPTION, from Latin *intus,* within, inside; **b.** ENTO-, from Greek *entos,* within. **9.** Suffixed form **en-tero-.* (ENTERIC), ENTERO-, ENTERON; DYSENTERY, EXENTERATE, MESENTERY, from Greek *enteron,* intestine. **10.** Extended form **ens.* **a.** EPISODE, from Greek *eis,* into; **b.** suffixed form **ens-ō.* ESOTERIC, from Greek *esō,* within. **11.** Possibly suffixed zero-grade form **n̥-dha.* AND, from Old English *and,* and, from Germanic **anda, *unda.* [Pokorny 1. *en* 311.]

---

epi. An important derivative is *epi-.*

epi. Also **opi.** Near, at, against. **1.** OB-, from Latin *ob, ob-,* before, to, against. **2.** EPI-, from Greek *epi,* on, over, at. **3.** OPISTHOBRANCH, OPISTHOGNATHOUS, from Greek *opisthen,* behind, at the back. **4.** Zero-grade **pi,* on. (see **sed-**) Greek *piezein,* to press tight. **5.** OBLAST, from Russian *oblast',* oblast, from Old Church Slavonic *ob,* on. **6.** Prefix **op-* in **op-wer-yo-,* to cover over (see **wer-[4]**). [Pokorny *epi* 323.]

---

er-[1]. Important derivatives are *are[1], earnest[1], orient, origin, original,* and *abort.*

er-[1]. To move, set in motion. **1.** ARE[1], ART[2], from Old English *eart* and *aron,* second person singular and plural present of *bēon,* to be, from Germanic **ar-, *or-, *art(a),* to be, exist, probably from **er-[1]**. **2.** EARNEST[1], from Old English *eornoste,* zealous, serious, from Germanic suffixed form **er-n-os-ti-,* perhaps from **er-[1]**. **3.** Suffixed form **or-yo-.* ORIENT, ORIGIN, (ORIGINAL); ABORT, from Latin *orīrī,* to arise, appear, be born. **4.** Suffixed form **or-smā-.* HORMONE, from Greek *hormē,* impulse, onrush. [Pokorny 3. *er-* 326; *ergh-* 339.]

---

er-[2]. An important derivative is *earth.*

er-[2]. Earth, ground. Extended form **ert-.* **a.** EARTH, from Old English *eorthe,* earth; **b.** AARDVARK, AARDWOLF, from Middle Dutch *aerde, eerde,* earth. Both **a** and **b** from Germanic **erthō.* [Pokorny 4. *er-* 332.]

---

erə-. Important derivatives are *row[2]* and *rudder.*

erə-. To row. **1.** Variant form **rē-* (< **reə-*). **a.** ROW[2], from Old English *rōwan,* to row, from Germanic **rō-;* **b.** suffixed form **rō-tro-.* RUDDER, RUSSIAN, from Old English *rōther* and Old Norse *rōdhr,* steering oar, both from Germanic **rōthra,* rudder; **c.** suffixed form **rē-smo-.* BIREME, REMEX, TRIREME, from Latin *rēmus,* oar. **2.** Oldest variant form **əreə-* becoming **erē-.* TRIERARCH, from Greek *triērēs,* trireme. [Pokorny 1. *erə-* 338.]

---

ers-. Important derivatives are *race[2], erratic,* and *error.*

ers-. To be in motion. **1.** Variant form **rēs-.* RACE[2], from Old Norse *rās,* rushing, from Germanic **rēs-.* **2.** Form **ers-ā-.* ERR, ERRATIC, ERRATUM, ERRONEOUS, ERROR; ABERRATION, from Latin *errāre,* to wander. [Pokorny 2. *eres-s-* 336.]

es-. Important derivatives are *am*[1], *is, yes, soothe, sin*[1], *essence, absent, interest, present*[1], and *proud.*

es-. To be. **1.** Athematic first person singular form **es-mi.* AM[1], from Old English *eam, eom,* am, from Germanic **izm(i).* **2.** Athematic third person singular form **es-ti.* IS, from Old English *is,* is, from Germanic **ist(i).* **3.** Optative stem **sī-.* YES, from Old English *gēse,* yes, (*gēa,* yea; see **i-** + *sīe*), from *sīe,* may it be (so), from Germanic **sijai-.* **4.** Participial form **sont-,* being, existing, hence real, true. **a.** SOOTH, SOOTHE, from Old English *sōth,* true, from Germanic **santhaz;* **b.** suffixed (collective) zero-grade form **sn̥t-yā,* "that which is." SIN[1], from Old English *synn,* sin, from Germanic **sun(d)jō,* sin (< "it is true," "the sin is real"); **c.** SUTTEE; BODHISATTVA, SATYAGRAHA, from Sanskrit *sat-, sant-,* existing, true, virtuous. **5.** Basic form **es-.* ENTITY, ESSENCE; ABSENT, (IMPROVE), INTEREST, OSSIA, PRESENT[1], (PRESENT[2]), PROUD, (QUINTESSENCE), (REPRESENT), from Latin *esse,* to be. **6.** Basic form **es-.* -ONT, ONTO-; (-BIONT), HOMOIOUSIAN, PAROUSIA, (SCHIZONT), from Greek *einai* (present participle *ont-,* being), to be (in *pareinai,* to be present). **7.** Suffixed form **es-ti-.* SWASTIKA, from Sanskrit *sv-as-ti-,* "well-being" (see **su-**). [Pokorny *es-* 340.] See extension **(e)su-**.

(e)su-. A derivative is *eu-*.

(e)su-. Good. Suffixed form of **es-**. EU-, from Greek *eu-,* well, combining form of *eus,* good. [Pokorny *esu-s* 342.] See **su-**.

eu-¹. A derivative is *endue.*

eu-¹. To dress. **1.** ENDUE, from Latin *induere,* to don (*ind-,* variant of *in-,* in, on; see **en**). **2.** EXUVIAE, from Latin *exuere,* to doff (*ex-,* off; see **eghs**). **3.** REDUVIID, from Latin *reduvia,* fragment (*red-,* back, in reverse; see **re-**). [Pokorny 2. *eu-* 346.] See extension **wes-²**.

eu-². Important derivatives are *wane, want, vanish, vacant, vacation, vacuum, void, avoid, evacuate,* and *waste.*

eu-². Lacking, empty. Extended forms **euə-, *wā-, *wə-.* **1.** Suffixed form **wə-no-.* **a.** WANE, from Old English *wanian,* to lessen, and *wana,* lack, from Germanic **wanēn;* **b.** WANT, from Old Norse *vanta,* to lack, from North Germanic **wanatōn.* **2.** Suffixed form **wā-no-.* VAIN, VANITY, VAUNT; EVANESCE, VANISH, from Latin *vānus,* empty. **3.** Extended form **wak-.* VACANT, VACATE, VACATION, (VACUITY), VACUUM, VOID; (AVOID), (DEVOID), EVACUATE, from Latin *vacāre* (variant *vocāre*), to be empty. **4.** Extended and suffixed form **wās-to-.* WASTE; DEVASTATE, from Latin *vāstus,* empty, waste. [Pokorny 1. *eu-* 345.]

euə-dh-r̥. Derivatives are *udder* and *exuberant.*

euə-dh-r̥. Udder. Related to **wē-r-**. **1.** Suffixed zero-grade form **ūdh-r̥.* UDDER, from Old English *ūder,* udder, from Germanic **ūdr-.* **2.** Suffixed o-grade form **oudh-r̥.* (EXUBERANT), EXUBERATE, from Latin adjective *über,* fertile, derived from *über,* "breast." [Pokorny *ēudh-* 347.]

gal-. Important derivatives are *call* and *clatter.*

gal-. To call, shout. **1.** CALL, from Old Norse *kalla,* to call, from Germanic expressive form **kall-.* **2.** CLATTER, from Old English **clatrian,* to clatter, from Germanic **klat-.* **3.** Expressive form **gall-.* GALLINACEOUS, (GALLINULE), from Latin *gallus,* cock (< "the calling bird"; but probably also associated with *Gallus,* Gallic, as if to mean "the bird of Gaul," the cock being archaeologically attested as an important symbol in the iconography of Roman and pre-Roman Gaul). **4.** Suffixed form **gal-so-.* GLASNOST, from a Slavic source akin to Old Church Slavonic *glasŭ,* voice. **5.** Reduplicated form *gal-gal-.* GLAGOLITIC, from a Slavic source akin to Old Church Slavonic *glagolŭ,* word. [Pokorny 2. *gal-* 350.]

gāu-. Important derivatives are *gaudy*[1], *joy, enjoy,* and *rejoice.*

gāu-. To rejoice; also to have religious fear or awe. Contracted from **gaəu-.* **1.** Suffixed form **gau-d-ē-.* GAUD, (GAUDY[1]), GAUDY[2], JOY; ENJOY, REJOICE, from Latin *gaudēre,* to rejoice. **2.** Form (with nasal infix) **gə-n-u-.* GANOID, from Greek *ganusthai,* to rejoice. [Pokorny *gāu-* 353.]

gel-. Important derivatives are *chill, cold, cool, jelly,* and *glacier.*

gel-. Cold; to freeze. **1.** CHILL, from Old English *c(i)ele,* chill, from Germanic **kaliz,* coldness. **2.** COLD, from Old English *ceald,* cold, from Germanic **kaldaz,* cold. **3.a.** COOL, from Old English *cōl,* cold, cool; **b.** KEEL[3], from Old English *cēlan,* to cool, from Germanic **kōljan,* to cool. Both **a** and **b** from Germanic **kōl-,* cool. **4.** Suffixed form **gel-ā-.* GELATIN, GELATION, JELLY; CONGEAL, from Latin *gelāre,* to freeze. **5.** Suffixed form **gel-u-.* GELID, from Latin *gelū,* frost, cold. **6.** Probably suffixed zero-grade form **gl̥-k-.* (GLACÉ), GLACIAL, GLACIATE, GLACIER, GLACIS, from Latin *glaciēs,* ice. [Pokorny 3. *gel(ə)-* 365.]

gembh-. Important derivatives are *comb, unkempt,* and *gem.*

gembh-. Tooth, nail.
I. Suffixed o-grade form **gombh-o-.* **a.** COMB, KAME, from Old English *comb, camb,* comb; **b.** CAM, from Dutch *kam,* cog, comb; **c.** UNKEMPT, from Old English *cemban,* to comb, from Germanic denominative **kambjan,* to comb. **a, b,** and **c** all from Germanic **kambaz,* comb.
II. Suffixed zero-grade form **gm̥bh-ōn-.* OAKUM, from Old English *ā-cumba,* oakum.
III. CHIME[2], from Old English *cim-, cimb-,* rim (only in compounds), from Germanic **kimb-,* perhaps from **gembh-**.
IV. Possibly suffixed form **gembh-mā.* GEM, GEMMA, GEMMATE, GEMMULE, from Latin *gemma,* bud, hence gem. [Pokorny *ĝembh-* 369.]

gemə-. Derivatives are *gamete, -gamous,* and *-gamy.*

gemə-. To marry. Suffixed zero-grade form **gm̥ə-o-.* GAMETE, GAMO-, -GAMOUS, -GAMY, from Greek *gamos,* marriage. [Pokorny *ĝem(e)-* 369.]

genə-. Important derivatives are *kin, king, kind*[1], *kind*[2], *gentle, general, generate, genius, engine, genuine, germ, genital, pregnant, nation, native,* and *nature.*

genə-. Also **gen-**. To give birth, beget; with derivatives referring to aspects and results of procreation and to familial and tribal groups. **1.** Suffixed zero-grade form **gn̥-yo-.* **a.** KIN; KINDRED, from Old English *cyn(n),* race, family, kin; **b.** KING, from Old English *cyning,* king, from Germanic **kuningaz,* king. Both **a** and **b** from Germanic **kunjam,* family. **2.** Suffixed zero-grade form **gn̥-t-.* **a.** KIND[2], from Old English *cynd, gecynd(e),* origin, birth, race, family, kind, from Germanic **kundjaz,* family, race; **b.** KIND[1], from Old English *gecynde,* natural, native, fitting (*ge-,* collective prefix; see **kom**), from Germanic **kundiz,* natural, native; **c.** Suffixed form **gn̥-ti-.* GENS, (GENTEEL), (GENTILE), GENTLE; GENDARME, from Latin *gēns* (stem *gent-*), race, clan; **d.** KINDERGARTEN, KRISS KRINGLE, from Old High German *kind,* child, from Germanic secondary full-grade variant **kentham.* **3.** Suffixed full-grade form **gen-es-.* **a.** GENDER, GENERAL, GENERATE, (GENERATION), GENERIC, GENEROUS, GENRE, GENUS; CONGENER, DEGENERATE, (ENGENDER), MISCEGENATION, from Latin *genus* (stem *gener-*), race, kind; **b.** GENE; ALLOGENEIC, GENEALOGY, GENOCIDE, GENOTYPE, HETEROGENEOUS, from Greek *genos* and *genea,* race, family; **c.** -GEN, -GENY; EPIGENE, from Greek suffix *-genēs,* "-born." **4.** Suffixed full-grade form **gen-yo-.* **a.** GENIAL[1], GENIUS; (CONGENIAL), from Latin *genius,* procreative divinity, inborn tutelary spirit, innate quality; **b.** ENGINE, INGENIOUS, from Latin *ingenium,* inborn character (*in-,* in; see **en**). **5.** Suffixed full-grade form **gen-ā-.* INDIGEN, (INDIGENOUS), from Latin *indigena,* born in (a place), indigenous (*indu-,* within; see **en**). **6.** Suffixed full-grade form **genə-wo-.* (GENUINE), INGENUOUS, from Latin *ingenuus,* born in (a place), native, natural, freeborn (*in-,* in; see **en**). **7.** Suffixed full-grade form **gen-men-.* GERM, GERMAN[2], (GERMANE), GERMINAL, GERMINATE, from dissimilated Latin *germen,* shoot, bud, embryo, germ. **8.** Suffixed secondary zero-grade form **gn̥ə-ti-.* GENESIS, -GENESIS, from Greek *genesis,* birth, beginning. **9.** Reduplicated form **gi-gn-.* GENITAL, GENITIVE, GENITOR, GENT[1], (GINGERLY); CONGENITAL, PRIMOGENITOR, PRIMOGENITURE, PROGENITOR, (PROGENY), from Latin *gignere* (past participle *genitus*), to beget. **10.** Suffixed zero-grade form **-gn-o-.* BENIGN, MALIGN, from Latin *benignus,* good-natured, kindly (*bene,* well; see **deu-²**), and *malignus,* evil-natured, malevolent (*male,* ill; see **mel-³**). **11.** Zero-grade form **gn̥ə-* becoming **gnā-.* PREGNANT[1], from Latin *praegnās,* pregnant (*prae-,* before; see **per**[1]). **12.** Suffixed zero-grade form **gn̥ə-sko-* becoming **gnā-sko-.* NAIVE, NASCENT, NATAL, NATION, NATIVE, NATURE, NÉE, NOËL; (ADNATE), AGNATE, COGNATE, CONNATE, ENATE, INNATE, NEONATE, PUISNE, (PUNY), RENAISSANCE, from Latin *gnāscī, nāscī* (present participle *nāscēns,* past participle *gnātus, nātus*), to be born. **13.** Suffixed o-grade form **gon-o-.* GONAD, GONO-, -GONY; ARCHEGONIUM, EPIGONE, from Greek *gonos* (combining form *-gonos*), child, procreation, seed. **14.** Zero-grade form **gn̥-.* (see **kʷr̥mi-**) Sanskrit *kr̥mi-ja-,* "produced by worms," from *ja-.* [Pokorny 1. *ĝen-* 373.]

genu-¹. Important derivatives are *knee, kneel,* and *diagonal.*

genu-¹. Knee; also angle. **1.** Variant form **gneu-.* **a.** KNEE, from Old English *cnēo,* knee, from Germanic **knewam;* **b.** KNEEL, from Old English *cnēowlian,* to kneel, from Germanic **knewljan.* **2.** Basic form **genu-.* GENICULATE, GENUFLECT, from Latin *genū,* knee. **3.** O-grade form **gonu.* POLYGONUM, PYCNOGONID, from Greek *gonu,* knee. **4.** Suffixed variant form **gōnw-yə-.* -GON, GONION; AMBLYGONITE, DIAGONAL, GONIOMETER, ORTHOGONAL, from Greek *gōnia,* angle, corner. [Pokorny 1. *ĝenu-* 380.]

genu-². An important derivative is *chin.*

genu-². Jawbone, chin. **1.** Form **genw-.* CHIN, from Old English *cin(n),* chin, from Germanic **kinnuz.* **2.** Basic form **genu-.* GENIAL[2], from Greek *genus,* jaw, chin. **3.** Suffixed variant form **gnə-dho-.* GNATHIC, -GNATHOUS; CHAETOGNATH, from Greek *gnathos,* jaw. [Pokorny 2. *ĝenu-* 381.]

ger-. Important derivatives are *cram, congregate, segregate,* and *category.*

ger-. To gather. **1.** Extended form **grem-.* CRAM, from Old English *crammian,* to stuff, cram, from Germanic **kramm-.* **2.** Reduplicated form **gre-g-.* GREGARIOUS; AGGREGATE, CONGREGATE, EGREGIOUS, SEGREGATE, from Latin *grex* (stem *greg-*), herd, flock. **3.** Earliest forms **əger-, *əgor-ā-.* AGORA[1], AGORAPHOBIA, ALLEGORY, CATEGORY, PANEGYRIC, from Greek *ageirein,* to assemble, and *aguris, agora,* marketplace. [Pokorny 1. *ger-* 382.]

gerbh-. Important derivatives are *carve, crab*[1], *crawl*[1], *gram*[1], *grammar, diagram, paragraph,* and *program.*

gerbh-. To scratch. **1.** CARVE, from Old English *ceorfan,* to cut, from Germanic **kerban.* **2.** KERF, from Old English *cyrf,* a cutting (off), from zero-grade Germanic form **kurbiz.* **3.** Variant form **grebh-.* **a.** CRAB[1], from Old English *crabba,* a crab, from Germanic **krab(b)-;* **b.** CRAYFISH, from Old High German *krebiz,* edible crustacean, from Germanic **krabiz-;* **c.** CRAWL[1], from Old Norse *krafla,* to crawl, from Germanic **krab-,* perhaps from **gerbh-**. **4.** Zero-grade form **gr̥bh-.* GRAFFITO, GRAM[1], -GRAM, GRAMMAR, -GRAPH, -GRAPHER, GRAPHIC, -GRAPHY; AGRAPHA, AGRAPHIA, ANAGRAM, DIAGRAM, EPIGRAM, (EPIGRAPH), GRAPHITE, (ICONOGRAPHY), PARAGRAPH, PARALLELOGRAM, PROGRAM, PSEUDEPIGRAPHA, TETRAGRAMMATON, (TOPOGRAPHY), from Greek *graphein,* to scratch, draw, write, *gramma* (< **gr̥bh-mn̥*), a picture, written letter, piece of writing, and *grammē,* a line. [Pokorny *gerebh-* 392.]

gerə-¹. An important derivative is *geriatrics.*

gerə-¹. To grow old. **1.** Suffixed lengthened-grade form **gērə-s-.* AGERATUM, GERIATRICS, from Greek *gēras,* old age. **2.** Suffixed form **gerə-ont-.* GERONTO-, from Greek *gerōn* (stem *geront-*), old man. [Pokorny *ger-* 390.]

gerə-². Important derivatives are *crow*[1], *crack, crane, cranberry, pedigree,* and *geranium.*

gerə-[2]. To cry hoarsely; also the name of the crane.
I. Words meaning "to cry hoarsely"; also words denoting the crow. **1.a.** CROW[1], from Old English *crāwe,* a crow; **b.** CROW[2], from Old English *crāwan,* to crow; **c.** CRACK, from Old English *cracian,* to resound; **d.** CRACKNEL, from Middle Dutch *krāken,* to crack; **e.** CRAKE, from Old Norse *krāka,* a crow; **f.** CROON, from Middle Dutch *krōnen,* to groan, lament. **a, b, c, d, e,** and **f** all from Germanic _*krē-_. **2.** CUR, from Middle English *curre,* cur, akin to Old Norse *kurra,* to growl, from Germanic _*kur(r)-_, possibly from **gerə-[2]** (but more likely imitative).
II. Words denoting a crane. **1.a.** CRANE, from Old English *cran,* crane; **b.** CRANBERRY, from Middle Low German *kran,* crane. Both **a** and **b** from Germanic _*kran-_, crane. **2.** Extended form _*grū-_. GRUS; PEDIGREE, from Latin *grūs,* crane. **3.** Suffixed variant form _*grā-k-_. GRACKLE, from Latin *grāculus,* jackdaw. **4.** Suffixed extended form _*gerə-no-_. GERANIUM, from Greek *geranos,* crane. [Pokorny 2. *ger-* 383.]

geus-. Important derivatives are *choose, choice,* and *disgust.*

geus-. To taste, choose. **1.a.** CHOOSE, from Old English *cēosan, ceōsan,* to choose, from Germanic _*keusan_; **b.** CHOICE, from a Germanic source akin to Gothic *kausjan,* to test, taste, from Germanic causative _*kausjan_. **2.** Zero-grade _*gus-_. (see **welə-**) Old Norse *Valkyrja,* "chooser of the slain," Valkyrie (*valr,* the slain), from Germanic _*kur-_ from _*kuz-_. **3.** Suffixed zero-grade form _*gus-tu-_. **a.** (GUST[2]), GUSTO; RAGOUT, from Latin *gustus,* taste; **b.** DEGUST, DISGUST, from Latin *gustāre,* to taste. [Pokorny *ĝeus-* 399.]

ghabh-. Important derivatives are *give, forgive, gift, able, habit, exhibit, inhabit, malady, prohibit, debt, due, duty,* and *endeavor.*

ghabh-. Also **ghebh-.** To give or receive. **1.** Form _*ghebh-_. **a.** GIVE, from Old English *giefan,* to give, and Old Norse *gefa,* to give; **b.** FORGIVE, from Old English *forgi(e)fan,* to give, give up, leave off (anger), remit, forgive, from Germanic compound _*far-geban_, to give away (_*far-_, away; see **per[1]**). Both **a** and **b** from Germanic _*geban_. **2.** Suffixed form _*ghebh-ti-_, something given (or received). GIFT, from Old Norse *gipt, gift,* a gift, from Germanic _*giftiz_. **3.** O-grade form _*ghobh-_. GAVEL[2], from Old English *gafol,* tribute, tax, debt, from Germanic _*gabulam_, something paid (or received). **4.** Form _*ghabh-ē-_. **a.** ABLE, BINNACLE, HABILE, HABIT, HABITABLE, (HABITANT), (HABITAT); (COHABIT), EXHIBIT, INHABIT, INHIBIT, MALADY, PREBEND, PROHIBIT, (PROVENDER), from Latin *habēre,* to hold, possess, have, handle (> *habitāre,* to dwell); **b.** DEBENTURE, (DEBIT), DEBT, DEVOIR, DUE, (DUTY); (ENDEAVOR), from Latin *dēbēre,* to owe (*dē-,* away from; see **de-**). [Pokorny *ghabh-* 407.] Compare **kap-.**

ghans-. Important derivatives are *goose[1], gosling,* and *gander.*

ghans-. Goose. **1.a.** GOOSE[1]; (GOSHAWK), from Old English *gōs* (nominative plural *gēs*), goose; **b.** GOSLING, from Old Norse *gās,* goose; **c.** GUNSEL, from Old High German *gans,* goose; **d.** GONZO, from Spanish *ganso,* goose, from a Germanic source akin to Old High German *gans,* goose. **a, b, c,** and **d** all from Germanic _*gans-_ (nominative plural _*gansiz_). **2.** GANDER, from Old English *ganra, gandra,* gander, from Germanic _*gan(d)rōn-_. **3.** GANNET, from Old English *ganot,* gannet, from Germanic _*ganōtōn-_. **4.** Suffixed form _*ghans-er-_. ANSERINE; MERGANSER, from Latin *ānser* (< _*hanser_), goose. **5.** Basic form _*ghans-_. CHENOPOD, from Greek *khēn,* goose. [Pokorny *ĝhans-* 412.]

ghē-. Important derivatives are *go, ago, heir, heritage, inherit,* and *gait.*

ghē-. To release, let go; (in the middle voice) to be released, go. Contracted from _*gheə-_. **1.** GO; AGO, FOREGO[1], FORGO, from Old English *gān,* to go, from Germanic variant form _*gaian_. **2.** Suffixed form _*ghē-ro-_. HEIR, HEREDITAMENT, HEREDITY, (HERITAGE); INHERIT, from Latin *hērēs,* heir (? < "orphan" < "bereft"). **3.** Possibly suffixed o-grade form _*ghō-ro-_, "empty space." **a.** CHOROGRAPHY, from Greek *khōros,* place, country, particular spot; **b.** -CHORE; ANCHORITE, from Greek denominative *khōrein,* to move, go, spread about, make room for; **c.** CHORIPETALOUS, from Greek *khōris, khōri,* apart, separate. **4.** Possible suffixed zero-grade form _*ghə-t(w)ā-_. **a.** GAIT, GATE[2]; RUNAGATE, from Old Norse *gata,* path, street; **b.** (GANTLET[1]), GAUNTLET[2], from Old Swedish *gata,* lane. Both **a** and **b** from Germanic _*gatwōn-_, a going. **5.** Suffixed zero-grade form _*ghə-no-_. HINAYANA, from Sanskrit *hīna-,* inferior, verbal adjective of *jahāti,* he leaves, lets go (< reduplicated _*ghe-ghē-ti, *ghe-gheə-ti_). [Pokorny 1. *ĝhē-* 418.]

ghebh-el-. Derivatives are *gable* and *cephalic.*

ghebh-el-. Head. **1.** GABLE, from Old Norse *gafl,* gable, from Germanic _*gablaz_, top of a pitched roof. **2.** Form _*kephal-_, dissimilated from _*khephal-_. CEPHALIC, CEPHALO-, -CEPHALOUS; ENCEPHALO-, ENKEPHALIN, HYDROCEPHALUS, from Greek *kephalē,* head. [Pokorny *ghebh-el-* 423.]

ghedh-. Important derivatives are *good, together,* and *gather.*

ghedh-. To unite, join, fit. **1.** Lengthened o-grade form _*ghōdh-_. GOOD, from Old English *gōd,* good, from Germanic _*gōdaz_, "fitting, suitable." **2.** TOGETHER, from Old English *tōgædere,* together (*tō,* to; see **de-**), from Germanic _*gaduri_, "in a body." **3.** GATHER, from Old English *gad(e)rian,* to gather, from Germanic _*gadurōn_, "to come or bring together." [Pokorny *ghedh-* 423.]

ghei-. An important derivative is *hibernate.*

ghei-. Theoretical base of _*ghyem-, *ghiem-_, winter. **1.** Form _*ghiem-_. HIEMAL, from Latin *hiems,* winter. **2.** Suffixed variant form _*gheim-ri-no-_. HIBERNACULUM, HIBERNATE, from Latin *hībernus,* pertaining to winter. **3.** Suffixed zero-grade form _*ghim-r̥-yə_, "female animal one year (winter) old." CHIMERA, from Greek *khimaira,* she-goat. [Pokorny 2. *ĝhei-* 425.]

ghel-[1]. Important derivatives are *yell, yelp,* and *nightingale.*

ghel-[1]. To call. **1.a.** YELL, from Old English *gellan, giellan,* to sound, shout; **b.** YELP, from Old English *gielpan,* to boast, exult; **c.** NIGHTINGALE, from Old English *galan,* to sing. **a, b,** and **c** all from Germanic _*gel-, *gal-_. **2.** Reduplicated form _*ghi-ghl-_. CICHLID, from Greek *kikhlē,* thrush, later also the name for a kind of wrasse (a sea fish that has bright colors and jagged waving fins, reminiscent of the plumage of a bird). **3.** CELANDINE, from Greek *khelidwōn, khelidōn,* the swallow. [Pokorny *ghel-* 428.]

ghel-[2]. Important derivatives are *yellow, gold, arsenic, gall[1], melancholy, gleam, glimpse, glimmer, glitter, glass, glare[1], glad, glee, glow,* and *glide.*

ghel-[2]. To shine; with derivatives referring to colors, bright materials (probably "yellow metal"), and bile or gall.
I. Words denoting colors. **1.** Suffixed form _*ghel-wo-_. YELLOW, from Old English *geolu,* yellow, from Germanic _*gelwaz_. **2.** Suffixed variant form _*ghlō-ro-_. CHLORO-; CHLORITE[1], from Greek *khlōros,* green, greenish yellow. **3.** Suffixed variant form _*ghlo-wo-_. CHLOASMA, from Greek *khloos* (< _*khlo-wo-s_), greenish color. **4.** O-grade form _*ghol-_. PODZOL, from Russian *zola,* ashes (from their color). **5.** Suffixed form _*ghel-i-_. HARE KRISHNA, from Sanskrit *hari-,* tawny yellow. **6.** Possibly suffixed zero-grade form _*ghl̥-wo-_. GRISEOFULVIN, from Latin *fulvus,* tawny, perhaps from **ghel-[2]** (with dialectal *f-* as in *fel,* gall).
II. Words denoting gold. **1.** Suffixed zero-grade form _*ghl̥-to-_. **a.** GOLD, from Old English *gold,* gold; **b.** GILD[1], from Old English *gyldan,* to gild, from Germanic denominative verb _*gulthjan_; **c.** GUILDER, GULDEN, from Middle Dutch *gulden,* golden; **d.** GOWAN, from Middle English *gollan,* yellow flower, possibly from a source akin to Old Norse *gullinn,* golden. **a, b, c,** and **d** all from Germanic _*gultham_, gold. **2.** Suffixed o-grade form _*ghol-to-_. ZLOTY, from Polish *złoto,* gold. **3.** Suffixed full-grade form _*ghel-no-_. ARSENIC, from Syriac *zarnīkā,* orpiment, from Middle Iranian _*zarnik-_, from Old Iranian _*zarna-_, golden.
III. Words denoting bile. **1.** Suffixed o-grade form _*ghol-no-_. GALL[1], from Old English *gealla,* gall, from Germanic _*gallōn-_, bile. **2.** Suffixed o-grade form _*ghol-ā_. CHOLE-, CHOLER, (CHOLERA); ACHOLIA, MELANCHOLY, from Greek *kholē,* bile. **3.** Suffixed full-grade form _*ghel-n-_. FELON[2], from Latin *fel,* bile.
IV. A range of Germanic words (where no preforms are given, the words are late creations). **1.** GLEAM, from Old English *glǣm,* bright light, gleam, from Germanic _*glaimiz_. **2.** GLIMPSE, from Middle English *glimsen,* to glimpse, from a source akin to Middle High German *glimsen,* to gleam. **3.** GLANCE[1], GLINT, from Middle English *glent,* a glint, and *glenten,* to shine, from a source akin to Swedish dialectal *glinta,* to shine. **4.** GLIMMER, from Middle English *glimeren,* to glimmer, from a source akin to Swedish *glimra,* glimmer. **5.** GLITTER, from Old Norse *glitra,* to shine. **6.** GLITZ, from Old High German *glīzan,* to sparkle. **7.** GLISTEN, from Old English *glisnian,* to shine. **8.** GLISTER, from Middle Dutch *glinsteren* or Middle Low German *glisteren,* to shine. **9.** GLASS, GLAZE, (GLAZIER), from Old English *glæs,* glass, from Germanic _*glasam_, glass. **10.** GLARE[1], from Middle English *glaren,* to glitter, stare, from a source akin to Middle Low German *glaren,* to glisten, from Germanic _*glaz-_. **11.** GLOSS[1], from a source perhaps akin to Icelandic *glossi,* a spark. **12.** GLANCE[2], from Old High German *glanz,* bright. **13.** GLEG, from Old Norse *glöggr,* clear-sighted. **14.** GLAD, from Old English *glæd,* shining, joyful, from Germanic _*gladaz_. **15.** GLEE, from Old English *glēo,* sport, merriment, from Germanic _*gleujam_. **16.a.** GLEED, from Old English *glēd,* ember; **b.** GLOGG, from Swedish *glōd,* ember. Both **a** and **b** from Germanic _*glō-di-_. **17.a.** GLOW, from Old English *glōwan,* to glow; **b.** GLOWER, from Middle English *gloren,* to gleam, stare, probably from a source akin to Norwegian dialectal *glora,* to gleam, stare; **c.** GLOAT, from a source perhaps akin to Old Norse *glotta,* to smile (scornfully). **a, b,** and **c** all from Germanic _*glō-_. **18.** GLOAMING, from Old English *glōm,* twilight, from Germanic _*glō-m-_. **19.a.** GLIDE, from Old English *glīdan,* to slip, glide; **b.** GLISSADE, from Old French *glier,* to glide; **c.** GLITCH, from Old High German *glītan,* to glide; **d.** GLEDE, from Old English *glida,* kite (< "gliding, hovering bird"), from derivative Germanic _*glidōn-_. **a, b, c,** and **d** all from Germanic _*glīdan_, to glide, possibly distantly related to **ghel-[2].** **20.** GLIB, from a source possibly akin to Middle Low German *glibberich,* slippery. [Pokorny 1. *ĝhel-* 429.]

ghend-. Important derivatives are *get, forget, guess, prison, apprehend, comprehend, surprise,* and *prey.*

ghend-. Also **ghed-.** To seize, take. **1.a.** GET, from Old Norse *geta,* to get; **b.** BEGET, from Old English *beg(i)etan,* to get, beget, from Germanic compound _*bigetan_, to acquire (_*bi-_, intensive prefix; see **ambhi**); **c.** FORGET, from Old English *forg(i)etan,* to forget, from Germanic compound _*fer-getan_, "to lose one's hold," forget (_*fer-_, prefix denoting rejection; see **per[1]**). **a, b,** and **c** all from Germanic _*getan_. **2.** GUESS, from Middle English *gessen,* to guess, from a Scandinavian source akin to Old Swedish *gissa,* to guess, from Germanic _*getisōn_, "to try to get," aim at. **3.** Basic form _*ghend-_. PREHENSILE, PREHENSION, PRISON, PRIZE[2], (PRIZE[3]), (PRY[2]); APPREHEND, (APPRENTICE), (APPRISE), COMPREHEND, (COMPRISE), EMPRISE, ENTERPRISE, (ENTREPRENEUR), MISPRISION[1], PREGNABLE, REPREHEND, (REPRISAL), (REPRISE), SURPRISE, from Latin *prendere, prehendere,* to get hold of, seize, grasp (*pre-, prae-,* before; see **per[1]**). **4.** Form _*ghed-_. PREDATORY, PREY, SPREE; DEPREDATE, OSPREY, from Latin *praeda,* booty (< _*prai-heda_, "something seized before"; *prai-, prae-,* before; see **per[1]**). [Pokorny *ghend-* 437.]

gher-[1]. Important derivative are *girdle, yard[2], orchard, kindergarten, garden, court, courteous, choir,* and *choral.*

gher-[1]. To grasp, enclose; with derivatives meaning "enclosure." **1.** Suffixed zero-grade form _*ghr̥-dh-_. **a.** GIRD[1], from Old English *gyrdan,* to gird, from Germanic _*gurdjan_; **b.** GIRDLE, from

Old English *gyrdel,* girdle; **c.** GIRTH, from Old Norse *gjördh,* girdle, girth. **2.** Suffixed o-grade form **ghor-to-* or (in Germanic) **ghor-dho-,* an enclosure. **a.** *(i)* YARD[2]; ORCHARD, from Old English *geard,* enclosure, garden, yard; *(ii)* GARTH, from Old Norse *gardhr,* garden, yard; *(iii)* KINDERGARTEN, from Old High German *garto,* garden; *(iv)* GARDEN, from Old North French *gart,* garden; *(v)* HANGAR, from Old French *hangard,* shelter, possibly from Germanic **haimgardaz* (**haimaz,* home; see **tkei-**); *(vi)* (see **medhyo-**) Germanic compound **midja-gardaz,* "middle zone," earth. *(i), (ii), (iii), (iv), (v),* and *(vi)* all from Germanic **gardaz;* **b.** HORTICULTURE, ORTOLAN, from Latin *hortus,* garden. **3.** Prefixed and suffixed zero-grade form **ko(m)-ghr̥-ti-* (**ko(m)-,* collective prefix, "together"; see **kom**). COHORT, CORTEGE, COURT, (COURTEOUS), COURTESAN, (COURTESY), (COURTIER), (CURTILAGE), (CURTSY), from Latin *cohors* (stem *cohort-*), enclosed yard, company of soldiers, multitude. **4.** Perhaps suffixed o-grade form **ghor-o-.* (CHOIR), (CHORAL), (CHORALE), CHORIC, (CHORISTER), CHORUS, HORA; CHORAGUS, TERPSICHORE, from Greek *khoros,* dancing ground (? perhaps originally a special enclosure for dancing), dance, dramatic chorus. [Pokorny 4. *ĝher-* 442, *ĝherdh-* 444.]

gher-[2]. Important derivatives are *yearn, greedy, exhort,* and *charisma.*

gher-[2]. To like, want. **1.** Suffixed form **ghern-.* YEARN, from Old English *giernan, gyrnan,* to strive, desire, yearn, from Germanic **gernjan.* **2.** Possibly extended form **ghrē-.* **a.** GREEDY, from Old English *grǣdig,* hungry, covetous, greedy, from Germanic **grēdigaz,* hungry, formed from **grēduz,* hunger; **b.** CATACHRESIS, CHRESARD, CHRESTOMATHY, from Greek *khrēsthai,* to lack, want, use, from *khrē,* it is necessary. **3.** Suffixed zero-grade form **ghr̥-to-.* HORTATIVE; EXHORT, from Latin *hortārī,* to urge on, encourage (< "to cause to strive or desire"). **4.** Suffixed zero-grade form **ghr̥-i-.* CHARISMA; EUCHARIST, from Greek *kharis,* grace, favor. **5.** Suffixed zero-grade form **ghr̥-yo-.* CHERVIL, from Greek *khairein,* to rejoice, delight in. [Pokorny 1. *ĝher-* 440.]

gherə-. Important derivatives are *yarn, hernia,* and *cord.*

gherə-. Gut, entrail. **1.** Suffixed form **gherə-no-.* YARN, from Old English *gearn,* yarn, from Germanic **garnō,* string. **2.** Suffixed form **gherə-n-.* HERNIA, from Latin *hernia,* "protruded viscus," rupture, hernia. **3.** Suffixed o-grade form **ghorə-d-.* (CHORD[2]), CORD, (CORDON); HARPSICHORD, TETRACHORD, from Greek *khordē,* gut, string. **4.** O-grade form **ghorə-.* CHORION, from Greek *khorion,* intestinal membrane, afterbirth. **5.** Possible suffixed zero-grade form **ghr̥ə-u-.* HARUSPEX, from Latin *haruspex,* "he who inspects entrails," diviner (*-spex,* "he who sees" < **spek-,* "to see"; see **spek-**), but perhaps borrowed from Etruscan. [Pokorny 5. *ĝher-* 443.]

gheslo-. Important derivatives are *kilo-, mile,* and *million.*

gheslo-. Seen by some as a base for words meaning "thousand." **1.** Suffixed form **ghesl-yo-.* CHILIAD, KILO-, from Greek *khilioi,* thousand. **2.** MIL, MILE, MILLENARY, MILLESIMAL, MILLI-, MILLIARY, MILLIME, MILLION; MILFOIL, MILLENNIUM, MILLEPORE, MILLIPEDE, from Latin *mīlle,* thousand, which has been analyzed as **smī-,* "one" + a form **ghslī-,* but is of obscure origin. [Pokorny *ĝhéslo-* 446.]

ghesor-. Important derivatives are *surgeon* and *surgery.*

ghesor-. Hand. Reduced form **ghesr-.* CHIRO-; (CHIRURGEON), ENCHIRIDION, (SURGEON), SURGERY, from Greek *kheir,* hand. [Pokorny 1. *ĝhesor-* 447.]

gheu-. Important derivatives are *gut, funnel, fusion, confuse, refund[1],* and *refuse[1].*

gheu-. To pour, pour a libation.
I. Extended form **gheud-.* **1.** Zero-grade form **ghud-.* GUT, from Old English *guttas,* intestines, from Germanic **gut-.* **2.** Nasalized zero-grade form **ghu-n-d-.* FOISON, FONDANT, (FONDUE), (FONT[2]), FOUND[2], (FUNNEL), FUSE[2], FUSILE, FUSION; AFFUSION, CIRCUMFUSE, CONFOUND, (CONFUSE), DIFFUSE, EFFUSE, INFUSE, PERFUSE, PROFUSE, REFUND, (REFUSE[1]), (REFUSE[2]), SUFFUSE, TRANSFUSE, from Latin *fundere,* to melt, pour out.
II. Extended form **gheus-.* **1.a.** GUST[1], from Old Norse *gustr,* a cold blast of wind, from Germanic suffixed form **gustiz;* **b.** GUSH, from Middle English *gushen,* to gush, perhaps akin to Icelandic *gusa,* to gush. Both **a** and **b** from Germanic zero-grade form **gus-.* **2.** GEYSER, from Old Norse *geysa,* to gush, from Germanic suffixed o-grade form **gausjan.* **3.a.** Suffixed zero-grade form **ghus-mo-.* CHYME; ECCHYMOSIS, from Greek *khumos,* juice; **b.** suffixed zero-grade form **ghuslo-.* CHYLE, from Greek *khulos,* juice.
III. Suffixed form **gheu-ti-.* FUTILE, from Latin *fūtilis,* "(of a vessel) easily emptied, leaky," hence untrustworthy, useless.
IV. Basic form **gheu-.* CHOANOCYTE, PARENCHYMA, from Greek *khein,* to pour, with o-grade noun *khoanē,* funnel. [Pokorny *ĝheu-* 447.]

gheu(ə)-. Important derivatives are *god* and *giddy.*

gheu(ə)-. To call, invoke. Suffixed zero-grade form **ghu-to-,* "the invoked," god. **a.** GOD, from Old English *god,* god; **b.** GIDDY, from Old English *gydig, gidig,* possessed, insane, from Germanic **gud-igaz,* possessed by a god; **c.** GÖTTERDÄMMERUNG, from Old High German *got,* god. **a, b,** and **c** all from Germanic **gudam,* god. [Pokorny *ĝhau-* 413.]

ghos-ti-. Important derivatives are *guest, hostile, hospital, host[1],* and *hostage.*

ghos-ti-. Stranger, guest, host; properly "someone with whom one has reciprocal duties of hospitality." **1.** Basic form **ghos-ti-.* **a.** GUEST, from Old Norse *gestr,* guest, from Germanic **gastiz;* **b.** HOST[2], HOSTILE, from Latin *hostis,* enemy (< stranger). **2.** Compound **ghos-pot-, *ghos-po(d)-,* "guest-master," one who symbolizes the relationship of reciprocal obligation (**pot-,* master; see **poti-**). HOSPICE, HOSPITABLE, HOSPITAL, (HOSPITALITY), HOST[1], (HOSTAGE), (HOSTEL), (HOSTLER), from Latin *hospes* (stem *hospit-*), host, guest, stranger. **3.** Suffixed zero-grade form **ghs-enwo-.* XENO-; PYROXENE, from Greek *xenos,* guest, host, stranger. [Pokorny *ghosti-s* 453.]

ghrē-. Important derivatives are *grow, green,* and *grass.*

ghrē-. To grow, become green. Contracted from **ghreə-.* **1.** O-grade form **ghrō-.* GROW, from Old English *grōwan,* to grow, from Germanic **grō(w)an.* **2.** Suffixed o-grade form **ghrō-n-yo-.* GREEN, from Old English *grēne,* green, from Germanic **grōnjaz,* green. **3.** Suffixed zero-grade form **ghrə-so-.* GRASS, GRAZE[1], from Old English *græs,* grass, from Germanic **grasam,* grass. [Pokorny *ghrē-* 454.]

ghrebh-[1]. Important derivatives are *grasp* and *grab[1].*

ghrebh-[1]. To seize, reach. **1.** Zero-grade form **ghr̥bh-.* SATYAGRAHA, from Sanskrit *gr̥bhṇāti, gr̥h-ṇāti,* he seizes. **2.a.** GRASP, from Middle English *graspen,* to grasp; **b.** GRAB[1], from Middle Dutch or Middle Low German *grabben,* to seize. Both **a** and **b** from parallel (imitative) Germanic creations with base **grab-, *grap-.* [Pokorny 1 *ghrebh-* 455.]

ghrebh-[2]. Important derivatives are *engrave, grave[1], grub,* and *groove.*

ghrebh-[2]. To dig, bury, scratch. **1.** O-grade form **ghrobh-.* **a.** *(i)* GRAVE[3], (ENGRAVE), from Old English *grafan,* to dig, engrave, scratch, carve; *(ii)* GRABEN, from Old High German *graban,* to dig; *(iii)* GRAVLAX, from Swedish *grava,* to bury; *(iv)* GRAVURE, from Old French *graver,* to engrave. *(i), (ii), (iii),* and *(iv)* all from Germanic **graban;* **b.** GRAVE[1], from Old English *græf,* trench, grave, from Germanic **grabam.* **2.** GRUB, from Old English **grybban,* to dig, from Germanic **grub(b)jan* (with secondary ablaut). **3.** GROOVE, from Middle Dutch *groeve,* ditch, from Germanic **grōbō.* [Pokorny 2. *ghrebh-* 455.]

ghredh-. Important derivatives are *congress, progress, grade, degrade,* and *degree.*

ghredh-. To walk, go. Suffixed zero-grade form **ghr̥dh-yo-.* **a.** GRESSORIAL; AGGRESS, CONGRESS, DIGRESSION, DIGRESS, EGRESS, INGRESS, PLANTIGRADE, PROGRESS, REGRESS, RETROGRADE, RETROGRESS, TRANSGRESS, from Latin *gradī* (past participle *gressus*), to walk, go; **b.** GRADE, CENTIGRADE, DEGRADE, DEGREE, from Latin *gradus* (< deverbative **grad-u-*), step, stage, degree, rank. [Pokorny *ghredh-* 456.]

ghrēi-. Important derivatives are *grisly, grime, Christ, christen, Christian,* and *Christmas.*

ghrēi. To rub. **1.** GRISLY, from Old English *grislīc,* terrifying, from Germanic **gris-,* to frighten (< "to grate on the mind"). **2.** GRIME, from Middle English *grime,* grime, from a source akin to Middle Dutch *grīme,* grime, from Germanic **grīm-,* smear. **3.** Extended form **ghrīs-.* CHRISM, CHRIST, (CHRISTEN), (CHRISTIAN); (CHRISTMAS), CREAM, from Greek *khriein,* to anoint. [Pokorny *ghrēi-* 457.]

ghrendh-. Important derivatives are *grind, grist,* and *refrain[1].*

ghrendh-. To grind. **1.** GRIND, from Old English *grindan,* to grind, from Germanic **grindan.* **2.** GRIST, from Old English *grīst,* the action of grinding, from Germanic **grinst-,* a grinding. **3.** (FRAISE), (FRENULUM), FRENUM; REFRAIN[1], from Latin *frendere,* to grind. **4.** Variant form **ghrend-.* CHONDRO-; HYPOCHONDRIA, MITOCHONDRION, from Greek *khondros,* granule, groats, hence cartilage, sometimes but improbably regarded as from **ghrendh-.** [Pokorny *ghren-* 459.]

ghwer-. Important derivatives are *feral, fierce, ferocious,* and *treacle.*

ghwer-. Wild beast. **1.** Suffixed form **ghwer-o-.* FERAL, FIERCE, from Latin *ferus,* wild. **2.** Compound **ghwero-əkʷ-,* "of wild aspect" (**-əkʷ-,* "-looking"; see **okʷ-**). FEROCIOUS, from Latin *ferōx* (stem *ferōc-*), fierce. **3.** Lengthened-grade form **ghwēr-.* TREACLE; CHALICOTHERE, DINOTHERE, THEROPOD, from Greek *thēr,* wild beast. [Pokorny *ĝhu̯ēr-* 493.]

gleubh-. Important derivatives are *cleave[1], clove[2], clever,* and *hieroglyphic.*

gleubh-. To tear apart, cleave.
I. Basic form **gleubh-.* **1.** CLEAVE[1], from Old English *clēofan,* to split, cleave, from Germanic **kleuban.* **2.** Probably o-grade **gloubh-.* CLEVER, from Middle English *cliver,* nimble, skillful, perhaps akin to East Frisian *klüfer, klifer,* skillful, and Old Norse *kleyfr,* easy to split, from Germanic **klaubri-.*
II. Zero-grade form **glubh-.* **1.a.** CLOVE[2], from Old English *clufu,* clove (of garlic); **b.** KLOOF, from Middle Dutch *clove,* a cleft; **c.** CLEVIS, from a Scandinavian source akin to Old Norse *klofi,* a cleft. **a, b,** and **c** all from Germanic **klub-,* a splitting. **2.** CLEFT, from Old English *geclyft,* fissure, from Germanic **klufti-* (**klub-ti-*). **3.** GLYPH, GLYPTIC; ANAGLYPH, HIEROGLYPHIC, from Greek *gluphein,* to carve. **4.** Suffixed zero-grade form **glubh-mā-.* GLUME, from Latin *glūma,* husk of grain. [Pokorny *gleubh-* 401.]

gnō-. Important derivatives are *know, can[1], cunning, uncouth, notice, recognize, ignore, noble, diagnosis,* and *narrate.*

gnō-. To know. Contracted from **gnoə-.* **1.** Variant form **gnē-,* contracted from **gnēə-.* KNOW, from Old English *cnāwan,* to know, from Germanic **knē(w)-.* **2.** Zero-grade form **gn̥ə-.* **a.** CAN[1], CON[2], CUNNING, from Old English *cunnan,* to know, know how to, be able to, from Germanic **kunnan* (Old English first and third singular *can* from Germanic **kann* from o-grade **gonə-*); **b.** KEN, KENNING, from Old English *cennan,* to declare, and Old Norse *kenna,* to know, name (in a formal poetic metaphor), from Germanic causative verb **kannjan,* to make known; **c.** (COUTH); UNCOUTH, from Old English *cūth,* known, well-known, usual, excellent, familiar, from Germanic **kunthaz;* **d.** KITH AND KIN, from Old English *cȳth(the), cȳththu,* knowledge, acquaintance, friendship, kinfolk, from Germanic **kunthithō.* **3.** Suffixed form **gnō-sko-.* NOTICE, NOTIFY, NOTION, NOTORIOUS; (ACQUAINT), COGNITION, (COGNIZANCE), (CONNOISSEUR), (QUAINT), RECOGNIZE, from Latin *(g)nōscere, cognōscere,* to get to know, get acquainted with. **4.** Suffixed form **gnō-ro-.* IG-

NORANT, IGNORE, from Latin *ignōrāre,* not to know, to disregard (*i-* for *in-*, not; see **ne**). **5.** Suffixed form *gnō-dhli-. NOBLE, from Latin *nōbilis,* knowable, known, famous, noble. **6.** Reduplicated and suffixed form *gi-gnō-sko-. GNOME[2], GNOMON, GNOSIS; AGNOSIA, DIAGNOSIS, PATHOGNOMONIC, PHYSIOGNOMY, PROGNOSIS, from Greek *gignōskein,* to know, think, judge, with *gnōsis* (< *gnō-ti-), knowledge, inquiry, and *gnōmōn,* judge, interpreter. **7.** Suffixed zero-grade form *gn̥ə-ro-. NARRATE, from Latin *narrāre* (< *gnarrāre), to tell, relate, from *gnārus,* knowing, expert. **8.** Traditionally but improbably referred here are: **a.** NOTE; ANNOTATE, CONNOTE, PROTHONOTARY, from Latin *nota,* a mark, note, sign, cipher, shorthand character; **b.** NORM, NORMA, NORMAL; ABNORMAL, ENORMOUS, from Latin *norma,* carpenter's square, rule, pattern, precept, possibly from an Etruscan borrowing of Greek *gnōmōn,* carpenter's square, rule. [Pokorny 2. ĝen- 376.]

gr̥ə-no-. Important derivatives are *corn[1], kernel, grain, granite,* and *grenade.*

gr̥ə-no-. Grain. **1.a.** CORN[1], from Old English *corn,* grain; **b.** KERNEL, from Old English derivative noun *cyrnel,* seed, pip; **c.** EINKORN, from Old High German *korn,* grain. **a, b,** and **c** all from Germanic *kornam. **2.** (GARNER), GRAIN, GRAM[2], GRANADILLA, GRANARY, GRANGE, GRANITE, GRANULE, (GRENADE); FILIGREE, POMEGRANATE, from Latin *grānum,* grain. [In Pokorny ĝer- 390.]

g^{w}ā-. Important derivatives are *come, welcome, become, adventure, convene, convenient, event, invent, prevent, revenue, souvenir, base[1], basis, acrobat,* and *diabetes.*

g^{w}ā-. Contracted from *g^{w}aə-. Also **g^{w}em-.** To go, come. **1.a.** COME, from Old English *cuman,* to come; **b.** WELCOME, from Old English *wilcuma,* a welcome guest, and *wilcume,* the greeting of welcome, from Germanic compound *wil-kumōn-, a desirable guest (*wil-, desirable; see **wel-[1]**), from *kumōn-, he who comes, a guest; **c.** BECOME, from Old English *becuman,* to become, from Germanic compound *bi-kuman, to arrive, come to be (*bi-, intensive prefix; see **ambhi**). **a, b,** and **c** all from Germanic *kuman. **2.** Suffixed form *g^w(e)m-yo-. VENUE; ADVENT, (ADVENTITIOUS), (ADVENTURE), (AVENUE), CIRCUMVENT, CONTRAVENE, CONVENE, (CONVENIENT), (CONVENT), (CONVENTICLE), (CONVENTION), (COVEN), (COVENANT), EVENT, INTERVENE, INVENT, (MISADVENTURE), PARVENU, PREVENIENT, PREVENT, PROVENANCE, (PROVENIENCE), (REVENANT), REVENUE, SOUVENIR, SUBVENTION, SUPERVENE, from Latin *venīre,* to come. **3.** Suffixed zero-grade form *g^{w}m̥-yo-. BASE[1], BASIS; ABASIA, ACROBAT, ADIABATIC, AMPHISBAENA, ANABAENA, (DIABASE), DIABETES, HYPERBATON, KATABATIC, STEREOBATE, STYLOBATE, from Greek *bainein,* to go, walk, step, with *basis* (< *g^{w}m̥-ti-), a stepping, tread, base, *-batos* (< *g^{w}m̥-to-), going, and *-batēs* (< *g^{w}ə-to-, zero-grade of *g^{w}ā-), agential suffix, "one that goes or treads, one that is based." **4.** Suffixed zero-grade form *g^w(ə)-u- in compound form *pres-g^{w}u-, "going before" (see **per[1]**). **5.** Basic form *g^{w}ā-. BEMA, from Greek *bēma,* step, seat, raised platform. **6.** JUGGERNAUT, from Sanskrit *jigāti,* he goes. [Pokorny g^{u}ā- 463.]

g^{w}ei-. Important derivatives are *quick, vivid, revive, survive, vital, vitamin, whiskey, bio-, amphibious, microbe,* and *hygiene.*

g^{w}ei-. Also **g^{w}eiə-.** To live.

I. Suffixed zero-grade form *g^{w}i-wo-, *g^{w}ī-wo- (< *g^{w}iə-wo-), living. **1.a.** QUICK, QUICKSILVER, from Old English *cwic, cwicu,* living, alive; **b.** (COUCH GRASS), QUITCH GRASS, from Old English *cwice,* couch grass (so named from its rapid growth). Both **a** and **b** from Germanic *kwi(k)waz. **2.a.** VIVIFY, VIVIPAROUS, from Latin *vīvus,* living, alive; **b.** VIAND, VICTUAL, VIVA, VIVACIOUS, VIVID; CONVIVIAL, REVIVE, SURVIVE, VIPER, from Latin denominative *vīvere,* to live. **3.** AZOTH, from Sanskrit *jīva-,* alive. **4.** Further suffixed form *g^{w}ī-wo-tā. VIABLE, VITAL; VITAMIN, from Latin *vīta,* life. **5.** Further suffixed form *g^{w}i-wo-tūt-. USQUEBAUGH, (WHISKEY), from Old Irish *bethu,* life.

II. Suffixed zero-grade form *g^{w}iə-o-. BIO-, BIOTA, BIOTIC; AEROBE, AMPHIBIAN, ANABIOSIS, CENOBITE, MICROBE, RHIZOBIUM, SAPROBE, SYMBIOSIS, from Greek *bios,* life (> *biotē,* way of life).

III. Variant form *g^{w}yō- (< *g^{w}yoə-). **1.** AZO-, (DIAZO), from Greek *zoē,* life. **2.** Suffixed form *g^{w}yō-yo-. -ZOIC, ZOO-, ZOON[1], -ZOON, from Greek *zōon, zōion,* living being, animal.

IV. Prefixed and suffixed form *su-g^{w}iə-es-, "having good life" (*su-, well; see **su-**). HYGIENE, from Greek *hugiēs,* healthy.

V. QUIVER[1], from Old English *cwifer-,* nimble, possibly from **g^{w}ei-.** [Pokorny 3. g^{u}ei̯- 467.]

g^{w}elə-. Important derivatives are *devil, emblem, metabolism, parable, parliament, parlor, problem, symbol, ball[2], ballad, ballet,* and *kill[1].*

g^{w}elə-. Also **g^{w}el-.** To throw, reach, with further meaning to pierce.

I. Words denoting to throw, reach. Variant *g^{w}lē-, contracted from *g^{w}leə-. **1.** Suffixed zero-grade form *g^{w}l̥-n-ə-. **a.** BALLISTA; AMPHIBOLE, ASTROBLEME, BOLIDE, DEVIL, (DIABOLIC), EMBLEM, EPIBOLY, (HYPERBOLA), HYPERBOLE, METABOLISM, (PALAVER), PARABLE, (PARABOLA), (PARLEY), (PARLIAMENT), (PARLOR), (PAROL), (PAROLE), PROBLEM, SYMBOL, from Greek *ballein,* to throw (with o-grade *bol- and variant *blē-); **b.** BALL[2], (BALLAD), (BALLET), BAYADERE, from Greek *ballizein,* to dance. **2.** Suffixed o-grade form *g^{w}olə-ā. BOLOMETER, from Greek *bolē,* beam, ray. **3.** Possible suffixed o-grade form g^{w}ol(ə)-sā. BOULE[1], ABULIA, from Greek *boulē,* determination, will (< "throwing forward of the mind"), council. **4.** Suffixed variant zero-grade form *g^{w}elə-mno-. BELEMNITE, from Greek *belemnon,* dart, javelin.

II. Words denoting to pierce. **1.** Suffixed o-grade form *g^{w}ol-eyo-. **a.** QUELL, from Old English *cwellan,* to kill, destroy; **b.** QUAIL[2], from Middle Dutch *quelen,* to be ill, suffer. Both **a** and **b** from Germanic *kwaljan. **2.** Suffixed zero-grade form *g^{w}l̥-yo-. KILL[1], from Middle English *killen,* to kill, perhaps from Old English *cyllan, to kill, from Germanic *kuljan. **3.** Full-grade form *g^{w}el-. BELONEPHOBIA, from Greek *belonē,* needle. [Pokorny 2. g^{u}el- 471, 1. g^{u}el- 470.]

g^{w}en-. An important derivative is *queen.*

g^{w}en-. Woman. **1.** Suffixed form *g^{w}en-ā-. **a.** QUEAN, from Old English *cwene,* woman, prostitute, wife, from Germanic *kwenōn-; **b.** BANSHEE, from Old Irish *ben,* woman; **c.** ZENANA, from Persian *zan,* woman. **2.** Suffixed lengthened-grade form *g^{w}ēn-i-. QUEEN, from Old English *cwēn,* woman, wife, queen, from Germanic *kwēniz, woman, wife, queen. **3.** Suffixed zero-grade form *g^{w}n̥-ā-. -GYNE, GYNO-, -GYNOUS, -GYNY; GYNECOCRACY, (GYNECOLOGY), GYNOECIUM, from Greek *gunē,* woman. [Pokorny g^{u}enā 473.]

g^{w}erə-[1]. Important derivatives are *grave[2], grief, aggravate, baritone, guru, brute,* and *blitzkrieg.*

g^{w}erə-[1]. Heavy.

I. Zero-grade form *g^{w}r̥ə-. **1.** Suffixed form *g^{w}r̥ə-u-i-. GRAVE[2], GRAVID, GRAVITY, (GRIEF), GRIEVE; AGGRAVATE, (AGGRIEVE), from Latin *gravis,* heavy, weighty. **2.** Suffixed form *g^{w}r̥ə-u-. **a.** BARITE, (BARIUM), BARYON, BARYTA; BARITONE, BARYCENTER, BARYSPHERE, CHARIVARI, from Greek *barus,* heavy; **b.** GURU, from Sanskrit *guru-,* heavy, venerable. **3.** Suffixed form *g^{w}r̥ə-es-. BAR[2], BARO-; CENTROBARIC, ISALLOBAR, ISOBAR, from Greek *baros,* weight. **4.** Possibly *g^{w}rī-. (see **ud-**) Greek compound *u(d)-bri- from *bri-.

II. Suffixed extended form *g^{w}rū-to-. BRUT, BRUTE, from Latin *brūtus,* heavy, unwieldy, dull, stupid, brutish.

III. Suffixed extended form g^{w}rī-g-. **a.** BRIO, from Spanish *brio* or Provençal *briu,* vigor, from Celtic *brīg-o-, strength; **b.** (BRIG), BRIGADE, (BRIGAND), (BRIGANTINE), from Old Italian *briga,* strife, from Celtic *brīg-ā-, strife; **c.** BLITZKRIEG, from Old High German *krēg, chrēg,* stubbornness, from Germanic *krīg-.

IV. Suffixed full-grade form *g^{w}erə-nā-, millstone. QUERN, from Old English *cweorn,* quern. [Pokorny 2. g^{u}er- 476.]

g^{w}erə-[2]. Important derivatives are *grace, grateful, gratitude, agree, congratulate,* and *bard[1].*

g^{w}erə-[2]. To favor. **1.** Suffixed zero-grade form *g^{w}r̥ə-to-. GRACE, GRATEFUL, GRATIFY, GRATIS, GRATITUDE, GRATUITOUS, (GRATUITY); AGREE, CONGRATULATE, DISGRACE, INGRATE, INGRATIATE, MAUGRE, from Latin *grātus,* pleasing, beloved, agreeable, favorable, thankful, with related suffixed forms *g^{w}r̥ə-ti-, *g^{w}r̥ə-t-ā-, *g^{w}r̥ə-t-olc-. **2.** Possible suffixed zero-grade form *g^{w}r̥ə-d(h)o-, "he who praises." BARD[1], from Welsh *barad* and Scottish and Irish Gaelic *bard,* bard, from Celtic *bardo-, bard (but this is possibly from **g^{w}erə-[1]**). [Pokorny 4. g^{u}er(ə)- 478.]

g^{w}et-. Derivatives are *bequeath* and *quoth.*

g^{w}et-. To say, speak. **1.** Basic form *g^{w}et-. BEQUEATH, QUOTH, from Old English *cwethan,* to say, speak, from Germanic *kwithan. **2.** Suffixed form *g^{w}et-ti-. BEQUEST, from Old English *-cwis,* will, from Germanic *kwessiz. [Pokorny 2. g^{u}et- 480.]

g^{w}hedh-. Important derivatives are *bid* and *bead.*

g^{w}hedh-. To ask, pray. **1.** Suffixed form *g^{w}hedh-yo-. BID, from Old English *biddan,* to ask, pray, from Germanic *bidjan, to pray, entreat. **2.** BEAD, from Old English *bed(u), gebed,* prayer (*ge-,* intensive and collective prefix; see **kom**), from Germanic *bidam, entreaty. **3.** Suffixed form *g^{w}hedh-to-. INFEST, MANIFEST, from Latin *-festus,* probably in *infestus,* hostile (< *n̥-g^{w}hedh-to-, "inexorable"; *n̥-, not; see **ne**), and perhaps in *manifestus,* caught in the act, red-handed (*manus,* hand; see **man-[2]**). [Pokorny g^{u}hedh- 488, 2. bhedh- 114.]

g^{w}hen-. Important derivatives are *bane, gun, defend, fence,* and *offend.*

g^{w}hen-. To strike, kill. **1.** O-grade *g^{w}hon-. **a.** BANE, from Old English *bana,* slayer, cause of ruin or destruction; **b.** AUTOBAHN, from Middle High German *ban, bane,* way, road (? < "path hewn through woods"). Both **a** and **b** from Germanic suffixed form *ban-ōn-. **2.** Suffixed zero-grade form *g^{w}hn̥-tyā-. **a.** GUN, from Old Norse *gunnr,* war; **b.** GONFALON, from Italian *gonfalone,* standard, from Germanic compound *gundfanōn-, "battle flag" (*fanōn-, flag; see **pan-**). Both **a** and **b** from Germanic *gundjō, war, battle. **3.** Suffixed form *g^{w}hen-do-. **a.** DEFEND, (DEFENSE), (FENCE), from Latin *dēfendere,* to ward off (*dē-,* away; see **de-**); **b.** OFFEND, (OFFENSE), from Latin *offendere,* to strike against, be offensive, offend (*ob-,* against; see **epi**). **4.** Suffixed zero-grade form *g^{w}hn̥-tro-. BEZOAR, from Persian *zahr,* poison, from Old Iranian *jathra-. [Pokorny 2. g^{u}hen-(ə)- 491, bhen- 126.]

g^{w}her-. Important derivatives are *burn[1], brand, brandy, brandish, forceps,* and *furnace.*

g^{w}her-. To heat, warm. **1.** Zero-grade *g^{w}hr̥-. **a.** BURN[1], from Old English *beornan, byrnan* (intransitive) and *bærnan* (transitive), to burn; **b.** BRIMSTONE, from late Old English *brynstān,* "burning mineral," sulfur (*stān,* stone; see **stei-**); **c.** BRINDLED, from Old Norse *brenna,* to burn. **a, b,** and **c** all from Germanic *brennan (intransitive) and *brannjan (transitive), formed from *brenw- with nasal suffix and analogical vocalism. **2.a.** BRAND, from Old English *brand,* piece of burning wood, sword; **b.** BRANDY, from Dutch *branden,* to burn, distill; **c.** BRANDISH, from Old French *brand,* sword. **a, b,** and **c** all from Germanic *brandaz, a burning, a flaming torch, hence also a sword. **3.** Suffixed form *g^{w}her-mo-. THERM, -THERM, THERMO-, -THERMY; HYPOTHERMIA, from Greek *thermos,* warm, hot, and *thermē,* heat. **4.** O-grade form *g^{w}hor-. FORCEPS, from Latin *forceps,* pincers, fire tongs (< "that which holds hot things"; *-ceps,* agential suffix, "-taker"; see **kap-**). **5.** Suffixed o-grade form *g^{w}hor-no-. **a.** FORNAX, FURNACE, HORNITO, from Latin *furnus, fornus, fornāx,* oven; **b.** FORNICATE, FORNIX, from Latin *fornix,* arch, vault (< "vaulted brick oven"), probably from **g^{w}her-.** [Pokorny g^{u}her- 493, bhereu- 143.]

g^{w}hī-. Important derivatives are *filament, file[1],* and *profile.*

g^{w}hī-. Thread, tendon. Contracted from *g^{w}hiə-. Suffixed form *g^{w}hī-slo-. FILAMENT, FILAR, FILARIA, FILE[1], FILLET, FILOSE, FILUM; (DEFILE[2]), ENFILADE, FILIFORM, FILIGREE, FILOPLUME, PROFILE, PURFLE, from Latin *fīlum,* thread. [Pokorny g^{u}hei̯ə- 489.]

g^{w}hrē-. Important derivatives are *breath* and *breathe.*

gʷhrē-. To smell, breathe. Contracted from *g^whreə-. BREATH, (BREATHE), from Old English *brǣth,* odor, exhalation, from Germanic suffixed form **brē-thaz.*

gʷhren-. Important derivatives are *frantic, frenetic, frenzy, phrase,* and *paraphrase.*

gʷhren-. To think. **1.** (FRANTIC), FRENETIC, (FRENZY), -PHRENIA, PHRENO-; (PHRENITIS), from Greek *phrēn,* the mind, also heart, midriff, diaphragm. **2.** Extended zero-grade root form *g^whrn̥-d-. PHRASE; HOLOPHRASTIC, METAPHRASE, PARAPHRASE, PERIPHRASIS, from Greek *phrazein,* to point out, show. [Pokorny *gʷhren-* 496.]

gʷou-. Important derivatives are *cow*[1], *beef, bugle*[1], *bucolic,* and *butter.*

gʷou-. Ox, bull, cow. Nominative singular form *g^wōu-s. **1.** COW[1], (KINE); COWSLIP, from Old English *cū, cȳ, cȳe,* cow, from Germanic **kōuz* (> **kūz*). **2.** BEEF, BOVINE, BUGLE[1], from Latin *bōs* (stem *bov-*), ox, bull, cow. **3.** BOÖTES, BOUSTROPHEDON, BUCOLIC, BUGLOSS, BULIMIA, BUPRESTID, BUTTER, (BUTYRIC), from Greek *bous,* ox, bull, cow. **4.** GAYAL, from Sanskrit *go-, gauḥ,* cow. **5.** Suffixed form *g^wōu-ro-. GAUR, from Sanskrit *gauraḥ,* wild ox. **6.** Zero-grade suffixed form *g^ww-ā-. HECATOMB, from Greek *hekatombē,* "sacrifice of a hundred oxen" (*hekaton,* hundred; see **dekm̥**). [Pokorny *gʷou-* 482.]

i-. Important derivatives are *yonder, yea, yes, yet, if, identity,* and *item.*

i-. Pronominal stem. **1.** ILK[1], from Old English *ilca,* same, from Germanic **is-lik-,* same (**līk-,* like; see **līk-**). **2.** YON, from Old English *geon,* that, from Germanic **jaino-, *jeno-.* **3.a.** YOND, (YONDER), from Old English *geond,* as far as, yonder, from Germanic **jend-;* **b.** BEYOND, from Old English *geondan,* beyond, from Germanic **jendana-.* **4.** Extended forms **yām, *yāi.* YEA, YES, from Old English *gēa,* affirmative particle, and *gēse,* yes (see **es-**), from Germanic **jā, *jai.* **5.** YET, from Old English *gīet, gīeta* (preform uncertain), still. **6.** Relative stem **yo-* plus particle. IF, from Old English *gif,* if, from Germanic **ja-ba.* **7.** Basic form **i-,* with neuter **id-em.* ID, IDEM, (IDENTICAL), IDENTITY; (IDENTIFY), from Latin *is,* he (neuter *id,* it), and *īdem,* same. **8.** Suffixed form **i-tero-.* ITERATE; (REITERATE), from Latin *iterum,* again. **9.** Suffixed and extended form **it(ə)-em.* ITEM, from Latin *item,* thus, also. **10.** Stem **i-* plus locatival particle **-dha-i.* IBIDEM, from Latin *ibī-dem,* in the same place. **11.** Suffixed variant form **e-tero-.* (see **ko-**). [Pokorny 3. *e-* 281.]

kā-. Important derivatives are *whore, caress, charity,* and *cherish.*

kā-. To like, desire. Contracted from **kaə-.* **1.** Suffixed form **kā-ro-.* **a.** *(i)* WHORE, from Old English *hōre,* whore; *(ii)* WHOREDOM, from Old Norse compound *hōrdōmr,* whoredom (*-dōmr,* "condition"; see **dhē-**). Both *(i)* and *(ii)* from Germanic **hōraz* (feminine **hōrōn-*), "one who desires," adulterer; **b.** CARESS, CHARITY, CHERISH, from Latin *cārus,* dear. **2.** Suffixed form **kā-mo-.* KAMA; KAMASUTRA, from Sanksrit *kāmaḥ,* love, desire. [Pokorny *kā-* 515.]

kad-. Important derivatives are *cadaver, cadence, cascade, case*[1], *chance, chute, accident, decay, incident,* and *occasion.*

kad-. To fall. CADAVER, CADENCE, CADENT, CADUCOUS, CASCADE, CASE[1], CHANCE, CHUTE; ACCIDENT, DECAY, DECIDUOUS, ESCHEAT, INCIDENT, OCCASION, RECIDIVISM, from Latin *cadere,* to fall, die. [Pokorny 1. *kad-* 516.]

kaə-id-. Important derivatives are *cement, chisel, scissors, circumcise, concise, decide,* and *precise.*

kaə-id-. To strike. **1.** CAESURA, CEMENT, CESTUS[2], CHISEL, -CIDE, SCISSOR; ABSCISE, CIRCUMCISE, CONCISE, DECIDE, EXCISE[2], INCISE, PRECISE, RECISION, from Latin *caedere,* to cut, strike. **2.** CAELUM, from Latin *caelum* (? < **caedum*), sculptor's chisel. [Pokorny *(s)k(h)ai-* 917.]

kai-. Important derivatives are *hot* and *heat.*

kai-. Heat. Extended form **kaid-.* **a.** HOT, from Old English *hāt,* hot, from Germanic **haitaz;* **b.** HEAT, from Old English *hǣtu,* from Germanic **haitī-.* [Pokorny *kai̯-* 519.]

kailo-. Important derivatives are *whole, wholesome, health, heal, holy,* and *hallow.*

kailo-. Whole, uninjured, of good omen. **1.a.** HALE[1], WHOLE, from Old English *hāl,* hale, whole; **b.** WHOLESOME, from Old English **hālsum* (> Middle English *holsom*), wholesome; **c.** (HAIL[2]); WASSAIL, from Old Norse *heill,* healthy. **a, b,** and **c** all from Germanic **hailaz.* **2.** HEALTH, from Old English *hǣlth,* health, from Germanic **hailithō.* **3.** HEAL, from Old English *hǣlan,* to heal, from Germanic **hailjan.* **4.a.** HOLY, from Old English *hālig,* holy, sacred; **b.** HALLOW, from Old English *hālgian,* to consecrate, bless, from Germanic derivative verb **hailagōn.* Both **a** and **b** from Germanic **hailagaz.* [Pokorny *kai-lo-* 520.]

kaito-. Important derivatives are *heath* and *heathen.*

kaito-. Forest, uncultivated land. **1.** HEATH, from Old English *hǣth,* heath, untilled land, from Germanic **haithiz.* **2.a.** HEATHEN, from Old English *hǣthen,* heathen, "savage" (< "one inhabiting uncultivated land"); **b.** HOYDEN, from Middle Dutch *heiden,* heathen. Both **a** and **b** from Germanic **haithinaz.* [Pokorny *kaito-* 521.]

kakka-. Derivatives are *poppycock* and *cacophony.*

kakka-. Also **kaka-**. To defecate. Root imitative of glottal closure. **1.** CUCKING STOOL, from Middle English *cukken,* to defecate, from a source akin to Old Norse **kūka,* to defecate. **2.** POPPYCOCK, from Latin *cacāre,* to defecate. **3.** CACO-; CACODYL, CACOËTHES, CACOPHONOUS, (CACOPHONY), from Greek *kakos,* bad. [Pokorny *kakka-* 521.]

kan-. Important derivatives are *hen, chant, accent, enchant, incentive,* and *charm.*

kan-. To sing. **1.** HEN, from Old English *hen(n),* hen, from Germanic **han(e)nī.* **2.** CANOROUS, CANT[2], CANTABILE, CANTATA, CANTICLE, CANTILLATE, (CANTO), CANTOR, CANZONE, CHANT; ACCENT, DESCANT, ENCHANT, (INCANTATION), INCENTIVE, PRECENTOR, RECANT, from Latin *canere,* to sing (> *cantāre,* to sing, frequentative of *canere*). **3.** OSCINE, from Latin *oscen,* a singing bird used in divination (< **obs-cen,* "one that sings before the augurs"; *ob-,* before; see **epi-**). **4.** Suffixed form **kan-men-.* CHARM, from Latin *carmen,* song, poem. [Pokorny *kan-* 525.]

kand-. Important derivatives are *candid, candidate, candle, candor, incandesce,* and *incense.*

kand-. To shine. **1.** Suffixed (stative) form **kand-ē-.* CANDENT, CANDID, (CANDIDA), (CANDIDATE), CANDLE, CANDOR; INCANDESCE, from Latin *candēre* to shine. **2.** (INCENDIARY), INCENSE[1], INCENSE[2] from Latin compound *incendere,* to set fire to, kindle (*in-,* in; see **en**), from transitive **candere,* to kindle. [Pokorny *kand-* 526.]

kap-. Important derivatives are *have, heavy, haven, hawk*[1], *heave, cable, capable, caption, captive, catch, chase*[1], *accept, conceive, deceive, except, intercept, municipal, occupy, participate, perceive, receive, recover, capsule,* and *chassis.*

kap-. To grasp.
I. Basic form **kap-.* **1.** HEDDLE, from Old English *hefeld,* thread used for weaving, heddle (a device which grasps the thread), from Germanic **haf-.* **2.** HAFT, from Old English *hæft,* handle, from Germanic **haftjam.* **3.** Form **kap-o-.* HAVE, from Old English *habban,* to have, hold, from Germanic **habai-, *habēn.* **4.** HEAVY, from Old English *hefig,* heavy, from Germanic **hafigaz,* "containing something," having weight. **5.** HAVEN, from Old English *hæfen,* a haven, from Germanic **hafnō-,* perhaps "place that holds ships." **6.** HAWK[1], from Old English *h(e)afoc,* hawk, from Germanic **habukaz.* **7.** (see **per**[1]) Latin combining form *-ceps* (< **kap-s*), "taker." **8.** GAFF[1], from Provençal *gafar,* to seize, from Germanic **gaf-,* probably akin to **kap-**.
II. Suffixed form **kap-yo-.* **1.** HEAVE, from Old English *hebban,* to lift, from Germanic **hafjan.* **2.** CABLE, CAPABLE, CAPACIOUS, CAPIAS, CAPSTAN, CAPTION, CAPTIOUS, (CAPTIVATE), CAPTIVE, CAPTOR, CAPTURE, CATCH, (CHASE[1]), ACCEPT, ANTICIPATE, CONCEIVE, DECEIVE, EXCEPT, INCEPTION, (INCIPIENT), INTERCEPT, INTUSSUSCEPTION, MUNICIPAL, NUNCUPATIVE, OCCUPY, PARTICIPATE, PERCEIVE, PRECEPT, RECEIVE, (RECOVER), RECUPERATE, (Rx), SUSCEPTIBLE, from Latin *capere,* to take, seize, catch.
III. Lengthened-grade variant form **kōp-.* **1.a.** BEHOOF, from Old English *behōf,* use, profit, need; **b.** BEHOOVE, from Old English *behōfian,* to have need of. Both **a** and **b** from Germanic compound **bi-hōf,* "that which binds," requirement, obligation (**bi-,* intensive prefix; see **ambhi**), from **hōf-.* **2.** COPEPOD, from Greek *kōpē,* oar, handle. [Pokorny *kap-* 527.] Compare **ghabh-**.

kaput-. Important derivatives are *head, cadet, capital*[1], *caprice, captain, cattle, chapter, chief, biceps, decapitate, kerchief,* and *mischief.*

kaput-. Head. **1.a.** HEAD, from Old English *hēafod,* head; **b.** HETMAN, from Old High German *houbit,* head. Both **a** and **b** from Germanic **haubudam, *haubidam.* **2.** CADET, CAPE[2], CAPITAL[1], CAPITAL[2], CAPITATE, CAPITATION, CAPITELLUM, (CAPITULATE), CAPITULUM, CAPO[1], (CAPO[2]), CAPRICE, CAPTAIN, CATTLE, CAUDILLO, (CHAPITER), CHAPTER, CHIEF, CHIEFTAIN, CORPORAL[2]; BICEPS, DECAPITATE, KERCHIEF, MISCHIEF, OCCIPUT, PRECIPITATE, RECAPITULATE, SINCIPUT, TRICEPS, from Latin *caput,* head [Pokorny *kap-ut-* 529.]

kar-. Important derivatives are *hard, standard, hardy*[1], *cancer,* and *canker.*

kar-. Hard.
I. Variant form **ker-.* **1.** Suffixed o-grade form **kor-tu-.* **a.** HARD, from Old English *hard, heard,* hard; **b.** -ARD, from Germanic **-hart, *-hard,* bold, hardy; **c.** STANDARD, from Old French *estandard,* rallying place, perhaps from Frankish **hard,* hard; **d.** HARDY[1], from Old French *hardir,* to make hard. **a, b, c,** and **d** all from Germanic **harduz.* **2.** Suffixed zero-grade form **kr̥t-es-,* from earlier full-grade form **kret-es-.* -CRACY, from Greek *kratos,* strength, might, power.
II. Possible basic form **kar-* in derivatives referring to things with hard shells. **1.** CAREEN, CARINA, from Latin *carīna,* keel of a ship, nutshell, possibly from **kar-**. **2.** KARYO-; EUCARYOTE, GILLYFLOWER, SYNKARYON, from Greek *karuon,* nut, possibly from **kar-**. **3.** Reduplicated form **kar-kr-o-.* (CANCER), CANKER, CHANCRE, from dissimilated Latin *cancer,* crab, cancer, constellation Cancer. **4.** Suffixed form **kar-k-ino-.* CARCINO-, CARCINOMA, from Greek *karkinos,* cancer, crab. [Pokorny 3. *kar-* 531.]

kas-. An important derivative is *hare.*

kas-. Gray. **1.a.** HARE, from Old English *hara,* hare; **b.** HASENPFEFFER, from Old High German *haso,* rabbit. Both **a** and **b** from Germanic **hazōn-, *hasōn-.* **2.** Suffixed form **kas-no-.* CANESCENT, from Latin *cānus,* white, gray, grayed hair. [Pokorny *k̂as-* 533.]

kat-. A derivative is *cata-.*

kat-. Down. **1.** CATA-, from Greek *kata,* down, possibly from **kat-**. **2.** Suffixed form **kat-olo-.* CADELLE, from Latin *catulus,* young puppy, young of animals ("dropped"). [Pokorny 2. *kat-* 534.]

kau-. Important derivatives are *hew, haggle, hoe,* and *hay.*

kau-. To hew, strike. **1.a.** HEW, from Old English *hēawan,* to hew; **b.** HAGGLE, from Old Norse *högg-va,* to cut; **c.** HOE, from Old French *houe,* a hoe. **a, b,** and **c** all from Germanic **hawwan.* **2.** HAG[2], from a source akin to Old Norse *högg,* a gap, a cutting blow, from Germanic **hawwō.* **3.** HAY, from Old English *hīeg,* hay, cut grass, from Germanic **haujam.* **4.** Suffixed form **kau-do-.* INCUS, from Latin *cūdere* (< **caudere*), to strike, beat. [Pokorny *kāu-* 535.]

ked-. Important derivatives are *cease, cede, abscess, access, ancestor, concede, decease, exceed, precede, proceed, succeed,* and *necessary.*

ked-. To go, yield. **1.** Lengthened-grade form **kēd-.* CEASE, CEDE, CESSION; ABSCESS, ACCEDE, ACCESS, ANCESTOR, ANTECEDE, CONCEDE, (CONCESSION), DECEASE, EXCEED, INTERCEDE, PRECEDE, PREDECESSOR, PROCEED, RE-

CEDE, RETROCEDE, SECEDE, SUCCEED, from Latin *cēdere,* to go, withdraw, yield. **2.** Prefixed and suffixed form **ne-ked-ti-,* "(there is) no drawing back" (**ne-,* not; see **ne**). NECESSARY, from Latin *necesse,* inevitable, unavoidable. [In Pokorny *sed-* 884.]

keg-. Important derivatives are *hook, heckle,* and *hack*[1].

keg-. Hook, tooth. **1.a.** HAKE, from Old English *haca,* hook, akin to Old Norse *haki,* hook; **b.** HARQUEBUS, from Middle Dutch *hake,* hook. Both **a** and **b** from Germanic **hakan-.* **2.a.** HOOK, from Old English *hōc,* hook; **b.** HOOKER[1], from Middle Dutch *hōk, hoec,* hook; **c.** HAČEK, from Old High German *hāko,* hook. **a, b,** and **c** all from Germanic lengthened form **hōka-.* **3.** HECKLE, from Middle Dutch *hekel,* hatchel, a flax comb with long metal hooklike teeth, from Germanic **hakila-.* **4.** HACK[1], from Old English *-haccian,* to hack to pieces as with a hooked instrument, from Germanic **hakkijan.* [Pokorny *keg-* 537.]

kei-[1]. Important derivatives are *city, civic, civil,* and *cemetery.*

kei-[1]. To lie; bed, couch; beloved, dear.
I. Basic form **kei-.* **1.** Suffixed form **kei-wo-.* **a.** HIND[3], from Old English *hīwan,* members of a household, from Germanic **hīwa-;* **b.** HIDE[3], from Old English *hīgid, hīd,* a measure of land (< "household"), from suffixed Germanic form **hī-widō.* **2.** Suffixed form **kei-wi-.* CITY, CIVIC, CIVIL, from Latin *cīvis,* citizen (< "member of a household").
II. O-grade form **koi-.* **1.** Suffixed form **koi-nā.* INCUNABULUM, from Latin *cūnae,* a cradle. **2.** Suffixed form **koi-m-ā.* CEMETERY, from Greek *koiman,* to put to sleep.
III. Suffixed zero-grade form **ki-wo-.* SHIVA, from Sanskrit *śiva-,* auspicious, dear. [Pokorny 1. *ḱei-* 539.]

kei-[2]. Important derivatives are *cite, excite, incite, resuscitate, solicitous,* and *kinetic.*

kei-[2]. To set in motion.
I. Possibly extended o-grade from **koid-.* **1.** HIGHT, from Old English *hātan,* to call, summon, order, from Germanic **haitan.* **2.** Suffixed form **koid-ti-.* **a.** HEST, from Old English *hǣs,* a command, a bidding; **b.** BEHEST, from Old English compound *behǣs,* a vow, promise, command (*be-,* intensive prefix; see **ambhi**). Both **a** and **b** from Germanic **haissiz* from **hait-ti-* (but Germanic **hait-* of **1** and **2** is perhaps to be referred to a separate root **kaid-*).
II. Zero-grade form **ki-.* Suffixed iterative form **ki-eyo-.* CITE; EXCITE, INCITE, OSCITANCY, RESUSCITATE, SOLICITOUS, from Latin *ciēre* (past participle *citus*), with its frequentative *citāre,* to set in motion, summon.
III. Extended root **kyeu-.* Nasal infixed form **ki-n-eu-.* KINEMATICS, KINESICS, -KINESIS, KINETIC; CINEMATOGRAPH, HYPERKINESIA, KINESIOLOGY, KINESTHESIA, KININ, (TELEKINESIS), from Greek *kinein,* to move. [Pokorny *kēi-* 538.]

kekʷ-. A derivative is *copro-.*

kekʷ-. To excrete. Suffixed o-grade form **kokʷ-ro-.* COPRO-, from Greek *kopros,* dung. [Pokorny *ḱeku̯-* 544.]

kel-[1]. Important derivatives are *hell, hall, hull, hole, hollow, holster, apocalypse, eucalyptus, helmet, occult, color, cell, cellar,* and *conceal.*

kel-[1]. To cover, conceal, save.
I. O-grade form **kol-.* **1.a.** HELL, from Old English *hell,* hell; **b.** HEL, from Old Norse *Hel,* the underworld, goddess of death. Both **a** and **b** from Germanic **haljō,* the underworld (< "concealed place"). **2.a.** HALL, from Old English *heall,* hall; **b.** VALHALLA, from Old Norse *höll,* hall. Both **a** and **b** from Germanic **hallō,* covered place, hall. **3.** Suffixed form **kol-eyo-.* COLEUS; COLEOPTERAN, COLEOPTILE, COLEORHIZA, from Greek *koleon, koleos,* sheath.
II. Zero-grade form **kl̥-.* **1.a.** HOLD[2], HULL, from Old English *hulu,* husk, pod (< "that which covers"); **b.** HOLE, from Old English *hol,* a hollow; **c.** HOLLOW, from Old English *holh,* hole, hollow. **a, b,** and **c** all from Germanic **hul-.* **2.a.** HOLSTER, from Old High German *hulft,* covering; **b.** HOUSING[2], from Medieval Latin *hultia,* protective covering. Both **a** and **b** from suffixed Germanic form **hulftī-.* **3.** Suffixed form **kl̥-to-.* (see **III. 2.** below) Latin *occultus.* **4.** Extended form **klā* (< **kl̥ə-*). CLANDESTINE, from Latin *clam,* in secret. **5.** Suffixed variant form **kal-up-yo-.* CALYPSO[1], CALYPTRA; APOCALYPSE, EUCALYPTUS, from Greek *kaluptein,* to cover, conceal.
III. Full-grade form **kel-.* **1.a.** HELM[2], from Old English *helm,* protection, covering; **b.** HELMET, from Middle English *helmet,* helmet, from a source akin to Frankish **helm,* helmet. Both **a** and **b** from Germanic **helmaz,* "protective covering." **2.** OCCULT, from Latin *occulere* < **ob-kel-* (past participle *occultus* < *ob-kl̥-to-;* see **II. 3.** above), to cover over (*ob-,* over; see **epi**). **3.** Suffixed form **kel-os-.* COLOR, from Latin *color,* color, hue (< "that which covers"). **4.** Suffixed form **kel-nā-.* CELL, CELLA, CELLAR, CELLARER; (RATHSKELLER), from Latin *cella,* storeroom, chamber. **5.** Suffixed form **kel-yo-.* CILIUM, SEEL; SUPERCILIOUS, from Latin *cilium,* lower eyelid.
IV. Lengthened-grade form **kēl-ā-.* CONCEAL, from Latin *cēlāre,* to hide. [Pokorny 4. *ḱel-* 553.]

kel-[2]. Important derivatives are *hill, excel, culminate, colonel,* and *column.*

kel-[2]. To be prominent; hill. **1.** Zero-grade form **kl̥-.* **a.** HILL, from Old English *hyll,* hill, from suffixed Germanic form **hul-ni-;* **b.** HOLM, from Old Norse *hōlmr,* islet in a bay, meadow, from suffixed Germanic form **hul-ma-.* **2.** Suffixed form **kel-d-.* EXCEL, from Latin *excellere,* to raise up, elevate, also to be eminent (*ex-,* up out of; see **eghs**). **3.** O-grade form **kol-.* **a.** COLOPHON, from Greek *kolophōn,* summit; **b.** suffixed form **kol(u)men-.* CULMINATE, from Latin *culmen,* top, summit; **c.** extended and suffixed form **kolumnā.* COLONEL, COLONNADE, COLUMN, from Latin *columna,* a projecting object, column. [Pokorny 1. *kel-* 544.]

kelə-[1]. Important derivatives are *lee, chafe, caldron, chowder, scald*[1], and *calorie.*

kelə-[1]. Warm. Variant **klē-,* contracted from **kleə-.* **1.** Suffixed variant form **klē-wo-.* **a.** LEE, from Old English *hlēo, hlēow,* covering, protection (as from cold); **b.** LUKEWARM, from Old English *-hlēow,* warm. Both **a** and **b** from Germanic **hlēwaz.* **2.** Suffixed zero-grade form **kl̥ə-ē-.* **a.** CALENTURE, CHAFE; DECALESCENCE, INCALESCENT, NONCHALANT, RECALESCENCE, from Latin *calēre,* to be warm; **b.** CALDRON, CAUDLE, (CHOWDER); SCALD[1], from Latin derivative adjective *calidus,* warm. **3.** Suffixed zero-grade form **kl̥ə-os-.* CALORIC, CALORIE; CALORECEPTOR, CALORIFIC, CALORIMETER, CALORIMETRY, from Latin *calor,* heat. [Pokorny 1. *ḱel-* 551.]

kelə-[2]. Important derivatives are *claim, clamor, acclaim, exclaim, reclaim, haul, council, calendar, clear, declare,* and *class.*

kelə-[2]. To shout.
I. Variant form **klā-* (< **klaə-*). **1.** LOW[2], from Old English *hlōwan,* to roar, low, from Germanic **hlō-.* **2.** Suffixed form **klā-mā-.* CLAIM, CLAMANT, CLAMOR; ACCLAIM, DECLAIM, EXCLAIM, PROCLAIM, RECLAIM, from Latin *clāmāre,* to call, cry out.
II. O-grade form **kolə-.* **a.** KEELHAUL, from Middle Dutch *halen,* to haul, pull (? < "to call together, summon"); **b.** HALE[2], HAUL, from Old French *haler,* to haul. Both **a** and **b** from Germanic **halōn,* to call.
III. Zero-grade form **kl̥ə-* (> **kal-*). **1.** Suffixed form **kal-yo-.* CONCILIATE, COUNCIL, from Latin *concilium,* a meeting, gathering (< "a calling together"; *con-,* together; see **kom**). **2.** Suffixed form **kal-end-.* CALENDAR, CALENDS, from Latin *kalendae,* the calends, the first day of the month, when it was publicly announced on which days the nones and ides of that month would fall. **3.** Suffixed form **kal-e-.* ECCLESIA, PARACLETE, from Greek *kalein* (variant *klē-*), to call. **4.** Suffixed form **kal-ā-.* INTERCALATE, NOMENCLATOR, from Latin *calāre,* to call, call out. **5.** Suffixed form **kl̥ə-ro-* or suffixed variant form **klaə-ro-* contracted to **klā-ro-.* CLEAR, GLAIR; CHIAROSCURO, CLAIRVOYANT, DECLARE, ÉCLAIR, (ECLAIRCISSEMENT), from Latin *clārus,* bright, clear.
IV. Possibly extended zero-grade form **kl̥d-,* becoming **klad-* in suffixed form **klad-ti-.* CLASS, from Latin *classis,* summons, division of citizens for military draft, hence army, fleet, also class in general. [Pokorny 6. *kel-* 548.]

ken-. An important derivative is *recent.*

ken-. Fresh, new, young. **1.** Suffixed form **ken-t-.* RECENT, from Latin *recēns,* young, fresh, new (*re-,* again; see **re-**). **2.** Suffixed zero-grade form **kn̥-yo-.* -CENE; CAINOTOPHOBIA, CENOZOIC, KAINITE, from Greek *kainos,* new, fresh. [Pokorny 3. *ken-* 563.]

kenk-. Important derivatives are *cinch, precinct,* and *succinct.*

kenk-. To gird, bind. Variant form **keng-.* CINCH, CINCTURE, CINGULUM; ENCEINTE[1], ENCEINTE[2], PRECINCT, SHINGLES, SUCCINCT, from Latin *cingere,* to gird. [Pokorny 1. *kenk-* 565.]

kens-. Important derivatives are *censor* and *census.*

kens-. To proclaim, speak solemnly. Form **kens-ē-.* CENSOR, CENSUS; RECENSION, from Latin *cēnsēre,* to judge, assess, estimate, tax. [Pokorny *ḱens-* 566.]

kent-. Important derivatives are *center* and *eccentric.*

kent-. To prick, jab. **1.** CENTER; AMNIOCENTESIS, DICENTRA, ECCENTRIC, from Greek *kentein,* to prick. **2.** Suffixed form **kent-to-.* CESTUS[1], from Greek *kestos,* belt, girdle. [Pokorny *ḱent-* 567.]

ker-[1]. Important derivatives are *horn, cornea, corner, cornet, Capricorn, unicorn, hornet, reindeer, cranium, migraine, cheer, carrot, cervix, carat, rhinoceros,* and *cerebrum.*

ker-[1]. Horn, head; with derivatives referring to horned animals, horn-shaped objects, and projecting parts.
I. Zero-grade form **kr̥-.* **1.** Suffixed form **kr̥-n-.* **a.** *(i)* HORN, (HORNBEAM), from Old English *horn,* horn; *(ii)* ALPENHORN, ALTHORN, FLÜGELHORN, HORNBLENDE, from Old High German *horn,* horn. Both *(i)* and *(ii)* from Germanic **hurnaz;* **b.** CORN[2], CORNEA, CORNEOUS, CORNER, CORNET, CORNICULATE, CORNU; BICORNUATE, CAPRICORN, CORNIFICATION, LAMELLICORN, LONGICORN, TRICORN, UNICORN, from Latin *cornū,* horn. **2.** Suffixed and extended form **kr̥s-n-.* HORNET, from Old English *hyrnet,* hornet, from Germanic **hurznuta-.* **3.** Suffixed form **kr-ei-.* **a.** REINDEER, from Old Norse *hreinn,* reindeer, from Germanic **hraina-;* **b.** RINDERPEST, from Old High German *hrind,* ox, from Germanic **hrinda-.* **4.** Suffixed extended form **kr̥əs-no-.* CRANIUM; MIGRAINE, OLECRANON, from Greek *kranion,* skull, upper part of the head. **5.** Suffixed form **kr̥-ə-.* **a.** CHARIVARI; CHEER, from Greek *karē, kara,* head; **b.** CAROTID, from Greek *karoun,* to stupefy, be stupefied (< "to feel heavy-headed"); **c.** CARROT, from Greek *karōton,* carrot (from its hornlike shape). **6.** Possibly extended form **krī-.* CRIOSPHINX, from Greek *krios,* ram.
II. Suffixed form **ker-wo-.* **1.** CERVINE, SERVAL, from Latin *cervus,* deer. **2.** CERVIX, from Latin *cervīx,* neck.
III. Extended and suffixed form **keru-do-.* **a.** HART, from Old English *heorot,* hart, stag; **b.** HARTEBEEST, from Middle Dutch *hert,* deer, hart. Both **a** and **b** from Germanic **herutaz.*
IV. Extended form **kerəs-.* **1.** CARAT, CERASTES, KERATO-; CERATODUS, CHELICERA, CLADOCERAN, KERATIN, MONOCEROS, RHINOCEROS, TRICERATOPS, from Greek *keras,* horn. **2.** SIRDAR, from Persian *sar,* head. **3.** Suffixed form **kerəs-ro.* CEREBELLUM, CEREBRUM, SAVELOY, from Latin *cerebrum,* brain.
V. Extended o-grade form **koru-.* **1.** CORYMB, from Greek *korumbos,* uppermost point (< "head"). **2.** CORYPHAEUS, from Greek *koruphē,* head. **3.** Suffixed form **koru-do-.* CORYDALIS, from Greek *korudos,* crested lark. **4.** Suffixed form **koru-nā.* CORYNEBACTERIUM, from Greek *korunē,* club, mace. [Pokorny 1. *ḱer-* 574.]

ker-[2]. Important derivatives are *cereal, create, Creole, crescent, crew*[1], *concrete, decrease, increase, recruit,* and *sincere.*

ker-[2]. To grow. **1.** Suffixed form **ker-es-.* CEREAL, CERES, from Latin *Cerēs,* goddess of agriculture, especially the growth of grain. **2.** Extended form **krē-* (< **kreə-*). **a.** suffixed form **krē-yā-*. CREATE, CREOLE; PROCREATE, from Latin *creāre,* to bring forth, create, produce (< "to cause to grow); **b.** suffixed form **krē-sko-*. CRESCENDO, CRESCENT, CREW[1]; ACCRUE, (CONCRESCENCE), CONCRETE, DECREASE, EXCRESCENCE, INCREASE, RECRUIT, from Latin *crēscere,* to grow, increase. **3.** Suffixed o-grade form **kor-wo-*, "growing," adolescent. DIOSCURI, HYPOCORISM, from Greek *kouros, koros,* boy, son, and *korē,* girl. **4.** Compound **sm̥-kēro-*, "of one growth" (**sm̥-*, same, one; see **sem-**[1]). SINCERE, from Latin *sincērus,* pure, clean. [Pokorny 2. *k̂er-* 577.]

ker-[3]. Important derivatives are *hearth, carbon, cremate,* and *ceramic.*

ker-[3]. Heat, fire. **1.** Suffixed form **ker-tā*. HEARTH, from Old English *heorth,* hearth, from Germanic **herthō*. **2.** Zero-grade form **kr̥-*. **a.** CARBON, CARBUNCLE, from Latin *carbō,* charcoal, ember; **b.** extended form **krem-*. CREMATE, from Latin *cremāre,* to burn. **3.** Possibly suffixed and extended form **kerə-mo-*. CERAMIC, from Greek *keramos,* potter's clay, earthenware. **4.** Possibly variant extended form **krās-*. CRASH[2], from Russian *krasit',* to color. [Pokorny 3. *ker(ə)-* 571.]

kerd-. Important derivatives are *heart, cordial, courage, quarry*[1]*, accord, discord, record, cardiac, credence, credible, credit,* and *grant.*

kerd-. Heart. **1.** Suffixed form **kerd-en-*. HEART, from Old English *heorte,* heart, from Germanic **hertōn-*. **2.** Zero-grade form **kr̥d-*. **a.** CORDATE, CORDIAL, COURAGE, QUARRY[1]; ACCORD, CONCORD, CORDIFORM, DISCORD, MISERICORD, RECORD, from Latin *cor* (stem *cord-*), heart; **b.** suffixed form **kr̥d-yā-*. CARDIA, CARDIAC, CARDIO-; ENDOCARDIUM, EPICARDIUM, MYOCARDIUM, PERICARDIUM, from Greek *kardia,* heart, stomach, orifice. **3.** Possibly **kred-dhə-*, "to place trust" (an old religious term; **dhə-*, to do, place; see **dhē-**). CREDENCE, CREDIBLE, CREDIT, CREDO, CREDULOUS, GRANT; MISCREANT, RECREANT, from Latin *crēdere,* to believe. [Pokorny *k̂ered-* 579.]

kerə-. Important derivatives are *rare*[2]*, uproar,* and *crater.*

kerə-. To mix, confuse, cook. **1.** Variant form **krā-* (< **kraə-*). **a.** RARE[2], from Old English *hrēr,* lightly boiled, half-cooked, possibly from **kerə-**; **b.** UPROAR, from Middle Low German *rōr,* motion. Both **a** and **b** from Germanic **hrōr-*. **2.** Zero-grade form **kr̥ə-*. **a.** suffixed form **kr̥ə-ti-*. IDIOSYNCRACY; DYSCRASIA, from Greek *krasis,* a mixing; **b.** suffixed form **kr̥ə-ter-*. CRATER, from Greek *kratēr,* mixing vessel. [Pokorny *k̂erə-* 582.]

kerp-. Important derivatives are *harvest, carpet, excerpt,* and *scarce.*

kerp-. To gather, pluck, harvest. Variant **karp-*. **1.** HARVEST, from Old English *hærfest,* harvest, from Germanic **harbistaz.* **2.** CARPET; EXCERPT, (SCARCE), from Latin *carpere,* to pluck. **3.** -CARP, CARPEL, CARPO-, -CARPOUS, from Greek *karpos,* fruit. [In Pokorny 4. *sker-* 938.]

kers-. Important derivatives are *corridor, courier, course, current, cursive, cursor, concur, discourse, excursion, incur, intercourse, occur, recur, car, career, cargo, carry, charge,* and *carpenter.*

kers-. To run. Zero-grade form **kr̥s-*. **1.** CORRAL, CORRIDA, CORRIDOR, (CORSAIR), COURANTE, COURIER, COURSE, CURRENT, CURSIVE, CURSOR, CURULE; CONCOURSE, CONCUR, DECURRENT, DISCOURSE, EXCURSION, (HUSSAR), INCUR, INTERCOURSE, OCCUR, PRECURSOR, RECOURSE, RECUR, SUCCOR, from Latin *currere,* to run. **2.** Suffixed form **kr̥s-o-*. **a.** CAR, CAREER, CARGO, CARICATURE, CARIOLE, (CARK), CAROCHE, (CARRY), CHARGE, CHARIOT; (DISCHARGE), from Latin *carrus,* a two-wheeled wagon; **b.** CARPENTER, from Latin *carpentum,* a two-wheeled carriage. Both **a** and **b** from Gaulish *carros,* a wagon, cart. [Pokorny 2. *k̂ers-* 583.]

kes-. Important derivatives are *castrate, castle, caste, chaste, incest,* and *cashier.*

kes-. To cut. Variant **kas-*. **1.** Suffixed form **kas-tro-*. **a.** CASTRATE, from Latin *castrāre,* to castrate; **b.** ALCAZAR, CASTLE, from Latin *castrum,* fortified place, camp (perhaps "separated place"). **2.** Suffixed form **kas-to-*. CASTE, CHASTE; CASTIGATE, INCEST, from Latin *castus,* chaste, pure (< "cut off from or free of faults"). **3.** Suffixed (stative) form **kas-ē-*. CARET, from Latin *carēre,* "to be cut off from," lack. **4.** Extended geminated form **kasso-*. (CASHIER), QUASH[1], from Latin *cassus,* empty, void. [Pokorny *k̂es-* 586.]

keu-. Important derivatives are *hear, acoustic, show, scavenger,* and *sheen.*

keu-. Also **əkeu-**. To perceive, see, hear. O-grade form **əkou-*. **1.** Extended form **kous-*. **a.** *(i)* HEAR, from Old English *hīeran,* to hear; *(ii)* HEARKEN, from Old English *he(o)rcnian,* to harken. Both *(i)* and *(ii)* from Germanic **hausjan;* **b.** suffixed form **əkous-yo-*. ACOUSTIC, from Greek *akouein,* to hear. **2.** Variant **skou-*. **a.** *(i)* SHOW, from Old English *scēawian,* to look at; *(ii)* SCAVENGER, from Flemish *scauwen,* to look at; *(iii)* WELTANSCHAUUNG, from Old High German *scouwōn,* to look at. *(i), (ii),* and *(iii)* all from Germanic **skauwōn;* **b.** SCONE, from Middle Dutch *schoon,* beautiful, bright (< "conspicuous, attractive"); **c.** SHEEN, from Old English*sciēne,* bright, sheen, from Germanic **skauniz.* [Pokorny 1. *keu-* 587.]

keuə-. Important derivatives are *cave, cavern, concave, excavate, cumulus, accumulate,* and *church.*

keuə-. To swell; vault, hole.

I. O-grade form **kouə-*. **1.** Basic form **kouə-* becoming **kaw-*. CAVE, CAVERN, CAVETTO, CAVITY; CONCAVE, EXCAVATE, from Latin *cavus,* hollow. **2.** Suffixed form **kow-ilo-*.(-CELE[2]), CELIAC, -COEL, COELOM, from Greek *koilos,* hollow. **3.** Suffixed lengthened-grade form **kōw-o-*. CODEINE, from Greek *kōos,* hollow place, cavity.

II. Zero-grade form **kū-* (< **kuə-*). **1.** Suffixed shortened form **ku-m-olo*. CUMULATE, CUMULUS; ACCUMULATE, from Latin *cumulus,* heap, mass. **2.** Basic form **kū-*. **a.** suffixed form **kū-ro-*, "swollen," strong, powerful. CHURCH, (KIRK), KYRIE, from Greek *kurios* (vocative *kurie*), master, lord; **b.** suffixed form **kuw-eyo-*. CYMA; PSEUDOCYESIS, from Greek *kuein,* to swell, and derivative *kuma* (< **kū-mn̥*), " a swelling," wave; **c.** suffixed form **en-kū-yo-* (**en,* in; see **en-**). ENCEINTE[1]; from Latin *inciēns,* pregnant. [Pokorny 1. *k̂eu-* 592.]

klei-. Important derivatives are *decline, incline, recline, proclivity, lid, lean*[1]*, client, clinic, climax, climate,* and *ladder.*

klei-. To lean.

I. Full-grade form **klei-*. **1.** Suffixed form **klei-n-*. DECLINE, INCLINE, RECLINE, from Latin *-clīnāre,* to lean, bend. **2.** Suffixed form **klei-tro-*. CLITELLUM, from Latin *clītellae,* packsaddle, from diminutive of **clītra,* litter. **3.** Suffixed form **klei-wo-*. ACCLIVITY, DECLIVITY, PROCLIVITY, from Latin *clīvus,* a slope. **4.** Suffixed form **klei-tor-*, "incline, hill." CLITORIS, from Greek feminine diminutive *kleitoris.*

II. Zero grade form **kli-*. **1.** LID, from Old English *hlid,* cover, from Germanic **hlid-*, "that which bends over," cover. **2.** Suffixed form **kli-n-*. LEAN[1], from Old English *hlinian* and *hleonian,* to lean, from Germanic **hlinēn.* **3.** Suffixed form **kli-ent-*. CLIENT, from Latin *cliēns,* dependent, follower. **4.** Suffixed form **kli-to-*. (see **ous-**) Latin *auscultāre,* "to hold one's ear inclined," to listen to, from **aus-klit-ā-*. **5.** Suffixed form **kli-n-yo-*. -CLINAL, CLINE, (-CLINE), (-CLINIC), CLINO-; ACLINIC LINE, ANACLISIS, CLINANDRIUM, ENCLITIC, PERICLINE, (PROCLITIC), from Greek *klinein,* to lean. **6.** Lengthened form **klī-*. **a.** suffixed form **klī-n-ā*. CLINIC; DICLINOUS, MONOCLINOUS, TRICLINIUM, from Greek *klinē,* bed; **b.** suffixed form **klī-m-*. CLIMAX, from Greek *klimax,* ladder; **c.** suffixed form **klī-mn̥*. CLIMATE, from Greek *klima,* sloping surface of the earth.

III. Suffixed o-grade form **kloi-tr-*. LADDER, from Old English *hlǣd(d)er,* ladder, from Germanic **hlaidri-*. [Pokorny *klei-* 600.]

kleu-. Important derivatives are *leer, listen,* and *loud.*

kleu-. To hear.

I. Extended form **kleus-*. LEER, from Old English *hlēor,* cheek (< "side of the face" <-"ear"), from Germanic **hleuza-*.

II. Zero-grade form **klu-*. **1.** LIST[4], from Old English *hlystan,* to listen, from Germanic **hlustjan.* **2.** LISTEN, from Old English *hlysnan,* to listen, from Germanic **hlusinōn.* **3.** Suffixed lengthened form **klū-to-*. **a.** LOUD, from Old English *hlūd,* loud; **b.** ABLAUT, UMLAUT, from Old High German *hlūt,* sound. Both **a** and **b** from Germanic **hlūdaz,* "heard," loud.

III. Full-grade form **kleu-*. **1.** Suffixed form **klew-yo-*. CLIO, from Greek *kleiein,* to praise, tell. **2.** Suffixed form **klew-es-*. HERCULES, from Latin *Herculēs,* from Greek *Hēraklēs, Hērakleēs.* **3.** Suffixed form **kleu-to-*. SAROD, from Old Iranian *srauta-*. [Pokorny 1. *k̂leu-* 605.]

ko-. Important derivatives are *he*[1]*, him, his, her, it, here, hence,* and *et cetera.*

ko-. Stem of demonstrative pronoun meaning "this."

I. Variant form **ki-*. **1.a.** HE[1], from Old English *hē,* he; **b.** HIM, from Old English *him,* him (dative of *hē*); **c.** HIS, from Old English *his,* his (genitive of *hē*); **d.** HER, from Old English *hire,* her (dative and genitive of *heo,* she); **e.** IT, from Old English *hit,* it (neuter of *hē*); **f.** HERE, from Old English *hēr,* here; **g.** HENCE, from Old English *heonane, heonon,* from here. **a, b, c, d, e, f,** and **g** all from Germanic **hi-*, **2.** Suffixed form **ki-tro-*. HITHER, from Old English *hider,* hither, from Germanic **hi-thra-*. **3.** Suffixed form **ki-s*. CIS-, from Latin *cis,* on this side of.

II. Variant form **ke-*. **1.** Preposed in **ke-etero-* (**e-tero-* , a second time, again; see **i-**). ET CETERA, from Latin *cēterus* (neuter plural *cētera*), the other part, that which remains. **2.** (see **nu-**) Postposed in Latin *-ce.*

III. **1.** BEHIND, HIND[1], from Old English *behindan,* in the rear, behind (*bi,* at; see **ambhi**). **2.** HINTERLAND, from Old High German *hintar,* behind. **3.** HINDER[1], from Old English *hindrian,* to check, hinder, from Germanic derivative verb **hindrōn,* to keep back. **1, 2,** and **3** all from Germanic root **hind-*, behind, attributed by some to this root (but more likely of obscure origin). [Pokorny 1. *ko-* 609.]

kō-. An important derivative is *cone.*

kō-. To sharpen, whet. Contracted from **koə-*. **1.** Suffixed extended form **koəi-no-*. HONE[1], from Old English *hān,* stone, from Germanic **hainō.* **2.** CONE, CONIC; CONIFER, CONODONT, from Greek *kōnos,* cone, conical object (< "a sharp-pointed object"), perhaps from **kō-**. [Pokorny *k̂ēi-* 541.]

kob-. Important derivatives are *happen, happy, hapless,* and *mishap.*

kob-. To suit, fit, succeed. HAP, (HAPPEN), (HAPPY); (HAPLESS), (MISHAP), from Old Norse *happ,* chance, good luck, from Germanic **hap-*. [Pokorny *kob-* 610.]

kom. Important derivatives are *enough, co-, contra-, contrary, counter*[1]*, country,* and *encounter.*

kom. Beside, near, by, with. **1.** ENOUGH, GEMOT, HANDIWORK, YCLEPT; WITENAGEMOT, from Old English *ge-*, with, also participial, collective, and intensive prefix, from Germanic **ga-*, together, with (collective and intensive prefix and marker of the past participle). **2.** CUM; COONCAN, from Latin *cum, co-*, with. **3.** (CO-), COM-, from Old Latin *com,* with (collective and intensive prefix). **4.** (see **merg-**) British Celtic **kombrogos,* fellow countryman, from Celtic **kom-*, collective prefix. **5.** Suffixed form **kom-trā*. (CON[1]), CONTRA-, CONTRARY, (COUNTER[1]), COUNTER-, COUNTRY; ENCOUNTER, from Latin *contrā,* against, opposite. **6.** Suffixed form **kom-yo-*. COENO-; CENOBITE, EPICENE, KOINE, from Greek *koinos,* common, shared. **7.** Reduced form **ko-* (see **gher-**[1]**, mei-**[1]**, smei-**). [Pokorny *kom* 612.]

konk-. Important derivatives are *hang* and *hinge.*

konk-. To hang. **1.a.** HANG, from Old English *hōn,* to hang; **b.** HANKER, from Dutch (dialectal) *hankeren,* to long for; **c.** HINGE, from Middle English *he(e)ng, hinge,* hinge, possibly related (ultimately from the base of Old English *hangian,* to hang). **a**, **b**, and **c** all from Germanic **hanhan* (transitive), *hangēn* (intransitive), hang. **2.** Suffixed form **konk-t-ā-*. CUNCTATION, from Latin *cūnctārī,* to delay. [Pokorny *k̑enk-* 566, *k̑onk-* 614.]

koro-. Important derivatives are *harbor, harbinger, herald, harry,* and *harangue.*

koro-. War; also war-band, host, army.
I. 1. HERIOT, from Old English *here,* army. **2.** ARRIÈRE-BAN, from Old French *herban,* a summoning to military service (*ban,* proclamation, summons; see **bhā-**[2]). **3.a.** HARBOR, from Old English *herebeorg,* lodging; **b.** HARBINGER, from Old French *herberge,* lodging. Both **a** and **b** from Germanic compound **harja-bergaz,* "army hill," hill-fort, later shel-ter, lodging, army quarters (**bergaz,* hill; see **bhergh-**[2]). **4.** HERALD, from Anglo-Norman *herald,* from Germanic compound **harja-waldaz,* "army commander" (**wald-,* rule, power; see **wal-**). **5.** HARNESS, from Old French *harneis,* harness, from Germanic compound **harja-nestam,* "army provisions" (**nestam,* food for a journey; see **nes-**[1]). **1, 2, 3, 4,** and **5** all from Germanic **harjaz,* army.
II. HARRY, from Old English *hergian,* to ravage, plunder, raid, from Germanic denominative **harjōn.*
III. HARANGUE, from Old Italian *aringo, arringa,* public square, from Germanic compound **hari-hring,* assembly, "host-ring" (**hringaz,* ring; see **sker-**[2]). [Pokorny *koro-s* 615.]

kost-. Important derivatives are *coast, cutlet,* and *accost.*

kost-. Bone. Probably related to **ost-**. COAST, COSTA, COSTARD, COSTREL, CUESTA, CUTLET; ACCOST, INTERCOSTAL, STERNOCOSTAL, from Latin *costa,* rib, side. [Pokorny *kost-* 616.]

krei-. Important derivatives are *riddle*[1]*, garble, crime, criminal, discriminate, certain, concern, decree, discern, excrement, secret, crisis, critic,* and *hypocrisy.*

krei-. To sieve, discriminate, distinguish. **1.** Basic form with variant instrumental suffixes. **a.** suffixed form **krei-tro-*. RIDDLE[1], from Old English *hridder, hriddel,* sieve, from Germanic **hridra-,* a sieve; **b.** suffixed form **krei-dhro-*. CRIBRIFORM, GARBLE, from Latin *crībrum,* a sieve. **2.** Suffixed form **krei-men-*. **a.** CRIME, (CRIMINAL); RECRIMINATE, from Latin *crīmen,* judgment, crime; **b.** DISCRIMINATE, from Latin *discrīmen,* distinction (*dis-,* apart). **3.** Suffixed zero-grade form **kri-no-* (participial form **kri-to-*). CERTAIN; CONCERN, DECREE, DISCERN, (EXCREMENT), EXCRETE, (INCERTITUDE), RECREMENT, SECERN, SECRET, from Latin *cernere* (perfect *crēvī;* past participle *crētus*), to sift, separate, decide. **4.** Suffixed zero-grade form **kri-n-yo-*. CRISIS, CRITIC, CRITERION; APOCRINE, DIACRITIC, ECCRINE, ENDOCRINE, EPICRITIC, EXOCRINE, HEMATOCRIT, HYPOCRISY, from Greek *krinein,* to separate, decide, judge (> *krinesthai,* to explain). [Pokorny 4. *sker-,* Section II. 945.]

kreuə-. Important derivatives are *raw, pancreas, crude,* and *cruel.*

kreuə-. Raw flesh. **1.** Lengthened-grade form **krēw-*. RAW, from Old English *hrēaw,* raw, from Germanic **hrēwaz.* **2.** Suffixed form **krewə-s-*. CREATINE, CREODONT, CREOSOTE, PANCREAS, from Greek *kreas,* flesh. **3.** Suffixed zero-grade form **krū-do-* (< **kruə-do-*). **a.** CRUDE; ECRU, RECRUDESCE, from Latin *crūdus,* bloody, raw; **b.** CRUEL, from Latin *crūdēlis,* cruel. [Pokorny 1. A. *kreu-* 621.]

kreus-. Important derivatives are *crust, crustacean,* and *crystal.*

kreus-. To begin to freeze, form a crust. **1.** Suffixed zero-grade form **krus-to-*. **a.** CROUTON, CRUST, CRUSTACEAN, CRUSTACEOUS, CRUSTOSE; ENCRUST, from Latin *crusta,* crust; **b.** CRYSTAL, CRYSTALLINE, CRYSTALLO-, from Greek *krustallos,* ice, crystal. **2.** Suffixed zero-grade form **krus-es-*. CRYO-, from Greek *kruos,* icy cold, frost. [Pokorny 1. B. *kreu-* 621.]

ksun. Important derivatives are *syn-* and *sputnik.*

ksun. Preposition and preverb meaning "with." **1.** SYN-, from Greek *sun, xun,* together, with. **2.** Basic form **su(n)-*. **a.** SOVIET, from Old Russian compound *sŭvětŭ,* assembly, from *sŭ(n)-,* with, together; **b.** SPUTNIK, from Russian *sputnik,* fellow traveler, sputnik (see **pent-**), from *so-, s-,* with, together, from *sŭ(n).* [In Pokorny 2. *sem-* 902.]

kʷe. Derivatives are *sesqui-* and *ubiquity.*

kʷe. And (enclitic). SESQUI-, UBIQUITY, from Latin *-que,* and. [Pokorny *k̯ʷe* 635.]

kʷei-[1]**.** Important derivatives are *pain, penalty, punish, impunity,* and *subpoena.*

kʷei-[1]**.** To pay, atone, compensate. Suffixed o-grade form **kʷoi-nā.* PAIN, PENAL, (PENALTY), PINE[2], PUNISH; IMPUNITY, PENOLOGY, (PUNITORY), (REPINE), SUBPOENA, from Greek *poinē,* fine, penalty. [Pokorny *k̯ʷei-(t-)* 636.]

kʷei-[2]**.** Important derivatives are *cheetah, poem,* and *poet.*

kʷei-[2]**.** To pile up, build, make. O-grade form **kʷoi-*. **a.** CHEETAH, from Sanskrit *kāyaḥ,* body; **b.** suffixed form **kʷoi-wo-,* making, in denominative verb **kʷoiw-eyo-*. POEM, POESY, POET, POETIC, -POIESIS, -POIETIC; EPOPEE, MYTHOPOEIC, ONOMATOPOEIA, PHARMACOPOEIA, PROSOPOPEIA, from Greek *poiein,* to make, create. [Pokorny 2. *k̯ʷei-* 637.]

kʷeiə-. Important derivatives are *while, tranquil, coy, quiet,* and *acquiesce.*

kʷeiə-. To rest, be quiet.
I. Suffixed zero-grade variant form **kʷī-lo-* (< **kʷiə-lo-*). **1.a.** WHILE, from Old English *hwīl,* while; **b.** WHILOM, from Old English *hwīlum,* sometimes. Both **a** and **b** from Germanic **hwīlō.* **2.** TRANQUIL, from Latin *tranquillus,* tranquil (*trāns,* across, beyond; see **terə-**[2]), possibly from **kʷeiə-**.
II. Variant form **kʷyē-* (< **kʷyeə-*). COY, QUIET; ACQUIESCE, REQUIEM, REQUIESCAT, from Latin *quiēs,* quiet, *requiēs,* rest, and *requiēscere,* to rest. [Pokorny *k̯ʷei-* 638.]

kweit-. Important derivatives are *white* and *wheat.*

kweit-. White; to shine. **1.** Suffixed form **kweit-o-*. **a.** WHITE, from Old English *hwīt,* white; **b.** WITLOOF, from Middle Dutch *wit,* white; **c.** WHITING[2], from Middle Dutch *wijting,* whiting; **d.** EDELWEISS, from Old High German *hwīz, wīz,* white. **a, b, c,** and **d** all from Germanic **hwītaz.* **2.** Suffixed o-grade form **kwoit-yo-*. WHEAT, from Old English *hwǣte,* wheat (from the fine white flour it yields), from Germanic **hwait-jaz.* [Pokorny 3. *k̑uei-* 628.]

kʷel-[1]**.** Important derivatives are *colony, cult, cultivate, culture, wheel, cycle, cyclone, bicycle, collar, pole*[1]*, pulley,* and *bucolic.*

kʷel-[1]**.** To revolve, move around, sojourn, dwell.
I. Basic form **kʷel-*. COLONY, CULT, CULTIVATE, (CULTURE); INCULT, INQUILINE, from Latin *colere,* to till, cultivate, inhabit.
II. Suffixed form **kʷel-es-*. TELIC, (TELIUM), TELO-; ENTELECHY, TALISMAN, TELEOLOGY, (TELEOST), TELEUTOSPORE, from Greek *telos,* "completion of a cycle," consummation, perfection, end, result.
III. Suffixed reduplicated form **kʷ(e)-kʷl-o-,* circle. **1.** WHEEL, from Old English *hwēol, hweogol,* wheel, from Germanic **hwewlaz.* **2.** CYCLE, CYCLO-, CYCLOID, CYCLONE, CYCLOSIS; (BICYCLE), ENCYCLICAL, EPICYCLE, from Greek *kuklos,* circle, wheel. **3.** CHAKRA, CHUKKER, from Sanskrit *cakram,* circle, wheel. **4.** Metathesized form **kʷe-lkʷ-o-*. CHARKHA, from Old Persian **carka-*.
IV. O-grade form **kʷol-*. **1.** Suffixed form **kʷol-so-,* "that on which the head turns," neck. **a.** *(i)* HAWSE, from Old Norse *hāls,* neck, ship's bow; *(ii)* RINGHALS, from Middle Dutch *hals,* neck; *(iii)* HAUBERK, from Old French *hauberc,* hauberk, from Germanic compound **h(w)als-berg-,* "neck-protector," gorget (**bergan,* to protect; see **bhergh-**[1]). *(i), (ii),* and *(iii)* all from Germanic **h(w)alsaz;* **b.** COL, COLLAR, COLLET, CULLET; ACCOLADE, DECOLLATE[1], DÉCOLLETÉ, MACHICOLATE, (MACHICOLATION), TORTICOLLIS, from Latin *collum,* neck. **2.** Suffixed form **kʷol-ā.* -COLOUS; PRATINCOLE, from Latin *-cola* and *incola,* inhabitant (*in-,* in; see **en**). **3.** Suffixed form **kʷol-o-*. **a.** ANCILLARY, from Latin *anculus,* "he who bustles about," servant (*an-,* short for *ambi-,* around, about; see **ambhi**); **b.** POLE[1], PULLEY, from Greek *polos,* axis of a sphere; **c.** BUCOLIC, from Greek *boukolos,* cowherd, from *-kolos,* herdsman. **4.** Suffixed form **kwol-es-* (probably a blend of o-grade **kʷol-o-* and expected e-grade **kʷel-es-*). CALASH, from Slavic *kolo, koles-,* wheel. **5.** Suffixed o-grade form **kʷol-eno-*. (see **wes-**[3]) Old Iranian **vahā-carana-,* "sale-traffic," from **carana-,* trade, traffic. **6.** Suffixed zero-grade form **kʷl̥-i-*. PALIMPSEST, PALINDROME, PALINGENESIS, PALINODE, from Greek *palin,* again (< "revolving"). [Pokorny 1. *k̯ʷel-* 639.]

kʷel-[2]**.** Derivatives are *tele-* and *paleo-.*

kʷel-[2]**.** Far (in space and time). **1.** Lengthened-grade form **kʷēl-*. TELE-, from Greek *tēle,* far off. **2.** Suffixed zero-grade form **kʷl̥-ai.* PALEO-, from Greek *palai,* long ago. [Pokorny 2. *k̯ʷel-* 640.]

kʷent(h)-. Important derivatives are *pathetic, pathos,* and *sympathy.*

kʷent(h)-. To suffer. **1.** Suffixed form **kʷenth-es-*. NEPENTHE, from Greek *penthos,* grief. **2.** Zero-grade form **kʷn̥th-*. PATHETIC, PATHO-, PATHOS, -PATHY; APATHY, (PATHOGNOMONIC), SYMPATHY, from Greek *pathos,* suffering, passion, emotion, feelings. [Pokorny *k̯ʷenth-* 641.]

kʷer-. An important derivative is *karma.*

kʷer-. To make. **1.** SANSKRIT, from Sanskrit *karoti,* he makes. **2.** Suffixed form **kʷer-ōr* with dissimilated form **kʷel-ōr*. PELORIA, from Greek *pelōr,* monster (perhaps "that which does harm"). **3.** Suffixed form **kʷer-əs-*. TERA-; (TERATOCARCINOMA), TERATOGEN, TERATOID, TERATOMA, from Greek *teras,* monster. **4.** Suffixed form **kʷer-mn̥.* KARMA, from Sanskrit *karma,* act, deed. [Pokorny *k̯ʷer-* 641.]

kwes-. Important derivatives are *wheeze, quarrel*[1]*, querulous,* and *cyst.*

kwes-. To pant, wheeze. **1.** WHEEZE, from Old Norse *hvæsa,* to hiss, from Germanic **hwēsjan.* **2.** QUARREL[1], QUERULOUS, from Latin *querī,* to complain. **3.** Suffixed zero-grade form **kus-ti-*. CYST, CYSTO-, from Greek *kustis,* bladder, bag (< "bellows"). [Pokorny *k̑ues-* 631.]

kwēt-. Important derivatives are *squash*[2]*, discuss,* and *rescue.*

kwēt-. To shake. Zero-grade form **kwət-,* becoming **kwat-*. **a.** CASCARA, SCUTCH, SQUASH[2]; CONCUSS, DISCUSS, PERCUSS, RESCUE, SUCCUSSION, from Latin *quatere* (past participle *quassus,* in composition *-cussus*), to shake, strike; **b.** PASTE[1], from Greek *passein,* to sprinkle. [Pokorny *k̑uēt-* 632.]

kʷetwer-. Important derivatives are *four, forty, fourteen, quatrain, squad, square, quadri-, quadrant, quarantine, tetra-, trapezium, fourth, farthing, quart,* and *quarter.*

kʷetwer-. Four.
I. O-grade form **kʷetwor-*. **1.a.** FOUR, from Old English *fēower,* four; **b.** FORTY, from Old English *fēowertig,* forty; **c.** FOURTEEN, from Old English *fēowertēne,* fourteen (*-tēne,* ten; see **dekm̥**). **a, b,** and **c** all from Germanic **fe(d)wor-,* probably from **kʷetwor-*. **2.** QUATRAIN; CATER-CORNERED, QUATTROCENTO, from Latin *quattuor,* four. **3.** CZARDAS, from Old Iranian *cathwārō,* four.
II. Multiplicatives **kʷeturs, *kʷetrus,* and combining forms **kʷetur-, *kʷetru-*. **1.** CAHIER, (CARILLON), (CARNET), QUATERNARY, QUATERNION, QUIRE[1], from Latin *quater,* four times. **2.** CADRE, QUADRATE, QUADRILLE[1], QUARREL[2], QUARRY[2]; (SQUAD), SQUARE, TROCAR, from Latin *quadrum,* square. **3.** QUADRI-, from Latin *quadri-,* four. **4.** QUADRANT, from Latin *quadrāns,* a fourth part. **5.** QUARANTINE, from Latin *quadrāgintā,* forty (*-gintā,* ten times; see **dekm̥**). **6.** Variant form **kʷet(w)r̥-*. **a.** TETRA-, from Greek *tetra-,* four; **b.** TESSERA; DIATESSARON, from Greek *tessares, tettares* (genitive *tessarōn*), four; **c.** TETRAD, from Greek *tetras,* group of four; **d.** zero-grade form **kʷt(w)r̥-*. TRAPEZIUM, from Greek *tra-,* four.

III. Ordinal adjective *kʷetur-to-. **1.a.** FOURTH, from Old English *fēortha, fēowertha,* fourth; **b.** FIRKIN, from Middle Dutch *veerde,* fourth; **c.** FARTHING, from Old English *fēorthing, fēorthung,* fourth part of a penny. **a, b,** and **c** all from Germanic *fe(d)worthōn-. **2.** QUADRILLE[2], QUADROON, QUART, QUARTAN, QUARTER, QUARTO, from Latin *quārtus,* fourth, quarter. [Pokorny *kʷetu̯er-* 642.]

kʷo-. Important derivatives are *who, what, why, which, how, when, where, whether, neither, either, quorum, quip, quasi, quote, quotient, quantity, quality, neuter,* and *alibi.*

kʷo-. Also **kʷi-**. Stem of relative and interrogative pronouns. **1.a.** WHO, WHOSE, WHOM, from Old English *hwā, hwæs, hwǣm,* who, whose, whom, from Germanic personal pronouns *hwas, *hwasa, *hwam; **b.** WHAT, from Old English *hwæt,* what, from Germanic pronoun *hwat; **c.** WHY, from Old English *hwȳ,* why, from Germanic adverb *hwī; **d.** WHICH, from Old English *hwilc, hwelc,* which, from Germanic relative pronoun *hwa-līk- (*līk-, body, form; see **līk-**); **e.** HOW, from Old English *hū,* how, from Germanic adverb *hwō; **f.** *(i)* WHEN, from Old English *hwenne, hwanne,* when; *(ii)* WHENCE, from Old English *hwanon,* whence. Both *(i)* and *(ii)* from Germanic adverb *hwan-; **g.** WHITHER, from Old English *hwider,* whither, from Germanic adverb *hwithrē; **h.** WHERE, from Old English *hwǣr,* where, from Germanic adverb *hwar-. **a, b, c, d, e, f, g,** and **h** all from Germanic *hwa-, *hwi-. **2.a.** WHETHER; NEITHER, from Old English *hwæther, hwether,* which of two, whether; **b.** EITHER, from Old English *ǣghwæther, ǣther,* either, from Germanic phrase *aiwo gihwatharaz, "ever each of two" (*aiwo, *aiwi, ever; see **aiw-**; *gi- from *ga-, collective prefix; see **kom**). Both **a** and **b** from Germanic *hwatharaz. **3.** QUA, QUIBBLE, QUORUM, from Latin *quī* (genitive plural *quōrum*), who. **4.** HIDALGO, QUIDDITY, QUIDNUNC, QUIP, from Latin *quid,* what, something. **5.** QUASI, from Latin *quasi,* as if (*quam* + *sī,* if; see **swo-**), from *quam,* as, than, how. **6.** QUODLIBET, from Latin *quod,* what. **7.** QUOTE, QUOTIDIAN, QUOTIENT; ALIQUOT, from Latin *quot,* how many. **8.** QUONDAM, from Latin *quom,* when. **9.** COONCAN, from Latin *quem,* whom. **10.** QUANTITY, from Latin *quantus,* how great. **11.** QUALITY, from Latin *quālis,* of what kind. **12.** CUE[2], from Latin *quandō,* when (from *kʷām + -*dō,* to, til; see **de-**). **13.** NEUTER, from Latin *uter,* either of two. **14.** ALIBI, UBIQUITY, from Latin *ubi,* where, and *ibi,* there. **15.** CHEESE[3], from Old Persian *ciš-ciy, something (< *kʷid-kʷid). [Pokorny *kʷo-* 644.]

kwon-. Important derivatives are *cynic, hound, dachshund, canary, canine,* and *kennel*[1].

kwon-. Dog. **1.** CYNIC; CYNOSURE, PROCYON, QUINSY, from Greek *kuōn,* dog. **2.** Suffixed zero-grade form *kwn̥-to-. **a.** HOUND, from Old English *hund,* dog; **b.** DACHSHUND, from Old High German *hunt,* dog; **c.** KEESHOND, from Middle Dutch *hond,* dog. **a, b,** and **c** all from Germanic *hundaz. **3.** Nominative form *kwō. CORGI, from Welsh *ci,* dog. **4.** Variant *kan-i-. CANAILLE, CANARY, CANICULAR, CANINE, CHENILLE, KENNEL[1], from Latin *canis,* dog. [Pokorny *ku̯on-* 632.]

kʷrep-. Important derivatives are *midriff, corporal*[1]*, corporate, corporeal, corps, corpse, corpuscle, corsage, corset,* and *leprechaun.*

kʷrep-. Body. **1.** Suffixed form *kʷrep-es-. MIDRIFF, from Old English *hrif,* belly from Germanic *hrefiz-. **2.** Suffixed zero-grade form *kʷr̥p-es-. CORPORAL[1], CORPORAL[3], CORPORATE, CORPOREAL, CORPOSANT, CORPS, CORPSE, CORPULENCE, CORPUS, CORPUSCLE, CORSAGE, CORSE, CORSET; LEPRECHAUN, from Latin *corpus,* body, substance. [Pokorny 1. *krep-* 620.]

kʷr̥mi-. An important derivative is *crimson.*

kʷr̥mi-. Worm. Rhyme word to *wr̥mi-, worm (see **wer-**[2]). (CRIMSON), KERMES, from Arabic *qirmiz,* kermes, borrowed from Sanskrit compound *kr̥mi-ja-,* "(red dye) produced by worms" (*ja-,* produced; see **genə-**), from *kr̥mi-,* worm. [Pokorny *kʷr̥mi-* 649.]

laks-. A derivative is *lox*[1].

laks-. Salmon. Suffixed form *laks-o-. **a.** LOX[1], from Old High German *lahs,* salmon; **b.** GRAVLAX, from Swedish *lax,* salmon. Both **a** and **b** from Germanic *lahsaz. [Pokorny *lak-* 653.]

las-. Important derivatives are *lust, wanderlust,* and *lascivious.*

las-. To be eager, wanton, or unruly. **1.a.** LUST, from Old English *lust,* lust; **b.** WANDERLUST, from Old High German *lust,* desire; **c.** LIST[5], from Old English *lystan,* to please, satisfy a desire, from Germanic denominative verb *lustjan. **a, b,** and **c** all from suffixed Germanic zero-grade form *lustuz. **2.** Suffixed form *las-ko-. LASCIVIOUS, from Latin *lascīvus,* wanton, lustful. [Pokorny *las-* 654.]

lau-. An important derivative is *lucrative.*

lau-. Gain, profit. **1.** Suffixed form *lau-no-. GUERDON, from Old High German *lōn,* reward from Germanic *launam. **2.** Suffixed zero-grade form *lu-tlo-. LUCRATIVE, LUCRE, from Latin *lucrum,* gain, profit. [Pokorny *lāu-* 655.]

lē-. Important derivatives are *let*[1]*, liege, late, latter, last*[1]*, alas,* and *lenient.*

lē-. To let go, slacken. Contracted from *leə-. **I.** Extended form *lēd-. **1.a.** LET[1], from Old English *lǣtan,* to allow, leave undone, from Germanic *lētan; **b.** LIEGE, from Late Latin *laetus,* semifree colonist, from Germanic derivative *lēthigaz, freed. **2.** Zero-grade form *ləd-. **a.** LATE, LATTER, LAST[1], from Old English *læt,* late, with its comparative *lætra,* latter, and its superlative *latost,* last, from Germanic *lataz; **b.** LET[2], from Old English *lettan,* to hinder, impede (< "to make late"), from Germanic *latjan; **c.** suffixed form *ləd-to-. LASSITUDE; ALAS, from Latin *lassus,* tired, weary.

II. Suffixed basic form *lē-ni-. LENIENT, LENIS, LENITIVE, LENITY, from Latin *lēnis,* soft, gentle. [Pokorny 3. *lē(i)-* 666.]

leb-. Important derivatives are *lip* and *labial.*

leb-. Lip. **1.** LIP, from Old English *lippa,* lip, from Germanic *lep-. **2.** Variant form *lab-. **a.** suffixed form *lab-yo-. LABIAL, LABIUM, from Latin *labium,* lip; **b.** suffixed form *lab-ro-. LABELLUM, LABRET, LABRUM, from Latin *labrum,* lip. [Pokorny *lĕb-* 655.]

leg-. Important derivatives are *leech*[1]*, lectern, lecture, legend, legible, legion, lesson, coil*[1]*, collect*[1]*, diligent, elect, intelligent, neglect, sacrilege, select, lexicon, catalog, dialect, dialogue, eclectic, legal, legitimate, loyal, legislator, privilege, legacy, allege, colleague, delegate, relegate, logic, analogous, apology, epilogue, logarithm, prologue,* and *syllogism.*

leg-. To collect; with derivatives meaning "to speak." **1.** LEECH[1], from Old English *lǣce,* physician, from Germanic *lēkjaz, enchanter, one who speaks magic words, perhaps from **leg-**. **2.** LECTERN, (LECTION), LECTURE, LEGEND, LEGIBLE, LEGION, LESSON; (COIL[1]), COLLECT[1], DILIGENT, ELECT, INTELLIGENT, NEGLECT, PRELECT, SACRILEGE, SELECT, SORTILEGE, from Latin *legere,* to gather, choose, pluck, read. **3.** LEXICON, LOGION, -LOGUE, -LOGY; ALEXIA, ANALECTS, ANTHOLOGY, CATALOG, DIALECT, (DIALOGUE), DYSLEXIA, ECLECTIC, HOROLOGE, PROLEGOMENON, from Greek *legein,* to gather, speak, with *logos,* speech (see **6**). **4.** Suffixed form *leg-no-. LIGNEOUS, LIGNI-, from Latin *lignum,* wood, firewood (< "that which is gathered"). **5.** Possibly lengthened-grade form *lēg-. **a.** LEGAL, LEGIST, LEGITIMATE, LEX, LOYAL; LEGISLATOR, PRIVILEGE, from Latin *lēx,* law (? < "collection of rules"); **b.** LEGACY, LEGATE; COLLEAGUE, (COLLEGIAL), DELEGATE, RELEGATE, from Latin denominative *lēgāre,* to depute, commission, charge (< "to engage by contract"); but possibly from **legh-**). **6.** Suffixed o-grade form *log-o-. LOGIC, LOGISTIC, LOGO-, LOGOS, -LOGY; ANALOGOUS, APOLOGUE, APOLOGY, DECALOGUE, EPILOGUE, HOMOLOGOUS, LOGARITHM, PARALOGISM, PROLOGUE, SYLLOGISM, from Greek *logos,* speech, word, reason. [Pokorny *leĝ-* 658.]

legh-. Important derivatives are *lie*[1]*, lay*[1]*, ledge, ledger, lair, beleaguer, lees, low*[1]*, litter, law, fellow,* and *outlaw.*

legh-. To lie, lay. **1.** Suffixed form *legh-yo-. **a.** LIE[1], from Old English *licgan,* to lie, from Germanic *ligjan; **b.** *(i)* LAY[1], LEDGE, (LEDGER), from Old English *lecgan,* to lay; *(ii)* BELAY, from Old English *belecgan,* to cover, surround (*be-,* over; see **ambhi**). Both *(i)* and *(ii)* from Germanic *lagjan. **2.** Suffixed form *legh-ro-. **a.** LAIR, from Old English *leger,* lair; **b.** LEAGUER[1]; BELEAGUER, from Middle Dutch *leger,* lair, camp; **c.** LAAGER, LAGER; (STALAG), from Old High German *legar,* bed, lair. **a, b,** and **c** all from Germanic *legraz. **3.** LEES, from Medieval Latin *lia,* sediment, from Celtic *leg-yā-. **4.** Lengthened-grade form *lēgh-. LOW[1], from Old Norse *lāgr,* low, from Germanic *lēgaz, "lying flat," low. **5.** Suffixed form *legh-to-. COVERLET, LITTER; WAGON-LIT, from Latin *lectus,* bed. **6.** Suffixed o-grade form *logh-o-. **a.** LAW; BYLAW, (DANELAW), from Old Norse *lagu, *lag-,* law, "that which is set down"; **b.** FELLOW, from Old Norse *lag,* a laying down; **c.** OUTLAW, from Old Norse *lög,* law; **d.** ANLAGE, VORLAGE, from Old High German *lāga,* act of laying. **a, b, c,** and **d** all from Germanic *lagam. **7.** LAGAN, from Old Norse *lögn,* dragnet (< "that which is laid down"), from Germanic *lag-inō-. **8.** Suffixed o-grade form *logh-o-. LOCHIA, from Greek *lokhos,* childbirth, place for lying in wait. [Pokorny *legh-* 658, 2. *lēgh-* 660.]

legʷh-. Important derivatives are *light*[2]*, leaven, lever, levity, alleviate, carnival, elevate, relieve, leprechaun,* and *lung.*

legʷh-. Light, having little weight. **1.** Suffixed form *legʷh-t-. **a.** LIGHT[2], from Old English *līht, lēoht,* light; **b.** LIGHTER[2], from Old English *līhtan,* to lighten. Both **a** and **b** from Germanic *līht(j)az. **2.** Suffixed form *legʷh-u-i-. LEAVEN, LEVER, LEVITY; ALLEVIATE, CARNIVAL, ELEVATE, LEGERDEMAIN, (MEZZO-RELIEVO), RELIEVE, from Latin *levis,* light, with its derivative *levāre,* to lighten, raise. **3.** Variant form *lagʷh-. LEPRECHAUN, from Old Irish *lū-,* small. **4.** Nasalized form *l(e)ngʷh-. LUNG, from Old English *lungen,* lungs (from their lightness), from Germanic *lung-. **5.** (see **lei-**) Latin *oblīvīscī,* to forget, attributed by some to this root, is more likely from **lei-**. [Pokorny *legᵘ̯h-* 660.]

lei-. Important derivatives are *slime, slippery, slick, loam, slight, slip*[1]*, oblivion,* and *liniment.*

lei-. Also **slei-**. Slimy. **1.a.** SLIME, from Old English *slīm,* slime; **b.** SLIPPERY, from Old English *slipor,* slippery; **c.** SLICK, from Old English *slice, smooth; **d.** LIME[3], from Old English *līm,* cement, birdlime; **e.** LOAM, from Old English *lām,* loam; **f.** SLIGHT, from Middle English *slight,* slender, probably from a Scandinavian source akin to Old Norse *slēttr,* smooth, sleek; **g.** SLIP[1], from Middle English *slippen,* to slip, probably from a source akin to Middle Dutch and Middle Low German *slippen,* to slip, slip away; **h.** SCHLEP, from Middle Low German *slēpen,* to drag. **a, b, c, d, e, f, g,** and **h** all from Germanic *slī- with various extensions. **2.** Suffixed form *lei-mo-. LIMACINE, LIMICOLINE, from Latin *līmus,* slime. **3.** Suffixed form *lei-w-. OBLIVION, OUBLIETTE, from Latin *oblīvīscī,* to forget (< "to wipe, let slip from the mind"; *ob-,* away; see **epi**). **4.** Extended form *(s)leiə-, with metathesis *(s)leə(i)-. **a.** Zero-grade form with nasal infix *li-n-ə-. LINIMENT, from Latin *linere* (perfect *lēvī*), to anoint; **b.** suffixed zero-grade form *lī- (< *liə-). LITOTES, from Greek *litos,* plain, simple; **c.** suffixed metathesized form *leə-wo-, whence *lē-wo-. LEVIGATE, from Latin *lēvis,* smooth. [Pokorny 3. *lei-* 662.]

leid-. Important derivatives are *ludicrous, allude, collude, delude, elude, illusion, interlude,* and *prelude.*

leid-. To play, jest. Suffixed o-grade form *loid-o-. LUDIC, LUDICROUS; ALLUDE, COLLUDE, DELUDE, ELUDE, ILLUSION, INTERLUDE, PRELUDE, PROLUSION, from Latin *lūdus,* game, play, with its derivative *lūdere,* to play (but both words may possibly be from Etruscan). [Pokorny *leid-* 666.]

leig-. Important derivatives are *league*[1]*, liable, lien, alloy, ally, furl, oblige, rally,* and *rely.*

leig-. To bind. **1.** LEECH[2], from Middle Low German *līk,* leech line, from Germanic *līk-. **2.** Suffixed agent noun *l(e)ig-tor-. LICTOR, from Latin *lictor,* lictor. **3.** Zero-grade form **lig-ā-.* LEAGUE[1], LEGATO, LIABLE, LIEN, LIGASE, LIGATE, LIGATURE; ALLOY, (ALLY), COLLIGATE, FURL, OBLIGE, (RALLY[1]), (RELIGION), RELY, from Latin *ligāre,* to bind. [Pokorny 4. *leig-* 668.]

leigh-. Important derivatives are *lick* and *lecher.*

leigh-. To lick. **1.** ELECTUARY, LICHEN, from Greek *leikhein,* to lick. **2.** Zero-grade form **ligh-.* **a.** LICK, from Old English *liccian,* to lick; **b.** LECHER, from Old French *lechier,* to live in debauchery. Both **a** and **b** from Germanic **likkōn.* **3.** Nasalized zero-grade form **li-n-gh-.* ANILINGUS, CUNNILINGUS, from Latin *lingere,* to lick. [Pokorny *leigh-* 668.]

leikʷ-. Important derivatives are *eclipse, ellipsis, lend, loan, delinquent, derelict,* and *relinquish.*

leikʷ-. To leave. **1.** Basic form **leikʷ-.* ECLIPSE, ELLIPSIS, from Greek *leipein,* to leave. **2.** O-grade form **loikʷ-.* **a.** suffixed form **loikʷ-nes-.* LOAN, from Old Norse *lān,* loan, from Germanic **laihwniz;* **b.** LEND, from Old English *lǣnan,* to lend, loan from Germanic denominative **laihwnjan.* **3.** Zero-grade form **likʷ-.* **a.** (see **oi-no-**) Old English *endleofan,* eleven, from Germanic **ain-lif-,* "one left (beyond ten)"; **b.** (see **dwo-**) Old English *twelf,* twelve, from Germanic **twa-lif-,* "two left (beyond ten)." Both **a** and **b** from Germanic **-lif-,* left. **4.** Nasalized zero-grade form **li-n-kʷ-.* DELINQUENT, (DERELICT), RELINQUISH, from Latin *linquere,* to leave. [Pokorny *leikᵘ-* 669.]

leip-. Important derivatives are *life, lively, live*[1], *leave*[1], and *liver*[1].

leip-. To stick, adhere; fat. **1.** LIFE, LIVELY, from Old English *līf,* life (< "continuance"), from Germanic **lībam.* **2.a.** LIVE[1], from Old English *lifian, libban,* to live; **b.** LEBENSRAUM, from Old High German *lebēn,* to live. Both **a** and **b** from Germanic **libēn.* **3.a.** LEAVE[1], from Old English *lǣfan,* to leave, have remaining; **b.** DELAY, RELAY, from Old French *laier,* to leave, from Frankish **laibjan.* Both **a** and **b** from o-grade Germanic causative **-laibjan.* **4.** LIVER[1], from Old English *lifer,* liver (formerly believed to be the blood-producing organ), from Germanic **librō.* **5.** Zero-grade form **lip-.* LIPO-, from Greek *lipos,* fat. **6.** Variant form **əleibh-.* ALIPHATIC; SYNALEPHA, from Greek *aleiphein,* to anoint with oil. [Pokorny *leip-* 670.]

leis-[1]. Important derivatives are *last*[2], *lore*[1], *learn,* and *delirium.*

leis-[1]. Track, furrow. **1.** O-grade form **lois-.* **a.** LAST[3], from Old English *lāst, lǣst,* sole, footprint, from Germanic **laist-;* **b.** LAST[2], from Old English *lǣstan,* to continue, from Germanic **laistjan,* "to follow a track"; **c.** suffixed form **lois-ā.* LORE,[1] from Old English *lār,* learning, from Germanic **laizō.* **2.** LEARN, from Old English *leornian,* to learn, from Germanic zero-grade form **liznōn,* "to follow a course (of study)." **3.** Suffixed full-grade form **leis-ā.* DELIRIUM, from Latin *līra,* a furrow. [Pokorny *leis-* 671.]

leis-[2]. Important derivatives are *least* and *less.*

leis-[2]. Small. LEAST, LESS, from Old English comparative *lǣs, lǣssa* and superlative *lǣst, lǣrest,* from Germanic comparative **lais-izō* and superlative **lais-ista-.*

leit-. Important derivatives are *lead*[1], *load, lode,* and *livelihood.*

leit-. To go forth, die. **1.** Suffixed o-grade form **loit-eyo-.* **a.** LEAD[1], from Old English *lǣdan,* to lead; **b.** LEITMOTIF, from Old High German *leitan,* to lead. Both **a** and **b** from Germanic **laidjan.* **2.** Suffixed variant o-grade form **loit-ā.* LOAD, LODE; LIVELIHOOD, from Old English *lād,* course, way, from Germanic **laidō.* [Pokorny *leit(h)-* 672.]

lendh-. Important derivatives are *land, landscape, hinterland,* and *lawn*[1].

lendh-. Open land. **a.** LAND; ISLAND, from Old English *land,* land; **b.** LANDSCAPE, UITLANDER, from Middle Dutch *land,* land; **c.** AUSLANDER, GELÄNDESPRUNG, HINTERLAND, LANDSMAN[2], from Old High German *lant,* land; **d.** LANDGRAVE, (LANDGRAVINE), from Middle Low German *lant,* country; **e.** LANDSMÅL, from Old Norse *land,* land; **f.** LAWN[1], from Old French *launde,* heath, pasture. **a, b, c, d,** and **e** all from Germanic **landam;* **f** from Germanic, or from Celtic **landā.* [Pokorny 3. *lendh-* 675.]

leu-. Important derivatives are *forlorn, -less, lose, loss, loose, analysis, paralysis, soluble, solve, absolute, absolve, dissolve,* and *resolve.*

leu-. To loosen, divide, cut apart.
I. Extended Germanic root **leus-.* **1.a.** LORN, (LOSEL), from Old English *-lēosan,* to lose; **b.** *(i)* FORLORN, from Old English *forlēosan,* to forfeit, lose; *(ii)* FORLORN HOPE, from Dutch *verliezen* (past participle *verloren*), to lose. Both *(i)* and *(ii)* from Germanic **fer-leusan, *far-leusan* (**fer-, *far-,* prefix denoting rejection or exclusion; see **per**[1]). Both **a** and **b** from Germanic **leusan.* **2.a.** LEASING, -LESS, from Old English *lēas,* "loose," free from, without, untrue, lacking; **b.** LOSE, (LOSS), from Old English *los,* loss; **c.** LOOSE, from Old Norse *lauss, louss,* loose; **d.** LOESS, from German dialectal *lösch,* loose. **a, b, c,** and **d** all from Germanic **lausaz.*
II. Basic form **leu-.* **1.** LAG[2], probably from a source akin to Swedish *lagg,* barrel stave (< "split piece of wood"), from Germanic **lawwō.* **2.** Zero-grade form **lu-.* **a.** LYO-, LYSIS, LYSO-, -LYTE, (LYTIC), -LYTIC; ANALYSIS, CATALYSIS, DIALYSIS, PARALYSIS, TACHYLYTE, from Greek *luein,* to loosen, release, untie; **b.** LUES, from Latin *luēs,* plague, pestilence (< "dissolution, putrefaction"); **c.** prefixed form **se-lu-* (*se-,* apart; see **s(w)e-**). SOLUBLE, SOLUTE, SOLVE; ABSOLUTE, (ABSOLVE), ASSOIL, CONSOLUTE, DISSOLVE, RESOLVE, from Latin *solvere,* to loosen, untie. [Pokorny 2. *leu-* 681.]

leubh-. Important derivatives are *livelong, furlough, belief, believe, love,* and *libido.*

leubh-. To care, desire; love.
I. Suffixed form **leubh-o-.* LIEF; LEMAN, LIVELONG, from Old English *lēof,* dear, beloved, from Germanic **leubaz.*
II. O-grade form **loubh-.* **1.a.** LEAVE[2], from Old English *lēaf,* permission (< "pleasure, approval"); **b.** FURLOUGH, from Middle Dutch *verlof,* leave, permission (*ver-,* intensive prefix, from Germanic **fer-;* see **per**[1]); **c.** BELIEF, from Old English *gelēafa,* belief, faith (*bi-,* about; see **ambhi**), from Germanic **galaubō* (**ga-,* intensive prefix; see **kom**). **a, b,** and **c** all from Germanic **laubō.* **2.** BELIEVE, from Old English *gelēfan, belēfan,* to believe, trust (*be-,* about; see **ambhi**), from Germanic **galaubjan,* "to hold dear," esteem, trust (**ga-,* intensive prefix; see **kom**).
III. Zero-grade form **lubh-.* **1.** Suffixed form **lubh-ā-.* LOVE, from Old English *lufu,* love, from Germanic **lubō.* **2.** Suffixed (stative) form **lubh-ē-.* QUODLIBET, from Latin *libēre,* to be dear, be pleasing. **3.** LIBIDO, from Latin *libīdō,* pleasure, desire. [Pokorny *leubh-* 683.]

leudh-. Important derivatives are *liberal, liberate, liberty, livery,* and *deliver.*

leudh-. To mount up, grow. **1.** Basic form **leudh-.* LANDSLEIT, from Old High German *liut,* person, people, from Germanic **liud-i-.* **2.** Suffixed form **leudh-ero-.* LIBERAL, LIBERATE, LIBERTINE, LIBERTY, LIVERY; DELIVER, from Latin *līber,* free (the precise semantic development is obscure). [Pokorny 1. *leudh-* 684.]

leu(ə)-. Important derivatives are *lye, lather, lotion, deluge, dilute,* and *latrine.*

leu(ə)-. To wash. **1.** Suffixed form **lou-kā.* LYE, from Old English *lēag,* lye, from Germanic **laugō.* **2.** Suffixed form **lou-tro-.* LATHER, from Old English *lēthran, līthran,* to lather. **3.** Variant form **law-.* **a.** LOMENT, LOTION; ABLUTION, ALLUVION, COLLUVIUM, DELUGE, DILUTE, (ELUANT), ELUTE, (ELUVIUM), from Latin *lavere,* to wash, with its derivative *-luere,* to wash; **b.** form **law-ā-.* LAVE, from Latin *lavāre,* to wash; **c.** LATRINE, from Latin *lavātrīna, lātrīna,* a bath, privy. **4.** O-grade form **lou-.* PYROLUSITE, from Greek *louein,* to wash. [Pokorny *lou-* 692.]

leugh-. Important derivatives are *warlock, belie,* and *lie*[2].

leugh-. To tell a lie. **1.a.** WARLOCK, from Old English *lēogan,* to lie; **b.** BELIE, from Old English *belēogan,* to deceive (*be-,* about; see **ambhi**). Both **a** and **b** from Germanic **leugan.* **2.** LIE[2], from Old English *lyge,* a lie, falsehood, from Germanic **lugiz.* [Pokorny *leugh-* 686.]

leuk-. Important derivatives are *light*[1], *luminary, luminous, illuminate, lunar, lunatic, luster, illustrate, lea, lucid, elucidate, translucent,* and *lynx.*

leuk-. Light, brightness.
I. Basic form **leuk-.* **1.** Suffixed form **leuk-to-.* **a.** LIGHT[1], from Old English *lēoht, līht,* light; **b.** LIGHTNING, from Old English *lihtan,* to shine, from Germanic **leuht-jan,* to make light. Both **a** and **b** from Germanic **leuhtam.* **2.** Unsuffixed form **leuk-.* LUCINA, LUCULENT, LUX; LUCIFER, (LUCIFERIN), from Latin *lūx,* light. **3.** Suffixed form **leuk-smen-.* LIMN, LUMEN, LUMINARY, LUMINOUS; ILLUMINATE, PHILLUMENIST, from Latin *lūmen,* light, opening. **4.** Suffixed form **leuk-snā-.* LUNA, LUNAR, LUNATE, LUNATIC, LUNE, LUNULA; SUBLUNARY, from Latin *lūna,* moon. **5.** Suffixed form **leuk-stro-.* **a.** LUSTER, (LUSTRUM), from Latin *lūstrum,* purification; **b.** ILLUSTRATE, from Latin *lūstrāre,* to purify, illuminate. **6.** Suffixed form **leuko-dhro-.* LUCUBRATE, from Latin *lūcubrāre,* to work by lamplight. **7.** Suffixed form **leuk-o-.* LEUKO-, from Greek *leukos,* clear, white.
II. O-grade form **louk-.* **1.** Suffixed form **louk-o-.* **a.** LEA, from Old English *lēah,* meadow (< "place where light shines"), from Germanic **lauhaz;* **b.** LEVIN, from Middle English *levin,* lightning, from Germanic **lauh-ubni-.* **2.** Suffixed (iterative) form **louk-eyo-.* LUCENT, LUCID; ELUCIDATE, NOCTILUCA, PELLUCID, RELUCENT, TRANSLUCENT, from Latin *lūcēre,* to shine.
III. Zero-grade form **luk-.* **1.** Suffixed form **luk-sno-.* LINK[2], LYCHNIS, from Greek *lukhnos,* lamp. **2.** LYNX, OUNCE[2], from Greek *lunx,* lynx (as if from its shining eyes), attributed by some to this root (but more likely of obscure origin). [Pokorny *leuk-* 687.]

[līk-. Important derivatives are *-ly*[1], *-ly*[2], *alike, like*[2], *each, likely, frolic,* and *like*[1].

līk-. Body, form; like, same. Germanic root. **1.** LYCH-GATE, from Old English *līc,* form, body. **2.** -LY[1], -LY[2], from Old English *-līc,* having the form of. **3.a.** ALIKE, LIKE[2], LIKELY, from Old English *gelīc,* similar, and Old Norse *(g)līkr,* like, both from Germanic **galīkaz;* **b.** EACH; EVERY, from Old English *ǣlc,* each, from Germanic phrase **aiwo galīkaz,* "ever alike" (**aiwo, *aiwi,* ever; see **aiw-**). **4.** (see **i-**) Old English *ilca,* the same, from Germanic **is-līk-.* **5.** ALIKE, from Old English *onlīc,* from Germanic **ana-līkaz.* **6.** FROLIC, from Middle Dutch *-lijc,* -like. **7.** LIKE[1], from Old English *līcian,* to please, from Germanic **līkjan.* **8.** (see **kʷo-**) Germanic **hwa-līk-,* which. [Pokorny 2. *lēig-* 667.] **]**

līno-. Important derivatives are *line*[1], *linen, lingerie, lint,* and *linseed.*

līno-. Flax. **1.** Form **lino-.* LINOLEIC ACID, from Greek *linon,* flax. **2.** Form **līno-.* LINE[1], LINE[2], LINEN, LINGERIE, LINNET, LINT; CRINOLINE, LINSEED, from Latin *līnum,* flax, linen, thread. [Pokorny *li-no-* 691.]

lūs-. An important derivative is *louse.*

lūs-. Louse. LOUSE, from Old English *lūs* louse, from Germanic **lūs-.* [Pokorny *lūs-* 692.]

mā-[1]. Important derivatives are *mature, premature,* and *matinee.*

mā-[1]. Good; with derivatives meaning "occurring at a good moment, timely, seasonable, early." **1.** Suffixed form **mā-tu-.* **a.** further suffixed form **mā-tu-ro-.* MATURE; IMMATURE, PREMATURE, from Latin *mātūrus,* seasonable, ripe, mature; **b.** further suffixed form **mā-tu-to-.* (MATINEE), MATINS, (MATUTINAL), from Latin *Mātūta,* name of the goddess of dawn. **2.** Suffixed form **mā-ni-.* **a.** MAÑANA, from Latin *māne,* (in) the morning; **b.** MANES, from Latin *mānis, mānus,* good. [Pokorny 2. *mā-* 693.]

mā-[2]. An important derivative is *mammal.*

mā-[2]. Mother. A linguistic near-universal found in many of the world's languages, often in reduplicated form. **1.** MAMMA[2], MAMMAL, MAMMILLA, from Latin *mamma,* breast. **2.** MAIA, MAIEUTIC, from Greek *Maia,* "good mother" (respectful form of address to old women), also nurse, probably from **mā-**[2]. **3.** MAMA, more recently formed in the same way. [Pokorny 3. *mā-* 694.]

---

mag-. Important derivatives are *make, mason, match*[1], *mingle, among, mongrel, magma, mass,* and *amass.*

mag-. Also **mak-.** To knead, fashion, fit. **1.a.** *(i)* MAKE, from Old English *macian,* to make; *(ii)* MASON, from Old French *masson,* mason; *(iii)* MAQUILLAGE, from Middle Dutch *maken,* to make. *(i), (ii),* and *(iii)* all from Germanic verb **makōn,* to fashion, fit; **b.** MATCH[1], from Old English *gemæcca,* mate, spouse, from Germanic compound noun **ga-mak-(j)ōn-,* "one who is fitted with (another)" (**ga-,* with, together; see **kom**). Both **a** and **b** from Germanic **mak-.* **2.a.** MINGLE, from Old English *mengan,* to mix; **b.** AMONG, MONGREL, from Old English *gemang,* mixture, crowd (*ge-,* together; see **kom**). Both **a** and **b** from Germanic nasalized form **mangjan,* to knead together. **3.** Suffixed form **mak-yo-.* MAGMA, from Greek *magma,* unguent, from *massein* (aorist stem *mag-*), to knead. **4.** Suffixed lengthened-grade form **māg-ya-.* MASS; (AMASS), from Greek *maza,* a (kneaded) lump, barley cake. **5.** Suffixed lengthened-grade form **māk-ero-.* MACERATE, from Latin *mācerāre,* to tenderize, to soften (food) by steeping. [Pokorny *maĝ-* 696, 2. *māk-* 698, *men(ə)k-* 730.]

---

magh-. Important derivatives are *may*[1], *dismay, might*[1], *main, machine, mechanic,* and *magic.*

magh-. To be able, have power. **1.a.** MAY[1], from Old English *magan,* to be able; **b.** DISMAY, from Old French *esmaier,* to frighten. Both **a** and **b** from Germanic **magan,* to be able. **2.** MIGHT[1], from Old English *miht,* power, from Germanic suffixed form **mah-ti-,* power. **3.** MAIN, from Old English *mægen,* power, from Germanic suffixed form **mag-inam,* power. **4.** Suffixed lengthened-grade form **māgh-anā-,* "that which enables." MACHINE, MECHANIC, (MECHANISM), (MECHANO-), from Greek (Attic) *mēkhanē,* (Doric) *mākhanā,* device. **5.** Possibly suffixed form **magh-u-.* (MAGIC), MAGUS, from Old Persian *maguš,* member of a priestly caste (< "mighty one"). [Pokorny *magh-* 695.]

---

maghu-. Important derivatives are *maid* and *maiden.*

maghu-. Young person of either sex. Suffixed form **magho-ti-.* **a.** MAID, MAIDEN, from Old English *mægden,* virgin; **b.** MATJES HERRING, from Dutch *maagd,* maid. Both **a** and **b** from Germanic **magadi-,* with diminutive **magadin-.* [Pokorny *maghos* 696.]

---

māk-. Important derivatives are *meager, emaciate,* and *macro-.*

māk-. Long, thin. Contracted from **maək-.* **1.** Zero-grade form **mək-* becoming **mak-* in suffixed form **mak-ro-.* **a.** MEAGER; EMACIATE, from Latin *macer,* thin; **b.** MACRO-, MACRON; AMPHIMACER, from Greek *makros,* long, large. **2.** Suffixed form **māk-es-.* MECOPTERAN, PARAMECIUM, from Greek *mēkos,* length. [Pokorny *māk-* 699.]

---

man-[1]. Important derivatives are *man, Norman*[1], mannequin, and *ombudsman.*

man-[1]. Also **mon-.** Man. **1.** Extended forms **manu-, *manw-.* **a.** MAN; NORMAN, from Old English *man(n)* (plural *menn*), man; **b.** FUGLEMAN, LANDSMAN[2], from Old High German *man,* man; **c.** MANIKIN, (MANNEQUIN), from Middle Dutch *man,* man; **d.** NORMAN[1], OMBUDSMAN, from Old Norse *madhr, mannr,* man; **e.** ALEMANNI, possibly from Germanic **Ala-manniz,* tribal name (< *"all men": **ala-,* all; see **al-**[3]). **a, b, c, d,** and **e** all from Germanic **manna-* (plural **manniz*). **2.** MENSCH, from Old High German *mennisco,* human, from Germanic adjective **manniska-,* human. **3.** MUZHIK, from Russian *muzh,* man, male, from Slavic suffixed form **mon-gyo-.* [Pokorny *manu-s* 700.]

---

man-[2]. Important derivatives are *manacle, manage, manner, manual, maintain, maneuver, manicure, manifest, manipulation, manufacture, manure, manuscript, mastiff, emancipate, mandate, command, commando, commend, countermand, demand,* and *recommend.*

man-[2]. Hand. **1.** MANACLE, MANAGE, (MANÈGE), MANNER, MANUAL, MANUBRIUM, MANUS; AMANUENSIS, MAINTAIN, MANEUVER, MANICOTTI, MANICURE, MANIFEST, MANIPLE, MANIPULATION, MANSUETUDE, MANUFACTURE, MANUMIT, MANURE, MANUSCRIPT, MASTIFF, MORTMAIN, QUADRUMANOUS, from Latin *manus,* hand. **2.** Suffixed form **man-ko-,* maimed in the hand. MANQUÉ, from Latin *mancus,* maimed, defective. **3.** EMANCIPATE, from Latin compound *manceps,* "he who takes by the hand," purchaser (*-ceps,* agential suffix, "taker"; see **kap-**). **4.** MANDAMUS, MANDATE; COMMAND, (COMMANDO), COMMEND, COUNTERMAND, DEMAND, (RECOMMEND), REMAND, from Latin compound *mandāre,* "to put into someone's hand," entrust, order (*-dere,* to put; see **dhē-**). [Pokorny *mə-r* 740.]

---

marko-. An important derivative is *mare*[1].

marko-. Horse. MARE[1], from Old English *mere, miere,* mare, from Germanic feminine **marhjōn-.* [Pokorny *marko-* 700.]

---

māter-. Important derivatives are *mother*[1], *maternal, maternity, matriculate, matrix, matron, matrimony, metropolis, material,* and *matter.*

māter-. Mother. Based ultimately on the baby-talk form **mā-**[2], with the kinship term suffix **-ter-.* **1.a.** MOTHER[1], from Old English *mōdor,* mother; **b.** MOTHER[2], from Middle Dutch *moeder,* mother. Both **a** and **b** from Germanic **mōdar-.* **2.** MATER, MATERNAL, MATERNITY, (MATRICULATE), MATRIX, MATRON; MADREPORE, MATRIMONY, from Latin *māter,* mother. **3.** METRO-; METROPOLIS, from Greek *mētēr,* mother. **4.** MATERIAL, MATTER, from Latin *māteriēs, māteria,* tree trunk (< "matrix," the tree's source of growth), hence hard timber used in carpentry, hence (by a calque on Greek *hulē,* wood, matter) substance, stuff, matter. **5.** DEMETER, from Greek compound *Dēmētēr,* name of the goddess of produce, especially cereal crops (*dē-,* possibly meaning "earth"). [Pokorny *māter-* 700.]

---

me-[1]. Important derivatives are *me, myself, mine*[2], and *my.*

me-[1]. Oblique form of the personal pronoun of the first person singular. For the nominative see **eg.** **1.** ME, MYSELF, from Old English *mē̆* (dative and accusative), from Germanic **mē̆-.* **2.** Possessive adjective **mei-no-.* **a.** MINE[2], MY, from Old English *mīn,* my; **b.** MYNHEER, from Middle Dutch *mijn,* my. Both **a** and **b** from Germanic **mīn-.* **3.** Possessive adjective **me-yo-.* MADAME, MONSIEUR, from Latin *meus,* mine. **4.** Genitive form **me-wo.* MAVOURNEEN, from Old Irish *mo,* my. [Pokorny 1. *me-* 702.]

---

me-[2]. Derivatives are *midwife* and *meta-.*

me-[2]. In the middle of. **1.** Suffixed form **medhi.* MIDWIFE, from Old English *mid,* among, with, from Germanic **mid-.* **2.** Suffixed form **me-ta.* META-, from Greek *meta,* between, with, beside, after. [Pokorny 2. *me-* 702.] See also **medhyo-.**

---

mē-[1]. Important derivatives are *mood*[1], *moral, morale,* and *morose.*

mē-[1]. Expressing certain qualities of mind. Contracted from **meə-.* **1.** Suffixed o-grade form **mō-to-.* *(i)* MOOD[1], from Old English *mōd,* mind, disposition; *(ii)* GEMÜTLICH, (GEMÜTLICHKEIT); BISMUTH, from Old High German *muot,* mind, spirit. Both *(i)* and *(ii)* from Germanic **mōthaz.* **2.** MORAL, (MORALE), MORES, MOROSE, from Latin *mōs* (< **mō-s-*), wont, humor, manner, custom, perhaps from **mē-**[1]. [Pokorny 5. *mē-* 704.]

---

mē-[2]. Important derivatives are *meal*[2], *piecemeal, measure, dimension, immense, meter*[1], *diameter, geometry, moon, Monday, month, menopause, menstruate,* and *semester.*

mē-[2]. To measure. Contracted from **meə-.*
I. Basic form *mē-.* **1.** Suffixed form **mē-lo-.* MEAL[2]; PIECEMEAL, from Old English *mǣl,* "measure, mark, appointed time, time for eating, meal," from Germanic **mēlaz.* **2.** Suffixed form **mē-ti-.* **a.** MEASURE, (MENSURAL); (COMMENSURATE), DIMENSION, IMMENSE, from Latin *mētīrī,* to measure; **b.** METIS, from Greek *mētis,* wisdom, skill. **3.** METER[1], METER[2], (METER[3]), -METER, METRICAL, -METRY; DIAMETER, GEOMETRY, ISOMETRIC, METROLOGY, METRONOME, SYMMETRY, from Greek *metron,* measure, rule, length, proportion, poetic meter, possibly from **mē-**[2] (but this is referred by some to **med-**).
II. Extended and suffixed forms **mēn-, *mēnen-, *mēn-ōt-, *mēn-s-,* moon, month (an ancient and universal unit of time measured by the moon). **1.** MOON; (MONDAY), from Old English *mōna,* moon, from Germanic **mēnōn-.* **2.** MONTH, from Old English *mōnath,* month, from Germanic **mēnōth-.* **3.** AMENORRHEA, CATAMENIA, DYSMENORRHEA, EMMENAGOGUE, (MENARCHE), MENISCUS, MENOPAUSE, from Greek *mēn, mēnē,* month. **4.** MENSES, MENSTRUAL, (MENSTRUATE); BIMESTRIAL, SEMESTER, TRIMESTER, from Latin *mēnsis,* month. [Pokorny 3. *mē-* 703, *mēnōt-* 731.]

---

mē-[3]. Important derivatives are *more* and *most.*

mē-[3]. Big. Contracted from **meə-.* **1.** Suffixed (comparative) form **mē-is-.* MORE, from Old English *māra,* greater, and *māre* (adverb), more, from Germanic **maizōn-.* **2.** Suffixed (superlative) form **mē-isto-.* MOST, from Old English *mǣst,* most, from Germanic **maista-.* **3.** Suffixed form **mē-ro-, *mē-ri-.* MÄRCHEN, from Old High German *māri,* news, narration. **4.** Suffixed o-grade form **mō-ro-.* CLAYMORE, from Gaelic *mōr,* big, great. [Pokorny 4. *mē-* 704.]

---

mē-[4]. Important derivatives are *mow*[2], *aftermath,* and *meadow.*

mē-[4]. To cut down grass or grain with a sickle or scythe. Contracted from **meə-.* **1.** MOW[2], from Old English *māwan,* to mow, from Germanic **mē-.* **2.** Suffixed form **mē-ti-.* AFTERMATH, from Old English *mǣth,* a mowing, a mown crop, from Germanic **mēdiz.* **3.** Suffixed form **mē-twā-,* a mown field. MEAD[2], MEADOW, from Old English *mǣd* (oblique case *mǣdwe*), meadow, from Germanic **mēdwō.* [Pokorny 2. *mē-* 703.]

---

med-. Important derivatives are *mete*[1], *medicine, remedy, meditate, modest, moderate, mode, model, modern, modify, module, mold*[1], *accomodate, commodity, must*[1], and *empty.*

med-. To take appropriate measures. **1.a.** METE[1], from Old English *metan,* to measure (out), from Germanic **metan;* **b.** MEET[2], from Old English *gemǣte,* "commensurate," fit (*ge-,* with; see **kom**), from Germanic derivative **mǣtō,* measure. **2.a.** MEDICAL, MEDICATE, (MEDICINE), (MEDICO); METHEGLIN, REMEDY, from Latin *medērī,* to look after, heal, cure; **b.** MEDITATE, from Latin *meditārī,* to think about, consider, reflect. **3.** Suffixed form **medes-.* **a.** MODEST; IMMODEST, from Latin *modestus,* "keeping to the appropriate measure," moderate; **b.** MODERATE; IMMODERATE, from Latin *moderārī,* "to keep within measure," to moderate, control. Both **a** and **b** from Latin **modes-,* replacing **medes-* by influence of *modus* (see **5** below). **4.** MEDUSA, from Greek *medein,* to rule (feminine participle *medousa* < **med-ont-ia*). **5.** Suffixed o-grade form **mod-o-.* MODAL, MODE, MODEL, MODERN, MODICUM, MODIFY, MODULATE, MODULE, MODULUS, MOLD[1], (MOOD[2]), (MOULAGE); (ACCOMODATE), (COMMODE), COMMODIOUS, (COMMODITY), from Latin *modus,* measure, size, limit, manner, harmony, melody. **6.** Suffixed o-grade form **mod-yo-.* MODIOLUS, MUTCHKIN, from Latin *modius,* a measure of grain. **7.** Possibly lengthened o-grade form **mōd-.* **a.** MOTE[2], MUST[1], from Old English *mōtan,* to have occasion, to be permitted or obliged; **b.** EMPTY, from Old English *ǣmetta,* rest, leisure, from Germanic compound **ē-mōt-ja-* (prefix **ē-,* meaning uncertain, from Indo-European **ē, *ō,* to). Both **a** and **b** from Germanic **mōt-,* ability, leisure. [Pokorny 1. *med-* 705.]

---

medhu-. Important derivatives are *mead*[1] and *amethyst.*

medhu-. Honey; also mead. **1.** MEAD[1], from Old English *meodu,* mead, from Germanic **medu.* **2.** AMETHYST, METHYLENE, from Greek *methu,* wine. [Pokorny *médhu-* 707.]

medhyo-. Important derivatives are *mid[1], amid, middle, mean[3], medial, mediate, medium, intermediate, medieval, mediocre, mediterranean,* and *meridian.*

medhyo-. Middle. **1.a.** MID[1]; AMID, from Old English *midd(e),* middle; **b.** MIDDLE, from Old English *middel,* middle, from West Germanic diminutive form *middila-; **c.** MIDGARD, from Old Norse *Midhgardhr,* Midgard, from Germanic compound *midja-gardaz, "middle zone," name of the earth conceived as an intermediate zone lying between heaven and hell (*gardaz, enclosure, yard; see **gher-[1]**). **a, b,** and **c** all from Germanic *midja-. **2.** MEAN[3], MEDIAL, MEDIAN, MEDIASTINUM, MEDIATE, MEDIUM, MIZZEN, MOIETY, MULLION; INTERMEDIATE, MEDIEVAL, MEDIOCRE, MEDITERRANEAN, MERIDIAN, MILIEU, from Latin *medius,* middle, half. **3.** MESO-, from Greek *mesos,* middle. [Pokorny *medhi-* 706.] See also **me-[2]**.

meg-. Important derivatives are *much, magnate, magnitude, magnum, magnanimous, magnificent, magnify, major, majority, mayor, majesty, maestro, magistrate, master, mister, mistress, maximum, May, mega-,* and *maharajah.*

meg-. Great. **1.a.** MICKLE, MUCH, from Old English *micel, mycel,* great; **b.** MICKLE, from Old Norse *mikill.* Both **a** and **b** from Germanic suffixed form *mik-ila-. **2.** Suffixed form *mag-no-. MAGNATE, MAGNITUDE, MAGNUM; MAGNANIMOUS, MAGNIFIC, (MAGNIFICENT), (MAGNIFICO), (MAGNIFY), MAGNILOQUENT, from Latin *magnus,* great. **3.** Suffixed (comparative) form *mag-yos-. **a.** MAJOR, MAJOR-DOMO, MAJORITY, MAJUSCULE, MAYOR, from Latin *māior,* greater; **b.** MAESTOSO, MAJESTY, from Latin *māiestās,* greatness, authority; **c.** MAESTRO, MAGISTERIAL, MAGISTRAL, MAGISTRATE, MASTER, (MISTER), MISTRAL, (MISTRESS), from Latin *magister,* master, high official (< "he who is greater"). **4.** Suffixed (superlative) form *mag-samo-. MAXIM, MAXIMUM, from Latin *maximus,* greatest. **5.** Suffixed (feminine) form *mag-ya-, "she who is great." MAY, from Latin *Maia,* name of a goddess. **6.** Suffixed form *meg-ə-(l-). MEGA-, MEGALO-; ACROMEGALY, ALMAGEST, OMEGA, from Greek *megas* (stem *megal-*), great. **7.** Variant form *megh- (< *meg-ə-). MAHARAJAH, MAHARANI, MAHARISHI, MAHATMA, MAHAYANA, from Sanskrit *mahā-, mahat-,* great. [Pokorny *meĝ(h)-* 708.]

mei-[1]. Important derivatives are *permeate, mad, molt, mutate, commute, mutual, mis-[1], amiss, mistake, miss[1], common, communicate, communism, municipal, remunerate, immune, amoeba, migrate,* and *emigrate.*

mei-[1]. To change, go, move; with derivatives referring to the exchange of goods and services within a society as regulated by custom or law. **1.** MEATUS; CONGÉ, IRREMEABLE, PERMEATE, from Latin *meāre,* to go, pass. **2.** Suffixed o-grade form *moi-to-. **a.** MAD, from Old English *gemǣdan, to make insane or foolish, from Germanic *ga-maid-jan, denominative from *ga-maid-az, "changed (for the worse)," abnormal (*ga-, intensive prefix; see **kom**); **b.** MEW[1], MOLT, MUTATE; COMMUTE, PERMUTE, REMUDA, TRANSMUTE, from Latin *mūtāre,* to change; **c.** MUTUAL, from Latin *mūtuus,* "done in exchange," borrowed, reciprocal, mutual. **3.** Suffixed extended zero-grade form *mit-to-. **a.** MIS-[1], from Old English *mis-,* mis-, and Old French *mes-* (from Frankish *miss-); **b.** AMISS, MISTAKE, from Old Norse *mis(s), mis(s)-,* miss, mis-; **c.** MISS[1], from Old English *missan,* to miss, from Germanic *missjan, to go wrong. **a, b,** and **c** all from Germanic *missa-, "in a changed manner," abnormally, wrongly. **4.** Suffixed o-grade form *moi-n- in compound adjective *ko-moin-i-, "held in common" (*ko-, together; see **kom**). **a.** MEAN[2], (DEMEAN[2]), from Old English *gemǣne,* common, public, general, from Germanic *gamainiz; **b.** COMMON, (COMMUNE[1]), COMMUNE[2], COMMUNICATE, (COMMUNISM), from Latin *commūnis,* common, public, general. **5.** Suffixed o-grade form *moi-n-es-. **a.** MUNICIPAL, MUNIFICENT, REMUNERATE, from Latin *mūnus,* "service performed for the community," duty, work, "public spectacle paid for by a magistrate," gift; **b.** IMMUNE, from Latin *immūnis,* exempt from public service (*in-,* negative prefix; see **ne**). **6.** Extended form *(ə)meig^w-. **a.** AMOEBA, from Greek *ameibein,* to change; **b.** MIGRATE; EMIGRATE, from Latin *migrāre,* to change one's place of living. [Pokorny 2. *mei-,* 3. *mei-* 710, *meig^u-* 713, 2. *meit(h)-* 715.]

mei-[2]. Important derivatives are *menu, mince, minute[2], diminish, minor, minus, minimum, minestrone,* and *minister.*

mei-[2]. Small. **1.** MEIOSIS; MIOCENE, from Greek *meiōn,* less, lesser. **2.** (see **ne**) Latin *nimis,* too much, very (< *ne-mi-s, "not little"; *ne-,* negative prefix). **3.** Suffixed zero-grade form *mi-nu-. **a.** MENU, (MINCE), MINUEND, MINUTE[2]; COMMINUTE, DIMINISH, from Latin *minuere,* to reduce, diminish; **b.** MINOR, MINUS; MINUSCULE, from Latin *minor* (influenced by the comparative suffix *-or*), less, lesser, smaller; **c.** further suffixed (superlative) form *minu-mo-. MINIMUM, from Latin *minimus,* least; **d.** MINESTRONE, MINISTER, MINISTRY, MYSTERY[2], from Latin *minister,* an inferior, servant (formed after *magister,* master; see **meg-**); **e.** MENSHEVIK, from Russian *men'she,* less. [Pokorny 5. *mei-* 711.]

meigh-. Important derivatives are *mist* and *mistletoe.*

meigh-. To urinate. **1.a.** MIST, from Old English *mist,* mist; **b.** MIZZLE[1], from Middle English *misellen,* to drizzle, from a source perhaps akin to Dutch dialectal *mieselen,* to drizzle; **c.** (MISSEL THRUSH), MISTLETOE, from Old English *mistel,* mistletoe, from Germanic diminutive form *mihst-ila-, mistletoe (which is propagated through the droppings of the missel thrush). **a, b,** and **c** all from Germanic suffixed form *mih-stu-, urine, hence mist, fine rain. **2.** Suffixed form *migh-tu-. MICTURATE, from Latin *micturīre,* to want to urinate (desiderative of *meiere,* to urinate). [Pokorny *meigh-* 713.]

meik-. Important derivatives are *meddle, medley, mestizo, miscellaneous, mix, mixture, pell-mell, promiscuous,* and *mash.*

meik-. To mix. **1.** Variant form *meig-. AMPHIMIXIS, APOMIXIS, PANMICTIC, PANMIXIA, from Greek *mignunai,* to mix, with zero-grade noun *mixis* (< *mig-ti-), a mingling. **2.** Suffixed zero-grade form *mik-sk-. MEDDLE, (MEDLEY), (MELANGE), MESTIZO, MISCELLANEOUS, MISCIBLE, MIX, MIXTURE, MUSTANG; ADMIX, COMMIX, IMMIX, MISCEGENATION, (PELL-MELL), PROMISCUOUS, from Latin *miscēre* (past participle *mixtus*), to mix. **3.** MASH, from Old English *māsc, *mācs, māx-, mashed malt, from a possible Germanic form *maisk-. [Pokorny *meiḱ-* 714.]

mei-no-. Important derivatives are *moan, bemoan,* and *mean[1].*

mei-no-. Opinion, intention. **1.** MOAN, from Old English *mān, opinion, complaint, from Germanic *main-. **2.** MEAN[1]; BEMOAN, from Old English *mǣnan,* to signify, tell, complain of, moan, from Germanic *mainjan. [Pokorny *mei-no-* 714.]

mel-[1]. Important derivatives are *melt, malt, mollify, mollusk, bland, smelt[1], enamel, mild,* and *mulch.*

mel-[1]. Soft; with derivatives referring to soft or softened materials of various kinds.

I. Extended form *meld-. **1.** MELT, from Old English *meltan,* to melt, from Germanic *meltan. **2.** MILT, from Old English *milte,* spleen, and Middle Dutch *milte,* milt, from Germanic *miltja-, possibly from **mel-[1]**. **3.** MALT, from Old English *mealt,* malt, from Germanic *malta-, possibly from **mel-[1]**. **4.** Suffixed variant form *mled-sno-. BLENNY, from Greek *blennos,* slime, also a name for the blenny. **5.** Suffixed zero-grade form *ml̥d-wi-. MOIL, MOLLIFY, MOLLUSK, (MOUILLÉ); EMOLLIENT, from Latin *mollis,* soft. **6.** Possibly nasalized variant form *mlad-. BLAND, BLANDISH, from Latin *blandus,* smooth, caressing, flattering, soft-spoken.

II. Variant form *smeld-. **a.** SMELT[1], from Middle Dutch or Middle Low German *smelten,* to smelt; **b.** SCHMALTZ, from Old High German *smalz,* animal fat; **c.** SMALT, from Italian *smalto,* enamel, glaze; **d.** ENAMEL, from Old French *esmail,* enamel; **e.** SMELT[2], from Old English *smelt, smylt,* a marine fish, smelt, perhaps from **mel-[1]**. **a, b, c, d,** and **e** all from Germanic *smelt-.

III. Extended form *meldh-. **1.** MILD, from Old English *milde,* mild, from Germanic *mildja-. **2.** MALTHA, from Greek *maltha,* a mixture of wax and pitch, possibly from **mel-[1]**.

IV. Suffixed form *mel-sko-. MULCH, from Old English *mel(i)sc, mylsc,* mild, mellow, from Germanic *mil-sk-.

V. Extended form *ml̥ək-. BONANZA, CHONDROMALACIA, MALACOLOGY, OSTEOMALACIA, from Greek *malakos,* soft.

VI. MUTTON, from Old French *moton,* sheep, from Celtic *molto-, sheep, possibly from **mel-[1]**.

VII. Suffixed zero-grade form *(ə)ml-u-. AMBLYGONITE, AMBLYOPIA, from Greek *amblus,* blunt, dull, dim. [Pokorny 1. *mel-* 716.]

mel-[2]. Important derivatives are *ameliorate, multi-,* and *multitude.*

mel-[2]. Strong, great. **1.** Suffixed (comparative) form *mel-yos-. (AMELIORATE), MELIORATE, MELIORISM, from Latin *melior,* better. **2.** Suffixed zero-grade form *ml̥-to-. MOLTO, MULTI-, MULTITUDE, from Latin *multus,* much, many. [Pokorny 4. *mel-* 720.]

mel-[3]. Important derivatives are *mal-, malice, malign, dismal, malady,* and *malevolent.*

mel-[3]. Bad. MAL-, MALICE, (MALIGN); DISMAL, MALADY, MALARIA, MALEDICT, MALEFACTOR, MALEFIC, MALENTENDU, MALEVOLENCE, MALVERSATION, from Latin *malus,* bad, and *male,* ill (> *malignus,* harmful). [Pokorny *mĕlo-* 724.]

melə-. Important derivatives are *maelstrom, meal[1], mill[1], immolate, millet, malleable, mallet,* and *maul.*

melə-. Also **mel-.** To crush, grind; with derivatives referring to various ground or crumbling substances (such as flour) and to instruments for grinding or crushing (such as millstones). **1.** O-grade form *mol-. MAELSTROM, from Middle Dutch *malen,* to whirl, from Germanic *mal-. **2.** Full-grade form *mel-. MEAL[1], from Old English *melu,* flour, meal, from Germanic suffixed form *mel-wa-. **3.** Zero-grade form *ml̥-. MOLD[3], (MOLDER), from Old English *molde,* soil, from Germanic suffixed form *mul-dō. **4.** Full-grade form *mel-. **a.** MILL[1], MOLA[2], MOLAR[2], MOLE[4], (MOULIN); EMOLUMENT, IMMOLATE, ORMOLU, from Latin *molere,* to grind (grain), and its derivative *mola,* a millstone, mill, coarse meal customarily sprinkled on sacrificial animals; **b.** possible suffixed form *mel-iyo-. MEALIE, MILIUM, MILLET, from Latin *milium,* millet. **5.** Suffixed variant form *mal-ni-. MALLEABLE, (MALLET), MALLEUS, MAUL; PALL-MALL, from Latin *malleus,* hammer, mallet. **6.** Zero-grade form *ml̥-. AMYLUM, MYLONITE, from Greek *mulē, mulos,* millstone, mill. **7.** Possibly extended form *mlī-. BLINTZ, from Old Russian *blinŭ,* pancake. [Pokorny 1. *mel-* 716.]

melg-. Important derivatives are *emulsion, milk, galaxy, lacto-,* and *lettuce.*

melg-. To rub off; also to milk.

I. 1. Zero-grade form *ml̥g-. EMULSION, from Latin *mulgēre,* to milk. **2.** Full-grade form *melg-. **a.** MILK, from Old English *meolc, milc,* milk; **b.** MILCH, from Old English *-milce,* milch, from Germanic suffixed form *meluk-ja-, giving milk; **c.** MILCHIG, from Old High German *miluh,* milk. **a, b,** and **c** all from Germanic *melkan, to milk, contaminated with an unrelated noun for milk, cognate with the Greek and Latin forms given in **II** below, to form the blend *meluk-.

II. Included here to mark the unexplained fact that no common Indo-European noun for milk can be reconstructed is another root *g(a)lag-, *g(a)lakt-, milk, found only in: **a.** (GALACTIC), GALACTO-, GALAXY; AGALACTIA, POLYGALA, from Greek *gala* (stem *galakt-*), milk; **b.** (LACTATE), LACTEAL, LACTESCENT, LACTO-, LATTE, LETTUCE, from Latin *lac* (stem *lact-*), milk; **c.** the blended Germanic form cited in **I. 2.** above. [Pokorny *mĕlĝ-* 722, *glag-* 400.]

melit-. Important derivatives are *marmalade, mellifluous, molasses,* and *mildew.*

melit-. Honey. **1.** HYDROMEL, MARMALADE, MELILOT, OENOMEL, from Greek *meli,* honey. **2.a.** MELLIFEROUS, MELLIFLUOUS, MOLASSES, from Latin *mel* (stem *mell-*), honey, from *meld-, syncopated from *melid-; **b.** suffixed zero-grade form *ml̥d-to-, "honied." MOUSSE, from Latin *mulsus,* honey-sweet. **3.** MILDEW, from Old English *mildēaw,* honeydew, nectar, from Germanic compound **melith-dauwaz,* honeydew (a substance secreted by aphids on leaves; it was formerly imagined to be distilled from the air like dew; **dauwaz,* dew; see **dheu-**[1]), from **melith-.* [Pokorny *melit-* 723.]

men-[1]. Important derivatives are *mind, mental, mention, automatic, memento, comment, reminiscent, mania, mandarin, mint*[1]*, money, monitor, monster, monument, muster, admonish, demonstrate, premonition, summon, mosaic, Muse, museum, music, amnesia,* and *amnesty.*

men-[1]. To think; with derivatives referring to various qualities and states of mind and thought.
I. Zero-grade form **mn̥-.* **1.** Suffixed form **mn̥-ti-.* **a.** MIND, from Old English *gemynd,* memory, mind, from Germanic **ga-mundi-* (**ga-,* intensive prefix; see **kom**); **b.** MENTAL[1]; AMENT[2], DEMENT, from Latin *mēns* (stem *ment-*), mind; **c.** MENTION, from Latin *mentiō,* remembrance, mention. **2.** Suffixed form **mn̥-to-.* AUTOMATIC, from Greek *-matos,* "willing." **3.** Suffixed form **mn̥-yo-.* **a.** MAENAD, from Greek *mainesthai,* to be mad; **b.** AHRIMAN, from Avestan *mainiiuš,* spirit.
II. Full-grade form **men-.* **1.** Suffixed form **men-ti-.* **a.** MINNESINGER, from Old High German *minna,* love; **b.** MINIKIN, from Middle Dutch *minne,* love. Both **a** and **b** from Germanic **minthjō.* **2.a.** MEMENTO, from Latin reduplicated form *meminisse,* to remember; **b.** COMMENT, from Latin *comminīscī,* to contrive by thought (*com-,* intensive prefix; see **kom**); **c.** REMINISCENT, from Latin *reminīscī,* to recall, recollect (*re-,* again, back; see **re-**); **d.** MINERVA, from Latin *Minerva,* name of the goddess of wisdom, possibly from **men-**[1]. **3.a.** MENTOR, from Greek *Mentōr,* Mentor, man's name (probably meaning "adviser"); **b.** MANIA, MANIAC, MANIC, from Greek *mania,* madness; **c.** -MANCY, MANTIC, MANTIS, from Greek *mantis,* seer. **4.** MANDARIN, MANTRA, from Sanskrit *mantraḥ,* counsel, prayer, hymn.
III. O-grade form **mon-.* **1.** Suffixed (causative) form **mon-eyo-.* MONISH, MONITION, MONITOR, MONSTER, MONUMENT, MUSTER; ADMONISH, DEMONSTRATE, PREMONITION, SUMMON, from Latin *monēre,* to remind, warn, advise. **2.** Suffixed o-grade form **mon-twə.* MOSAIC, MUSE, MUSEUM, MUSIC, from Greek *Mousa,* a Muse.
IV. Extended form **mnā-,* contracted from **mnaə-.* **1.** AMNESIA, AMNESTY, ANAMNESIS, from Greek reduplicated form *mimnēskein,* to remember. **2.** MNEMONIC, from Greek *mnēmōn,* mindful.
V. Indo-European verb phrase **mens dhē-,* "to set mind" (see **dhē-**), underlying compound **mn̥s-dhē-.* AHURA MAZDA, (ORMAZD), from Avestan *mazdā-,* wise. [Pokorny 3. *men-* 726, *mendh-* 730.]

men-[2]. Important derivatives are *mouth, menace, amenable, demean*[1]*, promenade, eminent, imminent, prominent, mount*[1]*, mountain,* and *amount.*

men-[2]. To project. **1.** Suffixed zero-grade form **mn̥-to-* in a western Indo-European word for a projecting body part, variously "chin, jaw, mouth." **a.** MOUTH, from Old English *mūth,* mouth, from Germanic **munthaz;* **b.** MENTAL[2], from Latin *mentum,* chin. **2.** MENACE, MINACIOUS; AMENABLE, DEMEAN[1], PROMENADE, from Latin *minae,* projecting points, threats. **3.** EMINENT, IMMINENT, PROMINENT, (PROMONTORY), from Latin *-minēre,* to project, jut, threaten. **4.** Suffixed o-grade form **mon-ti-.* MONS, (MONTAGNARD), MONTANE, MONTE, MONTICULE, MOUNT[1], MOUNT[2], MOUNTAIN; AMOUNT, ULTRAMONTANE, from Latin *mōns* (stem *mont-*), mountain. [Pokorny 1. *men-* 726, 2. *menth-* 732.]

men-[3]. Important derivatives are *manor, mansion, ménage, permanent,* and *remain.*

men-[3]. To remain. Variant suffixed (stative) form **man-ē-.* MANOR, MANSE, MANSION, (MÉNAGE); IMMANENT, PERMANENT, REMAIN, from Latin *manēre,* to remain. [Pokorny 5. *men-* 729.]

men-[4]. Important derivatives are *monastery, monk, mono-,* and *minnow.*

men-[4]. Small, isolated. **1.** MANOMETER, from Greek *manos,* rare, sparse. **2.** Suffixed o-grade form **mon-wo-.* MONAD, MONASTERY, MONK, MONO-; PSEUDOMONAD, from Greek *monos,* alone, single, sole. **3.** Possibly also suffixed form **men-i-,* a small fish. MINNOW, from Middle English *meneu,* a small fish, from a source akin to Old English *myne, mynwe,* minnow. [Pokorny 4. *men-* 728, *meni-* 731.]

mendh-. Important derivatives are *mathematical* and *mathematics.*

mendh-. To learn. Zero-grade form **mn̥dh-.* MATHEMATICAL, (MATHEMATICS); CHRESTOMATHY, POLYMATH, from Greek *manthanein* (aorist stem *math-*), to learn. [Pokorny *mendh-* 730.]

menegh-. An important derivative is *many.*

menegh-. Copious. MANY, from Old English *manig, mænig,* many, from Germanic **managa-.* [Pokorny *men(e)gh-* 730.]

mer-. Important derivatives are *nightmare, mortar, mordant, morsel, remorse, morbid, murder, mortal, mortuary, mortgage, mortify, postmortem,* and *ambrosia.*

mer-. To rub away, harm.
I. 1. NIGHTMARE, from Old English *mare, mære,* goblin, incubus, from Germanic **marōn-,* goblin. **2.** MARASMUS; AMARANTH, from Greek *marainein,* to waste away, wither. **3.** Probably suffixed zero-grade form **mr̥- to-,* "ground down." MORTAR, from Latin *mortārium,* mortar. **4.** Possibly extended root **merd-.* MORDACIOUS, MORDANT, MORDENT, MORSEL; PREMORSE, REMORSE, from Latin *mordēre,* to bite. **5.** Possibly suffixed form **morbho-.* MORBID, from Latin *morbus,* disease (but this is more likely of unknown origin).
II. Possibly the same root, but more likely distinct, is **mer-,* "to die," with derivatives referring to death and to human beings as subject to death. **1.** Zero-grade form **mr̥-.* **a.** suffixed form **mr̥-tro-.* MURDER, from Old English *morthor,* murder, from Germanic suffixed form **mur-thra-;* **b.** suffixed form **mr̥-ti-.* MORT[1], MORTAL; AMORTIZE, MORTIFY, POSTMORTEM, from Latin *mors* (stem *mort-*), death; **c.** suffixed form **mr̥-yo-.* MORIBUND, MORTUARY, MURRAIN, MORTGAGE, (MORTMAIN), from Latin *morī,* to die, with irregular past participle *mortuus* (< **mr̥-two-*), replacing older **mr̥-to-* (for which see **d**); **d.** prefixed and suffixed form **n̥-mr̥-to-,* "undying, immortal." (**n̥-,* negative prefix; see **ne**). *(i)* IMMORTAL, from Latin *immortālis; (ii)* AMBROSIA, from Greek *ambrotos,* immortal, divine (*a-* + *-mbrotos, brotos,* mortal); *(iii)* AMRITA, from Sanskrit *amr̥tam,* immortality (*a-* + *mr̥ta-,* dead). **2.** Suffixed o-grade form **mor-t-yo-.* MANTICORE, from Greek *mantikhōras* (corrupted from *martiokhōras*), manticore, probably from Iranian compound **martiya-khvāra-,* "man-eater" (**khvāra-,* eating; see **swel-**), from Old Persian *martiya-* , a mortal man. [Pokorny 4. *mer-,* 5. *mer-* 735.]

merg-. Important derivatives are *mark*[1]*, marquee, marquis, demarcation, mark*[2]*, remark, march*[1]*,* and *margin.*

merg-. Boundary, border. **1.a.** MARK[1], from Old English *mearc,* boundary, landmark, sign, trace; **b.** MARGRAVE, from Middle Dutch *marc,* border; **c.** MARCH[2], (MARQUEE), MARQUIS, (MARQUISE), from Old French *marc, marche,* border country; **d.** MARCHESE, MARCHIONESS, from Medieval Latin *marca,* boundary, border; **e.** DEMARCATION, from Old Italian *marcare,* to mark out; **f.** MARK[2], from Old English *marc,* a mark of weight or money; **g.** MARKKA, from Swedish *mark,* a mark of money. **a, b, c, d, e, f,** and **g** all from Germanic **mark-,* boundary, border territory; also to mark out a boundary by walking around it (ceremonially "beating the bounds"); also a landmark, boundary marker, and a mark in general (and in particular a mark on a metal currency bar, hence a unit of currency); these various meanings are widely represented in Germanic descendants and in Romance borrowings. **2.** MARQUETRY; REMARK, from Old Norse *merki,* a mark, from Germanic **markja-,* mark, border. **3.** MARC, MARCH[1], from Frankish **markōn,* to mark out, from Germanic denominative verb **markōn.* **4.** MARGIN; EMARGINATE, from Latin *margō,* border, edge. **5.** Celtic variant form **mrog-,* territory, land. CYMRY, from Welsh *Cymro,* Wales, from British Celtic **kombrogos,* fellow countryman (**kom-,* collective prefix; see **kom**), from *-brogos,* district. [Pokorny *merĝ-* 738.]

meuə-. Important derivatives are *mob, mobile, moment, momentous, momentum, motif, motion, motive, motor, move, movement, commotion, emotion, promote, remote,* and *remove.*

meuə-. To push away. (MOB), MOBILE, MOMENT, (MOMENTOUS), MOMENTUM, MOSSO, (MOTIF), MOTION, MOTIVE, MOTOR, MOVE, (MOVEMENT); COMMOTION, EMOTION, PROMOTE, (REMOTE), (REMOVE), from Latin *movēre,* to move. [Pokorny 2. *meu-* 743.]

mori-. Important derivatives are *mere*[2]*, mermaid, meerschaum, marsh, morass, marine, maritime,* and *ultramarine.*

mori-. Body of water; lake (?), sea (?). **1.a.** MERE[2]; (MERMAID), from Old English *mere,* sea, lake, pond; **b.** MARRAM, from a Scandinavian source akin to Old Norse *marr,* sea; **c.** MEERSCHAUM, from Old High German *mari,* sea. **a, b,** and **c** all from Germanic **mari-.* **2.a.** MARSH, from Old English *mersc, merisc,* marsh; **b.** MORASS, from Old French *maresc, mareis,* marsh. Both **a** and **b** from Germanic **mariska-,* water-logged land. **3.** MARE[2], (MARINARA), MARINE, MARITIME; BÊCHE-DE-MER, MARICULTURE, ORMER, ULTRAMARINE, from Latin *mare,* sea. [Pokorny *mori* 748.]

mregh-u-. Important derivatives are *brief, abbreviate, abridge, merry, mirth, brace, brassiere, pretzel,* and *embrace.*

mregh-u-. Short.
I. Suffixed form **mregh-w-i-.* BRIEF, BRUMAL; ABBREVIATE, (ABRIDGE), from Latin *brevis,* short.
II. Zero-grade form **mr̥ghu-.* **1.a.** MERRY, from Old English *myrge, mirige,* pleasant; **b.** MIRTH, from Old English *myrgth,* pleasure, joy, from Germanic **murgithō,* pleasantness. Both **a** and **b** from Germanic **murgja-,* short, also pleasant, joyful. **2.** BRACHY-; AMPHIBRACH, TRIBRACH, from Greek *brakhus,* short. **3.** BRACE, BRACERO, BRACHIUM, BRASSARD, BRASSIERE, PRETZEL; (EMBRACE), from Greek comparative *brakhiōn,* shorter, hence also "upper arm" (as opposed to the longer forearm). [Pokorny *mreghu-* 750.]

mūs-. Important derivatives are *mouse* and *muscle.*

mūs-. A mouse; also a muscle (from the resemblance of a flexing muscle to the movements of a mouse). **1.** MOUSE, from Old English *mūs* (plural *mȳs*), mouse, from Germanic **mūs-* (plural **mūsiz*). **2.** MURINE, MUSCLE, MUSTELINE, from Latin *mūs,* mouse. **3.** MYELO-, MYO-; EPIMYSIUM, MYOSOTIS, MYSTICETE, PERIMYSIUM, SYRINGOMYELIA, from Greek *mus,* mouse, muscle. [Pokorny *mūs* 752.]

nas-. Important derivatives are *nose, nuzzle, nostril, nasal, nasturtium,* and *pince-nez.*

nas-. Nose. **1.** NOSE, (NUZZLE); NOSTRIL, from Old English *nosu,* nose, from Germanic zero-grade form **nusō.* **2.** NESS, from Old English *næss,* headland, from Germanic **nasja-.* **3.** Lengthened-grade form **nās-.* **a.** NARIS, from Latin *nāris,* nostril; **b.** expressive form **nāss-.* NASAL, NASO-; NASTURTIUM, PINCE-NEZ, from Latin *nāsus,* nose. **4.** NARK[2], from Romany *nāk,* nose, from expressive Indo-Aryan form **nakka-.* [Pokorny *nas-* 755, *neu-ks-* 768.]

nāu-. Important derivatives are *naval, navigate, navy, nausea, nautical, nautilus, noise,* and *astronaut.*

nāu-. Boat. Contracted from **naəu-.* **1.** NACELLE, NAVAL, NAVE[1], NAVICULAR, NAVIGATE, (NAVY), from Latin *nāvis,* ship. **2.** NAUSEA, NAUTICAL, NAUTILUS, (NOISE); AERONAUT, AQUANAUT, ARGONAUT, ASTRONAUT, COSMONAUT, from Greek *naus,* ship, and *nautēs,* sailor. [Pokorny 1. *nāu-* 755.]

n̥dher-. Important derivatives are *under, inferior, infernal, inferno,* and *infra-.*

n̥dher-. Under. **1.a.** UNDER, UNDER-, from Old English *under,* under; **b.** U-BOAT, from Old High German *untar,* under. Both **a** and **b** from Germanic *under-. **2.** INFERIOR, from Latin *īnferus,* lower. **3.** INFERNAL, (INFERNO), from Latin *īnfernus,* lower. **4.** INFRA-, from Latin *īnfrā,* below. [Pokorny *n̥dhos* 771.]

ne. Important derivatives are *naught, naughty, neither, never, no*[1], *no*[2], *none, nor*[1], *not, nothing, nay, annul, nefarious, neuter, nice, null, nullify, annihilate, non-, neglect, negligee, negotiate, negate, deny,* and *renegade.*

ne. Not. **1.a.** NAUGHT, (NAUGHTY), NEITHER, NEVER, NILL, NO[1], NO[2], NONE, (NOR[1]), (NOT), (NOTHING), from Old English *ne,* not, and *nā,* no; **b.** NAY, from Old Norse *ne,* not; **c.** NIX[2], from Old High German *ne, ni,* not. **a, b,** and **c** all from Germanic **ne-, *na-.* **2.** ANNUL, NEFARIOUS, NESCIENCE, NEUTER, (NICE), NULL, NULLIFY, NULLIPARA, from Latin *ne-,* not, and *nūllus,* none (*ne-* + *ūllus,* any; see **oi-no-**). **3.** NIMIETY, from Latin *nimis,* too much, excessively, very (< **ne-mi-s,* "not little"; **mi-,* little; see **mei-**[2]). **4.** NIHILISM, (NIHILITY), NIL; ANNIHILATE, from Latin *nihil, nīl,* nothing, contracted from *nihilum,* nothing (< **ne-hīlum,* "not a whit, nothing at all"; *hīlum,* a thing, trifle; origin unknown). **5.** NON-, from Latin *nōn,* not (< **ne-oinom,* not one thing"; **oino-,* one; see **oi-no-**). **6.** NISI, from Latin *nisī,* unless (*nī,* not, from **nei* + *sī,* if; see **swo-**). **7.a.** NEGLECT, (NEGLIGEE), NEGOTIATE, from Latin prefix *neg-,* not; **b.** NEGATE; ABNEGATE, DENY, RENEGADE, (RENEGE), from Latin *negāre,* to deny. Both **a** and **b** from Italic **nek,* not. **8.** NEPENTHE, from Greek *nē-,* not. **9.** Zero-grade combining form **n̥-.* **a.** UN-[1], from Old English *un-,* not, from Germanic **un-;* **b.** IN-[1], from Latin *in-,* not; **c.** A-[1], (AN-), from Greek *a-, an-,* not; **d.** AHIMSA, AMRITA, from Sanskrit *a-, an-,* not. [Pokorny *ne* 756.]

nebh-. Important derivatives are *nebula, nebulous,* and *nimbus.*

nebh-. Cloud. **1.** Suffixed form **nebh-(e)lo-.* **a.** NIFLHEIM, from Old Norse *nifl-,* "mist" or "dark," probably from Germanic **nibila-;* **b.** NIBELUNG, from Old High German *Nibulunc, Nibilung,* from Germanic suffixed patronymic form **nibul-unga-,* beside Old High German *nebul,* mist, fog, from Germanic **nebla-.* **2.** Suffixed form **nebh-elā-.* **a.** NEBULA, NEBULOUS, from Latin *nebula,* cloud; **b.** NEPHELINE; NEPHELOMETER, from Greek *nephelē,* cloud. **3.** Nasalized form **ne-m-bh-.* NIMBUS, from Latin *nimbus,* rain, cloud, aura. [Pokorny *(enebh-)* 315.]

ned-. Important derivatives are *net*[1], *nettle, node, nodule, annex,* and *connect.*

ned-. To bind, tie. **1.** O-grade form **nod-.* **a.** NET[1], from Old English *net(t),* a net, from Germanic **nati-;* **b.** NETTLE, from Old English *netel(e), netle,* nettle, from Germanic **nat-ilo,* a nettle (nettles or plants of closely related genera such as hemp were used as a source of fiber); **c.** OUCH[2], from Anglo- Norman *nouch,* brooch, from Germanic **nat-sk-.* **2.** Lengthened o-grade form **nōdo-.* NODE, NODULE, NODUS; DÉNOUEMENT, from Latin *nōdus,* a knot. **3.** With re-formation of the root. NEXUS; (ADNEXA), ANNEX, CONNECT, from Latin *nectere* (past participle *nexus*), to tie, bind, connect. [Pokorny 1. *ned-* 758.]

[nēhw-iz. Important derivatives are *near, neighbor, next,* and *nigh.*

nēhw-iz. Near. Germanic root. NEAR, NEIGHBOR, NEXT, NIGH, from Old English *nēah,* near.**]**

nek-[1]**.** Important derivatives are *pernicious, nuisance, innocent, innocuous, noxious, obnoxious, necrosis, necromancy, nectar,* and *nectarine.*

nek-[1]**.** Death. **1.** INTERNECINE, PERNICIOUS, from Latin *nex* (stem *nec-*), death. **2.** Suffixed (causative) o-grade form **nok-eyo-.* NOCENT, NOCUOUS, NUISANCE; INNOCENT, INNOCUOUS, from Latin *nocēre,* to injure, harm. **3.** Suffixed o-grade form **noks-.* NOXIOUS; OBNOXIOUS, from Latin *noxa,* injury, hurt, damage entailing liability. **4.** Suffixed full-grade form **nek-ro-.* NECRO-, NECROSIS; NECROMANCY, from Greek *nekros,* corpse. **5.** NECTAR, (NECTARINE), from Greek *nektar,* the drink of the gods, "overcoming death" (**tar-,* overcoming; see **terə-**[2]). [Pokorny *nek̂-* 762.]

nek-[2]**.** Important derivatives are *enough* and *oncology.*

nek-[2]**.** To reach, attain.
I. O-grade form **nok-.* ENOUGH, from Old English *genōg,* enough, from Germanic **ganōga-,* sufficient, from **ga-nah,* "suffices" (**ga-,* intensive prefix; see **kom**).
II. Variant form **enk-.* **1.** ONCOGENESIS, ONCOLOGY, from Greek *onkos,* a burden, mass, hence a tumor, from reduplicated *enenkein,* to carry. **2.** Compound root **bhrenk-* (see **bher**[1]). [Pokorny *enek̂-* 316.]

nekʷ**-t-.** Important derivatives are *night, nocturnal,* and *equinox.*

nekʷ**-t-.** Night. O-grade form **nok*ʷ*-t-.* **1.** NIGHT, from Old English *niht, neaht,* night, from Germanic **naht-.* **2.** NOCTI-, (NOCTURN), NOCTURNAL, EQUINOX, from Latin *nox* (stem *noct-*), night. **3.** NOCTUID, NOCTULE, from Latin *noctua,* night owl. **4.** NYCTALOPIA, NYCTITROPISM, from Greek *nux* (stem *nukt-*), night. [Pokorny *nek*ᵘ*(t)-* 762.]

nem-. Important derivatives are *numb, nimble, nemesis, economy, astronomy, autonomous, metronome, nomad, number,* and *enumerate.*

nem-. To assign, allot; also to take. **1.a.** NIM, NUMB; (BENUMB), from Old English *niman,* to take, seize; **b.** NIMBLE, from Old English *nǣmel,* quick to seize, and *numol,* quick at learning, seizing; **c.** NIM[2], from Old High German *nëman,* to take. **a, b,** and **c** all from Germanic **nem-.* **2.** NEMESIS; ECONOMY, from Greek *nemein,* to allot. **3.** O-grade form **nom-.* **a.** NOME, -NOMY; ANOMIE, ANTINOMIAN, ANTINOMY, (ASTRONOMER), (ASTRONOMY), AUTONOMOUS, DEUTERONOMY, METRONOME, NOMOGRAPH, NOMOLOGY, NOMOTHETIC, NUMISMATIC, from Greek *nomos,* portion, usage, custom, law, division, district; **b.** NOMA, from Greek *nomē,* pasturage, grazing, hence a spreading, a spreading ulcer; **c.** NOMAD, from Greek *nomas,* wandering in search of pasture; **d.** NUMMULAR, NUMMULITE, from Greek *nomimos,* legal. **4.** Perhaps suffixed o-grade form **nom-eso-.* NUMBER; ENUMERATE, SUPERNUMERARY, from Latin *numerus,* number, division. [Pokorny 1. *nem-* 763.]

nepōt-. Important derivatives are *nephew, nepotism,* and *niece.*

nepōt-. Grandson, nephew. Feminine **neptī-.* NEPHEW, NEPOTISM, NIECE, from Latin *nepōs,* grandson, nephew, and *neptis,* granddaughter, niece. [Pokorny *nepōt-* 764.]

ner-[1]**.** Important derivatives are *Nordic, north, Norman*[1], northern, and *Norse.*

ner-[1]**.** Under, also on the left; hence, with an eastward orientation, north. Suffixed zero-grade form **nr̥-t(r)o-.* **a.** NORDIC, NORTH, from Old English *north,* north; **b.** NORTHERN, from Old English *northerne,* northern; **c.** NORSE, from Middle Dutch *nort,* north; **d.** NORMAN[1], NORWEGIAN, from Old Norse *nordhr,* north. [Pokorny 2. *ner-* 765.]

ner-[2]**.** A derivative is *andro-.*

ner-[2]**.** Also **əner-.** Man; basic sense "vigorous, vital, strong." Oldest root form **əner-.* ANDRO-, -ANDROUS, -ANDRY; PHILANDER, from Greek *anēr* (stem *andr-,* from zero-grade **ənr-*), man. [Pokorny 1. *ner-(t)-* 765.]

nes-[1]**.** Important derivatives are *harness* and *nostalgia.*

nes-[1]**.** To return safely home. **1.** HARNESS, from Old French *harneis,* harness, possibly from a Germanic source akin to Old English, Old High German (in composition), and Old Norse *nest,* food for a journey, from Germanic **nes-tam.* **2.** Suffixed o-grade form **nos-to-.* NOSTALGIA, from Greek *nostos,* a return home. [Pokorny *nes-* 766.]

nes-[2]**.** Important derivatives are *us, our,* and *ours.*

nes-[2]**.** Oblique cases of the personal pronoun of the first person plural. For the nominative see **we-. 1.** Zero-grade form **n̥s-.* US, from Old English *ūs,* us (accusative), from Germanic **uns.* **2.** Suffixed (possessive) zero-grade form **n̥s-ero-.* OUR, OURS, from Old English *ūser, ūre,* our, from Germanic **unsara-.* **3.** O-grade form **nos-,* with suffixed (possessive) form *nos-t(e,)ro-.* NOSTRUM; PATERNOSTER, from Latin *nōs,* we, and *noster,* our. [Pokorny 3. *ne-* 758.]

neu-. Important derivatives are *announce, denounce, enunciate, pronounce,* and *renounce.*

neu-. To shout. Suffixed (participial) o-grade form **now-ent-(yo-),* "shouting." NUNCIO; ANNOUNCE, DENOUNCE, ENUNCIATE, PRONOUNCE, RENOUNCE, from Latin *nūntius,* "announcing," hence a messenger, also a message, and *nūntium,* message. [Pokorny 1. *neu-* 767.]

newn̥. Important derivatives are *nine, nineteen, ninety, ninth, November, novena,* and *noon.*

newn̥. Nine. **1.** NINE, NINETEEN, NINETY, NINTH, from Old English *nigon,* nine, with derivatives *nigontig,* ninety, and *nigontēne,* nineteen (*-tēne,* ten; see **dekm̥**), from Germanic **nigun,* variant of **niwun.* **2.** NOVEMBER, NOVENA; (NONAGENARIAN), from Latin *novem,* nine (< **noven,* with *m* for *n* by analogy with the *m* of *septem,* seven, and *decem,* ten). **3.** Ordinal form **neweno-.* NONA-, NONES, NOON; (NONAGON), (NONANOIC ACID), from Latin *nōnus,* ninth. **4.** Prothetic or prefixed forms **enewn̥, *enwn̥.* ENNEAD, from Greek *ennea,* nine (< **ennewa, *enwa-*). [Pokorny *e-neu̯en* 318.]

newo-. Important derivatives are *new, neo-, neon, nova, novel*[1], *novel*[2], *novelty, novice, innovate,* and *renovate.*

newo-. New. Related to **nu-. 1.** Suffixed form **new-yo-.* **a.** NEW, from Old English *nēowe, nīwe,* new; **b.** SPAN-NEW, from Old Norse *nȳr,* new. Both **a** and **b** from Germanic **neuja-.* **2.** Basic form **newo-.* NEO-, NEON, NEOTERIC; MISONEISM, from Greek *newos, neos,* new. **3.** Suffixed form **new-aro-.* ANEROID, from Greek *nēron,* water, from *nēros,* fresh (used of fish and of water), contracted from *nearos,* young, fresh. **4.** Basic form **newo-.* NOVA, NOVATION, NOVEL[1], NOVEL[2], (NOVELTY), NOVICE; INNOVATE, RENOVATE, from Latin *novus,* new. **5.** Suffixed form **new-er-ko-.* NOVERCAL, from Latin *noverca,* stepmother (< "she who is new"). [Pokorny *neu̯os* 709.]

nobh-. Important derivatives are *nave*[2], *navel,* and *umbilicus.*

nobh-. Also **ombh-.** Navel; later also "central knob," boss of a shield, hub of a wheel. **1.a.** NAVE[2], from Old English *nafu, nafa,* hub of a wheel; **b.** AUGER, from Old English *nafogār,* auger, from Germanic compound **nabō-gaizaz,* tool for piercing wheel hubs (**gaizaz,* spear, piercing tool). Both **a** and **b** from Germanic **nabō.* **2.** Variant form **ombh-.* UMBO, from Latin *umbō,* boss of a shield. **3.** Suffixed form **nobh-alo-.* NAVEL, from Old English *nafela,* navel, from Germanic **nabalō.* **4.** Suffixed variant form **ombh-alo-.* **a.** UMBILICUS; NOMBRIL, from Latin *umbilīcus,* navel; **b.** OMPHALOS, from Greek *omphalos,* navel. [Pokorny 1. *(enebh-)* 314.]

nogh-. An important derivative is *nail.*

nogh-. Also **ənogh-, ongh-.** Nail, claw. **1.** Suffixed (diminutive) form **nogh-ela-.* NAIL, from Old English *nægl,* nail, from Germanic **nagla-.* **2.** Form **ənogh-.* ONYX; PARONYCHIA, PERIONYCHIUM, SARDONYX, from Greek *onux* (stem *onukh-*), nail. **3.** Variant form **ongh-.* UNGUIS, from Latin *unguis,* nail, claw, hoof, with diminutive *ungula,* hoof, claw, talon (< **ongh-elā-*). [Pokorny *onogh-* 780.]

nogʷ**-.** Important derivatives are *naked, nude, denude, gymnasium,* and *gymnast.*

nogʷ**-.** Naked. **1.** Suffixed forms **nog*ʷ*-eto-, *nog*ʷ*-oto-.* NAKED, from Old English *nacod,* naked, from Germanic **nakweda-, *nakwada-.* **2.** Suffixed form **nog*ʷ*-edo-.* NUDE, NUDI-; DENUDE, from Latin *nūdus,* naked. **3.** Suffixed form **nog*ʷ*-mo-.* GYMNASIUM, (GYMNAST); GYMNOSOPHIST, GYMNOSPERM, from Greek *gumnos,* naked. [Pokorny *nogᵘ-* 769.]

nŏ-men-. Important derivatives are *name, nominal, nominate, noun, ignominy, misnomer, pronoun, renown, anonymous, eponym, homonymous, metonymy, pseudonym,* and *synonymous.*

nō-men-. Name. Earlier form **(ə)noə-mn̥,* zero-grade form **(ə)nə-men-.* **1.** NAME, from Old English *nama,* name, from Germanic **namōn-.* **2.** NOMINAL, NOMINATE, NOUN; AGNOMEN, (BINOMIAL), COGNOMEN, DENOMINATE, IGNOMINY, MISNOMER, NOMENCLATOR, NUNCUPATIVE, PRAENOMEN, (PRONOUN), RENOWN, from Latin *nōmen,* name, reputation. **3.** ONOMASTIC, -ONYM, -ONYMY; ALLONYM, ANONYMOUS, ANTONOMASIA, EPONYM, (EPONYMOUS), EUONYMUS, HETERONYMOUS, HOMONYMOUS, METONYMY, METRONYMIC, ONOMATOPOEIA, (PARONOMASIA), PARONYMOUS, PATRONYMIC, PSEUDONYM, SYNONYMOUS, from Greek *onoma, onu-ma,* name. **4.** MONIKER, from Old Irish *ainm,* name. [Pokorny *en(o)mn̥-* 321.]

nu-. An important derivative is *now.*

nu-. Now. Related to **newo-**. **1.** NOW, from Old English *nū,* now. **2.** QUIDNUNC, from Latin *nunc,* now (< **nun-ce; -ce,* a particle meaning "this," "here"; see **ko-**). [Pokorny *nu-* 770.]

od-. Important derivatives are *annoy, ennui, noisome,* and *odium.*

od-. To hate. ANNOY, ENNUI, (NOISOME), ODIUM, from Latin *ōdī,* I hate, and *odium,* hatred. [Pokorny 2. *od-* 773.]

oi-no-. Important derivatives are *a*[1], *an*[1], *once, one, alone, atone, lone, lonely, none, eleven, inch*[1], *ounce*[1], *union, unite, unity, unanimous, unicorn, universe, any,* and *unique.*

oi-no-. One, unique.
I. Basic form **oi-no-.* **1.a.** (A[1]), AN[1], ONCE, ONE; (ALONE), ANON, (ATONE), (LONE), (LONELY), NONE, from Old English *ān,* one; **b.** ELEVEN, from Old English *endleofan,* eleven, from Germanic compound **ain-lif-,* "one left (beyond ten)," eleven (**lif-,* left over; see **leik^w-**); **c.** EINKORN, TURNVEREIN, from Old High German *ein,* one. **a, b,** and **c** all from Germanic **ainaz.* **2.** UNI-, UNION, UNITE, UNITY; COADUNATE, TRIUNE, UNANIMOUS, UNICORN, UNIVERSE, from Latin *ūnus,* one. **3.** (see **ne**) Latin *nōn,* not (< **ne-oinom,* "not one thing"; *ne,* not).
II. Suffixed form **oino-ko-.* **a.** ANY, from Old English *ǣnig,* one, anyone, from Germanic **ainigaz;* **b.** UNIQUE, from Latin *ūnicus,* sole, single. **c.** INCH[1], OUNCE[1], UNCIAL; (QUINCUNX), from Latin *uncia,* one twelfth of a unit (*unc-,* shortened form of **ūnc-*).
III. Suffixed form **oino-lo-.* (see **ne**) Latin *ūllus,* any. [In Pokorny *e-* 281.]

oktō(u). Important derivatives are *eight, octave, octet, October, octogenarian,* and *octopus.*

oktō(u). Eight. **1.a.** EIGHT, EIGHTEEN, EIGHTY, from Old English *eahta,* eight, with derivatives *eahtatig,* eighty, and *eahtatēne,* eighteen (*-tēne,* ten; see **dekm̥**); **b.** ATTO-, from Old Norse *āttjān,* eighteen (*tjān,* ten; see **dekm̥**). Both **a** and **b** from Germanic **ahtō.* **2.** OCTANS, OCTANT, OCTAVE, OCTAVO, OCTET, OCTO-, OCTOBER, OCTONARY; OCTODECIMO, OCTOGENARIAN, from Latin *octō,* eight. **3.** OCTAD, OCTO-; OCTOPUS, from Greek *oktō,* eight. [Pokorny *oktō* 775.]

ōku-. A derivative is *accipiter.*

ōku-. Swift. **1.** OXYTOCIC, from Greek *ōkus,* swift. **2.** Possibly altered zero-grade form **aku-* in compound **aku-petro-,* "swift-flying" (**pet-ro-,* flying; see **pet-**). ACCIPITER, from Latin *accipiter,* hawk. [Pokorny *ōku-s* 775.] See also **ekwo-**.

ok^w-. Important derivatives are *eye, daisy, window, eyelet, ocular, inoculate, monocle, myopia, autopsy, synopsis, optic,* and *optometry.*

ok^w-. To see. **1.a.** EYE; DAISY, from Old English *ēage,* eye; **b.** WALLEYED, WINDOW, from Old Norse *auga,* eye; **c.** OGLE, from Low German *oog, oge,* eye. **a, b,** and **c** all from Germanic **augōn-* (with taboo deformation). **2.** Suffixed form **ok^w-olo-.* **a.** EYELET, OCELLUS, OCULAR, OCULIST, ULLAGE; INOCULATE, MONOCLE, OCULOMOTOR, PINOCHLE, from Latin *oculus,* eye; **b.** INVEIGLE, from French *aveugle,* blind, from Gallo-Latin compound **ab-oculus,* blind, modeled on Gaulish *ex-ops,* blind. **3.** Form **ok^w-s.* METOPIC, MYOPIA, NYCTALOPIA, PELOPS, PHLOGOPITE, PYROPE, TRICERATOPS, from Greek *ōps,* eye (and stem **op-,* to see). **4.** Suffixed form **ok^w-ti-.* (OPSIN), -OPSIS, -OPSY; AUTOPSY, (IODOPSIN), (RHODOPSIN), SYNOPSIS, from Greek *opsis,* sight, appearance. **5.** Suffixed form **ok^w-to-.* OPTIC; DIOPTER, OPTOMETRY, PANOPTIC, from Greek *optos,* seen, visible. **6.** Suffixed form **ok^w-ā.* METOPE, from Greek *opē,* opening. **7.** Suffixed form **ok^w-mn̥.* OMMATIDIUM, from Greek *omma* (< **opma*), eye. **8.** Suffixed form **ok^w-tro-.* CATOPTRIC, from Greek *katoptron,* "back-looker," mirror (*kata-,* down, back; see **kat-**). **9.** OPHTHALMO-; EXOPHTHALMOS, from Greek *ophthalmos,* eye (with taboo deformation). **10.** Zero-grade form **ək^w-* (of oldest full-grade form **əok^w-*). **a.** (see **ant-**) Latin *antīquus,* "appearing before, having prior aspect," former (**anti-,* before); **b.** (see **āter-**) Latin *ătrōx,* "black-looking," frightful (**atro-,* black); **c.** (see **ghwer-**) *ferōx,* "wild-looking," fierce (**ghwero-,* wild). [Pokorny *oku-* 775.]

op-. Important derivatives are *opera*[1], *operate, opus, cooperate, inure, maneuver, manure, opulent, omni-, optimum, copious, copy,* and *cornucopia.*

op-. To work, produce in abundance. **1.** Suffixed form **op-es-.* OPERA[1], OPERATE, OPEROSE, OPUS; COOPERATE, INURE, MANEUVER, MANURE, OFFICINAL, from Latin *opus* (stem *oper-*), work, with its denominative verb *operārī,* to work, and secondary noun *opera,* work. **2.** (see **dhē-**) Latin *officium,* service, duty, business (< **opi-fici-om,* "performance of work"; **-fici-,* doing). **3.** Suffixed form **op-en-ent-.* OPULENT, from Latin dissimilated *opulentus,* rich, wealthy. **4.** Suffixed form **op-ni-.* OMNI-, OMNIBUS; OMNIUM-GATHERUM, from Latin *omnis,* all (< "abundant"). **5.** Suffixed (superlative) form **op-tamo-.* OPTIMUM, from Latin *optimus,* best (< "wealthiest"). **6.** COPIOUS, COPY; CORNUCOPIA, from Latin *cōpia,* profusion, plenty, from prefixed form **co-op-* (*co-,* collective and intensive prefix; see **kom**). [Pokorny 1. *op-* 780.]

or-. Derivatives are *erne* and *ornitho-.*

or-. Large bird. **1.** Suffixed form **or-n-.* ERNE, from Old English *earn,* eagle, from Germanic **arnuz,* eagle. **2.** Suffixed form **or-n-īth-.* ORNITHO-; AEPYORNIS, ICHTHYORNIS, NOTORNIS, from Greek *ornis* (stem *ornith-*), bird. [Pokorny 1. *er-* 325.]

orbh-. Important derivatives are *orphan* and *robot.*

orbh-. To put asunder, separate. Suffixed form **orbh-o-,* "bereft of father," also "deprived of free status." **a.** ORPHAN, from Greek *orphanos,* orphaned; **b.** ROBOT, from Czech *robota,* compulsory labor, drudgery, from Old Church Slavonic *rabota,* servitude, from *rabŭ,* slave, from Old Slavic **orbŭ.* [Pokorny *orbho-* 781.]

ors-. Important derivatives are *ass*[2] and *squirrel.*

ors-. Buttocks, backside. **1.** Suffixed form **ors-o-.* **a.** ASS[2], from Old English *ærs, ears,* backside; **b.** DODO, from Middle Dutch *ærs,* backside, tail. Both **a** and **b** from Germanic **arsaz.* **2.** Suffixed form **ors-ā-.* **a.** URO-[2], -UROUS; ANTHURIUM, ANURAN, CYNOSURE, DASYURE, EREMURUS, OXYURIASIS, SQUIRREL, from Greek *oura,* tail; **b.** SILURID, from Greek *silouros,* sheatfish (< obscure first element + *oura*), probably from **ors-**. [Pokorny *ers-* 340.]

ōs-. Important derivatives are *oral* and *usher.*

ōs-. Mouth. **1.** ORAL, OS[1], OSCILLATE, OSCULATE, OSCULUM, OSTIUM, USHER; INOSCULATE, ORIFICE, ORINASAL, OROTUND, OSCITANCY, (PERORAL), from Latin *ōs* (stem *ōr-*), mouth, face, orifice, and derivative *ōstium* (< suffixed form **ōs-to-*), door. **2.** AURIGA, from Latin *aurīga,* charioteer (< **ōr-ig-,* "he who manages the (horse's) bit"; *-īg-,* lengthened from *ig-,* driving, from **ag-;* see **ag-**), possibly from **ōs-**. [Pokorny 1. *ōus-* 784.]

ost-. Important derivatives are *ossify, osteo-, ostracize,* and *oyster.*

ost-. Bone. **1.** OS[2], OSSEOUS, OSSICLE, OSSUARY; OSSIFRAGE, OSSIFY, from Latin *os* (stem *oss-*), bone. **2.** OSTEO-; ENDOSTEUM, EXOSTOSIS, PERIOSTEUM, SYNOSTOSIS, TELEOST, from Greek *osteon,* bone. **3.** Suffixed form **ost-r-.* **a.** OSTRACIZE, OSTRACOD, from Greek *ostrakon,* shell, potsherd; **b.** OYSTER, from Greek *ostreon,* oyster; **c.** ASTRAGAL, ASTRAGALUS, from variant form in Greek *astragalos,* vertebra, ball of the ankle joint, knucklebone, Ionic molding. [Pokorny *ost(h)-* 783.]

ous-. Important derivatives are *ear*[1], *aural*[1], and *scout*[1].

ous-. Also **aus-**. Ear. **1.** Suffixed form **ous-en-.* EAR[1], from Old English *ēare,* ear, from Germanic **auzōn-.* **2.** Suffixed form **aus-i-.* AURAL[1], AURICLE; AURIFORM, ORMER, from Latin *auris,* ear. **3.** AUSCULTATION, SCOUT[1], from Latin *auscultāre,* to listen to (**aus-* + **kli-to-,* inclined; see **klei-**). **4.** Suffixed basic form **ous-os-.* **a.** OTIC, OTO-; MYOSOTIS, PAROTID GLAND, from Greek *ous* (stem *ōt-*), ear; **b.** (see **slēg-**) Greek *lagōs,* hare (< **lag-ous-,* "with drooping ears"; **lag-,* to droop). [Pokorny *ōus-* 785.]

owi-. Important derivatives are *ewe* and *ovine.*

owi-. Sheep. **1.** EWE, from Old English *ēwe, eōwu,* ewe, from Germanic **awi-.* **2.** OVINE, from Latin *ovis,* sheep. [Pokorny *oui-s* 784.]

pā-. Important derivatives are *fodder, forage, fur, pabulum, food, feed, foster, pasture, antipasto, pester, repast, pastor, pantry, companion,* and *company.*

pā-. To protect, feed. Contracted from **paə-.* **1.** Suffixed form **pā-trom.* **a.** FODDER, from Old English *fōdor,* fodder; **b.** FORAGE, from Old French *feurre,* fodder; **c.** FUR, from Old French *forre, fuerre,* trimming made from animal skin, fur (< "sheath, case, lining"). **a, b,** and **c** all from Germanic **fōdram.* **2.** Suffixed form **pā-dhlom* (doublet of **pā-trom*). PABULUM, from Latin *pābulum,* food, fodder. **3.** Extended form **pāt-.* **a.** FOOD, from Old English *fōda,* food, from Germanic **fōd-,* food; **b.** FEED, from Old English *fēdan,* to feed, from Germanic denominative **fōd-jan,* to give food to; **c.** suffixed form **pāt-tro-.* FOSTER, from Old English *fōstor,* food, nourishment, from Germanic **fōstra-.* **4.** Extended form **pās-.* **a.** suffixed form **pās-sko-.* PASTURE; ANTIPASTO, REPAST, from Latin *pāscere,* to feed; **b.** suffixed form **pās-tor-.* PASTOR, PESTER, from Latin *pāstor,* shepherd; **c.** suffixed form **pās-t-ni-.* PANADA, PANATELA, PANNIER, (PANOCHA), PANTRY, PASTILLE, (PENUCHE); APPANAGE, COMPANION[1], (COMPANY), from Latin *pānis,* bread. **5.** Suffixed form **pā-tor-.* BEZOAR, from Persian *pād,* protecting against, from Iranian **pātar-* (Avestan *pātar-*). **6.** Suffixed form **pā-won-,* protector. SATRAP, from Old Persian *khshathra-pāvā,* protector of the province. [Pokorny *pā-* 787, 1. *pō(i)-* 839.]

pag-. Important derivatives are *fang, compact*[1], *impinge, pay*[1], *peace, appease, pacific, pacify, pact, pale*[1], *palisade, pole*[2], *impale, travail, travel, palette, pagan, peasant, page*[1], *pageant, propagate,* and *pectin.*

pag-. Also **pak-**. To fasten. **1.** Lengthened-grade form **pāk-.* FAY[1], from Old English *fēgan,* to fit closely, from Germanic **fōgjan,* to join, fit. **2.** Nasalized form **pa-n-g-,* also **pa-n-k-.* **a.** *(i)* FANG, from Old English *fang, feng,* plunder, booty, from Germanic **fangam, *fangiz; (ii)* VANG, from Dutch *vangen,* to catch, from remade Germanic verb **fangan; (iii)* NEWFANGLED, from Middle English **-fangel,* taken, akin to Old High German *-fangolon,* to close, from Germanic **fanglōn,* to grasp. *(i), (ii),* and *(iii)* all derivatives of Germanic **fanhan,* to seize; **b.** COMPACT[1], IMPINGE, from Latin *pangere,* to fasten. **3.** Root form **păk-.* **a.** PACE[2], PAY[1], PEACE; APPEASE, PACIFIC, PACIFY, from Latin *pāx,* peace (< "a binding together by treaty or agreement"); **b.** PACT, from Latin *pacīscī,* to agree. **4.** Suffixed form **pak-slo-.* **a.** PALE[1], PALISADE, PAWL, PEEL[3], POLE[2]; IMPALE, TRAVAIL, (TRAVEL), from Latin *pālus,* stake (fixed in the ground); **b.** PALETTE, PEEL[2], from Latin *pāla,* spade, probably from **pag-**. **5.** Lengthened-grade form **pāg-.* **a.** PAGAN, PEASANT, from Latin *pāgus,* "boundary staked out on the ground," district, village, country; **b.** PAGE[1], PAGEANT, from Latin *pāgina,* "trellis to which a row of vines is fixed," hence (by metaphor) column of writing, page; **c.** PROPAGATE, from Latin *prōpāgāre,* to propagate (< "to fix before"; *prō-,* before, in front; see **per**[1]); **d.** PECTIN, PEGMATITE; AREOPAGUS, from Greek *pēgnunai,* to fasten, coagulate, with derivative *pagos* (< **pag-o-*), mass, hill. [Pokorny *păk-* 787.]

pan-. Important derivatives are *vane, pane,* and *panel.*

pan-. Fabric. **1.a.** VANE, from Old English *fana,* flag, banner, weathercock; **b.** (see **g[w]hen-**) Germanic compound **gund-fanōn-,* "battle-flag." Both **a** and **b** from Germanic **fanōn.* **2.** Extended form **panno-.* PANE, PANEL, from Latin *pannus,* piece of cloth, rag. [Pokorny *pan-* 788.]

pant-. Derivatives are *pan-* and *pancreas.*

pant-. All. Attested only in Tocharian and Greek. PAN-; DIAPASON, PANCRATIUM, PANCREAS, from Greek *pas* (neuter *pan,* stem *pant-*), all. [In Pokorny 1. *k̂eu-* 592.]

papa. Important derivatives are *papa* and *pope.*

papa. A child's word for "father," a linguistic near-universal found in many languages. **1.** PAPA, from French *papa,* father. **2.** PAPPUS, POPE, from Greek *pappas,* father, and *pappos,* grandfather. [Pokorny *pap(p)a* 789.]

past-. Important derivatives are *fast[1], steadfast, fasten, fast[2],* and *breakfast.*

past-. Solid, firm. **1.a.** FAST[1]; STEADFAST, from Old English *fæst,* fixed, firm; **b.** AVAST, from Middle Dutch *vast,* firm, fast. Both **a** and **b** from Germanic **fastuz,* firm, fast. **2.** FASTEN, from Old English *fæstnian,* to fasten, establish, from Germanic **fastinōn,* to make firm or fast. **3.** HANDFAST, from Old Norse *festa,* to fix, affirm, from Germanic causative **fastjan,* to make firm. **4.a.** FAST[2], from Old English *fæstan,* to abstain from food; **b.** BREAKFAST, from Old Norse *fasta,* to abstain from food. Both **a** and **b** from Germanic **fastēn,* to hold fast, observe abstinence. [Pokorny *pasto-* 789.]

pau-. Important derivatives are *few, paucity, paraffin, pauper, poor, poverty, foal, filly, pony, pullet, puerile, encyclopedia,* and *orthopedics.*

pau-. Few, little.
I. Adjectival form **pau-,* few, little. **1.** FEW, from Old English *fēawe,* few, from Germanic **fawaz.* **2.** Suffixed form **pau-ko-.* PAUCITY, POCO, from Latin *paucus,* little, few. **3.** Suffixed form **pau-ro-* in metathetical form **par-wo-.* PARAFFIN, PARVOVIRUS, from Latin *parvus,* little, small, neuter *parvum,* becoming *parum,* little, rarely. **4.** Compound **pau-paros,* producing little, poor (**par-os,* producing; see **perə-[1]**). PAUPER, POOR, POVERTY, from Latin *pauper,* poor.
II. Suffixed reduced variant form **pu-lo-,* young of an animal. **1.** FOAL, from Old English *fola,* young horse, colt, from Germanic **fulōn-.* **2.** FILLY, from Old Norse *fylja,* young female horse, from Germanic derivative **fuljō.*
III. Basic form **pau-* and variant form **pŭ-,* boy, child. **1.** Suffixed form **pu-ero-.* PUERILE, PUERPERAL, from Latin *puer,* child. **2.** Extended form **put-.* **a.** POLTROON, PONY, POOL[2], POULARD, PULLET; CATCHPOLE, from Latin *pullus* (< **putslo-*), young of an animal, chicken; **b.** PUSILLANIMOUS, from Latin *pusillus* (< **putslo-lo*), old diminutive of *pullus.* **3.** Suffixed form **paw-id-.* PEDO-[2]; ENCYCLOPEDIA, ORTHOPEDICS, from Greek *pais* (stem *paid-*), child (> *paideia,* education). [Pokorny *pōu-* 842.]

ped-. Important derivatives are *foot, fetter, fetlock, pawn[2], pedal, pedestrian, peon, pioneer, millipede, trivet, expedite, impede, impeach, pew, podium, octopus, platypus, podiatry, pajamas, fetch[1], impair, pessimism,* and *impeccable.*

ped-. Foot.
I. Nominal root. **1.** Lengthened o-grade form **pōd-.* FOOT, from Old English *fōt,* foot, from Germanic **fōt-.* **2.** Suffixed form **ped-ero-.* FETTER, from Old English *fetor, feter,* leg iron, fetter, from Germanic **feterō.* **3.** Suffixed form **ped-el-.* FETLOCK, from Middle English *fitlock, fetlock,* fetlock, from a Germanic source akin to Old High German *vizzelach,* fetlock, from Germanic **fetel-.* **4.** Basic form **ped-.* PAWN[2], -PED, PEDAL, PEDATE, PEDESTRIAN, PEDI-, PEDICEL, PEDUNCLE, (PEON), PES, PIONEER; MILLIPEDE, SESQUIPEDAL, (TRIPEDAL), TRIVET, VAMP[1], from Latin *pēs* (stem *ped-*), foot. **5.** Form **ped-yo-.* **a.** EXPEDITE, from Latin *expedīre,* to free from a snare (*ex-,* out of; see **eghs**); **b.** IMPEDE, from Latin *impedīre,* "to put in fetters, hobble, shackle," entangle, hinder (*in-,* in; see **en**). **6.** Suffixed form **ped-ikā.* IMPEACH, from Latin *pedica,* fetter, snare. **7.** O-grade form **pod-.* **a.** (PEW), -POD, PODITE, PODIUM; ANTIPODES, APODAL, APPOGGIATURA, APUS, LYCOPODIUM, MONOPODIUM, OCTOPUS, (PELECYPOD), PHALAROPE, PLATYPUS, PODAGRA, PODIATRY, PODOPHYLLIN, POLYP, (POLYPOD), SYMPODIUM, from Greek *pous* (stem *pod-*), foot; **b.** PODZOL, from Russian *pod,* under. **8.** Suffixed form **ped-ya.* TRAPEZIUM, from Greek *peza,* foot. **9.** Suffixed form **ped-o-.* **a.** PEDO-[1]; PARALLELEPIPED, from Greek *pedon,* ground, soil; **b.** (PAISA), (PICE), PIE[3], PUG[3], from Sanskrit *padam,* footstep, foot, and *pāt,* foot; **c.** PAJAMA, TEAPOY, from Middle Persian *pāī,* leg, foot; **d.** lengthened-grade form **pēd-o-.* *(i)* PILOT, from Greek *pēdon,* rudder, steering oar; *(ii)* DIAPEDESIS, from Greek *pēdan,* to leap. **10.** Suffixed form *ped-ī-.* CYPRIPEDIUM, from Greek *pedilon,* sandal.
II. Verbal root **ped-,* to walk, stumble, fall. **1.** FETCH[1], from Old English *fetian, feccean,* to bring back, from Germanic **fetēn.* **2.a.** Suffixed (comparative) form **ped-yos-.* PEJORATION; IMPAIR, from Latin *pēior,* worse (< "stumbling"); **b.** suffixed (superlative) form **ped-samo-.* PESSIMISM, from Latin *pessimus,* worst; **c.** suffixed form **ped-ko-.* PECCABLE, PECCADILLO, PECCANT; IMPECCABLE, from Latin *peccāre,* to stumble, sin. **a, b,** and **c** all from Latin **ped-.* [Pokorny 2. *pĕd-* 790.]

pē(i)-. Important derivatives are *fiend, passion, passive, patient,* and *compassion.*

pē(i)-. Also **pē-, pī-.** To hurt. Contracted from **peə(i)-.* **1.** Suffixed (participial) form **pī-ont-* (< **piə-ont-*). FIEND, from Old English *fēond, fīond,* enemy, devil, from Germanic **fījand-,* hating, hostile. **2.** Possibly **pē-* in suffixed zero-grade **pə-to-.* PASSIBLE, PASSION, PASSIVE, PATIENT; COMPASSION, from Latin *patī,* to suffer. [Pokorny *pē(i)-* 792.]

peiə-. Important derivatives are *fat, pituitary, pine[1],* and *Irish.*

peiə-. To be fat, swell. **1.** Extended o-grade form **poid-.* FAT, from Old English *fǣt(t),* fat, from Germanic past participle **faitidaz,* fattened, from derivative verb **faitjan,* to fatten, from **faitaz,* plump, fat. **2.** Possibly suffixed zero-grade form **pī-tu-.* PIP[5], PITUITARY, from Latin *pītuīta,* moisture exuded from trees, gum, phlegm. **3.** Possibly suffixed zero-grade form **pī-nu-.* PINE[1], PINEAL, PINNACE, PIÑON, PINOT; PIÑA CLOTH, from Latin *pīnus,* pine tree (yielding a resin). **4.** Suffixed zero-grade form **pī-won-.* PROPIONIC ACID, from Greek *piōn,* fat. **5.** Suffixed zero-grade form **pī-wer-,* "fat, fertile." **a.** (ERSE), IRISH, from Old English *Īras,* the Irish, from **Īwer-iū,* the prehistoric Celtic name for Ireland; **b.** PIERIAN SPRING, from Greek *Pieria,* a region of Macedonia, from **Pīwer-iā.* [Pokorny *pei̯(ə)-* 793.]

peig-. Important derivatives are *file[2], paint, picture, picturesque, pigment, pimento, pinto,* and *depict.*

peig-. Also **peik-.** To cut, mark (by incision). **1.** Alternate form **peik-.* FILE[2], from Old English *fīl,* file, from Germanic **fīhala,* cutting tool. **2.** Nasalized zero-grade form **pi-n-g-.* PAINT, PICTOR, PICTURE, PICTURESQUE, PIGMENT, PIMENTO, PINT, PINTO; DEPICT, PICTOGRAPH, from Latin *pingere,* to embroider, tattoo, paint, picture. **3.** Suffixed zero-grade form **pik-ro-.* PICRO-, from Greek *pikros,* sharp, bitter. **4.** O-grade form **poik-.* PLATY[2], POIKILOTHERM, from Greek *poikilos,* spotted, pied, various. [Pokorny 1. *peig-* 794.]

peku-. Important derivatives are *fellow, fee, pecuniary,* and *peculiar.*

peku-. Wealth, movable property. **1.a.** FELLOW, from Old Norse *fē,* property, cattle; **b.** FEE, from Old French *fie,* fief; **c.** FEUD[2], from Medieval Latin *feudum,* feudal estate. **a, b,** and **c** all from Germanic **fehu-.* **2.** PECORINO, from Latin *pecus,* cattle. **3.** Suffixed form **peku-n-.* PECUNIARY; IMPECUNIOUS, from Latin *pecūnia,* property, wealth. **4.** Suffixed form **peku-l-.* PECULATE, PECULIAR, from Latin *pecūlium,* riches in cattle, private property. [In Pokorny 2. *pek̂-* 797.]

pek[w]-. Important derivatives are *cook, cuisine, kitchen, apricot, biscuit, concoct, precocious, culinary, kiln, pumpkin, peptic,* and *dyspepsia.*

pek[w]-. To cook, ripen. **1.** Assimilated form (in Italic and Celtic) **k[w]ek[w]-.* **a.** COOK, CUISINE, KITCHEN, QUITTOR; APRICOT, BISCUIT, CONCOCT, DECOCT, PRECOCIOUS, RICOTTA, TERRA COTTA, from Latin *coquere,* to cook; **b.** CULINARY, KILN, from Latin *culīna,* kitchen, deformed from *coquīna.* **2.** PEPO; PUMPKIN, from Greek *pepōn,* ripe. **3.** PEPTIC, PEPTIZE; DRUPE, EUPEPTIC, PEPSIN, PEPTONE, from Greek *peptein,* to cook, ripen, digest (> *peptos,* cooked). **4.** DYSPEPSIA, from Greek *-pepsia,* digestion. **5.** PUKKA, from Sanskrit *pakva-,* ripe. [Pokorny *pek[u]-* 798.]

pel-[1]. Important derivatives are *pale[1], pallid, pallor, appall, palomino, falcon,* and *poliomyelitis.*

pel-[1]. Pale. **1.** Suffixed variant form **pal-wo-.* **a.** *(i)* FALLOW DEER, from Old English *fealu, fealo,* reddish yellow; *(ii)* FAUVISM, from Frankish *falw-,* reddish-yellow. Both *(i)* and *(ii)* from Germanic **falwaz;* **b.** PALE[2], PALLID, PALLOR; APPALL, from Latin *pallēre,* to be pale; **c.** PALOMINO, from Latin *palumbēs* (influenced in form by Latin *columbus,* dove), ringdove, "gray-bird." **2.** Probably suffixed form **pel-ko-.* FALCON; (GYRFALCON), from Late Latin *falcō,* falcon, from Germanic **falkōn-,* falcon (< "gray bird"; but this is also possibly from the Late Latin). **3.** Suffixed extended form **peli-wo-.* **a.** PELOPS, from Greek *pelios,* dark; **b.** o-grade form **poli-wo-.* POLIOMYELITIS, from Greek *polios,* gray. **4.** PELARGONIUM, from Greek *pelargos* (< **pelawo-argos*), stork (< "black-white bird"; *argos,* white; see **arg-**), perhaps from **pel-[1].** [Pokorny 6. *pel-* 804.]

pel-[2]. Important derivatives are *fold[1], -fold, multiple,* and *triple.*

pel-[2]. To fold. **1.** Extended o-grade form **polt-.* **a.** FOLD[1], from Old English *fealdan, faldan,* to fold; **b.** FALTBOAT, from Old High German *faldan,* to fold; **c.** FURBELOW, from Italian *falda,* fold, flap, pleat; **d.** *(i)* FALDSTOOL, from Medieval Latin compound *faldistolium,* folding chair; *(ii)* FAUTEUIL, from Old French *faldestoel,* faldstool. Both *(i)* and *(ii)* from Germanic compound **faldistōlaz,* "folding stool" (**stōlaz,* stool; see **stā-**); **e.** -FOLD, from Old English *-feald, -fald,* -fold, from Germanic combining form **-falthaz, *-faldaz.* **a, b, c, d,** and **e** all from Germanic **falthan, *faldan.* **2.** Combining form **-plo-.* **a.** DECUPLE, MULTIPLE, OCTUPLE, QUADRUPLE, QUINTUPLE, SEPTUPLE, (SEXTUPLE), TRIPLE, from Latin *-plus,* -fold (as in *triplus,* threefold); **b.** (-PLOID); TRIPLOBLASTIC, from Greek *-plos, -ploos,* -fold (as in *haploos, haplous,* single, and *triploos,* triple). [Pokorny 3. a. *pel-* 802.]

pel-[3]. Important derivatives are *film, pelt[1],* and *surplice.*

pel-[3]. Skin, hide. **1.** Suffixed form **pel-no-.* FELL[3], from Old English *fel,* skin, hide, from Germanic **felnam.* **2.** FILM, from Old English *filmen,* membrane, from Germanic suffixed form **felman-ja-.* **3.** Suffixed form **pel-ni-.* PELISSE, PELLICLE, PELT[1], (PELTRY), PILLION; PELLAGRA, SURPLICE, from Latin *pellis,* skin. **4.** ERYSIPELAS, from Greek *-pelas,* skin. **5.** Suffixed form **pel-to-.* PELTATE, from Greek *peltē,* a shield (made of hide). [Pokorny 3. b. *pel-* 803.]

pel-[4]. An important derivative is *monopoly.*

pel-[4]. To sell. Lengthened o-grade form **pōl-.* BIBLIOPOLE, MONOPOLY, from Greek *pōlein,* to sell. [Pokorny 5. *pel-* 804.]

pel-[5]. Important derivatives are *anvil, felt[1], filter, pulsate, pulse[1], push, compel, expel, propel, repel, polish,* and *appeal.*

pel-[5]. To thrust, strike, drive.
I. Suffixed form **pel-de-.* **1.a.** ANVIL, from Old English *anfilt(e), anfealt,* anvil ("something beaten on"); **b.** *(i)* FELT[1], from Old English *felt,* felt; *(ii)* FILTER, from Medieval Latin *filtrum,* filter, piece of felt. Both *(i)* and *(ii)* from Germanic **feltaz, *filtiz,* compressed wool. Both **a** and **b** from Germanic **felt-, *falt-,* to beat. **2.** PELT[2], POUSSETTE, PULSATE, PULSE[1], PUSH; COMPEL, DISPEL, EXPEL, IMPEL, PROPEL, REPEL, from Latin *pellere* (past participle *pulsus*), to push, drive, strike. **3.a.** Suffixed o-grade form **pol-o-,* fuller of cloth. POLISH, from Latin *polīre,* to make smooth, polish (< "to full cloth");

b. suffixed o-grade form **pol-o-* (with different accentuation from the preceding), fulled (of cloth). INTERPOLATE, from Latin compound adjective *inter-polis* (also *interpolus*), refurbished (*inter-*, between; see **en**).
II. Extended form **pelə-*. **1.** Present stem **pelnā-*. **a.** APPEAL, from Latin *appellāre,* "to drive to," address, entreat, appeal, call (*ad-*, to; see **ad-**); **b.** COMPELLATION, from Latin *compellāre,* to accost, address (*com-*, intensive prefix; see **kom**). **2.** Possible suffixed zero-grade extended adverbial form **plə-ti-*, or locative plural **plə-si.* PLESIOSAUR, from Greek *plēsios,* near (< "pushed toward"), from pre-Greek **plāti* or **plāsi.* [Pokorny 2. a. *pel-* 801.]

---

pelə-[1]**.** Important derivatives are *full*[1]*, fill, plenitude, plenty, replenish, folk, plural, plus, surplus, poly-, accomplish, complete, compliment, comply, deplete, expletive, implement, supply, plebeian,* and *plethora.*

pelə-[1]**.** To fill; with derivatives referring to abundance and multitude. Variant **plē-*, contracted from **pleə-*.
I. Zero-grade form **pl̥ə-*. **1.** Suffixed form **pl̥ə-no-* FULL[1], from Old English *full,* full, from Germanic **fulnaz, *fullaz,* full. **2.** FILL, from Old English *fyllan,* to fill (from Germanic derivative verb **fulljan,* to fill), and *fyllu,* full amount (from Germanic abstract noun **full-īnō-*, fullness). **3.** PLENARY, PLENITUDE, PLENTY, PLENUM; PLENIPOTENTIARY, REPLENISH, TERREPLEIN, from Latin *plēnus,* full, from Latin stem **plēno-*, replacing **plāno-* (influenced by Latin verb *plēre,* to fill; see **III. 1.** below). **4.** Suffixed form **pl̥ə-go-*. **a.** FOLK, from Old English *folc,* people; **b.** VOLKSLIED, from Old High German *folc,* people. Both **a** and **b** from Germanic **folkam.*
II. Suffixed form **p(e)lə-u-*. **1.** Obscure comparative form. PIÙ, PLURAL, PLUS; NONPLUS, PLUPERFECT, SURPLUS, from Latin *plūs,* more (Old Latin *plous*). See also **III. 4.** below. **2.** O-grade form **pol(ə)-u-*. POLY-; HOI POLLOI, from Greek *polus,* much, many. **3.** PALUDAL, PALUDISM, from Latin *palūs,* marsh, possibly from **pelə-**[1] (? < "inundated"; but probably rather from **pel-**[1]).
III. Variant form **plē-*. **1.** (ACCOMPLISH), COMPLETE, COMPLIMENT, (COMPLY), DEPLETE, EXPLETIVE, IMPLEMENT, REPLETE, SUPPLY, from Latin *plēre,* to fill. **2.** Possibly suffixed form **plē-dhw-*. (PLEBE), PLEBEIAN, PLEBS; PLEBISCITE, from Latin *plēbs, plēbēs,* the people, multitude. **3.** Suffixed form **plē-dhwo-*. PLETHORA; PLETHYSMOGRAPH, from Greek derivative verb *plēthein,* to be full. **4.** Suffixed adjective (positive) form **plē-ro-*. PLEROCERCOID, from Greek *plērēs,* full. **5.** Suffixed (comparative) form **plē-i(s)on-*. PLEO-, PLEONASM; PLEIOTAXY, PLEIOTROPISM, PLIOCENE, from Greek *pleōn, pleiōn,* more. **6.** Suffixed (superlative) form **plē-isto-*. PLEISTOCENE, from Greek *pleistos,* most.
IV. POORI, from Sanskrit *pūraḥ,* cake (< "that which fills or satisfies"), possibly from **pelə-**[1]. [Pokorny 1. *pel-* 798.]

---

pelə-[2]**.** Important derivatives are *field, floor, plain, plane*[1]*, plane*[2]*, explain, palm*[1]*, palm*[2]*, planet, plasma, plaster, plastic,* and *polka.*

pelə-[2]**.** Flat; to spread. Variant **plā-*, contracted from **plaə-*. **1.** Suffixed form **pel(ə)-tu-*. FIELD, from Old English *feld,* open field, from Germanic **felthuz,* flat land. **2.** Suffixed form **pel(ə)-t-es-* (by-form of **pel(ə)-tu-*). **a.** FELDSPAR, from Old High German *feld,* field; **b.** VELDT, from Middle Dutch *veld, velt,* field. Both **a** and **b** from Germanic **feltha-*, flat land. **3.** Variant form **plā-*. **a.** suffixed form **plā-ru-*. FLOOR, from Old English *flōr,* floor, from Germanic **flōruz,* floor; **b.** suffixed form **plā-no-*. LLANO, PIANO[2], PLAIN, PLANARIAN, PLANE[1], PLANE[2], PLANE[3], PLANISH, PLANO-, PLANULA; EXPLAIN, (PIANOFORTE), from Latin *plānus,* flat, level, even, plain, clear. **4.** Suffixed zero-grade form **pl̥ə-mā.* PALM[1], PALM[2], from Latin *palma* (< **palama*), palm of the hand. **5.** Possibly extended variant form **plan-*. **a.** PLANET; APLANATIC, from Greek *planasthai,* to wander (< "to spread out"); **b.** FLÂNEUR, from French *flâner,* to walk the streets idly, from a Germanic source akin to Old Norse *flana,* to wander aimlessly, from Germanic **flan-*, possibly from **pelə-**[2]. **6.** Suffixed zero-grade form **plə-dh-*. -PLASIA, PLASMA, -PLAST, PLASTER, PLASTIC, (PLASTID), -PLASTY; (DYSPLASIA), METAPLASM, (TOXOPLASMA), from Greek *plassein* (< **plath-yein*), to mold, "spread out." **7.** O-grade form **polə-*. **a.** POLYNYA, from Russian *polyĭ,* open; **b.** POLACK, POLKA, from Slavic *polje,* broad flat land, field. [Pokorny *pelə-* 805.] See also extensions **plāk-**[1] and **plat-**.

---

pelə-[3]**.** Important derivatives are *police, policy*[1]*, politic,* and *metropolis.*

pelə-[3]**.** Citadel, fortified high place. POLICE, (POLICY[1]), POLIS, POLITIC, (POLITY); ACROPOLIS, COSMOPOLIS, COSMOPOLITE, MEGALOPOLIS, METROPOLIS, NECROPOLIS, POLICLINIC, PROPOLIS, from Greek *polis,* city. [In Pokorny 1. *pel-* 798.]

---

penk^{w}e. Important derivatives are *five, fifteen, penta-, pentad, pentagon, pentathlon, Pentecost, fifth, quintet, quintessence, finger, fist,* and *foist.*

penk^{w}e. Five.
I. Basic form **penk^{w}e.* **1.** Assimilated form **pempe.* **a.** FIVE; FIFTY, from Old English *fīf,* five, with derivative *fiftig,* fifty (*-tēne,* ten; see **dek̑m̥**); **b.** FIN[2], from Old High German *finf, funf,* five. Both **a** and **b** from Germanic **fimf.* **2.a.** FIFTEEN, from Old English *fīftēne,* fifteen; **b.** FEMTO-, from Old Norse *fimmtān,* fifteen. Both **a** and **b** from Germanic compound **fimftehun,* fifteen (**tehun,* ten; see **dek̑m̥**). **3.** Assimilated form **k^{w}enk^{w}e.* **a.** CINQUAIN, CINQUE, QUINQUE-; CINQUECENTO, (CINQUEFOIL), QUINCUNX, from Latin *quīnque,* five; **b.** KENO, QUINATE, from Latin distributive *quīnī,* five each; **c.** QUINDECENNIAL, from Latin compound *quīndecim,* fifteen (*decem,* ten; see **dek̑m̥**). **4.** PENTA-, PENTAD; PENSTEMON, (PENTAGON), (PENTAMETER), (PENTATHLON), from Greek *pente,* five. **5.** PUNCH[3]; PACHISI, from Sanskrit *pañca,* five.
II. Compound **penk^{w}e-(d)konta,* "five tens," fifty (**-(d)konta,* group of ten; see **dek̑m̥**). **1.** QUINQUAGENARIAN, from Latin *quīnquāginta,* fifty. **2.** PENTECOST, from Greek *pentēkonta,* fifty.
III. Ordinal adjective **penk^w-to-*. **1.** FIFTH, from Old English *fīfta,* fifth, from Germanic **fimftōn-*. **2.** QUINT[1], QUINTAIN, QUINTET, QUINTILE; QUINTESSENCE, QUINTILLION, QUINTUPLE, from Latin *quīntus* (< **quinc-tos*), feminine *quīnta,* fifth.
IV. Suffixed form **penk^w-ro-*. FINGER, from Old English *finger,* finger, from Germanic **fingwraz,* finger (< "one of five").
V. Suffixed reduced zero-grade form **pn̥k-sti-*. **a.** FIST, from Old English *fȳst,* fist; **b.** FOIST, from Dutch *vuist,* fist. Both **a** and **b** from Germanic **funhstiz* [Pokorny *penk^{u}e* 808, *pn̥ksti-* 839.]

---

pent-. Important derivatives are *find, pontiff, pontoon, punt*[1]*, sputnik,* and *path.*

pent-. To tread, go. **1.** FIND, from Old English *findan,* to find, from Germanic **finthan,* to come upon, discover. **2.** Suffixed o-grade form **pont-i-*. **a.** PONS, PONTIFEX, PONTIFF, PONTINE, PONTOON, PUNT[1]; (TRANSPONTINE), from Latin *pōns* (stem *pont-*), bridge (earliest meaning, "way, passage," preserved in the priestly title *pontifex,* "he who prepares the way"; *-fex,* maker; see **dhē-**); **b.** SPUTNIK, from Russian *sputnik,* fellow traveler, sputnik, from *put',* path, way. **3.** Zero-grade form **pn̥t-*. PERIPATETIC, from Greek *patein,* to tread, walk. **4.** Suffixed zero-grade form **pn̥t-ə-*. **a.** PATH, from Old English *pæth,* path; **b.** FOOTPAD, from Middle Dutch *pad,* way, path. Both **a** and **b** from Germanic **patha-*, way, path, probably borrowed (? via Scythian) from Iranian **path-*. [Pokorny *pent-* 808.]

---

per[1]**.** Important derivatives are *far, paramount, paradise, for, forth, afford, further, foremost, former*[2]*, first, prow, protein, proton, fore, forefather, before, from, furnish, veneer, purchase, prone, reciprocal, approach, reproach, approximate, probable, probe, proof, prove, approve, improve, pre-, private, privilege, privy, deprive, proper, property, appropriate, premier, primal, primary, primate, prime, primitive, prince, principal, principle, pristine,* and *priest.*

per[1]**.** Base of prepositions and preverbs with the basic meanings of "forward," "through," and a wide range of extended senses such as "in front of," "before," "early," "first," "chief," "toward," "against," "near," "at," "around."
I. Basic form **per* and extended form **peri.* **1.a.** TURNVEREIN, from Middle High German *vereinen,* to unite, from Old High German *far-;* **b.** VEER[2], from Middle Dutch *vieren,* to let out, slacken; **c.** (see **ghend-**) Germanic compound **fer-getan,* "to lose one's hold," forget. **d.** FRUMP, from Middle Dutch *verrompelen,* to wrinkle. **a, b, c,** and **d** all from Germanic **fer-, *far-*, used chiefly as an intensive prefix denoting destruction, reversal, or completion. **2.** Suffixed (comparative) form **per-ero-*, farther away. FAR, from Old English *feor(r),* far, from Germanic **fer(e)ra.* **3.** PER, PER-; PARAMOUNT, PARAMOUR, PARGET, PARVENU, from Latin *per,* through, for, by. **4.** PERI-; PERISSODACTYL, from Greek *peri,* around, near, beyond. **5.a.** PARADISE, from Avestan *pairi-*, around; **b.** PURDAH, from Old Persian *pari,* around, over; **c.** (see **wer-**) Old Iranian **pari-vāraka-*, protective. **a, b,** and **c** all from Old Iranian **pari-*, around. **6.** PERESTROIKA, from Old Russian *pere-*, around, again, from Slavic **per-*.
II. Zero-grade form **pr̥-*. **1.a.** FOR, from Old English *for,* before, instead of, on account of; **b.** FOR-, from Old English *for-*, prefix denoting destruction, pejoration, exclusion, or completion. Both **a** and **b** from Germanic **fur,* before, in. **2.** Extended form **pr̥t-*. FORTH; AFFORD, from Old English *forth,* from Germanic **furth-*, forward. **3.** Suffixed (comparative) form **pr̥-tero-*. FURTHER, from Old English *furthra, furthor,* farther away, from Germanic **furthera-*. **4.a.** Compound **pr̥-st-i-* (or **por-st-i-*, with o-grade form **por-*), "that which stands before," stake, post (see **stā-**); **b.** PORRECT, from Latin *por-*, forth, forward. Both **a** and **b** from Latin *por-* from **pr̥-*. **5.** Suffixed form **pr̥-sōd.* PARGET, from Latin *porrō,* forward.
III. Extended zero-grade form **pr̥ə-*. **1.** Suffixed (superlative) form **pr̥ə-mo-*. **a.** FOREMOST, FORMER[2], from Old English *forma,* first, foremost, from Germanic **fruma-, *furma-;* **b.** (see **ed-**) Latin compound *prandium,* "first meal," late breakfast, lunch (probably < **prām-d-ium* < **pr̥əm-(e)d-yo-;* second element **-(e)d-*, to eat). **2.** Suffixed (superlative) form **pr̥ə-isto-*. FIRST, from Old English *fyrst, fyrest,* first, from Germanic **furista-*, foremost. **3.** Suffixed form **pr̥ə-wo-*. **a.** PROW, from Greek *prōira,* forward part of a ship, from analogically suffixed form **prōw-arya;* **b.** PROTEIN, PROTIST, PROTO-, PROTON, from Greek *prōtos,* first, foremost, from suffixed (superlative) form **prōw-ato-*. Both **a** and **b** from Greek **prōwo-*, first, foremost. **4.** Suffixed form **pr̥ə-i.* ARPENT, from Latin *arepennis,* half-acre (second element obscure), from Gaulish *ari* (combining form *are-*), before, from Celtic **(p)ari, *are.*
IV. Extended form **prəǟ.* **1.a.** FORE, FORE-; (FOREFATHER), from Old English *fore, for,* before; **b.** VORLAGE, from Old High German *fora,* before; **c.** BEFORE, from Old English *beforan,* before, from Germanic prefixed and suffixed form **bi-fora-na,* in the front (**bi-*, at, by; see **ambhi**). **a, b,** and **c** all from Germanic **fura,* before. **2.** PARA-[1]; PALFREY, from Greek *para,* beside, alongside of, beyond.
V. Extended form **prŏ.* **1.a.** FRO; (FROWARD), from Old Norse *frā,* from, from Germanic **fra,* forward, away from; **b.** (see **ed-, ēik-**) Germanic **fra-*, completely. **2.** Suffixed form **prŏ-mo-*. **a.** FROM, from Old English *from,* from, from Germanic **fram,* from; **b.** FURNISH, VENEER, from Old French *f(o)urnir,* to supply, provide, from Germanic derivative verb **frumjan,* to further, from Germanic **frum,* forward; **c.** PRAM[2], from Czech *prám,* raft. **3.** Suffixed form **prō-wo-*. FRAU, (FRÄULEIN), from Old High German *frouwa,* lady, from Germanic **frōwō-*, lady, lengthened-grade feminine of **frawan-*, lord. **4.** PRO[1], PRO-[1], (PROUD); (IMPROVE), PURCHASE, from Latin *prō, prŏ-*, before, for, instead of. **5.** Suffixed form **prō-no-*. PRONE, from Latin *prōnus,* leaning forward. **6.** Possible suffixed form **pro-ko-*. RECIPROCAL, from Latin compound *reciprocus,* alternating, "backward and forward" (**re-ko-*, backward; see **re-**). **7.** Suffixed adverb **pro-k^{w}e.* **a.** APPROACH, (RAPPROCHEMENT), REPROACH, from Latin *prope,* near; **b.** suffixed form **prok^w-ink^{w}o-*. PROPINQUITY, from Latin *propinquus,* near; **c.** suffixed (superlative) form **prok^w-samo-*. PROXIMATE; APPROXIMATE, from Latin *proximus,* nearest. **8.** Com-

pound _*pro-bhw-o-_, growing well or straightforward (_*bhw-o-_, to grow; see **bheuə-**). (PROBABLE), PROBE, PROBITY, (PROOF), PROVE; APPROVE, IMPROBITY, (REPROVE), from Latin _probus,_ upright, good, virtuous. **9.** PRO-^{2}, from Greek _pro,_ before, in front, forward. **10.** Suffixed (comparative) form _*pro-tero-_. HYSTERON PROTERON, PROTEROZOIC, from Greek _proteros,_ before, former. **11.** PRAKRIT, from Sanskrit _pra-_ , before, forth. **12.** (see **wēro-**) Celtic _*ro-_, intensive prefix, in _*ro-wero-_, sufficiency.

VI. Extended forms _*prai-_, _*prei-_. **1.** PRE-; PRETERIT, from Latin _prae,_ before. **2.** Suffixed (comparative) form _*prei-yos-_. PRIOR^{2}, from Latin _prior,_ former, higher, superior. **3.** Suffixed form _*prei-wo-_. **a.** PRIVATE, PRIVILEGE, PRIVITY, PRIVY; DEPRIVE, from Latin _prīvus,_ single, alone (< "standing in front," "isolated from others"); **b.** PROPER, PROPERTY; APPROPRIATE, PROPRIOCEPTION, PROPRIOCEPTOR, from Latin _proprius,_ one's own, particular (< _prō prīvō,_ in particular, from the ablative of _prīvus,_ single; _prō,_ for; see **V. 5.**). **4.** Extended form _*preis-_. **a.** Suffixed (superlative) form _*preis-mo-_. _(i)_ PREMIER, PRIMAL, PRIMARY, PRIMATE, PRIME, PRIMITIVE, PRIMO, PRIMUS; IMPRIMIS, PRIMAVERA^{1}, PRIMEVAL, PRIMIPARA, PRIMOGENITOR, PRIMOGENITURE, PRIMORDIAL, from Latin _prīmus_ (< _*prīsmus;_ ablative plural _prīmīs_), first, foremost; _(ii)_ PRINCE, PRINCIPAL, PRINCIPLE, from Latin compound _prīnceps,_ "he who takes first place," leader, chief, emperor (_-ceps,_ "-taker"; see **kap-**); **b.** suffixed form _*preis-tano-_. PRISTINE, from Latin _prīstinus,_ former, earlier, original.

VII. Extended form _*pres-_ in compound _*pres-g^{w}u-_, "going before" (_*g^{w}-u-_, going; see **g^{w}ā-**). PRESBYTER, (PRIEST); PRESBYOPIA, from Greek _presbus,_ old, old man, elder.

VIII. Extended form _*proti_. PROS-, from Greek _pros,_ against, toward, near, at. [Pokorny 2. A. _per_ 810.] Other possibly related forms are grouped under **per-^{2}, per-^{3}, per-^{4}, and per-^{5}.**

---

per-^{2}. Important derivatives are _firth, fjord, fare, wayfarer, welfare, pore^{2}, emporium, ferry, fern, ford, port^{1}, opportune, porch, portal, portable, portage, porter^{1}, export, import, important, portfolio, rapport, report, sport, support,_ and _transport._

per-^{2}. To lead, pass over. A verbal root belonging to the group of **per^{1}.**

I. Full-grade form _*per-_. **1.** Suffixed form _*per-tu-_. FIRTH, FJORD, from Old Norse _fjördhr,_ an inlet, estuary, from Germanic _*ferthuz,_ place for crossing over, ford. **2.** Suffixed form _*per-onā_. PERONEAL, from Greek _peronē,_ pin of a brooch, buckle (< "that which pierces through"). **3.** Suffixed form _*per-yo-_. DIAPIR, from Greek _peirein,_ to pierce.

II. O-grade form _*por-_. **1.a.** _(i)_ FARE; WAYFARER, WAYFARING, (WELFARE), from Old English _faran,_ to go on a journey, get along; _(ii)_ FIELDFARE, from Old English _faran,_ possibly altered by folk etymology in Old English, from an uncertain original; **b.** GABERDINE, from Old High German _faran,_ to go, travel. Both **a** and **b** from Germanic _*faran,_ to go. **2.** Suffixed form _*por-o-_, passage, journey. PORE^{2}; EMPORIUM, from Greek _poros,_ journey, passage. **3.** Suffixed (causative) form _*por-eyo-_, to cause to go, lead, conduct. FERRY, from Old English _ferian,_ to transport, from Germanic _*farjan,_ to ferry. **4.** Lengthened-grade form _*pōr-_. **a.** FERE, from Old English _(ge)fēra,_ "fellow-traveler," companion (_ge-,_ together, with; see **kom**), from Germanic suffixed form _*fōr-ja-;_ **b.** FÜHRER, from Old High German _fuoren,_ to lead, from Germanic suffixed (causative) form _*fōr-jan._ **5.** Possibly suffixed form _*por-no-_, feather, wing (< "that which carries a bird in flight"). **a.** FERN, from Old English _fearn,_ fern (having feathery fronds), from Germanic _*farnō,_ feather, leaf; **b.** PAN^{2}, from Sanskrit _parṇam,_ leaf, feather.

III. Zero-grade form _*pr̥-_. **1.** Suffixed form _*pr̥-tu-_, passage. **a.** FORD, from Old English _ford,_ shallow place where one may cross a river, from Germanic _*furdu-;_ **b.** PORT^{1}; IMPORTUNE, OPPORTUNE, from Latin _portus,_ harbor (< "passage"). **2.** Suffixed form _*pr̥-tā_. PORCH, PORT^{3}, PORTAL, PORTCULLIS, PORTER^{2}, PORTICO, PORTIÈRE, PORTULACA, from Latin _porta,_ gate. **3.** Suffixed (denominative) form _*pr̥-to-_. PORT^{5}, PORTABLE, PORTAGE, PORTAMENTO, PORTATIVE, PORTER^{1}; COMPORT, DEPORT, EXPORT, IMPORT, (IMPORTANT), PORTFOLIO, PURPORT, RAPPORT, REPORT, (SPORT), SUPPORT, TRANSPORT, from Latin _portāre,_ to carry. [Pokorny 2. B. _per_ 816.]

---

per-^{3}. Important derivatives are _fear, peril, experience, experiment, expert, pirate,_ and _empiric._

per-^{3}. To try, risk (< "to lead over," "press forward"). A verbal root belonging to the group of **per^{1}.** **1.** Lengthened grade _*pēr-_. FEAR, from Old English _fǣr,_ danger, sudden calamity, from Germanic _*fēraz,_ danger. **2.** Suffixed form _*perī-tlo-_. (PARLOUS), PERIL, from Latin _perīclum, perīculum,_ trial, danger. **3.** Suffixed form _*per-yo-_. EXPERIENCE, EXPERIMENT, EXPERT, from Latin _experīrī,_ to try, learn by trying (_ex-,_ from; see **eghs**). **4.** Suffixed form _*per-ya_. PIRATE; EMPIRIC, from Greek _peira,_ trial, attempt. [Pokorny 2. E. _per_ 818.]

---

per-^{4}. Important derivatives are _press^{1}, pressure, print, compress, depress, express, imprint, oppress, repress, reprimand,_ and _suppress._

per-^{4}. To strike. A verbal root possibly belonging to the group of **per^{1}.** Extended forms _*prem-_, _*pres-_. PREGNANT^{2}, PRESS^{1}, PRESSURE, PRINT; APPRESSED, COMPRESS, DEPRESS, EXPRESS, IMPRESS^{1}, (IMPRINT), OPPRESS, REPRESS, (REPRIMAND), SUPPRESS, from Latin _premere_ (past participle _pressus_), to press. [Pokorny 3. _per-_ 818.]

---

per-^{5}. Important derivatives are _interpret, praise, precious, price, appraise, appreciate, depreciate,_ and _pornography._

per-^{5}. To traffic in, sell (< "to hand over," "distribute"). A verbal root belonging to the group of **per^{1}.** Base of two distinct extended roots.

I. Root form _*pret-_. **1.** INTERPRET, from Latin compound _inter-pres_ (stem _inter-pret-_), go-between, negotiator (_inter-,_ between; see **en**). **2.** Suffixed form _*pret-yo-_. PRAISE, PRECIOUS, PRICE; APPRAISE, (APPRECIATE), DEPRECIATE, from Latin _pretium,_ price.

II. Root form _*perə-_. Suffixed form _*p(e)r-n-ə-_, with o-grade _*por(ə)-nā_. PORNOGRAPHY, from Greek _pornē,_ prostitute, from _pernanai,_ to sell. [In Pokorny 2. C. _per_ 817.]

---

perd-. Important derivatives are _fart_ and _partridge._

perd-. To fart. **1.** FART, from Old English _*feortan,_ to fart, from Germanic _*fertan, *fartōn._ **2.** PARTRIDGE, from Greek _perdix,_ partridge (which makes a sharp whirring sound when suddenly flushed). [Pokorny _perd-_ 819.] See also **pezd-.**

---

perə-^{1}. Important derivatives are _parade, pare, parry, apparatus, apparel, disparate, emperor, imperative, imperial, parachute, parasol, prepare, rampart, repair^{1}, separate, sever, several, parent,_ and _repertory._

perə-^{1}. To produce, procure. Possibly the same root as **perə-^{2}.** See also **per-^{5} II.** Zero-grade form _*pr̥ə-_ (becoming _*par-_ in Latin). **a.** root form _*par-ā-_. PARADE, PARE, (PARLAY), PARRY, (PARURE); APPARATUS, (APPAREL), COMPRADOR, DISPARATE, EMPEROR, (IMPERATIVE), (IMPERIAL), (PARACHUTE), PARASOL, PREPARE, RAMPART, REPAIR^{1}, SEPARATE, (SEVER), (SEVERAL), from Latin _parāre,_ to try to get, prepare, equip; **b.** suffixed form _*par-yo-_. -PARA, PARENT, PARITY^{2}, -PAROUS, PARTURIENT, POSTPARTUM, REPERTORY, VIPER, from Latin _parere, parīre,_ to get, beget, give birth; **c.** suffixed form _*par-o-_, producing, in compound _*pau-paros,_ producing little, poor (see **pau-**); **d.** suffixed form _*par-ikā_. PARCAE, from Latin _Parcae,_ the Fates (who assign one's destiny). [Pokorny 2. D. _per_ 818.]

---

perə-^{2}. Important derivatives are _parcel, parse, part, impart, repartee, portion, proportion, pair, par, parlay, peer^{2}, compare,_ and _nonpareil._

perə-^{2}. To grant, allot (reciprocally, to get in return). Possibly the same root as **perə-^{1}.** See also **per-^{5} II.** Zero-grade form _*pr̥ə-_ (becoming _*par-_ in Latin). **a.** suffixed form _*par-ti-_. PARCEL, (PARCENER), PARSE, PART; BIPARTITE, COMPART, IMPART, REPARTEE, from Latin _pars_ (stem _part-_), a share, part; **b.** possibly suffixed form _*par-tiō_. PORTION, PROPORTION, from Latin _portiō,_ a part (first attested in the phrase _prō portiōne,_ in proportion, according to each part, perhaps assimilated from _*prō partiōne_); **c.** PAIR, PAR, (PARITY^{1}), PEER^{2}; COMPARE, IMPARITY, NONPAREIL, PARI-MUTUEL, from Latin _pār,_ equal, perhaps from **perə-^{2}.** [Pokorny 2. _per,_ Section C. 817.]

---

perk^{w}u-. Important derivatives are _fir_ and _cork._

perk^{w}u-. Oak. **1.** Zero-grade form _*pr̥k^{w}-_. FIR, probably from a Scandinavian source akin to Old Icelandic _fȳri,_ fir, from Germanic _*furh-jōn-_. **2.** Assimilated form _*k^{w}erk^{w}u-_. CORK, QUERCETIN; QUERCITRON, from Latin _quercus,_ oak. [Pokorny _perk^{w}u-s_ 822.]

---

pes-. Important derivatives are _pencil, penicillium,_ and _penis._

pes-. Penis. Suffixed form _*pes-ni-_. PENCIL, (PENICILLIUM), PENIS, from Latin _pēnis_ (< _*pesnis_), penis, tail. [Pokorny 3. _pes-_ 824.]

---

pet-. Important derivatives are _feather, petition, appetite, compete, perpetual, repeat, pen^{1}, propitious, ptomaine, symptom,_ and _hippopotamus._

pet-. Also **petə-.** To rush, fly. Variant _*ptē-_, contracted from _*pteə-_. **1.** Suffixed form _*pet-rā_. FEATHER, from Old English _fether,_ feather, from Germanic _*fethrō,_ feather. **2.** -PETAL, PETITION, PETULANT; APPETITE, COMPETE, IMPETUS, PERPETUAL, REPEAT, from Latin _petere,_ to go toward, seek. **3.** Suffixed form _*pet-nā_. PANACHE, PEN^{1}, PENNA, PENNATE, PENNON, PIN, PINNA, PINNACLE, PINNATE, (PINNATI-), PINNULE; EMPENNAGE, from Latin _penna, pinna,_ feather, wing. **4.** Suffixed form _*pet-ro_ (see **ōku-**). **5.** Suffixed form _*pet-yo-_. PROPITIOUS, from Latin _propitius,_ favorable, gracious, originally a religious term meaning "falling or rushing forward," hence "eager," "well-disposed" (said of the gods; _prō-,_ forward; see **per^{1}**). **6.** Suffixed zero-grade form _*pt-ero-_. -PTER; ACANTHOPTERYGIAN, APTERYX, ARCHAEOPTERYX, COLEOPTERAN, MECOPTERAN, ORTHOPTERAN, PERIPTERAL, PLECOPTERAN, PTERIDOLOGY, PTERYGOID, from Greek _pteron,_ feather, wing, and _pterux,_ wing. **7.** Suffixed zero-grade form _*pt-ilo-_. COLEOPTILE, from Greek _ptilon,_ soft feathers, down, plume. **8.** Reduplicated form _*pi-pt-_. PTOMAINE, PTOSIS; ASYMPTOTE, PERIPETEIA, PROPTOSIS, SYMPTOM, from Greek _piptein,_ to fall, with nominal derivatives _ptō-to-, ptō-ti-, ptō-ma._ **9.** O-grade form _*pot-_. HIPPOPOTAMUS, from Greek _potamos_ "rushing water," river (_-amo-,_ Greek suffix). **10.** Suffixed form _*pet-tro-_. TALIPOT, from Sanskrit _pattram,_ feather, leaf. [Pokorny 2. _pet-_ 826.]

---

petə-. Important derivatives are _fathom, patent, pace^{1}, pass, compass, expand, petal,_ and _pan^{1}._

petə-. To spread. **1.** Suffixed o-grade form _*pot(ə)-mo-_. FATHOM, from Old English _fæthm,_ fathom, from Germanic _*fathmaz,_ "length of two arms stretched out." **2.** Suffixed (stative) variant zero-grade form _*pat-ē-_. PATENT, PATULOUS, from Latin _patēre,_ to be open. **3.** Probably variant zero-grade form in remade nasalized form _*pat-no-_. PACE^{1}, (PAS), (PASS), PASSIM; (COMPASS), EXPAND, REPAND, from Latin _pandere_ (past participle _passus_ < _*pat-to-_), to spread out. **4** Suffixed form _*pet-alo-_. PETAL, from Greek _petalon,_ leaf. **5.** Suffixed form _*pet-ano-_. (PAELLA), PAN^{1}, PATEN, (PATINA^{1}), (PATINA^{2}), from Greek _patanē_ (? < _*petanā_), platter, "thing spread out." **6.** PETASOS, from Greek _petasos,_ broad-brimmed hat from Greek suffixed form _*peta-so-_. [Pokorny 1. _pet_ 824.]

---

peu-. Important derivatives are _putative, account, amputate, compute, count^{1}, dispute, impute, repute,_ and _pave._

peu-. To cut, strike, stamp **1.** Suffixed (participial) zero-grade form _*pu-to,_ cut, struck. **a.** PUTAMEN, PUTATIVE; (ACCOUNT), AMPUTATE, COMPUTE, COUNT^{1}, DEPUTE, DISPUTE, IMPUTE, REPUTE, from Latin _putāre,_ to prune, clean, settle an account, think over, reflect; **b.** PIT^{1}, from Latin _puteus,_ well, possibly from **peu-.** **2.** Variant form _*pau-_. **a.** suffixed form _*pau-yo_. PAVE, (PAVÉ), from Latin _pavīre,_ to beat; **b.** suffixed (stative) form _*paw-ē-_. PAVID, from Latin _pavēre,_ to fear (< "to be struck"); **c.** ANAPEST, from Greek _paiein,_ to beat, perhaps from **peu-.** [Pokorny 3. _pēu-_ 827.]

---

peuə-. Important derivatives are _pure, purge, Puritan,_ and _expurgate._

peuə-. To purify, cleanse. Suffixed zero-grade form **pū-ro-* (< **puə-ro*). POUR, PURE, PURÉE, PURGE, PURITAN; COMPURGATION, DEPURATE, EXPURGATE, (SPURGE), from Latin *pūrus,* pure, and *pūrgāre,* to purify (< **pūr-igāre;* second element *agere,* to drive; see **ag-**). [Pokorny 1. *peu-* 827.]

peuk-. Important derivatives are *pugilism, pugnacious, impugn, poignant, point, pounce*[1], *punctuate, puncture, pungent, expunge,* and *pygmy.*

peuk-. Also **peug-**. To prick. Zero-grade form **pug-*. **1.** Suffixed form **pug-no-*. PONIARD, PUGILISM, PUGIL STICK, PUGNACIOUS; IMPUGN, OPPUGN, REPUGN, from Latin *pugil,* pugilist, and *pugnus,* fist, with denominative *pugnāre,* to fight with the fist. **2.** Nasalized zero-grade form **pu-n-g-*. BUNG, POIGNANT, POINT, POINTILLISM, PONTIL, (POUNCE[1]), (POUNCE[3]), PUNCHEON[1], PUNCTILIO, PUNCTUAL, PUNCTUATE, PUNCTURE, PUNGENT; COMPUNCTION, EXPUNGE, SPONTOON, TRAPUNTO, from Latin *pungere,* to prick. **3.** (PYGMAEAN), PYGMY, from Greek *pugmē,* fist. [Pokorny *peuk-* 828.]

pezd-. Derivatives are *fizzle* and *petard.*

pezd-. To fart. **1.** Suffixed form **pezd-i-*. FEIST, FIZZLE, from Middle English *fisten,* to fart, from Germanic **fistiz,* a fart. **2.** PETARD, from Latin *pēdere,* to fart. **3.** PEDICULAR, from Latin *pēdis,* louse (? < "foul-smelling insect"), possibly from **pezd-**. [Pokorny *pezd-* 829, 2. *peis-* 796.] See also **perd-**.

pəter-. Important derivatives are *father, forefather, padre, paternal, patrician, patrimony, patron, expatriate, perpetrate, patriot,* and *patriarch.*

pəter-. Father. **1.** FATHER; (FOREFATHER), from Old English *fæder,* father, from Germanic **fadar.* **2.** PADRE, PATER, PATERNAL, PATRI-, PATRICIAN, PATRIMONY, PATRON, PÈRE; EXPATRIATE, PERPETRATE, from Latin *pater,* father. **3.** PATRI-, PATRIOT; ALLOPATRIC, EUPATRID, PATRIARCH, SYMPATRIC, from Greek *patēr,* father. [Pokorny *pətḗ(r)* 829.]

plāk-[1]. Important derivatives are *fluke*[1], *flake*[1], *flaw*[1], *placebo, placid, plea, plead, pleasant, please, complacent, placate, plank, placenta,* and *archipelago.*

plāk-[1]. Also **plak-**. To be flat. Extension of **pelə-**[2]. **1.** FLOE, from Old Norse *flō,* layer, coating, from Germanic **flōhō.* **2.** Variant form **plāg-*. **a.** FLUKE[1], from Old English *flōc,* flatfish, from Germanic **flōk-;* **b.** FLAKE[1], from Middle English *flake,* flake, from a Scandinavian source probably akin to Norwegian *flak,* flat piece, flake, from Germanic **flakaz;* **c.** FLAKE[2], from Old Norse *flaki, fleki,* hurdle, from Germanic **flak-*. **3.** Extended form **plakā.* FLAG[4], FLAW[1], from Old Norse *flaga,* layer of stone, from Germanic **flagō.* **4.** Possibly suffixed (stative) form **plak-ē-,* to be calm (as of the flat sea). PLACEBO, PLACID, PLEA, (PLEAD), PLEASANT, PLEASE; COMPLACENT, from Latin *placēre,* to please, be agreeable. **5.** Root noun **plak-*. (SUPPLICATE), SUPPLE, from Latin *supplex,* suppliant (whence denominative *supplicāre,* to beg humbly, first attested in Archaic Latin as *sub vos placō,* I entreat you; *sub,* under; see **upo**.) **6.** Lengthened suffixed form **plāk-ā-*. PLACABLE, PLACATE, from Latin *plācāre,* to calm (causative of *placēre*). **7.** Nasalized form **pla-n-k-*. PLANCHET, PLANK, from Latin *plancus,* flat, flat-footed. **8.** Variant form **plag-*. **a.** PLAGIARY, from Latin *plaga,* net (? < "something extended"), perhaps from **plāk-**[1]; **b.** PLAGAL, PLAGIO-, PLAYA, from Greek *plagos,* side. **9.** Root form **plak-*. PLACENTA, PLACOID; LEUKOPLAKIA, from Greek *plax,* flat, flat land, surface. **10.** Possible variant form **pelag-*. PELAGIC; ARCHIPELAGO, from Greek *pelagos,* sea. [Pokorny 1. *plā-k-* 831.]

plāk-[2]. Important derivatives are *fling, plaint, complain, plankton, plague, apoplexy,* and *paraplegia.*

plāk-[2]. To strike. **1.** Nasalized variant forms **pla-n-k-, *pla-n-g-*. **a.** FLING, from Middle English *flingen* to fling, from a Scandinavian source akin to Old Norse *flengja,* to flog, whip, from Germanic **flang-;* **b.** PLAINT, PLANGENT; COMPLAIN, from Latin *plangere,* to strike (one's own breast), lament; **c.** suffixed form **plang-yo-*. PLANKTON, from Greek *plazein,* to drive away, turn aside. **2.** Variant form **plāg-*. PLAGUE, from Latin *plāga,* a blow, stroke. **3.** Suffixed form **plāk-yo-*. PLECTRUM, -PLEGIA, PLEXOR; APLOPLEXY, PARAPLEGIA, from Greek *plēssein,* to beat, strike. [Pokorny 2. *plāk-* 832.]

plat-. Important derivatives are *flat*[1], *flatter*[1], *flat*[2], *flounder*[2], *clan, plan, plant, supplant, place, plate, plateau, platitude,* and *plaza.*

plat-. To spread. Also **plet-*. Extension of **pelə-**[2]. **1.** Variant form **plad-*. **a.** FLAT[1], from Old Norse *flatr,* flat; **b.** FLATTER[1], from Old French *flater,* to flatter. Both **a** and **b** from Germanic **flataz,* flat. **2.** Suffixed variant form **plad-yo-*. FLAT[2], from Old English *flet(t),* floor, dwelling, from Germanic **flatjam.* **3.** Basic form **plat-*. FLAN, from Late Latin *fladō,* flat cake, pancake, from Germanic **flathō(n),* flat cake. **4.** FLOUNDER[2], from Anglo-Norman *floundre,* flounder, from a Scandinavian source probably akin to Old Swedish *flundra,* flatfish, flounder, from Germanic nasalized suffixed form **flu-n-th-r-jō-*. **5.** Nasalized form **pla-n-t-*. CLAN, PLAN, PLANT, PLANTAIN[1], PLANTAR; PLANTIGRADE, SUPPLANT, TRANSPLANT, from Latin *planta,* sole of the foot, and denominative *plantāre,* to drive in with the sole of the foot, plant, whence *planta,* a plant. **6.** Suffixed zero-grade form **pl̥t-u-*. PIAZZA, PLACE, PLAICE, PLANE[4], (PLANE TREE), PLATE, (PLATEAU), (PLATITUDE), (PLATY[2]), PLATY-, (PLAZA), from Greek *platus,* flat, broad. [Pokorny *plat-* 833.]

plek-. Important derivatives are *flax, multiplex, plait, pliant, plight*[1], *ply*[1], *apply, complicate, deploy, display, employ, implicate, reply, complex,* and *perplex.*

plek-. To plait. Extension of **pel-**[2]. **1.** Suffixed o-grade form **plok-so-*. FLAX, from Old English *fleax,* flax, from Germanic **flahsam,* flax. **2.** Full-grade form **plek-*. MULTIPLEX, from Latin *-plex,* -fold (in compounds such as *duplex,* twofold; see **dwo-**). **3.** PLAIT, PLIANT, PLICA, PLICATE, PLIGHT[1], PLISSÉ, PLY[1]; APPLY, COMPLICATE, COMPLICE, DEPLOY, DISPLAY, EMPLOY, EXPLICATE, IMPLICATE, REPLICATE, (REPLY), from Latin *plicāre,* to fold (also in compounds used as denominatives of words in *-plex,* genitive *-plicis*). **4.** Suffixed forms **plek-to-* and **plek-t-to-*. PLEACH, PLEXUS; AMPLEXICAUL, COMPLECT, (COMPLEX), PERPLEXED, from Latin *plectere* (past participle *plexus*), to weave, plait, entwine. **5.** PLECOPTERAN, PLECTOGNATH, from Greek *plekein,* to plait, twine, and *plektos,* twisted. [Pokorny *plek-* 834.]

pleu-. Important derivatives are *plover, pulmonary, pneumonia, Pluto, flow, flood, fly*[1], *fly*[2], *flee, fledge, flight*[1], *fowl, fleet*[1], *fleet*[2], *float, flutter, flit,* and *fluster.*

pleu-. To flow.

I. Basic form **pleu-*. **1.** (PLOVER), (PLUVIAL), PLUVIOUS, from Latin *pluere,* to rain. **2.** PLEUSTON, from Greek *pleusis,* sailing. **3.** Suffixed zero-grade form **plu-elos.* PYELITIS, from Greek dissimilated *puelos,* trough, basin. **4.** Suffixed form **pl(e)u-mon-,* "floater," lung(s). **a.** PULMONARY, from Latin *pulmō* (< **plumonēs*), lung(s); **b.** PNEUMO-, PNEUMONIA, PNEUMONIC, from Greek *pleumōn, pneumōn* (influenced by *pneuma,* breath; see **pneu-**), lung. **5.** Suffixed o-grade form **plou-to.* PLUTO; PLUTOCRACY, PLUTOGRAPHY, from Greek *ploutos,* wealth, riches (< "overflowing"). **6.** Lengthened o-grade form **plō(u)-*. **a.** *(i)* FLOW, from Old English *flōwan,* to flow; *(ii)* FLUE[2], from Middle Dutch *vluwe,* fishnet, perhaps from **pleu-**. Both *(i)* and *(ii)* from Germanic **flōwan,* to flow; **b.** suffixed form **plō-tu-*. FLOOD, from Old English *flōd,* flood, from Germanic **flōduz,* flowing water, deluge.

II. Extended form **pleuk-*. **1.** FLY[1], from Old English *flēogan,* to fly, from Germanic **fleugan,* to fly. **2.** FLY[2], from Old English *flēoge,* a fly, from Germanic **fleugōn-,* flying insect, fly. **3.** FLEE, from Old English *flēon,* to flee, from Germanic **fleuhan,* to run away, probably from **pleu-**. **4.** FLEY, from Old English *flȳgan, flēgan,* to put to flight, from Germanic causative **flaugjan.* **5.** FLÈCHE, FLETCHER, from Old French *fleche,* arrow, from Germanic suffixed form **fleug-ika.* **6.** Zero-grade form **pluk-*. **a.** FLEDGE, from Old English **flycge,* with feathers (only in *unfligge,* featherless), from Germanic **flugja-,* feather; **b.** FLIGHT[1], FLIGHT[2], from Old English *flyht,* act of flying, and **flyht,* act of fleeing, escape, from Germanic suffixed form **flug-ti-;* **c.** FOWL, from Old English *fugol,* bird, from Germanic **fuglaz,* bird, dissimilated from possible (but unlikely) suffixed form **flug-laz;* **d.** FLÜGELHORN, FUGLEMAN, from Middle High German *vlügel,* wing, from Germanic suffixed form **flug-ila.*

III. Extended form **pleud-*. **1.** FLEET[1], FLEET[2], from Old English *flēotan,* to float, swim (from Germanic **fleutan*), and Old Norse *fliōtr,* fleet, swift (from Germanic **fleutaz*). **2.** Zero-grade form **plud-*. **a.** *(i)* FLOAT, from Old English *flotian,* to float; *(ii)* FLOTSAM, from Old French *floter,* to float. Both *(i)* and *(ii)* from Germanic derivative **flotōn,* to float; **b.** FLOTILLA, from Old Norse *floti,* raft, fleet; **c.** FLUTTER, from Old English *floterian, flotorian,* to float back and forth (*-erian,* iterative and frequentative suffix); **d.** FLIT, from Old Norse *flytja,* to further, convey, from Germanic **flutjan,* to float. **a, b, c,** and **d** all from Germanic **flut-, *flot-*. **3.** FLUSTER, probably from a Scandinavian source akin to Icelandic *flaustr,* hurry, and *flaustra,* to bustle, from Germanic **flausta-,* contracted from suffixed form **flaut-stā-,* probably from **pleud-,* o-grade **ploud-*. [Pokorny *pleu-* 835, *pl(e)u-mon-* 837.]

pneu-. Important derivatives are *sneeze, snore, snort,* and *pneumatic.*

pneu-. To breathe. Imitative root. **1.** SNEEZE, from Old English *fnēosan,* to sneeze, from Germanic **fneu-s-*. **2.** SNORE, (SNORT), from Old English *fnora,* sneezing, from Germanic **fnu-s-*. **3.** APNEA, DIPNOAN, DYSPNEA, EUPNEA, HYPERPNEA, HYPOPNEA, POLYPNEA, from Greek *pnein,* to breathe, with o-grade nouns *pnoia,* breathing, and *pnoē,* breath. **4.** Suffixed form **pneu-mn̥.* PNEUMA, PNEUMATIC, PNEUMATO-, PNEUMO-, from Greek *pneuma,* breath, wind, spirit. **5.** Germanic variant root **fnes-*. SNEER, from Old English *fnǣran,* to snort, gnash one's teeth. [Pokorny *pneu-* 838.]

pō(i)-. Important derivatives are *potable, poison, potion, beer, beverage, imbibe,* and *symposium.*

pō(i)-. To drink. Contracted from **poə(i)-*.

I. Basic form **pō(i)-*. **1.a.** Suffixed reduced form **pō-to-*. POTABLE, POTATION, POTATORY, from Latin *pōtus,* drunk; a drink (whence *pōtāre,* to drink); **b.** suffixed form **pō-ti-*. POISON, POTION, from Latin *pōtiō,* a drink. **2.** Reduplicated form **pi-pə-o-,* whence **pi-bo-,* assimilated to **bi-bo-*. BEER, BEVERAGE, BIB, BIBULOUS; IMBIBE, (IMBRUE), from Latin *bibere,* to drink. **3.** Suffixed zero-grade form **pə-ti-, *po-ti-*. SYMPOSIUM, from Greek *posis,* drink, drinking.

II. Zero-grade form **pī-* (< **piə-*). **1.** Suffixed form **pī-ro-*. PIROG, from Old Church Slavonic *pirŭ,* feast. **2.** Suffixed (nasal present) form **pī-no-*. PINOCYTOSIS, from Greek *pinein,* to drink. [Pokorny 2. *pō(i)-* 839.]

pōl-. Important derivatives are *feel, palpable, palpitate, catapult,* and *psalm.*

pōl-. To touch, feel, shake. **1.a.** FEEL, from Old English *fēlan,* to examine by touch, feel; **b.** SPRACHGEFÜHL, from Old High German *vuolen,* to feel. Both **a** and **b** from Germanic **fōljan,* to feel. **2.** Reduplicated zero-grade form **pal-p-*. **a.** PALP, from Latin *palpus,* a touching; **b.** PALPABLE, PALPATE[1], PALPITATE, from Latin *palpārī, palpāre,* to stroke gently, touch; **c.** PALPEBRA, from Latin *palpebra,* eyelid (< "that which shakes or moves quickly"). **3.** Perhaps suffixed zero-grade form **pal-yo-*. CATAPULT, from Greek *pallein,* to sway, brandish. **4.** Perhaps suffixed form **psal-yo-*. PSALM, PSALTERY, from Greek *psallein,* to pluck, play the harp (but more likely of imitative origin). [Pokorny 1. G. *pel-* 801.]

porko-. Important derivatives are *aardvark, porcelain, pork, porcupine,* and *porpoise.*

porko-. Young pig. **1.a.** FARROW[1], from Old English *fearh,* little pig; **b.** AARDVARK, from Middle Dutch diminutive form *varken,* small pig. Both **a** and **b** from Germanic **farhaz.* **2.** PORCELAIN, PORCINE, PORK; PORCUPINE, PORPOISE, from Latin *porcus,* pig. [Pokorny *porko-s* 841.]

poti-. Important derivatives are *possess, power, possible, potent,* and *impotent.*

poti-. Powerful; lord. **1.** PODESTA, POSSESS, POWER, from Latin *potis* (> *pots > pos-), powerful, able. **2.** POSSIBLE, POTENT; (IMPOTENT), OMNIPOTENT, PREPOTENT, from Latin compound *posse,* to be able (contracted from *potis,* able + *esse,* to be; see **es-**). **3.** Form *pot-. **a.** compound *ghos-pot-, "guest-master," host (see **ghos-ti-**); **b.** compound *dems-pot-, "house- master," ruler (see **dem-**). **4.** PADISHAH, from Old Persian *pati-,* master. [Pokorny *poti-s* 842.]

prek-. Important derivatives are *pray, prayer*[1], *precarious, deprecate,* and *postulate.*

prek-. To ask, entreat. **1.** Basic form *prek-. PRAY, PRAYER[1], PRECARIOUS; DEPRECATE, IMPRECATE, from *prex, prayer (attested only in the plural *precēs*), with Latin denominative *precārī,* to entreat, pray. **2.** Suffixed zero-grade form *pr̥k-sk- becoming *pork-sk-, contracted into *posk- in suffixed form *posk-to, contracted into *posto-. POSTULATE; EXPOSTULATE, from Latin *postulāre,* to ask, request. [Pokorny 4. *perk̂-* 821.]

preus-. Important derivatives are *freeze, frost,* and *prurient.*

preus-. To freeze, burn. **1.** FREEZE, from Old English *frēosan,* to freeze, from Germanic *freusan, to freeze. **2.** Suffixed zero-grade form *prus-to-. FROST, from Old English *forst, frost,* frost, from Germanic *frustaz, frost. **3.** Suffixed form *preus-i-. PRURIENT, PRURIGO, PRURITUS, from Latin denominative *prūrīre,* to burn, itch, yearn for, from *preusis, *preuris, act of burning. **4.** Suffixed zero-grade form *prus-wīnā. PRUINOSE, from Latin *pruīna,* hoarfrost. [Pokorny *preus-* 846.]

prī-. Important derivatives are *free, filibuster, friend, afraid,* and *Friday.*

prī-. To love. Contracted from *priə-. **1.** Suffixed form *priy-o-. **a.** FREE, from Old English *frēo,* free, and *frēon, freogan,* to love, set free; **b.** (FILIBUSTER), FREEBOOTER, from Dutch *vrij,* free. Both **a** and **b** from Germanic *frijaz, beloved, belonging to the loved ones, not in bondage, free, and *frijōn, to love. **2.** Suffixed (participial) form *priy-ont-, loving. FRIEND, from Old English *frīond, frēond,* friend, from Germanic *frijand-, lover, friend. **3.** Suffixed shortened form *pri-tu-. **a.** SIEGFRIED, from Old High German *fridu,* peace; **b.** AFFRAY, AFRAID, from Old French *esfreer,* to disturb, from Vulgar Latin *exfredāre, to break the peace, from *ex-,* out, away (see **eghs**) + *fridāre, to make peace, from Germanic *frithu-, peace; **c.** (see **bhergh-**[2]) Germanic compound *berg-frij-, "high place of safety," from *frij-, peace, safety. **a**, **b**, and **c** all from Germanic *frithuz, peace. **4.** Suffixed feminine form *priy-ā, beloved. **a.** FRIGG, from Old Norse *Frigg,* goddess of the heavens, wife of Odin; **b.** FRIDAY, from Old English *Frīgedæg,* Friday, from Germanic compound *frije-dagaz, "day of Frigg" (translation of Latin *Veneris diēs,* "Venus's day"). Both **a** and **b** from Germanic *frijjō, beloved, wife. [Pokorny *prāi-* 844.]

pū̆-. Important derivatives are *foul, filth, defile*[1], *fuzzy, putrid, potpourri, putrefy, purulent,* and *pus.*

pū̆-. To rot, decay. **1.** Suffixed form *pū-lo-. **a.** FOUL, from Old English *fūl,* unclean, rotten; **b.** FULMAR, from Old Norse *fūll,* foul; **c.** FILTH, from Old English *fȳlth,* foulness, from Germanic abstract noun *fūlithō; **d.** FILE[3]; DEFILE[1], from Old English *fȳlan,* to sully, from Germanic denominative *fūljan, to soil, dirty. **a**, **b**, **c**, and **d** all from Germanic *fūlaz, rotten, filthy. **2.** Extended form *pug-. FOG[2], from Middle English *fog, fogge,* aftermath grass, from a Scandinavian source probably akin to Icelandic *fūki,* rotten sea grass, and Norwegian *fogg,* rank grass, from Germanic *fuk-. **3.** Extended variant form *pous-. FUZZY, from Low German *fussig,* spongy, from Germanic *fausa-. **4.** Suffixed form *pu-tri-. PUTRESCENT, PUTRID; (OLLA PODRIDA), (POTPOURRI), PUTREFY, from Latin *puter* (stem *putri-*), rotten. **5.** Suffixed form *puw-os-. **a.** PURULENT, PUS; SUPPURATE, from Latin *pūs,* pus; **b.** PYO-, from Greek *puon, puos,* pus. **6.** EMPYEMA, from Greek compound *empuein,* to suppurate (*en-,* in; see **en**). [Pokorny 2. *pū̆-* 848.]

pūr-. Important derivatives are *fire* and *pyre.*

pūr-. Fire. Contracted from *puər-, zero-grade form of *paəwr̥. **1.** FIRE, from Old English *fȳr,* fire, from Germanic suffixed form *fūr-i-. **2.** PYRE, PYRETIC, PYRITES, PYRO-, PYRRHOTITE, PYROSIS; EMPYREAL, from Greek *pur,* fire. [Pokorny *peu̯ōr* 828.]

[re-. Important derivatives are *re-, retro-,* and *arrears.*

re-. Also **red-**. Backward. Latin combining form conceivably from Indo-European *wret-, metathetical variant of *wert-, to turn (< "turned back"), an extended form of **wer-**[2]. **1.** RE-, from Latin *re-, red-,* backward, again. **2.** Suffixed form *re(d)-tro-. RETRAL, RETRO-; ARREARS, REAR GUARD, REARWARD[2], REREDOS, from Latin *retrō,* backward, back, behind. **3.** Suffixed form *re-ko-. (see **per**[1]) Latin *reciprocus,* "backward and forward."**]**

rē-. Important derivatives are *real*[1] and *republic.*

rē-. To bestow, endow. Contracted from *reə-. Suffixed form *reə-i-, goods, wealth, property. RE[2], REAL[1], REBUS, REIFY, REPUBLIC, from Latin *rēs,* thing. [Pokorny 4. *rei-* 850.]

rēd-. Important derivatives are *rodent, corrode, erode, rostrum, rash*[2], *abrade,* and *erase.*

rēd-. To scrape, scratch, gnaw. **1.** O-grade form *rōd-. **a.** RODENT; CORRODE, ERODE, from Latin *rōdere,* to gnaw; **b.** suffixed (instrumental) form *rōd-tro-. ROSTRUM, from Latin *rōstrum,* beak, ship's bow. **2.** Possibly variant form *rād-. **a.** RADULA, RASH[2], RASORIAL; ABRADE, CORRADE, ERASE, from Latin *rādere,* to scrape; **b.** suffixed (instrumental) form *rād-tro-. RACLETTE, from Latin *rāstrum,* rake. [Pokorny 2. *rēd-* 854.]

reg-. Important derivatives are *right, realm, rector, rectum, regent, regime, regiment, region, correct, direct, erect, rectangle, rectify, surge, rich, regal, reign, royal, maharajah, rail*[1], *regular, regulate, rule, rake*[1], *rack*[1], *reckon, interrogate, prerogative,* and *reckless.*

reg-. To move in a straight line, with derivatives meaning "to direct in a straight line, lead, rule."
I. Basic form *reg-. **1.** Suffixed form *reg-to-. RIGHT, from Old English *riht,* right, just, correct, straight, from Germanic *rehtaz. **2.** REALM, RECTITUDE, RECTO, RECTOR, RECTUM, RECTUS, REGENT, REGIME, REGIMENT, REGION; CORRECT, DIRECT, ERECT, (PORRECT), RECTANGLE, RECTIFY, RECTILINEAR, (RESURGE), (RISORGIMENTO), SURGE, from Latin *regere,* to lead straight, guide, rule (past participle *rēctus,* hence adjective *rēctus,* right, straight). **3.** ANORECTIC, ANOREXIA, from Greek *oregein,* to stretch out, reach out for (with prothetic vowel from oldest root form *əreg-).
II. Lengthened-grade form *rēg-, Indo-European word for a tribal king. **1.a.** BISHOPRIC, ELDRITCH, from Old English *rīce,* realm; **b.** RIKSMÅL, from Old Norse *rīki,* realm; **c.** REICHSMARK, from Old High German *rīchi,* realm; **d.** RICH, from Old English *rīce,* strong, powerful, and Old French *riche,* wealthy. **a**, **b**, **c**, and **d** all from Germanic *rīkja-, from Celtic suffixed form *rīg-yo-. **2.** REAL[2], REGAL, REGULUS, REIGN, ROYAL; REGICIDE, REGIUS PROFESSOR, VICEREINE, VICEROY, from Latin *rēx,* king (royal and priestly title). **3.** Suffixed form *rēgen-. RAJ, RAJAH, (RANI), (RYE[2]); MAHARAJAH, MAHARANI, from Sanskrit *rājā, rājan-,* king, rajah (feminine *rājñī,* queen, rani), and *rājati,* he rules.
III. Suffixed lengthened-grade form *rēg-olā. RAIL[1], REGLET, REGULAR, REGULATE, RULE, from Latin *rēgula,* straight piece of wood, rod.
IV. O-grade form *rog-. **1.** RAKE[1], from Old English *raca, racu,* rake (implement with straight pieces of wood), from Germanic *rakō. **2.** RACK[1], from Middle Dutch *rec,* framework, from Germanic *rak-. **3.** RANK[2], from Old English *ranc,* straight, strong, hence haughty, overbearing, from Germanic *rankaz (with nasal infix), possibly from **reg-**. **4.** RECKON, from Old English *gerecenian,* to arrange in order, recount (*ge-,* collective prefix; see **kom**), from Germanic *rakinaz, ready, straightforward. **5.** Suffixed form *rog-ā-. ROGATION, ROGATORY; ABROGATE, ARROGATE, CORVÉE, DEROGATE, INTERROGATE, PREROGATIVE, PROROGUE, SUBROGATE, SUPEREROGATE, from Latin *rogāre,* to ask (< "stretch out the hand"). **6.** Suffixed form *rog-o-. ERGO, from Latin *ergō,* therefore, in consequence of, perhaps contracted from a Latin phrase *ē rogō, "from the direction of" (*ē* < *ex,* out of; see **eghs**), from a possible Latin noun *rogus, "extension, direction."
V. Lengthened o-grade form *rōg-. **1.** RECK, Old English *rec(c)an,* to pay attention to, take care (formally influenced by Old English *reccan,* to extend, stretch out, from Germanic *rakjan), from Germanic *rōkjan. **2.** RECKLESS, from Old English *rēcelēas,* careless (*-lēas,* lacking; see **leu-**), from Germanic *rōkja-.* [Pokorny 1. *reĝ-* 854.]

rei-. Important derivatives are *run, rill, rival, rivulet,* and *derive.*

rei-. To flow, run. **1.** Suffixed zero-grade form *ri-nu-. **a.** RUN, RUNNEL, from Old English *rinnan,* to run, and Old Norse *rinna,* to run (from Germanic *rinnan, to run, from *ri-nw-an), and from Old English causative *ærnan, eornan,* to run (from secondary Germanic causative *rannjan); **b.** EMBER DAY, from Old English *ryne,* a running, from secondary Germanic derivative *runiz; **c.** RENNET, from Old English *rynet, from secondary Germanic derivative *runita-. **2.** Suffixed zero-grade form *ri-l-. RILL, from Dutch *ril* or Low German *rille,* running stream, from Germanic *ril-. **3.** Suffixed form *rei-wo-. RIVAL, RIVULET; DERIVE, from Latin *rīvus,* stream. [Pokorny 3. *er-* 326.]

reidh-. Important derivatives are *ride, raid, road, ready,* and *array.*

reidh-. To ride.
I. Basic form *reidh-. **1.** RIDE, from Old English *rīdan,* to ride, from Germanic *rīdan. **2.** PALFREY, from Latin *verēdus,* post horse, from Celtic *worēd- (*wo-, under; see **upo**).
II. O-grade form *roidh-. **1.a.** RAID, ROAD, from Old English *rād,* a riding, road; **b.** RADDLE[1], from Middle High German *reidel,* rod between upright stakes (< "wooden horse"), possibly from **reidh-**. Both **a** and **b** from Germanic *raid-. **2.** READY, from Old English *ræde, geræde,* ready (< "prepared for a journey"), from Germanic *raid-ja-, probably from **reidh-**. **3.** ARRAY, CURRY[1], from Vulgar Latin *-rēdāre, to arrange, from Germanic *raidjan, probably from **reidh-**. [Pokorny *reidh-* 861.]

reig-. Important derivatives are *reach, rigid,* and *rigor.*

reig-. To reach, stretch out. **1.** O-grade form *roig-. REACH, from Old English *rǣcan,* to stretch out, reach, from Germanic *raikjan. **2.** Possibly suffixed (stative) zero-grade form *rig-ē-. RIGID, RIGOR, from Latin *rigēre,* to be stiff (? < "be stretched out"). [Pokorny *(reiĝ-)* 862.]

rep-. Important derivatives are *rape*[1], *rapid, rapt, ravish,* and *surreptitious.*

rep-. To snatch. Suffixed zero-grade form *rapyo-. RAPACIOUS, RAPE[1], RAPID, RAPINE, RAPT, (RAVEN[2]), RAVIN, RAVISH; EREPSIN, (SUBREPTION), SURREPTITIOUS, from Latin *rapere,* to seize. [Pokorny *rep-* 865.]

ret-. Important derivatives are *Tory, rodeo, roll, rotary, rotate, rotund, roulette, round*[1], *control,* and *prune*[2].

ret-. To run, roll. **1.** Prefixed form *to-wo-ret-, "a running up to" (*to-,* to; *wo,* under, up, up from under; see **upo**). TORY, from Old Irish *tōir,* pursuit. **2.** Suffixed o-grade form *rot-ā-. RODEO, ROLL, ROTA, ROTARY, ROTATE, ROTUND, (ROTUNDA), ROULETTE, ROUND[1], ROWEL; BAROUCHE, CONTROL, PRUNE[2], ROTIFORM, ROTOGRAVURE, from Latin *rota,* wheel. **3.** Suffixed (participial) form *ret-ondo-. ROTUND, from Latin *rotundus,* round, probably from *retundus, "rolling." [Pokorny *ret(h)-* 866.]

reudh-. Important derivatives are *red, rufous, robust, corroborate, rambunctious, ruddy, rust, rouge, rubeola, ruby, rubric,* and *russet.*

reudh-. Red, ruddy.

I. O-grade form *roudh-. **1.a.** RED, from Old English *rēad,* red; **b.** RORQUAL, from Old Norse *raudhr,* red. Both **a** and **b** from Germanic *raudaz. **2.** ROWAN, from a source akin to Old Norse *reynir,* mountain ash, rowan (from its red berries), from Germanic *raudnia-. **3.** RUFESCENT, RUFOUS, from Latin *rūfus* (of dialectal Italic origin), reddish. **4.** RUBIGINOUS, from Latin *rōbus,* red. **5.** ROBLE, ROBORANT, ROBUST; CORROBORATE, (RAMBUNCTIOUS), from Latin *rōbur, rōbus,* red oak, hardness, and *rōbustus,* strong.
II. Zero-grade form *rudh-. **1.** Form *rudh-ā-. **a.** RUDDLE, from Old English *rudu,* red color; **b.** RUDDOCK, from Old English *rudduc,* robin; **c.** RUDDY, from Old English *rudig,* ruddy. **a, b,** and **c** all from Germanic *rudō. **2.** Suffixed form *rudh-sto-. RUST, from Old English *rūst* (also *rust?*), rust, from Germanic *rust-. **3.** ROUGE, RUBEOLA, RUBY; RUBEFACIENT, from Latin *rubeus,* red. **4.** RUBICUND, from Latin *rubicundus,* red, ruddy. **5.** RUBIDIUM, from Latin *rubidus,* red. **6.** Suffixed (stative) form *rudh-ē-. RUBESCENT, from Latin *rubēre,* to be red. **7.** Suffixed form *rudh-ro-. **a.** RUBELLA, RUBRIC; BILIRUBIN, from Latin *ruber,* red; **b.** RUTILANT, from Latin *rutilus,* reddish; **c.** ERYTHEMA, ERYTHRO-, from Greek *eruthros,* red (with prothetic vowel, from oldest root form *əreudh-); **d.** ERYSIPELAS, from possibly remade Greek *erusi-,* red, reddening. **8.** Suffixed form *rudh-to-. RISSOLE, ROUX, RUSSET, from Latin *russus,* red. [Pokorny *reudh-* 872.]

reuə-. Important derivatives are *room, rummage, rural,* and *rustic.*

reuə-. To open; space. **1.** Suffixed variant form *rū-mo- (< *ruə-mo-). **a.** ROOM, from Old English *rūm,* space; **b.** LEBENSRAUM, from Old High German *rūm,* space; **c.** RUMMAGE, from Old Provençal *run,* ship's hold, space. **a, b,** and **c** all from Germanic *rūmaz; **d.** REAM[2], from Old English *ryman,* to widen, open up, from Germanic denominative *rūmjan. **2.** Suffixed form *reu(ə)-es-. RURAL, RUSTIC, from Latin *rūs,* "open land," the country. [Pokorny *reuə-, rū-* 874.]

reug-. An important derivative is *reek.*

reug-. To vomit, belch; smoke, cloud. **1.** REEK, from Old English *rēocan,* to smoke, reek, and *rēcan,* to fumigate, from Germanic *reukan. **2.** Suffixed zero-grade form *rug-to-. ERUCT, from Latin *ructāre,* to belch. [Pokorny 4. *reu-* 871.]

reup-. Important derivatives are *rip*[1], *bereave, rover, rob, robe, loot, usurp, rout*[1], *rupture, abrupt, bankrupt, corrupt, disrupt, erupt,* and *interrupt.*

reup-. Also **reub-.** To snatch.
I. Basic form *reub-. RIP[1], from Flemish *rippen,* to rip, from Germanic *rupjan.
II. O-grade form *roup-. **1.a.** REAVE[1], from Old English *rēafian,* to plunder; **b.** BEREAVE, from Old English *berēafian,* to take away (*be-, bi-,* intensive prefix; see **ambhi**); **c.** ROVER[2], from Middle Dutch and Middle Low German *roven,* to rob. **a, b,** and **c** all from Germanic *(bi-)raubōn. **2.a.** ROB, from Old French *rober,* to rob; **b.** RUBATO, from Italian *rubare,* to rob. Both **a** and **b** from a Romance borrowing from Germanic *raubōn, to rob. **3.** ROBE, from Old French *robe,* robe (< "clothes taken as booty"), from Germanic *raubō, booty. **4.** Suffixed form *roup-tro-. LOOT, from Sanskrit *loptram,* booty. **5.** RUBLE, from Old Russian *rubiti,* to chop, hew, from Slavic *rubjela-.
III. Zero-grade form *rup-. **1.** USURP, from Latin *ūsūrpāre* (< *ūsu-rup-; *ūsus,* use, usage, from *ūtī,* to use), originally "to interrrupt the orderly acquisition of something by the act of using," whence to take into use, usurp. **2.** Nasalized form *ru-m-p-. ROUT[1], RUPTURE; ABRUPT, BANKRUPT, CORRUPT, DISRUPT, ERUPT, INTERRUPT, IRRUPT, RUPICOLOUS, from Latin *rumpere,* to break. [Pokorny 2. *reu-* 868.]

r̥tko-. An important derivative is *Arthur.*

r̥tko-. Bear. **1.** URSINE, from Latin *ursus,* bear (< *orcsos). **2.** ARCTIC, ARCTURUS, from Greek *arktos,* bear. [Pokorny *r̥k̑þo-s* 875.]

sā-. Important derivatives are *sad, sate*[1], *satiate, asset, satisfy, satire,* and *saturate.*

sā-. To satisfy. Contracted from *saə-. **1.** Suffixed zero-grade form *sə-to-. **a.** SAD, from Old English *sæd,* sated, weary, from Germanic *sadaz, sated; **b.** SATE[1], from Old English *sadian,* to sate, from derivative Germanic verb *sadōn, to satisfy, sate. **2.** Suffixed zero-grade form *sə-ti-. SATIATE, SATIETY; (ASSAI[2]), ASSET, SATISFY, from Latin *satis,* enough, sufficient. **3.** Suffixed zero-grade form *sə-tu-ro-. SATIRE, SATURATE, from Latin *satur,* full (of food), sated. **4.** Suffixed zero-grade form *sə-d-ro-. HADRON, from Greek *hadros,* thick. [Pokorny *sā-* 876.]

sāg-. Important derivatives are *seek, sake*[1], *forsake, ransack, presage, sagacious,* and *hegemony.*

sāg-. To seek out. Contracted from *saəg-. **1.** Suffixed form *sāg-yo-. SEEK, from Old English *sǣcan, sēcan,* to seek, from Germanic *sōkjan. **2.** Suffixed form *sāg-ni-. SOKE, from Old English *sōcn,* attack, inquiry, right of local jurisdiction, from Germanic *sōkniz. **3.** Zero-grade form *səg-. **a.** SAKE[1], from Old English *sacu,* lawsuit, case, from Germanic derivative noun *sakō, "a seeking," accusation, strife; **b.** *(i)* FORSAKE, from Old English *forsacan,* to renounce, refuse (*for-,* prefix denoting exclusion or rejection; see **per**[1]); *(ii)* RANSACK, from Old Norse *saka, to seek. Both *(i)* and *(ii)* from Germanic *sakan, to seek, accuse, quarrel. Both **a** and **b** from Germanic *sak-. **4.** Independent suffixed form *sāg-yo-. PRESAGE, from Latin *sāgīre,* to perceive, "seek to know." **5.** Zero-grade form *səg-. SAGACIOUS, from Latin *sagāx,* of keen perception. **6.** Suffixed form *sāg-eyo-. EXEGESIS, HEGEMONY, from Greek *hēgeisthai,* to lead (< "to track down"). [Pokorny *sāg-* 876.]

sak-. Important derivatives are *sacred, consecrate, execrate, saint, sanctum,* and *sanctify.*

sak-. To sanctify. **1.** Suffixed form *sak-ro-. **a.** SACRED; CONSECRATE, EXECRATE, from Latin *sacer,* holy, sacred, dedicated; **b.** compound *sakro-dhōt-, "performer of sacred rites" (*-dhōt-, doer; see **dhē-**). SACERDOTAL, from Latin *sacerdōs,* priest. **2.** Nasalized form *sa-n-k-. SAINT, (SANCTUM); CORPOSANT, SACROSANCT, SANCTIFY, from Latin *sancīre* (past participle *sanctus*), to make sacred, consecrate. [Pokorny *sak-* 878.]

sal-. Important derivatives are *salt, silt, sauce, salad, salami, salary, saline, saltcellar,* and *saltpeter.*

sal-. Salt. **1.** Extended form *sald-. **a.** suffixed form *sald-o-. SALT, from Old English *sealt,* salt, from Germanic *saltam; **b.** *(i)* SOUSE[1], from Old French *sous,* pickled meat; *(ii)* SILT, from Middle English *cylte,* fine sand, from a source probably akin to Danish and Norwegian *sylt,* salt marsh. Both *(i)* and *(ii)* from Germanic zero-grade suffixed extended form *sult-jō; **c.** (SALSA), SAUCE, from Latin *sallere* (past participle *salsus* < *sald-to-*), to salt. **2.** SAL, SALAD, SALAMI, SALARY, SALI-, SALINE; SALTCELLAR, SALTPETER, from Latin *sāl* (genitive *salis*), salt. **3.** HALO-, from Greek *hals* (stem *hal-*), salt, sea. [Pokorny 1. *sal-* 878.]

sāwel-. Important derivatives are *sun, Sunday, south, southern, solar, parasol, solstice,* and *helium.*

sāwel-. Also **s(u)wel-, su(ə)el-, su(ə)en-, sun-.** The sun. Contracted from *saəwel-. **1.** Variant forms *swen-, *sun-. **a.** *(i)* SUN, from Old English *sunne,* sun; *(ii)* SUNDEW, from Middle Dutch *sonne,* sun. Both *(i)* and *(ii)* from Germanic *sunnōn-; **b.** SUNDAY, from Old English *sunnandæg,* Sunday, from Germanic compound *sunnōn-dagaz, "day of the sun" (translation of Latin *diēs sōlis*); **c.** SOUTH, SOUTHERN, from Old English *sūth,* south, and *sūtherne,* southern, from Germanic derivative *sunthaz, "sun-side," south. **2.** Variant form *s(ə)wōl-. SOL[3], SOL, SOLAR, SOLARIUM; GIRASOL, INSOLATE, PARASOL, SOLANINE, SOLSTICE, TURNSOLE, from Latin *sōl,* the sun. **3.** Suffixed form *sāwel-yo-. HELIACAL, HELIO-, HELIUM; ANTHELION, APHELION, ISOHEL, PARHELION, PERIHELION, from Greek *hēlios,* sun. [Pokorny *sāwel-* 881.]

sē-. Important derivatives are *sow*[1], *seed, season, semen, seminary,* and *disseminate.*

sē-. To sow. Contracted from *seə-. **1.** SOW[1], from Old English *sāwan,* to sow, from Germanic *sēan. **2.** Suffixed form *sē-ti-, sowing. **a.** SEED, from Old English *sǣd,* seed; **b.** COLZA, from Middle Dutch *saet* and Middle Low German *sāt,* seed. Both **a** and **b** from Germanic *sēdiz, seed. **3.** Reduplicated zero-grade form *si-s(ə)-. SEASON, from Latin *serere,* to sow, *satiō* (< *sə-tiō), sowing. **4.** Suffixed form *sē-men-, seed. SEMÉ, SEMEN, SEMINARY; DISSEMINATE, from Latin *sēmen,* seed. [In Pokorny 2. *sē(i)-* 889.]

sed-. Important derivatives are *sit, set*[1], *ersatz, settle, saddle, soot, seat, séance, sedentary, sediment, session, siege, assess, dissident, obsess, possess, preside, reside, subsidy, supersede, subside, sedate*[1], *soil*[1], and *chair.*

sed-. To sit. **1.** Suffixed form *sed-yo-. **a.** SIT, from Old English *sittan,* to sit; **b.** SITZ BATH, SITZMARK, from Old High German *sizzen,* to sit. Both **a** and **b** from Germanic *sitjan. **2.** Suffixed (causative) o-grade form *sod-eyo-. **a.** SET[1], from Old English *settan,* to place; **b.** BESET, from Old English *besettan,* to set near; **c.** ERSATZ, from Old High German *irsezzan,* to replace, from *sezzan,* to set. **a, b,** and **c** all from Germanic *(bi-)satjan, to cause to sit, set. **3.** Suffixed form *sed-lo-, seat. SETTLE, from Old English *setl,* seat, from Germanic *setlaz. **4.** O-grade form *sod-. SADDLE, from Old English *sadol,* saddle, from Germanic *sadulaz, seat, saddle (perhaps from *sod-dhlo-). **5.** Suffixed lengthened o-grade form *sōd-o-. SOOT, from Old English *sōt,* soot (< "that which settles"), from Germanic *sōtam. **6.** Suffixed lengthened-grade form *sēd-i-,* settler. COSSET, possibly from Old English *sǣta, -sǣte,* inhabitant(s), from Germanic *sāti-. **7.** Suffixed lengthened-grade form *sēd-yo-. SEAT, from Old Norse *sæti,* seat, from Germanic *(ge)sētjam, seat (*ge-, *ga-, collective prefix; see **kom**). **8.** Form *sed-ē-. SÉANCE, SEDENTARY, SEDILE, SEDIMENT, SESSILE, SESSION, SEWER[2], SIEGE; ASSESS, ASSIDUOUS, DISSIDENT, (INSESSORIAL), INSIDIOUS, OBSESS, POSSESS, PRESIDE, RESIDE, SUBSIDY, SUPERSEDE, from Latin *sedēre,* to sit. **9.** Reduplicated form *si-zd-. **a.** SUBSIDE, from Latin *sīdere,* to sit down, settle; **b.** SYNIZESIS, from Greek *hizein,* to sit down, settle down. **10.** Lengthened-grade form *sēd-. SEE[2], from Latin *sēdēs,* seat, residence. **11.** Lengthened-grade form *sēd-ā-. SEDATE[1], from Latin *sēdāre,* to settle, calm down. **12.** Suffixed o-grade form *sod-yo-. SOIL[1], from Latin *solium,* throne, seat. **13.** Suffixed form *sed-rā-. -HEDRON; CATHEDRA, (CHAIR), EPHEDRINE, EXEDRA, SANHEDRIN, TETRAHEDRON, from Greek *hedra,* seat, chair, face of a geometric solid. **14.** Prefixed and suffixed form *pi-sed-yo-, to sit upon (*pi, on; see **epi**). PIEZO-; ISOPIESTIC, from Greek *piezein,* to press tight. **15.** Basic form *sed-. **a.** EDAPHIC, from Greek *edaphos,* ground, foundation (with Greek suffix *-aphos*); **b.** UPANISHAD, from Sanskrit *upaniṣad,* Upanishad, from *sad-;* **c.** TANIST, from Old Irish *tānaise,* designated successor, from Celtic *tānihessio-, "one who is waited for," from *to-ad-ni-sed-tio, from *to-ad-ni-sed-, to wait for. **16.** Suffixed form *sed-o-, sitting. EISTEDDFOD, from Welsh *eistedd,* sitting, from Celtic *eks-dī-sedo- (see **eghs, de-**). [Pokorny *sed-* 884.]

segh-. Important derivatives are *hectic, eunuch, epoch, scheme, scholar, scholastic,* and *school*[1].

segh-. To hold. **1.** Suffixed form *segh-es-. SIEGFRIED, from Old High German *sigu, sigo,* victory, from Germanic *sigiz-, victory (< "a holding or conquest in battle"). **2.** HECTIC; CACHEXIA, CATHEXIS, ENTELECHY, EUNUCH, OPHIUCHUS, from Greek *ekhein,* to hold, possess, be in a certain condition, and *hexis,* habit, condition. **3.** O-grade form *sogh-. EPOCH, from Greek *epokhē,* "a holding back," pause, cessation, position in time (*epi-,* on, at; see **epi**). **4.** Zero-grade form *sgh-. **a.** SCHEME, from Greek *skhēma,* "a holding," form, figure; **b.** (SCHOLAR), SCHOLASTIC, SCHOLIUM, SCHOOL[1], from Greek *skholē,* "a holding back," stop, rest, leisure, employment of leisure in disputation, school. **5.** Reduplicated form *si-sgh-. ISCHEMIA, from Greek *iskhein,* to keep back. [Pokorny *seĝh-* 888.]

sek-. Important derivatives are *scythe, saw*[1], *sedge, Saxon, skin, secant, section, sector, segment, dissect, insect, intersect,* and *sickle.*

sek-. To cut. **1.** SCYTHE, from Old English *sīthe, sigthe,* sickle, from Germanic *segithō, sickle.

2. Suffixed o-grade form **sok-ā-*. SAW[1], from Old English *sagu, sage,* saw, from Germanic **sagō,* a cutting tool, saw. **3.** Suffixed o-grade form **sok-yo-*. SEDGE, from Old English *secg,* sedge, from Germanic **sagjaz,* "sword," plant with a cutting edge. **4.** Suffixed o-grade form **sok-so-*. SAXON, from Late Latin *Saxō,* (plural *Saxonēs*), a Saxon, from West Germanic tribal name **Saxon-,* Saxon, traditionally (but doubtfully) regarded as from Germanic **sahsam,* knife, sword (as if "warrior with knives"). **5.** Extended root **skend-,* to peel off, flay. SKIN, from Old Norse *skinn,* skin, from Germanic **skinth-*. **6.** Basic form **sek-*. SECANT, -SECT, SECTILE, SECTION, SECTOR, SEGMENT; DISSECT, INSECT, INTERSECT, RESECT, (TRANSECT), from Latin *secāre,* to cut. **7.** Lengthened-grade form **sēk-*. SICKLE, from Latin *sēcula,* sickle. **8.** Possible suffixed variant form **sak-so-*. SAXATILE; SAXICOLOUS, SAXIFRAGE, from Latin *saxum,* stone (< "broken-off piece"?). [Pokorny 2. *sĕk-* 895, *sken-(d-)* 929.] See also extended roots **skei-**, **sker-[1]**, **sker-[3]**.

---

sek^w-[1]. Important derivatives are *sect, sequel, sequence, sue, suitor, consequent, ensue, execute, persecute, prosecute, pursue, subsequent, sequester, second[2], intrinsic, seal[1], sign, assign, designate, insignia, resign, social, society, associate,* and *dissociate.*

sek^w-[1]. To follow. **1.** SECT, SEGUE, SEGUIDILLA, SEQUACIOUS, SEQUEL, SEQUENCE, SUE, SUITOR; CONSEQUENT, ENSUE, EXECUTE, OBSEQUIOUS, PERSECUTE, PROSECUTE, (PURSUE), SUBSEQUENT, from Latin *sequī,* to follow. **2.** SEQUESTER, SEQUESTRUM, from Latin *sequester,* "follower," mediator, depositary. **3.** Suffixed (participial) form **sek^w-ondo-*. SECOND[2], SECONDO, SECUND, from Latin *secundus,* following, coming next, second. **4.** Suffixed form **sek^w-os,* following. EXTRINSIC, INTRINSIC, from Latin *secus,* along, alongside of. **5.** Suffixed form **sek^w-no-*. SEAL[1], SEGNO, SIGN; ASSIGN, CONSIGN, DESIGNATE, INSIGNIA, RESIGN, from Latin *signum,* identifying mark, sign (< "standard that one follows"). **6.** Suffixed o-grade form **sok^w-yo-*. SOCIABLE, SOCIAL, SOCIETY, SOCIO-; ASSOCIATE, CONSOCIATE, DISSOCIATE, from Latin *socius,* ally, companion (< "follower"). [Pokorny 1. *seku̯-* 896.]

---

sek^w-[2]. Important derivatives are *see[1]* and *sight.*

sek^w-[2]. To perceive, see. **1.** SEE[1], from Old English *sēon,* to see, from Germanic **sehwan,* to see. **2.** SIGHT, from Old English *sihth, gesiht,* vision, spectacle, from Germanic abstract noun **sih-tiz.* [Pokorny 2. *seku̯-* 897.]

---

sek^w-[3]. Important derivatives are *say, saw[2], saga,* and *scold.*

sek^w-[3]. To say, utter. **1.** O-grade form **sok^w-*. **a.** suffixed form **sok^w-yo-*. SAY, from Old English *secgan,* to say, from Germanic **sagjan;* **b.** suffixed form **sok^w-ā-*. *(i)* SAW[2], from Old English *sagu,* a saying, speech; *(ii)* SAGA, from Old Norse *saga,* a saying, narrative. Both *(i)* and *(ii)* from Germanic **sagō,* a saying. **2.** Perhaps suffixed zero-grade form **sk^w-e-tlo-,* narration. SCOLD, SKALD, from Middle English *scolde,* an abusive person, and Old Norse *skāld,* poet, "satirist" (to which the probable Scandinavian source of Middle English *scolde* is perhaps akin), from North Germanic **skathla.* [In Pokorny 2. *seku̯-* 897.]

---

sel-. Important derivatives are *salient, sally, sauté, assail, desultory, exult, insult, result, somersault,* and *salmon.*

sel-. To jump. **1.** Suffixed zero-grade form **sal-yo-*. **a.** SALACIOUS, SALIENT, SALLY, (SAUTÉ); ASSAIL, DESULTORY, EXULT, INSULT, RESILE, RESULT, SOMERSAULT, from Latin *salīre,* to leap; **b.** HALTER[2], from Greek *hallesthai,* to leap, jump. **2.** SALMON, from Latin *salmō* (borrowed from Gaulish), salmon (< "the leaping fish"), perhaps from **sel-**. [Pokorny 4. *sel-* 899.]

---

sem-[1]. Important derivatives are *simultaneous, assemble, ensemble, single, Sanskrit, same, anomalous, seem, seemly, some, similar, assimilate, resemble, simplicity,* and *simple.*

sem-[1]. One; also adverbially "as one," together with.

I. Full-grade form **sem-*. **1.a.** HENDECASYLLABIC, HENDIADYS, HENOTHEISM, HYPHEN, from Greek *heis* (< nominative singular masculine **hen-s* < **hem-s*), one; **b.** (see **dekm̥**) Greek *he-* in *hekaton,* one hundred (? dissimilated from **hem-katon*). Both **a** and **b** from Greek **hem-*. **2.** Suffixed form **sem-el-*. SIMULTANEOUS; ASSEMBLE, ENSEMBLE, from Latin *simul,* at the same time. **3.** Suffixed form **sem-golo-*. SINGLE, from Latin *singulus,* alone, single. **4.** Compound **sem-per-* (**per,* during, for; see **per[1]**). SEMPRE; SEMPITERNAL, from Latin *semper,* always, ever (< "once for all").

II. O-grade form **som-*. **1.** SAMSARA, SANDHI, SANSKRIT, from Sanskrit *sam,* together. **2.** Suffixed form **som-o-*. **a.** SAME, from Old Norse *samr,* same, from Germanic **samaz,* same; **b.** HOMEO-, HOMO-; ANOMALOUS, from Greek *homos,* same; **c.** HOMILY, from Greek *homilos,* crowd. **3.** Suffixed form **som-alo-*. HOMOLOGRAPHIC, from Greek *homalos,* like, even, level.

III. Lengthened o-grade form **sōm-*. **1.** Suffixed form **sōm-i-*. SEEM, SEEMLY, from Old Norse *sœmr,* fitting, agreeable (< "making one," "reconciling"), from Germanic **sōmiz.* **2.** Suffixed lengthened o-grade form **sōm-o-*. SAMIZDAT, SAMOVAR, from Russian *sam(o)-,* self.

IV. Zero-grade form **sm̥-*. **1.** (ACOLYTE), ANACOLUTHON, from Greek compound *a-kolouthos,* accompanying (*a-* + *keleuthos,* way, path), from *ha-, a-,* together. **2.** Compound form **sm̥-plo-* (**-plo-,* -fold; see **pel-[2]**). HAPLOID, from Greek *haploos, haplous,* single, simple. **3.** Suffixed form **sm̥m-o-*. **a.** SOME, from Old English *sum,* one, a certain one; **b.** -SOME[1], from Old English *-sum,* -like. Both **a** and **b** from Germanic **sumaz.* **4.** Suffixed form **sm̥m-alo-*. SIMILAR; ASSIMILATE, RESEMBLE, from Latin *similis,* of the same kind, like. **5.** Compound **sm̥-kēro-,* of one growing (see **ker-[2]**). **6.** Suffixed form **sm̥-tero-*. HETERO-, from Greek *heteros* (earlier *hateros*), one of two, other. **7.** Compound **sm̥-plek-,* "one-fold," simple (**plek-,* -fold; see **plek-**). SEMPLICE, SIMPLEX, SIMPLICITY, from Latin *simplex,* simple. **8.** Compound **sm̥-plo-,* "one-fold," simple (**-plo-,* -fold; see **pel-[2]**). SIMPLE, from Latin *simplus,* simple. **9.** Extended form **sm̥ma.* HAMADRYAD, from Greek *hama,* together with, at the same time. [Pokorny 2. *sem-* 902.]

---

sem-[2]. An important derivative is *summer[1].*

sem-[2]. Also **semə-**. Summer. Suffixed zero-grade form **sm̥ə-aro-*. SUMMER[1], from Old English *sumor,* summer, from Germanic **sumaraz.* [Pokorny 3. *sem-* 905.]

---

sēmi-. An important derivative is *semi-.*

sēmi-. Half. **1.** SAND-BLIND, from Old English *sām-,* half, from Germanic **sēmi-*. **2.** SEMI-, from Latin *sēmi-,* half. **3.** SESQUI-, SESTERCE, from Latin *sēmis,* half. **4.** HEMI-, from Greek *hēmi-,* half. [Pokorny *sēmi-* 905.]

---

sen-. Important derivatives are *senate, senescent, senile, senior, sir, sire,* and *surly.*

sen-. Old. SEIGNIOR, SENATE, SENECTITUDE, SENESCENT, SENILE, SENIOR, SENOPIA, (SIGNORY), (SIR), SIRE, (SURLY), from Latin *senex,* old, an elder. [Pokorny *sen(o)-* 907.]

---

seng^wh-. Important derivatives are *sing* and *song.*

seng^wh-. To sing, make an incantation. **1.a.** SING, from Old English *singan,* to sing; **b.** MEISTERSINGER, MINNESINGER, SINGSPIEL, from Old High German *singan,* to sing. Both **a** and **b** from Germanic **singan.* **2.** Suffixed o-grade form **song^wh-o-,* singing, song. SONG, from Old English *sang, song,* song, from Germanic **sangwaz.* [Pokorny *sengu̯h-* 906.]

---

sent-. Important derivatives are *send[1], godsend, scent, sense, sentence, sentinent, sentiment, sentinel, assent, consent, dissent,* and *resent.*

sent-. To head for, go. **1.** WIDDERSHINS, from Old High German *sin(d),* direction, from Germanic form **sinthaz.* **2.** Suffixed (causative) o-grade form **sont-eyo-*. SEND[1], from Old English *sendan,* to send, from Germanic **sandjan,* to cause to go. **3.** Suffixed o-grade form **sont-o-*. GODSEND, from Old English *sand,* message, messenger, from Germanic **sandaz,* that which is sent. **4.** Perhaps suffixed form **sent-yo-*. SCENT, SENSE, (SENSILLIUM), SENTENCE, SENTIENT, SENTIMENT, SENTINEL; ASSENT, CONSENT, DISSENT, PRESENTIMENT, RESENT, from Latin *sentīre,* to feel (< "to go mentally"). [Pokorny *sent-* 908.]

---

sep-. Important derivatives are *sage[1], sapient, savant, savor, savvy,* and *insipid.*

sep-. To taste, perceive. Suffixed zero-grade form **sap-yo-*. SAGE[1], SAPID, SAPIENT, SAPOR, SAVANT, SAVOR, SAVVY; INSIPID, from Latin *sapere,* to taste, have taste, be wise. [Pokorny *sap-* 880.]

---

septm̥. Important derivatives are *seven, September,* and *septet.*

septm̥. Seven. **1.** SEVEN; SEVENTEEN, SEVENTY, from Old English *seofon,* seven, with derivatives *(hund) seofontig,* seventy, and *seofontīne,* seventeen (*-tīne,* ten; see **dekm̥**), from Germanic **sebum.* **2.** SEPTEMBER, SEPTENNIAL, SEPTET, SEPTUAGINT, SEPTUPLE; SEPTENTRION, from Latin *septem,* seven. **3.** HEBDOMAD, HEPTA-, HEPTAD, from Greek *hepta,* seven. [Pokorny *septm̥* 909.]

---

ser-[1]. Important derivatives are *conserve, observe, preserve, reserve, reservoir,* and *hero.*

ser-[1]. To protect. **1.** Extended form **serw-*. CONSERVE, OBSERVE, PRESERVE, RESERVE, (RESERVOIR), from Latin *servāre,* to keep, preserve. **2.** Perhaps suffixed lengthened-grade form **sēr-ōs-*. HERO, from Greek *hērōs,* "protector," hero. [Pokorny 2. *ser-* 910.]

---

ser-[2]. Important derivatives are *series, assert, exert, insert, sermon, sorcerer, sort, assort,* and *consort.*

ser-[2]. To line up. **1.** SERIES, SERTULARIAN; ASSERT, DESERT[3], DISSERTATE, EXERT, INSERT, from Latin *serere,* to arrange, attach, join (in speech), discuss. **2.** Suffixed form **ser-mon-*. SERMON, from Latin *sermō* (stem *sermōn-*), speech, discourse. **3.** Perhaps suffixed form **ser-ā-*. SEAR[2], (SERRIED), from Latin *sera,* a lock, bolt, bar (? < "that which aligns"). **4.** Suffixed zero-grade form **sr̥-ti-*. SORCERER, SORT; ASSORT, CONSORT, SORTILEGE, from Latin *sors* (stem *sort-*), lot, fortune (probably from the lining up of lots before drawing). [Pokorny 4. *ser-* 911.]

---

seuə-[1]. An important derivative is *son.*

seuə-[1]. To give birth. Suffixed zero-grade form in derivative noun **su(ə)-nu-,* son. SON, from Old English *sunu,* son, from Germanic **sunuz.* [Pokorny 2. *seu-* 913.] See also **sū-**.

---

seuə-[2]. Important derivatives are *soup, sup[2], sop, sip, suck, soak, suction,* and *succulent.*

seuə-[2]. To take liquid.

I. Suffixed zero-grade form **suə-yo-,* contracted to **sū-yo.* HYETAL; ISOHYET, from Greek *huetos,* rain, from *huein,* to rain.

II. Possible extended zero-grade form **sūb-*. **1.a.** SUP[1], from Old English *sūpan, sūpian,* to drink, sip; **b.** SOUP, (SUP[2]), from Old French *soup(e),* soup. Both **a** and **b** from Germanic **sūp-*. **2.a.** SOP, from Old English *sopp-* in *soppcuppe,* cup for dipping bread in; **b.** SIP, from Middle English *sippen,* to sip, from a source probably akin to Low German *sippen,* to sip, possibly from **seuə-[2]**. Both **a** and **b** from Germanic **supp-*.

III. Possible extended zero-grade form **sūg-*. **1.** SUCK, from Old English *sūcan,* to suck, from Germanic **sūk-*. **2.** SOAK, from Old English *socian,* to steep, from Germanic shortened form **sukōn.* **3.** SUCTION, SUCTORIAL, from Latin *sūgere,* to suck. **4.** Variant form **sūk-*. SUCCULENT, from Latin *sūcus, succus,* juice. [Pokorny 1. *seu-* 912.]

---

skand-. Important derivatives are *scan, scansion, ascend, descend, transcend, scandal,* and *scale[2].*

skand-. Also **skend-**. To leap, climb. **1.** SCAN, SCANDENT, SCANSION, SCANSORIAL, SCANTLING; ASCEND, (CONDESCEND), DESCEND, TRANSCEND, from Latin *scandere,* to climb. **2.** Suffixed form **skand-alo-*. SCANDAL, from Greek *skandalon,* a snare, trap, stumbling block. **3.** Suffixed form **skand-slā-*. ECHELON, ESCALADE, SCALE[2], from Latin *scālae,* steps, ladder.

---

skei-. Important derivatives are *shin[1], science, conscious, nice, shit, schism, rescind, shed[1], sheath, ski, esquire,* and *squire.*

skei-. To cut, split. Extension of **sek-**. **1.a.** SHIN[1], from Old English *scinu,* shin, shinbone (< "piece cut off"); **b.** CHINE, from Old French *eschine,* backbone, piece of meat with part of the backbone. Both **a** and **b** from Germanic suffixed form **ski-nō-*. **2.** SCIENCE, SCILICET, SCIOLISM; ADSCITITIOUS, CONSCIENCE, CONSCIOUS, NESCIENCE, (NICE), OMNISCIENT, PLEBISCITE, PRESCIENT, from Latin *scīre,* to know (< "to separate one thing from another," "discern.") **3.** Suffixed zero-grade form **skiy-enā*. SKEAN, from Old Irish *scīan,* knife. **4.** Extended root **skeid-*. **a.** *(i)* SHIT, from Old English **scītan,* to defecate; *(ii)* SKATE[3], from Old Norse *skīta,* to defecate; *(iii)* SHYSTER, from Old High German *skīzzan,* to defecate. *(i), (ii),* and *(iii)* all from Germanic **skītan,* to separate, defecate; **b.** suffixed zero-grade form **sk(h)id-yo-*. SCHISM, SCHIST, SCHIZO-, from Greek *skhizein,* to split; **c.** nasalized zero-grade form **ski-n-d-*. SCISSION; EXSCIND, PRESCIND, RESCIND, from Latin *scindere,* to split. **5.** Extended root **skeit-*. **a.** *(i)* SHED[1], from Old English *scēadan,* to separate; *(ii)* SHEATH, from Old English *scēath,* sheath (< "split stick"), perhaps from **skei-**. Both *(i)* and *(ii)* from Germanic **skaith-, *skaidan;* **b.** SKI, from Old Norse *skīdh,* log, stick, snowshoe, from Germanic **skīdam;* **c.** o-grade form **skoit-*. ÉCU, ESCUDO, ESCUTCHEON, ESQUIRE, SCUDO, SCUTUM, (SQUIRE), from Latin *scūtum,* shield (< "board"). **6.** Extended root **skeip-*. **a.** SHEAVE[2], from Middle English *sheve,* pulley (< "piece of wood with grooves"); **b.** SKIVE, from a Scandinavian source akin to Old Norse *skīfa,* to slice, split; **c.** SHIVER[2], from Middle English *shivere, scivre,* splinter, possibly from a Low German source akin to Middle Low German *schever,* splinter. **a, b,** and **c** all from Germanic **skif-*. [Pokorny *skei-* 919.]

skel-[1]. Important derivatives are *shell, shale, scale[1], scalp, shield, skill, cutlass, shelf, half, scalpel,* and *sculpture.*

skel-[1]. Also **kel-**. To cut. **1.a.** SHELL, from Old English *scell, sciel,* shell; **b.** SCAGLIOLA, from Italian *scaglia,* chip. Both **a** and **b** from Germanic **skaljō,* piece cut off, shell, scale. **2.a.** SHALE, from Old English *sc(e)alu,* husk, shell; **b.** SCALE[1], from Old French *escale,* husk, shell. Both **a** and **b** from Germanic **skalō*. **3.a.** SCALL, from Old Norse *skalli,* bald head (< "closely shaved skull"); **b.** SCALP, from Middle English *scalp,* top of the head, from a source akin to Old Norse *skalpr,* sheath, shell. Both **a** and **b** from Germanic **skal-*. **4.** SCALE[3], SKOAL, from Old Norse *skāl,* bowl, drinking vessel (made from a shell), from Germanic **skēlō*. **5.** SHIELD, from Old English *scield,* shield (< "board"), from Germanic **skelduz*. **6.a.** SKILL, from Old Norse *skil,* reason, discernment, knowledge (< "incisiveness"); **b.** SHELDRAKE, from Middle English *scheld,* variegated, from a Low German source akin to Middle Dutch *schillen,* to diversify, with past participle *schillede,* separated, variegated. Both **a** and **b** from Germanic **skeli-*. **7.** SCHOOL[2], SHOAL[2], from Middle Low German *schōle,* troop, or Middle Dutch *scōle,* both from Germanic **skulō,* a division. **8.** Suffixed variant form **kel-tro-*. COULTER, CULTRATE, CUTLASS, from Latin *culter,* knife. **9.** Suffixed zero-grade form **skl̥-yo-*. SCALENE, from Greek *skallein,* to stir up, hoe (> *skalenos,* uneven). **10.** Extended root **skelp-*. **a.** SHELF, from Middle Low German *schelf,* shelf (< "split piece of wood"), from Germanic **skelf-;* **b.** HALF, from Old English *healf,* half, from Germanic **halbaz* (< variant root **kelp-*), divided possibly from **skel-[1]**; **c.** perhaps variant **skalp-*. SCALPEL, SCULPTURE, from Latin *scalpere,* to cut, scrape, with derivative *sculpere* (originally as the combining form of *scalpere*), to carve [Pokorny 1. *(s)kel-* 923.]

skel-[2]. An important derivative is *shall.*

skel-[2]. To be under an obligation. O-grade (perfect) form **skol-*. SHALL, from Old English *sceal* (used with the first and third person singular pronouns), shall, from Germanic **skal,* I owe, hence I ought. [Pokorny 2. *(s)kel-* 927.]

sker-[1]. Important derivatives are *shear, share[1], shears, scabbard, score, shard, short, shirt, skirt, skirmish, screen, carnage, carnal, carnation, carnival, carrion, carnivorous, incarnate, curt, cortex, sharp, scrap[1], scrape, scrub[1], shrub[1],* and *screw.*

sker-[1]. Also **ker-**. To cut.
I. Basic form **sker-, *ker-*. **1.a.** SHEAR, from Old English *scieran, sceran,* to cut; **b.** SHEER[1], from Low German *scheren,* to move to and fro, and Dutch *scheren,* to withdraw, depart. Both **a** and **b** from Germanic **skeran*. **2.a.** SHARE[2], from Old English *scēar,* plowshare; **b.** SHARE[1], from Old English *scearu, scaru,* portion, division (but recorded only in the sense of "fork of the body," "tonsure"). Both **a** and **b** from Germanic **skeraz*. **3.a.** SHEAR, from Old English *scēar,* scissors, from Germanic **skēr-ō-* and **sker-ez-;* **b.** compound **skēr-berg-,* "sword protector," scabbard (see **bhergh-[1]**). SCABBARD, from Old French *escauberc,* scabbard, possibly from a Germanic source akin to Old High German *scarberc,* scabbard. Both **a** and **b** from Germanic **skēr-*. **4.** SCORE, from Old Norse *skor,* notch, tally, twenty, from Germanic **skur-*. **5.** SCAR[2], SKERRY, from Old Norse *sker,* low reef (< "something cut off"), from Germanic suffixed form **skar-jam*. **6.** Suffixed o-grade extended form **skorp-o-*. SCARF[2], from Old Norse *skarfr,* diagonally-cut end of a board, from Germanic **skarfaz*. **7.** Suffixed o-grade extended form **skord-o-*. SHARD, from Old English *sceard,* a cut, notch, from Germanic **skardaz*. **8.** Extended form **skerd-* in suffixed zero-grade form **skr̥d-o-*. **a.** SHORT, from Old English *scort, sceort,* "cut," short; **b.** SHIRT, from Old English *scyrte,* skirt (< "cut piece"); **c.** SKIRT, from Old Norse *skyrta,* shirt. **a, b,** and **c** all from Germanic **skurtaz*. **9.a.** SKIRMISH, from Old French *eskermir,* to fight with a sword, fence, and Old Italian *scaramuccia,* skirmish, from a source akin to Old High German *skirmen,* to protect; **b.** SCREEN, from Middle Dutch *scherm,* shield. Both **a** and **b** from Germanic extended form **skerm-*. **10.** Variant form **kar-*. CARNAGE, CARNAL, CARNASSIAL, CARNATION, CARNIVAL, CARRION, CARUNCLE, CHARNEL, CRONE; CARNIVOROUS, INCARNATE, from Latin *carō* (stem *carn-*), flesh. **11.** Suffixed o-grade form **kor-yo*. CORIACEOUS, CORIUM, CUIRASS, CURRIER; EXCORIATE, from Latin *corium,* leather (originally "piece of hide"). **12.** Suffixed zero-grade form **kr̥-to-*. CURT, CURTAL, KIRTLE, from Latin *curtus,* short. **13.** Suffixed o-grade form **kor-mo-*. CORM, from Greek *kormos,* a trimmed tree trunk. **14.** Suffixed o-grade form **kor-i-*. COREOPSIS, from Greek *koris,* bedbug (< "cutter"). **15.** Suffixed zero-grade form. SHORE[1], from Old English *scora,* shore, from Germanic **skur-ō*.
II. Extended roots **skert-, *kert-*. **1.** Zero-grade form **kr̥t-* or o-grade form **kort-*. CORTEX; DECORTICATE, from Latin *cortex,* bark (< "that which can be cut off"). **2.** Suffixed form **kert-snā-*. CENACLE, from Latin *cēna,* meal (< "portion of food").
III. Extended root **skerp-*. SCURF, probably from a Scandinavian source akin to Old English *sceorf,* scab, scurf, from Germanic **skerf-*.
IV. Extended root **skerb(h)-, *skreb(h)-*. **1.a.** SHARP, from Old English *scearp,* slope; **b.** SCARP, from Italian *scarpa,* embankment, possibly from a Germanic source akin to Gothic *skarpō,* pointed object. Both **a** and **b** from Germanic **skarpaz,* cutting, sharp. **2.a.** SCRAP[1], from Old Norse *skrap,* "pieces," remains; **b.** SCRAPE, from Old Norse *skrapa,* to scratch. Both **a** and **b** from Germanic **skrap-*. **3.a.** SCRABBLE, from Middle Dutch *schrabben,* to scrape; **b.** SCRUB[1], from Middle Dutch *schrobben,* to scrape. Both **a** and **b** from Germanic **skrab-*. **4.** SHRUB[1], from Old English *scrybb,* shrub (< "rough plant"), from Germanic **skrub-*. **5.** SCROBICULATE, from Latin *scrobis,* trench, ditch. **6.** SCREW, SCROFULA, from Latin *scrōfa,* a sow (< "rooter, digger"). [Pokorny 4. *sker-,* Section I. 938.]

sker-[2]. Important derivatives are *shrink, ring[1], ranch, range, rank[1], rink, arrange, ridge, curb, curve, crest, crepe, crisp, circle, search,* and *crown.*

sker-[2]. Also **ker-**. To turn, bend. Presumed base of a number of distantly related derivatives. **1.** Extended form **(s)kreg-* in nasalized form **(s)kre-n-g-*. **a.** SHRINK, from Old English *scrincan,* to wither, shrivel up, from Germanic **skrink-;* **b.** variant **kre-n-g-*. *(i)* RUCK[2], from Old Norse *hrukka,* a crease, fold; *(ii)* FLOUNCE[1], from Old French *fronce,* pleat, from Frankish **hrunkjan,* to wrinkle. Both *(i)* and *(ii)* from Germanic **hrunk-*. **2.** Extended form **(s)kregh-* in nasalized form **skre-n-gh-*. **a.** RING[1], from Old English *hring,* a ring; **b.** RANCH, RANGE, RANK[1], RINK; ARRANGE, DERANGE, from Old French *renc, reng,* line, row; **c.** RINGHALS, from Middle Dutch *rinc* (combining form *ring-*), a ring. **a, b,** and **c** all from Germanic **hringaz,* something curved, circle. **3.** Extended form **kreuk-*. **a.** RIDGE, from Old English *hrycg,* spine, ridge; **b.** RUCKSACK, from Old High German *hrukki,* back. Both **a** and **b** from Germanic *hrugjaz*. **4.** Suffixed variant form **kur-wo-*. CURB, CURVATURE, CURVE, CURVET, from Latin *curvus,* bent, curved. **5.** Suffixed extended form **kris-ni-*. CRINOLINE, from Latin *crīnis* (< **crisnis*), hair. **6.** Suffixed extended form **kris-tā-*. CREST, CRISTA, CRISTATE, from Latin *crista,* tuft, crest. **7.** Suffixed extended form **krip-so-*. CREPE, CRISP, CRISPATE, from Latin *crispus* (metathesized from **cripsus*), curly. **8.** Extended expressive form **krīss-*. CRISSUM, from Latin *crisāre,* (of women) to wiggle the hips during copulation. **9.** Perhaps reduplicated form **ki-kr-o-*. (CIRCA), CIRCLE, (CIRCUM-), SEARCH; CRICOID, from Greek *krikos* (with metathesis), a ring. **10.** Suffixed o-grade form **kor-ōno-*. (CORONA), CROWN, from Greek *korōnos,* curved. **11.** Suffixed variant form **kur-to*. KURTOSIS, from Greek *kurtos,* bent. [Pokorny 3. *(s)ker-* 935.]

sker-[3]. A derivative is *dreck.*

sker-[3]. Excrement, dung. Extension of **sek-**, "to cut, separate," hence "to void excrement." **1.** Suffixed unextended form **sk-ōr/n-*. SCATO-, SCORIA, SKATOLE, from Greek *skōr* (genitive *skatos* < **sk-n̥t-*), dung. **2.** Extended form **skert-* in taboo metathesis **sterk-os-*. **a.** STERCORACEOUS, from Latin *stercus,* dung; **b.** variant forms **(s)terg-, *(s)treg-*. DRECK, from Middle High German *drëc,* dung, from Germanic **threkka-*. [Pokorny *sker-d-* 947, 8. *(s)ter-* 1031.]

(s)keu-. Important derivatives are *sky, meerschaum, scum, obscure, hide[2], cuticle, recoil, hose, hoard, hide[1],* and *hut.*

(s)keu-. To cover, conceal. Zero-grade form **(s)ku-*. Variant **(s)keuə-,* zero-grade form **(s)kuə-,* contracted to **(s)kū-*. **1.** Suffixed basic form. **a.** SKY, from Old Norse *skȳ,* cloud; **b.** SKEWBALD, from a Scandinavian source akin to Old Norse *skȳ,* cloud. Both **a** and **b** from Germanic **skeu-jam,* cloud ("cloud cover"). **2.** Zero-grade form **skū-*. **a.** suffixed form **skū-mo-*. *(i)* SKIM, from Old French *escume,* scum; *(ii)* MEERSCHAUM, from Old High German *scūm,* scum; *(iii)* SCUM, from Middle Dutch *schūm,* scum. *(i), (ii),* and *(iii)* all from Germanic **skūmaz,* foam, scum (< "that which covers the water"); **b.** suffixed form **skū-ro-*. OBSCURE; CHIAROSCURO, from Latin *obscūrus,* "covered," dark (*ob-,* away from; see **epi**). **3.** Zero-grade form **kŭ-*. **a.** suffixed form **kū-ti-*. HIDE[2], from Old English *hȳd,* skin, hide, from Germanic **hūdiz;* **b.** suffixed form **ku-ti-*. CUTANEOUS, CUTICLE, CUTIS; CUTIN, from Latin *cutis* skin; **c.** possibly suffixed form **kū-lo-*. CULET, CULOTTE; BASCULE, RECOIL, from Latin *cūlus,* the rump, backside; **d.** suffixed form **kuto-*. -CYTE, CYTO-, from Greek *kutos,* a hollow, vessel. **4.** Extended zero-grade form **kus-*. **a.** *(i)* HOSE, from Old English *hosa, hose,* covering for the leg; *(ii)* LEDERHOSEN, from Old High German *hosa,* leg covering. Both *(i)* and *(ii)* from Germanic **husōn-;* **b.** suffixed form **kus-dho-* (or suffixed extended form **kudh-to-*). HOARD, from Old English *hord,* stock, store, treasure (< "thing hidden away"), from Germanic **huzdam;* **c.** KISHKE, from Russian *kishka,* gut (< "sheath"). **5.** Suffixed extended zero-grade form **kut-no-*. CUNNILINGUS, from Latin *cunnus,* vulva (< "sheath"). **6.** Extended root **keudh-*. **a.** HIDE[1], from Old English *hȳdan,* to hide, cover up, from Germanic suffixed lengthened zero-grade form **hūd-jan;* **b.** HUT, from French *hutte,* hut, from Germanic suffixed zero-grade form **hūd-jōn-;* **c.** HUDDLE, from Low German *hudeln,* to crowd together, probably from Germanic *hūd-. **7.** SHIELING, from a Scandinavian source akin to Old Norse *skāli,* hut, from Germanic suffixed o-grade form **skawala-.* [Pokorny 2. *(s)keu-* 951.]

skeud-. Important derivatives are *shoot, shot[1], shut, shuttle, sheet[1],* and *scuttle[1].*

skeud-. To shoot, chase, throw. **1.** SHOOT, from Old English *scēotan,* to shoot, from Germanic **skeutan,* to shoot. **2.a.** SHOT[1], from Old English *sceot, scot,* shooting, a shot; **b.** SCHUSS, from Old High German *scuz,* shooting, a shot; **c.** SCOT, (SCOT AND LOT), from Old Norse *skot* and Old French *escot,* contribution, tax (< "money thrown down"); **d.** WAINSCOT, from Middle Dutch *sc(h)ot,* crossbar, wooden partition. **a, b, c,** and **d** all from Germanic **skutaz,* shooting, shot. **3.** SHUT, from Old English *scyttan,* to shut (by pushing a crossbar), probably from Germanic **skutjan.* **4.** SHUTTLE, from Old English *scytel,* a dart, missile, from Germanic **skutilaz.* **5.a.** SHEET[2], from Old English *scēata,* corner of a sail; **b.** SHEET[1], from Old English *scēte,* piece of cloth. Both **a** and **b** from Germanic **skautjōn-.* **6.a.** SCOUT[2], from a Scandinavian source akin to Old Norse *skūta,* mockery (< "shooting of words"); **b.** SHOUT, from Old Norse *skūta,* a taunt. Both **a** and **b** from Germanic **skut-.* [Pokorny 2. *(s)keud-* 956.]

skrībh-. Important derivatives are *scribble, scribe, script, Scripture, ascribe, circumscribe, conscript, describe, inscribe, manuscript, postscript, prescribe, subscribe,* and *transcribe.*

skrībh-. To cut, separate, sift. Extension of **sker-[1].** **1.** SCRIBBLE, SCRIBE, SCRIPT, SCRIPTORIUM, SCRIPTURE, SERIF, SHRIVE; ASCRIBE, CIRCUMSCRIBE, CONSCRIPT, DESCRIBE, FESTSCHRIFT, INSCRIBE, MANUSCRIPT, POSTSCRIPT, PRESCRIBE, PROSCRIBE, RESCRIPT, SUBSCRIBE, SUPERSCRIBE, TRANSCRIBE, from Latin *scrībere,* to scratch, incise, write. **2.** SCARIFY[1], from Greek *skariphos,* scratching, sketch, pencil. [Pokorny 4. *sker-,* Section II. 945.]

slēb-. An important derivative is *sleep.*

slēb-. To be weak, sleep. Possibly related to **slēg-** through a hypothetical base **slē-* (< **sleə-*). SLEEP, from Old English *slǣpan,* to sleep, and *slǣp,* sleep, from Germanic **slēpan, *slēpaz.* [In Pokorny 1. *leb-* 655.]

slēg-. Important derivatives are *slack[1], lax, relax,* and *languish.*

slēg-. To be slack, be languid. Possibly related to **slēb-** through a hypothetical base **slē-* (< **sleə-*). Zero-grade form **slag-,* becoming **slag-.* **1.** SLACK[1], from Old English *slæc,* "loose," indolent, careless, from Germanic **slak-.* **2.** Suffixed form **lag-so-.* LAX; RELAX, from Latin *laxus,* loose, slack. **3.** Suffixed nasalized form **la-n-g-u-.* LANGUISH, from Latin *languēre,* to be languid. **4.** Compound **lag-ous-,* "with drooping ears" (**ous-,* ear; see **ous-**). LAGOMORPH, from Greek *lagōs, lagos,* hare. **5.** Suffixed form **lag-no-.* ALGOLAGNIA, from Greek *lagnos,* lustful, lascivious. **6.** Basic form **slēg-.* CATALECTIC, from Greek *lēgein,* to leave off. [Pokorny *(s)lēg-* 959.]

sleubh-. Important derivatives are *sleeve, lubricate, cowslip, slop[1],* and *sloop.*

sleubh-. To slide, slip.
I. Basic form **sleubh-.* **1.** SLEEVE, from Old English *slēf, slīf, slīef,* sleeve (into which the arm slips), from Germanic **sleub-.* **2.** SLOVEN, from Middle Low German *slôven,* to put on clothes carelessly, from Germanic **slaubjan.* **3.** Suffixed form **sleubh-ro-.* LUBRICATE, LUBRICITY, LUBRICIOUS, from Latin *lūbricus,* slippery.
II. **1. a.** SLIP[3]; COWSLIP, OXLIP, from Old English *slypa, slyppe, slipa,* slime, slimy substance; **b.** SLOP[1], from Old English **sloppe,* dung; **c.** SLOP[2], from Old English *(ofer)slop,* surplice. **a, b,** and **c** all from Germanic **slup-.* **2.** SLOOP, from Middle Dutch *slūpen,* to glide. Both **1** and **2** from variant Germanic root form **sleup-.* [Pokorny *sleub(h)-* 963.]

slī-. Derivatives are *sloe* and *livid.*

slī-. Bluish. Contracted from **sliə-.* **1.** O-grade form **sloi-.* SLOE, from Old English *slāh, slā,* sloe (< "bluish fruit"), from Germanic **slaihwōn.* **2.** Suffixed form **slī-wo-.* LIVID, from Latin *līvēre,* to be bluish. **3.** Suffixed form **slī-wā-.* SLIVOVITZ, from Serbo-Croatian *šljiva,* plum [Pokorny *(s)lī-* 965.]

smei-. Important derivatives are *smirk, smile, marvel, miracle, mirage, mirror,* and *admire.*

smei-. To laugh, smile. **1.** SMIRK, from Old English *smercian,* to smile (with *-k-* formative), from Germanic reshaped forms **smer-, *smar-.* **2.** SMILE, from Middle English *smilen,* to smile, from a Scandinavian source probably akin to Swedish *smila,* to smile, from Germanic extended form **smīl-.* **3.** Suffixed form **smei-ro-.* MARVEL, MIRACLE, MIRAGE, MIRROR; ADMIRE, from Latin *mīrus,* wonderful. **4.** Prefixed zero-grade form **ko(m)-smi-,* smiling with (**ko-, *kom-,* together; see **kom**). COMITY, from Latin *cōmis* (< *cosmis*), courteous. [Pokorny 1. *(s)mei-* 967.]

(s)mer-[1]. Important derivatives are *mourn, memorable, mermorandum, memory, commemorate,* and *remember.*

(s)mer-[1]. To remember. **1.** Suffixed zero-grade form **mr̥-no-.* MOURN, from Old English *murnan,* to mourn, from Germanic **murnan,* to remember sorrowfully. **2.** Reduplicated form **me-mor-.* **a.** MIMIR, from Old Norse *Mimir,* a giant who guards the well of wisdom, from Germanic **mimer-;* **b.** MEMORABLE, (MEMORANDUM), MEMORY; COMMEMORATE, REMEMBER, from Latin *memor,* mindful. [Pokorny *(s)mer-* 969.]

(s)mer-[2]. Important derivatives are *merit* and *emeritus.*

(s)mer-[2]. To get a share of something. **1.** Suffixed (stative) form **mer-ē-.* MERETRICIOUS, MERIT; EMERITUS, TURMERIC, from Latin *merēre, merērī,* to receive a share, deserve, serve. **2.** Suffixed form **mer-o-.* -MERE, MERISTEM, MERO-, -MEROUS; (ALLOMERISM), (DIMER), (ISOMER), (MONOMER), (TRIMER), from Greek *meros* (feminine *meris*), a part, division. [In Pokorny *(s)mer-* 969.]

snā-. Derivatives are *natant* and *natation.*

snā-. To swim. Contracted from **snaə-.* **1.** Extended form **snāgh-.* NEKTON, from Greek *nēkhein,* to swim. **2.** Suffixed zero-grade form **(s)nə-to-.* NATANT, NATATION, NATATORIAL, (NATATORIUM); SUPERNATANT, from Latin *natāre,* to swim. **3.** CHERSONESE, from Greek *nēsos,* island, attributed by some to this root (but more likely obscure). [Pokorny *snā-* 971.] See **(s)nāu-.**

(s)nāu-. Important derivatives are *nourish, nurse, nutrient,* and *nutrition.*

(s)nāu-. To swim, flow, let flow, whence suckle. Contracted from **snaəu-;* extension of **snā-.** **1.** Suffixed basic form **nāw-yo-.* NAIAD, from Greek *Naias,* fountain nymph, probably from *naein,* to flow. **2.** Variant root form **(s)neu(ə)-.* NEUSTON, from Greek *nein,* to swim. **3.** Zero-grade form **(s)nū-* (< **snuə-*) in suffixed form **nū-trī* (with feminine agent suffix). NOURISH, NURSE, NURTURE, NUTRIENT, NUTRIMENT, NUTRITION, NUTRITIOUS, NUTRITIVE, from Latin *nūtrīx,* nurse, and *nūtrīre,* to suckle, nourish. [In Pokorny *snā-* 971.]

(s)nē-. An important derivative is *needle.*

(s)nē-. Also **nē-.** To spin, sew. Contracted from **(s)neə-.* **1.** Suffixed form **nē-tlā.* NEEDLE, from Old English *nǣdl,* needle, from Germanic **nēthlō.* **2.** Suffixed form **snē-mn̥.* NEMATO-; AXONEME, CHROMONEMA, PROTONEMA, TREPONEMA, from Greek *nēma,* thread. **3.** Suffixed o-grade form **snō-tā-.* SNOOD, from Old English *snōd,* headband, from Germanic **snōdō.* [Pokorny *(s)nē-* 973.]

(s)neəu-. Important derivatives are *neuron* and *nerve.*

(s)neəu-. Tendon, sinew. Extension of **(s)nē-.** Suffixed form **(s)neəw-r̥-,* with further suffixes. **a.** **neu-r-o-.* NEURO-, NEURON; APONEUROSIS, from Greek *neuron,* sinew; **b.** metathesized form **nerwo-.* NERVE; ENERVATE, from Latin *nervus,* sinew. [Pokorny *snēu-* 977.]

so-. Important derivatives are *the[1]* and *she.*

so-. This, that (nominative). For other cases see **to-.** **1.** THE[1], from Late Old English *the,* masculine demonstrative pronoun, replacing *se* (with *th-* from oblique forms; see **to-**). **2.** HOI POLLOI, from Greek *ho,* the. **3.** Feminine form **syā.* SHE, from Old English *sēo, sīe,* she, from Germanic **sjō.* **4.** Compound variant form **sei-ke* (**-ke,* "that"; see **ko-**). SIC[1], from Latin *sīc,* thus, so, in that manner. [Pokorny *so(s), sā, sī* 978.]

sol-. Important derivatives are *solid, consolidate, catholic, solicitous, solemn, salute, safe, salvage, salvo,* and *save[1].*

sol-. Also **solə-.** Whole.
I. Basic form **sol-.* **1.** Suffixed form **sol-ido-.* SOLID; CONSOLIDATE, from Latin *solidus,* solid. **2.** Suffixed form **sol-wo-.* HOLO-; CATHOLIC, from Greek *holos,* whole. **3.** Dialectal geminated form **soll-o-.* **a.** SOLICITOUS, from Latin *sollus,* whole, entire, unbroken; **b.** SOLEMN, from Latin *sollemnis* (second element obscure), celebrated at fixed dates (said of religious rites), established, religious, solemn.
II. Variant form **solə-.* **1.** Suffixed zero-grade form *slə-u-* giving **sal-u-.* SALUBRIOUS, SALUTARY, SALUTE, from Latin *salūs,* health, a whole or sound condition. **2.** Suffixed zero-grade form **sl̥ə-wo-* giving **sala-wo-.* SAFE, SAGE[2], SALVAGE, SALVO, SAVE[1], SAVE[2], from Latin *salvus,* whole, safe, healthy, uninjured. [Pokorny *solo-* 979.]

spē-. Important derivatives are *speed, despair,* and *prosper.*

spē-. To thrive, prosper. Contracted from **speə-.* **1.** Suffixed o-grade form **spō-ti-.* SPEED, from Old English *spēd,* success, from Germanic **spōdiz.* **2.** Suffixed form **spē-s-.* DESPAIR, ESPERANCE, from Latin *spērāre,* to hope, denominative of *spēs* (plural *spērēs*), hope. **3.** Suffixed zero-grade form **spə-ro-.* PROSPER, from Latin *prosperus,* favorable, prosperous (traditionally regarded as from *prō spērē,* according to one's hope; *pro-,* according to; see **per[1]**). [Pokorny 3. *sp(ē)ēi-* 983.]

spek-. Important derivatives are *spy, espionage, specimen, spectacle, spectrum, speculate, aspect, circumspect, conspicuous, despise, expect, inspect, perspective, prospect, respect, respite, suspect, species, especial, despicable, skeptic, bishop,* and *telescope.*

spek-. To observe.
I. Basic form **spek-.* **1.a.** ESPY, SPY, from Old French *espier,* to watch; **b.** ESPIONAGE, from Old Italian *spione,* spy, from Germanic derivative **speh-ōn-,* watcher. Both **a** and **b** from Germanic **spehōn.* **2.** Suffixed form **spek-yo-.* SPECIMEN, SPECTACLE, SPECTRUM, SPECULATE, SPECULUM; ASPECT, CIRCUMSPECT, CONSPICUOUS, DESPISE, EXPECT, FRONTISPIECE, INSPECT, INTROSPECT, PERSPECTIVE, PROSPECT, RESPECT, (RESPITE), RETROSPECT, SUSPECT, TRANSPICUOUS, from Latin *specere,* to look at. **3.** SPECIES, SPECIOUS; ESPECIAL, from Latin *speciēs,* a seeing, sight, form. **4.a.** (see **gherə-**) Latin *haruspex,* diviner; **b.** (see **awi-**) Latin *auspex,* augur. Both **a** and **b** from Latin *-spex* (< **-spek-*), "he who sees." **5.** Suffixed form **spek-ā-.* DESPICABLE, from Latin (denominative) *dēspicārī,* to despise, look down on (*dē-,* down; see **de-**). **6.** Suffixed metathetical form **skep-yo-.* SKEPTIC, from Greek *skeptesthai,* to examine, consider.
II. Extended o-grade form **spoko-.* SCOPE, -SCOPE, -SCOPY; BISHOP, EPISCOPAL, HOROSCOPE, TELESCOPE, from metathesized Greek *skopos,* one who watches, also object of attention, goal, and its denominative *skopein* (< **skop-eyo-*), to see. [Pokorny *spek-* 984.]

(s)pen-. Important derivatives are *spider, spin, spindle, pansy, pendant[1], pension[1], pensive, poise[1], append, appendix, compensate, depend, dispense, expend, penthouse, perpendicular, suspend, span[1], pound[1], ponder,* and *spontaneous.*

(s)pen-. To draw, stretch, spin.
I. Basic form **spen-.* **1.** Suffixed form **spen-wo-.* **a.** SPIDER, SPIN, from Old English *spinnan,* to spin, and *spīthra,* spider, contracted from Germanic derivative **spin-thrōn-,* "the spinner"; **b.** SPINDLE, from Old English *spinel,* spindle, from Germanic derivative **spin-ilōn-.* Both **a** and **b** from Germanic **spinnan,* to spin. **2.** Extended form **pend-.* PAINTER[2], (PANSY), PENCHANT, PENDANT[1], PENDENTIVE, PENDULOUS, PENSILE, PENSION[1], PENSIVE, PESO,

poise[1]; antependium, append, (appendix), avoirdupois, compendium, compensate, depend, dispense, expend, impend, (penthouse), perpend, perpendicular, prepense, propend, suspend, vilipend, from Latin *pendēre,* to hang (intransitive), and *pendere,* to cause to hang, weigh, with its frequentative *pēnsāre,* to weigh, consider. **3.** Perhaps suffixed form _*pen-ya-_. -penia, from Greek *penia,* lack, poverty (< "a strain, exhaustion"). **4.** geoponic, lithopone, from Greek *ponos,* toil, and *ponein,* to toil, o-grade derivatives of *penesthai,* to toil.
II. O-grade forms _*spon-_, _*pon-_. **1.a.** span[2], from Middle Dutch *spannen,* to bind; **b.** spanner, from Old High German *spannan,* to stretch. Both **a** and **b** from Germanic _*spannan_. **2.** span[1], from Old English *span(n),* distance, from Germanic _*spanno-_. **3.** spangle, from Middle Dutch *spange,* clasp, from Germanic _*spangō_, perhaps from **(s)pen-**. **4.** Suffixed and extended form _*pond-o-_. pound[1], from Latin *pondō,* by weight. **5.** Suffixed and extended form _*pond-es-_. ponder, ponderous; equiponderate, preponderate, from Latin *pondus* (stem *ponder-*), weight, and its denominative *ponderāre,* to weigh, ponder. **6.** Suffixed o-grade form _*spon-t-_. spontaneous, from Latin *sponte,* of one's own accord, spontaneously, possibly from **(s)pen-**, but more likely to a homophonous Germanic verb _*spanan_, to entice. [Pokorny *(s)pen-(d)-* 988.]

spend-. Important derivatives are *sponsor, spouse,* and *respond.*

spend-. To make an offering, perform a rite, hence to engage oneself by a ritual act. O-grade from _*spond-_. **1.** Suffixed form _*spond-eyo-_. sponsor, spouse; despond, espouse, respond, from Latin *spondēre,* to make a solemn promise, pledge, betroth. **2.** Suffixed form _*spond-ā_. spondee, from Greek *spondē,* libation, offering. [Pokorny *spend-* 989.]

sper-. Important derivatives are *sprawl, sprout, spurt, spread, Diaspora, sperm[1], spore, sporadic,* and *spray[1].*

sper-. To strew.
I. Zero-grade form _*spr̥-_. **1.** sprawl, from Old English *sprēawlian,* to sprawl, from Germanic _*spr-_. **2.** Extended form _*spreud-_. **a.** sprout, from Old English *sprūtan,* to sprout; **b.** spritz, spritzer, from Middle High German *sprützen,* to spurt, spray; **c.** sprit, from Old English *sprēot,* pole (< "sprout, stem"); **d.** bowsprit, from Middle Low German *bōchsprēt,* bowsprit. **a, b, c,** and **d** all from Germanic _*sprūt-_. **3.** Extended form _*spreit-_. spray[2], spread, from Old English *-sprǣdan,* to spread, from Germanic _*spraidjan_.
II. Basic form _*sper-_. **1.** Suffixed form _*sper-yo-_. Diaspora, from Greek *speirein,* to scatter, with derivative *spora,* a scattering, sowing (see **III. 1.**). **2.** Suffixed form _*sper-mn̥_. sperm[1], from Greek *sperma,* sperm, seed (< "that which is scattered").
III. O-grade form _*spor-_. **1.** Suffixed form _*spor-ā-_. spore, sporo-, from Greek *spora,* a sowing, seed. **2.** Suffixed form _*spor-n̥d-_. sporadic, from Greek *sporas* (stem *sporad-*), scattered, dispersed.
IV. Extended Germanic root _*sprē(w)-_. spray[1], from Middle Dutch *spraeien, sprayen,* to sprinkle, from Germanic _*sprēwjan_. [Pokorny 2. *(s)p(h)er-* 993.]

sperə-. Important derivatives are *spur, spurn,* and *spoor.*

sperə-. Ankle. Zero-grade form _*spr̥(ə)-_. **1.** spur, from Old English *spura, spora,* spur, from Germanic suffixed form _*spur-ōn-_. **2.** Nasalized form _*spr̥-n-ə-_. spurn, from Old English *spurnan, spornan,* to kick, strike against, from Germanic _*spurnōn_. **3.** spoor, from Middle Dutch *spor, spoor,* track of an animal, from Germanic suffixed form _*spur-am_. [Pokorny 1. *sp(h)er-* 992.]

sreu-. Important derivatives are *stream, diarrhea, hemorrhoid,* and *rhythm.*

sreu-. To flow. **1.** Suffixed o-grade form _*srou-mo-_. **a.** stream, from Old English *strēam,* stream; **b.** maelstrom, from Middle Dutch *stroom,* stream. Both **a** and **b** from Germanic _*straumaz_, stream. **2.** Basic form _*sreu-_. **a.** rheo-, -rrhea; catarrh, diarrhea, hemorrhoid, rhyolite, from Greek *rhein,* to flow, with o-grade *rhoos,* flowing, a flowing; **b.** suffixed form _*sreu-mn̥_. rheum, from Greek *rheuma,* stream, humor of the body. **3.** Suffixed zero-grade form _*sru-dhmo-_. rhythm, from Greek *rhuthmos,* measure, recurring motion, rhythm. **4.** Zero-grade extended form _*srug-_. sastruga, from Russian *struga,* deep place, perhaps from **sreu-**. [Pokorny *sreu-* 1003.]

stā-. Important derivatives are *steed, stud[2], stool, stage, stance, stanza, stay[1], arrest, circumstance, constant, contrast, cost, distant, instant, obstacle, obstetric, rest[2], substance, stand, understand, standard, stem[1], station, static, destine, obstinate, state, statue, statute, institute, prostitute, substitute, superstition, establish, stable[1], assist, exist, insist, resist, ecstasy, system, post[1], store, steer[1],* and *steer[2].*

stā-. To stand; with derivatives meaning "place or thing that is standing." Contracted from _*staə-_.
I. Basic form _*stā-_. **1.** Extended form _*stādh-_. **a.** steed, from Old English *stēda,* stallion, stud-horse (< "place for breeding horses"), from Germanic _*stōd-jōn-_; **b.** stud[2], from Old English *stōd,* establishment for breeding horses, from Germanic _*stōdō_. **2.** Suffixed form _*stā-lo-_. **a.** stool, from Old English *stōl,* stool; **b.** (see **pel-[2]**) Germanic compound _*faldistōlaz_. Both **a** and **b** from Germanic _*stōlaz_. **3.** estancia, stage, stance, stanch[1], stanchion, (stanza), stator, stay[1], stet; arrest, circumstance, constant, contrast, (cost), distant, extant, instant, obstacle, obstetric, (oust), rest[2], restive, substance, from Latin *stāre,* to stand. **4.** Suffixed form _*stā-men-_. etamine, stamen, stammel, from Latin *stāmen,* thread of the warp (a technical term). **5.** Suffixed form _*stā-mon-_. penstemon, from Greek *stēmōn,* thread. **6.** Suffixed form _*stā-ro-_. starets, from Old Church Slavonic *starŭ,* old ("long-standing").
II. Zero-grade form _*stə-_ (before consonants). **1.** Nasalized extended form _*stə-n-t-_. **a.** stand, from Old English *standan,* to stand; **b.** understand, from Old English *understandan,* to know, stand under (*under-,* under-; see **n̥dher**); **c.** standard, from Frankish _*standan_, to stand; **d.** stound, from Old English *stund,* a fixed time, while, from secondary zero-grade form in Germanic _*stund-ō_. **a, b, c,** and **d** all from Germanic _*standan_. **2.** Suffixed form _*stə-tyo-_. stithy, from Old Norse *stedhi,* anvil, from Germanic _*stathjōn-_. **3.** Suffixed form _*stə-tlo-_. staddle, starling[2], from Old English *stathol,* foundation, from Germanic _*stathlaz_. **4.** Suffixed form _*stə-mno-_. stem[1], from Old English *stefn,* stem, tree trunk, from Germanic _*stamniz_. **5.** Suffixed form _*stə-ti-_. **a.** *(i)* stead, from Old English *stede,* place; *(ii)* shtetl, from Old High German *stat,* place. Both *(i)* and *(ii)* from Germanic _*stadiz_; **b.** stat[2], from Latin *statim,* at once; **c.** station, from Latin *statiō,* a standing still; **d.** armistice, solstice, from Latin *-stitium,* a stoppage; **e.** stasis, from Greek *stasis* (see **III. 1. b.**), a standing, a standstill. **6.** Suffixed form _*stə-to-_. **a.** bestead, from Old Norse *stadhr,* place, from Germanic _*stadaz_, placed; **b.** -stat, static, statice, stato-; astasia, (astatine), from Greek *statos,* placed, standing. **7.** Suffixed form _*stə-no-_. **a.** destine, from Latin *dēstināre,* to make firm, establish (*dē-,* thoroughly; see **de-**); **b.** obstinate, from Latin *obstināre,* to set one's mind on, persist (*ob-,* on; see **epi**). **8.** Suffixed form _*stə-tu-_. state, statistics, (statue), stature, status, statute; constitute, destitute, institute, prostitute, restitute, substitute, superstition, from Latin *status,* manner, position, condition, attitude, with derivatives *statūra,* height, stature, *statuere,* to set up, erect, cause to stand, and *superstes* (< _*-stə-t-_), witness ("who stands beyond"). **9.** Suffixed form _*stə-dhlo-_. stable[2]; constable, from Latin *stabulum,* "standing place," stable. **10.** Suffixed form _*stə-dhli-_. establish, stable[1], from Latin *stabilis,* standing firm. **11.** Suffixed form _*stə-tā_. -stat; enstatite, from Greek *-statēs,* one that causes to stand, a standing.
III. Zero-grade form _*st-_, _*st(ə)-_ (before vowels). **1.** Reduplicated form _*si-st(ə)-_. **a.** assist, consist, desist, exist, insist, interstice, persist, resist, subsist, from Latin *sistere,* to set, place, stop, stand; **b.** apostasy, catastasis, diastase, ecstasy, epistasis, epistemology, hypostasis, iconostasis, isostasy, metastasis, prostate, system, from Greek *histanai* (aorist *stanai*), to set, place, with *stasis* (_*stə-ti-_), a standing (see **II. 5. e.**); **c.** histo-; histiocyte, from Greek *histos,* web, tissue (< "that which is set up"). **2.** Compound form _*tri-st-i-_, "third person standing by" (see **trei-**). **3.** Compound form _*por-st-i-_, "that which stands before" (_*por-_, before, forth; see **per[1]**). post[1], from Latin *postis,* post. **4.** Suffixed form _*st-o-_ in compound _*upo-st-o-_, "one who stands under" (see **upo**).
IV. Extended root _*stāu-_ (< _*staəu-_), becoming _*stau-_ before consonants, _*stāw-_ before vowels; basic meaning "stout-standing, strong." **1.** Suffixed extended form _*stāw-ā_. stow, from Old English *stōw,* place, from Germanic _*stōwō_. **2.** Probable o-grade suffixed extended form _*stōw-yā_. stoa, stoic, from Greek *stoa,* porch. **3.** Suffixed extended form _*stau-ro-_. **a.** *(i)* store; instauration, from Latin *īnstaurāre,* to restore, set upright again (*in-,* on; see **en**); *(ii)* restore, from Latin *restaurāre,* to restore, rebuild (*re-,* anew, again; see **re-**); **b.** staurolite, from Greek *stauros,* cross, post, stake. **4.** Variant _*tau-ro-_, bull (see **tauro-**).
V. Zero-grade extended root _*stū-_ (< _*stuə-_). Suffixed form _*stū-lo-_. stylite; amphistylar, astylar, epistyle, hypostyle, peristyle, prostyle, stylobate, from Greek *stulos,* pillar.
VI. Secondary full-grade form _*steuə-_. Suffixed form _*steuə-ro-_. Theravada, from Sanskrit *sthavira-,* thick, stout, old.
VII. Variant zero-grade extended root _*stu-_. Suffixed form _*stu-t-_. stud[1], from Old English *stuthu, studu,* post, prop.
VIII. Secondary full-grade form _*steu-_. **1.** Suffixed form _*steu-rā_. starboard, from Old English *stēor-,* a steering, from Germanic _*steurō_, "a steering." **2.a.** steer[1], from Old English *stīeran, stēran,* to steer; **b.** stern[2], from Middle English *sterne,* stern of a boat, possibly from a source akin to Old Norse *stjōrn,* a rudder, a steering, derivative of *stȳra,* to steer. Both **a** and **b** from Germanic denominative _*steurjan_. **3.** Suffixed form _*steu-ro-_, a larger domestic animal. steer[2], from Old English *stēor,* steer, from Germanic _*steuraz_, ox. **4.** stirk, from Old English *stirc, stierc,* calf, from Germanic diminutive _*steur-ika-_, probably from **stā-**. [Pokorny *stā-* 1004.]

(s)teg-. Important derivatives are *thatch, deck[2], deck[1], thug, tile, detect,* and *protect.*

(s)teg-. To cover.
I. O-grade form _*tog-_. **1.a.** thatch, from Old English *theccan,* to cover; **b.** deck[2], from Middle Dutch *decken,* to cover; **c.** deckle, from Old High German *decchen,* to cover. **a, b,** and **c** all from Germanic _*thakjan_. **2.a.** thatch, from Old English *thæc,* thatch; **b.** deck[1], from Middle Dutch *dec, decke,* roof, covering. Both **a** and **b** from Germanic _*thakam_. **3.** Suffixed form _*tog-ā-_, covering. toga, from Latin *toga,* toga. **4.** thug, from Sanskrit *sthagayati,* he covers, possibly from **(s)teg-**.
II. Basic form _*steg-_. stegodon, from Greek *stegein,* to cover.
III. Basic form _*teg-_. tectrix, tectum, tegmen, tegmentum, tegular, tegument, tile, tuille; detect, integument, obtect, protect, from Latin *tegere,* to cover, and *tēgula,* tile (with lengthened-grade root). [Pokorny 1. *(s)teg-* 1013.]

stegh-. Important derivatives are *sting* and *stag.*

stegh-. To stick, prick; pointed. **1.** Perhaps nasalized form _*stengh-_. sting, from Old English *stingan,* to sting, from Germanic _*stingan_. **2.** O-grade form _*stogh-_. **a.** stag, from Old English *stagga,* stag, from Germanic _*stag-_; **b.** stochastic, from Greek *stokhos,* pointed stake or pillar (used as a target for archers), goal. [Pokorny *stegh-* 1014.]

stei-. Important derivatives are *stone, tungsten,* and *stein.*

stei-. Stone. Possibly contracted from _*staəi-_. **1.** Suffixed o-grade form _*stoi-no-_. **a.** stone, from Old English *stān;* **b.** steenbok, from Middle Dutch *steen,* stone; **c.** tungsten, from Old Norse *steinn,* stone; **d.** stein, from Old High German *stein,* stone. **a, b, c,** and **d** all from Germanic _*stainaz_. **2.** Possibly suffixed form _*stāy-r̥_ (earlier *staəi-r̥). STEARIC, STEARIN, STEATITE, STEATO-; STEAPSIN, from Greek *stear,* solid fat, suet. [Pokorny *stāi-* 1010.]

---

steig-. Important derivatives are *stitch, stick, etiquette, ticket, distinguish, instinct, stigma, tiger, instigate,* and *steak.*

steig-. To stick; pointed. Partly blended with **stegh-**.
I. Zero-grade form **stig-*. **1.** STICKLEBACK, from Old English *sticel,* a prick, sting, from Germanic suffixed form **stik-ilaz.* **2.** Suffixed form **stig-i-*. STITCH, from Old English *stice,* a sting, prick, from Germanic **stikiz.* **3.** STICK, from Old English *sticca,* stick, from Germanic expressive form **stikkōn-*. **4.** (ETIQUETTE), TICKET, from Old French *estiquier,* to stick, from Germanic stative **stikkēn,* "to be stuck." **5.** SNICKERSNEE, from Middle Dutch *steken,* to stick, stab, from Germanic blended variant **stekan.* **6.** Nasalized form **sti-n-g-*. DISTINGUISH, EXTINGUISH, INSTINCT, from Latin *stinguere,* to quench, perhaps originally to prick, and its apparent derivative *dīstinguere,* to separate (phonological and semantic transitions obscure). **7.** Suffixed form **stig-yo-*. STIGMA; ASTIGMATISM, from Greek *stizein,* to prick, tattoo. **8.** Suffixed reduced form **tig-ro-*. TIGER, from Greek *tigris,* tiger (from its stripes), from the same Iranian source as Old Persian *tigra-,* sharp, pointed, and Avestan *tighri-,* arrow.
II. Basic form **steig-*. INSTIGATE, from Latin *īnstīgāre,* to urge, from *-stīgāre,* to spur on, prod.
III. Suffixed o-grade form **stoig-ā-*. STEAK, from Old Norse *steik,* roast, steak, and *steikja,* to roast (on a spit), from Germanic **staikō.* [Pokorny *steig-* 1016.]

---

steigh-. Important derivatives are *stirrup, acrostic* and *stair.*

steigh-. To stride, step, rise.
I. Basic form **steigh-*. STY[2]; STIRRUP, from Old English *stīgan,* to go up, rise, from Germanic **stīgan.*
II. Zero-grade form **stigh-*. **1.** STILE[1], from Old English *stigel,* series of steps, from Germanic **stigila-*. **2.** Suffixed form **stigh-to-*. STICKLE, from Old English *stiht(i)an,* to settle, arrange, from Germanic **stihtan,* "to place on a step or base." **3.** Suffixed form **stigh-o-*. STICH; ACROSTIC, CADASTRE, DISTICH, HEMISTICH, PENTASTICH, STICHOMETRY, STICHOMYTHIA, from Greek *stikhos,* row, line, line of verse.
III. O-grade form **stoigh-*. **1.** Suffixed form **stoigh-ri-*. STAIR, from Old English *stǣger,* stair, step, from Germanic **staigrī.* **2.** STOICHIOMETRY, from Greek *stoikheion,* shadow line, element. [Pokorny *steigh-* 1017.]

---

stel-. Important derivatives are *still*[1], *apostle, epistle, stall*[1], installment[1], stallion, pedestal, install, gestalt, stole[1], stalk[1], stilt, and *stout.*

stel-. To put, stand; with derivatives referring to a standing object or place.
I. Basic form **stel-*. **1.** Suffixed form **stel-ni-*. STILL[1], from Old English *stille,* quiet, fixed, from Germanic **stilli-*. **2.** Suffixed form **stel-yo-*. APOSTLE, DIASTOLE, EPISTLE, PERISTALSIS, SYSTALTIC, from Greek *stellein,* to put in order, prepare, send, make compact (with o-grade and zero-grade forms *stol-* and *stal-*).
II. O-grade form **stol-*. **1.** Suffixed form **stol-no-*. **a.** STALL[1]; FORESTALL, from Old English *steall,* standing place, stable; **b.** STALE[1]; INSTALLMENT[1], from Old French *estal,* place; **c.** STALLION, from Anglo-Norman *estaloun,* stallion; **d.** PEDESTAL, from Old Italian *stallo,* stall; **e.** INSTALL, from Medieval Latin *stallum,* stall; **f.** GESTALT, from Old High German *stellen,* to set, place, from Germanic denominative **stalljan.* **a, b, c, d, e,** and **f** all from Germanic **stalla-*. **2.** Suffixed form **stol-ōn-*. STOLON, from Latin *stolō,* branch, shoot. **3.** Suffixed form **stol-ido-*. STOLID, from Latin *stolidus,* "firm-standing," stupid. **4.** Suffixed form **stol-ā-*. **a.** STALK[1], from Old English *stalu,* upright piece, stalk, from Germanic **stalō-;* **b.** STOLE[1], from Greek *stolē,* garment, array, equipment.
III. Zero-grade form **stl̥-*. **1.** Suffixed form **stl̥-to-*. STULTIFY, from Latin *stultus,* foolish (< "unmovable, uneducated"). **2.** Suffixed zero-grade form **stl̥-no-*. STULL, (STOLLEN), from Old High German *stollo,* post, support, from Germanic **stullōn-*. **3.** Suffixed zero-grade form **stal-nā-*. STELE, from Greek *stēlē,* pillar.
IV. Extended form **steld-*. **a.** STILT, from Middle English *stilte,* crutch, stilt, from a source akin to Low German and Flemish *stilte,* stick, from Germanic **stiltjōn-;* **b.** zero-grade form **stl̥d-*. STOUT, from Old French *estout,* stout, from Germanic **stult-,* "walking on stilts," strutting. [Pokorny 3. *stel-* 1019.]

(s)tenə-. Important derivatives are *thunder, Thursday, tornado, astonish, detonate,* and *stun.*

(s)tenə-. To thunder. **1.** Zero-grade form **stn̥ə-*. **a.** THUNDER; THURSDAY, from Old English *thunor,* thunder, Thor; **b.** BLUNDERBUSS, DUNDERHEAD, from Middle Dutch *doner, donder,* thunder. **c.** THOR, from Old Norse *Thōrr* (older form *Thunarr*), "thunder," thunder god. **a, b,** and **c** all from Germanic **thunaraz.* **2.** O-grade form **tonə-*. TORNADO; ASTONISH, DETONATE, STUN, from Latin *tonāre,* to thunder. [Pokorny 1. *(s)ten-* 1021.]

---

ster-[1]. Important derivatives are *stare, stark, starch, stern*[1], *stereo-, stork, strut, start, startle, starve, torpedo,* and *torpor.*

ster-[1]. Stiff.
I. O-grade form **stor-*. **1.** Suffixed form **stor-ē-*. STARE, from Old English *starian,* to stare, from Germanic **staren.* **2.** Extended form **stor-g-*. **a.** STARK, from Old English *stearc,* hard, severe, from Germanic **starkaz;* **b.** STARCH, from Old English **stercan,* to stiffen, from Germanic denominative **starkjan.*
II. Full-grade form **ster-*. **1.** STERN[1], from Old English *stierne, styrne,* firm, from Germanic **sternjaz.* **2.** Suffixed form **ster-ewo-*. STERE, STEREO-; CHOLESTEROL, from Greek *stereos,* solid. **3.** Lengthened-grade form **stēr-*. STERIGMA, from Greek *stērizein,* to support.
III. Zero-grade form **str̥-*. **1.** Extended form **str̥g-*. STORK, from Old English *storc,* stork (probably from the stiff movements of the bird), from Germanic **sturkaz.* **2.** STRUT, from Old English *strūtian,* to stand out stiffly, from Germanic **strūt-*.
IV. Extended form **sterd-*. **1.** REDSTART, from Old English *steort,* tail, from Germanic **stertaz.* **2.a.** START, from Old English **styrtan,* to leap up (< "move briskly, move stiffly"); **b.** STARTLE, from Old English *steartlian,* to kick, struggle. Both **a** and **b** from Germanic **stert-*.
V. Extended form **sterbh-*. STARVE, from Old English *steorfan,* to die (< "become rigid"), from Germanic **sterban.*
VI. Extended form **(s)terp-* in suffixed (stative) zero-grade form **tr̥p-ē-*. TORPEDO, TORPID, TORPOR, from Latin *torpēre,* to be stiff. [Pokorny 1. *(s)ter-* 1022.]

---

ster-[2]. Important derivatives are *structure, construct, destroy, instruct, obstruct, industry, strew, straw, street,* and *stratagem.*

ster-[2]. Also **sterə-**. To spread.
I. Extended form **streu-*. **1.** STRAIN[2], from Old English *strēon,* something gained, offspring, from Germanic suffixed form **streu-nam.* **2.** STRUCTURE; CONSTRUCT, DESTROY, INSTRUCT, OBSTRUCT, SUBSTRUCTION, from Latin *struere,* to pile up, construct. **3.** Zero-grade form **stru-*. INDUSTRY, from Latin *industrius,* diligent, from Old Latin *indostruus* (*endo-,* within; see **en**). **4.** BREMSSTRAHLUNG, from Old High German *strāla,* arrow, lightning bolt, from Germanic **strēlō.*
II. O-grade extended form **strou-*. **1.** Suffixed form **strou-eyo-*. **a.** STREW, from Old English *strē(o)wian,* to strew; **b.** STREUSEL, from Old High German *strouwen, strowwen,* to sprinkle, strew. Both **a** and **b** from Germanic **strawjan.* **2.** Suffixed form **strow-o.* STRAW, from Old English *strēaw,* straw, from Germanic **strawam,* "that which is scattered."
III. O-grade extended form **stroi-*. PERESTROIKA, from Old Russian *stroĭĭ,* order.
IV. Basic forms **ster-, *sterə-*. **1.** Nasalized form **ster-n-ə-*. STRATUS, STREET; CONSTERNATE, PROSTRATE, SUBSTRATUM, from Latin *sternere* (past participle *strātus* from zero-grade **strə-to-*), to stretch, extend. **2.** Suffixed form **ster-no-*. STERNUM, from Greek *sternon,* breast, breastbone.
V. Zero-grade form **str̥-, *str̥ə-*. **1.** Suffixed form **str̥-to-*. STRATAGEM; STRATOCRACY, from Greek *stratos,* multitude, army, expedition. **2.** Suffixed form **str̥ə-to-*. STRATH, from Old Irish *srath,* a wide river valley, from Celtic **s(t)rato-*. **3.** Suffixed extended form **str̥ə-mn̥.* STROMA; (STROMATOLITE), from Greek *strōma,* mattress, bed. [Pokorny 5. *ster-* 1029.]

---

ster-[3]. Important derivatives are *star, stellar, constellation, aster, asterisk, asteroid,* and *disaster.*

ster-[3]. Star. **1.** Suffixed form **ster-s-*. STAR, from Old English *steorra,* star, from Germanic **sterzōn-*. **2.** Suffixed form **stēr-lā-*. STELLAR, STELLATE; CONSTELLATION, from Latin *stēlla,* star. **3.** Oldest root form **əste-*. ASTER, ASTERIATED, ASTERISK, ASTERISM, ASTEROID, ASTRAL, ASTRO-; ASTRAPHOBIA, DISASTER, from Greek *astēr,* star, with its derivative *astron,* star, and possible compound *astrapē, asteropē,* lightning, twinkling (< "looking like a star"; *ōps,* stem *op-,* eye, appearance; see **okʷ-**). **4.** ESTHER, from Persian *sitareh,* star, from Iranian stem **stār-*. [Pokorny 2. *ster-* 1027.]

---

streb(h)-. Important derivatives are *strop, strophe, apostrophe*[1], *catastrophe,* and *stroboscope.*

streb(h)-. To wind, turn. **1.** STREPTO-, STROP, STROPHE, STROPHOID; ANASTROPHE, APOSTROPHE[1], BOUSTROPHEDON, CATASTROPHE, DIASTROPHISM, from Greek *strephein,* to wind, turn, twist, with o-grade derivatives *strophē,* a turning, and *strophion,* headband. **2.** Unaspirated o-grade form **strob-*. STROBILUS; STROBOSCOPE, from Greek *strobos,* a whirling, whirlwind. **3.** Unaspirated zero-grade form **str̥b-*. STRABISMUS, from Greek *strabos,* squinting. [Pokorny *strebh-* 1025.]

---

streig-. Important derivatives are *strike, streak, stroke*[1], *strain*[1], *strict, stringent, constrain, prestige,* and *restrict.*

streig-. To stroke, rub, press.
I. Basic form **streig-*. **1.a.** STRIKE, from Old English *strīcan,* to stroke; **b.** TRICOT, from Old French *estriquier,* to strike. Both **a** and **b** from Germanic **strīkan.* **2.** STRICKLE, from Old English *stricel,* implement for leveling grain, from Germanic diminutive **strik-ila-*. **3.** STREAK, from Old English *strica,* stroke, line, from Germanic **strikōn-*.
II. O-grade form **stroig-*. STROKE[1], from Old English **strāc,* stroke, from Germanic **straik-*.
III. Zero-grade form **strig-*. **1.** Suffixed form **strig-ā-*. STRIGOSE, from Latin *striga,* row of grain, furrow drawn lengthwise over the field. **2.** Suffixed form **strig-yā-*. STRIA, from Latin *stria,* furrow, channel. **3.** Nasalized form **stri-n-g-*. STRAIN[1], STRAIT, STRICT, STRINGENDO, STRINGENT; ASTRINGENT, CONSTRAIN, DISTRAIN, PRESTIGE, RESTRICT, from Latin *stringere,* to draw tight, press together. **4.** STRIGIL, from Latin *strigilis,* strigil, possibly akin to *stringere.* [Pokorny 1. *streig-* 1036; 4. *ster-* 1028.]

---

su-. A derivative is *swastika.*

su-. Well, good. **1.** SWASTIKA, from Sanskrit *svasti,* well-being, good luck, from *su-,* well- (see **es-**). **2.** Compound **su-gʷiə-es-,* "having good life" (see **gʷei-**). [Pokorny *su-* 1037.]

---

sū-. Important derivatives are *swine, hog, socket, sow*[2], and *hyena.*

sū-. Pig. Contracted from **suə-;* probably a derivative of **seuə-**[1]. **1.** Suffixed form **suə-īno-*. **a.** SWINE, from Old English *swīn,* swine; **b.** KEELSON, from Old Norse *svīn,* swine. Both **a** and **b** from Germanic **swīnam.* **2.** Suffixed form **su-kā.* **a.** HOG, from Old English *hogg,* hog, from British **hukk-;* **b.** SOCKET, from Anglo-Norman *soc,* plowshare, perhaps from **sū-**. Both **a** and **b** from Celtic expressive form **sukko-,* swine, snout of a swine, plowshare; **c.** SOW[2], from Old English *sugu,* sow, from Germanic **sugō.* **3.** Basic form **sū-*. SOW[2], from Old English *sū,* from Germanic **sū-*. **4.** SOIL[2], from Latin *sūs,* pig. **5.** HYENA; HYOSCINE, from Greek *hus,* swine. [Pokorny *sŭ-s* 1038.]

---

swād-. Important derivatives are *sweet, dissuade, persuade, suave,* and *hedonism.*

swād-. Sweet, pleasant. **1.** SWEET, from Old English *swēte,* sweet, from Germanic **swōtja-.* **2.** Suffixed form **swād-ē-.* SUASION; (ASSUASIVE), DISSUADE, PERSUADE, from Latin *suādēre,* to advise, urge (< "recommend as good"). **3.** Suffixed form **swād-w-i-.* SOAVE, SUAVE; ASSUAGE, from Latin *suāvis,* delightful. **4.** Suffixed form **swād-es-.* AEDES, from Greek *ēdos,* pleasure. **5.** Suffixed form **swād-onā.* HEDONIC, HEDONISM, from Greek *hēdonē,* pleasure. [Pokorny *su̯ād-* 1039.]

s(w)e-. Important derivatives are *self, gossip, bustle*[1]*, suicide, secede, seclude, secret, secure, sedition, seduce, segregate, select, separate, sure, sober, sole*[2]*, solitary, solitude, solo, sullen, desolate, soliloquy, custom, ethic, ethnic, idiom, idiot,* and *idiosyncrasy.*

s(w)e-. Pronoun of the third person and reflexive (referring back to the subject of the sentence); further appearing in various forms referring to the social group as an entity, "(we our-)selves." **1.** Suffixed extended form **sel-bho-.* SELF, from Old English *self, sylf,* self, same, from Germanic **selbaz,* self. **2.** Suffixed form **s(w)e-bh(o)-.* SIB; GOSSIP, from Old English *sibb,* relative, from Germanic **sibja-,* "one's own," blood relation, relative. **3.** Suffixed form **se-ge.* BUSTLE[1], from Old Norse *-sk,* reflexive suffix, as in *būask,* to make oneself ready, from *sik,* oneself (reflexive pronoun), from Germanic **sik,* self. **4.** Suffixed form **swoi-no-.* SWAIN; (BOATSWAIN), from Old Norse *sveinn,* herdsman, boy, from Germanic **swainaz,* "one's own (man)," attendant, servant. **5.** Suffixed form **s(u)w-o-,* one's own. **a.** SUICIDE, from Latin *suī* (genitive), of oneself; **b.** SWAMI, from Sanskrit *svāmin,* "one's own master," owner, prince, from *sva-* (< **swo-*), one's own. **6.** Extended form **sed.* SECEDE, SECERN, SECLUDE, SECRET, SECURE, SEDITION, SEDUCE, SEDULOUS, SEGREGATE, SELECT, SEPARATE, (SURE), from Latin *sēd, sē, sē-* , without, apart (< "on one's own"); **c.** SOBER, from Latin compound *sōbrius,* not drunk (*ēbrius,* drunk; see **ēgʷh-**). **7.** Possibly suffixed lengthened o-grade form **sō-lo.* SOLE[2], SOLITARY, SOLITUDE, SOLO, SULLEN; DESOLATE, SOLILOQUY, SOLIPSISM, from Latin *sōlus,* by oneself alone. **8.** Extended root **swĕdh-,* "that which is one's own," peculiarity, custom. **a.** SODALITY, from Latin *sodālis,* companion (< "one's own," "relative"); **b.** suffixed form **swēdh-sko-.* (CONSUETUDE), CUSTOM, DESUETUDE, MANSUETUDE, MASTIFF, from Latin *suēscere,* to accustom, get accustomed; **c.** ETHIC, ETHOS; CACOETHES, from Greek *ēthos,* custom, disposition, trait; **d.** suffixed form **swedh-no-.* ETHNIC, ETHNO-, from Greek *ethnos,* band of people living together, nation, people (< "people of one's own kind"). **9.** Suffixed extended form **swet-aro-.* HETAERA, from Greek *hetairos,* comrade, companion, earlier *hetaros.* **10.** Suffixed extended form **swed-yo-.* IDIO-, IDIOM, IDIOT; (IDIOPATHY), (IDIOSYNCRASY), from Greek *idios,* personal, private ("particular to oneself"). **11.** Suffixed form **swei-no-.* SINN FEIN, from Old Irish *fēin,* self. **12.** Suffixed (ablatival) form **swe-tos,* from oneself. KHEDIVE, from Old Iranian *khvadāta-,* lord, by haplology from compound form **khvatō-dāta-,* created from oneself (*dāta-,* created; see **dhē-**). [Pokorny *se-* 882.]

sweid-. An important derivative is *sweat.*

sweid-. Sweat; to sweat.
I. O-grade form **swoid-.* **1.** SWEAT, from Old English *swǣtan,* to sweat, from Germanic **swaitaz,* sweat, with its denominative **swaitjan,* to sweat. **2.** Suffixed form **swoid-os-.* SUDORIFIC; SUDORIFEROUS, from Latin *sūdor,* sweat. **3.** O-grade form **swoid-ā-.* SUDATORIUM, SUINT; EXUDE, TRANSUDE, from Latin *sūdāre,* to sweat.
II. Suffixed zero-grade form **swid-r-os-.* HIDROSIS, from Greek *hidrōs,* sweat. [Pokorny 2. *su̯eid-* 1043.]

s(w)eks. Important derivatives are *six, semester, sestet, sextant,* and *hexa-.*

s(w)eks. Six.
I. Form **seks.* **1.** SIX; SIXTEEN, SIXTY, from Old English *s(i)ex, six,* with derivatives *sixtig,* sixty, and *sixtȳne,* sixteen (*-tȳne,* ten; see **dekm̥**), from Germanic **seks.* **2.** SENARY, SEX-; SEICENTO, SEMESTER, from Latin *sex,* six. **3.** Suffixed form **seks-to-.* SESTET, SESTINA, SEXT, SEXTANT, SEXTILE; SEXTODECIMO, from Latin *sextus,* sixth.
II. Form **sweks.* HEXA-, HEXAD, from Greek *hex,* six. [Pokorny *su̯eks* 1044.]

swel-. Important derivatives are *swill* and *swallow*[1].

swel-. To eat, drink. **1.** SWILL, from Old English *swilian,* to wash out, gargle, from Germanic **swil-,* perhaps from **swel-.** **2.** Extended form **swelk-.* SWALLOW[1]; GROUNDSEL[1], from Old English *swelgan,* to swallow, from Germanic **swelgan, *swelhan.* **3.** MANTICORE, from Greek *mantikhōras,* manticore, probably from Iranian **khvāra-,* eating. [Pokorny 1. *su̯el(k)-* 1045.]

swen-. Important derivatives are *swan, sonic, sonnet, sound*[1]*, unison, sonata, sonorous, consonant, dissonant,* and *resound.*

swen-. To sound. **1.** Suffixed o-grade form **swon-o-.* **a.** SWAN, from Old English *swan,* swan, from Germanic **swanaz, *swanōn-,* "singer"; **b.** SONE, SONIC, SONNET, SOUND[1]; UNISON, from Latin *sonus,* a sound. **2.** Form **swen-ā-.* SONANT, SONATA, SONOROUS; ASSONANCE, CONSONANT, DISSONANT, RESOUND, from Latin *sonāre,* to sound. [Pokorny *su̯en-* 1046.]

swep-. Important derivatives are *insomnia* and *hypnosis.*

swep-. To sleep. **1.** Suffixed form **swep-os-.* SOPOR; (SOPORIFIC), from Latin *sopor,* a deep sleep. **2.** Suffixed form **swep-no-.* SOMNI-, SOMNOLENT; INSOMNIA, from Latin *somnus,* sleep. **3.** Suffixed zero-grade form **sup-no-.* HYPNO-, (HYPNOSIS), HYPNOTIC, from Greek *hupnos,* sleep. [Pokorny 1. *su̯ep-* 1048.]

swer-. Important derivatives are *swear* and *answer.*

swer-. To speak, talk. O-grade form **swor-.* **a.** SWEAR, from Old English *swerian,* to swear, proclaim, from Germanic **swarjan;* **b.** ANSWER, from Old English *andswaru,* answer, from Germanic **and-swarō,* "a swearing against," "rebuttal" (**andi-,* against; see **ant-**). [Pokorny 1. *su̯er-* 1049.]

swesor-. Important derivatives are *sister, cousin,* and *sorority.*

swesor-. Sister. **1.** Zero-grade form **swesr-.* **a.** SISTER, from Old English *sweostor,* sister, and Old Norse *systir,* sister, both from Germanic **swestr-;* **b.** suffixed form **swesr-īno-.* COUSIN, from Latin *sobrinus,* maternal cousin. **2.** SORORAL, SORORITY, from Latin *soror,* sister. [Pokorny *su̯esor-* 1051.]

swo-. Important derivatives are *so*[1] and *such.*

swo-. Pronominal stem; so. Derivative of **s(w)e-.** **1.a.** SO[1], from Old English *swā,* so; **b.** SUCH, from Old English *swylc,* such, from Germanic compound **swa-līk-,* "so like," of the same kind (**līk-,* same; see **līk-**). **2.** Adverbial form **swai.* NISI, QUASI, from Latin *sī,* if, in *nisi,* unless (*nī,* not; see **ne-** + *sī,* if), *quasi* (*quam,* as; see **kʷo-** + *sī,* if). [In Pokorny 2. *seu-* 882.]

syū-. Important derivatives are *sew, seam, suture, couture,* and *hymen.*

syū-. To bind, sew.
I. Basic form **syū-.* SEW, from Old English *seowian, siowan,* to sew, from Germanic **siwjan.*
II. Variant form **sū-.* **1.** SEAM, from Old English *sēam,* seam, from Germanic **saumaz.* **2.** SUTURE; COUTURE, from Latin *suere* (past participle *sūtus*), to sew. **3.** Suffixed form **sū-dhlā-.* SUBULATE, from Latin *sūbula,* awl (< "sewing instrument"). **4.** Suffixed form **sū-tro-.* SUTRA; KAMASUTRA, from Sanskrit *sūtram,* thread, string.
III. Suffixed shortened form **syu-men-.* HYMEN, from Greek *humēn,* thin skin, membrane. [Pokorny *sī̆u̯-* 915.]

tag-. Important derivatives are *tact, tangent, tangible, taste, tax, attain, contact, intact, entire, integer,* and *contaminate.*

tag-. To touch, handle. **1.** Nasalized form **ta-n-g-.* TACT, TANGENT, TANGIBLE, TASTE, TAX; ATTAIN, CONTACT, INTACT, from Latin *tangere,* to touch, with derivatives *taxāre,* to touch, assess (possibly a frequentative of *tangere,* but probably influenced by Greek *tassein, taxai,* to arrange, assess), and *tāctus,* touch. **2.** Compound form **n̥-tag-ro-,* "untouched, intact" (**n̥-,* negative prefix; see **ne**). ENTIRE, INTEGER, INTEGRATE, INTEGRITY, from Latin *integer,* intact, whole, complete, perfect, honest. **3.** Suffixed form **tag-smen-.* CONTAMINATE, from Latin *contāmināre,* to corrupt by mixing or contact (< **con-tāmen-,* "bringing into contact with"; *con-, com-,* with; see **kom**). [Pokorny *tag-* 1054.]

tauro-. Important derivatives are *Taurus, toreador,* and *torero.*

tauro-. Bull. Derivative of **stā-**, but an independent word in Indo-European. **1.** TAURINE[1], TAURUS, TOREADOR, TORERO; BITTERN[1], from Latin *taurus,* bull. **2.** TAURINE[2]; TAUROCHOLIC ACID, from Greek *tauros,* bull. [In Pokorny *tēu-* 1083.]

tegu-. An important derivative is *thick.*

tegu-. Thick. THICK, from Old English *thicce,* thick, from Germanic **thiku-.* [Pokorny *tegu-* 1057.]

tek-. A derivative is *thane.*

tek-. To beget, give birth to. **1.** Suffixed form **tek-no-,* child. THANE, from Old English *thegn,* freeman, nobleman, military vassal, warrior, from Germanic **thegnaz,* boy, man, servant, warrior. **2.** Suffixed o-grade form **tok-o-.* OXYTOCIC, POLYTOCOUS, TOCOLOGY, from Greek *tokos,* birth. [Pokorny 1. *tek-* 1057.]

teks-. Important derivatives are *text, tissue, context, pretext, subtle, architect, technical,* and *technology.*

teks-. To weave; also to fabricate, especially with an ax; also to make wicker or wattle fabric for (mud-covered) house walls. **1.** TEXT, TISSUE; CONTEXT, PRETEXT, from Latin *texere,* to weave, fabricate. **2.** Suffixed form **teks-lā.* **a.** TILLER[2], TOIL[2], from Latin *tēla,* web, net, warp of a fabric, also weaver's beam (to which the warp threads are tied); **b.** SUBTLE, from Latin *subtīlis,* thin, fine, precise, subtle (< **sub-tēla,* "thread passing under the warp," the finest thread; *sub,* under; see **upo**). **3.** Suffixed form **teks-ōn,* weaver, maker of wattle for house walls, builder (possibly contaminated with **teks-tōr,* builder). TECTONIC; ARCHITECT, from Greek *tektōn,* carpenter, builder. **4.** Suffixed form **teks-nā-,* craft (of weaving or fabricating). TECHNICAL, (POLYTECHNIC), TECHNOLOGY, from Greek *tekhnē,* art, craft, skill. **5.a.** DACHSHUND, from Old High German *dahs,* badger; **b.** DASSIE, from Middle Dutch *das,* badger. Both **a** and **b** from Germanic **thahsu-,* badger, possibly from **teks-** ("the animal that builds," referring to its burrowing skill) but more likely borrowed from the same pre-Indo-European source as the Celtic totemic name *Tazgo-,* Gaelic *Tadhg,* originally "badger." [Pokorny *tekp-* 1058.]

telə-. Important derivatives are *toll*[1]*, philately, tolerate, retaliate, talent, tantalize, Atlantic, Atlas, collate, elate, legislator, relate, superlative, translate,* and *extol.*

telə-. To lift, support, weigh; with derivatives referring to measured weights and thence to money and payment. **1.** Suffixed form **telə-mon-.* TELAMON, from Greek *telamōn,* supporter, bearer. **2.** Suffixed form **tel(ə)-es-.* **a.** TOLL[1]; PHILATELY, from Greek *telos,* tax, charge; **b.** TOLERATE, from Latin *tolerāre,* to bear, endure. **3.** Suffixed zero-grade form **tl̥ə-i-.* TALION; RETALIATE, from Latin *tāliō,* reciprocal punishment in kind, possibly "something paid out," from **tali-* (influenced by *tālis,* such). **4.** Suffixed variant zero-grade form **tala-nt-.* TALENT, from Greek *talanton,* balance, weight, any of several specific weights of gold or silver, hence the sum of money represented by such a weight. **5.** Perhaps (but unlikely) intensive reduplicated form **tantal-.* (TANTALIZE), TANTALUS, from Greek *Tantalos,* name of a legendary king, "the sufferer." **6.** Perhaps (but unlikely) zero-grade form **tl̥ə-.* ATLANTIC, ATLAS, from Greek *Atlas* (stem *Atlant-*), name of the Titan supporting the world. **7.** Suffixed zero-grade form **tl̥ə-to-.* ABLATION, COLLATE, DILATORY, ELATE, ILLATION, LEGISLATOR, OBLATE[1], PRELATE, PROLATE, RELATE, SUB-

LATE, SUPERLATIVE, TRANSLATE, from Latin _lātus,_ “carried, borne,” used as the suppletive past participle of _ferre,_ to bear (see **bher-**[1]), with its compounds. **8.** Suffixed zero-grade form *tl̥ə-ā-. TOLA, from Sanskrit _tulā,_ scales, balance, weight. **9.** Nasalized zero-grade form *tl̥-n-ə-. EXTOL, from Latin _tollere,_ to lift. [Pokorny 1. _tel-_ 1060.]

tem-. Important derivatives are _tome, anatomy, atom, diatom, epitome, temple_[1], and _contemplate._

tem-. Also **temə-**. To cut.
I. Form *temə-. Nasalized form *t(e)m-n-ə-. TMESIS, TOME, (-TOME), -TOMY; ANATOMY, ATOM, DIATOM, DICHOTOMY, ENTOMO-, EPITOME, from Greek _temnein,_ to cut, with o-grade forms _tomos,_ cutting, a cut, section, volume, and _tomē,_ a cutting.
II. Form *tem-. **1.** Suffixed form *tem-lo-. TEMPLE[1], TEMPLE[3]; CONTEMPLATE, from Latin _templum,_ temple, shrine, open place for observation (augury term < “place reserved or cut out”), small piece of timber. **2.** Extended root *tem-d- becoming *tend- in o-grade suffixed (iterative) form *tond-eyo-. TONSORIAL, TONSURE, from Latin _tondēre,_ to shear, shave. [Pokorny 1. _tem-, tend-_ 1062.]

ten-. Important derivatives are _tend_[1], _tendon, tense_[1], _tent_[1], _attend, contend, extend, intend, pretend, hypotenuse, sitar, tenacious, tenant, tenement, tenor, tenure, contain, continue, detain, entertain, lieutenant, maintain, obtain, pertain, retain, sustain, thin, tenuous, tender_[1], and _tone._

ten-. To stretch.
I. Derivatives with the basic meaning. **1.** Suffixed form *ten-do-. **a.** TEND[1], TENDER[2], TENSE[1], TENT[1]; ATTEND, CONTEND, DETENT, DISTEND, EXTEND, INTEND, OSTENSIBLE, PRETEND, SUBTEND, from Latin _tendere,_ to stretch, extend; **b.** PORTEND, from Latin _portendere,_ “to stretch out before” (_por-_, variant of _pro-,_ before; see **per**[1]), a technical term in augury, “to indicate, presage, foretell.” **2.** Suffixed form *ten-yo-. TENESMUS; ANATASE, BRONCHIECTASIS, CATATONIA, EPITASIS, HYPOTENUSE, PERITONEUM, PROTASIS, TELANGIECTASIA, from Greek _teinein,_ to stretch, with o-grade form _ton-_ and zero-grade noun _tasis_ (< *tn̥-ti-), a stretching, tension, intensity. **3.** Reduplicated zero-grade form *te-tan-o-. TETANUS, from Greek _tetanos,_ stiff, rigid. **4.** Suffixed full-grade form *ten-tro-. **a.** TANTRA, from Sanskrit _tantram,_ loom; **b.** SITAR, from Persian _tār,_ string. **5.** Basic form (with stative suffix) *ten-ē-. TENABLE, TENACIOUS, TENACULUM, TENANT, TENEMENT, TENET, TENON, TENOR, TENURE, TENUTO; ABSTAIN, CONTAIN, (CONTINUE), DETAIN, ENTERTAIN, LIEUTENANT, MAINTAIN, OBTAIN, PERTAIN, PERTINACIOUS, RETAIN, (RETINACULUM), SUSTAIN, from Latin _tenēre,_ to hold, keep, maintain (< “to cause to endure or continue, hold on to”).
II. Derivatives meaning “stretched,” hence “thin.” **1.** Suffixed zero-grade form *tn̥-u-. THIN, from Old English _thynne,_ thin, from Germanic *thunniz, from *thunw-. **2.** Suffixed full-grade form *ten-u-. TENUOUS; ATTENUATE, EXTENUATE, from Latin _tenuis,_ thin, rare, fine. **3.** Suffixed full-grade form *ten-ero-. TENDER[1], (TENDRIL), from Latin _tener,_ tender, delicate.
III. Derivatives meaning “something stretched or capable of being stretched, a string.” **1.** Suffixed form *ten-ōn-. TENDON, TENO-, from Greek _tenōn,_ tendon. **2.** Suffixed o-grade form *ton-o-. TONE; (BARITONE), TONOPLAST, from Greek _tonos,_ string, hence sound, pitch. **3.** Suffixed zero-grade form *tn̥-ya-. TAENIA, from Greek _tainia,_ band, ribbon. [Pokorny 1. _ten-_ 1065.]

terə-[1]. Important derivatives are _trite, detriment, thrash, thresh, threshold, turn, contour, return, drill_[1], _throw, thread, trauma,_ and _truant._

terə-[1]. To rub, turn; with some derivatives referring to twisting, boring, drilling, and piercing; and others referring to the rubbing of cereal grain to remove the husks, and thence to the process of threshing either by the trampling of oxen or by flailing with flails. Variant *trē-, contracted from *treə-.
I. Full-grade form *ter(ə)-. **1.a.** TRITE, TRITURATE; ATTRITION, CONTRITE, DETRIMENT, from Latin _terere_ (past participle _trītus_), to rub away, thresh, tread, wear out; **b.** TEREDO, from Greek _terēdōn,_ a kind of biting worm. **2.** Suffixed form *ter-et-. TERETE, from Latin _teres_ (stem _teret-_), rounded, smooth. **3.** Suffixed form *ter-sko-. **a.** (THRASH), THRESH, from Old English _therscan,_ to thresh; **b.** THRESHOLD, from Old English _therscold, threscold,_ sill of a door (over which one treads; second element obscure). Both **a** and **b** from Germanic *therskan, *threskan, to thresh, tread.
II. O-grade form *tor(ə)-. **1.** TOREUTICS, from Greek _toreus,_ a boring tool. **2.** Suffixed form *tor(ə)-mo-, hole. DERMA[2], from Old High German _darm,_ gut, from Germanic *tharma-. **3.** Suffixed form *tor(ə)-no-. TURN; CONTOUR, (DETOUR), (RETURN), from Greek _tornos,_ tool for drawing a circle, circle, lathe.
III. Zero-grade form *tr-. DRILL[1], from Middle Dutch _drillen,_ to drill, from Germanic *thr-.
IV. Variant form *trē- (< *treə-). **1.** THROW, from Old English _thrāwan,_ to turn, twist, from Germanic *thrēw-. **2.** Suffixed form *trē-tu-. THREAD, from Old English _thrǣd,_ thread, from Germanic *thrēdu-, twisted yarn. **3.** Suffixed form *trē-mn̥ (< *treə- or *tr̥ə-). MONOTREME, TREMATODE, from Greek _trēma,_ perforation. **4.** Suffixed form *trē-ti- (< *treə- or *tr̥ə-). ATRESIA, from Greek _trēsis,_ perforation.
V. Extended form *trī- (< *triə-). **1.** Probably suffixed form *trī-ōn-. SEPTENTRION, from Latin _triō,_ plow ox. **2.** Suffixed form *trī-dhlo-. TRIBULATION, from Latin _trībulum,_ a threshing sledge.
VI. Various extended forms **1.** Forms *trō-, *trau-. TRAUMA, from Greek _trauma,_ hurt, wound. **2.** Form *trīb-. DIATRIBE, TRIBOELECTRICITY, TRIBOLOGY, TRYPSIN, from Greek _tribein,_ to rub, thresh, pound, wear out. **3.** Form *trōg-, *trag-. **a.** TROGON, TROUT, from Greek _trōgein,_ to gnaw; **b.** DREDGE[2], from Greek _tragēma,_ sweetmeat. **4.** Form *trup-. TREPAN[1]; TRYPANOSOME, from Greek _trupē,_ hole. **5.** Possible form *trūg-. TRUANT, from Old French _truant,_ beggar. [Pokorny 3. _ter-_ 1071.]

terə-[2]. Important derivatives are _thrill, nostril, thorough, through, trans-, transient, trench,_ and _trunk._

terə-[2]. To cross over, pass through, overcome. Variant *trā-, contracted from *traə-.
I. Zero-grade form *tr̥(ə)-. **1.** THRILL; NOSTRIL, from Old English _thyr(e)l, thȳrel,_ a hole (< “a boring through”), from Germanic suffixed form *thur-ila-. **2.** Suffixed form *tr̥ə-k^{w}e. THOROUGH, THROUGH, from Old English _thurh, thuruh,_ through, from Germanic *thurh. **3.** (see **nek-**[1]) Greek _nek-tar,_ overcoming death. **4.** Zero-grade form *tr̥ə- and full-grade form *ter(ə)-. AVATAR, from Sanskrit _tirati, tarati,_ he crosses over.
II. Variant form *trā- (< *traə-). **1.** TRANS-, TRANSIENT, (TRANSOM), from Latin _trāns,_ across, over, beyond, through (perhaps originally the present participle of a verb *trāre, to cross over). **2.** Suffixed form *trā-yo-. CARAVANSARY, from Persian _sarāy,_ inn, from Middle Persian _srāyīdhan,_ to protect, from Iranian _thrāya-,_ to protect.
III. Possible extended form *tru-. **1.** Suffixed form *tru-k-. TRUCULENT, from Latin _trux_ (stem _truc-_), savage, fierce, grim (< “overcoming,” “powerful,” “penetrating”). **2.** Suffixed nasalized form *tru-n-k-o-. TRENCH, TRUNCATE, TRUNK, from Latin _truncus,_ deprived of branches or limbs, mutilated, hence trunk (? < “overcome, maimed”). [Pokorny 5. _ter-_ 1075.]

terk^w-. Important derivatives are _queer, thwart, torch, torment, torque_[1], _tortuous, distort, extort, nasturtium,_ and _retort_[1].

terk^w-. To twist. Extension of **terə-**[1]. **1.** Possible variant form *t(w)erk-. **a.** QUEER, from Middle Low German _dwer,_ oblique; **b.** THWART, from Old Norse _thverr,_ transverse. Both **a** and **b** from Germanic *thwerh-, twisted, oblique. **2.** Suffixed (causative) o-grade form *tork^w-eyo-. TORCH, TORMENT, TORQUE[1], TORQUE[2], TORSADE, TORT, TORTUOUS, TORTURE, TRUSS; CONTORT, DISTORT, EXTORT, NASTURTIUM, RETORT[1], TORTICOLLIS, from Latin _torquēre,_ to twist. [Pokorny _terk-_ 1077.]

ters-. Important derivatives are _thirst, terrace, terrain, terrier, territory, inter, mediterranean, subterranean, toast_[1], _torrent,_ and _torrid._

ters-. To dry. **1.** Suffixed zero-grade form *tr̥s-. **a.** THIRST, from Old English _thurst,_ dryness, thirst, from Germanic suffixed form *thurs-tu-; **b.** CUSK, from Old Norse _thorskr,_ cod (< “dried fish”). Both **a** and **b** from Germanic *thurs-. **2.** Suffixed basic form *ters-ā-. TERRACE, (TERRAIN), TERRAN, TERRENE, TERRESTRIAL, TERRIER, TERRITORY, TUREEN; FUMITORY, INTER, MEDITERRANEAN, PARTERRE, SUBTERRANEAN, TERRAQUEOUS, TERREPLEIN, TERRE-VERTE, TERRICOLOUS, TERRIGENOUS, TURMERIC, VERDITER, from Latin _terra,_ “dry land,” earth. **3.** Suffixed o-grade form *tors-eyo-. TOAST[1], TORRENT, TORRID, from Latin _torrēre,_ to dry, parch, burn. **4.** Suffixed zero-grade form *tr̥s-o-. TARSUS, from Greek _tarsos,_ frame of wickerwork (originally for drying cheese), hence a flat surface, sole of the foot, ankle. [Pokorny _ters-_ 1078.]

teuə-. Important derivatives are _thigh, thousand, thimble, thumb, tumor, truffle, tuber, butter,_ and _tomb._

teuə-. Also **teu-**. To swell. **1.** Extended form *teuk-. THIGH, from Old English _thēoh,_ thigh, from Germanic *theuham, “the swollen or fat part of the leg,” thigh. **2.** Extended form *tūs-. THOUSAND, from Old English _thūsend,_ thousand, from Germanic compound *thūs-hundi-, “swollen hundred,” thousand (*hundi-, hundred; see **dekm̥**). **3.** Probably suffixed zero-grade form *tu-l-. THOLE PIN, from Old English _thol(l),_ oar pin, oarlock (< “a swelling”), from Germanic *thul-. **4.** Extended zero-grade form *tūm-. **a.** THIMBLE, THUMB, from Old English _thūma,_ thumb (< “the thick finger”), from Germanic *thūmōn-; **b.** suffixed (stative) form *tum-ē-. TUMESCENT, TUMID, TUMOR; DETUMESCENCE, INTUMESCE, TUMEFACIENT, (TUMEFY), from Latin _tumēre,_ to swell, be swollen, be proud; **c.** suffixed form *tum-olo-. TUMULUS, from Latin _tumulus,_ raised heap of earth, mound. **5.** Extended zero-grade form *tūbh-. TRUFFLE, TUBER; PROTUBERATE, from Latin _tūber,_ lump, swelling. **6.** Suffixed zero-grade form *tū-ro- (< *tuə-ro-). **a.** BUTTER, TYROSINE, from Greek _turos,_ cheese (< “a swelling,” “coagulating”); **b.** OBTURATE, from Latin _-tūrāre,_ to stop up, possibly from *tūros swollen, coagulated, stopped up. **7.** Suffixed variant form *twō-ro-. SORITES, SORUS, from Greek _sōros,_ heap, pile. **8.** Suffixed variant form *twō-mn̥. SOMA, SOMATO-, -SOME[3]; PROSOMA, from Greek _sōma,_ body (< “a swelling,” “stocky form”). **9.** Suffixed zero-grade form *twə-wo-. CREOSOTE, SOTERIOLOGY, from Greek _sōzein,_ to save, rescue, derivative of _saos, sōs,_ safe, healthy (< “swollen,” “strong”). **10.** Perhaps nasalized extended form *tu-m-b(h)- (or extended zero-grade form *tum-). TOMB, from Greek _tumbos,_ barrow, tomb. [Pokorny _tēu-_ 1080.]

teutā-. Important derivatives are _Dutch, Teuton,_ and _total._

teutā-. Tribe. **1.a.** DUTCH, from Middle Dutch _duutsch,_ German, of the Germans or Teutons; **b.** PLATTDEUTSCH, from Old High German _diutisc,_ of the people. Both **a** and **b** from Germanic *theudiskaz, of the people, derivative of *theudā-, people. **2.** Suffixed form *teut-onōs, “they of the tribe.” TEUTON, from Latin _Teutonī,_ the Teutons, borrowed via Celtic from Germanic tribal name *theudanōz. **3.** TOTAL, TUTTI; FACTOTUM, TEETOTUM, from Latin _tōtus,_ all, whole, possibly from _teutā-_ (? < “of the whole tribe”). [In Pokorny _tēu-_ 1080.]

tkei-. Important derivatives are _home, hamlet, haunt, hangar,_ and _situate._

tkei-. To settle, dwell, be home. **1.** Suffixed o-grade form *(t)koi-mo-. **a.** HOME, from Old English _hām,_ home; **b.** NIFLHEIM, from Old Norse _heimr,_ home; **c.** HAIMISH, from Old High German _heim,_ home; **d.** HAME, from Middle Dutch _hame,_ hame (< “covering”); **e.** HAMLET, from Old French _ham,_ village, home; **f.** HAUNT, from Old French _hanter,_ to frequent, haunt, from Germanic *haimatjan, to go or bring home; **g.** HANGAR, from Old French _hangard,_ shelter, possibly from Germanic *haimgardaz (*gardaz, enclosure; see **gher-**[1]). **a, b, c, d, e, f,** and **g** all from Germanic *haimaz, home. **2.** Zero-grade form *tki-. **a.** AMPHICTYONY, from Greek _ktizein,_ to found, settle, from metathesized _kti-;_ **b.** SITUATE, SITUS, from Latin _situs,_ location, from suffixed form *si-tu- from _si-,_ probably from *tki-. [Pokorny 1. _ḱei-_ 539, _ḱpei-_ 626.]

to-. Important derivatives are _the[1], decoy, though, these, this, than, then, there, they, their, them, that, those, thus,_ and _tandem._

to-. Demonstrative pronoun. For the nominative singular see **so-**. **1.a.** THE[2]; NATHELESS, from Old English _thē, thȳ_ (instrumental case), by the; **b.** DECOY, from Middle Dutch _de,_ the. Both **a** and **b** from Germanic _*thē-._ **2.** THOUGH, from Middle English _though,_ though, from a Scandinavian source akin to Old Norse _thō,_ though, from Germanic _*thauh,_ "for all that." **3.** THESE, THIS, (THOSE), from Old English _thes, this,_ this, from Germanic _*thasi-._ **4.** THAN, THEN, from Old English _thanne, thænne, thenne,_ than, then, from Germanic _*thana-._ **5.** THENCE, from Old English _thanon,_ thence, from Germanic _*thanana-._ **6.** THERE, from Old English _thǣr, thēr,_ there, from Germanic _*thēr._ **7.** THITHER, from Old English _thæder, thider,_ thither, from Germanic _*thathro._ **8.** THEY, from Old Norse _their,_ they, from Germanic nominative plural _*thai._ **9.** THEIR, from Old Norse _their(r)a,_ theirs, from Germanic genitive plural _*thaira._ **10.** THEM, from Old Norse _theim_ and Old English _thǣm,_ them, from Germanic dative plural _*thaimiz._ **11.** Extended neuter form _*tod-._ THAT, from Old English _thæt,_ that, from Germanic _*that._ **12.** THUS, from Old English _thus,_ thus, from Germanic _*thus-._ **13.** Adverbial (originally accusative) form _*tam._ TANDEM, TANTAMOUNT, from Latin _tandem,_ at last, so much, and _tantus,_ so much. **14.** Suffixed reduced form _*t-āli-._ TALES, from Latin _tālis,_ such. **15.** TAUTO-, from Greek _to,_ the. [Pokorny 1. _to-_ 1086.]

tolk^{w}-. Important derivatives are _loquacious, circumlocution, colloquium, elocution, soliloquy,_ and _ventriloquism._

tolk^{w}-. To speak. Metathesized form _*tlok^{w}-._ LOCUTION, LOQUACIOUS; ALLOCUTION, CIRCUMLOCUTION, COLLOQUIUM, (COLLOQUY), ELOCUTION, GRANDILOQUENCE, INTERLOCUTION, MAGNILOQUENT, OBLOQUY, SOLILOQUY, VENTRILOQUISM, from Latin _loquī,_ to speak. [Pokorny _tolk^{w}-_ 1088.]

tong-. Important derivatives are _thank, think,_ and _thought._

tong-. To think, feel. **1.** THANK, from Old English _thanc,_ thought, good will, and _thancian,_ to thank, from Germanic _*thankaz,_ thought, gratitude, and _*thankōn,_ to think of, thank. **2.** BETHINK, THINK, from Old English _(bi)thencan,_ to think, from Germanic _*(bi-)thankjan._ **3.** THOUGHT, from Old English _(ge)thōht,_ thought, from Germanic _*(ga)thanht-_ (_*ga-,_ collective prefix; see **kom**). **4.** METHINKS, from Old English _thyncan,_ (third person singular present indicative _thyncth_), to seem, from Germanic _*thunkjan._ [Pokorny 1. _tong-_ 1088.]

treb-. Derivatives are _thorp_ and _trave._

treb-. Dwelling. **1.** Zero-grade form _*tr̥b-._ THORP, from Old English _thorp,_ village, hamlet, from Germanic _*thurp-._ **2.** TRABEATED, TRABECULA, TRAVE; ARCHITRAVE, from Latin _trabs,_ beam, timber. [Pokorny _treb-_ 1090.]

trei-. Important derivatives are _three, thrice, thirteen, thirty, trio, third, tertiary, triple, testament, testimony, attest, contest, detest, protest, testify, sitar,_ and _trinity._

trei-. Three.

I. Nominative plural form _*treyes._ **1.a.** THREE, THRICE; THIRTEEN, THIRTY, from Old English _thrie, thrēo, thrī,_ three, with its derivatives _thrīga, thriwa,_ thrice, _thrītig,_ thirty, and _thrēotīne,_ thirteen (_-tīne,_ ten; see **dekm̥**); **b.** TRILLIUM, from Old Swedish _thrīr,_ three. Both **a** and **b** from Germanic _*thrijiz,_ **2.** TREY; TRAMMEL, TRECENTO, TREPHINE, TRIUMVIR, TROCAR, from Latin _trēs,_ three. **3.** TRISKAIDEKAPHOBIA, from Greek _treis, tris,_ three.

II. Zero-grade form _*tri-._ **1.** Suffixed form _*trityo-._ **a.** _(i)_ THIRD, from Old English _thrid(d)a, thirdda,_ third; _(ii)_ RIDING[2], from Old Norse _thridhi,_ third. Both _(i)_ and _(ii)_ from Germanic _*thridjaz,_ third; **b.** TERCEL, TERCET, TERTIAN, TERTIARY, TIERCE; SESTERCE, from Latin _tertius_ (neuter _tertium_), third. **2.** Combining form _*tri-._ **a.** TRI-, TRIBE, TRIO, TRIPLE, from Latin _tri-,_ three; **b.** TRI-; TRICLINIUM, TRICROTIC, TRIDACTYL, TRIGLYPH, TRITONE, from Greek _tri-,_ three; **c.** TRIMURTI, from Sanskrit _tri-,_ three. **3.** TRIAD, from Greek _trias,_ the number three. **4.** TRICHOTOMY, from Greek _trikha,_ in three parts. **5.** TRIERARCH, from Greek compound _triērēs,_ galley with three banks of oars, trireme (_-ērēs,_ oar; see **erə-**). **6.** Suffixed form _*tri-to-._ TRITIUM, from Greek _tritos,_ third. **7.** Compound form _*tri-pl-,_ "threefold" (_*-pl-_ < combining form _*-plo-;_ see **pel-[2]**). TRIPLOBLASTIC, from Greek _triploos,_ triple. **8.** Compound form _*tri-plek-,_ "threefold" (_*-plek-,_ -fold; see **plek-**). TRIPLEX, from Latin _triplex,_ triple. **9.** Compound form _*tri-st-i-,_ "third person standing by" (see **stā-**). TESTAMENT, (TESTIMONY); ATTEST, CONTEST, DETEST, OBTEST, PROTEST, TESTIFY, from Latin _testis,_ a witness. **10.** SITAR, from Persian _si,_ three.

III. Extended zero-grade form _*tris,_ "thrice." **1.** TERN[2]; TERPOLYMER, from Latin _ter,_ thrice. **2.** TRISOCTAHEDRON, from Greek _tris,_ thrice. **3.** Suffixed form _*tris-no-._ TRINE, (TRINITY), from Latin _trīnī,_ three each.

IV. Suffixed o-grade form _*troy-o-._ TROIKA, from Russian _troje,_ group of three. [Pokorny _trei-_ 1090.]

trep-. Important derivatives are _trope, contrive, retrieve, trophy, tropic,_ and _entropy._

trep-. To turn. **1.** -TROPOUS; APOTROPAIC, (ATROPOS), TREPONEMA, from Greek _trepein,_ to turn, with o-grade _tropos,_ turning. **2.** O-grade form _*trop-._ **a.** suffixed form _*trop-o-._ TROPE, (TROUBADOUR), (TROVER); CONTRIVE, (RETRIEVE), from Greek _tropos,_ a turn, way, manner; **b.** suffixed form _*trop-ā-._ TROPHY, TROPIC, TROPO-; ENTROPY, from Greek _tropē,_ a turning, change. [Pokorny 2. _trep-_ 1094.]

treud-. Important derivatives are _threat, thrust, intrude,_ and _protrude._

treud-. To squeeze. **1.** Suffixed o-grade form _*troud-o-._ THREAT, from Old English _thrēat,_ oppression, use of force, from Germanic _*thrautam._ **2.** Variant form _*trūd-._ THRUST, from Old Norse _thrȳsta,_ to squeeze, compress, from Germanic _*thrūstjan._ **3.** ABSTRUSE, EXTRUDE, INTRUDE, OBTRUDE, PROTRUDE, from Latin _trūdere,_ to thrust, push. [Pokorny _tr-eu-d_ 1095.]

tu-. Important derivatives are _thee, thou[1], thine,_ and _thy._

tu-. Second person singular pronoun; you, thou. **1.** Lengthened form _*tū_ (accusative _*te, *tege_). (THEE), THOU[1], from Old English _thū_ (accusative _thec, thē_), thou, from Germanic _*thū_ (accusative _*theke_). **2.** Suffixed extended form _*t(w)ei-no-._ THINE, THY, from Old English _thīn,_ thine, from Germanic _*thīnaz._ [Pokorny _tu-_ 1097.]

ud-. Important derivatives are _out, utmost, carouse, outlaw, utter[1], utter[2], but, about, ersatz,_ and _hubris._

ud-. Also **ūd-**. Up, out. **1.a.** OUT; UTMOST, from Old English _ūt,_ out; **b.** CAROUSE; AUSLANDER, from Old High German _ūz,_ out; **c.** OUTLAW, from Old Norse _ūt,_ out; **d.** UITLANDER, from Middle Dutch _ute, uut,_ out; **e.** UTTER[1], from Middle Low German _ūt,_ out; **f.** UTTER[2], from Old English _ūtera,_ outer, from Germanic suffixed (comparative) form _*ūt-era-;_ **g.** BUT; ABOUT, from Old English _būtan, būte,_ outside (adverb), from Germanic compound _*bi-ūtana,_ "at the outside" (_*bi-,_ by, at; see **ambhi**). **a, b, c, d, e, f,** and **g** all from Germanic _*ūt-,_ out. **2.** Extended form _*uds._ **a.** ERSATZ, from Old High German _irsezzan,_ to replace, from _ir-,_ out; **b.** ORT, from Middle Dutch _oor,_ out; **c.** (see **dail-**) Germanic _*uz-dailjam,_ "a portioning out," judgment; **d.** URSPRACHE, from Old High German _ur-,_ out of, original. **a, b, c,** and **d** all from Germanic _*uz, *uz-,_ out. **3.** Suffixed (comparative) form _*ud-tero-._ HYSTERESIS, HYSTERON PROTERON, from Greek _husteros,_ later, second, after. **4.** HUBRIS, from Greek compound _hubris,_ violence, outrage, insolence (_bri-,_ perhaps "heavy," "violent"; see **g^{w}erə-[1]**), from _hu-._ **5.** VIGORISH, from Russian _vy-,_ out. [Pokorny _ŭd-_ 1103.]

uper. Important derivatives are _over, sovereign, super-, superior, supreme, sirloin, superb, sum, summit, soprano, somersault,_ and _hyper-._

uper. Over. **1.** Extended form _*uperi._ **a.** OVER, from Old English _ofer,_ over; **b.** ORLOP, from Middle Low German _over,_ over. Both **a** and **b** from Germanic _*uberi._ **2.** Variant form _*(s)uper._ **a.** SOUBRETTE, SOVEREIGN, SUPER-, SUPERABLE, SUPERIOR, SUPREME, (SUPREMO), SUR-; SIRLOIN, from Latin _super, super-,_ above, over; **b.** suffixed form _*(s)uper-no-._ SUPERNAL, from Latin _supernus,_ above, upper, top; **c.** suffixed form _*super-bhw-o-,_ "being above" (_*bhw-o-,_ being; see **bheuə-**). SUPERB, from Latin _superbus,_ superior, excellent, arrogant; **d.** suffixed (superlative) reduced form _*sup-mo-._ SUM, SUMMIT, from Latin _summus,_ highest, topmost; **e.** suffixed form _*super-o-._ (SOPRANINO), SOPRANO, SUPRA-; SOMERSAULT, from Latin _suprā_ (feminine ablative singular), above, beyond. **3.** Basic form _*uper._ HYPER-, from Greek _huper,_ over. [Pokorny _uper_ 1105.]

upo. Important derivatives are _up, uproar, open, above, often, eaves, eavesdrop, sub-, supine[1], supple, hypo-, valet, vassal,_ and _opal._

upo. Under, up from under, over. **1.a.** UP, from Old English _up, uppe,_ up; **b.** UP-, from Old English _ūp-, upp-,_ up; **c.** UPROAR, from Middle Low German _up,_ up; **d.** AUFKLÄRUNG, from Old High German _ūf,_ up. **a, b, c,** and **d** all from Germanic _*upp-,_ up. **2.** OPEN, from Old English _open,_ open, from Germanic _*upanaz,_ "put or set up," open. **3.** ABOVE, from Old English _būfan,_ above, over, from Germanic compound _*bi-ufana,_ "on, above" (_*bi-,_ by, at; see **ambhi**). **4.** Possibly suffixed form _*up-t-._ OFT, OFTEN, from Old English _oft,_ often, from Germanic _*ufta,_ frequently. **5.** Extended form _*upes-._ **a.** EAVES, from Old English _efes,_ eaves; **b.** EAVESDROP, from Old English _yfesdrype,_ water from the eaves, from Germanic _*obisdrup-,_ dripping water from the eaves (_*drup-,_ to drip, from _*dhrub-;_ see **dhreu-**). Both **a** and **b** from Germanic _*ubaswō, *ubizwō,_ vestibule, porch, eaves (< "that which is above or in front"). **6.** Variant form _*(s)up-._ **a.** SOUTANE, SUB-, from Latin _sub,_ under; **b.** SUPINE, from Latin _supīnus,_ lying on the back (< "thrown backward or under"); **c.** suffixed form _*sup-ter._ SUBTERFUGE, from Latin _subter,_ secretly; **d.** (see **plāk-[1]**) Latin _supplex,_ suppliant, from _sub,_ under. **7.** Basic form _*upo._ HYPO-, from Greek _hupo,_ under. **8.** Suffixed variant form _*ups-o-._ HYPSO-, from Greek _hupsos,_ height, top. **9.** Basic form _*upo-._ (see **reidh-**) Latin _verēdus,_ post horse, from Celtic _*wo-,_ under. **10.** Probably compound _*upo-st-o-._ (VALET), (VARLET), VASSAL, from Vulgar Latin _*vassus,_ vassal, from Celtic _*wasso-,_ "one who stands under," servant, young man (_*sto-,_ standing; see **stā-**). **11.** OPAL, UPANISHAD, from Sanskrit _upa,_ near to, under (in _upaniṣad,_ Upanishad). [Pokorny _upo_ 1106.]

wal-. Important derivatives are _valence, valiant, valid, valor, value, avail, convalesce, equivalent, invalid[1], prevail,_ and _wield._

wal-. To be strong. **1.** Suffixed (stative) form _*wal-ē-._ VALE[2], VALENCE, VALETUDINARIAN, VALIANT, VALID, VALOR, VALUE; AMBIVALENCE, AVAIL, CONVALESCE, COUNTERVAIL, EQUIVALENT, (INVALID[1]), INVALID[2], PREVAIL, (VALEDICTION), from Latin _valēre,_ to be strong. **2.** Extended o-grade form _*wold(h)-._ **a.** WIELD, from Old English _wealdan,_ to rule, and _wieldan,_ to govern, from Germanic _*waldan,_ to rule; **b.** (see **koro-**) Germanic _*harja-waldaz,_ "army commander," from _*wald-,_ power, rule. **3.** Suffixed extended o-grade form _*wold-ti-._ OBLAST, from Old Church Slavonic _vlastĭ,_ rule. [Pokorny _u̯al-_ 1111.]

we-. An important derivative is _we._

we-. We. For oblique cases of the pronoun see **nes-[2]**. Suffixed variant form _*wey-es._ WE, from Old English _wē, we,_ we, from Germanic _*wīz._ [Pokorny _u̯ē-_ 1114.]

wē-. Important derivatives are _weather, wind[1], window, vent, ventilate, wing,_ and _nirvana._

wē-. To blow. Contracted from _*weə-;_ oldest basic form _*əwē-_ (< _*əweə-_). **1.** Suffixed irregular shortened form _*we-dhro-._ WEATHER, from Old English _weder,_ weather, storm, wind, from Germanic _*wedram_ wind, weather. **2.** Suffixed (participial) form _*wē-nt-o-,_ blowing. **a.** _(i)_ WIND[1], from Old English _wind,_ wind; _(ii)_ WINDOW, from Old Norse _vindr,_ wind. Both _(i)_ and _(ii)_ from Germanic _*windaz;_ **b.** VENT[1], VENTAIL, VENTILATE, from Latin *ventus,* wind. **3.** WING, from Middle English *wenge,* wing, from a Scandinavian source akin to Old Norse *vængr,* wing, from suffixed Germanic form _*wē-ingjaz._ **4.** Basic form _*wē-._ NIRVANA, from Sanskrit *vāti* (stem _*vā-_), it blows. [Pokorny 10. *au̯(ē)-* 81.]

webh-. Important derivatives are *weave, web, weevil, wafer, waffle*[1], *wave,* and *wobble.*

webh-. To weave, also to move quickly. **1.** WEAVE, WOOF[1], from Old English *wefan,* to weave, from Germanic _*weban._ **2.** WEFT, from Old English *wefta, weft,* cross thread, from Germanic _*wefta-._ **3.** Suffixed o-grade form _*wobh-yo-._ WEB, WEBSTER, from Old English *web(b),* web, from Germanic _*wabjam,_ fabric, web. **4.** WEEVIL, from Old English *wifel,* weevil (< "that which moves briskly"), from suffixed Germanic form _*webila-._ **5.a.** *(i)* GOFFER, from Old French *gaufre,* honeycomb, waffle; *(ii)* WAFER, from Old North French *waufre,* wafer. Both *(i)* and *(ii)* from a source akin to Middle Low German *wāfel,* honeycomb; **b.** WAFFLE[1], from Middle Dutch *wāfel,* waffle. Both **a** and **b** from suffixed Germanic form _*wabila-,_ web, honeycomb. **6.a.** WAVE, from Old English *wafian,* to move (the hand) up and down; **b.** WAVER, from Middle English *waveren,* to waver; **c.** WOBBLE, from Low German *wabbeln,* to move from side to side, sway. **a, b,** and **c** all from Germanic _*wab-,_ to move back and forth as in weaving, possibly from **webh-**. **7.** Suffixed zero-grade form _*ubh-ā-._ HYPHA, from Greek *huphē,* web. [Pokorny *u̯ebh-* 1114.]

wed-[1]. Important derivatives are *water, wet, wash, winter, hydrant, hydro-, undulate, abound, inundate, redundant, surround, otter, Hydra, whiskey,* and *vodka.*

wed-[1]. Water; wet. **1.** Suffixed o-grade form _*wod-ōr._ **a.** WATER, from Old English *wæter,* water; **b.** KIRSCHWASSER, from Old High German *wassar,* water. Both **a** and **b** from Germanic _*watar._ **2.** Suffixed lengthened-grade form _*wēd-o-._ WET, from Old English *wǣt, wēt,* from Germanic _*wēd-._ **3.** O-grade form _*wod-._ WASH, from Old English *wæscan, wacsan,* to wash, from Germanic suffixed form _*wat-skan,_ to wash. **4.** Nasalized form _*we-n-d-._ WINTER, from Old English *winter,* winter, from Germanic _*wintruz,_ winter, "wet season." **5.** Suffixed zero-grade form _*ud-ōr._ (HYDRANT), HYDRO-, (HYDROUS), UTRICLE; ANHYDROUS, CLEPSYDRA, DROPSY, HYDATHODE, HYDATID, from Greek *hudōr,* water. **6.** Suffixed nasalized zero-grade form _*u-n-d-ā-._ UNDINE, UNDULATE; ABOUND, INUNDATE, (REDOUND), REDUNDANT, SURROUND, from Latin *unda,* wave. **7.** Suffixed zero-grade form _*ud-ro-, *ud-rā-,_ water animal. **a.** OTTER, from Old English *otor,* otter, from Germanic _*otraz,_ otter; **b.** NUTRIA, from Latin *lutra,* otter (with obscure *l-*); **c.** HYDRUS, from Greek *hudros,* a water snake; **d.** HYDRA, from Greek *hudra,* a water serpent, Hydra. **8.** Suffixed zero-grade form _*ud-skio-._ USQUEBAUGH, (WHISKEY), from Old Irish *uisce,* water. **9.** Suffixed o-grade form _*wod-ā-._ VODKA, from Russian *voda,* water. [Pokorny 9. *au̯(e)-* 78.]

wed-[2]. Important derivatives are *ode, comedy, melody, parody, rhapsody,* and *tragedy.*

wed-[2]. To speak. **1.** Oldest root form _*əwed-_ becoming _*awed-_ in possible reduplicated form _*awe-ud-,_ dissimilated to _*aweid-,_ with suffixed o-grade form _*awoid-o-_ (but more likely a separate root _*əweid-_ becoming Greek _*aweid-,_ to sing). ODE; COMEDY, EPODE, HYMNODY, MELODY, MONODY, PARODY, RHAPSODY, TRAGEDY, from Greek *aeidein* (Attic *aidein*), to sing, and *aoidē* (Attic *ōidē*), song, ode, with *aoidos* (Attic *ōidos*), a singer, singing. **2.** THERAVADA, from Sanskrit *vādaḥ,* sound, statement. [Pokorny 6. *au-* 76.]

weg-. Important derivatives are *wake*[1], *waken, watch, bivouac, wait, vegetable, vigor, vigil, vigilante, reveille,* and *velocity.*

weg-. To be strong, be lively. **1.** Suffixed o-grade form _*wog-ē-._ WAKE[1], from Old English *wacan,* to wake up, arise, and *wacian,* to be awake, from Germanic _*wakēn._ **2.** Suffixed o-grade form _*wog-no-._ WAKEN, from Old English *wæcnan, wæcnian,* to awake, from Germanic _*waknan._ **3.** WATCH, from Old English *wæccan,* to be awake, from Germanic _*wakjan._ **4.** Suffixed form _*weg-yo-._ (WICCA), (WICKED), WITCH; (BEWITCH), from Old English *wicca,* sorcerer, wizard (feminine *wicce,* witch), from Germanic _*wikkjaz,_ necromancer (< "one who wakes the dead"). **5.** BIVOUAC, from Old High German *wahta,* watch, vigil, from Germanic _*wahtwō._ **6.a.** WAIT, from Old North French *waitier,* to watch; **b.** WAFT, from Middle Dutch and Middle Low German *wachten,* to watch, guard. Both **a** and **b** from Germanic _*waht-._ **7.** Suffixed (causative) o-grade form _*wog-eyo-._ VEGETABLE, from Latin *vegēre,* to be lively. **8.** Suffixed (stative) form _*weg-ē-._ VIGOR, from Latin *vigēre,* to be lively. **9.** Suffixed form _*weg-(e)li-._ VEDETTE, VIGIL, (VIGILANT), VIGILANTE; REVEILLE, SURVEILLANT, from Latin *vigil,* watchful, awake. **10.** Suffixed form _*weg-slo-._ VELOCITY, from Latin *vēlōx,* fast, "lively." [Pokorny *u̯eĝ-* 1117.]

wegh-. Important derivatives are *weigh*[1], *wee, weight, way, always, away, wagon, wag*[1], *vogue, earwig, wiggle, vector, vehicle, convection, via, voyage, convey, deviate, devious, envoy*[1], *obvious, previous, trivial, vex,* and *convex.*

wegh-. To go, transport in a vehicle. **1.** WEIGH[1], from Old English *wegan,* to carry, balance in a scale, from Germanic _*wegan._ **2.** WEE, from Old English *wǣg(e),* weight, unit of weight, from Germanic lengthened-grade form _*wēgō._ **3.** Suffixed form _*wegh-ti-._ WEIGHT, from Old English *wiht, gewiht,* weight, from Germanic _*wihti-._ **4.a.** WAY; ALWAYS, AWAY, from Old English *weg,* way; **b.** NORWEGIAN, from Old Norse *vegr,* way. Both **a** and **b** from Germanic _*wegaz,_ course of travel, way. **5.** Suffixed o-grade form _*wogh-no-._ **a.** WAIN, from Old English *wæ(g)n,* wagon; **b.** WAGON, from Middle Dutch *wagen,* wagon. Both **a** and **b** from Germanic _*wagnaz._ **6.** Suffixed o-grade form _*wogh-lo-._ **a.** WALLEYED, from Old Norse *vagl,* chicken roost, perch, beam, eye disease, from Germanic _*waglaz;_ **b.** OCHLOCRACY, OCHLOPHOBIA, from Greek *okhlos,* populace, mob (< "moving mass"). **7.** Distantly related to this root are: **a.** *(i)* WAG[1], from Middle English *waggen,* to wag, possibly from **wegh-**; *(ii)* GRAYWACKE, from Old High German *waggo, wacko,* boulder rolling on a riverbed. Both *(i)* and *(ii)* from Germanic _*wag-,_ "to move about"; **b.** VOGUE, from Old French *voguer,* to row, sail, from Old Low German _*wogōn,_ to rock, sway, from Germanic _*wēga-,_ water in motion; **c.** *(i)* EARWIG, from Old English *wicga,* insect (< "thing that moves quickly"); *(ii)* WIGGLE, from Middle Dutch and Middle Low German *wiggelen,* to move back and forth, wag. Both *(i)* and *(ii)* from Germanic _*wig-._ **8.** Basic form _*wegh-._ VECTOR, VEHEMENT, VEHICLE; ADVECTION, CONVECTION, EVECTION, INVEIGH, from Latin *vehere* (past participle *vectus*), to carry. **9.** Suffixed basic form _*wegh-yā._ FOY, VIA, VOYAGE; CONVEY, DEVIATE, DEVIOUS, (ENVOI), ENVOY[1], OBVIOUS, PERVIOUS, PREVIOUS, (TRIVIAL), TRIVIUM, (VIADUCT), from Latin *via,* way, road. **10.** Suffixed form _*wegh-s-._ VEX, from Latin *vexāre,* to agitate (< "to set in motion"). **11.** Probably suffixed form _*wegh-so-._ CONVEX, from Latin *convexus,* "carried or drawn together (to a point)," convex (*com-,* together; see **kom**). [Pokorny *u̯eĝh-* 1118.]

wei-. Important derivatives are *wire, ferrule, vise, viticulture,* and *iris.*

wei-. Also **weiə-**. To turn, twist; with derivatives referring to suppleness or binding.
I. Form _*wei-._ **1.a.** WIRE, from Old English *wīr,* wire; **b.** GARLAND, from Old French *garlande,* wreath, from Frankish _*wiara, *weara,_ wire. Both **a** and **b** from Germanic suffixed form _*wī-ra-, *wē-ra-._ **2.** SEAWARE, from Old English *wār,* seaweed, from suffixed Germanic form _*wai-ra-,_ probably from **wei-**. **3.** Suffixed zero-grade form _*wi-ria-._ FERRULE, from Latin *viriae,* bracelets (of Celtic origin). **4.** Suffixed form _*wei-ti-._ WITHY, from Old English *wīthig,* willow, withy, from Germanic _*wīth-,_ willow. **5.** Suffixed zero-grade form _*wi-t-._ WITHE, from Old English *withthe,* supple twig, from Germanic _*withjōn-._
II. Form _*weiə-,_ zero-grade _*wī-_ (< _*wiə-_). **1.** Suffixed form _*wī-ti-._ VISE; VITICULTURE, from Latin *vītis,* vine. **2.** Suffixed form _*wī-tā-_ becoming _*wittā._ VITTA, from Latin *vitta,* headband. **3.** Probably suffixed form _*wī-ri-._ (IRIDACEOUS), IRIDO-, IRIS, IRIS; (IRIDIUM), (IRITIS), from Greek *iris,* rainbow, and *Iris,* rainbow goddess. **4.** Perhaps suffixed form _*wī-n-._ INION; EXINE, INOSITOL, INOTROPIC, from Greek *is* (genitive *inos*), sinew. [Pokorny 1. *u̯ei-* 1120.]

weid-. Important derivatives are *guide, wise*[1], *wisdom, guise, idol, kaleidscope, Hades, wit*[1], *unwitting, view, visa, vision, advice, clairvoyance, envy, evident, interview, provide, review, supervise, survey, idea, history, story*[1], and *penguin.*

weid-. To see.
I. Full-grade form _*weid-._ **1.a.** TWIT, from Old English *wītan,* to reproach; **b.** GUIDE, from Old Provençal *guidar,* to guide; **c.** GUY[1], from Old French *guier,* to guide; **d.** WITE, from Old English *wīte,* fine, penalty, from Germanic derivative noun _*wītī-._ **a, b, c,** and **d** all from Germanic _*wītan,_ to look after, guard, ascribe to, reproach. **2.** Suffixed form _*weid-to-._ **a.** WISE[1], from Old English *wīs,* wise; **b.** WISDOM, from Old English *wīsdōm,* learning, wisdom (*-dōm,* abstract suffix; see **dhē-**); **c.** WISEACRE, from Old High German *wīssago,* seer, prophet; **d.** *(i)* WISE[2], from Old English *wīse, wīs,* manner; *(ii)* GUISE, from Old French *guise,* manner. Both *(i)* and *(ii)* from Germanic _*wīssōn-,_ appearance, form, manner. **a, b, c,** and **d** all from Germanic _*wīssaz._ **3.** Suffixed form _*weid-es-._ EIDETIC, EIDOLON, IDOL, IDYLL, -OID; IDOCRASE, KALEIDOSCOPE, from Greek *eidos,* form, shape.
II. Zero-grade form _*wid-._ **1.a.** WIT[1], from Old English *wit, witt,* knowledge, intelligence; **b.** WITENAGEMOT, from Old English *wita,* wise man, councilor. Both **a** and **b** from Germanic _*wit-._ **2.** WIT[2]; UNWITTING, from Old English *witan,* to know, from Germanic _*witan._ **3.** Suffixed form _*wid-to-._ IWIS, from Old English *gewis, gewiss,* certain, sure, from Germanic _*wissaz,_ known. **4.** Form _*wid-ē-_ (with participial form _*weid-to-_). VIDE, VIEW, VISA, VISAGE, VISION, VISTA, VOYEUR; ADVICE, (ADVISE), BELVEDERE, CLAIRVOYANT, ENVY, EVIDENT, INTERVIEW, PREVISE, PROVIDE, REVIEW, SUPERVISE, SURVEY, from Latin *vidēre,* to see, look. **5.** Suffixed form _*wides-ya._ IDEA, IDEO-, from Greek *idea,* appearance, form, idea. **6.** Suffixed form _*wid-tor-._ HISTORY, (STORY[1]); POLYHISTOR, from Greek *histōr,* wise, learned, learned man. **7.** HADAL, HADES, from Greek *Haidēs* (also *Aidēs*), the underworld, perhaps "the invisible" and from _*wid-._ **8.** Suffixed nasalized form _*wi-n-d-o-._ **a.** COLCANNON, from Old Irish *find,* white (< "clearly visible"); **b.** PENGUIN, from Welsh *gwyn, gwynn,* white. **9.** (see **deru-**) Celtic compound _*dru-wid-,_ "strong seer" (_*dru-,_ strong).
III. Suffixed o-grade form _*woid-o-._ VEDA; RIG-VEDA, from Sanskrit *vedaḥ,* knowledge. [Pokorny 2. *u̯(e)di-* 1125.]

weiə-. Important derivatives are *vim, violate,* and *violent.*

weiə-. Vital force. Related to **wī-ro-**. Zero-grade form _*wī-_ (< _*wiə-_). VIM, VIOLATE, VIOLENT, from Latin *vīs,* force, with irregular derivatives *violāre,* to treat with force, and *violentus,* vehement. [In Pokorny 3. *u̯ei-* 1123.]

weik-[1]. Important derivatives are *village, villain, vicinity, diocese, ecology, economy,* and *parish.*

weik-[1]. Clan (social unit above the household). **1.** Suffixed form _*weik-slā._ VILLA, VILLAGE, VILLAIN, VILLANELLE, (VILLEIN); (BIDONVILLE), from Latin *vīlla,* country house, farm. **2.** Suffixed o-grade form _*woik-o-._ **a.** (VICINAGE), VICINITY; (BAILIWICK), from Latin *vīcus,* quarter or district of a town, neighborhood; **b.** ANDROECIUM, AUTOECIOUS, DIOCESE, DIOECIOUS, DIOICOUS, ECESIS, ECOLOGY, ECONOMY, ECUMENICAL, HETEROECIOUS, MONOECIOUS, PARISH, from Greek *oikos,* house, and its derivatives *oikia,* a dwelling, and *oikēsis,* dwelling, administration. **3.** Zero-grade form _*wik-._ VAISYA, from Sanskrit *viśaḥ,* dwelling, house. [Pokorny *u̯eik̂-* 1131.]

weik-[2]. Important derivatives are *wicker, wicket, weak, week, vicar,* and *vicarious.*

weik-[2]. Also **weig-**. To bend, wind.
I. Form _*weig-._ **1.a.** WYCH ELM, from Old English *wice,* wych elm (having pliant branches);

b. WICKER, from Middle English _wiker,_ wicker, from a Scandinavian source akin to Swedish _viker,_ willow twig, wand; c. WICKET, from Old North French _wiket,_ wicket (< "door that turns"), from a Scandinavian source probably akin to Old Norse _vikja,_ to bend, turn. a, b, and c all from Germanic _*wik-._ 2.a. WEAK, from Old Norse _veikr,_ pliant; b. WEAKFISH, from Middle Dutch _weec,_ weak, soft. Both a and b from Germanic _*waikwaz._ 3. WEEK, from Old English _wicu, wice,_ week, from Germanic _*wikōn-,_ "a turning," series.

II. Form _*weik-._ Zero-grade form _*wik-._ a. VICAR, (VICARIOUS), VICE-; VICISSITUDE, from Latin _*vix_ (genitive _vicis_), turn, situation, change; b. VETCH, from Latin _vicia,_ vetch (< "twining plant"). [Pokorny 4. _ṷeik-_ 1130.]

weik-[3]. Important derivatives are _vanquish, victor, convince,_ and _evict._

weik-[3]. To fight, conquer. 1. WIGHT[2], from Old Norse _vīgr,_ able in battle, from Germanic _*wīk-._ 2. Nasalized zero-grade form _*wi-n-k-._ VANQUISH, VICTOR, VINCIBLE; CONVINCE, EVICT, from Latin _vincere,_ to conquer. 3. Zero-grade form _*wik-._ ORDOVICIAN, from Celtic _Ordovices_ (_*ordo-wik-_), "those who fight with hammers" (_*ordo-,_ hammer). [Pokorny 2. _ṷeik-_ 1128.]

weip-. Important derivatives are _waive, wipe, whip,_ and _vibrate._

weip-. To turn, vacillate, tremble ecstatically. 1. O-grade form _*woip-._ WAIF[1], WAIF[2], (WAIVE), (WAIVER), from Anglo-Norman _waif,_ ownerless property, from a Scandinavian source probably akin to Old Norse _veif,_ waving thing, flag, from Germanic _*waif-._ 2. Variant form _*weib-._ a. WIPE, from Old English _wīpian,_ to wipe; b. GUIPURE, from Old French _guiper,_ to cover with silk; c. WHIP, from Middle English _wippen,_ to whip. a, b, and c all from Germanic _*wīpjan,_ to move back and forth. 3. Perhaps suffixed nasalized zero-grade form _*wi-m-p-ila-._ a. WIMPLE, from Old English _wimpel,_ covering for the neck (< "something that winds around"); b. (GIMP[1]), GUIMPE, from Old High German _wimpal,_ guimpe; c. WIMBLE, from Middle Dutch _wimmel,_ auger (< "that which turns in boring"), perhaps from **weip-**. 4. Suffixed zero-grade variant form _*wib-ro-._ VIBRATE, from Latin _vibrāre,_ to vibrate. [Pokorny _ṷeip-_ 1131.]

wekti-. Important derivatives are _wight[1], aught[2], naught,_ and _not._

wekti-. Thing, creature. a. WIGHT[1]; (AUGHT[2]), NAUGHT, (NOT), from Old English _wiht,_ person, thing; b. NIX[2], from Old High German _wiht,_ thing, being. Both a and b from Germanic _*wihti-._ [Pokorny _ṷek-ti-_ 1136.]

wek^{w}-. Important derivatives are _vocal, voice, vowel, equivocal, vocation, vouch, advocate, avocation, evoke, invoke, provoke, revoke,_ and _epic._

wek^{w}-. To speak. 1. O-grade form _*wōk^{w}-._ a. VOCAL, VOICE, VOWEL; EQUIVOCAL, UNIVOCAL, from Latin _vōx_ (stem _vōc-_), voice; b. CALLIOPE, from Greek _ops,_ voice. 2. Suffixed o-grade form _*wok^{w}-ā-._ VOCABLE, VOCATION, VOUCH; ADVOCATE, AVOCATION, CONVOKE, EVOKE, INVOKE, PROVOKE, REVOKE, from Latin _vocāre,_ to call. 3. Suffixed form _*wek^{w}-es-._ EPIC, EPOS; EPOPEE, ORTHOEPY, from Greek _epos,_ song, word. [Pokorny _ṷek^{ṷ}-_ 1135.]

wel-[1]. Important derivatives are _well[2], wealth, will[1], will[2], gallop, gallant, volition, voluntary, benevolent, malevolent,_ and _voluptuous._

wel-[1]. To wish, will. 1. WELL[2], from Old English _wel,_ well (< "according to one's wish"), from Germanic _*wel-._ 2. WEAL[1], WEALTH, from Old English _wela, weola,_ well-being, riches, from Germanic _*welōn-._ 3. WILL[1], from Old English _willa,_ desire, will power, from Germanic _*wiljōn-._ 4. WILL[2]; NILL, from Old English _willan,_ to desire, from Germanic _*wil(l)jan._ 5. (see **gwā-**) Germanic compound _*wil-kumōn-._ 6. O-grade form _*wol-._ a. GALLOP, from Old French _galoper,_ to gallop; b. WALLOP, from Old North French _*waloper,_ to gallop; c. GALLANT, from Old French _galer,_ to rejoice, from Frankish Latin _*walāre,_ to take it easy, from Frankish _*wala,_ good, well. a, b, and c all from Germanic _*wal-._ 7. Basic form _*wel-._ VELLEITY, VOLITION, VOLUNTARY; BENEVOLENT, MALEVOLENCE, from Latin _velle_ (present stem _vol-_), to wish, will. 8. Suffixed form _*wel-up-._ VOLUPTUARY, VOLUPTUOUS, from Latin _voluptās,_ pleasure. [Pokorny 2. _ṷel-_ 1137.]

wel-[2]. Important derivatives are _waltz, willow, walk, well[1], wallow, vault[1], vault[2], volume, evolve, involve, revolve, vulva, valve, valley,_ and _helix._

wel-[2]. To turn, roll; with derivatives referring to curved, enclosing objects. 1.a. WALTZ, from Old High German _walzan,_ to roll, waltz; b. WELTER, from Middle Low German or Middle Dutch _welteren,_ to roll. Both a and b from Germanic _*walt-._ 2. WHELK[1], from Old English _weoluc, weoloc,_ mollusk (having a spiral shell), whelk, from Germanic _*weluka-._ 3. WILLOW, from Old English _welig,_ willow (with flexible twigs), from Germanic _*wel-,_ perhaps from **wel-[2]**. 4. WALK, from Old English _wealcan,_ to roll, toss, and _wealcian,_ to muffle up, from Germanic _*welk-,_ perhaps from **wel-[2]**. 5. O-grade form _*wol-._ a. WELL[1], from Old English _wiella, wælla, welle,_ a well (< "rolling or bubbling water," "spring"); b. GABERDINE, from Old High German _wallōn,_ to roam; c. WALLET, possibly from Old North French _*walet,_ roll, knapsack. a, b, and c all from Germanic _*wall-._ 6. Perhaps suffixed o-grade form _*wol-ā-._ a. WALE, from Old English _walu,_ streak on the skin, weal, welt; b. (see **wrād-**) Old High German _*wurzwalu,_ rootstock, from _*-walu,_ a roll, round stem. Both a and b from Germanic _*walō._ 7. Extended form _*welw-._ a. WALLOW, from Old English _wealwian,_ to roll (in mud), from Germanic _*walwōn;_ b. VAULT[1], VAULT[2], (VOLT[2]), VOLUBLE, VOLUME, VOLUTE, VOLVOX, VOUSSOIR; CIRCUMVOLVE, CONVOLVE, DEVOLVE, EVOLVE, INVOLVE, REVOLVE, from Latin _volvere,_ to roll; c. suffixed o-grade form _*wolw-ā-._ VOLVA, VULVA, from Latin _vulva, volva,_ covering, womb; d. suffixed zero-grade form _*wl̥w-ā-._ VALVE, from Latin _valva,_ leaf of a door (< "that which turns"); e. Suffixed zero-grade form _*wl̥u-ti-._ ALYCE CLOVER, from Greek _halusis,_ chain; f. suffixed form _*welu-tro-._ ELYTRON, from Greek _elutron,_ sheath, cover. 8. Suffixed form _wel-n-._ ILEUS; NEURILEMMA, from Greek _eilein_ (< _*welnein_), to turn, squeeze. 9. Perhaps variant _*wall-._ VAIL[1], VALE[1], VALLEY, from Latin _vallēs, vallis,_ valley (< "that which is surrounded by hills"). 10. Possibly suffixed form _*wel-enā._ ELECAMPANE, INULIN, from Greek _helenion,_ elecampane, from the Greek name _Helenē_ (earliest form _Welenā_), Helen. 11. Suffixed form _*wel-ik-._ HELIX, from Greek _helix,_ spiral object. 12. Suffixed form _*wel-mi-nth-._ HELMINTH; ANTHELMINTIC, PLATYHELMINTH, from Greek _helmis, helmins_ (stem _helminth-_), parasitic worm. [Pokorny 7. _ṷel-_ 1140.]

welə-. An important derivative is _vulnerable._

welə-. To strike, wound. 1. Suffixed o-grade form _*wol(ə)-o-._ a. VALHALLA, from Old Norse _Valhöll,_ Valhalla; b. VALKYRIE, from Old Norse _Valkyrja,_ "chooser of the slain," name of one of the twelve war goddesses (_-kyrja,_ chooser; see **geus-**). Both a and b from Old Norse _valr,_ the slain in battle, from Germanic _*walaz._ 2. Suffixed basic form _*welə-nes-._ VULNERABLE, from Latin _vulnus_ (stem _vulner-_), a wound. 3. Suffixed zero-grade form _*wl̥ə-to-._ BERDACHE, from Old Iranian _*varta-_ (Avestan _varəta-_), seized, prisoner. [In Pokorny 8. _ṷel-_ 1144.]

wemə-. Important derivatives are _vomit_ and _emetic._

wemə-. To vomit. 1. WAMBLE, from Middle English _wam(e)len,_ to feel nausea, stagger, from a Scandinavian source probably akin to Old Norse _vamla,_ qualm, and Danish _vamle,_ to become sick, from Germanic _*wam-._ 2. NUX VOMICA, VOMIT, from Latin _vomere,_ to vomit. 3. EMESIS, EMETIC, from Greek _emein,_ to vomit. [Pokorny _ṷem-_ 1146.]

wen-[1]. Important derivatives are _win, winsome, wont, wean[1], wish, venerate, venereal, Venus, venom, venial,_ and _venison._

wen-[1]. To desire, strive for. 1. Suffixed form _*wen-w-._ WIN, from Old English _winnan,_ to win, from Germanic _*winn(w)an,_ to seek to gain. 2. Suffixed zero-grade form _*wn̥-yā._ WYNN, WINSOME, from Old English _wynn, wen,_ pleasure, joy, from Germanic _*wunjō._ 3. Suffixed (stative) zero-grade form _*wn̥-ē-,_ to be contented. WON[1], (WONT), from Old English _wunian,_ to become accustomed to, dwell, from Germanic _*wunēn._ 4. Suffixed (causative) o-grade form _*won-eyo-._ WEAN, from Old English _wenian,_ to accustom, train, wean, from Germanic _*wanjan._ 5. WEEN, from Old English _wēnan,_ to expect, imagine, think, from Germanic denominative _*wēnjan,_ to hope, from _*wēniz,_ hope. 6. Suffixed zero-grade form _*wn̥-sko-._ WISH, from Old English _wȳscan,_ to desire, wish, from Germanic _*wunsk-._ 7. Perhaps o-grade _*won-._ a. VANIR, from Old Norse _Vanir,_ the Vanir; b. VANADIUM, from Old Norse _Vanadīs,_ name of the goddess Freya. Both a and b from Germanic _*wana-._ 8. Suffixed form _*wen-es-._ a. VENERATE, VENEREAL, VENERY[1], VENUS, from Latin _venus,_ love; b. suffixed form _*wen-es-no-._ VENOM, from Latin _venēnum,_ love potion, poison. 9. Possibly suffixed form _*wen-eto-,_ "beloved." WEND, from Old High German _Winid,_ Wend, from Germanic _*Weneda-,_ a Slavic people. 10. Suffixed form _*wen-yā._ VENIAL, from Latin _venia,_ favor, forgiveness. 11. Lengthened-grade form _*wēn-ā-._ VENERY[2], VENISON, from Latin _vēnārī,_ to hunt. 12. Possibly zero-grade suffixed form _*wn̥-ig-._ BANYAN, from Sanskrit _vaṇik, vāṇijaḥ,_ merchant (? < "seeking to gain"). [Pokorny 1. _ṷen-_ 1146.]

wen-[2]. An important derivative is _wound[1]._

wen-[2]. To beat, wound. 1. Suffixed zero-grade form _*wn̥-to-._ WOUND[1], from Old English _wund,_ a wound, from Germanic _*wundaz._ 2. Suffixed o-grade form _*won-yo-._ WEN[1], from Old English _wen(n), wæn(n),_ wen, from Germanic _*wanja-,_ a swelling. [In Pokorny 1. _ṷā-_ 1108.]

wep-. An important derivative is _evil._

wep-. Bad, evil. From earlier _*əwep-._ Suffixed zero-grade form _*up-elo-._ EVIL, from Old English _yfel,_ evil, from Germanic _*ubilaz,_ evil.

wer-[1]. Important derivatives are _artery, aerial, air, aria, malaria,_ and _aura._

wer-[1]. To raise, lift, hold suspended. Earlier form _*əwer-._ 1. Basic form _*awer-._ AORTA, ARSIS, ARTERIO-, ARTERIOLE, ARTERY, from Greek _aeirein,_ to raise, and _artēria,_ windpipe, artery. 2. (Obscure basic form _*āwer-_). AERIAL, AERO-, AIR, ARIA; MALARIA, from Greek _aēr,_ air, possibly referred to this root. 3. Zero-grade form _*aur-._ AURA, from Greek _aura,_ breath, vapor (related to Greek _aēr,_ air). [Pokorny 1. _ṷer-_ 1151.]

wer-[2]. Important derivatives are _inward, worth[1], stalwart, weird, versatile, verse[1], version, versus, vertebra, vertex, adverse, anniversary, avert, controversy, convert, divert, invert, pervert, prose, universe, wreath, writhe, wrath, worry, wring, wrong, wrench, wrinkle, converge, wry, wriggle, wrist, wrestle, briar[1], warp, reverberate, wrap, rhapsody, worm,_ and _vermin._

wer-[2]. Conventional base of various Indo-European roots; to turn, bend.

I. Root _*wert-,_ to turn, wind. 1.a. _(i)_ -WARD, from Old English _-weard,_ toward (< "turned toward"); _(ii)_ INWARD, from Old English _inweard,_ inward, from Germanic _*inwarth,_ inward (_*in,_ in; see **en**). Both _(i)_ and _(ii)_ from Germanic variant _*warth;_ b. WORTH[1]; STALWART, from Old English _weorth,_ worth, valuable, and derivative noun _weorth, wierth,_ value, from Germanic derivative _*werthaz,_ "toward, opposite," hence "equivalent, worth," perhaps from **wer-[2]**. Both a and b from Germanic _*werth-._ 2. WORTH[2], from Old English _weorthan,_ to befall, from Germanic _*werthan,_ to become (< "to turn into"). 3. Zero-grade form _*wr̥t-._ WEIRD, from Old English _wyrd,_ fate, destiny (< "that which befalls one"), from Germanic _*wurthi-._ 4. VERSATILE, VERSE[1], VERSION, VERSUS, VERTEBRA, VERTEX, VERTIGO, VORTEX; ADVERSE, ANNIVERSARY, AVERT, BOULEVERSEMENT, CONTROVERSY, CONVERSE[1], CONVERT, DEXTRORSE, DIVERT, EVERT, EXTRORSE, (EXTROVERSION), EXTROVERT, INTRORSE, INTROVERT, INVERT, MALVERSATION, OBVERT, PERVERT, PROSE, RETRORSE, REVERT, SINISTRORSE, SUBVERT, TERGIVERSATE, TRANSVERSE,

UNIVERSE, from Latin *vertere,* to turn, with its frequentative *versāre,* to turn, and passive *versārī,* to stay, behave (< "to move around a place, frequent"). **5.** VERST, from Russian *versta,* line, from Balto-Slavic **wirstā-,* a turn, bend.
II. Root **wreit-,* to turn. **a.** WREATH, from Old English *writha,* band (< "that which is wound around"); **b.** WRITHE, from Old English *wrīthan,* to twist, torture; **c.** WRATH, WROTH, from Old English *wrāth,* angry (< "tormented, twisted"). **a, b,** and **c** all from Germanic **wrīth-, *wraith-.*
III. Root **wergh-,* to turn. **1.** WORRY, from Old English *wyrgan,* to strangle, from Germanic **wurgjan.* **2.** Nasalized variant **wrengh-.* **a.** WRING, from Old English *wringan,* to twist, from Germanic **wreng-;* **b.** *(i)* WRONG, from Middle English *wrong,* wrong, from a Scandinavian source akin to Old Norse **vrangr, rangr,* curved, crooked, wrong; *(ii)* WRANGLE, from Middle English *wranglen,* to wrangle, from a Low German source akin to *wrangeln,* to wrestle. Both *(i)* and *(ii)* from Germanic **wrang-.*
IV. Root **werg-,* to turn. **1.** Nasalized variant form **wreng-.* **a.** WRENCH, from Old English *wrencan,* to twist; **b.** WRINKLE, from Old English *gewrinclian,* to wind (*ge-,* collective prefix; see **kom**). Both **a** and **b** from Germanic **wrankjan.* **2.** VERGE[2]; CONVERGE, DIVERGE, from Latin *vergere,* to turn, tend toward.
V. Root **wreik-,* to turn. **1.a.** WRY, from Old English *wrīgian,* to turn, bend, go; **b.** WRIGGLE, from Middle Low German *wriggeln,* to wriggle. Both **a** and **b** from Germanic **wrig-.* **2.a.** WRIST, from Old English *wrist,* wrist; **b.** GAITER, from Old French *guietre,* gaiter, from Frankish **wrist-.* Both **a** and **b** from Germanic **wristiz,* from **wrihst-.* **3.** WREST, WRESTLE, from Old English *wrǣstan,* to twist, from secondary Germanic derivative **wraistjan.* **4.** Possibly o-grade form **wroik-.* BRIAR[1], (BRUSQUE), from Late Latin *brūcus,* heather, from Gaulish **brūko-.*
VI. RIBALD, from Old French *riber,* to be wanton, from Germanic root **wrib-.*
VII. Root **werb-,* also **werbh-,* to turn, bend. **1.** WARP, from Old English *weorpan,* to throw away, from Germanic **werp-, *warp-,* "to fling by turning the arm." **2.** REVERBERATE, from Latin *verber,* whip, rod. **3.** VERBENA, (VERVAIN), from Latin *verbēna,* sacred foliage. **4.** Zero-grade form **wr̥b-.* RHABDOMANCY, RHABDOVIRUS, from Greek *rhabdos,* rod. **5.** Nasalized variant form **wrembh-.* RHOMBUS, from Greek *rhombos,* magic wheel, rhombus.
VIII. Root **werp-,* to turn, wind. **1.** Metathesized form **wrep-.* WRAP, from Middle English *wrappen,* to wrap, from a source akin to Danish dialectal *vravle,* to wind, from Germanic **wrap-.* **2.** Zero-grade form **wr̥p-.* RAPHE, RHAPHIDE; RHAPSODY, TENORRHAPHY, from Greek *rhaptein,* to sew.
IX. Root **wr̥mi-,* worm; rhyme word to **kʷr̥mi-. 1.** WORM, from Old English *wyrm,* worm, from Germanic **wurmiz.* **2.** VERMEIL, VERMI-, VERMICELLI, VERMICULAR, VERMIN, from Latin *vermis,* worm. [Pokorny 3. *u̯er-* 1152.]

wer-3. Important derivatives are *wary, aware, ward, lord, steward, warden, award, reward, wardrobe, guard, panorama,* and *revere[1].*

wer-3. To perceive, watch out for.
I. O-grade form **wor-.* **1.** Suffixed form **wor-o-.* **a.** WARY, from Old English *wær,* watchful; **b.** AWARE, from Old English *gewær,* aware (*ge-,* collective and intensive prefix; see **kom**); **c.** WARE[2], from Old English *warian,* to beware. **a, b,** and **c** all from Germanic **waraz.* **2.** Suffixed form *wor-to-.* **a.** *(i)* WARD; LORD, STEWARD, from Old English *weard,* a watching, keeper; *(ii)* WARDER[2], from Old English *weardian,* to ward, guard; **b.** WARDEN; AWARD,REWARD, WARDROBE, from Old North French *warder,* to guard; **c.** GUARD, from Old French *guarder,*to guard; **d.** REARWARD[2], from Anglo-Norman *warde,* guard. **a, b, c,** and **d** all from Germanic **wardaz,* guard, and **wardōn,* to guard. **3.** WARE[1], from Old English *waru,* goods, protection, guard, from Germanic **warō.* **4.** Suffixed form **wor-wo-.* ARCTURUS, PYLORUS, from Greek *ouros,* a guard. **5.** Probably variant **(s)wor-, *s(w)or-.* EPHOR, PANORAMA, from Greek *horan,* to see.
II. Suffixed (stative) form **wer-ē-.* REVERE[1], from Latin *verērī,* to respect, feel awe for. [Pokorny 8. *u̯er-* 1164.]

wer-4. Important derivatives are *weir, aperture, overt, overture, cover, warn, warrant, warranty, garage, garret, garrison, warren, garment,* and *garnish.*

wer-4. To cover.
I. Basic form **wer-.* **1.** WEIR, from Old English *wer,* dam, fish trap, from Germanic **wer-jōn-.* **2.** Compound form **ap-wer-yo-* (**ap-,* off, away; see **apo-**). APERIENT, APÉRITIF, APERTURE; OVERT, OVERTURE, PERT, from Latin *aperīre,* to open, uncover. **3.** Compound form **op-wer-yo-* (**op-,* over; see **epi**). COVER, OPERCULUM, from Latin *operīre,* to cover.
II. O-grade form **wor-.* **1.** WARN, from Old English **war(e)nian,* to take heed, warn, from Germanic **war-nōn.* **2.a.** *(i)* GUARANTY, from Old French *garant,* warrant, authorization; *(ii)* WARRANT, (WARRANTEE), WARRANTY, from Old North French *warant,* warrant, and *warantir,* to guarantee; **b.** GARAGE, from Old French *garer,* to guard, protect; **c.** GARRET, GARRISON, from Old French *g(u)arir,* to defend, protect; **d.** WARREN, from Old North French *warenne,* enclosure, game preserve; **e.** GARMENT, GARNISH, from Old French *g(u)arnir,* to equip. **a, b, c, d,** and **e** all from Germanic **war-.* **3.** Suffixed form **wor-o-.* BARBICAN, from Old Iranian compound **pari-vāraka-,* protective (**pari-,* around; see **per[1]**). [Pokorny 5. *u̯er-* 1160.]

wer-5. Important derivatives are *word, verb, verve, adverb, proverb,* and *irony.*

wer-5. Also **werə-.** To speak. Variant **wrē-,* contracted from **wreə-.* **1.** Suffixed zero-grade form **wr̥-dho-.* WORD, from Old English *word,* word, from Germanic **wurdam.* **2.** Suffixed form **wer-dho-.* VERB, VERVE; ADVERB, PROVERB, from Latin *verbum,* word. **3.** Suffixed form **wer-yo-.* IRONY, from Greek *eirein,* to say, speak. **4.** Variant form **wrē-* in suffixed form **wrē-tor-.* RHETOR, from Greek *rhētōr,* public speaker. [Pokorny 6. *u̯er-* 1162.]

wē-r-. An important derivative is *urine.*

wē-r-. Contracted from **weə-r-.* Water, liquid, milk. Related to **eue-dh-r̥.** Suffixed zero-grade form **ūr-inā-.* URINE, from Latin *ūrīna,* urine. [In Pokorny 9. *au̯(e)-* 78.]

werg-. Important derivatives are *work, boulevard, allergy, dramaturge, energy, liturgy, metallurgy, surgery, wrought, wright, organ,* and *orgy.*

werg-. To do.
I. Suffixed form **werg-o-.* **1.a.** WORK, from Old English *weorc, werc,* work; **b.** (BOULEVARD), BULWARK, from Old High German *werc,* work. Both **a** and **b** from Germanic **werkam,* work. **2.** ERG, -URGY; ADRENERGIC, ALLERGY, ARGON, CHOLINERGIC, DEMIURGE, DRAMATURGE, ENDERGONIC, ENDOERGIC, ENERGY, ERGOGRAPH, ERGOMETER, ERGONOMICS, EXERGONIC, EXERGUE, EXOERGIC, GEORGIC, LITURGY, METALLURGY, SURGERY, (SYNERGID), SYNERGISM, THAUMATURGE, from Greek *ergon,* work, action.
II. Zero-grade form **wr̥g-.* **1.** Suffixed forms **wr̥g-yo-, *wr̥g-to-.* **a.** WROUGHT, from Old English *wyrcan,* to work; **b.** IRK, from Old Norse *yrkja,* to work. Both **a** and **b** from Germanic **wurkjan,* to work, participle **wurhta-.* **2.** Suffixed form **wr̥g-t-.* WRIGHT, from Old English *wryhta,* maker, wright, from Germanic **wurhtjō-.*
III. O-grade form **worg-.* **a.** ORGAN, ORGANON, from Greek *organon* (with suffix *-ano-*), tool; **b.** ORGY, from Greek *orgia,* secret rites, worship (< "service"). [Pokorny 2. *u̯erĝ-* 1168.]

wēro-. Important derivatives are *warlock, verity, very, verdict, verify, severe,* and *persevere.*

wēro-. True. **1.** WARLOCK, from Old English *wǣr,* faith, pledge, from Germanic **wēra-.* **2.** VERACIOUS, VERISM, VERITY, VERY; AVER, VERDICT, VERIDICAL, VERIFY, VERISIMILAR, VOIR DIRE, from Latin *vērus,* true. **3.** SEVERE; ASSEVERATE, PERSEVERE, from Latin *sevērus,* grave, serious; regarded by some as a compound of *se-, sed,* without (see **s(w)e-**), and *vērus,* true, but the semantic difficulties make this explanation improbable. **4.** Normal grade **wero-,* from **werə-o-.* GALORE, from Old Irish *roar,* enough, from **ro-wero-,* sufficiency (**ro-,* intensive prefix, from **pro-;* see **per[1]**). [Pokorny 11. *u̯er-* 1165.]

wers-. Important derivatives are *war, guerrilla, worse, worst,* and *liverwurst.*

wers-. To confuse, mix up. Compare **ers-.**
I. Suffixed basic form. **1.a.** WAR, from Old North French *werre,* war; **b.** GUERRILLA, from Spanish *guerra,* war. Both **a** and **b** from Germanic **werra-,* from **werz-a-.* **2.** WORSE, from Old English *wyrsa,* worse, from Germanic comparative **wers-izōn-.* **3.** WORST, from Old English *wyrsta,* worst, from Germanic superlative **wers-istaz.*
II. Suffixed zero-grade form **wr̥s-ti-.* WURST; (LIVERWURST), from Old High German *wurst,* sausage (< "mixture"), from Germanic **wursti-.* [Pokorny *u̯ers-* 1169.]

wes-1. Important derivatives are *was, were,* and *astute.*

wes-1. To stay, dwell, pass the night, with derivatives meaning "to be." **1.** O-grade form **wos-.* WAS, from Old English *wæs,* was, from Germanic **was-.* **2.** Lengthened-grade form **wēs-.* WERE, from Old English *wǣre* (subjunctive), *wǣron* (plural), were, from Germanic **wēz-.* **3.** WASSAIL, from Old Norse *vesa, vera,* to be, from Germanic **wesan.* **4.** Perhaps suffixed form **wes-tā-.* VESTA, from Latin *Vesta,* household goddess. **5.** Possibly suffixed variant form **was-tu-.* ASTUTE, from Latin *astus,* skill, craft (practiced in a town), from Greek *astu,* town (< "place where one dwells"). **6.** Suffixed form **wes-eno-.* DIVAN, from Old Persian *vahanam,* house. [Pokorny 1. *u̯es-* 1170.]

wes-2. Important derivatives are *wear, vest, invest,* and *travesty.*

wes-2. To clothe. Extension of **eu-1. 1.** Suffixed o-grade form **wos-eyo-.* WEAR, from Old English *werian,* to wear, carry, from Germanic **wazjan.* **2.** Suffixed form **wes-ti-.* VEST; DEVEST, INVEST, REVET, TRAVESTY, from Latin *vestis,* garment. **3.** Suffixed form **wes-nu-.* HIMATION, from Greek *hennunai,* to clothe, with nominal derivative *heima, hima* (< **wes-mn̥*), garment. [Pokorny 5. *u̯es-* 1172.]

wes-3. Important derivatives are *vend* and *bazaar.*

wes-3. To buy. **1.** Suffixed form **wes-no-.* VENAL, VEND, from Latin *vēnum,* sale. **2.** Suffixed o-grade form **wos-no-.* MONOPSONY, from Greek *ōneisthai,* to buy. **3.** Suffixed form **wes-ā-.* BAZAAR, from Persian *bāzār,* from Old Iranian **vahā-carana-,* "sale-traffic." [Pokorny 8. *u̯es-* 1173.]

wes-pero-. Important derivatives are *west, western, Visigoth,* and *vesper.*

wes-pero-. Evening, night.
I. Reduced form **wes-.* **1.** Suffixed form **wes-to-.* **a.** WEST, from Old English *west,* west; **b.** WESTERN, from Old English *westerne,* western; **c.** WESTERLY, from Old English *westra,* more westerly. **a, b,** and **c** all from Germanic **west-.* **2.** VISIGOTH, from Late Latin *Visigothī,* "West Goths" (*Gothī,* the Goths), from Germanic **wis-,* possibly from **wes-pero-.**
II. Basic form **wespero-.* **1.** VESPER, VESPERTILIONID, from Latin *vesper,* evening. **2.** HESPERIAN, from Greek *hesperos,* evening. [Pokorny *u̯esperos* 1173.]

wesr̥. An important derivative is *vernal.*

wesr̥. Spring. VERNAL; PRIMAVERA[1], from Latin *vēr,* spring (phonologically irregular). [Pokorny *u̯es-r̥* 1174.]

wet-1. Important derivatives are *Wednesday, fan[1],* and *atmosphere.*

wet-1. To blow, inspire, spiritually arouse. Related to **wē-. 1.** Lengthened-grade form **wōt-.* **a.** WODEN, from Old English *Wōden,* Woden; **b.** WEDNESDAY, from Old English *Wōdnesdæg,* "Woden's day"; **c.** ODIN, from Old Norse *Ōdhinn,* Odin; **d.** WOTAN, from Old High German *Wuotan.* **a, b, c,** and **d** all from Germanic suffixed form **wōd-eno-, *wōd-ono-,* "raging," "mad," "inspired," hence "spirit," name of the chief Teutonic god **Wōd-enaz;* **e.** WOOD[2], from Old English *wōd,* mad, insane, from Germanic **wōdaz.* **2.** Lengthened variant form **wāt-.* VAT-

IC, from Latin _vātēs_, prophet, poet. **3.** Variant form _*wat-_. WEDELN, from Old High German _wedil_, fan, from Germanic suffixed form _*wath-ila-_. **4.** Suffixed variant form _*wat-no-_. FAN^1, VAN^3, from Latin _vannus_, a winnowing fan. **5.** Oldest basic form _*əwet-_ becoming _*awet-_ in suffixed form _*awet-mo-_. ATMOSPHERE, from Greek _atmos_ (< _*aetmos_), breath, vapor. [Pokorny _u̯āt-_ 1113.]

wet-^{2}. Important derivatives are _wether, veteran, inveterate, veterinary,_ and _veal._

wet-^{2}. Year. **1.** Suffixed form _*wet-ru-_. WETHER, from Old English _wether_, wether, from Germanic _*wethruz_, perhaps "yearling." **2.** Suffixed form _*wet-es-_. **a.** VETERAN; INVETERATE, from Latin _vetus_, old (< "having many years"); **b.** VETERINARY, from Latin _veterīnus_, of beasts of burden, of cattle (perhaps chiefly old cattle); **c.** ETESIAN, from Greek _etos_, year. **3.** Suffixed form _*wet-olo-_. VEAL, VITELLUS, from Latin _vitulus_, calf, yearling. [Pokorny _u̯et-_ 1175.]

wi-. Important derivatives are _wide_ and _with_.

wi-. Apart, in half. **1.** Suffixed form _*wi-itos_. WIDE, from Old English _wīd_, wide (< "far apart"), from Germanic _*wīdaz_. **2.** Suffixed (comparative) form _*wi-tero-_. **a.** WITH, WITHERS, from Old English _wither_, against, with its derivative _with_, with, against; **b.** GUERDON; WIDDERSHINS, from Old High German _widar_, against. Both **a** and **b** from Germanic _*withrō_, against. [Pokorny 1. _u̯ī̆-_ 1175.]

wīkm̥tī. A derivative is _vigesimal_.

wīkm̥tī. Twenty. Compound of **wi-**, in half, hence two, and _*(d)km̥t-ī_ (nominative dual), decade, reduced zero-grade form of **dekm̥**. **1.** VICENARY, VIGESIMAL, from Latin _vīgintī_, twenty. **2.** ICOSAHEDRON, from Greek _eikosi_, twenty. **3.** PACHISI, from Sanskrit _viṁśatiḥ_, twenty. [Pokorny _u̯ī-km̥t-ī_ 1177.]

wī-ro-. Important derivatives are _werewolf, world, virile, virtue,_ and _virtuoso_.

wī-ro-. Man. Derivative of **weiə-**. **1.a.** WEREWOLF, WERGELD, from Old English _wer_, man; **b.** _(i)_ WORLD, from Old English _weorold_, world; _(ii)_ WELTANSCHAUUNG, from Old High German _weralt_, world. Both _(i)_ and _(ii)_ from Germanic compound _*wer-ald-_, "life or age of man" (_*-ald-_, age; see **al-^{2}**); **c.** LOUP-GAROU, from Old French _garoul_, werewolf, from Frankish _*wer-wulf_, "man-wolf" (_*wulf_, wolf; see **wl̥kʷo-**). Both **a** and **b** from Germanic _*weraz_, from shortened form _*wiraz_. **2.** VIRAGO, VIRILE, VIRTUE, (VIRTUOSA), (VIRTUOSO); DECEMVIR, DUUMVIR, TRIUMVIR, from Latin _vir_, man. **3.** CURIA, from Latin _cūria_, curia, court, possibly from **wī-ro-**, if regarded as from _*co-vir_, "men together" (_*co-_, together; see **kom**). [Pokorny _u̯iro-s_ 1177.]

wl̥kʷo-. An important derivative is _wolf_.

wl̥kʷo-. Wolf. **1.a.** WOLF, from Old English _wulf_, wolf; **b.** AARDWOLF, from Middle Dutch _wolf_, _wulf_, wolf; **c.** WOLFRAM, from Old High German _wolf_, wolf; **d.** (see **wī-ro-**) Frankish _*wulf_, wolf. **a, b, c,** and **d** all from Germanic _*wulfaz_. **2.** Taboo variant _*lupo-_. LOBO, (LUPINE^1), LUPINE^2, LUPUS; LOUP-GAROU, from Latin _lupus_, wolf. **3.** Taboo variant _*lukʷo-_. **a.** LYCANTHROPE, LYCOPODIUM, from Greek _lukos_, wolf; **b.** suffixed form _*lukʷ-ya_. LYTTA; ALYSSUM, from Greek _lussa_, martial rage, madness, rabies ("wolf-ness"). [Pokorny _u̯l̥kʷos_ 1178.]

wl̥p-ē-. A derivative is _vulpine_.

wl̥p-ē-. Fox. **1.** VULPINE, from Latin _vulpēs_, fox. **2.** Taboo variant _*əlōpĕk-_. ALOPECIA, from Greek _alōpēx_, fox. [Pokorny _u̯l̥p-_, _lup-_ 1179.]

wōs. An important derivative is _rendezvous_.

wōs. You (plural). RENDEZVOUS, from Latin _vōs_, you. [In Pokorny 1. _i̯u-_ 513.]

wrād-. Important derivatives are _root^1, wort, radical, radish, eradiate, ramify,_ and _licorice_.

wrād-. Branch, root.
I. Basic form _*wrād-_. ROOT^1; RUTABAGA, from Old Norse _rōt_, root, from Germanic _*wrōt-_.
II. Zero-grade form _*wr̥əd-_. **1.a.** WORT^1, from Old English _wyrt_, plant, herb; **b.** GEWÜRZTRAMINER, from Old High German _wurz_, plant, root; **c.** MANGEL-WURZEL, from German _Wurzel_, root (< _*wurzwala_, rootstock; _*-wala_, a roll, round stem; see **wel-^{2}**). **a, b,** and **c** all from Germanic _*wurtiz_. **2.** Suffixed form _*wr̥əd-yā-_. WORT^2, from Old English _wyrt_, brewer's wort, from Germanic _*wurtjō-_. **3.** RADICAL, RADICLE, RADISH, RADIX; DERACINATE, ERADICATE, from Latin _rādīx_, root. **4.** Suffixed form _*wrəd-mo-_. RAMOSE, RAMUS; RAMIFY, from Latin _rāmus_, branch. **5.** Perhaps suffixed reduced form _*wr̥(ə)d-ya_. RHIZO-, RHIZOME; COLEORHIZA, LICORICE, MYCORRHIZA, from Greek _rhiza_, root. [Pokorny _u̯(e)rād-_ 1167.]

yē-. Important derivatives are _jet^2, abject, adjacent, adjective, conjecture, ease, eject, inject, object, project, reject, subject, catheter,_ and _enema_.

yē-. To throw. Contracted from _*yeə-_. **1.** Extended zero-grade forms _*yak-yo-_ and _*yak-ē-_ (stative). GIST, (GITE), JACTITATION, JESS, JET^2, JOIST; ABJECT, ADJACENT, ADJECTIVE, AMICE, CONJECTURE, DEJECT, (EASE), EJACULATE, EJECT, INJECT, INTERJECT, OBJECT, PARGET, PROJECT, REJECT, SUBJACENT, SUBJECT, SUPERJACENT, TRAJECT, from Latin _iacere_, to throw, lay, and _iacēre_, to lie down (< "to be thrown") and _iaculum_, dart. **2.** Basic form _*yē-_ and zero-grade form _*yə-_. CATHETER, DIESIS, ENEMA, PARESIS, SYNESIS, from Greek _hienai_, to send, throw. [Pokorny _i̯ē-_ 502.]

yeg-. An important derivative is _icicle_.

yeg-. Ice. ICICLE, from Old English _gicel_, icicle, ice, from Germanic _*jakilaz_, _*jekilaz_. [Pokorny _i̯eg-_ 503.]

yek-. Important derivatives are _jewel, jocular, joke, juggle,_ and _jeopardy_.

yek-. To speak. Suffixed o-grade form _*yok-o-_. JEWEL, JOCOSE, JOCULAR, JOKE, JUGGLE, (JUGGLER); JEOPARDY, from Latin _iocus_, joke. [Pokorny _i̯ek-_ 503.]

yĕkʷr̥. An important derivative is _hepatitis_.

yĕkʷr̥. Liver. **1.** HEPATIC, HEPATO-; HEPARIN, (HEPATITIS), from Greek _hēpar_, liver. **2.** GIZZARD, from Persian _jigar_, liver. [Pokorny _i̯ekʷ-r̥t_ 504.]

yēr-. Important derivatives are _year, hour,_ and _horoscope_.

yēr-. Year, season. **1.** Suffixed basic form _*yēr-o-_. YEAR, from Old English _gēar_, year, from Germanic _*jēram_. **2.** Suffixed o-grade form _*yōr-ā-_. HOUR; HOROLOGE, HOROLOGY, HOROSCOPE, from Greek _hōra_, season. [In Pokorny 1. _ei-_ 293.]

yes-. Important derivatives are _yeast_ and _eczema_.

yes-. To boil, foam, bubble. **1.** YEAST, from Old English _gist_, yeast, from Germanic _*jest-_. **2.** KIESELGUHR, from Old High German _jësan_, to ferment, and _jerian_, to cause to ferment, from Germanic _*jes-_. **3.** ECZEMA, ZEOLITE, from Greek _zeein_, _zein_, to boil. [Pokorny _i̯es-_ 506.]

yeu-. Important derivatives are _youth, young, junior, juvenile,_ and _rejuvenate_.

yeu-. Vital force, youthful vigor. Earliest form _*əyeu-_; variant of **aiw-**. Suffixed zero-grade form _*yuwen-_ (< _*yu-əen-_), "possessing youthful vigor," young. **1.** Further suffixed form _*yuwn̥-ti-_. YOUTH, from Old English _geoguth_, youth, from Germanic _*jugunthi-_, _*jugunthā-_. **2.** Further suffixed form _*yuwn̥-ko-_. **a.** _(i)_ YOUNG, from Old English _geong_, young; _(ii)_ JUNKER, from Old High German _junc_, young; _(iii)_ YOUNKER, from Middle Dutch _jonc_, young. _(i), (ii),_ and _(iii)_ all from Germanic _*jungaz_ from _*juwungaz_; **b.** GALLOWGLASS, from Old Irish _ōac_, from Celtic _*yowanko-_. **3.** JUNIOR, JUVENILE; REJUVENATE, from Latin _iuvenis_, young. [Pokorny 3. _i̯eu-_ 510.]

yeug-. Important derivatives are _yoke, jugular, subjugate, joust, adjust, juxtapose, join, junction, juncture, junta, conjugal, injunction,_ and _yoga_.

yeug-. To join.
I. Zero-grade form _*yug-_. **1.** Suffixed form _*yug-o-_. **a.** YOKE, from Old English _geoc_, yoke, from Germanic _*yukam_; **b.** JUGATE, JUGULAR, JUGUM; CONJUGATE, SUBJUGATE, from Latin _iugum_, yoke; **c.** ZYGO- ZYGOMA, ZYGOTE, -ZYGOUS; (AZYGOUS), SYZYGY, from Greek _zugon_, yoke, and _zugoun_, to join; **d.** YUGA, from Sanskrit _yugam_, yoke. **2.** Suffixed (superlative) form _*yug-istos_. JOUST; ADJUST, JUXTAPOSE, (JUXTAPOSITION), from Latin _iuxtā_, close by, from _*iugistā (viā)_, "on a nearby (road). **3.** Nasalized form _*yu-n-g-_. JOIN, JUNCTION, JUNCTURE, JUNTA; ADJOIN, CONJOIN, (CONJUGAL), (CONJUNCT), ENJOIN, INJUNCTION, SUBJOIN, from Latin _iungere_, to join.
II. Suffixed form _*yeug-mn̥_. ZEUGMA, from Greek _zeugma_, a bond.
III. Suffixed o-grade form _*youg-o-_. YOGA, from Sanskrit _yogaḥ_, union. [Pokorny 2. _i̯eu-_ 508.]

yewes-. Important derivatives are _jurist, jury^1, conjure, injury, perjure, judge, prejudice,_ and _just^1_.

yewes-. Law. **1.** JURAL, JURIST, JURY^1; ABJURE, ADJURE, CONJURE, INJURY, JURIDICAL, JURISCONSULT, JURISDICTION, JURISPRUDENCE, (NONJUROR), OBJURGATE, PERJURE, from Latin _iūs_ (stem _iūr-_), law, and its derivative _iūrāre_, "to pronounce a ritual formula," swear. **2.** Compound form _*yewes-dik-_, "one who shows or pronounces the law." (see **deik-**) Latin _iūdex_, judge. **3.** Suffixed from _*yewes-to-_. JUST^1, from Latin _iūstus_, just. [Pokorny _i̯eu̯os_ 512.]

yewo-. A derivative is _zein_.

yewo-. Grain. Suffixed form _*yew-ya_. ZEIN, from Greek _zeia_, one-seeded wheat. [Pokorny _i̯eu̯o-_ 512.]

yu-. Important derivatives are _ye^2_ and _you_.

yu-. You. Second person (plural) pronoun. YE^2, YOU, from Old English _gē_ and _ēow_, you, from Germanic _*jūz_ (nominative) and _*iwwiz_ (oblique). [Pokorny 1. _i̯u-_ 513.]

Picture Credits

The editorial and production staff wishes to thank the many individuals, organizations, and agencies that have contributed to the art program of the Dictionary.

Credits on the following pages are arranged alphabetically by boldface entry word. When two or more illustrations complement an entry, the sources are separated by slashes and follow the order of the illustrations. Locator maps were rendered by Francis & Shaw, Inc., and by Publication Services, Inc.

The following abbreviations are used throughout: AA/Animals Animals; BA/Bettmann Archive, Inc.; CC/Chris Costello; CDB/Cecile Duray-Bito; EPJCo./E.P. Jones Company; ES/©Houghton Mifflin Company-Photograph by Evelyn Shafer; GEP/Gail Piazza; GHP/Grant Heilman Photography, Inc.; GP/Globe Photos, Inc.; HAR/H. Armstrong Roberts; HPSM/Historical Pictures-Stock Montage, Inc.; KAMD/*Knight's American Mechanical Dictionary*; LC/Laurel Cook; LOC/Library of Congress; LW/Lightwave; MMA/Metropolitan Museum of Art; NASA/National Aeronautics and Space Administration; NGA/National Gallery of Art, Smithsonian Institution, Washington, D.C.; NMAI/National Museum of the American Indian, Smithsonian Institution; NYZS/NYZS-The Wildlife Conservation Society; PC/The Picture Cube; PI/Positive Images; PR/Photo Researchers, Inc.; San Diego Zoo/Zoological Society of San Diego; SB/Stock, Boston; SLAM/The Saint Louis Art Museum; TG/Tech-Graphics (Susan Coons); TSI/Tony Stone Images; USDA/United States Department of Agriculture; WCFTR/Wisconsin Center for Film and Theater Research; WWP/AP-Wide World Photos.

---

aardwolf PR - Des Bartlett & Armand Denis **abacus** BA **Kareem Abdul-Jabbar** Courtesy of Kareem Abdul-Jabbar **abelmosk** CC **Aberdeen Angus** GHP **abracadabra** TG **abscissa** TG **absinthe** CC **abstract expressionism** SLAM, Museum Purchase **Abu Simbel** Russell A. Thompson **acanthus** CC **acciaccatura** TG **accordion** SB - Jean-Claude Lejeune **acerose** CC **achene** GEP **aconite** CC **acorn** LC **acrobat** WWP **acropolis** BA **actinoid** PR - Jack Dermid **action painting** The Museum of Modern Art, New York, Gift of Mr. and Mrs. Ronald Lauder in honor of Eliza Parkinson Cobb **Abigail Adams** LOC **John Adams** LOC **John Quincy Adams** LOC **addax** San Diego Zoo - Ron Garrison **adder's tongue-fern** CC **Adélie penguin** Comstock - Russ Kinne **adjacent angle** TG **admiral** GHP - Runk & Schoenberger **adobe** Eric Kroll **adrenal gland** CDB **adz** Courtesy of The Oriental Institute of The University of Chicago/CC **aerialist** HAR **Afghan hound** LW - © 1988 Oscar Palmquist **A-frame** HAR **African violet** LC **agaric** LC **agave** CC **James Agee** BA **agitator** CC **agouti** San Diego Zoo - Ron Garrison **Agrippina the Younger** Anderson - Art Resource, New York **aileron** LC **Airedale** LW - Oscar Palmquist **air rifle** LW - Oscar Palmquist **Akbar the Great** SLAM, Gift of J. Lionberger Davis **Akhenaton** BA **albatross** PR - George Holton/PR - Karl W. Kenyon **alcazar** SB - Peter Menzel **Louisa May Alcott** Chicago Historical Society, neg. no. ICHi-09394 **alembic** CC **Alexander the Great** HPSM **alfalfa** LC **alga** PR - Hugh Spencer **Muhammad Ali** GP - Camera Press **alimentary canal** LC **Gracie Allen** BA **Woody Allen** WWP **alligator** HAR **allium** CC **allspice** CDB **almond** LC **alpaca** PR - Andrew Rakoczy **altar** PC - Franz Kraus **altazimuth** BA **alternate angle** TG **amanita** GEP **amaryllis** W. Atlee Burpee & Company, Warminster, Pennsylvania **ammonite** PR - Bucky & W.S. Reeves **amoeba** GHP - Runk & Schoenberger **amphipod** CDB **amphitheater** BA **amphora** MMA, Rogers Fund, 1917 **amulet** Jewish Museum - Art Resource, New York **Roald Amundsen** BA **amusement park** PC - Emilio A. Mercado **anchor** LC **Marian Anderson** LOC **anemone** GEP/PR - Jack Dermid **aneroid barometer** TG **angelfish** © 1991 Judith Winters **angiogram** © 1986 Martin M. Rotker, Deltona, Florida **angle[2]** LC **Angora goat** GHP **anhinga** AA - M. Krishnan **Anne of Cleves** LOC **annual ring** GHP - Runk & Schoenberger **annular eclipse** NASA **anorak** SB - Ellis Herwig **ansate cross** BA **antefix** GEP **anthemion** Alinari - Art Resource, New York **anther** LC **Susan B. Anthony** National Portrait Gallery, Smithsonian Institution, Washington, D.C. **anthurium** LC **antibody** LC **anticipation** TG **anticline** GEP **antler** GEP **Anubis** MMA, Museum Excavations, 1928–1929 and Rogers Fund, 1930 (30.3.31) **ao dai** WWP **aperture** TG **aphid** CDB **apiarist** GHP **Apis** Alinari - Art Resource, New York **apogee** TG **appaloosa** *Appaloosa Journal*/Crown Center Farms, Columbia, Missouri **appliqué** SB - Tom Cheek **apricot** LC **Aquarius** TG **aqueduct** HAR **arabesque** Boston Ballet - John Burke **Arabian horse** EPJCo. **Yasir Arafat** WWP **arch[1]** HAR/PC - Stanley Rowin **archaeopteryx** TG **archery** GP - Newton Nelson **architrave** LC **arctic fox** AA - Irene Vandermolen **argyle** GEP **Aries** TG **armadillo** PR - Keith Gunnar **armoire** MMA, Fletcher Fund, 1959 (59.108) **armor** MMA, Rogers Fund and Pratt Gift, 1933 (33.164 a-x) **Louis Armstrong** WCFTR **Neil Armstrong** WWP **arrowhead** GHP/GEP **Artemis** LOC **artesian well** GEP **Chester A. Arthur** LOC **artichoke** LC **art nouveau** MMA, Sansbury Mills Fund, 1980 (1980.299) **ascender** CC **ascidium** CDB **ash[2]** CC **asparagus** LC **aspergillum** Comstock - Russ Kinne **ass[1]** PR - Tom McHugh **assassin bug** CDB **Fred Astaire** BA **astigmatism** CDB **astragal** CC **astrolabe** Courtesy of The Oriental Institute of The University of Chicago **astronaut** NASA **asymptote** TG **Athena** BA **Atlas** WWP **atmosphere** TG **atoll** LC **atom bomb** LC **atrium** PC - Betty Barry **attaché case** EPJCo. **John James Audubon** PR **auger** GEP **auk** PR - Gösta Håkansson Visby **auscultation** © 1990 Walter Silver, Boston, Massachusetts **avocado** LC **avocet** AA - Leonard Lee Rue III **awl** NMAI **ax** CC **azalea** GEP **azimuthal equidistant projection** © 1986 by the American Congress on Surveying and Mapping **babirusa** NYZS **Johann Sebastian Bach** LOC **backgammon** The Pierpont Morgan Library, New York (M.763, f.241v-242) **backhand** WWP **backsaw** LC **bacterium** LC **Robert Baden-Powell** LOC **Joan Baez** WWP **balalaika** MMA, Gift of Mr. Ustin Smolensky, 1948 (48.146) **balance beam** SB - Cary Wolinsky **bald eagle** AA - Irene Vandermolen **James Baldwin** National Portrait Gallery, Smithsonian Institution, Washington, D.C.; © of 1955 negative, Estate of Carl Van Vechten; © of 1983 photogravure, Eakins Press Foundation **ballet** Comstock - Billy Brown Photography **balloon** PC - Stanley Rowin **balsam fir** GEP **balustrade** Image Photos - Clemens Kalischer **Honoré de Balzac** The Granger Collection, New York **banana** PC - Foto du Monde **band shell** HAR **banjo** SB - Jean-Claude Lejeune **banquette** The Cleveland Museum of Art, John L. Severance Fund (54.385) **baobab** CC **baptistery** Italian Government Travel Office, New York/Courtesy, Museum of Fine Arts, Boston, Sarah F. Gorham & Alice H. Goddard Fund **barbell** BA **bard[2]** Anderson - Art Resource, New York **bargeboard** The Preservation Society of Newport County **Barlow knife** PI - Jerry Howard **Christiaan Barnard** BA **barouche** From the collections of Henry Ford Museum & Greenfield Village, neg. no. B5240 **barracuda** PR - Ron Church **bartizan** Russell A. Thompson **Clara Barton** LOC **Mikhail Baryshnikov** GP **bascule** British Tourist Authority, New York **basenji** ES **Count Basie** GP - Dmitri Kasterine **basilica** CC **basket star** PR - C. Ray **bass clef** TG **bat[2]** PR - S. Bisserot **bathyscaph** Office of Information, Dept. of the Navy, Washington, D.C. **battering ram** HPSM **bay window** PI - Jerry Howard **beagle** ES **beak** CDB **beaker** Image Photos - Clemens Kalischer **bearskin** PC - Cynthia W. Sterling **Beatrix** BA **Simone de Beauvoir** PR - Gisele Freund **Thomas à Becket** Walters Art Gallery, Baltimore, Maryland **Bedlington terrier** EPJCo. **beefeater** British Tourist Authority, New York **Ludwig van Beethoven** LOC **belaying pin** GEP **belfry** Russell A. Thompson **Alexander Graham Bell** HPSM **Bellerophon** Culver Pictures Inc. **bellows** CC **bench-press** PC - Sarah Putnam **bend[2]** GEP **bend sinister** GEP **David Ben Gurion** BA **benzene ring** TG **beret** SB - Owen Franken **Bernese mountain dog** ES **Sarah Bernhardt** LOC **Leonard Bernstein** GP **Mary McLeod Bethune** HPSM **betony** CC **bevel gear** LC **bias-ply tire** GEP **biceps** LC **bicycle** SB - Owen Franken **bighorn** AA - Leonard Lee Rue III **billy club** PR - Fred Lombardi **binocular** SB - Gale Zucker **birch** CC **bireme** GEP **biretta** SB - Donald Dietz **bisector** TG **bishop** GEP **Otto von Bismarck** WWP **bison** AA - C.W. Perkins **bit[2]** GEP **bittern[1]** PR - Karl H. Maslowski **black bear** AA - Leonard Lee Rue III **blackberry** LC **black-eyed Susan** LC **black letter** CC **blacksmith** SB - Jean-Claude Lejeune **black widow** PR - Bucky Reeves **blastoff** NASA **bleeding heart** LC **blimp** The Goodyear Tire & Rubber Company **blinders** PC - Judith Sedwick **block and tackle** GEP **blockhouse** LOC **bloodhound** ES **bloomer[2]** LOC **blueberry** GEP **blue grouse** PR - Allan D. Cruickshank **blue whale** CC **blunderbuss** LC **boa constrictor** PR - Dade W. Thornton **boat** TG **boatbill** PR - Arthur W. Ambler **bobwhite** PR - Nell Bolen **bodkin** Mystic Seaport Museum, Inc. All rights reserved. **Humphrey Bogart** WWP **boiler** TG **Anne Boleyn** National Portrait Gallery, London **Simón Bolívar** LOC **bollard** SB - Joseph Schuyler **boll weevil** CDB **bongo[1]** NYZS **bongo[2]** PC - Frank Siteman **bontebok** PR - Arthur W. Ambler **booby[1]** SB - Ira Kirschenbaum **boojum tree** PR - Jen & Des Bartlett **Daniel Boone** National Portrait Gallery, Smithsonian Institution, Washington, D.C. **Boötes** TG **John Wilkes Booth** LOC **borage** GEP **Lizzie Borden** The Granger Collection, New York **borzoi** © 1991 Judith Winters **boss[2]** CC **Boston rocker** Courtesy, Museum of Fine Arts, Boston **bouzouki** PI - Martin Miller **bowie knife** CC **boxer[3]** ES **boxing[2]** SB - Peter Southwick **box turtle** GHP **brace** CC **Mathew Brady** LOC **Johannes Brahms** BA **Braille** TG/EPJCo. **brain** LC **brake[1]** TG **brass knuckles** PI - Jerry Howard **brazier[2]** KAMD **Brazil nut** CDB **breastplate** BA **Leonid Brezhnev** WWP **bridge[1]** SB - Jeff Albertson/Cunard Line Ltd. **bridle** EPJCo. **bristlecone pine** CDB **Brittany spaniel** PR - Leonard Lee Rue III **broccoli** CC **Brontë** National Portrait Gallery, London **brontosaur** CC **Gwendolyn Brooks** BA **brougham** From the collections of Henry Ford Museum & Greenfield Village, neg. no. A2081 **brown recluse spider** CDB **brown thrasher** PR - Allan D. Cruickshank **Pieter Brueghel the Elder** BA **Brussels sprouts** CC **James Buchanan** LOC **buckboard** Carriage Association of America, New Jersey **bucksaw** KAMD **Buddha** PC - Bruce Rosenblum **buffing wheel** PI - Jerry Howard **bull[1]** AA - Leonard Lee Rue III **bulldozer** GHP **bullet train** SB - J.R. Holland **bull terrier** PR - Mary Eleanor Browning **bumblebee** LC **Bunsen burner** SB - Jeffrey Dunn **Luis Buñuel** BA **burdock** GEP **burette** LC **Martha Jane Burk** LOC **burnoose** SB - Frank Siteman **George Burns** WWP **burying beetle** CDB **Barbara Bush** The White House - David Valdez **George Bush** The White House - David Valdez **bustard** PR - Mark Boulton **butte** PC - Mike Rizza **butterfly valve** GEP **butternut** GEP **butt hinge** GEP **buzzard** PR - Allan D. Cruickshank **Richard E. Byrd** BA **cab[1]** HAR **cable car** SB - Judy Canty **Mother Cabrini** LOC **cachepot** Cooper-Hewitt National Museum of Design, Smithsonian Institution - Art Resource, New York **caddis fly** CDB **caduceus** LC **cairn** Comstock - Richard Harrington **calash** Shelburne Museum, Shelburne, Vermont **calceolaria** LC **caliper** GEP **Maria Callas** HPSM **calliope** BA **calumet** Peabody Museum, Harvard University - © 1987 Hillel Burger **camel** PR - George Holton **cameo** Walters Art Gallery, Baltimore, Maryland **camera** TG **Albert Camus** WWP **Canada goose** GHP - Hal Harrison **Cancer** TG **Canis Major** TG **Canis Minor** TG **canoe** SB - Fredrik Bodin **canopy** MMA **cantaloupe** CC **cantilever bridge** TG **canvasback** AA - Leonard Lee Rue III **Capricorn** TG **capsule** PC - Stanley Rowin **capuchin** PR - Robert C. Hermes **carabiner** LC **caravel** Culver Pictures Inc. **carboy** GEP **carburetor** TG **cardinal** PR - Karl H. Maslowski **cardioid** TG **carpus** LC **carrel** © 1983 Walter Silver, Boston, Massachusetts **carriage** EPJCo. **carrick bend** TG **Kit Carson** Courtesy, Colorado Historical Society **Jimmy Carter** Courtesy, Jimmy Carter Library **Rosalynn Carter** Courtesy, Jimmy Carter Library **Enrico Caruso** LOC **George Washington Carver** HPSM **caryatid** Greek National Tourist Organization - Cyril Morris **cashew** LC **Mary Cassatt** National Portrait Gallery, Smithsonian Institution, Washington, D.C. **casserole** Phototake - Yoav Levy **cassowary** PR - Len Rue, Jr. **castanet** GEP **castle** EPJCo. **Fidel Castro** GP **cat-**

amaran WWP catapult BA catboat Mystic Seaport Museum, Inc. All rights reserved. catenary Tech-Graphics TG caterpillar CDB catfish GHP - Runk & Schoenberger cathedral EPJCo. Catherine of Aragon National Portrait Gallery, London cathode-ray tube TG CAT scanner WWP causeway GHP - William Felger C clef TG cecropia moth CDB cedar of Lebanon CC cedar waxwing PR - Karl H. Maslowski cell LC cello[1] Jeroboam, Inc. - Kent Reno Celtic cross Comstock - Russ Kinne censer BA centaur BA centipede PI - Martin Miller cerebellum LC Ceres *Museum of Antiquity* by L.W. Yaggy and T.L. Haines, Standard Publishing House, © 1882 cesta Florida Dept. of Commerce, Division of Tourism Cetus TG Paul Cézanne Giraudon - Art Resource, New York chafing dish Courtesy, Museum of Fine Arts, Boston, Gift of Leverett, Muriel, and Richard Saltonstall Marc Chagall WWP chain saw SB - Peter Menzel chair lift PI - Jerry Howard chalice Marburg - Art Resource, New York chameleon PR - George Porter chamois PR - Toni Angermayer chandelier MMA, American Wing Restricted Building Fund, 1968 (68.143.5) chanterelle CDB chapel WWP Charlie Chaplin WCFTR chariot MMA, Rogers Fund, 1903 (03.23.1) Charles British Information Services, New York chasuble PR - Ray Ellis chateau Swiss National Tourist Office chatelaine MMA, Gift of Miss Sarah Lazarus in memory of Moses Lazarus, 1890 (90.22.7 ab) Cesar Chavez SB - Jon Chase cheetah AA - Leonard Lee Rue III cherimoya CDB chess[1] SB - Eric Neurath cheval glass MMA, Gift of Ginsburg and Levy, Inc., in memory of John Ginsburg and Isaac Levy, 1969 (69.183) chevron PR - Bettye Lane Chiang Kai-shek BA Chichén Itzá © 1984 Walter Silver, Boston, Massachusetts chignon Palmer/Brilliant, Boston, Massachusetts Chihuahua[2] EPJCo. chimney sweep PI - Martin Miller Chincoteague pony AA - Robert Redden chin-up SB - Thomas Cheek chipmunk AA - Irene Vandermolen Chi-Rho GEP chisel LC chiton HPSM chock PI - Martin Miller choker LW - Oscar Palmquist Frédéric Chopin WWP chopine MMA, Purchase, Irene Lewisohn Bequest, 1973 (1973.114.4ab) chopstick PR - Susan Woog-Wagner chow[1] ES Agatha Christie WWP chromosome GHP - Runk & Schoenberger church GHP Winston S. Churchill BA churn New York Public Library ciborium Courtesy, Museum of Fine Arts, Boston, Theodora Wilbour Fund, in memory of Charlotte B. Wilbour cinquefoil CC circle LC circuit GEP circular saw SB - Donald C. Dietz cirrocumulus GHP - Grant Heilman cirrus GHP cithara MMA, Gift of Mr. and Mrs. Leon Pomerance, 1953 cittern MMA, The Crosby Brown Collection of Musical Instruments, 1889 civet San Diego Zoo clamp CC clarinet Comstock - Russ Kinne William Clark Independence National Historical Park clavichord Courtesy, Museum of Fine Arts, Boston, Gift of William Lindsey as a memorial to his daughter, Mrs. Leslie Lindsey Mason clavicle LC claymore MMA, Gift of Mrs. Alexander McMillan Welch, in memory of Alexander McMillan Welch, 1945 (45.160.2) clean room PR - Spencer Grant Cleopatra The Granger Collection, New York clerestory CC clerical collar SB - John Maher Grover Cleveland LOC clevis KAMD cliff dweller EPJCo. Bill Clinton The White House - Bob McNeely Hillary Rodham Clinton The White House - Bob McNeely clipper Peabody Museum of Salem, Massachusetts clitellum GEP cloche BA cloister Palmer/Brilliant, Boston, Massachusetts clove hitch TG cloverleaf HPSM Clumber spaniel ES Clydesdale AA - Robert L. Miller coati NYZS coat of arms BA cobblestone LW - © 1988 Jeff Thiebauth cobra AA - M. Krishnan coccyx LC Jacqueline Cochran WWP cockatoo BA cock-of-the-rock NYZS cockpit PR - Jeannine Niepce/Rapho cockroach LC William F. Cody National Portrait Gallery, Smithsonian Institution, Washington, D.C. coelacanth GEP coffee LC cog railway Image Photos - Clemens Kalischer coliseum SB - Elizabeth Hamlin collage Photograph © The Solomon R. Guggenheim Foundation, New York - Gift, Katherine S. Dreier Estate from Marcel Duchamp (FN 53.1348) - Robert E. Mates collie Mrs. Kathy Peters - Gulie Krook colonnade Marburg - Art Resource, New York Colorado potato beetle CDB colossus Comstock - Richard Harrington columbarium Jeroboam, Inc. - Werner Hiebel columbine LC Christopher Columbus LOC column LC combine HPSM comet Lick Observatory Photograph comma GHP - Runk & Schoenberger command module NASA commode MMA, Fletcher Fund, 1928 (28.154) compact disk LW - Oscar Palmquist compass LW - Oscar Palmquist complementary angles LC compote SLAM, Bequest of Mrs. Christine Graham Long compound eye PR - Dr. Jeremy Burgess, Science Photo Library computer EPJCo. concave LC concession LW - S.E. Byrne conch PC - Frank Siteman condor USDA condyle LC cone TG/Phototake - CNRI Conestoga wagon Shelburne Museum, Shelburne, Vermont confessional EPJCo. Confucius WWP conga drums LW - Oscar Palmquist Congo eel CDB Jimmy Connors WWP console[2] CC console table Spencer Museum of Art, Lawrence, Kansas, The Williams Bridges Thayer Memorial (28.2053) contact lens LW - Oscar Palmquist continental code TG continental shelf GEP contortionist SB - Michael Grecco convection TG convertible WWP convex LC conveyer Olof Källström Calvin Coolidge LOC Grace Coolidge LOC coop EPJCo. coping saw PC - Frank Siteman John Singleton Copley LOC copperhead PR - Karl H. Maslowski coral GHP - Runk & Schoenberger coral snake PR - Jack Dermid corbel Comstock - Stuart Cohen corbie-step Netherlands Board of Tourism, New York core LC Corinthian order LC cormorant PR - Arthur W. Ambler cornet From the collections of Henry Ford Museum & Greenfield Village cornrow PI - Jerry Howard cornucopia MMA, Rogers Fund, 1916 (16.112) Corona Borealis TG corsage Palmer/Brilliant, Boston, Massachusetts Hernando Cortés American Museum of Natural History, Courtesy Department Library Services, neg. no. 286846 Corvus TG cosecant TG cosine TG cotangent TG cottonwood CC cotyledon CDB countersink CC Gustave Courbet International Museum of Photography at George Eastman House, neg. no. 17527 course SB - Dean Abramson Jacques Cousteau GP - Jerry Watson covalent bond TG covered wagon Carriage Association of America, New Jersey cowcatcher HPSM cowrie GEP coxswain SB - Arthur Grace crab[1] GHP - Runk & Schoenberger cradle Courtesy, Museum of Fine Arts, Boston/PI - Jerry Howard crag PC - Read D. Brugger crampon LC crane AA - Miriam Austerman/PC - David S. Strickler crater NASA creamcups CC creamer MMA, Edgar J. Kaufmann Charitable Foundation, 1969 (69.128.1,2) creel PC - Jeffrey Dunn crenate CC crew[1] PC - Rick Friedman cribbage SB - Tom Cheek crinkleroot GEP crochet CC Davy Crockett LOC crocodile NYZS Oliver Cromwell LOC crossbow HPSM cross-country skiing PR - Keith Gunnar crosse Comstock - Sven Martson crow's-nest BA Crucifixion LOC cruet MMA, Gift of Audrey Love in memory of C. Ruxton Love, Jr., 1978 (1978.524.1a-e) crust LC crutch LC ctenophore CDB cube TG cubism MMA, The Alfred Stieglitz Collection, 1949 (49.70.34) cuckoo clock EPJCo. cue ball PI - Patricia J. Bruno cumulonimbus GHP cumulus SB - J.R. Holland cuneiform Comstock - Georg Gerster cupola SB - Peter Southwick Marie Curie BA Pierre Curie The Granger Collection, New York currycomb LW - Oscar Palmquist cutaway SB - Jeff Albertson cuttlefish CDB cycloid TG cyclotron TG cylinder TG cymbal Jeroboam, Inc. - Philip Jon Bailey cypress CC dachshund PR - Ylla daffodil LC Salvador Dali BA Dalmatian ES dalmatic MMA, Rogers Fund, 1954 (54.176.1) Father Damien WWP dandelion CDB dapple-gray PR Darius I Courtesy of The Oriental Institute of The University of Chicago Charles Darwin HPSM datura CC davit SB - Fredrik D. Bodin Moshe Dayan GP - Yvonne Plaut day lily CDB dead bolt LW - Oscar Palmquist James Dean WWP death cup CDB decoy PC - Edward Bishop deer AA - Len Rue, Jr. deer fly CC Charles de Gaulle HPSM dehumidify TG Eugène Delacroix International Museum of Photography at George Eastman House, neg. no. 17527 delft Jewish Museum - Art Resource, New York Delphinus TG demijohn Jeffrey Dunn demoiselle crane AA - Irene Vandermolen demolition WWP Deng Xiaoping WWP dentin LC dentist Comstock - Stuart Cohen Denver boot SB - Peter Southwick deodar CDB derailleur TG derby SB - Jeff Albertson derrick GHP - Alan Pitcairn dervish Turkish Culture and Information Office, New York descender CC desert[1] GHP - Alan Pitcairn Hernando de Soto BA destroying angel CDB detector SB - Peter Vandermark devilwood CC Thomas Dewey WWP dhow Mystic Seaport Museum, Inc. All rights reserved. diagonal LC Diana Courtesy, Museum of Fine Arts, Boston Diana British Information Service, New York diatom CDB dibble CC Charles Dickens BA Emily Dickinson HPSM Babe Didrikson WWP diesel engine TG dig Comstock - Georg Gerster digestive system LC dihedral angle TG dikdik AA - D. Fawcett dill GEP Joe DiMaggio BA dingo PR - Des Bartlett Dionysus MMA, Purchase, Joseph Pulitzer Bequest, 1955 (55.1.5) dirndl Austrian National Tourist Office dirt bike GP - Mark Stoddard disc brake TG disc jockey PR - Spencer Grant discus SB - Barbara Alper dish antenna National Center for Atmospheric Research, National Science Foundation dislocate Martin M. Rotker, Deltona, Florida/Martin M. Rotker, Deltona, Florida Walt Disney WWP Benjamin Disraeli BA distaff BA distillation LC diver EPJCo. divi-divi CC DNA LC Doberman pinscher ES dobsonfly CDB dock[1] SB - Peter Vandermark dodecagon LC dodecahedron TG Charles Dodgson HPSM dodo TG dogtooth CC dogwood GEP dolphin EPJCo. domino[1] LW - Oscar Palmquist donkey PI - Jerry Howard donor PR - Christopher Morrow Dorado TG Doric order LC dormer HPSM dory[1] Mystic Seaport Museum, Inc. All rights reserved. double bass Jeroboam, Inc. - Emilio A. Mercado double-decker TSI - Michael Bertan double dutch SB - Gale Zucker doublet Yale Center for British Art, Paul Mellon Collection Frederick Douglass Sophia Smith Collection, Smith College dovetail TG downspout LW - Oscar Palmquist Draco[2] TG draft AA - Harry Cutting/PI - Jerry Howard dragonfly CDB dragon tree CC Sir Francis Drake LOC drawknife GEP dreadnought GHP - Alan Pitcairn dredge KAMD dreidel PI - Martin Miller drill press LW - Oscar Palmquist dromedary NYZS drop leaf From the collections of Henry Ford Museum & Greenfield Village, neg. no. B25492 W.E.B. Du Bois BA ducking stool HPSM Daphne du Maurier WWP dumbwaiter BA dummy PC - Steve Takatsuno Isadora Duncan BA dune buggy SB - Virginia L. Blaisdell dunk shot PR - Jim Zerschling Jimmy Durante WWP Albrecht Dürer BA Dutchman's breeches LC Dutch oven PI - Karen Bussolini 'Papa Doc' Duvalier BA Mary Dyer Margaret Anne Miles ear LC Amelia Earhart WWP earwig CDB easel SB - Barbara Alper Easter Island Comstock - Richard Harrington George Eastman WWP eaves PI - Martin Miller eccentric TG echeveria CC echidna NYZS Mary Baker Eddy LOC edelweiss LC Gertrude Ederle BA Thomas Edison Snark - Art Resource, New York Edward VIII Globe Photos, Inc. - Camera Press eel CDB egg-and-dart CC eggplant CC Albert Einstein HPSM Dwight D. Eisenhower Dwight D. Eisenhower Library - U.S. Navy Mamie Eisenhower Dwight D. Eisenhower Library eland San Diego Zoo Eleanor of Aquitaine Walters Art Gallery, Baltimore, Maryland electric guitar Comstock - Russ Kinne electrocardiogram Martin M. Rotker, Deltona, Florida electrocardiograph SB - Paul Fortin electromagnetic spectrum TG elephant AA - Leonard Lee Rue III/AA - Irene Vandermolen George Eliot Sophia Smith Collection, Smith College Elizabeth II GP ellipsoid TG emblem WWP embroidery LW - Oscar Palmquist Empire © The Frick Collection, New York/From the collections of Henry Ford Museum & Greenfield Village, neg. no. B49284 enamel LC encaustic Virginia Museum of Fine Arts, The Adolph D. and Wilkins C. Williams Fund endive CC endocrine gland LC Friedrich Engels BA English saddle GEP English setter TSI - Leonard Lee Rue III entablature CC eohippus LC epaulet Culver Pictures Inc. epicycloid TG Jacob Epstein WWP equator LC equestrian PR - Richard Dibon-Smith Erasmus LOC Erlenmeyer flask EPJCo. eruption EPJCo. escalator SB - Peter Menzel/TG escapement CC escritoire Courtesy, Museum of Fine Arts, Boston, Forsyth Wicks Collection escutcheon GEP étagère Courtesy, Museum of Fine Arts, Boston, H.E. Bolles Fund eucalyptus LC Eugénie LOC Chris Evert WWP ewer MMA, Rogers Fund, 1944 (44.15) expansion bolt LC expressionism NGA, Smithsonian Institution, Washington, D.C., Rosenwald Collection exterior angle TG extinguisher PI - Jerry Howard extravehicular activity NASA - Lyndon B. Johnson Space Center eye LC eye chart HPSM eyelet SB - T.A. Rothschild eyespot WWP eyestalk PR - Jen & Des Bartlett facemask PC - Rick Friedman/ Comstock - Steve Martson fairlead KAMD fairy shrimp CDB falchion MMA, Gift of Mrs. K.H. Schmidt, 1937 (37.186.1) fallow deer PR - Leonard Lee Rue III fan[1] © 1989 Denver Art Museum fang PR - Leonard Lee Rue III fantail Comstock - Russ Kinne farkleberry GEP Fannie Farmer BA farthingale MMA, Irene Lewisohn Bequest, 1962 fasces GEP faucet GEP William Faulkner WWP fault LC Faust BA feather CDB featherstitch GEP Federal Courtesy, Winterthur Museum fedora The Granger Collection, New York feedbag EPJCo. felucca PR - Chester Higgins, Jr. femur LC fender SB - Ákos Szilvasi fennel CC ferret[1] WWP - National Geographic Society Ferris wheel Chicago Historical Society, neg. no. ICHi-02442 ferrule LC fess[1] GEP festoon LC fetlock GEP fibula LC fid Mystic Seaport Museum, Inc. All rights reserved. fiddlehead PR - Hugh Spencer Arthur Fiedler WWP field hockey SB - Jean-Claude Lejeune fig[1] CDB figurehead SB - Jeff Albertson figure skating WWP filigree LW - Oscar Palmquist Millard Fillmore LOC fingerprint EPJCo. Vigdís Finnbogadóttir WWP fire ant CDB fire tower SB - Bohdan Hrynewych firkin Hancock Shaker Village, Pittsfield, Massachusetts - Paul Rocheleau fish CDB fisherman's knot TG fish ladder PR - H.B. Carr Ella Fitzgerald BA F. Scott Fitzgerald BA flagellum CDB flagon Yale University Art Gallery, Gift of Mr. Donald R. Hyde flamenco PC - Jeffrey Dunn flamingo CC flange CC flask The Museum of Fine Arts, Houston, Museum purchase with funds provided by Dr. and Mrs. John R. Kelsey, Jr. flatboat LOC flatworm CDB flax CC flèche Art Resource, New York fleur-de-lis SCALA - Art Resource, New York flintlock MMA, Gift of Wilfred Wood, 1956 (42.22) floe PR - George Holton floppy disk PI - Jerry Howard flotilla Official U.S. Navy Photograph - PHz Robert D. Bunge fluke[2] CDB fluorescent lamp LC flute PI - Jerry Howard fluting SB - Frank Wing flycatcher PR - Peter & Stephen Maslowski flying bridge SB - Dean Abramson flying buttress PR - Omikron flying squirrel Leonard Rue Enterprises - Leonard Lee Rue III foil[3] PC - Jeffrey Dunn folding door GEP folium TG Henry Fonda GP fondue SB - Owen Franken font[1] Comstock - Russ Kinne food processor PI - Jerry Howard fool's cap GEP footbridge Comstock - Michael S. Thompson footpath Comstock - Stuart Cohen footrope PC - Jonathan Goell forceps LC Betty Ford WWP Gerald Ford LOC forehand Frank Siteman foreshorten Alinari - Art Resource, New York forklift EPJCo. fossil GHP - Runk & Schoenberger Stephen Foster National Portrait Gallery, Smithsonian Institution, Washington, D.C. - Art Resource, New York Foucault pendulum PR - J.J. Barton fountain Image Photos - Clemens Kalischer fourposter Image Photos - Clemens Kalischer foxglove LC fracture LC Jean Fragonard HPSM Francis I Cincinnati Art Museum, Bequest of Mary M. Emery, © Forth 1/82 (1927.384) Francis Ferdinand BA Benjamin Franklin National Portrait Gallery, Smithsonian Institution, Washington, D.C., Gift of the Morris and Gwendolyn Cafritz Foundation Franklin stove CC freesia LC French curve GEP French door Palmer/Brilliant, Boston, Massachusetts French horn PR - John Bova French knot GEP fret[3] LC Sigmund Freud HPSM frieze[1] CC frigate PC - Jaye R. Phillips/WWP fringe PI - Karen Bussolini frog BA frustum LC f-stop TG Carlos Fuentes GP - Reg Gray funicular BA fur seal PR - Jen & Des Bartlett fuse[2] LC futon LW - Oscar Palmquist futurism The Museum of Modern Art, New York, Acquired through the Lillie P. Bliss Bequest. gable roof BA gaff[1] LC Yuri Gagarin LOC Thomas Gainsborough HPSM galaxy Lick Observatory Photograph Galileo LOC gambrel roof USDA gamopetalous GEP Indira Gandhi BA Mahatma Gandhi WWP Federico García Lorca GP James A. Garfield LOC gargoyle SB - Barbara Alper Giuseppe Garibaldi New York Public Library gas mask SB - Lionel Delevingne gas turbine TG gate[1] HAR gatehouse EPJCo. gauntlet[1] BA gaur NYZS gavel[1] EPJCo. gecko GHP - Hal Harrison Lou Gehrig WWP Gemini TG gemsbok SB - Ira Kirschenbaum Genghis Khan The Granger Collection, New York geode GHP geodesic dome Jeroboam, Inc. - Ilka Hartman Saint George Yale University Art Gallery, Purchased by the University, from James Jackson Jarves George III LOC German shepherd ES Geronimo National Portrait Gallery, Smithsonian Institution, Washington, D.C. George and Ira Gershwin WWP geta LW - Oscar Palmquist geyser Russell A. Thompson gibbon PR - Arthur W. Ambler Gibson girl BA Gila monster AA - Miriam Austerman gimbal TG gimlet LC gingko CC giraffe AA - Leonard Lee Rue III girandole Photograph © 1991, The Art Institute of Chicago. All rights reserved. Gift of the Antiquarian Society, Jesse Spalding Landon Fund (1952.169) glass blowing EPJCo. John Glenn NASA globe EPJCo. glockenspiel PC - Carol Palmer glove LC glowworm CDB glyph LOC/LOC gnu PR - Clem Haagner goalkeeper PC - J.D. Sloan goblet Jewish Museum - Art Resource, New York goggles SB - Jonathan Rawle golden eagle United States Dept. of the Interior - Karl H. Maslowski golf HAR gondola PC - Franz Kraus gonfalon SB - Mike Mazzaschi goose SB - Lionel J-M Delevingne goose step Comstock - Robert Houser Mikhail Gorbachev BA Gorgon BA gorilla PR - Arthur W. Ambler goshawk PR - G. Ronald Austing Gothic SB - Owen Franken gouge LC Francisco Goya LOC graben GEP graffito E.P. Jones Company EPJCo. graft[1] LC grain elevator GHP Grand Canyon EPJCo. grand piano BA Ulysses S. Grant LOC grape LC grapeshot KAMD grapple PC - Jeffrey Dunn grasshopper LC grater LW - Oscar Palmquist gray wolf AA - Pat Crowe great seal The White House Great Wall of China WWP El Greco Brown Brothers greyhound BA griffin The Nelson-Atkins Museum of Art, Kansas City, Missouri, Nelson Fund 47-47 D.W. Griffith WWP grindstone LW - Oscar Palmquist groin CDB grotesque Alinari - Art Resource, New York Grus TG gueridon White House Historical Association Guernsey[2] GHP guide dog PC - Spencer Grant guinea fowl PR - R. Van Nostrand guitar SB - Elizabeth Crews gullwing © 1991 Judith Winters/Gullwing Service Company, Inc., Essex, Mass. Johann Gutenberg LOC gypsy moth BA gyroscope GHP - Runk & Schoenberger hacksaw PC - Frank Siteman Hadrian Giraudon - Art Resource, New York hadrosaur TG haku Comstock - Richard Harrington halberd MMA, Gift of Mary Alice Dyckman Dean, in memory of Alexander McMillan Welch, 1949 (49.120.12) Edmund Halley LOC Halley's comet WWP halo LOC halter[1] GHP hame KAMD hammer CC Hampshire Ewing Galloway George Frederick Handel LOC hand press LOC hang glider WWP hansom Shelburne Museum, Shelburne, Vermont **hardhat** LW - Aldo Mastrocola **Florence Harding** LOC **Warren G. Harding** LOC **hardy**[2] GEP **hare** AA - Robert Maier **harp** Lyon & Healy Harps, Inc., Chicago, Illinois/GEP **Benjamin Harrison**[2] LOC **George Harrison** BA **William Henry Harrison** LOC **hartebeest** San Diego Zoo - Ron Garrison **hatchet** National Museum of American History, Smithsonian Institution, Washington, D.C. **Hatshepsut** MMA, Museum Excavations 1926–1928, Rogers Fund, 1931 (31.3.163) **hauberk** HPSM **havelock** GEP **Nathaniel Hawthorne** LOC **Rutherford B. Hayes** LOC **headdress** SB - Ira Kirschenbaum/SB - John Running **headset** PI - Jerry Howard **headstand** SB - Elizabeth Hamlin **heart** LC **hedgehog** PR - Eric Hosking **Jascha Heifetz** WWP **Heimlich maneuver** LC **helicopter** Comstock - Russ Kinne **helix** TG **hellebore** CC **helmet** PC - Paul Nurnberg/ SLAM, Museum Purchase **Ernest Hemingway** GP - Hy Simon **hemlock** CC **Jimi Hendrix** BA **Henry VIII** LOC **Hercules** Courtesy, Museum of Fine Arts, Boston, Perkins Collection/TG **Woody Herman** BA **heron** PR - Allan D. Cruickshank **heterocercal** CDB **hex sign** GHP **Thor Heyerdahl** GP **hibiscus** CC **Wild Bill Hickok** BA **hieroglyphic** Marburg - Art Resource, New York **high-hat cymbal** LW - Oscar Palmquist **high jump** SB - Barbara Alper **high relief** Courtesy Museum of Fine Arts, Boston **hinge** GEP **Hirohito** BA **hitch** TG **Alfred Hitchcock** BA **Adolf Hitler** HPSM **hoe** LC **holly** LC **Oliver Wendell Holmes** Sophia Smith Collection, Smith College **Holstein**[2] GHP **Homburg** BA **Winslow Homer** BA **homocercal** CDB **homolosine projection** TG **honeycomb** AA - Stephen Dalton **hoof** GEP **hoopoe** NYZS **Herbert Hoover** LOC **Lou Hoover** LOC **hopper** LW - Oscar Palmquist **hornbill** PR - Jen & Des Bartlett **Lena Horne** WWP **Vladimir Horowitz** Archive Photos **horse chestnut** LC **horst** GEP **hot dog** PR - Bill Bachman **Harry Houdini** LOC **hound's-tongue** CDB **houndstooth check** LW - Oscar Palmquist **hourglass** EPJCo. **Sam Houston** International Museum of Photography at George Eastman House, neg. no. 25540 **huarache** PI - Jerry Howard **Henry Hudson** WWP **Langston Hughes** National Portrait Gallery, Smithsonian Institution, Washington, D.C., © 1981 Center for Creative Photography, Arizona Board of Regents **hula** GP - Ric Robinson **humerus** CC **hummingbird** AA - Len Rue, Jr. **hurdle** WWP **hurdy-gurdy** Courtesy, Museum of Fine Arts, Boston, Mary Smith Fund **hurricane lamp** EPJCo. **Hussein** BA **Aldous Huxley** WWP **hydra** PR - Omikron **hydrant** LW - © 1989 Aldo Mastrocola **hydroelectric** TG **hyena** NYZS **hyoid** LC **hyperbola** LC **hyperboloid** TG **hyperopia** CDB **hypocycloid** TG **hypotenuse** LC **hyrax** PR - Jen & Des Bartlett **ibis** AA - C.C. Lockwood **Henrik Ibsen** HPSM **iceboat** HAR **ice hockey** SB - Frank Siteman **ichthyosaur** TG **icosahedron** TG **idle wheel** GEP **Ignatius of Loyola** BA **iguana** AA - Len Rue, Jr. **iguanodon** TG **ikebana** © 1991 Judith Winters **ileum** CC **illumination** MMA, The Cloisters Collection, 1954 (54.1.2) **imbricate** SB - Owen Franken **impala** AA - Len Rue, Jr. **impatiens** CC **imperial** Culver Pictures Inc. **implosion** PC - George Mars Cassidy **impressionism** © The Frick Collection, New York **incandescent lamp** LC **incuse** SB - James R. Holland **Indian club** LW - Oscar Palmquist **Indian tobacco** CDB **Indra** BA **infanta** Marburg - Art Resource, New York **inflatable** PR - Herman Emmet **inflorescence** GEP **Jean Auguste Dominique Ingres** HPSM **inhaler** LW - Oscar Palmquist **initial** BA **inky cap** GEP **inlay** Deborah Buckley **Innocent III** BA **Ismet Inönü** WWP **inro** Cummer Gallery of Art, Jacksonville, Florida **instrument panel** PC - Frank Siteman **intarsia** SEF - Art Resource, New York **intercept** TG **internal-combustion engine** LC **intestine** LC **inverness** The Granger Collection, New York **involute** TG **io moth** AA - Stan Schroeder **Eugène Ionesco** BA - John Foraste **Ionic order** LC **Irish moss** GEP **Irish setter** ES **Irish wolfhound** ES **ironwork** SB - Mike Mazzaschi **Washington Irving** National Portrait Gallery, Smithsonian Institution, Washington, D.C. **Isabella I** The Granger Collection, New York **Isis**[1] HPSM **issuant** GEP **ivory** MMA, The Michael C. Rockefeller Memorial Collection, Gift of Nelson A. Rockefeller, 1972 (1978.412.323) **ivy** PI - Jerry Howard **jackal** AA - Leonard Lee Rue III **Andrew Jackson** LOC **Jesse Jackson** BA **jaguar** San Diego Zoo **jai alai** BA **jalousie** LW - © 1989 S.E. Byrne **Japanese beetle** CDB **jasmine** CC **javelin** SB - Jean-Claude Lejeune **Thomas Jefferson** LOC **jejunum** CC **jellyfish** GHP - Runk & Schoenberger **Jersey** LW - © 1989 Feza D. Oktay **Jerusalem artichoke** CC **jet engine** CC **jib**[1] TG **jimsonweed** CC **jinriksha** Hong Kong Tourist Association **Joan of Arc** Giraudon - Art Resource, New York **jodhpurs** Palmer/Brilliant, Boston, Massachusetts **Andrew Johnson** National Portrait Gallery, Smithsonian Institution, Washington, D.C. **Lady Bird Johnson** GP **Lyndon B. Johnson** BA **joist** LC **Jolly Roger** LC **jonquil** LC **Chief Joseph** National Anthropological Archives at the National Museum of Natural History, Smithsonian Institution, Washington, D.C. **James Joyce** The Granger Collection, New York **Juan Carlos** GP - Richard Open **judo** HPSM **jumping jack** Museum of the City of New York, Gift of Dewitt Clinton Cohen (35.248.14) **Carl Jung** Mary Evans Picture Library - Photo Researchers, Inc. **juniper** CC **junk**[2] HPSM **Jupiter** NASA **Justinian I** BA **kachina** PC - Jon Goell **kaffiyeh** PC - Jeffrey Dunn **kalimba** LW - Oscar Palmquist **Kamehameha I** National Portrait Gallery, Smithsonian Institution, Washington, D.C., Gift of the Bernice Pauahi Bishop Museum **karate** SB - James R. Holland **katydid** PR - John R. Clawson **kazoo** GEP **Buster Keaton** WCFTR **Helen Keller** The Schlesinger Library, Radcliffe College **kelp** LC **Jacqueline Kennedy** BA **John F. Kennedy** GP **kepi** Jeroboam, Inc. - Jeffrey Blankfort **kettledrum** Comstock - Russ Kinne **keystone** CDB **Nikita Khrushchev** United Nations **kickboxing** PC - Lauren Lantos **killdeer** Leonard Rue Enterprises - Leonard Lee Rue III **kiln** SB - J. Berndt **kilt** LW - Oscar Palmquist **kimono** WWP **king** GEP **Martin Luther King, Jr.** BA **king post** TG **kinkajou** NYZS **kiosk** SB - Owen Franken **Henry Kissinger** GP - Jeff Taylor **kiwi** PR - R. Van Nostrand/ CC **Paul Klee** BA **knight** GEP **knit** LC **knot**[1] TG/PC - Frank Siteman **John Knox** BA **koala** HAR **kookaburra** AA - Ann Sanfedele **Kublai Khan** LOC **Kufic** LOC **kumquat** LC **kylix** Museum of Fine Arts, Boston, William E. Nickerson Fund **labyrinth** Comstock - Georg Gerster **lacrosse** SB - Bruce M. Wellman **ladder-back** Yale University Art Gallery, The Mabel Brady Garvan Collection **ladybug** CDB **Marquis de Lafayette** National Portrait Gallery, Smithsonian Institution, Washington, D.C. **lag screw** CC **lamb** PR - Arthur W. Ambler **lamprey** PR - Karl H. Maslowski/CDB **lancet window** CC **landau** Shelburne Museum, Shelburne, Vermont **Lillie Langtry** WCFTR **lantern wheel** GEP **lap joint** TG **large intestine** LC **largemouth bass** PR - Treat Davidson **La Salle** LOC **Lascaux** PR - J.J. Languepin **laser** LC **last**[3] Palmer/Brilliant, Boston, Massachusetts **lateen** CC **Latin cross** GEP **lattice** Image Photos - Clemens Kalischer **launch pad** NASA **laver**[1] MMA, The Cloisters Collection (47.101.56 a,b) **Antoine Lavoisier** MMA, Purchase, Mr. and Mrs. Charles Wrightsman Gift, 1977 (1977.10) **T.E. Lawrence** GP **lazy tongs** LC **leaf** LC **leaf spring** CC **leatherback** HPSM **Leda** MMA, Wildenstein Fund, 1970 (1970.140) **Le Duc Tho** BA **Robert E. Lee** LOC **leeboard** CC **leg-of-mutton** HPSM **leg warmer** LW - Oscar Palmquist **lemur** AA - George Roos **Vladimir Lenin** WWP **John Lennon** GP - Tom Hanley **lens** LC **Leo** TG **Leonardo da Vinci** BA **lesser celandine** CC **levee**[1] LOC **lever** LC **Meriwether Lewis** Independence National Historical Park **Libra** TG **lichen** PR - Jack Dermid **lierne** CC **life jacket** SB - George Bellerose **ligature** TG **lighthouse** GHP - Hal Harrison **lightning** AA - Michael Fredericks, Jr. **Liliuokalani** National Portrait Gallery, Smithsonian Institution, Washington, D.C., Gift of the Bernice Pauahi Bishop Museum **lily pad** PI - Jerry Howard **limpet** GEP **Abraham Lincoln** LOC **Mary Todd Lincoln** LOC **Charles Lindbergh** LOC **linden** CC **lion** AA - Len Rue, Jr. **Franz Liszt** HPSM **litchi** LC **live oak** CC **liver**[1] LC **llama** HPSM **loblolly pine** CC **lobster pot** Frank Siteman **lock**[1] LC/EPJCo. **John Locke** BA **locomotive** PC - William A. Todd, Jr. **locust** GP - Anthony Bannister/LC **loganberry** LC **Lombardy poplar** CC **Henry Wadsworth Longfellow** National Portrait Gallery, Smithsonian Institution, Washington, D.C. **longhorn** PR - Clint Grant **long jump** Jeroboam, Inc. - Cheryl A. Traendly **loom**[2] Comstock - Stuart Cohen **loon**[1] Cornell Laboratory of Ornithology - Grimes **loosestrife** CC **loquat** CC **lorgnette** BA **lotus** PI - Jerry Howard **lotus position** SB - Jean-Claude Lejeune **Louis XIV** Giraudon - Art Resource, New York **Juliette Low** BA **lowboy** From the collections of Henry Ford Museum & Greenfield Village, neg. no. A3837 **low relief** The Nelson-Atkins Museum of Art, Kansas City, Missouri, Nelson Fund **Clare Boothe Luce** WWP **Henry Luce** WWP **luna moth** CDB **lune** TG **luster** The Currier Gallery of Art, Manchester, New Hampshire, The Murray Collection of Glass (1974.45.1-.2) **lute**[1] Courtesy, Museum of Fine Arts, Boston, Leslie Lindsey Mason Fund **Martin Luther** Alinari - Art Resource, New York **lynx** AA - Leonard Lee Rue III **Lyra** TG **lyre** Courtesy, Museum of Fine Arts, Boston, William Francis Warden Fund (62.362) **Douglas MacArthur** HPSM **Niccolò Machiavelli** BA **machicolation** CC **mackerel** CC **Dolley Madison** LOC **James Madison** LOC **madroña** CC **Magen David** SB - Richard Sobol **magic square** TG **magnetic field** GHP - Runk & Schoenberger **magpie** PR - Allan D. Cruickshank **maidenhair fern** CDB **mainspring** LC **maintop** SB - Frances M. Cox **majolica** SLAM, Museum Purchase **major scale** TG **malamute** ES **Malcolm X** BA **mammoth** Tech-Graphics TG **Manchester terrier** ES **manchineel** GEP **mandala** Los Angeles County Museum of Art, From the Nasli and Alice Heeramaneck Collection, Museum Associates Purchase **mandarin duck** AA - Leonard Lee Rue IV **Nelson Mandela** GP - Jan Kopec **mandolin** Courtesy, Museum of Fine Arts, Boston, Leslie Lindsey Mason Collection **mangle**[2] KAMD **manhole** SB - Rudolph Robinson **manometer** TG **mansard** LW - © 1990 S.E. Byrne **mantel** SB - Peter Southwick **manual alphabet** TG **Mao Zedong** WWP **marabou** PR - Arthur W. Ambler **maraca** LW - © 1990 S.E. Byrne **Jean Paul Marat** Giraudon - Art Resource, New York **Marcel Marceau** WCFTR **Margrethe II** GP - Camera Press **mariachi** SB - Jean-Claude Lejeune **Marie Antoinette** Walters Art Gallery, Baltimore, Maryland **marionette** Courtesy of Cooper-Hewitt National Museum of Design, Smithsonian Institution - Art Resource, New York **markhor** San Diego Zoo - Ron Garrison **marmot** Comstock - Phyllis Greenberg **marquee** PI - Martin Miller **marquetry** Peter Vandermark **martlet** GEP **Marx Brothers** WCFTR **Mary Queen of Scots** MMA, Gift of J. Pierpont Morgan, 1917 (17.190.2) **mask** Cincinnati Art Museum, Gift of Dr. and Mrs. W.W. Seely **mast**[1] Courtesy of the Society for the Preservation of New England Antiquities, Boston, Massachusetts - N.L. Stebbins **mastaba** LC **mastiff** ES **matilija poppy** CC **Henri Matisse** WWP **Matterhorn** Swiss National Tourist Office **Somerset Maugham** WWP **mausoleum** SB - Ira Kirschenbaum **Maximilian** LOC **Mayan** PC - Cynthia W. Sterling **May apple** CC **Willie Mays** WWP **Paul McCartney** WWP **William McKinley** LOC **Margaret Mead** WWP **meadowlark** PR - Allan D. Cruickshank **meander** GHP **measure** TG **Mecca** Globe Photos, Inc. - Camera Press **medal** SB - James R. Holland **Lorenzo de Medici** National Gallery of Art, Smithsonian Institution, Washington, D.C., Samuel H. Kress Collection **medlar** LC **megakaryocyte** PR - Biophoto Assoc. **megaphone** SB - Arthur Grace **meiosis** CDB **Golda Meir** GP **Herman Melville** Bettmann Archive, Inc. BA **memorial** PC - Dennis MacDonald **meniscus** LC **menorah** Peter Vandermark **Mercury** Courtesy of The Bostonian Society and Old State House/NASA **merganser** TSI - Leonard Lee Rue III **meridian** TG **merlon** CC **mesa** SB - Ira Kirschenbaum **metacarpus** LC **metamorphosis** LC **metatarsus** LC **metate** NMAI - Edward H. Davis **metronome** LW - © 1990 S.E. Byrne **mews** Marilyn Root **Michelangelo** BA **micrometer**[1] GHP - Runk & Schoenberger **microreader** Russ Kinne **microscope** AA - George F. Godfrey **mihrab** Leo de Wys, Inc. - Alon Reininger **milestone** PI - Jerry Howard **milkweed** PI - Martin Miller **Edna Saint Vincent Millay** WWP **Glenn Miller** WWP **millinery** Palmer/Brilliant, Boston, Massachusetts **millipede** CDB **miniature** The Nelson-Atkins Museum of Art, Kansas City, Missouri, Gift of Mr. and Mrs. John W. Starr through the Starr Foundation **miniature golf** PI - Jerry Howard **minor scale** TG **minuteman** SB - Lionel J-M Delevingne **misericord** Marburg - Art Resource, New York **mission** Russell A. Thompson **mistletoe** LC **mitosis** CDB **François Mitterrand** WWP **mobcap** Collection of The J.B. Speed Art Museum, Louisville, Kentucky **mobile** Photograph © The Solomon R. Guggenheim Foundation, New York, Collection Mary Reynolds, Gift of her brother (FN54.1388) - Robert E. Mates **Möbius strip** LC **moccasin** NMAI **modular** Image Photos - Clemens Kalischer **mola**[1] LW - Jim Cronk **molar**[2] LC **moloch** CC **monarch butterfly** AA - Stan Schroeder **Thelonious Monk** WWP **monkey bars** Jeroboam, Inc. - Suzanne Arms **monkey wrench** CC **monocle** EPJCo. **monolith** PR - David Moore **James Monroe** LOC **monstrance** Courtesy of the Hispanic Society of America, New York City **Montezuma II** LOC **monument** HPSM **moon** Lick Observatory Photographs **moose** PR - Leonard Lee Rue III **moped** Palmer/Brilliant, Boston, Massachusetts **Sir Thomas More** © The Frick Collection, New York **morel** CDB **Morgan** American Morgan Horse Association, Inc. **Samuel F.B. Morse** LOC **Morse code** TG **mortarboard** PC - Kincra Clineff **Grandma Moses** GP **mosque** GP - Photo Trends **motorboat** EPJCo. **motorcycle** EPJCo. **motor scooter** Wolfgang Kaehler Photography **mountain ash** CDB **mouth** LC **Wolfgang Amadeus Mozart** GP **muff**[2] Culver Pictures Inc. **muffler** LC **mule**[1] PR - Joe Munroe **mummer** Palmer/Brilliant, Boston, Massachusetts **Edvard Munch** The Art Museum, Princeton University, Gift of James R. Epstein **mural** WWP **Musca** TG **musk ox** AA - Leonard Lee Rue III **Benito Mussolini** BA **mute** Peter Vandermark **myopia** CDB **nail** CC **Napoleon I** NGA, Samuel H. Kress Collection **narwhal** PR - Richard Ellis **Gamal Abdel Nasser** WWP **nasturtium** LC **nativity** NGA, Samuel H. Kress Collection **nautilus** GHP - Runk & Schoenberger **nave**[1] CC **nebula** Lick Observatory Photograph **neckerchief** Jeroboam, Inc. - Laimute Druskis **needle** LC **needlepoint** Allen Moore **Nefertiti** Art Resource, New York **nene** AA - Irene Vandermolen **neoclassicism** HPSM **Neptune**[1] BA/ NASA **nest** PR - Hal H. Harrison/Museum of Art, Rhode Island School of Design, Gift of Mrs. Harold Brown **netsuke** MMA, Rogers Fund, 1913 (13.67.52)/Cummer Gallery of Art, Jacksonville, Florida **neuron** LC **newel** TG/Allen Moore **Newfoundland**[2] ES **newt** PR - Treat Davidson **Isaac Newton** HPSM **Nicholas II** WWP **Jack Nicklaus** WWP **Friedrich Nietzsche** HPSM **Florence Nightingale** National Portrait Gallery, London **Nike** MMA, Rogers Fund, 1907 **nimbostratus** SB - George W. Gardner **Pat Nixon** LOC **Richard M. Nixon** GP - Larry Stevens **No**[1] Japan National Tourist Organization **Noah** The Pierpont Morgan Library, New York (PML 17593, July 1488, f.34r) **Norfolk Island pine** Comstock - Richard Harrington **noria** KAMD **Norway spruce** CDB **Norwegian elkhound** ES **nose** LC **Rudolf Nureyev** © 1986 Martha Swope, New York City **nut** LC **nuthatch** AA - Leonard Lee Rue III **nutmeg** LC **oasis** PR - E.A. Weber **obelisk** Margaret Anne Miles **oboe** Comstock - Russ Kinne **observatory** GHP - Runk & Schoenberger **obtuse angle** LC **ocarina** PI - Martin Miller **ocelot** NYZS **Sandra Day O'Connor** WWP **ocotillo** PR - Art Bilsten **octahedron** TG **octopus** GHP - Runk & Schoenberger **Oedipus** Alinari - Art Resource, New York **ogee** CC **okapi** PR - Frank Stevens **Georgia O'Keeffe** WWP **okra** LC **Old English sheepdog** AA - Terence A. Gili **olecranon** CDB **Laurence Olivier** The Granger Collection, New York **olla** Museum of Fine Arts, Houston, Gift of Miss Ima Hogg **omasum** CDB **Eugene O'Neill** WWP **onion** LC **open-hearth** TG **Ophiuchus** TG **ophthalmoscope** PC - Richard Wood **opium poppy** CC **opossum** GHP - Runk & Schoenberger **orach** *Field Guide to Wildflowers* by Roger Tory Peterson and Margaret McKenny. © 1968 by Roger Tory Peterson and Margaret McKenny. Reprinted by permission of Houghton Mifflin Company. All rights reserved. **orangutan** AA - Miriam Austerman **orb** Marburg - Art Resource, New York **orbicular** CC **organ** Comstock - Russ Kinne **organ-pipe cactus** GHP - John Colwell **oriel** SB - Ellis Herwig **Orion** TG **José Orozco** WWP **orrery** The Granger Collection, New York **José Ortega y Gasset** WWP **George Orwell** WWP **osprey** PR - Jen & Des Bartlett **ostrich** AA - Stewart D. Halperin **ostrich fern** CC **otter** San Diego Zoo **ottoman** High Museum of Art, Atlanta, Georgia, Virginia Carroll Crawford Collection (1981.1000.42) **outboard motor** Jeroboam, Inc. - Laimute Druskis **outrigger** Wolfgang Kaehler Photography **overalls** SB - Jeffry W. Myers **overpass** HPSM **Jesse Owens** BA **owl** PR - Karl H. Maslowski **ox** PR - Tom McHugh **Seiji Ozawa** BA **pacemaker** SB - Harry Wilks **paddle**[1] LC **paddy** BA **pagoda** SCALA - Art Resource, New York **Mohammed Reza Pahlavi** WWP **paisley** Allen Moore **palapa** Comstock - Richard Harrington **pale**[1] GEP **palette** PR - David M. Grossman **Palladian**[2] SEF - Art Resource, New York **pallet**[1] PC - Spencer Grant **palmate** CC **Olaf Palme** WWP **palmette** Alinari - Art Resource, New York **Pan** © 1898 *Bulfinch's Age of Fable or Beauties of Mythology* **pancreas** LC **panda** GP - Popperfoto **Pangaea** TG **panpipe** GEP **Pantheon** Alinari - Art Resource, New York **papaya** CC **papillote** CC **parabola** LC **paraboloid** TG **parachute** GHP **parallax** CC **paramecium** CDB **parasol** GP - Alex Waskinski **parbuckle** CC **parget** BA **Rosa Parks** BA **parquetry** Comstock - Russ Kinne **Catherine Parr** National Portrait Gallery, London **parsnip** CC **parterre** BA **Parthenon** Marburg - Art Resource, New York **partisan**[2] MMA, Gift of William H. Riggs, 1913 (14.25.454) **Blaise Pascal** Giraudon - Art Resource, New York **passant** GEP **passionflower** LC **Louis Pasteur** HPSM **pasture** PI - Jerry Howard **patchwork** SB - Peter Southwick **patella** LC **patriarchal cross** GEP **Linus Pauling** Archive Photos **Luciano Pavarotti** GP - Jane Bown **pavis** MMA, Rogers Fund, 1923 (23.42.2) **Anna Pavlova** BA **Pavo** TG **pawl** LC **pawn**[2] GEP **peacock** PR - Arthur W. Ambler **pear** LC **Robert E. Peary** National Portrait Gallery, Smithsonian Institution, Washington, D.C. **peavey** GEP **peccary** PR - Leonard Lee Rue III **Pegasus** National Museum of American History, Smithsonian Institution, Washington, D.C., National Numismatics Collection **pelican** AA - Irene Vandermolen **peltate** CC **pelvis** LC **pendentive** CDB **pendulum** GEP **William Penn** The Historical Society of Pennsylvania **pentagon** LC/WWP **pepper** LC **peppermint** CDB **peregrine falcon** PR - G. Ronald Austing **pergola** LW - Oscar Palmquist **Pericles** Alinari - Art Resource, New York **periodical cicada** PR - Alvin E. Staffan **peristyle** CC **periwinkle**[2] CC **Frances Perkins** HPSM **Persian cat** PR - Ylla **persimmon** LC **peruke** Worcester Art Museum, Worcester, Massachusetts **pestle** BA **Peter the Great** The Granger Collection, New York **Petrarch** Alinari - Art Resource, New York **petri dish** PC - Tom McHugh **petroglyph** GHP - Alan Pitcairn **pew** EPJCo. **phaeton** Shelburne Museum, Shelburne, Vermont **phalanx** LC **pheasant** AA - Robert Maier **Prince Philip** GP - John Lawrence **phlox** GEP **phoenix** BA **phonograph** From the collections of Henry Ford Museum & Greenfield Village, neg. no. B67920 **photoelectric cell** TG

phylactery LOC **Edith Piaf** BA **piano[1]** Steinway & Sons, New York **Pablo Picasso** BA **pickax** GEP **Mary Pickford** GP **pier** GHP - Runk & Schoenberger/PI - Jerry Howard **Franklin Pierce** LOC **pietà** LOC **pike[2]** PR - Tom McHugh **pilaster** PC - Jeffrey Dunn **pillory** EPJCo. **piñata** PI - Jerry Howard **pince-nez** BA **pine[1]** CC **pineapple** LC **pinnace** Peabody Museum of Salem, Massachusetts - Mark Sexton **pintail** AA - Leonard Lee Rue III **pinto** Comstock - Russ Kinne **piolet** PR - Rapho Agence **pipeline** GHP **pipkin** Museum of the City of New York, Gift of Mrs. Thomas K. Gale - John Parnell **piranha** PR - John H. Gerard **Pisces** TG **Piscis Austrinus** TG **pistachio** LC **pistil** LC **pitcher plant** CC **pith helmet** PI - Martin Miller **Francisco Pizarro** The Granger Collection, New York **placard** PR - Barbara Rios **plaid** LW - © 1990 S.E. Byrne **plane[2]** PC - Frank Siteman **planetary nebula** Lick Observatory Photograph **plastron** Comstock - M. Stuckey **Sylvia Plath** Sophia Smith Collection, Smith College **Plato** BA **platypus** CDB **player piano** Marilyn Root **Pleiades** Lick Observatory Photograph **plexor** PI - Jerry Howard **pliers** CC **plinth** PC - Jeffrey Dunn **plover** AA - M. Krishnan **plow** GHP/USDA - John McConnell **plunger** GEP **plus fours** PR **Plymouth Rock** GHP - John Colwell **Pocahontas** LOC **pocketknife** LW - © 1990 S.E. Byrne **podium** PI - Jerry Howard **pointer** PR - Stan Wayman **pointillism** Giraudon - Art Resource, New York **poison ivy** LC **Poland China** GHP - John Colwell **polar bear** Leonard Rue Enterprises - Leonard Lee Rue III **pole vault** SB - George Bellerose **James K. Polk** LOC **polo** SB - Pamela Schuyler **Polyphemus** Courtesy, Museum of Fine Arts, Boston, Gift in honor of Edward W. Forbes from his friends (63.120) **polyphemus moth** CDB **pomegranate** LC **Pomeranian** AA - Paula Wright **Madame de Pompadour** Portland Art Museum, Portland, Oregon **pop art** The Museum of Modern Art, New York, Philip Johnson Fund. **poppy** CC **porcupine** PR - Des Bartlett **porcupine fish** PR - Omnikron **porringer** Gift of Mrs. L.A. di Zarega - John Parnell **portcullis** CC **Portuguese man-of-war** GHP - Runk & Schoenberger **potato** LC **potbelly stove** EPJCo. **potter's wheel** PR - Fritz Henle **powder horn** MMA, Gift of Mrs. J.H. Grenville, 1940 (40.105) **prairie dog** AA - Harry Engels **prayer rug** SLAM, Gift of James F. Ballard **prayer wheel** Collection of The Newark Museum, Purchase 1971, C. Suydam Cutting Endowment Fund - Bob Hanson **praying mantis** CDB **pre-Columbian** MMA, The Michael C. Rockefeller Memorial Collection, Bequest of Nelson A. Rockefeller, 1979 (1979.206.497) **prefab** PI - Jerry Howard **prehensile** AA - Leonard Lee Rue III **Pre-Raphaelite** The Art Museum, Princeton University, Museum Purchase, Surdna Fund **present arms** Official U.S. Navy Photograph - PHC Kirby Harrison **Elvis Presley** GP - Rangefinders **Leontyne Price** BA **pricket** MMA, The Cloisters Collection (55.40.1) **prickly pear** GEP **prie-dieu** Lloyd's Woodworking, Inc. **printed circuit** PR - Robert A. Isaacs **proboscis** AA - Leonard Lee Rue III **profile** NGA **Prohibition** LOC **prominence** PR - Science Source **promontory** GHP - Alan Pitcairn **pronghorn** AA - Tom Edwards **propeller** National Center for Atmospheric Research, National Science Foundation **prop root** LC **prospector** SB - Peter Southwick **prosthesis** BA **protozoan** GHP - Runk & Schoenberger **protractor** TG **prow** PI - Jerry Howard **ptarmigan** AA - Charles G. Summers, Jr. **pterodactyl** TG **pterygoid** LC **puffball** CDB **puffin** AA - Leonard Lee Rue III **pug[1]** PR - Mary Eleanor Browning **Joseph Pulitzer** Brown Brothers **pulpit** Jeroboam, Inc. - Frank Siteman **pump[1]** GEP **pumpkinseed** PR - Treat Davidson **punt[1]** Mystic Seaport Museum, Inc. All rights reserved. **punty** PR - Paolo Koch **pupa** CC **Puppis** TG **Purple Heart** Official U.S. Navy Photograph **pushup** PC - Spencer Grant **pussy willow** LC **pylon** CC **pyramid** SB - Peter Menzel **pyrrhuloxia** PR - Robert H. Wright **python** PR - Dade W. Thornton **pyx** MMA, The Cloisters Collection (54.117.3a,b) **quadriga** Wadsworth Atheneum, Hartford, Connecticut, Bequest of Mrs. Gurdon Trumbull **quagga** TG **quail[1]** TSI - Len Rue, Jr. **quarrel[2]** GEP **quarter horse** AA- George F. Godfrey **quatrefoil** PC - William A. Todd, Jr. **queen** GEP **Queen Anne** Museum of Fine Arts, Houston, The Bayou Bend Collection, Gift of Miss Ima Hogg **Queen Anne's lace** LC **quetzal** PR - Robert Hermes **quilt** © 1991 Judith Winters **quince** LC **Josiah Quincy** National Portrait Gallery, Smithsonian Institution, Washington, D.C., Gift of Mr. and Mrs. Paul Mellon **quipu** American Museum of Natural History, Courtesy Department of Library Services, neg. no. 321934 - Rota **quiver[2]** NMAI **quoin** CC **Ra[1]** Leo de Wys, Inc. - Gunter Reitz **rabbit** GHP **raccoon** American Museum of Natural History, Courtesy Department Library Services, neg. no. 336665 - Jim Coxe **Sergei Rachmaninoff** BA **racket[1]** LC **radial symmetry** GHP - Runk & Schoenberger **radiometer** Peter Vandermark **radio telescope** National Radio Astronomy Observatory, operated by Associated University, Inc., under cooperative agreement with the National Science Foundation **radish** LC **radius** LC **radula** PR - David M. Phillips **rafflesia** CDB **rainbow trout** GHP **rake[1]** CC **Sir Walter Raleigh** BA **Rameses II** The Granger Collection, New York **ramp[1]** SB - George W. Cardner **rampant** BA **Jeannette Rankin** Sophia Smith Collection, Smith College **rappel** EPJCo. **rasp** CC **Rasputin** BA **ratchet** LC **ratel** PR - Mark Boulton **rattlesnake** GHP - Hal Harrison **ray[2]** © 1991 by Sea World, Inc. **Nancy Reagan** GP - Lord Snowdon **Ronald Reagan** SB - Peter Southwick **reamer** CC/© 1991 Judith Winters **receptacle** LC **recorder** SB - Jean-Claude Lejeune **Red Cloud** Smithsonian Institution National Anthropological Archives, Bureau of American Ethnology Collection **red fox** PR - Leonard Lee Rue III **redingote** New York Public Library, Special Collections **red squirrel** PR - Leonard Lee Rue III **red-tailed hawk** National Agricultural Library, Forest Service Photo Collection **reed** EPJCo. **referee** PC - Henry Horenstein **refracting telescope** LC **register** EPJCo. **reindeer** NYZS **relay race** PR - Kenneth Murray **relief** Courtesy of The Oriental Institute of The University of Chicago/Virginia Museum of Fine Arts, Richmond, Purchase, The Williams Fund, 1960/MMA, Fletcher Fund, 1936 (36.11.1) **reliquary** SLAM, Museum Purchase **Rembrandt** BA **Frederic Remington** Courtesy of the R.W. Norton Art Gallery, Shreveport, Louisiana **remora** BA **reniform** CC **respiratory system** LC **rest[1]** TG **reticulum** CDB **retinoscope** LW - Oscar Palmquist **retort[2]** LC **revolver** LW - © 1990 Oscar Palmquist **revolving door** PC - Sarah Putnam **rhea** PR - Leonard Lee Rue III **rhesus monkey** AA - M. Krishnan **rhinoceros** PC - Lynn McLaren **Rhodesian ridgeback** ES **rhododendron** LC **rhombus** LC **rhubarb** CC **rib** LC **Richard the Lion-Hearted** PR - Fritz Henle **Richard III** BA **Duc de Richelieu** BA **Sally Ride** BA **rifle[1]** LW - © 1990 Oscar Palmquist **rig** PC - D.D. Morrison **rigging** GP - Camera Press **right angle** LC **Charles Ringling** HPSM **ring-necked pheasant** Comstock - Phyllis Greenberg **ringtail** PR - Jen & Des Bartlett **ripple[2]** KAMD **RNA** LC **roadrunner** PR - Allan D. Cruickshank **Paul Robeson** HPSM **Robespierre** Giraudon - Art Resource, New York **robin** Stephen J. Krasemann **Jackie Robinson** BA **robot** SB - Phyllis Graber Jensen **Norman Rockwell** SB - James R. Holland **rococo** MMA, Rogers Fund, 1927 (27.184.2-3) **rodeo** GHP **rolamite** TG **roller coaster** PC - Stanley Rowin **rolling mill** TG **rolling pin** SB - Joseph Schuyler **rook[2]** LC **Edith Roosevelt** BA **Eleanor Roosevelt** National Portrait Gallery, Smithsonian Institution, Washington, D.C., Bequest of Phyllis Fenner **Franklin D. Roosevelt** HPSM **Theodore Roosevelt** HPSM **rorqual** CDB **rose[1]** Massachusetts Historical Society **rosemary** CDB **rose window** BA **rottweiler** ES **rotunda** BA **rowel** CC **row house** Ewing Galloway **ruddy duck** PR - Len Rue, Jr. **Rugby shirt** LW - Oscar Palmquist **rumen** CDB **running board** BA **runway** SB - Arthur Grace **Mount Rushmore** GHP **rutabaga** GEP **Babe Ruth** BA **saber-toothed tiger** TG **sabot** BA **sacrum** LC **Anwar el-Sadat** BA **safety net** PR - Tom Hollyman **Sagittarius** TG **saguaro** AA - Leonard Lee Rue III **saiga** PR - Tom McHugh **Saint Andrew's cross** GEP **Saint Bernard** ES **Andrei Sakharov** BA **salamander** GHP - Hal Harrison **J.D. Salinger** WWP **sallet** SLAM, Museum Purchase **saltbox** LC **saltire** GEP **saluki** PR - Jeanne White **samara** CDB **samisen** BA **samovar** BA **sampan** SB - Ira Kirschenbaum **George Sand** LOC **Carl Sandburg** GP - Nat Dallinger **sand dollar** GHP - Runk & Schoenberger **sandwich board** PC - Gary Goodman **Margaret Sanger** BA **sansevieria** LC **Antonio López de Santa Anna** Courtesy of The New-York Historical Society, New York City **Santa Claus** Courtesy of The New-York Historical Society, New York City **sapsucker** PR - G. Ronald Austing **sari** HAR **sarong** TSI - Donald Smetzer **Jean Paul Sartre** PR - D. Berretty-Rapho **Saturn** NASA - Jet Propulsion Laboratory Photo **satyr** BA **sauropod** TG **Savonarola** SEF - Art Resource, New York **sawfish** PR - Karl H. Maslowski **sawfly** CDB **sawhorse** CC **saxophone** PC - J.D. Sloan **scaffold** GHP **scallop** PR - Jack Dermid/National Museum of American History, Smithsonian Institution, Washington D.C. **scalpel** EPJCo. **scapula** LC **scarecrow** EPJCo. **scarf[2]** GEP **scarlet tanager** PR - Karl H. & Stephen Maslowski **scepter** Chicago Historical Society **schipperke** ES **Helmut Schmidt** WWP **schnauzer** PR - Mary Eleanor Browning **schooner** SB - Fredrik D. Bodin **Franz Schubert** PR **scimitar** National Museum of American History, Smithsonian Institution, Washington, D.C. **scissors** LC **scoliosis** Peter Arnold, Inc. Dr. Freiburger **scoreboard** PC - Henry Horenstein **scorpion** CDB **Scorpius** TG **scotch[2]** LW - Oscar Palmquist **Dred Scott** Missouri Historical Society, neg. no. 001-007694 **screech owl** AA - Tom Edwards **screw** CC **scrimshaw** Mystic Seaport Museum, Inc. All rights reserved. **script** The Art Museum, Princeton University, Gift of John B. Elliott **scroll** SB - Virginia Blaisdell **scuba diver** HAR **scuffle[2]** CC **sculptor** SB - Bohdan Hrynewych **scythe** GHP **sea fan** HAR **sea horse** CDB **seal[1]** MMA, Bequest of A.T. Clearwater, 1933 **Sealyham terrier** American Sealyham Terrier Club **Elizabeth Seaman** Courtesy of The New-York Historical Society, New York City **sea turtle** © 1991 Sea World, Inc. **secant** TG **secretary** The Connecticut Historical Society, Hartford, Connecticut **secretary bird** PR - Jen & Des Bartlett **Seder** Palmer/Brilliant, Boston, Massachusetts **Andrés Segovia** GP - Richard Open **self-heal** *Field Guide to the Wildflowers* by Roger Tory Peterson and Margaret McKenny. © 1968 by Roger Tory Peterson and Margaret McKenny. Reprinted by permission of Houghton Mifflin Company. All rights reserved. **David O. Selznick** WWP **semidome** LC **sennit** KAMD **sentry box** HAR **sepal** LC **Sequoya** LOC **serape** PR - Carl Frank **seriema** PR - Arthur W. Ambler **serif** CC **serpent** Cincinnati Art Museum, Gift of William H. Doane (1914.228)/Walters Art Gallery, Baltimore, Maryland **serval** PR - Mark Boulton **sesame** CDB **sessile** CC **Elizabeth Seton** Mount St. Vincent-on-Hudson, Sisters of Charity Center, Bronx, New York **settee** The Baltimore Museum of Art, Gift of Lydia Howard de Roth and Nancy H. De Ford Venable, in memory of their mother, Lydia Howard De Ford; and Purchase Fund **settle** The Connecticut Historical Society, Hartford, Connecticut **Sèvres** Huntington Library **sexpartite** CDB **sextant** LC **Anne Sexton** WWP **Jane Seymour** The Granger Collection, New York **shadoof** KAMD **shaggymane** CDB **William Shakespeare** The Folger Shakespeare Library, Washington, D.C. **shallop** Peabody Museum of Salem, Massachusetts - Mark Sexton **shallot** CC **sharpie** Mystic Seaport Museum, Inc. All rights reserved. **sharp-shinned hawk** PR - G. Ronald Austing **George Bernard Shaw** WCFTR **shay** From the collections of Henry Ford Museum & Greenfield Village, neg. no. A2811 **shears** LC **sheath** NMAI **sheet bend** TG **sheldrake** PR - Arthur W. Ambler **Mary Wollstonecraft Shelley** National Portrait Gallery, London **Percy Bysshe Shelley** National Portrait Gallery, London **Alan Shepard** BA **William Tecumseh Sherman** LOC **Shetland pony** EPJCo. **Shetland sheepdog** ES **shillelagh** American Museum of Natural History, Courtesy Department Library Services, neg. no. 410658 **shinleaf** CDB **Shiva** The Nelson-Atkins Museum of Art, Kansas City, Missouri, Nelson Fund **shock absorber** TG **shoofly** PI - Martin Miller **shoot-the-chute** SB - Mike Mazzaschi **shovel** CC **shrike** PR - G. Ronald Austing **shrimp** GHP - Runk & Schoenberger **shrine** SB - Judy Canty **Shropshire[2]** Marilyn Root **shuttlecock** CC **Siamese cat** PR - Ylla **sickle** CC **sickle cell** LC **sideboard** Courtesy of the Rhode Island Historical Society **sidecar** Allen Moore **side chair** Johns Hopkins University, The Halstead Collection (L.23.013.023) **sieve** PC - Frank Siteman **signpost** Comstock - Georg Gerster **silhouette** From *Silhouettes: A Pictorial Archive of Varied Illustrations.* Dover Publications, Inc. **silk-cotton tree** LC **Beverly Sills** GP - Reg Wilson **silo** SB - Daniel Brody **silverfish** CC **Neil Simon** WWP **O.J. Simpson** WWP **Sinai Peninsula** NASA **sine** TG **sine curve** TG **Isaac Bashevis Singer** WWP **sinusoidal projection** © 1986 by the American Congress on Surveying and Mapping **siphon** LC **David Siqueiros** WWP **sisal** Comstock - Georg Gerster **sistrum** Metropolitan Museum of Art, Purchase, 1955, Joseph Pulitzer Bequest (55.137.1) **sitar** PC - Mikki Ansin Ehrenfeld **Sitting Bull** NMAI **skeleton** LC **skewback** CC **ski** SB - Dean Abramson **skiff** Mystic Seaport Museum, Inc. All rights reserved. **skimmer** AA - Irene Vandermolen **skink** GHP - Hal Harrison **skull** LC **skunk** AA - Leonard Lee Rue III **skyscraper** TSI - Michael Bertan **slalom** PC - Phaneuf/Gurdziel **slash** Yale Center for British Art, Paul Mellon Collection **sled** © 1991 W. Hal Stewart **sledge** EPJCo. **sledgehammer** CC **sleigh** EPJCo. **slingshot** CC **slipknot** TG **sloop** Courtesy of the Commonwealth of Massachusetts, Metropolitan District Commission **sloth** PR - Jen & Des Bartlett **slug[2]** American Museum of Natural History, Courtesy Department Library Services, neg. no. 127917 **sluice** SB - Lionel J-M Delevingne **smack[3]** Mystic Seaport Museum, Inc. All rights reserved. **small intestine** LC **Joseph Smith** The National Portrait Gallery, Smithsonian Institution, Washington, D.C., Gift of the Reorganized Church of Jesus Christ of Latter-Day Saints, Independence, Missouri **Margaret Chase Smith** GP **smock** PC - Bob Kramer **snaffle** GEP **snail** GP **snake** LC **snapdragon** LC **snorkel** Comstock - Russ Kinne **snowboard** Comstock - David Lokey **snow goose** PR - Allan D. Cruickshank **snowshoe** The Brooklyn Museum, Nathan Sturges Jarvis Collection **soccer** GP **socket wrench** PI - Jerry Howard **Socrates** HPSM **sofa** SLAM, Museum Purchase, Funds donated by the Friends of the Saint Louis Art Museum,/The Sycamore Tree Trust and Decorative Arts Society funds, donated in memory of Mrs. Arthur B. Shepley, Jr. **soft-shelled turtle** PR - Alvin E. Staffan **solar panel** NASA **solleret** MMA, Rogers Fund, 1904 (04.3.295) **Solomon's seal** LC **sombrero** SB - Jean-Claude Lejeune **Sophocles** Alinari - Art Resource, New York **sorrel[1]** *Field Guide to the Wildflowers* by Roger Tory Peterson and Margaret McKenny. © 1968 by Roger Tory Peterson and Margaret McKenny. Reprinted by permission of Houghton Mifflin Company. All rights reserved. **sousaphone** Brent Jones, Chicago, Illinois **soybean** Laurel Cook LC **Wole Soyinka** GP - Horst Tappe **space shuttle** NASA **spadix** CC **spanker** TG **spark plug** LC **sparrow hawk** GHP - Hal Harrison **spathe** CC **spearmint** *Field Guide to the Wildflowers* by Roger Tory Peterson and Margaret McKenny. © 1968 by Roger Tory Peterson and Margaret McKenny. Reprinted by permission of Houghton Mifflin Company. All rights reserved. **spectacled** San Diego Zoo **spectroscope** TG **sphinx** MMA, Hewitt Fund, 1911, Rogers Fund, 1921, Munsey Fund, 1936, 1938, and Anonymous gift, 1951 (11.185) **sphygmomanometer** PC - Kindra Clineff **spinal column** LC **spinnaker** PR - Fritz Henle **spinning wheel** PC - Edward Bishop **spiral** EPJCo. **spirillum** GHP - Runk & Schoenberger **spittlebug** CDB **splat[1]** Courtesy The Strong Museum, Rochester, New York **splice** TG **splint** PR - Peter G. Aitken **split rail** PI - Jerry Howard **Benjamin Spock** SB - Lionel J-M Delevingne **spoonbill** GHP **spotter** PC - Steve Takatsuno **spread eagle** Shelburne Museum, Shelburne, Vermont **spring** TG **springer spaniel** GHP - John Colwell **spruce[1]** USDA **spur** Worcester Art Museum, Worcester, Massachusetts **square knot** TG **squash[1]** LC **squeegee** PI - Jerry Howard **squid** GHP - Runk & Schoenberger **squinch[1]** CDB **Madame de Staël** Giraudon - Art Resource, New York **stagecoach** From the collections of Henry Ford Museum & Greenfield Village, neg. no. A2768 **stained glass** PR - Jim Goodwin **stalactite and stalagmite** GHP - Runk & Schoenberger **Joseph Stalin** WWP **stamen** LC **standard** Courtesy of The Bostonian Society and Old State House - Richard Merrill **Elizabeth Cady Stanton** Sophia Smith Collection, Smith College **star-nosed mole** PR - Roy Pinney **Ringo Starr** EPJCo. **steamboat** LOC **steam engine** TG **steamroller** SB - Owen Franken **steel band** Comstock - Russ Kinne **steelyard** GEP **steeple** GHP - Alan Pitcairn **John Steinbeck** GP **Gloria Steinem** BA **stencil** PI - Jerry Howard **stentor** CC **Isaac Stern** WWP **stickleback** PR - Laurence Perkins **still life** The Brooklyn Museum, Bequest of Mrs. W. Sterling Peters (50.143.1) **stilt** GP **stinkbug** CDB **stirrup** GEP **stocks** The Pierpont Morgan Library, New York (M.763, f.134v detail) **stock saddle** GEP **stole[1]** Jeroboam, Inc. - Bob Clay **stomach** LC **stomacher** SLAM, Gift of Edward Mallinckrodt **stoneware** From the collections of Henry Ford Museum & Greenfield Village, neg. no. B16963 **stonework** EPJCo. **stopwatch** Peter Vandermark **stork** SB - Ira Kirschenbaum **stovepipe** Culver Pictures Inc. **Harriet Beecher Stowe** Sophia Smith Collection, Smith College **straight razor** Peter Vandermark **strainer** Museum of the Historical Society of Delaware, Bequest of Miss Henrietta Jane Bedford (1827.10) **Johann Strauss the Younger** BA **strawberry** LC **streetcar** LW - © 1990 S.E. Byrne **stroller** PI - Jerry Howard **Gilbert Stuart** BA **J.E.B. Stuart** LOC **sturgeon** PR - Tom McHugh **Peter Stuyvesant** Courtesy of The New-York Historical Society, New York City **William Styron** WWP **submersible** Woods Hole Oceanographic Institution **subway** GP - Camera Press **suffragist** BA **Sugarloaf Mountain** PR - George Holton **sugar maple** CC **Suleiman I** Turkish Culture and Information Office **sulky[2]** EPJCo. **sumac** CDB **sunburst** SB - Mike Mazzaschi **sundial** EPJCo. **sunflower** PI - Jerry Howard **Sun Yat-sen** BA **surcoat** The Pierpont Morgan Library (M.52, f.558v) **surfboard** SB - T.D. Lovering **surplice** Comstock - Russ Kinne **Mary Surratt** BA **surrealism** The Museum of Modern Art, New York, Purchase. **suspender** PC - Thomas Craig **suspension** TG **suspension bridge** SB - Peter Menzel **Joan Sutherland** GP - Vivienne **swallowtail** GHP - Runk & Schoenberger **swan** USDA - Soil Conservation Service **swift** Shelburne Museum, Shelburne, Vermont/ PR - G. Ronald Austing **Jonathan Swift** National Portrait Gallery, London **swimmeret** CDB **sword** BA **sycamore** CC **symbiosis** Leonard Rue Enterprises - Leonard Lee Rue III **synagogue** LW - © 1990 S.E. Byrne **synapse** CC **syncline** GEP **syncopation** TG **John Millington Synge** The Granger Collection, New York **synthesizer** SB - Judy Gelles **Henrietta Szold** WWP **tabard** BA **table tennis** PI - Patricia J. Bruno **taboret** Giraudon - Art Resource, New York **tachina fly** PR - Richard Parker **taco** Palmer/Brilliant, Boston, Massachusetts **tadpole** CDB **Helen Taft** GP **William Howard Taft** LOC **talisman** Bowdoin College Museum of Art, Florence C. Quinby in Memory of Henry Cole Quinby **talon** CC **tamarind** LC **tambourine** PI - Martin Miller **tangent** TG **tank** EPJCo./Department of Defense **tankard** Museum of Fine Arts, Houston, The Bayou Bend Collection,

Gift of Miss Ima Hogg **tapa**[1] Denver Art Museum - Otto Nelson **tapir** PR - Jen & Des Bartlett **tarantula** AA - Karen Tweedy-Holmes **targe** MMA, Gift of William H. Riggs, 1913 (14.25.742) **target** LW - Oscar Palmquist **tarragon** CC **tarsus** LC **tartan**[1] EPJCo. **tassel** PR - Steve Kagan **tau cross** GEP **Taurus** TG **Zachary Taylor** LOC **Peter Ilich Tchaikovsky** BA **tea caddy** Huntington Library **teasel** CC **teem**[2] EPJCo. **telephone booth** Image Photos - Clemens Kalischer **telescope** LC **template** LW - S.E. Byrne **temple**[1] SB - Ira Kirschenbaum **Ten Commandments** LOC **Tennessee walking horse** Tennessee Walking Horse Breeders and Exhibitors Association, Lewisburg, Tennessee **tennis** PC - Jaye R. Phillips **tent**[1] GEP **tepee** American Museum of Natural History, Courtesy Department Library Services, neg. no. 317248 - Rodman Wanamaker **Mother Teresa** GP - Camera Press **Valentina Tereshkova** GP - Camera Press **termitarium** PR - Bill Bachman **terrace** Comstock - Georg Gerster **terrapin** PR - Jack Dermid **tesseract** TG **testudo** TG **tetrahedron** TG **U Thant** BA **thatch** Image Photos - Clemens Kalischer **Margaret Thatcher** GP - Norman Parkinson **thermometer** LC **Theseus** MMA, Bequest of John Cadwalader, 1914 (14.58.131) **thimble** LW - Oscar Palmquist **thistle** CC **thoroughbred** PR - Josephus Daniels **Jim Thorpe** BA **Thoth** Cincinnati Art Museum, John J. Emery Fund **three-decker** SEF - Art Resource, New York **throne** EPJCo. **thunderbird** NMAI **thyme** CC **thyroid gland** CC **thyrsus** CC **tiara** Valentine Museum, Richmond, Virginia **tibia** LC **tide**[1] SB - Fredrik D. Bodin/SB - Fredrik D. Bodin **Tiffany glass** William Doyle Galleries, New York **tightrope** BA **tile** LOC/Courtesy of Cooper-Hewitt National Museum of Design, Smithsonian Institution - Art Resource, New York **tinamou** NYZS **tippet** Courtesy, Museum of Fine Arts, Boston, Gift of Amelia Peabody and William S. Eaton **tit**[1] PR - Russ Kinne **Titian** Marburg - Art Resource, New York **Tito** BA **toboggan** LC **toby** Shelburne Museum, Shelburne, Vermont **toggle bolt** CC **tokamak** TG **Leo Tolstoy** BA **tomahawk** NMAI **tom-tom** EPJCo. **tongs** Huntington Library **tooth** LC **top hat** SB - Owen Franken **topiary** BA **Torah** Jewish Museum - Art Resource, New York **torchère** Collection of Cranbrook Academy of Art Museum (1972.23) **torii** Leo de Wys, Inc. - Leo de Wys **tornado** PR - Max & Kit Hunn **torque**[2] Walters Art Gallery, Baltimore, Maryland **tortoise** TSI - Irene Vandermolen **totem pole** AA - Leonard Lee Rue III **totipalmate** CDB **toucan** PR - Arthur W. Ambler **François Dominique Toussaint L'Ouverture** HPSM **tower** PR - Jane Latta **towhee** PR - Karl H. Maslowski **tracery** Marburg - Art Resource, New York **tracheid** CDB **track and field** PC - Mac Donald/BA **tractor** SB - Cary Wolinsky **tragopan** PR - Arthur W. Ambler **transept** LC **transformer** TG **transit** SB - Spencer Grant **transom** © 1981 Walter Silver, Boston, Massachusetts **trap**[1] GEP **trapezoid** LC **trawler** Mystic Seaport Museum, Inc. All rights reserved. **treadmill** SB - Ellis Herwig **treble clef** TG **tree frog** GHP - Hal Harrison **trellis** LW - Oscar Palmquist **trephine** LC **triangle** LC/Comstock - Russ Kinne **triceps** LC **triceratops** LC **tricorn** SB - Charles Gatewood **trident** Alinari - Art Resource, New York **triforium** CC **trilithon** SB - Spencer Grant **trilobite** CC **Trinity** The Pierpont Morgan Library, New York **triplane** BA **tripod** SLAM, Gift of J. Lionberger Davis **triptych** MMA, Gift of J. Pierpont Morgan, 1917 (17.190.211) **triskelion** Alinari - Art Resource, New York **Triton** Courtesy, Museum of Fine Arts, Boston Edwin E. Jack Fund **Trojan horse** BA **trombone** PI - Jerry Howard **trophy** SB - Phyllis Graber Jensen **tropic** LC **Leon Trotsky** BA **trowel** CC **Bess Truman** Courtesy the Harry S. Truman Library - Hessler Studio of Washington, D.C. **Harry S. Truman** Courtesy the Harry S. Truman Library - U.S. Army Photo **trumpet** PC - Dan Walsh **truss bridge** LW - © 1990 Aldo Mastrocola **Sojourner Truth** National Portrait Gallery, Smithsonian Institution, Washington, D.C. **tsetse fly** CDB **T-square** GEP **tuberose**[1] CC **Harriet Tubman** LOC **tulip** LC **tulip tree** CC **tuning fork** LW - Oscar Palmquist **turban** SB - Rick Smolan **tureen** Courtesy, Museum of Fine Arts, Boston, Bequest of Forsyth Wickes, Forsyth Wickes Collection **turnbuckle** CC **turtle**[1] GHP - Hal Harrison **tusk** AA - Leonard Lee Rue III **Tutankhamen** MMA - Harry Burton **tutu** SB - Jean-Claude Lejeune **Desmond Tutu** GP - Godfrey Argent **twinflower** LC **John Tyler** In the Collection of The Corcoran Gallery of Art, Museum Purchase **tympanum** Comstock - Stuart Cohen **type** TG **Tyr** *Encyclopedia of Source Illustrations, vol. II* **Tzu Hsi** BA **Galina Ulanova** BA **ulna** LC **ultrasonograph** National Institutes of Health, Bethesda, Maryland **umbrella** PI - Martin Miller **umbrella bird** NYZS **Uncle Sam** LOC **underhand** PI- Jerry Howard **unicorn** Courtesy, Winterthur Museum **unicycle** Aristide Abrahams, Courtesy of The International Unicycling Federation **Union Jack** EPJCo. **unitard** © 1991 Judith Winters **universal joint** LC **John Updike** BA **upland sandpiper** PR - Hugh M. Halliday **upright piano** PI - Martin Miller **uraeus** Wolfgang Kaehler Photography **Urania** Alinari - Art Resource, New York **Urban II** The Granger Collection, New York **urn** SLAM, Museum Purchase **Ursa Major** TG **Ursa Minor** TG **utensil** GEP **Maurice Utrillo** The Granger Collection, New York **Rudolf Valentino** WCFTR **Valhalla** Icelandic Manuscript Institute, Reykjavick, Iceland **vambrace** MMA, John Stoneacre Ellis and Augustus van Horne Ellis, 1896 (96.5.85) **vampire bat** CDB **Martin Van Buren** LOC **Van de Graaff generator** TG **vane** CDB **vanilla** CC **Sarah Vaughan** Archive Photos **vault**[1] CC **VDT** SB - Tim Barnwell **vector product** TG **veil** SB - Peter Menzel **velocipede** Smithsonian Institution, Washington, D.C., Cycle Collection **vender** SB - David Carmack **Venus's-flytrap** LC **Giuseppe Verdi** Art Resource, New York **verdin** PR - Allan D. Cruickshank **vermiform appendix** LC **vernier caliper** GHP - Runk & Schoenberger **veronica**[2] NGA, Samuel H. Kress Collection **Giovanni da Verrazano** LOC **vervet** PR - Leonard Lee Rue III **vesper sparrow** PR - Allan D. Cruickshank **Amerigo Vespucci** SCALA - Art Resource, New York **vest** LW - © 1990 S.E. Byrne **vetch** *Field Guide to the Wildflowers* by Roger Tory Peterson and Margaret McKenny. © 1968 by Roger Tory Peterson and Margaret McKenny. Reprinted by permission of Houghton Mifflin Company. All rights reserved. **viaduct** LOC **victoria** Shelburne Museum, Shelburne, Vermont **Victoria**[1] BA **vicuña** San Diego Zoo **video game** PI - Jerry Howard **Élisabeth Vigée-Lebrun** Kimbell Art Museum, Fort Worth, Texas **Pancho Villa** Brown Brothers **vinegarroon** CDB **viola da gamba** Courtesy, Museum of Fine Arts, Boston, William Lindsey Fund **violet** *Field Guide to the Wildflowers* by Roger Tory Peterson and Margaret McKenny. © 1968 by Roger Tory Peterson and Margaret McKenny. Reprinted by permission of Houghton Mifflin Company. All rights reserved. **violin** SB - Gale Zucker **vireo** PR - Steve Maslowski **virginal**[2] Cincinnati Art Museum, Gift of William H. Doane **Virgo** TG **Vishnu** SLAM, Museum Purchase **visor** Comstock - Georg Gerster/LC **vitrine** LW - Oscar Palmquist **Volans** TG **volcano** LC **volleyball** PC - Ellis Herwig **voltaic pile** KAMD **Voltaire** NGA, Widener Collection **volva** CDB **V sign** GP **Vulcan** *Encyclopedia of Source Illustrations, vol. II* **vulture** AA - Leonard Lee Rue III **waders** Ewing Galloway **Richard Wagner** HPSM **waistcoat** Photograph © 1991, The Art Institute of Chicago. All rights reserved. Gift of Mrs. Guy Antrobus through the Antiquarian Society of The Art Institute of Chicago (1924.1223). **wake**[2] Official U.S. Navy Photograph - PH2 Robert D. Bunge **Alice Walker** AP/Wide World Photos WWP **walkie-talkie** SB - Rhoda Sidney **walking stick** PI - Jerry Howard/CDB **wallaby** NYZS **walnut** CC **wampum** NMAI **wapiti** USDA - Chester F. Fry **warbler** Cornell Laboratory of Ornithology - Wilson Bloomer **war bonnet** American Museum of Natural History Courtesy Department Library Services, neg. no. 324440 **Andy Warhol** GP - Deborah K. O'Brien **warming pan** Courtesy, Winterthur Museum **wart hog** PR - Tomas D.W. Friedman **washboard** Allen Moore **Booker T. Washington** National Portrait Gallery, Smithsonian Institution, Washington, D.C., Transfer from the National Gallery of Art **George Washington** NGA, Gift of Andrew W. Mellon, 1942 **Martha Washington** National Portrait Gallery, Smithsonian Institution, Washington, D.C. **wasp** CDB **wasp waist** LOC **waterbuck** SB - Ira Kirschenbaum **water lily** PI - Jerry Howard **water polo** SB - Ellis Herwig **water spaniel** ES **water tower** Ewing Galloway **Watson-Crick model** LW - Oscar Palmquist **wattle** GHP **Evelyn Waugh** GP - Yevonde **John Wayne** BA **weasel** AA - Irene Vandermolen **weathering** EPJCo. **weathervane** EPJCo. **weave** SB - Charles Kennard/GEP **Daniel Webster** LOC **wedge** LW - © 1990 Aldo Mastrocola **weeping willow** LC **weevil** CDB **Weimaraner** ES **Orson Welles** GP - Camera Press **Duke of Wellington** National Portrait Gallery, London **Welsh corgi** AA - Jayne Langdon **Welsh terrier** EPJCo. **Mae West** BA **Western Wall** PC - Stanley Rowin **West Highland white terrier** ES **wet suit** PC - Herb Snitzer **Phillis Wheatley** LOC **Wheatstone bridge** TG **wheelchair** PC - Spencer Grant **wheelie** PC - Sarah Putnam **whelk**[1] LC **whippet** ES **whisk** UCLA Museum of Cultural History **whisker** TSI - Peter Pearson **white admiral** CDB **White House** USDA/ The White House - Mary Anne Fackelman **white pine** CC **white snakeroot** CC **whitewall tire** GP **Eli Whitney** BA **whorl** CC **wicket** PI - Jerry Howard **wickiup** NMAI **widow's walk** Allen Moore **Elie Wiesel** SB - Owen Franken **wigwam** NMAI **Oscar Wilde** BA **wild ginger** CC **wild turkey** PR - Jeanne White **Tennessee Williams** GP **willowware** Spencer Museum of Art, The University of Kansas, William Bridges Thayer Memorial **Edith Wilson** LOC **Ellen Wilson** LOC **Woodrow Wilson** HPSM **winch** PI - Jerry Howard **windmill** BA/USDA **Duchess of Windsor** GP - Cecil Beaton **Windsor chair** Northampton Historical Society **windsurfing** SB - Peter Menzel **wing chair** Art Resource, New York **wire fox terrier** EPJCo. **wisteria** LC **wolf** NYZS **wombat** NYZS **woodchuck** EPJCo. **Victoria Woodhull** Sophia Smith Collection, Smith College **woodpecker** PR - Leonard Lee Rue III **wood tick** CDB **Virginia Woolf** BA **woolly bear** GHP **worktable** The Valentine Museum, Richmond, Virginia **worm gear** LC **Christopher Wren** National Portrait Gallery, London **wrench** LC **wrestling** Lou Jones Studio **Frank Lloyd Wright** BA **Wright Brothers** HPSM/HPSM **wrought iron** EPJCo. **Wyandotte**[2] USDA **Andrew Wyeth** BA **Saint Francis Xavier** Walters Art Gallery, Baltimore, Maryland **Xerxes I** Courtesy of The Oriental Institute of The University of Chicago **xylem** CDB **xylophone** Comstock - Russ Kinne **yam** CC **yang** LC **yashmak** Turkish Government Tourism and Information Office **William Butler Yeats** BA **yellow jacket** CDB **yew** LC **yoke** CC **Yorkshire terrier** AA - Paula Wright **Andrew Young** BA **Brigham Young** Brigham Young University Photoarchives **yucca** SB - Eric Neurath **yurt** PR - Paolo Koch **Emiliano Zapata** BA **zebra** AA - Leonard Lee Rue III **Zhou Enlai** BA **zinnia** LC **zither** Smithsonian Institution, Washington, D.C., Division of Musical Instruments **zizith** Marilyn Root **zodiac** BA **Émile Zola** BA **zucchini** LC **Ulrich Zwingli** LOC **zygodactyl** CDB

ABCDEFGHIJKL-RMV-9976543